Collins

柯林斯COBUILD 高级英汉双解词典

Collins COBUILD ADVANCED DICTIONARY of English

Grace.

CONTENTS

Acknowledgements

总策划	刘　援				
前期筹划	周　龙	白震坤	张毅达		
项目编辑	洪志娟	陈　进			

（以下人员按姓氏拼音字母顺序）

专家组	李正栓	任晓晋	杨信彰	翟象俊	张柏然
审订组	冯　梅	韩江洪	黄宗英	姬生雷	杨信彰
	朱宾忠	朱章华			
译者	蔡小容	邓小红	丁秉伟	段文静	高兰芳
	韩江洪	韩莉妲	黄　忠	李典秀	李　力
	李丽辉	李琼花	李素英	栗文达	梁鲁晋
	林记明	刘　纯	刘荣强	彭贵菊	乔建珍
	宋润娟	孙海影	郤庆燕	唐青叶	童慧萍
	王晋军	王慧敏	王　瑛	肖　薇	杨翠英
	杨丽华	杨萍萍	杨小蓉	杨信彰	张国庆
	张　洁	张淑艳	张　苇	赵丽华	赵　霞
	朱　骅	朱章华			
特邀编辑	曹根望	陈　凯	李子亮	孙亦丽	田文琪
编辑审校	艾　斌	白震坤	陈　进	陈　丽	常少华
	邓中杰	甘红娜	贺伟华	洪志娟	贾巍巍
	康冬婷	康黎君	李　宁	李　欣	李锡奎
	梁　玫	梁　宇	蔺启东	吕艳萍	马文敏
	闵　阅	秦彬彬	宋亚昆	孙云鹏	唐灵依
	王琳琳	谢玉春	徐艳梅	张慧勇	张　凯
	张维华	张歆秋	张毅达	朱晓军	

Collins COBUILD

Founding Editor-in-Chief: John Sinclair
Publisher: Elaine Higgleton
Project Manager: Lisa Sutherland
Senior Editor: Yueshi Gu

For the English text
Contributors: Maree Airlee, Carol Braham, Carol-June Cassidy, Rosalind Combley, Pat Cook, Helen Forrest, Robert Grossmith, Penny Hands, Orin Hargraves, Dana Darby Johnson, Cindy Mitchell, Marianne Noble, Susan Norton, Sue Ogden, Enid Pearsons, Elizabeth Potter, Maggie Seaton, Laura Wedgeworth

For the Chinese Text
Contributors: Lingzhi Gu, Hellen Hu, Min-Hsiu Liao, Lou Zhao, Ning Sun, Youling Sun, Lulu Wang, Weiqing Zhu

Computing Support: Thomas Callan
Typesetting: Davidson Pre-Press

Heinle

President: Dennis Hogan
Publisher: Sherrise Roehr
Senior Development Editor: Katherine Carroll
Technology Publisher: Mac Mendelsohn
Director of Global Marketing: Ian Martin
Director of U.S. Marketing: Jim McDonough
Senior Content Project Manager: Dawn Marie Elwell
Front and End Matter Typeset: Parkwood Composition Service, Inc.

The publishers would like to thank everyone who worked on the original COBUILD concept, in particular: John Sinclair.

Guide to Key Features

Through a collaborative initiative, Collins COBUILD and Heinle are co-publishing a dynamic new line of learner's dictionaries offering unparalleled pedagogy and learner resources.

Band 4 and Band 6 Words

The *Collins COBUILD Advanced Dictionary of English, English/Chinese* marks vocabulary commonly found in the College English Test (CET) bands four and six. CET-4 words are magenta. CET-6 words are magenta and are marked with ★. CET-6+ words are magenta and are marked with ▲.

With innovations such as Definitions*PLUS* and Vocabulary Builders, the *Collins COBUILD Advanced Dictionary of English, English/Chinese* transforms the learner's dictionary from an occasional reference into the ultimate resource and must-have dictionary for language learners.

Definitions*PLUS*

- **Definitions*PLUS* Collocations**—Each definition is written in simple, natural English and shows which words are most typically used with the target word.
- **Definitions*PLUS* Grammar**—Each definition includes the most representative grammatical patterns to help the learner use English correctly.
- **Definitions*PLUS* Natural English**—Each definition is a model of how to use the language appropriately and idiomatically.

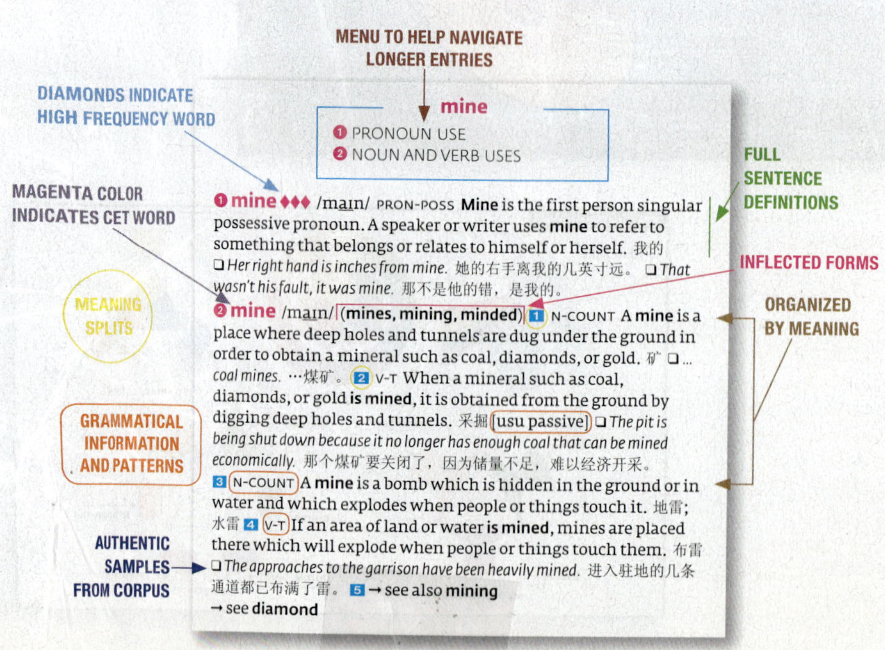

MENU TO HELP NAVIGATE LONGER ENTRIES
DIAMONDS INDICATE HIGH FREQUENCY WORD
mine
❶ PRONOUN USE
❷ NOUN AND VERB USES
FULL SENTENCE DEFINITIONS
MAGENTA COLOR INDICATES CET WORD
❶ mine ♦♦♦ /maɪn/ PRON-POSS Mine is the first person singular possessive pronoun. A speaker or writer uses mine to refer to something that belongs or relates to himself or herself. 我的 ❑ Her right hand is inches from mine. 她的右手离我的几英寸远。 ❑ That wasn't his fault, it was mine. 那不是他的错，是我的。
INFLECTED FORMS
MEANING SPLITS
❷ mine /maɪn/ (mines, mining, minded) 1 N-COUNT A mine is a place where deep holes and tunnels are dug under the ground in order to obtain a mineral such as coal, diamonds, or gold. 矿 ❑ ... coal mines. …煤矿。 2 V-T When a mineral such as coal, diamonds, or gold is mined, it is obtained from the ground by digging deep holes and tunnels. 采掘 [usu passive] ❑ The pit is being shut down because it no longer has enough coal that can be mined economically. 那个煤矿要关闭了，因为储量不足，难以经济开采。 3 N-COUNT A mine is a bomb which is hidden in the ground or in water and which explodes when people or things touch it. 地雷；水雷 4 V-T If an area of land or water is mined, mines are placed there which will explode when people or things touch them. 布雷 ❑ The approaches to the garrison have been heavily mined. 进入驻地的几条通道都已布满了雷。 5 → see also mining
→ see diamond
ORGANIZED BY MEANING
GRAMMATICAL INFORMATION AND PATTERNS
AUTHENTIC SAMPLES FROM CORPUS

The Bank of English™ is the original and the most current computerized corpus of authentic American English. This robust research tool was used to create each definition. All sample sentences are drawn from the rich selection that the corpus offers.

Vocabulary Builders

Over 3,000 pedagogical features encourage curiosity and exploration, which in turn builds the learner's bank of active and passive vocabulary knowledge. The "Vocabulary Builders" outlined here enhance vocabulary acquisition, increase language fluency, and improve accurate communication. They provide the learner with a greater depth and breadth of knowledge of the English language. The *Collins COBUILD Advanced Dictionary of English, English/Chinese* offers a level of content and an overall learning experience unmatched in other dictionaries.

"Picture Dictionary" boxes illustrate vocabulary and concepts. The words are chosen for their usefulness in an academic setting, frequently showing a concept or process that benefits from a visual presentation.

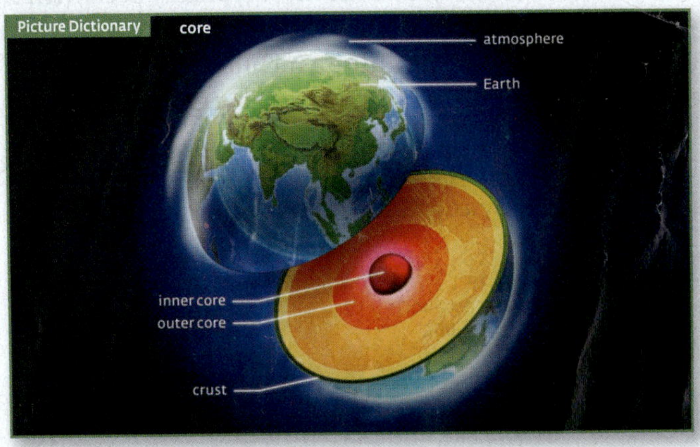

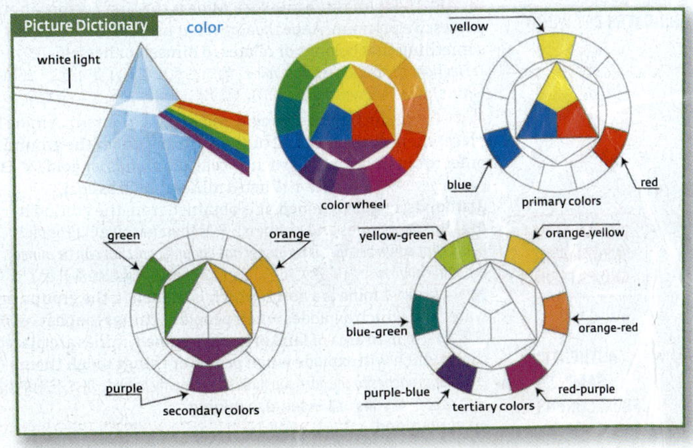

"Word Webs" present topic-related vocabulary through encyclopedia-like readings combined with stunning art, creating opportunities for deeper understanding of the language and concepts. All key words in bold are defined in the dictionary. Upon looking up one word, learners discover other related words that draw them further into the dictionary and the language. The more sustained time learners spend exploring words, the greater and richer their language acquisition is. The "Word Webs" encourage language exploration.

Word Web spice

While researching the use of **spices** in cooking, scientists discovered that many of them have strong disease-prevention properties. Bacteria can grow quickly on food and cause a variety of serious illnesses in humans. The researchers found that many spices are extremely antibacterial. For example, **garlic**, **onion**, allspice, and oregano kill almost all common germs. **Cinnamon**, tarragon, cumin, and **chili peppers** also eliminate about 75% of bacteria. And even common, everyday **black pepper** destroys about 25% of all microbes. The research also found a connection between hot climates and **spicy** food and cold climates and **bland** food.

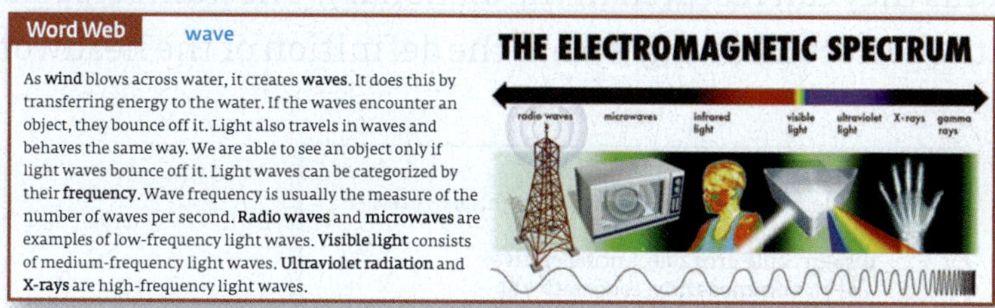
Word Web wave

As **wind** blows across water, it creates **waves**. It does this by transferring energy to the water. If the waves encounter an object, they bounce off it. Light also travels in waves and behaves the same way. We are able to see an object only if light waves bounce off it. Light waves can be categorized by their **frequency**. Wave frequency is usually the measure of the number of waves per second. **Radio waves** and **microwaves** are examples of low-frequency light waves. **Visible light** consists of medium-frequency light waves. **Ultraviolet radiation** and **X-rays** are high-frequency light waves.

Chosen based on frequency in the Bank of English™, **"Word Partnerships"** show high-frequency word patterns, giving the complete collocation with the headword in place to clearly demonstrate use. The numbers refer the student to the correct meaning within the definition of the word that collocates with the headword.

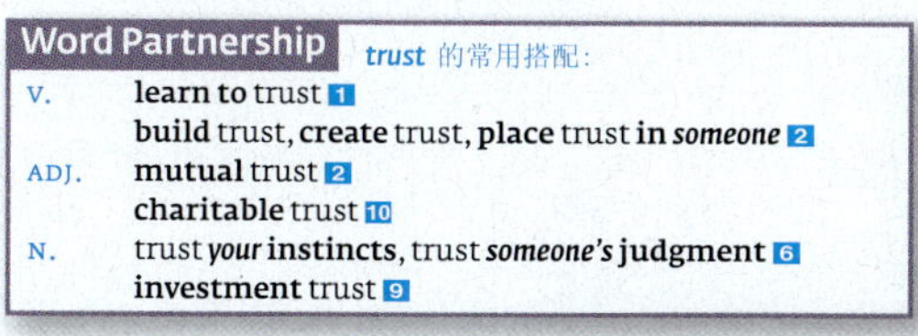
Word Partnership *trust* 的常用搭配:

V. **learn to** trust 1
build trust, **create** trust, **place** trust **in** *someone* 2
ADJ. **mutual** trust 2
charitable trust 10
N. trust *your* **instincts**, trust *someone's* **judgment** 6
investment trust 9

Word Partnership *moment* 的常用搭配:

ADV. **a** moment **ago**, **just a** moment 1
N. moment **of silence**, moment **of thought** 1
V. **stop for a** moment, **take a** moment, **think for a** moment, **wait a** moment 1
ADJ. **an awkward** moment, **a critical** moment, **the right** moment 2

"Word Links" exponentially increase language awareness by showing how words are built in English, something that will be useful for learners in all areas of academic work as well as in daily communication. Focusing on prefixes, sufxes, and word roots, each "Word Link" provides a simple definition of the building block and then gives three examples of it used in a word. Providing three examples encourages learners to look up these words to further solidify understanding.

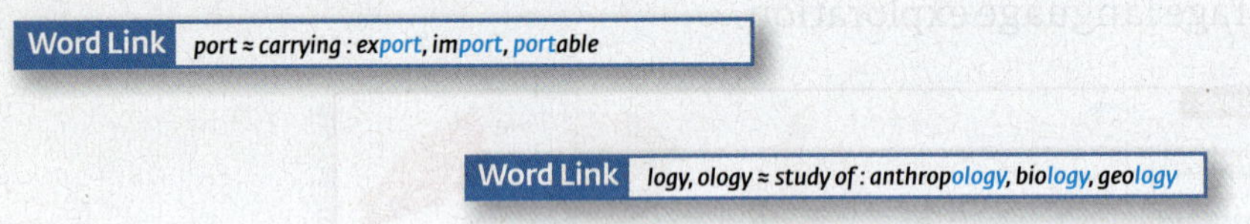

"Thesaurus" entries offer both synonyms and antonyms for high frequency words. An extra focus on synonyms offers learners an excellent way to expand vocabulary knowledge and usage by directing them to other words they can research in the dictionary. The numbers refer the student to the correct meaning within the definition of the headword.

CD-ROM

A valuable enhancement to the learning experience, the *Collins COBUILD Advanced Dictionary of American English* CD-ROM offers learners a fast and simple way to explore words and their meanings while working on a computer.

- **Search** definitions, sample sentences, Word Webs, and Picture Dictionary boxes.
- **"Mini-View" Dictionary:** Allows easy access while working on other computer applications.
- **Audio playback** allows students to review the pronunciation of headwords.
- **"My Dictionary"** allows learners to create a personalized tool by adding their own words, definitions, and sample sentences.
- **Bookmarks** allow learners to save and organize vocabulary. There are 75 bookmark folders already created with topic-related vocabulary to act as a springboard for vocabulary learning.

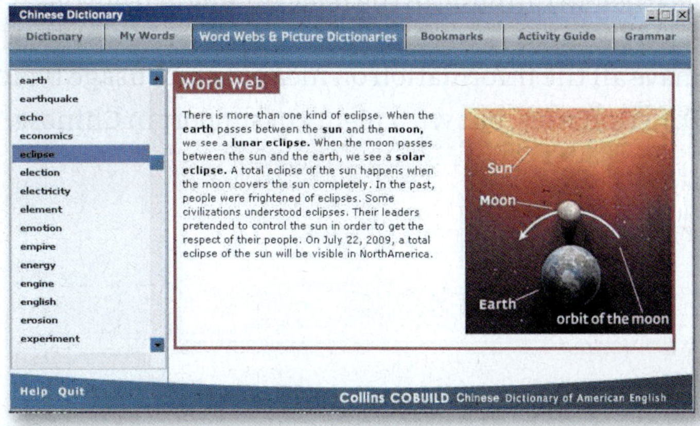

By using the resources found in this volume, learners will discover that the *Collins COBUILD Advanced Dictionary of English, English/Chinese* is something that they want to delve into and spend time exploring, not just something to flip through for a quick answer. As they investigate options for words that will best serve their individual communicative needs at any given point, learners will find more opportunities for learning than they have ever seen in a traditional reference tool. This will become their ultimate resource and partner in their language learning journey.

Benefits of Semibilingual Dictionary

Collins COBUILD and Heinle are pleased to offer a new type of dictionary for Chinese learners of English. The *Collins COBUILD Advanced Dictionary of English, English/Chinese* is a semibilingual dictionary designed for high intermediate or advanced level learners of English.

- This semibilingual dictionary includes all the features of a COBUILD monolingual dictionary, such as full sentence definitions and corpus-based examples.
- Additionally, for learners who feel they would benefit from access to Chinese translations, they are included for all definitions, senses, and examples.
- Chinese translations are included to complement the English material and provide additional support to the learner when they encounter a difficult word or expression.
- The index lists the translations found in the dictionary and directs the learner, in Chinese, to the relevant English entry.

Thus users have all the information on meaning and usage typically found in COBUILD dictionaries, but with plenty of support in Chinese.

John Sinclair

Founding Editor-in-Chief, Collins COBUILD Dictionaries

1933-2007

John Sinclair was Professor of Modern English Language at the University of Birmingham for most of his career; he was an outstanding scholar, one of the very first modern corpus linguists, and one of the most open-minded and original thinkers in the field. The COBUILD project in lexical computing, funded by Collins, revolutionized lexicography in the 1980s, and resulted in the creation of the largest corpus of English language texts in the world.

Professor Sinclair personally oversaw the creation of this very first electronic corpus, and was instrumental in developing the tools needed to analyze the data. Having corpus data allowed Professor Sinclair and his team to find out how people really use the English language, and to develop new ways of structuring dictionary entries. Frequency information, for example, allowed him to rank senses by importance and usefulness to the learner (thus the most common meaning should be put first); and the corpus highlights collocates (the words which go together), information which had only been sketchily covered in previous dictionaries. Under his guidance, his team also developed a full-sentence defining style, which not only gave the user the sense of a word, but showed that word in grammatical context.

When the first *Collins COBUILD Dictionary of English* was published in 1987, it revolutionized dictionaries for learners, completely changed approaches to dictionary-writing, and led to a new generation of corpus-driven dictionaries and reference materials for English language learners.

Professor Sinclair worked on the Collins COBUILD range of titles until his retirement, when he moved to Florence, Italy and became president of the Tuscan Word Centre, an association devoted to promoting the scientific study of language. He remained interested in dictionaries until his death, and the Collins COBUILD range of dictionaries remains a testament to his revolutionary approach to lexicography and English language learning. Professor Sinclair will be sorely missed by everyone who had the great pleasure of working with him.

Introduction

A dictionary is probably the single most important reference book that a learner of English can buy. At Collins we do our best to ensure that our dictionaries live up to all expectations. This **Collins Cobuild Advanced Dictionary of English, English/Chinese** is a new type of dictionary. It is especially designed for Chinese learners who already have a good working knowledge of English, but who may not be entirely comfortable using a monolingual English dictionary. All the features of a monolingual dictionary are included, with Chinese translations provided for all senses and examples. Translations of explanatory terms are provided in the introduction. The dictionary also includes an index which lists alphabetically the translations found in the dictionary and which directs you to the relevant English entry through the medium of Chinese.

The corpus

The **Collins Cobuild Advanced Dictionary of English, English/Chinese** like all Collins dictionaries, is based on a corpus, the Bank of English ™, part of the Collins Word Web, which now contains over 650 million words of contemporary English. The corpus is central to the compilation of COBUILD dictionaries. It enables the dictionary editors to look at how the language works and make evidence-based statements about the meanings, patterns, and uses of words with confidence and accuracy.

Content

A dictionary must present the most important facts about language, and dictionary compilers need good evidence to be able to make their selections. It is much easier to decide which words to include, and which to omit, when we have accurate statistical information from such a vast database of language as the Bank of English ™. This enables the compilers to look at the relative frequency of words and to identify and highlight the 2,500 most frequently used words in English. These words account for over 75% of all English usage, so it is easy to see why they are important.

Definitions

One of the most distinctive feature of all COBUILD dictionaries is the use of full English sentences in the definitions, explaining the meaning in the way that one person might explain it to another. They give the user much more than the meaning of the word they are looking up, and also contain information on usage, register, typical context, and syntax. The fullness of the definitions will give learners of English confidence as they learn what words and phrases mean and how they are used.

Examples

All of the examples in this dictionary have been selected from the Bank of English ™, and have been chosen carefully to show the collocates of a word—other words that are frequently used with the word we are defining—and the patterns in which it is used. Since the examples are genuine pieces of text, you can be sure that they show the word in use in a natural context.

Set structures

For each definition, the word or phrase being defined is printed in **bold**. In addition, we have identified and highlighted in **bold** words which combine with the headword to make a very important or set grammatical structure or collocational pattern, for example, *A* **band of** *people is . . . If you say something* **to yourself**, *you think it . . . If you are* **unable to** *do something, it is . . .*

Coverage

Today's learners of English need to be aware of the variation of language in different parts of the English-speaking world. The **Collins Cobuild Advanced Dictionary of English, English/Chinese** includes useful notes to identify vocabulary and expressions from those parts of the world, particularly American and British English.

Usage notes

Throughout the text we have included a number of notes which give additional information about how words are used. There is a variety of useful information contained in these notes, which help to clarify important distinctions in usage and in grammar.

Culture notes

Extra information on culturally significant events, institutions, traditions and customs is given in the form of a note following the relevant entry. These notes are intended to help you gain a greater understanding of life and culture in English-speaking countries.

Complex entries

Entries which are long or complex are given a special treatment to make them easier to navigate. A menu shows what sections the entry is divided into, and how they are ordered, so that you can immediately go to the correct section to find the meaning you want. For example, **mean** is divided into three sections, corresponding to its verb, adjective, and noun uses. The same principle is used for **hold**, where there is an important sense distinction running through its uses.

Grammatical information

Where relevant, useful information about the grammatical patterns is provided. This information appears immediately before the examples which further clarify the patterns.

Guide to the Dictionary Entries

Definitions

One of the features of the **Collins Cobuild Advanced Dictionary of English, English/Chinese** is that the definitions are written in full sentences, using vocabulary and grammatical structures that occur naturally with the word being explained. This enables us to give a lot of information about the way a word or meaning is used by speakers of the language. Whenever possible, words are explained using simpler and more common words. This gives us a natural defining vocabulary with most words in our definitions being among the 2,500 commonest words of English. A Chinese translation is given for each sense of each word. For example, the verb **bask** has two senses, each of which has a Chinese translation:

If you **bask in** the sunshine, you lie somewhere sunny and enjoy the heat.
If you **bask in** someone's approval, favor, or admiration, you greatly enjoy their positive reaction toward you.

An individual sense of an English word may have more than one Chinese translation. For example, the noun **jealousy** has two different Chinese translations.

Information about collocates and structure

In our definitions, we show the typical collocates of a word: that is, the other words that are used with the word we are defining. For example, the definition of meaning 1 of the adjective **savory** says:

> **Savory** food has a salty or spicy flavor rather than a sweet one.

This shows that you use the adjective **savory** to describe food, rather than other things.

Meaning 1 of the verb **wag** says:

> When a dog **wags** its tail, it repeatedly waves its tail from side to side.

This shows that the subject of meaning 1 of **wag** refers to a dog, and the object of the verb is "tail".

Information about Chinese collocations, if any, is given in brackets.

> If you are **aboard** a ship or plane, you are on it or in it: 在（船或飞机）上

Information about grammar

The definitions also give information about the grammatical structures in which a word is used. For example, meaning 1 of the adjective **candid** says:

> When you are **candid** about something or with someone, you speak honestly.

This shows that you use **candid** with the preposition "about" with something and "with" with someone.

Other definitions show other kinds of structure. Meaning 1 of the verb **soften** says:

> If you **soften** something or if it **softens**, it becomes less hard, stiff, or firm.

This shows that the verb is used both transitively and intransitively. In the transitive use, you have a human subject and a non-human object. In the intransitive use, you have a non-human subject.

Finally, meaning 1 of **compel** says:

> If a situation, a rule, or a person **compels** you to do something, they force you to do it.

This shows you what kinds of subject and object to use with **compel**, and it also shows that you typically use the verb in a structure with a to-infinitive.

Information about context and usage

In addition to information about collocation and grammar, definitions also can be used to convey your evaluation of something, for example to express your approval or disapproval. For example, here is the definition of **unhelpful**:

> If you say that someone or something is **unhelpful**, you mean that they do not help you or improve a situation, and may even make things worse.

In this definition, the expressions "if you say that", and "you mean that" indicate that these words are used subjectively, rather than objectively.

Other kinds of definition

We sometimes explain grammatical words and other function words by paraphrasing the word in context. For example, meaning 3 of **through** says:

> To go **through** a town, area, or country means to travel across it or in it.

In many cases, it is impossible to paraphrase the word, and so we explain its function instead. For example, the definition of **unfortunately** says:

> You can use **unfortunately** to introduce or refer to a statement when you consider that it is sad or disappointing, or when you want to express regret.

Lastly, some definitions are expressed as if they are cross-references. For example:

> **rd.** is a written abbreviation for **road**.
> **e-commerce** is the same as **e-business**.

If you need to know more about the words **road** or **e-business**, you look at those entries.

Style and Usage

Some words or meanings are used mainly by particular groups of people, or in particular social contexts. In this dictionary, where relevant, the definitions also give information about the kind of people who are likely to use a word or expression, and the type of social situation in which it is used.

In terms of geographical diversity, this dictionary focuses on American and British English using evidence from the Bank of English ™. Where relevant, the American or British form is shown at its equivalent word or meaning.

This information is usually placed at the end of the definition, in small capitals and within square brackets. If more than one type of information is provided, they are given in a list. If an equivalent term is provided, it is given in a blue box. The Chinese translation of this information is provided in the introduction.

Geographical labels

AM (美国英语): used mainly by speakers and writers in the US, and in other places where American English is used or taught. Where relevant the British equivalent is provided.

BRIT (英国英语): used mainly by speakers and writers in Britain, and in other places where British English is used or taught. Where relevant the American equivalent is provided.

Other geographical labels are used in the text to refer to English as it is spoken in other parts of the world, e.g. AUSTRALIAN (澳大利亚英语), SCOTTISH (苏格兰英语).

Style labels

BUSINESS (商业): used mainly when talking about the field of business, e.g. **annuity**

COMPUTING (计算机): used mainly when talking about the field of computing, e.g. **chat room**

DIALECT (方言): used in some dialects of English, e.g. **ain't**

FORMAL (正式): used mainly in official situations, or by political and business organizations, or when speaking or writing to people in authority, e.g. **gracious**

HUMOROUS (幽默): used mainly to indicate that a word or expression is used in a humorous way, e.g. **gents**

INFORMAL (非正式): used mainly in informal situations, conversations, and personal letters, e.g. **pep talk**

JOURNALISM (新闻): used mainly in journalism, e.g. **glass ceiling**

LEGAL (法律): used mainly in legal documents, in law courts, and by the police in official situations, e.g. **manslaughter**

LITERARY (文学性): used mainly in novels, poetry, and other forms of literature, e.g. **plaintive**

MEDICAL (医学): used mainly in medical texts, and by doctors in official situations, e.g. **psychosis**

MILITARY (军事): used mainly when talking or writing about military terms, e.g. **armor**

OFFENSIVE (侮辱): likely to offend people, or to insult them; words labeled OFFENSIVE should therefore usually be avoided, e.g. **cripple**

OLD-FASHIONED (老式): generally considered to be old-fashioned, and no longer in common use, e.g. **dashing**

SPOKEN (口语): used mainly in speech rather than in writing, e.g. **pardon**

TECHNICAL (技术): used mainly when talking or writing about objects, events, or processes in a specialist subject, such as business, science, or music, e.g. **biotechnology**

TRADEMARK (商标): used to show a designated trademark, e.g. **hoover**

VULGAR (粗话): used mainly to describe words which could be considered taboo by some people; words labeled VULGAR should therefore usually be avoided, e.g. **bloody**

WRITTEN (书面): used mainly in writing rather than in speech, e.g. **avail**

FREQUENCY BANDING

Information on the frequency of words in this dictionary is given using three frequency bands, shown as diamonds in the headword line. The most frequent words have three diamonds, the next most frequent two, and the ones which are less frequent have one diamond. Words which occur less frequently still, but which deserve an entry in the dictionary, do not have any diamonds.

PRAGMATICS LABELS

Many uses of words need more than a statement of meaning to be properly explained. People use words to do many things: give invitations, express their feelings, emphasize what they are saying, and so on. The study and description of the way in which people use language to do these things is called **pragmatics**.

In the dictionary, we draw attention to certain pragmatic aspects of words and phrases of English, paying special attention to those that, for cultural and linguistic reasons, we feel may be confusing to learners. The following labels are used:

APPROVAL (表赞许): used to show that you approve of the person or thing you are talking about, e.g. **angelic**

DISAPPROVAL (表不满): used to show that you disapprove of the person or thing you are talking about, e.g. **brat**

EMPHASIS (强调): used to emphasize the point you are making, e.g. **never-ending**

FEELINGS (情感): used to express your feelings about something, or towards someone, e.g. **unfortunately**

FORMULAE (套语): used in particular situations such as greeting and thanking people, or acknowledging something, e.g. **hi, congratulations**

POLITENESS (礼貌): used to express politeness, sometimes even to the point of being euphemistic. e.g. **elderly**

VAGUENESS (含糊): used to show how certain you are about the truth or validity of your statements; this is sometimes called "hedging" or "modality", e.g. **presumably**

Pronunciation

The basic principle underlying the suggested pronunciations is "If you pronounce it like this, most people will understand you." The pronunciations are therefore broadly based on the two most widely taught accents of English, GenAm or General American for American English, and RP or Received Pronunciation for British English.

For the majority of words, a single pronunciation is given, as most differences between American and British pronunciation are systematic. Where the usual British pronunciation differs from the usual American pronunciation more significantly, a separate transcription is given after the code BRIT. Where more than one pronunciation is common in either American or British English, alternative pronunciations are given.

The pronunciations are the result of a program of monitoring spoken English and consulting leading reference works. The transcription system has developed from original work by Dr David Brazil for the Collins COBUILD English Language Dictionary. The symbols used in the dictionary are adapted from those of the International Phonetic Alphabet (IPA), as standardized in the English Pronouncing Dictionary by Daniel Jones (14th Edition, revised by AC Gimson and SM Ramsaran 1988).

IPA Symbols

Vowel Sounds	
ɑ	calm, ah
æ	act, mass
ɑɪ	dive, cry
ɑʊ	out, down
ɛ	met, lend, pen
eɪ	say, weight
ɪ	fit, win
i	feed, me
ɒ	lot, spot
oʊ	note, coat
ɔ	claw, maul
ɔɪ	boy, joint
ʊ	could, stood
u	you, use
ʌ	fund, must
ə	first vowel in about
i	second vowel in very
u	second vowel in actual

Consonant Sounds	
b	bed, rub
d	done, red
f	fit, if
g	good, dog
h	hat, horse
k	king, pick
l	lip, bill
ᵊl	handle, panel
m	mat, ram
n	not, tin
ᵊn	hidden, written
p	pay, lip
r	run, read
s	soon, bus
t	talk, bet
v	van, love
w	win, wool
x	loch
y	yellow, you
z	zoo, buzz
ʃ	ship, wish
ʒ	measure, leisure
ŋ	sing, working
tʃ	cheap, witch
θ	thin, myth
ð	then, bathe
dʒ	joy, bridge

Notes

/æ/ or /ɑ/

There are a number of words which use the /æ/ sound in GenAm and in most accents of English, but /ɑ/ in RP, such as 'bath' which is pronounced /bæθ/ in GenAm and /bɑθ/ in RP. This affects some words in which this vowel is followed by the sounds /f/, /nd/, /ns/, /nt/, /ntʃ/, /s/, /θ/. For example, 'graph', 'command', 'answer', 'can't', 'ranch', 'class' and 'bath' are pronounced /græf/, /kəmænd/, /ænsər/, /kænt/, /ræntʃ/, /klæs/ and /bæθ/ in GenAm, but /grɑf/, /kəmɑnd/, /ɑ̈nsəʳ/, /kɑnt/, /rɑntʃ/, /klɑs/ and /bɑθ/ in RP. However, there are exceptions to this such as "land" /lænd/. In these cases, we show only the GenAm version as it is a common and acceptable pronunciation for British English, even though it is not RP.

/r/

In most accents of English, including GenAm, 'r' is always pronounced. One of the main ways in which RP differs is that 'r' is only pronounced as /r/ when the next sound is a vowel. Thus, in RP, 'far gone' is pronounced /fɑ̈ gɒn/ but 'far out' is pronounced /fɑ̈r aʊt/. Similarly, 'fire', 'flour', 'fair', 'near' and 'pure' are pronounced /faɪər/, /flaʊər/, /fɛər/, /nɪər/ and /pyʊər/ in GenAm, but /faɪə/, /flaʊə/, /fɛə/, /nɪə/ and /pyʊə/ in RP.

/oʊ/

This symbol is used to represent the sound /oʊ/ in GenAm, and also the sound /əʊ/ in RP, as these sounds are almost entirely equivalent.

/ᵊl/ and /ᵊn/

These show that /l/ and /n/ are pronounced as separate syllables:

handle /hændᵊl/

hidden /hɪdᵊn/

Stress

Stress is shown by underlining the vowel in the stressed syllable:

two /tu/

result /rɪzʌlt/

disappointing /dɪsəpɔɪntɪŋ/

When a word is spoken in isolation, stress falls on the syllables which have vowels which are underlined. If there is one syllable underlined, it will have primary stress.

'TWO'

'reSULT'

If two syllables are underlined, the first will have secondary stress, and the second will have primary stress:

'DISapPOINTing'

A few words are shown with three underlined syllables, for example 'disqualification' /dɪskwɒlɪfɪkeɪʃᵊn/. In this case, the third underlined syllable will have primary stress, while the secondary stress may be on the first or second syllable:

'DISqualifiCAtion' or 'disQUALifiCAtion'

GenAm usually prefers 'dis-', while RP tends to prefer 'DIS-'.

In the case of compound words, where the pronunciation of each part is given separately, the stress pattern is shown by underlining the headword: 'off-peak', 'first-class', but 'cake pan'.

Stressed syllables

When words are used in context, the way in which they are pronounced depends upon the information units that are constructed by the speaker. For example, a speaker could say:

1 'the reSULT was disapPOINTing'
2 'it was a DISappointing reSULT'
3 'it was VERy disappointing inDEED'

In (3), neither of the two underlined syllables in disappointing /dɪsəpɔ̲ɪntɪŋ/ receives either primary or secondary stress. This shows that it is not possible for a dictionary to predict whether a particular syllable will be stressed in context.

It should be noted, however, that in the case of adjectives with two stressed syllables, the second syllable often loses its stress when it is used before a noun:
'an OFF-peak FARE'
'a FIRST-class SEAT'

Two things should be noted about the marked syllables:

1 They can take primary or secondary stress in a way that is not shared by the other syllables.
2 Whether they are stressed or not, the vowel must be pronounced distinctly; it cannot be weakened to /ə/, /ɪ/ or /ʊ/.

These features are shared by most of the one-syllable words in English, which are therefore transcribed in this dictionary as stressed syllables:
two /tu̲/
inn /ɪ̲n/
tree /tri̲/

Unstressed syllables

It is an important characteristic of English that vowels in unstressed syllables tend not to be pronounced clearly. Many unstressed syllables contain the vowel /ə/, a neutral vowel which is not found in stressed syllables. The vowels /ɪ/ , or /ʊ/, which are relatively neutral in quality, are also common in unstressed syllables.

Single-syllable grammatical words such as 'shall' and 'at' are often pronounced with a weak vowel such as /ə/. However, some of them are pronounced with a more distinct vowel under certain circumstances, for example when they occur at the end of a sentence. This distinct pronunciation is generally referred to as the strong form, and is given in this dictionary after the word STRONG.

shall /ʃəl, STRONG ʃæl/
at /ət, STRONG æt/

List of Grammatical Notations

Word classes

adjective	ADJ	形容词
adverb	ADV	副词
auxiliary verb	AUX	助动词
color word	COLOR	色彩词
combining form	COMB	复合词
conjunction	CONJ	连词
convention	CONVENTION	习惯表达
determiner	DET	限定词
exclamation	EXCLAM	感叹词
fraction	FRACTION	分数词
modal verb	MODAL	情态动词
count noun	N-COUNT	可数名词
collective count noun	N-COUNT-COLL	集体可数名词
family noun	N-FAMILY	家庭成员名词
noun in names	N-IN-NAMES	名称名词
mass noun	N-MASS	集合名词
plural noun	N-PLURAL	复数型名词
proper noun	N-PROPER	专有名词
collective proper noun	N-PROPER-COLL	专有集体名词
singular noun	N-SING	单数型名词
collective singular noun	N-SING-COLL	单数型集体名词
title noun	N-TITLE	头衔名词
uncount noun	N-UNCOUNT	不可数名词
collective uncount noun	N-UNCOUNT-COLL	不可数集体名词
variable noun	N-VAR	有变体名词
collective variable noun	N-VAR-COLL	有变体集体名词
vocative noun	N-VOC	称呼名词
negative	NEG	否定词
number	NUM	数词
ordinal	ORD	序数词
phrasal verb	PHRASAL VERB	动词词组
phrase	PHRASE	习语
predeterminer	PREDET	前置限定词
prefix	PREFIX	前缀
preposition	PREP	介词
pronoun	PRON	代词
emphatic pronoun	PRON-EMPH	强调代词
indefinite pronoun	PRON-INDEF	不定代词
negative indefinite pronoun	PRON-INDEF-NEG	否定不定代词
negative pronoun	PRON-NEG	否定代词
plural pronoun	PRON-PLURAL	复数型代词
possessive pronoun	PRON-POSS	所有格代词
reciprocal pronoun	PRON-RECIP	相互代词
reflexive pronoun	PRON-REFL	反身代词
emphatic reflexive pronoun	PRON-REFL-EMPH	强调反身代词
relative pronoun	PRON-REL	关系代词
singular pronoun	PRON-SING	单数型代词
quantifier	QUANT	数量词
negative quantifier	QUANT-NEG	否定数量词
plural quantifier	QUANT-PLURAL	复数型数量词
question word	QUEST	疑问词
sound word	SOUND	表音词
intransitive verb	V-I	不及物动词
link verb	V-LINK	连系动词
passive verb	V-PASSIVE	被动及物动词
reciprocal verb	V-RECIP	相互动词
passive reciprocal verb	V-RECIP-PASSIVE	被动相互动词
transitive verb	V-T	及物动词
passive transitive verb	V-T PASSIVE	被动及物动词
intransitive or transitive verb	V-T/V-I	及物动词/不及物动词

Words and abbreviations used in patterns

adjective group	**adj**
superlative form	**adj-superl**
adverb group	**adv**
word or phrase indicating an amount of something	**amount**
broad negative	**brd-neg**
clause	**cl**
color word	**color**
comparative form	**compar**
continuous	**cont**
definite noun group	**def-n**
definite noun group with an uncount noun	**def-n-uncount**
definite noun group with a noun in the plural	**def-pl-n**
determiner	**det**
past participle of a verb	**-ed**
noun group, adjective, adverb, or prepositional phrase	**group**
imperative	**imper**
infinitive form of a verb	**inf**
present participle of a verb	**-ing**
interrogative	**interrog**
clause beginning with *like*	**like**
noun or noun group	**n**
names of places or institutions	**names**
negative word	**neg**
proper noun	**n-proper**
number	**num**
uncount noun or noun group with an uncount noun	**n-uncount**
ordinal	**ord**
particle, part of a phrasal verb	**P**
passive voice	**passive**
plural	**pl**
noun in the plural, plural noun group, co-ordinated noun group	**pl-n**
plural number	**pl-num**
possessive	**poss**
prepositional phrase or preposition	**prep**
pronoun	**pron**
indefinite pronoun	**pron-indef**
reflexive pronoun	**pron-refl**
relative pronoun	**pron-rel**
question word	**quest**
singular	**sing**
noun in the singular	**sing-n**
supplementary information accompanying a noun	**supp**
'that'-clause	**that**
the to-infinitive form of a verb	**to-inf**
usually	**usu**
verb or verb group	**v**
continuous verb	**v-cont**
link verb	**v-link**
wh-word, clause beginning with a wh-word	**wh**

Explanation of Grammatical Terms

Introduction

For each use of each word in this dictionary, grammar information is provided. For a very few words, such as abbreviations, contractions and some words of foreign origin, no grammar is given, because the words do not belong to any word class, or are used so freely that every example could be given a different word class, e.g. *AD, ditto, must've.*

The grammar information that is given is of three types:

1 the word class of the word: e.g. **PHRASAL VERB, N-COUNT, ADJ, QUANT**
2 restrictions or extensions to its behavior, compared to other words of that word class: e.g. **usu passive, usu sing, also no det**
3 the patterns that the word most frequently occurs in: e.g. **N *of* n, ADJ that, ADV with v**

For all word classes, the patterns are given immediately before the examples they accompany.

The word class of the word being explained is in CAPITAL LETTERS. The order of items in a pattern is the order in which they normally occur in a sentence. Words in *italics* are words (not word classes) that occur in the pattern. Alternatives are separated by a slash (/).

Word classes

ADJ

An **adjective** can be graded or ungraded, or be in the comparative or the superlative form, e.g. *He has been absent from his desk for two weeks . . . the most accurate description of the killer to date . . . The eldest child was a daughter called Fatiha.*

Adjective patterns

ADJ n The adjective is always used before a noun, e.g. *. . . a governmental agency.*

usu ADJ n The adjective is usually used before a noun. It is sometimes used after a link verb.

v-link ADJ The adjective is used after a link verb such as *be* or *feel*, e.g. *He felt unwell.* Adjectives with this label are sometimes used in other positions such as after the object of a verb such as *make* or *keep*, but never before a noun.

usu v-link ADJ The adjective is usually used after a link verb. It is sometimes used before a noun.

ADJ after v The adjective is used after a verb that is not a link verb, e.g. *I wore a white dress and was barefoot.*

n ADJ The adjective comes immediately after a noun, e.g. *between archaeology proper and science-based archaeology.*

det ADJ The adjective comes immediately after a determiner and before any other adjectives, and sometimes comes before numbers, e.g. *You owe a certain person a sum of money.* If the dictionary does not show that an adjective is used only or mainly in the pattern **ADJ n** and **v-link ADJ**, this means that the adjective is used freely in both patterns.

These main adjective patterns are sometimes combined with other patterns.

ADV

An **adverb** can be graded or ungraded, or be in the comparative or the superlative form. e.g. *Much of our behavior is biologically determined . . . I'll work hard . . . Inflation is below 5% and set to fall further . . . those areas furthest from the coast.*

AUX

An **auxiliary verb** is used with another verb to add particular meanings to that verb, for example, to form the continuous aspect or the passive voice, or to form negatives and interrogatives. The verbs *be, do, get* and *have* have some senses in which they are auxiliary verbs.

COLOR

A **color word** refers to a color. It is like an adjective, e.g. *the blue sky . . . The sky was blue*, and also like a noun, e.g. *She was dressed in red . . . several shades of yellow.*

COMB

A **combining form** is a word which is joined with another word, usually with a hyphen, to form compounds, e.g. *strawberry-flavored, business-speak*. The word class of the compound is also given, e.g. **COMB in ADJ, COMB in N-UNCOUNT.**

CONJ

A **conjunction** usually links elements of the same grammatical type, such as two words or two clauses, e.g. *She and Simon had already gone . . . I sat on the chair to unwrap the package while he stood by.*

CONVENTION

A **convention** is a word or a fixed phrase which is used in conversation, for example when greeting someone, apologizing, or replying, e.g. *hello, sorry, no comment.*

DET

A **determiner** is a word that is used at the beginning of a noun group, e.g. *a tray, more time, some books, this amount*. It can also be used to say who or what something belongs or relates to e.g. *his face, my house*, or to begin a question e.g. *Whose car were they in?*

EXCLAM

An **exclamation** is a word or phrase which is spoken suddenly, loudly, or emphatically in order to express a strong emotion such as shock or anger. Exclamations are often followed by exclamation marks, e.g. *good heavens! Ouch!*

FRACTION

A **fraction** is used in numbers, e.g. *five and a half, two and two thirds;* before *of* and a noun group, e.g. *half of the money, a third of the children, an eighth of* Russia's *grain;* after *in* or *into*, e.g. *in half, into thirds*. A fraction is also used like a count noun, e.g. *two halves, the first quarter of the year.*

MODAL

A **modal** is used before the infinitive form of a verb, e.g. *You may go*. In questions, it comes before the subject, e.g. *Must you speak?* In negatives, it comes before the negative word, e.g. *They would not like this*. It does not inflect, for example, it does not take an *-s* in the third person singular, e.g. *She can swim.*

N-COUNT

A **count noun** has a plural form, usually made by adding -s. When it is singular, it must have a determiner in front of it, such as *the, her,* or *such*, e.g. *My cat is getting fatter . . . She's a good friend.*

N-COUNT-COLL

A **collective count noun** is a count noun which refers to a group of people or things. It behaves like a count noun, but when it is in the singular form it can be used with either a singular or plural verb, e.g. *Their audience are much younger than the average . . . The British audience has a huge appetite for serials . . . Audiences are becoming more selective.*

N-FAMILY

A **family noun** refers to a member of a family, e.g. *father, mommy,* and *granny.* Family nouns are count nouns which are typically used in the singular, and usually follow a possessive determiner. They are also vocative nouns. They are also proper nouns, used with no determiner, e.g. *My mommy likes marzipan . . . Tell them I didn't do it, Mommy . . . Mommy's always telling me I'm too old for dolls.*

N-IN-NAMES

The **noun** occurs **in names** of people, things, or institutions.

N-MASS

A **mass noun** typically combines the behavior of both count and uncount nouns in the same sense. It is used like an uncount noun to refer to a substance. It is used like a count noun to refer to a brand or type, e.g. *Rinse in cold water to remove any remaining detergent . . . Wash it in hot water with a good detergent . . . We used several different detergents in our stain-removal tests.*

N-PLURAL

A **plural noun** is always plural, and is used with plural verbs. If a pronoun is used to stand for the noun, it is a plural pronoun such as *they* or *them*, e.g. *These clothes are ready to wear . . . He expressed his condolences to the families of people who died in the incident.* Plural nouns which end in *-s* usually lose the *-s* when they come in front of another noun, e.g. *pants, pants leg.* If they refer to a single object which has two main parts, such as *jeans* and *glasses,* the expression *a pair of* is sometimes used, e.g. *a pair of jeans.* This is shown as **N-PLURAL: also** *a pair of* **N**.

N-PROPER

A **proper noun** refers to one person, place, thing, or institution, and begins with a capital letter. Many proper nouns are used without a determiner, e.g. . . . *Earth*; some must be used with *the*, and this is indicated: **N-PROPER,** *the* **N**, e.g. *the* UK.

N-PROPER-COLL

A **collective proper noun** is a proper noun which refers to a group of people or things. It can be used with either a singular or a plural verb, e.g. *The Senate is expected to pass the bill shortly . . . The Houses of Parliament are the British parliament.*

N-SING

A **singular noun** is always singular, and needs a determiner, e.g. . . . *to respect the environment . . . Maureen was the epitome of sophistication.* When only *a* or *the* is used, this is indicated: **N-SING: a N** or **N-SING:** *the* **N**, e.g. *The traffic slowed to a crawl . . . We dropped to the ground.*

N-SING-COLL

A **collective singular noun** is a singular noun which refers to a group of people or things. It behaves like a singular noun, but can be used with either a singular or plural verb, e.g. *The enemy were pursued for two miles . . . Their defense has now conceded 12 goals in six games.*

N-TITLE

A **title noun** is used to refer to someone who has a particular role or position. Titles come before the name of the person and begin with a capital letter, e.g. *The Chancellor of the Exchequer.*

N-UNCOUNT

An **uncount noun** refers to things that are not normally counted or considered to be individual items. Uncount nouns do not have a plural form, and are used with a singular verb. They do not need determiners, e.g. . . . *an area of outstanding natural beauty.*

N-UNCOUNT-COLL

A **collective uncount noun** is an uncount noun which refers to a group of people or things. It behaves like an uncount noun, but can be used with either a singular or plural verb, e.g. . . . *Hearts is one of the four suits in a pack of playing cards . . . Hearts are trumps.*

N-VAR

A **variable noun** typically combines the behavior of both count and uncount nouns in the same sense (see **N-COUNT, N-UNCOUNT**). The singular form occurs freely both with and without determiners. Variable nouns also have a plural form, usually made by adding *-s*. Some variable nouns when used like uncount nouns refer to abstract things like *hardship* and *technology,* and when used like count nouns refer to individual examples or instances of that thing, e.g. *Technology is changing fast . . . They should be allowed to wait for cheaper technologies to be developed.* Others refer to objects which can be mentioned either individually or generally, like *potato* and *salad:* you can talk about *a potato, potatoes,* or *potato.*

N-VAR-COLL

A **collective variable noun** is a variable noun which refers to a group of people or things. It behaves like a variable noun, but when it is singular it can be used with either a singular or a plural verb, e.g. *The management is doing its best to improve the situation.*

N-VOC

A **vocative noun** is used when speaking directly to someone or writing to them. Vocative nouns do not need a determiner, but some may be used with a possessive determiner, e.g. *Thank you, darling . . . How are you, my darling?*

NEG see PRON-INDEF-NEG, PRON-NEG, QUANT-NEG

NUM

A **number** is a word such as *three* and *hundred.* Numbers such as *one, two, three* are used like determiners, e.g. *three bears;* like adjectives, e.g. *the four horsemen;* like pronouns, e.g. *She has three cases and I have two*; and like quantifiers, e.g. *Six of the boys stayed behind.* Numbers such as *hundred, thousand, million* always follow a determiner or another number, e.g. *two hundred people, the thousand horsemen, She has a thousand dollars and I have a million, A hundred of the boys stayed behind.*

ORD

An **ordinal** is a type of number. Ordinals are used like adjectives, e.g. *He was the third victim;* like pronouns, e.g. *the second of the two teams;* like adverbs, e.g. *The other team came first*; and like determiners, e.g. *Fourth place goes to Timmy.*

PHRASAL VERB

A **phrasal verb** consists of a verb and one or more particles e.g. *look after, look back, look down on.* Some phrasal verbs are reciprocal, link or passive verbs.

PHRASE

Phrases are groups of words which are used together with little variation and which have a meaning of their own, e.g. *The emergency services were working against the clock.*

PREDET

A **predeterminer** is used in a noun group before *a, the,* or another determiner, e.g. *What a terrific idea! . . . both the children . . . all his life.*

PREFIX

A **prefix** is a letter or group of letters, such as *un-* or *ultra-*, which is added to the beginning of a word in order to form another word. For example, the prefix *un-* is added to *happy* to form *unhappy*

PREP

A **preposition** begins a prepositional phrase and is followed by a noun group or a present participle. Patterns for prepositions are shown in the dictionary only if they are restricted in some way. For example, if a preposition occurs only before a present participle, it is shown as **PREP -ing**.

PREP-PHRASE

A **phrasal preposition** is a phrase which behaves like a preposition, e.g. *Prices vary <u>according to</u> the quantity ordered.*

PRON

Pronouns are used like noun groups, to refer to someone or something that has already been mentioned or whose identity is known, e.g. *They produced their own shampoos and hair-care products, <u>all</u> based on herbal recipes . . . two bedrooms, <u>each</u> with three beds.* Some pronouns are further classified, for example as **PRON-EMPH, PRON-INDEF,** and so on.

PRON-EMPH

Emphatic pronouns are words like *all*, *both*, and *each*, when they are used to emphasize another noun or pronoun, e.g. *We <u>each</u> have different needs and interests . . . I wish you both a good trip.*

PRON-INDEF

Indefinite pronouns are words like *anyone*, *anything*, *everyone*, and *something*, e.g. *Why would <u>anyone</u> want that job? . . . after <u>everything</u> else in his life had changed.*

PRON-INDEF-NEG

Negative indefinite pronouns are words like *none*, *no-one*, and *nothing*, e.g. *He searched for a sign of recognition on her face, but there was <u>none</u> . . . Do our years together mean <u>nothing</u>?*

PRON-NEG

Negative pronouns are words like *neither*, e.g. *Neither seemed likely to be aware of my absence for long.*

PRON-PLURAL

Plural pronouns are the plural personal pronouns, which include *we*, *us*, *they*, and *them*, e.g. *Neither of <u>us</u> forgot about it.*

PRON-POSS

A **possessive pronoun** is used to say who or what something belongs to or relates to. The possessive pronouns are *mine*, *yours*, *his*, *hers*, *ours* and *theirs*, e.g. *That wasn't his fault, it was <u>mine</u> . . . The author can report other people's results which more or less agree with <u>hers</u>.*

PRON-RECIP

The **reciprocal pronouns** are *each other* and *one another*, e.g. *We looked at <u>each other</u> in silence.*

PRON-REFL

Reflexive pronouns are pronouns which are used as the object of a verb or preposition when they refer to the same person or thing as the subject of the verb. They are used in the same positions as other pronouns. The reflexive pronouns are *myself*, *yourself*, *himself*, *herself*, *itself*, *oneself*, *ourselves*, *yourselves*, and *themselves*, e.g. *I asked <u>myself</u> what I would have done in such a situation . . . One must apply <u>oneself</u> to the present.*

PRON-REFL-EMPH

Emphatic reflexive pronouns are reflexive pronouns which are used for emphasis, often after another pronoun or at the end of a clause, e.g. *A wealthy man like yourself is bound to make an enemy or two along the way . . . The president himself is on a visit to Beijing . . . I made it myself.*

PRON-REL

Relative pronouns are words like *which* and *who*, that introduce relative clauses. They are the subject or object of the verb in the relative clause, or the object of a preposition, e.g. *. . . those who eat out for a special occasion . . . The largest asteroid is Ceres, which is about a quarter the size of the moon.*

PRON-SING

Singular pronouns are the singular personal pronouns, which include *I, me, he, him, she, her, it,* and *one*, e.g. *He didn't mean to be cruel but I cried my eyes out.*

QUANT

A **quantifier** comes before *of* and a noun group, e.g. *most of the house.* If there are any restrictions on the type of noun group, this is indicated: **QUANT** *of* **def-n** means that the quantifier occurs before *of* and a definite noun group, e.g. *Most of the kids have never seen the sea.*

QUANT-NEG

Negative quantifiers are words like *neither*, e.g. *Neither of us felt like going out.*

QUANT-PLURAL

Plural quantifiers are words like *billions* and *millions* which are followed by *of* and a noun group, e.g. *. . . for billions of years.*

QUEST

A **question word** is a wh-word that is used to begin a question, e.g. *Why didn't he stop me?*

SOUND

Sound words are used before or after verbs such as *go* and *say*, e.g. *Suddenly there was a loud crack.*

SUFFIX

A **suffix** is a letter or group of letters such as *-ly* or *-ness*, which is added to the end of a word in order to form a new word, usually of a different word class, e.g. *quick, quickly.*

V-I

An **intransitive verb** is one which takes an indirect object or no object, e.g. *The problems generally fall into two categories . . . As darkness fell outside, they sat down to eat.*

V-LINK

A **link verb** connects a subject and a complement. Most link verbs do not occur in the passive voice, e.g. *be, become, taste, feel.*

V-RECIP

Reciprocal verbs describe processes in which two or more people, groups, or things interact mutually: they do the same thing to each other, or participate jointly in the same action or event. Reciprocal verbs are used where the subject is both participants, e.g. *Fred and Sally met . . .* The participants can also be referred to separately, e.g. *Fred met Sally . . . Fred argued with Sally.* These patterns are reciprocal because they also mean that *Sally met Fred* and *Sally argued with Fred.* Note that many reciprocal verbs can also be used in a way that is not reciprocal. For example, *Fred and Sally kissed* is reciprocal, but *Fred kissed Sally* is not reciprocal (because it does not mean that Sally also kissed Fred).

V-RECIP-PASSIVE

A **passive reciprocal verb** behaves like both a passive verb and a reciprocal verb, e.g. *He never believed he and Susan would be reconciled.*

V-T

A **transitive verb** is one which takes a direct object, e.g. *He mailed me the contract.*

V-T PASSIVE

A **passive verb** occurs in the passive voice only, e.g. *The company is rumored to be a takeover target.*

V-T/V-I

Some verbs may be **transitive** or **intransitive** depending on how they are used, e.g. *He opened the window and looked out... The flower opens to reveal a bee.*

Words and abbreviations used in patterns

In a pattern, the element in capital letters represents the word in the entry. All the other elements are in small letters. Items in *italics* show the actual word that is used, such as *of*. Items in roman print show the word class or type of clause that is used. For example:

> **N** *of* **n** means that the word being explained is a noun (**N**), and it is followed in the sentence by the word *of* and another noun or noun group (**n**).
> **ADV adj/adv** means that the word being explained is an adverb (**ADV**), and it is followed in the sentence by an adjective (**adj**) or (/) another adverb (**adv**).

When the word in the entry occurs in a pattern, the element in capital letters is **N** for any kind of noun, **ADJ** for any kind of adjective, and so on. **PHR** is used for a phrase, and **N** is used to represent a noun in a phrase.

Words used to structure information in patterns

after: **after v** means after a verb. The word is used either immediately after the verb, or after the verb and another word or phrase, or in a marked position at the beginning of the clause. For example, the adverb **mildly** is used:

> immediately after a verb: *Have a nice time, dear, and drive carefully.*
> after a verb and its object: *Use a flash and position the camera carefully.*
> at the beginning of a clause: *Carefully make a cut with a small knife.*

The phrase **on hold** is used:

> immediately after a verb: *Everything is on hold until we know more.*
> after a verb and its object: *He put his retirement on hold.*

also: used with some nouns to show that the word is used in a way that is not typical of that type of noun. For example, **also N in pl** means that unlike most uncount nouns, this noun also has a plural form and use. **Also** is used with some adverbs and adjectives to show a pattern that is less common than the other patterns mentioned. For example, **usu ADV with v, also ADV adj** means that the adverb is usually used with a verb but is also used before an adjective.

before: **before v** means before a verb. The word is used before the main element in a verb group. For example, the adverb **already** is used:

> before the whole verb group: *those who already know of the delights of skiing.*
> immediately before the main element in the group: *They had already voted for him at the first ballot.*

no: used to indicate that a verb is not used in a particular way, for example **no passive**, or that a singular noun is also used without a determiner: **also no det.**

oft: used to indicate that a word or phrase often occurs in a particular pattern or behaves in a particular way.

only: used to indicate that a verb is always used in a particular way, for example **only cont.**

usu: used to indicate that a word or phrase usually occurs in a particular pattern or behaves in a particular way.

with: **with** is used when the position of a word or phrase is not fixed. This means that the word or phrase sometimes comes before the named word class and sometimes comes after it. For example, **quickly** at **quick 1** has the pattern **ADV** *with* **v**. It occurs:

after the verb: *Cussane worked quickly and methodically;*
before the verb: *She quickly looked away and stared down at her hands.*

In addition, **with cl** is used when the word sometimes occurs at the beginning of the clause, sometimes at the end, and sometimes in the middle. For example, **seriously** has the pattern **ADV with cl.** It occurs:

at the beginning of the clause: *Seriously, I only watch TV in the evenings.*
at the end of the clause: *All of us react favorably to those who take our views seriously.*
in the middle of the clause: *This approach is now seriously out of step with the times.*

Elements used in patterns

adj: stands for **adjective group.** This may be one word, such as "happy", or a group of words, such as "very happy" or "as happy as I have ever been".

e.g. **adj N: read** 8 . . . *Ben Okri's latest novel is a good read.*

adj-compar: stands for **comparative adjective.** This is used to indicate an adjective group with the comparative form of the adjective.

e.g. ADJ-compar *than*: **old** 2 . . . *Bill was six years older than David.*

adj-superl: stands for **superlative adjective**. It is used to indicate an adjective group with the superlative form of the adjective.

e.g. **ADV adj-superl: positively** 1 . . . *This is positively the last chance for the industry to establish such a system.*

e.g. **ORD adj-superl: second** 2 . . . *the party is still the second strongest in Italy.*

adv: stands for **adverb group.** This may be one word, such as "slowly", or a group of words, such as "extremely slowly" or "more slowly than ever".

e.g. **adv ADV: else** 1 . . . *I never wanted to live anywhere else.*

amount: means **word or phrase indicating an amount of something,** such as "a lot", "nothing", "three percent", "four hundred pounds", "more", or "much".

e.g. **amount** *and* **ADV: above** 2 . . . *Banks have been charging 25 percent and above for unsecured loans.*

brd-neg: stands for **broad negative,** that is, a clause which is negative in meaning. It may contain a negative element such as "no-one", "never", or "hardly", or may show that it is negative in some other way.

e.g. **oft with brd-neg: approve** 1 . . . *Not everyone approves of the festival.*

cl: stands for **clause.**

e.g. **cl ADV: anyway** 4 . . . *What do you want from me, anyway?*

color: means **color word**, such as "red", "green", or "blue".

e.g. **ADJ color: pastel** . . . *pastel pink, blue, peach, and green.*

compar: stands for **comparative form of an adjective or adverb.**

e.g. **ADV compar: even** 2 . . . *On television he made an even stronger impact as an interviewer.*

cont: stands for **continuous.** It is used when indicating that a verb is always, usually, or never used in the continuous.

e.g. **only cont: die** 4 . . . *I'm dying for a breath of fresh air.*

no cont: adore 1 . . . *She adored her parents and would do anything to please them.*

def-n: stands for **definite noun group.** A definite noun group is a noun group that refers to a specific person or thing, or a specific group of people or things, that is known and identified.

e.g. **QUANT** *of* **def-n: whole** 1 . . . *I was cold throughout the whole of my body.*

def-pl-n: stands for **definite noun group with a noun in the plural.**

e.g. **QUANT** *of* **def-pl-n: many** 1 . . . *It seems there are not very many of them left in the sea.*

det: stands for **determiner.** A determiner is a word that comes at the beginning of a noun group, such as "the", "her", or "those".

e.g. **det ADJ: following** 2 . . . *We went to dinner the following Monday evening.*

-ed: stands for **past participle of a verb,** such as "decided", "gone", or "taken".

e.g. **ADV -ed: freshly** . . . *freshly baked bread.*

group: stands for **noun group, adjective, adverb, or prepositional phrase.**

e.g. **ADV group: strictly** . . . *He seemed fond of her in a strictly professional way.*

imper: stands for **imperative.** It is used when indicating that a verb is always or usually used in the imperative.

e.g. **only imper** and **inf: beware** . . . *Beware of being too impatient with others.*

inf: stands for **infinitive form of a verb,** such as "decide", "go", or "sit".

e.g. **ADJ to-inf: duty-bound** . . . *I felt duty-bound to help.*

ADV to-inf: yet 7: . . . *She has yet to spend a Christmas with her husband.*

-ing: stands for **present participle of a verb,** such as "deciding", "going", or "taking".

e.g. **PREP -ing: before** 2 . . . *He spent his early life in Sri Lanka before moving to Canada.*

it : means an "introductory" or "dummy" *it*. It does not refer to anything in a previous sentence or in the world; it may refer to what is coming later in the clause or it may refer to things in general.

e.g. **oft** *it* **v-link ADJ to-inf: nice** 7 . . . *It's nice to meet you.*

n: stands for **noun** or **noun group.** If the **n** element occurs in a pattern with something that is part of a noun group, such as an adjective or another noun, it represents a noun. If the **n** element occurs in a pattern with something that is not part of a noun group, such as a verb or preposition, it represents a noun group. The noun group can be of any kind, including a pronoun.

e.g. **ADJ n: abiding:** . . . *He has a genuine and abiding love of the craft.*

names: means **names of places or institutions.**

e.g. **oft in names: requiem** 2 . . . *a performance of Verdi's Requiem.*

neg: stands for **negative words,** such as "not", or "never".

e.g. **with neg: dream** 6 . . . *I wouldn't dream of making fun of you.*

n-proper: stands for **proper noun.** A proper noun is the name of a particular person or thing.

e.g. usu **n-proper N: lookalike** . . . a Marilyn Monroe lookalike.

num: stands for **number.**

e.g. **num ADV: odd** 3 . . . *How many pages was it, 500 odd?*

n-uncount: stands for **uncount noun** or **noun group with an uncount noun.** An uncount noun is a noun which has no plural form and which is sometimes used with no determiner.

e.g. **QUANT** of **n-uncount: touch** 13 . . . *She thought she just had a touch of flu.*

ord: stands for **ordinal**, such as "first", or "second".

e.g. **ord ADJ n: generation** 4 . . . *second generation Jamaicans in New York.*

passive: stands for **passive voice.** It is used when indicating that a verb usually or never occurs in the passive voice.

e.g. **usu passive: expel** 1 . . . *More than five-thousand high school students have been expelled for cheating.*

pl: stands for **plural.**

pl-n: stands for **noun in the plural, plural noun group**, or **co-ordinate noun group** (two or more noun groups joined by a co-ordinating conjunction).

e.g. **PREP pl-n: between** 2 . . . *I spent a lot of time in the early Eighties travelling between Waco and El Paso.*

pl-num: stands for **plural number.** A plural number is a number which is used only in the plural.

e.g. **PREP poss pl-num: in** 5 . . . *young people in their twenties.*

poss: stands for **possessive.** Possessives which come before the noun may be a possessive determiner, such as "my", "her", or "their", or a possessive formed from a noun group, such as "the horse's". Possessives which come after the noun are of the form "*of* n", such as "of the horse".

e.g. **usu pl, with poss: ancestor** 1 . . . *our daily lives, so different from those of our ancestors.*

prep: stands for **prepositional phrase** or **preposition.**

prep PRON: him 1 . . . *Is Sam there? Let me talk to him.*

pron: stands for **pronoun.** A pronoun is a word such as "I", "it", or "them" which is used like a noun group. It refers to someone or something that has already been mentioned or whose identity is known.

e.g. **PREP pron: before** 12 . . . *Everyone in the room knew it was the single hardest task before them.*

pron-indef: stands for **indefinite pronoun**. An indefinite pronoun is a word like *anyone, anything, everyone* and *something.*

e.g. **pron-indef ADJ: else** 2 . . . *I expect everyone else to be truthful.*

pron-refl: stands for **reflexive pronoun,** such as "yourself", "herself", or "ourselves".

e.g. **PREP pron-refl: among** 9 . . . *The girls stood aside, talking among themselves.*

quest: stands for **question word.** A question word is a wh-word such as "what", "how", or "why" which is used to begin a question.

e.g. **quest ADV: ever** 6 . . . *Why ever didn't you tell me?*

sing: stands for **singular**.

sing-n: stands for **noun in the singular**.

e.g. **PREDET det sing-n: all** 2 . . . *She's worked all her life.*

supp: stands for **supplementary information accompanying a noun.** Supplementary information that comes before a noun may be given by a determiner, possessive, adjective, or noun modifier. Supplementary information that comes after the noun may be given by a prepositional phrase or a clause.

e.g. **supp N: park** 2 . . . *a science and technology park.*

that: stands for **"that"-clause**. The clause may begin with the word "that", but does not necessarily do so.

e.g. **usu N that: conviction** 1 . . . *It is our conviction that a step forward has been taken.*

to-inf: stands for **to-infinitive form of a verb**.

e.g. **v-link ADJ to-inf: inclined** 2 . . . *I am inclined to agree with Alan.*

v: stands for **verb or verb group**. It is not used to represent a link verb. See also the explanations of **after, before** and **with**.

e.g.**v PRON: her** 1 . . . *I told her I had something to say.*

v PREP n: at 10 . . . *She opened the door and stood there, frowning at me.*

v-link: stands for **link verb**. A link verb is a verb such as "be" which connects a subject and a complement.

e.g. **v-link ADJ: down** 3 . . . *The computer's down again.*

wh: stands for **wh-word**, or **clause beginning with a wh-word**, such as "what", "why", "when", "how", "if", or "whether".

e.g. **ADJ** *about* **n/wh: tight-lipped** 1 . . . *Military officials are still tight-lipped about when their forces will launch a ground offensive.*

Activity Guide Contents

1. USING YOUR BRAIN

Word Web Activities Choosing the Right Definition	Word Link Activities Practice with Pragmatics

1. Word Web Activities

Use the Word Web feature entitled *brain* to answer the following questions about the brain.

a. Which part tells you it's time to eat? ________

b. Which part helps you learn to speak? ________

c. Which part makes sure you stand up straight? ________

d. Which part controls your heartbeat? ________

e. Which part is wrapped around the outside of the brain? ________

2. Choosing the Right Definition

Study definitions 1–4 for "brain." Then write the number of the definition that relates to each sentence below.

a. ____ Angela mastered the new computer program in one day. She has brains!

b. ____ Some studies show that people with larger brains are more intelligent than people with smaller brains.

c. ____ They say that Martin is the brains behind the success of the company.

d. ____ If you'll just use your brain you'll make the right decision.

e. ____ In proportion to the size of its body, the elephant's brain is very small.

3. Word Link Activities

a. The definition of brain says that it "enables you to think." The prefix in the word *enable* is ________.

b. Find the Word Link for this prefix. What does the prefix mean? ________

c. What two other words with this prefix do you find?

________ ________

Guess what each word means. Then check your answers by looking up the words.

4. **Practice with Pragmatics**

Study the information about the fourth meaning in the definition of *brain*.
Read the four sentences below. Write *Yes* if the sentence uses the term appropriately, and *No* if the usage is inappropriate.

a. _____ I think Anna was the brains behind the kids' plan to skip school on Friday.

b. _____ History states that Einstein was the brains behind the discovery of the theory of relativity.

c. _____ The president said that the governor was the brains behind the economic recovery in her state.

d. _____ I supplied the money, but Mike was the brains behind the surprise party.

ANSWER KEY:

1. **a.** medulla oblongata; **b.** cerebrum; **c.** cerebellum; **d.** medulla oblongata; **e.** cerebrum
2. **a.** 3; **b.** 1; **c.** 4; **d.** 2; **e.** 1
3. **a.** -en; **b.** making, putting; **c.** enact, encode
4. **a.** Yes; **b.** No; **c.** No; **d.** Yes

2. GOING IN CIRCLES

Grammar Activities Picture Dictionary Activities	Word Link Activities

1. Grammar Activities

Many different words are based on the word *circle*. Write the part of speech of each underlined word—noun, verb, or adjective. Use your dictionary to check your answers.

a. The moon was perfectly circular last night. ______

b. The students arranged the chairs in a circle. ______

c. Vitamin E improves the circulation of the blood. ______

d. Airplanes sometimes circle several times before landing. ______

e. Please open the window so the air can circulate. ______

f. What is the circulation of the *New York Times*? ______

g. Did the teacher circle your mistakes? ______

h. I like circular eyeglasses, not square ones. ______

2. Picture Dictionary Activities—A

a. How many other shapes can you think of besides the circle? Write your list below.

____

Look at the Picture Dictionary feature for *shapes* and check your answers.

b. Which two shapes most closely resemble the circle?

______ ______

3. Picture Dictionary Activities—B

Study the Picture Dictionary feature titled *area*. Pay special attention to how to find the area of a circle.

a. What do you call the distance from the center of the circle to the outside edge? ______

b. What do you call the line that runs around the outside of the circle? ______

c. What do you call the line that runs across the circle from one side to the other? ______

d. What is the formula for finding the area of a circle? ______

e. If a circle has a radius of 3 inches, what is its area? Use $\pi = 3.14$. ______

4. **Word Link Activities**

a. The first four letters of the word *circle* form a Word Link. Look at the information in the Word Link for *circ-*.
What words besides *circle* appear there? __________ __________

b. Rewrite each word below. Then look it up in the dictionary and identify it as *verb*, *noun*, or *adjective*.

__________, __________ __________, __________
(word) (part of speech) (word) (part of speech)

c. Complete each sentence below with the correct word from **b.**

1. Blood __________ around the body.
2. A tree fell on the power lines and broke the electrical __________.

ANSWER KEY:

1. **a.** adjective; **b.** noun; **c.** noun; **d.** verb; **e.** verb; **f.** noun; **g.** verb; **h.** adjective
2. **a.** Answers will vary; **b.** ellipse, oval
3. **a.** radius; **b.** circumference; **c.** diameter; **d.** πr^2; **e.** 28.26 inches
4. **a.** circuit, circulate; **b.** circuit, noun; circulate, verb; **c1.** circulates; **c2.** circuit

3. TRANSPORTATION

Choosing the Right Definition Word Web Activities	Dictionary Research Word Link Activities

1. **Choosing the Right Definition**

   Study the numbered definitions for *transportation*. Then write the number of the definition that relates to each sentence below.

   a. _____ The transportation of nuclear waste through large cities can be dangerous.

   b. _____ Using mass transportation helps the environment.

   c. _____ Many schools provide transportation for children in the form of school buses.

   d. _____ Subways provide rapid transportation.

   e. _____ Bad weather slows down most forms of transportation.

2. **Word Web Activities**

   Use the Word Web feature titled *ship* to answer the following questions. Look up these words in the dictionary to check your answers.

   a. What do you call things other than people that are carried on ships? _________

   b. What do you call the place where a ship stops? _________

   c. What do you call the person who steers a large ship? _________

   d. What do you call the place where a plane can land on a large ship? _________

3. **Dictionary Research**

   a. Reread the definition of *transportation*. Write your own definition of the word *goods* as it is used in the definition.

   ____

   b. Look up the word *goods* in the dictionary and complete these sentences.

   Goods are things that people make and then later _________.

   Goods are things that people _________ and can move from one place to another.

4. **Word Link Activities**

The first four letters of the word *transportation* form a Word Link. Look at the information in the Word Link for *trans-*.

a. What does the Word Link *trans-* mean? ________

b. What are the three Word Links for *trans*?

________ ________ ________

c. Complete each sentence below with the correct word from b. Check your answers by looking up each word in the dictionary.

1. I don't know how to read Chinese. Can you ________ this letter for me?
2. After the president of the college left, there was a period of ________ before a new one was appointed.
3. You'll have to take two buses to get there. You can ________ from the 101 to the 145 at Main Street.

ANSWER KEY:

1. **a.** 3; **b.** 2; **c.** 1; **d.** 2; **e.** 3
2. **a.** cargo; **b.** port; **c.** captain; **d.** flight deck
3. **a.** Answers will vary.; **b.** sell, own
4. **a.** across; **b.** transfer, transition, translate; **c1.** translate; **c2.** transition; **c3.** transfer

4. TRIAL BY JURY

Dictionary Research Word Web Activities Word Partnership Activities	Word Link Activities Choosing the Right Definition

1. Dictionary Research

Study the first numbered definition for the word *trial*. Think about the meaning of the four words listed below. Then match each word with the correct definition. Look up these words in the dictionary if you are not sure.

_____ **a.** judge
_____ **b.** guilty
_____ **c.** jury
_____ **d.** evidence

1. something you see that causes you to believe something is true
2. a person who decides how a law is applied
3. responsible for a crime
4. group of people who decide if a person is guilty or not

If a person is accused of a crime and a grand jury calls for a trial, the defendant must appear in court. Study the information in the definitions for *appear*. Then write the number of the definition that relates to each sentence below.

_____ **e.** The sun finally appeared at about 11:00 in the morning.
_____ **f.** Clive appeared in court on Monday morning at 9:00.
_____ **g.** My favorite band appeared at the Roxy last weekend.
_____ **h.** Linda appears to be very healthy.

2. Word Web Activities

Study the Word Web feature titled *trial*. Then use bold words from this Word Web feature to complete the following sentences. Look up any words you aren't sure of.

a. The defendant will get a trial by _________.
b. The defendant may or may not _________ guilty.
c. The person who accused the defendant is the _________.
d. The _________ will tell what they know about the crime.
e. The words the witnesses say is called their _________.
f. In the end, the judge will deliver a _________.

3. **Word Partnership Activities**

Study the Word Partnerships feature for the word *jury*. Pay special attention to the phrases below. Then match each phrase with the correct definition. Look up the words in the dictionary if you are not sure.

_____ **a.** jury convicts
_____ **b.** hung jury
_____ **c.** jury duty

1. a jury that can't agree on a verdict
2. a jury finds someone guilty
3. a citizen's obligation to serve on a jury

4. **Word Link Activities**

Look up the word *illegal*. Then, study the Word Link feature for the root *il-*.

a. What definition do you find for the root *il-*? ____________

Which of the words means the following?
Look up the words in the dictionary if you are not sure.

b. a person who is unable to read ____________
c. something that is against the law ____________

5. **Choosing the Right Definition**

Study definitions 1–4 for *trial*. Then write the number of the definition that relates to each sentence below.

a. _____ Sitting through that movie was a real trial for me.
b. _____ You should give aspirin a trial before you ask for anything stronger.
c. _____ The murderer's trial lasted for six weeks.
d. _____ The boss gave me a three-week trial to see if I could handle the responsibilities.

ANSWER KEY:

1. **a.** 2; **b.** 3; **c.** 4; **d.** 1; **e.** 3; **f.** 7; **g.** 6; **h.** 2
2. **a.** jury; **b.** plead; **c.** plaintiff; **d.** witnesses; **e.** testimony; **f.** verdict
3. **a.** 2; **b.** 1; **c.** 3
4. **a.** not; **b.** illiterate; **c.** illegal
5. **a.** 3; **b.** 2; **c.** 1; **d.** 2

5. NEWSPAPER

Word Web Activities	Word Link Activities
Thesaurus Activities	Choosing the Right Definition
Dictionary Research	Grammar Activities

1. Word Web Activities

Study the information in the Word Web feature entitled *newspaper*.
Then answer the questions below. Write T for *true* or F for *false*.

_____ **a.** The *Weekly Journal* was a British newspaper.
_____ **b.** This newspaper contained some anti-British stories.
_____ **c.** The British governor went to prison.
_____ **d.** Zenger was found guilty.
_____ **e.** The first amendment to the Constitution guarantees the freedom of the press.

2. Thesaurus Activities

The two words below are sometimes used to describe an article in a newspaper:

- story
- report

Read the dictionary definition for the word *story*. Then study the thesaurus feature for this word.

a. Which numbered meanings of the word *story* apply to a newspaper story? _________

b. What two words does the thesaurus give relating to the second definition? _________

Look up any of these words that you don't understand.

Read the dictionary definition for the word *report*. Then study the thesaurus feature for this word.

c. Which numbered meanings of the word *report* apply to a newspaper story? _________

3. Dictionary Research

Review the Word Web feature entitled *newspaper*. Then look up the word *article*. Study the five meanings. Write the number of the meaning that relates to the underlined word in each sentence.

_____ **a.** Some people disagreed with several articles in the U.S. Constitution.
_____ **b.** The use of the definite article can be confusing at times.
_____ **c.** There were two articles about the football game in today's newspaper.
_____ **d.** Words starting with a consonant sound take the article *a*.
_____ **e.** We left several articles in the trunk of our rental car.

4. **Word Link Activities**

Read the definitions of the following item as it appears in the dictionary after the word *news*:

- news conference

Then answer the questions about these words.

a. Look up the Word Link for *con-* as in *convene*. What does *con-* mean? ______

b. Which of the example words after *con-* means "to call a meeting together?" ______

c. Which of the example words means "general agreement?" ______

5. **Choosing the Right Definition**

Look up the word *news* and study definitions 1–4. Write the number of the definition that relates to how the word *news* is used in each sentence below.

_____ **a.** The fire in the public library was big news.

_____ **b.** I saw a full report on the news last night.

_____ **c.** News about the economy is always on page 2.

_____ **d.** I have some good news to tell you.

6. **Grammar Activities**

Read the dictionary entry for *report* and also read the surrounding entries that contain the word *report*. Then write the word forms described below using the root word *report*.

a. A noun that means the same as "newspaper article." ______

b. An adjective form of the word *report* as in the phrase "a ________ fire." ______

c. A noun that describes a person who writes newspaper stories. ______

d. A verb that tells what a reporter does. A reporter ________. ______

ANSWER KEY:

1. **a.** F; **b.** T; **c.** F; **d.** F; **e.** T
2. **a.** 2, 5; **b.** account, report; **c.** 2, 3
3. **a.** 3; **b.** 4; **c.** 1; **d.** 4; **e.** 2
4. **a.** together; **b.** convene; **c.** consensus
5. **a.** 4; **b.** 3; **c.** 2; **d.** 1
6. **a.** report; **b.** reported; **c.** reporter; **d.** reports

6. THE HUMAN BODY

Choosing the Right Definition Picture Dictionary Activities	Word Partnership Activities Word Link Activities

1. Choosing the Right Definition

Study the definitions for the word *body*. Then write the number of the definition that relates to each sentence below.

_____ **a.** Congress is the largest law-making body in the country.
_____ **b.** My arms and legs got sunburned, but my body didn't.
_____ **c.** The introduction was interesting, but the body of the essay was boring.
_____ **d.** This beer has real body!
_____ **e.** When you dive into a pool, your whole body goes under the water.
_____ **f.** The Library of Congress contains a large body of information about American history.
_____ **g.** The body of the plane was painted blue, but the wings were bright red.
_____ **h.** The police found a body buried in the back yard.
_____ **i.** The Pacific Ocean is the largest body of water in the world.
_____ **j.** There is a small body of sports fans who like to watch violent wrestling matches.

2. Picture Dictionary Activities

a. How many parts of the human body can you name? Start with the head and finish with the foot. Write your list below.

____

Look at the Picture Dictionary feature for *body*. Which parts of the body did you miss?

____

b. What are the four parts of the leg shown in the picture?

____

c. What are the three parts of the arm shown in the picture?

____

3. Word Partnership Activities

Look up the word *knee* in the dictionary.

a. What is the plural form of the word *knee*? ________
b. What is the past tense form of the verb *knee*? ________

Study the Word Partnership feature for *knee*. Then complete the four sentences below using the word *knee* before or after one of these words: *bent*, *injury*, *left*, *weak*. Use each of these words one time.

c. Luke sprained his ________ ________ skiing.
d. I'm getting sick. I feel dizzy and ________ ________.
e. He suffered a minor ________ ________ at Friday's game.
f. My trainer says it's important to keep my ________ ________ when lifting weights.

4. **Word Link Activities**

The definition of *body* says that it is all of your "physical" parts. Read the definition of *physical* and then study the Word Link that accompanies it.

a. What does the Word Link *physi* mean? ________

b. What synonym for *doctor* appears in the Word Link? ________

ANSWER KEY:

1. **a.** 4; **b.** 2; **c.** 6; **d.** 10; **e.** 1; **f.** 9; **g.** 7; **h.** 3; **i.** 8; **j.** 5
2. **a.** Answers will vary.; **b.** foot, ankle, knee, thigh; **c.** hand, wrist, elbow
3. **a.** knees; **b.** kneed; **c.** left knee; **d.** weak-kneed; **e.** knee injury; **f.** knees bent
4. **a.** of nature; **b.** physician

7. ORCHESTRA

Word Web Activities Word Partnership Activities Word Link Activities	Choosing the Right Definition Dictionary Research

1. **Word Web Activities**

   Study the information in the Word Web feature entitled *orchestra*. Then answer the questions below. Write T for *true* or F for *false*.

   _____ **a.** A symphony orchestra usually has more than 100 players.
   _____ **b.** The largest section of the orchestra is the string section.
   _____ **c.** The double bass plays in the string section.
   _____ **d.** The brass section needs to play very loud.
   _____ **e.** The timpani is part of the brass section.

2. **Word Partnership Activities**

   The job of a symphony orchestra is to *perform* for the public. Look up the word *perform* in the dictionary.

   a. Write the number of the definition that applies to music. _________

   Study the Word Partnership feature for *perform*. Then complete the four sentences below using the word perform before or after one of these words or phrases: *tasks*, *ability to*, *miracles*, *well*. Use each of these words or phrases one time.

   b. Some people believe holy people can _________ _________.
   c. The violinist's cold affected his _________ _________.
   d. The new truck _________ _________ on the icy roads.
   e. Doctors believe the brains of adults and children _________ _________ in different ways.

3. **Word Link Activities**

   a. Look up the Word Link for *sym*. What does *sym* mean? _________
   b. Look up the Word Link for *phon*. What does *phon* mean? _________
   c. A symphony is a piece of music for an orchestra to perform to make _________ all _________.

4. Choosing the Right Definition

Reread the Word Web feature for the word *orchestra*. Several of the words in this feature have multiple meanings.

Study the definitions for the word *composition*. Then write the number of the definition that relates to each sentence below.

_____ **a.** The composition of furniture in the store window was very attractive.

_____ **b.** Have you written any new compositions for the piano lately?

Study the definitions for the word *section*. Then write the number of the definition that relates to each sentence below.

_____ **c.** Did you read the section that tells how much interest you have to pay?

_____ **d.** Which section of the city do you live in?

Study the definitions for the word *instrument*. Then write the number of the definition that relates to each sentence below.

_____ **e.** The piano is my favorite instrument.

_____ **f.** The dentist placed the instruments on the shelf.

5. Dictionary Research

a. Study the definitions for the word *string*. Then find the one that applies to musical instruments. Complete the sentence with the correct phrase.
The brass section needs to play softer. I can't hear _________ _________.

b. Find the dictionary entries that contain the word *symphony*.
Symphony orchestras usually play _________ music.

ANSWER KEY:

1. **a.** F; **b.** T; **c.** T; **d.** F; **e.** F
2. **a.** 3; **b.** perform miracles; **c.** ability to perform; **d.** performed well; **e.** perform tasks
3. **a.** together; **b.** sound; **c.** sound together
4. **a.** 1; **b.** 2; **c.** 1; **d.** 2; **e.** 2; **f.** 1
5. **a.** the strings; **b.** classical

8. COOKING

Word Web Activities Picture Dictionary Activities	Thesaurus Activities Grammar Activities Dictionary Research

1. **Word Web Activities**
As you complete this activity, look up any words you aren't sure of.

Read the definitions for the words *cook* and *cooking*. Then study the Word Web feature entitled *cooking* to answer the following questions.
a. Which bold word means the opposite of *tough*? ________
b. Which bold word means *absorb food* into your body? ________

Now study the Word Web feature entitled *spice* to answer the following questions.
c. Which spice is the least effective in killing germs? ________
d. What kind of food do people in cold climates usually like? ________

Now study the Word Web feature entitled *pan* to answer the following questions.
e. Cooking pans made of what material are very heavy? ________
f. Copper pans are usually covered with a thin layer of what metal? ________

2. **Picture Dictionary Activities—A**
Look at the Picture Dictionary feature for *cook*. Then complete the sentences.
a. If you want to make coffee, you have to ________ the water.
b. You need an oven if you want to ________, ________, or ________ food.
c. When you put food in a wire container with boiling water under it, you ________ the food.
d. When you turn a slice of bread brown by cooking it you ________ it.
e. When you cook food in an oven very close to the flame, you ________ it.

3. **Picture Dictionary Activities—B**
Look at the Picture Dictionary feature for *egg*. Then answer the questions below. Look up any words you aren't sure of. Write T for *true* or F for *false*.
_____ a. The scrambled eggs have peppers in them.
_____ b. The omelet has meat in it.
_____ c. The hard-boiled egg has a round yolk.
_____ d. The quiche is in a frying pan.

4. **Thesaurus Activities**
Find the Thesaurus feature with the word *cook*. Then complete the sentences using words from the feature. Look up any words you aren't sure of.

a. The noun meaning is ________.
b. Yeast is the ingredient that ________ bread rise.
c. If the meal is cooked but it has gotten cold, you might just ________ the food.
d. Busy people tend to eat meals that are simple to ________.

5. **Grammar Activities**

Read the definitions for *cook* and *cooking*. Identify the part of speech of each underlined word below—noun, verb, or adjective.

a. My sister's <u>cooking</u> is fantastic. ________

b. When you make pies, you should use <u>cooking</u> apples. ________

c. On Sunday I <u>cooked</u> dinner for my family. ________

d. My husband is a very good <u>cook</u>. ________

6. **Dictionary Research**

Look at other words and phrases that follow the word *cook* in the dictionary.

a. Which one describes a collection of recipes? ________

b. Which one describes the food of a certain nation? ________

ANSWER KEY:

1. **a.** tender; **b.** digest; **c.** black pepper; **d.** bland; **e.** cast iron; **f.** tin
2. **a.** boil; **b.** roast, bake, broil; **c.** steam; **d.** toast; **e.** broil
3. **a.** F; **b.** T; **c.** T; **d.** F
4. **a.** chef; **b.** makes; **c.** heat up; **d.** prepare
5. **a.** noun; **b.** adjective; **c.** verb; **d.** noun
6. **a.** cookbook; **b.** cooking

9. ENERGY

Choosing the Right Definition Word Web Activities	Word Link Activities Grammar Activities

1. Choosing the Right Definition

Study the four numbered definitions for *energy*. Then write the number of the definition that relates to each sentence below.

a. ____ She's putting all her energies into her children instead of going back to work.
b. ____ My children have more energy than I do.
c. ____ One problem with nuclear energy is that it produces radioactive waste.
d. ____ You should put more energy into your homework.
e. ____ Which energy source do you think is the cleanest?
f. ____ Conserve your energy. Go to bed early.

2. Word Web Activities

Use the Word Web feature titled *energy* to answer the following questions. Answer each question with one of the bold words in the Word Web feature.

a. What kind of power plants were built in the 1970s? ________
b. What kind of gas is still used for home heating? ________
c. What was the primary energy source for American settlers? ________
d. What was the source of electrical power in the early 1900s? ________

3. Word Link Activities

Look up the words in the first column. Study the accompanying Word Links. Then match each Word Link with the correct definition.

Word	Word Link	Link Meaning
hydraulic	____ a. hydr	1. without
carefree	____ b. free	2. cause to be
electron	____ c. electr	3. one who acts as
motivate	____ d. ate	4. water
liar	____ e. ar	5. electric

4. Grammar Activities

Review the dictionary entry for *energy* as well as the entry that appears just before it. Then complete each sentence with the correct form of a word starting with the letters *energ-*. Identify the part of speech of each word you use—noun, verb, adjective, or adverb.

Sentences	Part of Speech
a. Celia is very ________ today.	________
b. I don't know what happened to all my ________. I'm really tired.	________
c. David washed the car ________.	________

ANSWER KEY:

1. **a.** 3; **b.** 1; **c.** 4; **d.** 2; **e.** 4; **f.** 1
2. **a.** nuclear; **b.** natural; **c.** wood; **d.** coal
3. **a.** 4; **b.** 1; **c.**5; **d.** 2; **e.** 3
4. **a.** energetic, adjective; **b.** energy, noun; **c.** energetically, adverb

10. UNION

Word Web Activities Word Link Activities	Choosing the Right Definition Style and Pragmatics

1. **Word Web Activities**
Use the Word Web feature titled *union* to answer the following questions. Each answer is one of the bold words in the feature. Look up each word in the dictionary to check your answer.
   - **a.** What do you call people who work in offices? __________ employees
   - **b.** What do you call an increase in someone's pay? a __________
   - **c.** What do you call the money workers take home each week? __________
   - **d.** What do you call the action workers take when they refuse to work? a __________
   - **e.** What do you call the hours an employee works each day? a __________

2. **Word Link Activities**
The first three letters of the word *union* form a Word Link. Look at the information in the Word Link for *uni*.
   - **a.** What does the word link *uni* mean? __________
   - **b.** What are the three word links for *uni*?

     __________ __________ __________
   - **c.** Complete each sentence below with the correct word from b. Check your answers by looking up each word in the dictionary.
     1. The police officers were all wearing the same dark blue __________.
     2. The boss made a __________ decision that the workday would begin at 8:00 AM.
     3. Leaders of the __________ asked to meet with the company's managers.

3. **Choosing the Right Definition**
Review the Word Web feature entitled *union* and notice how the word *strike* is used. Then look up the word *strike* in the dictionary. The categories (shown by 1 and 2) define labor union activity. Study the other numbered definitions in categories 2 and 3. Then write the number of the category and definition that relates to each sentence below.
   - **a.** _____ The tsunami struck without warning.
   - **b.** _____ When the hammer struck the rock, it broke into several pieces.
   - **c.** _____ The injured man had been struck on the head.

4. **Style and Pragmatics**

Look at the dictionary definition of *strike* again. Three of the meanings contain a boxed note like this: BUSINESS Read all the definitions and find as many of these pragmatics notes as you can. Write the category and definition numbers below.

a. Which two definitions relate to business situations? ________ and ________

b. Which definition relates to literary situations? ________

c. Which uses of *strike* are considered formal? ________

ANSWER KEY:

1. **a.** white-collar; **b.** raise; **c.** wages; **d.** strike; **e.** workday
2. **a.** one; **b.** uniform, unilateral, union; **c.** **1.** uniform; **2.** unilateral; **3.** union
3. **a.** 2 5; **b.** 2 4; **c.** 2 2
4. **a.** 1 2, 2 1; **b.** 2 13; **c.** 2 2, 3, 4, 15

11. BANK

Word Web Activities Choosing the Right Definition Dictionary Research	Word Partnership Activities Thesaurus Activities

1. **Word Web Activities**

Study the Word Web feature entitled *bank*. Answer each question with one of the bold words in the feature.

a. What is the verb that means "to take money out?" ________

b. What two things does a borrower pay back? ________ and ________

c. What do you use to get money out of an ATM? a ________

d. Which word means the same as *loan*? ________

2. **Choosing the Right Definition**

Look up the word *bank* in the dictionary. The circled numbers indicate three very different uses of the word *bank*. Write the category and definition number of the usage that relates to each sentence below.

_____ **a.** The airplane banked before it landed.

_____ **b.** The park was located on the banks of the Genesee River.

_____ **c.** Most banks are closed on Sunday.

Study the three noun meanings in category ❶ of *bank*. Write the number of the usage that relates to each sentence below.

_____ **d.** A new bank just opened on the corner.

_____ **e.** There is a large bank of vocabulary words in a dictionary.

_____ **f.** The World Bank helps poor countries develop new businesses.

3. **Dictionary Research**

Look at other words and phrases that follow the word *bank* in the dictionary. Several of them include the word *bank* followed by another word. Use the correct word to fill in the blanks after the word *bank* in the sentences below.

a. My bank ________ is $352.25.

b. I've lost my bank ________ so I can't use the ATM.

c. I opened a new bank ________ and received a checkbook and check register.

4. **Word Partnership Activities**

Study the Word Partnerships feature for the word *borrow*. Use one of the phrases in this feature to complete each sentence below. If necessary, look up new words in these phrases in the dictionary.

a. When his business burned down, Michael had to ________ ________ to put up a new building.

b. To get money to pay for college, parents sometimes ________ ________ the value of their house.

c. Your ________ ________ ________ money can be limited if you have a bad credit rating.

d. I decided to ________ ________ my brother instead of going to a bank.

5. **Thesaurus Activities**

a. Look up the word *money*. Find the Thesaurus feature with this word. What five words and phrases do you find?

________ ________ ________ ________ ________

b. Guess which of these words and phrases go with each definition below. Then look up the definition the words in the dictionary and check your answers.

1. Which two items mean "coins and bills that you can use to pay for things"?

________ ________

2. Which item means "a large amount of money and property"? ________
3. Which item means "money used to start a business"? ________
4. Which item means "amounts of money available to be spent"? ________

ANSWER KEY:

1. **a.** withdraw; **b.** principal, interest; **c.** bank card; **d.** lend
2. **a.** 3 1; **b.** 2 1; **c.** 1 1; **d.** 2; **e.** 4; **f.** 1
3. **a.** balance; **b.** card; **c.** account
4. **a.** borrow heavily; **b.** borrow against; **c.** ability to borrow; **d.** borrow from
5. **a.** capital, cash, currency, funds, wealth;
b. **1.** cash, currency; **2.** wealth; **3.** capital; **4.** funds

12. WATER

Word Web Activities Choosing the Right Definition	Word Link Activities

1. **Word Web Activities**

   Use the Word Web feature entitled *water* to answer the following questions.

   a. What happens when the sun warms lakes and rivers?
   Some of the water in them ______________________.

   b. What is the gas that is created during evaporation called?
   It's called ______________________.

   c. What happens to water when it forms clouds?
   It ______________________.

   d. What are the three types of precipitation?
   They are rain, ______________________, and snow.

2. **Choosing the Right Definition**

   Study the numbered definitions for *cloud*. Then write the number of the definition that relates to each sentence below.

   ______ a. The ongoing argument between the couple clouded their vacation fun.
   ______ b. There wasn't a cloud in the sky.
   ______ c. The glass quickly clouded after I added ice cubes to my drink.
   ______ d. His anxiety clouded his understanding of the situation.
   ______ e. A cloud of smoke rose from the volcano.

3. **Work Link Activities**

   The first four letters of the word *cycle* form a Word Link. Look up the word *cycle* and study the information in the Word Link for *cycl*.

   a. What does the Word Link *cycl* mean? ______
   b. Which sample word describes a series of things? ______
   c. Which sample word describes a pattern that repeats over and over? ______
   d. Which sample word describes a vehicle with two wheels? ______

ANSWER KEY:

1. **a.** evaporates; **b.** water vapor; **c.** condenses; **d.** sleet
2. **a.** 4; **b.** 1; **c.** 5; **d.** 3; **e.** 2
3. **a.** circle; **b.** cycle; **c.** cyclical; **d.** bicycle

13. PARK

Word Web Activities Grammar Activities Picture Dictionary Activities	Choosing the Right Definition Word Partnership Activities Thesaurus Activities

1. Word Web Activities

Study the Word Web feature entitled *park*. Answer each question with one of the bold words in the feature. Look up any words you aren't sure of.

a. Which part of the park features animals? the ________

b. Which part of the park do older people seem to prefer? the ________

c. What do you call food eaten while sitting on a blanket in the park? a ________

d. Where do people play tennis? on a tennis ________

2. Grammar Activities

Read the definitions for *park* and *parking*. Write the part of speech of each underlined word below—noun, verb, or adjective.

a. We couldn't find <u>parking</u> on the street, so we had to use a parking garage. ________

b. Where did you <u>park</u> the car? ________

c. We left the car on a street near the <u>park</u>. ________

d. Sarah <u>parked</u> the car at a parking meter. ________

3. Picture Dictionary Activities

Study the Picture Dictionary feature entitled *baseball* and answer these questions.

a. What does the catcher use to catch the ball? a ________

b. What does the pitcher stand on? the pitcher's ________

Study the Picture Dictionary feature entitled *tennis* and answer these questions.

c. What do you call the person who supervises the game? the ________

d. What long feature is in the middle of the tennis court? a ________

e. What is the line at the side of the tennis court called? a ________

4. Choosing the Right Definition

Study the numbered dictionary definitions for *diamond*. Then write the number of the definition that relates to each sentence below.

_____ a. Tony put a <u>diamond</u> on my three of hearts.

_____ b. Baseball is played on a <u>diamond</u>.

_____ c. I love my <u>diamond</u> earrings.

Study the numbered dictionary definitions for *court*. Then write the number of the category and definition that relates to each sentence below.

_____ d. I'll meet you at the tennis <u>court</u>.

_____ e. The King of France had his <u>court</u> at Versailles.

_____ f. After his accident, Roy had to appear in <u>court</u>.

5. **Word Partnership Activities**

Study the Word Partnership feature for *catch*. Then complete the four sentences below using the word *catch* before or after one of these words or phrases: *ball*, *play*, *the train*, *a fish*, *my eye*. Use each item one time.

a. In baseball you will hurt your hand if you try to catch a ________ without a glove.

b. I have to catch ________ to Fairfield right after class.

c. Many baseball players ________ catch between innings in a game.

d. I wanted to catch ________ for our dinner.

e. The waiter was trying to catch ________ because he finally had a free table.

6. **Thesaurus Activities**

In an athletic competition, one player or team tries to *beat* the other. Study the synonyms in the thesaurus for the three other meanings for the word *beat*. Then write the number of the meaning in the thesaurus that relates to each sentence below.

_____ **a.** Beat the eggs until they are stiff.

_____ **b.** I could hear the baby's heart beat.

_____ **c.** He was so angry he beat on the door with his fists.

ANSWER KEY:

1. **a.** zoo; **b.** gardens; **c.** picnic; **d.** court
2. **a.** noun; **b.** verb; **c.** noun; **d.** verb
3. **a.** glove; **b.** mound; **c.** referee; **d.** net; **e.** sideline
4. **a.** 3; **b.** 4; **c.** 1; **d.** ❷ 3; **e.** ❶ 4; **f.** ❶ 5
5. **a.** ball; **b.** the train; **c.** play; **d.** a fish; **e.** my eye, my attention
6. **a.**5; **b.** 3; **c.** 1

14. STARS AND ASTRONOMERS

Word Web Activities Choosing the Right Definition Word Partnership Activities	Thesaurus Activities Word Link Activities

1. Word Web Activities

Use the Word Web feature entitled *star* to answer the following questions. Look up these words in the dictionary to check your answers.

a. What is a group of stars called? a ______

b. What do people call the idea that the stars control our lives? ______

c. What is the scientific study of the stars called? ______

d. Which star is used to guide ships on the sea? the ______

Use the Word Web feature entitled *astronomer* to answer this question:

e. Copernicus was an astronomer who thought that the center of the universe was the ______.

2. Choosing the Right Definition

Study definitions 1–5 for *star*. Then write the number of the definition that relates to each sentence below.

a. ______ I only eat in restaurants that get at least four stars.

b. ______ Eric is starring in a new TV comedy called " Just for You."

c. ______ It was cloudy last night and we couldn't see any stars.

d. ______ Madonna is my favorite singing star.

e. ______ The flag of the United States has 50 stars on it.

3. Word Partnership Activities

Reread the Word Web feature for *star*. Find the word *object* in the second sentence. Look up the word *object* in the dictionary and read the definitions.

a. The first meaning of *object* is *something that has a fixed* ______ or ______.

b. The second meaning of *object* is ______ or ______.

Study the Word Partnership feature for the noun form of *object*. Then complete the four sentences below using the word *object* and one of these words: *foreign*, *inanimate*, *moving*, *solid*. Use each of these words one time. Look up any words you aren't sure of.

c. Dogs are not usually interested in an ______ ______.

d. We watched as the magician passed a ______ ______ through a mirror.

e. A fast-______ ______ has a high speed.

f. If a child swallows a ______ ______ call a doctor for advice.

4. **Thesaurus Activities**

Reread the Word Web feature entitled *astronomer*. Notice the word *observe* near the end of the feature. Look up *observe* in the dictionary and study the Thesaurus entry that accompanies it. Which of the words in the box goes with each sentence below?

notice	celebrate	study

a. Americans observe Independence Day on July 4th. ________

b. I checked the level of the water every hour, but I didn't observe any change. ________

c. Jane Goodall would observe the chimps carefully for hours without moving. ________

5. **Word Link Activities**

The first four letters of the word *astronomer* form a Word Link. Look at the information in the Word Links for *astro*.

a. What does the Word Link *astro* mean? ________

b. What are the three Word Links for *astro*? ________ ________ ________

c. Complete each sentence below with the correct word from b. Check your answers by looking up each word in the dictionary.

1. This symbol (*) is called the ________.
2. You need a telescope to study ________.
3. You have to know how to fly a plane before you can study to become an ________.

ANSWER KEY:

1. **a.** constellation; **b.** astrology; **c.** astronomy; **d.** North Star; **e.** sun
2. **a.** 3; **b.** 5; **c.** 1; **d.** 4; **e.** 2
3. **a.** shape, form; **b.** aim, purpose; **c.** inanimate object; **d.** solid object; **e.** moving object; **f.** foreign object
4. **a.** celebrate; **b.** notice; **c.** study
5. **a.** star; **b.** asterisk, astronaut, astronomy; **c1.** asterisk; **c2.** astronomy; **c3.** astronaut

15. FOOD

Word Web Activities Thesaurus Activities	Picture Dictionary Activities Choosing the Right Definition

1. **Word Web Activities**

Study the information in the Word Web feature entitled *food*. Then answer the questions below. Write T for *true* or F for *false*.

_____ **a.** Snakes are herbivores.

_____ **b.** Mice are predators.

_____ **c.** Green plants store energy from the sun.

2. **Thesaurus Activities**

The Word Web feature for *food* says that a hawk is a top predator. Find the Thesaurus feature with the word *top*. Then complete the sentences using words from the feature. Look up any words you aren't sure of.

a. The adjective meanings for *top* are ________, ________, and ________.

b. Which adjective best describes the hawk's position as a top predator? ________

c. Which two noun meanings describe the top of a mountain? ________ and ________

3. **Picture Dictionary Activities**

Study the Picture Dictionary feature for *dessert*. Then answer the questions below. Look up any words you aren't familiar with.

a. Which three desserts don't have to be cooked? ________, ________, and ________

b. Which dessert is usually very cold? ________

c. Which dessert is always brown? ________

d. Which dessert is made mostly of eggs? ________

4. **Choosing the Right Definition**

The word *feed* is related to the word *food*. Look up the word *feed* in the dictionary. Then write the number of the definition that relates to each sentence below.

a. _____ My mother always feeds the children dinner early on Friday nights.

b. _____ The squirrels in our yard like to feed on the seed we leave for the birds.

c. _____ Newborn babies usually feed every three hours.

d. _____ We collected money to feed the hurricane victims in Louisiana.

ANSWER KEY:

1. **a.** F; **b.** F; **c.** T
2. **a.** best, first-rate, finest; **b.** best; **c.** peak, summit
3. **a.** ice cream, fruit salad; **b.** ice cream; **c.** chocolate mousse; **d.** custard
4. **a.** 1; **b.** 3; **c.** 4; **d.** 2

16. ECONOMICS AND BUSINESS

Word Web Activities Word Partnership Activities Picture Dictionary Activities	Word Link Activities Choosing the Right Definition

1. **Word Web Activities**

   Study the Word Web feature entitled *economics*. Then use bold words from this Word Web feature to complete the following sentences. Look up any words you aren't sure of.

   a. Tasks that a worker performs are called ________.

   b. The word that describes how much of something is available on the market is ________.

   c. Products manufactured in a factory are called ________.

   d. The amount of money a country possesses is called its ________.

2. **Word Partnership Activities**

   Study the Word Partnerships feature for the word *business*. Pay special attention to the phrases below. Then match each word with the correct definition. Look up these words in the dictionary if you are not sure.

   _____ **a.** business casual
   _____ **b.** business owner
   _____ **c.** online business
   _____ **d.** unfinished business
   _____ **e.** go out of business

   1. Internet orders
   2. person who owns a company
   3. an appropriate but informal way to dress
   4. close a business permanently
   5. a situation that is still a problem

3. **Picture Dictionary Activities**

   Most businesses require an office. Study the Picture Dictionary feature for *office*. Use the words in this feature to answer these questions.

   a. What do you need if you make a mistake in typing a name on an envelope? ________

   b. Where do people keep old letters and other documents? in a ________

   c. What do you use to make an important word or name stand out in your notes? a ________

   d. What do you use to permanently attach two pieces of paper together? a ________

   e. What is the name of a worker's space that has only three walls? a ________

4. **Word Link Activities**

Review the Word Web feature for *economics*. This feature contains two words with important Word Links. Look up the Word Links below and answer the following questions. Look up any words you don't know in the dictionary.

a. What does *micro* mean? ________

b. Which word in this link names an instrument used to look at tiny objects? ________

c. What does *tribute* as in the word *distribute* mean? ________

d. Which word in this link means the same as "give"? ________

e. Which word means "a quality or characteristic that someone possesses"? ________

5. **Choosing the Right Definition**

Reread the Word Web feature for *economics*. Several words in this feature have multiple meanings.

Study the definitions for the word *capital*. Then write the number of the category and the definition that relates to each sentence below.

_____ **a.** The capital of New York State is Albany.

_____ **b.** They need a lot of capital to start their business.

_____ **c.** Always begin a proper name with a capital letter.

Study the definitions for the word *service*. Then write the number of the definition that relates to each sentence below.

_____ **d.** The service in this restaurant is usually very good.

_____ **e.** We attended a service in memory of the flood victims.

Study the definitions for the word *demand*. Then write the number of the category and the definition that relates to each sentence below.

_____ **f.** The demand for fresh water is high in desert areas.

_____ **g.** I demand an explanation for you actions last night.

ANSWER KEY:

1. **a.** services; **b.** supply; **c.** goods; **d.** wealth
2. **a.** 3; **b.** 2; **c.** 1; **d.** 5; **e.** 4
3. **a.** correction fluid; **b.** file cabinet; **c.** highlighter; **d.** stapler; **e.** cubicle
4. **a.** small; **b.** microscope; **c.** giving; **d.** contribute; **e.** attribute
5. **a.** 4; **b.** 1; **c.** 6; **d.** 1 11; **e.** 1 12; **f.** 4; **g.** 1

17. ART

Word Web Activities Thesaurus Activities	Word Link Activities Style and Pragmatics Choosing the Right Definition

1. **Word Web Activities**

   Use the Word Web feature titled *art* to answer the following questions.

   a. What inspired the term "Impressionism"? a painting by ________
   b. In what part of the world did Impressionism start? in ________
   c. What did the Impressionists usually paint? ________
   d. What elements did they emphasize in their paintings? ________ and color
   e. The art of what country influenced the Impressionists? ________

2. **Thesaurus Activities**

   The Word Web feature for *art* says that the Impressionists were interested in light and color. Find the Thesaurus feature with the word *light*. Then complete the sentences using words from the feature. Look up any words you aren't sure of.

   a. The noun meanings for *light* are ________, ________, ________, ________, and ________.
   b. Which noun meaning best describes the soft light of a fire when there are no flames? ________
   c. Which noun meaning describes the happiness on a person's face? ________
   d. Which adjective describes a room with a lot of windows facing south? ________

3. **Word Link Activities**

   Review the Word Web feature for *art* noting the words *realistic* and *depict*.
   Look up the Word Link below and answer the questions. Look up any words you don't know in the dictionary.

   a. Look up the word *reality*. What does the Word Link *real* mean? ________
   b. Which word in this link means "to make something happen"? ________
   c. Which word in this link means "actually"? ________
   d. Look up the word *artist*. What does *-ist* mean? ________
   e. Which word describes someone who works in a drugstore? ________
   f. Look up the word *picture*. What does the Word Link *pict* mean? ________
   g. Which word in this link means "charming and pretty"? ________
   h. Which word in this link means "show or illustrate"? ________

4. **Style and Pragmatics**

Here are several words that use the root *real: real, realize, really.* Look up each word in the dictionary. Look for notes about pragmatics in a box following sample sentences that include these words. Locate the following notes and copy the sample sentence below.

a. Describe how much something sold for. FORMAL

____

b. Emphasize a description by using *real* + adjective. AM, INFORMAL

____

5. **Choosing the Right Definition**

The Word Web feature for *art* says that the Impressionists stopped painting in their *studios*. Study the four numbered definitions for *studio.* Then write the number of the definition that relates to each sentence below.

a. ____ The TV show originated in a studio in New York City.

b. ____ Because he couldn't afford a one-bedroom apartment, he lived in a studio.

c. ____ The photographer has a large studio with large windows.

d. ____ Most of the large movie studios are located in Hollywood.

ANSWER KEY:

1. **a.** Monet; **b.** Europe; **c.** landscapes; **d.** light; **e.** Japan
2. **a.** brightness, gleam, glow, radiance, shine; **b.** glow; **c.** radiance/glow; **d.** sunny
3. **a.** actual; **b.** realize; **c.** really; **d.** one who practices; **e.** pharmacist; **f.** painting; **g.** picturesque; **h.** depict
4. **a.** A selection of correspondence from P.G. Wodehouse realized 2,000 dollars.; **b.** He is finding prison life real tough.
5. **a.** 2; **b.** 4; **c.** 1; **d.** 3

18. TELEVISION

Word Web Activities	Choosing the Right Definition
Thesaurus Activities	Grammar Activities
Word Link Activities	Dictionary Research

1. Word Web Activities

Use the Word Web feature entitled *television* to answer the following questions. Look up any words you don't know in the dictionary.

a. What kind of tube was used in old-fashioned televisions? a ________ tube

b. What are the tiny dots of light on a TV screen called? ________

c. What are the three sources of TV signals? ________, ________, and ________.

d. How many pixels per square inch does a high-definition TV have? ________

2. Thesaurus Activities

The Word Web feature for *television* says that high-definition televisions have a very *clear picture*.

a. Read the dictionary definition for the word *clear*. *Clear* is used to describe a TV picture that is easy to ________.

Study the thesaurus feature for *clear*.

b. Which numbered definition of *clear* relates to the weather? ________

c. Which word in the thesaurus entry means the opposite of *dark*? ________

Read the dictionary definition for the word *picture*. Then study the thesaurus feature for this word.

d. Which meaning of the word *picture* applies to a television picture? ________

e. Look at the verb meanings of *picture* in the thesaurus entry. They describe a picture that exists only in a person's ________.

3. Word Link Activities

Look up the word *television*. Study the Word Link for *tele*.

a. What does *tele* mean? ________

b. What does the word *vision* mean? ________

c. So television is something that lets you ________ things at a ________.

4. **Choosing the Right Definition**

Reread the Word Web feature for *television*. Pay special attention to the words *screen* and *station*.

Study the numbered definitions for *screen*. Then write the number of the definition that relates to each sentence below.

_____ **a.** We put a screen in front of the window to keep out the light.

_____ **b.** Did they screen your luggage at the airport?

Study the numbered definitions for *station*. Then write the number of the definition that relates to each sentence below.

_____ **c.** We live only three blocks from the subway station.

_____ **d.** Which station is showing the soccer game tonight?

5. **Grammar Activities**

The Word Web feature says that cathode-ray tubes are used to *produce* a television picture. Many different words are based on the word *produce*. Write the part of speech of each underlined word—noun, verb, adjective, or adverb. Use your dictionary to check your answers.

a.	I always buy my produce in the fruit market on the corner.	_____
b.	There are so many new products on the market, I don't know which to buy.	_____
c.	A lot of movie production takes place on the streets of New York.	_____
d.	I am the most productive early in the morning.	_____
e.	The thief produced a gun from his pocket.	_____

6. **Dictionary Research**

Look at the words and phrases that follow the word *screen* in the dictionary.

a. Which one describes something you find on a computer? _____

b. Which one describes something that will later become a movie? _____

ANSWER KEY:

1. **a.** cathode-ray; **b.** pixels; **c.** ground stations, satellites, cables; **d.** two million
2. **a.** see; **b.** 3; **c.** bright; **d.** image; **e.** mind
3. **a.** distance; **b.** see; **c.** see, distance
4. **a.** 4; **b.** 8; **c.** 1; **d.** 3
5. **a.** noun; **b.** noun; **c.** noun; **d.** adjective; **e.** verb
6. **a.** screensaver; **b.** screenplay

19. MONEY

Word Web Activities Word Partnership Activities Thesaurus Activities	Choosing the Right Definition Dictionary Research

1. **Word Web Activities**

Study the Word Web feature entitled *money* and answer the following questions.

a. Which word in the feature means the same as *trade*? ________

b. What form of ocean life was used as money at one time? ________

c. Were the first coins round? ________

d. What country had the first circular coins? ________

e. Which two metals were used by the Lydians to make coins? ________ and ________

2. **Word Partnership Activities**

Look up the word *buy* in the dictionary.

a. What is the past tense of the verb *buy*?

b. Which meaning of *buy* is found in this sentence?

I bought myself a few minutes by raising my hand and asking questions.

meaning number ________

Study the Word Partnership feature for *buy*. Then complete the three sentences below using the word *buy* before or after one of these words or phrases: *online, and sell, afford to*. Use each of these items one time.

c. I can't ________ ________ a flat screen TV. I don't have enough money.

d. If you ________ ________ stocks at the right time, you can get rich.

e. Is it safe to ________ ________?

3. **Thesaurus Activities**

Study the Thesaurus feature for *money*. Look up each synonym given in order to understand the differences in meaning. Then complete each sentence below with the correct word.

a. A single ________ is now in use in all European countries.

b. I never use ________. I prefer to pay by credit card or check.

c. I don't have the amount of ________ I need to start my own business.

d. The group decided to raise ________ to help people with AIDS.

e. The discovery of oil brought great ________ to the Middle East.

4. Choosing the Right Definition

Study the numbered definitions for *bill*. Then write the number of the definition that relates to each sentence below.

_____ **a.** Please ask the waiter to bring the bill.
_____ **b.** The duck put its bill into the water.
_____ **c.** My electric bill this month was over $100.
_____ **d.** My favorite band is billed to perform at Madison Square Garden next summer.
_____ **e.** He handed me three crisp, new dollar bills.
_____ **f.** The singer was billed as the next Madonna.
_____ **g.** The mechanic billed us for some work he didn't do.
_____ **h.** Congress passed a bill that prohibited smoking in hospitals.

5. Dictionary Research

The Word Web feature for *money* says that the Lydians *minted* three types of coins. Look up the word *mint* in the dictionary. Then write the number of the definition that relates to each sentence below.

a. Which numbered meaning of *mint* is used in the Word Web feature? _____
b. Which meaning names a spice people cook with? _____
c. Which meaning names a type of candy? _____
d. Which meaning tells where money is manufactured? _____

ANSWER KEY:

1. **a.** barter; **b.** cowrie shells; **c.** no; **d.** China; **e.** gold, silver
2. **a.** bought; **b.** 3; **c.** afford to buy; **d.** buy and sell; **e.** buy online
3. **a.** currency; **b.** cash; **c.** capital; **d.** funds; **e.** wealth
4. **a.** 6; **b.** 9; **c.** 1; **d.** 7; **e.** 3; **f.** 8; **g.** 2; **h.** 4
5. **a.** 4; **b.** 1; **c.** 2; **d.** 3

20. POLLUTION AND THE GREENHOUSE EFFECT

Word Web Activities Word Partnership Activities	Word Link Activities Choosing the Right Definition Dictionary Research

1. Word Web Activities

Use the Word Web feature entitled *pollution* to answer the following questions. Look up any words you aren't familiar with.

a. *Smog* is a combination of smoke and ________.
b. Factories in the Midwest cause ________ that falls in the East.
c. A substance used to kill insects is called a ________.

Use the Word Web feature entitled *the greenhouse effect* to answer these questions.

d. Energy that comes from the sun is called ________ radiation.
e. Gasoline is an example of a ________ fuel.
f. The average temperature of the earth is going ________.

2. Word Partnership Activities

Notice how the word *cause* is used in the Word Web features for *pollution* and *the greenhouse effect*. Next study the Word Partnerships feature for the word *cause*. Use the correct Word Partnership phrase to complete each sentence below. If necessary, look up new words in the dictionary.

a. Scientists are looking for answers. They want to ____________ global warming.
b. My cold isn't serious at all. There's no ____________.
c. Doctors say cigarette smoking may ____________.
d. They want to know why their dog died. The vet is looking for the ____________.

3. Word Link Activities

The Word Web feature for *pollution* talks about *exhaust*.

a. The prefix in the word *exhaust* is ________.
b. Find the Word Link for this prefix at the word *exit*. What does the prefix mean?

____

Which of the words means the same as the following? Look up the words in the dictionary if you are not sure.

c. to leave ________
d. to break into many pieces ________
e. to go beyond ________

4. **Choosing the Right Definition**

The Word Web feature for *the greenhouse effect* mentions carbon dioxide and other *gases*. Study definitions 1–5 for *gas*. Then write the number of the definition that best relates to each sentence below.

_____ **a.** I need to put some gas in the car before we leave this afternoon.
_____ **b.** The soldiers were gassed by a small group of enemy troops.
_____ **c.** Our new stove uses gas instead of electricity.
_____ **d.** Cigarette smoke contains poisonous gases.
_____ **e.** Oxygen is a gas that plants give off.

5. **Dictionary Research**

The Word Web feature for *the greenhouse effect* says that global average *temperature* has risen over the past hundred years. Search the Word Webs to find the answers to the following questions about temperature.

	Word Web feature	Question	Answer
a.	sun	The temperature of the sun is _________.	_________
b.	climate	In the last 100 years, the earth's temperature has increased by _______.	_________
c.	wind	Air flows from one place to another because of the _______ in temperature from one area to another.	_________
d.	element	Oxygen is a gas at _______ temperature.	_________
e.	cooking	Heating food to a high temperature kills _________.	_________

ANSWER KEY:

1. **a.** fog; **b.** acid rain; **c.** pesticide; **d.** solar; **e.** fossil; **f.** up
2. **a.** determine the cause of; **b.** cause for concern; **c.** cause cancer; **d.** cause of death
3. **a.** ex; **b.** away, from, out; **c.** exit; **d.** explode; **e.** exceed
4. **a.** 4; **b.** 5; **c.** 1; **d.** 3; **e.** 2
5. **a.** 15 million degrees Celsius; **b.** about 1° Fahrenheit; **c.** difference; **d.** room; **e.** bacteria

21. BRIDGES AND DAMS

Word Web Activities Thesaurus Activities Grammar Activities	Word Partnership Activities Word Link Activities Practice with Pragmatics

1. Word Web Activities

Study the Word Web feature for *bridge*. Then match each number below with the correct description.

Word Link	Definition
____ **a.** 1+ mile	**1.** The height in feet of the Akashi Kaikyo Bridge
____ **b.** 1883	**2.** When the Brooklyn Bridge was built
____ **c.** 120,000	**3.** The length of the Evergreen Point Floating Bridge
____ **d.** 1,000	**4.** How many cars cross the Brooklyn Bridge every day
____ **e.** 8.5	**5.** The strength of an earthquake that the Akashi Kaikyo Bridge can withstand
____ **f.** 12,828	**6.** The length of the Akashi Kaikyo Bridge

Read the Word Web feature for *dam*. Then answer the questions below. Write T for *true* or F for *false*.

____ **g.** The world's first dam was built near Memphis.
____ **h.** The world's first dam prevented flooding.
____ **i.** Hydroelectric dams provide 20% of the world's electricity.
____ **j.** The Itapu Dam took 10 years to build.

2. Thesaurus Activities

The Word Web feature for *dam* states that dams help protect valuable forest *lands*. Find the Thesaurus feature with the word *land*. Then complete the sentences below using words from this thesaurus feature. Look up any words you aren't sure of.

a. Someday I will return to the _________ of my birth.
b. Harry doesn't own a house, but he does own some _________ outside of town.
c. We weren't sure when the train would _________.
d. Do you live in a safe _________ ?

3. Grammar Activities

The Word Web feature for *dam* describes the world's longest *suspension* bridge. Study the list of words that are formed from the word *suspend*. Identify the part of speech of each underlined word below—noun, verb, or adjective. Use the dictionary to check any you aren't sure of.

a. I drove over a large rock and damaged the car's suspension. _________
b. The airline suspends flights during storms. _________
c. I use suspenders instead of a belt. _________
d. I couldn't stand the suspense so I asked the teacher what my grade was. _________

4. **Word Partnership Activities**

Study the Word Partnerships feature for the word *build*. Use one of the phrases in this feature to complete each sentence below. If necessary, look up new words in these phrases in the dictionary.

a. Students need to speak English as much as possible to ________________.

b. Leo works out at the gym and has a very _____________.

c. Many female ballet dancers have a _________________.

d. The government will _____________ to connect all the major cities in the country.

e. Tax revenue often helps to ___________ and ___________.

5. **Word Link Activities**

Reread the Word Web feature entitled *dam*. Notice the words *constructed* and *endanger*. Look these words up in the dictionary.

a. Which one relates to building something? _________

b. Which one relates to destroying something? _________

There are two Word Links in the word *constructed*—*con* and *struct*. Look up these Word Links.

c. What does the Word Link *con* mean? _________

d. What does the Word Link *struct* mean? _________

e. So the word *construct* means to _________ something _________.

The first two letters of *endanger* are a Word Link. Look at the Word Link for *en*.

f. What does the word link *en* mean? _________

g. So the word *endanger* means to _________ someone or something in danger.

6. **Practice with Pragmatics**

Study the information about the fourth meaning in the definition of *bridge*. Read the four sentences below. Write *Yes* if the sentence uses the term appropriately, and *No* if the usage is inappropriate.

a. ___ Some scientists believe that it is possible to bridge the gap between human and machine.

b. ___ Museums are a bridge between past and present.

c. ___ The summit failed to bridge differences on free trade between the two nations.

d. ___ The president tried to build bridges with Europe.

ANSWER KEY:

1. **a.** 3; **b.** 2; **c.** 4; **d.** 1; **e.** 5; **f.** 6; **g.** T; **h.** F; **i.** T; **j.** F

2. **a.** country; **b.** acreage/real estate; **c.** arrive; **d.** area

3. **a.** noun; **b.** verb; **c.** noun; **d.** noun

4. **a.** build confidence; **b.** athletic/strong build; **c.** slender build; **d.** build roads; **e.** build bridges, build schools

5. **a.** constructed; **b.** endanger; **c.** together, with; **d.** building; **e.** building, together; **f.** making, putting; **g.** put

6. **a.** yes; **b.** no; **c.** yes; **d.** no

22. CLONE

Word Web Activities Thesaurus Activities	Word Link Activities Choosing the Right Definition Grammar Activities

1. **Word Web Activities**

Study the Word Web feature entitled *clone*. Then use bold words from this feature to complete the following sentences. Look up any words you aren't sure of.

a. Maria's computer is ________ to mine.
b. I need to give them a ________ of my driver's license.
c. The girls look like ________, but they were born a year apart.
d. Each ________ in your body contains DNA.
e. Scientists use ________ to create new types of plants.

2. **Thesaurus Activities**

Find the Thesaurus feature for the word *natural*. Then complete the sentences using words from the feature. Look up any words you aren't sure of.

a. It is ________ for new students to be a little nervous at first.
b. This doesn't look like ________ leather to me. I think it's plastic.
c. Please accept my ________ apology for what I said.
d. Farm-grown strawberries are good, but ________ strawberries are better.

3. **Word Link Activities**

Find the word *identical* in the Word Web feature for *clone*. Study the Word Link feature for the root *ident*.

a. What does the Word Link *ident* mean? ________

Write the word in this Word Link that matches each definition below. Look up the words in the dictionary if you are not sure.

b. your passport or driver's license ________
c. exactly the same ________
d. unknown or nameless ________

Find the word *donate* in the Word Web feature for *clone*. Study the Word Link feature for the root *don*.

e. What does the Word Link *don* mean? ________

Write the word in this Word Link that matches each definition below. Look up the words in the dictionary if you are not sure.

f. to forgive someone ________
g. someone who gives something away ________
h. to give money or goods to an organization ________

4. **Choosing the Right Definition**

Clones are produced by *genetic engineering*. Study the numbered definitions for *engineer*. Then write the number of the definition that relates to each sentence below.

____ **a.** A famous civil engineer designed that bridge.

____ **b.** The building engineer repaired the water heater.

____ **c.** The engineer told the captain that the ship would never make it back to port.

____ **d.** They engineered the car in such a way that it would get good gas mileage.

____ **e.** My "accidental" meeting with Rosa was actually engineered by her sister.

5. **Grammar Activities**

Review the dictionary entry for *genetic* as well as the five entries that follow it. Then complete each sentence with the correct word or phrase.

a. The study of how characteristics are passed from parents to children is called ________.

b. The science of changing the genetic structure of a plant or animal is called ________.

c. Plants and animals whose genes have been changed have ________ genes.

ANSWER KEY:

1. **a.** identical; **b.** copy; **c.** twins; **d.** cell; **e.** genetic engineering
2. **a.** normal; **b.** genuine; **c.** sincere; **d.** wild
3. **a.** same; **b.** identification; **c.** identical; **d.** unidentified; **e.** giving; **f.** pardon; **g.** donor; **h.** donate
4. **a.** 1; **b.** 2; **c.** 3; **d.** 4; **e.** 5
5. **a.** genetics; **b.** genetic engineering; **c.** genetically modified

Aa

A also **a** /eɪ/ (**A's, a's**) N-VAR **A** is the first letter of the English alphabet. 英语字母表中第1个字母

a ◆◆◆ /ə, STRONG eɪ/ or **an** /ən, STRONG æn/

A or **an** is the indefinite article. It is used at the beginning of noun groups that refer to only one person or thing. The form **an** is used in front of words that begin with vowel sounds.

1 DET You use **a** or **an** when you are referring to someone or something for the first time or when people may not know which particular person or thing you are talking about. (用于首次提及或泛指某人或某物) 一(个) ❑ *A waiter entered with a tray bearing a glass and a bottle of whiskey.* 一名服务员端着一个放有一只玻璃杯和一瓶威士忌酒的托盘进来了。 ❑ *He started eating an apple.* 他开始吃苹果。 2 DET You use **a** or **an** when you are referring to any person or thing of a particular type and do not want to be specific. 用于指一类人或物，不需要特指 ❑ *I suggest you leave it to an expert.* 我建议你把它留给专家来处理。 ❑ *Bring a sleeping bag.* 带个睡袋来。 3 DET You use **a** or **an** in front of an uncount noun when that noun follows an adjective, or when the noun is followed by words that describe it more fully. 一种 (用于前有形容词或后有修饰语的不可数名词前) ❑ *The islanders exhibit a constant happiness with life.* 这些岛民表现出一种对生活的持久的幸福感。 4 DET You use **a** or **an** in front of a mass noun when you want to refer to a single type or make of something. 一种 (用于物质名词前，特指某物的种类或成分) ❑ *Bollinger "RD" is a rare, highly prized wine.* **Bollinger "RD"**是一种罕见的、非常名贵的葡萄酒。 5 DET You use **a** in quantifiers such as **a lot**, **a little**, and **a bit**. 用在量化词组中，如**a lot**，**a little**，**a bit**等 ❑ *I spend a lot on expensive jewelry and clothing.* 我在昂贵的首饰和衣服上开销很大。 6 DET You use **a** or **an** to refer to someone or something as a typical member of a group, class, or type. 指某人或某物是一个团队、阶层或类型中典型的一员或一部分 ❑ *Some parents believe a boy must learn to stand up and fight like a man.* 一些家长认为一个男孩必须学会像男子汉一样奋起战斗。 7 DET You use **a** or **an** in front of the names of days, months, or festivals when you are referring to one particular instance of that day, month, or festival. 用于某一天、某一月份或某节日前，特指在该天、该月或该节日发生的事件 ❑ *The interview took place on a Friday afternoon.* 该面谈是在一个星期五下午进行的。 8 DET You use **a** or **an** when you are saying what someone is or what job they have. 用于说明某人的职业 ❑ *I explained that I was an artist.* 我解释说我是一位艺术家。 9 DET You use **a** or **an** instead of the number "one," especially with words of measurement such as "hundred," "hour," and "meter," and with fractions such as "half," "quarter," and "third." 一 (代替**one**，尤与量词**hundred, hour, meter**和分数词**half, quarter, third**合用) ❑ *...more than a thousand acres of land.* …一千多英亩的土地。 10 DET You use **a** or **an** in expressions such as **eight hours a day** to express a rate or ratio. 每一 (用于速率或比率的表达中) ❑ *Prices start at $13.95 a yard for printed cotton.* 印花棉布开价为$13.95一码。

A & E /eɪ ən i/ N-UNCOUNT **A & E** is the same as the **ER**. 急诊室 [BRIT]

aback /əbæk/ PHRASE If you are **taken aback by** something, you are surprised or shocked by it and you cannot respond at once. 被…所震惊 ❑ *Roland was taken aback by our strength of feeling.* 罗兰对我们感情的强烈程度感到很吃惊。

aba·cus /æbəkəs/ (**abacuses**) N-COUNT An **abacus** is a frame used for counting. It has rods with sliding beads on them. 算盘

aban·don ◆◇◇ /əbændən/ (**abandons, abandoning, abandoned**) 1 V-T If you **abandon** a place, thing, or person, you leave the place, thing, or person permanently or for a long time, especially when you should not do so. 抛弃 ❑ *He claimed that his parents had abandoned him.* 他声称他的父母抛弃了他。 2 V-T If you **abandon** an activity or piece of work, you stop doing it before it is finished. 中途放弃 ❑ *The authorities have abandoned any attempt to distribute food in an orderly fashion.* 当局中途放弃了任何有序地分发食品的尝试。 3 V-T If you **abandon** an idea or way of thinking, you stop having that idea or thinking in that way. 放弃 (想法或思想方式) ❑ *Logic had prevailed and he had abandoned the idea.* 理性占了上风，他放弃了该想法。 4 N-UNCOUNT If you say that someone does something **with abandon**, you mean that they behave in a wild, uncontrolled way and do not think or care about how they should behave. 放纵 [usu "with" N] [DISAPPROVAL] ❑ *He approached life with reckless abandon–I don't think he himself knew what he was going to do next.* 他以不计后果的放纵态度对待生活——我想他自己都不知道他接下来要做什么。 5 → see also **abandoned** 6 PHRASE If people **abandon ship**, they get off a ship because it is sinking. (因船舶下沉而) 弃船 ❑ *At the captain's order, they abandoned ship.* 在船长的命令下，他们弃船离开了。

Thesaurus *abandon* 另参见：

v. desert, leave, quit; *(ant.)* stay 1
break off, give up, quit, stop; *(ant.)* continue 2

aban·doned ◆◇◇ /əbændənd/ ADJ An **abandoned** place or building is no longer used or occupied. 废弃的 ❑ *The digging had left a network of abandoned mines and tunnels.* 挖掘留下了满地密布的废弃矿井和隧道。

aban·don·ment /əbændənmənt/ 1 N-UNCOUNT The **abandonment of** a place, thing, or person is the act of leaving it permanently or for a long time, especially when you should not do so. 抛弃 ❑ *...memories of her father's complete abandonment of her.* …她父亲对她的彻底抛弃的那些记忆。 2 N-UNCOUNT The **abandonment of** a piece of work or activity is the act of stopping doing it before it is finished. 中途放弃 ❑ *Constant rain forced the abandonment of the next day's competitions.* 持续降雨迫使了第二天各项比赛的中途停止。

abate /əbeɪt/ (**abates, abating, abated**) V-I If something bad or undesirable **abates**, it becomes much less strong or severe. 减弱 [FORMAL] ❑ *The storms had abated by the time they rounded Cape Horn.* 暴风在他们绕过好望角时已经减弱了。

▲ **ab·bey** /æbi/ (**abbeys**) N-COUNT An **abbey** is a church with buildings attached to it in which monks or nuns live or used to live. 修道院

ab·bre·vi·ate /əbriviert/ (**abbreviates, abbreviating, abbreviated**) V-T If you **abbreviate** something, especially a word or a piece of writing, you make it shorter. 缩写 ❑ *The creators of the original X-Men abbreviated the title of its sequel to simply X2.* 第1部《X战警》的创作者们把其续集的片名缩写成简单的《X2》。

▲ **ab·bre·via·tion** /əbrivieɪʃ^{ə}n/ (**abbreviations**) N-COUNT An **abbreviation** is a short form of a word or phrase, made by leaving out some of the letters or by using only the first letter of each word. 缩写 ❑ *The abbreviation for Kansas is KS.* **Kansas**的缩写是**KS**。

ab·di·cate /æbdɪkeɪt/ (**abdicates, abdicating, abdicated**) 1 V-I If a king or queen **abdicates**, he or she gives up being king or queen. 退位 ❑ *The last French king was Louis Philippe, who abdicated in 1848.* 最后一位法国国王是路易斯·菲利普，退位于1848年。 ● **ab·di·ca·tion** /æbdɪkeɪʃ^{ə}n/ N-UNCOUNT 退位 ❑ *...the most serious royal crisis since the abdication of Edward VIII.* …自从爱德华八世退位以来最严重的皇室危机。 2 V-T If you say that someone has **abdicated** responsibility for something, you disapprove of them because they have refused to accept responsibility for it any longer. 推卸 (职责) [FORMAL, DISAPPROVAL] ❑ *Many parents simply abdicate all responsibility for their children.* 很多父母干脆推卸掉他们对孩子的所有责任。 ● **ab·di·ca·tion** N-UNCOUNT 推卸 ❑ *There had been a complete abdication of responsibility.* 曾有个彻底推卸责任的情况。

ab·do·men /æbdəʊmən/ (**abdomens**) N-COUNT Your **abdomen** is the part of your body below your chest where your stomach and intestines are. 腹部 [FORMAL] ❑ *He went into the hospital to undergo tests for a pain in his abdomen.* 他去了医院接受对他的腹部疼痛进行的各项检查。

A

ab·domi·nal /æbdɒmɪnᵊl/ ADJ **Abdominal** is used to describe something that is situated in the abdomen or forms part of it. 腹部的 [ADJ n] [FORMAL] ❑ *...vomiting, diarrhea, and abdominal pain.* …呕吐、腹泻和腹部疼痛。

▲ **ab·duct** /æbdʌkt/ (**abducts, abducting, abducted**) V-T If someone **is abducted** by another person, he or she is taken away illegally, usually using force. 绑架 ❑ *He was on his way to the airport when his car was held up and he was abducted by four gunmen.* 在去机场的路上，他的车遭到拦截，他被 4 名持枪歹徒绑架了。 ● **ab·duc·tion** /æbdʌkʃᵊn/ N-VAR (**abductions**) 绑架 ❑ *The U.N. World Food Program confirmed the abduction of eight of its workers in northern Darfur.* 联合国世界粮食计划署证实其 8 名工作人员在达尔富尔北部遭到绑架。

ab·er·ra·tion /æbəreɪʃᵊn/ (**aberrations**) N-VAR An **aberration** is an incident or way of behaving that is not typical. 失常 [FORMAL] ❑ *It became very clear that the incident was not just an aberration; it was not just a single incident.* 已经很明确这次事件并不仅仅是一次失常，也不只是一个单独的事件。

▲ **abide** /əbaɪd/ (**abides, abiding, abided**) **1** PHRASE If you **can't abide** someone or something, you dislike them very much. 无法容忍 ❑ *I can't abide people who can't make up their minds.* 我无法容忍下定不了决心的人。 **2** → see also **abiding, law-abiding**

▸ **abide by** PHRASAL VERB If you **abide by** a law, agreement, or decision, you do what it says you should do. 遵守 ❑ *They have got to abide by the rules.* 他们必须要遵守规定。

abid·ing /əbaɪdɪŋ/ ADJ An **abiding** feeling, memory, or interest is one that you have for a very long time. 持久的 (感情、记忆、兴趣) [ADJ n] ❑ *He has a genuine and abiding love of the craft.* 他对这门手艺有着一种发自内心和持久不变的热爱。

abil·ity ♦♦◇ /əbɪlɪti/ (**abilities**) **1** N-SING Your **ability to** do something is the fact that you can do it. 能力 ❑ *The public never had faith in his ability to handle the job.* 公众从来都不相信他有处理这个工作的能力。 **2** N-VAR Your **ability** is the quality or skill that you have which makes it possible for you to do something. 才能 ❑ *Her drama teacher spotted her ability.* 她的戏剧老师发现了她的才能。 ❑ *Does the school cater to all abilities?* 这所学校满足各水平才能的人吗? **3** PHRASE If you do something **to the best of** your **abilities** or **to the best of** your **ability**, you do it as well as you can. 尽某人所能 ❑ *I take care of them to the best of my abilities.* 我尽全力照顾他们。

> Do not confuse **ability** with **capability** and **capacity**. You often use **ability** to say that someone can do something well. ❑ *He had remarkable ability as a musician. ...the ability to bear hardship.* A person's **capability** is the amount of work they can do and how well they can do it. ❑ *...a job that was beyond the capability of one man. ...the director's ideas of the capability of the actor.* If someone has a particular **capacity**, a **capacity** for something, or a **capacity** to do something, they have the qualities required to do it. **Capacity** is a more formal word than **ability**. ❑ *...their capacity for hard work. ...his capacity to see the other person's point of view.*

Thesaurus *ability* 另参见：

N. capability, competence **1**
knack, skill, talent, technique **2**

Word Partnership *ability* 的常用搭配：

N. **lack of** ability **1**
V. ability **to handle, have the** ability, **lack the** ability **1 2**
ADJ. **natural** ability **2**

ab·ject /æbdʒɛkt/ ADJ You use **abject** to emphasize that a situation or quality is extremely bad. 糟糕透顶的 [EMPHASIS] ❑ *Both of them died in abject poverty.* 他们两个人都死于穷困潦倒。

ablaze /əbleɪz/ **1** ADJ Something that is **ablaze** is burning very fiercely. 熊熊燃烧的 [v n ADJ, v-link ADJ] ❑ *Stores, houses, and vehicles were set ablaze.* 商店、房子和车辆被大火烧着了。 **2** ADJ If a place is **ablaze with** lights or colors, it is very bright because of them. 光彩夺目的 [v-link ADJ] ❑ *The chamber was ablaze with light.* 该大厅当时灯火辉煌。

able ♦♦♦ /eɪbᵊl/ (**abler** /eɪblər/, **ablest** /eɪblɪst/) **1** PHRASE If you **are able to** do something, you have skills or qualities which make it possible for you to do it. (因具有某技能或素质而) 能够 ❑ *The older child should be able to prepare a simple meal.* 这个大点儿的孩子应该能做顿简单的饭菜。 ❑ *The company says they're able to keep pricing competitive.* 这个公司说他们能够保持价格竞争力。

> **Can, could,** and **be able to** are all used to talk about a person's ability to do something. They are followed by the infinitive form of a verb. You use **can** or a present form of **be able to** to refer to the present, although **can** is more common. ❑ *They can all read and write... The snake is able to catch small mammals.* You use **could** or a past form of **be able to** to refer to the past, and "will" or "shall" with **be able to** to refer to the future. **Be able to** is used if you want to refer to doing something at a particular time. ❑ *After treatment he was able to return to work.* **Can** and **could** are used to talk about possibility. **Could** refers to a particular occasion and **can** to more general situations. ❑ *Many jobs could be lost... Too much salt can be harmful.* When talking about the past, you use **could have** and a past participle. ❑ *It could have been much worse.* You also use **can** for the present and **could** for the past to talk about rules or what people are allowed to do. ❑ *They can leave at any time.* Note that when making requests either **can** or **could** may be used. ❑ *Can I have a drink?... Could we put the fire on?* However, **could** is always used for suggestions. ❑ *You could phone her and ask.*

2 PHRASE If you **are able to** do something, you have enough freedom, power, time, or money to do it. (因有足够的自由、权力、时间或财力而) 可以 ❑ *You'll be able to read in peace.* 你将可以安静地看书。 ❑ *Have you been able to have any kind of contact?* 你取得任何联系了吗?

> Note that **able** and **capable** are both used to say that someone can do something. When you say that someone is **able** to do something, you mean that they can do it either because of their knowledge or skill, or because it is possible. ❑ *He wondered if he would be able to climb over the rail... They were able to use their profits for new investments.* Note that if you use a past tense, you are saying that someone has actually done something. ❑ *We were able to reduce costs.* When you say that someone is **capable** of doing something, you mean either that they have the knowledge and skill to do it, or that they are likely to do it. ❑ *The workers are perfectly capable of running the organization themselves... She was quite capable of falling asleep.* You can say that someone is **capable** of a particular feeling or action. ❑ *He's capable of loyalty... Bowman could not believe him capable of murder.* You can also use "**capable** of" when talking about what something such as a car or machine can do. ❑ *The car was capable of 110 miles per hour.* If you describe someone as **able** or **capable**, you mean that they do things well. ❑ *He's certainly a capable gardener.*

3 ADJ Someone who is **able** is very intelligent or very good at doing something. 有才能的 ❑ *...one of the brightest and ablest members of the government.* …最聪明、最有才能的政府成员之一。

able-bodied /eɪbᵊlbɒdid/ ADJ An **able-bodied** person is physically strong and healthy, rather than weak or disabled. 体格健全的 ❑ *The gym can be used by both able-bodied and disabled people.* 该健身房既可以让体格健全的人使用也可以让残疾人使用。 ● N-PLURAL **The able-bodied** are people who are able-bodied. 体格健全的人 ❑ *No doubt such robots would be very useful in the homes of the able-bodied, too.* 毫无疑问，这样的机器人在健全人的家里也会非常有用。

ably /eɪbli/ ADV **Ably** means skillfully and successfully. 能干地 [ADV with v] ❑ *He was ably assisted by a number of members from other branches.* 他得到了其他部门的几个成员的得力协助。

ab·nor·mal /æbnɔrmᵊl/ ADJ Someone or something that is **abnormal** is unusual, especially in a way that is troublesome. 异常的 [FORMAL] ❑ *...abnormal heart rhythms and high anxiety levels.* …异常的心律和高度焦虑。 ● **ab·nor·mal·ly** ADV 异常地 ❑ *...abnormally high levels of glucose.* …异常高的葡萄糖指标。

ab·nor·mal·ity /æbnɔrmælɪti/ (**abnormalities**) N-VAR An **abnormality** in something, especially in a person's body or behavior, is an unusual part or feature of it that may be worrying or dangerous. 异常 (尤指人的身体或行为中令人担忧或危险性的特征) [FORMAL] ❑ *Further scans are required to confirm the diagnosis of an abnormality.* 需要做进一步的扫描来确诊异常情况。

aboard /əbɔrd/ PREP If you are **aboard** a ship or plane, you are on it or in it. 在 (船或飞机) 上 ❑ *She invited 750 people aboard the luxury yacht, the Savarona.* 她邀请了750人登上这艘豪华游艇，萨瓦罗纳号。 ● ADV **Aboard** is also an adverb. 在 (船或飞机) 上 [ADV after v]

❑ *It had taken two hours to load all the people aboard.* 用了两个小时才让所有的人上了船。

abol·ish /əbɒlɪʃ/ (**abolishes, abolishing, abolished**) V-T If someone in authority **abolishes** a system or practice, they formally put an end to it. 废除 ❑ *An Illinois House committee voted Thursday to abolish the death penalty.* 伊利诺伊州议院的一个委员会在星期四投票废除了死刑。

Thesaurus *abolish* 另参见:
v. eliminate, end; (*ant.*) continue

abo·li·tion /æbəlɪʃən/ N-UNCOUNT The **abolition of** something such as a system or practice is its formal ending. 废除 ❑ *The abolition of slavery in Brazil and the Caribbean closely followed the pattern of the United States.* 巴西和加勒比海地区对奴隶制的废除很大程度上遵循了美国的模式。

abomi·nable /əbɒmɪnəbəl/ ADJ Something that is **abominable** is very unpleasant or bad. 恶劣的 ❑ *The president described the killings as an abominable crime.* 总统称这系列杀戮为恶劣的罪行。

Abo·rigi·nal /æbərɪdʒɪnəl/ (**Aboriginals**) or **aboriginal** 1 N-COUNT An **Aboriginal** is an Australian Aborigine. 澳大利亚的土著人 ❑ *He remained fascinated by the Aboriginals' tales.* 他一直对澳大利亚土著人的故事很着迷。 2 ADJ **Aboriginal** means belonging or relating to the Australian Aborigines. 澳大利亚土著的 [ADJ n] ❑ *...Aboriginal art.* …土著艺术。

Abo·rigi·ne /æbərɪdʒɪni/ (**Aborigines**) N-COUNT **Aborigines** are members of the tribes that were living in Australia when Europeans arrived there. 澳大利亚土著居民 ❑ *...Bigge Island, an area sacred to Aborigines for more than 20,000 years.* …比格岛，两万多年来被澳大利亚土著居民认为神圣的地区。

★ **abort** /əbɔrt/ (**aborts, aborting, aborted**) 1 V-T If an unborn baby **is aborted**, the pregnancy is ended deliberately and the baby is not born alive. 使流产 ❑ *Her lover walked out on her after she had aborted their child.* 在她打掉了他们的孩子之后，她的情人离开了她。 2 V-T If someone **aborts** a process, plan, or activity, they stop it before it has been completed. 中途放弃 ❑ *When the decision was made to abort the mission, there was great confusion.* 中途放弃这次任务的决定引起了严重混乱。

abor·tion ♦◇◇ /əbɔrʃən/ (**abortions**) N-VAR If a woman has an **abortion**, she ends her pregnancy deliberately so that the baby is not born alive. 流产 ❑ *He and his girlfriend had been going out together for a year when she had an abortion.* 他的女友流产时，他和她已经交往了一年时间。

abor·tive /əbɔrtɪv/ ADJ An **abortive** attempt or action is unsuccessful. 失败的 [FORMAL] ❑ *...an abortive attempt to prevent the current president from taking office.* …一次阻止现任总统就职的不成功的尝试。

▲ **abound** /əbaʊnd/ (**abounds, abounding, abounded**) V-I If things **abound**, or if a place **abounds with** things, there are very large numbers of them. 充满 [FORMAL] ❑ *Stories abound about when he was in charge.* 他负责时传闻很多。

about ♦♦♦ /əbaʊt/

> In addition to the uses shown below, **about** is used after some verbs, nouns, and adjectives to introduce extra information. **About** is also often used after verbs of movement, such as "walk" and "drive," especially in British English, and in phrasal verbs such as "set about."

1 PREP You use **about** to introduce who or what something relates to or concerns. 关于；对于 ❑ *She knew a lot about food.* 她对食品懂得很多。 ❑ *He never complains about his wife.* 他对他妻子从不抱怨。 2 PREP When you mention the things that an activity or institution is **about**, you are saying what it involves or what its aims are. 涉及；旨在 ❑ *Leadership is about the ability to implement change.* 领导才能是一种实行变革的能力。 3 PREP You use **about** after some adjectives to indicate the person or thing that a feeling or state of mind relates to. 为…感到(用在某些形容词后，表示与某种感觉或心态有关的人或事) ❑ *"I'm sorry about Patrick," she said.* "我为帕特里克感到难过，"她说道。 4 PREP If you do something **about** a problem, you take action in order to solve it. 针对 ❑ *Rachel was going to do something about Jacob.* 雷切尔要对雅各布采取行动。 5 PREP When you say that there is a particular quality **about** someone or something, you mean that they have this quality. 在…(具有某种品质) ❑ *There was a warmth and passion about him I never knew existed.* 他身上有一种我从来没有认识到的热情和激情。 6 PREP If you put something **about** a person or thing, you put it around them. 围绕 [mainly BRIT]

in AM, usually use **around**

7 ADV **About** is used in front of a number to show that the number is not exact. 大约 [ADV num] ❑ *The rate of inflation is running at about 2.7 percent.* 通货膨胀率大约在2.7%。 8 ADV If someone or something moves **about**, they keep moving in different directions. 到处 [ADV after v] [mainly BRIT]

in AM, usually use **around**

● PREP **About** is also a preposition. 各处 [v PREP n] [mainly BRIT]

in AM, usually use **around**

9 ADJ If someone or something is **about**, they are present or available. 在场的；可得到的 [v-link ADJ] [mainly BRIT]

in AM, usually use **around**

10 ADJ If you are **about to** do something, you are going to do it very soon. If something is **about to** happen, it will happen very soon. 就要…的 [v-link ADJ to-inf] ❑ *I think he's about to leave.* 我想他就要离开。 ❑ *Argentina has lifted all restrictions on trade and visas are about to be abolished.* 阿根廷已经取消了所有的贸易限制，签证就要被废除了。 11 **how about** → see **how** 12 **what about** → see **what** 13 **just about** → see **just** 14 PHRASE If someone is **out and about**, they are going out and doing things, especially after they have been unable to for a while. 到外面活动 ❑ *Despite considerable pain she has been getting out and about almost as normal.* 尽管很疼，她已经在几乎像正常人一样到外面活动了。

above ♦♦◇ /əbʌv/ 1 PREP If one thing is **above** another one, it is directly over it or higher than it. 在…上方 ❑ *He lifted his hands above his head.* 他双手举过头顶。 ❑ *Apartment 46 was a quiet apartment, unlike the one above it.* 46号公寓是一套安静的公寓，不像它上面的那一套。 ● ADV **Above** is also an adverb. 在上面 ❑ *A long scream sounded from somewhere above.* 从上面什么地方传来一声长长的尖叫。 ❑ *...a picture of the new plane as seen from above.* …一张该新型飞机的俯瞰图片。 2 PREP If an amount or measurement is **above** a particular level, it is greater than that level. (数量或度量) 高于 ❑ *The temperature crept up to just above 40 degrees.* 气温慢慢升至刚过40度。 ❑ *Victoria Falls has had above average levels of rainfall this year.* 维多利亚瀑布今年的降雨量高于平均水平。 ● ADV **Above** is also an adverb. 高于 [amount "and" ADV] ❑ *Banks have been charging 25 percent and above for unsecured loans.* 银行一直以来对无担保贷款收取25%或更高的费用。 3 PREP If you hear one sound **above** another, it is louder or clearer than the second one. (声音) 高过 ❑ *Then there was a woman's voice, rising shrilly above the barking.* 然后是一个女人的声音，尖利刺耳，高过了狗吠声。 4 PREP If someone is **above** you, they are in a higher social position than you or in a position of authority over you. (职位或社会地位) 高于 ❑ *I married above myself.* 我和比我地位高的人结了婚。 ● ADV **Above** is also an adverb. (职位或社会地位) 在上 ["from" ADV] ❑ *The policemen admitted beating the student, but said they were acting on orders from above.* 警察承认打了这个学生，但是说他们是根据上级命令行事的。 5 PREP If you say that someone thinks they are **above** something, you mean that they act as if they are too good or important for it. 不屑于；不至于 [DISAPPROVAL] ❑ *This was clearly a failure by someone who thought he was above failure.* 这显然是一个自以为不会失败的人所经历的一次失败。 6 PREP If someone is **above** criticism or suspicion, they cannot be criticized or suspected because of their good qualities or their position. 不受(批评或怀疑) [v-link PREP n] ❑ *He was a respected academic and above suspicion.* 他是一位受敬重的学者，不能受怀疑。 7 PREP If you value one person or thing **above** any other, you value them more or consider that they are more important. 胜过 ❑ *...his tendency to put the team above everything.* …他的一切以团队为重的倾向。 8 **over and above** → see **over** 9 **above the law** → see **law** 10 **above board** → see **board** 11 ADV In writing, you use **above** to refer to something that has already been mentioned or discussed. 以上 ❑ *Several conclusions could be drawn from the results described above.* 几个结论可从上述的那些结果中得出。 ● N-SING-COLL **Above** is also a noun. 上述内容 ❑ *For additional information, contact any of the above.* 欲知详情，请与上述任一人联系。 ● ADJ **Above** is also an adjective. 上述的 [ADJ n] ❑ *For a copy of their brochure, write to the above address.* 欲取得一份他们的宣传手册，写信到上述地址。

A

Above and over are both used to talk about position and height. If something is higher than something else and the two things are imagined as being positioned along a vertical line, you can use either **above** or **over**. ❑ *He opened a cupboard above the sink... She leaned forward until her face was over the basin.* However, if something is higher than something else but the two things are regarded as being wide or horizontal rather than tall or vertical, you have to use **above**. ❑ *The trees rose above the row of houses.* **Above** and **over** are both used to talk about measurements, for example, when you are talking about a point that is higher than another point on a scale. ❑ *Any money earned over that level is taxed. ...everybody above five feet eight inches in height.* You use **over** to say that a distance or period of time is longer than the one mentioned. ❑ *...a height of over twelve thousand feet... Our relationship lasted for over a year.*

abra·sive /əbreɪsɪv/ **1** ADJ Someone who has an **abrasive** manner is unkind and rude. 粗鲁的 ❑ *His abrasive manner has won him an unenviable notoriety.* 他粗鲁的态度已经为他招来了一个无可羡慕的恶名。 **2** ADJ An **abrasive** substance is rough and can be used to clean hard surfaces. 有研磨作用的 ❑ *...a new all-purpose, non-abrasive cleaner that cleans and polishes all metals.* …一种可以清洁、抛光各种金属的万能无磨损新型清洁剂。

▲ **abreast** /əbrɛst/ **1** ADV If people or things walk or move **abreast**, they are next to each other, side by side, and facing in the same direction. 并排地 ❑ *The steep sidewalk was too narrow for them to walk abreast.* 这个很陡的人行道窄得不能让他们并排走。 **2** PHRASE If you **keep abreast of** a subject, you know all the most recent facts about it. 及时了解 ❑ *He will be keeping abreast of the news.* 他会不断及时了解最新消息。

abroad ♦◇◇ /əbrɔd/ ADV If you go **abroad**, you go to a foreign country, usually one that is separated from the country where you live by an ocean or a sea. 到国外 ❑ *I would love to go abroad this year, perhaps to the South of France.* 我今年想去国外，可能去法国南部。 ❑ *He will stand in for Mr. Goh when he is abroad.* 当高先生在国外时他将代行其职。

ab·rupt /əbrʌpt/ **1** ADJ An **abrupt** change or action is very sudden, often in a way that is unpleasant. 骤然的 ❑ *Rosie's idyllic world came to an abrupt end when her parents' marriage broke up.* 当她的父母婚姻破裂后，罗茜的田园诗一般的世界骤然结束了。 ● **ab·rupt·ly** ADV 骤然地 [ADV with v] ❑ *He stopped abruptly and looked my way.* 他突然停住，向我看了过来。 **2** ADJ Someone who is **abrupt** speaks in a rude, unfriendly way. 唐突的 ❑ *He was abrupt to the point of rudeness.* 他唐突到了无礼的地步。 ● **ab·rupt·ly** ADV 唐突地 ❑ *"Good night, then," she said abruptly.* "那么，晚安"，她唐突地说道。

ab·sence ♦◇◇ /æbsᵊns/ (**absences**) **1** N-VAR Someone's **absence** from a place is the fact that they are not there. 缺席 ❑ *...a bundle of letters which had arrived for me in my absence.* …我不在的时候寄给我的一捆信。 **2** N-SING The **absence** of something from a place is the fact that it is not there or does not exist. 不存在 ❑ *The presence or absence of clouds can have an important impact on temperature.* 云的有无对气温会产生重要影响。

ab·sent /æbsᵊnt/ **1** ADJ If someone or something is **absent from** a place or situation where they should be or where they usually are, they are not there. 缺席的 ❑ *He has been absent from his desk for two weeks.* 他已经两个星期没来了。 ❑ *The pictures, too, were absent from the walls.* 那些照片也不在那些墙上了。 **2** ADJ If someone appears **absent**, they are not paying attention because they are thinking about something else. 心不在焉的 ❑ *"Nothing," Rosie said in an absent way.* "没什么，"罗茜心不在焉地说。 ● **ab·sent·ly** /æbsᵊntli/ ADV 心不在焉地 ❑ *He nodded absently.* 他心不在焉地点了点头。 **3** ADJ An **absent** parent does not live with his or her children. 不与孩子同住的 [ADJ n] ❑ *...absent fathers who fail to pay toward the costs of looking after their children.* …未能支付抚养费的不与孩子同住的父亲们。 **4** PREP If you say that **absent** one thing, another thing will happen, you mean that if the first thing does not happen, the second thing will happen. 倘若没有… [AM, FORMAL] ❑ *Absent a solution, people like Sue Godfrey will just keep on fighting.* 若没有个解决方案，像休・戈弗雷这样的人就会继续争斗。

ab·sen·tee /æbsᵊnti/ (**absentees**) **1** N-COUNT An **absentee** is a person who is expected to be in a particular place but who is not there. 缺席者 ❑ *At least two of the three other absentees also had justifiable reasons for being away.* 其他三个缺席者中至少两个人也有合理的缺席理由。 **2** ADJ **Absentee** is used to describe someone who is not there to do a particular job in person. 缺席的 [ADJ n] ❑ *Absentee fathers will be forced to pay child support.* 不和孩子在一起的父亲会被强制支付子女抚养费。 **3** ADJ In elections in the United States, if you vote by **absentee** ballot or if you are an **absentee** voter, you vote in advance because you will be unable to go to the polling place. 缺席投票的 [ADJ n] [AM] ❑ *He has already voted by absentee ballot.* 他已经通过缺席投票的方式投了票。

→ see **election**

absent-minded ADJ Someone who is **absent-minded** forgets things or does not pay attention to what they are doing, often because they are thinking about something else. 心不在焉的 ❑ *In his later life he became even more absent-minded.* 在晚年他变得更加心不在焉了。 ● **absent-mindedly** ADV 心不在焉地 [ADV with v] ❑ *Elizabeth absent-mindedly picked a thread from his lapel.* 伊丽莎白心不在焉地从他的翻领上拈起了一根线。

ab·so·lute ♦◇◇ /æbsəlut/ (**absolutes**) **1** ADJ **Absolute** means total and complete. 完全的 ❑ *It's not really suited to absolute beginners.* 这对于纯粹的初学者们不太适合。 **2** ADJ You use **absolute** to emphasize something that you are saying. 绝对的 [ADJ n] [EMPHASIS] ❑ *About 12 inches wide is the absolute minimum you should consider.* 12英寸左右的宽度是你应该考虑的绝对最小尺寸。 **3** ADJ An **absolute** ruler has complete power and authority over his or her country. 独裁的 [ADJ n] ❑ *He ruled with absolute power.* 他实行独裁统治。 **4** ADJ **Absolute** is used to say that something is definite and will not change even if circumstances change. 确凿的 ❑ *John brought the absolute proof that we needed.* 约翰拿出了我们需要的确凿证据。 **5** ADJ An amount that is expressed in **absolute** terms is expressed as a fixed amount rather than referring to variable factors such as what you earn or the effects of inflation. 绝对的 [ADJ n] ❑ *In absolute terms their wages remain low by national standards.* 他们工资的绝对值根据国家标准仍然是低的。 **6** ADJ **Absolute** rules and principles are believed to be true, right, or relevant in all situations. 绝对的 ❑ *There are no absolute rules.* 没有绝对的准则。 **7** N-COUNT An **absolute** is a rule or principle that is believed to be true, right, or relevant in all situations. 绝对原则 ❑ *This is one of the few absolutes in U.S. constitutional law.* 这是美国宪法中少有的几项绝对原则之一。

ab·so·lute·ly ♦♦◇ /æbsəlutli/ **1** ADV **Absolutely** means totally and completely. 绝对地 [EMPHASIS] ❑ *Joan is absolutely right.* 琼绝对正确。 ❑ *I absolutely refuse to get married.* 我绝对拒绝结婚。 **2** ADV Some people say **absolutely** as an emphatic way of saying yes or of agreeing with someone. They say **absolutely not** as an emphatic way of saying no or of disagreeing with someone. 绝对地 [ADV as reply] [EMPHASIS] ❑ *"It's worrying that they're doing things without training though, isn't it?"—"Absolutely."* "可是他们未经培训就干，这真让人担忧，是不是？"——"绝对是。"

ab·sorb /æbsɔrb, -zɔrb/ (**absorbs, absorbing, absorbed**) **1** V-T If something **absorbs** a liquid, gas, or other substance, it soaks it up or takes it in. 吸收（液体、气体等） ❑ *Plants absorb carbon dioxide from the air and moisture from the soil.* 植物从空气中吸收二氧化碳，从泥土中吸收水分。 **2** V-T If something **absorbs** light, heat, or another form of energy, it takes it in. 吸取（光、热等能量） ❑ *A household radiator absorbs energy in the form of electric current and releases it in the form of heat.* 家用暖气以电流的形式吸收能量，然后以热量的形式将其释放出去。 **3** V-T If a group **is absorbed into** a larger group, it becomes part of the larger group. 使并入 ❑ *City schools were absorbed into the countywide school district.* 市立学校被并入了郡学区。 **4** V-T If something **absorbs** a force or shock, it reduces its effect. 使缓冲 ❑ *...footwear which does not absorb the impact of the foot striking the ground.* …不能缓冲脚踏在地面上所产生的冲击力的鞋子。 **5** V-T If a system or society **absorbs** changes, effects, or costs, it is able to deal with them. 能应付 ❑ *The banks would be forced to absorb large losses.* 这些银行将被迫承担那些巨大的损失。 **6** V-T If something **absorbs** something valuable such as money, space, or time, it uses up a great deal of it. 大量消耗 ❑ *It absorbed vast amounts of capital that could have been used for investment.* 它消耗掉了原本可以用作投资的大量资本。 **7** V-T If you **absorb** information, you learn and understand it. 理解 ❑ *Too often he only absorbs half the information in the manual.* 通常，他对手册里的信息只是一知半解。 **8** V-T If something **absorbs** you, it interests you a great deal and takes up all your attention and energy. 使专注 ❑ *...a second career which absorbed her more completely than her acting ever had.* …一个比其演艺事

业更让她全身心投入的第二职业。 9 → see also **absorbed**, **absorbing**

ab·sorbed /əbsɔrbd, -zɔrbd/ ADJ If you are **absorbed in** something or someone, you are very interested in them and they take up all your attention and energy. 专心致志的 [v-link ADJ] ❑ *They were completely absorbed in each other.* 他们完全专注于对方。

ab·sor·bent /əbsɔrbənt, -zɔrbənt/ ADJ **Absorbent** material soaks up liquid easily. 有吸收力的 ❑ *The towels are highly absorbent.* 这些毛巾吸水力很强。

ab·sorb·ing /əbsɔrbɪŋ, -zɔrbɪŋ/ ADJ An **absorbing** task or activity interests you a great deal and takes up all your attention and energy. 让人专注的 ❑ *"Two Sisters" is an absorbing read.* 《两姊妹》是一本引人入胜的读物。

ab·sorp·tion /əbsɔrpʃən, -zɔrpʃən/ 1 N-UNCOUNT The **absorption of** a liquid, gas, or other substance is the process of it being soaked up or taken in. 吸收 ❑ *This controls the absorption of liquids.* 这可以控制液体的吸收。 2 N-UNCOUNT The **absorption** of a group **into** a larger group is the process of it becoming part of the larger group. 收并 ❑ *...Serbia's absorption into the Ottoman Empire.* …塞尔维亚被奥斯曼帝国的兼并。

▲ **ab·stain** /æbsteɪn/ (**abstains, abstaining, abstained**) 1 V-I If you **abstain from** something, usually something you want to do, you deliberately do not do it. 对…节制 [FORMAL] ❑ *Abstain from sex or use condoms.* 节制性生活或使用避孕套。 2 V-I If you **abstain** during a vote, you do not use your vote. 弃权 ❑ *Three countries abstained in the vote.* 三个国家在投票中弃权了。

ab·sten·tion /æbstɛnʃən/ (**abstentions**) N-VAR **Abstention** is a formal act of not voting either for or against a proposal. 弃权 ❑ *...a vote of sixteen in favor, three against, and one abstention.* …一轮16人赞同、3人反对、1人弃权的投票。

ab·sti·nence /æbstɪnəns/ N-UNCOUNT **Abstinence** is the practice of abstaining from something such as alcoholic drink or sex, often for health or religious reasons. (常指因健康或宗教等原因对饮酒或性事等的) 禁欲 ❑ *...six months of abstinence.* …6个月的禁欲。

ab·stract /æbstrækt/ (**abstracts**) 1 ADJ An **abstract** idea or way of thinking is based on general ideas rather than on real things and events. 抽象的 ❑ *...starting with a few abstract principles.* …以几条抽象的原则开始。 ❑ *It's not a question of some abstract concept of justice.* 这不是一个有关正义的某一抽象概念的问题。 2 ADJ In grammar, an **abstract** noun refers to a quality or idea rather than to a physical object. 抽象的 (名词) [ADJ n] ❑ *...abstract words such as glory, honor, and courage.* …诸如光荣、荣誉、勇气这样的抽象词汇。 3 ADJ **Abstract** art makes use of shapes and patterns rather than showing people or things. 抽象的 (艺术) ❑ *A modern abstract painting takes over one complete wall.* 一幅现代抽象画占了整整一面墙。 4 PHRASE When you talk or think about something **in the abstract**, you talk or think about it in a general way, rather than considering particular things or events. 在抽象意义上 ❑ *Money was a commodity she never thought about except in the abstract.* 金钱是她从未具体想过的一种商品。 5 N-COUNT An **abstract** is an abstract work of art. 抽象作品 ❑ *His abstracts are held in numerous collections.* 他的抽象画被纳入到很多收藏中。 6 N-COUNT An **abstract of** an article, document, or speech is a short piece of writing that gives the main points of it. 摘要 ❑ *It might also be necessary to supply an abstract of the review of the literature as well.* 可能也有必要提供这篇文学评论的摘要。

ab·strac·tion /æbstrækʃən/ (**abstractions**) N-VAR An **abstraction** is a general idea rather than one relating to a particular object, person, or situation. 抽象概念 [FORMAL] ❑ *Is it worth fighting a big war, in the name of an abstraction like sovereignty?* 以象主权这样一个抽象概念的名义，值得打一场大战吗？

★ **ab·surd** /əbsɜrd, -zɜrd/ ADJ If you say that something is **absurd**, you are criticizing it because you think that it is ridiculous or that it does not make sense. 荒谬的 [DISAPPROVAL] ❑ *That's absurd.* 那是荒谬的。 ❑ *It's absurd to suggest that they knew what was going on but did nothing.* 暗示说他们知道怎么回事但却袖手旁观是荒谬的。 ● N-SING **The absurd** is something that is absurd. 荒谬之事 ["the" N] [FORMAL] ❑ *Connie had a sharp eye for the absurd.* 康妮对荒谬之事有敏锐的眼光。 ● **ab·surd·ly** ADV 荒谬地 ❑ *Prices were still absurdly low, in his opinion.* 在他看来，价格依然低得荒谬。 ● **ab·surd·ity** /əbsɜrdɪti, -zɜrd-/ N-VAR (**absurdities**) 荒谬性 ❑ *I find myself growing increasingly angry at the absurdity of the situation.* 我发觉自己对这种情况的荒谬性越来越气愤。

Thesaurus *absurd* 另参见：
ADJ. crazy, foolish, idiotic

★ **abun·dance** /əbʌndəns/ N-SING-COLL An **abundance of** something is a large quantity of it. 丰富 [usu N "of" n, also "in" N] ❑ *This area of Mexico has an abundance of safe beaches and a pleasing climate.* 墨西哥的这个地区有大量的安全沙滩与宜人的气候。

abun·dant /əbʌndənt/ ADJ Something that is **abundant** is present in large quantities. 丰富的 ❑ *There is an abundant supply of cheap labor.* 有丰富的廉价劳动力供应。

abuse ♦♦◇ (**abuses, abusing, abused**)

The noun is pronounced /əbyus/. The verb is pronounced /əbyuz/.

名词读作 /əbyus/，动词读作 /əbyuz/。

1 N-UNCOUNT **Abuse** of someone is cruel and violent treatment of them. 虐待 [also N in pl] ❑ *...investigation of alleged child abuse.* …对涉嫌虐待儿童的调查。 ❑ *...victims of sexual and physical abuse.* …性虐待和肉体摧残的受害者们。 2 N-UNCOUNT **Abuse** is extremely rude and insulting things that people say when they are angry. 辱骂 ❑ *I was left shouting abuse as the car sped off.* 当车加速离去时，我在那里破口大骂。 3 N-VAR **Abuse** of something is the use of it in a wrong way or for a bad purpose. 滥用 [with supp] ❑ *What went on here was an abuse of power.* 这里发生的情况是职权的滥用。 4 V-T If someone **is abused**, they are treated cruelly and violently. 虐待 ❑ *Janet had been abused by her father since she was eleven.* 詹妮特自从11岁起就被她的父亲虐待。 ❑ *...parents who feel they cannot cope or might abuse their children.* …感到自己不能应付或可能虐待孩子的家长们。 5 V-T You can say that someone **is abused** if extremely rude and insulting things are said to them. 侮辱 ❑ *He alleged that he was verbally abused by other soldiers.* 他声称他被其他士兵们口头侮辱了。 6 V-T If you **abuse** something, you use it in a wrong way or for a bad purpose. 滥用 ❑ *He showed how the rich and powerful can abuse their position.* 他揭露了有钱有势的人会如何滥用他们的地位。

Thesaurus *abuse* 另参见：
N. damage, harm, injury, violation 1
blame, injury, insult; *(ant.)* compliment 2
V. damage, harm, injure, mistreat; *(ant.)* care for, protect, respect 4
insult, offend, pick on, put down; *(ant.)* compliment, flatter, praise 5

▲ **abu·sive** /əbyusɪv/ 1 ADJ Someone who is **abusive** behaves in a cruel and violent way toward other people. 恶毒残暴的 ❑ *He became violent and abusive toward Ben's mother.* 他对待本的妈妈变得粗暴而又残酷。 2 ADJ **Abusive** language is extremely rude and insulting. 侮辱的 ❑ *I did not use any foul or abusive language.* 我没有使用过任何粗话或侮辱性的语言。

abys·mal /əbɪzməl/ ADJ If you describe a situation or the condition of something as **abysmal**, you think that it is very bad or poor in quality. 糟透的 ❑ *The general standard of racing was abysmal.* 比赛的总体水平糟透了。 ● **abys·mal·ly** ADV 糟透地 ❑ *The group for the most part found the standard of education abysmally low.* 这个小组总体上认为这里的教育水准低得可怜。

abyss /əbɪs/ (**abysses**) 1 N-COUNT An **abyss** is a very deep hole in the ground. 深渊 [LITERARY] ❑ *The torrent, swollen by the melting snow, plunges into a tremendous abyss.* 因融化的雪水而高涨的急流泻入一个巨大的深渊之中。 2 N-COUNT If someone is on the edge or brink of an **abyss**, they are about to enter into a very frightening or threatening situation. 深渊 (指危险处境) [LITERARY] ❑ *...a warning that the Middle East was on the brink of an abyss.* …一则有关中东已经濒临深渊的警告。

aca·dem·ic ♦◇◇ /ækədɛmɪk/ (**academics**) 1 ADJ **Academic** is used to describe things that relate to the work done in schools, colleges, and universities, especially work that involves studying and reasoning rather than practical or technical skills. 学术上的 [ADJ n] ❑ *Their academic standards are high.* 他们的学术水平很高。 ● **aca·dem·ical·ly** /ækədɛmɪkli/ ADV 学术上地 ❑ *He is academically gifted.* 他在学术方面有天份。 2 ADJ **Academic** is used to describe things that relate to schools, colleges, and universities. 学校的 [ADJ n] ❑ *...the start of the last academic year.* …上一个学年的开始。 3 ADJ **Academic** is used to describe work, or a school, college, or university, that places emphasis on studying and reasoning rather than on practical or technical skills. 学术的 ❑ *The author has settled for a more academic approach.* 该作者已经确定了一种更学术的方法。 **4** ADJ Someone who is **academic** is good at studying. 学习好的 ❑ *The system is failing most disastrously among less academic children.* 这种制度在学习不太好的学生中最失败。 **5** ADJ You can say that a discussion or situation is **academic** if you think it is not important because it has no real effect or cannot happen. 空谈的 ❑ *Who wants to hear about contracts and deadlines that are purely academic?* 谁想听那些完全不切实际的合同和最后期限呢? **6** N-COUNT An **academic** is a member of a university or college who teaches or does research. 学者 ❑ *A group of academics say they can predict house prices through a computer program.* 一批学者声称，他们可以通过一种电脑程序预测房价。

★ **acad·emi·cian** /ækədəmɪʃən, əkædəmɪʃən/ (**academicians**) N-COUNT An **academician** is a member of an academy, usually one that has been formed to improve or maintain standards in a particular field. 院士

acad·emy /əkædəmi/ (**academies**) **1** N-COUNT **Academy** is sometimes used in the names of schools and colleges, especially those specializing in particular subjects or skills, or private high schools in the United States. 有时用于(尤为专科)院校或美国私立中学名称中 ❑ *He is an English teacher at the Seattle Academy for Arts and Sciences.* 他是西雅图文理学院的一名英语老师。 **2** N-IN-NAMES **Academy** appears in the names of some societies formed to improve or maintain standards in a particular field. 用于专业学术团体名称中 ❑ *...the American Academy of Psychotherapists.* …美国心理治疗师学会。

ac·cel·er·ate /æksɛləreɪt/ (**accelerates, accelerating, accelerated**) **1** V-T/V-I If the process or rate of something **accelerates** or if something **accelerates** it, it gets faster and faster. 使加速；加速 ❑ *Growth will accelerate to 2.9 percent next year.* 增长明年将加快到2.9%。 **2** V-I When a moving vehicle **accelerates**, it goes faster and faster. 加速 ❑ *Suddenly the car accelerated.* 突然车加速了。

ac·cel·era·tion /æksɛləreɪʃən/ **1** N-UNCOUNT The **acceleration of** a process or change is the fact that it is getting faster and faster. 增速 ❑ *He has also called for an acceleration of political reforms.* 他也已呼吁加速政治改革。 **2** N-UNCOUNT **Acceleration** is the rate at which a car or other vehicle can increase its speed, often seen in terms of the time that it takes to reach a particular speed. 加速幅度 ❑ *Acceleration to 60 mph takes a mere 5.7 seconds.* 加速到每小时60英里仅用5.7秒。 **3** N-UNCOUNT **Acceleration** is the rate at which the speed of an object increases. 加速度 [TECHNICAL]
→ see **motion**

ac·cel·era·tor /æksɛləreɪtər/ (**accelerators**) N-COUNT The **accelerator** in a car or other vehicle is the pedal that you press with your foot in order to make the vehicle go faster. 油门 ❑ *He eased his foot off the accelerator.* 他把脚慢慢移离了油门。

ac·cent /æksent/ (**accents**) **1** N-COUNT Someone who speaks with a particular **accent** pronounces the words of a language in a distinctive way that shows which country, region, or background they come from. 口音 ❑ *He had developed a slight southern accent.* 他有了一点南方口音。 **2** N-COUNT An **accent** is a short line or other mark which is written above certain letters in some languages and which indicates the way those letters are pronounced. 变音符号 ❑ *...an acute accent.* …一个尖音符。

Word Partnership *accent* 的常用搭配：

ADJ.	**American/French** accent, **regional** accent, **thick** accent **1**
ADV.	**heavily** accented **1**
V.	**have an** accent **1**
	put the accent **on 2**

ac·cen·tu·ate /æksɛntʃueɪt/ (**accentuates, accentuating, accentuated**) V-T To **accentuate** something means to emphasize it or make it more noticeable. 使突出 ❑ *His shaven head accentuates his large round face.* 他剃了的光头突出了他的大圆脸。

ac·cept ♦♦♦ /æksɛpt/ (**accepts, accepting, accepted**) **1** V-T/V-I If you **accept** something that you have been offered, you say yes to it or agree to take it. 接受 ❑ *Eventually Esteban persuaded her to accept an offer of marriage.* 最终埃斯特班说服她接受了求婚。 ❑ *All those invited to next week's peace conference have accepted.* 所有应邀参加下周和平会议的人都已接受了邀请。 **2** V-T If you **accept** an idea, statement, or fact, you believe that it is true or valid. 相信 ❑ *I do not accept that there is any kind of crisis in American science.* 我不相信美国科学有任何危机。 ❑ *I don't think they would accept that view.* 我不认为他们会相信那个观点。 **3** V-T If you **accept** a plan or an intended action, you agree to it and allow it to happen. 接受 ❑ *The Council will meet to decide if it should accept his resignation.* 委员会将开会来决定是否应该接受他的辞呈。 **4** V-T If you **accept** an unpleasant fact or situation, you get used to it or recognize that it is necessary or cannot be changed. 容忍 ❑ *People will accept suffering that can be shown to lead to a greater good.* 人们将会容忍能被证明会带来更大利益的苦难。 ❑ *Urban dwellers often accept noise as part of city life.* 城市居民常常将噪音作为城市生活的一部分来容忍。 **5** V-T If a person, company, or organization **accepts** something such as a document, they recognize that it is genuine, correct, or satisfactory and agree to consider it or handle it. 接受 ❑ *We took the unusual step of contacting newspapers to advise them not to accept the advertising.* 我们采取了联系各家报社的非常规做法来劝阻他们不要承接这则广告。 **6** V-T If an organization or person **accepts** you, you are allowed to join the organization or use the services that are offered. 接纳 ❑ *All-male groups will not be accepted.* 全男性的组合不会被接纳。 **7** V-T If a person or a group of people **accepts** you, they begin to be friendly toward you and are happy with who you are or what you do. 接纳 ❑ *As far as my grandparents were concerned, they've never had a problem accepting me.* 至于我的祖父母，接纳我对他们来说从来就不是问题。 ❑ *Many men still have difficulty accepting a woman as a business partner.* 很多男性依然难以接受女性作为自己的生意伙伴。 **8** V-T If you **accept** the responsibility or blame for something, you recognize that you are responsible for it. 承担(责任等) ❑ *The company cannot accept responsibility for loss or damage.* 该公司不能承担遗失或损坏的责任。 **9** V-T If you **accept** someone's advice or suggestion, you agree to do what they say. 接受 ❑ *The army refused to accept orders from the political leadership.* 军队拒绝接受政界领导的命令。 **10** V-T If a machine **accepts** a particular kind of thing, it is designed to take it and deal with it or process it. 接受 ❑ *The new parking meters don't accept dollar bills.* 这种新型停车计时器不接受美元纸钞。 **11** → see also **accepted**

Thesaurus *accept* 另参见：

V.	receive, take; *(ant.)* refuse, reject **1**
	acknowledge, agree to, recognize; *(ant.)* object, oppose, refuse **2 3**
	endure, live with, tolerate; *(ant.)* disallow, reject **4**

ac·cept·able ♦◇◇ /æksɛptəbəl/ **1** ADJ **Acceptable** activities and situations are those that most people approve of or consider to be normal. 可接受的 ❑ *It is becoming more acceptable for women to drink.* 女性饮酒越来越为人接受。 ● **ac·cept·abil·ity** /æksɛptəbɪlɪti/ N-UNCOUNT 可接受性 ❑ *This assumption played a considerable part in increasing the social acceptability of divorce.* 这种假设对增加社会对离婚的接纳起了相当大的作用。 ● **ac·cept·ably** /æksɛptəbli/ ADV 可接受地 ❑ *The aim of discipline is to teach children to behave acceptably.* 纪律的宗旨是教孩子举止得体。 **2** ADJ If something is **acceptable to** someone, they agree to consider it, use it, or allow it to happen. 可接受的 ❑ *They have thrashed out a compromise formula acceptable to Moscow.* 他们反复讨论确定了一个莫斯科可以接受的妥协方案。 **3** ADJ If you describe something as **acceptable**, you mean that it is good enough or fairly good. 足够好的；相当好的 ❑ *On the far side of the street was a restaurant that looked acceptable.* 在这条街的另一头有家餐馆看起来还可以。 ● **ac·cept·ably** ADV 足够好地；相当好地 ❑ *...a method that provides an acceptably accurate solution to a problem.* …一个可以足以准确地解决问题的方法。

Thesaurus *acceptable* 另参见：

ADJ.	adequate, decent, passable, satisfactory **3**

ac·cept·ance /æksɛptəns/ (**acceptances**) **1** N-VAR **Acceptance of** an offer or a proposal is the act of saying yes to it or agreeing to it. 接受 ❑ *The Party is being degraded by its acceptance of secret donations.* 该党因接受秘密捐款而遭贬低。 ❑ *...his acceptance speech for the Nobel Peace Prize.* …他的诺贝尔和平奖受奖演说。 **2** N-UNCOUNT If there is **acceptance** of an idea, most people believe or agree that it is true. 承认 ❑ *...a theory that is steadily gaining acceptance.* …一个正稳步得到承认的理论。 **3** N-UNCOUNT Your **acceptance of** a situation, especially an unpleasant or difficult one, is an attitude or feeling that you cannot change it and that you must get used to it. 容忍 ❑ *The most impressive thing about him is his calm acceptance of whatever* *comes his way.* 他给人最深刻的印象是他对任何事情的从容接纳。 **4** N-UNCOUNT **Acceptance** of someone into a group means beginning to think of them as part of the group and to act in a friendly way toward them. 接纳 ❑ *A very determined effort by society will ensure that the disabled achieve real acceptance and integration.* 社会坚定不移的努力将会确保残障人员获得真正的接纳与融入。

ac·cept·ed ♦♦◇ /æksɛptɪd/ **1** ADJ **Accepted** ideas are agreed by most people to be correct or reasonable. 公认的 ❑ *There is no generally accepted definition of life.* 没有一个对生活的普遍公认的定义。 **2** → see also **accept**

ac·cess ♦◇◇ /æksɛs/ (**accesses, accessing, accessed**) **1** N-UNCOUNT If you have **access to** a building or other place, you are able or allowed to go into it. 进入手段；进入权 ❑ *The facilities have been adapted to give access to wheelchair users.* 这些设施已经过改装，使轮椅使用者们能够进入。 ❑ *For logistical and political reasons, scientists have only recently been able to gain access to the area.* 因后勤与政治原因，科学家们直到最近才得以进入该地区。 **2** N-UNCOUNT If you have **access to** something such as information or equipment, you have the opportunity or right to see it or use it. 使用权 ❑ *...a Code of Practice that would give patients access to their medical records.* …一个给病人们使用自己病历权利的行业守则。 **3** N-UNCOUNT If you have **access to** a person, you have the opportunity or right to see them or meet them. 接触的机会；接触的权利 ❑ *He was not allowed access to a lawyer.* 他未被允许接触律师。 **4** V-T If you **access** something, especially information held on a computer, you succeed in finding or obtaining it. 获取（尤其电脑信息） ❑ *You've illegally accessed and misused confidential security files.* 你已经非法获取并盗用了机密文件。

ac·ces·sible /æksɛsɪbᵊl/ **1** ADJ If a place or building is **accessible to** people, it is easy for them to reach it or get into it. If an object is **accessible**, it is easy to reach. （地方）易于进入的；（物品）易于接近的 ❑ *The center is easily accessible to the general public.* 该中心对于广大公众来讲很便利。 ● **ac·ces·sibil·ity** /æksɛsɪbɪlɪti/ N-UNCOUNT （地方）易于进入性；（物品）易于接近性 ❑ *...the easy accessibility of the area.* …该地区的交通便利性。 **2** ADJ If something is **accessible to** people, they can easily use it or obtain it. 易使用的；易得到的 ❑ *The aim of any reform of legal aid should be to make the system accessible to more people.* 任何法律援助改革的目标都应该是让该体系服务于更多的人。 ● **ac·ces·sibil·ity** N-UNCOUNT 易使用性；可及性 ❑ *...growing public concern about the cost, quality and accessibility of health care.* …公众对医疗保健的费用、质量与可及性的日益关注。 **3** ADJ If you describe a book, painting, or other work of art as **accessible**, you think it is good because it is simple enough for people to understand and appreciate easily. 浅显易懂的 [APPROVAL] ❑ *Both say they want to write literary books that are accessible to a general audience.* 两个人都说他们要写对于普通读者浅显易懂的文学书籍。 ● **ac·ces·sibil·ity** N-UNCOUNT 易懂性 ❑ *Seminar topics are chosen for their accessibility to a general audience.* 专题讨论会的话题是根据普通听众的理解力来选定的。
→ see **disability**

★ **ac·ces·sion** /æksɛʃᵊn/ N-UNCOUNT **Accession** is the act of taking up a position as the ruler of a country. 继位 [with poss, oft N "to" n] [FORMAL] ❑ *...the anniversary of the king's accession to the throne.* …国王继承王位周年纪念。

★ **ac·ces·so·ry** /æksɛsəri/ (**accessories**) **1** N-COUNT **Accessories** are items of equipment that are not usually essential, but can be used with or added to something else in order to make it more efficient, useful, or decorative. 附件 ❑ *...an exclusive range of hand-made bedroom and bathroom accessories.* …一个高档系列的手工制作的卧室及卫生间设备附件。 **2** N-COUNT **Accessories** are articles such as belts and scarves which you wear or carry but which are not part of your main clothing. 配饰 ❑ *It also has a good range of accessories, including sunglasses, handbags and belts.* 它还有多种配饰，包括墨镜、手包和皮带。 **3** N-COUNT If someone is guilty of being an **accessory to** a crime, they helped the person who committed it, or knew it was being committed but did not tell the police. 从犯 [LEGAL] ❑ *She had been charged with being an accessory to the embezzlement of funds from a cooperative farm.* 她已被指控为挪用一个合作农场资金的一个从犯。

ac·cess time (**access times**) N-COUNT **Access time** is the time that is needed to get information that is stored in a computer. 读取数据的时间 [COMPUTING] ❑ *This system helps speed up access times.* 这个系统有助于加快读取数据的时间。

ac·ci·dent ♦◇◇ /æksɪdənt/ (**accidents**) **1** N-COUNT An **accident** happens when a vehicle hits a person, an object, or another vehicle, causing injury or damage. 交通事故 ❑ *She was involved in a serious car accident last week.* 她上个星期卷入了一场严重的车祸。 **2** N-COUNT If someone has an **accident**, something unpleasant happens to them that was not intended, sometimes causing injury or death. 事故 ❑ *5,000 people die every year because of accidents in the home.* 每年有5千人死于家庭意外事故。 **3** N-VAR If something happens **by accident**, it happens completely by chance. 偶然 ❑ *She discovered the problem by accident during a visit to a nearby school.* 她在去附近一所学校参观时偶然发现了这个问题。

Thesaurus *accident* 另参见：

N. casualty, mishap **2**
chance **3**

Word Partnership *accident* 的常用搭配：

N. **car** accident **1**
the cause of an accident **1** **2**
ADJ. **bad** accident, **a tragic** accident **1** **2**
V. **cause an** accident, **insure against** accident, **killed in** the accident, **report an** accident **1** **2**
PREP. **without** accident **2**
by accident **3**

ac·ci·den·tal /æksɪdɛntᵊl/ ADJ An **accidental** event happens by chance or as the result of an accident, and is not intended. 意外的 ❑ *...the tragic accidental shooting of his younger brother.* …对他弟弟的悲剧性意外枪击。 ● **ac·ci·den·tal·ly** /æksɪdɛntli/ ADV 意外地 [ADV with v] ❑ *A policeman accidentally killed his two best friends with a single bullet.* 一位警察意外地用一颗子弹杀死了他的两个最好的朋友。

ac·ci·dent and emer·gen·cy (**accident and emergencies**) N-COUNT **Accident and emergency** is the same as **emergency room.** 急诊室 [BRIT]

Word Link *claim, clam ≈ shouting : acclaim, clamor, exclaim*

▲ **ac·claim** /əkleɪm/ (**acclaims, acclaiming, acclaimed**) **1** V-T If someone or something **is acclaimed**, they are praised enthusiastically. 热烈称赞 [usu passive] [FORMAL] ❑ *The restaurant has been widely acclaimed for its excellent French cuisine.* 这个餐馆因出众的法式烹调而受到广泛赞扬。 ❑ *He was acclaimed as America's greatest filmmaker.* 他被赞誉为美国最伟大的电影制片人。 ● **ac·claimed** ADJ 受到高度赞扬的 ❑ *She has published six highly acclaimed novels.* 她已经出版了6本受到高度赞扬的小说。 **2** N-UNCOUNT **Acclaim** is public praise for someone or something. 赞扬 [FORMAL] ❑ *Angela Bassett has won critical acclaim for her excellent performance.* 安杰拉·巴西特因她出色的表演而赢得了评论界的赞扬。

ac·cli·mate /æklɪmeɪt, əklaɪmɪt/ (**acclimates, acclimating, acclimated**) V-T/V-I When you **acclimate** or **are acclimated to** a new situation, place, or climate, you become used to it. 使适应；适应 [AM] ❑ *I help them acclimate to living in the U.S.* 我帮助他们适应在美国的生活。 ❑ *I hadn't had any time to acclimate myself.* 我那时没有时间来适应环境。 ❑ *It does take time to acclimate, especially for guys who haven't grown up in an urban environment.* 这确实需要时间适应，特别是对于那些不在城市长大的人。 ❑ *Some ethnic groups can't become acclimated to the mainstream.* 一些种族群体不能适应主流。 ● **ac·cli·ma·tion** /æklɪmeɪʃən/ N-UNCOUNT 适应 ❑ *...gradual acclimation to strenuous exercise.* …对高强度训练的逐渐适应。

ac·cli·ma·tise /əklaɪmətaɪz/ [BRIT] → see **acclimatize**

ac·cli·ma·tize /əklaɪmətaɪz/ (**acclimatizes, acclimatizing, acclimatized**)

in BRIT, also use **acclimatise**

V-T/V-I **Acclimatize** means the same as **acclimate.** 使适应；对…适应 [FORMAL] ❑ *The athletes are acclimatizing to the heat by staying in Monte Carlo.* 运动员通过住在蒙特卡罗来适应高温。 ❑ *This year he has left for St. Louis early to acclimatize himself.* 今年他已早早地前往圣路易斯去适应环境。

ac·co·lade /ækəleɪd/ (**accolades**) N-COUNT If someone is given an **accolade**, something is done or said about them which shows how much people admire them. 荣誉 [FORMAL] ❑ *The Nobel Prize has become the ultimate accolade in the sciences.* 诺贝尔奖已成为科学界的最高荣誉。 ❑ *He won accolades as one of America's top test pilots.* 他作为美国顶级试飞员之一赢得了众多荣誉。

A

★ **ac·com·mo·date** /əkɒmədeɪt/ (**accommodates, accommodating, accommodated**) **1** V-T If a building or space can **accommodate** someone or something, it has enough room for them. 容纳 [no cont] ❑ *The school was not big enough to accommodate all the children.* 学校没有足够的地方容纳所有的学生。 **2** V-T To **accommodate** someone means to provide them with a place to live or stay. 为…提供住宿 ❑ *...a hotel built to accommodate guests for the wedding of King Alfonso.* …一个为来参加阿方索国王婚礼的客人提供住宿而建造的宾馆。 **3** V-T If something is planned or changed to **accommodate** a particular situation, it is planned or changed so that it takes this situation into account. 使…适应 [FORMAL] ❑ *The roads are built to accommodate gradual temperature changes.* 这些道路是为适应气温的逐渐变化而建的。

ac·com·mo·dat·ing /əkɒmədeɪtɪŋ/ ADJ If you describe someone as **accommodating**, you like the fact that they are willing to do things in order to please you or help you. 乐于助人的 [APPROVAL] ❑ *Eddie was among the most approachable athletes on the team, always very accommodating to me.* 艾迪是队里最容易接近的运动员之一，总是很乐于帮助我。

ac·com·mo·da·tion /əkɒmədeɪʃən/ (**accommodations**) **1** N-UNCOUNT **Accommodations** are buildings or rooms where people live or stay. 住所 [also N in pl] [AM]

in BRIT, use **accommodation**

❑ *The government will provide temporary accommodations for up to three thousand homeless people.* 政府将为多达三千无家可归的人提供临时住所。 **2** N-UNCOUNT **Accommodation** is space in buildings or vehicles that is available for certain things, people, or activities. (楼内或车内等) 专用空间 [FORMAL] ❑ *Their offices are housed in rented accommodation in a modernized wing of the Mathematics Institute.* 他们的办公室坐落在数学研究所的现代化侧楼的租赁楼层中。

ac·com·pa·ni·ment /əkʌmpənɪmənt/ (**accompaniments**) **1** N-COUNT The **accompaniment** to a song or tune is the music that is played at the same time as it and forms a background to it. 伴奏 ❑ *He sang "My Funny Valentine" and "Wanted" to musical director Jim Steffan's piano accompaniment.* 他在音乐总监吉姆·斯蒂芬的钢琴伴奏下演唱了《我可爱的情人》与《需要有人爱》。 **2** N-COUNT An **accompaniment** is something that goes with another thing. 相配物 ❑ *This recipe makes a good accompaniment to ice cream.* 这个食谱与冰激凌很相配。 ● PHRASE If one thing happens **to the accompaniment** of another, they happen at the same time. 在…的伴随下

ac·com·pa·ny ♦◊◊ /əkʌmpəni/ (**accompanies, accompanying, accompanied**) **1** V-T If you **accompany** someone, you go somewhere with them. 陪伴 [FORMAL] ❑ *Ken agreed to accompany me on a trip to Africa.* 肯同意陪我去非洲旅行。 ❑ *She was accompanied by her younger brother.* 她由她的弟弟陪着。 **2** V-T If one thing **accompanies** another, it happens or exists at the same time, or as a result of it. 与…相伴 [FORMAL] ❑ *This volume of essays was designed to accompany an exhibition in Seattle.* 这部论文集是为配合西雅图的展览设计的。 **3** V-T If you **accompany** a singer or a musician, you play one part of a piece of music while they sing or play the main tune. 为…伴奏 ❑ *On Meredith's new recording, Eddie Higgins accompanies her on all but one song.* 在梅瑞迪斯的新唱片中，艾迪·希金斯为她伴奏了除一首歌以外的所有歌曲。

▲ **ac·com·plice** /əkɒmplɪs/ (**accomplices**) N-COUNT Someone's **accomplice** is a person who helps them to commit a crime. 同犯 ❑ *Witnesses said the gunman immediately ran to a motorcycle being ridden by an accomplice.* 证人们说该枪手立即向由一名同犯驾驶的摩托车跑去。

ac·com·plish /əkɒmplɪʃ/ (**accomplishes, accomplishing, accomplished**) V-T If you **accomplish** something, you succeed in doing it. 完成 ❑ *If we'd all work together, I think we could accomplish our goal.* 如果我们齐心协力，我想我们能实现我们的目标。

Thesaurus *accomplish* 另参见:

v. achieve, complete, gain, realize, succeed

ac·com·plished /əkɒmplɪʃt/ ADJ If someone is **accomplished** at something, they are very good at it. 精通的 [FORMAL] ❑ *She is an accomplished painter and a prolific author of stories for children.* 她是位技艺精湛的画家和多产的儿童文学作家。

ac·com·plish·ment /əkɒmplɪʃmənt/ (**accomplishments**) N-COUNT An **accomplishment** is something remarkable that has been done or achieved. 成就 ❑ *For a novelist, that's quite an accomplishment.* 对于一个小说家来说，那是一个了不起的成就。

ac·cord ♦♦♦ /əkɔrd/ (**accords, according, accorded**) **1** N-COUNT An **accord** between countries or groups of people is a formal agreement; for example, to end a war. 协议 ❑ *UNITA was legalized as a political party under the 1991 peace accords.* 根据1991年和平协议，安盟作为一个政党被合法化了。 **2** V-T If you **are accorded** a particular kind of treatment, people act toward you or treat you in that way. 给予 (某种待遇) [FORMAL] ❑ *His predecessor was accorded an equally tumultuous welcome.* 他的前任受到了同样热烈的欢迎。 ❑ *On his return home, the government accorded him the rank of Colonel.* 在他回国时，该国政府授予他上校军衔。 **3** → see also **according to** **4** PHRASE If something happens **of its own accord**, it seems to happen by itself, without anyone making it happen. 自动地 ❑ *In many cases the disease will clear up of its own accord.* 在很多情况下这种疾病会自动地痊愈。 **5** PHRASE If you do something **of your own accord**, you do it because you want to, without being asked or forced. 自愿地 ❑ *He did not quit as France's prime minister of his own accord.* 他不是自愿地辞去法国总理一职的。

ac·cord·ance /əkɔrdᵊns/ PHRASE If something is done **in accordance with** a particular rule or system, it is done in the way that the rule or system says that it should be done. 按照 ❑ *Entries which are illegible or otherwise not in accordance with the rules will be disqualified.* 难以辨认的或不符合这些规定的参赛作品将被取消资格。

ac·cord·ing·ly /əkɔrdɪŋli/ **1** ADV You use **accordingly** to introduce a fact or situation that is a result or consequence of something that you have just referred to. 因此 ❑ *We have a different background, a different history. Accordingly, we have the right to different futures.* 我们拥有不同的背景、不同的历史。因此，我们有权获得不一样的前途。 **2** ADV If you consider a situation and then act **accordingly**, the way you act depends on the nature of the situation. 相应地 [ADV after V] ❑ *It is a difficult job and they should be paid accordingly.* 它是一项艰巨的工作，他们应该相应地获得报酬。

ac·cord·ing to ♦♦♦ **1** PHRASE If someone says that something is true **according to** a particular person, book, or other source of information, they are indicating where they got their information. 根据 ❑ *The van raced away, according to police reports, and police gave chase.* 根据警方的报告，这辆货车飞驰而去，警方进行了追赶。 **2** PHRASE If something is done **according to** a particular set of principles, these principles are used as a basis for the way it is done. 按照 ❑ *They both played the game according to the rules.* 他们两个都按照那些规则进行了这场游戏。 **3** PHRASE If something varies **according to** a changing factor, it varies in a way that is determined by this factor. 根据…(变化) ❑ *Prices vary according to the quantity ordered.* 价格根据所订数量而变化。 **4** PHRASE If something happens **according to plan**, it happens in exactly the way that it was intended to happen. 按照计划 ❑ *If all goes according to plan, the first concert will be Tuesday evening.* 如果一切按照计划进行，首场音乐会将是在周二晚上。

ac·count ♦♦♦ /əkaʊnt/ (**accounts, accounting, accounted**) **1** N-COUNT If you have an **account** with a bank or a similar organization, you have an arrangement to leave your money there and take some out when you need it. 账户 ❑ *Some banks make it difficult to open an account.* 有些银行使开一个账户困难重重。 **2** N-COUNT In business, a regular customer of a company can be referred to as an **account**, especially when the customer is another company. 客户 [BUSINESS] ❑ *All three Internet agencies boast they've won major accounts.* 所有的三家网络代理公司都夸口说他们已赢得了大客户。 **3** N-COUNT **Accounts** are detailed records of all the money that a person or business receives and spends. 账目 [BUSINESS] ❑ *He kept detailed accounts.* 他保存了详细的账目。 **4** N-COUNT An **account** is a written or spoken report of something that has happened. 报道 ❑ *He gave a detailed account of what happened on the fateful night.* 他对那个决定命运的夜晚所发生的事情做了一个详细的报道。 **5** → see also **accounting, bank account, checking account, deposit account**

Do not confuse **account** and **bill**. When you have an **account** with a bank, you leave your money in the bank and take it out when you need it. When you have to pay for things such as electricity or work done by a repairman, you get a **bill**.

6 PHRASE If you say that something is true **by all accounts** or **from all accounts**, you believe it is true because other people say so. 据说 ❑ *He is, by all accounts, a superb teacher.* 据说，他是一名优秀的教师。 **7** PHRASE If you say that something is **of no account** or **of little account**, you mean that it is very unimportant and is not

worth considering. 无足轻重的 [FORMAL] ❑ *These obscure groups were of little account in either national or international politics.* 这些无名的组织在国内或国际政治中都是无足轻重的。 **8** PHRASE If you buy or pay for something **on account**, you pay nothing or only part of the cost at first, and pay the rest later. 以赊账方式 ❑ *He was ordered to pay the company $500,000 on account pending a final assessment of his liability.* 在对他的债务做最后的评估期间，他被命令先付这家公司50万美元。 **9** PHRASE You use **on account of** to introduce the reason or explanation for something. 由于 ❑ *The president declined to deliver the speech himself, on account of a sore throat.* 那位总统由于嗓子疼拒绝亲自发表演讲。 **10** PHRASE Your feelings **on** someone's **account** are the feelings you have about what they have experienced or might experience, especially when you imagine yourself to be in their situation. 为（某人的）缘故（而感到…）❑ *Mollie told me what she'd done and I was really scared on her account.* 莫丽告诉了我她做过的事情，我真为她感到害怕。 **11** PHRASE If you tell someone not to do something **on** your **account**, you mean that they should do it only if they want to, and not because they think it will please you. （不）为（某人的）缘故（而做某事）[SPOKEN] ❑ *Don't leave on my account.* 不要因为我而离开。 **12** PHRASE If you say that something should **on no account** be done, you are emphasizing that it should not be done under any circumstances. 绝对不 [EMPHASIS] ❑ *On no account should the mixture come near boiling.* 这种混合物绝对不应当接近沸点。 **13** PHRASE If you do something **on** your **own account**, you do it because you want to and without being asked, and you take responsibility for your own action. 随（某人）自己 ❑ *I told him if he withdrew it was on his own account.* 我告诉他，如果他退出那么他要自负其则。 **14** PHRASE If you **take** something **into account**, or **take account of** something, you consider it when you are thinking about a situation or deciding what to do. 考虑到 ❑ *The defendant asked for 21 similar offenses to be taken into account.* 该被告请求将21项相似的犯罪罪行考虑在内。 **15** PHRASE If someone **is called, held,** or **brought to account** for something they have done wrong, they are made to explain why they did it, and are often criticized or punished for it. 追究 ❑ *Individuals who repeatedly provide false information should be called to account for their actions.* 反复提供虚假情报的人应为其行为而受到追究。 **16** PHRASE If you say that someone **gave a good account of** themselves in a particular situation, you mean that they performed well, although they may not have been completely successful. 表现很好 [BRIT] ❑ *We have been hindered by our lack of preparation, but I'm sure we will give a good account of ourselves.* 我们曾经为缺乏准备所阻，但我肯定我们会表现很好的。
→ see **bank, history**

▸ **account for** **1** PHRASAL VERB If a particular thing **accounts for** a part or proportion of something, that part or proportion consists of that thing, or is used or produced by it. （数量、比例上）占 ❑ *Computers account for 5% of the country's commercial electricity consumption.* 电脑占了这个国家商业用电的5%。 **2** PHRASAL VERB If something **accounts for** a particular fact or situation, it causes or explains it. 导致；解释 ❑ *The gene they discovered today doesn't account for all those cases.* 他们今天发现的那种基因解释不了所有的那些情况。 **3** PHRASAL VERB If you can **account for** something, you can explain it or give the necessary information about it. 解释 ❑ *How do you account for the company's alarmingly high staff turnover?* 你怎么解释这家公司高得惊人的人员流动率？ **4** PHRASAL VERB If someone has to **account for** an action or policy, they are responsible for it, and may be required to explain it to other people or be punished if it fails. 对…负责 ❑ *The president and the president alone must account for his government's reforms.* 该总统并且只有总统一个人必须对他的这些政府改革负责。 **5** PHRASAL VERB If a sum of money **is accounted for** in a budget, it has been included in that budget for a particular purpose. 列入预算 ❑ *The really heavy costs have been accounted for.* 这些确实巨大的花费已被列入预算。

Word Partnership *account* 的常用搭配：

N.	account **balance**, **bank** account, account **number**, **savings** account **1**
V.	**access your** account, **open an** account **1** **give a detailed** account **4** **take** *something* **into** account **14**
ADJ.	**blow-by-blow** account **4**

★ **ac·count·able** /əkaʊntəbᵊl/ ADJ If you are **accountable to** someone **for** something that you do, you are responsible for it and must be prepared to justify your actions to that person. 负有责任的 ❑ *Public officials can finally be held accountable for their actions.* 政府官员最终是要对他们的行为负责任的。 ● ★ **ac·count·abil·ity** /əkaʊntəbɪlɪti/ N-UNCOUNT 责任心 ❑ *...a drive toward democracy and greater accountability.* …一场促进民主和增强责任心的运动。

★ **ac·count·an·cy** /əkaʊntənsi/ N-UNCOUNT **Accountancy** is the theory or practice of keeping financial accounts. 会计学 [BRIT] in AM, use **accounting**

ac·count·ant /əkaʊntənt/ (**accountants**) N-COUNT An **accountant** is a person whose job is to keep financial accounts. 会计师

★ **ac·count·ing** /əkaʊntɪŋ/ **1** N-UNCOUNT **Accounting** is the activity of keeping detailed records of the amounts of money a business or person receives and spends. 会计 ❑ *...the accounting firm of Leventhal & Horwath.* …利文撒尔与霍瓦特会计事务所。 **2** → see also **account**

ac·cru·al /əkruəl/ (**accruals**) N-COUNT In finance, the **accrual** of something such as interest or investments is the adding together of interest or different investments over a period of time. 积累 [BUSINESS] ❑ *After an employee has 25 years of service, there is no further accrual of benefits.* 在一位雇员工作了25年之后，就没有更多的补助积累了。

ac·crue /əkru/ (**accrues, accruing, accrued**) V-T/V-I If money or interest **accrues**, it gradually increases in amount over a period of time. 累积（过程）[BUSINESS] ❑ *I owed $5,000 – part of this was accrued interest.* 我欠$5000——这其中的一部分是累积的利息。 ❑ *While they may use a credit card for convenience, affluent people never let interest charges accrue.* 虽然有钱人可能为了方便而使用信用卡，他们从来不让利息费累积。

ac·cu·mu·late /əkyumyəleɪt/ (**accumulates, accumulating, accumulated**) V-T/V-I When you **accumulate** things or when they **accumulate**, they collect or are gathered over a period of time. 积聚 ❑ *Lead can accumulate in the body until toxic levels are reached.* 铅可以在体内积聚直至到达有毒的程度。

ac·cu·mu·la·tion /əkyumyəleɪʃᵊn/ (**accumulations**) **1** N-COUNT An **accumulation of** something is a large number of things that have been collected together or acquired over a period of time. 积累 ❑ *...an accumulation of experience and knowledge.* …经验和知识的一种积累。 **2** N-UNCOUNT **Accumulation** is the collecting together of things over a period of time. 积聚 ❑ *...the accumulation of capital and the distribution of income.* …资金的积聚和收入的分配。

ac·cu·ra·cy /ækyərəsi/ **1** N-UNCOUNT The **accuracy of** information or measurements is their quality of being true or correct, even in small details. 精确（性）；准确（性）❑ *Every care has been taken to ensure the accuracy of all information given in this leaflet.* 已经采取了一切措施来保证这张传单上所有信息的准确。 **2** N-UNCOUNT If someone or something performs a task, for example, hitting a target, **with accuracy**, they do it in an exact way without making a mistake. 准确无误 ❑ *...weapons that could fire with accuracy at targets 3,000 yards away.* …那些可以准确无误地射中3000码以外的目标的武器。

ac·cu·rate ♦◇◇ /ækyərɪt/ **1** ADJ **Accurate** information, measurements, and statistics are correct to a very detailed level. An **accurate** instrument is able to give you information of this kind. 精确的 ❑ *Police have stressed that this is the most accurate description of the killer to date.* 警方已强调这是到目前为止对这名杀人犯最精确的描述。 ● **ac·cu·rate·ly** ADV 精确地 ❑ *The test can accurately predict what a bigger explosion would do.* 这项测试能精确地预测一场更大的爆炸可能产生的后果。 **2** ADJ An **accurate** statement or account gives a true or fair judgment of something. 准确的 ❑ *Stalin gave an accurate assessment of the utility of nuclear weapons.* 斯大林对核武器的效用作了一个准确的评估。 ● **ac·cu·rate·ly** ADV 准确地 [ADV with v] ❑ *What many people mean by the word "power" could be more accurately described as "control."* 许多人对“权力”这个词的理解可以更为准确地用“控制”来形容。 **3** ADJ You can use **accurate** to describe the results of someone's actions when they do or copy something correctly or exactly. 正确无误的 ❑ *We require grammar and spelling to be accurate.* 我们要求语法与拼写正确无误。 **4** ADJ An **accurate** weapon or throw reaches the exact point or target that it was intended to reach. You can also describe a person as **accurate** if they fire a weapon or throw something in this way. 精准的 ❑ *His throws were long, hard and accurate, as always.* 像往常一样，他的投掷远、有力又精准。 ● **ac·cu·rate·ly** ADV 精准地 [ADV with v] ❑ *He hit the golf ball powerfully and accurately.* 他有力而准确地击中了那个高尔夫球。

A

Thesaurus *accurate* 另参见：
ADJ. right, true; *(ant.)* inaccurate 2
correct, precise, rigorous 3

★ **ac·cu·sa·tion** /ækyʊzeɪʃ^{ə}n/ (**accusations**) 1 N-VAR If you make an **accusation** against someone, you criticize them or express the belief that they have done something wrong. 指责 ❏ *Kim rejects accusations that country music is over-sentimental.* 金姆反驳了那些说乡村音乐过于伤感的指责。 2 N-COUNT An **accusation** is a statement or claim by a witness or someone in authority that a particular person has committed a crime, although this has not yet been proved. 指控 ❏ *...people who have made public accusations of rape.* …对强奸进行了公开指控的人们。

ac·cuse ♦♦◇ /əkyuz/ (**accuses, accusing, accused**) 1 V-T If you **accuse** someone **of** doing something wrong or dishonest, you say or tell them that you believe that they did it. 指责 ❏ *My mom was really upset because he was accusing her of having an affair with another man.* 我妈妈真的很难过，因为他指责她和另一个男人有暧昧关系。 2 V-T If you **are accused of** a crime, a witness or someone in authority states or claims that you did it, and you may be formally charged with it and put on trial. 指控 ❏ *Her assistant was accused of theft and fraud by the police.* 她的助手被警方指控偷窃和诈骗。 ❏ *He faced a total of seven charges, all accusing him of lying in his testimony.* 他面临共7项控告，都指控他作伪证。 3 → see also **accused**
4 PHRASE If someone **stands accused of** something, they have been accused of it. 被谴责 ❏ *The candidate stands accused of breaking promises even before he's in office.* 这位候选人甚至在他就职前就因违背诺言而被谴责。

Thesaurus *accuse* 另参见：
V. blame, charge, implicate; *(ant.)* absolve, exonerate, vindicate 1 2

ac·cused /əkyuzd/ (**accused**)

Accused is both the singular and the plural form.

N-COUNT You can use **the accused** to refer to a person or a group of people charged with a crime or on trial for it. 被告 [LEGAL] ❏ *The accused is alleged to be a member of a right-wing gang.* 这名被告据称是一个右翼团伙中的一员。

★ **ac·cus·tom** /əkʌstəm/ (**accustoms, accustoming, accustomed**) 1 V-T If you **accustom yourself** or another person **to** something, you make yourself or them become used to it. 使习惯 [FORMAL] ❏ *She tried to accustom herself to the tight bandages.* 她尝试着使自己习惯那些紧绷的绷带。 2 → see also **accustomed**

ac·cus·tomed /əkʌstəmd/ 1 ADJ If you are **accustomed to** something, you know it so well or have experienced it so often that it seems natural, unsurprising, or easy to deal with. 习惯的 [v-link ADJ "to" n/-ing] ❏ *I was accustomed to being the only child at a table full of adults.* 我习惯了作为惟一的孩子坐在满是成年人的桌旁。 2 ADJ When your eyes become **accustomed to** darkness or bright light, they adjust so that you start to be able to see things, after not being able to see properly at first. 适应的 [v-link ADJ "to" n] ❏ *My eyes were becoming accustomed to the gloom and I was able to make out a door at one side of the room.* 我的双眼逐渐适应了这种昏暗，能够看到那个房间的一侧有一扇门。

Word Partnership *accustomed* 的常用搭配：
N. accustomed **to the heat** 1
accustomed **to the dark(ness)** 2
V. **become** accustomed, **get** accustomed, **grow** accustomed 1 2
ADV. **gradually** accustomed, **long** accustomed 1 2

▲ **ace** /eɪs/ (**aces**) 1 N-COUNT An **ace** is a playing card with a single symbol on it. In most card games, the ace of a particular suit has either the highest or the lowest value of the cards in that suit. (纸牌) A ❏ *...the ace of hearts.* …红桃A。 2 N-COUNT If you describe someone such as a sports player as an **ace**, you mean that they are very good at what they do. 一流选手 [JOURNALISM] ❏ *Despite the loss of their ace early in the game, Seattle beat the Brewers 6-5.* 尽管在那场比赛开始不久就失去了一流队员，西雅图队仍以6比5击败了酿酒人队。 ● ADJ **Ace** is also an adjective. 一流的 [ADJ n] ❏ *...ace horror-film producer Lawrence Woolsey.* …一流的恐怖片制片人劳伦斯·伍希。 3 N-COUNT In tennis, an **ace** is a serve which is so fast that the other player cannot reach the ball. Ace球(网球比赛中直接得分的发球) ❏ *Agassi believed he had served an ace at 5-3 (40-30) in the deciding set.* 阿加西认为他在决胜盘中5-3(40-30)时曾发出过一记Ace球。 4 PHRASE Something that is an **ace in the hole** is an advantage which you have over an opponent or rival, and which you can use if necessary. 手中的王牌 [v-link PHR, PHR after v] ❏ *Our superior technology is our ace in the hole.* 我们的优越技术是我们手中的王牌。

ache /eɪk/ (**aches, aching, ached**) 1 V-I If you **ache** or a part of your body **aches**, you feel a steady, fairly strong pain. 疼痛 ❏ *The glands in her neck were swollen, her head was throbbing and she ached all over.* 她脖子里的淋巴腺肿了，头一跳一跳地作痛而且全身疼痛。 ❏ *My leg is giving me much less pain but still aches when I sit down.* 我的腿疼痛减轻了许多，但是当我坐下时还是会疼。 2 N-COUNT An **ache** is a steady, fairly strong pain in a part of your body. 疼痛 ❏ *You feel nausea and aches in your muscles.* 你觉得恶心而且肌肉疼痛。 3 PHRASE You can use **aches and pains** to refer in a general way to any minor pains that you feel in your body. (泛指不严重的) 疼痛 ❏ *It seems to ease all the aches and pains of a hectic and tiring day.* 它似乎可以减轻繁忙疲劳的一天带来的所有疼痛。 4 → see also **headache, heartache, stomach ache**

Thesaurus *ache* 另参见：
V. hurt, throb 1
N. pain, pang, sore 2

achieve ♦♦◇ /ətʃiv/ (**achieves, achieving, achieved**) V-T If you **achieve** a particular aim or effect, you succeed in doing it or causing it to happen, usually after a lot of effort. 实现 ❏ *There are many who will work hard to achieve these goals.* 有很多人会努力工作来实现这些目标。

Thesaurus *achieve* 另参见：
V. accomplish, bring about; *(ant.)* fail, lose, miss

achieve·ment ♦◇◇ /ətʃivmənt/ (**achievements**) 1 N-COUNT An **achievement** is something that someone has succeeded in doing, especially after a lot of effort. 成就 ❏ *It was a great achievement that a month later a global agreement was reached.* 一个月后一个全球协议达成了，这是一个巨大的成就。 2 N-UNCOUNT **Achievement** is the process of achieving something. 实现 ❏ *It is only the achievement of these goals that will finally bring lasting peace.* 只有这些目标的实现才会最终带来持久的和平。

achiev·er /ətʃivər/ (**achievers**) N-COUNT A high **achiever** is someone who is successful in their studies or their work, usually as a result of their efforts. A low **achiever** is someone who achieves less than those around them. 成功者 ❏ *High achievers at the company are in line for cash bonuses.* 公司里那些业绩突出的人有望获得现金分红。

acid ♦◇◇ /æsɪd/ (**acids**) 1 N-MASS An **acid** is a chemical substance, usually a liquid, which contains hydrogen and can react with other substances to form salts. Some acids burn or dissolve other substances that they come into contact with. 酸 ❏ *...citric acid.* …柠檬酸。 2 ADJ An **acid** substance contains acid. 酸性的 ❏ *These shrubs must have an acid, lime-free soil.* 这些灌木必须要有酸性、无石灰的土壤。 ● **acid·ity** /əsɪdɪti/ N-UNCOUNT 酸性 [oft N "of" n] ❏ *...the acidity of rainwater.* …雨水的酸性。

acid·ic /əsɪdɪk/ ADJ **Acidic** substances contain acid. 酸性的 ❏ *Dissolved carbon dioxide makes the water more acidic.* 溶解的二氧化碳使水更具酸性。

acid rain N-UNCOUNT **Acid rain** is rain polluted by acid that has been released into the atmosphere from factories and other industrial processes. Acid rain is harmful to the environment. 酸雨
→ see **pollution**

ac·knowl·edge ♦◇◇ /æknɒlɪdʒ/ (**acknowledges, acknowledging, acknowledged**) 1 V-T If you **acknowledge** a fact or a situation, you accept or admit that it is true or that it exists. 承认(事实或情况) [FORMAL] ❏ *Naylor acknowledged, in a letter to the judge, that he was a drug addict.* 在一封写给法官的信中，内勒承认他是一个吸毒者。 ❏ *Belatedly, the government has acknowledged the problem.* 政府过晚地承认了这个问题。 2 V-T If someone's achievements, status, or qualities **are acknowledged**, they are known about and recognized by a lot of people, or by a particular group of people. 认可(某人的成就、地位或品质) ❏ *He is also acknowledged as an excellent goalkeeper.* 他还被认可为一名优秀的守门员。 3 V-T If you acknowledge a message or letter, you write to the person who sent it in order to say that you have received it. 确认收到 ❑ *The army sent me a postcard acknowledging my request.* 军方寄给我一张明信片以确认收到了我的请求。 **4** V-T If you **acknowledge** someone, for example, by moving your head or smiling, you show that you have seen and recognized them. (点头或微笑) 向…致意 ❑ *He saw her but refused to even acknowledge her.* 他看到了她，但甚至都拒绝向她致意。

Thesaurus	*acknowledge* 另参见:
v.	accept, admit, grant **1** recognize; *(ant.)* ignore **2**–**4**

ac·knowl·edg·ment /æknɒlɪdʒmənt/ (**acknowledgments**) also **acknowledgement** **1** N-SING An **acknowledgment** is a statement or action which recognizes that something exists or is true. (对某物存在或属实的) 承认 [also no det] ❑ *The president's resignation appears to be an acknowledgment that he has lost all hope of keeping the country together.* 该总统的辞职看起来是对他已经放弃将国家团结起来的所有希望的一种承认。 **2** N-PLURAL The **acknowledgments** in a book are the section in which the author thanks all the people who have helped him or her. 致谢辞 ❑ *...two whole pages of acknowledgments.* …整整两页的致谢辞。 **3** N-UNCOUNT A gesture of **acknowledgment**, such as a smile, shows someone that you have seen and recognized them. 致意 [also "a" N] ❑ *Farling smiled in acknowledgment and gave a bow.* 法林微笑致意并鞠了一躬。

acne /ækni/ N-UNCOUNT If someone has **acne**, they have a skin condition which causes a lot of pimples on their face and neck. 粉刺 ❑ *She wore no makeup, and her face was dotted with acne.* 她没有化妆，脸上长满了粉刺。

acorn /eɪkɔrn/ (**acorns**) N-COUNT An **acorn** is a pale oval nut that is the fruit of an oak tree. 橡实

▲ **acous·tic** /əkustɪk/ (**acoustics**) **1** ADJ An **acoustic** guitar or other instrument is one whose sound is produced without any electrical equipment. 自然声的 [ADJ n] **2** N-COUNT If you refer to the **acoustics** of a space, you are referring to the structural features which determine how well you can hear music or speech in it. 传声效果 ❑ *In this performance, Rattle had the acoustics of the Symphony Hall on his side.* 在这场演出中，拉特尔有着交响音乐厅传声效果的襄助。 **3** N-UNCOUNT **Acoustics** is the scientific study of sound. 声学 ❑ *...his work in acoustics.* …他在声学方面的工作。

ac·quaint /əkweɪnt/ (**acquaints, acquainting, acquainted**) **1** V-T If you **acquaint** someone **with** something, you tell them about it so that they know it. If you **acquaint yourself with** something, you learn about it. 使了解 [FORMAL] ❑ *Have steps been taken to acquaint breeders with their right to apply for licenses?* 已经采取措施让饲养动物者了解他们申请执照的权利了吗？ **2** → see also **acquainted**

ac·quaint·ance /əkweɪntəns/ (**acquaintances**) **1** N-COUNT An **acquaintance** is someone who you have met and know slightly, but not well. 相识之人 ❑ *He exchanged a few words with the proprietor, an old acquaintance of his.* 他跟一位业主，他的一位老相识交谈了几句。 **2** N-VAR If you have an **acquaintance with** someone, you have met them and you know them. 结识 ❑ *...a writer who becomes involved in a real murder mystery through his acquaintance with a police officer.* …一位通过他同一名警官的结识而卷入一起真正的谋杀谜案的作家。 **3** PHRASE When you **make** someone's **acquaintance**, you meet them for the first time and get to know them a little. 与某人初次相识 [FORMAL] ❑ *I first made his acquaintance in the early 1960s.* 我在20世纪60年代初第一次认识了他。

ac·quaint·ed /əkweɪntɪd/ **1** ADJ If you are **acquainted with** something, you know about it because you have learned it or experienced it. 了解的 [v-link ADJ "with" n] [FORMAL] ❑ *He was well acquainted with the literature of Latin America.* 他对拉丁美洲文学是十分了解的。 **2** ADJ If you get or become **acquainted with** someone that you do not know, you talk to each other or do something together so that you get to know each other. You can also say that two people get or become **acquainted**. 认识的 [v-link ADJ] ❑ *At first the meetings were a way to get acquainted with each other.* 起初这些会议是相互认识的一种方式。 **3** → see also **acquaint**

ac·quire ♦◇◇ /əkwaɪər/ (**acquires, acquiring, acquired**) **1** V-T If you **acquire** something, you buy or obtain it for yourself, or someone gives it to you. 获得 [FORMAL] ❑ *General Motors acquired a 50% stake in Saab for about $400m.* 通用汽车公司以大约4亿美元获得了萨博50%的股份。 **2** V-T If you **acquire** something such as a skill or a habit, you learn it, or develop it through your daily life or experience. 习得 ❑ *I've never acquired a taste for wine.* 我从未养成对葡萄酒的爱好。 **3** V-T If someone or something **acquires** a certain reputation, they start to have that reputation. 获得 (名声) ❑ *During her film career, she acquired a reputation as a strong-willed, outspoken woman.* 在她的银幕生涯中，她获得了一个意志坚定、坦率直言的名声。

ac·quir·er /əkwaɪərər/ (**acquirers**) N-COUNT In business, an **acquirer** is a company or person who buys another company. 收购方 [BUSINESS] ❑ *...the ability of corporate acquirers to finance large takeovers.* 收购团体为大规模收购提供资金的能力。

ac·qui·si·tion ♦◇◇ /ækwɪzɪʃən/ (**acquisitions**) **1** N-VAR If a company or business person makes an **acquisition**, they buy another company or part of a company. 收购 [BUSINESS] ❑ *...the acquisition of a profitable paper recycling company.* 对一家有利润的废纸回收公司的收购。 **2** N-COUNT If you make an **acquisition**, you buy or obtain something, often to add to things that you already have. 获得 ❑ *How did you go about making this marvelous acquisition then?* 那么你是怎么着手进行这宗不可思议的购置的？ **3** N-UNCOUNT The **acquisition** of a skill or a particular type of knowledge is the process of learning it or developing it. 习得 ❑ *...language acquisition.* …语言习得。

▲ **ac·quit** /əkwɪt/ (**acquits, acquitting, acquitted**) V-T If someone **is acquitted of** a crime in a court of law, they are formally declared not to have committed the crime. 宣判…无罪 [usu passive] ❑ *Mr. Castorina was acquitted of attempted murder.* 卡斯托瑞纳先生被宣判谋杀未遂罪不成立。

ac·quit·tal /əkwɪtəl/ (**acquittals**) N-VAR **Acquittal** is a formal declaration in a court of law that someone who has been accused of a crime is innocent. 无罪的判决 ❑ *...the acquittal of six police officers charged with beating up a suspect.* …对被控殴打一嫌疑犯的 6 名警官作出的无罪判决。 ❑ *The jury voted 8-to-4 in favor of acquittal.* 该陪审团以8票比4票投票赞成无罪判决。

acre ♦◇◇ /eɪkər/ (**acres**) N-COUNT An **acre** is an area of land measuring 4,840 square yards or 4,047 square meters. 英亩 ❑ *The property consists of two acres of land.* 这片地产有两英亩。

ac·ri·mo·ni·ous /ækrɪmoʊniəs/ ADJ **Acrimonious** words or quarrels are bitter and angry. (言辞或争辩) 激烈的 [FORMAL] ❑ *The acrimonious debate on the agenda ended indecisively.* 对这项议程的激烈辩论无果而终。

Word Link	*onym ≈ name : acronym, anonymous, synonym*

ac·ro·nym /ækrənɪm/ (**acronyms**) N-COUNT An **acronym** is a word composed of the first letters of the words in a phrase, especially when this is used as a name. An example of an acronym is NATO which is made up of the first letters of the "North Atlantic Treaty Organization." 首字母缩略词

across ♦♦♦ /əkrɔs/

> In addition to the uses shown below, **across** is used in phrasal verbs such as "come across," "get across," and "put across."

1 PREP If someone or something goes **across** a place or a boundary, they go from one side of it to the other. 过 ❑ *She walked across the floor and lay down on the bed.* 她走过地板躺在了床上。 ❑ *He watched Karl run across the street to Tommy.* 他看着卡尔横穿那条街道向汤米跑去。 ● ADV **Across** is also an adverb. 从一边到另一边 [ADV after v] ❑ *Richard stood up and walked across to the window.* 理查德站起来，走到了窗户那边。 **2** PREP If something is situated or stretched **across** something else, it is situated or stretched from one side of it to the other. 跨越 ❑ *...the floating bridge across Lake Washington in Seattle.* …横跨西雅图华盛顿湖的浮桥。 ❑ *He scrawled his name across the bill.* 他在账单上草草地写了他的名字。 ● ADV **Across** is also an adverb. 跨越 [ADV after v] ❑ *Trim toenails straight across using nail clippers.* 用指甲刀整块地剪脚指甲。 **3** PREP If something is lying **across** an object or place, it is resting on it and partly covering it. 在…上 ❑ *She found her clothes lying across the chair.* 她发现她的衣服平放在椅子上。 **4** PREP Something that is **across** something such as a street, river, or area is on the other side of it. 在…另一边 ❑ *Anyone from the houses across the road could see him.* 在路另一边的那些房子里的任何一个人都能看到他。 ● ADV **Across** is also an adverb. 在对面 ❑ *They parked across from the Castro Theater.* 他们在卡斯特罗剧院对面停了车。 **5** PREP You use **across** to say that a particular expression is shown on someone's face. (表情) 在(某人脸) 上 ❑ *An enormous grin spread across his face.* 一个灿烂的笑容绽开在他的脸上。 **6** PREP If someone hits you **across** the face or head, they hit you on that part. (击打) 在…上 ❑ *Graham hit him across the face with the gun, then pushed him against the wall.* 格林厄姆用枪打在他的脸上，然后把他推到墙上。 **7** PREP When something happens **across** a place or organization, it happens equally everywhere within it. 在…各处 ❑ *The movie opens across the country on December 11.* 这部电影于12月11日在全国各地上映。 **8** PREP When something happens **across** a political, religious, or social barrier, it involves people in different groups. 在…里 ❑ *...parties competing across the political spectrum.* …在政治领域里竞争的党派。 **9** **across the board** → see **board** **10** ADV If you look **across** at a place, person, or thing, you look toward them. 向 ❑ *He glanced across at his sleeping wife.* 他瞥向睡着的妻子。 ❑ *She rose from the chair and gazed across at him.* 她从椅子上站起凝目朝他望去。 **11** ADV **Across** is used in measurements to show the width of something. …宽 [amount ADV] ❑ *This hand-decorated plate measures 14 inches across.* 这个手绘盘子有14英寸宽。

acryl·ic /ækrɪlɪk/ N-UNCOUNT **Acrylic** material is artificial and is manufactured by a chemical process. 丙烯酸纤维 ❑ *...her pink acrylic sweater.* …她那件粉红色的丙烯酸纤维毛衣。

act ♦♦♦ /ækt/ (**acts, acting, acted**) **1** V-T/V-I When you **act**, you do something for a particular purpose. 行动 ❑ *The deaths occurred when police acted to stop widespread looting and vandalism.* 当警方行动起来去制止大范围的洗劫和蓄意破坏时，死亡事件发生了。 **2** V-I If you **act on** advice or information, you do what has been advised or suggested. (按照建议或信息) 行动 ❑ *A patient will usually listen to the doctor's advice and act on it.* 病人通常会听从医生的建议并且按照它行动。 **3** V-I If someone **acts** in a particular way, they behave in that way. 表现 ❑ *...a gang of youths who were acting suspiciously.* …一帮表现可疑的年轻人。 ❑ *He acted as if he hadn't heard any of it.* 他表现得好像一点都没有听过这件事一样。 **4** V-I If someone or something **acts as** a particular thing, they have that role or function. 担任 ❑ *Among his other duties, he acted both as the ship's surgeon and as chaplain for the men.* 另外，他兼任船上的外科医生以及船员们的牧师。 **5** V-I If someone **acts** in a particular way, they pretend to be something that they are not. 假装 ❑ *Chris acted astonished as he examined the note.* 在克里斯检查这张便条时，他假装很吃惊。 **6** V-I When professionals such as lawyers **act for** you, or **act on** your **behalf**, they are employed by you to deal with a particular matter. 代理 ❑ *Daniel Webster acted for Boston traders while still practicing in New Hampshire.* 丹尼尔·韦伯斯特还在新罕布什尔州实习时，就为波斯顿的商人们代理过。 **7** V-I If a force or substance **acts on** someone or something, it has a certain effect on them. 作用(于) ❑ *He's taking a dangerous drug: it acts very fast on the central nervous system.* 他在使用一种危险的药物——这种药物很快作用于中枢神经系统。 **8** V-I If you **act** in a play or film, you have a part in it. 表演 ❑ *She confessed to her parents her desire to act.* 她向父母承认了她想表演的欲望。 **9** N-COUNT An **act** is a single thing that someone does. 行为 [oft N "of" n] [FORMAL] ❑ *Language interpretation is the whole point of the act of reading.* 语言诠释是阅读行为的全部意义。 **10** N-COUNT An **Act** is a law passed by the government. 法案 ❑ *...an Act of Congress.* …一项议会法案。 **11** N-COUNT An **act** in a play, opera, or ballet is one of the main parts into which it is divided. 幕 [oft N num] ❑ *Act II contained one of the funniest scenes I have ever witnessed.* 第二幕包含了我所看过的最为可笑的场景之一。 **12** N-COUNT An **act** in a show is a short performance which is one of several in the show. 节目 ❑ *This year numerous bands are playing, as well as comedy acts.* 今年有许多乐队在表演，也有喜剧节目。 **13** N-SING If you say that someone's behavior is an **act**, you mean that it does not express their real feelings. 装样子 ❑ *His anger was real. It wasn't an act.* 他的生气是真的，不是装样子。 **14** PHRASE If you **catch** someone **in the act**, you discover them doing something wrong or committing a crime. 逮个正着 ❑ *The men were caught in the act of digging up buried explosives.* 这些人在挖掩埋起来的炸药时被逮了个正着。 **15** PHRASE If someone who has been behaving badly **cleans up** their **act**, they start to behave in a more acceptable or responsible way. 检点(某人的) 行为 [INFORMAL] ❑ *The nation's advertisers need to clean up their act.* 该国的广告商们需要检点他们的行为。 **16** PHRASE If you **get in on the act**, you take part in or take advantage of something that was started by someone else. 插手其中 [INFORMAL] ❑ *In the 1970s Kodak, anxious to get in on the act, launched its own instant camera.* 在20世纪70年代，急于插手其中的柯达公司推出了自己的即时成像照相机。 **17** PHRASE You say that someone was **in the act of** doing something to indicate what they were doing when they were seen or interrupted. 在(做某事的) 行动中 ❑ *Ken was in the act of paying his bill when Neil came up behind him.* 当尼尔走到他身后时，肯正在付账单。 **18** PHRASE If you **get** your **act together**, you organize your life or your affairs so that you are able to achieve what you want or to deal with something effectively. 有条理地安排(生活或事务) [INFORMAL] ❑ *The government should get its act together.* 政府应该有条理地安排其事务。 **19** **to act the fool** → see **fool**

Word Partnership *act* 的常用搭配:

PREP.	**act like** 5
N.	**an acting career** 8
	acts of vandalism, act of violence 9
	act one/two/three 11
V.	**caught in the act** 14
	get in on the act 16

act·ing /æktɪŋ/ **1** N-UNCOUNT **Acting** is the activity or profession of performing in plays or films. 表演 [oft N n] ❑ *She returned to London to pursue her acting career.* 她返回伦敦去从事她的表演事业。 **2** ADJ You use **acting** before the title of a job to indicate that someone is doing that job temporarily. 临时代理的 [ADJ n] ❑ *The new acting president has a reputation of being someone who is independent.* 这位新的临时代理总裁有极有主见的名声。

ac·tion ♦♦♦ /ækʃ^{ə}n/ (**actions, actioning, actioned**) **1** N-UNCOUNT **Action** is doing something for a particular purpose. 行动 ❑ *The government is taking emergency action to deal with a housing crisis.* 该政府正在采取紧急行动来处理一次住房危机。 **2** N-UNCOUNT The fighting which takes place in a war can be referred to as **action**. (军事) 行动 ❑ *Our leaders have generally supported military action if it proves necessary.* 我们的领导者们一般都支持必要军事行动的。 **3** N-COUNT An **action** is something that you do on a particular occasion. 行为 ❑ *As always, Peter had a reason for his action.* 如往常一样，彼得对他的行为总有理由。 **4** N-VAR To take legal **action** or to bring a legal **action** against someone means to bring a case against them in a court of law. 诉讼 [LEGAL] ❑ *Two leading law firms are to prepare legal actions against tobacco companies.* 两大律师事务所准备对烟草公司提起法律诉讼。 **5** ADJ An **action** movie is a film in which a lot of dangerous and exciting things happen. An **action** hero is the main character in one of these films. 动作(影片、演员) [ADJ n] **6** V-T If you **action** something that needs to be done, you deal with it. 处理 [usu passive] [BUSINESS] ❑ *Documents can be actioned, or filed immediately.* 这些文件可以立即得到处理或被存档。 **7** PHRASE If someone or something is **out of action**, they are injured or damaged and cannot work or be used. (人) 无法工作; (物体) 无法使用 ❑ *He's been out of action for 16 months with a serious knee injury.* 他因严重的膝伤已经16个月不能活动了。 **8** PHRASE If someone wants to have **a piece of the action** or **a slice of the action**, they want to take part in an exciting activity or situation, usually in order to make money or become more important. 插手 ❑ *In the late 1990s, investors big and small wanted a piece of the dot.com action.* 在20世纪90年代末，投资者们无论大小都想在网络概念股中插一手。 **9** PHRASE If you **put** an idea or policy **into action**, you begin to use it or cause it to operate. 将…付诸行动 ❑ *They have excelled in learning the lessons of business management theory, and putting them into action.* 他们在学习商业管理理论并将其付诸实践方面表现优异。
→ see **genre, motion**

Word Partnership *action* 的常用搭配:

N.	**course of action, plan of action** 1
V.	**take action** 1
ADJ.	**disciplinary action** 1
	military action 2
	legal action 4

★ **ac·ti·vate** /æktɪveɪt/ (**activates, activating, activated**) V-T If a device or process **is activated**, something causes it to start working. 激活 [usu passive] ❑ *Video cameras with night vision can be activated by movement.* 有夜视功能的摄像机能被物体的活动激活。

ac·tive ♦♦◊ /æktɪv/ **1** ADJ Someone who is **active** moves around a lot or does a lot of things. 好动的 ❑ *With three active little kids running around, there was plenty to keep me busy.* 有3个好动的小孩到处跑，就够让我忙的了。 **2** ADJ If you have an **active** mind or imagination, you are always thinking of new things. (思维或想像力) 活跃的 ❑ *...the tragedy of an active mind trapped by failing physical*

health. …活跃的头脑被衰弱的生理健康所困扰的悲剧。 3 ADJ If someone is **active** in an organization, cause, or campaign, they do things for it rather than just giving it their support. 积极主动的 ❑ *We should play an active role in politics, both at the national and local level.* 我们应该在国家和地方层面的政治生活中扮演积极主动的角色。
● **ac·tive·ly** ADV 积极主动地 ❑ *They actively campaigned for the vote.* 他们积极主动地为争取选票而活动。 4 ADJ **Active** is used to emphasize that someone is taking action in order to achieve something, rather than just hoping for it or achieving it in an indirect way. 积极的 [ADJ n] [EMPHASIS] ❑ *Companies need to take active steps to increase exports.* 那些公司需要采取积极的措施来增加出口。
● **ac·tive·ly** ADV 积极地 ❑ *They have never been actively encouraged to take such risks.* 他们从未被积极地鼓励去冒这样的风险。 5 ADJ If you say that a person or animal is **active** in a particular place or at a particular time, you mean that they are performing their usual activities or performing a particular activity. 活动的 ❑ *Guerrilla groups are active in the province.* 游击队组织在该省活动。 6 ADJ An **active** volcano has erupted recently or is expected to erupt soon. (火山) 活的 ❑ *...molten lava from an active volcano.* …一座活火山的熔岩。 7 ADJ An **active** substance has a chemical or biological effect on things. 活性的 ❑ *The active ingredient in some of the mouthwashes was simply detergent.* 某些漱口剂中的活性成分只是清洁剂而已。 8 N-SING In grammar, **the active** or **the active voice** means the forms of a verb which are used when the subject refers to a person or thing that does something. For example, in "I saw her yesterday," the verb is in the active. Compare **passive**. 主动语态

Word Partnership *active* 的常用搭配:
N. active **imagination** 2
active **role** 4
active **ingredient** 7
ADV. **politically** active 3

▲ **ac·tiv·ist** ♦◇◇ /æktɪvɪst/ (**activists**) N-COUNT An **activist** is a person who works to bring about political or social changes by campaigning in public or working for an organization. 激进分子 ❑ *The police say they suspect the attack was carried out by animal rights activists.* 警方说他们怀疑这次袭击是由保护动物权利的激进分子实施的。 ❑ *Dobson blames activist judges for undermining families with favorable gay-marriage rulings.* 多布森责备激进派法官们通过赞成同性婚姻的裁决破坏家庭。

ac·tiv·ity ♦♦◇ /æktɪvɪti/ (**activities**) 1 N-UNCOUNT **Activity** is a situation in which a lot of things are happening or being done. 活跃状况 ❑ *Changes in the money supply affect the level of economic activity and the interest rate.* 货币供给的变化影响经济活动水平和利率。 ❑ *Children are supposed to get 60 minutes of physical activity every day.* 儿童应该每天获得60分钟的体育活动。 2 N-COUNT An **activity** is something that you spend time doing. (个体性的) 活动 ❑ *For lovers of the great outdoors, activities range from canoeing to bird watching.* 对于户外活动的爱好者们来说，有从划船到观鸟的各种活动。 3 N-PLURAL The **activities** of a group are the things that they do in order to achieve their aims. (群体性的) 活动 ❑ *...a jail term for terrorist activities.* …一个针对恐怖主义活动的刑期。

Word Partnership *activity* 的常用搭配:
N. **level of** activity 1
ADJ. **criminal** activity, **extra-curricular** activity, **physical** activity 2

ac·tor ♦◇◇ /æktər/ (**actors**) N-COUNT An **actor** is someone whose job is acting in plays or films. "Actor" in the singular usually refers to a man, but some women who act prefer to be called "actors" rather than "actresses." 演员 ❑ *His father was an actor in the Cantonese Opera Company.* 他父亲曾是粤剧团的一名演员。 → see **theater**

Word Link *ess ≈ female : actress, heiress, princess*

ac·tress ♦◇◇ /æktrɪs/ (**actresses**) N-COUNT An **actress** is a woman whose job is acting in plays or films. 女演员 ❑ *She's not only a great dramatic actress but she's also very funny.* 她不仅是一位伟大的女戏剧演员，而且也很幽默。

ac·tual ♦◇◇ /æktʃuəl/ 1 ADJ You use **actual** to emphasize that you are referring to something real or genuine. 真实的 [ADJ n] [EMPHASIS] ❑ *The segments are filmed using either local actors or the actual people involved.* 这些片段是用当地的演员或真实的当事人拍摄的。 2 ADJ You use **actual** to contrast the important aspect of something with a less important aspect. 实际的 [ADJ n] [EMPHASIS] ❑ *She had compiled pages of notes, but she had not yet gotten down to doing the actual writing.* 她已辑录了多篇笔记，但她还没有着手实际的写作。

Do not confuse **actual** and **real**. You use **actual** to emphasize that what you are referring to is real or genuine, or to contrast different aspects of something. You use **real** to describe things that exist rather than being imagined or theoretical. ❑ *Robert squealed in mock terror, then in real pain.* Note that you only use **actual** in front of a noun. You do not say that something "is actual." Note also that **actual** is not used to refer to something which is happening now, at the present time. For this meaning, you need to use adjectives such as **current** or **present**.

★ **ac·tu·al·ity** /æktʃuælɪti/ (**actualities**) 1 PHRASE You can use **in actuality** to emphasize that what you are saying is true, when it contradicts or contrasts with what you have previously said. 事实上 [PHR with cl] [WRITTEN, EMPHASIS] ❑ *In actuality, Ted did not have a disorder but merely a difficult temperament.* 事实上，特德并没有什么异常而只是脾气不好。 2 N-UNCOUNT **Actuality** is the state of really existing rather than being imagined. 实际 ❑ *It exists in dreams rather than actuality.* 它于梦想而非实际中存在。

ac·tu·al·ly ♦♦♦ /æktʃuəli/ 1 ADV You use **actually** to indicate that a situation exists or happened, or to emphasize that it is true. 实际上 (指某种情形真实存在) [EMPHASIS] ❑ *One afternoon, I got bored and actually fell asleep for a few minutes.* 一天下午，我感到很无聊，实际上有几分钟还睡着了。 2 ADV You use **actually** when you are correcting or contradicting someone. 事实上 (用于纠正或反驳他人) [ADV with cl] [EMPHASIS] ❑ *No, I'm not a student. I'm a doctor, actually.* 不，我不是一名学生。事实上，我是一名医生。 3 ADV You can use **actually** when you are politely expressing an opinion that other people might not have expected from you. (用于礼貌地表达观点) 说实话 [ADV with cl] [POLITENESS] ❑ *"Do you think it's a good idea to socialize with one's patients?"—"Actually, I do, I think it's a great idea."* "你觉得和病人交往是个好主意吗?" —— "说实话，我觉得是，我觉得这是一个非常好的主意。" 4 ADV You use **actually** to introduce a new topic into a conversation. (用于开始新话题) 其实 [ADV with cl] ❑ *Well actually, John, I called you for some advice.* 嗯，约翰，其实我打电话给你是寻求一些建议。

Note that **actually** and **really** are both used to emphasize statements. **Actually** is used to emphasize what is true or genuine in a situation, often when this is surprising, or a contrast with what has just been said. ❑ *All the characters in the novel actually existed... He actually began to cry.* It can also be used to be precise or to correct someone. ❑ *No one was actually drunk... We couldn't actually see the garden.* You use **really** in conversation to emphasize something that you are saying. ❑ *I really think he's sick.* When you use **really** in front of an adjective or adverb, it has a similar meaning to "very." ❑ *This is really serious.*

acu·men /əkyumən/ N-UNCOUNT **Acumen** is the ability to make good judgments and quick decisions. 敏锐；精明

▲ **acu·punc·ture** /ækyupʌŋktʃər/ N-UNCOUNT **Acupuncture** is the treatment of a person's illness or pain by sticking small needles into their body at certain places. 针灸 ❑ *I had acupuncture in my lower back.* 我在后腰上做了针灸。

acute /əkyut/ 1 ADJ You can use **acute** to indicate that an undesirable situation or feeling is very severe or intense. 严峻的 ❑ *The war has aggravated an acute economic crisis.* 这场战争加剧了一场严峻的经济危机。 ❑ *The report has caused acute embarrassment to the government.* 这份报告使政府极其尴尬。 2 ADJ An **acute** illness is one that becomes severe very quickly but does not last very long. Compare **chronic**. 急性的 [ADJ n] [MEDICAL] ❑ *...a patient with acute rheumatoid arthritis.* …一位患急性风湿性关节炎的病人。 3 ADJ If a person's or animal's sight, hearing, or sense of smell is **acute**, it is sensitive and powerful. 敏锐的 ❑ *When she lost her sight, her other senses grew more acute.* 失明以后，她的其他感官变得更加敏锐了。 4 ADJ An **acute** angle is less than 90°. Compare **obtuse** angle. 锐 (角) 5 ADJ An **acute** accent is a symbol that is placed over vowels in some languages in order to indicate how that vowel is pronounced or over one letter in a word to indicate where it is stressed. You refer to a letter with this accent as, for example,

A

e **acute**. For example, there is an acute accent over the letter "e" in the French word "café." 尖音符的 (如**café**中**e**上的符号) [ADJ n, n ADJ]

acute·ly /əkyutli/ ADV If you feel or notice something **acutely**, you feel or notice it very strongly. 强烈地 ❑ *He was acutely aware of the odor of cooking oil.* 他强烈地觉察到了烹调油的味道。

ad ♦◇◇ /æd/ (**ads**) N-COUNT An **ad** is an advertisement. 广告 [INFORMAL] ❑ *She replied to a lonely hearts ad she spotted in the New York Times.* 她回复了在《纽约时报》上看到的一则求友广告。

AD /eɪ di/ You use **AD** in dates to indicate the number of years or centuries that have passed since the year in which Jesus Christ is believed to have been born. Compare **BC**. 公元 ❑ *The original castle was probably built about AD 860.* 原先的城堡可能是在公元860年前后修建的。 ❑ *The cathedral was destroyed by the Great Fire of 1136 AD.* 这座大教堂被公元1136年的大火烧毁了。

ada·mant /ædəmənt/ ADJ If someone is **adamant about** something, they are determined not to change their mind about it. 坚决的 ❑ *The president is adamant that he will not resign.* 该总统坚决不辞职。 ● **ada·mant·ly** ADV 坚决地 ❑ *She was adamantly opposed to her husband taking this trip.* 她坚决地反对她丈夫进行这次旅行。

a·dapt /ədæpt/ (**adapts, adapting, adapted**) **1** V-T/V-I If you **adapt to** a new situation or **adapt yourself to** it, you change your ideas or behavior in order to deal with it successfully. 适应 ❑ *The world will be different, and we will have to be prepared to adapt to the change.* 这个世界将会不同，所以我们必须准备好适应变化。 **2** V-T If you **adapt** something, you change it to make it suitable for a new purpose or situation. 改装 ❑ *Shelves were built to adapt the library for use as an office.* 做了个书架，以便将这个图书馆改作一个办公室用。 **3** → see also **adapted**

Thesaurus *adapt* 另参见：
V. acclimate, adjust, conform **1**
modify, revise **2**

adapt·able /ədæptəbᵊl/ ADJ If you describe a person or animal as **adaptable**, you mean that they are able to change their ideas or behavior in order to deal with new situations. 能适应的 ❑ *By making the workforce more adaptable and skilled, he hopes to attract foreign investment.* 通过使劳动力更具适应力并且更具技能，他希望吸引到外资。 ● **adapt·abil·ity** /ədæptəbɪlɪti/ N-UNCOUNT 适应性 ❑ *The adaptability of wool is one of its great attractions.* 羊毛的适应性是其巨大的吸引力之一。

ad·ap·ta·tion /ædæpteɪʃᵊn/ (**adaptations**) **1** N-COUNT An **adaptation** of a book or play is a film or a television program that is based on it. 改编 ❑ *Branagh won two awards for his screen adaptation of Shakespeare's Henry the Fifth.* 布拉纳因他对莎士比亚的《亨利五世》的荧幕改编而获了两次奖。 **2** N-UNCOUNT **Adaptation** is the act of changing something or changing your behavior to make it suitable for a new purpose or situation. 适应 ❑ *Most living creatures are capable of adaptation when compelled to do so.* 大多数生物在为情势所迫时都能适应。

Thesaurus *adaptation* 另参见：
N. adjustment, alteration, modification **2**

a·dapt·ed /ədæptɪd/ ADJ If something is **adapted to** a particular situation or purpose, it is especially suitable for it. 适合的 [v-link ADJ "to/for" n] ❑ *The camel's feet, well adapted for dry sand, are useless on mud.* 骆驼的脚十分适合干旱沙地，但在泥地上毫无用处。

add ♦♦♦ /æd/ (**adds, adding, added**) **1** V-T If you **add** one thing **to** another, you put it in or on the other thing, to increase, complete, or improve it. 添加 ❑ *Add the grated cheese to the sauce.* 把磨碎的奶酪加进那种酱中。 ❑ *Since 1908, chlorine has been added to drinking water.* 自从1908年起，氯就被添加到饮用水当中了。 **2** V-T If you **add** numbers or amounts **together**, you calculate their total. 加 ❑ *Banks add all the interest and other charges together.* 银行把所有利息和其他费用加在一起。 **3** V-I If one thing **adds to** another, it makes the other thing greater in degree or amount. 增加 ❑ *This latest incident will add to the pressure on the White House.* 最近的这起事件会给白宫增加更多的压力。 **4** V-T To **add** a particular quality **to** something means to cause it to have that quality. 增添 (某种特性) ❑ *The generous amount of garlic adds flavor.* 大量的蒜会增添滋味。 **5** V-T If you **add** something when you are speaking, you say something more. (讲话) 补充 ❑ *"You can tell that he is extremely embarrassed," Mr. Montoya added.* "你可以看出他是非常尴尬的，"蒙托亚先生补充道。 **6** V-I If you can **add**, you are able to calculate the total of numbers or amounts. 做加法

in BRIT, usually use **add up**

[AM] ❑ *More than a quarter of seven-year-olds cannot add properly.* 超过1/4的7岁儿童不会正确地做加法。

▸ **add in** PHRASAL VERB If you **add in** something, you include it as a part of something else. 加入 ❑ *Once the vegetables start to cook add in a couple of tablespoons of water.* 一旦蔬菜开始加热烹调，就加入几汤匙水。

▸ **add on** **1** PHRASAL VERB If one thing **is added on** to another, it is attached to the other thing, or is made a part of it. 加上 ❑ *Vacationers can also add on a week in Florida before or after the cruise.* 度假者们还可以在游船旅行前后加上在佛罗里达的一周。 **2** PHRASAL VERB If you **add on** an extra amount or item to a list or total, you include it. 附加 ❑ *Many loan application forms automatically add on insurance.* 许多贷款申请表自动附加保险。 **3** PHRASAL VERB If you **add on**, you increase the size of a house or other building by constructing one or more extra rooms. 扩建 [AM] ❑ *Investors who cannot afford a larger property now can add on when they have more money.* 现在买不起更大房产的投资者们可以在他们有更多钱时进行扩建。

▸ **add up** **1** PHRASAL VERB If you **add up** numbers or amounts, or if you **add** them **up**, you calculate their total. 把…加起来 ❑ *Add up the total of those six games.* 把那 6 场比赛的总分加起来。 ❑ *We just added all the numbers up and divided one by the other.* 我们只是把所有的数加起来，然后用一个除以另一个。 **2** PHRASAL VERB If facts or events do not **add up**, they make you confused about a situation because they do not seem to be consistent. If something that someone has said or done **adds up**, it is reasonable and sensible. 合乎情理 ❑ *Police said they arrested Olivia because her statements did not add up.* 警方说他们逮捕了奥丽维娅，因为她的陈述不合乎情理。 **3** PHRASAL VERB If small amounts of something **add up**, they gradually increase. 积少成多 ❑ *Even small savings, 5 cents here or 10 cents there, can add up.* 即使少量的节省，这儿5美分那儿10美分，也能积少成多。

▸ **add up to** PHRASAL VERB If amounts **add up to** a particular total, they result in that total when they are put together. 总计为 ❑ *For a hit show, profits can add up to millions of dollars.* 对于一个热门节目，利润可达上百万美元。

Thesaurus *add* 另参见：
V. put on, throw in **1**
calculate, tally, total; *(ant.)* reduce, subtract **2**
augment, increase; *(ant.)* lessen, reduce **3**

add·ed /ædɪd/ ADJ You use **added** to say that something has more of a particular thing or quality. 额外的 [ADJ n] ❑ *For added protection choose moisturizing lipsticks with a sunscreen.* 要额外的保护，请选择有防晒成分的保湿唇膏。

add·ed value N-UNCOUNT In marketing, **added value** is something that makes a product more appealing to customers. 附加价值 [BUSINESS] ❑ *We can create significant added value by pushing the brand into other areas.* 我们可以通过把这个品牌推向其他领域而创造出巨大的附加价值。

★ **ad·dict** /ædɪkt/ (**addicts**) **1** N-COUNT An **addict** is someone who takes harmful drugs and cannot stop taking them. (吸毒) 上瘾者 ❑ *He's only 24 years old and a drug addict.* 他只有24岁，可已经是一个瘾君子。 **2** N-COUNT If you say that someone is an **addict**, you mean that they like a particular activity very much and spend as much time doing it as they can. 对…入迷的人 ❑ *She is a TV addict and watches as much as she can.* 她是一个电视迷，看尽可能多的电视。

★ **ad·dict·ed** /ədɪktɪd/ **1** ADJ Someone who is **addicted to** a harmful drug cannot stop taking it. (吸食毒品) 成瘾的 ❑ *Many of the women are addicted to heroin and cocaine.* 这些妇女中的很多吸食海洛因和可卡因成瘾。 **2** ADJ If you say that someone is **addicted to** something, you mean that they like it very much and want to spend as much time doing it as possible. 入迷的 ❑ *She had become addicted to golf.* 她已经对高尔夫球入迷了。

ad·dic·tion /ədɪkʃᵊn/ (**addictions**) **1** N-VAR **Addiction** is the condition of taking harmful drugs and being unable to stop taking them. (毒品) 瘾 ❑ *She helped him fight his drug addiction.* 她帮助了他对抗自己的毒瘾。 **2** N-VAR An **addiction to** something is a very strong desire or need for it. 瘾 ❑ *He needed money to feed his addiction to gambling.* 他需要钱来满足他的赌瘾。

a

Word Partnership *addiction* 的常用搭配:

N. **drug** addiction 1
V. **feed an** addiction, **fight against** addiction 2
ADJ. **long-term** addiction 2
PREP. addiction **to** ***something*** 2

★ **ad·dic·tive** /ədɪktɪv/ 1 ADJ If a drug is **addictive**, people who take it cannot stop taking it. 使人上瘾的 ❑ *Cigarettes are highly addictive.* 香烟非常容易使人上瘾。 2 ADJ Something that is **addictive** is so enjoyable that it makes you want to do it or have it a lot. 使人着迷的 ❑ *Video movie-making can quickly become addictive.* 视频电影制作能迅速让人着迷。

ad·di·tion ♦♦◇ /ədɪʃən/ (**additions**) 1 PHRASE You use **in addition** when you want to mention another item connected with the subject you are discussing. 另外 ❑ *The web site provides regional weather reports, a shipping forecast and gale warnings. In addition, visitors can download satellite images of the U.S.* 这个网站提供地区天气报道、出航预测和大风警报。另外，访客可以下载美国的卫星图像。 2 N-COUNT An **addition to** something is a thing which is added to it. 添加物 ❑ *This is a fine book; a worthy addition to the series.* 这是一本好书——是对这套丛书有价值的增补。 3 N-COUNT An **addition** is a new room or building which is added to an existing building or group of buildings. 扩建部分 [oft N "to" n] [AM] ❑ *The couple said they spent $20,000 on building an addition to their kitchen.* 这对夫妻说他们花了2万美元扩建他们的厨房。 4 N-UNCOUNT The **addition of** something is the fact that it is added to something else. 增添部分 ❑ *It was completely refurbished in 1987, with the addition of a picnic site.* 它于1987年被完全翻修，增添了一个野餐场所。 5 N-UNCOUNT **Addition** is the process of calculating the total of two or more numbers. 加法 ❑ *...simple addition and subtraction problems using whole numbers.* …运用整数的简单加法和减法题。
→ see **mathematics**

ad·di·tion·al ♦◇◇ /ədɪʃənəl/ ADJ **Additional** things are extra things apart from the ones already present. 额外的 ❑ *The U.S. is sending additional troops to the region.* 美国正在往该地区派遣额外的部队。

ad·di·tion·al·ly /ədɪʃənəli/ ADV You use **additionally** to introduce something extra such as an extra fact or reason. 另外 [ADV with cl] ❑ *All teachers are qualified to teach their native language. Additionally, we select our teachers for their engaging personalities.* 所有教师都具备教授其母语的资格。另外，我们还根据富有魅力的个性来选择我们的教师。

▲ **ad·di·tive** /ædɪtɪv/ (**additives**) N-COUNT An **additive** is a substance which is added in small amounts to foods or other things in order to improve them or to make them last longer. 添加剂 ❑ *Strict safety tests are carried out on food additives.* 对食品添加剂进行了严格的安全检测。

add-on (**add-ons**) N-COUNT An **add-on** is an extra piece of equipment, especially computer equipment, that can be added to a larger one which you already own in order to improve its performance or its usefulness. (尤指电脑的) 附带装置 ❑ *To use this software, you don't need a CD-ROM drive or any expensive add-ons for your computer.* 使用这种软件，你不需要为你的电脑装光盘驱动器或者任何昂贵的附带装置。

ad·dress ♦♦◇ (**addresses, addressing, addressed**)

The noun is pronounced /ədrɛs/ or /ædrɛs/. The verb is pronounced /ədrɛs/.

名词读作 /ədrɛs/或 /ædrɛs/。动词读作 /ədrɛs/。

1 N-COUNT Your **address** is the number of the house or apartment and the name of the street and the town where you live or work. 地址 ❑ *The address is 2025 M Street, NW, Washington, DC, 20036.* 地址是华盛顿哥伦比亚特区，华盛顿西北，M街2025号，邮编20036。 2 N-COUNT The **address** of a website is its location on the Internet, for example, http://www.thomson.com. 网址 [COMPUTING] ❑ *Full details, including the website address to log on to, are at the bottom of this page.* 包括要登陆的网址的完整信息在本页下端。 3 V-T If a letter, envelope, or parcel **is addressed to** you, your name and address have been written on it. 写(收信人的) 姓名地址 [usu passive] ❑ *Applications should be addressed to: The business affairs editor.* 申请信应该寄给商务编辑。 4 V-T If you **address** a group of people, you give a speech to them. 作演讲 ❑ *He is due to address a conference on human rights next week.* 他下周要在一个人权会议上发言。 ● N-COUNT **Address** is also a noun. 演讲 ❑ *He had scheduled an address to the American people for the evening of May 27.* 他已经安排在5月27日晚向美国人民作一个演讲。

Thesaurus *address* 另参见:

N. lecture, speech, talk 4

Word Partnership *address* 的常用搭配:

N. **name and** address, **street** address 1
address **remarks to** 4
ADJ. **permanent** address 1
inaugural address, **public** address 4

ad·dress book (**address books**) 1 N-COUNT An **address book** is a book in which you write people's names and addresses. 地址簿 2 N-COUNT An **address book** is a computer file which contains a list of e-mail addresses. (电脑) 通讯簿 [COMPUTING]

▲ **adept** /ədɛpt/ ADJ Someone who is **adept at** something can do it skillfully. 娴熟的 ❑ *He's usually very adept at keeping his private life out of the media.* 他通常十分擅长于使他的私生活远离媒体。

ad·equa·cy /ædɪkwəsi/ N-UNCOUNT **Adequacy** is the quality of being good enough or great enough in amount to be acceptable. 足够 ❑ *There are questions to be raised about the adequacy of the inmates' legal representation.* 关于监犯的法定代表是否够格会有一些问题被提出。

ad·equate ♦◇◇ /ædɪkwɪt/ ADJ If something is **adequate**, there is enough of it or it is good enough to be used or accepted. 足够的 ❑ *One in four people worldwide are without adequate homes.* 世界上1/4的人没有足够的住房。 ❑ *She is prepared to offer me an amount adequate to purchase another house.* 她准备好了给我一笔足以购买另一所房子的钱。 ● **ad·equate·ly** ADV 足够地 [ADV with v] ❑ *Many students are not adequately prepared for higher education.* 很多学生没有为高等教育做足准备。

★ **ad·here** /ædhɪər/ (**adheres, adhering, adhered**) 1 V-I If you **adhere to** a rule or agreement, you act in the way that it says you should. 遵守 ❑ *All members of the association adhere to a strict code of practice.* 所有该协会的成员都遵守严格的业务守则。 2 V-I If something **adheres to** something else, it sticks firmly to it. 紧贴 ❑ *Small particles adhere to the seed.* 微小的粒子紧贴着种子。

★ **ad·her·ence** /ædhɪərəns/ N-UNCOUNT **Adherence** is the fact of adhering to a particular rule, agreement, or belief. 遵守 [usu N "to" n] ❑ *...strict adherence to the constitution.* …对宪法的严格遵守。

▲ **ad·he·sive** /ædhisɪv/ (**adhesives**) 1 N-MASS An **adhesive** is a substance such as glue, which is used to make things stick firmly together. 黏合剂 ❑ *Glue the mirror in with a strong adhesive.* 用一种强力黏合剂把镜子粘进去。 2 ADJ An **adhesive** substance is able to stick firmly to something else. 带黏性的 ❑ *...adhesive tape.* …胶布。

ad hoc /æd hɒk/ ADJ An **ad hoc** activity or organization is not planned in advance, but is done or formed only because a particular situation has made it necessary. 特别的 ❑ *"I would accept opportunities in TV on an ad hoc basis," he said.* "在特别需要时我会接受在电视上露面的机会，"他说道。

★ **ad·ja·cent** /ədʒeɪsənt/ ADJ If one thing is **adjacent to** another, the two things are next to each other. 相邻的 ❑ *He sat in an adjacent room and waited.* 他坐在一间相邻的房间里等。 ❑ *The schools were adjacent but there were separate doors.* 这些学校相邻，但是有各自的门。

ad·jec·tive /ædʒɪktɪv/ (**adjectives**) N-COUNT An **adjective** is a word such as "big," "dead," or "financial" that describes a person or thing, or gives extra information about them. Adjectives usually come before nouns or after linking verbs. 形容词

★ **ad·join** /ədʒɔɪn/ (**adjoins, adjoining, adjoined**) V-T If one room, place, or object **adjoins** another, they are next to each other. 紧邻 [FORMAL] ❑ *The doctor's bedroom adjoined his wife's and the door between the rooms was always open.* 这位医生的卧室紧邻他妻子的卧室，两间房之间的门总是开着的。

▲ **ad·journ** /ədʒɜrn/ (**adjourns, adjourning, adjourned**) V-T/V-I If a meeting or trial **is adjourned** or if it **adjourns**, it is stopped for a short time. (会议或审判) 暂停 ❑ *The proceedings have now been adjourned until next week.* 法律诉讼延至下周进行。

ad·journ·ment /ədʒɜrnmənt/ (**adjournments**) N-COUNT An **adjournment** is a temporary stopping of a trial, inquiry, or other meeting. 暂停 ❑ *The court ordered a four month adjournment.* 该法庭宣布了4个月的休庭。

A

ad·just ◆◇◇ /ədʒʌst/ (**adjusts, adjusting, adjusted**) 1 V-T/V-I When you **adjust to** a new situation, you get used to it by changing your behavior or your ideas. 调整以适应 ❑ *We have been preparing our fighters to adjust themselves to civil society.* 我们一直在让我们的战士们准备好自我调整以适应普通社会。 ❑ *I felt I had adjusted to the idea of being a mother very well.* 我感到我已经很好地适应了做母亲的想法。 2 V-T If you **adjust** something, you change it so that it is more effective or appropriate. 调整 ❑ *To attract investors, Panama has adjusted its tax and labor laws.* 为了吸引投资者，巴拿马已经调整了其税务及劳动法规。 3 V-T If you **adjust** something such as your clothing or a machine, you correct or alter its position or setting. 调节 ❑ *Liz adjusted her mirror and then edged the car out of its parking space.* 莉兹调节了她的后视镜，然后把车慢慢地开出了停车位。 4 V-T/V-I If you **adjust** your vision or if your vision **adjusts**, the muscles of your eye or the pupils alter to cope with changes in light or distance. 适应 ❑ *He stopped to try to adjust his vision to the faint starlight.* 他停下来，试着使眼睛适应昏暗的星光。

ad·just·able /ədʒʌstəbᵊl/ ADJ If something is **adjustable**, it can be changed to different positions or sizes. (位置、大小等) 可调整的 ❑ *The bags have adjustable shoulder straps.* 这些包有可调肩带。

→ see **interest rate**

Thesaurus *adjustable* 另参见：
ADJ. adaptable, adaptive, changeable; (*ant.*) fixed

ad·just·ment /ədʒʌstmənt/ (**adjustments**) 1 N-COUNT An **adjustment** is a small change that is made to something such as a machine or a way of doing something. (对机器、做事方法等的) 调整 ❑ *Compensation could be made by adjustments to taxation.* 补偿可由调税实现。 ❑ *Investment is up by 5.7% after adjustment for inflation.* 投资在通货膨胀调整之后增长了5.7%。 2 N-COUNT An **adjustment** is a change in a person's behavior or thinking. (对行为、思想等的) 调整 ❑ *He will have to make major adjustments to his thinking if he is to survive in office.* 他要想继续任职的话，就得对他的思维方式作大的调整。

ad·man /ædmæn/ (**admen**) N-COUNT An **adman** is someone who works in advertising. 广告人 [INFORMAL] ❑ *He was the most brilliant adman that any of us knew.* 他曾是我们任何人都知道的最出色的广告人。

ad·min /ædmɪn/ 1 ADJ **Admin** is an abbreviation of **administrative.** 行政的 2 N-UNCOUNT **Admin** is the activity or process of organizing an institution or organization. **Admin** is an abbreviation of **administration.** 行政工作 [BRIT, INFORMAL]

★ **ad·min·is·ter** /ædmɪnɪstər/ (**administers, administering, administered**) 1 V-T If someone **administers** something such as a country, the law, or a test, they take responsibility for organizing and supervising it. 监管 (国家、法律、考试等) ❑ *The plan calls for the UN to administer the country until elections can be held.* 该计划呼吁联合国监管该国直至选举可以举行。 2 V-T If a doctor or a nurse **administers** a drug, they give it to a patient. (医生、护士) 派发 (药物) [FORMAL] ❑ *The physician may prescribe but not administer the drug.* 内科医师可以开处方但不可发药。

★ **ad·min·is·trate** /ædmɪnɪstreɪt/ (**administrates, administrating, administrated**) VERB To **administrate** an organization's business activities means to manage or direct them. 管理 (商业活动) ❑ *The Internet opens up new ways of administrating the tax system.* 互联网开拓了管理税收系统的一些新途径。

ad·min·is·tra·tion ◆◆◇ /ædmɪnɪstreɪʃᵊn/ (**administrations**) 1 N-UNCOUNT **Administration** is the range of activities connected with organizing and supervising the way that an organization or institution functions. 行政工作；管理工作 ❑ *Too much time is spent on administration.* 太多的时间花在了管理工作上。 2 N-UNCOUNT The **administration** of something is the process of organizing and supervising it. 监管 ❑ *Standards in the administration of justice have degenerated.* 司法监管的标准已退化了。 3 N-SING **The administration** of a company or institution is the group of people who organize and supervise it. 管理层；行政部门 ❑ *They would like the college administration to exert more control over the fraternity.* 他们希望该学院行政部门加大对该兄弟会的控制力度。 4 N-COUNT You can refer to a country's government as **the administration**; used especially in the United States. 政府 (尤用于美国) ❑ *O'Leary served in federal energy posts in both the Ford and Carter administrations.* 奥利里在福特政府和卡特政府期间都任过联邦政府能源部门的职位。

ad·min·is·tra·tive /ædmɪnɪstreɪtɪv/ ADJ **Administrative** work involves organizing and supervising an organization or institution. 行政的；管理的 ❑ *Other industries have had to sack managers to reduce administrative costs.* 其他行业已不得不解雇管理人员来减少管理成本。

ad·min·is·tra·tor /ædmɪnɪstreɪtər/ (**administrators**) N-COUNT An **administrator** is a person whose job involves helping to organize and supervise the way that an organization or institution functions. 行政人员；管理人员 ❑ *On Friday the company's administrators sought permission from a Melbourne court to keep operating.* 在星期五，该公司的管理人员们从一家墨尔本法院取得了继续经营的许可。

ad·mi·rable /ædmɪrəbᵊl/ ADJ An **admirable** quality or action is one that deserves to be praised and admired. 值得钦佩的 ❑ *She did an admirable job of holding the audience's attention.* 她做了件值得钦佩的事：吸引了观众的注意力。 ● **ad·mi·rably** /ædmɪrəbli/ ADV 值得钦佩地 ❑ *Peter had dealt admirably with the sudden questions about Keith.* 彼得对关于基思的突如其来的问题处理得值得人钦佩。

▲ **ad·mi·ral** /ædmərəl/ (**admirals**) N-COUNT; N-TITLE An **admiral** is a very senior officer who commands a navy. 海军上将 ❑ *...Admiral Hodges.* …霍奇斯海军上将。

ad·mi·ra·tion /ædmɪreɪʃᵊn/ N-UNCOUNT **Admiration** is a feeling of great liking and respect for a person or thing. 钦佩 ❑ *I have always had the greatest admiration for him.* 我对他一直怀有最大的钦佩。

ad·mire ◆◇◇ /ædmaɪər/ (**admires, admiring, admired**) 1 V-T If you **admire** someone or something, you like and respect them very much. 钦佩 ❑ *I admired her when I first met her and I still think she's marvelous.* 我第一次见到她时就钦佩她，而且我现在依然认为她很了不起。 ❑ *He admired the way she had coped with life.* 他钦佩她应对生活的方式。 2 V-T If you **admire** someone or something, you look at them with pleasure. 欣赏 ❑ *We took time to stop and admire the view.* 我们特意停下来欣赏风景。

Thesaurus *admire* 另参见：
V. esteem, honor, look up to, respect 1

ad·mir·er /ædmaɪərər/ (**admirers**) N-COUNT If you are an **admirer** of someone, you like and respect them or their work very much. 仰慕者 ❑ *He was an admirer of her grandfather's paintings.* 他是她祖父画作的一个仰慕者。

ad·mis·sion /ædmɪʃᵊn/ (**admissions**) 1 N-VAR **Admission** is permission given to a person to enter a place, or permission given to a country to enter an organization. **Admission** is also the act of entering a place. 进入许可；加入许可；进入 ❑ *Students apply for admission to a particular college.* 学生们申请某学院的入学许可。 2 N-VAR An **admission** is a statement that something bad, unpleasant, or embarrassing is true. 承认 ❑ *By his own admission, he is not playing well.* 据他自己承认，他表现不佳。 3 N-PLURAL **Admissions** to a place such as a school or university are the people who are allowed to enter or join it. 获准入学者；获准加入者 ❑ *Each school sets its own admissions policy.* 每所学校都设立自己的入学政策。 4 N-UNCOUNT **Admission** at a park, museum, or other place is the amount of money that you pay to enter it. (公园、博物馆等地的) 门票价格 ❑ *Gates open at 10:30 a.m. and admission is free.* 上午10:30开门，免门费。 ● N-UNCOUNT **Admission** is also used before a noun. 门票价格 (用于名词前) ❑ *The admission price is $8 for adults.* 入场费成人是$8。

→ see **hospital**

ad·mit ◆◆◇ /ædmɪt/ (**admits, admitting, admitted**) 1 V-T/V-I If you **admit** that something bad, unpleasant, or embarrassing is true, you agree, often unwillingly, that it is true. 承认 (不好、不快或尴尬的事实) ❑ *I am willing to admit that I do make mistakes.* 我愿意承认我确实会犯错误。 ❑ *Up to two thirds of 14 to 16 year olds admit to buying alcohol illegally.* 14至16岁的少年中有多达2/3的少年承认非法买过酒。 ❑ *None of these people will admit responsibility for their actions.* 这些人中没有人愿意承认为他们的行为负有的责任。 2 V-T If someone **is admitted to** a hospital, they are taken into the hospital for treatment and kept there until they are well enough to go home. 接收 (入院) ❑ *She was admitted to the hospital with a soaring temperature.* 她因高烧被接收入院。 3 V-T If someone **is admitted to** an organization or group, they are allowed to join it. 接收 (加入) ❑ *He was admitted to the Académie Culinaire de France.* 他被接收加入法国厨艺学会。 4 V-T To **admit** someone **to** a place means to allow them to enter it. 准许进入 ❑ *Embassy security personnel refused to admit him or his wife.* 使馆保安人员拒绝让他或他的妻子进入。

Word Partnership *admit* 的常用搭配:

V. **ashamed to** admit, **be the first to** admit, **must** admit, **willing to** admit 1
N. admit **defeat** 1
CONJ. admit **that** 1

★ **ad·mit·tance** /ædmɪtᵊns/ N-UNCOUNT **Admittance** is the act of entering a place or institution or the right to enter it. 进入; 进入权 [oft N "into/to" n] [mainly BRIT] ❑ *We had not been able to gain admittance to the flat.* 我们还未能获得进入那所公寓的权利。

★ **ad·mit·ted·ly** /ædmɪtɪdli/ ADV You use **admittedly** when you are saying something that weakens the importance or force of your statement. 得承认 [ADV with cl/group] ❑ *It's only a theory, admittedly, but the pieces fit together.* 得承认这只是一种理论，但其各部分自成一体。

★ **ado·les·cence** /ædᵊlɛsᵊns/ N-UNCOUNT **Adolescence** is the period of your life in which you develop from being a child into being an adult. 青春期 ❑ *Some young people suddenly become self-conscious and tongue-tied in early adolescence.* 一些年青人在青春期早期突然变得害羞结舌。
→ see **child**

★ **ado·les·cent** /ædᵊlɛsᵊnt/ (**adolescents**) ADJ **Adolescent** is used to describe young people who are no longer children but who have not yet become adults. It also refers to their behavior. 青春期的 (少年、行为) ❑ *It is important that an adolescent boy should have an adult in whom he can confide.* 一个青春期男孩应该有一个他能倾吐心声的成年人，这是很重要的。 ● N-COUNT An **adolescent** is an adolescent boy or girl. 青春期少年 ❑ *Young adolescents are happiest with small groups of close friends.* 年轻的青春期少年们和一小圈亲近的朋友在一起时最高兴。
→ see **age**

Word Link *opt ≈ choosing : adopt, opt, optional*

adopt ♦♦◇ /ədɒpt/ (**adopts, adopting, adopted**) 1 V-T If you **adopt** a new attitude, plan, or way of behaving, you begin to have it. 采纳; 采用 ❑ *The United Nations General Assembly has adopted a resolution calling on all parties in the conflict to seek a political settlement.* 联合国大会已采纳了一项呼吁所有冲突各方寻求政治解决的决议。 ● **adop·tion** /ədɒpʃᵊn/ N-UNCOUNT 采纳; 采用 ❑ *The group is working to promote the adoption of broadband wireless access over long distances.* 该集团正在致力于推广远距离宽带无线访问的采用。 2 V-T/V-I If you **adopt** someone else's child, you take it into your own family and make it legally your son or daughter. 收养 ❑ *There are hundreds of people desperate to adopt a child.* 有数以百计的人极其渴望收养小孩。 ● **adop·tion** N-VAR (**adoptions**) 收养 ❑ *They gave their babies up for adoption.* 他们放弃了自己的婴儿让别人收养。

Thesaurus *adopt* 另参见:

V. approve, endorse, support; *(ant.)* refuse, reject 1
care for, raise, take in 2

adop·tive /ədɒptɪv/ ADJ Someone's **adoptive** family is the family that adopted them. 收养的 (家庭) [ADJ n] ❑ *He was brought up by adoptive parents in Kentucky.* 他是被他在肯塔基州的养父母抚养大的。

ador·able /ədɔrəbᵊl/ ADJ If you say that someone or something is **adorable**, you are emphasizing that they are very attractive and you feel great affection for them. 非常可爱的 [EMPHASIS] ❑ *By the time I was 30, we had three adorable children.* 到我30岁时，我们有了3个非常可爱的孩子。

ado·ra·tion /ædɔreɪʃᵊn/ N-UNCOUNT **Adoration** is a feeling of great admiration and love for someone or something. 爱慕之情 ❑ *She needs and wants to be loved with overwhelming passion and adoration.* 她需要并想要被人怀着排山倒海般的激情与爱慕爱着。
→ see **emotion**

★ **adore** /ədɔr/ (**adores, adoring, adored**) 1 V-T If you **adore** someone, you feel great love and admiration for them. 爱慕 (某人) [no cont] ❑ *She adored her parents and would do anything to please them.* 她深爱她的父母，愿做任何事来让他们高兴。 2 V-T If you **adore** something, you like it very much. 很喜欢 (某物) [no cont] [INFORMAL] ❑ *My mother adores bananas and eats two a day.* 我妈妈很喜欢香蕉，一天吃两根。

▲ **adorn** /ədɔrn/ (**adorns, adorning, adorned**) V-T If something **adorns** a place or an object, it makes it look more beautiful. 装饰 ❑ *His watercolor designs adorn a wide range of books.* 他的水彩设计装饰着各种各样的书籍。

adrena·lin /ədrɛnᵊlɪn/ also **adrenaline** N-UNCOUNT **Adrenalin** is a substance which your body produces when you are angry, scared, or excited. It makes your heart beat faster and gives you more energy. 肾上腺素 ❑ *That was my first big game in months and the adrenalin was going.* 那是我数月来第一场大赛，非常兴奋。

adrift /ədrɪft/ 1 ADJ If a boat is **adrift**, it is floating on the water and is not tied to anything or controlled by anyone. (船) 漂浮着的 [v-link ADJ, v n ADJ] ❑ *They were spotted after three hours adrift in a dinghy.* 3小时后他们被发现坐在一艘小艇里在漂着。 2 ADJ If someone is **adrift**, they feel alone with no clear idea of what they should do. (人) 茫然的 [v-link ADJ, v n ADJ] ❑ *Amy had the growing sense that she was adrift and isolated.* 埃米有越来越强的茫然与孤独感。

adult ♦♦◇ /ədʌlt/ (**adults**) 1 N-COUNT An **adult** is a mature, fully developed person. An adult has reached the age when they are legally responsible for their actions. 成年人 ❑ *Becoming a father signified that he was now an adult.* 成为一名父亲意味着他现在是一个成年人了。 2 N-COUNT An **adult** is a fully developed animal. 成年动物 ❑ *...a pair of adult birds.* …一对成鸟。 3 ADJ **Adult** means relating to the time when you are an adult, or typical of adult people. 成年人的 [ADJ n] ❑ *I've lived most of my adult life in Arizona.* 我已在亚利桑那州度过了我大部分的成年生活。 4 ADJ You can describe things such as films or books as **adult** when they deal with sex in a very clear and open way. (电影、书籍等) 只适合成人的 ❑ *...an adult movie.* …一部成人电影。
→ see **age**

Thesaurus *adult* 另参见:

N. grown-up, man, woman 1
ADJ. full-grown 2

adul·ter·ate /ədʌltəreɪt/ (**adulterates, adulterating, adulterated**) V-T If something such as food or drink **is adulterated**, someone has made its quality worse by adding water or cheaper products to it. (给食物、饮料等) 掺假 [usu passive] ❑ *The food had been adulterated to increase its weight.* 这种食物被掺了假以增加其重量。

adul·tery /ədʌltəri/ N-UNCOUNT If a married person commits **adultery**, they have sex with someone that they are not married to. 通奸 ❑ *She is going to divorce him on the grounds of adultery.* 她打算以通奸为由与他离婚。

Word Link *hood ≈ state, condition : adulthood, childhood, manhood*

adult·hood /ədʌlthʊd/ N-UNCOUNT **Adulthood** is the state of being an adult. 成年 ❑ *Few people nowadays are able to maintain friendships into adulthood.* 现今很少有人能够把友谊维持到成年。

ad·vance ♦♦◇ /ædvæns/ (**advances, advancing, advanced**) 1 V-I To **advance** means to move forward, often in order to attack someone. (常指为攻击而) 前进 ❑ *Reports from Chad suggest that rebel forces are advancing on the capital.* 来自乍得的报导指出叛军正在向首都挺进。 ❑ *According to one report, the water is advancing at a rate of between 8 and 10 inches a day.* 根据一份报告，大水在以每天8至10英寸的速度逼近。 2 V-I To **advance** means to make progress, especially in your knowledge of something. (尤指知识) 发展 ❑ *Medical technology has advanced considerably.* 医学技术已大大发展了。 3 → see also **advanced** 4 V-T If you **advance** someone a sum of money, you lend it to them, or pay it to them earlier than arranged. 提前借 (一笔钱给某人); 提前付 (一笔钱给某人) ❑ *I advanced him some money, which he would repay on our way home.* 我先借了些钱给他，他会在回家的路上还给我。 5 V-T To **advance** an event, or the time or date of an event, means to bring it forward to an earlier time or date. 使提前 ❑ *Too much protein in the diet may advance the aging process.* 饮食中过多的蛋白质会使衰老的过程提前。 6 V-T If you **advance** a cause, interest, or claim, you support it and help to make it successful. 造成; 促成 ❑ *When not producing art of his own, Oliver was busy advancing the work of others.* 没有创作自己的艺术品时，奥利弗就在忙于促成他人的作品。 7 N-COUNT An **advance** is money lent or paid to someone before they would normally receive it. 预付款 ❑ *She was paid a $100,000 advance for her next two novels.* 她得到了其接下来的两本小说的10万美元的预付款。 8 N-VAR An **advance** is a forward movement of people or vehicles, usually as part of a military operation. (常指军事行动中的) 前进 ❑ *In an exercise designed*

A

to be as real as possible, they simulated an advance on enemy positions. 在一次设计得尽可能逼真的演习中，他们模拟了一次向敌方阵地的前进。 **9** N-VAR An **advance** in a particular subject or activity is progress in understanding it or in doing it well. (在某科目、某活动中的) 发展 ❑ *Air safety has not improved since the dramatic advances of the 1970s.* 飞行安全自从20世纪70年代的急剧发展以来还没有得到改善。 **10** N-SING If something is an **advance on** what was previously available or done, it is better in some way. 改善 [usu "a" N "on" n] ❑ *This could be an advance on the present situation.* 这可能是对目前情况的一次改善。 **11** ADJ **Advance** booking, notice, or warning is done or given before an event happens. 事先的 (预定、通知、警告等) [ADJ n] ❑ *They don't normally give any advance notice about which building they're going to inspect.* 他们对要视察哪座大楼通常不作事先通知。 **12** PHRASE If you do something **in advance**, you do it before a particular date or event. 提前 ❑ *The subject of the talk is announced a week in advance.* 会谈的主题提前一周宣布。

Thesaurus *advance* 另参见：

V.	improve **2**
N.	allowance, credit, loan, pre-payment, retainer **7**
ADJ.	early, prior **11**
ADV.	beforehand, previously **12**

Word Partnership *advance* 的常用搭配：

V.	advance **and retreat** **1**
N.	advance **a cause** **6**
	cash advance **7**
	advance **knowledge**, advance **notice**, advance **purchase**, advance **reservations** **11**
ADJ.	**technological** advance **9**

ad·vanced ♦◇◇ /ædvænst/ **1** ADJ An **advanced** system, method, or design is modern and has been developed from an earlier version of the same thing. 先进的 (系统、方法、设计等) ❑ *...a superpower equipped with the most advanced military technology in the world.* …一个拥有世界上最先进的军事技术的超级大国。 **2** ADJ A country that is **advanced** has reached a high level of industrial or technological development. (国家) 发达的 ❑ *Agricultural productivity remained low by comparison with advanced countries like the United States.* 与美国等发达国家相比，农业生产率仍很低。 **3** ADJ An **advanced** student has already learned the basic facts of a subject and is doing more difficult work. An **advanced** course of study is designed for such students. 高阶的 (学生、课程) ❑ *The course is suitable for beginners and advanced students.* 该课程适合初学者和高阶学生。 **4** ADJ Something that is at an **advanced** stage or level is at a late stage of development. 晚期的 ❑ *Medicare is available to victims of advanced kidney disease.* 晚期肾病患者可获得医疗保障。

Thesaurus *advanced* 另参见：

ADJ.	cutting-edge, foremost, latest, sophisticated **1**

★ **ad·vance·ment** /ædvænsmənt/ (**advancements**) **1** N-UNCOUNT **Advancement** is progress in your job or in your social position. 晋升；升迁 ❑ *He cared little for social advancement.* 他几乎不在乎社会地位的升迁。 **2** N-VAR The **advancement of** something is the process of helping it to progress or the result of its progress. 促进 ❑ *Her work for the advancement of the status of women in India was recognized by the whole nation.* 她为促进印度妇女地位的提升所做的工作得到了全国人民的认可。

ad·van·tage ♦♦◇ /ædvɑntɪdʒ, -væn-/ (**advantages**) **1** N-COUNT An **advantage** is something that puts you in a better position than other people. 有利条件 ❑ *They are breaking the law in order to obtain an advantage over their competitors.* 他们为了获得超越其竞争对手的有力条件在违犯法律。 **2** N-COUNT An **advantage** is a way in which one thing is better than another. 优势 ❑ *The great advantage of home-grown oranges is their magnificent flavor.* 自产橙子的巨大优势是其极好的味道。 **3** N-UNCOUNT **Advantage** is the state of being in a better position than others who are competing against you. 占优势 ❑ *Men have created a social and economic position of advantage for themselves over women.* 男性创造了相对于女性的社会和经济上的优势地位。 **4** PHRASE If you **take advantage of** something, you make good use of it while you can. 利用 (某事物) ❑ *I intend to take full advantage of this trip to buy the things we need.* 我打算充分利用这次旅行来购买我们需要的物品。 **5** PHRASE If someone **takes advantage of** you, they treat you unfairly for their own benefit, especially when you are trying to be kind or to help them. 利用 (某人) ❑ *She took advantage of him even after they were divorced.* 她甚至在他们离婚以后仍然利用他。 **6** PHRASE If you use or turn something **to your advantage**, you use it in order to benefit from it, especially when it might be expected to harm or damage you. 对 (某人) 有利 ❑ *The government has not been able to turn today's demonstration to its advantage.* 政府还未能将今天的游行示威转化为对其有利。

Word Partnership *advantage* 的常用搭配：

ADJ.	**competitive** advantage, **unfair** advantage **1**
V.	**have an** advantage **1**
	take advantage **of** *someone/something* **4**
	use to *someone's* advantage **6**

★ **ad·van·ta·geous** /ædvənteɪdʒəs/ ADJ If something is **advantageous to** you, it is likely to benefit you. 有利的 ❑ *Free exchange of goods was advantageous to all.* 自由商品交易对大家都有利。

▲ **ad·vent** /ædvɛnt/ N-UNCOUNT **The advent of** an important event, invention, or situation is the fact of it starting or coming into existence. 出现 [FORMAL] ❑ *The advent of the computer has brought this sort of task within the bounds of possibility.* 电脑的出现使这种任务的完成成为可能。

ad·ven·ture /ædvɛntʃər/ (**adventures**) **1** N-COUNT If someone has an **adventure**, they become involved in an unusual, exciting, and somewhat dangerous trip or series of events. 冒险经历 ❑ *I set off for a new adventure in Alaska on the first day of the new year.* 我在新年第一天出发去阿拉斯加进行一次新的冒险。 **2** N-UNCOUNT **Adventure** is excitement and willingness to do new, unusual, or somewhat dangerous things. 冒险精神 ❑ *Their cultural backgrounds gave them a spirit of adventure.* 他们的文化背景赋予了他们一种冒险精神。

★ **ad·ven·tur·er** /ædvɛntʃərər/ (**adventurers**) N-COUNT An **adventurer** is a person who enjoys going to new, unusual, and exciting places. 探险者

★ **ad·ven·tur·ous** /ædvɛntʃərəs/ **1** ADJ Someone who is **adventurous** is willing to take risks and to try new methods. Something that is **adventurous** involves new things or ideas. (人) 有冒险精神的；(事物) 冒险性的 ❑ *Warren was an adventurous businessman.* 沃伦是一位有冒险精神的商人。 **2** ADJ Someone who is **adventurous** is eager to visit new places and have new experiences. (人) 爱冒险的 ❑ *He had always wanted an adventurous life in the tropics.* 他一直都想要一种在热带丛林里的冒险生活。

ad·verb /ædvɜrb/ (**adverbs**) N-COUNT An **adverb** is a word such as "slowly," "now," "very," "politically," or "fortunately" which adds information about the action, event, or situation mentioned in a clause. 副词

ad·verb phrase (**adverb phrases**) N-COUNT An **adverb phrase** or **adverbial phrase** is a group of words based on an adverb, such as "very slowly" or "fortunately for us." An adverb phrase can also consist simply of an adverb. 副词短语

ad·ver·sar·ial /ædvərsɛəriəl/ ADJ If you describe something as **adversarial**, you mean that it involves two or more people or organizations who are opposing each other. 对立的 [FORMAL] ❑ *In our country there is an adversarial relationship between government and business.* 在我们的国家，在政府和商界之间存有一种敌对关系。

▲ **ad·ver·sary** /ædvərsɛri/ (**adversaries**) N-COUNT Your **adversary** is someone you are competing with, or arguing or fighting against. 对手 ❑ *His political adversaries would like to discredit him.* 他的政敌想破坏他的声誉。

★ **ad·verse** /ædvɜrs/ ADJ **Adverse** decisions, conditions, or effects are unfavorable to you. 不利的 ❑ *The police said Mr. Hadfield's decision would have no adverse effect on the progress of the investigation.* 警方说哈德菲尔德先生的决定对于调查进展不会有任何不利的影响。 ● **ad·verse·ly** ADV 不利地 [ADV with v] ❑ *Price changes must not adversely affect the living standards of the people.* 价格变化一定不能负面地影响人们的生活水平。

▲ **ad·ver·sity** /ædvɜrsɪti/ (**adversities**) N-VAR **Adversity** is a very difficult or unfavorable situation. 困境；逆境 ❑ *He showed courage in adversity.* 他在逆境中显示出了勇气。

ad·vert /ædvɜrt/ (**adverts**) N-COUNT An **advert** is an announcement in a newspaper, on television, or on a poster about something such as a product, event, or job. 广告 [BRIT]

in AM, use **ad**

a

Word Web advertising

It's impossible to avoid **advertisements**. In our homes, **newspaper, magazine,** and **television** ads compete for our attention. **Posters, billboards,** and **flyers** greet us the moment we walk out the door. **Advertising agencies** stay busy thinking up new ways to get our attention. We have company **logos** on our clothes. Our email is full of **spam**, and pop-ups slow us down as we surf the Web. Product **placements** sneak into movies and TV shows. "Ad wrapping" turns cars into moving signboards. Advertisers have even tried **subliminal** advertising in TV **commercials**. It's no wonder that this is called the **consumer** age.

ad·ver·tise ♦◇◇ /ædvərtaɪz/ (**advertises, advertising, advertised**) **1** V-T/V-I If you **advertise** something such as a product, an event, or a job, you tell people about it in newspapers, on television, or on posters in order to encourage them to buy the product, go to the event, or apply for the job. 为…做广告；做广告 ❑ *The company is spending heavily to advertise its strongest brands.* 该公司在花重金为其最强势的品牌做广告。 ❑ *In 1991, the house was advertised for sale at $49,000.* 在1991年，这所房子登出以4.9万美元出售的广告。 **2** V-I If you **advertise for** someone to do something for you, for example, to work for you or share your accommodation, you announce it in a newspaper, on television, or on a bulletin board. 登广告（寻求职员、合住者等）❑ *We advertised for staff in a local newspaper.* 我们在一份地方报纸上登了广告招聘员工。 **3** V-T If you do not **advertise** the fact that something is the case, you try not to let other people know about it. 宣传 [usu with brd-neg] ❑ *There is no need to advertise the fact that you are a single woman.* 没必要宣传你是个单身女性这一事实。 **4** → see also **advertising**

ad·ver·tise·ment /ædvərtaɪzmənt/ (**advertisements**) **1** N-COUNT An **advertisement** is an announcement in a newspaper, on television, or on a poster about something such as a product, event, or job. 广告；启事 [WRITTEN] ❑ *Miss Parrish recently placed an advertisement in the local newspaper.* 帕里什小姐最近在当地报纸上登出了一则启事。 **2** N-COUNT If you say that an example of something is **an advertisement for** that thing in general, you mean that it shows how good that thing is. 宣传 ❑ *The Treviso team was an effective advertisement for the improving state of Italian club rugby.* 特雷维索队是意大利俱乐部橄榄球改进状况的一个有效展示。

ad·ver·tis·er /ædvərtaɪzər/ (**advertisers**) N-COUNT An **advertiser** is a person or company that pays for a product, event, or job to be advertised in a newspaper, on television, or on a poster. 广告客户 ❑ *When will advertisers stop bombarding women with images of unattainable beauty?* 什么时候广告客户们才会停止用不可企及的美丽形象来持续轰炸女性？

ad·ver·tis·ing /ædvərtaɪzɪŋ/ N-UNCOUNT **Advertising** is the activity of creating advertisements and making sure people see them. 广告业 ❑ *I work in advertising.* 我在广告业工作。 → see Word Web: **advertising**

ad·ver·tis·ing agen·cy (**advertising agencies**) N-COUNT An **advertising agency** is a company whose business is to create advertisements for other companies or organizations. 广告代理公司

ad·ver·tis·ing cam·paign (**advertising campaigns**) N-COUNT An **advertising campaign** is a planned series of advertisements. 广告计划

ad·vice ♦♦◇ /ædvaɪs/ N-UNCOUNT If you give someone **advice**, you tell them what you think they should do in a particular situation. 建议 ❑ *Don't be afraid to ask for advice about ordering the meal.* 别怕就点餐寻求建议。 ❑ *Take my advice and stay away from him!* 听我的忠告，离他远点！

Thesaurus *advice* 另参见：

N. counsel, guidance, help, information, input, opinion, recommendation, suggestion

Word Partnership *advice* 的常用搭配：

PREP. **against** advice
V. **ask for** advice, **give** advice, **need some** advice, **take** advice
ADJ. **bad/good** advice, **expert** advice

Note that **advice** is an uncount noun. You can say **a piece of advice** or **some advice**, but you cannot say "an advice" or "advices." Do not confuse **advice** and **advise**. **Advise** is the verb that is connected with **advice**.

ad·vice col·umn·ist (**advice columnists**) N-COUNT An **advice columnist** is a person who writes a column in a newspaper or magazine in which they reply to readers who have written to them for advice on their personal problems. 忠告专栏作家 [AM] in BRIT, use **agony aunt** ❑ *...the advice columnist at the local paper.* …当地报纸的忠告专栏作家。

ad·vis·able /ædvaɪzəbəl/ ADJ If you tell someone that **it is advisable to** do something, you are suggesting that they should do it, because it is sensible or is likely to achieve the result they want. 可取的 [v-link ADJ] [FORMAL] ❑ *Because of the popularity of the region, it is advisable to book hotels or camp sites in advance.* 鉴于该地区的受欢迎度，事先预订旅馆或露营地是可取的。

ad·vise ♦◇◇ /ædvaɪz/ (**advises, advising, advised**) **1** V-T If you **advise** someone **to** do something, you tell them what you think they should do. 建议 ❑ *The minister advised him to leave as soon as possible.* 部长建议他尽快离开。 ❑ *I would strongly advise against it.* 我会强烈建议不要这样做。 **2** V-T If an expert **advises** people **on a** particular subject, he or she gives them help and information on that subject. （就某话题向某人）提供咨询 ❑ *...an officer who advises undergraduates from the University on money matters.* …一位在钱的问题上向该大学本科生提供咨询的官员。

Word Partnership *advise* 的常用搭配：

PREP. advise **against** **1**
N. advise ***someone*** **to** **1**
ADV. **strongly** advise **1**

Do not confuse **advise** and **advice**. **Advice** is the noun that is connected with the verb **advise**. If you **advise** someone to do something, you tell them what you think they should do. If you **suggest** something, however, you mention it as an idea or plan for someone to think about, perhaps together with other ideas or plans. You can also **suggest** doing something, or **suggest** that someone does something. ❑ *Your bank manager will probably suggest a loan... I suggested inviting Jim... I suggest that you leave this to me.*

ad·vis·er ♦◇◇ /ædvaɪzər/ (**advisers**) also **advisor** N-COUNT An **adviser** is an expert whose job is to give advice to another person or to a group of people. 顾问 ❑ *In Washington, the president and his advisers spent the day in meetings.* 在华盛顿，总统和他的顾问们开了一天的会。

Word Link *ory ≈ relating to : advisory, contradictory, predatory*

ad·vi·so·ry /ædvaɪzəri/ (**advisories**) **1** N-COUNT An **advisory** is an official announcement or report that warns people about bad weather, diseases, or other dangers or problems. 警告 [AM] ❑ *26 states have issued health advisories.* 26个州已经发布了卫生警告。 **2** ADJ An **advisory** group regularly gives suggestions and help to people or organizations, especially about a particular subject or area of activity. 咨询性的（团体）[FORMAL] ❑ *...members of the advisory committee on the safety of nuclear installations.* …核设施安全咨询委员会的成员们。

ad·vo·ca·cy /ædvəkəsi/ **1** N-SING Someone's **advocacy of a** particular action or plan is their act of recommending it publicly. 倡议 [FORMAL] ❑ *I support your advocacy of free trade.* 我支持你的自由贸

A

易倡议。 2 N-UNCOUNT An **advocacy** group or organization is one that tries to influence the decisions of a government or other authority. 游说 (组织) [AM] ❑ *Consumer advocacy groups are not so enthusiastic about removing restrictions on the telephone companies.* 各顾客游说组织对于取消对电话公司的限制不是那么热衷。

Word Link *voc ≈ speaking : advocate, vocabulary, vocal*

ad·vo·cate ♦◇◇ (**advocates, advocating, advocated**)

The verb is pronounced /ædvəkeɪt/. The noun is pronounced /ædvəkɪt/.

动词读作 /ædvəkeɪt/。名词读作 /ædvəkɪt/。

1 V-T If you **advocate** a particular action or plan, you recommend it publicly. 提倡 [FORMAL] ❑ *Mr. Williams is a conservative who advocates fewer government controls on business.* 威廉斯先生是一位提倡减少政府对商业的控制的保守人士。 2 N-COUNT An **advocate of** a particular action or plan is someone who recommends it publicly. 倡导者 [FORMAL] ❑ *He was a strong advocate of free market policies and a multi-party system.* 他是自由市场政策以及多党制的坚定倡导者。 3 N-COUNT An **advocate** for a particular group is a person who works for the interests of that group. 为 (某团体) 谋利益者 [AM] ❑ *...advocates for the homeless.* …为无家可归者谋利益的人。 4 N-COUNT An **advocate** is a lawyer who speaks in favor of someone or defends them in a court of law. 辩护律师 [LEGAL]

Word Partnership *advocate* 的常用搭配：

ADJ. **leading** advocate, **strong** advocate 2
PREP. advocate **of** *something* 2
advocate **for** *something/someone* 3

Word Link *aer ≈ air : aerial, aerobics, aerosol*

★ **aer·ial** /ɛəriəl/ (**aerials**) 1 ADJ You talk about **aerial** attacks and **aerial** photographs to indicate that people or things on the ground are attacked or photographed by people in airplanes. 从空中的 (袭击等) [ADJ n] ❑ *Weeks of aerial bombardment had destroyed factories and highways.* 数周的空袭已经摧毁了各工厂和公路。 ❑ *Patterns that are invisible on the ground can be the most striking part of an aerial photograph.* 在地面上看不见的图案可能是空中照片中最为醒目的部分。 2 N-COUNT An **aerial** is a device that receives television or radio signals. 天线 [mainly BRIT]

in AM, usually use **antenna**

aero·bics /ɛəroʊbɪks/ N-UNCOUNT **Aerobics** is a form of exercise which increases the amount of oxygen in your blood, and strengthens your heart and lungs. The verb that follows **aerobics** may be either singular or plural. 有氧运动 (可接单数或复数形式的谓语动词) [oft N n] ❑ *I'd like to join an aerobics class to improve my fitness.* 我想进一个有氧运动班来增强我的体质。

aero·dy·nam·ic /ɛəroʊdaɪnæmɪk/ ADJ If something such as a car has an **aerodynamic** shape or design, it goes faster and uses less fuel than other cars because the air passes over it more easily. (汽车等) 流线型的 ❑ *The secret of the machine lies in the aerodynamic shape of the one-piece, carbon-fiber frame.* 该机器的秘密在于其一体式碳纤维外壳的流线型设计。

aero·plane /ɛərəpleɪn/ (**aeroplanes**) N-COUNT An **aeroplane** is a vehicle with wings and one or more engines that enable it to fly through the air. 飞机 [BRIT]

in AM, use **airplane**

aero·sol /ɛərəsɔl/ (**aerosols**) N-COUNT An **aerosol** can or spray is a small container in which a liquid such as paint or deodorant is kept under pressure. When you press a button, the liquid is forced out as a fine spray or foam. (涂料、除臭剂等) 喷雾器; 喷雾罐 [usu N n] ❑ *...an aerosol can of insecticide.* …一个杀虫剂喷雾罐。

★ **aero·space** /ɛəroʊspeɪs/ N-UNCOUNT **Aerospace** companies are involved in developing and making rockets, missiles, space vehicles, and related equipment. 航空航天 [usu N n] ❑ *...the U.S. aerospace industry.* …美国航空航天工业。

★ **aes·thet·ic** /ɛsθɛtɪk/ also **esthetic** ADJ **Aesthetic** is used to talk about beauty or art, and people's appreciation of beautiful things. 审美的 ❑ *...products chosen for their aesthetic appeal as well as their durability and quality.* …因其审美吸引力以及耐用性和质量好而被挑选的产品。 ● N-SING **The aesthetic** of a work of art is its aesthetic quality. (艺术品的) 审美特质 ❑ *He responded very strongly to the aesthetic of this particular work.* 他对这部作品的审美特质反应十分强烈。 ● **aes·theti·cal·ly** /ɛsθɛtɪkli/ ADV 审美上地 ❑ *A statue which is aesthetically pleasing to one person, however, may be repulsive to another.* 从审美角度令一个人满意的一尊雕像可能令另一个人反感。

★ **aes·thet·ics** /ɛsθɛtɪks/ also **esthetics** N-UNCOUNT **Aesthetics** is a branch of philosophy concerned with the study of the idea of beauty. 美学

af·fable /æfəbᵊl/ ADJ Someone who is **affable** is pleasant and friendly. 和蔼的 ❑ *Mr. Brooke is an extremely affable and approachable man.* 布鲁克先生是一个极为和蔼可亲的人。

af·fair ♦♦◇ /əfɛər/ (**affairs**) 1 N-SING If an event or a series of events has been mentioned and you want to talk about it again, you can refer to it as **the affair**. 事件 ❑ *The administration has mishandled the whole affair.* 政府错误地处理了整个事件。 2 N-SING You can refer to an important or interesting event or situation as "**the ... affair**." (…) 事件 [mainly JOURNALISM] ❑ *...the damage caused to the CIA and FBI in the aftermath of the Watergate affair.* …水门事件过后对中情局和美国联邦调查局造成的损害。 3 N-SING You can describe the main quality of an event by saying that it is a particular kind of **affair**. (某种性质的) 事 ❑ *Michael said that his planned 10-day visit would be a purely private affair.* 迈克尔说他计划的10天的访问将是一件纯粹私事。 4 N-COUNT If two people who are not married to each other have an **affair**, they have a sexual relationship. 不正当关系 ❑ *Married male supervisors were carrying on affairs with female subordinates in the office.* 已婚男上司和办公室里的女下级在搞不正当关系。 5 → see also **love affair** 6 N-PLURAL You can use **affairs** to refer to all the important facts or activities that are connected with a particular subject. (有关某话题的) 事务 ❑ *He does not want to interfere in the internal affairs of another country.* 他不想干涉他国的内部事务。 7 → see also **current affairs, state of affairs** 8 N-PLURAL Your **affairs** are all the matters connected with your life that you consider to be private and normally deal with yourself. (个人的) 事情 ❑ *The unexpectedness of my father's death meant that his affairs were not entirely in order.* 我父亲的意外过世意味着他的个人事情不是完全有序。

af·fect ♦♦◇ /əfɛkt/ (**affects, affecting, affected**) 1 V-T If something **affects** a person or thing, it influences them or causes them to change in some way. (某事物) 影响 (某人或物) ❑ *Nicotine adversely affects the functioning of the heart and arteries.* 尼古丁负面地影响心脏和动脉的功能。 ❑ *More than seven million people have been affected by drought.* 七百多万多人受到了干旱的影响。 2 V-T If a disease **affects** someone, it causes them to become ill. (疾病) 困扰 (某人) ❑ *Arthritis is a crippling disease which affects people all over the world.* 关节炎是一种严重影响健康的、困扰世界各地人们的疾病。 3 V-T If something or someone **affects** you, they make you feel a strong emotion, especially sadness or pity. (某事物或人) 影响 (某人) ❑ *If Jim had been more independent, the divorce would not have affected him as deeply.* 如果吉姆曾更为独立的话，离婚就不会这样深深地影响他了。

Note that the noun that comes from **affect** is **effect**. You can say that something **affects** you, or that it has an **effect** on you. ❑ *...the effect that noise has on people in factories.* You can also talk about the **effect** of something. ❑ *...the effect of the anesthetic.* **Effect** can also be a verb. If you **effect** something such as a change or a repair, you make it happen or do it. This is a fairly formal word. ❑ *She had effected a few hasty repairs.*

af·fec·tion /əfɛkʃᵊn/ (**affections**) 1 N-UNCOUNT If you regard someone or something with **affection**, you like them and are fond of them. 喜爱 ❑ *She thought of him with affection.* 她怀着喜爱想起了他。 2 N-PLURAL Your **affections** are your feelings of love or fondness for someone. 感情 ❑ *Caroline is the object of his affections.* 卡罗琳是他感情的归属。 → see **love**

Word Link *ate ≈ filled with : affectionate, compassionate, considerate*

af·fec·tion·ate /əfɛkʃənɪt/ ADJ If you are **affectionate**, you show your love or fondness for another person in the way that you behave toward them. 显露感情的 ❑ *They seemed devoted to each other and were openly affectionate.* 他们似乎很相爱，公然含情脉脉。 ● **af·fec·tion·ate·ly** ADV 显露感情地 [ADV with v] ❑ *He looked affectionately at his niece.* 他慈爱地看着他的侄女。

af·fi·da·vit /æfɪdeɪvɪt/ (**affidavits**) N-COUNT An **affidavit** is a written statement that you swear is true and that may be used as evidence in a court of law.（经陈述者本人宣誓、可用作法庭证据的）书面陈述 [LEGAL] ❑ *In his sworn affidavit, Roche outlined a history of actions against him by the church.* 在其宣誓了的书面陈述中，罗奇罗列了教会反对他的行动经过。

★ **af·fili·ate** (**affiliates, affiliating, affiliated**)

The noun is pronounced /əfɪliɪt/. The verb is pronounced /əfɪlieɪt/.

名词读作 /əfɪliɪt/，动词读作 /əfɪlieɪt/。

1 N-COUNT An **affiliate** is an organization which is officially connected with another, larger organization or is a member of it. 分支机构；成员组织 [FORMAL] ❑ *The World Chess Federation has affiliates in around 120 countries.* 世界象棋联盟在大约一百二十个国家内设有分支机构。 2 V-I If an organization **affiliates with** another larger organization, it forms a close connection with the larger organization or becomes a member of it. 成为隶属机构；成为会员组织 [FORMAL] ❑ *He wanted to affiliate with a U.S. firm because he needed expert advice in legal affairs.* 他想成为一家美国公司的会员，因为他需要法律事务方面的专家意见。

▲ **af·filia·tion** /əfɪlieɪʃən/ (**affiliations**) N-VAR If one group has an **affiliation** with another group, it has a close or official connection with it. 紧密联系；官方联系 [FORMAL] ❑ *The kidnappers had no affiliation with any militant group.* 这些绑架者与任何军事组织都没有紧密联系。

▲ **af·fin·ity** /əfɪnɪti/ N-SING If you have an **affinity** with someone or something, you feel that you are similar to them or that you know and understand them very well. 亲切感 ❑ *He has a close affinity with the landscape and people he knew when he was growing up.* 他对他成长过程中所熟悉的景色和人们有一种很强的亲切感。

Word Link *firm ≈ making strong : affirm, confirm, infirm*

★ **af·firm** /əfɜrm/ (**affirms, affirming, affirmed**) 1 V-T If you **affirm** that something is true or that something exists, you state firmly and publicly that it is true or exists. 公开肯定 [FORMAL] ❑ *The court affirmed that the information can be made public under the Freedom of Information Act.* 法院公开肯定了此信息能依据《自由信息法案》公之于众。 ❑ *...a speech in which he affirmed a commitment to lower taxes.* …在其中他公开肯定了减税承诺的一次演讲。 ● **af·fir·ma·tion** /æfərmeɪʃən/ N-VAR (**affirmations**) 公开肯定 ❑ *The North Atlantic Treaty begins with the affirmation that its parties "reaffirm their faith in the purposes and principles of the Charter of the United Nations."* 《北大西洋公约》以公开肯定其成员"重申其对《联合国宪章》的目的以及原则的信念"开头。 2 V-T If an event **affirms** something, it shows that it is true or exists. 证实 [FORMAL] ❑ *Everything I had accomplished seemed to affirm that opinion.* 我所做成的每件事似乎都证实了那个观点。 ● **af·fir·ma·tion** N-UNCOUNT 证实 [also "a" N] ❑ *The ruling was a welcome affirmation of the constitutional right to free speech.* 此裁决是对言论自由这一宪法权利的受人欢迎的肯定。

af·firma·tive /əfɜrmətɪv/ 1 ADJ An **affirmative** word or gesture indicates that you agree with what someone has said or that the answer to a question is "yes." 肯定的（言辞、手势）[FORMAL] ❑ *Haig was desperately eager for an affirmative answer.* 黑格极渴望得到一个肯定的回答。 2 ADJ In grammar, an **affirmative** clause is positive and does not contain a negative word. （语法中）肯定的（分句） 3 PHRASE If you reply to a question **in the affirmative**, you say "yes" or make a gesture that means "yes." （回答问题）肯定地 [FORMAL] ❑ *He asked me if I was ready. I answered in the affirmative.* 他问我是否准备好了。我肯定地回答了。

af·firma·tive ac·tion N-UNCOUNT **Affirmative action** is the policy of giving jobs and other opportunities to members of groups such as racial minorities or women who might not otherwise have them. 平权举措 [AM]

in BRIT, use **positive discrimination**

❑ *Despite nearly a decade of affirmative action since apartheid was dismantled, few black sportsmen have reached the top level.* 尽管种族隔离被取消后采取了近十年的平权举措，几乎没有黑人运动员达到过顶极。

Word Link *fix ≈ fastening : affix, prefix, suffix*

★ **af·fix** /æfɪks/ (**affixes**) N-COUNT An **affix** is a letter or group of letters, for example, "un-" or "-y," which is added to either the beginning or the end of a word to form a different word with a different meaning. For example, "un-" is added to "kind" to form "unkind." Compare **prefix** and **suffix**. 词缀

★ **af·flict** /əflɪkt/ (**afflicts, afflicting, afflicted**) V-T If you **are afflicted by** pain, illness, or disaster, it affects you badly and makes you suffer. 困扰 [FORMAL] ❑ *Italy has been afflicted by political corruption for decades.* 意大利受政治腐败困扰已数十年了。 ❑ *There are two main problems which afflict people with hearing impairments.* 有两大问题困扰有听觉障碍的人。

Word Link *flict ≈ striking : affliction, conflict, inflict*

af·flic·tion /əflɪkʃən/ (**afflictions**) N-VAR An **affliction** is something that causes physical or mental suffering. 折磨人的事物 [FORMAL] ❑ *Hay fever is an affliction that arrives at an early age.* 花粉热是一种早年易患的病。

af·flu·ence /æfluəns/ N-UNCOUNT **Affluence** is the state of having a lot of money or a high standard of living. 富裕 [FORMAL] ❑ *The postwar era was one of new affluence for the working class.* 战后时期是工人阶级新富期。

▲ **af·flu·ent** /æfluənt/ ADJ If you are **affluent**, you have a lot of money. 富裕的 ❑ *Cigarette smoking used to be more common among affluent people.* 吸烟过去在富人中更为普遍。 ● N-PLURAL **The affluent** are people who are affluent. 富人 ❑ *The diet of the affluent has not changed much over the decades.* 富人的饮食数十年来没怎么变。

af·ford ♦◇◇ /əfɔrd/ (**affords, affording, afforded**) 1 V-T If you **cannot afford** something, you do not have enough money to pay for it. 支付得起 ❑ *My parents can't even afford a new refrigerator.* 我父母甚至买不起一台新冰箱。 ❑ *The arts should be available to more people at prices they can afford.* 艺术品应该以人们支付得起的价格提供给更多人。 2 V-T If you say that you cannot **afford to** do something or allow it to happen, you mean that you must not do it or must prevent it from happening because it would be harmful or embarrassing to you. 承担得起 ❑ *We can't afford to wait.* 我们等不起。

Word Partnership *afford* 的常用搭配：

V.	afford **to buy/pay** 1
	can/could afford, **can't/couldn't** afford 1 2
	afford **to lose** 2
ADJ.	**able/unable to** afford 1 2

★ **af·ford·able** /əfɔrdəbəl/ ADJ If something is **affordable**, most people have enough money to buy it. 多数人支付得起的 ❑ *...the availability of affordable housing.* …多数人支付得起的房产的供应。

af·front /əfrʌnt/ (**affronts, affronting, affronted**) 1 V-T If something **affronts** you, you feel insulted and hurt because of it. 侮辱 [FORMAL] ❑ *One recent example, which particularly affronted Kasparov, was at the European team championship in Hungary.* 近期的一个尤其使卡斯帕罗夫受辱的例子是在匈牙利的欧洲团体锦标赛上。 2 N-COUNT If something is an **affront to** you, it is an obvious insult to you. 侮辱 ❑ *It's an affront to human dignity to keep someone alive like this.* 让一个人如此活着是对人类尊严的一种侮辱。

afield /əfild/ PHRASE **Further afield** or **farther afield** means in places or areas other than the nearest or most obvious one. 在更远处 ❑ *They enjoy participating in a wide variety of activities, both locally and further afield.* 他们喜欢参加种类繁多的活动，无论是在当地还是在更远的地方。

▲ **afloat** /əfloʊt/ 1 ADV If someone or something is **afloat**, they remain partly above the surface of water and do not sink. 漂浮着地 ❑ *They talked modestly of their valiant efforts to keep the tanker afloat.* 他们谦虚地谈论了他们为让油轮保持不沉而付出的英勇努力。 2 ADV If a person, business, or country stays **afloat** or is kept **afloat**, they have just enough money to pay their debts and continue operating. （人、企业、国家等）仅够还债维持下去地 [BUSINESS] ❑ *A number of efforts were being made to keep the company afloat.* 在做多种努力以保持公司继续维持下去。

afoot /əfʊt/ ADJ If you say that a plan or scheme is **afoot**, it is already happening or being planned, but you do not know much about it. 在进行中的；在酝酿中的 [v-link ADJ] ❑ *Everybody knew that something awful was afoot.* 每个人都知道糟糕的事在酝酿之中。

afore·men·tioned /əfɔrmɛnʃənd/ ADJ If you refer to **the aforementioned** person or subject, you mean the person or subject that has already been mentioned. 此前提及的 [det ADJ, usu "the" ADJ n] [FORMAL] ❑ *This is the draft of a declaration that will be issued at the end of the aforementioned U.N. conference.* 这是将在上述联合国会议结束时发布的宣言的草稿。

afore·said /əfɔrsɛd/ ADJ **Aforesaid** means the same as **aforementioned**. 此前提及的（同**aforementioned**）[det ADJ, usu

A

"the" ADJ n] [FORMAL] ❑ *...the aforesaid organizations and institutions.* ···上述组织和机构。

afraid ♦◇◇ /əfreɪd/ **1** ADJ If you are **afraid of** someone or **afraid to** do something, you are frightened because you think that something very unpleasant is going to happen to you. 害怕的 [v-link ADJ] ❑ *She did not seem at all afraid.* 她一点儿也没显得害怕。 ❑ *I was afraid of the other boys.* 我害怕其他的男孩子们。 **2** ADJ If you are **afraid for** someone else, you are worried that something horrible is going to happen to them. (为某人) 担心的 [v-link ADJ] ❑ *She's afraid for her family in Somalia.* 她为她在索马里的家人担心。 **3** ADJ If you are **afraid** that something unpleasant will happen, you are worried that it may happen and you want to avoid it. (对令人不快的事情会发生) 担心的 [v-link ADJ] ❑ *I was afraid that nobody would believe me.* 我担心没有人会相信我的话。 **4** PHRASE If you want to apologize to someone or to disagree with them in a polite way, you can say **I'm afraid.** 恐怕 [SPOKEN, POLITENESS] ❑ *We don't have anything like that, I'm afraid.* 我们恐怕没有任何像那样的东西。

Thesaurus *afraid* 另参见:

ADJ. alarmed, fearful, frightened, petrified, scared, terrified **1**
worried **3**

Word Partnership *afraid* 的常用搭配:

PREP. afraid of ***someone/something*** **1**
V. be afraid **1** – **3**

▲ **afresh** /əfrɛʃ/ ADV If you do something **afresh**, you do it again in a different way. 重新地 [ADV after v] ❑ *They believe that the only hope for the French left is to start afresh.* 他们认为留下来的法国人的惟一希望是重新开始。

African-American (African-Americans) N-COUNT **African-Americans** are black people living in the United States who are descended from families that originally came from Africa. 非裔美国人 ❑ *Today African-Americans are 12 percent of the population.* 如今非裔美国人占美国人口的12%。 ● ADJ **African-American** is also an adjective. 非裔美国人的 ❑ *...a group of African-American community leaders.* ···一群非裔美国人的社区领导人。

> The term **African-American** is used in the USA to describe people whose ancestors came from Africa. Some people prefer to use the term **black**.

aft /æft/ ADV If you go **aft** in a boat or plane, you go to the back of it. If you are **aft**, you are in the back. 向 (船、飞机) 尾部; 在 (船、飞机) 尾部 ❑ *I went aft to take my turn at the helm.* 我到船尾去接班掌舵。

af·ter ♦♦♦ /æftər/

> In addition to the uses shown below, **after** is used in phrasal verbs such as "ask after," "look after," and "take after."

1 PREP If something happens **after** a particular date or event, it happens during the period of time that follows that date or event. 在 (某日、某事件) 以后 ❑ *After May 19, strikes were occurring on a daily basis.* 在5月19日以后，罢工每天都在发生。 ❑ *After breakfast Amy took a taxi to the station.* 早饭以后，埃米乘出租车去了车站。 ● CONJ **After** is also a conjunction. (某事) 以后 ❑ *After Don told me this, he spoke of his mother.* 唐告诉我这件事以后，他谈到了他的母亲。 **2** PREP If you do one thing **after** doing another, you do it during the period of time that follows the other thing. 在 (做某事) 以后 [PREP -ing] ❑ *After completing and signing it, please return the form to us in the envelope provided.* 填完并且签名以后，请将表格装入所提供的信封中返还给我们。 **3** PREP You use **after** when you are talking about time. For example, if something is going to happen during **the day after** or **the weekend after** a particular time, it is going to happen during the following day or during the following weekend. 在 (某日、某周) 以后 [n PREP n] ❑ *She's leaving the day after tomorrow.* 她定于后天离开。 ● ADV **After** is also an adverb. (某日、某周) 以后地 [ADV after v] ❑ *Tomorrow. Or the day after.* 明天。或者后天。 **4** PREP If you go **after** someone, you follow or chase them. (追随) 在 (某人) 之后 ❑ *Alice said to Gina, "Why don't you go after him, he's your son."* 艾丽斯对吉娜说："你为什么不追他，他是你儿子。" **5** PREP If you are **after** something, you are trying to get it. 以···为目标 ❑ *They were after the money.* 他们想得到这笔钱。 **6** PREP If you call, shout, or stare **after** someone, you call, shout, or stare at them as they move away from you. 在 (某人) 身后 (喊、叫、瞪眼等) ❑ *"Come back!" he called after me.* "回来！"他在我身后冲我喊。 **7** PREP If you tell someone that one place is a particular distance **after** another, you mean that it is situated beyond the other place and further away from you. 在 (某地) 以外 (某距离处) ❑ *...a station 134 miles after the train starts its journey.* ···在火车出发后的134英里以外的一个车站。 **8** PREP If one thing is written **after** another thing on a page, it is written following it or underneath it. (写) 在 (某物) 之后 ❑ *I wrote my name after Penny's at the bottom of the page.* 我把我的名字写在了这页最下面彭尼的名字之后。 **9** PREP You use **after** in order to give the most important aspect of something when comparing it with another aspect. (重要性) 在···之后 ❑ *After Germany, America is Britain's second-biggest customer.* 仅次于德国，美国是英国的第二大客户。 **10** PREP To be named **after** someone means to be given the same name as them. 以 (同样的名字命名) ❑ *He persuaded Virginia to name the baby after him.* 他劝弗吉尼亚给孩子命以他的名字。 **11** PREP **After** is used when telling the time. If it is, for example, **ten after six**, the time is ten minutes past six. (···点) 过 (···分) [AM] **12** CONVENTION If you say **"after you"** to someone, you are being polite and allowing them to go in front of you or through a doorway before you do. 您先走 [POLITENESS] **13** **after all** → see **all**

> You use **after, afterward,** and **later** to talk about things that happen following the time when you are speaking, or following a particular event. Expressions such as "not long" and "shortly" can also be used with **after.** ❑ *After dinner she spoke to him... I returned to England after visiting India... Shortly after, she called me.* **Afterward** can be used when you do not need to mention the particular time or event. ❑ *Afterward we went to a night club.* You can also use words such as "soon" and "shortly" with **afterward.** ❑ *Soon afterward, he came to the clinic.* You can use **later** to refer to a time or situation that follows the time when you are speaking. ❑ *I'll go and see her later.* "A little," "much," and "not much" can also be used with **later.** ❑ *A little later, the lights went out... I learned all this much later.* You can use **after, afterward,** or **later** following a phrase that mentions a period of time, in order to say when something happens. ❑ *...five years after his death... She wrote about it six years afterward... Ten minutes later he left the house.*

14 PHRASE If you do something to several things **one after the other** or **one after another**, you do it to one, then the next, and so on, with no break between your actions. 一个接一个地 ❑ *...a lawyer who wins three cases, one after another.* ···一位连赢 3 个案子的律师。 **15** PHRASE If something happens **day after day** or **year after year**, it happens every day or every year, for a long time. 日复一日地/年复一年地 ❑ *...people who'd been coming here year after year.* ···年复一年地来这里的人们。

after- /æftər-/ COMB IN ADJ **After-** is added to nouns to form adjectives which indicate that something takes place or exists after an event or process. ···后的 (加于名词前构成形容词) [ADJ n] ❑ *...an after-dinner speech.* ···一场餐后讲话。

after·care /æftərkɛər/

in BRIT, also use **after-care**

N-UNCOUNT **Aftercare** is the nursing and care of people who have been treated in a hospital, and who are now recovering. (住院治疗之后康复期的) 护理 ❑ *Individualized aftercare is given to each patient.* 每个病人都得到针对自己的康复护理。 ❑ *...a 14-week aftercare program.* ···一个为期14周的康复护理服务。

after·effect /æftəɪfɛkt/ (aftereffects)

in BRIT, use **after-effect**

N-COUNT The **aftereffects** of an event, experience, or substance are the conditions which result from it. 事后影响 [usu pl] ❑ *...people still suffering from the aftereffects of the world's worst nuclear accident.* ···人们还在遭受那次世界上最严重的核事件的影响。

after·market /æftərmɑrkɪt/ **1** N-SING The **aftermarket** is all the related products that are sold after an item, especially a car, has been bought. 售后市场 [BUSINESS] ❑ *The company serves the national automotive aftermarket with a broad range of accessory and recreational-vehicle products.* 该公司为全国机动车售后市场提供各种配件和休闲车产品。 **2** N-SING The **aftermarket** in stocks and bonds is the buying and selling of them after they have been issued. (股市中的) 后市 [BUSINESS] ❑ *It's illegal to get into a formal agreement with investors that they'll buy in the aftermarket.* 与投资人达成正式协议允许其在后市买入是非法的。

▲ **after·math** /æftərmæθ/ N-SING **The aftermath of** an important event, especially a harmful one, is the situation that results from it. (灾难性大事件的) 后果 ❑ *In the aftermath of the coup, the troops opened fire on the demonstrators.* 在那次政变的余波之中，军队向示威者开了枪。

after·noon ♦♦◊ /æftərnu̲n/ (**afternoons**) N-VAR The **afternoon** is the part of each day that begins at lunchtime and ends at about six o'clock. 下午 ❑ *He's arriving in the afternoon.* 他将于下午到达。 ❑ *He had stayed in his room all afternoon.* 他整个下午都呆在他的房间里。

after-school ADJ **After-school** activities are those that are organized for children in the afternoon or evening after they have finished school. 课外的 [ADJ n] ❑ *...an after-school program for advanced students.* …一项针对高年级学生的课外项目。

after·shave /æftərʃeɪv/ (**aftershaves**) also **after-shave** N-MASS **Aftershave** is a liquid with a pleasant smell that men sometimes put on their faces after shaving. (男人剃须后用的) 须后水 ❑ *...a bottle of aftershave.* …一瓶须后水。

after·ward ♦◊◊ /æftərwərd/ also **afterwards** ADV If you do something or if something happens **afterward**, you do it or it happens after a particular event or time that has already been mentioned. (某事件、某时间) 之后 [ADV with cl] ❑ *Shortly afterward, police arrested four suspects.* 之后不久，警方逮捕了 4 名嫌疑犯。

again ♦♦♦ /əge̲n, əge̲ɪn/ **1** ADV You use **again** to indicate that something happens a second time, or after it has already happened before. 再一次 (发生)；又 ❑ *He kissed her again.* 他再一次亲了她。 ❑ *Again there was a short silence.* 又有一阵短暂的沉默。 **2** ADV You use **again** to indicate that something is now in a particular state or place that it used to be in. 又 (回到过去的状态或地方) [ADV after v] ❑ *He opened his attaché case, removed a folder, then closed it again.* 他打开了他的公文包，拿出了一个文件夹，然后又把它合上了。 **3** ADV You can use **again** when you want to point out that there is a similarity between the subject that you are talking about now and a previous subject. 又 (和以前类似) [ADV cl] ❑ *Again the pregnancy was very similar to my previous two.* 这次怀孕又和我前两次怀孕非常类似。 **4** ADV You can use **again** in expressions such as **but again, then again,** and **there again** when you want to introduce a remark that contrasts with or weakens something that you have just said. (但是、然后) 又 (用以对比前后所说的话) [ADV with cl] ❑ *You may be happy to buy imitation leather, and then again, you may wonder what you're getting for your money.* 你可能乐于买仿制皮革，然后你也许又想知道你花的钱买到的是什么。 **5** ADV You can add **again** to the end of your question when you are asking someone to tell you something that you have forgotten or that they have already told you. 再 (问一次) [cl ADV] [SPOKEN] ❑ *Sorry, what's your name again?.* 对不起，你叫什么名字来着？ **6** ADV You use **again** in expressions such as **half as much again** when you are indicating how much greater one amount is than another amount that you have just mentioned or are about to mention. 又一个 (同样的量) [amount ADV] [BRIT] ❑ *A similar wine from France would cost you half as much again.* 类似的法国葡萄酒会花你多一半的钱。 **7** PHRASE You can use **again and again** or **time and again** to emphasize that something happens many times. 一再 [EMPHASIS] ❑ *He would go over his work again and again until he felt he had it right.* 他会反复检查他的工作直到他觉得准确无误为止。 **8** **now and again** → see **now** **9** **once again** → see **once**

against ♦♦♦ /əge̲nst, əge̲ɪnst/

In addition to the uses shown below, **against** is used in phrasal verbs such as "come up against," "guard against," and "hold against."

1 PREP If one thing is leaning or pressing **against** another, it is touching it. 靠着 (某物) ❑ *She leaned against him.* 她靠在他身上。 ❑ *On a table pushed against a wall there were bottles of beer and wine.* 在靠着墙的一张桌子上有数瓶啤酒和葡萄酒。 **2** PREP If you are **against** something such as a plan, policy, or system, you think it is wrong, bad, or stupid. 反对 (某计划、政策、体制等) ❑ *Taxes are unpopular – it is understandable that voters are against them.* 税收是不受欢迎的——选民们反对是可以理解的。 ❑ *Joan was very much against commencing drug treatment.* 琼非常反对开始药物治疗。 ● ADV **Against** is also an adverb. 反对地 [ADV after v] ❑ *The vote for the suspension of the party was 283 in favor with 29 against.* 就暂时取缔该党而进行的投票结果是283票支持，29票反对。 **3** PREP If you compete **against** someone in a game, you try to beat them. (在比赛中) 与 (某人) 对阵 ❑ *This is the first of two games against Denver in the next five days.* 这是接下来的 5 天里两场与丹佛对阵的比赛中的第一场。 **4** PREP If you take action **against** someone or something, you try to harm them. 对付 (某人、某事物) ❑ *Security forces are still using violence against opponents of the government.* 保安部队还在使用武力对付反政府者。 **5** PREP If you take action **against** a possible future event, you try to prevent it. 防止 (可能发生的事件) ❑ *Experts have been discussing how to improve the fight against crime.* 专家们一直在讨论如何加强打击犯罪的斗争。 **6** PREP If you do something **against** someone's wishes, advice, or orders, you do not do what they want you to do or tell you to do. 违背 (某人意愿、建议、命令等) ❑ *He discharged himself from the hospital against the advice of doctors.* 他违背医生们的建议自行出院了。 **7** PREP If you do something in order to protect yourself **against** something unpleasant or harmful, you do something that will make its effects on you less serious if it happens. 防备 (令人不快或有害的事物) ❑ *Any business needs insurance against ordinary risks such as fire, flood, and breakage.* 任何企业都需要保险来防备诸如火灾、洪灾和破损等常见风险。 **8** PREP If something is **against** the law or **against** the rules, there is a law or a rule which says that you must not do it. 违反 (法律、规定等) ❑ *It is against the law to detain you against your will for any length of time.* 违反你的意愿拘留你无论多久都是违法的。 **9** PREP If you are moving **against** a current, tide, or wind, you are moving in the opposite direction to it. 逆着 (水流、潮流、风等) ❑ *...swimming upstream against the current.* …逆流向上游。 **10** PREP If something happens or is considered **against** a particular background of events, it is considered in relation to those events, because those events are relevant to it. 在 (某事件背景) 下 ❑ *The profits rise was achieved against a backdrop of falling metal prices.* 利润的增长是在金属价格下降的背景下取得的。 **11** PREP If something is measured or valued **against** something else, it is measured or valued by comparing it with the other thing. 比照 (某事物) ❑ *Our policies have to be judged against a clear test: will it improve the standard of education?* 我们的政策得比照一个明确的检验，即会提高教育水准吗？ **12** PREP The odds **against** something happening are the chances or odds that it will not happen. 逆着 (机会、可能性的发生) [n PREP] ❑ *The odds against him surviving are incredible.* 他生还的可能性太小。 ● ADV **Against** is also an adverb. (对机会、可能性的发生) 逆着地 [n ADV] ❑ *What were the odds against?* 赔率是多少？ **13** PHRASE If you **have** something **against** someone or something, you dislike them. 以某种原因不喜欢某人、某物 ❑ *Have you got something against women, Les?* 你对女性有什么不满吗，莱斯？ **14** **up against** → see **up** **15** **against the clock** → see **clock**

age ♦♦♦ /e̲ɪdʒ/ (**ages, aging** or **ageing, aged**) **1** N-VAR Your **age** is the number of years that you have lived. (人的) 年龄 ❑ *She has a nephew who is just ten years of age.* 她有个才满10岁的侄子。 ❑ *At the age of sixteen he qualified for a place at the University of North Carolina.* 16岁时他取得了北卡罗来纳大学的入学资格。 **2** N-VAR The **age** of a thing is the number of years since it was made. (物的) 年代 ❑ *Everything in the room looks in keeping with the age of the building.* 该房间里的一切看起来都和该楼的年代相符。 **3** N-UNCOUNT **Age** is the state of being old or the process of becoming older. 年长；成长 ❑ *Perhaps he has grown wiser with age.* 或许他已经随着年龄的增长变得更睿智了。 ❑ *This cologne, like wine, improves with age.* 这种科隆香水像葡萄酒一样越陈越香。 **4** V-T/V-I When someone **ages,** or when something **ages** them, they seem much older and less strong or less alert. 使显老；显老 ❑ *He had always looked so young, but he seemed to have aged in the last few months.* 他曾一直显得很年轻，但是在过去的几个月里他似乎显得老了。 **5** N-COUNT An **age** is a period in history. 时代 ❑ *...the age of steam and steel.* …蒸汽与钢铁时代。 **6** N-COUNT You can say **an age** or **ages** to mean a very long time. 很长时间 [INFORMAL] ❑ *He waited what seemed an age.* 他等了似乎很长时间。 **7** → see also **aged, aging, middle age**
→ see Picture Dictionary: **age**

aged

Pronounced /e̲ɪdʒd/ for meaning **1**, and /e̲ɪdʒɪd/ for meanings **2** and **3**.

义项**1**读作 /e̲ɪdʒd/，义项**2**和**3**读作 /e̲ɪdʒɪd/。

1 ADJ You use **aged** followed by a number to say how old someone is. 岁数为…的 ❑ *Alan has two children, aged eleven and nine.* 艾伦有两个孩子，岁数为11岁和9岁。 **2** ADJ **Aged** means very old. 年迈的 [ADJ n] ❑ *She has an aged parent who's capable of being very difficult.* 她有个年迈的、很难伺候的父亲。 **3** N-PLURAL You can refer to all people who are very old as **the aged.** 老年人 ❑ *The American*

A

Picture Dictionary age

Society on Aging provides resource services to those dealing with the aged. 美国老年协会为那些处理老年人问题的人提供资源服务。 4 → see also **middle-aged**

age·ing [BRIT] → see **age, aging**

agen·cy ♦♦◇ /eɪdʒənsi/ (**agencies**) 1 N-COUNT An **agency** is a business that provides a service on behalf of other businesses. 代理公司 [BUSINESS] ❑ *We had to hire maids through an agency.* 我们得通过代理公司雇用女佣。 2 → see also **ad agency, employment agency** 3 N-COUNT An **agency** is a government organization responsible for a certain area of administration. 地区政府 ❑ *She is calling for a collaboration of local, state and federal agencies to deal with the problem.* 她在呼吁地方、州和联邦等各级政府通力合作来处理这个问题。 → see **advertising**

agen·da ♦◇◇ /ədʒɛndə/ (**agendas**) 1 N-COUNT You can refer to the political issues that are important at a particular time as an **agenda**. (政治) 议题 ❑ *Does television set the agenda on foreign policy?* 电视安排了有关外交政策的议题了吗？ 2 → see also **hidden agenda** 3 N-COUNT An **agenda** is a list of the items that have to be discussed at a meeting. 议事日程 ❑ *This is sure to be an item on the agenda next week.* 这必将成为下周议事日程上的一项议题。

Word Partnership *agenda* 的常用搭配：

ADJ.	**domestic/legislative/political** agenda, **hidden** agenda 1
V.	**set the** agenda 1 3
PREP.	**on the** agenda 3

agent ♦♦◇ /eɪdʒənt/ (**agents**) 1 N-COUNT An **agent** is a person who looks after someone else's business affairs or does business on their behalf. 代理商 [BUSINESS] ❑ *You are buying direct, rather than through an agent.* 你在直接购买，而不是通过代理商购买。 2 → see also **travel agent** 3 N-COUNT An **agent** in the arts world is a person who gets work for an actor or musician, or who sells the work of a writer to publishers. (艺术界的) 经纪人 ❑ *My literary agent thinks it is not unreasonable to expect $500,000 in total.* 我的文学经纪人认为预期总共50万美元并非不合情理。 4 N-COUNT An **agent** is a person who works for a country's secret service. 间谍 ❑ *All these years he's been an agent for the East.* 这些年来他一直为东方国家做间谍。 5 N-COUNT A chemical that has a particular effect or is used for a particular purpose can be referred to as a particular kind of **agent**. 剂 ❑ *...the bleaching agent in white flour.* …白面粉中的漂白剂。 → see **concert**

age of con·sent N-SING **The age of consent** is the age at which a person can legally agree to having a sexual relationship. 同意年龄 (指女性可以合法性交的年龄) ["the" N] ❑ *He was under the age of consent.* 他那时还不到同意年龄。

age-old ADJ An **age-old** story, tradition, or problem has existed for many generations or centuries. (故事、传统、问题等) 存在了数世纪的 [WRITTEN] ❑ *This age-old struggle for control had led to untold bloody wars.* 这种由来已久的对控制权的争夺已经导致了无数的血腥战争。

★ **ag·gra·vate** /ægrəveɪt/ (**aggravates, aggravating, aggravated**) 1 V-T If someone or something **aggravates** a situation, they make it worse. 使恶化 ❑ *Stress and lack of sleep can aggravate the situation.* 紧张和缺少睡眠会使情况恶化。 2 V-T If someone or something **aggravates** you, they make you annoyed. 使恼火 [INFORMAL] ❑ *What aggravates you most about this country?* 这个国家最让你恼火的是什么？ ● **ag·gra·vat·ing** ADJ 恼人的 ❑ *You don't realize how aggravating you can be.* 你没意识到你有多烦人。 ● **ag·gra·va·tion** /ægrəveɪʃᵊn/ N-VAR (**aggravations**) 恼人的事 ❑ *I just couldn't take the aggravation.* 我就受不了这种烦恼人的事。

★ **ag·gre·gate** /ægrɪgɪt/ ADJ An **aggregate** amount or score is made up of several smaller amounts or scores added together. 合计的 [ADJ n] ❑ *The rate of growth of GNP will depend upon the rate of growth of aggregate demand.* 国民生产总值的增长率将依赖于总需求的增长率。

ag·gres·sion /əgrɛʃᵊn/ (**aggressions**) 1 N-UNCOUNT **Aggression** is a quality of anger and determination that makes you ready to attack other people. 攻击性 ❑ *Aggression is by no means a male-only trait.* 攻击性决不是男性独有的特征。 2 N-VAR **Aggression** is violent and attacking behavior. 攻击 ❑ *...the threat of massive military aggression.* …大规模军事攻击的威胁。 → see **anger**

Word Partnership *aggression* 的常用搭配：

N.	**act of** aggression 1
PREP.	aggression **against** 2
ADJ.	**military** aggression, **physical** aggression 2

ag·gres·sive ♦◇◇ /əgrɛsɪv/ 1 ADJ An **aggressive** person or animal has a quality of anger and determination that makes them ready to attack other people. 好斗的 ❑ *Some children are much more aggressive than others.* 一些孩子比其他孩子好斗得多。 ❑ *These fish are very aggressive.* 这些鱼十分好斗。 ● **ag·gres·sive·ly** ADV 好斗地 ❑ *They'll react aggressively.* 他们会凶猛地作出反应。 2 ADJ People who are **aggressive** in their work or other activities behave in a forceful way because they are very eager to succeed. 好强的 ❑ *He is respected as a very aggressive and competitive executive.* 他被尊认为一位十分好强好胜的主管。 ● **ag·gres·sive·ly** ADV 好强地 ❑ *...countries noted for aggressively pursuing energy efficiency.* …以拼命追求能效著称的国家。

ag·gres·sor /əgre̱sər/ (**aggressors**) N-COUNT The **aggressor** in a fight or battle is the person, group, or country that starts it. 挑衅者 ❑ *They have been the aggressors in this conflict.* 他们一直是这场冲突中的挑衅者。

Word Link *griev ≈ heavy, serious : aggrieved, grievance, grieve*

ag·grieved /əgri̱vd/ ADJ If you feel **aggrieved**, you feel upset and angry because of the way in which you have been treated. 愤愤不平的 ❑ *I really feel aggrieved at this sort of thing.* 我对这种事真地感到愤愤不平。

aghast /əgɑ̱st, əgæ̱st/ ADJ If you are **aghast**, you are filled with horror and surprise. 惊骇的 [ADJ after v] [FORMAL] ❑ *While she watched, aghast, his eyes glazed over as his life flowed away.* 她惊骇地看着，他的眼睛随着他的生命逐渐消失而变得呆滞无神。

ag·ile /æ̱dʒəl/ 1 ADJ Someone who is **agile** can move quickly and easily. 敏捷的 ❑ *At 20 years old he was not as strong, as fast, as agile as he is now.* 在他20岁时，他没有现在这样强壮、迅速、敏捷。 ● **agil·ity** /ədʒɪ̱lɪti/ N-UNCOUNT 敏捷 ❑ *She blinked in surprise at his agility.* 她对他的敏捷惊愕地眨了眨眼睛。 2 ADJ If you have an **agile** mind, you think quickly and intelligently. 机敏的 ❑ *She was quick-witted and had an extraordinarily agile mind.* 她很机智并且有一个特别敏锐的头脑。 ● **agil·ity** N-UNCOUNT 机敏 ❑ *His intellect and mental agility have never been in doubt.* 他的才智和头脑的敏锐从未被受到怀疑。

ag·ing /e̱ɪdʒɪŋ/ also **ageing** 1 ADJ Someone or something that is **aging** is becoming older and less healthy or efficient. (人) 变衰老的; (物) 老化的 ❑ *John lives with his aging mother.* 约翰和他日渐衰老的母亲住在一起。 2 N-UNCOUNT **Aging** is the process of becoming old or becoming worn out. 变老; 变旧 ❑ *The only signs of aging are the flecks of gray that speckle his dark hair.* 他变老的惟一迹象是散布在黑发中的几缕银丝。

▲ **agi·tate** /æ̱dʒɪteɪt/ (**agitates, agitating, agitated**) 1 V-I If people **agitate for** something, they protest or take part in political activity in order to get it. 抗争 ❑ *The women who worked in these mills had begun to agitate for better conditions.* 在这些工厂里工作的女工开始为更佳的条件而抗争。 2 V-T If you **agitate** something, you shake it so that it moves about. 搅动 [FORMAL] ❑ *All you need to do is gently agitate the water with a finger or paintbrush.* 你只需要用手指或刷子轻轻搅动水。 3 V-T If something **agitates** you, it worries you and makes you unable to think clearly or calmly. 使焦虑不安 ❑ *Carl and Martin may inherit their grandmother's possessions when she dies. The thought agitates her.* 他们的祖母去世后，卡尔和马丁可能会继承她的财产。这个念头令她焦虑不安。

agi·tat·ed /æ̱dʒɪteɪtɪd/ ADJ If someone is **agitated**, they are very worried or upset, and show this in their behavior, movements, or voice. 焦虑不安的 ❑ *Susan seemed agitated about something.* 苏姗像是对什么事感到不安。

agi·ta·tion /æ̱dʒɪteɪʃən/ N-UNCOUNT If someone is in a state of **agitation**, they are very worried or upset, and show this in their behavior, movements, or voice. 焦虑不安 ❑ *Danny returned to Father's house in a state of intense agitation.* 丹尼在一种极为焦虑不安的状态下回到了父亲的家。

ag·nos·tic /ægnɒ̱stɪk/ (**agnostics**) N-COUNT An **agnostic** believes that it is not possible to know whether God exists or not. Compare **atheist**. 不可知论者 ❑ *For the last twenty-three or twenty-four years I have been an agnostic.* 在过去的23或24年的时间里我一直是一个不可知论者。

→ see **religion**

ag·nos·ti·cism /ægnɒ̱stɪsɪzəm/ N-UNCOUNT **Agnosticism** is the belief that it is not possible to say definitely whether or not there is a God. Compare **atheism**. 不可知论

ago ♦♦♦ /əgo͟ʊ/ ADV You use **ago** when you are referring to past time. For example, if something happened one year **ago**, it is one year since it happened. If it happened a long time **ago**, it is a long time since it happened. 以前 ❑ *He was killed a few days ago in a skiing accident.* 他几天以前在一次滑雪事故中丧生。 ❑ *The meeting is the first ever between the two sides since the war there began 14 years ago.* 这是自从14年前双方爆发战争以来的第一次会晤。

You only use **ago** when you are talking about a period of time measured back from the present. If you are talking about a period measured back from some earlier time, you use **before** or **previously**. ❑ *He had died a month before... She had rented the apartment some fourteen months previously.* You use **for** to say how long a period lasts in the past, present, or future, or how much time passes without something happening. ❑ *She slept for eight hours... He will be away for three weeks... I hadn't seen him for four years.* You use **since** to say when a period of time started. ❑ *She has been with the group since it began. ...the first civilian president since the coup 17 years ago.* You also use **since** to refer to the last time that something happened, or to how much time passes without something happening. ❑ *She hadn't eaten since breakfast... It was a long time since she had been to church.*

ago·nise /æ̱gənaɪz/ [BRIT] → see **agonize**

ago·nis·ing /æ̱gənaɪzɪŋ/ [BRIT] → see **agonizing**

Word Link *agon ≈ struggling : agonize, antagonist, protagonist*

ago·nize /æ̱gənaɪz/ (**agonizes, agonizing, agonized**)

in BRIT, also use **agonise**

V-I If you **agonize over** something, you feel very anxious about it and spend a long time thinking about it. 伤脑筋 ❑ *Perhaps he was agonizing over the moral issues involved.* 或许他正在为牵涉到的道德问题伤脑筋。

ago·niz·ing /æ̱gənaɪzɪŋ/

in BRIT, also use **agonising**

1 ADJ Something that is **agonizing** causes you to feel great physical or mental pain. 令人痛苦的 ❑ *He did not wish to die the agonizing death of his mother and brother.* 他不希望像他母亲和他兄弟那样痛苦地死去。 2 ADJ **Agonizing** decisions and choices are very difficult to make. 痛苦的 ❑ *He now faced an agonizing decision about his immediate future.* 他现在面临着一项关系到他不久的将来的痛苦抉择。

ago·ny /æ̱gəni/ N-UNCOUNT **Agony** is great physical or mental pain. 极大痛苦 ❑ *A new machine may save thousands of animals from the agony of drug tests.* 一种新机器可能使成千上万只动物免于药物试验的极大痛苦。

ago·ny aunt [BRIT] → see **advice columnist**

agree ♦♦♦ /əgri͟/ (**agrees, agreeing, agreed**) 1 V-RECIP If people **agree with** each other about something, they have the same opinion about it or say that they have the same opinion. 同意 ❑ *Both have agreed on the need for the money.* 双方都同意需要那笔钱。 ❑ *So we both agree there's a problem?* 那么我们两个人都同意是有一个问题啦？ ❑ *I agree with you that the open system is by far the best.* 我同意你的观点，开放的系统是目前最好的。 ❑ *"It's appalling."—"It is. I agree."* "这糟透了。" —— "对。我同意。" ❑ *I agree with every word you've just said.* 我同意你刚刚说的每个字。 2 V-RECIP If people **agree on** something, they all decide to accept or do something. 达成一致意见 ❑ *The warring sides have agreed on an unconditional ceasefire.* 交战各方已经对无条件停火达成了一致意见。 3 V-RECIP In grammar, if a word **agrees with** a noun or pronoun, it has a form that is appropriate to the number or gender of the noun or pronoun. For example, in "He hates it," the singular verb agrees with the singular pronoun "he." 一致 [v "with" n, pl-n v] 4 V-T/V-I If you **agree to** do something, you say that you will do it. If you **agree to** a proposal, you accept it. 答应; 接受 ❑ *He agreed to pay me for the drawings.* 她答应为这些画付给我钱。 5 V-I If you **agree with** an action or suggestion, you approve of it. 赞同 ❑ *You didn't want to ask anybody whether they agreed with what you were doing.* 你不想问任何人他们是否赞同你在做的事情。 6 V-RECIP If one account of an event or one set of figures **agrees with** another, the two accounts or sets of figures are the same or are consistent with each other. 一致 ❑ *His second statement agrees with facts as stated by the other witnesses.* 他的第二项陈述和其他证人所陈述的事实一致。 7 PHRASE If two people who are arguing about something **agree to disagree** or **agree to differ**, they decide to stop arguing because neither of them is going to change their opinion. 同意各自保留意见 (以停止争论) ❑ *You and I are going to have to agree to disagree then.* 那么你和我将同意各自保留意见。

8 → see also **agreed**

Thesaurus *agree* 另参见：

v. concur; (ant.) disagree 1
consent, OK/okay 4

A

agree·able /əgriəbəl/ **1** ADJ If something is **agreeable**, it is pleasant and you enjoy it. 怡人的 ❑ *...workers in more agreeable and better paid occupations.* …从事更舒适并且报酬更好的职业的工作人员们。 **2** ADJ If someone is **agreeable**, they are pleasant and try to please people. 讨人喜欢的 ❑ *...sharing a bottle of wine with an agreeable companion.* …和一个令人愉快的同伴共享一瓶葡萄酒。

agreed /əgrid/ **1** ADJ If people are **agreed on** something, they have reached a joint decision on it or have the same opinion about it. 同意的 [v-link ADJ] ❑ *Okay, so are we agreed on going north?* 好吧，那么我们同意了向北走吗？ **2** → see also **agree**

Word Link *ment ≈ state, condition : agreement, management, movement*

agree·ment ♦♦◇ /əgrimənt/ (**agreements**) **1** N-COUNT An **agreement** is a formal decision about future action that is made by two or more countries, groups, or people. 协议 ❑ *It looks as though a compromise agreement has now been reached.* 看起来好像现在已经达成了一个妥协协议。 **2** N-UNCOUNT **Agreement on** something is a joint decision that a particular course of action should be taken. 共识 ❑ *A spokesman said, however, that the two men had not reached agreement on the issues discussed.* 但是，一位发言人说这两个人对讨论的问题还未达成共识。 **3** N-UNCOUNT **Agreement** with someone means having the same opinion as they have. 同意 ❑ *The judge kept nodding in agreement.* 法官不断点头表示同意。 ● PHRASE If you are **in agreement with** someone, you have the same opinion as they have. 意见相同 **4** N-UNCOUNT **Agreement** to a course of action means allowing it to happen or giving it your approval. 许可 ❑ *The clinic doctor will then write to your doctor to get his agreement.* 临床医生会给你的大夫写信取得他的许可。 ● PHRASE If you are **in agreement with** a plan or proposal, you approve of it. 赞同

Word Partnership *agreement* 的常用搭配：

V.	**enter into an** agreement, **reach an** agreement, **sign an** agreement **1**
N.	**peace** agreement, **terms of an** agreement, **trade** agreement **1**

ag·ri·busi·ness /ægribiznis/ N-UNCOUNT **Agribusiness** is the various businesses that produce, sell, and distribute farm products, especially on a large scale. 农业综合企业 [BUSINESS] ❑ *Many of the old agricultural collectives are now being turned into agribusiness corporations.* 很多从前的农业合作社现在被转变成了农业综合企业公司。

ag·ri·cul·tur·al ♦◇◇ /ægrɪkʌltʃərəl/ ADJ **Agricultural** means involving or relating to agriculture. 农业的 ❑ *Farmers struggling for survival strip the forests for agricultural land.* 为生存而挣扎的农民们把森林伐光来作农业用地。
→ see **farm**

ag·ri·cul·ture ♦◇◇ /ægrɪkʌltʃər/ N-UNCOUNT **Agriculture** is farming and the methods that are used to raise and take care of crops and animals. 农业 ❑ *Strong both in industry and agriculture, Ukraine produces much of the grain for the nation.* 工业与农业双强的乌克兰为其国民生产大部分谷物。
→ see **industry**

aground /əgraund/ ADV If a ship runs **aground**, it touches the ground in a shallow part of a river, lake, or the sea, and gets stuck. 搁浅地 [ADV after v] ❑ *The ship ran aground where there should have been a depth of 35 ft.* 这条船在本应该有35英尺深的地方搁浅了。

ah ♦◇◇ /ɑ/ EXCLAM **Ah** is used in writing to represent a noise that people make in conversation, for example, to acknowledge or draw attention to something, or to express surprise, relief or disappointment. 啊 [FEELINGS] ❑ *Ah, so many questions, so little time.* 啊，这么多问题，这么少的时间。

ahead
❶ ADVERB USES
❷ PREPOSITION USES

❶ ahead ♦♦◇ /əhɛd/

In addition to the uses shown below, **ahead** is used in phrasal verbs such as "get ahead," "go ahead," and "press ahead."

1 ADV Something that is **ahead** is in front of you. If you look **ahead**, you look directly in front of you. 在前面地；笔直向前地 ❑ *Brett looked straight ahead.* 布瑞特向前直视。 ❑ *The road ahead was now blocked solid.* 前方道路现在被堵死了。 **2** ADV You use **ahead** with verbs such as "push," "move," and "forge" to indicate that a plan, program, or organization is making fast progress. 向前地 [ADV after v] ❑ *Western countries were moving ahead with plans to send financial aid to all of the former Soviet republics.* 西方国家正推行对所有前苏联国家提供经济援助的计划。 **3** ADV If you are **ahead** in your work or achievements, you have made more progress than you expected to and are performing well. 提前地 ❑ *First half profits have charged ahead from $127.6m to $134.2m.* 上半年利润已经提前从1.276亿美元提升到了1.342亿美元。 **4** ADV If a person or a team is **ahead** in a competition, they are winning. 领先地 ❑ *Australia was ahead throughout the game.* 澳大利亚队在整场比赛中一直领先。 ❑ *The Communists are comfortably ahead in the opinion polls.* 共产党在民意调查中遥遥领先。 **5** ADV **Ahead** also means in the future. 在将来 ❑ *A much bigger battle is ahead for the president.* 总统还将面临一场更大的战斗。 **6** ADV If you prepare or plan something **ahead**, you do it some time before a future event so that everything is ready for that event to take place. 提前地 [ADV after v] ❑ *The government wants figures that help it to administer its policies and plan ahead.* 政府想要可以助其提前实施其政策和计划的数据。 **7** ADV If you go **ahead**, or if you go on **ahead**, you go in front of someone who is going to the same place so that you arrive there some time before they do. 提前地 [ADV after v] ❑ *I went ahead and waited with Sean.* 我提前去了，和肖恩一起等。

❷ ahead ♦◇◇ /əhɛd/

➪ **Please look at meanings 6 and 7 to see if the expression you are looking for is shown under another headword.** **1** PHRASE If someone is **ahead of** you, they are directly in front of you. If someone is moving **ahead of** you, they are in front of you and moving in the same direction. 在前面 ❑ *I saw a man in a blue jacket thirty yards ahead of me.* 我看见在我前面30码处有一个穿蓝色夹克的男人。 **2** PHRASE If an event or period of time lies **ahead of** you, it is going to happen or take place soon or in the future. 在将来 ❑ *I tried to think about all the problems that were ahead of me tomorrow.* 我试着想考虑一下明天要面对的所有问题。 ❑ *Heather had been awake all night thinking about the future that lay ahead of her.* 海瑟整夜未眠，考虑着她所要面临的未来。 **3** PHRASE In a competition, if a person or team does something **ahead of** someone else, they do it before the second person or team. (竞赛中) 领先于 ❑ *Robert Millar finished 1 minute and 35 seconds ahead of the Frenchman.* 罗伯特·米拉尔领先法国选手1分35秒完成比赛。 **4** PHRASE If something happens **ahead of** schedule or **ahead of** time, it happens earlier than was planned. 提前 ❑ *The election was held six months ahead of schedule.* 选举比计划日程提前了6个月举行。 **5** PHRASE If someone is **ahead of** someone else, they have made more progress and are more advanced in what they are doing. 领先于 ❑ *Henry generally stayed ahead of the others in the academic subjects.* 亨利的文化课成绩上通常都领先于其他人。 **6** **one step ahead of** someone or something → see **step** **7** **ahead of** your **time** → see **time**

Word Partnership *ahead* 的常用搭配：

ADV.	**straight** ahead ❶ **1**
V.	**lie** ahead, **look** ahead ❶ **1** **5**
	move ahead ❶ **2**
	get ahead ❶ **3**
	plan ahead ❶ **6**
	go ahead ❶ **7**
PREP.	**in the days/months/years** ahead ❷ **5**
	ahead **of schedule/time** ❷ **4**

aid ♦♦♦ /eɪd/ (**aids, aiding, aided**) **1** N-UNCOUNT **Aid** is money, equipment, or services that are provided for people, countries, or organizations who need them but cannot provide them for themselves. 援助 ❑ *...regular flights carrying humanitarian aid to Cambodia.* …向柬埔寨运送人道主义援助的定期班机。 ❑ *They have already pledged billions of dollars in aid.* 他们已经承诺了数十亿美元的援助。 **2** N-UNCOUNT If you perform a task **with the aid of** something, you need or use that thing to perform that task. 帮助 ❑ *He succeeded with the aid of a completely new method he discovered.* 借助于一个他所发现的全新方法，他取得了成功。 **3** V-T To **aid** a country, organization, or person means to provide them with money, equipment, or services that they need. 援助 ❑ *...U.S. efforts to aid Kurdish refugees.* …美国援助库尔德难民的努力。 ● **-aided** COMB IN ADJ 援助的 ❑ *...government-aided research.* …政府援助的研究。 **4** V-T To

aid someone means to help or assist them. 帮助 [WRITTEN] ❑ *...a software system to aid managers in advanced decision-making.* …一个帮助经理们做高级决策的软件系统。● N-UNCOUNT **Aid** is also a noun. 帮助 ❑ *He was forced to turn for aid to his former enemy.* 他被迫向他以前的敌人寻求帮助。 **5** V-T/V-I If something **aids** a process, it makes it easier or more likely to happen. 促使；有助于（事情发生）❑ *The survey suggests that the export sector will continue to aid the economic recovery.* 该调查表明出口产业将继续促进经济复苏。 ❑ *Calcium may aid in the prevention of colon cancer.* 钙可能有助于预防结肠癌。 **6** N-COUNT An **aid** is an object, device, or technique that makes something easier to do. 辅助工具 ❑ *The book is an invaluable aid to teachers of literature.* 这本书对文学教师是一个非常有用的辅助工具。 **7** → see also **first aid** **8** PHRASE If you **come** or **go to** someone's **aid**, you try to help them when they are in danger or difficulty. 向某人提供帮助 ❑ *Dr. Fox went to the aid of the dying man despite having been injured in the crash.* 尽管他自己在撞车事故中也受了伤，福克斯医生仍然去救助那个奄奄一息的男子。

▲ **aide** /eɪd/ (**aides**) **1** N-COUNT An **aide** is an assistant to someone who has an important job, especially in government or in the armed forces. 助手 ❑ *A close aide to the prime minister repeated that Israel would never accept it.* 首相身边的一个助手重申了以色列绝不会接受。 **2** → see also **teacher's aide**

AIDS ♦♦◇ /eɪdz/ N-UNCOUNT **AIDS** is a disease that destroys the natural system of protection that the body has against other diseases. **AIDS** is an abbreviation for **acquired immune deficiency syndrome**. 艾滋病 ❑ *...people suffering from AIDS.* …患有艾滋病的人们。

Word Partnership *AIDS* 的常用搭配：

N.	AIDS **activists**, AIDS **epidemic**, AIDS **patient**, AIDS **research**, **spread of** AIDS, AIDS **victims**
V.	**infected with** AIDS

ail·ing /eɪlɪŋ/ ADJ An **ailing** organization or society is in difficulty and is becoming weaker. 每况愈下的 ❑ *The rise in overseas sales is good news for the ailing American economy.* 海外销售的增长对每况愈下的美国经济是一个好消息。

▲ **ail·ment** /eɪlmənt/ (**ailments**) N-COUNT An **ailment** is an illness, especially one that is not very serious. 小病 ❑ *The pharmacist can assist you with the treatment of common ailments.* 药剂师能帮助你治疗平常小病。

aim ♦♦◇ /eɪm/ (**aims, aiming, aimed**) **1** V-T/V-I If you **aim for** something or **aim to** do something, you plan or hope to achieve it. 以…为目标 ❑ *He said he would aim for the 100 meter world record at the world championships in August.* 他说他将以在8月举行的世界锦标赛上打破100米世界纪录为目标。 ❑ *Businesses will have to aim at long-term growth.* 企业必须以长期增长为目标。 ❑ *The program aims to educate and prepare students for a challenging career.* 这个项目旨在教育学生使其为一个具有挑战性的职业做好准备。 **2** V-T/V-I If you **aim to** do something, you decide or want to do it. 打算 [AM, INFORMAL] ❑ *I didn't aim to get caught.* 我并不想被抓到。 **3** V-T If your actions or remarks **are aimed at** a particular person or group, you intend that the person or group should notice them and be influenced by them. 针对 [usu passive] ❑ *His message was aimed at the undecided middle ground of Israeli politics.* 他所传达的信息针对的是以色列政坛中尚未表态的中间派。 **4** V-T/V-I If you **aim** a weapon or object **at** something or someone, you point it toward them before firing or throwing it. 对…瞄准 ❑ *When he appeared again, he was aiming the rifle at Wade.* 他再次出现时，他正将步枪瞄准维德。 ❑ *...a missile aimed at the arms factory.* …一枚瞄准了军工厂的导弹。 **5** V-T If you **aim** a kick or punch at someone, you try to kick or punch them. 对准 ❑ *They set on him, punching him in the face and aiming kicks at his shins.* 他们袭击了他，猛打他的脸，并对准他的胫骨猛踢。 **6** N-COUNT The **aim** of something that you do is the purpose for which you do it or the result that it is intended to achieve. 目的 ❑ *The aim of the festival is to increase awareness of Hindu culture and traditions.* 这个庆祝活动的目的是增强人们对印度文化和传统的认识。 **7** V-T If an action or plan **is aimed at** achieving something, it is intended or planned to achieve it. 旨在 ❑ *The new measures are aimed at tightening existing sanctions.* 这些新措施旨在加强现行的制裁。 **8** N-SING Your **aim** is your skill or action in pointing a weapon or other object at its target. 瞄准 ❑ *He stood with the gun gripped in his right hand and his left hand steadying his aim.* 他站着用右手紧握住枪，用左手把稳瞄准。 **9** PHRASE When you **take aim**, you point a weapon or object at someone or something, before firing or throwing it. 瞄准 ❑ *She had spotted a man with a shotgun taking aim.* 她看见了一个正在用手持猎枪瞄准的男子。

Word Partnership *aim* 的常用搭配：

PREP.	aim **for**, aim **to** **1** **2**
	aim **at** **3** **4**
	aim **of** **6**
ADJ.	**primary/sole/ultimate** aim **6**
V.	**take** aim **9**

Word Link *less ≈ without : aimless, harmless, worthless*

aim·less /eɪmləs/ ADJ A person or activity that is **aimless** has no clear purpose or plan. 漫无目的的 ❑ *After several hours of aimless searching they were getting low on fuel.* 在经历了几个小时的漫无目的的搜寻之后，他们的燃料不足了。 ● **aim·less·ly** ADV 漫无目的地 [ADV after v] ❑ *I wandered around aimlessly.* 我漫无目的地徘徊。

ain't /eɪnt/ People sometimes use **ain't** instead of "am not," "aren't," "isn't," "haven't," and "hasn't." Many people consider this use to be incorrect. **ain't**可被用来替代**am not**、**aren't**、**isn't**、**haven't**和**hasn't**。许多人认为该用法不规范 [DIALECT, SPOKEN] ❑ *Well, it's obvious, ain't it?* 嗯，这很明显，不是吗？

air ♦♦♦ /ɛər/ (**airs, airing, aired**) **1** N-UNCOUNT **Air** is the mixture of gases that forms the Earth's atmosphere and that we breathe. 空气 ❑ *Drafts help to circulate air.* 通风有助于循环空气。 ❑ *Keith opened the window and leaned out into the cold air.* 基斯打开窗户，探出身到冷风中。 **2** N-UNCOUNT **Air** is used to refer to travel in aircraft. 空运 ❑ *Air travel will continue to grow at about 6% per year.* 乘飞机旅行的人数将以每年大约6%的速度持续增加。 **3** N-SING **The air** is the space around things or above the ground. 空中 ❑ *Government troops broke up the protest by firing their guns in the air.* 政府军通过朝天鸣枪驱散了这场抗议示威。 **4** V-T If a broadcasting company **airs** a television or radio program, they show it on television or broadcast it on the radio. 播放 [mainly AM] ❑ *Tonight PBS will air a documentary called "Democracy In Action".* 今晚PBS电台将播放一部名为《民主进行时》的纪录片。 ● **air·ing** N-SING 播放 ❑ *...the airing of a new television commercial that attacked the president's war record.* …一个对总统的战争记录进行攻击的新电视广告片的播放。 **5** V-T If you **air** a room or building, you let fresh air into it. 使通风 ❑ *One day a week her mother cleaned and aired each room.* 每周一天，她的母亲给每一个房间进行清扫并通风。 **6** PHRASE If you do something to **clear the air**, you do it in order to resolve any problems or disagreements that there might be. 澄清视听 ❑ *...an inquiry just to clear the air and settle the facts of the case.* …一个只是澄清视听并确认事实的调查。 **7** PHRASE If something **is in the air** it is felt to be present, but it is not talked about. 可感觉到

Word Web air

The **air** we breathe contains seventeen different **gases**. Surprisingly, it is composed mostly of **nitrogen**, not **oxygen**. Recently, human activities have created imbalances in the earth's **atmosphere**. The widespread burning of coal and oil increased levels of **carbon dioxide** gas. Scientists believe this air **pollution** may be responsible for **global warming**. Certain chemical compounds used in air conditioners, agricultural processes, and manufacturing are the problem. With less protection from the sun, the air temperature rises. This leads to harmful effects on people, agriculture, animals, and the natural environment.

Composition of Air

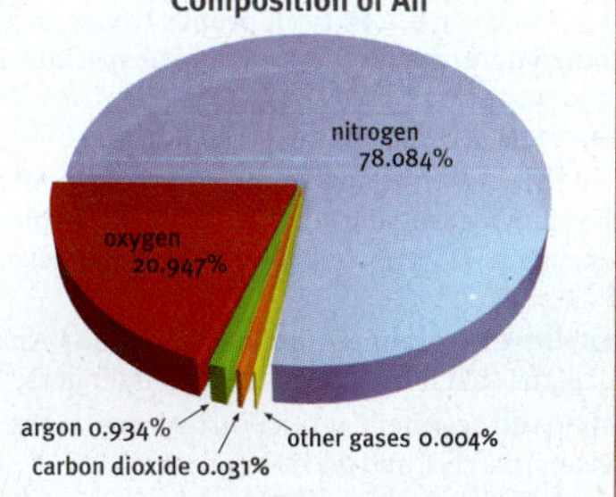

A

(但不说出来) ❑ *There was great excitement in the air.* 人人都感到了无比的激动。 **8** PHRASE If someone is **on the air**, they are broadcasting on radio or television. If a program is **on the air**, it is being broadcast on radio or television. If it is **off the air**, it is not being broadcast. (人) 播报; (节目) 播放 ❑ *We go on the air, live, at 11:30 a.m.* 我们上午11:30进行现场直播。 **9** PHRASE If someone or something disappears **into thin air**, they disappear completely. If someone or something appears **out of thin air**, they appear suddenly and mysteriously. 完全消失/突然神秘出现 ❑ *He had materialized out of thin air; I had not seen or heard him coming.* 他突然神秘地出现了；我既没看到也没听到他进来。

→ see Word Web: **air**

→ see **erosion, flight, fly, respiratory, wind**

air·bag /ɛərbæg/ (**airbags**) also **air bag** N-COUNT An **airbag** is a safety device in a car that automatically fills with air if the car crashes, and is designed to protect the people in the car when they are thrown forward in the crash. 安全气囊

→ see **car**

air base (**air bases**) also **airbase** N-COUNT An **air base** is a center where military aircraft take off or land and are serviced, and where many of the center's staff live. 空军基地 ❑ *...the largest U.S. air base in Saudi Arabia.* …沙特阿拉伯最大的美国空军基地。

★ **air·borne** /ɛərbɔrn/ **1** ADJ If an aircraft is **airborne**, it is in the air and flying. 在飞行中的 [v-link ADJ] ❑ *The pilot did manage to get airborne.* 这位飞行员的确使飞机升空了。 **2** ADJ **Airborne** troops use parachutes to get into enemy territory. 空降的 [ADJ n] ❑ *The allies landed thousands of airborne troops.* 同盟国投下了成千上万的空降部队。 **3** ADJ **Airborne** means in the air or carried in the air. 空气中的 ❑ *Many people are allergic to airborne pollutants such as pollen.* 许多人对空气中花粉之类的污染物质过敏。

→ see **pollution**

air-conditioned ADJ If a room or vehicle is **air-conditioned**, the air in it is kept cool and dry by means of a special machine. 有空气调节设备的 ❑ *...our new air-conditioned trains.* …我们装有空调的新火车。

air-condition·ing N-UNCOUNT **Air-conditioning** is a method of providing buildings and vehicles with cool dry air. 空调系统

air·craft ♦♦◊ /ɛərkræft/ (**aircraft**)

> **Aircraft** is both the singular and the plural form.

N-COUNT An **aircraft** is a vehicle that can fly, for example, an airplane or a helicopter. 飞机 ❑ *The return flight of the aircraft was delayed.* 飞机的返回航程被推迟了。

→ see **fly**

air·field /ɛərfild/ (**airfields**) N-COUNT An **airfield** is an area of ground where aircraft take off and land. It is smaller than an airport. 停机坪

air force ♦◊◊ (**air forces**) N-COUNT An **air force** is the part of a country's armed forces that is concerned with fighting in the air. 空军 ❑ *...the United States Air Force.* …美国空军。

▲ **air host·ess** (**air hostesses**) N-COUNT An **air hostess** is a woman whose job is to look after the passengers in an airplane. 航空小姐 [BRIT]

> in AM, use **stewardess**

air·lift /ɛərlɪft/ (**airlifts, airlifting, airlifted**) **1** N-COUNT An **airlift** is an operation to move people, troops, or goods by air, especially in a war or when land routes are closed. 空运 ❑ *President Garcia has ordered an airlift of food, medicines and blankets.* 加西亚总统已经下令空运食品、药品和毛毯。 **2** V-T If people, troops, or goods **are airlifted** somewhere, they are carried by air, especially in a war or when land routes are closed. 空运 ❑ *The injured were airlifted to a hospital in Dayton.* 伤员被空运到代顿的一所医院。

air·line ♦♦◊ /ɛərlaɪn/ (**airlines**) N-COUNT An **airline** is a company that provides regular services carrying people or goods in airplanes. 航空公司 ❑ *...the world's largest discount airline.* …世界上最大的折扣航空公司。

air·lin·er /ɛərlaɪnər/ (**airliners**) N-COUNT An **airliner** is a large airplane that is used for carrying passengers. 客机

air·mail /ɛərmeɪl/ N-UNCOUNT **Airmail** is the system of sending letters, parcels, and goods by air. 航空邮递 ❑ *...an airmail letter.* …一封航空信。

air·man /ɛərmən/ (**airmen**) N-COUNT An **airman** is a man who flies aircraft, especially one who serves in his country's air force. 飞行员 ❑ *...an American airman.* …一位美国飞行员。

air·plane /ɛərpleɪn/ (**airplanes**) N-COUNT An **airplane** is a vehicle with wings and one or more engines that enable it to fly through the air. 飞机 [AM]

> in BRIT, use **aeroplane**

→ see **fly**

air·port ♦♦◊ /ɛərpɔrt/ (**airports**) N-COUNT An **airport** is a place where aircraft land and take off, and that has buildings and facilities for passengers. 飞机场 ❑ *...Heathrow Airport, the busiest international airport in the world.* …希斯罗飞机场——世界上最繁忙的国际机场。

air·port tax (**airport taxes**) N-VAR **Airport tax** is a tax that airline passengers have to pay in order to use an airport. 机场税 ❑ *Overnight return flights cost from $349 including airport taxes.* 当夜往返的航班含机场税至少需要349美元。

air rage N-UNCOUNT **Air rage** is aggressive or violent behavior by airline passengers. 空中愤怒 (飞机上的乘客出现的攻击或暴力行为) ❑ *Most air rage incidents involve heavy drinking.* 大多数空中愤怒事件都与酗酒有关。

air raid (**air raids**) N-COUNT An **air raid** is an attack by military aircraft in which bombs are dropped. 空袭 ❑ *The war began with overnight air raids on Baghdad and Kuwait.* 这场战争以对巴格达和科威特的连夜空袭开始。

air·space /ɛərspeɪs/ also **air space** N-UNCOUNT A country's **airspace** is the part of the sky that is over that country and is considered to belong to it. 空域 ❑ *Forty minutes later, they left Colombian airspace.* 40分钟之后，他们离开了哥伦比亚的空域。

▲ **air strike** (**air strikes**) also **airstrike** N-COUNT An **air strike** is an attack by military aircraft in which bombs are dropped. 空袭 ❑ *A senior defense official said last night that they would continue the air strikes.* 一位高级国防官员昨晚说他们将继续空袭。

air·tight /ɛərtaɪt/ also **air-tight** **1** ADJ If a container is **airtight**, its lid fits so tightly that no air can get in or out. 密封的 ❑ *Store the cookies in an airtight container.* 把饼干存放在一个密封的容器里。 **2** ADJ An **airtight** alibi, case, argument, or agreement is one that has been so carefully put together that nobody will be able to find a fault in it. 无懈可击的 [AM]

> in BRIT, use **watertight**

❑ *If she could just establish the time the picture had been taken, Mick would have an airtight alibi.* 只要她能确定拍这张照片的时间，米克就可以有一个无懈可击的不在现场的证据。

→ see **can**

air traf·fic con·trol·ler (**air traffic controllers**) N-COUNT An **air traffic controller** is someone whose job is to organize the routes that aircraft should follow, and to tell pilots by radio which routes they should take. 空中交通管理员

air·waves /ɛərweɪvz/ also **air waves** N-PLURAL **The airwaves** is used to refer to the activity of broadcasting on radio and television. For example, if someone says something over **the airwaves**, they say it on the radio or television. 无线电波 [JOURNALISM] ❑ *The election campaign has been fought not in street rallies but on the airwaves.* 这场竞选大战不是在街头集会中进行，而是在无线电波中交锋。

air·way /ɛərweɪ/ (**airways**) **1** N-COUNT A person's **airways** are the passages from their nose and mouth down to their lungs, through which air enters and leaves their body. 呼吸道 ❑ *...an inflammation of the airways.* …一次呼吸道发炎 **2** N-PLURAL **The airways** are all the routes that planes can travel along. 飞机航线 [usu "the" N] ❑ *How does a private pilot get access to the airways?* 一个私人飞机的飞行员如何获得航线使用权呢？ **3** N-PLURAL **Airways** means the same as **airwaves**. 无线电波 [usu "the" N] ❑ *The interview went out over the airways.* 访谈通过无线电波传了出去。

airy /ɛəri/ (**airier, airiest**) ADJ If a building or room is **airy**, it has a lot of fresh air inside, usually because it is large. 通风的 ❑ *The bathroom has a light and airy feel.* 这个浴室给人以明亮通风之感。

★ **aisle** /aɪl/ (**aisles**) N-COUNT An **aisle** is a long narrow gap that people can walk along between rows of seats in a public building such as a church or between rows of shelves in a supermarket. (座位间或货架间的) 通道 ❑ *...the frozen food aisle.* …冷冻食品的货架通道。

a.k.a. /eɪ keɪ eɪ/ also **aka** **a.k.a.** is an abbreviation for "also known as." **a.k.a.** is used especially when referring to someone's nickname or stage name. **also known as**的缩写，亦称做，尤其当指外号或艺名时 ❑ *From the very beginning, Stuart Leslie Goddard, a.k.a. Adam Ant, knew he was going to be a star.* 从一开始，斯图尔特·莱斯利·戈达德，又叫蚂蚁亚当，就知道他将会成为明星。

▲ **akin** /əkɪn/ ADJ If one thing is **akin to** another, it is similar to it in some way. 相似的 [v-link ADJ "to" n] [FORMAL] ❑ *Listening to his life story is akin to reading a good adventure novel.* 听他的生活故事就像读一部好的探险小说。

alarm ♦◇◇ /əlɑrm/ (**alarms, alarming, alarmed**) **1** N-UNCOUNT **Alarm** is a feeling of fear or anxiety that something unpleasant or dangerous might happen. 惊恐 ❑ *The news was greeted with alarm by senators.* 议员们对这一消息报以恐慌。 **2** V-T If something **alarms** you, it makes you afraid or anxious that something unpleasant or dangerous might happen. 使惊恐 ❑ *We could not see what had alarmed him.* 我们不明白是什么吓着他了。 **3** N-COUNT An **alarm** is an automatic device that warns you of danger, for example, by ringing a bell. 警报器 ❑ *He heard the alarm go off.* 他听见警报器响了。 **4** N-COUNT An **alarm** is the same as an **alarm clock**. 闹钟 ❑ *Dad set the alarm for eight the next day.* 爸爸把闹钟设到了第2天8点。 **5** → see also **alarmed, alarming, car alarm, false alarm, fire alarm** **6** PHRASE If you say that something sets **alarm bells** ringing, you mean that it makes people feel worried or concerned about something. 危险信号 ❑ *This has set the alarm bells ringing in Moscow.* 这已给莫斯科拉响了警报。 **7** PHRASE If you **raise the alarm** or **sound the alarm**, you warn people of danger. 发出警报 ❑ *His family raised the alarm when he had not come home by 9 p.m.* 当他到晚上9点还没回家时，他的家人报了警。

Word Partnership *alarm* 的常用搭配：
V. **cause** alarm **1**
set the alarm **3** **4**
raise/sound the alarm **7**
N. alarm **system** **3**

alarm clock (**alarm clocks**) N-COUNT An **alarm clock** is a clock that you can set to make a noise so that it wakes you up at a particular time. 闹钟 ❑ *I set my alarm clock for 4:30.* 我把闹钟定在4:30。

alarmed /əlɑrmd/ ADJ If someone is **alarmed**, they feel afraid or anxious that something unpleasant or dangerous might happen. 恐慌的 ❑ *They should not be too alarmed by the press reports.* 他们不应该被媒体报道搞得过于恐慌。

alarm·ing /əlɑrmɪŋ/ ADJ Something that is **alarming** makes you feel afraid or anxious that something unpleasant or dangerous might happen. 令人惊恐的 ❑ *The disease has spread at an alarming rate.* 这种疾病已经以惊人的速度传播开来。 ● **alarm·ing·ly** ADV 令人惊恐地 ❑ *...the alarmingly high rate of heart disease.* …高得惊人的心脏病发病率。

alas /əlæs/ ADV You use **alas** to say that you think that the facts you are talking about are sad or unfortunate. 唉（表示难过或不幸的惊叹声）[ADV with cl] [FORMAL, FEELINGS] ❑ *Such scandals have not, alas, been absent.* 唉，这样的丑闻也不是没有。

al·be·it /ɔlbiɪt/ ADV You use **albeit** to introduce a fact or comment that reduces the force or significance of what you have just said. 尽管 [ADV with cl/group] [FORMAL] ❑ *Charles's letter was indeed published, albeit in a somewhat abbreviated form.* 查尔斯的信确实被刊登了出来，尽管有些删节。

al·bum ♦♦◇ /ælbəm/ (**albums**) **1** N-COUNT An **album** is a collection of songs that is available on a CD, record, or cassette. 唱片专辑 ❑ *Chris likes music and has a large collection of albums and cassettes.* 克里斯喜欢音乐，并且收藏了大量的唱片和磁带。 ❑ *Oasis release their new album on July 1.* 绿洲乐队将于7月1日发行他们的新专辑。 **2** N-COUNT An **album** is a book in which you keep things such as photographs or stamps that you have collected. （收存照片或邮票的）册子 ❑ *Theresa showed me her photo album.* 特雷莎给我看了她的相册。

Word Partnership *album* 的常用搭配：
ADJ. **debut/first/latest/new** album, **live** album, **solo** album **1**
V. **produce/release an** album **1**
N. **photo** album **2**

al·co·hol ♦◇◇ /ælkəhɔl/ (**alcohols**) **1** N-UNCOUNT Drinks that can make people drunk, such as beer, wine, and whiskey, can be referred to as **alcohol**. 酒 ❑ *Do either of you smoke cigarettes or drink alcohol?* 你们两个人有人抽烟喝酒吗？ **2** N-MASS **Alcohol** is a colorless liquid that is found in drinks such as beer, wine, and whiskey. It is also used in products such as perfumes and cleaning fluids. 酒精 ❑ *...low-alcohol beer.* …低酒精度啤酒。

▲ **al·co·hol·ic** /ælkəhɔlɪk/ (**alcoholics**) **1** N-COUNT An **alcoholic** is someone who cannot stop drinking large amounts of alcohol, even when this is making them ill. 酗酒者 ❑ *He showed great courage by admitting on television that he is an alcoholic.* 他在电视上承认他是个酒鬼，表现出了极大的勇气。 **2** ADJ **Alcoholic** drinks are drinks that contain alcohol. 含酒精的 ❑ *The serving of alcoholic drinks was forbidden after six o'clock.* 在6点以后供应酒精饮料是被禁止的。

al·co·hol·ism /ælkəhɒlɪzəm/ N-UNCOUNT People who suffer from **alcoholism** cannot stop drinking large quantities of alcohol. 酗酒 ❑ *...a physician who specialized in the problems of alcoholism.* …一位专攻酗酒问题的医生。

★ **ale** /eɪl/ (**ales**) N-MASS **Ale** is a kind of strong beer. 麦芽酒 ❑ *...our selection of ales and spirits.* …我们精选的麦芽酒和烈性酒。

alert ♦◇◇ /əlɜrt/ (**alerts, alerting, alerted**) **1** ADJ If you are **alert**, you are paying full attention to things around you and are able to deal with anything that might happen. 警觉的 ❑ *We all have to stay alert.* 我们都必须保持警觉。 ● **alert·ness** N-UNCOUNT 警觉性 ❑ *The drug improved mental alertness.* 这种药物提高了大脑的灵敏度。 **2** ADJ If you are **alert to** something, you are fully aware of it. 充分意识到的 [v-link ADJ "to" n] ❑ *The bank is alert to the danger.* 该银行对这种危险有警觉。 **3** N-COUNT An **alert** is a situation in which people prepare themselves for something dangerous that might happen soon. 戒备状态 ❑ *There has been criticism of how his administration handled last week's terrorism alert.* 对他的政府对待上周恐怖主义戒备状态的方式有批评之辞。 **4** V-T If you **alert** someone **to** a situation, especially a dangerous or unpleasant situation, you tell them about it. 向…发出警报 ❑ *He wanted to alert people to the activities of the group.* 他想警告人们注意这个组织的行动。 **5** PHRASE If you are **on the alert for** something, you are ready to deal with it if it happens. 准备应对 ❑ *They want to be on the alert for similar buying opportunities.* 他们要准备应对类似的购买机会。
→ see **hypnosis**

al·gae /ældʒi, ælgaɪ/ N-PLURAL **Algae** are plants with no stems or leaves that grow in water or on damp surfaces. 水藻 ❑ *...an effort to control toxic algae in Green Lake.* …控制绿湖里有毒水藻的努力。
→ see **plant**

▲ **al·ge·bra** /ældʒɪbrə/ N-UNCOUNT **Algebra** is a type of mathematics in which letters are used to represent possible quantities. 代数
→ see **mathematics**

Word Link *ali ≈ other : alias, alibi, alien*

ali·as /eɪliəs/ (**aliases**) **1** N-COUNT An **alias** is a false name, especially one used by a criminal. 化名 ❑ *Using an alias, he had rented a house in Des Moines.* 通过使用一个化名，他已在得梅因租了一所房子。 **2** PREP You use **alias** when you are mentioning another name that someone, especially a criminal or an actor, is known by. 化名为 ❑ *Richard Thorp, alias Alan Turner, said yesterday: "It is a sad time for both of us."* 理查德·索普，又名为阿伦·特纳，昨天说道："这对我们两个人来说都是一个悲伤的时刻"。

ali·bi /ælɪbaɪ/ (**alibis**) N-COUNT If you have an **alibi**, you can prove that you were somewhere else when a crime was committed. 不在现场证明 ❑ *He manages to persuade both his wife and girlfriend to provide him with an alibi.* 他设法说服他的妻子和女友都为他提供不在场的证明。

★ **al·ien** /eɪliən/ (**aliens**) **1** ADJ **Alien** means belonging to a different country, race, or group, usually one you do not like or are frightened of. 外国的 [FORMAL, DISAPPROVAL] ❑ *He said they were opposed to what he described as the presence of alien forces in the region.* 他说他们反对他所描述的在该地区有外国军队的存在。 **2** ADJ If something is **alien to** you or **to** your normal feelings or behavior, it is not the way you would normally feel or behave. 陌生的 [v-link ADJ "to" n] [FORMAL] ❑ *Such an attitude is alien to most businessmen.* 这种态度对大多数商人都很陌生。 **3** N-COUNT An **alien** is someone who is not a legal citizen of the country in which they live. 外国人 [LEGAL] ❑ *Both women had hired illegal aliens for child care.* 这两个女人都

A

雇佣了非法入境者来照看孩子。4 N-COUNT In science fiction, an **alien** is a creature from outer space. 外星人 ❑ *...aliens from another planet.* …从另一个行星来的外星人。

★ **al·ien·ate** /eɪliəneɪt/ (**alienates, alienating, alienated**) 1 V-T If you **alienate** someone, you make them become unfriendly or unsympathetic toward you. 冷落 ❑ *The government cannot afford to alienate either group.* 该政府承担不起冷落两个组织中的任何一个。 2 V-T To **alienate** a person **from** someone or something that they are normally linked with means to cause them to be emotionally or intellectually separated from them. 使疏远 ❑ *His second wife, Alice, was determined to alienate him from his two boys.* 他的第2个妻子阿丽丝决心让他疏远他的两个儿子。

alight /əlaɪt/ (**alights, alighting, alighted**) 1 ADJ If something is **alight**, it is burning. 燃烧着的 [v n ADJ, v-link ADJ] ❑ *Several buildings were set alight.* 几栋大楼着了火。 2 ADJ If someone's eyes are **alight** or if their face is **alight**, the expression in their eyes or on their face shows that they are feeling a strong emotion such as excitement or happiness. 洋溢着的 [v-link ADJ] [LITERARY] ❑ *She paused and turned, her face alight with happiness.* 她停住并且转过身来，满脸洋溢着幸福。 3 V-I If a bird or insect **alights** somewhere, it lands there. (鸟虫) 飞落 [LITERARY] ❑ *A thrush alighted on a branch of the pine tree.* 一只画眉落在这棵松树的一根树枝上。 4 V-I When you **alight** from a train, bus, or other vehicle, you get out of it after a trip. (从车上) 下来 [FORMAL]

▲ **align** /əlaɪn/ (**aligns, aligning, aligned**) 1 V-T If you **align yourself with** a particular group, you support them because you have the same political aim. 与…结盟 ❑ *When war broke out, they aligned themselves with the rebel forces.* 战争爆发以后，他们与叛军结了盟。 2 V-T If you **align** something, you place it in a certain position in relation to something else, usually parallel to it. 使对齐 ❑ *A tripod will be useful to align and steady the camera.* 三脚架会有助于对齐稳住照相机。

align·ment /əlaɪnmənt/ (**alignments**) 1 N-VAR An **alignment** is support for a particular group, especially in politics, or for a side in a quarrel or struggle. 结盟 ❑ *The church should have no political alignment.* 教会不应该有政治结盟。 2 N-UNCOUNT The **alignment** of something is its position in relation to something else or to its correct position. 位置 ❑ *They shunned the belief that there is a link between the alignment of the planets and events on the Earth.* 他们回避了在行星的排列和地球上发生的事件之间有联系的看法。

Word Link *like ≈ similar : alike, childlike, likeness*

alike /əlaɪk/ 1 ADJ If two or more things are **alike**, they are similar in some way. 相似的 [v-link ADJ] ❑ *We looked very alike.* 我们长得很相像。 2 ADV **Alike** means in a similar way. 相似地 [ADV after v] ❑ *They even dressed alike.* 他们甚至连穿着都相像。

Thesaurus *alike* 另参见：

ADJ. comparable, equal, equivalent, matching, parallel, similar; *(ant.)* different 1

alive ♦◇◇ /əlaɪv/ 1 ADJ If people or animals are **alive**, they are not dead. 活着的 [v-link ADJ] ❑ *She does not know if he is alive or dead.* 她不知道他是活还是死。 2 ADJ If you say that someone seems **alive**, you mean that they seem to be very lively and to enjoy everything that they do. 有活力的 ❑ *She seemed more alive and looked forward to getting up in the morning.* 她似乎更有活力，并且期待着一早就起来。 3 ADJ If an activity, organization, or situation is **alive**, it continues to exist or function. 继续存在的 [v-link ADJ, "keep" n ADJ] ❑ *The big factories are trying to stay alive by cutting costs.* 大工厂试图通过减少开支以维持生存。 4 ADJ If a place is **alive with** something, there are a lot of people or things there and it seems busy or exciting. 满是(人或物，显得繁忙或兴奋的) 的 [v-link ADJ] ❑ *The river was alive with birds.* 这条河流周围满是各种鸟类。 5 PHRASE If people, places, or events **come alive**, they start to be lively again after a quiet period. If someone or something **brings** them **alive**, they cause them to come alive. 恢复生机；使变活跃 ❑ *The doctor's voice had come alive and his small eyes shone.* 医生的声音变得响亮起来，两只小眼睛也有了神采。 6 PHRASE If a story or description **comes alive**, it becomes interesting, lively, or realistic. If someone or something **brings** it **alive**, they make it seem more interesting, lively, or realistic. 使变得有趣；使显得生动 ❑ *She made history come alive with tales from her own memories.* 她用自己记忆中的往事使历史变得生动有趣起来。

Word Partnership *alive* 的常用搭配：

ADJ.	**dead or alive** 1
ADV.	**alive and well** 1
	still alive 1 3
V.	**found alive, keep** *someone/something* **alive** 1
	stay alive 1 3
	feel alive 2 5
	come alive 5 6

all

1 EVERYTHING, THE WHOLE OF SOMETHING
2 EMPHASIS
3 OTHER PHRASES

❶ **all** ♦♦♦ /ɔl/ 1 PREDET You use **all** to indicate that you are referring to the whole of a particular group or thing or to everyone or everything of a particular kind. 所有的 ❑ *...the restaurant that Hugh and all his friends go to.* …休和他所有的朋友们去的那家饭馆。 ❑ *He lost all his money gambling in Las Vegas.* 他在拉斯维加斯赌博输光了他所有的钱。 ● DET **All** is also a determiner. 所有的 ❑ *There is built-in storage space in all bedrooms.* 所有卧室里都有内置储藏空间。 ❑ *He was passionate about all literature.* 他对所有文学作品都有热情。 ❑ *85 percent of all American households owe money on mortgages.* 全美国85%的家庭欠抵押贷款。 ● QUANT **All** is also a quantifier. 全部的 ❑ *He was told to pack up all of his letters and personal belongings.* 他被告知整理好他的全部信件和个人物品。 ● PRON **All** is also a pronoun. 全部 ❑ *The only salon produces its own shampoos and hair-care products, all based on herbal recipes.* 这惟一的发廊全部使用草本配方生产自己的洗发水和护发用品。 ● PRON-EMPH **All** is also an emphasizing pronoun. 全都 [n PRON v] ❑ *Milk, oily fish and eggs all contain vitamin D.* 牛奶、油性鱼类和鸡蛋全都含维他命D。

> **All** is often used to mean the same as **whole** but when used in front of plurals, **all** and **whole** have different meanings. For example, if you say "**All the buildings have been destroyed**," you mean that every building has been destroyed. If you say "**Whole buildings have been destroyed**," you mean that some buildings have been destroyed completely. Note that when **all** is used to consider a group, this means that the group has more than two members. To refer to two people or things, you use **both**. ❑ *Tony and Bob both laughed.* You use **every** to refer to all the members of a group that has more than two members. ❑ *He listened to every news bulletin. ...an equal chance for every child.* You use **each** to refer to every person or thing in a group when you are thinking about them as individuals. Note that **each** can be used to refer to both members of a pair. ❑ *Each apartment has two bedrooms... We each carried a suitcase.* Note that **each** and **every** are only used with singular nouns.

2 DET You use **all** to refer to the whole of a particular period of time. 整个 ❑ *George had to cut grass all afternoon.* 乔治不得不整个下午都割草。 ● PREDET **All** is also a predeterminer. 整个 [PREDET det sing-n] ❑ *She's worked all her life.* 她已经工作了一辈子。 ● QUANT **All** is also a quantifier. 整个 [QUANT "of" def-n] ❑ *He spent all of that afternoon polishing the silver.* 他花了那整个一下午擦银器。 3 PRON You use **all** to refer to a situation or to life in general. 一切 ❑ *All is silent on the island now.* 现在这个岛上一片寂静。 4 PHRASE **All but a** particular person or thing means everyone or everything except that person or thing. 除了…都 ❑ *The general was an unattractive man to all but his most ardent admirers.* 除了他的那些最热切的仰慕者以外，这位将军对于其他人并无吸引力。 5 PHRASE You use **all but** to say that something is almost the case. 差不多 ❑ *The concrete wall that used to divide this city has now all but gone.* 这堵曾经被用来分隔这座城市的水泥墙现在差不多不存在了。 6 PHRASE **In all** means in total. 总共 ❑ *There was evidence that thirteen people in all had taken part in planning the murder.* 有证据表明总共有13个人参与策划了这起谋杀。 7 PHRASE You use **all in all** to introduce a summary or general statement. 总之 ❑ *We both thought that all in all it might not be a bad idea.* 我们俩都认为总的来说这可能不是个坏主意。

❷ **all** ♦♦♦ /ɔl/ 1 DET You use **all** in expressions such as **in all sincerity** and **in all probability** to emphasize that you are being sincere or that something is very likely. 完全 (用来强调) [EMPHASIS]

❏ *In all fairness he had to admit that she was neither dishonest nor lazy.* 公正地说，他不得不承认她既非不诚实也非懒惰。 **2** PRON You use **all** at the beginning of a clause when you are emphasizing that something is the only thing that is important. 只是 (用在从句句首，表示强调) [EMPHASIS] ❏ *He said all that remained was to agree to a time and venue.* 他说剩下的只是同意一个时间和地点。 ❏ *All you ever want to do is going shopping!* 你想做的事情就是购物！ **3** ADV You use **all** to emphasize that something is completely true, or happens everywhere or always, or on every occasion. 完全地 [ADV prep/adv] [EMPHASIS] ❏ *He loves animals and he knows all about them.* 他热爱动物，并且对动物无所不知。 ❏ *He was doing it all by himself.* 全都是他独自一个人干的。 **4** ADV **All** is used in structures such as **all the more** or **all the better** to mean even more or even better than before. 更加 ❏ *The living room is decorated in pale colors that make it all the more airy.* 这个客厅用浅色装饰，显得更加清爽通风。 **5** PRON-EMPH You use **all** in expressions such as **seen it all** and **done it all** to emphasize that someone has had a lot of experience of something. 全都 [EMPHASIS] ❏ *They've seen it all, so it takes a lot to rattle them.* 他们已经全都见识过了，所以要费很大的劲儿才能让他们感到紧张。 **6** PHRASE You say **above all** to indicate that the thing you are mentioning is the most important point. 首先 [EMPHASIS] ❏ *Above all, chairs should be comfortable.* 首先椅子应该舒适。 **7** PHRASE You use **and all** when you want to emphasize that what you are talking about includes the thing mentioned, especially when this is surprising or unusual. 等等 [EMPHASIS] ❏ *He dropped his hot dog on the pavement and someone's dog ate it, mustard and all.* 他把热狗掉在了街上，然后不知谁的狗给吃了，连带芥末全都吃了个精光。 **8** PHRASE You use **at all** at the end of a clause to give emphasis in negative statements, conditional clauses, and questions. 根本 [EMPHASIS] ❏ *Robin never really liked him at all.* 罗宾根本从来没有真正喜欢过他。 **9** PHRASE You use **for all** in phrases such as **for all I know**, and **for all he cares**, to emphasize that you do not know something or that someone does not care about something. 强调对某事不了解、不在乎、无所谓 [EMPHASIS] ❏ *For all we know, he may not even be in this country.* 说不准，他或许都已不在这个国家了。 **10** PHRASE You use **of all** to emphasize the words "first" or "last," or a superlative adjective or adverb. 用来强调 **first**、**last**，或者最高级形容词或副词 [EMPHASIS] ❏ *First of all, answer these questions.* 首先，回答这些问题。 **11** PHRASE You use **of all** in expressions such as **of all people** or **of all things** when you want to emphasize someone or something surprising. 偏偏 [EMPHASIS] ❏ *One group of women, sitting on the ground, was singing, of all things, "Greensleeves."* 一群席地而坐的妇女偏偏在唱《绿袖子》。 **12** PHRASE You use **of all** in expressions like **of all the nerve** or **of all the luck** to emphasize how angry or surprised you are at what someone else has done or said. 竟然如此 [FEELINGS] ❏ *Of all the lazy, indifferent, unbusinesslike attitudes to have!* 竟然有如此懒惰、冷漠、不认真的态度！ **13** PHRASE You use **all of** before a number to emphasize how small or large an amount is. 足足有 [EMPHASIS] ❏ *It took him all of 41 minutes to score his first goal.* 用了足足有41分钟他才进了第一个球。

Word Partnership *all* 的常用搭配：

V.	**have** it all, **have seen** it all ❶ **1**
N.	all **ages**, all **kinds/sorts**, all **the way** ❶ **1**
	all **day/night**, all **the time** ❶ **2**
ADJ.	all **alone**, all **clear**, all **right** ❶ **3**
PREP.	**in** all ❶ **6**
	above all ❷ **6**
	at all ❷ **8**
	of all ❷ **10** – **12**
	all **of** ❷ **13**
	after all ❸ **2** **3**

❸ **all** ♦♦♦ /ɔl/ **1** ADV You use **all** when you are talking about an equal score in a game. For example, if the score is three **all**, both players or teams have three points. 打平地 [amount ADV] **2** PHRASE You use **after all** when introducing a statement that supports or helps explain something you have just said. 毕竟 ❏ *I thought you might know somebody. After all, you're the man with connections.* 我想你可能认识什么重要人物。毕竟，你交游甚广。 **3** PHRASE You use **after all** when you are saying that something that you thought might not be the case is in fact the case. 竟然 ❏ *I came out here on the chance of finding you at home after all.* 我到这儿来心想也许会在家找到你，没想到竟然还真是。

> Note that you do not use **after all** if you want to talk about what happens at the end of a long period, instead you use **at last**, **finally**, **in the end**, **lastly**, or **last of all**. You use **at last** or **finally** when you have been waiting for or expecting something for a long time. **At last** usually comes at the end of a sentence. ❏ *The storm that had threatened came at last.* **Finally** usually comes at the beginning of a sentence or before a verb. ❏ *After another search they finally located the house.* You also use **finally** to talk about something that is the last in a series of things. ❏ *He lived in Turkey, France, Norway, and finally Mexico.* You use **in the end** when talking about something that happens after a long time or a long process. ❏ *Perhaps the police got him in the end... In the end, Peter seemed quite happy.* You use **lastly** to talk about the last of a series of people or things. ❏ *I went through the bathroom, the bedroom, and lastly the living room.* You use **last of all** to emphasize that there is nobody or nothing else after the person or thing you mention. ❏ *Last of all came the cat.*

4 PHRASE You use **for all** to indicate that the thing mentioned does not affect or contradict the truth of what you are saying. 尽管 ❏ *For all its beauty, Prague could soon lose some of the individuality that the communist years helped to preserve.* 尽管布拉格美不胜收，但是它可能会很快失去在共产主义时期存留下来的一些特色。 **5** PHRASE You use **all that** in statements with negative meaning when you want to weaken the force of what you are saying. (没) 那么 [SPOKEN, VAGUENESS] ❏ *He wasn't all that much older than we were.* 他当时并不比我们大多少。 **6** PHRASE You can say **that's all** at the end of a sentence when you are explaining something and want to emphasize that nothing more happens or is the case. 就是这样 ❏ *"Why do you want to know that?" he demanded.—"Just curious, that's all."* "你为什么想了解它？"他索问道。——"只是好奇，仅此而已。" **7** PHRASE You use **all very well** to suggest that you do not really approve of something or you think that it is unreasonable. 好倒是好 [DISAPPROVAL] ❏ *It is all very well to urge people to give more to charity when they have less, but is it really fair?* 这样好倒是好，敦促人们给慈善机构更多东西，当他们自己却没那么多东西的时候，但是这真的公平吗？

all- /ɔl-/ **1** COMB IN ADJ **All-** is added to nouns or adjectives in order to form adjectives that describe something as consisting only of the thing mentioned or as having only the quality indicated. 全… (用于名词或形容词前构成形容词) [USU ADJ n] ❏ *The all-star cast includes Jeremy Irons.* 全明星演员阵容包括杰瑞米·艾恩斯在内。 **2** COMB IN ADJ **All-** is added to present participles or adjectives in order to form adjectives that describe something as including or affecting everything or everyone. 全面的 (用于现在分词或形容词前构成形容词) [USU ADJ n] ❏ *Nursing a demented person is an all-consuming task.* 护理一个精神错乱的人是一项非常耗力的任务。 **3** COMB IN ADJ **All-** is added to nouns in order to form adjectives that describe something as being suitable for or including all types of a particular thing. 适合或包括各种 (用于名词前构成形容词) [USU ADJ n] ❏ *He wanted to form an all-party government of national unity.* 他想要组建一个维护国家统一的多党执政政府。

Allah /ælə, ælɑ/ N-PROPER **Allah** is the name of God in Islam. 安拉 ❏ *Allah be praised!* 赞美安拉！

all-around **1** ADJ An **all-around** person is good at a lot of different skills, academic subjects, or sports. 全能的 [ADJ n] ❏ *He is a great all-around player.* 他是一位杰出的全能运动员。 **2** ADJ **All-around** means doing or relating to all aspects of a job or activity. 全面的 [ADJ n] ❏ *He demonstrated the all-around skills of a quarterback.* 他展示了一个四分卫的全面技能。

al·lay /əleɪ/ (**allays, allaying, allayed**) V-T If you **allay** someone's fears or doubts, you stop them feeling afraid or doubtful. 消除 (恐惧、疑虑) [FORMAL] ❏ *He did what he could to allay his wife's myriad fears.* 他尽其所能来消除他妻子的各种恐惧。

▲ **al·le·ga·tion** ♦◇◇ /ælɪgeɪʃᵊn/ (**allegations**) N-COUNT An **allegation** is a statement saying that someone has done something wrong. 指控 ❏ *The company has denied the allegations.* 该公司否认了这些指控。

Word Partnership *allegation* 的常用搭配：

V.	**deny an** allegation, **make an** allegation
PREP.	allegation **of**
CONJ.	allegation **that**

A

★ **al·lege** /əlɛ́dʒ/ (**alleges, alleging, alleged**) V-T If you **allege that** something bad is true, you say it but do not prove it. 指称(但还未被证实) [FORMAL] ❑ *She alleged that there was rampant drug use among the male members of the group.* 她指称该组织中有大量的男性成员吸毒。 ❑ *The accused is alleged to have killed a man.* 该被告据称杀了一个男子。

al·leged ◆◆◇ /əlɛ́dʒd/ ADJ An **alleged** fact has been stated but has not been proved to be true. 指称的 [ADJ n] [FORMAL] ❑ *They have begun a hunger strike in protest at the alleged beating.* 他们已经开始了绝食以抗议所指称的打人事件。 ● **al·leg·ed·ly** ★ /əlɛ́dʒɪdli/ ADV 指称地 ❑ *His van allegedly struck the two as they were crossing a street.* 据称，他的货车在这两个人过马路时撞上了他们。

Thesaurus *alleged* 另参见：
ADJ. questionable, supposed, suspicious; (*ant.*) certain, definite, sure

▲ **al·le·giance** /əlíːdʒəns/ (**allegiances**) N-VAR Your **allegiance** is your support for and loyalty to a particular group, person, or belief. 拥护 ❑ *My allegiance to Kendall and his company ran deep.* 我对肯达尔和他的公司的拥戴持久深厚。

al·ler·gic /əlɜ́rdʒɪk/ 1 ADJ If you are **allergic to** something, you become ill or get a rash when you eat it, smell it, or touch it. 过敏的 [v-link ADJ "to" n] ❑ *I'm allergic to cats.* 我对猫过敏。 2 ADJ If you have an **allergic** reaction to something, you become ill or get a rash when you eat it, smell it, or touch it. (反应) 过敏的 [ADJ n] ❑ *Soy milk can cause allergic reactions in some children.* 豆奶会导致有些儿童起过敏反应。

→ see **peanut**

▲ **al·ler·gy** /ǽlərdʒi/ (**allergies**) N-VAR If you have a particular **allergy**, you become ill or get a rash when you eat, smell, or touch something that does not normally make people ill. 过敏 ❑ *Food allergies can result in an enormous variety of different symptoms.* 食物过敏会导致大量不同种类的症状。

★ **al·le·vi·ate** /əlíːvieɪt/ (**alleviates, alleviating, alleviated**) V-T If you **alleviate** pain, suffering, or an unpleasant condition, you make it less intense or severe. 减轻(不适) [FORMAL] ❑ *Nowadays, a great deal can be done to alleviate back pain.* 如今，很多方法可以被用来减轻背部疼痛。 ● **al·le·via·tion** /əlìːvieɪʃən/ N-UNCOUNT 减轻 [usu N "of" n] ❑ *Their energies were focused on the alleviation of the refugees' misery.* 他们把精力集中在了对难民苦难的减轻上。

▲ **al·ley** /ǽli/ (**alleys**) N-COUNT An **alley** is a narrow passage or street with buildings or walls on both sides. 小巷

al·li·ance ◆◇◇ /əláɪəns/ (**alliances**) 1 N-COUNT An **alliance** is a group of countries or political parties that are formally united and working together because they have similar aims. 联盟 ❑ *The two parties were still too much apart to form an alliance.* 这两个党派分歧大得还不能形成联盟。 2 N-COUNT An **alliance** is a relationship in which two countries, political parties, or organizations work together for some purpose. 结盟 [oft N "with/between" n] ❑ *The Socialists' electoral strategy has been based on a tactical alliance with the Communists.* 社会党人的参选策略一直以和共产党人的战略性结盟为基础。

Word Partnership *alliance* 的常用搭配：
PREP. alliance **between**, alliance **with** 1 2
V. **form an** alliance 1 2
N. **members of an** alliance 1 2
ADJ. **military/political** alliance 1 2

al·lied ◆◇◇ /əláɪd/ 1 ADJ **Allied** forces or troops are armies from different countries who are fighting on the same side in a war. 盟国的 [ADJ n] ❑ *...the approaching Allied forces.* …正在逼近的同盟国军队。 2 ADJ **Allied** countries, troops, or political parties are united by a political or military agreement. 结盟的 [ADJ n, v-link ADJ "to" n] ❑ *...forces from three allied nations.* …三国同盟的军队。 3 ADJ If one thing or group is **allied to** another, it is related to it because the two things have particular qualities or characteristics in common. 有关联的 [v-link ADJ "to/with" n, ADJ n] ❑ *...lectures on subjects allied to health, beauty and fitness.* …与健康、美丽和健身主题相关的讲座。

al·li·ga·tor /ǽlɪgeɪtər/ (**alligators**) N-COUNT An **alligator** is a large reptile with short legs, a long tail, and very powerful jaws. 短吻鳄 ❑ *There are numerous signs warning people not to feed the alligators in the area.* 有很多标识警告人们不要在这个区域喂这些短吻鳄。

★ **al·lo·cate** /ǽləkeɪt/ (**allocates, allocating, allocated**) V-T If one item or share of something **is allocated to** a particular person or **for** a particular purpose, it is given to that person or used for that purpose. 分配 ❑ *Tickets are limited and will be allocated to those who apply first.* 票数有限，将分配给那些先申请的人。 ❑ *The 1985 federal budget allocated $7.3 billion for development programs.* 1985年联邦预算拨了73亿美元用于开发项目。

al·lo·ca·tion /æ̀ləkeɪʃən/ (**allocations**) 1 N-COUNT An **allocation** is an amount of something, especially money, that is given to a particular person or used for a particular purpose. (尤指经费) 配置 ❑ *A State Department spokeswoman said that the aid allocation for Pakistan was still under review.* 国务院的一位女发言人说对巴基斯坦的援助配置仍在审核之中。 2 N-UNCOUNT The **allocation** of something is the decision that it should be given to a particular person or used for a particular purpose. 分配决定 ❑ *Town planning and land allocation had to be coordinated.* 城镇规划和土地分配决定必须要协调。

▲ **al·lot** /əlɒ́t/ (**allots, allotting, allotted**) V-T If something **is allotted to** someone, it is given to them as their share. 分配 [usu passive] ❑ *The seats are allotted to the candidates who have won the most votes.* 这些席位被分配给了赢得了最多选票的候选人。

★ **al·lot·ment** /əlɒ́tmənt/ (**allotments**) N-COUNT An **allotment of** something is a share or amount of it that is given to someone. 份额 [oft N "of" n] ❑ *His meager allotment of gas had to be saved for emergencies.* 他的天然气的微薄份额必须省下以备急用。

all-out also **all out** ADJ You use **all-out** to describe actions that are carried out in a very energetic and determined way, using all the resources available. 竭尽全力的 [ADJ n] ❑ *He launched an all-out attack on his critics.* 他对他的批评者们发动了一场全力的攻击。

al·low ◆◆◆ /əláʊ/ (**allows, allowing, allowed**) 1 V-T If someone **is allowed to** do something, it is all right for them to do it and they will not get into trouble. 允许 ❑ *The children are allowed to watch TV after school.* 孩子们被允许在放学后看电视。 ❑ *Smoking will not be allowed.* 吸烟将被禁止。 2 V-T If you **are allowed** something, you are given permission to have it or are given it. 准许 ❑ *Gifts like chocolates or flowers are allowed.* 像巧克力或者花这样的礼物是准许的。 3 V-T If you **allow** something **to** happen, you do not prevent it. 容许 ❑ *He won't allow himself to fail.* 他不容许自己失败。 4 V-T If one thing **allows** another thing **to** happen, the first thing creates the opportunity for the second thing to happen. 使能够(发生) ❑ *The compromise will allow him to continue his free market reforms.* 这个妥协将使他得以继续他的自由市场改革。 ❑ *...an attempt to allow the Muslim majority a greater share of power.* …使穆斯林多数派分享更多权力的一种尝试。 5 V-T If you **allow** a particular length of time or a particular amount of something **for** a particular purpose, you include it in your planning. (在计划中) 酌留 ❑ *Please allow 28 days for delivery.* 请留出28天的送货时间。

▸ **allow for** PHRASAL VERB If you **allow for** certain problems or expenses, you include some extra time or money in your planning so that you can deal with them if they occur. (在计划中) 考虑到 ❑ *You have to allow for a certain amount of error.* 你必须考虑到一定数量的错误。

Thesaurus *allow* 另参见：
V. approve, consent, support, tolerate; (*ant.*) disallow, forbid, prohibit, prevent
let 3

Word Partnership *allow* 的常用搭配：
V. allow ***someone* to do *something*** 1
continue to allow, **refuse to** allow 1–3
N. allow **time** 5

al·low·ance /əláʊəns/ (**allowances**) 1 N-COUNT An **allowance** is money that is given to someone, usually on a regular basis, in order to help them pay for the things that they need. 补贴 ❑ *She gets an allowance for taking care of Amy.* 她因为照顾艾米而得到一笔补贴。 2 N-COUNT A child's **allowance** is money that is given to him or her every week or every month by his or her parents. 零花钱 [mainly AM]

in BRIT, use **pocket money**

❑ *When you give kids an allowance make sure they save some of it.* 给孩子们零花钱时，你一定要确保他们攒下一部分。 3 N-COUNT A particular type of **allowance** is an amount of something that you are allowed in particular circumstances. 限额 ❑ *Most of our flights have a baggage allowance of 44 lbs per passenger.* 我们大多数的航班行李限重为每位乘客44磅。 **4** N-COUNT Your tax **allowance** is the amount of money that you are allowed to earn before you have to start paying income tax. 免税额 [BRIT]

in AM, use **personal exemption**

5 PHRASE If you **make allowances for** something, you take it into account in your decisions, plans, or actions. 考虑到某事 ❑ *They'll make allowances for the fact it's affecting our performance.* 他们会将影响我们表现的事实情况考虑进去的。 ❑ *She tried to make allowances for his age.* 她试着顾及到他的年纪。 **6** PHRASE If you **make allowances for** someone, you accept behavior from them that you would not normally accept, because of a problem that they have. 体谅某人 ❑ *He's tired so I'll make allowances for him.* 他累了，所以我会体谅他的。

★ **al·loy** /ælɔɪ/ (**alloys**) N-MASS An **alloy** is a metal that is made by mixing two or more types of metal together. 合金 ❑ *Bronze is an alloy of copper and tin.* 青铜是一种铜锡合金。

all right ♦♦◇

in BRIT, also use **alright**

1 ADJ If you say that someone or something is **all right**, you mean that you find them satisfactory or acceptable. 还成的；认为可以的 [v-link ADJ] ❑ *I consider you a good friend, and if it's all right with you, I'd like to keep it that way.* 我把你看成一个好朋友，如果你认为可以的话，我想继续保持这样。 ● ADJ **All right** is also used before a noun. (在名词前) 还成的；认为可以的 [ADJ n] [INFORMAL] ❑ *He's an all right kind of guy really.* 其实他这个人还可以。 **2** ADJ If someone or something is **all right**, they are well or safe. 都好的；没事的 [v-link ADJ] ❑ *All she's worried about is whether he is all right.* 她所担心的只有他是否都好。 **3** ADV If you say that something happens or goes **all right**, you mean that it happens in a satisfactory or acceptable manner. (事情发生或进展) 令人满意地；可接受地 [ADV after v] ❑ *Things have thankfully worked out all right.* 谢天谢地事情的结果还可以。 **4** CONVENTION You say **"all right"** when you are agreeing to something. 好吧 [FORMULAE] ❑ *"I think you should go now."—"All right."* "我想你现在应该走了。"——"好吧。" **5** CONVENTION You say **"all right?"** after you have given an instruction or explanation to someone when you are checking that they have understood what you have just said, or checking that they agree with or accept what you have just said. 明白吗 ❑ *Peter, you get half the fees. All right?* 彼得，你得一半的钱。明白吗？ **6** CONVENTION If someone in a position of authority says **"all right,"** and suggests talking about or doing something else, they are indicating that they want you to end one activity and start another. 就这样吧 ❑ *All right, Bob. You can go now.* 鲍勃，就这样吧。你现在可以走了。 **7** CONVENTION You say **"all right"** during a discussion to show that you understand something that someone has just said, and to introduce a statement that relates to it. 好吧 ❑ *I said there was no room in my mother's house, and he said, "All right, come to my studio and paint."* 我说在我妈妈的家没有地方，然后他说："那好吧，到我的画室来画吧。" **8** CONVENTION You say **all right** before a statement or question to indicate that you are challenging or threatening someone. 哎 (用于陈述或疑问之前，表示责难或威胁某人) ❑ *All right, who are you and what are you doing in my office?* 哎，你是谁，在我的办公室干什么呢？

all-round [BRIT] → see **all-around**

all-time ADJ You use **all-time** when you are comparing all the things of a particular type that there have ever been. For example, if you say that something is the **all-time** best, you mean that it is the best thing of its type that there has ever been. 空前的 [ADJ n] ❑ *The president's popularity nationally is at an all-time low.* 总统在全国的声望处于历史最低点。

▲ **al·lude** /əlu̲d/ (**alludes, alluding, alluded**) V-I If you **allude to** something, you mention it in an indirect way. 暗指 [FORMAL] ❑ *With friends, she sometimes alluded to a feeling that she herself was to blame for her son's predicament.* 和朋友们一起时，她有时暗示她感到儿子的困境要怪她自己。

▲ **al·lure** /əlu̲ər/ N-UNCOUNT The **allure** of something or someone is the pleasing or exciting quality that they have. 魅力 ❑ *It's a game that has really lost its allure.* 这是一场已经真正失去其魅力的比赛。

al·lu·sion /əlu̲ʒən/ (**allusions**) N-VAR An **allusion** is an indirect reference to someone or something. 暗指 ❑ *This last point was understood to be an allusion to the long-standing hostility between the two leaders.* 这最后一点曾被理解为对这两位领导人之间长久敌意的一种影射。

ally ♦♦◇ (**allies, allying, allied**)

The noun is pronounced /ælaɪ/. The verb is pronounced /əla̲ɪ/.

名词读作 /ælaɪ/，动词读作 /əla̲ɪ/。

1 N-COUNT A country's **ally** is another country that has an agreement to support it, especially in war. 同盟国 ❑ *Washington would not take such a step without its allies' approval.* 没有其同盟国的赞同，华盛顿不会迈出这样的一步。 **2** N-COUNT If you describe someone as your **ally**, you mean that they help and support you, especially when other people are opposing you. 盟友 ❑ *He is a close ally of the president.* 他是总统的一位亲密盟友。 **3** N-PLURAL **The Allies** were the armed forces that fought against Germany and Japan in World War II. (二战时的) 同盟国 ❑ *...Germany's surrender to the Allies.* …德国向同盟国的投降。 **4** V-T If you **ally yourself with** someone or something, you give your support to them. 使结盟 ❑ *He will have no choice but to ally himself with the new movement.* 他将别无选择，只能与这个新运动结盟。 **5** → see also **allied**

▲ **al·mighty** /ɔlma̲ɪti/ **1** N-PROPER **The Almighty** is another name for God. You can also refer to **Almighty God**. 上帝 ❑ *Adam sought guidance from the Almighty.* 亚当向上帝寻求指导。 **2** EXCLAM People sometimes say **God Almighty** or **Christ Almighty** to express their surprise, anger, or horror. These expressions could cause offense. 天哪！ [FEELINGS]

al·mond /ɑ̲mənd, æm-, ælm-/ (**almonds**) **1** N-VAR **Almonds** are pale oval nuts. They are often used in cooking. 杏仁 ❑ *...sponge cake flavored with almonds.* …带杏仁味的松糕。 **2** N-VAR An **almond** or an **almond tree** is a tree on which almonds grow. 杏树 ❑ *On the left was a plantation of almond trees.* 在左边曾是一个杏树种植园。

al·most ♦♦♦ /ɔ̲lmoʊst/ ADV You use **almost** to indicate that something is not completely the case but is nearly the case. 差不多；几乎 ❑ *The couple had been dating for almost three years.* 这对情侣谈恋爱差不多三年了。 ❑ *The effect is almost impossible to describe.* 这影响几乎无法言表。 ❑ *He contracted Spanish flu, which almost killed him.* 他传染上了西班牙型流感，那几乎要了他的命。

Thesaurus *almost* 另参见：
ADV. about, most, practically, virtually

★ **aloft** /əlɔ̲ft/ ADV Something that is **aloft** is in the air or off the ground. 在空中 [ADV after v, "be" ADV] [LITERARY] ❑ *He held the trophy proudly aloft.* 他骄傲地把奖杯举向空中。

alone ♦♦◇ /əlo̲ʊn/ **1** ADJ When you are **alone**, you are not with any other people. 独自的 [v-link ADJ] ❑ *There is nothing so fearful as to be alone in a combat situation.* 没有比独自一人处于战斗环境中更可怕的事了。 ● ADV **Alone** is also an adverb. 独自地 [ADV after v] ❑ *She has lived alone in this house for almost five years now.* 她现在已经独自在这所房子里住了差不多五年了。 **2** ADJ If one person is **alone with** another person, or if two or more people are **alone**, they are together, without anyone else present. 独处的 [v-link ADJ] ❑ *I couldn't imagine why he would want to be alone with me.* 我想像不出他为什么想要和我独处。 **3** ADJ If you say that you are **alone** or feel **alone**, you mean that nobody who is with you, or nobody at all, cares about you. 孤独的 [v-link ADJ] ❑ *Never in her life had she felt so alone, so abandoned.* 她一辈子从没有感到过如此孤独、如此被抛弃。 **4** ADJ If someone is **alone in** doing something, they are the only person doing it, and so are different from other people. 惟一的 [v-link ADJ] ❑ *Am I alone in recognizing that these two statistics have quite different implications?* 惟独我看出这两个统计有完全不同含意吗？ ● ADV **Alone** is also an adverb. 惟一地 ❑ *I alone was sane, I thought, in a world of crazy people.* 我以为在这个狂人的世界中我是惟一清醒的。 **5** ADV You say that one person or thing **alone** does something when you are emphasizing that only one person or thing is involved. 只有 [n ADV] [EMPHASIS] ❑ *You alone should determine what is right for you.* 只有你应该决定什么对你是合适的。 **6** ADV If you say that one person or thing **alone** is responsible for part of an amount, you are emphasizing the size of that part and the size of the total amount. 单单 [n ADV] [EMPHASIS] ❑ *CNN alone is sending 300 technicians, directors and commentators.* 仅有线电视新闻网就派了300名技师、导演和实况播音员。 **7** ADV When someone does something **alone**, they do it without help from other people. 独力地 [ADV after v] ❑ *Bringing up a child alone should give you a sense of achievement.* 独力一人养大一个孩子会给你一种成就感。 **8** PHRASE If you **go it alone**, you do something without any help from other people. 单干 [INFORMAL] ❑ *I missed the stimulation of*

A

working with others when I tried to go it alone. 当我试着自己单干时，我想念和别人一起工作的那种刺激。 **9** to **leave** someone or something **alone** → see **leave** **10** **let alone** → see **let**

Thesaurus *alone* 另参见：
ADJ. solitary, unaccompanied; *(ant.)* crowded, together **1** friendless **3**

along ♦♦♦ /əlɔŋ/

In addition to the uses shown below, **along** is used in phrasal verbs such as "go along with," "play along," and "string along."

1 PREP If you move or look **along** something such as a road, you move or look toward one end of it. 沿着 ❑ *Pedro walked along the street alone.* 佩德罗独自一人沿着这条街走。 ❑ *The young man led Mark Ryle along a corridor.* 那个青年男子带着马克・赖尔沿着一条走廊走。 **2** PREP If something is situated **along** a road, river, or corridor, it is situated in it or beside it. 在…里；在…边上 ❑ *...enormous traffic jams all along the roads.* …各条道路上严重的交通堵塞。 **3** ADV When someone or something moves **along**, they keep moving in a particular direction. 向前地 [ADV after v] ❑ *She skipped and danced along.* 她向前蹦跳着、舞蹈着。 ❑ *He raised his voice a little, talking into the wind as they walked along.* 当他们向前走时，他提高了一点儿嗓门，迎风讲着话。 **4** ADV If you say that something is going **along** in a particular way, you mean that it is progressing in that way. 一直 [ADV after v] ❑ *...the negotiations which have been dragging along interminably.* …这场一直以来无限地拖沓着的谈判。 **5** ADV If you take someone or something **along** when you go somewhere, you take them with you. 一起地 [ADV after v] ❑ *This is open to women of all ages, so bring along your friends and colleagues.* 这对所有年龄的妇女开放，所以带你的朋友和同事一起来。 **6** ADV If someone or something is coming **along** or is sent **along**, they are coming or being sent to a particular place. 与"来"或"去"搭配，表示来或去某一地方 [ADV after v] ❑ *She invited everyone she knew to come along.* 她邀请了所有认识的人过来。 **7** PHRASE You use **along with** to mention someone or something else that is also involved in an action or situation. 同…一起 ❑ *The baby's mother escaped from the fire along with two other children.* 这个婴儿的母亲和其他两个孩子一起从火里逃了出来。 **8** PHRASE If something has been true or been present **all along**, it has been true or been present throughout a period of time. 一直 ❑ *I've been fooling myself all along.* 我一直在骗我自己。 **9** **along the way** → see **way**

along·side ♦◇◇ /əlɔŋsaɪd/ **1** PREP If one thing is **alongside** another thing, the first thing is next to the second. 在…旁边 ❑ *He crossed the street and walked alongside Central Park.* 他过了马路，然后在中央公园旁边走着。 ● ADV **Alongside** is also an adverb. 在旁边 [ADV after v] ❑ *He waited several minutes for a car to pull up alongside.* 他等了几分钟等一辆车停靠在旁边。 **2** PREP If you work **alongside** other people, you all work together in the same place. 与…并肩（工作） ❑ *He had worked alongside Frank and Mark and they had become friends.* 他曾与弗兰克和马克并肩工作过，他们已经成为朋友了。

aloof /əluf/ ADJ Someone who is **aloof** is not very friendly and does not like to spend time with other people. 冷淡的 [DISAPPROVAL] ❑ *He seemed aloof and detached.* 他看起来冷淡且超然。

aloud /əlaʊd/ **1** ADV When you say something, read, or laugh **aloud**, you speak or laugh so that other people can hear you. 大声地 [ADV after v] ❑ *When we were children, our father read aloud to us.* 当我们是孩子时，我们的父亲大声地朗读给我们听。 **2** PHRASE If you **think aloud**, you express your thoughts as they occur to you, rather than thinking first and then speaking. 边想边说出 ❑ *He really must be careful about thinking aloud. Who knew what he might say?* 他真地得对自言自语小心点。谁知道他可能会说什么？

al·pha·bet /ælfəbɛt, -bɪt/ **(alphabets)** N-COUNT An **alphabet** is a set of letters usually presented in a fixed order which is used for writing the words of a particular language or group of languages. 字母表 ❑ *The modern Russian alphabet has 31 letters.* 现代俄语字母表有31个字母。

al·pha·beti·cal /ælfəbɛtɪkᵊl/ ADJ **Alphabetical** means arranged according to the normal order of the letters in the alphabet. 按字母顺序的 [ADJ n] ❑ *Their herbs and spices are arranged in alphabetical order on narrow open shelves.* 他们的草药和调味品按照字母顺序列在狭窄、开放的架子上。

al·pine /ælpaɪn/ ADJ **Alpine** means existing in or relating to mountains, especially the ones in Switzerland. （尤指瑞士境内的）高山的 ❑ *...grassy, alpine meadows.* …绿草茂盛的高山草甸。

al·ready ♦♦♦ /ɔlrɛdi/ **1** ADV You use **already** to show that something has happened, or that something had happened before the moment you are referring to. Some speakers use **already** with the simple past tense of the verb instead of a perfect tense. 已经 ❑ *They had already voted for him at the first ballot.* 他们已经在第一轮投票中投了他的票。 ❑ *She says she already told the neighbors not to come over for a couple of days.* 她说她已经告诉了邻居们这两天不要过来。 **2** ADV You use **already** to show that a situation exists at this present moment or that it exists at an earlier time than expected. You use **already** after the verb "be" or an auxiliary verb, or before a verb if there is no auxiliary. When you want to add emphasis, you can put **already** at the beginning of a sentence. 早已 ❑ *The authorities believe those security measures are already paying off.* 当局相信那些安全措施已经在起作用了。 ❑ *He was already rich.* 他早就富了。 ❑ *Already, she is thinking ahead.* 她早就在考虑未来了。

Already is often used to add emphasis or to suggest that it is surprising that something has happened so soon. ❑ *They were already eating their lunch.* If you say that something is **still** happening or is **still** the case, you are usually emphasizing your surprise that it has been happening or has been the case for so long. ❑ *She was still looking at me... There are still plenty of horses around here.* You use **yet** in negative sentences and in questions. It is often used to add emphasis, to suggest surprise that something has not happened, or to say that it will happen later. ❑ *Have you seen it yet?... The troops could not yet see the shore... It isn't dark yet.* In British English, **already** and **yet** are usually used with the present perfect tense. ❑ *I have already started knitting baby clothes... Have they said sorry yet?* In American English, a past tense is commonly used. ❑ *She already told the neighbors not to come... I didn't get any sleep yet.* This usage is becoming more common in British English.

al·right /ɔlraɪt/ [BRIT] → see **all right**

also ♦♦♦ /ɔlsoʊ/ **1** ADV You can use **also** to give more information about a person or thing, or to add another relevant fact. 还 ❑ *The book also includes an appendix with a listing of all U.S. presidents.* 这本书还包含一个列有所有美国总统的附录。 ❑ *He is an asthmatic who is also anemic.* 他是一个哮喘病人，并且还贫血。 **2** ADV You can use **also** to indicate that something you have just said about one person or thing is true of another person or thing. 也 ❑ *General Geichenko was a survivor. His father, also a top-ranking officer, had perished during the war.* 格晨科将军是一位幸存者。他的父亲也是一位高级军官，在战争中丧生了。 ❑ *This rule has also been applied in the case of a purchase of used tires and tubes.* 这个规定也已经用于购买使用过的轮胎和内胎。

Also and **too** are similar in meaning. **Also** never comes at the end of a clause, whereas **too** usually comes at the end. ❑ *He was also an artist and lived in Cleveland... He's a singer and an actor too.*

Thesaurus *also* 另参见：
ADV. additionally, furthermore, plus, still **1** and, likewise, too **2**

Word Link *alt ≈ high : altar, altitude, exalted*

al·tar /ɔltər/ **(altars)** N-COUNT An **altar** is a holy table in a church or temple. 圣坛 ❑ *...the high altar of the cathedral.* …这个大教堂的高耸的圣坛。

al·ter ♦◇◇ /ɔltər/ **(alters, altering, altered)** V-T/V-I If something **alters** or if you **alter** it, it changes. 更改 ❑ *Nothing has altered and the deadline still stands.* 什么也没有更改，最后期限依然有效。

al·tera·tion /ɔltəreɪʃᵊn/ **(alterations)** **1** N-COUNT An **alteration** is a change in or to something. 改动 ❑ *Making some simple alterations to your diet will make you feel fitter.* 对你的饮食做一些简单的改变会使你感觉更健康。 **2** N-UNCOUNT The **alteration** of something is the process of changing it. 改变 ❑ *Her jacket was at the boutique waiting for alteration.* 她的夹克在服装精品店里等待修改。

★ **al·ter·nate** **(alternates, alternating, alternated)**

The verb is pronounced /ɔltərneɪt/. The adjective and noun are pronounced /ɔltɜrnɪt/.

动词读作 /ɔltərneɪt/。形容词和名词读作 /ɔltɜrnɪt/。

1 V-RECIP When you **alternate** two things, you keep using one then the other. When one thing **alternates with** another, the first regularly occurs after the other. 交替 ❑ *Her aggressive moods alternated with gentle or more cooperative states.* 她的挑衅情绪与温和或更为合作的情绪互相交替。 ❑ *Now you just alternate layers of that mixture and eggplant.* 现在你只用把那种混合物与茄子一层层交叠起来。 **2** ADJ **Alternate** actions, events, or processes regularly occur after each other. 交替的 [ADJ n] ❑ *They were streaked with alternate bands of color.* 他们都带有色彩交替相间的条纹。 ●**al·ter·nate·ly** ADV 交替地 ❑ *He could alternately bully and charm people.* 他能时而欺负人，时而吸引人。 **3** ADJ If something happens on **alternate** days, it happens on one day, then happens on every second day after that. In the same way, something can happen in **alternate** weeks, years, or other periods of time. 间隔的 [ADJ n] ❑ *Lesley had agreed to Jim going skiing in alternate years.* 莱斯丽已经同意了吉姆隔年去滑雪。 **4** ADJ You use **alternate** to describe a plan, idea, or system which is different from the one already in operation and can be used instead of it. 供替换的 [ADJ n] ❑ *His group was forced to turn back and take an alternate route.* 他的小组被迫返回并采用了替代路线。 **5** N-COUNT An **alternate** is a person or thing that replaces another, and can act or be used instead of them. 替补 [AM] ❑ *In most jurisdictions, twelve jurors and two alternates are chosen.* 在大多数审判中，12名陪审员和2名替补人员会被选出。

al·ter·na·tive ♦♦◊ /ɔltɜrnətɪv/ **(alternatives)** **1** N-COUNT If one thing is an **alternative to** another, the first can be found, used, or done instead of the second. 替代品 ❑ *New ways to treat arthritis may provide an alternative to painkillers.* 治疗关节炎的新方法可能会提供一种止痛药的替代品。 **2** ADJ An **alternative** plan or offer is different from the one that you already have, and can be done or used instead. 另外的 [ADJ n] ❑ *There were alternative methods of travel available.* 有另外的旅行方式可采用。 **3** ADJ **Alternative** is used to describe something that is different from the usual things of its kind, or the usual ways of doing something, in modern Western society. For example, an **alternative** lifestyle does not follow conventional ways of living and working. 另类的 [ADJ n] ❑ *...unconventional parents who embraced the alternative lifestyle of the Sixties.* …信奉60年代另类生活方式的与众不同的家长们。 **4** ADJ **Alternative** medicine uses traditional ways of curing people, such as medicines made from plants, massage, and acupuncture. 替代性的（疗法）[ADJ n] ❑ *...alternative health care.* …替代性保健。 **5** ADJ **Alternative** energy uses natural sources of energy such as the sun, wind, or water for power and fuel, rather than oil, coal, or nuclear power. 可再生的（能源）[ADJ n]

al·ter·na·tive·ly /ɔltɜrnətɪvli/ ADV You use **alternatively** to introduce a suggestion or to mention something different from what has just been stated. 或者 [ADV with cl] ❑ *Hotels are generally of a good standard and not too expensive. Alternatively you could stay in an apartment.* 旅馆一般标准高并且不太贵。或者你可以住公寓。

al·though ♦♦♦ /ɔlðoʊ/ **1** CONJ You use **although** to introduce a subordinate clause which contains a statement that contrasts with the statement in the main clause. 尽管 ❑ *Although he is known to only a few, his reputation among them is very great.* 尽管只有几个人知道他，但是他在他们之中的名声很大。 **2** CONJ You use **although** to introduce a subordinate clause which contains a statement that makes the main clause of the sentence seem surprising or unexpected. 虽然 ❑ *Although I was only six, I can remember seeing it on TV.* 虽然当时我只有6岁，我还能记得在电视上看见过它。 **3** CONJ You use **although** to introduce a subordinate clause which gives some information that is relevant to the main clause but modifies the strength of that statement. 虽然 ❑ *He was in love with her, although a man seldom puts that name to what he feels.* 他爱上了她，虽然一个男人很少用这个词来形容他的感受。 **4** CONJ You use **although** when admitting a fact about something that you regard as less important than a contrasting fact. 尽管 ❑ *Although they're expensive, they last forever and never go out of style.* 尽管它们贵，它们永远耐用并且永不过时。

Thesaurus *although* 另参见：
CONJ. despite, though, while **1** – **4**

al·ti·tude /æltɪtud/ **(altitudes)** N-VAR If something is at a particular **altitude**, it is at that height above sea level. 海拔高度 ❑ *The aircraft had reached its cruising altitude of about 39,000 feet.* 那架飞机已经达到了大约三万九千英尺的巡航高度。

al·to·geth·er ♦◊◊ /ɔltəgɛðər/ **1** ADV You use **altogether** to emphasize that something has stopped, been done, or finished completely. 完全地 [ADV after v] [EMPHASIS] ❑ *When Artie stopped calling altogether, Julie found a new man.* 当阿蒂彻底不再来拜访后，朱莉又找了个男人。 **2** ADV You use **altogether** in front of an adjective or adverb to emphasize a quality that someone or something has. 全然地 [ADV adj/adv] [EMPHASIS] ❑ *The choice of language is altogether different.* 语言的选择全然不同。 **3** ADV You use **altogether** to modify a negative statement and make it less forceful. （修饰否定陈述以减轻语气）十分 ❑ *We were not altogether sure that the comet would miss the Earth.* 我们不太确定这颗彗星是否会错过地球。 **4** ADV You can use **altogether** to introduce a summary of what you have been saying. 总体上讲 [ADV with cl] ❑ *Altogether, it was a delightful town garden, peaceful and secluded.* 总体来说，这是一个赏心悦目的城市花园，安静而幽僻。 **5** ADV If several amounts add up to a particular amount **altogether**, that amount is their total. 总共地 [ADV with amount] ❑ *Brando received eight Oscar nominations altogether.* 白兰度总共获得了8次奥斯卡提名。

al·tru·ism /æltruɪzəm/ N-UNCOUNT **Altruism** is unselfish concern for other people's happiness and welfare. 利他主义 ❑ *Fortunately, volunteers are not motivated by self-interest, but by altruism.* 幸运的是，志愿者们不是被自身利益而是被利他主义推动。

alu·min·ium /ælyumɪniəm/ [BRIT] → see **aluminum**

alu·mi·num /əluminəm/ N-UNCOUNT **Aluminum** is a lightweight metal used, for example, for making cooking equipment and aircraft parts. 铝 [AM] ❑ *...aluminum cans.* …一些铝罐。

al·ways ♦♦♦ /ɔlweɪz/ **1** ADV If you **always** do something, you do it whenever a particular situation occurs. If you **always** did something, you did it whenever a particular situation occurred. 总是；每次 [ADV before v] ❑ *She's always late for everything.* 她总是每件事都迟到。 ❑ *Always lock your garage.* 每次都要锁好你的车库。 **2** ADV If something is **always** the case, was **always** the case, or will **always** be the case, it is, was, or will be the case all the time, continuously. 永远地 ❑ *We will always remember his generous hospitality.* 我们将永远记住他的慷慨好客。 ❑ *He has always been the family solicitor.* 他一直是这个家的律师。 **3** ADV If you say that something is **always** happening, especially something that annoys you, you mean that it happens repeatedly. 老是 [ADV before v-cont] ❑ *She was always moving things around.* 她老是把东西挪来挪去。 **4** ADV You use **always** in expressions such as **can always** or **could always** when you are making suggestions or suggesting an alternative approach or method. （用于提出建议或替换方案）总还 ["can/could" ADV inf] ❑ *If you can't find any decent apples, you can always try growing them yourself.* 如果你找不到任何像样的苹果，你总还可以试着自己种。 **5** ADV You can say that someone **always** was, for example, awkward or lucky to indicate that you are not surprised about what they are doing or have just done. 一向以来地 [ADV before v] ❑ *She's going to be fine. She always was pretty strong.* 她一切都会好的。她一向以来都挺坚强。

Do not confuse **always** and **ever**. If something **always** happens, it happens regularly or on every occasion. ❑ *I would always ask for the radio to be turned down... He's always been an active person.* If something is **always** the case, it is true at all times. ❑ *No matter what she did, she would always be forgiven.* You use **ever**, for example in negative sentences, questions, and with superlatives, to talk about any time at all when referring to the past, present, or future. ❑ *No one ever came... Will I ever see France? ...the nicest thing anyone's ever said to me.*

Thesaurus *always* 另参见：
ADV. consistently, constantly, regularly, repeatedly **1** **3**
continuously, endlessly; *(ant.)* never, rarely **2**

am /əm, STRONG æm/ **Am** is the first person singular of the present tense of **be**. **Am** is often shortened to **'m** in spoken English. The negative forms are "I am not" and "I'm not." In questions and tags in spoken English, these are usually changed to "aren't I." **be**的现在时第一人称单数形式

AM /eɪ ɛm/ **AM** is a method of transmitting radio waves that can be used to broadcast sound. **AM** is an abbreviation for 'amplitude modulation.' 调幅

a.m. /eɪ ɛm/ also **am** **a.m.** is used after a number to show that you are referring to a particular time between midnight and

A

noon. Compare **p.m.** 上午 ❑ *The program starts at 9 a.m.* 这个节目上午9点开始。

amal·gam·ate /əmælgəmeɪt/ (**amalgamates, amalgamating, amalgamated**) V-RECIP When two or more things, especially organizations, **amalgamate** or **are amalgamated**, they become one large thing. 合并 ❑ *The firm has amalgamated with another company.* 这家公司已经与另一家公司合并了。❑ *The chemical companies had amalgamated into a vast conglomerate.* 这些化学公司已经合并成了一个巨型企业集团。● **amal·gama·tion** /əmælgəmeɪʃᵊn/ N-VAR (**amalgamations**) 合并 ❑ *Athletics South Africa was formed by an amalgamation of two organizations.* 南非体育委员会是由两个组织的合并形成的。

▲ **amass** /əmæs/ (**amasses, amassing, amassed**) V-T If you **amass** something such as money or information, you gradually get a lot of it. 聚集 ❑ *How had he amassed his fortune?* 他是如何聚集起他的财富的?

Word Link *eur ≈ one who does : amateur, chauffeur, entrepreneur*

ama·teur ♦◇◇ /æmətʃɜr, -tʃʊər/ (**amateurs**) 1 N-COUNT An **amateur** is someone who does something as a hobby and not as a job. 业余爱好者 ❑ *Jerry is an amateur who dances because he feels like it.* 杰瑞是一位业余舞蹈爱好者，他跳舞因为他喜欢跳。 2 ADJ **Amateur** sports or activities are done by people as a hobby and not as a job. 业余的 [ADJ n] ❑ *...professional athletes and amateur runners.* …专业运动员和业余赛跑运动员。

amaze /əmeɪz/ (**amazes, amazing, amazed**) V-T/V-I If something **amazes** you, it surprises you very much. 使吃惊；感到惊讶 ❑ *He amazed us by his knowledge of Colorado history.* 他对于科罗拉多州历史的了解让我们吃惊。❑ *The "Riverside" restaurant promises a variety of food that never ceases to amaze!* "河畔"餐厅承诺提供永远给人惊奇的多种食品。● **amazed** ADJ 吃惊的 ❑ *Most of the cast was amazed by the play's success.* 演员班子中的大多数人对这出戏的成功感到吃惊。

Word Partnership *amaze* 的常用搭配:
V. **continue to** amaze, **never cease to** amaze
N. amaze **your friends**

amaze·ment /əmeɪzmənt/ N-UNCOUNT **Amazement** is the feeling you have when something surprises you very much. 吃惊 [oft "in" N] ❑ *I stared at her in amazement.* 我惊讶地盯着她。

amaz·ing ♦◇◇ /əmeɪzɪŋ/ ADJ You say that something is **amazing** when it is very surprising and makes you feel pleasure, approval, or wonder. 令人惊诧的 ❑ *It's amazing what we can remember with a little prompting.* 只需一点提示我们就能想起很多东西真是令人吃惊。● **amaz·ing·ly** ADV 令人惊诧地 ❑ *She was an amazingly good cook.* 她曾是个好得惊人的厨师。

Thesaurus *amazing* 另参见:
ADJ. astonishing, astounding, extraordinary, incredible, stunning, wonderful

am·bas·sa·dor ♦◇◇ /æmbæsədər/ (**ambassadors**) N-COUNT An **ambassador** is an important official who lives in a foreign country and represents his or her own country's interests there. 大使 ❑ *...the German ambassador to Poland.* …德国驻波兰大使。

am·ber /æmbər/ 1 N-UNCOUNT **Amber** is a hard yellowish-brown substance used for making jewelry. 琥珀 [usu N n] ❑ *...an amber choker with matching earrings.* …一条琥珀贴颈短项链和相配的耳环。 2 COLOR **Amber** is used to describe things that are yellowish-brown in color. 琥珀色(的) ❑ *A burst of sunshine sent a beam of amber light through the window.* 一道阳光透过窗户射进了一束琥珀色的光。 3 COLOR An **amber** traffic light is yellow. 黄色(的) ❑ *Cars did not stop when the lights were on amber.* 当交通灯是黄色时汽车没有停下来。

am·bi·ence /æmbiəns/ also **ambiance** N-SING The **ambience** of a place is the character and atmosphere that it seems to have. 氛围 [LITERARY] ❑ *The overall ambience of the room is cozy.* 这个房间的整体氛围是舒适的。

★ **am·bi·gu·ity** /æmbɪgyuɪti/ (**ambiguities**) N-VAR If you say that there is **ambiguity** in something, you mean that it is unclear or confusing, or it can be understood in more than one way. 模棱两可 ❑ *There is considerable ambiguity about what this part of the agreement actually means.* 关于协议这一部分到底是什么意思存在着相当大的含混不清。

★ **am·bigu·ous** /æmbɪgyuəs/ ADJ If you describe something as **ambiguous**, you mean that it is unclear or confusing because it can be understood in more than one way. 模棱两可的 ❑ *This agreement is very ambiguous and open to various interpretations.* 这个协议非常模棱两可，可以有多种解释。● **am·bigu·ous·ly** ADV 模棱两可地 ❑ *The national conference on democracy ended ambiguously.* 这次全国民主大会含糊其词地结束了。

am·bi·tion ♦◇◇ /æmbɪʃᵊn/ (**ambitions**) 1 N-COUNT If you have an **ambition to** do or achieve something, you want very much to do it or achieve it. 理想 ❑ *His ambition is to sail around the world.* 他的理想是航行环游世界。 2 N-UNCOUNT **Ambition** is the desire to be successful, rich, or powerful. 雄心 ❑ *Even when I was young I never had any ambition.* 即使当我年轻的时候我也从未有过什么雄心。

am·bi·tious /æmbɪʃəs/ 1 ADJ Someone who is **ambitious** has a strong desire to be successful, rich, or powerful. 雄心勃勃的 ❑ *Chris is so ambitious, so determined to do it all.* 克里斯是如此雄心勃勃，如此坚决地要把它做完。 2 ADJ An **ambitious** idea or plan is on a large scale and needs a lot of work to be carried out successfully. 宏大的 ❑ *The ambitious project was completed in only nine months.* 这个宏大的项目在仅仅9个月之内就完成了。

Thesaurus *ambitious* 另参见:
ADJ. aspiring 1
challenging, difficult 2

am·biva·lent /æmbɪvələnt/ ADJ If you say that someone is **ambivalent about** something, they seem to be uncertain whether they really want it, or whether they really approve of it. 暧昧的 ❑ *She remained ambivalent about her marriage.* 她对她的婚姻保持暧昧的态度。

am·bu·lance /æmbyələns/ (**ambulances**) N-COUNT An **ambulance** is a vehicle for taking people to and from a hospital. 救护车 [also "by" N]

▲ **am·bush** /æmbʊʃ/ (**ambushes, ambushing, ambushed**) 1 V-T If a group of people **ambush** their enemies, they attack them after hiding and waiting for them. 伏击 ❑ *The Guatemalan army says rebels ambushed and killed 10 patrolmen.* 危地马拉军方称叛军伏击并杀死了10名巡逻兵。 2 N-VAR An **ambush** is an attack on someone by people who have been hiding and waiting for them. 伏击 ❑ *Three civilians were killed in guerrilla ambushes.* 3名平民在游击队的伏击中丧生。

amen /ɑmɛn, eɪ-/ CONVENTION **Amen** is said by Christians at the end of a prayer. 阿门 ❑ *In the name of the Father and of the Son and of the Holy Ghost, amen.* 以圣父、圣子和圣灵的名义，阿门。

ame·nable /əminəbᵊl, əmɛnə-/ ADJ If you are **amenable to** something, you are willing to do it or accept it. 愿意的 ❑ *The Jordanian leader seemed amenable to attending a conference.* 约旦的领袖看起来愿意去参加一个会议。

★ **amend** /əmɛnd/ (**amends, amending, amended**) 1 V-T If you **amend** something that has been written such as a law, or something that is said, you change it in order to improve it or make it more accurate. 修正 ❑ *The president agreed to amend the constitution and allow multi-party elections.* 总统同意了修正宪法并且允许多党选举。 2 PHRASE If you **make amends** when you have harmed someone, you show that you are sorry by doing something to please them. 做补偿 ❑ *He wanted to make amends for causing their marriage to fail.* 他想为一手造成他们婚姻的破裂做出补偿。

amend·ment ♦◇◇ /əmɛndmənt/ (**amendments**) 1 N-VAR An **amendment** is a section that is added to a law or rule in order to change it. 修正案 ❑ *...an amendment to the defense bill.* …对辩护法案的一条修正案。 2 N-COUNT An **amendment** is a change that is made to a piece of writing. 修改

amen·ity /əmɛnɪti/ (**amenities**) N-COUNT **Amenities** are things such as shopping centers or sports facilities that are provided for people's convenience, enjoyment, or comfort. 便利设施 [usu pl] ❑ *The hotel amenities include health clubs, conference facilities, and banqueting rooms.* 这家旅馆的设施包括健身俱乐部、会议设备和宴会厅。→ see **hotel**

Ameri·can foot·ball (**American footballs**) 1 N-UNCOUNT **American football** is a game that is played by two teams of eleven players using an oval-shaped ball. Players try to score points by passing or carrying the ball to their opponents' end of the field, or by kicking it over a bar fixed between two posts. 美式橄榄球运动 [BRIT] in AM, use **football**

2 N-COUNT An **American football** is an oval-shaped ball used for playing American football. 美式橄榄球 [BRIT]

in AM, use **football**

▲ **ami·able** /eɪmiəbᵊl/ ADJ Someone who is **amiable** is friendly and pleasant to be with. 和蔼可亲的 [WRITTEN] ❑ *She had been surprised at how amiable and polite he had been.* 她对他如此和蔼可亲、彬彬有礼感到了惊讶。

ami·cable /æmɪkəbᵊl/ ADJ When people have an **amicable** relationship, they are pleasant to each other and solve their problems without quarreling. 友好的 ❑ *The meeting ended on reasonably amicable terms.* 这次会议在相当友好的氛围中结束。

● **ami·cably** /æmɪkəbli/ ADV 友好地 [ADV with v] ❑ *He hoped the dispute could be settled amicably.* 他希望这次纠纷能友好地得到解决。

amid ♦◊◊ /əmɪd/

The form **amidst** is also used, but is old-fashioned.

PREP If something happens **amid** noises or events of some kind, it happens while the other things are happening. 在…当中 ❑ *Workers are sifting through the wreckage of the airliners amid growing evidence that the disasters were the work of terrorists.* 在越来越多证据证明这些灾难是恐怖分子所为的同时，工人们正在仔细检查那些客机的残骸。

amiss /əmɪs/ ADJ If you say that something is **amiss**, you mean there is something wrong. 出差错的 [v-link ADJ] ❑ *Their instincts warned them something was amiss.* 他们的直觉警告他们某些地方不对头。

am·mo·nia /əmoʊniə/ N-UNCOUNT **Ammonia** is a colorless liquid or gas with a strong, sharp smell. It is used in making household cleaning substances. 氨; 氨水

★ **am·mu·ni·tion** /æmyunɪʃᵊn/ 1 N-UNCOUNT **Ammunition** is bullets and rockets that are made to be fired from weapons. 弹药 ❑ *He had only seven rounds of ammunition for the revolver.* 他只有7发左轮手枪的弹药。 2 N-UNCOUNT You can describe information that you can use against someone in an argument or discussion as **ammunition**. (可用于争辩的) 论据 ❑ *The improved trade figures have given the government fresh ammunition.* 增长的贸易数据为政府提供了新的论据。

am·ne·sia /æmniʒə/ N-UNCOUNT If someone is suffering from **amnesia**, they have lost their memory. 失忆症 ❑ *People suffering from amnesia don't forget their general knowledge of objects.* 患有失忆症的人不会忘记他们对物品的常识。

am·nes·ty /æmnɪsti/ (**amnesties**) 1 N-VAR An **amnesty** is an official pardon granted to a group of prisoners by the state. 赦免 ❑ *Activists who were involved in crimes of violence will not automatically be granted amnesty.* 参与暴力犯罪的活跃分子不会被自动地给予赦免。 2 N-COUNT An **amnesty** is a period of time during which people can admit to a crime or give up weapons without being punished. 赦免时段 ❑ *The government has announced an immediate amnesty for rebel fighters.* 政府已经宣布了一个对叛军战士的即刻赦免时段。

among ♦♦♦ /əmʌŋ/

The form **amongst** is also used, but is more old-fashioned.

1 PREP Someone or something that is situated or moving **among** a group of things or people is surrounded by them. 在…当中 ❑ *...youths in their late teens sitting among adults.* …坐在成年人当中的十八九岁的青年们。 ❑ *They walked among the crowds in Red Square.* 他们走在红场上的人群之中。 2 PREP If you are **among** people of a particular kind, you are with them and having contact with them. 与…在一起 ❑ *Things weren't so bad, after all. I was among friends again.* 情况毕竟没有那么糟。我又和朋友们在一起了。 3 PREP If someone or something is **among** a group, they are a member of that group and share its characteristics. …之一 ❑ *A fifteen year old girl was among the injured.* 一个15岁的女孩是受伤人员之一。 4 PREP If you want to focus on something that is happening within a particular group of people, you can say that it is happening **among** that group. 在…中间 ❑ *Homicide is the leading cause of death among black men.* 凶杀在黑人男子中是主要死因。 5 PREP If something happens **among** a group of people, it happens within the whole of that group or between the members of that group. 在…之中 ❑ *The calls for reform come as intense debate continues among the leadership over the next five-year economic plan.* 当围绕下一个五年经济计划的激烈争论在领导层中继续时，改革的呼声到来了。 6 PREP If something such as a feeling, opinion, or situation exists **among** a group of people, most of them have it or experience it. 为…所共有 ❑ *There was some concern among book and magazine retailers after last Wednesday's news.* 上周三的新闻之后，图书与杂志零售商都有了些担忧。 7 PREP If something applies to a particular person or thing **among others**, it also applies to other people or things. 以及 ❑ *...a news conference attended among others by our foreign affairs correspondent.* …有我们的驻外记者和其他人参加的一个新闻发布会。 8 PREP If something is shared **among** a number of people, some of it is given to all of them. 在…中 ❑ *Most of the furniture was left to the neighbors or distributed among friends.* 大多数家具留给了邻居们或者分给了朋友们。 9 PREP If people talk, fight, or agree **among themselves**, they do it together, without involving anyone else. 在(他们自己)之间 [PREP pron-refl] ❑ *The girls stood aside, talking among themselves, looking over their shoulders at the boys.* 这些女孩子站在一边，互相交谈着并且扭过头去看着那些男孩子。

If there are more than two people or things, you should use **among**. If there are only two people or things you should use **between** ❑ *...an area between Mars and Jupiter.* You can also talk about relationships **between** or **among** people or things, and discussions **between** or **among** people. ❑ *...an argument between his mother and another woman.* Note that if you are **between** things or people, the things or people are on either side of you. If you are **among** things or people, they are all around you ❑ *...the bag standing on the floor between us. ...the sound of a pigeon among the trees.*

amongst /əmʌŋst/ PREP **Amongst** means the same as **among**. 同**among** 在…当中 [OLD-FASHIONED]

amor·tise /əmɔːˈtaɪz/ [BRIT] → see **amortize**

amor·tize /æmərtaɪz/ (**amortizes, amortizing, amortized**)

in BRIT, also use **amortise**

V-T In finance, if you **amortize** a debt, you pay it back in regular payments. 分期偿还 [BUSINESS] ❑ *There's little advantage to amortizing the loan, especially on a 30 or 40-year basis.* 分期偿还这项贷款没有什么好处，尤其是按30或40年偿还。

amount ♦♦◊ /əmaʊnt/ (**amounts, amounting, amounted**)

1 N-VAR The **amount of** something is how much there is, or how much you have, need, or get. 数量 ❑ *He needs that amount of money to survive.* 他需要那笔钱来维持生活。 ❑ *I still do a certain amount of work for them.* 我仍旧为他们做一定数量的工作。 2 V-I If something **amounts to** a particular total, all the parts of it add up to that total. 总计 ❑ *Consumer spending on sports-related items amounted to $9.75 billion.* 消费者在体育相关用品上的消费总共达到了97.5亿美元。

You should avoid using a plural noun after **amount of**; instead you should use **number of** with a plural noun. ❑ *...the number of people out of work.*

▶ **amount to** PHRASAL VERB If you say that one thing **amounts to** something else, you consider the first thing to be the same as the second thing. 等同于 ❑ *The banks have what amounts to a monopoly.* 这些银行几乎接近于垄断。

amp /æmp/ (**amps**) 1 N-COUNT An **amp** is the same as an **ampere**. 安培 ❑ *Use a 3 amp fuse for equipment up to 720 watts.* 最高720瓦的设备可用3安培的保险丝。 2 N-COUNT An **amp** is the same as an **amplifier**. 扩音器 [INFORMAL]

am·pere /æmpɪər, æmpɪər/ (**amperes**)

in BRIT, also use **ampre**

N-COUNT An **ampere** is a unit used for measuring electric current. The abbreviation **amp** is also used. 安培

am·pheta·mine /æmfɛtəmin/ (**amphetamines**) N-MASS **Amphetamine** is a drug that increases people's energy, makes them excited, and reduces their desire for food. 安非他明

Word Link *ampl ≈ large : ample, amplifier, amplify*

★ **am·ple** /æmpᵊl/ (**ampler, amplest**) ADJ If there is an **ample** amount of something, there is enough of it and usually some extra. 充足的 ❑ *There'll be ample opportunity to relax, swim and soak up some sun.* 将会有充足的机会来放松、游泳和接受一些阳光。 ● **am·ply** ADV 充足地 ❑ *This collection of his essays and journalism amply demonstrates his commitment to democracy.* 他的这部散文和新闻报道集充分地证明了他对民主的奉献。

A

Word Link ampl ≈ large : ample, amplifer, amplify

am·pli·fi·er /æmplɪfaɪər/ (amplifiers) N-COUNT An **amplifier** is an electronic device in a radio or stereo system that causes sounds or signals to get louder. 扩音器

★ **am·pli·fy** /æmplɪfaɪ/ (amplifies, amplifying, amplified) **1** V-T If you **amplify** a sound, you make it louder, usually by using electronic equipment. 扩大(声音) ❑ *This landscape seemed to trap and amplify sounds.* 这种地形好像能聚拢和扩大声音。❑ *The music was amplified with microphones.* 那音乐被麦克风扩大了。 • **am·pli·fi·ca·tion** /æmplɪfɪkeɪʃən/ N-UNCOUNT 扩音 ❑ *...a voice that needed no amplification.* …一个不需要扩音的嗓门。 **2** V-T To **amplify** something means to increase its strength or intensity. 增强 ❑ *The mist had been replaced by a kind of haze that seemed to amplify the heat.* 这薄雾已经被一种热汽代替了，这似乎加重了炎热的程度。

ampre /æmpeər/ [BRIT] → see **ampere**

am·pu·tate /æmpyʊteɪt/ (amputates, amputating, amputated) V-T To **amputate** someone's arm or leg means to cut all or part of it off in an operation because it is diseased or badly damaged. 截(肢) ❑ *To save his life, doctors amputated his legs.* 为了救他的命，医生们截去了他的双腿。 • **am·pu·ta·tion** /æmpyʊteɪʃən/ (amputations) N-VAR 截肢 ❑ *He lived only hours after the amputation.* 他在截肢后只活了几个小时。

amuse /əmyuz/ (amuses, amusing, amused) **1** V-T If something **amuses** you, it makes you want to laugh or smile. 使发笑 ❑ *The thought seemed to amuse him.* 这个想法好像让他觉得好笑。 **2** V-T If you **amuse yourself**, you do something in order to pass the time and not become bored. 使消遣 ❑ *I need distractions. I need to amuse myself so I won't keep thinking about things.* 我需要娱乐。我需要自我消遣，这样我才不会一直想事情。 **3** → see also **amused**, **amusing**

amused /əmyuzd/ ADJ If you are **amused by** something, it makes you want to laugh or smile. 逗笑的 ❑ *Sara was not amused by Franklin's teasing.* 莎拉没有被弗兰克林的逗趣儿逗笑。

amuse·ment /əmyuzmənt/ (amusements) **1** N-UNCOUNT **Amusement** is the feeling that you have when you think that something is funny or amusing. 兴味 ❑ *He stopped and watched with amusement to see the child so absorbed.* 他停下来饶有兴味地看这个孩子如此全神贯注的样子。 **2** N-UNCOUNT **Amusement** is the pleasure that you get from being entertained or from doing something interesting. 欢乐 ❑ *I stumbled sideways before landing flat on my back, much to the amusement of the rest of the guys.* 我向侧面绊了一下，然后仰面摔倒了，这让其余人乐不可支。 **3** N-COUNT **Amusements** are ways of passing the time pleasantly. 消遣方式 ❑ *People had very few amusements to choose from. There was no radio, or television.* 那时人们可选择的消遣方式很少。没有收音机，也没有电视。 **4** N-PLURAL **Amusements** are games, rides, and other things that you can enjoy, for example, at an amusement park or resort. 娱乐活动 ❑ *...a place full of swings and amusements.* …一个满是秋千和娱乐活动的地方。

amus·ing /əmyuzɪŋ/ ADJ Someone or something that is **amusing** makes you laugh or smile. 令人发笑的 ❑ *He had a terrific sense of humor and could be very amusing.* 他有极好的幽默感，能非常搞笑。 • **amus·ing·ly** ADV 令人发笑地 ❑ *The article must be amusingly written.* 这篇文章肯定写得好笑。

an /ən, STRONG æn/ DET **An** is used instead of "a," the indefinite article, in front of words that begin with vowel sounds. 代替不定冠词a，用在元音字母开头的词之前

anaemia /ənimiə/ [BRIT] → see **anemia**

anaemic /ənimɪk/ [BRIT] → see **anemic**

an·aes·thet·ic /ænɪsθɛtɪk/ [BRIT] → see **anesthetic**

anaes·the·tist /ænɛsθətɪst/ (anaesthetists) N-COUNT An **anaesthetist** is a doctor who specializes in giving anesthetics to patients. 麻醉师 [BRIT]

in AM, use **anesthesiologist**

anal /eɪnəl/ ADJ **Anal** means relating to the anus of a person or animal. 肛门的 ❑ *...anal injuries.* …肛门损伤。

▲ **ana·log** /ænəlɔg/ (analogs)

The spelling **analogue** is sometimes used for the adjective, and usually used for the noun.

1 ADJ **Analog** technology involves measuring, storing, or recording an infinitely variable amount of information by using physical quantities such as voltage. 模拟的 ❑ *The analog signals from the videotape are converted into digital code.* 该录像带的模拟信号被转换成数字代码。 **2** ADJ An **analog** watch or clock shows what it is measuring with a pointer on a dial rather than with a number display. Compare **digital**. 指针式的 **3** N-COUNT If one thing is an **analog of** another, it is similar in some way. 模拟物 [FORMAL] ❑ *No model can ever be a perfect analog of nature itself.* 没有任何模型能是自然本身的完美模拟。

analo·gous /ənæləgəs/ ADJ If one thing is **analogous to** another, the two things are similar in some way. 类似的 [FORMAL] ❑ *Marine construction technology like this is very complex, somewhat analogous to trying to build a bridge under water.* 像这样的海洋建筑技术非常复杂，有些类似于尝试在水下建筑一座桥。

★ **anal·ogy** /ənælədʒi/ (analogies) N-COUNT If you make or draw an **analogy between** two things, you show that they are similar in some way. 类比 ❑ *The analogy between music and fragrance has stuck.* 音乐与香味的类比已经深入人心了。

Word Partnership *analogy* 的常用搭配：

PREP.	analogy **between**
V.	**draw an** analogy, **make an** analogy
ADJ.	**false** analogy

ana·lyse /ænəlaɪz/ [BRIT] → see **analyze**

analy·sis ♦◇◇ /ənælɪsɪs/ (analyses /ənælɪsiz/) **1** N-VAR **Analysis** is the process of considering something carefully or using statistical methods in order to understand it or explain it. 分析 ❑ *Sporting greatness defies analysis – but we know it when we see it.* 运动的伟大无法进行分析——但是我们一看就知道。 **2** N-VAR **Analysis** is the scientific process of examining something in order to find out what it consists of. 化验分析 ❑ *They collect blood samples for analysis at a national laboratory.* 他们收集血样以在一个国家实验室做化验分析。 **3** N-COUNT An **analysis** is an explanation or description that results from considering something carefully. 分析报告 ❑ *Coming up after the newscast, an analysis of the president's domestic policy.* 在新闻广播之后是一个对总统国内政策的分析报告。

▲ **ana·lyst** ♦♦◇ /ænəlɪst/ (analysts) **1** N-COUNT An **analyst** is a person whose job is to analyze a subject and give opinions about it. 分析师 ❑ *...a political analyst.* …一位政治分析家。 **2** N-COUNT An **analyst** is someone, usually a doctor, who examines and treats people who have emotional problems. 心理分析师 ❑ *My analyst warned me that I liked married men too much.* 我的心理分析师警告过我太喜欢已婚男人。

ana·lyt·ic /ænəlɪtɪk/ ADJ **Analytic** means the same as **analytical**. 分析的 [mainly AM]

★ **ana·lyti·cal** /ænəlɪtɪkəl/ ADJ An **analytical** way of doing something involves the use of logical reasoning. 分析的 ❑ *I have an analytical approach to every survey.* 我对每项调查都采用一种分析的方法。

ana·lyze /ænəlaɪz/ (analyzes, analyzing, analyzed)

in BRIT, use **analyse**

1 V-T If you **analyze** something, you consider it carefully or use statistical methods in order to fully understand it. 分析 ❑ *McCarthy was asked to analyze the data from the first phase of trials of the vaccine.* 麦卡西被要求分析从这种疫苗试验的第一阶段取得的数据。 **2** V-T If you **analyze** something, you examine it using scientific methods in order to find out what it consists of. 化验分析 ❑ *We haven't had time to analyze those samples yet.* 我们还没有时间化验分析那些样本。

Thesaurus *analyze* 另参见：

V.	consider, examine, inspect **1** break down, dissect **2**

an·ar·chic /ænɑrkɪk/ ADJ If you describe someone or something as **anarchic**, you disapprove of them because they do not recognize or obey any rules or laws. 无政府的 [DISAPPROVAL] ❑ *...anarchic attitudes and complete disrespect for authority.* …无政府的态度以及对权威的全然蔑视。

an·ar·chism /ænərkɪzəm/ N-UNCOUNT **Anarchism** is the belief that the laws and power of governments should be replaced by people working together freely. 无政府主义 ❑ *He advocated anarchism as the answer to social problems.* 他鼓吹无政府主义作为解决社会问题的答案。

▲ **an·ar·chist** /ænərkɪst/ (**anarchists**) 1 N-COUNT An **anarchist** is a person who believes in anarchism. 无政府主义者 [oft N n] ❑ *West Berlin always had a large anarchist community.* 西柏林一直存在一个大的无政府主义群体。 2 ADJ If someone has **anarchist** beliefs or views, they believe in anarchism. 无政府主义的 [ADJ n] ❑ *He was apparently quite converted from his anarchist views.* 他显然已经从他的无政府主义观点大大地转变了。

Word Link *arch ≈ rule : anarchy, hierarchy, monarch*

an·ar·chy /ænərki/ N-UNCOUNT If you describe a situation as **anarchy**, you mean that nobody seems to be paying any attention to rules or laws. 无政府状态 [DISAPPROVAL] ❑ *The school's liberal, individualistic traditions were in danger of slipping into anarchy.* 这所学校的自由主义和个人主义的传统有滑入无政府状态的危险。

ana·tomi·cal /ænətɒmɪkᵊl/ ADJ **Anatomical** means relating to the structure of the bodies of people and animals. 身体结构的 ❑ *...minute anatomical differences between insects.* …昆虫之间微小的身体结构上的区别。

anato·my /ənætəmi/ 1 N-UNCOUNT **Anatomy** is the study of the structure of the bodies of people or animals. 解剖学 ❑ *...a course in anatomy.* …一门解剖学课程。 2 N-COUNT You can refer to your body as your **anatomy**. 身体 [HUMOROUS] ❑ *The ball hit him in the most sensitive part of his anatomy.* 这个球打中了他身体的最敏感部位。
→ see **medicine**

an·ces·tor /ænsɛstər/ (**ancestors**) 1 N-COUNT Your **ancestors** are the people from whom you are descended. 祖先 [usu pl, with poss] ❑ *...our daily lives, so different from those of our ancestors.* …我们的日常生活，与我们祖先的生活如此不同。 2 N-COUNT An **ancestor of** something modern is an earlier thing from which it developed. 物种原型 ❑ *The direct ancestor of the modern cat was the Kaffir cat of ancient Egypt.* 现代猫的直系物种原型是古代埃及的卡菲尔猫。

an·ces·tral /ænsɛstrəl/ ADJ You use **ancestral** to refer to a person's family in former times, especially when the family is important and has property or land that they have had for a long time. 祖先的 ❑ *...the family's ancestral home in southern Germany.* …这一家在德国南部的祖宅。

▲ **an·ces·try** /ænsɛstri/ (**ancestries**) N-COUNT Your **ancestry** is the fact that you are descended from certain people. 家世 ❑ *...a family who could trace their ancestry back to the sixteenth century.* …一个家世能追溯回16世纪的家庭。

an·chor /æŋkər/ (**anchors, anchoring, anchored**) 1 N-COUNT An **anchor** is a heavy hooked object that is dropped from a boat into the water at the end of a chain in order to make the boat stay in one place. 锚 2 N-COUNT The **anchor** on a television or radio program, especially a news program, is the person who presents it. 节目主持人 [mainly AM] ❑ *He worked in the news division of ABC – he was the anchor of its 15-minute evening newscast.* 他以前在美国广播公司的新闻部工作——他是该公司15分钟晚间新闻节目的主持人。 3 V-T/V-I When a boat **anchors** or when you **anchor** it, its anchor is dropped into the water in order to make it stay in one place. 抛锚 ❑ *We could anchor off the pier.* 我们可以在码头抛锚。 4 V-T If an object **is anchored** somewhere, it is fixed to something to prevent it moving from that place. 使固定 ❑ *The roots anchor the plant in the earth.* 根须把这植物固定在土里。 5 V-T The person who **anchors** a television or radio program, especially a news program, is the person who presents it and acts as a link between interviews and reports that come from other places or studios. 主持 [mainly AM] ❑ *Viewers saw him anchoring a five-minute summary of regional news.* 观众们看到了他主持地区新闻的5分钟综述。 6 N-COUNT An **anchor** is the main store in a mall or shopping center. 主体商店 [AM] ❑ *A clothing store is to be a key anchor in a new development planned on the vacant lot.* 一个服装店将成为在这块空地上计划新开发项目中的一个关键主体商店。 7 PHRASE If a boat is **at anchor**, it is floating in a particular place and is prevented from moving by its anchor. 停泊 ❑ *Sailboats lay at anchor in the narrow waterway.* 帆船停泊在狭窄的水道里。

an·cient ♦◇◇ /eɪnʃənt/ 1 ADJ **Ancient** means belonging to the distant past, especially to the period in history before the end of the Roman Empire. 古代的 [ADJ n] ❑ *They believed ancient Greece and Rome were vital sources of learning.* 他们认为古希腊和古罗马是至关重要的知识来源。 2 ADJ **Ancient** means very old, or having existed for a long time. 古老的 ❑ *...ancient Jewish tradition.* …古老的犹太传统。
→ see **history**

an·cil·lary /ænsəlɛri/ ADJ The **ancillary** workers in an institution are the people such as cleaners and cooks whose work supports the main work of the institution. 后勤的 [ADJ n] ❑ *...ancillary staff.* …后勤职工。

and ♦♦♦ /ənd, STRONG ænd/ 1 CONJ You use **and** to link two or more words, groups, or clauses. 和；并且 ❑ *When he returned, she and Simon had already gone.* 当他回来时，她和西蒙已经走了。 ❑ *I'm going to write good jokes and become a good comedian.* 我要创作出好的笑话并且成为一个优秀的喜剧演员。 2 CONJ You use **and** to link two words or phrases that are the same in order to emphasize the degree of something, or to suggest that something continues or increases over a period of time. 用于强调程度，或者表示某事持续或增长了一段时间 [EMPHASIS] ❑ *Learning becomes more and more difficult as we get older.* 当我们年纪越大，学习就变得越来越困难。 ❑ *We talked for hours and hours.* 我们谈了好多个小时。 3 CONJ You use **and** to link two statements about events when one of the events follows the other. 然后 ❑ *I waved goodbye and went down the stone harbor steps.* 我挥手告别，然后走下了港口的石头台阶。 4 CONJ You use **and** to link two statements when the second statement continues the point that has been made in the first statement. (表示延续上个陈述的意思) 而 ❑ *You could only really tell the effects of the disease in the long term, and five years wasn't long enough.* 这种疾病的影响只有在长期内才能真正看清楚，而5年是不够长的。 5 CONJ You use **and** to link two clauses when the second clause is a result of the first clause. 结果 ❑ *All through yesterday crowds have been arriving and by midnight thousands of people packed the square.* 昨天一整天人们一直不断地到达，结果到午夜的时候成千上万的人挤满了这个广场。 6 CONJ You use **and** to interrupt yourself in order to make a comment on what you are saying. (表示对自己的话加以评价) 而且 ❑ *Danielle was among the last to find out, and as often happens, too, she learned of it only by chance.* 丹妮尔是最后一个才知道的人之一，而且同往常一样，她也只是偶然听到的。 7 CONJ You use **and** at the beginning of a sentence to introduce something else that you want to add to what you have just said. Some people think that starting a sentence with **and** is ungrammatical, but it is now quite common in both spoken and written English. 此外 ❑ *Commuter airlines fly to out-of-the-way places. And business travelers are the ones who go to those locations.* 通勤航空公司飞往偏僻的地方。此外，商务旅客就是去那些地方的人。 8 CONJ You use **and** to introduce a question that follows logically from what someone has just said. 那么 ❑ *"He used to be so handsome."—"And now?"* "他过去曾经那么英俊。"——"那么现在呢？" 9 CONJ **And** is used by broadcasters and people making announcements to change a topic or to start talking about a topic they have just mentioned. 接下来 ❑ *And now the drought in Sudan.* 现在接下来是关于苏丹的干旱。 10 CONJ You use **and** to indicate that two numbers are to be added together. 加 ❑ *What does two and two make?* 2加2是多少？ 11 CONJ **And** is used before a fraction that comes after a whole number. 用于连接整数后的分数 ❑ *McCain spent five and a half years in a prisoner-of-war camp in Vietnam.* 麦凯恩在越南的一所战俘营里度过了五年半。 12 CONJ You use **and** in numbers larger than one hundred, after the words "hundred" or "thousand" and before other numbers. 用于大于100的数字，在百位或千位数和紧跟的数之间 ❑ *We printed two hundred and fifty invitations.* 我们印了250份请柬。

an·ec·do·tal /ænɪkdoʊtᵊl/ ADJ **Anecdotal** evidence is based on individual accounts, rather than on reliable research or statistics, and so may not be valid. 轶闻的 ❑ *Anecdotal evidence suggests that sales in the Southwest have slipped.* 传闻的证据表明西南部的销售量有所下滑。

▲ **an·ec·dote** /ænɪkdoʊt/ (**anecdotes**) N-VAR An **anecdote** is a short, amusing account of something that has happened. 趣闻轶事 ❑ *Pete was telling them an anecdote about their mother.* 皮特正告诉他们一个关于他们母亲的趣闻轶事。

anemia /əniːmiə/
in BRIT, use **anaemia**
N-UNCOUNT **Anemia** is a medical condition in which there are too few red cells in your blood, causing you to feel tired and look pale. 贫血症 ❑ *She suffered from anemia and even required blood transfusions.* 她患有贫血症而且甚至需要输血。

anemic /əniːmɪk/
in BRIT, use **anaemic**
ADJ Someone who is **anemic** suffers from anemia. 贫血的 ❑ *Tests showed that she was very anemic.* 化验表明她非常贫血。

A

Word Web anger

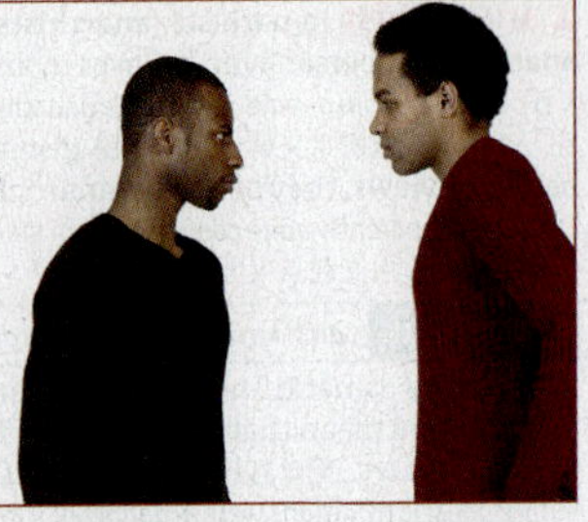

Anger can be a positive thing. Until it surfaces, we may not realize how **upset** we are about a situation. Anger can give us a sense of our own power. Showing someone how **annoyed** we are with them may lead them to change their behavior. Anger also helps release **tension** in **frustrating** situations. This allows us to move on with our lives. But anger has its downside. It's hard to think clearly when we're **furious**. We may use bad judgment. **Rage** can also prevent us from seeing the truth about ourselves. And when anger turns into **aggression**, people get hurt.

an·es·thesi·olo·gist /ænɪsθiziɒlədʒɪst/ (**anesthesiologists**) N-COUNT An **anesthesiologist** is a doctor who specializes in giving anesthetics to patients. 麻醉科医师 [AM]

in BRIT, use **anaesthetist**

Word Link *a, an ≈ not, without : anesthetic, anorexia, atheism*

an·es·thet·ic /ænɪsθɛtɪk/ (**anesthetics**)

in BRIT, use **anaesthetic**

N-MASS **Anesthetic** is a substance that doctors use to stop you feeling pain during an operation, either in the whole of your body when you are unconscious, or in a part of your body when you are awake. 麻醉药 ❑ *The operation is carried out under a general anesthetic.* 这个手术是在全身麻醉下进行的。

anes·the·tist /ənɛsθətɪst/ (**anesthetists**) N-COUNT An **anesthetist** is a nurse or other person who gives an anesthetic to a patient. 麻醉师 [AM]

★ **anew** /ənu/ ADV If you do something **anew**, you do it again, often in a different way from before. 重新地 [ADV after v] [WRITTEN] ❑ *She's ready to start anew.* 她准备好重新来过。 ❑ *He began his work anew.* 他重新开始了他的工作。

★ **an·gel** /eɪndʒ^əl/ (**angels**) **1** N-COUNT **Angels** are spiritual beings that some people believe are God's servants in heaven. 天使 ❑ *The artist usually painted his angels with multi-colored wings.* 这位艺术家通常给他的天使画上多彩的翅膀。 **2** N-COUNT You can call someone you like very much an **angel** in order to show affection, especially when they have been kind to you or done you a favor. 天使 [FEELINGS] ❑ *Thank you a thousand times, you're an angel.* 千恩万谢了，你是个天使。 **3** N-COUNT If you describe someone as an **angel**, you mean that they seem to be very kind and good. 大好人 [APPROVAL] ❑ *Papa thought her an angel.* 爸爸认为她是个大好人。

an·gel·ic /ændʒɛlɪk/ **1** ADJ You can describe someone as **angelic** if they are, or seem to be, very good, kind, and gentle. 天使般的 [APPROVAL] ❑ *...an angelic face.* …一张天使般的脸庞。 **2** ADJ **Angelic** means like angels or relating to angels. 天使般的 [ADJ n] ❑ *...angelic choirs.* …天使般的合唱团。

an·ger ♦◇◇ /æŋgər/ (**angers, angering, angered**) **1** N-UNCOUNT **Anger** is the strong emotion that you feel when you think that someone has behaved in an unfair, cruel, or unacceptable way. 愤怒 ❑ *He cried with anger and frustration.* 他愤怒而沮丧地哭了。 **2** V-T If something **angers** you, it makes you feel angry. 使气愤 ❑ *The decision to allow more offshore oil drilling angered some Californians.* 这个允许更多海底石油钻探的决定激怒了一些加利福尼亚人。

→ see Word Web: **anger**
→ see **emotion**

an·gle ♦◇◇ /æŋg^əl/ (**angles**) **1** N-COUNT An **angle** is the difference in direction between two lines or surfaces. Angles are measured in degrees. 角 ❑ *The boat is now leaning at a 30 degree angle.* 这条船现在正以30度角倾斜着。 **2** → see also **right angle** **3** N-COUNT An **angle** is the shape that is created where two lines or surfaces join together. 角 ❑ *...the angle of the blade.* …刀刃的尖角。 **4** N-COUNT An **angle** is the direction from which you look at something. 角度 ❑ *Thanks to the angle at which he stood, he could just see the sunset.* 多亏他站的角度，他刚好能看到日落。 **5** N-COUNT You can refer to a way of presenting something or thinking about it as a particular **angle**. 视角 ❑ *He was considering the idea from all angles.* 他从各个视角考虑着这个观点。 **6** PHRASE If something is **at an angle**, it is leaning in a particular direction so that it is not straight, horizontal, or vertical. 成一定角度 ❑ *An iron bar stuck out at an angle.* 一根铁条成一定角度地突出来。

→ see **mathematics**

an·gler /æŋglər/ (**anglers**) N-COUNT An **angler** is someone who fishes with a fishing rod as a hobby. 垂钓爱好者

an·gling /æŋglɪŋ/ N-UNCOUNT **Angling** is the activity or sport of fishing with a fishing rod. 垂钓

an·gry ♦◇◇ /æŋgri/ (**angrier, angriest**) ADJ When you are **angry**, you feel strong dislike or impatience about something. 生气的 ❑ *Are you angry with me for some reason?* 你是因为某个原因生我的气了吗？ ❑ *I was angry about the rumors.* 我对这些谣言感到生气。 ❑ *An angry mob gathered outside the courthouse.* 一群愤怒的民众聚集到了法院外面。

● **an·gri·ly** /æŋgrɪli/ ADV 生气地 [ADV with v] ❑ *Officials reacted angrily to those charges.* 官员们愤怒地回应了那些指控。

> **Angry** is normally used to talk about someone's mood or feelings on a particular occasion. If someone is often angry, you can describe them as **bad-tempered**. ❑ *She's a bad-tempered young lady.* If someone is very angry, you can describe them as **furious**. ❑ *Senior police officers are furious at the blunder.* If they are less angry, you can describe them as **annoyed** or **irritated**. ❑ *The premier looked annoyed but calm.* *...a man irritated by the barking of his neighbor's dog.* Typically, someone is **irritated** by something because it happens constantly or continually. If someone is often irritated, you can describe them as **irritable**.

Thesaurus *angry* 另参见：

ADJ. bitter, enraged, mad; *(ant.)* content, happy, pleased

Word Partnership *angry* 的常用搭配：

PREP. angry **about** *something*, angry **at** *someone/something*, angry **with someone**
V. **get** angry, **make** *someone* angry
N. angry **mob**

angst /æŋst/ N-UNCOUNT **Angst** is a feeling of anxiety and worry. 焦虑 [JOURNALISM] ❑ *Many kids suffer from acne and angst.* 许多孩子深受粉刺和焦虑之苦。

▲ **an·guish** /æŋgwɪʃ/ N-UNCOUNT **Anguish** is great mental suffering or physical pain. 极度痛苦 ❑ *Mark looked at him in anguish.* 马克极为痛苦地看着他。

an·guished /æŋgwɪʃt/ ADJ **Anguished** means showing or feeling great mental suffering or physical pain. 极为痛苦的 [WRITTEN] ❑ *She let out an anguished cry.* 她发出了一声极为痛苦的叫喊。

an·gu·lar /æŋgyʊlər/ ADJ **Angular** things have shapes that seem to contain a lot of straight lines and sharp points. 有棱角的 ❑ *He had an angular face with prominent cheekbones.* 他有一张颧骨突出、棱角分明的脸。

Word Link *anim ≈ alive, mind : animal, animated, unanimous*

ani·mal ♦♦◇ /ænɪm^əl/ (**animals**) **1** N-COUNT An **animal** is a living creature such as a dog, lion, or rabbit, rather than a bird, fish, insect, or human being. 动物（不包括鸟类、鱼类、昆虫和人类） ❑ *He was attacked by wild animals.* 他被野兽袭击了。 **2** N-COUNT Any living creature other than a human being can be referred to as an **animal**. 兽类；动物（不包括人类） ❑ *Language is something that fundamentally distinguishes humans from animals.* 语言是从根本上把人类与动物区分开的事物。 **3** N-COUNT Any living creature, including a human being, can be referred to as an **animal**. （包括人类在内的）动物 ❑ *Watch any young human being, or any other young animal.* 观察任意一个年少的人，或者任意其他幼小的动物。 **4** ADJ **Animal** products come from animals rather than from plants. 动物的 ❑ *...food high in animal fats such as red meat and dairy products.* …富含动物脂肪的食物，如红色肉类和奶制品。

→ see **earth, pet**

a

Word Partnership *animal* 的常用搭配：

N. **plant and** animal 1
cruelty to animals, animal **hide**, animal **kingdom**, animal **noises**, animal **shelter** 2
ADJ. **domestic** animal, **stuffed** animal, **wild** animal 2

★ **ani·mate** (animates, animating, animated)

The adjective is pronounced /ænɪmət/. The verb is pronounced /ænɪmeɪt/.

形容词读作 /ænɪmət/。动词读作 /ænɪmeɪt/。

1 ADJ Something that is **animate** has life, in contrast to things like stones and machines which do not. 有生命的 ❑ *Natural philosophy involved the study of all aspects of the material world, animate and inanimate.* 自然哲学涉及到了对包括有生命体与无生命体的物质世界的全面研究。 2 V-T To **animate** something means to make it lively or more cheerful. 使有生气 ❑ *There was precious little about the cricket to animate the crowd.* 这场板球比赛极少有让观众兴奋的地方。

★ **ani·mat·ed** /ænɪmeɪtɪd/ 1 ADJ Someone who is **animated** or who is having an **animated** conversation is lively and is showing their feelings. 热烈的 ❑ *She was seen in animated conversation with the singer Yuri Marusin.* 她被看见与歌手尤里・马鲁辛进行热烈的交谈。 2 ADJ An **animated** film is one in which puppets or drawings appear to move. 动画的 [ADJ n] ❑ *Disney has returned to what it does best: making full-length animated feature films.* 迪斯尼电影公司回到他们最拿手的事情：制作长篇动画故事片。

ani·ma·tion /ænɪmeɪʃən/ (animations) 1 N-UNCOUNT **Animation** is the process of making films in which drawings or puppets appear to move. 动画制作 ❑ *The films are a mix of animation and full-length features.* 这些电影是动画和情节长片的混合体。 2 N-COUNT An **animation** is a film in which drawings or puppets appear to move. 动画片 ❑ *This film is the first British animation sold to an American network.* 这部电影是卖给一家美国电视网的第一部英国动画片。
→ see Word Web: **animation**

ani·mos·ity /ænɪmɒsɪti/ (animosities) N-UNCOUNT **Animosity** is a strong feeling of dislike and anger. **Animosities** are feelings of this kind. 强烈敌意 [also N in pl] ❑ *There's a long history of animosity between the two nations.* 在那两个国家间存在着历史悠久的强烈敌意。

an·kle /æŋkəl/ (ankles) N-COUNT Your **ankle** is the joint where your foot joins your leg. 脚踝 ❑ *John twisted his ankle badly.* 约翰的脚踝严重扭伤。
→ see **body, foot**

▲ **an·nex** (annexes, annexing, annexed)

The verb is pronounced /ænɛ̱ks/. The noun is pronounced /ænɛks/.

动词读作 /ænɛ̱ks/。名词读作 /ænɛks/。

1 V-T If a country **annexes** another country or an area of land, it seizes it and takes control of it. 并吞 ❑ *Rome annexed the Nabatean kingdom in AD 106.* 罗马帝国于公元106年并吞了纳巴泰王国。
• **an·nexa·tion** /ænekseɪʃən/ N-COUNT (annexations) 并吞 ❑ *Indonesia's annexation of East Timor never won the acceptance of the United Nations.* 印度尼西亚对东帝汶的并吞从未获得联合国的认可。
2 N-COUNT An **annex** is a building joined to or next to a larger main building. 侧楼 [AM]
in BRIT, use **annexe**

❑ *...setting up a museum in an annex to the theater.* …在这所剧院的一个侧楼里建一个博物馆。

▲ **an·nexe** /ænɛks/ [BRIT] → see **annex**

an·ni·hi·late /ənaɪɪleɪt/ (annihilates, annihilating, annihilated) 1 V-T To **annihilate** something means to destroy it completely. 毁灭 ❑ *There are lots of ways of annihilating the planet.* 有很多毁灭那个星球的方式。 • **an·ni·hi·la·tion** /ənaɪɪleɪʃən/ N-UNCOUNT 毁灭 ❑ *...the threat of nuclear war and annihilation of the human race.* …核战争与人类毁灭的威胁。 2 V-T If you **annihilate** someone in a contest or argument, you totally defeat them. 彻底击败 ❑ *The Dutch annihilated the Olympic champions 5-0.* 荷兰队以5-0彻底打败了奥运会冠军队。

Word Link *ann ≈ year : anniversary, annual, annum*

an·ni·ver·sa·ry ♦◇◇ /ænɪvɜrsəri/ (anniversaries) N-COUNT An **anniversary** is a date that is remembered or celebrated because a special event happened on that date in a previous year. 周年纪念日 ❑ *Vietnam is celebrating the one hundredth anniversary of the birth of Ho Chi Minh.* 越南正在庆祝胡志明的百年诞辰。

an·no·tate /ænoʊteɪt/ (annotates, annotating, annotated) V-T If you **annotate** written work or a diagram, you add notes to it, especially in order to explain it. 为…做注释 ❑ *Historians annotate, check and interpret the diary selections.* 历史学家们对这些日记选段进行注释、核对和阐释。

Word Link *nounce ≈ reporting : announce, denounce, pronounce*

an·nounce ♦♦♦ /ənaʊns/ (announces, announcing, announced) 1 V-T If you **announce** something, you tell people about it publicly or officially. 宣布 ❑ *He will announce tonight that he is resigning from office.* 他今晚将宣布他要辞职。 ❑ *She was planning to announce her engagement to Peter.* 她在计划宣布她与彼得的婚约。 2 V-T If you **announce** a piece of news or an intention, especially something that people may not like, you say it loudly and clearly, so that everyone you are with can hear it. 声明 ❑ *Peter announced that he had no intention of wasting his time at any university.* 彼得声明他无意在任何一所大学里浪费他的时间。 3 V-T If an airport or rail employee **announces** something, they tell the public about it by means of a loudspeaker system. 广播 ❑ *The loudspeaker announced the arrival of the train.* 扬声器宣布了那列火车的到达。

Thesaurus *announce* 另参见：
V. advertise, declare, make public, reveal; (*ant.*) withhold 1

an·no·ta·tion /ænoʊteɪʃən/ (annotations) N-UNCOUNT **Annotation** is the activity of annotating something. 注解 ❑ *She retained a number of copies for further annotation.* 她留下了许多份以添加注解。

an·nounce·ment ♦◇◇ /ənaʊnsmənt/ (announcements) 1 N-COUNT An **announcement** is a statement made to the public or to the media that gives information about something that has happened or that will happen. 公告 ❑ *She made her announcement after talks with the president.* 她在与总统的会谈后发布了公告。 2 N-COUNT An **announcement** in a public place, such as a newspaper or the window of a store, is a short piece of writing telling people about something or asking for something. 通告 ❑ *The Seattle Times publishes brief announcements of religious events every Saturday.* 《西雅图时报》每周六刊登简短的宗教活动通告。 3 N-SING The **announcement of** something that has happened is the act of telling people about it. 宣布 ❑ *...the announcement of their engagement.* …他们婚约的宣布。

Word Web animation

TV **cartoons** are one of the most popular forms of **animation**. Each **episode** begins with a storyline. Once the **script** is final, cartoonists make up storyboards. The director uses them to plan how the **artists** will **illustrate** the episode. First the illustrators **draw** some **sketches**. Next they draw a few key **frames** for each **scene**. Animators turn these into moving storyboards. This version of the cartoon looks unfinished. The producers review it and suggest changes. After they make these changes, the artists fill in the missing frames. This makes the movements of the characters look smooth and natural.

A

Word Partnership *announcement* 的常用搭配：

ADJ. **formal** announcement, **official** announcement, **public** announcement, **surprise** announcement 1

V. **make an** announcement 1

an·nounc·er /ənaʊnsər/ (**announcers**) 1 N-COUNT An **announcer** is someone who introduces programs on radio or television or who reads the text of a radio or television advertisement. 播音员 ❑ *The radio announcer said it was nine o'clock.* 电台播音员报了9点。 2 N-COUNT The **announcer** at a train station or airport is the person who makes the announcements. (火车站、机场的) 广播员 ❑ *The announcer apologized for the delay.* 广播员为晚点道了歉。

an·noy /ənɔɪ/ (**annoys, annoying, annoyed**) 1 V-T If someone or something **annoys** you, it makes you fairly angry and impatient. 使心烦 ❑ *Try making a note of the things that annoy you.* 试着把让你心烦的事记下来。 ❑ *It annoyed me that I didn't have time to do more ironing.* 没有时间熨更多的衣服让我心烦了。 2 → see also **annoyed, annoying**

★ **an·noy·ance** /ənɔɪəns/ (**annoyances**) 1 N-UNCOUNT **Annoyance** is the feeling that you get when someone makes you feel fairly angry or impatient. 厌烦 ❑ *To her annoyance the stranger did not go away.* 让她厌烦的是这个陌生人没有离开。 2 N-COUNT An **annoyance** is something that makes you feel angry or impatient. 烦人的事物 ❑ *Snoring can be more than an annoyance.* 打呼噜不只是一桩烦人的事。

an·noyed /ənɔɪd/ 1 ADJ If you are **annoyed**, you are fairly angry about something. 恼怒的 ❑ *She is hurt and annoyed that the authorities have banned her from working with children.* 她因当局禁止她做儿童工作而伤心恼怒。 2 → see also **annoy**

→ see **anger**

an·noy·ing /ənɔɪɪŋ/ ADJ Someone or something that is **annoying** makes you feel fairly angry and impatient. 烦人的 ❑ *You must have found my attitude annoying.* 你一定觉得我的态度让人烦。

Word Link *ann ≈ year : anniversary, annual, annum*

an·nual ♦♦◊ /ænyuəl/ (**annuals**) 1 ADJ **Annual** events happen once every year. 每年一次的 [ADJ n] ❑ *The issues will be voted on at the company's annual meeting on April 21 in Wilmington.* 这些问题将在该公司4月21日在威尔明顿的年会上投票表决。 ● **an·nual·ly** ADV 每年一次地 [ADV with v] ❑ *Companies report to their shareholders annually.* 各公司每年向其股东们汇报一次。 2 ADJ **Annual** quantities or rates relate to a period of one year. 年度的 [ADJ n] ❑ *The electronic and printing unit has annual sales of about $80 million.* 电子与印刷部有约八千万美元的年度销售额。 ● **an·nual·ly** ADV 年度地 ❑ *El Salvador produces 100,000 tons of refined copper annually.* 萨尔瓦多一年生产10万吨精炼铜。 3 N-COUNT An **annual** is a book or magazine that is published once a year. 年鉴；年刊 ❑ *I looked for Wyman's picture in my high-school annual.* 我在我的中学年鉴里找过怀曼的照片。 4 N-COUNT An **annual** is a plant that grows and dies within one year. 一年生植物 ❑ *Maybe this year I'll sow brilliant annuals everywhere.* 也许今年我会到处种上鲜艳的一年生植物。

→ see **plant**

an·nu·ity /ənuɪti/ (**annuities**) N-COUNT An **annuity** is an investment or insurance policy that pays someone a fixed sum of money each year. 年金 [BUSINESS] ❑ *He received a paltry annuity of $100.* 他收到了微不足道的100美元年金。

an·nul /ənʌl/ (**annuls, annulling, annulled**) V-T If an election or a contract **is annulled**, it is declared invalid, so that legally it is considered never to have existed. 宣布…无效 [usu passive] ❑ *Opposition party leaders are now pressing for the entire election to be annulled.* 反对党领袖们现在正在迫切要求宣布整个选举无效。

an·num /ænəm/ → see **per annum**

anoma·ly /ənɒməli/ (**anomalies**) N-COUNT If something is an **anomaly**, it is different from what is usual or expected. 反常的事物 [FORMAL] ❑ *The space shuttle had stopped transmitting data, a very serious anomaly for the mission.* 这架航天飞机已经停止了传输数据，这是这次任务中一个十分严重的反常现象。

Word Link *onym ≈ name : acronym, anonymous, synonym*

★ **anony·mous** /ənɒnɪməs/ 1 ADJ If you remain **anonymous** when you do something, you do not let people know that you were the person who did it. 匿名的 ❑ *You can remain anonymous if you wish.* 如果你愿意你可以保持匿名。 ❑ *An anonymous benefactor stepped in to provide the prize money.* 一位匿名捐助人参与进来提供了奖金。 ● **ano·nym·ity** ▲ /ænɒnɪmɪti/ N-UNCOUNT 匿名 ❑ *Both mother and daughter, who have requested anonymity, are doing fine.* 要求匿名的母女情况都好。 ● **anony·mous·ly** ADV 匿名地 ❑ *The latest photographs were sent anonymously to the magazine's headquarters.* 最新的照片匿名寄给了该杂志总部。 2 ADJ Something that is **anonymous** does not reveal who you are. 不记名的 ❑ *Of course, that would have to be by anonymous vote.* 当然，那得是通过不记名投票。 ● **ano·nym·ity** N-UNCOUNT 不记名 ❑ *He claims many more people would support him in the anonymity of a voting booth.* 他声称在投票站不记名的情况下更多的人会支持他。

ano·rak /ænəræk/ (**anoraks**) N-COUNT An **anorak** is a warm waterproof jacket, usually with a hood. 带帽防水夹克 [mainly BRIT]

Word Link *a, an ≈ not, without : anesthetic, anorexia, atheism*

ano·rexia /ænərɛksiə/ N-UNCOUNT **Anorexia** or **anorexia nervosa** is an illness in which a person has an overwhelming fear of becoming fat, and so refuses to eat enough and becomes thinner and thinner. 厌食症

ano·rex·ic /ænərɛksɪk/ (**anorexics**) ADJ If someone is **anorexic**, they are suffering from anorexia and so are very thin. 患厌食症的 ❑ *Claire had been anorexic for three years.* 克莱尔已经患厌食症3年了。 ● N-COUNT An **anorexic** is someone who is anorexic. 厌食症患者 ❑ *Not eating makes an anorexic feel in control.* 不进食让厌食症患者感到安然。

an·oth·er ♦♦♦ /ənʌðər/ 1 DET **Another** thing or person means an additional thing or person of the same type as one that already exists. 又一的 ❑ *Divers this morning found the body of another American sailor drowned during yesterday's ferry disaster.* 潜水员们今天早晨发现了在昨天渡轮失事中淹死的又一名美国水手的尸体。 ● PRON-SING **Another** is also a pronoun. 又一个 ❑ *The demand generated by one factory required the construction of another.* 一家工厂提出的需要再建一家工厂的要求。 2 DET You use **another** when you want to emphasize that an additional thing or person is different from one that already exists. 另一的 ❑ *I think he's just going to deal with this problem another day.* 我想他只是打算改天再处理这个问题。 ● PRON-SING **Another** is also a pronoun. 另一个 ❑ *He didn't really believe that any human being could read another's mind.* 他并不真地相信一个人能够看出另一个人的心思。 3 DET You use **another** at the beginning of a statement to link it to a previous statement. 另一的 (用于一陈述句的开头以使之与前一陈述句衔接) ❑ *Another time of great excitement for us boys was when war broke out.* 另一个对于我们小伙子来讲极为兴奋的时刻是在战争爆发的时候。 4 DET You use **another** before a word referring to a distance, length of time, or other amount, to indicate an additional amount. 再加的 (用于表示距离、时长、数量等的词前) ❑ *Continue down the same road for another 2 miles until you reach the church of Santa Maria.* 沿着同一条路继续走2英里直到你到达圣玛丽亚教堂。 5 PRON-RECIP You use **one another** to indicate that each member of a group does something to or for the other members. 相互 [V PRON, prep PRON] ❑ *...women learning to help themselves and one another.* …学习自助和互助的女人们。

> Do not confuse **another** and **other**. When you are talking about **another** thing or person, you often mean one more of the same type. ❑ *Rick's got another camera... I waited another few minutes.* You use **other** to refer to more than one type of person or thing, usually followed by a plural count noun but sometimes by an uncount noun. ❑ *Other boys were arriving now... There was certainly other evidence.* When you are talking about two people or things and have already referred to one of them, you refer to the second one as **the other** or **the other one.** ❑ *One daughter was a baby, the other a girl of twelve.* When you are talking about several people or things and have already referred to one or more of them, you usually refer to the remaining ones as **the others.** ❑ *Jack and the others paid no attention.* More people or things of the same type are referred to simply as **others.** ❑ *Some writers are better than others.* **Other** can also be used after words such as "the," "few," or "any," and after numbers. ❑ *...the other side of the room... I love my son, like any other mother. ...the Hogans and three other couples.*

6 PHRASE If you talk about **one** thing **after another**, you are referring to a series of repeated or continuous events. 一个接一个的 ❑ *They had faced one difficulty after another with bravery and dedication.*

他们曾以勇敢与执著面对了一个又一个困难。 **7** PHRASE You use **or another** in expressions such as **one kind or another** when you do not want to be precise about which of several alternatives or possibilities you are referring to. 或那种的 ❑ *...family members and visiting artists of one kind or another crowding the huge kitchen.* …挤满了这间巨大的厨房的家庭成员以及这类或那类的访问艺术家们。

Word Partnership *another* 的常用搭配:
ADV. yet another **1**
N. another **chance**, another **day**, another **one** **1**
another **man/woman**, another **thing** **2**
V. **tell one from** another **2**
PRON. **one** another **5**

an·swer ♦♦♦ /ænsər/ (**answers, answering, answered**) **1** V-T/V-I When you **answer** someone who has asked you something, you say something back to them. (口头) 回答 ❑ *Just answer the question.* 只回答这个问题。 ❑ *He paused before answering.* 他在回答前停了下来。 ❑ *Williams answered that he had no specific proposals yet.* 威廉斯回答说他还没有具体的提议。 **2** V-T/V-I If you **answer** a letter or advertisement, you write to the person who wrote it. 回复 ❑ *Did he answer your letter?* 他回复你的信了吗? **3** V-T/V-I When you **answer** the telephone, you pick it up when it rings. When you **answer** the door, you open it when you hear a knock or the bell. 应答 ❑ *She answered her phone on the first ring.* 她在响第一声铃时就接了电话。 ● N-COUNT **Answer** is also a noun. 应答 ❑ *I knocked at the front door and there was no answer.* 我敲了前门, 没有应答。 **4** V-T When you **answer** a question in a test or quiz, you write or say something in an attempt to give the facts that are asked for. (书面) 回答 ❑ *Always read an exam all the way through at least once before you start to answer any questions.* 在开始回答任何问题之前总是把试卷从头到尾读至少一遍。 **5** V-T/V-I If someone or something **answers** a particular description or **answers to** it, they have the characteristics described. 符合 ❑ *Two men answering the description of the suspects tried to enter Switzerland.* 符合嫌疑犯特征的两个男人试图进入瑞士。 **6** N-COUNT An **answer** is something that you say when you answer someone. 回答 [also "in" N "to" n] ❑ *Without waiting for an answer, he turned and went in through the door.* 他没有等候应答, 转身进了门。 **7** N-COUNT An **answer** is a letter that you write to someone who has written to you. 回信 [also "in" N "to" n] ❑ *I wrote to him but I never had an answer back.* 我给他写了信, 但是我从未收到回信。 **8** N-COUNT An **answer to** a problem is a solution to it. 解决方法 ❑ *There are no easy answers to the problems facing the economy.* 经济所面临的问题没有简单的解决方法。 **9** N-COUNT Someone's **answer to** a question in a test or quiz is what they write or say in an attempt to give the facts that are asked for. The **answer to** a question is the fact that was asked for. 解答 ❑ *Simply marking an answer wrong will not help the student to get future examples correct.* 只将某个解答判为错误不会帮助学生答对以后的例题。 **10** N-COUNT Your **answer to** something that someone has said or done is what you say or do in response to it or in defense of yourself. 回应 [also "in" N "to" n] ❑ *In answer to speculation that she wouldn't finish the race, she boldly declared her intention of winning it.* 作为对她不会完成赛程的推测的回应, 她大胆地宣布了她获胜的意图。 **11** PHRASE If you say that someone will not **take no for an answer**, you mean that they go on trying to make you agree to something even after you have refused. 不答应不罢休 ❑ *She is tough, unwilling to take no for an answer.* 她很难对付, 不答应不肯罢休。

▸ **answer back** PHRASAL VERB If someone, especially a child, **answers back**, they speak rudely to you when you speak to them. 顶嘴 [BRIT] ❑ *My youngest child is eight and she has started answering back too.* 我最小的孩子8岁, 也已经开始顶嘴了。

▸ **answer for** **1** PHRASAL VERB If you have to **answer for** something bad or wrong you have done, you are punished for it. (为所做的不好或错误的事) 付出代价 ❑ *He must be made to answer for his terrible crimes.* 必须让他为他的深重罪行付出代价。 **2** PHRASE If you say that someone **has a lot to answer for**, you are saying that their actions have led to problems which you think they are responsible for. 负有很大责任 ["have" inflects]

Thesaurus *answer* 另参见:
V. reply, respond **1** **2**

Word Partnership *answer* 的常用搭配:
V. **refuse to** answer **1**–**3**
have an answer **6**–**10**
wait for an answer **6** **7** **10**
find the answer **8** **10**
N. answer **a question** **1** **4**
answer **the door/telephone** **3**
DET. **no** answer **3**
ADJ. **correct/right** answer, **wrong** answer **8** **9**
straight answer **10**

an·swer·ing ma·chine (**answering machines**) N-COUNT An **answering machine** is a device that you connect to your telephone to record telephone calls while you are out. 电话答录机

ant /ænt/ (**ants**) N-COUNT **Ants** are small crawling insects that live in large groups. 蚂蚁 ❑ *Ants swarmed up out of the ground and covered her shoes and legs.* 蚂蚁从地里成群地爬出来, 爬满了她的鞋和腿。

an·tago·nise /æntægənaɪz/ [BRIT] → see **antagonize**

▲ **an·tago·nism** /æntægənɪzəm/ (**antagonisms**) N-UNCOUNT **Antagonism** between people is hatred or dislike between them. **Antagonisms** are instances of this. 敌意 [also N in pl] ❑ *There is still much antagonism between environmental groups and the oil companies.* 环境组织与石油公司之间仍有很多敌意。

Word Link *agon ≈ struggling : agonize, antagonist, protagonist*

▲ **an·tago·nist** /æntægənɪst/ (**antagonists**) N-COUNT Your **antagonist** is your opponent or enemy. 敌手 ❑ *Spassky had never previously lost to his antagonist.* 斯帕斯基以前从未败给过他的敌手。

Word Link *ant ≈ not, opposite : antagonize, Antarctic, antonym*

an·tago·nize /æntægənaɪz/ (**antagonizes, antagonizing, antagonized**)

in BRIT, also use **antagonise**

V-T If you **antagonize** someone, you make them feel angry or hostile toward you. 使(某人)对自己产生敌意 ❑ *He didn't want to antagonize her.* 他不想使她对自己产生敌意。

Ant·arc·tic /æntɑrktɪk/ N-PROPER **The Antarctic** is the area around the South Pole. 南极洲
→ see **globe**

ante /ænti/ **1** N-SING In card games such as poker, the **ante** is the sum of money staked by the players before the cards are dealt. (扑克等牌类游戏中的) 底注 **2** PHRASE If you **up the ante** or **raise the ante**, you increase your demands when you are in dispute or fighting for something. (在争斗中) 加高要求 [JOURNALISM] ❑ *Whenever they reached their goal, they upped the ante, setting increasingly complex challenges for themselves.* 每当他们达到了目标, 他们就加高要求, 为他们自己设置越来越复杂的挑战。

▲ **an·ten·na** /æntɛnə/ (**antennae** /æntɛni/ or **antennas**)

Antennas is the usual plural form for meaning **2**.

1 N-COUNT The **antennae** of something such as an insect or crustacean are the two long, thin parts attached to its head that it uses to feel things with. 触角 **2** N-COUNT An **antenna** is a device or a piece of wire that sends and receives television or radio signals and is usually attached to a radio, television, car, or building. 天线

an·them /ænθəm/ (**anthems**) N-COUNT An **anthem** is a song that is used to represent a particular nation, society, or group and that is sung on special occasions. 国歌; 会歌 ❑ *The band played the Czech anthem.* 这支乐队演奏了捷克国歌。

an·thol·ogy /ænθɒlədʒi/ (**anthologies**) N-COUNT An **anthology** is a collection of writings by different writers published together in one book. 选集 ❑ *...an anthology of poetry.* …一本诗歌选集。

Word Link *logy, ology ≈ study of : anthropology, biology, geology*

an·thro·pol·ogy /ænθrəpɒlədʒi/ N-UNCOUNT **Anthropology** is the scientific study of people, society, and culture. 人类学
● **an·thro·polo·gist** ▲ /ænθrəpɒlədʒɪst/ N-COUNT (**anthropologists**) 人类学家 ❑ *...an anthropologist who had been in China for three years.* …一位在中国呆过3年的人类学家。

Word Link *anti ≈ against : antibiotic, antibody, antidote*

★ **anti·bi·ot·ic** /æntibaɪɒtɪk, -taɪ-/ (**antibiotics**) N-COUNT **Antibiotics** are medical drugs used to kill bacteria and treat

A

infections. 抗生素 ❑ *Your doctor may prescribe antibiotics.* 你的大夫可能会开抗生素。
→ see **medicine**

Word Link *anti ≈ against : antibiotic, antibody, antidote*

anti·body /æntibɒdi, æntaɪ-/ (**antibodies**) N-COUNT **Antibodies** are substances that a person's or an animal's body produces in their blood in order to destroy substances that carry disease. 抗体 ❑ *Such women carry antibodies which make their blood more likely to clot during pregnancy.* 这样的女性携带在孕期使她们的血液更可能凝结的抗体。

an·tici·pate /æntɪsɪpeɪt/ (**anticipates, anticipating, anticipated**) **1** V-T If you **anticipate** an event, you realize in advance that it may happen and you are prepared for it. 预期 ❑ *At the time we couldn't have anticipated the result of our campaigning.* 当时我们不可能预期到我们活动的结果。 ❑ *It is anticipated that the equivalent of 192 full-time jobs will be lost.* 据预测相当于192个全职的工作将会丧失。 **2** V-T If you **anticipate** a question, request, or need, you do what is necessary or required before the question, request, or need occurs. 预先准备 ❑ *What Jeff did was to anticipate my next question.* 杰夫所做的是预先准备我的下一个问题。

an·tici·pa·tion /æntɪsɪpeɪʃ°n/ **1** N-UNCOUNT **Anticipation** is a feeling of excitement about something pleasant or exciting that you know is going to happen. 期待 ❑ *There's been an atmosphere of anticipation around here for a few days now.* 一种期待的氛围在这儿已存在几天了。 **2** PHRASE If something is done **in anticipation of** an event, it is done because people believe that event is going to happen. 预期某事的发生 ❑ *Troops in the Philippines have been put on full alert in anticipation of trouble during a planned general strike.* 预期在计划的总罢工期间会有麻烦，在菲律宾的军队已处于完全戒备状态。

anti·clock·wise /æntiklɒkwaɪz, æntaɪ-/ also **anti-clockwise** ADV If something is moving **anticlockwise**, it is moving in the opposite direction to the direction in which the hands of a clock move. 逆时针方向地 [BRIT]

in AM, use **counterclockwise**

● ADJ **Anticlockwise** is also an adjective. 逆时针方向的 [ADJ n] ❑ *...an anticlockwise route around the coast.* ……一条环绕海岸的逆时针路线。

an·tics /æntɪks/ N-PLURAL **Antics** are funny, silly, or unusual ways of behaving. 滑稽反常的举止 ❑ *Elizabeth tolerated Sarah's antics.* 伊丽莎白容忍了萨拉的滑稽反常的举止。

anti·dote /æntidoʊt/ (**antidotes**) **1** N-COUNT An **antidote** is a chemical substance that stops or controls the effect of a poison. 解毒药 ❑ *When he returned, he noticed their sickness and prepared an antidote.* 当他返回时，他注意到了他们的病情，准备了解毒药。 **2** N-COUNT Something that is an **antidote to** a difficult or unpleasant situation helps you to overcome the situation. 克服…的良方 ❑ *Massage is a wonderful antidote to stress.* 按摩是一种极妙的对抗压力的良方。

▲ **anti·mis·sile** /æntimɪs°l, æntaɪ-/ (**antimissiles**) **1** ADJ **Antimissile** defenses are weapons and equipment that are used for stopping and destroying missiles before they reach their target. 反导弹的 [ADJ n] ❑ *The military is expanding its antimissile defense system.* 军方正在扩大其反导弹防御系统。 **2** N-COUNT An **antimissile** is a type of weapon that is used to stop and destroy missiles before they reach their target. 反导弹 ❑ *The attacks allowed the coalition to display its shield of antimissiles.* 该进攻令联盟得以展示其反导弹屏障。

an·tipa·thy /æntɪpəθi/ N-UNCOUNT **Antipathy** is a strong feeling of dislike or hostility toward someone or something. 憎恶 [FORMAL] ❑ *...the voting public's antipathy toward the president.* ……投票民众对总统的憎恶。

Word Link *antiq ≈ old : antiquated, antique, antiquity*

anti·quat·ed /æntɪkweɪtɪd/ ADJ If you describe something as **antiquated**, you are criticizing it because it is very old or old-fashioned. 陈旧的；过时的 [DISAPPROVAL] ❑ *Many factories are so antiquated they are not worth saving.* 许多工厂太陈旧以致不值得保留。

an·tique ♦◇◇ /æntik/ (**antiques**) N-COUNT An **antique** is an old object such as a piece of china or furniture that is valuable because of its beauty or rarity. 古董 ❑ *...a genuine antique.* ……一件真古董。

▲ **an·tiq·uity** /æntɪkwɪti/ (**antiquities**) **1** N-UNCOUNT **Antiquity** is the distant past, especially the time of the ancient Egyptians, Greeks, and Romans. 古代（尤指古埃及、古希腊和古罗马时期）❑ *...famous monuments of classical antiquity.* ……古典时期的著名纪念碑。 **2** N-COUNT **Antiquities** are things such as buildings, statues, or coins that were made in ancient times and have survived to the present day. 古物 ❑ *...collectors of Roman antiquities.* ……罗马古物的收藏者们。

anti·sep·tic /æntəsɛptɪk/ (**antiseptics**) N-MASS **Antiseptic** is a substance that kills germs and harmful bacteria. 消毒剂 ❑ *She bathed the cut with antiseptic.* 她用消毒剂浸洗了伤口。
→ see **medicine**

anti·so·cial /æntisoʊʃ°l, æntaɪ-/ ADJ Someone who is **antisocial** is unwilling to meet and be friendly with other people. 孤僻的 ❑ *...a generation of teenagers who will become aggressive and antisocial.* ……将会变得好斗、孤僻的青少年一代。

an·tith·esis /æntɪθəsɪs/ (**antitheses** /æntɪθəsiz/) N-COUNT **The antithesis of** something is its exact opposite. 对立面 [FORMAL] ❑ *The antithesis of the Middle Eastern buyer is the Japanese.* 与中东买主截然相反的是日本买主。

anti·trust /æntitrʌst, æntaɪ-/ ADJ In the United States, **antitrust** laws are intended to stop big companies taking over their competitors, fixing prices with their competitors, or interfering with free competition in any way. 反垄断的 [ADJ n] ❑ *The jury found that the NFL had violated antitrust laws.* 该陪审团判定全美橄榄球联盟违反了反垄断法规。

anti-virus also **antivirus** ADJ **Anti-virus** software is software that protects a computer against viruses. 杀电脑病毒的 [ADJ n]

Word Link *ant ≈ not, opposite : antagonize, Antarctic, antonym*

▲ **an·to·nym** /æntənɪm/ (**antonyms**) N-COUNT The **antonym** of a word is a word that means the opposite. 反义词 [FORMAL]

anus /eɪnəs/ (**anuses**) N-COUNT A person's **anus** is the hole from which feces leaves their body. 肛门 [MEDICAL]

anxi·ety ♦◇◇ /æŋzaɪɪti/ (**anxieties**) N-UNCOUNT **Anxiety** is a feeling of nervousness or worry. 焦虑 [also N in pl] ❑ *Her voice was full of anxiety.* 她的声音饱含焦虑。

anx·ious ♦◇◇ /æŋkʃəs/ **1** ADJ If you are **anxious to** do something or **anxious that** something should happen, you very much want to do it or very much want it to happen. 焦急的 [v-link ADJ] ❑ *Both the Americans and the Russians are anxious to avoid conflict in South Asia.* 美国人与俄国人都急于避免南亚冲突。 ❑ *He is anxious that there should be no delay.* 他急切希望不会有任何延误。 **2** ADJ If you are **anxious**, you are nervous or worried about something. 焦虑的 ❑ *The foreign minister admitted he was still anxious about the situation in the country.* 外交部长承认他对该国的局势依然感到焦虑。
● **anx·ious·ly** ADV 焦虑地 [ADV with v] ❑ *They are waiting anxiously to see who will succeed him.* 他们在焦虑不安地等着看谁将接替他。

Word Partnership *anxious* 的常用搭配：

PREP.	anxious **for** *something* **1**
	anxious **about** *something* **2**
V.	anxious **to do** *something* **1**
	become/feel/get/seem anxious, **make** *someone* anxious **2**

any ♦♦♦ /ɛni/ **1** DET You use **any** in statements with negative meaning to indicate that no thing or person of a particular type exists, is present, or is involved in a situation. 任何的（用于含否定意义的陈述句中）❑ *I'm not making any promises.* 我不是在作任何承诺。 ❑ *We are doing this all without any support from the hospital.* 我们在没有来自医院的任何支持的情况下做着这一切。 ❑ *It is too early to say what effect, if any, there will be on the workforce.* 说对职工会有什么影响，如果有的话，也还为时过早。 ● QUANT **Any** is also a quantifier. 任何一个 ❑ *You don't know any of my friends.* 你不认识任何一个我的朋友。 ● PRON **Any** is also a pronoun. 任何一个 [PRON after v] ❑ *The children needed new school clothes and Kim couldn't afford any.* 孩子们需要新校服，金买不起任何一件。 **2** DET You use **any** in questions and conditional clauses to ask whether there is some of a particular thing or some of a particular group of people, or to suggest that there might be. 某个的（用于疑问句和条件分句中）❑ *Do you speak any foreign languages?* 你说某种外语吗？ ● QUANT **Any** is also a quantifier. 某个 ❑ *Introduce foods one at a time and notice if you feel uncomfortable with any of them.* 一次尝一种食物，看你是否对其中某种食物感到不适。 ● PRON **Any** is also a pronoun. 某个 [PRON after v] ❑ *If any bright thoughts occur to you pass them straight to me. Have you got any?* 如果你想到某个好主意就直接告诉我。你有什么好主意吗？ **3** DET You use **any** in positive statements when you are referring to someone or something of a particular kind that might exist, occur, or be involved in a situation, when their exact identity or nature is not important. 任何一个的(用于肯定陈述句中) ❑ *Any actor will tell you that it is easier to perform than to be themselves.* 任何演员都会告诉你表演比做自己更容易。 ● QUANT **Any** is also a quantifier. 任何一个 ❑ *Nealy disappeared two days ago, several miles away from any of the fighting.* 尼利两天前失踪了，离任何一个战场都有几英里。 ● PRON **Any** is also a pronoun. 任何一个 ❑ *Clean the mussels and discard any that do not close.* 清洗这些蚌，并且丢掉任何合不上的。 4 ADV You can also use **any** to emphasize a comparative adjective or adverb in a negative statement. 任何地(用于否定陈述句中以强调某比较级形容词或副词) [ADV compar] [EMPHASIS] ❑ *I can't see things getting any easier for graduates.* 我看不到对于毕业生们事情有任何变容易的趋势。 5 PHRASE If you say that someone or something is **not just any** person or thing, you mean that they are special in some way. 并非任何的 ❑ *Finzer is not just any East Coast businessman.* 芬泽并非一般的东海岸商人。

> **Any** is mainly used in questions and negative sentences. You use **not any** instead of **some** in negative sentences. ❑ *There isn't any money.*

6 PHRASE If something does not happen or is not true **any longer**, it has stopped happening or is no longer true. (不) 再 ❑ *I couldn't keep the tears hidden any longer.* 我再也藏不住泪水了。 7 **in any case** → see **case** 8 **by any chance** → see **chance** 9 **in any event** → see **event** 10 **any old** → see **old** 11 **at any rate** → see **rate**

Word Partnership *any* 的常用搭配：

ADV. **almost** any, any **better**, any **further**, **hardly** any, any **longer**, any **more**, **without** any 1
N. any **difference**, any **good**, any **idea**, any **kind**, any **luck**, any **minute/moment (now)**, any **number of *something***, any **questions** 3
PREP. any **(one) of *something***, at any **point/time**, at any **rate**, by any **chance**, by any **means**, in any **case**, in any **way** 3

any·body ♦◇◇ /ɛnibɒdi, -bʌdi/ PRON-INDEF **Anybody** means the same as **anyone**. 任何人

any·how /ɛnihaʊ/ 1 ADV **Anyhow** means the same as **anyway**. 反正 (同**anyway**) 2 ADV If you do something **anyhow**, you do it in a careless or untidy way. 马虎随便地 [ADV after v] ❑ *Her discarded books were piled up just anyhow.* 她丢弃的书被胡乱地堆了起来。

any·more ♦♦◇ /ɛnimɔr/ also **any more** ADV If something does not happen or is not true **anymore**, it has stopped happening or is no longer true. (不) 再 [ADV after v] ❑ *I don't ride my motorbike much anymore.* 我不再常骑我的摩托车了。 ❑ *I couldn't trust him anymore.* 我再不能相信他了。

any·one ♦♦◇ /ɛniwʌn/

> The form **anybody** is also used.

1 PRON-INDEF You use **anyone** or **anybody** in statements with negative meaning to indicate in a general way that nobody is present or involved in an action. 任何人(用于含否定意义的陈述句中) ❑ *I won't tell anyone I saw you here.* 我不会告诉任何人我在这儿看见了你。 ❑ *You needn't talk to anyone if you don't want to.* 如果你不想你就不需要和任何人说话。 2 PRON-INDEF You use **anyone** or **anybody** in questions and conditional clauses to ask or talk about whether someone is present or doing something. 某个人(用于疑问句和条件分句中) ❑ *Why would anyone want that job?* 为什么会有人想要那份工作？ ❑ *How can anyone look sad at an occasion like this?* 在像这样的一个场合怎么会有人看上去悲伤呢？ 3 PRON-INDEF You use **anyone** or **anybody** before words that indicate the kind of person you are talking about. 任何…的人(接后置修饰语) [PRON cl/group] ❑ *I always had been the person who achieved things before anyone else at my age.* 我过去一直是那种在任何同龄人之前达成目标的人。 ❑ *It's not a job for anyone who is slow with numbers.* 这不是一种适合任何对数字反应慢的人的工作。 4 PRON-INDEF You use **anyone** or **anybody** to refer to a person when you are emphasizing that it could be any person out of a very large number of people. 任何一个人 [EMPHASIS] ❑ *Anyone could be doing what I'm doing.* 任何一个人都可以做我在做的事。 5 PHRASE You use **anyone who is anyone** and **anybody who is anybody** to refer to people who are important or influential. 任何要人 ❑ *It seems anyone who's anyone in business is going to the conference.* 似乎商界的任何要人都要来参加这次会议。

> Do not confuse **anyone** with **any one**. **Anyone** always refers to people. In the phrase **any one**, "one" is a pronoun or a determiner that can refer to either a person or a thing, depending on the context. It is often followed by the word **of**. ❑ *Parting from any one of you for even a short time is hard... None of us stay in any one place for a very long time.* In these examples, **any one** is a more emphatic way of saying **any**. **Anyone** or **anybody** is mainly used in questions and negative sentences. You use **not anyone** instead of **someone** in negative sentences. ❑ *There isn't anyone here... There isn't anybody here.*

any·place /ɛnipleɪs/ ADV **Anyplace** means the same as **anywhere**. 任何地方 [ADV after v] [AM, INFORMAL] ❑ *She didn't have anyplace to go.* 她没有任何地方可去。

any·thing ♦♦♦ /ɛniθɪŋ/ 1 PRON-INDEF You use **anything** in statements with negative meaning to indicate in a general way that nothing is present or that an action or event does not or cannot happen. 任何事物(用于含有否定意义的陈述句中) ❑ *We can't do anything.* 我们什么也做不了。 ❑ *She couldn't see or hear anything at all.* 她根本什么也看不见、听不见。 2 PRON-INDEF You use **anything** in questions and conditional clauses to ask or talk about whether something is present or happening. 某事物(用于疑问句和条件分句中) ❑ *What happened, is anything wrong?* 发生什么了，有什么问题吗？ ❑ *Did you find anything?* 你发现什么了吗？ 3 PRON-INDEF You can use **anything** before words that indicate the kind of thing you are talking about. 任何…的事物(接后置修饰语) [PRON cl/group] ❑ *More than anything else, he wanted to become a teacher.* 比起任何别的职业，他更想当老师。 ❑ *Anything that's cheap this year will be even cheaper next year.* 今年任何便宜的东西明年甚至会更便宜。 4 PRON-INDEF You use **anything** to emphasize a possible thing, event, or situation, when you are saying that it could be any one of a very large number of things. 任一事物 [EMPHASIS] ❑ *He is young, fresh, and ready for anything.* 他年轻、未经世故，任何事都愿意尝试。 5 PRON-INDEF You use **anything** in expressions such as **anything near**, **anything close to** and **anything like** to emphasize a statement that you are making. 任何(接近、像…的) 事物 [PRON prep] [EMPHASIS] ❑ *Doctors have decided the only way he can live anything near a normal life is to give him an operation.* 医生们已经确定了他能过任何接近正常生活的惟一方法是给他做个手术。 6 PRON-INDEF When you do not want to be exact, you use **anything** to talk about a particular range of things or quantities. (某范围的) 任何事物 [PRON "from" n "to" n, PRON "between" n "and" n] ❑ *...Chinese herbs that have cured anything from colds to broken bones.* …治愈了从感冒到骨折的任何病的中草药。

> **Anything** is mainly used in questions and negative sentences. You use **not anything** instead of **something** in negative sentences. ❑ *There isn't anything here.*

7 PHRASE You use **anything but** in expressions such as **anything but quiet** and **anything but attractive** to emphasize that something is not the case. 绝对不 [EMPHASIS] ❑ *There's no evidence that Christopher told anyone to say anything but the truth.* 没有证据证明克里斯托弗叫任何人绝对不说真相。 8 PHRASE You can say that you **would not** do something **for anything** to emphasize that you definitely would not want to do or be a particular thing. 决不会做某事/决不会是某事 [INFORMAL, SPOKEN, EMPHASIS] ❑ *I wouldn't want to move for anything in the world.* 说什么我也不会搬走。 9 PHRASE You use **if anything**, especially after a negative statement, to introduce a statement that adds to what you have just said. 如果有什么的话 ❑ *I never had to clean up after the lodgers. If anything, they did most of the cleaning.* 我从来不必在房客们走后做打扫。要做的话，他们做大部分的清扫。 10 PHRASE You can add **or anything** to the end of a clause or sentence in order to refer vaguely to other things that are or may be similar to what you just mentioned. 或什么的 [INFORMAL, SPOKEN, VAGUENESS] ❑ *Listen, if you talk to Elizabeth or anything make sure you let everyone know, will you.* 听着，如果你和伊丽莎白讲话或什么的，一定要让每个人都知道，你能做到吧。

Word Partnership *anything* 的常用搭配：

ADJ. anything **left**, anything **more** 2
ready for anything 4
PREP. anything **like** 5
anything **but** 7

any·time /ɛnitaɪm/ ADV You use **anytime** to mean a point in time that is not fixed or set. 任何时候 ❑ *The college admits students anytime during the year.* 这所学院在全年里任何时间都接收学生。 ❑ *He can leave anytime he wants.* 他可以在任何他想要的时间离开。

any·way ♦♦◇ /ɛniweɪ/

The form **anyhow** is also used.

1 ADV You use **anyway** or **anyhow** to indicate that a statement explains or supports a previous point. 反正（用以表示某陈述解释或支撑前一观点）[ADV with cl] ❑ *I'm certain David's told you his business troubles. Anyway, it's no secret that he owes money.* 我肯定戴维已经告诉了你他生意上的麻烦。反正他欠钱不是什么秘密。 2 ADV You use **anyway** or **anyhow** to suggest that a statement is true or relevant in spite of other things that have been said. 不管怎样（用以表示某陈述是事实）[ADV with cl] ❑ *I don't know why I settled on Miami, but anyway I did.* 我不知道为什么我落户到了迈阿密，但不管怎样我做了。 3 ADV You use **anyway** or **anyhow** to correct or modify a statement, for example, to limit it to what you definitely know to be true. 用以纠正或限定某陈述 [cl/group ADV] ❑ *Mary Ann doesn't want to have children. Not right now, anyway.* 玛丽・安不想要孩子。至少眼下不要。 4 ADV You use **anyway** or **anyhow** to indicate that you are asking what the real situation is or what the real reason for something is. 究竟 [cl ADV] ❑ *What do you want from me, anyway?* 你究竟想从我这儿得到什么？ 5 ADV You use **anyway** or **anyhow** to indicate that you are leaving out some details in a story and are passing on to the next main point or event. 如此这般之后（用以表示略掉一些细节进入下一要点或事件）[ADV with cl] ❑ *I was told to go to Denver for this interview. It was a very amusing affair. Anyhow, I got the job.* 我被告知去丹佛参加这个面试。那是件非常有意思的事。如此这般之后，我得到了这份工作。 6 ADV You use **anyway** or **anyhow** to change the topic or return to a previous topic. 用以转换话题或回到先前的话题 [ADV cl] ❑ *"I've got a terrible cold."—"Have you? Oh dear. Anyway, so you're not going to go away this weekend?"* "我得了重感冒。"——"是吗？哦，真是的。如此的话，你这个周末就不走了吧？" 7 ADV You use **anyway** or **anyhow** to indicate that you want to end the conversation. 好了（用以表示想结束对话）[ADV cl] ❑ *"Anyway, I'd better let you have your dinner. Bye."* "好了，我最好让你吃晚餐了。再见！"

any·ways /ɛniweɪz/ ADV **Anyways** is a nonstandard or dialectal form of **anyway**. **anyway**的非标准或方言形式 [AM, SPOKEN] ❑ *Well, anyways, she said it wasn't safe.* 嗯，不管怎样，她说不安全。

any·where ♦◇◇ /ɛniwɛər/ 1 ADV You use **anywhere** in statements with negative meaning to indicate that a place does not exist. 任何地方（用于含有否定意义的陈述句中）❑ *I haven't got anywhere to live.* 我没有任何地方住。 2 ADV You use **anywhere** in questions and conditional clauses to ask or talk about a place without saying exactly where you mean. 某个地方（用于疑问句或条件从句中）❑ *Did you try to get help from anywhere?* 你有没有试着从某个地方获得帮助？ 3 ADV You use **anywhere** before words that indicate the kind of place you are talking about. 任何…的地方 [ADV cl/group] ❑ *He'll meet you anywhere you want.* 他会在任何你希望的地点见你。 4 ADV You use **anywhere** to refer to a place when you are emphasizing that it could be any of a large number of places. 任何一个地方 [EMPHASIS] ❑ *...jokes that are so funny they always work anywhere.* …如此有趣以致在哪里都奏效的笑话。 5 ADV When you do not want to be exact, you use **anywhere** to refer to a particular range of things. （某范围内的）任何地方 ❑ *His shoes cost anywhere from $200 up.* 他的鞋价钱在$200以上。 6 ADV You use **anywhere** in expressions such as **anywhere near** and **anywhere close to** to emphasize a statement that you are making. 任何（接近…的）地方 [ADV adj/adv] [EMPHASIS] ❑ *There weren't anywhere near enough empty boxes.* 根本没有足够的空盒子。

Anywhere is mainly used in questions and negative sentences. You use **not anywhere** instead of **somewhere** in negative sentences. ❑ *He isn't going anywhere.*

Word Partnership *anywhere* 的常用搭配:

V. **can/could happen** anywhere, **get** anywhere, **go** anywhere 2–4

PREP. anywhere **in the world** 2–4
anywhere **near** 6

apart
1 POSITIONS AND STATES
2 INDICATING EXCEPTIONS AND FOCUSING

1 apart ♦♦◇ /əpɑrt/

In addition to the uses shown below, **apart** is used in phrasal verbs such as "grow apart" and "take apart."

1 ADV When people or things are **apart**, they are some distance from each other. 分开地 ❑ *He was standing a bit apart from the rest of us, watching us.* 他和我们其余人分开一点站着看着我们。 ❑ *Ray and sister Renee lived just 25 miles apart from each other.* 雷和姊妹勒妮住得彼此仅隔25英里。 2 ADV If two people or things move **apart** or are pulled **apart**, they move away from each other. 分离地 [ADV after v] ❑ *John and Isabelle moved apart, back into the sun.* 约翰和伊莎贝尔彼此分开了，回到阳光下。 3 ADV If two people are **apart**, they are no longer living together or spending time together, either permanently or just for a short time. 不在一起地 ❑ *It was the first time Jane and I had been apart for more than a few days.* 这是我和简第一次分开超过了几天。 4 ADV If you take something **apart**, you separate it into the pieces that it is made of. If it comes or falls **apart**, its parts separate from each other. 散开地 [ADV after v] ❑ *When the clock stopped he took it apart, found what was wrong, and put the whole thing together again.* 钟停了之后他把它拆开，找出了问题，然后又全部装好了。 5 ADV If something such as an organization or relationship falls **apart**, or if something tears it **apart**, it can no longer continue because it has serious difficulties. 破裂地 [ADV after v] ❑ *Any manager knows that his company will start falling apart if his attention wanders.* 任何经理都知道如果他的注意力分散了他的公司将会开始分崩离析。 6 ADV If something sets someone or something **apart**, it makes them different from other people or things. 区分开地 ❑ *What really sets Mr. Thaksin apart is that he comes not from Southern China, but from northern Thailand.* 真正使他信先生与众不同的是他并非来自中国南方，而是来自泰国北方。 7 ADJ If people or groups are a long way **apart** on a particular topic or issue, they have completely different views and disagree about it. 有分歧的 [v-link amount ADJ, oft ADJ "on" n] ❑ *Their concept of a performance and our concept were miles apart.* 他们对一场表演的概念和我们的概念相去甚远。 8 PHRASE If you can't **tell** two people or things **apart**, they look exactly the same to you. 不能区分 ❑ *I can still only tell Mark and Dave apart by the color of their shoes!* 我依然只能通过马克和戴夫的鞋的颜色区分他们。

Word Partnership *apart* 的常用搭配:

ADV. **far** apart 1 1
N. **miles** apart 1 1
V. **take** apart 1 4
drive apart, **fall** apart, **tear** apart 1 5
set *someone/something* apart 1 6
tell apart 1 8

2 apart ♦◇◇ /əpɑrt/ 1 PHRASE **Apart from** means the same as **aside from**. 除…以外（同**aside from**）2 ADV You use **apart** when you are making an exception to a general statement. 除…以外 [n ADV] ❑ *This was, New York apart, the first American city I had ever been in where people actually lived downtown.* 这是除纽约以外我所呆过的居民实际住在市中心的第一座美国城市。

apart·heid /əpɑrthaɪt/ N-UNCOUNT **Apartheid** was a political system in South Africa in which people were divided into racial groups and kept apart by law. 种族隔离制 ❑ *He praised her role in the struggle against apartheid.* 他赞扬了她在反对种族隔离制的斗争中所起的作用。

apart·ment ♦◇◇ /əpɑrtmənt/ (**apartments**) N-COUNT An **apartment** is a separate set of rooms for living in, in a house or a building with other apartments. 公寓 [mainly AM]

in BRIT, usually use **flat**

❑ *Christina has her own apartment, with her own car.* 克里斯蒂娜有她自己的公寓，有自己的车。

→ see **city**

apart·ment build·ing (**apartment buildings**) or **apartment house** N-COUNT An **apartment building** or **apartment house** is a tall building that contains different apartments. 公寓楼 [AM]

in BRIT, use **block of flats**

❑ *...the Manhattan apartment house where they live.* …他们居住的曼哈顿公寓楼。

apa·thet·ic /æpəθɛtɪk/ ADJ If you describe someone as **apathetic**, you are criticizing them because they do not seem to be interested in or enthusiastic about doing anything. 漠不关心的 [DISAPPROVAL] ❑ *Even the most apathetic students are beginning to sit up and listen.* 即使最漠不关心的学生都开始坐直身子听了。

Word Link *path ≈ feeling : apathy, empathy, sympathy*

apa·thy /æpəθi/ N-UNCOUNT You can use **apathy** to talk about someone's state of mind if you are criticizing them because they do not seem to be interested in or enthusiastic about anything. 漠不关心 [DISAPPROVAL] ❑ *They told me about isolation and public apathy.* 他们向我讲述了孤立感与公众的冷漠。

▲ **ape** /eɪp/ (apes, aping, aped) 1 N-COUNT **Apes** are chimpanzees, gorillas, and other animals in the same family. 猿 ❑ *...chimpanzees and other apes.* …黑猩猩和其他猿。 2 V-T If you **ape** someone's speech or behavior, you imitate it. 模仿 ❑ *Modeling yourself on someone you admire is not the same as aping all they say or do.* 以你仰慕的某个人为榜样并不等于模仿他们的全部言行。

→ see **primate**

ap·er·ture /æpərtʃər/ (apertures) 1 N-COUNT An **aperture** is a narrow hole or gap. 孔隙 [FORMAL] ❑ *Through the aperture he could see daylight.* 通过这个孔隙他能看到日光。 2 N-COUNT In photography, the **aperture** of a camera is the size of the hole through which light passes to reach the film. (相机镜头的) 孔径 ❑ *Use a small aperture and position the camera carefully.* 使用小孔径并且小心地安放好照相机。

apex /eɪpɛks/ (apexes) 1 N-SING **The apex of** an organization or system is the highest and most important position in it. (机构、体系的) 最上层 ❑ *At the apex of the party was its central committee.* 该党的最高机构是其中央委员会。 2 N-COUNT **The apex of** something is its pointed top or end. 尖端; 顶点 ❑ *The hangar is 103 feet high at the apex of its roof.* 飞机库顶最高点高103英尺。

apiece /əpis/ 1 ADV If people have a particular number of things **apiece**, they have that number each. 每人地 [amount ADV] ❑ *He and I had two fish apiece.* 我和他每人有两条鱼。 2 ADV If a number of similar things are for sale at a certain price **apiece**, that is the price for each one of them. 各 [amount ADV] ❑ *Entire roast chickens were sixty cents apiece.* 烤全鸡每只60美分。

apolo·get·ic /əpɒlədʒɛtɪk/ ADJ If you are **apologetic**, you show or say that you are sorry for causing trouble for someone, for hurting them, or for disappointing them. 表达歉意的 ❑ *The hospital staff were very apologetic but that couldn't really compensate.* 医院员工都深表歉意，但那不能真正补偿。 ● **apolo·geti·cal·ly** /əpɒlədʒɛtɪkli/ ADV 表达歉意地 [ADV with v] ❑ *"It's of no great literary merit," he said, almost apologetically.* "它不具有重要的文学价值，"他几乎抱歉地说道。

apolo·gise /əpɒlədʒaɪz/ [BRIT] → see **apologize**

apolo·gize /əpɒlədʒaɪz/ (apologizes, apologizing, apologized)

in BRIT, also use **apologise**

V-I When you **apologize to** someone, you say that you are sorry that you have hurt them or caused trouble for them. You can say **"I apologize"** as a formal way of saying sorry. 表达歉意 ❑ *I apologize for being late, but I have just had a message from the hospital.* 我为迟到表示歉意，但我刚得到了来自医院的一个消息。 ❑ *He apologized to the people who had been affected.* 他向受到了影响的人道了歉。

Word Link *log ≈ reason, speech : apology, dialogue, logic*

apol·ogy /əpɒlədʒi/ (apologies) 1 N-VAR An **apology** is something that you say or write in order to tell someone that you are sorry that you have hurt them or caused trouble for them. 表达歉意的言辞 ❑ *I didn't get an apology.* 我没有得到道歉之词。 ❑ *We received a letter of apology.* 我们收到了一封致歉信。 2 N-PLURAL If you offer or make your **apologies**, you apologize. (表达) 歉意 [FORMAL] ❑ *When Mary finally appeared, she made her apologies to Mrs. Velasquez.* 当玛丽最终露面时，她向委拉斯开兹夫人道了歉。

Word Partnership *apology 的常用搭配:*

ADJ. **formal/public** apology 1
N. **letter of** apology 1
V. **demand** apologies, **owe** *someone* apologies 1
make apologies 2

apos·tro·phe /əpɒstrəfi/ (apostrophes) N-COUNT An **apostrophe** is the mark ' when it is written to indicate that one or more letters have been left out of a word, as in "isn't" and "we'll." It is also added to nouns to form possessives, as in "Mike's car." 撇号

▲ **ap·pal** /əpɔːl/ [BRIT] → see **appall**

▲ **ap·pall** /əpɔl/ (appalls, appalling, appalled)

in BRIT, use **appal**

V-T If something **appalls** you, it disgusts you because it seems so bad or unpleasant. 使厌恶 ❑ *The new-found strength of local militancy appalls many observers.* 新发现的地方军事行动战斗力让很多观察员厌恶。

ap·palled /əpɔld/ ADJ If you are **appalled** by something, you are shocked or disgusted because it is so bad or unpleasant. 感到厌恶的 ❑ *She said that the Americans are appalled at the statements made at the conference.* 她说美国人对在该大会中作的声明感到震惊。

★ **ap·pal·ling** /əpɔlɪŋ/ 1 ADJ Something that is **appalling** is so bad or unpleasant that it shocks you. 骇人听闻的 ❑ *They have been living under the most appalling conditions for two months.* 他们在最骇人听闻的条件下生活了两个月。 ● **ap·pal·ling·ly** ADV 骇人听闻地 ❑ *He says that he understands why they behaved so appallingly.* 他说他明白为什么他们表现得如此让人震惊。 2 ADJ You can use **appalling** to emphasize that something is very extreme or severe. 极度的; 严重的 [EMPHASIS] ❑ *I developed an appalling headache.* 我得了严重头疼。 ● **ap·pal·ling·ly** ADV 极度地; 严重地 ❑ *It's been an appallingly busy morning.* 那是个极其繁忙的早晨。 3 → see also **appall**

★ **ap·pa·rat·us** /æpərætəs, -reɪ-/ (apparatuses) 1 N-VAR The **apparatus** of an organization or system is its structure and method of operation. (机构、体系的) 组织和运作方式 ❑ *For many years, the country had been buried under the apparatus of the regime.* 多年来，该国一直处于这种政体的统治下。 2 N-VAR **Apparatus** is the equipment, such as tools and machines, which is used to do a particular job or activity. 设备 ❑ *One of the boys had to be rescued by firemen wearing breathing apparatus.* 其中的一个男孩得由戴着呼吸设备的消防队员们营救。

ap·par·ent ◆◇◇ /əpærənt/ 1 ADJ An **apparent** situation, quality, or feeling seems to exist, although you cannot be certain that it does exist. 未必真实的 [ADJ n] ❑ *I was a bit depressed by our apparent lack of progress.* 我对我们表面上的缺乏进展感到有点沮丧。 2 ADJ If something is **apparent** to you, it is clear and obvious to you. 明显的 [v-link ADJ] ❑ *It has been apparent that in other areas standards have held up well.* 显然在其他领域标准保持得良好。 3 PHRASE If you say that something happens **for no apparent reason**, you cannot understand why it happens. 莫名其妙地 ❑ *The person may become dizzy for no apparent reason.* 此人可能会莫名其妙地变得头晕目眩。

ap·par·ent·ly ◆◆◇ /əpærəntli/ 1 ADV You use **apparently** to indicate that the information you are giving is something that you have heard, but you are not certain that it is true. 据说 [VAGUENESS] ❑ *Apparently the girls are not at all amused by the whole business.* 据说这些女孩们完全不觉得这整件事好笑。 2 ADV You use **apparently** to refer to something that seems to be true, although you are not sure whether it is or not. 貌似地 ❑ *The recent deterioration has been caused by an apparently endless recession.* 最近的恶化是由貌似没完没了的萧条造成的。

ap·peal ◆◆◇ /əpil/ (appeals, appealing, appealed) 1 V-I If you **appeal to** someone **to** do something, you make a serious and urgent request to them. 呼吁 ❑ *He appealed to voters to go to the polls tomorrow.* 他呼吁选民们明天去投票站。 ❑ *He will appeal to the state for an extension of unemployment benefits.* 他将呼吁国家延长失业救济。 2 V-T If you **appeal** a decision **to** someone in authority, you formally ask them to change it. 申诉 ❑ *We intend to appeal the verdict.* 我们打算对此裁决提出申诉。 3 V-I If something **appeals to** you, you find it attractive or interesting. 有吸引力 ❑ *On the other hand, the idea appealed to him.* 另一方面，这个主意对他有吸引力。 4 N-COUNT An **appeal** is a serious and urgent request. 呼吁 ❑ *He has a message from King Fahd, believed to be an appeal for Arab unity.* 他有个来自法赫德国王的口信，相信是对阿拉伯团结的呼吁。 5 N-COUNT An **appeal** is an attempt to raise money for a charity or for a good cause. (为慈善或好的事业所做的) 筹款努力 ❑ *...an appeal to save a library containing priceless manuscripts.* …为挽救一个藏有无价手稿图书馆的一次筹款努力。 6 N-VAR An **appeal** is a formal request for a decision to be changed. 申诉 ❑ *They took their appeal to the Supreme*

Court. 他们上诉到了最高法院。 7 N-UNCOUNT The **appeal** of something is a quality that people find attractive or interesting. 吸引力 ❑ *Its new title was meant to give the party greater public appeal.* 其新的名字意在给予该党更大的公众吸引力。 8 → see also **appealing** → see **trial**

Word Partnership *appeal* 的常用搭配：

PREP. appeal **to** *someone* 1 2
appeal **to a court** 2
appeal **for** *something* 4 5
N. **make an** appeal 4 5
V. appeal **a case/decision** 2 6

ap·peal·ing /əpiːlɪŋ/ 1 ADJ Someone or something that is **appealing** is pleasing and attractive. 吸引人的 ❑ *There was a sense of humor to what he did that I found very appealing.* 他所做的带有一种我发现很迷人的幽默感。 2 ADJ An **appealing** expression or tone of voice indicates to someone that you want help, advice, or approval. 恳求的（表情、语气） ❑ *She gave him a soft appealing look that would have melted solid ice.* 她向他投去一种会融化坚冰的温柔恳求的表情。 3 → see also **appeal**

ap·pear ♦♦♦ /əpɪər/ (**appears, appearing, appeared**) 1 V-LINK If you say that something **appears to** be the way you describe it, you are reporting what you believe or what you have been told, though you cannot be sure it is true. 似乎 [no cont] [VAGUENESS] ❑ *There appears to be increasing support for the leadership to take a more aggressive stance.* 似乎有不断增长的对领导层采取更强立场的支持。 2 V-LINK If someone or something **appears to** have a particular quality or characteristic, they give the impression of having that quality or characteristic. 表现得 [no cont] ❑ *She did her best to appear more self-assured than she felt.* 她竭力表现得比她感觉的更为自信。 ❑ *He is anxious to appear a gentleman.* 他急于表现得像一位绅士。 3 V-I When someone or something **appears**, they move into a position where you can see them. 出现 ❑ *A woman appeared at the far end of the street.* 一个女人在街那端出现了。 4 V-I When something new **appears**, it begins to exist or reaches a stage of development where its existence can be noticed. 显现 ❑ *...small white flowers which appear in early summer.* …在初夏出现的小白花。 5 V-I When something such as a book **appears**, it is published or becomes available for people to buy. 出版 ❑ *I could hardly wait for "Boys' Life" to appear each month.* 我每个月几乎都等不及《男孩生活》出版。 6 V-I When someone **appears in** something such as a play, a show, or a television program, they take part in it. （在戏剧、访谈、电视节目等中）露面 ❑ *Jill Bennett became John Osborne's fourth wife, and appeared in several of his plays.* 吉尔・贝纳特成为了约翰・奥斯本的第4任妻子，并在他的几部戏剧中出演角色。 7 V-I When someone **appears before** a court of law or **before** an official committee, they go there in order to answer charges or to give information as a witness. （在法庭上、正式委员会中）出席 ❑ *The defendants are expected to appear in federal court today.* 被告们今天预期会在联邦法院出庭。

Thesaurus *appear* 另参见：

V. seem 1
look like, resemble, seem 2
arrive, show up, turn up; *(ant.)* disappear, vanish 3

ap·pear·ance ♦♦◇ /əpɪərəns/ (**appearances**) 1 N-COUNT When someone makes an **appearance** at a public event or in a broadcast, they take part in it. （在公共活动或广播中的）露面 ❑ *It was the president's second public appearance to date.* 这是迄今该总统的第二次公开露面。 2 N-SING Someone's or something's **appearance** is the way that they look. 外表；外观 ❑ *She used to be so fussy about her appearance.* 她过去过分在意自己的外表。 3 N-SING The **appearance of** someone or something in a place is their arrival there, especially when it is unexpected. （尤指出人意料的）出现 ❑ *The sudden appearance of a few bags of rice could start a riot.* 几袋大米的突然出现会引起一场骚乱。 4 N-SING The **appearance of** something new is its coming into existence or use. 问世 ❑ *Flowering plants were making their first appearance, but were still a rarity.* 有花植物初现，但是依然少见。 5 N-SING If something has the **appearance of** a quality, it seems to have that quality. 表象 ❑ *We tried to meet both children's needs without the appearance of favoritism or unfairness.* 我们试图在没有偏爱或不公平的表象下满足两个孩子的需要。 6 PHRASE If something is true **by all appearances, from all appearances,** or **to all appearances,** it seems from what you observe or know about it that it is true. 从一切表象来看 ❑ *He was a small and by all appearances an unassuming man.* 他是个个子小并且从一切表象看来不装腔作势的人。

Word Partnership *appearance* 的常用搭配：

N. **court** appearance 1
ADJ. **public** appearance 1
physical appearance 2
sudden appearance 3
V. **make an** appearance 1 3
change *your* appearance 2
give/have an appearance **of** 5

★ **ap·pease** /əpiːz/ (**appeases, appeasing, appeased**) V-T If you try to **appease** someone, you try to stop them from being angry by giving them what they want. 姑息 [DISAPPROVAL] ❑ *Gandhi was accused by some of trying to appease both factions of the electorate.* 甘地被一些人指责试图对两派选民都加以姑息。

ap·pease·ment /əpiːzmənt/ N-UNCOUNT **Appeasement** means giving people what they want to prevent them from harming you or being angry with you. 姑息 [FORMAL, DISAPPROVAL] ❑ *He denied there is a policy of appeasement.* 他否认有姑息政策。

Word Link *pend ≈ hanging : appendix, depend, pendant*

★ **ap·pen·dix** /əpɛndɪks/ (**appendixes**)

The plural form **appendices** /əpɛndɪsiːz/ is usually used for meaning 2.

1 N-COUNT Your **appendix** is a small closed tube inside your body that is attached to your digestive system. 阑尾 ❑ *...a burst appendix.* …一个爆裂的阑尾。 2 N-COUNT An **appendix to** a book is extra information that is placed after the end of the main text. 附录 ❑ *The survey results are published in full as an appendix to Mr. Barton's discussion paper.* 该调查结果作为巴顿先生的讨论报告的附录被全文刊出。

ap·pe·tis·ing /æpɪtaɪzɪŋ/ [BRIT] → see **appetizing**

ap·pe·tite /æpɪtaɪt/ (**appetites**) 1 N-VAR Your **appetite** is your desire to eat. 胃口 ❑ *He has a healthy appetite.* 他有健康的胃口。 2 N-COUNT Someone's **appetite for** something is their strong desire for it. 欲望 ❑ *...his appetite for success.* …他的成功欲望。

ap·pe·tiz·ing /æpɪtaɪzɪŋ/

in BRIT, also use **appetising**

ADJ **Appetizing** food looks and smells good, so that you want to eat it. 引起食欲的 ❑ *...the appetizing smell of freshly baked bread.* …新出炉的面包的引起食欲的气味。

ap·plaud /əplɔːd/ (**applauds, applauding, applauded**) 1 V-T/V-I When a group of people **applaud**, they clap their hands in order to show approval, for example, when they have enjoyed a play or concert. 鼓掌 ❑ *The audience laughed and applauded.* 观众欢笑并且鼓掌。 2 V-T When an attitude or action **is applauded**, people praise it. 称赞 ❑ *He should be applauded for his courage.* 他应该因其勇气而受到称赞。 ❑ *This last move can only be applauded.* 这最后的举措不得不受到称赞。

ap·plause /əplɔːz/ N-UNCOUNT **Applause** is the noise made by a group of people clapping their hands to show approval. 掌声 ❑ *They greeted him with thunderous applause.* 他们以雷鸣般的掌声欢迎了他。

ap·ple ♦◇◇ /æpᵊl/ (**apples**) N-VAR An **apple** is a round fruit with smooth red, yellow, or green skin and firm white flesh. 苹果 ❑ *I want an apple.* 我要一个苹果。 ❑ *...his ongoing search for the finest varieties of apple.* …他对最佳品种苹果的不断寻找。

This fruit has been used as a nickname for New York City: The Big Apple. Other nicknames include: The Windy City (Chicago), Mile High City (Denver), The Motor City (Detroit), Beantown (Boston), and Tinseltown (Hollywood).

ap·plet /æplɪt/ (**applets**) N-COUNT An **applet** is a computer program contained within a page on the World Wide Web that transfers itself to your computer and runs automatically while you are looking at that Web page. （万维网上的）小应用程序

ap·pli·ance /əplaɪəns/ (**appliances**) N-COUNT An **appliance** is a device or machine in your home that you use to do a job such as cleaning or cooking. Appliances are often electrical. （常为用电的）家用器械 [FORMAL] ❑ *He could also learn to use the vacuum cleaner, the washing machine and other household appliances.* 他还能学习使用吸尘器、洗衣机和其他家用电器。

ap·pli·cable /æplɪkəᵊl, əplɪkə-/ ADJ Something that is **applicable to** a particular situation is relevant to it or can be applied to it. 适用的 ❑ *What is a reasonable standard for one family is not applicable for another.* 对一个家庭合理的标准对于另一个家庭并不适用。

ap·pli·cant /æplɪkənt/ (**applicants**) N-COUNT An **applicant for** something such as a job or a college is someone who makes a formal written request to be considered for it. 申请人 ❑ *We have had lots of applicants for these positions.* 对这些职位我们已有了很多申请人。

ap·pli·ca·tion ♦◊◊ /æplɪkeɪʃᵊn/ (**applications**) **1** N-COUNT An **application for** something such as a job or membership of an organization is a formal written request for it. 申请 ❑ *His application for membership of the organization was rejected.* 他对该组织会员资格的申请被拒绝了。 **2** N-COUNT In computing, an **application** is a piece of software designed to carry out a particular task. 应用软件 ❑ *The service works as a software application that is accessed via the internet.* 该业务是一个可以通过因特网访问的软件应用程序。 **3** N-VAR The **application of** a rule or piece of knowledge is the use of it in a particular situation. 应用 ❑ *Students learned the practical application of the theory they had learned in the classroom.* 学生们学会了课堂上学到的理论的实际应用。 **4** N-UNCOUNT **Application** is hard work and concentration on what you are doing over a period of time. 勤奋 ❑ *...his immense talent, boundless energy and unremitting application.* …他的巨大天资、无限精力与不懈努力。

Word Partnership *application* 的常用搭配：

V.	**accept/reject an** application, **file/submit an** application, **fill out an** application **1**
N.	**college** application, application **form**, **grant/loan** application, **job** application, **membership** application **1**
	application **software** **2**
ADJ.	**practical** application **3**

ap·plied /əplaɪd/ ADJ An **applied** subject of study has a practical use, rather than being concerned only with theory. 应用的 [ADJ n] ❑ *...Applied Physics.* …应用物理学。
→ see **science**

ap·ply ♦♦◊ /əplaɪ/ (**applies, applying, applied**) **1** V-T/V-I If you **apply for** something such as a job or membership of an organization, you write a letter or fill out a form in order to ask formally for it. 申请 ❑ *I am continuing to apply for jobs.* 我在继续申请工作。 ❑ *They may apply to join the organization.* 他们可能申请加入该组织。 **2** V-T If you **apply yourself to** something or **apply** your mind **to** something, you concentrate hard on doing it or on thinking about it. 将…投入 ❑ *Scymanski has applied himself to this task with considerable energy.* 赛曼斯基已经花了相当多的精力致力于这项任务。 **3** V-I If something such as a rule or a remark **applies to** a person or in a situation, it is relevant to the person or the situation. (对…) 适用 [no cont] ❑ *The convention does not apply to us.* 该协定对我们不适用。 ❑ *The rule applies where a person owns stock in a corporation.* 该规定对于在公司里拥有股份的人适用。 **4** V-T If you **apply** something such as a rule, system, or skill, you use it in a situation or activity. 运用 ❑ *The government appears to be applying the same principle.* 政府似乎在运用同样的原则。 **5** V-T A name that **is applied to** someone or something is used to refer to them. (在…上) 使用 ❑ *...a biological term that cannot be applied to a whole culture.* …一个不能用于整个培养物的生物学术语。 **6** V-T If you **apply** something **to** a surface, you put it on or rub it into the surface. 施用 ❑ *The right thing would be to apply direct pressure to the wound.* 正确的做法会是在伤口上施加直接压力。 **7** → see also **applied**
→ see **makeup**

Word Partnership *apply* 的常用搭配：

PREP.	apply **for admission**, apply **for a job** **1**
N.	**laws/restrictions/rules** apply **3**
	apply **make-up**, apply **pressure** **6**

ap·point ♦◊◊ /əpɔɪnt/ (**appoints, appointing, appointed**) **1** V-T If you **appoint** someone **to** a job or official position, you formally choose them for it. 任命 ❑ *It made sense to appoint a banker to this job.* 任命一位银行家做这项工作是合理的。 ❑ *The president has appointed a civilian as defense secretary.* 总统任命了一位平民做国防部长。 **2** → see also **appointed**

Word Partnership *appoint* 的常用搭配：

N.	appoint **judges**, appoint **a leader**, appoint **members** **1**

ap·point·ed /əpɔɪntɪd/ ADJ If something happens at the **appointed** time, it happens at the time that was decided in advance. 指定的 [ADJ n] [FORMAL] ❑ *The appointed hour of the ceremony was drawing nearer.* 该仪式的指定时间正在临近。

ap·point·ment ♦◊◊ /əpɔɪntmənt/ (**appointments**) **1** N-VAR The **appointment** of a person **to** a particular job is the choice of that person to do it. 任命 ❑ *His appointment to the cabinet would please the right wing.* 他进入内阁的任命会令右翼高兴。 **2** N-COUNT An **appointment** is a job or position of responsibility. 职务；职位 ❑ *Mr. Fay is to take up an appointment as a researcher.* 费伊先生将担任研究员的职务。 **3** N-COUNT If you have an **appointment with** someone, you have arranged to see them at a particular time, usually in connection with their work or for a serious purpose. 约会 ❑ *She has an appointment with her accountant.* 她和她的会计师有个约会。 **4** PHRASE If something can be done **by appointment**, people can arrange in advance to do it at a particular time. 通过预约 ❑ *Viewing is by appointment only.* 参观须预约。

Thesaurus *appointment* 另参见：

N.	date, engagement, meeting **1** **3**

Word Partnership *appointment* 的常用搭配：

PREP.	appointment **to *something*** **1**
	appointment **with *someone*** **3**
	by appointment **4**
N.	appointment **book** **3**
V.	**have/make/schedule an** appointment **3**

★ **ap·prais·al** /əpreɪzᵊl/ (**appraisals**) **1** N-VAR If you make an **appraisal of** something, you consider it carefully and form an opinion about it. 估计 ❑ *What is needed in such cases is a calm appraisal of the situation.* 在此类情况下需要的是对形势的冷静估计。 **2** N-VAR **Appraisal** is the official or formal assessment of the strengths and weaknesses of someone or something. Appraisal often involves observation or some kind of testing. 评估 ❑ *One of the most important tools for organizational improvement is the performance appraisal.* 组织改进的最重要手段之一是业绩评估。 **3** N-COUNT An **appraisal** is a judgement that someone makes about how much money something such as a house or a company is worth. 估价 [AM] ❑ *It may also be necessary to get a new appraisal of the property.* 可能还需要对该房产做个新的估价。

★ **ap·praise** /əpreɪz/ (**appraises, appraising, appraised**) **1** V-T If you **appraise** something or someone, you consider them carefully and form an opinion about them. 评价 [FORMAL] ❑ *This prompted many employers to appraise their selection and recruitment policies.* 这促使很多雇主评价其人才选聘政策。 **2** V-T When experts **appraise** something, they decide how much money it is worth. 估价 [AM] ❑ *His estate is now appraised at a figure near $1,000,000.* 他的财产现在被估价的数额接近$1000000。

ap·pre·ci·ate ♦◊◊ /əpriʃieɪt/ (**appreciates, appreciating, appreciated**) **1** V-T If you **appreciate** something, for example, a piece of music or good food, you like it because you recognize its good qualities. 欣赏 ❑ *Anyone can appreciate our music.* 任何人都能欣赏我们的音乐。 **2** V-T If you **appreciate** a situation or problem, you understand it and know what it involves. 理解 ❑ *She never really appreciated the depth and bitterness of the family's conflict.* 她从未真正理解该家庭矛盾的深度与激烈程度。 **3** V-T If you **appreciate** something that someone has done for you or is going to do for you, you are grateful for it. 感激 ❑ *Peter stood by me when I most needed it. I'll always appreciate that.* 彼得在我最需要时支持了我。我对此将永远感激。 **4** V-I If something that you own **appreciates** over a period of time, its value increases. 增值 ❑ *They don't have any confidence that houses will appreciate in value.* 他们对房屋增值没有一点信心。

Word Partnership *appreciate* 的常用搭配：

V.	**fail to** appreciate **1** – **3**
ADV.	**fully** appreciate **1** – **3**
N.	appreciate ***someone's* concern/support** **3**
	appreciate **in value** **4**

ap·pre·cia·tion /əpriʃieɪʃᵊn/ **1** N-SING **Appreciation of** something is the recognition and enjoyment of its good qualities. 欣赏 [also no det, oft N "of" n] ❑ *...an investigation into children's understanding and appreciation of art.* …关于孩子对艺术的理解与欣赏的一个调查。 **2** N-SING Your **appreciation for** something

A

that someone does for you is your gratitude for it. 感激 [also no det] ❑ *He expressed his appreciation for what he called Saudi Arabia's moderate and realistic oil policies.* 他表达了对他所称的沙特阿拉伯温和而务实的石油政策的感激。 **3** N-SING An **appreciation of** a situation or problem is an understanding of what it involves. 了解 [also no det] ❑ *They have a stronger appreciation of the importance of economic incentives.* 他们对经济激励的重要性有了更深的了解。 **4** N-UNCOUNT **Appreciation** in the value of something is an increase in its value over a period of time. 增值 ❑ *You have to take capital appreciation of the property into account.* 你得将那个房产的资本增值考虑进来。

ap·pre·cia·tive /əpriʃiətɪv, -ʃətɪv/ **1** ADJ An **appreciative** reaction or comment shows the enjoyment that you are getting from something. 欣赏的 ❑ *There is a murmur of appreciative laughter.* 有一阵低低的赞赏的笑声。 **2** ADJ If you are **appreciative of** something, you are grateful for it. 感激的 ❑ *We have been very appreciative of their support.* 我们对他们的支持一直非常感激。

▲ **ap·pre·hend** /æprɪhɛnd/ (**apprehends, apprehending, apprehended**) V-T If the police **apprehend** someone, they catch them and arrest them. 逮捕 [FORMAL] ❑ *Police have not apprehended her killer.* 警方尚未逮捕杀害她的凶手。

ap·pre·hen·sion /æprɪhɛnʃ°n/ (**apprehensions**) N-VAR **Apprehension** is a feeling of fear that something bad may happen. 忧虑 [FORMAL] ❑ *It reflects real anger and apprehension about the future.* 这反映出对未来真正的愤怒和忧虑。

ap·pre·hen·sive /æprɪhɛnsɪv/ ADJ Someone who is **apprehensive** is afraid that something bad may happen. 担心的 ❑ *People are still terribly apprehensive about the future.* 人们对未来依旧极为担心。

▲ **ap·pren·tice** /əprɛntɪs/ (**apprentices, apprenticing, apprenticed**) **1** N-COUNT An **apprentice** is a young person who works for someone in order to learn their skill. 学徒 ❑ *I started off as an apprentice and worked my way up.* 我从学徒做起，然后一步一步做上来的。 **2** V-T If a young person **is apprenticed to** someone, they go to work for them in order to learn their skill. 使做学徒 [usu passive] ❑ *I was apprenticed to a plumber when I was fourteen.* 我14岁时给一个管子工做学徒。

ap·pren·tice·ship /əprɛntɪsʃɪp/ (**apprenticeships**) N-VAR Someone who has an **apprenticeship** works for a fixed period of time for a person who has a particular skill in order to learn the skill. **Apprenticeship** is the system of learning a skill like this. 学徒期；学徒制 ❑ *After serving his apprenticeship as a toolmaker, he became a manager.* 在完成了工具匠的学徒期之后，他当上了经理。

ap·proach ♦♦◇ /əproʊtʃ/ (**approaches, approaching, approached**) **1** V-T/V-I When you **approach** something, you get closer to it. 走近 ❑ *He didn't approach the front door at once.* 他没有立即走近前门。 ❑ *When I approached, they grew silent.* 当我走近时，他们变得沉默了。 ● N-COUNT **Approach** is also a noun. 走近 ❑ *At their approach the little boy ran away and hid.* 当他们走近时，那个小男孩跑开了并藏了起来。 **2** V-T If you **approach** someone **about** something, you speak to them about it for the first time, often making an offer or request. 与…接洽 [no cont] ❑ *When Brown approached me about the job, my first reaction was of disbelief.* 当布朗为这份工作找我时，我的第一反应是不相信。 ❑ *He approached me to create and design the restaurant.* 他来找我创办并设计那餐馆。 ● N-COUNT **Approach** is also a noun. 接洽 ❑ *There had already been approaches from buyers interested in the whole of the group.* 已经有一些对整个集团感兴趣的买主来接洽了。 **3** V-T When you **approach** a task, problem, or situation in a particular way, you deal with it or think about it in that way. 处理 ❑ *The Bank has approached the issue in a practical way.* 该银行已经务实地处理了这个问题。 **4** V-I As a future time or event **approaches**, it gradually gets nearer as time passes. 临近 ❑ *As autumn approached, the plants and colors in the garden changed.* 秋天渐近，花园里的植物与色调发生了变化。 ● N-SING **Approach** is also a noun. 临近 ❑ *...the festive spirit that permeated the house with the approach of Christmas.* …随着圣诞节的临近而弥漫在这所房子里的节日气氛。 **5** V-T As you **approach** a future time or event, time passes so that you get gradually nearer to it. 逐渐接近(某时间或事件) ❑ *There is a need for understanding and cooperation as we approach the summit.* 在我们即将参加峰会之际需要理解与合作。 **6** V-T If something **approaches** a particular level or state, it almost reaches that level or state. 几乎达到(某水平或状态) ❑ *Oil prices have approached their highest level for almost ten years.* 石油价格已几乎达到近十年来的最高水平。 **7** N-COUNT An **approach to** a place is a road, path, or other route that leads to it. 路径 ❑ *The path serves as an approach to the boathouse.* 这条小路是通向那个船库的一条路径。 **8** N-COUNT Your **approach to** a task, problem, or situation is the way you deal with it or think about it. 方式 ❑ *We will be exploring different approaches to gathering information.* 我们将探索收集信息的不同方法。

Thesaurus *approach* 另参见：

V.	close in, near; *(ant.)* go away, leave **1**
N.	attitude, method, technique **8**

Word Partnership *approach* 的常用搭配：

N.	approach **a problem** **3**
PREP.	approach **to** ***something*** **7** **8**
V.	**adopt/take an** approach **8**
ADJ.	**different/new/novel** approach, **hands-on** approach **8**

ap·pro·pri·ate ♦◇◇ /əproʊpriɪt/ ADJ Something that is **appropriate** is suitable or acceptable for a particular situation. 适当的 ❑ *It is appropriate that Hispanic names dominate the list.* 西班牙人的名字在这个名单中占主导地位是适当的。 ❑ *Dress neatly and attractively in an outfit appropriate to the job.* 穿适合于这份工作的整洁美观的套装。 ● **ap·pro·pri·ate·ly** ADV 适当地 ❑ *Behave appropriately and ask intelligent questions.* 举止要得体，提问要机智。

Thesaurus *appropriate* 另参见：

ADJ.	correct, fitting, relevant, right; *(ant.)* improper, inappropriate, incorrect

★ **ap·pro·pria·tion** /əproʊprieɪʃ°n/ (**appropriations**) **1** N-COUNT An **appropriation** is an amount of money that a government or organization reserves for a particular purpose. 拨款 [usu with supp] [FORMAL] ❑ *The government raised defense appropriations by 12 percent.* 政府将国防拨款提高了12%。 **2** N-UNCOUNT **Appropriation of** something that belongs to someone else is the act of taking it, usually without having the right to do so. 占用 [also "a" N, usu N "of" n] [FORMAL] ❑ *Other charges include fraud and illegal appropriation of land.* 其他指控包括诈骗和非法占用土地。

ap·prov·al ♦◇◇ /əpruv°l/ (**approvals**) **1** N-UNCOUNT If you win someone's **approval for** something that you ask for or suggest, they agree to it. 赞同 ❑ *...efforts to win congressional approval for an aid package for Moscow.* …为赢得国会赞同对莫斯科的一揽子援助计划而做的努力。 ❑ *The chairman has also given his approval for an investigation into the case.* 该主席也对此案的调查表示赞同。 **2** N-UNCOUNT If someone or something has your **approval**, you like and admire them. 赞赏 ❑ *His son had an obsessive drive to gain his father's approval.* 他儿子渴望得到他的赞赏。 **3** N-VAR **Approval** is a formal or official statement that something is acceptable. 批准 ❑ *The testing and approval of new drugs will be speeded up.* 新药的检测与审批将会加速。

Word Partnership *approval* 的常用搭配：

V.	**gain** approval, **meet with** approval, **seek** approval, **subject to** approval, **win** approval **1** – **3**
N.	approval **rating** **2**
	approval **process** **3**
ADJ.	**final** approval **3**

ap·prove ♦♦◇ /əpruv/ (**approves, approving, approved**) **1** V-I If you **approve of** an action, event, or suggestion, you like it or are pleased about it. 喜欢 [oft with brd-neg] ❑ *Not everyone approves of the festival.* 不是每个人都喜欢这个节日。 **2** V-I If you **approve of** someone or something, you like and admire them. 赞赏 [oft with brd-neg] ❑ *You've never approved of Henry, have you?* 你从未赞赏过亨利，是吧？ **3** V-T If someone in a position of authority **approves** a plan or idea, they formally agree to it and say that it can happen. 批准 ❑ *The Russian Parliament has approved a program of radical economic reforms.* 俄罗斯议会已经批准了一项重大经济改革计划。 **4** → see also **approved**

Thesaurus *approve* 另参见：

V.	agree to, authorize, permit; *(ant.)* disapprove, reject **3**

Word Partnership *approve* 的常用搭配：

ADJ.	**likely** to approve **1** **3**
PREP.	approve **of** ***someone/something*** **2**
N.	approve **a plan** **3**

ap·proved /əpruvd/ ADJ An **approved** method or course of action is officially accepted as appropriate in a particular situation. 得到正式认可的 ❑ *The approved method of cleaning is industrial sand-blasting.* 得到正式认可的清洁方法是工业喷砂处理。 ❑ *Approved methods might include destruction of nests and eggs, and the trapping and destruction of geese.* 得到正式认可的方法可能包括对巢和蛋的捣毁以及对鹅的捕杀。

Word Link *proxim ≈ near : approximate, approximation, proximity*

ap·proxi·mate (**approximates, approximating, approximated**)

The adjective is pronounced /əprɒksɪmət/. The verb is pronounced /əprɒksɪmeɪt/.

形容词读作 /əprɒksɪmət/。动词读作 /əprɒksɪmeɪt/。

1 ADJ An **approximate** number, time, or position is close to the correct number, time, or position, but is not exact. 大概的（数字、时间或方位等） ❑ *The approximate cost varies from around $150 to $250.* 大致的费用在$150至$250之间不等。 ● **ap·proxi·mate·ly** ADV 大概地 [ADV num] ❑ *Approximately $150 million is to be spent on improvements.* 大概1.5亿美元将花在改进上。 **2** ADJ An idea or description that is **approximate** is not intended to be precise or accurate, but to give some indication of what something is like. 大概的（观点或描述等） ❑ *They did not have even an approximate idea what the Germans really wanted.* 他们对于德国人真正想要什么甚至没有一个大致概念。 **3** V-T If something **approximates** something else, it is similar to it but is not exactly the same. 近似于 ❑ *The mixture described below will approximate it, but is not exactly the same.* 下面所描述的混合物会与之近似，但不完全一样。

ap·proxi·ma·tion /əprɒksɪmeɪʃən/ (**approximations**) **1** N-COUNT An **approximation** is a fact, object, or description which is similar to something else, but which is not exactly the same. 近似物 ❑ *That is a fair approximation of the way in which the next boss is being chosen.* 那是一个挑选下任老板的大体近似方式。 **2** N-COUNT An **approximation** is a number, calculation, or position that is close to a correct number, time, or position, but is not exact. 近似值 ❑ *Clearly that's an approximation, but my guess is there'll be a reasonable balance.* 显然那是一个近似值，但是我的猜测是会有不少余额。 ❑ *As we know, 365.25 is only an approximation.* 如我们所知，365.25只是一个近似值。

Apr. **Apr.** is a written abbreviation for **April**. 四月

apri·cot /eɪprɪkɒt/ (**apricots**) **1** N-VAR An **apricot** is a small, soft, round fruit with yellowish-orange flesh and a large seed inside. 杏 ❑ *...12 oz apricots, halved and pitted.* …12盎司的杏，切成了两半并去了核。 **2** COLOR **Apricot** is used to describe things that are yellowish-orange in color. 杏色的 ❑ *The bridesmaids wore apricot and white organza.* 女傧相们穿着杏色和白色的透明硬纱。

April ◆◆◆ /eɪprɪl/ (**Aprils**) N-VAR **April** is the fourth month of the year in the Western calendar. 4月 ❑ *The changes will be introduced in April.* 这些变更将于4月实施。

On April 1 people in Britain and America play all sorts of tricks and practical jokes on each other. People who fall for these tricks are called **April Fools**. Sometimes even the media join in the fun, inventing news stories and publishing spoof reports, for example, about spaghetti growing on trees in Italy.

▲ **apron** /eɪprən/ (**aprons**) N-COUNT An **apron** is a piece of clothing that you put on over the front of your normal clothes and tie around your waist, especially when you are cooking, in order to prevent your clothes from getting dirty. 围裙

★ **apt** /æpt/ **1** ADJ An **apt** remark, description, or choice is especially suitable. 恰当的 ❑ *The words of this report are as apt today as in 1929.* 这份报告的措词在当今如在1929年一样恰当。 ● **apt·ly** ADV 恰当地 ❑ *...the beach in the aptly named town of Oceanside.* …命名贴切的"海边镇"上的沙滩。 **2** ADJ If someone is **apt to** do something, they often do it and so it is likely that they will do it again. 易于…的 [v-link ADJ to-inf] ❑ *She was apt to raise her voice and wave her hands about.* 她常常提高嗓门并挥舞双手。 **3** ADJ An **apt** student is intelligent and able to understand things easily. 聪慧的 [ADJ n] ❑ *She had taught him French and he had been an apt student.* 她教过他法语，他一直是个聪慧的学生。

apt. /æpt/ **Apt.** is a written abbreviation for **apartment**. 公寓套房

▲ **ap·ti·tude** /æptɪtud/ (**aptitudes**) N-VAR Someone's **aptitude for** a particular kind of work or activity is their ability to learn it quickly and to do it well. 天资 ❑ *He drifted into publishing and discovered an aptitude for working with accounts.* 他俱入出版界，发现自己具有管账的天资。

aquat·ic /əkwætɪk/ **1** ADJ An **aquatic** animal or plant lives or grows on or in water. 水生的 ❑ *The pond is small but can support many aquatic plants and fish.* 这个池塘虽小，但是能养活许多水生植物和鱼。 **2** ADJ **Aquatic** means relating to water. 与水相关的 ❑ *...our aquatic resources.* …我们的水资源。

Arab /ærəb/ (**Arabs**) **1** N-COUNT **Arabs** are people who speak Arabic and who come from the Middle East and parts of North Africa. 阿拉伯人 **2** ADJ **Arab** means belonging or relating to Arabs or to their countries or customs. 阿拉伯的；阿拉伯人的 ❑ *On the surface, it appears little has changed in the Arab world.* 表面上，似乎阿拉伯世界没有什么变化。

ar·able /ærəbəl/ ADJ **Arable** farming involves growing crops such as wheat and barley rather than keeping animals or growing fruit and vegetables. **Arable** land is land that is used for arable farming. 耕种的 ❑ *...arable farmers.* …从事农耕的农场主们。

ar·bi·trage /ɑrbɪtrɑʒ/ N-UNCOUNT In finance, **arbitrage** is the activity of buying securities or currency in one financial market and selling it at a profit in another. 套利 [BUSINESS] ❑ *Astute Singaporeans quickly spotted an arbitrage opportunity.* 精明的新加坡人很快看到了一个套利机会。

ar·bi·trary /ɑrbɪtrɛri/ ADJ If you describe an action, rule, or decision as **arbitrary**, you think that it is not based on any principle, plan, or system. It often seems unfair because of this. 随意的 [DISAPPROVAL] ❑ *Arbitrary arrests and detention without trial were common.* 不经审讯随意扣押是常有的。 ● **ar·bi·trari·ly** /ɑrbɪtrɛərɪli/ ADV 随意地 [ADV with v] ❑ *The victims were not chosen arbitrarily.* 这些受害者不是被随意选的。

ar·bi·trate /ɑrbɪtreɪt/ (**arbitrates, arbitrating, arbitrated**) V-I When someone in authority **arbitrates between** two people or groups who are in dispute, they consider all the facts and make an official decision about who is right. 仲裁 ❑ *He arbitrates between investors and members of the association.* 他在投资者与该协会成员之间做仲裁。

▲ **ar·bi·tra·tion** /ɑrbɪtreɪʃən/ N-UNCOUNT **Arbitration** is the judging of a dispute between people or groups by someone who is not involved. 仲裁 ❑ *The matter is likely to go to arbitration.* 这件事可能要交付仲裁。

★ **arc** /ɑrk/ (**arcs**) **1** N-COUNT An **arc** is a smoothly curving line or movement. 弧线；弧线运动 ❑ *The helicopter made a slow arc, passing over the mound but not stopping.* 这架直升飞机做了一个缓慢的弧线运行，飞过那座小丘，但没停下来。 **2** N-COUNT In geometry, an **arc** is a part of the line that forms the outside of a circle. 弧 [TECHNICAL]

ar·cade /ɑrkeɪd/ (**arcades**) **1** N-COUNT An **arcade** is a place where you can play games on machines which work when you put money in them. 游戏厅 **2** → see also **video arcade** **3** N-COUNT An **arcade** is a covered passage where there are stores or market stalls. （购物）拱廊 [mainly BRIT] ❑ *...a shopping arcade.* …一条购物拱廊。

★ **arch** /ɑrtʃ/ (**arches, arching, arched**) **1** N-COUNT An **arch** is a structure that is curved at the top and is supported on either side by a pillar, post, or wall. 拱形结构 ❑ *When she passed under the arch leading out of the park, Mira whooped with delight.* 从通向公园外的拱门下走过时，米拉高兴地喊叫起来。 **2** N-COUNT An **arch** is a curved line or movement. 弧线；弧线运动 ❑ *...the arch of the fishing rods.* …钓鱼竿的弧线。 **3** N-COUNT The **arch** of your foot is the curved section at the bottom in the middle. （足）弓 ❑ *"Good girl," said Frank, winding the bandages around the arch of her foot.* "好姑娘，"弗兰克说道，一边把绷带缠在她的足弓上。 **4** → see also **arched** **5** V-T/V-I If you **arch** a part of your body such as your back or if it **arches**, you bend it so that it forms a curve. 弓着 ❑ *Don't arch your back, keep your spine straight.* 别弓着背，挺直脊梁。

→ see **architecture, foot**

arch- /ɑrtʃ-/ COMB IN N-COUNT **Arch-** combines with nouns referring to people to form new nouns that refer to people who are extreme examples of something. For example, your **archrival** is the rival you most want to beat. 主要的 ❑ *Neither he nor his archrival, Giuseppe De Rita, won.* 他和他的头号对手朱塞佩·德·丽塔都没有赢。

A

Word Web architecture

The Colosseum (sometimes spelled Coliseum) in Rome is a great **architectural** triumph of the ancient world. This amphitheater, built in the first century BC, could hold 50,000 spectators. It was used for animal fights, human executions, and staged combat. The elliptical shape allowed spectators to be closer to the action. It also prevented participants from hiding in the corners. The **arches** are an important part of the **building**. They are an example of a Roman improvement to the simple arch. Each arch is supported by a **keystone** in the top center. The **design** of the Colosseum has influenced the design of thousands of other public venues. Many modern day sports stadiums are the same shape.

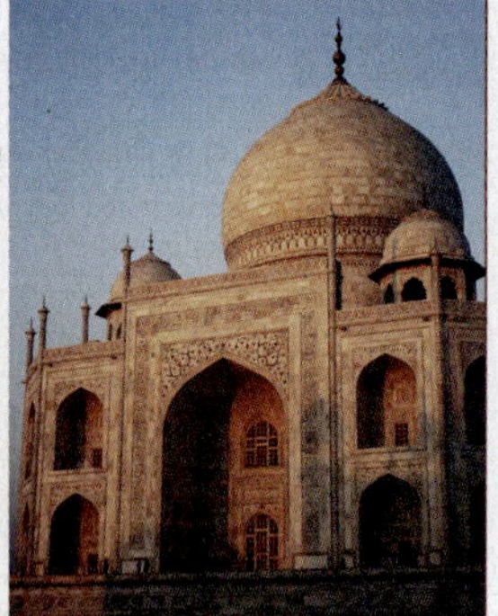

▲ **ar·chae·ol·ogy** /ɑrkiɒlədʒi/ also **archeology** N-UNCOUNT **Archaeology** is the study of the societies and peoples of the past by examining the remains of their buildings, tools, and other objects. 考古学 ● **ar·chaeo·logi·cal** /ɑrkiəlɒdʒɪkᵊl/ ADJ 考古学的 [ADJ n] ❑ *...one of the region's most important archaeological sites.* …该地区最重要的考古遗址之一。 ● **ar·chae·olo·gist** ▲ /ɑrkiɒlədʒɪst/ N-COUNT (**archaeologists**) 考古学家 ❑ *The archaeologists found a house built around 300 BC, with a basement and attic.* 考古学家们找到了一所大约建于公元前300年的、带地下室和阁楼的房子。

ar·cha·ic /ɑrkeɪɪk/ ADJ **Archaic** means extremely old or extremely old-fashioned. 陈旧的; 早已过时的 ❑ *...archaic laws that are very seldom used.* …现在极少使用的早已过时的法律。

arch·bishop /ɑrtʃbɪʃəp/ (**archbishops**) N-COUNT; N-TITLE In the Roman Catholic, Orthodox, and Anglican Churches, an **archbishop** is a bishop of the highest rank, who is in charge of all the bishops and priests in a particular country or region. 大主教 ❑ *...the Roman Catholic archbishop of Colorado Springs.* …科罗拉多斯普林斯的罗马天主教大主教。

arched /ɑrtʃt/ **1** ADJ An **arched** roof, window, or doorway is curved at the top. 拱形的 ❑ *From the television room an arched doorway leads in to the hall.* 一个拱形门廊从电视房通向大厅。 **2** ADJ An **arched** bridge has arches as part of its structure. 拱形结构的 ❑ *She led them up some stairs and across a little arched stone bridge.* 她带他们上了些台阶，然后走过了一座小石拱桥。

▲ **ar·che·ol·ogy** /ɑrkiɒlədʒi/ → see **archaeology**

ar·che·typ·al /ɑrkɪtaɪpᵊl/ ADJ Someone or something that is **archetypal** has all the most important characteristics of a particular kind of person or thing and is a perfect example of it. 典型的 [FORMAL] ❑ *...the archetypal American middle-class family living in the suburbs.* …住在郊区的典型美国中产阶级家庭。

→ see **myth**

ar·che·type /ɑrkɪtaɪp/ (**archetypes**) N-COUNT An **archetype** is something that is considered to be a perfect or typical example of a particular kind of person or thing, because it has all their most important characteristics. 典型 [FORMAL] ❑ *He came to this country 20 years ago and is the archetype of the successful Asian businessman.* 他20年前来到这个国家，是成功的亚裔商人的典型。

archi·tect /ɑrkɪtɛkt/ (**architects**) **1** N-COUNT An **architect** is a person who designs buildings. 建筑师 **2** N-COUNT The **architect** of an idea, event, or institution is the person who invented it or made it happen. 设计师; 缔造者 [oft N "of" n] ❑ *James Madison was the principal architect of the constitution.* 詹姆斯·麦迪逊是该宪法的主设计师。

archi·tec·tur·al /ɑrkɪtɛktʃərəl/ ADJ **Architectural** means relating to the design and construction of buildings. 有关建筑的 ❑ *...Tibet's architectural heritage.* …西藏的建筑遗产。

● **archi·tec·tur·al·ly** ADV 建筑上 ❑ *The old city center is architecturally rich.* 这座古老的市中心在建筑上多姿多彩。

archi·tec·ture /ɑrkɪtɛktʃər/ **1** N-UNCOUNT **Architecture** is the art of planning, designing, and constructing buildings. 建筑艺术 ❑ *He studied classical architecture and design in Rome.* 他在罗马学过古典建筑艺术和设计。 **2** N-UNCOUNT The **architecture** of a building is the style in which it is designed and constructed. 建筑风格 ❑ *...modern architecture.* …现代建筑风格。

→ see Word Web: **architecture**

▲ **ar·chive** /ɑrkaɪv/ (**archives, archiving, archived**) **1** N-COUNT **Archives** are a collection of documents and records that contain historical information. You can also use **archives** to refer to the place where archives are stored. 档案; 档案馆 ❑ *...the State Library's archives.* …国立图书馆的档案。 **2** ADJ **Archive** material is information that comes from archives. 记入档案的 [ADJ n] ❑ *...archive material.* …档案资料。 **3** V-T If you **archive** material such as documents or data, you store it in an archive. 把…存档 ❑ *The system will archive the information so agencies can review it in detail.* 该系统会将该信息存档，以便各代理机构能对其详细审阅。

arc·tic /ɑrktɪk/ **1** N-PROPER **The Arctic** is the area of the world around the North Pole. It is extremely cold and there is very little light in winter and very little darkness in summer. 北极 ❑ *...winter in the Arctic.* …北极的冬天。 **2** ADJ If you describe a place or the weather as **arctic**, you are emphasizing that it is extremely cold. 极冷的 [INFORMAL, EMPHASIS] ❑ *The bathroom, with its spartan pre-war facilities, is positively arctic.* 这个有简陋战前设施的浴室实在冷极了。

→ see Picture Dictionary: **Arctic**

→ see **globe**

▲ **ar·dent** /ɑrdᵊnt/ ADJ **Ardent** is used to describe someone who has extremely strong feelings about something or someone. 热烈的 ❑ *He's been one of the most ardent supporters of the administration's policy.* 他是政府政策的最热烈的支持者之一。

▲ **ar·du·ous** /ɑrdʒuəs/ ADJ Something that is **arduous** is difficult and tiring, and involves a lot of effort. 艰难的 ❑ *...a long, hot and arduous trip.* …一段漫长、灼热、艰难的旅程。

are /ər, STRONG ɑr/ **Are** is the plural and the second person singular of the present tense of the verb **be**. **Are** is often shortened to -'**re** after pronouns in spoken English. 是 (**be**的现在时复数以及第二人称单数形式)

area ♦♦♦ /ɛəriə/ (**areas**) **1** N-COUNT An **area** is a particular part of a town, a country, a region, or the world. 地区 ❑ *...the large number of community groups in the area.* …该地区大量的社团。 ❑ *The survey was carried out in both urban and rural areas.* 该调查在城市和乡村地区都开展了。 **2** N-COUNT Your **area** is the part of a town, country, or region where you live. An organization's **area** is the part of a town, country, or region that it is responsible for. 居住区域; 管辖区域 ❑ *Local authorities have been responsible for the running of schools in their areas.* 地方政府一直负责其辖区内各校的运作。 **3** N-COUNT A particular **area** is a piece of land or part of a building that is used for a particular activity. (作某用途的) 区域 ❑ *...a picnic area.* …一个野餐区。 **4** N-COUNT An **area** is a particular place on a surface or object, for example, on your body. 部位 ❑ *You will notice*

Picture Dictionary **Arctic**

snow
polar bear
arctic fox
ice
seal
iceberg
whale

that your baby has two soft areas on the top of his head. 你会注意到你孩子的头顶有两个柔软的部位。 **5** N-COUNT You can use **area** to refer to a particular subject or topic, or to a particular part of a larger, more general situation or activity. 话题; 方面 ❑ *...the politically sensitive area of social security.* …社保这个政治敏感话题。 **6** N-VAR The **area** of a surface such as a piece of land is the amount of flat space or ground that it covers, measured in square units. 面积 ❑ *The islands cover a total area of 400 square miles.* 这些岛屿的总面积为400平方英里。 **7** → see also **gray area**

→ see Picture Dictionary: **area**

Thesaurus *area* 另参见：

N. district, place, region, vicinity **1** **2**

Word Partnership *area* 的常用搭配：

ADJ. **metropolitan** area, **rural/suburban/urban** area, **surrounding** area **1**
local area, **remote** area **2**
residential area, **restricted** area **3**
N. **downtown** area **1** **2**
tourist area **3**
PREP. **throughout the** area **1** **2**
area **of expertise** **5**

area code (area codes) N-COUNT The **area code** for a particular place is the series of numbers that you have to dial before someone's personal number if you are making a telephone call to that place from a different area. (电话) 区域代码 [mainly AM]

in BRIT, use **dialling code**

❑ *The area code for western Pennsylvania is 412.* 西宾夕法尼亚的区号是412。

★ **arena** /ərinə/ (**arenas**) **1** N-COUNT An **arena** is a place where sports, entertainments, and other public events take place. It has seats around it where people sit and watch. 竞技场 ❑ *...the largest indoor sports arena in the world.* …世界上最大的室内体育竞技场。 **2** N-COUNT You can refer to a field of activity, especially one where there is a lot of conflict or action, as an **arena** of a particular kind. 斗争场所 ❑ *He made it clear he had no intention of withdrawing from the political arena.* 他明确表示他没有退出政治舞台的意图。

aren't ◆◆◇ /ɑrnt, ɑrənt/ **1** **Aren't** is the usual spoken form of "are not." **are not**的常用口语形式 **2** **Aren't** is the form of "am not" that is used in questions or tags in spoken English. 口语中疑问句或附加疑问句里**am not**的缩略形式

ar·gu·ably /ɑrgyuəbli/ ADV You can use **arguably** when you are stating your opinion or belief, as a way of giving more authority to it. 可以说 ❑ *They are arguably the most important band since The Rolling Stones.* 他们可以说是自滚石以来最重要的乐队。

ar·gue ◆◆◇ /ɑrgyu/ (**argues, arguing, argued**) **1** V-RECIP If one person **argues with** another, they speak angrily to each other about something that they disagree about. You can also say that two people **argue.** 争吵 ❑ *The committee is concerned about players' behavior, especially arguing with referees.* 该委员会担心运动员的表现，尤其担心他们与裁判争吵。 **2** V-RECIP If you **argue with** someone **about** something, you discuss it with them, with each of you giving your different opinions. 讨论 ❑ *He was arguing with the king about the need to maintain the cavalry at full strength.* 他在和国王讨论保留骑兵全部兵力的必要性。 ❑ *They are arguing over foreign policy.* 他们在讨论外交政策。 **3** V-I If you tell someone not to **argue with** you, you want them to do or believe what you say without protest or disagreement. 争辩 [usu imper with neg] ❑ *Don't argue with me.* 不要和我争辩。 **4** V-T If you **argue**

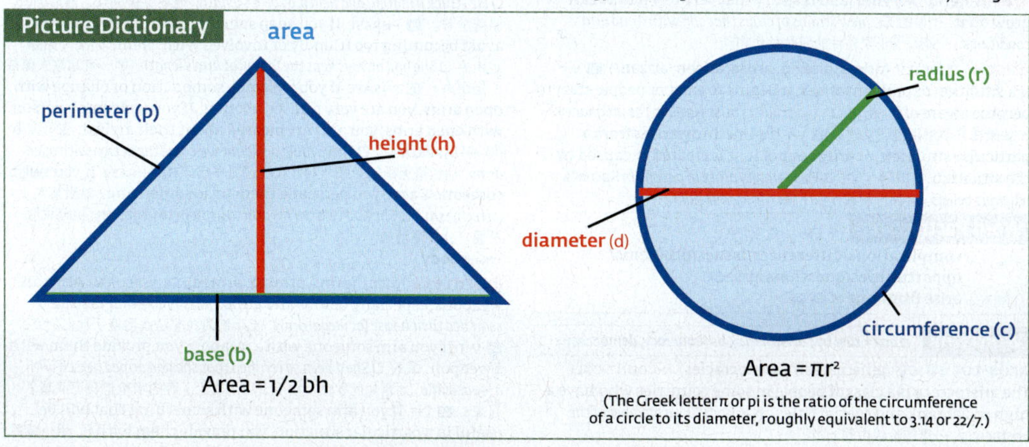

A

that something is true, you state it and give the reasons why you think it is true. 辩论 ❑ *His lawyers are arguing that he is unfit to stand trial.* 他的律师们在辩称他不适宜受审。 **5** V-I If you **argue for** something, you say why you agree with it, in order to persuade people that it is right. If you **argue against** something, you say why you disagree with it, in order to persuade people that it is wrong. 陈述理由 ❑ *The report argues against tax increases.* 该报告陈述理由反对增税。

Thesaurus *argue* 另参见：
V. bicker, disagree, fight, quarrel; *(ant.)* agree **1**
debate, discuss, dispute **2**
claim **4**

Word Partnership *argue* 的常用搭配：
PREP. argue **with *someone/something*** **1**–**3**
argue **about/over *something*** **1** **2**
argue **against/for *something*** **5**
N. argue **a case, critics** argue, **officials** argue, **opponents/supporters** argue **5**

ar·gu·ment ♦♦◇ /ɑrgyəmənt/ (**arguments**) **1** N-VAR An **argument** is a statement or set of statements that you use in order to try to convince people that your opinion about something is correct. 论据 ❑ *There's a strong argument for lowering the price.* 有一个支持降低价格的有力论据。 ❑ *The doctors have set out their arguments against the proposals.* 医生们已经说明了反对这些提案的理由。 **2** N-VAR An **argument** is a discussion or debate in which a number of people put forward different or opposing opinions. 讨论；辩论 ❑ *The incident has triggered fresh arguments about the role of the extreme right in U.S. politics.* 该事件引发了有关美国政治中极右势力角色的新讨论。 **3** N-COUNT An **argument** is a conversation in which people disagree with each other angrily or noisily. 争吵 ❑ *Anny described how she got into an argument with one of the marchers.* 安妮描述了她是如何与游行者中的一个人争吵起来的。 **4** N-UNCOUNT If you accept something without **argument**, you do not question it or disagree with it. 争辩 ❑ *He complied without argument.* 他没有争辩就服从了。

Do not confuse **argument** and **dispute**. An **argument** is a disagreement between people who may or may not know each other. ❑ *She had an argument with her father about practicing the piano... Travis got in an argument with another motorist.* A **dispute** is a serious argument that can last for a long time. **Disputes** generally occur between organizations, political parties, or countries. ❑ *...a 10-year-old dispute over crude oil.* Note that **dispute** can also be a verb. ❑ *Opponents dispute the value of Japan's research.*

Word Partnership *argument* 的常用搭配：
ADJ. **persuasive** argument **1**
heated argument **3**
V. **support an** argument **1**
get into an argument, **have an** argument **3**
PREP. argument **against/for** **2**
without argument **4**

▲ **arid** /ærɪd/ ADJ **Arid** land is so dry that very few plants can grow on it. 干旱的 ❑ *...new strains of crops that can withstand arid conditions.* …能经受干旱条件的新品种作物。

arise ♦◇◇ /əraɪz/ (**arises, arising, arose, arisen** /ərɪzən/) **1** V-I If a situation or problem **arises**, it begins to exist or people start to become aware of it. 出现 ❑ *...if a problem arises later in the pregnancy.* …如果在怀孕后期出现问题。 **2** V-I If something **arises from** a particular situation, or **arises out of** it, it is created or caused by the situation. (由…) 产生 ❑ *This serenity arose in part from Rachel's religious beliefs.* 这种平和部分由于雷切尔的宗教信仰。

Word Partnership *arise* 的常用搭配：
N. **complications/differences/issues/problems/opportunities/questions** arise **1**
PREP. arise **from/out of** **1** **2**

Word Link *cracy ≈ rule by : aristocracy, bureaucracy, democracy*

ar·is·toc·ra·cy /ærɪstɒkrəsi/ (**aristocracies**) N-COUNT-COLL **The aristocracy** is a class of people in some countries who have a high social rank and special titles. 贵族阶级 ❑ *...a member of the aristocracy.* …贵族阶级中的一员。

Word Link *crat ≈ power : aristocrat, bureaucrat, democrat*

▲ **aris·to·crat** /ærɪstəkræt, ərɪst-/ (**aristocrats**) N-COUNT An **aristocrat** is someone whose family has a high social rank, especially someone who has a title. 贵族 ❑ *...a wealthy southern aristocrat.* …一位富有的南方贵族。

aris·to·crat·ic /ərɪstəkrætɪk/ ADJ **Aristocratic** means belonging to or typical of the aristocracy. 贵族的 ❑ *...a wealthy, aristocratic family.* …一个富有的贵族家庭。

arith·me·tic /ərɪθmɪtɪk/ **1** N-UNCOUNT **Arithmetic** is the part of mathematics that is concerned with the addition, subtraction, multiplication, and division of numbers. 算术 ❑ *...teaching the basics of reading, writing and arithmetic.* …教授读、写、算的基本知识。 **2** N-UNCOUNT You can use **arithmetic** to refer to the process of doing a particular sum or calculation. 计算 ❑ *4,000 women put in ten rupees each, which if my arithmetic is right adds up to 40,000 rupees.* 4千名妇女每人交10卢比，如果我的计算准确的话加起来总共是4万卢比。 **3** N-UNCOUNT If you refer to **the arithmetic** of a situation, you are concerned with those aspects of it that can be expressed in numbers, and how they affect the situation. (某形势的) 数据 ❑ *The arithmetic was discouraging. In less than two months, they had used up six months' worth of food.* 数据不容乐观。在不到两个月里，他们已经吃完了6个月的食物。
→ see **mathematics**

arm
❶ PART OF YOUR BODY OR OF SOMETHING ELSE
❷ WEAPONS

❶ **arm** ♦♦♦ /ɑrm/ (**arms**) **1** N-COUNT Your **arms** are the two long parts of your body that are attached to your shoulders and that have your hands at the end. 手臂 ❑ *She stretched her arms out.* 她伸开了双臂。 **2** N-COUNT **The arm** of a chair is the part on which you rest your arm when you are sitting down. (椅子的) 扶手 ❑ *Mack gripped the arms of the chair.* 麦克抓紧了那把椅子的一对扶手。 **3** N-COUNT An **arm of** an object is a long thin part of it that sticks out from the main part. (物体的) 臂状物 ❑ *...the lever arm of the machine.* …该机器的杠杆臂。 **4** N-COUNT An **arm of** land or water is a long thin area of it that is joined to a broader area. (陆地、水域的) 狭长区域 ❑ *...a small area of woodland between two arms of a small stream.* …一条小溪的两条支流之间的一小块林地。 **5** N-COUNT An **arm of** an organization is a section of it that operates in a particular country or that deals with a particular activity. 部门；分支机构 ❑ *The agency is the central research and development arm of the Department of Defense.* 该机构是国防部的核心研究与开发部门。 **6** N-COUNT The **arm** of a piece of clothing is the part of it that covers your arm. 袖子 ❑ *...coats that were short in the arms.* …袖子短的几件大衣。 **7** PHRASE If two people are walking **arm in arm**, they are walking together with their arms linked. 臂挽臂地 ❑ *He walked from the court arm in arm with his wife.* 他和他妻子臂挽着臂从法院走来了。 **8** PHRASE If you hold something **at arm's length**, you hold it away from your body with your arm straight. 以一臂之距 ❑ *He struck a match, and held it at arm's length.* 他划了根火柴，然后伸长胳膊举着。 **9** PHRASE If you **keep** someone **at arm's length**, you avoid becoming too friendly or involved with them. 同某人保持一定距离 ❑ *She had always kept the family at arm's length.* 她一直和家人保持一定距离。 **10** PHRASE If you welcome some action or change **with open arms**, you are very pleased about it. If you welcome a person **with open arms**, you are very pleased about their arrival. 张开双臂(欢迎) [APPROVAL] ❑ *They would no doubt welcome the action with open arms.* 他们毫无疑问会张开双臂欢迎这项举措。 **11** PHRASE If you **twist** someone's **arm**, you persuade them to do something. 说服某人 [INFORMAL] ❑ *She had twisted his arm to get him to invite her.* 她已说服了他，让他邀请她。
→ see **body**

❷ **arm** ♦♦♦ /ɑrm/ (**arms, arming, armed**) **1** N-PLURAL **Arms** are weapons, especially bombs and guns. 武器 [FORMAL] ❑ *Soldiers searched their house for illegal arms.* 士兵们为找非法武器搜了他们的家。 **2** V-T If you **arm** someone **with** a weapon, you provide them with a weapon. 武装 ❑ *She'd been so terrified that she had armed herself with a loaded rifle.* 她是如此害怕，以至于用一支上了膛的步枪把自己武装了起来。 **3** V-T If you **arm** someone **with** something that will be useful in a particular situation, you provide them with it. 用…装备

❑ *She thought that if she armed herself with all the knowledge she could gather she could handle anything.* 她曾以为，如果她用其所能搜集到的所有知识充实自己，她就能处理任何事。 **4** → see also **armed** **5** PHRASE A person's right to **bear arms** is their right to own and use guns, as a means of defense. 持有武器 ❑ *...a country where the right to bear arms is enshrined in the constitution.* …把武器持有权载入宪法的一个国家。 **6** PHRASE If one group or country **takes up arms against** another, they prepare to attack and fight them. 拿起武器 ❑ *They threatened to take up arms against the government if their demands were not met.* 他们威胁说，如果要求得不到满足就拿起武器对抗政府。 **7** PHRASE If people are **up in arms about** something, they are very angry about it and are protesting strongly against it. 愤怒抗议 ❑ *Patient advocates are up in arms over the possible closure of the psychiatric hospital.* 病人的支持者们愤怒抗议该精神病院的可能关闭。
→ see **war**

Word Partnership *arms* 的常用搭配：

PREP.	arms **around** ❶ **1**
V.	arms **crossed/folded, hold/take in *your*** arms, **join/link** arms ❶ **1**
ADJ.	**open/outstretched** arms ❶ **1**
V.	**bear** arms ❷ **1**
N.	arms **control**, arms **embargo**, arms **sales** ❷ **1**

▲ **ar·ma·ments** /ɑrməmənts/ N-PLURAL **Armaments** are weapons and military equipment belonging to an army or country. 军备 ❑ *...global efforts to reduce nuclear and other armaments.* …旨在减少核武器及其他军备的全球性努力。

arm·chair /ɑrmtʃɛər/ (**armchairs**) **1** N-COUNT An **armchair** is a big comfortable chair that has a support on each side for your arms. 扶手椅 ❑ *She was sitting in an armchair with blankets wrapped around her.* 她当时正裹着毯子坐在一把扶手椅里。 **2** ADJ An **armchair** critic, fan, or traveler knows about a particular subject from reading or hearing about it rather than from practical experience. 足不出户的 [ADJ n] ❑ *This great book is ideal for both the traveling supporter and the armchair fan.* 这本了不起的书对于旅行的和足不出户的支持者们都是理想的。

armed ♦♦◊ /ɑrmd/ **1** ADJ Someone who is **armed** is carrying a weapon, usually a gun. 持有武器的 ❑ *City police said the man was armed with a revolver.* 市警方说那名男子持有一支左轮手枪。 ❑ *...a barbed-wire fence patrolled by armed guards.* …一个由武装卫兵巡查的带刺铁丝网围栏。 **2** ADJ An **armed** attack or conflict involves people fighting with guns or carrying weapons. 使用武器的 [ADJ n] ❑ *They had been found guilty of armed robbery.* 他们被判犯有持械抢劫罪。 **3** → see also **arm**

armed forces ♦◊◊ N-PLURAL The **armed forces** or the **armed services** of a country are its military forces, usually the army, navy, marines, and air force. 武装部队 ❑ *Every member of the armed forces is a hero.* 武装部队的每个人都是英雄。

★ **ar·mor** /ɑrmər/
in BRIT, use **armour**
1 N-UNCOUNT In former times, **armor** was special metal clothing that soldiers wore for protection in battle. 盔甲 ❑ *...knights in armor.* …身穿盔甲的骑士们。 **2** N-UNCOUNT **Armor** consists of tanks and other military vehicles used in battle. 装甲部队 [MILITARY] ❑ *U.S. Army troops and armor blocked access to the main palace grounds.* 美国陆军部队和装甲部队阻断了进入主殿庭院的通道。 **3** N-UNCOUNT **Armor** is a hard, usually metal, covering that protects a vehicle against attack. (车辆的) 护甲 ❑ *...a formidable warhead that can penetrate the armor of most tanks.* …一种很有威力的、能穿透大多数坦克护甲的弹头。 **4** **knight in shining armor** → see **knight**
→ see **army**

ar·mored /ɑrmərd/
in BRIT, use **armoured**
1 ADJ **Armored** vehicles are equipped with a hard metal covering in order to protect them from gunfire and other missiles. 装甲的 (车辆) ❑ *More than forty armored vehicles carrying troops have been sent into the area.* 四十多辆载有士兵的装甲车已经被派往该地区。 **2** ADJ **Armored** troops are troops in armored vehicles. 配备装甲车的 (部队) ❑ *These front-line defenses are backed up by armored units in reserve.* 前线防御有后备装甲部队的支援。

ar·mory /ɑrməri/ (**armories**)
in BRIT, use **armoury**
1 N-COUNT A country's **armory** is all the weapons and military equipment that it has. 军械 ❑ *Nuclear weapons will play a less prominent part in NATO's armory in the future.* 核武器将来在北约的军械中会起较次要的作用。 **2** N-COUNT An **armory** is a place where weapons, bombs, and other military equipment are stored. 军械库 ❑ *...a failed attempt to steal weapons from an armory.* …从军械库中盗窃武器的一次失败尝试。 **3** N-COUNT In the United States, an **armory** is a building used by the National Guard or Army Reserve for meetings and training. (美国) 军务楼 ❑ *The National Guard says an armory in Fairmont has opened to shelter stranded motorists.* 国民警卫队声称费尔蒙特的一个军务楼已经开放，以收容受困的汽车司机们。

★ **ar·mour** /ɑrmər/ [BRIT] → see **armor**

ar·moured /ɑːʳməʳd/ [BRIT] → see **armored**

ar·moury /ɑːʳməri/ [BRIT] → see **armory**

arm·pit /ɑrmpɪt/ (**armpits**) N-COUNT Your **armpits** are the areas of your body under your arms where your arms join your shoulders. 腋窝 ❑ *I shave my armpits every couple of days.* 我每隔几天刮一次腋毛。

army ♦♦♦ /ɑrmi/ (**armies**) **1** N-COUNT-COLL An **army** is a large organized group of people who are armed and trained to fight on land in a war. Most armies are organized and controlled by governments. 陆军 ❑ *Perkins joined the Army in 1990.* 珀金斯于1990年加入了陆军。 **2** N-COUNT-COLL An **army of** people, animals, or things is a large number of them, especially when they are regarded as a force of some kind. 大群 ❑ *...data collected by an army of volunteers.* …由一大群志愿者搜集的数据。
→ see Word Web: **army**

aro·ma /əroʊmə/ (**aromas**) N-COUNT An **aroma** is a strong, pleasant smell. 芳香 ❑ *...the wonderful aroma of freshly baked bread.* …新烤面包的美妙香味。

aroma·thera·py /əroʊməθɛrəpi/ N-UNCOUNT **Aromatherapy** is a type of treatment which involves massaging the body with special fragrant oils. 芳香疗法

aro·mat·ic /ærəmætɪk/ ADJ An **aromatic** plant or food has a strong, pleasant smell of herbs or spices. 芳香的 ❑ *...an evergreen shrub with deep green, aromatic leaves.* …一种有深绿色芳香叶子的常青灌木。

Word Web army

The first Roman **army** was a poorly organized **militia band**. Its members had no **weapons** such as **swords** or **spears**. After the Etruscans, an advanced society from west-central Italy, **conquered** Rome, things changed. Then the Roman army became a powerful force. They learned how to **deploy** their **troops** to **fight** more effective **battles**. By the first century BC, the Roman army realized the importance of protective equipment. They started using bronze **helmets**, chain mail **armor**, and wooden **shields**. They fought many **military campaigns** and won many **wars**.

A

arose /ərouz/ **Arose** is the past tense of **arise**. **arise**的过去式

around ◆◆◆ /əraund/

> **Around** is an adverb and a preposition. In British English, the word "round" is often used instead. **Around** is often used with verbs of movement, such as "walk" and "drive," and also in phrasal verbs such as "get around" and "turn around."

1 PREP To be positioned **around** a place or object means to surround it or be on all sides of it. To move **around** a place means to go along its edge, back to your starting point. 在…四周 ❑ *She looked at the papers around her.* 她看了看她四周的报纸。 ❑ *Today she wore her hair down around her shoulders.* 今天她把头发披在了肩上。 ● ADV **Around** is also an adverb. 在…四周地 [n ADV] ❑ *...a village with a rocky river, a ruined castle and hills all around.* …一个有一条多石的河流和一座被毁的城堡、四面环山的村庄。 **2** PREP If you move **around** a corner or obstacle, you move to the other side of it. If you look **around** a corner or obstacle, you look to see what is on the other side. 绕过 ❑ *The photographer stopped clicking and hurried around the corner.* 该摄影师停止按动快门，匆匆绕过那个拐角。 **3** PREP If you move **around** a place, you travel through it, going to most of its parts. If you look **around** a place, you look at every part of it. 四处（走动、看） ❑ *I've been walking around Moscow and the town is terribly quiet.* 我一直在莫斯科四处走动，城里极其安静。 ● ADV **Around** is also an adverb. 四处地 [ADV after v] ❑ *He backed away from the edge, looking all around at the flat horizon.* 他从那边上退了回来，环视着平坦的地平线。 **4** PREP If someone moves **around** a place, they move through various parts of that place without having any particular destination. 在…四处（闲转） ❑ *These days much of my time is spent weaving my way around cocktail parties.* 这些日子我的很多时间花在闲转于各鸡尾酒会上。 ● ADV **Around** is also an adverb. 四处地 [ADV after v] ❑ *My mornings are spent rushing around after him.* 我的那些上午都花在跟着他四处奔波上。 **5** PREP You use **around** to say that something happens in different parts of a place or area. 在各处 ❑ *Police in South Africa say ten people have died in scattered violence around the country.* 南非警方称，该国各地的暴力事件中已有10人死亡。 ❑ *Elephants were often to be found in swamp in eastern Kenya around the Tana River.* 大象经常会在肯尼亚东部沼泽塔纳河各处被发现。 ● ADV **Around** is also an adverb. 在各处地 ❑ *What the hell do you think you're doing following me around?* 你到处跟着我究竟是在干什么？ **6** PREP The people **around** you are the people whom you come into contact with, especially your friends and relatives, and the people you work with. 在…周围的 ❑ *We change our behavior by observing the behavior of those around us.* 我们通过观察周围人的行为举止来改变自己的行为举止。 **7** PREP If something such as a film, a discussion, or a plan is based **around** something, that thing is its main theme. 围绕（某主题） ❑ *The novel is a political thriller loosely based around current political issues.* 这部小说是一本在一定程度上围绕当前政治问题撰写的政治惊悚小说。 **8** PREP When you are giving measurements, you can use **around** to talk about the distance along the edge of something round. 绕…一周（的长度） ❑ *She was 5 foot 4 inches, 38 around the chest, 28 around the waist and 40 around the hips.* 她身高5英尺4英寸，胸围38英寸，腰围28英寸，臀围40英寸。 **9** ADV If you turn **around**, you turn so that you are facing in the opposite direction. 朝相反方向地 [ADV after v] ❑ *I turned around and wrote the title on the blackboard.* 我转过身将标题写在了黑板上。 **10** ADV If you go **around** to someone's house, you visit them. （去）拜访地 [ADV after v] ❑ *She helped me unpack my things and then we went around to see the other girls.* 她帮助我打开行李，然后我们去看望别的女孩。 **11** ADV You use **around** in expressions such as **sit around** and **hang around** when you are saying that someone is spending time in a place and not doing anything very important. 无所事事地 [ADV after v] ❑ *I'm just going to be hanging around twiddling my thumbs.* 我正要无所事事地旋弄拇指。 ● PREP **Around** is also a preposition. 在…（无所事事） ❑ *He used to skip lessons and hang around the harbor with some other boys.* 他过去经常逃课，和其他一些男孩子在码头上闲荡。 **12** ADV If you move things **around**, you move them so that they are in different places. 别处地 [ADV after v] ❑ *Furniture in the classroom should not be changed around without warning the blind child.* 该教室里的设施未经告知该盲童不得挪动。 **13** ADV If a wheel or object turns **around**, it turns. 绕圈地 [ADV after v] ❑ *The boat started to spin around in the water.* 那条船开始在水里打转。 **14** ADV If someone or something is **around**, they exist or are present in a place. 在某处 ❑ *You haven't seen my publisher anywhere around, have you?* 你还没有在哪儿看见我的出版商，是吧？ **15** ADV You use **around** in expressions such as **this time around** or **to come around** when you are describing something that has happened before or things that happen regularly. 又一次地 ❑ *Senator Bentsen has declined to get involved this time around.* 参议员本特森这次又拒绝了介入。 **16** ADV **Around** means approximately. 大约地 ❑ *My salary was around $45,000 plus a car and expenses.* 我的工资大约是$45000，外加一辆车和各种报销。 ● PREP **Around** is also a preposition. 在…左右 ❑ *He expects the elections to be held around November.* 他期待选举在11月左右举行。

> When you are talking about movement in no particular direction, you can use **around** or **about**. **Around** is more common in American English. ❑ *It's so romantic up here, flying around in a small plane... Police officers walk about with guns on their hips.* When you are talking about something being generally present or available, you can use **around** or **about**: again, **around** is more common in American English. ❑ *There is a lot of talent around at the moment... There are not that many jobs about.*

17 PHRASE **Around about** means approximately. 大约 [SPOKEN] ❑ *There is an outright separatist party but it only scored around about 10 percent in the vote.* 有一个极端分离主义党派，但是该党在选举中只取得了大约10%的选票。 **18** **the other way around** → see **way**

arous·al /ərauzᵊl/ **1** N-UNCOUNT **Arousal** is the state of being sexually excited. 性兴奋 ❑ *...sexual arousal.* …性兴奋。 **2** N-UNCOUNT **Arousal** is a state in which you feel excited or very alert, for example, as a result of fear, stress, or anger. 兴奋 ❑ *Thinking angry thoughts can provoke strong physiological arousal.* 想生气的事情能激起强烈的生理兴奋。

arouse /ərauz/ (**arouses, arousing, aroused**) **1** V-T If something **arouses** a particular reaction or attitude in people, it causes them to have that reaction or attitude. 引起 ❑ *His revolutionary work in linguistics has aroused intense scholarly interest.* 他在语言学方面的革命性著作引起了强烈的学术兴趣。 **2** V-T If something **arouses** a particular feeling or instinct that exists in someone, it causes them to experience that feeling or instinct strongly. 激起 ❑ *The smell of frying bacon aroused his hunger.* 煎咸肉的味道激起了他的饥饿感。 **3** V-T If you **are aroused** by something, it makes you feel sexually excited. 激起性欲 [usu passive] ❑ *Some men are aroused when their partner says erotic words to them.* 一些男人在性伙伴对他们说色情话时会被撩起性欲。

ar·range ◆◇◇ /əreɪndʒ/ (**arranges, arranging, arranged**) **1** V-T If you **arrange** an event or meeting, you make plans for it to happen. 安排（活动、会议） ❑ *She arranged an appointment for Friday afternoon at four-fifteen.* 她安排了一个星期五下午四点一刻的约会。 **2** V-T/V-I If you **arrange** with someone **to** do something, you make plans with them to do it. 安排；筹划 ❑ *I've arranged to see him on Friday morning.* 我已经安排了星期五早上见他。 ❑ *It was arranged that the party would gather for lunch in Grant Park.* 已经安排好这一行人在格兰特公园聚集吃午餐。 ❑ *The city had arranged for the National Guard to be brought in.* 该市已筹划调入国民警卫队。 **3** V-T/V-I If you **arrange** something **for** someone, you make it possible for them to have it or to do it. 安排好 ❑ *I will arrange for someone to take you around.* 我会安排好人领你转转。 ❑ *The hotel manager will arrange for a babysitter.* 宾馆经理会安排一位保姆。 ❑ *Mr. Dambar had arranged a dinner for the three of them.* 丹姆巴尔先生已经为他们3人安排好了一顿晚餐。 **4** V-T If you **arrange** things somewhere, you place them in a particular position, usually in order to make them look attractive or neat. 布置 ❑ *When she has a little spare time she enjoys arranging dried flowers.* 她有一点闲暇时间就喜欢插干花。 **5** V-T If a piece of music **is arranged by** someone, it is changed or adapted so that it is suitable for particular instruments or voices, or for a particular performance. 改编（乐曲） [usu passive] ❑ *The songs were arranged by another well-known bass player, Ron Carter.* 这些歌曲由另一位著名的贝司手罗恩·卡特改编。

ar·range·ment ◆◇◇ /əreɪndʒmənt/ (**arrangements**) **1** N-COUNT **Arrangements** are plans and preparations that you make so that something will happen or be possible. 安排 ❑ *The staff is working frantically on final arrangements for the summit.* 工作人员在紧张忙碌地为该峰会做最后的安排。 ❑ *She telephoned Ellen, but made no arrangements to see her.* 她给埃伦打了电话，但没安排见她。 **2** N-COUNT An **arrangement** is an agreement that you make with someone to do something. 商定 [also "by" N] ❑ *The caves can be visited only by prior arrangement.* 这些洞穴只能预约参观。 **3** N-COUNT An **arrangement** of things, for example, flowers or furniture, is a group of them displayed in a particular way. 布置 ❑ *The house was* always decorated with imaginative flower arrangements. 该房子那时经常装饰着富有创意的插花。 4 N-COUNT If someone makes an **arrangement** of a piece of music, they change it so that it is suitable for particular voices or instruments, or for a particular performance. (乐曲的) 改编 ❑ *...an arrangement of a well-known piece by Mozart.* …对莫扎特的一首名曲的改编。

Word Partnership *arrangement* 的常用搭配:

ADJ. **formal** arrangement, **informal** arrangement, **permanent** arrangement, **special** arrangement, **temporary** arrangement 1 – 3
N. **flower** arrangement, **seating** arrangement 3

ar·rant /ærənt/ ADJ **Arrant** is used to emphasize that something or someone is very bad in some way. 彻头彻尾的 [ADJ n] [FORMAL, EMPHASIS] ❑ *That's arrant nonsense.* 那是一派胡言。 ❑ *...an arrant coward.* …一个彻头彻尾的懦夫。

★ **ar·ray** /əreɪ/ (**arrays**) 1 N-COUNT-COLL An **array of** different things or people is a large number or wide range of them. 大量; 各种 ❑ *As the deadline approached she experienced a bewildering array of emotions.* 随着最后期限的临近，她心绪变得纷繁复杂起来。 2 N-COUNT An **array of** objects is a collection of them that is displayed or arranged in a particular way. 陈列 ❑ *We visited the local markets and saw wonderful arrays of fruit and vegetables.* 我们参观了当地的市场，看到了漂亮地摆放着的水果蔬菜。

Word Partnership *array* 的常用搭配:

ADJ. **broad/vast/wide** array, **dizzying** array, **impressive** array 1 2
PREP. array **of** ***something*** 1 2

ar·rears /ərɪərz/ 1 N-PLURAL **Arrears** are amounts of money that you owe, especially regular payments that you should have made earlier. 逾期欠款 ❑ *They have promised to pay the arrears over the next five years.* 他们已经保证在接下来的5年里付清逾期债款。 2 PHRASE If someone is **in arrears with** their payments, or falls **into arrears**, they have not paid the regular amounts of money that they should have paid. 拖欠中 ❑ *...the 300,000 households who are more than six months in arrears with their mortgages.* …拖欠按揭贷款超过6个月的30万户家庭。 3 PHRASE If sums of money such as wages or taxes are paid **in arrears**, they are paid at the end of the period of time to which they relate, for example, after a job has been done and the wages have been earned. 在(某段时间) 之后 (支付) ❑ *Interest is paid in arrears after you use the money.* 利息在你使用了这笔钱之后支付。

ar·rest ♦♦◊ /ərɛst/ (**arrests, arresting, arrested**) 1 V-T If the police **arrest** you, they take charge of you and take you to a police station, because they believe you may have committed a crime. 逮捕 ❑ *Police arrested five young men in connection with one of the attacks.* 警方逮捕了与其中一起袭击事件有关的5名年轻男子。 ● N-VAR **Arrest** is also a noun. 逮捕 ❑ *...a substantial reward for information leading to the arrest of the bombers.* …用于奖励为抓捕爆炸犯提供有效信息的一大笔赏金。 ❑ *Police chased the fleeing terrorists and later made two arrests.* 警方追赶逃窜的恐怖分子，后来逮捕了两个人。 2 V-T If something or someone **arrests** a process, they stop it from continuing. 抑制 [FORMAL] ❑ *The sufferer may have to make major changes in his or her life to arrest the disease.* 患者可能得对自身生活作大的调整以抑制病情。 3 → see also **house arrest**

ar·ri·val ♦◊◊ /əraɪvᵊl/ (**arrivals**) 1 N-VAR When a person or vehicle arrives at a place, you can refer to their **arrival**. 到达 ❑ *...the day after his arrival in Wichita.* …他到达威奇托的第二天。 ❑ *He was dead on arrival at the nearby hospital.* 他在到达附近的医院时已死。 2 N-VAR When someone starts a new job, you can refer to their **arrival** in that job. 到任 ❑ *...the power vacuum created by the arrival of a new president.* …由一位新总统到任造成的权力真空。 3 N-SING When something is brought to you or becomes available, you can refer to its **arrival**. 到达 ❑ *I was flicking idly through a newspaper while awaiting the arrival of orange juice and coffee.* 我在等橙汁和咖啡送达的同时漫不经心地翻阅一份报纸。 4 N-SING When a particular time comes or a particular event happens, you can refer to its **arrival**. 来临 ❑ *He celebrated the arrival of the New Year with a bout of drinking that nearly killed him.* 他以一番狂饮庆祝新年的来临，这几乎要了他的命。 5 N-COUNT You can refer to someone who has just arrived at a place as a new **arrival**. 到来者 ❑ *A high proportion of the new arrivals are skilled professionals.* 很大一部分新来的人们是技术熟练的专业人士。

Word Partnership *arrival* 的常用搭配:

N. **time of** arrival 1
PREP. arrival **at** ***someplace***, **on** arrival 1
arrival **of** ***something*** 1 3 4
ADJ. **early/late** arrival 1
new arrival, **recent** arrival 5
V. **awaiting the** arrival 1 3 4

ar·rive ♦♦◊ /əraɪv/ (**arrives, arriving, arrived**) 1 V-I When a person or vehicle **arrives** at a place, they come to it from somewhere else. 到达 ❑ *Fresh groups of guests arrived.* 新客成批到达了。 ❑ *...a small group of commuters waiting for their train, which arrived on time.* …几个等候火车准点到达的通勤者。 2 V-I When you **arrive** at a place, you come to it for the first time in order to stay, live, or work there. 初次抵达 ❑ *...in the old days before the European settlers arrived in the country.* …在欧洲定居者们初次到达这个国家之前的古老岁月。 3 V-I When something such as letter or meal **arrives**, it is brought or delivered to you. 送达 ❑ *Breakfast arrived while he was in the bathroom.* 早餐在他在浴室里时送到了。 4 V-I When something such as a new product or invention **arrives**, it becomes available. (产品、发明) 问世 ❑ *Several long-awaited movies will finally arrive in the stores this month.* 几部期盼已久的影片最终将于本月在各家商店露面。 5 V-I When a particular moment or event **arrives**, it happens, especially after you have been waiting for it or expecting it. 到来 ❑ *The time has arrived when I need to give up smoking.* 我需要戒烟的时候到了。 6 V-I When you **arrive at** something such as a decision, you decide something after thinking about it or discussing it. 达成 ❑ *...if the jury cannot arrive at a unanimous decision.* …如果陪审团不能达成一致判决。

You use both **arrive** and **reach** to talk about coming to a particular place. You can use **arrive** to emphasize being in a place rather than traveling to it. ❑ *When I arrived in England I was exhausted.* **Reach** is always followed by a noun or pronoun referring to a place and you can use it to emphasize the effort required to get there. ❑ *To reach the capital might not be easy.* **Arrive at** and **reach** can also be used to say that someone eventually makes a decision or finds the answer to something. ❑ *It took hours to arrive at a decision... They were unable to reach a decision.*

Thesaurus *arrive* 另参见:

V. enter, land, pull in, reach; (*ant.*) depart 1

★ **ar·ro·gant** /ærəgənt/ ADJ Someone who is **arrogant** behaves in a proud, unpleasant way toward other people because they believe that they are more important than others. 傲慢的 [DISAPPROVAL] ❑ *He was so arrogant.* 他是如此傲慢。 ❑ *That sounds arrogant, doesn't it?* 那听起来很傲慢，不是吗? ● **ar·ro·gance** ★ N-UNCOUNT 傲慢 ❑ *At times the arrogance of those in power is quite blatant.* 有时那些当权者的傲慢很露骨。

ar·row /ærou/ (**arrows**) 1 N-COUNT An **arrow** is a long thin weapon that is sharp and pointed at one end and that often has feathers at the other end. An arrow is shot from a bow. 箭 ❑ *Warriors armed with bows and arrows and spears have invaded their villages.* 佩有弓箭和长矛的武士们已入侵了他们的村庄。 2 N-COUNT An **arrow** is a written or printed sign that consists of a straight line with another line bent at a sharp angle at one end. This is a printed arrow: ➜. The arrow points in a particular direction to indicate where something is. 箭头 ❑ *A series of arrows points the way to the modest grave of Andrei Sakharov.* 一系列箭头指示着通往简朴的安德烈·萨哈罗夫之墓的路。

arse /ɑrs/ (**arses**) N-COUNT Your **arse** is your buttocks. 屁股 [BRIT, INFORMAL, VULGAR]

▲ **ar·senal** /ɑrsənᵊl/ (**arsenals**) 1 N-COUNT An **arsenal** is a large collection of weapons and military equipment held by a country, group, or person. 武器 ❑ *Russia is committed to destroying most of its nuclear arsenals.* 俄国承诺销毁其大部分核武器。 2 N-COUNT An **arsenal** is a building where weapons and military equipment are stored. 军火库

▲ **ar·son** /ɑrsᵊn/ N-UNCOUNT **Arson** is the crime of deliberately setting fire to a building or vehicle. 纵火罪 ❑ *...a terrible wave of rioting, theft and arson.* …一波可怕的骚乱、盗窃和纵火事件。

art ♦♦♦ /ɑrt/ (**arts**) 1 N-UNCOUNT **Art** consists of paintings, sculpture, and other pictures or objects that are created for people to look at and admire or think deeply about. 艺术品 ❑ *...the first*

A

Word Web art

The **Impressionist** movement in **painting** began in Europe during the second half of the 19th century. The Impressionists abandoned traditional **realistic** depictions of people and objects painted in **studios**. They often painted **landscapes**,

emphasizing light and color in their **interpretations** of everyday life. Among these **painters** were French artists Paul Cézanne, Pierre Renoir, and Claude Monet. The word "Impressionist" has its origin in the name of a Monet **painting**, "Impression, Sunrise." Japanese prints had an effect on the Impressionist movement. The Impressionists appreciated the use of contrasting dark and bright colors found in these prints.

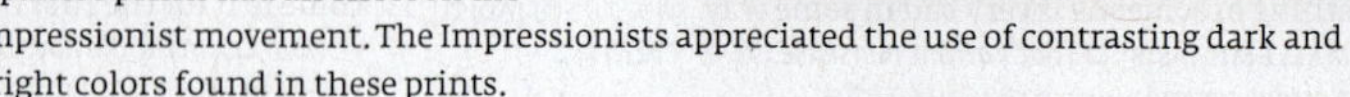

exhibition of such art in the West. …这种艺术品在西方的初次展出。❏ *...contemporary and modern American art.* …美国当代与现代的艺术品。**2** N-UNCOUNT **Art** is the activity or educational subject that consists of creating paintings, sculptures, and other pictures or objects for people to look at and admire or think deeply about. 艺术 ❏ *...a painter, content to be left alone with her all-absorbing art.* …一个乐于独自沉浸在她的迷人艺术中的画家。❏ *...Savannah College of Art and Design.* …萨瓦纳艺术设计学院。**3** N-VAR **The arts** are activities such as music, painting, literature, film, and dance, which people can take part in for enjoyment, or to create works that express certain meanings or ideas of beauty. 艺术活动 ❏ *Catherine the Great was a patron of the arts and sciences.* 叶卡捷琳娜大帝是艺术和科学活动的赞助人。**4** N-PLURAL At a university or college, **arts** are subjects such as history, literature, or languages in contrast to scientific subjects. 人文学科 ❏ *...arts and social science graduates.* …人文与社会科学的毕业生们。**5** ADJ **Arts** or **art** is used to describe theaters that show plays or films that are intended to make the audience think deeply about the content, and not simply to entertain them. 艺术性的 [ADJ n] ❏ *...a lower Manhattan art theater.* …下曼哈顿区的一座艺术剧院。**6** N-COUNT If you describe an activity as an **art**, you mean that it requires skill and that people learn to do it by instinct or experience, rather than by learning facts or rules. 技艺 ❏ *...pioneers who transformed clinical medicine from an art to a science.* …把临床医学从技艺转化成科学的先驱们。**7** → see also **fine art, martial art, state-of-the-art, work of art**
→ see Word Web: **art**
→ see **culture, drawing, gallery**

ar·te·fact /ɑrtɪfækt/ [mainly BRIT] → see **artifact**

★ **ar·tery** /ɑrtəri/ (**arteries**) **1** N-COUNT **Arteries** are the tubes in your body that carry blood from your heart to the rest of your body. Compare **vein**. 动脉 ❏ *...patients suffering from blocked arteries.* …患动脉堵塞的病人们。**2** N-COUNT You can refer to an important main route within a complex road, railroad, or river system as an **artery**. 干线 ❏ *...Connecticut Ave., one of the main arteries of Washington.* …康涅狄格大道，华盛顿的主干道之一。

★ **art·ful** /ɑrtfəl/ **1** ADJ If you describe someone as **artful**, you mean that they are clever and skillful at achieving what they want, especially by deceiving people. 狡猾的 [usu ADJ n] ❏ *Some politicians have realized that there are more artful ways of subduing people than shooting or jailing them.* 一些政客已经意识到有比开枪镇压或监禁更狡猾的征服人民的办法。**2** ADJ If you use **artful** to describe the way someone has done or arranged something, you approve of it because it is clever or elegant. 巧妙的；精巧的 [usu ADJ n] [FORMAL, APPROVAL] ❏ *There is also an artful contrast of shapes.* 还有一种不同形状的巧妙对比。

ar·thrit·ic /ɑrθrɪtɪk/ **1** ADJ **Arthritic** is used to describe the condition, the pain, or the symptoms of arthritis. 关节炎的 [ADJ n] ❏ *I developed serious arthritic symptoms and chronic sinusitis.* 我有了严重的关节炎症状和慢性鼻窦炎。**2** ADJ An **arthritic** person is suffering from arthritis, and cannot move very easily. **Arthritic** joints or hands are affected by arthritis. 患关节炎的 ❏ *...an elderly lady who suffered with arthritic hands.* …一位手部患有关节炎的老妇人。

Word Link *itis ≈ inflammation : arthritis, hepatitis, meningitis*

ar·thri·tis /ɑrθraɪtɪs/ N-UNCOUNT **Arthritis** is a medical condition in which the joints in someone's body are swollen and painful. 关节炎 ❏ *I have a touch of arthritis in the wrist.* 我的手腕有轻微关节炎。

ar·ti·choke /ɑrtɪtʃoʊk/ (**artichokes**) N-VAR **Artichokes** or **globe artichokes** are round green vegetables that have fleshy leaves arranged like the petals of a flower. 洋蓟

Word Link *cle ≈ small : article, cubicle, particle*

ar·ti·cle ♦♦◇ /ɑrtɪkəl/ (**articles**) **1** N-COUNT An **article** is a piece of writing that is published in a newspaper or magazine. 文章 ❏ *...a newspaper article.* …一篇报上的文章。❏ *According to an article in Newsweek the drug could have side effects.* 据一篇《新闻周刊》上的文章，这种药物可能有副作用。**2** N-COUNT You can refer to objects as **articles** of some kind. 物品 ❏ *...articles of clothing.* …衣物。❏ *He had stripped the house of all articles of value.* 他已把那所房子里值钱的东西洗劫一空。**3** N-COUNT An **article of** a formal agreement or document is a section of it that deals with a particular point. 条款 ❏ *The country appears to be violating several articles of the convention.* 该国看来正在违反该公约中的数个条款。**4** N-COUNT In grammar, an **article** is a kind of determiner. In English, "a" and "an" are called **the indefinite article**, and "the" is called **the definite article**. 冠词 **5** PHRASE If you describe something as **the genuine article**, you are emphasizing that it is genuine, and often that it is very good. 真品 [EMPHASIS] ❏ *The vodka was the genuine article.* 这伏特加是真品。
→ see **newspaper**

★ **ar·ticu·late** (**articulates, articulating, articulated**)

The adjective is pronounced /ɑrtɪkyəlɪt/. The verb is pronounced /ɑrtɪkyəleɪt/.

形容词读作 /ɑrtɪkyəlɪt/。动词读作 /ɑrtɪkyəleɪt/。

1 ADJ If you describe someone as **articulate**, you mean that they are able to express their thoughts and ideas easily and well. 善表达的 [APPROVAL] ❏ *She is an articulate young woman.* 她是个善表达的年轻女子。**2** V-T When you **articulate** your ideas or feelings, you express them clearly in words. 清楚地表述 [FORMAL] ❏ *The president has been accused of failing to articulate an overall vision in foreign affairs.* 总统被指责没能清楚地表述对外交事务的总体设想。**3** V-T If you **articulate** something, you say it very clearly, so that each word or syllable can be heard. 清楚地说出 ❏ *He articulated each syllable.* 他清楚地说出了每个音节。

ar·ticu·lat·ed /ɑrtɪkyəleɪtɪd/ ADJ An **articulated** vehicle, especially a bus, is made in two or more sections that are joined together by metal bars, so that the vehicle can turn more easily. 铰接式的（车辆）

Word Link *fact, fic ≈ making : artifact, artificial, factor*

★ **ar·ti·fact** /ɑrtɪfækt/ (**artifacts**)

in BRIT, usually use **artefact**

N-COUNT An **artifact** is an ornament, tool, or other object that is made by a human being, especially one that is historically or culturally interesting. （尤指有历史或文化价值的）手工艺品 ❏ *They also repair broken religious artifacts.* 他们也修补破损的宗教手工艺品。
→ see **history**

ar·ti·fi·cial /ɑrtɪfɪʃəl/ **1** ADJ **Artificial** objects, materials, or processes do not occur naturally and are created by human beings, often using science or technology. 人造的（物体、材料、

工艺等) ❑ *The city is dotted with small lakes, natural and artificial.* 这座城市满是天然和人造的小湖泊。 ❑ *...a wholefood diet free from artificial additives, colors and flavors.* …一种无人造添加剂、色素及味素的全天然食物饮食。 ● **ar·ti·fi·cial·ly** ADV 人造地 ❑ *...artificially sweetened lemonade.* …人工加了糖的柠檬汽水。 **2** ADJ An **artificial** state or situation exists only because someone has created it, and therefore often seems unnatural or unnecessary. 人为的（状态、状况） ❑ *Even in the artificial environment of an office, our body rhythms continue to affect us.* 即便在办公室的人为环境中，我们的身体节律继续影响我们。 ● **ar·ti·fi·cial·ly** ADV 人为地 ❑ *...state subsidies that have kept retail prices artificially low.* …人为地将零售价格保持在低水平的国家补贴。

Thesaurus *artificial* 另参见：
ADJ. manmade, manufactured, synthetic, unnatural; (*ant.*) natural **1** **2**

ar·ti·fi·cial in·tel·li·gence N-UNCOUNT **Artificial intelligence** is a type of computer technology concerned with making machines work in an intelligent way, similar to the way that the human mind works. 人工智能

★ **ar·til·lery** /ɑrtɪləri/ **1** N-UNCOUNT **Artillery** consists of large, powerful guns that are transported on wheels and used by an army. 大炮 ❑ *Using tanks and heavy artillery, they seized the town.* 他们使用坦克和重炮攻下了这座城市。 **2** N-SING-COLL **The artillery** is the section of an army that is trained to use large, powerful guns. 炮兵部队 ❑ *From 1935 to 1937 he was in the artillery.* 从1935年到1937年他在炮兵部队。

Word Link *ist ≈ one who practices : artist, chemist, pharmacist*

art·ist ♦♦◇ /ɑrtɪst/ (**artists**) **1** N-COUNT An **artist** is someone who draws or paints pictures or creates sculptures as a job or a hobby. 美术家 ❑ *...the studio of a great artist.* …一位伟大美术家的工作室。 ❑ *Each poster is signed by the artist.* 每张海报都由这位美术家签了名。 **2** N-COUNT An **artist** is a person who creates novels, poems, films, or other things which can be considered as works of art. 文学艺术家 ❑ *His books are enormously easy to read, yet he is a serious artist.* 他的书极易读，然而他却是一位严肃的文学艺术家。 **3** N-COUNT An **artist** is a performer such as a musician, actor, or dancer. 表演艺术家 ❑ *...a popular artist who has sold millions of records.* …一位卖了上百万张唱片的、受人欢迎的表演艺术家。
→ see **animation**

ar·tis·tic /ɑrtɪstɪk/ **1** ADJ Someone who is **artistic** is good at drawing or painting, or arranging things in a beautiful way. 有美术才能的 ❑ *They encourage boys to be sensitive and artistic.* 他们鼓励男孩子们要反应敏感并有美术才能。 **2** ADJ **Artistic** means relating to art or artists. 艺术的；艺术家的 ❑ *...the campaign for artistic freedom.* …艺术自由运动。 ● **ar·tis·ti·cal·ly** /ɑrtɪstɪkli/ ADV 艺术方面地 ❑ *...artistically gifted children.* …有艺术天赋的儿童。 **3** ADJ An **artistic** design or arrangement is beautiful. （设计、布局）有艺术性的 ❑ *...an artistic arrangement of stone paving.* …石头铺路的艺术性布局。 ● **ar·tis·ti·cal·ly** ADV 有艺术性地 ❑ *...artistically carved vessels.* …艺术性地刻成的船只。

art·ist·ry /ɑrtɪstri/ N-UNCOUNT **Artistry** is the creative skill of an artist, writer, actor, or musician. 艺术技艺 ❑ *...his artistry as a cellist.* …他作为大提琴家的艺术技艺。

art·work /ɑrtwɜrk/ (**artworks**) **1** N-UNCOUNT **Artwork** is drawings and photographs that are prepared in order to be included in something such as a book or advertisement. 图片 ❑ *The artwork for the poster was done by my sister.* 该海报的图片是我妹妹制作的。 **2** N-VAR **Artworks** are paintings or sculptures of high quality. 艺术品 ❑ *The museum contains 6,000 contemporary and modern artworks.* 该博物馆藏有6000件现当代艺术作品。 ❑ *...a magnificent collection of priceless artwork.* …一个无价艺术珍品的极佳收藏。

as
❶ CONJUNCTION AND PREPOSITION USES
❷ USED WITH OTHER PREPOSITIONS AND CONJUNCTIONS

❶ **as** ♦♦♦ /əz, STRONG æz/
⇨ **Please look at meanings 12 – 22 to see if the expression you are looking for is shown under another headword.** **1** CONJ If something happens **as** something else happens, it happens at the same time. 在（某事发生的）同时 ❑ *Another policeman has been injured as fighting continued this morning.* 又一名警察在今天上午打斗继续过程中受了伤。 ❑ *All the jury's eyes were on him as he continued.* 所有陪审员的目光在他继续下去时都集中在了他身上。 ❑ *The play started as I got there.* 演出在我到达时开始了。 **2** CONJ You use **as** to say how something happens or is done, or to indicate that something happens or is done in the same way as something else. 像（做某事、某事发生）一样 ❑ *I'll behave toward them as I would like to be treated.* 我会像希望别人怎样对待我那样对待他们。 ❑ *Today, as usual, he was wearing a three-piece suit.* 今天他像往常一样穿着一套三件套西装。 **3** CONJ You use **as** to introduce short clauses that comment on the truth of what you are saying. 如…（用于引导评注性短从句） ❑ *As you can see, we're still working.* 如你能看到的，我们仍在工作。 **4** CONJ You can use **as** to mean "because" when you are explaining the reason for something. 由于 ❑ *Enjoy the first hour of the day. This is important as it sets the mood for the rest of the day.* 享受一天中的第一个小时。这很重要，因为这第一个小时奠定当天其余时间的情绪。 **5** PHRASE You use the structure **as...as** when you are comparing things. 像…一样 ❑ *I never went through a final exam that was as difficult as that one.* 我从未经历过像那次一样难的期末考试。 ● PHRASE **As** is also a conjunction. 像 …一样 ❑ *Being a mother isn't as bad as I thought at first!* 做一位母亲并不像我当初想的那样糟！ ❑ *I don't think he was ever as fit as he should have been.* 我认为他从来没有过他应该有的健康。 **6** PHRASE You use **as...as** to emphasize amounts of something. （数量）多达 [EMPHASIS] ❑ *She gets as many as eight thousand letters a month.* 她每月收到多达8千封信。 ❑ *You can look forward to a significant cash return by saving from as little as $10 a month.* 每月只要存哪怕像10美元这么小的数目，你就可以期待着收回一笔可观的现金收入。

You can use **as**, **because**, **since**, or **for** to give an explanation for something. **Because** is the most common of these, and is used when answering a question beginning with 'why'. You can use **as** or **since** instead of **because** to introduce a clause containing a reason for something, especially in writing. ❑ *The size of the room is important as it will dictate the type of desk you choose... Since the juice is quite strong, you should always dilute it.* In stories, **for** is sometimes used to explain or justify something. ❑ *He seemed to be in need of company, for he suddenly went back into the house.* Note that **because** is a conjunction, and is used to link two ideas within one sentence. ❑ *I just forgot because I was nervous.*

7 PHRASE You say **as it were** in order to make what you are saying sound less definite. 好像是 [VAGUENESS] ❑ *I'd understood the words, but I didn't, as it were, understand the question.* 我已经理解了这些词，但我似乎还不理解这个问题。 **8** PHRASE You use expressions such as **as it is**, **as it turns out**, and **as things stand** when you are making a contrast between a possible situation and what actually happened or is the case. （比较可能性与事实）事实是/结果是/情况是 ❑ *I want to work at home on a Tuesday but as it turns out sometimes it's a Wednesday or a Thursday.* 我想在某个星期二在家里工作，但结果是有时是在星期三或星期四。 **9** PREP You use **as** when you are indicating what someone or something is or is thought to be, or what function they have. 作为 ❑ *He has worked as a diplomat in the U.S., Sudan and Saudi Arabia.* 他曾做过驻美国、苏丹和沙特阿拉伯的外交官。 ❑ *The news apparently came as a complete surprise.* 这消息显然来得是个彻头彻尾的意外。 **10** PREP If you do something **as** a child or **as** a teenager, for example, you do it when you are a child or a teenager. 还是（小孩）时 ❑ *She loved singing as a child and started vocal training at 12.* 她还是个小孩的时候就爱唱歌，12岁就开始了声乐训练。 **11** PREP You use **as** in expressions like **as a result** and **as a consequence** to indicate how two situations or events are related to each other. 作为（结果等） ❑ *As a result of the growing fears about home security, more people are arranging for someone to stay in their home when they're away.* 由于日益增长的对家庭安全的担心，更多人在外出时会安排个人呆在他们家里。 **12** **as ever** → see **ever** **13** **as a matter of fact** → see **fact** **14** **as follows** → see **follow** **15** **as long as** → see **long** **16** **as opposed to** → see **opposed** **17** **as regards** → see **regard** **18** **as soon as** → see **soon** **19** **as such** → see **such** **20** **as well** → see **well** **21** **as well as** → see **well** **22** **as yet** → see **yet**

❷ **as** ♦♦♦ /əz, STRONG æz/ **1** PHRASE You use **as for** and **as to** at the beginning of a sentence in order to introduce a slightly different subject that is still connected to the previous one. 至于

❑ *I don't know why the guy yelled at me. And as for going back there, certainly I would never go back, for fear of receiving further abuse.* 我不知道为什么这个家伙冲我吼叫。至于回到那儿去，我肯定永远也不会回去了，生怕遭到进一步虐待。 **2** PHRASE You use **as to** to indicate what something refers to. 就… ❑ *They should make decisions as to whether the student needs more help.* 他们应该就该学生是否需要更多帮助作决定。 **3** PHRASE If you say that something will happen **as of** a particular date or time, you mean that it will happen from that time on. 从（某日、某时）起 ❑ *The border, effectively closed since 1981, will be opened as of January the 1st.* 自1981年以来实际上关闭了的边境将从1月1日起开放。 **4** PHRASE You use **as if** and **as though** when you are giving a possible explanation for something or saying that something appears to be the case when it is not. 好像 ❑ *Anne shrugged, as if she didn't know.* 安妮耸了耸肩，好像她不知道。

Word Partnership *as* 的常用搭配：

V.	**act as, (also) known as, describe as, perceived/seen as, serve/use as, treat as** ❶ **2**
ADJ.	**as good** ❶ **2**
N.	**reputation as** ❶ **9**
	as a result ❶ **11**
PREP.	**as for/to** ***something*** ❷ **1** **2**
	as of ❷ **3**
CONJ.	**as if/though** ❷ **4**

asap /eɪ ɛs eɪ piː/ ADV **asap** is an abbreviation for "as soon as possible." 尽快（**as soon as possible** 的缩略）[ADV after v] ❑ *The colonel ordered, "I want two good engines down here asap."* 上校命令道："我要两台好的发动机尽快到这儿"。

as·bes·tos /æsbɛstəs, æz-/ N-UNCOUNT **Asbestos** is a gray material that does not burn and that was used in the past as a protection against fire or heat. Clothing and mats are sometimes made from it. 石棉 ❑ *...asbestos gloves.* …石棉手套。

Word Link *scend ≈ climbing : ascend, condescend, descend*

★ **as·cend** /əsɛnd/ (**ascends, ascending, ascended**) **1** V-T If you **ascend** a hill or staircase, you go up it. 上（山、楼梯）[WRITTEN] ❑ *Mrs. Clayton had to hold Lizzie's hand as they ascended the steps.* 上台阶时克莱顿夫人不得不抓着莉齐的手。 **2** V-I If a staircase or path **ascends**, it leads up to a higher position. （楼梯或路）向上延伸 [WRITTEN] ❑ *A number of staircases ascend from the cobbled streets onto the ramparts.* 若干个阶梯从鹅卵石街道向上延伸到城墙上。 **3** V-I If something **ascends**, it moves up, usually vertically or into the air. （通常垂直地）向上移动 [WRITTEN] ❑ *Keep the drill centered in the borehole while it ascends and descends.* 当钻头上下钻时，要把钻孔保持在中心。 **4** → see also **ascending**

as·cend·ancy /əsɛndənsi/ also **ascendency** N-UNCOUNT If one group has **ascendancy** over another group, it has more power or influence than the other group. 支配地位 [FORMAL] ❑ *Although geographically linked, the two provinces have long fought for political ascendancy.* 尽管位置上相邻，这两个省长期以来都在争夺政治上的支配地位。

as·cend·ing /əsɛndɪŋ/ **1** ADJ If a group of things is arranged in **ascending** order, each thing is bigger, greater, or more important than the thing before it. 升（序）的 [ADJ n] ❑ *Now draw or trace ten dinosaurs in ascending order of size.* 现在按大小以升序画或描出10只恐龙。 **2** → see also **ascend**

as·cent /əsɛnt/ (**ascents**) **1** N-COUNT An **ascent** is an upward journey, especially when you are walking or climbing. 攀登 ❑ *In 1955 he led the first ascent of Kangchenjunga, the world's third highest mountain.* 1955年他率领了对世界第三高峰干城章嘉峰的首次攀登。 **2** N-COUNT An **ascent** is an upward slope or path, especially when you are walking or climbing. 上坡；上坡路 ❑ *It was a tough course over a gradual ascent before the big climb of Bluebell Hill.* 这是蓝钟山大攀登之前在一段缓坡上的艰难路程。 **3** N-COUNT An **ascent** is an upward, vertical movement. 垂直上升运动 ❑ *Burke pushed the button and the elevator began its slow ascent.* 伯克按下按钮，电梯开始了其缓慢的上升。

Word Link *cert ≈ determined, true : ascertain, certificate, certify*

★ **as·cer·tain** /æsərteɪn/ (**ascertains, ascertaining, ascertained**) V-T If you **ascertain** the truth about something, you find out what it is, especially by making a deliberate effort to do so. （尤指经过努力）查明 [FORMAL] ❑ *Through doing this, the teacher will be able to ascertain the extent to which the child understands what he is reading.* 通过这样做，老师将能确定这个孩子对他正在读的内容的理解程度。 ❑ *Once they had ascertained that he was not a spy, they agreed to release him.* 一查明他不是间谍，他们就同意了释放他。

★ **as·cribe** /əskraɪb/ (**ascribes, ascribing, ascribed**) **1** V-T If you **ascribe** an event or condition **to** a particular cause, you say or consider that it was caused by that thing. 将…归因于 [FORMAL] ❑ *An autopsy eventually ascribed the baby's death to sudden infant death syndrome.* 一次尸检最终把这名婴儿的死亡归因于婴儿猝死综合症。 **2** V-T If you **ascribe** a quality **to** someone, you consider that they possess it. 将…归属（于某人）[FORMAL] ❑ *We do not ascribe a superior wisdom to government or the state.* 我们并不将胜人一筹的智慧归属于政府或国家。

ash /æʃ/ (**ashes**) **1** N-UNCOUNT **Ash** is the gray or black powdery substance that is left after something is burned. You can also refer to this substance as **ashes**. 灰 [also N in pl] ❑ *A cloud of volcanic ash is spreading across wide areas of the Philippines.* 一大片火山灰正在扩散到菲律宾的大片区域。 ❑ *He brushed the cigarette ash from his sleeve.* 他掸掉了袖子上的烟灰。 **2** N-PLURAL A dead person's **ashes** are their remains after their body has been cremated. 骨灰 ❑ *And she asks him to go back there after her death and scatter her ashes on the lake.* 她还要求他在她死后回到那里并把她的骨灰撒在那个湖上。 **3** N-VAR An **ash** is a tree that has smooth gray bark and loses its leaves in winter. 梣树 ● N-UNCOUNT **Ash** is the wood from this tree. 梣木 ❑ *The rafters are made from ash.* 这些椽是用梣木做的。 → see **fire, glass, volcano**

ashamed /əʃeɪmd/ **1** ADJ If someone is **ashamed**, they feel embarrassed or guilty because of something they do or they have done, or because of their appearance. 尴尬的；惭愧的 [v-link ADJ] ❑ *I felt incredibly ashamed of myself for getting so angry.* 我为自己发了这么大的脾气而感到极为惭愧。 **2** ADJ If you are **ashamed of** someone, you feel embarrassed to be connected with them, often because of their appearance or because you disapprove of something they have done. 感到羞耻的 [v-link ADJ "of" n] ❑ *I've never told this to anyone, but it's true, I was terribly ashamed of my mom.* 我从未告诉过任何人，但这是真的，我特别以自己的母亲为耻。

★ **ashore** /əʃɔr/ ADV Someone or something that comes **ashore** comes from the sea onto the shore. 到岸上地 ❑ *Oil has come ashore on a ten mile stretch to the east of Anchorage.* 连绵10英里的浮油已经到达安克雷齐东面的海岸上。

ash·tray /æʃtreɪ/ (**ashtrays**) N-COUNT An **ashtray** is a small dish in which smokers can put the ash from their cigarettes and cigars. 烟灰缸

Asian ♦♦◇ /eɪʒᵊn/ (**Asians**) **1** ADJ Someone or something that is **Asian** comes from or is associated with Asia. Americans use this term especially to refer to China, Korea, Thailand, Japan, or Vietnam. British people use this term especially to refer to India, Pakistan, and Bangladesh. 亚洲的 ❑ *...Asian music.* …亚洲音乐。 ● N-COUNT An **Asian** is a person who comes from or is associated with a country or region in Asia. 亚洲人 ❑ *Many of the shops were run by Asians.* 这些商店中有许多是由亚洲人经营的。

> The word **Asian** is used to describe people from Asia, but the word **Oriental** is considered a derogatory term, and should be used only to refer to inanimate objects such as art, music, or history.

aside ♦◇◇ /əsaɪd/

> In addition to the uses shown below, **aside** is used in phrasal verbs such as "cast aside," "stand aside," and "step aside."

1 ADV If you move something **aside**, you move it to one side of you. （把某物移或放）到一边地 [ADV after v] ❑ *Sarah closed the book and laid it aside.* 萨拉合上书并将其放到了一边。 **2** ADV If you take or draw someone **aside**, you take them a little way away from a group of people in order to talk to them in private. （把某人带或拉）到一旁地 [ADV after v] ❑ *Latoya grabbed him by the elbow and took him aside.* 拉托亚抓住他的胳膊肘把他带到了一旁。 **3** ADV If you move **aside**, you get out of someone's way. 向一旁地 [ADV after v] ❑ *She had been standing in the doorway, but now she stepped aside to let them pass.* 她一直站在门道里，不过现在她让到一边让他们过去。 **4** ADV If you set something such as time, money, or space **aside** for a particular purpose, you save it and do not use it for anything else. （存留）在一边地 [ADV after v] ❑ *While many parents are putting money aside for college tuition, some are taking on another big expense: buying cars for their teenagers.* 许多父母在将钱留作大学学费时，然而有些则在进行

另一项巨大开支：为他们十几岁的孩子们买车。 5 ADV If you brush or sweep **aside** a feeling or suggestion, you reject it. (拒绝而) 置于一旁地 [ADV after V] ❑ *Talk to a friend who will really listen and not brush aside your feelings.* 跟一个愿意真正倾听并不会置你的感受于不顾的朋友谈谈。 6 ADV You use **aside** to indicate that you have finished talking about something, or that you are leaving it out of your discussion, and that you are about to talk about something else. 除了 ❑ *Leaving aside the tiny minority who are clinically depressed, most people who have bad moods also have very good moods.* 先不谈极少数患有临床抑郁症的人，大多数有坏情绪的人也有很好的情绪。 7 PHRASE You use **aside from** when you are making an exception to a general statement. 除…以外 ❑ *The room was empty aside from one man seated beside the fire.* 这个房间别无他人，除了一个坐在炉火旁的男人。 8 PHRASE You use **aside from** to indicate that you are aware of one aspect of a situation, but that you are going to focus on another aspect. 除…以外还 ❑ *Quite aside from her tiredness, Amanda seemed unnaturally abstracted.* 除了疲惫不堪，阿曼达看上去还一反常态地心不在焉。

ask ♦♦♦ /ɑsk, æsk/ (**asks, asking, asked**) 1 V-T/V-I If you **ask** someone something, you say something to them in the form of a question because you want to know the answer. 问 ❑ *"How is Frank?" he asked.* "弗兰克怎么样？"他问道。 ❑ *I asked him his name.* 我问了他的名字。 ❑ *She asked me if I'd enjoyed my dinner.* 她问我是否喜欢我的晚餐。 ❑ *Maybe we should adopt the policy of "don't ask, don't tell."* 或许我们应该采用"不问不提"的政策。 2 V-T If you **ask** someone **to** do something, you tell them that you want them to do it. 让 (某人做某事) ❑ *We had to ask him to leave.* 我们不得不让他离开。 3 V-T If you **ask to** do something, you tell someone that you want to do it. 要求 ❑ *I asked to see the Director.* 我要求见总经理。 4 V-I If you **ask for** something, you say that you would like it. 索要 ❑ *I decided to go to the next house and ask for food.* 我决定到隔壁房子去要吃的。 5 V-I If you **ask for** someone, you say that you would like to speak to them. 求见 ❑ *There's a man at the gate asking for you.* 大门口有个男人要见你。 6 V-T If you **ask** someone's permission, opinion, or forgiveness, you try to obtain it by making a request. 征求 (意见); 请求 (许可、原谅) ❑ *Please ask permission from whoever pays the phone bill before making your call.* 打电话前请先征得话费支付人的许可。 7 V-T If you **ask** someone **to** an event or place, you invite them to go there. 邀请 ❑ *Couldn't you ask Juan to the party?* 你不能邀请胡安参加这个聚会吗？ 8 V-T If someone **is asking** a particular price **for** something, they are selling it for that price. 要 (价) ❑ *Mr. Pantelaras was asking $6,000 for his collection.* 潘特莱拉斯先生在为他的藏品要价$6000。 9 CONVENTION You reply **"don't ask me"** when you do not know the answer to a question, usually when you are annoyed or surprised that you have been asked. 别问我 [FEELINGS] ❑ *"She's got other things on her mind, wouldn't you think?" "Don't ask me," murmured Chris. "I've never met her."* "她脑子里想着别的事，你不认为吗？""别问我，"克里斯咕哝道，"我从未见过她。" 10 PHRASE You can say **"if you ask me"** to emphasize that you are stating your personal opinion. 依我看 [EMPHASIS] ❑ *He was nuts, if you ask me.* 依我看，他当时是疯了。 11 PHRASE If you say that someone **is asking for trouble** or **is asking for it**, you mean that they are behaving in a way that makes it very likely that they will get into trouble. 自找麻烦 ❑ *To go ahead with the match after such clear advice had been asking for trouble.* 在得到如此明确的忠告之后还要继续比赛是在自找麻烦。

Thesaurus *ask* 另参见：

V.	demand, interrogate, question, quiz; *(ant.)* answer, reply, respond 1
	beg, plead, request; *(ant.)* command, insist 6

Word Partnership *ask* 的常用搭配：

ADJ.	afraid to ask 1
DET.	ask **how/what/when/where/who/why** 1
CONJ.	ask **if/whether** 1
N.	ask **a question** 1
	ask **for help** 4
	ask **forgiveness**, ask ***someone's*** **opinion**, ask **permission** 6
PREP.	ask **about** 1
	ask **to** 2 3 7
	ask **for** 4 5
V.	**come to** ask, **have to** ask 1
	don't ask **me** 9

ask·ing price (**asking prices**) N-COUNT The **asking price** of something is the price that the person selling it says that they want for it, although they may accept less. 要价 ❑ *Offers 15% below the asking price are unlikely to be accepted.* 低于要价15%的出价不太可能被接受。

asleep /əsli̲p/ 1 ADJ Someone who is **asleep** is sleeping. 睡着的 [v-link ADJ] ❑ *My four-year-old daughter was asleep on the sofa.* 我4岁的女儿在沙发上睡着了。 2 ADJ If you say that your arm or leg is **asleep**, you mean that it is numb, for example because you have been sitting in an awkward position. (胳膊、腿等) 麻木的 ["be" ADJ] [mainly AM] ❑ *Her left leg was asleep from sitting on the floor.* 她的左腿在地板上坐得麻木了。 3 PHRASE When you **fall asleep**, you start sleeping. 入睡 ❑ *Sam snuggled down in his pillow and fell asleep.* 萨姆舒适地枕着枕头睡着了。 4 PHRASE Someone who is **fast asleep** or **sound asleep** is sleeping deeply. 熟睡的 ❑ *They were both fast asleep in their beds.* 他们俩在各自的床上都熟睡了。
→ see **sleep**

as·para·gus /əspæ̲rəgəs/ N-UNCOUNT **Asparagus** is a vegetable that is long and green and has small shoots at one end. It is cooked and usually served whole. 芦笋

as·pect ♦♦◊ /æ̲spɛkt/ (**aspects**) 1 N-COUNT An **aspect** of something is one of the parts of its character or nature. 方面 ❑ *Climate and weather affect every aspect of our lives.* 气候和天气影响我们生活的每个方面。 ❑ *He was interested in all aspects of the work here.* 他对这里工作的各方面都感兴趣。 2 N-COUNT The **aspect** of a building or window is the direction in which it faces. (建筑物或窗子的) 朝向 [FORMAL] ❑ *The house had a southwest aspect.* 这房子为西南朝向。

Word Partnership *aspect* 的常用搭配：

DET.	**another/any/every** aspect 1
ADJ.	**most important** aspect, **particular** aspect 1
PREP.	aspect **of *something*** 1 2

as·pi·ra·tion /æ̲spɪreɪ̲ʃ°n/ (**aspirations**) N-VAR Someone's **aspirations** are their desire to achieve things. 志向 ❑ *...the needs and aspirations of our pupils.* …我们学生的需求和志向。 ❑ *He is unlikely to send in the army to quell nationalist aspirations.* 他不大可能派军队来压制民族主义倾向。

Word Link *spir ≈ breath : aspire, inspire, respiratory*

▲ **as·pire** /əspaɪ̲ər/ (**aspires, aspiring, aspired**) 1 V-I If you **aspire to** something such as an important job, you have a strong desire to achieve it. 有志 (于) ❑ *...people who aspire to public office.* …志在获得公职的人们。 ❑ *Rice aspired to go to college.* 赖斯渴望上大学。
2 → see also **aspiring**

as·pi·rin /æ̲spərɪn, -prɪn/ (**aspirins**)

The form **aspirin** can also be used for the plural.

N-VAR **Aspirin** is a mild drug that reduces pain and fever. 阿司匹林

as·pir·ing /əspaɪ̲ərɪŋ/ 1 ADJ If you use **aspiring** to describe someone who is starting a particular career, you mean that they are trying to become successful in it. 有志向的 [ADJ n] ❑ *Many aspiring young artists are advised to learn by copying the masters.* 许多有志向的年轻艺术家们被建议通过临摹大师们的作品来学习。 2 → see also **aspire**

▲ **ass** /æs/ (**asses**) 1 N-COUNT Your **ass** is your buttocks. 屁股 [AM, INFORMAL, VULGAR]
in BRIT, use **arse, bum**
❑ *I jumped back and fell on my ass.* 我往后一跳，摔了个屁股墩。 2 N-COUNT If you describe someone as an **ass**, you think that they are silly or do silly things. 蠢货 [INFORMAL, DISAPPROVAL] ❑ *He was generally disliked and regarded as a pompous ass.* 他普遍不受喜欢且被认为是个自命不凡的蠢货。 3 N-COUNT An **ass** is an animal related to a horse but that is smaller and has long ears. 驴 4 **cover your ass** → see **cover** 5 **a pain in the ass** → see **pain**

as·sail·ant /əseɪ̲lənt/ (**assailants**) N-COUNT Someone's **assailant** is a person who has physically attacked them. 攻击者 [FORMAL] ❑ *Other partygoers rescued the injured man from his assailant.* 其他参加聚会的人从攻击者手中救出了这名受伤的男子。

★ **as·sas·sin** /əsæ̲sɪn/ (**assassins**) N-COUNT An **assassin** is a person who assassinates someone. 杀手 ❑ *He saw the shooting and memorized the license plate of the assassin's car.* 他目睹了那起枪击事件并且记住了杀手的车牌。

★ **as·sas·si·nate** /əsæ̲sɪneɪt/ (**assassinates, assassinating, assassinated**) V-T When someone important **is assassinated**,

A

they are murdered as a political act. (因政治原因而) 刺杀 ❑ *Would the U.S. be radically different today if Kennedy had not been assassinated?* 如果肯尼迪没有被刺杀，今天的美国会大不相同吗？

● **as·sas·si·na·tion** ★ /əsæsɪneɪʃᵊn/ N-VAR (**assassinations**) 刺杀 ❑ *She would like an investigation into the assassination of her husband.* 她想要对其丈夫的遇刺进行调查。 ❑ *He lives in constant fear of assassination.* 他一直生活在对刺杀的恐惧之中。

★ **as·sault** ♦◇◇ /əsɔ̲lt/ (**assaults, assaulting, assaulted**) **1** N-COUNT An **assault** by an army is a strong attack made on an area held by the enemy. 猛攻 ❑ *The rebels are poised for a new assault on the government garrisons.* 叛乱分子作好了对政府卫戍部队的新一轮猛攻的准备。 **2** ADJ **Assault** weapons such as rifles are intended for soldiers to use in battle rather than for purposes such as hunting. 用于战争的 (武器) [ADJ n] **3** N-VAR An **assault on** a person is a physical attack on them. 袭击 [oft N "on/upon" n] ❑ *The attack is one of a series of savage sexual assaults on women in the university area.* 这次袭击是一系列在大学区对女性的野蛮性侵犯之一。 **4** V-T To **assault** someone means to physically attack them. 袭击 ❑ *The gang assaulted him with iron bars.* 该团伙用铁棒袭击了他。

as·sem·ble /əsɛ̲mbᵊl/ (**assembles, assembling, assembled**) **1** V-T/V-I When people **assemble** or when someone **assembles** them, they come together in a group, usually for a particular purpose such as a meeting. 集合 ❑ *There wasn't even a convenient place for students to assemble between classes.* 甚至没有一个学生们课间集合的方便的地方。 **2** V-T To **assemble** something means to collect it together or to fit the different parts of it together. 聚集；组装 ❑ *Greenpeace managed to assemble a small flotilla of inflatable boats to waylay the ship at sea.* 绿色和平组织设法聚集了一支充气艇小舰队去拦截海上的那艘船。

→ see **industry**

as·sem·bly ♦◇◇ /əsɛ̲mbli/ (**assemblies**) **1** N-COUNT An **assembly** is a large group of people who meet regularly to make decisions or laws for a particular region or country. 议会 ❑ *...the campaign for the first free election to the National Assembly.* …为首次自由选举入国民议会而进行的运动。 **2** N-COUNT An **assembly** is a group of people gathered together for a particular purpose. 集会者 ❑ *He waited until complete quiet settled on the assembly.* 他等到集会者完全安静下来。 **3** N-UNCOUNT When you refer to rights of **assembly** or restrictions on **assembly**, you are referring to the legal right that people have to gather together. 集会 [FORMAL] ❑ *The U.S. Constitution guarantees free speech, freedom of assembly and equal protection.* 美国宪法保证自由言论、集会自由和平等保护权。 **4** N-UNCOUNT The **assembly** of a machine, device, or object is the process of fitting its different parts together. 组装 ❑ *For the rest of the day, he worked on the assembly of an explosive device.* 在那天余下的时间里，他在进行一个爆炸装置的组装。 **5** N-VAR In a school, an **assembly** is a gathering of all the teachers and students for a particular purpose. (学校师生的) 大会 ❑ *Recently named the nation's top girls' basketball player, she will be honored this morning at a school assembly.* 最近被命名为全国顶级女子篮球运动员的她将于今天上午在学校大会上被表彰。

→ see **mass production**

as·sent /əsɛ̲nt/ (**assents, assenting, assented**) **1** N-UNCOUNT If someone gives their **assent to** something that has been suggested, they formally agree to it. 正式的认可 ❑ *He gave his assent to the proposed legislation.* 他对这项拟议法案给予了正式认可。 **2** V-I If you **assent to** something, you agree to it or agree with it. 同意 ❑ *I assented to the request of the American publishers to write this book.* 我同意了美国出版商们写这本书的请求。

as·sert /əsɜ̲rt/ (**asserts, asserting, asserted**) **1** V-T If someone **asserts** a fact or belief, they state it firmly. 坚定地陈述 [FORMAL] ❑ *Mr. Helm plans to assert that the bill violates the First Amendment.* 赫尔姆先生计划坚定地陈述该法案有违《第一修正案》。 ❑ *The defendants, who continue to assert their innocence, are expected to appeal.* 那些继续宣称其清白的被告预计会上诉。 ● **as·ser·tion** /əsɜ̲rʃᵊn/ (**assertions**) N-VAR 断言 ❑ *There is no concrete evidence to support assertions that the recession is truly over.* 没有任何确凿的证据支持经济衰退已真正结束的断言。 **2** V-T If you **assert** your authority, you make it clear by your behavior that you have authority. 显示 (权威) ❑ *After the war, the army made an attempt to assert its authority in the south of the country.* 战后，军队试图在该国南部显示其权威。 ● **as·ser·tion** N-UNCOUNT (权威的) 显示 ❑ *The decision is seen as an assertion of his authority within the company.* 这一决定被看作是公司内他的权威的显示。 **3** V-T If you **assert** your right or claim to something, you insist that you have the right to it. 坚持 (权利或要求) ❑ *The republics began asserting their right to govern themselves.* 各共和国开始坚持他们自治的权利。 ● **as·ser·tion** N-UNCOUNT 坚持 ❑ *These institutions have made the assertion of ethnic identity possible.* 这些机构已使种族身份的坚持成为可能。 **4** V-T If you **assert yourself**, you speak and act in a forceful way, so that people take notice of you. 彰显 (自己) ❑ *He's speaking up and asserting himself and doing things he enjoys.* 他现在直言不讳、彰显自我，做着他喜欢做的事。

★ **as·ser·tive** /əsɜ̲rtɪv/ ADJ Someone who is **assertive** states their needs and opinions clearly, so that people take notice. 坚定自信的 ❑ *Women have become more assertive in the past decade.* 妇女在过去十年已变得更坚定自信。 ● **as·ser·tive·ness** N-UNCOUNT 坚定自信 ❑ *Chantelle's assertiveness stirred up his deep-seated sense of inadequacy.* 仙黛尔的坚定自信激起了他根深蒂固的自卑感。

as·sess ♦◇◇ /əsɛ̲s/ (**assesses, assessing, assessed**) **1** V-T When you **assess** a person, thing, or situation, you consider them in order to make a judgment about them. 评估 ❑ *The test was to assess aptitude rather than academic achievement.* 该测试将评估能力而不是学业成绩。 ❑ *It would be a matter of assessing whether she was well enough to travel.* 这将是个评估她是否身体好到可以旅行的问题。 **2** V-T When you **assess** the amount of money that something is worth or should be paid, you calculate or estimate it. 计算；估算 ❑ *Ask them to send you information on how to assess the value of your belongings.* 叫他们把如何估算你的财产价值的资料寄给你。

as·sess·ment ♦◇◇ /əsɛ̲smənt/ (**assessments**) **1** N-VAR An **assessment** is a consideration of someone or something and a judgment about them. 评估 ❑ *There is little assessment of the damage to the natural environment.* 几乎没有有关自然环境破坏的评估。 **2** N-VAR An **assessment** of the amount of money that something is worth or that should be paid is a calculation or estimate of the amount. 估算 ❑ *Tax assessment is all about comparing values of similar properties.* 税金估算就是比较类似房产的价值。

as·ses·sor /əsɛ̲sər/ (**assessors**) N-COUNT An **assessor** is a person who is employed to calculate the value of something, or the amount of money that should be paid, for example, in tax. 估算员 [BUSINESS]

as·set ♦♦◇ /æsɛt/ (**assets**) **1** N-COUNT Something or someone that is an **asset** is considered useful or helps a person or organization to be successful. 资本 ❑ *Our creativity in the field of technology is our greatest asset.* 我们在技术领域的创造力是我们最大的资本。 **2** N-PLURAL The **assets** of a company or a person are all the things that they own. 资产 [BUSINESS] ❑ *By the end of 1989 the group had assets of $3.5 billion.* 到1989年底该集团已有35亿美元的资产。

asset-stripping N-UNCOUNT If a person or company is involved in **asset-stripping**, they buy companies cheaply, sell off their assets to make a profit, and then close the companies down. 资产倒卖 [BUSINESS, DISAPPROVAL]

as·sign /əsaɪ̲n/ (**assigns, assigning, assigned**) **1** V-T If you **assign** a piece of work **to** someone, you give them the work to do. 布置 (任务) ❑ *When I taught, I would assign a topic to children that they would write about.* 教书时，我会给孩子们布置个写作题。 ❑ *Later in the year, she'll assign them research papers.* 今年晚些时候，她将给他们布置论文。 **2** V-T If you **assign** something **to** someone, you say that it is for their use. 分配 (某物) ❑ *The selling broker is then required to assign a portion of the commission to the buyer broker.* 卖方经纪人则被要求分给买方经纪人一部分佣金。 **3** V-T If someone **is assigned to** a particular place, group, or person, they are sent there, usually in order to work at that place or for that person. 分派 [usu passive] ❑ *I was assigned to Troop A of the 10th Cavalry.* 我被分派到了第10装甲部队的A大队。 ❑ *Did you choose Russia or were you simply assigned there?* 你选择了俄罗斯还是只是被派到了那里？ **4** V-T If you **assign** a particular function or value **to** someone or something, you say they have it. 赋予 (某功能或价值) ❑ *Under the system, each business must assign a value to each job.* 在这种制度下，每家企业必须赋予每份工作某种价值。

as·sign·ment /əsaɪ̲nmənt/ (**assignments**) N-COUNT An **assignment** is a task or piece of work that you are given to do, especially as part of your job or studies. 任务；作业 ❑ *The assessment for the course involves written assignments and practical tests.* 这门课程的评估包括各种书面作业和实践测试。

Thesaurus *assignment* 另参见：

N. chore, duty, job, task

Word Link *simil ≈ similar : assimilate, dissimilar, similarity*

★ **as·simi·late** /əsɪmɪleɪt/ (**assimilates, assimilating, assimilated**) 1 V-T/V-I When people such as immigrants **assimilate into** a community or when that community **assimilates** them, they become an accepted part of it. 同化；被同化 ❑ *There is every sign that new Asian-Americans are just as willing to assimilate.* 各种迹象表明新的亚裔美籍人简直一样愿意被同化。 ❑ *His family tried to assimilate into the white and Hispanic communities.* 他的家人努力融入到白人和拉美人社区。 ● **as·simi·la·tion** /əsɪmɪleɪʃən/ N-UNCOUNT 同化 ❑ *They promote social integration and assimilation of minority ethnic groups into the culture.* 他们提倡少数民族团体与该文化的社会融合及同化。 2 V-T If you **assimilate** new ideas, customs, or techniques, you learn them or adopt them. 吸纳 ❑ *My mind could only assimilate one impossibility at a time.* 我的头脑一次只能吸纳一件不可能的事情。 ● **as·simi·la·tion** N-UNCOUNT 吸纳 ❑ *This technique brings life to instruction and eases assimilation of knowledge.* 这种技术给教学带来活力，并使知识的吸收更加容易。

→ see **culture**

as·sist ♦◇◇ /əsɪst/ (**assists, assisting, assisted**) 1 V-T If you **assist** someone, you help them to do a job or task by doing part of the work for them. (通过分担一部分工作以) 帮助 ❑ *The family decided to assist me with my chores.* 家人决定分担我的琐事。 2 V-T/V-I If you **assist** someone, you give them information, advice, or money. (提供信息、建议、资金等以) 协助 ❑ *The public is urgently requested to assist police in tracing this man.* 公众被紧急要求协助警方追踪这名男子。 ❑ *International organizations intensified their activities to locate victims and assist with relief efforts.* 各国际组织加强了他们的活动以寻找受害者并协助救援工作。 3 V-T/V-I If something **assists in** doing a task, it makes the task easier to do. (在做某任务中) 有助益 ❑ *...a chemical that assists in the manufacture of proteins.* …一种有助于蛋白质的制造的化学物。 ❑ *Our sales representatives can assist you in selecting suitable investments.* 我们的销售代表在选择合适的投资方面能帮到您。

as·sis·tance ♦◇◇ /əsɪstəns/ 1 N-UNCOUNT If you give someone **assistance**, you help them do a job or task by doing part of the work for them. (通过分担一部分任务而给予的) 帮助 [oft with poss] ❑ *Since 1976 he has been operating the shop with the assistance of volunteers.* 自1976年以来他一直在志愿者的帮助下经营着这家商店。 2 N-UNCOUNT If you give someone **assistance**, you give them information or advice. (通过提供信息或建议而给予的) 协助 ❑ *Any assistance you could give the police will be greatly appreciated.* 您能给警方的任何帮助都将受到不胜感谢。 3 N-UNCOUNT If someone gives a person or country **assistance**, they help them by giving them money. (通过给予资金而提供的) 援助 [oft supp N] ❑ *...a viable program of economic assistance.* …一项切实可行的经济援助计划。 4 N-UNCOUNT If something is done **with the assistance of** a particular thing, that thing is helpful or necessary for doing it. (某物提供的) 帮助 ❑ *The translations were carried out with the assistance of a medical dictionary.* 这些翻译是在一本医学词典的帮助下完成的。 5 PHRASE Someone or something that **is of assistance** to you is helpful or useful to you. 有助益 ❑ *Can I be of any assistance?* 我能有所帮助吗？ 6 PHRASE If you **come to** someone's **assistance**, you take action to help them. 来援助某人 ❑ *They are appealing to the world community to come to Jordan's assistance.* 他们正呼吁国际社会来援助约旦。

Word Partnership *assistance* 的常用搭配：

V. **need/require** assistance 1
provide assistance 1 – 3
ADJ. **emergency** assistance, **medical** assistance, **technical** assistance 2
financial assistance 3

as·sis·tant ♦◇◇ /əsɪstənt/ (**assistants**) 1 ADJ **Assistant** is used in front of titles or jobs to indicate a slightly lower rank. For example, an assistant director is one rank lower than a director in an organization. 助理的 (用在头衔或职位前，表示级别略低) [ADJ n] ❑ *...the assistant secretary of defense.* …助理国防部长。 2 N-COUNT Someone's **assistant** is a person who helps them in their work. 助理 ❑ *Kalan called his assistant, Hashim, to take over while he went out.* 卡兰打电话给他的助理哈什姆以在他外出时接管。 3 N-COUNT An **assistant** is a person who works in a store selling things to customers. 售货员 ❑ *The assistant took the book and checked the price on the back cover.* 售货员拿起书，核对了封底上的价格。

Word Link *soci ≈ companion : associate, social, sociology*

as·so·ci·ate ♦◇◇ (**associates, associating, associated**)

The verb is pronounced /əsoʊʃieɪt, -sieɪt/. The noun and adjective are pronounced /əsoʊʃiɪt, -siɪt/.

动词读作 /əsoʊʃieɪt, -sieɪt/。名词和形容词读作 /əsoʊʃiɪt, -siɪt/。

1 V-T If you **associate** someone or something **with** another thing, the two are connected in your mind. 将 (…和…) 联系起来 ❑ *Through science we've got the idea of associating progress with the future.* 通过科学我们已有了将进步与未来联系起来的观念。 2 V-T If you **are associated with** a particular organization, cause, or point of view, or if you **associate yourself with** it, you support it publicly. 使 (某人与某组织、事业、观点等) 有关联 ❑ *I haven't been associated with the project over the last year.* 我过去一年不曾跟这个项目有关联。 3 V-I If you say that someone **is associating with** another person or group of people, you mean they are spending a lot of time in the company of people you do not approve of. (与某个或某群人) 混在一起 ❑ *What would they think if they knew that they were associating with a murderer?* 如果他们知道了他们正与一个杀人犯打成一片，他们会怎么想？ 4 N-COUNT Your **associates** are the people you are closely connected with, especially at work. (尤指工作中的) 伙伴 ❑ *...the restaurant owner's business associates.* …该餐馆老板的商业伙伴们。 5 N-COUNT An **associate** is a retail worker who does not have previous experience or qualifications. 准零售工 ❑ *Be sure to get help from the sales associates before buying.* 在购买前一定要得到准销售人员的帮助。 6 ADJ **Associate** is used before a rank or title to indicate a slightly different or lower rank or title. 副的 (用在级别或头衔前，表示稍有不同或略低的) [ADJ n] ❑ *Mr. Lin is associate director of the Institute.* 林先生是该研究所的副主任。

as·so·ci·at·ed ♦◇◇ /əsoʊʃieɪtɪd, -sieɪ-/ 1 ADJ If one thing is **associated with** another, the two things are connected with each other. (与…) 相关联的 ❑ *These symptoms are particularly associated with migraine headaches.* 这些症状尤其与偏头痛相关联。 2 ADJ **Associated** is used in the name of a company that is made up of a number of smaller companies that have joined together. 联合的 (用于由若干小公司组成的公司名称中) [ADJ n] ❑ *...the Associated Press.* …联合通讯社。

as·so·cia·tion ♦♦◇ /əsoʊʃieɪʃən, -sieɪ-/ (**associations**) 1 N-COUNT An **association** is an official group of people who have the same job, aim, or interest. 协会 ❑ *...the National Basketball Association.* …全国篮球协会。 2 N-COUNT Your **association with** a person or a thing such as an organization is the connection that you have with them. (与某人、某物的) 关联 ❑ *...the company's six-year association with retailer J.C. Penney Co.* …这家公司与零售商彭尼公司6年的业务往来。 3 N-COUNT If something has particular **associations** for you, it is connected in your mind with a particular memory, idea, or feeling. (与某记忆、观念、情感的) 关联 ❑ *He has a shelf full of things, each of which has associations for him.* 他有一个摆满了东西的架子，每一样都与他的内心世界有关联。 4 PHRASE If you do something **in association with** someone else, you do it together. 与…联合 ❑ *The changes I instigated in association with the board 18 months ago were because I love this company.* 18个月前我联合董事会发起的这些变革是出于我爱这家公司。

→ see **memory**

▲ **as·sort·ed** /əsɔrtɪd/ ADJ A group of **assorted** things is a group of similar things that are of different sizes or colors or have different qualities. 各式各样的 ❑ *It should be a great week, with overnight stops in assorted hotels in the Adirondacks.* 那该是很棒的一周，可以在阿迪朗达克山各式各样的旅馆里停留过夜。

as·sort·ment /əsɔrtmənt/ (**assortments**) N-COUNT An **assortment** is a group of similar things that are of different sizes or colors or have different qualities. 花色品种 ❑ *...an assortment of cheese.* …一堆各式各样的奶酪。

Word Link *sume ≈ taking : assume, consume, presume*

as·sume ♦♦◇ /əsum/ (**assumes, assuming, assumed**) 1 V-T If you **assume that** something is true, you imagine that it is true, sometimes wrongly. 假设 ❑ *It is a misconception to assume that the two continents are similar.* 假设这两块大陆类似是种错误概念。 ❑ *If mistakes occurred, they were assumed to be the fault of the commander on the spot.* 如果出现了错误，它们就被以为是现场指挥官的错。 2 V-T If someone **assumes** power or responsibility, they take power or responsibility. 接受 (权利、责任) ❑ *Mr. Cross will assume the role of CEO*

A

with a team of four directors. 克罗斯先生将担任由 4 位执行官组成的一个团队的首席执行官一职。 3 V-T If you **assume** a particular expression or way of behaving, you start to look or behave in this way. 做出(某表情); 采取(某行为方式) ❑ *He managed to assume an air of calm.* 他设法表现出一幅平静的样子。

Word Partnership *assume* 的常用搭配:
V. **let's** assume **that**, **tend to** assume 1
ADV. assume **so** 1
automatically assume 1 2
N. assume **the worst** 1
assume **control/power**, assume **responsibility**, assume **a role** 2

as·sum·ing /əsuːmɪŋ/ CONJ You use **assuming** or **assuming that** when you are considering a possible situation or event, so that you can think about the consequences. 假定 ❑ *"Assuming you're right," he said, "there's not much I can do about it, is there?"* "假定你是对的,"他说, "我对此能做的也不多,对吗?"

Word Link *sumpt ≈ taking : assumption, consumption, presumption*

as·sump·tion ♦◇◇ /əsʌmpʃn/ (**assumptions**) N-COUNT If you make an **assumption that** something is true or will happen, you accept that it is true or will happen, often without any real proof. 假设 ❑ *You would be making an assumption that's not based on any fact that you could report.* 你会做出不以你能报道的任何事实为依据的一种假设。

Word Partnership *assumption* 的常用搭配:
ADJ. assumption **based on**, **common** assumption, **underlying** assumption
V. **challenge an** assumption, **make an** assumption

★ **as·sur·ance** /əʃʊərəns/ (**assurances**) 1 N-VAR If you give someone an **assurance that** something is true or will happen, you say that it is definitely true or will definitely happen, in order to make them feel less worried. 保证 ❑ *He would like an assurance that other forces will not move into the territory that his forces vacate.* 他想要其他部队不会进入他的部队撤出的那个领地的一个保证。 2 N-UNCOUNT If you do something **with assurance**, you do it with a feeling of confidence and certainty. 信心 ❑ *Masur led the orchestra with assurance.* 马苏尔很有信心地带领了那个管弦乐队。

as·sure /əʃʊər/ (**assures, assuring, assured**) 1 V-T If you **assure** someone **that** something is true or will happen, you tell them that it is definitely true or will definitely happen, often in order to make them less worried. (向…)保证 ❑ *He hastened to assure me that there was nothing traumatic to report.* 他急忙向我保证没有任何不快的事要报告。 ❑ *"Are you sure the raft is safe?" she asked anxiously. "Couldn't be safer," Max assured her confidently.* "你确定这筏子安全吗?"她不安地问。"再安全不过了,"马克斯自信地向她保证。 2 → see also **assured** 3 V-T To **assure** someone **of** something means to make certain that they will get it. 确保得到 ❑ *His performance yesterday morning assured him of a record eighth medal.* 他昨天上午的成绩确保了他得到创纪录的第8枚奖牌。 4 PHRASE You use phrases such as **I can assure you** or **let me assure you** to emphasize the truth of what you are saying. 我可以向你保证/让我向你保证 [EMPHASIS] ❑ *I can assure you that the animals are well cared for.* 我可以向你保证这些动物都被照看得很好。

as·sured ♦◇◇ /əʃʊərd/ 1 ADJ Someone who is **assured** is very confident and relaxed. 雄有成竹的 ❑ *He was infinitely more assured than in his more recent concert appearances.* 比起他之后的音乐会上露面他那次要有信心得多。 2 ADJ If something is **assured**, it is certain to happen. 确定的 [v-link ADJ] ❑ *Our victory is assured; nothing can stop us.* 我们的胜利是确定无疑的;没有什么能阻挡我们。 3 ADJ If you are **assured of** something, you are certain to get it or achieve it. 有把握得到的 [v-link ADJ "of" n] ❑ *Laura Davies is assured of a place in the Olympic team.* 劳拉·戴维斯有把握得到奥林匹克队中的一席。 4 PHRASE If you say that someone **can rest assured that** something is the case, you mean that it is definitely the case, so they do not need to worry about it. 尽管放心 [EMPHASIS] ❑ *Their parents can rest assured that their children's safety will be of paramount importance.* 他们的家长们可以尽管放心,他们孩子们的安全将是最为重要的。

Word Link *aster, astro ≈ star : asterisk, astronaut, astronomy*

as·ter·isk /æstərɪsk/ (**asterisks**) N-COUNT An **asterisk** is the sign *. It is used especially to indicate that there is further information about something in another part of the text. 星号(*)

▲ **asth·ma** /æzmə/ N-UNCOUNT **Asthma** is a lung condition that causes difficulty in breathing. 哮喘

asth·mat·ic /æzmætɪk/ (**asthmatics**) 1 N-COUNT People who suffer from asthma are sometimes referred to as **asthmatics**. 哮喘病人 ❑ *I have been an asthmatic from childhood and was never able to play any sports.* 我从小就是个哮喘病人,从来不能参加任何体育运动。 ● ADJ **Asthmatic** is also an adjective. 患哮喘病的 ❑ *One child in ten is asthmatic.* 每10个孩子中有1个是患哮喘病的。 2 ADJ **Asthmatic** means relating to asthma. 哮喘性的 [ADJ n] ❑ *...asthmatic breathing.* …哮喘性呼吸。

aston·ish /əstɒnɪʃ/ (**astonishes, astonishing, astonished**) V-T If something or someone **astonishes** you, they surprise you very much. 使十分惊讶 ❑ *My news will astonish you.* 我的消息会令你十分惊讶。

aston·ished /əstɒnɪʃt/ ADJ If you are **astonished** by something, you are very surprised about it. 感到十分惊讶的 ❑ *They were astonished to find the driver was a six-year-old boy.* 他们当时很感意外,发现司机是个 6 岁的男孩。

aston·ish·ing /əstɒnɪʃɪŋ/ ADJ Something that is **astonishing** is very surprising. 令人惊讶的 ❑ *...an astonishing display of physical strength.* …令人惊讶的体力展现。 ● **aston·ish·ing·ly** ADV 令人惊讶地 ❑ *Andrea was an astonishingly beautiful young woman.* 安德烈亚是个惊人美丽的年轻女子。

aston·ish·ment /əstɒnɪʃmənt/ N-UNCOUNT **Astonishment** is a feeling of great surprise. 惊讶 ❑ *I spotted a shooting star which, to my astonishment, was bright green in color.* 我看见了一颗划过长空的流星,让我惊讶的是,它是鲜绿色的。

astound /əstaʊnd/ (**astounds, astounding, astounded**) V-T If something **astounds** you, you are very surprised by it. 使震惊 ❑ *He used to astound his friends with feats of physical endurance.* 他过去常以身体耐力之好令其朋友们震惊。

astound·ing /əstaʊndɪŋ/ ADJ If something is **astounding**, you are shocked or amazed that it could exist or happen. 令人震惊的 ❑ *The results are quite astounding.* 这些结果非常令人震惊。

▲ **astray** /əstreɪ/ 1 PHRASE If you **are led astray** by someone or something, you behave badly or foolishly because of them. 引某人偏离正道 ❑ *The judge thought he'd been led astray by older children.* 法官认为他是被更大的孩子们引入了歧途。 2 PHRASE If someone or something **leads** you **astray**, they make you believe something that is not true, causing you to make a wrong decision. 引某人偏离真相 ❑ *The testimony would inflame the jurors, and lead them astray from the facts of the case.* 这证词会惹怒陪审员们,让他们偏离案件事实。 3 PHRASE If something **goes astray**, it gets lost while it is being taken or sent somewhere. 丢失 ❑ *Many items of mail being sent to her have gone astray.* 很多寄给她的邮件都丢失了。

astride /əstraɪd/ PREP If you sit or stand **astride** something, you sit or stand with one leg on each side of it. 跨着(某物)地 ❑ *...three youths who stood astride their bicycles and stared.* …3个跨着自行车站着盯着看的年轻人。

as·trolo·ger /əstrɒlədʒər/ (**astrologers**) N-COUNT An **astrologer** is a person who uses astrology to try to tell you things about your character and your future. 占星家

as·trol·ogy /əstrɒlədʒi/ N-UNCOUNT **Astrology** is the study of the movements of the planets, sun, moon, and stars in the belief that these movements can have an influence on people's lives. 占星学
→ see **star**

▲ **as·tro·naut** /æstrənɔt/ (**astronauts**) N-COUNT An **astronaut** is a person who is trained for traveling in a spacecraft. 宇航员

Word Link *er, or ≈ one who does, that which does : astronomer, author, writer*

as·trono·mer /əstrɒnəmər/ (**astronomers**) N-COUNT An **astronomer** is a scientist who studies the stars, planets, and other natural objects in space. 天文学家
→ see Word Web: **astronomer**
→ see **galaxy, telescope**

as·tro·nomi·cal /æstrənɒmɪkl/ 1 ADJ If you describe an amount, especially the cost of something as **astronomical**, you are emphasizing that it is very large. 天文数字般的(数量,尤指花费) [EMPHASIS] ❑ *Houses in the subdivision are going for astronomical prices.* 该小区里的房子在以天价出售。 2 ADJ **Astronomical** means relating

Word Web astronomer

The Italian **astronomer** Galileo Galilei did not invent the telescope. However, he was the first person to use it to study **celestial** bodies. He recorded his findings. What Galileo saw through the telescope supported the theory that the **planet** Earth is not the center of the universe. This theory was written by the Polish astronomer Nicolaus Copernicus in 1530. Copernicus said that all the planets in the universe revolve around the **sun**. In 1609, Galileo used a telescope to observe the **craters** on Earth's **moon**. He also discovered the four largest **satellites** of the planet Jupiter. These four bodies are called the Galilean moons.

to astronomy. 天文学的 ❑ *...the American Astronomical Society.* …美国天文学会。

★ **as·trono·my** /əstrɒnəmi/ N-UNCOUNT **Astronomy** is the scientific study of the stars, planets, and other natural objects in space. 天文学
→ see **star**

as·tute /əstut/ ADJ If you describe someone as **astute**, you think they show an understanding of behavior and situations, and are skillful at using this knowledge to their own advantage. 精明的 ❑ *She was politically astute.* 她政治上很精明。

▲ **asy·lum** /əsaɪləm/ (**asylums**) **1** N-UNCOUNT If a government gives a person from another country **asylum**, they allow them to stay, usually because they are unable to return home safely for political reasons. (给予通常因政治原因不能回国的人的) 避难许可 ❑ *He applied for asylum in 1987 after fleeing the police back home.* 他于1987年逃脱本国的警察之后申请了避难许可。 **2** N-COUNT An **asylum** is a psychiatric hospital. 精神病院 [OLD-FASHIONED]

asy·lum seek·er (**asylum seekers**) N-COUNT An **asylum seeker** is a person who is trying to get asylum in a foreign country. 寻求避难者 ❑ *Fewer than 7% of asylum seekers are accepted as political refugees.* 不足7%的寻求避难者被接受为政治难民。

at ◆◆◆ /ət, STRONG æt/

> In addition to the uses shown below, **at** is used after some verbs, nouns, and adjectives to introduce extra information. **At** is also used in phrasal verbs such as "have at" and "play at".

1 PREP You use **at** to indicate the place or event where something happens or is situated. 在(某地) ❑ *He will be at the airport to meet her.* 他将在机场见她。 ❑ *I didn't like being alone at home.* 我不喜欢独自在家。 ❑ *They agreed to meet at a restaurant in Soho.* 他们约定了在索霍区的一家餐馆里见面。 **2** PREP If you are **at** something such as a table, a door, or someone's side, you are next to it or them. 在…旁边 ❑ *An assistant sat typing away at a table beside him.* 一名助手坐在他身边的一张桌子旁在打字。 ❑ *At his side was a beautiful young woman.* 在他身边是一位漂亮的年轻女子。 **3** PREP When you are describing where someone or something is, you can say that they are **at** a certain distance. You can also say that one thing is **at** an angle in relation to another thing. 以(某距离、某角度) ❑ *The two journalists followed at a discreet distance.* 那两名记者保持一段恭敬的距离跟在后面。 **4** PREP If something happens **at** a particular time, that is the time when it happens or begins to happen. 在(某时刻) ❑ *The funeral will be carried out this afternoon at 3:00.* 葬礼将在今天下午3点举行。 **5** PREP If you do something **at** a particular age, you do it when you are that age. 在(某岁时) ❑ *Zachary started playing violin at age 4.* 扎卡里4岁开始拉小提琴。 **6** PREP If someone is **at** a particular school or college, they go there regularly to study. 在(某学校) ❑ *Their daughter is a sophomore at Yale.* 他们的女儿是耶鲁大学的一名二年级学生。 **7** PREP You use **at** to express a rate, frequency, level, or price. 以(某速度、频率、水平或价格) ❑ *I drove back down the highway at normal speed.* 我以正常速度沿高速公路往回开。 ❑ *Check the oil at regular intervals, and have the car serviced regularly.* 以固定的时间间隔检查油量，且定期对汽车进行维护。 **8** PREP You use **at** before a number or amount to indicate a measurement. 在(某数量) [PREP amount] ❑ *...as unemployment stays pegged at three million.* …由于失业人数维持在300万。 **9** PREP If you look **at** someone or something, you look toward them. If you direct an object or a comment **at** someone, you direct it toward them. 朝(…看) ❑ *He looked at Michael and laughed.* 他朝迈克尔看去，笑了。 **10** PREP You can use **at** after verbs such as "smile" or "wave" and before nouns referring to people to indicate that you have put on an expression or made a gesture that someone is meant to see or understand. 冲(某人…) [V PREP n] ❑ *She opened the door and stood there, frowning at me.* 她打开门站在那里，冲我皱着眉头。 **11** PREP If you point or gesture **at** something, you move your arm or head in its direction so that it will be noticed by someone you are with. 向(某物指或示意) [V PREP n] ❑ *He pointed at the empty bottle and the waitress quickly replaced it.* 他向那个空瓶指了指，女服务员迅速换了它。 **12** PREP If you are working **at** something, you are dealing with it. If you are aiming **at** something, you are trying to achieve it. 在(某事物上) ❑ *She has worked hard at her marriage.* 她在其婚姻上已经很努力了。 **13** PREP If something is done **at** someone's invitation or request, it is done as a result of it. 应(某人的邀请或要求) [PREP n with poss] ❑ *She left the light on in the bathroom at his request.* 她应他的要求让浴室里的灯开着。 **14** PREP You use **at** to say that someone or something is in a particular state or condition. 在(某状态或情况下) [v-link PREP n] ❑ *I am afraid we are not at liberty to disclose that information.* 恐怕我们无权透露那信息。 **15** PREP You use **at** before a possessive pronoun and a superlative adjective to say that someone or something has more of a particular quality than at any other time. 在(某人、某事物最…的时候) ❑ *When I'm on the soccer field, I'm at my happiest.* 当我在足球场上时，我最开心了。 **16** PREP You use **at** to say how something is being done. 以(某方式) ❑ *Three people were killed by shots fired at random from a minibus.* 3个人被从一辆小巴里乱射出的子弹打死了。 **17** PREP You use **at** to show that someone is doing something repeatedly. 在(某物上反复做某事) [V PREP n] ❑ *She lowered the handkerchief which she had kept dabbing at her eyes.* 她放下了那块她一直在用其反复擦眼睛的手绢。 **18** PREP You use **at** to indicate an activity or task when saying how well someone does it. 在(某方面) ❑ *I'm good at my work.* 我擅长我的工作。 **19** PREP You use **at** to indicate what someone is reacting to. 因(某事物) ❑ *Elena was annoyed at having had to wait so long for him.* 埃琳娜因不得不等他那么长的时间而恼火。 **20** **at all** → see **all**

ate /eɪt/ **Ate** is the past tense of **eat**. eat的过去式

Word Link *a, an ≈ not, without : anesthetic, anorexia, atheism*

athe·ism /eɪθiɪzəm/ N-UNCOUNT **Atheism** is the belief that there is no God. Compare **agnosticism**. 无神论

athe·ist /eɪθiɪst/ (**atheists**) N-COUNT An **atheist** is a person who believes that there is no God. Compare **agnostic**. 无神论者

ath·lete ◆◇◇ /æθlit/ (**athletes**) **1** N-COUNT An **athlete** is a person who does any kind of physical sports, exercise, or games, especially in competitions. 运动员 ❑ *Mark Spitz was a great athlete.* 马克・斯皮茨是一名伟大的运动员。 **2** N-COUNT You can refer to someone who is fit and athletic as an **athlete**. 运动型人 ❑ *I was no athlete.* 我完全不是运动型的人。

★ **ath·let·ic** /æθlɛtɪk/ **1** ADJ **Athletic** means relating to athletes and athletics. 运动的；运动员的 [ADJ n] ❑ *They have been given college scholarships purely on athletic ability.* 他们完全凭他们的运动才能获得了大学奖学金。 **2** ADJ An **athletic** person is fit, and able to perform energetic movements easily. 运动型的(人) ❑ *Xandra is an athletic 36-year-old with a 21-year-old's body.* 赞德拉是位36岁却有着21岁人体格的运动型人。

ath·let·ics /æθlɛtɪks/ **1** N-UNCOUNT **Athletics** refers to any kind of physical sports, exercise, or games. 体育运动 [AM] ❑ *...students who play intercollegiate athletics.* …参加大学校际体育运动的学生们。 **2** N-UNCOUNT **Athletics** refers to track and field

A

sports such as running, the high jump, and the javelin. 田径运动 [mainly BRIT]

in AM, use **track and field**

★ **at·las** /ætləs/ (**atlases**) N-COUNT An **atlas** is a book of maps. 地图册

ATM /eɪ ti ɛm/ (**ATMs**) N-COUNT An **ATM** is a machine that allows people to take out money from their bank account by using a special card. **ATM** is an abbreviation for "automated teller machine." 自动取款机 [mainly AM]

in BRIT, usually use **cash dispenser**

❑ *Keep your ATM card in a safe place.* 把你的自动取款卡放在一个安全的地方。

→ see **bank**

Word Link *sphere ≈ ball : atmosphere, hemisphere, sphere*

at·mos·phere ◆◇◇ /ætməsfɪər/ (**atmospheres**) **1** N-COUNT A planet's **atmosphere** is the layer of air or other gases around it. (行星的) 大气层 ❑ *The shuttle Columbia will re-enter Earth's atmosphere tomorrow morning.* 哥伦比亚号航天飞机将在明天上午重进地球大气层。 **2** N-COUNT The **atmosphere** of a place is the air that you breathe there. (某地的) 空气 ❑ *These gases pollute the atmosphere of towns and cities.* 这些气体污染城镇的空气。 **3** N-SING The **atmosphere** of a place is the general impression that you get of it. 气氛 ❑ *There's still an atmosphere of great hostility and tension in the city.* 在这座城市里依然有一种极其敌对和紧张的气氛。 **4** N-UNCOUNT If a place or an event has **atmosphere**, it is interesting. 神韵 ❑ *The old harbor is still full of atmosphere and well worth visiting.* 旧港口依然充满神韵，很值得参观。

→ see **air, core, earth, greenhouse effect, meteor, moon, water**

★ **at·mos·pher·ic** /ætməsfɛrɪk/ **1** ADJ **Atmospheric** is used to describe something that relates to the Earth's atmosphere. 大气层的 ❑ *...atmospheric gases.* …大气层中的气体。 **2** ADJ If you describe a place or a piece of music as **atmospheric**, you like it because it has a particular quality that is interesting or exciting and makes you feel a particular emotion. (某地、某音乐) 有独特氛围的 [APPROVAL] ❑ *One of the most atmospheric corners of Prague is the old Jewish ghetto.* 布拉格最具神韵的街角之一是老犹太人区。

atom /ætəm/ (**atoms**) N-COUNT An **atom** is the smallest amount of a substance that can take part in a chemical reaction. 原子 ❑ *...the news that Einstein's former colleagues Otto Hahn and Fritz Strassmann had split the atom.* …爱因斯坦的前同事奥托・哈恩和弗里茨・斯特拉斯曼曾分裂了原子的消息。

→ see **element**

atom·ic /ətɒmɪk/ **1** ADJ **Atomic** means relating to power that is produced from the energy released by splitting atoms. 原子能的 ❑ *...atomic energy.* …原子能。 **2** ADJ **Atomic** means relating to the atoms of substances. 原子的 [ADJ n] ❑ *...the atomic number of an element.* …一种元素的原子序数。

atro·cious /ətroʊʃəs/ **1** ADJ If you describe something as **atrocious**, you are emphasizing that its quality is very bad. (质量) 极差的 [EMPHASIS] ❑ *I remain to this day fluent in Hebrew, while my Arabic is atrocious.* 我直到今天希伯来语仍很流利，而我的阿拉伯语则极差。 **2** ADJ If you describe someone's behavior or their actions as **atrocious**, you mean that it is unacceptable because it is extremely violent or cruel. (行为) 残暴的 ❑ *The judge said he had committed atrocious crimes against women.* 该法官称他对妇女犯下了残暴的罪行。

▲ **atroc·ity** /ətrɒsɪti/ (**atrocities**) N-VAR An **atrocity** is a very cruel, shocking action. 暴行 ❑ *The killing was cold-blooded, and those who committed this atrocity should be tried and punished.* 这场杀戮非常残酷，那些犯下此暴行的人应该受到审判和惩罚。

at·tach ◆◇◇ /ətætʃ/ (**attaches, attaching, attached**) **1** V-T If you **attach** something **to** an object, you join it or fasten it to the object. 附; 贴; 系 ❑ *We attach labels to things before we file them away.* 我们在把东西归档前先给它们贴上标签。 ❑ *For further information, please contact us on the attached form.* 如需更多信息，请凭附表联系我们。 **2** V-T In computing, if you **attach** a file **to** a message that you send to someone, you send it with the message but separate from it. (在计算机中) 附上 (文件) ❑ *It is possible to attach executable program files to e-mail.* 可以在电子邮件上附上可执行程序文件。 **3** → see also **attached** **4** **no strings attached** → see **string**

at·tached /ətætʃt/ **1** ADJ If you are **attached to** someone or something, you like them very much. 非常喜欢…的 [v-link ADJ "to" n] ❑ *She is very attached to her family and friends.* 她非常喜欢她的家人和朋友。 **2** ADJ If someone is **attached to** an organization or group of people, they are working with them, often only for a short time. (临时) 从属于…的 [v-link ADJ "to" n] ❑ *Ford was attached to the 101st Airborne Division.* 福特曾属于第101空降师。

at·tach·ment /ətætʃmənt/ (**attachments**) **1** N-VAR If you have an **attachment to** someone or something, you are fond of them or loyal to them. 爱慕; 忠诚 ❑ *As a teenager she formed a strong attachment to one of her teachers.* 十几岁时她曾对自己的一位老师产生了强烈的爱慕之情。 **2** N-COUNT An **attachment** is a device that can be fixed onto a machine in order to enable it to do different jobs. (机器的) 附加装置 ❑ *Some models come with attachments for dusting.* 一些模型带有附加的除尘装置。 **3** N-COUNT In computing, an **attachment** is a file which is attached separately to a message that you send to someone. (电子邮件的) 附件 ❑ *When you send an e-mail you can also send a file as an attachment and that file can be a graphic, a program, a sound or whatever.* 当发送电子邮件时，你还可以把一份文件作为附件发送，该文件可以是图片、程序、或声音文件等。

at·tack ◆◆◆ /ətæk/ (**attacks, attacking, attacked**) **1** V-T/V-I To **attack** a person or place means to try to hurt or damage them using physical violence. 攻击 ❑ *Fifty civilians in Masawa were killed when government planes attacked the town.* 马萨瓦50名平民在政府飞机袭击该市时丧生。 ❑ *He bundled the old lady into her hallway and brutally attacked her.* 他把老太太推进她家门厅里，并且野蛮地袭击了她。 ❑ *They found the least defended area and attacked.* 他们找到了防守最薄弱的地区发动了攻击。 ● N-VAR **Attack** is also a noun. 攻击 ❑ *...a campaign of air attacks on strategic targets.* …对战略目标的空袭行动。 **2** V-T If you **attack** a person, belief, idea, or act, you criticize them strongly. 抨击 ❑ *He publicly attacked the people who've been calling for secret ballot nominations.* 他公开抨击了那些一直要求秘密投票提名的人。 ● N-VAR **Attack** is also a noun. 抨击 [usu with supp] ❑ *The role of the state as a prime mover in planning social change has been under attack.* 国家作为规划社会变革发起者的角色已经遭到抨击。 **3** V-T If something such as a disease, a chemical, or an insect **attacks** something, it harms or spoils it. (疾病、化学药品或昆虫等) 侵害 ❑ *The virus seems to have attacked his throat.* 病毒似乎已侵害到他的咽喉。 ● N-UNCOUNT **Attack** is also a noun. 侵害 [also N in pl] ❑ *The virus can actually destroy those white blood cells, leaving the body wide open to attack from other infections.* 该病毒实际上能破坏那些白血球，使身体极易受到其他感染。 **4** V-T If you **attack** a job or a problem, you start to deal with it in an energetic way. 积极处理 ❑ *Any attempt to attack the budget problem is going to have to in some way deal with those issues.* 要想妥善处理预算问题，从某方面来说必须先解决那些问题。 **5** V-T/V-I In games such as soccer, when one team **attacks** the opponent's goal, they try to score a goal. (在足球等比赛中) 进攻 ❑ *Now the U.S. is controlling the ball and attacking the opponent's goal.* 现在美国队在控球，正向对方球门发起进攻。 ❑ *The goal was just reward for their decision to attack constantly in the second half.* 这粒进球正是他们决定在下半场连续进攻的回报。 ● N-COUNT **Attack** is also a noun. 进攻 ❑ *Lee was at the hub of some incisive attacks in the second half.* 李是下半场几次犀利进攻中的主角。 **6** N-COUNT An **attack of** an illness is a short period in which you suffer badly from it. (疾病急性) 发作 ❑ *It had brought on an attack of asthma.* 这引起了一次哮喘发作。 **7** → see also **counterattack, heart attack**

→ see **war**

Thesaurus *attack* 另参见：

V.	assault, hit, invade; (*ant.*) defend **1**
	abuse, blame, criticize; (*ant.*) defend, praise **2**
	deal with, tackle; (*ant.*) avoid, ignore, put off **4**
N.	invasion **1**
	abuse, criticism, libel, slander; (*ant.*) defense **2**
	bout, fit **6**

Word Partnership *attack* 的常用搭配：

N.	**terrorist** attack **1**
ADJ.	**sudden/surprise** attack **1**
	personal attack **2**
V.	**launch/lead/plan an** attack **1 2**
PREP.	attack **against/on, under** attack **1 2**
	attack **of** *something* **6**

at·tack·er /ətækər/ (**attackers**) N-COUNT You can refer to a person who attacks someone as their **attacker**. 袭击者 ❑ *There were signs that she struggled with her attacker before she was stabbed.* 有迹象表明，她在被刺前曾与袭击者进行过搏斗。

at·tain /ətein/ (**attains, attaining, attained**) V-T If you **attain** something, you gain it or achieve it, often after a lot of effort. (常指经过努力) 获得 [FORMAL] ❑ *Jim is halfway to attaining his pilot's license.* 吉姆快要拿到他的飞行员执照了。

at·tain·ment /əteinmənt/ (**attainments**) 1 N-UNCOUNT The **attainment of** an aim is the achieving of it. 获得 [FORMAL] ❑ *...the attainment of independence.* …获得独立。 2 N-COUNT An **attainment** is a skill you have learned or something you have achieved. 技能; 成就 [FORMAL] ❑ *...their educational attainments.* …他们的教育成就。

Word Link *tempt ≈ trying : attempt, temptation, tempted*

at·tempt ♦♦♦ /ətɛmpt/ (**attempts, attempting, attempted**) 1 V-T If you **attempt to** do something, especially something difficult, you try to do it. 试图 (尤指做困难的事) ❑ *The only time that we attempted to do something like that was in the city of Philadelphia.* 我们惟一一次试图做那样的事是在费城。 2 N-COUNT If you make an **attempt to** do something, you try to do it, often without success. (常指不成功的) 企图 ❑ *...a deliberate attempt to destabilize the defense.* …蓄意削弱防御的企图。 3 N-COUNT An **attempt on** someone's life is an attempt to kill them. (杀人) 企图 ❑ *...an attempt on the life of the former Iranian prime minister.* …刺杀伊朗前总理的企图。

Thesaurus *attempt* 另参见:
- V. strive, tackle, take on, try 1
- N. effort, try, venture 2

Word Partnership *attempt* 的常用搭配:
- V. attempt **suicide** 1
  attempt **to control/find/prevent/solve** 1
  make an attempt 2
- N. **assassination** attempt 3
- ADJ. **any** attempt, **desperate** attempt, **failed/successful** attempt 2

at·tempt·ed /ətɛmptɪd/ ADJ An **attempted** crime or unlawful action is an unsuccessful effort to commit the crime or action. (犯罪或非法行为)未遂的 [ADJ n] ❑ *...a case of attempted murder.* …一起谋杀未遂案件。

at·tend ♦♦◇ /ətɛnd/ (**attends, attending, attended**) 1 V-T/V-I If you **attend** a meeting or other event, you are present at it. 参加; 出席 ❑ *Thousands of people attended the funeral.* 数千人参加了葬礼。 ❑ *The meeting will be attended by finance ministers from many countries.* 这次会议将有许多国家的财政部长出席。 ❑ *The senator was invited but was unable to attend.* 参议员受到了邀请，但是未能出席。 2 V-T If you **attend** an institution such as a school, college, or church, you go there regularly. 上(学); 去(教堂) ❑ *They attended college together at the University of Pennsylvania.* 他们一起就读于宾夕法尼亚大学。 3 V-I If you **attend to** something, you deal with it. If you **attend to** someone who is hurt or injured, you care for them. 处理; 照料 ❑ *He took a short leave of absence to attend to personal business.* 他休了一个短假去处理私事。

at·tend·ance /ətɛndəns/ (**attendances**) 1 N-UNCOUNT Someone's **attendance** at an event or an institution is the fact that they are present at the event or go regularly to the institution. 出勤; 出席 ❑ *Her attendance in school was sporadic.* 她在学校的出勤率很低。 2 N-VAR The **attendance** at an event is the number of people who are present at it. 出席人数 ❑ *Rain played a big part in the air show's drop in attendance.* 下雨是这次飞行表演观众数量下降的主要原因。

★ **at·tend·ant** /ətɛndənt/ (**attendants**) 1 N-COUNT An **attendant** is someone whose job is to serve or help people in a place such as a gas station or a parking lot. (加油站或停车场的)服务员 ❑ *Tony Williams was working as a parking lot attendant in Los Angeles.* 托尼·威廉斯当时在洛杉矶的一个停车场做服务生。 2 → see also **flight attendant** 3 N-COUNT The **attendants** at a wedding are people such as the bridesmaids and the ushers, who accompany or help the bride and groom. 婚礼随员 (如迎宾招待员、傧相) ❑ *If the bride pays, she has the right to decide on the style of dress worn by her attendants.* 如果新娘付费，她有权决定她的婚礼随员穿什么款式。

at·ten·tion ♦♦◇ /ətɛnʃᵊn/ 1 N-UNCOUNT If you give someone or something your **attention**, you look at it, listen to it, or think about it carefully. 注意力 ❑ *You have my undivided attention.* 我全部的注意力都在你身上。 ❑ *Later he turned his attention to the desperate state of housing in the city.* 后来他把注意力转向了该市极为严重的住房状况。 2 N-UNCOUNT **Attention** is great interest that is shown in someone or something, particularly by the general public. (尤指公众的) 关注 ❑ *Volume Two, subtitled "The Lawyers," will also attract considerable attention.* 副标题为《律师》的第2卷也将会引起极大的关注。 3 N-UNCOUNT If someone or something is getting **attention**, they are being dealt with or cared for. 照料 ❑ *Each year more than two million household injuries need medical attention.* 每年有二百多万起在家受伤、需要医疗救治的案例。 4 N-UNCOUNT If you **bring** something **to** someone's **attention** or **draw** their **attention to** it, you tell them about it or make them notice it. (引起某人) 注意 ❑ *If we don't keep bringing this to the attention of the people, nothing will be done.* 如果我们无法让公众保持对此事的关注，那就将一事无成。 5 PHRASE If someone or something **attracts** your **attention** or **catches** your **attention**, you suddenly notice them. 突然引起某人的注意 ❑ *A faint aroma of coffee attracted his attention.* 一股淡淡的咖啡香味吸引了他的注意。 6 PHRASE If you **pay attention to** someone, you watch them, listen to them, or take notice of them. If you **pay no attention to** someone, you behave as if you are not aware of them or as if they are not important. 注意 ❑ *More than ever before, the food industry is paying attention to young consumers.* 现在，食品业比以往任何时候都更加关注年轻的消费者。 7 PHRASE When people **stand at attention**, they stand straight with their feet together and their arms at their sides. 立正 ❑ *Soldiers in full combat gear stood at attention.* 全副武装的士兵们立正站着。

Word Partnership *attention* 的常用搭配:
- PREP. attention **to detail** 1
- ADJ. **careful/close/undivided** attention 1
  special attention 1–3
  unwanted attention 2
  medical attention 3
- V. **catch *someone's*** attention, **focus** attention, **turn** attention **to *someone/something*** 1 5
  call/direct *someone's* attention 4
  draw attention 4
  attract attention 5
  pay attention 6
- N. **center of** attention 2

at·ten·tive /ətɛntɪv/ 1 ADJ If you are **attentive**, you are paying close attention to what is being said or done. 注意的 ❑ *He wishes the government would be more attentive to detail in their response.* 他希望政府在回应时能更注意细节。 ● **at·ten·tive·ly** ADV 注意地 ❑ *He questioned Chrissie, and listened attentively to what she told him.* 他询问了克丽茜，专注地听了她的讲述。 2 ADJ Someone who is **attentive** is helpful and polite. 体贴的; 殷勤的 ❑ *At society parties he is attentive to his wife.* 在社交聚会上，他对妻子体贴殷勤。

at·test /ətɛst/ (**attests, attesting, attested**) V-T/V-I To **attest** something or **attest to** something means to say, show, or prove that it is true. 证明 [FORMAL] ❑ *Police records attest to his long history of violence.* 警方记录证明他有长期的暴力史。

▲ **at·tic** /ætɪk/ (**attics**) N-COUNT An **attic** is a room at the top of a house just below the roof. 阁楼
→ see **house**

at·ti·tude ♦♦◇ /ætɪtud/ (**attitudes**) N-VAR Your **attitude to** something is the way that you think and feel about it, especially when this shows in the way you behave. 态度 ❑ *...the general change in attitude toward handicapped people.* …对残疾人态度的普遍转变。 ❑ *Being unemployed produces negative attitudes to work.* 失业会对工作产生消极态度。

Word Partnership *attitude* 的常用搭配:
- PREP. attitude **about/toward**
- ADJ. **bad** attitude, **negative/positive** attitude, **new** attitude, **progressive** attitude
- V. **change your** attitude

at·tor·ney ♦◇◇ /ətɜrni/ (**attorneys**) 1 N-COUNT In the United States, an **attorney** or **attorney-at-law** is a lawyer. 律师 ❑ *...a prosecuting attorney.* …一位公诉律师。 ❑ *At the hearing, her attorney did not enter a plea.* 在听证会上，她的律师没有提出申诉。 2 → see also **state's attorney**
→ see **trial**

A

Attorney General (Attorneys General) N-COUNT A country's **Attorney General** is its chief law officer, who advises its government or ruler. 检察总长；司法部长

at·tract ♦♦◊ /ətrækt/ (attracts, attracting, attracted) **1** V-T If something **attracts** people or animals, it has features that cause them to come to it. 吸引 ❑ *The Cardiff Bay project is attracting many visitors.* 加的夫湾工程吸引着众多的参观者。 **2** V-T If someone or something **attracts** you, they have particular qualities which cause you to like or admire them. If a particular quality **attracts** you **to** a person or thing, it is the reason why you like them. 引起…的兴趣 ❑ *He wasn't sure he'd got it right, although the theory attracted him by its logic.* 他不能确定自己理解是否正确，尽管该理论的逻辑推理引起了他的兴趣。 **3** V-T If you **are attracted to** someone, you are interested in them sexually. (性的) 吸引 ❑ *In spite of her hostility, she was attracted to him.* 尽管心存敌意，她还是被他吸引住了。
● **at·tract·ed** ADJ 被吸引的 [v-link ADJ] ❑ *He was nice looking, but I wasn't deeply attracted to him.* 他长得挺好看，但我并没有被他深深吸引。
4 V-T If something **attracts** support, publicity, or money, it receives support, publicity, or money. 吸引 (支持或资金等) ❑ *President Mwinyi said his country would also like to attract investment from private companies.* 姆维尼总统说他的国家也愿意吸引私企的投资。
5 to **attract** someone's **attention** → see **attention**
→ see **magnet**

at·trac·tion /ətrækʃ^{ə}n/ (attractions) **1** N-UNCOUNT **Attraction** is a feeling of liking someone, and often of being sexually interested in them. 吸引 (常指异性) ❑ *Our level of attraction to the opposite sex has more to do with our inner confidence than how we look.* 我们对异性的吸引程度更多地与我们内心的自信有关，而不是外貌。
2 N-COUNT An **attraction** is a feature that makes something interesting or desirable. 吸引力 ❑ *...the attractions of living on the waterfront.* …滨水生活的吸引力。 **3** N-COUNT An **attraction** is something that people can go to for interest or enjoyment, for example, a famous building. 游览胜地 ❑ *The walled city is an important tourist attraction.* 这座城墙围绕的城市是一个重要的旅游胜地。

at·trac·tive ♦◊◊ /ətræktɪv/ **1** ADJ A person who is **attractive** is pleasant to look at. 有魅力的 ❑ *She's a very attractive woman.* 她是一个非常有魅力的女人。 ❑ *I thought he was very attractive and obviously very intelligent.* 我认为他很有魅力，而且显然也很聪明。
● **at·trac·tive·ness** N-UNCOUNT 魅力 ❑ *Most of us would maintain that physical attractiveness does not play a major part in how we react to the people we meet.* 我们中大多数人都会认为，外表的魅力在我们待人接物方面并不起主要作用。

> When you are describing someone's appearance, you generally use **pretty** and **beautiful** to describe women, girls, and babies. **Beautiful** is a much stronger word than **pretty**. The equivalent word for a man is **handsome**. **Good-looking** and **attractive** can be used to describe people of either sex. **Pretty** can also be used to modify adjectives and adverbs but is less strong than **very**. In this sense, **pretty** is informal.

2 ADJ Something that is **attractive** has a pleasant appearance or sound. 外表漂亮的；声音优美的 ❑ *The apartment was small but attractive, if rather shabby.* 这套公寓不大却满漂亮，尽管已相当陈旧。
3 ADJ You can describe something as **attractive** when it seems worth having or doing. 有诱惑力的 ❑ *Smoking is still attractive to many young people who see it as glamorous.* 吸烟仍然对很多年轻人有诱惑力，他们将之视为魅力标志。

> **Thesaurus** *attractive* 另参见：
> ADJ. appealing, charming, good-looking, pleasant; *(ant.)* repulsive, ugly, unappealing, unattractive **1** **2**

★ **at·trib·ut·able** /ətrɪbyətəb^{ə}l/ ADJ If something **is attributable to** an event, situation, or person, it is likely that it was caused by that event, situation, or person. 很可能由于…导致的 [v-link ADJ "to" n] ❑ *10,000 deaths a year from chronic lung disease are attributable to smoking.* 每年1万个慢性肺病患者的死亡可能是由于吸烟导致的。

> **Word Link** *tribute* ≈ *giving* : *attribute, contribute, distribute*

at·trib·ute (attributes, attributing, attributed)

> The verb is pronounced /ətrɪbyut/. The noun is pronounced /ætrɪbyut/.

> 动词读作 /ətrɪbyut/。名词读作 /ætrɪbyut/。

1 V-T If you **attribute** something **to** an event or situation, you think that it was caused by that event or situation. 把…归因于 ❑ *Women tend to attribute their success to external causes such as luck.* 女性往往把她们的成功归因于外因，如运气。 **2** V-T If you **attribute** a particular quality or feature **to** someone or something, you think that they have it. 赋予 (某品质或特点) ❑ *People were beginning to attribute superhuman qualities to him.* 人们开始赋予他超人的品质。
3 V-T If a piece of writing, a work of art, or a remark **is attributed to** someone, people say that they wrote it, created it, or said it. 认为 (文章、作品等) 出自… [usu passive] ❑ *This, and the remaining frescoes, are not attributed to Giotto.* 这个，还有那些残存的壁画，被认为不是乔托的作品。 **4** N-COUNT An **attribute** is a quality or feature that someone or something has. 特性 ❑ *Cruelty is a normal attribute of human behavior.* 残忍是人类行为的一种正常的特性。

auber·gine /oʊbərʒin/ N-VAR [BRIT] → see **eggplant**

auburn /ɔbərn/ COLOR **Auburn** hair is reddish brown. 红棕色的 ❑ *...a tall woman with long auburn hair.* …一个红棕色长发的高个子女人。

auc·tion ♦◊◊ /ɔkʃ^{ə}n/ (auctions, auctioning, auctioned) **1** N-VAR An **auction** is a public sale where items are sold to the person who offers the highest price. 拍卖 ❑ *The painting is expected to fetch up to $400,000 at auction.* 这幅画预计在拍卖会上能卖到40万美元。 **2** V-T If something **is auctioned**, it is sold in an auction. 被拍卖 ❑ *Eight drawings by French artist Jean Cocteau will be auctioned next week.* 法国艺术家让・科克托的8幅画作将在下周拍卖。
▸ **auction off** PHRASAL VERB If you **auction off** something, you sell it to the person who offers most for it, often at an auction. 拍卖掉 ❑ *Any fool could auction off a factory full of engineering machinery.* 任何傻瓜都能把一个满是工程机械设备的工厂拍卖掉。

> **Word Link** *eer* ≈ *one who does* : *auctioneer, mountaineer, volunteer*

auc·tion·eer /ɔkʃənɪər/ (auctioneers) N-COUNT An **auctioneer** is a person in charge of an auction. 拍卖师

auda·cious /ɔdeɪʃəs/ ADJ Someone who is **audacious** takes risks in order to achieve something. 大胆的 ❑ *...an audacious plan to win the presidency.* …一个为赢得总统大选而订的大胆计划。 ❑ *He was known for risky tactics that ranged from audacious to outrageous.* 他以大胆甚至是骇人听闻的冒险战术而闻名。

audac·ity /ɔdæsɪti/ N-UNCOUNT **Audacity** is audacious behavior. 大胆行为 ❑ *I was shocked at the audacity of the gangsters.* 我为这些匪帮的大胆行为感到震惊。

> **Word Link** *ible* ≈ *able to be* : *audible, flexible, possible*

audible /ɔdɪb^{ə}l/ ADJ A sound that is **audible** is loud enough to be heard. 听得见的 ❑ *The Colonel's voice was barely audible.* 上校的声音几乎听不见。 ● **audibly** /ɔdɪbli/ ADV 听得见地 ❑ *Frank sighed audibly.* 弗兰克出声地叹了口气。

> **Word Link** *audi* ≈ *hearing* : *audience, audition, auditorium*

audi·ence ♦♦◊ /ɔdiəns/ (audiences) **1** N-COUNT-COLL The **audience** at a play, concert, film, or public meeting is the group of people watching or listening to it. 观众 ❑ *The entire audience broke into loud applause.* 全场观众爆发出响亮的掌声。 **2** N-COUNT-COLL The **audience** for a television or radio program consists of all the people who watch or listen to it. 观众；听众 ❑ *The concert will be broadcast to a worldwide television audience estimated at one billion.* 这场音乐会将向全世界大约十亿电视观众转播。 **3** N-COUNT-COLL The **audience** of a writer or artist is the people who read their books or look at their work. 读者；欣赏者 ❑ *Say's writings reached a wide audience during his lifetime.* 塞伊的作品在他有生之年就拥有了广泛读者。
→ see **concert**, **theater**

> **Word Partnership** *audience* 的常用搭配：
> PREP. **before/in front of an** audience **1**
> ADJ. **captive** audience, **live** audience **1**
> **large** audience **1** – **3**
> **general** audience, **target** audience, **wide** audience **2**
> N. audience **participation**, **studio** audience **1**
> **television** audience **2**
> V. **reach an** audience **2** **3**

audio ♦♦◊ /ɔdioʊ/ ADJ **Audio** equipment is used for recording and reproducing sound. 录音的 [ADJ n] ❑ *The software was the first to offer access to audio and video files.* 这是第一种可以访问音视频文件的软件。

audio·tape /ɔdioʊteɪp/ also **audio tape** N-UNCOUNT **Audiotape** is magnetic tape used to record sound. 录音磁带 ❑ *Unfortunately, fewer than 5 percent of books are now available in Braille or audiotape.* 遗憾的是，现在只有不足5%的图书有布莱叶盲文版或录音磁带。

Word Link *vid, vis ≈ seeing : audiovisual, videotape, visible*

audio·visual /ɔdioʊvɪʒuəl/ also **audio-visual** ADJ **Audio-visual** equipment and materials involve both recorded sound and pictures. 视听的 [ADJ n]

▲ **audit** /ɔdɪt/ (**audits, auditing, audited**) V-T When an accountant **audits** an organization's accounts, he or she examines the accounts officially in order to make sure that they have been done correctly. 审计 ❑ *Each year they audit our accounts and certify them as being true and fair.* 每年他们都会审核我们的账目，以证明其准确合理。● N-COUNT **Audit** is also a noun. 审计 ❑ *The bank first learned of the problem when it carried out an internal audit.* 银行是在进行内部审计时最先得知这个问题的。

audi·tion /ɔdɪʃ°n/ (**auditions, auditioning, auditioned**) **1** N-COUNT An **audition** is a short performance given by an actor, dancer, or musician so that a director or conductor can decide if they are good enough to be in a play, film, or orchestra. 试(镜、演) ❑ *...an audition for a Broadway musical.* …一部百老汇歌舞剧的试演。 **2** V-T/V-I If you **audition** or if someone **auditions** you, you do an audition. 试(镜、演) ❑ *I was auditioning for the part of a jealous girlfriend.* 我试演了一个有妒忌心的女友角色。 ❑ *They're auditioning new members for the cast of "Miss Saigon" today.* 他们今天在为《西贡小姐》剧组的新演员试镜。

▲ **audi·tor** /ɔdɪtər/ (**auditors**) N-COUNT An **auditor** is an accountant who officially examines the accounts of organizations. 审计员

▲ **audi·to·rium** /ɔdɪtɔriəm/ (**auditoriums** or **auditoria** /ɔdɪtɔriə/) **1** N-COUNT An **auditorium** is the part of a theater or concert hall where the audience sits. 观众席 ❑ *Anderson was to sing at the Constitution Hall auditorium.* 安德森将要在宪法厅的观众席演唱。 **2** N-COUNT An **auditorium** is a large room, hall, or building that is used for events such as meetings and concerts. 礼堂 [AM] ❑ *...a high school auditorium.* …一所中学的礼堂。

▲ **audi·tory** /ɔdɪtɔri/ ADJ **Auditory** means related to hearing. 听觉的 [usu ADJ n] [TECHNICAL] ❑ *...the limits of the human auditory range.* …人类听觉范围的局限。

Aug. **Aug.** is a written abbreviation for **August**. 8月

▲ **aug·ment** /ɔgmɛnt/ (**augments, augmenting, augmented**) V-T To **augment** something means to make it larger, stronger, or more effective by adding something to it. 增加 [FORMAL] ❑ *While searching for a way to augment the family income, she began making dolls.* 为求增加家庭收入，她开始做起了玩具娃娃。

august /ɔgʌst/ ADJ Someone or something that is **august** is dignified and impressive. 庄严的 [usu ADJ n] [FORMAL] ❑ *...that august body, the United States Senate.* …那庄严的团体，美国参议院。

August ♦♦♦ /ɔgəst/ (**Augusts**) N-VAR **August** is the eighth month of the year in the Western calendar. 8月 ❑ *The world premiere took place in August 1956.* 全球首映是在1956年8月。 ❑ *The trial will resume on August the twenty-second.* 审讯将于8月22日继续进行。

aunt ♦♦◊ /ænt, ɑnt/ (**aunts**) N-FAMILY; N-TITLE Someone's **aunt** is the sister of their mother or father, or the wife of their uncle. 姨母；舅母；姑母；伯母；婶母 ❑ *She wrote to her aunt in Alabama.* 她给在阿拉巴马州的姑母写了信。
→ see **family**

auntie /ænti, ɑnti/ (**aunties**) also **aunty** N-FAMILY; N-TITLE Someone's **auntie** is their aunt. 姨妈；舅妈；姑姑；伯母；婶娘 [INFORMAL] ❑ *His uncle is dead, but his auntie still lives here.* 他舅舅死了，但他舅妈还住在这儿。

au pair /oʊ pɛər/ (**au pairs**) N-COUNT An **au pair** is a young person from a foreign country who lives with a family in order to learn the language and who helps to take care of the children. 互惠生(为学习语言而住在当地人家里并照看小孩的外国年轻人)

aura /ɔrə/ (**auras**) N-COUNT An **aura** is a quality or feeling that seems to surround a person or place or to come from them. 气质；氛围 ❑ *She had an aura of authority.* 她有一种权威气质。

aus·pices /ɔspɪsɪz/ PHRASE If something is done **under the auspices of** a particular person or organization, or **under** someone's **auspices**, it is done with their support and approval. 在…的支持下 [FORMAL] ❑ *... to meet and discuss peace under the auspices of the United Nations.* …在联合国的支持下开会并且讨论和平问题。

▲ **aus·tere** /ɔstɪər/ **1** ADJ If you describe something as **austere**, you approve of its plain and simple appearance. 朴素的 [APPROVAL] ❑ *...a cream linen suit and austere black blouse.* …一套奶油色的亚麻西装和一件朴素的黑衬衫。 **2** ADJ If you describe someone as **austere**, you disapprove of them because they are strict and serious. 严厉的 [DISAPPROVAL] ❑ *I found her a rather austere, distant, somewhat cold person.* 我发觉她是一个相当严厉、难以亲近、有些冷漠的人。 **3** ADJ An **austere** way of life is one that is simple and without luxuries. 简朴的 ❑ *The life of the troops was still comparatively austere.* 部队生活相对而言仍然简朴。 **4** ADJ An **austere** economic policy is one that reduces people's living standards sharply. (经济政策) 紧缩的 ❑ *...a set of very austere economic measures to control inflation.* …一系列控制通货膨胀的、大力度的紧缩经济措施。

aus·ter·ity /ɔstɛrɪti/ N-UNCOUNT **Austerity** is a situation in which people's living standards are reduced because of economic difficulties. 经济紧缩 ❑ *...the years of austerity which followed the war.* …战后的经济紧缩年代。

authen·tic /ɔθɛntɪk/ **1** ADJ An **authentic** person, object, or emotion is genuine. 真实的 ❑ *...authentic Italian food.* …正宗的意大利食品。 ❑ *She has authentic charm whereas most people simply have nice manners.* 她有真正的魅力，而大多数人只是有礼貌而已。 ● **au·then·tic·ity** ★ /ɔθɛntɪsɪti/ N-UNCOUNT 真实性 ❑ *There are factors, however, that have cast doubt on the statue's authenticity.* 然而，有些因素已经让人们对这座雕像的真实性产生了怀疑。 **2** ADJ If you describe something as **authentic**, you mean that it is such a good imitation that it is almost the same as or as good as the original. 逼真的 [APPROVAL] ❑ *...patterns for making authentic frontier-style clothing.* …制作地道的边疆风格服装的图样。 **3** ADJ An **authentic** piece of information or account of something is reliable and accurate. 可靠的 ❑ *I had obtained the authentic details about the birth of the organization.* 我已经弄到了有关该组织成立的可靠的详细资料。

Word Link *er, or ≈ one who does, that which does : astronomer, author, writer*

author ♦♦◊ /ɔθər/ (**authors**) **1** N-COUNT The **author of** a piece of writing is the person who wrote it. 作者 [oft N "of" n] ❑ *...Jill Phillips, author of the book "Give Your Child Music."* …吉尔·菲利浦斯，《把音乐给你的孩子》一书的作者。 **2** N-COUNT An **author** is a person whose job is writing books. 作家 ❑ *Haruki Murakami is Japan's best-selling author.* 村上春树是日本的畅销书作家。

author·ise /ɔθəraɪz/ [BRIT] → see **authorize**

Word Link *arian ≈ believing in, having : authoritarian, humanitarian, vegetarian*

authori·tar·ian /əθɔrɪtɛəriən/ ADJ If you describe a person or an organization as **authoritarian**, you are critical of them controlling everything rather than letting people decide things for themselves. 独裁的 [DISAPPROVAL] ❑ *Senior officers could be considering a coup to restore authoritarian rule.* 高级军官们可能会考虑发动一场政变来恢复独裁统治。

★ **authori·ta·tive** /əθɔrɪteɪtɪv/ **1** ADJ Someone or something that is **authoritative** gives an impression of power and importance and is likely to be obeyed. 有权威的 ❑ *He has a commanding presence and deep, authoritative voice.* 他仪态威严，声音深沉而有权威。 **2** ADJ Someone or something that is **authoritative** has a lot of knowledge of a particular subject. (关于某一学科) 权威性的 ❑ *The first authoritative study of polio was published in 1840.* 关于小儿麻痹症的首篇权威研究报告发表于1840年。

author·ity ♦♦♦ /əθɔrɪti/ (**authorities**) **1** N-PLURAL **The authorities** are the people who have the power to make decisions and to make sure that laws are obeyed. 当局 ❑ *This provided a pretext for the authorities to cancel the elections.* 这给当局提供了一个取消选举的借口。 **2** N-COUNT An **authority** is an official organization or government department that has the power to make decisions. 官方机构 ❑ *...the Philadelphia Parking Authority.* …费城停车管理局。 **3** → see also **local authority** **4** N-COUNT Someone who is an **authority on** a particular subject knows a lot about it. (某一学科的) 权威人士 ❑ *He's universally recognized as an authority on Russian affairs.* 他被公认为是俄罗斯事务的权威。 **5** N-UNCOUNT **Authority** is the right to command and control other people. 职权 ❑ *A family member in a family business has a position of authority and power.* 家庭成员在家族企业中都有职权。 **6** N-UNCOUNT If someone has **authority**, they have a quality which makes other people take notice of what they say. 威信 ❑ *He had no natural authority and no capacity for imposing his will on others.* 他天生没有威信，

A

也没有将其意志强加于他人的能力。 7 N-UNCOUNT **Authority** is official permission to do something. 官方的许可 ❑ *The prison governor has refused to let him go, saying he must first be given authority from his own superiors.* 监狱长已拒绝释放他，说他必须首先得到上级的许可。

★ **author·ize** /ɔθəraɪz/ (**authorizes, authorizing, authorized**)
in BRIT, also use **authorise**
V-T If someone in a position of authority **authorizes** something, they give their official permission for it to happen. 批准 ❑ *It would certainly be within his power to authorize a police raid like that.* 他肯定有权批准那种警方突袭行动。 ● **authori·za·tion** /ɔθərɪzeɪʃən/ N-VAR (**authorizations**) 批准 ❑ *The United Nations will approve his request for authorization to use military force to deliver aid.* 联合国将同意他的请求，批准他动用军队来运送救援物资。

autism /ɔtɪzəm/ N-UNCOUNT **Autism** is a severe mental disorder that makes someone unable to respond to other people. 自闭症

auto ♦◇◇ /ɔtoʊ/ (**autos**) N-COUNT An **auto** is a car. 汽车 [AM] ❑ *...the auto industry.* …汽车工业。

auto·bio·graphi·cal /ɔtoʊbaɪəgræfɪkəl/ ADJ An **autobiographical** piece of writing relates to events in the life of the person who has written it. 自传性的 ❑ *...a highly autobiographical novel of a woman's search for identity.* …一部关于一位女性寻找自我、自传性色彩浓厚的长篇小说。

▲ **auto·bi·og·ra·phy** /ɔtəbaɪɒgrəfi/ (**autobiographies**) N-COUNT Your **autobiography** is an account of your life, which you write yourself. 自传 ❑ *He published his autobiography last fall.* 他去年秋天出版了他的自传。

Word Link *graph ≈ writing : autograph, biography, graph*

auto·graph /ɔtəgræf/ (**autographs, autographing, autographed**) 1 N-COUNT An **autograph** is the signature of someone famous that is specially written for a fan to keep. (名人的) 签名 ❑ *He went backstage and asked for her autograph.* 他到后台去要她的签名。 2 V-T If someone famous **autographs** something, they put their signature on it. 在…签名 ❑ *I autographed a copy of one of my books.* 我在我的一本书上签了名。

auto·mate /ɔtəmeɪt/ (**automates, automating, automated**) V-T To **automate** a factory, office, or industrial process means to put in machines that can do the work instead of people. 使自动化 ❑ *He wanted to use computers to automate the process.* 他想用电脑来使流程自动化。 ● **auto·ma·tion** ★ /ɔtəmeɪʃən/ N-UNCOUNT 自动化 ❑ *In the last ten years automation has reduced the work force here by half.* 在过去的10年中，自动化已经减少了这里一半的劳动力。
→ see **factory**

auto·mat·ed /ɔtəmeɪtɪd/ ADJ An **automated** factory, office, or industrial process uses machines to do the work instead of people. 自动化的 ❑ *The equipment was made on highly automated production lines.* 该设备是在高度自动化的生产线上制造的。

Word Link *auto ≈ self : automatic, automobile, autonomy*

auto·mat·ic ♦◇◇ /ɔtəmætɪk/ (**automatics**) 1 ADJ An **automatic** machine or device is one that has controls that enable it to perform a task without needing to be constantly operated by a person. **Automatic** methods and processes involve the use of such machines. (机器或装置) 自动的 ❑ *Modern trains have automatic doors.* 现代火车都有自动门。 2 ADJ An **automatic** weapon is one that keeps firing shots until you stop pulling the trigger. (武器) 自动的 [ADJ n] ❑ *Three gunmen with automatic rifles opened fire.* 3名手持自动步枪的歹徒开了火。 ● N-COUNT **Automatic** is also a noun. 自动枪 ❑ *He drew his automatic and began running in the direction of the sounds.* 他拔出自动枪，朝发出声音的方向跑去。 3 ADJ An **automatic** action is one that you do without thinking about it. (行动) 无意识的 ❑ *All of the automatic body functions, even breathing, are affected.* 所有无意识的身体功能，甚至呼吸，都受到影响。 ● **auto·mati·cal·ly** /ɔtəmætɪkli/ ADV 无意识地 ❑ *You will automatically wake up after this length of time.* 你将在这段时间之后自然醒来。 4 N-COUNT An **automatic** is a car in which the gears change automatically as the car's speed increases or decreases. 自动换档汽车

Word Link *mobil ≈ moving : automobile, mobile, mobilize*

auto·mo·bile /ɔtəməbil/ (**automobiles**) N-COUNT An **automobile** is a car. 汽车 [mainly AM] ❑ *...the automobile industry.* …汽车工业。
→ see **car**

★ **autono·mous** /ɔtɒnəməs/ 1 ADJ An **autonomous** country, organization, or group governs or controls itself rather than being controlled by anyone else. 自治的 ❑ *They proudly declared themselves part of a new autonomous province.* 他们自豪地宣布自己是新自治省的一部分。 2 ADJ An **autonomous** person makes their own decisions rather than being influenced by someone else. 独立自主的 ❑ *He treated us as autonomous individuals who had to make up our own minds about issues.* 他视我们为独立个体，必须学会自主处理问题。

★ **autono·my** /ɔtɒnəmi/ 1 N-UNCOUNT **Autonomy** is the control or government of a country, organization, or group by itself rather than by others. 自治 ❑ *Activists stepped up their demands for local autonomy last month.* 活动的积极分子上个月提高了其对地方自治的要求。 2 N-UNCOUNT **Autonomy** is the ability to make your own decisions about what to do rather than being influenced by someone else or told what to do. 独立自主 [FORMAL] ❑ *Each of the area managers enjoys considerable autonomy in the running of his own area.* 每一位地区经理在各自主管的区域都享有相当大的自主权。

autop·sy /ɔtɒpsi/ (**autopsies**) N-COUNT An **autopsy** is an examination of a dead body by a doctor who cuts it open in order to try to discover the cause of death. 验尸 ❑ *Macklin had the grim task of carrying out an autopsy on his friend.* 麦克林的可怕差事是为他的朋友验尸。

autumn ♦◇◇ /ɔtəm/ (**autumns**) N-VAR **Autumn** is the season between summer and winter when the weather becomes cooler and the leaves fall off the trees. 秋天 [mainly BRIT]
in AM, usually use **fall**

aux·ilia·ry /ɔgzɪlyəri, -zɪləri/ (**auxiliaries**) 1 ADJ **Auxiliary** equipment is extra equipment that is available for use when necessary. 备用的 [ADJ n] ❑ *...an auxiliary motor.* …一台备用的发动机。 2 ADJ **Auxiliary** staff and troops assist other staff and troops. 后备的 [ADJ n] ❑ *The government's first concern was to augment the army and auxiliary forces.* 政府首要关注的是扩充军队与后备军。 3 N-COUNT An **auxiliary** is a person who is employed to assist other people in their work. Auxiliaries are often medical workers or members of the armed forces. 助手 ❑ *Nursing auxiliaries provide basic care, but are not qualified nurses.* 助理护士们提供基本护理，但没有护士资格。 4 N-COUNT In grammar, an **auxiliary** or **auxiliary verb** is a verb that is used with a main verb, for example, to form different tenses or to make the verb passive. In English, the basic auxiliary verbs are "be," "have," and "do." Modal verbs such as "can" and "will" are also sometimes called auxiliaries. 助动词

★ **avail** /əveɪl/ (**avails, availing, availed**) 1 PHRASE If you do something **to no avail** or **to little avail**, what you do fails to achieve what you want. 徒劳 [WRITTEN] ❑ *His efforts were to no avail.* 他的努力是徒劳的。 2 V-T If you **avail yourself of** an offer or an opportunity, you accept the offer or make use of the opportunity. 利用 [FORMAL] ❑ *Guests should feel at liberty to avail themselves of your facilities.* 客人们应可以随意使用你们的设施。

avail·able ♦♦♦ /əveɪləbəl/ 1 ADJ If something you want or need is **available**, you can find it or obtain it. 可获得的 ❑ *Since 1978, the amount of money available to buy books has fallen by 17%.* 自1978年以来，可供买书的钱已减少了17%。 ❑ *The store has about 500 autographed copies of the book available for purchase.* 这家书店有大约500本该书的签名版本可供购买。 ● **avail·abil·ity** ★ /əveɪləbɪlɪti/ N-UNCOUNT 可获得性 ❑ *...the easy availability of guns.* …获取枪支的容易性。 2 ADJ Someone who is **available** is not busy and is therefore free to talk to you or to do a particular task. 有空的 [V-link ADJ] ❑ *Mr. Leach is on holiday and was not available for comment.* 利奇先生在休假，没空作评论。

Thesaurus *available* 另参见：
ADJ. accessible, handy, obtainable, usable 1
free, unoccupied 2

Word Partnership *available* 的常用搭配：
N. available **information**, available **opportunities/options**, available **resources** 1
ADV. **readily** available, **widely** available 1
currently/now available 1 2
PREP. available **on request** 1
available **for *something*** 2
V. **make *yourself*** available 2

ava·lanche /ævəlæntʃ/ (**avalanches**) N-COUNT An **avalanche** is a large mass of snow that falls down the side of a mountain. 雪崩

a

avant-garde /ævɒŋ gɑrd/ ADJ **Avant-garde** art, music, theater, and literature is very modern and experimental. 前卫的 ❑ *...avant-garde concert music.* …音乐会上的前卫音乐。

▲ **avenge** /əvɛndʒ/ (**avenges, avenging, avenged**) V-T If you **avenge** a wrong or harmful act, you hurt or punish the person who is responsible for it. 为…报仇 ❑ *He has devoted the past five years to avenging his daughter's death.* 他在过去的5年中一直在努力为他女儿的死报仇。

av·enue ♦♦◊ /ævinyu, -nu/ (**avenues**) 1 N-IN-NAMES **Avenue** is sometimes used in the names of streets. The written abbreviation **Ave.** is also used. 大街 ❑ *...the most expensive apartments on Park Avenue.* …派克大街上最昂贵的公寓。 2 N-COUNT An **avenue** is a wide, straight road, especially one with trees on either side. 林荫大道

av·er·age ♦♦◊ /ævərɪdʒ, ævrɪdʒ/ (**averages, averaging, averaged**) 1 N-COUNT An **average** is the result that you get when you add two or more numbers together and divide the total by the number of numbers you added together. 平均数 ❑ *Take the average of those ratios and multiply by a hundred.* 取那些比例的平均数再乘以100。 ● ADJ **Average** is also an adjective. 平均的 [ADJ n] ❑ *The average price of goods rose by just 2.2%.* 商品的平均价格仅上涨了2.2%。 2 N-SING You use **average** to refer to a number or size that varies but is always approximately the same. 平均值 ❑ *It takes an average of ten weeks for a house sale to be completed.* 平均需要10周的时间才能完成一幢房子的销售。 3 N-SING An amount or quality that is **the average** is the normal amount or quality for a particular group of things or people. 一般水平 ❑ *35% of staff time was being spent on repeating work, about the average for a service industry.* 员工35%的时间花费在重复劳动上，大约是服务业的一般水平。 ● ADJ **Average** is also an adjective. 正常标准的 ❑ *$2.20 for a beer is average.* 一瓶啤酒$2.20是一般价位。 4 ADJ An **average** person or thing is typical or normal. 普通的 [ADJ n] ❑ *The average adult man burns 1,500 to 2,000 calories per day.* 一个普通成年男子每天消耗1500到2000卡路里热量。 5 ADJ Something that is **average** is neither very good nor very bad, usually when you had hoped it would be better. 平平的 ❑ *I was only average academically.* 我的学业成绩只能算平平。 6 V-T To **average** a particular amount means to do, get, or produce that amount as an average over a period of time. 平均为 ❑ *We averaged 42 miles per hour.* 我们平均时速为42英里。 7 PHRASE You say **on average** or **on the average** to indicate that a number is the average of several numbers. 按平均值 ❑ *Shares rose, on average, by 38%.* 股值平均上涨了38%。

aver·sion /əvɜrʒən/ (**aversions**) N-VAR If you have an **aversion to** someone or something, you dislike them very much. 厌恶 ❑ *Many people have a natural and emotional aversion to insects.* 很多人对昆虫有一种天生的厌恶之感。

★ **avert** /əvɜrt/ (**averts, averting, averted**) 1 V-T If you **avert** something unpleasant, you prevent it from happening. 防止 ❑ *Talks with the teachers' union over the weekend have averted a strike.* 周末与教师工会的会谈避免了一次罢工。 2 V-T If you **avert** your eyes or gaze **from** someone or something, you look away from them. 转移（视线） ❑ *He avoids any eye contact, quickly averting his gaze when anyone approaches.* 他避免任何目光接触，任何人接近他时，他都会迅速转移视线。

a·vi·an flu /eɪviən flu/ N-UNCOUNT **Avian flu** is a serious illness that can be transmitted to people from chickens, ducks, and other birds. 禽流感

aviary /eɪvieri/ (**aviaries**) N-COUNT An **aviary** is a large cage or covered area in which birds are kept. 大鸟笼；鸟舍

★ **avia·tion** /eɪvieɪʃən/ N-UNCOUNT **Aviation** is the operation and production of aircraft. 航空；飞机制造业 ❑ *...the aviation industry.* …航空工业。

avid /ævɪd/ ADJ You use **avid** to describe someone who is very enthusiastic about something that they do. 热切的 ❑ *He misses not having enough books because he's an avid reader.* 他遗憾没有足够的书，因为他是一个热爱读书的人。 ● **av·id·ly** ADV 热切地 [ADV with v] ❑ *Thank you for a most entertaining magazine, which I read avidly each month.* 感谢你们出了这本极为有趣的杂志，我每个月都如饥似渴地读它。

avo·ca·do /ævəkɑdoʊ/ (**avocados**)

in BRIT, also use **avocado pear**

N-VAR **Avocados** are pear-shaped vegetables, with hard skins and large seeds, which are usually eaten raw. 鳄梨

avo·ca·do pear [BRIT] → see **avocado**

avoid ♦♦◊ /əvɔɪd/ (**avoids, avoiding, avoided**) 1 V-T If you **avoid** something unpleasant that might happen, you take action in order to prevent it from happening. 避免（坏事的发生） ❑ *The pilots had to take emergency action to avoid a disaster.* 飞行员们不得不采取紧急措施以避免灾难的发生。 2 V-T If you **avoid** doing something, you choose not to do it, or you put yourself in a situation where you do not have to do it. 避免 ❑ *By borrowing from dozens of banks, he managed to avoid giving any of them an overall picture of what he was up to.* 通过向几十家银行借钱，他得以避免让任何一家了解他要做事情的全貌。 3 V-T If you **avoid** a person or thing, you keep away from them. When talking to someone, if you **avoid** the subject, you keep the conversation away from a particular topic. 避开 ❑ *She eventually had to lock herself in the women's restroom to avoid him.* 她最后不得不把自己锁在女厕所里避开他。 4 V-T If a person or vehicle **avoids** someone or something, they change the direction they are moving in, so that they do not hit them. （人或车）避让 ❑ *The driver had ample time to brake or swerve and avoid the woman.* 该司机有足够的时间刹车或急转来避让那女子。

Thesaurus	*avoid* 另参见：
V.	abstain, bypass, evade, shun; (*ant.*) confront, embrace, face, seek 1 – 3

★ **avoid·ance** /əvɔɪdəns/ N-UNCOUNT **Avoidance of** someone or something is the act of avoiding them. 避免 [usu N "of" n] ❑ *...the avoidance of stress.* …对压力的避免。

await ♦◊◊ /əweɪt/ (**awaits, awaiting, awaited**) 1 V-T If you **await** someone or something, you wait for them. 等候 [FORMAL] ❑ *Very little was said as we awaited the arrival of the chairman.* 我们在等候主席的到来时几乎没说什么话。 2 V-T Something that **awaits** you is going to happen or come to you in the future. 将发生在…身上 [FORMAL] ❑ *A surprise awaited them in Wal-Mart.* 一件意想不到的事情正在沃尔玛里等待着他们。

Thesaurus	*await* 另参见：
V.	anticipate, count on, expect, hope 1

Word Link *wak ≈ being awake : awake, awakening, wake*

awake /əweɪk/ 1 ADJ Someone who is **awake** is not sleeping. 醒着的 [v-link ADJ, ADJ after v] ❑ *I don't stay awake at night worrying about that.* 我才不会彻夜不眠为那事儿担心呢。 2 PHRASE Someone who is **wide awake** is fully awake and unable to sleep. 毫无睡意的 ❑ *I could not relax and still felt wide awake.* 我不能放松下来，仍然觉得没有一点儿睡意。

→ see **dream, sleep**

Word Partnership	*awake* 的常用搭配：
V.	**keep** *someone* awake, **lie** awake, **stay** awake 1
ADV.	**fully** awake, **half** awake 1
	wide awake 2

awak·en·ing /əweɪkənɪŋ/ (**awakenings**) 1 N-COUNT The **awakening** of a feeling or realization is the start of it. 觉醒 ❑ *...the awakening of national consciousness in people.* …人民民族意识的觉醒。 2 PHRASE If you have a **rude awakening**, you are suddenly made aware of an unpleasant fact. （对不愉快事情）猛然醒悟 ❑ *It was a rude awakening to learn after I left home that I wasn't so special anymore.* 离家之后我猛然醒悟到自己不再那么特殊了。

award ♦♦◊ /əwɔrd/ (**awards, awarding, awarded**) 1 N-COUNT An **award** is a prize or certificate that a person is given for doing something well. 奖 ❑ *The Institute's annual award is presented to organizations that are dedicated to democracy and human rights.* 该协会的年度奖授予致力于民主与人权的组织。 2 N-COUNT In law, an **award** is a sum of money that a court decides should be given to someone. （赔偿金等的）裁定额 ❑ *...worker's compensation awards.* …工人的赔偿金裁定额。 3 V-T If someone **is awarded** something such as a prize or an examination mark, it is given to them. 被授予 ❑ *She was awarded the prize for both films.* 她因这两部电影而获奖。 4 V-T To **award** something **to** someone means to decide that it will be given to that person. 给予 ❑ *We have awarded the contract to a New York-based company.* 我们已经把这份合同给了一家总部设在纽约的公司。

Word Link *war ≈ watchful : aware, beware, wary*

aware ♦♦◊ /əwɛər/ 1 ADJ If you are **aware of** something, you know about it. 意识到…的 [v-link ADJ] ❑ *Smokers are well aware of the dangers to their own health.* 吸烟者们都很清楚吸烟对其自身健康的那些危害。 ❑ *He should have been aware of what his junior officers were*

A

doing. 他本该意识到自己部下在做什么。● **aware·ness** N-UNCOUNT 意识 ❑ *The 1980s brought an awareness of green issues.* 20世纪80年代有了环保意识。 2 ADJ If you are **aware of** something, you realize that it is present or is happening because you hear it, see it, smell it, or feel it. 感受到…的 [v-link ADJ] ❑ *She was acutely aware of the noise of the city.* 她敏锐地感受到了城市的噪音。 ❑ *Jane was suddenly aware that she was digging her nails into her thigh.* 简突然意识到她正在把指甲戳进大腿。 3 ADJ Someone who is **aware** notices what is happening around them or happening in the place where they live. 察觉的 ❑ *They are politically very aware.* 他们在政治上很明白。● **aware·ness** N-UNCOUNT 意识 ❑ *He introduced radio to the school to increase the children's awareness.* 他在学校连接了无线电广播，以提高孩子们的意识。

Word Partnership *aware* 的常用搭配：
ADV. **acutely/vaguely** aware, **fully** aware, **painfully** aware, **well** aware 1 2
V. **become** aware 1 2
PREP. aware **of *someone/something***, aware **that** 1 2

awash /əwɒʃ/ 1 ADJ If a place is **awash with** something, it contains a large amount of it. 有大量…的 [v-link ADJ] ❑ *This is a company that is awash with cash.* 这是一家有大量现金的公司。 2 ADJ If the ground or a floor is **awash**, it is covered in water, often because of heavy rain or as the result of an accident. 被水覆盖的 [v-link ADJ] ❑ *The bathroom floor was awash.* 浴室地板浸在水中。

away ◆◆◆ /əweɪ/

Away is often used with verbs of movement, such as "go" and "drive," and also in phrasal verbs such as "do away with" and "fade away."

1 ADV If someone or something moves or is moved **away from** a place, they move or are moved so that they are no longer there. If you are **away from** a place, you are not in the place where people expect you to be. 离开 ❑ *An injured policeman was led away by colleagues.* 一位受伤的警察被同事们带走了。 ❑ *He walked away from his car.* 他从他的车边走开了。 ❑ *Jason was away on a business trip.* 贾森出差在外。 2 ADV If you look or turn **away from** something, you move your head so that you are no longer looking at it. (目光)移开地 ❑ *She quickly looked away and stared down at her hands.* 她迅速转移目光，低头盯着自己的双手。 3 ADV If you put something **away**, you put it where it should be. If you hide someone or something **away**, you put them in a place where nobody can see them or find them. (收藏) 好 [ADV after v] ❑ *I put my journal away and prepared for bed.* 我把日记收好，准备睡觉。 ❑ *All her letters were carefully filed away in folders.* 她所有的信件都被仔细地归档在文件夹里。 4 ADV You use **away** to talk about future events. For example, if an event is a week **away**, it will happen after a week. 距离 (某事件的时间) ["be" amount ADV] ❑ *...the Washington summit, now only just over two weeks away.* …现在离华盛顿峰会的召开只有两个多星期。 5 ADV When a sports team plays **away**, it plays on its opponents' playing court or field. (比赛) 在客场地 [ADV after v] ❑ *...a sensational 4-3 victory for the team playing away.* …该队在客场4-3轰动性的胜利。● ADJ **Away** is also an adjective. 客场的 [ADJ n] ❑ *Pittsburgh is about to play an important away game.* 匹兹堡队将要打一场重要的客场比赛。 6 ADV You can use **away** to say that something slowly disappears, becomes less significant, or changes so that it is no longer the same. 渐逝地 [ADV after v] ❑ *So much snow has already melted away.* 那么多雪已经逐渐融化掉了。 ❑ *His voice died away in a whisper.* 他的声音渐渐放低成了耳语。 7 ADV You use **away** to show that there has been a change or development from one state or situation to another. 变化发展地 ❑ *British courts are increasingly moving away from sending young offenders to prison.* 英国法庭逐渐地不再将犯法的年轻人送进监狱。 8 ADV You can use **away** to emphasize a continuous or repeated action. 持续不断地 [ADV after v] [EMPHASIS] ❑ *He would often be working away on his word processor late into the night.* 他经常会在他的文字处理机上持续工作到深夜。 9 ADV You use **away** to show that something is removed. 拿走 [ADV after v] ❑ *If you take my work away I can't be happy anymore.* 如果你带走了我的工作，那我就再也高兴不起来了。 10 PHRASE If something is **away from** a person or place, it is at a distance from that person or place. 离 (某人或某地) 一段距离 ❑ *The two women were sitting as far away from each other as possible.* 那两个女人坐得离对方尽可能地远。 11 **right away** → see **right**

Word Partnership *away* 的常用搭配：
V. **back** away, **blow** away, **break** away, **chase *someone*** away, **drive** away, **hide** away, **move** away, **walk** away 1
get away, **go** away 1 6
stay away 1 9 10
look/turn away 2
put away, **throw** away 3
pull/take/wash *something* away 6
ADJ. **far** away 1 4 10
N. away **from home** 1 10

▲ **awe** /ɔ/ (**awes, awed**) 1 N-UNCOUNT **Awe** is the feeling of respect and amazement that you have when you are faced with something wonderful and often rather frightening. 敬畏 ❑ *She gazed in awe at the great stones.* 她敬畏地凝视着那些巨石。 2 V-T If you **are awed by** someone or something, they make you feel respectful and amazed, though often rather frightened. 对…感到敬畏 [usu passive, no cont] ❑ *I am still awed by David's courage.* 我依然对戴维的勇气感到敬佩。

Word Link *some* ≈ *causing* : *awesome, fearsome, troublesome*

★ **awe·some** /ɔsəm/ 1 ADJ An **awesome** person or thing is very impressive and often frightening. 令人畏惧的 ❑ *...the awesome responsibility of sending men into combat.* …派士兵去打仗的令人畏惧的责任。 2 ADJ If you describe someone or something as **awesome**, you are emphasizing that you think that they are very impressive or extraordinary. 棒极了的 [INFORMAL, EMPHASIS] ❑ *Melvill called the flight "mind-blowing" and "awesome."* 梅尔维尔说这次飞行令人"无比兴奋"、"棒极了"。

aw·ful ◆◇◇ /ɔfəl/ 1 ADJ If you say that someone or something is **awful**, you dislike that person or thing or you think that they are not very good. 令人讨厌的 ❑ *We met and I thought he was awful.* 我们见了面，我觉得他令人讨厌。 ❑ *...an awful smell of paint.* …一股难闻的油漆味。 ❑ *Even if the weather's awful there's lots to do.* 即使天气很恶劣也有很多事做。 ❑ *Jeans look awful on me.* 我穿牛仔裤很难看。 2 ADJ If you say that something is **awful**, you mean that it is extremely unpleasant, shocking, or bad. 糟透的 ❑ *Her injuries were massive. It was awful.* 她的伤势很严重，糟透了。 3 ADJ If you look or feel **awful**, you look or feel ill. 难受的 [v-link ADJ] ❑ *I hardly slept at all and felt pretty awful.* 我几乎没睡，感觉挺难受。 4 ADJ You can use **awful** with noun groups that refer to an amount in order to emphasize how large that amount is. 极度的 [ADJ n] [EMPHASIS] ❑ *I've got an awful lot of work to do.* 我有极多的工作要做。● **aw·ful·ly** ADV 极度地 ❑ *The caramel looks awfully good.* 这种黄油奶糖看上去棒极了。

Thesaurus *awful* 另参见：
ADJ. bad, dreadful, horrible, terrible; *(ant.)* good, nice, pleasing 1 2

awhile /əwaɪl/ ADV **Awhile** means for a short time. 一会儿 ❑ *He worked awhile as a pharmacist in Cincinnati.* 他在辛辛那提做了一阵子的药剂师。

awk·ward /ɔkwərd/ 1 ADJ An **awkward** situation is embarrassing and difficult to deal with. 令人尴尬的 ❑ *I was the first to ask him awkward questions but there'll be harder ones to come.* 我是第一个问他尴尬问题的人，但后面还会有更棘手的问题。● **awk·ward·ly** ADV 令人尴尬地 [ADV adj/-ed] ❑ *There was an awkwardly long silence.* 有一段令人尴尬的长时间的沉默。 2 ADJ Something that is **awkward to** use or carry is difficult to use or carry because of its design. A job that is **awkward** is difficult to do. (使用) 不便的；棘手的 (工作) ❑ *It was small but heavy enough to make it awkward to carry.* 它虽然小，却沉重得不便携带。● **awk·ward·ly** ADV 不便地；棘手地 [ADV -ed] ❑ *The front window switches are awkwardly placed on the dashboard.* 前窗的开关安装在仪表板上，使用不便。 3 ADJ An **awkward** movement or position is uncomfortable or clumsy. 笨拙的 ❑ *Amy made an awkward gesture with her hands.* 艾米用双手做了一个笨拙的手势。● **awk·ward·ly** ADV 笨拙地 [ADV with v] ❑ *He fell awkwardly and went down in agony clutching his right knee.* 他笨拙地摔倒了，紧抓住右膝盖痛苦地蹲了下去。 4 ADJ Someone who feels **awkward** behaves in a shy or embarrassed way. 难为情的 ❑ *Women frequently say that they feel awkward taking the initiative in sex.* 女性经常说她们觉得在性方面采取主动令人难为情。● **awk·ward·ly** ADV 难为情地 [ADV with v] ❑ *"This is Malcolm," the girl said awkwardly, to fill the silence.* "这是马尔科姆，"女孩子为了打破沉默难为情地说道。

Thesaurus *awkward* 另参见:

ADJ. delicate, embarrassing, sticky, uncomfortable 1
bulky, cumbersome, difficult 2
blundering, bumbling, uncoordinated, ungraceful 3

awoke /əwo͟ʊk/ **Awoke** is the past tense of **awake**. **awake**的过去式

awok·en /əwo͟ʊkən/ **Awoken** is the past participle of **awake**. **awake**的过去分词

ax /æks/ (**axes, axing, axed**)

in BRIT, and sometimes in AM, use **axe**

1 N-COUNT An **ax** is a tool used for cutting wood. It consists of a heavy metal blade that is sharp at one edge and attached by its other edge to the end of a long handle. 斧子 2 V-T If someone's job or something such as a public service or a television program **is axed**, it is ended suddenly and without discussion. 被砍掉 [usu passive] ❑ *Community projects are being axed by hard-pressed social services departments.* 社区项目正遭到受困社会服务部门的削减。

axe /æks/ [BRIT] → see **ax**

axes

Pronounced /æksɪz/ for meaning 1, and /æksiz/ for meaning 2.

义项1读作 /æksɪz/，义项2读作 /æksiz/。

1 **Axes** is the plural of **ax**. **ax**的复数形式 2 **Axes** is the plural of **axis**. **axis**的复数形式

★ **axis** /æksɪs/ (**axes**) 1 N-COUNT An **axis** is an imaginary line through the middle of something. 轴 ❑ *...the tilt of the Earth's axis.* …地轴的倾斜。 2 N-COUNT An **axis** of a graph is one of the two lines on which the scales of measurement are marked. 坐标轴 ❑ *The level of spiritual achievement is plotted along the Y axis, and the degree of physical health is plotted along the X axis.* 精神成就水平沿Y轴标出，身体健康程度沿X轴标出。

→ see **graph, moon**

Bb

B also **b** /bi̲/ **(B's, b's)** N-VAR **B** is the second letter of the English alphabet. 英语字母表中的第2个字母

B2B /bi̲ tə bi̲/ N-UNCOUNT **B2B** is the selling of goods and services by one company to another using the Internet. **B2B** is an abbreviation for "business to business." 企业间电子商务 [BUSINESS] ❑ *American analysts have been somewhat cautious in estimating the size of the B2B market.* 美国分析家们对评估企业间电子商务的市场规模颇为谨慎。

B2C /bi̲ tə si̲/ N-UNCOUNT **B2C** is the selling of goods and services by businesses to consumers using the Internet. **B2C** is an abbreviation for "business to consumer." 企业对消费者的电子商务 [BUSINESS] ❑ *B2C companies look particularly vulnerable with 19 per cent of them now worth little more than the cash on their balance sheets.* 面向消费者的网络直销公司看上去尤为脆弱，它们其中有19%的公司价值现在不比其资产负债表上的现金额多多少。

bab·ble /bæbᵊl/ **(babbles, babbling, babbled)** **1** V-I If someone **babbles**, they talk in a confused or excited way. 含糊不清地说；兴奋地说 ❑ *Momma babbled on and on about how he was ruining me.* 妈妈喋喋不休地数说他在如何毁我。 ❑ *They all babbled simultaneously.* 他们全都异口同声地唧唧喳喳起来。 **2** N-SING You can refer to people's voices as a **babble of** sound when they are excited and confused, preventing you from understanding what they are saying. 嘈杂的说话声 ❑ *Kemp knocked loudly so as to be heard above the high babble of voices.* 肯普大声地敲门，以压过唧唧喳喳的高声喧哗而让人听见。

baby ♦♦◊ /be̲ɪbi/ **(babies)** **1** N-COUNT A **baby** is a very young child, especially one that cannot yet walk or talk. 婴儿 ❑ *She used to take care of me when I was a baby.* 她曾在我还是婴儿的时候照看过我。 ❑ *My wife has just had a baby.* 我妻子刚生小孩。 **2** N-COUNT A **baby** animal is a very young animal. 幼崽 [usu N n] ❑ *...a baby elephant.* …一头幼象。 **3** N-COUNT If you refer to someone as a **baby**, you mean that they are behaving in a cowardly way or they are being too sensitive about something. 孩子气的人 [DISAPPROVAL] ❑ *I know he's an ex-champion boxer, but he can be a big baby sometimes! He hates spiders.* 我知道他是前拳击冠军，但有时他像个大孩子！他怕蜘蛛。 **4** ADJ **Baby** vegetables are vegetables picked when they are very small. (蔬菜) 小的 [ADJ n] ❑ *Cook the baby potatoes in their skins.* 把这些小土豆连皮煮。 **5** N-VOC, N-COUNT Some people use **baby** as an affectionate way of addressing someone, especially a young woman, or referring to them. 宝贝儿 (尤用于称呼年轻姑娘) [INFORMAL] ❑ *You have to wake up now, baby.* 你现在得醒了，宝贝儿。
→ see **child**

Word Partnership	*baby* 的常用搭配:
N.	baby **boy/girl/sister**, baby **clothes**, baby **food**, baby **names**, baby **talk** **1**
V.	**deliver a** baby, **have a** baby **1**
ADJ.	**new/newborn** baby, **unborn** baby **1**

baby car·riage **(baby carriages)** N-COUNT A **baby carriage** is a small vehicle in which a baby can lie as it is pushed along. 婴儿车 [AM]
in BRIT, use **pram**

baby·sit /be̲ɪbisɪt/ **(babysits, babysitting, babysat)** V-T/V-I If you **babysit for** someone or **babysit** their children, you look after their children while they are out. 代人临时照看 (别人的孩子)；代人临时照看小孩 ❑ *I promised to babysit for Mrs. Plunkett.* 我答应了为普伦基特太太临时照看孩子。 ❑ *She had been babysitting him and his four-year-old sister.* 她曾一直代为临时照看他和他4岁的妹妹。
● **baby·sitter** N-COUNT 临时保姆 ❑ *It can be difficult to find a good babysitter.* 可能难以找到一个好的临时保姆。

bach·elor /bætʃələr/ **(bachelors)** N-COUNT A **bachelor** is a man who has never married. 单身汉 ❑ *...America's most eligible bachelor.* …美国最适合做夫婿的单身汉。
→ see **wedding**

back
1 ADVERB USES
2 OPPOSITE OF FRONT; NOUN AND ADJECTIVE USES
3 VERB USES

1 **back** ♦♦♦ /bæk/

In addition to the uses shown below, **back** is also used in phrasal verbs such as "date back" and "fall back on."

➪ **Please look at meaning 17 to see if the expression you are looking for is shown under another headword.** **1** ADV If you move **back**, you move in the opposite direction to the one in which you are facing or in which you were moving before. 向后 ❑ *She stepped back from the door expectantly.* 她充满期待地从门口往后退。 ❑ *He pushed her away and she fell back on the wooden bench.* 他把她推开，然后她向后跌坐在长木椅上。 **2** ADV If you go **back** somewhere, you return to where you were before. 回到原处 ❑ *I went back to bed.* 我回到床上。 ❑ *I'll be back as soon as I can.* 我会尽快回来。 **3** ADV If someone or something is **back** in a particular state, they were in that state before and are now in it again. 恢复原状 ❑ *The rail company said it expected services to get slowly back to normal.* 铁路公司称，预计服务会慢慢恢复正常。 **4** ADV If you give or put something **back**, you return it to the person who had it or to the place where it was before you took it. If you get or take something **back**, you then have it again after not having it for a while. (放、取) 回 ❑ *She handed the knife back.* 她把小刀递了回去。 ❑ *Put it back in the freezer.* 把它放回到冰柜里。 **5** ADV If you put a clock or watch **back**, you change the time shown on it so that it shows an earlier time, for example, when the time changes to standard time. (将钟、表等拨) 回 [ADV after v] ❑ *The clocks go back at 2 o'clock tomorrow morning.* 钟明天早上往回拨到2点。 **6** ADV If you write or call **back**, you write to or telephone someone after they have written to or telephoned you. If you look **back** at someone, you look at them after they have started looking at you. 作为回复；往回 (望) ❑ *They wrote back to me and told me I didn't have to do it.* 他们给我回信告诉我不必做它。 ❑ *If the phone rings, say you'll call back after dinner.* 如果有电话，就说你晚饭后打回去。 **7** ADV You can say that you go or come **back to** a particular point in a conversation to show that you are mentioning or discussing it again. 回到 (先前谈论的地方) ❑ *Can I come back to the question of policing once again?* 我能回过头来再说说治安问题吗？ **8** ADV If something is or comes **back**, it is fashionable again after it has been unfashionable for some time. 再度 (流行) ❑ *Short skirts are back.* 短裙又流行起来了。 **9** ADV If someone or something is kept or situated **back from** a place, they are at a distance away from it. 在一段距离之外 ❑ *Keep back from the edge of the platform.* 请勿靠近站台边缘。 ❑ *I'm a few miles back from the border.* 我离边境有几英里远。 **10** ADV If something is held or tied **back**, it is held or tied so that it does not hang loosely over something. 收拢地 [ADV after v] ❑ *The curtains were held back by tassels.* 窗帘用流苏扎了起来。 **11** ADV If you lie or sit **back**, you move your body backward into a relaxed sloping or flat position, with your head and body resting on something. 后仰地；后靠地 [ADV after v] ❑ *She lay back and stared at the ceiling.* 她躺下来，盯着天花板。 **12** ADV If you look or shout **back** at someone or something, you turn to look or shout at them when they are behind you. 回头向后 (看或喊) ❑ *Nick looked back over his shoulder and then stopped, frowning.* 尼克扭过头朝后看，然后皱着眉头停了下来。 **13** ADV You use **back** in expressions like **back in Chicago** or **back at the house** when you are giving an account, to show that you are going to start talking about what happened or was happening in the place you mention. 在 (某地) ❑ *Meanwhile, back in Everett, Marc Fulmer is busy raising money to help get the project off the ground.* 此时在埃弗里特，马克·富尔默正忙着筹资来帮助该项目启动。

14 ADV If you talk about something that happened **back** in the past or several years **back**, you are emphasizing that it happened quite a long time ago. 早在 [EMPHASIS] ❑ *The story starts back in 1950, when I was five.* 这件事始于1950年，当时我5岁。 15 ADV If you think **back to** something that happened in the past, you remember it or try to remember it. 回(想) ❑ *I thought back to the time in 1975 when my son was desperately ill.* 我回想起1975年的时候，当时我儿子病得很重。 16 PHRASE If someone moves **back and forth**, they repeatedly move in one direction and then in the opposite direction. 来回地 ❑ *He paced back and forth.* 他来回踱步。 17 to **cast** your **mind back** → see **mind**

❷ **back** ♦♦♦ /bæk/ (**backs**)
➪ **Please look at meaning 12 to see if the expression you are looking for is shown under another headword.** 1 N-COUNT A person's or animal's **back** is the part of their body between their head and their legs that is on the opposite side to their chest and stomach. 背部 ❑ *Her son was lying peacefully on his back.* 她儿子正静静地仰面躺着。 ❑ *She turned her back to the audience.* 她转过身背对着观众。 2 N-COUNT The **back of** something is the side or part of it that is toward the rear or farthest from the front. The back of something is normally not used or seen as much as the front. 后面；后部 ❑ *...a room at the back of the shop.* …商店后部的一个房间。 ❑ *She raised her hands to the back of her neck.* 她把双手伸到后脖子上。 3 ADJ **Back** is used to refer to the side or part of something that is toward the rear or farthest from the front. 后面的；后部的 [ADJ n] ❑ *He opened the back door.* 他打开了后门。 ❑ *Ann could remember sitting in the back seat of their car.* 安能记得曾坐在他们车子的后座上。 4 N-COUNT The **back** of a chair or sofa is the part that you lean against when you sit on it. 靠背 ❑ *There was a pink sweater on the back of the chair.* 在椅背上有一件粉色毛线衫。 5 N-COUNT The **back** of something such as a piece of paper or an envelope is the side that is less important. (纸、信封等的) 背面 ❑ *Send your answers on the back of a postcard or sealed, empty envelope.* 把你的答案写在明信片或封好的空信封背面寄来。 6 N-COUNT The **back** of a book is the part nearest the end, where you can find the index or the notes, for example. (书的) 末尾 ❑ *The index at the back of the book lists both brand and generic names.* 书末尾的索引把商标名和通用名都列了出来。 7 N-UNCOUNT You use **out back** to refer to the area behind a house or other building. You also use **in back** to refer to the rear part of something, especially a car or building. (房屋等建筑物的) 后面；(车、建筑物等的) 后部 [AM] ❑ *Dan informed her that he would be out back on the patio cleaning his shoes.* 丹告诉她说，他要到后面露台上弄干净他的鞋子。 ❑ *...the trees in back of the building.* …大楼后面的树。 8 PHRASE If you say that something was done **behind** someone's **back**, you disapprove of it because it was done without them knowing about it, in an unfair or dishonest way. 背地里 [DISAPPROVAL] ❑ *You eat her food, enjoy her hospitality and then criticize her behind her back.* 你吃她的饭菜，享受她的热情款待，然后在背地里却批评她。 9 PHRASE If two or more things are done **back to back**, one follows immediately after the other without any interruption. 接连相继地 ❑ *...two half-hour shows, which will be screened back to back.* …将被相继播放的两场半小时的表演。 10 → see also **back-to-back** 11 PHRASE If you are wearing something **back to front**, you are wearing it with the back of it at the front of your body. If you do something **back to front**, you do it the wrong way around, starting with the part that should come last. (穿) 反；(做事) 首尾颠倒 [mainly BRIT]

in AM, usually use **backward**

12 to **take a back seat** → see **seat**
→ see **body**

❸ **back** ♦♦♦ /bæk/ (**backs, backing, backed**) 1 V-I If a building **backs onto** something, the back of it faces in the direction of that thing or touches the edge of that thing. (指建筑物) 背朝；背靠 ❑ *He lives in a loft that backs onto Friedman's Bar.* 他住在一间背朝弗里德曼酒吧的阁楼里。 2 V-T/V-I When you **back** a car or other vehicle somewhere or when it **backs** somewhere, it moves backward. 倒(车)；(车) 倒退 ❑ *He backed his car out of the drive.* 他把车倒出车道。 3 V-T If you **back** a person or a course of action, you support them, for example, by voting for them or giving them money. 支持 ❑ *His defense says it has found a new witness to back his claim that he is a victim of mistaken identity.* 他的辩词称已经找到一位新的证人来证实他是弄错了身份的受害者。 4 V-T If you **back** a particular person, team, or horse in a competition, you predict that they will win, and usually you bet money that they will win. 下赌注于 ❑ *She backed the Detroit Lions to beat the Chicago Bears by at least 20-10.* 她下注赌底特律狮队至少会以20-10击败芝加哥熊队。 5 V-T If a singer **is backed by** a band or by other singers, they provide the musical background for the singer. 为…伴奏；为…伴唱 [usu passive] ❑ *She chose to be backed by a classy trio of acoustic guitar, bass and congas.* 她选择了用原声吉他、低音吉他和康茄鼓组成的经典三重奏组合为自己伴奏。

▶ **back away** 1 PHRASAL VERB If you **back away from** a commitment that you made or something that you were involved with in the past, you try to show that you are no longer committed to it or involved with it. 放弃 ❑ *The company backed away from plans to cut their pay by 15%.* 该公司放弃了对他们减薪15%的方案。 2 PHRASAL VERB If you **back away**, you walk backward away from someone or something, often because you are frightened of them. (因害怕而) 后退；退缩 ❑ *James got to his feet and started to come over, but the girls hastily backed away.* 詹姆斯站起身，开始走过来，而女孩子们却慌忙后退。

▶ **back down** PHRASAL VERB If you **back down**, you withdraw a claim, demand, or commitment that you made earlier, because other people are strongly opposed to it. (因他人反对而) 放弃 ❑ *It's too late to back down now.* 现在打退堂鼓为时已晚。

▶ **back off** 1 PHRASAL VERB If you **back off**, you move away in order to avoid problems or a fight. 避开 (问题或争斗) ❑ *They backed off in horror.* 他们吓得躲开了。 2 PHRASAL VERB If you **back off from** a claim, demand, or commitment that you made earlier, or if you **back off** it, you withdraw it. 撤回 (原来的主张、要求、承诺) ❑ *A spokesman says the president has backed off from his threat to boycott the conference.* 一位发言人说，总统已经撤回了他抵制这次会谈的威胁。

▶ **back out** PHRASAL VERB If you **back out**, or if you **back out of** something, you decide not to do something that you previously agreed to do. 退出；变卦 ❑ *The Hungarians backed out of the project in 1989 on environmental grounds.* 匈牙利人在1989年以环境问题为由退出了该项目。

▶ **back up** 1 PHRASAL VERB If someone or something **backs up** a statement, they supply evidence to suggest that it is true. 证实 ❑ *Radio signals received from the galaxy's center back up the black hole theory.* 从该星系中心接收到的无线电信号证实了黑洞理论。 2 PHRASAL VERB If you **back up** a computer file, you make a copy of it that you can use if the original file is damaged or lost. 备份 [COMPUTING] ❑ *Make a point of backing up your files at regular intervals.* 要特别注意定期备份你的文档。 3 PHRASAL VERB If an idea or intention **is backed up** by action, action is taken to support or confirm it. (以行动) 支持 ❑ *The secretary general says the declaration must now be backed up by concrete and effective actions.* 秘书长说现在必须以具体有效的行动来支持这个宣言。 4 PHRASAL VERB If you **back** someone **up**, you show your support for them. 支持 (某人) ❑ *His employers backed him up.* 他的雇主们支持了他。 5 PHRASAL VERB If you **back** someone **up**, you help them by confirming that what they are saying is true. 证实…的话 ❑ *The girl denied being there, and the man backed her up.* 这女孩否认去过那儿，并且这位男子证实了她的话。 6 PHRASAL VERB If you **back up**, the car or other vehicle that you are driving moves back a short distance. 倒车 ❑ *Back up, Hans.* 倒车，汉斯。 7 PHRASAL VERB If you **back up**, you move backward a short distance. 后退 (一小段距离) ❑ *I backed up carefully until I felt the wall against my back.* 我小心翼翼地后退了几步，直到感觉到后背贴上了墙。 8 PHRASAL VERB When a car **backs up** or when you **back it up**, the car is driven backward. (车) 向后倒；倒 (车) [AM]

in BRIT, usually use **reverse**

9 → see also **backup**

back·bone /bækboʊn/ (**backbones**) 1 N-COUNT Your **backbone** is the column of small linked bones down the middle of your back. 脊骨 2 N-UNCOUNT If you say that someone has no **backbone**, you think that they do not have the courage to do things which need to be done. 骨气 [oft with brd-neg] ❑ *You might be taking drastic measures and you've got to have the backbone to do that.* 你可能在采取极端措施，而且你得有骨气做它。

back·date /bækdeɪt/ (**backdates, backdating, backdated**) also **back-date** V-T If a document or an arrangement **is backdated**, it is valid from a date before the date when it is completed or signed. (实际生效日) 追溯到 ❑ *The contract that was signed on Thursday morning was backdated to March 11.* 星期四上午所签的合同从3月11日起生效。

back·er /bækər/ (**backers**) N-COUNT A **backer** is someone who helps or supports a project, organization, or person, often by giving or lending money. 赞助人 ❑ *I was looking for a backer to assist*

b

me in the attempted buyout. 我当时正在寻找一位赞助人来帮助我进行这次全面收购。

back·fire /bækfaɪər/ (**backfires, backfiring, backfired**) **1** V-I If a plan or project **backfires**, it has the opposite result to the one that was intended. 事与愿违 ❑ *The president's tactics could backfire.* 总统的策略可能会事与愿违。 **2** V-I When a motor vehicle or its engine **backfires**, it produces an explosion in the exhaust pipe. (机动车或引擎) 回火 ❑ *The car backfired.* 这辆车回火了。

Word Link *ground ≈ bottom : background, grounding, groundwork*

back·ground ♦◇◇ /bækgraʊnd/ (**backgrounds**) **1** N-COUNT Your **background** is the kind of family you come from and the kind of education you have had. It can also refer to such things as your social and racial origins, your financial status, or the type of work experience that you have. (家庭、职业) 出身 ❑ *The Warners were from a Jewish working-class background.* 沃纳一家人是犹太工人阶级出身。 **2** N-COUNT The **background** to an event or situation consists of the facts that explain what caused it. 背景 ❑ *The background to the current troubles is provided by the dire state of the country's economy.* 目前这些问题的背景是严峻的国家经济形势。 ❑ *The meeting takes place against a background of continuing political violence.* 这次会议是在持续的政治暴力背景下召开的。 **3** N-SING **The background** is sounds, such as music, that you can hear but that you are not listening to with your full attention. 背景声音 ❑ *I kept hearing the sound of applause in the background.* 我不断听到背景音中有掌声。 **4** N-COUNT You can use **background** to refer to the things in a picture or scene that are less noticeable or important than the main things or people in it. (图画、布景等的) 背景 ❑ *...roses patterned on a blue background.* …印在蓝色背景上的玫瑰。

Word Partnership *background* 的常用搭配:

ADJ.	**cultural/ethnic/family** background, **educational** background **1**
N.	background **check** **1**
	background **information/knowledge** **1** **2**
	background **story** **2**
	background **music/noise** **3**
PREP.	**in the** background **3** **4**
	against a background **4**
V.	**blend into the** background **4**

back·ing ♦◇◇ /bækɪŋ/ (**backings**) **1** N-UNCOUNT If someone has the **backing of** an organization or an important person, they receive support or money from that organization or person in order to do something. 支持; 资助 ❑ *He said the president had the full backing of his government to negotiate a deal.* 他说总统得到了他的政府的全力支持来交涉一份协议。 **2** N-VAR A **backing** is a layer of something such as cloth that is put onto the back of something in order to strengthen or protect it. 背衬 ❑ *The table mats and coasters have a non-slip, soft green backing.* 这些桌垫和杯垫下都有一层绿色防滑软衬。

back·lash /bæklæʃ/ N-SING A **backlash against** a tendency or recent development in society or politics is a sudden, strong reaction against it. (对政治或社会变化的) 强烈反应 ❑ *...the male backlash against feminism.* …男性对女权主义的强烈反应。

back·log /bæklɔg/ (**backlogs**) N-COUNT A **backlog** is a number of things which have not yet been done but which need to be done. 积压待办的事务 ❑ *There is a backlog of repairs and maintenance in schools.* 学校里有积压下来等待处理的维修和养护工作。

back pay N-UNCOUNT **Back pay** is money which an employer owes an employee for work that he or she did in the past. 欠薪 [BUSINESS] ❑ *He will receive $6,000 in back pay.* 他将收到$6000的欠薪。

back·side /bæksaɪd/ (**backsides**) N-COUNT Your **backside** is the part of your body that you sit on. 屁股 [INFORMAL] ❑ *The lad fell backwards, landing on his backside.* 那个男孩向后倒下去，屁股着地。

back·stage /bæksteɪdʒ/ ADV In a theater, **backstage** refers to the areas behind the stage. 在后台 [ADV after v] ❑ *He went backstage and asked for her autograph.* 他到后台去请她签名。 ● ADJ **Backstage** is also an adjective. 后台的 [ADJ n] ❑ *...a backstage pass.* …一张后台通行证。
→ see **theater**

back·stroke /bækstroʊk/ N-UNCOUNT **Backstroke** is a swimming stroke that you do lying on your back. 仰泳 [also "the" N] ❑ *"I see you know how to swim very well," she said, watching him do the backstroke.* "看来你很会游泳啊"，她一边说一边看他仰泳。

back·up /bækʌp/ (**backups**) also **back-up** **1** N-VAR **Backup** consists of extra equipment, resources, or people that you can get help or support from if necessary. 后备 (设备、物资或人力) ❑ *There is no emergency back-up immediately available.* 没有立即就能获得的后备。 **2** N-VAR If you have something such as a second piece of equipment or set of plans as **backup**, you have arranged for them to be available for use in case the first one does not work. 备用物 (如设备、计划) ❑ *Every part of the system has a backup.* 这套系统的每个部分都有备件。 **3** N-COUNT The **backup** of a song is the music that is sung or played to accompany the main tune. 伴奏; 伴唱 ❑ *Sharon also sang backup for Barry Manilow.* 莎伦还为巴里·马尼洛伴唱了伴唱。 **4** N-COUNT A **backup** is a long line of traffic stretching back along a road, which moves very slowly or not at all, for example, because of roadwork or an accident. (拥堵造成的) 汽车长龙 [AM] ❑ *There was a seven-mile backup on the freeway* 在高速公路上有7英里的汽车长龙。

in BRIT, use **tailback**

→ see **concert**

Word Link *ward ≈ in the direction of : backward, forward, inward*

back·ward /bækwərd/

In British English, **backwards** is much more common than **backward** when used as an adverb.

1 ADJ A **backward** movement or look is in the direction that your back is facing. 向后的 [ADJ n] ❑ *He unlocked the door of apartment two and disappeared inside after a backward glance at Larry.* 他打开2号公寓的门锁，向后瞥了拉里一眼之后走进去就不见了。 **2** ADJ If someone takes a **backward** step or a step **backward**, they do something that does not change or improve their situation, but causes them to go back a stage. 退步的 ❑ *The current U.S. farm bill, however, is a big step backward.* 然而，目前的美国农业法却倒退了一大步。 **3** ADJ A **backward** country or society does not have modern industries and machines. 落后的 ❑ *We need to accelerate the pace of change in our backward country.* 我们需要在我们这个落后的国家加快变革的步伐。 **4** ADJ A **backward** child has difficulty in learning. (后进的) 学习 [OFFENSIVE] ❑ *...research into teaching techniques to help backward children.* …对帮助后进生的教学技巧的研究。 **5** ADV If you move or look **backward**, you move or look in the direction that your back is facing. 向后 [ADV after v] ❑ *The diver flipped over backward into the water.* 跳水运动员向后翻转跳入水中。 ❑ *He took two steps backward.* 他往后退了两步。 **6** ADV If you do something **backward**, you do it in the opposite way to the usual way. 倒着地 [ADV after v] ❑ *He works backward, building a house from the top downward.* 他倒着干活，从上往下盖房子。 **7** ADV You use **backward** to indicate that something changes or develops in a way that is not an improvement, but is a return to old ideas or methods. 倒退地 ❑ *This country is going backward.* 这个国家正在倒退。 **8** PHRASE If someone or something moves **backward and forward**, they move repeatedly first in one direction and then in the opposite direction. 来回地 ❑ *Using a gentle, sawing motion, draw the floss backward and forward between the teeth.* 用轻柔的拉锯的动作把牙线在牙齿间来回拉动。

back·wards /bækwərdz/ → see **backward**

back·water /bækwɔtər/ (**backwaters**) **1** N-COUNT A **backwater** is a place that is isolated. 荒僻处 ❑ *...a quiet rural backwater.* …一处宁静的乡下偏僻之地。 **2** N-COUNT If you refer to a place or institution as a **backwater**, you think it is not developing properly because it is isolated from ideas and events in other places and institutions. 闭塞落后的地方 [DISAPPROVAL] ❑ *The state's high schools remain an educational backwater where dropout rates are rising.* 该州的高中仍旧是教育封闭落后之所，辍学率在上升。 ❑ *This agency will be relegated to the backwaters of Washington.* 这个机构将被移到华盛顿闭塞落后的地方。

back·yard /bækyɑrd/ (**backyards**) also **back yard** **1** N-COUNT A **backyard** is an area of land at the back of a house. 后院 **2** N-COUNT If you refer to a country's own **backyard**, you are referring to its own territory or to somewhere that is very close and where that country wants to influence events. (国家的) 后院 ❑ *They seem to think that if it isn't happening in their own backyard, it isn't worth worrying about.* 他们似乎认为，如果事情不是发生在他们本国的后院，就不值得担心。

ba·con /beɪkən/ N-UNCOUNT **Bacon** is salted or smoked meat which comes from the back or sides of a pig. 腌猪肉; 熏猪肉 ❑ *...bacon and eggs.* …腌猪肉和鸡蛋。

bac·te·ria /bæktɪəriə/ N-PLURAL **Bacteria** are very small organisms. Some bacteria can cause disease. 细菌 ❑ *Chlorine is added to kill bacteria.* 加入氯以杀菌。

→ see **can**

bac·te·rial /bæktɪəriəl/ ADJ **Bacterial** is used to describe things that relate to or are caused by bacteria. 细菌的; 细菌引起的 [ADJ n] ❑ *Cholera is a bacterial infection.* 霍乱是一种由细菌引起的感染。

bac·te·ri·ol·ogy /bæktɪəriɒlədʒi/ N-UNCOUNT **Bacteriology** is the science and the study of bacteria. 细菌学 ● **bac·te·rio·logi·cal** /bæktɪəriəlɒdʒɪkəl/ ADJ 细菌学的 [ADJ n] ❑ *...the national bacteriological laboratory.* …国家细菌学实验室。

bad ♦♦♦ /bæd/ (**worse, worst**)

> In meaning 9, the comparative form is **badder** and the superlative form is **baddest**.

1 ADJ Something that is **bad** is unpleasant, harmful, or undesirable. 坏的 ❑ *The bad weather conditions prevented the plane from landing.* 恶劣的天气使飞机无法着陆。 ❑ *Divorce is bad for children.* 离婚对孩子不好。 2 ADJ You use **bad** to indicate that something unpleasant or undesirable is severe or great in degree. 严重的 ❑ *Glick had a bad accident two years ago and had to give up farming.* 格利克两年前遭遇了一次严重事故，不得不放弃务农。 ❑ *The floods are described as the worst in nearly fifty years.* 这场洪水被描述为差不多五十年来最严重的一次。 3 ADJ A **bad** idea, decision, or method is not sensible or not correct. 糟糕的; 错误的 ❑ *Giving your address to a man you don't know is a bad idea.* 把你的地址告诉一个你不认识的男人是个坏主意。 ❑ *The worst thing you can do is underestimate an opponent.* 最糟的做法就是低估对手。 4 ADJ If you describe a piece of news, an action, or a sign as **bad**, you mean that it is unlikely to result in benefit or success. 不利的 ❑ *The closure of the project is bad news for her staff.* 该项目的结束对她的员工来说是个坏消息。 ❑ *It was a bad start in my relationship with Warr.* 这对我和沃尔的关系是个不好的开端。 5 ADJ Something that is **bad** is of an unacceptably low standard, quality, or amount. 低劣的 ❑ *Many old people in the United States are living in bad housing.* 在美国的许多老年人住房条件恶劣。 ❑ *The schools' main problem is that teachers' pay is so bad.* 这些学校的主要问题是教师的工资太低。 6 ADJ Someone who is **bad at** doing something is not skillful or successful at it. 不擅长的 ❑ *Howard was so bad at basketball.* 霍华德篮球打得真臭。 ❑ *He was a bad driver.* 他是个烂司机。 7 ADJ If you say that it is **bad** that something happens, you mean it is unacceptable, unfortunate, or wrong. 糟糕的; 不幸的; 错的 ❑ *Not being able to hear doesn't seem as bad to the rest of us as not being able to see.* 对我们其他人来说，听不见似乎不像看不见那么糟。 8 ADJ You can say that something is **not bad** to mean that it is quite good or acceptable, especially when you are rather surprised about this. 很好的 (与not同用) [with neg] ❑ *"How much is he paying you?"—"Oh, five thousand."—"Not bad."* "他付你多少工资？" —— "哦，5千。" —— "还不错。" ❑ *That's not a bad idea.* 那个主意不错。 9 ADJ If you describe someone or something as **bad**, you mean that they are very good. 非常好的 [usu ADJ n] [INFORMAL] ❑ *...the baddest bass music from Miami, featuring Dr. Boom & The Dominator.* …来自迈阿密最棒的以霸主布姆博士为代表的低音音乐。 10 ADJ A **bad** person has morally unacceptable attitudes and behavior. (指人) 恶的 ❑ *I was selling drugs, but I didn't think I was a bad person.* 我卖毒品，但我不认为自己是坏人。 11 ADJ A **bad** child disobeys rules and instructions or does not behave in a polite and correct way. 不听话的; 没规矩的 ❑ *You are a bad boy for repeating what I told you.* 你是个没规矩的男孩，重复我对你讲的话。 12 ADJ If you are in a **bad** mood, you are angry and behave unpleasantly to people. (情绪) 糟的 ❑ *She is in a bit of a bad mood because she's just given up smoking.* 因为刚戒烟，她心情有点糟。 13 ADJ If you **feel bad about** something, you feel sorry or guilty about it. 内疚的 ❑ *You don't have to feel bad about relaxing.* 你不必因休息而感到内疚。 ❑ *I feel bad that he's doing most of the work.* 让我感到愧疚的是，他在做大部分的工作。 14 ADJ If you have a **bad** back, heart, leg, or eye, it is injured, diseased, or weak. (身体某部位) 不适的 ❑ *Joe has a bad back so we have a hard bed.* 乔背不好，所以我们睡硬板床。 15 ADJ Food that has **gone bad** is not suitable to eat because it has started to decay. 变质的 ❑ *They bought so much beef that some went bad.* 他们买了这么多牛肉，有些都变质了。 16 ADJ **Bad** language is language that contains offensive words such as swear words. (语言) 带脏字的 ❑ *I don't like to hear bad language in the street.* 我不喜欢听大街上的脏话。 17 → see also **worse, worst** 18 **bad blood** → see **blood** 19 **bad luck** → see **luck** 20 to **get a bad press** → see **press**

> **Thesaurus** bad 另参见:
>
> ADJ. damaging, dangerous, harmful; *(ant.)* good 1
> inferior, poor, unsatisfactory; *(ant.)* acceptable, good, satisfactory 5 6
> disobedient, naughty; *(ant.)* nice, obedient, well-behaved 11
> rancid, rotten, spoiled; *(ant.)* fresh, good 15

bad debt (**bad debts**) N-COUNT A **bad debt** is a sum of money that has been lent but is not likely to be repaid. 坏账 ❑ *The bank set aside 1.1 billion dollars to cover bad debts from business failures.* 银行留出11亿美元来支付生意失败导致的坏账。

badge /bædʒ/ (**badges**) 1 N-COUNT A **badge** is a piece of metal, cloth or plastic which you wear or carry to show that you work for a particular organization, or that you have achieved something. (表明身份的) 徽章 ❑ *...a police officer's badge.* …警官的徽章。 2 N-COUNT A **badge** is a small piece of metal or plastic which you wear in order to show that you support a particular movement, organization, or person. You fasten a badge to your clothes with a pin. (表明支持对象的) 徽章 [BRIT]

> in AM, use **button**

badg·er /bædʒər/ (**badgers, badgering, badgered**) 1 N-COUNT A **badger** is a wild animal which has a white head with two wide black stripes on it. Badgers live underground and usually come up to feed at night. 獾 2 V-T If you **badger** someone, you repeatedly tell them to do something or repeatedly ask them questions. 纠缠 ❑ *She badgered her doctor time and again, pleading with him to do something.* 她一再纠缠医生，恳求他做点什么。 ❑ *They kept phoning and writing, badgering me to go back.* 他们不断打电话、写信，缠着要我回去。

bad·ly ♦◇◇ /bædli/ (**worse, worst**) 1 ADV If something is done **badly** or goes **badly**, it is not very successful or effective. 不令人满意地 [ADV with v] ❑ *I was angry because I played so badly.* 我生气因为我弹得这么糟。 ❑ *The whole project was badly managed.* 整个项目管理得差劲。 2 ADV If someone or something is **badly** hurt or **badly** affected, they are severely hurt or affected. 严重地 ❑ *The bomb destroyed a police station and badly damaged a church.* 炸弹炸毁了一个警察局，还严重毁坏了一座教堂。 ❑ *One man was killed and another badly injured.* 一男子死亡，另一个受重伤。 3 ADV If you want or need something **badly**, you want or need it very much. 非常 [ADV with v] ❑ *Why do you want to go so badly?* 你为什么要这么急着走？ 4 ADV If someone behaves **badly** or treats other people **badly**, they act in an unkind, unpleasant, or unacceptable way. 不友善地; (待人) 恶劣地 [ADV with v] ❑ *They have both behaved very badly and I am very hurt.* 他们俩都表现得极不友善，这令我很伤心。 5 ADV If something reflects **badly** on someone or makes others think **badly** of them, it harms their reputation. 不利地 [ADV after v] ❑ *Teachers know that low exam results will reflect badly on them.* 老师们知道低的考试成绩会对他们不利。 6 ADV If a person or their job is **badly** paid, they are not paid very much for what they do. (支付薪水) 低地 ❑ *You may have to work part-time, in a badly paid job.* 你也许不得不做兼职，干报酬低的工作。 7 → see also **worse, worst**

> **Thesaurus** badly 另参见:
>
> ADV. carelessly, poorly, unsuccessfully; *(ant.)* well 1
> deeply, desperately, seriously; *(ant.)* mildly 2
> greatly 3

bad·ly off [BRIT] → see **bad off**

▲ **bad·min·ton** /bædmɪntən/ N-UNCOUNT **Badminton** is a game played by two or four players on a rectangular court with a high net across the middle. The players try to score points by hitting a small object called a shuttlecock across the net using a racket. 羽毛球运动

bad off (**worse off, worst off**) [mainly AM]

> in BRIT, usually use **badly off**

1 ADJ If you are **bad off**, you are in a bad situation. 情况糟糕的 [usu v-link ADJ] ❑ *But there were other people worse off than me at the hospital, linked up to respirators and unable to walk.* 但是，医院里有些人情况比我还糟，他们接着人工呼吸机，无法走动。 2 ADJ If you are **bad off**, you do not have much money. 穷困的 [usu v-link ADJ] ❑ *An independent study found that the owners are not as bad off as they say, and most are making money.* 一项独立的研究发现，企业主们并不像他们说的那么经济困难，大部分都在赚钱。

B

bad-tempered ADJ Someone who is **bad-tempered** is not very cheerful and gets angry easily. 脾气坏的 ❑ *When his headaches developed, Nick became bad-tempered and even violent.* 尼克的头疼起来时，他变得焦躁易怒，甚至暴躁。

> **Angry** is normally used to talk about someone's mood or feelings on a particular occasion. If someone is often angry, you can describe them as **bad-tempered**. ❑ *She's a bad-tempered young lady.* If someone is very angry, you can describe them as **furious**. ❑ *Senior police officers are furious at the blunder.* If they are less angry, you can describe them as **annoyed** or **irritated**. ❑ *The premier looked annoyed but calm.* ... *a man irritated by the barking of his neighbor's dog.* Typically, someone is **irritated** by something because it happens constantly or continually. If someone is often irritated, you can describe them as **irritable**.

★ **baf·fle** /bæf^əl/ (**baffles, baffling, baffled**) V-T If something **baffles** you, you cannot understand it or explain it. 使困惑 ❑ *An apple tree producing square fruit is baffling experts.* 一棵结方形果实的苹果树正令专家们感到困惑。● **baf·fling** ADJ 令人困惑的 ❑ *I was constantly ill, with a baffling array of symptoms.* 我不断地生病，还伴有一大堆莫名其妙的症状。

bag ♦♦◇ /bæg/ (**bags**) **1** N-COUNT A **bag** is a container made of thin paper or plastic, for example, one that is used in stores to put things in that a customer has bought. (薄纸或塑料做的) 袋子 **2** N-COUNT You can use **bag** to refer to a bag and its contents, or to the contents only. (纸、塑料) 袋；一袋之物 ❑ *...a bag of candy.* …一袋糖果。 **3** N-COUNT A **bag** is a strong container with one or two handles, used to carry things in. (有手柄的结实的) 袋子 ❑ *She left the hotel carrying a shopping bag.* 她拎着一个购物袋离开了宾馆。 **4** N-COUNT You can use **bag** to refer to a bag and its contents, or to the contents only. 一袋；一袋之物 ❑ *Mama came in the back door carrying two bags of groceries.* 妈妈提着两袋食品走进了后门。 **5** N-COUNT A **bag** is the same as a **handbag**. 手提包 **6** N-PLURAL If you have **bags** under your eyes, you have folds of skin there, usually because you have not had enough sleep. 眼袋 ❑ *The bags under his eyes have grown darker.* 他眼袋的颜色变得更深了。 **7** → see also **pocketbook, purse, sleeping bag**
→ see **tea**

bag·gage /bægɪdʒ/ **1** N-UNCOUNT Your **baggage** consists of the bags that you take with you when you travel. 行李 ❑ *The passengers went through immigration control and collected their baggage.* 乘客们通过了移民管理站然后领取了行李。 **2** N-UNCOUNT You can use **baggage** to refer to someone's emotional problems, fixed ideas, or prejudices. (感情或思想上的) 包袱 ❑ *How much emotional baggage is he bringing with him into the relationship?* 他正把多少感情包袱带入这个关系？

> **Baggage** is an uncount noun. You can have **a piece of baggage** or **some baggage** but you cannot have "a baggage" or "some baggages." Both British and American speakers can refer to everything that travelers carry as their **bags**. American speakers can also call an individual suitcase a **bag**. In British English, people normally use **luggage** when they are talking about everything that travelers carry. **Baggage** is a more technical word and is used for example when discussing airports or travel insurance. In American English, **luggage** refers to empty bags and suitcases and **baggage** refers to bags and suitcases with their contents.

bag·gage car (**baggage cars**) N-COUNT A **baggage car** is a railroad car, often without windows, which is used to carry luggage, goods, or mail. 行李车厢 [AM]
in BRIT, use **van**
❑ *The coffin was loaded into the baggage car of the train.* 棺材被装进了火车的行李车厢内。

bag·gy /bægi/ (**baggier, baggiest**) ADJ If a piece of clothing is **baggy**, it hangs loosely on your body. 宽松的 ❑ *...a baggy sweater.* …一件宽松的毛线衫。

▲ **bail** /beɪl/ (**bails, bailing, bailed**)

> The spelling **bale** is also used for meaning **4**, and for meanings **1** and **3** of the phrasal verb.

1 N-UNCOUNT **Bail** is a sum of money that an arrested person or someone else puts forward as a guarantee that the arrested person will attend their trial in a law court. If the arrested person does not attend it, the money will be lost. 保释金 ❑ *He was freed on bail pending an appeal.* 他被保释释放，等候上诉。 **2** N-UNCOUNT **Bail** is permission for an arrested person to be released after bail has been paid. 保释许可 ❑ *Bilal was held without bail after a court appearance in Detroit.* 比拉尔在底特律的一次出庭后，被扣押不予保释。 **3** V-T If someone **is bailed**, they are released while they are waiting for their trial, after paying an amount of money to the court. 保释 [usu passive] ❑ *He was bailed to appear on 26 August.* 他被保释，要于8月26日出庭。 **4** V-I If you **bail**, you use a container to remove water from a boat or from a place which is flooded. (从船里或某处) 往外舀水 ❑ *We kept her afloat for a couple of hours by bailing frantically.* 我们拼命往外舀水让船漂浮了几个小时。● PHRASAL VERB **Bail out** means the same as **bail**. (从船里或某处) 往外舀水 ❑ *A crew was sent down the shaft to close it off and bail out all the water.* 一队工作人员被派下竖井去将其封闭，并把所有积水舀出来。 **5** PHRASE If someone who has been arrested **makes bail**, or if another person **makes bail** for them, the arrested person is released on bail. 保释 ❑ *Guerrero was ultimately arrested, but he made bail and fled to Colombia.* 格雷罗最终被捕了，可他被保释释放了，逃到了哥伦比亚。 **6** PHRASE If a prisoner **jumps bail**, he or she does not come back for his or her trial after being released on bail. 弃保潜逃 ❑ *He had jumped bail last year while being tried on drug charges.* 他去年在因毒品罪受审时弃保潜逃了。

▶ **bail out** **1** PHRASAL VERB If you **bail** someone **out**, you help them out of a difficult situation, often by giving them money. (常通过提供资金) 帮助…摆脱困境 ❑ *They will discuss how to bail the economy out of its slump.* 他们将讨论如何使经济走出低谷。 **2** → see also **bailout** **3** PHRASAL VERB If you **bail** someone **out**, you pay bail on their behalf. 把…保释出来 ❑ *He has been jailed eight times. Each time, friends bailed him out.* 他已经蹲过八次监狱。每次，朋友们都把他保释出来。 **4** PHRASAL VERB If a pilot **bails out of** an aircraft that is crashing, he or she jumps from it, using a parachute to land safely. 跳伞逃生 ❑ *Reid was forced to bail out of the crippled aircraft.* 里德被迫从严重受损的飞机中跳伞逃生。 **5** → see **bail 4**

bail·iff /beɪlɪf/ (**bailiffs**) N-COUNT A **bailiff** is an official in a court of law who deals with tasks such as keeping control in court. 法警 [AM] ❑ *The court bailiff said jurors did not wish to speak to news media until the sentencing.* 法院法警说，陪审员不想在宣判之前接受新闻媒体采访。

▲ **bait** /beɪt/ (**baits, baiting, baited**) **1** N-VAR **Bait** is food which you put on a hook or in a trap in order to catch fish or animals. 饵 ❑ *Vivien refuses to put down bait to tempt wildlife to the waterhole.* 维维恩拒绝放饵到水坑引诱野生动物。 **2** V-T If you **bait** a hook or trap, you put bait on it or in it. 放诱饵于 ❑ *He baited his hook with pie.* 他把馅饼放在钓钩上作饵。 ❑ *The boys dug pits and baited them so that they could spear their prey.* 男孩子们挖了陷阱，在里面放上诱饵，以便用矛刺杀猎物。 **3** N-UNCOUNT To use something as **bait** means to use it to trick or persuade someone to do something. 诱饵 [also "a" N] ❑ *Television programs are essentially bait to attract an audience for commercials.* 电视节目本质上是用来吸引观众看商业广告的诱饵。 **4** V-T If you **bait** someone, you deliberately try to make them angry by teasing them. 故意惹怒 ❑ *He delighted in baiting his mother.* 他以惹他妈妈生气为乐。 **5** **Bait and switch** is used to refer to a sales technique in which goods are advertised at low prices in order to attract customers, although only a small number of the low-priced goods are available. 诱导转向法 (以廉价商品诱使顾客上门的销售方法) ❑ *The classy piano bar next to Maddalena's really sells 11 dishes for the advertised price at lunch. There's no bait and switch here.* 马达莱纳隔壁的高级钢琴酒吧按广告中的价位售卖11道午餐菜肴。在这没有用廉价品招揽生意的幌子。

bake ♦◇◇ /beɪk/ (**bakes, baking, baked**) **1** V-T/V-I If you **bake**, you spend some time preparing and mixing together ingredients to make bread, cakes, pies, or other food which is cooked in the oven. 烤制 (面包等食品) [no passive] ❑ *How did you learn to bake cakes?* 你是怎么学会烤蛋糕的？ ❑ *I love to bake.* 我喜欢烤点心。● **bak·ing** N-UNCOUNT 烘烤 [also "the" N] ❑ *On a Thursday she used to do all the baking.* 她以前每个星期四做所有烘烤的活儿。 **2** V-T/V-I When a cake or bread **bakes** or when you **bake** it, it cooks in the oven without any extra liquid or fat. (指蛋糕或面包) 烘烤 ❑ *Bake the cake for 35 to 50 minutes.* 把蛋糕烘烤35至50分钟。 ❑ *The batter rises as it bakes.* 面糊烘烤时膨胀。 **3** → see also **baking**
→ see **cook**

bak·er /beɪkər/ (**bakers**) 1 N-COUNT A **baker** is a person whose job is to bake and sell bread, pastries, and cakes. 面包师 2 N-COUNT A **baker** or a **baker's** is a store where bread and cakes are sold. 面包店 [mainly BRIT]

in AM, usually **bakery**

Word Link *ery ≈ place where something happens : bakery, fishery, refinery*

bak·ery /beɪkəri, beɪkri/ (**bakeries**) N-COUNT A **bakery** is a building where bread, pastries, and cakes are baked, or the store where they are sold. 面包房；面包店 ❑ *A smell of bread drifted from some distant bakery.* 一股面包的味道从远处的某个面包店飘来。

bake·ware /beɪkwɛər/ N-UNCOUNT Pans, trays, and dishes that are used for baking can be referred to as **bakeware**. 烘烤用具

bak·ing /beɪkɪŋ/ 1 ADJ You can use **baking** to describe weather or a place that is very hot indeed. 炎热的 ❑ *...a baking July day.* …一个炎热的7月天。 ❑ *The coffins stood in the baking heat surrounded by mourners.* 这些棺材停在炙热的高温之下，四周围着哀悼的人们。 2 → see also **bake**

bak·ing pow·der (**baking powders**) N-MASS **Baking powder** is an ingredient used in cake making. It causes cakes to rise when they are in the oven. 发酵粉

bal·ance ♦♦◇ /bæləns/ (**balances, balancing, balanced**) 1 V-T/V-I If you **balance** something somewhere, or if it **balances** there, it remains steady and does not fall. 使平衡；平衡 ❑ *I balanced on the ledge.* 我在岩脊上站稳。 2 N-UNCOUNT **Balance** is the ability to remain steady when you are standing up. 平衡能力 ❑ *The medicines you are currently taking could be affecting your balance.* 你现在吃的药可能会影响你的平衡能力。 3 V-RECIP If you **balance** one thing **with** something different, each of the things has the same strength or importance. 使均衡 ❑ *Balance spicy dishes with mild ones.* 使辛辣的菜和清淡的菜均衡。 ❑ *The government has to find some way to balance these two needs.* 政府得找到某种方法来平衡这两种需求。 ❑ *Supply and demand on the currency market will generally balance.* 货币市场上的供需关系将会大致平衡。 ● **bal·anced** ADJ 均衡的 ❑ *This book is a well balanced biography.* 这是一本很公正的传记。 4 N-SING A **balance** is a situation in which all the different parts are equal in strength or importance. 均衡 ❑ *...the ecological balance of the forest.* …森林的生态平衡。 5 N-SING If you say that **the balance** tips in your favor, you start winning or succeeding, especially in a conflict or contest. (表示冲突中的形势) 天平 ❑ *...a powerful new gun which could tip the balance of the war in their favor.* …可能会使战争的天平向他们那边倾斜的一种威力强大的新型炮。 6 V-T If you **balance** one thing **against** another, you consider its importance in relation to the other one. 权衡；使协调 ❑ *She carefully tried to balance religious sensitivities against democratic freedom.* 她小心翼翼地试着协调宗教敏感性与民主自由。 7 V-T If someone **balances** their budget or if a government **balances** the economy of a country, they make sure that the amount of money that is spent is not greater than the amount that is received. 使(收支) 平衡 ❑ *He balanced his budgets by rigid control over public expenditure.* 他通过严格控制公共开支来平衡预算。 8 V-T/V-I If you **balance** your books or make them **balance**, you prove by calculation that the amount of money you have received is equal to the amount that you have spent. 使(账目) 平衡；(账目) 平衡 ❑ *...teaching them to balance the books.* …教他们平衡账目。 9 N-COUNT The **balance** in your bank account is the amount of money you have in it. (账户上的) 余额 ❑ *I'd like to check the balance in my account please.* 我想查一下我账户的余额。 10 N-SING **The balance** of an amount of money is what remains to be paid for something or what remains when part of the amount has been spent. 余款；结余 ❑ *They were due to pay the balance on delivery.* 他们定在货到时支付余款。 11 → see also **bank balance** 12 PHRASE If you **keep** your **balance**, for example, when standing in a moving vehicle, you remain steady and do not fall over. If you **lose** your **balance**, you become unsteady and fall over. 保持/失去平衡 ❑ *She was holding onto the rail to keep her balance.* 她抓着栏杆来保持身体平衡。 13 PHRASE If you are **off balance**, you are in an unsteady position and about to fall. 失去平衡 ❑ *A gust of wind knocked him off balance and he fell face down in the mud.* 一阵大风吹得他失去了平衡，脸朝下摔在了泥里。 14 PHRASE You can say **on balance** to indicate that you are stating an opinion after considering all the relevant facts or arguments. 总的说来 ❑ *On balance he agreed with Christine.* 总的说来，他同意克里斯蒂娜的看法。 → see **bank, brain**

Word Partnership *balance* 的常用搭配：

V. **keep/lose your** balance, **restore** balance 2 4
check a balance, **maintain a** balance 9 10
pay a balance 10
ADJ. **delicate** balance 2 4
balance **due, outstanding** balance 10
N. balance **a budget** 7
account balance, balance **transfer** 9

bal·anced /bælənst/ 1 ADJ A **balanced** report, book, or other document takes into account all the different opinions on something and presents information in a fair and reasonable way. 全面公正的 [APPROVAL] ❑ *...a fair, balanced, comprehensive report.* …一份公平、公正、全面的报告。 2 ADJ Something that is **balanced** is pleasing or useful because its different parts or elements are in the correct proportions. 均衡的 [APPROVAL] ❑ *...a balanced diet.* …均衡的饮食。 3 ADJ Someone who is **balanced** remains calm and thinks clearly, even in a difficult situation. 沉着冷静的 [APPROVAL] ❑ *I have to prove myself as a respectable, balanced person.* 我得证明自己是一个可敬、沉稳的人。 4 → see also **balance**

bal·ance of pay·ments (**balances of payments**) N-COUNT A country's **balance of payments** is the difference, over a period of time, between the payments it makes to other countries for imports and the payments it receives from other countries for exports. 国际收支差额 [BUSINESS] ❑ *...the chronic American balance-of-payments deficit of the 1960s.* …20世纪60年代美国长期的国际收支赤字。

bal·ance of trade (**balances of trade**) N-COUNT A country's **balance of trade** is the difference in value, over a period of time, between the goods it imports and the goods it exports. 贸易差额 [usu sing] [BUSINESS] ❑ *As other nations grow and spend more money on American products, the balance of trade should even out.* 随着其他国家的发展，并且花更多钱来购买美国产品，贸易差额应该会拉平。

bal·ance sheet (**balance sheets**) N-COUNT A **balance sheet** is a written statement of the amount of money and property that a company or person has, including amounts of money that are owed or are owing. **Balance sheet** is also used to refer to the general financial state of a company. 资产负债表 [BUSINESS] ❑ *Rolls-Royce needed a strong balance sheet.* 劳斯莱斯公司需要良好的财务状况。

bal·co·ny /bælkəni/ (**balconies**) 1 N-COUNT A **balcony** is a platform on the outside of a building, above ground level, with a wall or railing around it. 阳台 2 N-SING The **balcony** in a theatre or cinema is an area of seats above the main seating area. (戏院或电影院里的) 楼座

★ **bald** /bɔld/ (**balder, baldest**) 1 ADJ Someone who is **bald** has little or no hair on the top of their head. 秃顶的 ❑ *The man's bald head was beaded with sweat.* 这位男子的秃头上满是汗珠。 ● **bald·ness** N-UNCOUNT 秃顶 ❑ *He wears a cap to cover a spot of baldness.* 他戴一顶帽子来遮住一小块秃顶。 2 ADJ If a tire is **bald**, its surface has worn down and it is no longer safe to use. (轮胎表面) 磨平的 3 ADJ A **bald** statement is in plain language and contains no extra explanation or information. (陈述等) 直白的 [ADJ n] ❑ *The bald truth is he's just not happy.* 明摆着的事实是他就是不高兴。 ● **bald·ly** ADV (陈述等) 直白地 [ADV with v] ❑ *"The leaders are outdated," he stated baldly. "They don't relate to young people."* "领导们落伍了。" 他直白地说，"他们不理解年轻人。"

bald·ing /bɔldɪŋ/ ADJ Someone who is **balding** is beginning to lose the hair on the top of their head. 开始秃顶的 ❑ *He wore a straw hat to keep his balding head from getting sunburned.* 他戴了一顶草帽，以防止开始变秃的头被晒伤。

▲ **bale** /beɪl/ (**bales, baling, baled**) 1 N-COUNT A **bale** is a large quantity of something such as hay, cloth, or paper, tied together tightly. 大捆 ❑ *...bales of hay.* …大捆大捆的干草。 2 V-T If something such as hay, cloth, or paper **is baled**, it is tied together tightly. 把…捆紧 ❑ *Once hay has been cut and baled, it has to go through some chemical processes.* 干草一旦被割下来扎成捆，必须经过一些化学处理。 3 → see also **bail**

ball ♦♦◇ /bɔl/ (**balls, balling, balled**) 1 N-COUNT A **ball** is a round or oval object that is used in games such as tennis, baseball, football, basketball, and soccer. 球 ❑ *...a golf ball.* …一个高尔夫球。 2 N-COUNT A **ball** is something or an amount of something that has a round shape. 球状物 ❑ *Thomas screwed the letter up into a ball.*

B

托马斯把信揉成一团。 3 V-T/V-I When you **ball** something or when it **balls**, it becomes round. 使成球状；成球状 ❑ *He picked up the sheets of paper, and balled them tightly in his fists.* 他捡起那几张纸，在手里把它们紧紧地攥成团。 4 N-COUNT **The ball of** your foot or **the ball of** your thumb is the rounded part where your toes join your foot or where your thumb joins your hand. (脚趾与脚掌相接或大拇指与手掌相接的) 球状部位 5 N-COUNT A **ball** is a large formal social event at which people dance. (正式的) 舞会 ❑ *My Mama and Daddy used to have a grand Christmas ball every year.* 我妈妈和爸爸以前每年都要办一场盛大的圣诞节舞会。 6 PHRASE If you **are having a ball**, you are having a very enjoyable time. 玩得高兴 [INFORMAL] ❑ *Outside the boys were sitting on the ground and, judging by the gales of laughter, they were having a ball.* 在外面，男孩子们正坐在地上，从他们发出的阵阵笑声来看，他们玩得很开心。

→ see **foot, golf, soccer**

▸ **ball up** PHRASAL VERB If you **ball up** a task or activity, you do it very badly, making a lot of mistakes. 把…弄得一团糟 [AM, INFORMAL, VULGAR] ❑ *The government has totally balled up the whole assessment process by going to the system they did.* 政府通过使用其所选的体系，把整个评估过程弄得一团糟。

Word Partnership *ball* 的常用搭配：

V. **bounce/catch/hit/kick/throw a** ball 1
roll into a ball 2
N. **bowling/golf/soccer/tennis** ball, ball **field**, ball **game** 1
crystal ball, **snow** ball 2
PREP. ball **of *something*** 2

bal·lad /bæləd/ (**ballads**) 1 N-COUNT A **ballad** is a long song or poem which tells a story in simple language. 叙事歌；民间叙事诗 ❑ *...an eighteenth century ballad about some lost children called the Babes in the Wood.* …一首关于迷路儿童的名为《丛林中的宝贝》的18世纪民间叙事诗。 2 N-COUNT A **ballad** is a slow, romantic, popular song. 流行情歌 ❑ *"You Don't Know Paris" is one of the most beautiful ballads that he ever wrote.* 《你不了解巴黎》是他写过的最优美的流行情歌之一。

★ **bal·let** /bæleɪ/ (**ballets**) 1 N-UNCOUNT **Ballet** is a type of very skilled and artistic dancing with carefully planned movements. 芭蕾舞 [also "the" N, oft N n] ❑ *I trained as a ballet dancer.* 我受过做芭蕾舞演员的训练。 2 N-COUNT A **ballet** is an artistic work that is performed by ballet dancers. 芭蕾舞剧 ❑ *The performance will include the premiere of three new ballets.* 这次演出将包括3部新芭蕾舞剧的首演。

bal·loon /bəlu̲n/ (**balloons, ballooning, ballooned**) 1 N-COUNT A **balloon** is a small, thin, rubber bag that you blow air into so that it becomes larger and rounder or longer. Balloons are used as toys or decorations. 气球 ❑ *She popped a balloon with her fork.* 她用叉子把气球砰的一声戳爆了。 2 N-COUNT A **balloon** is a large, strong bag filled with gas or hot air, which can carry passengers in a container that hangs underneath it. 热气球 ❑ *They are to attempt to be the first to circle the Earth non-stop by balloon.* 他们将试图成为首批乘热气球不间断环球飞行的人。 3 V-I When something **balloons**, it increases rapidly in amount. (数量上) 猛增 ❑ *The jail's female and minority populations have both ballooned in recent years.* 该监狱的女性及少数民族犯人在近几年都猛增了。

→ see **fly**

bal·loon mort·gage (**balloon mortgages**) N-COUNT A **balloon mortgage** is a mortgage on which the repayments are relatively small until the large final payment. 气球式按揭 (即大额尾付贷款) [AM]

★ **bal·lot** ♦◇◇ /bælət/ (**ballots, balloting, balloted**) 1 N-COUNT A **ballot** is a secret vote in which people select a candidate in an election, or express their opinion about something. 无记名投票 ❑ *The result of the ballot will not be known for two weeks.* 本次无记名投票的结果将在两周后才会揭晓。 2 N-COUNT A **ballot** is a piece of paper on which you indicate your choice or opinion in a secret vote. 无记名选票 ❑ *Election boards will count the ballots by hand.* 选举委员会将手工清点选票。 3 V-T If you **ballot** a group of people, you find out what they think about a subject by organizing a secret vote. 组织…进行秘密投票 ❑ *The union said they will ballot members on whether to strike.* 工会称他们将组织会员们秘密投票表决是否罢工。

→ see **election, vote**

ball·park /bɔlpark/ (**ballparks**) also **ball park** 1 N-COUNT A **ballpark** is a park or stadium where baseball is played. 棒球场 ❑ *...one of the oldest and most beautiful ballparks in baseball.* …最古老、最美丽的棒球场之一。 2 ADJ A **ballpark** figure or **ballpark** estimate is an approximate figure or estimate. 大概的 [ADJ n] ❑ *I can't give you anything more than just sort of a ballpark figure.* 我只能给你一个大概的数字。

balm /bɑm/ (**balms**) 1 N-MASS **Balm** is a sweet-smelling oil that is obtained from some tropical trees and used to make creams that heal wounds or reduce pain. (做疗伤或镇痛药膏的) 香树油 ❑ *...a jar of lip balm.* …一罐唇膏。 2 N-UNCOUNT If you refer to something as **balm**, you mean that it makes you feel better. 慰藉物 [also "a" N] [APPROVAL] ❑ *The place is balm to the soul.* 这个地方是对心灵的抚慰。

bam·boo /bæmbu̲/ (**bamboos**) N-VAR **Bamboo** is a tall tropical plant with hard, hollow stems. The young shoots of the plant can be eaten and the stems are used to make furniture. 竹子 ❑ *...huts with walls of bamboo.* …竹墙小屋。

ban ♦♦◇ /bæn/ (**bans, banning, banned**) 1 V-T To **ban** something means to state officially that it must not be done, shown, or used. (官方) 明令禁止 ❑ *Canada will ban smoking in all offices later this year.* 加拿大将于今年晚些时候禁止在所有办公场所吸烟。 ❑ *Last year arms sales were banned.* 去年军火交易被明令禁止了。 2 N-COUNT A **ban** is an official ruling that something must not be done, shown, or used. 官方禁令 ❑ *The general lifted the ban on political parties.* 将军解除了对政党的官方禁令。 3 V-T If you **are banned from** doing something, you are officially prevented from doing it. 禁止 ❑ *He was banned from driving for three years.* 他被禁止驾驶3年。

Thesaurus *ban* 另参见：

V. bar, forbid, prohibit; *(ant.)* allow, legalize, permit 1
N. prohibition; *(ant.)* approval, sanction 2

ba·nal /bənɑ̲l, -næl, beɪnᵊl/ ADJ If you describe something as **banal**, you do not like it because you think it is so ordinary that it is not at all effective or interesting. 平庸乏味的 [DISAPPROVAL] ❑ *The text is banal.* 这篇文章乏味得很。

ba·na·na /bənænə/ (**bananas**) N-VAR **Bananas** are long curved fruit with yellow skins. 香蕉 ❑ *...a bunch of bananas.* …一串香蕉。

band ♦♦◇ /bænd/ (**bands, banding, banded**) 1 N-COUNT-COLL A **band** is a small group of musicians who play popular music such as jazz, rock, or pop. (演奏流行音乐的) 乐队 ❑ *He was a drummer in a rock band.* 他曾是一支摇滚乐队里的鼓手。 2 N-COUNT-COLL A **band** is a group of musicians who play brass and percussion instruments. (演奏铜管乐和打击乐的) 乐队 ❑ *Bands played German marches.* 管乐队演奏了德国的进行曲。 3 N-COUNT-COLL A **band of** people is a group of people who have joined together because they share an interest or belief. (趣味相投的人) 群 ❑ *Bands of government soldiers, rebels and just plain criminals have been roaming some neighborhoods.* 一群群政府士兵、叛乱分子和纯属一般的罪犯一直在一些街区里游荡。 4 N-COUNT A **band** is a flat, narrow strip of cloth which you wear around your head or wrists, or which forms part of a piece of clothing. (指服饰) 带子 ❑ *Almost all hospitals use a wrist-band of some kind with your name and details on it.* 几乎所有医院都使用某种腕带，上面有你的名字和详细信息。 5 N-COUNT A **band** is a strip of something such as color, light, land, or cloth that contrasts with the areas on either side of it. 带状物 ❑ *...bands of natural vegetation between strips of crops.* …在带状的庄稼地之间的条条天然植物带。 6 N-COUNT A **band** is a strip or loop of metal or other strong material which strengthens something, or which holds several things together. (用以加固或捆绑的) 箍；带 ❑ *Surgeon Geoffrey Horne placed a metal band around the knee cap to help it knit back together.* 外科医生杰弗里·霍恩在膝盖骨上放了一个金属箍以帮助其愈合。 7 → see also **elastic band, rubber band** 8 N-COUNT A **band** is a range of numbers or values within a system of measurement. (测量的) 范围 ❑ *For an initial service, a 10 megahertz-wide band of frequencies will be needed.* 初期制动将需要10兆赫兹宽的频带。

→ see **army, concert, radio**

▸ **band together** PHRASAL VERB If people **band together**, they meet and act as a group in order to try and achieve something. 联合 ❑ *Women banded together to protect each other.* 妇女们联合起来互相保护。

band·age /bændɪdʒ/ (**bandages, bandaging, bandaged**) 1 N-COUNT A **bandage** is a long strip of cloth that is wrapped around a wounded part of someone's body to protect or support it. 绷带 ❑ *We put some ointment and a bandage on his knee.* 我们在他的膝盖上涂了些药膏，还缠了一条绷带。 2 V-T If you **bandage** a wound or part of someone's body, you tie a bandage around it. 用绷带包扎

❑ *Apply a dressing to the wound and bandage it.* 在伤口上敷上敷料并用绷带包扎起来。● PHRASAL VERB **Bandage up** means the same as **bandage.** 用绷带包扎 ❑ *I bandaged the leg up and gave her aspirin for the pain.* 我用绷带把她的腿包扎起来，又给她阿斯匹林镇痛。

Band-Aid (**Band-Aids**) **1** N-VAR A **Band-Aid** is a small piece of sticky tape that you use to cover small cuts or wounds on your body. (邦迪) 创可贴 [mainly AM, TRADEMARK]

in BRIT, use **plaster**

2 ADJ If you refer to a **Band-Aid** solution to a problem, you mean that you disapprove of it because you think that it will only be effective for a short period. 权宜的 [ADJ n] [DISAPPROVAL] ❑ *We need long-term solutions, not short-term Band-Aid ones.* 我们需要长远的解决方法，而不是短期的权宜之计。

B & B /bi ən bi/ (**B&Bs**) → see **bed and breakfast**

▲ **ban·dit** /bændɪt/ (**bandits**) N-COUNT Robbers are sometimes called **bandits**, especially if they are found in areas where the law has broken down. 土匪 ❑ *This is real bandit country.* 这是真正的强盗之地。

band·wagon /bændwægən/ (**bandwagons**) **1** N-COUNT You can refer to an activity or movement that has suddenly become fashionable or popular as a **bandwagon**. (指活动或运动) 潮流 ❑ *...the environmental bandwagon.* …环保潮流。 **2** N-COUNT If someone, especially a politician, jumps or climbs **on the bandwagon**, they become involved in an activity or movement because it is fashionable or likely to succeed and not because they are really interested in it. (尤指政客追赶的) 浪头 [DISAPPROVAL] ❑ *In recent months many conservative politicians have jumped on the anti-immigrant bandwagon.* 最近几个月，许多保守党政客赶上了反移民的浪头。

band·width /bændwɪdθ/ (**bandwidths**) N-VAR A **bandwidth** is the range of frequencies used for a particular telecommunications signal, radio transmission, or computer network. 带宽 ❑ *To cope with this amount of data, the system will need a bandwidth of around 100mhz.* 要处理这样的数据量，这个系统将需要约100兆赫兹的带宽。

bang /bæŋ/ (**bangs, banging, banged**) **1** N-COUNT; SOUND A **bang** is a sudden loud noise such as the noise of an explosion. (突然的) 巨响 ❑ *I heard four or five loud bangs.* 我听到四五声巨响。 ❑ *She slammed the door with a bang.* 她砰地一声关上门。 **2** V-I If something **bangs**, it makes a sudden loud noise, once or several times. 砰然作响 ❑ *The engine spat and banged.* 引擎发出劈啪声和砰砰巨响。 **3** V-T/V-I If you **bang** a door or if it **bangs**, it closes suddenly with a loud noise. 砰地关上 ❑ *...the sound of doors banging.* …砰砰的关门声。 ❑ *All up and down the street the windows bang shut.* 整条街的窗户都砰砰关上了。 **4** V-T/V-I If you **bang on** something or if you **bang** it, you hit it hard, making a loud noise. 大声猛击 ❑ *We could bang on the desks and shout till they let us out.* 我们会大声猛拍桌子，大声喊叫，直到他们放我们出去。 **5** V-T If you **bang** something on something or if you **bang** it down, you quickly and violently put it on a surface, because you are angry. (因生气而) 猛然用力放 ❑ *She banged his dinner on the table.* 她猛地用力把他的晚饭砸在桌上。 **6** V-T If you **bang** a part of your body, you accidentally knock it against something and hurt yourself. (无意中) 撞伤 ❑ *She'd fainted and banged her head.* 她晕了过去，撞伤了头部。 ● N-COUNT **Bang** is also a noun. 撞伤 ❑ *...a nasty bang on the head.* …头部可恶的撞伤。 **7** V-I If you **bang into** something or someone, you bump or knock them hard, usually because you are not looking where you are going. (不小心) 猛撞上 ❑ *I didn't mean to bang into you.* 我不是故意撞你的。 **8** ADV You can use **bang** to emphasize expressions that indicate an exact position or an exact time. 正好 [ADV prep] [EMPHASIS] ❑ *...bang in the middle of the track.* …在路的正中央。 **9** PHRASE If something begins or ends **with a bang**, it begins or ends with a lot of energy, enthusiasm, or success. 轰轰烈烈地 [PHR after v] ❑ *Her career began with a bang in 1986.* 她的事业在1986年轰轰烈烈地开始了。

Word Partnership *bang* 的常用搭配：

V.	**hear** a bang **1**
ADJ.	**loud** bang **1**
PREP.	**with** a bang **1 9**
	bang **on** *something* **4**
	bang **into 7**
ADV.	bang **down 5**
N.	bang *your* **head 6**

bangs /bæŋz/ N-PLURAL **Bangs** are hair that is cut so that it hangs over your forehead. 刘海 [AM]

in BRIT, use **fringe**

❑ *My bangs were cut short, but the rest of my hair was long.* 我的刘海剪得短，但其余的头发长。

▲ **ban·ish** /bænɪʃ/ (**banishes, banishing, banished**) **1** V-T If someone or something **is banished from** a place or area of activity, they are sent away from it and prevented from entering it. 驱逐 ❑ *John was banished from England.* 约翰被逐出英国。 ❑ *I was banished to the small bedroom upstairs.* 我被赶到楼上的小卧室。 **2** V-T If you **banish** something unpleasant, you get rid of it. 消除 ❑ *...a public investment program intended to banish the recession.* …一项旨在消除经济衰退的公共投资计划。

Thesaurus *banish* 另参见：

V. ban, deport, evict, exile; *(ant.)* embrace, invite, welcome **1**

bank
1. FINANCE AND STORAGE
2. AREAS AND MASSES
3. OTHER VERB USES

1 bank ◆◆◆ /bæŋk/ (**banks, banking, banked**) **1** N-COUNT A **bank** is an institution where people or businesses can keep their money. 银行 (机构) ❑ *Students should look to see which bank offers them the service that best suits their financial needs.* 学生们应该去了解哪家银行提供最适合他们财务需求的服务。 **2** N-COUNT A **bank** is a building where a bank offers its services. 银行 (大楼) **3** V-I If you **bank with** a particular bank, you have an account with that bank. (在某银行) 设有账户 ❑ *I have banked with Coutts & Co. for years.* 我已经使用雇资银行很多年了。 **4** N-COUNT You use **bank** to refer to a store of something. For example, a blood **bank** is a store of blood that is kept ready for use. 库 ❑ *...a national data bank of information on hospital employees.* …一个有关医院职工信息的国家数据库。
→ see Word Web: **bank**

2 bank /bæŋk/ (**banks**) **1** N-COUNT The **banks of** a river, canal, or lake are the raised areas of ground along its edge. 岸 ❑ *We pedaled north along the east bank of the river.* 我们沿着这条河的东岸骑车北上。 **2** N-COUNT A **bank** of ground is a raised area of it with a flat top and one or two sloping sides. 堤 ❑ *...lounging on the grassy bank.*

Word Web bank

Most people deposit **money** into **checking accounts** and **savings accounts.** Money can be **withdrawn** from a checking account by writing a **check** or using a **bank card** at an automated teller machine **(ATM).** People record these **transactions** in a **check register.** People **balance** their accounts using their monthly **bank statements.** Customers can also **bank online** at their bank's website. When people **deposit** money into a savings account they earn **interest** from the bank for the use of the money. A bank uses its customers' money to make **loans.** Banks **lend** money for mortgages, car loans, student loans, and business loans. The **borrower** pays back the **principal** amount **borrowed,** plus interest.

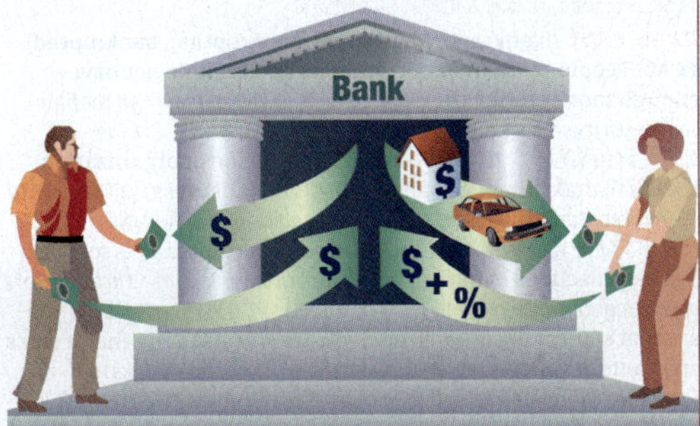

B

…懒洋洋地躺在长满草的堤岸上。 **3** N-COUNT A **bank of** something is a long high mass of it. 长堆 ❑ *A bank of clouds had built up along the western horizon.* 一长团云已经沿着西边的地平线积聚起来。 **4** N-COUNT A **bank of** things, especially machines, switches, or dials, is a row of them, or a series of rows. 一排 (机器、开关或仪表盘) ❑ *The typical laborer now sits in front of a bank of dials.* 现在典型的劳动者坐在一排仪表盘面前。

❸ bank /bæŋk/ (**banks, banking, banked**) V-I When an aircraft **banks**, one of its wings rises higher than the other, usually when it is changing direction. (飞机) 倾斜着飞行 ❑ *A single-engine plane took off and banked above the highway in front of him.* 一架单引擎飞机起飞了，倾斜地飞行在他前面的公路上空。

▸ **bank on** PHRASAL VERB If you **bank on** something happening, you expect it to happen and rely on it happening. 指望 ❑ *Everyone is banking on an economic rebound to help ease the state's fiscal problems.* 每个人都指望经济反弹来帮助缓解国家的财政问题。

bank ac·count (**bank accounts**) N-COUNT A **bank account** is an arrangement with a bank which allows you to keep your money in the bank and to take some out when you need it. 银行账户 ❑ *Paul had at least 17 different bank accounts.* 保罗至少有17个不同的银行账户。

bank bal·ance (**bank balances**) N-COUNT Your **bank balance** is the amount of money that you have in your bank account at a particular time. 银行存款余额 ❑ *Do you wish to use the Internet simply to check your bank balance?* 你只想用因特网来查询你的银行存款余额吗？

bank card (**bank cards**) also **bankcard** **1** N-COUNT A **bank card** is a plastic card that your bank gives you so you can get money from your bank account using a cash machine. It is also called an ATM card. 银行自动提款卡 **2** N-COUNT A **bank card** is a credit card that is supplied by a bank. 银行信用卡 [AM]
→ see **bank**

bank check (**bank checks**) N-COUNT A **bank check** is a check that you can buy from a bank in order to pay someone who is not willing to accept a personal check. 银行支票 ❑ *Payments should be made by credit card or bank check in U.S. dollars.* 应使用信用卡或银行支票以美元付款。

bank·er ♦◇◇ /bæŋkər/ (**bankers**) N-COUNT A **banker** is someone who works in banking at a senior level. 银行家 ❑ *...an investment banker.* …一位投资银行家。

bank holi·day (**bank holidays**) N-COUNT A **bank holiday** is a public holiday. 法定假日；银行假日 [mainly BRIT]
in AM, usually use **national holiday**

bank·ing ♦◇◇ /bæŋkɪŋ/ N-UNCOUNT **Banking** is the business activity of banks and similar institutions. 银行业务 ❑ *...the online banking revolution.* …在线银行业务改革。
→ see **industry**

★ **bank·note** /bæŋknoʊt/ (**banknotes**) also **bank note** N-COUNT **Banknotes** are pieces of paper money. 钞票 ❑ *...a shopping bag full of banknotes.* …一只装满钞票的购物袋。

bank rate (**bank rates**) N-COUNT The **bank rate** is the rate of interest at which a bank lends money, especially the minimum rate of interest that banks are allowed to charge, which is decided from time to time by the country's central bank. (中央银行规定的) 银行利率 ❑ *The United States reduced its main bank rate ten days ago.* 美国10天前降低了其主要银行利率。

bank·roll /bæŋkroʊl/ (**bankrolls, bankrolling, bankrolled**) V-T To **bankroll** a person, organization, or project means to provide the financial resources that they need. 为…提供资金 [mainly AM, INFORMAL] ❑ *The company has bankrolled a couple of local movies.* 这家公司已经为几部地方电影提供了资金。

bank·rupt /bæŋkrʌpt/ (**bankrupts, bankrupting, bankrupted**) **1** ADJ People or organizations that go **bankrupt** do not have enough money to pay their debts. 破产的 [BUSINESS] ❑ *If the firm cannot sell its products, it will go bankrupt.* 如果这家公司无法销售其产品，它将面临破产。 **2** V-T To **bankrupt** a person or organization means to make them go bankrupt. 使破产 [BUSINESS] ❑ *The move to the market nearly bankrupted the firm and its director.* 走向市场的行动几乎使这家公司及其董事破产。 **3** N-COUNT A **bankrupt** is a person who has been declared bankrupt by a court of law. 破产者 ❑ *In total, 80% of bankrupts are men.* 总体来看，有80%的破产者为男性。 **4** ADJ If you say that something is **bankrupt**, you are emphasizing that it lacks any value or worth. 无价值的 [EMPHASIS] ❑ *He really thinks that European civilization is morally bankrupt.* 他确实认为欧洲文明在道德上全无价值。

★ **bank·rupt·cy** /bæŋkrʌptsi/ (**bankruptcies**) **1** N-UNCOUNT **Bankruptcy** is the state of being bankrupt. 破产 (状态) [BUSINESS] ❑ *Pan Am is the second airline in two months to file for bankruptcy.* 泛美航空公司是两个月内第二家申请破产的航空公司。 **2** N-COUNT A **bankruptcy** is an instance of an organization or person going bankrupt. 破产 (事件) [BUSINESS] ❑ *The number of corporate bankruptcies climbed in August.* 企业破产的数量在8月份增加了。

Word Partnership *bankruptcy* 的常用搭配：

V. **avoid** bankruptcy, **declare** bankruptcy, **file for** bankruptcy, **force into** bankruptcy **1**
N. bankruptcy **law**, bankruptcy **protection** **1** **2**

bank state·ment (**bank statements**) N-COUNT A **bank statement** is a printed document showing all the money paid into and taken out of a bank account. Bank statements are usually sent by a bank to a customer at regular intervals. 银行结单

ban·ner /bænər/ (**banners**) **1** N-COUNT A **banner** is a long strip of cloth with something written on it. Banners are usually attached to two poles and carried during a protest or rally. (游行或集合用的) 横幅 ❑ *A large crowd of students followed the coffin, carrying banners and shouting slogans denouncing the government.* 一大群学生跟在灵柩的后面，举着横幅，高喊口号谴责政府。 **2** PHRASE If someone does something **under the banner of** a particular cause, idea, or belief, they do it saying that they support that cause, idea, or belief. 在…旗帜下；在…名义下 ❑ *Russia was the first country to forge a new economic system under the banner of Marxism.* 苏联是第一个在马克思主义的旗帜下建立新的经济体制的国家。

ban·ner ad (**banner ads**) N-COUNT A **banner ad** is a rectangular advertisement on a web page that contains a link to the advertiser's website. (网页上的) 广告条 ❑ *See our banner ad at this site!* 看看这家网站上我们的广告条！

ban·quet /bæŋkwɪt/ (**banquets**) N-COUNT A **banquet** is a grand formal dinner. 正式宴会 ❑ *...this week's Greater Cleveland Sports Commission awards banquet.* …本周的大克利夫兰体育委员会的颁奖宴会。 ❑ *...a wedding banquet.* …一场婚宴。

ban·ter /bæntər/ N-UNCOUNT **Banter** is teasing or joking talk that is amusing and friendly. 无恶意的玩笑 ❑ *As she closed the door, she heard Tom exchanging good-natured banter with Jane.* 她关门时听见汤姆与简在开着善意的玩笑。

bap·tise /bæptaɪz/ [BRIT] → see **baptize**

bap·tism /bæptɪzəm/ (**baptisms**) N-VAR A **baptism** is a Christian ceremony in which a person is baptized. Compare **christening**. (基督教的) 洗礼 ❑ *Infants prepared for baptism should be dressed in pure white.* 准备受洗礼的婴儿应穿纯白色的衣服。

▲ **bap·tize** /bæptaɪz/ (**baptizes, baptizing, baptized**)
in BRIT, also use **baptise**
V-T When someone **is baptized**, water is put on their heads or they are covered with water as a sign that their sins have been forgiven and that they have become a member of the Christian church. Compare **christen**. 给…施洗礼 [usu passive] ❑ *At this time she decided to become a Christian and was baptized.* 这时她决定成为一名基督教徒，并受了洗礼。

bar ♦♦◇ /bɑr/ (**bars, barring, barred**) **1** N-COUNT A **bar** is a place where you can buy and drink alcoholic drinks. 酒吧 [mainly AM] ❑ *...Devil's Herd, the city's most popular country and western bar.* …"魔鬼群"，全城最受欢迎的西部乡村酒吧。 **2** → see also **snack bar, wine bar** **3** N-COUNT A **bar** is a room in a hotel or other establishment where alcoholic drinks are served. (旅馆等的) 酒吧间 ❑ *Last night in the hotel there was some talk in the bar about drugs.* 昨天晚上，在旅馆的酒吧间里有人谈起了毒品。 **4** N-COUNT A **bar** is a counter on which alcoholic drinks are served. 吧台 ❑ *Michael was standing alone by the bar when Brian rejoined him.* 布赖恩回来的时候，迈克尔正独自站在吧台旁。

There are a number of names that can be applied to businesses serving alcohol. The most common is **bar**. In the UK, there are **pubs**, which sometimes also serve light meals. **Nightclubs** also serve drinks along with music or entertainment. However, a **snack bar** does not serve alcohol, just food and soft drinks.

5 N-COUNT A **bar** is a long, straight, stiff piece of metal. 金属棒 ❑ *...a brick building with bars across the ground floor windows.* …一楼窗户穿装有铁栅的一座砖楼。 **6** PHRASE If you say that someone is **behind bars**, you mean that they are in prison. 在狱中 ❑ *Fisher was* *behind bars last night, charged with attempted murder.* 由于被指控犯有谋杀未遂罪，费希尔昨晚进了监狱。 **7** N-COUNT A **bar of** something is a piece of it which is roughly rectangular. (长方形的) 条 ❑ *What is your favorite chocolate bar?* 你最喜爱的巧克力棒是什么？ **8** V-T If you **bar** a door, you place something in front of it or a piece of wood or metal across it in order to prevent it from being opened. 闩(门) ❑ *For added safety, bar the door to the kitchen.* 为了更加安全，把厨房的门闩上。 **9** V-T If you **bar** someone's way, you prevent them from going somewhere or entering a place, by blocking their path. 挡(路) ❑ *Harry moved to bar his way.* 哈里挪过去挡住了他的路。 **10** V-T If someone **is barred from** a place or **from** doing something, they are officially forbidden to go there or to do it. 禁止 [usu passive] ❑ *Amnesty workers have been barred from the country since 1982.* 自1982年以来特赦的工人被禁止进入该国。 **11** N-COUNT If something is a **bar to** doing a particular thing, it prevents someone from doing it. 障碍 ❑ *One of the fundamental bars to communication is the lack of a universally spoken, common language.* 沟通的根本障碍之一就是缺乏一种通用的共同语言。 **12** PREP You can use **bar** when you mean "except." For example, all the work **bar** the laundry means all the work except the laundry. 除…外 [mainly BRIT] ❑ *Bar a plateau in 1989, there has been a rise in inflation ever since the mid-1980s.* 自20世纪80年代中期以来，除了1989年稳定之外，通货膨胀一直在增长。 **13** → see also **barring** **14** N-SING **The bar** is used to refer to the profession of any kind of lawyer in the United States, or of a barrister in England. 律师职业 [oft N n]

in BRIT, use **Bar**

❑ *Less than a quarter of graduates from the law school pass the bar exam on the first try.* 不到1/4的法学院毕业生能一次就通过律师考试。

15 N-COUNT In music, a **bar** is one of the several short parts of the same length into which a piece of music is divided. (音乐的) 小节 ❑ *She sat down at the piano and played a few bars of a Chopin Polonaise.* 她坐在钢琴边弹奏了肖邦的波洛奈兹舞曲的几个小节。

→ see **gymnastics, soap**

Word Partnership *bar* 的常用搭配:

ADJ.	**full** bar, **gay** bar, **local** bar **1** **candy/chocolate** bar **7**
N.	bar **and grill**, bar **and lounge**, bar **owner**, **restaurant and** bar, **sports** bar, bar **stool** **1** bar **of soap** **7** bar **a door** **8** bar **exam** **14**
PREP.	**behind a** bar **4** bar ***someone*** **from** **10**

bar·bar·ic /bɑrbærɪk/ ADJ If you describe someone's behavior as **barbaric**, you strongly disapprove of it because you think that it is extremely cruel or uncivilized. 残酷的; 野蛮的 [DISAPPROVAL] ❑ *This barbaric treatment of animals has no place in any decent society.* 对动物的这种虐待在任何文明的社会里都是无法容忍的。

bar·ba·rism /bɑrbərɪzəm/ N-UNCOUNT If you refer to someone's behavior as **barbarism**, you strongly disapprove of it because you think that it is extremely cruel or uncivilized. 野蛮行为 [DISAPPROVAL] ❑ *We do not ask for the death penalty: barbarism must not be met with barbarism.* 我们并不要求死刑：不能以暴制暴。

▲ **bar·becue** /bɑrbɪkyu/ (**barbecues, barbecuing, barbecued**) also **barbeque, Bar-B-Q** **1** N-COUNT A **barbecue** is a piece of equipment which you use for cooking on in the open air. (户外使用的) 烤架 **2** N-COUNT If someone has a **barbecue**, they cook food on a barbecue in the open air. 烧烤 ❑ *On New Year's Eve we had a barbecue on the beach.* 除夕那天我们在海滩上举行了烧烤野餐。 **3** V-T If you **barbecue** food, especially meat, you cook it on a barbecue. (用烤架) 烧烤 ❑ *Tuna can be grilled, fried or barbecued.* 金枪鱼可以烤、煎或烧烤着吃。 ❑ *Here's a way of barbecuing corn-on-the-cob that I learned from my uncle.* 这是我向我叔叔学的一种烤玉米棒的方法。

→ see **cook**

A **barbecue** is a popular style of cooking during the summer. Meat with a spicy sauce is cooked on a metal grill over an open fire. Some food may not be spiced, such as hamburgers, hot dogs, or corn on the cob, and this is cooked over the fire as well. North Americans may also call this event a **cookout**. In South Africa a barbecue is called a **braai** (pronounced like the word "cry"), and is a very common social or family gathering.

barbed wire /bɑrbd waɪər/ N-UNCOUNT **Barbed wire** is strong wire with sharp points sticking out of it, and is used to make fences. 带刺铁丝网 ❑ *The factory was surrounded by barbed wire.* 工厂被带刺铁丝网围着。

bar·bell /bɑrbɛl/ (**barbells**) N-COUNT A **barbell** is a long bar with adjustable weights on either side that people lift to strengthen their arm and shoulder muscles. 杠铃 ❑ *She lifted the barbell in her left hand.* 她用左手举起了杠铃。

bar·ber /bɑrbər/ (**barbers**) **1** N-COUNT A **barber** is a man whose job is cutting men's hair. 理发师 ❑ *My father marched me over to Otto, the local barber, to have my hair cut short.* 爸爸把我拽到当地理发师奥托跟前，让他把我的头发剪短。 **2** N-SING A **barber's** is a store where a barber works. 理发店 [mainly BRIT]

in AM, usually use **barber shop**

bar chart (**bar charts**) N-COUNT A **bar chart** is the same as a **bar graph**. 条形图

bar code (**bar codes**) also **barcode** N-COUNT A **bar code** is an arrangement of numbers and parallel lines that is printed on products to be sold in stores. The bar code can be read by computers. 条形码

→ see **laser**

bare ♦◇◇ /bɛər/ (**barer, barest, bares, baring, bared**) **1** ADJ If a part of your body is **bare**, it is not covered by any clothing. 赤裸的 ❑ *She was wearing only a thin robe over a flimsy nightgown, and her feet were bare.* 她只在薄薄的睡衣外面穿了件薄袍子，还光着双脚。 **2** ADJ A **bare** surface is not covered or decorated with anything. 无遮盖的; 无装饰的 ❑ *They would have liked bare wooden floors throughout the house.* 他们本想把整个房子都铺不加装饰的原木地板。 **3** ADJ If a tree or a branch is **bare**, it has no leaves on it. (树或树枝) 没有树叶的 ❑ *...an old, twisted tree, many of its limbs brittle and bare.* …一棵扭曲的老树，它的树枝很多是脆弱而光秃的。 **4** ADJ If a room, cupboard, or shelf is **bare**, it is empty. 空的 ❑ *His fridge was bare apart from three very withered tomatoes.* 他的冰箱里除了3个干瘪的番茄之外什么也没有。 **5** ADJ An area of ground that is **bare** has no plants growing on it. (土地) 光秃的 ❑ *That's probably the most bare, bleak, barren and inhospitable island I've ever seen.* 那可能是我见过的最光秃、最荒凉、最贫瘠和最不适合居住的岛屿。 **6** ADJ If someone gives you the **bare** facts or the **barest** details of something, they tell you only the most basic and important things. 最简要的 [det ADJ n] ❑ *Newspaper reporters were given nothing but the bare facts by the superintendent in charge of the investigation.* 报社记者们只提供了负责该项调查的监管人所提供的一些简要事实。 **7** ADJ If you talk about the **bare** minimum or the **bare** essentials, you mean the very least that is necessary. 基本的 [det ADJ n] ❑ *The army would try to hold the western desert with a bare minimum of forces.* 军队将尽量用最少的兵力控制西部沙漠。 **8** ADJ **Bare** is used in front of an amount to emphasize how small it is. 仅仅的 ["a" ADJ amount] [EMPHASIS] ❑ *Sales are growing for premium wines, but at a bare 2 percent a year.* 优质葡萄酒的销量在上涨，但每年仅涨2%。 **9** V-T If you **bare** something, you uncover it and show it. 使露出 [WRITTEN] ❑ *Walsh bared his teeth in a grin.* 沃尔什一笑露出了牙齿。 **10** PHRASE If someone does something **with** their **bare hands**, they do it without using any weapons or tools. 徒手 ❑ *Police believe the killer punched her to death with his bare hands.* 警方认为凶手是徒手击她至死的。 **11** **bare bones** → see **bone**

Thesaurus *bare* 另参见:

ADJ.	naked, nude, undressed; *(ant.)* clothed, dressed **1** arid, barren, bleak **5**
V.	disclose, expose, reveal, show; *(ant.)* cover, hide **9**

bare-bones **1** ADJ If you describe something as **bare-bones**, you mean that it is reduced to the smallest size, amount, or number that you need. 降到最低限度的 [usu ADJ n] ❑ *The mayor will have to slash the city's already bare-bones budget.* 市长将不得不削减该市已经降到最低限度的预算。 **2** → see also **bone 4**

bare·foot /bɛərfʊt/ ADJ Someone who is **barefoot** is not wearing anything on their feet. 赤足的 ❑ *I wore a white dress and was barefoot.* 我穿了件白色连衣裙，光着脚。

bare·ly ♦◇◇ /bɛərli/ **1** ADV You use **barely** to say that something is only just true or only just the case. 仅仅; 几乎不 ❑ *Anastasia could barely remember the ride to the hospital.* 阿纳斯塔西娅只勉强记得被送到了医院。 ❑ *It was 90 degrees and the air conditioning barely cooled the room.* 气温是90度，空调几乎没有使房间凉快下来。 **2** ADV If you say that one thing had **barely** happened when

B

something else happened, you mean that the first event was followed immediately by the second. 刚刚 [ADV before v] ❑ *The water had barely come to a simmer when she cracked four eggs into it.* 水刚开她就打了4个鸡蛋进去。

bar·gain ♦◇◇ /bɑrgɪn/ (**bargains, bargaining, bargained**) 1 N-COUNT Something that is a **bargain** is good value, usually because it has been sold at a lower price than normal. 物美价廉的商品 ❑ *At this price the wine is a bargain.* 以这个价格，这葡萄酒算是物美价廉了。 2 N-COUNT A **bargain** is an agreement, especially a formal business agreement, in which two people or groups agree what each of them will do, pay, or receive. 协议（尤指正式商业合同） ❑ *I'll make a bargain with you. I'll play hostess if you'll include Matthew in your guest list.* 我想和你达成个协议：如果你把马修列入客人名单，我就充当女主人。 3 V-I When people **bargain with** each other, they discuss what each of them will do, pay, or receive. 谈判；讨价还价 ❑ *They prefer to bargain with individual clients, for cash.* 他们更愿意同个人客户洽谈，做现金交易。 ● **bar·gain·ing** N-UNCOUNT 谈判；讨价还价 ❑ *The government has called for sensible pay bargaining.* 政府已呼吁进行理性的工资谈判。 4 PHRASE You use **into the bargain** or **in the bargain** when mentioning an additional quantity, feature, fact, or action, to emphasize the fact that it is also involved. 而且还 [EMPHASIS] ❑ *This machine is designed to save you effort, and keep your work surfaces tidy into the bargain.* 这种机器是为了省力而设计的，而且它还会使你的工作台面保持整洁。

▸ **bargain for** or **bargain on** PHRASAL VERB If you have not **bargained for** or **bargained on** something that happens, you did not expect it to happen and so feel surprised or worried by it. 预料 ❑ *The effects of this policy were more than the government had bargained for.* 这项政策的影响出乎政府的预料。

Thesaurus *bargain* 另参见：

N. deal, discount, markdown 1
agreement, deal, understanding 2
V. barter, haggle, negotiate 3

Word Partnership *bargain* 的常用搭配：

V. **find/get a** bargain 1
make/strike a bargain 2
N. bargain **hunter**, bargain **price**, bargain **rates** 1
part of the bargain 2
PREP. bargain **with** *someone* 3

▲ **barge** /bɑrdʒ/ (**barges, barging, barged**) 1 N-COUNT A **barge** is a long, narrow boat with a flat bottom. Barges are used for carrying heavy loads, especially on rivers and canals. 平底载货船 [also "by" N] ❑ *Carrying goods by train costs nearly three times more than carrying them by barge.* 用火车运货的费用几乎比用货船高出3倍。 2 V-I If you **barge into** a place or **barge through** it, you rush or push into it in a rough and rude way. 闯入 [INFORMAL] ❑ *Students tried to barge into the secretariat buildings.* 学生们试图闯进秘书处大楼。 3 V-I If you **barge into** someone or **barge past** them, you bump against them roughly and rudely. 撞 [INFORMAL] ❑ *He would barge into them and kick them in the shins.* 他会冲撞他们，踢他们的小腿。
→ see **ship**

▸ **barge in** PHRASAL VERB If you **barge in** or **barge in on** someone, you rudely interrupt what they are doing or saying. 插一杠子 [INFORMAL] ❑ *I'm sorry to barge in like this, but I have a problem I hope you can solve.* 抱歉这样插进来，不过我有个问题希望你能解决。

bar graph (**bar graphs**) N-COUNT A **bar graph** is a graph that uses parallel rectangular shapes to represent changes in the size, value, or rate of something or to compare the amount of something relating to a number of different countries or groups. 条形图 ❑ *They made a bar graph to display the results.* 他们用条形图来显示结果。
→ see **graph**

bar-hop (**bar-hops, bar-hopping, bar-hopped**) V-I If a person **bar-hops**, they go from one bar to another having drinks in each one. 从一家酒吧喝到另一家酒吧 [AM, INFORMAL] ❑ *...a yearly rite-of-passage in which graduating seniors bar-hop from morning until late afternoon.* …一年一度的毕业庆祝活动，即将毕业的四年级学生从上午到傍晚从一家酒吧喝到另一家酒吧。

bari·tone /bærɪtoʊn/ (**baritones**) N-COUNT In music, a **baritone** is a man with a fairly deep singing voice that is lower than that of a tenor but higher than that of a bass. 男中音歌手 ❑ *...the young American baritone Monte Pederson.* …年轻的美国男中音歌手蒙特·佩德森。

bark /bɑrk/ (**barks, barking, barked**) 1 V-I When a dog **barks**, it makes a short, loud noise, once or several times. （狗）吠 ❑ *Don't let the dogs bark.* 别让狗叫。 ● N-COUNT **Bark** is also a noun. 吠声 ❑ *The Doberman let out a string of roaring barks.* 那条德国短毛猎犬发出一连串的吼叫声。 2 V-I If you **bark at** someone, you shout at them aggressively in a loud, rough voice. 咆哮 ❑ *I didn't mean to bark at you.* 我不是有意吼你。 3 N-UNCOUNT **Bark** is the tough material that covers the outside of a tree. 树皮 4 **to be barking up the wrong tree** → see **tree**

▲ **bar·ley** /bɑrli/ N-UNCOUNT **Barley** is a grain that is used to make food, beer, and whiskey. 大麦 ❑ *...fields of ripening wheat and barley.* …快要成熟的小麦和大麦田。

bar·maid /bɑrmeɪd/ (**barmaids**) N-COUNT A **barmaid** is a woman who serves drinks behind a bar. 酒吧间女招待 [mainly BRIT]

in AM, use **bartender**

bar·man /bɑrmən/ (**barmen**) N-COUNT A **barman** is a man who serves drinks behind a bar. 酒吧间男招待 [mainly BRIT]

in AM, use **bartender**

barn /bɑrn/ (**barns**) N-COUNT A **barn** is a building on a farm in which animals, animal food, or crops can be kept. 谷仓；牲口房
→ see Picture Dictionary: **barn**

▲ **ba·rom·eter** /bərɒmɪtər/ (**barometers**) 1 N-COUNT A **barometer** is an instrument that measures air pressure and shows when the weather is changing. 气压计 ❑ *A man in camp took a barometer reading at half-hour intervals.* 营地里的一个人每半小时看一次气压计。 2 N-COUNT If something is a **barometer of** a particular situation, it indicates how things are changing or how things are likely to develop. 发展变化的指示计 ❑ *In past presidential elections, Missouri has been a barometer of the rest of the country.* 在过去的总统大选中，密苏里州一直是该国其余各州的晴雨表。

baro·met·ric /bærəmɛtrɪk/ **Barometric** pressure is the atmospheric pressure that is shown by a barometer. 气压表的 ADJ
→ see **forecast, weather**

bar·on /bærən/ (**barons**) 1 N-COUNT; N-TITLE A **baron** is a man who is a member of the lowest rank of the nobility. 男爵（英国贵族的最低爵位） [BRIT] ❑ *...their stepfather, Baron Michael Distemple.* …他们的继父迈克尔·迪斯坦普尔男爵 2 N-COUNT You can use **baron** to refer to someone who controls a large part of a particular industry or activity and who is therefore extremely powerful. 大亨 ❑ *...the battle against the drug barons.* …与大毒枭们的斗争。

▲ **bar·racks** /bærəks/ (**barracks**)

Barracks is both the singular and plural form.

N-COUNT A **barracks** is a building or group of buildings where soldiers or other members of the armed forces live and work. 营房 [oft in names] ❑ *...an army barracks in the north of the city.* …一所在那个城市北面的军营。

bar·rage /bərɑʒ/ (**barrages, barraging, barraged**)

Pronounced /bɑrɪdʒ/ for meaning 4.

义项4读作 /bɑrɪdʒ/。

1 N-COUNT A **barrage** is continuous firing on an area with large guns and tanks. 连续炮击 ❑ *The artillery barrage on the city was the heaviest since the ceasefire.* 此次对城市的连续炮击是自停战以来最猛烈的。 2 N-COUNT A **barrage of** something such as criticism or complaints is a large number of them directed at someone, often in an aggressive way. 一连串（问题，抱怨等） ❑ *He was faced with a barrage of angry questions from the floor.* 他面临着听众一连串的愤怒质问。 3 V-T If you **are barraged** by people or things, you have to deal with a great number of people or things you would rather avoid. 不断骚扰 [usu passive] ❑ *Doctors are complaining about being barraged by drug-company salesmen.* 医生们抱怨总是受到医药公司销售人员的骚扰。 4 N-COUNT A **barrage** is a structure that is built across a river to control the level of the water. 堰堤；水坝 ❑ *...a hydro-electric tidal barrage.* …一座水力发电潮汐拦河坝。

bar·rel ♦◇◇ /bærəl/ (**barrels, barreling** or **barrelling, barreled** or **barrelled**) 1 N-COUNT A **barrel** is a large, round container for liquids or food. 桶 ❑ *The wine is aged for almost a year in oak barrels.* 这葡萄酒在橡木桶里陈了将近一年。 2 N-COUNT In the oil industry, a **barrel** is a unit of measurement equal to 42 gallons (159 liters). 桶（石油计量单位，等于42加仑或159升） ❑ *In 1989, Kuwait was exporting 1.5 million barrels of oil a day.* 1989年，科威特每天出口150万桶石油。

b

3 N-COUNT The **barrel** of a gun is the tube through which the bullet moves when the gun is fired. 枪管；炮管 ❑ *He pushed the barrel of the gun into the other man's open mouth.* 他把枪管插入另一个人张开着的嘴里。 4 V-I If a vehicle or person **is barreling** in a particular direction, they are moving very quickly in that direction. 高速行驶 [mainly AM] ❑ *The car was barreling down the street at a crazy speed.* 汽车沿着街道发疯一般地高速行驶。 5 PHRASE If you say, for example, that someone moves or buys something **lock, stock, and barrel**, you are emphasizing that they move or buy every part or item of it. 完全 [EMPHASIS] ❑ *They received a verbal offer to buy the company lock, stock and barrel.* 他们收到全盘收购公司的口头承诺。

Word Partnership *barrel* 的常用搭配：

N. **bottom of the** barrel, **wine** barrel 1
barrel **of oil** 2
barrel **of a gun** 3
PREP. barrel **down toward** ***somewhere*** 4

barrel-chested ADJ A **barrel-chested** man has a large, rounded chest. 胸部厚实发达的 ❑ *A barrel-chested young man entered the bedroom.* 一位胸部厚实发达的年轻男子走进了卧室。

★ **bar·ren** /bærən/ 1 ADJ A **barren** landscape is dry and bare, and has very few plants and no trees. 荒芜的 ❑ *...the Tibetan landscape of high barren mountains.* …西藏荒芜的高山景观。 2 ADJ **Barren** land consists of soil that is so poor that plants cannot grow in it. 贫瘠的 ❑ *He wants to use the water to irrigate barren desert land.* 他想用该水来灌溉贫瘠的沙漠土地。 3 ADJ If you describe something such as an activity or a period of your life as **barren**, you mean that you achieve no success during it or that it has no useful results. 无成就的；不成功的 [oft ADJ "of" n] [WRITTEN] ❑ *...an empty exercise barren of utility.* …一项毫无效用的无聊训练。 4 ADJ If you describe a room or a place as **barren**, you do not like it because it has almost no furniture or other objects in it. 空荡荡的 [oft ADJ "of" n] [WRITTEN, DISAPPROVAL] ❑ *The room was austere, nearly barren of furniture or decoration.* 这个房间很简朴，几乎没有什么家具或装饰。

Thesaurus *barren* 另参见：

ADJ. desolate, empty, infertile, sparse, sterile; *(ant.)* fertile, lush, rich 1 2

▲ **bar·ri·cade** /bærɪkeɪd/ (**barricades, barricading, barricaded**) 1 N-COUNT A **barricade** is a line of vehicles or other objects placed across a road or open space to stop people from getting past, for example, during street fighting or as a protest. 街垒；路障 ❑ *Large areas of the city have been closed off by barricades set up by the demonstrators.* 城里的大部分地区都被示威者设置的路障给封锁了。 2 V-T If you **barricade** something such as a road or an entrance, you place a barricade or barrier across it, usually to stop someone from getting in. 在…设路障 ❑ *The rioters barricaded streets with piles of blazing tires.* 闹事者用成堆燃烧着的轮胎挡住了街道。 3 V-T If you **barricade** yourself inside a room or building, you place barriers across the door or entrance so that other people cannot get in. 把…堵在 ❑ *The students have barricaded themselves into their dormitory building.* 学生们将自己堵在宿舍楼里。

bar·ri·er ♦◇◇ /bæriər/ (**barriers**) 1 N-COUNT A **barrier** is something such as a rule, law, or policy that makes it difficult or impossible for something to happen or be achieved. 障碍 ❑ *Duties and taxes are the most obvious barrier to free trade.* 关税及其他各种税是自由贸易最明显的障碍。 2 N-COUNT A **barrier** is a problem that prevents two people or groups from agreeing, communicating, or working with each other. 障碍；隔阂 ❑ *There is no reason why love shouldn't cross the age barrier.* 爱情没有理由不应跨越年龄障碍。 ❑ *She had been waiting for Simon to break down the barrier between them.* 她一直在等着西蒙来破除他们之间的隔阂。 3 N-COUNT A **barrier** is something such as a fence or wall that is put in place to prevent people from moving easily from one area to another. 栅栏；围墙 ❑ *The demonstrators broke through heavy police barriers.* 示威者们冲破了警方的重重关卡。 4 N-COUNT A **barrier** is an object or layer that physically prevents something from moving from one place to another. 屏障 ❑ *A severe storm destroyed a natural barrier between the house and the lake.* 一场猛烈的暴风雨摧毁了房屋和湖泊之间的天然屏障。 5 N-SING You can refer to a particular number or amount as a **barrier** when you think it is significant, because it is difficult or unusual to go above it. (数量) 大关 ❑ *They are fearful that unemployment will soon break the barrier of three million.* 他们担心失业人数不久将突破300万大关。

Word Partnership *barrier* 的常用搭配：

ADJ. **psychological** barrier, **racial** barrier 2
N. **language** barrier 2
police barrier 3
barrier **islands/reef** 4
PREP. barrier **between** 2 – 4
V. **break down a** barrier, **cross a** barrier 2 – 4

bar·ring /bɑrɪŋ/ PREP You use **barring** to indicate that the person, thing, or event that you are mentioning is an exception to your statement. 除…之外 ❑ *Barring accidents, I believe they will succeed.* 不出意外的话，我相信他们会成功。

B

Word Link *ster ≈ one who does : barrister, gangster, youngster*

bar·ris·ter /bærɪstər/ (**barristers**) N-COUNT In England and Wales, a **barrister** is a lawyer who represents clients in the higher courts of law. Compare **solicitor.** (英格兰和威尔士的) 大律师

bar·room /bɑrrum/ (**barrooms**) also **bar-room** N-COUNT A **barroom** is a room or building in which alcoholic drinks are served over a counter. 酒吧间 [mainly AM]

in BRIT, usually use **bar, pub**

❑ *...a barroom brawl.* …一场发生在酒吧间的斗殴。

bar·tender /bɑrtɛndər/ (**bartenders**) N-COUNT A **bartender** is a person who serves drinks behind a bar. 酒吧侍者 [AM]

in BRIT, use **barmaid, barman**

bar·ter /bɑrtər/ (**barters, bartering, bartered**) V-T/V-I If you **barter** goods, you exchange them for other goods, rather than selling them for money. 以物交换; 以物易物 ❑ *They have been bartering wheat for cotton and timber.* 他们一直在用小麦交换棉花和木材。 ❑ *The market-place and street were crowded with those who'd come to barter.* 市场和街道上挤满了来进行物物交换的人。 ● N-UNCOUNT **Barter** is also a noun. 物物交换 ❑ *Overall, barter is a very inefficient means of organizing transactions.* 总的说来，物物交换是一种非常低效的组织交易的方式。

→ see **money**

base ♦♦♦ /beɪs/ (**bases, basing, based, baser, basest**) **1** N-COUNT The **base** of something is its lowest edge or part. 底边; 底部 ❑ *There was a bike path running along this side of the wall, right at its base.* 沿着墙的这一边，就在墙脚下，有一条自行车道。 **2** N-COUNT The **base** of something is the lowest part of it, where it is attached to something else. 基部 ❑ *The surgeon placed catheters through the veins and arteries near the base of the head.* 医生把导管插入靠近大脑底部附近的血管和动脉。 **3** N-COUNT The **base** of an object such as a box or vase is the lower surface of it that touches the surface it rests on. (箱、瓶等器皿的) 底部 ❑ *Remove from the heat and plunge the base of the pan into a bowl of very cold water.* 把烤盘从高温中取出，把盘的底部浸泡在一盆极冷的水中。 **4** N-COUNT The **base** of an object that has several sections and that rests on a surface is the lower section of it. 底座 ❑ *The mattress is best on a solid bed base.* 床垫最好放在结实的床座上。 **5** N-COUNT A **base** is a layer of something which will have another layer added to it. 底层 ❑ *Mix together the cream cheese, yogurt and honey, and spread over the meringue base.* 把干酪、酸奶和蜂蜜拌在一起，然后涂在蛋白甜饼底层上。 **6** N-COUNT A position or thing that is a **base** for something is one from which that thing can be developed or achieved. 基础 ❑ *The post will give him a powerful political base from which to challenge the Kremlin.* 这个职位将为他挑战克里姆林宫提供一个有力的政治基础。 **7** V-T If you **base** one thing **on** another thing, the first thing develops from the second thing. 以…为基础 ❑ *He based his conclusions on the evidence given by the captured prisoners.* 他根据俘虏提供的证据得出了自己的结论。 ● **based** ADJ 以…为基础的 [v-link ADJ "on/upon" n] ❑ *Three of the new products are based on traditional herbal medicines.* 新产品中有三种是根据传统草药研制的。 **8** N-COUNT A company's client **base** or customer **base** is the group of regular clients or customers that the company gets most of its income from. (客户) 群 [BUSINESS] ❑ *The company has been expanding its customer base using trade magazine advertising.* 这家公司一直通过商业杂志广告来扩大客户群。 **9** N-COUNT A military **base** is a place that part of the armed forces works from. (军事) 基地 ❑ *Gunfire was heard at an army base close to the airport.* 在临近机场的一个军事基地听到了枪声。 **10** N-COUNT Your **base** is the main place where you work, stay, or live. 主要 (工作、逗留或生活) 地点 ❑ *For most of the spring and early summer her base was her home in Connecticut.* 春天和初夏的大部分时间她的主要活动地点是她在康涅狄格州的家。 **11** N-COUNT If a place is a **base** for a certain activity, the activity can be carried out at that place or from that place. (活动) 大本营 ❑ *The two hotels are attractive bases from which to explore southeast Tuscany.* 这两个旅馆是去托斯卡纳东南探险最有吸引力的大本营。 **12** N-COUNT The **base** of a substance such as paint or food is the main ingredient of it, to which other substances can be added. 主要配料 ❑ *Just before cooking, drain off any excess marinade and use it as a base for a sauce.* 临烹饪前，沥干多余的腌汁，用它做调味汁的主要配料。 **13** N-COUNT A **base** is a system of counting and expressing numbers. The decimal system uses base 10, and the binary system uses base 2. 基数 [also N num] **14** N-COUNT A **base** in baseball or softball is one of the places at each corner of the diamond on the field. A player who is at **first base, second base,** or **third base,** is standing at the first, second, or third base in a clockwise direction from home plate. (棒球、垒球中的) 垒 ❑ *The first runner to reach second base in the game was John Flaherty.* 比赛中首先到达二垒的跑垒员是约翰•弗莱厄蒂。 **15** ADJ **Base** is used to describe a price or someone's income when this does not include any additional amounts. 基本的 (价格或收入) [ADJ n] ❑ *...an increase of more than twenty percent on the base pay of a typical worker.* …一个典型工人的基本工资超过20%的增长。

→ see **area, baseball**

Word Partnership *base* 的常用搭配:

N. **knowledge** base, **tax** base **6**
client/customer base, **fan** base **8**
base **camp**, **home** base, base **of operation** **10** **11**
base **hit/run** **14**
ADJ. **military/naval** base **9**
stolen base **14**

base·ball ♦◇◇ /beɪsbɔl/ (**baseballs**) **1** N-UNCOUNT **Baseball** is a game played by two teams of nine players. Each player from one team hits a ball with a bat and then tries to run around three bases and get to home plate before the other team can get the ball back. Compare **softball.** 棒球运动 **2** N-COUNT A **baseball** is a small hard ball which is used in the game of baseball. 棒球

→ see Picture Dictionary: **baseball**

→ see **park**

Although it isn't the most watched sport anymore, **baseball** is still called "America's Pastime." A player who wants to reach his goal usually dreams of playing in the Major League and winning the World Series.

base·ball cap (**baseball caps**) N-COUNT A **baseball cap** is a close-fitting cap with a curved part at the front that sticks out above your eyes. 棒球帽 ❑ *He often wore a baseball cap.* 他经常戴顶棒球帽。

→ see **clothing**

based ♦♦♦ /beɪst/ ADJ If you are **based** in a particular place, that is the place where you live or do most of your work. See also **base.** 基地 (或总部) 在…的 [v-link ADJ] ❑ *Both firms are based in Kent.* 这两家公司的总部都位于肯特郡。

base·ment /beɪsmənt/ (**basements**) N-COUNT The **basement** of a building is a floor built partly or completely below ground level. 地下室 ❑ *They bought an old schoolhouse to live in and built a workshop in the basement.* 他们买了座旧校舍居住，还在地下室建了个作坊。

→ see **house**

bases

Pronounced /beɪsɪz/ for meaning **1**. Pronounced /beɪsiz/ and hyphenated ba·ses for meaning **2**.

义项**1**读作 /beɪsɪz/。义项**2**读作 /beɪsiz/且音节划分为ba·ses。

1 **Bases** is the plural of **base. base**的复数形式 **2** **Bases** is the plural of **basis. basis**的复数形式

bash /bæʃ/ (**bashes, bashing, bashed**) **1** N-COUNT A **bash** is a party or celebration, especially a large one held by an official organization or attended by famous people. (尤为官方举办的或名流出席的) 盛会; 庆典 [INFORMAL] ❑ *He threw one of the biggest showbiz bashes of the year as a 36th birthday party for Jerry Hall.* 他为杰里•霍耳的36岁生日举行了该年度娱乐界最盛大的名流派对。 **2** V-T If someone **bashes** you, they attack you by hitting or punching you hard. 痛打 [INFORMAL] ❑ *If someone tried to bash my best friend they would have to bash me as well.* 如果有人要打我最好的朋友，他们也要连我一起打才行。 ❑ *I bashed him on the head and dumped him in the water.* 我猛揍他的头，然后把他扔到了水里。 **3** V-T If you **bash** something, you hit it hard in a rough or careless way. 乱打 [INFORMAL] ❑ *Too many golfers try to bash the ball out of sand. That spells disaster.* 太多打高尔夫球的人试图把球胡乱打出沙坑。那就意味着灾难。

ba·sic ♦♦◇ /beɪsɪk/ **1** ADJ You use **basic** to describe things, activities, and principles that are very important or necessary, and on which others depend. 基本的 ❑ *...the basic skills of reading, writing and communicating.* …阅读、写作和交际等基本技巧。 ❑ *Access to justice is a basic right.* 享有公正是一种基本权利。 **2** ADJ **Basic** goods and services are very simple ones which every human being needs. You can also refer to people's **basic** needs for such goods and services. 基本必需的 ❑ *...shortages of even the most basic foodstuffs.* …甚至最基本食品的短缺。 ❑ *Hospitals lack even basic drugs for surgical*

b

Picture Dictionary baseball

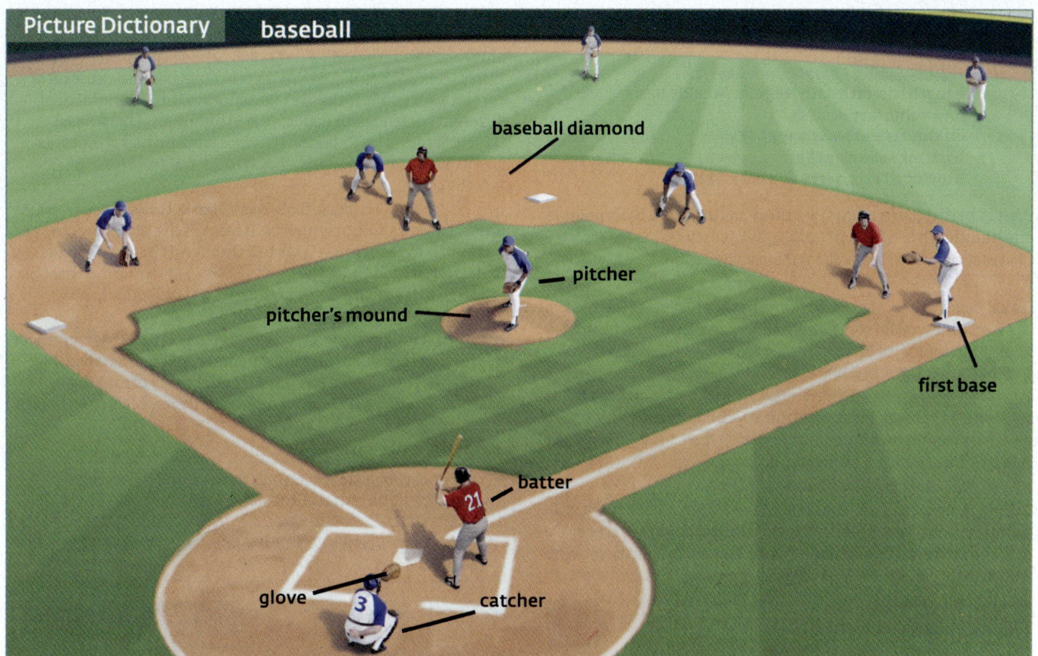

operations. 医院甚至缺乏外科手术的基本必需的药品。 3 ADJ If one thing is **basic to** another, it is absolutely necessary to it, and the second thing cannot exist, succeed, or be imagined without it. 必不可少的 [V-link ADJ "to" n] ❑ *...an oily liquid, basic to the manufacture of a host of other chemical substances.* …生产许多其它化学材料所必不可少的一种油状液体。 4 ADJ You can use **basic** to emphasize that you are referring to what you consider to be the most important aspect of a situation, and that you are not concerned with less important details. 主要的 [ADJ n] [EMPHASIS] ❑ *There are three basic types of tea.* 有3种主要的茶。 ❑ *The basic design changed little from that patented by Edison more than 100 years ago.* 这个主要设计与100多年前爱迪生取得专利的设计相比没什么变化。 5 ADJ You can use **basic** to describe something that is very simple in style and has only the most necessary features, without any luxuries. 简单的 ❑ *We provide 2-person tents and basic cooking and camping equipment.* 我们提供双人帐篷以及简单的烹饪和露营设备。 6 ADJ The **basic** rate of income tax is the lowest or most common rate, which applies to people who earn average incomes. (所得税) 最低标准额的 [ADJ n] ❑ *All this is to be done without big increases in the basic level of taxation.* 所有这一切将在没有大幅度提高最低所得税标准的情况下进行。

Thesaurus *basic* 另参见：

ADJ. essential, fundamental, key, main, necessary, principal, vital; (*ant.*) nonessential, secondary 1–4

Word Partnership *basic* 的常用搭配：

N. basic **right** 1
basic **idea**, basic **principles/values**, basic **problem**, basic **questions**, basic **skills**, basic **types of** *something*, basic **understanding** 1 4
basic **(health) care**, basic **needs** 2

ADJ. **most** basic 1–5

BA·SIC /beɪsɪk/ also **Basic** N-UNCOUNT **BASIC** is a computer language that uses common English words. **BASIC** is an abbreviation for "Beginner's All-Purpose Symbolic Instruction Code." BASIC语言 [COMPUTING, COMPUTING]

ba·si·cal·ly ♦◇◇ /beɪsɪkli/ 1 ADV You use **basically** for emphasis when you are stating an opinion, or when you are making an important statement about something. 基本上；主要地 [ADV with cl/group] [EMPHASIS] ❑ *This gun is designed for one purpose – it's basically to kill people.* 设计这把枪只有一个目的——主要用于杀人。 2 ADV You use **basically** to show that you are describing a situation in a simple, general way, and that you are not concerned with less important details. 简单来说；大致说来 ❑ *Basically you've got two choices.* 大致说来，你有两个选择。

ba·sics /beɪsɪks/ 1 N-PLURAL **The basics** of something are its simplest, most important elements, ideas, or principles, in contrast to more complicated or detailed ones. 基本要点 ❑ *They will concentrate on teaching the basics of reading, writing and arithmetic.* 他们将重点教授阅读、写作和算术的基本要点。 ❑ *A strong community cannot be built until the basics are in place.* 只有等到基本要素都已就位，一个牢固的社会才能建立。 2 N-PLURAL **Basics** are things such as simple food, clothes, or equipment that people need in order to live or to deal with a particular situation. 基本生活用品 ❑ *...supplies of basics such as bread and milk.* …面包、牛奶等基本食品的供给。

ba·sin /beɪsᵊn/ (**basins**) 1 N-COUNT A **basin** is a large or deep bowl that you use for holding liquids. 盆 ❑ *Water dripped into a basin at the back of the room.* 水滴入房间后面的一个盆里。 2 N-COUNT A **basin of** something such as water is an amount of it that is contained in a basin. 一盆之量 ❑ *We were given a basin of water to wash our hands in.* 我们得到了一盆水洗手。 3 N-COUNT A **basin** is a sink. 洗涤槽 ❑ *...a cast-iron bathtub with a matching basin.* …一个配有洗涤槽的铸铁浴缸。 4 N-COUNT The **basin** of a large river is the area of land around it from which streams run down into it. 流域 ❑ *...the Amazon basin.* …亚马孙流域 5 N-COUNT In geography, a **basin** is a particular region of the world where the Earth's surface is lower than in other places. 盆地 [TECHNICAL] ❑ *...countries around the Pacific Basin.* …太平洋盆地周围的国家。
→ see **lake, plumbing**

ba·sis ♦♦◇ /beɪsɪs/ (**bases** /beɪsiz/) 1 N-SING If something is done **on** a particular **basis**, it is done according to that method, system, or principle. 按…原则；以…方式 ❑ *We're going to be meeting there on a regular basis.* 我们将定期在那儿会面。 ❑ *They want all groups to be treated on an equal basis.* 他们要求所有的群体都能得到平等的对待。 2 N-SING If you say that you are acting **on the basis of** something, you are giving that as the reason for your action. 以…为由 ❑ *McGregor must remain confined, on the basis of the medical reports we have received.* 基于我们所收到的医疗报告，麦格雷戈必须继续卧床休息。 3 N-COUNT The **basis** of something is its starting point or an important part of it from which it can be further developed. 基础 ❑ *Both factions have broadly agreed that the U.N. plan is a possible basis for negotiation.* 两派已大致同意该联合国计划是谈判的可能基础。 4 N-COUNT The **basis** for something is a fact or argument that

B

you can use to prove or justify it. 依据 ❑ *...Japan's attempt to secure the legal basis to send troops overseas.* …日本取得派遣军队的法律依据的企图。

Word Partnership *basis* 的常用搭配:

ADJ.	**equal** basis, **on a daily/regular/weekly** basis, **on a voluntary** basis 1
PREP.	**on the** basis **of** ***something*** 2 – 4 basis **for** ***something*** 3 4
V.	**provide a** basis, **serve as a** basis 3 4

ba•sis point (**basis points**) N-COUNT In finance, a **basis point** is one hundredth of a percent (.01%). 基点 [BUSINESS] ❑ *The dollar climbed about 30 basis points during the morning session.* 在上午这段时间美元上升了大约30个基点。

bask /bɑsk, bæsk/ (**basks, basking, basked**) 1 V-I If you **bask in** the sunshine, you lie somewhere sunny and enjoy the heat. 晒太阳 ❑ *All through the hot, still days of their vacation Amy basked in the sun.* 在整个炎热、寂静的假期里埃米都在晒太阳。❑ *Crocodiles bask on the small sandy beaches.* 鳄鱼在小沙滩上晒太阳。2 V-I If you **bask in** someone's approval, favor, or admiration, you greatly enjoy their positive reaction toward you. 享受; 陶醉于 ❑ *He has spent a month basking in the adulation of the fans back in Jamaica.* 他一个月里都陶醉在牙买加崇拜者的吹捧之中。

bas•ket /bɑskɪt, bæs-/ (**baskets**) 1 N-COUNT A **basket** is a stiff container that is used for carrying or storing objects. Baskets are made from thin strips of materials such as straw, plastic, or wire woven together. 篮; 筐; 篓 ❑ *...big wicker picnic baskets filled with sandwiches.* …装满三明治的大的藤条野餐篮。2 N-COUNT You can use **basket** to refer to a basket and its contents, or to the contents only. 一篮(篓、筐); 一篮(篓、筐)之量 ❑ *...a small basket of fruit and snacks.* …一小篮水果和点心。3 N-COUNT In economics, a **basket of** currencies or goods is the average or total value of a number of different currencies or goods. 一篮子(货币或商品) [BUSINESS] ❑ *The dollar has fallen 6.5 percent this year against a basket of currencies from its largest trading partners.* 美元对其最大贸易伙伴们的一篮子货币今年贬值了6.5%。

basket•ball ♦♦◊ /bɑskɪtbɔl, bæs-/ (**basketballs**) 1 N-UNCOUNT **Basketball** is a game in which two teams of five players each try to score goals by throwing a large ball through a circular net fixed to a metal ring at each end of the court. 篮球运动 2 N-COUNT A **basketball** is a large ball which is used in the game of basketball. 篮球

→ see Picture Dictionary: **basketball**

bas•ket•ry /bæskɪtri/ 1 N-UNCOUNT **Basketry** is baskets made by weaving together thin strips of materials such as wood. 编织物品 2 N-UNCOUNT **Basketry** is the activity of making baskets. 编织活动 ❑ *Eva specializes in one of the most difficult techniques of basketry.* 伊娃专攻一种最难的编织篮筐的技艺。

▲ **bass** ♦◊◊ (**basses**)

Pronounced /beɪs/ for meanings 1 to 4, and /bæs/ for meaning 5. The plural of the noun in meaning 5 is **bass**.

义项1至4读作 /beɪs/, 义项5读作 /bæs/。义项5的名词复数形式是**bass**。

Picture Dictionary **basketball**

1 N-COUNT A **bass** is a man with a very deep singing voice. 男低音歌手 ❑ *...the great Russian bass Chaliapin.* …著名的俄罗斯男低音歌手夏里亚宾。 2 ADJ A **bass** drum, guitar, or other musical instrument is one that produces a very deep sound. (鼓、吉他等乐器) 低音的 [ADJ n] ❑ *...bass guitarist Dee Murray.* …低音吉他手迪伊•默里。 3 N-VAR In popular music, a **bass** is a bass guitar or a **double bass**. 低音吉他; 低音提琴 ❑ *...Dave Ranson on bass and Kenneth Blevins on drums.* …戴夫•兰森弹低音吉他，肯尼思•布莱文斯敲鼓。 4 N-UNCOUNT On a stereo system or radio, the **bass** is the ability to reproduce the lower musical notes. The **bass** is also the knob that controls this. 低音部; 低音旋钮 ❑ *Larger models give more bass.* 更大的型号能奏出更多的低音。 5 N-VAR **Bass** are edible fish that are found in rivers and the sea. There are several types of bass. 鲈鱼 ❑ *They unloaded their catch of cod and bass.* 他们卸下捕获的鳕鱼和鲈鱼。 ● N-UNCOUNT **Bass** is a piece of this fish eaten as food. 鲈鱼肉 ❑ *...a large fresh fillet of sea bass.* …一大块新鲜的海产无骨鲈鱼肉。

bas·si·net /bæsɪnɛt/ (**bassinets**) N-COUNT A **bassinet** is a small bed for a baby that is like a basket. 摇篮 ❑ *My baby slept safe from harm in her white wicker bassinet.* 我的小宝贝安稳地睡在白色的藤条摇篮里。

▲ **bas·tard** /bæstərd/ (**bastards**) 1 N-COUNT **Bastard** is an insulting word which some people use about a person, especially a man, who has behaved very badly. 杂种 [INFORMAL, OFFENSIVE, VULGAR, DISAPPROVAL] 2 N-COUNT A **bastard** is a person whose parents were not married to each other at the time that he or she was born. This use could cause offense. 私生子 [oft N n] [OLD-FASHIONED]

bas·ti·on /bæstʃən/ (**bastions**) N-COUNT If a system or organization is described as a **bastion of** a particular way of life, it is seen as being important and effective in defending that way of life. **Bastion** can be used both when you think that this way of life should be ended and when you think it should be defended. 堡垒; 精神支柱 [FORMAL] ❑ *...a town which had been a bastion of white prejudice.* …一个曾经是白人偏见的堡垒的小镇。 ❑ *...a bastion of spiritual freedom.* …一座精神自由的堡垒。

bat ♦◇◇ /bæt/ (**bats, batting, batted**) 1 N-COUNT A **bat** is a specially shaped piece of wood that is used for hitting the ball in baseball, softball, or cricket. (棒球、垒球、板球) 球棒 ❑ *...a baseball bat.* …一支棒球；球拍球棒。 2 V-I When you **bat**, you have a turn at hitting the ball with a bat in baseball, softball, or cricket. (在棒球、垒球、板球运动中) 击球 ❑ *Pettitte hurt an elbow tendon while batting.* 佩蒂特在击球时伤了肘腱。 3 N-COUNT A **bat** is a small flying animal that looks like a mouse with wings made of skin. Bats are active at night. 蝙蝠 4 PHRASE If something happens **right off the bat**, it happens immediately. 马上 [AM] ❑ *He learned right off the bat that you can't count on anything in this business.* 他马上就认识到在这件事上你不能指望任何事物。

→ see Word Web: **bat**

→ see **flower**

bat·boy /bætbɔɪ/ (**batboys**) N-COUNT A **batboy** is a boy whose job is to take care of equipment that belongs to a baseball team. 棒球队球童 [AM] ❑ *If you are a batboy, then you are holding the bat for the baseball players.* 如果你是棒球队球童，那么你就要为棒球队员拿球棒。

★ **batch** /bætʃ/ (**batches**) N-COUNT A **batch of** things or people is a group of things or people of the same kind, especially a group that is dealt with at the same time or is sent to a particular place at the same time. (一) 批 ❑ *...the current batch of trainee priests.* …当前的这一批受训牧师。 ❑ *She brought a large batch of newspaper clippings.* 她带来一大批剪报。 ❑ *I baked a batch of cookies.* 我烤了一批小甜饼。

bath ♦◇◇ /bæθ/ (**baths, bathing, bathed**)

> When the form **baths** is the plural of the noun it is pronounced /bæðz/. When it is used in the present tense of the verb, it is pronounced /bɑθs/ or /bæθs/.

> **baths**此词形是名词复数时读作 /bæðz/。用于动词现在时读作 /bɑθs/或 /bæθs/。

1 N-COUNT A **bath** is the process of washing your body in a bathtub. 泡澡 ❑ *The midwife gave him a warm bath.* 助产士给他洗了个温水澡。 2 N-COUNT When you take a **bath**, you sit or lie in a bathtub filled with water in order to wash your body. 盆浴

> in BRIT, also use **have a bath**

❑ *Take a shower instead of a bath.* 别泡澡了，洗淋浴吧。 3 V-T If you **bath** someone, especially a child, you wash them in a bathtub. 给…洗澡 [BRIT]

> in AM, use **bathe**

4 N-COUNT A **bath** is a container, usually a long rectangular one, which you fill with water and sit in while you wash your body. 浴缸 [BRIT]

> in AM, use **bathtub**

5 V-I When you **bath**, you take a bath. 洗盆浴 [BRIT]

> in AM, use **bathe**

6 N-COUNT A **bath** or a **baths** is a public building containing a swimming pool, and sometimes other facilities that people can use to wash or take a bath. 澡堂 ❑ *...a thriving town with houses, government buildings and public baths.* …一个有住宅、政府办公楼以及公共澡堂的繁荣城镇。 7 N-COUNT A **bath** is a container filled with a particular liquid, such as a dye or an acid, in which particular objects are placed, usually as part of a manufacturing or chemical process. (装有液体的) 容器 ❑ *...a developing photograph placed in a bath of fixer.* …一张正放在一盆定影液里显影的照片。

bathe /beɪð/ (**bathes, bathing, bathed**) 1 V-I When you **bathe**, you take a bath. 洗盆浴 [AM] ❑ *At least 60% of us now bathe or shower once a day.* 如今我们中至少有60%的人每天洗盆浴或冲淋浴一次。 2 V-T If you **bathe** someone, especially a child, you wash them in a bathtub. 给…洗澡 [AM] ❑ *Back home, Shirley plays with, feeds and bathes the baby.* 回到家里，雪莉逗婴儿玩，给婴儿喂饭并洗澡。 3 V-I If you **bathe** in a sea, river, or lake, you swim, play, or wash yourself in it. Birds and animals can also **bathe**. (在海、河、湖里) 游泳、戏水; 洗澡 [mainly BRIT, FORMAL] ❑ *The police have warned the city's inhabitants not to bathe in the polluted river.* 警方已经警告该市市民不要在受污染的河里游泳。 ● N-SING **Bathe** is also a noun. 游泳 ❑ *They took an early morning bathe in the lake.* 他们在湖里进行了晨泳。 ● **bath·ing** /beɪðɪŋ/ N-UNCOUNT 游泳; 戏水; 洗澡 ❑ *Bathing is not allowed.* 禁止游泳。 4 V-T If you **bathe** a part of your body or a wound, you wash it gently or soak it in a liquid. 浸洗; 浸泡 ❑ *Bathe the infected area in a salt solution.* 把感染的部位浸泡在盐水溶液里。 5 V-T If a place is **bathed in** light, it is covered with light, especially a gentle, pleasant light. 以 (尤为柔和、令人愉悦的光线) 覆盖 ❑ *The arena was bathed in warm sunshine.* 该运动场沐浴在温暖的阳光中。 ❑ *I was led to a small room bathed in soft red light.* 我被领进了一个被柔和的红光笼罩着的小房间。 6 → see also **sunbathe**

bath·room ♦◇◇ /bæθrum/ (**bathrooms**) 1 N-COUNT A **bathroom** is a room in a house that contains a bathtub or shower, a sink, and sometimes a toilet. 浴室 2 N-SING A **bathroom** is a room in a house or public building that contains a sink and toilet. 洗手间 [mainly AM]

> in BRIT, usually use **toilet**

❑ *She had gone in to use the bathroom.* 她已经去上洗手间了。 3 PHRASE People say that they **are going to the bathroom** when they want to say that they are going to use the toilet. 去洗手间 [POLITENESS] ❑ *Although he had been treated with antibiotics, he went to the bathroom repeatedly.* 尽管已经用抗菌素治疗过了，他还是频繁地去洗手间。 4 PHRASE You can say that someone **goes to the bathroom** to mean that they get rid of waste substances from their body, especially when you want to avoid using words that you think

Word Web **bat**

Bats fly like birds, but they are **mammals**. Female bats give birth to live young and produce milk. Bats are **nocturnal**, searching for food at night and sleeping during the day. They **roost** upside down in dark, quiet places such as caves and attics. People think that bats drink blood, but only **vampire bats** do this. Most bats eat fruit or insects. As bats fly they make high-pitched sounds that bounce off objects. This echolocation is a kind of **radar** that guides them.

b

B

may offend people. 去洗手间 [mainly AM, POLITENESS]

in BRIT, use **go to the toilet**

❑ *I had to go to the bathroom, but I didn't want to use that awful outhouse. So I went off in the woods.* 我不得不上卫生间，但是我不想用那糟糕的户外厕所，所以我到树林里去了。

→ see **house, plumbing**

Thesaurus *bathroom* 另参见：

N. lavatory, boys'/girls'/ladies'/men's/women's room, powder room, restroom, toilet, washroom 1 2

bath salts N-PLURAL You dissolve **bath salts** in bath water to make the water smell pleasant and as a water softener. 浴盐 ❑ *She poured all of the bath salts into the swirling water of the tub.* 她把所有的浴盐都倒进浴缸里旋动的水中。

bath·tub /bæθtʌb/ (**bathtubs**) N-COUNT A **bathtub** is a long, usually rectangular container that you fill with water and sit in to wash your body. 浴缸 [AM]

in BRIT, use **bath**

❑ *...a gigantic pink marble bathtub.* …一个巨大的粉红色大理石浴缸。

ba·ton /bætɒn/ (**batons**) 1 N-COUNT A **baton** is a light, thin stick used by a conductor to conduct an orchestra or a choir. (乐队)指挥棒 ❑ *The maestro raises his baton.* 大师举起他的指挥棒。 2 N-COUNT In track and field or track events, a **baton** is a short stick that is passed from one runner to another in a relay race. 接力棒 ❑ *...their biggest relay outing since dropping the baton in Edmonton last August.* …自去年8月在埃德蒙顿丢棒以来他们参加的最大的接力赛。 3 N-COUNT A **baton** is a short heavy stick which is sometimes used as a weapon by the police. 警棍 [BRIT]

in AM, use **billy, billy club, nightstick**

★ **bat·tal·ion** /bətælyən/ (**battalions**) 1 N-COUNT A **battalion** is a large group of soldiers that consists of three or more companies. 营(由三个或以上的连组成的) ❑ *Ten hours later Anthony was ordered to return to his battalion.* 10小时之后安东尼被命令回营。 2 N-COUNT A **battalion of** people is a large group of them, especially a well-organized, efficient group that has a particular task to do. (有组织的) 队伍 ❑ *There were battalions of highly paid publicists to see that such news didn't make the press.* 有数支由高薪宣传人员组成的队伍确保这样的消息不变成新闻。

★ **bat·ter** /bætər/ (**batters, battering, battered**) 1 V-T To **batter** someone means to hit them many times, using fists or a heavy object. 连续猛击(某人) ❑ *The passengers were battered by flying luggage and cargo as the cabin lost pressure.* 当机舱失去压力时，乘客们被飞落的行李和货物连续猛击。 ❑ *A karate expert battered a man to death.* 一位空手道高手将一名男子猛击致死。 ● **bat·tered** ADJ 遭殴打的 ❑ *Her battered body was discovered in a field.* 她被殴打过的尸体在一块田里被发现了。 2 V-T If someone **is battered**, they are regularly hit and badly hurt by a member of their family or by their partner. 虐待 ❑ *...evidence that the child was being battered.* …这个孩子那时正遭虐待的证据。 ❑ *...boys who witness fathers battering their mothers.* …亲眼目睹父亲虐待他们母亲的男孩们。 ● **bat·ter·ing** N-UNCOUNT 虐待 ❑ *Leaving the relationship does not mean that the battering will stop.* 脱离了这种关系并不意味着虐待会停止。 3 V-T If a place **is battered by** wind, rain, or storms, it is seriously damaged or affected by very bad weather. (风、雨或风暴等) 袭击 [usu passive] ❑ *The country has been battered by winds of between fifty and seventy miles an hour.* 这个国家一直受到时速50至70英里大风的袭击。 4 V-T If you **batter** something, you hit it many times, using your fists or a heavy object. 连续猛击 ❑ *They were battering the door, they were trying to break in.* 他们连续击门，试图破门而入。 5 N-VAR **Batter** is a mixture of flour, eggs, and milk that is used in cooking. (面粉、蛋、牛奶混合成的) 糊 ❑ *...pancake batter.* …做薄煎饼的面糊。 6 N-COUNT In sports such as baseball and softball, a **batter** is a person who hits the ball with a wooden bat. 击球员 ❑ *...batters and pitchers.* …击球员和投球手们。 7 → see also **battered, battering**

→ see **baseball**

bat·tered /bætərd/ ADJ Something that is **battered** is old and in poor condition because it has been used a lot. 用旧了的 ❑ *He drove up in a battered old car.* 他开着一辆破烂不堪的旧车过来了。

bat·ter·ing /bætərɪŋ/ (**batterings**) N-COUNT If something takes a **battering**, it suffers very badly as a result of a particular event or action. 打击 ❑ *The industry's reputation has taken a battering and its image needs to be restored.* 这一行业的声誉已受到了打击，需要重新恢复形象。

bat·tery /bætəri/ (**batteries**) 1 N-COUNT **Batteries** are small devices that provide the power for electrical items such as radios and children's toys. 电池 ❑ *The shavers come complete with batteries.* 这些电动剃须刀带有电池。 ❑ *...a battery-operated cassette player.* …用电池的磁带放音机。 2 N-COUNT A car **battery** is a rectangular box containing acid that is found in a car engine. It provides the electricity needed to start the car. (汽车) 蓄电池 ❑ *...a car with a dead battery.* …一辆蓄电池没电了的汽车。 3 N-UNCOUNT **Battery** is the crime of hitting or beating someone. 殴打罪 [mainly AM, LEGAL] ❑ *Lawrence punched a man in a Los Angeles nightclub and was charged with battery.* 劳伦斯在洛杉矶的一家夜总会里打了人，结果被指控犯了殴打罪。 4 → see also **assault and battery** 5 N-COUNT A **battery of** equipment such as guns, lights, or computers is a large set of it kept together in one place. 一排；一套 ❑ *They stopped beside a battery of abandoned guns.* 他们停在一排废弃的大炮旁。 6 N-COUNT A **battery of** people or things is a very large number of them. 一大群；一组 ❑ *...a battery of journalists and television cameras.* …一大群记者和电视摄像机。

→ see **cellphone**

Word Partnership *battery* 的常用搭配：

ADJ. **dead** battery, battery **operated/powered, rechargeable** battery 1
N. battery **charger**, battery **pack** 1
car battery 2
missile battery 5

bat·tle ◆◆◇ /bætᵊl/ (**battles, battling, battled**) 1 N-VAR A **battle** is a violent fight between groups of people, especially one between military forces during a war. 战役 ❑ *...the victory of King William III at the Battle of the Boyne.* …威廉三世国王在博因河战役中所取得的胜利。 ❑ *...a gun battle between police and drug traffickers.* …警察和毒品贩子之间的一场枪战。 2 N-COUNT A **battle** is a conflict in which different people or groups compete in order to achieve success or control. 斗争；较量 ❑ *...an unfolding political battle over jobs and the economy.* …一场正在展开的关于就业和经济的政治较量。 ❑ *...the eternal battle between good and evil in the world.* …世界上善恶之间永无休止的较量。 3 N-COUNT You can use **battle** to refer to someone's efforts to achieve something in spite of very difficult circumstances. 斗争 ❑ *...the battle against crime.* …制止犯罪的斗争。 ❑ *She has fought a constant battle with her weight.* 她一直在和自己的体重作斗争。 4 V-RECIP To **battle with** an opposing group means to take part in a fight or contest against them. You can also say that one group or person **is battling** another. 与…搏斗；与…较量 ❑ *In one town thousands of people battled with police and several were reportedly wounded.* 在一个镇子里，成千上万的人同警察展开搏斗，据报道有几人受伤。 ❑ *The sides must battle again for a quarter-final place on December 16.* 两队必须于12月16日再战一次，来争夺1/4决赛的位置。 5 V-T/V-I To **battle** means to try hard to do something in spite of very difficult circumstances. You can also **battle** something, or **battle against** something or **with** something. 与…作斗争；斗争 ❑ *Doctors battled throughout the night to save her life.* 医生们奋战了整个晚上来抢救她的生命。 ❑ *Firefighters are still battling the two blazes.* 消防队员们还在与两处大火作斗争。 6 PHRASE If one group or person **battles it out with** another, they take part in a fight or contest against each other until one of them wins or a definite result is reached. You can also say that two groups or two people **battle it out**. 战斗到底 ❑ *She will now battle it out with 50 other hopefuls for a place in the last 10.* 她现在将和另外50名有希望的候选人决战最后10个位置中的一个。

→ see **army**

Word Partnership *battle* 的常用搭配：

V. **prepare for** battle 1
fight a battle, **lose/win** a battle 1–3
ADJ. **bloody** battle, **major** battle 1
legal battle 2
constant battle, **losing** battle, **uphill** battle 2 3
N. battle **of wills** 2

bat·tle fa·tigue N-UNCOUNT **Battle fatigue** is a mental condition of anxiety and depression caused by the stress of fighting in a war. 战斗疲劳症 ❑ *...a man suffering from battle fatigue.* …一名患战斗疲劳症的男子。

battle·field /bætᵊlfild/ (**battlefields**) 1 N-COUNT A **battlefield** is a place where a battle is fought. 战场 ❑ *...the struggle to save*

America's Civil War battlefields. …保存美国内战战场的努力。 2 N-COUNT You can refer to an issue or field of activity over which people disagree or compete as a **battlefield**. 斗争的领域；争论的问题 ❑ *…the domestic battlefield of family life.* …家庭生活的内部问题。

battle·ground /bætᵊlgraʊnd/ [BRIT] → see **battlefield**

battle·ship /bætᵊlʃɪp/ (**battleships**) N-COUNT A **battleship** is a very large, heavily armed warship. 战列舰

bawl /bɔl/ (**bawls, bawling, bawled**) 1 V-I If you say that a child **is bawling**, you are annoyed because it is crying loudly. 放声大哭 ❑ *One of the toddlers was bawling, and the other had a runny nose.* 其中一个刚学会走路的孩子在放声大哭，另一个则流着鼻涕。 2 V-T/V-I If you **bawl**, you shout in a very loud voice, for example, because you are angry or you want people to hear you. 大声喊叫 ❑ *When I came back to the hotel Laura and Peter were shouting and bawling at each other.* 当我回到旅馆时，劳拉和彼得正在互相大喊大叫。 ❑ *Then a voice bawled: "Lay off! I'll kill you, you little rascal!"* 然后一个声音大叫道："停下！我要杀了你！你这个小捣蛋鬼！" ● PHRASAL VERB **Bawl out** means the same as **bawl**. 大声喊叫 ❑ *Someone in the audience bawled out "Not him again!"* 观众中有人大声喊道："不会又是他吧！"

▶ **bawl out** PHRASAL VERB If someone **bawls** you **out**, they tell you off angrily. 训 [INFORMAL] ❑ *I was bawled out at school for not doing my homework.* 我因为没做家庭作业在学校被训了一顿。

bay ♦◇◇ /beɪ/ (**bays, baying, bayed**) 1 N-COUNT A **bay** is a part of a coast where the land curves inward. 海湾 ❑ *…a short ferry ride across the bay.* …一趟跨海湾的短途渡轮旅程。 ❑ *…the Bay of Bengal.* …孟加拉湾。 2 N-COUNT A **bay** is a partly enclosed area, inside or outside a building, that is used for a particular purpose. (建筑物内或外辟作特定用途的) 隔区 ❑ *The animals are herded into a bay, then butchered.* 动物被赶到隔栏内，然后被屠宰。 3 N-COUNT A **bay** is an area of a room that extends beyond the main walls of a house, especially an area with a large window at the front of a house. (尤指位于房屋前端并装有大窗的) 凸出部分 4 ADJ A **bay** horse is reddish-brown in color. 红棕色的 ❑ *…a 10-year-old bay mare.* …一匹10岁的红棕色母马。 5 V-I If a number of people **are baying for** something, they are demanding something angrily, usually that someone should be punished. 愤怒地要求 [usu cont] ❑ *The referee ignored voices baying for a penalty.* 裁判对愤怒要求惩罚的呼声置之不理。 ❑ *Opposition politicians have been baying for his blood.* 反对派的政客们一直怒气冲冲地要他的命。 6 V-I If a dog or wolf **bays**, it makes loud, long cries. (犬或狼等) 嗥叫 ❑ *A dog suddenly howled, baying at the moon.* 一只狗忽然嗥叫起来，对月长嗥。 7 PHRASE If you **keep** something or someone **at bay**, or **hold** them **at bay**, you prevent them from reaching, attacking, or affecting you. 使无法近身 ❑ *Eating oranges keeps colds at bay.* 吃橘子可防感冒。

bayo·net /beɪənɪt, beɪənɛt/ (**bayonets**) N-COUNT A **bayonet** is a long, sharp blade that can be attached to the end of a rifle and used as a weapon. 刺刀

ba·zaar /bəzɑr/ (**bazaars**) 1 N-COUNT In areas such as the Middle East and India, a **bazaar** is a place where there are many small stores and stalls. (中东、印度等地的) 集市 ❑ *Kamal was a vendor in Cairo's open-air bazaar.* 卡莫尔曾是开罗露天集市的摊贩。 2 N-COUNT A **bazaar** is a sale to raise money for charity. 义卖会 ❑ *…a church bazaar.* …一场教会义卖会。

BBC ♦♦◇ /bi bi si/ N-PROPER **The BBC** is a British organization which broadcasts programs on radio and television. **BBC** is an abbreviation for "British Broadcasting Corporation." 英国广播公司 ["the" N] ❑ *The concert will be broadcast live by the BBC.* 这场音乐会将由英国广播公司实况转播。

BB gun /bi bi gʌn/ (**BB guns**) N-COUNT A **BB gun** is a type of airgun that fires small round bullets that are called **BBs**. (使用小而圆的BB气枪弹的) BB型气枪 [AM] ❑ *Sims was carrying a BB gun at the time he was shot.* 西姆斯被射杀时携带着一把BB型气枪

BC /bi si/ also **B.C.** You use **BC** in dates to indicate a number of years or centuries before the year in which Jesus Christ is believed to have been born. Compare **AD**. 公元前 ❑ *The brooch dates back to the fourth century BC.* 胸针可追溯至公元前4世纪。

BCE /bi si i/ also **B.C.E.** Non-Christians often use **BCE** instead of **BC** in dates. **BCE** indicates a number of years or centuries before the year in which Jesus Christ is believed to have been born. **BCE** is an abbreviation for "before the Common Era." Compare **AD, BC,** and **CE**. 公元前 ❑ *…Lao-tzu, a sixth-century BCE Chinese teacher.* …老子，一位公元前6世纪的中国教育者。 ❑ *The Babylonian Empire was conquered by the Persian Empire in 539 BCE.* 巴比伦帝国于公元前539年被波斯帝国征服。

be
1 AUXILIARY VERB USES
2 OTHER VERB USES

1 be ♦♦♦ /bi, STRONG bi/ (**am, are, is, being, was, were, been**)

In spoken English, forms of **be** are often shortened, for example "I am" can be shortened to "I'm" and "was not" can be shortened to "wasn't."

1 AUX You use **be** with a present participle to form the continuous tenses of verbs. 后接动词的现在分词，构成动词进行体 ❑ *This is happening in every school throughout the country.* 这在全国各校都正在发生。 ❑ *She didn't always think carefully about what she was doing.* 她不总是仔细思考自己正在做什么。 2 **be going to** → see **going** 3 AUX You use **be** with a past participle to form the passive voice. 后接动词的过去分词，构成被动语态 ❑ *Her husband was killed in a car crash.* 她丈夫在一场车祸中被夺去了性命。 ❑ *Similar action is being taken by the U.S. government.* 类似的行动正被美国政府所采取。 4 AUX You use **be** with an infinitive to indicate that something is planned to happen, that it will definitely happen, or that it must happen. 后接动词不定式，表"安排、注定、必然"等意 ❑ *The talks are to begin tomorrow.* 会谈将于明天开始。 ❑ *It was to be Johnson's first meeting with the board in nearly a month.* 那将是近一个月来约翰逊与董事会的首次会面。 5 **be about to** → see **about** 6 AUX You use **be** with an infinitive to say or ask what should happen or be done in a particular situation, how it should happen, or who should do it. 后接动词不定式，用于说明或询问特定情况下应该会怎样、怎样做、谁来做等 ❑ *What am I to do without him?* 没有他我该怎么办？ ❑ *Who is to say which of them had more power?* 谁知道他们当中谁有更大权利？ 7 AUX You use **was** and **were** with an infinitive to talk about something that happened later than the time you are discussing, and was not planned or certain at that time. **was**和**were**接不定式表示说话时间之后发生的事 ❑ *He started something that was to change the face of China.* 他发起了某项后来改变了中国面貌的行动。 8 AUX You can say that something is **to be** seen, heard, or found in a particular place to mean that people can see it, hear it, or find it in that place. 后接**seen**、**heard**、**found**，表"可见到、可听到、可发现"之意 ❑ *Little traffic was to be seen on the streets.* 路上几乎没有车辆可见。

2 be ♦♦♦ /bi, STRONG bi/ (**am, are, is, being, was, were, been**)

In spoken English, forms of **be** are often shortened, for example "I am" can be shortened to "I'm" and "was not" can be shortened to "wasn't."

1 V-LINK You use **be** to introduce more information about the subject, such as its identity, nature, qualities, or position. 用于补充说明主语，表示其身份、性质、品质、位置等 ❑ *She's my mother.* 她是我母亲。 ❑ *He is a very attractive man.* 他是个非常有吸引力的人。 ❑ *He is fifty and has been through two marriages.* 他50岁，已经经历了两次婚姻。 ❑ *The sky was black.* 天是黑的。 ❑ *His house is next door.* 他的房间在隔壁。 ❑ *He's still alive, isn't he?* 他还活着，是吗？ 2 V-LINK You use **be**, with "it" as the subject, in clauses where you are describing something or giving your judgment of a situation. 与主语**it**连用，用以描述事物或给出判断 ❑ *It was too chilly for swimming.* 游泳太冷了。 ❑ *Sometimes it is necessary to say no.* 有时候说"不"是必要的。 ❑ *It is likely that investors will face losses.* 那时投资者将面临亏损是很可能的。 ❑ *It's nice having friends to chat to.* 有朋友一起聊真好。 3 V-LINK You use **be** with the impersonal pronoun "there" in expressions like **there is** and **there are** to say that something exists or happens. 与非人称代名词**there**连用，表示存在或发生 ❑ *Clearly there is a problem here.* 显然这里有问题。 ❑ *There are very few cars on this street.* 这条马路上很少有车辆。 4 V-LINK You use **be** as a link between a subject and a clause and in certain other clause structures, as shown below. 用于连接主语和分句或其他分句结构 ❑ *Our greatest problem is convincing them.* 我们最重要的问题是说服他们。 ❑ *All she knew was that I'd had a broken marriage.* 她所知道的就是我曾有过一次破裂的婚姻。 ❑ *Local residents said it was as if there had been a nuclear explosion.* 当地居民说好像发生过核爆炸。 5 V-LINK You use **be** in expressions like **the thing is** and **the point is** to introduce a clause in which you make a statement or give your opinion. 用于**the thing is**和**the point is**等表达中，引导一个分句，以陈述事实或表达观点 [SPOKEN]

❑ *The fact is, the players gave everything they had.* 事实是，运动员们倾尽了所有。 **6** V-LINK The form "**be**" is used occasionally instead of the normal forms of the present tense, especially after "whether." **be**有时用来替代通常的现在时形式，尤其在**whether**之后 [FORMAL] ❑ *They should then be able to refer you to the appropriate type of practitioner, whether it be your GP, dentist, or optician.* 然后他们应当能够介绍你去见合适科别的执业医生，不管是你的全科医师、牙医还是配镜师。 **7** PHRASE If you talk about what would happen **if it wasn't for** someone or something, you mean that they are the only thing that is preventing it from happening. 若不是因为 ❑ *I could happily move back into an apartment if it wasn't for the fact that I'd miss my garden.* 若不是因为我会惦记着花园，我本可以高兴地搬回公寓。

beach ♦◇◇ /bitʃ/ (**beaches, beaching, beached**) **1** N-COUNT A **beach** is an area of sand or stones beside the ocean. 海滩 ❑ *...a beautiful sandy beach.* …一片美丽的沙滩。 **2** V-T/V-I If something such as a boat **beaches**, or if it **is beached**, it is pulled or forced out of the water and onto land. 使上岸；上岸 ❑ *We beached the canoe, running it right up the bank.* 我们把独木舟拖上了海滩，直朝堤岸拖去。 ❑ *The boat beached on a mud flat.* 船在泥沼上搁浅了。

→ see Word Web: **beach**

You can use **beach**, **coast**, and **shore** to talk about the piece of land beside a stretch of water. A **beach** is a flat area of sand or pebbles next to the ocean. The **coast** is the area of land that lies alongside the ocean. You may be referring just to the land close to the ocean, or to a wider area that extends further inland. The **shore** is the area of land along the edge of the ocean, a lake, or a wide river.

Word Partnership *beach* 的常用搭配：

PREP.	**along the** beach, **at/on the** beach **1**
N.	beach **chair**, beach **club/resort**, beach **vacation** **1**
V.	**lie on the** beach, **walk on the** beach **1**
ADJ.	**nude** beach, **private** beach, **rocky** beach, **sandy** beach **1**

beach chair (**beach chairs**) N-COUNT A **beach chair** is a simple chair with a folding frame, and a piece of canvas as the seat and back. **Beach chairs** are usually used on the beach, on a ship, or in the yard. 沙滩椅 [AM]

in BRIT, sometimes AM use **deckchair**

❑ *People sprawl in beach chairs or sit under umbrellas.* 人们四肢舒展地躺在沙滩椅上，或坐在遮阳伞下。

beach·wear /bitʃwɛər/ N-UNCOUNT **Beachwear** is the things people wear for swimming. 海滩装 [mainly AM] ❑ *There is a boutique where beachwear and sportswear are on sale.* 有家小店在卖海滩装和运动装。

bea·con /bikən/ (**beacons**) **1** N-COUNT A **beacon** is a light or a fire, usually on a hill or tower, that acts as a signal or a warning. 烽火；信号灯 ❑ *...a huge office tower with aircraft warning beacons on the roof.* …一个屋顶有航行警告灯的巨型办公塔。 **2** N-COUNT If someone acts as a **beacon to** other people, they inspire or encourage them. 指路人 ❑ *She is a beacon of hope for women navigating the darkest passage of their lives.* 她是个指引女性们穿越她们生活最黑暗时光的希望的灯塔。

▲ **bead** /bid/ (**beads**) **1** N-COUNT **Beads** are small pieces of colored glass, wood, or plastic with a hole through the middle. Beads are often put together on a piece of string or wire to make jewelry. 中间有孔的小珠子 ❑ *...a string of beads.* …一串珠子。 **2** N-COUNT A **bead of** liquid or moisture is a small drop of it. (液体或湿气的) 小滴 ❑ *...beads of blood.* …滴滴鲜血。

→ see **glass**

▲ **beak** /bik/ (**beaks**) N-COUNT A bird's **beak** is the hard curved or pointed part of its mouth. 喙 ❑ *...a black bird with a yellow beak.* …一只有着黄喙的黑鸟。

→ see **bird**

beak·er /bikər/ (**beakers**) **1** N-COUNT A **beaker** is a large cup or glass. 大口杯 [AM] **2** N-COUNT A **beaker** is a glass or plastic jar which is used in chemistry. (化学实验用的) 大口烧杯

beam /bim/ (**beams, beaming, beamed**) **1** V-T/V-I If you say that someone **is beaming**, you mean that they have a big smile on their face because they are happy, pleased, or proud about something. 绽开笑容 [WRITTEN] ❑ *Frances beamed at her friend with undisguised admiration.* 弗朗西丝用毫不掩饰的羡慕的神情朝她的朋友们绽开了笑容。 ❑ *"Welcome back," she beamed.* "欢迎回来，"她笑容满面地说。 **2** N-COUNT A **beam** is a line of energy, radiation, or particles sent in a particular direction. (能量、辐射、粒子) 束 ❑ *...high-energy laser beams.* …高能激光束。 **3** V-T/V-I If radio signals or television pictures **are beamed** somewhere, they are sent there by means of electronic equipment. 播送 ❑ *The interview was beamed live across America.* 那场访谈同步播送至全美。 ❑ *The Sci-Fi Channel began beaming into 10 million American homes this week.* 科幻频道本周已经开始播送到1000万个美国家庭。 **4** N-COUNT A **beam of** light is a line of light that shines from an object such as a lamp. (光) 束 ❑ *A beam of light slices through the darkness.* 一道光束划破了黑暗。 **5** N-COUNT A **beam** is a long thick bar of wood, metal, or concrete, especially one used to support the roof of a building. 梁 ❑ *The ceilings are supported by oak beams.* 天花板由橡木横梁支撑着。

→ see **laser**

Word Partnership *beam* 的常用搭配：

PREP.	beam **at** ***someone*** **1**
	beam **down** ***(on something)*** **3**
N.	**laser** beam **2**
	beam **of light** **4**
ADJ.	**steel/wooden** beam **5**

bean ♦◇◇ /bin/ (**beans**) **1** N-COUNT Beans such as green **beans**, French **beans**, or fava **beans** are the seeds of a climbing plant or the long thin cases which contain those seeds. 豆；豆荚 **2** N-COUNT Beans such as **soybeans** and kidney **beans** are the dried seeds of other types of bean plants. 干豆 **3** N-COUNT Beans such as coffee **beans** or cocoa **beans** are the seeds of plants that are used to produce coffee, cocoa, and chocolate. (供制作咖啡、可可等饮料的) 豆形种子

→ see **coffee**

bean·ie /bini/ (**beanies**) N-COUNT A **beanie** is a small, close-fitting cap. 无檐小便帽 ❑ *He bursts into a breakfast diner with his hair under a woolen beanie.* 他突然闯进早餐店，头发掖在羊毛小便帽下。

bear

❶ VERB USES
❷ NOUN USES

❶ **bear** ♦♦◇ /bɛər/ (**bears, bearing, bore, borne**)

➪ **Please look at meanings 15 – 18 to see if the expression you are looking for is shown under another headword.** **1** V-T If you **bear** something somewhere, you carry it there or take it there. 运送 [LITERARY] ❑ *They bore the oblong hardwood box into the kitchen and put it on the table.* 他们把那个长方形的硬木箱抬进了厨房，放在了餐桌上。 **2** V-T If you **bear** something such as a weapon, you hold it or carry it with you. 携带 [FORMAL] ❑ *...the constitutional right to bear arms.* …携带武器的宪法权。 **3** V-T If one thing **bears** the weight of

Word Web beach

Beaches have a natural cycle of build-up and **erosion**. **Ocean currents**, **wind**, and **waves** move **sand** along the **coast**. In certain spots, some of the sand gets left behind. The **surf** deposits it on the beach. Then the wind blows it into **dunes**. As currents change, they **erode** sand from the beach. High waves carry beach sand seaward. This process raises the seafloor. As the water gets shallower, the waves become smaller. Then they begin depositing sand on the beach. At the same time, small **pebbles** smash into each other. They break up and form new sand.

something else, it supports the weight of that thing. 承受；支撑 ❑ *The ice was not thick enough to bear the weight of marching men.* 冰的厚度不足以支撑行军队伍的重量。 **4** V-T If something **bears** a particular mark or characteristic, it has that mark or characteristic. 带有（某标记或特征） ❑ *The houses bear the marks of bullet holes and the streets are practically deserted.* 房屋带有子弹的痕迹，街道几乎是被废弃了。 ❑ *...notepaper bearing the presidential seal.* …盖有总统印章的信笺。 **5** V-T If you **bear** an unpleasant experience, you accept it because you are unable to do anything about it. 忍受 ❑ *They will have to bear the misery of living in constant fear of war.* 他们将不得不忍受生活在没完没了的战争恐惧中的痛苦。 **6** V-T If you can't **bear** someone or something, you dislike them very much. 容忍 [with neg] ❑ *I can't bear people who make judgements and label me.* 我受不了那些对我评头论足、乱贴标签的人。 **7** V-T When a woman **bears** a child, she gives birth to him or her. 生（孩子） [OLD-FASHIONED] ❑ *Emma bore a son called Karl.* 埃玛生了个儿子，取名卡尔。 ❑ *She bore him a daughter, Susanna.* 她给他生了个女儿，苏珊娜。 **8** V-T If someone **bears** the cost of something, they pay for it. 负担（费用） ❑ *Patients should not have to bear the costs of their own treatment.* 病人们不该需要负担他们自己的医疗费。 **9** V-T If you **bear** the responsibility for something, you accept responsibility for it. 承担（责任） ❑ *If a woman makes a decision to have a child alone, she should bear that responsibility alone.* 如果一名女子独自决定生养小孩，她就必须独自承担这一责任。 **10** V-T If one thing **bears** no resemblance or no relationship to another thing, they are not at all similar. 具有（相似处或关系） [usu with brd-neg] ❑ *Their daily menus bore no resemblance whatsoever to what they were actually fed.* 他们的日常菜单与他们每天实际吃的东西完全不一样。 **11** V-T When a plant or tree **bears** flowers, fruit, or leaves, it produces them. 开（花）；结（果）；长（枝叶） ❑ *As the plants grow and start to bear fruit they will need a lot of water.* 随着植物的生长及开始结果，它们将需要大量的水分。 **12** V-T If something such as a bank account or an investment **bears** interest, interest is paid on it. 产生（利息） [BUSINESS] ❑ *The eight-year bond will bear annual interest of 10.5%.* 这份8年期的债券将产生10.5%的年利息。 **13** V-I If you **bear** left or **bear** right when you are driving or walking along, you turn and continue in that direction. 向（左、右）转 ❑ *Traveling north on 309 to Center Valley, bear right at the fork onto Route 378 North.* 经309道向北去中央谷时，在378道北的岔口向右拐。 **14** → see also **bore**, **borne** **15** to **bear the brunt of** → see **brunt** **16** to **bear fruit** → see **fruit** **17** to **grin and bear it** → see **grin** **18** to **bear in mind** → see **mind**

▸ **bear out** PHRASAL VERB If someone or something **bears** a person **out** or **bears out** what that person is saying, they support what that person is saying. 支持；证实 ❑ *Recent studies have borne out claims that certain perfumes can bring about profound psychological changes.* 最近的研究已经证实了某些香水能导致深刻的心理变化的说法。

▸ **bear with** PHRASAL VERB If you ask someone to **bear with** you, you are asking them to be patient. 对（某人）有耐心 ❑ *If you'll bear with me, Frank, just let me try to explain.* 如果你对我有耐心，弗兰克，就让我试着解释。

Thesaurus *bear* 另参见：

V. carry, lug, move, transport ❶ **1**
endure, put up with, stand, tolerate ❶ **5**
produce, yield ❶ **7** **11** **12**

Word Partnership *bear* 的常用搭配：

N. bear **a burden/weight** ❶ **1** **3** **5**
bear **responsibility** ❶ **9**
bear **fruit** ❶ **11**
bear **interest** ❶ **12**
ADV. bear **left/right** ❶ **13**

❷ **bear** /bɛər/ (**bears**) **1** N-COUNT A **bear** is a large, strong wild animal with thick fur and sharp claws. 熊 **2** N-COUNT In the stock market, **bears** are people who sell shares in expectation of a drop in price, in order to make a profit by buying them back again after a short time. Compare **bull**. （股票市场上）卖空的人 [BUSINESS] → see **arctic**

bear·able /bɛərəbᵊl/ ADJ If something is **bearable**, you feel that you can accept it or deal with it. 可忍受的 ❑ *A cool breeze made the heat bearable.* 一阵凉爽的微风使得炎热可以忍受。

beard /bɪərd/ (**beards**) N-COUNT A man's **beard** is the hair that grows on his chin and cheeks. 胡须 ❑ *He's decided to grow a beard.* 他已经决定蓄胡须。

beard·ed /bɪərdɪd/ ADJ A **bearded** man has a beard. 有胡须的 ❑ *...a bearded 40-year-old sociology professor.* …一个留着胡子的40岁的社会学教授。

bear·er /bɛərər/ (**bearers**) **1** N-COUNT The **bearer of** something such as a message is the person who brings it to you. 捎信人；运送者 ❑ *I hate to be the bearer of bad news.* 我讨厌当坏消息的捎信人。 **2** N-COUNT A **bearer** of a particular thing is a person who carries it, especially in a ceremony. （尤指典礼中的）搬运者 [FORMAL] ❑ *He was the U.S. flag bearer at the 1976 Montreal Games.* 他是1976年蒙特利尔奥运会上美国的举旗手。 **3** N-COUNT The **bearer of** something such as a document, a right, or an official position is the person who possesses it or holds it. 持有者；拥有者 [FORMAL] ❑ *...the traditional bourgeois notion of the citizen as a bearer of rights.* …传统的中产阶级观念，认为公民是权利的所有者。

bear·ing ♦◇◇ /bɛərɪŋ/ (**bearings**) **1** PHRASE If something **has a bearing on** a situation or event, it is relevant to it. 与…有关系 ❑ *Experts generally agree that diet has an important bearing on your general health.* 专家们普遍认可饮食与你的总体健康有着重要关系。 **2** N-SING Someone's **bearing** is the way in which they move or stand. 举止 [LITERARY] ❑ *She later wrote warmly of his bearing and behavior.* 稍后她热情地写到了他的风度与举止。 **3** PHRASE If you **get** your **bearings** or **find** your **bearings**, you find out where you are or what you should do next. If you **lose** your **bearings**, you do not know where you are or what you should do next. 方位 ❑ *A sightseeing tour of the city is included to help you get your bearings.* 城市观光游包括在内，以帮助你们弄清方向。

bear·ish /bɛərɪʃ/ ADJ In the stock market, if there is a **bearish** mood, prices are expected to fall. Compare **bullish**. （股票市场）熊市的；行情看跌的 [BUSINESS] ❑ *Dealers said investors remain bearish.* 证券经纪人说投资者们依然看跌。

bear mar·ket (**bear markets**) N-COUNT A **bear market** is a situation in the stock market when people are selling a lot of shares because they expect the shares will decrease in value and they will be able to make a profit by buying them again after a short time. Compare **bull market**. （股票市场）熊市；下跌行情 [BUSINESS] ❑ *Is the bear market in equities over?* 股票熊市结束了吗？

beast /bist/ (**beasts**) N-COUNT You can refer to an animal as a **beast**, especially if it is a large, dangerous, or unusual one. （尤指罕见或巨大凶猛的）兽 [LITERARY] ❑ *...the threats our ancestors faced from wild beasts.* …我们祖辈所面临的来自野兽的威胁。

beat ♦♦♦ /bit/ (**beats, beating, beaten**)

> The form **beat** is used in the present tense and is the past tense.

1 V-T If you **beat** someone or something, you hit them very hard. 用力打 ❑ *My wife tried to stop them and they beat her.* 我妻子试图阻止他们，他们就猛打她。 **2** V-I To **beat on**, **at**, or **against** something means to hit it hard, usually several times or continuously for a period of time. （常指多次或连续地）重击 ❑ *There was dead silence but for a fly beating against the glass.* 若没有一只苍蝇在扑打着玻璃，便是一片死寂。 ❑ *Nina managed to free herself and began beating at the flames with a pillow.* 尼娜设法自救，开始用一个枕头连续地拍打着火焰。 ● N-SING **Beat** is also a noun. 击打 ❑ *...the rhythmic beat of the surf.* …海浪有韵律的拍击。 ● **beat·ing** N-SING 敲打 ❑ *The silence was broken only by the beating of the rain.* 唯有雨的敲击打破了宁静。 **3** V-I When your heart or pulse **beats**, it continually makes regular rhythmic movements. （心脏、脉搏）跳动 ❑ *I felt my heart beating faster.* 我感觉心脏跳得更快了。 ● N-COUNT **Beat** is also a noun. 跳动 ❑ *He could hear the beat of his heart.* 他能听到自己的心跳。 ● **beat·ing** N-SING 跳动 ❑ *I could hear the beating of my heart.* 我能听到自己心脏的跳动。 **4** V-T/V-I If you **beat** a drum or similar instrument, you hit it in order to make a sound. You can also say that a drum **beats**. 敲（乐鼓等）；（乐鼓等）敲打 ❑ *When you beat the drum, you feel good.* 当你击鼓时，你感觉良好。 ❑ *...drums beating and pipes playing.* …乐鼓在敲打，风笛在演奏。 ● N-SING **Beat** is also a noun. 敲打 ❑ *...the rhythmical beat of the drum.* …乐鼓的有节奏的敲打。 **5** N-COUNT The **beat** of a piece of music is the main rhythm that it has. （音乐的）节奏 ❑ *...the thumping beat of rock music.* …摇滚乐的强烈节奏。 **6** N-COUNT In music, a **beat** is a unit of measurement. The number of beats in a measure of a piece of music is indicated by two numbers at the beginning of the piece. （音乐的）节拍 ❑ *It's got four beats to a measure.* 1小节有4拍。 **7** V-T If you **beat** eggs, cream, or butter, you mix them thoroughly using a fork or beater. 搅打（蛋、奶油等） ❑ *Beat the eggs and sugar until they start to thicken.* 将蛋和奶油搅打到开

B

始变黏稠为止。 8 V-T/V-I When a bird or insect **beats** its wings or when its wings **beat**, its wings move up and down. 拍打（翅膀）；（翅膀）连续拍动 ❑ *Beating their wings they flew off.* 它们拍打着翅膀飞走了。 9 V-T If you **beat** someone in a competition or election, you defeat them. 打败 ❑ *In yesterday's game, Switzerland beat the United States two to one.* 在昨天的比赛中，瑞士以2比1击败了美国。 10 V-T If someone **beats** a record or achievement, they do better than it. 打破（纪录等）❑ *He was as eager as his Captain to beat the record.* 他和他的队长一样渴望打破纪录。 11 V-T If you **beat** something that you are fighting against, for example, an organization, a problem, or a disease, you defeat it. 战胜 ❑ *It became clear that the Union was not going to beat the government.* 情形变得很清楚，工会敌不过政府。 12 V-T If an attack or an attempt **is beaten off** or **is beaten back**, it is stopped, often temporarily. （常指暂时）击退 [usu passive] [usu passive] ❑ *The rescuers were beaten back by strong winds and currents.* 救助者被强风和水流击退了。 13 V-T If you say that one thing **beats** another, you mean that it is better than it. 好过；胜过 [no cont] [INFORMAL] ❑ *Being boss of a software firm beats selling insurance.* 当一家软件公司的老板好过卖保险。 14 V-T To **beat** a time limit or an event means to achieve something before that time or event. （在某时限前）完成 ❑ *They were trying to beat the midnight deadline.* 他们正在试图赶在午夜的最后期限前完成。 15 N-COUNT A police officer's or journalist's **beat** is the area for which he or she is responsible. （警察、记者等的）负责区 ❑ *A policeman was patrolling his regular beat, when he saw a group of boys milling about the street.* 一名警察在其辖区内巡逻时发现一群男孩子在街上瞎转。 16 → see also **beating** 17 PHRASE If you intend to do something but someone **beats** you **to it**, they do it before you do. 抢先做 ❑ *Don't be too long about it or you'll find someone has beaten you to it.* 别耽搁太久，否则你会发现已经有人抢在你前面了。 18 to **beat** someone **at their own game**
→ see **game**
→ see **drum**

▸ **beat up** PHRASAL VERB If someone **beats** a person **up**, they hit or kick the person many times. 毒打 ❑ *Then they actually beat her up as well.* 然后他们事实上也毒打了她一顿。

Thesaurus *beat* 另参见：

V. hit, pound, punch; *(ant.)* caress, pat, pet 1
flutter, quiver, vibrate 3 8
mix, stir, whip 7

Word Partnership *beat* 的常用搭配：

N. beat **a rug** 1
heart beat 3
beat **a drum** 4
beat **eggs** 7
beat **a deadline** 14
PREP. beat **against**, beat **on** 2
on/to a beat 5 6
PRON. beat **its/their wings** 8

beat·en ♦◇◇ /biːtᵊn/ 1 **Beaten** is the past participle of **beat**. **beat**的过去分词 2 PHRASE A place that is **off the beaten track** is in an area where not many people live or go. 人迹罕至 ❑ *Tiny secluded beaches can be found off the beaten track.* 极小的与世隔绝的海滩能在鲜有人至之处找到。

beat·ing ♦◇◇ /biːtɪŋ/ (**beatings**) 1 N-COUNT If someone is given a **beating**, they are hit hard many times, especially with something such as a stick. （尤指使用棍棒的）毒打 ❑ *...the investigation into the beating of an alleged car thief.* …对嫌疑偷车贼遭毒打事件的调查。 2 N-SING If something such as a business, a political party, or a team takes **a beating**, it is defeated by a large amount in a competition or an election. 惨败 ❑ *Our firm has taken a terrible beating in recent years.* 我们公司在近几年中败得很惨。

Beau·jo·lais /boʊʒəleɪ/ (**Beaujolais**) also **beaujolais** N-VAR **Beaujolais** is a type of red wine that comes from the region of eastern France called Beaujolais. （产于法国东部博若莱地区的）博若莱葡萄酒 ❑ *...a fruity Beaujolais.* …果味博若莱葡萄酒

Word Link *ful ≈ filled with : beautiful, careful, dreadful*

beau·ti·ful ♦♦◇ /byuːtɪfəl/ 1 ADJ A **beautiful** person is very attractive to look at. 美丽的 ❑ *She was a very beautiful woman.* 她是个非常美丽的女人。 2 ADJ If you describe something as **beautiful**, you mean that it is very attractive or pleasing. 迷人的 ❑ *New England is beautiful.* 新英格兰很迷人。 ❑ *It was a beautiful morning.* 那是个迷人的早晨。 ● **beau·ti·ful·ly** /byuːtɪfli/ ADV 迷人地 ❑ *The children behaved beautifully.* 孩子们表现甚佳。 3 ADJ You can describe something that someone does as **beautiful** when they do it very skillfully. 出色的 ❑ *That's a beautiful shot!* 那一射真漂亮！ ● **beau·ti·ful·ly** ADV 出色地 ❑ *The Sixers played beautifully.* 费城76人队打得很出色。

When you are describing someone's appearance, you usually use **beautiful** and **pretty** to describe women, girls, and babies. **Beautiful** is a much stronger word than **pretty**. The equivalent word for a man is **handsome**. **Good-looking** and **attractive** can be used to describe people of either sex.

Thesaurus *beautiful* 另参见：

ADJ. gorgeous, lovely, pretty, ravishing, stunning; *(ant.)* grotesque, hideous, homely, ugly 1

beau·ty ♦◇◇ /byuːti/ (**beauties**) 1 N-UNCOUNT **Beauty** is the state or quality of being beautiful. 美丽 ❑ *...an area of outstanding natural beauty.* …一处具有非凡自然之美的地区。 2 N-COUNT A **beauty** is a beautiful woman. 美人 [JOURNALISM] ❑ *She is known as a great beauty.* 她是个众所皆知的大美人。 3 N-COUNT You can say that something is a **beauty** when you think it is very good. 美的东西 [INFORMAL] ❑ *It was the one opportunity in the game – the pass was a real beauty, but the shot was poor.* 那是比赛中的一个机会——传球的确很漂亮，但射门却很糟。 4 N-COUNT The **beauties** of something are its attractive qualities or features. 丽质 [LITERARY] ❑ *He was beginning to enjoy the beauties of nature.* 他渐渐喜欢上了大自然的迷人之处。 5 ADJ **Beauty** is used to describe people, products, and activities that are concerned with making women look beautiful. 美容的 [ADJ n] ❑ *Additional beauty treatments can be booked in advance.* 额外的美容项目可以提前预订。 6 N-COUNT If you say that a particular feature is **the beauty of** something, you mean that this feature is what makes the thing so good. 优点；妙处 ❑ *There would be no effect on animals – that's the beauty of such water-based materials.* 它将不会对动物产生影响——这就是该种基于水的材料的优点所在。

beau·ty mark (**beauty marks**) N-COUNT A **beauty mark** is a small, dark spot on the skin that is supposed to add to a woman's beauty. 美人痣 [AM, AUSTRALIAN]

in BRIT, use **beauty spot**

❑ *...that cute little beauty mark on Teri Hatcher's lower lip.* …泰莉•哈彻下唇上那颗可爱的小美人痣。

beau·ty spot [BRIT] → see **beauty mark**

bea·ver /biːvər/ (**beavers**) 1 N-COUNT A **beaver** is a furry animal with a big flat tail and large teeth. Beavers use their teeth to cut wood and build dams in rivers. 海狸 2 N-UNCOUNT **Beaver** is the fur of a beaver. 海狸毛皮 [oft N n] ❑ *...a coat with a huge beaver collar.* …一件带有大的海狸毛皮领的外套。

be·came /bɪkeɪm/ **Became** is the past tense of **become**. **become**的过去式

be·cause ♦♦♦ /bɪkɔz, bɪkɒz/ 1 CONJ You use **because** when stating the reason for something. 因为（用以陈述理由）❑ *He is called Mitch, because his name is Mitchell.* 他被叫做米奇，因为他的名字是米切尔。 ❑ *Because it is an area of outstanding natural beauty, the number of boats available for hire on the river is limited.* 这是一个自然风景极美的地方，所以河上可供租用的船只数量有限。 2 CONJ You use **because** when stating the explanation for a statement you have just made. 因为（用以陈述解释）❑ *Maybe they just didn't want to ask too many questions, because they rented us a room without even asking to see our papers.* 也许他们只是不想问太多的问题，因为他们甚至没要求查看我们的证件就把房间租给了我们。 ❑ *The president has played a shrewd diplomatic game because from the outset he called for direct talks.* 总统玩了一场精明的外交游戏，因为从一开始他就要求进行直接对话。 3 PHRASE If an event or situation occurs **because of** something, that thing is the reason or cause. 由于 ❑ *Many families break up because of a lack of money.* 许多家庭因缺钱而破裂。

▲ **beck·on** /bɛkən/ (**beckons, beckoning, beckoned**) 1 V-T/V-I If you **beckon to** someone, you signal to them to come to you. 向…招手 ❑ *He beckoned to the waiter.* 他朝服务员招了招手。 ❑ *I beckoned her over.* 我招手叫她过来。 2 V-I If something **beckons**, it is so attractive to someone that they feel they must become involved in it. 召唤 ❑ *All the attractions of the peninsula beckon.* 那半岛上所有胜地都引人入胜。 3 V-I If something **beckons for** someone, it is very likely to happen to them. 向…召唤 ❑ *The big time beckons for Billy Dodds.* 伟大的时刻在向比利•多兹召唤。

be•come ♦♦♦ /bɪkʌm/ (**becomes, becoming, became**)

The form **become** is used in the present tense and is the past participle.

1 V-LINK If someone or something **becomes** a particular thing, they start to change and develop into that thing, or start to develop the characteristics mentioned. 变成 ❑ *I first became interested in Islam while I was doing my nursing training.* 我在进行护理训练的时候，我初次对伊斯兰教产生了兴趣。 2 V-T If something **becomes** someone, it makes them look attractive or it seems right for them. 适合；与…相称 [no passive, no cont] ❑ *Does khaki become you?* 卡其布适合你吗？ 3 PHRASE If you wonder **what** has **become of** someone or something, you wonder where they are and what has happened to them. (某人、某事物) 怎么样了 ❑ *She thought constantly about her family; she might never know what had become of them.* 她经常想着她的家人；她也许永远都不知道他们怎么样了。

bed ♦♦◊ /bɛd/ (**beds**) 1 N-COUNT A **bed** is a piece of furniture that you lie on when you sleep. 床 [also prep N] ❑ *We finally went to bed at about 4am.* 我们最后在凌晨四点左右上了床。 ❑ *By the time we got back from dinner, Nona was already in bed.* 等我们吃完饭回来，诺娜已经上床了。 2 N-COUNT If a place such as a hospital or a hotel has a particular number of **beds**, it is able to hold that number of patients or guests. (医院、旅馆等的) 床位 3 N-COUNT A **bed** in a garden or park is an area of ground that has been specially prepared so that plants can be grown in it. 苗床 ❑ *...beds of strawberries and rhubarb.* …草莓与大黄的苗床。 4 N-COUNT A **bed** of shellfish or plants is an area in the sea or in a lake where a particular type of shellfish or plant is found in large quantities. (某种贝类生物或植物密集的) 地带 ❑ *The whole lake was rimmed with thick beds of reeds.* 整个湖边长满了厚厚的芦苇丛。 5 N-COUNT The sea **bed** or a river **bed** is the ground at the bottom of the sea or of a river. 海床；河床 ❑ *For three weeks a big operation went on to recover the wreckage from the sea bed.* 一项大规模行动持续3周以从海床寻找残骸。 6 N-COUNT A **bed** of rock is a layer of rock that is found within a larger area of rock. (岩) 层 ❑ *Between the white limestone and the grayish pink limestone is a thin bed of clay.* 在白色石灰石与略带浅灰色的粉红色石灰石之间的是薄薄的黏土层。 7 N-COUNT If a recipe or a menu says that something is served on a **bed of** a food such as rice or vegetables, it means it is served on a layer of that food. (米饭、菜) 底 ❑ *Heat the curry thoroughly and serve it on a bed of rice.* 将咖喱加热透再浇到一层米饭上。 8 N-COUNT On a vehicle such a truck or a pickup, the **bed** is the long, flat part at the back where goods are carried. (车辆的) 拖斗 ❑ *They loaded about a ton of canned goods into the covered bed of a pickup truck.* 他们将约一吨重的罐装食品装到了小卡车的有篷拖斗里。 9 → see also **bedding** 10 PHRASE To **go to bed with** someone means to have sex with them. 发生性关系 ❑ *I went to bed with him once, just once.* 我有一次、仅有一次和他上过床。 11 PHRASE When you **make** the **bed**, you neatly arrange the sheets and covers of a bed so that it is ready to sleep in. 铺床 ❑ *He had made the bed after breakfast.* 早饭后他就把床铺好了。 12 **bed of roses** → see **rose**

→ see Picture Dictionary: **bed**

→ see **lake, sleep**

Word Partnership *bed* 的常用搭配:

ADJ.	**asleep in** bed, **double/single/twin** bed, **ready for** bed 1
V.	**be sick in** bed, **get into** bed, **go to** bed, **lie (down) in** bed, **put** *someone* **to** bed 1
PREP.	**in/out of** bed, **under the** bed 1 bed **of** *something* 3 4 6 7

bed and break•fast (**bed and breakfasts**) also **bed-and-breakfast** 1 N-UNCOUNT **Bed and breakfast** is a system of accommodations in a hotel or guest house, in which you pay for a room for the night and for breakfast the following morning. The abbreviation **B&B** is also used. 住宿加早餐 ❑ *Bed and breakfast costs from $50 per person per night.* 住宿加早餐每人每晚$50起。 2 N-COUNT A **bed and breakfast** is a guest house that provides bed and breakfast accommodations. The abbreviation **B&B** is also used. 住宿加早餐客栈 ❑ *The restored home is now a bed-and-breakfast.* 这座重建后的房子现在是一家住宿加早餐客栈。

bed•clothes /bɛdkloʊz, -kloʊðz/ N-PLURAL **Bedclothes** are the sheets and covers that you put over yourself when you get into bed. (睡觉时用的床单、被单等) 卧具 [OLD-FASHIONED] ❑ *Momma was cleaning inside, changing the bedclothes.* 妈妈在里面清扫，换卧具。

bed•ding /bɛdɪŋ/ N-UNCOUNT **Bedding** is sheets, blankets, and covers that are used on beds. 床上用品 ❑ *...a crib with two full sets of bedding.* …有两整套床单被褥的婴儿床。

bed•room ♦◊◊ /bɛdrum/ (**bedrooms**) 1 N-COUNT A **bedroom** is a room used for sleeping in. 卧室 ❑ *...the spare bedroom.* …那间空卧室。

Picture Dictionary bed

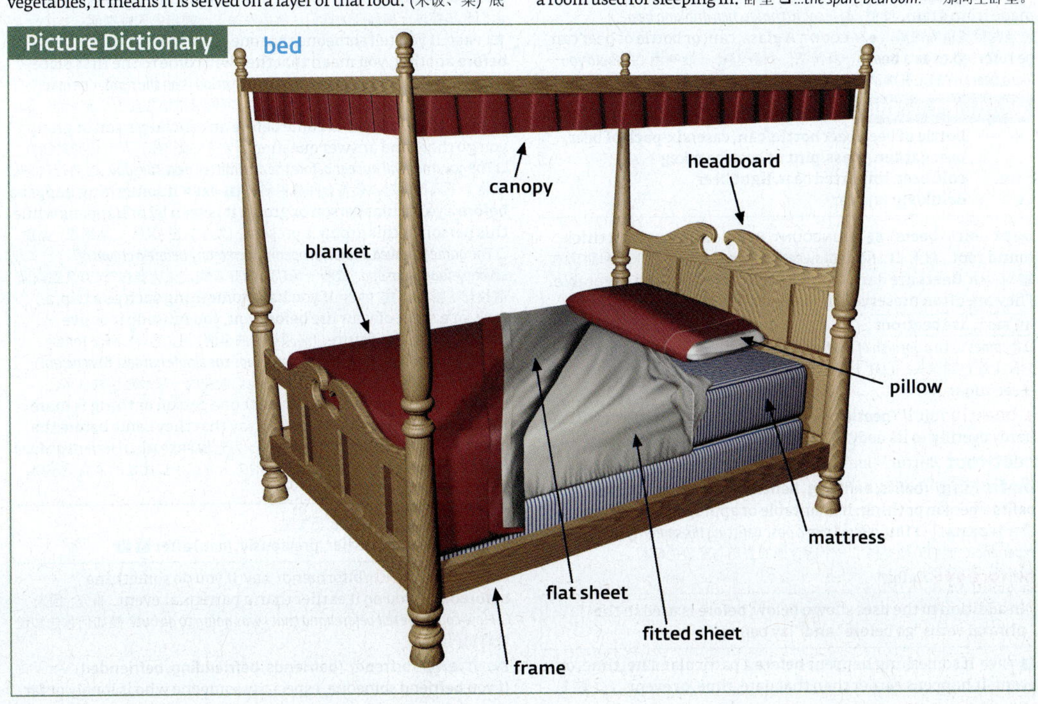

B

2 ADJ If you refer to a place as a **bedroom community** or **suburb**, you mean that most of the people who live there travel to work in a city or another, larger town a short distance away. (指通勤者居住的）卧室社区 [ADJ n] [AM]

in BRIT, use **dormitory**

❑ *This town is becoming a bedroom community of Columbus, 20 miles to the north.* 这座小镇正成为距此北面20英里处哥伦布市的卧室社区。

→ see **house**

bed·side /bɛdsaɪd/ **1** N-SING Your **bedside** is the area beside your bed. 床边 [usu N n] ❑ *She put a cup of tea down on the bedside table.* 她把一杯茶放在了床边的桌子上。 **2** N-SING If you talk about being at someone's **bedside**, you are talking about being near them when they are ill in bed. 病床边 ❑ *She kept vigil at the bedside of her critically ill son.* 她彻夜守护在病重儿子的病榻旁。

bee /bi/ (**bees**) N-COUNT A **bee** is an insect with a yellow-and-black striped body that makes a buzzing noise as it flies. Bees make honey, and can sting. 蜜蜂 ❑ *A bee buzzed in the flowers.* 一只蜜蜂在花丛中嗡嗡作响。

→ see **flower**

beef /bif/ (**beefs, beefing, beefed**) N-UNCOUNT **Beef** is the meat of a cow, bull, or ox. 牛肉 ❑ *...roast beef.* …烤牛肉。 ❑ *...beef stew.* …炖牛肉。

→ see **meat**

▸ **beef up** PHRASAL VERB If you **beef up** something, you increase, strengthen, or improve it. 加强 ❑ *...a campaign to beef up security.* …一场加强治安的运动。 ❑ *Both sides are still beefing up their military strength.* 双方仍在增强各自的军事力量。

Beem·er /bimər/ (**Beemers**) also **Beamer** N-COUNT Some people refer to a BMW automobile as a **Beemer**. 宝马（汽车）[INFORMAL] ❑ *The Beemer's door swung open and Markus Salkow stepped out.* 宝马车门打开了，马库斯•索尔寇跨了出来。

been /bɪn/ **1** **Been** is the past participle of **be**. **be**的过去分词 **2** V-I If you have **been** to a place, you have gone to it or visited it. 去过 ❑ *He's already been to Tunisia, and is to go on to Morocco and Mauritania.* 他已经去过了突尼斯，还将接着去摩洛哥和毛里塔尼亚。

beep·er /bipər/ (**beepers**) N-COUNT A **beeper** is a portable device that makes a beeping noise, usually to tell you to phone someone or to remind you to do something. 寻呼机 ❑ *His beeper sounded and he picked up the telephone.* 他的寻呼机响了，于是他拿起了电话。

beer ♦◇◇ /bɪər/ (**beers**) N-MASS **Beer** is an alcoholic drink made from grain. 啤酒 ❑ *He sat in the kitchen drinking beer.* 他坐在厨房里喝啤酒。 ● N-COUNT A glass, can, or bottle of beer can be referred to as a **beer**. 一杯啤酒；一罐啤酒；一瓶啤酒 ❑ *Would you like a beer?* 你想来杯啤酒吗？

Word Partnership *beer* 的常用搭配：

N.	**bottle of** beer, beer **bottle/can, case/six-pack of** beer, beer **garden, glass/pint of** beer, beer **keg**
ADJ.	**cold** beer, **imported** beer, **light** beer
V.	**drink/sip (a)** beer

beet /bit/ (**beets**) **1** N-UNCOUNT **Beet** is a crop with a thick round root. 甜菜 ❑ *...fields of sweet corn and beet.* …甜玉米和甜菜地 **2** N-VAR **Beets** are dark red roots that are eaten as a vegetable. They are often preserved in vinegar. 甜菜根 [AM]

in BRIT, use **beetroot**

❑ *It comes with a garnish of red beets, white cottage cheese and blueberries.* 它配上红色甜菜头、白软干酪和蓝莓等装饰。

→ see **sugar**

▲ **bee·tle** /bitᵊl/ (**beetles**) N-COUNT A **beetle** is an insect with a hard covering to its body. 甲虫

beet·root /bitrut/ [BRIT] → see **beet 2**

be·fit /bɪfɪt/ (**befits, befitting, befitted**) V-T If something **befits** a person or thing, it is suitable or appropriate for them. 适合 [FORMAL] ❑ *They offered him a post befitting his seniority and experience.* 他们给他提供了一个适合他的资历与经验的职位。

be·fore ♦♦♦ /bɪfɔr/

In addition to the uses shown below, **before** is used in the phrasal verbs "go before" and "lay before."

1 PREP If something happens **before** a particular date, time, or event, it happens earlier than that date, time, or event. 在（某日、某时、某事件）以前 ❑ *Annie was born a few weeks before Christmas.* 安妮在圣诞节前几个礼拜出生。 ❑ *Before World War II, women were not recruited as intelligence officers.* 二战前，女性不被征募为情报官。 ● CONJ **Before** is also a conjunction. 在（某日、某时、某事件）以前 ❑ *Stock prices have climbed close to the peak they'd registered before the stock market crashed in 1987.* 股票价格已经快爬升到了1987年股市崩溃前的最高纪录。 **2** PREP If you do one thing **before** doing something else, you do it earlier than the other thing. 在（做某事）之前 [PREP -ing] ❑ *He spent his early life in Sri Lanka before moving to Canada.* 移居加拿大前，他早年生活在斯里兰卡。 ● CONJ **Before** is also a conjunction. 在（做某事）之前 ❑ *He took a cold shower and then toweled off before he put on fresh clothes.* 他穿上干净衣服之前，冲了个冷水澡，再擦干身子。 **3** ADV You use **before** when you are talking about time. For example, if something happened the day **before** a particular date or event, it happened during the previous day. （某时、某事）以前 [n ADV] ❑ *The war had ended only a month or so before.* 战争大约在一个月前才结束。 ● PREP **Before** is also a preposition. （某时、某事）以前 [n PREP n] ❑ *It's interesting that he sent me the book twenty days before the deadline for my book.* 有趣的是，在距离我书的截止日期20天前他把那本书寄给了我。 ● CONJ **Before** is also a conjunction. （某时、某事）以前 ❑ *Kelman had a book published in the U.S. more than a decade before a British publisher would touch him.* 科尔曼在美国已经出版了一本书，十多年后英国的出版商才愿意出版他的作品。 **4** CONJ If you do something **before** someone else can do something, you do it when they have not yet done it. 在（某人能做某事）之前 ❑ *Before Gallacher could catch up with the ball, Nadlovu had beaten him to it.* 在加拉赫能接住球之前，纳德洛夫就已经比他先接到了。 **5** ADV If someone has done something **before**, they have done it on a previous occasion. If someone has not done something **before**, they have never done it. 以前（做过某事）[ADV after v] ❑ *I've been here before.* 我以前来过这儿。 ❑ *I had met Professor Lown before.* 我以前见过劳恩教授。 **6** CONJ If there is a period of time or if several things are done **before** something happens, it takes that amount of time or effort for this thing to happen. 经过（一段时间或努力）才 ❑ *It was some time before the door opened in response to his ring.* 他按过门铃后好一会儿门才打开。 **7** CONJ If a particular situation has to happen **before** something else happens, this situation must happen or exist in order for the other thing to happen. 在（某事发生）之前（另一情况必须发生） ❑ *There was additional work to be done before all the troops would be ready.* 在全军准备就绪之前还有些事情要做。 **8** PREP If someone is **before** something, they are in front of it. 在（某物）前面 [FORMAL] ❑ *They drove through a tall iron gate and stopped before a large white villa.* 他们开车穿过一扇高高的铁门，然后停在了一幢白色大别墅前。 **9** PREP If you tell someone that one place is a certain distance **before** another, you mean that they will come to the first place first. 在（某地）前方（某距离处） ❑ *The station is on the right, one mile before downtown Romney.* 车站在右侧，罗姆尼市中心前方一英里处。 **10** PREP If you appear or come **before** an official person or group, you go there and answer questions. 在（人或组织）面前（回答提问） ❑ *The governor will appear before the committee next Tuesday.* 这名行政官员将于下周二面对该委员会回答提问。 **11** PREP If something happens **before** a particular person or group, it is seen by or happens while this person or this group is present. （发生）在（某人、某组织）面前 ❑ *The game followed a colorful opening ceremony before a crowd of seventy-four thousand.* 紧随一场精彩的开幕式，该比赛在7.4万名观众面前拉开了帷幕。 **12** PREP If you have something such as a trip, a task, or a stage of your life **before** you, you must do it or live through it in the future. （必须经历的事情）在（某人）面前 [PREP pron] ❑ *Everyone in the room knew it was the single hardest task before them.* 屋子里每个人都知道这是摆在他们面前的一项最艰巨的任务。 **13** PREP When you want to say that one person or thing is more important than another, you can say that they come **before** the other person or thing. （重要性）以…为先 [V PREP n] ❑ *Her husband and her children came before her needs.* 她的丈夫和孩子们比她的需要更重要。 **14** **before long** → see **long**

Thesaurus *before* 另参见：

ADV.	already, earlier, previously; (*ant.*) after **3** **5**

★ **before·hand** /bɪfɔrhænd/ ADV If you do something **beforehand**, you do it earlier than a particular event. 事先；预先 ❑ *How could she tell beforehand that I was going to go out?* 她如何预先知道我将出门的？

be·friend /bɪfrɛnd/ (**befriends, befriending, befriended**) V-T If you **befriend** someone, especially someone who is lonely or far from home, you make friends with them. 和…交朋友; 友好对待 ❑ *The film's about an elderly woman and a young nurse who befriends her.* 该电影是关于一名年迈的妇女和一个待她友善的年轻护士的故事。

beg /bɛg/ (**begs, begging, begged**) 1 V-T/V-I If you **beg** someone **to** do something, you ask them very anxiously or eagerly to do it. 恳求 ❑ *I begged him to come back to New York with me.* 我请求他和我一起回纽约。❑ *We are not going to beg for help anymore.* 我们将不再请求帮助。❑ *They dropped to their knees and begged forgiveness.* 他们跪倒在地，祈求原谅。 2 V-I If someone who is poor **is begging**, they are asking people to give them food or money. 行乞 [oft cont] ❑ *I was surrounded by people begging for food.* 我被一群讨饭的人围住了。❑ *...homeless people begging on the streets.* …沿街乞讨的无家可归者。❑ *She was living alone, begging food from neighbors.* 她一个人生活，从邻居那儿讨些吃的。 3 **I beg your pardon** → see **pardon**

Word Partnership *beg* 的常用搭配:

V.	beg **and plead** 1
PREP.	beg **for** ***something*** 1 2
N.	beg **for help/mercy** 1 2
	beg **for food/money** 2
	beg ***(someone's)*** **forgiveness/pardon** 3

be·gan /bɪgæn/ **Began** is the past tense of **begin**. **begin**的过去式

beg·gar /bɛgər/ (**beggars**) N-COUNT A **beggar** is someone who lives by asking people for money or food. 乞丐 ❑ *There are no beggars on the street in Vienna.* 维也纳的街道上没有乞丐。

be·gin ♦♦♦ /bɪgɪn/ (**begins, beginning, began, begun**) 1 V-T To **begin to** do something means to start doing it. 开始(做某事) ❑ *He stood up and began to move around the room.* 他站了起来，开始在屋子里走来走去。 ❑ *The weight loss began to look more serious.* 体重的减轻开始显得更严重。 2 V-T/V-I When something **begins** or when you **begin** it, it takes place from a particular time onward. 使开始发生; 开始发生 ❑ *The problems began last November.* 问题于去年11月开始出现。 ❑ *He has just begun his fourth year in hiding.* 他刚刚开始他东躲西藏的生活的第4个年头。 3 V-T/V-I If you **begin with** something, or **begin by** doing something, this is the first thing you do. 以(某事、做某事)开始 ❑ *Could I begin with a few formalities?* 我可以从一些例行程序开始吗? ❑ *...a businessman who began by selling golf shirts from the trunk of his car.* …一个从销售汽车行李箱里的高尔夫衬衫起家的商人。 ❑ *He began his career flipping hamburgers.* 他以翻转汉堡包开始他的职业生涯。 4 V-T/V-I You use **begin** to mention the first thing that someone says. 开始说; 以…做开场白 [no cont] ❑ *"Professor Theron," he began, "I'm very pleased to see you."* "西伦教授，"他开始说道，"我非常高兴见到你。" ❑ *He didn't know how to begin.* 他不知道如何开场。 5 V-I If one thing **began as** another thing, it first existed as the other thing before it changed into its present form. 起初是 [no cont] ❑ *What began as a local festival has blossomed into an international event.* 起初的一个地方性的节日已经发展成了一项国际盛事。 6 V-I If you say that a thing or place **begins** somewhere, you are talking about one of its limits or edges. 起始于 [no cont] ❑ *The fate line begins close to the wrist.* 命运线始于接近手腕处。 7 V-I If a word **begins with** a particular letter, that is the first letter of that word. (某词) 以(某字母)开头 [no cont] ❑ *The first word begins with an F.* 第一个词以F开头。 8 PHRASE You use **to begin with** when you are talking about the first stage of a situation, event, or process. 起初; 刚开始 ❑ *It was great to begin with but now it's difficult.* 这起初很顺利，但现在难了。 9 PHRASE You use **to begin with** to introduce the first of several things that you want to say. 首先 ❑ *"What do scientists you've spoken with think about that?"—"Well, to begin with, they doubt it's going to work."* "和你交谈过的科学家们对此怎么看?"——"噢，首先，他们怀疑这是否会奏效。"

> **Begin**, **start**, and **commence** all have a similar meaning, although **commence** is more formal and is not normally used in conversation. ❑ *The meeting is ready to begin... He tore the list up and started a fresh one ... an alternative to commencing the process of European integration.* Note that **begin**, **start**, and **commence** can all be followed by an -ing form or a noun, but only **begin** and **start** can be followed by a "to" infinitive.

Thesaurus *begin* 另参见:

V.	commence, kick off, start; *(ant.)* end, stop 2

Word Partnership *begin* 的常用搭配:

ADV.	begin **again/anew**, begin **immediately/soon**, **suddenly** begin 1 2
V.	**expected/scheduled to** begin, begin **to show**, begin **to understand** 1 2
ADJ.	**ready to** begin 1 2
N.	begin **a process** 2
PREP.	begin **by doing** ***something*** 3
	to begin **with** 8 9

be·gin·ner /bɪgɪnər/ (**beginners**) N-COUNT A **beginner** is someone who has just started learning to do something and cannot do it very well yet. 初学者 ❑ *The course is suitable for both beginners and advanced students.* 这门课程对初学者和高阶学生都适合。

be·gin·ning ♦◊◊ /bɪgɪnɪŋ/ (**beginnings**) 1 N-COUNT The **beginning of** an event or process is the first part of it. (事情、过程的) 开始 ❑ *This was also the beginning of her recording career.* 这也是她灌片生涯的开始。 2 N-PLURAL **The beginnings of** something are the signs or events which form the first part of it. 序曲 ❑ *The discussions were the beginnings of a dialogue with Moscow.* 这些会谈是与莫斯科对话的序曲。 3 N-SING **The beginning of** a period of time is the time at which it starts. (某时段的) 初期 ❑ *The wedding will be at the beginning of March.* 婚礼将于3月初举行。 4 N-COUNT The **beginning of** a piece of written material is the first words or sentences of it. (文章的) 开头 ❑ *...the question that was raised at the beginning of this chapter.* …本章开头提出的问题。 5 N-PLURAL If you talk about the **beginnings** of a person, company, or group, you are referring to their backgrounds or origins. 背景; 出身 ❑ *His views come from his own humble beginnings.* 他的观点源自于他卑微的出身。

Thesaurus *beginning* 另参见:

N.	birth, conception, genesis; *(ant.)* conclusion, end 1
	inception, introduction, start; *(ant.)* conclusion, end 3

Word Partnership *beginning* 的常用搭配:

ADV.	**just the** beginning 1 3
PREP.	**in the** beginning 1 3
	beginning **of** ***something***, **from/since the** beginning 1–3
ADJ.	**a new** beginning 1 4

be·gun /bɪgʌn/ **Begun** is the past participle of **begin**. **begin**的过去分词

be·half ♦◊◊ /bɪhæf/ 1 PHRASE If you do something **on** someone's **behalf**, you do it for that person as their representative. 代表 ❑ *She made an emotional public appeal on her son's behalf.* 她代表儿子作了感动人心的公开呼吁。 2 PHRASE If you feel, for example, embarrassed or angry **on** someone's **behalf**, you feel embarrassed or angry for them. 替某人(感到害羞、愤怒等) ❑ *"What do you mean?" I asked, offended on Liddie's behalf.* "你什么意思?"我问道，很为莉迪生气。

be·have ♦◊◊ /bɪheɪv/ (**behaves, behaving, behaved**) 1 V-I The way that you **behave** is the way that you do and say things, and the things that you do and say. 行为; 表现 ❑ *I couldn't believe these people were behaving in this way.* 我无法相信这些人竟这样行事。 2 V-T/V-I If you **behave** or **behave yourself**, you act in the way that people think is correct and proper. 使…规矩; 规矩地行事 ❑ *You have to behave.* 你得守规矩。 3 V-I In science, the way that something **behaves** is the things that it does. (科学领域) 运动表现 ❑ *Under certain conditions, electrons can behave like waves rather than particles.* 在某些条件下，电子能像波而不是粒子那样运动。

Word Partnership *behave* 的常用搭配:

ADV.	behave **badly/well** 1
PREP.	behave **toward** ***someone*** 1
PRON.	behave ***themselves/yourself*** 1 2

be·hav·ior ♦♦◊ /bɪheɪvyər/ (**behaviors**)

in BRIT, use **behaviour**

1 N-VAR People's or animals' **behavior** is the way that they behave. You can refer to a typical and repeated way of behaving as a **behavior**. 行为 ❑ *Make sure that good behavior is rewarded.* 确保良好的行为受到嘉奖。 ❑ *...human sexual behavior.* …人类性行为。 2 N-UNCOUNT In science, the **behavior** of something is the way that it behaves. (科学领域) 运动表现 ❑ *It will be many years before anyone can predict a hurricane's behavior with much accuracy.* 要高精确度

B

地预测飓风的表现尚需要许多年。 **3** PHRASE If someone is **on** their **best behavior**, they are trying very hard to behave well. 尽全力好好表现 ❑ *The 1,400 fans were on their best behavior and filed out peacefully at the end.* 1400名支持者尽全力守着规矩，结束时排成队平静地离场。

Thesaurus *behavior* 另参见：
N. action, conduct **1**

Word Partnership *behavior* 的常用搭配：
V. **change** *someone's* behavior **1**
N. **human** behavior, behavior **pattern**, behavior **problems** **1**
ADJ. **aggressive/criminal** behavior, **bad/good** behavior **1** **learned** behavior **1** **2**

★ **be·hav·ior·al** /bɪheɪvyərəl/
in BRIT, use **behavioural**
ADJ **Behavioral** means relating to the behavior of a person or animal, or to the study of their behavior. 行为方面的；行为科学的 [ADJ n] ❑ *...emotional and behavioral problems.* …情感与行为上的问题。

be·hav·iour /bɪheɪvyər/ [BRIT] → see **behavior**

★ **be·hav·iour·al** /bɪheɪvyərəl/ [BRIT] → see **behavioral**

be·hind ♦♦♦ /bɪhaɪnd/ (**behinds**)

In addition to the uses shown below, **behind** is also used in a few phrasal verbs, such as "fall behind" and "lie behind."

1 PREP If something is **behind** a thing or person, it is on the other side of them from you, or nearer their back rather than their front. 在…后面 ❑ *I put one of the cushions behind his head.* 我把其中一个垫子放在了他脑后。 ❑ *They were parked behind the truck.* 它们被停在了卡车后面。 ● ADV **Behind** is also an adverb. 在后面 ❑ *Rising into the hills behind are 800 acres of parkland.* 往上延伸至后面小山的是800英亩的草木区。 **2** PREP If you are walking or traveling **behind** someone or something, you are following them. (跟随) 在…后面 ❑ *Keith wandered along behind him.* 基思跟在他后面闲逛。 ● ADV **Behind** is also an adverb. (跟随) 在后面 [ADV after v] ❑ *The troopers followed behind, every muscle tensed for the sudden gunfire.* 骑兵们跟在后面，每一块肌肉都因突如其来的炮火而绷得紧紧的。 **3** PREP If someone is **behind** a desk, counter, or bar, they are on the other side of it from where you are. 在…后面 (指另一侧) ❑ *The colonel was sitting behind a cheap wooden desk.* 上校坐在一张廉价的木质书桌后面。 **4** PREP When you shut a door or gate **behind** you, you shut it after you have gone through it. 在…身后 [PREP pron] ❑ *I walked out and closed the door behind me.* 我走了出来并关上了身后的门。 **5** N-COUNT Your **behind** is the part of your body that you sit on. 臀部 **6** PREP The people, reason, or events **behind** a situation are the causes of it or are responsible for it. 在背后；在幕后 ❑ *It is still not clear who was behind the killing.* 至今尚不清楚谁是这起谋杀案的幕后策划者。 **7** PREP If something or someone is **behind** you, they support you and help you. 在背后 (支持) [PREP pron] ❑ *He had the state's judicial power behind him.* 他有国家司法力量在其背后支持他。 **8** PREP If you refer to what is **behind** someone's outside appearance, you are referring to a characteristic which you cannot immediately see or is not obvious, but which you think is there. 在 (某人的外表) 背后 ❑ *What lay behind his anger was really the hurt he felt at Grace's refusal.* 在他的愤怒背后其实是遭格雷斯拒绝而感到的心痛。 **9** PREP If you are **behind** someone, you are less successful than them, or have done less or advanced less. (成就、业绩、进展等) 在 (某人) 之后 ❑ *She finished second behind the American, Ann Cody, in the 800 meters.* 她在800米赛跑中在美国的安•科迪之后跑到终点，位居第2。 ● ADV **Behind** is also an adverb. 在后面 ❑ *The rapid development of technology means that she is now far behind, and will need retraining.* 科技的快速发展意味着她现在已经远远落后了，将需要再训练。 **10** PREP If an experience is **behind** you, it happened in your past and will not happen again, or no longer affects you. (将经历抛) 到…脑后 [PREP pron] ❑ *Maureen put the nightmare behind her.* 莫琳将噩梦抛诸脑后。 **11** PREP If you have a particular achievement **behind** you, you have managed to reach this achievement, and other people consider it to be important or valuable. (成就) 在…背后 ["have/with" n PREP pron] ❑ *He has 20 years of loyal service to Barclays Bank behind him.* 他背后有20年忠心为巴克利银行工作的经历。 **12** PREP If something is **behind** schedule, it is not as far advanced as people had planned. If someone is **behind** schedule, they are not progressing as quickly at something as they had planned. (落) 在 (时间进度) 之后 ❑ *The work is 22 weeks behind schedule.* 这项工作比预计时间推迟了22周。 **13** ADV If you stay **behind**, you remain in a place after other people have gone. (留) 在后面 [ADV after v] ❑ *About 1,200 personnel will remain behind to take care of the air base.* 约有1200名人员将留下来照管空军基地。 **14** ADV If you leave something or someone **behind**, you do not take them with you when you go. (把…留) 在后面 [ADV after v] ❑ *The rebels fled into the mountains, leaving behind their weapons and supplies.* 叛乱者逃进了山里，丢下了武器和给养物资。 **15** to **do** something **behind** someone's **back** → see **back** **16** **behind bars** → see **bar** **17** **behind the scenes** → see **scene** **18** **behind the times** → see **time**

beige /beɪʒ/ COLOR Something that is **beige** is pale brown in color. 淡棕色的 ❑ *The walls are beige.* 墙是淡棕色的。

be·ing ♦◇◇ /biɪŋ/ (**beings**) **1** **Being** is the present participle of **be**. be的现在分词 **2** V-LINK **Being** is used in nonfinite clauses where you are giving the reason for something. 用于非限定分句，表示原因 ❑ *It being a Sunday, the old men had the day off.* 因为是星期天，老人们休了一天假。 ❑ *Little boys, being what they are, might decide to play on it.* 小男孩们也许会决定要弄它，因为他们就是这样。 **3** N-COUNT You can refer to any real or imaginary creature as a **being**. (任何真实或虚构的) 生物 ❑ *People expect a horse to perform like a car, with no thought for its feelings as a living being.* 人们期望一匹马能表现得像一辆车那样，却没考虑到它作为一个活的生物的感受。 **4** → see also **human being** **5** N-UNCOUNT **Being** is existence. Something that is **in being** or comes **into being** exists. 存在 ❑ *Abraham Maslow described psychology as "the science of being."* 亚伯拉罕•马斯洛将心理学描述为"存在科学"。 **6** → see also **well-being** **7** **other things being equal** → see **equal** **8** **for the time being** → see **time**

be·lat·ed /bɪleɪtɪd/ ADJ A **belated** action happens later than it should have. 迟来的 [FORMAL] ❑ *...the government's belated attempts to alleviate the plight of the poor.* …政府想减轻穷人的困苦的、为时已晚的尝试。

belch /bɛltʃ/ (**belches, belching, belched**) **1** V-I If someone **belches**, they make a sudden noise in their throat because air has risen up from their stomach. 打嗝 ❑ *Garland covered his mouth with his hand and belched discreetly.* 加兰用手捂住嘴，小心翼翼地打了个嗝。 ● N-COUNT **Belch** is also a noun. 打嗝 ❑ *He drank and stifled a belch.* 他喝了一口，强忍住打嗝。 **2** V-T/V-I If a machine or chimney **belches** smoke or fire, or if smoke or fire **belches** from it, large amounts of smoke or fire come from it. 喷出 (烟、火等)；(烟、火等) 喷出 ❑ *Tired old trucks were struggling up the road below us, belching black smoke.* 疲倦的旧卡车正喷着黑烟吃力地攀爬着我们脚下的路。 ● PHRASAL VERB **Belch out** means the same as **belch**. 喷出 ❑ *The power-generation plant belched out five tons of ash an hour.* 发电厂每小时喷出了5吨的灰。

be·lea·guered /bɪligərd/ ADJ A **beleaguered** person, organization, or project is experiencing a lot of difficulties, opposition, or criticism. 饱经曲折的 [FORMAL] ❑ *There have been seven coup attempts against the beleaguered government.* 已有过7次政变企图要颠覆这个饱经风霜的政府。

be·lie /bɪlaɪ/ (**belies, belying, belied**) **1** V-T If one thing **belies** another, it hides the true situation and so creates a false idea or image of someone or something. 掩饰 ❑ *Her looks belie her 50 years.* 她的容貌掩饰着她的50岁年龄。 **2** V-T If one thing **belies** another, it proves that the other thing is not true or genuine. 证明…为虚假 ❑ *The facts of the situation belie his testimony.* 事实情况证明他的证词是虚假的。

be·lief ♦◇◇ /bɪlif/ (**beliefs**) **1** N-UNCOUNT **Belief** is a feeling of certainty that something exists, is true, or is good. 信仰 ❑ *One billion people throughout the world are Muslims, united by belief in one god.* 全世界有10亿人是穆斯林，因为对一位神灵的信仰而团结在一起。 **2** N-PLURAL Your religious or political **beliefs** are your views on religious or political matters. (宗教或政治的) 观念 ❑ *He refuses to compete on Sundays because of his religious beliefs.* 由于他的宗教观念，他拒绝星期天进行比赛。 **3** N-SING If it is your **belief** that something is the case, it is your strong opinion that it is the case. 坚定的信念 ❑ *It is our belief that improvements in health care will lead to a stronger, more prosperous economy.* 我们坚定的信念是卫生保健的改善会带来更加茁壮、繁荣的经济。 **4** PHRASE You use **beyond belief** to emphasize that something is true to a very great degree or that it happened to a very great degree. 难以置信 [EMPHASIS] ❑ *We are devastated, shocked beyond belief.* 我们遭到了挫败，震惊得难以置信。 **5** PHRASE If you do one thing **in the belief that** another thing is true or will happen, you do it because you think, usually wrongly, that it is true or will happen. (通常错误地) 相信 ❑ *Civilians had broken into the*

building, apparently in the belief that it contained food. 老百姓已闯入这栋大楼，很明显他们错误地相信这儿有食物。
→ see religion

Thesaurus *belief* 另参见：
N. dogma, faith, ideology, principle 2
assumption, opinion 3

Word Partnership *belief* 的常用搭配：
N. belief **in God** 1
ADJ. **religious/spiritual** belief 1
(contrary to) popular belief, **firm** belief, **strong** belief, **widespread** belief 1 3
PREP. belief **in *something*** 1
beyond belief 4
V. **hold** a belief 1 3

be·liev·able /bɪliːvəbᵊl/ ADJ Something that is **believable** makes you think that it could be true or real. 可信的 ❑ *...believable evidence.* …可信的证据。

be·lieve ♦♦♦ /bɪliːv/ (**believes, believing, believed**) 1 V-T If you **believe** that something is true, you think it is true, but you are not sure. 认为 [FORMAL] ❑ *Experts believe that the coming drought will be extensive.* 专家们认为即将到来的干旱将会是大面积的。 ❑ *We believe them to be hidden here in this apartment.* 我们认为他们藏匿在这所公寓里。 2 V-T If you **believe** someone or if you **believe** what they say or write, you accept that they are telling the truth. 相信 ❑ *He did not sound as if he believed her.* 听起来他似乎不相信她的话。 ❑ *Never believe anything a married man says about his wife.* 永远别相信一个已婚男人说的关于自己妻子的话。 3 V-I If you **believe in** fairies, ghosts, or miracles, you are sure that they exist or happen. If you **believe in** a god, you are sure of the existence of that god. 相信…的存在 ❑ *I don't believe in ghosts.* 我不相信有鬼。 4 V-I If you **believe in** a way of life or an idea, you are in favor of it because you think it is good or right. 赞成 ❑ *He believed in marital fidelity.* 他赞成对婚姻忠实。 5 V-I If you **believe in** someone or what they are doing, you have confidence in them and think that they will be successful. 对…有信心 ❑ *If you believe in yourself you can succeed.* 对自己有信心，你就能成功。

Note that when you are using the verb **believe** with a **that**-clause in order to state a negative opinion or belief, you normally make **believe** negative, rather than the verb in the **that**-clause. For instance, it is more usual to say "*He didn't believe that she could do it...*" than "*He believed that she couldn't do it.*" The same applies to other verbs with a similar meaning, such as **consider**, **suppose**, and **think**. ❑ *I don't consider that you kept your promise ... I don't suppose he ever saw it ... I don't think he saw me.*

Thesaurus *believe* 另参见：
V. consider, guess, speculate, think 1
accept, buy, trust 2

be·liev·er /bɪliːvər/ (**believers**) 1 N-COUNT If you are a great **believer in** something, you think that it is good, right, or useful. 相信…的人 ❑ *Mom was a great believer in herbal medicines.* 妈妈是个深信草药的人。 2 N-COUNT A **believer** is someone who is sure that God exists or that their religion is true. 宗教信徒 ❑ *I made no secret of the fact that I was not a believer.* 我对自己不是一个宗教信徒的事实并不隐瞒。

bell ♦◇◇ /bɛl/ (**bells**) 1 N-COUNT A **bell** is a device that makes a ringing sound and is used to give a signal or to attract people's attention. 铃 ❑ *I had just enough time to finish eating before the bell rang and I was off to my first class.* 我在铃响前刚好有时间吃完，然后就去上第一节课了。 2 N-COUNT A **bell** is a hollow metal object shaped like a cup which has a piece hanging inside it that hits the sides and makes a sound. 钟 ❑ *My brother, Nick, was born on a Sunday, when all the church bells were ringing.* 我的弟弟尼克，出生在一个星期天，当时所有教堂的钟都在鸣响。 3 PHRASE If you say that something **rings a bell**, you mean that it reminds you of something, but you cannot remember exactly what it is. 引起模糊回忆 [INFORMAL] ❑ *The name doesn't ring a bell.* 这名字听上去没有印象。

bel·lig·er·ent /bɪlɪdʒərənt/ ADJ A **belligerent** person is hostile and aggressive. 好斗的 ❑ *...the belligerent statements from both sides which have led to fears of war.* …双方火药味十足的声明已造成了对战争爆发的担忧。 ● **bel·lig·er·ence** N-UNCOUNT 好斗性 ❑ *He could be accused of passion, but never belligerence.* 他也许可以被指责为性情冲动，但决不是生性好斗。

▲ **bel·low** /bɛloʊ/ (**bellows, bellowing, bellowed**) 1 V-T/V-I If someone **bellows**, they shout angrily in a loud, deep voice. (人)吼叫 ❑ *"I didn't ask to be born!" she bellowed.* "我没有请求被生下来！"她大声吼道。 ❑ *She prayed she wouldn't come in and find them there, bellowing at each other.* 她祈祷着她不会进去后就发现他们在那里冲着对方互相吼叫。 ● N-COUNT **Bellow** is also a noun. 吼叫声 ❑ *I was distraught and let out a bellow of tearful rage.* 我心烦意乱，发出了一声悲愤的吼叫。 2 V-I When a large animal such as a bull or an elephant **bellows**, it makes a loud and deep noise. (大型动物)低嚎 ❑ *A heifer bellowed in her stall.* 小母牛在牛棚里低嚎。 3 N-COUNT A **bellows** is or **bellows** are a device used for blowing air into a fire in order to make it burn more fiercely. 风箱 [also "a pair of" N]

bell pep·per (**bell peppers**) N-COUNT A **bell pepper** is a hollow green, red, or yellow vegetable with seeds. 甜椒 [mainly AM]

★ **bel·ly** /bɛli/ (**bellies**) N-COUNT The **belly** of a person or animal is their stomach or abdomen. 肚子；腹部 ❑ *She laid her hands on her swollen belly.* 她把手放在隆起的肚子上。 ❑ *...a horse with its belly ripped open.* …一匹被破开了肚子的马。

be·long ♦◇◇ /bɪlɔŋ/ (**belongs, belonging, belonged**) 1 V-I If something **belongs to** you, you own it. 属于 [no cont] ❑ *The house had belonged to her family for three or four generations.* 这座房子属于她家已有三四代了。 2 V-I You say that something **belongs to** a particular person when you are guessing, discovering, or explaining that it was produced by or is part of that person. (某人)所做；所有 [no cont] ❑ *The handwriting belongs to a male.* 这笔迹出自一名男子之手。 3 V-I If someone **belongs to** a particular group, they are a member of that group. 是…的成员 [no cont] ❑ *I used to belong to a youth club.* 我曾是一个青年俱乐部的成员。 4 V-I If something or someone **belongs in** or **to** a particular category, type, or group, they are of that category, type, or group. 属(某一类别、类型、群) [no cont] ❑ *The judges could not decide which category it belonged in.* 法官们无法决定它属于哪一类别。 5 V-I If something **belongs to** a particular time, it comes from that time. 源自于；属于(某一时期) [no cont] ❑ *The pictures belong to an era when there was a preoccupation with high society.* 这些图片源于上层社会占据主流的时代。 6 V-I If you say that something **belongs to** someone, you mean that person has the right to it. 有权拥有 [no cont] ❑ *...but the last word belonged to Rosanne.* …但最后的决定权归罗桑所有。 7 V-I If you say that a time **belongs to** a particular system or way of doing something, you mean that that time is or will be characterized by it. (时代)具有…的特征 [no cont] ❑ *The future belongs to democracy.* 未来将是民主的时代。 8 V-I If a baby or child **belongs to** a particular adult, that adult is his or her parent or the person who is looking after him or her. (小孩)为…所监护 [no cont] ❑ *He deduced that the two children belonged to the couple.* 他推断这两个孩子是那对夫妇的。 9 V-I If a person or thing **belongs** in a particular place or situation, that is where they should be. 属于(某地或环境情形) [no cont] ❑ *You don't belong here.* 你不属于这里。 ❑ *They need to feel they belong.* 他们需要有归属感。

Word Partnership *belong* 的常用搭配：
PREP. belong **to *someone*** 1 2 8
belong **to a club/group/organization** 3
ADV. belong **together** 4 5
back where you belong 9
V. ***someone/something* doesn't** belong 9

be·long·ings /bɪlɔŋɪŋz/ N-PLURAL Your **belongings** are the things that you own, especially things that are small enough to be carried. 所有物 ❑ *I collected my belongings and left.* 我收拾好行李就离开了。

be·lov·ed /bɪlʌvɪd/ ADJ A **beloved** person, thing, or place is one that you feel great affection for. 深爱的 [ADJ n] ❑ *He lost his beloved wife last year.* 他去年痛失爱妻。

be·low ♦♦◇ /bɪloʊ/ 1 PREP If something is **below** something else, it is in a lower position. 在…下面 ❑ *He appeared from the apartment directly below Leonard's.* 他从伦纳德家正下方的公寓里走了出来。 ❑ *The sun had already sunk below the horizon.* 太阳已沉下地平线。 ● ADV **Below** is also an adverb. 在下面 ❑ *We climbed rather perilously down a rope-ladder to the boat below.* 我们冒着危险沿着绳梯爬到了下边的小船上。 ❑ *...a view to the street below.* …楼下街景。 2 PHRASE

B

If something is **below ground** or **below the ground**, it is in the ground. 在地表下 ❑ *They have designed a system which pumps up water from nearly 1,000 feet below ground.* 他们设计了一个能从地表以下1000英尺处抽水的系统。 3 ADV You use **below** in a piece of writing to refer to something that is mentioned later. 在下文中 ❑ *Please write to me at the address below.* 请按以下地址给我写信。 4 PREP If something is **below** a particular amount, rate, or level, it is less than that amount, rate, or level. (数量、比率、水平等) 在…下面 ❑ *Night temperatures can drop below 15 degrees Celsius.* 夜间温度可能会降到15摄氏度以下。 ● ADV **Below** is also an adverb. 在下面 ❑ *...temperatures at zero or below.* …零度或零度以下。 5 PREP If someone is **below** you in an organization, they are lower in rank. (地位) 低于 ❑ *Such people often experience less stress than those in the ranks immediately below them.* 这些人经受的压力通常比那些职位刚好低于他们的人要小。 6 **below par** → see **par**

Word Partnership *below* 的常用搭配:

ADV. **directly** below, **far/significantly/substantially/well** below, **just/slightly** below 1
N. below **the belt/waist**, below **the surface** 1
below **ground** 2
below **cost**, below **freezing**, below **the poverty level/line**, below **zero** 4
V. **dip/drop/fall** below 1 4
described below, **listed** below, **see** below 3
ADJ. below **average**, below **normal** 4

below the belt → see **belt**

belt ♦◇◇ /bɛlt/ (**belts, belting, belted**) 1 N-COUNT A **belt** is a strip of leather or cloth that you fasten around your waist. 腰带; 皮带 ❑ *He wore a belt with a large brass buckle.* 他系着一条缀有一颗大铜扣的皮带。 2 → see also **safety belt, seat belt** 3 N-COUNT A **belt** in a machine is a circular strip of rubber that is used to drive moving parts or to move objects along. 输送带 ❑ *The turning disk is connected by a drive belt to an electric motor.* 转盘与电动马达之间由一条输送带连接。 4 → see also **conveyor belt** 5 N-COUNT A **belt** of land or sea is a long, narrow area of it that has some special feature. 狭长地带 ❑ *Miners in Zambia's northern copper belt have gone on strike.* 赞比亚北部铜矿区的矿工们举行了罢工。 6 → see also **commuter belt, green belt** 7 V-T If someone **belts** you, they hit you very hard. If someone **belts** something, they hit it very hard. 狠揍; 猛打 [INFORMAL] ❑ *"Is it right she belted old George in the gut?" she asked.* "她狠揍老乔治的肚子对吗?"她质问道。 ❑ *Torrealba belted the ball into the left-field bleachers.* 托雷尔巴把球猛打到左边的看台上。 ● N-COUNT **Belt** is also a noun. 狠揍; 猛打 ❑ *Father would give you a belt over the head with the scrubbing brush.* 父亲会拿板刷狠狠地敲你的头。 8 V-I If you **belt** somewhere, you move or travel there very fast. 飞奔 [INFORMAL] ❑ *Darren and I belted down the stairs and ran out of the house.* 达伦和我飞奔下楼, 跑出了屋子。 9 PHRASE Something that is **below the belt** is cruel and unfair. 不公正的 ❑ *Do you think it's a bit below the belt what they're doing?* 你认为他们的所作所为有点不太公正吗? 10 PHRASE If you have to **tighten** your **belt**, you have to spend less money and manage without things because you have less money than you used to have. 省吃俭用 ❑ *Clearly, if you are spending more than your income, you'll need to tighten your belt.* 很显然, 如果你现在花钱就入不敷出, 以后就不得不勒紧腰带了。 11 PHRASE If you have something **under** your **belt**, you have already achieved it or done it. 已成囊中之物 ❑ *Clare is now a full-time author with six books, including four novels, under her belt.* 克莱尔现在是个名下有6本书的专职作家, 其中包括4本小说。

▸ **belt out** PHRASAL VERB If you **belt out** a song, you sing or play it very loudly. 大声演唱; 大声演奏 [INFORMAL] ❑ *He belted out Sinatra and Beatles hits.* 他高唱着西纳特拉和甲壳虫乐队的热门歌曲。

belt·way /bɛltweɪ/ (**beltways**) N-COUNT A **beltway** is a road that goes around a city or town, to keep traffic away from the center. 环形公路 [AM]

in BRIT, use **ring road**

❑ *Interstate 295 is a 20-mile beltway that bypasses Jacksonville's busy downtown area.* 295号州际公路是一条20英里长、绕过了杰克逊维尔的繁华市区的环路。

be·mused /bɪmyuzd/ ADJ If you are **bemused**, you are puzzled or confused. 困惑不解的 ❑ *He was rather bemused by children.* 他被孩子们弄糊涂了。

bench /bɛntʃ/ (**benches**) 1 N-COUNT A **bench** is a long seat of wood or metal that two or more people can sit on. 长凳 ❑ *He sat down on a park bench.* 他在一条公园的长凳上坐下来。 2 N-COUNT A **bench** is a long, narrow table in a factory or laboratory. (工厂、实验室的) 工作台 ❑ *...the laboratory bench.* …实验室工作台。 3 N-SING-COLL In a court of law, **the bench** is the judge or magistrates. 法官 ❑ *The chairman of the bench adjourned the case until October 27.* 首席法官将该案延至到10月27日。

Word Link *mark ≈ boundary, sign : benchmark, bookmark, trademark*

▲ **bench·mark** /bɛntʃmɑrk/ (**benchmarks**) also **bench mark** N-COUNT A **benchmark** is something whose quality or quantity is known and which can therefore be used as a standard with which other things can be compared. 衡量基准 ❑ *The truck industry is a benchmark for the economy.* 卡车产业是衡量经济发展的基准。

bend ♦◇◇ /bɛnd/ (**bends, bending, bent**) 1 V-I When you **bend**, you move the top part of your body downward and forward. Plants and trees also **bend**. 弯下 ❑ *I bent over and kissed her cheek.* 我俯身亲吻了她的面颊。 ❑ *She bent and picked up a plastic bucket.* 她弯下身拎起一个塑料桶。 2 V-T When you **bend** your head, you move your head forward and downward. 低下 (头) ❑ *Rick appeared, bending his head a little to clear the top of the door.* 里克出来了, 他稍微低头躲开了门框。 3 V-T/V-I When you **bend** a part of your body such as your arm or leg, or when it **bends**, you change its position so that it is no longer straight. 弯曲 (身体某个部位); 弯曲 ❑ *These cruel devices are designed to stop prisoners from bending their legs.* 这些残酷的刑具是设计来限制犯人弯腿的。 ● **bent** ADJ 弯曲的 ❑ *Keep your knees slightly bent.* 保持两膝微屈。 4 V-T If you **bend** something that is flat or straight, you use force to make it curved or to put an angle in it. 使…弯曲 ❑ *Bend the bar into a horseshoe.* 把钢条弯卷成马蹄形。 ● **bent** ADJ 弯的 ❑ *...a length of bent wire.* …一截弯曲的铁丝。 5 V-T/V-I When a road, beam of light, or other long thin thing **bends**, or when something **bends** it, it changes direction to form a curve or angle. 弯向; 拐弯 ❑ *The road bent slightly to the right.* 公路微微向右弯。 6 N-COUNT A **bend** in a road, pipe, or other long thin object is a curve or angle in it. (道路、管子等的) 弯曲处 ❑ *The crash occurred on a sharp bend.* 碰撞发生在一个急转弯处。 7 V-T If you **bend** rules or laws, you interpret them in a way that allows you to do something they would not normally allow you to do. 篡改; 歪曲 (规则等) ❑ *A minority of officers were prepared to bend the rules.* 少数官员准备篡改规则。 8 N-PLURAL If deep-sea divers suffer from **the bends**, they experience severe pain and difficulty in breathing as a result of coming to the surface of the ocean too quickly. (潜水员浮出水面过急而引起的) 潜涵病; 呼吸减压病 ❑ *New evidence suggests that exercise could protect divers from the bends.* 新证据表明锻炼可以防止潜水员得潜函病。 9 → see also **bent**

Thesaurus *bend* 另参见:

V. arch, bow, hunch, lean; *(ant.)* straighten 1
contort, curl, twist 4
N. angle, curve, deviation, turn 6

Word Partnership *bend* 的常用搭配:

ADV. bend **backward/forward**, bend **down**, bend **over** 1
N. bend **your arms/knees** 3
bend **the rules** 7
PREP. **around the** bend, bend **in a river/road/trail** 6

be·neath ♦◇◇ /bɪniθ/ 1 PREP Something that is **beneath** another thing is under the other thing. 在…之下 ❑ *She could see the muscles of his shoulders beneath his T-shirt.* 她可以看到他T恤衫下的肩部肌肉。 ❑ *Four levels of parking beneath the theater was not enough.* 剧院底下的四层停车库还不够。 ● ADV **Beneath** is also an adverb. 在下方 ❑ *On a shelf beneath he spotted a photo album.* 在下方的书架上他发现了一本相册。 2 PREP If you talk about what is **beneath** the surface of something, you are talking about the aspects of it which are hidden or not obvious. 在 (表面) 之下 ❑ *...emotional strains beneath the surface.* …表面下的情感压力。 ❑ *Somewhere deep beneath the surface lay a caring character.* 在其外表下心灵深处的某个地方保留着一种关爱别人的品格。 3 PREP If you say that someone or something is **beneath** you, you feel that they are not good enough for you or not suitable for you. 不如; 配不上 ❑ *They decided she was marrying beneath her.* 他们认定她嫁的是一个配不上她的人。

ben·efac·tor /bɛnɪfæktər/ (**benefactors**) N-COUNT A **benefactor** is someone who helps a person or organization by giving them money. 捐助人 ❑ *In his old age he became a benefactor of the arts.* 他晚年成了一位艺术赞助人。

ben·efi·cial /bɛnɪfɪʃᵊl/ ADJ Something that is **beneficial** helps people or improves their lives. 有帮助的 ❑ *...vitamins that are beneficial to our health.* …有益我们健康的维生素。

★ **bene·fi·ciary** /bɛnɪfɪʃieri/ (**beneficiaries**) 1 N-COUNT Someone who is a **beneficiary of** something is helped by it. 受益者 ❑ *One of the main beneficiaries of the early election is thought to be the former president.* 前总统被认为是早期选举的主要受益者之一。 2 N-COUNT The **beneficiaries** of a will are legally entitled to receive money or property from someone when that person dies. (遗嘱的) 受益人 ❑ *...one of the beneficiaries of the will made by the late Mr. Steil.* …已故的斯泰尔先生的遗嘱受益人之一。

ben·efit ♦♦◊ /bɛnɪfɪt/ (**benefits, benefiting** or **benefitting, benefited** or **benefitted**) 1 N-VAR The **benefit of** something is the help that you get from it or the advantage that results from it. 益处；成效 ❑ *Each family farms individually and reaps the benefit of its labor.* 每个家庭独立耕作，收获各自的劳动成果。 ❑ *I'm a great believer in the benefits of this form of therapy.* 我对这种疗法的益处深信不疑。 2 N-UNCOUNT If something is **to** your **benefit** or is **of benefit to** you, it helps you or improves your life. 好处 ❑ *This could now work to Albania's benefit.* 这可能现在对阿尔巴尼亚有利。 3 V-T/V-I If you **benefit from** something or if it **benefits** you, it helps you or improves your life. 有益于；得益 ❑ *Both sides have benefited from the talks.* 双方都从会谈中获益。 4 N-UNCOUNT If you have the **benefit of** some information, knowledge, or equipment, you are able to use it so that you can achieve something. 优势 ❑ *Steve didn't have the benefit of a formal college education.* 史蒂夫没有接受过正规大学教育的优势。 5 N-VAR **Benefits** are money or other advantages which come from your job, the government, or an insurance company. 福利 ❑ *McCary will receive about $921,000 in retirement benefits.* 麦克卡里将获得大约九十二万一千美元的退休福利。 ❑ *...the skyrocketing cost of health care and medical benefits.* …一路飚升的健康保健和医疗保险福利金。 6 N-COUNT A **benefit**, or a **benefit** concert or dinner, is an event that is held in order to raise money for a particular charity or person. 义演 [oft N n] ❑ *...a memorial benefit concert for the Bonhoeffer endowment.* …一场纪念邦赫费尔基金的慈善音乐会。 7 → see also **fringe benefit** 8 PHRASE If you give someone **the benefit of the doubt**, you treat them as if they are telling the truth or as if they have behaved properly, even though you are not sure that this is the case. 姑且信其为真 ❑ *At first I gave him the benefit of the doubt.* 起初我姑且信了他。 9 PHRASE If you say that someone is doing something **for the benefit of** a particular person, you mean that they are doing it for that person. 为了某人的利益 ❑ *You need people working for the benefit of the community.* 你需要一些为公众利益服务的人。

Word Partnership *benefit* 的常用搭配：

PREP.	benefit **from** *something* 1 3
	benefit **of** *something* 1 4
	for *someone's* benefit 1 9
	to *someone's* benefit 2
N.	benefit **programs** 5
	benefit **concert/performance** 6

Word Link *vol ≈ will : benevolent, involuntary, volunteer*

▲ **be·nevo·lent** /bɪnɛvələnt/ ADJ If you describe a person in authority as **benevolent**, you mean that they are kind and fair. 仁慈的 ❑ *The company has proved to be a most benevolent employer.* 结果证明该公司是一个非常仁慈的雇主。 ● **be·nevo·lence** ▲ N-UNCOUNT 仁慈 ❑ *A bit of benevolence from people in power is not what we need.* 来自当权者的一点点仁慈不是我们所需要的。

▲ **be·nign** /bɪnaɪn/ 1 ADJ You use **benign** to describe someone who is kind, gentle, and harmless. 和善的 ❑ *They are normally a more benign audience.* 他们通常是更为和善的观众。 ● **be·nign·ly** ADV 和善地 ❑ *I just smiled benignly and stood back.* 我只是和善地笑了笑，就退到了后边。 2 ADJ A **benign** substance or process does not have any harmful effects. 无害的 ❑ *We're taking relatively benign medicines and we're turning them into poisons.* 我们拿相对无害的药品，把它们转化成毒药。 3 ADJ A **benign** tumor will not cause death or serious harm. 良性的 [MEDICAL] ❑ *It wasn't cancer, only a benign tumor.* 这不是癌，只是良性肿瘤。 4 ADJ **Benign** conditions are pleasant or make it easy for something to happen. 宜人的 ❑ *They enjoyed an especially benign climate.* 他们那里的气候十分宜人。

bent /bɛnt/ 1 **Bent** is the past tense and past participle of **bend**. **bend**的过去式和过去分词 2 ADJ If an object is **bent**, it is damaged and no longer has its correct shape. 弄弯的 ❑ *The trees were all bent and twisted from the wind.* 那些树全都被风吹得东倒西歪的。 3 ADJ If a person is **bent**, their body has become curved because of old age or disease. 驼背的 [WRITTEN] ❑ *...a bent, frail, old man.* …一个驼背、体弱的老人。 4 ADJ If someone is **bent on** doing something, especially something harmful, they are determined to do it. 执意的 [v-link ADJ "on/upon" n/-ing] [DISAPPROVAL] ❑ *He's bent on suicide.* 他一心想自杀。 5 N-SING If you have a **bent for** something, you have a natural ability to do it or a natural interest in it. 天生的本领；天生的喜好 ❑ *His bent for natural history directed him towards his first job.* 他对自然历史天生的爱好指引他找到了他的第一份工作。 6 N-SING If someone is **of** a particular **bent**, they hold a particular set of beliefs. 有…思想倾向 ❑ *...economists of a socialist bent.* …有社会主义思想倾向的经济学家。

be·queath /bɪkwið/ (**bequeaths, bequeathing, bequeathed**) V-T If you **bequeath** your money or property **to** someone, you legally state that they should have it when you die. 遗赠 [FORMAL] ❑ *He bequeathed all his silver to his children.* 他把所有的银币都留给了他的孩子们。

be·reaved /bɪrivd/ ADJ A **bereaved** person is one who has a relative or close friend who has recently died. 新近丧失亲人的 ❑ *Mr. Dinkins visited the bereaved family to offer comfort.* 丁金斯先生拜访了丧失亲人的家庭，给予安慰。

be·reave·ment /bɪrivmənt/ (**bereavements**) N-VAR **Bereavement** is the sorrow you feel or the state you are in when a relative or close friend dies. 丧亲；丧亲之痛 ❑ *When Mary died Anne did not share her brother's sense of bereavement.* 玛丽死后，安妮并没有同她哥哥一样的丧亲之痛。

be·reft /bɪrɛft/ ADJ If a person or thing is **bereft of** something, they no longer have it. 失去…的 [FORMAL] ❑ *The place seemed to be utterly bereft of human life.* 看起来，这地方人迹罕至。

ber·ry /bɛri/ (**berries**) N-COUNT **Berries** are small, round fruit that grow on a bush or a tree. Some berries are edible, for example, blackberries and raspberries. 莓

berth /bɜrθ/ (**berths, berthing, berthed**) 1 PHRASE If you **give** someone or something **a wide berth**, you avoid them because you think they are unpleasant or dangerous, or simply because you do not like them. 躲避 ❑ *She gives showbiz parties a wide berth.* 她对娱乐聚会敬而远之。 2 N-COUNT A **berth** is a bed on a ship or train. (轮船、火车的) 卧铺 ❑ *Goldring booked a berth on the first boat he could.* 戈德林在第一艘他能订到卧铺的船上订了个位子。 3 N-COUNT A **berth** is a space in a harbor where a ship stays for a period of time. 泊位 ❑ *...the slow passage through the docks to the ship's berth.* …缓缓通过码头到达轮船停泊处。 4 V-I When a ship **berths**, it sails into harbor and stops at the quay. 停泊 ❑ *As the ship berthed in New York, McClintock was with the first immigration officers aboard.* 当那艘轮船停泊在纽约时，麦克林托克正和第一批上船的移民官员们在船上。

▲ **be·set** /bɪsɛt/ (**besets, besetting**)

> The form **beset** is used in the present tense and is the past tense and past participle.

V-T If someone or something **is beset by** problems or fears, they have many problems or fears which affect them severely. 困扰 ❑ *The country is beset by severe economic problems.* 该国为严重的经济问题所困。 ❑ *The discussions were beset with difficulties.* 会谈困难重重。

be·side ♦◊◊ /bɪsaɪd/ 1 PREP Something that is **beside** something else is at the side of it or next to it. 在…旁边 ❑ *On the table beside an empty plate was a pile of books.* 桌上的空碟子旁摆着一摞书。 2 → see also **besides** 3 PHRASE If you are **beside yourself with** anger or excitement, you are extremely angry or excited. 发狂 ❑ *He had shouted down the phone at her, beside himself with anxiety.* 他在电话里冲她大吼大叫，急得要发狂了。 4 **beside the point** → see **point**

be·sides ♦◊◊ /bɪsaɪdz/ 1 PREP **Besides** something or **beside** something means in addition to it. 除了 ❑ *I think she has many good qualities besides being very beautiful.* 我觉得她除了非常漂亮之外，还有许多好的品质。 ● ADV **Besides** is also an adverb. 此外 [cl ADV] ❑ *You get to sample lots of baked things and take home masses of cookies besides.*

B

你可以品尝许多烘烤食品，此外还能带许多饼干回家。 **2** ADV **Besides** is used to emphasize an additional point that you are making, especially one that you consider to be important. 而且 ❑ *The house was out of our price range and too big anyway. Besides, I'd grown fond of our little rented house.* 反正这个房子超出了我们的预算范围，而且也太大了。再说，我已经渐渐喜欢上我们租的小房子了。

Do not confuse **besides**, **except**, **except for**, and **unless**. You use **besides** to introduce extra things in addition to the ones you are mentioning already. ❑ *Fruit will give you, besides enjoyment, a source of vitamins.* However, note that if you talk about "the only thing" or "the only person" **besides** a particular person or thing, **besides** means the same as "apart from." ❑ *He was the only person besides Gertrude who talked to Guy.* You use **except** to introduce the only things, situations, people, or ideas that a statement does not apply to. ❑ *All of his body relaxed except his right hand... Travelling was impossible, except in the cool of the morning.* You use **except for** before something that prevents a statement from being completely true. ❑ *The classrooms were silent, except for the scratching of pens on paper... I had absolutely no friends except for Tom.* **Unless** is used to introduce the only situation in which something will take place or be true. ❑ *In the 1940s, unless she wore gloves a woman was not properly dressed... You must not give compliments unless you mean them.*

▲ **be·siege** /bɪsi͟dʒ/ (**besieges, besieging, besieged**) **1** V-T If you **are besieged by** people, many people want something from you and continually bother you. 不断打扰 [usu passive] ❑ *She was besieged by the press and the public.* 她不断被媒体和公众打扰。 **2** V-T If soldiers **besiege** a place, they surround it and wait for the people in it to stop fighting or resisting. 围攻 ❑ *The main part of the army moved to Sevastopol to besiege the town.* 这支部队的主力前往塞瓦斯托波尔去围攻那个小镇。

best ♦♦♦ /bɛ̱st/ **1** **Best** is the superlative of **good**. 最好的 (**good** 的最高级形式) ❑ *If you want further information the best thing to do is have a word with the driver as you get on the bus.* 如果你想了解得更清楚，最好的办法就是上公共汽车后向司机询问。 **2** **Best** is the superlative of **well**. 最好地 (**well**的最高级形式) ❑ *James Fox is best known as the author of "White Mischief," and he is currently working on a new book.* 詹姆斯·福克斯以其作品《欲望城》最为知名，目前他正在写一本新书。 **3** N-SING **The best** is used to refer to things of the highest quality or standard. 最好的东西 ❑ *We offer only the best to our clients.* 我们只提供最好的东西给顾客。 **4** N-SING Someone's **best** is the greatest effort or highest achievement or standard that they are capable of. 最佳状态; 最大努力 ❑ *Miss Blockey was at her best when she played the piano.* 布洛基小姐弹钢琴那会儿正处于最佳状态。 **5** N-SING If you say that something is **the best** that can be done or hoped for, you think it is the most pleasant, successful, or useful thing that can be done or hoped for. 最好的事物 ❑ *A draw seems the best they can hope for.* 看来平局已经是他们所能期盼的最好结局了。 **6** ADV If you like something **best** or like it **the best**, you prefer it. 最大程度地 ❑ *The thing I liked best about the show was the music.* 这场演出中我最喜欢的是音乐。 ❑ *Mother liked it best when Daniel got money.* 丹尼尔挣到钱是母亲最喜欢的事。 **7** **Best** is used to form the superlative of compound adjectives beginning with "good" and "well." For example, the superlative of "well-known" is "best-known." 用于构成由**good**或**well**开头的复合词的最高级形式 **8** → see also **second best** **9** PHRASE You use **best of all** to indicate that what you are about to mention is the thing that you prefer or that has most advantages out of all the things you have mentioned. 最好的是 ❑ *It was comfortable and cheap: best of all, most of the rent was being paid by two American friends.* 这里又舒适又便宜，最好的是，大部分租金由两个美国朋友付了。 **10** PHRASE If someone does something **as best** they **can**, they do it as well as they can, although it is very difficult. 尽最大努力 ❑ *Let's leave people to get on with their jobs and do them as best they can.* 放手让人们去开展工作并尽最大努力做好。 **11** PHRASE You use **at best** to indicate that even if you describe something as favorably as possible or if it performs as well as it possibly can, it is still not very good. 充其量 ❑ *This policy, they say, is at best confused and at worst non-existent.* 他们说这项政策说好听点是混乱不清，说不好听点就是根本不存在。 **12** PHRASE If you **do** your **best** or **try** your **best to do** something, you try as hard as you can to do it, or do it as well as you can. 尽自己最大努力 ❑ *I'll do my best to find out.* 我将尽最大努力查清楚。 **13** PHRASE If you say that something is **for the best**, you mean it is the most desirable or helpful thing that could have happened or could be done, considering all the circumstances. (所有因素考虑在内) 能产生的最好结果 ❑ *Whatever the circumstances, parents are supposed to know what to do for the best.* 不论情况如何，父母应该知道做什么才能达到最佳效果。 **14** PHRASE If you say that a particular person **knows best**, you mean that they have a lot of experience and should therefore be trusted to make decisions for other people. 最具权威性 ❑ *He was convinced that doctors and dentists knew best.* 他对医生的权威性深信不疑。 **15** **to the best of your ability** → see **ability** **16** **to hope for the best** → see **hope** **17** **to the best of your knowledge** → see **knowledge** **18** **best of luck** → see **luck** **19** **the best of both worlds** → see **world**

▲ **be·stow** /bɪsto͟ʊ/ (**bestows, bestowing, bestowed**) V-T To **bestow** something **on** someone means to give or present it to them. 授予 [FORMAL] ❑ *The United States bestowed honorary citizenship upon England's World War II prime minister, Sir Winston Churchill.* 美国授予了二战期间的英国首相温斯顿·丘吉尔爵士荣誉公民的称号。

best·sell·er /bɛ̱stsɛ̱lər/ (**bestsellers**) N-COUNT A **bestseller** is a book of which a great number of copies has been sold. 畅销书 ❑ *By mid-August the book was a bestseller.* 到8月中旬，这本书已经是畅销书了。

best-selling also **bestselling** **1** ADJ A **best-selling** product such as a book is very popular and a large quantity of it has been sold. 畅销的 [ADJ n] **2** ADJ A **best-selling** author is an author who has sold a very large number of copies of his or her book. 有畅销作品的 (作者) [ADJ n]

bet ♦◇◇ /bɛ̱t/ (**bets, betting**)

The form **bet** is used in the present tense and is the past tense and past participle.

1 V-T/V-I If you **bet on** the result of a horse race, football game, or other event, you give someone a sum of money which they give you back with extra money if the result is what you predicted, or which they keep if it is not. 对…下注; 下赌注 ❑ *Jockeys are forbidden to bet on the outcome of races.* 职业赛马骑师们被禁止对比赛结果下注。 ❑ *I bet $20 on a horse called Premonition.* 我在那匹名叫"预言"的赛马身上下了$20的赌注。 ● N-COUNT **Bet** is also a noun. 下注 ❑ *Do you always have a bet on the Kentucky Derby?* 你总是在肯塔基赛马大会上赌马吗? ● **bet·ting** N-UNCOUNT 赌注 ❑ *...his thousand-dollar fine for illegal betting.* …他因非法赌博而受的千元罚款。 **2** N-COUNT A **bet** is a sum of money which you give to someone when you bet. 赌金 ❑ *You can put a bet on almost anything these days.* 如今，你几乎可以就任何事下赌注。 **3** V-T/V-I If someone **is betting** that something will happen, they are hoping or expecting that it will happen. 希望; 期待 [only cont] [JOURNALISM] ❑ *The party is betting that the presidential race will turn into a battle for younger voters.* 该党希望这场总统竞选会演变成对年轻选民的争夺。 ❑ *People were betting on a further easing of credit conditions.* 人们期待信贷条件的进一步放宽。 **4** PHRASE You use expressions such as "**I bet**," "**I'll bet**," and "**you can bet**" to indicate that you are sure something is true. 我确信; 我敢说 [INFORMAL] ❑ *I bet you were good at games when you were at school.* 我敢说你上学时很擅长比赛。 ❑ *I'll bet they'll taste out of this world.* 我相信它们的味道一定鲜美极了。 **5** PHRASE If you tell someone that something is a **good bet**, you are suggesting that it is the thing or course of action that they should choose. 好的做法; 好的选择 [INFORMAL] ❑ *Your best bet is to choose a guest house.* 你最好的选择就是找一家宾馆。 **6** PHRASE If you say that it is **a good bet** or **a safe bet** that something is true or will happen, you are saying that it is extremely likely to be true or to happen. 极有可能 [INFORMAL] ❑ *It is a safe bet that the current owners will not sell.* 现在的主人极有可能不卖了。 **7** PHRASE You use **I bet** or **I'll bet** in reply to a statement to show that you agree with it or that you expected it to be true, usually when you are annoyed or amused by it. 说的是 [INFORMAL, SPOKEN, FEELINGS] ❑ *"I'd like to ask you something," I said. "I bet you would," she grinned.* "我想问你一件事，"我说道。"我猜你就会问的，"她笑道。 **8** PHRASE You say **I bet** or **I'll bet** in reply to a statement to show that you do not believe it or you doubt that it is true. 谁信啊 ❑ *"I only kiss girls," said John. Then he blushed. "I'll bet," said Lisa.* "我只吻女孩们，"约翰说着，脸就红了。"谁信啊，"莉萨说。 **9** PHRASE You can use **my bet is** or **it's my bet** to give your personal opinion about something, when you are fairly sure that you are right. 我认定 [INFORMAL] ❑ *My bet is that next year will be different.* 我确信明年将有所不同。
→ see **lottery**

Word Partnership *bet* 的常用搭配：

N.	bet **money** 1
PREP.	bet **against** ***someone/something***, bet **on** ***something*** 1 2
V.	**lose/win a** bet, **make a** bet, **place a** bet 1 2
ADJ.	**willing to** bet 4
	best bet, **good** bet, **safe** bet 5 6

be·tray /bɪtreɪ/ (**betrays, betraying, betrayed**) 1 V-T If you **betray** someone who loves or trusts you, your actions hurt and disappoint them. 辜负 ❑ *When I tell someone I will not betray his confidence I keep my word.* 当我对人说我不会辜负他的信任时，我会说到做到。 2 V-T If someone **betrays** their country or their friends, they give information to an enemy, putting their country's security or their friends' safety at risk. 出卖；背叛 ❑ *They offered me money if I would betray my associates.* 如果我出卖自己的同伴，他们就会给我钱。 3 V-T If you **betray** an ideal or your principles, you say or do something which goes against those beliefs. 违背 ❑ *We betray the ideals of our country when we support capital punishment.* 我们赞同死刑就会违背我们国家的理想。 4 V-T If you **betray** a feeling or quality, you show it without intending to. (无意中) 流露 ❑ *She studied his face, but it betrayed nothing.* 她审视着他的脸，但他却丝毫不露声色。

be·tray·al /bɪtreɪəl/ (**betrayals**) N-VAR A **betrayal** is an action which betrays someone or something, or the fact of being betrayed. 背叛行为 ❑ *She felt that what she had done was a betrayal of Patrick.* 她觉得自己的所作所为是对帕特里克的背叛。

better

❶ COMPARING STATES AND QUALITIES
❷ GIVING ADVICE
❸ VERB USES

❶ **bet·ter** ♦♦♦ /bɛtər/
➪ **Please look at meaning 15 to see if the expression you are looking for is shown under another headword.** 1 **Better** is the comparative of **good**. 更好的 (**good**的比较级形式) 2 **Better** is the comparative of **well**. 更好地 (**well**的比较级形式) 3 ADV If you like one thing **better than** another, you like it more. 更大程度地 [ADV after v] ❑ *I like your interpretation better than the one I was taught.* 与我所学的相比，我更喜欢你这种解释。 ❑ *They liked it better when it rained.* 他们更喜欢下雨天。 4 ADJ If you are **better** after an illness or injury, you have recovered from it. If you feel **better**, you no longer feel so ill. 痊愈的 [v-link ADJ] ❑ *He is much better now, he's fine.* 他现在病好多了，他没什么事了。 5 PRON If you say that you expect or deserve **better**, you mean that you expect or deserve a higher standard of achievement, behavior, or treatment from people than they have shown you. 更高标准 (的成就、表现、待遇等) ❑ *We expect better of you in the future.* 我们期待你将来有更好的表现。 6 **Better** is used to form the comparative of compound adjectives beginning with "good" and "well." For example, the comparative of "well-off" is "better-off." 用于构成由**good**或**well**开头的复合词的比较级形式 7 PHRASE If something changes **for the better**, it improves. 变好 ❑ *He dreams of changing the world for the better.* 他梦想将世界变得更美好。 8 PHRASE If a feeling such as jealousy, curiosity, or anger **gets the better of** you, it becomes too strong for you to hide or control. 某人让 (妒忌、好奇心、愤怒等情绪) 打败 ❑ *She didn't allow her emotions to get the better of her.* 她没有让情绪打败自己。 9 PHRASE If you **get the better of** someone, you defeat them in a contest, fight, or argument. 击败 ❑ *He is used to tough defenders, and he usually gets the better of them.* 他习惯了强悍的防守队员，而且通常都能击败他们。 10 PHRASE If someone **knows better than to** do something, they are old enough or experienced enough to know it is the wrong thing to do. 明事理而不至于 ❑ *She knew better than to argue with Adeline.* 她不会糊涂到和阿德琳争论。 11 PHRASE If you **know better than** someone, you have more information, knowledge, or experience than them. 懂得更多；更有头脑 ❑ *He thought he knew better than I did, though he was much less experienced.* 他认为他比我懂得更多，虽然他经验远不如我。 12 CONVENTION You say **"That's better"** in order to express your approval of what someone has said or done, or to praise or encourage them. 这样好多了 ❑ *"I came to ask your advice – no, to ask for your help."—"That's better. And how can I help you?"* "我来向你请教——不，请你帮个忙。"——"这就对了，我能为你做什么？" 13 PHRASE You can say **"so much the better"** or **"all the better"** to indicate that it is desirable that a particular thing is used, done, or available. 要是…就好了 ❑ *The fog had come in; so much the better when it came to sneaking away.* 起雾了；如果雾慢慢散去就好了。 14 PHRASE If you intend to do something and then **think better of it**, you decide not to do it because you realize it would not be sensible. 重新考虑后决定不做 ❑ *Alberg opened his mouth, as if to protest. But he thought better of it.* 阿尔伯格张口像是要抗议，但转念一想就放弃了。 15 to **be better than nothing** → see **nothing**

Word Partnership *better* 的常用搭配：

N.	better **idea**, **nothing** better ❶ 1
V.	**make** ***something*** better ❶ 1
	look better ❶ 1 4
	feel better, **get** better ❶ 2 4
	deserve better ❶ 5
ADV.	**any** better, **even** better, better **than** ❶ 1 2
	much better ❶ 1 3 4

❷ **bet·ter** ♦♦♦ /bɛtər/ 1 PHRASE You use **had better** or **'d better** when you are advising, warning, or threatening someone, or expressing an opinion about what should happen. 最好 ❑ *It's half past two. I think we had better go home.* 现在两点半了，我想我们该回家了。 ❑ *You'd better run if you're going to get your ticket.* 如果你要去拿你的票，最好抓紧。 ● ADV In spoken English, people sometimes use **better** without 'had' or 'be' before it. It has the same meaning. 口语中，**had**或**be**经常省略，意思不变 ❑ *Better not say too much aloud.* 说话声最好不要太大。 2 PHRASE You can say that someone **is better** doing one thing than another, or **it is better** doing one thing than another, to advise someone about what they should do. (做某事) 更好 ❑ *Wouldn't it be better putting a time-limit on the task?* 给任务定个截止期限不是更好吗？ 3 PHRASE If you say that someone would **be better off** doing something, you are advising them to do it or expressing the opinion that it would benefit them to do it. 最好是 ❑ *If you've got bags you're better off taking a taxi.* 如果你有行李，最好是坐出租车。

❸ **bet·ter** ♦♦♦ /bɛtər/ (**betters, bettering, bettered**) 1 V-T If someone **betters** a high achievement or standard, they achieve something higher. 超过 ❑ *His throw bettered the American junior record set in 2003.* 他的这一投超越了2003年美国少年组的记录。 2 V-T If you **better** your situation, you improve your social status or the quality of your life. If you **better yourself**, you improve your social status. 改善 ❑ *He had dedicated his life to bettering the lot of the oppressed people of South Africa.* 他一生致力于改善南非被压迫人民的命运。

be·tween ♦♦♦ /bɪtwin/

In addition to the uses shown below, **between** is used in a few phrasal verbs, such as "come between."

1 PREP If something is **between** two things or is **in between** them, it has one of the things on one side of it and the other thing on the other side. 在…中间 ❑ *She left the table to stand between the two men.* 她离开桌子，站在两个男人中间。 2 PREP If people or things travel **between** two places, they travel regularly from one place to the other and back again. (往返) 于…之间 [PREP pl-n] ❑ *I spent a lot of time in the early Eighties traveling between Waco and El Paso.* 在八十年代早期，我花了很多时间往返于韦科和埃尔帕索之间。 3 PREP A relationship, discussion, or difference **between** two people, groups, or things is one that involves them both or relates to them both. (表示相互关系) 在…之间 [PREP pl-n] ❑ *I think the relationship between patients and doctors has got a lot less personal.* 我认为医生和患者之间的关系已经少了许多人情味。 ❑ *There have been intensive discussions between the two governments in recent days.* 最近两国政府之间进行了集中的会谈。 4 PREP If something stands **between** you and what you want, it prevents you from having it. 在…之间 (阻碍) [PREP n "and" n] ❑ *His sense of duty often stood between him and the enjoyment of life.* 他的责任感常使他不能安心地享受生活。 5 PREP If something is **between** two amounts or ages, it is greater or older than the first one and smaller or younger than the second one. (数量、年龄) 介乎…之间 [PREP num "and" num] ❑ *Increase the amount of time you spend exercising by walking between 15 and 20 minutes.* 步行15到20分钟来增加你用于运动的时间。 6 PREP If something happens **between** or **in between** two times or events, it happens after the first time or event and before the second one. (指时间) 在…之间 ❑ *The canal was built between 1793 and 1797.* 该运河建于1793至1797年之间。 ● ADV **Between** or **in between** is also an adverb. (指时间)

B

在…之间 [ADV with cl/group] ❑ *My life had been a journey from crisis to crisis with only a brief time in between.* 我的生活总是从一个危机到另一个危机，其间间隔的时间都很短。 7 PREP If you must choose **between** two or more things, you must choose just one of them. 在…之中（选择一个）[PREP pl-n] ❑ *Students will be able to choose between English, French and Russian as their first foreign language.* 学生们将可以在英语、法语和俄语中任选一门作为他们的第一外语。 8 PREP If people or places have a particular amount of something **between** them, this is the total amount that they have. 共有 [PREP pron] ❑ *The three sites employ 12,500 people between them.* 3个工地共雇佣12500个人。 9 PREP When something is divided or shared **between** people, they each have a share of it. 共同享有 [PREP pl-n] ❑ *There is only one bathroom shared between eight bedrooms.* 只有一个供8个卧室共同使用的卫生间。

If there are only two people or things you should use **between**. If there are more than two people or things, you should use **among**. You can also talk about relationships **between** or **among** people or things, and discussions **between** or **among** people. ❑ *...an argument between his mother and another woman. ...an opportunity to discuss these issues among themselves.* Note that if you are **between** things or people, the things or people are on either side of you. If you are **among** things or people, they are all around you. ❑ *...the bag standing on the floor between us. ...the sound of a pigeon among the trees.*

Word Partnership *between* 的常用搭配：

N. **line** between, **link** between 1
between **countries/nations**, **difference** between, **relationship** between 3
choice between 7
V. **caught** between 1
choose/decide/distinguish between 7
ADV. ***somewhere*** **in** between 1 6

▲ **bev·er·age** /bɛvərɪdʒ/ (**beverages**) N-COUNT **Beverages** are drinks. 饮料 [WRITTEN] ❑ *Alcoholic beverages are served in the hotel lounge.* 宾馆的休息室供应酒类饮料。 ❑ *...artificially sweetened beverages.* …人工甜味饮料。
→ see **sugar**

Word Link *war ≈ watchful : aware, beware, wary*

▲ **be·ware** /bɪwɛər/ V-I If you tell someone to **beware of** a person or thing, you are warning them that the person or thing may harm them or be dangerous. 当心；提防 [only imper and inf] ❑ *Beware of being too impatient with others.* 谨防对别人过于急噪。 ❑ *Motorists were warned to beware of slippery conditions.* 汽车驾驶者被提醒小心路滑。

★ **be·wil·der** /bɪwɪldər/ (**bewilders, bewildering, bewildered**) V-T If something **bewilders** you, it is so confusing or difficult that you cannot understand it. 使迷惑 ❑ *The silence from Alex had hurt and bewildered her.* 亚历克斯的沉默令她伤心和迷惑不解。

be·wil·dered /bɪwɪldərd/ ADJ If you are **bewildered**, you are very confused and cannot understand something or decide what you should do. 不知所措的 ❑ *Some shoppers looked bewildered by the sheer variety of goods for sale.* 一些顾客看上去对种类十分繁多的销售货品感到不知所措了。

be·wil·der·ing /bɪwɪldərɪŋ/ ADJ A **bewildering** thing or situation is very confusing and difficult to understand or to make a decision about. 令人迷惑的 ❑ *A glance along his bookshelves reveals a bewildering array of interests.* 扫一眼他的书架就可以看出他杂七杂八的兴趣爱好。

be·wil·der·ment /bɪwɪldərmənt/ N-UNCOUNT **Bewilderment** is the feeling of being bewildered. 迷惑 ❑ *He shook his head in bewilderment.* 他不解地摇了摇头。

be·witch /bɪwɪtʃ/ (**bewitches, bewitching, bewitched**) V-T If someone or something **bewitches** you, you are so attracted to them that you cannot think about anything else. 使着魔 ❑ *She was not moving, as if someone had bewitched her.* 她一动也不动，好像有人让她着了魔。 ● **be·witch·ing** ADJ 令人着魔的 ❑ *Frank was a quiet young man with bewitching brown eyes.* 弗兰克是一个文静的年轻人，长着一双令人着魔的褐色眼睛。

be·yond ◆◆◇ /bɪyɒnd/ 1 PREP If something is **beyond** a place or barrier, it is on the other side of it. 在…的另一边 ❑ *On his right was a thriving vegetable garden and beyond it a small orchard of apple trees.* 在他的右边是一片长势旺盛的菜园，另一头是一小片苹果树林。 ● ADV **Beyond** is also an adverb. 在…的另一边 ❑ *The house had a fabulous view out to the Strait of Georgia and the Rockies beyond.* 这座房子有很棒的景观，可以看到乔治亚海峡以及另一头的落基山脉。 2 PREP If something happens **beyond** a particular time or date, it continues after that time or date has passed. (时间) 在…之后 ❑ *Few jockeys continue race-riding beyond the age of 40.* 很少有骑师在40岁以后还继续赛马。 ● ADV **Beyond** is also an adverb. (时间) 在…之后 [cl "and" ADV] ❑ *The financing of home ownership will continue through the 1990s and beyond.* 房屋产权的融资将持续到20世纪90年代及以后。 3 PREP If something extends **beyond** a particular thing, it affects or includes other things. 超出 ❑ *His interests extended beyond the fine arts to international politics and philosophy.* 他的兴趣不仅限于美术，还包括国际政治和哲学。 4 PREP You use **beyond** to introduce an exception to what you are saying. 除了 ❑ *He appears to have almost no personal staff, beyond a secretary who can't make coffee.* 他看来似乎没有任何雇员，除了一个连咖啡都不会煮的秘书。 5 PREP If something goes **beyond** a particular point or stage, it progresses or increases so that it passes that point or stage. 超过 ❑ *Their five-year relationship was strained beyond breaking point.* 他们长达5年的关系紧张得超过了极限。 6 PREP If something is, for example, **beyond** understanding or **beyond** belief, it is so extreme in some way that it cannot be understood or believed. 超出（理解或信任的范围）❑ *What Jock had done was beyond my comprehension.* 乔克的所作所为让我摸不着头脑。 7 PREP If you say that something is **beyond** someone, or **beyond** their control, you mean that they cannot deal with it. 超出（能力所及）❑ *The situation was beyond her control.* 局势非她所能控制。 8 **beyond** your **wildest dreams** → see **dream**

Word Link *bi ≈ two : biannual, bicycle, bilingual*

bi·an·nual /baɪænyuəl/ ADJ A **biannual** event happens twice a year. 每年两次的 ❑ *You will need to have a routine biannual examination.* 你需要做一年两次的常规检查。 ● **bi·an·nu·al·ly** ADV 每年两次地 [ADV after v] ❑ *Only since 1962 has the show been held biannually.* 从1962以后，这个节目才开始每年举行两次。

★ **bias** /baɪəs/ (**biases, biasing, biased**) 1 N-VAR **Bias** is a tendency to prefer one person or thing to another, and to favor that person or thing. 偏见 ❑ *...his desire to avoid the appearance of bias in favor of one candidate or another.* …他想避免表现出对这个或那个候选人有偏好。 2 V-T To **bias** someone means to influence them in favor of a particular choice. (影响某人) 使偏心；使产生偏见 ❑ *We mustn't allow it to bias our teaching.* 我们不允许它使我们的教学产生偏见。

bi·ased /baɪəst/ 1 ADJ If someone is **biased**, they prefer one group of people to another, and behave unfairly as a result. You can also say that a process or system is **biased**. 有偏见的 ❑ *He seemed a bit biased against women in my opinion.* 我认为他好像对妇女有点偏见。 2 ADJ If something is **biased toward** one thing, it is more concerned with it than with other things. 偏重于…的 [v-link ADJ "toward" n] ❑ *University funding was tremendously biased toward scientists.* 大学资助金是极度偏重于科学家的。

Bi·ble /baɪbəl/ (**Bibles**) 1 N-PROPER **The Bible** is the holy book on which the Jewish and Christian religions are based. 《圣经》 2 N-COUNT A **bible** is a copy of the Bible. (一本)《圣经》 ❑ *...a publisher of bibles and hymn books.* …一家《圣经》册本和圣歌集出版商。
→ see **religion**

bib·li·cal /bɪblɪkəl/ ADJ **Biblical** means contained in or relating to the Bible. 《圣经》中的；与《圣经》有关的 ❑ *The community, whose links with Syria date back to biblical times, is mainly elderly.* 这个村落与叙利亚的关联可以追溯到圣经时代，其中大部分是上了年纪的人。

★ **bib·li·og·ra·phy** /bɪbliɒgrəfi/ (**bibliographies**) 1 N-COUNT A **bibliography** is a list of books on a particular subject. 书目 ❑ *At the end of this chapter there is a select bibliography of useful books.* 本章末尾附着有用书籍的精选书目。 2 N-COUNT A **bibliography** is a list of the books and articles that are referred to in a particular book. 参考书目 ❑ *...the full bibliography printed at the end of the second volume.* …印在第二卷最后的完整参考书目。

bick·er /bɪkər/ (**bickers, bickering, bickered**) V-RECIP When people **bicker**, they argue or quarrel about unimportant things. (为琐事的) 吵嘴 ❑ *I went into medicine to care for patients, not to waste time bickering over budgets.* 我从医是为了治病救人，不是为了预算争吵而浪费时间。 ❑ *...as states bicker over territory.* …当国与国之间为领土而争执不断时。 ● **bick·er·ing** N-UNCOUNT (为琐事) 吵嘴 ❑ *The election will end months of political bickering.* 这场选举将结束几个月以来的政治争论。

b

Word Web bicycle

A Scotsman named Kirkpatrick MacMillan invented the first **bicycle** with **pedals** around 1840. Early bicycles had wooden or metal **wheels**. However, by the mid-1800s **tires** with tubes appeared. Modern **racing bikes** are very lightweight and aerodynamic. The wheels have fewer **spokes** and the tires are very thin and smooth. **Mountain bikes** allow riders to ride up and down steep hills on dirt trails. These bikes have fat, knobby tires for extra traction. The **tandem** is a bicycle for two people. It has about the same **wind resistance** as a one-person bike. But with twice the power, it goes faster.

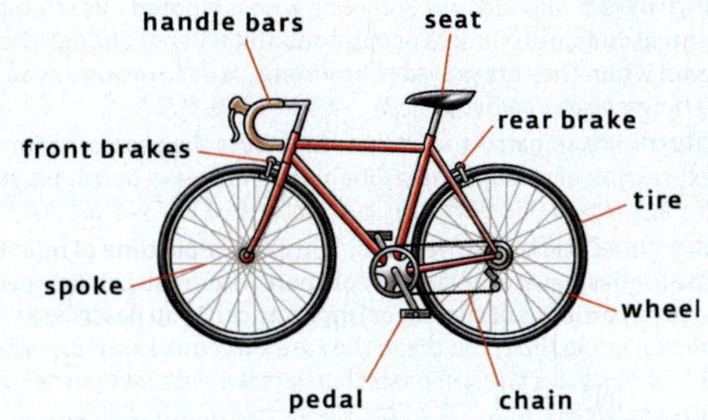

Word Link *cycl ≈ circle : bicycle, cycle, cyclical*

bi·cy·cle /baɪsɪkəl/ (**bicycles**) N-COUNT A **bicycle** is a vehicle with two wheels which you ride by sitting on it and pushing two pedals with your feet. You steer it by turning a bar that is connected to the front wheel. 自行车
→ see Word Web: **bicycle**

bid ◆◆◇ /bɪd/ (**bids, bidding**)

> The form **bid** is used in the present tense and is the past tense and past participle.

1 N-COUNT A **bid for** something or a **bid to** do something is an attempt to obtain it or do it. 努力尝试 [JOURNALISM] ❑ *...Sydney's successful bid for the 2000 Olympic Games.* …悉尼对2000年奥林匹克运动会成功的申办。 **2** N-COUNT A **bid** is an offer to pay a particular amount of money for something that is being sold. 出价 ❑ *Hanson made an agreed takeover bid of $351 million.* 汉森按约定出价3.51亿美元进行收购。 **3** V-T/V-I If you **bid for** something or **bid to** do something, you try to obtain it or do it. 力求获得; 努力争取 ❑ *Singapore Airlines is rumored to be bidding for a management contract to run both airports.* 据传，新加坡航空公司正在努力争取这两个机场的管理合约。 **4** V-I If you **bid for** something that is being sold, you offer to pay a particular amount of money for it. 出价 ❑ *She wanted to bid for it.* 她想出价买下它。 ❑ *The bank announced its intention to bid.* 银行宣布了其投标意向。

bid·der /bɪdər/ (**bidders**) **1** N-COUNT A **bidder** is someone who offers to pay a certain amount of money for something that is being sold. If you sell something to the highest **bidder**, you sell it to the person who offers the most money for it. 出价者 ❑ *The sale will be made to the highest bidder subject to a reserve price being attained.* 在保证底价的条件下，出售给出价最高者。 **2** N-COUNT A **bidder for** something is someone who is trying to obtain it or do it. 努力争取的人 ❑ *Vodafone is among successful bidders for two licenses to develop cellphone systems in Greece.* 沃达丰是成功获得了两个经营许可证来在希腊发展手机系统的的公司之一。

bid price (**bid prices**) N-COUNT The **bid price** of a particular stock or share is the price that investors are willing to pay for it. 买价 [BUSINESS] ❑ *Investors feel that the bid price undervalues the company.* 投资者们觉得这个买价对公司的估价过低。

big ◆◆◆ /bɪg/ (**bigger, biggest**) **1** ADJ A **big** person or thing is large in physical size. (体积、体态) 大的 ❑ *Australia's a big country.* 澳大利亚是一个幅员辽阔的国家。 ❑ *Her husband was a big man.* 她丈夫是个身材高大的男人。 **2** ADJ Something that is **big** consists of many people or things. (数量) 多的 ❑ *The crowd included a big contingent from Cleveland.* 人群中包括一个来自克利夫兰的大型代表团。 **3** ADJ If you describe something such as a problem, increase, or change as a **big** one, you mean it is great in degree, extent, or importance. 重大的; 严重的 ❑ *Her problem was just too big for her to tackle on her own.* 她的问题太严重了，她无法独力应付。 **4** ADJ A **big** organization employs many people and has many customers. (规模) 大的 ❑ *...one of the biggest companies in Italy.* …意大利规模最大的公司之一。 **5** ADJ If you say that someone is **big in** a particular organization, activity, or place, you mean that they have a lot of influence or authority in it. 有影响力的 [ADJ n, v-link ADJ "in" n] [INFORMAL] ❑ *Their father was very big in the army.* 他们的父亲在军界很有威望。 **6** ADJ If you call someone a **big** bully or a **big** coward, you are emphasizing your disapproval of them. (用以强调厌恶等语气) 大的 [ADJ n] [INFORMAL, EMPHASIS] ❑ *His personality changed. He turned into a big bully.* 他性格变了，成了一个大坏蛋。 **7** ADJ Children often refer to their older brother or sister as their **big** brother or sister. 年龄较大的 [ADJ n] ❑ *She always introduces me as her big sister.* 她总对别人介绍我是她的姐姐。 **8** ADJ **Big** words are long or rare words which have meanings that are difficult to understand. 艰深难懂的 (词) [INFORMAL] ❑ *They use a lot of big words.* 他们用许多难懂的大词。 **9** PHRASE If you **make it big**, you become successful or famous. 获得巨大成功 [INFORMAL] ❑ *Capone was an underdog hero, a poor boy who made it big.* 卡彭是个草莽英雄，一个飞黄腾达了的穷小子。 **10** PHRASE If you **think big**, you make plans on a large scale, often using a lot of time, effort, or money. 着眼大局 ❑ *Maybe we're not thinking big enough.* 也许我们不够着眼大局。

> **Big**, **large**, and **great** are all used to talk about size. In general, **large** is more formal than **big**, and **great** is more formal than **large**. **Big** and **large** are normally used to describe objects, but you can also use **big** to suggest that something is important or impressive. ❑ *...his influence over the big advertisers.* You normally use **great** to emphasize the importance of someone or something. ❑ *...the great English architect, Inigo Jones.* However, you can also use **great** to suggest that something is impressive because of its size. ❑ *The great bird of prey was a dark smudge against the sun.* You can use **large** or **great**, but not **big**, to describe amounts. ❑ *...a large amount of blood on the floor. ...the coming of tourists in great numbers.* Both **big** and **great** can be used to emphasize the intensity of something, although **great** is more formal. ❑ *It gives me great pleasure to welcome you... Most of them act like big fools.* Remember that **great** has several other meanings, when it does not refer to size, but to something that is remarkable, very good, or enjoyable.

Thesaurus *big* 另参见：

ADJ. enormous, huge, large, massive; *(ant.)* little, small, tiny **1**
considerable, significant, substantial; *(ant.)* insignificant, unimportant **3**
important, influential, prominent **5**

big busi·ness **1** N-UNCOUNT **Big business** is business which involves very large companies and very large sums of money. 大企业 ❑ *Big business will never let petty nationalism get in the way of a good deal.* 大公司绝不会因为狭隘的民族主义而耽误一笔大买卖。 **2** N-UNCOUNT Something that is **big business** is something which people spend a lot of money on, and which has become an important commercial activity. 大生意 ❑ *Online dating is big business in the United States.* 网上约会在美国是桩大生意。

big deal **1** N-SING If you say that something is a **big deal**, you mean that it is important or significant in some way. 至关重要的事情 [INFORMAL] ❑ *I felt the pressure on me, winning was such a big deal for the whole family.* 我感到了身上的压力，取胜对全家人是这么至关重要的事。 **2** PHRASE If someone **makes a big deal out of** something, they make a fuss about it or treat it as if it were very important. 小题大做 [INFORMAL] ❑ *The Joneses make a big deal out of being "different."* 琼斯一家子把 "与众不同" 看作是了不得的事。 **3** CONVENTION You can say "**big deal**" to someone to show that you are not impressed by something that they consider important or impressive. 没什么大不了 [INFORMAL, FEELINGS] ❑ *"You'll miss The Brady Bunch."—"Big deal."* "你会错过《布雷迪家庭》的。" —— "没什么大不了的。"

big·ot /bɪgət/ (**bigots**) N-COUNT If you describe someone as a **bigot**, you mean that they are bigoted. 偏执的人 [DISAPPROVAL] ❑ *Anyone who opposes them is branded a racist, a bigot, or a homophobe.* 任何反对他们的人都被冠以种族主义者，偏执狂或同性恋憎恨者的污名。

B

big·ot·ed /bɪɡətɪd/ ADJ Someone who is **bigoted** has strong, unreasonable prejudices or opinions and will not change them, even when they are proved to be wrong. 偏执的 [DISAPPROVAL] ❑ *He was bigoted and racist.* 他是一个偏执的种族主义者。

big·ot·ry /bɪɡətri/ N-UNCOUNT **Bigotry** is the possession or expression of strong, unreasonable prejudices or opinions. 偏执态度；偏执行为 ❑ *He deplored religious bigotry.* 他谴责了宗教偏执的行为。

big time also **big-time** 1 ADJ You can use **big time** to refer to the highest level of an activity or sport where you can achieve the greatest amount of success or importance. If you describe a person as **big time**, you mean they are successful and important. 第一流的；最高级别的 [INFORMAL] ❑ *He took a long time to settle in to big-time football.* 他花了很长时间才在第一流的足球运动中立足。 2 N-SING If someone hits **the big time**, they become famous or successful in a particular area of activity. (活动、职业等的) 顶峰 [INFORMAL] ❑ *He hit the big time with films such as Ghost and Dirty Dancing.* 他因《人鬼情未了》和《热舞》两部影片而到达了顶峰。 3 ADV You can use **big time** if you want to emphasize the importance or extent of something that has happened. 极度 [ADV after V] [INFORMAL, EMPHASIS] ❑ *Mike Edwards has tasted success big time.* 迈克·爱德华兹已尝过飞黄腾达的滋味。

bike ♦◇◇ /baɪk/ (**bikes, biking, biked**) 1 N-COUNT A **bike** is a bicycle. 自行车 [INFORMAL] ❑ *When you ride a bike, you exercise all of the leg muscles.* 骑自行车时，你可以锻炼腿部的全部肌肉。 2 N-COUNT A **bike** is a motorcycle. 摩托车 [INFORMAL] ❑ *She parked her bike in the alley.* 她把摩托车停在巷子里。 3 V-I To **bike** somewhere means to go there on a bicycle. 骑自行车 [INFORMAL] ❑ *I biked home from the beach.* 我从海滩骑自行车回家。

→ see **bicycle**

bik·er /baɪkər/ (**bikers**) 1 N-COUNT **Bikers** are people who ride around on motorcycles, usually in groups. 骑摩托车的人 (尤指团体) ❑ *There are always fights going on between rival bikers.* 在敌对的摩托车手之间总是发生着冲突。 2 N-COUNT People who ride bicycles are called **bikers**. 骑自行车的人 [AM]

in BRIT, use **cyclist**

❑ *And as the morning begins moving toward noon, look out for more bikers and pedestrians.* 当早上快到中午的时候，要小心更多骑自行车的人和行人。

bi·ki·ni /bɪkiːni/ (**bikinis**) N-COUNT A **bikini** is a two-piece swimsuit worn by women. 比基尼泳装

▲ **bi·lat·er·al** /baɪlætərəl/ ADJ **Bilateral** negotiations, meetings, or agreements, involve only the two groups or countries that are directly concerned. 双边的 [ADJ n] [FORMAL] ❑ *...bilateral talks between Britain and America.* …英美之间的双边会谈。 ● **bi·lat·er·al·ly** ADV 双边地 ❑ *The agreement provided for disputes and differences between the two neighbors to be solved bilaterally.* 协议规定相邻两国的争议由双边协商解决。

Word Link *bi ≈ two : biannual, bicycle, bilingual*

Word Link *lingu ≈ language : bilingual, linguist, linguistic*

★ **bi·lin·gual** /baɪlɪŋɡwəl/ 1 ADJ **Bilingual** means involving or using two languages. 双语的 [ADJ n] ❑ *...bilingual education.* …双语教育。 2 ADJ Someone who is **bilingual** can speak two languages equally well, usually because they learned both languages as a child. 使用双语的 ❑ *He is bilingual in an Asian language and English.* 他是通晓一种亚洲语言和英语的双语使用者。

bill ♦♦◇ /bɪl/ (**bills, billing, billed**) 1 N-COUNT A **bill** is a written statement of money that you owe for goods or services. 账单 ❑ *They couldn't afford to pay the bills.* 他们付不起账。

> Do not confuse **account** and **bill**. When you have an **account** with a bank, you leave your money in the bank and take it out when you need it. When you have to pay for things such as electricity or a work done by a repairman, you get a **bill**.

2 V-T If you **bill** someone **for** goods or services you have provided them with, you give or send them a bill stating how much money they owe you for these goods or services. 给…开账单 [no cont] ❑ *Are you going to bill me for this?* 你会为这开帐单给我吗？ 3 N-COUNT A **bill** is a piece of paper money. 纸币 [AM]

in BRIT, use **note**

❑ *The case contained a large quantity of U.S. dollar bills.* 盒子里装有大量美钞。 4 N-COUNT In government, a **bill** is a formal statement of a proposed new law that is discussed and then voted on. 议案 ❑ *This is the toughest crime bill that Congress has passed in a decade.* 这是十年来国会通过的最强硬的有关犯罪的议案。 5 N-SING The **bill** of a show or concert is a list of the entertainers who will take part in it. 演出人员名单 ❑ *Bob Dylan topped the bill.* 鲍勃·迪伦排在演员表的最前端。 6 N-SING **The bill** in a restaurant is a piece of paper on which the price of the meal you have just eaten is written and which you are given before you pay. (餐馆的) 账单 [mainly BRIT]

in AM, usually use **check**

7 V-T If someone **is billed to** appear in a particular show, it has been advertised that they are going to be in it. 宣传 (某人出演某戏) [usu passive] ❑ *She was billed to play the Wicked Queen in "Snow White."* 她已被宣布将出演《白雪公主》里狠毒的王后。 ● **bill·ing** N-UNCOUNT 演员表 ❑ *...their quarrels over star billing.* …他们就演员表排名顺序的争吵。 8 V-T If you **bill** a person or event **as** a particular thing, you advertise them in a way that makes people think they have particular qualities or abilities. 把…宣传为 ❑ *They bill it as California's most exciting museum.* 他们把这宣传为加利福尼亚最令人激动的博物馆。 9 N-COUNT A bird's **bill** is its beak. 喙 10 PHRASE If you say that someone or something **fits the bill** or **fills the bill**, you mean that they are suitable for a particular job or purpose. 符合要求 ❑ *If you fit the bill, send a CV to Rebecca Rees.* 如果你符合这些要求，送一份履历给丽贝卡·里斯。

Word Partnership *bill* 的常用搭配：

N.	**electricity/gas/phone** bill, **hospital/hotel** bill 1
	dollar bill 3
V.	**pay** a bill 1
	pass a bill, **sign** a bill, **vote on** a bill 4

★ **bill·board** /bɪlbɔrd/ (**billboards**) N-COUNT A **billboard** is a very large board on which advertising is displayed. 广告牌

→ see **advertising**

bill·fold /bɪlfoʊld/ (**billfolds**) N-COUNT A **billfold** is a small wallet, usually made of leather or plastic, where you can keep paper money and credit cards. 小钱包 [AM] ❑ *...a billfold containing fifteen dollars.* …一个装有15美元的钱包。

▲ **bil·liards** /bɪliərdz/

> The form **billiard** is used as a modifier.

1 N-UNCOUNT **Billiards** is a game played on a large table, in which you use a long stick called a cue to hit balls against each other or against the walls around the sides of the table. 撞球戏；桌球戏 [AM] 2 N-UNCOUNT **Billiards** is a game played on a large table, in which you use a long stick called a cue to hit balls against each other or into pockets around the sides of the table. 台球戏；落袋弹子戏 [BRIT]

in AM, use **pool**

bil·lion ♦♦♦ /bɪlyən/ (**billions**)

> The plural form is **billion** after a number, or after a word or expression referring to a number, such as "several" or "a few."

1 NUM A **billion** is a thousand million. 10亿 ❑ *The Ethiopian foreign debt stands at 3 billion dollars.* 埃塞俄比亚的外债达30亿美元。 2 QUANT-PLURAL If you talk about **billions of** people or things, you mean that there is a very large number of them but you do not know or do not want to say exactly how many. 亿万 [QUANT "of" pl-n] ❑ *Biological systems have been doing this for billions of years.* 生物系统亿万年来都在这样做。 ● PRON You can also use **billions** as a pronoun. 亿万 ❑ *He thought that it must be worth billions.* 他认为它一定值亿万元。 3 → see also **trillion**

★ **bil·lion·aire** /bɪlyənɛər/ (**billionaires**) N-COUNT A **billionaire** is an extremely rich person who has money or property worth at least a thousand million dollars. 亿万富翁

Bill of Rights N-SING A **Bill of Rights** is a written list of citizens' rights which is usually part of the constitution of a country. (英) 权利法案；(美) 人权法案 ❑ *And what are your rights according to the Bill of Rights?* 根据《权利法案》你的权利是什么？

▲ **bil·low** /bɪloʊ/ (**billows, billowing, billowed**) 1 V-I When something made of cloth **billows**, it swells out and moves slowly in the wind. 在风中鼓胀着飘动 ❑ *The curtains billowed in the breeze.* 窗帘在微风中鼓胀着飘动。 ❑ *Her pink dress billowed out around her.* 她粉红色的连衣裙随身飘了起来。 2 V-I When smoke or cloud **billows**, it moves slowly upward or across the sky. (烟、云等) 升腾 ❑ *...thick plumes of smoke billowing from factory chimneys.* …从工厂烟囱里

冒出来的滚滚浓烟。❑ *Steam billowed out from under the hood.* 蒸汽从机罩下冒了出来。 **3** N-COUNT A **billow of** smoke or dust is a large mass of it rising slowly into the air. 缓缓升起的大团(烟、灰尘) ❑ *...smoke stacks belching billows of almost solid black smoke.* …喷吐着滚滚黑色浓烟的大烟囱。

bil·ly /bɪli/ (**billies**) N-COUNT A **billy** or **billy club** is a short heavy stick which is sometimes used as a weapon by the police. 警棍 [AM]

in BRIT, use **baton**

bi·month·ly /baɪmʌnθli/ **1** ADJ A **bimonthly** event or publication happens or appears every two months. 两月一次的 [usu ADJ n]

in BRIT, also use **bi-monthly**

❑ *...bimonthly assemblies.* …两月一次的聚会。 ● ADV **Bimonthly** is also an adverb. 两月一次地

in BRIT, also use **bi-monthly**

❑ *Under the new plan, customers would pay $45 bimonthly, instead of $18 a month – a substantial increase.* 根据新方案，顾客将每两个月支付$45，而不是每个月$18——一个相当大的增长。 **2** ADJ A **bimonthly** event or publication happens or appears twice every month. 每月两次的 [AM]

in BRIT, use **fortnightly**

❑ *In November, it will start bimonthly publication, and in January it goes weekly.* 从11月开始，它将每月出版两次，到了1月则每周1次。 ● ADV **Bimonthly** is also an adverb. 每月两次地

in BRIT, use **fornightly**

❑ *...people who get paid weekly, bimonthly and monthly.* …每周一次、每月两次、每月一次领取报酬的人。

▲ **bin** /bɪn/ (**bins**) **1** N-COUNT A **bin** is a container that you keep or store things in. 贮物容器 ❑ *...big steel storage bins.* …钢制大贮藏箱。 **2** N-COUNT A **bin** is a container that you put garbage or trash in. 垃圾箱 [mainly BRIT]

in AM, usually use **garbage can**, **trash can**

bi·na·ry /baɪnəri/ **1** ADJ The **binary** system expresses numbers using only the two digits 0 and 1. It is used especially in computing. 二进制的 [usu ADJ n] ❑ *The message contains Unicode characters and has been sent as a binary attachment.* 这条信息含有统一码字符，已经以二进制附件形式发送。 **2** N-UNCOUNT **Binary** is the binary system of expressing numbers. 二进制 ❑ *The machine does the calculations in binary.* 这台机器用二进制做计算。

bi·na·ry code (**binary codes**) N-VAR **Binary code** is a computer code that uses the binary number system. 二进制代码 [COMPUTING] ❑ *The instructions are translated into binary code, a form that computers can easily handle.* 这些指令被翻译成二进制代码，这是计算机容易处理的一种形式。

bind /baɪnd/ (**binds, binding, bound**) **1** V-T If something **binds** people **together**, it makes them feel as if they are all part of the same group or have something in common. 使结合 ❑ *It is the memory and threat of persecution that binds them together.* 是受迫害的记忆和威胁将他们紧紧联系在一起。 ❑ *...the social and political ties that bind the U.S. to Britain.* …使美国与英国紧密联系在一起的社会与政治纽带。 **2** V-T If you **are bound** by something such as a rule, agreement, or restriction, you are forced or required to act in a certain way. 约束 ❑ *All pharmacists are bound by the society's rules of confidentiality.* 所有药剂师都受到保密性这一社会规则的约束。 ❑ *The authorities will be legally bound to arrest any suspects.* 当局将依法逮捕任何可疑人员。 ● **bound** ADJ 受约束的 [v-link ADJ "by" n] ❑ *The world of advertising is obviously less bound by convention than the world of banking.* 与银行业相比，广告业显然较少受常规的约束。 **3** V-T If you **bind** something or someone, you tie rope, string, tape, or other material around them so that they are held firmly. 捆绑 ❑ *Bind the ends of the cord together with thread.* 把细绳的两端用线系在一起。 ❑ *...the red tape which was used to bind the files.* …曾用来捆绑文件的红色带子。 **4** V-T When a book **is bound**, the pages are joined together and the cover is put on. 装订 ❑ *Each volume is bound in bright-colored cloth.* 每一册都用颜色鲜亮的布料装订。 ❑ *Their business came from a few big publishers, all of whose books they bound.* 他们的生意来自几家大出版社，这些出版社所有的书都由其装订。

★ **bind·er** /baɪndər/ (**binders**) N-COUNT A **binder** is a hard cover with metal rings inside, which is used to hold loose pieces of paper. 活页夹

bind·ing /baɪndɪŋ/ (**bindings**) **1** ADJ A **binding** promise, agreement, or decision must be obeyed or carried out. 有约束力的 ❑ *...proposals for a legally binding commitment on nations to stabilize emissions of carbon dioxide.* …关于就稳定二氧化碳排放各国做出有法律约束力的承诺的建议。 **2** N-VAR The **binding** of a book is its cover. (书的) 封面 ❑ *Its books are noted for the quality of their paper and bindings.* 其书籍以纸张和封面的品质而著称。 **3** N-VAR **Binding** is a strip of material that you put around the edge of a piece of cloth or other object in order to protect or decorate it. 滚条；镶边 ❑ *...the Regency mahogany dining table with satinwood binding.* …摄政时期有椴木镶边的桃花心木餐桌 **4** → see also **bind**

binge /bɪndʒ/ (**binges, bingeing, binged**) **1** N-COUNT If you go on a **binge**, you do too much of something, such as drinking alcohol, eating, or spending money. 放纵 [INFORMAL] ❑ *She went on occasional drinking binges.* 她偶尔狂饮一番。 **2** V-I If you **binge**, you do too much of something, such as drinking alcohol, eating, or spending money. 放纵 [INFORMAL] ❑ *I haven't binged since 1986.* 我从1986年以来从未放纵过自己。

★ **bin·go** /bɪŋgoʊ/ **1** N-UNCOUNT **Bingo** is a game in which each player has a card with numbers on it. Someone calls out numbers and if you are the first person to have all your numbers called out, you win the game. 宾戈游戏 (一种赌博游戏) ❑ *...a bingo hall.* …一间宾戈游戏厅。 **2** EXCLAM You can say **"bingo!"** when something pleasant happens, especially in a surprising, unexpected, or sudden way, or to show that you have just achieved or discovered something. 因突然出现的好事或成功所发出的叫声 ❑ *She grinned. "Wow, bingo! Got it in one."* 她咧嘴笑了。“哇，好！一下就中了。”

▲ **bin·ocu·lars** /bɪnɒkyələrz/ N-PLURAL **Binoculars** consist of two small telescopes joined together side by side, which you look through in order to look at things that are a long distance away. 双筒望远镜 [also "a pair of" N]

bio·chemi·cal /baɪoʊkɛmɪkᵊl/ ADJ **Biochemical** changes, reactions, and mechanisms relate to the chemical processes that happen in living things. 生物化学的 [ADJ n] ❑ *Starvation brings biochemical changes in the body.* 饥饿引起体内的生化变化。

Word Link *chem ≈ chemical : biochemist, chemical, chemistry*

bio·chem·ist /baɪoʊkɛmɪst/ (**biochemists**) N-COUNT A **biochemist** is a scientist or student who studies biochemistry. 生物化学家；学习生物化学的学生

★ **bio·chem·is·try** /baɪoʊkɛmɪstri/ **1** N-UNCOUNT **Biochemistry** is the study of the chemical processes that occur in living things. 生物化学 **2** N-UNCOUNT The **biochemistry** of a living thing is the chemical processes that occur in it or are involved in it. 生物化学过程 ❑ *...the effects of air pollutants on the biochemistry of plants or animals.* …大气污染物对植物或动物生化过程的影响。

Word Link *bio ≈ life : biodegradable, biography, biology*

bio·degrad·able /baɪoʊdɪgreɪdəbᵊl/ ADJ Something that is **biodegradable** breaks down or decays naturally without any special scientific treatment, and can therefore be thrown away without causing pollution. 能进行生物降解的 ❑ *...a natural and totally biodegradable plastic.* …一种天然的完全能进行生物降解的塑料。

bi·o·die·sel /baɪoʊdizᵊl/ N-UNCOUNT **Biodiesel** is fuel made from natural sources such as plant oils, that can be used in diesel engines. 生物柴油

bi·o·fu·el /baɪoʊfyuəl/ N-VAR A **biofuel** is a gas, liquid, or solid from natural sources such as plants that is used as a fuel. 生物燃料 ❑ *Biofuels can be mixed with conventional fuels.* 生物燃料能够和传统燃料混合。

bi·og·raph·er /baɪɒgrəfər/ (**biographers**) N-COUNT Someone's **biographer** is a person who writes an account of their life. 传记作者 ❑ *...Picasso's biographer.* …毕加索的传记作者。

bio·graphi·cal /baɪəgræfɪkᵊl/ ADJ **Biographical** facts, notes, or details are concerned with the events in someone's life. 传记的 ❑ *The book contains few biographical details.* 此书包含的生平细节很少。

Word Link *graph ≈ writing : autograph, biography, graph*

★ **bi·og·ra·phy** /baɪɒgrəfi/ (**biographies**) **1** N-COUNT A **biography** of someone is an account of their life, written by someone else. 传记 ❑ *...recent biographies of Stalin.* …近年的斯大林传记。 **2** N-UNCOUNT **Biography** is the branch of literature which deals with accounts of people's lives. 传记文学 ❑ *...a volume of biography and criticism.* …一册传记文学与评论。

→ see **library**

B

bio·logi·cal /baɪəlɒdʒɪkᵊl/ **1** ADJ **Biological** is used to describe processes and states that occur in the bodies and cells of living things. 与生命过程和状态有关的 ❑ *The living organisms somehow concentrated the minerals by biological processes.* 活的有机物以某种方式随其生命过程聚集了矿物质。● **bio·logi·cal·ly** /baɪəlɒdʒɪkli/ ADV 与生命过程和状态有关地 ❑ *Much of our behavior is biologically determined.* 我们的许多行为是由生命过程和状态所决定的。**2** ADJ **Biological** is used to describe activities concerned with the study of living things. 生物学的 [ADJ n] ❑ *...all aspects of biological research associated with leprosy.* …与麻风病有关的生物学研究的方方面面。**3** ADJ **Biological** weapons and **biological** warfare involve the use of bacteria or other living organisms in order to attack human beings, animals, or plants. 生物性的（武器、战争）❑ *Such a war could result in the use of chemical and biological weapons.* 这样一场战争可能导致生化武器的使用。**4** ADJ **Biological** pest control is the use of bacteria or other living organisms in order to destroy other organisms which are harmful to plants or crops. (利用细菌或其他生物对有害生物进行) 生物控制的 [ADJ n] ❑ *...a consultant on biological control of agricultural pests.* …一位农作物害虫生物防治顾问。**5** ADJ A child's **biological** parents are the man and woman who caused him or her to be born, rather than other adults who raise him or her. (指父母亲) 生身的 [ADJ n] ❑ *...foster parents for young teenagers whose biological parents have rejected them.* …被亲生父母抛弃的十几岁青少年的养父母们。
→ see **war, zoo**

Word Link *logy, ology ≈ study of : anthropology, biology, geology*

bi·ol·ogy /baɪɒlədʒi/ **1** N-UNCOUNT **Biology** is the science which is concerned with the study of living things. 生物学 ● **bi·olo·gist** /baɪɒlədʒɪst/ N-COUNT (**biologists**) 生物学家 ❑ *...biologists studying the fruit fly.* …研究果蝇的生物学家。**2** N-UNCOUNT The **biology** of a living thing is the way in which its body or cells behave. (机体、细胞的) 作用方式 ❑ *The biology of these diseases is terribly complicated.* 这些疾病的作用方式极其复杂。

★ **bio·medi·cal** /baɪoʊmɛdɪkᵊl/ ADJ **Biomedical** research examines the effects of drugs and medical techniques on the biological systems of living creatures. 生物医学的 [ADJ n] ❑ *Biomedical research will enable many individuals infected with HIV to live longer, more comfortable lives.* 生物医学研究将使许多感染艾滋病病毒的人们能够活得时间更长、更舒适。

bi·op·sy /baɪɒpsi/ (**biopsies**) N-VAR A **biopsy** is the removal and examination of fluids or tissue from a patient's body in order to discover why they are ill. 活组织检查 ❑ *James had a biopsy of the tumor over his right ear.* 詹姆斯做了一次右耳肿块的活组织检查。

Word Link *techn ≈ art, skill : biotechnology, technical, technician*

bio·tech·nol·ogy /baɪoʊtɛknɒlədʒi/ N-UNCOUNT **Biotechnology** is the use of living parts such as cells or bacteria in industry and technology. 生物技术 [TECHNICAL] ❑ *...the Scottish biotechnology company that developed Dolly the cloned sheep.* …培育出克隆羊多利的苏格兰生物技术公司。
→ see **technology**

birch /bɜrtʃ/ (**birches**) N-VAR A **birch** is a type of tall tree with thin branches. 桦树

bird ♦♦◇ /bɜrd/ (**birds**) **1** N-COUNT A **bird** is a creature with feathers and wings. Female birds lay eggs. Most birds can fly. 鸟 **2** → see also **early bird** **3** PHRASE If you refer to two people as **birds of a feather**, you mean that they have the same interests or are very similar. 志趣相同的人 ❑ *We're birds of a feather, you and me, Mr. Plimpton.* 我们志趣相投，我和你，普林顿先生。**4** PHRASE **A bird in the hand** is something that you already have and do not want to risk losing by trying to get something else. 已到手的东西 ❑ *Another temporary discount may not be what you want, but at least it is a bird in the hand.* 再一次临时打折可能达不到你所希望的，但至少这是已经到手的东西。**5** PHRASE If you say that a **little bird** told you about something, you mean that someone has told you about it, but you do not want to say who it was. 消息灵通的人 ❑ *Incidentally, a little bird tells me that your birthday's coming up.* 顺便提一句，有个消息灵通的人告诉我你的生日快到了。**6** PHRASE If you say that doing something will **kill two birds with one stone**, you mean that it will enable you to achieve two things that you want to achieve, rather than just one. 一箭双雕 ❑ *We can talk about Union Hill while I get this business over with. Kill two birds with one stone, so to speak.* 我们可以谈谈尤宁山，同时我把这件事干完。可以说是一举两得吧。
→ see Word Web: **bird**
→ see **pet**

bird flu N-UNCOUNT **Bird flu** is a virus that can be transmitted from chickens, ducks, and other birds to people. 禽流感

Biro /baɪroʊ/ (**Biros**) N-COUNT A **Biro** is the same as a **ballpoint**. 圆珠笔 [BRIT, TRADEMARK]

birth ♦◇◇ /bɜrθ/ (**births**) **1** N-VAR When a baby is born, you refer to this event as his or her **birth**. 出生 ❑ *It was the birth of his grandchildren that gave him greatest pleasure.* 是孙儿孙女们的降生给了他最大的欢乐。❑ *She weighed 5lb 7oz at birth.* 她出生时重5磅7盎司。**2** N-UNCOUNT You can refer to the beginning or origin of something as its **birth**. 开始；起源 ❑ *...the birth of popular democracy.* …人民民主的开始 **3** N-UNCOUNT Some people talk about a person's **birth** when they are referring to the social position of the person's family. 出身 ❑ *...men of low birth.* …出身低微的男人们。**4** → see also **date of birth** **5** PHRASE If, for example, you are French **by birth**, you are French because your parents are French, or because you were born in France. 在血统上 ❑ *Sadrudin was an Iranian by birth.* 萨德鲁丁在血统上是伊朗人。**6** PHRASE When a woman **gives birth**, she produces a baby from her body. 分娩 ❑ *She's just given birth to a baby girl.* 她刚刚生下一个女婴。**7** PHRASE To **give birth to** something such as an idea means to cause it to start to exist. 使产生 ❑ *In 1980, strikes at the Lenin shipyards gave birth to the Solidarity trade union.* 1980年，列宁造船厂的罢工导致团结工会的建立。**8** PHRASE The country, town, or village **of** your **birth** is the place where you were born. 出生地 ❑ *He left the town of his birth five years later for Australia.* 他5年后离开故乡去了澳大利亚。

Word Partnership *birth* 的常用搭配：

ADJ.	**premature** birth **1**
N.	birth **of a baby/child**, birth **certificate**, birth **control**, birth **and death**, birth **defect**, birth **rate** **1** **date of** birth **1** **4** birth **of a nation** **2**
PREP.	**at** birth, **before** birth **1** **by** birth **3** **5**
V.	**give** birth **6** **7**

birth cer·tifi·cate (**birth certificates**) N-COUNT Your **birth certificate** is an official document that gives details of your birth, such as the date and place of your birth, and the names of your parents. 出生证

birth con·trol N-UNCOUNT **Birth control** means planning whether to have children, and using contraception to prevent having them when they are not wanted. 节育 ❑ *Today's methods of birth control make it possible for a couple to choose whether or not to have a child.* 如今的节育措施使一对夫妇可以选择是否要生育孩子。

birth·day ♦◇◇ /bɜrθdeɪ, -di/ (**birthdays**) N-COUNT Your **birthday** is the anniversary of the date on which you were born. 生日 ❑ *On his birthday she sent him presents.* 他生日那天，她送了他礼物。

Word Web bird

Many scientists today believe that birds evolved from avian dinosaurs. Recently many links have been found. Like birds, these dinosaurs laid their **eggs** in **nests**. Some had **wings**, **beaks**, and **claws** similar to modern birds. But perhaps the most dramatic link was found in 2001. Scientists in China discovered a well-preserved *Sinornithosaurus*, a bird-like dinosaur with **feathers**. This dinosaur is believed to be related to a prehistoric bird, the *Archaeopteryx*.

b

birth·place /bɜrθpleɪs/ (**birthplaces**) **1** N-COUNT Your **birthplace** is the place where you were born. 出生地 [WRITTEN] ❑ *...Bob Marley's birthplace in the village of Nine Mile.* …在九里村鲍勃・马利的出生地。 **2** N-COUNT The **birthplace of** something is the place where it began. 发源地 ❑ *...Athens, the birthplace of the ancient Olympics.* …雅典，古代奥林匹克运动的发祥地。

birth rate (**birth rates**) also **birth-rate** N-COUNT The **birth rate** in a place is the number of babies born there for every 1000 people during a particular period of time. 出生率 ❑ *America's birth rate fell to a record low last year.* 美国去年的出生率降到了创纪录的最低点。
→ see **population**

birth·right /bɜrθraɪt/ (**birthrights**) N-COUNT Something that is your **birthright** is something that you feel you have a basic right to have, simply because you are a human being. 基本人权 [usu sing] ❑ *Freedom is the natural birthright of every human.* 自由是每个人与生俱来的基本权利。

bis·cuit /bɪskɪt/ (**biscuits**) **1** N-COUNT A **biscuit** is a small round dry cake that is made with baking powder, baking soda, or yeast. 小圆饼干 [AM] **2** N-COUNT A **biscuit** is a small flat cake that is crisp and usually sweet. (扁平、松脆的) 小甜饼 [BRIT]

in AM, use **cookie**

3 PHRASE **Take the biscuit** means the same as **take the cake**. 差劲到极点 [BRIT]

bi·sex·ual /baɪsɛkʃuəl/ (**bisexuals**) ADJ Someone who is **bisexual** is sexually attracted to both men and women. 双性恋的 ● N-COUNT **Bisexual** is also a noun. 双性恋者 ❑ *He was an active bisexual.* 他是一个有实际双性恋行为的双性恋者。

★ **bish·op** /bɪʃəp/ (**bishops**) **1** N-COUNT; N-TITLE; N-VOC A **bishop** is a clergyman of high rank in the Roman Catholic, Anglican, and Orthodox churches. (天主教、英国圣公会、东正教的) 主教 **2** N-COUNT In chess a **bishop** is a piece that can be moved diagonally across the board on squares that are the same color. (国际象棋中的) 象
→ see **chess**

bis·tro /bistroʊ/ (**bistros**) N-COUNT A **bistro** is a small, informal restaurant or a bar where food is served. 小餐馆；小酒吧

bit ♦♦♦ /bɪt/ (**bits**) **1** QUANT **A bit of** something is a small amount of it. 一点儿 [QUANT "of" n-uncount] ❑ *All it required was a bit of work.* 它所需要的只是少量工作。 **2** PHRASE **A bit** means to a small extent or degree. It is sometimes used to make a statement less extreme. 有点儿 [VAGUENESS] ❑ *This girl was a bit strange.* 这个女孩有点儿古怪。 ❑ *I think people feel a bit more confident.* 我认为人们感觉更自信一点儿了。 **3** PHRASE You can use **a bit of** to make a statement less forceful. For example, the statement "It's a bit of a nuisance." is less forceful than "It's a nuisance." 有点儿 (用于使陈述不那么强烈) [VAGUENESS] ❑ *It's all a bit of a mess.* 它整个有点儿乱。 ❑ *Students have always been portrayed as a bit of a joke.* 学生们总是被描述得有些荒唐可笑。 **4** PHRASE **Quite a bit** means quite a lot. 相当多 ❑ *They're worth quite a bit of money.* 它们值很多钱。 ❑ *Things have changed quite a bit.* 情况大有改观。 **5** PHRASE You use **a bit** before "more" or "less" to mean a small amount more or a small amount less. (多或少) 一点儿 ❑ *I still think I have a bit more to offer.* 我仍然认为我可以多提供一点儿。 ❑ *Maybe we'll hear a little bit less noise.* 也许我们听见的噪音会少一点。 **6** PHRASE If you do something **a bit** or do something **for a bit**, you do it for a short time. 一会儿 ❑ *Let's wait a bit.* 我们稍等片刻。 ❑ *I hope there will be time to talk a bit—or at least ask you about one or two things this evening.* 我希望今晚能有时间和你谈一会儿，——或者至少能问你一两件事儿。 **7** N-COUNT **A bit of** something is a small part or section of it. 小部分 ❑ *Only a bit of the barley remained.* 只有一小部分大麦保留了下来。 ❑ *Now comes the really important bit.* 现在到了非常重要的一小部分。 **8** N-COUNT **A bit of** something is a small piece of it. 小块儿 ❑ *Only a bit of string looped round a nail in the doorpost held it shut.* 仅凭一小段绕在门框钉子上的绳子将门关住。 **9** N-COUNT You can use **bit** to refer to a particular item or to one of a group or set of things. For example, **a bit of** information is an item of information. (一组东西中的) 一个 ❑ *There was one bit of vital evidence which helped win the case.* 有一项至关重要的证据帮助赢了这场官司。 **10** N-COUNT In computing, **a bit** is the smallest unit of information that is held in a computer's memory. It is either 1 or 0. Several bits form a byte. 比特 (计算机存储的最小信息单位) **11** N-COUNT **A bit** is 12½ cents; mainly used in expressions such as two **bits**, which means 25 cents, or **four bits**, which means 50 cents. 12.5美分 [AM, INFORMAL or OLD-FASHIONED] ❑ *They weren't worth four bits.* 它们不值50美分了。 **12** **Bit** is the past tense of **bite**. bite的过去式 **13** PHRASE If something happens **bit by bit**, it happens in stages. 逐渐地 ❑ *Bit by bit I began to understand what they were trying to do.* 渐渐地，我开始明白了他们正在努力做什么。 **14** PHRASE If you **do your bit**, you do something that, to a small or limited extent, helps to achieve something. 尽本分 [BRIT]

in AM, use **do your part**

15 PHRASE You say that one thing is **every bit as** good, interesting, or important **as** another to emphasize that the first thing is just as good, interesting, or important as the second. 同样 [EMPHASIS] ❑ *My dinner jacket is every bit as good as his.* 我的小礼服和他的一样好。 **16** PHRASE If you say that something is **a bit much**, you are annoyed because you think someone has behaved in an unreasonable way. 太过分 [INFORMAL, FEELINGS] ❑ *Her stage outfit of hot pants, over-the-knee boots and a tube top was a bit much.* 她在舞台上的装扮是热裤、过膝长靴加紧身抹胸，太过分了。 **17** PHRASE You use **not a bit** when you want to make a strong negative statement. 一点也不 [EMPHASIS] ❑ *I'm really not a bit surprised.* 我确实毫不吃惊。 **18** PHRASE You can use **bits and pieces** to refer to a collection of different things. 零碎的东西 [INFORMAL] ❑ *The drawers are full of bits and pieces of armor.* 抽屉里满是零零碎碎的盔甲片。

▲ **bitch** /bɪtʃ/ (**bitches, bitching, bitched**) **1** N-COUNT If someone calls a woman a **bitch**, they are saying in a very rude way that they think she behaves in a very mean or unkind way. 泼妇 [INFORMAL, OFFENSIVE, VULGAR, DISAPPROVAL] **2** → see also **son of a bitch** **3** V-I If you say that someone **is bitching about** something, you mean that you disapprove of the fact that they are complaining about it in an unpleasant way. 发牢骚 [oft cont] [INFORMAL, DISAPPROVAL] ❑ *They're forever bitching about everybody else.* 他们总是在埋怨其他的每个人。 **4** N-COUNT A **bitch** is a female dog. 母狗

bite ♦♦♦ /baɪt/ (**bites, biting, bit, bitten**) **1** V-T/V-I If you **bite** something, you use your teeth to cut into it, for example, in order to eat it or break it. If an animal or person **bites** you, they use their teeth to hurt or injure you. 咬；咬伤 ❑ *Both sisters bit their nails as children.* 这两姐妹在孩童时都啃指甲。 ❑ *He bit into his sandwich.* 他咬了一口三明治。 ❑ *Every year in this country more than 50,000 children are bitten by dogs.* 每年这个国家有五万多个孩子被狗咬伤。 **2** N-COUNT A **bite** of something, especially food, is the action of biting it. 咬 ❑ *He took another bite of apple.* 他又咬了一口苹果。 **3** N-COUNT A **bite** of food is the amount of food you take into your mouth when you bite it. 一口的量 ❑ *Look forward to eating the food and enjoy every bite.* 盼望吃到那个食品并享受吃它的每一口。 **4** N-SING If you have **a bite** to eat, you have a small meal or a snack. 少量吃的东西 [INFORMAL] ❑ *It was time to go home for a little rest and a bite to eat.* 是该回家休息一会儿，吃点东西了。 **5** V-T/V-I If a snake or a small insect **bites** you, or if it **bites**, it makes a mark or hole in your skin, and often causes the surrounding area of your skin to become painful or itchy. (蛇、虫等) 叮咬 ❑ *When an infected mosquito bites a human, spores are injected into the blood.* 受感染的蚊子叮人时，孢子就被注入人体血液。 **6** N-COUNT A **bite** is an injury or a mark on your body where an animal, snake, or small insect has bitten you. (叮、咬的) 伤痕 ❑ *Any dog bite, no matter how small, needs immediate medical attention.* 任何狗咬的伤口，无论多小，都需要立即就医。 **7** V-I When an action or policy begins to **bite**, it begins to have a serious or harmful effect. 产生严重影响 ❑ *As the sanctions begin to bite there will be more political difficulties ahead.* 随着制裁真正开始起作用，今后将会有更多的政治困难。 **8** V-I If an object **bites** into a surface, it presses hard against it or cuts into it. 咬住；切入 ❑ *There may even be some wire or nylon biting into the flesh.* 甚至可能有金属丝或尼龙勒进肉里。 **9** N-UNCOUNT If you say that a food or drink has **bite**, you like it because it has a strong or sharp taste. (食物、饮料等) 够刺激的味道 ❑ *The olive salad has to have bite and tang.* 橄榄色拉的味道一定要够足够冲。 **10** V-I If a fish **bites** when you are fishing, it takes the hook or bait at the end of your fishing line in its mouth. 上钩 ❑ *After half an hour, the fish stopped biting and we moved on.* 过了半小时，鱼不再上钩，我们就走开了。 ● N-COUNT **Bite** is also a noun. 上钩 ❑ *If I don't get a bite in a few minutes I lift the rod and twitch the bait.* 如果好几分钟也不见鱼上钩，我就提起鱼竿猛拉钓饵。 **11** PHRASE If someone **bites the hand that feeds** them, they behave badly or in an ungrateful way toward someone who they depend on. 恩将仇报 ❑ *She may be cynical about the film industry, but ultimately she has no intention of biting the hand that feeds her.* 她也许会对电影业冷嘲热讽，但终究不打算恩将仇报。

B

12 PHRASE If you **bite** your **lip** or your **tongue**, you stop yourself from saying something that you want to say, because it would be the wrong thing to say in the circumstances. 忍住不说 ❑ *I must learn to bite my lip.* 我必须学会不随便说话。 **13** **to bite the bullet** → see **bullet** **14** **to bite the dust** → see **dust**

bit·ing /baɪtɪŋ/ **1** ADJ **Biting** wind or cold is extremely cold. 严寒刺骨的 ❑ *...a raw, biting northerly wind.* …湿冷刺骨的北风。 **2** ADJ **Biting** criticism or wit is very harsh or unkind, and is often caused by such feelings as anger or dislike. 尖刻的 ❑ *...the author's biting satire on the church.* …作者对教会的尖锐讽刺。

bit·map /bɪtmæp/ (**bitmaps, bitmapping, bitmapped**) N-COUNT A **bitmap** is a type of graphics file on a computer. 位图（计算机的一种图形文件）[COMPUTING] ❑ *...bitmap graphics for representing complex images such as photographs.* …表示诸如照片等复杂图像的位图图形。 ● V-T **Bitmap** is also a verb. 位元映射 ❑ *Bitmapped maps require huge storage space.* 位元映射地图需要巨大的存储空间。

bit·ten /bɪtᵊn/ **Bitten** is the past participle of **bite**. **bite**的过去分词

bit·ter ♦◇◇ /bɪtər/ (**bitterest**) **1** ADJ In a **bitter** argument or conflict, people argue very angrily or fight very fiercely. 激烈的 ❑ *...the scene of bitter fighting during the Second World War.* …第二次世界大战期间激烈的战斗场面。 ❑ *...a bitter attack on the government's failure to support manufacturing.* …对政府未能支持制造业的猛烈抨击。 ● **bit·ter·ly** ADV 激烈地 ❑ *Any such thing would be bitterly opposed by most of the world's democracies.* 任何此类事件都将受到世界上绝大多数民主国家的强烈反对。 ● **bit·ter·ness** N-UNCOUNT 激烈 ❑ *The rift within the organization reflects the growing bitterness of the dispute.* 该组织内部的分裂反映了争端的日趋激烈。 **2** ADJ If someone is **bitter** after a disappointing experience or after being treated unfairly, they continue to feel angry about it. 依然愤怒的 ❑ *She is said to be very bitter about the way she was fired.* 据说她对自己被解雇的方式仍很气愤。 ● **bit·ter·ly** ADV 依然愤怒地 ❑ *"And he sure didn't help us," Grant said bitterly.* "他确实没有帮助过我们，"格兰特仍很气愤地说。 ● **bit·ter·ness** N-UNCOUNT 愤懑 ❑ *I still feel bitterness and anger towards the person who knocked me down.* 我仍对撞倒我的那个人感到气愤和恼怒。 **3** ADJ A **bitter** taste is sharp, not sweet, and often slightly unpleasant. 苦的 ❑ *The leaves taste rather bitter.* 这些叶子尝起来相当苦。 **4** ADJ A **bitter** experience makes you feel very disappointed. You can also use **bitter** to emphasize feelings of disappointment. 惨痛的 ❑ *The decision was a bitter blow from which he never quite recovered.* 这个决定是个沉重的打击，他一直没有完全恢复过来。 ❑ *A great deal of bitter experience had taught him how to lose gracefully.* 大量痛苦的经历已经教会了他如何体面地认输。 ● **bit·ter·ly** ADV 惨痛地 ❑ *I was bitterly disappointed to have lost yet another race so near the finish.* 我感到痛心沮丧，在那么接近终点的情形下又输掉了一场比赛。 **5** ADJ **Bitter** weather, or a **bitter** wind, is extremely cold. 严寒的；刺骨的 ❑ *Outside, a bitter east wind was accompanied by flurries of snow.* 外面，凛冽的东风挟着阵阵小雪。 ● **bit·ter·ly** ADV 严寒地；刺骨地 [ADV adj] ❑ *It's been bitterly cold here in Moscow.* 在莫斯科这里，天气一直极其寒冷。 **6** **a bitter pill** → see **pill** → see **taste**

bit·ter·ly /bɪtərli/ ADV You use **bitterly** when you are describing an attitude which involves strong, unpleasant emotions such as anger or dislike. 强烈地 [ADV adj] ❑ *We are bitterly upset at what has happened.* 我们对发生的事感到极其难过。

bi·week·ly /baɪwikli/ ADJ A **biweekly** event or publication happens or appears once every two weeks. 每两周一次的 [ADJ n] [AM] ❑ *He used to see them at the biweekly meetings.* 他过去常常在每两周一次的会议上见到他们。 ❑ *...Beverage Digest, the industry's biweekly newsletter.* …《饮料文摘》，该行业的双周简讯。 ● ADV **Biweekly** is also an adverb. 每两周一次地 [ADV with v]

in BRIT, use **fortnightly**

❑ *The group meets on a regular basis, usually weekly or biweekly.* 该小组定期会面，通常每周或每两周一次。

★ **bi·zarre** /bɪzɑr/ ADJ Something that is **bizarre** is very odd and strange. 怪异的 ❑ *The game was also notable for the bizarre behavior of the team's manager.* 这场比赛另一值得注意的地方是该队经理人异乎寻常的表现。 ● **bi·zarre·ly** ADV 怪异地 ❑ *She dressed bizarrely.* 她穿着怪异。

black ♦♦♦ /blæk/ (**blacker, blackest, blacks, blacking, blacked**) **1** COLOR Something that is **black** is of the darkest color that there is, the color of the sky at night when there is no light at all. 黑色的 ❑ *She was wearing a black coat with a white collar.* 她穿着一件白领黑上衣。 ❑ *He had thick black hair.* 他有着浓密乌黑的头发。 **2** ADJ A **black** person belongs to a race of people with dark skins, especially a race originally from Africa. 黑色人种的 ❑ *He worked for the rights of black people.* 他为黑人的权利而工作。 ❑ *Sherry is black, tall, slender and soft-spoken.* 谢里是黑人，个头高挑，身材苗条，说话柔声细气。 **3** N-COUNT Black people are sometimes referred to as **blacks**. This use could cause offense. 黑人 ❑ *There are about thirty-one million blacks in the U.S.* 美国大约有三千一百万黑人。 **4** ADJ **Black** coffee or tea has no milk or cream added to it. （咖啡、茶）不加牛奶或奶油的 [ADJ n, V n ADJ] ❑ *A cup of black tea or black coffee contains no calories.* 一杯红茶或黑咖啡不含任何卡路里。 **5** ADJ If you describe a situation as **black**, you are emphasizing that it is very bad indeed. 糟糕的 [EMPHASIS] ❑ *It was, he said later, one of the blackest days of his political career.* 后来他说，那一天是他政治生涯中最糟糕的日子之一。 **6** ADJ If someone is in a **black** mood, they feel very miserable and depressed. 郁闷的 ❑ *In late 1975, she fell into a black depression.* 1975年末，她陷入极度消沉中。 **7** PHRASE If a person or an organization is **in the black**, they do not owe anyone any money. 不欠债 ❑ *Remington's operations in Japan are now in the black.* 雷明顿在日本的经营现在没有赤字。

▸ **black out** **1** PHRASAL VERB If you **black out**, you lose consciousness for a short time. 暂时失去知觉 ❑ *I could feel blood draining from my face. I wondered whether I was about to black out.* 我能感到血从脸上淌下来。我不知道自己是不是要昏过去了。 **2** PHRASAL VERB If a place **is blacked out**, it is in darkness, usually because it has no electricity supply. 使变成一片漆黑 ❑ *Large parts of Lima were blacked out after electricity pylons were blown up.* 电缆塔被炸后，利马城的大部分地区陷入一片黑暗。 **3** PHRASAL VERB If a film or a piece of writing **is blacked out**, it is prevented from being broadcast or published, usually because it contains information which is secret or offensive. 禁止播放；禁止出版 ❑ *TV pictures of the demonstration were blacked out.* 这次示威游行的电视报道被禁播了。 **4** PHRASAL VERB If you **black out** a piece of writing, you color over it in black so that it cannot be seen. 用黑色涂掉（文字等）❑ *U.S. government specialists went through each page, blacking out any information a foreign intelligence expert could use.* 美国政府的专家们检查了每一页，用黑色涂掉任何可能被外国情报专家利用的信息。 **5** PHRASAL VERB If you **black out** the memory of something, you try not to remember it because it upsets you. 试图抹掉（记忆）❑ *I tried not to think about it. I blacked it out. It was the easiest way of coping.* 我试图不去想它，将其从记忆中抹去。这是最容易的处理办法了。 **6** → see also **blackout** → see **coffee**

black and white also **black-and-white** **1** COLOR In a **black and white** photograph or film, everything is shown in black, white, and gray. （照片、电影）黑白的 ❑ *...old black and white film footage.* …老的黑白电影镜头。 ❑ *...a black-and-white photo of the two of us together.* …一张我们俩在一起的黑白照片。 **2** ADJ A **black and white** television set shows only black and white pictures. （电视机）黑白图像的 **3** ADJ A **black and white** issue or situation is one that involves issues that seem simple and therefore easy to make decisions about. 黑白分明的；容易判明的 ❑ *But this isn't a simple black and white affair, Marianne.* 但这不是一件简单的非对即错的事情，玛丽安娜。 **4** PHRASE You say that something is **in black and white** when it has been written or printed, and not just said. 以书面形式 ❑ *He'd seen the proof in black and white.* 他已经见到书面证据了。

black·berry /blækbɛri/ (**blackberries**) **1** N-COUNT A **blackberry** is a small, soft black or dark purple fruit. 黑莓果 **2** N-COUNT A **Blackberry** is a portable, wireless computing device that allows you to send and receive email. （可收发电子邮件的）黑莓手机 [COMPUTING, TRADEMARK]

black·board /blækbɔrd/ (**blackboards**) N-COUNT A **blackboard** is a dark-colored board that you can write on with chalk. Blackboards are often used by teachers in the classroom. 黑板

in AM, also use **chalkboard**

black·en /blækən/ (**blackens, blackening, blackened**) **1** V-T/V-I To **blacken** something means to make it black or very dark in color. Something that **blackens** becomes black or very dark in color. 使变黑；变黑 ❑ *The married women of Shitamachi maintained the custom of blackening their teeth.* 下町的已婚妇女保留了染黑牙齿的习俗。 **2** V-T If someone **blackens** your character, they make other people believe that you are a bad person. 诋毁 ❑ *They're trying to blacken our name.* 他们在设法败坏我们的名声。

black eye (**black eyes**) N-COUNT If someone has a **black eye**, they have a dark-colored bruise around their eye. 青肿的眼眶

b

❏ *He punched her in the face, giving her a black eye.* 他朝她脸上就是一拳，打得她眼眶都青了。

black·list /blæklɪst/ (**blacklists, blacklisting, blacklisted**) **1** N-COUNT If someone is on a **blacklist**, they are seen by a government or other organization as being one of a number of people who cannot be trusted or who have done something wrong. 黑名单 ❏ *A government official disclosed that they were on a secret blacklist.* 一位政府官员透露说，他们被列入了秘密黑名单。 **2** V-T If someone **is blacklisted** by a government or organization, they are put on a blacklist. 把…列入黑名单 [usu passive] ❏ *He has been blacklisted since being convicted of possessing marijuana in 1969.* 因在1969年被判拥有大麻，他已被列入黑名单。

▲ **black·mail** /blækmeɪl/ (**blackmails, blackmailing, blackmailed**) **1** N-UNCOUNT **Blackmail** is the action of threatening to reveal a secret about someone, unless they do something you tell them to do, such as giving you money. 敲诈 ❏ *It looks like the pictures were being used for blackmail.* 看来这些照片正被用于敲诈勒索。 **2** N-UNCOUNT If you describe an action as emotional or moral **blackmail**, you disapprove of it because someone is using a person's emotions or moral values to persuade them to do something against their will. 要挟 [DISAPPROVAL] ❏ *The tactics employed can range from overt bullying to subtle emotional blackmail.* 使用的手段从公开恐吓到情感要挟花样百出。 **3** V-T If one person **blackmails** another person, they use blackmail against them. 敲诈 ❏ *He told her their affair would have to stop, because Jack Smith was blackmailing him.* 他告诉她他们俩的风流韵事不得不到此为止，因为杰克・史密斯正在借此敲诈他。 ❏ *The government insisted that it would not be blackmailed by violence.* 政府坚称不会受暴力要挟。● **black·mail·er** N-COUNT (**blackmailers**) 敲诈者 ❏ *The nasty thing about a blackmailer is that his starting point is usually the truth.* 讨厌的事情在于，敲诈者开始借以要挟的把柄往往是事实。

black mar·ket (**black markets**) N-COUNT If something is bought or sold **on the black market**, it is bought or sold illegally. 黑市 ❏ *There is a plentiful supply of arms on the black market.* 黑市上有大量的武器供应。

black·out /blækaʊt/ (**blackouts**) also **black-out** **1** N-COUNT A **blackout** is a period of time during a war in which towns and buildings are made dark so that they cannot be seen by enemy planes. (战时为防止空袭而实施的) 灯火管制期 ❏ *...blackout curtains.* …灯火管制时用的窗帘。 **2** N-COUNT If a **blackout** is imposed on a particular piece of news, journalists are prevented from broadcasting or publishing it. (新闻等的) 封锁 ❏ *...a media blackout imposed by the Imperial Palace.* …皇宫强制实行的新闻封锁。 **3** N-COUNT If there is a power **blackout**, the electricity supply to a place is temporarily cut off. 停电 ❏ *There was an electricity black-out in a large area in the north of the country.* 该国北方有一大片地区都停电了。 **4** N-COUNT If you have a **blackout**, you temporarily lose consciousness. 暂时失去知觉 ❏ *I suffered a black-out which lasted for several minutes.* 我昏过去好几分钟。

▲ **black·smith** /blæksmɪθ/ (**blacksmiths**) N-COUNT A **blacksmith** is a person whose job is making things by hand out of metal that has been heated to a high temperature. 铁匠

black·top /blæktɒp/ N-UNCOUNT **Blacktop** is a hard black substance which is used as a surface for roads. (铺路面用的) 沥青 [AM]

in BRIT, use **tarmac**

❏ *...waves of heat rising from the blacktop.* …沥青路面上升起的热浪。

▲ **blad·der** /blædər/ (**bladders**) N-COUNT Your **bladder** is the part of your body where urine is stored until it leaves your body. See also **gall bladder**. 膀胱 ❏ *...an opportunity to empty a full bladder.* …将涨满的膀胱排空的机会。

blade /bleɪd/ (**blades**) **1** N-COUNT The **blade** of a knife, ax, or saw is the edge, which is used for cutting. 刃 ❏ *Many of them will have sharp blades.* 他们很多都会有锋利的刃。 **2** N-COUNT The **blades** of a propeller are the long, flat parts that turn around. (螺旋桨的) 桨叶 **3** N-COUNT The **blade** of an oar is the thin flat part that you put into the water. (船桨的) 桨叶 **4** N-COUNT A **blade** of grass is a single piece of grass. 草叶 ❏ *Brian began to tear blades of grass from between the bricks.* 布赖恩开始从砖缝儿里拔草叶。

→ see **silverware**

blame ◆◆◇ /bleɪm/ (**blames, blaming, blamed**) **1** V-T If you **blame** a person or thing **for** something bad, or if you **blame** something bad **on** somebody, you believe or say that they are responsible for it or that they caused it. 指责；把…归咎于 ❏ *The commission is expected to blame the army for many of the atrocities.* 该委员会预计会将大量暴行归咎于军队。 ❏ *Ms. Carey appeared to blame her breakdown on EMI's punishing work schedule.* 凯丽女士看来是将自己的崩溃归咎于百代公司紧张的工作安排。● N-UNCOUNT **Blame** is also a noun. 责备 ❏ *Nothing could relieve my terrible sense of blame.* 没什么能把我从极度自责中解脱出来。 **2** N-UNCOUNT The **blame for** something bad that has happened is the responsibility for causing it or letting it happen. (事故、过失等的) 责任 ❏ *I'm not going to sit around and take the blame for a mistake he made.* 我不会闲坐着，为他犯的错误承担责任。 **3** V-T If you say that you do not **blame** someone **for** doing something, you mean that you consider it was a reasonable thing to do in the circumstances. 责怪 [usu with brd-neg] ❏ *I do not blame them for trying to make some money.* 我不怪他们想要挣些钱。 **4** PHRASE If someone is **to blame for** something bad that has happened, they are responsible for causing it. 该受责备 ❏ *If their forces were not involved, then who is to blame?* 如果他们的军队没有参与，那么谁应该受到指责呢？ **5** PHRASE If you say that someone **has only** themselves **to blame** or **has no one but** themselves **to blame**, you mean that they are responsible for something bad that has happened to them and that you have no sympathy for them. 只能责怪自己 ❏ *My life is ruined and I suppose I only have myself to blame.* 我的一生都毁了，我想这只能怪我自己。

Word Partnership *blame* 的常用搭配：

N. blame **the victim** **1**
V. **tend to** blame **1**
lay blame, **share the** blame **1** **2**
can hardly blame *someone* **3**

blanch /blæntʃ/ (**blanches, blanching, blanched**) **1** V-I If you **blanch**, you suddenly become very pale. 突然变苍白 ❏ *Simon's face blanched as he looked at Sharpe's blood-drenched uniform.* 当西蒙看见夏普被血浸透的制服时，脸一下子就白了。 **2** V-I If you say that someone **blanches at** something, you mean that they find it unpleasant and do not want to be involved with it. 感到很不安 ❏ *Everything he had said had been a mistake. He blanched at his miscalculations.* 他所说过的一切都是错的。他对自己的失算感到懊恼不已。

▲ **bland** /blænd/ (**blander, blandest**) **1** ADJ If you describe someone or something as **bland**, you mean that they are rather dull and unexciting. 没精打采的；平淡乏味的 ❏ *Serle has a blander personality than Howard.* 塞尔在个性上比霍华德更沉闷。 ❏ *It sounds like a commercial: easy on the ear but bland and forgettable.* 它听起来像句广告语：顺耳却平淡易忘。 **2** ADJ Food that is **bland** has very little flavor. (食物) 淡而无味的 ❏ *It tasted bland and insipid, like warmed cardboard.* 它吃起来淡而无味，像加热过的卡纸板。

→ see **spice**

blank /blæŋk/ (**blanks**) **1** ADJ Something that is **blank** has nothing on it. 空白的；空的 ❏ *We could put some of the pictures over on that blank wall over there.* 我们可以在那边的空墙上贴一些画。 ❏ *He tore a blank page from his notebook.* 他从笔记本上撕下一页白纸。 **2** N-COUNT A **blank** is a space which is left in a piece of writing or on a printed form for you to fill in particular information. (表格等的) 空白处 ❏ *Put a word in each blank to complete the sentence.* 在每个空格处填一个单词完成句子。 **3** ADJ If you look **blank**, your face shows no feeling, understanding, or interest. 茫然的；无表情的；漠然的 ❏ *Abbot looked blank. "I don't quite follow, sir."* 阿博特一脸茫然，"我不太明白，先生。"● **blank·ly** ADV 茫然地；面无表情地；漠然地 [ADV with v] ❏ *She stared at him blankly.* 她面无表情地盯着他。 **4** N-SING If your mind or memory is **a blank**, you cannot think of anything or remember anything. (头脑、记忆等的) 一片空白 ❏ *I'm sorry, but my mind is a blank.* 很抱歉，可是我脑子里一片空白。 **5** N-COUNT **Blanks** are gun cartridges which contain explosive but do not contain a bullet, so that they cause no harm when the gun is fired. (有炸药而无弹头的) 空包弹 ❏ *...a starter pistol which only fires blanks.* …只发射空包弹的发令枪。 **6** → see also **point-blank** **7** PHRASE If your mind **goes blank**, you are suddenly unable to think of anything appropriate to say, for example in reply to a question. (头脑) 突然出现一片空白

blank check (**blank checks**)

in BRIT, use **blank cheque**

1 N-COUNT If someone is given a **blank check**, they are given the authority to spend as much money as they need or want. 空额签名

支票 ❑ *We are not prepared to write a blank check for companies that have run into trouble.* 我们不愿给那些陷入困境的公司开空额签名支票。 **2** N-COUNT If someone is given a **blank check**, they are given the authority to do what they think is best in a particular situation. 自由处理权 ❑ *He has, in a sense, been given a blank check to negotiate the new South Africa.* 从某种意义上说，他已被允许全权洽谈新南非问题。

blank cheque [BRIT] → see **blank check**

blan·ket /blæŋkɪt/ (**blankets, blanketing, blanketed**) **1** N-COUNT A **blanket** is a large square or rectangular piece of thick cloth, especially one that you put on a bed to keep you warm. 毯子 **2** N-COUNT A **blanket of** something such as snow is a continuous layer of it which hides what is below or beyond it. 覆盖层 ❑ *The mud disappeared under a blanket of snow.* 泥地在一层白雪的覆盖下消失不见了。 **3** V-T If something such as snow **blankets** an area, it covers it. 覆盖 ❑ *More than a foot of snow blanketed parts of Michigan.* 一英尺多厚的白雪覆盖了密歇根州的部分地区。 **4** ADJ You use **blanket** to describe something when you want to emphasize that it affects or refers to every person or thing in a group, without any exceptions. 适用于全体的 [ADJ n] [EMPHASIS] ❑ *There's already a blanket ban on foreign unskilled labor in Japan.* 日本已经有一项禁止使用外国非熟练工人的通用禁令。

→ see **bed**

blare /blɛər/ (**blares, blaring, blared**) V-I If something such as a siren or radio **blares**, it makes a loud, unpleasant noise. 发出响亮刺耳的声音 ❑ *The fire engines were just pulling up, sirens blaring.* 救火车刚刚停下，警笛声还在尖利地响着。 ❑ *Music blared from the apartment behind me.* 音乐声响亮刺耳，从我身后的房间传了出来。 ● N-SING **Blare** is also a noun. 刺耳的鸣响 ❑ *...the blare of a radio through a thin wall.* …透过一堵薄墙传来的收音机刺耳的声音。 ● PHRASAL VERB **Blare out** means the same as **blare.** 发出响亮刺耳的声音 ❑ *Music blares out from every cafe.* 每一间咖啡馆都传出刺耳的音乐声。

blas·phe·my /blæsfəmi/ (**blasphemies**) N-VAR You can describe something that shows disrespect for God or a religion as **blasphemy**. (对上帝或宗教的) 亵渎 ❑ *He has acted out every kind of blasphemy, including dressing up as the pope in Rome.* 他做过各种亵渎行为，包括在罗马装扮成教皇。

blast ♦◇◇ /blæst/ (**blasts, blasting, blasted**) **1** N-COUNT A **blast** is a big explosion, especially one caused by a bomb. (尤指炸弹引起的)大爆炸 ❑ *250 people were killed in the blast.* 250人在这次大爆炸中丧生。 **2** V-T If something **is blasted** into a particular place or state, an explosion causes it to be in that place or state. If a hole **is blasted** in something, it is created by an explosion. 由爆炸生成; 由爆炸引起 ❑ *There is a risk that toxic chemicals might be blasted into the atmosphere.* 有毒化学品有爆炸后进入空气的危险。 ❑ *The explosion which followed blasted out the wall of her apartment.* 随后的爆炸炸开了她房间的那面墙。 **3** V-T If workers **are blasting** rock, they are using explosives to make holes in it or destroy it, for example, so that a road or tunnel can be built. 用炸药炸 ❑ *Local workmen were blasting the rock face beside the track in order to make it wider.* 当地工人正在用炸药炸开小路旁边的岩石面以便将其拓宽。 **4** V-T To **blast** someone means to shoot them with a gun. 向…射击 [JOURNALISM] ❑ *A son blasted his father to death after a lifetime of bullying, a court was told yesterday.* 昨天有人告知法庭，一个儿子因长期受欺凌而开枪打死了其父亲。 ● N-COUNT **Blast** is also a noun. 枪击 ❑ *Anthony died from a shotgun blast to the face.* 安东尼因被猎枪击中面部而死。 **5** V-T If someone **blasts** their way somewhere, they get there by shooting at people or causing an explosion. 借助射击或爆炸打开 (通道) ❑ *The police were reported to have blasted their way into the house using explosives.* 据报道，警察已经借助炸药开道冲进了那所房子。 **6** V-T If something **blasts** water or air somewhere, it sends out a sudden, powerful stream of it. 强速喷射 (水流或气流) ❑ *Blasting cold air over it makes the water evaporate.* 向它上面快速喷冷气可使水蒸发掉。 ● N-COUNT **Blast** is also a noun. 强劲的 (气或水) 流 ❑ *Blasts of cold air swept down from the mountains.* 阵阵强冷气流从山上席卷下来。 **7** V-T/V-I If you **blast** something such as a car horn, or if it **blasts**, it makes a sudden, loud sound. If something **blasts** music, or music **blasts**, the music is very loud. 突然大声按响; 大声放 (音乐); 突然发出巨响; (音乐) 大声播放 ❑ *...drivers who do not blast their horns.* …那些没有狂按喇叭的驾驶员。 ● N-COUNT **Blast** is also a noun. (喇叭或音乐等的) 大声鸣响 ❑ *The buzzer suddenly responded in a long blast of sound.* 蜂鸣器突然以一声长长的鸣响做出回应。 **8** N-SING If you say that something was a **blast**, you mean that you enjoyed it very much. 奇妙的感受 [INFORMAL] ❑ *He went sledding with his daughter. "It was a blast," he said later.* 他和女儿去坐雪橇玩了。"那真是一次奇妙的感受，"他后来说。 **9** PHRASE If something such as a radio or a heater is on **full blast**, or on **at full blast**, it is producing as much sound or power as it is able to. 最大音量; 最大限量 ❑ *In many of those homes the television is on full blast 24 hours a day.* 许多家庭一天24小时都把电视开到最大音量。

▸ **blast off** PHRASAL VERB When a space rocket **blasts off**, it leaves the ground at the start of its journey. (火箭等) 发射升空 ❑ *Columbia is set to blast off at 1:20 a.m. Eastern Time tomorrow.* 哥伦比亚号定于东部时间明晨1:20点火起飞。

bla·tant /bleɪtᵊnt/ ADJ You use **blatant** to describe something bad that is done in an open or very obvious way. 公然的 [EMPHASIS] ❑ *Outsiders will continue to suffer the most blatant discrimination.* 圈外人将继续遭受极其明目张胆的歧视。 ❑ *...a blatant attempt to spread the blame for the fiasco.* …公然想要分摊这次惨败的责任的企图。 ● **bla·tant·ly** ADV 公然地 ❑ *...a blatantly sexist question.* …一个毫不掩饰的性别歧视问题。

bla·tant·ly /bleɪtᵊntli/ ADV **Blatantly** is used to add emphasis when you are describing states or situations that you think are bad. 极其 [EMPHASIS] ❑ *It became blatantly obvious to me that the band wasn't going to last.* 我看得再清楚不过，这个乐队存在不了多久。 ❑ *For years, blatantly false assertions have gone unchallenged.* 很多年来，极其错误的断言从未曾受到质疑。

★ **blaze** /bleɪz/ (**blazes, blazing, blazed**) **1** V-I When a fire **blazes**, it burns strongly and brightly. 熊熊燃烧 ❑ *Three people died as wreckage blazed, and rescuers fought to release trapped drivers.* 三个人丧生于熊熊燃烧的残骸，营救人员奋力去解救被困的司机。 ❑ *The log fire was blazing merrily.* 篝火正在欢快地熊熊燃烧着。 **2** N-COUNT A **blaze** is a large fire which is difficult to control and which destroys a lot of things. 大火 [JOURNALISM] ❑ *Some 4,000 firefighters are battling the blaze.* 约有四千名消防人员正在与大火搏斗。 **3** V-I If something **blazes with** light or color, it is extremely bright. 闪耀 [LITERARY] ❑ *The gardens blazed with color.* 公园里色彩缤纷，艳丽夺目。 ● N-COUNT **Blaze** is also a noun. 灿烂 ❑ *I wanted the front garden to be a blaze of color.* 我想把前花园装点得五彩缤纷。 **4** N-SING **A blaze of** publicity or attention is a great amount of it. 大量 ❑ *He was arrested in a blaze of publicity.* 他在铺天盖地的报道中被捕。 **5** V-I If guns **blaze**, or **blaze away**, they fire continuously, making a lot of noise. 连续射击 ❑ *Guns were blazing, flares going up and the sky was lit up all around.* 枪声响个不停，照明弹升起来，周围的天空都被照亮了。 **6** **with all guns blazing** → see **gun**

blaz·er /bleɪzər/ (**blazers**) N-COUNT A **blazer** is a kind of light jacket for men or women that is also often worn by members of a particular group. (一般男女或某特别群体成员穿的) 轻便短上衣

blaz·ing /bleɪzɪŋ/ ADJ The **blazing** sun or **blazing hot** weather is very hot. 炽热的 [ADJ n] ❑ *Quite a few people were eating outside in the blazing sun.* 相当多的人正在外面烈日下吃东西。

▲ **bleach** /blitʃ/ (**bleaches, bleaching, bleached**) **1** V-T If you **bleach** something, you use a chemical to make it white or pale in color. 漂白; 使脱色 ❑ *These products don't bleach the hair.* 这些产品不会使头发脱色。 ❑ *...bleached pine tables.* …褪色的松木桌。 **2** V-T/V-I If the sun **bleaches** something, or something **bleaches**, its color gets paler until it is almost white. 晒白; 逐渐变白 ❑ *The tree's roots are stripped and hung to season and bleach.* 这些树根被剥去皮并挂起来风干晒白。 ❑ *He has hair which is naturally black but which has been bleached by the sun.* 他有着一头天生的黑发，但已经被太阳晒得变淡了。 **3** N-MASS **Bleach** is a chemical that is used to make cloth white, or to clean things thoroughly and kill germs. 漂白剂

★ **bleak** /blik/ (**bleaker, bleakest**) **1** ADJ If a situation is **bleak**, it is bad, and seems unlikely to improve. 黯淡的 ❑ *The immediate outlook remains bleak.* 最近的前景依然很黯淡。 ● **bleak·ness** N-UNCOUNT 黯淡 ❑ *The continued bleakness of the American job market was blamed.* 美国就业市场的持续低迷被认为是其根源。 **2** ADJ If you describe a place as **bleak**, you mean that it looks cold, empty, and unattractive. 荒凉的 ❑ *The island's pretty bleak.* 这个岛很荒凉。 **3** ADJ When the weather is **bleak**, it is cold, dull, and unpleasant. 阴冷的 ❑ *The weather can be quite bleak on the coast.* 沿海一带的天气可能会十分阴冷。 **4** ADJ If someone looks or sounds **bleak**, they look or sound depressed, as if they have no hope or energy. 沮丧的 ❑ *His face was bleak.* 他面容沮丧。 ● **bleak·ly** ADV 沮丧地 ❑ *"There is nothing left," she says bleakly.* "一点也不剩了，"她沮丧地说。

bleed /blid/ (**bleeds, bleeding, bled**) **1** V-I When you **bleed**, you lose blood from your body as a result of injury or illness. 流血 ❑ *His head had struck the sink and was bleeding.* 他的头撞到了洗脸池上，

正在流血。 ❑ *He was bleeding profusely.* 他正大量流血。 ● **bleed·ing** N-UNCOUNT 出血 ❑ *This results in internal bleeding.* 这导致内部出血。 **2** V-I If the color of one substance **bleeds into** the color of another substance that it is touching, it goes into the other thing so that its color changes in an undesirable way. (颜色) 掺混 ❑ *The coloring pigments from the skins are not allowed to bleed into the grape juice.* 这些果皮的色素不允许掺混进葡萄汁中。 **3** V-T If someone **is being bled**, money or other resources are gradually being taken away from them. 榨取 (钱财) [DISAPPROVAL] ❑ *We have been gradually bled for twelve years.* 12年来，我们被逐渐榨尽了钱财。

blem·ish /blɛmɪʃ/ (**blemishes, blemishing, blemished**) **1** N-COUNT A **blemish** is a small mark on something that spoils its appearance. 瑕疵 ❑ *Every piece is closely scrutinized, and if there is the slightest blemish on it, it is rejected.* 每一件都经过仔细检查，如果上面有哪怕最微小的瑕疵，都会被拒绝。 **2** N-COUNT A **blemish on** something is a small fault in it. 小缺点 ❑ *This is the one blemish on an otherwise resounding success.* 这就是惟一那点小缺陷，否则将是圆满的成功。 **3** V-T If something **blemishes** someone's character or reputation, it spoils it or makes it seem less good than it was in the past. 损害 ❑ *He wasn't about to blemish that pristine record.* 他不想破坏那完美的记录。

blend /blɛnd/ (**blends, blending, blended**) **1** V-RECIP If you **blend** substances together or if they **blend**, you mix them together so that they become one substance. 混合 ❑ *Blend the butter with the sugar and beat until light and creamy.* 把黄油和糖混合起来，快速搅拌成松软的糊状。 ❑ *Blend the ingredients until you have a smooth cream.* 把这些配料调成均匀的糊状。 **2** N-COUNT A **blend of** things is a mixture or combination of them that is useful or pleasant. 调配；美妙的结合 ❑ *The public areas offer a subtle blend of traditional charm with modern amenities.* 这些公共场所表现出对传统魅力与现代设施的巧妙结合。 ❑ *...a blend of wine and sparkling water.* …葡萄酒与汽水的调配。 **3** V-RECIP When colors, sounds, or styles **blend**, they come together or are combined in a pleasing way. (色彩、声音或风格) 交融 ❑ *You could paint the walls and ceilings the same color so they blend together.* 你可以把这些墙和天花板漆成相同的颜色，这样它们就浑然一体。 **4** V-T If you **blend** ideas, policies, or styles, you use them together in order to achieve something. 融合 (不同的思想、政策或风格) ❑ *His vision is to blend Christianity with "the wisdom of all world religions."* 他的梦想是把世界上各种宗教的智慧融入到基督教。

★ **bless** /blɛs/ (**blesses, blessing, blessed**) **1** V-T When someone such as a priest **blesses** people or things, he or she asks for God's favor and protection for them. 祈求上帝祝福 ❑ *...asking for all present to bless this couple and their loving commitment to one another.* …请所有在场的人祈求上帝祝福这对夫妇及其对彼此爱的承诺。 **2** CONVENTION **Bless** is used in expressions such as "God bless" or "bless you" to express affection, thanks, or good wishes. 用于**God bless**，**bless you**等短句中，以表达友爱、谢意或祝福 [INFORMAL, SPOKEN, FEELINGS] ❑ *"Bless you, Eva," he whispered.* "愿上帝保佑你，伊娃，"他低声说道。 **3** CONVENTION You can say "**bless you**" to someone who has just sneezed. 长命百岁 (对打喷嚏的人说的话) [SPOKEN, FORMULAE] **4** → see also **blessed, blessing**

bless·ed

Pronounced /blɛst/ for meaning **1**, and /blɛsɪd/ for meaning **2**.

义项**1**读作 /blɛst/，义项**2**读作 /blɛsɪd/。

1 ADJ If someone is **blessed with** a particular good quality or skill, they have that good quality or skill. 有幸具有的 [v-link ADJ "with" n] ❑ *Both are blessed with an uncommon ability to fix things.* 俩人都有幸具有不寻常的修理东西的能力。 **2** ADJ You use **blessed** to describe something that you think is wonderful, and that you are grateful for or relieved about. 幸运的 [ADJ n] [APPROVAL] ❑ *The birth of a live healthy baby is a truly blessed event.* 生一个活泼健康的孩子确实是一件幸运的事。 ● **bless·ed·ly** ADV 幸运地 ❑ *...a wall still blessedly warm from the day's sun.* …一堵受到了日间阳光照晒依然温暖的墙。 **3** → see also **bless**

bless·ing /blɛsɪŋ/ (**blessings**) **1** N-COUNT A **blessing** is something good that you are grateful for. 幸事 ❑ *Rivers are a blessing for an agricultural country.* 河流是农业国的福祉。 **2** N-COUNT If something is done with someone's **blessing**, it is done with their approval and support. 同意；支持 [with poss] ❑ *With the blessing of the White House, a group of Democrats in Congress is meeting to find additional budget cuts.* 经白宫同意，国会中的一组民主党人正开会寻求进一步削减预算。 **3** N-COUNT A **blessing** is a prayer asking God to look kindly upon the people who are present or the event that is taking place. 祈福祷告 ❑ *The Reverend Chris Long led the prayers and pronounced the blessing.* 克里斯・朗牧师带领祷告并宣讲了祈福祷词。 **4** → see also **bless**

blew /blu/ **Blew** is the past tense of **blow**. **blow**的过去式

▲ **blight** /blaɪt/ (**blights, blighting, blighted**) **1** N-VAR You can refer to something as a **blight** when it causes great difficulties, and damages or spoils other things. 祸因 ❑ *This discriminatory policy has really been a blight on America.* 这项歧视政策一直以来确实是美国的一个祸因。 **2** V-T If something **blights** your life or your hopes, it damages and spoils them. If something **blights** an area, it spoils it and makes it unattractive. 使损害；使 (地区) 遭殃 ❑ *An embarrassing blunder nearly blighted his career before it got off the ground.* 他的事业还未起步，就差点因一次难堪的失误断送了。 ❑ *...thousands of families whose lives were blighted by unemployment.* …生活遭失业打击的数以千计的家庭。 **3** N-UNCOUNT **Blight** is a disease which makes plants dry up and die. 枯萎病 ❑ *All you can do to prevent potato blight is keep an eye on your crops.* 为预防马铃薯枯萎病你惟一能做的就是留意你的庄稼。

blind ♦◇◇ /blaɪnd/ (**blinds, blinding, blinded**) **1** ADJ Someone who is **blind** is unable to see because their eyes are damaged. 失明的 ❑ *I started helping him run the business when he went blind.* 他失明以后，我就开始帮他打理生意。 ● N-PLURAL **The blind** are people who are blind. 盲人 ❑ *He was a teacher of the blind.* 他过去是位教盲人的老师。 ● **blind·ness** N-UNCOUNT 失明 ❑ *Early diagnosis and treatment can usually prevent blindness.* 早期诊断和治疗通常可以防止失明。 **2** V-T If something **blinds** you, it makes you unable to see, either for a short time or permanently. 使看不见；使失明 ❑ *The sun hit the windshield, momentarily blinding him.* 阳光射在挡风玻璃上，使他一时看不见。 **3** ADJ If you are **blind with** something such as tears or a bright light, you are unable to see for a short time because of the tears or light. 因 (眼泪或强光) 而暂时看不见的 [v-link ADJ, usu ADJ "with" n] ❑ *Her mother groped for the back of the chair, her eyes blind with tears.* 她妈妈摸索着椅背，她的眼睛被眼泪遮住了视线。 ● **blind·ly** ADV 暂时看不见地 ❑ *Lettie groped blindly for the glass.* 莱蒂瞎子似地摸索着找杯子。 **4** ADJ If you say that someone is **blind to** a fact or a situation, you mean that they ignore it or are unaware of it, although you think that they should take notice of it or be aware of it. 视而不见的；没有觉察到的 [v-link ADJ "to" n] [DISAPPROVAL] ❑ *David's good looks and impeccable manners had always made her blind to his faults.* 大卫俊朗的外表和完美的风度总是令她对他的缺点视而不见。 ● **blind·ness** N-UNCOUNT 忽视 ❑ *...blindness in government policy to the very existence of the unemployed.* …政府政策中对失业人员的存在这一事实的忽视。 **5** V-T If something **blinds** you **to** the real situation, it prevents you from realizing that it exists or from understanding it properly. 使觉察不到；使理解不当 ❑ *He never allowed his love of Australia to blind him to his countrymen's faults.* 他从来不因自己对澳大利亚的热爱而无视同胞的过错。 **6** ADJ You can describe someone's beliefs or actions as **blind** when you think that they seem to take no notice of important facts or behave in an unreasonable way. 盲目的 [DISAPPROVAL] ❑ *...her blind faith in the wisdom of the church.* …她对教会箴言的盲目信仰。 **7** N-COUNT A **blind** is a roll of cloth or paper which you can pull down over a window as a covering. 窗帘；百叶窗帘 ❑ *Pulling the blinds up, she let some of the bright sunlight in.* 她拉起窗帘，让一些明媚的阳光照进来。 **8** → see also **blinding, blindly** **9** PHRASE If you say that someone **is turning a blind eye to** something bad or illegal that is happening, you mean that you think they are pretending not to notice that it is happening so that they will not have to do anything about it. 视而不见 [DISAPPROVAL] ❑ *Teachers are turning a blind eye to pupils smoking at school, a report reveals today.* 今天的一篇报道称，教师对学生在校抽烟视而不见。

→ see **disability**

Word Partnership *blind* 的常用搭配：

ADJ.	blind **and deaf** **1**
ADV.	**legally** blind, **partially** blind **1**
N.	blind **person** **1**
	blind **faith** **6**

blind·fold /blaɪndfoʊld/ (**blindfolds, blindfolding, blindfolded**) **1** N-COUNT A **blindfold** is a strip of cloth that is tied over someone's eyes so that they cannot see. 蒙眼布 **2** V-T If you

B

blindfold someone, you tie a blindfold over their eyes. 用布蒙住眼睛 ❑ *His abductors blindfolded him and drove him to an apartment in southern Beirut.* 绑架者们用布蒙住了他的眼睛，把他载到了贝鲁特南部的一套公寓。

blind·ing /bl<u>aɪ</u>ndɪŋ/ **1** ADJ A **blinding** light is extremely bright. 耀眼的 ❑ *The doctor worked busily beneath the blinding lights of the delivery room.* 医生在产房耀眼的灯光下忙碌地工作。 **2** ADJ You use **blinding** to emphasize that something is very obvious. 极为明显的 [ADJ n] [EMPHASIS] ❑ *The miseries I went through made me suddenly realize with a blinding flash what life was all about.* 我所经受的苦难令我豁然顿悟生命的意义。 **3** ADJ **Blinding** pain is very strong pain. (疼痛) 剧烈的 ❑ *There was a pain then, a quick, blinding agony that jumped along Danlo's spine.* 接下来，一阵急剧的疼痛穿过了丹娄的脊椎。

blind·ly /bl<u>aɪ</u>ndli/ **1** ADV If you say that someone does something **blindly**, you mean that they do it without having enough information, or without thinking about it. 盲目地 [DISAPPROVAL] ❑ *Don't just blindly follow what the banker says.* 不要盲目地听从这位银行家的话。 ❑ *Without adequate information, many students choose a college almost blindly.* 由于没有足够的信息，很多学生几乎都是盲目地选择大学。 **2** → see also **blind**

blind trust (**blind trusts**) N-COUNT A **blind trust** is a financial arrangement in which someone's investments are managed without the person knowing where the money is invested. **Blind trusts** are used especially by people in public office, so that they cannot be accused of using their position to make money unfairly. 保密信托 [BUSINESS] ❑ *Yang transferred the shares into a blind trust earlier this week.* 这个星期的早些时候杨把股票转成了保密信托。

bling /blɪŋ/ or **bling-bling** N-UNCOUNT Some people refer to expensive or fancy jewelry or clothes as **bling** or **bling-bling**. 奢华高档的首饰或服装 [INFORMAL] ❑ *Big-name jewelers are battling it out to get celebrities to wear their bling.* 大牌珠宝商们为了让名人们戴他们的高档首饰正在一争高下。 ❑ *...gangsta rap's love of bling-bling.* …匪帮说唱乐手对奢华高档服饰的热爱。

★ **blink** /blɪŋk/ (**blinks, blinking, blinked**) **1** V-T/V-I When you **blink** or when you **blink** your eyes, you shut your eyes and very quickly open them again. 眨 (眼睛) ❑ *Kathryn blinked and forced a smile.* 凯瑟琳眨了眨眼，挤出了一丝微笑。 ❑ *She was blinking her eyes rapidly.* 她一直在快速地眨眼。 ● N-COUNT **Blink** is also a noun. 眨眼 ❑ *He kept giving quick blinks.* 他不停地快速眨眼。 **2** V-I When a light **blinks**, it flashes on and off. 闪烁 ❑ *Green and yellow lights blinked on the surface of the harbor.* 绿色和黄色的灯光在港湾水面上闪烁。 ❑ *The plane was flying normally for about 15 minutes before a warning light blinked on.* 飞机正常飞行15分钟后警示灯开始闪烁。

▲ **bliss** /blɪs/ N-UNCOUNT **Bliss** is a state of complete happiness. 极乐 ❑ *It was a scene of such domestic bliss.* 这是一幅天伦之乐的场景。

bliss·ful /blɪsfəl/ **1** ADJ A **blissful** situation or period of time is one in which you are extremely happy. 极乐的 ❑ *We spent a blissful week together.* 我们在一起度过了极为幸福的一周。 ● **bliss·ful·ly** /blɪsfəli/ ADV 极幸福地 ❑ *We're blissfully happy.* 我们非常幸福快乐。 **2** ADJ If someone is in **blissful** ignorance of something unpleasant or serious, they are totally unaware of it. (由于对不快之事或严重事态毫无察觉而) 无忧无虑的 [ADJ n] ❑ *Many country towns were still living in blissful ignorance of the post-war crime wave.* 很多乡间小镇对战后的犯罪潮一无所知，依然生活在无忧无虑中。 ● **bliss·ful·ly** ADV 无忧无虑地 ❑ *At first, he was blissfully unaware of the conspiracy against him.* 起初，他对反对自己的阴谋全不知情，还在优哉游哉。

▲ **blis·ter** /blɪstər/ (**blisters, blistering, blistered**) **1** N-COUNT A **blister** is a painful swelling on the surface of your skin. Blisters contain a clear liquid and are usually caused by heat or by something repeatedly rubbing your skin. (皮肤上的) 水疱 **2** V-T/V-I When your skin **blisters** or when something **blisters** it, blisters appear on it. 使起水疱；起水疱 ❑ *The affected skin turns red and may blister.* 受感染的皮肤会变红，并可能起水疱。 ❑ *The sap of this plant blisters the skin.* 这种植物的汁液会使皮肤起水疱。

blis·ter·ing /blɪstərɪŋ/ **1** ADJ **Blistering** heat is very great heat. 酷热的 ❑ *...a blistering summer day.* …一个酷热的夏日。 **2** ADJ A **blistering** remark expresses great anger or dislike. 愤怒的；憎恶的 ❑ *The president responded to this with a blistering attack on his critics.* 总统对此愤怒地回击了他的批评者们。 **3** ADJ **Blistering** is used to describe actions in sports to emphasize that they are done with great speed or force. 风驰电掣般的 [ADJ n] [JOURNALISM, EMPHASIS] ❑ *Sharon Wild set a blistering pace to take the lead.* 莎伦·王尔德以风驰电掣般的速度居于领先位置。

blithe /bl<u>aɪ</u>ð/ ADJ You use **blithe** to indicate that something is done casually, without serious or careful thought. 漫不经心的 [DISAPPROVAL] ❑ *Acts of trespass and petty theft often grew out of the blithe disregard that boys had for private property.* 擅自侵入和小偷小摸的行为经常出自于男孩子们对私有财物漫不经心的轻视态度。 ● **blithe·ly** ADV 漫不经心地 ❑ *Your editorial blithely ignores the hard facts.* 你们的社论轻率地忽略了铁的事实。

blitz /blɪts/ (**blitzes, blitzing, blitzed**) **1** N-COUNT If you have a **blitz on** something, you make a big effort to deal with it or to improve it. 突击处理；大力改进 [INFORMAL] ❑ *Regional accents are still acceptable but there is to be a blitz on incorrect grammar.* 地方口音还可以接受，但错误语法必须要大力改进。 **2** N-PROPER The heavy bombing of British cities by German aircraft in 1940 and 1941 is referred to as **the Blitz**. 在1940至1941年间德国空军对英国城市的大空袭 **3** V-T If a city or building **is blitzed** during a war, it is attacked by bombs dropped by enemy aircraft. 空袭 ❑ *In the autumn of 1940 London was blitzed by an average of two hundred aircraft a night.* 1940年秋，伦敦平均每晚被两百架飞机空袭。

bliz·zard /blɪzərd/ (**blizzards**) N-COUNT A **blizzard** is a very bad snowstorm with strong winds. 暴风雪
→ see **storm, weather**

bloat·ed /bl<u>oʊ</u>tɪd/ **1** ADJ If someone's body or a part of their body is **bloated**, it is much larger than normal, usually because it has a lot of liquid or gas inside it. 肿胀的 ❑ *...the bloated body of a dead bullock.* …一头小公牛的肿胀尸体。 **2** ADJ If you feel **bloated** after eating a large meal, you feel very full and uncomfortable. 饱胀的 [V-link ADJ] ❑ *Diners do not want to leave the table feeling bloated.* 用餐者们不想离开餐桌的时候感到肚胀。

blob /blɒb/ (**blobs**) **1** N-COUNT A **blob of** thick or sticky liquid is a small, often round, amount of it. (粘稠的) 一滴；一团 [INFORMAL, INFORMAL] ❑ *...a blob of chocolate mousse.* …一团巧克力奶油冻。 **2** N-COUNT You can use **blob** to refer to something that you cannot see very clearly, for example because it is in the distance. 模糊不清的一团东西 [INFORMAL] ❑ *You could just see vague blobs of faces.* 你只能看到一张张模模糊糊的脸。

★ **bloc** /blɒk/ (**blocs**) N-COUNT A **bloc** is a group of countries that have similar political aims and interests and that act together over some issues. (具有相似政治目标和利益的国家结成的) 阵营 ❑ *...the former Soviet bloc.* …前苏联阵营。

block ◆◆◇ /blɒk/ (**blocks, blocking, blocked**) **1** N-COUNT A **block of** a substance is a large rectangular piece of it. 大块 ❑ *...a block of ice.* …一大块冰。 **2** N-COUNT A **block** of apartments or offices is a large building containing them. 大楼 ❑ *...a white-painted apartment block.* …一幢漆成白色的公寓楼。 **3** N-COUNT A **block** in a town or city is an area of land with streets on all its sides, or the area or distance between such streets. 街区 ❑ *He walked around the block three times.* 他绕着这个街区走了3圈。 ❑ *She walked four blocks down High Street.* 她沿着高街走了4个街区。 **4** N-COUNT **Blocks** are wooden or plastic cubes, such as those used as toys by children. 积木 **5** V-T To **block** a road, channel, or pipe means to put an object across it or in it so that nothing can pass through it or along it. 堵塞；封锁 ❑ *Some students today blocked a highway that cuts through the center of the city.* 一些学生今天封锁了穿过市中心的公路。 **6** V-T If something **blocks** your view, it prevents you from seeing something because it is between you and that thing. 挡住 ❑ *...a row of spruce trees that blocked his view of the long north slope of the mountain.* …挡住了他看向山北长坡视线的一排云杉。 **7** V-T If you **block** someone's way, you prevent them from going somewhere or entering a place by standing in front of them. 阻挡 ❑ *I started to move around him, but he blocked my way.* 我开始绕开他走，但他挡着我的路。 **8** V-T If you **block** something that is being arranged, you prevent it from being done. 阻止 ❑ *For years the country has tried to block imports of various cheap foreign products.* 多年以来，这个国家曾试图阻止多种外国廉价产品的进口。 **9** N-COUNT A **block of** something such as tickets or shares is a large quantity of them, especially when they are all sold at the same time and are in a particular sequence or order. 一大叠 (一次大量购买的入场券、股票等) [usu N "of" n] ❑ *Those booking a block of seats get them at reduced rates.* 那些一次预订大量座位的人可以享受折扣价。 **10** N-COUNT If you have a **mental block** or a **block**, you are temporarily unable to do something that you can normally do which involves using, thinking about, or remembering something. (思维、记忆等的) 阻滞 ❑ *I cannot do math. I've got a mental block about it.* 我做不了数学。我一做就大脑一片空白。 **11** → see also **stumbling block**

▸ **block out** 1 PHRASAL VERB If someone **blocks out** a thought, they try not to think about it. 排除（想法）❑ *She accuses me of having blocked out the past.* 她指责我忘记了过去。 2 PHRASAL VERB Something that **blocks out** light prevents it from reaching a place. 遮挡（光线）❑ *He pulled down the shades, blocking out the bright sunlight.* 他拉下了窗帘，遮挡住强烈的阳光。

▲ **block·ade** /blɒkeɪd/ (**blockades, blockading, blockaded**) 1 N-COUNT A **blockade** of a place is an action that is taken to prevent goods or people from entering or leaving it. 封锁 ❑ *It's not yet clear who will actually enforce the blockade.* 目前还不清楚到底谁会来执行封锁。 2 V-T If a group of people **blockade** a place, they stop goods or people from reaching that place. If they **blockade** a road or a port, they stop people from using that road or port. 封锁 ❑ *About 50,000 people are trapped in the town, which has been blockaded for more than 40 days.* 约有五万人被困在这个已经被封锁了40多天的小镇里。

block·age /blɒkɪdʒ/ (**blockages**) N-COUNT A **blockage in** a pipe, tube, or tunnel is an object which blocks it, or the state of being blocked. 堵塞物；堵塞 ❑ *The logical treatment is to remove this blockage.* 合理的处理方法是清除这种堵塞物。

block·bust·er /blɒkbʌstər/ (**blockbusters**) N-COUNT A **blockbuster** is a movie or book that is very popular and successful, usually because it is very exciting. 大片；畅销书 [INFORMAL] ❑ *...the latest Hollywood blockbuster.* …最新的好莱坞大片。

block of flats [BRIT] → see **apartment building**

blog /blɒg/ (**blogs**) N-COUNT A **blog** is a website containing a diary or journal on a particular subject. 博客；网络日志 [COMPUTING] ❑ *When Barbieux started his blog, his aspirations were small; he simply hoped to communicate with a few people.* 当巴布开始他的博客时，他的期望并不大。他只是希望能与几个人交流。 ● **blog·ger** N-COUNT (**bloggers**) ❑ *While most bloggers comment on news reported elsewhere, some do their own reporting.* 虽然大多博客对别处报道的新闻发表意见，有些却做他们自己的报道。 ● **blog·ging** N-UNCOUNT ❑ *...the explosion in the popularity of blogging.* …博客流行的急速扩张。
→ see Word Web: **blog**

blogo·sphere /blɒgəsfɪər/ or **blogsphere** /blɒgsfɪər/ N-SING In computer technology, **the blogosphere** or **the blogsphere** is all the weblogs on the Internet, considered collectively. 博客空间；网志空间 ["the" N] ❑ *Consequently, even as the blogosphere continues to expand, only a few blogs are likely to emerge as focal points.* 因此，虽然博客空间继续扩大，但只有少数博客有可能脱颖而出成为焦点。 ❑ *The blogsphere has changed a lot in the past few years.* 网志空间在过去的几年变了许多。
→ see **blog**

▲ **blonde** /blɒnd/ (**blondes, blonder, blondest**)

> The form **blonde** is usually used to refer to women, and **blond** to refer to men.

1 COLOR A woman who has **blonde** hair has pale-colored hair. Blonde hair can be very light brown or light yellow. The form **blond** is used when describing men. 浅色的；（头发）金黄色的 ❑ *...a little girl with blonde hair.* …一头金发的小女孩。 2 ADJ Someone who is **blonde** has blonde hair. 金发的 ❑ *He was blonder than his brother.* 他的头发比哥哥的还黄。 3 N-COUNT A **blonde** is a woman who has blonde hair. 金发女子 ❑ *...a stunning blonde in her early thirties.* …一位美貌惊人的三十出头的金发女郎。

blood ♦♦◊ /blʌd/ 1 N-UNCOUNT **Blood** is the red liquid that flows inside your body, which you can see if you cut yourself. 血液 ❑ *His shirt was covered in blood.* 他的衬衫沾满了血。 2 N-UNCOUNT You can use **blood** to refer to the race or social class of someone's parents or ancestors. 血统 ❑ *There was Greek blood in his veins: his ancestors originally bore the name Karajannis.* 他有希腊血统——他的祖先原来姓卡拉扬尼斯。 3 PHRASE If you say that there is **bad blood between** people, you mean that they have argued about something and dislike each other. 积怨 ❑ *There is, it seems, some bad blood between Mills and the Baldwins.* 米尔和鲍德温两家看上去好像有积怨。 4 PHRASE If something violent and cruel is done **in cold blood**, it is done deliberately and in an unemotional way. 残忍蓄意地 [DISAPPROVAL] ❑ *The crime had been committed in cold blood.* 这起案件是蓄意犯罪。 5 → see also **cold-blooded** 6 PHRASE If you say that someone has a person's **blood on** their **hands**, you mean that they are responsible for that person's death. 应对某人的死亡负责 ❑ *He has my son's blood on his hands. I hope it haunts him for the rest of his days.* 他应该对我儿子的死负责，但愿他终生不得安宁。 7 PHRASE If a quality or talent is **in your blood**, it is part of your nature, and other members of your family have it too. 天生遗传的 ❑ *Diplomacy was in his blood: his ancestors had been feudal lords.* 他的外交能力是天生的：他的祖上曾是封建王侯。 8 PHRASE You can use the expressions **new blood, fresh blood**, or **young blood** to refer to people who are brought into an organization to improve it by thinking of new ideas or new ways of doing things. 新生力量 ❑ *There's been a major reshuffle of the cabinet to bring in new blood.* 内阁进行了重大改组以吸纳新生力量。 9 **flesh and blood** → see **flesh** 10 **own flesh and blood** → see **flesh**
→ see **donor**

Word Partnership *blood* 的常用搭配:

N.	**(red/white)** blood **cells**, blood **clot**, blood **disease**, blood **loss**, **pool of** blood, blood **sample**, blood **supply**, blood **test**, blood **transfusion** 1
V.	**donate/give** blood 1
ADJ.	**covered in** blood, blood **stained** 1
	related by blood 2
	bad blood 3
PREP.	**in** *someone's* blood 2 7

blood pres·sure N-UNCOUNT Your **blood pressure** is the amount of force with which your blood flows around your body. 血压 ❑ *Your doctor will monitor your blood pressure.* 你的医生会监测你的血压。
→ see **diagnosis**

blood·shed /blʌdʃɛd/ N-UNCOUNT **Bloodshed** is violence in which people are killed or wounded. 流血暴力 ❑ *The government must increase the pace of reforms to avoid further bloodshed.* 政府必须加快改革的步伐以避免更多的流血事件。

blood·stream /blʌdstrim/ (**bloodstreams**) N-COUNT Your **bloodstream** is the blood that flows around your body. （体内循环的）血流 ❑ *The disease releases toxins into the bloodstream.* 这种疾病将毒素释放进血流中。

blood test (**blood tests**) N-COUNT A **blood test** is a medical examination of a small amount of your blood. 验血

blood ves·sel (**blood vessels**) N-COUNT **Blood vessels** are the narrow tubes through which your blood flows. 血管

Word Web blog

The word **blog** is a combination of the words **web** and **log**. It is a **website** containing a series of dated **entries**. A blog can focus on a single subject of interest. Most blogs are written by individuals. But sometimes a political committee, corporation, or other group maintains a blog. Many blogs invite readers to leave **comments** on the site. This often results in a community of **bloggers** who write back and forth to each other. The total group of web logs is the **blogosphere**. A blogstorm occurs when there is a lot of blog activity on a certain topic.

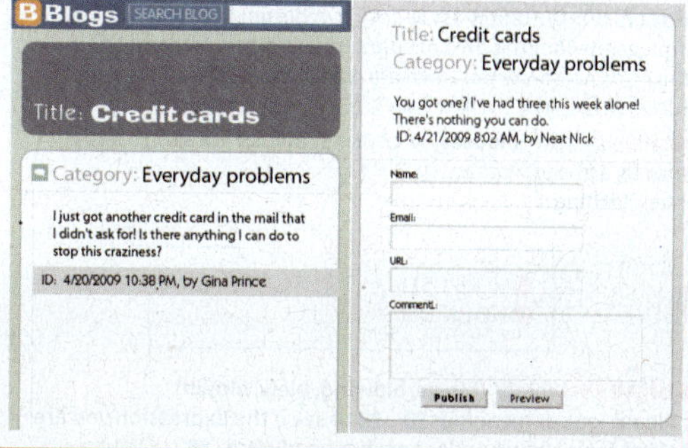

B

bloody ◆◇◇ /blʌdi/ (**bloodier, bloodiest, bloodies, bloodying, bloodied**) 1 ADJ If you describe a situation or event as **bloody**, you mean that it is very violent and a lot of people are killed. 血腥的 ❑ *Forty-three demonstrators were killed in bloody clashes.* 43名示威者在血腥冲突中丧命。 2 ADJ You can describe someone or something as **bloody** if they are covered in a lot of blood. 沾满血迹的 ❑ *He was arrested last October still carrying a bloody knife.* 他去年10月被捕时还拿着一把血迹斑斑的刀。 3 V-T If you have **bloodied** part of your body, there is blood on it, usually because you have had an accident or you have been attacked. 使流血 ❑ *One of our children fell and bloodied his knee.* 我们的一个孩子摔得膝盖流血了。

bloom /blum/ (**blooms, blooming, bloomed**) 1 N-COUNT A **bloom** is the flower on a plant. 花 [LITERARY] ❑ *The sweet fragrance of the white blooms makes this climber a favorite.* 白色花朵散发出的甜香使这株藤蔓成了宠儿。 2 PHRASE A plant or tree that is **in bloom** has flowers on it. 开花 ❑ *...a pink climbing rose in full bloom.* …一朵盛开的粉色攀缘玫瑰。 3 V-I When a plant or tree **blooms**, it produces flowers. When a flower **blooms**, it opens. 开花；(花) 开 ❑ *This plant blooms between May and June.* 这种植物在五六月间开花。 4 V-I If someone or something **blooms**, they develop good, attractive, or successful qualities. 蓬勃发展 ❑ *Not many economies bloomed in 1990, least of all gold exporters like Australia.* 没有几个国家的经济在1990年蓬勃发展，尤其是像澳大利亚这样的金矿出口国。 5 N-UNCOUNT If something such as someone's skin has a **bloom**, it has a fresh and healthy appearance. 红润 [also "a" N] ❑ *The skin loses its youthful bloom.* 皮肤失去了年轻时的红润。

blos·som /blɒsəm/ (**blossoms, blossoming, blossomed**) 1 N-VAR **Blossom** is the flowers that appear on a tree before the fruit. (果树的) 花 ❑ *The cherry blossom came out early in Washington this year.* 华盛顿的樱花今年开得早。 2 V-I If someone or something **blossoms**, they develop good, attractive, or successful qualities. 成功发展 ❑ *Why do some people take longer than others to blossom?* 为什么有些人比其他人大器晚成呢？ ❑ *What began as a local festival has blossomed into an international event.* 开始时的一个地方节日已经发展成了一个国际盛会。 3 V-I When a tree **blossoms**, it produces blossom. (树) 开花 ❑ *Rain begins to fall and peach trees blossom.* 雨开始下，桃树就开花了。

▲ **blot** /blɒt/ (**blots, blotting, blotted**) 1 N-COUNT If something is a **blot on** a person's or thing's reputation, it spoils their reputation. (名誉上的) 污点 ❑ *...a blot on the reputation of the architectural profession.* …建筑业名声上的污点。 2 N-COUNT A **blot** is a drop of liquid that has fallen on to a surface and has dried. 污渍 ❑ *...an ink blot.* …一滴墨水渍。 3 V-T If you **blot** a surface, you remove liquid from it by pressing a piece of soft paper or cloth onto it. (用纸、布) 吸干 ❑ *Before applying makeup, blot the face with a tissue to remove any excess oils.* 化妆之前，用纸巾吸干脸上所有过多的油。

▸ **blot out** 1 PHRASAL VERB If one thing **blots out** another thing, it is in front of the other thing and prevents it from being seen. 遮挡 ❑ *About the time the three climbers were halfway down, clouds blotted out the sun.* 当3位登山者下到半山腰的时候，云层遮住了太阳。 ❑ *The victim's face was blotted out by a camera blur.* 受害者的面部图像被做了模糊处理。 2 PHRASAL VERB If you try to **blot out** a memory, you try to forget it. If one thought or memory **blots out** other thoughts or memories, it becomes the only one that you can think about. 抹掉 (记忆)；(思想、记忆) 占据全部大脑 ❑ *Are you saying that she's trying to blot out all memory of the incident?* 你是说她想抹掉对那次事件的一切记忆吗？ ❑ *The boy has gaps in his mind about it. He is blotting certain things out.* 这个男孩对此事的记忆有缺失，他对有些事情不记得了。

blotch /blɒtʃ/ (**blotches**) N-COUNT A **blotch** is a small unpleasant-looking area of color, for example, on someone's skin. 色斑 ❑ *His face was covered in red blotches, seemingly a nasty case of acne.* 他脸上布满了红斑，看起来像是严重的痤疮。

blouse /blaʊs/ (**blouses**) N-COUNT A **blouse** is a kind of shirt worn by a girl or woman. 女式衬衫
→ see **clothing**

blow
❶ VERB USES
❷ NOUN USES

❶ **blow** ◆◆◇ /bloʊ/ (**blows, blowing, blew, blown**)
➪ **Please look at meanings 12 – 15 to see if the expression you are looking for is shown under another headword.** 1 V-I When a wind or breeze **blows**, the air moves. 刮风 ❑ *A chill wind blew at the top of the hill.* 山顶上刮了一阵凉飕飕的风。 2 V-T/V-I If the wind **blows** something somewhere or if it **blows** there, the wind moves it there. 把…吹到；吹 ❑ *The wind blew her hair back from her forehead.* 风把她额头上的头发向后吹。 ❑ *Sand blew in our eyes.* 沙子吹进了我们眼里。 3 V-I If you **blow**, you send out a stream of air from your mouth. 呵气 ❑ *Danny rubbed his arms and blew on his fingers to warm them.* 丹尼搓着胳膊，向他的手指上呵气来暖手。 4 V-T If you **blow** something somewhere, you move it by sending out a stream of air from your mouth. (人) 把…吹到 ❑ *He picked up his mug and blew off the steam.* 他端起杯子吹掉蒸汽。 5 V-T If you **blow** bubbles or smoke rings, you make them by blowing air out of your mouth through liquid or smoke. 吹出 (肥皂泡、烟圈等) ❑ *He blew a ring of blue smoke.* 他吐出了一圈蓝烟。 6 V-T/V-I When a whistle or horn **blows** or someone **blows** it, they make a sound by blowing into it. 吹 (口哨、喇叭)；吹响 ❑ *The whistle blew and the train slid forward.* 汽笛吹响，火车向前滑动。 7 V-T When you **blow** your nose, you force air out of it through your nostrils in order to clear it. 擤 (鼻子) ❑ *He took out a handkerchief and blew his nose.* 他掏出手帕擤鼻子。 8 V-T To **blow** something **out**, **off**, or **away** means to remove or destroy it violently with an explosion. 炸毁 ❑ *The can exploded, wrecking the kitchen and bathroom and blowing out windows.* 罐子爆炸了，毁了厨房和浴室，也炸掉了窗户。 9 V-T If you **blow** a chance or attempt to do something, you make a mistake which wastes the chance or causes the attempt to fail. 使 (机会) 告吹 [INFORMAL] ❑ *One careless word could blow the whole deal.* 一句不经意的话可能使整笔交易告吹。 ❑ *Oh you fool! You've blown it!* 傻瓜！你把它搞砸了！ 10 V-T If you say that something **blows** an event, situation, or argument into a particular extreme state, especially an uncertain or unpleasant state, you mean that it causes it to be in that state. 搞成 (极端局面) ❑ *Someone took an inappropriate use of words on my part and tried to blow it into a major controversy.* 有人不当借用了我说的话，想要挑起一场大争端。 11 V-T If you **blow** a large amount of money, you spend it quickly on luxuries. 挥霍 [INFORMAL] ❑ *My brother lent me some money and I went and blew it all.* 我哥哥借给我一些钱，我全都挥霍掉了。 12 → see also **full-blown**
13 to **blow hot and cold** → see **hot** 14 to **blow a kiss** → see **kiss**
15 to **blow the whistle** → see **whistle**
→ see **glass, wind**

▸ **blow away** PHRASAL VERB If you say that you **are blown away** by something, or if it **blows** you **away**, you mean that you are very impressed by it. 给…留下深刻印象；深深打动 [INFORMAL] ❑ *I was blown away by the tone and the quality of the story.* 我深深地被故事的基调和格调所打动。 ❑ *Everyone I met overwhelmed me and kind of blew me away.* 我遇到的每个人都让我很感动，可以说给我留下了深刻的印象。

▸ **blow off** PHRASAL VERB If you **blow** something **off**, you ignore it or choose not to deal with it. 不理会 [AM, INFORMAL] ❑ *I don't think we can afford just to blow this off.* 我想我们担负不起对此置之不理。

▸ **blow out** PHRASAL VERB If you **blow out** a flame or a candle, you blow at it so that it stops burning. 吹灭 ❑ *I blew out the candle.* 我吹灭了蜡烛。

▸ **blow over** PHRASAL VERB If something such as trouble or an argument **blows over**, it ends without any serious consequences. (麻烦、争论等) 平息 ❑ *Wait, and it'll all blow over.* 等等吧，事情总会过去的。

▸ **blow up** 1 PHRASAL VERB If someone **blows** something **up** or if it **blows up**, it is destroyed by an explosion. 爆炸 ❑ *He was jailed for 45 years for trying to blow up a plane.* 他因图谋炸飞机而被监禁了45年。 2 PHRASAL VERB If you **blow up** something such as a balloon or a tire, you fill it with air. 给…充气 ❑ *Other than blowing up a tire I hadn't done any car maintenance.* 除了给一个轮胎充气外，我没有做过任何汽车保养。 3 PHRASAL VERB If a wind or a storm **blows up**, the weather becomes very windy or stormy. (风、暴风雨) 大作 ❑ *A storm blew up over the mountains.* 山上狂风大作。 4 PHRASAL VERB If you **blow up at** someone, you lose your temper and shout at them. 大发脾气 [INFORMAL] ❑ *I'm sorry I blew up at you.* 对不起，我冲你发脾气了。 5 PHRASAL VERB If someone **blows** an incident **up** or if it **blows up**, it is made to seem more serious or important than it really is. 夸大 ❑ *Newspapers blew up the story.* 报纸夸大了这个故事。 ❑ *The media may be blowing it up out of proportion.* 媒体可能对此事很大程度地夸大其词。 6 PHRASAL VERB If a photographic image **is blown up**, a large copy is made of it. 放大 ❑ *The image is blown up on a large screen.* 图像在大屏幕上被放大了。

❷ **blow** ♦◇◇ /bloʊ/ (**blows**) **1** N-COUNT If someone receives a **blow**, they are hit with a fist or weapon. (用拳或武器的) 击打 ❑ *He went to the hospital after a blow to the face.* 他脸上挨了一拳后就去了医院。 **2** N-COUNT If something that happens is a **blow to** someone or something, it is very upsetting, disappointing, or damaging to them. 打击 ❑ *That ruling comes as a blow to environmentalists.* 那项规定对环境保护主义者是一个打击。

Word Partnership *blow* 的常用搭配:

ADV.	blow **away** ❶ 2 8
N.	blow **bubbles**, blow **smoke** ❶ 5
	blow **a whistle** ❶ 6
	blow *your* **nose** ❶ 7
V.	**deliver/strike a** blow ❷ 1
	cushion/soften a blow, **suffer a** blow ❷ 1 2
ADJ.	**crushing/devastating/heavy** blow ❷ 1 2
PREP.	blow **to the head** ❷ 1
	blow **to** *someone* ❷ 2

bludg·eon /blʌdʒ°n/ (**bludgeons, bludgeoning, bludgeoned**) V-T To **bludgeon** someone means to hit them several times with a heavy object. (用重器) 连击 ❑ *He broke into the old man's house and bludgeoned him with a hammer.* 他闯进那位老人的家，用锤子连打他。

blue ♦♦♦ /blu/ (**bluer, bluest, blues**) **1** COLOR Something that is **blue** is the color of the sky on a sunny day. 蓝色的; 天蓝色的 ❑ *There were swallows in the cloudless blue sky.* 燕子在无云的蓝天上飞翔。 ❑ *She fixed her pale blue eyes on her father's.* 她用那蔚蓝色的双眼盯着父亲的眼睛。 **2** N-PLURAL **The blues** is a type of music which was developed by African American musicians in the southern United States. It is characterized by a slow tempo and a strong rhythm. 蓝调音乐 ❑ *Can white girls sing the blues?* 白人女孩会唱蓝调吗? **3** ADJ If you are feeling **blue**, you are feeling sad or depressed, often when there is no particular reason. 心情低落的 [v-link ADJ] [INFORMAL] ❑ *There's no earthly reason for me to feel so blue.* 我完全没有理由感到如此低落。 **4** ADJ If a U.S. state is described as **blue**, it means that the majority of its residents vote for the Democratic Party in elections, especially in the presidential elections. 蓝色阵营的 (美国总统大选时民主党的主要选区) ❑ *This issue could drive an even bigger wedge between the red and blue states.* 这个问题可能会进一步造成红色选区和蓝色选区之间的不和。
→ see **color, rainbow**

blue·berry /bluberi/ (**blueberries**) N-COUNT A **blueberry** is a small dark blue fruit that is found in North America. 蓝莓

blue chip (**blue chips**) N-COUNT **Blue chip** stocks and shares are an investment which are considered fairly safe to invest in while also being profitable. 蓝筹股 [BUSINESS] ❑ *Blue chip issues were sharply higher, but the rest of the market actually declined slightly by the end of the day.* 蓝筹股急剧上涨，但其他上市股票收盘时实际上均有小幅下跌。

blue-collar ADJ **Blue-collar** workers work in industry, doing physical work, rather than in offices. 蓝领的 [ADJ n] ❑ *It wasn't just the blue-collar workers who lost their jobs, it was everyone.* 不只是蓝领工人失去了工作，而是每一个人。

★ **blue·print** /bluprɪnt/ (**blueprints**) **1** N-COUNT A **blueprint for** something is a plan or set of proposals that shows how it is expected to work. 蓝图 ❑ *The president will offer delegates his blueprint for the country's future.* 总统将向代表们提出他的国家未来蓝图。 **2** N-COUNT A **blueprint** of an architect's building plans or a designer's pattern is a photographic print consisting of white lines on a blue background. Blueprints contain all of the information that is needed to build or make something. (建筑师的) 蓝图 ❑ *...a blueprint of the whole place, complete with heating ducts and wiring.* …整个地方的蓝图，连带暖气管道和线路。 **3** N-COUNT A genetic **blueprint** is a pattern that is contained within all living cells. This pattern decides how the organism develops and what it looks like. (基因的) 图谱 ❑ *The offspring contain a mixture of the genetic blueprint of each parent.* 后代体内含有父母亲基因图谱的混合。
→ see **copy**

Blue·tooth /blutuθ/ N-UNCOUNT **Bluetooth** is a type of short-range wireless technology that allows portable devices such as cell phones, laptops, and PDAs to communicate with each other. 蓝牙 [oft N n] [TRADEMARK] ❑ *...the latest Bluetooth technology.* …最新的蓝牙技术。

▲ **bluff** /blʌf/ (**bluffs, bluffing, bluffed**) **1** N-VAR A **bluff** is an attempt to make someone believe that you will do something when you do not really intend to do it. 虚张声势 ❑ *The letter was a bluff.* 这封信是虚张声势。 ❑ *It is essential to build up the military option and show that this is not a bluff.* 重要的是准备军事解决途径来证明这并不是虚张声势。 **2** PHRASE If you **call** someone's **bluff**, you tell them to do what they have been threatening to do, because you are sure that they will not really do it. 要某人摊牌 ❑ *The socialists have decided to call the opposition's bluff.* 社会党人已经决定让反对党摊牌了。 **3** V-T/V-I If you **bluff**, you make someone believe that you will do something when you do not really intend to do it, or that you know something when you do not really know it. 用…虚张声势; 招摇撞骗 ❑ *Either side, or both, could be bluffing.* 任何一方或者双方都可能是在虚张声势。 ❑ *In each case the hijackers bluffed the crew using fake grenades.* 每一次，劫机者都是用假手榴弹骗机组人员。

★ **blun·der** /blʌndər/ (**blunders, blundering, blundered**) **1** N-COUNT A **blunder** is a stupid or careless mistake. 愚蠢错误 ❑ *I think he made a tactical blunder by announcing it so far ahead of time.* 我认为他如此提早宣布消息是犯了战术上的错误。 **2** V-I If you **blunder**, you make a stupid or careless mistake. 犯愚蠢错误 ❑ *No doubt I had blundered again.* 不用说我又犯了个蠢错。 **3** V-I If you **blunder into** a dangerous or difficult situation, you get involved in it by mistake. 误入 (危险境地或困境) ❑ *People wanted to know how they had blundered into war, and how to avoid it in the future.* 人们想弄清他们怎么会错误地卷入战争，将来如何才能避免这样的事。 **4** V-I If you **blunder** somewhere, you move there in a clumsy and careless way. 跌跌撞撞地走 ❑ *He had blundered into the table, upsetting the flowers.* 他撞上了桌子，打翻了花。

★ **blunt** /blʌnt/ (**blunter, bluntest, blunts, blunting, blunted**) **1** ADJ If you are **blunt**, you say exactly what you think without trying to be polite. 直言不讳的 ❑ *She is blunt about her personal life.* 她对自己的私生活直言不讳。 ● **blunt·ly** ADV 直言不讳地 [ADV with v] ❑ *"I don't believe you!" Jeanne said bluntly.* "我不信你!" 珍妮直言不讳地说。 ● **blunt·ness** N-UNCOUNT 率直 ❑ *His bluntness got him into trouble.* 他的率直给他招惹了麻烦。 **2** ADJ A **blunt** object has a rounded or flat end rather than a sharp one. 钝的 [ADJ n] ❑ *One of them had been struck 13 times over the head with a blunt object.* 他们其中一人的头部被钝器砸了13下。 **3** ADJ A **blunt** knife or blade is no longer sharp and does not cut well. 不锋利的 ❑ *The edge is as blunt as an old butter knife.* 刃钝得跟一把老黄油刀一样。 **4** V-T If something **blunts** an emotion, a feeling or a need, it weakens it. 使减弱 ❑ *The constant repetition of violence has blunted the human response to it.* 持续不断的暴力事件使人们对它的反应减弱了。

blur /blɜr/ (**blurs, blurring, blurred**) **1** N-COUNT A **blur** is a shape or area which you cannot see clearly because it has no distinct outline or because it is moving very fast. 模糊不清 ❑ *Out of the corner of my eye I saw a blur of movement on the other side of the glass.* 从眼角我看见了玻璃窗另一边一个移动的模糊身影。 **2** V-T/V-I When a thing **blurs** or when something **blurs** it, you cannot see it clearly because its edges are no longer distinct. 使变模糊; 变模糊 ❑ *This creates a spectrum of colors at the edges of objects which blurs the image.* 这在物体的边缘产生了一系列颜色，使图像变得模糊不清。 ● **blurred** ADJ 模糊不清的 ❑ *...blurred black and white photographs.* …模糊的黑白照片。 **3** V-T If something **blurs** an idea or a distinction between things, that idea or distinction no longer seems clear. 使…变模糊 ❑ *...her belief that scientists are trying to blur the distinction between "how" and "why" questions.* …她认为科学家们正试图模糊"如何"与"为什么"问题之间的区别的想法。 ● **blurred** ADJ 使变模糊的 ❑ *The line between fact and fiction is becoming blurred.* 事实和虚构之间的界线正在变得模糊起来。 **4** V-T/V-I If your vision **blurs**, or if something **blurs** it, you cannot see things clearly. 使 (视力) 模糊; (视力) 变模糊 ❑ *Her eyes, behind her glasses, began to blur.* 她戴着眼镜的眼睛开始看不清了。 ● **blurred** ADJ (视觉) 模糊的 ❑ *...visual disturbances like eye-strain and blurred vision.* …诸如眼睛疲劳和视力模糊的视觉紊乱。

▲ **blurt** /blɜrt/ (**blurts, blurting, blurted**) V-T If someone **blurts** something, they say it suddenly, after trying hard to keep quiet or to keep it secret. (将秘密) 脱口说出 ❑ *"I was looking for Sally," he blurted, and his eyes filled with tears.* 他眼含热泪，突然脱口说道："我在找莎丽。"

▸ **blurt out** PHRASAL VERB If someone **blurts** something **out**, they blurt it. 脱口说出 [INFORMAL] ❑ *"You're mad," the driver blurted out.* 司机脱口说道："你疯了。"

★ **blush** /blʌʃ/ (**blushes, blushing, blushed**) V-I When you **blush**, your face becomes redder than usual because you are ashamed or

embarrassed. (因害羞、窘困等) 脸红 ❑ *"Hello, Maria," he said, and she blushed again.* 他说道："玛丽亚，你好！"然后她的脸又红了。
● N-COUNT **Blush** is also a noun. 脸红 ❑ *"The most important thing is to be honest," she says, without the trace of a blush.* "最重要的是要诚实。"她说道，丝毫不脸红。

B

Thesaurus *blush* 另参见：
V. redden, turn red

boar /bɔr/ (**boars**)

The plural **boar** can also be used for meaning 1.

1 N-COUNT A **boar** or a **wild boar** is a wild pig. 野猪 ❑ *Wild boar are numerous in the valleys.* 这些山谷里有无数的野猪。 2 N-COUNT A **boar** is a male pig. 公猪

board ♦♦◇ /bɔrd/ (**boards, boarding, boarded**) 1 N-COUNT A **board** is a flat, thin, rectangular piece of wood or plastic which is used for a particular purpose. (木头的或塑料的) 板 ❑ *...a cutting board.* …一块砧板。 2 N-COUNT A **board** is a square piece of wood or stiff cardboard that you use for playing games such as chess. (棋) 盘 ❑ *...a checkers board.* …一个跳棋盘。 3 N-COUNT You can refer to a blackboard or a bulletin board as a **board**. 黑板；布告栏 ❑ *He wrote a few more notes on the board.* 他在黑板上多写了几条笔记。 4 N-COUNT **Boards** are long flat pieces of wood which are used, for example, to make floors or walls. (建筑用的) 长条木板 ❑ *The floor was drafty bare boards.* 地板是有缝隙的裸板。 5 N-COUNT The **board** of a company or organization is the group of people who control it and direct it. 董事会 [BUSINESS] ❑ *Arthur has made a recommendation, which he wants her to put before the board at a special meeting scheduled for tomorrow afternoon.* 阿瑟提了个建议，要她在明天下午拟定召开的特别会议上向董事会提出。 6 → see also **board of directors** 7 N-COUNT **Board** is used in the names of various organizations which are involved in dealing with a particular kind of activity. 委员会；局 ❑ *The Scottish tourist board said 33,000 Japanese visited Scotland last year.* 苏格兰旅游局称，33000名日本游客去年到苏格兰旅游。 8 V-T When you **board** a train, ship, or aircraft, you get on it in order to travel somewhere. 登上 (火车、船或飞机) [FORMAL] ❑ *I boarded the plane bound for Boston.* 我登上了飞往波士顿的航班。 9 N-UNCOUNT **Board** is the food which is provided when you stay somewhere, for example in a hotel. (在外住宿的) 膳食 ❑ *Free room and board are provided for all hotel staff.* 旅馆的所有工作人员可以免费食宿。 10 PHRASE If a policy or a situation applies **across the board**, it affects everything or everyone in a particular group. 全体地 ❑ *There are hefty charges across the board for one-way rental.* 对所有人的单程租都收高费。 11 PHRASE If something **goes by the board**, it is rejected or ignored, or is no longer possible. 被拒绝；落空 ❑ *It's a case of not what you know but who you know in this world today and qualifications quite go by the board.* 现在社会的情形不是看你知道什么，而是看你认识谁，学位也基本被忽略了。 12 PHRASE When you are **on board** a train, ship, or aircraft, you are on it or in it. 在 (火车、轮船或飞机) 上 ❑ *All 269 people on board the plane were killed.* 机上269人全部遇难。 13 PHRASE If someone **sweeps the board** in a competition or election, they win nearly everything that it is possible to win. (在比赛或选举中) 大获全胜 ❑ *Spain swept the board in boys' team competitions.* 西班牙队在男子组的竞赛中大获全胜。 14 PHRASE If you **take on board** an idea or a problem, you begin to accept it or understand it. 接受；理解 ❑ *You may have to accept their point of view, but hope that they will take on board some of what you have said.* 你可能得接受他们的观点，但是希望他们也会理解你讲的一些话。
▶ **board up** PHRASAL VERB If you **board up** a door or window, you fix pieces of wood over it so that it is covered up. 用木板封住 ❑ *Shopkeepers have boarded up their windows.* 店主们已经用木板封住了他们的窗户。

Word Partnership *board* 的常用搭配：
N. **cutting** board, **diving** board 1
board **game** 2
bulletin board, **message** board 3
chair/member of the board, board **of directors**, board **meeting** 5 6
board **a flight/plane/ship** 8
room and board 9

board·ing card [BRIT] → see **boarding pass**

board·ing pass (**boarding passes**) N-COUNT A **boarding pass** is a card that a passenger must have when boarding a plane or a boat. 登机卡；登船卡

board·ing school (**boarding schools**) also **boarding-school** N-VAR A **boarding school** is a school that some or all of the students live in during the school term. Compare **day school**. 寄宿学校

board of di·rec·tors (**boards of directors**) N-COUNT A company's **board of directors** is the group of people elected by its shareholders to manage the company. 董事会 [BUSINESS] ❑ *The board of directors has approved the decision unanimously.* 董事会一致通过了这项决定。

board·room /bɔrdrum/ (**boardrooms**) also **board room** N-COUNT The **boardroom** is a room where the board of a company meets. 董事会议室 [BUSINESS] ❑ *Everyone had already assembled in the boardroom for the 9:00 a.m. session.* 每个人都到了董事会议室参加上午9:00的会议。

boast /boʊst/ (**boasts, boasting, boasted**) 1 V-T/V-I If someone **boasts** about something that they have done or that they own, they talk about it very proudly, in a way that other people may find irritating or offensive. 吹嘘 [DISAPPROVAL] ❑ *Witnesses said Furci boasted that he took part in killing them.* 证人们说富尔西曾吹嘘说他参与了杀人。 ❑ *Carol boasted about her costume.* 卡罗尔吹嘘着她的戏装。 ● N-COUNT **Boast** is also a noun. 吹嘘 ❑ *It is the charity's proud boast that it has never yet turned anyone away.* 该慈善机构自吹自擂，声称从来没有拒绝过任何人。 2 V-T If someone or something can **boast** a particular achievement or possession, they have achieved or possess that thing. 取得 (成功)；拥有 ❑ *The houses will boast the latest energy-saving technology.* 这些房屋将采用最新节能技术。

★ **boast·ful** /boʊstfəl/ ADJ If someone is **boastful**, they talk too proudly about something that they have done or that they own. 自夸的 [DISAPPROVAL] ❑ *I'm not being boastful.* 我不是在自夸。 ❑ *...boastful predictions.* …自吹的那些预言。

boat ♦♦◇ /boʊt/ (**boats**) 1 N-COUNT A **boat** is something in which people can travel across water. 船 [also "by" N] ❑ *One of the best ways to see the area is in a small boat.* 参观这一地区的最好方式之一是乘小船。 2 N-COUNT You can refer to a passenger ship as a **boat**. 客船 ❑ *When the boat reached Cape Town, we said goodbye.* 客船抵达开普敦后，我们就分手了。 3 PHRASE If you say that someone has **missed the boat**, you mean that they have missed an opportunity and may not get another. 坐失良机 ❑ *If you don't want to miss the boat, the auction is scheduled for 2:30 p.m. on June 26.* 如果你不想坐失良机，拍卖会定在6月26日下午2:30。
→ see Word Web: **boat**
→ see **ship**

Thesaurus *boat* 另参见：
N. craft, ship, vessel 1 2

boat·ing /boʊtɪŋ/ N-UNCOUNT **Boating** is traveling on a lake or river in a small boat for pleasure. 划船 ❑ *You can go boating or play tennis.* 你可以去划船，也可以打网球。

bob /bɒb/ (**bobs, bobbing, bobbed**) 1 V-I If something **bobs**, it moves up and down, like something does when it is floating on water. 上下浮动 ❑ *Huge balloons bobbed about in the sky above.*

Word Web boat

People once used **boats** only for transportation. But today they are a favorite form of recreation for millions. Weekend **captains** enjoy quietly **sailing** their skiffs along the shore. However, other boaters prefer to ride around in motorboats. Any rowboat can become a motorboat just by attaching an outboard **motor** to the back. Inboard motors are quieter, but they're more expensive. Fishermen usually prefer using a rowboat with **oars**. That way they don't scare the fish. For an even more peaceful ride, some people **paddle** around in **canoes**. But really adventurous folks like the thrill of white-water **rafting**.

b

巨大的气球在上空上下浮动。 2 V-I If you **bob** somewhere, you move there quickly so that you disappear from view or come into view. 快速移动 ❑ *She handed over a form, then bobbed down again behind a typewriter.* 她递过来一张表格，又快速坐回到打字机后面。

bob·by pin /bɒbi pɪn/ (**bobby pins**) N-COUNT A **bobby pin** is a small piece of metal or plastic bent back on itself that someone uses to hold their hair in position. 发夹 [AM]

in BRIT, use **hairgrip**

bode /boʊd/ (**bodes, boding, boded**) V-I If something **bodes** ill, it makes you think that something bad will happen in the future. If something **bodes** well, it makes you think that something good will happen. 为…的预兆 [FORMAL] ❑ *She says the way the bill was passed bodes ill for democracy.* 她说议案通过的方式预示民主的恶运。

★ **bodi·ly** /bɒdɪli/ 1 ADJ Your **bodily** needs and functions are the needs and functions of your body. 身体的 [ADJ n] ❑ *...descriptions of natural bodily functions.* …对身体自然机能的描述。 2 ADV You use **bodily** to indicate that an action involves the whole of someone's body. 整个身体地 [ADV with v] ❑ *I was hurled bodily to the deck.* 我整个人被扔到了甲板上。

body ♦♦♦ /bɒdi/ (**bodies**) 1 N-COUNT Your **body** is all your physical parts, including your head, arms, and legs. 身体 ❑ *The largest organ in the body is the liver.* 体内最大的器官是肝脏。 2 N-COUNT You can also refer to the main part of your body, except for your arms, head, and legs, as your **body**. 躯干 ❑ *Lying flat on the floor, twist your body on to one hip and cross your upper leg over your body.* 平躺在地板上，躯干扭向胯一侧，将上边的腿跨过躯干。 3 N-COUNT You can refer to a person's dead body as a **body**. 尸体 ❑ *Officials said they had found no traces of violence on the body of the politician.* 官方说他们在这位政治家的尸体上没有发现任何暴力痕迹。 4 N-COUNT A **body** is an organized group of people who deal with something officially. 团体；组织 ❑ *She was elected student body president at the University of North Carolina.* 她当选为北卡罗莱纳大学学生社团主席。 5 N-COUNT A **body of** people is a group of people who are together or who are connected in some way. 一群（人） ❑ *...that large body of people which teaches other people how to teach.* …教别人如何教学的那一大群人。 6 N-SING **The body of** something such as a building or a document is the main part of it or the largest part of it. 主体；正文 ❑ *The main body of the church had been turned into a massive television studio.* 教堂的主体已经被改建成了巨型电视演播室。 7 N-COUNT The **body** of a car or airplane is the main part of it, not including its engine, wheels, or wings. 车身；机身 ❑ *The only shade was under the body of the plane.* 惟一的阴凉处是机身下面。 8 N-COUNT A **body of** water is a large area of water, such as a lake or an ocean. （水域）一大片 ❑ *It is probably the most polluted body of water in the world.* 这也许是世界上最为污染的一片水域。 9 N-COUNT A **body of** information is a large amount of it. 大量 ❑ *An increasing body of evidence suggests that all of us have cancer cells in our bodies at times during our lives.* 越来越多的证据表明在一生中我们所有人有时在体内都会出现癌细胞。 10 N-UNCOUNT If you say that an alcoholic drink has **body**, you mean that it has a full and strong flavor. （酒的）醇味 ❑ *...a dry wine with good body.* …醇味佳的干葡萄酒。

→ see Picture Dictionary: **body**

body·guard /bɒdigɑrd/ (**bodyguards**) N-COUNT A **bodyguard** is a person or a group of people employed to protect someone. 保镖 ❑ *Three of his bodyguards were injured in the attack.* 他的三名保镖在袭击中受了伤。

body lan·guage N-UNCOUNT Your **body language** is the way in which you show your feelings or thoughts to other people by means of the position or movements of your body, rather than with words. 身体语言 ❑ *I can tell by your body language that you're happy with the decision.* 我能从你的身体语言看出来你对这个决定感到满意。

▲ **bog** /bɒg/ (**bogs**) N-COUNT A **bog** is an area of land that is very wet and muddy. 沼泽

→ see **wetland**

bogged down ADJ If you get **bogged down in** something, it prevents you from making progress or getting something done. 陷入停滞状态的 ❑ *But why get bogged down in legal details?* 可是为什么要被法律细节裹足不前呢？

bog·gle /bɒgəl/ (**boggles, boggling, boggled**) V-T/V-I If you say that the mind **boggles at** something, or that something **boggles** the mind, you mean that it is so strange or amazing that it is difficult to imagine or understand. 使困惑；困惑 ❑ *The mind boggles at the possibilities that could be in store for us.* 一想到我们将要面临的各种可能，脑子里就一片混乱。

bo·gus /boʊgəs/ ADJ If you describe something as **bogus**, you mean that it is not genuine. 伪造的 ❑ *...their bogus insurance claim.* …他们伪造的保险索赔。

boil ♦◇◇ /bɔɪl/ (**boils, boiling, boiled**) 1 V-T/V-I When a hot liquid **boils** or when you **boil** it, bubbles appear in it and it starts to change into steam or vapor. 使…沸腾；沸腾 ❑ *I stood in the kitchen, waiting for the water to boil.* 我站在厨房里等水开。 ❑ *Boil the water in the saucepan and add the sage.* 把汤锅里的水烧开，然后放进鼠尾草叶。 2 V-T/V-I When you **boil** a pot or a kettle, or put it on to **boil**, you heat the water inside it until it boils. 烧开 ❑ *He had nothing to do but boil the kettle and make the tea.* 他除了烧开水和沏茶以外无事可做。 3 V-I When a pot **is boiling**, the water inside it has reached boiling point. 烧沸 [only cont] ❑ *The pot was boiling.* 锅里的水烧开了。 4 V-T/V-I When you **boil** food, or when it **boils**, it is cooked in boiling water. 煮 ❑ *Boil the chick peas, add garlic and lemon juice.* 把鹰嘴豆煮了，加进蒜和柠檬汁。 ❑ *I'd peel potatoes and put them on to boil.* 我会削土豆皮，然后把它们煮了。 5 V-I If you **are boiling with** anger, you are very angry. 发怒 [usu cont] ❑ *I used to be all sweetness and light on the outside, but inside I would be boiling with rage.* 我过去虽然表面上笑呵呵的，可是心里却怒火中烧。 6 N-COUNT A **boil** is a red, painful swelling on your skin that contains a thick yellow liquid called pus. 疖子 7 → see also **boiling** 8 PHRASE When you **bring** a liquid **to a boil**, you heat it until it boils. When it **comes to a boil**, it begins to boil. 烧沸/开始沸腾 ❑ *Put water, butter and lard into a saucepan and bring slowly to the boil.* 在汤锅里加入水、黄油和猪油，慢慢煮开。

→ see **cook, egg**

▸ **boil down to** PHRASAL VERB If you say that a situation or problem **boils down to** a particular thing or can **be boiled down to** a particular thing, you mean that this is the most important or

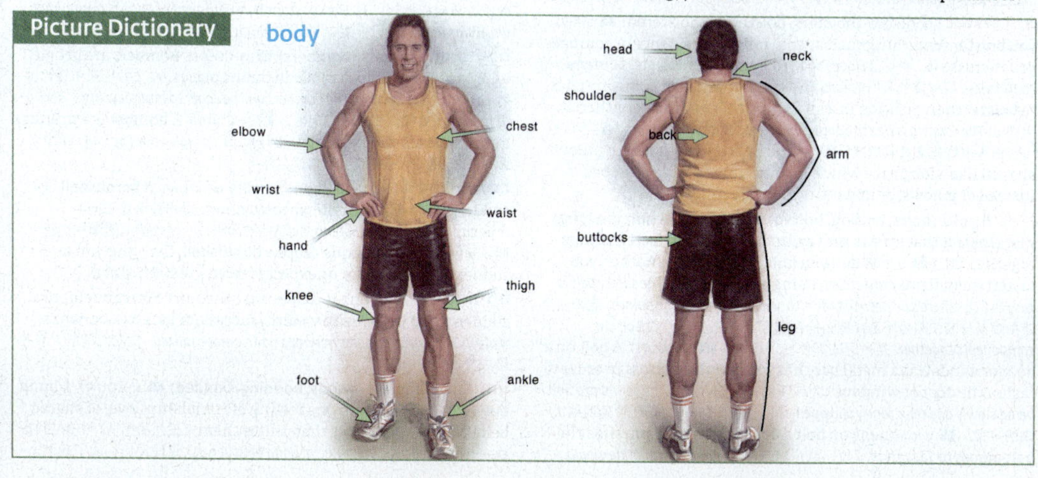

B

the most basic aspect of it. (情况或问题) 归根结底 ❑ *What they want boils down to just one thing. It is land.* 他们想要的归根结底只有一样东西，那就是土地。

▸ **boil over** 1 PHRASAL VERB When a liquid that is being heated **boils over**, it rises and flows over the edge of the container. 煮沸而溢出 ❑ *Heat the liquid in a large, wide container rather than a high narrow one, or it can boil over.* 液体加热时要放进宽大的容器里，不要放进细长的容器里，否则它会溢出来。 2 PHRASAL VERB When someone's feelings **boil over**, they lose their temper or become violent. (情绪) 失去控制 ❑ *Sometimes frustration and anger can boil over into direct and violent action.* 有时无奈和愤怒会失去控制，变成直接的暴力行为。

boil·er /bɔɪlər/ (**boilers**) N-COUNT A **boiler** is a device that burns gas, oil, electricity, or coal in order to provide hot water, especially for the central heating in a building. 锅炉

boil·ing /bɔɪlɪŋ/ 1 ADJ Something that is **boiling** or **boiling hot** is very hot. 炙热的 ❑ *"It's boiling in here," complained Miriam.* "这里热死了！"，米瑞尔姆抱怨道。 2 ADJ If you say that you are **boiling** or **boiling hot**, you mean that you feel very hot, usually unpleasantly hot. 感到热得难受的 [v-link ADJ] ❑ *When everybody else is boiling hot, I'm freezing!* 当每一个人都热得不行时，我却冻得发抖！

> In informal English, if you want to emphasize how hot the weather is, you can say that it is **boiling** or **scorching**. In winter, if the temperature is above average, you can say that it is **mild**. In general, **hot** suggests a higher temperature than **warm**, and **warm** things are usually pleasant. ❑ *...a warm evening.*

bois·ter·ous /bɔɪstərəs, -strəs/ ADJ Someone who is **boisterous** is noisy, lively, and full of energy. 喧闹的；欢闹的 ❑ *...a boisterous but good-natured crowd.* …喧闹却和善的一群人。

bold /boʊld/ (**bolder, boldest**) 1 ADJ Someone who is **bold** is not afraid to do things that involve risk or danger. 无畏的；大胆的 ❑ *Amrita becomes a bold, daring rebel.* 阿莫瑞塔成了一位英勇无畏的反叛者。 ❑ *In 1960 this was a bold move.* 在1960年，这是一个大胆的举动。 ● **bold·ly** ADV 无畏地；大胆地 [ADV with v] ❑ *You must act boldly and confidently.* 你必须表现得大胆、自信。 ● **bold·ness** N-UNCOUNT 勇敢；大胆 ❑ *Don't forget the boldness of his economic program.* 别忘了他的经济方案的大胆。 2 ADJ Someone who is **bold** is not shy or embarrassed in the company of other people. 大胆的 ❑ *I don't feel I'm being bold, because it's always been natural for me to just speak out about whatever disturbs me.* 我并不认为自己莽撞，因为无论什么事令我不安我就说出来，对我这一直以来是很自然的事。 ● **bold·ly** ADV 大胆地 ❑ *"You should do it," the girl said, boldly.* 这个女孩大胆地说道："你应该这么做。" 3 ADJ A **bold** color or pattern is very bright and noticeable. (色彩或图案) 鲜明的；醒目的 ❑ *...bold flowers in various shades of red, blue or white.* …各种深浅不同的红色、蓝色和白色的醒目的花朵。 4 ADJ **Bold** lines or designs are drawn in a clear, strong way. 清晰的；(线条、轮廓) 刚劲的；大胆的 ❑ *Each picture is shown in color on one page and as a bold outline on the opposite page.* 每幅画在一页上是彩色的，在相对的一页上则是清晰刚劲的轮廓。 5 N-UNCOUNT **Bold** is print which is thicker and looks blacker than ordinary printed letters. 粗体 [TECHNICAL] ❑ *When a candidate is elected his or her name will be highlighted in bold.* 当候选人被选中时，他或她的名字就用粗体来突出。

▲ **bol·ster** /boʊlstər/ (**bolsters, bolstering, bolstered**) 1 V-T If you **bolster** something such as someone's confidence or courage, you increase it. 增强 ❑ *Hopes of an early cut in interest rates bolstered confidence.* 提前降低利率的希望增强了信心。 2 V-T If someone tries to **bolster** their position in a situation, they try to strengthen it. 巩固 ❑ *The country is free to adopt policies to bolster its economy.* 这个国家可自由采取措施来巩固经济。 3 N-COUNT A **bolster** is a firm pillow shaped like a long tube which is sometimes put across a bed instead of pillows, or under the ordinary pillows. 长枕

bolt /boʊlt/ (**bolts, bolting, bolted**) 1 N-COUNT A **bolt** is a long metal object that screws into a nut and is used to fasten things together. 螺钉 2 V-T When you **bolt** one thing to another, you fasten them firmly together, using a bolt. 栓牢 ❑ *The safety belt is easy to fit as there's no need to bolt it to seat belt anchorage points.* 这种安全带很容易安装，因为不需要把它拴在安全带固定点上。 ❑ *Bolt the components together.* 把所有的部件栓接起来。 3 N-COUNT A **bolt** on a door or window is a metal bar that you can slide across in order to fasten the door or window. (门或窗的) 闩 ❑ *I heard the sound of a bolt being slowly and reluctantly slid open.* 我听到门闩被人缓慢而费劲地抽出来的声音。 4 V-T When you **bolt** a door or window, you slide the bolt across to fasten it. 闩 (门或窗) ❑ *He reminded her that he would have to lock and bolt the kitchen door after her.* 他提醒她，他得在她离开后锁上厨房的门并插上门闩。 5 V-I If a person or animal **bolts**, they suddenly start to run very fast, often because something has frightened them. (因受惊吓) 突然快跑 ❑ *The pig rose squealing and bolted.* 那头猪尖叫着站起来，飞快地跑开了。 6 V-T If you **bolt** your food, you eat it so quickly that you hardly chew it or taste it. 吞吃 ❑ *Being under stress can cause you to miss meals, eat on the move, or bolt your food.* 压力之下会造成错过进餐、边做事边吃、或者吞吃食物。 ● PHRASAL VERB **Bolt down** means the same as **bolt**. 吞吃 ❑ *I like to think back to high school, when I could bolt down three or four burgers and a pile of French fries.* 我喜欢回想高中时，那时我可以一气吞下三四个汉堡和一大堆炸薯条。 7 N-COUNT A **bolt of** lightning is a flash of lightning that is seen as a white line in the sky. (闪电) 道 ❑ *Suddenly a bolt of lightning crackled through the sky.* 突然，一道闪电划破天空。 8 PHRASE If someone is sitting or standing **bolt upright**, they are sitting or standing very straight. 笔直地 ❑ *When I pushed his door open, Trevor was sitting bolt upright in bed.* 我推开他的门时，发现特雷弗正笔直地坐在床上。
→ see **lightning**

bomb ◆◆◇ /bɒm/ (**bombs, bombing, bombed**) 1 N-COUNT A **bomb** is a device that explodes and damages or destroys a large area. 炸弹 ❑ *Bombs went off at two London train stations.* 炸弹在伦敦的两个火车站爆炸了。 ❑ *It's not known who planted the bomb.* 不知是谁放置了这颗炸弹。 2 N-SING Nuclear weapons are sometimes referred to as **the bomb**. 核武器 ❑ *They are generally thought to have the bomb.* 他们被普遍认为拥有核武器。 3 V-T When people **bomb** a place, they attack it with bombs. 轰炸 ❑ *Air force jets bombed the airport.* 空军喷气机轰炸了机场。 ● **bomb·ing** N-VAR (**bombings**) 轰炸 ❑ *Aerial bombing of rebel positions is continuing.* 对叛军阵地的空中轰炸仍在继续。

Word Partnership *bomb* 的常用搭配：

N.	bomb **blast**, **car** bomb, **pipe** bomb, bomb **shelter**, bomb **squad**, bomb **threat** 1
V.	**drop/plant a** bomb, **set off a** bomb 1
ADJ.	**atomic/nuclear** bomb, **live** bomb 1 2

bom·bard /bɒmbɑrd/ (**bombards, bombarding, bombarded**) 1 V-T If you **bombard** someone **with** something, you make them face a great deal of it. For example, if you **bombard** them **with** questions or criticism, you keep asking them a lot of questions or you keep criticizing them. 连珠炮似地提问；不断批评 ❑ *He bombarded Catherine with questions to which he should have known the answers.* 他不停地追问凯瑟琳他本该知道答案的问题。 2 V-T When soldiers **bombard** a place, they attack it with continuous heavy gunfire or bombs. 连续轰炸 ❑ *Rebel artillery units have regularly bombarded the airport.* 叛军的炮兵部队经常炮轰机场。

bom·bard·ment /bɒmbɑrdmənt/ (**bombardments**) 1 N-VAR A **bombardment** is a strong and continuous attack of gunfire or bombing. 轰击；轰炸 ❑ *The city has been flattened by heavy artillery bombardments.* 该城市因遭重炮轰击而夷为平地。 2 N-VAR A **bombardment of** ideas, demands, questions, or criticisms is an aggressive and exhausting stream of them. 连珠炮式 (想法、要求、质问或批评) ❑ *...the constant bombardment of images urging that work was important.* …持续的连珠炮式的比喻，强调工作是重要的。

bomb·er /bɒmər/ (**bombers**) 1 N-COUNT **Bombers** are people who cause bombs to explode in public places. 在公共场所引爆炸弹者 ❑ *Detectives hunting the bombers will be eager to interview him.* 追踪引爆炸弹者的警探们将急于审问他。 2 N-COUNT A **bomber** is a military aircraft which drops bombs. 轰炸机 ❑ *...a high-speed bomber with twin engines.* …一架双引擎高速轰炸机。

bomb·shell /bɒmʃel/ (**bombshells**) N-COUNT A **bombshell** is a sudden piece of bad or unexpected news. 爆炸性消息 ❑ *His resignation is a political bombshell.* 他的辞职是一件政治上的爆炸性新闻。 ● PHRASE If someone **drops a bombshell**, they give you a sudden piece of bad or unexpected news. 说出爆炸性消息

bo·nan·za /bənænzə/ (**bonanzas**) N-COUNT You can refer to a sudden great increase in wealth, success, or luck as a **bonanza**. 鸿运 ❑ *The expected sales bonanza hadn't materialized.* 预期的销售大涨并未成为现实。

bond ◆◆◇ /bɒnd/ (**bonds, bonding, bonded**) 1 N-COUNT A **bond between** people is a strong feeling of friendship, love, or shared beliefs and experiences that unites them. (强烈的感情) 纽带 ❑ *The experience created a very special bond between us.* 这段经历构成了我们之

间一条非常特殊的纽带。 **2** V-RECIP When people **bond with** each other, they form a relationship based on love or shared beliefs and experiences. You can also say that people **bond** or that something **bonds** them. 建立关系 ❑ *Belinda was having difficulty bonding with the baby.* 贝琳达难以和这个婴儿建立亲密关系。 ❑ *They all bonded while writing graffiti together.* 他们在一起涂鸦时相识。 **3** N-COUNT A **bond between** people or groups is a close connection that they have with each other, for example because they have a special agreement. 密切联系 ❑ *...the strong bond between church and nation.* …教会与国家的紧密联系。 **4** N-COUNT A **bond between** two things is the way in which they stick to one another or are joined in some way. 黏合 ❑ *If you experience difficulty with the superglue not creating a bond with dry wood, moisten the surfaces with water.* 如果你用强力胶难以粘上干燥的木头，就用水润湿木头表面。 **5** V-RECIP When one thing **bonds with** another, it sticks to it or becomes joined to it in some way. You can also say that two things **bond together**, or that something **bonds** them **together**. (使) 黏合 ❑ *In graphite sheets, carbon atoms bond together in rings.* 在石墨片中，碳原子以环状黏合在一起。 **6** N-COUNT When a government or company issues a **bond**, it borrows money from investors. The certificate that is issued to investors who lend money is also called a **bond**. (政府或公司发行的) 债券 [BUSINESS] ❑ *Most of it will be financed by government bonds.* 其主要资金来源于政府债券。 **7** → see also **junk bond**
→ see **love**

▲ **bond·age** /bɒndɪdʒ/ **1** N-UNCOUNT **Bondage** is the condition of being someone's property and having to work for them. 奴役 ❑ *Masters sometimes allowed their slaves to buy their way out of bondage.* 主人们有时候允许奴隶赎身。 **2** N-UNCOUNT **Bondage** is the condition of not being free because you are strongly influenced by something or someone. 束缚 [FORMAL] ❑ *All people, she said, lived their lives in bondage to hunger, pain and lust.* 她说所有人都生活在饥饿、痛苦和欲望的束缚之中。

bond·ed /bɒndɪd/ ADJ A **bonded** company has entered into a legal agreement that offers its customers some protection if the company does not fulfill its contract with them. 有担保的 [BUSINESS] ❑ *They are a fully bonded and licensed company.* 他们是一家有全面担保和经营许可的公司。

bond·holder /bɒndhoʊldər/ (**bondholders**) also **bond holder** N-COUNT A **bondholder** is a person who owns one or more investment bonds. 债券持有者 [BUSINESS]

bone ♦◇◇ /boʊn/ (**bones, boning, boned**) **1** N-VAR Your **bones** are the hard parts inside your body that together form your skeleton. 骨头 ❑ *Many passengers suffered broken bones.* 许多乘客骨折了。 ❑ *The body is made up primarily of bone, muscle, and fat.* 人体主要由骨、肌肉和脂肪组成。 **2** V-T If you **bone** a piece of meat or fish, you remove the bones from it before cooking it. 去 (肉、鱼) 骨或刺 ❑ *Make sure that you do not pierce the skin when boning the chicken thighs.* 给鸡腿去骨时，确保不要刺破皮。 **3** ADJ A **bone** tool or ornament is made of bone. 骨制的 [ADJ n] ❑ *...a small, expensive pocketknife with a bone handle.* …一把昂贵的、带骨制刀把的小刀。 **4** PHRASE The **bare bones of** something are its most basic parts or details. 基本要素 ❑ *There are not even the bare bones of a garden here – I've got nothing.* 这儿连花园的最基本的东西都没有——我一无所获。 **5** → see also **bare-bones** **6** PHRASE If something such as costs are cut **to the bone**, they are reduced to the minimum possible. 减到最低 ❑ *It has survived by cutting its costs to the bone.* 把成本降到最低，它才撑了过来。
→ see **skeleton**

▸ **bone up on** PHRASAL VERB If you **bone up on** a subject, you try to find out about it or remind yourself what you have already learned about it. 钻研；温习 ❑ *I had spent the last few months boning up on neurology.* 我前几个月都在钻研神经病学。

bone of con·ten·tion (**bones of contention**) N-COUNT If a particular matter or issue is a **bone of contention**, it is the subject of a disagreement or argument. 争议点 ❑ *The main bone of contention is the temperature level of the air-conditioners.* 主要的争议点是空调温度。

bon·fire /bɒnfaɪər/ (**bonfires**) N-COUNT A **bonfire** is a fire that is made outdoors, usually to burn waste. Bonfires are also sometimes lit as part of a celebration. (燃烧废物的) 火堆；篝火 ❑ *With bonfires outlawed in urban areas, gardeners must cart their refuse to a dump.* 市区禁止户外焚烧垃圾，园林工人必须用推车把垃圾运到垃圾场。

bon·net /bɒnɪt/ (**bonnets**) **1** N-COUNT A **bonnet** is a hat with ribbons that are tied under the chin. Bonnets are now worn by babies. In the past, they were also worn by women. 在颌下系带的帽子 **2** N-COUNT The **bonnet** of a car is the metal cover over the engine at the front. (汽车) 引擎盖 [BRIT]

in AM, use **hood**

bo·nus /boʊnəs/ (**bonuses**) **1** N-COUNT A **bonus** is an extra amount of money that is added to someone's pay, usually because they have worked very hard. 奖金 ❑ *Workers in big firms receive a substantial part of their pay in the form of bonuses and overtime.* 大公司的工人，工资很大一部分是奖金和加班费。 ❑ *...a $60 bonus.* …一笔$60的奖金。 **2** N-COUNT A **bonus** is something good that you get in addition to something else, and which you would not usually expect. 额外收获 ❑ *We felt we might finish third. Any better would be a bonus.* 我们觉得我们可能得第三名。任何更好的结果都是意外收获。

bony /boʊni/ **1** ADJ Someone who has a **bony** face or **bony** hands, for example, has a very thin face or very thin hands, with very little flesh covering their bones. 瘦削的 ❑ *...an old man with a bony face and white hair.* …一个面部瘦削、白发苍苍的老人。 **2** ADJ The **bony** parts of a person's or animal's body are the parts made of bone. 骨的 ❑ *...the bony ridge of the eye socket.* …眼窝的骨架。

boo /buː/ (**boos, booing, booed**) **1** V-T/V-I If you **boo** a speaker or performer, you shout "boo" or make other loud sounds to indicate that you do not like them, their opinions, or their performance. 发出嘘声 (以示不满) ❑ *People were booing and throwing things at them.* 人们发出嘘声，并朝他们扔东西。 ❑ *Demonstrators booed and jeered him.* 示威者发出嘘声嘲笑他。 ● N-COUNT **Boo** is also a noun. 嘘声 ❑ *She was greeted with boos and hisses.* 迎接她的是一片喝倒彩的嘘声。 ● **boo·ing** N-UNCOUNT 发出嘘声 ❑ *The fans are entitled to their opinion but booing doesn't help anyone.* 狂热爱好者们有权表达自己的看法，但发出嘘声对任何人都没有好处。 **2** EXCLAM You say "**Boo!**" loudly and suddenly when you want to surprise someone who does not know that you are there. 为吓唬人而发出的声音

book ♦♦♦ /bʊk/ (**books, booking, booked**) **1** N-COUNT A **book** is a number of pieces of paper, usually with words printed on them, which are fastened together and fixed inside a cover of stronger paper or cardboard. Books contain information, stories, or poetry, for example. 书 ❑ *His eighth book came out earlier this year and was an instant best-seller.* 他的第8本书今年早些时候出版了，并很快成为了一本畅销书。 ❑ *...the author of a book on politics.* …一本政治书的作者。 ❑ *...a new book by Rosella Brown.* …罗赛拉・布朗写的一本新书。 **2** N-COUNT A **book of** something such as stamps, matches, or tickets is a small number of them fastened together between thin cardboard covers. (邮票) 册；(火柴) 纸板；(票) 版 ❑ *Can I have a book of first class stamps please?* 请给我一版一等邮票，好吗？ **3** V-T When you **book** something such as a hotel room or a ticket, you arrange to have it or use it at a particular time. 预订 ❑ *American officials have booked hotel rooms for the women and children.* 美国官员已经为这些妇女和儿童预订了宾馆房间。 ❑ *Laurie booked herself a flight home.* 劳里为自己预订了回家的机票。 **4** N-PLURAL A company's or organization's **books** are its records of money that has been spent and earned or of the names of people who belong to it. (公司或机构的) 帐簿；名册 [BUSINESS] ❑ *For the most part he left the books to his managers and accountants.* 他大多把账簿留给他的经理和会计们处理。 **5** V-T When a police officer **books** someone, he or she officially records their name and the offense that they may be charged with. 把…记录在案 ❑ *They took him to the station and booked him for assault with a deadly weapon.* 他们把他带回警察局，以使用致命武器进行攻击的罪名将他记录在案。 **6** N-COUNT In a very long written work such as the Bible, a **book** is one of the sections into which it is divided. 卷 ❑ *...the last book of the Bible.* …《圣经》的最后一卷。 **7** → see also **booking, checkbook, phone book** **8** PHRASE If you say that someone or something is a **closed book**, you mean that you do not know anything about them. 不被知晓的人或事 ❑ *Frank Spriggs was a very able man but something of a closed book.* 弗兰克・斯普里格斯是个非常能干的人，却不被人所知晓。 **9** PHRASE If transportation or a hotel, restaurant, or theater is **booked up**, **fully booked**, or **booked solid**, it has no tickets, rooms, or tables left for a particular time or date. 预订一空的 ❑ *The car ferries from the mainland are often fully booked by February.* 从大陆出发的汽车渡轮常常到2月底前就被预订一空。
→ see Word Web: **book**
→ see **concert, library**

b

B

Word Web book

Before the invention of the book in first century Rome, **literary works** were recorded on **scrolls**. The earliest examples of bookbinding used sheets of parchment. Workers folded them in half and then sewed through the fold. Scribes copied books by hand until the invention of the **printing press** in the fifteenth century. Today, most books come from factories. High-speed presses print thousands of pages every hour. The pages are then folded into signatures* and trimmed to size. Finally, machines sew or glue the signatures onto the cover. Today's **e-books** provide pages on a computer screen instead of paper.

signature: a group of pages.

Word Partnership book 的常用搭配:

N. **address** book, book **award**, **children's** book, book **club**, **comic** book, **copy of a** book, book **cover**, **library** book, **phone** book, book **review**, **subject of a** book, **title of a** book 1
ADJ. **latest/new/recent** book 1
V. **publish a** book, **read a** book, **write a** book 1

book·case /bʊkkeɪs/ (**bookcases**) N-COUNT A **bookcase** is a piece of furniture with shelves that you keep books on. 书橱

book·ing /bʊkɪŋ/ (**bookings**) N-COUNT A **booking** is the arrangement that you make when you book something such as a hotel room, a table at a restaurant, or a theater seat. 预订 ❏ *There was a mistake over his booking.* 他的预订中有个错误。

book·keeper /bʊkkipər/ (**bookkeepers**) also **book-keeper** N-COUNT A **bookkeeper** is a person whose job is to keep an accurate record of the money that is spent and received by a business or other organization. 簿记员 [BUSINESS]

book·keeping /bʊkkipɪŋ/ also **book-keeping** N-UNCOUNT **Bookkeeping** is the job or activity of keeping an accurate record of the money that is spent and received by a business or other organization. 簿记 [BUSINESS]

Word Link *let ≈ little : booklet, droplet, pamphlet*

book·let /bʊklɪt/ (**booklets**) N-COUNT A **booklet** is a very thin book that has a paper cover and that gives you information about something. 小册子 ❏ *...a 48-page booklet of notes for the completion of the form.* …一本48页的表格填写说明小册子。

Word Link *mark ≈ boundary, sign : benchmark, bookmark, trademark*

book·mark /bʊkmɑrk/ (**bookmarks, bookmarking, bookmarked**) 1 N-COUNT A **bookmark** is a narrow piece of card or leather that you put between the pages of a book so that you can find a particular page easily. 书签 2 N-COUNT In computing, a **bookmark** is the address of an Internet site that you put into a list on your computer so that you can return to it easily. 电子书签 [COMPUTING] ❏ *This makes it extremely simple to save what you find with an electronic bookmark so you can return to it later.* 用一个电子书签保存找到的内容使以后再次访问变得非常简单。 ● V-T **Bookmark** is also a verb. 为…设定电子书签 [COMPUTING] ❏ *This site is definitely worth bookmarking.* 这个网站绝对值得设电子书签。

book·shop /bʊkʃɒp/ (**bookshops**) N-COUNT A **bookshop** is a store where books are sold. 书店 [mainly BRIT]

in AM, usually use **bookstore**

book·store /bʊkstɔr/ (**bookstores**) N-COUNT A **bookstore** is a store where books are sold. 书店 [mainly AM]

in BRIT, usually use **bookshop**

book value (**book values**) N-COUNT In business, the **book value** of an asset is the value it is given in the account books of the company that owns it. 账面价值 [BUSINESS] ❏ *The insured value of the airplane was greater than its book value.* 该飞机的保险价值高于账面价值。

boom ♦◇◇ /bum/ (**booms, booming, boomed**) 1 N-COUNT If there is a **boom** in the economy, there is an increase in economic activity, for example, in the number of things that are being bought and sold. (经济) 繁荣 ❏ *An economic boom followed, especially in housing and construction.* 接着是一个经济的繁荣，尤其在住房和建筑方面。 ❏ *The 1980s were indeed boom years.* 20世纪80年代确实是繁荣的时代。 2 N-COUNT A **boom in** something is an increase in its amount, frequency, or success. 增长 ❏ *The boom in the sport's popularity has meant more calls for stricter safety regulations.* 该项运动普及程度的大幅提高带来了更多要求更严格安全法规的呼声。 3 V-I If the economy or a business **is booming**, the number of things being bought or sold is increasing. 激增 ❏ *By 1988 the economy was booming.* 到1988年为止经济一直很繁荣。 ❏ *Sales are booming.* 销售量在激增。 4 V-T/V-I When something such as someone's voice, a cannon, or a big drum **booms**, it makes a loud, deep sound that lasts for several seconds. 发出低沉洪亮的声音 ❏ *"Ladies," boomed Helena, without a microphone, "we all know why we're here tonight."* "女士们"，海伦娜没用话筒朗声说道，"我们都知道今晚我们为什么在这儿。" ❏ *Thunder boomed over Crooked Mountain.* 雷声在克鲁克德山上空轰鸣。 ● PHRASAL VERB **Boom out** means the same as **boom**. 发出低沉洪亮的声音 ❏ *Music boomed out from loudspeakers.* 扬声器传出了低沉响亮的音乐。 ❏ *A megaphone boomed out, "This is the police."* 扩音器传出了低沉而响亮的声音："我们是警察。" ● N-COUNT; SOUND **Boom** is also a noun. 轰鸣声 ❏ *The stillness of the night was broken by the boom of a cannon.* 夜晚的寂静被大炮的轰鸣声打破了。

Thesaurus boom 另参见:

V. flourish, prosper, succeed, thrive; *(ant.)* fail 3
N. explosion, roar 4

boom-bust cy·cle (**boom-bust cycles**) N-COUNT A **boom-bust cycle** is a series of events in which a rapid increase in business activity in the economy is followed by a rapid decrease in business activity, and this process is repeated again and again. (经济的) 繁荣-萧条周期 [BUSINESS] ❏ *We must avoid the damaging boom-bust cycles which characterized the 1980s.* 我们必须避免类似20世纪80年代那样破坏性的繁荣-萧条周期。

boon /bun/ (**boons**) N-COUNT You can describe something as a **boon** when it makes life better or easier for someone. 福音 ❏ *It is for this reason that television proves such a boon to so many people.* 正是这个原因电视机成为这么多人的一大福音。

boost ♦◇◇ /bust/ (**boosts, boosting, boosted**) 1 V-T If one thing **boosts** another, it causes it to increase, improve, or be more successful. 促进 ❏ *Lower interest rates can boost the economy by reducing borrowing costs for consumers and businesses.* 低利率可以通过为消费者和商家降低借贷成本来促进经济发展。 ● N-COUNT **Boost** is also a noun. 推动力 ❏ *It would get the economy going and give us the boost that we need.* 这会推动经济发展并带给我们所需要的推动力。 2 V-T If something **boosts** your confidence or morale, it improves it. 增强 (信心、士气) ❏ *We need a big win to boost our confidence.* 我们需要一个大的胜利来增强我们的自信心。 ● N-COUNT **Boost** is also a noun. (信心、士气的) 增强 ❏ *It did give me a boost to win such a big event.* 赢了这么一场大型比赛，的确使我士气大振。 3 N-COUNT If you give someone a **boost**, you push or lift them from behind so that they can reach something. 推; 托 [usu sing] ❏ *He cupped his hands and gave her a boost up to the ledge.* 他双手拢作杯状把她托上了窗台。

boot ♦◇◇ /but/ (**boots, booting, booted**) 1 N-COUNT **Boots** are shoes that cover your whole foot and the lower part of your leg. 靴子 ❏ *He sat in a kitchen chair, reached down and pulled off his boots.* 他坐在厨房的椅子上，弯腰脱掉了靴子。 2 N-COUNT **Boots** are strong, heavy shoes that cover your ankle and that have thick soles. You wear them to protect your feet, for example, when you are walking or taking part in sports. (步行或运动时穿的) 厚底靴 ❏ *The soldiers' boots resounded in the street.* 士兵们的厚底靴在街道上发出回响。

3 V-T To **boot** an illegally parked car means to fit a device to one of its wheels so that it cannot be driven away. 锁扣(违章停放的车辆) [AM]

in BRIT, use **clamp**

❑ *Though the city will no longer boot cars, illegally parked vehicles will be towed.* 尽管该城将不再锁扣车辆，违规停放的车辆将被拖走。 4 V-T/V-I If a computer **boots** or you **boot** it, it is made ready to use by putting in the instructions it needs in order to start working. 启动 [COMPUTING] ❑ *The computer won't boot.* 计算机无法启动。 ❑ *Put the CD into the drive and boot the machine.* 把光盘放进驱动器，然后启动机器。 ● PHRASAL VERB **Boot up** means the same as **boot**. 启动 ❑ *Go over to your PC and boot it up.* 到你的个人电脑那儿，启动它。 5 N-COUNT The **boot** of a car is the same as the **trunk**. 后备箱 [BRIT] 6 PHRASE If you **get the boot** or **are given the boot**, you are told that you are not wanted anymore, either in your job or by someone you are having a relationship with. 被解雇；被抛弃 [INFORMAL] ❑ *She was a disruptive influence, and after a year or two she got the boot.* 她是个捣乱分子，一两年后就被解雇了。

→ see **clothing**

★ **booth** /buθ/ (**booths**) 1 N-COUNT A **booth** is a small area separated from a larger public area by screens or thin walls where, for example, people can make a telephone call or vote in private. 小隔间(如公用电话亭、投票间) ❑ *I called her from a public phone booth near the entrance to the bar.* 我在酒吧入口附近的一个公用电话亭给她打了电话。 2 N-COUNT A **booth** in a restaurant or café consists of a table with long fixed seats on two or sometimes three sides of it. 隔开的用餐区(固定的长座围绕着餐桌) ❑ *They sat in a corner booth, away from other diners.* 他们坐在角落里的分隔用餐区，远离其他就餐者。

booze /buz/ (**boozes, boozing, boozed**) 1 N-UNCOUNT **Booze** is alcoholic drink. 酒 [also "the" N] [INFORMAL] ❑ *...booze and cigarettes.* …酒和烟。 2 V-I If people **booze**, they drink alcohol. 喝酒 [INFORMAL] ❑ *...a load of drunken businessmen who had been boozing all afternoon.* …一群整个下午都在喝酒、醉醺醺的商人。

bor·der ♦♦◊ /bɔrdər/ (**borders, bordering, bordered**) 1 N-COUNT The **border** between two countries or regions is the dividing line between them. Sometimes **the border** also refers to the land close to this line. 边界；边界地区 ❑ *They fled across the border.* 他们越过边界逃走了。 ❑ *Soldiers had temporarily closed the border between the two countries.* 士兵们已暂时封闭了两国的边界。 2 V-T A country that **borders** another country, a sea, or a river is next to it. 与…接壤 ❑ *...the European and Arab countries bordering the Mediterranean.* …地中海沿岸的欧洲国家和阿拉伯国家。 ● PHRASAL VERB **Border on** means the same as **border**. 与…接壤 ❑ *Both republics border on the Black Sea.* 这两个共和国都与黑海毗邻。 3 N-COUNT A **border** is a strip or band around the edge of something. 饰边 ❑ *...pillowcases trimmed with a hand-crocheted border.* …镶有一道手工钩制花边的枕套。 4 N-COUNT In a garden, a **border** is a long strip of ground planted with flowers, along the edge of a path or lawn. (小路或草地边) 狭长花坛 ❑ *...a lawn flanked by wide herbaceous borders.* …一片两侧有草本植物花坛的草坪。 5 V-T If something **is bordered** by another thing, the other thing forms a line along the edge of it. 给…镶边 ❑ *...the mile of white sand beach bordered by palm trees and tropical flowers.* …环绕着棕榈树和热带花卉的一英里白色沙滩。

Thesaurus *border* 另参见：

V. abut, surround, touch 2
N. boundary, end, extremity, perimeter; *(ant.)* center, inside, middle 3

border·line /bɔrdərlaɪn/ (**borderlines**) 1 N-COUNT The **borderline between** two different or opposite things is the division between them. 分界线 ❑ *...a task which involves exploring the borderline between painting and photography.* …一项涉及探索绘画与摄影之间界线的任务。 2 ADJ Something that is **borderline** is only just acceptable as a member of a class or group. 勉强合格的 ❑ *Some were obviously unsuitable and could be ruled out at once. Others were borderline cases.* 一些显然不合适，可以马上被排除。另一些勉强合格。

bore ♦◊◊ /bɔr/ (**bores, boring, bored**) 1 V-T If someone or something **bores** you, you find them dull and uninteresting. 使厌烦 ❑ *Dickie bored him all through the meal with stories of the navy.* 迪基整整一顿饭都在讲海军的故事，让他厌烦。 2 PHRASE If someone or something **bores** you **to tears**, **bores** you **to death**, or **bores** you **stiff**, they bore you very much. 使…厌烦至极 [INFORMAL, EMPHASIS] ❑ *Monuments and museums bore him to tears.* 纪念碑和博物馆让他厌烦透了。 3 N-COUNT You describe someone as a **bore** when you think that they talk in a very uninteresting way. 无聊的家伙 ❑ *There is every reason why I shouldn't enjoy his company – he's a bore and a fool.* 我有充分的理由不和他在一起——他是个无聊的家伙，一个傻瓜。 4 N-SING You can describe a situation as **a bore** when you find it annoying. 令人讨厌的事 ❑ *It's a bore to be sick, and the novelty of lying in bed all day wears off quickly.* 生病是件无趣的事，整天躺在床上的新鲜感很快就没了。 5 V-T If you **bore** a hole in something, you make a deep round hole in it using a special tool. 钻(孔) ❑ *Get the special drill bit to bore the correct size hole for the job.* 找个特殊的钻头，钻个尺寸合适的孔。 6 **Bore** is the past tense of **bear**. **bear**的过去式 7 → see also **bored, boring**

bored /bɔrd/ ADJ If you are **bored**, you feel tired and impatient because you have lost interest in something or because you have nothing to do. 厌烦的 ❑ *I am getting very bored with this entire business.* 我开始对整件事感到非常厌倦。

Word Link *dom ≈ state of being : boredom, freedom, wisdom*

bore·dom /bɔrdəm/ N-UNCOUNT **Boredom** is the state of being bored. 厌烦 ❑ *He had given up attending lectures out of sheer boredom.* 他已经不再去听讲座了，纯粹出于厌倦。

bor·ing /bɔrɪŋ/ ADJ Someone or something **boring** is so dull and uninteresting that they make people tired and impatient. 乏味的 ❑ *Not only are mothers not paid but also most of their boring or difficult work is unnoticed.* 母亲们不仅得不到报酬，而且所干的乏味艰辛的活儿也很少被留意。

Thesaurus *boring* 另参见：

ADJ. dull, tedious, unexciting, uninteresting; *(ant.)* exciting, fun, interesting, lively

born ♦♦◊ /bɔrn/ 1 V-T PASSIVE When a baby **is born**, it comes out of its mother's body at the beginning of its life. In formal English, if you say that someone **is born of** someone or **to** someone, you mean that person is their parent. 出生 ❑ *She was born in Milan on April 29, 1923.* 她1923年4月29日生于米兰。 ❑ *He was born of German parents and lived most of his life abroad.* 他的父母是德国人，他一生大部分时间生活在国外。 2 V-T PASSIVE If someone **is born with** a particular disease, problem, or characteristic, they have it from the time they are born. 先天的 [no cont] ❑ *He was born with only one lung.* 他生下来就只有一个肺。 ❑ *Some people are born brainy.* 有些人生来就聪明。 3 V-T PASSIVE You can use **be born** in front of a particular name to show that a person was given this name at birth, although they may be better known by another name. 出生取名 [no cont] [FORMAL] ❑ *She was born Jenny Harvey on June 11, 1946.* 1946年6月11日她出生时取名珍妮・哈维。 4 ADJ You use **born** to describe someone who has a natural ability to do a particular activity or job. For example, if you are a **born** cook, you have a natural ability to cook well. 天生的 [ADJ n] ❑ *Jack was a born teacher.* 杰克是个天生的教师。 5 V-T PASSIVE When an idea or organization **is born**, it comes into existence. If something **is born of** a particular emotion or activity, it exists as a result of that emotion or activity. (思想或组织) 产生；诞生 [FORMAL] ❑ *The idea for the show was born in his hospital room.* 这个演出的想法是在他医院病房里产生的。 ❑ *Congress passed the National Security Act, and the CIA was born.* 国会通过了《国家安全法案》，中央情报局由此诞生。 6 → see also **newborn**

borne /bɔrn/ **Borne** is the past participle of **bear**. **bear**的过去分词

▲ **bor·ough** /bɜroʊ/ (**boroughs**) N-COUNT A **borough** is a town, or a district within a large city, which has its own council, government, or local services. 自治市；(大城市中的) 自治区 ❑ *...the New York City borough of Brooklyn.* …纽约市的布鲁克林自治区。

bor·row ♦◊◊ /bɒroʊ/ (**borrows, borrowing, borrowed**) 1 V-T If you **borrow** something that belongs to someone else, you take it or use it for a period of time, usually with their permission. 借 ❑ *Can I borrow a pen please?* 我可以借支笔吗？ 2 V-T/V-I If you **borrow** money **from** someone or **from** a bank, they give it to you and you agree to pay it back at some time in the future. 借(钱) ❑ *Morgan borrowed $5,000 from his father to form the company 20 years ago.* 摩根20年前向他父亲借了$5000来建立这家公司。 ❑ *It's so expensive to borrow from finance companies.* 向金融公司借款费用真够高的。 3 V-T If you **borrow** a book **from** a library, you take it away for a fixed period of time. 借(书) ❑ *I couldn't afford to buy any, so I borrowed them from the library.* 我一本也买不起，所以从图书馆借了这些。 4 V-T If you **borrow** something such as a word or an idea from another

language or from another person's work, you use it in your own language or work. 借用(思想、词等) ❑ *I borrowed his words for my book's title.* 我借用他的话作为我的书名。
→ see **bank, library**

Do not confuse **borrow** and **lend**. You say that you **borrow** something **from** another person. However, if you allow someone to **borrow** something that belongs to you, you say that you **lend** it **to** them. **Lend** is often followed by two objects. ❑ *Betty lent him some blankets... He lent Tim the money.* Both **borrow** and **lend** can be used without objects. ❑ *The poor had to borrow from the rich... Banks will not lend to them.* The noun related to **lend** is **loan**. ❑ *...a government loan of $3m.* **Loan** can also be used as a verb in the same way as **lend**, especially in American English. ❑ *I'll loan you fifty dollars.*

Word Partnership *borrow* 的常用搭配:
V. **forced to** borrow 1 2
PREP. borrow **from** 1 – 4
borrow **against** *something* 2
N. **ability to** borrow, borrow **cash/funds/money** 2
borrow **a phrase** 4
ADV. borrow **heavily** 2 4

bor·row·er /bɒroʊər/ (**borrowers**) N-COUNT A **borrower** is a person or organization that borrows money. 借方 ❑ *Borrowers with a big mortgage should go for a fixed rate.* 有大额抵押贷款的借款人应选择固定利率。
→ see **bank, interest rate**

bor·row·ing /bɒroʊɪŋ/ (**borrowings**) N-UNCOUNT **Borrowing** is the activity of borrowing money. 借钱 [also N in pl] ❑ *We have allowed spending and borrowing to rise in this recession.* 我们在这个经济衰退期允许增加支出和借款。

▲ **bos·om** /bʊzəm/ (**bosoms**) 1 N-COUNT A woman's breasts are sometimes referred to as her **bosom** or her **bosoms**. 乳房 [OLD-FASHIONED] ❑ *...a young mother with a baby resting against her ample bosom.* …婴儿依偎在其丰满乳房上的一位年轻母亲。 2 ADJ A **bosom** buddy is a friend who you know very well and like very much. 知心的 [ADJ n] ❑ *They were bosom buddies.* 他们曾是知心的伙伴。

boss ♦♦◇ /bɒs/ (**bosses, bossing, bossed**) 1 N-COUNT Your **boss** is the person in charge of the organization or department where you work. 老板 ❑ *He cannot stand his boss.* 他受不了他的老板。 2 N-COUNT If you are **the boss** in a group or relationship, you are the person who makes all the decisions. 头儿 [INFORMAL] ❑ *He thinks he's the boss.* 他自以为是头儿。 3 V-T If you say that someone **bosses** you, you mean that they keep telling you what to do in a way that is irritating. 支使 ❑ *We cannot boss them into doing more.* 我们不能再支使他们干其他事了。 ● PHRASAL VERB **Boss around** means the same as **boss**. 支使 ❑ *He started bossing people around.* 他开始支使大家了。

Thesaurus *boss* 另参见:
N. chief, director, employer, foreman, manager, owner, superintendent, supervisor 1 2

bossy /bɒsi/ ADJ If you describe someone as **bossy**, you mean that they enjoy telling people what to do. 好支使人的 [DISAPPROVAL] ❑ *She remembers being a rather bossy little girl.* 她记得自己曾是个爱支使人的小女孩。

Word Link *botan ≈ plant : botanical, botanist, botany*

★ **bo·tani·cal** /bətænɪkəl/ ADJ **Botanical** books, research, and activities relate to the scientific study of plants. 植物学的 [ADJ n] ❑ *The area is of great botanical interest.* 该地区很有植物学研究价值。

bota·nist /bɒtənɪst/ (**botanists**) N-COUNT A **botanist** is a scientist who studies plants. 植物学家

★ **bota·ny** /bɒtəni/ N-UNCOUNT **Botany** is the scientific study of plants. 植物学

botch /bɒtʃ/ (**botches, botching, botched**) 1 V-T If you **botch** something that you are doing, you do it badly or clumsily. 使…糟糕 [INFORMAL] ❑ *...a botched job.* …一项拙劣的工作。 ● PHRASAL VERB **Botch up** means the same as **botch**. 使…糟糕 ❑ *I hate having builders botch up repairs on my house.* 我痛恨建筑工人笨手笨脚地修理我的房子。 2 N-COUNT If you **make a botch of** something that you are doing, you botch it. 弄得一团糟 [INFORMAL]

both ♦♦♦ /boʊθ/ 1 DET You use **both** when you are referring to two people or things and saying that something is true about each of them. 两个(都) ❑ *She cried out in fear and flung both arms up to protect her face.* 她害怕得哭起来，急忙伸出双臂以保护自己的脸。 ● QUANT **Both** is also a quantifier. 两个 [QUANT "of" pl-n] ❑ *Both of these women have strong memories of the Vietnam War.* 两个女人对越南战争有着深刻的记忆。 ● PRON **Both** is also a pronoun. 两者 ❑ *Miss Brown and her friend, both from Brooklyn, were arrested on the 8th of June.* 布朗小姐和她的朋友，两人来自布鲁克林，于6月8日被捕了。 ● PRON-EMPH **Both** is also an emphasizing pronoun. 两者都 [n PRON] ❑ *He visited the Institute of Neurology in Havana where they both worked.* 他在哈瓦那参观了他们俩都曾工作过的神经病学研究所。 ● PREDET **Both** is also a predeterminer. 两者 [PREDET det pl-n] [EMPHASIS] ❑ *Both the horses were out, tacked up and ready to ride.* 两匹马都在门外被套上了马鞍，随时可以骑。 2 CONJ You use the structure **both...and** when you are giving two facts or alternatives and emphasizing that each of them is true or possible. …和…都 ❑ *Now women work both before and after having their children.* 如今，女性在生孩子前和生孩子后都工作。

Notice that all these sentences mean the same thing: "**Both boys have been ill**," "**Both the boys have been ill**," "**Both of the boys have been ill**," "**The boys have both been ill**." You cannot say "Both of boys have been ill," although when a pronoun is used, you can say "**Both of them have been ill**." See also note at **all**.

both·er ♦◇◇ /bɒðər/ (**bothers, bothering, bothered**) 1 V-T/V-I If you do not **bother to** do something or if you do not **bother with** it, you do not do it, consider it, or use it because you think it is unnecessary or because you are too lazy. 费心 [with brd-neg] ❑ *Lots of people don't bother to go through a marriage ceremony these days.* 很多人如今不费心举办婚礼了。 ❑ *Nothing I do makes any difference anyway, so why bother?* 不管我做什么都没有区别，那为什么还要费心去做呢？ 2 N-UNCOUNT **Bother** means trouble or difficulty. You can also use **bother** to refer to an activity which causes this, especially when you would prefer not to do it or get involved with it. 麻烦 [also "a" N] ❑ *I usually buy sliced bread – it's less bother.* 我通常买切片面包——这样可以少些麻烦。 ❑ *The courts take too long and going to the police is a bother.* 庭审太费时间，去警察局是件麻烦事。 3 V-T/V-I If something **bothers** you, or if you **bother** about it, it worries, annoys, or upsets you. 使烦恼；烦恼 ❑ *Is something bothering you?* 有什么事让你烦恼吗？ ❑ *It bothered me that boys weren't interested in me.* 让我烦恼的是，男孩们对我不感兴趣。 ● **both·ered** ADJ 烦恼的 [v-link ADJ] ❑ *I was bothered about the blister on my hand.* 我为手上的水疱感到很心烦。 4 V-T If someone **bothers** you, they talk to you when you want to be left alone or interrupt you when you are busy. 打扰 ❑ *We are playing a trick on a man who keeps bothering me.* 我们正在捉弄那个总是打搅我们的人。 5 PHRASE If you say that you **can't be bothered to** do something, you mean that you are not going to do it because you think it is unnecessary or because you are too lazy. 懒得 ❑ *I just can't be bothered to look after the house.* 我只是懒得照看那房子。 6 **hot and bothered** → see **hot**

bot·tle ♦♦◇ /bɒtəl/ (**bottles, bottling, bottled**) 1 N-COUNT A **bottle** is a glass or plastic container in which drinks and other liquids are kept. Bottles are usually round with straight sides and a narrow top. 瓶子 ❑ *There were two empty beer bottles on the table.* 桌上有两个空啤酒瓶。 ❑ *He was pulling the cork from a bottle of wine.* 他在拔一瓶葡萄酒的瓶塞。 2 N-COUNT You can use **bottle** to refer to a bottle and its contents, or to the contents only. 瓶 ❑ *She had drunk half a bottle of whiskey.* 她已经喝了半瓶威士忌。 3 V-T To **bottle** a drink or other liquid means to put it into bottles after it has been made. 使装瓶 ❑ *This is a large truck which has equipment to automatically bottle the wine.* 这是辆有葡萄酒自动装瓶设备的大卡车。 4 N-COUNT A **bottle** is a drinking container used by babies. It has a special rubber part at the top through which they can suck their drink. 奶瓶 ❑ *Gary was holding a bottle to the baby's lips.* 加里正把奶瓶放到婴儿的嘴边。 5 → see also **bottled**
→ see **glass**

bot·tled /bɒtəld/ ADJ **Bottled** gas is kept under pressure in special metal cylinders which can be moved from one place to another. 瓶装的

bot·tom ♦♦◇ /bɒtəm/ (**bottoms**) 1 N-COUNT **The bottom of** something is the lowest or deepest part of it. 底部 ❑ *He sat at the* *bottom of the stairs.* 他坐在楼梯底部。 ❑ *Answers can be found at the bottom of page 8.* 答案可以在第8页下端找到。 **2** ADJ The **bottom** thing or layer in a series of things or layers is the lowest one. 最下面的 [ADJ n] ❑ *There's an extra duvet in the bottom drawer of the cupboard.* 在柜子最下层的抽屉里还有一床羽绒被。 **3** N-COUNT **The bottom of** an object is the flat surface at its lowest point. You can also refer to the inside or outside of this surface as the **bottom**. 底 ❑ *Spread the onion slices on the bottom of the dish.* 把洋葱丝铺在盘底。 ❑ *...the bottom of their shoes.* …他们的鞋底。 **4** N-SING If you say that **the bottom** has dropped or fallen out of a market or industry, you mean that people have stopped buying the products it sells. (市场、行业)底部 [BUSINESS, JOURNALISM] ❑ *The bottom had fallen out of the city's property market.* 该市的房地产市场暴跌。 **5** N-SING **The bottom of** an organization or career structure is the lowest level in it, where new employees often start. 最底层 ["the" N, of t N "of" n] ❑ *He had worked in the theater for many years, starting at the bottom.* 他从最底层做起，在这个剧院工作了很多年。 **6** N-SING If someone is **bottom** or at **the bottom** in a survey, test, or league, their performance is worse than that of all the other people involved. 最后一名 ["the" N, also no det] ❑ *He was always bottom of the class.* 他总是班上的最后一名。 **7** N-COUNT The lower part of a swimsuit, tracksuit, or pair of pajamas can be referred to as the **bottoms** or the **bottom**. 服装的下半部 ❑ *She wore blue tracksuit bottoms.* 她下穿蓝色田径裤。 **8** N-SING **The bottom of** a street or yard is the end farthest away from you or from your house. (街道或庭院的) 尽头 [mainly BRIT]

in AM, usually use **end**

9 N-SING **The bottom of** a table is the end farthest away from where you are sitting. **The bottom of** a bed is the end where you usually rest your feet. (桌子或床的) 末端 [mainly BRIT]

in AM, usually use **end**

10 N-COUNT Your **bottom** is the part of your body that you sit on. 臀部 [mainly BRIT]

in AM, usually use **behind**

11 → see also **rock bottom** **12** PHRASE You use **at bottom** to emphasize that you are stating what you think is the real nature of something or the real truth about a situation. 实际上 [EMPHASIS] ❑ *The two systems are, at bottom, conceptual models.* 这两个系统实际上是概念模型。 **13** PHRASE If something is **at the bottom of** a problem or an unpleasant situation, it is the real cause of it. 某事的实际原因 ❑ *Often I find that anger and resentment are at the bottom of the problem.* 我经常发现愤怒与不满是问题的实际原因。 **14** PHRASE If you want to **get to the bottom of** a problem, you want to solve it by finding out its real cause. 彻底查明某事 ❑ *I have to get to the bottom of this.* 我必须把此事一查到底。

Thesaurus *bottom* 另参见：

N. base, floor, foundation, ground; *(ant.)* peak, top **1**

Word Partnership *bottom* 的常用搭配：

V. **reach the** bottom, **sink to the** bottom **1**
N. bottom **of a hill**, bottom **of the page/screen** **1**
bottom **drawer**, bottom **of the pool**, bottom **of the sea**, **river** bottom **1** **2**
bottom **lip**, bottom **rung** **2**
PREP. **along the** bottom, **on the** bottom **1** **3**
at/near the bottom **1** – **3** **5** **8**

★ **bot·tom·less** /bɒtəmlɪs/ **1** ADJ If you describe a supply of something as **bottomless**, you mean that it seems so large that it will never run out. 无穷无尽的 ❑ *...big supermarkets and multinationals with apparently bottomless pockets.* …表面上取之不尽的那些大超市和跨国公司们。 **2** ADJ If you describe something as **bottomless**, you mean that it is so deep that it seems to have no bottom. 深不见底的 ❑ *His eyes were like bottomless brown pools.* 他的眼睛像两汪深不见底的褐色水潭。 **3** PHRASE If you describe something as a **bottomless pit**, you mean that it seems as if you can take things from it and it will never be empty or put things in it and it will never be full. 取之不尽的事物；无底洞 ❑ *A gold mine is not a bottomless pit, the gold runs out.* 一个金矿不是无限的，黄金采光了。 ❑ *The problem is we don't have a bottomless pit of resources.* 问题是我们没有取之不尽的资源。

bot·tom line (**bottom lines**) **1** N-COUNT **The bottom line** in a decision or situation is the most important factor that you have to consider. 最重要的因素 ❑ *The bottom line is that it's not profitable.* 最重要的是这无利可图。 **2** N-COUNT The **bottom line** in a business deal is the least a person is willing to accept. 底线 ❑ *She says $95,000 is her bottom line.* 她说$95000是她的底线。 **3** N-COUNT The **bottom line** is the total amount of money that a company has made or lost over a particular period of time. 盈亏底线 [BUSINESS] ❑ *...to force chief executives to look beyond the next quarter's bottom line.* …迫使首席执行官们考虑下季度的盈亏底线。

bought /bɔt/ **Bought** is the past tense and past participle of **buy**. **buy**的过去式和过去分词

boul·der /boʊldər/ (**boulders**) N-COUNT A **boulder** is a large rounded rock. 圆形巨石 ❑ *It is thought that the train hit a boulder that had fallen down a cliff on to the track.* 人们认为这列火车撞到了从悬崖滚到铁轨上的大圆石。

boule·vard /bʊləvɑrd/ (**boulevards**) N-COUNT A **boulevard** is a wide street in a city, usually with trees along each side. 林荫大道 ❑ *...Lenton Boulevard.* …伦特林荫大道。

bounce /baʊns/ (**bounces, bouncing, bounced**) **1** V-T/V-I When an object such as a ball **bounces** or when you **bounce** it, it moves upward from a surface or away from it immediately after hitting it. 使…弹起；弹起 ❑ *My father would burst into the kitchen bouncing a tennis ball.* 我父亲会拍打着网球闯进厨房。 ❑ *...a falling pebble, bouncing down the eroded cliff.* …弹跳着滚下被蚀悬崖的一块卵石。 ● N-COUNT **Bounce** is also a noun. 弹 ❑ *The wheelchair tennis player is allowed two bounces of the ball.* 残疾网球运动员可以有两次弹球的机会。 **2** V-T/V-I If sound or light **bounces off** a surface or **is bounced off** it, it reaches the surface and is reflected back. 使…反射；反射 ❑ *Your arms and legs need protection from light bouncing off glass.* 你的双臂和双腿需要保护，免受玻璃反射光的照射。 **3** V-T/V-I If something **bounces** or if something **bounces** it, it swings or moves up and down. 使…跳动；跳动 ❑ *Her long black hair bounced as she walked.* 她长长的黑发在她走路时摆动着。 ❑ *The car was bouncing up and down as if someone were jumping on it.* 车上下颠簸，仿佛有人正在上面跳动。 **4** V-I If you **bounce** on a soft surface, you jump up and down on it repeatedly. 蹦跳 ❑ *She lets us do anything, even bounce on our beds.* 她允许我们做任何事，甚至是在床上蹦跳。 **5** V-I If someone **bounces** somewhere, they move there in an energetic way, because they are feeling happy. (因为开心) 蹦跳着走 ❑ *Moira bounced into the office.* 莫伊拉蹦蹦跳跳地走进办公室。 **6** V-T If you **bounce** your ideas **off** someone, you tell them to that person, in order to find out what they think about them. 征求别人的看法 ❑ *It was good to bounce ideas off another mind.* 征求别人的看法是好的。 **7** V-T/V-I If a check **bounces** or if someone **bounces** it, the bank refuses to accept it and pay out the money, because the person who wrote it does not have enough money in their account. 拒付 (支票) ❑ *Our only complaint would be if the check bounced.* 如果支票被拒收，这会是我们惟一的抱怨。 **8** V-I If an e-mail or other electronic message **bounces**, it is returned to the person who sent it because the address was wrong or because of a problem with one of the computers involved in sending it. 退回 [COMPUTING] ❑ *...a message saying that your mail has bounced or was unable to be delivered.* …一条说明你的邮件被退回或无法递送的信息。

▸ **bounce back** PHRASAL VERB If you **bounce back** after a bad experience, you return very quickly to your previous level of success, enthusiasm, or activity. 重新振作 ❑ *We lost two or three early games but we bounced back.* 我们之前输了两三场比赛，但又重新振作了起来。 ❑ *He is young enough to bounce back from this disappointment.* 他非常年轻，会从这次失望中振作起来。

Word Partnership *bounce* 的常用搭配：

ADJ. **a big/high/little** bounce **1**
N. bounce **a ball** **1**
bounce **a check** **7**
bounce **ideas off *someone*** **6**
ADV. bounce **off** **1** **2** **6**
bounce **along** **1** **3**
bounce **around** **1** **3** **5**

bounc·er /baʊnsər/ (**bouncers**) N-COUNT A **bouncer** is someone who stands at the door of a club, prevents unwanted people from coming in, and makes people leave if they cause trouble. (夜总会) 保安

bouncy /baʊnsi/ **1** ADJ Someone or something that is **bouncy** is very lively. 有活力的 ❑ *She was bouncy and full of energy.* 她生气勃勃，精力充沛。 **2** ADJ A **bouncy** thing can bounce very well or makes other things bounce well. 弹力大的 ❑ *...a children's paradise filled with bouncy toys.* …一个满是弹力玩具的儿童乐园。

b

B

bound
❶ BE BOUND
❷ OTHER USES

❶ **bound** ♦◇◇ /baʊnd/ 1 **Bound** is the past tense and past participle of **bind**. **bind**的过去式和过去分词 2 PHRASE If you say that something **is bound to** happen, you mean that you are sure it will happen, because it is a natural consequence of something that is already known or exists. 必然会 ❑ *There are bound to be price increases next year.* 明年价格必然会上涨。 3 PHRASE If you say that something **is bound to** happen or be true, you feel confident and certain of it, although you have no definite knowledge or evidence. 应该会 [SPOKEN] ❑ *I'll show it to Benjamin. He's bound to know.* 我要让本杰明瞧瞧，他该知道。 4 ADJ If one person, thing, or situation is **bound to** another, they are closely associated with each other, and it is difficult for them to be separated or to escape from each other. 与…密切相关的 [v-link ADJ "to" n] ❑ *We are as tightly bound to the people we dislike as to the people we love.* 我们与我们喜欢的以及不喜欢的人都一样密切相关。 5 ADJ If a vehicle or person is **bound for** a particular place, they are traveling toward it. 前往 [v-link ADJ "for" n] ❑ *The ship was bound for Italy.* 这艘船是开往意大利的。 ● COMB IN ADJ **Bound** is also a combining form. 开往 ❑ *...a Texas-bound oil freighter.* …一艘开往得克萨斯州的油轮。

Word Partnership *bound* 的常用搭配：

ADV.	**legally** bound, **tightly** bound ❶ 1
V.	bound **and gagged** ❶ 1
	bound **to fail** ❶ 2 3
N.	bound **by duty**, **feet/hands/wrists** bound, **leather** bound, **spiral** bound, bound **with tape** ❶ 1
	a flight/plane/ship/train bound **for** ❶ 5
PREP.	bound **together**, bound **up with** ❶ 4

❷ **bound** ♦◇◇ /baʊnd/ (**bounds, bounding, bounded**) 1 N-PLURAL **Bounds** are limits which normally restrict what can happen or what people can do. 界限；限制；范围 ❑ *Changes in temperature occur slowly and are constrained within relatively tight bounds.* 温度变化得很慢，而且被控制在相对严格的范围内。 ❑ *...a forceful personality willing to go beyond the bounds of convention.* …想要打破世俗束缚的坚强个性。 2 V-T If an area of land **is bounded by** something, that thing is situated around its edge. 位于…的界线周围 ❑ *Kirgizia is bounded by Uzbekistan, Kazakhstan and Tajikistan.* 吉尔吉斯与乌兹别克斯坦，哈萨克斯坦和塔吉克斯坦相毗邻。 ❑ *...the trees that bounded the parking lot.* …停车场周围的树。 3 V-T PASSIVE If someone's life or situation **is bounded by** certain things, those are its most important aspects and it is limited or restricted by them. 约束 ❑ *Our lives are bounded by work, family and television.* 我们的生活受到工作、家庭及电视的约束。 4 V-I If a person or animal **bounds** in a particular direction, they move quickly with large steps or jumps. 跳跃着前行 ❑ *He bounded up the steps and pushed the bell of the door.* 他跳上了台阶，按了门铃。 5 N-COUNT A **bound** is a long or high jump. 跳跃 [LITERARY] ❑ *With one bound Jack was free.* 纵身一跃，杰克自由了。 6 V-I If the quantity or performance of something **bounds** ahead, it increases or improves quickly and suddenly. 骤升 ❑ *Shares in the company bounded ahead by almost 3 percent.* 公司的股份几乎骤升了3%。 7 PHRASE If a place is **out of bounds**, people are not allowed to go there. 禁止进入 ❑ *For the last few days the area has been out of bounds to foreign journalists.* 过去几天，这个地区禁止外国记者入内。 8 PHRASE If something is **out of bounds**, people are not allowed to do it, use it, see it, or know about it. 禁止的 ❑ *American parents may soon be able to rule violent TV programs out of bounds.* 美国父母也许很快就能禁止暴力电视节目的播放。

bounda·ry /baʊndəri/ (**boundaries**) 1 N-COUNT The **boundary** of an area of land is an imaginary line that separates it from other areas. 边界 ❑ *The Bow Brook forms the western boundary of the wood.* 鲍溪成了树林的西边界。 2 N-COUNT The **boundaries of** something such as a subject or activity are the limits that people think that it has. 界限 ❑ *The boundaries between history and storytelling are always being blurred and muddled.* 历史与故事的界限一直模糊不清。

Word Partnership *boundary* 的常用搭配：

N.	boundary **dispute**, boundary **line** 1
PREP.	boundary **around places/things**, boundary **between places/things**, **beyond a** boundary, boundary **of** ***someplace/something*** 1 2
V.	**cross a** boundary, **mark/set a** boundary 1 2

▲ **boun·ty** /baʊnti/ (**bounties**) 1 N-VAR You can refer to something that is provided in large amounts as **bounty**. 丰富的 [LITERARY] ❑ *...autumn's bounty of fruits, seeds and berries.* …秋天丰收的水果、种子和浆果。 2 N-COUNT A **bounty** is money that is offered as a reward for doing something, especially for finding or killing a particular person. 奖金（尤用于寻人或杀人） ❑ *A bounty of $50,000 was put on Dr. Alvarez's head.* 一笔5万美元的赏金用以悬赏阿尔瓦雷斯博士的人头。

▲ **bou·quet** /boʊkeɪ, bu-/ (**bouquets**) 1 N-COUNT A **bouquet** is a bunch of flowers which is attractively arranged. 花束 ❑ *The woman carried a bouquet of dried violets.* 那个女子拿着一束干紫罗兰花。 2 N-VAR The **bouquet** of something, especially wine, is the pleasant smell that it has. 芳香 ❑ *...a Sicilian wine with a light red color and a bouquet of cloves.* …一杯浅红色并带着丁香芬芳的西西里酒。

▲ **bour·geois** /bʊərʒwa/ ADJ If you describe people, their way of life, or their attitudes as **bourgeois**, you disapprove of them because you consider them typical of conventional middle-class people. 中产阶级的 [DISAPPROVAL] ❑ *He's accusing them of having a bourgeois and limited vision.* 他谴责他们有中产阶级的短浅目光。

▲ **bout** /baʊt/ (**bouts**) 1 N-COUNT If you have a **bout of** an illness or of an unpleasant feeling, you have it for a short period. （疾病或不愉快情绪）发作 ❑ *He was recovering from a severe bout of flu.* 他当时正从一次严重的流感中康复。 2 N-COUNT A **bout of** something that is unpleasant is a short time during which it occurs a great deal. 爆发 ❑ *The latest bout of violence has claimed twenty four lives.* 最近的一次暴力事件造成了24人死亡。 3 N-COUNT A **bout** is a boxing or wrestling match. 拳击（或摔跤）比赛 ❑ *This will be his eighth title bout in 19 months.* 这将是他19个月中的第八次比赛夺冠。

bou·tique /butik/ (**boutiques**) N-COUNT A **boutique** is a small store that sells fashionable clothes, shoes, or jewelry. 时尚精品小店 .

bow
❶ BENDING OR SUBMITTING
❷ PART OF A SHIP
❸ OBJECTS

❶ **bow** /baʊ/ (**bows, bowing, bowed**) 1 V-I When you **bow to** someone, you briefly bend your body toward them as a formal way of greeting them or showing respect. 鞠躬 ❑ *They bowed low to Louis and hastened out of his way.* 他们向路易斯深深地鞠躬并迅速给他让路。 ● N-COUNT **Bow** is also a noun. 鞠躬 ❑ *I gave a theatrical bow and waved.* 我夸张地鞠了一躬，然后挥了挥手。 2 V-T If you **bow** your head, you bend it downward so that you are looking toward the ground, for example, because you want to show respect or because you are thinking deeply about something. 低下（头） ❑ *The Colonel bowed his head and whispered a prayer of thanksgiving.* 上校低下头，低声感恩祷告。 3 V-I If you **bow to** pressure or to someone's wishes, you agree to do what they want you to do. 屈从 ❑ *Some stores are bowing to consumer pressure and stocking organically grown vegetables.* 有些商店屈于消费者的压力，供应有机蔬菜。

▶ **bow out** PHRASAL VERB If you **bow out** of something, you stop taking part in it. 退出 [WRITTEN] ❑ *He had bowed out gracefully when his successor had been appointed.* 当他的继任者被任命时，他很有风度地退出了。

❷ **bow** /baʊ/ (**bows**) N-COUNT The front part of a ship is called **the bow** or **the bows**. The plural **bows** can be used to refer either to one or to more than one of these parts. 船头 ❑ *The waves were about five feet high now, and the bow of the boat was leaping up and down.* 浪头现在约有五英尺高，船头上下颠簸。

❸ **bow** /boʊ/ (**bows**) 1 N-COUNT A **bow** is a knot with two loops and two loose ends that is used in tying shoelaces and ribbons. 蝴蝶结 ❑ *Add a length of ribbon tied in a bow.* 加一段打成蝴蝶结的缎带。 2 N-COUNT A **bow** is a weapon for shooting arrows that consists of a long piece of curved wood with a string attached to both its ends. 弓 ❑ *Some of the raiders were armed with bows and arrows.* 有些偷袭者配备了弓箭。 3 N-COUNT The **bow** of a violin or other stringed instrument is a long thin piece of wood with fibers stretched along it that you move across the strings of the instrument in order to play it. 琴弓

bowed

Pronounced /boʊd/ for meaning 1, and /baʊd/ for meaning 2.

义项1读作 /boʊd/，义项2读作 /baʊd/。

1 ADJ Something that is **bowed** is curved. 弯曲的 ❑ *...an old lady with bowed legs.* …一个弯着双腿的老太太。 2 ADJ If a person's body is **bowed**, it is bent forward. 弓着的 ❑ *He walked aimlessly along the street, head down and shoulders bowed.* 他低着头，缩着肩膀，漫无目的地在街上走着。

bow·el /baʊəl/ (**bowels**) N-COUNT Your **bowels** are the tubes in your body through which digested food passes from your stomach to your anus. 肠 ❑ *Symptoms such as stomach pains and irritable bowels can be signs of bowel cancer.* 胃痛和肠易激等症状都可能是肠癌的征兆。

bowl ♦◊◊ /boʊl/ (**bowls, bowling, bowled**) 1 N-COUNT A **bowl** is a round container with a wide uncovered top. Some kinds of bowl are used, for example, for serving or eating food from, or in cooking, while other larger kinds are used for washing or cleaning. 碗 ❑ *Put all the ingredients into a large bowl.* 把所有的配料放进一个大碗里。 2 N-COUNT The contents of a bowl can be referred to as a **bowl of** something. 一碗的量 ❑ *...a bowl of soup.* …一碗汤。 3 N-COUNT You can refer to the hollow rounded part of an object as its **bowl**. 碗状物 ❑ *He smacked the bowl of his pipe into his hand.* 他在手里磕了磕烟斗。 4 V-T In a sport such as bowling or lawn bowling, when a bowler **bowls** a ball, he or she rolls it down a narrow track or field of grass. (保龄球或草地滚球运动中) 滚球 ❑ *Neither finalist bowled a particularly strong game.* 两位决赛选手滚球得分都不是特别高。 5 V-T/V-I In a sport such as cricket, when a bowler **bowls** a ball, he or she throws it down the field toward a batsman. (板球等) 投球 ❑ *I can't see the point of bowling a ball like that.* 我不能理解那样的投球。 6 V-I If you **bowl along** in a car or on a boat, you move along very quickly, especially when you are enjoying yourself. (乘车、船) 飞驰 ❑ *Veronica looked at him, smiling, as they bowled along.* 在他们一路飞驰的当儿，韦罗妮卡微笑着看他。 7 → see also **bowling**

→ see **dish**

bow·ler /boʊlər/ (**bowlers**) 1 N-COUNT A **bowler** is someone who plays bowls or goes bowling. 保龄球手 2 N-COUNT The **bowler** in a sport such as cricket is the player who is bowling the ball. 投球手

▲ **bowl·ing** /boʊlɪŋ/ 1 N-UNCOUNT **Bowling** is a game in which you roll a heavy ball down a narrow track toward a group of wooden objects and try to knock down as many of them as possible. 保龄球 ❑ *I go bowling for relaxation.* 我玩保龄球放松自己。 2 N-UNCOUNT In a sport such as cricket, **bowling** is the action or activity of bowling the ball toward the batsman. 投球 ❑ *Much of the bowling today will be done by Phil Tufnell.* 大多数投球今天将由菲尔·塔夫内尔完成。

box ♦♦◊ /bɒks/ (**boxes, boxing, boxed**) 1 N-COUNT A **box** is a square or rectangular container with hard or stiff sides. Boxes often have lids. 盒子；箱子 ❑ *He reached into the cardboard box beside him.* 他把手伸进他旁边的纸板箱。 ❑ *They sat on wooden boxes.* 他们坐在木箱上。 2 N-COUNT You can use **box** to refer to a box and its contents, or to the contents only. 一盒的量 ❑ *She ate two boxes of chocolates.* 她吃了两盒巧克力。 3 N-COUNT A **box** is a square or rectangle that is printed or drawn on a piece of paper, a road, or on some other surface. 方格 ❑ *For more information, just check the box and send us the form.* 若需更多信息，在方框内打勾，然后把表格寄给我们。 4 N-COUNT A **box** is a small separate area in a theater or at a sports arena or stadium, where a small number of people can sit to watch the performance or game. 包厢 ❑ *Jim watched the game from a private box.* 吉姆在私人包厢里观看比赛。 5 N-COUNT **Box** is used before a number as a mailing address by people or organizations that rent a post office box. 邮箱 ❑ *...Country Crafts, Box 111, Landisville.* …兰迪斯维尔克拉福特斯地区111号邮箱。 6 N-UNCOUNT **Box** is a small evergreen tree with dark leaves that is often used to form hedges. 黄杨 [oft N n] ❑ *...box hedges.* …黄杨树篱。 7 V-I To **box** means to fight someone according to the rules of boxing. 拳击 ❑ *At school I boxed and played rugby.* 在学校，我打拳击并玩英式橄榄球。 8 → see also **boxing, post office box**

▸ **box in** 1 PHRASAL VERB If you **are boxed in**, you are unable to move from a particular place because you are surrounded by other people or cars. 围堵 ❑ *The cabs cut in front of them, trying to box them in.* 出租车超车跑在他们前面，试图堵住他们。 2 PHRASAL VERB If something **boxes** you **in**, it puts you in a situation where you have very little choice about what you can do. 约束 ❑ *We are not trying to box anybody in, we are trying to find a satisfactory way forward.* 我们不想限制任何人，我们在试图找到一个令人满意的解决方案。

box·er /bɒksər/ (**boxers**) N-COUNT A **boxer** is someone who takes part in the sport of boxing. 拳击手

box·ing /bɒksɪŋ/ N-UNCOUNT **Boxing** is a sport in which two people wearing large padded gloves fight according to special rules. 拳击

box lunch (**box lunches**) N-COUNT A **box lunch** is food packed in a box, for example a sandwich, that you buy and eat as your lunch. 盒装午餐；盒饭 [AM]

in BRIT, use **packed lunch**

❑ *Box lunches can be arranged to take with you on day trips into the valley.* 可以准备盒饭让你们带着，在峡谷一日游的路上吃。

box num·ber (**box numbers**) N-COUNT A **box number** is a number used as an address, for example one given by a newspaper for replies to a private advertisement, or one used by an organization for the letters sent to it. 邮政信箱号码 ❑ *He produced 1000 leaflets tagged with his phone number and a post office box number.* 他做了一千份标有他的电话号码和邮箱号码的传单。

box of·fice (**box offices**) also **box-office** 1 N-COUNT The **box office** in a theater or concert hall is the place where the tickets are sold. 售票处 ❑ *...the long line of people outside the box-office.* …售票处外的长队。 2 N-SING When people talk about **the box office**, they are referring to the degree of success of a film or play in terms of the number of people who go to watch it or the amount of money it makes. 票房 ❑ *The film has taken $180 million at the box office.* 这部电影的票房收入已达到1.8亿美元。

boy ♦♦♦ /bɔɪ/ (**boys**) 1 N-COUNT A **boy** is a child who will grow up to be a man. 男孩 ❑ *He was still just a boy.* 他还只是个男孩。 2 N-COUNT You can refer to a young man as a **boy**, especially when talking about relationships between boys and girls. 小伙子 ❑ *...the age when girls get interested in boys.* …女孩儿开始对小伙子感兴趣的年纪。 3 N-COUNT Someone's **boy** is their son. 儿子 [INFORMAL] ❑ *Eric was my cousin Edward's boy.* 埃里克是我堂兄爱德华的儿子。 4 N-COUNT You can refer to a man as a **boy**, especially when you are talking about him in an affectionate way. 小伙儿 [INFORMAL, FEELINGS] ❑ *...the local boy who made president.* …那个当上总统的本地小伙儿。 5 EXCLAM Some people say "**boy**" or "**oh boy**" in order to express feelings of excitement or admiration. 好家伙 (表示兴奋或羡慕) [mainly AM, INFORMAL, FEELINGS] ❑ *Oh boy! what resourceful children I have.* 好家伙！我的孩子们多机智啊。

★ **boy·cott** /bɔɪkɒt/ (**boycotts, boycotting, boycotted**) V-T If a country, group, or person **boycotts** a country, organization, or activity, they refuse to be involved with it in any way because they disapprove of it. 联合抵制 ❑ *The main opposition parties are boycotting the elections.* 主要的反对党派正在联合抵制选举。 ● N-COUNT **Boycott** is also a noun. 联合抵制 ❑ *Opposition leaders had called for a boycott of the vote.* 反对派领导者号召联合抵制投票。

boy·friend /bɔɪfrɛnd/ (**boyfriends**) N-COUNT Someone's **boyfriend** is a man or boy with whom they are having a romantic or sexual relationship. 男朋友 ❑ *...Brenda and her boyfriend Anthony.* …布伦达和她的男朋友安东尼。

A **boyfriend** is the male person in a romantic relationship. It is not used to describe friendship between men. This is different from **girlfriend**, which can describe either a friendship or a romance.

★ **boy·hood** /bɔɪhʊd/ N-UNCOUNT **Boyhood** is the period of a male person's life during which he is a boy. 少年时代 ❑ *They are rivals who have known each other since boyhood.* 他们是少年时代就相识的对手。

boy·ish /bɔɪɪʃ/ ADJ If you describe a man as **boyish**, you mean that he is like a boy in his appearance or behavior, and you find this characteristic quite attractive. 男孩子气的 [APPROVAL] ❑ *She was relieved to see his face light up with a boyish grin.* 看到他脸上显出孩子气的笑容，她松了一口气。 ● **boy·ish·ly** ADV 男孩子气地 ❑ *John grinned boyishly.* 约翰孩子气地咧嘴一笑。

b

B

bps /bi pi ɛs/ **bps** is a measurement of the speed at which computer data is transferred, for example, by a modem. **bps** is an abbreviation for "bits per second." 比特/秒 [COMPUTING] ❑ *A minimum 28,800 bps modem is probably the slowest you'll want to put up with.* 一个最低28800比特/秒的调制解调器可能是你能愿意忍受的最慢的了。

bra /brɑ/ (**bras**) N-COUNT A **bra** is a piece of underwear that women wear to support their breasts. 胸罩

★ **brace** /breɪs/ (**braces, bracing, braced**) 1 V-T If you **brace yourself for** something unpleasant or difficult, you prepare yourself for it. 准备(面对不愉快或困难之事) ❑ *He braced himself for the icy plunge into the black water.* 他准备跳入冰冷的黑水。 2 V-T If you **brace yourself against** something or **brace** part of your body **against** it, you press against something in order to steady your body or to avoid falling. 抵住 ❑ *Elaine braced herself against the dresser and looked in the mirror.* 伊莱恩身体抵住梳妆台，照了照镜子 3 V-T If you **brace** your shoulders or knees, you keep them stiffly in a particular position. 绷紧(肩或膝盖) ❑ *He braced his shoulders defiantly as another squall of wet snow slashed across his face.* 当又一阵雨雪呼啸着划过他的脸庞时，他毫无畏惧地绷紧双肩。 4 V-T To **brace** something means to strengthen or support it with something else. 支撑 ❑ *Overhead, the lights showed the old timbers, used to brace the roof.* 在头顶上，光线照射出支撑屋顶的旧木头。 5 N-COUNT A **brace** is a device attached to a part of a person's body, for example, to a weak leg, in order to strengthen or support it. 支架 ❑ *He wore leg braces after he had polio in childhood.* 小时候患小儿麻痹症后，他使用了腿部支架。 6 N-PLURAL **Braces** are a metal device that can be fastened to a person's teeth in order to help them grow straight. 牙箍 ❑ *I used to have to wear braces.* 我以前不得不戴牙箍。 7 N-COUNT **Braces** are a pair of written marks {} that you place around words, numbers, or parts of a computer code, for example, to indicate that they are connected in some way or are separate from other parts of the writing or code. 括弧 [AM]

in BRIT, usually use **curly brackets**

8 N-PLURAL **Braces** are a pair of straps that pass over your shoulders and fasten to your pants at the front and back in order to stop them from falling down. (裤子的) 背带 [BRIT]

in AM, use **suspenders**

→ see **teeth**

▲ **brace·let** /breɪslɪt/ (**bracelets**) N-COUNT A **bracelet** is a chain or band, usually made of metal, that you wear around your wrist as jewelry. 手镯

→ see **jewelry**

brac·ing /breɪsɪŋ/ ADJ If you describe something, especially a place, climate, or activity as **bracing**, you mean that it makes you feel fresh and full of energy. 令人心神气爽的 ❑ *...a bracing walk.* …一次令人心神气爽的散步。

★ **brack·et** /brækɪt/ (**brackets, bracketing, bracketed**) 1 N-COUNT If you say that someone or something is in a particular **bracket**, you mean that they come within a particular range, for example, a range of incomes, ages, or prices. (收入、年龄、价格等的) 范围 ❑ *...a 33% top tax rate on everyone in these high-income brackets.* …这些高收入范围内每个人的33%的最高税率。 2 N-COUNT **Brackets** are pieces of metal, wood, or plastic that are fastened to a wall in order to support something such as a shelf. (固定在墙上的) 支架 ❑ *Fix the beam with the brackets and screws.* 用支架和螺丝固定横梁。 3 V-T If two or more people or things **are bracketed together**, they are considered to be similar or related in some way. 归为一类 ❑ *The Magi, Brahmins, and Druids were bracketed together as men of wisdom.* 三贤人、婆罗门、德鲁伊特教僧侣一起被归为智者。 4 N-COUNT **Brackets** are pair of marks ( ) that are placed around a series of symbols in a mathematical expression to indicate that those symbols function as one item within the expression. (数学中用以表示整体的) 括号 5 N-COUNT **Brackets** are a pair of written marks ( ) that you place around a word, expression, or sentence in order to indicate that you are giving extra information. (用以给出额外信息的) 括号 [BRIT]

in AM, use **parentheses**

▲ **brag** /bræg/ (**brags, bragging, bragged**) V-T/V-I If you **brag**, you say in a very proud way that you have something or have done something. 吹嘘说; 吹嘘 [DISAPPROVAL] ❑ *He's always bragging that he's a great martial artist.* 他总是吹嘘说他是伟大的武术家。 ❑ *He'll probably go around bragging to his friends.* 他可能会到处去向他的朋友们吹嘘。 ❑ *Winn bragged that he had spies in the department.* 温吹嘘说他在这个部门里有密探。

braid /breɪd/ (**braids, braiding, braided**) 1 N-UNCOUNT **Braid** is a narrow piece of decorated cloth or twisted threads, which is used to decorate clothes or curtains. 流穗 ❑ *...a plum-colored uniform with lots of gold braid.* …一套带很多金色流穗的梅色制服。 2 V-T If you **braid** hair or a group of threads, you twist three or more lengths of the hair or threads over and under each other to make one thick length. 把…编成辫子 [AM]

in BRIT, use **plait**

❑ *She had almost finished braiding Louisa's hair.* 她已差不多给路易莎编完发辫了。 3 N-COUNT A **braid** is a length of hair that has been divided into three or more lengths and then braided. 发辫 [AM]

in BRIT, use **plait**

❑ *...a short, energetic woman with her hair in braids.* …一个梳着发辫、充满活力的矮个女人。

brain ♦♦◇ /breɪn/ (**brains**) 1 N-COUNT Your **brain** is the organ inside your head that controls your body's activities and enables you to think and to feel things such as heat and pain. 脑 ❑ *Her father died of a brain tumor.* 他的父亲死于脑瘤。 2 N-COUNT Your **brain** is your mind and the way that you think. 脑筋 ❑ *Once you stop using your brain you soon go stale.* 一旦你停止动脑筋，你很快就会变迟钝。 3 N-COUNT If someone has **brains** or a good **brain**, they have the ability to learn and understand things quickly, to solve problems, and to make good decisions. 头脑 ❑ *They were not the only ones to have brains and ambition.* 他们并非仅有的有头脑、有抱负的人。 4 N-COUNT If someone is **the brains** behind an idea or an organization, he or she had that idea or makes the important decisions about how that organization is managed. 智囊 [INFORMAL] ❑ *Mr. White was the brains behind the scheme.* 怀特先生是这项计划后面的智囊。 5 **to rack** your **brains** → see **rack**

→ see Word Web: **brain**

→ see **nervous system**

brain·child /breɪntʃaɪld/ N-SING Someone's **brainchild** is an idea or invention that they have thought up or created. 智慧结晶 ❑ *The record was the brainchild of rock star Bob Geldof.* 这张唱片是摇滚明星鲍勃·格尔多夫的智慧结晶。

brain·storm /breɪnstɔrm/ (**brainstorms, brainstorming, brainstormed**) 1 N-COUNT If you have a **brainstorm**, you suddenly have a clever idea. 突发的灵感 [AM]

in BRIT, use **brainwave**

❑ *"Look," she said, getting a brainstorm, "why don't you invite them here?"* "嘿，"她突发灵感，"你为什么不邀请他们来这里呢？" 2 V-T/V-I If a group of people **brainstorm**, they have a meeting in which they all put forward as many ideas and suggestions as they can think of. 开头脑风暴法讨论会 ❑ *The women meet twice a month to brainstorm*

Word Web brain

The human **brain** weighs about three pounds. It contains seven distinct sections. The largest are the cerebrum, the cerebellum, and the medulla oblongata. The cerebrum wraps around the outside of the brain. It handles **learning**, **communication**, and voluntary **movement**. The cerebellum controls **balance**, **posture**, and movement. The medulla oblongata links the **spinal cord** with other parts of the brain. This part of the brain controls automatic actions such as breathing, heartbeat, and swallowing. It also tells us when we are hungry and when we need to sleep.

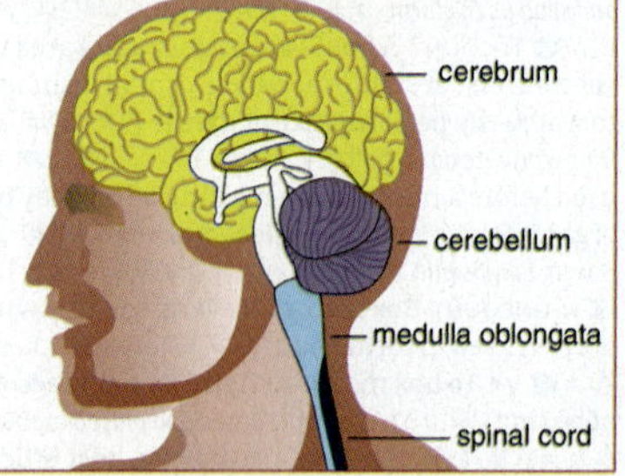

and set business goals for each other. 这些妇女们一个月聚头两次来开头脑风暴会议，为彼此设定商业目标。 ❑ *She brainstormed the possible approaches she might take.* 她用头脑风暴法想出了她可以采取的可能方法。 ● **brain·storming** N-UNCOUNT 头脑风暴法讨论 ❑ *Hundreds of other ideas had been tried and discarded during two years of brainstorming.* 数百个其它点子在两年的头脑风暴集体讨论中被尝试过但又被摒弃了。

brain·wash /breɪnwɒʃ/ (**brainwashes, brainwashing, brainwashed**) V-T If you **brainwash** someone, you force them to believe something by continually telling them that it is true, and preventing them from thinking about it properly. 给…洗脑 ❑ *They brainwash people into giving up all their money.* 他们给人们洗脑，使他们放弃他们所有的钱。

brain·wave /breɪnweɪv/ (**brainwaves**) N-COUNT If you have a **brainwave**, you suddenly have a clever idea. 突发的灵感 [BRIT]

in AM, use **brainstorm**

brake /breɪk/ (**brakes, braking, braked**) **1** N-COUNT **Brakes** are devices in a vehicle that make it go slower or stop. 刹车 ❑ *A seagull swooped down in front of her car, causing her to slam on the brakes.* 一只海鸥突然飞扑到她的车前，导致她猛踩刹车。 **2** V-T/V-I When a vehicle or its driver **brakes**, or when a driver **brakes** a vehicle, the driver makes it slow down or stop by using the brakes. 刹车 ❑ *He heard tires squeal as the car braked to avoid a collision.* 他听到当汽车刹车为避免撞车时轮胎发出了刺耳的尖声。 ❑ *He braked the car slightly.* 他稍稍刹车。 **3** N-COUNT You can use **brake** in a number of expressions to indicate that something has slowed down or stopped. 停止；减速 ❑ *Illness had put a brake on his progress.* 疾病中止了他的进展。

bran /bræn/ N-UNCOUNT **Bran** is the outer skin of grain that is left when the grain has been used to make flour. 麸 ❑ *...oat bran.* …燕麦麸。

branch ♦◇◇ /bræntʃ/ (**branches, branching, branched**) **1** N-COUNT The **branches** of a tree are the parts that grow out from its trunk and have leaves, flowers, or fruit growing on them. 树枝 ❑ *...the upper branches of a row of pines.* …一排松树的上部枝条。 **2** N-COUNT A **branch of** a business or other organization is one of the offices, stores, or groups which belong to it and which are located in different places. (企业或机构的) 分支 ❑ *The local branch of Bank of America is handling the accounts.* 美国银行的本地分行正在处理这些账目。 **3** N-COUNT A **branch of** an organization such as the government or the police force is a department that has a particular function. 分支部门 ❑ *Senate employees could take their employment grievances to another branch of government.* 参议院的雇员可以将他们对工作的不满向另一政府分支部门申诉。 ❑ *He had a fascination for submarines and joined this branch of the service.* 他迷恋潜艇并加入了海军的这个分支。 **4** N-COUNT A **branch of** a subject is a part or type of it. (学科的) 分科 ❑ *Whole branches of science may not receive any grants.* 很多整个科学分科可能都得不到拨款。 **5** N-COUNT A **branch of** your family is a group of its members who are descended from one particular person. (家族的) 支系 ❑ *This is one of the branches of the Roosevelt family.* 这是罗斯福家族的一个支系。

▶ **branch off** PHRASAL VERB A road or path that **branches off** from another one starts from it and goes in a slightly different direction. If you **branch off** somewhere, you change the direction in which you are going. 岔开 ❑ *After a few miles, a small road branched off to the right.* 过了几英里后，一条小路向右岔开了。

▶ **branch out** PHRASAL VERB If a person or an organization **branches out**, they do something that is different from their normal activities or work. 朝新的方向拓展 ❑ *I continued studying moths, and branched out to other insects.* 我继续研究飞蛾，同时也开始研究其它昆虫。

brand ♦◇◇ /brænd/ (**brands, branding, branded**) **1** N-COUNT A **brand** of a product is the version of it that is made by one particular manufacturer. 品牌 ❑ *Winston is a brand of cigarette.* 云斯顿是一种香烟品牌。 ❑ *I bought one of the leading brands.* 我买了知名品牌中的一种。 **2** N-COUNT A **brand of** something such as a way of thinking or behaving is a particular kind of it. (思维或行为方式等的) 独特类型 ❑ *Joel Hatch brings his own unique brand of humor to the role.* 乔尔·哈奇把他自己独具一格的幽默带进了这个角色。 **3** V-T If someone **is branded** as something bad, people think they are that thing. 归为 (不好的事物) ❑ *I was instantly branded as a rebel.* 我立刻被归为造反者。 ❑ *The company has been branded racist by some of its own staff.* 这家公司被它自己的一些职员归为种族主义者。 **4** V-T When you **brand** an animal, you put a permanent mark on its skin in order to show who it belongs to, usually by burning a mark onto its skin. 给…打上烙印 ❑ *The owner couldn't be bothered to brand the cattle.* 主人懒得给这牛打上烙印。 ● N-COUNT **Brand** is also a noun. 烙印 ❑ *A brand was a mark of ownership burned into the hide of an animal with a hot iron.* 烙印是用烙铁烧在牲畜皮上的所有权标记。

> The **brand** of a product such as jeans, tea, or soap is its name, which can also be the name of the company that makes or sells it. The **make** of a car or electrical appliance such as a radio or washing machine is the name of the company that produces it. If you talk about what **type** of product or service you want, you are talking about its quality and what features it should have. You can also talk about **types** of people or of abstract things. ❑ *...which type of coffeemaker to choose. ...a new type of bank account. ...looking for a certain type of actor.* A **model** of car or of some other devices is a name that is given to a particular **type**, for example, a Ford Escort. Note that **type** can also be used informally to mean either **make** or **model**. For example, if someone asks what **type** of car you have got, you could reply "an SUV," "a Ford," or perhaps "an Escort."

brand·ed /brændɪd/ ADJ A **branded** product is one that is made by a well-known manufacturer and has the manufacturer's label on it. 有品牌的 [ADJ n] [BUSINESS] ❑ *Supermarket lines are often cheaper than branded goods.* 超市里的产品常常比品牌商品便宜。

brand im·age (**brand images**) N-COUNT The **brand image** of a particular brand of a product is the image or impression that people have of it, usually created by advertising. 品牌形象 [BUSINESS] ❑ *Few products have brand images anywhere near as strong as Levi's.* 没有几个产品的品牌形象能跟李维斯的相提并论。

bran·dish /brændɪʃ/ (**brandishes, brandishing, brandished**) V-T If you **brandish** something, especially a weapon, you hold it in a threatening way. 挥舞 (尤指武器) ❑ *He appeared in the lounge brandishing a knife.* 他出现在休息室，挥舞着一把刀。

brand lead·er (**brand leaders**) N-COUNT The **brand leader** of a particular product is the brand of it that most people choose to buy, or the manufacturer that makes that brand. 品牌先锋 [BUSINESS] ❑ *In office supplies, we're the brand leader.* 在办公用品中，我们是品牌先锋。

brand name (**brand names**) N-COUNT The **brand name** of a product is the name the manufacturer gives it and under which it is sold. 商标 [BUSINESS] ❑ *The drug is marketed under the brand name Viramune.* 这种药品以维乐命商标销售。

> The maker of a product may come to be identified so closely with it that all products of that sort are called by the same name. For example, tissue paper for blowing your nose is branded as Kleenex and so people often call all brands of tissue "Kleenex" rather than "tissue." ❑ *My nose is running. Please give me a Kleenex.* The "Trademark" label in this dictionary will show you brands which are commonly used in this way.

brand-name prod·uct (**brand-name products**) N-COUNT A **brand-name product** is one which is made by a well-known manufacturer and has the manufacturer's label on it. 品牌产品 [BUSINESS] ❑ *In buying footwear, 66% prefer brand-name products.* 买鞋时，66%的人更喜欢品牌产品。

brand-new ADJ A **brand-new** object is completely new. 全新的 ❑ *Yesterday he went off to buy himself a brand-new car.* 昨天他去给自己买了一辆崭新的车。

▲ **bran·dy** /brændi/ (**brandies**) **1** N-MASS **Brandy** is a strong alcoholic drink. It is often drunk after a meal. 白兰地酒 **2** N-COUNT A **brandy** is a glass of brandy. (一杯) 白兰地酒 ❑ *After a couple of brandies Michael started telling me his life story.* 几杯白兰地酒过后，迈克尔开始向我讲述他的人生故事。

brash /bræʃ/ (**brasher, brashest**) ADJ If you describe someone or their behavior as **brash**, you disapprove of them because you think that they are too confident and aggressive. 自以为是的 [DISAPPROVAL] ❑ *On stage she seems hard, brash and uncompromising.* 在舞台上，她显得冷酷、自以为是而且不妥协。 ● **brash·ly** ADV 自以为是地 ❑ *I brashly announced to the group that NATO needed to be turned around.* 我自以为是地向小组宣布北约需要彻底转变。

brass /bræs/ **1** N-UNCOUNT **Brass** is a yellow-colored metal made from copper and zinc. It is used especially for making ornaments and musical instruments. 黄铜 ❑ *The instrument is*

B

beautifully made in brass. 这个乐器是用黄铜精致铸造成的。 2 N-SING **The brass** is the section of an orchestra which consists of brass wind instruments such as trumpets and horns. 铜管乐器 ❑ *Consequently even this vast chorus was occasionally overwhelmed by the brass.* 结果连这个大合唱偶尔也被铜管乐所压倒。
→ see **orchestra**

brat /bræt/ (**brats**) N-COUNT If you call someone, especially a child, a **brat**, you mean that he or she behaves badly or annoys you. 臭小子 [INFORMAL, DISAPPROVAL] ❑ *He's a spoiled brat.* 他是个被宠坏的臭小子。

bra·va·do /brəvɑdoʊ/ N-UNCOUNT **Bravado** is an appearance of courage or confidence that someone shows in order to impress other people. 故作勇敢；佯装自信 ❑ *"You won't get away with this," he said with unexpected bravado.* "你逃脱不了的，"他带着出人意料的假自信说道。

brave ♦◊◊ /breɪv/ (**braver, bravest, braves, braving, braved**) 1 ADJ Someone who is **brave** is willing to do things that are dangerous, and does not show fear in difficult or dangerous situations. 勇敢的 ❑ *He was not brave enough to report the loss of the documents.* 他当时不够勇敢去报失文件的丢失。 ● **brave·ly** ADV 勇敢地 ❑ *Our men wiped them out, but the enemy fought bravely and well.* 我们的人歼灭了敌人，不过敌人也打得很勇猛顽强。 2 V-T If you **brave** unpleasant or dangerous conditions, you deliberately expose yourself to them, usually in order to achieve something. 勇于置身(恶劣或危险的环境) [WRITTEN] ❑ *Thousands have braved icy rain to demonstrate their support.* 数千人曾顶着冰冷的雨表示他们的支持。
→ see **hero**

Thesaurus *brave* 另参见：
ADJ. courageous, fearless, unafraid; (*ant.*) afraid, cowardly 1
V. dare, endure, risk 2

brav·ery /breɪvəri/ N-UNCOUNT **Bravery** is brave behavior or the quality of being brave. 勇敢之举；勇敢 ❑ *He deserves the highest praise for his bravery.* 他为其勇敢应该得到至高的赞扬。

▲ **brawl** /brɔl/ (**brawls, brawling, brawled**) 1 N-COUNT A **brawl** is a rough or violent fight. 斗殴 ❑ *He had been in a drunken street brawl.* 他曾参与了一场街头醉酒斗殴。 2 V-RECIP If someone **brawls**, they fight in a very rough or violent way. 斗殴 ❑ *He was suspended for a year from the university after brawling with police over a speeding ticket.* 他在就一张超速罚单与警察斗殴后被该大学停学一年。

bra·zen /breɪzᵊn/ ADJ If you describe a person or their behavior as **brazen**, you mean that they are very bold and do not care what other people think about them or their behavior. 无所顾忌的 ❑ *They're quite brazen about their bisexuality, it doesn't worry them.* 他们对自己的双性恋无所顾忌，这并不使他们担心。 ● **bra·zen·ly** ADV 无所顾忌地 ❑ *He was brazenly running a $400,000-a-month drug operation from the prison.* 他那时肆无忌惮地在监狱里经营着每个月$400000的毒品交易。

★ **breach** /britʃ/ (**breaches, breaching, breached**) 1 V-T If you **breach** an agreement, a law, or a promise, you break it. 违反 ❑ *The newspaper breached the code of conduct on privacy.* 这家报纸违反了隐私保护行为准则。 2 N-VAR A **breach of** an agreement, a law, or a promise is an act of breaking it. 违反 ❑ *The congressman was accused of a breach of secrecy rules.* 这个国会议员被指控违反保密条例。 3 N-COUNT A **breach in** a relationship is a serious disagreement which often results in the relationship ending. (关系中的) 裂痕 [FORMAL] ❑ *Their actions threatened a serious breach in relations between the two countries.* 他们的行动有威胁两国关系分裂的危险。 4 V-T If someone or something **breaches** a barrier, they make an opening in it, usually leaving it weakened or destroyed. 使破开 [FORMAL] ❑ *The limestone is sufficiently fissured for tree roots to have breached the roof of the cave.* 石灰岩裂开了足以让树根突破洞顶。 5 V-T If you **breach** someone's security or their defenses, you manage to get through and attack an area that is heavily guarded and protected. 攻破(某人的防范) ❑ *The bomber had breached security by hurling his dynamite from a roof overlooking the building.* 爆破手从一个俯瞰这幢楼房的屋顶上投掷了炸药，攻破了安全防卫。 ● N-COUNT **Breach** is also a noun. 攻破 ❑ *...serious breaches of security at Camp Delta.* …三角洲军营安全防御的严重破坏。

bread ♦◊◊ /brɛd/ (**breads**) N-MASS **Bread** is a very common food made from flour, water, and usually yeast. 面包 ❑ *...a loaf of bread.* …一条面包 ❑ *...bread and butter.* …面包和黄油。

breadth /brɛtθ/ 1 N-UNCOUNT The **breadth of** something is the distance between its two sides. 宽度 ❑ *The breadth of the whole camp was 400 paces.* 整个营地的宽度为400步。 2 N-UNCOUNT The **breadth of** something is its quality of consisting of or involving many different things. 广度 ❑ *Older people have a tremendous breadth of experience.* 年长的人们有极其广泛的经验。

bread·winner /brɛdwɪnər/ (**breadwinners**) also **bread-winner** N-COUNT The **breadwinner** in a family is the person in it who earns the money that the family needs for essential things. 养家糊口的人 ❑ *I've always paid the bills and been the breadwinner.* 我一直支付家庭开销，并且一直是养家的人。

break
❶ DAMAGE OR DESTROY
❷ STOP OR CHANGE SOMETHING
❸ OTHER USES
❹ PHRASAL VERBS

❶ **break** ♦♦♦ /breɪk/ (**breaks, breaking, broke, broken**) 1 V-T/V-I When an object **breaks** or when you **break** it, it suddenly separates into two or more pieces, often because it has been hit or dropped. 打碎；破碎 ❑ *He fell through the window, breaking the glass.* 他打破玻璃，从窗口摔了出去。 ❑ *The plate broke.* 盘子碎了。 ❑ *The plane broke into three pieces.* 那架飞机碎成了3块。 2 V-T/V-I If you **break** a part of your body such as your leg, your arm, or your nose, or if a bone **breaks**, you are injured because a bone cracks or splits. 弄折(骨头)；骨折 ❑ *She broke a leg in a skiing accident.* 她在一次滑雪事故中摔断了一条腿。 ❑ *Old bones break easily.* 老骨头容易骨折。 ● N-COUNT **Break** is also a noun. 骨折 ❑ *It has caused a bad break to Gabriella's leg.* 这导致了加布里埃拉的一条腿严重骨折。 3 V-T/V-I If a surface, cover, or seal **breaks** or if something **breaks** it, a hole or tear is made in it, so that a substance can pass through. 拆裂；开裂 ❑ *Once you've broken the seal of a bottle there's no way you can put it back together again.* 一旦你撕开瓶子的封口，就没法将它重新合上。 ❑ *The bandage must be put on when the blister breaks.* 水疱破口后必须包扎上绷带。 4 V-T/V-I When a tool or piece of machinery **breaks** or when you **break** it, it is damaged and no longer works. 损坏 ❑ *When the clutch broke, the car was locked into second gear.* 离合器损坏了后，那辆轿车被锁在了二档。
→ see **crash**

❷ **break** ♦♦♦ /breɪk/ (**breaks, breaking, broke, broken**) 1 V-T If someone **breaks** something, especially a difficult or unpleasant situation that has existed for some time, they end it or change it. 结束；打破(困难或不快的情形) ❑ *We need to break the vicious cycle of violence and counterviolence.* 我们需要结束暴力和反暴力的恶性循环。 ❑ *New proposals have been put forward to break the deadlock among rival factions.* 新的提议已被提出来以打破对立派之间的僵局。 ● N-COUNT **Break** is also a noun. 结束；(对困难或不快的情形的) 打破 ❑ *Nothing that might lead to a break in the deadlock has been discussed yet.* 任何可能促成僵局破除的举措尚未被讨论。 2 V-T If someone or something **breaks** a silence, they say something or make a noise after a long period of silence. 打破(沉默) ❑ *Hugh broke the silence. "Is she always late?" he asked.* 休打破了沉默。问道："她总是迟到吗？" 3 V-T/V-I If you **break with** a group of people or a traditional way of doing things, or you **break** your connection with them, you stop being involved with that group or stop doing things in that way. 断绝(关系)；打破(传统) ❑ *In 1959, Akihito broke with imperial tradition by marrying a commoner.* 1959年，明仁天皇打破皇室传统，与一个平民结了婚。 ❑ *They were determined to break from precedent.* 他们决心打破先例。 ● N-COUNT **Break** is also a noun. (对关系的) 断绝；(对传统的) 打破 ❑ *Making a completely clean break with the past, the couple got rid of all their old furniture.* 为了与过去断得一干二净，这对夫妻丢弃了他们所有的旧家具。 4 V-T If you **break** a habit or if someone **breaks** you of it, you no longer have that habit. 戒除(习惯) ❑ *If you continue to smoke, keep trying to break the habit.* 如果你继续吸烟，继续试着戒掉这一习惯吧。 5 V-I If someone **breaks for** a short period of time, they rest or change from what they are doing for a short period. (短暂) 休息 ❑ *They broke for lunch.* 他们停下来吃午饭。 6 N-COUNT A **break** is a short period of time when you have a rest or a change from what you are doing, especially if you are working or if you are in a boring or unpleasant situation. 短暂休息 ❑ *They may be able to help with childcare so that you can have a break.* 他们或许能帮忙看孩子，这样你可以歇歇。 ❑ *I thought a 15 minute break from his work would do him good.* 我认为15分钟的工作休息对他会有好处。 7 N-COUNT A **break** is a short vacation. 短假 ❑ *They are currently taking a short break in Spain.*

他们目前在西班牙休短假。 8 V-T If you **break** your journey somewhere, you stop there for a short time so that you can have a rest. (旅行中) 使歇脚 ❑ *We broke our journey at a small country hotel.* 我们在一家小乡村旅店歇了歇脚。

→ see **factory**

Word Partnership *break* 的常用搭配:

N. break **a bone**, break **your arm/leg/neck** ❶ 2
break **the silence** ❷ 2
break **a habit** ❷ 4
coffee/lunch break ❷ 6
break **the law**, break **a promise**, break **a rule** ❸ 1
break **a record** ❸ 7
V. **need a** break, **take a** break ❷ 6

❸ **break** ♦♦♦ /breɪk/ (**breaks, breaking, broke, broken**)
➪ **Please look at meanings** 15 – 21 **to see if the expression you are looking for is shown under another headword.** 1 V-T If you **break** a rule, promise, or agreement, you do something that you should not do according to that rule, promise, or agreement. 违反 ❑ *We didn't know we were breaking the law.* 我们那时不知道我们在违法。 ❑ *The company has consistently denied it had knowingly broken arms embargoes.* 该公司始终否认故意违反了武器禁运规定。 2 V-I If you **break** free or loose, you free yourself from something or escape from it. 挣脱 ❑ *She broke free by thrusting her elbow into his chest.* 她用胳膊肘猛杵他的胸部挣脱了开来。 3 V-T To **break** the force of something such as a blow or fall means to weaken its effect, for example, by getting in the way of it. 减弱 (打击、坠落等的力度) ❑ *He sustained serious neck injuries after he broke someone's fall.* 他被坠落的人砸中之后受了严重颈伤。 4 V-I When a piece of news **breaks**, people hear about it from the newspapers, television, or radio. (消息) 传开 ❑ *The news broke that Montgomery was under investigation.* 消息传出说蒙哥马利在受到调查。 5 V-T When you **break** a piece of bad news to someone, you tell it to them, usually in a kind way. (常指善意地) 说出 (不好的消息) ❑ *Then Louise broke the news that she was leaving me.* 之后路易丝说出了她要离开我的消息。 6 N-COUNT A **break** is a lucky opportunity that someone gets to achieve something. 时来运转 [INFORMAL] ❑ *Her first break came when she was chosen out of 100 guitarists auditioning for a spot on Michael Jackson's tour.* 她的第一次时来运转是被从100名吉他手的试奏中选出来参加迈克尔・杰克逊的巡演。 7 V-T If you **break** a record, you beat the previous record for a particular achievement. 打破 (记录) ❑ *Carl Lewis has broken the world record in the 100 meters.* 卡尔・刘易斯打破了百米赛跑的世界纪录。 8 V-I When day or dawn **breaks**, it starts to grow light after the night has ended. 破晓 ❑ *They continued the search as dawn broke.* 他们在天亮之后继续搜寻。 9 V-I When a wave **breaks**, it passes its highest point and turns downward, for example, when it reaches the shore. (波浪) 落下 ❑ *Danny listened to the waves breaking against the shore.* 丹尼听着波浪拍岸的声音。 10 V-T If you **break** a secret code, you work out how to understand it. 破解 (密码) ❑ *It was feared they could break the Allies' codes.* 只怕他们能破解盟军的密码。 11 V-I If someone's voice **breaks** when they are speaking, it changes its sound, for example, because they are sad or afraid. (嗓音因悲伤、害怕等而) 变调 ❑ *Godfrey's voice broke, and he halted.* 戈弗雷的嗓音变了调, 然后停了下来。 12 V-I When a boy's voice **breaks**, it becomes deeper and sounds more like a man's voice. (男孩) 变声 ❑ *He sings with the strained discomfort of someone whose voice hasn't quite broken.* 他紧张不适地唱着, 嗓音像个还未完全变声的人。 13 V-I If the weather **breaks** or a storm **breaks**, it suddenly becomes rainy or stormy after a period of sunshine. (天气) 突变; (暴风雨) 骤起 ❑ *I've been waiting for the weather to break.* 我一直在等待下雨。 14 → see also **broke, broken, heartbreak, heartbreaking, heartbroken, outbreak** 15 **to break even** → see **even** 16 **to break new ground** → see **ground** 17 **to break** someone's **heart** → see **heart** 18 **all hell breaks loose** → see **hell** 19 **to break the ice** → see **ice** 20 **to break ranks** → see **rank** 21 **to break wind** → see **wind**

❹ **break** ♦♦♦ /breɪk/ (**breaks, breaking, broke, broken**)
▸ **break down** 1 PHRASAL VERB If a machine or a vehicle **breaks down**, it stops working. (机器、车辆等) 出故障 ❑ *Their car broke down.* 他们的车抛锚了。 2 PHRASAL VERB If a discussion, relationship, or system **breaks down**, it fails because of a problem or disagreement. (讨论、关系) 失败; (系统) 瘫痪 ❑ *Talks with business leaders broke down last night.* 与商界领导人的谈判于昨晚失败了。 3 PHRASAL VERB To **break down** something such as an idea or statement means to separate it into smaller parts in order to make it easier to understand or deal with. (对观点、陈述等) 分门别类 ❑ *The report breaks down the results region by region.* 该报告将结果按地区一一分类。 4 PHRASAL VERB When a substance **breaks down** or when something **breaks it down**, a biological or chemical process causes it to separate into the substances which make it up. 分解 ❑ *Over time, the protein in the eggshell breaks down into its constituent amino acids.* 随着时间的推移, 蛋壳中的蛋白质分解成其构成成分氨基酸。 5 PHRASAL VERB If someone **breaks down**, they lose control of themselves and start crying. 失控痛哭 ❑ *Because he was being so kind and concerned, I broke down and cried.* 因为他那时对我那般友善关心, 我失控哭了起来。 6 PHRASAL VERB If you **break down** a door or barrier, you hit it so hard that it falls to the ground. 砸倒 (门、障碍物) ❑ *An unruly mob broke down police barricades and stormed the courtroom.* 一群无法无天的暴徒捣毁了警障冲进了法庭。 7 PHRASAL VERB To **break down** barriers or prejudices that separate people or restrict their freedom means to change people's attitudes so that the barriers or prejudices no longer exist. 破除 (障碍、偏见等) [APPROVAL] ❑ *Women's sports are breaking down the barriers in previously male-dominated domains.* 女子体育运动正在打破障碍进入一些先前由男子占主导地位的领域。 8 → see also **breakdown**

▸ **break in** 1 PHRASAL VERB If someone, usually a thief, **breaks in**, they get into a building by force. (常指盗贼) 破门而入 ❑ *Masked robbers broke in and made off with $8,000.* 蒙面盗贼们破门而入偷走了$8000。 2 → see also **break-in** 3 PHRASAL VERB If you **break in** on someone's conversation or activity, you interrupt them. 打断 (谈话、活动) ❑ *O'Leary broke in on his thoughts.* 奥利里打断了他的思路。 ❑ *Mrs. Southern listened keenly, occasionally breaking in with pertinent questions.* 萨瑟恩夫人兴致勃勃地听着, 偶尔插入一个相关的问题。 4 PHRASAL VERB If you **break** someone **in**, you get them used to a new job or situation. 使适应 (新工作或新情况) ❑ *The band is breaking in a new backing vocalist, who sounds great.* 该乐队在让一名听上去很棒的新伴奏歌手适应。 5 PHRASAL VERB If you **break in** something new, you gradually use or wear it for longer and longer periods until it is ready to be used or worn all the time. 磨合 ❑ *When breaking in an engine, you should refrain from high speeds for the first thousand miles.* 磨合发动机时, 你应当避免在最初的1千英里高速行驶。

▸ **break into** 1 PHRASAL VERB If someone **breaks into** a building, they get into it by force. 强行闯入 ❑ *There was no one nearby who might see him trying to break into the house.* 当时附近没有人可能看见他试图闯进那所房子。 2 PHRASAL VERB If someone **breaks into** something they suddenly start doing it. For example, if someone **breaks into** a run they suddenly start running, and if they **break into** song they suddenly start singing. 突然开始 (做某事) ❑ *The moment she was out of sight she broke into a run.* 她一走出视线就突然开始跑。 3 PHRASAL VERB If you **break into** a profession or area of business, especially one that is difficult to succeed in, you manage to have some success in it. 成功打入 (某行业、某领域) ❑ *She finally broke into films after an acclaimed stage career.* 她在备受赞赏的舞台生涯后终于成功打入了电影界。

▸ **break off** 1 PHRASAL VERB If part of something **breaks off** or if you **break** it **off**, it comes off or is removed by force. 脱落; 用力移除 ❑ *The two wings of the aircraft broke off on impact.* 该飞机的两个机翼因受到撞击而脱落。 ❑ *Grace broke off a large piece of the clay.* 格雷斯使劲掰掉了一大块陶土。 2 PHRASAL VERB If you **break off** when you are doing or saying something, you suddenly stop doing it or saying it. 突然停止 ❑ *Barry broke off in mid-sentence.* 巴里话说到一半突然停止了。 3 PHRASAL VERB If someone **breaks off** a relationship, they end it. 终止 (关系) ❑ *The two West African states had broken off relations two years ago.* 这两个西非国家两年前已终止了关系。

▸ **break out** 1 PHRASAL VERB If something such as war, fighting, or disease **breaks out**, it begins suddenly. (战争、殴斗、疾病等) 爆发 ❑ *He was 29 when war broke out.* 战争爆发时他29岁。 2 PHRASAL VERB If a prisoner **breaks out of** a prison, they escape from it. 逃出 (监狱) ❑ *The two men broke out of their cells and cut through a perimeter fence.* 那两个男人逃出牢房并穿过了一道围墙。 3 → see also **breakout** 4 PHRASAL VERB If you **break out of** a dull situation or routine, you manage to change it or escape from it. 摆脱 (沉闷的处境、常规) ❑ *It's taken a long time to break out of my own conventional training.* 摆脱我自己的传统训练花了很长一段时间。 5 PHRASAL VERB If you **break out in** a rash or a sweat, a rash or sweat appears on your skin. 出 (疹子、汗) ❑ *A person who is allergic to cashews may break out in a rash when he consumes these nuts.* 对腰果过敏的人吃了这些坚果可能会出疹子。

▸ **break through** 1 PHRASAL VERB If you **break through** a barrier, you succeed in forcing your way through it. 冲破 (障碍) ❑ *Protesters tried to break through a police cordon.* 抗议者们试图冲破警察的封锁线。

2 PHRASAL VERB If you **break through**, you achieve success even though there are difficulties and obstacles. (克服困难和障碍而)获得成功 ❑ *There is still scope for new writers to break through.* 新作家们还有取得成功的空间。 **3** → see also **breakthrough**

▸ **break up** **1** PHRASAL VERB When something **breaks up** or when you **break** it **up**, it separates or is divided into several smaller parts. 分裂 ❑ *Civil war could come if the country breaks up.* 如果国家分裂，内战就会来临。 ❑ *Break up the chocolate and melt it.* 把巧克力弄碎，使其融化。 **2** PHRASAL VERB If you **break up with** your boyfriend, girlfriend, husband, or wife, your relationship with that person ends. 分手 ❑ *My girlfriend has broken up with me.* 我的女友已和我分手了。 ❑ *He felt appalled by the idea of marriage so we broke up.* 他恨透了结婚的念头，所以我们分手了。 **3** PHRASAL VERB If a marriage or romantic relationship **breaks up** or if someone **breaks** it **up**, it ends and the partners separate. (婚姻、恋爱关系)破裂 ❑ *His first marriage broke up.* 他的第一次婚姻破裂了。 **4** PHRASAL VERB When a meeting or gathering **breaks up** or when someone **breaks** it **up**, it is brought to an end and the people involved in it leave. (会议、聚会) 解散 ❑ *A neighbor asked for the music to be turned down and the party broke up.* 一位邻居要求调小音乐，聚会便散了。 ❑ *Police used tear gas to break up a demonstration.* 警察使用了催泪瓦斯来驱散示威活动。

★ **break·age** /breɪkɪdʒ/ (**breakages**) **1** N-VAR **Breakage** is the act of breaking something. 损坏 ❑ *Brushing wet hair can cause stretching and breakage.* 梳刷湿的头发会导致拉抻和破损。 ❑ *Check that your insurance policy covers breakages and damage when moving.* 检查你的保险是否涵盖搬运中的破损和毁坏。 **2** N-COUNT A **breakage** is something that has been broken. 破碎物品 [usu pl] ❑ *We arrived to find the staff cleaning up some breakages, and they asked us where we had been when the earthquake hit.* 我们到达时发现工作人员正在清理一些破碎物品，他们问地震时我们在哪里。

break·away /breɪkəweɪ/ ADJ A **breakaway** group is a group of people who have separated from a larger group, for example, because of a disagreement. 分裂出来的 [ADJ n] ❑ *A breakaway faction of the rebel group has claimed responsibility for the killing.* 反叛团体的一个分裂出来的派别已宣称对那次凶杀负责。

★ **break·down** /breɪkdaʊn/ (**breakdowns**) **1** N-COUNT The **breakdown of** something such as a relationship, plan, or discussion is its failure or ending. (关系、计划、讨论等的) 失败；结束 ❑ *...the breakdown of talks between the U.S. and E.U. officials.* …美国与欧盟官员会谈的失败。 ❑ *...the irretrievable breakdown of a marriage.* …无法挽回的一场婚姻的破裂。 **2** N-COUNT If you have a **breakdown**, you become very depressed, so that you are unable to cope with your life. 精神崩溃 ❑ *My personal life was terrible. My mother had died, and a couple of years later I had a breakdown.* 我的个人生活糟透了。母亲去世了，几年后我精神崩溃了。 **3** → see also **nervous breakdown** **4** N-COUNT If a car or a piece of machinery has a **breakdown**, it stops working. 故障 ❑ *Her old car was unreliable, so the trip was plagued by breakdowns.* 她的旧车性能不可靠，所以旅途被故障所困扰。 **5** N-COUNT A **breakdown of** something is a list of its separate parts. 细目列表 ❑ *The organizers were given a breakdown of the costs.* 组织者们被给了一份花销细目。
→ see **traffic**

break·fast ♦◇◇ /brɛkfəst/ (**breakfasts, breakfasting, breakfasted**) **1** N-VAR **Breakfast** is the first meal of the day. It is usually eaten in the early part of the morning. 早餐 ❑ *What's for breakfast?* 早餐吃什么？ **2** → see also **bed and breakfast** **3** V-I When you **breakfast**, you have breakfast. 用早餐 [FORMAL] ❑ *All the ladies breakfasted in their rooms.* 所有女士在她们房间里用了早餐。
→ see **meal**

break-in (**break-ins**) N-COUNT If there has been a **break-in**, someone has got into a building by force. 强行闯入 ❑ *The break-in had occurred just before midnight.* 这起强行闯入事件刚好发生在午夜之前。

break·ing point N-UNCOUNT If something or someone has reached **breaking point**, they have so many problems or difficulties that they can no longer cope with them, and may soon collapse or be unable to continue. 崩溃边缘 [also "the/a" N] ❑ *The report on the riot exposed a prison system stretched to breaking point.* 关于这场暴乱的报道暴露了一个被逼到崩溃边缘的监狱体制。

break·neck /breɪknɛk/ ADJ If you say that something happens or travels at **breakneck** speed, you mean that it happens or travels very fast. 极快的 [ADJ n] ❑ *Jack drove to the hospital at breakneck speed.* 杰克以飞快的速度驾车到了医院。

break·out /breɪkaʊt/ (**breakouts**) N-COUNT If there has been a **breakout**, someone has escaped from prison. 越狱 ❑ *He is thought to have planned a prison breakout of militants suspected of the July bombing.* 他被认为曾经策划了7月轰炸事件的嫌疑武力份子的越狱。

break·through /breɪkθru/ (**breakthroughs**) N-COUNT A **breakthrough** is an important development or achievement. 突破 ❑ *The company looks poised to make a significant breakthrough in China.* 该公司看上去稳将在中国实现一次重大突破。

break·up /breɪkʌp/ (**breakups**) **1** N-COUNT The **breakup of** a marriage, relationship, or association is the act of it finishing or coming to an end because the people involved decide that it is not working successfully. (婚姻、关系、联系等的) 破裂 ❑ *...the acrimonious breakup of the meeting's first session.* …恶言相向后该会议第一轮的破裂。 **2** N-COUNT The **breakup of** an organization or a country is the act of it separating or dividing into several parts. (组织、国家的) 解体 ❑ *The Justice Department advocated a breakup of Microsoft.* 司法部主张微软公司解体。

breast ♦◇◇ /brɛst/ (**breasts**) **1** N-COUNT A woman's **breasts** are the two soft, round parts on her chest that can produce milk to feed a baby. (女性的) 乳房 ❑ *She wears a low-cut dress which reveals her breasts.* 她穿着一件低胸露乳的连衣裙。 **2** N-COUNT A person's **breast** is the upper part of his or her chest. (人的) 胸部 [LITERARY] ❑ *He struck his breast in a dramatic gesture.* 他以戏剧性的姿态捶他的胸。 **3** N-COUNT A bird's **breast** is the front part of its body. (鸟的) 胸脯 ❑ *The cock's breast is tinged with chestnut.* 这只公鸡的胸脯带点栗色。 **4** N-SING The **breast** of a shirt, jacket, or coat is the part which covers the top part of the chest. (衬衫、外套、大衣等的) 胸部 **5** N-VAR You can refer to a piece of meat that is cut from the front of a bird or lamb as **breast**. (禽类或羔羊的) 胸脯肉 ❑ *...a chicken breast with vegetables.* …配着蔬菜的一块鸡胸肉。

breast·stroke /brɛststroʊk, brɛsstroʊk/ N-UNCOUNT **Breaststroke** is a swimming stroke that you do lying on your front, moving your arms and legs horizontally in a circular motion. 蛙泳 [also "the" N] ❑ *I do not yet know how to swim breaststroke effectively.* 我还不知道如何有效地进行蛙泳。

breath ♦◇◇ /brɛθ/ (**breaths**) **1** N-VAR Your **breath** is the air that you let out through your mouth when you breathe. If someone has **bad breath**, their breath smells unpleasant. 呼气 ❑ *I could smell the whiskey on his breath.* 我能从他的呼气中闻到威士忌酒味。 **2** N-VAR When you take a **breath**, you breathe in once. 呼吸 ❑ *He took a deep breath, and began to climb the stairs.* 他深深地吸了一口气，然后开始爬楼梯。 ❑ *Gasping for breath, she leaned against the door.* 她靠在门上，大口喘着气。 **3** PHRASE If you go outside **for a breath of fresh air** or **for a breath of air**, you go outside because it is unpleasantly warm indoors. (到户外) 透口气 ❑ *I had to step outside for a breath of fresh air.* 我得到外面去透口气。 **4** PHRASE If you describe something new or different as **a breath of fresh air**, you mean that it makes a situation or subject more interesting or exciting. 带来新气象 [APPROVAL] ❑ *Her brisk treatment of an almost taboo subject was a breath of fresh air.* 她对一个几乎是禁忌话题的干脆处理令人耳目一新。 **5** PHRASE When you **get** your **breath back** after doing something energetic, you start breathing normally again. 缓过气来 ❑ *I reached out a hand to steady myself against the house while I got my breath back.* 我伸出一只手撑在房子上使自己站稳，缓口气。 **6** PHRASE If you are **out of breath**, you are breathing very quickly and with difficulty because you have been doing something energetic. 喘不过气 ❑ *She was slightly out of breath from running.* 她跑过后有点上气不接下气。 **7** PHRASE You can use **in the same breath** or **in the next breath** to indicate that someone says two very different or contradictory things, especially when you are criticizing them. 自相矛盾 [DISAPPROVAL] ❑ *He hailed this week's arms agreement but in the same breath expressed suspicion about the motivations of the United States.* 他赞扬了这周的武器协定，可自相矛盾的是又表示了对美国的动机的怀疑。 **8** PHRASE If you are **short of breath**, you find it difficult to breathe properly, for example, because you are ill. You can also say that someone suffers from **shortness of breath**. 气短 ❑ *She felt short of breath and flushed.* 她感到气短，脸也红了。 **9** PHRASE If you say something **under** your **breath**, you say it in a very quiet voice, often because you do not want other people to hear what you are saying. 低声地 ❑ *Walsh muttered something under his breath.* 沃尔什低声嘀咕了什么。

Word Partnership *breath* 的常用搭配：

ADJ. **bad** breath, **fresh** breath 1
deep breath 2
V. **hold** *your* breath 1
gasp for breath, **take a** breath 2
catch *your* breath 5

breatha·lyse /brɛθəlaɪz/ [BRIT] → see **breathalyze**

Breatha·lys·er /brɛθəlaɪzəʳ/ [BRIT] → see **Breathalyzer**

breatha·lyze /brɛθəlaɪz/ (**breathalyzes, breathalyzing, breathalyzed**) V-T If the driver of a car **is breathalyzed** by the police, they ask him or her to breathe into a special bag or device in order to test whether he or she has drunk too much alcohol. 对…作呼气酒精检测 [usu passive]
in BRIT, also use **breathalyse**
❑ *She was breathalyzed and found to be over the limit.* 她接受了呼气酒精检测，被发现超过了上限。

Breatha·lyz·er /brɛθəlaɪzər/ (**Breathalyzers**) N-COUNT A **Breathalyzer** is a bag or electronic device that the police use to test whether a driver has drunk too much alcohol. 呼气酒精测量仪 [TRADEMARK]
in BRIT, also use **Breathalyser**
❑ *Luckily I was never stopped for a Breathalyzer.* 幸运的是我从未被拦下来做呼气酒精检测。

breathe ♦◇◇ /brið/ (**breathes, breathing, breathed**) 1 V-T/V-I When people or animals **breathe**, they take air into their lungs and let it out again. When they **breathe** smoke or a particular kind of air, they take it into their lungs and let it out again as they breathe. 呼吸 ❑ *He stood there breathing deeply and evenly.* 他站在那里深深地、均匀地呼吸。 ❑ *No American should have to drive out of town to breathe clean air.* 任何美国人都不应非得开车出城去呼吸清洁的空气。 ● **breath·ing** N-UNCOUNT 呼吸 ❑ *Her breathing became slow and heavy.* 她的呼吸变得缓慢而沉重。 2 **to be breathing down** someone's **neck** → see **neck** 3 **to breathe a sigh of relief** → see **sigh**
→ see **respiratory**

▸ **breathe in** PHRASAL VERB When you **breathe in**, you take some air into your lungs. 吸气 ❑ *She breathed in deeply.* 她深深地吸了气。

▸ **breathe out** PHRASAL VERB When you **breathe out**, you send air out of your lungs through your nose or mouth. 呼气 ❑ *Breathe out and ease your knees in toward your chest.* 呼气，将你的膝盖放松、收向胸部。

breath·er /briðər/ (**breathers**) N-COUNT If you take a **breather**, you stop what you are doing for a short time in order to rest. 歇息 [INFORMAL] ❑ *Relax and take a breather whenever you feel that you need one.* 放松，你什么时候需要休息就歇一下。

breath·ing space (**breathing spaces**) N-VAR A **breathing space** is a short period of time between two activities in which you can recover from the first activity and prepare for the second one. (两项活动之间的) 喘息时间 ❑ *Firms need a breathing space if they are to recover.* 各公司要复苏就需要个喘息时间。 ❑ *We hope that it will give us some breathing space.* 我们希望它能给我们些喘息时间。

breath·less /brɛθlɪs/ ADJ If you are **breathless**, you have difficulty in breathing properly, for example, because you have been running or because you are afraid or excited. 上气不接下气的 ❑ *I was a little breathless and my heartbeat was bumpy and fast.* 我有点上气不接下气，我的心跳不稳并且很快。 ● **breath·less·ly** ADV 上气不接下气地 ❑ *"I'll go in," he said breathlessly.* "我要进去，"他上气不接下气地说。 ● **breath·less·ness** N-UNCOUNT 呼吸困难 ❑ *Asthma causes wheezing and breathlessness.* 哮喘导致气喘和呼吸困难。

breath·taking /brɛθteɪkɪŋ/ also **breath-taking** ADJ If you say that something is **breathtaking**, you are emphasizing that it is extremely beautiful or amazing. 令人惊叹的 [EMPHASIS] ❑ *The house has breathtaking views from every room.* 这房子从各个房间都能看到令人惊叹的风景。 ❑ *Some of their football was breathtaking, a delight to watch.* 他们踢的足球赛有些场次令人惊叹，看起来赏心悦目。

breed ♦◇◇ /brid/ (**breeds, breeding, bred**) 1 N-COUNT A **breed** of a pet animal or farm animal is a particular type of it. For example, terriers are a breed of dog. (动物的) 品种 ❑ *...rare breeds of cattle.* …稀有牛种。 2 V-T If you **breed** animals or plants, you keep them for the purpose of producing more animals or plants with particular qualities, in a controlled way. 养殖 ❑ *He lived alone, breeding horses and dogs.* 他独自生活，养殖马和狗。 ❑ *He used to breed dogs for the police.* 他过去为警察部门养殖狗。 ● **breed·ing** N-UNCOUNT 养殖 ❑ *There is potential for selective breeding for better yields.* 以优产为目的的精选养殖是有潜力的。 3 V-I When animals **breed**, they have babies. 繁殖 ❑ *Frogs will usually breed in any convenient pond.* 青蛙通常在任何适宜的水塘里繁殖。 ● **breed·ing** N-UNCOUNT 繁殖 ❑ *During the breeding season the birds come ashore.* 在繁殖期鸟儿们上岸。 4 V-T If you say that something **breeds** bad feeling or bad behavior, you mean that it causes bad feeling or bad behavior to develop. 酿成(不良情绪或不良行为) ❑ *If they are unemployed it's bound to breed resentment.* 如果他们失业了，一定会酿成怨恨。 5 → see also **breeding**
→ see **gene**

breed·er /bridər/ (**breeders**) N-COUNT **Breeders** are people who breed animals or plants. 饲养者；培育者 ❑ *Her father was a well-known racehorse breeder.* 她的父亲是一位有名的赛马驯养者。

breed·ing /bridɪŋ/ 1 N-UNCOUNT If someone says that a person has **breeding**, they mean that they think the person is from a good social background and has good manners. 教养 ❑ *It's a sign of good breeding to know the names of all your staff.* 知道你所有职员的名字是有良好教养的表现。 2 → see also **breed**
→ see **zoo**

breeze /briz/ (**breezes, breezing, breezed**) 1 N-COUNT A **breeze** is a gentle wind. 微风 ❑ *...a cool summer breeze.* …一阵凉爽的夏风。 2 V-I If you **breeze into** a place or a position, you enter it in a very casual or relaxed manner. 轻而易举 ❑ *Lopez breezed into the quarter-finals of the tournament.* 洛佩斯轻松进入了那次锦标赛的四分之一决赛。 3 V-I If you **breeze through** something such as a game or test, you cope with it easily. 轻松应付 ❑ *John seems to breeze effortlessly through his many commitments at work.* 约翰似乎对他工作中的许多职责应付自如。
→ see **wind**

breezy /brizi/ ADJ If you describe someone as **breezy**, you mean that they behave in a casual, cheerful, and confident manner. 轻松活泼的 ❑ *...his bright and breezy personality.* …他聪明又活泼的个性。

breth·ren /brɛðrɪn/ N-PLURAL You can refer to the members of a particular organization or group, especially a religious group, as **brethren**. 同胞 [OLD-FASHIONED] ❑ *We must help our brethren, it is our duty.* 我们必须帮助我们的同胞，这是我们的职责。

★ **brew** /bru/ (**brews, brewing, brewed**) 1 V-T If you **brew** tea or coffee, you make it by pouring hot water over tea leaves or ground coffee. 冲泡(茶、咖啡等) ❑ *He brewed a pot of coffee.* 他冲了一壶咖啡。 2 N-COUNT A **brew** is a particular kind of tea or coffee. It can also be a particular pot of tea or coffee. (茶或咖啡的) 种类 ❑ *She swallowed a mouthful of the hot strong brew, and wiped her eyes.* 她咽下一大口热浓茶，然后擦了擦眼睛。 3 V-T If a person or company **brews** beer, they make it. 酿造(啤酒) ❑ *I brew my own beer.* 我酿造自己的啤酒。 4 V-I If a storm **is brewing**, large clouds are beginning to form and the sky is becoming dark because there is going to be a storm. (暴风雨) 酝酿 [usu cont] ❑ *We'd seen the storm brewing when we were out in the boat.* 我们乘船外出时看到了暴风雨正在酝酿之中。 5 V-I If an unpleasant or difficult situation **is brewing**, it is starting to develop. (危机、困境等) 酝酿 [usu cont] ❑ *At home a crisis was brewing.* 家里一场危机正在酝酿着。
→ see **coffee, tea**

brew·er /bruər/ (**brewers**) N-COUNT **Brewers** are people or companies who make beer. 啤酒酿造者；啤酒酿造公司

★ **brew·ery** /bruəri/ (**breweries**) N-COUNT A **brewery** is a place where beer is made. 啤酒厂

bribe /braɪb/ (**bribes, bribing, bribed**) 1 N-COUNT A **bribe** is a sum of money or something valuable that one person offers or gives to another in order to persuade him or her to do something. 贿赂 ❑ *He was being investigated for receiving bribes.* 他那时因为接收贿赂在受到调查。 2 V-T If one person **bribes** another, they give them a bribe. 贿赂 ❑ *He was accused of bribing a senior bank official.* 他被控贿赂一位银行高级职员。

★ **brib·ery** /braɪbəri/ N-UNCOUNT **Bribery** is the act of offering someone money or something valuable in order to persuade them to do something for you. 贿赂行为 ❑ *He was jailed on charges of bribery.* 他因贿赂指控被监禁。

brick /brɪk/ (**bricks**) 1 N-VAR **Bricks** are rectangular blocks of baked clay used for building walls, which are usually red or brown. **Brick** is the material made up of these blocks. 砖 ❑ *She built bookshelves out of bricks and planks.* 她用砖和厚木板制作了书架。
2 PHRASE If you **hit a brick wall** or **come up against a brick wall**,

B

you are unable to continue or make progress because something stops you. 碰壁 [INFORMAL] ❑ *After that my career just seemed to hit a brick wall.* 从那以后我的事业似乎碰了壁。

brid·al /braɪdᵊl/ ADJ **Bridal** is used to describe something that belongs or relates to a bride, or to both a bride and her bridegroom. 新娘的; 新郎新娘的 [ADJ n] ❑ *She wore a floor length bridal gown.* 她穿了一件拖地婚纱。

bride /braɪd/ (**brides**) N-COUNT A **bride** is a woman who is getting married or who has just gotten married. 新娘 ❑ *Guests toasted the bride and groom with champagne.* 客人们以香槟为新娘新郎敬酒。
→ see **wedding**

bride·groom /braɪdgrum/ (**bridegrooms**) N-COUNT A **bridegroom** is a man who is getting married. 新郎

brides·maid /braɪdzmeɪd/ (**bridesmaids**) N-COUNT A **bridesmaid** is a woman or a girl who helps and accompanies a bride on her wedding day. 伴娘
→ see **wedding**

bridge ♦♦◊ /brɪdʒ/ (**bridges, bridging, bridged**) **1** N-COUNT A **bridge** is a structure that is built over a railroad, river, or road so that people or vehicles can cross from one side to the other. 桥 ❑ *He walked back over the railroad bridge.* 他从铁路桥上走了回去。 **2** N-COUNT A **bridge** between two places is a piece of land that joins or connects them. (连接两地的) 陆桥 ❑ *...a land bridge linking Serbian territories.* …连接塞尔维亚领土的陆桥。 **3** V-T To **bridge** the gap between two people or things means to reduce it or get rid of it. 克服 (障碍) ❑ *It is unlikely that the two sides will be able to bridge their differences.* 双方不太可能会克服彼此间的分歧。 **4** V-T Something that **bridges** the gap between two very different things has some of the qualities of each of these things. 结合 (极为不同的两者) ❑ *...the singer who bridged the gap between pop music and opera.* …结合了流行音乐和歌剧的歌手。 **5** N-COUNT If something or someone acts as a **bridge** between two people, groups, or things, they connect them. 纽带 ❑ *We hope this book will act as a bridge between doctor and patient.* 我们希望这本书将成为沟通医生与病人的纽带。 **6** N-COUNT **The bridge** is the place on a ship from which it is steered. 舰桥 ❑ *Captain Ronald Warwick was on the bridge when the wave hit.* 浪打来时, 罗纳德·沃里克船长正在舰桥上。 **7** N-COUNT The **bridge** of your nose is the thin top part of it, between your eyes. (鼻) 梁 ❑ *On the bridge of his hooked nose was a pair of gold rimless spectacles.* 在他的鹰勾鼻梁上是一副镀金无边眼镜。 **8** N-COUNT The **bridge** of a pair of glasses is the part that rests on your nose. (眼镜的) 鼻梁架 **9** N-COUNT The **bridge** of a violin, guitar, or other stringed instrument is the small piece of wood under the strings that holds them up. (小提琴、吉他等弦乐器的) 琴马 **10** N-UNCOUNT **Bridge** is a card game for four players in which the players begin by declaring how many tricks they expect to win. 桥牌
→ see Word Web: **bridge**
→ see **ship**

bridge loan (**bridge loans**) N-COUNT A **bridge loan** is money that a bank lends you for a short time, for example, so that you can buy a new house before you have sold the one you already own. 过桥贷款; 过渡贷款 [AM]

in BRIT, use **bridging loan**

bridg·ing loan [BRIT] → see **bridge loan**

bri·dle /braɪdᵊl/ (**bridles**) N-COUNT A **bridle** is a set of straps that is put around a horse's head and mouth so that the person riding or driving the horse can control it. 马勒
→ see **horse**

brief ♦♦◊ /brif/ (**briefer, briefest, briefs, briefing, briefed**) **1** ADJ Something that is **brief** lasts for only a short time. 短暂的 ❑ *She once made a brief appearance on television.* 她曾在电视上短暂露面。 **2** ADJ A **brief** speech or piece of writing does not contain too many words or details. (讲话、文章) 简短的 ❑ *In a brief statement, he concentrated entirely on international affairs.* 在一个简短的陈述中, 他完全集中在了国际事务上。 **3** ADJ If you are **brief**, you say what you want to say in as few words as possible. (说话) 简明扼要的 [v-link ADJ] ❑ *Now please be brief – my time is valuable.* 现在请长话短说——我的时间很宝贵。 **4** ADJ You can describe a period of time as **brief** if you want to emphasize that it is very short. 短暂的 [EMPHASIS] ❑ *For a few brief minutes we forgot the anxiety and anguish.* 短短的几分钟, 我们忘却了忧伤和痛苦。 **5** N-PLURAL Men's or women's underpants can be referred to as **briefs**. 短内裤 [also "a pair of" N] ❑ *A bra and a pair of briefs lay on the floor.* 一件胸罩和一条短内裤放在地板上。 **6** V-T If someone **briefs** you, especially about a piece of work or a serious matter, they give you information that you need before you do it or consider it. 介绍; 提供 (信息) ❑ *A Defense Department spokesman briefed reporters.* 一位国防部发言人向记者们介绍了情况。 **7** N-COUNT A **brief** is a document containing all the information relating to a particular legal case, which is used by a lawyer to defend his or her client in court. 案情摘要 ❑ *Griffith's expertise is in writing legal briefs.* 格里菲思的专长在于撰写法律案情摘要。 **8** N-COUNT If someone gives you a **brief**, they officially give you responsibility and instructions for dealing with a particular thing. 职责 [mainly BRIT, FORMAL] ❑ *...customs officials with a brief to stop foreign porn coming into Britain.* …身担阻止外国淫秽物品进入英国的职责的海关管员们。 **9** → see also **briefing** **10** PHRASE You can say **in brief** to indicate that you are about to say something in as few words as possible or to give a summary of what you have just said. 简言之 ❑ *In brief, take no risks.* 简言之, 别冒险。

Word Partnership *brief* 的常用搭配:

N. brief **appearance**, brief **conversation**, brief **pause** **1**
brief **description**, brief **explanation**, brief **history**,
brief **speech**, brief **statement** **2**

brief·case /brifkeɪs/ (**briefcases**) N-COUNT A **briefcase** is a case used for carrying documents in. 公文包

★ **brief·ing** /brifɪŋ/ (**briefings**) **1** N-VAR A **briefing** is a meeting at which information or instructions are given to people, especially before they do something. 信息发布会; 指示传达会 ❑ *They're holding a press briefing tomorrow.* 他们明天将召开新闻发布会。 **2** → see also **brief**

brief·ly /brifli/ **1** ADV Something that happens or is done **briefly** happens or is done for a very short period of time. 短暂地 [ADV with v] ❑ *He smiled briefly.* 他短促地微微一笑。 **2** ADV If you say or write something **briefly**, you use very few words or give very few details. 简洁地 [ADV with v] ❑ *There are four basic alternatives; they are described briefly below.* 有4种基本选择, 简略描述如下。 **3** ADV You can say **briefly** to indicate that you are about to say something in as few words as possible. 简言之 [ADV with cl] ❑ *Briefly, no less than nine of our agents have passed information to us.* 简言之, 至少已经有9位我们的代理商将信息传递给了我们。

▲ **bri·gade** /brɪgeɪd/ (**brigades**) N-COUNT-COLL A **brigade** is one of the groups which an army is divided into. 旅 ❑ *...the soldiers of the 173rd Airborne Brigade.* …第173空降旅的士兵们。

bright ♦♦◊ /braɪt/ (**brights, brighter, brightest**) **1** ADJ A **bright** color is strong and noticeable, and not dark. 鲜艳的 (颜色) ❑ *...a bright red dress.* …一条鲜艳的红色连衣裙。 ● **bright·ly** ADV 鲜艳地

Word Web bridge

The world's longest and tallest **suspension bridge** is the Akashi Kaikyo Bridge. It is 12,828 feet long and almost 1,000 feet tall. It can withstand an 8.5 magnitude earthquake. Another famous **span**, the Brooklyn Bridge in New York City, dates from 1883. It was the first suspension bridge to use **steel** for its **cable** wire. Over 120,000 vehicles still use the bridge every day. The Evergreen Point Floating Bridge near Seattle, Washington, floats on pontoons. It's more than a mile long. During windy weather the drawbridge in the middle must remain open. This prevents damage to the span.

❑ ...a display of brightly colored flowers. …色彩鲜艳的花卉的一次展示。 ● **bright·ness** N-UNCOUNT 鲜艳 ❑ *You'll be impressed with the brightness and the beauty of the colors.* 你会对色彩的鲜艳和美丽感到吃惊。 **2** ADJ A **bright** light, object, or place is shining strongly or is full of light. 明亮的 ❑ *...a bright October day.* …一个明媚的10月天。 ● **bright·ly** ADV 明亮地 [ADV with v] ❑ *...a warm, brightly lit room.* …一间温暖的、灯光明亮的房间。 ● **bright·ness** N-UNCOUNT 明亮 ❑ *An astronomer can determine the brightness of each star.* 天文学家可以测定每颗星的亮度。 **3** ADJ If you describe someone as **bright**, you mean that they are quick at learning things. 聪明的 ❑ *I was convinced that he was brighter than average.* 我确信他比一般人聪明。 **4** ADJ A **bright** idea is clever and original. 巧妙新颖的 (主意) ❑ *There are lots of books crammed with bright ideas.* 有很多书都充满了巧妙新颖的点子。 **5** ADJ If someone looks or sounds **bright**, they look or sound cheerful and lively. 欢快活泼的 ❑ *The boy was so bright and animated.* 这个男孩非常欢快活泼、有生气。 ● **bright·ly** ADV 欢快活泼地 [ADV with v] ❑ *He smiled brightly as Ben approached.* 当本走近时，他欢快地笑了。 **6** ADJ If the future is **bright**, it is likely to be pleasant or successful. (未来) 光明的 ❑ *Both had successful careers and the future looked bright.* 两人都有过成功的事业，前途看上去很光明。 **7** N-PLURAL The **brights** on a vehicle are its headlights when they are set to shine their brightest. (开到最亮的) 车头灯 [AM] ❑ *...a Bronco with its brights on, parked in the middle of the street.* …一辆烈马牌的汽车打着开到最亮的头灯，停在街中央。

★ **bright·en** /braɪtᵊn/ (**brightens, brightening, brightened**) **1** V-I If someone **brightens** or their face **brightens**, they suddenly look happier. 变得开心；面露喜色 ❑ *Seeing him, she seemed to brighten a little.* 看见他她似乎高兴点了。 ● PHRASAL VERB **Brighten up** means the same as **brighten**. 变得开心；面露喜色 ❑ *He brightened up a bit.* 他微露喜色。 **2** V-I If your eyes **brighten**, you suddenly look interested or excited. (眼睛) 变亮 ❑ *His eyes brightened and he laughed.* 他眼睛一亮，笑了起来。 **3** V-T If someone or something **brightens** a place, they make it more colorful and attractive. 使增辉 ❑ *Tubs planted with flowers brightened the area outside the door.* 盆里种上了花给门外的那块地增辉了。 ● PHRASAL VERB **Brighten up** means the same as **brighten**. 使增辉 ❑ *David spotted the pink silk lampshade in a shop and thought it would brighten up the room.* 大卫在一家商店发现了这个粉色的丝绸灯罩，他想它会使房间生辉。 **4** V-T/V-I If someone or something **brightens** a situation or the situation **brightens**, it becomes more pleasant, enjoyable, or favorable. 改善；转好 ❑ *That does not do much to brighten the prospects of kids in the city.* 那并没怎么改善城里孩子们的前途。 **5** V-T/V-I When a light **brightens** a place or when a place **brightens**, it becomes brighter or lighter. 照亮；变亮 ❑ *The sky above the ridge of mountains brightened.* 山脊上方的天空变亮了。 **6** V-I If the weather **brightens**, it becomes less cloudy or rainy, and the sun starts to shine. (天气) 放晴 ❑ *By early afternoon the weather had brightened.* 午后不久，天气已经放晴了。

bril·liant ♦◇◇ /brɪliənt/ **1** ADJ A **brilliant** person, idea, or performance is extremely clever or skillful. 极有才智的；绝妙的 ❑ *She had a brilliant mind.* 她有极聪明的头脑。 ● **bril·liant·ly** ADV 极有才智地；绝妙地 ❑ *It is a very high quality production, brilliantly written and acted.* 这是一部非常高质量的演出，绝妙地编写而成并被表演出来。 ● **bril·liance** N-UNCOUNT 才智；绝妙 ❑ *He was a deeply serious musician who had shown his brilliance very early.* 他是一位极为严肃的音乐家，很早就展现了才华。 **2** ADJ A **brilliant** career or success is very successful. 非常成功的 ❑ *He served four years in prison, emerging to find his brilliant career in ruins.* 他在监狱服了4年刑，出狱后发现他的辉煌事业已经毁了。 ● **bril·liant·ly** ADV 非常成功地 ❑ *The strategy worked brilliantly.* 这项策略非常成功。 **3** ADJ A **brilliant** color is extremely bright. 鲜亮的 [ADJ n] ❑ *The woman had brilliant green eyes.* 这个女人有一双亮晶晶的绿眼睛。 ● **bril·liant·ly** ADV 鲜亮地 [ADV adj/-ed] ❑ *Many of the patterns show brilliantly colored flowers.* 许多图案都有绚丽多彩的花。 ● **bril·liance** N-UNCOUNT 鲜亮 ❑ *...an iridescent blue butterfly in all its brilliance.* …一只色彩斑斓的闪亮的蓝蝴蝶。 **4** ADJ You describe light, or something that reflects light, as **brilliant** when it shines very brightly. 灿烂的 ❑ *The event was held in brilliant sunshine.* 这次活动在灿烂的阳光下举行。 ● **bril·liant·ly** ADV 灿烂地 ❑ *It's a brilliantly sunny morning.* 这是个阳光灿烂的早晨。 ● **bril·liance** N-UNCOUNT 灿烂光辉 ❑ *His eyes became accustomed to the dark after the brilliance of the sun outside.* 他的眼睛经过了户外的灿烂阳光后开始适应了黑暗。 **5** ADJ You can say that something is **brilliant** when you are very pleased about it or think that it is very good. 真棒的 [mainly BRIT, INFORMAL, SPOKEN] ❑ *If you get a chance to see the show, do go – it's brilliant.* 如果你有机会去看那场演出，一定要去——它太棒了。

▲ **brim** /brɪm/ (**brims, brimming, brimmed**) **1** N-COUNT The **brim** of a hat is the wide part that sticks outward at the bottom. (帽) 檐 ❑ *Rain dripped from the brim of his baseball cap.* 雨水从他的棒球帽檐上滴下来。 **2** V-I If someone or something **is brimming with** a particular quality, they are full of that quality. 充满 [usu cont] ❑ *The team is brimming with confidence after two straight wins in the tournament.* 锦标赛连胜两场后，这支队伍充满自信。 **3** V-I When your eyes **are brimming with** tears, they are full of fluid because you are upset, although you are not actually crying. 充盈 ❑ *Michael looked at him imploringly, eyes brimming with tears.* 迈克尔恳求地望着他，眼里充满了泪水。 **4** PHRASE If something, especially a container, **is filled to the brim** or **full to the brim with** something, it is filled right up to the top. 盛满 ❑ *Her glass was filled right up to the brim.* 她的玻璃杯被装得满满的。

brine /braɪn/ (**brines**) N-MASS **Brine** is salty water, especially salty water that is used for preserving food. (尤指用于保存食物的) 盐水

bring ♦♦♦ /brɪŋ/ (**brings, bringing, brought**) **1** V-T If you **bring** someone or something **with** you when you come to a place, they come with you or you have them with you. 带来 ❑ *Remember to bring an apron or an old shirt to protect your clothes.* 记着带一条围裙或一件旧衬衫来保护你的衣服。 ❑ *Someone went upstairs and brought down a huge kettle.* 有人上楼拿下来一个巨大的水壶。 **2** V-T If you **bring** something somewhere, you move it there. 把…移动到 ❑ *Reaching into her pocket, she brought out a cigarette.* 她把手伸进口袋，拿出一根香烟。 **3** V-T If you **bring** something that someone wants or needs, you get it for them or carry it to them. 拿给 ❑ *He went and poured a brandy for Dena and brought it to her.* 他去给德娜倒了杯白兰地并拿给了她。 **4** V-T To **bring** something or someone to a place or position means to cause them to come to the place or move into that position. 把…引到 ❑ *I told you about what brought me here.* 我告诉过你是什么把我引到这里来的。 ❑ *The shock of her husband's arrival brought her to her feet.* 丈夫的到来惊得她不由自主地站了起来。

> **Bring** and **take** are both used to talk about carrying something or accompanying someone somewhere, but **bring** is used to suggest movement toward the speaker and **take** is used to suggest movement away from the speaker. ❑ *Bring your calculator to every lesson... Anna took the book to school with her.*
> In the first sentence, **bring** suggests that the person and the calculator should come to the place where the speaker is.
> In the second sentence, **take** suggests that Anna left the speaker when she went to school. You could also say "take your calculator to every lesson" to suggest that the speaker will not be present at the lesson, and "Anna brought the book to school with her" to suggest that Anna and the speaker were both at school.

5 V-T If you **bring** something new **to** a place or group of people, you introduce it to that place or cause those people to hear or know about it. 把…引入 (某地)；把…介绍给 (某些人) ❑ *...the drive to bring art to the public.* …把艺术介绍给大众的动力。 **6** V-T To **bring** someone or something into a particular state or condition means to cause them to be in that state or condition. 使处于 (某种状态、情势等) ❑ *He brought the car to a stop in front of the square.* 他在广场前把车停了下来。 ❑ *They have brought down income taxes.* 他们已经降低了所得税。 **7** V-T If something **brings** a particular feeling, situation, or quality, it makes people experience it or have it. 带来 ❑ *He called on the United States to play a more effective role in bringing peace to the region.* 他呼吁美国在给该地区带来和平的问题上发挥更加有效的作用。 ❑ *Her three children brought her joy.* 她的3个孩子给她带来了快乐。 **8** V-T If a period of time **brings** a particular thing, it happens during that time. 带来 ❑ *For Sandro, the new year brought disaster.* 对桑德罗来说，新年给他带来了灾难。 **9** V-T When you are talking, you can say that something **brings** you **to** a particular point in order to indicate that you have now reached that point and are going to talk about a new subject. 带入 (某话题) ❑ *And that brings us to the end of this special report from Germany.* 那我们就此结束这篇来自德国的特别报道。 **10** V-T If you cannot **bring yourself to** do something, you cannot do it because you find it too upsetting, embarrassing, or disgusting. 使自己 (做某事) [with brd-neg] ❑ *It is all very tragic and I am afraid I just cannot bring myself to talk about it at the moment.* 太悲惨了，恐怕我现在还无法让自己去谈论它。 **11** to **bring** something **alive** → see **alive** **12** to **bring the house down** → see **house** **13** to **bring up the rear** → see **rear**

B

Do not confuse the verbs **bring up** and **grow up**. **Bring up** is a transitive verb, and describes the process of looking after and socializing a child. ❑ *...we both felt the town was the perfect place to bring up a family*. **Grow up** is an intransitive verb, and describes the process of becoming an adult. ❑ *I grew up in rural southern Colorado*. Note then, that parents do not "grow up" their children, they "bring them up." See also note at **educate**.

▸ **bring about** PHRASAL VERB To **bring** something **about** means to cause it to happen. 引起 ❑ *The only way they can bring about political change is by putting pressure on the country.* 他们能引起政治变化的惟一办法就是向该国施加压力。

▸ **bring along** PHRASAL VERB If you **bring** someone or something **along**, you bring them with you when you come to a place. 把…带来 ❑ *They brought baby Michael along in a carrier.* 他们把小迈克尔放在婴儿车上一起带来了。❑ *Dad brought a notebook along to the beach, in case he was seized by sudden inspiration.* 爸爸把一个笔记本带到了海滩，以备他万一突发灵感时用。

▸ **bring back** 1 PHRASAL VERB Something that **brings back** a memory makes you think about it. 使回想起 ❑ *Your article brought back sad memories for me.* 你的文章勾起了我悲伤的回忆。 2 PHRASAL VERB When people **bring back** a practice or fashion that existed at an earlier time, they introduce it again. 恢复 ❑ *Pennsylvania brought back the death penalty in 1978.* 宾夕法尼亚州于1978年恢复了死刑。

▸ **bring down** 1 PHRASAL VERB When people or events **bring down** a government or ruler, they cause the government or ruler to lose power. 使垮台 ❑ *They were threatening to bring down the government by withdrawing from the ruling coalition.* 他们威胁要退出统治联盟以让政府垮台。 2 PHRASAL VERB If someone or something **brings down** a person or airplane, they cause them to fall, usually by shooting them. 击落 ❑ *Military historians may never know what brought down the jet.* 军事史学家们也许永远不会知道是什么击落了那架喷气式飞机。

▸ **bring forward** PHRASAL VERB If you **bring forward** a meeting or event, you arrange for it to take place at an earlier date or time than had been planned. 使…提前 ❑ *He had to bring forward an 11 o'clock meeting so that he could get to the funeral on time.* 他不得不把11点的会议提前，以便他能按时参加葬礼。

▸ **bring in** 1 PHRASAL VERB When a government or organization **brings in** a new law or system, they introduce it. 推行 ❑ *The government brought in a controversial law under which it could take any land it wanted.* 政府推行了一条颇有争议的法律，根据这条法律，政府可以占据任何它想要的土地。 2 PHRASAL VERB Someone or something that **brings in** money makes it or earns it. 赚得 ❑ *I have three part-time jobs, which bring in about $24,000 a year.* 我有3份兼职工作，一年能赚大约$24000。 3 PHRASAL VERB If you **bring in** someone from outside a team or organization, you invite them to do a job or join in an activity or discussion. 请来 ❑ *The firm decided to bring in a new management team.* 该公司决定请一支新的管理队伍。

▸ **bring out** 1 PHRASAL VERB When a person or company **brings out** a new product, especially a new book or CD, they produce it and put it on sale. 生产出 ❑ *A journalist all his life, he's now brought out a book.* 他做了一辈子的记者，现在已经出版了一本书。 2 PHRASAL VERB Something that **brings out** a particular kind of behavior or feeling in you causes you to show it, especially when it is something you do not normally show. 激发 ❑ *He is totally dedicated and brings out the best in his pupils.* 他全身心地投入，激发学生们最优秀的品质。

▸ **bring up** 1 PHRASAL VERB When someone **brings up** a child, they look after it until it is an adult. If someone has **been brought up** in a certain place or with certain attitudes, they grew up in that place or were taught those attitudes when they were growing up. 养育 ❑ *She brought up four children.* 她养育了4个孩子。 ❑ *He was brought up in Nebraska.* 他在内布拉斯加州被抚养大。 ❑ *We'd been brought up to think that borrowing money was bad.* 我们从小所受的教育都是说借钱是坏事。 2 PHRASAL VERB If you **bring up** a particular subject, you introduce it into a discussion or conversation. 提出 ❑ *He brought up a subject rarely raised during the course of this campaign.* 他提出了一个在该运动进程中很少被提及的话题。

Thesaurus *bring* 另参见：

V. accompany, bear, carry, take; (*ant.*) drop, leave 1
move, take, transfer 2

Word Partnership *bring* 的常用搭配：

N. bring **bad/good luck**, bring ***someone/something* home** 1
bring **to a boil**, bring **to life**, bring **together** 6
bring **to *someone's* attention**, bring **to justice**,
bring **to mind** 7

★ **brink** /brɪŋk/ N-SING If you are **on the brink of** something, usually something important, terrible, or exciting, you are just about to do it or experience it. 边缘 ❑ *Their economy is teetering on the brink of collapse.* 他们的经济正摇摆于崩溃的边缘。

★ **brisk** /brɪsk/ (**brisker, briskest**) 1 ADJ A **brisk** activity or action is done quickly and in an energetic way. 轻快的 ❑ *Taking a brisk walk can often induce a feeling of well-being.* 轻快的散步经常能使人心旷神怡。 ● **brisk·ly** ADV 轻快地 [ADV with v] ❑ *Eve walked briskly down the corridor to her son's room.* 伊芙轻快地沿着走廊走到她儿子的房间。 2 ADJ If trade or business is **brisk**, things are being sold very quickly and a lot of money is being made. (买卖、生意) 兴隆的 ❑ *Vendors were doing a brisk trade in souvenirs.* 小贩们的纪念品生意很兴隆。 ● **brisk·ly** ADV 兴隆地 [ADV after v] ❑ *A trader said gold sold briskly on the local market.* 一位贸易商说黄金在当地市场的销售很兴旺。 3 ADJ If the weather is **brisk**, it is cold and fresh. 寒冷而清新的 ❑ *...a typically brisk winter's day on the south coast.* …南海岸典型的寒冷而清新的冬日。 4 ADJ Someone who is **brisk** behaves in a busy, confident way which shows that they want to get things done quickly. 干脆利索的 ❑ *The Chief summoned me downstairs. He was brisk and businesslike.* 上司召我到楼下。他做事干脆利索而有效率。 ● **brisk·ly** ADV 脆利索地 [ADV with v] ❑ *"Anyhow," she added briskly, "it's none of my business."* "无论如何"，她干脆利索地加了一句："这不关我的事。"

▲ **bris·tle** /brɪsᵊl/ (**bristles**) 1 N-COUNT **Bristles** are the short hairs that grow on a man's face after he has shaved. The hairs on the top of a man's head can also be called **bristles** when they are cut very short. 胡子茬；(男子头顶处的) 短发 ❑ *...two days' growth of bristles.* …两天没剃长出的胡子茬儿。 2 N-COUNT The **bristles** of a brush are the thick hairs or hairlike pieces of plastic which are attached to it. (刷子的) 毛 ❑ *As soon as the bristles on your toothbrush begin to wear, throw it out.* 牙刷毛一旦磨损就扔掉。 3 N-COUNT **Bristles** are thick, strong animal hairs that feel hard and rough. 刚毛 ❑ *It has a short stumpy tail covered with bristles.* 它有一条又短又粗、长满了刚毛的尾巴。

Brit·on /brɪtᵊn/ (**Britons**) N-COUNT A **Briton** is a British citizen, or a person of British origin. 英国人 [FORMAL] ❑ *The role is played by seventeen-year-old Briton Jane March.* 那个角色由17岁的英国人简·马奇扮演。

▲ **brit·tle** /brɪtᵊl/ ADJ An object or substance that is **brittle** is hard but easily broken. 硬脆易碎的 ❑ *Pine is brittle and breaks.* 松木硬脆易折。

broach /broʊtʃ/ (**broaches, broaching, broached**) V-T When you **broach** a subject, especially a sensitive one, you mention it in order to start a discussion on it. 提出 ❑ *Eventually I broached the subject of her early life.* 最后我提出她早年生活的话题。

broad ◆◆◇ /brɔd/ (**broader, broadest**) 1 ADJ Something that is **broad** is wide. 宽的 ❑ *His shoulders were broad and his waist narrow.* 他肩宽腰细。 ❑ *The hills rise green and sheer above the broad river.* 群山青翠，陡然屹立于宽阔的大河之上。 2 ADJ A **broad** smile is one in which your mouth is stretched very wide because you are very pleased or amused. 咧开大嘴的 (笑) ❑ *He greeted them with a wave and a broad smile.* 他咧嘴笑着挥手和他们打招呼。 ● **broad·ly** ADV 咧开大嘴地 ❑ *Charles grinned broadly.* 查尔斯咧大嘴笑。 3 ADJ You use **broad** to describe something that includes a large number of different things or people. 广泛的 ❑ *A broad range of issues was discussed.* 广泛的问题得到了讨论。 ● **broad·ly** ADV 广泛地 [ADV with v] ❑ *Such policies will do little to resolve long-standing problems more broadly affecting America's global competitiveness.* 这些政策对于解决长久以来更广泛地影响美国全球竞争力的问题将没什么作用。 4 ADJ You use **broad** to describe a word or meaning which covers or refers to a wide range of different things. 宽泛的 ❑ *...restructuring in the broad sense of the word.* …以该词的广义而言的调整。 ● **broad·ly** ADV 宽泛地 [ADV with v] ❑ *We define education very broadly and students can study any aspect of its consequences for society.* 我们对教育的定义很宽泛，学生们可以研究它对社会任何一面的影响。 5 ADJ You use **broad** to describe a feeling or opinion that is shared by many people, or by people of many different kinds. 普遍的 [ADJ n] ❑ *The agreement won broad*

support in the U.S. Congress. 这项协议在美国议会赢得了普遍的支持。
● **broad·ly** ADV 普遍地 [ADV with v] ❑ *The new law has been broadly welcomed by road safety organizations.* 新法律得到了道路安全组织的普遍欢迎。 **6** **in broad daylight** → see **daylight**

Word Partnership *broad* 的常用搭配:
N. broad **expanse**, broad **shoulders** **1**
broad **smile** **2**
broad **range**, broad **spectrum** **3**
broad **definition**, broad **strokes**, broad **view** **5**

★ **broad·band** /brɔdbænd/ N-UNCOUNT **Broadband** is a method of sending many electronic messages at the same time by using a wide range of frequencies. 宽带 [oft N n] [COMPUTING] ❑ *A recent study shows many broadband services lack basic security features.* 最近研究表明许多宽带服务缺少基本的安全特性。

broad·cast ♦◇◇ /brɔdkæst/ (**broadcasts, broadcasting**)

The form **broadcast** is used in the present tense and is the past tense and past participle of the verb.

1 N-COUNT A **broadcast** is a program, performance, or speech on the radio or on television. (无线电或电视) 广播节目 ❑ *In a broadcast on state radio the government announced that it was willing to resume peace negotiations.* 在国家电台的广播节目中，政府宣布愿意恢复和平谈判。 **2** V-T/V-I To **broadcast** a program means to send it out by radio waves, wires, or satellites so that it can be heard on the radio or seen on television. (由无线电或电视) 播放 ❑ *The concert will be broadcast live on television and radio.* 音乐会将通过电视和电台现场直播。 ❑ *CNN also broadcasts in Europe.* 美国有线新闻网络也在欧洲进行广播。

broad·cast·er /brɔdkæstər/ (**broadcasters**) N-COUNT A **broadcaster** is someone who gives talks or takes part in interviews and discussions on radio or television programs. 广播员 ❑ *...the prominent naturalist and broadcaster, Sir David Attenborough.* …著名的博物学家兼广播员大卫・阿滕伯勒爵士。

broad·cast·ing ♦◇◇ /brɔdkæstɪŋ/ N-UNCOUNT **Broadcasting** is the making and sending out of television and radio programs. (电视、无线电节目的) 广播 ❑ *If this happens it will change the face of religious broadcasting.* 如果此事发生，它将改变宗教广播的面貌。

broad·en /brɔdᵊn/ (**broadens, broadening, broadened**) **1** V-I When something **broadens**, it becomes wider. 变宽 ❑ *The trails broadened into roads.* 小径变宽成大路了。 **2** V-T/V-I When you **broaden** something such as your experience or popularity, or when it **broadens**, the number of things or people that it includes becomes greater. 扩宽；开阔 ❑ *We must broaden our appeal.* 我们必须扩大我们的吸引力。 ❑ *I thought you wanted to broaden your horizons.* 我以为你想拓宽自己的视野。

broad·ly /brɔdli/ **1** ADV You can use **broadly** to indicate that something is generally true. 大体上；一般地 [ADV with cl] ❑ *The president broadly got what he wanted out of his meeting.* 总统大体上得到了他想从会议中得到的东西。 **2** → see also **broad**

broad·sheet /brɔdʃit/ (**broadsheets**) N-COUNT A **broadsheet** is a newspaper that is printed on large sheets of paper. Broadsheets are generally considered to be more serious than other newspapers. Compare **tabloid**. (通常比其他报纸严肃的) 大幅报纸 [mainly BRIT] ❑ *Even the broadsheets made it their lead story.* 就连大幅报纸都把它作为头条新闻报道。

broc·co·li /brɒkəli/ N-UNCOUNT **Broccoli** is a vegetable with green stalks and green or purple tops. 花椰菜
→ see **vegetable**

★ **bro·chure** /broʊʃʊr/ (**brochures**) N-COUNT A **brochure** is a thin magazine with pictures that gives you information about a product or service. 小册子 ❑ *...travel brochures.* …旅游小册子。

broil /brɔɪl/ (**broils, broiling, broiled**) V-T When you **broil** food, you cook it using very strong heat directly above it. 烤 [AM]

in BRIT, use **grill**

❑ *I'll broil the lobster.* 我来烤龙虾。
→ see **cook**

broil·er /brɔɪlər/ (**broilers**) **1** N-COUNT A **broiler** is a part of an oven that produces strong heat and cooks food placed underneath it. 烘烤用具 [AM]

in BRIT, use **grill**

❑ *Remove from heat and finish off under the broiler until cheese melts.* 把它从火上拿开，放在烘烤器下面烤到奶酪熔化为止。 **2** N-COUNT A **broiler** or a **broiler chicken** is a young chicken that is suitable for broiling, roasting, or frying. 童子鸡 [AM]

broke /broʊk/ **1** **Broke** is the past tense of **break**. **break**的过去式 **2** ADJ If you are **broke**, you have no money. 一文不名的 [v-link ADJ] [INFORMAL] ❑ *What do you mean, I've got enough money? I'm as broke as you are.* 你什么意思啊，我有足够的钱？我和你一样一文不名。 **3** PHRASE If a company or person **goes broke**, they lose money and are unable to continue in business or to pay their debts. 破产 [INFORMAL] ❑ *Balton went broke twice in his career.* 伯顿在他的职业生涯中破产过两次。

Thesaurus *broke* 另参见:
ADJ. bankrupt, destitute, impoverished, penniless, poor; (ant.) rich, wealthy, well-to-do **2**

bro·ken /broʊkən/ **1** **Broken** is the past participle of **break**. **break**的过去分词 **2** ADJ A **broken** line is not continuous but has gaps or spaces in it. 虚的 (线) [ADJ n] ❑ *A broken blue line means the course of a waterless valley.* 蓝色虚线代表无水流过的山谷走向。 **3** ADJ You can use **broken** to describe a marriage that has ended in divorce, or a home in which the parents of the family are divorced, when you think this is a sad or bad thing. (婚姻) 破裂的 [ADJ n] [DISAPPROVAL] ❑ *She spoke for the first time about the traumas of a broken marriage.* 她第一次说起婚姻破裂之痛。 **4** ADJ If someone talks in **broken** English, for example, or in **broken** French, they speak slowly and make a lot of mistakes because they do not know the language very well. 蹩脚的 [ADJ n] ❑ *Eric could only respond in broken English.* 埃里克只能用蹩脚的英语应答。

★ **bro·ker** ♦◇◇ /broʊkər/ (**brokers, brokering, brokered**) **1** N-COUNT A **broker** is a person whose job is to buy and sell securities, foreign money, real estate, or goods for other people. 经纪人；掮客 [BUSINESS] **2** V-T If a country or government **brokers** an agreement, a ceasefire, or a round of talks, they try to negotiate or arrange it. 斡旋 ❑ *The United Nations brokered a peace in Mogadishu at the end of March.* 联合国于3月底在摩加迪沙促成了一场和平谈判。

▲ **bro·ker·age** /broʊkərɪdʒ/ (**brokerages**) N-COUNT A **brokerage** or a **brokerage** firm is a company of brokers. 经纪公司 [BUSINESS] ❑ *...Japan's four biggest brokerages.* …日本的4大经纪公司。 ❑ *...the nation's largest brokerage firms.* …全国最大的经纪公司。

Bronx cheer /brɒŋks tʃɪər/ (**Bronx cheers**) N-COUNT A **Bronx cheer** is a sound that people make by vibrating their lips in order to express disapproval or contempt. (表示反对、轻视等的) 嘘嘘声 [AM, INFORMAL]

in BRIT, use **raspberry**

★ **bronze** /brɒnz/ **1** N-UNCOUNT **Bronze** is a yellowish-brown metal which is a mixture of copper and tin. 青铜 ❑ *...a bronze statue of Giorgi Dimitrov.* …一座乔治・季米特洛夫铜像。 **2** COLOR Something that is **bronze** is yellowish-brown in color. 青铜色的 ❑ *Her hair shone bronze and gold.* 她的头发闪耀着青铜色和金黄色的光彩。

bronze med·al (**bronze medals**) N-COUNT A **bronze medal** is a medal made of bronze or bronze-colored metal that is given as a prize to the person who comes third in a competition, especially a sports contest. 铜牌

brooch /broʊtʃ/ (**brooches**) N-COUNT A **brooch** is a piece of jewelry that has a pin at the back so it can be fastened on a dress, blouse, or coat. (可以别在衣服上的) 饰针
→ see **jewelry**

★ **brood** /brud/ (**broods, brooding, brooded**) **1** N-COUNT A **brood** is a group of baby birds that were born at the same time to the same mother. 一窝幼雏 ❑ *...a hungry brood of fledglings.* …一窝饥饿的雏鸟。 **2** N-COUNT You can refer to someone's young children as their **brood** when you want to emphasize that there are a lot of them. 一家子 [EMPHASIS] ❑ *...a large brood of children.* …一大家子小孩。 **3** V-I If someone **broods** over something, they think about it a lot, seriously and often unhappily. 担忧 ❑ *She constantly broods about her family.* 她一直在为她的家人担忧。

brood·ing /brudɪŋ/ ADJ **Brooding** is used to describe an atmosphere or feeling that makes you feel anxious or slightly afraid. 令人担忧的；令人有些恐惧的 [LITERARY] ❑ *The same heavy, brooding silence descended on them.* 同样沉重、阴森的寂静笼罩着他们。

▲ **brook** /brʊk/ (**brooks, brooking, brooked**) **1** N-COUNT A **brook** is a small stream. 小溪 **2** V-T If someone in a position of authority will **brook no** interference or opposition, they will not accept any interference or opposition from others. 允许 ❑ *From childhood on, she'd had a plan of action, one that would brook no interference.* 从儿时起，她已有了一个行动计划，不容干预。

B

broom /brum/ (**brooms**) 1 N-COUNT A **broom** is a kind of brush with a long handle. You use a broom for sweeping the floor. 扫帚 2 N-UNCOUNT **Broom** is a wild bush with a lot of tiny yellow flowers. 金雀花

Bros. **Bros.** is a written abbreviation for **brothers**. It is usually used as part of the name of a company. **brothers**的缩写，常用于公司名 [BUSINESS]

broth /brɔθ/ (**broths**) N-VAR **Broth** is a kind of soup made by boiling meat or vegetables. 肉汤；蔬菜清汤

broth·el /brɒθəl/ (**brothels**) N-COUNT A **brothel** is a building where men can go to pay to have sex with prostitutes. 妓院

broth·er ♦♦♦ /brʌðər/ (**brothers**)

> The old-fashioned form **brethren** is still sometimes used as the plural for meanings 2 and 3.

1 N-COUNT Your **brother** is a boy or a man who has the same parents as you. 兄弟 ❑ *Oh, so you're Peter's younger brother.* 噢，这么说你是彼得的弟弟。 2 → see also **half brother, stepbrother** 3 N-COUNT You can describe a man as your **brother** if he belongs to the same race, religion, country, or profession as you, or if he has similar ideas to you. 弟兄（用于指同一种族、宗教、国家、职业或有相同思想的人）❑ *He told reporters he'd come to be with his Latvian brothers.* 他告诉记者他将和他的拉脱维亚弟兄们在一起。 4 N-TITLE; N-COUNT; N-VOC **Brother** is a title given to a man who belongs to a religious community such as a monastery. 修士 ❑ *...Brother Otto.* …奥托修士。 5 N-IN-NAMES **Brothers** is used in the names of some companies and stores. 用于公司、商店名 ❑ *...the movie company Warner Brothers.* 华纳兄弟影业公司
→ see **family**

brother·hood /brʌðərhʊd/ (**brotherhoods**) 1 N-UNCOUNT **Brotherhood** is the affection and loyalty that you feel for people who you have something in common with. 兄弟情谊；手足情谊 ❑ *People threw flowers into the river between the two countries as a symbolic act of brotherhood.* 人们把花扔进两国之间的河里，以此作为兄弟情谊的象征性的行为。 2 N-COUNT A **brotherhood** is an organization whose members all have the same political aims and beliefs or the same job or profession. 兄弟会；同业会 ❑ *...the Brotherhood of Locomotive Engineers.* …机车工程师同业会。

brother-in-law (**brothers-in-law**) N-COUNT Someone's **brother-in-law** is the brother of their husband or wife, or the man who is married to their sister. 姐夫；妹夫
→ see **family**

★ **broth·er·ly** /brʌðərli/ ADJ A man's **brotherly** feelings are feelings of love and loyalty which you expect a brother to show. 兄弟般的 [usu ADJ n] ❑ *...family loyalty and brotherly love.* …家人般的忠诚和兄弟般的爱。 ❑ *He gave her a brief, brotherly kiss.* 他给了她短促、兄弟般的一吻。

brought /brɔt/ **Brought** is the past tense and past participle of **bring**. **bring**的过去式和过去分词

brow /braʊ/ (**brows**) 1 N-COUNT Your **brow** is your forehead. 额头 ❑ *He wiped his brow with the back of his hand.* 他用手背擦了擦额头。 2 N-COUNT Your **brows** are your eyebrows. 眉毛 [usu pl] ❑ *He had thick brown hair and shaggy brows.* 他长着浓密褐色的头发和浓粗杂乱的眉毛。 3 N-COUNT The **brow of** a hill is the top part of it. 顶部 ❑ *He was on the lookout just below the brow of the hill.* 他就在山顶之下放哨。

brown ♦♦♦ /braʊn/ (**browner, brownest, browns, browning, browned**) 1 COLOR Something that is **brown** is the color of earth or of wood. 褐色的 ❑ *...her deep brown eyes.* …她深邃的褐色眼睛。 2 ADJ You can describe a white-skinned person as **brown** when they have been sitting in the sun until their skin has become darker than usual. 晒黑了的 3 ADJ **Brown** is used to describe grains that have not had their outer layers removed, and foods made from these grains. （谷物）未去壳的；全粮制作的 ❑ *...brown bread.* …全麦面包。 ❑ *...spicy tomato sauce served over a bed of brown rice.* …放在一层糙米饭上的辣番茄酱。 4 V-T/V-I When food **browns** or when you **brown** food, you cook it, usually for a short time on a high flame. 使呈褐色；呈褐色 ❑ *Cook for ten minutes until the sugar browns.* 烹调10分钟直到糖变成褐色。

brown·field /braʊnfild/ ADJ **Brownfield** land is land in a town or city where houses or factories have been built in the past, but which is not being used at the present time. （指城市里建过的楼房或工厂）已开发但是而今闲置的 [ADJ n]

browse /braʊz/ (**browses, browsing, browsed**) 1 V-I If you **browse** in a store, you look at things in a fairly casual way, in the hope that you might find something you like. 浏览；逛 ❑ *I stopped in several bookstores to browse.* 我去了几家书店，随便浏览了一下。 ❑ *She browsed in an upscale antiques shop.* 她逛了一家上等的古玩店。 ● N-COUNT **Browse** is also a noun. 浏览；逛 ❑ *...a browse around the shops.* …在商店的一番闲逛。 2 V-I If you **browse through** a book or magazine, you look through it in a fairly casual way. 随意翻阅 ❑ *...sitting on the sofa browsing through the TV pages of the paper.* …坐在沙发上随意翻看报纸上的电视版面。 3 V-I If you **browse** on a computer, you search for information in computer files or on the Internet, especially on the World Wide Web. （在电脑或网络上）搜索 [COMPUTING] ❑ *Try browsing around in the network bulletin boards.* 在网络布告栏里搜索一下试试。 4 V-T/V-I When animals **browse**, they feed on plants. （动物）嚼食植物 ❑ *...three red deer stags browsing on the fringes of the forest.* …在森林边上吃嫩枝嫩叶的3头红色雄鹿。

brows·er /braʊzər/ (**browsers**) N-COUNT A **browser** is a piece of computer software that you use to search for information on the Internet, especially on the World Wide Web. 浏览器 [COMPUTING] ❑ *You need an up-to-date Web browser.* 你需要一个最新的网络浏览器。

★ **bruise** /bruz/ (**bruises, bruising, bruised**) 1 N-COUNT A **bruise** is an injury that appears as a purple mark on your body, although the skin is not broken. 瘀伤 ❑ *How did you get that bruise on your cheek?* 你脸颊上怎么有一块瘀伤？ 2 V-T/V-I If you **bruise** a part of your body, a bruise appears on it, for example, because something hits you. If you **bruise** easily, bruises appear when something hits you only slightly. 使受瘀伤；受瘀伤 ❑ *I had only bruised my knee.* 我只是膝盖受了瘀伤。 ● **bruised** ADJ 受了瘀伤的 ❑ *I escaped with severely bruised legs.* 我拖着受了严重瘀伤的腿逃走了。 3 V-T/V-I If a fruit, vegetable, or plant **bruises** or **is bruised**, it is damaged by being handled roughly, making a mark on the skin. （水果、蔬菜等）碰伤 ❑ *Choose a warm, dry day to cut them off the plants, being careful not to bruise them.* 选择暖和干燥的一天把它们从植物上剪下来，小心不要碰伤它们。 ❑ *...bruised tomatoes and cucumbers.* …碰伤了的西红柿和黄瓜。 ● N-COUNT **Bruise** is also a noun. （水果、蔬菜等表皮上）碰的伤痕 ❑ *...bruises on the fruit's skin.* …水果表皮上的碰的伤痕。 4 V-T If you **are bruised** by an unpleasant experience, it makes you feel unhappy or upset. 受伤 [usu passive] ❑ *The government will be severely bruised by yesterday's events.* 政府将因昨天的事件而严重受挫。

brunch /brʌntʃ/ (**brunches**) N-VAR **Brunch** is a meal that is eaten in the late morning. It is a combination of breakfast and lunch. 早午餐

brunt /brʌnt/ PHRASE To **bear the brunt** or **take the brunt of** something unpleasant means to suffer the main part or force of it. 受主要冲击 ❑ *Young people are bearing the brunt of unemployment.* 失业对年轻人的冲击最大。

brush ♦◇◇ /brʌʃ/ (**brushes, brushing, brushed**) 1 N-COUNT A **brush** is an object that has a large number of bristles or hairs fixed to it. You use brushes for painting, for cleaning things, and for making your hair neat. 画笔；刷子 ❑ *We gave him paint and brushes.* 我们给了他颜料和画笔。 ❑ *Stains are removed with buckets of soapy water and scrubbing brushes.* 污点用一桶桶的肥皂水和擦洗的刷子除掉了。 2 V-T If you **brush** something or **brush** something such as dirt off it, you clean it or make it neat using a brush. 刷；梳理 ❑ *Have you brushed your teeth?* 你刷过牙了吗？ ❑ *She brushed the powder out of her hair.* 她把粉末从头发中梳掉。 ● N-SING **Brush** is also a noun. 刷；梳理 ❑ *I gave it a quick brush with my hairbrush.* 我用发刷对它进行了一番迅速的梳理。 3 V-T If you **brush** something **with** a liquid, you apply a layer of that liquid using a brush. 用…涂刷 ❑ *Brush the dough with beaten egg yolk.* 在生面团上刷一层打好的蛋黄。 4 V-T If you **brush** something somewhere, you remove it with quick light movements of your hands. （用手）轻轻拭去 ❑ *He brushed his hair back with both hands.* 他用双手把头发轻轻地捋到后面去。 ❑ *She brushed away tears as she spoke of him.* 她在谈起他的时候轻轻拭去眼泪。 5 V-T/V-I If one thing **brushes against** another or if you **brush** one thing **against** another, the first thing touches the second thing lightly while passing it. 轻轻擦过 ❑ *Something brushed against her leg.* 有什么东西轻轻从她腿上擦过。 ❑ *I felt her dark brown hair brushing the back of my shoulder.* 我感觉到她深褐色的头发轻轻拂过我的肩后。

6 N-COUNT If you have a **brush with** a particular situation, usually an unpleasant one, you almost experience it. 擦肩而过 ❑ *...the trauma of a brush with death.* …与死神擦肩而过后的创伤。 7 N-UNCOUNT **Brush** is an area of rough open land covered with small bushes and trees. You also use **brush** to refer to the bushes and trees on this land. 灌木丛地带；灌木丛 ❑ *...the brush fire that destroyed nearly 500 acres.* …烧毁了近五百英亩的灌木丛火灾。

→ see **hair, teeth**

▸ **brush aside** or **brush away** PHRASAL VERB If you **brush aside** or **brush away** an idea, remark, or feeling, you refuse to consider it because you think it is not important or useful, even though it may be. 对(主意、评论、感情)置之不理 ❑ *Perhaps you shouldn't brush the idea aside too hastily.* 或许你不该太草率地对那个想法置之不理。

▸ **brush off** PHRASAL VERB If someone **brushes** you **off** when you speak to them, they refuse to talk to you or be nice to you. 不予理睬；冷落 ❑ *When I tried to talk to her about it she just brushed me off.* 我试图与她谈谈那件事，她就是不理我。

▸ **brush up** or **brush up on** PHRASAL VERB If you **brush up** something or **brush up on** it, you practice it or improve your knowledge of it. 温习；加强…知识 ❑ *I had hoped to brush up my Spanish.* 我曾希望提高一下我的西班牙语。

brusque /brʌsk/ ADJ If you describe a person or their behavior as **brusque**, you mean that they deal with things, or say things, quickly and shortly, so that they seem to be rude. 简短生硬的；唐突的 ❑ *The doctors are brusque and busy.* 医生们十分忙碌，说话简短生硬。

brus·sels sprout /brʌsəlz spraʊt/ (**brussels sprouts**) also **Brussels sprout** N-COUNT **Brussels sprouts** are vegetables that look like tiny cabbages. 抱子甘蓝

★ **bru·tal** /brutᵊl/ 1 ADJ A **brutal** act or person is cruel and violent. 残暴的 ❑ *He was the victim of a very brutal murder.* 他是一桩异常残暴的谋杀案的受害者。 ❑ *...the brutal suppression of anti-government protests.* …对反政府抗议行动的残酷镇压。 ● **bru·tal·ly** ADV 残暴地 ❑ *Her real parents had been brutally murdered.* 她的亲生父母已被残暴地杀害了。 2 ADJ If someone expresses something unpleasant with **brutal** honesty or frankness, they express it in a clear and accurate way, without attempting to disguise its unpleasantness. 不留情面的(诚实、直白) ❑ *It was refreshing to talk about themselves and their feelings with brutal honesty.* 不留情面的诚实地谈论他们自己和他们的感情令人耳目一新。 ● **bru·tal·ly** ADV 不留情面地 ❑ *The talks had been brutally frank.* 那些谈话不留情面地坦率。

★ **bru·tal·ity** /brutælɪti/ (**brutalities**) N-VAR **Brutality** is cruel and violent treatment or behavior. A **brutality** is an instance of cruel and violent treatment or behavior. 残暴；残暴行为 ❑ *Her experience of men was of domination and brutality.* 男人留给她的感受是支配一切，野蛮残暴。 ❑ *...police brutality.* …警察的暴行。

brute /brut/ (**brutes**) N-COUNT If you call someone, usually a man, a **brute**, you mean that they are rough, violent, and insensitive. 粗暴的人(通常指男性) [DISAPPROVAL] ❑ *Custer was an idiot and a brute and he deserved his fate.* 卡斯特是个愚蠢而粗暴的人，他应该有这样的下场。

BSE /bi ɛs i/ N-UNCOUNT **BSE** is a disease that affects the nervous system of cattle and kills them. **BSE** is an abbreviation for "bovine spongiform encephalopathy." 牛绵状脑病 ❑ *...meat from cattle infected with BSE, or mad cow disease.* …感染了牛绵状脑病或疯牛病的牛肉。

BTW BTW is the written abbreviation for "by the way," often used in e-mail. 顺便提一句 ❑ *BTW, the machine is simply amazing.* 顺便提一句，这台机器简直太了不起了。

bub·ble /bʌbᵊl/ (**bubbles, bubbling, bubbled**) 1 N-COUNT **Bubbles** are small balls of air or gas in a liquid. (液体中的) 气泡 ❑ *Ink particles attach themselves to air bubbles and rise to the surface.* 墨点吸附在气泡上，升到表面。 2 N-COUNT A **bubble** is a hollow ball of soapy liquid that is floating in the air or standing on a surface. 肥皂泡 ❑ *With soap and water, bubbles and boats, children love bathtime.* 因为有肥皂、水、肥皂泡和小船，孩子们都喜欢洗澡。 3 N-COUNT In a cartoon, a speech **bubble** is the shape which surrounds the words which a character is thinking or saying. (圈注漫画中人物心理活动或对白的) 泡状框 ❑ *All that was missing were speech bubbles saying, "Golly!" and "Wow!"* 漏掉的都是写着"呀！"和"哇！"的泡状话框。 4 V-I When a liquid **bubbles**, bubbles move in it, for example, because it is boiling or moving quickly. 冒泡；沸腾 ❑ *Heat the seasoned stock until it is bubbling.* 把这些调了味的汤汁加热至沸腾为止。 ❑ *The fermenting wine has bubbled up and over the top.* 这些发酵的酒已经冒泡溢出来了。 5 V-I A feeling, influence, or activity that is **bubbling** away continues to occur. 继续发生 [usu cont] ❑ *...political tensions that have been bubbling away for years.* …持续了若干年的政治紧张局势。

→ see **soap**

bub·bly /bʌbli/ 1 ADJ Someone who is **bubbly** is very lively and cheerful and talks a lot. 活泼、欢快而爱讲话的 [APPROVAL] ❑ *...a bubbly girl who loves to laugh.* …一个爱笑爱讲话的活泼女孩。 ❑ *She had a bright and bubbly personality.* 她曾经有愉快和阳光的个性。 2 ADJ If something is **bubbly**, it has a lot of bubbles in it. 多泡的 ❑ *Melt the butter over a medium-low heat. When it is melted and bubbly, put in the flour.* 用中低火把黄油加热。待黄油熔化起泡后，放入面粉。

★ **buck** /bʌk/ (**bucks, bucking, bucked**) 1 N-COUNT A **buck** is a U.S. or Australian dollar. 美元；澳元 [INFORMAL] ❑ *That would probably cost you about fifty bucks.* 那可能会花费你大约五十美元。 ❑ *Why can't you spend a few bucks on a coat?* 为什么你不能花几美元买件外套呢？ 2 N-COUNT A **buck** is the male of various animals, including the deer, antelope, rabbit, and kangaroo. (雄鹿、公羊、雄兔、雄袋鼠等) 雄性动物 3 ADJ If someone has **buck** teeth, their upper front teeth stick forward out of their mouth. 外龅的 [ADJ n] 4 V-I If a horse **bucks**, it kicks both of its back legs wildly into the air, or jumps into the air wildly with all four feet off the ground. (马) 狂蹬后腿跃起；四蹄离地狂跳 ❑ *The stallion bucked as he fought against the reins holding him tightly in.* 那匹种马四蹄离地狂跳，试图挣脱紧紧拴住它的缰绳。 5 V-T If you **buck** the trend, you obtain different results from others in the same area. If you **buck** the system, you get what you want by breaking or ignoring the rules. 违逆 (潮流)；抗拒 (体制) ❑ *While other newspapers are losing circulation, we are bucking the trend.* 其他报纸发行量在下降，而我们却逆势而进。 ❑ *He wants to be the tough rebel who bucks the system.* 他想成为抗拒体制的强硬叛逆者。 6 PHRASE If you **pass the buck**, you refuse to accept responsibility for something, and say that someone else is responsible. 推诿责任 [INFORMAL] ❑ *David says the responsibility is Mr. Smith's and it's no good trying to pass the buck.* 大卫说责任应该由史密斯先生承担，试图推诿责任毫无益处。

buck·et /bʌkɪt/ (**buckets**) 1 N-COUNT A **bucket** is a round metal or plastic container with a handle attached to its sides. Buckets are often used for holding and carrying water. (有提梁的) 桶 ❑ *We drew water in a bucket from the well outside the door.* 我们用水桶从门外的井里提水。 2 N-COUNT A **bucket of** something such as water is the amount of it that is contained in a bucket. 一桶之量 ❑ *She threw a bucket of water over them.* 她向他们泼了一桶水。

▲ **buck·le** /bʌkᵊl/ (**buckles, buckling, buckled**) 1 N-COUNT A **buckle** is a piece of metal or plastic attached to one end of a belt or strap, which is used to fasten it. (皮带等的) 带扣 ❑ *He wore a belt with a large brass buckle.* 他系了一根有很大黄铜扣的皮带。 2 V-T When you **buckle** a belt or strap, you fasten it. 扣紧 ❑ *A door slammed in the house and a man came out buckling his belt.* 屋子里门砰地关上了，一名男子一边扣着皮带一边走了出来。 3 V-T/V-I If an object **buckles** or if something **buckles** it, it becomes bent as a result of very great heat or force. 使弯曲；(因受热或受压而) 变弯 ❑ *The door was beginning to buckle from the intense heat.* 由于高温，门正开始变弯。 4 V-I If your legs or knees **buckle**, they bend because they have become very weak or tired. (腿、膝) 发软弯曲 ❑ *Mcanally's knees buckled and he crumpled down onto the floor.* 麦卡纳利双膝发软弯了下去，瘫倒在地板上。

→ see **crash**

▸ **buckle up** PHRASAL VERB When you **buckle up** in a car or airplane, you fasten your seat belt. 系上安全带 [INFORMAL] ❑ *A sign just ahead of me said, "Buckle Up. It's the Law in Illinois."* 在我前面的一个告示牌上写着"系上安全带，这是伊利诺伊州的法律"。

bud /bʌd/ (**buds**) 1 N-COUNT A **bud** is a small pointed lump that appears on a tree or plant and develops into a leaf or flower. 芽；花蕾 ❑ *Rosanna's favorite time is early summer, just before the buds open.* 罗莎娜最喜欢的时节是初夏，就在花蕾开放之前。 2 → see also **budding** 3 PHRASE If you **nip** something such as bad behavior **in the bud**, you stop it before it can develop very far. 把某事物掐灭于萌芽状态 [INFORMAL] ❑ *It is important to recognize jealousy and to nip it in the bud before it gets out of hand.* 意识到嫉妒并在它发展到无法控制之前就把它消灭于萌芽状态，这一点至关重要。

→ see **taste**

▲ **Bud·dhism** /budɪzəm, bud-/ N-UNCOUNT **Buddhism** is a religion which teaches that the way to end suffering is by overcoming your desires. 佛教

→ see **religion**

B

▲ **Bud·dhist** /bʊdɪst, bu̲d-/ (**Buddhists**) **1** N-COUNT A **Buddhist** is a person whose religion is Buddhism. 佛教徒 **2** ADJ **Buddhist** means relating or referring to Buddhism. 佛教的 ❏ *...Buddhist monks.* …和尚。

bud·ding /bʌdɪŋ/ **1** ADJ If you describe someone as, for example, a **budding** businessman or a **budding** artist, you mean that they are starting to succeed or become interested in business or art. 崭露头角的 [ADJ n] ❏ *The forum is now open to all budding entrepreneurs.* 该论坛现在向所有崭露头角的企业家开放。 **2** ADJ You use **budding** to describe a situation that is just beginning. 萌发中的 [ADJ n] ❏ *Our budding romance was over.* 我们刚刚萌发的浪漫爱情结束了。

bud·dy /bʌdi/ (**buddies**) N-COUNT A **buddy** is a close friend, usually a male friend of a man. 好朋友 (常用于男子之间) [mainly AM] ❏ *We became great buddies.* 我们成了很好的哥们。

budge /bʌdʒ/ (**budges, budging, budged**) **1** V-T/V-I If someone will not **budge** on a matter, or if nothing **budges** them, they refuse to change their mind or to come to an agreement. 使让步；做让步 [with brd-neg] ❏ *The Americans will not budge on this point.* 这些美国人在这一点上不会让步的。 **2** V-T/V-I If someone or something will not **budge**, they will not move. If you cannot **budge** them, you cannot make them move. 使移动；移动 [with brd-neg] ❏ *Her mother refused to budge from Omaha.* 她母亲拒绝离开奥马哈。 ❏ *The window refused to budge.* 窗子怎么也动不了。

budg·et ♦♦◊ /bʌdʒɪt/ (**budgets, budgeting, budgeted**) **1** N-COUNT Your **budget** is the amount of money that you have available to spend. The **budget** for something is the amount of money that a person, organization, or country has available to spend on it. 预算 [BUSINESS] ❏ *She will design a fantastic new kitchen for you – and all within your budget.* 她将为你设计一个崭新的漂亮厨房——所有的花费都将在你的预算之内。 ❏ *Someone had furnished the place on a tight budget.* 有人用不多的钱把那个地方布置了一下。 **2** N-COUNT The **budget** of an organization or country is its financial situation, considered as the difference between the money it receives and the money it spends. (机构、政府等的) 财政收支状况 [BUSINESS] ❏ *The hospital obviously needs to balance the budget each year.* 该医院显然每年都需要平衡其财务收支。 **3** V-T/V-I If you **budget** certain amounts of money for particular things, you decide that you can afford to spend those amounts on those things. 安排开支；编制预算 ❏ *The company has budgeted $10 million for advertising.* 公司已经安排了1千万美元的广告预算。 ❏ *The movie is only budgeted at $10 million.* 这部电影的预算只有1千万美元。 ❏ *I'm learning how to budget.* 我正在学习怎样编制预算。 ● **budg·et·ing** N-UNCOUNT 预算 ❏ *We have continued to exercise caution in our budgeting for the current year.* 在今年的预算方面，我们继续小心谨慎。 **4** ADJ **Budget** is used in advertising to suggest that something is being sold cheaply. 价格低廉的 [ADJ n] ❏ *Cheap flights are available from budget travel agents from $240.* 起价$240的廉价机票可从一些经济旅行社那里买到。

▸ **budget for** PHRASAL VERB If you **budget for** something, you take account of it when you are deciding how much you can afford to spend on different things. 在预算中考虑到 ❏ *The authorities had budgeted for some non-payment.* 政府部门在预算中已考虑到一些未付款项。

Word Partnership *budget* 的常用搭配:

V.	**balance** a budget **1** **2**
PREP.	**over** budget, **under** budget **1** **2**
N.	budget **crunch** **1** **2**
	budget **crisis**, budget **cuts**, budget **deficit** **2**
ADJ.	**tight** budget **1** **2**
	federal budget **2**

▲ **budg·et·ary** /bʌdʒɪteri/ ADJ A **budgetary** matter or policy is concerned with the amount of money that is available to a country or organization, and how it is to be spent. 预算的 [ADJ n] [FORMAL] ❏ *There are huge budgetary pressures on all governments in Europe to reduce their armed forces.* 欧洲各国政府都面临着巨大的裁军预算压力。

▲ **buff** /bʌf/ (**buffs**) **1** COLOR Something that is **buff** is pale brown in color. 浅棕色的 ❏ *He took a largish buff envelope from his pocket.* 他从口袋里拿出一个相当大的浅棕色信封。 **2** N-COUNT You use **buff** to describe someone who knows a lot about a particular subject. For example, if you describe someone as a movie **buff**, you mean that they know a lot about movies. 爱好者 [INFORMAL] ❏ *Judge Lanier is a real movie buff.* 拉尼尔法官是个真正的电影迷。

▲ **buf·fa·lo** /bʌfəloʊ/ (**buffalo**)

> The plural can be either **buffaloes** or **buffalo**.

N-COUNT A **buffalo** is a wild animal like a large cow with horns that curve upwards. Buffalo are usually found in southern and eastern Africa. 水牛

▲ **buff·er** /bʌfər/ (**buffers, buffering, buffered**) **1** N-COUNT A **buffer** is something that prevents something else from being harmed or that prevents two things from harming each other. 缓冲物 ❏ *Keep savings as a buffer against unexpected cash needs.* 备有存款来作为急需现金时的缓冲。 **2** V-T If something **is buffered**, it is protected from harm. 受保护 ❏ *The company is buffered by long-term contracts with growers.* 这家公司受到了与种植者签订长期合同的保护。 **3** N-COUNT A **buffer** is an area in a computer's memory where information can be stored for a short time. 缓冲区 [COMPUTING]

▲ **buf·fet** (**buffets, buffeting, buffeted**)

> Pronounced /bʊfe̲ɪ/ for meanings **1** and **2**, and /bʌfɪt/ for meaning **3**.

> 义项**1**和**2**读作 /bʊfe̲ɪ/，义项**3**读作 /bʌfɪt/。

1 N-COUNT A **buffet** is a meal of food that is displayed on a long table at a party or public occasion. Guests usually serve themselves. 自助餐 ❏ *...a buffet lunch.* …自助午餐。 **2** N-COUNT A **buffet** is a café, usually in a hotel or station. (旅馆、车站等处的) 餐饮部 ❏ *We sat in the station buffet sipping tea.* 我们坐在车站餐饮部喝茶。 **3** V-T If something **is buffeted** by strong winds or by stormy seas, it is repeatedly struck or blown around by them. (强风、狂浪) 反复袭击 ❏ *Their plane had been severely buffeted by storms.* 他们的飞机遭到了暴风雨的猛烈袭击。

bug /bʌg/ (**bugs, bugging, bugged**) **1** N-COUNT A **bug** is an insect or similar small creature. 小虫 [INFORMAL] ❏ *We noticed tiny bugs that were all over the walls.* 我们发现墙上爬满了小虫。 **2** N-COUNT A **bug** is an illness which is caused by small organisms such as bacteria. (由细菌引起的) 疾病 [INFORMAL] ❏ *I think I've got a bit of a stomach bug.* 我觉得我有点肠胃感染。 **3** N-COUNT If there is a **bug** in a computer program, there is a mistake in it. (计算机程序的) 故障 [COMPUTING] ❏ *There is a bug in the software.* 软件出了故障。 **4** N-COUNT A **bug** is a tiny hidden microphone that transmits what people are saying. 微型窃听器 ❏ *There was a bug on the phone.* 那部电话里装有一个微型窃听器。 **5** V-T If someone **bugs** a place, they hide tiny microphones in it that transmit what people are saying. (在某处) 装窃听器 ❏ *He heard that they were planning to bug his office.* 他听说他们正计划在他的办公室安装窃听器。 **6** V-T If someone or something **bugs** you, they worry or annoy you. 使烦恼 [INFORMAL] ❏ *I only did it to bug my parents.* 我那样做只不过是为了烦扰我父母。

Thesaurus *bug* 另参见:

N.	disease, germ, infection, microorganism, virus **2**
	breakdown, defect, error, glitch, hitch, malfunction **3**

build ♦♦♦ /bɪ̲ld/ (**builds, building, built**) **1** V-T If you **build** something, you make it by joining things together. 建造 ❏ *Developers are now proposing to build a hotel on the site.* 开发商们现在正提议在这个地方建造一座宾馆。 ❏ *The house was built in the early 19th century.* 这座房子建于19世纪早期。 ● **build·ing** N-UNCOUNT 建造 ❏ *In Japan, the building of Kansai airport continues.* 在日本，关西机场的建设仍在继续。 ● **built** ADJ 建造好的 [adv ADJ, ADJ "for" n, ADJ to-inf] ❏ *Even newly built houses can need repairs.* 甚至新建造好的房屋也会需要维修。 ❏ *It's a product built for safety.* 这是一个为安全而造的产品。 **2** V-T If you **build** something **into** a wall or object, you make it in such a way that it is in the wall or object, or is part of it. 把…嵌入 (墙壁、物体等) ❏ *If the TV was built into the ceiling, you could lie there while watching your favorite program.* 如果把电视嵌入天花板，你就能躺着观看你喜爱的节目了。 **3** V-T If people **build** an organization, a society, or a relationship, they gradually form it. 建立 (机构、社团、关系等) ❏ *He and a partner set up on their own and built a successful fashion company.* 他和一个合伙人依靠自己的力量创建了一家成功的时装公司。 ❏ *Their purpose is to build a fair society and a strong economy.* 他们的目的是建立一个公平的社会和一种强大的经济。 ● **build·ing** N-UNCOUNT 建立 ❏ *...the building of the great civilizations of the ancient world.* …古代世界伟大文明的创建。 **4** V-T If you **build** an organization, system, or product **on** something, you base it on it. 以…为基础 ❏ *We will then*

have a firmer foundation of fact on which to build theories. 那时我们将有更坚实的事实根据来作为理论的基础。 5 V-T If you **build** something **into** a policy, system, or product, you make it part of it. 使成为组成部分 ❑ *We have to build computers into the school curriculum.* 我们必须计算机知识纳入学校的课程。 6 V-T To **build** someone's confidence or trust means to increase it gradually. 逐步增强 ❑ *Diplomats hope the meetings will build mutual trust.* 外交官们希望这些会议能逐步增强彼此的信任。 ● PHRASAL VERB **Build up** means the same as **build.** 逐步增强 ❑ *The delegations had begun to build up some trust in one another.* 各代表团已经开始逐步增强相互的信任。 7 V-I If you **build on** the success of something, you take advantage of this success in order to make further progress. (在…的基础上) 继续发展 ❑ *The new regime has no successful economic reforms on which to build.* 新政权没有成功实施可赖以为继的经济改革。 8 V-I If pressure, speed, sound, or excitement **builds**, it gradually becomes greater. (压力、速度、声音等) 逐渐增大 ❑ *Pressure built yesterday for postponement of the ceremony.* 要求推迟庆典的压力昨天逐渐增大了。 ● PHRASAL VERB **Build up** means the same as **build.** (压力、速度、声音等) 逐渐增大 ❑ *We can build up the speed gradually and safely.* 我们可以逐步安全地加快速度。 9 N-VAR Someone's **build** is the shape that their bones and muscles give to their body. 体格 ❑ *He's described as around thirty years old, six feet tall and of medium build.* 他被描述为大约三十岁，身高6英尺，体格中等。 10 → see also **building, built**
→ see **muscle**

▸ **build up** 1 PHRASAL VERB If you **build up** something or if it **builds up**, it gradually becomes bigger, for example, because more is added to it. 使逐渐变大；逐渐变大 ❑ *The regime built up the largest army in Africa.* 该政权逐渐建立起一支在非洲规模最大的军队。 ❑ *The collection has been built up over the last seventeen years.* 这些收藏是在过去的17年里逐渐收集的。 2 PHRASAL VERB If you **build** someone **up**, you help them to feel stronger or more confident, especially when they have had a bad experience or have been ill. 使振作 ❑ *Build her up with kindness and a sympathetic ear.* 用友善和富有同情心的倾听来使她振作起来。 3 PHRASAL VERB If you **build** someone or something **up**, you make them seem important or exciting, for example, by talking about them a lot. 吹捧；大肆宣传 ❑ *The media will report on it and the tabloids will build it up.* 媒体将对它进行报导，小报将对其大肆宣传。 ❑ *The soccer community built him up as the savior of the sport.* 足球界曾把他吹捧为这项运动的救星。 4 → see also **build 6, 8, build-up, built-up**

Thesaurus *build* 另参见：
V. assemble, make, manufacture, produce, put together, set up; *(ant.)* demolish, destroy, knock down 1

Word Partnership *build* 的常用搭配：
V. **plan to** build 1
N. build **bridges**, build **roads**, build **schools** 1
build **confidence** 6
build **momentum** 8
ADJ. **athletic** build, **slender** build, **strong** build 9

build·er /bɪldər/ (**builders**) N-COUNT A **builder** is a person whose job is to build or repair houses and other buildings. 建筑工人 ❑ *The builders have finished the roof.* 建筑工人们已经完成了屋顶的建造。

build·ing ◆◆◆ /bɪldɪŋ/ (**buildings**) N-COUNT A **building** is a structure that has a roof and walls, for example, a house or a factory. 建筑物 ❑ *They were on the upper floor of the building.* 他们在该建筑物的上层。
→ see **architecture, skyscraper**

build-up (**build-ups**) also **buildup, build up** 1 N-COUNT A **build-up** is a gradual increase in something. 逐渐增加 ❑ *There has been a build-up of troops on both sides of the border.* 边境两边的军队都在逐渐增兵。 2 N-COUNT The **build-up** to an event is the way that journalists, advertisers, or other people talk about it a lot in the period of time immediately before it, and try to make it seem important and exciting. 大肆宣传 ❑ *The exams came, almost an anticlimax after the build-up that the students had given them.* 在学生们一番大造声势之后，随之而来的考试却出乎意料地平淡。

built /bɪlt/ 1 **Built** is the past tense and past participle of **build.** **build**的过去式和过去分词 2 ADJ If you say that someone is **built** in a particular way, you are describing the kind of body they have. 有…体格的 ❑ *...a strong, powerfully-built man of 60.* …一位体格健壮的60岁男子。 3 → see also **well-built**

built-in ADJ **Built-in** devices or features are included in something as a part of it, rather than being separate. 内置的 [ADJ n] ❑ *...modern cameras with built-in flash units.* …有内置闪光灯的新式照相机。

built-up ADJ A **built-up** area is an area such as a town or city which has a lot of buildings in it. 建筑物密集的 ❑ *A speed limit of 30 mph was introduced in built-up areas.* 在建筑物密集区域，限速为每小时30英里。

bulb /bʌlb/ (**bulbs**) 1 N-COUNT A **bulb** is the glass part of an electric light or lamp, which gives out light when electricity passes through it. 电灯泡 ❑ *The stairwell was lit by a single bulb.* 楼梯间只有一盏灯照明。 2 N-COUNT A **bulb** is a root shaped like an onion that grows into a flower or plant. 球茎 ❑ *...tulip bulbs.* …郁金香球茎。

▲ **bulge** /bʌldʒ/ (**bulges, bulging, bulged**) 1 V-I If something such as a person's stomach **bulges**, it sticks out. 鼓起 ❑ *Jiro waddled closer, his belly bulging and distended.* 吉罗大腹便便地蹒跚而来。 ❑ *He bulges out of his black T-shirt.* 他臃肿的身体在黑色T恤下面鼓了出来。 2 V-I If someone's eyes or veins **are bulging**, they seem to stick out a lot, often because the person is making a strong physical effort or is experiencing a strong emotion. (眼睛或血管因用力或激动而) 凸出 ❑ *He shouted at his brother, his neck veins bulging.* 他冲着弟弟大喊大叫，脖子上的血管都凸起来了。 3 V-I If you say that something **is bulging with** things, you are emphasizing that it is full of them. 塞满 [oft cont] [EMPHASIS] ❑ *They returned home with the car bulging with boxes.* 他们开着那辆塞满了盒子的车回到了家。 4 N-COUNT **Bulges** are lumps that stick out from a surface which is otherwise flat or smooth. (平面上) 凸起的一块 ❑ *Why won't those bulges on your hips and thighs go?* 为什么你臀部和大腿上的赘肉不能消失呢？ 5 N-COUNT If there is a **bulge in** something, there is a sudden large increase in it. 骤增 ❑ *...a bulge in aircraft sales.* …飞机销量的骤增。

bu·limia /bulɪmiə, -lɪm-/ N-UNCOUNT **Bulimia** or **bulimia nervosa** is an illness in which a person has a very great fear of becoming fat, and so they make themselves vomit after eating. 贪食症

bu·limic /bulɪmɪk, -lɪm-/ (**bulimics**) ADJ If someone is **bulimic**, they are suffering from bulimia. 贪食症的 ❑ *...bulimic patients.* …贪食症病人。 ● N-COUNT A **bulimic** is someone who is bulimic. 贪食症患者 ❑ *...a former bulimic.* …曾经得过贪食症的人。

bulk /bʌlk/ (**bulks, bulking, bulked**) 1 N-SING You can refer to something's **bulk** when you want to emphasize that it is very large. 大块 [WRITTEN, EMPHASIS] ❑ *The truck pulled out of the lot, its bulk unnerving against the dawn.* 拂晓时分，卡车驶出了停车场，庞大的车身看起来有点儿可怕。 2 N-SING You can refer to a large person's body or to their weight or size as their **bulk.** 庞大肥硕的身躯 ❑ *Bannol lowered his bulk carefully into the chair.* 班诺尔那肥硕的身躯小心地坐落到了椅子上。 3 QUANT The **bulk of** something is most of it. 大部分 [QUANT "of" def-n] ❑ *The bulk of the text is essentially a review of these original documents.* 正文的大部分基本上是对这些原始文献的回顾。 ● PRON **Bulk** is also a pronoun. 大部分 ❑ *They come from all over the world, though the bulk is from the Indian subcontinent.* 他们来自世界各地，但其中大部分人还是来自印度次大陆。 4 PHRASE If you buy or sell something **in bulk**, you buy or sell it in large quantities. 大批地 (买卖) ❑ *Buying in bulk is more economical than shopping for small quantities.* 大批采购比少量购买更经济实惠。

▸ **bulk up** PHRASAL VERB If someone **bulks up** or if they **bulk up** their body, they put on weight in the form of extra muscle. 使变粗壮；变粗壮 ❑ *They feel I need to bulk up, and to improve my upper body strength.* 他们觉得我需要变粗壮些，并增强上身的力量。 ❑ *My friend is obsessed with going to the gym and has really bulked up her arms.* 我朋友迷上了去健身房，她确实把胳膊练得粗壮了。

bulky /bʌlki/ (**bulkier, bulkiest**) ADJ Something that is **bulky** is large and heavy. Bulky things are often difficult to move or deal with. 大而笨重的 ❑ *...bulky items like lawn mowers.* …割草机这样笨重的东西。

bull /bʊl/ (**bulls**) 1 N-COUNT A **bull** is a male animal of the cow family. 公牛 2 N-COUNT Some other male animals, including elephants and whales, are called **bulls.** 巨大的雄性动物 ❑ *Suddenly a massive bull elephant with huge tusks charged us.* 突然，一只体形壮硕、长着巨型象牙的雄象朝我们冲了过来。 3 N-COUNT In the stock market, **bulls** are people who buy shares in expectation of a price rise, in order to make a profit by selling the shares again after a short time. Compare **bear.** (股票市场上) 买空的人 [BUSINESS] ❑ *The bulls argue stock prices are low and there are bargains to be had.* 那些买空者

B

认为股价很低，有些便宜股可以买进。**4** N-COUNT In the Roman Catholic church, a papal **bull** is an official statement on a particular subject that is issued by the pope. 教皇训谕 **5** N-UNCOUNT If you say that something is **bull** or a load of **bull**, you mean that it is complete nonsense or absolutely untrue. 胡说八道 [INFORMAL] ❑ *I think it's a load of bull.* 我觉得那是一派胡言。

bull·doze /bʊldoʊz/ (**bulldozes, bulldozing, bulldozed**) **1** V-T If people **bulldoze** something such as a building, they knock it down using a bulldozer. (用推土机) 推倒 ❑ *She defeated developers who wanted to bulldoze her home to build a supermarket.* 她打败了那些企图推倒她的家园建造超市的开发商。 **2** V-T If people **bulldoze** earth, stone, or other heavy material, they move it using a bulldozer. (用推土机) 推走 ❑ *They have been cutting down the trees and bulldozing the land.* 他们正砍倒树木，推整土地。 **3** V-T If someone **bulldozes** a plan **through** or **bulldozes** another person **into** doing something, they get what they want in an unpleasantly forceful way. 胁迫 [DISAPPROVAL] ❑ *Dropping all pretense of reason, they began to bulldoze through the democratic reforms.* 他们抛开一切佯装的理性，开始胁迫进行民主改革。 ❑ *...to sway public opinion and bulldoze them into adopting uneconomic practices.* …左右公众的观点，胁迫他们接受没有效益的做法。

bull·doz·er /bʊldoʊzər/ (**bulldozers**) N-COUNT A **bulldozer** is a large vehicle with a broad metal blade at the front, which is used for knocking down buildings or moving large amounts of earth. 推土机

bul·let /bʊlɪt/ (**bullets**) **1** N-COUNT A **bullet** is a small piece of metal with a pointed or rounded end, which is fired out of a gun. 子弹 ❑ *Two of the police fired 16 bullets each.* 两名警察各发射了16枚子弹。 **2** PHRASE If someone **bites the bullet**, they accept that they have to do something unpleasant but necessary. 硬着头皮接受 [JOURNALISM] ❑ *Tour operators may be forced to bite the bullet and cut prices.* 旅游社的经营者们不得不忍痛降价。

bul·letin /bʊlɪtɪn/ (**bulletins**) **1** N-COUNT A **bulletin** is a short news report on the radio or television. (电台、电视台的) 新闻快报 ❑ *...the early morning news bulletin.* …早间新闻快报。 **2** N-COUNT A **bulletin** is a short official announcement made publicly to inform people about an important matter. 公告 ❑ *At 3:30 p.m. a bulletin was released announcing that the president was out of immediate danger.* 下午3:30发布了公告，宣布总统暂时脱离了危险。 **3** N-COUNT A **bulletin** is a regular newspaper or leaflet that is produced by an organization or group such as a school or church. (学校、教堂等机构发行的) 简报或小册子

bul·letin board (**bulletin boards**) **1** N-COUNT A **bulletin board** is a board that is usually attached to a wall in order to display notices giving information about something. 布告栏 [mainly AM]

in BRIT, use **noticeboard**

2 N-COUNT In computing, a **bulletin board** is a system that enables users to send and receive messages of general interest. 电子布告栏 ❑ *The Internet is the largest computer bulletin board in the world, and it's growing.* 因特网是世界上最大的电子布告栏，并且仍在不断扩大。

bul·let point (**bullet points**) N-COUNT A **bullet point** is one of a series of important items for discussion or action in a document, usually marked by a square or round symbol. (文件中用符号标记的) 重点句 ❑ *Use bold type for headings and bullet points for noteworthy achievements.* 标题使用粗体，显著的成就用着重号。

bullet·proof /bʊlɪtpruf/ also **bullet-proof** ADJ Something that is **bulletproof** is made of a strong material that bullets cannot pass through. 防弹的 ❑ *...bulletproof glass.* …防弹玻璃。
→ see **glass**

bull·horn /bʊlhɔrn/ (**bullhorns**) N-COUNT A **bullhorn** is a device for making your voice sound louder in the open air. 扩音器 [AM]

in BRIT, use **loudhailer, megaphone**

❑ *A bullhorn blared warnings of a bomb scare.* 扩音器大声播报炸弹恐吓的警告。

bul·lion /bʊliən/ N-UNCOUNT **Bullion** is gold or silver, usually in the form of bars. 金条；银条 ❑ *The Japanese are busy buying up gold bullion.* 日本人正忙着大批收购金条。

bull·ish /bʊlɪʃ/ ADJ In the stock market, if there is a **bullish** mood, prices are expected to rise. Compare **bearish**. (股票市场) 牛市的；行情看涨的 (比较**bearish**) [BUSINESS] ❑ *The market opened in a bullish mood.* 股市开盘呈上涨趋势。

bull mar·ket (**bull markets**) N-COUNT A **bull market** is a situation in the stock market when people are buying a lot of shares because they expect the shares will increase in value and they will be able to make a profit by selling them again after a short time. Compare **bear market**. (股市等) 牛市；上涨行情 (比较**bear market**) [BUSINESS] ❑ *...the decline in prices after the bull market peaked in April 2000.* …2000年4月股市涨到顶峰后股价的下滑。

bull·ock /bʊlək/ (**bullocks**) N-COUNT A **bullock** is a young bull that has been castrated. 小阉牛

★ **bul·ly** /bʊli/ (**bullies, bullying, bullied**) **1** N-COUNT A **bully** is someone who uses their strength or power to hurt or frighten other people. 恃强凌弱者 ❑ *I fell victim to the office bully.* 我成了这个办公室霸王欺负的对象。 **2** V-T If someone **bullies** you, they use their strength or power to hurt or frighten you. 欺负 ❑ *I wasn't going to let him bully me.* 我可不会让他欺负我。 ● **bul·ly·ing** N-UNCOUNT 欺凌行为 ❑ *...schoolchildren who were victims of bullying.* …遭受欺凌的小学生。 **3** V-T If someone **bullies** you **into** something, they make you do it by using force or threats. 威逼 ❑ *We think an attempt to bully them into submission would be counterproductive.* 我们认为威逼他们屈服的尝试可能会适得其反。 ❑ *She used to bully me into doing my schoolwork.* 她过去总逼我做作业。

bum /bʌm/ (**bums, bumming, bummed**) **1** N-COUNT A **bum** is a person who has no permanent home or job and who gets money by working occasionally or by asking people for money. 流浪者 [AM, INFORMAL] ❑ *...the bums on the corner fighting over beers.* …在街角争抢啤酒的流浪者们。 **2** N-COUNT If someone refers to another person as a **bum**, they think that person is worthless or irresponsible. 无赖 [INFORMAL, DISAPPROVAL] ❑ *You're all a bunch of bums.* 你们这伙人是一帮无赖。 **3** ADJ Some people use **bum** to describe a situation that they find unpleasant or annoying. 糟糕的 [ADJ n] [INFORMAL] ❑ *He knows you're getting a bum deal.* 他知道你遇上了糟糕的买卖。 **4** V-T If you **bum** something off someone, you ask them for it and they give it to you. 讨要 [INFORMAL] ❑ *Mind if I bum a cigarette?* 讨根烟抽，不介意吧？ **5** N-COUNT Someone's **bum** is the part of their body which they sit on. 屁股 [BRIT, INFORMAL]

in AM, use **ass**

6 **a bum rap** → see **rap**

bump /bʌmp/ (**bumps, bumping, bumped**) **1** V-T/V-I If you **bump** into something or someone, you accidentally hit them while you are moving. 撞上 ❑ *They stopped walking and he almost bumped into them.* 他们停下了脚步，这下他几乎撞到他们。 ❑ *She bumped her head against a low branch.* 她的头撞到一根低矮的树枝上。 ● N-COUNT **Bump** is also a noun. 碰撞 ❑ *Small children often cry after a minor bump.* 小孩子们在轻微的碰撞后常常会哭。 **2** N-COUNT A **bump** is the action or the dull sound of two heavy objects hitting each other. 碰撞；碰撞声 ❑ *I felt a little bump and I knew instantly what had happened.* 我感到了一下轻轻的撞击，立刻就明白发生了什么。 **3** N-COUNT A **bump** is a minor injury or swelling that you get if you bump into something or if something hits you. 肿块 ❑ *She fell against our coffee table and got a large bump on her forehead.* 她撞到了我们的咖啡桌跌倒了，前额起了一个大包。 **4** N-COUNT A **bump** on a road is a raised, uneven part. (路面) 隆起部分 ❑ *The truck hit a bump and bounced.* 卡车开到了路面上一块隆起的地方，颠簸起来。 **5** V-I If a vehicle **bumps over** a surface, it travels in a rough, bouncing way because the surface is very uneven. 颠簸行驶 ❑ *We left the road, and again bumped over the mountainside.* 我们离开公路，又一次在山坡上颠簸行驶。
▶ **bump into** PHRASAL VERB If you **bump into** someone you know, you meet them unexpectedly. 碰见 [INFORMAL] ❑ *I happened to bump into Mervyn Johns in the hallway.* 我碰巧在走廊里撞见了默文·约翰斯。

▲ **bump·er** /bʌmpər/ (**bumpers**) **1** N-COUNT **Bumpers** are bars at the front and back of a vehicle that protect it if it bumps into something. 保险杠 ❑ *What stickers do you have on the bumper or the back windshield?* 你在汽车保险杠或后挡风玻璃上用的是什么贴纸？ **2** ADJ A **bumper** crop or harvest is one that is larger than usual. 丰收的 [ADJ n] ❑ *...a bumper crop of rice.* …水稻的大丰收。 **3** ADJ If you say that something is **bumper** size, you mean that it is very large. 巨大的 [ADJ n] ❑ *...bumper profits.* …巨额收益。 **4** PHRASE If traffic is **bumper-to-bumper**, the vehicles are so close to one another that they are almost touching and are moving very slowly. (车辆) 首尾相接的 ❑ *...bumper-to-bumper rush-hour traffic.* …汽车首尾相接的高峰时间的交通。

bumpy /bʌmpi/ (**bumpier, bumpiest**) **1** ADJ A **bumpy** road or path has a lot of bumps on it. 崎岖不平的 ❑ *...bumpy cobbled streets.* …崎岖不平的铺满卵石的街道。 **2** ADJ A **bumpy** ride is uncomfortable and rough, usually because you are traveling over an uneven surface. 颠簸的 ❑ *...a hot and bumpy ride across the desert.* …穿过沙漠的炎热、颠簸的车程。

▲ **bun** /bʌn/ (**buns**) **1** N-COUNT **Buns** are small bread rolls. They are sometimes sweet and may contain dried fruit or spices. 小圆面包 ❑ *...a currant bun.* …一块含葡萄干的小圆面包。 **2** N-COUNT If a woman has her hair in a **bun**, she has fastened it tightly on top of her head or at the back of her head in the shape of a ball. 圆髻 **3** N-PLURAL Your **buns** are your buttocks. 屁股 [mainly AM, INFORMAL] ❑ *I'd pinch his buns and kiss his neck.* 我要拧他的屁股，亲他的脖子。

bunch ♦◇◇ /bʌntʃ/ (**bunches, bunching, bunched**) **1** N-COUNT A **bunch of** people is a group of people who share one or more characteristics or who are doing something together. 伙 [INFORMAL] ❑ *My neighbors are a bunch of busybodies.* 我的邻居们都是一伙爱管闲事的人。 ❑ *We were a pretty inexperienced bunch of people really.* 我们实际上是一群相当没有经验的人。 **2** N-COUNT A **bunch of** flowers is a number of flowers with their stalks held or tied together. 束 ❑ *He had left a huge bunch of flowers in her hotel room.* 他在她的宾馆房间里留了一大束花。 **3** N-COUNT A **bunch of** bananas or grapes is a group of them growing on the same stem. 串 ❑ *Lili had fallen asleep clutching a fat bunch of grapes.* 莉莉手里抓着一大串葡萄睡着了。 **4** N-COUNT A **bunch of** keys is a set of keys kept together on a metal ring. 串 ❑ *George took out a bunch of keys and went to work on the complicated lock.* 乔治掏出一串钥匙，去设法开这把复杂的锁。

▸ **bunch up** or **bunch together** PHRASAL VERB If people or things **bunch up** or if you **bunch** them **up**, they move close to each other so that they form a small tight group. **Bunch together** means the same as **bunch up.** 聚集 ❑ *They were bunching up, almost stepping on each other's heels.* 他们正挤在一起，几乎踩着彼此的脚跟。 ❑ *People were bunched up at all the exits.* 人们都被聚集在各个出口处。

bun·dle /bʌndᵊl/ (**bundles, bundling, bundled**) **1** N-COUNT A **bundle of** things is a number of them that are tied together or wrapped in a cloth or bag so that they can be carried or stored. 包；捆；束 ❑ *Lance pulled a bundle of papers out of a folder.* 兰斯从一个文件夹中拉出一叠文件。 ❑ *He gathered the bundles of clothing into his arms.* 他把一捆捆衣物抱起来。 **2** N-SING If you describe someone as, for example, a **bundle of** fun, you are emphasizing that they are full of fun. If you describe someone as a **bundle of** nerves, you are emphasizing that they are very nervous. (强调人的特点) 非常 [EMPHASIS] ❑ *I remember Mickey as a bundle of fun, great to have around.* 我记得米基是个非常有趣的人，有他在身边很开心。 ❑ *Life at high school wasn't a bundle of laughs.* 高中生活并不是充满了笑声。 **3** V-T If someone **is bundled** somewhere, someone pushes them there in a rough and hurried way. 塞 ❑ *He was bundled into a car and driven 50 miles to a police station.* 他被塞进一辆小汽车，被带到50英里外的警察局。 **4** V-T To **bundle** software means to sell it together with a computer, or with other hardware or software, as part of a set. 捆绑销售 [COMPUTING] ❑ *It's cheaper to buy software bundled with a PC than separately.* 购买与计算机捆绑销售的软件比单独买更便宜。

▲ **bun·ga·low** /bʌŋgəloʊ/ (**bungalows**) N-COUNT A **bungalow** is a house that has only one level, and no stairs. 平房

bun·gle /bʌŋgᵊl/ (**bungles, bungling, bungled**) V-T If you **bungle** something, you fail to do it properly, because you make mistakes or are clumsy. 搞砸 ❑ *Two prisoners bungled an escape bid after running either side of a lamppost while handcuffed.* 两个囚犯手铐在一起时却分别往灯柱两边跑，结果没跑成。 ● N-COUNT **Bungle** is also a noun. 办砸的事 ❑ *...an appalling administrative bungle.* …一次令人震惊的管理失误。 ● **bun·gling** ADJ 笨拙的 ❑ *...a bungling burglar.* …一个笨拙的窃贼。

▲ **bunk** /bʌŋk/ (**bunks**) N-COUNT A **bunk** is a narrow bed that is usually attached to a wall, especially in a ship. (轮船等的) 铺位 ❑ *He left his bunk and went up on deck again.* 他离开自己的铺位，再次上了甲板。

bun·ker /bʌŋkər/ (**bunkers**) **1** N-COUNT A **bunker** is a place, usually underground, that has been built with strong walls to protect it against heavy gunfire and bombing. 地堡 ❑ *...an extensive network of fortified underground bunkers.* …一个大范围的地下防御工事网络。 **2** N-COUNT A **bunker** is a container for coal or other fuel. 燃料舱 **3** N-COUNT On a golf course, a **bunker** is a large area filled with sand that is deliberately put there as an obstacle that golfers must try to avoid. (高尔夫球场的) 沙坑 ❑ *He put his second shot in a bunker to the left of the green.* 他把第二杆球打进了草地左边的沙坑。

bun·ny /bʌni/ (**bunnies**) N-COUNT A **bunny** or a **bunny rabbit** is a child's word for a rabbit. 兔子 (儿童语言) [INFORMAL]

buoy /bui/ (**buoys, buoying, buoyed**) **1** N-COUNT A **buoy** is a floating object that is used to show ships and boats where they can go and to warn them of danger. 浮标 **2** V-T If someone in a difficult situation **is buoyed** by something, it makes them feel more cheerful and optimistic. 使振奋 ❑ *In May they danced in the streets, buoyed by their victory.* 5月他们在街上跳舞，为胜利而振奋。 ● PHRASAL VERB **Buoy up** means the same as **buoy.** 使振奋 ❑ *They are buoyed up by a sense of hope.* 一线希望使他们振作起来。

buoy·an·cy /bɔɪənsi/ **1** N-UNCOUNT **Buoyancy** is the ability that something has to float on a liquid or in the air. 浮力 ❑ *Air can be pumped into the diving suit to increase buoyancy.* 可以往潜水衣中打气增加浮力。 **2** N-UNCOUNT **Buoyancy** is a feeling of cheerfulness. 愉快 ❑ *...a mood of buoyancy and optimism.* …愉快、乐观的情绪。 **3** N-UNCOUNT There is economic **buoyancy** when the economy is growing. 繁荣 ❑ *The likelihood is that the slump will be followed by a period of buoyancy.* 有可能在衰退之后出现一段繁荣时期。

buoy·ant /bɔɪənt/ **1** ADJ If you are in a **buoyant** mood, you feel cheerful and behave in a lively way. 快活的 ❑ *You will feel more buoyant and optimistic about the future than you have for a long time.* 对于未来，你会比很久以来所感受到的更加快活、乐观。 **2** ADJ A **buoyant** economy is a successful one in which there is a lot of trade and economic activity. 繁荣的 ❑ *We have a buoyant economy and unemployment is considerably lower than the regional average.* 我们有繁荣的经济，失业率远远低于区域平均值。 **3** ADJ A **buoyant** object floats on a liquid. 浮起的 ❑ *While there is still sufficient trapped air within the container to keep it buoyant, it will float.* 只要容器中仍然有足够的空气使它能浮起，它就能漂浮。

bur·den ♦◇◇ /bɜrdᵊn/ (**burdens, burdening, burdened**) **1** N-COUNT If you describe a problem or a responsibility as a **burden**, you mean that it causes someone a lot of difficulty, worry, or hard work. 负担 ❑ *The developing countries bear the burden of an enormous external debt.* 发展中国家背负着巨额外债的负担。 ❑ *Her death will be an impossible burden on Paul.* 她的去世会成为保罗难以承受的负担。 **2** N-COUNT A **burden** is a heavy load that is difficult to carry. 重负 [FORMAL] ❑ *...African women carrying burdens on their heads.* …头顶重物的非洲妇女。 **3** V-T If someone **burdens** you **with** something that is likely to worry you, for example, a problem or a difficult decision, they tell you about it. 使烦恼 ❑ *We decided not to burden him with the news.* 我们决定不拿这个消息去烦他。

bur·dened /bɜrdᵊnd/ **1** ADJ If you are **burdened** with something, it causes you a lot of worry or hard work. 受…困扰的 [v-link ADJ "with/by" n] ❑ *Nicaragua was burdened with a foreign debt of $11 billion.* 尼加拉瓜受110亿美元外债的困扰。 **2** ADJ If you describe someone as **burdened** with a heavy load, you are emphasizing that it is very heavy and that they are holding it or carrying it with difficulty. 负担沉重的 [v-link ADJ "with/by" n] [EMPHASIS] ❑ *Anna arrived burdened by bags and food baskets.* 安娜带着一些沉甸甸的袋子和食物篮子来了。

★ **bur·den·some** /bɜrdᵊnsəm/ ADJ If you describe something as **burdensome**, you mean it is worrying or hard to deal with. 繁重的 [WRITTEN] ❑ *...a burdensome debt.* …一笔沉重的债务。 ❑ *The load was too burdensome.* 负担太繁重了。

bu·reau /byʊəroʊ/ (**bureaus**) **1** N-COUNT; N-IN-NAMES A **bureau** is an office, organization, or government department that collects and distributes information. 局 ❑ *...the Federal Bureau of Investigation.* …联邦调查局。 **2** N-COUNT A **bureau** is an office of a company or organization that has its main office in another city or country. 分公司 [mainly AM, BUSINESS] ❑ *...the Wall Street Journal's Washington bureau.* …《华尔街日报》的华盛顿分社。 **3** N-COUNT A **bureau** is a chest of drawers. 五斗橱 [AM] **4** N-COUNT A **bureau** is a writing desk with shelves and drawers and a lid that opens to form the writing surface. 写字台 [BRIT]

Word Link *cracy ≈ rule by : aristocracy, bureaucracy, democracy*

★ **bu·reau·cra·cy** /byʊrɒkrəsi/ (**bureaucracies**) **1** N-COUNT A **bureaucracy** is an administrative system operated by a large number of officials. 官僚体制 ❑ *State bureaucracies can tend to stifle enterprise and initiative.* 国家官僚体制会压抑人的进取心和积极性。 **2** N-UNCOUNT **Bureaucracy** refers to all the rules and procedures followed by government departments and similar organizations, especially when you think that these are complicated and cause long delays. 官僚作风 [DISAPPROVAL] ❑ *People usually complain about too much bureaucracy.* 人们通常会抱怨过多的官僚作风。

B

Word Link *crat ≈ power : aristocrat, bureaucrat, democrat*

★ **bu·reau·crat** /byʊərəkræt/ (**bureaucrats**) N-COUNT **Bureaucrats** are officials who work in a large administrative system. You can refer to officials as bureaucrats especially if you disapprove of them because they seem to follow rules and procedures too strictly. 官僚 [DISAPPROVAL] ❑ *The economy is still controlled by bureaucrats.* 经济依然被官僚们所控制。

★ **bu·reau·crat·ic** /byʊərəkrætɪk/ ADJ **Bureaucratic** means involving complicated rules and procedures which can cause long delays. 官僚主义的 [DISAPPROVAL] ❑ *Bureaucratic delays are inevitable.* 官僚主义所致的延误是不可避免的。

bur·geon /bɜrdʒᵊn/ (**burgeons, burgeoning, burgeoned**) V-I If something **burgeons**, it grows or develops rapidly. 迅速生长 [LITERARY] ❑ *Plants burgeon from every available space.* 植物能从任何可获得的空间中迅速生长。 ❑ *My confidence began to burgeon later in life.* 我的信心到了晚年开始迅速增长。

burg·er /bɜrgər/ (**burgers**) N-COUNT A **burger** is a flat round mass of ground meat or minced vegetables that is fried and often eaten in a bread roll. 汉堡 ❑ *...burger and fries.* …汉堡和炸薯条。

▲ **bur·glar** /bɜrglər/ (**burglars**) N-COUNT A **burglar** is a thief who enters a house or other building by force. 强行入室的窃贼 ❑ *Burglars broke into their home.* 窃贼闯进了他们家。

bur·glar·ize /bɜrgləraɪz/ (**burglarizes, burglarizing, burglarized**) V-T If a building **is burglarized**, a thief enters it by force and steals things. 闯入…行窃 [usu passive] [AM]

in BRIT, use **burgle**

❑ *Her home was burglarized.* 她的家被盗了。

bur·gla·ry /bɜrgləri/ (**burglaries**) N-VAR If someone commits a **burglary**, they enter a building by force and steal things. **Burglary** is the act of doing this. 入室盗窃罪 ❑ *An 11-year-old boy committed a burglary.* 一个11岁的男孩犯了入室盗窃罪。

bur·gle /bɜrgᵊl/ (**burgles, burgling, burgled**) V-T If a building **is burgled**, a thief enters it by force and steals things. 遭入室行窃 [BRIT]

in AM, use **burglarize**

❑ *I thought we had been burgled.* 我本以为我们被盗了。

bur·ial /bɛriəl/ (**burials**) N-VAR A **burial** is the act or ceremony of putting a dead body into a grave in the ground. 埋葬；葬礼 ❑ *The priest prepared the body for burial.* 牧师为尸体做好了下葬的准备。

bur·ly /bɜrli/ (**burlier, burliest**) ADJ A **burly** man has a broad body and strong muscles. 魁梧的 ❑ *He was a big, burly man.* 他是个高大魁梧的男人。

burn ♦♦◇ /bɜrn/ (**burns, burning, burned** or **burnt**) **1** V-I If there is a fire or a flame somewhere, you say that there is a fire or flame **burning** there. 燃烧 ❑ *Fires were burning out of control in the center of the city.* 火在市中心燃烧着，失去了控制。 ❑ *There was a fire burning in the fireplace.* 壁炉里有火正燃着。 **2** V-I If something **is burning**, it is on fire. 燃烧 ❑ *When I arrived one of the vehicles was still burning.* 我到达时，其中的一辆车还在燃烧。 ❑ *The building housed 1,500 refugees and it burned for hours.* 这栋楼住着1500个难民，它烧了好几个小时。 ● **burn·ing** N-UNCOUNT 燃烧 ❑ *When we arrived in our village there was a terrible smell of burning.* 我们到达村子的时候，那里有一股难闻的燃烧的味道。 **3** V-T If you **burn** something, you destroy or damage it with fire. 烧毁 ❑ *Protesters set cars on fire and burned a building.* 抗议者们焚烧汽车，烧毁了一栋建筑。 ❑ *Incineration plants should be built to burn household waste.* 应该建焚化厂来焚烧生活垃圾。 ● **burn·ing** N-UNCOUNT 烧毁 ❑ *The French government has criticized the burning of a U.S. flag outside the American embassy.* 法国政府谴责了在美国大使馆外焚毁美国国旗的行为。 **4** V-T/V-I If you **burn** a fuel or if it **burns**, it is used to produce heat, light, or energy. 烧 燃烧；❑ *The power stations burn coal from the Ruhr region.* 这些电厂烧产自鲁尔地区的煤。 **5** V-T/V-I If you **burn** something that you are cooking or if it **burns**, you spoil it by using too much heat or cooking it for too long. 烧煳 ❑ *I burned the toast.* 我烤煳了面包片。 ● **burnt** ADJ 烧煳的 ❑ *...the smell of burnt toast.* …面包片烤煳的气味。 **6** V-T If you **burn** part of your body, **burn yourself**, or **are burned** or **burnt**, you are injured by fire or by something very hot. 烧伤 ❑ *Take care not to burn your fingers.* 小心别烧着你的手指。 ● N-COUNT **Burn** is also a noun. 烧伤 ❑ *She suffered appalling burns to her back.* 她背部受了严重烧伤。 **7** V-T If someone **is burned** or **burned** to death, they are killed by fire. 烧死 [usu passive] ❑ *Women were burned as witches in the Middle Ages.* 在中世纪女人被当作巫婆烧死。 **8** V-I If a light **is burning**, it is shining. 发光 [LITERARY] ❑ *The building was darkened except for a single light burning in a third-story window.* 除了三楼的一扇窗户透出一丝光亮，整栋楼一片漆黑。 **9** V-T/V-I If you **burn** or get **burned** in the sun, the sun makes your skin become red and sore. 晒伤 ❑ *Build up your tan slowly and don't allow your skin to burn.* 将你的皮肤慢慢晒黑，不要让皮肤晒伤。 **10** V-T/V-I If a part of your body **burns** or if something **burns** it, it has a painful hot or stinging feeling. 灼痛 ❑ *My eyes burn from staring at the needle.* 因为盯着针看，我的眼睛灼痛。 ❑ *His face was burning with cold.* 他的脸冻得灼痛。 **11** V-T To **burn** a CD means to write or copy data onto it. 刻录 [COMPUTING] ❑ *You can use this software to burn custom compilations of your favorite tunes.* 你可以用这个软件刻制你最喜欢曲子的自选曲集。 **12** → see also **burning** **13** **to burn something to the ground** → see **ground** **14** **to burn the midnight oil** → see **midnight** **15** **to have money to burn** → see **money** → see **calorie, fire**

▸ **burn down** PHRASAL VERB If a building **burns down** or if someone **burns** it **down**, it is completely destroyed by fire. 烧毁 ❑ *Six months after Bud died, the house burned down.* 巴德死后6个月时房子烧毁了。

Thesaurus *burn* 另参见：

V. ignite, incinerate, kindle, scorch, singe; (*ant.*) extinguish, put out **1** – **5**

Word Partnership *burn* 的常用搭配：

N. **fires** burn **1**
burn **calories**, burn **coal**, burn **fat**, burn **fuel**, burn **oil** **4**
burn **victim** **6**
burn **a CD** **11**

V. **watch** *something* burn **1** **2**

ADJ. **first/second/third degree** burn **6**

burned-out or **burnt-out**

in BRIT, also use **burnt-out**

1 ADJ **Burned-out** vehicles or buildings have been so badly damaged by fire that they can no longer be used. 烧毁的 ❑ *...a burned-out car.* …一辆烧毁的车。 **2** ADJ If someone is **burned-out**, they exhaust themselves at an early stage in their life or career because they have achieved too much too quickly. 早衰的 [INFORMAL] ❑ *Everyone I know who kept it up at that intensity is burned-out.* 我所认识的一直保持那样工作强度的人都早衰了。

burn·er /bɜrnər/ (**burners**) N-COUNT A **burner** is a device which produces heat or a flame, especially as part of a stove or heater. 炉灶 ❑ *He put the frying pan on the gas burner.* 他把煎锅放到煤气灶上。

burn·ing /bɜrnɪŋ/ **1** ADJ You use **burning** to describe something that is extremely hot. 炙热的 ❑ *...the burning desert of central Asia.* …中亚地区炙热的沙漠。 ● ADV **Burning** is also an adverb. ADV 火热地 [ADV adj] ❑ *He touched the boy's forehead. It was burning hot.* 他摸了摸男孩的前额，热得发烫。 **2** ADJ If you have a **burning** interest in something or a **burning** desire to do something, you are extremely interested in it or want to do it very much. 强烈的 [ADJ n] ❑ *I had a burning ambition to become a journalist.* 我有强烈的愿望要成为一名记者。 **3** ADJ A **burning** issue or question is a very important or urgent one that people feel very strongly about. 重要的；迫切的 [ADJ n] ❑ *The burning question in this year's debate over the federal budget is: whose taxes should be raised?* 今年联邦预算的辩论中最迫切的问题是：应该提高哪些人的税？

burnt /bɜrnt/ **Burnt** is a past tense and past participle of **burn**. **burn**的过去式和过去分词

burnt-out → see **burned-out**

▲ **bur·row** /bɜroʊ/ (**burrows, burrowing, burrowed**) **1** N-COUNT A **burrow** is a tunnel or hole in the ground that is dug by an animal such as a rabbit. 洞穴 ❑ *Normally timid, they rarely stray far from their burrows.* 它们通常很胆小，极少远离自己的洞穴。 **2** V-I If an animal **burrows** into the ground or into a surface, it moves through it by making a tunnel or hole. 掘地洞 ❑ *The larvae burrow into cracks in the floor.* 幼虫钻进地板的裂缝中。 **3** V-I If you **burrow** in a container or pile of things, you search there for something using your hands. 翻找 ❑ *...the enthusiasm with which he burrowed through old records in search of facts.* …他为了弄清事实在老档案中翻查的热情。 **4** V-I If you **burrow** into something, you move underneath it or press against it, usually in order to feel warmer or safer. 钻进

❑ *She turned her face away from him, burrowing into her heap of covers.* 她从他那边背过脸去，钻进她的被窝里。

burst ♦◇◇ /bɜrst/ (**bursts, bursting**)

> The form **burst** is used in the present tense and is the past tense and past participle.

1 V-T/V-I If something **bursts** or if you **burst** it, it suddenly breaks open or splits open and the air or other substance inside it comes out. 使爆裂；爆裂 ❑ *The driver lost control when a tire burst.* 一只轮胎爆裂时司机失去了控制。 ❑ *It is not a good idea to burst a blister.* 把水疱弄破不是个好主意。 2 V-T/V-I If a dam **bursts**, or if something **bursts** it, it breaks apart because the force of the river is too great. 使溃决；溃决 ❑ *A dam burst and flooded their villages.* 一个大坝决堤，淹没了他们的村子。 3 V-T If a river **bursts** its banks, the water rises and goes on to the land. 决（堤） ❑ *Monsoons caused the river to burst its banks.* 雨季使这条河决堤。 4 V-I When a door or lid **bursts** open, it opens very suddenly and violently because someone pushes it or there is great pressure behind it. （门、盖子等）猛然打开 ❑ *The door burst open and an angry young nurse appeared.* 门突然开了，一个生气的年轻护士出现了。 5 V-I To **burst into** or **out** of a place means to enter or leave it suddenly with a lot of energy or force. 闯 ❑ *Gunmen burst into his home and opened fire.* 持枪歹徒闯入他家，开了枪。 6 V-I If you say that something **bursts** onto the scene, you mean that it suddenly starts or becomes active, usually after developing quietly for some time. 突然活跃起来 [JOURNALISM] ❑ *He burst onto the fashion scene in the early 1980s.* 20世纪80年代初他突然在时尚界活跃起来。 7 N-COUNT A **burst of** something is a sudden short period of it. （突然的）一阵 ❑ *...a burst of machine-gun fire.* …一阵机枪射击。
→ see **crash**

▸ **burst into** 1 PHRASAL VERB If you **burst into** tears, laughter, or song, you suddenly begin to cry, laugh, or sing. 突然（哭、笑、唱）起来 ❑ *She burst into tears and ran from the kitchen.* 她突然哭起来，跑出了厨房。 2 PHRASAL VERB If you say that something **bursts into** a particular situation or state, you mean that it suddenly changes into that situation or state. 突然进入（某种状态） ❑ *This weekend's fighting is threatening to burst into full-scale war.* 这个周末的战斗有突然升级为全面战争的危险。 3 to **burst into flames** → see **flame**

▸ **burst out** PHRASAL VERB If someone **bursts out** laughing, crying, or making another noise, they suddenly start making that noise. You can also say that a noise **bursts out**. 突然爆发出 ❑ *The class burst out laughing.* 全班爆发出笑声。 ❑ *Then the applause burst out.* 随后爆发出掌声。
→ see **cry, laugh**

Thesaurus *burst* 另参见：
V. blow, explode, pop, rupture 1

Word Partnership *burst* 的常用搭配：
N. burst **appendix**, **bubble** burst, **pipe** burst 1
burst **of air**, burst **of energy**, burst **of laughter** 7
ADJ. **ready to** burst 1
sudden burst 7

burst·ing /bɜrstɪŋ/ 1 ADJ If a place is **bursting with** people or things, it is full of them. 充满的 [v-link ADJ] ❑ *The place appears to be bursting with women directors.* 这个地方好像挤满了女主管。 2 ADJ If you say that someone is **bursting with** a feeling or quality, you mean that they have a great deal of it. 满怀着的 [v-link ADJ "with" n] ❑ *I was bursting with curiosity.* 我满怀好奇。 3 → see also **burst**

bury ♦◇◇ /bɛri/ (**buries, burying, buried**) 1 V-T To **bury** something means to put it into a hole in the ground and cover it up with earth. 埋 ❑ *They make the charcoal by burying wood in the ground and then slowly burning it.* 他们制作木炭时要把木头埋进地里，然后让它慢慢燃烧。 ❑ *...squirrels who bury nuts and seeds.* …将坚果和种子埋起来的松鼠。 2 V-T To **bury** a dead person means to put their body into a grave and cover it with earth. 埋葬 ❑ *Soldiers helped to bury the dead in large communal graves.* 士兵们协助将死者埋葬在大型公共墓地里。 ❑ *I was horrified that people would think I was dead and bury me alive.* 人们会以为我死了而将我活埋的想法让我极度恐惧。 3 V-T If someone says they **have buried** one of their relatives, they mean that one of their relatives has died. 丧失（亲人） ❑ *He had buried his wife some two years before he retired.* 他大约在退休前两年丧妻。 4 V-T If you **bury** something under a large quantity of things, you put it there, often in order to hide it. 埋藏 ❑ *She buried it under some leaves.* 她把它埋藏在一些树叶下。 5 V-T If something **buries** a place or person, it falls on top of them so that it completely covers them and often harms them in some way. 掩埋 ❑ *Latest reports say that mud slides buried entire villages.* 最新的报道说泥石流将好几个村庄整个吞没。 ❑ *Their house was buried by a landslide.* 他们的房子被一次山体滑坡掩埋了。 6 V-T If you **bury** your head or face in something, you press your head or face against it, often because you are unhappy. 埋进…中 ❑ *She buried her face in the pillows.* 她把脸埋进枕头中。 7 V-T If something **buries itself** somewhere, or if you **bury** it there, it is pushed very deeply in there. 嵌入 ❑ *The missile buried itself deep in the grassy hillside.* 导弹深深地嵌入绿色的山坡中。 8 **to bury the hatchet**
→ see **hatchet**

bus ♦◇◇ /bʌs/ (**buses, busing, bused**)

> The spellings **busses, bussing, bussed** are also used for the verb.

1 N-COUNT A **bus** is a large motor vehicle that carries passengers from one place to another. Buses drive along particular routes, and you usually have to pay to travel in them. 公共汽车 [also "by" N] ❑ *He missed his last bus home.* 他没赶上回家的末班公共汽车。 2 V-T/V-I When someone is **bused** to a particular place or when they **bus** there, they travel there on a bus. 用公共汽车运送；乘公共汽车 ❑ *On May Day hundreds of thousands used to be bused in to parade through East Berlin.* 昔日每逢五一劳动节，成千上万的人们通常会被公共汽车载着游行穿过东柏林。 ❑ *To get our Colombian visas we bused back to Medellin.* 为了获得哥伦比亚签证，我们又乘公共汽车回到麦德林。 3 V-T To **bus** tables means to clear away dirty dishes and reset the tables. 收拾（餐桌） [AM] ❑ *As a fund-raiser, police officers will don aprons, take orders and bus tables today.* 作为募捐方，警官们今天将穿上围裙，接受点菜，收拾餐桌。
→ see **transportation**

bush /bʊʃ/ (**bushes**) 1 N-COUNT A **bush** is a large plant which is smaller than a tree and has a lot of branches. 灌木 ❑ *Trees and bushes grew down to the water's edge.* 树和灌木丛一直向下长到了水边。 2 N-SING The wild, uncultivated parts of some hot countries are referred to as **the bush**. 灌木丛区 ❑ *They walked through the dense Mozambican bush for thirty-six hours.* 他们步行穿过茂密的莫桑比克灌木丛区，走了36个小时。

bushy /bʊʃi/ (**bushier, bushiest**) 1 ADJ **Bushy** hair or fur is very thick. 浓密的 ❑ *...bushy eyebrows.* …浓密的眉毛。 2 ADJ A **bushy** plant has a lot of leaves very close together. 茂密的 ❑ *...strong, sturdy, bushy plants.* …顽强、茁壮、茂密的植物。

busi·ly /bɪzɪli/ ADV If you do something **busily**, you do it in a very active way. 忙碌地 [ADV with v] ❑ *The two saleswomen were busily trying to keep up with the demand.* 这两个女售货员正忙着尽力满足顾客的需求。

busi·ness ♦♦♦ /bɪznɪs/ (**businesses**) 1 N-UNCOUNT **Business** is work relating to the production, buying, and selling of goods or services. 商业 ❑ *Jennifer has an impressive academic and business background.* 詹妮弗有着了不起的学术和商业背景。 ❑ *...Harvard Business School.* …哈佛商学院。 2 N-UNCOUNT **Business** is used when talking about how many products or services a company is able to sell. If **business** is good, a lot of products or services are being sold and if **business** is bad, few of them are being sold. 生意 ❑ *They worried that German companies would lose business.* 他们担心德国公司会失去生意。 3 N-COUNT A **business** is an organization that produces and sells goods or that provides a service. 企业 ❑ *The company was a family business.* 这家公司是一个家族企业。 ❑ *The majority of small businesses fail within the first twenty-four months.* 大多数小企业在最初的两年内倒闭。 4 N-UNCOUNT **Business** is work or some other activity that you do as part of your job and not for pleasure. 工作 ❑ *I'm here on business.* 我在这里出差。 ❑ *You can't mix business with pleasure.* 你不能把工作和娱乐混在一起。 5 N-SING You can use **business** to refer to a particular area of work or activity in which the aim is to make a profit. 行业 ❑ *May I ask you what business you're in?* 您能告诉我您从事哪个行业吗？ 6 N-SING You can use **business** to refer to something that you are doing or concerning yourself with. 事务 ❑ *...recording Ben as he goes about his business.* …摄录本做自己的事的样子。 7 N-UNCOUNT You can use **business** to refer to important matters that you have to deal with. 要事 ❑ *The most important business was left to the last.* 最重要的事留到最后做。 8 N-UNCOUNT If you say that something is your **business**, you mean that it concerns you personally and that other people have no right to ask questions about it or disagree with it. 私事 [poss N] ❑ *My sex life is my business.* 我的性生活是我的私事。 ❑ *If she doesn't want the police involved, that's her business.* 如果她不想让警察牵扯进来，

B

那是她自己的事。 9 N-SING You can use **business** to refer in a general way to an event, situation, or activity. For example, you can say something is "a wretched business" or you can refer to "this assassination business." 事件 ❑ *We have sorted out this wretched business at last.* 我们终于处理了这起恶劣的事件。 10 → see also **big business, show business** 11 PHRASE If two people or companies **do business with** each other, one sells goods or services to the other. 做生意 ❑ *I was fascinated by the different people who did business with me.* 我对跟我做生意的各种不同的人感到着迷。 12 PHRASE If you say that someone **has no business to** be in a place or **to** do something, you mean that they have no right to be there or to do it. 无权 ❑ *Really I had no business to be there at all.* 其实我根本无权在那儿。 13 PHRASE A company that is **in business** is operating and trading. 运行 ❑ *You can't stay in business without cash.* 没有现金你无法继续营业。 14 PHRASE If a store or company goes **out of business** or is put **out of business**, it has to stop trading because it is not making enough money. 停业 ❑ *Thousands of firms could go out of business.* 数千家商号可能倒闭。 15 PHRASE In a difficult situation, if you say it is **business as usual**, you mean that people will continue doing what they normally do. 一切照常 ❑ *For the time being it's business as usual for consumers.* 对于消费者来说暂时一切照常。 → see **city**

Thesaurus *business* 另参见:

N. company, corporation, firm, organization

Word Partnership *business* 的常用搭配:

N. **close of** business, business **opportunity**, business **school** 1
business **administration**, business **decision**, business **expenses**, business **hours**, business **owner**, business **partner**, business **practices** 1 3

ADJ. business **casual** 1
family business, **online** business, **small** business 3
your own business 1 6 – 8
unfinished business 7

V. **go out of** business, **run a** business 3 5

busi·ness card (business cards) N-COUNT A person's **business card** or their **card** is a small card that they give to other people, and that has their name and details of their job and company printed on it. 名片 ❑ *When we met, he gave me his business card.* 我们见面时，他给了我他的名片。

busi·ness class ADJ **Business class** seating on an airplane costs less than first class but more than economy class. 商务舱的 [ADJ n] ❑ *You can pay to be upgraded to a business class seat.* 你可以花钱调换到商务舱的座位。 ● ADV **Business class** is also an adverb. 乘坐商务舱地 [ADV after v] ❑ *They flew business class.* 他们乘坐商务舱旅行。 ● N-UNCOUNT **Business class** is the business class seating on an airplane. 商务舱 ❑ *The Australian team will be seated in business class.* 澳大利亚队将乘坐商务舱。

busi·ness hours N-PLURAL **Business hours** are the hours of the day in which a store or a company is open for business. 营业时间 ❑ *All showrooms are staffed during business hours.* 所有样品陈列室在营业时间都配备了人手。

business·like /bɪznɪslaɪk/ ADJ If you describe someone as **businesslike**, you mean that they deal with things in an efficient way without wasting time. 高效的 ❑ *Mr. Penn sounds quite businesslike.* 佩恩先生听起来效率蛮高的。

business·man ♦◇◇ /bɪznɪsmæn/ (**businessmen**) N-COUNT A **businessman** is a man who works in business. 商人 ❑ *...a wealthy businessman who owns a printing business in Orlando.* …一个在奥兰多拥有印刷企业的富有商人。

business·person /bɪznɪspɜrsᵊn/ (**businesspeople**) also **business person** N-COUNT **Businesspeople** are people who work in business. 生意人 ❑ *...businesspeople who serve or supply the security forces.* …为保安部队提供服务或给养的生意人。

busi·ness plan (business plans) N-COUNT A **business plan** is a detailed plan for setting up or developing a business, especially one that is written in order to borrow money. 企划书 ❑ *She learned how to write a business plan for the catering business she wanted to launch.* 她学会了如何为自己想要开办的餐饮生意写企划书。

busi·ness school (business schools) N-COUNT A **business school** is a school or college which teaches business subjects such as economics and management. 商学院

business·woman /bɪznɪswʊmən/ (**businesswomen**) N-COUNT A **businesswoman** is a woman who works in business. 女商人 ❑ *...a successful businesswoman who runs her own international cosmetics company.* …一个经营着自己的国际化妆品公司的成功的女商人。

★ **bust** /bʌst/ (**busts, busting, busted**)

> The form **bust** is used as the present tense of the verb, and can also be used as the past tense and past participle.

1 V-T If you **bust** something, you break it or damage it so badly that it cannot be used. 打碎 [INFORMAL] ❑ *They will have to bust the door to get him out.* 他们将不得不砸碎门把他弄出来。 2 V-T If someone **is busted**, the police arrest them. 逮捕 [usu passive] [INFORMAL] ❑ *They were busted for possession of cannabis.* 他们因持有大麻而被逮捕。 3 V-T If police **bust** a place, they go to it in order to arrest people who are doing something illegal. 突袭 [INFORMAL] ❑ *Police busted an underground network of illegal sports gambling.* 警察突袭了一个非法体育赌博的地下网络。 ● N-COUNT **Bust** is also a noun. 突袭行动 ❑ *Six tons of cocaine were seized last week in Panama's biggest drug bust.* 上周在巴拿马最大的毒品突袭行动中收缴了6吨可卡因。 4 ADJ A company or fund that is **bust** has no money left and has been forced to close down. 破产的 [INFORMAL] ❑ *It is taxpayers who will pay most of the bill for bailing out bust banks.* 帮助破产银行摆脱困境的大部分费用将由纳税人支付。 5 PHRASE If a company **goes bust**, it loses so much money that it is forced to close down. 倒闭 [INFORMAL] ❑ *...a Swiss company which went bust last May.* …去年5月倒闭的一家瑞士公司。 6 N-COUNT A **bust** is a statue of the head and shoulders of a person. 半身像 ❑ *...a bronze bust of Thomas Jefferson.* …一座托马斯・杰斐逊的半身铜像。 7 N-COUNT You can use **bust** to refer to a woman's breasts, especially when you are describing their size. (女性的) 胸部 ❑ *Good posture helps your bust look bigger.* 好的姿势可以使你的胸部看起来更丰满。

▲ **bus·tle** /bʌsᵊl/ (**bustles, bustling, bustled**) 1 V-I If someone **bustles** somewhere, they move there in a hurried way, often because they are very busy. 奔忙 ❑ *My mother bustled around the kitchen.* 我母亲在厨房里忙得团团转。 2 V-I A place that **is bustling** or **bustling with** people or activity is full of people who are very busy or lively. 熙熙攘攘的 ❑ *The sidewalks are bustling with people.* 两侧的人行道上人来人往。 3 N-UNCOUNT **Bustle** is busy, noisy activity. 忙碌; 喧嚣 ❑ *...the hustle and bustle of modern life.* …现代生活的忙碌喧嚣。

busy ♦◇◇ /bɪzi/ (**busier, busiest, busies, busying, busied**) 1 ADJ When you are **busy**, you are working hard or concentrating on a task, so that you are not free to do anything else. 忙碌的 ❑ *What is it? I'm busy.* 你说什么？我正忙着呢。 ❑ *They are busy preparing for a hectic day's activity on Saturday.* 他们正忙着为星期六这一天热闹的活动做准备。 2 ADJ A **busy** time is a period of time during which you have a lot of things to do. 繁忙的 ❑ *It'll have to wait. This is our busiest time.* 不得不等一等。这是我们最繁忙的时候。 ❑ *Even with her busy schedule she finds time to watch TV.* 即使有着繁忙的日程安排，她还是抽时间看看电视。 3 ADJ If you say that someone is **busy** thinking or worrying about something, you mean that it is taking all their attention, often to such an extent that they are unable to think about anything else. 全神贯注的 [v-link ADJ] ❑ *Companies are so busy analyzing the financial implications that they overlook the effect on workers.* 公司太专注于分析其财务影响，而忽略了对工人的影响。 4 V-T If you **busy yourself** with something, you occupy yourself by dealing with it. 使忙于 ❑ *He busied himself with the camera.* 他忙于摆弄这部相机。 ❑ *She busied herself getting towels ready.* 她忙着准备好毛巾。 5 ADJ A **busy** place is full of people who are doing things or moving around. 热闹的 ❑ *...a busy commercial street.* …热闹的商业街。 6 ADJ When a telephone line is **busy**, you cannot make your call because the line is already being used by someone else. 占线的 [mainly AM]

> in BRIT, usually use **engaged**

❑ *I tried to reach him, but the line was busy.* 我试过联系他，但电话占线。 7 → see also **busily**

but ♦♦♦ /bət, STRONG bʌt/ 1 CONJ You use **but** to introduce something that contrasts with what you have just said, or to introduce something that adds to what you have just said. 但是 ❑ *"You said you'd stay till tomorrow."—"I know, Bel, but I think I would rather go back."* "你说过要待到明天。" —— "我知道，贝尔，但我想我还是要回去。" ❑ *Place the saucepan over moderate heat until the cider is very hot but not boiling.* 将炖锅置于中火上，直到把苹果酒煮热，但不要煮沸。

2 CONJ You use **but** when you are about to add something further in a discussion or to change the subject. 但是 ❑ *After three weeks, they gradually reduced their sleep to about eight hours. But another interesting thing happened.* 3周后，他们把睡眠时间逐渐缩短到8小时。但是另一件有趣的事发生了。 **3** CONJ You use **but** after you have made an excuse or apologized for what you are just about to say. (表示歉意) 不过 ❑ *Please excuse me, but there is something I must say.* 请原谅，不过有件事我必须说一下。 ❑ *I'm sorry, but it's nothing to do with you.* 对不起，不过这和你无关。 **4** CONJ You use **but** to introduce a reply to someone when you want to indicate surprise, disbelief, refusal, or protest. 可是 [FEELINGS] ❑ *"I don't think I should stay in this house."—"But why?"* "我想我不应该再呆在这栋房子里了" —— "可这是为什么？" **5** PREP **But** is used to mean "except." 除了 [n PREP n] ❑ *Europe will be represented in all but two of the seven races.* 7场比赛中除了2场之外，都将有欧洲的代表参加。 ❑ *He didn't speak anything but Greek.* 他除了希腊语之外不会说其他任何语言。 **6** ADV **But** is used to mean "only." 仅仅 [FORMAL] ❑ *Zach insists that he is but one among many who are fighting for equality.* 扎克坚持认为他仅仅是许多为平等而战的人们中的一个。 **7** PHRASE You use **but for** to introduce the only factor that causes a particular thing not to happen or not to be completely true. 要不是 ❑ *...the small square below, empty but for a dirty white van and a clump of palm trees.* …下面那个小小的、要不是有一辆肮脏的白色货车和一丛棕榈树将空无一物的广场。 **8** PHRASE You use **but then** or **but then again** before a remark which slightly contradicts what you have just said. 不过话说回来 ❑ *My husband spends hours in the bathroom, but then again so do I.* 我丈夫总在浴室泡数小时，不过话说回来，我也一样。 **9** PHRASE You use **but then** before a remark which suggests that what you have just said should not be regarded as surprising. 不过 ❑ *He was a fine young man, but then so had his father been.* 他是个不错的年轻人，不过他父亲也曾是这样。 **10** **all but** → see **all** **11** **anything but** → see **anything**

butch·er /bʊtʃər/ (**butchers, butchering, butchered**)
1 N-COUNT A **butcher** is a storekeeper who cuts up and sells meat. Some butchers also kill animals for meat and make foods such as sausages and meat pies. 屠夫；肉商 **2** N-COUNT A **butcher** or a **butcher's** is a store where meat is sold. 肉铺 [mainly BRIT] ❑ *He worked in a butcher's.* 他在肉铺工作。
in AM, usually use **butcher shop**
3 V-T To **butcher** an animal means to kill it and cut it up for meat. 宰杀 ❑ *Pigs were butchered, hams were hung to dry from the ceiling.* 猪被宰杀了，火腿吊在屋顶下风干。 **4** V-T You can say that someone **has butchered** people when they have killed a lot of people in a very cruel way, and you want to express your horror and disgust. 屠杀 [DISAPPROVAL] ❑ *...rebels who butchered eight tourists in Bwindi national park.* …在布文迪国家公园屠杀了8名游客的叛乱分子。

but·ler /bʌtlər/ (**butlers**) N-COUNT A **butler** is the most important male servant in a wealthy house. 男管家 ❑ *I called for the butler to clear up the broken crockery.* 我叫来男管家清理摔碎的陶瓷。

▲ **butt** /bʌt/ (**butts, butting, butted**) **1** N-COUNT Someone's **butt** is their bottom. 屁股 [AM, INFORMAL] ❑ *Frieda grinned, pinching him on the butt.* 弗里达咧嘴笑了，在他屁股上拧了一把。 **2** N-COUNT The **butt** or the **butt end of** a weapon or tool is the thick end of its handle. (武器或工具的) 柄较粗的一端 ❑ *Troops used tear gas and rifle butts to break up the protests.* 军队使用催泪弹和气枪托驱散抗议者。 **3** N-COUNT The **butt of** a cigarette or cigar is the small part of it that is left when someone has finished smoking it. 烟蒂 ❑ *He dropped his cigarette butt into the street below.* 他把烟蒂扔到了下面的街上。 **4** N-COUNT A **butt** is a large barrel used for collecting or storing liquid. 大桶 ❑ *Make sure your water butt has a top to exclude sunlight.* 确保你的水桶有个盖子遮挡阳光。 **5** N-SING If someone or something is **the butt of** jokes or criticism, people often make fun of them or criticize them. 笑柄 ❑ *He is still the butt of cruel jokes about his humble origins.* 他卑微的身世仍然是一些恶意玩笑的嘲弄对象。 **6** V-T If a person or animal **butts** you, they hit you with the top of their head. 用头撞 ❑ *Lawrence kept on butting me but the referee did not warn him.* 劳伦斯不断用头撞我，可裁判没有警告他。
▶ **butt in** PHRASAL VERB If you say that someone **is butting in**, you are criticizing the fact that they are joining in a conversation or activity without being asked to. 插进来 [DISAPPROVAL] ❑ *Sorry, I don't mean to butt in.* 对不起，我不是故意要插一杠子。

but·ter ♦◇◇ /bʌtər/ (**butters, buttering, buttered**) **1** N-MASS **Butter** is a soft yellow substance made from cream. You spread it on bread or use it in cooking. 黄油 ❑ *...bread and butter.* …面包和黄油。 **2** V-T If you **butter** something such as bread or toast, you spread butter on it. 涂黄油 ❑ *She spread pieces of bread on the counter and began buttering them.* 她放了几片面包在柜台上，开始给它们涂黄油。
→ see **dish**

butter·fly /bʌtərflaɪ/ (**butterflies**) N-COUNT A **butterfly** is an insect with large colorful wings and a thin body. 蝴蝶 ❑ *Butterflies and moths are attracted to the wild flowers.* 蝴蝶和飞蛾为野花所吸引。
→ see **flower**

but·tock /bʌtək/ (**buttocks**) N-COUNT Your **buttocks** are the two rounded fleshy parts of your body that you sit on. 臀部 ❑ *There were marks on his buttocks I hadn't seen before.* 他的臀部有些我从没有见过的疤。
→ see **body**

but·ton ♦◇◇ /bʌtᵊn/ (**buttons, buttoning, buttoned**)
1 N-COUNT **Buttons** are small hard objects sewn onto shirts, coats, or other pieces of clothing. You fasten the clothing by pushing the buttons through holes called buttonholes. 纽扣 ❑ *...a coat with brass buttons.* …有铜纽扣的大衣。 **2** V-T If you **button** a shirt, coat, or other piece of clothing, you fasten it by pushing its buttons through the buttonholes. 扣上 ❑ *Ferguson stood up and buttoned his coat.* 弗格森站起来，扣上大衣。 ● PHRASAL VERB **Button up** means the same as **button**. 扣上 ❑ *I buttoned up my coat; it was chilly.* 我扣上大衣；天冷嗖嗖的。 ❑ *The young man slipped on the shirt and buttoned it up.* 年轻人迅速套上衬衫，扣上扣子。 **3** N-COUNT A **button** is a small object on a machine or electrical device that you press in order to operate it. 按钮 ❑ *He reached for the remote control and pressed the "play" button.* 他伸手去拿遥控器，按下播放按钮。 **4** N-COUNT A **button** is a small piece of metal or plastic that you wear in order to show that you support a particular movement, organization, or person. You fasten a button to your clothes with a pin. 小徽章 [AM]
in BRIT, use **badge**
❑ *Wear a campaign button to show support for mothers in prison.* 佩上活动徽章，以支持坐牢的母亲们。
→ see **photography**
▶ **button up** → see **button 2**

Word Partnership	*button* 的常用搭配：
N.	**shirt** button **1**
PREP.	button **up something** **2**
V.	**sew on a** button **1**
	press a button, **push a** button **3**

button·hole /bʌtᵊnhoʊl/ (**buttonholes**) N-COUNT A **buttonhole** is a hole that you push a button through in order to fasten a shirt, coat, or other piece of clothing. 扣眼

but·tress /bʌtrɪs/ (**buttresses**) N-COUNT **Buttresses** are supports, usually made of stone or brick, that support a wall. 扶壁 ❑ *...the neo-Gothic buttresses of Riverside Church in Manhattan.* …曼哈顿的里弗赛德教堂中的新哥特式扶壁。

buy ♦♦♦ /baɪ/ (**buys, buying, bought**) **1** V-T If you **buy** something, you obtain it by paying money for it. 购买 ❑ *He could not afford to buy a house.* 他买不起房子。 ❑ *Lizzie bought herself a mountain bike.* 莉齐给自己买了一辆山地自行车。 **2** V-T If you talk about the quantity or standard of goods an amount of money **buys**, you are referring to the price of the goods or the value of the money. 买得到 ❑ *About $70,000 buys a habitable house.* 大约七万美元才买得到一栋适合居住的房子。 **3** V-T If you **buy** something like time, freedom, or victory, you obtain it but only by offering or giving up something in return. 换取 ❑ *It was a risky operation, but might buy more time.* 这是一项冒险的举动，但也许能换得更多的时间。 **4** V-T If you say that a person can **be bought**, you are criticizing the fact that they will give their help or loyalty to someone in return for money. 收买 [usu passive] [DISAPPROVAL] ❑ *Any number of our military and government officials can be bought.* 我们的军官和政府官员中有许多可以被收买。 **5** V-T If you **buy** an idea or a theory, you believe and accept it. 相信 [INFORMAL] ❑ *I'm not buying any of that nonsense.* 我一点也不相信那些废话。 ● PHRASAL VERB **Buy into** means the same as **buy**. 相信 ❑ *I bought into the popular myth that when I got the new car or the next house, I'd finally be happy.* 我相信了这种大众神话，以为只要买上新车或再买栋房子就会最终幸福起来。 **6** N-COUNT If something is a good **buy**, it is of good quality and not very expensive. 买得合算的东西 ❑ *This was still a good buy even at the higher price.* 即便价格再高些，这仍买得合算。

B

Do not confuse **buy** and **pay**. If you **buy** something, you obtain it by paying money for it. ❑ *Gary's bought a bicycle.* If you **pay** someone, **pay** them money, or **pay for** something, you give someone money for something they are selling to you. ❑ *I paid the taxi driver ... I need some money to pay the window cleaner ... Some people are forced to pay for their own health insurance.* If you **pay** a bill or debt, you pay the amount of money that is owed. ❑ *He paid his bill and left... We were paying $50 for a single room.*

▶ **buy into** 1 PHRASAL VERB If you **buy into** a company or an organization, you buy part of it, often in order to gain some control of it. 买进(公司或组织的)一部分 [BUSINESS] ❑ *Other companies could buy into the firm.* 其他公司可以买进这家企业的一部分。 2 → see also **buy** 5

▶ **buy out** 1 PHRASAL VERB If you **buy** someone **out**, you buy their share of something such as a company or piece of property that you previously owned together. 买断 [BUSINESS] ❑ *The bank had to pay to buy out most of the 200 former partners.* 银行不得不花钱买断200个前合伙人的多数股权。 2 → see also **buyout**

▶ **buy up** PHRASAL VERB If you **buy up** land, property, or a commodity, you buy large amounts of it, or all that is available. 全部(或尽量)买下 ❑ *The mention of price increases sent citizens out to buy up as much as they could.* 价格上涨的风声使得民众外出抢购尽可能多的东西。

Thesaurus *buy* 另参见:

V. acquire, bargain, barter, get, obtain, pay, purchase 1

Word Partnership *buy* 的常用搭配:

V. **afford to** buy, buy **and/or sell** 1
N. buy **in bulk**, buy **clothes**, buy **a condo/house**, buy **food**, buy **shares/stocks**, buy **tickets** 1
ADV. buy **direct**, buy **online**, buy **retail**, buy **secondhand**, buy **wholesale** 1

buy-back (**buy-backs**) N-COUNT A **buy-back** is a situation in which a company buys shares back from its investors. 回购 [BUSINESS] ❑ *...a share buy-back plan.* …一个股份回购计划。

Word Link *ar, er ≈ one who acts as : buyer, liar, seller*

buy·er ♦◇◇ /baɪər/ (**buyers**) 1 N-COUNT A **buyer** is a person who is buying something or who intends to buy it. 买主 ❑ *Car buyers are more interested in safety and reliability than speed.* 比起速度,汽车买主更关注安全性和可靠性。 2 N-COUNT A **buyer** is a person who works for a large store deciding what goods will be bought from manufacturers to be sold in the store. 采购员 ❑ *Diana is a buyer for a chain of furniture stores.* 戴安娜是一家连锁家具商店的采购员。

buy·er's mar·ket N-SING When there is a **buyer's market** for a particular product, there are more of the products for sale than there are people who want to buy them, so buyers have a lot of choice and can make prices come down. 买方市场 [BUSINESS] ❑ *Real estate remains a buyer's market.* 房地产依然是买方市场。

buy·out /baɪaʊt/ (**buyouts**) 1 N-COUNT A **buyout** is the buying of a company, especially by its managers or employees. (尤指管理层或雇员做出的)公司收购 [BUSINESS] ❑ *It is thought that a management buyout is one option.* 管理权收购被认为是一个选择。 2 → see also **MBO**

★ **buzz** /bʌz/ (**buzzes, buzzing, buzzed**) 1 V-I If something **buzzes** or **buzzes** somewhere, it makes a long continuous sound, like the noise a bee makes when it is flying. 嗡嗡地响 ❑ *The intercom buzzed and he pressed down the appropriate switch.* 对讲机嗡嗡地响起来,他按下了相应的开关。 ● N-COUNT; SOUND **Buzz** is also a noun. 嗡嗡声 ❑ *...the irritating buzz of an insect.* …一只昆虫的烦人的嗡嗡声。 2 V-I If people **are buzzing around**, they are moving around quickly and busily. 匆忙地跑来跑去 [WRITTEN] ❑ *A few tourists were buzzing around.* 几名游客在匆忙地跑来跑去。 3 V-I If questions or ideas **are buzzing around** your head, or if your head **is buzzing with** questions or ideas, you are thinking about a lot of things, often in a confused way. 翻腾 ❑ *Many more questions were buzzing around in my head.* 更多的问题在我头脑中翻腾。 4 V-I If a place **is buzzing with** activity or conversation, there is a lot of activity or conversation there, especially because something important or exciting is about to happen. 充满兴奋 [usu cont] ❑ *The rehearsal studio is buzzing with lunchtime activity.* 排练场被午餐时段活动搞得很热闹。 5 N-SING You can use **buzz** to refer to a long continuous sound, usually caused by lots of people talking at once. 嘈杂声 ❑ *A buzz of excitement filled the courtroom as the defendant was led in.* 被告被带进来时,法庭内充满激动的嘈杂声。 6 ADJ You can use **buzz** to refer to a word, idea, or activity which has recently become extremely popular. 流行的 [ADJ n] ❑ *...the latest buzz phrase in garden design circles.* …园林设计圈子里的最新流行语。 7 N-SING If a place or event has a **buzz** around it, it has a lively, interesting, and modern atmosphere. 活跃气氛 ["a" N] ❑ *There is a real buzz around the place. Everyone is really excited.* 这地方实在充满活力,大家真的很兴奋。 8 V-T If an aircraft **buzzes** a place, it flies low over it, usually in a threatening way. 低空掠过 ❑ *American fighter planes buzzed the city.* 美国战机低空掠过该城市。

buzz·er /bʌzər/ (**buzzers**) N-COUNT A **buzzer** is an electrical device that is used to make a buzzing sound, for example, to attract someone's attention. 电子蜂鸣器 ❑ *She rang a buzzer at the information desk.* 她按响了信息台上的一只蜂鸣器。

buzz·word /bʌzwɜrd/ (**buzzwords**) also **buzz word** N-COUNT A **buzzword** is a word or expression that has become fashionable in a particular field and is being used a lot by the media. 某领域的时髦用语 ❑ *Biodiversity was the buzzword of the Rio Earth Summit.* 生物多样性是里约地球峰会上的时髦用语。

by

❶ WHO DOES SOMETHING OR HOW IT IS DONE
❷ POSITION OR PLACE
❸ TIMES AND AMOUNTS

❶ **by** ♦♦♦ 1 PREP If something is done **by** a person or thing, that person or thing does it. 被 ❑ *The feast was served by his mother and sisters.* 宴席由他的母亲和姐妹们招待。 ❑ *I was amazed by their discourtesy and lack of professionalism.* 我为他们的无礼和职业精神的缺乏所震惊。 2 PREP If you say that something such as a book, a piece of music, or a painting is **by** a particular person, you mean that this person wrote it or created it. 由…创作 ❑ *A painting by Van Gogh has been sold in New York for more than eighty-two million dollars.* 一幅由梵高创作的画在纽约卖到超过八千二百万美元。

When you are talking about the author of a book or play, the composer of a piece of music, or the painter of a painting, you say that the piece of work is **by** that person or is written or painted **by** him or her. ❑ *... three books by Michael Moorcock ... a collection of piano pieces by Mozart.* When you are talking about the person who has written you a letter or sent a message to you, you say that the letter or message is **from** that person. ❑ *He received a message from Vito Corleone.*

3 PREP If you do something **by** a particular means, you do it using that thing. 以…方式 ❑ *If you're traveling by car, ask whether there are parking facilities nearby.* 如果你开汽车旅行,问问附近是否有停车设施。 4 PREP If you achieve one thing **by** doing another thing, your action enables you to achieve the first thing. 通过 [PREP -ing] ❑ *Make the sauce by boiling the cream and stock together in a pan.* 通过将乳酪和高汤一起放在平底锅里煮来制作调味料。 ❑ *The all-female yacht crew made history by becoming the first to sail round the world.* 全部由女性组成的游艇船员通过首次环球航行而创造了历史。 5 PREP You use **by** in phrases such as "by chance" or "by accident" to indicate whether or not an event was planned. 由于 ❑ *I met him by chance out walking yesterday.* 昨天出去散步时我无意中遇到了他。 ❑ *He opened Ingrid's letter by mistake.* 他误拆了英格丽德的信。 6 PREP If someone is a particular type of person **by** nature, **by** profession, or **by** birth, they are that type of person because of their nature, their profession, or the family they were born into. 就…而言 [adj/n PREP n] ❑ *I am certainly lucky to have a kind wife who is loving by nature.* 我的确幸运有一位仁慈的妻子,她天生富有爱心。 ❑ *She's a nurse by profession and now runs a counseling service for women.* 她是护士出身,现在经营着一家针对女性的咨询服务公司。 7 PREP If something must be done **by** law, it happens according to the law. If something is the case **by** particular standards, it is the case according to the standards. 根据 ❑ *Pharmacists are required by law to give the medicine prescribed by the doctor.* 根据法律,药剂师被要求只配医生开列的药。 8 PREP If you say what someone means **by** a particular word or expression, you are saying what they intend the word or expression to refer to. 通过(说某词或某话) ❑ *Stella knew what he meant by "start again."* 斯特拉知道他说"再次开始"是什么意思。

9 PREP If you hold someone or something **by** a particular part of them, you hold that part. 通过 ❑ *He caught her by the shoulder and turned her around.* 他抓住她的肩膀，使她转过身。 ❑ *She was led by the arm to a small room at the far end of the corridor.* 她被抓着胳膊带到走廊另一头的一个小屋里。 10 PHRASE If you are **by yourself**, you are alone. 独自地 ❑ *...a dark-haired man sitting by himself in a corner.* …一个独自坐在角落里的、深色头发的男子。 11 PHRASE If you do something **by yourself**, you succeed in doing it without anyone helping you. 独立地 ❑ *I didn't know if I could raise a child by myself.* 我不知道是否能独立抚养一个孩子。

❷ **by** ♦♦♦ 1 PREP Someone or something that is **by** something else is beside it and close to it. 在…旁边 ❑ *Judith was sitting in a rocking chair by the window.* 朱迪丝坐在窗边的摇椅上。 ❑ *Felicity Maxwell stood by the bar and ordered a glass of wine.* 费利西蒂·马克斯韦尔站在吧台旁，叫了一杯葡萄酒。 ● ADV **By** is also an adverb. 在旁边 [ADV after v] ❑ *Large numbers of security police stood by.* 许多秘密警察站在旁边。 2 PREP If a person or vehicle goes **by** you, they move past you without stopping. 经过 [V PREP n] ❑ *A few cars passed close by me.* 几辆车从我近旁驶过。 ● ADV **By** is also an adverb. 经过 [ADV after v] ❑ *The bomb went off as a police patrol went by.* 炸弹在巡警队经过时爆炸了。 3 PREP If you stop **by** a place, you visit it for a short time. 暂时（拜访） ❑ *We had made arrangements to stop by her house in Pacific Grove.* 我们已安排好顺道去她在太平洋路的家拜访。 ● ADV **By** is also an adverb. 暂时地 [ADV after v] ❑ *I'll stop by after dinner and we'll have that talk.* 晚餐后我会过来待会儿，我们可以谈谈那件事。

❸ **by** ♦♦♦ /baɪ/ 1 PREP If something happens **by** a particular time, it happens at or before that time. 到…时；在…之前 ❑ *By eight o'clock he had arrived at my hotel.* 他八点前已到了我住的旅馆。 2 PREP If you do something **by** day, you do it during the day. If you do it **by** night, you do it during the night. 在…期间 ❑ *By day a woman could safely walk the streets.* 白天，妇女可以安全地在街上走。 3 PREP In arithmetic, you use **by** before the second number in a multiplication or division sum. 用于乘除法中 [PREP num] ❑ *...an annual rate of 22.8 percent (1.9 multiplied by 12).* …每年22.8%的比率（1.9乘以12）。 4 PREP You use **by** to talk about measurements of area. For example, if a room is twenty feet **by** fourteen feet, it measures twenty feet in one direction and fourteen feet in the other direction. 表示面积尺寸 [PREP num] ❑ *Three prisoners were sharing one small cell 3 meters by 2½ meters.* 3名囚犯共住一间3米长2.5米宽的小牢房。 5 PREP If something increases or decreases **by** a particular amount, that amount is gained or lost. （表示数量、程度等）以…之差 [PREP amount] ❑ *Violent crime has increased by 10 percent since last year.* 暴力犯罪自去年以来已上升了10%。 6 PREP Things that are made or sold **by** the million or **by** the dozen are made or sold in those quantities. 按…计算 [PREP "the" n] ❑ *Packages arrived by the dozen from America.* 成打的包裹从美国寄来。 7 PREP You use **by** in expressions such as "minute by minute" and "drop by drop" to talk about things that happen gradually, not all at once. 表示循序渐进的速度 [n PREP n] ❑ *His father began to lose his memory bit by bit, becoming increasingly forgetful.* 他父亲的记忆力开始一点点衰退，变得越来越健忘。

> In addition to the uses shown here, **by** is used in phrasal verbs such as "abide by," "put by," and "stand by."

> The preposition is pronounced /baɪ/. The adverb is pronounced /baɪ/.

> 介词读作 /baɪ/。副词读作 /baɪ/。

bye ♦◇◇ /baɪ/ or **bye-bye** CONVENTION **Bye** and **bye-bye** are informal ways of saying goodbye. 再见 ❑ *Bye, Daddy.* 再见，爸爸。

by-election (**by-elections**) N-COUNT A **by-election** is an election that is held to choose a new member of parliament or another legislature when a member has resigned or died. 补缺选举 [mainly BRIT]

by·gone /baɪgɒn/ ADJ **Bygone** means happening or existing a very long time ago. 很久以前的 [ADJ n] ❑ *The book recalls other memories of a bygone age.* 这本书勾起了人们对遥远岁月的其他回忆。

★ **by·pass** /baɪpæs/ (**bypasses, bypassing, bypassed**) 1 V-T If you **bypass** someone or something that you would normally have to get involved with, you ignore them, often because you want to achieve something more quickly. （为了更快地达成某事而）不顾 ❑ *A growing number of employers are trying to bypass the unions altogether.* 越来越多的雇主试图完全置工会于不顾。 2 N-COUNT A **bypass** is a surgical operation performed on or near the heart, in which the flow of blood is redirected so that it does not flow through a part of the heart that is diseased or blocked. 心脏分流手术 ❑ *...heart bypass surgery.* …心脏搭桥手术。 3 N-COUNT A **bypass** is a main road that takes traffic around the edge of a town or city rather than through its center. （绕过城镇中心的）旁道 ❑ *A new bypass around the city is being built.* 一条绕城而过的新旁路正在修建之中。 4 V-T If a road **bypasses** a place, it goes around it rather than through it. 绕过 ❑ *...money for new roads to bypass cities.* …修建绕城新路的款项。 5 V-T If you **bypass** a place when you are traveling, you avoid going through it. 避开 ❑ *The rebel forces simply bypassed the town on their way further south.* 叛军在向南推进时仅仅避开了该镇。

by·product /baɪprɒdʌkt/ (**byproducts**) also **by-product** N-COUNT A **byproduct** is something that is produced during the manufacture or processing of another product. 副产品 ❑ *The raw material for the tire is a byproduct of gasoline refining.* 这种轮胎的原料是汽油提炼的副产品。

by·stander /baɪstændər/ (**bystanders**) N-COUNT A **bystander** is a person who is present when something happens and who sees it but does not take part in it. 旁观者 ❑ *It looks like an innocent bystander was killed instead of you.* 看样子一位无辜的旁观者当了你的替死鬼。

byte /baɪt/ (**bytes**) N-COUNT In computing, a **byte** is a unit of storage approximately equivalent to one printed character. 字节 ❑ *...two million bytes of data.* …200万字节的数据。

Cc

C also **c** /siː/ (**C's, c's**) **1** N-VAR **C** is the third letter of the English alphabet. 英文字母表中的第3个字母 **2** N-VAR In music, **C** is the first note in the scale of C major. C大调音阶中的第1个音符 **3** N-VAR If you get a **C** as a mark for a piece of work or in an exam, your work is average. 指学业成绩第3等，即中等 **4** **c.** is written in front of a date or number to indicate that it is approximate. **c.** is an abbreviation for "circa." 约 ❑ *...the museum's re-creation of a New York dining room (c. 1825-35).* …该博物馆对纽约一家餐厅（约1825年至1835年）的重建。 **5** **C** or **c** is used as an abbreviation for words beginning with c, such as "copyright" or "Celsius." C打头的单词的缩写形式 ❑ *Heat the oven to 180°C.* 把烤箱加热至摄氏180度。 **6** → see also **C-in-C, c/o**

cab /kæb/ (**cabs**) **1** N-COUNT A **cab** is a taxi. 出租汽车 ❑ *Could I use your phone to call a cab?* 我能用你的电话叫一辆出租车吗？ **2** N-COUNT The **cab** of a truck or train is the front part in which the driver sits. (卡车或列车的) 驾驶室 ❑ *The van has additional load space over the driver's cab.* 该货车在驾驶室上方有额外的载货空间。

caba·ret /kæbəreɪ/ N-UNCOUNT **Cabaret** is live entertainment consisting of dancing, singing, or comedy acts that are performed in the evening in restaurants or nightclubs. 卡巴莱歌舞表演 (餐馆或夜总会中的歌舞或滑稽短剧等现场表演) [oft N n] ❑ *Helen made a successful career in cabaret.* 海伦的卡巴莱歌舞表演生涯曾非常成功。

cab·bage /kæbɪdʒ/ (**cabbages**) N-VAR A **cabbage** is a round vegetable with white, green, or purple leaves that is usually eaten cooked. 卷心菜
→ see **vegetable**

cab·in /kæbɪn/ (**cabins**) **1** N-COUNT A **cabin** is a small wooden house, especially one in an area of forests or mountains. 小木屋 ❑ *...a log cabin.* …一间小木屋。 **2** N-COUNT A **cabin** is a small room in a ship or boat. 船舱 ❑ *He showed her to a small cabin.* 他把她带到一间小房舱。 **3** N-COUNT A **cabin** is one of the areas inside a plane. 机舱 ❑ *He sat quietly in the first class cabin of the flight looking tired.* 他静静地坐在班机的头等舱内，看上去有些疲惫。

cabi·net ♦♦◇ /kæbɪnɪt/ (**cabinets**) **1** N-COUNT A **cabinet** is a cupboard used for storing things such as medicine or alcoholic drinks or for displaying decorative things in. 贮藏橱；陈列柜 ❑ *She looked in the medicine cabinet and found some aspirin.* 她在药橱中翻看了一下，找到几片阿司匹林。 **2** N-COUNT The **cabinet** is a group of the most senior advisers or ministers in a government, who meet regularly to discuss policies. 内阁 ❑ *The announcement came after a three-hour cabinet meeting.* 这项公告是在3小时的内阁会议之后发布的。

ca·ble ♦◇◇ /keɪbᵊl/ (**cables**) **1** N-VAR A **cable** is a kind of very strong, thick rope, made of wires twisted together. 缆绳 ❑ *The miners rode a conveyance attached to a cable made of braided steel wire.* 矿工们乘坐连着钢索的缆车。 **2** N-VAR A **cable** is a thick wire, or a group of wires inside a rubber or plastic covering, which is used to carry electricity or electronic signals. 电缆 ❑ *...overhead power cables.* …高架电缆。 **3** N-UNCOUNT **Cable** is used to refer to television systems in which the signals are sent along underground wires rather than by radio waves. 有线电视 ❑ *They ran commercials on cable systems across the country.* 他们在全国范围内的有线电视上做广告。
→ see **bridge, laser, television**

cache /kæʃ/ (**caches**) **1** N-COUNT A **cache** is a quantity of things such as weapons that have been hidden. (武器等) 一批隐藏物 ❑ *A huge arms cache was discovered by police.* 一大批私藏武器遭警方查获。 **2** N-COUNT A **cache** or **cache memory** is an area of computer memory that is used for temporary storage of data and can be accessed more quickly than the main memory. 高速缓冲存储器 [COMPUTING] ❑ *In your Web browser's cache are the most recent Web files that you have downloaded.* 在你的网络浏览器的高速缓冲存储器里是你最新下载的网络文档。

cac·tus /kæktəs/ (**cactuses** or **cacti** /kæktaɪ/) N-COUNT A **cactus** is a thick, fleshy plant that grows in many hot, dry parts of the world. Cacti have no leaves and many of them are covered in prickles. 仙人掌属植物
→ see **desert**

CAD /kæd/ N-UNCOUNT **CAD** refers to the use of computer software in the design of things such as cars, buildings, and machines. **CAD** is an abbreviation for "computer aided design." 计算机辅助设计 [COMPUTING] ❑ *...CAD software.* …计算机辅助设计软件。

ca·det /kədɛt/ (**cadets**) N-COUNT A **cadet** is a young man or woman who is being trained in the armed services or the police force. (军校或警校的) 学员 ❑ *...army cadets.* …陆军军校学员们。

café /kæfeɪ/ (**cafés**) also **cafe** **1** N-COUNT A **café** is a place where you can buy drinks, simple meals, and snacks. 小餐馆 **2** N-COUNT A street **café** or a sidewalk **café** is a café which has tables and chairs on the sidewalk outside it where people can eat and drink. 街边小餐馆 [n N] ❑ *...an Italian street café.* …一家意大利街边小餐馆。 ❑ *...sidewalk cafés and boutiques.* …街边小餐馆和精品店。

★ **caf·eteria** /kæfɪtɪəriə/ (**cafeterias**) N-COUNT A **cafeteria** is a restaurant where you choose your food from a counter and take it to your table after paying for it. Cafeterias are usually found in public buildings such as hospitals, colleges, and offices. 自助餐厅
→ see **restaurant**

▲ **caf·feine** /kæfiːn/ N-UNCOUNT **Caffeine** is a chemical substance found in coffee, tea, and cocoa, which affects your brain and body and makes you more active. 咖啡因
→ see **coffee**

cage /keɪdʒ/ (**cages**) N-COUNT A **cage** is a structure of wire or metal bars in which birds or animals are kept. 笼子 ❑ *I hate to see birds in cages.* 我不喜欢看到鸟在笼子里。

caged /keɪdʒd/ ADJ A **caged** bird or animal is inside a cage. 关在笼子中的 ❑ *Mark was still pacing like a caged animal.* 马克仍在像笼中的困兽一样踱来踱去。

ca·jole /kədʒoʊl/ (**cajoles, cajoling, cajoled**) V-T If you **cajole** someone **into** doing something, you get them to do it after persuading them for some time. 说服 ❑ *It was he who had cajoled Garland into doing the film.* 是他说服加兰去拍电影的。

cake ♦◇◇ /keɪk/ (**cakes**) **1** N-VAR A **cake** is a sweet food made by baking a mixture of flour, eggs, sugar, and fat in an oven. Cakes may be large and cut into slices or small and intended for one person only. 蛋糕 ❑ *...a piece of cake.* …一块蛋糕。 ❑ *Would you like some chocolate cake?* 你想来点儿巧克力蛋糕吗？ ❑ *...a birthday cake.* …一个生日蛋糕。 **2** N-COUNT Food that is formed into flat round shapes before it is cooked can be referred to as **cakes**. (未煮的) 饼状食物 ❑ *...fish cakes.* …鱼糜饼。 **3** N-COUNT A **cake of soap** is a small block of it. 一块 (肥皂) ❑ *...a small cake of lime-scented soap.* …一小块酸橙味香皂。 **4** PHRASE If someone has done something very stupid, rude, or selfish, you can say that they **take the cake** or that what they have done **takes the cake**, to emphasize your surprise at their behavior. 糟糕透顶 [AM, EMPHASIS]

in BRIT, use **take the biscuit**

5 **the icing on the cake** → see **icing**
→ see **dessert**

cake pan (**cake pans**) N-COUNT A **cake pan** is a metal container that you bake a cake in. 蛋糕烤盘 [AM] ❑ *Lightly grease and flour a 13-by-9-inch cake pan.* 在一个长13英寸宽9英寸的蛋糕烤盘上涂少许油脂，并洒上一些面粉。

in BRIT, use **cake tin**

cake tin (**cake tins**) N-COUNT [BRIT] → see **cake pan**

▲ **ca·lam·ity** /kəlæmɪti/ (**calamities**) N-VAR A **calamity** is an event that causes a great deal of damage, destruction, or personal distress. 灾难 [FORMAL] ❑ *He described drugs as the greatest calamity of the age.* 他形容毒品是这个时代最大的灾难。

★ **cal·cium** /kælsiəm/ N-UNCOUNT **Calcium** is a soft white chemical element which is found in bones and teeth, and also in limestone, chalk, and marble. 钙

cal·cu·late /kælkyəleɪt/ (**calculates, calculating, calculated**) 1 V-T If you **calculate** a number or amount, you discover it from information that you already have, by using arithmetic, mathematics, or a special machine. 计算 ❑ *From this you can calculate the total mass in the Galaxy.* 据此，你可以计算出银河系的总质量。❑ *We calculate that the average size farm in Lancaster County is 65 acres.* 我们算出兰开斯特郡的农场平均面积为65英亩。 2 V-T If you **calculate** the effects of something, especially a possible course of action, you think about them in order to form an opinion or decide what to do. 估计；推测 ❑ *I believe I am capable of calculating the political consequences accurately.* 我认为自己能够正确地预测出各种政治后果。

cal·cu·lat·ed /kælkyəleɪtɪd/ 1 ADJ If something is **calculated to** have a particular effect, it is specially done or arranged in order to have that effect. 故意作出的；有意安排的 [v-link ADJ to-inf] ❑ *Their movements through the region were calculated to terrify landowners into abandoning their holdings.* 他们在整个地区的行动意在恐吓地主们放弃其财产。 2 ADJ If you say that something is not **calculated to** have a particular effect, you mean that it is unlikely to have that effect. 很可能的 [with brd-neg, v-link ADJ to-inf] ❑ *The liberal agenda is not calculated to help minority groups.* 自由党的议题是不太可能帮助少数派的。 3 ADJ You can describe a clever or dishonest action as **calculated** when it is very carefully planned or arranged. 精心安排的 ❑ *Irene's use of the mop had been a calculated attempt to cover up her crime.* 艾琳使用拖把是个精心安排的举动，意在掩盖她的罪行。 4 ADJ If you take a **calculated** risk, you do something which you think might be successful, although you have fully considered the possible bad consequences of your action. 全盘衡量过的（风险）[ADJ n] ❑ *The president took a calculated political risk in throwing his full support behind the rebels.* 总统在全盘计算过后，冒着风险全力支持反叛分子。

cal·cu·lat·ing /kælkyəleɪtɪŋ/ ADJ If you describe someone as **calculating**, you disapprove of the fact that they deliberately plan to get what they want, often by hurting or harming other people. 精明的；会算计的 [DISAPPROVAL] ❑ *Northbridge is a cool, calculating, and clever criminal who could strike again.* 诺思布里奇是个冷静、精明、机灵的罪犯，他有可能再犯。

★ **cal·cu·la·tion** /kælkyəleɪʃ°n/ (**calculations**) N-VAR A **calculation** is something that you think about and work out mathematically. **Calculation** is the process of working something out mathematically. 计算 ❑ *Leonard made a rapid calculation: he'd never make it in time.* 伦纳德做了个快速的估算：他不可能及时做完。→ see **mathematics**

cal·cu·la·tor /kælkyəleɪtər/ (**calculators**) N-COUNT A **calculator** is a small electronic device that you use for making mathematical calculations. 计算器 ❑ *...a pocket calculator.* …一个袖珍计算器。→ see **office**

cal·en·dar /kælɪndər/ (**calendars**) 1 N-COUNT A **calendar** is a chart or device which displays the date and the day of the week, and often the whole of a particular year divided up into months, weeks, and days. 日历 ❑ *There was a calendar on the wall above, with large squares around the dates.* 墙的上方曾有一本日历，日期框在大方格里。 2 N-COUNT A **calendar** is a particular system for dividing time into periods such as years, months, and weeks, often starting from a particular point in history. 历法 ❑ *The Christian calendar was originally based on the Julian calendar of the Romans.* 公历最初是基于罗马的儒略历的。 3 N-COUNT You can use **calendar** to refer to a series or list of events and activities which take place on particular dates, and which are important for a particular organization, community, or person. 日程表 ❑ *It is one of the hottest tickets on Washington's social calendar.* 这是华盛顿社交日程表上最热门的入场券之一。→ see **year**

cal·en·dar year (**calendar years**) N-COUNT A **calendar year** is a period of twelve months from January 1 to December 31. **Calendar year** is often used in business to compare with the **fiscal year**. 日历年度 ❑ *In the last calendar year the company had a turnover of $426m.* 在上一个日历年度里，该公司的营业额为4.26亿美元。

▲ **calf** /kæf/ (**calves** /kævz/) 1 N-COUNT A **calf** is a young cow. 牛犊 2 N-COUNT Some other young animals, including elephants and whales, are called **calves**. （大象、鲸鱼等的）幼兽 3 N-COUNT Your **calf** is the thick part at the back of your leg, between your ankle and your knee. 腓；小腿肚 ❑ *...a calf injury.* …一处小腿的伤。

calf-length ADJ **Calf-length** skirts, dresses, and coats come to halfway between your knees and ankles. （裙子、外套等）长及小腿的 [ADJ n] ❑ *...a black, calf-length coat.* …一件长及小腿的黑色外套。

cali·ber /kælɪbər/

in BRIT, use **calibre**

1 N-UNCOUNT The **caliber of** a person is the quality or standard of their ability or intelligence, especially when this is high. 能力；才干 ❑ *I was impressed by the high caliber of the researchers and analysts.* 我对这些研究员和分析员的优秀才干印象深刻。 2 N-UNCOUNT The **caliber of** something is its quality, especially when it is good. 质量 ❑ *The caliber of teaching was very high.* 教学质量非常高。 3 N-COUNT The **caliber** of a gun is the width of the inside of its barrel. （枪、炮的）口径 [TECHNICAL] ❑ *...a small-caliber rifle.* …一把小口径步枪。 4 N-COUNT The **caliber** of a bullet is its diameter. （子弹的）直径 [TECHNICAL] ❑ *She was hit in the head by a .22-caliber bullet.* 她的头部被一颗直径为0.22的子弹击中。

cali·brate /kælɪbreɪt/ (**calibrates, calibrating, calibrated**) V-T If you **calibrate** an instrument or tool, you mark or adjust it so that you can use it to measure something accurately. 校准 [TECHNICAL] ❑ *...instructions on how to calibrate a thermometer.* …校准温度计的说明。

cali·bre /kælɪbər/ [BRIT] → see **caliber**

call

1 NAMING
2 DECLARING, ANNOUNCING, AND DEMANDING
3 TELEPHONING AND VISITING
4 PHRASAL VERBS

❶ **call** ♦♦♦ /kɔl/ (**calls, calling, called**)

➪ **Please look at meanings 4 and 5 to see if the expression you are looking for is shown under another headword.** 1 V-T If you **call** someone or something **by** a particular name or title, you give them that name or title. 称呼 ❑ *I always wanted to call the dog Mufty for some reason.* 出于某种原因，我总想叫那条狗穆夫蒂。❑ *"Doctor..."—"Will you please call me Sarah?"* "…医生"——"请叫我萨拉好吗？" 2 V-T If you **call** someone or something a particular thing, you suggest they are that thing or describe them as that thing. 把…描述为；把…说成 ❑ *The speech was interrupted by members of the Republican Party, who called him a traitor.* 演讲被称他为叛徒的共和党成员们打断了。❑ *She calls me lazy and selfish.* 她说我又懒又自私。 3 → see also **so-called** 4 **to call** something **your own** → see **own** 5 **to call it quits** → see **quit**

❷ **call** ♦♦♦ /kɔl/ (**calls, calling, called**)

➪ **Please look at meanings 12 – 15 to see if the expression you are looking for is shown under another headword.** 1 V-T If you **call** something, you say it in a loud voice, because you are trying to attract someone's attention. 喊 ❑ *He could hear the others downstairs calling his name.* 他能听到其他人在楼下喊他的名字。● PHRASAL VERB **Call out** means the same as **call**. 喊 ❑ *The butcher's son called out a greeting.* 那屠夫的儿子声音洪亮地招呼了一声。 2 V-T If you **call** someone, you ask them to come to you by shouting to them. 喊某人过来 ❑ *She called her young son: "Here, Stephen, come and look at this!"* 她喊她的小儿子过来，"这儿，斯蒂芬，来看这个！" 3 V-T If you **call** someone such as a doctor or the police, you ask them to come to you, usually by telephoning them. （打电话）叫…来 ❑ *He screamed for his wife to call an ambulance.* 他尖叫着，要妻子叫辆救护车来。 4 V-T If someone in authority **calls** something such as a meeting, rehearsal, or election, they arrange for it to take place at a particular time. 安排召开；安排举行 ❑ *We're going to call a meeting and discuss how we can work with other groups.* 我们打算开个会，讨论如何与其他团队协作。 5 V-T If someone **is called** before a court or committee, they are ordered to appear there, usually to give evidence. 传讯；传唤 [usu passive] ❑ *The child waited two hours before she was called to give evidence.* 那个小孩等了2个小时才被传唤去做证。 6 V-T To **call** a game or sporting event means to cancel it, for example because of rain or bad light. 取消 [AM] ❑ *We called the next game.* 我们取消了下一场比赛。

C

C

If you **cancel** or **call off** an arrangement or an appointment, you stop it from happening. ❑ *His failing health forced him to cancel the meeting... The European Community has threatened to call off peace talks.* If you **postpone** or **put off** an arrangement or an appointment, you make another arrangement for it to happen at a later time. ❑ *Elections have been postponed until next year... The senate put off a vote on the nomination for one week.* If you **delay** something that has been arranged, you make it happen later than planned. ❑ *Space agency managers decided to delay the launch of the space shuttle.* If something **delays** you or **holds** you **up**, you start or finish what you are doing later than you planned. ❑ *He was delayed in traffic... Delivery of equipment had been held up by delays and disputes.*

7 N-COUNT If there is a **call for** something, someone demands that it should happen. 要求 ❑ *There have been calls for a new kind of security arrangement.* 有人要求采用新型的安保措施。 **8** N-COUNT The **call** of a particular bird or animal is the characteristic sound that it makes. (鸟、兽的) 叫声 ❑ *...a wide range of animal noises and bird calls.* …动物和鸟的各种各样叫声。 **9** N-UNCOUNT If there is little or no **call for** something, very few people want it to be done or provided. 要求; 需求 ❑ *"Have you got just plain chocolate?"—"No, I'm afraid there's not much call for that."* "有纯巧克力吗？" —— "没有，恐怕对这种巧克力的需求不多。" **10** N-SING The **call of** something such as a place is the way it attracts or interests you strongly. 吸引力; 魅力 ❑ *But the call of the wild was simply too strong and so he set off once more.* 但大自然的吸引力实在太大了，所以他又一次出发了。 **11** PHRASE If someone is **on call**, they are ready to go to work at any time if they are needed, especially if there is an emergency. 随叫随到 ❑ *In theory I'm on call day and night.* 理论上，我不分昼夜随叫随到。 **12** to **call** someone's **bluff** → see **bluff** **13** to **call a halt** → see **halt** **14** to **call** something **into question** → see **question** **15** to **call the tune** → see **tune**

Thesaurus *call* 另参见:
V. cry, holler, scream, shout **2** **1** **2**

3 call ♦♦♦ /kɔːl/ (**calls, calling, called**) **1** V-T If you **call** someone, you telephone them. 给…打电话 ❑ *Would you call me as soon as you find out? My number's in the phone book.* 你一查清就给我打电话好吗？我的号码在电话簿里。 ❑ *A friend of mine gave me this number to call.* 我的一个朋友让我打这个号码。 **2** V-I If you **call** somewhere, you make a short visit there. 短暂访问 ❑ *A market researcher called at the house where my uncle was living.* 一位市场调查员到过我叔叔的住处。 ● N-COUNT **Call** is also a noun. 短暂访问 ❑ *He decided to pay a call on Tommy Cummings.* 他决定去拜访汤米·卡明斯。 **3** V-I When a train, bus, or ship **calls** somewhere, it stops there for a short time to allow people to get on or off. (火车、公共汽车或船只) 停靠 ❑ *The steamer calls at several palm-fringed ports along the way.* 汽船一路上停靠过好几个棕榈树掩映的港口。 **4** N-COUNT When you make a telephone **call**, you telephone someone. 打电话 ❑ *I made a phone call to the United States to talk to a friend.* 我打电话到美国同一个朋友交谈。 ❑ *I've had hundreds of calls from other victims.* 我已经接到几百个其他受害者打来的电话。

Word Partnership *call* 的常用搭配:
N. call ***someone*** **names** **1** **2**
call **an ambulance**, call **a doctor**, call **the police** **2** **3**
call **a meeting** **2** **4**
a number to call **3** **1**
conference call, **emergency** call, **(tele)phone** call **3** **4**
ADJ. **collect** call **3** **4**
V. **make a** call, **receive a** call, **return a** call, **take a** call, **wait for a** call **3** **4**

4 call ♦♦♦ /kɔːl/ (**calls, calling, called**)
▸ **call around**
in BRIT, usually use **ring round, ring around**
PHRASAL VERB If you **call around**, you phone several people, usually when you are trying to organize something or to find some information. 四处打电话 [mainly AM] ❑ *Call around to find the best bargains.* 多打几个电话，找最便宜的。
▸ **call back** PHRASAL VERB If you **call** someone **back**, you telephone them again or in return for a telephone call that they have made to you. 给…回电话 ❑ *If we're not around, she'll take a message and we'll call you back.* 如果我们不在，她会帮忙传话，我们会给你回电话的。

▸ **call for** **1** PHRASAL VERB If something **calls for** a particular action or quality, it needs it or makes it necessary. 须有; 需要 ❑ *It's a situation that calls for a blend of delicacy and force.* 这种情况下需要的是刚柔并济。 **2** PHRASAL VERB If you **call for** someone, you go to the building where they are, so that you can both go somewhere. 前往接某人 ❑ *I'll call for you at seven o'clock.* 我7点钟去接你。 **3** PHRASAL VERB If you **call for** something, you demand that it should happen. 要求 ❑ *They angrily called for Robinson's resignation.* 他们愤怒地要求罗滨逊辞职。
▸ **call in** **1** PHRASAL VERB If you **call** someone **in**, you ask them to come and help you or do something for you. 叫…来 (帮忙) ❑ *Call in an architect or engineer to oversee the work.* 找一名建筑师或工程师来监督这项工程。 **2** PHRASAL VERB If you **call in**, you phone a place, such as the place where you work, or a radio or TV station. (给工作单位、电台或电视台) 打电话 ❑ *She reached for the phone to call in sick.* 她伸手拿起话机打电话请病假。 ❑ *24 million viewers called in to cast their final votes last night.* 昨晚，有2400万观众打进电话进行了最后的投票。 **3** → see also **call-in** **4** PHRASAL VERB If you **call in** somewhere, you make a short visit there. 短暂访问 ❑ *He just calls in occasionally.* 他只是偶尔来坐坐。
▸ **call off** PHRASAL VERB If you **call off** an event that has been planned, you cancel it. 取消 ❑ *He has called off the trip.* 他取消了这次旅行。
▸ **call on** or **call upon** **1** PHRASAL VERB If you **call on** someone **to** do something or **call upon** them **to** do it, you say publicly that you want them to do it. 呼吁; 公开请求 ❑ *One of Kenya's leading churchmen has called on the government to resign.* 肯尼亚宗教界的一位重要人物已呼吁政府下台。 **2** PHRASAL VERB If you **call on** someone or **call upon** someone, you pay them a short visit. 短暂访问 ❑ *Sofia was intending to call on Miss Kitts.* 索菲娅打算去拜访基茨小姐。
▸ **call out** **1** PHRASAL VERB If you **call** someone **out**, you order or request that they come to help, especially in an emergency. 召集 ❑ *Colombia has called out the army and imposed emergency measures.* 哥伦比亚已下令召集军队，并强制执行了紧急措施。 **2** → see also **call** **2** 1
▸ **call up** **1** PHRASAL VERB If you **call** someone **up**, you telephone them. 打电话给 [mainly AM] ❑ *When I'm in Pittsburgh, I call him up.* 到匹兹堡后，我会给他打电话。 ❑ *He called up the museum.* 他往博物馆打了电话。 **2** PHRASAL VERB If someone **is called up**, they are ordered to join the army, navy, or air force. 征召…入伍 ❑ *The United States has called up some 150,000 military reservists.* 美国已招募了约十五万预备役军人。
▸ **call upon** → see **call on**

call cen·ter (**call centers**)
in BRIT, use **call centre**
N-COUNT A **call center** is an office where people work answering or making telephone calls for a particular company. 电话服务中心

call cen·tre [BRIT] → see **call center**

call·er /kɔːlər/ (**callers**) **1** N-COUNT A **caller** is a person who is making a telephone call. 打电话者 ❑ *An anonymous caller told police what had happened.* 一个打匿名电话的人告知了警方所发生的一切。 **2** N-COUNT A **caller** is a person who comes to see you for a short visit. 来访者; 来客 ❑ *She ushered her callers into a cluttered living room.* 她把来客们带到一间杂乱的客厅。

call-in (**call-ins**) N-COUNT A **call-in** is a program on radio or television in which people telephone with questions or opinions and their calls are broadcast. (听众或观众) 来电参与互动的节目 [AM]
in BRIT, use **phone-in**
❑ *...a call-in show on Los Angeles radio station KABC.* …一个洛杉矶KABC电台的来电互动节目。

★ **call·ing** /kɔːlɪŋ/ (**callings**) N-COUNT A **calling** is a profession or career which someone is strongly attracted to, especially one which involves helping other people. 使命 [usu sing] ❑ *He was a consultant physician, a serious man dedicated to his calling.* 他是一名顾问医生，一个专注于其使命的严肃认真的人。

call·ing card (**calling cards**) **1** N-COUNT A **calling card** is a small card with personal information about you on it, such as your name and address, which you can give to people when you go to visit them. 名片 [mainly AM, OLD-FASHIONED] ❑ *Don't forget to give your calling card to those you'd like to see again.* 别忘了把你的名片留给还想再见面的人。 **2** N-COUNT If you say that someone has left a **calling card**, you mean that they have left evidence that shows they have been in a particular place, especially at the scene of a crime. 在场证据 ❑ *John was studying the medallion in the evidence bag – the killer's* calling card. 约翰正在研究证据袋里的徽章——凶手留在犯罪现场的证物。

cal·lous /kæləs/ ADJ A **callous** person or action is very cruel and shows no concern for other people or their feelings. 麻木不仁的；冷酷无情的 ❑ *...his callous disregard for human life.* …他对人命的漠视。 ● **cal·lous·ness** N-UNCOUNT 麻木不仁；冷酷无情 ❑ *...the callousness of Raymond's murder.* …雷蒙德凶杀案的冷酷无情。 ● **cal·lous·ly** ADV 麻木不仁地；冷酷无情地 [ADV with v] ❑ *He is accused of callously ill-treating his wife.* 他被指控冷酷无情地虐待妻子。

call wait·ing N-UNCOUNT **Call waiting** is a telephone service that sends you a signal if another call arrives while you are already on the phone. 呼叫等待 ❑ *The service includes caller ID, voice mail, and call waiting.* 这项服务包括呼叫方身份识别、语音邮件和呼叫等待。

calm ♦◇◇ /kɑm/ (**calmer, calmest, calms, calming, calmed**) **1** ADJ A **calm** person does not show or feel any worry, anger, or excitement. 冷静的；平静的 ❑ *She is usually a calm and diplomatic woman.* 她通常是个冷静而圆滑的女人。 ❑ *Try to keep calm and just tell me what happened.* 试着保持冷静，告诉我发生了什么。 ● N-UNCOUNT **Calm** is also a noun. 冷静；平静 [also "a" N] ❑ *He felt a sudden sense of calm, of contentment.* 他突然感受到了内心的平静和满足。 ● **calm·ly** ADV 冷静地；平静地 ❑ *Alan looked at him and said calmly, "I don't believe you."* 艾伦看着他，平静地说，"我不相信你。" **2** ADJ If someone says that a place is **calm**, they mean that it is free from fighting or public disorder, when trouble has recently occurred there or had been expected. 平静的 [JOURNALISM] ❑ *The city of Sarajevo appears relatively calm today.* 萨拉热窝市今天显得相对平静了些。 ● N-UNCOUNT **Calm** is also a noun. 平静 [also "a" N] ❑ *Community and church leaders have appealed for calm and no retaliation.* 社区和教会领袖呼吁人们保持冷静，不要采取报复行动。 **3** ADJ If the sea or a lake is **calm**, the water is not moving very much and there are no big waves. 平静无波的 ❑ *...the safe, calm waters protected by an offshore reef.* …由近海礁脉保护的安全、平静无波的海域。 **4** ADJ **Calm** weather is pleasant weather with little or no wind. 风和日丽的 ❑ *Tuesday was a fine, clear and calm day.* 星期二是晴空万里、风和日丽的一天。 **5** N-UNCOUNT **Calm** is used to refer to a quiet, still, or peaceful atmosphere in a place. 安宁 ❑ *The house projects an atmosphere of calm and order.* 整幢房子呈现出一种宁静祥和、井然有序的氛围。 **6** V-T If you **calm** someone, you do something to make them feel less angry, worried, or excited. 使冷静；使镇静 ❑ *The ruling party's veterans know how to calm their critics.* 执政党中的资深官员们深谙安抚批评者之道。 ❑ *She was breathing quickly and tried to calm herself.* 她呼吸急促，试图使自己镇定下来。 ● **calm·ing** ADJ 使人镇静的 ❑ *...a fresh, cool fragrance which produces a very calming effect on the mind.* …有镇静作用的清新香气。 **7** V-T To **calm** a situation means to reduce the amount of trouble, violence, or panic there is. 使平静；平息 ❑ *Officials hoped admitting fewer foreigners would calm the situation.* 官方希望通过招收较少的外国人来平息局面。 **8** V-I When the sea **calms**, it becomes still because the wind stops blowing strongly. When the wind **calms**, it stops blowing strongly. (海或风) 平静下来 ❑ *Dawn came, the sea calmed but the cold was as bitter as ever.* 破晓时分，大海平静下来，但寒冷依然。

→ see **hypnosis**

▸ **calm down** **1** PHRASAL VERB If you **calm down**, or if someone **calms** you **down**, you become less angry, upset, or excited. 使冷静下来；冷静下来 ❑ *Calm down for a minute and listen to me.* 冷静一下，听我说。 ❑ *I'll try a herbal remedy to calm him down.* 我会尝试用一种香草疗法使他平静下来。 **2** PHRASAL VERB If things **calm down**, or someone or something **calms** things **down**, the amount of activity, trouble, or panic is reduced. 使平息下来；平息下来 ❑ *We will go back to normal when things calm down.* 一切平息下来后，我们将恢复正常。

Thesaurus *calm* 另参见：

ADJ. cool-headed, laid-back, relaxed; *(ant.)* excited, upset **1**
mild, peaceful, placid, serene, tranquil; *(ant.)* rough **1**–**4**

Word Link *cal, caul ≈ hot, heat : calorie, cauldron, scald*

★ **calo·rie** /kæləri/ (**calories**) N-COUNT **Calories** are units used to measure the energy value of food. People who are on diets try to eat food that does not contain many calories. 卡路里 (食物的热量单位) ❑ *Sweetened drinks contain a lot of calories.* 含糖的饮料热量很高。

→ see Word Web: **calories**

→ see **diet**

cam·cord·er /kæmkɔrdər/ (**camcorders**) N-COUNT A **camcorder** is a portable video camera which records both pictures and sound. 便携式摄像机

came /keɪm/ **Came** is the past tense of **come**. come的过去式

cam·el /kæməl/ (**camels**) **1** N-COUNT A **camel** is a large animal that lives in deserts and is used for carrying goods and people. Camels have long necks and one or two lumps on their backs called humps. 骆驼 **2** **the straw that broke the camel's back**

→ see **straw**

cameo /kæmioʊ/ (**cameos**) **1** N-COUNT A **cameo** is a short description or piece of acting which expresses cleverly and neatly the nature of a situation, event, or person's character. 精彩片段；小品 ❑ *...a succession of memorable cameos of American history.* …一系列美国历史上难忘的精彩片段。 **2** N-COUNT A **cameo** is a piece of jewelry, usually oval in shape, consisting of a raised stone figure or design fixed on to a flat stone of another color. 浮雕宝石 ❑ *...a cameo brooch.* …一个浮雕宝石饰针。

cam·era ♦♦◇ /kæmrə/ (**cameras**) **1** N-COUNT A **camera** is a piece of equipment that is used for taking photographs, making movies, or producing television pictures. 照相机；摄影机 ❑ *Her grandmother lent her a camera for a school trip to Venice and Egypt.* 她的祖母借给她一部相机，让她在学校组织的到威尼斯和埃及的旅行中使用。 **2** PHRASE If someone or something is **on camera**, they are being filmed. 在拍摄中；上镜头 ❑ *Fay was so impressive on camera that a special part was written in for her.* 镜头中的费伊太令人印象深刻了，因此有一个专门写给她的角色。 **3** PHRASE If you do something or if something happens **off camera**, you do it or it happens when not being filmed. 不在拍摄中 ❑ *They were anything but friendly off camera, refusing even to take the same elevator.* 不拍摄时他们根本称不上友好，甚至拒绝乘同一部电梯。 **4** PHRASE If a trial is held **in camera**, the public and the press are not allowed to attend. 不对外公开的 [FORMAL] ❑ *This morning's appeal was held in camera.* 今天上午的上诉是不对外公开的。

→ see **photography**

camera·man /kæmrəmæn/ (**cameramen**) N-COUNT A **cameraman** is a person who operates a camera for television or movies. (电视或电影) 摄影师

camou·flage /kæməflɑʒ/ (**camouflages, camouflaging, camouflaged**) **1** N-UNCOUNT **Camouflage** consists of things such as leaves, branches, or brown and green paint, which are used to make it difficult for an enemy to see military forces and equipment. (军事) 伪装 [also "a" N, oft N n] ❑ *They were dressed in camouflage and carried automatic rifles.* 他们身着迷彩服，手持自动步枪。 ❑ *...a camouflage jacket.* …一件迷彩夹克衫。 **2** N-UNCOUNT **Camouflage** is the way in which some animals are colored and shaped so that they cannot easily be seen in their natural

Word Web calories

Calories are a measure of **energy**. One calorie of heat raises the **temperature** of 1 gram of water by 1°C*. However, we usually think of calories in relation to food and exercise. A person eating a cup of vanilla ice cream **takes in** 270 calories. Walking a mile **burns** 66 calories. Different types of foods store different amounts of energy. **Proteins** and **carbohydrates** contain 4 calories per gram. However **fat** contains 9 calories per gram. Our bodies store extra calories in the form of fat. For every 3,500 excess calories we take in, we gain a pound of fat.

*0°Celsius = 32° Fahrenheit

C

surroundings. (某些动物的) 保护色; 伪装手段 [also "a" N] ❑ *Confident in its camouflage, being the same color as the rocks, the lizard stands still when it feels danger.* 蜥蜴对自己和石头颜色相同的保护色很自信，即便感觉危险也不动。 **3** V-T If military buildings or vehicles **are camouflaged**, things such as leaves, branches, or brown and green paint are used to make it difficult for an enemy to see them. 伪装 [usu passive] ❑ *The entrance was camouflaged with bricks and dirt.* 入口处用砖块和泥土伪装了起来。 **4** V-T If you **camouflage** something such as a feeling or a situation, you hide it or make it appear to be something different. 掩饰 ❑ *He has never camouflaged his desire to better himself.* 他从不掩饰自己想不断提升的愿望。 ● N-UNCOUNT **Camouflage** is also a noun. 掩饰 [also "a" N] ❑ *There was much laughter – a perfect camouflage for the anxiety of waiting for the verdict in the trial.* 笑声不断——审判中等待裁决时焦虑的最佳掩饰。

camp ♦♦◇ /kæmp/ (**camps, camping, camped**) **1** N-COUNT A **camp** is a collection of huts and other buildings that is provided for a particular group of people, such as refugees, prisoners, or soldiers, as a place to live or stay. (难民、囚犯、士兵等的) 集中生活营 ❑ *...a refugee camp.* …一个难民营。 **2** N-COUNT You can refer to a group of people who all support a particular person, policy, or idea as a particular **camp**. 阵营 ❑ *The press release provoked furious protests from the Gore camp and other top Democrats.* 这篇新闻稿引发了戈尔阵营和民主党其他高层的激烈抗议。 **3** N-VAR A **camp** is an outdoor area with cabins, tents, or trailers where people stay on vacation. 度假营 **4** N-VAR A **camp** is a collection of tents or trailers where people are living or staying, usually temporarily while they are traveling. 营地 ❑ *...gypsy camps.* …吉普赛人的营地。 **5** V-I If you **camp** somewhere, you stay or live there for a short time in a tent or trailer, or in the open air. 宿营; 露营 ❑ *We camped near the beach.* 我们在海滩附近宿营。 ● PHRASAL VERB **Camp out** means the same as **camp**. 宿营; 露营 ❑ *For six months they camped out in a meadow at the back of the house.* 他们在房子后面的草地上露宿了6个月。 ● **camp·ing** N-UNCOUNT 宿营; 露营 ❑ *They went camping in the wild.* 他们在野外露营。 **6** ADJ If you describe someone's behavior, performance, or style of dress as **camp**, you mean that it is exaggerated and amusing, often in a way that is thought to be typical of some male homosexuals. 装模作样的; 忸怩作态的 [INFORMAL] ❑ *James Barron turns in a delightfully camp performance.* 詹姆斯・巴伦忸怩作态的表演令人忍俊不禁。 **7** → see also **concentration camp**

cam·paign ♦♦♦ /kæmpeɪn/ (**campaigns, campaigning, campaigned**) **1** N-COUNT A **campaign** is a planned set of activities that people carry out over a period of time in order to achieve something such as social or political change. (有计划的) 活动; 运动 ❑ *During his election campaign he promised to put the economy back on its feet.* 竞选活动期间，他许诺要致力于恢复经济。 ❑ *...a campaign to improve the training of staff.* …改进员工培训的一个活动。 **2** N-COUNT In a war, a **campaign** is a series of planned movements carried out by armed forces. 一系列军事行动; 战役 ❑ *The allies are intensifying their air campaign.* 盟军在加强他们的空中军事活动。 **3** V-I If someone **campaigns for** something, they carry out a planned set of activities over a period of time in order to achieve their aim. 从事运动 ❑ *We are campaigning for law reform.* 我们正从事法律改革运动。 **4** → see also **ad campaign**
→ see **army, election**

Word Partnership *campaign* 的常用搭配:

N. **election** campaign, campaign **slogan** **1**
advertising/marketing campaign **3** **4**
PREP. campaign **against *someone/something***, campaign **for *something*** **3**

cam·paign·er /kæmpeɪnər/ (**campaigners**) N-COUNT A **campaigner** is a person who campaigns for social or political change. 从事活动者 ❑ *...anti-war campaigners.* …反战活动家们。

camp bed (**camp beds**) N-COUNT A **camp bed** is a small bed that you can fold up. [BRIT]
in AM, use **cot**

camp·er /kæmpər/ (**campers**) **1** N-COUNT A **camper** is someone who is camping somewhere. 露营者; 野营者 ❑ *My fellow campers were already packing up their tents.* 我的露营同伴已经在收起他们的帐篷了。 **2** N-COUNT A **camper** is a motor vehicle which is equipped with beds and cooking equipment so that you can live, cook, and sleep in it. 野营车 [mainly AM] **3** → see also **RV**
in BRIT, usually use **camper van**

camp·er van [BRIT] → see **camper**

Word Link ***site, situ ≈ position, location : campsite, situation, website***

camp·site /kæmpsaɪt/ (**campsites**) N-COUNT A **campsite** is a place where people who are on vacation can stay in tents. 露营地

cam·pus /kæmpəs/ (**campuses**) N-COUNT A **campus** is an area of land that contains the main buildings of a university or college. (大学的) 校园 [also prep N] ❑ *...during a rally at the campus.* …在一次校园集会时。

can
❶ MODAL USES
❷ CONTAINER

❶ can ♦♦♦ /kən, STRONG kæn/

Can is a modal verb. It is used with the base form of a verb. The form **cannot** is used in negative statements. The usual spoken form of **cannot** is **can't**, pronounced /kænt/.

1 MODAL You use **can** when you are mentioning a quality or fact about something which people may make use of if they want to. 可以 ❑ *Tickets can be purchased at the Madstone Theater box office.* 票可在麦德斯通剧院售票处买到。 ❑ *A central reservation number can direct you to accommodations that best suit your needs.* 预订总机可以帮你找到最适合你需求的住处。 **2** MODAL You use **can** to indicate that someone has the ability or opportunity to do something. 能够; 会 ❑ *Don't worry yourself about me, I can take care of myself.* 别为我担心，我会照顾好自己的。 ❑ *I can't give you details because I don't actually have any details.* 我无法告诉你详情，因为我确实不了解具体情况。 ❑ *The United States will do whatever it can to help Greece.* 美国将尽一切所能帮助希腊。 **3** MODAL You use **cannot** to indicate that someone is not able to do something because circumstances make it impossible for them to do it. 无法 ❑ *We cannot buy food and clothes and pay for rent and utilities on $20 a week.* 我们无法靠每星期$20来购买食品、衣物，付房租和水电费。 **4** MODAL You use **can** to indicate that something is true sometimes or is true in some circumstances. 可能 ❑ *...long-term therapy that can last five years or more.* …可能要持续5年或者更长时间的长期治疗。 ❑ *Exercising alone can be boring.* 独自一个人锻炼可能会很无聊。 **5** MODAL You use **cannot** and **can't** to state that you are certain that something is not the case or will not happen. 不可能; 不会 ❑ *From her knowledge of Douglas's habits, she feels sure that that person can't have been Douglas.* 根据她对道格拉斯的习惯的了解，她肯定那人不会是道格拉斯。 ❑ *Things can't be that bad.* 情况不会那么糟。 **6** MODAL You use **can** to indicate that someone is allowed to do something. You use **cannot** or **can't** to indicate that someone is not allowed to do something. 可以 ❑ *Can I really have your jeans when you go?* 你走后，我真的可以穿你的牛仔裤吗？ ❑ *We can't answer any questions, I'm afraid.* 我们恐怕不能再回答任何问题了。 **7** MODAL You use **cannot** or **can't** when you think it is very important that something should not happen or that someone should not do something. 不应该 [EMPHASIS] ❑ *It is an intolerable situation and it can't be allowed to go on.* 这种情形令人无法容忍，不应该被允许继续下去。 **8** MODAL You use **can**, usually in questions, in order to make suggestions or to offer to do something. 可以; 能 (用于表示建议或给予) ❑ *What can I do around here?* 在这里我能做什么？ ❑ *This elderly woman was struggling out of the train and I said, "Oh, can I help you?"* 这位老妇人力图挤出列车时，我问道，"哦，我能帮忙吗？" **9** MODAL You use **can** in questions in order to make polite requests. You use **can't** in questions in order to request strongly that someone does something. 可以; 能 (用于表示请求) [POLITENESS] ❑ *Can I have a look at that?* 我能看看那个东西吗？ ❑ *Why can't you leave me alone?* 你为什么不能别管我的事情？ **10** MODAL You use **can** as a polite way of interrupting someone or of introducing what you are going to say next. 可不可以 (打断谈话或插嘴时) [FORMAL, SPOKEN] ❑ *Can I interrupt you just for a minute?* 我可不可以打断你一会儿？ ❑ *But if I can interrupt, Joe, I don't think anybody here is personally blaming you.* 恕我打断你，乔，我认为这里并没有人在怪你。 **11** MODAL You use **can** with verbs such as "imagine," "think," and "believe" in order to emphasize how you feel about a particular situation. 能够 (与imagine, think, believe连用，表示强调) [INFORMAL or SPOKEN, EMPHASIS] ❑ *You can imagine he was terribly upset.* 你能想像他有多苦恼。 ❑ *You can't think how glad I was to see them all go.* 你想不到看到他们都走掉我有多开心。 **12** MODAL You use **can** in questions with "how" to

Word Web can

A Frenchman named Nicholas Appert* invented the process of canning in 1795. First he pre-**cooked** the **food**. Then he placed it in glass **jars** with cork **lids** to make an **airtight seal**. The final step was a boiling water bath to kill **bacteria**. Food **preserved** in this way lasted for a least a year. In 1804, Appert opened the world's first factory to produce **vacuum-packed** foods. In 1810, an Englishman, Peter Durance, began to use **metal containers** to can food. Today's canning factories use steel cans covered with a thin coating of **tin**.

Nicholas Appert (1750-1840): a confectioner.

indicate that you feel strongly about something. 与**how**连用，表示强烈的感受 [SPOKEN, EMPHASIS] ❑ *How can millions of dollars go astray?* 数百万美元怎么会丢失了呢？ ❑ *How can you say such a thing?* 你怎么能说这样的话？

> **Can**, **could**, and **be able to** are all used to talk about a person's ability to do something. They are followed by the infinitive form of a verb. You use **can** or a present form of **be able to** to refer to the present, although **can** is more common. ❑ *They can all read and write... The snake is able to catch small mammals.* You use **could** or a past form of **be able to** to refer to the past, and "will" or "shall" with **be able to** to refer to the future. **Be able to** is used if you want to refer to doing something at a particular time. ❑ *After treatment he was able to return to work.* **Can** and **could** are used to talk about possibility. **Could** refers to a particular occasion and **can** to more general situations. ❑ *Many jobs could be lost... Too much salt can be harmful.* When talking about the past, you use **could have** and a past participle. ❑ *It could have been much worse.* You also use **can** for the present and **could** for the past to talk about rules or what people are allowed to do. ❑ *They can leave at any time.* Note that when making requests either **can** or **could** may be used. ❑ *Can I have a drink?... Could we put the fire on?* However, **could** is always used for suggestions. ❑ *You could phone her and ask.*

❷ **can** ♦♦♦ /kæn/ (**cans, canning, canned**) **1** N-COUNT A **can** is a metal container in which something such as food, drink, or paint is put. The container is usually sealed to keep the contents fresh. 罐；罐头 ❑ *Several young men were kicking a tin can along the middle of the road.* 几个小伙子正在马路中间踢着一个锡罐。 ❑ *...empty beer cans.* …空啤酒罐。 **2** N-COUNT You can use **can** to refer to a can and its contents, or to the contents only. 一罐 ❑ *She grabbed a can of soda out of the refrigerator.* 她从冰箱里取出一罐汽水。 **3** V-T When food or drink **is canned**, it is put into a metal container and sealed so that it will remain fresh. 把…装罐 [usu passive] ❑ *...fruits and vegetables that will be canned, skinned, diced, or otherwise processed.* …将要经过装罐、去皮、切块或其他加工程序的水果和蔬菜。 **4** V-T If you **are canned**, you are dismissed from your job. 解雇 [AM, INFORMAL] ❑ *The extremists prevailed, and the security chief was canned.* 极端分子占了上风，那名安全主管被解雇。 **5** N-SING **The can** is the toilet. 厕所 [AM, INFORMAL]
→ see Word Web: **can**

ca·nal /kənæl/ (**canals**) **1** N-COUNT A **canal** is a long, narrow stretch of water that has been made for boats to travel along or to bring water to a particular area. 运河 ❑ *...the Grand Union Canal.* …大联盟运河。 **2** N-COUNT A **canal** is a narrow tube inside your body for carrying food, air, or other substances. (体内的) 管道 ❑ *...delaying its progress through the alimentary canal.* …通过消化道延迟它的作用。

can·cel ♦◇◇ /kænsᵊl/ (**cancels, canceling** or **cancelling, canceled** or **cancelled**) **1** V-T/V-I If you **cancel** something that has been arranged, you stop it from happening. If you **cancel** an order for goods or services, you tell the person or organization supplying them that you no longer wish to receive them. 取消 ❑ *The Russian foreign minister yesterday canceled his visit to Washington.* 俄外交部长昨天取消了对华盛顿的访问。 ❑ *Many trains have been cancelled and a limited service is operating on other lines.* 许多列车都被取消了，少数班次在其他路线运行。 ❑ *The customer called to cancel.* 顾客打电话来取消了。 ● **can·cel·la·tion** /kænsəleɪʃᵊn/ N-VAR (**cancellations**) 取消 ❑ *Outbursts of violence forced the cancellation of Haiti's first free elections in 1987.* 暴力事件的爆发迫使海地取消了1987年的首次自由选举。

> If you **cancel** or **call off** an arrangement or an appointment, you stop it from happening. ❑ *His failing health forced him to cancel the meeting... The European Community has threatened to call off peace talks.* If you **postpone** or **put off** an arrangement or an appointment, you make another arrangement for it to happen at a later time. ❑ *Elections have been postponed until next year... The senate put off a vote for one week.* If you **delay** something that has been arranged, you make it happen later than planned. ❑ *Space agency managers decided to delay the launch of the space shuttle.* If something **delays** you or **holds** you **up**, you start or finish what you are doing later than you planned. ❑ *He was delayed in traffic... Delivery of equipment had been held up by delays and disputes.*

2 V-T If someone in authority **cancels** a document, an insurance policy, or a debt, they officially declare that it is no longer valid or no longer legally exists. 废止；废除 ❑ *He intends to try to leave the country, in spite of a government order canceling his passport.* 他不顾废止他的护照的政府命令，仍打算要离开这个国家。 ● **can·cel·la·tion** N-UNCOUNT 废止；废除 ❑ *...a march by groups calling for cancellation of Third World debt.* …要求解除第三世界的债务的一场集体游行。 **3** V-T To **cancel** a stamp or a check means to mark it to show that it has already been used and cannot be used again. 盖销；使作废 ❑ *The new device can also cancel the check after the transaction is complete.* 这种新设备还能在交易结束后将支票注销。

▸ **cancel out** PHRASAL VERB If one thing **cancels out** another thing, the two things have opposite effects, so that when they are combined no real effect is produced. 抵消 ❑ *He wonders if the different influences might not cancel each other out.* 他想知道不同的影响是否不会相互抵消。

Thesaurus *cancel* 另参见：
V. annul, break, call off, scrap, trash, undo **1**

can·cer ♦♦◇ /kænsər/ (**cancers**) N-VAR **Cancer** is a serious disease in which cells in a person's body increase rapidly in an uncontrolled way, producing abnormal growths. 癌症 ❑ *Her mother died of breast cancer.* 她母亲死于乳腺癌。 ❑ *Jane was just 25 when she learned she had cancer.* 珍妮得知自己患了癌症时才25岁。
→ see Word Web: **cancer**

can·cer·ous /kænsərəs/ ADJ **Cancerous** cells or growths are cells or growths that are the result of cancer. 癌的 ❑ *The production of these cancerous cells suppresses the production of normal white blood cells.* 这些癌细胞的产生抑制了正常白血球的生成。

Word Web cancer

The traditional **treatments** for **cancer** are **surgery**, **radiation therapy**, and chemotherapy. However, a new type of treatment called targeted therapy has emerged in the past few years. This treatment uses new drugs that target specific types of cancer cells. Targeted therapy also eliminates many of the **toxic** effects on healthy **tissue** that often result from traditional chemotherapy. One of these drugs helps prevent blood vessels that feed a tumor from growing. Another drug kills cancer cells.

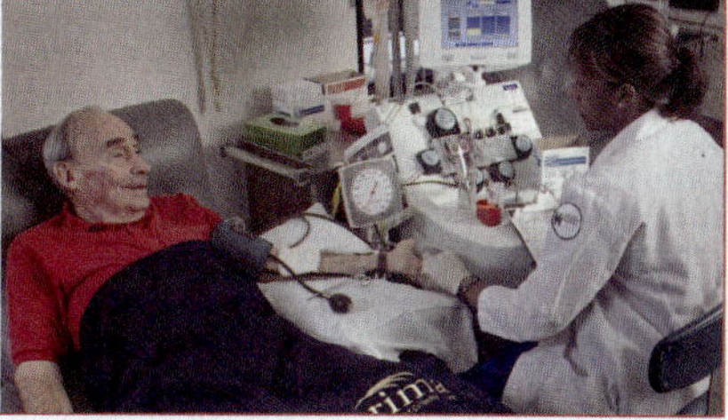

C

can·did /kændɪd/ **1** ADJ When you are **candid** about something or with someone, you speak honestly. 直言不讳的；坦率的 ❑ *Natalie is candid about the problems she is having with Steve.* 纳塔莉对她与史蒂夫的问题直言不讳。❑ *I haven't been completely candid with him.* 我没有完全对他说实话。**2** ADJ A **candid** photograph of someone is one that was taken when the person did not know they were being photographed. 偷拍的 [ADJ n] ❑ *...candid snaps of off-duty film stars.* …偷拍的荧幕下影星们的照片。

can·di·da·cy /kændɪdəsi/ (**candidacies**) N-VAR Someone's **candidacy** is their position of being a candidate in an election. 候选资格；候选人之身份 ❑ *Today he is formally announcing his candidacy for president.* 今天他正式宣布他的总统候选人身份。

can·di·date ♦♦◊ /kændɪdeɪt/ (**candidates**) **1** N-COUNT A **candidate** is someone who is being considered for a position, for example someone who is running in an election or applying for a job. 候选人 ❑ *The Democratic candidate is still leading in the polls.* 那名民主党候选人仍在民意测验中领先。❑ *He is a candidate for the office of governor.* 他是州长的候选人。**2** N-COUNT A **candidate** is someone who is studying for a degree at a college. 攻读学位者 [AM] ❑ *He is now a candidate for a Master's degree in social work at San Francisco State University.* 他目前在旧金山州立大学攻读社会工作硕士学位。**3** N-COUNT A **candidate** is a person or thing that is regarded as being suitable for a particular purpose or as being likely to do or be a particular thing. 有望做…的人；有望成为…的事 ❑ *Those who are overweight or indulge in high-salt diets are candidates for hypertension.* 那些身体超重或饮食偏咸的人属于易患高血压症的人群。

→ see **election, vote**

can·dle /kændᵊl/ (**candles**) N-COUNT A **candle** is a stick of hard wax with a piece of string called a wick through the middle. You light the wick in order to give a steady flame that provides light. 蜡烛 ❑ *The bedroom was lit by a single candle.* 卧室被一支蜡烛照亮。

can·dor /kændər/

in BRIT, use **candour**

N-UNCOUNT **Candor** is the quality of speaking honestly and openly about things. 直率；直言不讳 ❑ *...a brash, forceful man, noted both for his candor and his quick temper.* …以其坦率和性急出名的一个性情鲁莽、行为强势的人。

can·dour /kændəʳ/ [BRIT] → see **candor**

can·dy /kændi/ (**candies**) N-VAR **Candy** is sweet foods such as chocolate or taffy. 糖果 [AM]

in BRIT, usually use **sweets**

❑ *...a piece of candy.* …一块糖果。

can·dy apple (**candy apples**) N-COUNT A **candy apple** is an apple coated with hard red sugar syrup and fixed on a stick. 焦糖苹果(棒上只带一个苹果的糖葫芦) [AM]

in BRIT, use **toffee apple**

candy cane (**candy canes**) N-COUNT A **candy cane** is a stick of red and white candy with a curve at one end. 一种红白相间的棒糖 [AM]

candy·floss /kændiflɔs/ N-UNCOUNT **Candyfloss** is the same as **cotton candy**. 棉花糖 [BRIT]

cane /keɪn/ (**canes**) **1** N-VAR **Cane** is used to refer to the long, hollow, hard stems of plants such as bamboo. Strips of cane are often used to make furniture, and some types of cane can be crushed and processed to make sugar. (竹或甘蔗的) 茎 ❑ *...cane furniture.* …藤制家具。❑ *...cane sugar.* …蔗糖。**2** N-COUNT A **cane** is a long thin stick with a curved or round top which you can use to support yourself when you are walking, or which in the past was fashionable to carry with you. 手杖 ❑ *He wore a gray suit and leaned heavily on his cane.* 他身着灰色西服，吃力地倚着手杖。

→ see **disability, sugar**

ca·nine /keɪnaɪn/ ADJ **Canine** means relating to dogs. 犬的 [ADJ n] ❑ *...research into canine diseases.* …犬类疾病的研究。❑ *The Canine Rescue Center is a charity that rescues and cares for unwanted and abandoned dogs.* 救犬中心是一个慈善机构旨在拯救并照顾没人要的和被遗弃的狗。

can·is·ter /kænɪstər/ (**canisters**) **1** N-COUNT A **canister** is a strong, metal container. It is used to hold gases or chemical substances. 强固金属罐 ❑ *Riot police hurled tear gas canisters and smoke bombs into the crowd.* 防暴警察朝人群猛掷催泪瓦斯罐和烟幕弹。**2** N-COUNT A **canister** is a metal, plastic, or china container with a lid. It is used for storing food such as sugar and flour. (罐、盒等) 有盖容器 ❑ *...a canister of tea.* …一罐茶叶。

can·na·bis /kænəbɪs/ N-UNCOUNT **Cannabis** is the hemp plant when it is used as a drug. 大麻 ❑ *...cannabis smokers.* …吸食大麻的人们。

canned /kænd/ **1** ADJ **Canned** music, laughter, or applause on a television or radio program has been recorded beforehand and is added to the program to make it sound as if there is a live audience. 预先录制的 [usu ADJ n] ❑ *However, the temptation is always there to add canned laughter in the editing.* 然而，人们总是忍不住要在剪辑中加入预先录制的笑声。**2** → see also **can**

can·ni·bal /kænɪbᵊl/ (**cannibals**) N-COUNT **Cannibals** are people who eat the flesh of other human beings. 食人族 ❑ *...a tropical island inhabited by cannibals.* …一个居住着食人族的热带岛屿。

can·ni·bal·ism /kænɪbəlɪzəm/ N-UNCOUNT If a group of people practice **cannibalism**, they eat the flesh of other people. 同类相食 ❑ *They were forced to practice cannibalism in order to survive.* 为了生存，他们被迫同类相食。

★ **can·non** /kænən/ (**cannons**) **1** N-COUNT A **cannon** is a large gun, usually on wheels, which used to be used in battles. 大炮 ❑ *The cannons boom, the band plays.* 炮声隆隆，鼓乐齐鸣。**2** N-COUNT A **cannon** is a heavy automatic gun, especially one that is fired from an aircraft. 机关炮 ❑ *Others carried huge cannons plundered from Russian aircraft.* 其他人扛着从俄国飞机上抢来的巨型机关炮。**3** PHRASE If someone is a **loose cannon**, they do whatever they want and nobody can predict what they are going to do. 随心所欲的人 ❑ *Max is a loose cannon politically.* 马克斯是个在政治上随心所欲的人。

can·not /kænɒt, kənɒt/ **Cannot** is the negative form of **can**. can的否定式

▲ **ca·noe** /kənu/ (**canoes**) N-COUNT A **canoe** is a small, narrow boat that you move through the water using a stick with a wide end called a paddle. 划子；独木舟

→ see **boat**

can·on /kænən/ (**canons**) **1** N-COUNT A **canon** is a member of the clergy who is on the staff of a cathedral. 大教堂教士 **2** N-COUNT A **canon** of texts is a list of them that is accepted as genuine or important. 真作全集 [oft N of n] [FORMAL] ❑ *...a canon of accepted literary texts.* …一本公认的真作文集。❑ *...the Irish literary canon.* …爱尔兰文学真作全集。

cano·py /kænəpi/ (**canopies**) **1** N-COUNT A **canopy** is a decorated cover, often made of cloth, which is placed above something such as a bed or a seat. 华盖；罩 **2** N-COUNT A **canopy** is a layer of something that spreads out and covers an area, for example the branches and leaves that spread out at the top of trees in a forest. 遮盖；(树) 冠 ❑ *The trees formed such a dense canopy that all beneath was a deep carpet of pine needles.* 这些树形成了浓密的冠盖，下面是一层厚厚的松针。

→ see **bed**

can't /kænt/ **Can't** is the usual spoken form of "cannot." cannot的常用口语形式

can·teen /kæntin/ (**canteens**) **1** N-COUNT A **canteen** is a place in a factory or military base where meals or snacks are served to the people who work there. 食堂 ❑ *Rennie had eaten his supper in the canteen.* 伦尼已在食堂吃过晚饭。**2** N-COUNT A **canteen** is a small metal or plastic bottle for carrying water and other drinks. Canteens are used by soldiers. (军用) 水壶 ❑ *...a full canteen of water.* …一整壶的水。

can·ter /kæntər/ (**canters, cantering, cantered**) V-I When a horse **canters**, it moves at a speed that is slower than a gallop but faster than a trot. 慢步小跑 ❑ *The competitors cantered into the arena to conclude the closing ceremony.* 赛手们慢跑进入比赛场地，结束了闭幕式。● N-COUNT **Canter** is also a noun. 慢步小跑 ❑ *Carnac set off at a canter.* 卡纳克以慢步小跑出发了。

★ **can·vas** /kænvəs/ (**canvases**) **1** N-UNCOUNT **Canvas** is a strong, heavy cloth that is used for making things such as tents, sails, and bags. 帆布 ❑ *...a canvas bag.* …一个帆布包。**2** N-VAR A **canvas** is a piece of canvas or similar material on which an oil painting can be done. 油画布 **3** N-COUNT A **canvas** is a painting that has been done on canvas. 帆布油画 ❑ *The show includes canvases by masters like Carpaccio, Canaletto and Guardi.* 展览包括卡巴杰、卡纳列托和瓜第等大师的帆布油画。

→ see **painting**

can·vass /kænvəs/ (**canvasses, canvassing, canvassed**) **1** V-I If you **canvass for** a particular person or political party, you go around an area trying to persuade people to vote for that person or party. 拉选票 ❑ *I'm canvassing for the Republican Party.* 我在为共和党拉选票。 **2** V-T If you **canvass** public opinion, you find out how people feel about a particular subject. 征求 (意见) ❑ *Members of Congress are spending the weekend canvassing opinion in their constituencies.* 国会议员利用周末在各自的选区征求意见。

▲ **can·yon** /kænyən/ (**canyons**) N-COUNT; N-IN-NAMES A **canyon** is a long, narrow valley with very steep sides. 峡谷 ❑ *...the Grand Canyon.* …大峡谷。

cap ♦◇◇ /kæp/ (**caps, capping, capped**) **1** N-COUNT A **cap** is a soft, flat hat with a curved part at the front which is called a visor. 软扁帽; 便帽 ❑ *...a dark blue baseball cap.* …一顶深蓝色的棒球帽。 **2** N-COUNT A **cap** is a special hat which is worn as part of a uniform. 制服帽 ❑ *...a border guard in olive gray uniform and a cap.* …一个穿橄榄绿军服、戴军帽的边防卫士。 **3** N-COUNT The **cap** of a bottle is its lid. 瓶盖 ❑ *She unscrewed the cap of her water bottle and gave him a drink.* 她拧开水瓶盖，给他喝了一口水。 **4** V-T If someone says that a good or bad event **caps** a series of events, they mean it is the final event in the series, and the other events were also good or bad. 成为…的结尾 [JOURNALISM] ❑ *The unrest capped a weekend of right-wing attacks on foreigners.* 整个周末右翼分子对外国人的袭击最终发展成为骚乱。

ca·pa·bil·ity /keɪpəbɪlɪti/ (**capabilities**) **1** N-VAR If you have the **capability** or the **capabilities** to do something, you have the ability or the qualities that are necessary to do it. 能力; 才能 ❑ *People experience differences in physical and mental capability depending on the time of day.* 视一天中的不同时候而定，人们会经历体能和智能上的差异。 **2** N-VAR A country's military **capability** is its ability to fight in a war. 军事力量 ❑ *Their military capability has gone down because their air force has proved not to be an effective force.* 他们的军事力量已经削弱了，因为其空军被证明不是一只有战斗力的队伍。

> Do not confuse **capability** with **ability** and **capacity**. A person's **capability** is the amount of work they can do and how well they can do it. ❑ *...a job that was beyond the capability of one man. ... the director's ideas of the capability of the actor.* You often use **ability** to say that someone can do something well. ❑ *He had remarkable ability as a musician. ...the ability to bear hardship.* If someone has a particular **capacity**, a **capacity** for something, or a **capacity** to do something, they have the qualities required to do it. **Capacity** is a more formal word than **ability** . ❑ *...their capacity for hard work. ...his capacity to see the other person's point of view.*

ca·pable ♦◇◇ /keɪpəbəl/ **1** ADJ If a person or thing is **capable of** doing something, they have the ability to do it. 有能力的 [v-link ADJ "of" -ing/n] ❑ *He appeared hardly capable of conducting a coherent conversation.* 他看起来几乎没有能力进行连贯的谈话。 ❑ *The kitchen is capable of catering for several hundred people.* 这间厨房可为数百人提供饮食。 **2** ADJ Someone who is **capable** has the skill or qualities necessary to do a particular thing well, or is able to do most things well. 有才能的; 有才干的 ❑ *She's a very capable speaker.* 她是一个非常有能力的演说者。 ● **ca·pably** /keɪpəbli/ ADV 有能力地; 能干地 [ADV with v] ❑ *It was all dealt with very capably by the police and security people.* 警方和治安人员极其出色地处理了这一切。

> Note that **capable** and **able** are both used to say that someone can do something. When you say that someone is **able** to do something, you mean that they can do it either because of their knowledge or skill, or because it is possible. ❑ *He wondered if he would be able to climb over the rail... They were able to use their profits for new investments.* Note that if you use a past tense, you are saying that someone has actually done something. ❑ *We were able to reduce costs.* When you say that someone is **capable** of doing something, you mean either that they have the knowledge and skill to do it, or that they are likely to do it. ❑ *The workers are perfectly capable of running the organization themselves... She was quite capable of falling asleep.* You can say that someone is **capable** of a particular feeling or action. ❑ *He's capable of loyalty... Bowman could not believe him capable of murder.* You can also use "**capable** of" when talking about what something such as a car or machine can do. ❑ *The car was capable of 110 miles per hour.* If you describe someone as **able** or **capable**, you mean that they do things well. ❑ *He's certainly a capable gardener.*

> **Thesaurus** *capable* 另参见:
> ADJ. able, competent, skillful, talented; *(ant.)* incapable, incompetent **2**

ca·pac·ity ♦◇◇ /kəpæsɪti/ (**capacities**) **1** N-VAR Your **capacity for** something is your ability to do it, or the amount of it that you are able to do. 能力 ❑ *Our capacity for giving care, love, and attention is limited.* 我们给予照顾、爱护和关心的能力是有限的。 ❑ *Her mental capacity and temperament are as remarkable as his.* 她的智慧和气质与他的同样出众。

> Do not confuse **capacity** with **ability** and **capability**. If someone has a particular **capacity**, a **capacity** for something, or a **capacity** to do something, they have the qualities required to do it. **Capacity** is a more formal word than **ability**. ❑ *...their capacity for hard work. ...his capacity to see the other person's point of view.* You often use **ability** to say that someone can do something well. ❑ *He had remarkable ability as a musician. ...the ability to bear hardship.* A person's **capability** is the amount of work they can do and how well they can do it. ❑ *...a job that was beyond the capability of one man. ...the director's ideas of the capability of the actor.*

2 N-VAR The **capacity** of a container is its volume, or the amount of liquid it can hold, measured in units such as quarts or gallons. 容量 ❑ *...containers with a maximum capacity of 200 gallons of water.* …最大容量为200加仑水的容器。 **3** N-UNCOUNT The **capacity** of something such as a factory, industry, or region is the quantity of things that it can produce or deliver with the equipment or resources that are available. 产量 ❑ *...the amount of spare capacity in the economy.* …经济中的过剩产能。 ❑ *Bread factories are working at full capacity.* 面包厂正在满负荷进行生产。 **4** N-COUNT The **capacity** of a piece of equipment is its size or power, often measured in particular units. 负载量 ❑ *...an aircraft with a bomb-carrying capacity of 1000 pounds.* …一架炸弹装载量达1000磅的飞机。 **5** N-COUNT If you do something **in** a particular **capacity**, you do it as part of a particular job or duty, or because you are representing a particular organization or person. 身份 [WRITTEN] ❑ *Ms. Halliwell visited the Philippines in her capacity as a Special Representative of UNICEF.* 哈利韦尔女士以联合国儿童基金会特使的身份访问了菲律宾。 **6** N-SING The **capacity** of a building, place, or vehicle is the number of people or things that it can hold. If a place is filled **to capacity**, it is as full as it can possibly be. 容纳力 [also no det, oft "to" N] ❑ *Each stadium had a seating capacity of about 50,000.* 每个运动场能容纳大约五万座席。 **7** ADJ A **capacity** crowd or audience completely fills a theater, sports stadium, or other place. 满座的 [ADJ n] ❑ *A capacity crowd of 76,000 people was at the stadium for the event.* 运动场内座无虚席，7.6万人观看了比赛。

★ **cape** /keɪp/ (**capes**) **1** N-COUNT; N-IN-NAMES A **cape** is a large piece of land that sticks out into the sea from the coast. 海角; 岬 ❑ *Naomi James became the first woman to sail solo around the world via Cape Horn.* 内奥米・詹姆斯成为第一位独自经合恩角进行环球航行的女子。 **2** N-COUNT A **cape** is a short cloak. 披肩 ❑ *...a woolen cape.* …一件羊毛披肩。

> **Word Link** *cap* ≈ *head* : *capital, capitulate, captain*

capi·tal ♦♦♦ /kæpɪtəl/ (**capitals**) **1** N-UNCOUNT **Capital** is a large sum of money which you use to start a business, or which you invest in order to make more money. 资本; 资金 [BUSINESS] ❑ *Companies are having difficulty in raising capital.* 各公司在融资方面遇到麻烦。 **2** N-UNCOUNT You can use **capital** to refer to buildings or machinery which are necessary to produce goods or to make companies more efficient, but which do not make money directly. 资产 [BUSINESS] ❑ *...capital equipment that could have served to increase production.* …可用于提高产量的资产设备。 **3** N-UNCOUNT **Capital** is the part of an amount of money borrowed or invested which does not include interest. 本金; 本钱 [BUSINESS] ❑ *With a conventional mortgage, the payments consist of both capital and interest.* 一般的抵押借款，偿还包括本金和利息两部分。 **4** N-COUNT The **capital** of a country is the city or town where its government or legislature meets. 首都 ❑ *...Kathmandu, the capital of Nepal.* …加德满都，尼泊尔的首都。 **5** N-COUNT If a place is **the capital of** a particular industry or activity, it is the place that is most famous for it, because it happens in that place more than anywhere else. (某一产业或活动的) 有名之地; …之都 ❑ *Colmar has long been considered* *the capital of the wine trade.* 科尔马长久以来一直被誉为葡萄酒贸易之都。 6 N-COUNT **Capitals** or **capital letters** are written or printed letters in the form which is used at the beginning of sentences or names. "T," "B," and "F" are capitals. 大写字母 ❑ *The name and address are written in capitals.* 姓名和地址都大写。

> Note that you must always use a capital letter with days of the week, months of the year, and festivals. ❑ *...on Monday the 13th of January. ...at Christmas.* Names of seasons, however, usually begin with a small letter. ❑ *...in spring.* Capitals must also be used with the names of countries and other places, as well as with the adjectives and nouns derived from them, such as those which refer to their inhabitants or languages. ❑ *...in Portugal. ...the Swiss police. ...thousands of Germans... He spoke fluent Arabic.*

7 ADJ A **capital** offense is one that is so serious that the person who commits it can be punished by death. 可处死刑的 [ADJ n] ❑ *Espionage is a capital offense in this country.* 间谍活动在这个国家是死罪。 8 PHRASE If you say that someone **is making capital out of** a situation, you disapprove of the way they are gaining an advantage for themselves through other people's efforts or bad luck. 利用 [FORMAL, DISAPPROVAL] ❑ *He rebuked the president for trying to make political capital out of the hostage situation.* 他指责总统想利用人质事件捞取政治资本。 9 → see also **working capital**
→ see **city, country, economics, stock market**

capi·tal ac·count (capital accounts) 1 N-COUNT A country's **capital account** is the part of its balance of payments that is concerned with the movement of capital. 资本账户 ❑ *...restrictions that affect the capital account of a country's balance of payments.* …影响一国国际收支资本账户的限制。 2 N-COUNT A **capital account** is a financial statement showing the capital value of a company on a particular date. (公司某日的) 资产净值 [BUSINESS] ❑ *No business can survive without a capital account.* 没有资产净值，任何公司都无法生存。

capi·tal gains N-PLURAL **Capital gains** are the profits that you make when you buy something and then sell it again at a higher price. 资本收益 [BUSINESS] ❑ *He called for the reform of capital gains tax.* 他呼吁改革资本收益税。

capi·tal goods N-PLURAL **Capital goods** are used to make other products. Compare **consumer goods**. 资本货物 [BUSINESS] ❑ *Most imports into Korea are raw materials and capital goods.* 韩国的大多数进口物品都是原材料和资本货物。

capital-intensive ADJ **Capital-intensive** industries and businesses need the investment of large sums of money. Compare **labor-intensive**. 资本密集型的 [BUSINESS] ❑ *...highly capital-intensive industries like auto manufacturing or petrochemicals.* …如汽车制造或石油化工这样的资本高度密集型产业。

capi·tal·ise /kæpɪtəlaɪz/ [BRIT] → see **capitalize**

▲ **capi·tal·ism** /kæpɪtəlɪzəm/ N-UNCOUNT **Capitalism** is an economic and political system in which property, business, and industry are owned by private individuals and not by the state. 资本主义 ❑ *...the two fundamentally opposed social systems, capitalism and socialism.* …两种根本对立的社会制度，资本主义与社会主义。

capi·tal·ist /kæpɪtəlɪst/ (capitalists) 1 ADJ A **capitalist** country or system supports or is based on the principles of capitalism. 基于资本主义原则的 ❑ *China has pledged to retain Hong Kong's capitalist system for 50 years.* 中国政府已保证维持香港的资本主义制度50年。 2 N-COUNT A **capitalist** is someone who believes in and supports the principles of capitalism. 资本主义者；资本主义拥护者 ❑ *Lenin had hoped to even have a working relationship with the capitalists.* 列宁甚至曾希望能与资本主义者建立合作关系。 3 N-COUNT A **capitalist** is someone who owns a business which they run in order to make a profit for themselves. 资本家 ❑ *They argue that only private capitalists can remake Poland's economy.* 他们争辩说只有个体资本家才能重振波兰的经济。

▲ **capi·tal·ize** /kæpɪtəlaɪz/ (capitalizes, capitalizing, capitalized)

in BRIT, also use **capitalise**

1 V-I If you **capitalize on** a situation, you use it to gain some advantage for yourself. 利用 ❑ *The rebels seem to be trying to capitalize on the public's discontent with the government.* 反叛者们似乎正试图利用公众对政府的不满情绪。 2 V-T In business, if you **capitalize** something that belongs to you, you sell it in order to make money. 使资本化 [BUSINESS] ❑ *Our intention is to capitalize the company by any means we can.* 我们的目的是尽一切可能把该公司资本化。 3 V-T If you **capitalize** a letter, you write it as a capital letter. If you **capitalize** a word, you spell it in capital letters, or with the first letter as a capital letter. 把…大写 ❑ *Capitalize all proper nouns but not the articles (a, an) that precede them.* 把所有的专有名词大写，它们之前的冠词(a, an)则不用。

capi·tal pun·ish·ment N-UNCOUNT **Capital punishment** is punishment which involves the legal killing of a person who has committed a serious crime such as murder. 死刑

Word Link *cap ≈ head : capital, capitulate, captain*

ca·pitu·late /kəpɪtʃəleɪt/ (**capitulates, capitulating, capitulated**) V-I If you **capitulate**, you stop resisting and do what someone else wants you to do. 让步 ❑ *The club eventually capitulated and now grants equal rights to women.* 该俱乐部最终让步，现在给予妇女同等的权利。

cap·size /kæpsaɪz/ (**capsizes, capsizing, capsized**) V-T/V-I If you **capsize** a boat or if it **capsizes**, it turns upside down in the water. 使(船) 倾覆；(船) 倾覆 ❑ *The sea got very rough and the boat capsized.* 海的风浪变得很大，船翻了。

★ **cap·sule** /kæpsəl/ (**capsules**) 1 N-COUNT A **capsule** is a very small tube containing powdered or liquid medicine, which you swallow. (装药的) 胶囊 ❑ *...cod liver oil capsules.* …鳕鱼肝油胶囊。 2 N-COUNT A **capsule** is a small container with a drug or other substance inside it, which is used for medical or scientific purposes. (用于医学或科学目的的) 小容器 ❑ *They first implanted capsules into the animals' brains.* 他们先将胶囊植入那些动物的大脑。 3 N-COUNT A space **capsule** is the part of a spacecraft in which people travel, and which often separates from the main rocket. 太空舱 ❑ *A Russian space capsule is currently orbiting the Earth.* 一个俄罗斯太空舱目前正环绕地球飞行。 4 N-COUNT A time **capsule** is a container into which people put typical everyday objects from their lives. The container is buried so that people in the future can dig it up, and find out about what life was like in the past. 时光宝盒(指装入日常用品后埋于地下，有待后来人挖掘以便了解过去的盒子) ❑ *Twenty-five years ago they filled a time capsule and buried it.* 25年前，他们装满一个时光宝盒并把它埋了起来。

cap·tain ♦♦◇ /kæptɪn/ (**captains, captaining, captained**) 1 N-TITLE; N-COUNT; N-VOC In the army, navy, and some other armed forces, a **captain** is an officer of middle rank. (陆军、海军及其他军种的) 上尉 ❑ *...Captain Mark Phillips.* …马克・菲利普斯上尉。 ❑ *...a captain in the army.* …一名陆军上尉。 2 N-COUNT The **captain** of a sports team is the player in charge of it. (体育运动队) 队长 ❑ *...Mickey Thomas, the captain of the tennis team.* …米奇・托马斯，这支网球队的队长。 3 N-COUNT The **captain** of a ship is the sailor in charge of it. 船长 ❑ *...the captain of an excursion boat.* …一艘游船的船长。 4 N-COUNT; N-TITLE The **captain** of an airplane is the pilot in charge of it. 机长 5 N-COUNT; N-TITLE In the United States and some other countries, a **captain** is a police officer or firefighter of fairly senior rank. 警察局副巡官；消防中队长 ❑ *...a former Honolulu police captain.* …火奴鲁鲁警察局前任巡官。 6 V-T If you **captain** a team or a ship, you are the captain of it. 率队；指挥 ❑ *He captained the winning team in 1991.* 他于1991年率队夺得胜利。
→ see **boat, ship**

cap·tain·cy /kæptɪnsi/ N-UNCOUNT The **captaincy** of a team is the position of being captain. 队长之职 ❑ *His captaincy of the team was ended by mild eye trouble.* 他的队长生涯因轻微眼疾而结束。

★ **cap·tion** ♦♦◇ /kæpʃən/ (**captions**) N-COUNT A **caption** is the words printed underneath a picture or cartoon which explain what it is about. (图片或卡通的) 说明文字 ❑ *The local paper featured me standing on a stepladder with a caption, "Wendy climbs the ladder to success."* 当地的报纸刊登了一幅我站在活梯上的特写，下面写着："温迪登上了成功之梯。"

Word Link *cap ≈ seize : captivate, captive, capture*

cap·ti·vate /kæptɪveɪt/ (**captivates, captivating, captivated**) V-T If you **are captivated** by someone or something, you find them fascinating and attractive. 迷住 [usu passive] ❑ *I was captivated by her brilliant mind.* 我为她的聪慧所迷。

★ **cap·tive** /kæptɪv/ (**captives**) 1 ADJ A **captive** person or animal is being kept imprisoned or enclosed. 被囚禁的；被圈养的 [LITERARY] ❑ *Her heart had begun to pound inside her chest like a captive animal.* 她心如鹿撞，怦怦跳个不停。 ● N-COUNT A **captive** is someone who is captive. 被囚禁者 ❑ *He described the difficulties of* *surviving for four months as a captive.* 他讲述了沦为阶下囚的4个月中生存的种种不易。 2 ADJ A **captive** audience is a group of people who are not free to leave a certain place and so have to watch or listen. A **captive** market is a group of people who cannot choose whether or where to buy things. (观众) 不能随意离开的; (市场) 被垄断的 [ADJ n] ❑ *We all performed action songs, sketches, and dances before a captive audience of parents and patrons.* 我们都表演了带动作的歌曲、短剧和舞蹈给父母和赞助人这类被动观众看。 3 PHRASE If you **take** someone **captive** or **hold** someone **captive**, you take or keep them as a prisoner. 囚禁某人 ❑ *Richard was finally released on February 4, one year and six weeks after he'd been taken captive.* 理查德经历了1年零6周的囚禁之后，终于在2月4日被释放。

cap·tiv·i·ty /kæptɪvɪti/ N-UNCOUNT **Captivity** is the state of being kept imprisoned or enclosed. 囚禁; 圈养 ❑ *The great majority of barn owls are reared in captivity.* 绝大多数仓鸮是圈养的。

cap·ture ♦◇◇ /kæptʃər/ (**captures, capturing, captured**) 1 V-T If you **capture** someone or something, you catch them, especially in a war. 俘虏; 捕获 ❑ *The guerrillas shot down one airplane and captured the pilot.* 那些游击队员击落了一架飞机，并俘虏了飞行员。 ● N-UNCOUNT **Capture** is also a noun. 占领 ❑ *...the final battles which led to the army's capture of the town.* …部队夺取该镇的最后几场战斗。 2 V-T If something or someone **captures** a particular quality, feeling, or atmosphere, they represent or express it successfully. 充分体现 [no cont] ❑ *Chef Idris Caldora offers an inspired menu that captures the spirit of the Mediterranean.* 伊德里斯·卡尔多拉厨师的菜单很有创意，充分体现了地中海风情。 3 V-T If something **captures** your attention or imagination, you begin to be interested or excited by it. If someone or something **captures** your heart, you begin to love them or like them very much. 吸引 ❑ *...the great names of the past who usually capture the historian's attention.* …那些常常为史学家所关注的伟人们。 4 V-T If an event **is captured** in a photograph or on film, it is photographed or filmed. 拍摄 [usu passive] ❑ *The incident was captured on videotape.* 这一事件被拍摄下来。 ❑ *The images were captured by TV crews filming outside the base.* 这些镜头被正在基地外拍摄的电视台工作人员捕捉到了。

Word Partnership *capture* 的常用搭配:
V. **avoid** capture, **escape** capture, **fail to** capture 1
N. capture **territory** 1
capture **your attention**, capture **your imagination** 3

car ♦♦♦ /kɑr/ (**cars**) 1 N-COUNT A **car** is a motor vehicle with room for a small number of passengers. 小汽车 [also "by" N] ❑ *He had left his tickets in his car.* 他把票落在自己的小汽车里了。 2 N-COUNT A **car** is one of the separate, long sections of a train that carries passengers. 火车车厢 [mainly AM]

in BRIT, usually use **carriage**

❑ *The company manufactured elegant railroad cars.* 该公司生产雅致的火车车厢。 3 N-COUNT The separate sections of a train are called **cars** when they are used for a particular purpose. (有特殊用途的) 火车车厢 ❑ *He made his way into the dining car for breakfast.* 他挤进餐车吃早点。
→ see Word Web: **car**
→ see **train, transportation**

car alarm (**car alarms**) N-COUNT A **car alarm** is a device in a car which makes a loud noise if anyone tries to break into the vehicle. 汽车报警器 ❑ *He returned to the airport to find his car alarm going off.* 他回到机场，发现自己汽车的报警器响了。

cara·mel /kærəmɛl, -məl, kɑrməl/ (**caramels**) 1 N-VAR A **caramel** is a chewy sweet food made from sugar, butter, and milk. 黄油奶糖 2 N-UNCOUNT **Caramel** is burnt sugar used for coloring and flavoring food. (调色、调味用的) 焦糖

car·at /kærət/ (**carats**) N-COUNT A **carat** is a unit for measuring the weight of diamonds and other precious stones. It is equal to 0.2 grams. 克拉 (钻石等宝石的计重单位，相当于0.2克) ❑ *The gemstone is 28.6 millimeters high and weighs 139.43 carats.* 这颗宝石高28.6毫米，重达139.43克拉。
→ see **diamond**

▲ **cara·van** /kærəvæn/ (**caravans**) 1 N-COUNT A **caravan** is a group of people and animals or vehicles who travel together. 旅行队 ❑ *...the old caravan routes from Central Asia to China.* …从中亚到中国的古老旅行路线。 2 N-COUNT A **caravan** is the same as a **trailer**. 旅行拖车; 活动房屋 [BRIT] → see **trailer 2**

cara·van site (**caravan sites**) N-COUNT A **caravan site** is the same as a **trailer park**. 旅行拖车停车场 [BRIT]

▲ **car·bo·hy·drate** /kɑrboʊhaɪdreɪt/ (**carbohydrates**) N-VAR **Carbohydrates** are substances, found in certain kinds of food, that provide you with energy. Foods such as sugar and bread that contain these substances can also be referred to as **carbohydrates**. (为身体提供热量的) 碳水化合物; 含碳水化合物的食物 ❑ *...carbohydrates such as bread, pasta, or potatoes.* …含碳水化合物的食物，如面包、意大利面或马铃薯。
→ see **calorie, diet**

car·bon ♦◇◇ /kɑrbən/ N-UNCOUNT **Carbon** is a chemical element that diamonds and coal are made up of. (化学元素) 碳
→ see **diamond**

car·bon·at·ed /kɑrbəneɪtɪd/ ADJ **Carbonated** drinks are drinks that contain small bubbles of carbon dioxide. (饮料) 含二氧化碳的 [usu ADJ n] ❑ *...colas and other carbonated soft drinks.* …可乐及其他含二氧化碳的软饮料。

car·bon di·ox·ide /kɑrbən daɪɒksaɪd/ N-UNCOUNT **Carbon dioxide** is a gas. It is produced by animals and people breathing out, and by chemical reactions. 二氧化碳
→ see **air, dry-cleaning, greenhouse effect, respiratory**

car·bon foot·print N-COUNT Your **carbon footprint** is a measure of the amount of carbon dioxide released into the atmosphere by your activities over a particular period. 碳足迹; 碳排放量 [oft poss N] ❑ *We all need to look for ways to reduce our carbon footprint.* 我们都需要寻找减少我们碳足迹的办法。

car·bon mon·ox·ide /kɑrbən mənɒksaɪd/ N-UNCOUNT **Carbon monoxide** is a poisonous gas that is produced especially by the engines of vehicles. 一氧化碳 ❑ *The limit for carbon monoxide is 4.5 per cent of the exhaust gas.* 尾气中一氧化碳的排放量限制在4.5% 以下。

car·bon neu·tral ADJ A **carbon neutral** lifestyle, company, or activity does not cause an increase in the overall amount of carbon dioxide in the atmosphere. 碳中和的 ❑ *You can make your flights carbon neutral by planting trees to make up for the greenhouse gas emissions.* 你可以通过种树抵消温室气体排放，这样你的飞行就可以做到碳中和。

car·bon trad·ing N-UNCOUNT **Carbon trading** is the practice of buying and selling the right to produce carbon dioxide emissions, so that people, countries or companies who use a lot of fuel and electricity can buy rights from those that do not use so much. 碳排放权交易

▲ **car·case** /kɑːkəs/ [BRIT] → see **carcass**

Word Web car

The first mass-produced **automobile** in the U.S. was the Model T. In 1909, Ford sold over 10,000 of these **vehicles**. They all had the same basic **engine** and **chassis**. For years the only color choice was black. Three different bodies were available—roadster, **sedan**, and coupe. Today manufacturers offer many more options. These include **convertibles**, **sports cars**, **station wagons**, **vans**, **pickups**, and **SUVs**. Laws now require devices such as **seat belts** and **airbags** to make **driving** safer. Some car makers now offer **hybrid** vehicles. They combine an electrical engine with an **internal combustion engine** to improve **fuel** economy.

C

▲ **car·cass** /kɑrkəs/ (**carcasses**)
in BRIT, also use **carcase**
N-COUNT A **carcass** is the body of a dead animal. 动物尸体 ❑ *A cluster of vultures crouched on the carcass of a dead buffalo.* 一群秃鹫伏在一头水牛的尸体上啄食。

card ♦♦◇ /kɑrd/ (**cards**) **1** N-COUNT A **card** is a piece of stiff paper or thin cardboard on which something is written or printed. 卡片 ❑ *Check the numbers below against the numbers on your card.* 核对下面的数字是否和您卡片上的相符。 **2** N-COUNT A **card** is a piece of cardboard or plastic, or a small document, which shows information about you and which you carry with you, for example to prove your identity. 身份证明卡 ❑ *...they check my bag and press card.* …他们检查了我的包和记者证。 ❑ *...her membership card.* …她的会员卡。 **3** N-COUNT A **card** is a rectangular piece of plastic, issued by a bank, company, or store, which you can use to buy things or obtain money. 消费卡 ❑ *He paid the whole bill with an American Express card.* 他用美国运通卡支付了全款。 **4** N-COUNT A **card** is a folded piece of stiff paper with a picture and sometimes a message printed on it, which you send to someone on a special occasion. 贺卡 ❑ *She sends me a card on my birthday.* 她在我生日那天送了一张贺卡。 **5** N-COUNT A **card** is the same as a **postcard**. 明信片 ❑ *Send your details on a card to the following address.* 将你的详细信息写在明信片上，寄到下面的地址。 **6** N-COUNT A **card** is a piece of thin cardboard carried by someone such as a businessperson in order to give it to other people. A card shows the name, address, telephone number, and other details of the person who carries it. 名片 [BUSINESS] ❑ *Here's my card. You may need me.* 这是我的名片。你可能会需要我。 **7** N-COUNT **Cards** are thin pieces of cardboard with numbers or pictures printed on them which are used to play various games. 纸牌 ❑ *...a deck of cards.* …一副纸牌。 **8** N-UNCOUNT If you are playing **cards**, you are playing a game using cards. 纸牌游戏 ❑ *They enjoy themselves drinking wine, smoking, and playing cards.* 他们喝酒、抽烟、打牌，玩得不亦乐乎。 **9** N-UNCOUNT **Card** is strong, stiff paper or thin cardboard. 硬纸片 ❑ *She put the pieces of card in her pocket.* 她把那些硬纸片塞进口袋里。 **10** → see also **bank card, business card, calling card, credit card, debit card, gold card, greeting card, identity card, playing card, smart card, wild card** **11** PHRASE If you say that something is **in the cards**, you mean that it is very likely to happen. 很可能发生 ❑ *Last summer she began telling friends that a New Year marriage was in the cards.* 去年夏天她开始通知朋友们她很可能在新年结婚。 **12** PHRASE If you **have** your **cards read**, you have your fortune told by someone who uses playing cards or tarot cards to tell you about yourself and predict your future. 找人算命 ❑ *The shop had a sign in the window: "Have your cards read here, $25."* 那家商店的窗户上有个招牌，写着：“算命，$25”。

▲ **card·board** /kɑrdbɔrd/ N-UNCOUNT **Cardboard** is thick, stiff paper that is used, for example, to make boxes and models. 硬纸板

car·di·ac /kɑrdiæk/ ADJ **Cardiac** means relating to the heart. 心脏的 [ADJ n] [MEDICAL] ❑ *The man was suffering from cardiac weakness.* 这人当时正患心脏衰弱。
→ see **muscle**

car·di·gan /kɑrdɪgən/ (**cardigans**) N-COUNT A **cardigan** is a knitted woolen sweater that you can fasten at the front with buttons or a zipper. 开襟羊毛衫

★ **car·di·nal** /kɑrdᵊnᵊl/ (**cardinals**) **1** N-COUNT; N-TITLE A **cardinal** is a high-ranking priest in the Catholic church. (天主教的)红衣主教 ❑ *In 1448, Nicholas was appointed a cardinal.* 1448年，尼古拉斯被任命为红衣主教。 **2** ADJ A **cardinal** rule or quality is the one that is considered to be the most important. 首要的 [ADJ n] [FORMAL] ❑ *As a salesman, your cardinal rule is to do everything you can to satisfy a customer.* 作为一名推销员，首要原则就是要尽你所能使客户满意。 **3** N-COUNT A **cardinal** is a common North American bird. The male has bright red feathers. 红衣凤头鸟

card in·dex (**card indexes**) N-COUNT A **card index** is a number of cards with information written on them which are arranged in a particular order, usually alphabetical, so that you can find the information you want easily. 卡片索引 ❑ *Then he turned to the card index and tore out the entry for Matthew Holmwood.* 接着他转向卡片索引，撕下了有关马修・霍姆伍德的条目。

care ♦♦♦ /kɛər/ (**cares, caring, cared**) **1** V-T/V-I If you **care** about something, you feel that it is important and are concerned about it. 关注 [no cont] ❑ *...a company that cares about the environment.* …一家关心环境的公司。 ❑ *...young men who did not care whether they lived or died.* …一群不在乎自己死活的年轻人。 **2** V-I If you **care for** someone, you feel a lot of affection for them. 喜爱 [no cont] [APPROVAL] ❑ *He wanted me to know that he still cared for me.* 他想让我知道他仍然爱着我。 ● **car·ing** ★ N-UNCOUNT 体贴 ❑ *...the "feminine" traits of caring and compassion.* …体贴和同情这些“女性”的特质。 **3** V-I If you **care for** someone or something, you look after them and keep them in a good state or condition. 照顾 ❑ *They hired a nurse to care for her.* 他们雇了个护士来照顾她。 ❑ *...these distinctive cars, lovingly cared for by private owners.* …这些被私家车主精心呵护着的各具特色的汽车。 ● N-UNCOUNT **Care** is also a noun. 照顾 ❑ *Most of the staff specialize in the care of children.* 大部分员工都擅长照顾孩子。 ❑ *...sensitive teeth which need special care.* …需要特殊护理的敏感型牙齿。 **4** V-T/V-I You can ask someone if they would **care for** something or if they would **care to** do something as a polite way of asking if they would like to have or do something. 想要 [no cont] [POLITENESS] ❑ *Would you care for some orange juice?* 你想要些橙汁吗？ **5** N-UNCOUNT If you do something **with care**, you give careful attention to it because you do not want to make any mistakes or cause any damage. 谨慎 ❑ *Condoms are an effective method of birth control if used with care.* 避孕套如果谨慎使用，是一种有效的节育方法。 **6** N-COUNT Your **cares** are your worries, anxieties, or fears. 烦恼 ❑ *Lean back in a hot bath and forget all the cares of the day.* 躺下享受个热水浴，忘掉一天中所有的烦恼。 **7** → see also **caring, day care, intensive care** **8** PHRASE You can use **for all I care** to emphasize that it does not matter at all to you what someone does. 不关某人的事 [EMPHASIS] ❑ *You can go right now for all I care.* 你现在就可以走，我才不管呢。 **9** PHRASE If you say that you **couldn't care less about** someone or something, you are emphasizing that you are not interested in them or worried about them. You can also say that you **could care less**, with the same meaning. 不在乎 [EMPHASIS] ❑ *I couldn't care less about the woman.* 我才不在乎那个女人呢。 ❑ *I don't care if they respect me. I could care less.* 我不在乎他们是否尊重我。我一点都不在乎。 **10** PHRASE If someone sends you a letter or package **care of** or **in care of** a particular person or place, they send it to that person or place, and it is then passed on to you. 经某人转交 ❑ *Please write to me care of the publishers.* 写给我的信请通过出版商转交。 ❑ *He wrote to me in care of my publisher.* 他写信给我，经由我的出版商转交。 **11** PHRASE If you **take care of** someone or something, you look after them and prevent them from being harmed or damaged. 照顾某人/某事 ❑ *There was no one else to take care of their children.* 没有其他人照看他们的孩子了。 **12** PHRASE If you **take care to** do something, you make sure that you do it. 留意做某事 ❑ *Foley followed Albert through the gate, taking care to close the latch.* 福利随着艾伯特进了大门，留心地把门闩上。 **13** PHRASE To **take care of** a problem, task, or situation means to deal with it. 处理某事 ❑ *They leave it to the system to try and take care of the problem.* 他们把问题留给体制去设法解决。 **14** PHRASE You can say **"Who cares?"** to emphasize that something does not matter to you at all. 管它呢 [EMPHASIS] ❑ *"But we might ruin the stove."—"Who cares?"* “我们可能会毁了炉子。”——“管它呢！” ❑ *Who cares about some stupid vacation?* 谁在乎愚蠢地休假？

Word Partnership *care* 的常用搭配：

ADJ.	**good** care, **loving** care **3**
V.	**provide** care, **receive** care **3**

ca·reer ♦♦◇ /kərɪər/ (**careers, careering, careered**) **1** N-COUNT A **career** is the job or profession that someone does for a long period of their life. 职业 ❑ *She is now concentrating on a career as a fashion designer.* 她现在专注于时装设计这一行。 ❑ *...a career in journalism.* …新闻职业。 **2** N-COUNT Your **career** is the part of your life that you spend working. 职业生涯 ❑ *During his career, he wrote more than fifty plays.* 在他的创作生涯里，他共写了五十多部剧作。 **3** ADJ **Career** advice or guidance consists of information about different jobs and help with deciding what kind of job you want to do. 就业的 [ADJ n] ❑ *She received very little career guidance when young.* 她年轻时没受过什么就业指导。 **4** V-I If a person or vehicle **careers** somewhere, they move fast and in an uncontrolled way. 猛冲 [oft cont] ❑ *His car careered into a river.* 他的车猛地冲进了河里。

Thesaurus *career* 另参见：

N.	field, job, profession, specialty, vocation, work **1**

Word Partnership *career* 的常用搭配:

N. career **advancement**, career **goals**, career **opportunities**, career **path** 1 2
ADJ. **political** career, **professional** career 1 2
V. **pursue** a career 1 2

ca·reer wom·an (**career women**) N-COUNT A **career woman** is a woman with a career who is interested in working and progressing in her job, rather than staying at home taking care of the house and children. 职业女性

Word Link *free ≈ without : carefree, duty-free, tax-free*

★ **care·free** /kɛərfri/ ADJ A **carefree** person or period of time doesn't have or involve any problems, worries, or responsibilities. 无忧无虑的 ❑ *Chantal remembered carefree summers at the beach.* 香岱儿想起了在海滩上的那些无忧无虑的夏日。

Word Link *ful ≈ filled with : beautiful, careful, dreadful*

care·ful ♦♦◇ /kɛərfəl/ 1 ADJ If you are **careful**, you give serious attention to what you are doing, in order to avoid harm, damage, or mistakes. If you are **careful to** do something, you make sure that you do it. 谨慎的；注意的 ❑ *Be very careful with this stuff, it can be dangerous if it isn't handled properly.* 对这东西要小心，处理得不好可能会发生危险。 ❑ *Careful on those stairs!* 小心那些楼梯！ ● **care·ful·ly** ADV 小心地 [ADV with v] ❑ *Have a nice time, dear, and drive carefully.* 好好玩，亲爱的，要小心驾驶。 2 ADJ **Careful** work, thought, or examination is thorough and shows a concern for details. 仔细的 ❑ *He has decided to prosecute her after careful consideration of all the relevant facts.* 他仔细考虑了所有相关事实后，决定起诉她。 ● **care·ful·ly** ADV 仔细地 [ADV with v] ❑ *...a vast series of deliberate and carefully planned thefts.* …多起精心策划、周密安排的盗窃案件。 3 ADJ If you tell someone to be **careful about** doing something, you think that what they intend to do is probably wrong, and that they should think seriously before they do it. 当心的 [v-link ADJ "about/of" -ing] ❑ *I think you should be careful about talking of the rebels as heroes.* 我认为你还是当心点好，别把叛乱分子说成是英雄。 ● **care·ful·ly** ADV 当心地 [ADV after v] ❑ *He should think carefully about actions like this which play into the hands of his opponents.* 他应该留神这类对对手有利的行为。 4 ADJ If you are **careful with** something such as money or resources, you use or spend only what is necessary. 精打细算的 ❑ *Industries should be more careful with natural resources.* 各行业对自然资源应该更加精打细算。

Word Partnership *careful* 的常用搭配:

ADV. **better be** careful 1
extremely careful, **very** careful 1–4
N. careful **attention**, careful **consideration**, careful **observation**, careful **planning** 2

care·giv·er /kɛərgɪvər/ (**caregivers**) N-COUNT A **caregiver** is someone who is responsible for taking care of another person, for example, a person who is disabled, ill, or very young. 看护者 [mainly AM]

in BRIT, usually use **carer**

❑ *It is always women who are the primary caregivers.* 一直由妇女做主要的看护人。

care·less /kɛərlɪs/ 1 ADJ If you are **careless**, you do not pay enough attention to what you are doing, and so you make mistakes, or cause harm or damage. 粗心的 ❑ *I'm sorry. How careless of me.* 对不起，我太粗心了。 ❑ *Some parents are accused of being careless with their children's health.* 有些父母被指责对孩子的健康掉以轻心。 ● **care·less·ly** ADV 粗心地 [ADV with v] ❑ *She was fined $200 for driving carelessly.* 她由于粗心驾驶被罚$200。 ● **care·less·ness** N-UNCOUNT 粗心 ❑ *Errors are sometimes made from simple carelessness.* 错误有时是因为单纯的粗心而造成的。 2 ADJ If you say that someone is **careless of** something such as their health or appearance, you mean that they do not seem to be concerned about it, or do nothing to keep it in a good condition. 不在意的 ❑ *He had shown himself careless of personal safety where the life of his colleagues might be at risk.* 他在同事们有生命危险时表现出不顾个人安危之举。

Thesaurus *careless* 另参见:

ADJ. absent-minded, forgetful, irresponsible, reckless, sloppy; *(ant.)* attentive, careful, cautious 1

car·er /kɛərər/ (**carers**) N-COUNT A **carer** is the same as a **caregiver**. 看护者 [BRIT]

▲ **ca·ress** /kərɛs/ (**caresses, caressing, caressed**) V-T If you **caress** someone or something, you stroke them gently and affectionately. 抚摸 [WRITTEN] ❑ *He was gently caressing her golden hair.* 他正温柔地抚摸着她的金发。 ● N-COUNT **Caress** is also a noun. 抚摸 ❑ *Margaret took me to one side, holding my arm in a gentle caress.* 玛格丽特把我拉到一旁，轻轻地抚弄着我的手臂。

▲ **care·taker** /kɛərteɪkər/ (**caretakers**) 1 N-COUNT A **caretaker** is a person whose job it is to take care of a house or property when the owner is not there. (主人不在时看管房子或财产的) 看管人 ❑ *Slater remained at the house, acting as its caretaker when the family was not in residence.* 这家人不在的时候，斯莱特留在这幢房子里看家。 2 N-COUNT A **caretaker** is someone who is responsible for looking after another person, for example, a person who is disabled, ill, or very young. 看护者 [mainly AM]

in BRIT, use **carer**

❑ *His caretakers labeled him severely disabled.* 他的看护人说他严重残疾。 3 N-COUNT A **caretaker** is a person whose job it is to take care of a large building such as a school or an apartment house, and deal with small repairs to it. 物业管理员 [BRIT]

in AM, use **janitor**

4 ADJ A **caretaker** government or leader is in charge temporarily until a new government or leader is appointed. 临时的 (政府或领导人) [ADJ n] ❑ *The military intends to hand over power to a caretaker government and hold elections within six months.* 军方打算将权力移交给临时政府，并在6个月内进行选举。

car·go /kɑrgoʊ/ (**cargoes**) N-VAR The **cargo** of a ship or plane is the goods that it is carrying. 货物 ❑ *The boat calls at the main port to load its regular cargo of bananas.* 船停泊在那个大港，装载其常规货物香蕉。

→ see **ship**

Car·ib·bean ♦◇◇ /kærəbiən, kərɪbiən/ (**Caribbeans**) 1 N-PROPER **The Caribbean** is the sea which is between the West Indies, Central America and the north coast of South America. 加勒比海 2 ADJ **Caribbean** means belonging or relating to the Caribbean Sea and its islands, or to its people. 加勒比海的；加勒比海人的 ❑ *...the Caribbean island of St. Thomas.* …加勒比海上的圣・托马斯岛。 ● N-COUNT A **Caribbean** is a person from a Caribbean island. 加勒比海人

cari·ca·ture /kærɪkətʃər, -tʃʊər/ (**caricatures, caricaturing, caricatured**) 1 N-COUNT A **caricature of** someone is a drawing or description of them that exaggerates their appearance or behavior in a humorous or critical way. 漫画 ❑ *The poster showed a caricature of Hitler with a devil's horns and tail.* 这张招贴漫画里的希特勒长着魔鬼一样的犄角和尾巴。 2 N-COUNT If you describe something as a **caricature of** an event or situation, you mean that it is a very exaggerated account of it. 夸张的描述 [DISAPPROVAL] ❑ *Hall is angry at what he sees as a caricature of the training offered to modern-day social workers.* 霍尔看到对当前社会工作者培训的夸张描述，感到很气愤。 3 V-T If you **caricature** someone, you draw or describe them in an exaggerated way in order to be humorous or critical. 漫画化 ❑ *Her political career has been caricatured in the headlines.* 她的政治生涯在新闻头条里被夸张嘲弄了。

★ **car·ing** ♦◇◇ /kɛərɪŋ/ 1 ADJ If someone is **caring**, they are affectionate, helpful, and sympathetic. 体贴的 ❑ *He is a lovely boy, very gentle and caring.* 他是个可爱的男孩，既温柔又体贴。 2 ADJ The **caring** professions are those such as nursing and social work that are involved with looking after people who are ill or who need help in coping with their lives. 护理的 [ADJ n] ❑ *The course is also suitable for those in the caring professions.* 这门课同样适合护理行业从业者。

Word Link *carn ≈ flesh : carnage, incarnation, reincarnation*

car·nage /kɑrnɪdʒ/ N-UNCOUNT **Carnage** is the violent killing of large numbers of people, especially in a war. 大屠杀 [LITERARY] ❑ *...his strategy for stopping the carnage in Kosovo.* …他阻止科索沃大屠杀的策略。

car·na·tion /kɑrneɪʃən/ (**carnations**) N-COUNT A **carnation** is a plant with white, pink, or red flowers. 康乃馨

car·ni·val /kɑrnɪvəl/ (**carnivals**) 1 N-COUNT A **carnival** is a public festival during which people play music and sometimes dance in the streets. 狂欢节 2 N-COUNT A **carnival** is a traveling show which is held in a park or field and at which there are machines to ride on, entertainments, and games. 嘉年华 [AM]

in BRIT, use **funfair**

car·ol /kærəl/ (**carols**) N-COUNT **Carols** are Christian religious songs that are sung at Christmas. 圣诞颂歌 ❑ *The singing of Christmas carols is a custom derived from early dance routines of pagan origin.* 唱圣诞歌这一传统源自异教早期的舞蹈仪式。

carou·sel /kærəsɛl/ (**carousels**) **1** N-COUNT At an airport, a **carousel** is a moving surface from which passengers can collect their luggage. (机场的) 行李传送带 **2** N-COUNT A **carousel** is a large, circular machine with seats, often in the shape of animals or cars. People can sit on it and go around and around for fun. 旋转木马
→ see **park**

car park (**car parks**) also **carpark** N-COUNT A **car park** is an area or building where people can leave their cars. 停车场 [BRIT]

in AM, use **parking lot, parking garage**

car·pen·ter /kɑrpɪntər/ (**carpenters**) N-COUNT A **carpenter** is a person whose job is making and repairing wooden things. 木匠

car·pet /kɑrpɪt/ (**carpets, carpeting, carpeted**) **1** N-VAR A **carpet** is a thick covering of soft material which is laid over a floor or a staircase. 地毯 ❑ *They put down wooden boards, and laid new carpets on top.* 他们安装了木地板，还在上面铺了新地毯。 **2** V-T If a floor or a room **is carpeted**, a carpet is laid on the floor. 铺地毯 [usu passive] ❑ *The room had been carpeted and the windows glazed with colored glass.* 房间里铺上了地毯，彩色的玻璃令窗户闪闪发亮。

car phone (**car phones**) N-COUNT A **car phone** is a cellular phone which is designed to be used in a car. 车载电话

car·pool /kɑrpul/ (**carpools, carpooling, carpooled**) also **car pool, car-pool** **1** N-COUNT A **carpool** is an arrangement where a group of people take turns driving each other to work, or driving each other's children to school. A **carpool** also refers to the people traveling together in a car. 拼车; 拼车旅行的人 ❑ *His wife stays home to drive the children to school in the carpool.* 他妻子留在家里同别人拼车送孩子上学。 **2** N-COUNT A **carpool** is a number of cars that are owned by a company or organization for the use of its employees or members. (公司或机构供员工使用的) 车队 [BUSINESS] **3** V-I If a group of people **carpool**, they take turns driving each other to work, or driving each other's children to school. 拼车 [mainly AM or AUSTRALIAN] ❑ *The government says fewer Americans are carpooling to work.* 政府宣称拼车上班的美国人越来越少。

car·riage /kærɪdʒ/ (**carriages**) **1** N-COUNT A **carriage** is an old-fashioned vehicle, usually for a small number of passengers, which is pulled by horses. 马车 [also "by" N] ❑ *The president-elect followed in an open carriage drawn by six beautiful gray horses.* 新当选的总统紧随其后，坐着6匹灰色骏马开道的敞篷马车。 **2** N-COUNT A **carriage** is the same as a **car**. 火车车厢 [mainly BRIT] → see **car 2** **3** N-UNCOUNT **Carriage** is the same as a **delivery charge**. 送货费 [BRIT]

car·ri·er ♦◇◇ /kæriər/ (**carriers**) **1** N-COUNT A **carrier** is a vehicle that is used for carrying people, especially soldiers, or things. 运输工具 ❑ *There were armored personnel carriers and tanks on the streets.* 街上有装甲车和坦克。 **2** N-COUNT A **carrier** is a company that provides telecommunications services, such as telephone and Internet services. 电信运营商 ❑ *...Japan's top wireless carrier.* …日本头号无线通讯运营商。 ❑ *Regional carriers get paid for calls that pass through their switches.* 地方运营商向那些通过其转接台的电话收费。 **3** N-COUNT A **carrier** is a passenger airline. 客运航空公司 ❑ *American Airlines is the third-largest carrier at Denver International Airport.* 美国航空公司是丹佛国际机场第三大客运航空公司。 **4** N-COUNT A **carrier** is a company that transports goods from one place to another by truck. 卡车运输公司 ❑ *The Colorado Motor Carriers Association represents 450 trucking companies across the state.* 科罗拉多汽车运输协会代表了该州450家卡车运输公司。 **5** N-COUNT A **carrier** is a person or an animal that is infected with a disease and so can make other people or animals ill. 病毒携带者 ❑ *...an AIDS carrier.* …一名艾滋病毒携带者。
→ see **ship**

car·rot /kærət/ (**carrots**) **1** N-VAR **Carrots** are long, thin, orange-colored vegetables. They grow under the ground, and have green shoots above the ground. 胡萝卜 **2** N-COUNT Something that is offered to people in order to persuade them to do something can be referred to as a **carrot**. Something that is meant to persuade people not to do something can be referred to in the same sentence as a "stick." 诱饵 ❑ *Why the new emphasis on sticks instead of diplomatic carrots?* 为什么不再抛出外交诱饵，反而重新侧重大棒威胁？
→ see **vegetable**

car·ry ♦♦♦ /kæri/ (**carries, carrying, carried**) **1** V-T If you **carry** something, you take it with you, holding it so that it does not touch the ground. 提; 抱 ❑ *He was carrying a briefcase.* 他提着公文包。 ❑ *She carried her son to the car.* 她抱着儿子向车走去。 **2** V-T If you **carry** something, you have it with you wherever you go. 携带 ❑ *You have to carry a pager so that they can call you in at any time.* 你得带个传呼机，以便他们随时可以联系到你。

Do not confuse **carry** and **lift**. When you **carry** something, you move it from one place to another without letting it touch the ground. When you **lift** something, you move it upwards using your hands or a machine. After you have lifted it, you may **carry** it to a different place.

3 V-T If something **carries** a person or thing somewhere, it takes them there. 传送 ❑ *Flowers are designed to attract insects which then carry the pollen from plant to plant.* 花儿天生就能吸引昆虫，昆虫则在植物之间传递花粉。 ❑ *The delegation was carrying a message of thanks to President Mubarak.* 代表团向穆巴拉克总统传达谢意。 **4** V-T If a person or animal **is carrying** a disease, they are infected with it and can pass it on to other people or animals. 携带 (病毒) ❑ *The test could be used to screen healthy people to see if they are carrying the virus.* 这项测试可以用来检查健康人群，看他们是否携带该病毒。 **5** V-T If an action or situation has a particular quality or consequence, you can say that it **carries** it. 具有; 带有 [no passive, no cont] ❑ *Check that any medication you're taking carries no risk for your developing baby.* 要确保服用的药物不会对你正在发育的胎儿造成危险。 **6** V-T If a quality or advantage **carries** someone into a particular position or through a difficult situation, it helps them to achieve that position or deal with that situation. 使位居; 使通过 ❑ *He had the ruthless streak necessary to carry him into the cabinet.* 他有着跻身内阁所必需的冷酷品性。 **7** V-T If you **carry** an idea or a method to a particular extent, you use or develop it to that extent. 运用; 发挥 ❑ *It's not such a new idea, but I carried it to extremes.* 这不是什么新想法，但我却把它发挥到了极致。 **8** V-T If a newspaper or poster **carries** a picture or a piece of writing, it contains it or displays it. 刊登 ❑ *Several papers carry the photograph of Mr. Anderson.* 好几家报纸都刊登了安德森先生的照片。 **9** V-T In a debate, if a proposal or motion **is carried**, a majority of people vote in favor of it. 以多数票通过 [usu passive] ❑ *A motion backing its economic policy was carried by 322 votes to 296.* 一项支持其经济政策的动议以322票对296票获得通过。 **10** V-T If a crime **carries** a particular punishment, a person who is found guilty of that crime will receive that punishment. 受 (某种处罚) [no cont] ❑ *It was a crime of espionage and carried the death penalty.* 那是间谍罪，处了死刑。 **11** V-I If a sound **carries**, it can be heard a long way away. (声音) 传得远 ❑ *Even in this stillness Leaphorn doubted if the sound would carry far.* 即使置身如此的宁静之中，利普霍恩仍然怀疑声音是否可以传得很远。 **12** V-T If you **carry yourself** in a particular way, you walk and move in that way. 带…姿态 ❑ *They carried themselves with great pride and dignity.* 他们带着非常骄傲和高贵的姿态。 **13** PHRASE If you **get carried away** or **are carried away**, you are so eager or excited about something that you do something hasty or foolish. 忘乎所以 ❑ *I got completely carried away and almost cried.* 我差点忘乎所以地叫出声来。 **14** **to carry weight** → see **weight**

▸ **carry off** PHRASAL VERB If you **carry** something **off**, you do it successfully. 成功应对 ❑ *He's got the experience and the authority to carry it off.* 他的经验和威望足以成事。

▸ **carry on** **1** PHRASAL VERB If you **carry on** doing something, you continue to do it. 继续 ❑ *The assistant carried on talking.* 那个助理接着谈了下去。 ❑ *Her bravery has given him the will to carry on with his life and his work.* 她的勇气激发了他继续生活和工作下去的意愿。 ❑ *His eldest son Joseph carried on his father's traditions.* 长子约瑟夫继承了他父亲的传统。 **2** PHRASAL VERB If you **carry on** an activity, you do it or take part in it for a period of time. 开展; 参与 ❑ *The consulate will carry on a political dialogue with Indonesia.* 领事馆将与印度尼西亚展开政治对话。

▸ **carry out** PHRASAL VERB If you **carry out** a threat, task, or instruction, you do it or act according to it. 实行 ❑ *The Social Democrats could still carry out their threat to leave the government.* 社会民主党人仍然可能实现其脱离政府的威胁。 ❑ *Police say they believe the attacks were carried out by nationalists.* 警方称他们认为这些袭击行为是民族主义分子发动的。

▸ **carry through** PHRASAL VERB If you **carry** something **through**, you do it or complete it, often in spite of difficulties. (常指不顾困难)完成 ❑ *We don't have the confidence that the U.N. will carry through a sustained program.* 我们没有信心的是，联合国能否将该项目长期坚持下去。

Thesaurus *carry* 另参见：
v. bear, bring, cart, haul, lug, move, tote, truck 1

carry·all /kæriɔl/ (**carryalls**) N-COUNT A **carryall** is a large bag made of nylon, canvas, or leather, which you use to carry your clothes and other possessions, for example when you are traveling. 大手提包 [mainly AM] ❑ *He shivered, humping his canvas carryall higher onto his shoulder.* 他打着哆嗦，把帆布包往肩上又挪了挪。

in BRIT, usually use **holdall**

car·ry·over /kærioʊvər/ (**carryovers**) N-COUNT If something is a **carryover from** an earlier time, it began during an earlier time but still exists or happens now. 遗留物 [usu sing] [AM]

in BRIT, use **carry-over**

❑ *Her love of these sandwiches was a carryover from the Depression, when she sometimes had nothing else to eat.* 她对三明治的钟爱是大萧条时期留下的后遗症，她那时往往没有别的东西可吃。

cart /kɑrt/ (**carts, carting, carted**) 1 N-COUNT A **cart** is an old-fashioned wooden vehicle that is used for transporting goods or people. Some carts are pulled by animals. 老式板车 ❑ *...a country where horse-drawn carts far outnumber cars.* …一个马拉车远多于汽车的国家。 2 N-COUNT A **cart** is a small vehicle with a motor. 小型机动车 [AM] ❑ *Cars are prohibited, so transportation is by electric cart or by horse and buggy.* 由于汽车被禁止使用，交通依赖于电车或轻便马车。 3 N-COUNT A **cart** or a **shopping cart** is a large metal basket on wheels which is provided by stores such as supermarkets for customers to use while they are in the store. 购物推车 [AM]

in BRIT, use **trolley**

4 V-T If you **cart** things or people somewhere, you carry them or transport them there, often with difficulty. (常指费力地) 运送 [INFORMAL] ❑ *After their parents died, one of their father's relatives carted off the entire contents of the house.* 他们的父母死后，其父的一个亲戚把这所房子里所有的东西都运走了。 ❑ *...a neat tote bag for carting around your child's books or toys.* …用来装孩子的书本和玩具的精致手袋。
→ see **golf, hotel**

carte blanche /kɑrt blɒnʃ/ N-UNCOUNT If someone gives you **carte blanche**, they give you the authority to do whatever you think is right. 全权 ❑ *They gave him carte blanche to make decisions.* 他们让他全权决定。

car·tel /kɑrtɛl/ (**cartels**) N-COUNT A **cartel** is an association of similar companies or businesses that have grouped together in order to prevent competition and to control prices. 卡特尔；同业联盟 [BUSINESS] ❑ *...a drug cartel.* …药业联盟。

car·ti·lage /kɑrtɪlɪdʒ/ (**cartilages**) N-VAR **Cartilage** is a strong, flexible substance in your body, especially around your joints and in your nose. 软骨 ❑ *Andre Agassi has pulled out of next week's Grand Slam Cup after tearing a cartilage in his chest.* 安德烈・阿加西胸部软骨拉伤后已退出了下周的大满贯赛事。
→ see **shark**

▲ **car·ton** /kɑrtᵊn/ (**cartons**) 1 N-COUNT A **carton** is a plastic or cardboard container in which food or drink is sold. (盛装卖品的)盒 ❑ *A quart carton of milk is cheaper than two single pints.* 一夸脱的盒装牛奶比两盒一品脱的要便宜。 2 N-COUNT You can use **carton** to refer to the carton and its contents, or to the contents only. 盒；盒装物 ❑ *He went to the store for a carton of milk.* 他到店里买了一盒牛奶。 3 N-COUNT A **carton** is a large, strong cardboard box in which goods are stored and transported. 硬纸箱 [AM] ❑ *Those cartons contain the archives of The New Yorker for the years 1925 to 1980.* 那些纸箱里装着1925年到1980年的《纽约客》杂志存档。

car·toon /kɑrtun/ (**cartoons**) 1 N-COUNT A **cartoon** is a humorous drawing or series of drawings in a newspaper or magazine. 卡通；漫画 ❑ *Mickey Mouse, Donald Duck, and other Disney cartoon characters gave endless delight to millions of children.* 米老鼠、唐老鸭及其他迪斯尼卡通形象给数百万的儿童带来了无尽的欢乐。 2 N-COUNT A **cartoon** is a film in which all the characters and scenes are drawn rather than being real people or objects. 动画片 ❑ *...a TV set blares out a cartoon comedy.* …一台电视里播放着一部动画喜剧。
→ see **animation**

car·toon·ist /kɑrtunɪst/ (**cartoonists**) N-COUNT A **cartoonist** is a person whose job is to draw cartoons for newspapers and magazines. 漫画家

▲ **car·tridge** /kɑrtrɪdʒ/ (**cartridges**) 1 N-COUNT A **cartridge** is a metal or cardboard tube containing a bullet and an explosive substance. Cartridges are used in guns. 弹药筒 ❑ *Only four of the five spent cartridges were recovered by police.* 5个子弹壳中只有4个被警方收回。 2 N-COUNT A **cartridge** is part of a machine or device that can be easily removed and replaced when it is worn out or empty. (机器或装置中可替换的部分) 套筒 ❑ *Change the filter cartridge as often as instructed by the manufacturer.* 要按制造商要求的频率更换过滤套筒。

★ **carve** /kɑrv/ (**carves, carving, carved**) 1 V-T/V-I If you **carve** an object, you make it by cutting it out of a substance such as wood or stone. If you **carve** something such as wood or stone into an object, you make the object by cutting it out. 雕刻 ❑ *One of the prisoners has carved a beautiful wooden chess set.* 有名囚犯雕刻了一副精美的木制国际象棋。 ❑ *I picked up a piece of wood and started carving.* 我捡起一块木头，刻了起来。 2 → see also **carving** 3 V-T If you **carve** writing or a design **on** an object, you cut it into the surface of the object. 刻上 ❑ *He carved his name on his desk.* 他在书桌上刻了自己的名字。 4 V-T If you **carve** a piece of cooked meat, you cut slices from it so that you can eat it. 切 ❑ *Andrew began to carve the chicken.* 安德鲁动手切鸡肉。

▸ **carve out** PHRASAL VERB If you **carve out** a niche or a career, you succeed in getting the position or the career that you want by your own efforts. 凭自身努力获得 ❑ *Vick carved out his niche as the fastest quarterback in football.* 维克凭借自身努力成为了足球队中最快的四分卫。

▸ **carve up** PHRASAL VERB If you say that someone **carves** something **up**, you disapprove of the way they have divided it into small parts. 瓜分 [DISAPPROVAL] ❑ *He has set about carving up the company which Hammer created from almost nothing.* 他已着手瓜分哈默白手起家创办的公司。

carv·ing /kɑrvɪŋ/ (**carvings**) 1 N-COUNT A **carving** is an object or a design that has been cut out of a material such as stone or wood. 雕刻品 ❑ *...a wood carving of a human hand.* …一尊人手木雕。 2 N-UNCOUNT **Carving** is the art of carving objects, or of carving designs or writing on objects. 雕刻艺术 ❑ *I found wood carving satisfying, and painting fun.* 我从木雕中感到了满足，从绘画中体会到了乐趣。

cas·cade /kæskeɪd/ (**cascades, cascading, cascaded**) 1 N-COUNT If you refer to a **cascade of** something, you mean that there is a large amount of it. 大量 [LITERARY] ❑ *The women have lustrous cascades of black hair.* 这些女子长着浓密而有光泽的黑发。 2 V-I If water **cascades** somewhere, it pours or flows downward very fast and in large quantities. 倾泻 ❑ *She hung on as the freezing, rushing water cascaded past her.* 冰冷刺骨的急流冲刷着她，但她仍然坚持着。

case
1 INSTANCES AND OTHER ABSTRACT MEANINGS
2 CONTAINERS
3 GRAMMAR TERM

Word Link *cas ≈ box, hold : case, encase, suitcase*

1 **case** ♦♦♦ /keɪs/ (**cases**) 1 N-COUNT A particular **case** is a particular situation or incident, especially one that you are using as an individual example or instance of something. 状况 ❑ *Surgical training takes at least nine years, or 11 in the case of obstetrics.* 外科培训至少需要9年，产科则要11年。 ❑ *In extreme cases, insurance companies can prosecute for fraud.* 在极个别情况下，保险公司会起诉骗保行为。 2 N-COUNT A **case** is a person or their particular problem that a doctor, social worker, or other professional is dealing with. 事例 ❑ *Dr. Thomas Bracken describes the case of a 45-year-old Catholic priest much given to prayer whose left knee became painful.* 托马斯・布拉肯医生描述了那个病例：一名45岁天主教牧师由于经常祈祷导致左膝疼痛。 ❑ *Some cases of arthritis respond to a gluten-free diet.* 不含谷蛋白粘胶质的饮食对一些关节炎病例有疗效。 3 N-COUNT If you say that someone is a sad **case** or a hopeless **case**, you mean that they are in a sad situation or a hopeless situation. (可怜的、无可救药的) 人 ❑ *I knew I was going to make it – that I wasn't a hopeless case.* 我知道自己能行——我不是无药可救的人。 4 → see also **basket case** 5 N-COUNT A **case** is a crime or mystery that the police are investigating. 案件

C

❑ *The police have several suspects in the case of five murders committed in Gainesville, Florida.* 警方就佛罗里达州盖恩斯维尔市的5起谋杀案已经锁定了几名嫌疑人。 6 N-COUNT The **case for** or **against** a plan or idea consists of the facts and reasons used to support it or oppose it. 事实；根据 ❑ *He sat there while I made the case for his dismissal.* 他坐在那儿，听我讲着他被解雇的原因。 ❑ *Both these facts strengthen the case against hanging.* 这两大事实都是反对绞刑的充实理由。 7 N-COUNT In law, a **case** is a trial or other legal inquiry. 诉讼 ❑ *It can be difficult for public figures to win a libel case.* 公众人物要赢得诽谤诉讼是有难度的。 8 → see also **test case** 9 PHRASE You say **in any case** when you are adding something which is more important than what you have just said, but which supports or corrects it. 再者 [EMPHASIS] ❑ *The concert was sold out, and in any case, most of the people gathered in the square could not afford the price of a ticket.* 音乐会的票已售完，再说，聚在广场上的人也大都买不起票。 10 PHRASE If you do something **in case** or **just in case** a particular thing happens, you do it because that thing might happen. 以防 ❑ *In case anyone was following me, I made an elaborate detour.* 我特意绕了一圈，以防有人跟踪。 11 PHRASE If you do something or have something **in case of** a particular thing, you do it or have it because that thing might happen or be true. 以免 ❑ *Many stores along the route have been boarded up in case of trouble.* 沿途很多商店都用板封上了，以免招来麻烦。 12 PHRASE You use **in case** in expressions like "in case you didn't know" or "in case you've forgotten" when you are telling someone in a rather irritated way something that you think is either obvious or none of their business. 难道 [FEELINGS] ❑ *She's nervous about something, in case you didn't notice.* 她对某些事情神经兮兮的，难道你没注意到？ 13 PHRASE You say **in that case** or **in which case** to indicate that what you are going to say is true if the possible situation that has just been mentioned actually exists. 那样的话 ❑ *Perhaps you've some doubts about the attack. In that case it may interest you to know that Miss Woods witnessed it.* 或许你对本次袭击有些怀疑。要是那样的话，你可能会有兴趣了解伍兹小姐目睹了一切。 14 PHRASE You can say that you are doing something **just in case** to refer vaguely to the possibility that a thing might happen or be true, without saying exactly what it is. 以防万一 ❑ *I guess we've already talked about this but I'll ask you again just in case.* 我想我们已经讨论过了这个问题，但为保险起见，我再问你一次。 15 PHRASE If you say that a task or situation is **a case of** a particular thing, you mean that it consists of that thing or can be described as that thing. …的事 ❑ *It's not a case of whether anyone would notice or not.* 这不是人们会不会注意到的问题。 16 PHRASE If you say that something **is the case**, you mean that it is true or correct. 情况是那样 ❑ *You'll probably notice her having difficulty swallowing. If this is the case, give her plenty of liquids.* 你可能会发现她吞咽有困难，要真是那样，多给她一些流质食物。

→ see **hospital**

Word Partnership *case* 的常用搭配:

- N. **worst case scenario** 1 1
- **court case** 1 7
- V. **make a case** 1 6
- **argue a case** 1 6 7
- **lose/win a case** 1 7
- PREP. **in any case** 1 9
- **just in case** 1 12 14
- **in that case, in which case** 1 13

2 case /keɪs/ (**cases**) 1 N-COUNT A **case** is a container that is specially designed to hold or protect something. 容器；箱子；盒 ❑ *...a black case for his glasses.* …他的黑色眼镜盒。 2 → see also **bookcase, briefcase**

3 case /keɪs/ (**cases**) 1 N-COUNT In the grammar of many languages, the **case** of a group such as a noun group or adjective group is the form it has which shows its relationship to other groups in the sentence. (语法) 格 2 → see also **lowercase, uppercase**

case study (**case studies**) N-COUNT A **case study** is a written account that gives detailed information about a person, group, or thing and their development over a period of time. 个案研究 ❑ *...a large case study of malaria in West African children.* …一个关于西非儿童疟疾的大型个案研究。

cash ♦♦◊ /kæʃ/ (**cashes, cashing, cashed**) 1 N-UNCOUNT **Cash** is money in the form of bills and coins rather than checks. 现金 ❑ *...two thousand dollars in cash.* …2000美元现金。 2 → see also **hard cash, petty cash** 3 N-UNCOUNT **Cash** means the same as money, especially money which is immediately available. 现钱 [INFORMAL] ❑ *...a state-owned financial-services group with plenty of cash.* …一家有大量现钱的国有金融机构。 4 V-T If you **cash** a check, you exchange it at a bank for the amount of money that it is worth. 兑现 ❑ *There are similar charges if you want to cash a check or withdraw money at a branch other than your own.* 如果你在其他银行兑现支票或支取现金，也将收取类似的费用。

▸ **cash in** 1 PHRASAL VERB If you say that someone **cashes in on** a situation, you are criticizing them for using it to gain an advantage, often in an unfair or dishonest way. 从…中牟利 [DISAPPROVAL] ❑ *Residents said local gang leaders had cashed in on the violence to seize valuable land.* 居民们说地方帮会头目曾经从暴力掠取宝贵土地中牟利。 2 PHRASAL VERB If you **cash in** something such as an insurance policy, you exchange it for money. 兑现 ❑ *Avoid cashing in a policy early as you could lose out heavily.* 不要提前兑现保单，因为那样你会损失惨重。

cash bar (**cash bars**) N-COUNT A **cash bar** is a bar at a party or similar event where guests can buy drinks. 吧台 ❑ *At 6 p.m. there will be a reception and cash bar.* 下午6点钟有招待会和饮料吧台。

cash cow (**cash cows**) N-COUNT In business, a **cash cow** is a product or investment that steadily continues to be profitable. 摇钱树 [BUSINESS] ❑ *The retail division is BT's cash cow.* 零售部是英国电信公司的摇钱树。

cash dis·pens·er (**cash dispensers**) N-COUNT A **cash dispenser** is a machine built into the wall of a bank or other building, which allows people to take out money from their bank account using a special card. 取款机 [BRIT]

in AM, use **ATM**

cash flow also **cash-flow** N-UNCOUNT The **cash flow** of a firm or business is the movement of money into and out of it. 现金流通 [BUSINESS] ❑ *The company ran into cash-flow problems and faced liquidation.* 公司的现金流通出现了问题，面临清算。

cash·ier /kæʃɪər/ (**cashiers**) N-COUNT A **cashier** is a person who customers pay money to or get money from in places such as stores or banks. 出纳员；收银员

cash·ier's desk (**cashier's desks**) N-COUNT A **cashier's desk** is a place in a large store where you pay for the things you want to buy. 收银台 [AM]

cash·mere /kæʒmɪər/ N-UNCOUNT **Cashmere** is a kind of very fine, soft wool. 开士米羊绒 ❑ *...a big, soft cashmere sweater.* …一件又宽大又柔软的开士米羊绒衫。

cash·point /kæʃpɔɪnt/ (**cashpoints**) N-COUNT A **cashpoint** is the same as a **cash dispenser**. 取款机 [BRIT]

cash reg·is·ter (**cash registers**) N-COUNT A **cash register** is a machine in a store, bar, or restaurant that is used to add up and record how much money people pay, and in which the money is kept. 收银机

cash-starved ADJ A **cash-starved** company or organization does not have enough money to operate properly, usually because another organization, such as the government, is not giving them the money that they need. 缺乏资金的 [BUSINESS, JOURNALISM] ❑ *We are heading for a crisis, with cash-starved councils forced to cut back on vital community services.* 我们正面临危机，几个资金匮乏的理事会不得不削减一些重要的公共服务项目。

★ **ca·si·no** /kəsiːnoʊ/ (**casinos**) N-COUNT A **casino** is a building or room where people play gambling games such as roulette. 赌场

cas·se·role /kæsəroʊl/ (**casseroles**) 1 N-COUNT A **casserole** is a dish made of meat and vegetables that have been cooked slowly in a liquid. (由肉和蔬菜做成的) 炖菜 ❑ *...a huge beef casserole, full of herbs, vegetables, and wine.* …一大份的炖牛肉，里面满是香草、蔬菜和酒。 2 N-COUNT A **casserole** or a **casserole dish** is a large heavy container with a lid. You cook casseroles and other dishes in it. 砂锅 ❑ *Place all the chopped vegetables into a casserole dish.* 把切好的蔬菜全放进砂锅里。

cas·sette /kəsɛt/ (**cassettes**) N-COUNT A **cassette** is a small, flat, rectangular plastic case containing magnetic tape which is used for recording and playing back sound or film. 磁带 [also "on" N] ❑ *His two albums released on cassette have sold 10 million copies.* 他以磁带形式发行的两张专辑已售出1000万份。

cast ♦♦◇ /kæst/ (**casts, casting**)

The form **cast** is used in the present tense and is the past tense and past participle.

1 N-COUNT-COLL The **cast** of a play or movie is all the people who act in it. 全体演员 ❑ *The show is very amusing and the cast is very good.* 表演非常有趣，演员都很优秀。 2 V-T To **cast** an actor **in** a play or film means to choose them to act a particular role in it. 选…扮演角色 ❑ *The world premiere of Harold Pinter's new play casts Ian Holm in the lead role.* 哈罗德·品特新戏的首次全球公演选择伊恩·霍姆扮演主要角色。 ❑ *He was cast as a college professor.* 他被选扮演大学教授这个角色。 3 V-T If you **cast** your eyes or **cast** a look in a particular direction, you look quickly in that direction. 扫视 [WRITTEN] ❑ *He cast a stern glance at the two men.* 他严厉地瞪了那两名男子一眼。 ❑ *I cast my eyes down briefly.* 我往下瞅了瞅。 4 V-T If something **casts** a light or shadow somewhere, it causes it to appear there. 投射 [WRITTEN] ❑ *The moon cast a bright light over the yard.* 月亮在院子里撒下清辉。 5 V-T To **cast** doubt **on** something means to cause people to be unsure about it. 使人生疑 ❑ *Last night a top criminal psychologist cast doubt on the theory.* 昨晚，一位顶级的犯罪心理学家让人对该理论生疑。 6 V-T When you **cast** your vote in an election, you vote. 投票 ❑ *About ninety-five per cent of those who cast their votes approve the new constitution.* 95%的人投票赞成新宪法。 7 V-T To **cast** an object means to make it by pouring a liquid such as hot metal into a specially shaped container and leaving it there until it becomes hard. 铸造 ❑ *Our door knocker is cast in solid brass.* 我们的门环是纯铜铸造的。 8 N-COUNT A **cast** is a model that has been made by pouring a liquid such as plaster or hot metal onto something or into something, so that when it hardens it has the same shape as that thing. 模型 ❑ *An orthodontist took a cast of the inside of Billy's mouth to make a dental plate.* 正牙医师从比利的口腔内部取了模型来制作齿板。 9 N-COUNT A **cast** is the same as a **plaster cast.** 石膏模型 10 to **cast** your **mind back** → see **mind**
→ see **election, vote**

▸ **cast aside** PHRASAL VERB If you **cast aside** someone or something, you get rid of them because they are no longer necessary or useful to you. 消除；废除 ❑ *We need to cast aside outdated policies.* 我们要废除不合时宜的政策。

caste /kæst/ (**castes**) 1 N-COUNT A **caste** is one of the traditional social classes into which people are divided in a Hindu society. 印度的种姓 ❑ *Most of the upper castes worship the goddess Kali.* 大部分的印度上层种姓都信奉卡莉女神。 2 N-UNCOUNT **Caste** is the system of dividing people in a society into different social classes. 种姓制度 ❑ *Caste is defined primarily by social honor attained through personal lifestyle.* 种姓制度的定义源于通过个人生活方式而获取的社会荣誉。

cas·ti·gate /kæstɪgeɪt/ (**castigates, castigating, castigated**) V-T If you **castigate** someone or something, you speak to them angrily or criticize them severely. 谴责 [FORMAL] ❑ *Marx never lost an opportunity to castigate colonialism.* 马克思从不放过任何谴责殖民主义的机会。

cast·ing vote (**casting votes**) N-COUNT When a committee has given an equal number of votes for and against a proposal, the chairperson can give a **casting vote.** This vote decides whether or not the proposal will be passed. (指赞成票和反对票持平时会议主席所投的)决定票 ❑ *The vote was tied and a union leader used his casting vote in favor of the return to work.* 由于票数相同，一名工会领导投了决定票支持复工。

cast iron 1 N-UNCOUNT **Cast iron** is iron which contains a small amount of carbon. It is hard and cannot be bent so it has to be made into objects by casting. 铸铁 ❑ *Made from cast iron, it is finished in graphite enamel.* 该物由铸铁制成，表面以石墨搪瓷抛光。 2 ADJ A **cast-iron** guarantee or alibi is one that is absolutely certain to be effective and will not fail you. 确保有效的 ❑ *They would have to offer cast-iron guarantees to invest in long-term projects.* 他们不得不有效确保长期项目的投资。
→ see **pan**

cas·tle ♦◇◇ /kæsᵊl/ (**castles**) N-COUNT A **castle** is a large building with thick, high walls. Castles were built by important people, such as kings, in former times, especially for protection during wars and battles. 城堡

cas·trate /kæstreɪt/ (**castrates, castrating, castrated**) V-T To **castrate** a male animal or a man means to remove his testicles. 阉割 ❑ *In the ancient world, it was probably rare to castrate a dog or cat.* 古时候可能很少阉割猫或狗。 ● **cas·tra·tion** /kæstreɪʃᵊn/ N-VAR (**castrations**) 阉割 ❑ *...the castration of male farm animals.* …对农场雄性禽畜的阉割。

cas·ual /kæʒuəl/ 1 ADJ If you are **casual**, you are, or you pretend to be, relaxed and not very concerned about what is happening or what you are doing. 放松的 ❑ *It's difficult for me to be casual about anything.* 要我轻松待事有难度。 ● **casu·al·ly** ADV 放松地 [ADV with v] ❑ *"No need to hurry," Ben said casually.* "不必匆忙，"本轻松地说道。 2 ADJ A **casual** event or situation happens by chance or without planning. 不经意的 [ADJ n] ❑ *What you mean as a casual remark could be misinterpreted.* 你不经意所说的话可能会被误解。 3 ADJ **Casual** clothes are ones that you normally wear at home or on vacation, and not on formal occasions. (服装) 休闲的 [ADJ n] ❑ *I also bought some casual clothes for the weekend.* 我还买了些休闲服准备周末穿。 ● **casu·al·ly** ADV 休闲地 ❑ *They were casually dressed.* 他们穿着休闲。 4 ADJ **Casual** work is done for short periods and not on a permanent or regular basis. 临时的 [mainly BRIT]

in AM, use **temporary**

★ **casu·al·ty** ♦◇◇ /kæʒuəlti/ (**casualties**) 1 N-COUNT A **casualty** is a person who is injured or killed in a war or in an accident. 死伤者 ❑ *Troops fired on the demonstrators causing many casualties.* 军队向示威的人群开火，造成不少伤亡。 2 N-COUNT A **casualty of** a particular event or situation is a person or a thing that has suffered badly as a result of that event or situation. 受害者 ❑ *The car industry has been one of the greatest casualties of the recession.* 汽车工业是经济不景气最大的受害者之一。 3 N-UNCOUNT **Casualty** is the part of a hospital where people who have severe injuries or sudden illnesses are taken for emergency treatment. 急救室 [BRIT]

in AM, use **emergency room**

cat ♦◇◇ /kæt/ (**cats**) 1 N-COUNT A **cat** is a furry animal that has a long tail and sharp claws. Cats are often kept as pets. 猫 2 N-COUNT **Cats** are lions, tigers, and other wild animals in the same family. 猫科动物 ❑ *The lion is perhaps the most famous member of the cat family.* 狮子可能是猫科家族里最有名的成员了。 3 → see also **fat cat**
→ see **pet**

cata·log /kætᵊlɒg/ (**catalogs**) also **catalogue** 1 N-COUNT A **catalog** is a list of things such as the goods you can buy from a particular company, the objects in a museum, or the books in a library. 目录 ❑ *...the world's biggest seed catalog.* …世界上最大的种子目录。 2 N-COUNT A **catalog of** similar things, especially bad things, is a number of them considered or discussed one after another. 一连串 (尤指不幸的事) ❑ *His story is a catalog of misfortune.* 他的经历中充满了接二连三的厄运。
→ see **library**

cata·lyst /kætᵊlɪst/ (**catalysts**) 1 N-COUNT You can describe a person or thing that causes a change or event to happen as a **catalyst.** 催化剂 ❑ *I very much hope that this case will prove to be a catalyst for change.* 我非常希望这件事终将成为促成变化的催化剂。 2 N-COUNT In chemistry, a **catalyst** is a substance that causes a chemical reaction to take place more quickly. 催化剂

cata·pult /kætəpʌlt/ (**catapults, catapulting, catapulted**) 1 V-T/V-I If someone or something **catapults** or **is catapulted** through the air, they are thrown very suddenly, quickly, and violently through it. 弹射 ❑ *We've all seen enough dummies catapulting through windshields in TV warnings to know the dangers of not wearing seat belts.* 我们都已经看过将假人从挡风玻璃后弹射出来的电视节目，警告人们不系安全带会招致危险。 2 V-T/V-I If something **catapults** you into a particular state or situation, or if you **catapult** there, you are suddenly and unexpectedly caused to be in that state or situation. 使突然处于；突然处于 ❑ *"Basic Instinct" catapulted her to top status Hollywood.* 《本能》这部电影使她一跃成为好莱坞顶级明星。 3 N-COUNT A **catapult** is a device for shooting small stones. It is made of a Y-shaped stick with a piece of elastic tied between the two top posts. 弹弓 [BRIT]

in AM, use **slingshot**

cata·ract /kætərækt/ (**cataracts**) N-COUNT **Cataracts** are layers over a person's eyes that prevent them from seeing properly. Cataracts usually develop because of old age or illness. 白内障 ❑ *In one study, light smokers were found to be more than twice as likely to get cataracts as non-smokers.* 一项研究表明，轻度烟民患白内障的比例是不吸烟者的两倍以上。

C

★ **ca·tas·tro·phe** /kətæstrəfi/ (**catastrophes**) N-COUNT A **catastrophe** is an unexpected event that causes great suffering or damage. 灾难 ❑ *From all points of view, war would be a catastrophe.* 从各个方面来看，战争都会是一场灾难。

cata·stroph·ic /kætəstrɒfɪk/ 1 ADJ Something that is **catastrophic** involves or causes a sudden terrible disaster. 灾难性的 ❑ *A tidal wave caused by the earthquake hit the coast causing catastrophic damage.* 地震引发的海啸袭击了海岸，造成了灾难性的损失。❑ *The water shortage in this country is potentially catastrophic.* 该国水资源的匮乏很可能是灾难性的。 2 ADJ If you describe something as **catastrophic**, you mean that it is very bad or unsuccessful. 极糟的；失败的 ❑ *...another catastrophic attempt to arrest control from a rival Christian militia.* …和敌对基督徒民兵组织争夺控制权的再次惨败。

catch
❶ HOLD OR TOUCH
❷ MANAGE TO SEE, HEAR, OR TALK TO
❸ OTHER USES
❹ PHRASAL VERBS

❶ **catch** ♦♦◇ /kætʃ/ (**catches, catching, caught**)
➪ **Please look at meaning 6 to see if the expression you are looking for is shown under another headword.** 1 V-T If you **catch** a person or animal, you capture them after chasing them, or by using a trap, net, or other device. 捉住；捕获 ❑ *Police say they are confident of catching the gunman.* 警方说他们有信心抓获枪手。❑ *Where did you catch the fish?* 你在哪儿捕到了这条鱼？ 2 V-T If you **catch** an object that is moving through the air, you seize it with your hands. 接住 ❑ *I jumped up to catch a ball and fell over.* 我跳起来接球，结果摔倒了。● N-COUNT **Catch** is also a noun. 接住 ❑ *He missed the catch and the game was lost.* 他没接住球，输了这场比赛。 3 V-T If you **catch** a part of someone's body, you take or seize it with your hand, often in order to stop them from going somewhere. 抓住；握住 ❑ *Liz caught his arm.* 利兹抓住了他的胳膊。❑ *He knelt beside her and caught her hand in both of his.* 他跪在她旁边，双手握住她的手。 4 V-T If one thing **catches** another, it hits it accidentally or manages to hit it. 打击；击中 ❑ *The stinging slap almost caught his face.* 这狠狠的一巴掌差点打在他的脸上。❑ *I may have caught him with my elbow but it was just an accident.* 我的胳膊肘可能碰了他，不过那只是个意外。 5 V-I If something **catches on** or **in** an object, it accidentally becomes attached to the object or stuck in it. 绊住；卡住 ❑ *Her ankle caught on a root, and she almost lost her balance.* 她的脚踝绊到一个树根上，身体差点失去平衡。 6 **to catch hold of something** → see **hold**

Thesaurus *catch* 另参见：
V. apprehend, arrest, capture, grab, nab, seize, snatch, trap; *(ant.)* free, let go, let off, release ❶ 1

❷ **catch** ♦♦◇ /kætʃ/ (**catches, catching, caught**)
➪ **Please look at meaning 9 to see if the expression you are looking for is shown under another headword.** 1 V-T When you **catch** a bus, train, or plane, you get on it in order to travel somewhere. 搭上；赶上（车、飞机等）❑ *We were in plenty of time for Anthony to catch the ferry.* 我们有足够的时间等安东尼搭上渡船。 2 V-T If you **catch** someone doing something wrong, you see or find them doing it. 撞见；发现 ❑ *He caught a youth breaking into a car.* 他撞见一青年正在撬一辆车。❑ *I don't want to catch you pushing yourself into the picture to get some personal publicity.* 我不想看到你为出点风头而抢镜头。 3 V-T If you **catch yourself** doing something, especially something surprising, you suddenly become aware that you are doing it. （突然）发觉 ❑ *I caught myself feeling almost sorry for poor Mr. Laurence.* 我突然发觉自己几乎是在为可怜的劳伦斯先生感到难过了。 4 V-T If you **catch** something or **catch** a glimpse of it, you notice it or manage to see it briefly. 瞥见；突然看到 ❑ *As she turned back she caught the puzzled look on her mother's face.* 她转身时瞥到母亲一脸茫然的神情。 5 V-T If you **catch** something that someone has said, you manage to hear it. 听到 ❑ *His ears caught a faint cry.* 他的耳朵听到微弱的哭声。❑ *I do not believe I caught your name.* 我想我没听清你的名字。 6 V-T If you **catch** a TV or radio program or an event, you manage to see or listen to it. 收看；收听 ❑ *Bill turns on the radio to catch the local news.* 比尔打开收音机收听地方新闻。 7 V-T If you **catch** someone, you manage to contact or meet them to talk to them, especially when they are just about to go somewhere else. 联系上 ❑ *I dialed Elizabeth's number thinking I might catch her before she left for work.* 我拨了伊丽莎白的电话号码，心想我或许能赶在她动身上班前和她取得联系。 8 V-T If something or someone **catches** you by surprise or at a bad time, you were not expecting them or do not feel able to deal with them. 惊扰 ❑ *She looked as if the photographer had caught her by surprise.* 她看起来好像是被摄影师吓了一跳。❑ *I'm sorry but I just cannot say anything. You've caught me at a bad time.* 很抱歉我真的无可奉告。你找我找得很不是时候。 9 **to catch sight of something** → see **sight**

❸ **catch** ♦♦◇ /kætʃ/ (**catches, catching, caught**)
➪ **Please look at meaning 8 to see if the expression you are looking for is shown under another headword.** 1 V-T If something **catches** your attention or your eye, you notice it or become interested in it. 引起（注意、兴趣）；吸引住 ❑ *My shoes caught his attention.* 我的鞋子引起了他的注意。 2 V-T If you **catch** a cold or a disease, you become ill with it. 患上；染上（疾病）❑ *The more stress you are under, the more likely you are to catch a cold.* 你所受的压力越大，越有可能患感冒。 3 V-T If something **catches** the light or if the light **catches** it, it reflects the light and looks bright or shiny. 受（光）照射；（光）照射于 ❑ *They saw the ship's guns, catching the light of the moon.* 他们看到船上的枪支映着月光闪闪发亮。 4 V-T PASSIVE If you **are caught** in a storm or other unpleasant situation, it happens when you cannot avoid its effects. 遭遇（暴风雨、不幸）❑ *When he was fishing off the island he was caught in a storm and almost drowned.* 他离岛出海钓鱼时遭遇暴风雨袭击，差点被淹死。 5 V-T PASSIVE If you **are caught between** two alternatives or two people, you do not know which one to choose or follow. 左右为难 ❑ *The Jordanian leader is caught between both sides in the dispute.* 这位约旦元首夹在争执双方之间左右为难。 6 N-COUNT A **catch** on a window, door, or container is a device that fastens it. 窗钩；门闩；扣子 ❑ *She fiddled with the catch of her bag.* 她拨弄着提包的锁扣。 7 N-COUNT A **catch** is a hidden problem or difficulty in a plan or an offer that seems surprisingly good. 隐藏的困难；意料不到的情况 ❑ *The catch is that you work for your supper, and the food and accommodations can be very basic.* 问题在于你工作是为了顿饭，而且吃住条件非常一般。 8 **to catch fire** → see **fire**

Word Partnership *catch* 的常用搭配：
N. catch **a fish** ❶ 1
catch **a ball** ❶ 2
catch **a bus/flight/plane/train** ❷ 1
catch **a thief** ❷ 2
catch **your attention**, catch **your eye** ❸ 1
V. **play** catch ❶ 2
PREP. catch **on** ***something*** ❶ 5

❹ **catch** ♦♦◇ /kætʃ/ (**catches, catching, caught**)
▸ **catch on** 1 PHRASAL VERB If you **catch on to** something, you understand it, or realize that it is happening. 懂得；领悟 ❑ *He got what he could out of me before I caught on to the kind of person he'd turned into.* 他尽其所能从我处得到一切后，我才明白他已蜕变成什么样的人。 2 PHRASAL VERB If something **catches on**, it becomes popular. 流行 ❑ *The idea has been around for ages without catching on.* 这个观点由来已久，但一直未风行。
▸ **catch up** 1 PHRASAL VERB If you **catch up with** someone who is in front of you, you reach them by walking faster than they are walking. 赶上（某人）❑ *I stopped and waited for her to catch up.* 我停下来等她赶上。 2 PHRASAL VERB To **catch up with** someone means to reach the same standard, stage, or level that they have reached. （在标准、进度、水平上）追上 ❑ *Most late developers will catch up with their friends.* 绝大多数发育晚的人都将赶上他们的朋友们。❑ *John began the season better than me but I have fought to catch up.* 约翰起步的时机比我好，但我还是努力追赶上了。 3 PHRASAL VERB If you **catch up on** an activity that you have not had much time to do recently, you spend time doing it. 赶做；补做 ❑ *I was catching up on a bit of reading.* 我正赶着读点东西。 4 PHRASAL VERB If you **catch up** on friends who you have not seen for some time or on their lives, you talk to them and find out what has happened in their lives since you last talked together. 叙旧 ❑ *The ladies spent some time catching up on each other's health and families.* 女士们花了些时间聊聊彼此的健康和家庭情况。 5 PHRASAL VERB If you **are caught up in** something, you are involved in it, usually unwillingly. 被卷入（通常是不情愿地）❑ *The people themselves weren't part of the conflict; they were just caught up in it.* 这些人本身并未参与到这场冲突中，他们只是被卷进去而已。
▸ **catch up with** 1 PHRASAL VERB When people **catch up with** someone who has done something wrong, they succeed in

finding them in order to arrest or punish them. 逮捕 ❑ *The law caught up with him yesterday.* 他于昨日落入法网。 **2** PHRASAL VERB If something **catches up with** you, you are forced to deal with something unpleasant that happened or that you did in the past, which you have been able to avoid until now. 让(某人)尝到恶果 ❑ *Although he subsequently became a successful businessman, his criminal past caught up with him.* 虽然他后来成了一位成功的商人，但他的犯罪前科却让他尝到了恶果。

catch·word /kætʃwɜrd/ (**catchwords**) N-COUNT A **catchword** is a word or phrase that becomes popular or well-known, for example, because it is associated with a political campaign. 标语；口号(常用在政治运动中) ❑ *The catchword he and his supporters have been using is "consolidation."* 他和他的支持者们一直在用的口号是"统一"。

catchy /kætʃi/ (**catchier, catchiest**) ADJ If you describe a tune, name, or advertisement as **catchy**, you mean that it is attractive and easy to remember. (乐曲、名字、广告) 引人注意的；容易记住的 ❑ *The songs were both catchy and cutting.* 这些歌曲易上口且尖刻。

cat·egori·cal /kætɪgɔrɪkᵊl/ ADJ If you are **categorical** about something, you state your views very definitely and firmly. 断然的 ❑ *...his categorical denial of the charges of sexual harassment.* …他对性骚扰指控的断然否定。 ● **cat·egori·cal·ly** /kætɪgɔrɪkli/ ADV 断然地 [ADV with V] ❑ *They totally and categorically deny the charges.* 他们断然全盘否认了这些指控。

cat·ego·rise /kætɪgəraɪz/ [BRIT] → see **categorize**

cat·ego·rize /kætɪgəraɪz/ (**categorizes, categorizing, categorized**)

in BRIT, also use **categorise**

V-T If you **categorize** people or things, you divide them into sets or you say which set they belong to. 把…分类 ❑ *Lindsay, like his films, is hard to categorize.* 就像他演的电影难于归类一样，很难说林赛属于哪一类演员。 ❑ *Make a list of your child's toys and then categorize them as sociable or antisocial.* 把你孩子的玩具列个清单，然后将之分为交际型和非交际型。 ● **cat·ego·ri·za·tion** /kætɪgərɪzeɪʃᵊn/ N-VAR (**categorizations**) 分类 ❑ *Her first novel defies easy categorization.* 她的处女作小说不容易归类。

cat·ego·ry ♦◇◇ /kætɪgɔri/ (**categories**) N-COUNT If people or things are divided into **categories**, they are divided into groups in such a way that the members of each group are similar to each other in some way. 种类；范畴 ❑ *This book clearly falls into the category of fictionalized autobiography.* 这本书显然类属自传体小说。

Thesaurus *category* 另参见：

N. class, classification, grouping, kind, rank, sort, type

★ **ca·ter** /keɪtər/ (**caters, catering, catered**) **1** V-I To **cater to** a group of people means to provide all the things that they need or want. 满足…需要；迎合 ❑ *We cater to an exclusive clientele.* 我们满足一个特殊客户群的需求。 **2** V-I To **cater to** something means to take it into account. 考虑 ❑ *Exercise classes cater to all levels of fitness.* 训练课照顾到各种健康状况。 ❑ *...shops that cater to the needs of men.* … 经营男士用品的商店。 **3** V-T If a person or company **caters** an occasion such as a wedding or a party, they provide food and drink for all the people there. (在婚礼、派对等场合) 提供餐饮服务；承办酒席 ❑ *...a full-service restaurant equipped to cater large events.* …一家承办大型活动及提供全方位服务的饭店。 **4** → see also **catering**

ca·ter·er /keɪtərər/ (**caterers**) N-COUNT **Caterers** are people or companies that provide food and drink for a place such as an office or for special occasions such as weddings and parties. (为办公、婚礼、派对等的) 餐饮供应者；酒席承办者 ❑ *The caterers were already laying out the tables for lunch.* 酒宴承办者已经在摆午餐的饭桌了。

ca·ter·ing /keɪtərɪŋ/ N-UNCOUNT **Catering** is the activity of providing food and drink for a large number of people, for example, at weddings and parties. (婚礼、派对等的) 餐饮供应；酒席承办 [also "the" N, oft N n] ❑ *His catering business made him a millionaire at 41.* 他的酒宴承办生意使他在41岁时成为了百万富翁。

cat·er·pil·lar /kætərpɪlər/ (**caterpillars**) N-COUNT A **caterpillar** is a small, worm-like animal that feeds on plants and eventually develops into a butterfly or moth. 毛虫

★ **ca·thedral** /kəθidrəl/ (**cathedrals**) N-COUNT A **cathedral** is a very large and important church which has a bishop in charge of it. 大教堂；主教座堂 ❑ *...St. Paul's Cathedral.* …圣保罗大教堂。

★ **Catho·lic** ♦◇◇ /kæθlɪk/ (**Catholics**) **1** ADJ The **Catholic** Church is the branch of the Christian Church that accepts the Pope as its leader and is based in the Vatican in Rome. 天主教的 ❑ *...the Catholic Church.* …天主教会。 ❑ *...Catholic priests.* …天主教教士。 **2** ADJ If you describe a collection of things or people as **catholic**, you are emphasizing that they are very varied. 广泛的 ❑ *He was a man of catholic tastes, a lover of grand opera, history, and the fine arts.* 他是一个兴趣广泛的人，爱好大歌剧、历史和美术。 **3** N-COUNT A **Catholic** is a member of the Catholic Church. 天主教徒 ❑ *At least nine out of ten Mexicans are baptized Catholics.* 至少十分之九的墨西哥人是受过洗礼的天主教徒。

C

Ca·tholi·cism /kəθɒlɪsɪzəm/ N-UNCOUNT **Catholicism** is the traditions, the behavior, and the set of Christian beliefs that are held by Catholics. 天主教的教义 ❑ *...her conversion to Catholicism.* … 她对天主教的皈依。

cat·nip /kætnɪp/ N-UNCOUNT **Catnip** is an herb with scented leaves, which cats are fond of. 樟脑草(其香气吸引猫) ❑ *Catnip grows wild in much of the United States.* 樟脑草野生于美国的诸多地区。

cat·tle /kætᵊl/ N-PLURAL **Cattle** are cows and bulls. 牛 ❑ *...the finest herd of beef cattle for two hundred miles.* …方圆200英里内最佳的肉牛群。 → see **dairy**

cat·walk /kætwɔk/ (**catwalks**) **1** N-COUNT At a fashion show, the **catwalk** is a narrow platform that models walk along to display clothes. 时装表演台；T 形台 ❑ *On the catwalk the models stomped around in thigh-high leather boots.* T形台上，时装模特儿穿着长及大腿的皮靴，噔噔地走来走去。 **2** N-COUNT A **catwalk** is a narrow bridge high in the air, for example between two parts of a tall building, on the outside of a large structure, or over a stage. (连接两栋大楼的或设在舞台上方的) 天桥 ❑ *...a catwalk overlooking a vast room.* …俯瞰一个大房间的天桥。

Cau·ca·sian /kɔkeɪʒən/ (**Caucasians**) ADJ A **Caucasian** person is a white person. 白种人的 [FORMAL] ❑ *...a 25-year-old Caucasian male.* …一位25岁的白种男子。 ● N-COUNT A **Caucasian** is someone who is Caucasian. 白人 ❑ *Ann Hamilton was a Caucasian from New England.* 安·汉密尔顿是来自新英格兰的白人。

cau·cus /kɔkəs/ (**caucuses**) N-COUNT A **caucus** is a group of people within an organization who share similar aims and interests or who have a lot of influence. (机构中的) 核心组织 [FORMAL] ❑ *...the Black Caucus of minority congressmen.* …由少数派国会议员组成的黑人核心组织。

caught /kɔt/ **Caught** is the past tense and past participle of **catch**. **catch**的过去式和过去分词

Word Link *cal, caul ≈ hot, heat : calorie, cauldron, scald*

caul·dron /kɔldrən/ (**cauldrons**) N-COUNT A **cauldron** is a very large, round metal pot used for cooking over a fire. (金属) 大锅 [LITERARY] ❑ *...a witch's cauldron.* …一个女巫的大锅。

▲ **cau·li·flow·er** /kɔliflaʊər/ (**cauliflowers**) N-VAR **Cauliflower** is a large, round vegetable that has a hard, white center surrounded by green leaves. 花椰菜

cause ♦♦♦ /kɔz/ (**causes, causing, caused**) **1** N-COUNT The **cause** of an event, usually a bad event, is the thing that makes it happen. 起因；原因 ❑ *Smoking is the biggest preventable cause of death and disease.* 吸烟是造成不必要疾病和死亡的最大原因。 **2** N-COUNT A **cause** is an aim or principle which a group of people supports or is fighting for. 奋斗目标；事业 ❑ *Refusing to have one leader has not helped the cause.* 拒绝接受领导无益于该事业。 **3** V-T To **cause** something, usually something bad, means to make it happen. 引起 ❑ *The insecticide used on some weeds can cause health problems.* 喷洒在野草上的杀虫剂会引发各种健康问题。 ❑ *This was a genuine mistake, but it did cause me some worry.* 这纯属失误，但它确实令我有些不安。 **4** N-UNCOUNT If you have **cause for** a particular feeling or action, you have good reasons for feeling it or doing it. 理由 ❑ *Only a few people can find any cause for celebration.* 只有少数人能找到庆祝的理由。 **5** PHRASE If you say that something is **for a good cause**, you mean that it is worth doing or giving to because it will help other people, for example by raising money for charity. 为了高尚的事业(如慈善捐赠) ❑ *The Raleigh International Bike Ride is open to anyone who wants to raise money for a good cause.* 罗利国际自行车骑行会欢迎有志为慈善事业筹钱者参加。

Thesaurus *cause* 另参见：

V. generate, make, produce, provoke; *(ant.)* deter, prevent, stop **3**

C

Word Partnership *cause* 的常用搭配:

V. **determine the cause** 1
support a cause 2
N. **cause of death** 1
cause **an accident**, cause **cancer**, cause **problems**,
cause **a reaction** 3
cause **for concern** 4

'cause /kʌz, kɔz/ also **cause** CONJ **'Cause** is an informal way of saying **because**. **because**的非正式表达 [SPOKEN] ❑ *Hopefully everybody's well-rested 'cause it could be a long day.* 希望大家都休息好了，因为这一天会很漫长。

Word Link *caut ≈ taking care : caution, cautious, precaution*

★ **cau·tion** /kɔʃᵊn/ (**cautions, cautioning, cautioned**) 1 N-UNCOUNT **Caution** is great care which you take in order to avoid possible danger. 谨慎 ❑ *Extreme caution should be exercised when buying used tires.* 买二手轮胎时一定要极其谨慎。 2 V-T/V-I If someone **cautions** you, they warn you about problems or danger. 警告; 告诫 ❑ *Tony cautioned against misrepresenting the situation.* 托尼告诫说不要歪曲事实。 ❑ *The statement clearly was intended to caution Seoul against attempting to block the council's action again.* 很显然，这份声明用意在于警告首尔别再试图阻止委员会的行动。 ● N-UNCOUNT **Caution** is also a noun. 警告; 告诫 ❑ *There was a note of caution for the treasury in the figures.* 这些数据向财政部亮出了一个警告。 3 **to err on the side of caution** → see **err**

cau·tion·ary /kɔʃənɛri/ ADJ A **cautionary** story or a **cautionary** note to a story is one that is intended to give a warning to people. 警告的; 告诫的 ❑ *Barely fifteen months later, it has become a cautionary tale of the pitfalls of international mergers and acquisitions.* 15个月刚过，这便成了一个有关国际并购陷阱的警世故事。

cau·tious ♦◇◇ /kɔʃəs/ ADJ Someone who is **cautious** acts very carefully in order to avoid possible danger. 谨慎的 ❑ *The scientists are cautious about using enzyme therapy on humans.* 科学家们对于人体使用酶疗法持谨慎态度。 ● **cau·tious·ly** ADV 谨慎地 ❑ *David moved cautiously forward and looked over the edge.* 大卫小心翼翼地向前移动，视线越过边缘看过去。

Thesaurus *cautious* 另参见:

ADJ. alert, careful, guarded, watchful; (*ant.*) careless, rash, reckless

cava·lier /kævəlɪər/ ADJ If you describe a person or their behavior as **cavalier**, you are criticizing them because you think that they do not consider other people's feelings or take account of the seriousness of a situation. 目空一切的; 漫不经心的 [DISAPPROVAL] ❑ *The editor takes a cavalier attitude to the concept of fact checking.* 该编辑对事实核查持漫不经心的态度。

▲ **cav·al·ry** /kævᵊlri/ 1 N-SING **The cavalry** is the part of an army that uses armored vehicles for fighting. 装甲部队 ❑ *The 3rd Cavalry went on the offensive.* 第3装甲兵团继续发动进攻。 2 N-SING **The cavalry** is the group of soldiers in an army who ride horses. 骑兵团 ❑ *...a young cavalry officer.* …一位年轻的骑兵军官。

Word Link *cav ≈ hollow : cave, cavity, excavate*

cave ♦◇◇ /keɪv/ (**caves, caving, caved**) N-COUNT A **cave** is a large hole in the side of a cliff or hill, or one that is under the ground. 洞穴 ❑ *Outside the cave mouth the blackness of night was like a curtain.* 洞口外面，漆黑的夜晚宛如一块幕布。

▸ **cave in** 1 PHRASAL VERB If something such as a roof or a ceiling **caves in**, it collapses inward. (屋顶、天花板等) 坍塌 ❑ *Part of the roof has caved in.* 部分屋顶已经坍塌了。 2 PHRASAL VERB If you **cave in**, you suddenly stop arguing or resisting, especially when people put pressure on you to stop. 屈服; (在压力下) 突然停止争辩或反抗 ❑ *After a ruinous strike, the union caved in.* 在一次造成极大破坏的罢工之后，工会妥协了。 ❑ *The judge has caved in to political pressure.* 迫于政治压力，法官屈服了。

▲ **cav·ern** /kævərn/ (**caverns**) N-COUNT A **cavern** is a large, deep cave. 巨穴

cav·ern·ous /kævərnəs/ ADJ A **cavernous** room or building is very large inside, and so it reminds you of a cave. 巨穴般的; (房间或建筑物内) 如洞穴般空旷的 ❑ *Climbing steep stairs to the choir gallery you peer into a cavernous interior.* 登上陡峭的楼梯来到唱诗班楼座，你便可窥见如洞穴般空旷的内部。

cavi·ar /kæviar/ (**caviars**) also **caviare** N-MASS **Caviar** is the salted eggs of a fish called a sturgeon. 鱼子酱

★ **cav·ity** /kævɪti/ (**cavities**) 1 N-COUNT A **cavity** is a space or hole in something such as a solid object or a person's body. 洞; 腔 [FORMAL] ❑ *...a cavity in the roof.* …屋顶的一个洞。 2 N-COUNT In dentistry, a **cavity** is a hole in a tooth, caused by decay. (牙齿的) 龋洞 [TECHNICAL]
→ see **smell, teeth**

cc /si si/ 1 You use **cc** when referring to the volume or capacity of something such as the size of a car engine. **cc** is an abbreviation for "cubic centimeters." 立方厘米 ❑ *...1,500 cc sports cars.* …气缸容量为1500立方厘米的跑车。 2 **cc** is used in e-mail headers or at the end of a business letter to indicate that a copy is being sent to another person. (电子邮件或业务信函的) 转发 [BUSINESS] ❑ *...cc j.jones@harpercollins.co.uk.* …转发到j.jones@harpercollins.co.uk。 ❑ *...cc J. Chater, S. Cooper.* …转发给J.蔡特与S.库珀。

CCTV /si si ti vi/ N-UNCOUNT **CCTV** is an abbreviation for "closed-circuit television." 闭路电视 ❑ *...a CCTV camera.* …一台闭路电视摄像机。

CD ♦◇◇ /si di/ (**CDs**) N-COUNT **CDs** are small plastic discs on which sound, especially music, is recorded. **CDs** can also be used to store information which can be read by a computer. **CD** is an abbreviation for "compact disc." 激光唱片; 光盘 ❑ *The Beatles' Red and Blue compilations are issued on CD for the first time next month.* 甲壳虫乐队的《红与蓝》专辑中将在下个月首次以激光唱片形式发行。
→ see **DVD, laser**

CD burn·er (**CD burners**) N-COUNT A **CD burner** is a piece of computer equipment that you use for copying data from a computer onto a CD. 光盘刻录机 [COMPUTING] ❑ *Users can download MP3 music files and record them directly onto a CD audio disc using a PC CD burner.* 使用者可下载MP3音乐文件并用个人电脑光盘刻录机直接将其刻录到音频光盘上。

CD play·er (**CD players**) N-COUNT A **CD player** is a machine on which you can play CDs. 激光唱机; 光盘播放机

CD-ROM /si di rɒm/ (**CD-ROMs**) N-COUNT A **CD-ROM** is a CD on which a very large amount of information can be stored and then read using a computer. **CD-ROM** is an abbreviation for "compact disc read-only memory." 只读光盘 [COMPUTING] ❑ *A single CD-ROM can hold more than 500 megabytes of data.* 单单一张只读光盘就能存储500多兆的资料。

CD-ROM drive /si di rɒm draɪv/ (**CD-ROM drives**) N-COUNT A **CD-ROM drive** is the device that you use with a computer to play CD-ROMs. 光盘驱动器 [COMPUTING]

CD writ·er (**CD writers**) N-COUNT A **CD writer** is the same as a **CD burner**. 光盘刻录机 [COMPUTING]

cease ♦◇◇ /sis/ (**ceases, ceasing, ceased**) 1 V-I If something **ceases**, it stops happening or existing. 停止 [FORMAL] ❑ *At one o'clock the rain had ceased.* 一点钟时雨已经停了。 2 V-T If you **cease to** do something, you stop doing it. 停止; 不再 (做某事) [FORMAL] ❑ *He never ceases to amaze me.* 他总让我惊喜不断。 ❑ *The secrecy about the president's condition had ceased to matter.* 有关总统健康状况的秘密已经不再举足轻重了。 3 V-T If you **cease** something, you stop it happening or working. 停止 [FORMAL] ❑ *The Tundra Times, a weekly newspaper in Alaska, ceased publication this week.* 阿拉斯加的周报——《苔原时报》于本周停刊。

Thesaurus *cease* 另参见:

V. end, finish, halt, quit, shut down, stop; (*ant.*) begin, continue, start 1

cease·fire ♦◇◇ /sisfaɪər/ (**ceasefires**) N-COUNT A **ceasefire** is an arrangement in which countries or groups of people that are fighting each other agree to stop fighting. 停火; 休战 ❑ *They have agreed to a ceasefire after three years of conflict.* 他们在3年冲突之后同意停火。

▲ **ce·dar** /sidər/ (**cedars**) N-COUNT A **cedar** is a large evergreen tree with wide branches and small, thin leaves called needles. 雪松 ● N-UNCOUNT **Cedar** is the wood of this tree. 雪松木 ❑ *The yacht is built of cedar strip planking.* 这艘游艇用雪松木板材制成。

cede /sid/ (**cedes, ceding, ceded**) V-T If someone in a position of authority **cedes** land or power **to** someone else, they let them have the land or power, often as a result of military or political pressure. (迫于军事、政治压力) 割让; 让出 (领土、主权) [FORMAL] ❑ *Only a short campaign took place in Puerto Rico, but after the war Spain ceded the island to America.* 波多黎各岛仅经历了一场短暂的战斗，但大战后西班牙把该岛割让给了美国。

ceil·ing /siːlɪŋ/ (**ceilings**) **1** N-COUNT A **ceiling** is the horizontal surface that forms the top part or roof inside a room. 天花板 ❑ *The rooms were spacious, with tall windows and high ceilings.* 房间很宽敞，且窗户和屋顶都很高。 **2** N-COUNT A **ceiling on** something such as prices or wages is an official upper limit that cannot be broken. (价格、工资等的) 上限 ❑ *...an informal agreement to put a ceiling on salaries.* …一项规定工资上限的非正式协议。 **3** → see also **glass ceiling**

cel·ebrate ♦◇◇ /sɛlɪbreɪt/ (**celebrates, celebrating, celebrated**) **1** V-T/V-I If you **celebrate** an occasion or if you **celebrate**, you do something enjoyable because of a special occasion or to mark someone's success. 庆祝 ❑ *I was in a mood to celebrate.* 我很想庆祝一番。 ❑ *Dick celebrated his 60th birthday Monday.* 迪克星期一庆祝了他的60岁生日。 **2** V-T If an organization or country **is celebrating** an anniversary, it has existed for that length of time and is doing something special because of it. 庆祝 (周年纪念日) ❑ *The society is celebrating its tenth anniversary this year.* 该学会今年将举行10周年年庆。 **3** V-T When priests **celebrate** Holy Communion or Mass, they officially perform the actions and ceremonies that are involved. 主持 (圣餐或弥撒等宗教仪式) ❑ *Pope John Paul celebrated mass today in a city in central Poland.* 约翰·保罗教皇今天在位于波兰中心的一个城市主持了弥撒。

cel·ebrat·ed /sɛlɪbreɪtɪd/ ADJ A **celebrated** person or thing is famous and much admired. 著名的 ❑ *He was soon one of the most celebrated young painters in England.* 他很快就跻身于英国最著名的青年画家行列。

Word Link *ation ≈ state of : celebration, elevation, relaxation*

cel·ebra·tion ♦◇◇ /sɛlɪbreɪʃ°n/ (**celebrations**) **1** N-COUNT A **celebration** is a special enjoyable event that people organize because something pleasant has happened or because it is someone's birthday or anniversary. 庆祝活动 ❑ *I can tell you, there was a celebration in our house that night.* 跟你说吧，那天晚上我们在家里搞了个庆祝活动。 **2** N-SING The **celebration of** something is praise and appreciation which is given to it. 颂扬 ❑ *This was not a memorial service but a celebration of his life.* 这仪式不是追悼会，而是对他的生平的颂扬。

★ **ce·leb·rity** /sɪlɛbrɪti/ (**celebrities**) **1** N-COUNT A **celebrity** is someone who is famous, especially in areas of entertainment such as movies, music, writing, or sports. (尤指娱乐界的) 名人 ❑ *In 1944, at the age of 30, Hersey suddenly became a celebrity.* 1944年，30岁的赫西突然成了一位名人。 **2** N-UNCOUNT If a person or thing achieves **celebrity**, they become famous, especially in areas of entertainment such as movies, music, writing, or sports. (尤指娱乐界的) 名望 ❑ *He achieved celebrity as a sports commentator.* 他作为一名体育评论员而享誉四方。

cel·ery /sɛləri/ N-UNCOUNT **Celery** is a vegetable with long, pale green stalks. It is eaten raw in salads. 芹菜 ❑ *...a stick of celery.* …一根芹菜。

ce·les·tial /sɪlɛstʃəl/ ADJ **Celestial** is used to describe things relating to heaven or to the sky. 天上的; 天堂的 [LITERARY] ❑ *...the clusters of celestial bodies in the ever-expanding universe.* …不断扩展的宇宙中的这些天体群。

→ see **astronomer**

celi·ba·cy /sɛlɪbəsi/ N-UNCOUNT **Celibacy** is the state of being celibate. 独身; 禁欲 ❑ *...priests who violate their vows of celibacy.* …违反独身誓言的牧师们。

celi·bate /sɛlɪbɪt/ (**celibates**) **1** ADJ Someone who is **celibate** does not marry or have sex, because of their religious beliefs. (为宗教信仰而) 独身的; 禁欲的 ❑ *The Pope bluntly told the world's priests yesterday to stay celibate.* 教皇昨天直言告诫世界各地的牧师们要保持独身。 ● N-COUNT A **celibate** is someone who is celibate. (出于宗教信仰的) 独身者; 禁欲者 ❑ *...the U.S.A.'s biggest group of celibates.* …美国最大的独身宗教群体。 **2** ADJ Someone who is **celibate** does not have sex during a particular period of their life. (某段时间内) 禁欲的 ❑ *I was celibate for two years.* 我禁欲了两年。

cell ♦♦◇ /sɛl/ (**cells**) **1** N-COUNT A **cell** is the smallest part of an animal or plant that is able to function independently. Every animal or plant is made up of millions of cells. 细胞 ❑ *Those cells divide and give many other different types of cells.* 那些细胞分裂后形成许多其他不同类型的细胞。 ❑ *...blood cells.* …血细胞。 **2** N-COUNT A **cell** is a small room in which a prisoner is locked. A **cell** is also a small room in which a monk or nun lives. 小牢房; 小禅房 ❑ *Do you recall how many prisoners were placed in each cell?* 你记得每间牢房里关了多少犯人吗?

→ see **cellphone, clone, skin**

cel·lar /sɛlər/ (**cellars**) **1** N-COUNT A **cellar** is a room underneath a building, which is often used for storing things in. 地窖; 地下室 ❑ *The box of papers had been stored in a cellar at the family home.* 那盒文件已存放在家中的一个地窖里。 **2** N-COUNT A person's or restaurant's **cellar** is the collection of different wines that they have. 酒窖 ❑ *Choose a superb wine to complement your meal from our extensive wine cellar.* 从我们的大酒窖里挑一瓶上等好酒来配你这顿饭菜吧。

cel·list /tʃɛlɪst/ (**cellists**) N-COUNT A **cellist** is someone who plays the cello. 大提琴手

cel·lo /tʃɛloʊ/ (**cellos**) N-VAR A **cello** is a musical instrument with four strings that looks like a large violin. You play the cello with a bow while sitting down and holding it upright between your legs. 大提琴

→ see **orchestra, string**

cell·phone /sɛlfoʊn/ (**cellphones**) N-COUNT A **cellphone** is the same as a **cellular phone**. 移动电话 [mainly AM]

→ see Word Web: **cellphone**

★ **cel·lu·lar** /sɛlyələr/ ADJ **Cellular** means relating to the cells of animals or plants. 细胞的 ❑ *Many toxic effects can be studied at the cellular level.* 许多毒性作用在细胞阶段就可加以研究。

→ see Word Web: **cellphone**

cel·lu·lar phone (**cellular phones**) N-COUNT A **cellular phone** or **cellular telephone** is a type of telephone which does not need wires to connect it to a telephone system. 移动电话 [mainly AM]

in BRIT, usually use **mobile phone**

→ see **cellphone**

cel·lu·lite /sɛlyəlaɪt/ N-UNCOUNT **Cellulite** is lumpy fat which people may get under their skin, especially on their thighs. (尤指大腿部的) 皮下脂肪团 ❑ *...an Italian-made product that is said to eradicate cellulite within weeks.* …一种意大利生产的、据说可以在几周内消除赘肉的产品。

Celsius /sɛlsiəs/ ADJ **Celsius** is a scale for measuring temperature, in which water freezes at 0 degrees and boils at 100 degrees. It is represented by the symbol °C. 摄氏的 (简写为C) [n/num ADJ] ❑ *Highest temperatures 11° Celsius, that's 52° Fahrenheit.* 最高温度11摄氏度，即52华氏度。 ● N-UNCOUNT **Celsius** is also a noun. 摄氏温度 ❑ *The thermometer shows the temperature in Celsius and Fahrenheit.* 温度计显示摄氏温度和华氏温度。

ce·ment /sɪmɛnt/ (**cements, cementing, cemented**) **1** N-UNCOUNT **Cement** is a gray powder which is mixed with sand and water in order to make concrete. 水泥 ❑ *Builders have*

Word Web cellphone

The word **"cell"** does not refer to something inside the **cellular phone** itself. It describes the area around a **wireless transmitter**. The electrical system and **battery** in today's **mobile** phones are tiny. This makes their electronic **signals** weak. They can't travel very far. Therefore today's **cellular** phone systems need a lot of closely-spaced cells. When you make a call, your phone connects to the transmitter with the strongest signal. Then it chooses a **channel** and connects you to the number you dialed. If you are in a car, **stations** in several different cells may handle your call.

C

trouble getting the right amount of cement into their concrete. 建筑工人们不知道该往混凝土中加入多少水泥才合适。 **2** N-UNCOUNT **Cement** is the same as **concrete**. 混凝土 ❑ *...the hard, cold cement floor.* …坚硬冰冷的混凝土地面。 **3** N-UNCOUNT Glue that is made for sticking particular substances together is sometimes called **cement**. 胶合剂 ❑ *Stick the pieces on with tile cement.* 用瓷砖胶合剂把这些碎片粘上。 **4** V-T Something that **cements** a relationship or agreement makes it stronger. 巩固（关系、协约） ❑ *Nothing cements a friendship between countries so much as trade.* 没有任何东西能比贸易更能巩固国家间的友谊了。 **5** V-T If things **are cemented** together, they are stuck or fastened together. 使黏结 [usu passive] ❑ *Most artificial joints are cemented into place.* 绝大部分人造关节是被黏结复位的。

C

★ **cem·etery** /sɛmətɛri/ (**cemeteries**) N-COUNT A **cemetery** is a place where dead people's bodies or their ashes are buried. 墓地

cen·sor /sɛnsər/ (**censors, censoring, censored**) **1** V-T If someone in authority **censors** letters or the media, they officially examine them and cut out any information that is regarded as secret. 审查（信件或媒体） ❑ *The military-backed government has heavily censored the news.* 以军方为后盾的政府对新闻报道进行了严格审查。 **2** V-T If someone in authority **censors** a book, play, or movie, they officially examine it and cut out any parts that are considered to be immoral or inappropriate. 审查（书刊、剧本、电影） ❑ *The Late Show censored the band's live version of "Bullet in the Head."* 《深夜秀》节目组审查了该乐队现场演奏的曲目《脑里的子弹》。 **3** N-COUNT A **censor** is a person who has been officially appointed to examine letters or the media and to cut out any parts that are regarded as secret. （信件、媒体的官方）审查员 ❑ *The report was cleared by the American military censors.* 这篇报道被美国军方审查员删掉了。 **4** N-COUNT A **censor** is a person who has been officially appointed to examine plays, movies, and books and to cut out any parts that are considered to be immoral. （书刊、剧本、电影的官方）审查员 ❑ *The movie had to be cut before the board of censors accepted it.* 该电影得先进行剪切，才能得到审查委员会的认可。

Word Link *ship ≈ condition or state : censorship, citizenship, friendship*

★ **cen·sor·ship** /sɛnsərʃɪp/ N-UNCOUNT **Censorship** is the censoring of books, plays, movies, or reports, especially by government officials, because they are considered immoral or secret in some way. （官方对书刊、剧本、电影或新闻报道的）审查 ❑ *The government today announced that press censorship was being lifted.* 该政府今日宣告说正在撤销新闻审查。

▲ **cen·sure** /sɛnʃər/ (**censures, censuring, censured**) V-T If you **censure** someone **for** something that they have done, you tell them that you strongly disapprove of it. 谴责 [FORMAL] ❑ *The ethics committee may take a decision to admonish him or to censure him.* 道德规范委员会可能决定对他进行警告或批评。 ● N-UNCOUNT **Censure** is also a noun. 谴责 ❑ *It is a controversial policy which has attracted international censure.* 这是一条有争议的政策，已经遭到国际谴责。

★ **cen·sus** /sɛnsəs/ (**censuses**) N-COUNT A **census** is an official survey of the population of a country that is carried out in order to find out how many people live there and to obtain details of such things as people's ages and jobs. 人口普查 ❑ *The detailed assessment of the latest census will be ready in three months.* 有关最新人口普查的详细评估工作将在3个月内就绪。

→ see Word Web: **census**

Word Link *cent ≈ hundred : cent, century, percent*

cent /sɛnt/ (**cents**) N-COUNT A **cent** is a small unit of money worth one hundredth of some currencies, for example the dollar and the euro. 分（如美元、欧元等基本货币单位的1%） ❑ *A cup of rice which cost thirty cents a few weeks ago is now being sold for up to one dollar.* 几周前价值30美分的1杯米如今卖到了1美元。

cen·te·nary /sɛntɛnəri/ (**centenaries**) N-COUNT A **centenary** is the same as a **centennial**. 一百周年 [mainly BRIT]

Word Link *enn ≈ year : centennial, millennium, perennial*

cen·ten·nial /sɛntɛniəl/ N-SING The **centennial of** an event such as someone's birth is the 100th anniversary of that event. 一百周年纪念 [oft N n] [mainly AM] ❑ *The centennial Olympics was in Atlanta, Georgia.* 奥运会百年庆典在乔治亚州的亚特兰大举行。

cen·ter ◆◆◆ /sɛntər/ (**centers, centering, centered**)

in BRIT, use **centre**

1 N-COUNT The **center** of something is the middle of it. 中心 ❑ *A large, wooden table dominates the center of the room.* 一张大木桌占据了房间的中央。 **2** N-COUNT A **center** is a building where people have meetings, take part in a particular activity, or get help of some kind. （会议、活动、援助的）中心地点 ❑ *She now also does pottery classes at a community center.* 她现在还在社区中心上陶艺课。 **3** N-COUNT If an area or town is a **center** for an industry or activity, that industry or activity is very important there. （行业、活动的）中心；中枢 ❑ *New York is also a major international financial center.* 纽约也是一个重要的国际金融中心。 **4** N-COUNT The **center** of a town or city is the part where there are the most stores and businesses and where a lot of people come from other areas to work or shop. （镇、市的）中心区 ❑ *...the city center.* …市中心。 **5** N-COUNT If something or someone is at the **center of** a situation, they are the most important thing or person involved. 居中心地位的人或物 ❑ *...the man at the center of the controversy.* …处于争议中心的那位男子。 **6** N-SING If someone or something is the **center of** attention or interest, people are giving them a lot of attention. （关注、兴趣的）中心 ❑ *The rest of the cast was used to her being the center of attention.* 剧组的其他演员已经习惯了她成为众人关注的焦点。 **7** N-SING In politics, **the center** refers to groups and their beliefs, when they are considered to be neither left-wing nor right-wing. 中间派 ❑ *The Democrats have become a party of the center.* 民主党人士已经变成一个中间派团体。 **8** V-T/V-I If something **centers** or **is centered on** a particular thing or person, that thing or person is the main subject of attention. 使集中；集中 ❑ *...the improvement was the result of a plan which centered on academic achievement and personal motivation.* …该进步得益于一个强调学术成就和自我激励的方案。 ❑ *All his concerns were centered around himself rather than Rachel.* 他所有心思都集中在他自己而非雷切尔的身上。 ● **-centered** COMB IN ADJ 以…为中心的 ❑ *...a child-centered approach to teaching.* …以孩子为中心的教学方法。 **9** V-T/V-I If an industry or event **is centered** in a place, or if it **centers** there, it takes place to the greatest extent there. 使集中；集中 ❑ *The fighting has been centered around the town of Vucovar.* 战斗集中在武科瓦尔镇进行。 ❑ *The disturbances have centered around the two main university areas.* 骚乱集中发生在两所大学主校区。 **10** → see also **community center, shopping center**

→ see **soccer**

Word Web census

Every 10 years the U.S. government conducts a **census**. This **survey counts** the number of people and provides details about the way they live. It determines how many delegates each state sends to the House of Representatives. It also affects how the federal government spends its money. The census takes months to complete. In March, the Census Bureau* mails out around 100 million **questionnaires**. Government employees also deliver about 22 million more forms in person. In April, census workers visit people who haven't returned their forms. All the information must be pulled together by December 31 of that year.

Census Bureau: a part of the government that collects and reports data about the population and economy.

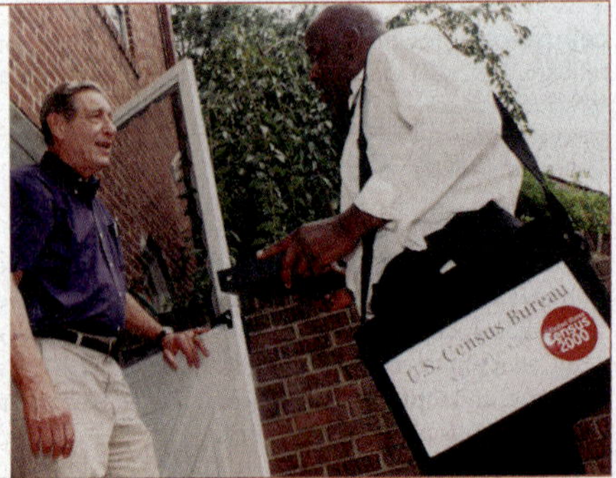

Word Partnership *center* 的常用搭配：

N. center **of a circle** 1
adult education center, **research** center 2
city/town center 4
center **of attention** 6

-centered /-sɛntərd/
in BRIT, use **-centred**
1 COMB IN ADJ **-centered** can be added to adjectives and nouns to indicate what kind of a center something has. 中心有…的；以…为中心的 ❑ *...lemon-centered white chocolates.* …柠檬夹心的白巧克力。
2 → see also **center, self-centered**

center·piece /sɛntərpis/ (**centerpieces**)
in BRIT, use **centrepiece**
1 N-COUNT The **centerpiece of** something is the best or most interesting part of it. (最佳的最具吸引力的) 部分 ❑ *The centerpiece of the plan is the idea of regular referendums, initiated by voters.* 投票人提出的方案中最好的一点就是公民定期投票。 2 N-COUNT A **centerpiece** is an ornament which you put in the middle of something, especially a dinner table. (尤指餐桌上) 放在中央的装饰物 ❑ *He was arranging floral centerpieces in the banquet hall.* 他正在宴会大厅摆放餐桌中央的装饰花束。

cen·ti·grade /sɛntɪgreɪd/ ADJ **Centigrade** is a scale for measuring temperature, in which water freezes at 0 degrees and boils at 100 degrees. It is represented by the symbol °C. 摄氏的 (简写为C) ❑ *...daytime temperatures of up to forty degrees centigrade.* …高达40摄氏度的日间气温。 ● N-UNCOUNT **Centigrade** is also a noun. 摄氏 ❑ *The number at the bottom is the recommended water temperature in centigrade.* 底部的数字为建议性摄氏度水温。

cen·ti·me·ter /sɛntɪmitər/ (**centimeters**)
in BRIT, use **centimetre**
N-COUNT A **centimeter** is a unit of length in the metric system equal to ten millimeters or one-hundredth of a meter. 厘米 ❑ *...a tiny fossil plant, only a few centimeters high.* …一块小小的植物化石，只有几厘米高。

cen·ti·me·tre /sɛntɪmiːtəʳ/ [BRIT] → see **centimeter**

Word Link *centr ≈ middle : central, concentrated, decentralized*

cen·tral ♦♦♦ /sɛntrəl/ 1 ADJ Something that is **central** is in the middle of a place or area. 中心的；中部的 ❑ *...Central America's Caribbean coast.* …美国中部的加勒比海岸。 ❑ *The disruption has now spread and is affecting a large part of central Liberia.* 分裂活动范围如今已扩大，正影响着利比里亚中部的大部分地区。 ● **cen·tral·ly** ADV 在中心；在中央 ❑ *The main cabin has its full-sized double bed centrally placed with plenty of room around it.* 主舱正中摆了一张标准的双人床，床周围空间很大。 2 ADJ A place that is **central** is easy to reach because it is in the center of a city, town, or particular area. (地点) 近市中心的；在中心地带的 ❑ *...a central location in the capital.* …首都的一个中心地带。 ● **cen·tral·ly** ADV 在中心地带 ❑ *...this centrally located hotel, situated on the banks of the river.* …地处中心位置的这家旅馆，座落在河岸边。
3 ADJ A **central** group or organization makes all the important decisions that are followed throughout a larger organization or a country. 中央的；首要的 [ADJ n] ❑ *There is a lack of trust toward the central government in Rome.* 对罗马中央政府缺乏信任。 ● **cen·tral·ly** ADV 中央地；首要地 ❑ *This is a centrally planned economy.* 这是一种中央计划经济。 4 ADJ The **central** person or thing in a particular situation is the most important one. 最重要的 ❑ *Black dance music has been central to mainstream pop since the early '60s.* 黑人舞蹈音乐自20世纪60年代初以来对主流流行音乐一直都是最重要的。

Word Partnership *central* 的常用搭配：

N. central **location** 2
central **government** 3

cen·tral heat·ing N-UNCOUNT **Central heating** is a heating system for buildings. Air or water is heated in one place and travels around a building through pipes and radiators. 中央供暖系统 ❑ *I am thinking of installing central heating.* 我在考虑安装中央供暖系统。

cen·tral·ise /sɛntrəlaɪz/ [BRIT] → see **centralize**

cen·tral·ize /sɛntrəlaɪz/ (**centralizes, centralizing, centralized**)
in BRIT, also use **centralise**
V-T To **centralize** a country, state, or organization means to create a system in which one central group of people gives instructions to regional groups. 使归中央控制；集权的 ❑ *In the mass production era, multinational firms tended to centralize their operations.* 在大规模生产时期，跨国公司倾向于集中运营。 ● **cen·trali·za·tion** ★ /sɛntrəlɪzeɪʃᵊn/ N-UNCOUNT 集权化 ❑ *...public hostility to central banks and the centralization of power.* …公众对中央银行及集权的敌意。

cen·tre /sɛntər/ [BRIT] → see **center**

cen·tred /sɛntərd/ [BRIT] → see **centered**

-centred /-sɛntərd/ [BRIT] → see **-centered**

centre·piece /sɛntərpis/ [BRIT] → see **centerpiece**

cen·tu·ry ♦♦♦ /sɛntʃəri/ (**centuries**) 1 N-COUNT A **century** is a period of a hundred years that is used when stating a date. For example, the 19th century was the period from 1801 to 1900. 世纪 ❑ *The material position of the Church had been declining since the late eighteenth century.* 自18世纪晚期以来，教堂的世俗地位一直在下降。
2 N-COUNT A **century** is any period of a hundred years. 百年 ❑ *The drought there is the worst in a century.* 那里的旱情百年不遇。

CEO /si i oʊ/ (**CEOs**) N-COUNT **CEO** is an abbreviation for **chief executive officer.** 首席执行官

▲ **ce·ram·ic** /sɪræmɪk/ (**ceramics**) 1 N-MASS **Ceramic** is clay that has been heated to a very high temperature so that it becomes hard. 陶瓷 ❑ *...ceramic tiles.* …瓷砖。 2 N-COUNT **Ceramics** are ceramic ornaments or objects. 陶瓷制品 [usu pl] ❑ *...a collection of Chinese ceramics.* …中国陶瓷收藏品。 3 N-UNCOUNT **Ceramics** is the art of making artistic objects out of clay. 制陶艺术 ❑ *...a degree in ceramics.* …陶艺学学位。
→ see **pottery**

ce·real /sɪəriəl/ (**cereals**) 1 N-MASS **Cereal** or **breakfast cereal** is a food made from grain. It is mixed with milk and eaten for breakfast. 麦片 ❑ *I have a bowl of cereal every morning.* 我每天早上吃一碗麦片粥。 2 N-COUNT **Cereals** are plants such as wheat, corn, or rice that produce grain. (小麦、高粱、米等) 谷类植物 ❑ *...the cereal-growing districts of the Midwest.* …中西部生产谷类植物的地区。

cere·bral /sərɪbrəl/ 1 ADJ If you describe someone or something as **cerebral**, you mean that they are intellectual rather than emotional. 理智的；理性的 [FORMAL] ❑ *Washington struck me as a precarious place from which to publish such a cerebral newspaper.* 我觉得要在华盛顿这个地方出版一份这么理性的报纸前途未卜。 2 ADJ **Cerebral** means relating to the brain. 大脑的 [ADJ n] [MEDICAL] ❑ *...a cerebral hemorrhage.* …脑溢血。

cer·emo·nial /sɛrɪmoʊniəl/ 1 ADJ Something that is **ceremonial** relates to a ceremony or is used in a ceremony. 仪式的；礼仪的 [ADJ n] ❑ *He represented the nation on ceremonial occasions.* 他在礼仪场合代表着国家。 2 ADJ A position, function, or event that is **ceremonial** is considered to be representative of an institution, but has very little authority or influence. 礼仪性的 ❑ *Up to now the post of president has been largely ceremonial.* 到目前为止，总统职位在很大程度上是礼仪性的。
→ see **funeral**

Word Link *mony ≈ resulting state : ceremony, harmony, testimony*

cer·emo·ny ♦◇◇ /sɛrɪmoʊni/ (**ceremonies**) 1 N-COUNT A **ceremony** is a formal event such as a wedding. 仪式；典礼 ❑ *...his grandmother's funeral, a private ceremony attended only by the family.* …他祖母的葬礼，一场只有家人参加的私人仪式。
2 N-UNCOUNT **Ceremony** consists of the special things that are said and done on very formal occasions. (全套) 仪式 ❑ *The republic was proclaimed with great ceremony.* 以隆重的仪式宣告共和国成立。
→ see **graduation, wedding**

certain
1 BEING SURE
2 REFERRING TO AND INDICATING AMOUNT

❶ **cer·tain** ♦◇◇ /sɜrtᵊn/ 1 ADJ If you are **certain** about something, you firmly believe it is true and have no doubt about it. If you are not **certain** about something, you do not have definite knowledge about it. 确信的 [v-link ADJ] ❑ *She's absolutely certain she's going to make it in the world.* 她确信自己将享誉全球。
❑ *We are not certain whether the appendix had already burst or not.* 我们不能确定阑尾破了没有。 2 ADJ If you say that something is **certain to** happen, you mean that it will definitely happen. 肯定的；有把握的

C

❑ *However, the scheme is certain to meet opposition from fishermen's leaders.* 不过这个计划肯定会遭到渔夫头领们的反对。 ❑ *It's not certain they'll accept that candidate if he wins.* 如果那位候选人胜出，无法肯定他们是否会接受他。 ❑ *The prime minister is heading for certain defeat if he forces a vote.* 如果首相强令大家投票表决，那他一定会遭遇失败。 3 ADJ If you say that something is **certain**, you firmly believe that it is true, or have definite knowledge about it. 确凿的 [v-link ADJ] ❑ *One thing is certain, both have the utmost respect for each other.* 有一点是确定无疑的，即两人对彼此都非常敬重。 4 PHRASE If you know something **for certain**, you have no doubt at all about it. 肯定地 ❑ *She couldn't know what time he'd go, or even for certain that he'd go at all.* 她不知道他何时要走，甚至于还不能确定他究竟要不要走。 5 PHRASE If you **make certain that** something is the way you want or expect it to be, you take action to ensure that it is. 确保 ❑ *Parents should make certain that the children spend enough time doing homework.* 父母应该确保孩子花足够多的时间做作业。

Thesaurus *certain* 另参见：
ADJ. definite, known, positive, sure, true, unmistakable ❶ 1 3

❷ **cer·tain** ♦♦◇ /sɜrtᵊn/ 1 ADJ You use **certain** to indicate that you are referring to one particular thing, person, or group, although you are not saying exactly which it is. 某 [det ADJ, ADJ n] ❑ *There will be certain people who'll say "I told you so!"* 会有某些人说，"我告诉过你了！" ❑ *You owe a certain person a sum of money.* 你欠着某人一笔钱。 2 ADJ You use **a certain** to indicate that something such as a quality or condition exists, and often to suggest that it is not great in amount or degree. 稍微的 ❑ *That was the very reason why he felt a certain bitterness.* 那正是他感到有点痛苦的原因。 3 QUANT When you refer to **certain of** a group of people or things, you are referring to some particular members of that group. 某些 [QUANT "of" def-pl-n] [FORMAL] ❑ *They'll have to give up completely on certain of their studies.* 他们将不得不完全放弃某些课程。

cer·tain·ly ♦♦◇ /sɜrtᵊnli/ 1 ADV You use **certainly** to emphasize what you are saying when you are making a statement. 的确；无疑地 [ADV with cl/group] [EMPHASIS] ❑ *The public is certainly getting tired of hearing about it.* 公众无疑厌倦了听这方面的事。 ❑ *The bombs are almost certainly part of a much bigger conspiracy.* 几乎可以确定这些炸弹是一个更大阴谋的一部分。 2 ADV You use **certainly** when you are agreeing with what someone has said. 当然 [ADV as reply] ❑ *"In any case you remained friends."—"Certainly."* "不管怎样，你们还是朋友。"——"那当然。" 3 ADV You say **certainly not** to say "no" in a strong way. 当然不 [ADV as reply] [EMPHASIS] ❑ *"Perhaps it would be better if I withdrew altogether."—"Certainly not!"* "我完全退出的话情况或许会好些。"——"当然不是。"

You use **certainly** to emphasize that what you say is definitely true. ❑ *His death was certainly not an accident.* You use **surely** to express disagreement or surprise. ❑ *Surely you care about what happens to her.* Both British and American speakers use **certainly** to agree with requests and statements. Note that American speakers also use **surely** in this way. ❑ *"Can I have a drink?"—"Why, surely."*

cer·tain·ty /sɜrtᵊnti/ (**certainties**) 1 N-UNCOUNT **Certainty** is the state of being definite or of having no doubts at all about something. 确定 ❑ *I have told them with absolute certainty there'll be no change of policy.* 我十分确定地告诉他们政策不会有变。 2 N-UNCOUNT **Certainty** is the fact that something is certain to happen. 必然的事 [also "a" N] ❑ *A general election became a certainty last week.* 普选上周已成必然。 ❑ *...the certainty of more violence and bloodshed.* …必然会有的更多的暴力和流血事件。 3 N-COUNT **Certainties** are things that nobody has any doubts about. 确定的事 [usu pl] ❑ *There are no certainties in modern Europe.* 现代欧洲无定事。

Word Link *cert ≈ determined : true : ascertain, certificate, certify*

cer·tifi·cate /sərtɪfɪkɪt/ (**certificates**) 1 N-COUNT A **certificate** is an official document stating that particular facts are true. 证明书 ❑ *...birth certificates.* …出生证明。 2 N-COUNT A **certificate** is an official document that you receive when you have completed a course of study or training. The qualification that you receive is sometimes also called a **certificate**. 结业证书 ❑ *To the right of the fireplace are various framed certificates.* 火炉右侧是各式各样加框的证书。
→ see **wedding**

★ **cer·ti·fy** /sɜrtɪfaɪ/ (**certifies, certifying, certified**) 1 V-T If someone in an official position **certifies** something, they officially state that it is true. 证明 ❑ *The president certified that the project would receive at least $650m from overseas sources.* 总统证实该工程将获得来自海外各种渠道的至少6.5亿美元的资金。 ❑ *The National Election Council is supposed to certify the results of the election.* 国家选举委员会将为选举结果作证。 ● **cer·ti·fi·ca·tion** ★ /sərtɪfɪkeɪʃᵊn/ N-VAR (**certifications**) 证明 ❑ *An employer can demand written certification that the relative is really ill.* 雇主可要求书面证明以证实这位亲属确实病了。 2 V-T If someone **is certified as** a particular kind of worker, they are given a certificate stating that they have successfully completed a course of training in their profession. 给…发证书 [usu passive] ❑ *They wanted to get certified as divers.* 他们想拿到潜水员资格证书。 ❑ *...a certified public accountant.* …一位注册会计师。 ● **cer·ti·fi·ca·tion** ★ N-UNCOUNT 合格证明 ❑ *Students would be offered on-the-job training leading to the certification of their skill in a particular field.* 学生将获得在职培训，他们也将因此得到在某一领域的技术合格证。

cer·vi·cal /sɜrvɪkᵊl/ 1 ADJ **Cervical** means relating to the cervix. 子宫颈的 [ADJ n] [MEDICAL] ❑ *Doctors aim to cut the number of women dying from cervical cancer by half this decade.* 医生们这十年的目标在于使死于宫颈癌的妇女人数减少一半。 2 ADJ **Cervical** means relating to the neck. 颈部的 [ADJ n] [MEDICAL] ❑ *...injury to the cervical spine from motor vehicle collisions.* …因机动车相撞导致的颈椎受伤。

cer·vix /sɜrvɪks/ (**cervixes** or **cervices** /sərvaɪsiz, sɜrvɪsiz/) N-COUNT The **cervix** is the entrance to the womb. 子宫颈 [MEDICAL]

cf. **cf.** is used in writing to introduce something that should be considered in connection with the subject you are discussing. 参阅 ❑ *For the more salient remarks on the matter, cf. "Isis Unveiled," Vol. I.* 关于此事更显著的评议可参阅《揭开面纱的伊西斯》第一卷。

CFC /si ɛf si/ (**CFCs**) N-COUNT **CFCs** are gases that are used in things such as aerosols and refrigerators and can cause damage to the ozone layer. **CFC** is an abbreviation for "chlorofluorocarbon." 含氯氟烃（用于冰箱、喷雾器等） ❑ *...the continued drop in CFC emissions.* …含氯氟烃释放量的持续下降。

chain ♦◇◇ /tʃeɪn/ (**chains, chaining, chained**) 1 N-COUNT A **chain** consists of metal rings connected together in a line. 链子 ❑ *His open shirt revealed a fat gold chain.* 他敞开的衬衣里露出一条粗大的金链子。 2 N-COUNT A **chain of** things is a group of them existing or arranged in a line. 一连串；一系列 ❑ *...a chain of islands known as the Windward Islands.* …被称为"向风群岛"的列岛。 3 N-COUNT A **chain of** stores, hotels, or other businesses is a number of them owned by the same person or company. 连锁店 ❑ *...a large supermarket chain.* …大型连锁超市。 4 N-PLURAL If prisoners are **in chains**, they have thick rings of metal around their wrists or ankles to prevent them from escaping. 镣铐 ❑ *He'd spent four and a half years in windowless cells, much of the time in chains.* 他在无窗的牢房里呆了4年半，大部分时间是镣铐加身。 5 V-T If a person or thing **is chained to** something, they are fastened to it with a chain. 用链条拴住 ❑ *The dogs were chained to a fence.* 狗被拴在栅栏上。 ❑ *We were sitting together in our cell, chained to the wall.* 我们一起坐在牢房里，还被铐在墙上。 ● PHRASAL VERB **Chain up** means the same as **chain**. 用链条拴住 ❑ *They kept me chained up every night and released me each day.* 他们每天晚上把我铐起来，白天再把我放出去。 6 N-SING A **chain of** events is a series of them happening one after another. 一连串；一系列 ❑ *...the bizarre chain of events that led to his departure in January 1938.* …导致他1938年1月离去的一连串怪异事件。
→ see **food**

Word Partnership *chain* 的常用搭配：

ADJ.	gold chain, silver chain 1
V.	break a chain 1 4 6
N.	department store chain, hotel chain, restaurant chain, supermarket chain 3

chair ♦♦◇ /tʃɛər/ (**chairs, chairing, chaired**) 1 N-COUNT A **chair** is a piece of furniture for one person to sit on, with a back and four legs. 椅子 ❑ *He rose from his chair and walked to the window.* 他从椅子上站起来走到窗户旁。 2 N-COUNT At a university, a **chair** is the position or job of professor. 大学教授 ❑ *He has been appointed to the chair of sociology.* 他受命任职社会学教授。 3 N-COUNT The person who is the **chair of** a committee or meeting is the person in charge of it. 主席 ❑ *She is the chair of the Defense Advisory Committee on Women in the Military.* 她是军队女兵国防顾问委员会的主席。 4 V-T If you **chair** a meeting or a committee, you are the person in charge of it. 担任（会议、委员会）主席 ❑ *He was about to chair a meeting in Venice of E.U. foreign ministers.* 他将担任威尼斯欧盟外交部长会议的主席。 **5** N-SING **The chair** is the same as the **electric chair**. 死刑电椅

chair·man ♦♦◊ /tʃɛərmən/ (**chairmen**) **1** N-COUNT The **chairman** of a committee, organization, or company is the head of it. （委员会、组织机构、公司的）主席 ❑ *Glyn Ford is chairman of the committee which produced the report.* 格林·福特是撰写该报告的委员会的主席。 **2** N-COUNT; N-VOC The **chairman** of a meeting or debate is the person in charge, who decides when each person is allowed to speak. （会议、辩论的）主持人 ❑ *The chairman declared the meeting open.* 主持人宣布会议开始。

chair·man·ship /tʃɛərmənʃɪp/ (**chairmanships**) N-VAR The **chairmanship** of a committee or organization is the fact of being its chairperson. Someone's **chairmanship** can also mean the period during which they are chairperson. 主席职位；主席任期 ❑ *The government has set up a committee under the chairmanship of Professor Roy Goode.* 该政府成立了一个委员会，由罗伊·古德教授担任主席。

chair·person /tʃɛərpɜrsᵊn/ (**chairpersons**) N-COUNT The **chairperson** of a meeting, committee, or organization is the person in charge of it. （会议）主持人；（委员会、组织的）主席 ❑ *She's the chairperson of the safety committee.* 她是安全委员会主席。

chair·woman /tʃɛərwʊmən/ (**chairwomen**) N-COUNT The **chairwoman** of a meeting, committee, or organization is the woman in charge of it. （会议）女主持人；（委员会、组织的）女主席 ❑ *Primakov was in Japan meeting with the chairwoman of the Socialist Party there.* 普里马科夫正在日本和那里的社会党女主席会面。

cha·let /ʃæleɪ/ (**chalets**) N-COUNT A **chalet** is a small wooden house, especially in a mountain area. （山区）小木屋 ❑ *...Swiss ski chalets.* …瑞士滑雪小木屋。

chalk /tʃɔk/ (**chalks, chalking, chalked**) **1** N-UNCOUNT **Chalk** is a type of soft, white rock. You can use small pieces of it for writing or drawing with. 白垩 ❑ *...white cliffs made of chalk.* …白垩绝壁。 **2** N-UNCOUNT **Chalk** is small sticks of chalk, or a substance similar to chalk, used for writing or drawing with. 粉笔 [also N in pl] ❑ *...somebody writing with a piece of chalk.* …正用粉笔写字的某人。 **3** V-T If you **chalk** something, you draw or write it using a piece of chalk. 用粉笔画；用粉笔写 ❑ *He chalked the message on the blackboard.* 他用粉笔把这条消息写在黑板上。

▸ **chalk up** PHRASAL VERB If you **chalk up** a success, a victory, or a number of points in a game, you achieve it. 取得（胜利、分）❑ *For almost 11 months, the Bosnian army chalked up one victory after another.* 在差不多十一个月的时间里，波斯尼亚军队取得了一个又一个的胜利。

chalk·board /tʃɔkbɔrd/ (**chalkboards**) N-COUNT A **chalkboard** is a dark-colored board that you can write on with chalk. Chalkboards are often used by teachers in the classroom. 黑板 [mainly AM]

in BRIT, use **blackboard**

❑ *The menu was on a chalkboard.* 菜单在黑板上。

chal·lenge ♦♦◊ /tʃælɪndʒ/ (**challenges, challenging, challenged**) **1** N-VAR A **challenge** is something new and difficult which requires great effort and determination. 挑战 ❑ *The new government's first challenge is the economy.* 新政府面临的第一项挑战是经济。 **2** N-VAR A **challenge to** something is a questioning of its truth or value. A **challenge to** someone is a questioning of their authority. 质疑 ❑ *The demonstrators have now made a direct challenge to the authority of the government.* 示威者现已对该政府的权威性提出了直截了当的质疑。 **3** PHRASE If someone **rises to the challenge**, they act in response to a difficult situation which is new to them and are successful. 奋起应对挑战 ❑ *The new Germany must rise to the challenge of its enhanced responsibilities.* 新德国必须奋起应对更艰巨的挑战。 **4** V-T If you **challenge** ideas or people, you question their truth, value, or authority. 质疑 ❑ *Democratic leaders have challenged the president to sign the bill.* 民主党领导人对总统签署这项法案存有质疑。 ❑ *The move was immediately challenged by two of the republics.* 这项提案立即遭到了这两个共和国的质疑。 **5** V-T If you **challenge** someone, you invite them to fight or compete with you in some way. 向…发出挑战 ❑ *Marsyas thought he could play the flute better than Apollo and challenged the god to a contest.* 玛息阿觉得他长笛吹得比阿波罗好，便向这位神发出挑战。 ❑ *He left a note at the scene of the crime, challenging detectives to catch him.* 他在作案现场留了一张纸条，挑衅侦探们去抓他。 ● N-COUNT **Challenge** is also a noun. 挑战 ❑ *A third presidential candidate emerged to mount a serious challenge and throw the campaign wide open.* 第3位总统候选人上场郑重发出挑战，令这次竞选充满悬念。 **6** → see also **challenging**

Word Partnership *challenge* 的常用搭配：

V.	**accept a** challenge, **present a** challenge **1** **5**
	dare to challenge **4** **5**
ADJ.	**biggest** challenge, **new** challenge **1** **5**
	legal challenge **5**

chal·leng·er /tʃælɪndʒər/ (**challengers**) N-COUNT A **challenger** is someone who competes with you for a position or title that you already have, for example being a sports champion or a political leader. 挑战者 ❑ *The strongest challenger, Texas Democrat Martin Frost, has withdrawn from the race.* 最强劲的挑战者，德克萨斯州的民主党人马丁·弗罗斯特已经退出了竞选。

chal·leng·ing /tʃælɪndʒɪŋ/ **1** ADJ A **challenging** task or job requires great effort and determination. 有挑战性的 ❑ *Mike found a challenging job as a computer programmer.* 迈克找到了一份富有挑战性的工作——当电脑程序师。 **2** ADJ If you do something in a **challenging** way, you seem to be inviting people to argue with you or compete against you in some way. 挑衅的 ❑ *Mona gave him a challenging look.* 莫娜挑衅地看了他一眼。

cham·ber ♦◊◊ /tʃeɪmbər/ (**chambers**) **1** N-COUNT A **chamber** is a large room, especially one that is used for formal meetings. 会议厅 ❑ *We are going to be in the council chamber every time he speaks.* 我们每次都在会议厅听他讲话。 **2** N-COUNT You can refer to a country's legislature or to one section of it as a **chamber**. 议院 ❑ *More than 80 parties are contesting seats in the two-chamber parliament.* 80多个政党在竞争该议会两院的席位。 **3** N-COUNT A **chamber** is a room designed and equipped for a particular purpose. （作特殊用途的）房间 ❑ *For many, the dentist's office remains a torture chamber.* 对许多人来说，牙科诊室仍是一间行刑室。

cham·ber of com·merce (**chambers of commerce**) N-COUNT A **chamber of commerce** is an organization of businesspeople that promotes local commercial interests. 商会 [BUSINESS]

champ /tʃæmp/ (**champs**) N-COUNT A **champ** is the same as a **champion**. 冠军 [oft n N] [INFORMAL] ❑ *...boxing champ Mike Tyson.* …拳击冠军迈克·泰森。

cham·pagne /ʃæmpeɪn/ (**champagnes**) N-MASS **Champagne** is an expensive French white wine with bubbles in. It is often drunk to celebrate something. 香槟酒

cham·pi·on ♦♦◊ /tʃæmpiən/ (**champions, championing, championed**) **1** N-COUNT A **champion** is someone who has won the first prize in a competition, contest, or fight. 冠军 ❑ *...a former Olympic champion.* …一位前奥运冠军。 ❑ *Kasparov became world champion.* 卡斯帕罗夫成了世界冠军。 **2** N-COUNT If you are a **champion of** a person, a cause, or a principle, you support or defend them. 拥护者；捍卫者 ❑ *He received acclaim as a champion of the oppressed.* 他作为被压迫者的捍卫者而受到了赞誉。 **3** V-T If you **champion** a person, a cause, or a principle, you support or defend them. 拥护；捍卫 ❑ *He passionately championed the poor.* 他曾热情地捍卫穷人。

Word Partnership *champion* 的常用搭配：

ADJ.	**defending** champion, **former** champion, **reigning** champion, **world** champion **1**
N.	champion **a cause** **3**

cham·pi·on·ship ♦♦◊ /tʃæmpiənʃɪp/ (**championships**) **1** N-COUNT A **championship** is a competition to find the best player or team in a particular sport. 锦标赛 ❑ *...the world chess championship.* …世界国际象棋锦标赛。 **2** N-SING **The championship** refers to the title or status of being a sports champion. 冠军称号 ❑ *He went on to take the championship.* 他继续卫冕了冠军称号。

chance ♦♦♦ /tʃæns/ (**chances, chancing, chanced**) **1** N-VAR If there is a **chance of** something happening, it is possible that it will happen. 可能性 ❑ *Do you think they have a chance of beating Australia?* 你认为他们有可能击败澳大利亚队吗？ ❑ *There was really very little chance that Ben would ever have led a normal life.* 那时本几乎不可能过上正常的生活。 **2** N-SING If you have a **chance to** do something, you have the opportunity to do it. 机会 ❑ *The electoral council announced that all eligible people would get a chance to vote.* 选举委员会曾宣布所有符合条件者都将获得投票机会。 ❑ *Most refugee doctors never get the chance to practice medicine in our hospitals.* 绝大部分难民医生在我们

C

C

的医院里从未得到行医的机会。 3 ADJ A **chance** meeting or event is one that is not planned or expected. 偶然的 [ADJ n] ❑ *...a chance meeting.* …一次邂逅。 ● N-UNCOUNT **Chance** is also a noun. 偶然;意外 ❑ *...a victim of chance and circumstance.* …一个时运不济的倒霉者。 4 V-T If you **chance** something, you do it even though there is a risk that you may not succeed or that something bad may happen. 冒…险 ❑ *Andy knew the risks. I cannot believe he would have chanced it.* 安迪知道那些风险，我不能相信他会冒那个险。 5 PHRASE Something that happens **by chance** was not planned by anyone. 偶然地;意外地 ❑ *He had met Mr. Maude by chance.* 他曾与莫德先生邂逅。 6 PHRASE You can use **by any chance** when you are asking questions in order to find out whether something that you think might be true is actually true. 可能 ❑ *Are they by any chance related?* 他们可能有关联吗? 7 PHRASE If you say that someone **stands a chance of** achieving something, you mean that they are likely to achieve it. If you say that someone doesn't **stand a chance of** achieving something, you mean that they cannot possibly achieve it. 有可能 ❑ *Being very good at science subjects, I stood a good chance of gaining high grades.* 我很擅长理科科目，所以很有可能得高分。 8 PHRASE When you **take a chance**, you try to do something although there is a large risk of danger or failure. 碰运气;冒险 ❑ *You take a chance on the weather if you vacation in Maine.* 你若在缅因州度假，对天气得碰运气。 ❑ *Retailers are taking no chances on unknown brands.* 零售商们不在无名品牌上冒险。

Word Partnership *chance* 的常用搭配:

N.	chance **of success**, chance **of survival**, chance **of winning** 1
	chance **encounter**, chance **meeting** 3
ADJ.	**fair** chance, **good** chance, **slight** chance 1 2
V.	**give** ***someone/something*** **a** chance, **have a** chance, **miss a** chance 1 2
	get a chance 2

▲ **chan·cel·lor** ◆◆◇ /tʃænsələr, -slər/ (**chancellors**) 1 N-TITLE; N-COUNT **Chancellor** is the title of the head of government in Germany and Austria. (德国、奥地利) 总理 ❑ *...Chancellor Gerhard Schröder of Germany.* …德国总理格哈德・施罗德。 2 N-COUNT The head of some American universities is called **the chancellor.** (美国) 大学校长 3 N-COUNT In Britain, the **chancellor** is the chancellor of the exchequer. (英国) 财政大臣

chan·cel·lor of the ex·cheq·uer (**chancellors of the exchequer**) N-COUNT The **chancellor of the exchequer** is the minister in the British government who makes decisions about finance and taxes. (英国) 财政大臣

chan·de·lier /ʃændəlɪər/ (**chandeliers**) N-COUNT A **chandelier** is a large, decorative frame which holds light bulbs or candles and hangs from the ceiling. 垂吊灯 ❑ *A crystal chandelier lit the room.* 一盏水晶吊灯照亮了房间。

change ◆◆◆ /tʃeɪndʒ/ (**changes, changing, changed**) 1 N-VAR If there is a **change in** something, it becomes different. 变化 ❑ *The ambassador appealed for a change in U.S. policy.* 该大使呼吁美国政策的变革。 ❑ *There are going to have to be some drastic changes.* 一定得有些重大变革。 2 → see also **sea change** 3 N-SING If you say that something is a **change** or **makes a change**, you mean that it is enjoyable because it is different from what you are used to. 改进 [APPROVAL] ❑ *It is a complex system, but it certainly makes a change.* 这是个复杂系统，但肯定有所改进。 4 V-I If you **change from** one thing **to** another, you stop using or doing the first one and start using or doing the second. 改换 ❑ *His physician modified the dosage but did not change to a different medication.* 他的医生调整了剂量，但没有改换成别的药方。 5 V-T/V-I When something **changes** or when you **change** it, it becomes different. 改变;变化 ❑ *We are trying to detect and understand how the climates change.* 我们在努力探测并了解气候是怎样变化的。 ❑ *In the union office, the mood gradually changed from resignation to rage.* 在工会办公室，情绪渐渐由依从变成了愤怒。 ❑ *She has now changed into a happy, self-confident woman.* 她现在已经变成了一个快乐、自信的女人。 ❑ *They should change the law to make it illegal to own replica weapons.* 他们应该修改法律，使拥有仿真武器非法。 6 V-T To **change** something means to replace it with something new or different. 更换 ❑ *I paid $80 to have my car radio fixed and I bet all they did was change a fuse.* 我付了$80修车里的收音机，我敢断定他们只是换了根保险丝。 ● N-COUNT **Change** is also a noun. 更换 ❑ *A change of leadership alone will not be enough.* 仅仅更换领导将是不够的。 7 V-T/V-I When you **change** your clothes or **change**, you take some or all of your clothes off and put on different ones. 更换 (衣服); 更衣 ❑ *Ben had merely changed his shirt.* 本只换了他的衬衫。 ❑ *They had allowed her to shower and change.* 他们已允许她沐浴更衣。 8 V-T When you **change** a bed or **change** the sheets, you take off the dirty sheets and put on clean ones. 更换 (床单) ❑ *After changing the bed, I would fall asleep quickly.* 更换床单后，我会很快入睡。 9 V-T When you **change** a baby or **change** its diaper, you take off the dirty one and put on a clean one. 给…换 (尿布) ❑ *She criticizes me for the way I feed or change him.* 她批评我喂他或给他换尿布的方法。 10 V-T/V-I When you **change** buses, trains, or planes or **change**, you get off one bus, train, or plane and get on to another in order to continue your journey. 换乘 ❑ *At Glasgow I changed trains for Greenock.* 在格拉斯哥我换乘去格里诺克的火车。 11 V-T/V-I When you **change** gear or **change** into another gear, you move the gear lever on a car, bicycle, or other vehicle in order to use a different gear. 换 (挡); (车挡) 变换 [mainly BRIT]

in AM, usually use **shift**

12 V-T When you **change** money, you exchange it for the same amount of money in a different currency, or in smaller bills or coins. 兑换 ❑ *You can expect to pay the bank a fee of around 1% to 2% every time you change money.* 每次兑换钱时，你要准备支付银行约1%至2%的费用。 13 N-COUNT A **change of** clothes is an extra set of clothes that you take with you when you go to stay somewhere or to take part in an activity. 替换 (衣服) [N "of" n] ❑ *He stuffed a bag with a few changes of clothing.* 他往包里塞了几件替换衣服。 14 N-UNCOUNT Your **change** is the money that you receive when you pay for something with more money than it costs because you do not have exactly the right amount of money. 找回的钱 ❑ *"There's your change."—"Thanks very much."* "那是找你的钱。" —— "非常感谢。" 15 N-UNCOUNT **Change** is coins, rather than paper money. 硬币 ❑ *Thieves ransacked the office, taking a sack of loose change.* 窃贼们洗劫了办公室，拿走了一袋散币。 16 N-UNCOUNT If you have **change for** larger bills or coins, you have the same value in smaller bills or coins, which you can give to someone in exchange. 零钱 ❑ *The courier had change for a $10 bill.* 快递员有$10的零钱。 ● PHRASE If you **make change**, you give someone smaller bills or coins, in exchange for the same value of larger ones. 换零钱 [AM] 17 PHRASE If you say that you are doing something or something is happening **for a change**, you mean that you do not usually do it or it does not usually happen, and you are happy to be doing it or that it is happening. 变换一下 ❑ *Now let me ask you a question, for a change.* 换一下，现在让我来问你一个问题。 18 **to change for the better** → see **better** 19 **to change hands** → see **hand** 20 **a change of heart** → see **heart** 21 **to change** your **mind** → see **mind** 22 **to change places** → see **place** 23 **to change the subject** → see **subject** 24 **to change tack** → see **tack** 25 **to change** your **tune** → see **tune** 26 **to change for the worse** → see **worse**

▸ **change over** PHRASAL VERB If you **change over from** one thing **to** another, you stop doing one thing and start doing the other. 换成 ❑ *We are gradually changing over to a completely metric system.* 我们正逐渐换成完全公制。

Thesaurus *change* 另参见:

N.	adjustment, alteration 1
V.	adapt, modify, transform, vary 5

Word Partnership *change* 的常用搭配:

V.	**adapt to** change, **resist** change 1
	make a change 1 3
N.	**policy** change 1
	change **of pace** 3
	change **direction** 5
	change **of address**, change **color**, change **the subject** 6
	change **clothes** 7
ADJ.	**gradual** change, **social** change, **sudden** change 1
	loose change, **spare** change 15

change purse (**change purses**) N-COUNT A **change purse** is a very small bag that people, especially women, keep their coins in. 零钱袋 [AM] ❑ *Eve searched her change purse and found thirty cents.* 伊芙翻了翻零钱袋，找到了30美分。

in BRIT, use **purse**

chan·nel ◆◆◇ /tʃænᵊl/ (**channels, channeling** or **channelling, channeled** or **channelled**) **1** N-COUNT; N-IN-NAMES A **channel** is a television station. 电视频道 ❑ *...the only serious current affairs program on either channel.* …任一频道上惟一严肃的时事节目。 ❑ *...the proliferating number of television channels in America.* …美国电视频道的激增数量。 **2** N-COUNT A **channel** is a band of radio waves on which radio messages can be sent and received. 波段 ❑ *The radio channels were filled with the excited, jabbering voices of men going to war.* 收音机各波段满是即将参战的男人们激动喧哗的声音。 **3** N-COUNT If you do something through a particular **channel**, or particular **channels**, that is the system or organization that you use to achieve your aims or to communicate. 渠道；途径 ❑ *The government will surely use the diplomatic channels available.* 政府肯定会采用现有的外交途径。 ❑ *The Americans recognize that the U.N. can be the channel for greater diplomatic activity.* 美国人承认联合国可以是更重要的外交活动的渠道。 **4** N-COUNT A **channel** is a passage along which water flows. 水渠 ❑ *Keep the drainage channel clear.* 保持排水管渠道畅通。 **5** N-COUNT A **channel** is a route used by boats. 航道 ❑ *...the busy shipping channels of the harbor.* …港口繁忙的船运航道。 **6** V-T If you **channel** money or resources into something, you arrange for them to be used for that thing, rather than for a wider range of things. 调拨（钱、资源） ❑ *Jacques Delors wants a system set up to channel funds to the poor countries.* 雅克·迪洛斯想要建立一种体制，以便调拨资金帮助穷国。 **7** V-T If you **channel** your energies or emotions **into** something, you concentrate on or do that one thing, rather than a range of things. 集中（精力、情感） ❑ *Stephen is channeling his energies into a novel called Blue.* 斯蒂芬正集中精力写一本名为《蓝色》的小说。
→ see **cellphone**

★ **chant** /tʃænt/ (**chants, chanting, chanted**) **1** N-COUNT A **chant** is a word or group of words that is repeated over and over again. 重复的话语 ❑ *He was greeted by the chant of "Judas! Judas!"* 他迎来的是不绝于耳的呼喊"叛徒！叛徒！"。 **2** N-COUNT A **chant** is a religious song or prayer that is sung on only a few notes. 圣歌；赞美诗 ❑ *...a Gregorian chant.* …一首格列高利圣歌。 **3** V-T/V-I If you **chant** something or if you **chant**, you repeat the same words over and over again. 反复地说 ❑ *Demonstrators chanted slogans.* 示威者们反复地喊着口号。 ❑ *The crowd chanted "We are with you."* 民众反复喊着"我们支持你。" ● **chant·ing** N-UNCOUNT 重复的呼声 ❑ *A lot of the chanting was in support of the deputy prime minister.* 很多不绝于耳的呼声都支持副总理。 **4** V-T/V-I If you **chant** or if you **chant** something, you sing a religious song or prayer. 吟诵；唱圣歌 ❑ *Muslims chanted and prayed.* 穆斯林唱了圣歌并祈祷了。 ● **chant·ing** N-UNCOUNT 吟诵声 ❑ *The chanting inside the temple stopped.* 寺庙里面的诵经声停止了。

cha·os ◆◇◇ /keɪɒs/ N-UNCOUNT **Chaos** is a state of complete disorder and confusion. 混乱 ❑ *The world's first transatlantic balloon race ended in chaos last night.* 世界首次横渡大西洋的气球比赛昨晚在混乱中结束了。

Word Partnership *chaos* 的常用搭配：

V.	**bring** chaos, **cause** chaos
N.	chaos **and confusion**
ADJ.	**complete** chaos, **total** chaos

cha·ot·ic /keɪɒtɪk/ ADJ Something that is **chaotic** is in a state of complete disorder and confusion. 混乱的 ❑ *My own house feels as filthy and chaotic as a bus terminal.* 我自己的房子感觉和公共汽车总站一样污浊混乱。

chap /tʃæp/ (**chaps**) **1** N-COUNT A **chap** is a man or boy. 男人；小伙 [mainly BRIT, INFORMAL] ❑ *"I am a very lucky chap," he commented. "The doctors were surprised that I was not paralysed."* "我是个非常幸运的家伙，"他解释说，"医生们都很惊奇我没有瘫痪。" **2** → see also **chapped**

★ **chap·el** /tʃæpᵊl/ (**chapels**) **1** N-COUNT A **chapel** is a part of a church which has its own altar and which is used for private prayer. （附属于大教堂的）小教堂 ❑ *...the chapel of the Virgin Mary.* …圣母玛丽亚的教堂。 **2** N-COUNT A **chapel** is a small church attached to a hospital, school, or prison. （附属于医院、学校或监狱的）小教堂 ❑ *We married in the college chapel.* 我们在学院的小教堂里结的婚。 **3** N-VAR A **chapel** is a building used for worship by members of some Christian churches. **Chapel** refers to the religious services that take place there. 礼拜堂；礼拜式 ❑ *...a Methodist chapel.* …一个卫理公会教徒的礼拜堂。

chap·lain /tʃæplɪn/ (**chaplains**) N-COUNT A **chaplain** is a member of the Christian clergy who does religious work in a place such as a hospital, school, prison, or in the armed forces. （医院、学校、监狱或军队中的）牧师 ❑ *He joined the 40th Division as an army chaplain.* 他加入了第40师当军队牧师。

chapped /tʃæpt/ ADJ If your skin is **chapped**, it is dry, cracked, and sore. 皲裂的 ❑ *...chapped hands.* …皲裂的双手。

chap·ter ◆◆◇ /tʃæptər/ (**chapters**) **1** N-COUNT A **chapter** is one of the parts that a book is divided into. Each chapter has a number, and sometimes a title. 章 [also N num] ❑ *Chromium supplements were used successfully in the treatment of diabetes (see Chapter 4).* 铬补充剂成功地用在了糖尿病的治疗上（参见第4章）。 **2** N-COUNT A **chapter in** someone's life or **in** history is a period of time during which a major event or series of related events takes place. （事件发生的）时期 [WRITTEN] ❑ *This had been a particularly difficult chapter in Lebanon's recent history.* 这是黎巴嫩近代史上的一个特别困难的时期。

char·ac·ter ◆◆◇ /kærɪktər/ (**characters**) **1** N-COUNT The **character** of a person or place consists of all the qualities they have that make them distinct from other people or places. 性格；特性 ❑ *Perhaps there is a negative side to his character that you haven't seen yet.* 或许他性格中有你还未看到的消极一面。 **2** N-COUNT You use **character** to say what kind of person someone is. For example, if you say that someone is a strange **character**, you mean they are strange. （具有某种特性的）人 ❑ *It's that kind of courage and determination that makes him such a remarkable character.* 正是那种勇气和决心使他成为这样卓越的人。 **3** N-COUNT The **characters** in a movie, book, or play are the people that it is about. （电影、书、戏剧中的）人物 ❑ *The film is autobiographical and the central character is played by Collard himself.* 这部影片是自传式的，主角由科勒德亲自扮演。 **4** N-COUNT A **character** is a letter, number, or other symbol that is written or printed. 字符 ❑ *...a shopping list written in Chinese characters.* …用汉字写的一张购物单。 **5** N-SING If something has a particular **character**, it has a particular quality. 性质 [usu supp N, also "in" N] ❑ *The financial concessions were of a precarious character.* 财政优惠具有不稳定性。 **6** N-SING You can use **character** to refer to the qualities that people from a particular place are believed to have. 特征 ❑ *Individuality is a valued and inherent part of the British character.* 个性是英国人重视并固有的特征。 **7** N-VAR Your **character** is your personality, especially how reliable and honest you are. If someone is **of good character**, they are reliable and honest. If they are **of bad character**, they are unreliable and dishonest. 人品 ❑ *He's begun a series of personal attacks on my character.* 他开始对我的人品进行一系列的人身攻击。 **8** N-UNCOUNT If you say that someone has **character**, you mean that they have the ability to deal effectively with difficult, unpleasant, or dangerous situations. 人格力量 [APPROVAL] ❑ *She showed real character in her attempts to win over the crowd.* 她在争取民众支持的努力中显示出了真正的人格力量。 **9** N-UNCOUNT If you say that a place has **character**, you mean that it has an interesting or unusual quality which makes you notice it and like it. 特色 [APPROVAL] ❑ *A soulless shopping center stands across from one of the few buildings with character, the town hall.* 一座毫无生气的购物中心对面就是少有的几个别具特色的建筑物之一：市政厅。 **10** N-COUNT If you say that someone is a **character**, you mean that they are interesting, unusual, or amusing. （风趣、与众不同的）人物 ❑ *He's a nut, a real character.* 他是个怪人，一个真正与众不同的人。
→ see **printing, theater**

Word Partnership *character* 的常用搭配：

N.	character **flaw**, character **trait** **1**
	character **in a book/movie**, **cartoon** character, character **development** **3**
ADJ.	**moral** character **1** **7**
	fictional character, **main** character, **minor** character **3**

char·ac·teri·sa·tion /kærɪktəraɪzeɪʃᵊn/ [BRIT] → see **characterization**

char·ac·ter·ise /kærɪktəraɪz/ [BRIT] → see **characterize**

char·ac·ter·is·tic ◆◇◇ /kærɪktərɪstɪk/ (**characteristics**) **1** N-COUNT The **characteristics** of a person or thing are the qualities or features that belong to them and make them recognizable. 特征 ❑ *Genes determine the characteristics of every living thing.* 基因决定每个生物的特征。 **2** ADJ A quality or feature that is **characteristic of** someone or something is one which is often seen in them and seems typical of them. 典型的 ❑ *...the absence of strife between the generations that was so characteristic of such societies.*

…代与代之间冲突的消失，而这种冲突曾是这些社会的典型特征。❑ *Windmills are a characteristic feature of the Mallorcan landscape.* 风车是马略卡岛风光的一个典型的特色。● **char·ac·ter·is·ti·cal·ly** /kærɪktərɪstɪkli/ ADV 典型地 ❑ *He replied in characteristically robust style.* 他以典型的坚定风格作答。

→ see **gene**

char·ac·teri·za·tion /kærɪktərɪzeɪʃən/ (**characterizations**)

in BRIT, also use **characterisation**

N-VAR **Characterization** is the way an author or an actor describes or shows what a character is like. (作家的) 人物刻画；(演员的) 人物塑造 ❑ *As a writer, I am interested in characterization.* 作为作家，我对人物刻画感兴趣。

char·ac·ter·ize /kærɪktəraɪz/ (**characterizes, characterizing, characterized**)

in BRIT, also use **characterise**

1 V-T If something **is characterized by** a particular feature or quality, that feature or quality is an obvious part of it. 以…为特征 [usu passive] [FORMAL] ❑ *This election campaign has been characterized by violence.* 这次竞选运动以暴力为特征。 2 V-T If you **characterize** someone or something **as** a particular thing, you describe them as that thing. 描述为 [FORMAL] ❑ *Both companies have characterized the relationship as friendly.* 两家公司都认为彼此的关系是友好的。

char·ac·ter rec·og·ni·tion N-UNCOUNT **Character recognition** is a process which allows computers to recognize written or printed characters such as numbers or letters and to change them into a form that the computer can use. 字符识别 [COMPUTING] ❑ *...optical character recognition software that allows you to convert a scanned document to an electronic file.* …能把扫描的文件转换成电子文件的光学字符识别软件。

cha·rade /ʃəreɪd/ (**charades**) 1 N-COUNT If you describe someone's actions as a **charade**, you mean that their actions are so obviously false that they do not convince anyone. 假样子 [DISAPPROVAL] ❑ *I wondered why he had gone through the elaborate charade.* 我想知道为什么他做出了那么夸张的假样子。 2 N-UNCOUNT **Charades** is a game for teams of players in which one team acts a word or phrase, syllable by syllable, until other players guess the whole word or phrase. 哑谜猜字游戏 ❑ *We are all going to play charades in the library.* 我们大家都将在图书馆玩哑谜猜字游戏。

▲ **char·coal** /tʃɑrkoʊl/ N-UNCOUNT **Charcoal** is a black substance obtained by burning wood without much air. It can be burned as a fuel, and small sticks of it are used for drawing. 木炭

→ see **drawing, firework**

charge ♦♦♦ /tʃɑrdʒ/ (**charges, charging, charged**) 1 V-T/V-I If you **charge** someone an amount of money, you ask them to pay that amount for something that you have sold to them or done for them. 要价；收费 ❑ *Even local nurseries charge $150 a week.* 即便当地的托儿所每周也要收$150的费用。 ❑ *Some banks charge if you access your account to determine your balance.* 如果你进入自己的账户查看余额，有些银行要收费。 ❑ *The architect charged us a fee of seven hundred and fifty dollars.* 建筑师向我们收取了750美元的费用。 2 V-T To **charge** something **to** a person or organization means to tell the people providing it to send the bill to that person or organization. To **charge** something **to** someone's account means to add it to their account so they can pay for it later. 开帐单；记在…的账上 ❑ *Go out and buy a pair of glasses, and charge it to us.* 出去买一副眼镜，记在我们的账上。 3 V-T When the police **charge** someone, they formally accuse them of having done something illegal. 指控 ❑ *They have the evidence to charge him.* 他们有证据来指控他。 4 V-I If you **charge** toward someone or something, you move quickly and aggressively toward them. 冲 ❑ *He charged through the door to my mother's office.* 他破门而入，进了我母亲的办公室。 ❑ *He ordered us to charge.* 他命令我们冲锋。● N-COUNT **Charge** is also a noun. 冲 ❑ *...a bayonet charge.* …一次刺刀冲锋。 5 V-T To **charge** a battery means to pass an electrical current through it in order to make it more powerful or to make it last longer. 给…充电 ❑ *Alex had forgotten to charge the battery.* 亚历克斯忘了给电池充电。● PHRASAL VERB **Charge up** means the same as **charge**. 给…充电 ❑ *There was nothing in the brochure about having to drive it every day to charge up the battery.* 手册里没写它要每天开，给电池充电。 6 N-COUNT A **charge** is an amount of money that you have to pay for a service. 费用 ❑ *We can arrange this for a small charge.* 我们收取少量的费用就可以安排这事 7 → see also **service charge** 8 N-COUNT A **charge** is a formal accusation that someone has committed a crime. 指控 ❑ *He may still face criminal charges.* 他也许仍旧要面对刑事指控。 9 N-COUNT If you describe someone as your **charge**, they have been given to you to be taken care of and you are responsible for them. 受照料者 ❑ *The coach tried to get his charges motivated.* 该教练设法激励他的队员们。 10 N-COUNT An electrical **charge** is an amount of electricity that is held in or carried by something. 负荷 [TECHNICAL] 11 N-UNCOUNT If you take **charge of** someone or something, you make yourself responsible for them and take control over them. If someone or something is **in your charge**, you are responsible for them. 掌管；负责 ❑ *A few years ago Bacryl took charge of the company.* 几年前巴克莱尔掌管这家公司。 ❑ *I have been given charge of this class.* 我受命负责这个班。 12 PHRASE If you are **in charge** in a particular situation, you are the most senior person and have control over something or someone. 负责 ❑ *Who's in charge here?* 这里谁负责？ 13 PHRASE If something is **free of charge**, it does not cost anything. 免费 ❑ *The leaflet is available free of charge from post offices.* 小册子可免费向邮局索取。

→ see **lightning, magnet, trial**

Word Partnership *charge* 的常用搭配：

N.	charge **a fee** 1 charge **a battery** 5
V.	**lead a** charge 4 **deny a** charge 8
ADJ.	**criminal** charge, **guilty of a** charge 8 **electrical** charge 10

charge·able /tʃɑrdʒəbəl/ 1 ADJ If something is **chargeable**, you have to pay a sum of money for it. 应付费的 [FORMAL] ❑ *The day of discharge is not chargeable if rooms are vacated by 12:00 noon.* 如果中午12点前房间被腾空，退房当天就免交费用。 2 ADJ If something is **chargeable**, you have to pay tax on it. 应征税的 [BRIT, FORMAL] ❑ *...the taxpayer's chargeable gain.* …纳税人的应税收入。

charge card (**charge cards**) 1 N-COUNT A **charge card** is a plastic card that you use to buy goods on credit from a particular store or group of stores. 签账卡 2 N-COUNT A **charge card** is the same as a **credit card**. 信用卡 [AM]

charg·er /tʃɑrdʒər/ (**chargers**) N-COUNT A **charger** is a device used for charging or recharging batteries. 充电器 ❑ *He forgot the charger for his cellphone.* 他忘了带手机充电器。

cha·ris·ma /kərɪzmə/ N-UNCOUNT You say that someone has **charisma** when they can attract, influence, and inspire people by their personal qualities. 魅力；感召力 ❑ *He has neither the policies nor the personal charisma to inspire people.* 他既没有谋略也没有个人魅力去鼓舞人。

char·is·mat·ic /kærɪzmætɪk/ ADJ A **charismatic** person attracts, influences, and inspires people by their personal qualities. 有魅力的 ❑ *With her striking looks and charismatic personality, she was noticed far and wide.* 她以出众的相貌和富有魅力的个性闻名遐迩。

★ **chari·table** /tʃærɪtəbəl/ 1 ADJ A **charitable** organization or activity helps and supports people who are ill, disabled, or very poor. 慈善的 [ADJ n] ❑ *...charitable work for the handicapped.* …为残疾人做的慈善工作。 2 ADJ Someone who is **charitable** to people is kind or understanding toward them. 仁慈的 ❑ *They were less than charitable toward the referee.* 他们对裁判员毫不仁慈。

char·ity ♦◇◇ /tʃærɪti/ (**charities**) 1 N-COUNT A **charity** is an organization which raises money in order to help people who are ill, disabled, or very poor. 慈善机构 ❑ *...an AIDS charity.* …一个艾滋病慈善机构。 2 N-UNCOUNT If you give money **to charity**, you give it to one or more charitable organizations. If you do something **for charity**, you do it in order to raise money for one or more charitable organizations. 慈善 ❑ *He made substantial donations to charity.* 他做了大量的慈善捐赠。 ❑ *Gooch will be raising money for charity.* 古奇将为慈善筹集款项。 3 N-UNCOUNT People who live on **charity** live on money or goods which other people give them because they are poor. 救济金；救济物 ❑ *Her husband is unemployed and the family depends on charity.* 她的丈夫失业了，全家靠救济度日。

Word Partnership *charity* 的常用搭配：

ADJ.	**local** charity, **private** charity 1
N.	charity **organization** 1 **donation to** charity, charity **event**, **money for** charity, charity **work** 2
V.	**collect for** charity, **donate to** charity, **give to** charity 2

charm /tʃɑrm/ (**charms, charming, charmed**) 1 N-VAR **Charm** is the quality of being pleasant or attractive. 魅力 ❑ *"Snow White and the Seven Dwarfs," the 1937 Disney classic, has lost none of its original charm.* 迪斯尼1937年的经典之作《白雪公主和七个小矮人》从未丧失其最初的魅力。 2 N-UNCOUNT Someone who has **charm** behaves in a friendly, pleasant way that makes people like them. (人的) 魅力 ❑ *He was a man of great charm and distinction.* 他是一个魅力十足、地位显赫的男人。 3 V-T If you **charm** someone, you please them, especially by using your charm. (用魅力) 取悦 ❑ *He even charmed Mrs. Prichard, carrying her groceries and flirting with her, though she's 83.* 他甚至去取悦普里查德夫人，帮她搬杂货、与她调情，虽然她已经83岁了。 4 N-COUNT A **charm** is a small ornament that is fixed to a bracelet or necklace. (手链或项链上的) 挂坠 ❑ *Inside was a gold charm bracelet, with one charm on it - a star.* 里面是个金制挂坠手链，上面有一个挂坠——一颗星星。 5 N-COUNT A **charm** is an act, saying, or object that is believed to have magic powers. 符咒 ❑ *They cross their fingers and spit over their shoulders as charms against the evil eye.* 他们交叉手指，往肩后吐口水，以此作为对抗凶眼的符咒。
→ see **jewelry**

charm·ing /tʃɑrmɪŋ/ 1 ADJ If you say that something is **charming**, you mean that it is very pleasant or attractive. 迷人的 ❑ *...a charming little fishing village.* …一个迷人的小渔村。
● **charm·ing·ly** ADV 迷人地 ❑ *There's something charmingly old-fashioned about his brand of entertainment.* 他的娱乐品牌有种迷人的传统味道。 2 ADJ If you describe someone as **charming**, you mean they behave in a friendly, pleasant way that makes people like them. 惹人喜欢的 ❑ *...a charming young man.* …一个惹人喜欢的年轻男子。 ❑ *He found her as smart and beautiful as she is charming.* 他发现她聪明、美丽而且惹人喜欢。 ● **charm·ing·ly** ADV 惹人喜欢地 [ADV after V] ❑ *Calder smiled charmingly and put out his hand. "A pleasure, Mrs. Talbot."* 考尔德迷人地微笑着并伸出手说："十分荣幸，塔尔博特夫人。"

charred /tʃɑrd/ ADJ **Charred** plants, buildings, or vehicles have been badly burned and have become black because of fire. 烧焦的 ❑ *...the charred remains of a tank.* …一辆烧焦的坦克的遗骸。

chart ♦◇◇ /tʃɑrt/ (**charts, charting, charted**) 1 N-COUNT A **chart** is a diagram, picture, or graph which is intended to make information easier to understand. 图表 ❑ *Male unemployment was 14.2%, compared with 5.8% for women (see chart on next page).* 男性失业率是14.2%，相比女性为5.8% (参见下页图表)。 2 → see also **bar chart, flow chart, pie chart** 3 N-COUNT A **chart** is a map of the sea or stars. 海图; 星图 ❑ *...charts of Greek waters.* …希腊水域图。 4 V-T If you **chart** an area of land, sea, or sky, or a feature in that area, you make a map of the area or show the feature in it. 绘制 ❑ *Ptolemy charted more than 1,000 stars in 48 constellations.* 托勒密绘制了48个星座中1000多颗星的星图。 5 V-T If you **chart** the development or progress of something, you observe it and record or show it. You can also say that a report or graph **charts** the development or progress of something. 用图表记录 ❑ *One doctor has charted a dramatic rise in local childhood asthma since the road was built.* 一位医生用图表记录的方式，说明道路建成后当地儿童哮喘发病率急剧上升。

char·ter ♦◇◇ /tʃɑrtər/ (**charters, chartering, chartered**) 1 N-COUNT A **charter** is a formal document describing the rights, aims, or principles of an organization or group of people. 宪章 ❑ *...Article 50 of the United Nations Charter.* …联合国宪章第50条。 2 ADJ A **charter** plane or boat is one which is rented for use by a particular person or group and which is not part of a regular service. 包租的 [ADJ n] ❑ *...the last charter plane carrying out foreign nationals.* …运出外国侨民的最后一班包机。 3 V-T If a person or organization **charters** a plane, boat, or other vehicle, they rent it for their own use. 包租 ❑ *He chartered a jet to fly her home from California to Switzerland.* 他包租了一架喷气式飞机把她从加利福尼亚送回瑞士家中。

char·tered /tʃɑrtərd/ ADJ **Chartered** is used to indicate that someone, such as an accountant or a surveyor, has formally qualified in their profession. 受特许的 [BRIT]

in AM, use **certified**

chase ♦◇◇ /tʃeɪs/ (**chases, chasing, chased**) 1 V-T/V-I If you **chase** someone, or **chase after** them, you run after them or follow them quickly in order to catch or reach them. 追赶 ❑ *She chased the thief for 100 yards.* 她追了小偷100码远。 ● N-COUNT **Chase** is also a noun. 追赶 ❑ *He was reluctant to give up the chase.* 他不愿意放弃追逐。 2 V-T/V-I If you **are chasing** something you want, such as work or money, or are **chasing after** it, you are trying hard to get it. 追求 (事业、金钱等) ❑ *In some areas, 14 people are chasing every job.* 在某些地区，14个人角逐每一个岗位。 ❑ *There are too many schools chasing after too few students.* 有太多的学校争抢太少的学生。 ● N-SING **Chase** is also a noun. (对事业、金钱等的) 追求 [N "for" n] ❑ *They took an invincible lead in the chase for the championship.* 他们在冠军角逐中遥遥领先。 3 V-T/V-I If someone **chases** someone that they are attracted to, or **chases after** them, they try hard to persuade them to have a sexual relationship with them. 追求 (异性) ❑ *Women also have another reason for not chasing men too hard, of course.* 当然，妇女还有另一个不紧追男人的理由。 ● N-SING **Chase** is also a noun. (对异性的) 追求 ❑ *The chase is always much more exciting than the conquest anyway.* 无论如何，追求总比征服更令人兴奋。 4 V-T If someone **chases** you from a place, they force you to leave by using threats or violence. 驱逐 ❑ *Many farmers will then chase you off their land quite aggressively.* 到那时，许多农民便会毫不留情地将你逐出他们的土地。 5 V-T To **chase** someone **from** a job or a position or **from** power means to force them to leave it. 逼迫卸职 ❑ *In the '70s he had been chased out of his job.* 在70年代他被迫离开了他的职位。 6 V-I If you **chase** somewhere, you run or rush there. 冲 ❑ *They chased down the stairs into the narrow, dirty street.* 他们冲下楼梯，跑到狭窄肮脏的街道上。 7 PHRASE If someone **cuts to the chase**, they start talking about or dealing with what is important, instead of less important things. 切入主题 ❑ *Hi everyone, we all know why we are here today, so let's cut to the chase.* 大家好，我们都知道今天为何来此，让我们切入主题吧。

Word Partnership *chase* 的常用搭配:

PREP.	chase **after** ***someone/something*** 1
ADJ.	**car** chase, **high-speed** chase 1

chasm /kæzəm/ (**chasms**) 1 N-COUNT A **chasm** is a very deep crack in rock, earth, or ice. (岩石、地面或冰上的) 大裂口 ❑ *...a yawning fourteen-foot-deep chasm which inexplicably had opened up in the riverbed.* …河床上莫名其妙地开了一个14英尺深的敞开的大裂口。 2 N-COUNT If you say that there is a **chasm** between two things or between two groups of people, you mean that there is a very large difference between them. 鸿沟; 巨大分歧 ❑ *...the chasm that divides the worlds of university and industry.* …隔开大学与产业之间的的鸿沟。

chas·sis /tʃæsi, ʃæsi/ (**chassis**)

Chassis /tʃæsiz, ʃæsiz/ is also the plural form.

N-COUNT A **chassis** is the framework that a vehicle is built on. (车辆) 底盘
→ see **car**

chat ♦◇◇ /tʃæt/ (**chats, chatting, chatted**) V-RECIP When people **chat**, they talk to each other in an informal and friendly way. 聊天 ❑ *The women were chatting.* 妇女们在聊天。 ❑ *I was chatting to him the other day.* 我那天正和他聊天。 ● N-COUNT **Chat** is also a noun. 聊天 ❑ *I had a chat with John.* 我和约翰聊了会儿天。

Word Partnership *chat* 的常用搭配:

V.	**have a** chat
ADJ.	**online** chat
N.	chat **site**

chat room (**chat rooms**) also **chatroom** N-COUNT A **chat room** is a site on the Internet where people can exchange messages about a particular subject. 聊天室 [COMPUTING] ❑ *...a woman I met in a chat room.* …我在一个聊天室遇到的一名女子。

chat show (**chat shows**) N-COUNT A **chat show** is the same as a **talk show**. 脱口秀 [BRIT]

▲ **chat·ter** /tʃætər/ (**chatters, chattering, chattered**) 1 V-I If you **chatter**, you talk quickly and continuously, usually about things which are not important. 喋喋不休地说 (不重要的事) ❑ *Everyone's chattering away in different languages.* 大家用不同的语言喋喋不休地说着。 ❑ *Erica was friendly and chattered about Andrew's children.* 埃丽卡很友好并絮叨起安德鲁的孩子们。 ● N-UNCOUNT **Chatter** is also a noun. 喋喋不休 ❑ *...idle chatter.* …闲聊。 2 V-I If your teeth **chatter**, they keep knocking together because you are very cold or very nervous. (牙齿) 格格作响 ❑ *She was so cold her teeth chattered.* 她冻得连牙齿都格格作响。 3 V-I When birds or animals **chatter**, they make high-pitched noises. (鸟类、动物) 鸣叫 [LITERARY] ❑ *Birds were chattering somewhere, and occasionally he could hear a vehicle pass by.* 鸟儿们在某处啁啾，偶尔他能听到一辆汽车经过。 ● N-UNCOUNT **Chatter** is also a noun. (鸟类、动物的) 鸣叫 ❑ *...almond trees vibrating with the chatter of crickets.* …伴随蟋蟀的鸣叫而颤动的杏树。

C

Word Link *eur ≈ one who does : amateur, chauffeur, entrepreneur*

▲ **chauf·feur** /ʃoʊfər, ʃoʊfɜr/ (**chauffeurs, chauffeuring, chauffeured**) 1 N-COUNT The **chauffeur** of a rich or important person is the man or woman who is employed to take care of their car and drive them around in it. (富人、要人的) 私人司机 2 V-T If you **chauffeur** someone somewhere, you drive them there in a car, usually as part of your job. 为…开车 (通常指受雇佣) ❑ *It was certainly useful to have her there to chauffeur him around.* 有她在那儿为他开车肯定是有用的。

chau·vin·ism /ʃoʊvɪnɪzəm/ N-UNCOUNT **Chauvinism** is a strong, unreasonable belief that your own country, sex, race, or religion, is better and more important than any other. 沙文主义 [DISAPPROVAL] ❑ *...it may also appeal to the latent chauvinism of many ordinary people.* …它可能也迎合了许多普通人潜在的沙文主义。 ● **chau·vin·ist** N-COUNT (**chauvinists**) 沙文主义者 ❑ *He is arrogant and a bit of a chauvinist.* 他傲慢，还有点儿沙文主义。

cheap ♦♦◊ /tʃip/ (**cheaper, cheapest**) 1 ADJ Goods or services that are **cheap** cost less money than usual or than you expected. 便宜的 ❑ *I'm going to live off campus if I can find somewhere cheap enough.* 如果我能找到一个足够便宜的地方，我打算住在校外。 ❑ *Operating costs are coming down because of cheaper fuel.* 经营成本在下降是因为燃料更便宜了。 ● **cheap·ly** ADV 便宜地 [ADV after v] ❑ *It will produce electricity more cheaply than a nuclear plant.* 它将以比核电厂更低廉的成本生产电力。 2 ADJ If you describe goods as **cheap**, you mean they cost less money than similar products but their quality is poor. 价廉质劣的 [ADJ n] ❑ *Don't resort to cheap imitations; save up for the real thing.* 不要买价廉质劣的赝品，把钱存起来买真货。 3 ADJ If you describe someone's remarks or actions as **cheap**, you mean that they are unkindly or insincerely using a situation to benefit themselves or to harm someone else. 损人利己的 [ADJ n] [DISAPPROVAL] ❑ *These tests will inevitably be used by politicians to make cheap political points.* 这些测试难免会被政客们利用以炮制损人利己的政治观点。 4 ADJ If you describe someone as **cheap**, you are criticizing them for being unwilling to spend money. 小气的 [AM, DISAPPROVAL] ❑ *Oh, please, Dad, just this once don't be cheap.* 哦，求求你，爸爸，就这一次，别小气嘛。

Thesaurus *cheap* 另参见：

ADJ. budget, economical, low-cost, reasonable; (*ant.*) costly, expensive 1
second-rate, shoddy 2

cheat /tʃit/ (**cheats, cheating, cheated**) 1 V-I When someone **cheats**, they do not obey a set of rules which they should be obeying, for example in a game or exam. 舞弊；作弊 ❑ *Students may be tempted to cheat in order to get into top schools.* 学生们可能禁不住会作弊，以便能进一流学校。 ● **cheat·ing** N-UNCOUNT 舞弊；作弊 ❑ *In an election in 1988, he was accused of cheating by his opponent.* 在1988年的一次竞选中，他被对手指控舞弊。 2 V-T If someone **cheats** you **out of** something, they get it from you by behaving dishonestly. 诈取 ❑ *The company engaged in a deliberate effort to cheat them out of their pensions.* 该公司曾蓄意诈取他们的养老金。 3 N-COUNT Someone who is a **cheat** does not obey a set of rules which they should be obeying. 舞弊者 ❑ *Cheats will be disqualified.* 舞弊者将被取消资格。

▸ **cheat on** 1 PHRASAL VERB If someone **cheats on** their husband, wife, or partner, they have a sexual relationship with another person. 不忠实于 (配偶或伴侣) [INFORMAL] ❑ *I'd found Philippe was cheating on me and I was angry and hurt.* 我发现菲利普对我不忠，我很愤怒并且受到了伤害。 2 PHRASAL VERB If someone **cheats on** something such as an agreement or their taxes, they do not do what they should do under a set of rules. 违背 (协议等) [mainly AM] ❑ *Their job is to check that none of the signatory countries is cheating on the agreement.* 他们的工作是检查以确认没有任一签署国违背该协议。

check ♦♦◊ /tʃɛk/ (**checks, checking, checked**) 1 V-T/V-I If you **check** something such as a piece of information or a document, you make sure that it is correct or satisfactory. 检查；核实 ❑ *Check the accuracy of everything in your résumé.* 核查你简历中每一项的准确性。 ❑ *I think there is an age limit, but I'd have to check.* 我觉得是有年龄限制的，但我得去核实一下。 ❑ *She hadn't checked whether she had a clean, ironed shirt.* 她没有查看自己是否有件干净并熨好的衬衣。 ● N-COUNT **Check** is also a noun. 检查；核实 ❑ *He is being constantly monitored with regular checks on his blood pressure.* 他一直受到持续地监测，接受定期的血压检测。 2 V-I If you **check on** someone or something, you make sure they are in a safe or satisfactory condition. 察看 ❑ *Stephen checked on her several times during the night.* 斯蒂芬夜间察看了她几次。 3 V-T If you **check** something that is written on a piece of paper, you put a mark, like a V with the right side extended, next to it to show that something is correct or has been selected or dealt with. 打勾 [mainly AM]

in BRIT, usually use **tick**

❑ *To request your free gift, please check the appropriate box below.* 需要免费礼品的，请在下面相关的框中打勾。 4 V-T To **check** something, usually something bad, means to stop it from spreading or continuing. 抑制 ❑ *Sex education is also expected to help check the spread of AIDS.* 性教育也有望抑制艾滋病的蔓延。 5 V-T When you **check** your luggage at an airport, you give it to an official so that it can be taken on to your plane. 托运 [AM] ❑ *We arrived at the airport, checked our baggage and wandered around the gift shops.* 我们到达了机场，托运了行李，然后逛了逛礼品店。 ● PHRASAL VERB To **check in** your luggage means the same as to **check** it. 托运 ❑ *They checked in their luggage and found seats in the departure lounge.* 他们托运了行李，然后在候机室找到了座位。 6 N-COUNT The **check** in a restaurant is a piece of paper on which the price of your meal is written and which you are given before you pay. (餐馆的) 账单 [mainly AM]

in BRIT, usually use **bill**

❑ *After coffee, Gastler asked for the check.* 喝完咖啡，加斯特勒要了账单。 7 N-COUNT A pattern of squares, usually of two colors, can be referred to as **checks** or a **check**. 格子图案 (通常双色) ❑ *Styles include stripes and checks.* 样式有条纹的和格子的。 8 N-COUNT A **check** is a printed form on which you write an amount of money and who it is to be paid to. Your bank then pays the money to that person from your account. 支票 ❑ *He handed me an envelope with a check for $1,500.* 他递给我一个信封，里面有一张$1500的支票。

in BRIT, use **cheque**

9 → see also **blank check, traveler's check** 10 PHRASE If something or someone **is held in check** or **is kept in check**, they are controlled and prevented from becoming too great or powerful. 抑制住某物 ❑ *Life on Earth will become unsustainable unless population growth is held in check.* 地球上的生命将无法延续，除非人口增长得到控制。 11 → see also **double-check, rain check**
→ see **bank**

▸ **check in** 1 PHRASAL VERB When you **check in** or **check into** a hotel or clinic, or if someone **checks** you **in**, you arrive and go through the necessary procedures before you stay there. 登记入住 ❑ *I'll call the hotel. I'll tell them we'll check in tomorrow.* 我会给旅馆打电话，通知他们明天我们将登记入住。 ❑ *He has checked into an alcohol treatment center.* 他已登记住进了一所戒酒治疗中心。 2 PHRASAL VERB When you **check in** at an airport, you arrive and show your ticket before going on a flight. 办理登机手续 ❑ *He had checked in at Amsterdam's Schiphol airport for a flight to Atlanta.* 他在阿姆斯特丹的斯希普霍尔机场已办理了飞往亚特兰大的航班的登机手续。 3 → see also **check-in, check 5**
→ see **hotel**

▸ **check off** PHRASAL VERB When you **check** things **off**, you check or count them while referring to a list of them, to make sure you have considered all of them. (对照列单) 核对 ❑ *Once you've checked off the items you ordered, put this record in your file.* 你一旦核对了所定货物，就把该记录存档。 ❑ *I haven't checked them off but I would say that's about the number.* 我还没有核对，但我想大概就是这个数。

▸ **check out** 1 PHRASAL VERB When you **check out of** a hotel or clinic where you have been staying, or if someone **checks** you **out**, you pay the bill and leave. 退房 ❑ *They packed and checked out of the hotel.* 他们收拾好行李，退了旅馆的房。 ❑ *I was disappointed to miss Bryan, who had just checked out.* 我很失望没见到布莱恩，他刚刚退房走了。 2 PHRASAL VERB If you **check out** something or someone, you find out information about them to make sure that everything is correct or satisfactory. 调查 ❑ *Maybe we ought to go down to the library and check it out.* 也许我们该去图书馆调查一下。 ❑ *We ought to check him out on the computer.* 我们应该在计算机上调查他的信息。 3 PHRASAL VERB If something **checks out**, it is correct or satisfactory. 成立 ❑ *She was in San Diego the weekend Jensen got killed. Her alibi checked out.* 詹森遇害的那个周末她在圣地亚哥。她不在现场的申辩成立。 4 PHRASAL VERB If you **check out** a library book, you borrow it for a fixed period of time. 借出 ❑ *No books can be checked out after 6 p.m. tomorrow.* 明天下午6点以后图书不可以借出。 5 → see also **checkout**

▸ **check up** 1 PHRASAL VERB If you **check up on** something, you find out information about it. 调查 ❑ *It is certainly worth checking up* *on your benefit entitlements.* 调查一下你的福利权益无疑是值得的。 2 → see also **checkup** 3 PHRASAL VERB If you **check up on** someone, you obtain information about them, usually secretly. (私底下) 调查 ❑ *I'm sure he knew I was checking up on him.* 我确信他知道我在私底下调查他。

Thesaurus *check* 另参见：

V. confirm, find out, make sure, verify; *(ant.)* ignore, overlook 1

Word Partnership *check* 的常用搭配：

PREP. check **for/that** *something*, check **with** *someone* 1

N. **background** check, **credit** check, **security** check 1
check **your baggage/luggage** 5

V. **cash a** check, **deposit a** check, **pay with a** check, **write a** check 8

check·book /tʃɛkbʊk/ (**checkbooks**)
in BRIT, use **chequebook**
N-COUNT A **checkbook** is a book of checks which your bank gives you so that you can pay for things by check. 支票簿 [AM] ❑ *The woman took out her checkbook and quickly made out four checks.* 那个女人拿出支票簿迅速开了4张支票。

checked /tʃɛkt/ ADJ Something that is **checked** has a pattern of small squares, usually of two colors. 有格子图案的 ❑ *He was wearing blue jeans and a checked shirt.* 他穿着蓝色牛仔裤和一件格子衬衫。

check·er /tʃɛkər/ (**checkers**) 1 N-UNCOUNT **Checkers** is a game for two people, played with 24 round pieces on a board. 西洋跳棋 [AM] ❑ *...a game of checkers.* …一盘西洋跳棋游戏。
in BRIT, use **draughts**
2 N-COUNT A **checker** is a person or machine that has the job of checking something. 检验员；检验器 ❑ *Modern word processors usually have spelling checkers and even grammar checkers.* 现代文字处理器通常有拼写检验器甚至语法检验器。

check-in (**check-ins**) N-COUNT At an airport, a **check-in** is the counter or desk where you check in. 登机手续办理处 ❑ *The line at the check-in was already dispersing.* 在登机手续办理处排的队已在散开了。

check·ing ac·count (**checking accounts**) N-COUNT A **checking account** is a personal bank account which you can take money out of at any time using your checkbook or bank card. 活期存款账户 [mainly AM]
in BRIT, usually use **current account**
❑ *...Commonwealth Bank, where he has his checking account.* …他开立活期存款账户的银行——联邦银行。
→ see **bank**

check·out /tʃɛkaʊt/ (**checkouts**) N-COUNT In a supermarket, a **checkout** is a counter where you pay for things you are buying. (超市里的) 收款台 ❑ *...the supermarket checkout counter.* …超市收款台。

check·point /tʃɛkpɔɪnt/ (**checkpoints**) N-COUNT A **checkpoint** is a place where traffic is stopped so that it can be checked. 检查站 ❑ *...a bomb explosion close to an army checkpoint.* …军队检查站附近的一次炸弹爆炸。

check·up /tʃɛkʌp/ (**checkups**) N-COUNT A **checkup** is a medical examination by your doctor or dentist to make sure that there is nothing wrong with your health. 体检 ❑ *The disease was detected during a routine checkup.* 这种疾病是在一次例行体检中查出来的。

cheek /tʃik/ (**cheeks**) 1 N-COUNT Your **cheeks** are the sides of your face below your eyes. 面颊 ❑ *Tears were running down her cheeks.* 眼泪顺着她面颊流下。 2 N-COUNT Your **cheeks** are your buttocks. 臀部 [usu pl] ❑ *My butt cheeks are sore from sitting on this bench too long.* 我屁股痛，因为在长凳上坐得太久了。 3 N-SING You say that someone has **cheek** when you are annoyed or shocked at something unreasonable that they have done. 厚脸皮 [also no det] [mainly BRIT, INFORMAL] ❑ *I'm amazed they had the cheek to ask in the first place.* 我很吃惊，他们最初竟有脸问。
→ see **face**, **kiss**

cheek·bone /tʃikboʊn/ (**cheekbones**) N-COUNT Your **cheekbones** are the two bones in your face just below your eyes. 颧骨 ❑ *She was very beautiful, with high cheekbones.* 她很美，颧骨高高的。

cheeky /tʃiki/ (**cheekier**, **cheekiest**) ADJ If you describe a person or their behavior as **cheeky**, you think that they are slightly rude or disrespectful but in a charming or amusing way. 嘻皮笑脸的 [mainly BRIT] ❑ *The boy was cheeky and casual.* 这个男孩嘻皮笑脸、随随便便。

cheer ♦◇◇ /tʃɪər/ (**cheers**, **cheering**, **cheered**) 1 V-T/V-I When people **cheer**, they shout loudly to show their approval or to encourage someone who is doing something such as taking part in a game. 欢呼 ❑ *The crowd cheered as she went up the steps to the bandstand.* 当她走上演奏台的台阶时，人群欢呼起来。 ❑ *Hundreds of thousands of jubilant Americans cheered him on his return.* 成千上万欢腾的美国人为他的归来而欢呼。 ● N-COUNT **Cheer** is also a noun. 欢呼 ❑ *The colonel was rewarded with a resounding cheer from the men.* 上校被这些人们报以一阵响亮的欢呼。 2 V-T If you **are cheered by** something, it makes you happier or less worried. 感到振奋 ❑ *Stephen noticed that the people around him looked cheered by his presence.* 斯蒂芬注意到周围的人因为他的到场而振奋起来。 ● **cheer·ing** ADJ 令人振奋的 ❑ *...very cheering news.* …非常令人振奋的消息。 3 CONVENTION People sometimes say "**Cheers**" to each other just before they drink an alcoholic drink. 干杯 [mainly BRIT]

▸ **cheer on** PHRASAL VERB When you **cheer** someone **on**, you shout loudly in order to encourage them, for example when they are taking part in a game. 为…加油 ❑ *A thousand supporters packed into the stadium to cheer them on.* 1000名支持者涌进体育场为他们加油。

▸ **cheer up** PHRASAL VERB When you **cheer up** or when something **cheers** you **up**, you stop feeling depressed and become more cheerful. (使) 振作起来 ❑ *I think he misses her terribly. You might cheer him up.* 我觉得他太想念她了。你也许能使他振作起来。 ❑ *I wrote that song just to cheer myself up.* 我写了那首歌只是让自己振作起来。

cheer·ful /tʃɪərfəl/ 1 ADJ Someone who is **cheerful** is happy and shows this in their behavior. 高兴的 ❑ *Paddy was always cheerful and jolly.* 帕迪总是很高兴，很开心。 ● **cheer·ful·ly** ADV 高兴地 [ADV with v] ❑ *"We've come with good news," Pat said cheerfully.* "我们带来了好消息。" 帕特高兴地说。 ● **cheer·ful·ness** N-UNCOUNT 高兴 ❑ *I remember this extraordinary man with particular affection for his unfailing cheerfulness.* 我记得这个不同寻常的人，他永远的开心快乐让我有特殊好感。 2 ADJ Something that is **cheerful** is pleasant and makes you feel happy. 令人愉快的 ❑ *The nursery is bright and cheerful, with plenty of toys.* 该托儿所明亮宜人，有许多玩具。 3 ADJ If you describe someone's attitude as **cheerful**, you mean they are not worried about something, and you think that they should be. 乐观的 [usu ADJ n] ❑ *There is little evidence to support his cheerful assumptions.* 几乎没有证据来支持他乐观的设想。 ● **cheer·ful·ly** ADV 乐观地 [ADV before v] ❑ *He cheerfully ignored medical advice which could have prolonged his life.* 他对本可能延长他寿命的医疗建议乐观地置之不理。

cheery /tʃɪəri/ (**cheerier**, **cheeriest**) ADJ If you describe a person or their behavior as **cheery**, you mean that they are cheerful and happy. 高兴的 ❑ *She was cheery and talked to them about their problems.* 她当时很高兴，还和他们谈论了他们的问题。 ● **cheeri·ly** ADV 高兴地 ❑ *"Come on in," she said cheerily.* "进来吧，" 她高兴地说。

cheese ♦◇◇ /tʃiz/ (**cheeses**) N-MASS **Cheese** is a solid food made from milk. It is usually white or yellow. 奶酪 ❑ *...bread and cheese.* …面包和奶酪 ❑ *...delicious French cheeses.* …美味的法式奶酪。

cheese·burg·er /tʃizbɜrgər/ (**cheeseburgers**) N-COUNT A **cheeseburger** is a hamburger with a slice of cheese on top, served on a bun. 奶酪汉堡

▲ **chef** /ʃɛf/ (**chefs**) N-COUNT A **chef** is a cook in a restaurant or hotel. 厨师 ❑ *...some of Australia's leading chefs.* …一些澳大利亚的顶尖厨师们。

Word Link *chem ≈ chemical : biochemist, chemical, chemistry*

chemi·cal ♦♦◇ /kɛmɪkəl/ (**chemicals**) 1 ADJ **Chemical** means involving or resulting from a reaction between two or more substances, or relating to the substances that something consists of. 化学的 [ADJ n] ❑ *...chemical reactions that cause ozone destruction.* …导致臭氧破坏的化学反应。 ❑ *...the chemical composition of the ocean.* …海洋的化学成分。 ● **chemi·cal·ly** /kɛmɪkli/ ADV 经化学方式 ❑ *...chemically treated foods.* …经化学方式处理过的食品。 2 N-COUNT **Chemicals** are substances that are used in a chemical process or made by a chemical process. 化学物；化学制品 ❑ *The whole food chain is affected by the overuse of chemicals in agriculture.* 整个食物链受到了化学物质在农业中过度使用的影响。 ❑ *...a chemical company.* …一家化学制品公司。
→ see **dry-cleaning**, **farm**, **firework**, **war**

Word Link *ist ≈ one who practices : artist, chemist, pharmacist*

chem·ist /kɛmɪst/ (**chemists**) 1 N-COUNT A **chemist** is a person who does research connected with chemistry or who studies

C

Word Web chess

Scholars disagree on the origin of **chess**. Some say it started in China around 570 AD. Others say it was invented in India sometime later. In early versions of the **game**, the **king** was the most powerful **chess piece**. But when the game was brought to Europe in the Middle Ages, a new form appeared. It was called Queen's Chess. Modern chess is based on this game. The king is the most important piece, but the **queen** is the most powerful. Chess **players** use rooks, **bishops**, **knights**, and **pawns** to protect their king and to put their **opponent** in checkmate.

chemistry. 化学家 ❑ *She worked as a research chemist.* 她是一名化学研究员。 **2** N-COUNT A **chemist** or a **chemist's** is the same as a **drugstore** or a **pharmacy**. 药房 [BRIT] **3** N-COUNT A **chemist** is the same as a **druggist** or a **pharmacist**. 药剂师 [BRIT]

In American English, the usual way of referring to a store where medicines are sold is a **drugstore**. ❑ *She went into a drugstore and bought some aspirin.* **Pharmacy** refers specifically to a part of the drugstore where you get prescription medicines. Pharmacies are often located in stores that mainly sell other merchandise, such as supermarkets and discount centers. In Britain, the nearest equivalent of a drugstore is a **chemist's**.

Word Link *chem ≈ chemical : biochemist, chemical, chemistry*

chem·is·try /kɛmɪstri/ **1** N-UNCOUNT **Chemistry** is the scientific study of the structure of substances and of the way that they react with other substances. 化学 **2** N-UNCOUNT The **chemistry** of an organism or a material is the chemical substances that make it up and the chemical reactions that go on inside it. 化学成分；化学反应 ❑ *We have literally altered the chemistry of our planet's atmosphere.* 我们实际上改变了地球大气层的化学成分。 **3** N-UNCOUNT If you say that there is **chemistry** between two people, you mean that it is obvious they are attracted to each other or like each other very much. (彼此间的) 吸引 ❑ *...the extraordinary chemistry between Ingrid and Bogart.* …英格丽德和博加特之间强烈的相互吸引。

cheque /tʃɛk/ (**cheques**) [BRIT] → see **check**

chequebook /tʃɛkbʊk/ (**chequebooks**) [BRIT] → see **checkbook**

★ **cher·ish** /tʃɛrɪʃ/ (**cherishes, cherishing, cherished**) **1** V-T If you **cherish** something such as a hope or a pleasant memory, you keep it in your mind for a long period of time. 珍藏 (希望、记忆等) ❑ *The president will cherish the memory of this visit to Ohio.* 总统将铭记这次对俄亥俄州的访问。 ● **cher·ished** ADJ (对希望、记忆等) 珍藏的 [ADJ n] ❑ *...the cherished dream of a world without wars.* …久藏心中的梦想：一个没有战争的世界。 **2** V-T If you **cherish** someone or something, you take good care of them because you love them. 珍爱 ❑ *He genuinely loved and cherished her.* 他真爱并珍惜过她。 ● **cher·ished** ADJ 珍爱的 [ADJ n] ❑ *He described the picture as his most cherished possession.* 他说这张照片是他最珍爱的财产。 **3** V-T If you **cherish** a right, a privilege, or a principle, you regard it as important and try hard to keep it. 珍视 ❑ *Chinese people cherish their independence and sovereignty.* 中国人民珍视他们的独立和主权。 ● **cher·ished** ADJ 珍视的 [ADJ n] ❑ *Freud called into question some deeply cherished beliefs.* 弗洛伊德对某些人们一直深信不疑的观念提出了质疑。

cher·ry /tʃɛri/ (**cherries**) **1** N-COUNT **Cherries** are small, round fruit with red skins. 樱桃 **2** N-COUNT A **cherry** or a **cherry tree** is a tree that cherries grow on. 樱桃树

cherry-pick (**cherry-picks, cherry-picking, cherry-picked**) V-T If someone **cherry-picks** people or things, they choose the best ones from a group of them, often in a way that other people consider unfair. 挑捡最好的 ❑ *The team is in debt while others are lining up to cherry-pick their best players.* 该队负了债，而别的队正在排队挑捡他们最好的运动员。

chess /tʃɛs/ N-UNCOUNT **Chess** is a game for two people, played on a chessboard. Each player has 16 pieces, including a king. Your aim is to move your pieces so that your opponent's king cannot escape being taken. 国际象棋 ❑ *He was playing chess with his uncle.* 他在和伯父下国际象棋。
→ see Word Web: **chess**

chest ♦◇◇ /tʃɛst/ (**chests**) **1** N-COUNT Your **chest** is the top part of the front of your body where your ribs, lungs, and heart are. 胸部 ❑ *He crossed his arms over his chest.* 他在胸前交叉双臂。 ❑ *He was shot in the chest.* 他胸部中弹。 **2** N-COUNT A **chest** is a large, heavy box used for storing things. 储物箱 ❑ *At the very bottom of the chest were his carving tools.* 在储物箱的最底部有他的雕刻工具。 ❑ *...a treasure chest.* …一个珍宝箱。
→ see **body**

chest·nut /tʃɛsnʌt, -nət/ (**chestnuts**) **1** N-COUNT A **chestnut** or **chestnut tree** is a tall tree with broad leaves. 栗子树 **2** N-COUNT **Chestnuts** are the reddish brown nuts that grow on chestnut trees. You can eat chestnuts. 栗子 **3** COLOR Something that is **chestnut** is dark reddish brown in color. 栗色 ❑ *...chestnut hair.* …栗色的头发。

chew /tʃu/ (**chews, chewing, chewed**) **1** V-T/V-I When you **chew** food, you use your teeth to break it up in your mouth so that it becomes easier to swallow. 咀嚼 ❑ *Be certain to eat slowly and chew your food extremely well.* 一定要慢慢吃，特别细地咀嚼食物。 ❑ *Daniel leaned back on the sofa, still chewing on his apple.* 丹尼尔仰靠在沙发上，还在嚼着苹果。 **2** V-T If you **chew** gum or tobacco, you keep biting it and moving it around your mouth to taste the flavor of it. You do not swallow it. 嚼 (口香糖、烟) ❑ *One girl was chewing gum.* 一个女孩在嚼口香糖。 **3** V-T If you **chew** your lips or your fingernails, you keep biting them because you are nervous. 咬 (嘴唇、手指) ❑ *He chewed his lower lip nervously.* 他紧张地咬着下唇。 **4** V-T/V-I If a person or animal **chews** an object or **chews on** it, they bite it with their teeth. 咬 ❑ *They pause and chew their pencils.* 他们停了下来，咬着铅笔。 ❑ *She chewed through the tape that bound her.* 她咬断了捆绑她的带子。

chic /ʃik/ **1** ADJ Something or someone that is **chic** is fashionable and sophisticated. 时髦且有品位的 ❑ *Her gown was very French and very chic.* 她的礼服是地道的法国风格，非常时髦有品位。 **2** N-UNCOUNT **Chic** is used to refer to a particular style or to the quality of being chic. 特种风格；时髦雅致 ❑ *...French designer chic.* …法国设计师的特有风格。

chick /tʃɪk/ (**chicks**) **1** N-COUNT A **chick** is a baby bird. 雏鸟 ❑ *...newly-hatched chicks.* …刚孵出的雏鸟。 **2** N-COUNT Some men refer to women as **chicks**. This use could cause offense. 妞 (这一称谓可能引起冒犯) [INFORMAL] ❑ *I'm madly in love with this hot biker chick.* 我疯狂地爱上了这个迷人的骑摩托车的妞。

chick·en ♦◇◇ /tʃɪkɪn/ (**chickens, chickening, chickened**) **1** N-COUNT **Chickens** are birds which are kept on a farm for their eggs and for their meat. 鸡 ❑ *Lionel built a coop so that they could raise chickens and have a supply of fresh eggs.* 莱昂内尔搭建了一个鸡笼，这样他们就可以养鸡，得到新鲜鸡蛋。 ● N-UNCOUNT **Chicken** is the flesh of this bird eaten as food. 鸡肉 ❑ *...roast chicken with wild mushrooms.* …烤鸡肉和野蘑菇。 **2** N-COUNT If someone calls you a **chicken**, they mean that you are afraid to do something. 胆小鬼

[INFORMAL, DISAPPROVAL] ❑ *I'm scared of the dark. I'm a big chicken.* 我很怕黑。我是个十足的胆小鬼。● ADJ **Chicken** is also an adjective. 胆小的 [v-link ADJ] ❑ *Why are you so chicken, Gregory?* 你为什么这么胆小，格雷戈里？ 3 PHRASE If you say that someone **is counting** their **chickens**, you mean that they are assuming that they will be successful or get something, when this is not certain. 蛋尚未孵出就数小鸡；指望得过早 ❑ *I don't want to count my chickens before they are hatched.* 我不想指望得过早。 4 **chickens come home to roost** → see **roost**
→ see **meat**

▸ **chicken out** PHRASAL VERB If someone **chickens out of** something they were intending to do, they decide not to do it because they are afraid. 因胆怯而决定不做 [INFORMAL] ❑ *He makes excuses to chicken out of family occasions such as weddings.* 他总是找借口逃避如婚礼这样的家庭聚会。 ❑ *I had never ridden on a motor-cycle before. But it was too late to chicken out.* 在那以前我从未骑过摩托车。但当时已来不及临阵脱逃。

chide /tʃaɪd/ (**chides, chiding, chided**) V-T If you **chide** someone, you speak to them angrily because they have done something bad or foolish. 斥责 [OLD-FASHIONED] ❑ *Jack chided himself for worrying.* 杰克责备自己多虑。

chief ♦♦♦ /tʃif/ (**chiefs**) 1 N-COUNT The **chief** of an organization is the person who is in charge of it. 长官 ❑ *...a commission appointed by the police chief.* …由警察局长任命的委员会。 2 N-COUNT; N-TITLE The **chief** of a tribe is its leader. (部落) 首领 ❑ *...Sitting Bull, chief of the Sioux tribes of the Great Plains.* …大平原苏人部落的首领西廷·布尔。 3 ADJ **Chief** is used in the job titles of the most senior worker or workers of a particular kind in an organization. 首席的 [ADJ n] ❑ *...the chief test pilot.* …首席试飞员。 4 ADJ The **chief** cause, part, or member of something is the most important one. 首要的 [ADJ n] ❑ *Financial stress is well established as a chief reason for divorce.* 经济压力被充分证实为导致离婚的一个首要因素。

Thesaurus *chief* 另参见：
N. boss, director, head, leader 1
ADJ. key, main, major; *(ant.)* minor, unimportant 4

chief ex·ecu·tive of·fic·er (**chief executive officers**) N-COUNT The **chief executive officer** of a company is the person who has overall responsibility for the management of that company. The abbreviation **CEO** is often used. 首席执行官 [BUSINESS]

chief jus·tice (**chief justices**) N-COUNT; N-TITLE A **chief justice** is the most important judge in a court of law, especially a supreme court. (尤指最高法院的) 首席法官

chief·ly /tʃifli/ ADV You use **chiefly** to indicate that a particular reason, emotion, method, or feature is the main or most important one. 首要地 ❑ *He joined the consular service in China, chiefly because this was one of the few job vacancies.* 他参加了驻华领事馆的工作，主要是因为这是为数不多的几个空缺职位之一。

chief of staff (**chiefs of staff**) N-COUNT The **chiefs of staff** are the highest-ranking officers of each service of the armed forces. 参谋长

chif·fon /ʃɪfɒn/ (**chiffons**) N-MASS **Chiffon** is a kind of very thin silk or nylon cloth that you can see through. 雪纺绸 (一种透明的薄绸或薄尼龙面料) ❑ *...floaty chiffon skirts.* …飘动的薄绸裙。

child ♦♦♦ /tʃaɪld/ (**children**) 1 N-COUNT A **child** is a human being who is not yet an adult. 小孩 ❑ *When I was a child I lived in a country village.* 小时候我住在乡村里。 ❑ *...a child of six.* …一个6岁的小孩。 2 N-COUNT Someone's **children** are their sons and daughters of any age. 子女 ❑ *How are the children?* 孩子们好吗？ ❑ *His children have left home.* 他的儿女们已经离开家了。
→ see Word Web: **child**
→ see **age**

Word Partnership *child* 的常用搭配：
N. child **abuse**, child **care** 1
V. **adopt** a child, **have** a child, **raise** a child 1
ADJ. **difficult** child, **happy** child, **small/young** child, **unborn** child 1

child·birth /tʃaɪldbɜrθ/ N-UNCOUNT **Childbirth** is the act of giving birth to a child. 分娩 ❑ *She died in childbirth.* 她死于分娩。

child·care /tʃaɪldkɛər/ N-UNCOUNT **Childcare** refers to taking care of children, and to the facilities which help parents to do so. 儿童保育；儿童保育设施 ❑ *Both partners shared childcare.* 父母双方一同分担照顾孩子的责任。

Word Link *hood ≈ state : condition : adulthood, childhood, manhood*

child·hood ♦◇◇ /tʃaɪldhʊd/ (**childhoods**) N-VAR A person's **childhood** is the period of their life when they are a child. 童年 ❑ *She had a happy childhood.* 她有过一个快乐的童年。 ❑ *He was remembering a story heard in childhood.* 他一直记着童年时听过的一个故事。
→ see **child**

child·ish /tʃaɪldɪʃ/ 1 ADJ **Childish** means relating to or typical of a child. 孩子的；孩子特有的 ❑ *...childish enthusiasm.* …孩子特有的热情。 2 ADJ If you describe someone, especially an adult, as **childish**, you disapprove of them because they behave in an immature way. 幼稚的 [DISAPPROVAL] ❑ *...Penny's selfish and childish behavior.* …佩尼自私而幼稚的行为。

child·less /tʃaɪldlɪs/ ADJ Someone who is **childless** has no children. 无子女的 ❑ *...childless couples.* …无子女的夫妇。

Word Link *like ≈ similar : alike, childlike, likeness*

child·like /tʃaɪldlaɪk/ ADJ You describe someone as **childlike** when they seem like a child in their character, appearance, or behavior. 像孩子的 ❑ *His most enduring quality is his childlike innocence.* 他最持久不变的特质是孩子般的天真无邪。

chil·dren /tʃɪldrən/ **Children** is the plural of **child**. 孩子们

chili /tʃɪli/ (**chilies** or **chilis**) 1 N-VAR **Chilies** are small, red or green peppers. They have a very hot taste and are used in cooking. 辣椒 2 N-UNCOUNT **Chili** is a dish made from meat or beans, or sometimes both, with a thick sauce of tomatoes, and powdered or fresh chilies. 由肉或/和豆加浓番茄酱和辣椒粉或鲜辣椒做成的一道菜肴
→ see **spice**

chill /tʃɪl/ (**chills, chilling, chilled**) 1 V-T/V-I When you **chill** something or when it **chills**, you lower its temperature so that it becomes colder but does not freeze. 使冷却；冷却 ❑ *Chill the fruit salad until serving time.* 上菜前把水果色拉冷却。 ❑ *These doughs can be rolled out while you wait for the pastry to chill.* 当你等待油酥面团冷却时，可以擀平这些生面团。 2 V-T When cold weather or something cold **chills** a person or a place, it makes that person or that place feel very cold. 使很冷 ❑ *The marble floor was beginning to chill me.* 大理石的地板开始让我感到很冷。 ❑ *Wade placed his chilled hands on the radiator and warmed them.* 韦德把他冰冷的双手放到散热器上取暖。 3 N-COUNT If something sends a **chill** through you, it gives you a sudden feeling of fear or anxiety. 害怕的感觉 ❑ *The violence used against the students sent a chill through Indonesia.* 对学生使用暴力使得整个印度尼西

Word Web child

In the Middle Ages, only **infants** and **toddlers** enjoyed the freedoms of **childhood**. A **child** of seven or eight was important to the survival of the family. In the countryside, **sons** started working on the family's farm. **Daughters** did essential housework. In cities, children became laborers and worked along with adults. Today **parents** treat children with special care. The toys **babies** play with help them learn. There are educational programs for preschoolers. The idea of **adolescence** as a separate phase of life appeared about 100 years ago. Today **teenagers** often have part-time jobs while they go to school.

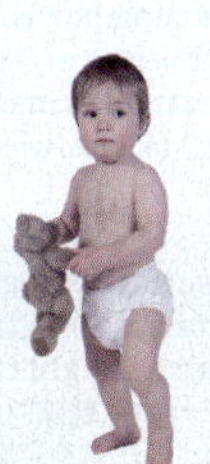

C

亚不寒而栗。 4 N-COUNT A **chill** is a mild illness which can give you a slight fever and headache. 风寒 ❑ *He caught a chill while performing at a rain-soaked open-air venue.* 他在一个被雨浸湿的露天场地表演时着了风寒。 5 ADJ **Chill** weather is cold and unpleasant. 寒冷的 [ADJ n] ❑ *...chill winds, rain and choppy seas.* …寒冷的风、雨以及波浪起伏的大海。 ● N-SING **Chill** is also a noun. 寒冷 ❑ *September is here, bringing with it a chill in the mornings.* 9月到了，带来了清晨的寒意。

→ see **illness, refrigerator**

▸ **chill out** PHRASAL VERB To **chill out** means to relax after you have done something tiring or stressful. 放松 [INFORMAL] ❑ *After school, we used to chill out in each others' bedrooms.* 放学后，我们常常到彼此的卧室里放松休息。

chill·er /tʃɪlər/ (**chillers**) N-COUNT A **chiller** is a very frightening movie or novel. 恐怖电影；恐怖小说

chil·li /tʃɪli/ (**chillies** or **chillis**) [mainly BRIT] → see **chili**

chill·ing /tʃɪlɪŋ/ ADJ If you describe something as **chilling**, you mean it is frightening. 令人恐惧的 ❑ *He described in chilling detail how he attacked her.* 他描述了他如何攻击她的恐怖细节。 ● **chill·ing·ly** ADV 令人恐惧地 ❑ *...the murder of a Chicago teenager in chillingly similar circumstances in February.* …2月份在惊人相似的场合下一位芝加哥青少年被害的凶杀案。

chil·ly /tʃɪli/ (**chillier, chilliest**) 1 ADJ Something that is **chilly** is unpleasantly cold. 阴冷的 ❑ *It was a chilly afternoon.* 那是一个阴冷的下午。 2 ADJ If you feel **chilly**, you feel rather cold. 寒冷的 [v-link ADJ] ❑ *I'm a bit chilly.* 我感到有点儿冷。

> If you want to emphasize how cold the weather is, you can say that it is **freezing**, especially in winter when there is ice or frost. In summer, if the temperature is below average, you can say that it is **cool**. In general, **cold** suggests a lower temperature than **cool**, and **cool** things may be pleasant or refreshing. ❑ *A cool breeze swept off the ocean; it was pleasant out there.* If it is very **cool** or too **cool**, you can also say that it is **chilly**.

chime /tʃaɪm/ (**chimes, chiming, chimed**) 1 V-T/V-I When a bell or a clock **chimes**, it makes ringing sounds. 鸣响 ❑ *He heard the front doorbell chime.* 他听见前门的门铃响了。 ❑ *...as the town hall clock chimed three o'clock.* …当市镇大厅的钟鸣报3点时。 2 N-COUNT A **chime** is a ringing sound made by a bell, especially when it is part of a clock. 钟声 ❑ *At that moment a chime sounded from the front of the house.* 那时从房子的前面传来了一阵钟声。 3 N-PLURAL **Chimes** are a set of small objects which make a ringing sound when they are blown by the wind. 风铃 ❑ *...the haunting sound of the wind chimes.* …萦绕心头的风铃声。

▸ **chime in** PHRASAL VERB If you **chime in**, you say something just after someone else has spoken. 插话 ❑ *"Why?" Pete asked impatiently.—"Yes, why?" Bob chimed in. "It seems like a good idea to me."* "为什么？"皮特不耐烦地问。——"是啊，为什么？"鲍勃插嘴说。"在我看来这好像是个好主意。"

chim·ney /tʃɪmni/ (**chimneys**) N-COUNT A **chimney** is a pipe through which smoke goes up into the air, usually through the roof of a building. 烟囱 ❑ *Thick, yellow smoke pours constantly out of the chimneys at the steel plant in Katowice.* 浓密的黄烟不断地从卡托维兹钢铁厂的烟囱里喷吐出来。

▲ **chim·pan·zee** /tʃɪmpænzi/ (**chimpanzees**) N-COUNT A **chimpanzee** is a kind of small African ape. 黑猩猩

→ see **primate, zoo**

chin /tʃɪn/ (**chins**) N-COUNT Your **chin** is the part of your face that is below your mouth and above your neck. 下巴 ❑ *...a double chin.* …双下巴。

chi·na /tʃaɪnə/ 1 N-UNCOUNT **China** is a hard white substance made from clay. It is used to make things such as cups, bowls, plates, and ornaments. 瓷 ❑ *...a small bowl made of china.* …一个小瓷碗。 2 N-UNCOUNT Cups, bowls, plates, and ornaments made of china are referred to as **china**. 瓷器 ❑ *Judy collects blue and white china.* 朱迪收集青花瓷器。

→ see **pottery**

chink /tʃɪŋk/ (**chinks**) 1 N-COUNT A **chink** in a surface is a very narrow crack or opening in it. 裂缝 ❑ *...a chink in the wall.* …墙上的一道裂缝。 2 N-COUNT A **chink of** light is a small patch of light that shines through a small opening in something. 一线(从缝隙间射入的光) ❑ *I noticed a chink of light at the end of the corridor.* 我注意到走廊的尽头有一线光亮。

chip ♦◇◇ /tʃɪp/ (**chips, chipping, chipped**) 1 N-COUNT **Chips** or **potato chips** are very thin slices of fried potato that are eaten as a snack. 炸薯片 [AM]

> in BRIT, use **crisps**

❑ *...a package of onion-flavored potato chips.* …一包洋葱味的薯片。 2 N-COUNT **Chips** are long, thin pieces of potato fried in oil or fat and eaten hot, usually with a meal. 炸薯条 [BRIT]

> in AM, use **French fries**

3 N-COUNT A silicon **chip** is a very small piece of silicon with electronic circuits on it which is part of a computer or other piece of machinery. 芯片(计算机或其他机器中带有电子电路的细小硅片) ❑ *...an electronic card containing a chip.* …一张带有芯片的电子卡。 4 N-COUNT A **chip** is a small piece of something or a small piece which has been broken off something. 小块东西；碎屑 ❑ *It contains real chocolate chips.* 它里面含有纯正的巧克力颗粒。 5 N-COUNT A **chip** in something such as a piece of china or furniture is where a small piece has been broken off it. 小缺口 ❑ *The cup had a small chip.* 这个杯子有个小缺口。 6 N-COUNT **Chips** are plastic counters used in gambling to represent money. (作赌注用的) 筹码 ❑ *He put the pile of chips in the center of the table and drew a card.* 他把那堆筹码放在桌子中间，然后抽了一张牌。 7 V-T/V-I If you **chip** something or if it **chips**, a small piece is broken off it. 把…碰掉一小块；碎掉一小块 ❑ *The blow chipped the woman's tooth.* 这一击把那个女人的牙齿打掉了一小块。 ● **chipped** ADJ 有缺口的；有缺损的 ❑ *The wagon's paint was badly chipped on the outside.* 这辆四轮马车外壳的油漆严重地剥落。 8 → see also **bargaining chip, blue chip**

→ see **computer**

▸ **chip in** PHRASAL VERB When a number of people **chip in**, each person gives some money so that they can pay for something together. 凑钱 [INFORMAL] ❑ *They chip in for the gas.* 他们凑钱买煤气。

chis·el /tʃɪzᵊl/ (**chisels, chiseling** or **chiselling, chiseled** or **chiselled**) 1 N-COUNT A **chisel** is a tool that has a long metal blade with a sharp edge at the end. It is used for cutting and shaping wood and stone. 凿子 ❑ *...a hammer and chisel.* …一把锤子和一把凿子。 2 V-T If you **chisel** wood or stone, you cut and shape it using a chisel. 用凿子雕切 ❑ *He set out to chisel a dog out of sandstone.* 他开始用凿子将砂岩雕刻成一只狗。

chlo·rine /klɔrin/ N-UNCOUNT **Chlorine** is a strong-smelling gas that is used to clean water and to make cleaning products. 氯气

choco·late ♦◇◇ /tʃɔkəlɪt, tʃɔklɪt/ (**chocolates**) 1 N-MASS **Chocolate** is a sweet, hard food made from cacao. It is usually brown in color and is eaten as a candy. 巧克力 ❑ *...a bar of chocolate.* …一条巧克力。 ❑ *Do you want some chocolate?* 你想吃点巧克力吗？ 2 N-UNCOUNT **Chocolate** or **hot chocolate** is a drink made from a powder containing chocolate. It is usually made with hot milk. 巧克力热饮 ❑ *...a small cafeteria where the visitors can buy tea, coffee and chocolate.* …一家小规模的自助快餐店，在那里游客们可以买到茶、咖啡和巧克力热饮。 3 N-COUNT **Chocolates** are small candies or nuts covered with a layer of chocolate. They are usually sold in a box. 巧克力糖 ❑ *...a box of chocolates.* …一盒巧克力糖。 4 COLOR **Chocolate** is used to describe things that are dark brown in color. 深褐色 ❑ *The curtains and the bedspread were chocolate velvet.* 窗帘和床罩是深褐色的天鹅绒。

→ see **dessert**

choice ♦♦◇ /tʃɔɪs/ (**choices, choicer, choicest**) 1 N-COUNT If there is a **choice of** things, there are several of them and you can choose the one you want. 选择 ❑ *It's available in a choice of colors.* 它有多种颜色可供选择。 ❑ *At lunchtime, there's a choice between the buffet or the set menu.* 午饭时，可以选择自助餐或套餐。 2 N-COUNT Your **choice** is someone or something that you choose from a range of things. 所挑选的人或物 ❑ *Although he was only grumbling, his choice of words made Rodney angry.* 尽管他只是在发牢骚，但他所用的字眼却让罗德尼很生气。 3 ADJ **Choice** means of very high quality. 优质的 [ADJ n] [FORMAL] ❑ *...a box of their choicest chocolates.* …他们的一盒上等巧克力。 4 PHRASE If you **have no choice but** to do something or **have little choice but** to do it, you cannot avoid doing it. 无选择余地 ❑ *They had little choice but to agree to what he suggested.* 除了同意他的意见，他们别无选择。 5 PHRASE The thing or person **of your choice** is the one that you choose. 自己挑选的 ❑ *...tickets to see the football team of your choice.* …观看你所中意的足球队的门票。 6 PHRASE The item **of choice** is the one that most people prefer. 受多数人欢迎的 ❑ *The drug is set to become the treatment of choice for asthma worldwide.* 这种药就要成为全世界治疗哮喘的首选药物。

C

Word Partnership *choice* 的常用搭配:

ADJ. best/good choice, wide choice 1
N. freedom of choice, choice of *something* 1
V. given a choice, have a choice, make a choice 1 2

▲ **choir** /kwaɪər/ (choirs) N-COUNT A **choir** is a group of people who sing together, for example in a church or school. 唱诗班; 合唱团 ❑ *He has been singing in his church choir since he was six.* 他从6岁起就开始在教堂的唱诗班咏唱了。

choke /tʃoʊk/ (chokes, choking, choked) 1 V-T/V-I When you **choke** or when something **chokes** you, you cannot breathe properly or get enough air into your lungs. 使窒息; 窒息 ❑ *A small child could choke on the doll's hair.* 小孩子可能会因玩具娃娃的头发而窒息。❑ *Dense smoke swirled and billowed, its rank fumes choking her.* 浓密的烟雾盘旋翻腾, 刺鼻的烟味使她窒息。❑ *The girl choked to death after breathing in smoke.* 那位女孩吸入烟雾后窒息而亡。 2 V-T To **choke** someone means to squeeze their neck until they are dead. (卡住喉咙) 使停止呼吸 ❑ *The men pushed him into the entrance of a nearby building, where they choked him with his tie.* 那些男人把他推进了附近一座大楼的入口处, 然后在那里用他的领带将他勒死了。 3 V-T If a place is **choked with** things or people, it is full of them and they prevent movement in it. 使阻塞 [usu passive] ❑ *The village's roads are choked with traffic.* 那个村庄的道路被车辆阻塞住了。 4 N-COUNT The **choke** in a car, truck, or other vehicle is a device that reduces the amount of air going into the engine and makes it easier to start. 阻气门 ❑ *It is like driving your car with the choke out all the time.* 就像一直松着阻气门在开车一样。

Word Partnership *choke* 的常用搭配:

N. choke **on** *something* 1
choke *someone* 2
V. make *someone* choke 1 2

chol·era /kɒlərə/ N-UNCOUNT **Cholera** is a serious disease that often kills people. It is caused by drinking infected water or by eating infected food. 霍乱 ❑ *...a cholera epidemic.* …一场霍乱疫情。

★ **cho·les·ter·ol** /kəlɛstərɔl/ N-UNCOUNT **Cholesterol** is a substance that exists in the fat, tissues, and blood of all animals. Too much cholesterol in a person's blood can cause heart disease. 胆固醇 ❑ *...a dangerously high cholesterol level.* …一个危险的高胆固醇水平。

choose ♦♦◊ /tʃuz/ (chooses, choosing, chose, chosen) 1 V-T/V-I If you **choose** someone or something **from** several people or things that are available, you decide which person or thing you want to have. 挑选; 选择 ❑ *They will be able to choose their own leaders in democratic elections.* 在民主选举中他们将可以选出他们自己的领导人。❑ *There are several patchwork cushions to choose from.* 有几种拼布工艺垫子可供选择。 2 V-T/V-I If you **choose to** do something, you do it because you want to or because you feel that it is right. 情愿; 觉得应该 (做某事) ❑ *They knew that discrimination was going on, but chose to ignore it.* 他们知道歧视仍然存在, 但他们情愿不去理会。❑ *You have the right to remain silent if you choose.* 如果你愿意, 你有权保持沉默。

Thesaurus *choose* 另参见:

V. decide on, opt for, prefer, settle on; *(ant.)* pass over, refuse, reject 1

chop ♦◊◊ /tʃɒp/ (chops, chopping, chopped) 1 V-T If you **chop** something, you cut it into pieces with strong, downward movements of a knife or an ax. (用力) 切; 砍 ❑ *Chop the butter into small pieces.* 把黄油切成小块。❑ *Visitors were set to work chopping wood.* 参观者们被安排去砍木头。 2 N-COUNT A **chop** is a small piece of meat cut from the ribs of a sheep or pig. 排骨 ❑ *...grilled lamb chops.* …烤羔羊排。

▸ **chop down** PHRASAL VERB If you **chop down** a tree, you cut through its trunk with an ax so that it falls to the ground. 砍倒 ❑ *Sometimes they have to chop down a tree for firewood.* 有时他们不得不砍倒一棵树来做木柴。
→ see **cut**

▸ **chop off** PHRASAL VERB To **chop off** something such as a part of someone's body means to cut it off. 割掉 ❑ *She chopped off her golden, waist-length hair.* 她剪掉了她那齐腰长的金发。

▸ **chop up** PHRASAL VERB If you **chop** something **up**, you chop it into small pieces. 切碎 ❑ *Chop up three firm tomatoes.* 把3个硬的西红柿切碎。
→ see **cut**

chop·per /tʃɒpər/ (choppers) N-COUNT A **chopper** is a helicopter. 直升飞机 [INFORMAL] ❑ *Overhead, the chopper roared and the big blades churned the air.* 直升飞机在头顶上轰响着, 巨大的桨叶搅动着空气。

chop·stick /tʃɒpstɪk/ (chopsticks) N-COUNT **Chopsticks** are a pair of thin sticks which people in China and the Far East use to eat their food. 筷子 [usu pl]

cho·ral /kɔrəl/ ADJ **Choral** music is sung by a choir. 合唱队的; 唱诗班的 ❑ *His collection of choral music from around the world is called "Voices."* 他那包含世界各地合唱音乐的合集叫做《声音》。

★ **chord** /kɔrd/ (chords) 1 N-COUNT A **chord** is a number of musical notes played or sung at the same time with a pleasing effect. 和弦 ❑ *I could play a few chords on the guitar and sing a song.* 我能弹着一些吉他和弦唱一首歌。 2 PHRASE If something **strikes a chord with** you, it makes you feel sympathy or enthusiasm. 引起同情; 引起共鸣 ❑ *Mr. Jenkins's arguments for stability struck a chord with Europe's two most powerful politicians.* 詹金斯先生支持稳定的观点引起了欧洲两位最有权力的政治家的共鸣。

▲ **chore** /tʃɔr/ (chores) N-COUNT A **chore** is a task that you must do but that you find unpleasant or boring. 琐事 ❑ *She sees exercise primarily as an unavoidable chore.* 她把锻炼主要看作是不得不做的琐事。

cho·reo·graph /kɔriəgræf/ (choreographs, choreographing, choreographed) V-T/V-I When someone **choreographs** a ballet or other dance, they invent the steps and movements and tell the dancers how to perform them. 设计舞蹈动作 ❑ *Achim had choreographed the dance in Act II himself.* 阿奇姆亲自为第二幕设计了舞蹈动作。

cho·reog·ra·phy /kɔriɒgrəfi/ N-UNCOUNT **Choreography** is the inventing of steps and movements for ballets and other dances. 舞蹈编排 ❑ *The choreography of Eric Hawkins is considered radical by ballet audiences.* 埃里克・霍金斯的舞蹈编排被芭蕾舞剧的观众认为是不同凡响的。

★ **cho·rus** /kɔrəs/ (choruses, chorusing, chorused) 1 N-COUNT A **chorus** is a part of a song which is repeated after each verse. 副歌 ❑ *Caroline sang two verses and the chorus of her song.* 卡罗琳唱了她歌中的两段主歌及副歌。 2 N-COUNT A **chorus** is a large group of people who sing together. 合唱团 ❑ *The chorus was singing "The Ode to Joy."* 合唱团那时正在唱着《欢乐颂》。 3 N-COUNT A **chorus** is a piece of music written to be sung by a large group of people. 合唱曲 ❑ *...the Hallelujah Chorus.* …哈利路亚合唱曲。 4 N-COUNT A **chorus** is a group of singers or dancers who perform together in a show, in contrast to the soloists. 合唱团; 舞蹈队 ❑ *Students played the lesser parts and sang in the chorus.* 学生们扮演了一些次要角色, 并参加了合唱团的演唱。 5 N-COUNT-COLL In drama, a **chorus** is an actor or a group of actors who comment on the action of the play. (戏剧中的) 剧情解说演员 ❑ *He decides to sort out her life for her, while a pushy Greek chorus dispenses advice from the sidelines.* 他决定帮她理顺一下生活, 而一位爱管闲事的希腊剧情解说演员则从旁观者的角度发表了建议。❑ *...commanding performances from Joe Savino as the chorus and Stephen Brennan as the ghost.* …由乔・萨维诺担任剧情解说演员、斯蒂芬・布伦南扮演幽灵的给人深刻印象的演出。 6 N-COUNT When there is a **chorus of** criticism, disapproval, or praise, that attitude is expressed by a lot of people at the same time. 齐声 (批评、反对或赞扬) ❑ *The government is defending its economic policies against a growing chorus of criticism.* 面对日益高涨的齐声批评, 政府还在为其经济政策辩护。 7 V-T When people **chorus** something, they say it or sing it together. 齐声说或唱 [WRITTEN] ❑ *"Hi," they chorused.* "嗨," 他们齐声说道。

chose /tʃoʊz/ **Chose** is the past tense of **choose**. **choose**的过去式

cho·sen /tʃoʊzᵊn/ **Chosen** is the past participle of **choose**. **choose**的过去分词

Christ /kraɪst/ N-PROPER **Christ** is one of the names of Jesus, whom Christians believe to be the son of God and whose teachings are the basis of Christianity. 耶稣 ❑ *...the teachings of Christ.* …耶稣的训导。

chris·ten /krɪsᵊn/ (christens, christening, christened) V-T When a baby **is christened**, he or she is given a name during the Christian ceremony of baptism. Compare **baptize**. 为…在洗礼时取名 [usu passive] ❑ *She was born in March and christened in June.* 她3月份出生, 6月洗礼时取了名。

chris·ten·ing /krɪsᵊnɪŋ/ (christenings) N-COUNT A **christening** is a Christian ceremony in which a baby is made a member of the

Christian church and is officially given his or her name. Compare **baptism**. 基督教的洗礼命名仪式 ❑ *...my granddaughter's christening.* …我孙女的洗礼命名仪式。

Word Link *an, ian ≈ one of, relating to : Christian, pedestrian, Roman*

Christian ♦♦◇ /krɪstʃən/ (**Christians**) **1** N-COUNT A **Christian** is someone who follows the teachings of Jesus Christ. 基督教徒 ❑ *He was a devout Christian.* 他曾是一个虔诚的基督教徒。 **2** ADJ **Christian** means relating to Christianity or Christians. 基督教的；基督教徒的 ❑ *...the Christian Church.* …基督教会。 ❑ *Most of my friends are Christian.* 我大多数朋友都信奉基督教。
→ see **religion**

Chris·ti·an·ity /krɪstʃiænɪti/ N-UNCOUNT **Christianity** is a religion that is based on the teachings of Jesus Christ and the belief that he was the son of God. 基督教 ❑ *He converted to Christianity that day.* 那天他改信了基督教。

Christian name (**Christian names**) N-COUNT Some people refer to their first names as their **Christian names**. 名字 ❑ *Despite my attempts to get him to call me by my Christian name, he insisted on addressing me as "Mr. Kennedy."* 尽管我试图让他直接叫我的名，可他还是坚持称呼我为"肯尼迪先生"。

Christ·mas ♦♦◇ /krɪsməs/ (**Christmases**) **1** N-VAR **Christmas** is a Christian festival when the birth of Jesus Christ is celebrated. Christmas is celebrated on the 25th of December. 圣诞节 ❑ *The day after Christmas is generally a busy one for retailers.* 圣诞节次日对零售商们来说通常都是繁忙的一天。 **2** N-VAR **Christmas** is the period of several days around and including Christmas Day. 圣诞节期间 ❑ *During the Christmas holidays there's a tremendous amount of traffic between the Northeast and Florida.* 在圣诞节期间，东北部和弗罗里达州之间的交通异常繁忙。

Christ·mas Day N-UNCOUNT **Christmas Day** is the 25th of December, when Christmas is celebrated. 圣诞节

Christ·mas Eve N-UNCOUNT **Christmas Eve** is the 24th of December, the day before Christmas Day. 圣诞节前夜

chrome /kroʊm/ N-UNCOUNT **Chrome** is metal plated with chromium. 铬合金 ❑ *...old-fashioned chrome taps.* …老式的铬合金水龙头。

chro·mium /kroʊmiəm/ N-UNCOUNT **Chromium** is a hard, shiny, metallic element, used to make steel alloys and to coat other metals. 铬 ❑ *...chromium-plated fire accessories.* …镀铬的消防配件。

chro·mo·some /kroʊməsoʊm/ (**chromosomes**) N-COUNT A **chromosome** is a part of a cell in an animal or plant. It contains genes which determine what characteristics the animal or plant will have. 染色体 ❑ *Each cell of our bodies contains 46 chromosomes.* 我们体内的每个细胞都有46条染色体。

Word Link *chron ≈ time : chronic, chronicle, synchronize*

★ **chron·ic** /krɒnɪk/ **1** ADJ A **chronic** illness or disability lasts for a very long time. Compare **acute**. 慢性的；长期的 ❑ *...chronic back pain.* …长期背痛。 ● **chroni·cal·ly** /krɒnɪkli/ ADV 慢性地；长期地 [ADV adj/-ed] ❑ *Most of them were chronically ill.* 他们中大部分人都有慢性病。 **2** ADJ You can describe someone's bad habits or behavior as **chronic** when they have behaved like that for a long time and do not seem to be able to stop themselves. 积习难改的 [ADJ n] ❑ *...a chronic worrier.* …一个老是发愁的人。 **3** ADJ A **chronic** situation or problem is very severe and unpleasant. 严重的 ❑ *One cause of the artist's suicide seems to have been chronic poverty.* 那位艺术家自杀的原因之一好像是极度贫困。 ● **chroni·cal·ly** ADV 严重地 [ADV adj/-ed] ❑ *Research and technology are said to be chronically underfunded.* 据说研究和技术资金严重不足。

★ **chroni·cle** /krɒnɪkᵊl/ (**chronicles, chronicling, chronicled**) **1** V-T To **chronicle** a series of events means to write about them or show them in broadcasts in the order in which they happened. 按发生时间顺序编写或播放 ❑ *The series chronicles the everyday adventures of two eternal bachelors.* 这部丛书按时间顺序记载了两个终生未婚男子每天的奇遇。 **2** N-COUNT A **chronicle** is an account or record of a series of events. 编年史 ❑ *...this vast chronicle of Napoleonic times.* …这本关于拿破仑时期的大部头编年史。 **3** N-IN-NAMES **Chronicle** is sometimes used as part of the name of a newspaper. …报 ❑ *...the San Francisco Chronicle.* …旧金山报。
→ see **diary**

chrono·logi·cal /krɒnᵊlɒdʒɪkᵊl/ ADJ If things are described or shown in **chronological** order, they are described or shown in the order in which they happened. 按时间顺序排列的 ❑ *I have arranged these stories in chronological order.* 我按时间顺序排列了这些故事。 ● **chrono·logi·cal·ly** ADV 按时间顺序排列地 ❑ *The exhibition is organized chronologically.* 展览品是按其时间顺序来安排的。

▲ **chry·san·themum** /krɪsænθəməm/ (**chrysanthemums**) N-COUNT A **chrysanthemum** is a large garden flower with many long, thin petals. 菊花

chub·by /tʃʌbi/ (**chubbier, chubbiest**) ADJ A **chubby** person is somewhat fat. 圆胖的 ❑ *Do you think I'm too chubby?* 你觉得我太胖了吗？

▲ **chuck** /tʃʌk/ (**chucks, chucking, chucked**) **1** V-T When you **chuck** something somewhere, you throw it there in a casual or careless way. 随意丢弃 [INFORMAL] ❑ *I took a great dislike to the clock, so I chucked it in the trash.* 我很不喜欢那个钟，所以我随手把它扔进了垃圾里。 **2** V-T If you **chuck** your job or some other activity, you stop doing it. 放弃；停止（工作或其他活动）[INFORMAL] ❑ *Last summer, he chucked his 10-year career as a stockbroker and headed for the mountains.* 去年夏天，他放弃了从事10年的股票经纪人的工作，前往高山地区。 **3** PHRASE If someone **chucks it all**, they stop doing their job, and usually move somewhere else. 放弃工作（并前往他处） ❑ *Sometimes I'd like to chuck it all and go fishing.* 有时我真想放弃工作去钓鱼。 **4** N-COUNT A **chuck** is a device for holding a tool in a machine such as a drill. （钻机等机器中固定工具的）卡盘 **5** N-UNCOUNT **Chuck** is a cut of beef. 牛颈部至肩部的肉

▲ **chuck·le** /tʃʌkᵊl/ (**chuckles, chuckling, chuckled**) V-I When you **chuckle**, you laugh quietly. 轻声地笑 ❑ *The banker chuckled and said, "Of course not."* 银行家轻声笑了，说道，"当然不。" ● N-COUNT **Chuckle** is also a noun. 轻声笑 ❑ *He gave a little chuckle.* 他轻声一笑。

chug /tʃʌg/ (**chugs, chugging, chugged**) **1** V-I When a vehicle **chugs** somewhere, it goes there slowly, noisily, and with difficulty. （车辆）发着嘎嚓声吃力地行驶 ❑ *The train chugs down the track.* 火车沿着轨道嘎嚓嘎嚓地缓慢行驶着。 **2** V-T If you **chug** something, you drink it very quickly without stopping. 一口气喝完 [AM, INFORMAL] ❑ *Nadine chugs her beer and orders another.* 内丁一口气喝完了她的啤酒后又要了一杯。

★ **chunk** /tʃʌŋk/ (**chunks**) **1** N-COUNT **Chunks of** something are thick, solid pieces of it. 厚块 ❑ *They had to be careful of floating chunks of ice.* 他们不得不小心漂浮着的厚冰块。 ❑ *...a chunk of meat.* …一大块肉。 **2** N-COUNT A **chunk of** something is a large amount or large part of it. 相当大的部分；相当大的数量 [INFORMAL] ❑ *The company owns a chunk of farmland near the airport.* 这家公司在机场附近拥有一大片农场。

chunky /tʃʌŋki/ (**chunkier, chunkiest**) **1** ADJ A **chunky** person is broad and heavy. （人）粗壮的 ❑ *The soprano was a chunky girl from California.* 这名女高音是一位来自加利福尼亚的粗壮女孩。 **2** ADJ A **chunky** object is large and thick. （物）大而厚的 ❑ *Her taste in fiction was for chunky historical romances.* 她以前喜欢的小说是大部头的历史爱情故事。 ❑ *...a chunky sweater.* …一件厚实的毛线衫。

church ♦♦◇ /tʃɜrtʃ/ (**churches**) **1** N-VAR A **church** is a building in which Christians worship. You usually refer to this place as **church** when you are talking about the time that people spend there. 教堂 ❑ *...one of the country's most historic churches.* …该国家历史上最著名的教堂之一。 ❑ *...St Helen's Church.* …圣海伦教堂。 ❑ *The family had gone to church.* 这家人都去教堂了。 **2** N-COUNT A **Church** is one of the groups of people within the Christian religion, for example Catholics or Methodists, that have their own beliefs, clergy, and forms of worship. （基督教的）教派 ❑ *...cooperation with the Catholic Church.* …与天主教派的合作。 ❑ *Church leaders said he was welcome to return.* 该教派领袖说欢迎他回皈。

churn /tʃɜrn/ (**churns, churning, churned**) **1** N-COUNT A **churn** is a container which is used for making butter. （制黄油的）搅乳器 **2** V-T If something **churns** water, mud, or dust, it moves it about violently. 剧烈搅动 ❑ *...dirt roads now churned into mud by the annual rains.* …土路现在被一年一度的雨水搅和得一片泥泞。 ● PHRASAL VERB **Churn up** means the same as **churn**. 剧烈搅动 ❑ *The recent rain had churned up the waterfall into a muddy whirlpool.* 近来的雨水把那条瀑布搅成了泥水漩涡。 ❑ *Occasionally dolphins slap the water with their tails or churn it up in play.* 海豚偶尔会在戏耍时用它们的尾巴拍打海水或剧烈地翻腾海水。 **3** V-T/V-I If you say that your stomach **is churning**, you mean that you feel sick. You can also say that something **churns**

your stomach. 使恶心 及物动词；恶心 不及物动词 ❑ *My stomach churned as I stood up.* 我站起身时，胃里一阵翻腾。

▸ **churn out** PHRASAL VERB To **churn out** something means to produce large quantities of it very quickly. 快速大量生产 [INFORMAL] ❑ *He began to churn out literary compositions in English.* 他开始用英文很快地创作出大量的文学作品。

▸ **churn up** → see **churn 2**

chute /ʃut/ (**chutes**) 1 N-COUNT A **chute** is a steep, narrow slope down which people or things can slide. 滑道 ❑ *Passengers escaped from the plane's front exits by sliding down emergency chutes.* 乘客们从飞机前面出口的紧急滑道滑下去得以逃生。 2 N-COUNT A **chute** is a parachute. 降落伞 [INFORMAL] ❑ *You can release the chute with either hand, but it is easier to do it with the left.* 你可用任意一只手打开降落伞，但用左手会更容易些。

chut·ney /tʃʌtni/ (**chutneys**) N-MASS **Chutney** is a cold sauce made from fruit, vinegar, sugar, and spices. It is sold in jars and you eat it with meat or cheese. 酸辣酱 ❑ *...mango chutney.* …芒果酸辣酱。

ci·der /saɪdər/ (**ciders**) N-MASS **Cider** is a drink made from apples. **Cider** does not usually contain alcohol, and if it does contain alcohol, it is usually called **hard cider**. In Britain, **cider** usually contains alcohol. 苹果汁；苹果酒 ● N-COUNT A glass of cider can be referred to as a **cider**. (一杯) 苹果汁 ❑ *At the bar he ordered a cider.* 他在酒吧点了一杯苹果汁。

ci·gar /sɪgɑr/ (**cigars**) N-COUNT **Cigars** are rolls of dried tobacco leaves which people smoke. 雪茄烟 ❑ *He was smoking a big cigar.* 他在抽一只大雪茄。

Word Link *ette ≈ small : cigarette, diskette, rosette*

ciga·rette ♦◇◇ /sɪgərɛt/ (**cigarettes**) also **cigaret** N-COUNT **Cigarettes** are small tubes of paper containing tobacco which people smoke. 香烟 ❑ *He went out to buy a packet of cigarettes.* 他出去买了一包香烟。

cin·ema ♦◇◇ /sɪnɪmə/ (**cinemas**) 1 N-UNCOUNT **Cinema** is the business and art of making movies. 电影业；电影制作艺术 ❑ *Contemporary African cinema has much to offer.* 当代非洲电影制作艺术有很多贡献。 2 N-COUNT A **cinema** is a place where people go to watch movies for entertainment. 电影院 [mainly BRIT]

in AM, usually use **movie theater, movie house**

3 N-SING You can talk about **the cinema** when you are talking about seeing a movie. 电影 [mainly BRIT]

in AM, usually use **the movies**

cin·ema-goer [BRIT] → see **moviegoer**

cin·emat·ic /sɪnɪmætɪk/ ADJ **Cinematic** means relating to movies made for movie theaters. 电影的 ❑ *...a cinematic masterpiece.* …一部电影杰作。

cin·na·mon /sɪnəmən/ N-UNCOUNT **Cinnamon** is a sweet spice used for flavoring food. 肉桂

→ see **spice**

cir·ca /sɜrkə/ PREP **Circa** is used in front of a particular year to say that this is the approximate date when something happened or was made. 大约 [FORMAL] ❑ *The story tells of a runaway slave girl in Louisiana, circa 1850.* 这个故事讲述的是路易斯安那州一个年轻的逃跑女奴，时间大约在1850年。

Word Link *circ ≈ around : circle, circuit, circulate*

cir·cle ♦♦◇ /sɜrkəl/ (**circles, circling, circled**) 1 N-COUNT A **circle** is a shape consisting of a curved line completely surrounding an area. Every part of the line is the same distance from the center of the area. 圆圈 ❑ *The flag was red, with a large white circle in the center.* 那面旗子是红色的，中间有一个白色的大圆圈。 2 N-COUNT A **circle of** something is a round, flat piece or area of it. 圆盘状物 ❑ *Cut out 4 circles of pastry.* 切出4块圆形油酥面饼。 3 N-COUNT A **circle of** objects or people is a group of them arranged in the shape of a circle. 圈 ❑ *...a circle of gigantic stones.* …一圈巨石。 4 N-COUNT You can refer to a group of people as a **circle** when they meet each other regularly because they are friends or because they belong to the same profession or share the same interests. (相同兴趣、职业等的人形成的) 圈子 ❑ *He has a small circle of friends.* 他有一个小小的朋友圈子。 5 V-T/V-I If something **circles** an object or a place, or **circles around** it, it forms a circle around it. 环绕 ❑ *This is the road that circles the city.* 这就是那条环城路。 6 V-T/V-I If an aircraft or a bird **circles** or **circles** something, it moves around in a circle in the air. 围着…转圈；盘旋 ❑ *The plane circled, awaiting permission to land.* 飞机盘旋着，等待着陆指令。 ❑ *There were two helicopters circling around.* 有两架直升飞机在周围盘旋。 7 V-T If you **circle** something on a piece of paper, you draw a circle around it. 把…圈出来 ❑ *Circle the words on this list that you recognize.* 把这张表上你认识的字圈出来。 8 → see also **inner circle, vicious circle**

→ see **globe, shape, soccer**

Word Partnership *circle* 的常用搭配:

V.	**draw** a circle 1 2
	form a circle, **make** a circle 1 – 3
ADV.	circle **around** 1 – 3
ADJ.	**big/large/small** circle 1 – 4
PREP.	**inside/outside/within** a circle 1 – 4
	circle **around** 5

cir·cuit ♦◇◇ /sɜrkɪt/ (**circuits**) 1 N-COUNT An electrical **circuit** is a complete route which an electric current can flow around. 电路 ❑ *Any attempts to cut through the cabling will break the electrical circuit.* 任何切断电缆的做法都会使电路中断。 2 → see also **closed-circuit** 3 N-COUNT A **circuit** is a series of places that are visited regularly by a person or group, especially as a part of their job. 巡回的场所 ❑ *It's a common problem, the one I'm asked about most when I'm on the lecture circuit.* 这是个常见问题，一个在我巡回演讲时人们最常问到的问题。

cir·cu·lar /sɜrkyələr/ (**circulars**) 1 ADJ Something that is **circular** is shaped like a circle. 圆形的 ❑ *...a circular hole twelve feet wide and two feet deep.* …一个12英尺宽、2英尺深的圆洞。 2 ADJ A **circular** journey or route is one in which you go to a place and return by a different route. (旅行或路线) 环行的 ❑ *Both sides of the river can be explored on this circular walk.* 沿着这条环形步行道走，河的两边就都可以看得到了。 3 N-COUNT A **circular** is an official letter or advertisement that is sent to a large number of people at the same time. 函件；通告 ❑ *The proposal has been widely publicized in press information circulars sent to 1,800 newspapers.* 通过向1800份报纸发送新闻通告，这项提议得到了广泛地宣传。

→ see **circle**

cir·cu·late /sɜrkyəleɪt/ (**circulates, circulating, circulated**) 1 V-T/V-I If a piece of writing **circulates** or **is circulated**, copies of it are passed around among a group of people. 散发；流传 ❑ *The document was previously circulated in New York at the United Nations.* 这份文件过去曾在纽约的联合国总部传阅过。 ❑ *Public employees, teachers and liberals are circulating a petition for his recall.* 公务员、教师和自由主义者们正在传签一份请求召回他的请愿书。 ● **cir·cu·la·tion** ★ /sɜrkyəleɪʃən/ N-UNCOUNT 流传 ❑ *...an inquiry into the circulation of "unacceptable literature."* …对于"不可接受的文学"的流传所进行的调查。 2 V-T/V-I If something such as a rumor **circulates** or **is circulated**, the people in a place tell it to each other. 散布；流传 ❑ *Rumors were already beginning to circulate that the project might have to be abandoned.* 有关这个项目可能被迫放弃的流言已经开始在四处传播。 3 V-I When something **circulates**, it moves easily and freely within a closed place or system. 循环 ❑ *...a virus which circulates via the bloodstream and causes ill health in a variety of organs.* …一种通过血流在体内循环而导致许多器官病变的病毒。 ● **cir·cu·la·tion** ★ N-UNCOUNT 循环 ❑ *The north pole is warmer than the south and the circulation of air around it is less well contained.* 北极比南极温暖，其周围的空气循环更为畅通。 4 V-I If you **circulate** at a party, you move among the guests and talk to different people. (在聚会上) 往来应酬 ❑ *If you'll excuse me, I really must circulate.* 对不起，我真得去应酬一下了。

★ **cir·cu·la·tion** /sɜrkyəleɪʃən/ (**circulations**) 1 N-COUNT The **circulation** of a newspaper or magazine is the number of copies that are sold each time it is produced. 发行量 ❑ *The Daily News once had the highest circulation of any daily in the country.* 《每日新闻报》一度在该国所有日报中拥有最高发行量。 2 N-UNCOUNT Your **circulation** is the movement of blood through your body. 血液循环 ❑ *Anyone with heart, lung, or circulation problems should seek medical advice before flying.* 任何有心、肺或血液循环问题的人都应该在飞行前寻求医生建议。 3 → see also **circulate** 4 PHRASE If something such as money is **in circulation**, it is being used by the public. If something is **out of circulation** or has been **withdrawn from circulation**, it is no longer available for use by the public. 流通/停止流通 ❑ *The supply of money in circulation was drastically reduced overnight.* 一夜之间流通货币的供应就急剧减少了。 ❑ *...a society like America, with perhaps 180 million guns in circulation.* …像美国这样的社会里，可能有1.8亿支枪在流通之中。

C

Word Link *circum ≈ around : circumcise, circumference, circumstance*

cir·cum·cise /sɜrkəmsaɪz/ (**circumcises, circumcising, circumcised**) **1** V-T If a boy or man **is circumcised**, the loose skin at the end of his penis is cut off. 割去包皮 [usu passive] ❑ *He had been circumcised within eight days of birth as required by Jewish law.* 根据犹太律法的规定，他在出生8天之内就被行了割礼。 ● **cir·cum·ci·sion** /sɜrkəmsɪʒᵊn/ N-UNCOUNT 包皮割除 [also "a" N] ❑ *Jews and Moslems practice circumcision for religious reasons.* 犹太人和穆斯林出于宗教的原因实行割礼。 **2** V-T In some cultures, if a girl or woman **is circumcised**, her clitoris is cut or cut off. 割除阴蒂 [usu passive] ❑ *An estimated number of 90 to 100 million women around the world living today have been circumcised.* 据估计，现今全世界活着的被割除了阴蒂的妇女数量大约为9000万至1亿。 ● **cir·cum·ci·sion** N-UNCOUNT 阴蒂割除 ❑ *...a campaigner against female circumcision.* …一个反对女性割礼的活动家。

cir·cum·fer·ence /sərkʌmfrəns/ **1** N-UNCOUNT The **circumference** of a circle, place, or round object is the distance around its edge. 周长 ❑ *...a scientist calculating the Earth's circumference.* …一位正在计算地球周长的科学家。 **2** N-UNCOUNT The **circumference** of a circle, place, or round object is its edge. 周边 ❑ *Cut the salmon into long strips and wrap it round the circumference of the bread.* 把鲑鱼切成长条，然后把它裹在面包的四周。

→ see **area**

cir·cum·stance ♦◇◇ /sɜrkəmstæns/ (**circumstances**) **1** N-COUNT The **circumstances** of a particular situation are the conditions which affect what happens. 情形 ❑ *Recent opinion polls show that 60 percent favor abortion under certain circumstances.* 最近的民意调查显示60%的人赞同特定情况下的流产。 ❑ *The strategy was too dangerous in the explosive circumstances of the times.* 在当时爆炸性的形势下，这一战略太危险了。 **2** N-PLURAL The **circumstances** of an event are the way it happened or the causes of it. 详情；原委 ❑ *I'm making inquiries about the circumstances of Mary Dean's murder.* 我正在调查玛丽·迪安谋杀案的原委。 **3** N-PLURAL Your **circumstances** are the conditions of your life, especially the amount of money that you have. 境况（尤指经济状况）❑ *...help and support for the single mother, whatever her circumstances.* …提供给单身母亲的帮助和支持，无论她们的境况如何。 **4** N-UNCOUNT Events and situations which cannot be controlled are sometimes referred to as **circumstance**. 命运；客观环境 ❑ *There are those, you know, who, by circumstance, end up homeless.* 你知道，有些人由于命运的原因最终变得无家可归。 **5** PHRASE You can emphasize that something must not or will not happen by saying that it must not or will not happen **under any circumstances**. 在任何情况下 [EMPHASIS] ❑ *Racism is wholly unacceptable under any circumstances.* 在任何情况下种族主义都是完全不能被接受的。 **6** PHRASE You can use **in the circumstances** or **under the circumstances** before or after a statement to indicate that you have considered the conditions affecting the situation before making the statement. 在那种情况下 ❑ *In the circumstances, Paisley's plans looked highly appropriate.* 在那种情况下，佩斯利的计划看起来非常合适。

Word Partnership *circumstances* 的常用搭配:

PREP. **under the** circumstances **1** **2**
ADJ. **certain** circumstances, **different/similar** circumstances, **difficult** circumstances, **exceptional** circumstances **1** – **3**

★ **cir·cus** /sɜrkəs/ (**circuses**) **1** N-COUNT A **circus** is a group that consists of clowns, acrobats, and animals that travels around to different places and performs shows. 马戏团 ❑ *My real ambition was to work in a circus.* 我真正的理想是去马戏团工作。 ● N-SING **The circus** is the show performed by these people. 马戏 ❑ *My dad took me to the circus.* 我爸爸带我去看马戏。 **2** N-SING If you describe a group of people or an event as a **circus**, you disapprove of them because they attract a lot of attention but do not achieve anything useful. 闹剧 [DISAPPROVAL] ❑ *It could well turn into some kind of a media circus.* 这很可能会发展成某种媒体闹剧。

ci·ta·tion /saɪteɪʃᵊn/ (**citations**) **1** N-COUNT A **citation** is an official document or speech which praises a person for something brave or special that they have done. 嘉奖；奖状 ❑ *His citation says he showed outstanding and exemplary courage.* 他的嘉奖令中写道他表现出了与众不同和堪为楷模的英勇。 **2** N-COUNT A **citation** from a book or other piece of writing is a passage or phrase from it. 引文 [FORMAL] ❑ *...a 50-minute manifesto with citations from the Koran.* …一段长达50分钟、带有《古兰经》引文的宣言。 **3** N-COUNT A **citation** is the same as a **summons**. 传票 [AM] ❑ *The court could issue a citation and fine Ms. Robbins.* 法庭可以发出传票并且罚罗宾斯女士的款。 **4** N-COUNT A **citation** is an official piece of paper which orders you to pay a fine or to appear in court because you have committed a traffic offense. 交通违规传票；交通罚单 [AM] ❑ *The Highway Patrol this year issued 1,018 speeding citations.* 高速公路巡警今年开出了1018张超速罚单。

cite ♦◇◇ /saɪt/ (**cites, citing, cited**) **1** V-T If you **cite** something, you quote it or mention it, especially as an example or proof of what you are saying. 引用 [FORMAL] ❑ *She cites a favorite poem by George Herbert.* 她引用了一首她所喜爱的乔治·赫伯特的诗。 ❑ *Domestic interest rates are often cited as a major factor affecting exchange rates.* 国内利率常常被援引为影响汇率的一个主要因素。 **2** V-T To **cite** a person means to officially name them in a legal case. To **cite** a reason or cause means to state it as the official reason for your case. 引证 ❑ *They cited Alex's refusal to return to the marital home.* 他们援引了亚历克斯拒绝重返婚后住所这一事实为证。 **3** V-T If someone **is cited**, they are officially ordered to appear before a court. 传讯 [usu passive] [AM, LEGAL]

in BRIT, use **be summonsed**

❑ *He is the owner of a restaurant chain that was cited for violations of child labor laws.* 他是那个因违反童工法而被传讯的餐饮连锁店的业主。 **4** V-T If a judge **cites** someone, he or she officially names them in a critical way in court. 指控 [AM, LEGAL] ❑ *The judge ruled a mistrial and cited the prosecutors for outrageous misconduct.* 法官裁定判决无效并且指控控方有极其不端的行为。

citi·zen ♦♦◇ /sɪtɪzᵊn/ (**citizens**) **1** N-COUNT Someone who is a **citizen** of a particular country is legally accepted as belonging to that country. 公民 ❑ *...American citizens.* …美国公民。 **2** N-COUNT The **citizens of** a town or city are the people who live there. 市民 ❑ *...the citizens of Buenos Aires.* …布宜诺斯艾利斯的市民。 **3** → see also **senior citizen**

→ see **election**

Word Link *ship ≈ condition or state : censorship, citizenship, friendship*

citi·zen·ship /sɪtɪzᵊnʃɪp/ **1** N-UNCOUNT If you have **citizenship** of a country, you are legally accepted as belonging to it. 公民身份 ❑ *After 15 years in the U.S., he has finally decided to apply for American citizenship.* 在美国住了15年后，他最终决定申请美国的公民身份。 **2** N-UNCOUNT **Citizenship** is the fact of belonging to a community because you live in it, and the duties and responsibilities that this brings. 公民义务和责任 ❑ *Their German peers had a more developed sense of citizenship.* 他们的德国同龄人对于公民的义务和责任有更成熟的认识。

cit·rus /sɪtrəs/ ADJ A **citrus** fruit is a juicy fruit with a sharp taste such as an orange, lemon, or grapefruit. 柑橘类的 [ADJ n] ❑ *...citrus groves.* …柑橘林。

city ♦♦♦ /sɪti/ (**cities**) N-COUNT A **city** is a large town. 城市 ❑ *...the city of Bologna.* …波洛尼亚市。

→ see Word Web: **city**

→ see **skyscraper**

Word Link *civ ≈ citizen : civic, civil, civilian*

★ **civ·ic** /sɪvɪk/ **1** ADJ You use **civic** to describe people or things that have an official status in a town or city. 市政的 [ADJ n] ❑ *...the businessmen and civic leaders of Manchester.* …曼彻斯特的商人们和市政领导。 **2** ADJ You use **civic** to describe the duties or feelings that people have because they belong to a particular community. 市民的；公民的 [ADJ n] ❑ *...a sense of civic pride.* …市民自豪感。

civ·il ♦♦◇ /sɪvᵊl/ **1** ADJ You use **civil** to describe events that happen within a country and that involve the different groups of people in it. 国民的 [ADJ n] ❑ *...civil unrest.* …民众的骚乱。 **2** ADJ You use **civil** to describe people or things in a country that are not connected with its armed forces. 民用的 ❑ *...the U.S. civil aviation industry.* …美国民用航空工业。 **3** ADJ You use **civil** to describe things that are connected with the state rather than with a religion. 民政的 [ADJ n] ❑ *They were married on August 9 in a civil ceremony in Venice.* 他们于8月9日在威尼斯通过民政仪式结了婚。 **4** ADJ You use **civil** to describe the rights that people have within a society. 公民的 [ADJ n] ❑ *...a United Nations covenant on civil and political rights.* …一份关于民权和政治权利的联合国公约。 **5** ADJ Someone

Word Web city

For the past 6,000 years people have been moving from the **countryside** to **urban** centers. The world's oldest **capital** is Damascus, Syria. People have lived there for over 2,500 years. Cities are usually economic, commercial, cultural, political, social, and transportation centers. **Tourists** travel to cities for shopping and **sightseeing**. In some big cities, **skyscrapers** contain **apartments, businesses, restaurants, theaters,** and **retail stores**. People never have to leave their building. Sometimes cities become overpopulated and **crime rates** soar. Then people move to the **suburbs**. In recent decades this trend has been reversed in some places and **inner cities** are being rebuilt.

who is **civil** is polite in a formal way, but not particularly friendly. 文明的 [FORMAL] ❑ *As visitors, the least we can do is be civil to the people in their own land.* 作为游客，我们至少要能做到文明地对待当地人民。 ● **ci·vil·ity** /sɪvɪlɪti/ N-UNCOUNT 礼貌 ❑ *...civility to underlings.* …对下属的礼待。

Word Partnership *civil* 的常用搭配：

N. civil **disobedience**, civil **unrest** 1
civil **liberties/rights** 1 4
civil **court (law)suit/trial** 3

ci·vil·ian ♦◇◇ /sɪvɪlyən/ (**civilians**) 1 N-COUNT In a military situation, a **civilian** is anyone who is not a member of the armed forces. 平民 ❑ *The safety of civilians caught up in the fighting must be guaranteed.* 卷入战斗中的平民的安全必须得到保障。 2 ADJ In a military situation, **civilian** is used to describe people or things that are not military. 平民的；民用的 ❑ *...the country's civilian population.* …这个国家的平民人口。 ❑ *...civilian casualties.* …平民伤亡。
→ see **war**

civi·li·sa·tion /sɪvɪlaɪzeɪʃən/ [BRIT] → see **civilization**

civi·lise /sɪvɪlaɪz/ [BRIT] → see **civilize**

civi·lised /sɪvɪlaɪzd/ [BRIT] → see **civilized**

ci·vil·ity /sɪvɪlɪti/ → see **civil**

civi·li·za·tion /sɪvɪlɪzeɪʃən/ (**civilizations**)
in BRIT, also use **civilisation**
1 N-VAR A **civilization** is a human society with its own social organization and culture. 文明社会 ❑ *The ancient civilizations of Central and Latin America were founded upon corn.* 中美洲和拉丁美洲的古代文明社会是建立在玉米之上的。 2 N-UNCOUNT **Civilization** is the state of having an advanced level of social organization and a comfortable way of life. 文明 ❑ *...our advanced state of civilization.* …我们高度的文明形态。
→ see **history**

civi·lize /sɪvɪlaɪz/ (**civilizes, civilizing, civilized**)
in BRIT, also use **civilise**
V-T To **civilize** a person or society means to educate them and improve their way of life. 使文明；教化 ❑ *...a comedy about a man who tries to civilize a woman – but she ends up civilizing him.* …一部关于一个男人试图去教化一个女人——结果却是那个女人教化了他的喜剧。

civi·lized /sɪvɪlaɪzd/
in BRIT, also use **civilised**
1 ADJ If you describe a society as **civilized**, you mean that it is advanced and has established laws and customs. 文明的 [APPROVAL] ❑ *I believed that in civilized countries, torture had ended long ago.* 我相信在文明国家酷刑早就废止了。 2 ADJ If you describe a person or their behavior as **civilized**, you mean that they are polite and reasonable. 有教养的；有礼貌的 ❑ *I wrote to my ex-wife last week. She was very civilized about it.* 上个星期我写信给我的前妻。对此她表现得彬彬有礼。

civ·il rights N-PLURAL **Civil rights** are the rights that people have in a society to equal treatment and equal opportunities, whatever their race, sex, or religion. 民权 ❑ *...the civil rights movement.* …民权运动。

civ·il serv·ant (**civil servants**) N-COUNT A **civil servant** is a person who works for the local, state, or federal government in the United States, or in the civil service in Britain and some other countries. 公务员 ❑ *...two senior civil servants.* …两位高级公务员。

civ·il ser·vice N-SING **The civil service** of a country consists of its government departments and all the people who work in them. In many countries, the departments concerned with military and legal affairs are not part of the civil service. 政务；公务 ❑ *...a job in the civil service.* …一份政务工作。

civ·il war ♦◇◇ (**civil wars**) N-COUNT A **civil war** is a war which is fought between different groups of people who live in the same country. 内战 ❑ *...the American Civil War.* …美国内战。

CJD /si dʒeɪ di/ N-UNCOUNT **CJD** is an incurable brain disease that affects human beings and is believed to be caused by eating beef from cows infected with BSE. **CJD** is an abbreviation for "Creutzfeldt-Jakob disease." 克雅氏症

clad /klæd/ 1 ADJ If you are **clad in** particular clothes, you are wearing them. 身着…服装的 [LITERARY] ❑ *...the figure of a woman, clad in black.* …一个身穿黑衣服的女子的身影。 ❑ *Johnson was clad casually in slacks and a light blue golf shirt.* 约翰逊随意地穿着一条休闲裤和一件淡蓝色的高尔夫衬衫。 ● COMB IN ADJ **Clad** is also a combining form. 身着…衣服的 ❑ *...the leather-clad biker.* …那个身着皮衣的摩托车手。 2 ADJ A building, part of a building, or mountain that is **clad with** something is covered by that thing. 被…覆盖的 [v-link ADJ "in/with" n] [LITERARY] ❑ *The walls and floors are clad with ceramic tiles.* 墙和地板都贴上了瓷砖。 ● COMB IN ADJ **Clad** is also a combining form. …覆盖的 ❑ *...the distant shapes of snow-clad mountains.* …白雪覆盖的群山的远景。

claim ♦♦♦ /kleɪm/ (**claims, claiming, claimed**) 1 V-T If you say that someone **claims that** something is true, you mean they say that it is true but you are not sure whether or not they are telling the truth. 声称 ❑ *He claimed that it was all a conspiracy against him.* 他声称这完全是一个针对他的阴谋。 ❑ *A man claiming to be a journalist threatened to reveal details about her private life.* 一个自称是记者的男人威胁要公开她的私生活细节。 2 V-T If you say that someone **claims** responsibility or credit for something, you mean they say that they are responsible for it, but you are not sure whether or not they are telling the truth. 声称（对某事负责或应得荣誉） ❑ *An underground organization has claimed responsibility for the bomb explosion.* 一个地下组织已声称对炸弹爆炸事件负责。 3 V-T If you **claim** something, you try to get it because you think you have a right to it. 索取 ❑ *Now they are returning to claim what was theirs.* 现在他们回来索要原本属于他们的东西。 4 V-T If someone **claims** a record, title, or prize, they gain or win it. 赢得 [JOURNALISM] ❑ *Zhuang claimed the record in 54.64 seconds.* 庄创造了54.64秒的纪录。 5 V-T If something or someone **claims** your attention, they need you to spend your time and effort on them. 需要 ❑ *There is already a long list of people claiming her attention.* 已经有太多人需要她的关注了。 6 V-T/V-I If you **claim** money from the government, an insurance company, or another organization, you officially apply to them for it, because you think you are entitled to it according to their rules. 索赔 ❑ *Some 25 percent of the people who are entitled to claim benefits do not do so.* 大约25％有资格索赔的人没有那样做。 ❑ *John had taken out insurance but when he tried to claim, the insurance company refused to pay.* 约翰拿出保险单，但当他试图索赔时，保险公司却拒绝赔付。 ● N-COUNT **Claim** is also a noun. 索赔 ❑ *Last time we made a claim on our insurance, they paid up really quickly.* 上次我们依据保险提出索赔时，他们赔付得很快。 7 V-T If you **claim** money or other benefits from your employers, you demand them because you think you deserve or need them. 索要 ❑ *The union claimed a raise worth four times the rate of inflation.* 工会要求增长4倍于通货膨胀率的工资。 ● N-COUNT **Claim** is also a noun. 索要 ❑ *They are making substantial claims for improved working conditions.* 他们就改善工作条件提出了实质性要求。 8 V-T If you say that a war, disease, or accident **claims** someone's

C

life, you mean that they are killed in it or by it. 夺走(生命) [FORMAL] ❑ *The civil war claimed the life of a U.N. interpreter yesterday.* 昨天内战夺走了一位联合国译员的生命。 9 N-COUNT A **claim** is something which someone says which they cannot prove and which may be false. 声称 ❑ *He repeated his claim that the people of Trinidad and Tobago backed his action.* 他再三重复他所声称的：特立尼达和多巴哥的人民支持他的行动。 10 N-COUNT A **claim** is a demand for something that you think you have a right to. 索要 ❑ *Rival claims to Macedonian territory caused conflict in the Balkans.* 对马其顿领土的争夺导致了巴尔干地区的冲突 11 N-COUNT If you have a **claim on** someone or their attention, you have the right to demand things from them or to demand their attention. 索求权 ❑ *She had no claims on him now.* 现在她无权向他索取什么了。 12 **to stake a claim** → see **stake**

claim·ant /kleɪmənt/ (**claimants**) N-COUNT A **claimant** is someone who asks to be given something which they think they are entitled to. 索取人 ❑ *The claimants allege that manufacturers failed to warn doctors that their drugs should be used only in limited circumstances.* 索赔人声称生产商没有警告医生他们生产的药品只能在特定的条件下使用。

claims ad·just·er (**claims adjusters**) also **claims adjustor** N-COUNT A **claims adjuster** is someone who is employed by an insurance company to decide how much money a person making a claim should receive. 保险理赔人 [AM, BUSINESS]

in BRIT, use **loss adjuster**

clair·voy·ant /klɛərvɔɪənt/ ADJ Someone who is believed to be **clairvoyant** is believed to know about future events or to be able to communicate with dead people. 能预卜未来的；通灵的 ❑ *...clairvoyant powers.* …未卜先知的能力

clam /klæm/ (**clams**) N-COUNT **Clams** are a kind of shellfish which can be eaten. 蛤蜊

clam·ber /klæmbər/ (**clambers, clambering, clambered**) V-I If you **clamber** somewhere, you climb there with difficulty, usually using your hands as well as your feet. (手脚并用，费劲地) 爬 ❑ *They clambered up the stone walls of a steeply terraced olive grove.* 他们费力地爬上陡峭的橄榄树丛梯地上的石头墙。

Word Link *claim, clam ≈ shouting : acclaim, clamor, exclaim*

clam·or /klæmər/ (**clamors, clamoring, clamored**) V-I If people **are clamoring for** something, they are demanding it in a noisy or angry way. 强烈要求 [JOURNALISM]

in BRIT, use **clamour**

❑ *...competing parties clamoring for the attention of the voter.* …竞争党派大声疾呼以吸引选民的关注。

clam·our [BRIT] → see **clamor**

★ **clamp** /klæmp/ (**clamps, clamping, clamped**) 1 N-COUNT A **clamp** is a device that holds two things firmly together. 夹具 ❑ *Many openers have a magnet or set of clamps to grip the open lid.* 许多开启器是用磁铁或夹具来夹紧要开启的盖子。 2 N-COUNT A **clamp** is the same as a **Denver boot**. (锁住违章停靠车辆的) 夹钳 [mainly BRIT] 3 V-T When you **clamp** one thing **to** another, you fasten the two things together with a clamp. 用(夹具)夹紧 ❑ *Somebody forgot to bring along the U-bolts to clamp the microphones to the pole.* 有人忘记带来把麦克风夹在支杆上的U型螺栓。 4 V-T To **clamp** something in a particular place means to put it or hold it there firmly and tightly. 把…夹紧；固定 ❑ *Simon finished dialing and clamped the phone to his ear.* 西蒙拨完号码，把话筒紧夹在耳朵上。 ❑ *He clamped his lips together.* 他紧闭双唇。 5 V-T To **clamp** a car means the same as to **boot** a car. 用车轮钳锁锁住(车辆) [BRIT]

▸ **clamp down** PHRASAL VERB To **clamp down on** people or activities means to take strong official action to stop or control them. 取缔；严加限制 [JOURNALISM] ❑ *If the government clamps down on the movement, that will only serve to strengthen it in the long run.* 如果政府要压制该运动，从长远来说那只会加强其力量。

★ **clan** /klæn/ (**clans**) 1 N-COUNT A **clan** is a group which consists of families that are related to each other. 家族 ❑ *...rival clans.* …敌对家族。 2 N-COUNT You can refer to a group of people with the same interests as a **clan**. 帮派 [INFORMAL] ❑ *...a powerful clan of industrialists from Monterrey.* …有权势的一帮来自于蒙特雷的实业家们。

→ see **society**

clan·des·tine /klændɛstɪn/ ADJ Something that is **clandestine** is hidden or kept secret, often because it is illegal. (常指非法地) 暗中的；秘密的 [FORMAL] ❑ *...their clandestine meetings.* …他们的秘密会晤。

clap /klæp/ (**claps, clapping, clapped**) 1 V-T/V-I When you **clap**, you hit your hands together to express appreciation or attract attention. 拍(手)；鼓掌 ❑ *The men danced and the women clapped.* 男人们跳舞，女人们鼓掌。 ❑ *Midge clapped her hands, calling them back to order.* 米琪拍手叫他们恢复秩序。 2 V-T If you **clap** your hand or an object onto something, you put it there quickly and firmly. 猛然放置 ❑ *I clapped a hand over her mouth.* 我猛地用一只手捂住了她的嘴。 3 N-COUNT A **clap of thunder** is a sudden and loud noise of thunder. 轰隆的雷声

Word Link *clar ≈ clear : clarify, clarity, declare*

Word Link *ify ≈ making : clarify, diversify, intensify*

clari·fy /klærɪfaɪ/ (**clarifies, clarifying, clarified**) V-T To **clarify** something means to make it easier to understand, usually by explaining it in more detail. 澄清 [FORMAL] ❑ *Thank you for writing and allowing me to clarify the present position.* 谢谢你来信并允许我澄清目前的状况。 ● ★ **clari·fi·ca·tion** /klærɪfɪkeɪʃən/ N-VAR (**clarifications**) 澄清 ❑ *The union has written to Detroit asking for clarification of the situation.* 工会已经写信给底特律，要求对此情况给予澄清。

clari·net /klærɪnɛt/ (**clarinets**) N-VAR A **clarinet** is a musical instrument in the shape of a pipe. You play the clarinet by blowing into it and covering and uncovering the holes with your fingers. 单簧管

→ see **orchestra**

★ **clar·ity** /klærɪti/ 1 N-UNCOUNT The **clarity** of something such as a book or argument is its quality of being well explained and easy to understand. 明晰；清楚 ❑ *...the ease and clarity with which the author explains difficult technical and scientific subjects.* …该作者用于解释难懂的科技主题的轻松与明晰。 2 N-UNCOUNT **Clarity** is the ability to think clearly. (思路的) 清晰 ❑ *In business circles he is noted for his flair and clarity of vision.* 在商界，他以其风度与犀利的眼光而闻名。 3 N-UNCOUNT **Clarity** is the quality of being clear in outline or sound. (指轮廓、声音等) 清晰 ❑ *This remarkable technology provides far greater clarity than conventional x-rays.* 这一非凡技术提供了比传统的X光要高得多的清晰度。

clash ♦◇◇ /klæʃ/ (**clashes, clashing, clashed**) 1 V-RECIP When people **clash**, they fight, argue, or disagree with each other. 发生冲突；产生矛盾 [JOURNALISM] ❑ *A group of 400 demonstrators ripped down the front gate and clashed with police.* 400名示威者推倒前面的大前门，与警察发生了冲突。 ❑ *Behind the scenes, Parsons clashed with almost everyone on the show.* 幕后，帕森斯几乎跟每个参与演出的人都产生过矛盾。 ● N-COUNT **Clash** is also a noun. 冲突 [oft N "between/with" n] ❑ *There have been a number of clashes between police in riot gear and demonstrators.* 穿防暴服的警察和示威者之间发生过多次冲突。 2 V-RECIP Beliefs, ideas, or qualities that **clash with** each other are very different from each other and therefore are opposed. (因信仰、观点或质量不同而) 产生分歧 ❑ *Don't make any policy decisions which clash with official company thinking.* 不要做与公司官方理念有分歧的任何政策性决定。 ● N-COUNT **Clash** is also a noun. 分歧 ❑ *Inside government, there was a clash of views.* 政府内部有意见分歧。 3 V-RECIP If one color or style **clashes with** another, the colors or styles look ugly together. You can also say that two colors or styles **clash**. (颜色、风格等) 不协调 ❑ *The red door clashed with the soft, natural tones of the stone walls.* 这红色的门与柔和自然色调的石墙不协调。 4 V-I If one event **clashes with** another, the two events happen at the same time so that you cannot attend both of them. (两件事因发生的时间相同而) 产生冲突 [BRIT]

in AM, use **conflict**

★ **clasp** /klæsp/ (**clasps, clasping, clasped**) 1 V-T If you **clasp** someone or something, you hold them tightly in your hands or arms. 握紧；抱紧 ❑ *She clasped the children to her.* 她紧紧地搂住孩子们。 2 N-COUNT A **clasp** is a small device that fastens something. (拴牢某物的) 扣子；勾子 ❑ *...the clasp of her handbag.* …她的手包扣。

class ♦♦♦ /klæs/ (**classes, classing, classed**) 1 N-COUNT A **class** is a group of students who are taught together. 班 ❑ *He had to spend about six months in a class with younger students.* 他不得不在一个比他小的学生的班上呆了大约六个月。 2 N-COUNT A **class** is a course of teaching in a particular subject. 课程 ❑ *He acquired a law degree by taking classes at night.* 他通过上晚上的课获得了法律学位。 3 N-COUNT A **class of** things is a group of them with similar characteristics. 种类 ❑ *Harbor staff noticed that measurements given for the same class of boats often varied.* 港口员工们注意到对同一类小船所给出的尺寸经常

不同。4 N-UNCOUNT If you do something **in class**, you do it during a lesson in school. 课 ❑ *There is lots of reading in class.* 课上有大量阅读。 5 N-UNCOUNT If you say that someone or something has **class**, you mean that they are elegant and sophisticated. 品位 [INFORMAL, APPROVAL] ❑ *The most elegant woman I've ever met – she had class in every sense of the word.* 我曾见过的最高雅的女人——从各种意义上讲她都有品位。 6 N-SING The students in a school or college who finish their course in a particular year are often referred to as the **class of** that year. 同届学生 ❑ *These two members of Yale's Class of '57 never miss a reunion.* 这两位耶鲁57届的同学从未错过一次重聚联欢会。 7 N-VAR **Class** refers to the division of people in a society into groups according to their social status. 阶级 ❑ *...the relationship between social classes.* …社会阶级间的关系。 ❑ *What it will do is create a whole new ruling class.* 它要做的就是创造一个全新的统治阶级。 8 → see also **middle class, upper class, working class** 9 V-T If someone or something **is classed as** a particular thing, they are regarded as belonging to that group of things. 把…归类为 ❑ *Since they can and do successfully inter-breed, they cannot be classed as different species.* 既然它们能够而且确实可以成功杂交繁殖，它们就不能被归为不同的物种。 ❑ *I class myself as an ordinary working person.* 我把自己归类为一名普通的劳动者。 10 → see also **business class, first-class, second-class, world-class**

Word Partnership *class* 的常用搭配:

- N. class **for beginners**, class **size**, **students in a** class 1
  freshman/senior class, **graduating** class 6
  leisure class, class **struggle**, **working** class 7
- V. **take a** class, **teach a** class 1 2
- ORD. **first/second** class 3 7
- ADJ. **social** class 7

clas·sic ♦♦♢ /klæsɪk/ (**classics**) 1 ADJ A **classic** example of a thing or situation has all the features which you expect such a thing or situation to have. 典型的 ❑ *The debate in the press has been a classic example of hypocrisy.* 新闻界的这场争论是虚伪的典型例子。 ● N-COUNT **Classic** is also a noun. 典范 ❑ *It was a classic of interrogation: first the bully, then the kind one who offers sympathy.* 这是审问的一种典范：开始是欺负人的人，然后那个和善的人再施予同情。 2 ADJ A **classic** movie, piece of writing, or piece of music is of very high quality and has become a standard against which similar things are judged. 经典的 [ADJ n] ❑ *...the classic children's film Huckleberry Finn.* …经典的儿童影片《哈克贝利•芬》。 ❑ *...a classic study of the American penal system.* …一项针对美国刑罚系统的典型研究。 ● N-COUNT **Classic** is also a noun. 经典 ❑ *The record won a gold award and remains one of the classics of modern popular music.* 该唱片获得过金奖，而且依旧是现代流行音乐的经典作品之一。 3 N-COUNT A **classic** is a book which is well-known and considered to be of a high literary standard. You can refer to such books generally as **the classics**. 文学名著 ❑ *As I grow older, I like to reread the classics regularly.* 随着我年龄的增长，我喜欢定期重读文学名著。 4 N-UNCOUNT **Classics** is the study of the ancient Greek and Roman civilizations, especially their languages, literature, and philosophy. 古典学 ❑ *...a Classics degree.* …古典学学位。

clas·si·cal ♦♢♢ /klæsɪkᵊl/ 1 ADJ You use **classical** to describe something that is traditional in form, style, or content. 传统的 ❑ *Fokine did not change the steps of classical ballet; instead he found new ways of using them.* 福金没有改变传统芭蕾的舞步；取而代之的是他发现了使用传统舞步的新方法。 2 ADJ **Classical** music is music that is considered to be serious and of lasting value. (指音乐) 古典的 ❑ *...a classical composer like Beethoven.* …诸如贝多芬的一名古典作曲家。 3 ADJ **Classical** is used to describe things which relate to the ancient Greek or Roman civilizations. (指古希腊罗马) 古典文化的 ❑ *...the healers of ancient Egypt and classical Greece.* …古埃及和古希腊的疗愈者们。
→ see **genre**

clas·si·cal·ly /klæsɪkli/ 1 ADV Someone who has been **classically** trained in something such as art, music, or ballet has learned the traditional skills and methods of that subject. 以传统技能 (训练) [ADV -ed] ❑ *Peter is a classically trained pianist.* 彼得是个受过传统技能训练的钢琴家。 2 ADV **Classically** is used to indicate that something is based on or reminds people of the culture of ancient Greece and Rome. (古希腊罗马) 古典文化地 [ADV adj/-ed] ❑ *...the classically inspired church of S. Francesco.* …受到古典文化灵感的圣弗朗西斯科教堂。

clas·si·fi·ca·tion /klæsɪfɪkeɪʃᵊn/ (**classifications**) 1 N-COUNT A **classification** is a division or category in a system which divides things into groups or types. 类别 ❑ *The government uses a classification system that includes both race and ethnicity.* 政府采用一种既包括人种又包括种族的类别体系。 2 → see also **classify**

★ **clas·si·fied** /klæsɪfaɪd/ ADJ **Classified** information or documents are officially secret. 机密的 ❑ *He has a security clearance that allows him access to classified information.* 他有安全许可，这准许他接触机密。

clas·si·fied ad (**classified ads**) N-COUNT **Classified ads** or **classified advertisements** are small advertisements in a newspaper or magazine. They are usually from a person or company. 分类广告

clas·si·fieds /klæsɪfaɪdz/ N-PLURAL **The classifieds** are the same as **classified ads**. 分类广告 ❑ *It's common for companies to post job openings on their websites and in newspaper classifieds.* 公司在其网站和报纸分类广告上公布招聘信息是家常便饭。

clas·si·fy /klæsɪfaɪ/ (**classifies, classifying, classified**) V-T To **classify** things means to divide them into groups or types so that things with similar characteristics are in the same group. 把…分类 ❑ *It is necessary initially to classify the headaches into certain types.* 起初把头疼分成若干类别是有必要的。 ● **clas·si·fi·ca·tion** /klæsɪfɪkeɪʃᵊn/ N-VAR (**classifications**) 分类 ❑ *...the arbitrary classification of knowledge into fields of study.* …把知识归入研究领域的任意分类。

class·less /klæslɪs/ ADJ When politicians talk about a **classless** society, they mean a society in which people are not affected by social status. 无阶级的 [APPROVAL] ❑ *...the new prime minister's vision of a classless society.* …新首相对无阶级社会的眼光。

class·mate /klæsmeɪt/ (**classmates**) N-COUNT Your **classmates** are students who are in the same class as you at school or college. 同班同学

class·room /klæsrum/ (**classrooms**) N-COUNT A **classroom** is a room in a school where lessons take place. 教室

class sched·ule (**class schedules**) N-COUNT In a school or college, a **class schedule** is a list that shows the times in the week at which particular subjects are taught. You can also refer to the range of subjects that a student learns or the classes that a teacher teaches as their **class schedule**. 课程表 [AM]
in BRIT, usually use **timetable**
❑ *They had to be back at their colleges this week to enroll and work out class schedules for the new term.* 他们这周必须回到学院注册，并制定出新学期的课程表。

classy /klæsi/ (**classier, classiest**) ADJ If you describe someone or something as **classy**, you mean they are stylish and sophisticated. 有品位的 [INFORMAL] ❑ *The German star put in a classy performance.* 那位德国明星献上了一场上乘的表演。

▲ **clat·ter** /klætər/ (**clatters, clattering, clattered**) V-I If you say that people or things **clatter** somewhere, you mean that they move there noisily. (指移动时) 出大声 ❑ *He turned and clattered down the stairs.* 他转过身，噔噔地下楼梯。

clause /klɔz/ (**clauses**) 1 N-COUNT A **clause** is a section of a legal document. (法律文件的) 条款 ❑ *He has a clause in his contract which entitles him to a percentage of the profits.* 他在他的合同里有一项条款保证他享有一定比例的利润。 ❑ *...a compromise document sprinkled with escape clauses.* …一份满是免责条款的妥协性文件。 2 N-COUNT In grammar, a **clause** is a group of words containing a verb. Sentences contain one or more clauses. 分句

claw /klɔ/ (**claws, clawing, clawed**) 1 N-COUNT The **claws** of a bird or animal are the thin, hard, curved nails at the end of its feet. (鸟、动物的) 爪 ❑ *The cat tried to cling to the edge by its claws.* 那只猫试图用爪子抓紧边沿。 2 N-COUNT The **claws** of a lobster, crab, or scorpion are the two pointed parts at the end of its legs which are used for holding things. (龙虾、蟹、蝎的) 钳子 3 V-I If an animal **claws at** something, it scratches or damages it with its claws. (用爪) 抓 ❑ *The wolf clawed at the tree and howled the whole night.* 那只狼在那颗树上抓挠，还嗥叫了整整一个晚上。 4 V-I To **claw at** something mean to try very hard to get hold of it. 用力抓住 ❑ *His fingers clawed at Blake's wrist.* 他的手指使劲抓住布莱克的手腕。 5 V-T If you **claw** your **way** somewhere, you move there with great difficulty, trying desperately to find things to hold on to. (抓着东西艰难地)挪到 ❑ *From the flooded depths of the ship, some did manage to claw their way up iron ladders to the safety of the upper deck.* 从被洪水淹了

C

的船的深处，一些人着实艰难地爬上铁梯来到上层甲板的安全处。
→ see **bird**

clay /kleɪ/ (**clays**) **1** N-MASS **Clay** is a kind of earth that is soft when it is wet and hard when it is dry. Clay is shaped and baked to make things such as pots and bricks. 黏土 ❑ *...the heavy clay soils of Georgia.* …佐治亚州厚重的黏土的土壤。❑ *As the wheel turned, the potter shaped and squeezed the lump of clay into a graceful shape.* 随着轮盘的转动，陶工把那块黏土塑造、挤捏成了一个优雅的造型。 **2** N-UNCOUNT In tennis, matches played on **clay** are played on courts whose surface is covered with finely crushed stones or brick. 红土网球场 ❑ *Most tennis is played on hard courts, but a substantial amount is played on clay.* 大多数网球是在硬地球场上打，但相当多的是在红土场地上打。
→ see **pottery**

clean ♦♦◊ /kliːn/ (**cleaner, cleanest, cleans, cleaning, cleaned**) **1** ADJ Something that is **clean** is free from dirt or unwanted marks. 清洁的 ❑ *The subway is efficient and spotlessly clean.* 地铁快，而且一尘不染。❑ *Tiled kitchen floors are easy to keep clean.* 铺了地砖的厨房地面容易保持清洁。 **2** ADJ You say that people or animals are **clean** when they keep themselves or their surroundings clean. 爱干净的 ❑ *We like pigs, they're very clean.* 我们喜欢猪，它们很爱干净。 **3** ADJ A **clean** fuel or chemical process does not create many harmful or polluting substances. 无污染的 ❑ *Fans of electric cars say they are clean, quiet, and economical.* 电动车爱好者说电动车无污染，无噪音，而且经济。 **4** ADJ If you describe something such as a book, joke, or lifestyle as **clean**, you think that they are not sexually immoral or offensive. 纯洁的；不淫秽的 [APPROVAL] ❑ *They're trying to show clean, wholesome, decent movies.* 他们在努力放纯洁、健康、正派的电影。❑ *Flirting is good clean fun.* 调情是谑而不虐。 **5** ADJ If someone has a **clean** reputation or record, they have never done anything illegal or wrong. 清白的 ❑ *Accusations of tax evasion have tarnished his clean image.* 逃税的指控玷污了他清廉的形象。 **6** ADJ A **clean** game or fight is carried out fairly, according to the rules. 公正的 ❑ *He called for a clean fight in the election and an end to "negative campaigning."* 他呼吁在竞选中公正交锋，停止"消极竞选"。 ● **clean·ly** ADV 公正地 ❑ *The game had been cleanly fought.* 这场比赛打得公平。 **7** ADJ A **clean** sheet of paper has no writing or drawing on it. （纸张）空白的 ❑ *Take a clean sheet of paper and down the left-hand side make a list.* 拿一张白纸，在左下边列个清单。 **8** V-T/V-I If you **clean** something or **clean** dirt off it, you make it free from dirt and unwanted marks, for example by washing or wiping it. If something **cleans** easily, it is easy to clean. 把…弄干净；清洁 ❑ *Her father cleaned his glasses with a paper napkin.* 她父亲用一张餐巾纸擦他的眼镜。❑ *It took half an hour to clean the orange powder off the bathtub.* 用了半个小时才把浴缸里的橙色粉末擦掉。 ● **clean·ing** N-UNCOUNT 清洁 ❑ *The windows will have to be given a thorough cleaning.* 窗户必须得做彻底的清洁。 **9** V-T/V-I If you **clean** a room or house, you make the inside of it and the furniture in it free from dirt and dust. 打扫（房间、房子）；打扫卫生 ❑ *Mary cooked and cleaned for them.* 玛丽为他们做饭、打扫卫生。 ● **clean·ing** N-UNCOUNT 打扫卫生的工作 ❑ *I do the cleaning myself.* 我自己做打扫卫生的工作。 **10** ADV **Clean** is used to emphasize that something was done completely. 彻底地 [INFORMAL, EMPHASIS] ❑ *It burned clean through the seat of my overalls.* 把我的连身工作服的臀部全给烧穿了。❑ *The thief got clean away with the money.* 贼偷了钱逃之夭夭了。 **11** **to clean up** your **act** → see **act** **12** **to keep** your **nose clean** → see **nose** **13** **a clean slate** → see **slate** **14** **a clean sweep** → see **sweep** **15** **clean as a whistle** → see **whistle**
→ see **dry-cleaning, soap**

▶ **clean out** PHRASAL VERB If you **clean out** something such as a closet, room, or container, you take everything out of it and clean the inside of it thoroughly. 全面清理 ❑ *Mr. Wall asked if I would help him clean out the barrels.* 沃尔先生问我能否帮他把桶彻底清扫了。

▶ **clean up** **1** PHRASAL VERB If you **clean up** a mess or **clean up** a place where there is a mess, you make things neat and free of dirt again. 收拾干净 ❑ *Police in the city have been cleaning up the debris left by a day of violent confrontation.* 城里的警察一直在收拾一天的暴力冲突留下的残骸。 **2** PHRASAL VERB To **clean up** something such as the environment or an industrial process means to make it free from substances or processes that cause pollution. 治理（污染）❑ *Under pressure from the public, many regional governments cleaned up their beaches.* 迫于公众的压力，许多地区政府治理了海滩污染。 **3** PHRASAL VERB If the police or authorities **clean up** a place or area of activity, they make it free from crime, corruption, and other unacceptable forms of behavior. 整治（犯罪、腐败和其他不良行为）❑ *After years of neglect and decline, the city was cleaning itself up.* 在多年的荒废和衰退之后，该城市在进行自我整治。 **4** PHRASAL VERB If you go and **clean up**, you make yourself clean and neat, especially after doing something that has made you dirty. 使（自己）整洁 ❑ *Johnny, go inside and get cleaned up.* 约翰尼，进去把自己收拾收拾。

Thesaurus	*clean* 另参见：
ADJ.	neat, pure; *(ant.)* dirty, filthy **1**
V.	launder, rinse, wash; *(ant.)* dirty, soil, stain **8**

clean·er /kliːnər/ (**cleaners**) **1** N-COUNT A **cleaner** is someone who is employed to clean the rooms and furniture inside a building. 清洁工 ❑ *...the prison hospital where Sid worked as a cleaner.* …锡德做清洁工的那家监狱医院。 **2** N-COUNT A **cleaner** is someone whose job is to clean a particular type of thing. （清扫特定物品的）清洁工 ❑ *He was a window cleaner.* 他是一名窗户清洁工。 **3** N-COUNT A **cleaner** is a device used for cleaning things. 清洁器 ❑ *...an air cleaner.* …空气清新器。 **4** → see also **vacuum cleaner** **5** N-COUNT A **cleaner** or a **cleaner's** is a store where things such as clothes are dry-cleaned. 干洗店 ❑ *Did you pick up my suit from the cleaner's?* 你顺便从干洗店取我的西装了吗？ **6** N-MASS A **cleaner** is a substance used for cleaning things. 去污剂 ❑ *...oven cleaner.* …烤箱去污剂。

Word Link	***ness ≈ state, condition : cleanliness, consciousness, kindness***

clean·li·ness /klɛnlinɪs/ N-UNCOUNT **Cleanliness** is the degree to which people keep themselves and their surroundings clean. 清洁 ❑ *Many of the state's beaches fail to meet minimum standards of cleanliness.* 该州的许多海滩没能达到最低清洁标准。

▲ **cleanse** /klɛnz/ (**cleanses, cleansing, cleansed**) **1** V-T To **cleanse** a place, person, or organization **of** something dirty, unpleasant, or evil means to make them free from it. 使清洁；使净化 ❑ *Right after your last cigarette, your body will begin to cleanse itself of tobacco toxins.* 在最后一根香烟后，你的身体将马上开始清除烟草毒素。 **2** V-T If you **cleanse** your skin or a wound, you clean it. 清洁（皮肤、伤口）❑ *Catherine demonstrated the proper way to cleanse the face.* 凯瑟琳演示了洁面的正确方法。 **3** → see also **ethnic cleansing**

cleans·er /klɛnzər/ (**cleansers**) **1** N-MASS A **cleanser** is a liquid or cream that you use for cleaning your skin. 洁面乳 ❑ *...an extremely effective cleanser for dry and sensitive skins.* …一种对干燥和过敏性皮肤极为有效的洁面乳。 **2** N-MASS A **cleanser** is a liquid or powder that you use in cleaning kitchens and bathrooms. 清洁剂；去污粉 [mainly AM] ❑ *...a certain kind of bathroom cleanser.* …某种浴室清洁剂。

clear
❶ FREE FROM CONFUSION
❷ FREE FROM PHYSICAL OBSTACLES
❸ MORALLY OR LEGALLY RIGHT, POSSIBLE, OR PERMITTED
❹ PHRASAL VERBS

❶ **clear** ♦♦♦ /klɪər/ (**clearer, clearest, clears, clearing, cleared**) **1** ADJ Something that is **clear** is easy to understand, see, or hear. 清楚的；明白易懂的 ❑ *The book is clear, readable, and adequately illustrated.* 这本书易懂易读，而且图解充足。❑ *The space telescope has taken the clearest pictures ever of Pluto.* 太空望远镜拍下了有史以来最清晰的冥王星的照片。 ● **clear·ly** ADV 清楚地；明白易懂地 ❑ *Whales journey up the coast of California, clearly visible from the beach.* 鲸鱼们朝着加利福尼亚海岸游过来，从海滩就能清楚地看见。 **2** ADJ Something that is **clear** is obvious and impossible to be mistaken about. 明显的 ❑ *It was a clear case of homicide.* 这是一起确信无疑的谋杀案。❑ *It became clear that I hadn't been able to convince Mike.* 显然我没能说服迈克。 ● **clear·ly** ADV 显然无疑地 [ADV with cl/group] ❑ *Clearly, the police cannot break the law in order to enforce it.* 显然地，警察不能为了执法而违法。 **3** ADJ If you are **clear about** something, you understand it completely. 彻底明白的 ❑ *It is important to be clear about what Chomsky is doing here.* 明确乔姆斯基在这干什么很重要。❑ *He is not entirely clear on how he will go about it.* 他不完全清楚要如何着手做这件事。 **4** ADJ If your mind or your way of thinking is **clear**, you are able to think sensibly and reasonably, and you are not affected by confusion or by a drug such as alcohol. （头脑）清醒的 ❑ *She needed a clear head to carry out her instructions.* 她需要一个清醒的头脑来执行命令。 ● **clear·ly** ADV 清醒地 [ADV after v] ❑ *The only time I can think clearly is when I'm* alone. 我能清醒思考的惟一时间就是当我独处时。 5 V-T To **clear** your mind or your head means to free it from confused thoughts or from the effects of a drug such as alcohol. 使清醒 ❑ *He walked up Fifth Avenue to clear his head.* 他在第五大街上走，让头脑清醒清醒。 ❑ *Our therapists will show you how to clear your mind of worries.* 我们的治疗师们将会告诉你怎样消除心中的疑虑。 6 CONVENTION You can say **"Is that clear?"** or **"Do I make myself clear?"** after you have told someone your wishes or instructions, to make sure that they have understood you, and to emphasize your authority. 清楚了吗?/我说明白了吗? ❑ *We're only going for half an hour, and you're not going to buy anything. Is that clear?* 我们只去半个小时，你不许买任何东西。明白了吗? 7 PHRASE If you **make** something **clear**, you say something in a way that makes it impossible for there to be any doubt about your meaning, wishes, or intentions. 把事情说明白 ❑ *Mr. O'Friel made it clear that further insults of this kind would not be tolerated.* 奥弗瑞尔先生把意思说得清清楚楚，以后这种侮辱是不会被容忍的。

❷ **clear ♦♦♦** /klɪər/ (**clearer, clearest, clears, clearing, cleared**) ➪ **Please look at meanings 9 and 10 to see if the expression you are looking for is shown under another headword.** 1 ADJ A **clear** substance is one which you can see through and which has no color, like clean water. 透明的 ❑ *...a clear glass panel.* …一块透明的玻璃镶板。 ❑ *...a clear gel.* …一种透明的凝胶。 2 ADJ If a surface, place, or view is **clear**, it is free of unwanted objects or obstacles. 无障碍物的; 开阔的 ❑ *The runway is clear – go ahead and land.* 跑道畅通无阻——继续前行并着陆。 ❑ *Caroline prefers her countertops to be clear of clutter.* 卡罗琳喜欢厨房台面上没有杂乱的东西。 3 ADJ If it is a **clear** day or if the sky is **clear**, there is no mist, rain, or cloud. 晴朗的 ❑ *On a clear day you can see the coast.* 天晴时你能看见海岸。 4 ADJ **Clear** eyes look healthy, attractive, and shining. (眼睛) 明亮的 ❑ *...clear blue eyes.* …明亮的蓝眼睛。 5 ADJ If your skin is **clear**, it is healthy and free from blemishes. (皮肤) 光洁的 ❑ *No amount of cleansing or mineral water consumption can guarantee a clear skin.* 再多的洁肤和矿泉水的消耗都不能确保光洁的皮肤。 6 ADJ If something or someone is **clear of** something else, it is not touching it or is a safe distance away from it. 不与…接触的; 不与…靠近的 ❑ *As soon as he was clear of the terminal building, he looked around.* 他一走出航站楼就四处张望。 7 V-T When you **clear** an area or place or **clear** something **from** it, you remove things from it that you do not want to be there. 清空; 清理出 ❑ *To clear the land and harvest the bananas, they decided they needed a male workforce.* 为了清理土地和收割香蕉，他们决定需要男劳力。 ❑ *Workers could not clear the tunnels of smoke.* 工人们无法把烟从隧道里全部排出去。 8 V-I When fog or mist **clears**, it gradually disappears. (烟雾等) 消散 ❑ *The early morning mist had cleared.* 清晨的雾气已经消散了。 9 **to clear the air** → see **air** 10 **to clear** your **throat** → see **throat** 11 → see also **clearing, crystal clear**

Thesaurus *clear* 另参见:
ADJ. obvious, plain; *(ant.)* straightforward ❶ 1
bright, cloudless, sunny ❷ 3

❸ **clear ♦♦♦** /klɪər/ (**clearer, clearest, clears, clearing, cleared**) 1 ADJ If you say that your conscience is **clear**, you mean you do not think you have done anything wrong. 问心无愧的 ❑ *Mr. Garcia said his conscience was clear over the jail incidents.* 加西亚先生说对监狱发生的事他问心无愧。 2 V-T/V-I When a bank **clears** a check or when a check **clears**, the bank agrees to pay the sum of money mentioned on it. 兑现 ❑ *Banks can still take two or three weeks to clear a check.* 银行还要两三周的时间才能兑现支票。 ❑ *Allow plenty of time for the check to clear.* 留出足够的时间让支票兑现。 3 V-T If something or someone **clears** the way or the path **for** something to happen, they make it possible. 使…成为可能 ❑ *The prime minister resigned today, clearing the way for the formation of a new government.* 首相今天辞职了，为新政府的组建铺平了道路。 4 V-T If a course of action **is cleared**, people in authority give permission for it to happen. 允许 [usu passive] ❑ *Linda Gradstein has this report from Jerusalem, which was cleared by an Israeli censor.* 琳达•格雷德斯坦从耶路撒冷报道，该报道已经被以色列审查员批准了。 5 V-T If someone **is cleared**, they are proved to be not guilty of a crime or mistake. 宣判无罪 ❑ *She was cleared of murder and jailed for just five years for manslaughter.* 她谋杀罪不成立，只为过失杀人罪坐了5年牢。 6 PHRASE If someone is **in the clear**, they are not in danger, or are not blamed or suspected of anything. 没有危险的; 无辜的 ❑ *It would be stupid to do anything until we know we're in the clear.* 在得知我们没有危险之前采取任何行动，那会是愚蠢的。

Word Partnership *clear* 的常用搭配:
V. **be** clear, **make it** clear, **seem** clear ❶ 1 2
N. clear **goals/purposes**, clear **picture** ❶ 1
clear **idea**, clear **understanding** ❶ 1 2
clear *someone's* **head** ❶ 5
clear **the way** ❸ 3
ADJ. **crystal** clear ❶ 1 – 3 ❷ 1 3

❹ **clear ♦♦♦** /klɪər/ (**clears, clearing, cleared**)
▸ **clear away** PHRASAL VERB When you **clear** things **away** or **clear away**, you put away the things that you have been using, especially for eating or cooking. 收拾 (餐具) ❑ *The waitress had cleared away the plates and brought coffee.* 女服务员收走盘子，端来了咖啡。 ❑ *Tania cooked, served and cleared away.* 塔妮娅做了饭，端上来，然后又收拾了餐具。
▸ **clear out** 1 PHRASAL VERB If you tell someone to **clear out of** a place or to **clear out**, you are telling them rather rudely to leave the place. 滚出去 [INFORMAL, DISAPPROVAL] ❑ *She turned to the others in the room. "The rest of you clear out of here."* 她转向房间里的其他人，“你们其余的人都滚出去！” ❑ *"Clear out!" he bawled. "Private property!"* “出去！”他大喊到。“私人住宅！” 2 PHRASAL VERB If you **clear out** a container, room, or house, you make it neat and throw away the things in it that you no longer want. 清理 ❑ *I took the precaution of clearing out my desk before I left.* 为了万全起见我离开前清理了我的桌子。
▸ **clear up** 1 PHRASAL VERB When you **clear up** or **clear** a place **up**, you make things neat and put them away. 收拾 ❑ *After breakfast they played while I cleared up.* 早餐后，他们玩的时候我在收拾。 2 PHRASAL VERB To **clear up** a problem, misunderstanding, or mystery means to settle it or find a satisfactory explanation for it. 澄清; 解决 ❑ *There should be someone to whom you can turn for any advice or to clear up any problems.* 应该有你可以征求意见或为你解决问题的人。 3 PHRASAL VERB To **clear up** a medical problem, infection, or disease means to cure it or get rid of it. If a medical problem **clears up**, it goes away. 治愈; 痊愈 ❑ *Antibiotics should be used to clear up the infection.* 抗生素应该用来治愈这种感染。 ❑ *Acne often clears up after the first three months of pregnancy.* 一般在怀孕三个月以后，痤疮就会愈合了。 4 PHRASAL VERB When the weather **clears up**, it stops raining or being cloudy. 转晴 ❑ *It all depends on the weather clearing up.* 这一切都取决于天气放晴。

★ **clear·ance** /klɪərəns/ (**clearances**) 1 N-VAR **Clearance** is the removal of old buildings, trees, or other things that are not wanted from an area. 拆除; 清除 ❑ *The U.N. pledged to help supervise the clearance of mines.* 联合国承诺帮助监督扫雷工作。 2 N-VAR If you get **clearance to** do or have something, you get official approval or permission to do or have it. 官方许可 ❑ *Thai Airways said the plane had been given clearance to land.* 泰国航空公司说该飞机已经被授予了着陆的官方许可。

★ **clear-cut** also **clear cut** ADJ Something that is **clear-cut** is easy to recognize and quite distinct. 明显的 ❑ *This was a clear-cut case of the original landowner being in the right.* 这是一起明显的原土地所有者有理的案件。

★ **clear·ing** /klɪərɪŋ/ (**clearings**) N-COUNT A **clearing** is a small area in a forest where there are no trees or bushes. 林中空地 ❑ *A helicopter landed in a clearing in the dense jungle.* 一架直升机在茂密丛林中的一片空地着陆了。

clearing·house /klɪərɪŋhaʊs/ (**clearinghouses**) 1 N-COUNT If an organization acts as a **clearinghouse**, it collects, sorts, and distributes specialized information. 专门信息搜集所 ❑ *The center will act as a clearinghouse for research projects for former nuclear scientists.* 该中心将作为前任核科学家研究项目的信息搜集所。 2 N-COUNT A **clearinghouse** is a central bank which deals with all business among the banks that use its services. (银行之间的) 结算所 [BUSINESS]

▲ **clem·ent** /klɛmənt/ ADJ **Clement** weather is pleasantly mild and dry. 温和的 (气候) [usu ADJ n] [FORMAL]

▲ **clench** /klɛntʃ/ (**clenches, clenching, clenched**) 1 V-T/V-I When you **clench** your fist or your fist **clenches**, you curl your fingers up tightly, usually because you are very angry. (常指因生气而) 握紧 (拳头) ❑ *Alex clenched her fists and gritted her teeth.* 亚丽克斯握紧拳头，咬紧牙。 ❑ *She pulled at his sleeve and he turned on her, fists clenching again before he saw who it was.* 她扯了扯他的袖子，他恶汹汹地转过身，在看见她是谁之前又再次握紧了拳头。 2 V-T/V-I When you **clench** your teeth or they **clench**, you squeeze your teeth together firmly, usually because you are angry or upset.

(常指因生气或不安而) 咬紧 (牙) ❏ *Patsy had to clench her jaw to suppress her anger.* 帕茜不得不咬紧牙关来压下怒火。 **3** V-T If you **clench** something in your hand or in your teeth, you hold it tightly with your hand or your teeth. 握紧; 咬紧 ❏ *I clenched the arms of my chair.* 我紧紧握住我的椅子扶手。

C

▲ **cler·gy** /klɜrdʒi/ N-PLURAL The **clergy** are the official leaders of the religious activities of a particular group of believers. 教士

clergy·man /klɜrdʒimən/ (**clergymen**) N-COUNT A **clergyman** is a male member of the clergy. 男牧师

cler·ic /klɛrɪk/ (**clerics**) N-COUNT A **cleric** is a member of the clergy. 牧师; 教士 ❏ *His grandfather was a Muslim cleric.* 他祖父是一位穆斯林教士。

cleri·cal /klɛrɪkᵊl/ **1** ADJ **Clerical** jobs, skills, and workers are concerned with routine work that is done in an office. 办公室文书工作的 [ADJ n] ❏ *...a strike by clerical staff in all government departments.* …一次所有政府部门文书职员的罢工。 **2** ADJ **Clerical** means relating to the clergy. 牧师的; 教士的 [ADJ n] ❏ *...Iran's clerical leadership.* …伊朗的教士领导层。

clerk /klɜrk/ (**clerks, clerking, clerked**) **1** N-COUNT A **clerk** is a person who works in an office, bank, or law court and whose job is to keep the records or accounts. 文书; (法庭) 书记员 ❏ *She was offered a job as a clerk with a travel agency.* 她找到了在一家旅行社做文书的工作。 **2** N-COUNT In a hotel, office, or hospital, a **clerk** is the person whose job is to answer the telephone and deal with people when they arrive. 接待员 [mainly AM] ❏ *...a hotel clerk.* …一名宾馆接待员。 **3** N-COUNT A **clerk** is someone who sells things to customers in a store. 售货员 [AM] ❏ *Now Thomas was working as a clerk in a shop that sold leather goods.* 现在托马斯在一家卖皮革品的店里做售货员。 **4** V-I To **clerk** means to work as a clerk. 做文书工作 [mainly AM] ❏ *Gene clerked at the auction.* 吉恩在拍卖行做文书工作。
→ see **hotel**

clev·er ♦◇◇ /klɛvər/ (**cleverer, cleverest**) **1** ADJ Someone who is **clever** is intelligent and able to understand things easily or plan things well. 聪明的 ❏ *He's a very clever man.* 他是个很聪明的人。 ● **clev·er·ly** ADV 聪明地 ❏ *She would cleverly pick up on what I said.* 她会很聪明地留心我说的话。 ● **clev·er·ness** N-UNCOUNT 聪明 ❏ *Her cleverness seems to get in the way of her emotions.* 她的聪明似乎妨碍了她的感情。 **2** ADJ A **clever** idea, book, or invention is extremely effective and shows the skill of the people involved. 巧妙的 ❏ *It is a clever and gripping novel, yet something is missing from its heart.* 这是一部构思巧妙、引人入胜的小说，不过在精神上还缺少点什么。 ● **clev·er·ly** ADV 巧妙地 [ADV -ed] ❏ *...a cleverly designed swimsuit.* …一件设计巧妙的游泳衣。

Thesaurus *clever* 另参见:
ADJ. bright, ingenious, smart; *(ant.)* dumb, stupid **1** **2**

▲ **cli·ché** /kliʃeɪ/ (**clichés**)
in BRIT, also use **cliche**
N-COUNT A **cliché** is an idea or phrase which has been used so much that it is no longer interesting or effective or no longer has much meaning. 陈词滥调 [DISAPPROVAL] ❏ *I've learned that the cliché about life not being fair is true.* 我已经体会到有关生活不公的老调是对的。

click /klɪk/ (**clicks, clicking, clicked**) **1** V-T/V-I If something **clicks** or if you **click** it, it makes a short, sharp sound. 使发咔嚓声; 发出咔嚓声 ❏ *The applause rose to a crescendo and cameras clicked.* 掌声越来越响，照相机咔嚓咔嚓地响。 ❏ *He clicked off the radio.* 他咔嗒一声关上了收音机。 ● N-COUNT **Click** is also a noun. 咔嚓声 ❏ *The telephone rang three times before I heard a click and then her recorded voice.* 电话响了3次后我听到了咔嗒一声响，然后是她的录音留言。 **2** V-T/V-I If you **click** on an area of a computer screen, you point the cursor at that area and press one of the buttons on the mouse in order to make something happen. (用鼠标) 点击 [no passive] [COMPUTING] ❏ *I clicked on a link and recent reviews of the production came up.* 我点击了一个链接，最近的演出评论就出来了。 ❏ *Click the link and see what happens.* 点击那个链接，看看会发生什么。 ● N-COUNT **Click** is also a noun. 点击 ❏ *You can check your e-mail with a click of your mouse.* 通过鼠标的一点你就能查电子邮件。 **3** V-I When you suddenly understand something, you can say that it **clicks**. 恍然大悟 [INFORMAL] ❏ *When I saw the television report, it all clicked.* 当我看到电视报道时，一下就恍然大悟了。 **4** to **click into place** → see **place**

click·able /klɪkəbᵊl/ ADJ A **clickable** image on a computer screen is one that you can point the cursor at and click on, in order to make something happen. (用来显示图像) 可用鼠标点击的 [COMPUTING] ❏ *...a website with clickable maps showing hotel locations.* …一个有显示饭店位置的可点击地图的网站。

cli·ent ♦◇◇ /klaɪənt/ (**clients**) N-COUNT A **client** of a professional person or organization is a person or company that receives a service from them in return for payment. 客户 [BUSINESS] ❏ *...a lawyer and his client.* …一位律师和他的委托人。
→ see **trial**

If you use the professional services of someone such as a lawyer or an accountant, you are one of their **clients**. When you buy goods from a particular shop or company, you are one of its **customers**. Doctors and hospitals have **patients**, while hotels have **guests**. People who travel on public transportation are referred to as **passengers**.

cli·en·tele /klaɪəntɛl, kliɒn-/ N-SING-COLL The **clientele** of a place or organization are its customers or clients. 顾客群; 客户群 ❏ *This pub had a mixed clientele.* 这家酒吧有混杂的顾客群。

cliff /klɪf/ (**cliffs**) N-COUNT A **cliff** is a high area of land with a very steep side, especially one next to the sea. (尤其指靠海的) 悬崖 ❏ *The car rolled over the edge of a cliff.* 汽车翻下了悬崖边。
→ see **mountain**

cliff·top /klɪftɒp/ (**clifftops**) N-COUNT A **clifftop** is the area of land around the top of a cliff. 峭壁顶部周边地段 ❏ *...a house on the clifftop.* …一所在峭壁顶部旁边的房子。 ❏ *...25 acres of spectacular clifftop scenery.* …峭壁顶部周围25英亩的壮观景色。

cli·mate ♦◇◇ /klaɪmɪt/ (**climates**) **1** N-VAR The **climate** of a place is the general weather conditions that are typical of it. 气候 ❏ *...the hot and humid climate of Florida.* …佛罗里达炎热潮湿的气候。 **2** N-COUNT You can use **climate** to refer to the general atmosphere or situation somewhere. 氛围; 形势 ❏ *The economic climate remains uncertain.* 经济气候依然是不确定。 ❏ *...the existing climate of violence and intimidation.* … 现有的暴力与恐吓的氛围。
→ see Word Web: **climate**

Word Web climate

During the past 100 years, the surface air **temperature** of the earth has increased by about 1° **Fahrenheit** (F). Alaska has warmed by about 4° F. At the same time, precipitation over the northern hemisphere increased by 10%. The global sea level also rose 4-8 inches. The years 1998, 2001, and 2002 were the three hottest ever recorded. This warm period followed what some scientists call the "Little Ice Age." Researchers found that from the 1400s to the 1800s the Earth cooled by about 6° F. Air and water temperatures were lower, **glaciers** grew quickly, and **ice** floes came further south than usual.

St. Mark's Square in Venice flooded 111 times in 2002.

★ **cli·max** /klaɪmæks/ (**climaxes, climaxing, climaxed**) 1 N-COUNT The **climax of** something is the most exciting or important moment in it, usually near the end. 高潮 ❑ *For Pritchard, reaching the Olympics was the climax of her career.* 对普里查德来说，进军奥林匹克运动会是她事业的巅峰。 ❑ *It was the climax to 24 hours of growing anxiety.* 这是24小时不断升温的焦虑的顶点。 2 V-T/V-I The event that **climaxes** a sequence of events is an exciting or important event that comes at the end. You can also say that a sequence of events **climaxes with** a particular event. 使达到高潮；达到高潮 [JOURNALISM] ❑ *The demonstration climaxed two weeks of strikes.* 游行示威达到了两周罢工的高潮。

climb ♦◇◇ /klaɪm/ (**climbs, climbing, climbed**) 1 V-T/V-I If you **climb** something such as a tree, mountain, or ladder, or **climb up** it, you move toward the top of it. If you **climb down** it, you move toward the bottom of it. 爬 ❑ *Climbing the first hill took half an hour.* 爬第一座山花了半个小时。 ❑ *I told her about him climbing up the drainpipe.* 我把他爬排水管的事告诉了她。 ● N-COUNT **Climb** is also a noun. 爬 ❑ *...an hour's leisurely climb through olive groves and vineyards.* …橄榄丛和葡萄园中的一个小时的悠闲攀爬。 2 V-I If you **climb** somewhere, you move there carefully, for example because you are moving into a small space or trying to avoid falling. 小心翼翼地爬 ❑ *The girls hurried outside, climbed into the car, and drove off.* 女孩子们赶紧跑了出去，爬进车里，开走了。 ❑ *He must have climbed out of his bed.* 他肯定已经爬下了床。 3 V-I When something such as an airplane **climbs**, it moves upward to a higher position. When the sun **climbs**, it moves higher in the sky. (飞机、太阳) 爬升 ❑ *The plane took off for L.A., lost an engine as it climbed, and crashed just off the runway.* 那架飞机起飞前往洛杉矶，在升空时掉了一个引擎，就在跑道边上坠机了。 4 V-I When something **climbs**, it increases in value or amount. (价值、数量) 上涨 ❑ *The nation's unemployment rate has been climbing steadily since last June.* 去年6月以来这个国家的失业率在稳步持续上升。 ❑ *Prices have climbed by 21% since the beginning of the year.* 今年年初以来价格已经上涨了21%。 5 → see also **climbing** 6 **a mountain to climb** → see **mountain**

Word Partnership *climb* 的常用搭配:

N.	climb **the stairs** 1
	prices climb 4
V.	**begin/continue to** climb 1 – 4
PREP.	climb **down/up**, climb **in/on** 1 2

climb·er /klaɪmər/ (**climbers**) 1 N-COUNT A **climber** is someone who climbs rocks or mountains as a sport or a hobby. 登山者；攀岩者 ❑ *She was an experienced climber, who had climbed several of the world's tallest mountains.* 她是一个经验丰富的登山者，已经攀登过好几座世界最高的山峰。 2 N-COUNT A **climber** is a plant that grows upward by attaching itself to other plants or objects. 攀缘植物 ❑ *All good garden centers carry a selection of climbers.* 所有好的花卉中心都有不同的攀缘植物可供挑选。

climb·ing /klaɪmɪŋ/ N-UNCOUNT **Climbing** is the activity of climbing rocks or mountains. 攀岩运动；登山运动 ❑ *I had done no skiing, no climbing, and no hiking.* 我从未滑过雪、攀过岩和徒步旅行过。

▲ **clinch** /klɪntʃ/ (**clinches, clinching, clinched**) 1 V-T If you **clinch** something you are trying to achieve, such as a business deal or victory in a contest, you succeed in obtaining it. 赢得 ❑ *Her second-place finish in the final race was enough to clinch the overall victory.* 她决赛中第二名的成绩足以能让她赢得整体的胜利。 2 V-T The thing that **clinches** an uncertain matter settles it or provides a definite answer. 解决 ❑ *Evidently this information clinched the matter.* 显然这一信息解决了这个问题。

cling /klɪŋ/ (**clings, clinging, clung**) 1 V-I If you **cling to** someone or something, you hold onto them tightly. 紧紧抓住 ❑ *Another man was rescued as he clung to the riverbank.* 另一个男人因为紧紧抓住了河堤而被救了。 ❑ *She had to cling onto the door handle until the pain passed.* 她不得不紧紧抓住门的把手，直到疼痛消失为止。 2 V-I If someone **clings to** a position or a possession they have, they do everything they can to keep it even though this may be very difficult. 固守 ❑ *Instead, he appears determined to cling to power.* 反而，他看来坚决要握紧权力不放。 ❑ *Another congressman clung on with a majority of only 18.* 另一位国会议员在获得仅仅18张多数票的情况下保住了位子。

cling·film /klɪŋfɪlm/ also **cling film** N-UNCOUNT **Clingfilm** is a thin, clear, stretchy plastic that you use to cover food in order to keep it fresh. 保鲜膜 [BRIT]

in AM, use **plastic wrap, Saran wrap**

clin·ic ♦◇◇ /klɪnɪk/ (**clinics**) N-COUNT A **clinic** is a building where people go to receive medical advice or treatment. 诊所 ❑ *...a family planning clinic.* …计划生育诊所。

Word Partnership *clinic* 的常用搭配:

N.	**abortion/family planning** clinic, **fertility** clinic
ADJ.	**free** clinic, **medical** clinic

clini·cal /klɪnɪkᵊl/ 1 ADJ **Clinical** means involving or relating to the direct medical treatment or testing of patients. 临床的 [ADJ n] [MEDICAL] ❑ *The first clinical trials were expected to begin next year.* 第一批临床试验预计明年开始。 ● **clini·cal·ly** /klɪnɪkli/ ADV 临床地 ❑ *She was diagnosed as being clinically depressed.* 她被诊断为患临床抑郁症。 2 ADJ You use **clinical** to describe thought or behavior that is very logical and does not involve any emotion. 无人情味的 [DISAPPROVAL] ❑ *All this questioning is so clinical – it kills romance.* 所有这些发问是如此如此无人情味——使浪漫荡然无存。

clip /klɪp/ (**clips, clipping, clipped**) 1 N-COUNT A **clip** is a small device, usually made of metal or plastic, that is specially shaped for holding things together. 夹子；回形针 ❑ *She took the clip out of her hair.* 她从头发里取出发夹。 2 N-COUNT A **clip** from a movie or a radio or television program is a short piece of it that is broadcast separately. (电影、广播、电视节目的) 片断 ❑ *...an historical film clip of Lenin speaking.* …一段列宁讲话的历史电影片断。 3 V-T/V-I When you **clip** things together or when things **clip** together, you fasten them together using a clip or clips. 用夹子夹住；夹紧 ❑ *He clipped his safety belt to a fitting on the deck.* 他把安全带扣在甲板的一个固定拴上。 4 V-T If you **clip** something, you cut small pieces from it, especially in order to shape it. 修剪 ❑ *I saw an old man out clipping his hedge.* 我看见一个老人正在外面修剪他的树篱。 5 V-T If you **clip** something out of a newspaper or magazine, you cut it out. (从报纸、杂志上) 剪下 ❑ *Kids in his neighborhood clipped his picture from the newspaper and carried it around.* 他的街区里的孩子们从报纸上剪下他的照片，随身携带。 6 V-T If something **clips** something else, it hits it accidentally at an angle before moving off in a different direction. 意外碰撞(使改变方向) ❑ *The truck clipped the rear of a tanker and then crashed into a second truck.* 卡车意外地撞上了燃料车的尾部，然后又撞上了另一辆卡车。 7 → see also **clipped, clipping, paper clip**

Word Partnership *clip* 的常用搭配:

V.	**play a** clip 2
N.	**audio/film/movie/music/video** clip, **a** clip **from a tape** 2
	clip **coupons** 5

clip·board /klɪpbɔrd/ (**clipboards**) 1 N-COUNT A **clipboard** is a board with a clip at the top. It is used to hold together pieces of paper that you need to carry around, and provides a firm base for writing. 带夹子的写字板 2 N-COUNT In computing, a **clipboard** is a file where you can temporarily store text or images from one document until you are ready to use them again. 剪贴板 [COMPUTING]

clipped /klɪpt/ 1 ADJ **Clipped** means neatly cut. 修剪整齐的 ❑ *...a quiet street of clipped hedges and flowering gardens.* …一条树篱修剪整齐、花园开满鲜花的安静街道。 2 ADJ If you say that someone has a **clipped** way of speaking, you mean they speak with quick, short sounds, and usually that they sound upper-class. (尤指上等阶级说话声音) 清脆快速的 ❑ *Her clipped tones crackled over the telephone line.* 她清脆快速的语调在电话线另一头响了起来。

clip·ping /klɪpɪŋ/ (**clippings**) 1 N-COUNT A **clipping** is an article, picture, or advertisement that has been cut from a newspaper or magazine. 剪报 ❑ *...bulletin boards crowded with newspaper clippings.* …贴满了剪报的布告栏。 2 N-PLURAL **Clippings** are small pieces of something that have been cut from something larger. 剪切物 ❑ *Having mown the lawn, there are all those grass clippings to get rid of.* 修剪完草坪，还要清除所有那些剪下来的草。

clique /klik, klɪk/ (**cliques**) N-COUNT If you describe a group of people as a **clique**, you mean that they spend a lot of time together and seem unfriendly towards people who are not in the group. 小团体 [DISAPPROVAL] ❑ *He was accepted into the most popular clique on campus.* 他被吸收到了校园里最受欢迎的小团体里。

▲ **cloak** /kloʊk/ (**cloaks**) 1 N-COUNT A **cloak** is a long, loose, sleeveless piece of clothing which people used to wear over their other clothes when they went out. 斗篷 2 N-SING A **cloak of** something such as mist or snow completely covers and hides

C

Word Web clone

Clones have always existed. For example, plant propagation using a leaf cutting produces an **identical** new plant. Identical **twins** are also natural clones of each other. Recently however, scientists have started using **genetic engineering** to produce artificial clones of animals. The first step involves removing the **DNA** from a **cell**. Next, a technician places this genetic information into an egg cell. The egg then matures into a **copy** of the donor animal. The first animal experiments in the 1970s involved tadpoles. In 1997 a sheep named Dolly became the first successfully cloned mammal.

something. (如雾雪的) 掩盖 ❑ *Today most of New England will be under a cloak of thick mist.* 今天新英格兰大部分地区会在浓雾的笼罩中。 **3** N-SING If you refer to something as a **cloak**, you mean that it is intended to hide the truth about something. 幌子 ❑ *Preparations for the wedding were made under a cloak of secrecy.* 婚礼的准备工作是在秘密的掩饰中进行的。

cloak·room /kloʊkrum/ (**cloakrooms**) N-COUNT A **cloakroom** is the same as a **coat check**. 衣帽间 [OLD-FASHIONED] ❑ *...a cloakroom attendant.* …一名衣帽间服务员。

clock ♦◊◊ /klɒk/ (**clocks, clocking, clocked**) **1** N-COUNT A **clock** is an instrument that shows what time of day it is. 钟 ❑ *He was conscious of a clock ticking.* 他意识到了时间正在消逝。 ❑ *...a digital clock.* …一个数字时钟。 **2** N-COUNT A time **clock** in a factory or office is a device that is used to record the hours that people work. Each worker puts a special card into the device when they arrive and leave, and the times are recorded on the card. 考勤刷卡机 ❑ *Government workers were made to punch time clocks morning, noon and night.* 政府工作人员被要求早晨、中午和晚上要在考勤机上打卡。 **3** V-T To **clock** a particular time or speed in a race means to reach that time or speed. 以…的速度竞赛 ❑ *Elliott clocked the fastest time this year for the 800 meters.* 埃利奥特跑出了今年800米的最快速度。 **4** V-T If something or someone **is clocked at** a particular time or speed, their time or speed is measured at that level. 测…的速度 [usu passive] ❑ *He has been clocked at 11 seconds for 100 meters.* 他100米跑的速度已被测出是11秒。 **5** → see also **alarm clock, o'clock** **6** PHRASE If you are doing something **against the clock**, you are doing it in a great hurry, because there is very little time. 争分夺秒 ❑ *The emergency services were working against the clock as the tide began to rise.* 潮水开始上涨，应急部门正在争分夺秒地工作着。 **7** PHRASE If something is done **around the clock** or **round the clock**, it is done all day and all night without stopping. 夜以继日 ❑ *Rescue services have been working round the clock to free stranded motorists.* 救援工作一直在昼夜不停地进行着，来解救被困的开车的人们。
→ see **time**

▸ **clock in** PHRASAL VERB When you **clock in** at work, you arrive there or put a special card into a device to show what time you arrived. 打卡上班 ❑ *I have to clock in by eight.* 我必须八点前打卡上班。

▸ **clock off** PHRASAL VERB When you **clock off** at work, you leave work or put a special card into a device to show what time you left. 打卡下班 ❑ *The night duty officer was ready to clock off.* 值夜班的警官准备打卡下班了。

▸ **clock on** PHRASAL VERB When workers **clock on** at a factory or office, they put a special card into a device to show what time they arrived. 打卡上班 ❑ *They arrived to clock on and found the factory gates locked.* 他们到了就去打卡上班，结果发现工厂大门锁了。

▸ **clock out** PHRASAL VERB **Clock out** means the same as **clock off**. 打卡下班 ❑ *She had clocked out of her bank at 5:02pm using her plastic card.* 她用她的塑料卡在下午5:02从银行打卡下班。

▸ **clock up** PHRASAL VERB If you **clock up** a large number or total of things, you reach that number or total. (某一数量) 达到 [BRIT] in AM, use **chalk up**

Word Partnership *clock* 的常用搭配：

N. **hands of a** clock, clock **radio** **1**
V. **look at a** clock, **put/turn the** clock **back/forward, set a** clock, clock **strikes**, clock **ticks** **1**

Word Link *wise ≈ in the direction or manner of : clockwise, likewise, otherwise*

clock·wise /klɒkwaɪz/ ADV When something is moving **clockwise**, it is moving in a circle in the same direction as the hands on a clock. 顺时针地 [ADV after v] ❑ *He told the children to start moving clockwise around the room.* 他告诉孩子们在房间里开始按顺时针方向移动。 ● ADJ **Clockwise** is also an adjective. 顺时针的 [ADJ n] ❑ *Gently swing your right arm in a clockwise direction.* 按顺时针方向轻轻摆动你的右臂。

clock·work /klɒkwɜrk/ **1** ADJ A **clockwork** toy or device has machinery inside it which makes it move or operate when it is wound up with a key. 带发条装置的 [ADJ n] ❑ *...a clockwork train set.* …一套带发条装置的火车玩具。 **2** PHRASE If you say that something happens **like clockwork**, you mean that it happens without any problems or delays, or happens regularly. 极为准确地；极有规律地 ❑ *The president's trip is arranged to go like clockwork, everything pre-planned to the minute.* 总统的行程安排得极其周密，每一件事情都事先安排到了分钟。

▲ **clog** /klɒg/ (**clogs, clogging, clogged**) **1** V-T When something **clogs** a hole or place, it blocks it so that nothing can pass through. 堵塞 ❑ *Dirt clogs the pores, causing blemishes.* 尘垢堵塞了毛孔，由此产生了瑕疵。 **2** N-COUNT **Clogs** are heavy leather or wooden shoes with thick, wooden soles. 木屐

clone /kloʊn/ (**clones, cloning, cloned**) **1** N-COUNT If someone or something is a **clone** of another person or thing, they are so similar to this person or thing that they seem to be exactly the same as them. 翻版 ❑ *Tom was in some ways a younger clone of his handsome father.* 汤姆在某些方面是他英俊父亲年轻时的翻版。 **2** N-COUNT A **clone** is an animal or plant that has been produced artificially, for example in a laboratory, from the cells of another animal or plant. A clone is exactly the same as the original animal or plant. 克隆 ❑ *...the world's first human clone.* …世界上第一个克隆人。 **3** V-T To **clone** an animal or plant means to produce it as a clone. 对…进行克隆 ❑ *The idea of cloning extinct life forms still belongs to science fiction.* 对绝种的生命形式进行克隆的想法仍然属于科学幻想。
→ see Word Web: **clone**

close
❶ SHUTTING OR COMPLETING
❷ NEARNESS; ADJECTIVE USES
❸ NEARNESS; VERB USES

❶ **close** ♦♦♦ /kloʊz/ (**closes, closing, closed**)
➪ **Please look at meanings 12 and 13 to see if the expression you are looking for is shown under another headword.** **1** V-T/V-I When you **close** something such as a door or lid or when it **closes**, it moves so that a hole, gap, or opening is covered. 关闭；闭合 ❑ *If you are cold, close the window.* 如果你冷就关上窗户。 ❑ *Zacharias heard the door close.* 札哈里亚斯听到门关上了。 **2** V-T When you **close** something such as an open book or umbrella, you move the different parts of it together. 把 (书、伞等) 合上 ❑ *Slowly he closed the book.* 慢慢地他把书合上了。 **3** V-T If you **close** something such as a computer file or window, you give the computer an instruction to remove it from the screen. 关闭 (计算机文件、窗口) [COMPUTING] ❑ *To close your document, press CTRL+W on your keyboard.* 要关闭你的文件同时按下键盘上的CTRL和W键。 **4** V-T/V-I When you **close** your eyes or your eyes **close**, your eyelids move downward, so that you can no longer see. 闭上眼睛 ❑ *Bess closed her eyes and fell asleep.* 贝丝闭上眼睛，睡着了。 **5** V-T/V-I When a place **closes** or **is closed**, work or activity stops there for a short period. (地方) 暂时关闭 ❑ *Shops close only on Christmas Day and New Year's Day.* 商店只在圣诞日和元旦停业。 ❑ *Government troops closed the airport.* 政府军队临时关闭了机场。 **6** V-T/V-I If a place such as a factory, store, or school **closes**, or if it **is closed**, all work or activity stops there permanently. 使永久关闭；永久关闭 ❑ *Many enterprises will be forced to close.* 许多企业将被迫关闭。 ● PHRASAL VERB **Close down** means the same as **close**.

永久关闭 ❑ *Minford closed down the business and went into politics.* 明福特关了买卖，进入了政界。● **clos·ing** N-SING 关闭 ❑ *...since the closing of the steel mill in 1984.* …自从1984年钢铁厂的关闭以来。 **7** V-T To **close** a road or border means to block it in order to prevent people from using it. 封锁(道路、边境) ❑ *They were cut off from the West in 1948 when their government closed that border crossing.* 当他们的政府于1948年封锁了那个那个边境通道以后，他们与西方国家的联系就被切断了。 **8** V-T To **close** a conversation, event, or matter means to bring it to an end or to complete it. 结束 ❑ *Judge Isabel Oliva said last night: "I have closed the case. There was no foul play."* 伊莎贝尔•奥莉芙法官昨晚说：“我已经结案了，其中没有违规做法。” ❑ *The governor is said to now consider the matter closed.* 据说州长认为此事已经了结了。 **9** V-T If you **close** a bank account, you take all your money out of it and inform the bank that you will no longer be using the account. 结清(银行账户) ❑ *He had closed his account with the bank five years earlier.* 他早在5年前就已经跟银行结清了户头。 **10** V-I On the stock market or the currency markets, if a share price or a currency **closes** at a particular value, that is its value at the end of the day's business. (股票) 收盘 [BUSINESS] ❑ *The U.S. dollar closed higher in Tokyo today.* 美元今天在东京的收盘价更高。 **11** → see also **closing** **12** to **close** your **eyes to** something → see **eye** **13** to **close ranks** → see **rank**

▸ **close down** → see **close** ❶ 6

▸ **close up** **1** PHRASAL VERB If someone **closes up** a building, they shut it completely and securely, often because they are going away. (指临行前) 锁好 ❑ *Just close up the shop.* 就把店锁好。 ❑ *The summer house had been closed up all year.* 避暑别墅全年都是门户紧闭的。 **2** PHRASAL VERB If an opening, gap, or something hollow **closes up**, or if you **close it up**, it becomes closed or covered. (缺口、缝隙) 闭合 ❑ *Don't use cold water as it shocks the blood vessels into closing up.* 不要用冷水，因为冷水会刺激血管，使之闭合。

Thesaurus *close* 另参见：

V. fasten, seal, shut, slam; *(ant.)* open ❶ **1**

❷ **close** ◆◆◆ /kloʊs/ (closer, closest)

➪ **Please look at meanings 16 and 17 to see if the expression you are looking for is shown under another headword.** **1** ADJ If one thing or person is **close to** another, there is only a very small distance between them. 靠近的 ❑ *Her lips were close to his head and her breath tickled his ear.* 她的嘴唇靠近他的头，她的气息轻挠他的耳朵。 ❑ *The man moved closer, lowering his voice.* 那个男人凑得更近了，压低了声音。 ● **close·ly** ADV 靠近地 ❑ *They crowded more closely around the stretcher.* 他们更近地围到担架旁。 **2** ADJ You say that people are **close to** each other when they like each other very much and know each other very well. 亲密的 ❑ *She and Linda became very close.* 她和琳达变得很亲密。 ❑ *I shared a house with a close friend from school.* 我和学校的一位密友共住一座房子 ● **close·ness** N-UNCOUNT 亲密关系 ❑ *I asked whether her closeness to her mother ever posed any problems.* 我问她与她母亲的亲密关系是否曾带来过问题。 **3** ADJ Your **close** relatives are the members of your family who are most directly related to you, for example your parents and your brothers or sisters. 直系的 [ADJ n] ❑ *...large changes such as the birth of a child or death of a close relative.* …如孩子的诞生或直系亲属的死亡之类的巨大变化。 **4** ADJ A **close** ally or partner of someone knows them well and is very involved in their work. (工作上) 关系密切的 ❑ *He was once regarded as one of Mr. Brown's closest political advisers.* 他曾一度被认为是与布朗先生关系最密切的政治顾问之一。 **5** ADJ **Close** contact or cooperation involves seeing or communicating with someone often. (接触、合作) 紧密的 [ADJ n] ❑ *Both nations are seeking closer links with the West.* 这两个国家都正在寻求与西方国家更紧密的联系。 ● **close·ly** ADV 紧密地 [ADV after v] ❑ *Our agencies work closely with local groups in developing countries.* 我们的机构与发展中国家的地方团体密切协作。 **6** ADJ If there is a **close** connection or resemblance between two things, they are strongly connected or are very similar. 紧密的 (关联); 相似的 ❑ *There is a close connection between pain and tension.* 疼痛和紧张之间有紧密的关联。 ● **close·ly** ADV 紧密地; 相似地 ❑ *...a pattern closely resembling a cross.* …一个酷似十字架的图案。 **7** ADJ **Close** inspection or observation of something is careful and thorough. 全面细致的 ❑ *He discovered, on closer inspection, that the rocks contained gold.* 通过更周密的探查，他发现那些岩石中含有黄金。 ● **close·ly** ADV 全面细致地 [ADV with v] ❑ *If you look closely at many of the problems in society, you'll see evidence of racial discrimination.* 如果你仔细思考社会中的很多问题，你就会发现种族歧视的证据。 **8** ADJ A **close** competition or election is won or seems likely to be won by only a small amount. 势均力敌的 ❑ *It is still a close contest between two leading opposition parties.* 两大主要反对党之间的较量仍然旗鼓相当。 ● **close·ly** ADV 势均力敌地 ❑ *This will be a closely fought race.* 这将是一场出手势均力敌的比赛。 **9** ADJ If you are **close to** something or if it is **close**, it is likely to happen or come soon. If you are **close to** doing something, you are likely to do it soon. 即将发生的; 在即的 [v-link ADJ, usu ADJ "to" n/-ing] ❑ *She sounded close to tears.* 她听起来就要哭了。 ❑ *A senior White House official said the agreement is close.* 一位白宫高级官员说协议就要达成了。 **10** ADJ If something is **close** or comes **close to** something else, it almost is, does, or experiences that thing. 几近的 [v-link ADJ, usu ADJ "to" n] ❑ *An airliner came close to disaster while approaching Kennedy Airport.* 一架客机在飞近肯尼迪机场时险些出事。 **11** ADJ If the atmosphere somewhere is **close**, it is unpleasantly warm with not enough air. 闷热的 **12** PHRASE Something that is **close by** or **close at hand** is near to you. 在附近; 在身边 ❑ *Did a new hair salon open close by?* 附近开了家新发廊吗？ **13** PHRASE **Close to** a particular amount or distance means slightly less than that amount or distance. (数量、距离) 接近于 ❑ *Sisulu spent close to 30 years in prison.* 西苏鲁在监狱里呆了近三十年。 **14** PHRASE If you look at something **close up**, you look at it when you are very near to it. 近距离地 ❑ *They always look smaller close up.* 它们从近处看总是更小。 **15** → see also **close-up** **16** **at close quarters** → see **quarter** **17** **at close range** → see **range**

Word Partnership *close* 的常用搭配：

N. close **a door** ❶ **1**
close ***your* eyes** ❶ **4**
close **friend**, close **to *someone*** ❷ **2**
close **family/relative** ❷ **2** **3**
close **attention/scrutiny** ❷ **7**
close **election**, close **race** ❷ **8**

ADV. close **enough, so/too/very** close ❷ **1** **9**

❸ **close** ◆◇◇ /kloʊz/ (closes, closing, closed) V-I If you **are closing on** someone or something that you are following, you are getting nearer and nearer to them. 接近 ❑ *I was within 15 seconds of the guy in second place and closing on him.* 我当时和第2名相距15秒，而且逐步向他接近。

▸ **close in** PHRASAL VERB If a group of people **close in on** a person or place, they come nearer and nearer to them and gradually surround them. 包围 ❑ *Hitler himself committed suicide as Soviet forces were closing in on Berlin.* 当苏联军队包围柏林时，希特勒自杀了。

closed-circuit ADJ A **closed-circuit** television or video system is one that operates within a limited area such as a building. 闭路式的 [ADJ n] ❑ *There's a closed-circuit television camera in the reception area.* 接待处有一台闭路电视摄像机。

closed shop (closed shops) N-COUNT If a factory, store, or other business is a **closed shop**, the employees must be members of a particular trade union. 只雇佣特定工会会员的工厂、商店或企业 [BUSINESS] ❑ *...the trade union which they are required to join under the closed shop agreement.* …要求他们依照特定雇佣制而加入的工会。

clos·et /klɒzɪt/ (closets) N-COUNT A **closet** is a very small room for storing things, especially one without windows. 储藏室 [mainly AM]
→ see **house**

close-up /kloʊs ʌp/ (close-ups) N-COUNT A **close-up** is a photograph or a picture in a film that shows a lot of detail because it is taken very near to the subject. 特写镜头 ❑ *...a close-up of Harvey's face.* …一张哈维的脸部特写。 ● PHRASE If you see something **in close-up**, you see it in great detail in a photograph or piece of film which has been taken very near to the subject. 特写

clos·ing /kloʊzɪŋ/ (closings) **1** ADJ The **closing** part of an activity or period of time is the final part of it. 结尾的 [ADJ n] ❑ *He entered the army in the closing stages of the war.* 他参军时，战争已接近尾声。 **2** N-COUNT A **closing** is the final meeting between the buyer and seller of a property. (买卖双方的) 交割会 [AM]

clos·ing price (closing prices) N-COUNT On the stock exchange, the **closing price** of a share is its price at the end of a day's business. 收盘价 [BUSINESS] ❑ *The price is slightly above yesterday's closing price.* 价格比昨天的收盘价略有上扬。

▲ **clo·sure** /kloʊʒər/ (closures) **1** N-VAR The **closure** of a place such as a business or factory is the permanent ending of the work or activity there. 倒闭; 关闭 ❑ *...the closure of the steel mill.* …这家钢厂

C

的关闭。 ❑ *...protests against the proposed pit closures.* …针对关闭矿井计划的抗议。 **2** N-COUNT The **closure** of a road or border is the blocking of it in order to prevent people from using it. (道路、边界等的) 封闭 ❑ *Overnight storms left many streets underwater and forced the closure of road tunnels in the city.* 一夜的暴风雨使城市里的许多街道都淹没在水中，公路隧道被迫封闭。 **3** N-UNCOUNT If someone achieves **closure**, they succeed in accepting something bad that has happened to them. 认栽 [mainly AM] ❑ *I asked McKean if the reunion was meant to achieve closure.* 我问迈可基恩再度联合是否意味着认栽。

clot /klɒt/ (**clots, clotting, clotted**) **1** N-COUNT A **clot** is a sticky lump that forms when blood dries up or becomes thick. (血液的) 凝块 ❑ *He needed emergency surgery to remove a blood clot from his brain.* 他需要紧急动手术以清除大脑中的一个血栓。 **2** V-I When blood **clots**, it becomes thick and forms a lump. (血液) 凝结成块 ❑ *The patient's blood refused to clot.* 病人的血液无法凝结。

cloth /klɔθ/ (**cloths**) **1** N-MASS **Cloth** is fabric which is made by weaving or knitting a substance such as cotton, wool, silk, or nylon. Cloth is used especially for making clothes. 布 ❑ *She began cleaning the wound with a piece of cloth.* 她开始用一块布清洁伤口。 **2** N-COUNT A **cloth** is a piece of cloth which you use for a particular purpose, such as cleaning something or covering something. (有特定用途的) 布 ❑ *Clean the surface with a damp cloth.* 用一块湿布清洗表面。

clothed /kloʊðd/ ADJ If you are **clothed in** a certain way, you are dressed in that way. 着衣的 ❑ *He lay down on the bed fully clothed.* 他合衣躺在床上。 ❑ *She was clothed in a flowered dress.* 她穿了一件碎花连衣裙。

clothes ◆◆◇ /kloʊz, kloʊðz/ N-PLURAL **Clothes** are the things that people wear, such as shirts, coats, pants, and dresses. 衣服 ❑ *Moira walked upstairs to change her clothes.* 莫伊拉上楼去换衣服了。
→ see **dry-cleaning**

> Note that there is no singular form of **clothes**, so you cannot talk about "a clothe." In formal English, you can talk about a **garment**. **Clothing** is a more formal word that is used to refer to a person's clothes. ❑ *He took off his wet clothing. ...prison clothing.* You can refer to a **garment** less formally as a **piece of clothing**, an **article of clothing**, or an **item of clothing**, but in ordinary conversation you usually just name the piece of clothing you are talking about. **Cloth** is material made from something such as cotton, wool, or nylon. A **cloth** is a piece of **cloth** that is used, for example, for cleaning or wiping things. Note that the plural, **cloths**, is used only for this sense. For the different verbs associated with clothes, see the note at **wear**.

clothes peg [BRIT] → see **clothespin**

clothes·pin /kloʊzpɪn, kloʊðz-/ (**clothespins**) N-COUNT A **clothespin** is a small device which you use to fasten clothes to a clothesline. (晾衣用的) 衣夹 [AM]

in BRIT, use **clothes peg**

cloth·ing ◆◇◇ /kloʊðɪŋ/ N-UNCOUNT **Clothing** is the things that people wear. 衣服 ❑ *Some locals offered food and clothing to the refugees.* 一些当地人向难民提供食物和衣服。 ❑ *...the clothing industry.* …服装业。
→ see Picture Dictionary: **clothing**

cloud ◆◇◇ /klaʊd/ (**clouds, clouding, clouded**) **1** N-VAR A **cloud** is a mass of water vapor that floats in the sky. Clouds are usually white or gray in color. 云 ❑ *...the varied shapes of the clouds.* …云朵的各种形状。 ❑ *...a black mass of cloud.* …一团乌云。 **2** N-COUNT A **cloud of** something such as smoke or dust is a mass of it floating in the air. (烟尘) 团 ❑ *The hens darted away on all sides, raising a cloud of dust.* 母鸡四处飞奔，扬起一团尘土。 **3** V-T If you say that something **clouds** your view of a situation, you mean that it makes you unable to understand the situation or judge it properly. 蒙蔽 ❑ *Perhaps anger had clouded his vision, perhaps his judgment had been faulty.* 也许怒火蒙蔽了他的眼睛，也许他的判断有误。 **4** V-T If you say that something **clouds** a situation, you mean that it makes it unpleasant. 使不快 ❑ *The atmosphere has already been clouded by the party's anger at the media.* 该党对媒体的愤怒已经使得气氛很不愉快。 **5** V-T/V-I If glass **clouds** or if moisture **clouds** it, tiny drops of water cover the glass, making it difficult to see through. 起雾 ❑ *The mirror clouded beside her cheek.* 紧贴她脸颊的镜子起了雾。
→ see **water**

Word Partnership *cloud* 的常用搭配：

ADJ.	black/dark cloud, white cloud **1**
N.	cloud of dust, cloud of smoke **2**

cloudy /klaʊdi/ (**cloudier, cloudiest**) **1** ADJ If it is **cloudy**, there are a lot of clouds in the sky. 多云的 ❑ *...a windy, cloudy day.* …有风多云的一天。 **2** ADJ A **cloudy** liquid is less clear than it should be. (液体) 浑浊的 ❑ *If the water's cloudy like that, it'll be hard to see anyone underwater.* 如果水浑浊成那样，就很难看得到水下的人。

clout /klaʊt/ (**clouts, clouting, clouted**) **1** V-T If you **clout** someone, you hit them. 打 [INFORMAL] ❑ *Rachel clouted him.* 雷切尔打了他。 ● N-COUNT **Clout** is also a noun. 打 ❑ *I was half tempted to give one of them a clout myself.* 我几乎都想亲自去把他们当中的一个打一顿。 **2** N-UNCOUNT A person or institution that has **clout** has influence and power. 影响力 [INFORMAL] ❑ *Mr. Sutherland may have the clout needed to push the two trading giants into a deal.* 萨瑟兰先生可能具有影响力来促使两大贸易巨头达成交易。

clove /kloʊv/ (**cloves**) **1** N-VAR **Cloves** are small dried flower buds which are used as a spice. (用作调料的) 干丁香花苞 ❑ *...chicken soup with cloves.* …加入干丁香花苞的鸡汤。 **2** N-COUNT A **clove of** garlic is one of the sections of a garlic bulb. 蒜瓣

▲ **clown** /klaʊn/ (**clowns, clowning, clowned**) **1** N-COUNT A **clown** is a performer in a circus who wears funny clothes and bright makeup, and does silly things in order to make people laugh. 小丑 **2** N-COUNT If you say that someone is a **clown**, you mean that they say funny things or do silly things to amuse people. 滑稽的人 ❑ *Chapman was the family clown, with a knack for making a joke out of any situation.* 查普曼是家里的诙谐人物，他有诀窍在任何场合开玩笑。 **3** V-I If you **clown**, you do silly things in order to make people laugh. 扮演小丑 ❑ *He clowned with John Belushi and Bill Murray in National Lampoon shows.* 他与约翰・贝鲁西和比尔・默里在全国讽刺作品表演会上一起扮演小丑。 ● PHRASAL VERB **Clown around** means the same as **clown**. 扮演小丑 ❑ *Bev made her laugh, the way she was always clowning around.* 贝芙令她大笑，用她常用的扮小丑手法。

club ◆◆◆ /klʌb/ (**clubs, clubbing, clubbed**) **1** N-COUNT A **club** is an organization of people interested in a particular activity or subject who usually meet on a regular basis. 会社 ❑ *...the Young Republicans Club.* … 青年共和党会社。 ❑ *...a youth club.* …青年会社。 **2** N-COUNT A **club** is a place where the members of a club meet. 俱乐部 ❑ *I stopped in at the club for a drink.* 我在俱乐部喝一杯歇歇脚。 **3** N-COUNT A **club** is a team which competes in sports competitions. 运动队 ❑ *...the New York Yankees baseball club.* …纽约扬基棒球队。 **4** N-COUNT A **club** is the same as a **nightclub**. 夜总会 ❑ *It's a big dance hit in the clubs.* 在各个夜总会这可是个热门舞。 **5** N-COUNT A **club** is a long, thin, metal stick with a piece of wood or metal at one end that you use to hit the ball in golf. 高尔夫球棒 ❑ *...a six-iron club.* …一把6号铁头球棒。 **6** N-COUNT A **club** is a thick, heavy stick that can be used as a weapon. 棍棒 ❑ *Men armed with*

Picture Dictionary **clothing**

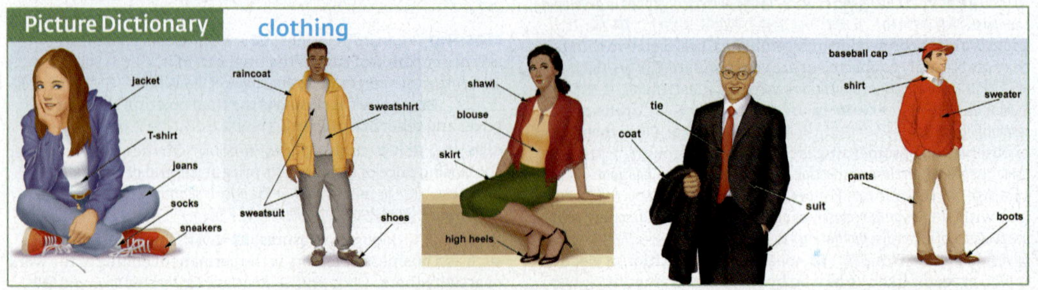

knives and clubs attacked his home. 一帮携刀带棍的人袭击了他的家。 7 V-T To **club** a person or animal means to hit them hard with a thick heavy stick or a similar weapon. (用棍棒或类似武器) 狠打 ❑ *Two thugs clubbed him with baseball bats.* 两名暴徒用棒球棍狠打了他。 8 N-UNCOUNT-COLL **Clubs** is one of the four suits in a pack of playing cards. Each card in the suit is marked with one or more black symbols: ♣. (纸牌的) 梅花 ❑ *...the ace of clubs.* …梅花幺。 ● N-COUNT A **club** is a playing card of this suit. (单张) 梅花 ❑ *The next player discarded a club.* 接下来的那位玩家出了张梅花牌。
→ see **golf**

club·house /klʌbhaʊs/ (**clubhouses**) N-COUNT A **clubhouse** is a place where the members of a club, especially a sports club, meet. (尤指运动俱乐部的) 俱乐部会所

clue /klu/ (**clues**) 1 N-COUNT A **clue to** a problem or mystery is something that helps you to find the answer to it. (解决问题或疑团时的) 线索 ❑ *Geneticists in Canada have discovered a clue to the puzzle of why our cells get old and die.* 加拿大的遗传学家已经发现了解开我们细胞衰老死亡之迷的线索。 2 N-COUNT A **clue** is an object or piece of information that helps someone solve a crime. (破案中的) 线索 ❑ *The vital clue to the killer's identity was his nickname, Peanuts.* 关于杀手身份的重大线索是他的绰号——花生。 3 N-COUNT A **clue** in a crossword or game is information which is given to help you to find the answer to a question. (纵横字谜或游戏中的) 提示 ❑ *Give me a clue. What's it begin with?* 给我点提示。是什么开头？ 4 PHRASE If you **haven't a clue** about something, you do not know anything about it or you have no idea what to do about it. 毫无头绪 [INFORMAL] ❑ *I haven't a clue what I'll give Carl for his birthday next year.* 对于明年该送什么生日礼物给卡尔我毫无头绪。

clump /klʌmp/ (**clumps**) 1 N-COUNT A **clump of** things such as trees or plants is a small group of them growing together. (树或植物的) 丛 ❑ *...a clump of trees bordering a side road.* …一丛长在小道边的树木。 2 N-COUNT A **clump** of things such as wires or hair is a group of them collected together in one place. (金属丝或毛发的) 簇 ❑ *I was combing my hair and it was just falling out in clumps.* 我当时正梳头，头发就一簇簇地掉了下来。

clum·sy /klʌmzi/ (**clumsier, clumsiest**) 1 ADJ A **clumsy** person moves or handles things in a careless, awkward way, often so that things are knocked over or broken. 笨拙的 ❑ *I'd never seen a clumsier, less coordinated boxer.* 我还从未见过更加笨拙、更不协调的拳击手。 ● **clum·si·ly** /klʌmzɪli/ ADV 笨拙地 [ADV with v] ❑ *In the sudden pitch darkness, she scrambled clumsily toward the ladder.* 在突如其来的一片漆黑中，她笨手笨脚地爬向梯子。 ● **clum·si·ness** N-UNCOUNT 笨拙 ❑ *His clumsiness and ineptitude with the wooden sticks did not embarrass him.* 他摆弄起木棍来笨拙和不熟练的样子并没有使他感到难为情。 2 ADJ A **clumsy** action or statement is not skillful or is likely to upset people. 笨拙的；不得当的 ❑ *The action seemed a clumsy attempt to topple the government.* 那个企图推翻政府的行动似乎并不得当。 ● **clum·si·ly** ADV 笨拙地；不得当地 ❑ *If the matter were handled clumsily, it could cost Miriam her life.* 如果问题处理不当，可能会断送米里亚姆的性命。 ● **clum·si·ness** N-UNCOUNT 笨拙；不得当 ❑ *I was ashamed at my clumsiness and insensitivity.* 我为我的笨拙和迟钝感到惭愧。

clung /klʌŋ/ **Clung** is the past tense and past participle of **cling**. **cling**的过去式和过去分词

★ **clus·ter** /klʌstər/ (**clusters, clustering, clustered**) 1 N-COUNT A **cluster of** people or things is a small group of them close together. (人或物的) 群 ❑ *...clusters of men in formal clothes.* …几组身着正装的男人。 2 V-I If people **cluster together**, they gather together in a small group. (人) 结成群 ❑ *The passengers clustered together in small groups.* 乘客们聚集成小群体。

★ **clutch** /klʌtʃ/ (**clutches, clutching, clutched**) 1 V-T/V-I If you **clutch at** something or **clutch** something, you hold it tightly, usually because you are afraid or anxious. (因为害怕或焦虑而) 抓牢 ❑ *I staggered and had to clutch at a chair for support.* 我踉跄了几步，不得不抓住一把椅子扶稳。 2 N-PLURAL If someone is in another person's **clutches**, that person has captured them or has power over them. 掌控 ❑ *Tony fell into the clutches of an attractive American who introduced him to drugs.* 托尼落入一个有魅力的美国人的掌控，那人给他介绍毒品。 3 N-COUNT In a vehicle, the **clutch** is the pedal that you press before you change gear. 离合器踏板 ❑ *Laura let out the clutch and pulled slowly away down the drive.* 劳拉松开离合器踏板，慢慢沿着车道把车开走了。 4 **to clutch at straws** → see **straw**

clut·ter /klʌtər/ (**clutters, cluttering, cluttered**) 1 N-UNCOUNT **Clutter** is a lot of things in a messy state, especially things that are not useful or necessary. 乱七八糟 ❑ *Caroline prefers her countertops to be clear of clutter.* 卡罗琳喜欢把她的厨房台面弄得整整齐齐。 2 V-T If things or people **clutter** a place, they fill it in a messy way. (物或人) 拥塞 ❑ *Empty soft-drink cans lie everywhere. They clutter the desks and are strewn across the floor.* 软饮料空罐到处都是，堆满了桌面，还扔了一地。 ● PHRASAL VERB **Clutter up** means the same as **clutter**. 拥塞 ❑ *The vehicles cluttered up the parking lot.* 车辆停满了停车场。

cm **cm** is the written abbreviation for **centimeter** or **centimeters**. 厘米 ❑ *His height had increased by 2.5 cm.* 他的身高增加了2.5厘米。

c/o You write **c/o** before an address on an envelope when you are sending it to someone who is staying or working at that address, often for only a short time. **c/o** is an abbreviation for "care of." 请转交

Co. ♦♦◊ 1 **Co.** is used as an abbreviation for **company** when it is part of the name of an organization. 公司 [BUSINESS] ❑ *...the Blue Star Amusement Co.* …蓝星娱乐公司。

coach ♦♦◊ /koʊtʃ/ (**coaches, coaching, coached**) 1 N-COUNT A **coach** is someone who trains a person or team of people in a particular sport. 教练 ❑ *Tony Woodcock has joined the team as coach.* 托尼·伍德科克已经作为教练加入了队伍。 2 N-COUNT A **coach** is a person who is in charge of a sports team. (体育队的) 领队 [mainly AM]

in BRIT, usually use **manager**

❑ *...the women's soccer coach at Rowan University.* …罗恩大学女子足球队的领队。 3 N-COUNT A **coach** is someone who gives people special teaching in a particular subject, especially in order to prepare them for an examination. (针对某科目，尤指进行考前指导的) 辅导员 ❑ *What you need is a drama coach.* 你需要的是一位戏剧指导。 4 N-COUNT A **coach** is an enclosed vehicle with four wheels which is pulled by horses, and in which people used to travel. Coaches are still used for ceremonial events in some countries, such as Britain. (用于外出旅行或仪式活动的) 四轮马车 ❑ *...a coach pulled by six black horses.* …一辆6匹黑马拉的4轮马车。 5 N-COUNT A **coach** is a large, comfortable bus that carries passengers on long trips. 长途公共汽车；大巴 [also "by" N] [BRIT]

in AM, use **bus**

6 N-COUNT A **coach** is one of the separate sections of a train that carries passengers. (火车的) 车厢 [BRIT]

in AM, use **car, train car**

7 V-T When someone **coaches** a person or a team, they help them to become better at a particular sport. (体育) 训练 ❑ *After her pro playing career, she coached a golf team in San Jose.* 在职业球员生涯结束之后，她在圣何塞训练一支高尔夫球队。 8 V-T If you **coach** someone, you give them special teaching in a particular subject, especially in order to prepare them for an examination. (针对某科目，尤指是考前进行的) 辅导 ❑ *He gently coached me in French.* 他和蔼地辅导我法语。

coal ♦◊◊ /koʊl/ (**coals**) 1 N-UNCOUNT **Coal** is a hard, black substance that is extracted from the ground and burned as fuel. 煤 ❑ *Gas is cheaper than coal.* 煤气比煤便宜。 2 N-PLURAL **Coals** are burning pieces of coal. 燃烧着的煤块 ❑ *The iron teakettle was hissing splendidly over live coals.* 铁茶壶在熊熊燃烧着的煤块上"嘶嘶"作响。
→ see **energy**

★ **coa·li·tion** ♦◊◊ /koʊəlɪʃən/ (**coalitions**) 1 N-COUNT A **coalition** is a government consisting of people from two or more political parties. 联合政府 ❑ *Since June the country has had a coalition government.* 从6月起，这个国家有了一个联合政府。 2 N-COUNT A **coalition** is a group consisting of people from different political or social groups who are cooperating to achieve a particular aim. 联盟 ❑ *He had been opposed by a coalition of about 50 civil rights, women's, and Latino organizations.* 他遭到一个联盟的反对，该联盟由大约五十个民权组织、妇女组织和拉美人组织构成。

coarse /kɔrs/ (**coarser, coarsest**) 1 ADJ **Coarse** things have a rough texture because they consist of thick threads or large pieces. 粗糙的 ❑ *...a jacket made of very coarse cloth.* …用非常粗糙的布做成的一件夹克衫。 ● **coarse·ly** ADV 粗糙地 ❑ *...coarsely ground black pepper.* …粗糙磨制的黑胡椒。 2 ADJ If you describe someone as **coarse**, you mean that he or she talks and behaves in a rude and offensive way. 粗鲁的；粗俗的 [DISAPPROVAL] ❑ *The soldiers did not bother to moderate their coarse humor in her presence.* 士兵们没有费神去约束他们的粗俗幽默，尽管她在场。 ● **coarse·ly** ADV 粗鲁地；粗俗地 [ADV with v] ❑ *The women laughed coarsely at some vulgar joke.* 女人们听到某个庸俗笑话后便粗俗地笑了起来。
→ see **coffee**

C

coast ♦♦◊ /koʊst/ (**coasts, coasting, coasted**) 1 N-COUNT The **coast** is an area of land that is next to the sea. 海岸 ❑ *Campsites are usually situated along the coast, close to beaches.* 宿营地通常都在海岸边，靠近沙滩的地方。

You can use **beach, coast,** and **shore** to talk about the piece of land beside a stretch of water. The **coast** is the area of land that lies alongside the ocean. You may be referring just to the land close to the ocean, or to a wider area that extends further inland. A **beach** is a flat area of sand or pebbles next to the ocean. The **shore** is the area of land along the edge of the ocean, a lake, or a wide river.

2 V-I If a vehicle **coasts** somewhere, it continues to move there with the motor switched off, or without being pushed or pedaled. (车辆的) 惯性滑行 ❑ *He pushed in the clutch and coasted to a halt.* 他踩下离合器，滑行了一会儿便停下来了。
→ see **beach**

coast·al /koʊstᵊl/ ADJ **Coastal** is used to refer to things that are in the sea or on the land near a coast. 沿海的 [ADJ n] ❑ *Local radio stations serving coastal areas often broadcast forecasts for yachtsmen.* 服务沿海地区的地方电台经常向驾驶快艇者播放天气预报。

coast guard (**coast guards**) also **Coast Guard, coastguard** N-COUNT The **coast guard** is a part of a country's military forces and is responsible for protecting the coast, carrying out rescues, and doing police work along the coast. 海岸警卫队 [AM] ❑ *The U.S. Coast Guard says it rescued more than 100 Haitian refugees.* 美国海岸警卫队称他们救起了一百多名海地难民。● N-COUNT A **coast guard** is a member of the coast guard. 海岸警卫队队员 [AM] ❑ *The boat was intercepted by U.S. Coast Guards.* 该船被美国海岸警卫队队员们拦截。

coast·line /koʊstlaɪn/ (**coastlines**) N-VAR A country's **coastline** is the outline of its coast. 海岸线 ❑ *This is some of the most exposed coastline in the world.* 这是世界上最无遮蔽的海岸线。

coat ♦◊◊ /koʊt/ (**coats, coating, coated**) 1 N-COUNT A **coat** is a piece of clothing with long sleeves which you wear over your other clothes when you go outside. 外套 ❑ *He turned off the television, put on his coat, and walked out.* 他关掉电视，穿上外套，走了出去。 2 N-COUNT An animal's **coat** is the fur or hair on its body. (动物的) 皮毛 ❑ *Vitamin B6 is great for improving the condition of dogs' and horses' coats.* 维生素B6对改善狗和马的皮毛非常有效。 3 N-COUNT A **coat of** paint or varnish is a thin layer of it on a surface. (油漆、清漆等的) 层 ❑ *The front door needs a new coat of paint.* 前门要新刷一层油漆。 4 V-T If you **coat** something **with** a substance or **in** a substance, you cover it with a thin layer of the substance. 涂上 ❑ *Coat the fish with seasoned flour.* 往鱼身上涂调好味道的面粉。
→ see **clothing, painting**

-coated /koʊtɪd/ 1 COMB IN ADJ **-coated** combines with color adjectives such as "white" and "red," or words for types of coat like "fur," to form adjectives that describe someone as wearing a certain sort of coat. 身着…服装的 [ADJ n] ❑ *At the top of the stairs stood the white-coated doctors.* 楼梯的顶端站着穿白大褂的医生们。 2 COMB IN ADJ **-coated** combines with names of substances such as "sugar" and "plastic" to form adjectives that describe something as being covered with a thin layer of that substance. 表面薄薄涂上…的 ❑ *...chocolate-coated strawberries.* …表面薄薄涂上一层巧克力的草莓。

coat hang·er (**coat hangers**) N-COUNT A **coat hanger** is a curved piece of wood, metal, or plastic that you hang a piece of clothing on. 衣架

coat·ing /koʊtɪŋ/ (**coatings**) N-COUNT A **coating of** a substance is a thin layer of it spread over a surface. 涂层 ❑ *Under the coating of dust and cobwebs, he discovered a fine French Louis XVI clock.* 在一层灰尘和蜘蛛网下面，他发现了一个精美的法国路易十六时期的钟。

▲ **coax** /koʊks/ (**coaxes, coaxing, coaxed**) 1 V-T If you **coax** someone **into** doing something, you gently try to persuade them to do it. 哄 ❑ *After lunch, she watched, listened and coaxed Bobby into talking about himself.* 午饭后，她察言观色，哄着博比谈谈他自己。 2 V-T If you **coax** something such as information out of someone, you gently persuade them to give it to you. 劝诱 ❑ *The officer spoke yesterday of her role in trying to coax vital information from the young victim.* 该官员昨天谈起她的职责：设法劝诱那个年轻受害人提供重要信息。

cob·ble /kɒbᵊl/ (**cobbles, cobbling, cobbled**) N-COUNT **Cobbles** are the same as **cobblestones**. 鹅卵石 [mainly BRIT]

▸ **cobble together** PHRASAL VERB If you say that someone has **cobbled** something **together**, you mean that they have made or produced it roughly or quickly. 粗制滥造 [DISAPPROVAL] ❑ *The group had cobbled together a few decent songs.* 这个小组竟然拼凑出了几首像样的歌。

cobble·stone /kɒbᵊlstoʊn/ (**cobblestones**) N-COUNT **Cobblestones** are stones with a rounded upper surface which used to be used for making streets. (铺设街道用的) 圆形鹅卵石 ❑ *...the narrow, cobblestone streets of the Left Bank.* …左岸狭窄的鹅卵石街道。

co·bra /koʊbrə/ (**cobras**) N-COUNT A **cobra** is a kind of poisonous snake that can make the skin on the back of its neck into a hood. 眼镜蛇

cob·web /kɒbwɛb/ (**cobwebs**) N-COUNT A **cobweb** is the net which a spider makes for catching insects. 蜘蛛网 ❑ *The windows are cracked and covered in cobwebs.* 窗户裂开了，上面布满蜘蛛网。

Coca-Cola /koʊkəkoʊlə/ (**Coca-Colas**) N-VAR **Coca-Cola** is a sweet brown nonalcoholic carbonated drink. 可口可乐 [TRADEMARK] ❑ *He bought a Hershey Bar and a bottle of Coca-Cola.* 他买了一块"好时"巧克力和一瓶可口可乐。● N-COUNT A **Coca-Cola** is a glass or a bottle of Coca-Cola. 可口可乐 ❑ *Eleanor bought him a Coca-Cola.* 埃莉诺给他买了瓶可口可乐。

★ **co·caine** /koʊkeɪn/ N-UNCOUNT **Cocaine** is a powerful drug which some people take for pleasure, but which they can become addicted to. 可卡因

cock /kɒk/ (**cocks**) N-COUNT A **cock** is an adult male chicken. 公鸡 [mainly BRIT]
in AM, use **rooster**

cock·a·ma·mie /kɒkəmeɪmi/ ADJ If you describe something as **cockamamie**, you mean that it is ridiculous or silly. 荒谬可笑的；愚蠢的 [usu ADJ n] [AM, INFORMAL] ❑ *...some cockamamie story about being late.* …关于迟到的可笑借口。

▲ **cock·pit** /kɒkpɪt/ (**cockpits**) N-COUNT In an airplane or racing car, the **cockpit** is the part where the pilot or driver sits. (飞行员或赛车手的) 座舱

cock·roach /kɒkroʊtʃ/ (**cockroaches**) N-COUNT A **cockroach** is a large brown insect that is sometimes found in warm places or where food is kept. 蟑螂

★ **cock·tail** /kɒkteɪl/ (**cocktails**) 1 N-COUNT A **cocktail** is an alcoholic drink which contains several ingredients. 鸡尾酒 ❑ *On arrival, guests are offered wine or a champagne cocktail.* 到达时，客人们可以享用葡萄酒或一份香槟鸡尾酒。 2 N-COUNT A **cocktail** is a mixture of a number of different things, especially ones that do not go together well. (尤指不太容易融合的几种物品的) 混合物 ❑ *The court was told she had taken a cocktail of drugs and alcohol.* 法庭被告知她服用了药酒混合剂。

cocky /kɒki/ (**cockier, cockiest**) ADJ Someone who is **cocky** is so confident and sure of their abilities that they annoy other people. 自以为是的 [INFORMAL, DISAPPROVAL] ❑ *He was a little bit cocky when he was about 11 because he was winning everything.* 他11岁的时候有点自以为是，因为那时他无往不胜。

co·coa /koʊkoʊ/ 1 N-UNCOUNT **Cocoa** is a brown powder made from the seeds of a tropical tree. It is used in making chocolate. 可可粉 ❑ *The Ivory Coast became the world's leading cocoa producer.* 象牙海岸成了世界上领先的可可粉生产地。 2 N-UNCOUNT **Cocoa** is a hot drink made from cocoa powder and milk or water. 热巧克力 ❑ *...a cup of cocoa.* …一杯热巧克力。

▲ **coco·nut** /koʊkənʌt/ (**coconuts**) 1 N-COUNT A **coconut** is a very large nut with a hairy shell, which has white flesh and milky juice inside it. 椰子 ❑ *...the smell of roasted meats mingled with spices, coconut oil, and ripe tropical fruits.* …烤肉夹杂着香料、椰子油和成熟的热带水果的味道。 2 N-UNCOUNT **Coconut** is the white flesh of a coconut. 椰子肉 ❑ *Put 2 cups of grated coconut into a blender or food processor.* 把两杯碎椰子肉放进搅拌器或食品加工机内。

co·coon /kəkuːn/ (**cocoons, cocooning, cocooned**) 1 N-COUNT A **cocoon** is a covering of silky threads that the larvae of moths and other insects make for themselves before they grow into adults. 茧 ❑ *...like a butterfly emerging from a cocoon.* …好似蝴蝶破茧而出。 2 N-COUNT If you are in a **cocoon of** something, you are wrapped up in it or surrounded by it. 包围层 ❑ *He stood there in a cocoon of golden light.* 他站在那儿，被一圈金色光环笼罩着。 3 N-COUNT If you are living in a **cocoon**, you are in an environment in which you feel protected and safe, and sometimes isolated from everyday life. 隔护层；与世隔绝 ❑ *...her innocent desire to envelop her beloved in a cocoon of love.* …她用爱呵护心上人的纯真愿望。 **4** V-T If something **cocoons** you **from** something, it protects you or isolates you from it. 把…保护或隔离起来 ❑ *There is nowhere to hide when things go wrong, no organization to cocoon you from blame.* 出了差错无处可躲，没有组织会庇护你免于责难。

cod /kɒd/ (**cod**)

The plural can be either **cod** or **cods**.

N-VAR **Cod** are a type of large edible fish. 鳕鱼 ● N-UNCOUNT **Cod** is this fish eaten as food. 鳕鱼肉 ❑ *A Catalan speciality is to serve salt cod cold.* 加泰罗尼亚的一道特色菜是冷食咸鳕鱼。
→ see **fish**

Word Link *cod ≈ writing : code, decode, encode*

code ♦◇◇ /koʊd/ (**codes, coding, coded**) **1** N-COUNT A **code** is a set of rules about how people should behave or about how something must be done. 法典；法规 ❑ *...Article 159 of the state's penal code.* …该国刑法第159条。 **2** N-COUNT A **code** is a system of replacing the words in a message with other words or symbols, so that nobody can understand it unless they know the system. 密码；代码 [also "in" N] ❑ *They used elaborate secret codes, as when the names of trees stood for letters.* 他们用的是精心设计的密码，用树木的名称代表字母。 **3** N-COUNT A **code** is a group of numbers or letters which is used to identify something, such as a mailing address or part of a telephone system. 编号 ❑ *Callers dialing the wrong area code will not get through.* 打电话的人拨错区号时电话就接不通。 **4** N-COUNT A **code** is any system of signs or symbols that has a meaning. 代码 ❑ *It will need other chips to reconvert the digital code back into normal TV signals.* 需要用其他芯片把数字代码重新转换成普通的电视信号。 **5** N-COUNT The genetic **code** of a person, animal, or plant is the information contained in DNA which determines the structure and function of cells, and the inherited characteristics of all living things. 遗传密码 ❑ *Scientists provided the key to understanding the genetic code that determines every bodily feature.* 科学家们提供了线索来了解决定每个身体特征的遗传密码。 **6** V-T To **code** something means to give it a code or to mark it with its code. 编码 ❑ *He devised a way of coding every statement uniquely.* 他设计出一种把每句话进行独特编码的方法。 **7** N-UNCOUNT Computer **code** is a system or language for expressing information and instructions in a form which can be understood by a computer. （电子计算机的）编码 [COMPUTING] ❑ *She began writing software code at the age of nine.* 她9岁就开始写软件编码。 **8** → see also **bar code, postcode, zip code**

Word Partnership *code 的常用搭配：*

N. code **of conduct**, **dress** code, code **of ethics** **1**
code **name**, code **word** **2**
ADJ. **secret** code **2**

cod·ed /koʊdɪd/ **1** ADJ **Coded** messages have words or symbols which represent other words, so that the message is secret unless you know the system behind the code. 加密码的 ❑ *In a coded telephone warning, the police were told four bombs had been planted in the area.* 通过一个加密的电话警告，警察得知4枚炸弹被放置在那个地区。 **2** ADJ If someone is using **coded** language, they are expressing their opinion in an indirect way, usually because that opinion is likely to offend people. 隐讳的 ❑ *They have sent barely coded messages to the secretary of education endorsing this criticism.* 他们毫不隐讳地把信息传达给教育部长，支持该批评意见。 **3** ADJ **Coded** electronic signals use a binary system of digits which can be decoded by an appropriate machine. 电码的 [ADJ n] [TECHNICAL] ❑ *The coded signal is received by satellite dishes.* 电码信号通过卫星天线接收。

cod·ing /koʊdɪŋ/ N-UNCOUNT **Coding** is a method of making something easy to recognize or distinct, for example by coloring it. 制码法 ❑ *...a color coding that will ensure easy reference for potential users.* …可以确保潜在用户轻松查询的色码。

co·erce /koʊɜrs/ (**coerces, coercing, coerced**) V-T If you **coerce** someone **into** doing something, you make them do it, although they do not want to. 胁迫 [FORMAL] ❑ *Potter had argued that the government coerced him into pleading guilty.* 波特曾争辩说是政府胁迫他认罪。

co·er·cion /koʊɜrʃən/ N-UNCOUNT **Coercion** is the act or process of persuading someone forcefully to do something that they do not want to do. 胁迫 ❑ *It was vital that the elections should be free of coercion or intimidation.* 至关重要的是，选举中不得有胁迫或威逼。

▲ **co·er·cive** /koʊɜrsɪv/ ADJ **Coercive** measures are intended to force people to do something that they do not want to do. 强制的 [usu ADJ n] ❑ *The eighteenth-century British Admiralty had few coercive powers over its officers.* 18世纪英国海军部对其官员有很小的强制权力。

★ **co·ex·ist·ence** /koʊɪgzɪstəns/

in BRIT, also use **co-existence**

N-UNCOUNT The **coexistence of** one thing **with** another is the fact that they exist together at the same time or in the same place. 共存 [oft N "of/with/between" n] ❑ *He also believed in coexistence with the West.* 他也赞成与西方共存。

cof·fee ♦◇◇ /kɔfi/ (**coffees**) **1** N-UNCOUNT **Coffee** is a hot drink made with water and ground or powdered coffee beans. 咖啡 ❑ *Would you like some coffee?* 你想喝点咖啡吗？ ● N-COUNT A **coffee** is a cup of coffee. 一杯咖啡 ❑ *I made a coffee.* 我冲了一杯咖啡。 **2** N-MASS **Coffee** is the roasted beans or powder from which the drink is made. 咖啡豆；咖啡粉 ❑ *Brazil harvested 28 million bags of coffee in 1991, the biggest crop for four years.* 1991年巴西收获了2800万袋咖啡豆，这是4年来的最大收成。
→ see Word Web: **coffee**

cof·fee shop (**coffee shops**) N-COUNT A **coffee shop** is an informal restaurant that sells food and drink, but not normally alcoholic drinks. 咖啡馆
→ see **restaurant**

cof·fin /kɔfɪn/ (**coffins**) **1** N-COUNT A **coffin** is a box in which a dead body is buried or cremated. 棺材 **2** PHRASE If you say that one thing is **a nail in the coffin of** another thing, you mean that it will help bring about its end or failure. 断送 ❑ *A fine would be the final nail in the coffin of the airline.* 一笔罚款将最终断送该航线。

cog·nac /koʊnyæk/ (**cognacs**) also **Cognac** N-MASS **Cognac** is a type of brandy made in the southwest of France. 科尼亚克白兰地 ❑ *...a bottle of Cognac.* …一瓶科尼亚克白兰地。 ● N-COUNT A **cognac** is a glass of cognac. （一杯）科尼亚克白兰地 ❑ *Phillips ordered a cognac.* 菲利普斯点了一杯科尼亚克白兰地。

Word Link *cogn ≈ knowing : cognitive, recognize, unrecognizable*

★ **cog·ni·tive** /kɒgnɪtɪv/ ADJ **Cognitive** means relating to the mental process involved in knowing, learning, and understanding things. 认知的 [ADJ n] [FORMAL] ❑ *As children grow older, their cognitive processes become sharper.* 随着孩子们长大，他们的认知过程也变得越来越敏锐了。

Word Web coffee

Coffee plants produce a bright red fruit. Inside each fruit is a single coffee **bean**. Workers pick the beans and dry them in the sun. Then the beans are roasted at 550°F* to bring out the true coffee flavor. Next the coffee is **ground**. It can be either **coarse** or **fine**. Many people **brew** coffee by putting it in a **filter** and **pouring** boiling water over it. Some people add **cream** or **sugar**, while others like it **black**. Many people drink coffee in the morning because the **caffeine** in it wakes them up. Others drink **decaffeinated** coffee, or decaf, which has little or no caffeine.

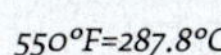
550°F=287.8°C

co·her·ence /koʊhɪərəns, -hɛrəns/ N-UNCOUNT **Coherence** is a state or situation in which all the parts or ideas fit together well so that they form a united whole. 连贯性 ❑ *The anthology has a surprising sense of coherence.* 该诗集的连贯性令人惊奇。

Word Link *co ≈ together : coherent, collaborate, cooperate*

C

★ **co·her·ent** /koʊhɪərənt, -hɛrənt/ 1 ADJ If something is **coherent**, it is well planned, so that it is clear and sensible and all its parts go well with each other. 连贯的 ❑ *He has failed to work out a coherent strategy for modernizing the service.* 他无法想出一个连贯的策略来使该服务现代化。 ● **co·her·ence** N-UNCOUNT 连贯性 ❑ *The campaign was widely criticized for making tactical mistakes and for a lack of coherence.* 该运动遭到广泛批评，因其有策略错误且缺乏连贯性。 2 ADJ If someone is **coherent**, they express their thoughts in a clear and calm way, so that other people can understand what they are saying. 条理清楚的 [v-link ADJ] ❑ *He's so calm when he answers questions in interviews. I wish I could be that coherent.* 他如此镇定地回答了访谈中的问题。我希望我也能那样有条不紊。 ● **co·her·ence** N-UNCOUNT 条理性 ❑ *This was debated eagerly at first, but with diminishing coherence as the champagne took hold.* 辩论一开始满热烈的，可是上了香槟后，条理性就降低了。

★ **co·he·sion** /koʊhiʒən/ N-UNCOUNT If there is **cohesion** within a society, organization, or group, the different members fit together well and form a united whole. 凝聚力 ❑ *By 1990, it was clear that the cohesion of the armed forces was rapidly breaking down.* 到1990年时，武装部队凝聚力明显地迅速瓦解。

▲ **co·he·sive** /koʊhisɪv/ ADJ Something that is **cohesive** consists of parts that fit together well and form a united whole. 有聚合力的 ❑ *"Daring Adventures" from '86 is a far more cohesive and successful album.* 1986年出的《勇敢的冒险》是一张极富凝聚力、极成功的唱片集。

coil /kɔɪl/ (**coils**) 1 N-COUNT A **coil of** rope or wire is a length of it that has been wound into a series of loops. (绳子或金属线的) 圈 ❑ *Tod shook his head angrily and slung the coil of rope over his shoulder.* 托德生气地摇摇头，把那圈绳索甩过肩头。 2 N-COUNT A **coil** is one loop in a series of loops. 一圈 ❑ *Pythons kill by tightening their coils so that their victim cannot breathe.* 蟒蛇捕杀时紧紧盘成一圈，使猎物无法呼吸。 3 N-COUNT A **coil** is a thick spiral of wire through which an electrical current passes. (电流通过的) 线圈

coin /kɔɪn/ (**coins, coining, coined**) 1 N-COUNT A **coin** is a small piece of metal which is used as money. 硬币 ❑ *...a few loose coins.* …几枚零钱。 2 V-T If you **coin** a word or a phrase, you are the first person to say it. 创造 (新词语) ❑ *Jaron Lanier coined the term "virtual reality" and pioneered its early development.* 加隆·雷尼尔首创"虚拟现实"一词，并率先进行早期开发。 3 PHRASE You say **"to coin a phrase"** to show that you realize you are making a pun or using a cliché. 套用一个双关语; 套用一句老话 ❑ *Fifty local musicians have, to coin a phrase, banded together to form the Jazz Umbrella.* 套用一句老话，50位当地的音乐家们联合在一起组成了爵士伞乐队。 4 PHRASE You use **the other side of the coin** to mention a different aspect of a situation. 另一方面 ❑ *On the other side of the coin, there'll be tax incentives for small businesses.* 另一方面，会有税收政策激励小型经营者。
→ see **English, money**

coin·age /kɔɪnɪdʒ/ 1 N-UNCOUNT **Coinage** is the coins which are used in a country. 钱币 ❑ *The city produced its own coinage from 1325 to 1864.* 该城在1325至1864年间自行铸造钱币。 2 N-UNCOUNT **Coinage** is the system of money used in a country. 币制 ❑ *In 1783 he secured the adoption of the decimal coinage in Congress.* 1783年他促使国会采纳了十进位币制。

★ **co·in·cide** /koʊɪnsaɪd/ (**coincides, coinciding, coincided**) 1 V-RECIP If one event **coincides with** another, they happen at the same time. 同时发生 ❑ *The exhibition coincides with the 50th anniversary of his death.* 展会与他50周年忌辰同日。 2 V-RECIP If the ideas or interests of two or more people **coincide**, they are the same. (观点或兴趣) 一致 ❑ *The kids' views on life don't always coincide, but they're not afraid of voicing their opinions.* 孩子们的生活观未必总是一致，但是他们不怕表达自己的观点。

★ **co·in·ci·dence** /koʊɪnsɪdəns/ (**coincidences**) N-VAR A **coincidence** is when two or more similar or related events occur at the same time by chance and without any planning. 巧合 ❑ *Mr. Berry said the timing was a coincidence and that his decision was unrelated to Mr. Roman's departure.* 贝里先生说时间的安排是个巧合，而且他的决策与罗曼先生的离去毫无关系。

co·in·ci·dent·al /koʊɪnsɪdɛntəl/ ADJ Something that is **coincidental** is the result of a coincidence and has not been deliberately arranged. 巧合的 ❑ *Any resemblance to actual persons, places, or events is purely coincidental.* 如与实际的人、地、事有所雷同，纯属巧合。

co·in·ci·dent·al·ly /koʊɪnsɪdɛntli/ ADV You use **coincidentally** when you want to draw attention to a coincidence. 巧合地 ❑ *Coincidentally, I had once found myself in a similar situation.* 碰巧的是，我有一次发现自己曾处于类似的境地。

coke /koʊk/ 1 N-UNCOUNT **Coke** is a solid, black substance that is produced from coal and is burned as a fuel. 焦炭 ❑ *...a coke-burning stove.* …一个烧焦炭的炉子。 2 N-UNCOUNT **Coke** is the same as **cocaine**. 可卡因 [INFORMAL]

cola /koʊlə/ (**colas**) N-MASS **Cola** is a sweet, brown, nonalcoholic carbonated drink. 可乐 ❑ *...a can of cola.* …一罐可乐。

col·an·der /kɒləndə, kʌl-/ (**colanders**) N-COUNT A **colander** is a container in the shape of a bowl with holes in it which you wash or drain food in. (洗、滤食物用的) 滤器

Word Link *er ≈ more : colder, higher, larger*

Word Link *est ≈ most : coldest, highest, largest*

cold ♦♦◇ /koʊld/ (**colder, coldest, colds**) 1 ADJ Something that is **cold** has a very low temperature or a lower temperature than is normal or acceptable. 冷的 ❑ *Rinse the vegetables under cold running water.* 用冷自来水冲洗蔬菜。 ❑ *He likes his tea neither too hot nor too cold.* 他喜欢茶不太烫也不太凉。 ● **cold·ness** N-UNCOUNT 冷 ❑ *She complained about the coldness of his hands.* 她抱怨他的那双手冷冰冰的。 2 ADJ If it is **cold**, or if a place is **cold**, the temperature of the air is very low. 寒冷的 ❑ *It was bitterly cold.* 天气冷得刺骨。 ❑ *The house is cold because I can't afford to turn the heat on.* 屋子冷冰冰的，因为我开不起暖气。 ● **cold·ness** N-UNCOUNT 寒冷 ❑ *Within a quarter of an hour, the coldness of the night had gone.* 一刻钟之内，夜晚的寒冷就消退了。

> If you want to emphasize how cold the weather is, you can say that it is **freezing**, especially in winter when there is ice or frost. In summer, if the temperature is below average, you can say that it is **cool**. In general, **cold** suggests a lower temperature than **cool**, and **cool** things may be pleasant or refreshing. ❑ *A cool breeze swept off the ocean; it was pleasant out there.* If it is very **cold** or too **cool**, you can also say that it is **chilly**.

3 ADJ If you are **cold**, your body is at an unpleasantly low temperature. 感觉冷的 ❑ *I was freezing cold.* 我快冻僵了。 4 ADJ **Cold** colors or **cold** light give an impression of coldness. (颜色或灯光) 冷的 ❑ *Generally, warm colors advance in painting and cold colors recede.* 一般来说，先上暖色调油漆，再上冷色调油漆。 5 ADJ A **cold** person does not show much emotion, especially affection, and therefore seems unfriendly and unsympathetic. If someone's voice is **cold**, they speak in an unfriendly, unsympathetic way. 冷漠的; 不友好的 [DISAPPROVAL] ❑ *What a cold, unfeeling woman she was.* 她是一个多么冷漠无情的女人啊。 ● **cold·ly** ADV 冷漠地; 不友好地 ❑ *"I'll see you in the morning," Hugh said coldly.* "我会在早上见你，"休冷冷地说。 ● **cold·ness** N-UNCOUNT 冷漠; 不友好 ❑ *His coldness angered her.* 他的冷漠惹恼了她。 6 N-UNCOUNT Cold weather or low temperatures can be referred to as **the cold**. (天气或气温的) 寒冷 [also "the" N] ❑ *He must have come inside to get out of the cold.* 他肯定进来避过寒。 7 **in cold blood** → see **blood** 8 **to get cold feet** → see **foot** 9 **to blow hot and cold** → see **hot** 10 **to pour cold water on** something → see **water** 11 N-COUNT If you have a **cold**, you have a mild, very common illness which makes you sneeze a lot and gives you a sore throat or a cough. 感冒 ❑ *I had a pretty bad cold.* 我得了很重的感冒。 12 PHRASE If you **catch cold**, or **catch a cold**, you become ill with a cold. 患感冒 ❑ *Let's dry our hair so we don't catch cold.* 我们把头发弄干吧，省得患感冒。 13 PHRASE If someone is **out cold**, they are unconscious or sleeping very heavily. 失去知觉的; 沉睡的 ❑ *She was out cold but still breathing.* 她失去了知觉，但还在呼吸。

Thesaurus *cold* 另参见：

ADJ. bitter, chilly, cool, freezing, frozen, raw; (*ant.*) hot, warm 1 2
cool, distant; (*ant.*) friendly, warm 5

Word Partnership cold 的常用搭配

N. cold **air**, **dark and** cold, cold **night**, cold **rain**, cold **water**, cold **weather**, cold **wind** 1 2
ADV. **bitterly** cold 1 2
freezing cold 1 – 3
V. **feel** cold, **get** cold 1 – 3
catch/get a cold 11

cold-blooded 1 ADJ Someone who is **cold-blooded** does not show any pity or emotion. 残酷无情的；冷血的 [DISAPPROVAL] ❑ *...a cold-blooded murderer.* …一个冷血杀手。 2 ADJ **Cold-blooded** animals have a body temperature that changes according to the surrounding temperature. Reptiles, for example, are cold-blooded. 冷血的 (动物)

cold call (**cold calls, cold calling, cold called**) 1 N-COUNT If someone makes a **cold call**, they telephone or visit someone they have never contacted, without making an appointment, in order to try and sell something. 陌生推销电话；陌生推销拜访 ❑ *She had worked as a call center operator making cold calls for time-share vacations.* 她曾经在一个呼叫中心担任话务员，打陌生推销电话推销分时度假。 2 V-T/V-I To **cold-call** means to make a cold call. 打陌生推销电话；进行陌生推销拜访 ❑ *You should refuse to meet anyone who cold-calls you with an offer of financial advice.* 你应该拒绝见任何通过陌生推销拜访来提供理财咨询的人。 ● **cold-calling** N-UNCOUNT 陌生推销电话；陌生推销拜访 ❑ *We will adhere to strict sales ethics, with none of the cold-calling that has given the industry such a bad name.* 我们将严格遵守销售道德，杜绝已败坏本行业名声的陌生推销。

Word Link *labor ≈ working : collaborate, elaborate, laboratory*

col·labo·rate /kəlæbəreɪt/ (**collaborates, collaborating, collaborated**) 1 V-RECIP When one person or group **collaborates with** another, they work together, especially on a book or on some research. (尤指著书或进行研究时的) 合作 ❑ *Much later he collaborated with his son Michael on the English translation of a text on food production.* 后来他和儿子迈克尔合作，把一个有关食品生产的文本翻译成英语。 ❑ *He turned his country house into a place where professionals and amateurs collaborated in the making of music.* 他把他的乡间小屋变成了业内外人士合作制作音乐的场所。 2 V-I If someone **collaborates with** an enemy that is occupying their country during a war, they help them. 通敌 [DISAPPROVAL] ❑ *He was accused of having collaborated with the Communist secret police.* 他被指控与纳粹党的秘密警察合作。

★ **col·labo·ra·tion** /kəlæbəreɪʃ^{ə}n/ (**collaborations**) 1 N-VAR **Collaboration** is the act of working together to produce a piece of work, especially a book or some research. (尤指著书或进行研究时的) 合作 ❑ *There is substantial collaboration with neighboring departments.* 相邻的几个院系进行了通力合作。 ❑ *...scientific collaborations.* …科学协作。 2 N-COUNT A **collaboration** is a piece of work that has been produced as the result of people or groups working together. 合作成果 ❑ *He was also a writer of beautiful stories, some of which are collaborations with his fiancée.* 他也撰写优美的故事，有些是和他的未婚妻合作的成果。 3 N-UNCOUNT **Collaboration** is the act of helping an enemy who is occupying your country during a war. 通敌行为 [DISAPPROVAL] ❑ *...rumors of his collaboration with the occupying forces during the war.* …关于他在战争期间与占领军勾结的谣传。

col·labo·ra·tive /kəlæbəreɪtɪv, -ərətɪv/ ADJ A **collaborative** piece of work is done by two or more people or groups working together. 合作的 [ADJ n] [FORMAL] ❑ *...a collaborative research project.* …一个合作研究项目。

col·labo·ra·tor /kəlæbəreɪtər/ (**collaborators**) 1 N-COUNT A **collaborator** is someone that you work with to produce a piece of work, especially a book or some research. (尤指著书或进行研究时的) 合作者 ❑ *The Irvine group and their collaborators are testing whether lasers do the job better.* 欧文小组和他们的合作者们正在测试是否用激光更好。 2 N-COUNT A **collaborator** is someone who helps an enemy who is occupying their country during a war. 通敌者 [DISAPPROVAL] ❑ *Two alleged collaborators were shot dead by masked activists.* 两名通敌嫌疑犯被蒙面激进主义分子枪杀。

col·lage /kəlɑʒ/ (**collages**) 1 N-COUNT A **collage** is a picture that has been made by sticking pieces of colored paper and cloth onto paper. 拼贴画 ❑ *...a collage of words and pictures from magazines.* …用杂志上的词语和图片做成的拼贴画。 2 N-UNCOUNT **Collage** is the method of making pictures by sticking pieces of colored paper and cloth onto paper. (把彩纸和布粘在纸上的) 拼贴法 ❑ *The illustrations make use of collage, watercolor, and other media.* 这些插图用上了拼贴法、水彩以及其他的手法。

Word Link *lapse ≈ falling : collapse, elapse, lapse*

col·lapse ◆◆◇ /kəlæps/ (**collapses, collapsing, collapsed**) 1 V-I If a building or other structure **collapses**, it falls down very suddenly. 坍塌 ❑ *A section of the Bay Bridge had collapsed.* 海湾大桥有一部分坍塌了。 ● N-UNCOUNT **Collapse** is also a noun. 坍塌 ❑ *The governor called for an inquiry into the freeway's collapse.* 州长要求对高速公路的坍塌进行调查。 2 V-I If something, for example a system or institution, **collapses**, it fails or comes to an end completely and suddenly. (系统或制度等) 崩溃；瓦解 ❑ *His business empire collapsed under a massive burden of debt.* 他的商业帝国由于债台高筑而瓦解。 ● N-UNCOUNT **Collapse** is also a noun. (系统或制度等的) 崩溃；瓦解 ❑ *The coup's collapse has speeded up the drive to independence.* 那次政变的失败加速推动了独立进程。 3 V-I If you **collapse**, you suddenly faint or fall down because you are very ill or weak. 晕倒；倒下 ❑ *He collapsed following a vigorous exercise session at his home.* 他在家中进行了一段时间的剧烈运动后倒下了。 ● N-UNCOUNT **Collapse** is also a noun. 晕倒；倒下 ❑ *A few days after his collapse he was sitting up in bed.* 他病倒后过了几天就在床上起身坐着了。 4 V-I If you **collapse** onto something, you sit or lie down suddenly because you are very tired. (因极度疲倦而) 瘫坐；瘫倒 ❑ *She arrived home exhausted and barely capable of showering before collapsing on her bed.* 她到家的时候累极了，几乎无法去淋浴就瘫倒在床上。

col·lar /kɒlər/ (**collars**) 1 N-COUNT The **collar** of a shirt or coat is the part which fits around the neck and is usually folded over. 衣领 ❑ *His tie was pulled loose and his collar hung open.* 他的领带被扯松了，衣领敞开着。 2 → see also **blue-collar, white-collar** 3 N-COUNT A **collar** is a band of leather or plastic which is put around the neck of a dog or cat. (狗或猫的) 项圈

collar·bone /kɒlərboun/ (**collarbones**) N-COUNT Your **collarbones** are the two long bones which run from throat to your shoulders. 锁骨 ❑ *Harold had a broken collarbone.* 哈罗德断了一根锁骨。

col·late /kəleɪt/ (**collates, collating, collated**) 1 V-T When you **collate** pieces of information, you gather them all together and examine them. 整理检点 (信息) ❑ *Roberts has spent much of his working life collating the data on which the study was based.* 罗伯茨花费很多工作时间来整理检点数据，以此作为该研究的基础。 2 V-T If someone, or something such as a photocopier, **collates** pieces of paper, they put them together in the correct order. 整理 (纸张) ❑ *They took sheets of paper off piles, collated them and put them into envelopes.* 他们从纸堆中拿出一沓一沓的纸，整理好并放入信封中。

col·lat·er·al /kəlætərəl/ N-UNCOUNT **Collateral** is money or property which is used as a guarantee that someone will repay a loan. 担保金；抵押品 [FORMAL] ❑ *Many people use personal assets as collateral for small business loans.* 许多人用个人资产作抵押，办理小额商业贷款。

col·lat·er·al dam·age N-UNCOUNT **Collateral damage** is accidental injury to nonmilitary people or damage to nonmilitary buildings which occurs during a military operation. (军事行动中对平民或非军事建筑造成的) 附带损害 ❑ *To minimize collateral damage, maximum precision in bombing was required.* 为使附带损害达到最小，要求在轰炸中使精确度达到最高。

col·league ◆◆◇ /kɒlig/ (**colleagues**) N-COUNT Your **colleagues** are the people you work with, especially in a professional job. 同事 ❑ *Without consulting his colleagues, he flew from Los Angeles to Chicago.* 在没有和同事商量的情况下，他从洛杉矶飞到了芝加哥。

col·lect ◆◆◇ /kəlɛkt/ (**collects, collecting, collected**) 1 V-T If you **collect** a number of things, you bring them together from several places or from several people. 采集；收集 ❑ *Two young girls were collecting firewood.* 两位年轻女孩在采集柴火。 ❑ *Elizabeth had been collecting snails for a school project.* 伊丽莎白为一个学校的项目在收集蜗牛。 2 V-T If you **collect** things, such as stamps or books, as a hobby, you get a large number of them over a period of time because they interest you. 收集 (邮票或书等) ❑ *I used to collect stamps.* 我过去曾经集邮。 ● **col·lect·ing** N-UNCOUNT 收集 ❑ *...hobbies like stamp collecting and fishing.* …诸如集邮和钓鱼之类的爱好。 3 V-T/V-I If a substance **collects** somewhere, or if something **collects** it, it keeps arriving over a period of time and is held in that place or thing. 积聚 ❑ *Methane gas does collect in the mines around here.* 沼气确实积聚在这周围的矿井中。 4 V-T If something **collects** light, energy, or heat, it attracts it. 聚集 (光、能量、热量等) ❑ *Like a*

C

telescope, it has a curved mirror to collect the sunlight. 和望远镜一样，它有一个曲面镜来聚集太阳光。 5 V-T/V-I If you **collect for** a charity or **for** a present for someone, you ask people to give you money for it. 募捐 ❑ *Are you collecting for charity?* 你是在为慈善募捐吗？ ❑ *The organization has collected $2.5 million for the relief effort.* 该组织已经募捐到了250万美元用于救济活动。 6 V-T When you **collect** someone or something, you go and get them from the place where they are waiting for you or have been left for you. 领走 [mainly BRIT]

in AM, usually use **pick up**

Thesaurus *collect* 另参见：
V. accumulate, compile, gather; *(ant.)* scatter 1

col·lect call (collect calls) N-COUNT A **collect call** is a telephone call which is paid for by the person who receives the call, rather than the person who makes the call. 对方付费电话 [AM] ❑ *"I want to make a collect call," she said as soon as a voice came on the line.* "我想打个对方付费的电话，"她一听到电话里传来声音就说道。 ● PHRASE If you **call collect** when you make a telephone call, the person who you are phoning pays the cost of the call and not you. 拨打对方付费的电话 [AM]

col·lec·tion ♦♦◇ /kəlɛkʃᵊn/ (collections) 1 N-COUNT A **collection of** things is a group of similar things that you have deliberately acquired, usually over a period of time. 收藏品 ❑ *Robert's collection of prints and paintings has been bought over the years.* 罗伯特的印刷收藏品和藏画是多年来花钱买的。 ❑ *The Art Gallery of Ontario has the world's largest collection of sculptures by Henry Moore.* 安大略美术馆关于亨利•摩尔的雕塑收藏品居世界之最。 2 N-COUNT A **collection of** stories, poems, or articles is a number of them published in one book. (作品) 集 ❑ *Two years ago he published a collection of short stories called "Facing The Music."* 两年前，他出版了一本题为《愿赌服输》的短篇小说集。 3 N-COUNT A **collection of** things is a group of things. 组群 ❑ *...a collection of modern glass office buildings.* …一组玻璃幕墙的现代办公楼群。 4 N-COUNT A fashion designer's new **collection** consists of the new clothes they have designed for the next season. 时装系列 ❑ *Her spring/summer collection for this year deliberately uses both simple and rich fabrics.* 她今年的春/夏装系列故意使用了既简单又华贵的材质。 5 N-COUNT If you organize a **collection** for charity, you collect money from people to give to charity. 募捐 ❑ *I asked my principal if he could arrange a collection for a refugee charity.* 我问我的校长能否为难民组织一次慈善募捐。 6 N-COUNT A **collection** is money that is given by people in church during some Christian services. (某些基督仪式中人们给教堂的) 捐款 7 N-UNCOUNT **Collection** is the act of collecting something from a place or from people. 收集；采集 ❑ *Money can be sent to any one of 22,000 agents worldwide for collection.* 钱款可以送交全世界22000个代理机构中的任何一个来收集。 ❑ *...computer systems to speed up collection of information.* …用于加快信息采集速度的电脑系统。

col·lec·tive ♦◇◇ /kəlɛktɪv/ (collectives) 1 ADJ **Collective** actions, situations, or feelings involve or are shared by every member of a group of people. 集体的 [ADJ n] ❑ *It was a collective decision.* 这是集体的决定。 ● **col·lec·tive·ly** ADV 集体地 ❑ *They collectively decided to recognize the changed situation.* 他们集体决定承认局势的变化。 2 ADJ A **collective** amount of something is the total obtained by adding together the amounts that each person or thing in a group has. 总体的 [ADJ n] ❑ *Their collective volume wasn't very large.* 他们总体的数量不太大。 ● **col·lec·tive·ly** ADV 总体地 [ADV with v] ❑ *In 1968 the states collectively spent $2 billion on it.* 1968年各州总体为此花了20亿美元。 3 ADJ The **collective** term for two or more types of thing is a general word or expression which refers to all of them. 总的 [ADJ n] ❑ *Social science is a collective name, covering a series of individual sciences.* 社会科学是一个总称，涵盖一系列独立学科。 ● **col·lec·tive·ly** ADV 总地 [ADV with v] ❑ *...other sorts of cells (known collectively as white corpuscles).* …其他几种细胞（总称白血球）。 4 N-COUNT A **collective** is a business or farm which is run, and often owned, by a group of people. 集体企业；集体农庄 [BUSINESS] ❑ *He will see that he is participating in all the decisions of the collective.* 他要确保他在参与集体企业的所有决策。

col·lec·tive bar·gain·ing N-UNCOUNT When a labor union engages in **collective bargaining**, it has talks with an employer about its members' pay and working conditions. (工会与雇主关于工资以及工作环境的) 集体谈判 [BUSINESS] ❑ *...a new collective-bargaining agreement.* …一个新的劳资双方集体谈判协议。
→ see **union**

col·lec·tor /kəlɛktər/ (collectors) 1 N-COUNT A **collector** is a person who collects things of a particular type as a hobby. 收藏家 ❑ *...a stamp collector.* …一位集邮者。 ❑ *...a respected collector of Indian art.* …一位受人尊敬的印第安艺术品收藏家。 2 N-COUNT You can use **collector** to refer to someone whose job is to take something such as money, tickets, or garbage from people. For example, a rent **collector** collects rent from people. (钱款、票据或垃圾的) 收取人 ❑ *He earned his living as a tax collector.* 他做收税员谋生。
→ see **gallery**

col·lege ♦♦◇ /kɒlɪdʒ/ (colleges) 1 N-VAR; N-IN-NAMES A **college** is an institution where students study after they have left secondary school. 大学；学院 ❑ *Their daughter Joanna is taking business courses at a local college.* 他们的女儿乔安娜正在当地一所大学修习商务课程。 ❑ *Stephanie took up making jewelry after leaving art college this summer.* 斯特凡妮今年夏天从艺术学院毕业以后开始从事珠宝的制作工作。 2 N-COUNT; N-IN-NAMES At some universities in the United States, **colleges** are divisions which offer degrees in particular subjects. (美国某些大学中的) 学院 ❑ *...a professor at the University of Florida College of Law.* …一位佛罗里达大学法学院的教授。

In North American education, students who have finished secondary school may go on to **college**, **university**, or **technical school**. College and university both offer baccalaureate degrees. Universities also have graduate schools for post-graduate education. Technical school provides training in a very specific area. In everyday speech a person will say they **go to college** regardless of which type of institution they attend.

3 N-COUNT A **college** is one of the institutions which some British universities are divided into. (英国某些大学中的) 学院 ❑ *He was educated at Balliol College, Oxford.* 他毕业于牛津大学贝列尔学院。
→ see **graduation**

★ **col·lide** /kəlaɪd/ (collides, colliding, collided) 1 V-RECIP If two or more moving people or objects **collide**, they crash into one another. If a moving person or object **collides with** a person or object that is not moving, they crash into them. 碰撞 ❑ *Two trains collided head-on in Ohio early this morning.* 两辆列车今天早晨在俄亥俄州迎头相撞。 ❑ *Racing up the stairs, he almost collided with Daisy.* 他冲上楼梯，几乎与戴西相撞。 2 V-RECIP If the aims, opinions, or interests of one person or group **collide with** those of another person or group, they are very different from each other and are therefore opposed. (目标、观点或利益等) 相抵触；相冲突 ❑ *The aims of the negotiators in New York again seem likely to collide with the aims of the warriors in the field.* 纽约谈判者的目标看起来可能再次与战场上勇士们的目标相冲突。

Thesaurus *collide* 另参见：
V. bump, clash, crash, hit, smash; *(ant.)* avoid 1

col·li·sion /kəlɪʒᵊn/ (collisions) 1 N-VAR A **collision** occurs when a moving object crashes into something. 碰撞 ❑ *They were on their way to the airport when their van was involved in a collision with a car.* 他们正往机场赶路的时候，其货车和一辆小汽车相撞了。 2 N-COUNT A **collision of** cultures or ideas occurs when two very different cultures or people meet and conflict. (文化或观点的) 冲突 ❑ *The play represents the collision of three generations.* 该剧表现了3代人之间的冲突。

Thesaurus *collision* 另参见：
N. accident, crash, pileup 1

col·lo·quial /kəloʊkwiəl/ ADJ **Colloquial** words and phrases are informal and are used mainly in conversation. 口语的 ❑ *...a colloquial expression.* …一个口语表达法。

col·lude /kəlud/ (colludes, colluding, colluded) V-RECIP If one person **colludes with** another, they cooperate with them secretly or illegally. (秘密或非法地) 串通 [DISAPPROVAL] ❑ *Several local officials are in jail on charges of colluding with the Mafia.* 几位地方官员因涉嫌串通黑手党而锒铛入狱。 ❑ *We all colluded in the myth of him as the swanky businessman.* 我们所有人串通一气，把他神化为一流的商人。

col·lu·sion /kəluʒᵊn/ N-UNCOUNT **Collusion** is secret or illegal cooperation, especially between countries or organizations. (尤指国家或组织间之间秘密或非法的) 串通；勾结 [usu N "between" pl-n, N "with" n, "in" N] [FORMAL, DISAPPROVAL] ❑ *He found no evidence of collusion between record companies and retailers.* 他找不出唱片公司与零售商互相勾结的证据。

▲ **co·lon** /koʊlən/ (colons) **1** N-COUNT A **colon** is the punctuation mark : which you can use in several ways. For example, you can put it before a list of things or before reported speech. 冒号 **2** N-COUNT Your **colon** is the part of your intestine above your rectum. 结肠 ❑ *In the U.S., there are 60,000 deaths a year from colon cancer.* 在美国，每年有 6 万人死于结肠癌。

▲ **colo·nel** ♦◇◇ /kɜrnᵊl/ (colonels) N-COUNT; N-TITLE; N-VOC A **colonel** is a senior officer in an army, air force, or the marines. (陆军、空军或海军的）上校 ❑ *This particular place was run by an ex-Army colonel.* 这个特别的地方归一位前陆军上校掌管。

co·lo·nial /kəloʊniəl/ **1** ADJ **Colonial** means relating to countries that are colonies, or to colonialism. 殖民地的；殖民主义的 [ADJ n] ❑ *...the 31st anniversary of Jamaica's independence from British colonial rule.* …牙买加摆脱英国殖民统治并获得独立的第31周年。 **2** ADJ A **colonial** building or piece of furniture was built or made in a style that was popular in America in the 17th and 18th centuries. (17和18世纪美洲）殖民地时期风格的 [mainly AM] ❑ *...the white colonial houses on the north side of the campus.* …校园北边的殖民地时期风格的白房子。

▲ **co·lo·ni·al·ism** /kəloʊniəlɪzəm/ N-UNCOUNT **Colonialism** is the practice by which a powerful country directly controls less powerful countries and uses their resources to increase its own power and wealth. 殖民主义 ❑ *...the bitter oppression of slavery and colonialism.* …奴隶制和殖民主义的残酷压迫。

★ **colo·nise** /kɒlənaɪz/ [BRIT] → see **colonize**

colo·nist /kɒlənɪst/ (colonists) N-COUNT **Colonists** are the people who start a colony or the people who are among the first to live in a particular colony. 殖民者；殖民地居民 ❑ *The apple was brought over here by the colonists when they came.* 这苹果是殖民者到这儿时带来的。

★ **colo·nize** /kɒlənaɪz/ (colonizes, colonizing, colonized)

in BRIT, also use **colonise**

1 V-T If people **colonize** a foreign country, they go to live there and take control of it. 把…变为殖民地 ❑ *The first British attempt to colonize Ireland was in the twelfth century.* 英国第一次企图把爱尔兰变成殖民地是在12世纪。 ❑ *Liberia was never colonized by the European powers.* 利比里亚从未沦为欧洲列强的殖民地。 **2** V-T When large numbers of animals **colonize** a place, they go to live there and make it their home. (动物）移居于 ❑ *Toads are colonizing the whole place.* 蟾蜍正移居到这整个地区。 **3** V-T When an area **is colonized by** a type of plant, the plant grows there in large amounts. (植物）在…大量繁殖 [usu passive] ❑ *The area was then colonized by scrub.* 那时该地区被大量低矮灌木所覆盖。

colo·ny /kɒləni/ (colonies) **1** N-COUNT A **colony** is a country which is controlled by a more powerful country. 殖民地 ❑ *In France's former North African colonies, anti-French feeling is growing.* 在法国的各前北非殖民地，反法情绪正在增长。 **2** N-COUNT You can refer to a place where a particular group of people lives as a particular kind of **colony**. (某一类人的）聚居区 ❑ *In 1932, he established a school and artists' colony in Stone City, Iowa.* 1932年，他在爱荷华州的小石城建立了一所学校和艺术家聚居区。 ❑ *...a penal colony.* …一个罪犯的流放地。 **3** N-COUNT A **colony of** birds, insects, or animals is a group of them that live together. (生物）居住在一起的群体 ❑ *The islands are famed for their colonies of sea birds.* 这些岛屿因有成群的海鸟居住而闻名。

col·or ♦♦♦ /kʌlər/ (colors, coloring, colored)

in BRIT, use **colour**

1 N-COUNT The **color** of something is the appearance that it has as a result of the way in which it reflects light. Red, blue, and green are colors. 颜色 ❑ *"What color is the car?"—"Red."* "那辆车是什么颜色？"——"红色。" ❑ *Judi's favourite color is pink.* 朱迪最喜欢的颜色是粉红色。 **2** N-COUNT Someone's **color** is the color of their skin. People often use **color** in this way to refer to a person's race. 肤色（常指人种）[POLITENESS] ❑ *I don't care what color she is.* 我不在乎她是什么人种。 **3** N-VAR A **color** is a substance you use to give something a particular color. Dyes and makeup are sometimes referred to as **colors**. 着色剂 ❑ *It is better to avoid all food colors.* 最好避开所有的食品着色剂。 ❑ *Her nail color was coordinated with her lipstick.* 她指甲上的染色与她的口红相配。 **4** V-T If you **color** something, you use something such as dyes or paint to change its color. 给…着色 ❑ *Many women begin coloring their hair in their mid-30s.* 许多妇女在三十五六岁时开始染发。 ❑ *We'd been making cakes and coloring the posters.* 我们一直在做蛋糕和给海报涂色。 ● **col·or·ing** N-UNCOUNT 着色 ❑ *They could not afford to spoil those maps by careless coloring.* 他们不敢用随意的涂色毁了那些地图。 **5** V-I If someone **colors**, their face becomes redder than it normally is, usually because they are embarrassed. 脸红 ❑ *Andrew couldn't help noticing that she colored slightly.* 安德鲁不禁注意到她微微有些脸红。 **6** V-T If something **colors** your opinion, it affects the way that you think about something. 影响 ❑ *All too often it is only the negative images of Ireland that are portrayed, coloring opinions and hiding the true nature of the country.* 通常只有爱尔兰的负面形象被加以描绘，从而影响了人们的看法并掩盖了这个国家的实质。 **7** ADJ A **color** television, photograph, or picture is one that shows things in all their colors, and not just in black, white, and gray. 彩色的 ❑ *In Japan 99 per cent of all households now have a color television set.* 日本99%的家庭如今都有彩电。 **8** N-UNCOUNT **Color** is a quality that makes something especially interesting or exciting. 趣味

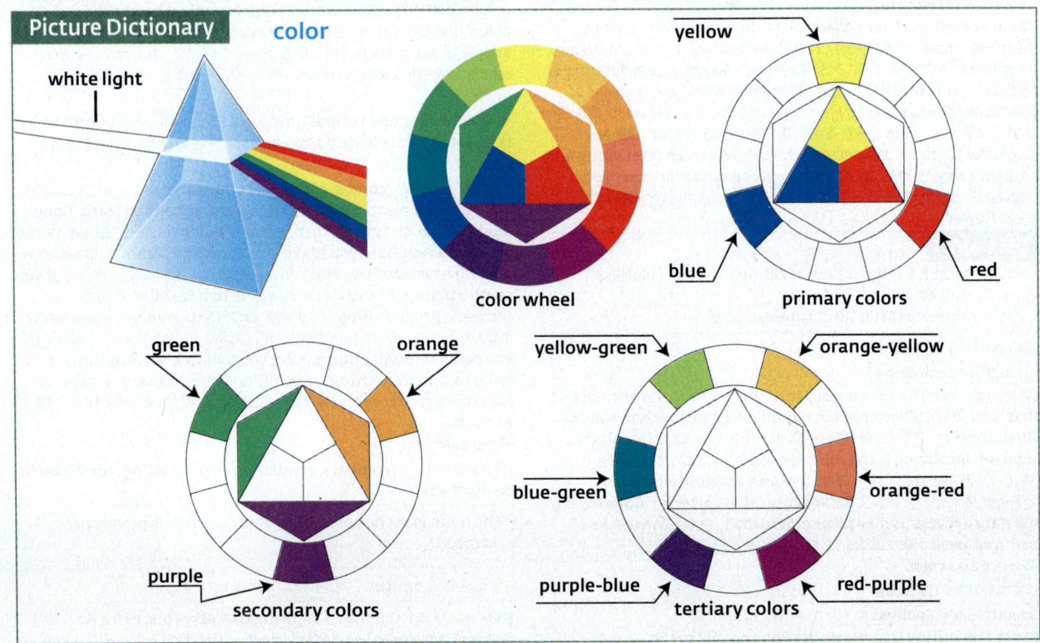

C

C

❑ *She had resumed the travel necessary to add depth and color to her novels.* 她重新开始旅行以给她的小说增加深度和趣味。 **9** N-PLURAL A country's national **colors** are the colors of its national flag. 国旗色 ❑ *The Opera House is decorated with the Hungarian national colors: green, red, and white.* 歌剧院饰以匈牙利的国旗色：绿，红，白。 **10** N-PLURAL People sometimes refer to the flag of a particular part of an army, navy, or air force, or the flag of a particular country as its **colors**. 军旗；国旗 ❑ *Troops raised the country's colors in a special ceremony.* 军队在一次特殊仪式上升了国旗。 **11** N-PLURAL A sports team's **colors** are the colors of the clothes they wear when they play. 队服颜色 ❑ *I was wearing the team's colors.* 我穿着该队队服的颜色。 **12** → see also **colored, coloring** **13** PHRASE If a movie or television program is **in color**, it has been made so that you see the picture in all its colors, and not just in black, white, or gray. (电影或电视节目) 彩色的 ❑ *Was he going to show the movie? Was it in color?* 他要去放电影吗？是彩色的吗？ **14** PHRASE People **of color** are people who belong to a race with dark skins. 有色的 [POLITENESS] ❑ *Black communities spoke up to defend the rights of all people of color.* 黑人社团为捍卫所有有色人种的权利大声疾呼。

→ see Picture Dictionary: color

→ see **flower, painting**

▶ **color in** PHRASAL VERB If you **color in** a drawing, you give it different colors using crayons or paints. 给…着色 ❑ *Someone had colored in all the black and white pictures.* 有人把所有的黑白图片绘成了彩色。

Word Partnership *color* 的常用搭配：

ADJ.	**bright** color, **favorite** color **1**
N.	color **blind**, **eye/hair** color **1**
	skin color **2**
	color **film/photograph**, color **television** **7**
PREP.	**in** color **13**

col·ored ♦◇◇ /kʌlərd/

in BRIT, use **coloured**

1 ADJ Something that is **colored** a particular color is that color. 呈…颜色的 ❑ *The illustration shows a cluster of five roses colored apricot orange.* 插图上展示了一簇杏黄色的5朵玫瑰。 **2** ADJ Something that is **colored** is a particular color or combination of colors, rather than being just white, black, or the color that it is naturally. 着了色的 ❑ *You can often choose between plain white or colored and patterned scarves.* 你通常可在原白色或彩色带图案的围巾中进行选择。 **3** ADJ A **colored** person belongs to a race of people with dark skins. 有色的 [OFFENSIVE, OLD-FASHIONED]

col·or·ful /kʌlərfəl/

in BRIT, use **colourful**

1 ADJ Something that is **colorful** has bright colors or a lot of different colors. 绚丽多彩的 ❑ *The flowers were colorful and the scenery magnificent.* 花儿绚丽多彩，风景美丽动人。 **2** ADJ A **colorful** story is full of exciting details. 生动的 ❑ *The story she told was certainly colorful, and extended over her life in England, Germany, and Spain.* 她讲述的故事的确很生动，包括了她在英国、德国和西班牙的生活。 **3** ADJ A **colorful** character is a person who behaves in an interesting and amusing way. 有趣的 ❑ *Casey Stengel was probably the most colorful character in baseball.* 凯西・斯坦格可能是棒球运动中最有趣的人物。

→ see **flower**

Thesaurus *colorful* 另参见：

ADJ. bright, lively, vibrant, vivid; *(ant.)* bland, colorless, dull **1**
animated, dramatic, interesting **2**

col·or·ing /kʌlərɪŋ/

in BRIT, use **colouring**

1 N-UNCOUNT The **coloring** of something is the color or colors that it is. 色彩 ❑ *Other countries vary the coloring of their bank notes as well as their size.* 其他各国钞票的色彩和大小各异。 **2** N-UNCOUNT Someone's **coloring** is the color of their hair, skin, and eyes. (头发、皮肤和眼睛的) 颜色 ❑ *None of them had their father's dark coloring.* 他们无一人具有父亲的黑肤色。 **3** N-UNCOUNT **Coloring** is a substance that is used to give color to food. 色素 ❑ *A few drops of green food coloring were added.* 几滴绿色的食品色素被加进去了。 **4** → see also **color**

col·or·less /kʌlərlɪs/

in BRIT, use **colourless**

1 ADJ Something that is **colorless** has no color at all. 无色的 ❑ *...a colorless, almost odorless liquid.* …一种无色的、几乎无味的液体。 **2** ADJ If someone's face is **colorless**, it is very pale, usually because they are frightened, shocked, or ill. 苍白的 ❑ *Her face was colorless, and she was shaking.* 她脸色苍白，全身发抖。 **3** ADJ **Colorless** people or places are dull and uninteresting. 平淡无趣的 ❑ *...the much more experienced but colorless general.* …这位经验更为丰富但平淡无趣的将军。

col·or line (**color lines**) N-COUNT A **color line** is the set of social, economic or political barriers that exist between different racial groups. 种族界限 [usu sing]

in BRIT, use **colour line**

❑ *...one of the first black players to break the color line in the deep South.* …最初在南方腹地打破种族界限的黑人球员之一。 ❑ *She made numerous efforts to break down color lines in public places.* 她为打破公共场所的种族界限做出过许多努力。

▲ **co·los·sal** /kəlɒsəl/ ADJ If you describe something as **colossal**, you are emphasizing that it is very large. 巨大的 [EMPHASIS] ❑ *There has been a colossal waste of public money.* 一直有巨大的公款浪费。

col·our /kʌlər/ [BRIT] → see **color**

col·oured /kʌlərd/ [BRIT] → see **colored**

col·our·ful /kʌlərfəl/ [BRIT] → see **colorful**

col·our·ing /kʌlərɪŋ/ [BRIT] → see **coloring**

col·our·less /kʌlərlɪs/ [BRIT] → see **colorless**

colt /koʊlt/ (**colts**) N-COUNT A **colt** is a young male horse. 小公马

col·umn ♦◇◇ /kɒləm/ (**columns**) **1** N-COUNT A **column** is a tall, often decorated cylinder of stone which is built to honor someone or forms part of a building. 纪念柱；圆形支柱 ❑ *Seven massive columns rise up from a marble floor.* 七根巨大的圆柱从大理石地面拔地而起。 **2** N-COUNT A **column** is something that has a tall, narrow shape. 柱状物 ❑ *The explosion sent a column of smoke thousands of feet into the air.* 爆炸造成的烟柱升入几千英尺的高空。 **3** N-COUNT A **column** is a group of people or animals which moves in a long line. (人或动物行进的) 长队 ❑ *There were reports of columns of military vehicles appearing on the streets.* 有报道称街道上出现了多列军车车队。 **4** N-COUNT On a printed page such as a page of a dictionary, newspaper, or printed chart, a **column** is one of two or more vertical sections which are read downward. (词典、报纸或图表等版面上的) 竖栏 ❑ *We had stupidly been looking at the wrong column of figures.* 我们真笨，一直看错了数字的栏。 **5** N-COUNT In a newspaper or magazine, a **column** is a section that is always written by the same person or is always about the same topic. (报刊的) 专栏 ❑ *His name features frequently in the social columns of the tabloid newspapers.* 他的名字常常显著出现在通俗小报的社会专栏中。

▲ **col·um·nist** /kɒləmnɪst, -əmɪst/ (**columnists**) N-COUNT A **columnist** is a journalist who regularly writes a particular kind of article in a newspaper or magazine. 专栏记者 ❑ *Clarence Page is a columnist for the Chicago Tribune.* 克拉伦斯・佩奇是《芝加哥论坛报》的专栏记者。

▲ **coma** /koʊmə/ (**comas**) N-COUNT Someone who is **in a coma** is in a state of deep unconsciousness. 昏迷 ❑ *She was in a coma for seven weeks.* 她昏迷了7周。

comb /koʊm/ (**combs, combing, combed**) **1** N-COUNT A **comb** is a flat piece of plastic or metal with narrow, pointed teeth along one side, which you use to make your hair neat. 梳子 **2** V-T When you **comb** your hair, you make it neat using a comb. 梳 ❑ *Salvatore combed his hair carefully.* 萨尔瓦多仔细地梳理了他的头发。 **3** V-T If you **comb** a place, you search everywhere in it in order to find someone or something. 彻底搜查 ❑ *Officers combed the woods for the murder weapon.* 警官们彻底搜查了那片树林，寻找杀人凶器。 **4** V-I If you **comb through** information, you look at it very carefully in order to find something. 仔细查看 ❑ *Eight policemen then spent two years combing through the evidence.* 8名警察后来用了两年的时间仔细审查那些证据。

→ see **hair**

com·bat ♦◇◇ (**combats, combating** or **combatting, combated** or **combatted**)

The noun is pronounced /kɒmbæt/. The verb is pronounced /kəmbæt/.

名词读作 /kɒmbæt/。动词读作 /kəmbæt/。

1 N-UNCOUNT **Combat** is fighting that takes place in a war. 战斗 ❑ *Over 16 million men had died in combat.* 一千六百多万人在战斗中阵亡。

❑ *Yesterday saw hand-to-hand combat in the city.* 昨天那座城里发生了肉搏战。 2 N-COUNT A **combat** is a battle, or a fight between two people. 搏斗 ❑ *It was the end of a long combat.* 那是一场长时间搏斗的结束。 3 V-T If people in authority **combat** something, they try to stop it from happening. 防止 ❑ *Congress has criticized new government measures to combat crime.* 国会批评了新政府防止犯罪的措施。

→ see **war**

Word Partnership *combat* 的常用搭配:

N. combat **forces/troops/units**, combat **gear** 1
combat **crime**, combat **disease**, combat **terrorism** 3

ADJ. **hand-to-hand** combat, **heavy** combat 1 2

com·bat·ant /kəmbætᵊnt/ (**combatants**) N-COUNT A **combatant** is a person, group, or country that takes part in the fighting in a war. 参战者 ❑ *I have never suggested that U.N. forces could physically separate the combatants in the region.* 我从未表示过联合国部队能将该地区的参战者们实际隔离开。

com·bat·ive /kəmbætɪv/ ADJ A person who is **combative** is aggressive and eager to fight or argue. 好斗的 ❑ *He conducted the meeting yesterday in his usual combative style, refusing to admit any mistakes.* 他昨天以他一贯的好斗风格主持了会议，拒绝承认任何错误。

com·bi·na·tion ♦◇◇ /kɒmbɪneɪʃᵊn/ (**combinations**) N-COUNT A **combination of** things is a mixture of them. 混合物 ❑ *...a fantastic combination of colors.* …一种奇妙的混合色。

Word Link *com ≈ with, together : combine, compact, companion*

com·bine ♦◇◇ /kəmbaɪn/ (**combines, combining, combined**) 1 V-RECIP If you **combine** two or more things or if they **combine**, they exist together. 使…结合; 结合 ❑ *The Church has something to say on how to combine freedom with responsibility.* 教会要讲一讲如何使自由和责任相结合。 ❑ *Relief workers say it's worse than ever as disease and starvation combine to kill thousands.* 援助人员说情况比以往任何时候都糟，因为疾病和饥饿致使数以千计的人死亡。 2 V-RECIP If you **combine** two or more things or if they **combine**, they join together to make a single thing. 使…合为一体; 合为一体 ❑ *David Jacobs was given the job of combining the data from these 19 studies into one giant study.* 大卫·雅各布斯分到的工作是把这19项研究中的数据合为一项大型研究。 ❑ *Combine the flour with 3 tablespoons water to make a paste.* 把面粉和3大汤匙的水混合起来做成一个面团。 3 V-RECIP If two or more groups or organizations **combine** or if someone **combines** them, they join to form a single group or organization. 使…合并; 合并 ❑ *...an announcement by Steetley and Tarmac of a joint venture that would combine their brick, tile, and concrete operations.* …一份由斯蒂特利和塔玛克公司发布的将要组建一个将他们的砖、瓦和混凝土生产业务合并起来的合资企业的通知。 4 V-T If someone or something **combines** two qualities or features, they have both those qualities or features at the same time. 同时具有 ❑ *Their system seems to combine the two ideals of strong government and proportional representation.* 他们的体制似乎同时具有强有力的政府与比例代表制这两种理想状况。 ❑ *...a clever, far-sighted lawyer who combines legal expertise with social concern.* …一位同时具有法律专业知识和社会责任感的聪明而有远见的律师。 5 V-T If someone **combines** two activities, they do them both at the same time. 同时做 ❑ *It is possible to combine a career with being a mother.* 同时既干事业又做母亲是可能的。

Thesaurus *combine* 另参见:

V. blend, fuse, incorporate, join, mix, unite; *(ant.)* detach, disconnect, divide, separate 1–3

com·bined /kəmbaɪnd/ 1 ADJ A **combined** effort or attack is made by two or more groups of people at the same time. 联合的 [ADJ n] ❑ *These refugees are taken care of by the combined efforts of the host countries and non-governmental organizations.* 这些难民得到东道国和非政府组织合力照顾。 2 ADJ The **combined** size or quantity of two or more things is the total of their sizes or quantities added together. 加在一起的 [ADJ n] ❑ *Such a merger would be the largest in U.S. banking history, giving the two banks combined assets of some $146 billion.* 考虑到两家银行加在一起的资产有约一千四百六十亿美元，这样的合并在美国银行史上将会是最大的。

com·bus·tion /kəmbʌstʃən/ N-UNCOUNT **Combustion** is the act of burning something or the process of burning. 燃烧 [TECHNICAL] ❑ *The energy is released by combustion on the application of a match.* 能量通过点火柴燃烧释放出来。

→ see **engine**

come

1 ARRIVE AT A PLACE
2 OTHER USES
3 PHRASES AND PHRASAL VERBS

C

1 **come** ♦♦♦ /kʌm/ (**comes, coming, came**)

The form **come** is used in the present tense and is the past participle.

1 V-I When a person or thing **comes** to a particular place, especially to a place where you are, they move there. 来(某地) ❑ *Two police officers came into the hall.* 两位警官来到大厅里。 ❑ *Come here, Tom.* 来这儿，汤姆。 ❑ *We heard the train coming.* 我们听见火车来了。 ❑ *The impact blew out some of the windows and the sea came rushing in.* 冲击力击碎了一些窗户，海水冲了进来。 2 V-T When someone **comes to** do something, they move to the place where someone else is in order to do it, and they do it. Someone can also **come** do something and **come and** do something. However, you always say that someone **came and** did something. 来(做某事) ❑ *Eleanor had come to see her.* 埃莉诺是来看她的。 ❑ *I want you to come visit me.* 我希望你来看我。 3 V-I When you **come to** a place, you reach it. 到达 ❑ *He came to a door that led into a passageway.* 他来到一扇通往走廊的门前。 4 V-I If something **comes up to** a particular point or **down to** it, it is tall enough, deep enough, or long enough to reach that point. 达到 ❑ *The water came up to my chest.* 水漫到了我的胸部。

2 **come** ♦♦♦ /kʌm/ (**comes, coming, came**)

The form **come** is used in the present tense and is the past participle.

1 V-I If something **comes apart** or **comes to pieces**, it breaks into pieces. If something **comes off** or **comes away**, it becomes detached from something else. 破碎; 脱离 ❑ *The lid won't come off.* 盖子不会脱掉。 ❑ *The pistol came to pieces, easily and quickly.* 手枪轻易地就破碎了。 2 V-T If someone **comes to** do something, they do it at the end of a long process or period of time. 达到(做某事的境界) ❑ *She said it so many times that she came to believe it.* 她说了如此多遍以致于最后她都相信了。 3 V-T You can ask how something **came to** happen when you want to know what caused it to happen or made it possible. 达到(做某事的地步) ❑ *How did you come to meet him?* 你怎么会遇见他的? 4 V-I When a particular event or time **comes**, it arrives or happens. 来临; 发生 ❑ *The announcement came after a meeting at the White House.* 通告是在白宫的一次会议后发布的。 ❑ *There will come a time when they will have to negotiate.* 他们终将会进行谈判的。 ● **com·ing** N-SING 来临; 发生 ❑ *Most of my patients welcome the coming of summer.* 我的大多数病人都喜欢夏天的来临。 5 V-I If a thought, idea, or memory **comes to** you, you suddenly think of it or remember it. (想法、主意或记忆等) 突然出现 ❑ *He was about to shut the door when an idea came to him.* 他正准备关门时，突然想起了一个主意。 6 V-I If money or property is going to **come to** you, you are going to inherit or receive it. (钱财) 降临(在某人身上) ❑ *He did have retirement money coming to him when the factory shut down.* 工厂倒闭时，他的确领到了退休金。 7 V-I If a case **comes before** a court or tribunal or **comes to** court, it is presented there so that the court or tribunal can examine it. (案子) 被提交到(法庭) ❑ *The membership application came before the committee in September.* 会员资格申请9月呈交给了委员会。 8 V-I If something **comes to** a particular number or amount, it adds up to it. 合计达 ❑ *Lunch came to $80.* 午餐合计达80美元。 9 V-I If someone or something **comes from** a particular place or thing, that place or thing is their origin, source, or starting point. 来自 ❑ *Nearly half the students come from overseas.* 几乎一半学生来自海外。 ❑ *Chocolate comes from the cacao tree.* 巧克力来自可可树。 10 V-I Something that **comes from** something else or **comes of** it is the result of it. 源自 ❑ *There is a feeling of power that comes from driving fast.* 开快车可以产生力量感。 ❑ *Some good might come of all this gloomy business.* 某种好的结果也许会从这种惨淡的经营中产生。 11 V-T If someone or something **comes** first, next, or last, they are first, next, or last in a series, list, or competition. 排在(第一、下一个或最后) ❑ *The two countries have been unable to agree which step should come next.* 这两个国家无法就下一步该怎么走达成一致。 ❑ *The alphabet might be more rational if all the vowels came first.* 要是所有的元音都排在前面，字母表也许会更合理些。 12 V-I If a type of thing **comes in** a particular range of colors, forms, styles, or sizes, it can

C

have any of those colors, forms, styles, or sizes. (以某些颜色、形式、样式、尺码) 出现 ❑ *Bikes come in all shapes and sizes.* 自行车有各种不同的形状和大小。 **13** V-I The next subject in a discussion that you **come to** is the one that you talk about next. 谈到 ❑ *Finally, I come to the subject of genetic engineering.* 最后，我来谈基因工程。 **14** V-LINK You use **come** in expressions such as **come to an end** or **come into operation** to indicate that someone or something enters or reaches a particular state or situation. 达到 (某种状态或情形) ❑ *The summer came to an end.* 夏天结束了。 ❑ *Their worst fears may be coming true.* 他们最恐惧的事也许会变成现实。 **15** PREP You can use **come** before a date, time, or event to mean when it arrives. For example, you can say **come spring** to mean "when the spring arrives." 到来 ❑ *Come the election on the 20th of May, we will have to decide.* 5月20日选举到来时，我们就不得不做出决定。

❸ come ♦♦♦ /kʌm/ (**comes, coming, came**)

> The form **come** is used in the present tense and is the past participle.

1 PHRASE You can use the expression **when it comes down to it** or **when you come down to it** for emphasis, when you are giving a general statement or conclusion. 归结起来 [EMPHASIS] ❑ *When you come down to it, however, the basic problems of life have not changed.* 然而，归结起来，生活的基本问题并未改变。 **2** PHRASE You use the expression **come to think of it** to indicate that you have suddenly realized something, often something obvious. 突然意识到 ❑ *He was his distant relative, as was everyone else on the island, come to think of it.* 我突然意识到，他像岛上的其他人一样是他的远亲。 **3** PHRASE When you refer to a time or an event **to come** or one that is still **to come**, you are referring to a future time or event. 未来的 ❑ *I hope in years to come he will reflect on his decision.* 我希望在未来的几年里他会反思他的决定。 **4** PHRASE You can use expressions like **I know where you're coming from** or **you can see where she's coming from** to say that you understand someone's attitude or point of view. 态度；观点 ❑ *To understand why they are doing it, it is necessary to know where they are coming from.* 要理解他们为什么这样做，有必要知道他们的想法。 **5** → see also **coming**

▸ **come about** PHRASAL VERB When you say how or when something **came about**, you say how or when it happened. 产生；发生 ❑ *The peace agreement came about through intense pressure by the international community.* 该和平协议是在国际社会的强大压力下产生的。 ❑ *That came about when we went to New York last year.* 那件事发生在去年我们去纽约时。

▸ **come across** **1** PHRASAL VERB If you **come across** something or someone, you find them or meet them by chance. 偶然发现；偶然遇见 ❑ *He came across the jawbone of a 4.5 million-year-old marsupial.* 他偶然发现了一个450万年前的有袋动物的颌骨。 **2** PHRASAL VERB If someone or what they are saying **comes across** in a particular way, they make that impression on people who meet them or are listening to them. 留下印象 ❑ *When sober, he can come across as an extremely pleasant and charming young man.* 在他不醉酒的时候，他给人的印象可能会是一位极其可爱迷人的年轻人。

▸ **come along** **1** PHRASAL VERB You tell someone to **come along** to encourage them in a friendly way to do something, especially to attend something. 一起来 ❑ *There's a barbecue tonight and you're very welcome to come along.* 今晚有个烧烤野餐，非常欢迎你一起来。 **2** PHRASAL VERB When something or someone **comes along**, they occur or arrive by chance. 偶然出现；不期而至 ❑ *I waited a long time until a script came along that I thought was genuinely funny.* 我等了很久才碰巧拿到一个我认为着实滑稽的剧本。 **3** PHRASAL VERB If something **is coming along**, it is developing or making progress. 在进展 ❑ *Pentagon spokesman Williams says those talks are coming along quite well.* 五角大楼的发言人威廉姆斯说那些会谈在顺利进展中。

> in BRIT, also use **come round**

▸ **come around** **1** PHRASAL VERB If someone **comes around to** your house, they come there to see you. 来访 ❑ *Beth came around, this morning to apologize.* 贝思今天上午来道歉了。 **2** PHRASAL VERB If you **come around to** an idea, you eventually change your mind and accept it or agree with it. 转而接受 ❑ *It looks like they're coming around to our way of thinking.* 好像他们正在转而接受我们的思维方式。 **3** PHRASAL VERB When something **comes around**, it happens as a regular or predictable event. 如期而至 ❑ *I hope to be fit when the World Championship comes around next year.* 希望明年世界锦标赛再度举行时我能身体健康。 **4** PHRASAL VERB When someone who is unconscious **comes around**, they become conscious again. 苏醒 ❑ *When I came around I was on the kitchen floor.* 当我苏醒时，我躺在厨房地板上。

▸ **come at** PHRASAL VERB If a person or animal **comes at** you, they move towards you in a threatening way and try to attack you. 逼向 ❑ *He maintained that he was protecting himself from Mr. Cox, who came at him with an ax.* 他坚持说他是在自我防卫，因为考克斯先生手持斧头向他逼过来。

▸ **come back** **1** PHRASAL VERB If someone comes back to a place, they return to it. 回来 ❑ *He wanted to come back to Washington.* 他想回到华盛顿。 ❑ *She just wanted to go home and not come back.* 她只想回家而且不再回来。 **2** PHRASAL VERB If something that you had forgotten **comes back** to you, you remember it. (遗忘后重又) 回忆起 ❑ *I'll think of his name in a moment when it comes back to me.* 我想一下，一会儿就能记起他的名字来。 **3** PHRASAL VERB When something **comes back**, it becomes fashionable again. 再度流行 ❑ *I'm glad hats are coming back.* 我很高兴帽子再度流行起来。 **4** → see also **comeback**

▸ **come between** PHRASAL VERB If someone or something **comes between** two people, or **comes between** a person and a thing, they make the relationship or connection between them less close or happy. 妨碍 ❑ *I don't want this misunderstanding to come between us.* 我不想让这种误解妨碍我们之间的关系。

▸ **come by** PHRASAL VERB To **come by** something means to obtain it or find it. 得到；找到 ❑ *How did you come by that check?* 你怎么得到那张支票的？

▸ **come down** **1** PHRASAL VERB If the cost, level, or amount of something **comes down**, it becomes less than it was before. 下降 ❑ *Interest rates should come down.* 利率应下降。 ❑ *If you buy three bottles, the bottle price comes down to $10.* 如果你买3瓶的话，每瓶价格就降为10美元。 **2** PHRASAL VERB If something **comes down**, it falls to the ground. 落下 ❑ *The cold rain came down for hours.* 冷雨下了几个小时。

▸ **come down on** **1** PHRASAL VERB If you **come down on** one side of an argument, you declare that you support that side. 宣布支持 (某一方) ❑ *He clearly and decisively came down on the side of the president.* 他明确而坚定地宣布支持总统一方。 **2** PHRASAL VERB If you **come down on** someone, you criticize them severely or treat them strictly. 抨击 ❑ *If Douglas came down hard enough on him, Dale would rebel.* 如果道格拉斯过于猛烈地抨击他，戴尔将会反击。

▸ **come down to** PHRASAL VERB If a problem, decision, or question **comes down to** a particular thing, that thing is the most important factor involved. 主要涉及到 ❑ *The problem comes down to money.* 这个问题主要涉及到钱的问题。 ❑ *I think that it comes down to the fact that people do feel very dependent on their automobiles.* 我认为这主要涉及到人们的确感到非常依赖他们的汽车这样一个事实。

▸ **come down with** PHRASAL VERB If you **come down with** an illness, you get it. 得 (病) ❑ *Thomas came down with the chickenpox.* 托马斯得了水痘。

▸ **come for** PHRASAL VERB If people such as soldiers or police **come for** you, they come to find you, usually in order to harm you or take you away, for example to prison. (军方或警察) 抓捕 ❑ *Tanya was getting ready to fight if they came for her.* 坦娅做好了若他们来抓她就反抗的准备。

▸ **come forward** PHRASAL VERB If someone **comes forward**, they make themselves known and offer to help. 站出来 ❑ *A vital witness came forward to say that she saw Tanner wearing the boots.* 一位关键证人站出来说她看见坦纳穿着那双靴子。

▸ **come in** **1** PHRASAL VERB If information, a report, or a telephone call **comes in**, it is received. 传到 ❑ *Reports are now coming in of trouble at yet another jail.* 另一所监狱也发生了麻烦的各种报告不断传来。 **2** PHRASAL VERB If you have some money **coming in**, you receive it regularly as your income. 定期收取 (钱) ❑ *She had no money coming in and no funds.* 她既无固定收入也无存款。 **3** PHRASAL VERB If someone **comes in on** a discussion, arrangement, or task, they join it. 加入 ❑ *Can I come in here too, on both points?* 在这两点上我也能加入讨论吗？ **4** PHRASAL VERB When a new idea, fashion, or product **comes in**, it becomes popular or available. 流行 ❑ *It was just when attitudes were really beginning to change and lots of new ideas were coming in.* 那时正值人们的态度开始变化，许多新思想正在流行。 **5** PHRASAL VERB If you ask where something or someone **comes in**, you are asking what their role is in a particular matter. 充当…角色 ❑ *Rose asked again, "But where do we come in, Henry?"* 罗斯又问道，“那我们充当什么角色呢，亨利？” **6** PHRASAL VERB When the tide **comes in**, the water in the sea gradually moves so that it covers more of the land. 涨 ❑ *She became trapped as the tide came in.* 她在潮涨时被困住了。

▸ **come in for** PHRASAL VERB If someone or something **comes in** for criticism or blame, they receive it. 受到 ❑ *The plans have already come in for fierce criticism.* 这些计划已遭到激烈的批评。

▸ **come into** 1 PHRASAL VERB If someone **comes into** some money, some property, or a title, they inherit it. 继承 [no passive] ❑ *My father has just come into a fortune in diamonds.* 我父亲刚刚继承了一笔钻石。 2 PHRASAL VERB If someone or something **comes into** a situation, they have a role in it. 充当…角色 [no passive] ❑ *We don't really know where Hortense comes into all this, Inspector.* 我们真不知道霍滕斯在整个事件中是什么角色，检查员。

▸ **come off** 1 PHRASAL VERB If something **comes off**, it is successful or effective. 成功; 奏效 ❑ *It was a good try but it didn't really come off.* 这是一次好的尝试但未真正奏效。 2 PHRASAL VERB If someone **comes off** worst in a contest or conflict, they are in the worst position after it. If they **come off** best, they are in the best position. 结果 (最差、最好) ❑ *Some Democrats still have bitter memories of how they came off worst during the investigation.* 一些民主党人仍留有他们在调查中如何惨败的痛苦记忆。 3 CONVENTION You say **'come off it'** to someone to show them that you think what they are saying is untrue or wrong. 别胡扯

▸ **come on** 1 CONVENTION You say **'Come on'** to someone to encourage them to do something they do not want to do. 来吧 [SPOKEN] ❑ *Come on Doreen, let's dance.* 来吧，多琳，我们跳舞吧。 2 CONVENTION You say **'Come on'** to someone to encourage them to hurry up. 快点 [SPOKEN] ❑ *Come on, darling, we'll be late.* 快点，亲爱的，我们要迟到了。 3 PHRASAL VERB If you have an illness or a headache **coming on**, you can feel it starting. (疾病或头痛) 开始 ❑ *Tiredness and fever are much more likely to be a sign of the flu coming on.* 疲倦和发烧很有可能是流感开始的征兆。 4 PHRASAL VERB If something or someone **is coming on** well, they are developing well or making good progress. 进展 ❑ *Leah is coming on very well now and it's a matter of deciding how to fit her into the team.* 利亚现在进展得很顺利，目前的问题只是决定如何使她融入团队中。 5 PHRASAL VERB When something such as a machine or system **comes on**, it starts working or functioning. 开始运转 ❑ *The central heating was coming on and the ancient wooden boards creaked.* 中央供热系统一开始工作，年久老化的木板就嘎吱作响。

▸ **come on to** If someone **comes on to** you, they show that they are interested in starting a sexual relationship with you. (对异性) 献殷勤 [INFORMAL] ❑ *I met a guy at a party and he came on to me real hard.* 我在聚会上遇见一个小伙子，他对我大献殷勤。

▸ **come out** 1 PHRASAL VERB When a new product such as a book or CD **comes out**, it becomes available to the public. 上市 ❑ *The book comes out this week.* 该书本周上市。 2 PHRASAL VERB If a fact **comes out**, it becomes known to people. 为大家所知 ❑ *The truth is beginning to come out about what happened.* 所发生的事情真相开始为大家所知。 3 PHRASAL VERB When a gay person **comes out**, they let people know that they are gay. (同性恋者) 公开表明身份 ❑ *...the few gay men there who dare to come out.* …那里极少几个敢于公开表明身份的男同性恋者。 4 PHRASAL VERB To **come out** in a particular way means to be in the position or state described at the end of a process or event. 结果是 ❑ *In this grim little episode of recent American history, few people come out well.* 在这一小段严酷的美国近代历史中，没几人结果很好。 ❑ *So what makes a good marriage? Faithfulness comes out top of the list.* 那么什么可以造就成功的婚姻呢？忠诚是第一位的。 5 PHRASAL VERB If you **come out for** something, you declare that you support it. If you **come out against** something, you declare that you do not support it. 宣布 (支持、反对) ❑ *Its members had come out virtually unanimously against the tests.* 其成员实质上已一致宣布反对这些试验。 6 PHRASAL VERB When the sun, moon, or stars **come out**, they appear in the sky. (太阳、星星或月亮) 出来 ❑ *Oh, look! The sun's coming out!* 噢，看！太阳出来啦！ 7 PHRASAL VERB When a group of workers **comes out** on strike, they go on strike. 出来 (罢工) [BRIT]

in AM, use **go on strike**

▸ **come over** 1 PHRASAL VERB If a feeling or desire, especially a strange or surprising one, **comes over** you, it affects you strongly. 攫住 [no passive] ❑ *As I entered the hallway which led to my room that eerie feeling came over me.* 当我走进通向我房间的过道时，那种怪异的感觉攫住了我。 2 PHRASAL VERB If someone or what they are saying **comes over** in a particular way, they make that impression on people who meet them or are listening to them. 留下印象 ❑ *You come over as a capable and amusing companion.* 你让人觉得是一个能干而有趣的同伴。 3 PHRASAL VERB If someone comes over to your house or another place, they visit you there. 拜访 ❑ *Maybe I could come over to your house before the party?* 也许我可以在聚会前拜访你？

▸ **come round** → see **come around**

▸ **come through** 1 PHRASAL VERB To **come through** a dangerous or difficult situation means to survive it and recover from it. 度过 [no passive] ❑ *The city had faced racial crisis and come through it.* 该城曾面临种族危机，但现已度过难关了。 2 PHRASAL VERB If a feeling or message **comes through**, it is clearly shown in what is said or done. (感情或消息) 传出 ❑ *The message that comes through is that taxes will have to be raised.* 传出的消息是税收会被提高。 3 PHRASAL VERB If something **comes through**, it arrives, especially after some procedure has been carried out. 批准下达 ❑ *The father of the baby was waiting for his divorce to come through.* 婴儿的父亲正等着离婚协议批下来。 4 PHRASAL VERB If you **come through** with what is expected or needed from you, you succeed in doing or providing it. 兑现; 提供 ❑ *He puts his administration at risk if he doesn't come through on these promises for reform.* 如果他不能兑现这些改革的承诺，他将使他的政府处于危险境地。

▸ **come to** PHRASAL VERB When someone who is unconscious **comes to**, they become conscious. 苏醒 ❑ *When he came to and raised his head, he saw Barney.* 当他苏醒过来抬起头时看见了巴尼。

▸ **come under** 1 PHRASAL VERB If you **come under** attack or pressure, for example, people attack you or put pressure on you. 遭受 [no passive] ❑ *The police came under attack from angry crowds.* 警察遭到来自愤怒群众的攻击。 2 PHRASAL VERB If something **comes under** a particular authority, it is managed or controlled by that authority. 受…管辖 [no passive] ❑ *They were neglected before because they did not come under NATO.* 他们先前被忽视是因为他们不受北大西洋公约组织的管辖。 3 PHRASAL VERB If something **comes under** a particular heading, it is in the category mentioned. 归入 [no passive] ❑ *Her articles come under the heading of human interest.* 她的文章被归入人文关怀类。

▸ **come up** 1 PHRASAL VERB If someone **comes up** or **comes up to** you, they approach you until they are standing close to you. 走上前来 ❑ *Her cat came up and rubbed itself against their legs.* 她的猫上前来蹭了他们的腿。 2 PHRASAL VERB If something **comes up** in a conversation or meeting, it is mentioned or discussed. 被提及; 被讨论 ❑ *The subject came up at work.* 这一话题在工作时被提及。 3 PHRASAL VERB If something **is coming up**, it is about to happen or take place. 将发生 ❑ *We do have elections coming up.* 我们的确有选举即将举行。 4 PHRASAL VERB If something **comes up**, it happens unexpectedly. 意外发生 ❑ *I was delayed – something came up at home.* 我耽搁了——家里有事意外发生。 5 PHRASAL VERB If a job **comes up** or if something **comes up for** sale, it becomes available. 出现 ❑ *A research fellowship came up and I applied for it and got it.* 一项研究奖金出台，我申请并得到了。 6 PHRASAL VERB When the sun or moon **comes up**, it rises. (太阳、月亮) 升起 ❑ *It will be so great watching the sun come up.* 看着太阳升起将会很美妙。 7 PHRASAL VERB In law, when a case **comes up**, it is heard in a court of law. 上庭受审 ❑ *He is one of the reservists who will plead not guilty when their cases come up.* 他是其中一个在案件审理时将申辩无罪的后备役军人。

▸ **come up against** PHRASAL VERB If you **come up against** a problem or difficulty, you are faced with it and have to deal with it. 面临 ❑ *We came up against a great deal of resistance in dealing with the case.* 我们在处理该案件时碰到了很多阻力。

Come is used in a large number of expressions which are explained under other words in this dictionary. For example, the expression "to come to terms with something" is explained at "term."

come·back (comebacks) 1 N-COUNT If someone such as an entertainer or sports personality makes a **comeback**, they return to their profession or sport after a period away. 复出 ❑ *Sixties singing star Petula Clark is making a comeback.* 60年代的歌星佩图拉・克拉克要复出了。 2 N-COUNT If something makes a **comeback**, it becomes fashionable again. 再度流行 ❑ *Tight fitting T-shirts are making a comeback.* 紧身短袖圆领T恤衫再度流行起来。

co·median /kəmiːdiən/ (comedians) N-COUNT A **comedian** is an entertainer whose job is to make people laugh, by telling jokes or funny stories. 喜剧演员 ❑ *...a stand-up comedian.* …一位单人喜剧表演员。

com·edy ♦◇◇ /kɒmədi/ (comedies) 1 N-UNCOUNT **Comedy** consists of types of entertainment, such as plays and movies, or particular scenes in them, that are intended to make people laugh. 喜剧 ❑ *Actor Dom Deluise talks about his career in comedy.* 演员多姆・德卢

C

斯谈论他的喜剧事业。 **2** N-COUNT A **comedy** is a play, movie, or television program that is intended to make people laugh. 喜剧 ❑ *The movie is a romantic comedy.* 这部电影是一个浪漫喜剧。
→ see **genre, theater**

★ **com·et** /kɒmɪt/ (**comets**) N-COUNT A **comet** is a bright object with a long tail that travels around the sun. 彗星 ❑ *Halley's Comet is going to come back in 2061.* 哈雷彗星将在2061年返回。
→ see **solar**

com·fort ♦◇◇ /kʌmfərt/ (**comforts, comforting, comforted**) **1** N-UNCOUNT If you are doing something **in comfort**, you are physically relaxed and contented, and are not feeling any pain or other unpleasant sensations. 舒服 ❑ *This will enable the audience to sit in comfort while watching the shows.* 这能使观众看演出时舒服地坐着。 **2** N-UNCOUNT **Comfort** is a style of life in which you have enough money to have everything you need. 舒适 ❑ *Surely there is some way of ordering our busy lives so that we can live in comfort and find spiritual harmony too.* 一定会有办法把我们繁忙的生活安排得既舒适又能找到内心平静。 **3** N-UNCOUNT **Comfort** is what you feel when worries or unhappiness stop. 安慰 ❑ *He welcomed the truce, but pointed out it was of little comfort to families spending Christmas without a loved one.* 他欢迎休战，但指出这对于没有亲人共度圣诞节的家庭并无多少安慰。 ❑ *They will be able to take some comfort from inflation figures due on Friday.* 他们将会从预定在周五发布的通货膨胀数字中得到些安慰。 **4** N-COUNT If you refer to a person, thing, or idea as a **comfort**, you mean that it helps you to stop worrying or makes you feel less unhappy. 安慰 ❑ *It's a comfort talking to you.* 与你谈谈是一种安慰。 **5** N-COUNT **Comforts** are things which make your life easier and more pleasant, such as electrical devices you have in your home. 使生活舒适的东西 ❑ *She enjoys the material comforts married life has brought her.* 她享受着婚姻生活带给她的物质上的舒适。 **6** V-T If you **comfort** someone, you make them feel less worried, unhappy, or upset, for example by saying kind things to them. 安慰 ❑ *Ned put his arm around her, trying to comfort her.* 内德搂着她，试图安慰她。 **7** PHRASE If you say that something is, for example, **too** close **for comfort**, you mean you are worried because it is closer than you would like it to be. 因(比如太近)而使人不安的 ❑ *The bombs fell in the sea, many too close for comfort.* 那些炸弹落进了海里，很多落得太近而使人不安。

Word Partnership *comfort* 的常用搭配：
V. **find/take** comfort, **give/offer/provide** comfort **3**
N. comfort **level/zone**, **source of** comfort **3**
comfort ***someone*** **6**

com·fort·able ♦◇◇ /kʌmftəbᵊl, -fərtəbᵊl/ **1** ADJ If a piece of furniture or an item of clothing is **comfortable**, it makes you feel physically relaxed when you use it, for example because it is soft. 令人舒服的 ❑ *...a comfortable fireside chair.* …一把令人舒服的炉边椅子。 **2** ADJ If a building or room is **comfortable**, it makes you feel physically relaxed when you spend time in it, for example because it is warm and has nice furniture. 令人舒适的 ❑ *A home should be comfortable and friendly.* 家应使人感到舒适与和睦。 ● **com·fort·ably** ADV 令人舒适地 ❑ *...the comfortably furnished living room.* …布置舒适的起居室。 **3** ADJ If you are **comfortable**, you are physically relaxed because of the place or position you are sitting or lying in. 感到舒服的 ❑ *Lie down on your bed and make yourself comfortable.* 躺在床上让你自己舒服些。 ● **com·fort·ably** ADV 感到舒服地 [ADV with v] ❑ *Are you sitting comfortably?* 你坐得舒服吗？ **4** ADJ If you say that someone is **comfortable**, you mean that they have enough money to be able to live without financial problems. 宽裕的 ❑ *"Is he rich?"—"He's comfortable."* "他富有吗？"——"他生活宽裕。" ● **com·fort·ably** ADV 宽裕地 ❑ *Cayton describes himself as comfortably well-off.* 凯顿把自己描述为生活很富裕。 **5** ADJ In a race, competition, or election, if you have a **comfortable** lead, you are likely to win it easily. If you gain a **comfortable** victory or majority, you win easily. 轻易的 [ADJ n] ❑ *By half distance we held a comfortable two-lap lead.* 赛程未过半我们就轻易领先了两圈。 ● **com·fort·ably** ADV 轻易地 [ADV with v] ❑ *...the Los Angeles Raiders, who comfortably beat the Bears earlier in the season.* …曾在本赛季的早些时候轻易地击败了熊队的洛杉矶袭击者队。 **6** ADJ If you feel **comfortable with** a particular situation or person, you feel confident and relaxed with them. 轻松的；自在的 [v-link ADJ] ❑ *Nervous politicians might well feel more comfortable with a step-by-step approach.* 紧张不安的政治家们也许会对逐步解决问题的方式感到更轻松些。 ❑ *He liked me and I felt comfortable with him.* 他喜欢我，而我和他在一起也感觉轻松自在。 ● **com·fort·ably** ADV 轻松地；自在地 [ADV after v] ❑ *They talked comfortably of their plans.* 他们轻松地讨论了他们的计划。 **7** ADJ When a sick or injured person is said to be **comfortable**, they are without pain. 无痛苦的 ❑ *He was described as comfortable in the hospital last night.* 据说昨晚他在医院里没有感到痛苦。

Thesaurus *comfortable* 另参见：
ADV. comfy, cozy, soft; (*ant.*) uncomfortable **1**
relaxed, untroubled **3**
well-off **4**

com·fort·ably /kʌmftəbli, -fərtəbli/ **1** ADV If you manage to do something **comfortably**, you do it easily. 容易地 [ADV with v] ❑ *Only take upon yourself those things that you know you can manage comfortably.* 只承担那些你知道你能轻松完成的事情。 **2** → see also **comfortable**

com·fort·er /kʌmfərtər/ (**comforters**) **1** N-COUNT A **comforter** is a person or thing that comforts you. 安慰者 ❑ *He became Vivien Leigh's devoted friend and comforter.* 他成了费雯丽的忠实朋友和安慰者。 **2** N-COUNT A **comforter** is a large cover filled with feathers or similar material that you use like a blanket. (羽绒或其他类似材料填充的) 夹被 [AM]

in BRIT, use **duvet, quilt**

com·fort·ing /kʌmfərtɪŋ/ ADJ If you say that something is **comforting**, you mean it makes you feel less worried or unhappy. 令人安慰的 ❑ *My mother had just died and I found the book very comforting.* 我母亲刚去世，我发现这本书能使我感到安慰。

com·fy /kʌmfi/ (**comfier, comfiest**) ADJ A **comfy** item of clothing, piece of furniture, room, or position is a comfortable one. 舒服的 [INFORMAL] ❑ *...a comfy chair.* …一把舒服的椅子

com·ic /kɒmɪk/ (**comics**) **1** ADJ If you describe something as **comic**, you mean that it makes you laugh, and is often intended to make you laugh. 喜剧的 ❑ *The novel is comic and tragic.* 这本小说兼有喜剧和悲剧的特点。 **2** ADJ **Comic** is used to describe funny entertainment, and the actors and entertainers who perform it. 滑稽的 [ADJ n] ❑ *Grodin is a fine comic actor.* 格罗丁是一位好的滑稽演员。 **3** N-COUNT A **comic** is an entertainer who tells jokes in order to make people laugh. 喜剧演员 ❑ *...the funniest comic in America.* …美国最有趣的喜剧演员。 **4** N-SING The **comics** is the part of a newspaper that contains the comic strips. (报刊的) 连环漫画栏 ❑ *She read the comics in the Philadelphia Inquirer.* 她看了《费城调查者报》的连环漫画。 **5** N-COUNT A **comic** is a magazine that contains stories told in pictures. 连环漫画 [mainly BRIT]

in AM, usually use **comic book**

comi·cal /kɒmɪkᵊl/ ADJ If you describe something as **comical**, you mean that it makes you laugh because it is funny or silly. 滑稽的 ❑ *Her expression is almost comical.* 她的表情几乎有点儿滑稽。

com·ic book (**comic books**) N-COUNT A **comic book** is a magazine that contains stories told in pictures. 连环漫画杂志 [mainly AM]

in BRIT, usually use **comic**

❑ *...comic book heroes such as Spider Man.* …连环漫画杂志中的男主角，如蜘蛛人。

com·ing ♦♦♦ /kʌmɪŋ/ **1** ADJ A **coming** event or time is an event or time that will happen soon. 即将发生的 [ADJ n] ❑ *This obviously depends on the weather in the coming months.* 这明显取决于接下来几个月的天气。 **2** → see also **come**

▲ **com·ma** /kɒmə/ (**commas**) N-COUNT A **comma** is the punctuation mark , which is used to separate parts of a sentence or items in a list. 逗号

com·mand ♦◇◇ /kəmænd/ (**commands, commanding, commanded**) **1** V-T If someone in authority **commands** you to do something, they tell you that you must do it. 命令 [mainly WRITTEN] ❑ *He commanded his troops to attack.* 他命令他的部队进攻。 ❑ *"Get in your car and follow me," she commanded.* "上车然后跟我来，"她命令道。 ● N-VAR **Command** is also a noun. 命令 ❑ *The tanker failed to respond to a command to stop.* 油轮未能对停止前进的指令做出反应。 ❑ *I closed my eyes at his command.* 我听从他的命令闭上了眼睛。 **2** V-T If you **command** something such as respect or obedience, you obtain it because you are popular, famous, or important. 博得 [no cont] ❑ *...an excellent physician who commanded the respect of all her colleagues.* …一位博得所有同事尊敬的杰出医生。 **3** V-T If an army or country **commands** a place, they have total control over it. 完全控制 ❑ *Yemen commands the strait at the southern end of the Red Sea.* 也门

完全控制着红海南端的海峡。 ● N-UNCOUNT **Command** is also a noun. 完全控制权 ❑ *...the struggle for command of the air.* …对制空权的争夺。 **4** V-T An officer who **commands** part of an army, navy, or air force is responsible for controlling and organizing it. 指挥 ❑ *...the French general who commands the U.N. troops in the region.* …指挥着这一地区联合国部队的法国将军。 ● N-UNCOUNT **Command** is also a noun. 指挥 ❑ *...a small garrison under the command of Major James Craig.* …一小支在詹姆斯·克雷格少校指挥下的卫戍部队。 **5** N-COUNT-COLL In the armed forces, a **command** is a group of officers who are responsible for organizing and controlling part of an army, navy, or air force. 指挥部 ❑ *He had authorization from the military command to retaliate.* 他得到了军事指挥部进行还击的授权。 **6** N-COUNT In computing, a **command** is an instruction that you give to a computer. 指令 ❑ *I entered the command into my navigational computer.* 我把指令输入了我的导航计算机。 **7** N-UNCOUNT If someone has **command** of a situation, they have control of it because they have, or seem to have, power or authority. 控制(局面等) ❑ *Mr. Baker would take command of the campaign.* 贝克先生将负责这次运动。 **8** N-UNCOUNT Your **command of** something, such as a foreign language, is your knowledge of it and your ability to use this knowledge. 掌握 ❑ *His command of English was excellent.* 他的英语相当出色。 **9** PHRASE If you have a particular skill or particular resources **at** your **command**, you have them and can use them fully. 掌控 ❑ *The country should have the right to defend itself with all legal means at its command.* 这个国家应该有权动用它所掌控的所有法律手段来捍卫自己。

com·man·dant /kɒməndænt/ (**commandants**) N-COUNT; N-TITLE A **commandant** is an army officer in charge of a particular place or group of people. 指挥官

com·mand econo·my (**command economies**) N-COUNT In a **command economy**, business activities and the use of resources are decided by the government, and not by market forces. 计划经济 [BUSINESS] ❑ *...the Czech Republic's transition from a command economy to a market system.* …捷克共和国从计划经济到市场体制的转变。

com·mand·er ♦◊◊ /kəmændər/ (**commanders**) **1** N-COUNT; N-TITLE; N-VOC A **commander** is an officer in charge of a military operation or organization. 指挥官；司令官 ❑ *The commander and some of the men had been released.* 指挥官和一些士兵已被释放。 **2** N-COUNT; N-TITLE; N-VOC A **commander** is an officer in the U.S. Navy or the Royal Navy. 海军军官

com·mand·ing /kəmændɪŋ/ **1** ADJ If you are in a **commanding** position or situation, you are in a strong or powerful position or situation. 支配的 ❑ *Right now you're in a more commanding position than you have been for ages.* 此刻你处于长久以来未达到的统治地位。 **2** ADJ If you describe someone as **commanding**, you mean that they are powerful and confident. 威严的 [APPROVAL] ❑ *Lovett was a tall, commanding man with a waxed gray mustache.* 洛维特是一位留着灰白短髭、高个子的威严男人。 **3** → see also **command**

com·man·do /kəmændoʊ/ (**commandos** or **commandoes**) **1** N-COUNT A **commando** is a group of soldiers who have been specially trained to carry out surprise attacks. 突击队 ❑ *...a small commando of marines.* …一小支海军突击队。 **2** N-COUNT A **commando** is a soldier who is a member of a commando. 突击队员 ❑ *...small groups of American commandos.* …美国突击队队员的几个小组。

Word Link *memor ≈ memory : commemorate, memorial, memory*

★ **com·memo·rate** /kəmɛməreɪt/ (**commemorates, commemorating, commemorated**) V-T To **commemorate** an important event or person means to remember them by means of a special action, ceremony, or specially created object. 纪念 ❑ *One room contained a gallery of paintings commemorating great moments in baseball history.* 有一间房间里有一个画廊，陈列着纪念棒球史上伟大时刻的绘画作品。 ● **com·memo·ra·tion** /kəmɛməreɪʃᵊn/ N-VAR (**commemorations**) 纪念 ❑ *...a march in commemoration of Malcolm X.* …一次为纪念马尔科姆·艾克斯而举行的游行。

com·memo·ra·tive /kəmɛmərətɪv, -əreɪtɪv/ ADJ A **commemorative** object or event is intended to make people remember a particular event or person. 纪念性的 [ADJ n] ❑ *A commemorative stamp will be issued October 15.* 一枚纪念邮票将于10月15日发行。

com·mence /kəmɛns/ (**commences, commencing, commenced**) V-T/V-I When something **commences** or you **commence** it, it begins. 使…开始；开始 [FORMAL] ❑ *The academic year commences at the beginning of October.* 该学年于10月初开始。 ❑ *They commenced a systematic search.* 他们开始了系统的搜查。

> **Commence**, **start**, and **begin** all have a similar meaning, although **commence** is more formal and is not normally used in conversation. ❑ *The meeting is ready to begin... He tore the list up and started a fresh one. ...an alternative to commencing the process of European integration.* Note that **begin**, **start**, and **commence** can all be followed by an -ing form or a noun, but only **begin** and **start** can be followed by a "to" infinitive.

▲ **com·mence·ment** /kəmɛnsmənt/ (**commencements**) **1** N-UNCOUNT The **commencement** of something is its beginning. 开始 [FORMAL] ❑ *All applicants should be at least 16 years of age at the commencement of this course.* 所有申请人在本课程开始时应至少年满16岁。 **2** N-VAR **Commencement** is a ceremony at a university, college, or high school at which students formally receive their degrees or diplomas. 毕业典礼 [AM]

in BRIT, use **graduation**

❑ *President Bush gave the commencement address today at the University of Notre Dame.* 布什总统今天在巴黎圣母院大学发表了毕业典礼演说。

★ **com·mend** /kəmɛnd/ (**commends, commending, commended**) **1** V-T If you **commend** someone or something, you praise them formally. 表扬；称赞 [FORMAL] ❑ *I commended her for that action.* 我表扬了她的那次表现。 ❑ *The reports commend her bravery.* 报告称赞她的英勇。 ● **com·men·da·tion** /kɒməndeɪʃᵊn/ N-COUNT (**commendations**) 表扬；称赞 ❑ *Clare won a commendation for bravery in 1998 after risking his life at the scene of a gas blast.* 1998年克莱尔因在一次瓦斯爆炸现场甘冒生命危险的勇敢行为而荣获嘉奖。 **2** V-T If someone **commends** a person or thing **to** you, they tell you that you will find them good or useful. 推荐 [FORMAL] ❑ *I can commend it to him as a realistic course of action.* 我可以把它作为一套现实的行动方案推荐给他。

com·mend·able /kəmɛndəbᵊl/ ADJ If you describe someone's behavior as **commendable**, you approve of it or are praising it. 值得称赞的 [FORMAL, APPROVAL] ❑ *He has acted with commendable speed.* 他以值得称赞的速度付诸了行动。

com·ment ♦♦◊ /kɒmɛnt/ (**comments, commenting, commented**) **1** V-T/V-I If you **comment on** something, you give your opinion about it or you give an explanation for it. 评论；解释 ❑ *So far, Mr. Cook has not commented on these reports.* 到目前为止，库克先生还未对这些报告进行过评论。 ❑ *You really can't comment until you know the facts.* 你的确不能在你知道事实之前进行评论。 ❑ *One student commented that she preferred literature to social science.* 一位学生解释说，较之于社会科学她更喜欢文学。

> If you **comment** on a situation, or make a **comment** about it, you give your opinion on it. ❑ *Mr. Cook has not commented on these reports... I was wondering whether you had any comments.* If you **mention** something, you say it, but only briefly, especially when you have not talked about it before. ❑ *He mentioned that he might go to New York.* If you **remark** on something, or make a **remark** about it, you say what you think or what you have noticed, often in a casual way. ❑ *Visitors remark on how well the children look.* ❑ *General Sutton's remarks about the conflict.*

2 N-VAR A **comment** is something that you say which expresses your opinion of something or which gives an explanation of it. 评论；解释 ❑ *He made his comments at a news conference in Amsterdam.* 他在阿姆斯特丹的一次记者招待会上做了评论。 ❑ *There's been no comment so far from police about the allegations.* 到目前为止还没有来自警方的对那些指控的任何解释。 **3** CONVENTION People say **"no comment"** as a way of refusing to answer a question, usually when it is asked by a journalist. 无可奉告 ❑ *No comment. I don't know anything.* 无可奉告。我什么也不知道。

Word Partnership *comment* 的常用搭配：

V.	**refuse to** comment **1**
	make a comment **2**
PREP.	comment **on** *someone/something* **1**
	comment **about** *something* **2**
ADJ.	**further** comment **2**

★ **com·men·tary** /kɒmənteri/ (**commentaries**) **1** N-VAR A **commentary** is a description of an event that is broadcast on radio or television while the event is taking place. 实况报道

❑ *He gave the listening crowd a running commentary.* 他为听众进行了实况报道。 **2** N-COUNT A **commentary** is an article or book which explains or discusses something. 评论性文章（或书籍） ❑ *Ms. Rich will be writing a twice-weekly commentary on American society and culture.* 里奇女士将就美国社会和文化每周写两篇评论文章。 **3** N-UNCOUNT **Commentary** is discussion or criticism of something. 评论 [also "a" N, with supp] ❑ *The show mixed comedy with social commentary.* 这个节目把喜剧和社会评论结合了起来。

C

com·men·tate /kɒmənteɪt/ (**commentates, commentating, commentated**) V-I To **commentate** means to give a radio or television commentary on an event. (电台或电视的) 解说 ❑ *They are in New Hampshire to commentate on the ice hockey.* 他们在新罕布什尔州解说冰球比赛。

com·men·ta·tor ♦◇◇ /kɒmənteɪtər/ (**commentators**) **1** N-COUNT A **commentator** is a broadcaster who gives a radio or television commentary on an event. (电台或电视的) 解说员 ❑ *...a sports commentator.* …一名体育解说员。 **2** N-COUNT A **commentator** is also someone who often writes or broadcasts about a particular subject. 评论员 ❑ *...a political commentator.* …一名政治评论员。

Word Link *merc ≈ trading : commerce, merchandise, merchant*

com·merce ♦◇◇ /kɒmɜrs/ **1** N-UNCOUNT **Commerce** is the activities and procedures involved in buying and selling things. 商业 ❑ *They have made their fortunes from industry and commerce.* 他们从工商业中发了财。 **2** → see also **chamber of commerce**
→ see **stock market**

com·mer·cial ♦♦◇ /kəmɜrʃəl/ (**commercials**) **1** ADJ **Commercial** means involving or relating to the buying and selling of goods. 商业的 ❑ *Baltimore in its heyday was a major center of industrial and commercial activity.* 巴尔的摩在其鼎盛时期曾是工商业活动的主要中心。 **2** ADJ **Commercial** organizations and activities are concerned with making money or profits, rather than, for example, with scientific research or providing a public service. 商业化的 ❑ *The company has indeed become more commercial over the past decade.* 这个公司在过去的十年里确实已变得越来越商业化了。 ❑ *Conservationists in Chile are concerned over the effect of commercial exploitation of forests.* 智利的自然保护者对森林商业化开发的后果感到担忧。 ● **com·mer·cial·ly** ADV 商业化地 ❑ *The plane will be commercially viable if 400 can be sold.* 这飞机若能售出400架从商业上看就可行。 **3** ADJ A **commercial** product is made to be sold to the public. 商业性的 [ADJ n] ❑ *They are the leading manufacturer in both defense and commercial products.* 他们在防御性和商业性的产品方面都是领先的制造商。 ● **com·mer·cial·ly** ADV 商业性地 ❑ *It was the first commercially available machine to employ artificial intelligence.* 这是第一台具有商业价值的人工智能机器。 **4** ADJ A **commercial** vehicle is a vehicle used for carrying goods, or passengers who pay. 商用的 ❑ *The route is used every day by many hundreds of commercial vehicles.* 这条路线每天都有成百辆商用车通过。 **5** ADJ **Commercial** television and radio are paid for by the broadcasting of advertisements, rather than by the government. 商业化的 (电视或广播) ❑ *There were no commercial radio stations until 1920.* 直到1920年才有了商业电台。 **6** ADJ **Commercial** is used to describe something such as a movie or a type of music that it is intended to be popular with the public, and is not very original or of high quality. 商业化的 (电影或音乐) ❑ *There's a feeling among a lot of people that music has become too commercial.* 许多人都感到音乐已变得太商业化了。 **7** N-COUNT A **commercial** is an advertisement that is broadcast on television or radio. 电视或电台广告 ❑ *Turn the channel – there are too many commercials.* 转换一下频道——太多广告了。
→ see **advertising**

> A **commercial** is a form of advertising done on the radio or television. **Advertisements** that appear in newspapers, magazines or on the internet are not called commercials. Newspapers allow individuals to post notices for selling items or announcing job vacancies. These are called **classified ads** or (in the US only) **want ads**.

com·mer·cial bank (**commercial banks**) N-COUNT A **commercial bank** is a bank whose main customers are businesses. 商业银行 [BUSINESS]

com·mer·cial break (**commercial breaks**) N-COUNT A **commercial break** is the interval during a commercial television program, or between programs, during which advertisements are shown. 插播广告时间 ❑ *The movie was aired without commercial breaks.* 该电影是无广告插播连续播出的。

com·mer·cial·ise /kəmɜːʃəlaɪz/ [BRIT] → see **commercialize**

★ **com·mer·cial·ism** /kəmɜrʃəlɪzəm/ N-UNCOUNT **Commercialism** is the practice of making a lot of money from things without caring about their quality. 商业主义 [DISAPPROVAL] ❑ *Koons has engrossed himself in a world of commercialism that most modern artists disdain.* 孔斯已沉醉于多数现代艺术家所鄙视的商业主义世界。

com·mer·cial·ize /kəmɜrʃəlaɪz/ (**commercializes, commercializing, commercialized**)

in BRIT, also use **commercialise**

V-T If something **is commercialized**, it is used or changed in such a way that it makes money or profits, often in a way that people disapprove of. 使…商业化 [usu passive] [DISAPPROVAL] ❑ *It seems such a pity that a distinguished and honored name should be commercialized in this way.* 一个著名的、受尊重的名字如此被商业化似乎太可惜了。 ● **com·mer·cial·ized** ADJ 商业化的 ❑ *Rock'n'roll has become so commercialized and safe since punk.* 摇滚乐自朋克摇滚出现以后已经变得非常商业化和安全了。 ● **com·mer·ciali·za·tion** /kəmɜrʃəlɪzeɪʃən/ N-UNCOUNT 商业化 ❑ *...the commercialization of Christmas.* …圣诞节的商业化。

com·mis·sion ♦♦◇ /kəmɪʃən/ (**commissions, commissioning, commissioned**) **1** V-T If you **commission** something or **commission** someone **to** do something, you formally arrange for someone to do a piece of work for you. 委托 ❑ *The Department of Agriculture commissioned a study into organic farming.* 农业部委托了一项有机耕作的研究。 ❑ *You can commission them to paint something especially for you.* 你可以委托他们专门为你画点什么。 ● N-VAR **Commission** is also a noun. 委托 ❑ *Our china can be bought off the shelf or by commission.* 我们的瓷器可以现货购买或委托定做。 **2** N-COUNT A **commission** is a piece of work that someone is asked to do and is paid for. 委托任务 ❑ *Just a few days ago, I finished a commission.* 就在几天之前我完成了一项委托任务。 **3** N-VAR **Commission** is a sum of money paid to a salesperson for every sale that he or she makes. If a salesperson is paid **on commission**, the amount they receive depends on the amount they sell. 销售佣金 ❑ *The salespeople work on commission only.* 推销员只拿销售佣金。 **4** N-UNCOUNT If a bank or other company charges **commission**, they charge a fee for providing a service, for example for exchanging money or issuing an insurance policy. 服务费 [BUSINESS] ❑ *Travel agents charge 1 per cent commission on tickets.* 旅行社收1%的购票服务费。 **5** N-COUNT-COLL A **commission** is a group of people who have been appointed to find out about something or to control something. 委员会 ❑ *The government has set up a commission to look into those crimes.* 政府已成立一个委员会调查那些罪行。 **6** N-COUNT If a member of the armed forces receives a **commission**, he or she becomes an officer. 任命 ❑ *He accepted a commission as a naval officer.* 他接受了海军军官的任命。

▲ **com·mis·sion·er** ♦◇◇ /kəmɪʃənər/ (**commissioners**) also **Commissioner** N-COUNT A **commissioner** is an important official in a government department or other organization. (政府部门等的) 重要官员 ❑ *...Alaska's commissioner of education.* …阿拉斯加州的教育要员。

com·mit ♦♦◇ /kəmɪt/ (**commits, committing, committed**) **1** V-T If someone **commits** a crime or a sin, they do something illegal or bad. 犯 (罪); 做 (坏事) ❑ *I have never committed any crime.* 我从没有犯过任何罪。 ❑ *This is a man who has committed murder.* 这是个犯了谋杀罪的男人。 **2** V-T If someone **commits suicide**, they deliberately kill themselves. 进行 (自杀) ❑ *There are unconfirmed reports he tried to commit suicide.* 有未经证实的报道说他曾企图自杀。 **3** V-T If you **commit** money or resources **to** something, you decide to use them for a particular purpose. 调拨 (钱、资源) ❑ *They called on Western nations to commit more money to the poorest nations.* 他们号召西方国家为最贫困国家拨更多的款。 ❑ *The company had committed thousands of dollars for a plan to reduce mercury emissions.* 该公司已经为了一项减少汞排放的计划调拨了数千美元。 **4** V-T/V-I If you **commit yourself to** something, you say that you will definitely do it. If you **commit yourself to** someone, you decide that you want to have a long-term relationship with them. 使 (自己) 致力于; 使 (自己) 承诺 (与某人的长期关系) ❑ *I would advise people to think very carefully about committing themselves to working Sundays.* 我会建议人们认真考虑答应周日工作。 ❑ *I'd like a friendship that might lead to something deeper, but I wouldn't want to commit myself too soon.* 我想要可

能发展到更深层关系的友谊，但我不想太快做出承诺。❑ *He won't commit.* 他不会承诺。 **5** V-T If you do not want to **commit yourself on** something, you do not want to say what you really think about it or what you are going to do. (就某事) 表态 [with brd-neg] ❑ *It isn't their diplomatic style to commit themselves on such a delicate issue.* 就如此微妙的问题表态不是他们的外交风格。 **6** V-T If someone **is committed to** a mental hospital, prison, or other institution, they are officially sent there for a period of time. 送交 (到精神病院、监狱等) [usu passive] ❑ *Arthur's drinking caused him to be committed to a psychiatric hospital.* 阿瑟酗酒导致他被关进了一家精神病院。 **7** V-T If you **commit** something **to** paper or **to** writing, you record it by writing it down. If you **commit** something **to** memory, you learn it so that you will remember it. 记 (在纸上、记忆中) ❑ *She had not committed anything to paper about it.* 她还没有把关于它的任何东西记在纸上。

Word Partnership *commit* 的常用搭配：

N. commit **a crime** 1
commit **suicide** 2
commit **resources** 3
commit **to** ***something*** 4
commit **to memory** 7

com·mit·ment ◆◆◇ /kəmɪtmənt/ (**commitments**) **1** N-UNCOUNT **Commitment** is a strong belief in an idea or system. 信奉 ❑ *...commitment to the ideals of democracy.* …对民主理想的信奉。 **2** N-COUNT A **commitment** is something which regularly takes up some of your time because of an agreement you have made or because of responsibilities that you have. 投身的事 ❑ *I've got a lot of commitments.* 我有很多要做的事。 **3** N-COUNT If you make a **commitment to** do something, you promise that you will do it. 承诺 ❑ *We made a commitment to keep working together.* 我们作了承诺要继续在一起工作。 **4** N-VAR **Commitment** is the process of officially sending someone to a prison or a hospital. 送交 (监狱、医院) [AM]

in BRIT, use **committal**

❑ *State law allows involuntary commitment for psychiatric evaluation.* 州法律允许强行送至医院进行精神病诊断。

Word Partnership *commitment* 的常用搭配：

ADJ. **deep/firm/strong** commitment 1
long-term commitment, **prior** commitment 3
N. ***someone's*** commitment 1 – 3
PREP. commitment **to** ***someone/something*** 2 3
V. **make a** commitment 3

com·mit·tal /kəmɪtᵊl/ (**committals**) N-VAR **1** **Committal** is the process of officially sending someone to a prison or a hospital. 收监；入 (医) 院 **2** → see also **commitment**

com·mit·tee ◆◆◆ /kəmɪti/ (**committees**) N-COUNT-COLL A **committee** is a group of people who meet to make decisions or plans for a larger group or organization that they represent. 委员会 ❑ *...the school yearbook committee.* …学校年鉴编委会。

★ **com·mod·ity** /kəmɒdɪti/ (**commodities**) N-COUNT A **commodity** is something that is sold for money. 商品 [BUSINESS] ❑ *Prices went up on several basic commodities like bread and meat.* 面包、肉等几种基本商品的价格上涨了。
→ see **economics, stock market**

com·mon ◆◆◆ /kɒmən/ (**commons**) **1** ADJ If something is **common**, it is found in large numbers or it happens often. 常见的 ❑ *His name was Hansen, a common name in Norway.* 他叫汉森，一个在挪威很常见的名字。 ❑ *Oil pollution is the most common cause of death for seabirds.* 石油污染是海鸟死亡的最常见的原因。 ● **com·mon·ly** ADV 常见地 [ADV with v] ❑ *Parsley is one of the most commonly used herbs.* 欧芹是最常用的草药之一。 **2** ADJ If something is **common to** two or more people or groups, it is done, possessed, or used by them all. 共同的；共有的；共用的 ❑ *Moldavians and Romanians share a common language.* 摩尔达维亚人和罗马尼亚人使用一种共同的语言。 **3** ADJ When there are more animals or plants of a particular species than there are of related species, then the first species is called **common**. (物种) 常见的 [ADJ n] ❑ *...the common house fly.* …常见的家蝇。 **4** ADJ **Common** is used to indicate that someone or something is of the ordinary kind and not special in any way. 普通的 [ADJ n] ❑ *Democracy might elevate the common man to a position of political superiority.* 民主可能会让普通人升至政治上优越的位置。 **5** ADJ **Common** decency or **common** courtesy is the decency or courtesy which most people have. You usually talk about this when someone has not shown these characteristics in their behavior to show your disapproval of them. 起码的 (修养、礼貌等) [DISAPPROVAL] ❑ *It is common decency to give your seat to anyone in greater need.* 把座位让给更需要的人是起码的修养。 **6** ADJ You can use **common** to describe knowledge, an opinion, or a feeling that is shared by people in general. 普遍的 (知识、观点、情感等) [ADJ n] ❑ *It is common knowledge that swimming is one of the best forms of exercise.* 游泳是最好的运动之一是普遍常识。 ● **com·mon·ly** ADV 普遍地 [ADV -ed] ❑ *A little adolescent rebellion is commonly believed to be healthy.* 少许青春期叛逆被普遍认为是一个健康的现象。 **7** ADJ If you describe someone or their behavior as **common**, you mean that they show a lack of taste, education, and good manners. 粗俗的 [mainly BRIT, DISAPPROVAL] ❑ *She might be a little common at times, but she was certainly not boring.* 她也许有时会有点儿粗俗，但她绝不令人厌烦。 **8** N-COUNT; N-IN-NAMES A **common** is an area of grassy land, usually in or near a village or small town, where the public is allowed to go. 公共草地 ❑ *We are warning women not to go out on to the common alone.* 我们在告诫女性不要单独去公共草地。 **9** PHRASE If two or more things have something **in common**, they have the same characteristic or feature. 共同的 (特点等) ❑ *The oboe and the clarinet have certain features in common.* 双簧管和单簧管有某些共同特点。 **10** PHRASE If two or more people have something **in common**, they share the same interests or experiences. 共同的 (兴趣或经历) ❑ *He had very little in common with his sister.* 他和他姐姐几乎没有相同之处。 **11** **common ground** → see **ground**

Thesaurus *common* 另参见：

ADJ. frequent, typical, usual 1
commonplace, everyday; *(ant.)* special 4
accepted, standard, universal 6

Word Partnership *common* 的常用搭配：

ADV. **fairly/increasingly/more/most** common 1
N. common **belief**, common **language**, common **practice**, common **problem** 1 2
V. **have** ***something*** **in** common 9 10

com·mon law **1** N-UNCOUNT **Common law** is the system of law which is based on judges' decisions and on custom rather than on written laws. 习惯法 ❑ *Canadian libel law is based on English common law.* 加拿大的诽谤法是以英国的习惯法为根据的。 **2** ADJ A **common law** relationship is regarded as a marriage because it has lasted a long time, although no official marriage contract has been signed. 按习惯法结合的 [ADJ n] ❑ *...his common law wife.* …他按习惯法结合的妻子。

com·mon noun (**common nouns**) N-COUNT A **common noun** is a noun such as "tree," "water," or "beauty" that is not the name of one particular person or thing. Compare **proper noun**. 普通名词

★ **common·place** /kɒmənpleɪs/ ADJ If something is **commonplace**, it happens often or is often found, and is therefore not surprising. 常见的 ❑ *Inter-racial marriages have become commonplace.* 不同种族间的通婚已经变得很常见。

com·mon sense also **commonsense** N-UNCOUNT Your **common sense** is your natural ability to make good judgments and to behave in a practical and sensible way. 直觉决断力 ❑ *Use your common sense.* 用用你的直觉决断力。 ❑ *She always had a lot of common sense.* 她总有很好的直觉决断力。

com·mon stock **1** N-UNCOUNT **Common stock** refers to the shares in a company that are owned by people who have a right to vote at the company's meetings and to receive part of the company's profits after the holders of preferred stock have been paid. 普通股 [AM, BUSINESS]

in BRIT, use **ordinary shares**

❑ *The company priced its offering of 2.7 million shares of common stock at 20 cents a share.* 该公司将所提供的270万份普通股定价为每股20美分。
2 → see also **preferred stock**

★ **common·wealth** /kɒmənwɛlθ/ **1** N-PROPER **The commonwealth** is an organization consisting of the United Kingdom and most of the countries that were previously under its rule. 英联邦 ❑ *...the Asian, Caribbean and African members of the commonwealth.* …英联邦在亚洲、加勒比海和非洲的成员国。 **2** N-IN-NAMES **Commonwealth** is used in the official names of

C

some countries, groups of countries, or parts of countries. 联邦 ❑ *...the Commonwealth of Australia.* …澳大利亚联邦。

▲ **com·mo·tion** /kəmoʊʃ°n/ (**commotions**) N-VAR A **commotion** is a lot of noise, confusion, and excitement. 骚动 ❑ *He heard a commotion outside.* 他听到外面一阵骚动。

▲ **com·mu·nal** /kəmyun°l/ 1 ADJ **Communal** means relating to particular groups in a country or society. 团体的 [ADJ n] ❑ *Communal violence broke out in different parts of the country.* 团体暴力冲突在该国不同地区爆发了。 2 ADJ You use **communal** to describe something that is shared by a group of people. 共有的 ❑ *The inmates ate in a communal dining room.* 同狱室的人在一个公共饭厅吃饭。

com·mune /kɒmyun/ (**communes**) N-COUNT A **commune** is a group of people who live together and share many of their possessions and responsibilities. 群居团体 ❑ *Mack lived in a commune.* 麦克住在一个群居团体里。

Word Link *commun ≈ sharing : communicate, communism, community*

com·mu·ni·cate ♦◇◇ /kəmyunɪkeɪt/ (**communicates, communicating, communicated**) 1 V-RECIP If you **communicate with** someone, you share or exchange information with them, for example by speaking, writing, or using equipment. You can also say that two people **communicate**. 交流 ❑ *My birth mother has never communicated with me.* 我的生母从未与我交流过。 ❑ *Officials of the CIA depend heavily on e-mail to communicate with each other.* 中情局的官员们很大程度上靠电子邮件相互交流。 ● **com·mu·ni·ca·tion** N-UNCOUNT 交流 [oft N "with/between" n] ❑ *Lithuania hasn't had any direct communication with Moscow.* 立陶宛与莫斯科还没有任何直接的交流。 ❑ *...use of the radio telephone for communication between controllers and pilots.* …无线电话在控制员和飞行员联络中的运用。 2 V-RECIP If one person **communicates with** another, they successfully make each other aware of their feelings and ideas. You can also say that two people **communicate**. 沟通 ❑ *He was never good at communicating with the players.* 他从不擅长和队员沟通。 ❑ *Family therapy showed us how to communicate with each other.* 家庭疗法向我们展示了如何相互沟通。 ● **com·mu·ni·ca·tion** N-UNCOUNT 沟通 ❑ *There was a tremendous lack of communication between us.* 我们之间极其缺乏沟通。 ❑ *Good communication with people around you could prove difficult.* 与你周围的人的良好沟通会被证明是很难的。 3 V-T If you **communicate** information, a feeling, or an idea **to** someone, you let them know about it. 传达 ❑ *They successfully communicate their knowledge to others.* 他们成功地把他们的知识传达给别人。

com·mu·ni·ca·tion ♦◇◇ /kəmyunɪkeɪʃ°n/ (**communications**) 1 N-PLURAL **Communications** are the systems and processes that are used to communicate or broadcast information, especially by means of electricity or radio waves. 通信 ❑ *...a communications satellite.* …一颗通信卫星。 2 N-COUNT A **communication** is a message. 信息 [FORMAL] ❑ *The ambassador has brought with him a communication from the president.* 该大使从总统那里带来了一则信息。 3 → see also **communicate**

→ see **brain, radio**

com·mun·ion /kəmyunyən/ 1 N-UNCOUNT **Communion** with nature or with a person is the feeling that you are sharing thoughts or feelings with them. 交融 [also "a" N, oft N "with" n] ❑ *...communion with nature.* …与大自然的交融。 2 N-UNCOUNT **Communion** is the Christian ceremony in which people eat bread and drink wine in memory of Christ's death. 圣餐仪式 ❑ *Most villagers took communion only at Easter.* 大多数村民只在复活节的时候领受圣餐。

▲ **com·mu·ni·qué** /kəmyunɪkeɪ/ (**communiqués**) N-COUNT A **communiqué** is an official statement or announcement. 公报 [FORMAL] ❑ *The communiqué said military targets had been hit.* 该公报说军事目标已被击中。

Word Link *ism ≈ action or state : communism, optimism, patriotism*

com·mun·ism /kɒmyənɪzəm/ also **Communism** N-UNCOUNT **Communism** is the political belief that all people are equal, that there should be no private ownership and that workers should control the means of producing things. 共产主义 ❑ *...the ultimate triumph of communism in the world.* …共产主义在全世界的最终胜利。

com·mun·ist ♦♦◇ /kɒmyənɪst/ (**communists**) also **Communist** 1 N-COUNT A **communist** is someone who believes in communism. 共产主义者 2 ADJ **Communist** means relating to communism. 共产主义的 ❑ *...the Communist Party.* …共产党。

com·mu·nity ♦♦♦ /kəmyunɪti/ (**communities**) 1 N-SING-COLL **The community** is all the people who live in a particular area or place. 社区 ❑ *He's well liked by people in the community.* 他很受社区人们的喜爱。 2 N-COUNT-COLL A particular **community** is a group of people who are similar in some way. 团体 ❑ *The police haven't really done anything for the black community in particular.* 警方并没有特别为黑人团体做什么。 3 N-UNCOUNT **Community** is friendship between different people or groups, and a sense of having something in common. 团体精神 ❑ *Two of our greatest strengths are diversity and community.* 我们的两个最大优点是多样性和团体精神。

Thesaurus *community* 另参见：
N. neighborhood, public, society 1

com·mu·nity cen·ter (**community centers**) N-COUNT A **community center** is a place that is specially provided for the people, groups, and organizations in a particular area, where they can go in order to meet one another and do things. 社区活动中心

com·mu·nity ser·vice 1 N-UNCOUNT **Community service** is unpaid work that criminals sometimes do as a punishment instead of being sent to prison. (作为犯罪惩罚的) 社区服务 ❑ *He was sentenced to 140 hours' community service for drunk driving.* 他因醉酒驾车被判140小时的社区服务。 2 N-UNCOUNT **Community service** is unpaid voluntary work that a person performs for the benefit of his or her local community. (自愿、无偿的) 社区服务 ❑ *I have been doing community service work in Oakland for the past several years.* 过去几年里我一直在奥克兰做社区服务工作。

Word Link *mut ≈ changing : commute, mutate, mutilate*

com·mute /kəmyut/ (**commutes, commuting, commuted**) 1 V-I If you **commute**, you travel a long distance every day between your home and your place of work. 通勤 ❑ *Mike commutes to Miami every day.* 迈克每天通勤去迈阿密。 ❑ *McLaren began commuting between Philadelphia and New York.* 麦克拉伦开始在费城和纽约之间通勤。 ● **com·mut·er** N-COUNT (**commuters**) 通勤者 ❑ *There are significant numbers of commuters using our streets.* 有相当多的通勤者使用我们的街道。 2 N-COUNT A **commute** is the journey that you make when you commute. 通勤的路程 ❑ *The average Los Angeles commute is over 60 miles a day.* 洛杉矶平均通勤路程每天超过60英里。

→ see **traffic, transportation**

com·mut·er belt (**commuter belts**) N-COUNT A **commuter belt** is the area surrounding a large city, where many people who work in the city live. (大城市周边的) 通勤者居住带 ❑ *...people who live in the commuter belt around the capital.* …居住在首都周边通勤者居住带的人们。

Word Link *com ≈ with : together : combine, compact, companion*

com·pact /kəmpækt/ (**compacts**) 1 ADJ **Compact** things are small or take up very little space. You use this word when you think this is a good quality. 小巧的 [APPROVAL] ❑ *...my compact office in Washington.* …我在华盛顿的小巧的办公室。 2 ADJ A **compact** person is small but looks strong. 矮小结实的 ❑ *He was compact, probably no taller than me.* 他矮小结实，大概没我高。 3 N-COUNT A **compact** or a **compact car** is a car that is smaller than the average car, and that is economical to run. 小型汽车

com·pact disc (**compact discs**) also **compact disk** N-COUNT **Compact discs** are small shiny discs that contain music or computer information. The abbreviation **CD** is also used. 光盘 [also "on" N]

→ see **DVD**

com·pan·ion /kəmpænyən/ (**companions**) N-COUNT A **companion** is someone who you spend time with or who you are traveling with. 同伴；旅伴 ❑ *Fred had been her constant companion for the last six years of her life.* 弗雷德曾是她生命里最后6年里的常伴。

→ see **pet**

★ **com·pan·ion·ship** /kəmpænyənʃɪp/ N-UNCOUNT **Companionship** is having someone you know and like with you, instead of being on your own. 陪伴 ❑ *I depended on his companionship and on his judgment.* 我依赖他的陪伴和他的判断。

com·pa·ny ♦♦♦ /kʌmpəni/ (**companies**) 1 N-COUNT-COLL; N-IN-NAMES A **company** is a business organization that makes money by selling goods or services. 公司 ❑ *Sheila found some work as a secretary in an insurance company.* 希拉在一家保险公司找到了一份做秘

Word Web company

In the United States most **companies** are **privately held corporations**. All of the **stock** in the company goes to the people who organized it. All the **profits** go to the same people. Some companies have publicly **traded stock**. This means that some or all of the start-up money came from **shares** of stock sold to the public. Such shares are **traded** on the **stock market**. People who own stock in a company receive **dividends**. They usually also have voting rights. This allows them to play a role in guiding the corporation.

书的工作。 2 N-COUNT-COLL; N-IN-NAMES A **company** is a group of opera singers, dancers, or actors who work together. 剧团 ❑ *...the Phoenix Dance Company.* …凤凰舞蹈团。 3 N-COUNT; N-IN-NAMES A **company** is a group of soldiers that is usually part of a battalion or regiment, and that is divided into two or more platoons. 连 ❑ *The division will consist of two tank companies and one infantry company.* 该师将由两个坦克连和一个步兵连组成。 4 N-UNCOUNT **Company** is having another person or other people with you, usually when this is pleasant or stops you feeling lonely. 陪伴 ❑ *"I won't stay long."—"No, please. I need the company."* "我不会呆很久。" —— "别，请别走。我需要陪伴。" ❑ *Ross had always enjoyed the company of women.* 罗斯总是喜欢女人的陪伴。 5 → see also **joint-stock company, public company** 6 PHRASE If you **have company**, you have a visitor or friend with you. 有客人 ❑ *He didn't say he had company.* 他没说他有客人。 7 PHRASE If you **keep** someone **company**, you spend time with them and stop them from feeling lonely or bored. 陪某人做伴 ❑ *Why don't you stay here and keep Emma company?* 你为什么不留在这儿陪埃玛做伴？

→ see Word Web: **company**

→ see **electricity**

Word Partnership *company* 的常用搭配：

ADJ. **foreign** company, **parent** company 1

V. **buy/own/sell/start a** company, company **employs**, company **makes** 1

have company, **keep** company, **part** company 6 7

com·pa·ny car (**company cars**) N-COUNT A **company car** is a car which an employer gives to an employee to use as their own, usually as a benefit of having a particular job, or because their job involves a lot of driving. 公车 [BUSINESS] ❑ *...changes to tax laws for company cars.* …公车税法的改变。

com·pa·rable /kɒmpərəbᵊl/ 1 ADJ Something that is **comparable** to something else is roughly similar, for example in amount or importance. (数量、重要性等) 相当的 ❑ *...paying the same wages to men and women for work of comparable value.* …对同等工作的男女支付同样的工薪。 ❑ *Farmers were supposed to get an income comparable to that of townspeople.* 农民应该获得与城镇人相当的收入。 2 ADJ If two or more things are **comparable**, they are of the same kind or are in the same situation, and so they can reasonably be compared. 可比的 ❑ *In other comparable countries, real wages increased much more rapidly.* 在其他可比的国家里实际工资增长快得多。 ❑ *By contrast, the comparable figure for Canada is 16 percent.* 对比之下，加拿大的可比数字是16%。

com·para·tive /kəmpærətɪv/ (**comparatives**) 1 ADJ You use **comparative** to show that you are judging something against a previous or different situation. For example, **comparative** calm is a situation which is calmer than before or calmer than the situation in other places. 比较的 (平静等) [ADJ n] ❑ *The task was accomplished with comparative ease.* 这项任务完成得比较容易。

● **com·para·tive·ly** ADV 比较地 [ADV adj/adv] ❑ *...a comparatively small nation.* …一个比较小的国家。 2 ADJ A **comparative** study is a study that involves the comparison of two or more things of the same kind. 比较的 (研究) [ADJ n] ❑ *...a comparative study of the dietary practices of people from various regions of India.* …对印度不同地区人们饮食习惯的比较研究。 3 ADJ In grammar, the **comparative** form of an adjective or adverb shows that something has more of a quality than something else has. For example, "bigger" is the comparative form of "big," and "more quickly" is the comparative form of "quickly." Compare **superlative**. 比较级的 ● N-COUNT **Comparative** is also a noun. 比较级 [ADJ n] ❑ *The comparative of "pretty" is "prettier."* "**pretty**" 的比较级是 "**prettier**"。

Word Link *par ≈ equal : compare, disparate, part*

com·pare ♦◇◇ /kəmpɛər/ (**compares, comparing, compared**) 1 V-T When you **compare** things, you consider them and discover the differences or similarities between them. 比较 ❑ *Compare the two illustrations in Figure 60.* 比较一下图60中的两个图示。 ❑ *Managers analyze their company's data and compare it with data on their competitors.* 经理们分析他们公司的数据并与其竞争者的数据进行比较。 2 V-T If you **compare** one person or thing **to** another, you say that they are like the other person or thing. 认为…像… ❑ *Some commentators compared his work to that of James Joyce.* 一些评论员认为他的作品像詹姆士・乔伊斯的作品。 3 V-I If you say that something does not **compare with** something else, you mean that it is much worse. 比得上 [usu with neg] ❑ *The flowers here do not compare with those at home.* 这儿的花比不上家里的花。 4 V-I If one thing **compares** favorably **with** another, it is better than the other thing. If it **compares** unfavorably, it is worse than the other thing. (与…) 比起来 (好、差) ❑ *Our road safety record compares favorably with that of other countries.* 我们的道路安全纪录比其他国家的好。 5 → see also **compared**

Thesaurus *compare* 另参见：

V. analyze, consider, contrast, examine 1

equate, match 2

com·pared ♦♦◇ /kəmpɛərd/ 1 PHRASE If you say, for example, that one thing is large or small **compared with** another or **compared to** another, you mean that it is larger or smaller than the other thing. 与某事物比起来 ❑ *The room was light and lofty compared to the basement.* 这个房间与地下室比起来更亮更高。 2 PHRASE You talk about one situation or thing **compared with** another or **compared to** another when contrasting the two situations or things. 与某事物相对比 ❑ *In 1800 Ireland's population was nine million, compared to Britain's 16 million.* 1800年爱尔兰的人口是900万，而英国人口是1600万。

com·pari·son ♦◇◇ /kəmpærɪsən/ (**comparisons**) 1 N-VAR When you make a **comparison**, you consider two or more things and discover the differences between them. 比较 ❑ *...a comparison of the Mexican and Guatemalan economies.* …墨西哥与危地马拉经济的比较。 ❑ *Its recommendations are based on detailed comparisons between the public and private sectors.* 其建议是以公有和私有部门之间的详细比较为根据的。 2 N-COUNT When you make a **comparison**, you say that one thing is like another in some way. 相似对比 ❑ *It is demonstrably an unfair comparison.* 这显然是一种不公平的相似对比。 3 PHRASE If you say, for example, that something is large or small **in comparison with, in comparison to,** or **by comparison with** something else, you mean that it is larger or smaller than the other thing. 相比之下 ❑ *The amount of carbon dioxide released by human activities such as burning coal and oil is small in comparison.* 相比之下人类燃烧煤、石油等活动所释放的二氧化碳的量是少的。

Word Partnership *comparison* 的常用搭配：

PREP. comparison **between/of/with** ***something*** 1 2

by comparison, **in** comparison 3

★ **com·part·ment** /kəmpɑrtmənt/ (**compartments**) 1 N-COUNT A **compartment** is one of the separate parts of an object that is used for keeping things in. 隔间 ❑ *The fire started in the baggage compartment.* 火是从行李舱着起来的。 2 → see also **glove compartment** 3 N-COUNT A **compartment** is one of the separate spaces into which a railroad car is divided. 火车车厢 ❑ *On the way home we shared our first class compartment with a group of businessmen.* 在回家的路上我们和一群商人共同乘坐头等车厢。

C

com·pass /kʌmpəs/ (**compasses**) N-COUNT A **compass** is an instrument that you use for finding directions. It has a dial and a magnetic needle that always points to the north. 罗盘 ❑ *We had to rely on a compass and a lot of luck to get here.* 我们只得靠罗盘和很大的运气到达这儿。
→ see **magnet, navigation**

▲ **com·pas·sion** /kəmpæʃ°n/ N-UNCOUNT **Compassion** is a feeling of pity, sympathy, and understanding for someone who is suffering. 同情 ❑ *Elderly people need time and compassion from their physicians.* 老年人需要医生的时间和同情心。

Word Link ate ≈ filled with : affection*ate*, compassion*ate*, consider*ate*

★ **com·pas·sion·ate** /kəmpæʃ°nɪt/ ADJ If you describe someone or something as **compassionate**, you mean that they feel or show pity, sympathy, and understanding for people who are suffering. 有同情心的; 表示同情的 [APPROVAL] ❑ *My father was a deeply compassionate man.* 我的父亲是个极富同情心的人。 ❑ *She has a wise, compassionate face.* 她有一张智慧和同情的脸。

com·pas·sion·ate leave N-UNCOUNT **Compassionate leave** is time away from your work that your employer allows you for personal reasons, especially when a member of your family dies or is seriously ill. (因亲人病、亡而特准的) 私事假 [BRIT, BUSINESS]
in AM, use **leave of absence**

com·pat·ible /kəmpætɪb°l/ 1 ADJ If things, for example systems, ideas, and beliefs, are **compatible**, they work well together or can exist together successfully. (系统、观点、信念等) 相容的 ❑ *Free enterprise, he argued, was compatible with Russian values and traditions.* 他辩称自由企业与俄罗斯的价值观和传统是相容的。
● **com·pat·ibil·ity** /kəmpætɪbɪlɪti/ N-UNCOUNT 相容性 ❑ *...the issue of Islam and its compatibility with democracy.* …伊斯兰教及其与民主体制的相容性问题。 2 ADJ If you say that you are **compatible** with someone, you mean that you have a good relationship with them because you have similar opinions and interests. 意趣相投的 ❑ *Mildred and I are very compatible. She's interested in the things that interest me.* 米尔德丽德和我非常意趣相投。我感兴趣的东西她也感兴趣。
● **com·pat·ibil·ity** N-UNCOUNT 意趣相投 ❑ *As a result of their compatibility, Haig and Fraser were able to bring about wide-ranging reforms.* 由于意趣相投，黑格和弗雷泽能带来广泛的改革。 3 ADJ If one brand of computer or computer equipment is **compatible with** another brand, they can be used together and can use the same software. (电脑品牌) 兼容的 ❑ *Fujitsu took over another American firm, Amdal, to help it to make and sell machines compatible with IBM in the United States.* 富士通接管了另一家美国公司安岛，以帮助其在美国生产并销售与IBM兼容的机器。

com·pat·ri·ot /kəmpeɪtriət/ (**compatriots**) N-COUNT Your **compatriots** are people from your own country. 同国人 ❑ *Chris Robertson of Australia beat his compatriot Chris Dittmar in the final.* 澳大利亚的克里斯・罗伯逊在决赛中击败了他的本国对手克里斯・迪特玛。

Word Link pel ≈ driving : forcing : com*pel*, ex*pel*, pro*pel*

com·pel /kəmpel/ (**compels, compelling, compelled**) 1 V-T If a situation, a rule, or a person **compels** you to do something, they force you to do it. 迫使 ❑ *...the introduction of legislation to compel cyclists to wear a helmet.* …强制骑车人戴头盔的法律的引入。 2 PHRASE If you **feel compelled to** do something, you feel that you must do it, because it is the right thing to do. 感到必须 (做某事) ❑ *Dickens felt compelled to return to the stage for a final goodbye.* 狄更斯感到必须返回舞台作最后的告别。

com·pel·ling /kəmpelɪŋ/ 1 ADJ A **compelling** argument or reason is one that convinces you that something is true or that something should be done. 令人信服的 ❑ *Factual and forensic evidence makes a suicide verdict the most compelling answer to the mystery of his death.* 事实和法庭证据使自杀的判定成为对他死亡之谜最令人信服的解答。 2 ADJ If you describe something such as a movie or book, or someone's appearance, as **compelling**, you mean you want to keep looking at it or reading it because you find it so interesting. 引人入胜的 ❑ *...a frighteningly violent yet compelling movie.* …一部充满恐怖暴力但却引人入胜的电影。

com·pen·sate /kɒmpənseɪt/ (**compensates, compensating, compensated**) 1 V-T To **compensate** someone **for** money or things that they have lost, means to pay them money or give them something to replace those things. 补偿 (损失) ❑ *The damages are designed to compensate victims for their direct losses.* 该赔偿金是用来补偿受害人的直接损失的。 2 V-I If you **compensate for** a lack of something or **for** something you have done wrong, you do something to make the situation better. 弥补 (过失) ❑ *The company agreed to keep up high levels of output in order to compensate for supplies lost.* 该公司同意保持高产出水平以补偿损失掉的供应品。 3 V-I Something that **compensates for** something else balances it or reduces its effects. 抵消 ❑ *Senators say it is crucial that a mechanism is found to compensate for inflation.* 参议员们说找到抵消通货膨胀的机制是至关重要的。 4 V-I If you try to **compensate for** something that is wrong or missing in your life, you try to do something that removes or reduces the harmful effects. 弥补 ❑ *Their sense of humor and ability to get along with people are two characteristics that compensate for their lack of experience.* 他们的幽默感和与人相处的能力是弥补他们经验不足的两个特质。

com·pen·sa·tion ♦◇◇ /kɒmpənseɪʃ°n/ (**compensations**) 1 N-UNCOUNT **Compensation** is money that someone who has experienced loss or suffering claims from the person or organization responsible, or from the state. 补偿金 ❑ *He received one year's salary as compensation for loss of office.* 他得到一年的薪水作为失去职位的补偿金。 ❑ *They want $20,000 in compensation for each of about 500 claimants.* 他们想要给约500个投诉者每人2万美元作为补偿金。 2 N-VAR If something is some **compensation for** something bad that has happened, it makes you feel better. 补偿 ❑ *Helen gained some compensation for her earlier defeat by winning the final open class.* 海伦通过赢得公开赛的决赛获得了对先前失利的一些补偿。

com·pete ♦◇◇ /kəmpit/ (**competes, competing, competed**) 1 V-RECIP When one firm or country **competes with** another, it tries to get people to buy its own goods in preference to those of the other firm or country. You can also say that two firms or countries **compete**. (与…) 竞争 ❑ *The banks have long competed with American Express's charge cards and various store cards.* 这些银行长期以来一直与美国运通公司的记账卡和各种商店卡竞争。 ❑ *Hardware stores are competing fiercely for business.* 各五金店正在为抢生意而激烈竞争。 2 V-RECIP If you **compete with** someone **for** something, you try to get it for yourself and stop the other person from getting it. You can also say that two people **compete for** something. 争夺 ❑ *Kangaroos compete with sheep and cattle for sparse supplies of food and water.* 袋鼠与绵羊和牛争夺为数不多的食物和水的供应。 ❑ *Young men compete with each other for membership in these societies and fraternities.* 年轻人为获取这些社团和兄弟会的会员身份而相互争夺。 3 V-I If you **compete** in a contest or a game, you take part in it. 参加 (竞赛或比赛) ❑ *He will be competing in the 100-meter race.* 他将参加100米比赛。

★ **com·pe·tence** /kɒmpɪtəns/ N-UNCOUNT **Competence** is the ability to do something well or effectively. 能力 ❑ *Many people have testified to his competence.* 很多人已证实了他的能力。

com·pe·tent /kɒmpɪtənt/ 1 ADJ Someone who is **competent** is efficient and effective. 有能力的 ❑ *He was a loyal, distinguished and very competent civil servant.* 他是一个忠诚、出色、很有能力的公务员。
● **com·pe·tent·ly** ADV 有能力地 ❑ *The government performed competently in the face of multiple challenges.* 政府在面临多重挑战时表现得很出色。 2 ADJ If you are **competent to** do something, you have the skills, abilities, or experience necessary to do it well. 能胜任的 ❑ *Most adults do not feel competent to deal with a medical emergency involving a child.* 多数成年人感到难以应付小孩医疗突发事件。

com·pe·ti·tion ♦♦◇ /kɒmpɪtɪʃ°n/ (**competitions**) 1 N-UNCOUNT **Competition** is a situation in which two or more people or groups are trying to get something which not everyone can have. (为获取难得之物而进行的) 竞争 ❑ *There's been some fierce competition for the title.* 已有一些为此头衔的激烈竞争。 2 N-UNCOUNT **Competition** is an activity involving two or more companies, in which each company tries to get people to buy its own goods in preference to the other companies' goods. (商业上的) 竞争 ❑ *The deal would have reduced competition in the commuter-aircraft market.* 该交易本可以减少通勤飞机市场的竞争。 ❑ *The farmers have been seeking higher prices as better protection from foreign competition.* 农场主们一直在寻求更高价格来作为对外来竞争的更好保护。 3 N-UNCOUNT The **competition** is the goods or services that a rival organization is selling. 竞争产品; 竞争服务 ❑ *The American aerospace industry has been challenged by some stiff competition.* 美国航空航天工业遭到了一些强劲竞争产品的挑战。 4 N-SING **The competition** is the person or people you are competing with. 竞争对手 ❑ *I have to change my approach, the competition is too good now.* 我得改变我的方法，竞争对手现在太好了。

5 N-VAR A **competition** is an event in which many people take part in order to find out who is best at a particular activity. 竞赛 ❑ *...a surfing competition.* ···一项冲浪比赛。

Word Partnership *competition* 的常用搭配:
PREP. competition **between** *something* 1
competition **for** *something*, competition **in** *something* 1 5
ADJ. **unfair** competition 1 2
stiff competition 1 – 4

com·peti·tive ♦◇◇ /kəmpɛtɪtɪv/ 1 ADJ **Competitive** is used to describe situations or activities in which people or companies compete with each other. 竞争的 ❑ *Only by keeping down costs will America maintain its competitive advantage over other countries.* 只有通过保持低成本美国才能保持对其他国家的竞争优势。 ❑ *Japan is a highly competitive market system.* 日本实行的是一个高度竞争的市场体制。 ● **com·peti·tive·ly** ADV 竞争地 [ADV after v] ❑ *He's now back up on the slopes again, skiing competitively in events for the disabled.* 他如今又回到了滑坡上，在残疾人赛事上赛滑雪。 2 ADJ A **competitive** person is eager to be more successful than other people. 好胜的 ❑ *He has always been ambitious and fiercely competitive.* 他一直很有抱负，极度好胜。 ● **com·peti·tive·ly** ADV 好胜地 [ADV after v] ❑ *They worked hard together, competitively and under pressure.* 他们一起努力工作，一心求胜，也承受压力。 ● **com·peti·tive·ness** N-UNCOUNT 好胜 ❑ *I can't stand the pace, I suppose, and the competitiveness, and the unfriendliness.* 我想我无法忍受这种节奏、争强好胜和不友善。 3 ADJ Goods or services that are at a **competitive** price or rate are likely to be bought, because they are less expensive than other goods of the same kind. (商品、服务) 有竞争力的 ❑ *Only those homes offered for sale at competitive prices will secure interest from serious purchasers.* 只有那些以具有竞争力的价格出售的房子才能抓住真正购买者的兴趣。 ● **com·peti·tive·ly** ADV 有竞争力地 ❑ *...a number of early Martin and Gibson guitars, which were competitively priced.* ···许多定价富有竞争力的早期马丁吉他和吉布森吉他。 ● **com·peti·tive·ness** N-UNCOUNT 竞争力 ❑ *It is only on the world market that we can prove the competitiveness and quality of our software.* 只有在世界市场上我们才能证明我们软件的竞争力和质量。

Word Partnership *competitive* 的常用搭配:
N. competitive **sport** 1
competitive **advantage** 1 3
competitive **person** 2
ADV. **fiercely** competitive, **highly** competitive, **more** competitive 1 2

com·peti·tor ♦◇◇ /kəmpɛtɪtər/ (**competitors**) 1 N-COUNT A company's **competitors** are companies who are trying to sell similar goods or services to the same people. 竞争对手 ❑ *The bank isn't performing as well as some of its competitors.* 这家银行没有它的一些竞争对手表现好。 2 N-COUNT A **competitor** is a person who takes part in a competition or contest. 参赛者 ❑ *One of the oldest competitors won the individual silver medal.* 其中一个年纪最大的参赛者赢得了个人银牌。

com·pi·la·tion /kɒmpɪleɪʃən/ (**compilations**) N-COUNT A **compilation** is a book, CD, or program that contains many different items that have been gathered together, usually ones which have already appeared in other places. 汇编; 合集 ❑ *His latest CD is a compilation of his jazz works over the past decade.* 他最新的CD是他过去十年的爵士乐作品集。

★ **com·pile** /kəmpaɪl/ (**compiles, compiling, compiled**) V-T When you **compile** something such as a report, book, or program, you produce it by collecting and putting together many pieces of information. 汇编; 汇集 ❑ *The book took 10 years to compile.* 这本书花了10年编写。

com·pla·cen·cy /kəmpleɪsənsi/ N-UNCOUNT **Complacency** is being complacent about a situation. 自满 [DISAPPROVAL] ❑ *...a worrying level of complacency about the risks of infection from AIDS.* ···对艾滋病感染危险的令人担忧的自满程度。

Word Link *plac ≈ pleasing : complacent, placate, placid*

▲ **com·pla·cent** /kəmpleɪsənt/ ADJ A **complacent** person is very pleased with themselves or feels that they do not need to do anything about a situation, even though the situation may be uncertain or dangerous. 自满的; 盲目乐观的 [DISAPPROVAL] ❑ *We cannot afford to be complacent about our health.* 我们对我们的健康自满不起。

com·plain ♦♦◇ /kəmpleɪn/ (**complains, complaining, complained**) 1 V-T/V-I If you **complain about** a situation, you say that you are not satisfied with it. 抱怨 ❑ *Miners have complained bitterly that the government did not fulfill their promises.* 矿工们已愤愤地抱怨政府没有兑现他们的承诺。 ❑ *The couple complained about the high cost of visiting Europe.* 这对夫妇抱怨了游览欧洲的高昂花费。 ❑ *I shouldn't complain, I've got a good job to go back to.* 我不该抱怨，我已有可回去干的一份好工作。 ❑ *"I wish someone would do something about it," he complained.* "我希望有人能对此做点什么，" 他抱怨道。 2 V-I If you **complain of** pain or illness, you say that you are feeling pain or feeling ill. 诉说 (病痛) ❑ *He complained of a headache.* 他说他头疼。

com·plaint ♦◇◇ /kəmpleɪnt/ (**complaints**) 1 N-VAR A **complaint** is a statement in which you express your dissatisfaction with a situation. 怨言; 投诉 ❑ *There's been a record number of complaints about the standard of service.* 已有对服务水准的创纪录数量的投诉。 ❑ *People have been reluctant to make formal complaints to the police.* 人们一直不愿正式向警方投诉。 2 N-COUNT A **complaint** is a reason for complaining. 抱怨的缘由 ❑ *My main complaint is that we can't go out on the racecourse anymore.* 我抱怨的主要缘由是我们无法再去外面的赛道了。 3 N-COUNT You can refer to an illness as a **complaint**, especially if it is not very serious. (尤指不严重的) 疾病 ❑ *Eczema is a common skin complaint which often runs in families.* 湿疹是一种常见的皮肤病，常会遗传。

Word Partnership *complaint* 的常用搭配:
PREP. complaint **about** *something*, complaint **against** *someone*, complaint **from** *someone* 1
V. **deal with** complaints, **file a** complaint, **make a formal** complaint 1

Word Link *ple ≈ filling : complement, complete, deplete*

★ **com·ple·ment** (**complements, complementing, complemented**)

The verb is pronounced /kɒmplɪmɛnt/. The noun is pronounced /kɒmplɪmənt/.

动词读作 /kɒmplɪmɛnt/。名词读作 /kɒmplɪmənt/。

1 V-T If one thing **complements** another, it goes well with the other thing and makes its good qualities more noticeable. 衬托 ❑ *Nutmeg, parsley and cider all complement the flavor of these beans well.* 肉豆蔻、欧芹和苹果酒都凸显这些菜豆的味道。 2 V-T If people or things **complement** each other, they are different or do something different, which makes them a good combination. 补充 ❑ *There will be a written examination to complement the practical test.* 会有一次书面考试来补充实践测试。 3 N-COUNT Something that is a **complement to** something else complements it. 衬托物; 补充物 ❑ *The green wallpaper is the perfect complement to the old pine of the dresser.* 绿色墙纸是旧松木梳妆台的完美衬托。

com·ple·men·tary /kɒmplɪmɛntəri, -mɛntri/ 1 ADJ **Complementary** things are different from each other but make a good combination. 互补的 [FORMAL] ❑ *To improve the quality of life through work, two complementary strategies are necessary.* 要通过工作提高生活质量，两个互补的策略很必要。 ❑ *He has done experiments complementary to those of Eigen.* 他已经做了与艾根的实验互补的实验。 2 ADJ **Complementary** medicine refers to ways of treating patients which are different from the ones used by most Western doctors, for example acupuncture and homeopathy. 辅助性的 [ADJ n] ❑ *...combining orthodox treatment with a wide range of complementary therapies.* ···结合传统治疗和各种辅助性疗法。

com·plete ♦♦♦ /kəmplit/ (**completes, completing, completed**) 1 ADJ You use **complete** to emphasize that something is as great in extent, degree, or amount as it possibly can be. 完全的 [EMPHASIS] ❑ *The house is a complete mess.* 这房子实在太乱了。 ❑ *The rebels had taken complete control.* 叛乱者已经取得了完全的控制。 ❑ *The resignation came as a complete surprise.* 该辞职来得十分意外。 ● **com·plete·ly** ADV 完全地 ❑ *Dozens of homes had been completely destroyed.* 数十家房屋已被完全毁坏了。 ❑ *Make sure that you defrost it completely.* 确保将其彻底除霜。 2 ADJ You can use **complete** to emphasize that you are referring to the whole of something and not just part of it. 整个的 [ADJ n] [EMPHASIS] ❑ *A complete apartment complex was burned to the ground.* 整座公寓大楼被烧成平地。 3 ADJ If something is **complete**, it contains all the parts that it should

C

contain. 完整的 ❑ *The list may not be complete.* 这份清单可能不完整。❑ *...a complete dinner service.* …一整套餐具。 4 ADJ The **complete** works of a writer are all their books or poems published together in one book or as a set of books. 全部的 (作品) [ADJ n] ❑ *...the Complete Works of William Shakespeare.* …威廉・莎士比亚全集。 5 ADJ If something is **complete**, it has been finished. 完成了的 [v-link ADJ] ❑ *The work of restoring the farmhouse is complete.* 修复该农舍的工作完成了。 6 V-T To **complete** a set or group means to provide the last item that is needed to make it a full set or group. 使齐全 [no cont] ❑ *Children don't complete their set of 20 baby teeth until they are two to three years old.* 孩子到两三岁时才长齐20颗乳牙。 7 V-T If you **complete** something, you finish doing, making, or producing it. 完成 ❑ *Peter Mayle has just completed his first novel.* 彼得・梅尔刚完成他的第一本小说。 ● **com·ple·tion** /kəmpliʃ°n/ N-VAR (**completions**) 完成 ❑ *The project is nearing completion.* 该项目快完成了。 8 V-T If you **complete** something, you do all of it. 完成 [no cont] ❑ *She completed her degree in two years.* 她在两年内修完了学位。 9 V-T If you **complete** a form or questionnaire, you write the answers or information asked for in it. 填写 (表格、问卷) ❑ *Simply complete part 1 of the application.* 只填写该申请表的第1部分即可。 10 PHRASE If one thing comes **complete with** another, it has that thing as an extra or additional part. 配有 ❑ *The diary comes complete with a gold ballpoint pen.* 该日记本还配有一支金圆珠笔。

Thesaurus *complete* 另参见：
ADJ. total, utter 1
entire, whole; *(ant.)* partial 2
unabridged; *(ant.)* abridged, selected 4

com·plex ♦♦◊ (**complexes**)

The adjective is pronounced /kəmplɛks/ or sometimes /kɒmplɛks/. The noun is pronounced /kɒmplɛks/.

形容词读作 /kəmplɛks/，有时读作 /kɒmplɛks/。名词读作 /kɒmplɛks/。

1 ADJ Something that is **complex** has many different parts, and is therefore often difficult to understand. 复杂的 ❑ *...in-depth coverage of today's complex issues.* …对当今复杂问题的深入报道。❑ *...a complex system of voting.* …一套复杂的选举体制。 2 N-COUNT A **complex** is a group of buildings designed for a particular purpose, or one large building divided into several smaller areas. 建筑群 ❑ *...a low-cost apartment complex.* …一个低价公寓楼群。

Thesaurus *complex* 另参见：
ADJ. complicated, intricate, involved; *(ant.)* obvious, plain, simple 1

Word Partnership *complex* 的常用搭配：
N. complex **issues**, complex **personality**, complex **problem/situation**, complex **process**, complex **system** 1

★ **com·plex·ion** /kəmplɛkʃ°n/ (**complexions**) N-COUNT When you refer to someone's **complexion**, you are referring to the natural color or condition of the skin on their face. 面色 ❑ *She had short brown hair and a pale complexion.* 她留棕色短发，面色苍白。
→ see **makeup**

com·plex·ities /kəmplɛksɪtiz/ N-PLURAL The **complexities** of something are the many complicated factors involved in it. 复杂因素 ❑ *...those who find it hardest to cope with the complexities of modern life.* …那些发现应付现代生活的复杂因素最难的人们。

★ **com·plex·ity** /kəmplɛksɪti/ N-UNCOUNT **Complexity** is the state of having many different parts connected or related to each other in a complicated way. 复杂性 ❑ *...a diplomatic tangle of great complexity.* …一场非常复杂的外交纠纷。

▲ **com·pli·ance** /kəmplaɪəns/ N-UNCOUNT **Compliance with** something, for example a law, treaty, or agreement, means doing what you are required or expected to do. 遵从 [FORMAL] ❑ *Inspectors were sent to visit nuclear sites and verify compliance with the treaty.* 监察员被派去参观核址并核实条约的遵守情况。

Word Link *ate ≈ causing to be : complicate, humiliate, motivate*

com·pli·cate /kɒmplɪkeɪt/ (**complicates, complicating, complicated**) V-T To **complicate** something means to make it more difficult to understand or deal with. 使复杂化 ❑ *What complicates the issue is the burden of history.* 使问题复杂化是历史的重负。❑ *The day's events, he said, would only complicate the task of the peacekeeping forces.* 他说那天的事件只会使维和部队的任务复杂化。

com·pli·cat·ed ♦◊◊ /kɒmplɪkeɪtɪd/ ADJ If you say that something is **complicated**, you mean it has so many parts or aspects that it is difficult to understand or deal with. 复杂的 ❑ *The situation in Lebanon is very complicated.* 黎巴嫩的形势非常复杂。

★ **com·pli·ca·tion** /kɒmplɪkeɪʃ°n/ (**complications**) 1 N-COUNT A **complication** is a problem or difficulty that makes a situation harder to deal with. 使情况复杂化的因素 ❑ *The age difference was a complication to the relationship.* 年龄差异是使该关系复杂化的一个因素。❑ *There are too many complications to explain now.* 现在有太多使情况复杂化的因素要解释。 2 N-COUNT A **complication** is a medical problem that occurs as a result of another illness or disease. 并发症 ❑ *Blindness is a common complication of diabetes.* 失明是糖尿病常有的一种并发症。

com·plic·ity /kəmplɪsɪti/ N-UNCOUNT **Complicity** is involvement with other people in an illegal activity or plan. 同谋 [FORMAL] ❑ *Recently a number of policemen were sentenced to death for their complicity in the murder.* 近来很多警察因参与这起谋杀而被判死刑。

★ **com·pli·ment** (**compliments, complimenting, complimented**)

The verb is pronounced /kɒmplɪmɛnt/. The noun is pronounced /kɒmplɪmənt/.

动词读作 /kɒmplɪmɛnt/。名词读作 /kɒmplɪmənt/。

1 N-COUNT A **compliment** is a polite remark that you make to someone to show that you like their appearance, appreciate their qualities, or approve of what they have done. 恭维话 ❑ *You can do no harm by paying a woman compliments.* 对女人讲恭维话不会有什么害处。 2 V-T If you **compliment** someone, you give them a compliment. 恭维 ❑ *They complimented me on the way I looked each time they saw me.* 他们每次见到我都就我的外貌恭维我。

com·pli·men·tary /kɒmplɪmɛntəri, -mɛntri/ 1 ADJ If you are **complimentary** about something, you express admiration for it. 赞赏的 ❑ *The staff have been very complimentary, and so have the customers.* 职员们一直非常赞赏，顾客们也是。 2 ADJ A **complimentary** seat, ticket, or book is given to you free. 免费赠送的 ❑ *He had complimentary tickets to take his wife to see the movie.* 他有赠票，可以带他妻子去看那部电影。

★ **com·ply** /kəmplaɪ/ (**complies, complying, complied**) V-I If someone or something **complies with** an order or set of rules, they do what is required or expected. 遵从 ❑ *The commander said that the army would comply with the ceasefire.* 指挥官说过部队会遵从停火协议。❑ *Some beaches had failed to comply with environmental regulations.* 一些海滩没能遵守环保规定。

com·po·nent ♦◊◊ /kəmpoʊnənt/ (**components**) 1 N-COUNT The **components** of something are the parts that it is made of. 组成部分 ❑ *Enriched uranium is a key component of a nuclear weapon.* 浓缩铀是核武器的一个关键组成部分。❑ *The management plan has four main components.* 该管理计划有4个主要组成部分。 2 ADJ The **component** parts of something are the parts that make it up. 组成的 [ADJ n] ❑ *Gorbachev failed to keep the component parts of the Soviet Union together.* 戈尔巴乔夫没能使苏联各组成部分保持在一起。
→ see **mass production**

Word Partnership *component* 的常用搭配：
ADJ. **key** component, **main** components, **separate** components 1
N. component **parts** 2

com·pose /kəmpoʊz/ (**composes, composing, composed**) 1 V-T The things that something **is composed of** are its parts or members. The separate things that **compose** something are the parts or members that form it. 组成 ❑ *The force would be composed of troops from NATO countries.* 该部队将由北约各国的军队组成。❑ *Protein molecules compose all the complex working parts of living cells.* 蛋白质分子构成了活细胞所有复杂的工作部件。 2 V-T/V-I When someone **composes** a piece of music or **composes**, they write music. 创作 (乐曲)；作曲 ❑ *Vivaldi composed a large number of very fine concertos.* 维瓦尔第创作了大量非常优美的协奏曲。 3 V-T If you **compose** something such as a letter, poem, or speech, you write

it, often using a lot of concentration or skill. (用心) 写(信、诗、演讲稿) [FORMAL] ❑ *He started at once to compose a reply to Anna.* 他立刻开始给安娜写回信。
→ see **music**

com·pos·er /kəmpoʊzər/ (**composers**) N-COUNT A **composer** is a person who writes music, especially classical music. (尤指古典音乐) 作曲家 ❑ *...music by Strauss, Mozart, Beethoven, and other great composers.* …施特劳斯、莫扎特、贝多芬及其他伟大作曲家创作的音乐。
→ see **music**

★ **com·po·site** /kəmpɑzɪt/ (**composites**) ADJ A **composite** object or item is made up of several different things, parts, or substances. 合成的 ❑ *Galton devised a method of creating composite pictures in which the features of different faces were superimposed over one another.* 高尔顿发明了一种将不同脸的部位相互叠加而创作合成图片的方法。 ● N-COUNT **Composite** is also a noun. 合成物 [usu sing, oft N "of" n] ❑ *Cuba is a composite of diverse traditions and people.* 古巴是一个不同传统和民族的融合体。

com·po·si·tion /kɒmpəzɪʃən/ (**compositions**) **1** N-UNCOUNT When you talk about the **composition** of something, you are referring to the way in which its various parts are put together and arranged. 构成 ❑ *Television has transformed the size and social composition of the audience at great sporting occasions.* 电视改变了大型体育赛事观众的数量及其社会构成。 **2** N-COUNT The **compositions** of a composer, painter, or other artist are the works of art that they have produced. (作曲家、画家等艺术家的) 作品 ❑ *Mozart's compositions are undoubtedly among the world's greatest.* 莫扎特的作品无疑位列于世界上最伟大的作品之中。 **3** N-COUNT A **composition** is a piece of written work that children write at school. (学生的) 作文 ❑ *We had to write a composition on the subject "My Pet."* 我们得就"我的宠物"这个主题写一篇作文。
→ see **orchestra**

com·post /kɒmpoʊst/ (**composts, composting, composted**) **1** N-UNCOUNT **Compost** is a mixture of decayed plants and vegetable waste which is added to the soil to help plants grow. 堆肥 ❑ *...a small compost heap.* …一小堆肥堆。 **2** N-MASS **Compost** is specially treated soil that you buy and use to grow seeds and plants in pots. (用于在盆中种种子和植物的) 特制土 ❑ *...a 75-pound bag of compost.* …一袋75磅重的栽种用土。 **3** V-T To **compost** things such as unwanted bits of plants means to make them into compost. 把…制成堆肥
→ see **dump**

com·po·sure /kəmpoʊʒər/ N-UNCOUNT **Composure** is the appearance or feeling of calm and the ability to control your feelings. 镇定; 定力 [FORMAL] ❑ *She was a little nervous at first but she soon regained her composure.* 她起初有点紧张但很快就恢复了镇定。

com·pound /kɒmpaʊnd/ (**compounds, compounding, compounded**)

> The noun is pronounced /kɒmpaʊnd/. The verb is pronounced /kəmpaʊnd/.

> 名词读作 /kɒmpaʊnd/。动词读作 /kəmpaʊnd/。

1 N-COUNT A **compound** is an enclosed area of land that is used for a particular purpose. 作特定用途的围地 ❑ *They took refuge in the embassy compound.* 他们在大使馆围区内避难。 ❑ *...a military compound.* …一个军事管辖区。 **2** N-COUNT In chemistry, a **compound** is a substance that consists of two or more elements. 化合物 ❑ *Organic compounds contain carbon in their molecules.* 有机化合物的分子里含碳。 **3** N-COUNT If something is a **compound of** different things, it consists of those things. 混合物 [FORMAL] ❑ *Honey is basically a compound of water, two types of sugar, vitamins and enzymes.* 蜂蜜主要是水、两种糖、维生素和酶的混合物。 **4** ADJ **Compound** is used to indicate that something consists of two or more parts or things. 复合的 [ADJ n] ❑ *...the big compound eyes of dragonflies.* …蜻蜓的大复眼。 **5** V-T To **compound** a problem, difficulty, or mistake means to make it worse by adding to it. 加剧 ❑ *Additional loss of life will only compound the tragedy.* 生命力的进一步丧失只会加重这一悲剧。 ❑ *The problem is compounded by the medical system here.* 这个问题被这里的医疗体制弄得更糟。 **6** ADJ In grammar, a **compound** noun, adjective, or verb is one that is made up of two or more words, for example "fire engine," "bottle-green," and "firelight." 合成的 (词) [ADJ n]
→ see **element, rock**

com·pound in·ter·est N-UNCOUNT **Compound interest** is interest that is calculated both on an original sum of money and on interest which has previously been added to the sum. Compare **simple interest**. 复利 [BUSINESS]

▲ **com·pre·hend** /kɒmprɪhɛnd/ (**comprehends, comprehending, comprehended**) V-T/V-I If you cannot **comprehend** something, you cannot understand it. 理解 [with brd-neg] [FORMAL] ❑ *I just cannot comprehend your attitude.* 我就是不能理解你的态度。

com·pre·hen·sion /kɒmprɪhɛnʃən/ **1** N-UNCOUNT **Comprehension** is the ability to understand something. 理解力 [FORMAL] ❑ *This was utterly beyond her comprehension.* 这完全超出了她的理解力。 **2** N-UNCOUNT **Comprehension** is full knowledge and understanding of the meaning of something. 理解 [FORMAL] ❑ *They turned to one another with the same expression of dawning comprehension, surprise, and relief.* 他们带着一样恍然大悟、惊奇、松了一口气的表情相互看了看。

com·pre·hen·sive ♦◇◇ /kɒmprɪhɛnsɪv/ ADJ Something that is **comprehensive** includes everything that is needed or relevant. 全面的 ❑ *The Rough Guide to Nepal is a comprehensive guide to the region.* 《尼泊尔概览》是介绍该地区的一本全面指南。

com·pre·hen·sive·ly /kɒmprɪhɛnsɪvli/ ADV Something that is done **comprehensively** is done thoroughly. 彻底地 ❑ *She was comprehensively outplayed by Coetzer.* 她被科泽尔彻底击败了。

com·press /kəmprɛs/ (**compresses, compressing, compressed**) **1** V-T/V-I When you **compress** something or when it **compresses**, it is pressed or squeezed so that it takes up less space. 压缩 ❑ *Poor posture, sitting or walking slouched over, compresses the body's organs.* 含胸坐、含胸走等不良姿势会压迫身体器官。 ● ▲ **com·pres·sion** /kəmprɛʃən/ N-UNCOUNT 压缩 ❑ *The compression of the wood is easily achieved.* 木材压缩容易实现。 **2** V-T If you **compress** something such as a piece of writing or a description, you make it shorter. 简缩 (文字、描述等) ❑ *He never understood how to organize or compress large masses of material.* 他从来不懂如何组织或简缩大篇材料。 **3** V-T If an event **is compressed into** a short space of time, it is given less time to happen than normal or previously. 压缩 (时间) [usu passive]

com·prise /kəmpraɪz/ (**comprises, comprising, comprised**) V-T If you say that something **comprises** or **is comprised of** a number of things or people, you mean it has them as its parts or members. 包含; 由…组成 [FORMAL] ❑ *The special cabinet committee comprises Mr. Brown, Mr. Mandelson, and Mr. Straw.* 这一特殊内阁委员会包括布朗先生、曼德尔森先生和斯特劳先生。 ❑ *The task force is comprised of congressional leaders, cabinet heads and administration officials.* 该任务队由国会领导人、内阁首脑和行政官员构成。

com·pro·mise ♦◇◇ /kɒmprəmaɪz/ (**compromises, compromising, compromised**) **1** N-VAR A **compromise** is a situation in which people accept something slightly different from what they really want, because of circumstances or because they are considering the wishes of other people. 折衷 ❑ *Encourage your child to reach a compromise between what he wants and what you want.* 鼓励你的孩子在他想要的和你想要的之间折衷。 **2** V-RECIP If you **compromise with** someone, you reach an agreement with them in which you both give up something that you originally wanted. You can also say that two people or groups **compromise**. 妥协 ❑ *The government has compromised with its critics over monetary policies.* 政府已经在货币政策上与其批评者们有了妥协。 ❑ *"Nine," I said. "Nine thirty," he replied. We compromised on 9:15.* "9点,"我说。"9: 30,"他回答道。我们各让一步定在9:15。 **3** V-T If someone **compromises** themselves or **compromises** their beliefs, they do something which damages their reputation for honesty, loyalty, or high moral principles. 使(自己、自己的信念) 降格 [DISAPPROVAL] ❑ *...members of the government who have compromised themselves by accepting bribes.* 收受贿赂而使其声誉受损的政府成员们。

> **Word Partnership** *compromise* 的常用搭配:
>
> V. **reach a** compromise **1**
> *to be* **willing to** compromise **2**
>
> PREP. compromise **between** *someone* **and** *someone else* **1 2**
> compromise **with** *someone* **2**

com·pro·mis·ing /kɒmprəmaɪzɪŋ/ ADJ If you describe information or a situation as **compromising**, you mean that it reveals an embarrassing or guilty secret about someone. 败坏名声的

C

❑ *How had this compromising picture come into the possession of the press?* 这张有损名声的照片是怎么到了媒体手里的？

comp·trol·ler /kəntroʊlər, kɒmp-/ (**comptrollers**) N-COUNT A **comptroller** is someone who is in charge of the accounts of a business or a government department; used mainly in official titles. (主要用于官衔中) 审计官 [BUSINESS] ❑ *...Robert Clarke, U.S. Comptroller of the Currency.* …美国货币审计官罗伯特・克拉克。

Word Link *puls ≈ driving, pushing : compulsion, expulsion, impulse*

com·pul·sion /kəmpʌlʃᵊn/ (**compulsions**) 1 N-COUNT A **compulsion** is a strong desire to do something, which you find difficult to control. 冲动 ❑ *He felt a sudden compulsion to drop the bucket and run.* 他感到一股突如其来的扔下桶跑掉的冲动。 2 N-UNCOUNT If someone uses **compulsion** in order to get you to do something, they force you to do it, for example by threatening to punish you if you do not do it. 逼迫 ❑ *Many universities argued that students learned more when they were in classes out of choice rather than compulsion.* 很多大学认为学生出于自愿比被逼迫上课能学到更多的东西。

com·pul·sive /kəmpʌlsɪv/ 1 ADJ You use **compulsive** to describe people or their behavior when they cannot stop doing something wrong, harmful, or unnecessary. 欲罢不能的 [ADJ n] ❑ *...a compulsive liar.* …一个禁不住说谎的人。 ❑ *He was a compulsive gambler and often heavily in debt.* 他是一个欲罢不能的赌徒，常常债台高筑。 2 ADJ If a book or television program is **compulsive**, it is so interesting that you do not want to stop reading or watching it. (书、电视节目) 使人着迷的 ❑ *Her new series is compulsive viewing.* 她的新系列节目引人入胜。

★ **com·pul·so·ry** /kəmpʌlsəri/ ADJ If something is **compulsory**, you must do it or accept it, because it is the law or because someone in a position of authority says you must. 强制性的

com·pu·ta·tion·al /kɒmpyʊteɪʃənᵊl/ ADJ **Computational** means using computers. 使用计算机的 ❑ *Students may pursue research in any aspect of computational linguistics.* 学生可以在计算机语言学的任何方面进行研究。

com·pute /kəmpyut/ (**computes, computing, computed**) V-T To **compute** a quantity or number means to calculate it. 计算 ❑ *To compute your scores, merely add or subtract your scores for each item.* 要计算你的分数，只需加减一下你每项上的得分。

Word Link *put ≈ thinking : computer, dispute, indisputable*

com·put·er ♦♦◇ /kəmpyutər/ (**computers**) 1 N-COUNT A **computer** is an electronic machine that can store and deal with large amounts of information. 计算机 [also "by/on" N] ❑ *The data are then fed into a computer.* 这些数据之后被输入一台计算机。 ❑ *The company installed a $650,000 computer system.* 该公司安装了一套65万美元的计算机系统。 2 → see also **personal computer**
→ see Word Web: **computer**
→ see **office**

com·put·er game (**computer games**) N-COUNT A **computer game** is a game that you play on a computer or on a small piece of electronic equipment. 电脑游戏

com·put·er·ise /kəmpjuːtəraɪz/ [BRIT] → see **computerize**

com·put·er·ised /kəmpjuːtəraɪzd/ [BRIT] → see **computerized**

com·put·er·ize /kəmpyutəraɪz/ (**computerizes, computerizing, computerized**)

in BRIT, also use **computerise**

V-T To **computerize** a system, process, or type of work means to arrange for a lot of the work to be done by computer. 使计算机化 ❑ *I'm trying to make a spreadsheet up to computerize everything that's done by hand at the moment.* 我正在试图作一个电子表格程序来使我们现在用手工做的一切工作计算机化。

com·put·er·ized /kəmpyutəraɪzd/

in BRIT, also use **computerised**

1 ADJ A **computerized** system, process, or business is one in which the work is done by computer. 计算机化的 ❑ *The National Cancer Institute now has a computerized system that can quickly provide information.* 国家癌症研究所现在拥有一套能快速提供信息的计算机化系统。 2 ADJ **Computerized** information is stored on a computer. 计算机存储的 ❑ *Computerized databases are proliferating fast.* 计算机存储数据库正在迅速发展。

computer-literate ADJ If someone is **computer-literate**, they have enough skill and knowledge to be able to use a computer. 懂电脑的 ❑ *We look for applicants who are good with numbers, computer-literate, and energetic self-starters.* 我们找精于计算、懂电脑、精力充沛、工作主动的申请人。

com·pu·ting /kəmpyutɪŋ/ 1 N-UNCOUNT **Computing** is the activity of using a computer and writing programs for it. 计算机应用；计算机编程 ❑ *Courses range from cooking to computing.* 课程从烹饪到计算机应用都有。 2 ADJ **Computing** means relating to computers and their use. 与计算机有关的 [ADJ n] ❑ *Many graduates are employed in the electronics and computing industries.* 许多毕业生受雇于电子与计算机行业。

com·rade /kɒmræd/ (**comrades**) N-COUNT Your **comrades** are your friends, especially friends that you share a difficult or dangerous situation with. (尤指共患难的) 同伴 [LITERARY] ❑ *Unlike so many of his comrades, he survived the war.* 不像他的许多战友，他在战争中幸存了下来。

con /kɒn/ (**cons, conning, conned**) 1 V-T If someone **cons** you, they persuade you to do something or believe something by telling you things that are not true. 哄骗 [INFORMAL] ❑ *He claimed that the businessman had conned him of $10,000.* 他声称那个商人骗了他1万美元。 ❑ *White conned his way into a job as a warehouseman with Dutch airline, KLM.* 怀特骗到了一份在荷兰皇家航空公司做仓库管理员的工作。 2 N-COUNT A **con** is a trick in which someone deceives you by telling you something that is not true. 骗局 [INFORMAL] ❑ *Snacks that offer miraculous weight loss are a con.* 那些可以神速减肥的快餐食品是个骗局。 3 **pros and cons** → see **pro**

con·ceal /kənsil/ (**conceals, concealing, concealed**) 1 V-T If you **conceal** something, you cover it or hide it carefully. 掩盖；隐藏 ❑ *Frances decided to conceal the machine behind a hinged panel.* 弗朗西丝决定把那台机器藏到一块可开合的镶板后面。 2 V-T If you **conceal** a piece of information or a feeling, you do not let other people know about it. 隐瞒 (信息)；掩饰 (情感) ❑ *Robert could not conceal his relief.* 罗伯特掩饰不住自己如释重负的心情。 3 V-T If something **conceals** something else, it covers it and prevents it from being seen. 遮盖 ❑ *...a pair of carved Indian doors which conceal a built-in cupboard.* …一对遮挡嵌入壁橱的印度式雕花门。

con·ceal·ment /kənsilmənt/ N-UNCOUNT **Concealment** is the state of being hidden or the act of hiding something. 隐藏 ❑ *The criminals vainly sought concealment from the searchlight.* 罪犯们试图躲开探照灯光，纯属徒劳。

con·cede ♦◇◇ /kənsid/ (**concedes, conceding, conceded**) 1 V-T If you **concede** something, you admit, often unwillingly, that it is true or correct. (常指不情愿地) 承认 ❑ *Bess finally conceded that Nancy was right.* 贝丝最终承认南希是对的。 ❑ *"Well," he conceded, "I do sometimes mumble a bit."* "嗯，"他承认道，"我有时说话确实有点儿含糊。" 2 V-T If you **concede** something **to** someone, you allow them to have it as a right or privilege. 给予 (权利或特权) ❑ *Poland's Communist government conceded the right to establish independent trade*

Word Web computer

Computers have revolutionized the way we live. Particularly exciting are the advances in the field of medicine. Computer **chips** allow deaf people to hear. Doctors recently placed an implant in the brain of a paralyzed man who could not speak. Soon he learned to move a **cursor** on a computer **screen** just by thinking. By pointing to letters and icons, he was able to express his ideas. Voice recognition **software** allows handicapped people to use a computer without a **keyboard**. Scientists are now experimenting with **devices** that will permit blind people to see.

unions. 波兰共产党政府给予了建立独立工会的权力。3 V-T If you **concede** something, you give it to the person who has been trying to get it from you. 让与 ❑ *The strike by bank employees ended after employers conceded some of their demands.* 银行雇员的罢工在雇主们答应了他们的一些要求之后停止了。4 V-T If you **concede** a game, contest, or argument, you end it by admitting that you can no longer win. (通过认输而) 使 (比赛、竞赛、争论等) 结束 ❑ *Reiner, 56, has all but conceded the race to his rival.* 56岁的赖纳差一点就向他的对手认输而使比赛结束。5 V-T If you **concede** defeat, you accept that you have lost a struggle. 承认 (失败) ❑ *She has conceded defeat in her bid for the Democratic Party's nomination for governor.* 她已经承认自己在民主党州长提名竞选中失败。

★ **con·ceit·ed** /kənsi̱tɪd/ ADJ If you say that someone is **conceited**, you are showing your disapproval of the fact that they are far too proud of their abilities or achievements. 自高自大的 [DISAPPROVAL] ❑ *I thought he was conceited and arrogant.* 我认为他自高自大而且傲慢。

con·ceiv·able /kənsi̱vəbᵊl/ ADJ If something is **conceivable**, you can imagine it or believe it. 可想像的；可相信的 ❑ *Without their support, the project would not have been conceivable.* 若没有他们的支持，这个项目是无法想像的。

★ **con·ceive** /kənsi̱v/ (**conceives, conceiving, conceived**) 1 V-T/V-I If you cannot **conceive of** something, you cannot imagine it or believe it. 想像；相信 [usu with brd-neg] ❑ *I just can't even conceive of that quantity of money.* 我简直无法想像那样一笔数量的钱。❑ *We could not conceive that he might soon be dead.* 我们无法相信他可能很快就会死去。2 V-T/V-I If you **conceive** something **as** a particular thing, you consider it to be that thing. 认为 ❑ *The ancients conceived the earth as afloat in water.* 古人认为地球漂浮在水里。❑ *We conceive of the family as being in a constant state of change.* 我们认为家庭是处于不断变化之中的。3 V-T If you **conceive** a plan or idea, you think of it and work out how it can be done. 构想出 ❑ *She had conceived the idea of a series of novels, each of which would reveal some aspect of Chinese life.* 她已经想出了一个关于一个系列小说的主意，每一部都将反映中国人生活的某一方面。4 V-T/V-I When a woman **conceives** a child or **conceives**, she becomes pregnant. 怀 (胎)；怀孕 ❑ *Women, he says, should give up alcohol before they plan to conceive.* 他说女人在计划怀孕前应该戒酒。

con·cen·trate ♦◇◇ /kɒ̱nsᵊntreɪt/ (**concentrates, concentrating, concentrated**) 1 V-T/V-I If you **concentrate on** something, or **concentrate** your mind **on** it, you give all your attention to it. 集中 (心思)；专心 ❑ *It was up to him to concentrate on his studies and make something of himself.* 他能否专心学习并有所成就取决于他自己。❑ *At work you need to be able to concentrate.* 工作时你要能专心。2 V-T If something **is concentrated in** an area, it is all there rather than being spread around. 集中 [usu passive] ❑ *Italy's industrial districts are concentrated in its north-central and northeastern regions.* 意大利的工业区集中在该国中北部和东北部地区。

Word Link *centr ≈ middle : central, concentrated, decentralized*

con·cen·trat·ed /kɒ̱nsᵊntreɪtɪd/ 1 ADJ A **concentrated** liquid has been increased in strength by having water removed from it. 浓缩的 ❑ *Sweeten dishes sparingly with honey, or concentrated apple or pear juice.* 用少许蜂蜜或浓缩苹果汁或梨汁使菜肴变甜。2 ADJ A **concentrated** activity is directed with great intensity in one place. 集中的 ❑ *...a more concentrated effort to reach out to troubled kids.* …更集中的帮助问题儿童的努力。

con·cen·tra·tion ♦◇◇ /kɒ̱nsᵊntre̱ɪʃᵊn/ (**concentrations**) 1 N-UNCOUNT **Concentration** on something involves giving all your attention to it. 专注 ❑ *Neal kept interrupting, breaking my concentration.* 尼尔不断打扰，打断我的注意力。2 N-VAR A **concentration of** something is a large amount of it or large numbers of it in a small area. 集中 ❑ *The area has one of the world's greatest concentrations of wildlife.* 该地区有世界上野生生物最集中的区域之一。3 N-VAR The **concentration of** a substance is the proportion of essential ingredients or substances in it. 浓度 ❑ *pH is a measure of the concentration of free hydrogen atoms in a solution.* pH值是溶液中游离氢原子浓度的计量单位。

con·cen·tra·tion camp (**concentration camps**) N-COUNT A **concentration camp** is a prison in which large numbers of ordinary people are kept in very bad conditions, usually during a war. 集中营 ❑ *...the ruins of the Nazi concentration camp at Buchenwald.* …布痕瓦尔德纳粹集中营废墟。

con·cept ♦◇◇ /kɒ̱nsɛpt/ (**concepts**) N-COUNT A **concept** is an idea or abstract principle. 概念；观念 ❑ *She added that the concept of arranged marriages is misunderstood in the west.* 她补充说包办婚姻的概念在西方被误解了。

★ **con·cep·tion** /kənsɛ̱pʃᵊn/ (**conceptions**) 1 N-VAR A **conception** of something is an idea that you have of it in your mind. (对某事物的) 概念 ❑ *My conception of a garden was based on gardens I had visited in England.* 我对花园的概念是基于我在英格兰参观过的一些花园的。2 N-VAR **Conception** is the process in which the egg in a woman is fertilized and she becomes pregnant. 受孕 ❑ *Six weeks after conception, your baby is the size of your little fingernail.* 受孕六周后你的孩子有你小手指甲那么大。

con·cern ♦♦♦ /kənsɜ̱rn/ (**concerns, concerning, concerned**) 1 N-UNCOUNT **Concern** is worry about a situation. 担忧 ❑ *The group has expressed concern about reports of political violence in Africa.* 该集团已对有关非洲政治暴力的报道表示担忧。❑ *The move follows growing public concern over the spread of the disease.* 该行动是针对公众日益增长的对该疾病传播的担忧而采取的。2 V-T If something **concerns** you, it worries you. 使担忧 [no cont] ❑ *The growing number of people seeking refuge in Thailand is beginning to concern Western aid agencies.* 日益增多的到泰国寻求避难的人数开始让西方援助机构感到担忧。● **con·cerned** ADJ 感到担忧的 ❑ *Academics and employers are concerned that students are not sufficiently prepared for college courses.* 学术界和用人单位都担心学生们对大学课程没有做好足够准备。3 V-T If you **concern yourself with** something, you give it attention because you think that it is important. 关心 ❑ *I didn't concern myself with politics.* 我不关心政治。● **con·cerned** ADJ 关心的 [v-link ADJ "with" n] ❑ *The agency is more concerned with making arty ads than understanding its clients' businesses.* 这家代理商更关心制作附庸风雅的广告而不是理解其客户的生意。4 V-T If something such as a book or a piece of information **concerns** a particular subject, it is about that subject. 有关于 [no cont] [no cont] ❑ *The bulk of the book concerns Sandy's two middle-aged children.* 这本书的主要部分讲的是桑迪的两个中年孩子。● **con·cerned** ADJ 有关于…的 [v-link ADJ "with" n] ❑ *Randolph's work was exclusively concerned with the effects of pollution on health.* 伦道夫的作品全部讲的是污染对健康的影响。5 V-T If a situation, event, or activity **concerns** you, it affects or involves you. (情况、事件、活动等) 与…有关 [no cont] ❑ *It was just a little unfinished business from my past, and it doesn't concern you at all.* 这只是我过去没有了结的一件小事，完全跟你没关。● **con·cerned** ADJ 有关的 [n ADJ, v-link ADJ "in/with" n] ❑ *It's a very stressful situation for everyone concerned.* 这对所有相关人员来说都是一个非常有压力的情况。6 N-COUNT A **concern** is a fact or situation that worries you. 令人担忧的事 ❑ *His concern was that people would know that he was responsible.* 他担忧的是人们会知道他应该负责任。7 N-COUNT You can refer to a company or business as a **concern**, usually when you are describing what type of company or business it is. 公司；生意 [FORMAL, BUSINESS] ❑ *If not a large concern, the Potomac Nursery was at least a successful one.* 虽不是一个大生意，波托马克幼儿园至少是一个成功的公司。8 N-VAR **Concern for** someone is a feeling that you want them to be happy, safe, and well. If you do something out of **concern for** someone, you do it because you want them to be happy, safe, and well. 关心 ❑ *Without her care and concern, he had no chance at all.* 没有她的照顾和关心，他根本就没有机会。9 N-SING If a situation or problem is your **concern**, it is something that you have a duty or responsibility to be involved with. 负责任的事 ❑ *The technical aspects were the concern of the Army.* 技术方面是军方负责的事。10 PHRASE If a company is a **going concern**, it is actually doing business, rather than having stopped trading or not yet having started trading. 在运营的公司 [BUSINESS] ❑ *The receivers will always prefer to sell a business as a going concern.* 接管人总是更希望出售仍然在运营的公司。

Word Partnership *concern* 的常用搭配：

N.	cause for concern 1
	health/safety concern 6
V.	express concern 1 8

con·cerned ♦◇◇ /kənsɜ̱rnd/ 1 → see **concern** 2 ADJ If you are **concerned to** do something, you want to do it because you think it is important. 想 (作某事) 的 [v-link ADJ to-inf] ❑ *We are deeply concerned to get out of this problematic situation.* 我们非常想摆脱这种问题重重的局面。

C

Word Web concert

A **rock concert** is much more than a group of **musicians** playing **music** on a **stage**. It is a full-scale **performance**. Each **band** must have a **manager** and an **agent** who **books** the **venue** and **promotes** the **show**. Roadies set up the stage, test the **microphones**, and tune the **instruments**. **Sound engineers** make sure the band sounds as good as possible. There's always **lighting** to **spotlight** the **lead singer** and **backup** singers. The bright, moving lights help to build excitement. The **fans** scream and yell when they hear their favorite **songs**. The **audience** never wants the show to end.

Word Partnership *concerned* 的常用搭配:

PREP. concerned **about** ***something***, concerned **for** ***something***, concerned **with** ***someone/something*** 1

con·cern·ing /kənsɜrnɪŋ/ 1 PREP You use **concerning** to indicate what a question or piece of information is about. 关于 [FORMAL] ❑ *For more information concerning the club, contact Mr. Coldwell.* 想了解更多有关该俱乐部的信息，请跟科德韦尔先生联系。 2 ADJ If something is **concerning**, it causes you to feel concerned about it. 令人担心的 [usu "it" v-link ADJ "that"] ❑ *It is particularly concerning that he is working for foreign companies while advising on foreign policy.* 尤其令人担心的是，他在为外交政策提供咨询的同时也在为外国公司工作。

con·cert ♦◇◇ /kɒnsərt/ (**concerts**) 1 N-COUNT A **concert** is a performance of music. 音乐会 ❑ *...a short concert of piano music.* …一场简短的钢琴音乐会。 ❑ *I've been to plenty of live rock concerts.* 我到过很多现场摇滚音乐会。 2 PHRASE If a musician or group of musicians appears **in concert**, they are giving a live performance. 现场演出 ❑ *I want people to remember Elvis in concert.* 我希望人们记住现场表演的埃尔维斯。

→ see Word Web: **concert**

▲ **con·cert·ed** /kənsɜrtɪd/ 1 ADJ A **concerted** action is done by several people or groups working together. 联合的 [ADJ n] ❑ *Martin Parry, author of the report, says it's time for concerted action by world leaders.* 这份报道的作者马丁•帕里说是各国领导人采取一致行动的时候了。 2 ADJ If you make a **concerted** effort to do something, you try very hard to do it. 极大的 [ADJ n] ❑ *He made a concerted effort to win me away from my steady, sweet but boring boyfriend.* 他作了极大的努力把我从踏实、可爱但令人乏味的男友手中赢走。

▲ **con·cer·to** /kəntʃɛərtoʊ/ (**concertos**) N-COUNT A **concerto** is a piece of music written for one or more solo instruments and an orchestra. 协奏曲 ❑ *...Tchaikovsky's First Piano Concerto.* …柴可夫斯基的《第一钢琴协奏曲》。

→ see **music**

con·ces·sion ♦◇◇ /kənsɛʃᵊn/ (**concessions**) 1 N-COUNT If you make a **concession to** someone, you agree to let them do or have something, especially in order to end an argument or conflict. 让步 ❑ *We made too many concessions and we got too little in return.* 我们作出了太多让步，而得到了太少回报。 2 N-COUNT A **concession** is a special right or privilege that is given to someone. 特许权 ❑ *Farmers were granted concessions from the government to develop the farms.* 农民已获得政府授权开发这些农场。 3 N-COUNT A **concession** is an arrangement where someone is given the right to sell a product or to run a business, especially in a building belonging to another business. (尤指在另一公司的建筑物内) 特许经营 [mainly AM, BUSINESS]

in BRIT, usually use **franchise**

❑ *...the man who ran the catering concession at the Rob Roy Links in Palominas.* …在帕罗米那斯的罗布罗依高尔夫球场特许经营饮食特许业务的人。

Word Partnership *concession* 的常用搭配:

V. **make** a concession 1
PREP. concessions **for** ***someone*** 1 2
N. **tax** concessions 2

con·ces·sion·aire /kənsɛʃənɛər/ (**concessionaires**) N-COUNT A **concessionaire** is a person or company that has the right to sell a product or to run a business, especially in a building belonging to another business. 特许经营者 [AM, BUSINESS]

in BRIT, use **franchisee**, **franchise-holder**

❑ *Concessionaires and shop owners report retail sales are up.* 特许经销商和店主们报告说零售额在增加。

con·cili·ation /kənsɪlieɪʃᵊn/ N-UNCOUNT **Conciliation** is willingness to end a disagreement or the process of ending a disagreement. 和解意愿；和解 ❑ *Resolving the dispute will require a mood of conciliation on both sides.* 解决这场争端需要双方都抱有和解的态度。 ❑ *The experience has left him sceptical about efforts of conciliation.* 那次经历让他对和解的努力有疑虑。

con·cilia·tory /kənsɪliətɔri/ ADJ When you are **conciliatory** in your actions or behavior, you show that you are willing to end a disagreement with someone. 愿意和解的 ❑ *The next time he spoke, he used a more conciliatory tone.* 再次说话时他换了一种更愿和解的口气。

★ **con·cise** /kənsaɪs/ 1 ADJ Something that is **concise** says everything that is necessary without using any unnecessary words. 简洁的 ❑ *Burton's text is concise and informative.* 伯顿的文章文字简洁、内容丰富。 ● **con·cise·ly** ADV 简洁地 [ADV with v] ❑ *He'd delivered his report clearly and concisely.* 他简洁明了地陈述了他的报告。 2 ADJ A **concise** edition of a book, especially a dictionary, is shorter than the original edition. 简明的 (版本) [ADJ n] ❑ *...Sotheby's Concise Encyclopedia of Porcelain.* …索思比的《简明瓷器百科全书》。

con·clude ♦◇◇ /kənklud/ (**concludes, concluding, concluded**) 1 V-T If you **conclude that** something is true, you decide that it is true using the facts you know as a basis. 断定 ❑ *Larry had concluded that he had no choice but to accept Paul's words as the truth.* 拉里断定他别无选择，只能相信保罗所说为实。 ❑ *So what can we conclude from this debate?* 那么从这场辩论中我们能推断出什么呢？ 2 V-T/V-I When you **conclude**, you say the last thing that you are going to say. 结束 (说话) [FORMAL] ❑ *"It's a waste of time," he concluded.* "这是浪费时间，"他最后说道。 3 V-T/V-I When something **concludes**, or when you **conclude** it, you end it. 使…结束 结束; [FORMAL] ❑ *The evening concluded with dinner and speeches.* 这个夜晚以晚宴和演讲告一段落。 4 V-T If one person or group **concludes** an agreement, such as a treaty or business deal, **with** another, they arrange it. You can also say that two people or groups **conclude** an agreement. 达成 (协议) [FORMAL] ❑ *Mexico and the Philippines have both concluded agreements with their commercial bank creditors.* 墨西哥和菲律宾双方都与他们的商业银行债权人达成了协议。

Word Partnership *conclude* 的常用搭配:

N. conclude ***something***, conclude **that** ***something*** 1 4
conclude **a deal** 4
PRON. **he/she** concluded 2 3

con·clu·sion ♦◇◇ /kənkluʒᵊn/ (**conclusions**) 1 N-COUNT When you come to a **conclusion**, you decide that something is true after you have thought about it carefully and have considered all the relevant facts. 结论 ❑ *Over the years I've come to the conclusion that she's a very great musician.* 这些年我得出的结论是，她是位非常伟大的音乐家。 2 N-SING The **conclusion** of something is its ending. 结束；结局 ❑ *At the conclusion of the program, I asked the children if they had any questions they wanted to ask me.* 节目结束时我问孩子们是否有要问我的问题。 3 N-SING The **conclusion** of a treaty or a business deal is the act of arranging it or agreeing on it. (条约、交易等的) 达成 ❑ *...the expected conclusion of a free-trade agreement between Mexico and the United States.* …墨西哥和美国之间自由贸易协议的如期达成。 4 PHRASE You say "**in conclusion**" to indicate that what you are about to say is the last thing that you want to say. 最后 (用以表明讲话即将结束) ❑ *In conclusion, walking is a cheap, safe, enjoyable, and readily available form of exercise.* 综上所述，散步是一种廉价、安全、有趣而又随时可以开展的运动形式。

Word Partnership *conclusion* 的常用搭配：
V. **come to a** conclusion, **draw a** conclusion, **reach a** conclusion 1
N. conclusion **of** *something* 2 3
PREP. **in** conclusion 4

con·clu·sive /kənklusɪv/ ADJ **Conclusive** evidence shows that something is certainly true. 确凿的 ❑ *Her attorneys claim there is no conclusive evidence that any murders took place.* 她的律师们声称没有任何发生过谋杀的确凿证据。

con·coct /kənkɒkt/ (**concocts, concocting, concocted**) 1 V-T If you **concoct** an excuse or explanation, you invent one that is not true. 编造 ❑ *Mr. Ferguson said the prisoner concocted the story to get a lighter sentence.* 费格森先生说该囚犯为了获轻罚编造了这个故事。 2 V-T If you **concoct** something, especially something unusual, you make it by mixing several things together. 调制 ❑ *Eugene was concocting Rossini Cocktails from champagne and pureed raspberries.* 尤金正在用香槟和覆盆子果泥调制罗西尼鸡尾酒。

con·coc·tion /kənkɒkʃᵊn/ (**concoctions**) N-COUNT A **concoction** is something that has been made out of several things mixed together. 调制品 ❑ *...a concoction of honey, yogurt, oats, and apples.* …一种加了蜂蜜、酸奶、燕麦和苹果的调制品。

con·crete ♦◇◇ /kɒŋkrit/ (**concretes, concreting, concreted**) 1 N-UNCOUNT **Concrete** is a substance used for building which is made by mixing together cement, sand, small stones, and water. 混凝土 ❑ *The posts have to be set in concrete.* 这些柱子必须固定在混凝土中。 ❑ *We sat on the concrete floor.* 我们坐在混凝土地板上。 2 V-T When you **concrete** something such as a path, you cover it with concrete. 给（道路等）浇混凝土 ❑ *He merely cleared and concreted the floors.* 他只是清理了地板并浇上了混凝土。 3 ADJ You use **concrete** to indicate that something is definite and specific. 明确具体的. ❑ *I had no concrete evidence.* 我当时没有明确而具体的证据。 ❑ *There were no concrete proposals on the table.* 没有提交讨论的具体提议。 4 ADJ A **concrete** object is a real, physical object. 实物的 ❑ *...using concrete objects to teach addition and subtraction.* …用实物教加减运算。 5 ADJ A **concrete** noun is a noun that refers to a physical object rather than to a quality or idea. 具体的（名词）[ADJ n]

con·cur /kənkɜr/ (**concurs, concurring, concurred**) V-RECIP If one person **concurs with** another person, the two people agree. You can also say that two people **concur**. 意见一致 [FORMAL] ❑ *Local feeling does not necessarily concur with the press.* 当地人的看法不一定和媒体一致。 ❑ *Daniels and Franklin concurred in an investigator's suggestion that the police be commended.* 丹尼尔斯和富兰克林对一位调查员提出的警方应受到表扬的提议意见一致。

Word Link *curr, curs ≈ running, flowing : concurrent, current, cursor*

con·cur·rent /kənkɜrənt/ ADJ **Concurrent** events or situations happen at the same time. 同时发生的 ❑ *Galerie St. Etienne is holding three concurrent exhibitions.* 圣・艾蒂安美术馆在同时举办3场展览。 ❑ *He will actually be serving three concurrent five-year sentences.* 实际上他要同期服3个5年的刑期。 ● **con·cur·rent·ly** ★ ADV 同时发生地 [ADV with v] ❑ *He was jailed for 33 months to run concurrently with a sentence he is already serving for burglary.* 他被关进监狱33个月，与因入室行窃已经在服的刑期同期执行。

con·cus·sion /kənkʌʃᵊn/ (**concussions**) N-VAR If you suffer a **concussion** after a blow to your head, you lose consciousness or feel sick or confused. 脑震荡 ❑ *Nicky was rushed to the hospital with a concussion.* 尼基由于脑震荡被迅速送往了医院。

Word Link *damn, demn ≈ harm, loss : condemn, damning, indemnify*

con·demn ♦◇◇ /kəndɛm/ (**condemns, condemning, condemned**) 1 V-T If you **condemn** something, you say that it is very bad and unacceptable. 谴责；责备 ❑ *Political leaders united yesterday to condemn the latest wave of violence.* 政治领袖们昨天联合谴责最近发生的一波暴力事件。 ❑ *Graham was right to condemn his players for lack of ability, attitude, and application.* 格雷厄姆责备他的队员缺乏能力、态度不端正以及不肯用功，这是对的。 2 V-T If someone **is condemned to** a punishment, they are given this punishment. 判（某人某罪）[usu passive] ❑ *He was condemned to life imprisonment.* 他被判终身监禁。 3 V-T If circumstances **condemn** you **to** an unpleasant situation, they make it certain that you will suffer in that way. 迫使（陷于不幸的境地） ❑ *Their lack of qualifications condemned them to a lifetime of boring, usually poorly-paid work.* 他们资历的缺乏迫使他们要一辈子做单调乏味且通常报酬很低的工作。 4 V-T If authorities **condemn** a building, they officially decide that it is not safe and must be pulled down or repaired. 确定（某建筑物）为危房 ❑ *The court's ruling clears the way to condemn buildings in the area.* 法院的裁决为确定这一地区的建筑物为危房扫清了障碍。 5 → see also **condemned**

★ **con·dem·na·tion** /kɒndɛmneɪʃᵊn/ (**condemnations**) N-VAR **Condemnation** is the act of saying that something or someone is very bad and unacceptable. 谴责；责备 ❑ *There was widespread condemnation of Saturday's killings.* 人们对星期六的几起杀人事件给予谴责。

con·demned /kəndɛmd/ ADJ A **condemned** man or woman is going to be executed. 判了死刑的 ❑ *...prison officers who had sat with the condemned man during his last days.* …在那个死囚临终前的日子看管他的狱警们。

con·dense /kəndɛns/ (**condenses, condensing, condensed**) 1 V-T If you **condense** something, especially a piece of writing or a speech, you make it shorter, usually by including only the most important parts. 简缩（尤指文章、演讲稿）❑ *When you summarize, you condense an extended idea or argument into a sentence or more in your own words.* 总结的时候，用自己的话把拓展了的观念或论据简缩成一句或几句话。 2 V-T/V-I When a gas or vapor **condenses**, or **is condensed**, it changes into a liquid. （气体、蒸汽）冷凝 ❑ *Water vapor condenses to form clouds.* 水蒸汽冷凝形成云。
→ see **matter, water**

Word Link *scend ≈ climbing : ascend, condescend, descend*

con·de·scend /kɒndɪsɛnd/ (**condescends, condescending, condescended**) 1 V-T If someone **condescends to** do something, they agree to do it, but in a way which shows that they think they are better than other people and should not have to do it. 屈尊 [DISAPPROVAL] ❑ *When he condescended to speak, he contradicted himself three or four times in the space of half an hour.* 当他屈尊讲话时，半小时内有三四次前后矛盾。 2 V-I If you say that someone **condescends to** other people, you are showing your disapproval of the fact that they behave in a way which shows that they think they are superior to other people. 摆出高人一等的架子 [DISAPPROVAL] ❑ *Don't condescend to me.* 不要对我摆出高人一等的样子。

con·de·scend·ing /kɒndɪsɛndɪŋ/ ADJ If you say that someone is **condescending**, you are showing your disapproval of the fact that they talk or behave in a way which shows that they think they are superior to other people. 显得高人一等的 [DISAPPROVAL] ❑ *I'm fed up with your money and your whole condescending attitude.* 我受够了你的钱和你整个高人一等的态度。

con·di·tion ♦♦♦ /kəndɪʃᵊn/ (**conditions, conditioning, conditioned**) 1 N-SING If you talk about the **condition** of a person or thing, you are talking about the state that they are in, especially how good or bad their physical state is. （尤指健康）状况 [also no det] ❑ *He remains in a critical condition in a California hospital.* 他在加利福尼亚的一家医院里，仍处于危急的状况。 ❑ *I received several compliments on the condition of my skin.* 我得到好几次有关我皮肤的状况的夸赞。 ❑ *The two-bedroom chalet is in good condition.* 这个有两间卧室的小屋状况良好。 2 N-PLURAL The **conditions** under which something is done or happens are all the factors or circumstances which directly affect it. （某事完成或发生的）条件 ❑ *It's easy to make a wrong turn here even under ideal weather conditions.* 即使在非常理想的天气条件下，也很容易在这里拐错弯。 3 N-PLURAL The **conditions** in which people live or work are the factors which affect their comfort, safety, or health. （生活或工作的）环境 ❑ *People are living in appalling conditions.* 人们生活在极其恶劣的环境中。 ❑ *I could not work in these conditions any longer.* 我再也不能在这样的环境中工作了。 4 N-COUNT A **condition** is something which must happen or be done in order for something else to be possible, especially when this is written into a contract or law. （尤指写进合同或法律中的某事发生的）条件 ❑ *Argentina failed to hit the economic targets set as a condition for loan payments.* 阿根廷没能达到作为贷款偿还条件而设的的经济目标。 ❑ *...terms and conditions of employment.* …雇用条款和条件。 5 N-COUNT If someone has a particular **condition**, they have an illness or other medical problem. 疾病；问题 ❑ *Doctors suspect he may have a heart condition.* 医生怀疑他可能有心脏病。 6 V-T If someone **is conditioned** by their experiences or environment, they are influenced by them over a period of time so that they do certain things or think in a particular way.

C

C

习惯于(以某种方式做事或思考) [usu passive] ❑ *We are all conditioned by early impressions and experiences.* 我们都受早年印象和经历的长期影响。❑ *I just feel women are conditioned into doing housework.* 我只是觉得女人习惯于做家务。● **con·di·tion·ing** N-UNCOUNT 长期影响 ❑ *Because of social conditioning, men don't expect to be managed by women.* 由于社会的长期影响，男人不希望被女人管。**7** PHRASE When you agree to do something **on condition that** something else happens, you mean that you will only do it if this other thing also happens. 在(某事发生的)条件下 ❑ *He agreed to speak to reporters on condition that he was not identified.* 他同意在不暴露身份的条件下和记者谈话。
→ see **factory**

Word Partnership *condition* 的常用搭配:
ADJ. **critical** condition **1 5**
N. **weather** conditions, **working** conditions **2 3**

con·di·tion·al /kəndɪʃənəl/ **1** ADJ If a situation or agreement is **conditional on** something, it will only happen or continue if this thing happens. 以…为条件的 ❑ *Their support is conditional on his proposals meeting their approval.* 他们的支持是以他的提议得到他们的批准为条件的。❑ *...a conditional offer.* …一项有条件的提议。**2** ADJ In grammar, a **conditional** clause is a subordinate clause which refers to a situation which may exist or happen. Most conditional clauses begin with "if" or "unless," for example "If that happens, we'll be in big trouble" and "You don't have to come unless you want to." 条件性的(分句) [ADJ n]

★ **con·do·lence** /kəndoʊləns/ (**condolences**) **1** N-UNCOUNT A message of **condolence** is a message in which you express your sympathy for someone because one of their friends or relatives has died recently. 吊唁 ❑ *Neil sent him a letter of condolence.* 尼尔给他发了一封吊唁信。**2** N-PLURAL When you offer or express your **condolences** to someone, you express your sympathy for them because one of their friends or relatives has died recently. 哀悼 ❑ *He expressed his condolences to the families of the people who died in the incident.* 他向那次事故遇难者家属表达了哀悼。

★ **con·dom** /kɒndəm/ (**condoms**) N-COUNT A **condom** is a covering made of thin rubber which a man can wear on his penis as a contraceptive or as protection against disease during sexual intercourse. 安全套

con·done /kəndoʊn/ (**condones, condoning, condoned**) V-T If someone **condones** behavior that is morally wrong, they accept it and allow it to happen. 纵容 [oft with brd-neg] ❑ *I have never encouraged nor condoned violence.* 我从来没有鼓励或纵容过暴力行为。

▲ **con·du·cive** /kəndusɪv/ ADJ If one thing is **conducive to** another thing, it makes the other thing likely to happen. (对某事)有助益的 ❑ *Make your bedroom as conducive to sleep as possible.* 把你的卧室尽可能地布置得有助于睡眠。

con·duct ♦♦◇ (**conducts, conducting, conducted**)

The verb is pronounced /kəndʌkt/. The noun is pronounced /kɒndʌkt/.

动词读作 /kəndʌkt/。名词读作 /kɒndʌkt/。

1 V-T When you **conduct** an activity or task, you organize it and do it. 组织并实施 ❑ *I decided to conduct an experiment.* 我决定做一项实验。**2** V-T If you **conduct** yourself in a particular way, you behave in that way. (以某种方式)表现 ❑ *The way he conducts himself reflects on the family.* 他的行为方式折射出他的家庭。**3** V-T/V-I When someone **conducts** an orchestra or choir, they stand in front of it and direct its performance. 指挥(交响乐、合唱等) ❑ *Dennis had recently begun a successful career conducting opera.* 丹尼斯最近成功地开始了指挥歌剧的生涯。❑ *Solti continued to conduct here and abroad.* 佐尔蒂继续在国内外指挥。**4** V-T If something **conducts** heat or electricity, it allows heat or electricity to pass through it or along it. 传导(热、电) [no cont] ❑ *Water conducts heat faster than air.* 水比空气导热快。**5** N-SING The **conduct of** a task or activity is the way in which it is organized and carried out. 进行实施 ❑ *Also up for discussion will be the conduct of free and fair elections.* 还需讨论的是公平自由的选举如何进行。**6** N-UNCOUNT Someone's **conduct** is the way they behave in particular situations. (某人在某情形中的)行为方式 ❑ *For Europeans, the law is a statement of basic principles of civilized conduct.* 对欧洲人来说，该法律是对基本文明行为原则的表述。

Thesaurus *conduct* 另参见:
V. control, direct, manage **1**
N. attitude, behavior, manner **6**

Word Partnership *conduct* 的常用搭配:
N. conduct **business**, conduct **an experiment 1**
code of conduct **6**

con·duc·tor /kəndʌktər/ (**conductors**) **1** N-COUNT A **conductor** is a person who stands in front of an orchestra or choir and directs its performance. (交响乐、合唱的)指挥 **2** N-COUNT On a train, a **conductor** is a person whose job is to travel on the train in order to help passengers and check tickets. 列车员 [AM]

in BRIT, use **guard**

3 N-COUNT On a streetcar or a bus, the **conductor** is the person whose job is to sell tickets to the passengers. (公共汽车等的)售票员 **4** N-COUNT A **conductor** is a substance that heat or electricity can pass through or along. (热、电的)导体 ❑ *Graphite is a highly efficient conductor of electricity.* 石墨是一种高效的电导体。
5 → see also **semiconductor**
→ see **metal**

▲ **cone** /koʊn/ (**cones**) **1** N-COUNT A **cone** is a shape with a circular base ending in a point at the top. 圆锥体 ❑ *...orange traffic cones.* …橙色的交通锥形警示标。❑ *...the streetlight's yellow cone of light.* …街灯的黄色锥形光柱。**2** N-COUNT A **cone** is the fruit of a tree such as a pine or fir. (松树、冷杉等的)球果 ❑ *...a bowl of fir cones.* …一碗冷杉球果。**3** N-COUNT A **cone** is a thin, cone-shaped cookie that is used for holding ice cream. You can also refer to ice cream that you eat in this way as a **cone**. 锥形蛋卷筒；蛋卷冰淇淋 ❑ *She stopped by the ice-cream shop and had a chocolate cone.* 她在冰淇淋店停下买了个巧克力蛋卷冰淇淋。
→ see **solid, volcano, volume**

con·fec·tion·ers' sug·ar N-UNCOUNT **Confectioners' sugar** is very fine white sugar that is used for making frosting and candy. (用于制作糖衣、糖果的)糖粉 [AM]

in BRIT, use **icing sugar**

★ **con·fed·era·tion** /kənfɛdəreɪʃən/ (**confederations**) N-COUNT; N-IN-NAMES A **confederation** is an organization or group consisting of smaller groups or states, especially one that exists for business or political purposes. (尤指为商业或政治目的而结成的)联邦；联盟 ❑ *...the Confederation of Indian Industry.* …印度工业联盟。

★ **con·fer** /kənfɜr/ (**confers, conferring, conferred**) **1** V-RECIP When you **confer with** someone, you discuss something with them in order to make a decision. You can also say that two people **confer**. 商议 ❑ *He conferred with Hill and the others in his office.* 他和希尔以及他办公室里的其他人进行了商议。**2** V-T To **confer** something such as power or an honor **on** someone means to give it to them. 授予 [FORMAL] ❑ *The constitution also confers large powers on Brazil's 25 constituent states.* 宪法还授予巴西25个成员州极大的权力。

con·fer·ence ♦♦♦ /kɒnfərəns, -frəns/ (**conferences**) **1** N-COUNT A **conference** is a meeting, often lasting a few days, which is organized on a particular subject or to bring together people who have a common interest. 专题讨论会 ❑ *The president took the unprecedented step of summoning all the state governors to a conference on education.* 总统采取了前所未有的举措，召集所有的州长参加一次教育讨论会。❑ *...the Alternative Energy conference.* …可替代能源讨论会。**2** N-COUNT A **conference** is a meeting at which formal discussions take place. (进行正式讨论的)会议 [also "in" N] ❑ *They sat down at the dinner table for a conference.* 他们在餐桌旁坐下开会。
3 → see also **press conference**

con·fer·ence call (**conference calls**) N-COUNT A **conference call** is a phone call in which more than two people take part. 电话会议 [BUSINESS] ❑ *There are daily conference calls with Washington.* 与华盛顿方面有每日电话会议。

con·fess /kənfɛs/ (**confesses, confessing, confessed**) **1** V-T/V-I If someone **confesses** to doing something wrong, they admit that they did it. 承认(做了某事) ❑ *He had confessed to seventeen murders.* 他已供认了17项谋杀罪。❑ *I had expected her to confess that she only wrote these books for the money.* 我曾期望她承认她写这些书仅仅是为了钱。❑ *Ray changed his mind, claiming that he had been forced into confessing.* 雷改变了主意，声称他是被迫承认的。**2** V-T/V-I If someone **confesses** or **confesses** their sins, they tell God or a priest about their sins so that they can be forgiven. 忏悔 ❑ *You just go to the church and confess your sins.* 你就去教堂忏悔你的罪过吧。

con·fes·sion /kənfɛʃən/ (**confessions**) 1 N-COUNT A **confession** is a signed statement by someone in which they admit that they have committed a particular crime. 供状 ❑ *They forced him to sign a confession.* 他们强迫他签了供状。 2 N-VAR **Confession** is the act of admitting that you have done something that you are ashamed of or embarrassed about. 承认 ❑ *I have a confession to make.* 我要作个坦白。 ❑ *The diaries are a mixture of confession and observation.* 这些日记混合着自白和一些观察。 3 N-VAR If you make a **confession** of your beliefs or feelings, you publicly tell people that this is what you believe or feel. (对信念、情感的) 表白 ❑ *...Tatyana's confession of love.* …塔蒂安娜的爱的表白。 4 N-VAR In the Catholic church and in some other churches, if you go to **confession**, you privately tell a priest about your sins and ask for forgiveness. (私下对神父的) 忏悔 ❑ *He never went to Father Porter for confession again.* 他再也没私下去向波特神父忏悔。

▲ **con·fide** /kənfaɪd/ (**confides, confiding, confided**) V-T/V-I If you **confide in** someone, you tell them a secret. 吐露 (秘密等) ❑ *I knew she had some fundamental problems in her marriage because she had confided in me a year earlier.* 我知道她的婚姻存在一些根本问题，因为她一年前曾向我吐露过。 ❑ *He confided to me that he felt like he was being punished.* 他私下跟我吐露过他觉得自己像在受惩罚。

con·fi·dence ♦♦◊ /kɒnfɪdəns/ 1 N-UNCOUNT If you have **confidence in** someone, you feel that you can trust them. 信任 ❑ *I have every confidence in you.* 我对你有完全的信任。 ❑ *This has contributed to the lack of confidence in the FDA.* 这导致了对食品与药品管理局信任的缺乏。 2 N-UNCOUNT If you have **confidence**, you feel sure about your abilities, qualities, or ideas. 自信心 ❑ *The band is in excellent form and brimming with confidence.* 该乐队处于极好的状态，表现得充满信心。 3 N-UNCOUNT If you can say something **with confidence**, you feel certain it is correct. 把握 ❑ *I can say with confidence that such rumors were totally groundless.* 我可以很有把握地说这些传言完全没有根据。 4 N-UNCOUNT If you tell someone something **in confidence**, you tell them a secret. 保密 ❑ *We told you all these things in confidence.* 我们告诉你的这些事情都是保密的。 ❑ *Even telling Lois seemed a betrayal of confidence.* 甚至告诉洛伊斯似乎也是对保密的背叛。 ● PHRASE If you **take** someone **into** your **confidence**, you tell them a secret. 向某人吐露秘密

→ see **stock market**

con·fi·dent ♦◊◊ /kɒnfɪdənt/ 1 ADJ If you are **confident** about something, you are certain that it will happen in the way you want it to. 有信心的 ❑ *I am confident that everything will come out right in time.* 我相信最终一切都会好起来的。 ❑ *Mr. Ryan is confident of success.* 瑞安先生对成功有信心。 ● **con·fi·dent·ly** ADV 有信心地 [ADV with v] ❑ *I can confidently promise that this year is going to be very different.* 我可以有信心地保证今年将大不一样。 2 ADJ If a person or their manner is **confident**, they feel sure about their own abilities, qualities, or ideas. 自信的 ❑ *In time he became more confident and relaxed.* 最终他变得更加自信而从容了。 ● **con·fi·dent·ly** ADV 自信地 ❑ *She walked confidently across the hall.* 她自信地走过大厅。 3 ADJ If you are **confident that** something is true, you are sure that it is true. A **confident** statement is one that the speaker is sure is true. 确信的 ❑ *She is confident that everybody is on her side.* 她确信每个人都在她那一边。 ● **con·fi·dent·ly** ADV 确信地 [ADV with v] ❑ *I can confidently say that none of them were or are racist.* 我可以确信地说他们当中没有人过去或现在是种族主义者。

★ **con·fi·den·tial** /kɒnfɪdɛnʃəl/ 1 ADJ Information that is **confidential** is meant to be kept secret or private. 保密的 ❑ *She accused them of leaking confidential information about her private life.* 她指责他们泄露了有关她的私生活的保密信息。 ● **con·fi·den·tial·ly** ADV 保密地 ❑ *People can phone in, knowing that any information they give will be treated confidentially.* 人们可以打电话进来，他们知道他们所提供的一切信息都会被保密。 ● **con·fi·den·ti·al·ity** /kɒnfɪdɛnʃiælɪti/ N-UNCOUNT 保密性 ❑ *...the confidentiality of the client-attorney relationship.* …客户与律师之间的保密。 2 ADJ If you talk to someone in a **confidential** way, you talk to them quietly because what you are saying is secret or private. 悄悄的 ❑ *"Look," he said in a confidential tone, "I want you to know that me and Joey are cops."* “喂，”他悄声说，“我想要你知道我和乔伊都是警察。” ● **con·fi·den·tial·ly** ADV 悄悄地 ❑ *Nash hadn't raised his voice, still spoke rather softly, confidentially.* 纳什没有提高嗓门，仍然很轻地、悄悄地说。

Thesaurus *confidential* 另参见:
ADJ. private, restricted; *(ant.)* public 1

con·fi·den·tial·ly /kɒnfɪdɛnʃəli/ 1 ADV **Confidentially** is used to say that what you are telling someone is a secret and should not be discussed with anyone else. 机密地 [ADV with cl] ❑ *Confidentially, I am not sure that it wasn't above their heads.* 私下里说，我不确定这没有超出他们的理解。 2 → see also **confidential**

★ **con·figu·ra·tion** /kənfɪgyəreɪʃən/ (**configurations**) 1 N-COUNT A **configuration** is an arrangement of a group of things. 布局；排列 [FORMAL] ❑ *...Stonehenge, in southwestern England, an ancient configuration of giant stones.* …史前巨石柱群，位于英国西南部，是一座古代巨石阵列。 2 N-UNCOUNT The **configuration** of a computer system is the way in which all its parts, such as the hardware and software, are connected together in order for the computer to work. (计算机系统的) 配置 [COMPUTING] ❑ *Prices range from $119 to $199, depending on the particular configuration.* 价格根据配置的不同从119美元到199美元不等。

Word Link *fig ≈ form : shape : configure, disfigure, figurative*

con·fig·ure /kənfɪgyər/ (**configures, configuring, configured**) V-T If you **configure** a piece of computer equipment, you set it up so that it is ready for use. 配置 (计算机设备) [COMPUTING] ❑ *How easy was it to configure the software?* 配置该软件有多容易呢？

con·fine /kənfaɪn/ (**confines, confining, confined**) 1 V-T To **confine** something **to** a particular place or group means to prevent it from spreading beyond that place or group. 将 (某事物) 控制 (在某地范围内) ❑ *Health officials have successfully confined the epidemic to the Tabatinga area.* 卫生官员们已经成功地将该传染病控制在塔巴廷加地区。 2 V-T If you **confine** somebody or something, you prevent them from leaving or escaping. 监禁 ❑ *He was confined in an internment camp in Utah.* 他被监禁在犹他州的一个拘留营里。 ❑ *They decided not to let their new dog run loose, confining it to a fenced enclosure during the day.* 他们决定不让他们的新狗乱跑，白天把它关在有围栏的围圈里。 3 V-T If you **confine yourself** or your activities **to** something, you do only that thing and are involved with nothing else. 将 (自己或自己的活动) 局限于 ❑ *He did not confine himself to the one language.* 他没把自己局限于这一门语言。

con·fined /kənfaɪnd/ 1 ADJ If something is **confined to** a particular place, it exists only in that place. If it is **confined to** a particular group, only members of that group have it. 只限于 (某地、某团体) 的 [v-link ADJ "to" n] ❑ *The problem is not confined to Georgia.* 这个问题不只限于佐治亚州。 2 ADJ A **confined** space or area is small and enclosed by walls. (空间、区域) 有限的 ❑ *His long legs bent up in the confined space.* 他长长的双腿蜷缩在有限的空间里。 3 ADJ If someone is **confined to** a wheelchair, bed, or house, they have to stay there, because they are disabled or ill. 被困在 (轮椅、床上、家里) 的 [v-link ADJ "to" n] ❑ *He had been confined to a wheelchair since childhood.* 他从孩童时起就被困在轮椅上了。

con·fine·ment /kənfaɪnmənt/ N-UNCOUNT **Confinement** is the state of being forced to stay in a prison or another place which you cannot leave. 关押 ❑ *She had been held in solitary confinement for four months.* 她曾被单独关押了4个月。

Word Link *firm ≈ making strong : affirm, confirm, infirm*

con·firm ♦♦◊ /kənfɜrm/ (**confirms, confirming, confirmed**) 1 V-T If something **confirms** what you believe, suspect, or fear, it shows that it is definitely true. 证实 (某人的观点、猜疑、担心的事) [no cont] ❑ *X-rays have confirmed that he has not broken any bones.* X光片已经证实他没有骨折。 ● **con·fir·ma·tion** /kɒnfərmeɪʃən/ N-UNCOUNT 证实 ❑ *They took her resignation as confirmation of their suspicions.* 他们认为她的辞职证实了他们的猜疑。 2 V-T If you **confirm** something that has been stated or suggested, you say that it is true because you know about it. 证实 (陈述或建议的事物) ❑ *The spokesman confirmed that the area was now in rebel hands.* 该发言人证实该地区现在处于反叛者的控制之中。 ● **con·fir·ma·tion** N-UNCOUNT 确认 ❑ *She glanced over at James for confirmation.* 她瞟了詹姆斯一眼寻求确认。 3 V-T If you **confirm** an arrangement or appointment, you say that it is definite, usually in a letter or on the telephone. (常指通过信件或电话) 确认 (安排、预约) ❑ *You make the reservation, and I'll confirm it in writing.* 你先预定，我再以书面形式确认。 ● **con·fir·ma·tion** N-UNCOUNT 确准 ❑ *Travel arrangements are subject to confirmation by the head office.* 旅行安排需经总公司确准。 4 V-T If someone **is confirmed**, they are formally accepted as a member of a Christian church during a ceremony in which they say they believe what the church teaches. 给…施坚信礼 [usu passive] ❑ *He was confirmed as a member of the Methodist Church.* 他受了坚信礼成为卫理公会的一员。 ● **con·fir·ma·tion** N-VAR (**confirmations**) 施坚信礼 ❑ *...when I was being prepared for Confirmation.* …当我为坚信礼作准备的时候。 5 V-T If something **confirms** you **in** your decision, belief, or opinion, it makes you think that you are definitely right. 使…坚信(其决定、信念、观点的正确性) [no cont] ❑ *It has confirmed me in my decision not to become a nun.* 这已让我坚信我不当修女的决定是正确的。 6 V-T If something **confirms** you **as** something, it shows that you definitely deserve a name, role, or position. 证明(某人是当之无愧的…) ❑ *Her new role could confirm her as one of our leading actors.* 她的新角色可以证明她是当之无愧的我们最好的演员之一。

▲ **con·fis·cate** /kɒnfɪskeɪt/ (**confiscates, confiscating, confiscated**) V-T If you **confiscate** something **from** someone, you take it away from them, usually as a punishment. 没收 ❑ *The law has been used to confiscate assets from people who have committed minor offenses.* 该法律已被用于没收那些犯了轻微过错的人的财产。 ● **con·fis·ca·tion** /kɒnfɪskeɪʃᵊn/ N-VAR (**confiscations**) 没收 ❑ *The new laws allow the confiscation of assets purchased with proceeds of the drugs trade.* 新法律允许通过毒品交易获益购置的财产的没收。

Word Link *flict ≈ striking : affliction, conflict, inflict*

con·flict ♦♦◇ (**conflicts, conflicting, conflicted**)

The noun is pronounced /kɒnflɪkt/. The verb is pronounced /kənflɪkt/.

名词读作 /kɒnflɪkt/。动词读作 /kənflɪkt/。

1 N-UNCOUNT **Conflict** is serious disagreement and argument about something important. If two people or groups are **in conflict**, they have had a serious disagreement or argument and have not yet reached agreement. 争执; 分歧 [oft "in/into" N] ❑ *Try to keep any conflict between you and your ex-partner to a minimum.* 尽量把你和前合伙人之间的争执控制到最少。 2 N-UNCOUNT **Conflict** is a state of mind in which you find it impossible to make a decision. 矛盾心态 ❑ *...the anguish of his own inner conflict.* …他自己内心矛盾的痛苦。 3 N-VAR **Conflict** is fighting between countries or groups of people. (国家或团体之间的) 冲突 [WRITTEN] ❑ *...talks aimed at ending four decades of conflict.* …旨在结束40年冲突的会谈。 4 N-VAR A **conflict** is a serious difference between two or more beliefs, ideas, or interests. If two beliefs, ideas, or interests are **in conflict**, they are very different. (信念、观点、利益之间的) 冲突 ❑ *There is a conflict between what they are doing and what you want.* 他们在做的和你想要的之间存在冲突。 5 V-RECIP If ideas, beliefs, or accounts **conflict**, they are very different from each other and it seems impossible for them to exist together or to each be true. (观点、信念、陈述等) 相冲突 ❑ *Personal ethics and professional ethics sometimes conflict.* 个人道德与职业道德之间有时会相冲突。 ❑ *He held firm opinions which usually conflicted with mine.* 他持有坚定的、通常跟我的相冲突的观点。

→ see war

Word Partnership *conflict* 的常用搭配:

N. conflict **resolution, source of** conflict 1
V. **end/resolve/settle a** conflict 1 3
avoid conflict 1 3 4
ADJ. **military** conflict 3

★ **con·form** /kənfɔrm/ (**conforms, conforming, conformed**) 1 V-I If something **conforms to** something such as a law or someone's wishes, it is of the required type or quality. (与法律、愿望等) 相符合 ❑ *The lamp has been designed to conform to new safety standards.* 该灯设计得符合新的安全标准。 2 V-I If you **conform**, you behave in the way that you are expected or supposed to behave. 守规矩 ❑ *Many children who can't or don't conform are bullied.* 许多不守规矩的孩子受欺负。

★ **con·form·ity** /kənfɔrmɪti/ 1 N-UNCOUNT If something happens **in conformity with** something such as a law or someone's wishes, it happens as the law says it should, or as the person wants it to. 依照 ❑ *The prime minister is, in conformity with their constitution, chosen by the president.* 首相是遵照宪法由总统选定的。 2 N-UNCOUNT **Conformity** means behaving in the same way as most other people. 随大流 ❑ *Excessive conformity is usually caused by fear of disapproval.* 过分随大流通常是由于担心不被认同造成的。

con·found /kənfaʊnd/ (**confounds, confounding, confounded**) V-T If someone or something **confounds** you, they make you feel surprised or confused, often by showing you that your opinions or expectations of them were wrong. 使吃惊; 使困惑 ❑ *He momentarily confounded his critics by his cool handling of the hostage crisis.* 他通过冷静处理人质危机顿时使他的批评者们大吃一惊。

con·front ♦◇◇ /kənfrʌnt/ (**confronts, confronting, confronted**) 1 V-T If you **are confronted with** a problem, task, or difficulty, you have to deal with it. 面临(问题、任务、困难等) ❑ *She was confronted with severe money problems.* 她面临严重的资金问题。 2 V-T If you **confront** a difficult situation or issue, you accept the fact that it exists and try to deal with it. 正视(困难局面或问题) ❑ *We are learning how to confront death.* 我们在学习如何正视死亡。 3 V-T If you **are confronted** by something that you find threatening or difficult to deal with, it is there in front of you. 面对(有威胁或难处理的事物) [usu passive] ❑ *I was confronted with an array of knobs, levers, and switches.* 我面对着一排旋钮、控制杆和开关。 4 V-T If you **confront** someone, you stand or sit in front of them, especially when you are going to fight, argue, or compete with them. 与(某人) 对峙(尤指准备打斗、争论或竞争) ❑ *She pushed her way through the mob and confronted him face to face.* 她从那群暴民中挤出来，与他当面对峙。 ❑ *They don't hesitate to open fire when confronted by police.* 他们一旦遭遇警察就毫不犹豫地开火。 5 V-T If you **confront** someone **with** something, you present facts or evidence to them in order to accuse them of something or force them to deal with a situation. (以某事物) 与(某人) 对质 ❑ *She had decided to confront Kathryn with the truth.* 她已决定用事实与凯瑟琳对质。 ❑ *I could not bring myself to confront him about it.* 我不能就此事让自己与他对质。

★ **con·fron·ta·tion** ♦◇◇ /kɒnfrʌnteɪʃᵊn/ (**confrontations**) N-VAR A **confrontation** is a dispute, fight, or battle between two groups of people. 争执; 对抗 ❑ *The commission remains so weak that it will continue to avoid confrontation with governments.* 该委员会依然如此弱小以致它将继续避免和各政府的冲突。

con·fron·ta·tion·al /kɒnfrʌnteɪʃənᵊl/ ADJ If you describe the way that someone behaves as **confrontational**, you are showing your disapproval of the fact that they are aggressive and likely to cause an argument or dispute. 对抗的 [DISAPPROVAL] ❑ *The committee's confrontational style of campaigning has made it unpopular.* 该委员会挑衅的宣传方式使之不得人心。

Con·fu·cian /kənfyuʃən/ (**Confucians**) 1 ADJ **Confucian** means relating to Confucianism. 儒家的 [ADJ n] ❑ *The government played a major role in promoting Confucian philosophy.* 该政府在推行儒家哲学上担当了一个重要角色。 2 N-COUNT A **Confucian** is someone who believes in Confucianism. 儒家人士 ❑ *It was a preference for naturalness and simplicity that separated the Taoists from the Confucians.* 正是对自然和质朴的偏爱把道家人士从儒家人士中区分开。

★ **Con·fu·cian·ism** /kənfyuʃənɪzᵊm/ N-UNCOUNT **Confucianism** is a Chinese religious philosophy that emphasizes human morality and correct personal behavior. 儒家; 儒学 ❑ *Confucianism and Taoism both stress the importance of compassion.* 儒家和道家都强调同情的重要性。

con·fuse /kənfyuz/ (**confuses, confusing, confused**) 1 V-T If you **confuse** two things, you get them mixed up, so that you think one of them is the other one. 混淆 ❑ *I always confuse my left with my right.* 我总是混淆左右。 ● **con·fu·sion** /kənfyuʒᵊn/ N-UNCOUNT 混淆 ❑ *Use different colors of felt pen on your sketch to avoid confusion.* 在草图上使用不同颜色的毡笔以免混淆。 2 V-T To **confuse** someone means to make it difficult for them to know exactly what is happening or what to do. 使困惑 ❑ *My words surprised and confused him.* 我的话使他既惊讶又困惑。 3 V-T To **confuse** a situation means to make it complicated or difficult to understand. 使复杂化 ❑ *To further confuse the issue, there is an enormous variation in the amount of sleep people feel happy with.* 使这个问题进一步复杂化的是，人们感觉愉快的睡眠时间相差很大。

con·fused /kənfyuzd/ 1 ADJ If you are **confused**, you do not know exactly what is happening or what to do. 困惑的 ❑ *A survey showed people were confused about what they should eat to stay healthy.* 一项调查表明人们对于保持健康该吃什么很困惑。 2 ADJ Something that is **confused** does not have any order or pattern and is difficult to understand. 混乱的 ❑ *The situation remains confused as both sides claim success.* 由于双方都声称自己获胜，形势依然混乱。

con·fus·ing /kənfyuzɪŋ/ ADJ Something that is **confusing** makes it difficult for people to know exactly what is happening or what to do. 令人困惑的 ❑ *The statement is really confusing.* 该声明确实令人困惑。

con·fu·sion /kənfyuʒᵊn/ (**confusions**) 1 N-VAR If there is **confusion** about something, it is not clear what the true situation is, especially because people believe different things. 不明朗 ❑ *There's still confusion about the number of students.* 学生的人数依然不清楚。 2 N-UNCOUNT **Confusion** is a situation in which everything is in disorder, especially because there are lots of things happening at the same time. 混乱 ❑ *There was confusion when a man fired shots.* 一名男子开了枪，出现了混乱。 3 → see also **confuse**

con·gen·ial /kəndʒinyəl/ ADJ A **congenial** person, place, or environment is pleasant. 令人愉快的 [FORMAL] ❑ *He is back in more congenial company.* 他回到了更令他愉快的同伴中。

con·gest·ed /kəndʒɛstɪd/ ADJ A **congested** road or area is extremely crowded and blocked with traffic or people. 拥塞的 ❑ *He promised to clear the city's congested roads.* 他承诺要清理城市拥塞的道路。

con·ges·tion /kəndʒɛstʃᵊn/ 1 N-UNCOUNT If there is **congestion** in a place, the place is extremely crowded and blocked with traffic or people. 拥塞 ❑ *The problems of traffic congestion will not disappear in a hurry.* 交通堵塞问题不会很快消失。 2 N-UNCOUNT **Congestion** in a part of the body is a medical condition in which the part becomes blocked. (身体部位的) 堵塞 ❑ *...nasal congestion.* …鼻塞 → see **traffic**

con·glom·er·ate /kənglɒmərɪt/ (**conglomerates**) N-COUNT A **conglomerate** is a large business firm consisting of several different companies. 企业集团 [BUSINESS] ❑ *...the world's second-largest media conglomerate.* …世界第二大传媒集团。

Word Link *grat ≈ pleasing : congratulate, gratify, gratitude*

con·gratu·late /kəngrætʃəleɪt/ (**congratulates, congratulating, congratulated**) 1 V-T If you **congratulate** someone, you say something to show you are pleased that something nice has happened to them. 祝贺 ❑ *She congratulated him on the birth of his son.* 她对他儿子的出生表示了祝贺。 ● **con·gratu·la·tion** /kəngrætʃəleɪʃᵊn/ N-UNCOUNT 祝贺 ❑ *We have received many letters of congratulation.* 我们收到了许多祝贺信。 2 V-T If you **congratulate** someone, you praise them for something good that they have done. 称赞 ❑ *I really must congratulate the organizers for a well run and enjoyable event.* 我真的必须称赞这次组织良好且有趣的活动的组织者们。

con·gratu·la·tions /kəngrætʃəleɪʃᵊnz/ 1 CONVENTION You say "**Congratulations**" to someone in order to congratulate them on something nice that has happened to them or something good that they have done. 祝贺；恭喜 ❑ *Congratulations, you have a healthy baby girl.* 恭喜你，有个健康的千金宝宝！ ❑ *Congratulations on your interesting article.* 祝贺你，文章写得很有趣！ 2 N-PLURAL If you offer someone your **congratulations**, you congratulate them on something nice that has happened to them or on something good that they have done. 祝贺的表示 ❑ *The club also offers its congratulations to D. Brown on her appointment as president.* 俱乐部还就布朗被任命为会长一事向她表示了祝贺。

▲ **con·gre·gate** /kɒŋgrɪgeɪt/ (**congregates, congregating, congregated**) V-I When people **congregate**, they gather together and form a group. 聚集 ❑ *Visitors congregated on Sunday afternoons to view public exhibitions.* 游客们周日下午聚集起来观看公开展览。

con·gre·ga·tion /kɒŋgrɪgeɪʃᵊn/ (**congregations**) N-COUNT-COLL The people who are attending a religious service or who regularly attend a religious service are referred to as the **congregation**. (教堂) 会众 ❑ *Most members of the congregation begin arriving a few minutes before services.* 多数会众成员在礼拜开始前几分钟陆续到达。

con·gress /kɒŋgrɪs/ (**congresses**) N-COUNT-COLL A **congress** is a large meeting that is held to discuss ideas and policies. 代表大会 ❑ *A lot has changed after the party congress.* 该党代表大会后很多都变了。

Con·gress ♦♦◊ N-PROPER-COLL **Congress** is the elected group of politicians that is responsible for making laws in the United States. It consists of two parts: the House of Representatives and the Senate. 美国国会 ❑ *We want to cooperate with both the administration and Congress.* 我们希望与政府和国会都合作。

con·gres·sion·al ♦◊◊ /kəngrɛʃənᵊl/ also **Congressional** ADJ A **congressional** policy, action, or person relates to the U.S. Congress. 美国国会的 [ADJ n] ❑ *The president explained his plans to congressional leaders.* 总统向国会领导人说明了他的计划。

★ **congress·man** /kɒŋgrɪsmən/ (**congressmen**) N-COUNT; N-TITLE A **congressman** is a male member of the U.S. Congress, especially of the House of Representatives. (尤指众议院的) 美国国会男议员

congress·woman /kɒŋgrɪswʊmən/ (**congresswomen**) N-COUNT; N-TITLE A **congresswoman** is a female member of the U.S. Congress, especially of the House of Representatives. 美国国会女议员 (尤指众议院的)

con·jec·ture /kəndʒɛktʃər/ (**conjectures, conjecturing, conjectured**) 1 N-VAR A **conjecture** is a conclusion that is based on information that is not certain or complete. 推测 [FORMAL] ❑ *That was a conjecture, not a fact.* 那是个推测，不是事实。 ❑ *There are several conjectures.* 有几种推测。 2 V-T/V-I When you **conjecture**, you form an opinion or reach a conclusion on the basis of information that is not certain or complete. 推测 [FORMAL] ❑ *He conjectured that some individuals may be able to detect major calamities.* 他推测有些人也许能察觉到重大灾难。

con·junc·tion /kəndʒʌŋkʃᵊn/ (**conjunctions**) 1 N-COUNT A **conjunction of** two or more things is the occurrence of them at the same time or place. 同时发生；同地发生 [FORMAL] ❑ *...the conjunction of two events.* …两事件的同时发生。 2 N-COUNT In grammar, a **conjunction** is a word or group of words that joins together words, groups, or clauses. In English, there are coordinating conjunctions such as "and" and "but," and subordinating conjunctions such as "although," "because," and "when." 连词 3 PHRASE If one thing is done **in conjunction with** another, the two things are done or used together. 与…一起 (做、用) [usu PHR "with" n] ❑ *Textbooks are designed to be used in conjunction with classroom teaching.* 教科书被设计成与课堂教学配合使用。

con·jure /kɒndʒər/ (**conjures, conjuring, conjured**) V-T If you **conjure** something out of nothing, you make it appear as if by magic. 使如变魔术般凭空出现 ❑ *Thirteen years ago she found herself having to conjure a career from thin air.* 十三年前她认识到自己得白手起家闯出一番事业来。 ● PHRASAL VERB **Conjure up** means the same as **conjure**. 使如变魔术般凭空出现 ❑ *Every day a different chef will be conjuring up delicious dishes in the restaurant.* 该饭店每天都有一位不同的厨师会像变戏法似地做出美味的菜肴。

▸ **conjure up** 1 PHRASAL VERB If you **conjure up** a memory, picture, or idea, you create it in your mind. 使在脑海中浮现 ❑ *When he closed his eyes, he could conjure up in exact color almost every event of his life.* 一闭上眼睛，他就能真真切切地回忆起他生命中几乎每一件事情。 2 → see **conjure**

con·nect /kənɛkt/ (**connects, connecting, connected**) 1 V-RECIP If something or someone **connects** one thing **to** another, or if one thing **connects to** another, or if two things **connect**, the two things are joined together. (某物、某人) 连接 (某物)；(一物与另一物) 相连 ❑ *You can connect the speakers to your CD player.* 你可以将这些扬声器与你的激光唱机连接起来。 ❑ *I connected the wires for the transformer.* 我给变压器接上了电线。 2 V-RECIP If two things or places **connect** or if something **connects** them, they are joined and people or things can pass between them. (两物或两地) 相连通 ❑ *...the long hallway that connects the rooms.* …连接这些房间的长长的过道。 ❑ *A pedestrian bridge now connects the parking garage with the mall.* 现在一座人行桥连通车库和购物中心。 3 V-I If one train or plane, for example, **connects with** another, it arrives at a time which allows passengers to change to the other one in order to continue their trip. (与火车、飞机等) 联运 ❑ *...a train connecting with a ferry to Ireland.* …一列与通往爱尔兰的渡船联运的火车。 4 V-T If a piece of equipment or a place **is connected to** a source of power or water, it is joined to that source so that it has power or water. 将 (设备、某地与水源、电源等) 接通 [usu passive] ❑ *These appliances should not be connected to power supplies.* 这些装置不应该接通电源。 ● PHRASAL VERB **Connect up** means the same as **connect**. 接通 ❑ *The shower is easy to install – it needs only to be connected up to the hot and cold water supply.* 淋浴器很容易安装——只需接上冷热水即可。 5 V-T If you **connect** a person or thing **with** something, you realize that there is a link or relationship between them. 将 (某人、某物与某事物) 联系起来 ❑ *I hoped he would not connect me with that now-embarrassing review I'd written seven years earlier.* 我希望他不会把我和我7

C

年前写的、现在读起来令人难堪的评论联系起来。 6 V-T Something that **connects** a person or thing **with** something else shows or provides a link or relationship between them. 显示（某人、某物与某事物）有关联 ❑ *A search of Brady's house revealed nothing that could connect him with the robberies.* 对布雷迪住处的搜查没有查出可以显示他同这些抢劫案有关联的任何线索。

con·nect·ed /kənɛktɪd/ 1 ADJ If one thing is **connected with** another, there is a link or relationship between them. 有关联的 ❑ *Have you ever had any skin problems connected with exposure to the sun?* 你曾有过与日晒有关联的皮肤问题吗？ ❑ *The dispute is not directly connected to the negotiations.* 此争论和那些谈判不直接相关。 2 → see also **connect, well-connected**

con·nec·tion ♦◇◇ /kənɛkʃ^ən/ (**connections**)

in BRIT, also use **connexion**

1 N-VAR A **connection** is a relationship between two things, people, or groups. 关系 ❑ *There was no evidence of a connection between BSE and the brain diseases recently confirmed in cats.* 没有有关疯牛病和最近证实的猫类脑部疾病之间的关系的证据。 ❑ *I felt a strong connection between us.* 我感觉到了我们之间的强烈关系。 2 N-COUNT A **connection** is a joint where two wires or pipes are joined together. 连接处 ❑ *Check all radiators for small leaks, especially round pipework connections.* 检查所有的暖气设备，尤其是圆形管道的接头处，看是否有小裂缝。 3 N-COUNT If a place has good road, rail, or air **connections**, many places can be directly reached from there by car, train, or plane. （道路、轨道、航道）连接 ❑ *Mexico City has excellent air and rail connections to the rest of the country.* 墨西哥城有很好的空运和铁路连接全国各地。 4 N-COUNT If you get a **connection** at a station or airport, you catch a train, bus, or plane, after getting off another train, bus, or plane, in order to continue your trip. （火车、轮船、飞机等的）联运 ❑ *My flight was late and I missed the connection.* 我乘坐的航班晚点了，因此我错过了联运航班。

con·nec·tiv·ity /kɒnɛktɪvəti/ N-UNCOUNT **Connectivity** is the ability of a computing device to connect to other computers or to the Internet. 连接性能 [COMPUTING] ❑ *...a DVD video and CD player with Internet connectivity.* …一台具有网络连接性能的DVD和CD机。

con·nex·ion /kənɛkʃ^ən/ [BRIT] → see **connection**

con·nois·seur /kɒnəsɜr, -sʊər/ (**connoisseurs**) N-COUNT A **connoisseur** is someone who knows a lot about the arts, food, drink, or some other subject. 鉴赏家；行家 ❑ *Sarah tells me you're something of an art connoisseur.* 萨拉告诉我你可以说是一位艺术鉴赏家。

▲ **con·no·ta·tion** /kɒnəteɪʃ^ən/ (**connotations**) N-COUNT The **connotations** of a particular word or name are the ideas or qualities which it makes you think of. 内涵意义 ❑ *It's just one of those words that's got so many negative connotations.* 它只是那些有很多负面内涵意义的词之一。

con·quer /kɒŋkər/ (**conquers, conquering, conquered**) 1 V-T If one country or group of people **conquers** another, they take complete control of their land. 征服；攻占 ❑ *During 1936, Mussolini conquered Abyssinia.* 1936年墨索里尼攻占了阿比西尼亚。 2 V-T If you **conquer** something such as a problem, you succeed in ending it or dealing with it successfully. 克服 ❑ *I was certain that love was quite enough to conquer our differences.* 我确信爱颇足以消除我们的分歧。 ❑ *He has never conquered his addiction to smoking.* 他从未戒除过烟瘾。 → see **army, empire**

★ **con·quer·or** /kɒŋkərər/ (**conquerors**) N-COUNT The **conquerors** of a country or group of people are the people who have taken complete control of that country or group's land. 征服者 ❑ *The people of an oppressed country obey their conquerors because they want to go on living.* 一个被压迫国家的人民顺从他们的征服者，是因为他们想活下去。

con·quest /kɒŋkwɛst/ (**conquests**) 1 N-UNCOUNT **Conquest** is the act of conquering a country or group of people. 征服 [also N in pl, oft N "of" n] ❑ *He had led the conquest of southern Poland in 1939.* 他曾于1939年统领对波兰南部的征服。 ❑ *...the Spanish conquest of Mexico.* …西班牙人对墨西哥的征服。 2 N-SING **The conquest of** something such as a problem is success in ending it or dealing with it. 克服 ❑ *The conquest of inflation has been the Government's overriding economic priority for nearly 15 years.* 对通货膨胀的克服一直是近15年以来政府的头等经济工作重点。

> **Word Link** *sci ≈ knowing : conscience, science, unconscious*

con·science /kɒnʃ^əns/ (**consciences**) 1 N-COUNT Your **conscience** is the part of your mind that tells you whether what you are doing is right or wrong. If you have a **guilty conscience**, you feel guilty about something because you know it was wrong. If you have a **clear conscience**, you do not feel guilty because you know you have done nothing wrong. 良知 ❑ *I have battled with my conscience over whether I should actually send this letter.* 我曾跟自己的良知斗争应否真的寄出这封信。 ❑ *What if he got a guilty conscience and brought it back?* 如果他问心有愧把它带回来呢？ 2 N-UNCOUNT **Conscience** is doing what you believe is right even though it might be unpopular, difficult, or dangerous. 凭良知行事 ❑ *He refused for reasons of conscience to eat meat.* 他为了良心好过而拒绝了吃肉。 3 N-UNCOUNT **Conscience** is a feeling of guilt because you know you have done something that is wrong. 负疚感 ❑ *I'm so glad he had a pang of conscience.* 我实在高兴他感到了一阵愧疚。 4 PHRASE If you have something **on** your **conscience**, you feel guilty because you know you have done something wrong. 引起内疚 ❑ *The drunk driver has two deaths on his conscience.* 这位醉酒的司机良心上背负着两条人命。

★ **con·sci·en·tious** /kɒnʃiɛnʃəs/ ADJ Someone who is **conscientious** is very careful to do their work properly. 认真的 ❑ *We are generally very conscientious about our work.* 我们一般对工作都是很认真的。 ● **con·sci·en·tious·ly** ADV 认真地 ❑ *He studied conscientiously and enthusiastically.* 他认真积极地学习。

con·scious ♦◇◇ /kɒnʃəs/ 1 ADJ If you are **conscious of** something, you notice it or realize that it is happening. 意识到的 [v-link ADJ] ❑ *He was conscious of the faint, musky aroma of aftershave.* 他留意到须后水那淡淡的、似麝香的芳香。 ❑ *She was very conscious of Max studying her.* 她十分清楚马克斯在仔细端详着她。 2 ADJ If you are **conscious of** something, you think about it a lot, especially because you are unhappy about it or because you think it is important. （尤指因为自认不满意或很重要而）在意的 [v-link ADJ] ❑ *I'm very conscious of my weight.* 我很在意自己的体重。 3 ADJ A **conscious** decision or action is made or done deliberately with you giving your full attention to it. 刻意的 ❑ *I don't think we ever made a conscious decision to have a big family.* 我不认为我们曾刻意下决定要成为一大家子。 ● **con·scious·ly** ADV 刻意地 [ADV with v] ❑ *Sophie was not consciously seeking a replacement after her father died.* 索菲在父亲去世后没有刻意地找一个代替的人。 4 ADJ Someone who is **conscious** is awake rather than asleep or unconscious. 神志清醒的 ❑ *She was fully conscious throughout the surgery and knew what was going on.* 她在整个手术过程中神志完全清醒，知道发生了什么。 5 ADJ **Conscious** memories or thoughts are ones that you are aware of. 清楚的（记忆、想法）[ADJ n] ❑ *He had no conscious memory of his four-week stay in the hospital.* 他对自己住院的4个星期记不大清了。 ● **con·scious·ly** ADV 清楚地（记得、想起）❑ *Most people cannot consciously remember much before the ages of 3 to 5 years.* 多数人不能清楚地记得3到5岁之前的多少事情。 → see **hypnosis**

> **Thesaurus** *conscious* 另参见：
> ADJ. calculated, deliberate, intentional, rational 3
> awake, aware, responsive; *(ant.)* unaware, unconscious 4

-conscious /kɒnʃəs/ COMB IN ADJ **-conscious** combines with words such as "health," "fashion," "politically," and "environmentally" to form adjectives which describe someone who believes that the aspect of life indicated is important. （用于构成复合词）注重…的 ❑ *We're all becoming increasingly health-conscious these days.* 如今我们都在变得日益注重健康。

> **Word Link** *ness ≈ state, condition : cleanliness, consciousness, kindness*

con·scious·ness ♦◇◇ /kɒnʃəsnɪs/ (**consciousnesses**) 1 N-COUNT Your **consciousness** is your mind and your thoughts. 思想头脑 ❑ *That idea has been creeping into our consciousness for some time.* 那个念头在我们脑子里渐渐产生已有一段时间了。 2 N-UNCOUNT The **consciousness** of a group of people is their set of ideas, attitudes, and beliefs. （群体的）观念体系 ❑ *The Green Party is attempting to shift the American consciousness.* 绿党在试图改变美国人的观念体系。 3 N-UNCOUNT You use **consciousness** to refer to an interest in and knowledge of a particular subject or idea. （对某话题或思想的）意识 ❑ *Her political consciousness sprang from her upbringing when her father's illness left the family short of money.* 她的政治觉悟源于她的成长背景，当时她父亲的病让家里缺钱。 4 N-UNCOUNT **Consciousness** is the state of being awake rather than being asleep or unconscious. If someone **loses consciousness**, they become unconscious, and if they **regain consciousness**, they become conscious after being unconscious. 知觉 ❑ *She banged her head and lost consciousness.* 她撞了头，失去了知觉。

con·script (**conscripts, conscripting, conscripted**)

The noun is pronounced /kɒnskrɪpt/. The verb is pronounced /kənskrɪpt/.

名词读作 /kɒnskrɪpt/。动词读作 /kənskrɪpt/。

1 N-COUNT A **conscript** is a person who has been made to join the armed forces of a country. 被征入伍者 ❑ *Most of the soldiers are reluctant conscripts.* 大部分士兵都是不情愿的被征服役者。 2 V-T If someone **is conscripted**, they are officially made to join the armed forces of a country. 征召入伍 [usu passive] ❑ *He was conscripted into the U.S. army.* 他被征入了美国陆军。

con·scrip·tion /kənskrɪpʃ[ə]n/ N-UNCOUNT **Conscription** is officially making people in a particular country join the armed forces. 征召入伍 [FORMAL] ❑ *All adult males will be liable for conscription.* 所有成年男子都将有义务服兵役。

con·se·crate /kɒnsɪkreɪt/ (**consecrates, consecrating, consecrated**) V-T When a building, place, or object **is consecrated**, it is officially declared to be holy. When a person **is consecrated**, they are officially declared to be a bishop. 正式宣告为神圣的; 正式宣告为主教 ❑ *The church was consecrated in 1234.* 这座教堂于1234年成为了神址。

★ **con·secu·tive** /kənsɛkyətɪv/ ADJ **Consecutive** periods of time or events happen one after the other without interruption. 连续的 ❑ *The Cup was won for the third consecutive year by the Toronto Maple Leafs.* 这个奖杯连续第三年由多伦多枫叶队赢去了。

Word Link *con ≈ together : with : consensus, contemporary, convene*

con·sen·sus /kənsɛnsəs/ N-SING A **consensus** is general agreement among a group of people. 共识 [also no det] ❑ *The consensus among the world's scientists is that the world is likely to warm up over the next few decades.* 全世界科学家的共识是地球可能在未来几十年中变暖。

con·sent /kənsɛnt/ (**consents, consenting, consented**) 1 N-UNCOUNT If you give your **consent to** something, you give someone permission to do it. 准许 [FORMAL] ❑ *At approximately 11:30 p.m., Pollard finally gave his consent to the search.* 大约晚上11:30的时候，波拉德终于对搜查予以同意。 2 V-T/V-I If you **consent to** something, you agree to do it or to allow it to be done. 同意 [FORMAL] ❑ *He finally consented to go.* 他最终同意去。 ❑ *He asked Ginny if she would consent to a small celebration after the christening.* 他问金尼她是否同意在洗礼仪式后来个小庆祝。 3 → see also **age of consent**

Word Link *sequ ≈ following : consequence, sequel, sequence*

con·se·quence ♦◇◇ /kɒnsɪkwɛns, -kwəns/ (**consequences**) 1 N-COUNT The **consequences of** something are the results or effects of it. 结果; 后果 ❑ *Her lawyer said she understood the consequences of her actions and was prepared to go to jail.* 她的律师说她明白自己行为的后果并准备去坐牢。 2 PHRASE If one thing happens and then another thing happens **in consequence** or **as a consequence**, the second thing happens as a result of the first. 结果 ❑ *His death was totally unexpected and, in consequence, no plans had been made for his replacement.* 他的死纯粹出乎意料，因此还没有为他的替代人定出计划。 ❑ *Maternity services were to be reduced as a consequence of falling birth rates.* 孕产服务因下降的出生率而将被削减。

Word Partnership *consequence 的常用搭配:*

ADJ.	**disastrous** consequence, **unfortunate** consequence 1
PREP.	consequence **for/of** *something* 1
V.	**suffer the** consequence 1

★ **con·se·quent** /kɒnsɪkwɛnt, -kwənt/ ADJ **Consequent** means happening as a direct result of an event or situation. 作为结果的 [FORMAL] ❑ *The warming of the Earth and the consequent climatic changes affect us all.* 全球变暖以及随之而来的气候变化影响我们每个人。

con·se·quent·ly /kɒnsɪkwɛntli, -kwəntli/ ADV **Consequently** means as a result. 结果 [ADV with cl] [FORMAL] ❑ *Grandfather had sustained a broken back while working in the mines. Consequently, he spent the rest of his life in a wheelchair.* 爷爷在矿上做工时受了背伤，结果，他在轮椅上度过了他的余生。

con·ser·va·tion /kɒnsərveɪʃ[ə]n/ 1 N-UNCOUNT **Conservation** is saving and protecting the environment. (对环境的) 保护 ❑ *...a four-nation regional meeting on elephant conservation.* …一次有关大象保护的4国区域性会议。 2 N-UNCOUNT **Conservation** is saving and protecting historical objects or works of art such as paintings, sculptures, or buildings. (对历史文物、艺术品等的) 保护 ❑ *Then he began his most famous work, the conservation and rebinding of the Book of Kells.* 接着，他就开始了他最著名的工作，即对《凯尔经》的维护和重新装订。 3 N-UNCOUNT The **conservation** of a supply of something is the careful use of it so that it lasts for a long time. 节约 ❑ *...projects aimed at promoting energy conservation.* …旨在促进能源节约的项目。

C

con·ser·va·tion·ist /kɒnsərveɪʃənɪst/ (**conservationists**) N-COUNT A **conservationist** is someone who cares very much about the conservation of the environment and who works to protect it. 环境保护主义者 ❑ *Conservationists say the law must be strengthened.* 环保主义者称必须加强法制。

con·serva·tism /kənsɜrvətɪzəm/ 1 N-UNCOUNT **Conservatism** is a political philosophy which believes that if changes need to be made to society, they should be made gradually. You can also refer to the political beliefs of a conservative party in a particular country as **conservatism**. (政治) 保守主义; (特指某国) 保守政党的政治主张 ❑ *...the philosophy of modern conservatism.* …现代保守主义哲学。 2 N-UNCOUNT **Conservatism** is unwillingness to accept changes and new ideas. 守旧性 ❑ *The conservatism of the literary establishment in this country is astounding.* 这个国家文学界的守旧态度令人震惊。

con·serva·tive ♦♦◇ /kənsɜrvətɪv/ (**conservatives**)

The spelling **Conservative** is also used for meaning 5.

1 ADJ Someone who is **conservative** has views that are toward the political right. In the U.S. the Republicans are more conservative than the Democrats, who are more liberal. 持政治右倾观点的 ❑ *...counties whose citizens invariably support the most conservative candidate in any election.* …公民们在任何选举中都千篇一律地支持最保守的候选人的县。 ● N-COUNT **Conservative** is also a noun. 右倾人士 ❑ *The new judge is 50-year-old David Suitor who's regarded as a conservative.* 这名新法官是50岁的、被视为右倾人士的戴维・休特。 2 ADJ Someone who is **conservative** or has **conservative** ideas is unwilling to accept changes and new ideas. (观点) 保守的 ❑ *People tend to be more liberal when they're young and more conservative as they get older.* 人们在年轻时常常更开放，年纪越大就越保守。 3 ADJ If someone dresses in a **conservative** way, their clothes are conventional in style. (衣着) 守旧的 ❑ *The girl was well dressed, as usual, though in a more conservative style.* 这个女孩像平常一样穿着得体，但式样则更守旧。 ● **con·ser·va·tive·ly** ADV 保守地 [ADV with v] ❑ *She was always very conservatively dressed when we went out.* 我们出门时她总是穿得很保守。 4 ADJ A **conservative** estimate or guess is one in which you are cautious and estimate or guess a low amount which is probably less than the real amount. 保守的 (估计、猜测) ❑ *The average fan spends $25 – a conservative estimate based on ticket price and souvenirs.* 平均球迷花费$25——根据票价和纪念品的一个保守估计。 ● **con·ser·va·tive·ly** ADV 保守地 (估计、猜测) [ADV with v] ❑ *The bequest is conservatively estimated at $30 million.* 这笔遗产被保守地估计为3000万美元。 5 ADJ A **Conservative** politician or voter is a member of or votes for the Conservative Party in Britain and in various other countries. (英国等) 保守党的 ❑ *Most Conservative MPs appear happy with the government's reassurances.* 大多数保守党的国会议员们看来对政府的保证感到满意。 ● N-COUNT **Conservative** is also a noun. 保守党 ❑ *In 1951 the Conservatives were returned to power.* 1951年保守党再度执政。

Thesaurus *conservative 另参见:*

ADJ.	right-wing; (*ant.*) left-wing, liberal, radical 1 conventional, traditional 2

Word Link *ory ≈ place where something happens : conservatory, factory, observatory*

con·serva·tory /kənsɜrvətɔri/ (**conservatories**) 1 N-COUNT; N-IN-NAMES A **conservatory** is an institution where musicians are trained. 音乐学院 ❑ *...the New England Conservatory of Music.* …新英格兰音乐学院。 2 N-COUNT A **conservatory** is a room with glass walls and a glass roof, which is attached to a house. People often grow plants in a conservatory. 温室

C

Word Link serv ≈ keeping : conserve, observe, preserve

★ **con·serve** /kənsɜːv/ (**conserves, conserving, conserved**)
1 V-T If you **conserve** a supply of something, you use it carefully so that it lasts for a long time. 节省 ❑ *The factories have closed for the weekend to conserve energy.* 这些工厂在那个周末关了厂以节省能源。
2 V-T To **conserve** something means to protect it from harm, loss, or change. 保护 ❑ *...a big increase in U.S. aid to help developing countries conserve their forests.* …美国对帮助发展中国家保护森林的援助的大幅增加。

con·sid·er ♦♦♦ /kənsɪdər/ (**considers, considering, considered**)
1 V-T If you **consider** a person or thing **to** be something, you have the opinion that this is what they are. 认为 ❑ *We don't consider our customers to be mere consumers; we consider them to be our friends.* 我们没有视我们的顾客为纯粹的消费者；我们视他们为我们的朋友。 ❑ *I had always considered myself a strong, competent woman.* 我曾一直以为自己是个坚强能干的女人。 ❑ *I consider activities such as jogging and weightlifting as unnatural.* 我认为类似慢跑和举重这样的活动是不自然的。 ❑ *Barbara considers that pet shops which sell customers these birds are very unfair..* 芭芭拉认为卖给消费者这些鸟的宠物店非常不公平。

Note that when you are using the verb **consider** with a "that" -clause in order to state a negative opinion or belief, you normally make **consider** negative, rather than the verb in the "that" -clause. For instance, it is more usual to say "I don't consider that you kept your promise" than "I consider that you didn't keep your promise." The same pattern applies to other verbs with a similar meaning, such as **believe**, **suppose**, and **think**.

2 V-T If you **consider** something, you think about it carefully. 仔细考虑（某事物）❑ *The administration continues to consider ways to resolve the situation.* 政府继续仔细考虑解决这种情况的办法。 ❑ *You do have to consider the feelings of those around you.* 你真的得仔细考虑你身边那些人的感受。 3 V-T If you **are considering** doing something, you intend to do it, but have not yet made a final decision whether to do it. 考虑（做某事）❑ *I had seriously considered telling the story from the point of view of the wives.* 我曾认真考虑过从妻子们的角度来讲述这个故事。 4 → see also **considering**

Thesaurus consider 另参见：
V. contemplate, examine, study, think about, think over; (ant.) dismiss, forget, ignore 2

con·sid·er·able ♦♦◊ /kənsɪdərəbᵊl/ ADJ **Considerable** means great in amount or degree. 相当多的；相当大的 [FORMAL] ❑ *To be without Pearce would be a considerable blow.* 要是缺了皮尔斯，那会是相当大的打击。 ❑ *Doing it properly makes considerable demands on our time.* 把这件事做得到位，要花我们相当多的时间。 ● **con·sid·er·ably** ADV 相当多地；相当大地 ❑ *Children vary considerably in the rate at which they learn these lessons.* 孩子们学习这些课的速度差别相当大。

Word Link ate ≈ filled with : affectionate, compassionate, considerate

con·sid·er·ate /kənsɪdərɪt/ ADJ Someone who is **considerate** pays attention to the needs, wishes, or feelings of other people. 体贴的 [APPROVAL] ❑ *I think he's the most charming, most considerate man I've ever known.* 我觉得他是我所认识的最有魅力、最体贴的男士。

con·sid·era·tion ♦◊◊ /kənsɪdəreɪʃᵊn/ (**considerations**)
1 N-UNCOUNT **Consideration** is careful thought about something. 仔细考虑 ❑ *There should be careful consideration about the use of such toxic chemicals.* 应有对这些有毒化学品的使用的慎重考虑。
2 N-UNCOUNT If something is **under consideration**, it is being discussed. 在讨论中 ❑ *Several proposals are under consideration by the state assembly.* 几项提案正由州议会审议。 3 N-UNCOUNT If you show **consideration**, you pay attention to the needs, wishes, or feelings of other people. 体贴 ❑ *Show consideration for your neighbors.* 要表示出对邻居们的体贴。 4 N-COUNT A **consideration** is something that should be thought about, especially when you are planning or deciding something. 考虑因素 ❑ *Price has become a more important consideration for shoppers in choosing which store to visit than it was before the recession.* 比起经济萧条前，价格已成为购物者们选择光顾哪家商店的一个更重要的考虑因素。 5 PHRASE If you **take** something **into consideration**, you think about it because it is relevant to what you are doing. 考虑到某事物 ❑ *Safe driving is good driving because it takes into consideration the lives of other people.* 安全驾驶是良好驾驶，因为它顾及到了他人的生命。

Word Partnership consideration 的常用搭配：
ADJ. **careful** consideration 1
an important consideration 1–4
PREP. **in** consideration **of** 1
under consideration 2
V. **show** consideration 3
take into consideration 5

con·sid·er·ing ♦◊◊ /kənsɪdərɪŋ/ 1 PREP You use **considering** to indicate that you are thinking about a particular fact when making a judgment or giving an opinion. 鉴于（某情况）❑ *He must be hoping, but considering the situation in June he may be hoping for too much too soon.* 他肯定正在期待着，但鉴于6月的情况，他可能期望得过多过早。 2 CONJ You use **considering that** to indicate that you are thinking about a particular fact when making a judgment or giving an opinion. 考虑到（某事实）❑ *Considering that you are no longer involved with this man, your response is a little extreme.* 考虑到你和这个男人不再有干系，你的反应有点过分。 3 ADV When you are giving an opinion or making a judgment, you can use **considering** to suggest that you have thought about all the circumstances, and often that something has succeeded in spite of these circumstances. 总的来看 [cl ADV] [SPOKEN] ❑ *I think you're pretty safe, considering.* 总的来看，我认为你很安全。

con·sign /kənsaɪn/ (**consigns, consigning, consigned**) V-T To **consign** something or someone **to** a place where they will be forgotten about, or **to** an unpleasant situation or place, means to put them there. 弃置（某物于某处或某境地）；发落（某人于某处或某境地）[FORMAL] ❑ *For decades, many of Malevich's works were consigned to the basements of Soviet museums.* 几十年来，马列维奇的许多作品都被弃置在苏联的博物馆的地下室里。

con·sign·ment /kənsaɪnmənt/ (**consignments**) 1 N-COUNT A **consignment of** goods is a load that is being delivered to a place or person. （货物）批 ❑ *The first consignment of food was flown in yesterday.* 第一批食品昨天空运到了。 2 PHRASE If goods are sold **on consignment**, the owner is given a percentage of the price once they are sold. 以代售方式 ❑ *She sold clothes on consignment to benefit homeless people.* 她以代售方式卖服装来施益于无家可归的人。

con·sist ♦◊◊ /kənsɪst/ (**consists, consisting, consisted**) 1 V-I Something that **consists of** particular things or people is formed from them. （以…）为组成部分 ❑ *My diet consisted almost exclusively of chocolate-covered cookies and glasses of milk.* 我的饮食几乎只包含裹上巧克力的曲奇饼和一杯杯牛奶。 2 V-I Something that **consists in** something else has that thing as its main or only part. （以…）为主要组成部分 ❑ *His work as a consultant consisted in advising foreign companies on the siting of new factories.* 他做顾问的工作主要包括就新工厂选址为外国公司提出意见。

con·sist·en·cy /kənsɪstənsi/ 1 N-UNCOUNT **Consistency** is the quality or condition of being consistent. 连贯性；一致性 ❑ *She scores goals with remarkable consistency.* 她以非凡的连贯性进球得分。
2 N-UNCOUNT The **consistency** of a substance is how thick or smooth it is. 黏稠度 ❑ *Dilute the paint with water until it is the consistency of milk.* 用水把颜料稀释到牛奶的黏稠度。

con·sist·ent ♦◊◊ /kənsɪstənt/ 1 ADJ Someone who is **consistent** always behaves in the same way, has the same attitudes towards people or things, or achieves the same level of success in something. 始终如一的 ❑ *Becker was never the most consistent of players anyway.* 贝克尔不管怎么说从来就不是一个很稳定的球员。 ● **con·sist·ent·ly** ADV 始终如一地 ❑ *It's something I have consistently denied.* 这是我始终否认的事。 2 ADJ If one fact or idea is **consistent with** another, they do not contradict each other. 相符的 [v-link ADJ, usu ADJ "with" n] ❑ *This result is consistent with the findings of Garnett & Tobin.* 该结果与加尼特和托宾的发现相符合。 3 ADJ An argument or set of ideas that is **consistent** is one in which no part contradicts or conflicts with any other part. （论点、观点）前后一致的 ❑ *A theory should be internally consistent.* 一套理论应当内在一致。

★ **con·sole** (**consoles, consoling, consoled**)

The verb is pronounced /kənsoʊl/. The noun is pronounced /kɒnsoʊl/.

动词读作 /kənsoʊl/。名词读作 /kɒnsoʊl/。

1 V-T If you **console** someone who is unhappy about something, you try to make them feel more cheerful. 安慰 ❑ *"Never mind, Ned,"*

he consoled me. “不要紧，内德”，他安慰我说。 ❑ *I can console myself with the fact that I'm not alone.* 我可以用不只我一个人的这种事实来安慰自己。 ● **con·so·la·tion** /kɒnsəleɪʃən/ N-VAR (**consolations**) 安慰 ❑ *The only consolation for the baseball team is that they look likely to get another chance.* 对这支棒球队的惟一安慰是他们看来可能会得到另一次机会。 2 N-COUNT A **console** is a panel with a number of switches or knobs that is used to operate a machine. 控制台 ❑ *Several nurses sat before a console of flickering lights and bleeping monitors.* 几名护士坐在灯光闪烁、监听器嘟嘟作响的控制台前。

★ **con·soli·date** /kənsɒlɪdeɪt/ (**consolidates, consolidating, consolidated**) 1 V-T If you **consolidate** something that you have, for example power or success, you strengthen it so that it becomes more effective or secure. 巩固 ❑ *The question is: will the junta consolidate its power by force?* 问题是，这个军政府会通过武力来巩固它的政权吗？ 2 V-T To **consolidate** a number of small groups or companies means to make them into one large organization. 合并 ❑ *Judge Charles Schwartz is giving the state 60 days to disband and consolidate Louisiana's four higher education boards.* 查尔斯・施瓦茨法官给该州60天解散且合并路易斯安那的4个高等教育委员会。

con·so·nant /kɒnsənənt/ (**consonants**) N-COUNT A **consonant** is a sound such as “p,” “f,” “n,” or “t” which you pronounce by stopping the air flowing freely through your mouth. Compare **vowel**. 辅音

con·sor·tium /kənsɔrʃiəm, -ti-/ (**consortia** /kənsɔrʃiə, -ti-/ or **consortiums**) N-COUNT-COLL A **consortium** is a group of people or firms who have agreed to cooperate with each other. 联盟 [FORMAL] ❑ *The consortium includes some of the biggest building contractors in North America.* 该联盟包括北美一些最大的建筑承包商。

★ **con·spicu·ous** /kənspɪkyuəs/ ADJ If someone or something is **conspicuous**, people can see or notice them very easily. 显眼的 ❑ *Most people don't want to be too conspicuous.* 大多数人不愿过于显眼。 ● **con·spicu·ous·ly** ADV 显眼地 ❑ *Britain continues to follow U.S. policy in this and other areas where American policies have most conspicuously failed.* 英国在这个以及其他领域继续跟随美国已经明显失败了的政策。

▲ **con·spira·cy** /kənspɪrəsi/ (**conspiracies**) 1 N-VAR **Conspiracy** is secret planning by a group of people to do something illegal. 合谋 ❑ *Seven men, all from North Carolina, admitted conspiracy to commit arson.* 全都来自于北卡罗来纳州的七名男子承认了合谋纵火。 2 N-COUNT A **conspiracy** is an agreement between a group of people which other people think is wrong or is likely to be harmful. 阴谋 ❑ *It's all part of a conspiracy to dispense with the town center all together and move everything out to the suburbs.* 这全都属于一个阴谋，以彻底放弃市中心而把一切搬到郊区。

con·spira·tor /kənspɪrətər/ (**conspirators**) N-COUNT A **conspirator** is a person who joins a conspiracy. 共谋者 ❑ *Julius Caesar was murdered by a group of conspirators famously headed by Marcus Junius Brutus.* 尤利乌斯・凯撒被以人所共知的马库斯・朱尼厄斯・布鲁特斯为首脑的一伙谋反者谋杀了。

▲ **con·spire** /kənspaɪər/ (**conspires, conspiring, conspired**) 1 V-RECIP If two or more people or groups **conspire to** do something illegal or harmful, they make a secret agreement to do it. 合谋 ❑ *They'd conspired to overthrow the government.* 他们曾合谋推翻政府。 ❑ *...a defendant accused of conspiring with his brother to commit robberies.* …被指控与其兄弟合谋抢劫的一名被告。 2 V-T/V-I If events **conspire to** produce a particular result, they seem to work together to cause this result. 协同 ❑ *History and geography have conspired to bring the country to a moment of decision.* 历史和地理情况共同将该国带到了做决定的时刻。

con·sta·ble /kʌnstəbəl, kɒn-/ (**constables**) 1 N-COUNT; N-TITLE In the United States, a **constable** is an official who helps keep the peace in a town. They are lower in rank than a sheriff. (美国乡镇的) 治安官 ❑ *Courts and magistrates may be set up but they cannot function without sheriffs and constables.* 法院和地方法院可以设立，但没有县治安官和乡镇治安官它们便无法运作。 2 N-COUNT; N-TITLE; N-VOC In Britain and some other countries, a **constable** is a police officer of the lowest rank. (英国等国家中级别最低的) 警官

con·stant ♦♦◇ /kɒnstənt/ 1 ADJ You use **constant** to describe something that happens all the time or is always there. 常发生的; 常存在的 ❑ *She suggests that women are under constant pressure to be abnormally thin.* 她提出女性受持续的压力之下要异常苗条。 ❑ *Inflation is a constant threat.* 通货膨胀是一种持续的威胁。 ● **con·stant·ly** ADV 持续不断地 ❑ *The direction of the wind is constantly changing.* 风的方向在不断地变。 2 ADJ If an amount or level is **constant**, it stays the same over a particular period of time. (在某时段内) 保持不变的 ❑ *The body feels hot and the temperature remains more or less constant at the new elevated level.* 身体感到热，可体温保持在升高后的新高度上差不多稳定不变。

> You can use **constant, continual**, and **continuous** to describe things that happen or exist without stopping. You describe something as **constant** when it happens all the time or never goes away. ❑ *He was in constant pain. ...Eva's constant criticism.* **Continual** is usually used to describe something that happens often over a period of time, especially something undesirable. ❑ *...his continual drinking. ...continual demands to cut costs.* If something is **continuous**, it happens all the time without stopping, or seems to do so. ❑ *...days of continuous rain. ...a continuous background noise.*

> **Thesaurus** *constant* 另参见:
> ADJ. continual, continuous, uninterrupted; *(ant.)* occasional 1
> consistent, permanent, stable; *(ant.)* changeable, variable 2

con·stel·la·tion /kɒnstəleɪʃən/ (**constellations**) N-COUNT A **constellation** is a group of stars which form a pattern and have a name. 星座 ❑ *...a planet orbiting a star in the constellation of Cepheus.* …绕仙王星座内一颗恒星运转的一颗行星。
→ see **star**

con·ster·na·tion /kɒnstərneɪʃən/ N-UNCOUNT **Consternation** is a feeling of anxiety or fear. 恐慌 [FORMAL] ❑ *His decision caused consternation in the art photography community.* 他的决定在艺术摄影界引起了恐慌。

con·sti·pa·tion /kɒnstɪpeɪʃən/ N-UNCOUNT **Constipation** is a medical condition which causes people to have difficulty getting rid of solid waste from their body. 便秘 ❑ *Do you suffer from constipation?* 你便秘吗？

▲ **con·stitu·en·cy** /kənstɪtʃuənsi/ (**constituencies**) 1 N-COUNT A particular **constituency** is a section of society that may give political support to a particular party or politician. (会支持某政党或政客的) 选民阵营 ❑ *In Iowa, farmers are a powerful political constituency.* 在爱荷华州，农民是一个强大的政治选民阵营。 2 N-COUNT A **constituency** is an area for which someone is elected as the representative in a legislature or government. 选区 ❑ *Voters in 17 constituencies are going back to the polls today.* 17个选区的投票人今天会回到那些投票站去。

★ **con·stitu·ent** /kənstɪtʃuənt/ (**constituents**) 1 N-COUNT A **constituent** is someone who lives in a particular constituency, especially someone who is able to vote in an election. 选民 ❑ *He told his constituents that he would continue to represent them to the best of his ability.* 他告诉他的选民们他会继续竭尽所能代表他们。 2 N-COUNT A **constituent of** a mixture, substance, or system is one of the things from which it is formed. 成分 [FORMAL] ❑ *Caffeine is the active constituent of drinks such as tea and coffee.* 咖啡因是茶和咖啡这类饮品的活性成分。 3 ADJ The **constituent** parts of something are the things from which it is formed. 构成的 [ADJ n] [FORMAL] ❑ *...a plan to split the company into its constituent parts and sell them separately.* …一项把公司拆分为各构成部分然后分别出售的计划。

con·sti·tute /kɒnstɪtut/ (**constitutes, constituting, constituted**) 1 V-LINK If something **constitutes** a particular thing, it can be regarded as being that thing. 构成 [no cont] ❑ *Testing patients without their consent would constitute a professional and legal offense.* 未得病人同意即对其进行试验会构成职业和法律犯罪。 2 V-LINK If a number of things or people **constitute** something, they are the parts or members that form it. (某数量的物或人) 构成 (某事物) [no cont] ❑ *China's ethnic minorities constitute less than 7 percent of its total population.* 中国的少数民族构成总人口的不到7%。

con·sti·tu·tion ♦◇◇ /kɒnstɪtuʃən/ (**constitutions**) 1 N-COUNT The **constitution** of a country or organization is the system of laws which formally states people's rights and duties. 宪法; 章程 ❑ *The king was forced to adopt a new constitution which reduced his powers.* 国王被迫通过了削减其权力的新宪法。 2 N-COUNT Your **constitution** is your health. 体格 ❑ *He must have an extremely strong constitution.* 他必有极为强健的体格。

★ **con·sti·tu·tion·al** ♦◇◇ /kɒnstɪtuʃənəl/ ADJ **Constitutional** means relating to the constitution of a particular country or

C

organization. 有关宪法的；有关章程的 ❑ *The issue is one of constitutional and civil rights.* 这问题涉及宪法的和民事的权利。

★ **con·strain** /kənstreɪn/ (**constrains, constraining, constrained**) V-T To **constrain** someone or something means to limit their development or force them to behave in a particular way. 限制；迫使 [FORMAL] ❑ *Women are too often constrained by family commitments and by low expectations.* 女性往往受家庭职责及低期望值约束。

▲ **con·straint** /kənstreɪnt/ (**constraints**) 1 N-COUNT A **constraint** is something that limits or controls what you can do. 限制 ❑ *Their decision to abandon the trip was made because of financial constraints.* 他们放弃这次旅行的决定是因财务限制而作出的。 2 N-UNCOUNT **Constraint** is control over the way you behave which prevents you from doing what you want to do. 约束 ❑ *Journalists were given the freedom to visit, investigate, and report without constraint.* 新闻记者被赋予在没有约束下参观、调查和报道的自由。

★ **con·strict** /kənstrɪkt/ (**constricts, constricting, constricted**) 1 V-T/V-I If a part of your body, especially your throat, **is constricted** or if it **constricts**, something causes it to become narrower. 使收缩；收缩 ❑ *Severe migraines can be treated with a drug that constricts the blood vessels.* 严重偏头痛可以用一种收缩血管的药物来治疗。 2 V-T If something **constricts** you, it limits your actions so that you cannot do what you want to do. 约束 ❑ *She objects to the constant testing because it constricts her teaching style.* 她反对频繁地测试，因为这约束了她的教学风格。

Word Link *struct ≈ building : construct, destructive, instruct*

con·struct /kənstrʌkt/ (**constructs, constructing, constructed**) 1 V-T If you **construct** something such as a building, road, or machine, you build it or make it. 建造 ❑ *His company recently constructed an office building in downtown Denver.* 他的公司最近在丹佛市中心建造了一座办公楼。 ❑ *The boxes should be constructed from rough-sawn timber.* 这些箱子应该用粗锯木材来做。 2 V-T If you **construct** something such as an idea, a piece of writing, or a system, you create it by putting different parts together. 构建 ❑ *He eventually constructed a huge business empire.* 他最终构建了一个庞大的商业王国。 ❑ *The novel is constructed from a series of on-the-spot reports.* 这部小说是由一系列现场报道构思而成的。

con·struc·tion ♦◇◇ /kənstrʌkʃən/ (**constructions**) 1 N-UNCOUNT **Construction** is the building of things such as houses, factories, roads, and bridges. 建造 ❑ *He'd already started construction on a hunting lodge.* 他已经开始建造一个狩猎用的小屋。 ❑ *...the downturn in the construction industry.* …建造业的衰退。 ❑ *Jim now works in construction.* 吉姆现在从事建造业。 2 N-UNCOUNT The **construction** of something such as a vehicle or machine is the making of it. (交通工具、机器等的) 制造 ❑ *...companies who have long experience in the construction of those types of equipment.* …在制造那种设备方面有长久经验的各公司。 3 N-UNCOUNT The **construction** of something such as a system is the creation of it. 创立 ❑ *...the construction of a just system of criminal justice.* …公正的刑事司法体制的建立。 4 N-UNCOUNT You use **construction** to refer to the structure of something and the way it has been built or made. 构造 ❑ *The Shakers believed that furniture should be plain, simple, useful, practical, and of sound construction.* 震颤派教徒认为家具应当朴素、简单、有用、实际，且构造很好。 5 N-COUNT You can refer to an object that has been built or made as a **construction**. 建造物 ❑ *...an impressive steel and glass construction.* …一座令人印象深刻的钢筋玻璃建造物。 6 N-COUNT A grammatical **construction** is a particular arrangement of words in a sentence, clause, or phrase. (语法) 结构 ❑ *Avoid complex verbal constructions.* 避免复杂的动词结构。
→ see **skyscraper**

con·struc·tive /kənstrʌktɪv/ ADJ A **constructive** discussion, comment, or approach is useful and helpful rather than negative and unhelpful. 建设性的 ❑ *She welcomes constructive criticism.* 她欢迎建设性的批评意见。 ❑ *After their meeting, both men described the talks as frank, friendly and constructive.* 会见之后，两位男士都形容这次会谈坦诚、友好且富有建设性。

▲ **con·strue** /kənstruː/ (**construes, construing, construed**) V-T If something **is construed** in a particular way, its nature or meaning is interpreted in that way. 诠释 [FORMAL] ❑ *What may seem helpful behavior to you can be construed as interference by others.* 在你看来似乎有助益的行为会被他人看作干涉。 ❑ *He may construe the approach as a hostile act.* 他可能把这种方法理解为一种不友善的行为。

▲ **con·sul** /kɒnsəl/ (**consuls**) N-COUNT; N-TITLE A **consul** is an official who is sent by his or her government to live in a foreign city in order to help other citizens from his or her country who are in that foreign city. 领事 ❑ *...Stephanie Sweet, the British Consul in Tangier.* …英国驻丹吉尔的领事斯蒂芬妮・斯威特。

con·su·lar /kɒnsələr/ ADJ **Consular** means involving or relating to a consul or the work of a consul. 领事的 [ADJ n] ❑ *U.S. consular officials have visited the men, although they have not yet had access to lawyers.* 美国领事馆的官员已经探望了那些男人，不过他们还没有机会见到律师们。

▲ **con·su·late** /kɒnsəlɪt/ (**consulates**) N-COUNT A **consulate** is the place where a consul works. 领事馆 ❑ *...the Canadian consulate in Seattle.* …驻西雅图的加拿大领事馆。

con·sult ♦◇◇ /kənsʌlt/ (**consults, consulting, consulted**) 1 V-T/V-I If you **consult** an expert or someone senior to you or **consult with** them, you ask them for their opinion, advice, or permission. 咨询 ❑ *Consult your doctor about how much exercise you should get.* 咨询你的医生你应做多少运动。 ❑ *He needed to consult with an attorney.* 他需要和律师咨询。 2 V-T If you **consult** a book or a map, you look in it or look at it in order to find some information. 查阅 ❑ *Consult the chart on page 44 for the correct cooking times.* 查阅第44页的图表找正确的烹调时间。 3 V-RECIP If a person or group of people **consults with** other people or **consults** them, or if two people or groups **consult**, they talk and exchange ideas and opinions about what they might decide to do. 商量 ❑ *After consulting with her daughter and manager, she decided to take on the part, on her terms.* 同她的女儿兼经纪人商量之后，她决定按她的要求接受那个角色。 ❑ *The two countries will have to consult their allies.* 两国得同各自的盟友协商。

★ **con·sul·tan·cy** /kənsʌltənsi/ (**consultancies**) 1 N-COUNT A **consultancy** is a company that gives expert advice on a particular subject. 咨询公司 ❑ *A survey of 57 hospitals by Newchurch, a consultancy, reveals striking improvements.* 纽彻奇咨询公司对57家医院的调查显示明显的改善。 2 N-UNCOUNT **Consultancy** is expert advice on a particular subject which a person or group is paid to provide to a company or organization. 咨询 [mainly BRIT]

con·sult·ant ♦◇◇ /kənsʌltənt/ (**consultants**) 1 N-COUNT A **consultant** is a person who gives expert advice to a person or organization on a particular subject. 顾问 ❑ *She is a consultant to the government.* 她是政府顾问。 2 N-COUNT A **consultant** is an experienced doctor with a high position, who specializes in one area of medicine. 顾问医生 [BRIT]
in AM, usually use **specialist**

con·sul·ta·tion /kɒnsəlteɪʃən/ (**consultations**) 1 N-VAR A **consultation** is a meeting to discuss something. **Consultation** is discussion about something. 磋商会议；磋商 ❑ *Next week he'll be in Florida for consultations with President Vicente Fox.* 下星期他将在佛罗里达同维森特・福克斯总统作磋商。 2 N-VAR A **consultation with** a doctor or other expert is a meeting with them to discuss a particular problem and get their advice. **Consultation** is the process of getting advice from a doctor or other expert. 咨询会；咨询 ❑ *A personal diet plan is devised after a consultation with a nutritionist.* 经向营养师作咨询后，一份个人饮食方案设计出来了。 3 N-COUNT A **consultation** is a meeting where several doctors discuss a patient and his or her condition and treatment. 会诊 [AM]

★ **con·sul·ta·tive** /kənsʌltətɪv/ ADJ A **consultative** committee or document gives advice or makes proposals about a particular problem or subject. 顾问的；咨询的 ❑ *...the consultative committee on local government finance.* …地方政府财政顾问委员会。

con·sum·able /kənsuməbəl/ (**consumables**) ADJ **Consumable** goods are items which are intended to be bought, used, and then replaced. 供消耗的 ❑ *...demand for consumable articles.* …对供消耗物品的需求。 ● N-COUNT **Consumable** is also a noun. 消耗品 ❑ *Suppliers add computer consumables, office equipment and furniture to their product range.* 供应商把计算机耗材、办公设备及家具加进他们的产品范围中。

Word Link *sume ≈ taking : assume, consume, presume*

con·sume /kənsum/ (**consumes, consuming, consumed**) 1 V-T If you **consume** something, you eat or drink it. 吃；喝 [FORMAL] ❑ *Martha would consume nearly a pound of cheese per day.* 玛莎那时每天吃将近一磅奶酪。 2 V-T To **consume** an amount of fuel, energy, or time means to use it up. 消耗 ❑ *Some of the most efficient refrigerators consume 70 percent less electricity than traditional models.* 一些能效最高的

冰箱比传统型号少消耗70%的电。 3 → see also **consuming**

con·sum·er ♦♦◇ /kənsuːmər/ (**consumers**) N-COUNT A **consumer** is a person who buys things or uses services. 消费者 ❑ *...claims that tobacco companies failed to warn consumers about the dangers of smoking.* …声称烟草公司没有就吸烟的种种危险警告消费者。 → see **advertising**

con·sum·er cred·it N-UNCOUNT **Consumer credit** is money that is lent to people by organizations such as banks and stores so that they can buy things. 消费信贷 ❑ *New consumer credit fell to $3.7 billion in August.* 8月份新的消费信贷下降至37亿美元。

con·sum·er du·rable (**consumer durables**) N-COUNT **Consumer durables** are goods which are expected to last a long time, and are bought infrequently. 耐用消费品 [BRIT, BUSINESS]

in AM, use **durable goods**

con·sum·er goods N-PLURAL **Consumer goods** are items bought by people for their own use, rather than by businesses. Compare **capital goods**. 消费用商品 [BUSINESS] ❑ *The choice of consumer goods available in local shops is small.* 本地商店中可供选择的消费用商品很少。

con·sum·er so·ci·ety (**consumer societies**) N-COUNT You can use **consumer society** to refer to a society where people think that spending money on goods and services is very important. 消费社会 ❑ *We live in a consumer society in which money is a massive preoccupation.* 我们生活在一个金钱是极大关注点的消费社会。

con·sum·ing /kənsuːmɪŋ/ 1 ADJ A **consuming** passion or interest is more important to you than anything else. 强烈的 ❑ *He has developed a consuming passion for chess.* 他对国际象棋已经产生了浓厚的兴趣。 2 → see also **consume, time-consuming**

Word Link *summ ≈ highest point : consummate, summary, summit*

▲ **con·sum·mate** (**consummates, consummating, consummated**)

The adjective is pronounced /kɒnsəmɪt, kənsʌmɪt/. The verb is pronounced /kɒnsəmeɪt/.

形容词读作 /kɒnsəmɪt, kənsʌmɪt/。动词读作 /kɒnsəmeɪt/。

1 ADJ You use **consummate** to describe someone who is extremely skillful. 炉火纯青的 [FORMAL] ❑ *He acted the part with consummate skill.* 他以精湛的演技饰演了这个角色。 2 V-T If two people **consummate** a marriage or relationship, they make it complete by having sex. (通过同房而) 完成 (婚姻) [FORMAL] ❑ *His wife divorced him for failing to consummate their marriage.* 他的妻子因为他未能完婚而跟他离婚了。

Word Link *sumpt ≈ taking : assumption, consumption, presumption*

con·sump·tion /kənsʌmpʃən/ 1 N-UNCOUNT The **consumption** of fuel or natural resources is the act of using them or the amount used. 消耗 ❑ *The laws have led to a reduction in fuel consumption in the U.S.* 这些法律已导致美国燃料消耗的降低。 2 N-UNCOUNT The **consumption** of food or drink is the act of eating or drinking something, or the amount eaten or drunk. 食用; 饮用 [FORMAL] ❑ *Most of the wine was unfit for human consumption.* 大多数酒都是不适合人类饮用的。 3 N-UNCOUNT **Consumption** is the act of buying and using things. 消费 ❑ *They were prepared to put people out of work and reduce consumption by strangling the whole economy.* 他们准备让人们失业、降低消费，由此来遏制整个经济。

cont. **Cont.** is an abbreviation for "continued," which is used at the bottom of a page to indicate that a letter or text continues on another page. 转下页

con·tact ♦♦◇ /kɒntækt/ (**contacts, contacting, contacted**) 1 N-UNCOUNT **Contact** involves meeting or communicating with someone, especially regularly. 往来 [also N in pl, oft N "with/between" n] ❑ *Opposition leaders are denying any contact with the government in Kabul.* 反对党领袖们在否认同喀布尔政府有任何往来。 2 N-UNCOUNT If you come **into contact with** someone or something, you meet that person or thing in the course of your work or other activities. (打) 交道 ❑ *Doctors I came into contact with voiced their concern.* 我打过交道的医生们表达了他们的关注。 3 N-UNCOUNT When people or things are in **contact**, they are touching each other. 接触 ❑ *They compared how these organisms behaved when left in contact with different materials.* 他们比较了这些有机物在接触不同材料时如何表现。 ❑ *The cry occurs when air is brought into contact with the baby's larynx.* 当空气接触到婴儿的喉咙时，哭声就会响起。 4 ADJ Your **contact** details or number are information such as a telephone number where you can be contacted. 联络用的 [ADJ n] ❑ *You must leave your full name and contact details when you phone.* 你打电话时必须留下自己的完整姓名及用于联络的详细资料。 5 PHRASE If you are **in contact with** someone, you regularly meet them or communicate with them. 与…有联络 ❑ *He was in direct contact with the kidnappers.* 他与绑匪有直接联络。 6 PHRASE If you **make contact with** someone, you find out where they are and talk or write to them. （与某人）联系 ❑ *How did you make contact with the author?* 你怎么跟这位作者联系的？ 7 PHRASE If you **lose contact with** someone who you have been friendly with, you no longer see them, speak to them, or write to them. （与某人）失去联系 ❑ *Though they all live nearby, I lost contact with them really quickly.* 虽然他们都住在附近，我真地很快就与他们失去了联系。 8 V-T If you **contact** someone, you telephone them, write to them, or go to see them in order to tell or ask them something. 联系 ❑ *Contact the Women's Alliance for further details.* 请联系妇女联合会获取详情。 9 N-COUNT A **contact** is someone you know in an organization or profession who helps you or gives you information. 联络人 ❑ *Their contact at the United States embassy was Phillip Norton.* 他们在美国大使馆的联络人是菲利普・诺顿。

con·tact lens (**contact lenses**) N-COUNT **Contact lenses** are small plastic lenses that you put on the surface of your eyes to help you see better, instead of wearing glasses. 隐形眼镜 → see **eye**

▲ **con·ta·gious** /kənteɪdʒəs/ 1 ADJ A disease that is **contagious** can be caught by touching people or things that are infected with it. Compare **infectious**. 接触传染的 ❑ *...a highly contagious disease of the lungs.* …一种高度接触传染的肺病。 2 ADJ A feeling or attitude that is **contagious** spreads quickly among a group of people. 有感染力的 ❑ *Laughing is contagious.* 笑是有感染力的。

con·tain ♦♦◇ /kənteɪn/ (**contains, containing, contained**) 1 V-T If something such as a box, bag, room, or place **contains** things, those things are inside it. 有…在里面 [no cont] ❑ *The envelope contained a Christmas card.* 该信封里装有一张圣诞贺卡。 ❑ *The first two floors of the building contain retail space and a restaurant.* 该大楼最底下两层有零售空间和一家餐馆。 2 V-T If a substance **contains** something, that thing is a part of it. 含有 [no cont] ❑ *Watermelon contains vitamins and also potassium.* 西瓜含有维生素也有钾。 3 V-T If writing, speech, or film **contains** particular information, ideas, or images, it includes them. (文章、演讲、电影) 包含 (某些信息、观点、图像等) [no cont] ❑ *This sheet contained a list of problems a patient might like to raise with the doctor.* 这张纸写有一个病人可能想向医生提出的问题清单。 4 V-T If a group or organization **contains** a certain number of people, those are the people that are in it. (团体、组织等) 包括 (某数量的成员) [no cont] ❑ *The committee contains 11 Democrats and nine Republicans.* 该委员会包括11名民主党人和9名共和党人。 5 V-T If you **contain** something, you control it and prevent it from spreading or increasing. 控制; 阻止 ❑ *More than a hundred firemen are still trying to contain the fire at the plant.* 一百多名消防队员仍在努力控制工厂火势。 6 → see also **self-contained**

con·tain·er /kənteɪnər/ (**containers**) 1 N-COUNT A **container** is something such as a box or bottle that is used to hold or store things in. 容器 ❑ *...the plastic containers in which fish are stored and sold.* …储藏和出售鱼的塑料容器。 2 N-COUNT A **container** is a very large metal or wooden box used for transporting goods so that they can be loaded easily onto ships and trucks. 集装箱 ❑ *The train, carrying loaded containers on flatcars, was 1.2 miles long.* 那列在平车上载着装得满满的集装箱的火车长1.2英里。 → see **can, ship**

▲ **con·tain·ment** /kənteɪnmənt/ 1 N-UNCOUNT **Containment** is the action or policy of keeping another country's power or area of control within acceptable limits or boundaries. 遏制 2 N-UNCOUNT The **containment of** something dangerous or unpleasant is the act or process of keeping it under control within a particular area or place. 控制 [usu N "of" n] ❑ *Fire crews are hoping they can achieve full containment of the fire before the winds pick up.* 消防队员们希望他们能够在起风前对大火做到完全控制。

C

con·tami·nate /kəntæmɪneɪt/ (**contaminates, contaminating, contaminated**) V-T If something **is contaminated by** dirt, chemicals, or radiation, they make it dirty or harmful. 污染 ❑ *Have any fish been contaminated in the Arctic Ocean?* 北冰洋里有鱼受到污染了吗？ ● **con·tami·na·tion** /kəntæmɪneɪʃᵊn/ N-UNCOUNT 污染 ❑ *The contamination of the ocean around Puget Sound may be just the beginning.* 普吉特海湾周围海域的污染可能才开始。

★ **con·tem·plate** /kɒntəmpleɪt/ (**contemplates, contemplating, contemplated**) **1** V-T If you **contemplate** an action, you think about whether to do it or not. 考虑 ❑ *For a time he contemplated a career as an army medical doctor.* 他曾一度考虑做一名军医。 **2** V-T If you **contemplate** an idea or subject, you think about it carefully for a long time. 对…考虑再三 ❑ *As he lay in his hospital bed that night, he cried as he contemplated his future.* 那天晚上他躺在医院病床上，当他反复考虑自己的未来时他哭了。 ● **con·tem·pla·tion** /kɒntəmpleɪʃᵊn/ N-UNCOUNT 考虑再三 ❑ *It is a place of quiet contemplation.* 这是一个适合静静深思的地方。 **3** V-T If you **contemplate** something or someone, you look at them for a long time. 凝视 ❑ *He contemplated his hands, still frowning.* 他凝视着他的双手，依然皱着眉头。 ● **con·tem·pla·tion** N-UNCOUNT 凝视 ❑ *He was lost in the contemplation of the landscape for a while.* 他沉湎在对风景的凝视中好一会儿。

Word Link *con ≈ together, with : consensus, contemporary, convene*

Word Link *tempo ≈ time : contemporary, temporal, temporary*

con·tem·po·rary ♦◇◇ /kəntɛmpərɛri/ (**contemporaries**) **1** ADJ **Contemporary** things are modern and relate to the present time. 当代的 ❑ *She writes a lot of contemporary music for people like Whitney Houston.* 她为惠特尼・休斯敦等人创作大量当代音乐作品。 **2** ADJ **Contemporary** people or things were alive or happened at the same time as something else you are talking about. 同时代的 ❑ *...drawing upon official records and the reports of contemporary witnesses.* …借助官方记录以及当时目击者的证言。 **3** N-COUNT Someone's **contemporary** is a person who is or was alive at the same time as them. 同时代的人 ❑ *Like most of my contemporaries, I grew up in a vastly different world.* 像我同时代的大多数人一样，我在一个非常不同的世界里长大。

★ **con·tempt** /kəntɛmpt/ N-UNCOUNT If you have **contempt for** someone or something, you have no respect for them or think that they are unimportant. 蔑视 ❑ *He has contempt for those beyond his immediate family circle.* 他对自己直系亲属以外的人都心怀蔑视。

con·temp·tu·ous /kəntɛmptʃuəs/ ADJ If you are **contemptuous of** someone or something, you do not like or respect them at all. 心怀蔑视的 ❑ *He was contemptuous of the poor.* 他那时对穷人是心怀蔑视的。 ❑ *He's openly contemptuous of all the major political parties.* 他对所有主要政党公然心怀蔑视。

★ **con·tend** /kəntɛnd/ (**contends, contending, contended**) **1** V-I If you have to **contend with** a problem or difficulty, you have to deal with it or overcome it. 解决 ❑ *It is time, once again, to contend with racism.* 又是对付种族主义的时候了。 **2** V-T If you **contend that** something is true, you state or argue that it is true. 辩称 [FORMAL] ❑ *The government contends that he is fundamentalist.* 政府辩称他是原教旨主义者。 **3** V-RECIP If you **contend with** someone **for** something such as power, you compete with them to try to get it. 争夺（权力等） ❑ *...the two main groups contending for power.* …争夺权力的两大主要集团。 ❑ *Small-market clubs such as the Kansas City Royals have had trouble contending with richer teams for championships.* 像堪萨斯城皇家队这样市场规模较小的俱乐部一直难以同财力更雄厚的球队争夺冠军。

con·tend·er /kəntɛndər/ (**contenders**) N-COUNT A **contender** is someone who takes part in a competition. 竞争者 [JOURNALISM] ❑ *Her trainer said yesterday that she would be a strong contender for a place on the Olympic team.* 她的教练昨天说，她会是取得奥运代表队里一个席位的一名强有力的竞争者。

content
❶ NOUN USES
❷ ADJECTIVE USES

❶ **con·tent** ♦◇◇ /kɒntɛnt/ (**contents**) **1** N-PLURAL The **contents** of a container such as a bottle, box, or room are the things that are inside it. （瓶子、盒子或房间的）所容之物 ❑ *Empty the contents of the pan into the sieve.* 将平锅里的东西全部倒入漏勺。 **2** N-PLURAL The **contents** of a book are its different chapters and sections, usually shown in a list at the beginning of the book. （书的）目录 ❑ *There is no Table of Contents.* 没有目录。 **3** N-UNCOUNT If you refer to the **content** or **contents** of something such as a book, television program, or website, you are referring to the subject that it deals with, the story that it tells, or the ideas that it expresses. （书、电视节目、网站等的）内容 [also N in pl, usu N "of" n] ❑ *She is reluctant to discuss the content of the play.* 她不愿讨论这部话剧的内容。 ❑ *Stricter controls were placed on the content of videos.* 对录像的内容有了更严格的控制。 **4** N-UNCOUNT The **content** of something such as an educational course or a program of action is the elements that it consists of. （课程、计划的）内容 ❑ *Previous students have had nothing but praise for the course content and staff.* 以前的学生们对该课程的内容和教师只有称赞。 **5** N-SING You can use **content** to refer to the amount or proportion of something that a substance contains. 含量 ❑ *Sunflower margarine has the same fat content as butter.* 葵花籽人造黄油有同黄油一样的脂肪含量。

❷ **con·tent** /kəntɛnt/
➪ **Please look at meaning 3 to see if the expression you are looking for is shown under another headword.** **1** ADJ If you are **content with** something, you are willing to accept it, rather than wanting something more or something better. 满足的 [v-link ADJ] ❑ *I am content to admire the mountains from below.* 我满足于从山下观赏群山。 ❑ *I'm perfectly content with the way the campaign has gone.* 我对这次活动开展的情况感到心满意足。 **2** ADJ If you are **content**, you are fairly happy or satisfied. 满意的 [v-link ADJ] ❑ *He says his daughter is quite content.* 他说他的女儿颇为满意。 **3** **to your heart's content** → see **heart**

con·tent·ed /kəntɛntɪd/ ADJ If you are **contented**, you are satisfied with your life or the situation you are in. 满意的 ❑ *Whenever he returns to this place, he is happy and contented.* 每次回到这里，他都是既高兴又满足。

★ **con·ten·tion** /kəntɛnʃᵊn/ (**contentions**) **1** N-COUNT Someone's **contention** is the idea or opinion that they are expressing in an argument or discussion. （辩论或讨论中表达的）观点 ❑ *It is my contention that death and murder always lurk as potentials in violent relationships.* 我的观点是，在暴力关系中总是潜伏着死亡和谋杀的可能。 **2** N-UNCOUNT If something is a cause **of contention**, it is a cause of disagreement or argument. 争论 ❑ *His case has become a source of contention between civil liberties activists and the government.* 他的案子已变成了公民自由活动家们和政府之间的争论缘由。 **3** → see also **bone of contention**

▲ **con·ten·tious** /kəntɛnʃəs/ ADJ A **contentious** issue causes a lot of disagreement or arguments. 引起争议的 [FORMAL] ❑ *Sanctions are expected to be among the most contentious issues.* 制裁预计位居最具有争议的问题之列。

con·tent·ment /kəntɛntmənt/ N-UNCOUNT **Contentment** is a feeling of quiet happiness and satisfaction. 满足 ❑ *I cannot describe the feeling of contentment that was with me at that time.* 我无法形容我当时的满足感。

con·test ♦◇◇ (**contests, contesting, contested**)

The noun is pronounced /kɒntɛst/. The verb is pronounced /kəntɛst/.

名词读作 /kɒntɛst/。动词读作 /kəntɛst/。

1 N-COUNT A **contest** is a competition or game that people try to win. 竞赛；比赛 ❑ *Few contests in the recent history of boxing have been as thrilling.* 在近期拳击史上没有几场比赛曾如此惊心动魄。 **2** N-COUNT A **contest** is a struggle to win power or control. 争夺 ❑ *The state election in November will be the last such ballot before next year's presidential contest.* 11月的州选举将是明年的总统竞选前最后一轮这类投票。 **3** V-T If you **contest** a statement or decision, you object to it formally because you think it is wrong or unreasonable. 对…提出抗辩 ❑ *Your former employer has to reply within 14 days in order to contest the case.* 你的前雇主得在14天内做出答复以对本案提出抗辩。 **4** V-T If someone **contests** an election or competition, they take part in it and try to win it. 参加（竞选或比赛） [BRIT] ❑ *He quickly won his party's nomination to contest the elections.* 他迅速赢得了其党派的提名来参加竞选。

Thesaurus *contest* 另参见：
N. competition, game, match **1**
fight, struggle **2**

con·test·ant /kəntɛstənt/ (**contestants**) N-COUNT A **contestant** in a competition or game show is a person who takes part in it. 参赛者 ❑ *Later he applied to be a contestant on the television show.* 之后他报了名做该电视秀的参赛者。

con·text ♦◇◇ /kɒntɛkst/ (**contexts**) **1** N-VAR The **context of** an idea or event is the general situation that relates to it, and which helps it to be understood. 背景 ❑ *We are doing this work in the context of reforms in the economic, social and cultural spheres.* 我们正在经济、社会和文化领域改革的背景下从事这项工作。 ❑ *It helps to understand the historical context in which Chaucer wrote.* 这有助于理解乔叟创作时的历史背景。 **2** N-VAR The **context** of a word, sentence, or text consists of the words, sentences, or text before and after it which help to make its meaning clear. 语境 ❑ *Without a context, I would have assumed it was written by a man.* 如果没有一个语境，我会以为这是由一个男人写的。 **3** PHRASE If something is seen **in context** or if it is put **into context**, it is considered together with all the factors that relate to it. 联系背景地 ❑ *Taxation is not popular in principle, merely acceptable in context.* 征税原则上不受大众欢迎，只是联系背景看是可接受的。 **4** PHRASE If a statement or remark is quoted **out of context**, the circumstances in which it was said are not correctly reported, so that it seems to mean something different from the meaning that was intended. 脱离语境地 ❑ *Thomas says that he has been quoted out of context.* 托马斯说，他的话被断章取义了。

con·ti·nent ♦◇◇ /kɒntɪnənt/ (**continents**) **1** N-COUNT A **continent** is a very large area of land, such as Africa or Asia, that consists of several countries. 大洲 ❑ *She loved the African continent.* 她热爱非洲大陆。 **2** N-PROPER People sometimes use **the Continent** to refer to the continent of Europe except for Britain. (除英国外的) 欧洲大陆 [mainly BRIT] ❑ *Its shops are among the most stylish on the Continent.* 其商店位列欧洲大陆最时尚的商店之中。

→ see Word Web: **continents**

→ see **earth**

con·ti·nen·tal /kɒntɪnɛntᵊl/ (**continentals**) **1** ADJ **Continental** is used to refer to something that belongs to or relates to a continent. 大陆的 [ADJ n] ❑ *The most ancient parts of the continental crust are 4000 million years old.* 该大陆地壳最古老的那些部分有40亿年了。 **2** ADJ The **continental** United States consists of all the states which are situated on the continent of North America, as opposed to Hawaii and territories such as the Virgin Islands. 内陆的 (美国) [mainly AM] ❑ *Shipping is included on orders sent within the continental U.S.* 运费含在美国内陆发出的订单中。 **3** ADJ **Continental** means existing or happening in the American colonies during the American Revolution. 大陆的 (指在美国独立战争期间的美国殖民地存在或发生的) [usu ADJ n] [AM] ❑ *...George Washington, Commander of the Continental Army.* …乔治・华盛顿，大陆军总司令。 **4** ADJ **Continental** means situated on or belonging to the continent of Europe except for Britain. (除英国外的) 欧洲大陆的 [ADJ n] [mainly BRIT] ❑ *He sees no signs of improvement in the U.K. and continental economy.* 他看不出英国和欧洲大陆的经济好转的迹象。 **5** N-COUNT **Continentals** were soldiers who fought in the Continental Army against the British in the American Revolution. (美国独立战争中的) 大陆军士兵 [AM]

→ see **continent**

con·tin·gen·cy /kəntɪndʒᵊnsi/ (**contingencies**) **1** N-VAR A **contingency** is something that might happen in the future. 可能发生的事 [FORMAL] ❑ *I need to examine all possible contingencies.* 我得查看所有可能发生的事。 **2** ADJ A **contingency** plan or measure is one that is intended to be used if a possible situation actually occurs. 应变的 [ADJ n] [FORMAL] ❑ *We have contingency plans.* 我们有应变计划。

▲ **con·tin·gent** /kəntɪndʒᵊnt/ (**contingents**) **1** N-COUNT A **contingent of** police, soldiers, or military vehicles is a group of them. (警察、士兵、军车) 批 [FORMAL] ❑ *Nigeria provided a large contingent of troops to the West African Peacekeeping Force.* 尼日利亚向西非维和部队派出了一大批部队。 **2** N-COUNT A **contingent** is a group of people representing a country or organization at a meeting or other event. 代表团 [FORMAL] ❑ *The American contingent will stay overnight in London.* 美国代表团将在伦敦留宿。

con·tin·ual /kəntɪnyuəl/ **1** ADJ A **continual** process or situation happens or exists without stopping. 持续不断的 [ADJ n] ❑ *The school has been in continual use since 1883.* 该校自1883年以来一直在不断使用中。 ❑ *They felt continual pressure to perform well.* 他们感受到持续不断的、要表演得好的压力。 ● **con·tinu·al·ly** ADV 持续不断地 ❑ *She cried almost continually and threw temper tantrums.* 她几乎哭个不停，还大发脾气。 **2** ADJ **Continual** events happen again and again. 频繁的 [ADJ n] ❑ *...the government's continual demands for cash to finance its chronic deficit.* …政府为负担其长期的财政赤字而对现金不断的需求。 ● **con·tinu·al·ly** ADV 频繁地 ❑ *Malcolm was continually changing his mind.* 马尔科姆频频改变其主意。

> You can use **continual**, **continuous**, and **constant** to describe things that happen or exist without stopping. **Continual** is usually used to describe something that happens often over a period of time, especially something undesirable. ❑ *...his continual drinking. ...continual demands to cut costs.* If something is **continuous**, it happens all the time without stopping, or seems to do so. ❑ *...days of continuous rain. ...a continuous background noise.* You describe something as **constant** when it happens all the time or never goes away. ❑ *He was in constant pain. ...Eva's constant criticism.*

Thesaurus *continual* 另参见:

ADJ. constant, ongoing, unending **1**
repeated **2**

★ **con·tinu·ance** /kəntɪnyuəns/ N-UNCOUNT The **continuance** of something is its continuation. 继续 [usu with poss] [FORMAL] ❑ *...thus ensuring the continuance of the human species.* …因此保证人种的延续。

con·tinu·ation /kəntɪnyueɪʃᵊn/ (**continuations**) **1** N-VAR The **continuation of** something is the fact that it continues, instead of stopping. 持续 ❑ *It's the coalition forces who are to blame for the continuation of the war.* 是联军应对战争的持续负责。 **2** N-COUNT Something that is a **continuation of** something else is closely connected with it or forms part of it. 延续 ❑ *This chapter is a continuation of Chapter 8.* 本章是第8章的延续。

Word Web continents

In 1912, Alfred Wegener* made an important discovery. The shapes of the various **continents** seemed to fit together like the pieces of a puzzle. He decided they had once been a single **land mass** which he called Pangaea. He thought the continents had slowly moved apart. Wegener called this theory **continental drift**. He said the earth's **crust** is not a single, solid piece. It's full of cracks which allow huge pieces to move around on the earth's mantle. The movement of these tectonic **plates** increases the distance between Europe and North America by about 20 millimeters every year.

Alfred Wegener (1880-1930): a German scientist.

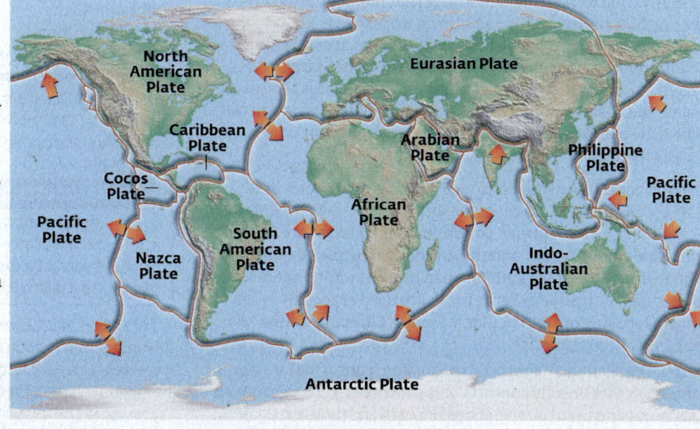

Major Plates of the Earth's Crust

C

con·tinue ◆◆◆ /kəntɪnyu/ (**continues, continuing, continued**) 1 V-T/V-I If someone or something **continues to** do something, they keep doing it and do not stop. 继续 ❑ *I hope they continue to fight for equal justice after I'm gone.* 我希望我走后他们继续为司法公正而奋斗。❑ *Diana and Roy Jarvis are determined to continue working when they reach retirement age.* 戴安娜・贾维斯和罗伊・贾维斯决心到退休年龄后还继续工作。 2 V-T/V-I If something **continues** or if you **continue** it, it does not stop. 使继续；继续 ❑ *He insisted that the conflict would continue until conditions were met for a ceasefire.* 他坚持认为冲突会持续下去，直至停火条件得到满足为止。❑ *Outside the building people continue their vigil, huddling around bonfires.* 在楼外，人们围聚在篝火旁继续守夜。 3 V-T/V-I If you **continue** something or **continue** with something, you start doing it again after a break or interruption. (某人在歇息或被打断后) 继续 (做某事或某事) ❑ *I went up to my room to continue with my packing.* 我上我房间去继续收拾行李。❑ *She looked up for a minute and then continued drawing.* 她抬头看了一会儿，然后继续画。 4 V-T/V-I If something **continues** or if you **continue** it, it starts again after a break or interruption. (某事在停顿或被打断后) 继续 ❑ *He denies 18 charges. The trial continues today.* 他否认18项指控。审判今天继续。 5 V-T/V-I If you **continue**, you begin speaking again after a pause or interruption. (在停顿或被打断后) 继续说 ❑ *"You have no right to intimidate this man," Alison continued.* "你无权威胁这个男人，"爱丽森继续说。❑ *Tony drank some coffee before he continued.* 托尼喝了些咖啡继续讲。 6 V-I If you **continue as** something or **continue** in a particular state, you remain in a particular job or state. 继续 (原有工作或状态) ❑ *He had hoped to continue as a full-time career officer.* 他原本希望继续当全职警官。 7 V-I If you **continue** in a particular direction, you keep walking or traveling in that direction. 继续走 ❑ *He continued rapidly up the path, not pausing until he neared the Chapter House.* 他继续快速地沿着那小径走，直到走近牧师会礼堂才停下脚步。

Thesaurus *continue* 另参见：
v. go on, persist; (*ant.*) stop 1 2
carry on, resume 3

con·tinu·ing edu·ca·tion N-UNCOUNT **Continuing education** is education for adults in a variety of subjects. 继续教育

con·ti·nu·ity /kɒntɪnuɪti/ (**continuities**) N-VAR **Continuity** is the fact that something continues to happen or exist, with no great changes or interruptions. 连续性；持续性 ❑ *...a tank designed to ensure continuity of fuel supply during aerobatics.* …为特技飞行中确保持续供油而设计的油箱。

con·tinu·ous /kəntɪnyuəs/ 1 ADJ A **continuous** process or event continues for a period of time without stopping. 持续的 (过程、事件) ❑ *Residents report that they heard continuous gunfire.* 居民们说他们听到了持续的枪声。● **con·tinu·ous·ly** ADV 持续地 ❑ *The civil war has raged almost continuously since 1976.* 自1976年以来，激烈的内战几乎持续不断。

You can use **continual, continuous**, and **constant** to describe things that happen or exist without stopping. **Continual** is usually used to describe something that happens often over a period of time, especially something undesirable. ❑ *...his continual drinking. ...continual demands to cut costs.* If something is **continuous**, it happens all the time without stopping, or seems to do so. ❑ *...days of continuous rain. ...a continuous background noise.* You describe something as **constant** when it happens all the time or never goes away. ❑ *He was in constant pain. ...Eva's constant criticism.*

2 ADJ A **continuous** line or surface has no gaps or holes in it. 连续的 (线条或平面) ❑ *...a continuous line of boats.* …络绎不绝的船只。 3 ADJ In English grammar, **continuous** verb groups are formed using the auxiliary "be" and the present participle of a verb, as in "I'm feeling a bit tired" and "She had been watching them for some time." Continuous verb groups are used especially when you are focusing on a particular moment. Compare **simple**. 进行 (时态) 的

con·tort /kəntɔrt/ (**contorts, contorting, contorted**) V-T/V-I If someone's face or body **contorts** or **is contorted**, it moves into an unnatural and unattractive shape or position. (面部或身体) 扭曲；使扭曲 ❑ *His face contorts as he screams out the lyrics.* 当他大声朗读这些抒情诗时，脸都变形了。❑ *The gentlest of her caresses would contort his already tense body.* 她温柔的爱抚会使他原本绷紧的身体更不自然。

con·tour /kɒntʊər/ (**contours**) 1 N-COUNT You can refer to the general shape or outline of an object as its **contours**. 轮廓；轮廓线 [LITERARY] ❑ *...the texture and color of the skin, the contours of the body.* …皮肤的肌理和颜色，身体的曲线。 2 N-COUNT A **contour** on a map is a line joining points of equal height and indicating hills, valleys, and the steepness of slopes. 等高线 ❑ *...a contour map showing two hills and this large mountain in the middle.* …一张显示有两座小山和其间一座大山的等高线图。

Word Link *contra* ≈ *against* : *contraception, contradict, contrary*

▲ **contra·cep·tion** /kɒntrəsɛpʃ^ən/ N-UNCOUNT **Contraception** refers to methods of preventing pregnancy. 避孕法 ❑ *Use a reliable method of contraception.* 使用可靠的避孕方法。

contra·cep·tive /kɒntrəsɛptɪv/ (**contraceptives**) 1 ADJ A **contraceptive** method or device is used to prevent pregnancy. 避孕的 [ADJ n] ❑ *...the contraceptive pill.* …避孕药丸。 2 N-COUNT A **contraceptive** is a device or drug that prevents a woman from becoming pregnant. 避孕药；避孕用品 ❑ *...oral contraceptives.* …口服避孕药。

Word Link *tract* ≈ *dragging, drawing* : *contract, subtract, tractor*

con·tract ◆◆◇ (**contracts, contracting, contracted**)

The noun is pronounced /kɒntrækt/. The verb is pronounced /kəntrækt/.

名词读作 /kɒntrækt/。动词读作 /kəntrækt/。

1 N-COUNT A **contract** is a legal agreement, usually between two companies or between an employer and employee, which involves doing work for a stated sum of money. 合同 ❑ *The company won a hefty contract for work on Chicago's tallest building.* 公司赢得了芝加哥最高建筑的重要施工合同。❑ *Have you read the contract?* 你看过这份合同了吗？ 2 V-T If you **contract with** someone **to** do something, you legally agree to do it for them or for them to do it for you. (与某人) 签订合同 [FORMAL] ❑ *You can contract with us to deliver your cargo.* 你们可以和我们签订合同，由我们负责运输你们的货物。 3 V-T/V-I When something **contracts** or when something **contracts** it, it becomes smaller or shorter. 缩小；缩短；使缩小；使缩短 ❑ *Blood is only expelled from the heart when it contracts.* 心脏收缩时，血液才从心脏射出。● **con·trac·tion** /kəntrækʃ^ən/ N-VAR (**contractions**) 收缩 ❑ *...the contraction and expansion of blood vessels.* …血管的收缩与扩张。 4 V-I When something such as an economy or market **contracts**, it becomes smaller. (经济、市场等) 萎缩 ❑ *The manufacturing economy contracted in October for the sixth consecutive month.* 制造业经济到10月份已连续萎缩6个月了。 5 V-T If you **contract** a serious illness, you become ill with it. 染 (重病) [no cont] [FORMAL] ❑ *He contracted AIDS from a blood transfusion.* 他因一次输血感染了艾滋病。 6 PHRASE If you are **under contract to** someone, you have signed a contract agreeing to work for them, and for no one else, during a fixed period of time. 已经与…签订合同 ❑ *The director wanted Olivia de Havilland, then under contract to Warner Brothers.* 导演想要奥莉维亚・德・哈维兰，但是那时她已经签约华纳兄弟公司。
→ see **illness, muscle**

▶ **contract out** PHRASAL VERB If a company **contracts out** work, they employ other companies to do it. 订立合同把 (工作) 包出去 [BUSINESS] ❑ *Firms can contract out work to one another.* 公司可以相互签订承包合同。❑ *When the bank contracted out its cleaning, the new company was cheaper.* 银行把清洁工作承包出去之后，才发现新的清洁公司报价更便宜。

Word Partnership *contract* 的常用搭配：
V. **sign** a contract 1
N. **terms of** a contract 1
contract **a disease** 5
PREP. contract **with** *someone* 2

con·trac·tion /kəntrækʃ^ən/ (**contractions**) 1 N-COUNT When a woman who is about to give birth has **contractions**, she experiences a very strong, painful tightening of the muscles of her womb. 宫缩 ❑ *The contractions were getting stronger.* 宫缩越来越强烈。 2 N-COUNT A **contraction** is a shortened form of a word or words. (单词的) 缩写形式 ❑ *"It's" (with an apostrophe) can be used as a contraction for "it is."* "**It's**" (带撇号) 是 "**it is**" 的缩写形式。
3 → see also **contract**

con·trac·tor /kɒntræktər, kəntræk-/ (**contractors**) N-COUNT A **contractor** is a person or company that does work for other people or organizations. 承包人；承包商 [BUSINESS] ❑ *We told the building contractor that we wanted a garage big enough for two cars.* 我们告诉建筑承包商，我们想要一个可以停放两辆汽车的车库。

con·trac·tual /kəntræktʃuəl/ ADJ A **contractual** arrangement or relationship involves a legal agreement between people. 合同的 [FORMAL] ❑ *The company has not fulfilled certain contractual obligations.* 这家公司还没有履行合同上的某些义务。 ● **con·trac·tu·al·ly** ADV 合同地 ❑ *He is contractually bound to another year in Los Angeles.* 他按照合同得在洛杉矶再呆一年。

Word Link *dict ≈ speaking : contradict, dictate, predict*

★ **contra·dict** /kɒntrədɪkt/ (**contradicts, contradicting, contradicted**) **1** V-T If you **contradict** someone, you tell them that what they have just said is wrong, or suggest that it is wrong by saying something different. 反驳 ❑ *She dared not contradict him.* 她不敢反驳他。 ❑ *His comments appeared to contradict remarks made earlier in the day by the chairman.* 他的评论好像在反驳主席当天早些时候的言论。 **2** V-T If one statement or piece of evidence **contradicts** another, the first one makes the second one appear to be wrong. 与…矛盾 ❑ *Her version contradicted her daughter's.* 她的说法与她女儿的说法相矛盾。

contra·dic·tion /kɒntrədɪkʃᵊn/ (**contradictions**) N-COUNT If you describe an aspect of a situation as a **contradiction**, you mean that it is completely different from other aspects, and so makes the situation confused or difficult to understand. 矛盾 ❑ *The militants see no contradiction in using violence to bring about a religious state.* 好战分子认为使用暴力与建立宗教国家不矛盾。

Word Link *ory ≈ relating to : advisory, contradictory, predatory*

contra·dic·tory /kɒntrədɪktəri/ ADJ If two or more facts, ideas, or statements are **contradictory**, they state or imply that opposite things are true. (事实、观点、陈述等) 相互矛盾的 ❑ *Customs officials have made a series of contradictory statements about the equipment.* 海关官员们对于这种设备做出了一系列相互矛盾的陈述。

con·tra·ry /kɒntreri/ **1** ADJ Ideas, attitudes, or reactions that are **contrary to** each other are completely different from each other. (观点、态度、反应) 相对立的 ❑ *This view is contrary to the aims of critical social research for a number of reasons.* 许多原因证明这种观点与批判性社会研究的目的截然相反。 **2** PHRASE If you say that something is true **contrary to** other people's beliefs or opinions, you are emphasizing that it is true and that they are wrong. 与…相反 [EMPHASIS] ❑ *Contrary to popular belief, moderate exercise actually decreases your appetite.* 与大部分人的想法相反，适度的运动实际上会降低食欲。 **3** PHRASE You use **on the contrary** when you have just said or implied that something is not true and are going to say that the opposite is true. 恰恰相反 ❑ *It is not an idea around which the community can unite. On the contrary, I see it as one that will divide us.* 这不是一个可以让我们的组织团结起来的主意。恰恰相反，我看它会分裂我们。 **4** PHRASE You can use **on the contrary** when you are disagreeing strongly with something that has just been said or implied, or are making a strong negative reply. 相反 (用于否定对方意见) [EMPHASIS] ❑ *"People just don't do things like that."—"On the contrary, they do them all the time."* "人们根本就不像那样做事。" —— "然而，他们却一直在那么做。"

> Do not confuse **on the contrary** with **on the other hand**. **On the contrary** is used to contradict someone, to say that they are wrong. **On the other hand** is used to state a different, often contrasting aspect of the situation you are considering.
> ❑ *Prices of other foods and consumer goods fell. Wages on the other hand increased.*

5 PHRASE When a particular idea is being considered, evidence or statements **to the contrary** suggest that this idea is not true or that the opposite is true. 相反 (用于否定前面的陈述) ❑ *He continued to maintain that he did nothing wrong, despite clear evidence to the contrary.* 他仍坚持认为自己没有做错，尽管有确凿的证据证明他做错了。

con·trast ♦◇◇ (**contrasts, contrasting, contrasted**)

> The noun is pronounced /kɒntræst/. The verb is pronounced /kəntræst/.

> 名词读作 /kɒntræst/。动词读作 /kəntræst/。

1 N-VAR A **contrast** is a great difference between two or more things which is clear when you compare them. (巨大的) 差别 ❑ *...the contrast between town and country.* …城乡差别。 ❑ *The two visitors provided a startling contrast in appearance.* 两位来访者的外貌有惊人的不同。 **2** PHRASE You say **by contrast** or **in contrast**, or **in contrast to** something, to show that you are mentioning a very different situation from the one you have just mentioned. 相比之下 ❑ *The private sector, by contrast, has plenty of money to spend.* 私营部门相比之下有很多钱可花。 ❑ *In contrast, the lives of girls in well-to-do families were often very sheltered.* 相比之下，富裕家庭的女孩子们通常都过着养尊处优的生活。 **3** PHRASE If one thing is **in contrast to** another, it is very different from it. 与…截然不同 ❑ *His public statements have always been in marked contrast to those of his son.* 他在公共场合的发言总是和他儿子的话截然不同。 **4** V-T If you **contrast** one thing **with** another, you point out or consider the differences between those things. 对比 (事物以指出不同点) ❑ *She contrasted the situation then with the present crisis.* 她把过去的情况与现在的危机进行了对比。 ❑ *Contrast that approach with what goes on in most organizations.* 对比这个方法与大多数组织运用的方法的不同之处。 **5** V-RECIP If one thing **contrasts with** another, it is very different from it. 与…形成对比 ❑ *Johnson's easy charm contrasted sharply with the prickliness of his boss.* 约翰的随和与他老板的挑剔形成了鲜明的对比。 **6** N-UNCOUNT **Contrast** is the degree of difference between the darker and lighter parts of a photograph, television picture, or painting. (图片、电视画面、绘画中深浅的) 对比度 ❑ *...a television with brighter colors, better contrast, and digital sound.* …一台色彩更亮丽、颜色对比度更好、配有数字音响的电视。

contra·vene /kɒntrəvin/ (**contravenes, contravening, contravened**) V-T To **contravene** a law or rule means to do something that is forbidden by the law or rule. 违反 (法律、规则) [FORMAL] ❑ *The board has banned the film on the grounds that it contravenes criminal libel laws.* 委员会已经禁播了那部电影，因为它违反了诽谤法。 ● **contra·ven·tion** /kɒntrəvenʃᵊn/ N-VAR (**contraventions**) 违反 ❑ *The government has lent millions of dollars to debt-ridden banks in contravention of local banking laws.* 政府把数百万美元借给了债台高筑的银行，违反了地方银行业法律。

Word Link *tribute ≈ giving : attribute, contribute, distribute*

con·trib·ute ♦◇◇ /kəntrɪbyut/ (**contributes, contributing, contributed**) **1** V-I If you **contribute to** something, you say or do things to help to make it successful. 贡献；做出贡献 ❑ *The three sons also contribute to the family business.* 3个儿子也为家族企业做贡献。 ❑ *I believe that each of us can contribute to the future of the world.* 我相信我们每一个人都能为世界的未来做出贡献。 **2** V-T/V-I To **contribute** money or resources **to** something means to give money or resources to help pay for something or to help achieve a particular purpose. 捐助 ❑ *The U.S. is contributing $4 billion in loans, credits, and grants.* 美国以信贷和赠与的方式捐助了40亿美元。 ❑ *Local businesses have agreed to contribute.* 当地的公司已经同意捐助了。 ● **con·tribu·tor** N-COUNT (**contributors**) 捐助者 ❑ *Candidates for Congress received 53 percent of their funds from individual contributors.* 国会候选人接受的捐款中有53%来自个人捐助者。 **3** V-I If something **contributes to** an event or situation, it is one of the causes of it. 是 (造成某情况) 的一个原因 ❑ *The report says design faults in both the vessels contributed to the tragedy.* 报道称两艘船在设计上的缺陷是造成悲剧的原因。

Thesaurus *contribute* 另参见：
v. aid, assist, chip in, commit, donate, give, grant, help, support; (*ant.*) neglect, take away **2**

con·tri·bu·tion ♦◇◇ /kɒntrɪbyuʃᵊn/ (**contributions**) **1** N-COUNT If you make a **contribution to** something, you do something to help make it successful or to produce it. 贡献 ❑ *American economists have made important contributions to the field of financial and corporate economics.* 美国经济学家在金融社团经济学领域做出了重要贡献。 **2** N-COUNT A **contribution** is a sum of money that you give in order to help pay for something. 捐款 ❑ *This list ranked companies that make charitable contributions of a half million dollars or more.* 这张清单列出了慈善捐款50万美元及50万美元以上的公司。

Word Partnership *contribution* 的常用搭配:

ADJ. **important** contribution, **significant** contribution 1 2
V. **make a** contribution, **send a** contribution 1 2

C

con·tribu·tor /kəntrɪbyətər/ (**contributors**) 1 N-COUNT You can use **contributor** to refer to one of the causes of an event or situation, especially if that event or situation is an unpleasant one. 造成(不良后果的)因素 ❑ *Old buses are major contributors to pollution in cities.* 旧公交车是造成城市污染的主要原因。 2 → see also **contribute**

★ **con·trive** /kəntraɪv/ (**contrives, contriving, contrived**) V-T If you **contrive** an event or situation, you succeed in making it happen, often by tricking someone. (常指用欺骗手段) 策划 [FORMAL] ❑ *The oil companies were accused of contriving a shortage of gasoline to justify price increases.* 一些石油公司为了找借口提高油价而策划谎报石油短缺，因而被起诉。

con·trived /kəntraɪvd/ ADJ If you say that something someone says or does is **contrived**, you think it is false and deliberate, rather than natural and not planned. 虚假人为的 [DISAPPROVAL] ❑ *There was nothing contrived about what he said.* 他说的话一点不假。

con·trol ♦♦♦ /kəntroʊl/ (**controls, controlling, controlled**) 1 N-UNCOUNT **Control of** an organization, place, or system is the power to make all the important decisions about the way that it is run. (对某组织机构的) 控制 ❑ *The restructuring involves Mr. Ronson giving up control of the company.* 公司重组需要罗森先生放弃对公司的控制。 ● PHRASE If you are **in control of** something, you have the power to make all the important decisions about the way it is run. 掌管 ❑ *Nobody knows who is in control of the club.* 没有人知道谁掌管这个俱乐部。 ● PHRASE If something is **under** your **control**, you have the power to make all the important decisions about the way that it is run. 处于…控制之下 ❑ *All the newspapers are under government control.* 所有的报纸都处在政府控制之下。 2 N-UNCOUNT If you have **control** of something or someone, you are able to make them do what you want them to do. (对某物或某人的) 控制 [oft N "of/over" n] ❑ *He lost control of his car.* 他失去了对他的车的控制。 ● **con·trolled** ADJ 受控制的 ❑ *...a controlled experiment.* …一个受控制的试验。 3 N-UNCOUNT If you show **control**, you prevent yourself behaving in an angry or emotional way. (对愤怒情绪等的) 克制 ❑ *He had a terrible temper, and sometimes he would completely lose control.* 他脾气暴躁，有时会完全失控。 4 V-T The people who **control** an organization or place have the power to make all the important decisions about the way that it is run. 管理 ❑ *He now controls the largest retail development empire in southern California.* 他现在管理着加利福尼亚南部最大的零售业帝国。 5 V-T To **control** a piece of equipment, process, or system means to make it work in the way that you want it to work. 控制(设备系统等) ❑ *...a computerized system to control the gates.* …一个控制大门的计算机系统。 ❑ *Scientists would soon be able to manipulate human genes to control the aging process.* 科学家将很快能够通过操控人类基因来控制衰老的过程。 6 V-T When a government **controls** prices, wages, or the activity of a particular group, it uses its power to restrict them. (政府) 管制(价格、工资、团体活动等) ❑ *The federal government tried to control rising health-care costs.* 联邦政府努力控制不断上涨的卫生保健费用。 ● N-UNCOUNT **Control** is also a noun. 管制 ❑ *Control of inflation remains the government's absolute priority.* 控制通货膨胀仍然是政府的第一要务。 7 V-T If you **control yourself**, or if you **control** your feelings, voice, or expression, you make yourself behave calmly even though you are feeling angry, excited, or upset. 抑制(感情、声音、表情) ❑ *Jo was advised to learn to control herself.* 人们建议乔要学会控制自己的情绪。 ● **con·trolled** ADJ 克制的 ❑ *Her manner was quiet and very controlled.* 她举止恬静很有涵养。 8 V-T To **control** something dangerous means to prevent it from becoming worse or from spreading. 抑制(危险物) ❑ *...the need to control environmental pollution.* …控制环境污染的需要。 9 N-COUNT A **control** is a device such as a switch or lever which you use in order to operate a machine or other piece of equipment. 控制装置 ❑ *I practiced operating the controls.* 我练习过操作这些控制装置。 10 N-VAR **Controls** are the methods that a government uses to restrict increases, for example in prices, wages, or weapons. (政府的) 调控 ❑ *Critics question whether price controls would do any good.* 批评家们怀疑物价调控的作用。 11 N-VAR **Control** is used to refer to a place where your documents or luggage are officially checked when you enter a foreign country. 海关检查处

You do not use **control** as a verb to talk about inspecting documents. The verb you use is **check**. ❑ *Police were searching cars and checking identity documents.* However, at an airport or port, the place where passports are checked is called **passport control**.

12 → see also **birth control, quality control, remote control, stock control** 13 PHRASE If something is **out of control**, no one has any power over it. 失控 ❑ *The fire is burning out of control.* 火势失控。 14 PHRASE If something harmful is **under control**, it is being dealt with successfully and is unlikely to cause any more harm. 处在控制之下 ❑ *The situation is under control.* 局面得到了控制。

Word Partnership *control* 的常用搭配:

V. **have** control **of/over** *something* 1 2
gain control, **lose** control 1 – 3
N. **self**-control 3
air traffic control 5
control **system** 9
birth control 12
PREP. **out of** control 13
under control 14

con·trol·ler /kəntroʊlər/ (**controllers**) 1 N-COUNT A **controller** is a person who has responsibility for a particular organization or for a particular part of an organization. 主管 [mainly BRIT] ❑ *...the job of controller of BBC1.* …BBC1的主管一职。 2 → see also **air traffic controller** 3 N-COUNT A **controller** is the same as a **comptroller**. 审计员

con·tro·ver·sial ♦◇◇ /kɒntrəvɜrʃᵊl/ ADJ If you describe something or someone as **controversial**, you mean that they are the subject of intense public argument, disagreement, or disapproval. 有争议的 ❑ *Immigration is a controversial issue in many countries.* 移民在很多国家都是一个有争议的问题。

Word Partnership *controversial* 的常用搭配:

N. controversial **bill**, controversial **drug**, controversial **issue/subject/topic**, controversial **law**, controversial **measure**, controversial **policy**
ADV. **highly** controversial

con·tro·ver·sy ♦◇◇ /kɒntrəvɜrsi/ (**controversies**) N-VAR **Controversy** is a lot of discussion and argument about something, often involving strong feelings of anger or disapproval. 论战 ❑ *The proposed cuts have caused considerable controversy.* 削减的提议引起了巨大的争议。

Word Partnership *controversy* 的常用搭配:

N. **center of the** controversy
V. **create** controversy
ADJ. **major** controversy, **political** controversy
PREP. controversy **over/surrounding** *something*

con·va·lesce /kɒnvəlɛs/ (**convalesces, convalescing, convalesced**) V-I If you **are convalescing**, you are resting and getting your health back after an illness or operation. 康复 [FORMAL] ❑ *After two weeks, I was allowed home, where I convalesced for three months.* 2星期后，我经允许回家静养，在家康复了3个月。

con·va·les·cence /kɒnvəlɛsᵊns/ N-UNCOUNT **Convalescence** is the period or process of becoming healthy and well again after an illness or operation. 康复期 [FORMAL] ❑ *Also thanks to Lucy and Guthrie Scott for inviting me to stay with them during my convalescence.* 也感谢露西和格思里·斯科特让我在他们家养病康复。

Word Link *con ≈ together, with : **con**sensus, **con**temporary, **con**vene*

★ **con·vene** /kənvin/ (**convenes, convening, convened**) V-T/V-I If someone **convenes** a meeting or conference, they arrange for it to take place. You can also say that people **convene** or that a meeting **convenes**. 召集(会议); 召开 [FORMAL] ❑ *Last August he convened a meeting of his closest advisers at Camp David.* 去年8月份，他在戴维营召集他最亲近的顾问开了一次会。

con·veni·ence /kənvinyəns/ (**conveniences**) 1 N-UNCOUNT If something is done for your **convenience**, it is done in a way that is useful or suitable for you. 便利 ❑ *He was happy to make a detour for her* convenience. 为了方便她，他乐意绕道而行。 2 N-COUNT If you describe something as a **convenience**, you mean that it is very useful. 方便 ❑ *Mail order is a convenience for buyers who are too busy to shop.* 邮购对于那些没有时间购物的人来说是很方便的。 3 N-COUNT **Conveniences** are pieces of equipment designed to make your life easier. 便利设施 ❑ *...an apartment with all the modern conveniences.* …一套配备了各种现代便利设施的公寓。 4 → see also **convenient**

con·veni·ent /kənviːniənt/ 1 ADJ If a way of doing something is **convenient**, it is easy, or very useful or suitable for a particular purpose. 方便的 ❑ *...a flexible and convenient way of paying for business expenses.* …一种灵活方便的支付商务费用的方式。 ● **con·veni·ence** N-UNCOUNT 方便 ❑ *They may use a credit card for convenience.* 他们可以为了方便而使用信用卡。 ● **con·veni·ent·ly** ADV 方便地 ❑ *The body spray slips conveniently into your sports bag for freshening up after a game.* 身体喷香器可以方便地放到你的运动包里，运动之后喷在身上使你神清气爽。 2 ADJ If you describe a place as **convenient**, you are pleased because it is near to where you are, or because you can reach another place from there quickly and easily. 近便的 [APPROVAL] ❑ *The town is well placed for easy access to Washington D.C. and convenient for Dulles Airport.* 这个小镇离华盛顿和杜勒斯机场都很近。 ● **con·veni·ent·ly** ADV 近便地 ❑ *It was very conveniently situated just across the road from the City Reference Library.* 它所处位置非常便利，就在市参考图书馆的马路对面。 3 ADJ A **convenient** time to do something, for example to meet someone, is a time when you are free to do it or would like to do it. 方便的 ❑ *She will try to arrange a mutually convenient time and place for an interview.* 她会尽量把面谈安排在一个双方都方便的时间和地点。

▲ **con·vent** /kɒnvent, -vənt/ (**convents**) N-COUNT A **convent** is a building in which a community of nuns live. 女修道院

con·ven·tion ♦◇◇ /kənvɛnʃən/ (**conventions**) 1 N-VAR A **convention** is a way of behaving that is considered to be correct or polite by most people in a society. 习俗 ❑ *It's just a social convention that men don't wear skirts.* 男人不穿裙子仅仅是一个社会习俗。 2 N-COUNT In art, literature, or the theater, a **convention** is a traditional method or style. 惯例 ❑ *We go offstage and come back for the convention of the encore.* 按照惯例，当要求我们再唱一次的时候，我们得先下台然后再返回台上。 3 N-COUNT A **convention** is an official agreement between countries or groups of people. 公约 ❑ *...the U.N. convention on climate change.* …关于气候变化的联合国公约。 4 N-COUNT A **convention** is a large meeting of an organization or political group. 大型会议 ❑ *...the annual convention of the Society of Professional Journalists.* …职业新闻工作者协会的年会。

con·ven·tion·al ♦◇◇ /kənvɛnʃənəl/ 1 ADJ Someone who is **conventional** has behavior or opinions that are ordinary and normal. (行为观念等) 传统的 ❑ *...a respectable married woman with conventional opinions.* …一个可敬的观念传统的已婚妇女。 ● **con·ven·tion·al·ly** ADV 传统地 ❑ *Men still wore their hair short and dressed conventionally.* 男人还是留着短发，着装传统。 2 ADJ A **conventional** method or product is one that is usually used or that has been in use for a long time. 传统的 (方法或产品等) ❑ *...the risks and drawbacks of conventional family planning methods.* …传统计划生育方法的风险和缺陷。 ● **con·ven·tion·al·ly** ADV 传统地 [ADV with v] ❑ *Organically grown produce does not differ greatly in appearance from conventionally grown crops.* 有机农产品与传统方法种植的农产品在外观上没有太大的区别。 3 ADJ **Conventional** weapons and wars do not involve nuclear explosives. 常规的 (武器); 不用核武器的 (战争) ❑ *We must reduce the danger of war by controlling nuclear, chemical, and conventional arms.* 我们必须通过控制核武器、化学武器和常规武器来降低战争的危险。

Word Link	*verg, vert ≈ turning : converge, diverge, subvert*

★ **con·verge** /kənvɜrdʒ/ (**converges, converging, converged**) 1 V-I If people or vehicles **converge on** a place, they move toward it from different directions. (人或车辆等) 聚集 ❑ *Hundreds of tractors will converge on the capital.* 成百上千的拖拉机将向首都聚集。 2 V-I If roads or lines **converge**, they meet or join at a particular place. (道路、江河等) 会合 [FORMAL] ❑ *As they flow south, the five rivers converge.* 这5条河向南流，最终汇合在一起。

con·ver·gence /kənvɜrdʒəns/ (**convergences**) N-VAR The **convergence** of different ideas, groups, or societies is the process by which they stop being different and become more similar. 趋同性 [FORMAL] ❑ *...the need to move towards greater economic convergence.* …迈向更高的经济趋同性的需要。

con·ver·sa·tion ♦◇◇ /kɒnvərseɪʃən/ (**conversations**) N-COUNT If you have a **conversation with** someone, you talk with them, usually in an informal situation. (非正式的) 交谈 ❑ *He's a talkative guy, and I struck up a conversation with him.* 他是一个健谈的人，我和他聊了起来。

con·ver·sa·tion·al /kɒnvərseɪʃənəl/ ADJ **Conversational** means relating to, or similar to, casual and informal talk. 谈话的 ❑ *What is refreshing is the author's easy, conversational style.* 使人耳目一新的是作者流畅的、谈话式的写作风格。

▲ **con·verse** (**converses, conversing, conversed**)

> The verb is pronounced /kənvɜrs/. The noun is pronounced /kɒnvɜrs/.

> 动词读作 /kənvɜrs/。名词读作 /kɒnvɜrs/。

1 V-RECIP If you **converse with** someone, you talk to them. You can also say that two people **converse**. 交谈 [FORMAL] ❑ *Luke sat directly behind the pilot and conversed with him.* 卢克坐在飞行员的正后方和他交谈。 2 N-SING **The converse** of a statement is its opposite or reverse. 相反的说法 [FORMAL] ❑ *What you do for a living is critical to where you settle and how you live – and the converse is also true.* 你的工作决定你在哪里定居和怎样生活——反之亦然。

con·verse·ly /kɒnvɜrsli, kənvɜrs-/ ADV You say **conversely** to indicate that the situation you are about to describe is the opposite or reverse of the one you have just described. 相反地 [ADV with cl] [FORMAL] ❑ *Malaysia and Indonesia rely on open markets for forest and fishery products. Conversely, some Asian countries are highly protectionist.* 马来西亚和印度尼西亚依靠开放的市场获取林业和渔业产品。与之相反的是，一些亚洲国家是高度的保护贸易论者。

★ **con·ver·sion** /kənvɜrʒən/ (**conversions**) 1 N-VAR **Conversion** is the act or process of changing something into a different state or form. (状态或形式的) 改变 ❑ *...the conversion of disused rail lines into cycle routes.* …把废弃的铁路改变成自行车道。 2 N-VAR If someone changes their religion or beliefs, you can refer to their **conversion to** their new religion or beliefs. 皈依 ❑ *...his conversion to Christianity.* …他对基督教的皈依。

con·vert ♦◇◇ (**converts, converting, converted**)

> The verb is pronounced /kənvɜrt/. The noun is pronounced /kɒnvɜrt/.

> 动词读作 /kənvɜrt/。名词读作 /kɒnvɜrt/。

1 V-T/V-I If one thing **is converted** or **converts into** another, it is changed into a different form. 转变 ❑ *The signal will be converted into digital code.* 信号将被转变成数字编码。 ❑ *...naturally occurring substances which the body can convert into vitamins.* …可以在身体内转化成维生素的天然物质。 2 V-T If someone **converts** a room or building, they alter it in order to use it for a different purpose. 改建 ❑ *By converting the attic, they were able to have two extra bedrooms.* 通过改建阁楼，他们又多出了两间卧室。 ❑ *...the entrepreneur who wants to convert County Hall into a hotel.* …想把县政大厅改建成旅馆的企业家。 3 V-T If you **convert** a vehicle or piece of equipment, you change it so that it can use a different fuel. 改装 ❑ *Save money by converting your car to run on used vegetable oil.* 通过改装你的汽车使其燃烧用过的植物油来省钱。 4 V-T If you **convert** a quantity **from** one system of measurement **to** another, you calculate what the quantity is in the second system. 换算 ❑ *Converting metric measurements to U.S. equivalents is easy.* 把公制度量衡换算成美制度量衡很容易。 5 V-T/V-I If someone **converts** you, they persuade you to change your religious or political beliefs. You can also say that someone **converts to** a different religion. 改变信仰 ❑ *If you try to convert him, you could find he just walks away.* 如果你想让他改变信仰，他会扭头就走。 ❑ *He was a major influence in converting Godwin to political radicalism.* 戈德温主要在他的影响下信仰了政治激进主义。 6 N-COUNT A **convert** is someone who has changed their religious or political beliefs. 改变信仰的人 [oft N "to" n] ❑ *She, too, was a convert to Roman Catholicism.* 她也改信罗马天主教了。 7 N-COUNT If you describe someone as a **convert** to something, you mean that they have recently become very enthusiastic about it. 热衷…的人 [usu N "to" n] ❑ *As recent converts to vegetarianism and animal rights, they now live with a menagerie of stray animals.* 作为最近开始热衷素食主义和动物权利保护的人们，他们现在和一群流浪动物生活在一起。

C

Thesaurus *convert* 另参见：
v. adapt, alter, change, modify, transform 1

★ **con·vert·ible** /kənvɜrtɪbᵊl/ (**convertibles**) 1 N-COUNT A **convertible** is a car with a soft roof that can be folded down or removed. 敞篷汽车 ❑ *Her own car is a convertible VW.* 她的车是一辆大众敞篷汽车。 2 ADJ In finance, **convertible** investments or money can be easily exchanged for other forms of investments or money. 可兑换的 [BUSINESS] ❑ *...the introduction of a convertible currency.* …可兑换货币的采用。 ● **con·vert·ibil·ity** /kənvɜrtɪbɪlɪti/ N-UNCOUNT 可兑换性 ❑ *...the convertibility of the peso.* …比索的可兑换性。
→ see **car**

con·vey /kənveɪ/ (**conveys, conveying, conveyed**) V-T To **convey** information or feelings means to cause them to be known or understood by someone. 传达 ❑ *When I returned home, I tried to convey the wonder of this machine to my husband.* 回到家之后，我设法让我丈夫知道这台机器的神奇之处。 ❑ *In every one of her pictures she conveys a sense of immediacy.* 她的每一张画都有一种直观性。

con·vey·or belt /kənveɪər bɛlt/ (**conveyor belts**) N-COUNT A **conveyor belt** or a **conveyor** is a continuously moving strip of rubber or metal which is used in factories for moving objects along so that they can be dealt with as quickly as possible. 传送带 ❑ *The damp bricks went along a conveyor belt into another shed to dry.* 潮湿的砖块沿着传送带进入另一个棚子进行干燥。

Word Link *vict, vinc ≈ conquering : convict, convince, invincible*

con·vict ♦◇◇ (**convicts, convicting, convicted**)

The verb is pronounced /kənvɪkt/. The noun is pronounced /kɒnvɪkt/.

动词读作 /kənvɪkt/。名词读作 /kɒnvɪkt/。

1 V-T If someone **is convicted of** a crime, they are found guilty of that crime in a court of law. 证明…有罪 ❑ *In 1977 he was convicted of murder and sentenced to life imprisonment.* 在1977年，他因谋杀被判处终生监禁。 ❑ *There was insufficient evidence to convict him.* 没有足够的证据证明他有罪。 2 N-COUNT A **convict** is someone who is in prison. 囚犯 [JOURNALISM] ❑ *...Neil Jordan's tale of two escaped convicts who get mistaken for priests.* …尼尔·乔丹的两个越狱囚犯被误认为是牧师的故事。

con·vic·tion ♦◇◇ /kənvɪkʃᵊn/ (**convictions**) 1 N-COUNT A **conviction** is a strong belief or opinion. 坚定的信念 [usu N that] ❑ *It is our firm conviction that a step forward has been taken.* 我们坚信已经向前迈进了一步。 2 N-COUNT If someone has a **conviction**, they have been found guilty of a crime in a court of law. 判罪 ❑ *He will appeal against his conviction.* 他将对判决进行上诉。 3 N-UNCOUNT If you have **conviction**, you have great confidence in your beliefs or opinions. 坚信 ❑ *"We shall, sir," said Thorne, with conviction.* 索恩坚定地说："先生，我们会的"。

con·vince ♦◇◇ /kənvɪns/ (**convinces, convincing, convinced**) 1 V-T If someone or something **convinces** you **to** do something, they persuade you to do it. 说服 ❑ *That weekend in Plattsburgh, he convinced her to go ahead and marry Bud.* 在普拉茨堡的那个周末，他说服了她嫁给巴德。 2 V-T If someone or something **convinces** you **of** something, they make you believe that it is true or that it exists. 使信服 ❑ *Although I soon convinced him of my innocence, I think he still has serious doubts about my sanity.* 尽管我很快就使他相信我是清白的，但是他还是非常怀疑我精神是否正常。

Thesaurus *convince* 另参见：
v. persuade, sell, talk into, win over; *(ant.)* discourage 1 2

con·vinced ♦◇◇ /kənvɪnst/ ADJ If you are **convinced that** something is true, you feel sure that it is true. 确信的 ❑ *He was convinced that I was part of the problem.* 他确信问题与我有关。 ❑ *He became convinced of the need for cheap editions of good quality writing.* 他确信需要高质量作品的简装本。

con·vinc·ing /kənvɪnsɪŋ/ ADJ If you describe someone or something as **convincing**, you mean that they make you believe that a particular thing is true, correct, or genuine. 有说服力的 ❑ *Scientists say there is no convincing evidence that power lines have anything to do with cancer.* 科学家称没有有力证据证明电线能致癌。 ● **con·vinc·ing·ly** ADV 有说服力地 ❑ *He argued forcefully and convincingly that they were likely to bankrupt the budget.* 他强有力地证明了他们的花费可能会超出预算。

▲ **con·voy** /kɒnvɔɪ/ (**convoys**) N-COUNT A **convoy** is a group of vehicles or ships traveling together. 同行的船队；同行的车队 [also "in" N] ❑ *...a U.N. convoy carrying food and medical supplies.* …一支联合国运输食品和药品的船队。 ❑ *...humanitarian relief convoys.* …人道主义救援车队。

con·vul·sion /kənvʌlʃᵊn/ (**convulsions**) N-COUNT If someone has **convulsions**, they suffer uncontrollable movements of their muscles. 抽搐 ❑ *Thirteen per cent said they became unconscious at night and 5 per cent suffered convulsions.* 13%的人说晚上他们失去知觉，5%的人说他们晚上抽搐。

cook ♦♦◇ /kʊk/ (**cooks, cooking, cooked**) 1 V-T/V-I When you **cook** a meal, you prepare food for eating by heating it. 烹调 ❑ *I have to go and cook dinner.* 我要去做饭了。 ❑ *Chefs at the restaurant once cooked for President Kennedy.* 这家饭店的厨师曾经给肯尼迪总统做过饭。 ● **cook·ing** N-UNCOUNT 烹饪 ❑ *Her hobbies include music, dancing, sport, and cooking.* 她的爱好包括音乐、跳舞、运动和烹饪。 2 V-T/V-I When you **cook** food, or when food **cooks**, it is heated until it is ready to be eaten. 烹制 ❑ *...some basic instructions on how to cook a turkey.* …火鸡的一些基本做法。 ❑ *Let the vegetables cook gently for about 10 minutes.* 把蔬菜小火煮约十分钟。

You often use a more specific verb instead of **cook** when you are talking about preparing food using heat. For example, you **roast** meat in an oven, but you **bake** bread and cakes. You can **boil** vegetables in hot water, or you can **steam** them over a pan of boiling water. You can **fry** meat and vegetables in oil or fat. You can also **broil** or, in British English, **grill** them directly under or over a flame. You do not normally talk about **grilling** bread. Instead, you **toast** it.

3 N-COUNT A **cook** is a person whose job is to prepare and cook food, especially in someone's home or in an institution. (职业)厨师 ❑ *They had a butler, a cook, and a maid.* 他们有一位管家、一位厨师和

Picture Dictionary cook

Word Web cooking

Anthropologists believe our ancestors began to experiment with **cooking** about 1.5 million years ago. Cooking made some toxic or **inedible** plants safe to **eat**. It made tough meat **tender** and easier to **digest**. It also improved the flavor of the food they ate. **Heating up food** to a high **temperature** killed dangerous bacteria. **Cooked** food could be stored longer. This all helped increase the amount of food available to our ancestors.

一位女仆。4 N-COUNT If you say that someone is a good **cook**, you mean they are good at preparing and cooking food. 厨师(指擅长烹调的人) ❑ *I'm a lousy cook.* 我是个蹩脚的厨师。

→ see Picture Dictionary: **cook**

→ see **can**

▸ **cook up** 1 PHRASAL VERB If someone **cooks up** a dishonest scheme, they plan it. 策划(骗局等) [INFORMAL] ❑ *He must have cooked up his scheme on the spur of the moment.* 他肯定是即兴策划了他的方案。2 PHRASAL VERB If someone **cooks up** an explanation or a story, they make it up. 编造 [INFORMAL] ❑ *She'll cook up a convincing explanation.* 她将编造一个有说服力的解释。

Thesaurus cook 另参见：

V. heat up, make, prepare 1

N. chef 3

cook·book /kʊ̱kbʊk/ (**cookbooks**) N-COUNT A **cookbook** is a book that contains recipes for preparing food. 食谱

▲ **cook·er** /kʊ̱kər/ (**cookers**) N-COUNT A **cooker** is a large metal device for cooking food using gas or electricity. A cooker usually consists of an oven, a broiler, and some gas burners or electric rings. 厨灶 [BRIT]

in AM, use **stove** or **range**

cook·ery /kʊ̱kəri/ N-UNCOUNT **Cookery** is the activity of preparing and cooking food. 烹饪 ❑ *The school runs cookery classes throughout the year.* 这个学校全年都开设烹饪课。

▲ **cookie** /kʊ̱ki/ (**cookies**) 1 N-COUNT A **cookie** is a small sweet cake. 小甜饼干 [mainly AM]

in BRIT, use **biscuit**

2 N-COUNT A **cookie** is a piece of computer software which enables a website you have visited to recognize you if you visit it again. 再次访问某一网站时，能令网站识别访问人的计算机软件 [COMPUTING]

→ see **dessert**

cook·ing ♦◇◇ /kʊ̱kɪŋ/ 1 N-UNCOUNT **Cooking** is food which has been cooked. 饭菜 ❑ *The menu is based on classic French cooking.* 这个菜单以传统法国菜为主。2 N-UNCOUNT **Cooking** is the activity of preparing food. 烹饪 ❑ *He did the cooking, cleaning, laundry, and home repairs.* 他做饭、打扫卫生、洗衣服，还在家修修补补。3 ADJ **Cooking** ingredients or equipment are used in cookery. 用于烹饪的 [ADJ n] ❑ *Finely slice the cooking apples.* 把做菜用的苹果切成薄片。4 → see also **cook**

→ see Word Web: **cooking**

cool ♦♦◇ /ku̱l/ (**cooler, coolest, cools, cooling, cooled**) 1 ADJ Something that is **cool** has a temperature which is low but not very low. 凉的 ❑ *I felt a current of cool air.* 我感觉到了一阵凉风。❑ *The water was slightly cooler than a child's bath.* 这水比小孩子的洗澡水稍微凉一点。2 ADJ If it is **cool**, or if a place is **cool**, the temperature of the air is low but not very low. 凉爽的 ❑ *Thank goodness it's cool in here.* 谢天谢地，这里很凉爽。❑ *Store grains and cereals in a cool, dry place.* 把谷物和杂粮储存在凉爽、干燥的地方。● N-SING **Cool** is also a noun. 凉爽 ❑ *She walked into the cool of the hallway.* 她走入了凉爽的过道。

If you want to emphasize how cold the weather is, you can say that it is **freezing**, especially in winter when there is ice or frost. In summer, if the temperature is below average, you can say that it is **cool**. In general, **cold** suggests a lower temperature than **cool**, and **cool** things may be pleasant or refreshing. ❑ *A cool breeze swept off the ocean; it was pleasant out there.* If it is very **cool** or too **cool**, you can also say that it is **chilly**.

3 ADJ Clothing that is **cool** is made of thin material so that you do not become too hot in hot weather. (衣服) 凉快的 ❑ *In warm weather, you should wear clothing that is cool and comfortable.* 天气热时，你应该穿凉快舒适的衣服。4 ADJ **Cool** colors are light colors which give an impression of coolness. 冷色的 [ADJ n] ❑ *Choose a cool color such as cream.* 选择一个冷色，比如乳白色。5 ADJ If you say that a person or their behavior is **cool**, you mean that they are calm and unemotional, especially in a difficult situation. 冷静的 [APPROVAL] ❑ *He was marvelously cool again, smiling as if nothing had happened.* 他又变得出奇的冷静，微笑着，似乎什么都没有发生过一样。● **cool·ly** ADV 冷静地 ❑ *Everyone must think this situation through calmly and coolly.* 每个人必须冷静沉着地考虑当前形势。6 ADJ If you say that a person or their behavior is **cool**, you mean that they are unfriendly or not enthusiastic. 冷漠的 ❑ *I didn't like him at all. I thought he was cool, aloof, and arrogant.* 我一点都不喜欢他。我认为他冷漠、不合群又狂妄。● **cool·ly** ADV 冷淡地 ❑ *"It's your choice, Nina," David said coolly.* 大卫冷淡地说："这是你的选择，尼娜"。7 ADJ If you say that a person or thing is **cool**, you mean that they are fashionable and attractive. 酷的 [INFORMAL, APPROVAL] ❑ *He was trying to be really cool and trendy.* 他总想变得又酷又时髦。❑ *That's a cool hat.* 那是一顶很酷的帽子。8 V-T/V-I When something **cools** or when you **cool** it, it becomes lower in temperature. 使变凉；变凉 ❑ *Drain the meat and allow it to cool.* 把肉晾干，让它冷却。❑ *Huge fans will have to cool the concrete floor to keep it below 150 degrees.* 为了让水泥地温度一直低于150度，必须用巨大的风扇来降温。● PHRASAL VERB To **cool down** means the same as to **cool**. 降温 ❑ *Avoid putting your car away until the engine has cooled down.* 等发动机冷却之后再把汽车放回原处。9 V-T/V-I When a feeling or emotion **cools**, or when you **cool** it, it becomes less powerful. (情绪等) 冷静下来 ❑ *Within a few minutes tempers had cooled.* 几分钟之内，就冷静了下来。10 ADJ If you say that someone is **cool about** something, you mean that they accept it and are not angry or upset about it. 冷静的 [v-link ADJ] [INFORMAL, APPROVAL] ❑ *Bev was really cool about it all.* 贝文对这整件事真的很冷静。11 ADJ If you say that something or someone is **cool**, you think they are excellent in some way. 很棒的 [INFORMAL] ❑ *Kathleen gave me a really cool dress.* 凯瑟琳给了我一件很漂亮的衣服。❑ *He's such a cool guy.* 他是一个很优秀的人。

→ see **refrigerator**

▸ **cool down** 1 PHRASAL VERB → see **cool 8** 2 PHRASAL VERB If someone **cools down** or if you **cool** them **down**, they become less angry than they were. 平静下来；使平静 ❑ *He has had time to cool down and look at what happened more objectively.* 他有时间平静下来，并且更加客观地考虑发生的一切。

▸ **cool off** 1 PHRASAL VERB If someone or something **cools off**, or if you **cool** them **off**, they become cooler after having been hot. 变凉；使变凉 ❑ *Maybe he's trying to cool off out there in the rain.* 可能他是想在外面的雨中凉快一下。❑ *She made a fanning motion, pretending to cool herself off.* 她做了一个扇扇子的动作，假装使自己凉快一些。2 PHRASAL VERB If someone **cools off**, they become less angry than they were. 变冷静 ❑ *We've got to give him some time to cool off.* 我们必须给他时间让他冷静下来。

Thesaurus cool 另参见：

ADJ. chilly, cold, nippy; (ant.) warm 1
easygoing, serene, tranquil 5
distant, unfriendly 6

Word Partnership cool 的常用搭配：

N. cool **air**, cool **breeze** 1 2

V. **play it** cool, **stay** cool 5 10 11

Word Link *co ≈ together : coherent, collaborate, cooperate*

Word Link *oper ≈ work : cooperate, opera, operation*

co·oper·ate ♦◇◇ /koʊɒ̱pəreɪt/ (**cooperates, cooperating, cooperated**)

in BRIT, also use **co-operate**

1 V-RECIP If you **cooperate with** someone, you work with them or

help them for a particular purpose. You can also say that two people **cooperate**. 合作 ❑ *The U.N. had been cooperating with the State Department on a plan to find countries willing to take the refugees.* 联合国和美国国务院合作，制定计划来寻找愿意接纳难民的国家。

● **co·opera·tion** /koʊɒpəreɪʃən/ N-UNCOUNT 合作 ❑ *A deal with Japan could open the door to economic cooperation with East Asia.* 与日本的交易可以打开与东亚经济合作的大门。 **2** V-I If you **cooperate**, you do what someone has asked or told you to do. 配合 ❑ *He agreed to cooperate with the police investigation.* 他同意配合警方调查。

● **co·opera·tion** N-UNCOUNT 协作 ❑ *The police underlined the importance of the public's cooperation in the hunt for the bombers.* 在寻找安置炸弹的人时，警察强调了公众协作的重要性。

Word Partnership *cooperate* 的常用搭配:

V.	**agree** to cooperate, **continue** to cooperate, **fail** to cooperate, **refuse** to cooperate **1** **2**
ADV.	cooperate **fully** **1** **2**
N.	**willingness** to cooperate **1** **2**

Word Partnership *cooperation* 的常用搭配:

ADJ.	**close** cooperation, **full** cooperation **1** **2**
N.	**lack of** cooperation **1** **2**

★ **co·opera·tive** /koʊɒpərətɪv/ (**cooperatives**)

in BRIT, also use **co-operative**

1 N-COUNT A **cooperative** is a business or organization run by the people who work for it, or owned by the people who use it. These people share its benefits and profits. 合作性企业；合作性组织 [BUSINESS] ❑ *They decided a housing cooperative was the way to regenerate the area.* 他们决定用合作建房的方式重建这一地区。 **2** ADJ A **cooperative** activity is done by people working together. 合作的 ❑ *He was transferred to FBI custody in a smooth cooperative effort between Egyptian and U.S. authorities.* 经埃及和美国政府的顺利合作，他被移交给了联邦调查局关押。 ● **co·opera·tive·ly** ADV 合作地 [ADV after v] ❑ *They agreed to work cooperatively to ease tensions wherever possible.* 他们同意尽可能合作以缓解紧张局面。 **3** ADJ If you say that someone is **cooperative**, you mean that they do what you ask them to without complaining or arguing. 乐意合作的 ❑ *I made every effort to be cooperative.* 我尽力配合。

Thesaurus *cooperative* 另参见:

ADJ.	combined, shared, united; *(ant.)* independent, private, separate **2**
	accommodating; *(ant.)* uncooperative **3**

co·or·di·nate (**coordinates, coordinating, coordinated**)

The verb is pronounced /koʊɔrdəneɪt/. The noun is pronounced /koʊɔrdənət/.

动词读作 /koʊɔrdəneɪt/。名词读作 /koʊɔrdənət/。

in BRIT, also use **co-ordinate**

1 V-T If you **coordinate** an activity, you organize the various people and things involved in it. 协调 ❑ *Government officials visited the earthquake zone on Thursday morning to coordinate the relief effort.* 政府官员星期四上午视察了地震灾区以协调救灾工作。

● **co·or·di·nat·ed** ADJ 协调的 ❑ *Coalition forces were planning a coordinated effort to attack the drug trade.* 联合部队正在计划共同打击毒品买卖。 ❑ *...a well-coordinated surprise attack.* …一次完美配合的突袭。

● **co·or·di·na·tor** N-COUNT (**coordinators**) 协调人 ❑ *...the party's campaign coordinator, Mr. Peter Mandelson.* …该党的竞选协调人，彼得·曼德尔森先生。 **2** V-T If you **coordinate** the different parts of your body, you make them work together efficiently to perform particular movements. 使(身体各部位)协调 ❑ *You need to coordinate legs, arms, and breathing for the front crawl.* 匍匐前进时，你要协调双腿、胳膊和呼吸。 **3** V-RECIP If you **coordinate** clothes or furnishings that are used together, or if they **coordinate**, they are similar in some way and look nice together. 搭配(衣服、饰品) ❑ *She'll show you how to coordinate pattern and colors.* 她会向你展示如何搭配款式和颜色。 ❑ *Tie it with fabric bows that coordinate with other furnishings.* 扎上和其他的饰品相配的布制蝴蝶结。 **4** N-COUNT The **coordinates** of a point on a map or graph are the two sets of numbers or letters that you need in order to find that point. 坐标 [TECHNICAL] ❑ *Can you give me your coordinates?* 能给我你的坐标吗？

Thesaurus *coordinate* 另参见:

V.	direct, manage, organize **1**

co·or·di·na·tion /koʊɔrdəneɪʃən/

in BRIT, also use **co-ordination**

1 N-UNCOUNT **Coordination** means organizing the activities of two or more groups so that they work together efficiently and know what the others are doing. 协作 ❑ *...the lack of coordination between the civilian and military authorities.* …民事机关和军事机关缺少协作。 ❑ *...the coordination of economic policy.* …经济政策的协作。

● PHRASE If you do something **in coordination with** someone else, you both organize your activities so that you work together efficiently. 与…协作 **2** N-UNCOUNT **Coordination** is the ability to use the different parts of your body together efficiently. (身体各部位的) 协调能力 ❑ *...clumsiness and lack of coordination.* …笨手笨脚，缺乏协调能力。

cop /kɒp/ (**cops, copping, copped**) N-COUNT A **cop** is a policeman or policewoman. 警察 [INFORMAL] ❑ *Frank didn't like having the cops know where to find him.* 弗兰克不愿意让警察知道他的去向。

▸ **cop out** PHRASAL VERB If you say that someone **is copping out**, you mean that they are avoiding doing something they should do. 逃避(应做的事) [INFORMAL] ❑ *The soldiers' families accused the government of copping out.* 士兵的家属谴责政府逃避责任。

▸ **cop to** PHRASAL VERB If you **cop to** something bad or wrong that you have done, you admit that you have done it. 认错 [AM, INFORMAL] ❑ *I left, but you told me to. I'd appreciate it if you'd cop to that.* 我离开了，但这是你让我这么做的。如果你认错的话我会很高兴。

cope ♦◇◇ /koʊp/ (**copes, coping, coped**) **1** V-I If you **cope with** a problem or task, you deal with it successfully. (妥善地) 处理 ❑ *It was amazing how my mother coped with bringing up three children on less than thirty dollars a week.* 让人惊叹的是我妈妈怎样以每周不到30美元的开销养大了3个孩子。 **2** V-I If you have to **cope with** an unpleasant situation, you have to accept it or bear it. 应付(困难局面) ❑ *Never before has the industry had to cope with war and recession at the same time.* 企业以前从来没有同时应付过战争和经济衰退。 **3** V-I If a machine or a system can **cope with** something, it is large enough or complex enough to deal with it satisfactorily. (用机器) 处理 ❑ *A giant washing machine copes with the mountain of laundry created by their nine boys and five girls.* 一台大容量洗衣机能够清洗他们9个男孩和5个女孩换下的堆积如山的脏衣服。

Word Partnership *cope* 的常用搭配:

ADV.	**how to** cope **1** **2**
V.	**learn to** cope, **manage to** cope **1** **2**
ADJ.	**unable to** cope **1** – **3**
N.	**ability to** cope **1** – **3**
	cope **with loss** **2**

co·pi·ous /koʊpiəs/ ADJ A **copious** amount of something is a large amount of it. 大量的 ❑ *I went out for dinner last night and drank copious amounts of red wine.* 昨晚我出去吃饭，喝了许多红酒。

● **co·pi·ous·ly** ADV 大量地 ❑ *The victims were bleeding copiously.* 受害者流了很多血。

cop·per /kɒpər/ (**coppers**) **1** N-UNCOUNT **Copper** is reddish brown metal that is used to make things such as coins and electrical wires. 铜 ❑ *Chile is the world's largest producer of copper.* 智利是世界上最大的产铜国。 **2** ADJ **Copper** is sometimes used to describe things that are reddish-brown in color. 铜色的 [LITERARY] ❑ *His hair has reverted back to its original copper hue.* 他的头发恢复到了原来的铜色。

→ see **metal, mineral, pan, plumbing**

copy ♦♦◇ /kɒpi/ (**copies, copying, copied**) **1** N-COUNT If you make a **copy of** something, you produce something that looks like the original thing. 复制品 ❑ *The reporter apparently obtained a copy of Steve's resignation letter.* 记者显然得到了史蒂夫辞职信的复件。 **2** N-COUNT A **copy of** a book, newspaper, or CD is one of many that are exactly the same. 一份(书籍、报纸、CD等) ❑ *I bought a copy of "USA Today" from a street-corner machine.* 我从售货机上买了一份《今日美国》。 **3** V-T If you **copy** something, you produce something that looks like the original thing. 复制 ❑ *...lawsuits against companies who have unlawfully copied computer programs.* …对非法复制计算机程序的公司的诉讼。 ❑ *He copied the chart from a book.* 他从书上复制了表格。 **4** V-T/V-I If you **copy**, or **copy** a piece of writing, you write it again exactly. 抄写 ❑ *He copied the data into a notebook.* 他把

Word Web copy

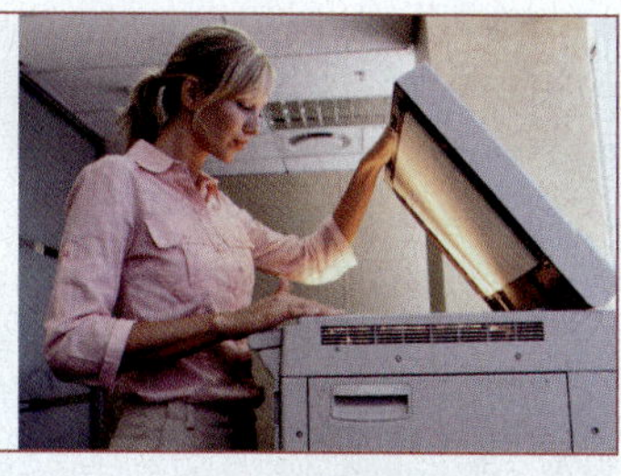

Making **copies** used to be difficult. Typists used sheets of carbon **paper** to make **multiple** copies. But the process was messy and the copies weren't very clear. Architects made photographic **blueprints**. But it was complicated and expensive. Modern **photocopiers** are completely different. You place your **document** on the glass and press a button. A bright light helps transfer the **image** from the paper onto a drum. Toner is spread over the drum. It sticks only to the image on the drum, not the blank spaces. A sheet of paper then passes over the drum and picks up the image.

C

资料抄在了笔记本上。 ❑ *We're copying from textbooks because we don't have enough to go round.* 我们在抄写课本，因为不够每人一本。 ● PHRASAL VERB **Copy out** means the same as **copy**. 抄写 ❑ *He wrote the title on the blackboard, then copied out the text, sentence by sentence.* 他把题目写在黑板上，然后一句一句地抄写了整篇课文。 5 V-T If you **copy** a letter, document, or e-mail to someone, you send them a copy of a letter or document that you have sent to someone else. 抄送 ❑ *He fired off a letter and copied it to the president.* 他发出了一封信，并且抄送给了总裁。 6 V-T If you **copy** someone's answer, you look at what that person has written and write the same thing yourself, in order to cheat in a test or exam. 抄袭 ❑ *He would allow John slyly to copy his answers to impossibly difficult algebra questions.* 对于那些特别难的代数题，他允许约翰偷偷抄袭他的答案。 7 V-T If you **copy** a person or what they do, you try to do what they do or try to be like them, usually because you admire them or what they have done. 效仿 ❑ *Children can be seen to copy the behavior of others whom they admire or identify with.* 可以看到儿童效仿那些他们崇拜或认同的人。 ❑ *He can claim to have been defeated by opponents copying his own tactics.* 他可能会宣称他已经被模仿他策略的对手打败了。 8 → see also **hard copy**

→ see Word Web: **copy**

→ see **clone**

▸ **copy in** PHRASAL VERB If you **copy** someone **in on** something, you send them a copy of something you have written to someone else. 抄送 [BRIT]

Thesaurus *copy* 另参见：

N. likeness, photocopy, replica, reprint; *(ant.)* master, original 1

V. replicate, reproduce; *(ant.)* originate 3
imitate, mimic 7

copy·right /kɒpiraɪt/ (**copyrights**) N-VAR If someone has the **copyright** on a piece of writing or music, it is illegal to reproduce or perform it without their permission. 版权 ❑ *Who owns the copyright on this movie?* 谁拥有这部电影的版权？

▲ **cor·al** /kɔrəl/ (**corals**) 1 N-VAR **Coral** is a hard substance formed from the bones of very small sea animals. It is often used to make jewelry. 珊瑚 ❑ *The women have elaborate necklaces of turquoise and pink coral.* 女士们拥有绿宝石和粉色珊瑚制成的精美项链。 2 N-COUNT **Corals** are very small sea animals. 珊瑚虫 ❑ *The seas around Bermuda are full of colorful corals and fantastic fish.* 百慕大周围的海域中到处都是五彩的珊瑚虫和奇异的鱼类。 3 COLOR Something that is **coral** is dark orangey-pink in color. 珊瑚色的 ❑ *...coral lipstick.* …珊瑚色的口红。

cord /kɔrd/ (**cords**) 1 N-VAR **Cord** is strong, thick string. 绳索 ❑ *The door had been tied shut with a length of nylon cord.* 这扇门已经被一段尼龙绳紧紧栓住了。 2 N-VAR **Cord** is wire covered in rubber or plastic which connects electrical equipment to an electricity supply. 电线 ❑ *...electrical cord.* …电源接线。 ❑ *...an extension cord.* …电源延长线。

→ see **nervous system, rope**

★ **cor·dial** /kɔrdʒəl/ ADJ **Cordial** means friendly. 友善的 [FORMAL] ❑ *He had never known him to be so chatty and cordial.* 他以前从来不知道他是这样一个健谈而友善的人。 ● **cor·di·al·ly** ADV 友善地 [ADV with V] ❑ *They all greeted me very cordially and were eager to talk about the new project.* 他们非常友善地和我打招呼，很想谈谈新项目。

cord·less /kɔrdlɪs/ ADJ A **cordless** telephone or piece of electric equipment is operated by a battery fitted inside it and is not connected to a supply of electricity. 无电线的 [usu ADJ n] ❑ *The waitress approached Picone with a cordless phone.* 女侍者拿着一个无绳电话走近培匡。

cor·don /kɔrdᵊn/ (**cordons, cordoning, cordoned**) N-COUNT A **cordon** is a line or ring of police, soldiers, or vehicles preventing people from entering or leaving an area. 警戒线 ❑ *Police formed a cordon between the two crowds.* 警察在两群人之间设置了一条警戒线。

▸ **cordon off** PHRASAL VERB If police or soldiers **cordon off** an area, they prevent people from entering or leaving an area. 封锁 ❑ *Police cordoned off part of the city center.* 警察封锁了市中心的部分地区。 ❑ *The police cordoned everything off.* 警察封锁了一切。

core ♦◇◇ /kɔr/ (**cores, coring, cored**) 1 N-COUNT The **core** of a fruit is the central part of it that contains seeds. 核 ❑ *Someone threw an apple core.* 有人扔了一个苹果核。 2 N-COUNT The **core** of an object, building, or city is the central part of it. 中心 [usu with poss] ❑ *...the Earth's core.* …地核。 3 V-T If you **core** a fruit, you remove its core. 去核 ❑ *...machines for peeling and coring apples.* …苹果削皮去核机。 4 N-SING **The core of** something such as a problem or an issue is the part of it that has to be understood or accepted before the whole thing can be understood or dealt with. (问题的)核心 ❑ *...the ability to get straight to the core of a problem.* …直击问题核心的能力。 5 ADJ A **core** team or a **core** group is a group of people who do the main part of a job or piece of work. Other people may also help, but only for limited periods of time. 核心(团体) ❑ *We already have our core team in place.* 我们的核心队伍已经就位。 6 ADJ In a school or college, **core** subjects are a group of subjects that have to be studied. 必修的(课程) ❑ *The core subjects are English, mathematics and science.* 必修课程为英语、数学和科学。 ❑ *I'm not opposed to a core curriculum in principle, but I think requiring a foreign language is unrealistic.* 原则上我不反对必修课程，但是我认为把外语列为必修课是不现实的。 7 N-SING The **core** businesses or the **core** activities of a company or organization are their most important ones. 核心(工作或活动) ❑ *The core activities of social workers were reorganized.* 社工的核心工作被重新安排了。

→ see Picture Dictionary: **core**

Word Partnership *core* 的常用搭配：

N. **apple** core 1
Earth's core 2
core **curriculum** 6
core **beliefs** 4
core **group** 5

★ **cork** /kɔrk/ (**corks**) 1 N-UNCOUNT **Cork** is a soft, light substance which forms the bark of a type of Mediterranean tree. 软木橡树皮 ❑ *...cork floors.* …软木地板。 2 N-COUNT A **cork** is a piece of cork or plastic that is pushed into the opening of a bottle to close it. 瓶塞 ❑ *He popped the cork and the champagne fizzed out over the bottle.* 他"砰"的一声打开瓶塞，香槟酒从瓶中喷出。

cork·screw /kɔrkskru/ (**corkscrews**) N-COUNT A **corkscrew** is a device for pulling corks out of bottles. (拔软木塞的)螺旋形开瓶器

corn /kɔrn/ 1 N-UNCOUNT **Corn** is a tall plant which produces long vegetables covered with yellow seeds. It can also be used to refer to the yellow seeds. 玉米；玉米粒 ❑ *...rows of corn in an Iowa field.* …爱荷华州农田里成排的玉米。 ❑ *We're having corn-on-the-cob for lunch.* 我们吃玉米棒子当午饭。 2 N-UNCOUNT **Corn** is used to refer to crops such as wheat and barley. It can also be used to refer to the seeds from these plants. 谷物(指小麦、燕麦等)；(小麦、燕麦等的)谷粒 [BRIT]

in AM, use **grain**

3 → see also **popcorn, sweetcorn**

→ see **grain**

cor·ner ♦♦◇ /kɔrnər/ (**corners, cornering, cornered**) 1 N-COUNT A **corner** is a point or an area where two or more edges, sides, or

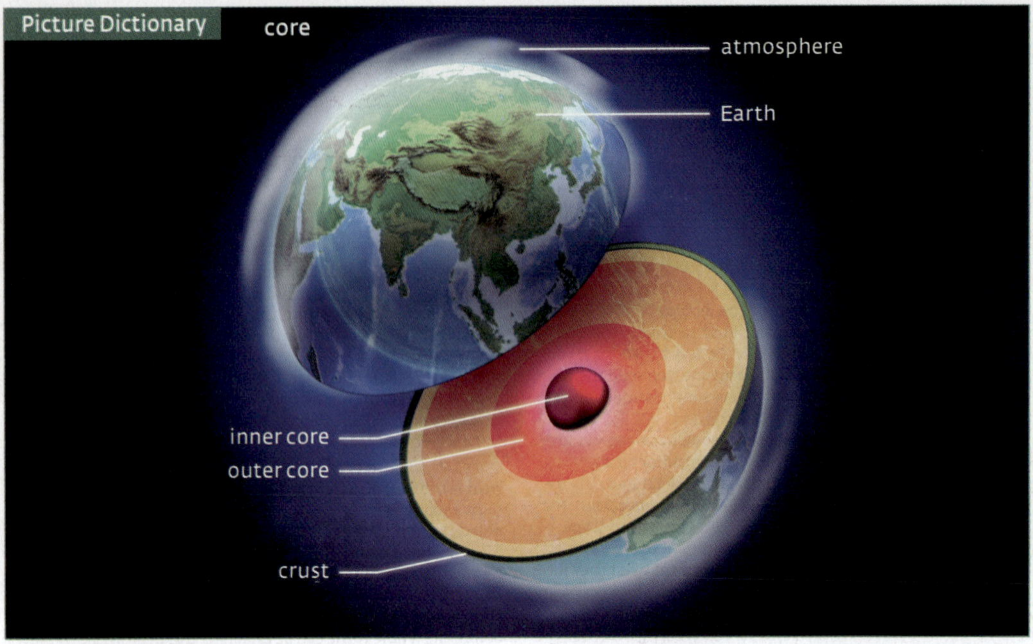

C

Picture Dictionary

core

atmosphere

Earth

inner core

outer core

crust

surfaces of something join. 角 ❑ *He saw the corner of a magazine sticking out from under the blanket.* 他看到毯子下露出了杂志的一角。 **2** N-COUNT The **corner** of a room, box, or similar space is the area inside it where its edges or walls meet. 角落 ❑ *...a card table in the corner of the living room.* …客厅角落里的一张牌桌。 ❑ *The ball hurtled into the far corner of the net.* 球直飞入球门的远角。 ❑ *Finally I spotted it, in a dark corner over by the piano.* 最终我发现了它，在钢琴旁边一个黑暗的角落。 **3** N-COUNT The **corner of** your mouth or eye is the side of it. (眼睛、嘴巴的) 角 ❑ *She flicked a crumb off the corner of her mouth.* 她轻轻擦去了嘴角的面包屑。 **4** N-COUNT The **corner** of a street is the place where one of its sides ends as it joins another street. (街道的) 拐角 ❑ *She would spend the day hanging around street corners.* 她常一整天在街头的各个角落闲逛。 ❑ *We can't have police officers on every corner.* 我们不可能在每一个路口都有警察。 **5** N-COUNT A **corner** is a bend in a road. (路的) 拐弯处 ❑ *...a sharp corner.* …一个急拐弯。 **6** N-COUNT In soccer, hockey, and some other sports, a **corner** is a free shot or kick taken from the corner of the field. (足球、曲棍球等的) 角球 ❑ *McPherson took the corner and James crashed his header off the crossbar and over the line.* 麦克弗森踢了个角球，詹姆斯头球顶出横梁后出界。 **7** V-T If you **corner** a person or animal, you force them into a place they cannot escape from. 使走投无路 ❑ *A police motorcycle chased his car twelve miles, and cornered him near Gainsborough.* 一辆警车追踪他的汽车12英里，在盖恩斯堡附近把他逼得走投无路。 **8** V-T If you **corner** someone, you force them to speak to you when they have been trying to avoid you. 强求与…交谈 ❑ *Thomas managed to corner the young producer-director for an interview.* 汤马斯缠着年轻的制片兼导演给了他一次面试的机会。 **9** V-T If a company or place **corners** an area of trade, they gain control over it so that no one else can have any success in that area. 垄断 [BUSINESS] ❑ *Sony has cornered the market in chic-looking MP3 players.* 索尼已经垄断了时尚MP3播放器市场。 **10** V-I If a car, or the person driving it, **corners** in a particular way, the car goes around bends in roads in this way. 转弯 ❑ *Peter drove jerkily, cornering too fast and fumbling the gears.* 彼得开车很不平稳，转弯太快，换档也不熟练。 **11** PHRASE If you say that something is **around the corner**, you mean that it will happen very soon. 即将到来 ❑ *Economic recovery is just around the corner.* 经济复苏即将到来。 **12** PHRASE If you say that something is **around the corner**, you mean that it is very near. 在附近 ❑ *My new place is just around the corner.* 我的新房子就在附近。 **13** PHRASE If you **cut corners**, you do something quickly by doing it in a less thorough way than you should. 走捷径 [DISAPPROVAL] ❑ *Take your time, don't cut corners, and follow instructions to the letter.* 慢慢来，不要走捷径。要严格按要求完成。

Word Partnership *corner* 的常用搭配：

ADJ.	**far** corner 1 2 4
	sharp corner 1 4 5
N.	corner **of a room** 2
	street corner 4 5
V.	**sit in a** corner 2
	round/turn a corner 4 5
PREP.	**in a** corner 2
	around the corner 4 5 11 12

★ **corner·stone** /kɔrnərstoʊn/ (**cornerstones**) N-COUNT The **cornerstone of** something is the basic part of it on which its existence, success, or truth depends. 基石 [FORMAL] ❑ *Research is the cornerstone of the profession.* 研究是该职业的基石。

corny /kɔrni/ (**cornier, corniest**) ADJ If you describe something as **corny**, you mean that it is obvious or sentimental and not at all original. 多愁善感的; 老一套的 [DISAPPROVAL] ❑ *I know it sounds corny, but I'm really not motivated by money.* 我知道这听起来有点俗，但是我真的不是为了钱。 ❑ *...a corny slapstick movie.* …一部老套的闹剧。

coro·nary /kɔrənɛri/ (**coronaries**) **1** ADJ **Coronary** means belonging or relating to the heart. 心脏的 [ADJ n] [MEDICAL] ❑ *If all the coronary arteries are free of significant obstructions, all parts of the heart will receive equal amounts of oxygen.* 如果冠状动脉没有重大堵塞，心脏的各个部位会收到等量的氧气。 **2** N-COUNT If someone has a **coronary**, they collapse because the flow of blood to their heart is blocked by a large lump of blood called a clot. 冠心病

coro·na·tion /kɔrəneɪʃ^ən/ (**coronations**) N-COUNT A **coronation** is the ceremony at which a king or queen is crowned. (国王或女王的) 加冕仪式

coro·ner /kɔrənər/ (**coroners**) N-COUNT A **coroner** is an official who is responsible for investigating the deaths of people who have died in a sudden, violent, or unusual way. 验尸官 ❑ *The coroner recorded a verdict of accidental death.* 验尸官记录下了意外死亡的判定。

Corp. ◆◆◇ **1** **Corp.** is a written abbreviation for **corporation**. 公司 [BUSINESS] ❑ *...Sony Corp. of Japan.* …日本索尼公司。

Word Link *corp* ≈ *body* : *corporal, corpse, incorporate*

▲ **cor·po·ral** /kɔrpərəl, -prəl/ (**corporals**) N-COUNT; N-TITLE A **corporal** is a noncommissioned officer in the army or United States Marines. 下士 ❑ *The corporal shouted an order at the men.* 下士对士兵们高声下令。

cor·po·ral pun·ish·ment N-UNCOUNT **Corporal punishment** is the punishment of people by hitting them. 体罚 ❑ *Corporal punishment in public schools is forbidden.* 体罚在公立学校是被禁止的。

★ **cor·po·rate** ♦◇◇ /kɔrpərɪt, -prɪt/ ADJ **Corporate** means relating to business corporations or to a particular business corporation. 公司的 [ADJ n] [BUSINESS] ❑ *...top U.S. corporate executives.* …美国公司的高层管理人员。 ❑ *...a corporate lawyer.* …一名公司律师。

Word Partnership *corporate* 的常用搭配:
N. corporate **clients**, corporate **culture**, corporate **hospitality**, corporate **image**, corporate **lawyer**, corporate **sector**, corporate **structure**

cor·po·rate raid·er (**corporate raiders**) N-COUNT **A corporate raider** is a person or organization that tries to take control of a company by buying a large number of its shares. 蓄意收购公司者 [BUSINESS] ❑ *Your present company could be taken over by corporate raiders.* 你现在的公司可能会被蓄意收购者收购。

cor·po·ra·tion ♦◇◇ /kɔrpəreɪʃᵊn/ (**corporations**) N-COUNT; N-IN-NAMES **A corporation** is a large business or company with special rights and powers. 大公司; 企业 [BUSINESS] ❑ *...multinational corporations.* …跨国公司。 ❑ *Many voters resented the power of big corporations.* 许多投票人憎恨大公司的权力。

cor·po·ra·tion tax N-UNCOUNT **Corporation tax** is a tax that companies have to pay on the profits they make. 公司税 [BUSINESS]

corps /kɔr/ (**corps**)

Corps is both the singular and the plural form.

1 N-COUNT; N-IN-NAMES **A corps** is a part of the army which has special duties. 特殊兵种 ❑ *...the Army Medical Corps.* …陆军医疗部队。 2 N-COUNT **The Corps** is the United States Marine Corps. 美国海军陆战队 [AM] ❑ *...seventy-five men, all combat veterans, all members of The Corps' most exclusive unit.* …75名士兵，全都是作战老手、海军陆战队最精锐部队的成员。 3 N-COUNT **A corps** is a small group of people who do a special job. 特别小组 ❑ *...the diplomatic corps.* …外交使团。

★ **corpse** /kɔrps/ (**corpses**) N-COUNT **A corpse** is a dead body, especially the body of a human being. 尸体 ❑ *Detectives placed the corpse in a body bag.* 刑警们把尸体装进了一个运尸袋。

Word Link *rect ≈ right, straight : correct, rectangle, rectify*

cor·rect ♦♦◇ /kərɛkt/ (**corrects, correcting, corrected**) 1 ADJ If something is **correct**, it is right and true. 正确的 ❑ *The correct answers can be found at the bottom of page 8.* 正确答案可以在第8页的底部找到。 ❑ *The following information was correct at time of going to press.* 以下信息在付印时是准确无误的。 ● **cor·rect·ly** ADV 正确地 [ADV with v] ❑ *Did I pronounce your name correctly?* 我把你的名字读对了吗? ● **cor·rect·ness** N-UNCOUNT 正确性 ❑ *Ask the investor to check the correctness of what he has written.* 让投资人核对一下他所写内容的正确性。 2 ADJ If someone is **correct**, what they have said or thought is true. 正确的 [v-link ADJ] [FORMAL] ❑ *You are absolutely correct. The leaves are from a bay tree.* 你的看法完全正确。这些是月桂树的叶子。 3 ADJ The **correct** thing or method is the thing or method that is required or is most suitable in a particular situation. 合适的; 恰当的 [ADJ n] ❑ *The use of the correct materials was crucial.* 使用合适材料是重要的。 ❑ *White was in no doubt the referee made the correct decision.* 怀特毫不怀疑裁判做出了恰当的判罚。 ● **cor·rect·ly** ADV 合适地 [ADV with v] ❑ *If correctly executed, this shot will give them a better chance of getting the ball close to the hole.* 如果处理得当，这一击将使他们更有机会使球接近球洞。 4 ADJ If you say that someone is **correct in** doing something, you approve of their action. 正确的 ❑ *You are perfectly correct in trying to steer your mother toward increased independence.* 你在试图引导你妈妈变得越来越独立这点上是完全正确的。 ● **cor·rect·ly** ADV 正确地 [ADV with cl] ❑ *I think the police commission acted correctly.* 我认为警方行动正确。 5 ADJ If a person or their behavior is **correct**, their behavior is in accordance with social or other rules. 符合公认准则的; 得体的 ❑ *He was very polite and very correct.* 他很有礼貌且举止得体。 ● **cor·rect·ly** ADV 得体地 [ADV with v] ❑ *She began speaking politely, even correctly.* 她开始礼貌地讲了起来，甚至还很得体。 ● **cor·rect·ness** N-UNCOUNT 得体性 ❑ *...his stiff-legged gait and formal correctness.* …他僵硬的步态和正式的矜持。 6 V-T If you **correct** a problem, mistake, or fault, you do something which puts it right. 矫正 ❑ *He may need surgery to correct the problem.* 他可能需要手术来矫正这一问题。 ● **cor·rec·tion** /kərɛkʃᵊn/ N-VAR (**corrections**) 改正 ❑ *...legislation to require the correction of factual errors.* …要求对事实上的错误做出改正的法规。 7 V-T If you **correct** someone, you say something which you think is more accurate or appropriate than what they have just said. 纠正 ❑ *"Actually, that isn't what happened," George corrects me.* "事实上，不是那样发生的，" 乔治纠正我。 8 V-T When someone **corrects** a piece of writing, they look at it and mark the mistakes in it. 批改 ❑ *It took an extraordinary effort to focus on preparing his classes or correcting his students' work.* 集中精力去备课或批改学生的作业费了他相当大的劲。

Thesaurus *correct* 另参见:
ADJ. accurate, legitimate, precise, right, true; *(ant.)* false, inaccurate, incorrect, wrong 1
V. fix, rectify, repair; *(ant.)* damage, hurt 6

Word Partnership *correct* 的常用搭配:
N. correct **answer**, correct **response** 1 2
correct **a situation** 6
correct **a mistake** 6 8
correct ***someone*** 7

cor·rec·tion /kərɛkʃᵊn/ (**corrections**) 1 N-COUNT **Corrections** are marks or comments made on a piece of work, especially school work, which indicate where there are mistakes and what are the right answers. 批改 ❑ *In a group, compare your corrections to Exercise 2A.* 以小组为单位，对比一下对练习2A的批改。 2 N-UNCOUNT **Correction** is the punishment of criminals. 惩罚; 改造 [mainly AM] ❑ *...jails and other parts of the correction system.* …监狱和劳教系统的其他部门。 3 → see also **correct**

cor·rec·tive /kərɛktɪv/ (**correctives**) 1 ADJ **Corrective** measures or techniques are intended to put right something that is wrong. 纠正性的 ❑ *Scientific institutions have been reluctant to take corrective action.* 科学机构一直都不愿采取纠正的行动。 2 N-COUNT If something is **a corrective to** a particular view or account, it gives a more accurate or fairer picture than there would have been without it. 匡正 [FORMAL] ❑ *...a useful corrective to the mistaken view that all psychologists are behaviorists.* …对所有心理学家都是行为主义者这一错误观点的有效匡正。

Word Link *cor ≈ with : correlate, correspond, corroborate*

★ **cor·re·late** /kɔrəleɪt/ (**correlates, correlating, correlated**) 1 V-RECIP If one thing **correlates with** another, there is a close similarity or connection between them, often because one thing causes the other. You can also say that two things **correlate**. 和…相关(尤指互有因果关系); 相近 [FORMAL] ❑ *Obesity correlates with increased risk for hypertension and stroke.* 过度肥胖与高血压和中风的发病风险增加密切相关。 ❑ *The political opinions of spouses correlate more closely than their heights.* 与身高匹配相比，配偶之间的政治观点更为接近。 2 V-T If you **correlate** things, you work out the way in which they are connected or the way they influence each other. 使…相互关联 [FORMAL] ❑ *Attempts to correlate specific language functions with particular parts of the brain have not advanced very far.* 试图把特定的语言功能和大脑特定区域相联系的努力还没有取得很大进展。

★ **cor·re·la·tion** /kɔrəleɪʃᵊn/ (**correlations**) N-COUNT **A correlation between** things is a connection or link between them. 相互关系; 关联 [FORMAL] ❑ *...the correlation between smoking and disease.* …吸烟和疾病之间的关联。

Word Partnership *correlation* 的常用搭配:
V. **find a** correlation
ADJ. **direct** correlation, **negative** correlation, **significant** correlation, **strong** correlation

cor·re·spond /kɔrɪspɒnd/ (**corresponds, corresponding, corresponded**) 1 V-RECIP If one thing **corresponds to** another, there is a close similarity or connection between them. You can also say that two things **correspond**. 相一致; 相对应 ❑ *Racegoers will be given a number which will correspond to a horse running in a race.* 观看赛马的观众将领到一个与参赛马匹相对应的号码。 ❑ *The two maps of the Rockies correspond closely.* 这两张落基山脉的地图极为相似。 ● **cor·re·spond·ing** ADJ 相应的 [ADJ n] ❑ *The rise in interest rates was not reflected in a corresponding rise in the dollar.* 利率上调没有反映在相应的美元增值上。 2 V-RECIP If you **correspond with** someone, you write letters to them. You can also say that two people **correspond**. 通信 ❑ *She still corresponds with friends she met in Majorca*

C

nine years ago. 她依然和9年前在马略卡岛遇到的朋友们通信。

cor·re·spond·ence /kɔrɪspɒndəns/ (**correspondences**) **1** N-UNCOUNT **Correspondence** is the act of writing letters to someone. 通信 [also "a" N, oft N "with" n] ❑ *The judges' decision is final and no correspondence will be entered into.* 法官们的判决为终审判决，所以再写信也不会付以审议。 **2** N-UNCOUNT Someone's **correspondence** is the letters that they receive or send. 信件 ❑ *He always replied to his correspondence.* 他总是来函必复。 **3** N-COUNT If there is a **correspondence between** two things, there is a close similarity or connection between them. 一致 ❑ *In African languages there is a close correspondence between sounds and letters.* 在非洲各语言中，语音和字母之间有着密切的对应关系。

cor·re·spond·ence course (**correspondence courses**) N-COUNT A **correspondence course** is a course in which you study at home, receiving your work by mail and sending it back by mail. 函授课程 ❑ *I took a correspondence course in computing.* 我学了一门计算机函授课程。

cor·re·spond·ent ♦♦◇ /kɔrɪspɒndənt/ (**correspondents**) N-COUNT A **correspondent** is a newspaper or television journalist, especially one who specializes in a particular type of news. (尤指对某一专题进行报道的) 记者 ❑ *As our Diplomatic Correspondent Mark Brayne reports, the president was given a sympathetic hearing.* 据我台外事记者马克・布雷恩报道，该总统获得了一个同情的申诉机会。

cor·re·spond·ing·ly /kɔrɪspɒndɪŋli/ ADV You use **correspondingly** when describing a situation which is closely connected with one you have just mentioned or is similar to it. 相应地 ❑ *As his political stature has shrunk, he has grown correspondingly more dependent on the army.* 随着政治声望不断降低，他相应地变得更依赖于军队了。

cor·ri·dor /kɔrɪdər, -dɔr/ (**corridors**) **1** N-COUNT A **corridor** is a long passage in a building, with doors and rooms on one or both sides. 走廊 [mainly BRIT] ❑ *There were doors on both sides of the corridor.* 走廊的两侧都有门。 **2** N-COUNT A **corridor** is a strip of land that connects one country to another or gives it a route to the sea through another country. 走廊地带 (与另一国家相连或穿越另一国取得出海通道的狭长地带) ❑ *East Prussia and the rest of Germany were separated, in 1919, by the Polish Corridor.* 1919年，波兰走廊把东普鲁士和德国其他地方分隔开了。 **3** N-COUNT A **corridor** is an area of land between 2 large cities. (两大城市之间的) 走廊地带 ❑ *...the Northeast corridor.* …东北走廊地带。

Word Link *cor ≈ with : correlate, correspond, corroborate*

cor·robo·rate /kərɒbəreɪt/ (**corroborates, corroborating, corroborated**) V-T To **corroborate** something that has been said or reported means to provide evidence or information that supports it. 证实 [FORMAL] ❑ *I had access to a wide range of documents which corroborated the story.* 我能取得大量文件来证实这个故事。

● **cor·robo·ra·tion** /kərɒbəreɪʃən/ N-UNCOUNT 确证 ❑ *He could not get a single witness to establish independent corroboration of his version of the accident.* 他找不到一个目击证人可以为他对事故的陈述提供独立的佐证。

★ **cor·rode** /kəroʊd/ (**corrodes, corroding, corroded**) V-T/V-I If metal or stone **corrodes**, or **is corroded**, it is gradually destroyed by a chemical or by rust. 腐蚀 ❑ *He has devised a process for making gold wires which neither corrode nor oxidize.* 他发明了一种制造程序，使金线既不会腐蚀也不会氧化。 ❑ *Engineers found the structure had been corroded by moisture.* 工程师们发现这个构件已经被湿气腐蚀了。

● **cor·rod·ed** ADJ 被腐蚀了的 ❑ *The investigators found that the underground pipes were badly corroded.* 调查人员发现地下管道已是严重腐蚀的。

cor·ro·sion /kəroʊʒən/ N-UNCOUNT **Corrosion** is the damage that is caused when something is corroded. 腐蚀 ❑ *Zinc is used to protect other metals from corrosion.* 锌被用来保护其他金属免受腐蚀。

cor·ru·gat·ed /kɔrəgeɪtɪd/ ADJ **Corrugated** metal or cardboard has been folded into a series of small parallel folds to make it stronger. 有瓦楞的; 波状的 ❑ *...a hut with a corrugated iron roof.* …一间有瓦楞铁顶的小屋。

★ **cor·rupt** /kərʌpt/ (**corrupts, corrupting, corrupted**) **1** ADJ Someone who is **corrupt** behaves in a way that is morally wrong, especially by doing dishonest or illegal things in return for money or power. 腐败的 ❑ *...to save the nation from corrupt politicians of both parties.* …把国家从两党腐败的政客们手中解救出来。 **2** V-T/V-I If someone **is corrupted by** something, it causes them to become dishonest and unjust and unable to be trusted. 使…腐化; 腐化 ❑ *It is sad to see a man so corrupted by the desire for money and power.* 看到一个人被金钱和权力欲望所腐蚀很可悲。 ❑ *Power tends to corrupt.* 权力容易造成腐化。 **3** V-T To **corrupt** someone means to cause them to stop caring about moral standards. 使…堕落 ❑ *...warning that television will corrupt us all.* …电视会使我们所有人堕落的警示。

cor·rup·tion ♦◇◇ /kərʌpʃən/ N-UNCOUNT **Corruption** is dishonesty and illegal behavior by people in positions of authority or power. 腐败 ❑ *The president faces 54 charges of corruption and tax evasion.* 总统面临着54项腐败和逃税的指控。

'cos ♦♦◇ /kəz, STRONG kʌz/ also **cos** CONJ **'Cos** is an informal way of saying **because**. 因为 (**because**的非正式说法) [BRIT, SPOKEN] in AM, use **cuz**

★ **cos·met·ic** /kɒzmɛtɪk/ (**cosmetics**) **1** N-COUNT **Cosmetics** are substances such as lipstick or powder, which people put on their face to make themselves look more attractive. 化妆品 ❑ *...the cosmetics counter of a department store.* …一个百货商店的化妆品专柜。 **2** ADJ If you describe measures or changes as **cosmetic**, you mean they improve the appearance of a situation or thing but do not change its basic nature, and you are usually implying that they are inadequate. 装门面的 [DISAPPROVAL] ❑ *It is a cosmetic measure which will do nothing to help the situation long term.* 这是装点门面的措施，无益于局势的长期发展。

→ see **makeup**

cos·met·ic sur·gery N-UNCOUNT **Cosmetic surgery** is surgery done to make a person look more attractive. 整形外科手术 ❑ *She is rumored to have had cosmetic surgery on nine different parts of her body.* 据传她的身体有9个部位做过整形手术。

▲ **cos·mic** /kɒzmɪk/ **1** ADJ **Cosmic** means occurring in, or coming from, the part of space that lies outside Earth and its atmosphere. 外层空间的 ❑ *...cosmic radiation.* …外层辐射。 **2** ADJ **Cosmic** means belonging or relating to the universe. 宇宙的 ❑ *...the cosmic laws governing our world.* …主宰我们世界的宇宙法则。

▲ **cos·mo·poli·tan** /kɒzməpɒlɪtən/ **1** ADJ A **cosmopolitan** place or society is full of people from many different countries and cultures. 世界性的 [APPROVAL] ❑ *...a cosmopolitan city.* …一个国际化都市。 **2** ADJ Someone who is **cosmopolitan** has had a lot of contact with people and things from many different countries and as a result is very open to different ideas and ways of doing things. 见多识广的 [APPROVAL] ❑ *The family is rich, and extremely sophisticated and cosmopolitan.* 这个家庭殷实富足，深谙世故，又见多识广。

cos·mos /kɒzməs, -moʊs/ N-SING **The cosmos** is the universe. 宇宙 [LITERARY] ❑ *...the natural laws of the cosmos.* …宇宙的自然法则。

cost ♦♦♦ /kɒst/ (**costs, costing**)

> The form **cost** is used in the present tense, and is also the past tense and participle, except for meaning **3**, where the form **costed** is used.

1 N-COUNT The **cost of** something is the amount of money that is needed in order to buy, do, or make it. 费用 ❑ *The cost of a loaf of bread has increased five-fold.* 一块面包的价格已经涨了5倍。 ❑ *In 1989 the price of coffee fell so low that in many countries it did not even cover the cost of production.* 1989年咖啡的价格跌得那么低，以致在许多国家还抵不上其生产成本。 **2** V-T If something **costs** a particular amount of money, you can buy, do, or make it for that amount. 要价 ❑ *This course is limited to 12 people and costs $150.* 这门课程限招12人，费用为$150。 ❑ *Painted walls look much more interesting and don't cost much.* 粉刷过的墙壁看上去更有趣，要价也不高。 **3** V-T When something that you plan to do or make **is costed**, the amount of money you need is calculated in advance. 估算…的费用 [usu passive] ❑ *The building work has not been fully costed but runs into millions of dollars.* 建筑工作的费用还未完全估算出来，但要高达几百万美元。 **4** V-T If an event or mistake **costs** you something, you lose that thing as the result of it. 使…付出 ❑ *...a six-year-old boy whose life was saved by an operation that cost him his sight.* …一个通过手术保住生命但双目失明的6岁男孩。 **5** N-PLURAL Your **costs** are the total amount of money that you must spend on running your home or business. (家庭或公司) 开销 ❑ *Costs have been cut by 30 to 50 percent.* 开销已经减少了30%到50%。

Do not confuse **cost** and **costs**. The **cost** of something is the amount of money that you need in order to buy it, do it, or make it. ❑ *...the cost of the telephone call. ...the total cost was over a million pounds.* The **costs** of a business or a home are the sums of money that have to be spent on running it. They include money spent on electricity, repairs, and taxes. ❑ *...attempts to cut costs and boost profits.* See also note at **price**.

6 N-PLURAL If someone is ordered by a court of law to pay **costs**, they have to pay a sum of money toward the expenses of a court case they are involved in. 诉讼费用 ❑ *He was jailed for 18 months and ordered to pay $550 costs.* 他被判入狱18个月，并支付$550的诉讼费。 7 N-UNCOUNT If something is sold **at cost**, it is sold for the same price as it cost the seller to buy it. 成本价格 ❑ *...a store that provided cigarettes and candy bars at cost.* …一家以成本价出售香烟和糖果的商店。 8 N-SING The **cost of** something is the loss, damage, or injury that is involved in trying to achieve it. 代价 ❑ *In March Mr. Salinas shut down the city's oil refinery at a cost of $500 million and 5,000 jobs.* 3月时萨利纳斯先生关闭了该市的炼油厂，损失了5亿美元和5000个工作岗位。 9 PHRASE If you say that something must be avoided **at all costs**, you are emphasizing that it must not be allowed to happen under any circumstances. 不惜任何代价地 [EMPHASIS] ❑ *They told Jacques Delors a disastrous world trade war must be avoided at all costs.* 他们告诉雅克·德洛斯，必须不惜一切代价避免灾难性的世界贸易大战。 10 PHRASE If you say that something must be done **at any cost**, you are emphasizing that it must be done, even if this requires a lot of effort or money. 无论如何 [EMPHASIS] ❑ *This book is of such importance that it must be published at any cost.* 这本书如此重要，无论如何也要出版。

Thesaurus *cost* 另参见：

N. fee, price 1
harm, loss, sacrifice 8

Word Partnership *cost* 的常用搭配：

ADJ. **additional** costs 1
N. cost **of living** 1
V. **cover** the cost, **cut** costs, **keep** costs **down** 1 5

cost ac·count·ing N-UNCOUNT **Cost accounting** is the recording and analysis of all the various costs of running a business. 成本会计 [BUSINESS] ❑ *But full cost accounting will be introduced without delay.* 但是，全面成本核算马上将被采用。

co·star /koʊstɑr/ (costars, costarring, costarred)

in BRIT, also use **co-star**

1 N-COUNT An actor's **costars** are the other actors who also have one of the main parts in a particular movie. 联合主演者 ❑ *During the filming, Curtis fell in love with his costar, Christine Kaufmann.* 在电影拍摄过程中，柯蒂斯爱上了他的搭档克里斯廷·考夫曼。 2 V-T If a movie **costars** particular actors, they have the main parts in it. 由…联袂主演 ❑ *Produced by Oliver Stone, "Wild Palms" costars Dana Delaney, Jim Belushi and Angie Dickinson.* 奥利弗·斯通制片的电影《野棕榈》由达纳·德拉尼、吉姆·贝鲁西和安吉·迪金森联袂主演。

cost-effective ADJ Something that is **cost-effective** saves or makes a lot of money in comparison with the costs involved. 有成本效益的 ❑ *The bank must be run in a cost-effective way.* 银行必须以有成本效益的方式经营。 ● **cost-effectively** ADV 有成本效益地 ❑ *The management tries to produce the magazine as cost-effectively as possible.* 管理部门尽可能最有成本效益地的方式制作杂志。 ● **cost-effectiveness** N-UNCOUNT 成本效益 ❑ *A report has raised doubts about the cost-effectiveness of the proposals.* 一个报告对这些建议的成本效益提出了质疑。

cost·ly /kɒstli/ (**costlier, costliest**) ADJ If you say that something is **costly**, you mean that it costs a lot of money, often more than you would want to pay. 昂贵的 ❑ *Having professionally made curtains can be costly, so why not make your own?* 买专业制造的窗帘可能很贵，你为什么不自己做呢？

cost of liv·ing N-SING The **cost of living** is the average amount of money that people in a particular place need in order to be able to afford basic food, housing, and clothing. 生活费用 ❑ *The cost of living has increased dramatically.* 生活费用已大幅增长了。

cost-plus ADJ A **cost-plus** basis for a contract for work to be done is one in which the buyer agrees to pay the seller or contractor all the cost plus a profit. 成本加利润的 [ADJ n] ❑ *All vessels were to be built on a cost-plus basis.* 所有船将根据成本加利润的原则建造。

cos·tume /kɒstum/ (**costumes**) 1 N-VAR An actor's or performer's **costume** is the set of clothes they wear while they are performing. 戏装 ❑ *Even from a distance, the effect of his fox costume was stunning.* 即使从远处看，他的狐装造型也非常漂亮。 ❑ *The performers, in costume and makeup, were walking up and down backstage.* 演员们穿着戏服化着妆，在后台走来走去。 2 N-UNCOUNT The clothes worn by people at a particular time in history, or in a particular country, are referred to as a particular type of **costume**. (某一历史时期或某一国家人们穿的) 服装 ❑ *...men and women in eighteenth-century costume.* …身着18世纪服装的男男女女。 3 ADJ A **costume** drama is one which is set in the past and in which the actors wear the type of clothes that were worn in that period. 古装的 [ADJ n] ❑ *...a lavish costume drama set in Ireland and the U.S. in the 1890s.* …以19世纪90年代的爱尔兰和美国为背景的一部大型古装戏。
→ see **theater**

cos·tume jew·el·ry

in BRIT, use **costume jewellery**

N-UNCOUNT **Costume jewelry** is jewelry made from cheap materials. (廉价材料制成的) 首饰

cosy /koʊzi/ [BRIT] → see **cozy**

cot /kɒt/ (**cots**) 1 N-COUNT A **cot** is a narrow bed, usually made of canvas fitted over a frame which can be folded up. 折叠床 [AM]

in BRIT, use **camp bed**

2 N-COUNT A **cot** is a bed for a baby. 婴儿床 [BRIT]

in AM, use **crib**

cot·tage ♦◇◇ /kɒtɪdʒ/ (**cottages**) N-COUNT; N-IN-NAMES A **cottage** is a small house, usually in the country. 村舍 ❑ *They used to have a cottage in N.W. Scotland.* 他们过去在苏格兰西北部有间村舍。

cot·tage in·dus·try (**cottage industries**) N-COUNT A **cottage industry** is a small business that is run from someone's home, especially one that involves a craft such as knitting or pottery. 家庭手工业 [BUSINESS] ❑ *Bookbinding is largely a cottage industry.* 装订业很大程度上属于家庭手工业。

cot·ton ♦◇◇ /kɒtᵊn/ (**cottons**) 1 N-MASS **Cotton** is a type of cloth made from soft fibers from a particular plant. 棉布 ❑ *...a cotton shirt.* …一件棉布衬衫。 2 N-UNCOUNT **Cotton** is a plant which is grown in warm countries and which produces soft fibers used in making cotton cloth. 棉花 ❑ *...a large cotton plantation in Tennessee.* …位于田纳西州的一个大棉花种植园。 3 N-UNCOUNT **Cotton** or **absorbent cotton** is a soft mass of cotton, used especially for applying liquids or creams to your skin. 脱脂棉；药棉 [AM]

in BRIT, use **cotton wool**

❑ *...cotton balls.* …脱脂棉球。 4 N-MASS **Cotton** is thread that is used for sewing, especially thread that is made from cotton. 棉线 [BRIT]

in AM, use **thread**

→ see Word Web: **cotton**

Word Web cotton

Some historians believe that **cotton** was first used in Egypt around 12,000 BC. Pieces of **fabric** containing a mixture of cotton and fur have been found in Mexico. They date back to about 5000 BC. Today's cotton **crop** in the U.S. totals about 20 billion dollars a year. The **textile industry** uses most of this cotton to make things like **denim** clothing, T-shirts, and bed sheets. However, many other products contain some cotton. For example, cotton fiber is used to make coffee filters, tents, stationery, and even U.S. currency.

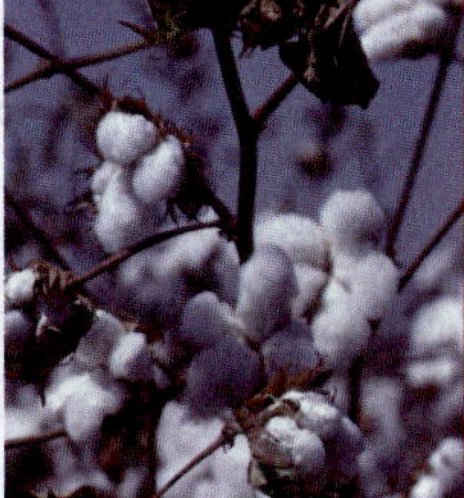

C

C

cot·ton can·dy N-UNCOUNT **Cotton candy** is a large pink or white mass of sugar threads that is eaten from a stick. It is sold at fairs or other outdoor events. 棉花糖 [AM]

in BRIT, use **candyfloss**

cot·ton wool N-UNCOUNT **Cotton wool** is a soft mass of cotton, used especially for applying liquids or creams to your skin. 脱脂棉; 药棉 [BRIT]

in AM, use **cotton**

couch /kaʊtʃ/ (**couches**) 1 N-COUNT A **couch** is a long, comfortable seat for two or three people. 长沙发 2 N-COUNT A **couch** is a narrow bed which patients lie on while they are being treated by a psychoanalyst. (精神科医生的) 诊察台 ❑ *Between films he often winds up spending every single morning on his psychiatrist's couch.* 在拍电影的间隔期间，他经常是在心理医生的诊察台上度过每一个早晨。

cough ♦◊◊ /kɒf/ (**coughs, coughing, coughed**) 1 V-I When you **cough**, you force air out of your throat with a sudden, harsh noise. You often cough when you are ill, or when you are nervous or want to attract someone's attention. 咳嗽 ❑ *Graham began to cough violently.* 格雷厄姆开始剧烈地咳嗽。 ● N-COUNT **Cough** is also a noun. 咳嗽 ❑ *Coughs and sneezes spread infections much faster in a warm atmosphere.* 咳嗽和喷嚏在温暖的空气里传播疾病快得多。 ● **cough·ing** N-UNCOUNT 咳嗽 ❑ *He was then overcome by a terrible fit of coughing.* 之后他一阵剧烈咳嗽，咳到无法控制。 2 V-T If you **cough** blood or mucus, it comes up out of your throat or mouth when you cough. 咳出 (血、痰等) ❑ *I started coughing blood so they transferred me to a hospital.* 我开始咳血，所以他们把我送到了一家医院。 ● PHRASAL VERB **Cough up** means the same as **cough**. 咳嗽 ❑ *On the chilly seas, Keats became feverish, continually coughing up blood.* 在寒冷的海边，济慈开始发烧，不断地咳血。 3 N-COUNT A **cough** is an illness in which you cough often and your chest or throat hurts. 咳嗽 ❑ *I had a persistent cough for over a month.* 我持续咳嗽已经一个多月了。

→ see **illness**

▸ **cough up** 1 PHRASAL VERB If you **cough up** an amount of money, you pay or spend that amount, usually when you would prefer not to. 勉强支付 [INFORMAL] ❑ *I'll have to cough up $10,000 a year for tuition.* 我将必须勉强支付每年$10000的学费。 2 → see also **cough 2**

could ♦♦♦ /kəd, STRONG kʊd/

Could is a modal verb. It is used with the base form of a verb. **Could** is sometimes considered to be the past form of **can**, but in this dictionary the two words are dealt with separately.

1 MODAL You use **could** to indicate that someone had the ability to do something. You use **could not** or **couldn't** to say that someone was unable to do something. 能; 会 ❑ *I could see that something was terribly wrong.* 我能看出有很大麻烦了。 ❑ *When I left school at 16, I couldn't read or write.* 我16岁离开学校时不会读也不会写。 2 MODAL You use **could** to indicate that something sometimes happened. 可能会 ❑ *Though he had a temper and could be nasty, it never lasted.* 尽管他有脾气，可能会粗暴，但从来不会持续很久。 3 MODAL You use **could have** to indicate that something was a possibility in the past, although it did not actually happen. 本可能 ❑ *He could have made a fortune as a lawyer.* 他本可能当律师挣大钱。 ❑ *You could have been killed!* 你本可能被杀了。 4 MODAL You use **could** to indicate that something is possibly true, or that it may possibly happen. 可能 ❑ *Doctors told him the disease could have been caused by years of working in smokey clubs.* 医生们告诉他，他的病可能是多年在烟雾弥漫的俱乐部工作所引起的。 ❑ *An improvement in living standards could be years away.* 生活水平的提高可能还要几年。 5 MODAL You use **could not** or **couldn't** to indicate that it is not possible that something is true. 可能 (与否定词**not**连用，表示不可能) ❑ *They argued all the time and thought it couldn't be good for the baby.* 他们一直在争论，认为这不可能对孩子有好处。 ❑ *Anne couldn't be expected to understand the situation.* 别指望安妮会理解这种形势。 6 MODAL You use **could** to talk about a possibility, ability, or opportunity that depends on other conditions. 能; 可能 ❑ *Their hope was that a new and better East Germany could be born.* 他们的希望是一个全新更好的东德能诞生。 7 MODAL You use **could** when you are saying that one thing or situation resembles another. 像 ❑ *The charming characters she draws look like they could have walked out of the 1920s.* 她画的那些可爱人物看上去像是从20世纪20年代走出来的。 8 MODAL You use **could**, or **couldn't** in questions, when you are making offers and suggestions. 可以 (用于建议) ❑ *I could call the local doctor.* 我可以给当地医生打电话。 ❑ *You could look for a career abroad where environmental jobs are better paid and more secure.* 你可以在国外找份工作，那里环保工作薪水更高，也更稳定。 ❑ *Couldn't we call a special meeting?* 我们不能召开一次特别会议吗？ 9 MODAL You use **could** in questions when you are making a polite request or asking for permission to do something. Speakers sometimes use **couldn't** instead of "could" to show that they realize that their request may be refused. 可以 [POLITENESS] ❑ *Could I stay tonight?* 今晚我可以待在这吗？ ❑ *He asked if he could have a cup of coffee.* 他问是否可以喝一杯咖啡。 ❑ *Couldn't I watch you do it?* 我不可以看着你做这件事吗？

Can, **could**, and **be able to** are all used to talk about a person's ability to do something. They are followed by the infinitive form of a verb. You use **can** or a present form of **be able to** to refer to the present, although **can** is more common. ❑ *They can all read and write... The snake is able to catch small mammals.* You use **could** or a past form of **be able to** to refer to the past, and "will" or "shall" with **be able to** to refer to the future. **Be able to** is used if you want to refer to doing something at a particular time. ❑ *After treatment he was able to return to work.* **Can** and **could** are used to talk about possibility. **Could** refers to a particular occasion and **can** to more general situations. ❑ *Many jobs could be lost... Too much salt can be harmful.* When talking about the past, you use **could have** and a past participle. ❑ *It could have been much worse.* You also use **can** for the present and **could** for the past to talk about rules or what people are allowed to do. ❑ *They can leave at any time.* Note that when making requests either **can** or **could** may be used. ❑ *Can I have a drink?... Could we put the fire on?* However, **could** is always used for suggestions. ❑ *You could phone her and ask.*

10 MODAL You use **could** to say emphatically that someone ought to do the thing mentioned, especially when you are annoyed because they have not done it. You use **why couldn't** in questions to express your surprise or annoyance that someone has not done something. 本可以 (对某人未做某事表示恼怒) [EMPHASIS] ❑ *We've come to see you, so you could at least stand and greet us properly.* 我们来是为了看你，因此你至少可以站起来适当地欢迎我们。 ❑ *Why couldn't she have said something?* 为什么她不能说点什么呢？ 11 MODAL You use **could** when you are expressing strong feelings about something by saying that you feel as if you want to do the thing mentioned, although you do not do it. 表示嘴上说要做实际上没有做 [EMPHASIS] ❑ *I could kill you! I swear I could!* 我要杀了你！我发誓我要。 ❑ *"Welcome back" was all they said. I could have kissed them!* "欢迎回来，"他们只说了这一句。我本想亲吻他们的。 12 MODAL You use **could** after "if" when talking about something that you do not have the ability or opportunity to do, but which you are imagining in order to consider what the likely consequences might be. 能 (与**if**连用，表示假设) ❑ *If I could afford it, I'd have four television sets.* 要是我买得起，我要有4台电视机。 13 MODAL You use **could not** or **couldn't** with comparatives to emphasize that someone or something has as much as is possible of a particular quality. For example, if you say "I couldn't be happier," you mean that you are extremely happy. 不可能再 (表示已达到极致) [EMPHASIS] ❑ *The rest of the players are great and I couldn't be happier.* 其他运动员都很优秀，我再高兴不过了。 14 MODAL In speech, you use **how could** in questions to emphasize that you feel strongly about something bad that has happened. 怎么能; 怎么会 [EMPHASIS] ❑ *How could you allow him to do something like that?* 你怎么能允许他做那样的事情？ ❑ *How could I have been so stupid?* 我怎么会这么傻？ 15 **could do with** → see **do**

couldn't /kʊdᵊnt/ **Couldn't** is the usual spoken form of "could not." **could not**的常用口语形式

could've /kʊdəv/ **Could've** is the usual spoken form of "could have," when "have" is an auxiliary verb. **could have**的常用口语形式

coun·cil ♦♦♦ /kaʊnsᵊl/ (**councils**) 1 N-COUNT-COLL; N-IN-NAMES A **council** is a group of people who are elected to govern a local area such as a city. 政务委员会 ❑ *The city council has voted almost unanimously in favor.* 市议会几乎全部投了赞成票。 2 N-COUNT-COLL **Council** is used in the names of some organizations. 委员会 ❑ *...the National Council for Civil Liberties.* …国家公民自由委员会。 ❑ *...the Arts Council.* …艺术委员会。 3 N-COUNT-COLL In some organizations, the **council** is the group of people that controls or governs it. 管理委员会 ❑ *The permanent council of the Organization of American States meets today here in Washington.* 美洲国家组织常务委员会今天在华盛顿召开会议。 4 N-COUNT A **council** is a specially organized, formal meeting that is attended by a particular group of people. 会议 ❑ *President Najibullah said he would call a grand council of all Afghans.* 纳吉布拉总统说他将召开全阿富汗人大会。

★ **coun·cil·lor** /kaʊnsələʳ/ [BRIT] → see **councilor**

★ **coun·ci·lor** /kaʊnsələr/ (**councilors**) N-COUNT; N-TITLE A **councilor** is a member of a local council. 政务会委员

in BRIT, use **councillor**

❑ ...*Councilor Michael Poulter.* …政务会委员迈克尔・保尔特。

coun·sel ♦◇◇ /kaʊnsᵊl/ (**counsels, counseling** or **counselling, counseled** or **counselled**) 1 N-UNCOUNT **Counsel** is advice. 劝告 [FORMAL] ❑ *He had always been able to count on her wise counsel.* 他总是能够指望她明智的忠告。 2 V-T If you **counsel** someone **to** take a course of action, or if you **counsel** a course of action, you advise that course of action. 建议；提议 [FORMAL] ❑ *My advisers counseled me to do nothing.* 我的顾问建议我不要做任何事情。 3 V-T If you **counsel** people, you give them advice about their problems. 提供建议 ❑ *...a psychologist who counsels people with eating disorders.* …一名向饮食紊乱症患者提供咨询的心理医生。 4 N-COUNT Someone's **counsel** is the lawyer who gives them advice on a legal case and speaks on their behalf in court. 辩护律师 ❑ *Singleton's counsel said after the trial that he would appeal.* 庭审之后辛格尔顿的辩护律师说他会上诉。

coun·sel·ing /kaʊnsəlɪŋ/ also **counselling** N-UNCOUNT **Counseling** is advice which a therapist or other expert gives to someone about a particular problem. 咨询 ❑ *She will need medical help and counseling to overcome the tragedy.* 她将需要医疗帮助和心理咨询来平复这场悲剧。

coun·se·lor /kaʊnsələr/ (**counselors**) also **counsellor** 1 N-COUNT A **counselor** is a person whose job is to give advice to people who need it, especially advice on their personal problems. 咨询师 ❑ *Children who have suffered like this should see a counselor experienced in bereavement.* 遭遇这种事情的孩子应该去看在丧亲之痛方面很有经验的心理咨询师。 2 N-COUNT A **counselor** is a young person who supervises children at a summer camp. (儿童夏令营的) 辅导员 ❑ *Hicks worked with children as a camp counselor.* 希克斯是一名和孩子打交道的夏令营辅导员。

count ♦♦◇ /kaʊnt/ (**counts, counting, counted**) 1 V-I When you **count**, you say all the numbers one after another up to a particular number. 数数 ❑ *He was counting slowly under his breath.* 他在低声慢慢地数数。 2 V-T If you **count** all the things in a group, you add them up in order to find how many there are. 数…的数目 ❑ *I counted the money. It was more than five hundred dollars.* 我数了数钱，有五百多美元。 ❑ *I counted 34 wild goats grazing.* 我数了有34只野山羊在吃草。 ● PHRASAL VERB **Count up** means the same as **count**. 数…的数目 ❑ *Couldn't we just count up our ballots and bring them to the courthouse?* 我们不能就数好我们的选票然后把它们送到法院吗？ 3 V-I If something or someone **counts for** something or **counts**, they are important or valuable. 有价值；有重要意义 ❑ *Surely it doesn't matter where charities get their money from: what counts is what they do with it.* 当然，慈善组织从哪里得到钱并不重要，重要的是他们用这些钱做什么。 4 V-T/V-I If something **counts** or **is counted as** a particular thing, it is regarded as being that thing, especially in particular circumstances or under particular rules. 看作 ❑ *No one agrees on what counts as a desert.* 没有人对于什么可以看作是荒漠有共识。 5 V-T If you **count** something when you are making a calculation, you include it in that calculation. 把…计算在内 ❑ *It's under 7 percent only because statistics don't count the people who aren't qualified to be in the work force.* 数字不到7%，这只是因为统计没有把未达劳动力标准的人算在内。 6 N-COUNT A **count** is the action of counting a particular set of things, or the number that you get when you have counted them. 点数；点出的数目 ❑ *The final count in last month's referendum showed 56.7 per cent in favor.* 上个月全民投票的最后计票显示支持率为56.7%。 7 N-COUNT You use **count** when referring to the level or amount of something that someone or something has. 数目；数量 ❑ *A glass or two of wine will not significantly add to the calorie count.* 一两杯酒不会显著增加卡路里的数量。 8 N-COUNT In law, a **count** is one of a number of charges brought against someone in court. 罪状 ❑ *He was indicted by a grand jury on two counts of murder.* 他被大陪审团以两项谋杀罪名正式起诉。 9 N-COUNT; N-TITLE; N-VOC A **count** is a European nobleman. 伯爵 ❑ *Her father was a Polish count.* 她父亲是波兰的一位伯爵。 10 PHRASE If you **keep count of** a number of things, you note or keep a record of how many have occurred. If you **lose count of** a number of things, you cannot remember how many have occurred. 计其数/无法计其数 ❑ *The authorities say they are not able to keep count of the bodies still being found as bulldozers clear the rubble.* 当局称他们不能记下推土机清理瓦砾时不断被找到的尸体数目。

→ see **census, mathematics, zero**

▸ **count against** PHRASAL VERB If something **counts against** you, it may cause you to be rejected or punished, or cause people to have a lower opinion of you. 算上去不利 ❑ *He is highly regarded, but his youth might count against him.* 他受人尊敬，但他很年轻这点可能对他不利。

▸ **count on** or **count upon** 1 PHRASAL VERB If you **count on** something or **count upon** it, you expect it to happen and include it in your plans. 指望 ❑ *What they did not know was how much support they could count on from Democrats.* 他们不知道能够指望从民主党人那里得到多少支持。 2 PHRASAL VERB If you **count on** someone or **count upon** them, you rely on them to support you or help you. 依靠 ❑ *Don't count on Lillian.* 别依靠莉莲了。

▸ **count out** PHRASAL VERB If you **count out** a sum of money, you count the bills or coins as you put them in a pile one by one. 逐一数出 ❑ *Mr. Rohmbauer counted out the money and put it in an envelope.* 罗默保尔先生把钱逐一数出并放入信封。

▸ **count up** → see **count 2**

▸ **count upon** → see **count on**

count·able noun /kaʊntəbᵊl naʊn/ (**countable nouns**) N-COUNT A **countable noun** is the same as a **count noun**. 可数名词

count·down /kaʊntdaʊn/ N-SING A **countdown** is the counting aloud of numbers in reverse order before something happens, especially before a spacecraft is launched. 倒计时 [also no det] ❑ *The countdown has begun for the launch of the space shuttle.* 航天飞机发射前的倒计时已经开始。

coun·te·nance /kaʊntɪnəns/ (**countenances, countenancing, countenanced**) 1 V-T If someone will not **countenance** something, they do not agree with it and will not allow it to happen. 赞同 [usu with brd-neg] [FORMAL] ❑ *Jake would not countenance Janis's marrying while still a student.* 杰克不会赞同贾尼斯还是个学生就结婚。 2 N-COUNT Someone's **countenance** is their face. 面孔 [FORMAL]

coun·ter ♦◇◇ /kaʊntər/ (**counters, countering, countered**) 1 N-COUNT In a place such as a store or café, a **counter** is a long narrow table or flat surface at which customers are served. 柜台 ❑ *...those guys we see working behind the counter at our local video rental store.* …我们所见在本地音像出租商店柜台后工作的那些家伙。 2 N-COUNT A **counter** is a mechanical or electronic device which keeps a count of something and displays the total. 计数器 ❑ *The new answering machine has a call counter.* 这种新型的电话答录机有一个通话计数器。 3 N-COUNT A **counter** is a small, flat, round object used in board games. 棋子 ❑ *...a versatile book which provides boards and counters for fifteen different games.* …一本为15种不同棋类游戏提供棋盘和棋子的多功能书。 4 V-T/V-I If you do something to **counter** a particular action or process, you do something which has an opposite effect to it or makes it less effective. 抵消；抗衡 ❑ *The leadership discussed a plan of economic measures to counter the effects of such a blockade.* 领导层讨论了一项经济措施计划来抵消如此封锁的影响。 ❑ *Sears countered by filing an antitrust lawsuit.* 西尔斯通过提交反垄断诉讼进行了反击。 5 N-SING Something that is **a counter to** something else has an opposite effect to it or makes it less effective. 抵消物 ❑ *...NATO's traditional role as a counter to the military might of the Warsaw Pact.* …北大西洋公约组织作为华沙公约组织军事力量的遏制力量的传统角色。 6 PHRASE If a medicine can be bought **over the counter**, you do not need a prescription to buy it. 不用开处方地 ❑ *Are you taking any other medicines whether on prescription or bought over the counter?* 你还要其他药吗，不管是处方药还是非处方药？ ❑ *...over-the-counter medicines.* …非处方药。 7 PHRASE **Over-the-counter** shares are bought and sold directly rather than on a stock exchange. 不通过交易所的 [BUSINESS] ❑ *In national over-the-counter trading yesterday, Clarcor shares tumbled $6.125 to close at $35.625.* 昨天在全国场外交易中，克拉克股票跌$6.125，以$35.625收盘。

Word Partnership *counter* 的常用搭配：

PREP.	**behind the** counter, **on the** counter 1
	over the counter 6 7
N.	counter **an argument** 4

▲ **counter·act** /kaʊntərækt/ (**counteracts, counteracting, counteracted**) V-T To **counteract** something means to reduce its effect by doing something that produces an opposite effect. 对…起反作用；抵消 ❑ *My husband has to take several pills to counteract high blood pressure.* 我丈夫不得不吃几片药来抵制高血压。

C

counter·at·tack /kaʊntərətæk/ (**counterattacks, counterattacking, counterattacked**) V-I If you **counterattack**, you attack someone who has attacked you. 反击 ❑ *The security forces counterattacked the following day and quelled the unrest.* 安全部队第二天进行了反击，平息了骚乱。● N-COUNT **Counterattack** is also a noun. 反攻 ❑ *The army began its counterattack this morning.* 今天早晨部队开始了反攻。

★ **counter·clockwise** /kaʊntərklɒkwaɪz/ ADV If something is moving **counterclockwise**, it is moving in the opposite direction to the direction in which the hands of a clock move. 逆时针方向地 [ADV after V] [AM] ❑ *Rotate the head clockwise and counterclockwise.* 使头顺时针转转，再逆时针转转。● ADJ **Counterclockwise** is also an adjective. 逆时针方向的 [ADJ n]

in BRIT, use **anticlockwise**

❑ *The dance moves in a counterclockwise direction.* 这个舞是逆时针移动的。

▲ **counter·feit** /kaʊntərfɪt/ (**counterfeits, counterfeiting, counterfeited**) **1** ADJ **Counterfeit** money, goods, or documents are not genuine, but have been made to look exactly like genuine ones in order to deceive people. 伪造的 ❑ *He admitted possessing and delivering counterfeit currency.* 他承认持有和运送了假币。● N-COUNT **Counterfeit** is also a noun. 仿制品；伪造品 ❑ *Levi Strauss says counterfeits of the company's jeans are flooding Europe.* 利瓦伊・斯特劳斯说该公司牛仔裤的仿冒品充斥着欧洲市场。 **2** V-T If someone **counterfeits** something, they make a version of it that is not genuine but has been made to look genuine in order to deceive people. 仿冒；伪造 ❑ *...the coins Davies is alleged to have counterfeited.* …这些据称是戴维斯伪造的硬币。

★ **counter·part** ♦◇◇ /kaʊntərpɑrt/ (**counterparts**) N-COUNT Someone's or something's **counterpart** is another person or thing that has a similar function or position in a different place. 对应的人或物 ❑ *As soon as he heard what was afoot, he telephoned his German and Italian counterparts to protest.* 他一听到在进行中的事，马上就给德国和意大利相应人员打电话抗议。

counter·pro·duc·tive /kaʊntərprədʌktɪv/ ADJ Something that is **counterproductive** achieves the opposite result from the one that you want to achieve. 产生相反结果的 ❑ *In practice, however, such an attitude is counterproductive.* 然而在实际中，这种态度会适得其反。

coun·ter·ter·ror·ism //kaʊntərtɛrərɪzəm// N-UNCOUNT **Counterterrorism** consists of activities that are intended to prevent terrorist acts or to get rid of terrorist groups. 反恐行动 ● **coun·ter·ter·ror·ist** ADJ 反恐的 ❑ *There were gaps in their counterterrorist strategy.* 他们的反恐策略曾有一些漏洞。

counter·top /kaʊntərtɒp/ (**countertops**) N-COUNT A **countertop** is a flat surface in a kitchen which is easily cleaned and on which you can prepare food. (厨房的) 工作台面 [AM] ❑ *She reached for a cloth and began scouring the countertop.* 她伸手拿了一块布，开始擦厨房的操作台面。

count·less /kaʊntlɪs/ ADJ **Countless** means very many. 数不清的 [ADJ n] ❑ *She brought joy to countless people through her music.* 她通过自己的音乐把快乐带给了无数人。

count noun (**count nouns**) N-COUNT A **count noun** is a noun such as "bird," "chair," or "year" which has a singular and a plural form and is always used after a determiner in the singular. 可数名词

coun·try ♦♦♦ /kʌntri/ (**countries**) **1** N-COUNT A **country** is one of the political units which the world is divided into, covering a particular area of land. 国家 ❑ *Indonesia is the fifth most populous country in the world.* 印度尼西亚是世界上人口第五大国。 ❑ *...the boundary between the two countries.* …这两个国家的分界线。

Country is the most usual word to use when you are talking about the major political units that the world is divided into. **State** is used when you are talking about politics or government institutions. ❑ *...the new German state created by the unification process. ...Italy's state-controlled telecommunications company.* **State** can also refer to a political unit within a particular country. ❑ *...the state of California.* **Nation** is often used when you are talking about a country's inhabitants, and their cultural or ethnic background. ❑ *Wales is a proud nation with its own traditions... A senior government spokesman will address the nation.* **Land** is a less precise and more literary word, which you can use, for example, to talk about the feelings you have for a particular country. ❑ *She was fascinated to learn about this strange land at the edge of Europe.*

2 N-SING The people who live in a particular country can be referred to as **the country**. 国民 ❑ *Finally the country got some much-needed good news.* 最后该国人民得到了一些他们最需要的好消息。 **3** N-SING **The country** consists of places such as farms, open fields, and villages which are away from towns and cities. 乡村 ❑ *...a healthy life in the country.* …在乡村的健康生活。 ❑ *She was cycling along a country road near Compiègne.* 她正沿着贡比涅附近的一条乡间小路骑车。 **4** N-UNCOUNT A particular kind of **country** is an area of land which has particular characteristics or is connected with a particular well-known person. 地区 ❑ *Varese Ligure is a small town in mountainous country east of Genoa.* 瓦雷泽・利古里亚是一座位于热那亚东部山区的小镇。 **5** N-UNCOUNT **Country** music is popular music from the southern United States. 乡村(音乐) ❑ *For a long time I just wanted to play country music.* 在过去的很长一段时间，我只想演奏乡村音乐。

→ see Word Web: **country**

country·man /kʌntrimən/ (**countrymen**) **1** N-COUNT Your **countrymen** are people from your own country. 同胞 ❑ *He beat his fellow countryman, Andre Agassi, 6-4, 6-3, 6-2.* 他以6-4，6-3，6-2战胜了他的同胞安德烈・阿加西。 **2** N-COUNT A **countryman** is a person who lives in the country rather than in a city or a town. 乡下人 ❑ *He had the red face of a countryman.* 他有着乡下人的红润脸庞。

country·side ♦◇◇ /kʌntrisaɪd/ N-UNCOUNT **The countryside** is land which is away from towns and cities. 乡村 ❑ *I've always loved the English countryside.* 我一直很喜欢英国的乡村。

→ see **city**

Do not confuse **countryside**, **scenery**, **landscape**, and **nature**. **Countryside** is land which is away from towns and cities. ❑ *...3,500 acres of mostly flat countryside.* With **landscape**, the emphasis is on the physical features of the land, while **scenery** includes everything you can see when you look out over an area of land. ❑ *...the landscape of steep woods and distant mountains. ...unattractive urban scenery.* **Nature** includes the landscape, the weather, animals, and plants. ❑ *These creatures roamed the Earth as the finest and rarest wonders of nature.*

coun·ty ♦♦◇ /kaʊnti/ (**counties**) N-COUNT A **county** is a region of the U.S., Britain, or Ireland, which has its own local government. (英国、爱尔兰的) 郡；(美国的) 县 ❑ *He arrived at the Palm Beach County courthouse with his mother.* 他和母亲来到了棕榈滩县法院大楼。

▲ **coup** ♦◇◇ /ku/ (**coups**) **1** N-COUNT When there is a **coup**, a group of people seize power in a country. 政变 ❑ *...a military coup.* …一次军事政变。 **2** N-COUNT A **coup** is an achievement which is thought to be especially good because it was very difficult. 极为难

Word Web country

The largest **country** in the world geographically is Russia. It has an area of six million square miles and a **population** of more than 142 million people. Russia is a federal state with a republican form of **government**. The government is based in Russia's **capital** city, Moscow. One of the smallest countries in the world is Nauru. This tiny island **nation** in the South Pacific Ocean is 8.1 square miles in size. Many of Nauru's more than 13,000 **residents** live in Yaren, which is the largest city, but not the capital. The Republic of Nauru is the only nation in the world without an official capital.

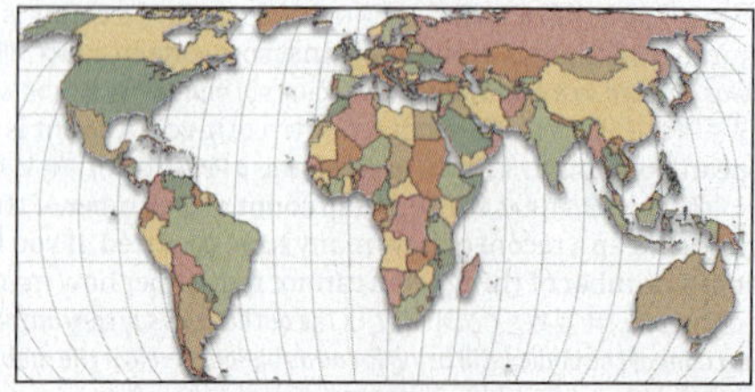

得的成就 ❑ *The sale is a big coup for the auction house.* 这次拍卖额对该拍卖行而言是极为难得的成就。

Word Partnership *coup* 的常用搭配：
N. coup **attempt**, **leader of the** coup **1**
V. **plot** a coup, **support the** coup **1**
ADJ. **bloodless** coup, **military** coup **1**
big coup **2**

coup d'état /kuː deɪtɑ/ (**coups d'état**) N-COUNT When there is a **coup d'état**, a group of people seize power in a country. 政变

cou·ple ♦♦◇ /kʌpᵊl/ (**couples, coupling, coupled**) **1** QUANT If you refer to **a couple of** people or things, you mean two or approximately two of them, although the exact number is not important or you are not sure of it. 一两个；几个 [QUANT "of" pl-n] ❑ *Across the street from me there are a couple of police officers standing guard.* 我所在的街对面有一两个警察在站岗。❑ *I think the trouble will clear up in a couple of days.* 我想几天内麻烦就会消除。● DET **Couple** is also a determiner in spoken American English, and is often used before "more" and "less." 几个 ❑ *...a couple weeks before the election.* …选举前的几周。● PRON **Couple** is also a pronoun. 几个 ❑ *I've got a couple that don't look too bad.* 我有几个，看上去还不错。**2** N-COUNT-COLL A **couple** is two people who are married, living together, or having a sexual relationship. 一对夫妇 ❑ *The couple have no children.* 这对夫妇没有孩子。❑ *Burglars ransacked an elderly couple's home.* 窃贼们洗劫了一对老夫妇的家。**3** N-COUNT-COLL A **couple** is two people that you see together on a particular occasion or that have some association. (特定场合或有特定联系的)一对人 ❑ *...as the four couples began the opening dance.* …随着4对舞伴跳起开场舞蹈。**4** V-T If you say that one thing produces a particular effect when it **is coupled with** another, you mean that the two things combine to produce that effect. 与…结合 [usu passive] ❑ *...a problem that is coupled with lower demand for the machines themselves.* …一个与对机器本身需求量减少连在一起的问题。

★ **cou·pon** /kuːpɒn, kyuː-/ (**coupons**) **1** N-COUNT A **coupon** is a piece of printed paper which allows you to pay less money than usual for a product, or to get it free. 优惠券 ❑ *...a money-saving coupon.* …一张省钱的优惠券。**2** N-COUNT A **coupon** is a small form, for example, in a newspaper or magazine, which you send off to ask for information, to order something, or to enter a competition. (报纸、杂志附的) 传单 ❑ *Mail this coupon with your check or money order.* 把这张表单和你的支票或汇款单一起邮寄。

Word Link *age ≈ state of, related to : courage, marriage, patronage*

cour·age ♦◇◇ /kɜrɪdʒ/ **1** N-UNCOUNT **Courage** is the quality shown by someone who decides to do something difficult or dangerous, even though they may be afraid. 勇气 ❑ *General Lewis Mackenzie has impressed everyone with his authority and personal courage.* 刘易斯·麦肯齐将军以其权威和个人勇气给每个人留下了深刻印象。**2** to **pluck up the courage** → see **pluck**

Word Partnership *courage* 的常用搭配：
V. **find the** courage, **have the** courage, **show** courage, courage **to do** *something* **1**
ADJ. **great** courage **1**

★ **cou·ra·geous** /kəreɪdʒəs/ ADJ Someone who is **courageous** shows courage. 勇敢的 ❑ *The children were very courageous.* 孩子们都很勇敢。

cour·gette /kʊrʒɛt/ (**courgettes**) N-VAR **Courgettes** are long thin vegetables with dark green skin. 密生西葫芦 [BRIT]
in AM, use **zucchini**

cou·ri·er /kʊəriər, kɜr-/ (**couriers, couriering, couriered**) **1** N-COUNT A **courier** is a person who is paid to take letters and packages direct from one place to another. 信使 ❑ *...a motorcycle courier.* …一名骑摩托车的信使。**2** V-T If you **courier** something somewhere, you send it there by courier. 让信使送 ❑ *I couriered it to Darren in New York.* 我让信使把它送给在纽约的达伦。

course ♦♦♦ /kɔrs/ (**courses**) **1** **Course** is often used in the expression "of course," or instead of "of course" in informal spoken English. See **of course**. 当然(在口语中代替**of course**) **2** N-UNCOUNT The **course** of a vehicle, especially a ship or aircraft, is the route along which it is traveling. 路线 [also "a" N] ❑ *Aircraft can avoid each other by altering course to left or right.* 飞行器可以通过向左或向右改变航线来避免相撞。**3** N-COUNT A **course of** action is an action or a series of actions that you can do in a particular situation. 做法 ❑ *My best course of action was to help Gill by being sympathetic.* 我最好的做法是通过表达同情去帮助吉尔。**4** N-COUNT A **course** is a series of lessons or lectures on a particular subject. 课程 ❑ *...a course in business administration.* …一门工商管理课程。**5** → see also **correspondence course, refresher course** **6** N-COUNT A **course of** medical treatment is a series of treatments that a doctor gives someone. 疗程 ❑ *He had a course of antibiotics to kill the bacterium.* 他服了一疗程的抗生素来杀死细菌。**7** N-COUNT A **course** is one part of a meal. 一道菜 ❑ *The lunch was excellent, especially the first course.* 午饭非常好吃，尤其是第一道菜。**8** N-COUNT In sports, a **course** is an area of land where races are held or golf is played, or the land over which a race takes place. 跑马场；跑道；高尔夫球场 ❑ *Only 12 seconds separated the first three riders on the course.* 跑道上的前3名选手12秒就拉开距离了。**9** N-COUNT The **course** of a river is the channel along which it flows. 河道 ❑ *Romantic castles overlook the river's twisting course.* 一座座传奇式的城堡俯瞰着小河蜿蜒曲折的河道。**10** **in due course** → see **due** **11** PHRASE If something happens **in the course of** a particular period of time, it happens during that period of time. 在…期间 ❑ *In the course of the 1930s steel production approximately doubled.* 20世纪30年代间，钢产量几乎翻了一番。**12** PHRASE If you do something **as a matter of course**, you do it as part of your normal work or way of life. 作为理所当然的事 ❑ *If police are carrying arms as a matter of course, then doesn't it encourage criminals to carry them?* 如果警察理所当然地携带武器，这难道不是鼓励罪犯也携带武器吗？**13** PHRASE If a ship or aircraft is **on course**, it is traveling along the correct route. If it is **off course**, it is no longer traveling along the correct route. 在正确路线上/偏离正确路线 ❑ *The ship was sent off course into shallow waters.* 轮船被驶出轨，进入了浅水区。**14** PHRASE If you are **on course for** something, you are likely to achieve it. 极有可能得到… ❑ *The company is on course for profits of $20m.* 这家公司的利润有望达到2000万美元。

Word Partnership *course* 的常用搭配：
N. course **of** *something* **2 3 6**
course **of action** **3**
course **on** *something* **4**
golf course **8**
ADJ. **full-time** course **4**
main course **7**

course book (**course books**) also **coursebook** N-COUNT A **course book** is a textbook that students and teachers use as the basis of a course. 教科书

course work also **coursework** N-UNCOUNT **Course work** is work that students do during a course, rather than in exams, especially work that counts toward a student's final grade. 课程作业 ❑ *Some 20 percent of grades are awarded for coursework.* 课程作业占分数的20%左右。

❶ **court** ♦♦♦ /kɔrt/ (**courts**) **1** N-COUNT A **court** is a place where legal matters are decided by a judge and jury or by a magistrate. 法庭 [oft n N, N n, also "in/at" N] ❑ *At this rate, we could find ourselves in the divorce courts!* 照这样下去，我们可能会在离婚法庭上对簿公堂！❑ *...a county court judge.* …一名县法院的法官。**2** N-COUNT You can refer to the people in a court, especially the judge, jury, or magistrates, as a **court**. (一次开庭的) 全体审判人员 ❑ *A court at Tampa, Florida has convicted five officials on charges of handling millions of dollars earned from illegal drug deals.* 佛罗里达州坦帕市的一个法庭宣布被指控通过非法毒品买卖获取上百万美元的5名官员罪名成立。**3** N-COUNT A **court** is an area in which you play a game such as tennis, basketball, badminton, or squash. 球场 [usu supp N, also "on/off" N] ❑ *The hotel has several tennis and squash courts.* 该旅馆有几个网球场和壁球场。**4** N-COUNT The **court** of a king or queen is the place where he or she lives and carries out ceremonial or administrative duties. 王宫 ❑ *She came to visit England, where she was presented at the court of James I.* 她来访问英格兰，在詹姆斯一世的王宫受到了接见。**5** PHRASE If you **go to court** or **take** someone **to court**, you take legal action against them. 起诉 ❑ *They have received at least twenty thousand dollars each but went to court to demand more.* 他们每人

C

至少已经得到了两万美元，但还起诉以求得到更多。 6 PHRASE If a legal matter is decided or settled **out of court**, it is decided without legal action being taken in a court of law. 不经法院庭审的 ❑ *The Government is anxious to keep the whole case out of court.* 政府急于把整个案子庭外了结。

→ see **park**

C

Word Partnership *court* 的常用搭配：
V. **appear in** court, **hold** court ❶ 1
go to court ❶ 1 5

❷ **court** /kɔrt/ (**courts, courting, courted**) 1 V-T To **court** a particular person, group, or country means to try to please them or improve your relations with them, often so that they will do something that you want them to do. 讨好；取悦 [JOURNALISM] ❑ *Both Democratic and Republican parties are courting former supporters of Ross Perot.* 民主党和共和党都在讨好以前罗斯・佩罗的支持者。 2 V-T If you **court** something such as publicity or popularity, you try to attract it. 设法获得 ❑ *Having spent a lifetime avidly courting publicity, Paul has suddenly become secretive.* 花了一生的时间狂热地追求出名之后，保罗突然变得遮遮掩掩起来了。 3 V-T If you **court** something unpleasant such as disaster or unpopularity, you act in a way that makes it likely to happen. 招致 ❑ *If he thinks he can remain in power by force, he is courting disaster.* 如果他认为可以通过武力维持权力的话，那就是在招灾惹祸。 4 V-RECIP If you **are courting** someone of the opposite sex, you spend a lot of time with them, because you are intending to get married. You can also say that a man and a woman **are courting**. 对…求爱；谈恋爱 [OLD-FASHIONED] ❑ *I was courting Billy at 19 and married him when I was 21.* 我19岁时和比利谈恋爱，21岁时嫁给了他。

▲ **cour·teous** /kɜrtiəs/ ADJ Someone who is **courteous** is polite and respectful to other people. 彬彬有礼的 ❑ *He was a kind and courteous man.* 他善良且彬彬有礼。 ● **cour·teous·ly** ADV 彬彬有礼地 ❑ *Then he nodded courteously to me and walked off to perform his unpleasant duty.* 他彬彬有礼地向我点点头，然后就走开去执行他令人讨厌的任务。

★ **cour·tesy** /kɜrtɪsi/ 1 N-UNCOUNT **Courtesy** is politeness, respect, and consideration for others. 彬彬有礼 [FORMAL] ❑ *...a gentleman who behaves with the utmost courtesy towards ladies.* …一位对女士极为彬彬有礼的绅士。 2 N-SING If you refer to **the courtesy of** doing something, you are referring to a polite action. 彬彬有礼的举止 [FORMAL] ❑ *By extending the courtesy of a phone call to my clients, I was building a personal relationship with them.* 通过给客户打电话这样有礼的行为，我渐渐和他们建立起私交。 3 ADJ **Courtesy** is used to describe services that are provided free of charge by an organization to its customers, or to the general public. 免费的 [ADJ n] ❑ *A courtesy shuttle bus operates between the hotel and the town.* 一辆免费运送班车在旅馆和小镇之间往返。 4 ADJ A **courtesy** call or a **courtesy** visit is a formal visit that you pay someone as a way of showing them politeness or respect. 出于礼节的 [ADJ n] ❑ *The president paid a courtesy call on Emperor Akihito.* 总统礼节性地拜访了明仁天皇。 5 PHRASE If something is provided **courtesy of** someone or **by courtesy of** someone, they provide it. You often use this expression in order to thank them. 蒙…的好意 ❑ *The waitress brings over some congratulatory glasses of champagne, courtesy of the restaurant.* 蒙饭店的好意，女侍者们送过来几杯表示祝贺的香槟酒。

court·house /kɔrthaʊs/ (**courthouses**) 1 N-COUNT A **courthouse** is a building in which a court of law meets. 法院大楼 [AM]

in BRIT, use **court**

❑ *The two were tried in the same courthouse at the same time, on separate floors.* 这两个人在同一时间、同一座法院大楼、不同的楼层接受了审判。 2 N-COUNT A **courthouse** is a building used by the government of a county. 县政府大楼 [AM] ❑ *They were married at the Los Angeles County Courthouse.* 他们在洛杉矶县政府大楼结的婚。

cour·ti·er /kɔrtiər/ (**courtiers**) N-COUNT **Courtiers** were noblemen and women who spent a lot of time at the court of a king or queen. 朝臣

court mar·tial (**court martials, court martialing** or **court martialling, court martialed** or **court martialled**) also **court-martial**

Courts martial is also used as a plural form for the noun.

1 N-VAR A **court martial** is a trial in a military court of a member of the armed forces who is charged with breaking a military law. 军事法庭的审判 ❑ *He is due to face a court martial on drugs charges.* 他将因毒品指控而面临军事法庭的审判。 2 V-T If a member of the armed forces **is court martialed**, he or she is tried in a military court. 受军法审判 [usu passive] ❑ *I was court martialed and sentenced to six months in a military prison.* 我受到了军事法庭的审判，被判在军事监狱服刑6个月。

court·room /kɔrtrum/ (**courtrooms**) N-COUNT A **courtroom** is a room in which a legal court meets. 审判室；法庭

court shoe (**court shoes**) 1 N-COUNT **Court shoes** are shoes worn for sports such as tennis or squash. (如网球、壁球) 球鞋 [usu pl] [AM] 2 N-COUNT **Court shoes** are the same as **pumps**. 短脸鞋 [BRIT]

court·yard /kɔrtyard/ (**courtyards**) N-COUNT A **courtyard** is an open area of ground which is surrounded by buildings or walls. 庭院 ❑ *They walked together through the arch and into the cobbled courtyard.* 他们一起走过拱门，来到了铺着鹅卵石的庭院。

cous·in ◆◆◇ /kʌzᵊn/ (**cousins**) N-COUNT Your **cousin** is the child of your uncle or aunt. 堂兄弟姐妹；表兄弟姐妹 ❑ *My cousin Mark helped me to bring in the bags.* 我表弟马克帮我把包提了进来。

cove /koʊv/ (**coves**) N-COUNT; N-IN-NAMES A **cove** is a part of a coast where the land curves inward so that the sea is partly enclosed. 小海湾 ❑ *The house is situated on a hillside overlooking Fairview Cove.* 这座房子位于山坡上，俯瞰费尔维尤海湾。

cov·enant /kʌvənənt/ (**covenants**) 1 N-COUNT A **covenant** is a formal written agreement between two or more people or groups of people which is recognized in law. 契约；公约 ❑ *...the International Covenant on Civil and Political Rights.* …公民权利和政治权利国际公约。 2 N-COUNT A **covenant** is a formal written promise to pay a sum of money each year for a fixed period, especially to a charity. (尤指定期向慈善机构捐款的) 契约 [also "by" N] [mainly BRIT]

in AM, usually use **pledge**

cover
❶ VERB USES
❷ NOUN USES

❶ **cov·er** ◆◆◆ /kʌvər/ (**covers, covering, covered**) 1 V-T If you **cover** something, you place something else over it in order to protect it, hide it, or close it. 盖 ❑ *Cover the casserole with a tight-fitting lid.* 用紧实的盖子把砂锅盖住。 ❑ *He whimpered and covered his face.* 他呜咽着捂住了脸。 2 V-T If one thing **covers** another, it has been placed over it in order to protect it, hide it, or close it. 盖住 ❑ *His finger went up to touch the black patch which covered his left eye.* 他的手指抬起来去摸盖在他左眼上的黑眼罩。 3 V-T If one thing **covers** another, it forms a layer over its surface. 覆盖 ❑ *The clouds had spread and covered the entire sky.* 乌云铺开，遮蔽了整个天空。 4 V-T To **cover** something **with** or **in** something else means to put a layer of the second thing over its surface. 铺盖 ❑ *The desk was covered with papers.* 书桌上铺了些报纸。 5 V-T If you **cover** a particular distance, you travel that distance. 走过 (一段距离) ❑ *It would not be easy to cover ten miles on that amount of gas.* 要靠那些数量的汽油跑10英里可不容易。 6 V-T An insurance policy that **covers** a person or thing guarantees that money will be paid by the insurance company in relation to that person or thing. 保险 ❑ *Their insurer paid the $900 bill, even though the policy did not strictly cover it.* 他们的保险公司赔付了他们$900，尽管保单并没有严格保到此项。 7 V-T If a law **covers** a particular set of people, things, or situations, it applies to them. 适用于 ❑ *The law covers four categories of experiments.* 这一原理适用于4类试验。 8 V-T If you **cover** a particular topic, you discuss it in a lecture, course, or book. 论及 ❑ *Introduction to Chemistry aims to cover important topics in organic chemistry.* 《化学入门》意在论及有机化学的重要问题。 9 V-T If a sum of money **covers** something, it is enough to pay for it. 足够支付 ❑ *Send it to the address given with $2.50 to cover postage and administration.* 把这封信寄到所给地址，$2.50足以支付邮资和手续费。 10 V-I If you **cover for** someone who is doing something secret or illegal, you give false information or do not give all the information you have, in order to protect them. 包庇 ❑ *Why would she cover for someone who was trying to kill her?* 她为何要包庇那个试图要杀死她的人呢？ 11 V-I If you **cover for** someone who is ill or away, you do their work for them while they are not there. 代替 ❑ *She did not have enough nurses to cover for those who were sick.* 她没有足够的护士来代替她们生病的同事的工作。 12 PHRASE If you **cover** your **ass** or

cover your **butt**, you do something in order to protect yourself, for example against criticism or against accusations of doing something wrong. 为自己开脱 [INFORMAL, VULGAR]

▸ **cover up** 1 PHRASAL VERB If you **cover** something or someone **up**, you put something over them in order to protect or hide them. 把…盖上 ❑ *He fell asleep in the front room so I covered him up with a duvet.* 他在前屋睡着了，所以我给他盖上了一床羽绒被。 2 PHRASAL VERB If you **cover up** something that you do not want people to know about, you hide the truth about it. 隐藏；掩盖 ❑ *He suspects there's a conspiracy to cover up the crime.* 他怀疑有掩盖这桩罪行的阴谋。 ❑ *They knew they had done something terribly wrong and lied to cover it up.* 他们知道已犯下了大错，并撒谎来掩盖这一错误。 3 → see also **cover-up**

Thesaurus *cover* 另参见：
V. conceal, drape, hide, screen; (*ant.*) uncover ❶ 1–3
guard, insure, protect ❶ 6

❷ **cov·er** ♦♦♦ /kʌvər/ (**covers**) 1 N-COUNT A **cover** is something which is put over an object, usually in order to protect it. 套子 ❑ *...a sofa with washable covers.* …一张沙发套可拆洗的沙发。 2 N-COUNT The **cover** of a book or a magazine is the outside part of it. 封面 ❑ *...a small book with a green cover.* …一本绿色封面的小册子。 3 N-UNCOUNT **Cover** is protection from enemy attack that is provided for troops or ships carrying out a particular operation, for example, by aircraft. 掩护 ❑ *They could not provide adequate air cover for ground operations.* 他们无法为地面作战行动提供足够的空中掩护。 4 N-UNCOUNT **Cover** is trees, rocks, or other places where you shelter from the weather or from an attack, or hide from someone. 掩蔽处 ❑ *Charles lit the fuses and they ran for cover.* 查尔斯点燃了导火索，大家跑向掩蔽处。 5 N-UNCOUNT Insurance **cover** is a guarantee from an insurance company that money will be paid by them if it is needed. (保险) 保障 ❑ *Make sure that the firm's insurance cover is adequate.* 要确保该公司的保险保障是足够的。 6 N-COUNT Something that is a **cover** for secret or illegal activities seems respectable or normal, and is intended to hide the activities. 掩护 ❑ *He ran a construction company as a cover for drug dealing.* 他经营了一家建筑公司，作为毒品交易的掩护。 7 N-PLURAL The **covers** on your bed are the things such as sheets and blankets that you have on top of you. 床上盖具 ❑ *She set her glass down and slid under the covers.* 她放下杯子，钻进了被子。 8 → see also **covering** 9 PHRASE If you **take cover**, you shelter from gunfire, bombs, or the weather. 躲避 ❑ *Shoppers took cover behind cars as the gunman fired.* 持枪歹徒开枪时，购物者们都躲到了汽车后面。 10 PHRASE If you do something **under cover of** a particular situation, you are able to do it without being noticed because of that situation. 在…的掩护下 ❑ *They move under cover of darkness.* 他们在黑夜的掩护下行进。

Word Partnership *cover* 的常用搭配：
N. cover *your face* ❶ 1 2
PREP. covered *in something* ❶ 4
under cover ❷ 10
V. **run for** cover ❷ 4
take cover ❷ 9

★ **cov·er·age** ♦◇◇ /kʌvərɪdʒ/ N-UNCOUNT The **coverage** of something in the news is the reporting of it. 报道 ❑ *Now a special TV network gives live coverage of most races.* 现在一个专门的电视网对大多数比赛进行现场报道。

cov·er·ing /kʌvərɪŋ/ (**coverings**) N-COUNT A **covering** is a layer of something that protects or hides something else. 保护层；遮盖层 ❑ *Leave a thin covering of fat.* 留下一层薄脂肪层。

cov·er·ing let·ter [BRIT] → see **cover letter**

cov·er let·ter (**cover letters**) N-COUNT A **cover letter** is a letter that you send with a package or with another letter in order to provide extra information. 附信 [AM] ❑ *Your cover letter creates the employer's first impression of you.* 你的附信会建立雇主对你的第一印象。

co·vert /koʊvɜrt, kʌvərt/ ADJ **Covert** activities or situations are secret or hidden. 隐秘的 [FORMAL] ❑ *They have been supplying covert military aid to the rebels.* 他们一直在为叛军提供隐秘的军事援助。 ● **co·vert·ly** ADV 隐秘地 ❑ *They covertly observed Lauren, who was sitting between Ned and Algie at a nearby table.* 他们秘密地观察着邻近桌子上坐在内德和阿尔吉之间的罗伦。

cov·er-up (**cover-ups**) also **coverup** N-COUNT A **cover-up** is an attempt to hide a crime or mistake. (对罪行、错误的) 掩盖 ❑ *General Schwarzkopf denied there'd been any cover-up.* 施瓦茨科夫将军否认有任何遮掩。

cov·et /kʌvɪt/ (**covets, coveting, coveted**) V-T If you **covet** something, you strongly want to have it for yourself. 对…垂涎三尺 [FORMAL] ❑ *She coveted his job so openly that their conversations were tense.* 她如此公开地对他的工作垂涎三尺，以至两人之间的谈话很紧张。

cov·et·ed /kʌvɪtɪd/ ADJ You use **coveted** to describe something that very many people would like to have. 令人垂涎的 ❑ *Allan Little from Radio 4 took the coveted title of reporter of the year.* 第4电台的艾伦·利特尔获得了令人垂涎的年度记者的头衔。 ❑ *...one of sport's most coveted trophies.* …体育界最令人向往的奖杯之一。

cow ♦◇◇ /kaʊ/ (**cows, cowing, cowed**) 1 N-COUNT A **cow** is a large female animal that is kept on farms for its milk. People sometimes refer to male and female animals of this species as **cows**. 母牛；奶牛 ❑ *He kept a few dairy cows.* 他养了几头奶牛。 ❑ *Dad went out to milk the cows.* 爸爸出去给牛挤奶去了。 2 N-COUNT Some female animals, including elephants and whales, are called **cows**. 大型雌兽 ❑ *...a cow elephant.* …一头母象。 3 V-T If someone **is cowed**, they are made afraid, or made to behave in a particular way because they have been frightened or badly treated. 胁迫；恐吓 [usu passive] [FORMAL] ❑ *The government, far from being cowed by these threats, has vowed to continue its policy.* 政府根本没有被这些威胁吓倒，发誓要继续执行自己的政策。 ● **cowed** ADJ 受到胁迫的；受到恐吓的 ❑ *By this time she was so cowed by the beatings that she meekly obeyed.* 到了这时候她被这些殴打吓得不行，以至温顺地服从。
→ see **barn, dairy, meat**

cow·ard /kaʊərd/ (**cowards**) N-COUNT If you call someone a **coward**, you disapprove of them because they are easily frightened and avoid dangerous or difficult situations. 胆小鬼 [DISAPPROVAL] ❑ *She accused her husband of being a coward.* 她指责自己的丈夫是个胆小鬼。

cow·ard·ice /kaʊərdɪs/ N-UNCOUNT **Cowardice** is cowardly behavior. 胆小；怯懦 ❑ *He openly accused his opponents of cowardice.* 他公开指责对手胆小怯懦。

cow·ard·ly /kaʊərdli/ ADJ If you describe someone as **cowardly**, you disapprove of them because they are easily frightened and avoid doing dangerous and difficult things. 胆小的；怯懦的 [DISAPPROVAL] ❑ *I was too cowardly to complain.* 我胆小得都不敢抱怨。

cow·boy /kaʊbɔɪ/ (**cowboys**) 1 N-COUNT A **cowboy** is a male character in a western. (美国西部的) 牛仔 ❑ *Boys used to play at cowboys and Indians.* 男孩子们过去常玩牛仔和印第安人的游戏。 2 N-COUNT A **cowboy** is a man employed to look after cattle in North America, especially in former times. (尤指旧时北美地区的) 牧牛工 ❑ *In his twenties Roosevelt had sought work as a cowboy on a ranch in the Dakota Territory.* 二十多岁时，罗斯福曾经到达科他地区的一个大牧场去找牧牛工的活儿。
→ see **horse**

★ **co·worker** /koʊwɜrkər/ (**coworkers**) also **co-worker** N-COUNT Your **coworkers** are the people you work with, especially people on the same job or project as you. 同事

coy /kɔɪ/ 1 ADJ A **coy** person is shy, or pretends to be shy, about love and sex. 腼腆的；扭怩作态的 ❑ *I was sickened by the way Carol charmed all the men by turning coy.* 我对卡罗尔扭怩作态哄诱男人的方式感到恶心。 ● **coy·ly** ADV 腼腆地；扭怩作态地 [ADV with v] ❑ *She smiled coyly at Algie as he took her hand and raised it to his lips.* 当阿尔吉拿起她的手举到他唇边时，她腼腆地对他微笑。 2 ADJ If someone is being **coy**, they are unwilling to talk about something that they feel guilty or embarrassed about. 不愿谈及的 ❑ *Mr. Alexander is not the slightest bit coy about his ambitions.* 亚历山大先生对自己的抱负一丁点也不保留。 ● **coy·ly** ADV 不愿谈及地 [ADV with v] ❑ *The administration coyly refused to put a firm figure on the war's costs.* 政府委婉地拒绝了就战争费用给出一个明确的数字。

★ **cozy** /koʊzi/ (**cozies, cozier, coziest**)
in BRIT, use **cosy**
1 ADJ A house or room that is **cozy** is comfortable and warm. (指房子或房间) 温暖舒适的 ❑ *Downstairs there's a breakfast room and guests can relax in the cozy bar.* 楼下有个早餐室，客人们可以在温暖舒适的酒吧间休息。 2 ADJ If you are **cozy**, you are comfortable and warm. (指人) 温暖舒适的 [v-link ADJ] ❑ *They like to make sure their guests are comfortable and cozy.* 他们喜欢保证客人们都舒适、惬意。 3 ADJ You use **cozy** to describe activities that are pleasant and friendly, and involve people who know each other well. 亲切的

❑ ...a cozy chat between friends. …朋友间亲切的交谈。 4 N-COUNT A **cozy** or a **tea cozy** is a soft knitted or fabric cover which you put over a teapot in order to keep the tea hot. 茶壶套 ❑ *...unusual miniature tea sets, elegant tea accessories, colorful cozies.* …与众不同的微型套装茶具，雅致的茶配件，色彩缤纷的茶壶套。 ❑ *...a whimsical tea cozy printed with a bright scene of the Tower of London.* …一个印有伦敦塔明快图景的别出心裁的茶壶套。

C

CPU /si pi yu/ (**CPUs**) N-COUNT In a computer, the **CPU** is the part that processes all the data and makes the computer work. **CPU** is an abbreviation for "central processing unit." 中央处理器 [COMPUTING]

▲ **crab** /kræb/ (**crabs**) N-COUNT A **crab** is a sea creature with a flat round body covered by a shell, and five pairs of legs with large claws on the front pair. Crabs usually move sideways. 螃蟹 ● N-UNCOUNT **Crab** is the flesh of this creature eaten as food. 蟹肉 ❑ *I can't remember when I last had crab.* 我不记得上次吃蟹是什么时候了。

crack
❶ VERB USES
❷ NOUN AND ADJECTIVE USES

❶ **crack** ♦◇◇ /kræk/ (**cracks, cracking, cracked**) 1 V-T/V-I If something hard **cracks**, or if you **crack** it, it becomes slightly damaged, with lines appearing on its surface. 使…破裂；破裂 ❑ *A gas main had cracked under my neighbor's garage and gas had seeped into our homes.* 邻居家车库下的煤气主管道破裂了，煤气渗漏进我们家。 2 V-T/V-I If something **cracks**, or if you **crack** it, it makes a sharp sound like the sound of a piece of wood breaking. 使…噼啪作响；发出辟裂声 ❑ *Thunder cracked in the sky.* 空中雷声炸响。 3 V-T If you **crack** a hard part of your body, such as your knee or your head, you hurt it by accidentally hitting it hard against something. 撞击 ❑ *He cracked his head on the pavement and was knocked cold.* 他的头撞着了路面，撞昏了。 4 V-T When you **crack** something that has a shell, such as an egg or a nut, you break the shell in order to reach the inside part. 叩开 ❑ *Crack the eggs into a bowl.* 把鸡蛋打到碗中。 5 V-T If you **crack** a problem or a code, you solve it, especially after a lot of thought. 破解（难题、密码） ❑ *He has finally cracked the system after years of painstaking research.* 经过数年的艰苦研究，他最终破译了该系统。 6 V-I If someone **cracks**, they lose control of their emotions or actions because they are under a lot of pressure. （精神）垮掉 [INFORMAL] ❑ *She's calm and strong, and she is just not going to crack.* 她冷静而坚强，决不会垮掉的。 7 V-I If your voice **cracks** when you are speaking or singing, it changes in pitch because you are feeling a strong emotion. （嗓音）突然变化 ❑ *Her voice cracked and she began to cry.* 她失声哭了起来。 8 V-T If you **crack** a joke, you tell it. 说（笑话） ❑ *He drove a Volkswagen, cracked jokes, and talked about beer and girls.* 那时他开着一辆大众牌汽车，讲着笑话，谈论着啤酒和女孩。
→ see **crash**

▶ **crack down** 1 PHRASAL VERB If people in authority **crack down on** a group of people, they become stricter in making the group obey rules or laws. 严加管制；严加治理 ❑ *The government has cracked down hard on those campaigning for greater democracy.* 政府严厉打击了那些争取更多民主的人。 2 → see also **crackdown**

▶ **crack up** 1 PHRASAL VERB If someone **cracks up**, they are under such a lot of emotional strain that they become mentally ill. 得精神病 [INFORMAL] ❑ *She would have cracked up if she hadn't allowed herself some fun.* 要不是她允许自己享受一些乐趣，她早就得精神病了。 2 PHRASAL VERB If you **crack up** or if someone or something **cracks you up**, you laugh a lot. 哈哈大笑；使…哈哈大笑 [INFORMAL] ❑ *She told stories that cracked me up and I swore to write them down so you could enjoy them too.* 她讲了些让我哈哈大笑的故事，我发誓要把那些故事写下来，以便你们也可以欣赏。

❷ **crack** /kræk/ (**cracks**) 1 N-COUNT A **crack** is a very narrow gap between two things, or between two parts of a thing. 裂缝 ❑ *Kathryn had seen him through a crack in the curtains.* 凯瑟琳曾从帘子的裂缝看到过他。 2 N-COUNT A **crack** is a line that appears on the surface of something when it is slightly damaged. 裂纹 ❑ *The plate had a crack in it.* 这盘子上有条裂纹。 3 N-SING If you open something such as a door, window, or curtain **a crack**, you open it only a small amount. 缝隙 ❑ *He went to the door, opened it a crack, and listened.* 他走到门边，把门打开一条缝，听了起来。 4 N-COUNT; SOUND A **crack** is a sharp sound, like the sound of a piece of wood breaking. 爆裂声 ❑ *Suddenly there was a loud crack and glass flew into the car.* 突然一阵巨大的爆裂声，碎玻璃飞溅进了车内。 5 N-UNCOUNT **Crack** is a very pure form of the drug cocaine. 强效纯可卡因 6 ADJ A **crack** soldier or sportsman is highly trained and very skillful. 训练有素的 [ADJ n] ❑ *...a crack undercover police officer.* …一名训练有素的卧底警察。 7 N-COUNT A **crack** is a slightly rude or cruel joke. （挖苦人的）笑话 ❑ *Tell Tracy you're sorry for that crack about her weight.* 告诉特蕾西你对那个有关她体重的玩笑感到抱歉。

Word Partnership *crack* 的常用搭配：

ADV.	crack **open** ❶ 1 4
N.	crack **a code**, crack **the system** ❶ 5
	crack **jokes** ❶ 8
ADJ.	**deep** crack ❷ 1 2
V.	**have a** crack ❷ 1 2

★ **crack·down** /krækdaʊn/ (**crackdowns**) N-COUNT A **crackdown** is strong official action that is taken to punish people who break laws. 严惩措施；镇压 ❑ *...anti-government unrest that ended with the violent army crackdown.* …因遭到暴力武装镇压而告终的反政府动乱。

▲ **crack·er** /krækər/ (**crackers**) N-COUNT A **cracker** is a thin, crisp piece of baked bread which is often eaten with cheese. 薄脆饼干

crack·le /krækᵊl/ (**crackles, crackling, crackled**) V-I If something **crackles**, it makes a rapid series of short, harsh noises. 发出连续急促刺耳的声音；发劈啪声 ❑ *The radio crackled again.* 收音机又吱吱地响了起来。 ● N-COUNT **Crackle** is also a noun. 噼啪声 ❑ *...the crackle of flames and gunfire.* …火焰和炮火的噼啪声。

★ **cra·dle** /kreɪdᵊl/ (**cradles, cradling, cradled**) 1 N-COUNT A **cradle** is a baby's bed with high sides. Cradles often have curved bases so that they rock from side to side. 摇篮 2 V-T If you **cradle** someone or something **in** your arms or hands, you hold them carefully and gently. （小心轻柔地）抱着 ❑ *I cradled her in my arms.* 我把她小心轻柔地抱在怀中。

craft ♦◇◇ /kræft/ (**crafts, crafting, crafted**)

Craft is both the singular and the plural form for meaning 1.

1 N-COUNT You can refer to a boat, a spacecraft, or an aircraft as a **craft**. 船；航天器；航空器 ❑ *With great difficulty, the fisherman maneuvered his small craft close to the reef.* 渔夫艰难地驾着小船靠近了礁石。 2 N-COUNT A **craft** is an activity such as weaving, carving, or pottery that involves making things skillfully with your hands. 工艺 ❑ *...the arts and crafts of the North American Indians.* …北美印第安人的美术工艺。 3 N-COUNT You can use **craft** to refer to any activity or job that involves doing something skillfully. 职业 ❑ *...the craft of writing.* …写作工作。 4 V-T If something **is crafted**, it is made skillfully. 精心制作 [usu passive] ❑ *The windows would probably have been crafted in the latter part of the Middle Ages.* 这些窗户可能是中世纪后期精制而成。 ❑ *...original, hand-crafted bags at affordable prices.* …价格适中的独创手工包。
→ see **fly, ship**

crafts·man /kræftsmən/ (**craftsmen**) N-COUNT A **craftsman** is a man who makes things skillfully with his hands. 手艺人；工匠 ❑ *The table in the kitchen was made by a local craftsman.* 厨房里的桌子是当地一名工匠做的。

crafts·man·ship /kræftsmənʃɪp/ N-UNCOUNT **Craftsmanship** is the skill that someone uses when they make beautiful things with their hands. 手艺 ❑ *It is easy to appreciate the craftsmanship of Armani.* 很容易鉴赏出阿玛尼的手艺。

crafty /kræfti/ (**craftier, craftiest**) ADJ If you describe someone as **crafty**, you mean that they achieve what they want in a clever way, often by deceiving people. 诡计多端的；狡猾的 ❑ *...a crafty, lying character who enjoys plotting against others.* …一个诡计多端、谎话连篇、好耍手段对付别人的家伙。 ❑ *A crafty look came to his eyes.* 他眼中露出狡猾的神情。

▲ **cram** /kræm/ (**crams, cramming, crammed**) 1 V-T If you **cram** things or people **into** a container or place, you put them into it, although there is hardly enough room for them. 把…塞进 ❑ *Terry crammed the dirty clothes into his bag.* 特里把脏衣服塞进了包里。 ❑ *She crammed her mouth with caviar.* 她塞了一嘴鱼子酱。 2 V-T/V-I If people **cram into** a place or vehicle or **cram** a place or vehicle, so many of them enter it at one time that it is completely full. 挤满；塞进 ❑ *We crammed into my car and set off.* 我们挤进我的汽车，出发了。 3 V-I If you **are cramming for** an examination, you are learning as much as possible in a short time just before you take the examination. 突击准备（考试）❑ *She was cramming for her Economics exam.* 她正为了应付经济学考试而临时抱佛脚。 ● **cram·ming** N-UNCOUNT（考试的）突击准备 ❑ *It would take two or three months of cramming to prepare for Vermont's bar exam.* 佛蒙特州的律师考试需要2到3个月时间的突击准备。

crammed /kræmd/ 1 ADJ If a place is **crammed with** things or people, it is full of them, so that there is hardly room for anything or anyone else. 塞满的 ❑ *The house is crammed with priceless furniture and works of art.* 这房子里堆满了价值连城的家具和艺术品。 2 ADJ If people or things are **crammed into** a place or vehicle, it is full of them. 挤满的 [v-link ADJ] ❑ *Between two and three thousand refugees were crammed into the church buildings.* 两到三千名难民挤进了教堂里。

▲ **cramp** /kræmp/ (**cramps, cramping, cramped**) 1 N-VAR A **cramp** is a sudden strong pain caused by a muscle suddenly contracting. You sometimes get cramps in a muscle after you have been making a physical effort over a long period of time. 抽筋 [also N in pl] ❑ *Hillsden was complaining of a cramp in his calf muscles.* 希尔斯登刚才一直在抱怨他小腿肌肉抽筋。 ❑ *...muscle cramps.* …肌肉痉挛。 2 PHRASE If someone or something **cramps** your **style**, their presence or existence restricts your behavior in some way. 束缚某人的行为方式 [INFORMAL] ❑ *Like more and more women, she believes wedlock would cramp her style.* 和越来越多的女性一样，她认为婚姻会束缚她的行为方式。

cramped /kræmpt/ ADJ A **cramped** room or building is not big enough for the people or things in it. 狭促的 ❑ *There are hundreds of families living in cramped conditions on the floor of the airport lounge.* 上百个家庭住在机场候机室地板上狭促的环境里。

crane /kreɪn/ (**cranes, craning, craned**) 1 N-COUNT A **crane** is a large machine that moves heavy things by lifting them in the air. 起重机 ❑ *The little prefabricated hut was lifted away by a huge crane.* 那间小小的预制棚屋被一台巨大的起重机吊走了。 2 N-COUNT A **crane** is a kind of large bird with a long neck and long legs. 鹤 3 V-T/V-I If you **crane** your neck or head, you stretch your neck in a particular direction in order to see or hear something better. 伸长（脖子）❑ *She craned her neck to get a better view.* 她伸长脖子以便看得清楚一些。 ❑ *Children craned to get close to him.* 孩子们伸长脖子想靠近他。

▲ **crank** /kræŋk/ (**cranks, cranking, cranked**) 1 N-COUNT If you call someone a **crank**, you think their ideas or behavior are strange. 怪人 [INFORMAL, DISAPPROVAL] ❑ *The man with a new idea is a crank until the idea succeeds.* 有新想法的人在想法实现前是怪人。 2 N-COUNT A **crank** is a device that you turn in order to make something move. 曲柄 ❑ *He was idly turning a crank on a strange mechanism strapped to his chest.* 他漫不经心地转着绑在他胸前的一个古怪装置上面的曲柄。 3 V-T If you **crank** an engine or machine, you make it move or function, especially by turning a handle. 用曲柄启动 ❑ *The chauffeur got out to crank the motor.* 司机下车用曲柄发动了引擎。

▸ **crank out** PHRASAL VERB If you say that a company or person **cranks out** a quantity of similar things, you mean they produce them quickly, in the same way, and are usually implying that the things are not original or are of poor quality. 迅速地大量滥制 ❑ *In 1933 the studio cranked out fifty-five feature films.* 1933年，这家电影公司粗制滥造了55部故事片。 ❑ *The writer must have cranked it out in his lunch-hour.* 作者一定是在午餐时间快速把它拼凑出来的。

▸ **crank up** PHRASAL VERB If you **crank up** a machine or device, you turn it on higher. 调高 ❑ *May's warm weather caused Americans to crank up their air conditioners.* 5月温暖的天气使美国人都调高了空调的力度。

▲ **crap** /kræp/ 1 ADJ If you describe something as **crap**, you think that it is wrong or of very poor quality. 狗屎不如的 [INFORMAL, VULGAR, DISAPPROVAL] ❑ *She later said the book was "crap."* 她后来说这本书"狗屎不如"。 ● N-UNCOUNT **Crap** is also a noun. 狗屁东西 ❑ *It is a tedious, humorless load of crap.* 这简直就是一堆乏味、无趣的臭狗屎。 2 N-UNCOUNT **Crap** is sometimes used to refer to feces. 屎 [INFORMAL, VULGAR] ❑ *I look down and I'm standing next to a pile of crap!* 我低头一看，我正站在一堆粪便旁边。 3 N-UNCOUNT **Craps** or **crap** is a gambling game, played mainly in North America, in which you throw two dice and bet what the total will be. 双骰赌博 ❑ *I'll shoot some craps or play some blackjack.* 我要掷几把双骰子或玩几把二十一点纸牌。

crash ♦♦◇ /kræʃ/ (**crashes, crashing, crashed**) 1 N-COUNT A **crash** is an accident in which a moving vehicle hits something and is damaged or destroyed. 撞车；坠机 ❑ *His elder son was killed in a car crash a few years ago.* 他大儿子几年前死于一次车祸。 2 N-COUNT A **crash** is a sudden, loud noise. 突然的巨响 ❑ *Two people recalled hearing a loud crash about 1:30 a.m.* 两人回忆说大约凌晨1：30时听到一声巨响。 3 V-T/V-I If a moving vehicle **crashes** or if the driver **crashes** it, it hits something and is damaged or destroyed. 使…撞毁；撞毁 ❑ *The plane crashed mysteriously near the island of Ustica.* 飞机在乌斯蒂卡岛附近神秘地坠毁了。 ❑ *Her car crashed into the rear of a van.* 她的汽车撞毁了一辆面包车的尾部。 4 V-I If something **crashes** somewhere, it moves and hits something else violently, making a loud noise. （发出巨响的）猛撞 ❑ *The door swung inwards to crash against a chest of drawers behind it.* 门摆向里面，砰的一声猛力撞上了门后的五斗橱。 ❑ *My words were lost as the walls above us crashed down, filling the cellar with brick dust.* 随着上面的墙体轰隆一声倒塌下来，地窖里充满砖灰，我吓得说不出话来。 5 V-I If a business or financial system **crashes**, it fails suddenly, often with serious effects. （企业、金融机构）突然垮台 [BUSINESS] ❑ *When the market crashed, they assumed the deal would be cancelled.* 市场崩盘时，他们以为那笔交易会取消。 ● N-COUNT **Crash** is also a noun. 崩溃 ❑ *He predicted correctly that there was going to be a stock market crash.* 他正确地预测到将出现股市崩溃。 6 V-I If a computer or a computer program **crashes**, it fails suddenly. （计算机或系统）死机 ❑ *The computer crashed for the second time in 10 days.* 计算机10天内第2次死机了。

→ see Word Web: **crash**
→ see **stock market**

Thesaurus *crash* 另参见：

N. collision, wreck 1
bang 2
V. collide, hit, smash 3
fail 5 6

crass /kræs/ (**crasser, crassest**) ADJ **Crass** behavior is stupid and does not show consideration for other people. 粗暴愚蠢的 ❑ *The government has behaved with crass insensitivity.* 政府表现得粗暴愚蠢，毫不体恤。

▲ **crate** /kreɪt/ (**crates, crating, crated**) 1 N-COUNT A **crate** is a large box used for transporting or storing things. 大货箱 ❑ *...a pile of wooden crates.* …一堆木制大货箱。 2 N-COUNT A **crate** is a plastic or wire box divided into sections that is used for carrying bottles. 隔条箱 3 N-COUNT You can use **crate** to refer to a crate and its contents, or to the contents only. 一箱；一箱的量 ❑ *...a crate of oranges.* …一箱橘子。 4 V-T If something **is crated** or **crated up**, it is packed in a crate so that it can be transported or stored

Word Web crash

Every year the National Highway Traffic Safety Administration* conducts crash tests on new cars. They evaluate exactly what happens during an accident. How fast do you have to be going to **buckel** a bumper during a collision? Does the gas tank **rupture**? Do the tires **burst**? What happens when the windshield **breaks**? Does it **crack**, or does it **shatter** into a thousand pieces? Does the force of the **impact crush** the front of the car completely? This is actually a good thing. It means that the engine and hood would protect the passengers during the crash.

National Highway Traffic Safety Administration: a U.S. government agency that sets safety standards.

C

somewhere safely. 把…装箱 [usu passive] ❑ *Equipment and office supplies were crated and shipped.* 设备及办公用品被装箱运走了。

▲ **cra·ter** /kreɪtər/ (**craters**) N-COUNT A **crater** is a very large hole in the ground, which has been caused by something hitting it or by an explosion. (撞击或爆炸形成的) 大坑 ❑ *The explosion, believed to be a car bomb, left a ten-foot crater in the street.* 这次爆炸，据说是一个汽车炸弹引起的，在街道上留下了一个10英尺的大坑。
→ see **astronomer, lake, meteor, moon, solar system**

▲ **crave** /kreɪv/ (**craves, craving, craved**) V-T If you **crave** something, you want to have it very much. 渴望得到 ❑ *There may be certain times of day when smokers crave their cigarette.* 一天中可能有那么几次吸烟者特别想叼上烟。 ● **crav·ing** N-COUNT (**cravings**) 渴求 ❑ *...a craving for sugar.* …对糖的渴求。

crawl /krɔl/ (**crawls, crawling, crawled**) **1** V-I When you **crawl**, you move forward on your hands and knees. 爬 ❑ *Don't worry if your baby seems a little reluctant to crawl or walk.* 如果你的小宝宝看起来有点不愿爬或走，不用担心。 ❑ *I began to crawl on my hands and knees toward the door.* 我开始手脚并用向门爬去。 **2** V-I When an insect **crawls** somewhere, it moves there quite slowly. 爬行 ❑ *I watched the moth crawl up the outside of the lampshade.* 我看着蛾子爬上灯罩表面。 **3** V-I If someone or something **crawls** somewhere, they move or progress slowly or with great difficulty. 缓慢行进 ❑ *I crawled out of bed at nine-thirty.* 9:30我才慢慢地爬下床。 ● N-SING **Crawl** is also a noun. 缓慢行进 ["a" N] ❑ *The traffic on the off-ramp slowed to a crawl.* 驶出匝道的交通慢得在爬进。 **4** V-I If you say that a place **is crawling with** people or animals, you are emphasizing that it is full of them. 到处都是 [only cont] [INFORMAL, EMPHASIS] ❑ *This place is crawling with police.* 这个地方警察到处都是。 **5** N-SING **The crawl** is a kind of swimming stroke which you do lying on your front, swinging one arm over your head, and then the other arm. 自由泳 ❑ *I expected him to do 50 lengths of the crawl.* 我希望他以自由泳游50趟。

▲ **cray·on** /kreɪɒn/ (**crayons**) N-COUNT A **crayon** is a rod of colored wax used for drawing. 彩色蜡笔

craze /kreɪz/ (**crazes**) N-COUNT If there is a **craze** for something, it is very popular for a short time. 一时的狂热 ❑ *...the craze for Mutant Ninja Turtles.* …风靡一时的忍者神龟热。

crazed /kreɪzd/ ADJ **Crazed** people are wild and uncontrolled, and perhaps insane. 疯狂的 [WRITTEN] ❑ *A crazed gunman slaughtered five people last night.* 昨晚一个疯狂的持枪歹徒杀了5人。

cra·zy ♦◇◇ /kreɪzi/ (**crazier, craziest, crazies**) **1** ADJ If you describe someone or something as **crazy**, you think they are very foolish or strange. 傻的；怪的 [INFORMAL, DISAPPROVAL] ❑ *People thought they were all crazy to try to make money from manufacturing.* 人们认为他们都试着从制造业中赚钱太傻了。 ● **cra·zi·ly** ADV 傻地；怪地 ❑ *The teenagers shook their long, black hair and gesticulated crazily.* 那群十几岁的青少年甩动着长长的黑发，怪怪地比着手势。 **2** ADJ Someone who is **crazy** is insane. 发疯的 [INFORMAL] ❑ *If I sat home and worried about all this stuff, I'd go crazy.* 要是我坐在家里为所有这些事发愁，我会发疯的。 ● N-COUNT **Crazy** is also a noun. 疯子 ❑ *Outside, mumbling, was one of New York's ever-present crazies.* 在外面喃喃自语的人是纽约常有的疯子之一。 **3** ADJ If you are **crazy about** something, you are very enthusiastic about it. If you are **not crazy about** something, you do not like it. 着迷的 [v-link ADJ "about" n] [INFORMAL] ❑ *He's still crazy about both his work and his hobbies.* 他依旧迷恋于自己的工作和业余爱好。 ● COMB IN ADJ **Crazy** is also a combining form. …狂热的 (用于词构成合成词) ❑ *Sports-crazy Coloradans will buy tickets to anything.* 运动狂热的科罗拉多人什么票都会买。 **4** ADJ If you are **crazy about** someone, you are deeply in love with them. 狂爱的 [v-link ADJ "about" n] [INFORMAL] ❑ *We're crazy about each other.* 我们为彼此疯狂。

▲ **creak** /krik/ (**creaks, creaking, creaked**) V-I If something **creaks**, it makes a short, high-pitched sound when it moves. 嘎吱作响 ❑ *The bed-springs creaked.* 床的弹簧嘎吱作响。 ❑ *The door creaked open.* 门嘎吱一声开了。 ● N-COUNT **Creak** is also a noun. 嘎吱声 ❑ *The door was pulled open with a creak.* 门嘎吱一声被拉开了。

cream ♦♦◇ /krim/ (**creams, creaming, creamed**) **1** N-UNCOUNT **Cream** is a thick yellowish-white liquid taken from milk. You can use it in cooking or put it on fruit or desserts. 奶油 ❑ *...strawberries and cream.* …草莓加奶油。 **2** N-UNCOUNT **Cream** is used in the names of soups that contain cream or milk. 奶油汤 [N "of" n] ❑ *...cream of mushroom soup.* …奶油蘑菇汤。 **3** N-VAR A **cream** is a substance that you rub into your skin, for example, to keep it soft or to heal or protect it. 膏；霜 ❑ *Gently apply the cream to the affected areas.* 轻轻地把药膏涂抹于患处。 **4** COLOR Something that is **cream** is yellowish-white in color. 奶油色 ❑ *...cream silk stockings.* …乳白色的长筒丝袜。 **5** → see also **ice cream**
→ see **coffee**

▸ **cream off** **1** PHRASAL VERB To **cream off** part of a group of people means to take them away and treat them in a special way, because they are better than the others. 挑走 (拔尖者) [DISAPPROVAL] ❑ *The private schools cream off many of the best pupils.* 私立学校挑走很多最优秀的学生。 **2** PHRASAL VERB If a person or organization **creams off** a large amount of money, they take it and use it for themselves. (大量钱) 入私帐 [INFORMAL, DISAPPROVAL] ❑ *This means smaller banks can cream off big profits during lending booms.* 这就意味着较小银行在贷款高峰期能将高额利润入私帐。

creamy /krimi/ (**creamier, creamiest**) **1** ADJ Food or drink that is **creamy** contains a lot of cream or milk. 含大量奶油的 ❑ *...rich, creamy coffee.* …浓郁的奶油咖啡。 **2** ADJ Food that is **creamy** has a soft smooth texture and appearance. 奶油般柔滑的 ❑ *...creamy mashed potato.* …细腻的土豆泥。

▲ **crease** /kris/ (**creases, creasing, creased**) **1** N-COUNT **Creases** are lines that are made in cloth or paper when it is crushed or folded. 折痕 ❑ *She stood up, frowning at the creases in her silk dress.* 她站起来，看着丝裙上的折痕皱起了眉。 ❑ *...cream-colored pants with sharp creases.* …裤缝笔挺的乳白色裤子。 **2** N-COUNT **Creases** in someone's skin are lines which form where their skin folds when they move. 皱纹 ❑ *...the tiny creases at the corners of his eyes.* …他眼角的细纹。 ● **creased** ADJ 有皱纹的 ❑ *Sweat poured down her deeply creased face.* 汗水从她布满深深皱纹的脸上哗哗地流下。 **3** V-T/V-I If cloth or paper **creases** or if you **crease** it, lines form in it when it is crushed or folded. 使…起皱；起皱 ❑ *Most outfits crease a bit when you are traveling.* 大多数的外套在旅行中都会有些起皱。 ● **creased** ADJ 起皱的 ❑ *His clothes were creased, as if he had slept in them.* 他的衣服皱巴巴的，好像穿着睡的一样。

cre·ate ♦♦♦ /krieɪt/ (**creates, creating, created**) **1** V-T To **create** something means to cause it to happen or exist. 创造；引起 ❑ *We set business free to create more jobs.* 我们让企业自由以创造更多的就业机会。 ❑ *She could create a fight out of anything.* 她可以为了任何事制造争斗。 ● **crea·tion** /krieɪʃᵊn/ N-UNCOUNT 创造 ❑ *These businesses stimulate the creation of local jobs.* 这些企业刺激了当地就业机会的产生。 **2** V-T When someone **creates** a new product or process, they invent it or design it. 创造；设计 ❑ *It is really great for a radio producer to create a show like this.* 一个电台节目制作人能设计出这样的节目真是太了不起了。

Thesaurus	*create* 另参见：
v.	make, produce; *(ant.)* destroy **1**
	compose, craft, design, invent **2**

Word Link *creat ≈ making : creation, creature, recreate*

crea·tion /krieɪʃᵊn/ (**creations**) **1** N-UNCOUNT In many religions, **creation** is the making of the universe, earth, and creatures by God. 上帝造物 [also "the" N] ❑ *...the Creation of the universe as told in Genesis Chapter One.* …如《创世纪》第一章中讲述的上帝创造天地万物。 **2** N-UNCOUNT People sometimes refer to the whole universe as **creation**. 全宇宙 [LITERARY] ❑ *The whole of creation is made up of energy.* 全宇宙是由能量构成的。 **3** N-COUNT You can refer to something that someone has made as a **creation**, especially if it shows skill, imagination, or artistic ability. 创作 ❑ *The bathroom is entirely my own creation.* 这个浴室完全是我个人的创作。 **4** → see also **create**

crea·tive ♦◇◇ /krieɪtɪv/ **1** ADJ A **creative** person has the ability to invent and develop original ideas, especially in the arts. 有创造力的 ❑ *Like so many creative people, he was never satisfied.* 正如许多有创造力的人一样，他永不满足。 ● **crea·tiv·ity** /krieɪtɪvɪti/ N-UNCOUNT 创造力 ❑ *American art reached a peak of creativity in the '50s and '60s.* 20世纪五六十年代，美国艺术的创造力达到了顶峰。 **2** ADJ **Creative** activities involve the inventing and making of new kinds of things. 创新性的 ❑ *...creative writing.* …创新写作。 ❑ *...creative arts.* …创新艺术。 **3** ADJ If you use something in a **creative** way, you use it in a new way that produces interesting and unusual results. 独创的 ❑ *...his creative use of words.* …他独创的词汇用法。

crea·tive ac·count·ing N-UNCOUNT **Creative accounting** is when companies present or organize their accounts in such a way that they gain money for themselves or give a false impression of their profits. 伪造账目 [DISAPPROVAL] ❑ *Much of the* *apparent growth in profits in the 1980s was the result of creative accounting.* 20世纪80年代利润的显著增长中，有很多都是伪造账目的结果。

Word Link *ator ≈ one who does : creator, innovator, spectator*

crea·tor /kriẹɪtər/ (**creators**) 1 N-COUNT The **creator** of something is the person who made it or invented it. 创作者 ❑ *...Ian Fleming, the creator of James Bond.* …伊恩・弗莱明，詹姆斯・邦德的创作者。 2 N-PROPER God is sometimes referred to as **the Creator.** 造物主 ❑ *This was the first object placed in the heavens by the Creator.* 这是造物主置于天上的第一个物体。

crea·ture /kritʃər/ (**creatures**) N-COUNT You can refer to any living thing that is not a plant as a **creature**, especially when it is of an unknown or unfamiliar kind. People also refer to imaginary animals and beings as **creatures.** (尤指不明的或想像中的）生物；动物 ❑ *Alaskan Eskimos believe that every living creature possesses a spirit.* 阿拉斯加的爱斯基摩人认为每个活着的动物都有灵魂。

crèche /krẹʃ/ (**crèches**) also **creche** N-COUNT A **crèche** is a place where small children can be left to be cared for while their parents are doing something else. 托儿所 [BRIT]

in AM, use **day care center**

cre·dence /krịdᵊns/ 1 N-UNCOUNT If something lends or gives **credence to** a theory or story, it makes it easier to believe. 信任 [FORMAL] ❑ *Good studies are needed to lend credence to the notion that genuine progress can be made in this important field.* 要有优秀的研究才能使人相信在这一重大领域能取得真正的进步。 2 N-UNCOUNT If you give **credence to** a theory or story, you believe it. 相信 [FORMAL] ❑ *You're surely not giving any credence to this story of Hythe's?* 你真的一点都不相信关于海斯的这个故事吗？

Word Link *cred ≈ to believe : credentials, credibility, incredible*

▲ **cre·den·tials** /krɪdẹnʃᵊlz/ 1 N-PLURAL Someone's **credentials** are their previous achievements, training, and general background, which indicate that they are qualified to do something. (表明某人有资格做某事的）资历 ❑ *...her credentials as a Bach specialist.* …她作为一名巴赫研究专家的资历。 2 N-PLURAL Someone's **credentials** are a letter or certificate that proves their identity or qualifications. (身份或资格的）证明文件 ❑ *The new ambassador to Lebanon has presented his credentials to the president.* 驻黎巴嫩新任大使已经向总统呈递了国书。

▲ **cred·ibil·ity** /krẹdɪbɪlɪti/ N-UNCOUNT If someone or something has **credibility**, people believe in them and trust them. 可信性 ❑ *The police have lost their credibility.* 警察已经失去了他们的可信性。

★ **cred·ible** /krẹdɪbᵊl/ 1 ADJ **Credible** means able to be trusted or believed. 可信的 ❑ *Her claims seem credible to many.* 她的说法似乎在许多人看来是可信的。 2 ADJ A **credible** candidate, policy, or system, for example, is one that appears to have a chance of being successful. 有可能成功 ❑ *Mr. Robertson would be a credible candidate.* 罗伯逊先生将是一名有希望成功的候选人。

cred·it ♦♦◊ /krẹdɪt/ (**credits, crediting, credited**) 1 N-UNCOUNT If you are given **credit**, you are allowed to pay for goods or services several weeks or months after you have received them. 赊购 ❑ *The group can't get credit to buy farming machinery.* 该集团无法以赊购方式购买农业机械。 2 N-UNCOUNT If you get **the credit for** something good, people praise you because you are responsible for it, or are thought to be responsible for it. 赞扬 ❑ *We don't mind who gets the credit so long as we don't get the blame.* 只要我们不挨批评，谁受到表扬我们都不在乎。 ❑ *It would be wrong for us to take all the credit.* 我们把所有的功劳都揽到自己身上就不对了。 3 V-T When a sum of money **is credited to** an account, the bank adds that sum of money to the total in the account. 存入 ❑ *She noticed that only $80,000 had been credited to her account.* 她注意到只有$80000存入了她的账户。 ❑ *Midland decided to change the way it credited payments to accounts.* 米德兰公司决定改变将所付款项存入账户的方式。 4 V-T If people **credit** someone **with** an achievement or if it **is credited to** them, people say or believe that they were responsible for it. 归功于 ❑ *The staff are crediting him with saving Hythe's life.* 海斯能得救全体人员都归功于他。 ❑ *The 74-year-old mayor is credited with helping make Los Angeles the financial capital of the West Coast.* 74岁的市长被归功为帮助洛杉矶成为西海岸金融中心的人。 5 N-COUNT A **credit** is a sum of money which is added to an account. 贷方款额 ❑ *The statement of total debits and credits is known as a balance.* 总的借贷报表称作借贷平衡表。 6 N-COUNT A **credit** is an amount of money that is given to someone. 补助 ❑ *Senator Bill Bradley outlined his own tax cut, giving families $350 in tax credits per child.* 参议员比尔・布拉德利简述了自己的减税计划，给家庭中每一个孩子$350税款补助。 7 N-PLURAL The list of people who helped to make a movie, a CD, or a television program is called **the credits.** 摄制人员名单 ❑ *It was fantastic seeing my name in the credits.* 在摄制人员名单中看到我的名字真是太好了。 8 N-COUNT A **credit** is a successfully completed part of a higher education course, representing about one hour of instruction a week. At universities and colleges you need a certain number of credits to be awarded a degree. 学分 ❑ *Through the AP program students can earn college credits in high school.* 通过大学预修课程计划，学生在中学就可以拿到大学的学分。 9 N-SING If you say that someone is **a credit to** someone or something, you mean that their qualities or achievements will make people have a good opinion of the person or thing mentioned. 为…增光的人 ❑ *He is one of the greatest players of recent times and is a credit to his profession.* 他是近年来最棒的选手之一，是为他的职业增光的人。 10 PHRASE To **give** someone **credit for** a good quality means to believe that they have it. 相信某人有 ❑ *Bratbakk had more ability than the media gave him credit for.* 布拉特巴克有比媒体所宣传的还要强的能力。 11 PHRASE If something is **to** someone's **credit**, they deserve praise for it. 值得赞扬 ❑ *She had managed to pull herself together and, to her credit, continued to look upon life as a positive experience.* 她努力使自己振作起来，并且值得称赞的是，她一如既往地积极面对人生。

Word Partnership *credit* 的常用搭配:

N.	credit **history**, **letter of** credit 1
	credit **an account** 3
V.	**provide** credit 1
	deserve credit, **take** credit 2
ADJ.	**personal** credit 1 6

cred·it·able /krẹdɪtəbᵊl/ 1 ADJ A **creditable** performance or achievement is of a reasonably high standard. 具有相当高水平的 ❑ *They turned out a quite creditable performance.* 他们做出了一场相当不错的演出。 2 ADJ If you describe someone's actions or aims as **creditable**, you mean that they are morally good. 值得称道的 ❑ *Not a very creditable attitude, I'm afraid.* 恐怕这不是一种值得称道的态度。

cred·it card (**credit cards**) N-COUNT A **credit card** is a plastic card that you use to buy goods on credit. Compare **charge card.** 信用卡

cred·it note [BRIT] → see **credit slip**

credi·tor /krẹdɪtər/ (**creditors**) N-COUNT Your **creditors** are the people who you owe money to. 债权人 ❑ *The company said it would pay in full all its creditors except Credit Suisse.* 该公司说将全额付款给除瑞士信贷以外的所有债权人。

cred·it rat·ing N-SING Your **credit rating** is a judgment of how likely you are to pay money back if you borrow it or buy things on credit. 信用等级 ❑ *But Cahoot's overdraft rate depends on your credit rating.* 然而合伙人的透支率取决于你的信用等级。

cred·it slip (**credit slips**) 1 N-COUNT A **credit slip** is a piece of paper that a shop gives you when you return goods that you have bought from it. It states that you are entitled to take goods of the same value without paying for them. 信用凭证 [AM]

in BRIT, use **credit note**

2 N-COUNT A **credit slip** is a piece of paper which shows that your account has been credited. 存款单

cred·it trans·fer (**credit transfers**) N-COUNT A **credit transfer** is a direct payment of money from one bank account into another. 银行转账 [BRIT]

in AM, use **money transfer**

Word Link *worthy ≈ deserving : suitable : creditworthy, trustworthy, unworthy*

credit·worthy /krẹdɪtwɜrði/ also **credit-worthy** ADJ A **creditworthy** person or organization is one who can safely be lent money or allowed to have goods on credit, for example, because in the past they have always paid back what they owe. 有信用的 ❑ *The Fed wants banks to continue to lend to creditworthy borrowers.* 联邦储备银行想让各家银行继续贷款给信用良好的借款人。
● **credit·worthi·ness** N-UNCOUNT 信用 ❑ *They now take extra steps to verify the creditworthiness of customers.* 他们现在采取额外措施来验证客户的信用。

▲ **creed** /krịd/ (**creeds**) 1 N-COUNT A **creed** is a set of beliefs, principles, or opinions that strongly influence the way people live or work. 信条 [FORMAL] ❑ *...their devotion to their creed of self-help.*

C

C

…他们对自助信条的奉献。 2 N-COUNT A **creed** is a religion. 信仰 [FORMAL] ❑ *The center is open to all, no matter what race or creed.* 该中心对所有人开放，不论其种族与信仰。

▲ **creek** /krik/ (**creeks**) N-COUNT A **creek** is a small stream or river. 小溪；小河 [AM] ❑ *Follow Austin Creek for a few miles.* 沿着奥斯汀河走上几英里。

creep /krip/ (**creeps, creeping, crept**) 1 V-I When people or animals **creep** somewhere, they move quietly and slowly. 悄悄地缓慢行进 ❑ *Back I go to the hotel and creep up to my room.* 我回到旅馆，蹑手蹑脚地进了房间。 2 V-I If something **creeps** somewhere, it moves very slowly. 渐渐蔓延 ❑ *Mist had crept in again from the sea.* 大雾再次从海上渐渐蔓延过来。 3 V-I If something **creeps** in or **creeps** back, it begins to occur or becomes part of something without people realizing or without them wanting it. 悄悄出现 ❑ *Insecurity might creep in.* 不安全感可能会悄然而生。 ❑ *An increasing ratio of mistakes, perhaps induced by tiredness, crept into her game.* 可能是因为疲劳，她在比赛中的错误率不知不觉地升高了。 4 V-I If a rate or number **creeps up** to a higher level, it gradually reaches that level. 攀升 ❑ *The inflation rate has been creeping up to 9.5 per cent.* 通货膨胀率已攀升至9.5%。 5 **to make** someone's **flesh creep** → see **flesh**

Word Partnership *creep* 的常用搭配：
PREP. creep **into**, creep **toward** 1 2
creep **in** 1 – 3
creep **up** 1 2 4
V. **give someone the** creeps 5

creepy /kripi/ (**creepier, creepiest**) ADJ If you say that something or someone is **creepy**, you mean they make you feel very nervous or frightened. 吓人的 [INFORMAL] ❑ *There were certain places that were really creepy at night.* 有些地方到了晚上真吓人。

cre·mate /krimeɪt/ (**cremates, cremating, cremated**) V-T When someone **is cremated**, their dead body is burned, usually as part of a funeral service. 火化 [usu passive] ❑ *She wants Chris to be cremated.* 她想要克里斯被火化。 ●**cre·ma·tion** /krɪmeɪʃən/ N-VAR (**cremations**) 火化 ❑ *At Miss Garbo's request, there was a cremation after a private ceremony.* 应加伯小姐的要求，私下举行仪式后就进行火化。

crept /krɛpt/ **Crept** is the past tense and past participle of **creep**. **creep**的过去式和过去分词

cre·scen·do /krɪʃɛndoʊ/ (**crescendos**) 1 N-COUNT A **crescendo** is a noise that gets louder and louder. Some people also use **crescendo** to refer to the point when a noise is at its loudest. 逐渐增强的响声；声音最响的一点 ❑ *She spoke in a crescendo: "You are a bad girl! You are a wicked girl! You are evil!"* 她嗓门越来越高地喊道："你这个坏丫头！你这个恶丫头！你真恶毒！" 2 N-COUNT People sometimes describe an increase in the intensity of something, or its most intense point, as a **crescendo**. 渐强；顶点 [JOURNALISM] ❑ *There was a crescendo of press criticism.* 媒体的批评逐渐升温。

Word Link *cresc, creas ≈ growing : crescent, decrease, increase*

▲ **cres·cent** /krɛsənt/ (**crescents**) 1 N-COUNT A **crescent** is a curved shape that is wider in the middle than at its ends, like the shape of the moon during its first and last quarters. It is the most important symbol of the Islamic faith. 新月（伊斯兰教最重要的标志） ❑ *A glittering Islamic crescent tops the mosque.* 一个闪闪发光的伊斯兰新月标志立于该清真寺之顶。 ❑ *...a narrow crescent of sand dunes.* …一个狭长的新月形沙丘。 2 N-IN-NAMES **Crescent** is sometimes used as part of the name of a street or row of houses that is usually built in a curve. 新月街（用于修成弧形的街道或房屋的地址单位） ❑ *The address is 44 Colville Crescent.* 地址是科尔维尔新月街44号。

▲ **crest** /krɛst/ (**crests**) 1 N-COUNT The **crest of** a hill or a wave is the top of it. 顶；峰 ● PHRASE If you say that you are **on the crest of a wave**, you mean that you are feeling very happy and confident because things are going well for you. 在巅峰 ❑ *The band is riding on the crest of a wave with the worldwide success of their number-one-selling single.* 这个乐队目前正处于巅峰，他们的单曲全球销量第一。 2 N-COUNT A bird's **crest** is a group of upright feathers on the top of its head. （鸟类的）羽冠 ❑ *Both birds had a dark blue crest.* 两只鸟都长着深蓝色的羽冠。 3 N-COUNT A **crest** is a design that is the symbol of a noble family, a town, or an organization. 饰章 ❑ *On the wall is the family crest.* 墙上是家族饰章。
→ see **sound**

crev·ice /krɛvɪs/ (**crevices**) N-COUNT A **crevice** is a narrow crack or gap, especially in a rock. 裂缝 ❑ *...a huge boulder with rare ferns growing in every crevice.* …一块每个裂缝中都长着稀有蕨类的巨石。

crew ♦◇◇ /kru/ (**crews, crewing, crewed**) 1 N-COUNT-COLL The **crew** of a ship, an aircraft, or a spacecraft is the people who work on and operate it. 全体船员；全体机务人员 ❑ *The mission for the crew of the space shuttle is essentially over.* 航天飞机全体机务人员的使命基本完成。 ❑ *Despite their size, these vessels carry small crews, usually of around twenty men.* 虽然个头大，这些轮船载船员却很少，一般只有二十人左右。 2 N-COUNT A **crew** is a group of people with special technical skills who work together on a task or project. 一组工作人员 ❑ *...a two-man film crew making a documentary.* …一个制作纪录片的两人摄制组。 3 V-T/V-I If you **crew** a boat, you work on it as part of the crew. 当船员；充当…的船员 ❑ *This neighbor crewed on a ferryboat.* 这位邻居在一艘渡船上当船员。 ❑ *There were to be five teams of three crewing the boat.* 将有5个3人组做这艘船的船员。

▲ **crib** /krɪb/ (**cribs**) N-COUNT A **crib** is a bed for a baby. 婴儿床 [mainly AM]
in BRIT, usually use **cot**

▲ **crick·et** ♦◇◇ /krɪkɪt/ (**crickets**) 1 N-UNCOUNT **Cricket** is an outdoor game played between two teams. Players try to score points, called runs, by hitting a ball with a wooden bat. 板球 ❑ *During the summer term we would play cricket at the village ground.* 夏季学期里我们常在村里的空地上玩板球。 2 N-COUNT A **cricket** is a small jumping insect that produces short, loud sounds by rubbing its wings together. 蟋蟀

crick·et·er /krɪkɪtər/ (**cricketers**) N-COUNT A **cricketer** is a person who plays cricket. 板球员

crime ♦♦◇ /kraɪm/ (**crimes**) 1 N-VAR A **crime** is an illegal action or activity for which a person can be punished by law. 罪行 ❑ *He and Lieutenant Cassidy were checking the scene of the crime.* 当时他正与卡西迪中尉一起检查犯罪现场。 ❑ *...the growing problem of organized crime.* …越来越严重的有组织犯罪问题。 2 N-COUNT If you say that doing something is a **crime**, you think it is very wrong or a serious mistake. 严重错误 [DISAPPROVAL] ❑ *It would be a crime to travel all the way to Australia and not stop in Sydney.* 如果千里迢迢去澳大利亚而不在悉尼停留，那就是大错特错。
→ see **city**

Word Partnership *crime* 的常用搭配：
V. **commit a** crime, **fight against** crime 1
ADJ. **organized** crime, **terrible** crime, **violent** crime 1
N. crime **prevention**, crime **scene**, crime **wave** 1
partner in crime 1 2

crimi·nal ♦♦◇ /krɪmɪnəl/ (**criminals**) 1 N-COUNT A **criminal** is a person who has committed a crime. 罪犯 ❑ *A group of gunmen attacked a prison and set free nine criminals.* 一伙持枪歹徒袭击了一所监狱并放走了9名罪犯。 2 ADJ **Criminal** means connected with crime. 犯罪的；刑事的 ❑ *Her husband faces various criminal charges.* 她丈夫面临多项刑事的指控。 3 ADJ If you describe an action as **criminal**, you think it is very wrong or a serious mistake. 严重错误的 [DISAPPROVAL] ❑ *He said a full-scale dispute involving strikes would be criminal.* 他说一个卷入罢工的全面抗争将是极其错误的。

▲ **crim·son** /krɪmzən/ (**crimsons**) COLOR Something that is **crimson** is deep red in color. 深红色的 ❑ *...a mass of crimson flowers.* …一团深红色的花。

cringe /krɪndʒ/ (**cringes, cringing, cringed**) V-I If you **cringe at** something, you feel embarrassed or disgusted, and perhaps show this feeling in your expression or by making a slight movement. 感到局促不安 ❑ *Molly had cringed when Ann started picking up the guitar.* 安伸手去拿吉他时，莫利感到局促不安。 ❑ *Chris had cringed at the thought of using her own family for publicity.* 克里斯一想到要利用家人做宣传就感到局促不安。

crip·ple /krɪpəl/ (**cripples, crippling, crippled**) 1 N-COUNT A person with a physical disability or a serious permanent injury is sometimes referred to as a **cripple**. 残疾人；残废人 [OFFENSIVE] ❑ *She has gone from being a healthy, fit, and sporty young woman to being a cripple.* 她从一个健康、强壮、爱好体育运动的年轻姑娘变成了一个残疾人。 2 V-T If someone **is crippled** by an injury, it is so serious that they can never move their body properly again. 使受伤致残 ❑ *Mr. Easton was crippled in an accident and had to leave his job.* 伊斯顿先生在一场事故中受伤致残，不得不离开了工作。 ❑ *He had been warned that another bad fall could cripple him for life.* 他被警告说再一次严重摔跤会使他终身残疾。

crip·pling /krɪplɪŋ/ 1 ADJ A **crippling** illness or disability is one that severely damages your health or your body. 严重损害健康的；致残的 [ADJ n] ❑ *Arthritis and rheumatism are prominent crippling diseases.* 关节炎和风湿病是常见致残的疾病。 2 ADJ If you say that an action, policy, or situation has a **crippling** effect on something, you mean it has a very serious, harmful effect. 极有害的 ❑ *The high cost of capital has a crippling effect on many small firms.* 高资本成本对许多小公司有着极坏的影响。

cri·sis ♦♦◊ /kraɪsɪs/ (**crises** /kraɪsiz/) N-VAR A **crisis** is a situation in which something or someone is affected by one or more very serious problems. 危机 ❑ *Natural disasters have obviously contributed to the continent's economic crisis.* 自然灾害显然促使了该大陆的经济危机。 ❑ *...someone to turn to in moments of crisis.* …在危机时刻可以向其求助的人。

Word Partnership *crisis* 的常用搭配：
N. **housing** crisis, crisis **management**, **solution to a** crisis
ADJ. **major** crisis, **political** crisis
V. **solve a** crisis

★ **crisp** /krɪsp/ (**crisper, crispest, crisps, crisping, crisped**) 1 ADJ Food that is **crisp** is pleasantly hard, or has a pleasantly hard surface. 脆的 [APPROVAL] ❑ *Bake the potatoes for 15 minutes, till they're nice and crisp.* 把土豆烤15分钟，直到变得香脆可口。 ❑ *...crisp bacon.* …香脆的熏肉。 2 ADJ Weather that is pleasantly fresh, cold, and dry can be described as **crisp**. 清爽的（天气）[APPROVAL] ❑ *...a crisp autumn day.* …一个清爽的秋日。 3 ADJ **Crisp** cloth or paper is clean and has no creases in it. 干净挺括的（纸、布等）❑ *He wore a panama hat and a crisp white suit.* 他戴着一顶巴拿马帽，穿着一身挺括的白西装。 ❑ *I slipped between the crisp clean sheets.* 我钻进了干净平整的被单中。 4 V-T/V-I If food **crisps** or if you **crisp** it, it becomes pleasantly hard, for example, because you have heated it at a high temperature. 变脆；使…变脆 ❑ *Cook the bacon until it begins to crisp.* 烤制熏肉直到变脆。 5 N-COUNT **Crisps** are very thin slices of fried potato that are eaten cold as a snack. 炸薯片 [BRIT]
in AM, use **chips, potato chips**

criss-cross /krɪs krɔs/ (**criss-crosses, criss-crossing, criss-crossed**) also **crisscross** 1 V-T If a person or thing **criss-crosses** an area, they travel from one side to the other and back again many times, following different routes. If a number of things **criss-cross** an area, they cross it, and cross over each other. 交叉往返 ❑ *They criss-crossed the country by bus.* 他们乘坐公共汽车在乡间交叉往返。 2 V-RECIP If two sets of lines or things **criss-cross**, they cross over each other. 交叉 ❑ *Wires criss-cross between the tops of the poles, forming a grid.* 电线在杆顶间交叉成网状。 3 ADJ A **criss-cross** pattern or design consists of lines crossing each other. 交错的 [ADJ n] ❑ *Slash the tops of the loaves with a serrated knife in a criss-cross pattern.* 用一把锯齿刀把面包顶部切成十字交叉状。

★ **cri·teri·on** /kraɪtɪəriən/ (**criteria** /kraɪtɪəriə/) N-COUNT A **criterion** is a factor on which you judge or decide something. （判断的）标准 ❑ *The most important criterion for entry is that applicants must design and make their own work.* 参加的最重要标准就是申请人必须设计并制作自己的作品。

Word Link *crit* ≈ *to judge* : *critic, critical, criticize*

crit·ic ♦♦◊ /krɪtɪk/ (**critics**) 1 N-COUNT A **critic** is a person who writes about and expresses opinions about things such as books, movies, music, or art. 评论家 ❑ *Mather was a film critic for many years.* 马瑟做过多年的电影评论家。 2 N-COUNT Someone who is a **critic** of a person or system disapproves of them and criticizes them publicly. 批评者 ❑ *The newspaper has been one of the most consistent critics ever of the government.* 该报纸是政府最坚持的批评者之一。

criti·cal ♦♦◊ /krɪtɪkᵊl/ 1 ADJ A **critical** time, factor, or situation is extremely important. 关键的 ❑ *The incident happened at a critical point in the campaign.* 该事件发生在运动的关键时刻。 ❑ *He says setting priorities is of critical importance.* 他说确定轻重缓急至关重要。 ● **criti·cal·ly** /krɪtɪkli/ ADV 关键地 ❑ *Economic prosperity depends critically on an open world trading system.* 经济繁荣关键取决于一个开放的世界贸易体系。 2 ADJ A **critical** situation is very serious and dangerous. 危急的 ❑ *The German authorities are considering an airlift if the situation becomes critical.* 德国当局正在考虑如果形势危急时进行空运。 ● **criti·cal·ly** ADV 危急地 ❑ *Moscow is running critically low on food supplies.* 莫斯科的食品供应正严重匮乏。 3 ADJ If a person is **critical** or in a **critical** condition in a hospital, they are seriously ill. 病危的 ❑ *Ten of the injured are said to be in critical condition.* 据说伤者中有十人情况危急。 ● **criti·cal·ly** ADV 病危地 ❑ *She was critically ill.* 她病情危急。 4 ADJ To be **critical of** someone or something means to criticize them. 批评的 ❑ *His report is highly critical of the trial judge.* 他的报道对承审法官是高度批判的。 ● **criti·cal·ly** ADV 批评地 ❑ *She spoke critically of Lara.* 她以批评的口吻谈到拉腊。 5 ADJ A **critical** approach to something involves examining and judging it carefully. 批判性的 [ADJ n] ❑ *We need to become critical text-readers.* 我们需要成为批判性的文本阅读者。 ● **criti·cal·ly** ADV 批判性地 ❑ *Wyman watched them critically.* 怀曼批判地注视着他们。 6 ADJ If something or someone receives **critical** acclaim, critics say that they are very good. 获好评的 [ADJ n] ❑ *The film met with considerable critical and public acclaim.* 这部电影深得评论和公众的赞扬。

Word Partnership *critical* 的常用搭配：
N. critical **issue**, critical **role** 1
critical **state** 1 – 3
critical **condition** 3
critical **acclaim** 6
V. **become** critical 1 2
PREP. critical **of** *someone/something* 4

criti·cise /krɪtɪsaɪz/ [BRIT] → see **criticize**

criti·cism ♦♦◊ /krɪtɪsɪzəm/ (**criticisms**) 1 N-VAR **Criticism** is the action of expressing disapproval of something or someone. A **criticism** is a statement that expresses disapproval. 批评；反对意见 ❑ *This policy had repeatedly come under strong criticism on Capitol Hill.* 这项政策在国会反复受到强烈批评。 2 N-UNCOUNT **Criticism** is a serious examination and judgment of something such as a book or play. 评论 ❑ *She has published more than 20 books including novels, poetry and literary criticism.* 她已出版了二十多本书，其中包括小说、诗歌和文学评论。

Thesaurus *criticism* 另参见：
N. disapproval, judgment, put-down; (*ant.*) approval, flattery, praise 1
commentary, critique, evaluation, review 2

Word Partnership *criticism* 的常用搭配：
PREP. criticism **against** *something*, criticism **from** *something*, criticism **of** *something* 1
ADJ. **constructive** criticism, **open to** criticism 1 2
N. **public** criticism 1 2
literary criticism 2

criti·cize ♦◊◊ /krɪtɪsaɪz/ (**criticizes, criticizing, criticized**)
in BRIT, also use **criticise**
V-T If you **criticize** someone or something, you express your disapproval of them by saying what you think is wrong with them. 批评 ❑ *His mother had rarely criticized him or any of her other children.* 他母亲很少批评他或她的其他孩子。

Thesaurus *criticize* 另参见：
V. knock; (*ant.*) applaud, praise

Word Partnership *criticize* 的常用搭配：
N. criticize **the government**
PREP. *be* criticized **about/by/for**

cri·tique /krɪtik/ (**critiques**) N-COUNT A **critique** is a written examination and judgment of a situation or of a person's work or ideas. 评论文章 [FORMAL] ❑ *She had brought a book, a feminist critique of Victorian lady novelists.* 她带来了一本书，一本从女权主义角度对维多利亚时期女小说家进行的评论。

croak /kroʊk/ (**croaks, croaking, croaked**) 1 V-I When a frog or bird **croaks**, it makes a harsh, low sound. （蛙或鸟）呱呱地叫 ❑ *Thousands of frogs croaked in the reeds by the riverbank.* 成千上万只青蛙在河岸的芦苇中呱呱地叫。 ● N-COUNT **Croak** is also a noun. 呱呱叫声 ❑ *...the guttural croak of the frogs.* …青蛙喉间发出的呱呱叫声。 2 V-T If someone **croaks** something, they say it in a low, rough voice. 以低沉沙哑的声音说 ❑ *Tiller moaned and managed to croak, "Help me."* 蒂勒呻吟着，勉强用低沉沙哑的声音说："帮帮我。" ● N-COUNT **Croak** is also a noun. 低沉而沙哑的声音 ❑ *His voice was just a croak.* 他的嗓音不过是个低沉而沙哑的声音。 3 V-I When someone croaks, they die. 断气 [INFORMAL] ❑ *I think the doctors were worried that I was going to croak on their watch.* 我想医生们都担心我会在他们当班的时候断气。

C

crock·ery /krɒkəri/ N-UNCOUNT **Crockery** is the plates, cups, saucers, and dishes that you use at meals. 陶制餐具 [mainly BRIT]

▲ **croco·dile** /krɒkədaɪl/ (**crocodiles**) N-COUNT A **crocodile** is a large reptile with a long body and strong jaws. Crocodiles live in rivers and eat meat. 鳄鱼

crois·sant /krwasɑn, krəsɑnt/ (**croissants**) N-VAR **Croissants** are bread rolls in the shape of a crescent that are eaten for breakfast. 牛角面包 ❑ *...coffee and croissants.* …咖啡和牛角面包。

cro·ny /kroʊni/ (**cronies**) N-COUNT You can refer to friends that someone spends a lot of time with as their **cronies**, especially when you disapprove of them. 狐朋狗友 [INFORMAL, DISAPPROVAL] ❑ *...lunchtime drinking sessions with his business cronies.* …同他那伙生意上的狐朋狗友们在午间进行的饮酒聚会。

crook /krʊk/ (**crooks, crooking, crooked**) **1** N-COUNT A **crook** is a dishonest person or a criminal. 无赖; 恶棍 [INFORMAL] ❑ *The man is a crook and a liar.* 这名男子是个恶棍和骗子。 **2** N-COUNT **The crook of** your arm or leg is the soft inside part where you bend your elbow or knee. 臂弯; 腿弯 ❑ *She hid her face in the crook of her arm.* 她把脸埋进了臂弯。 **3** N-COUNT A **crook** is a long pole with a large hook at the end. A crook is carried by a bishop in religious ceremonies, or by a shepherd. (主教在宗教仪式上所用的或牧羊人使用的) 曲柄手杖 **4** V-T If you **crook** your arm or finger, you bend it. 弯曲 ❑ *He crooked his finger: "Come forward," he said.* 他弯了弯手指，说："过来。"

▲ **crook·ed** /krʊkɪd/ **1** ADJ If you describe something as **crooked**, especially something that is usually straight, you mean that it is bent or twisted. 扭曲的 ❑ *...the crooked line of his broken nose.* …他折了的鼻梁的曲线。 **2** ADJ A **crooked** smile is uneven and bigger on one side than the other. 歪斜着嘴的 ❑ *Polly gave her a crooked grin.* 波莉给了她歪斜着嘴的一笑。 **3** ADJ If you describe a person or an activity as **crooked**, you mean that they are dishonest or criminal. 腐败的; 恶棍般的 [INFORMAL] ❑ *...a crooked cop.* …一名坏警察。

croon /krun/ (**croons, crooning, crooned**) **1** V-T/V-I If you **croon**, you sing or hum quietly and gently. 低唱; 轻哼 ❑ *He would much rather have been crooning in a smoky bar.* 他宁愿是在充满烟气的酒吧里低声哼唱。 **2** V-T/V-I If one person talks to another in a soft gentle voice, you can describe them as **crooning**, especially if you think they are being sentimental or insincere. 柔情地说 ❑ *"Dear boy," she crooned, hugging him heartily.* "亲爱的男孩儿，"她热烈地拥抱着他，柔情地说道。

crop ♦◇◇ /krɒp/ (**crops, cropping, cropped**) **1** N-COUNT **Crops** are plants such as wheat and potatoes that are grown in large quantities for food. 庄稼 ❑ *Rice farmers here still plant and harvest their crops by hand.* 这里的稻农仍然用手工种植和收割庄稼。 **2** N-COUNT The plants or fruits that are collected at harvest time are referred to as a **crop**. 收成 ❑ *Each year it produces a fine crop of fruit.* 每年这里的水果收成都不错。 ❑ *The U.S. government says that this year's corn crop should be about 8 percent more than last year.* 美国政府称今年的玉米产量应该比去年增长约8%。 **3** N-COUNT A **crop** is a short hairstyle. 短发 ❑ *She had her long hair cut into a boyish crop.* 她让人把她的长发剪成了像男孩子的短发。 **4** N-SING You can refer to a group of people or things that have appeared together as a **crop of** people or things. 一群 (人); 一堆 (物) [INFORMAL] ❑ *The present crop of books and documentaries about Marilyn Monroe exploit the thirtieth anniversary of her death.* 现在这批有关玛丽莲・梦露的书籍和记录片是借她去世三十周年纪念之机而发行的。 **5** V-I When a plant **crops**, it produces fruits or parts which people want. 收获 ❑ *Although these vegetables adapt well to our temperate climate, they tend to crop poorly.* 虽然这些蔬菜能够适应我们这里的温和气候，但它们的产量常常不高。 **6** V-T To **crop** someone's hair means to cut it short. 把…剪短 ❑ *She cropped her hair and dyed it blonde.* 她把头发剪短并染成了金色。 **7** V-T If you **crop a** photograph, you cut part of it off, in order to get rid of part of the picture or to be able to frame it. 裁切 ❑ *I decided to crop the picture just above the water line.* 我决定把这张照片裁切到刚刚高于水位线的地方。 → see **cotton, farm, grain, photography**

▸ **crop up** PHRASAL VERB If something **crops up**, it appears or happens, usually unexpectedly. 意外出现; 突然发生 ❑ *His name has cropped up at every selection meeting this season.* 他的名字出人意料地出现在了本季的每次选拔会上。

cro·quet /kroʊkeɪ/ N-UNCOUNT **Croquet** is a game played on grass in which the players use long wooden sticks called mallets to hit balls through metal arches. 槌球游戏

cross
❶ MOVING ACROSS
❷ ANGRY

❶ **cross** ♦♦◇ /krɔs/ (**crosses, crossing, crossed**)
➪ **Please look at meanings 13 – 16 to see if the expression you are looking for is shown under another headword.** **1** V-T/V-I If you **cross** something such as a room, a road, or an area of land or water, you move or travel to the other side of it. If you **cross to a** place, you move or travel over a room, road, or area of land or water in order to reach that place. 穿过; 穿过去 ❑ *She was partly to blame for failing to look as she crossed the road.* 她横穿马路时没有看车，应承担部分责任。 ❑ *Egan crossed to the drinks cabinet and poured a Scotch.* 伊根穿过去，来到酒柜旁，倒了一杯苏格兰威士忌。 **2** V-T A road, railroad, or bridge that **crosses** an area of land or water passes over it. 横跨 ❑ *The road crosses the river half a mile outside the town.* 这条路横跨城外半英里处的那条河。 **3** V-T If someone or something **crosses** a limit or boundary, for example, the limit of acceptable behavior, they go beyond it. 越过 (可以被容忍的限度) ❑ *I normally never write into magazines but Mr. Stubbs has finally crossed the line.* 我通常是从不给杂志写信的，但斯塔布斯先生最后太出格了。 **4** V-T If an expression **crosses** someone's face, it appears briefly on their face. 闪过 [WRITTEN] ❑ *Berg tilts his head and a mischievous look crosses his face.* 伯格歪着脑袋，一种淘气的表情在他的脸上一闪而过。 **5** V-T If you **cross** your arms, legs, or fingers, you put one of them on top of the other. 交叉 ❑ *Jill crossed her legs and rested her chin on one fist, as if lost in deep thought.* 吉尔两腿交叉，下巴抵在拳头上，似乎陷入了沉思。 **6** V-RECIP Lines or roads that **cross** meet and go across each other. 相交 ❑ *...the intersection where Main and Center streets cross.* …主干街和中心街相交的十字路口。 **7** N-COUNT A **cross** is a shape that consists of a vertical line or piece with a shorter horizontal line or piece across it. It is the most important Christian symbol. 十字架 (基督教最重要的标志) ❑ *Around her neck was a cross on a silver chain.* 她脖子上戴着一个垂挂着十字架的银链。 **8** N-COUNT A **cross** is a written mark in the shape of an X. You can use it, for example, to indicate that an answer to a question is wrong, to mark the position of something on a map, or to indicate your vote on a ballot. 叉形记号 (X) ❑ *Put a cross next to those activities you like.* 在你喜欢的活动旁边划个叉。 **9** N-COUNT In some team sports such as soccer and hockey, a **cross** is the passing of the ball from the side of the field to a player in the center, usually in front of the goal. (足球、曲棍球等的) 横传 ❑ *Johnson hit an accurate cross to Groves.* 约翰逊将球精准地横传给格罗夫斯。 **10** N-SING Something that is **a cross between** two things is neither one thing nor the other, but a mixture of both. 混合物 ❑ *"Ha!" It was a cross between a laugh and a bark.* "哈！"那是一种一半是笑一半是厉声喊叫的混杂声。 **11** ADJ A **cross** street is a road that crosses another more important road. (与主要道路) 交叉的 [ADJ n] [AM] ❑ *The Army boys had personnel carriers blockading the cross streets.* 士兵们用运兵车封堵了与主道交叉的道路。 **12** → see also **crossing** **13** **to cross your fingers** → see **finger** **14** **cross my heart** → see **heart** **15** **to cross your mind** → see **mind** **16** **to cross swords** → see **sword**

▸ **cross out** PHRASAL VERB If you **cross out** words on a page, you draw a line through them, because they are wrong or because you want to change them. 划掉 ❑ *He crossed out "fellow subjects," and instead inserted "fellow citizens."* 他划掉了"国民同胞们"，而写进了"公民同胞们"。

Word Partnership *cross* 的常用搭配:

N. cross **a street** ❶ **1** **2**
cross **your legs** ❶ **5**
cross ***someone's* mind** ❶ **15**

❷ **cross** /krɔs/ (**crosser, crossest**) ADJ Someone who is **cross** is angry or irritated. 愤怒的 ❑ *The women are cross and bored.* 这些妇女们感到愤怒和厌烦。 ❑ *I'm terribly cross with him.* 我对他非常生气。

● **cross·ly** ADV 愤怒地 [ADV with v] ❑ *"No, no, no," Morris said crossly.* "不，不，不，"莫里斯愤怒地说。

cross-country **1** N-UNCOUNT **Cross-country** is the sport of running, riding, or skiing across open countryside rather than along roads or around a running track. (跑步、骑车或滑雪等的) 越野赛 ❑ *She finished third in the world cross-country championships in Antwerp.* 她在安特卫普举行的世界越野锦标赛中夺得了第三名。 **2** ADJ A **cross-country** trip takes you from one side of a country to the other. 横穿全国的 [ADJ n] ❑ *...cross-country rail services.* …横穿全国的铁路运输服务。 ● ADV **Cross-country** is also an adverb. 横穿全国地 [ADV after v] ❑ *I drove cross-country in his van.* 我开着他的货车横穿了全国。

cross-examine (**cross-examines, cross-examining, cross-examined**) V-T When a lawyer **cross-examines** someone during a trial or hearing, he or she questions them about the evidence that they have already given. 盘问 (已提供证词的证人) ❑ *The accused's lawyers will get a chance to cross-examine him.* 被告的律师会有盘问他的机会。 ● **cross-examination** N-VAR (**cross-examinations**) 盘问 ❑ *...the cross-examination of a witness in a murder case.* …对一谋杀案的一个证人的盘问。
→ see **trial**

cross·ing /krɔsɪŋ/ (**crossings**) 1 N-COUNT A **crossing** is a journey by boat or ship to a place on the other side of an ocean, river, or lake. 横渡 ❑ *He made the crossing from Cape Town to Sydney in just over twenty-six days.* 他从开普敦横渡到悉尼只用了二十六天多时间。 2 N-COUNT A **crossing** is a place where two roads, paths, or lines cross. 交叉路口 ❑ *She sighed and squatted down next to the crossing of the two trails.* 她叹了口气，在两条小路的交叉口旁蹲了下来。 3 N-COUNT A **crossing** is the same as a **grade crossing** or a **level crossing**. 平交道口

cross·over /krɔsoʊvər/ (**crossovers**) 1 N-VAR A **crossover** of one style and another, especially in music or fashion, is a combination of the two different styles. 混合 ❑ *...the contemporary crossover of pop, jazz and funk.* …流行乐、爵士乐和乡土乐的当代混合音乐。 2 N-SING In music or fashion, if someone makes a **crossover from** one style **to** another, they become successful outside the style they were originally known for. 转型 ❑ *I told her the crossover from actress to singer is easier than singer to actress.* 我告诉过她从女演员到歌手的转型比从歌手到女演员要容易。

cross-reference (**cross-references**) N-COUNT A **cross-reference** is a note in a book which tells you that there is relevant or more detailed information in another part of the book. 相互参照 ❑ *It concludes with a very useful summary of key points, with cross-references to where each key point is dealt with in the book.* 它在结论中对要点进行了非常有用地总结，并标出了书中讲述每个要点的参照章节。

cross·roads /krɔsroʊdz/ (**crossroads**)

> **Crossroads** is both the singular and the plural form.

1 N-COUNT A **crossroads** is a place where two roads meet and cross each other. 十字路口 ❑ *Turn right at the first crossroads.* 在第一个十字路口向右转。 2 N-SING If you say that something is **at a crossroads**, you mean that it has reached a very important stage in its development where it could go one way or another. 紧要关头 ❑ *The company was clearly at a crossroads.* 这个公司显然正处于紧要关头。

cross-section (**cross-sections**) also **cross section** 1 N-COUNT If you refer to a **cross-section of** particular things or people, you mean a group of them that you think is typical or representative of all of them. 典型 ❑ *I was surprised at the cross-section of people there.* 我对那里人的典型性类型感到惊讶。 2 N-COUNT A **cross-section** of an object is what you would see if you could cut straight through the middle of it. 截面图；横断面 [also "in" N] ❑ *...a cross-section of an airplane.* …一架飞机的截面图。

cross·word /krɔswɜrd/ (**crosswords**) N-COUNT A **crossword** or **crossword puzzle** is a word game in which you work out the answers and write them in the white squares of a pattern of small black and white squares. 纵横字谜 ❑ *He could do the Times crossword in 15 minutes.* 他能在15分钟之内做完《泰晤士报》上的纵横字谜。

crotch /krɒtʃ/ (**crotches**) 1 N-COUNT Your **crotch** is the part of your body between the tops of your legs. 胯部 ❑ *Glover kicked him hard in the crotch.* 格拉弗朝他的胯部狠狠地踢了一脚。 2 N-COUNT The **crotch** of something such as a pair of pants is the part that covers the area between the tops of your legs. 裤裆 ❑ *They were too long in the crotch.* 裤裆太长了。

▲ **crouch** /kraʊtʃ/ (**crouches, crouching, crouched**) V-I If you **are crouching**, your legs are bent under you so that you are close to the ground and leaning forward slightly. 蹲伏 ❑ *We were crouching in the bushes.* 我们那时正蹲伏在灌木丛中。 ❑ *I crouched on the ground.* 我蹲伏在地上。 ● N-SING **Crouch** is also a noun. 蹲伏 ❑ *They walked in a crouch, each bent over close to the ground.* 他们蹲伏着行走，一个个弯着腰快要贴着地面了。 ● PHRASAL VERB **Crouch down** means the same as **crouch**. 蹲下

▲ **crow** /kroʊ/ (**crows, crowing, crowed**) 1 N-COUNT A **crow** is a large black bird which makes a loud, harsh noise. 乌鸦 ❑ *The crows roosted in Fonsa's Tower.* 那些乌鸦栖息在风萨塔里。 2 V-I When a cock **crows**, it makes a loud sound, often early in the morning. (公鸡的报晓) 啼叫 ❑ *The cock crows and the dawn chorus begins.* 公鸡叫了，众鸟的清晨鸣唱随之开始了。 3 PHRASE If someone **eats crow**, they admit that they have been wrong and apologize, especially in situations where this is humiliating or embarrassing for them. 被迫认错 [AM] ❑ *He wanted to make his critics eat crow.* 他想迫使批评他的人们认错。

crowd ◆◆◇ /kraʊd/ (**crowds, crowding, crowded**) 1 N-COUNT-COLL A **crowd** is a large group of people who have gathered together, for example, to watch or listen to something interesting, or to protest about something. 人群 ❑ *A huge crowd gathered in a square outside the Kremlin walls.* 一大群人聚集在了克里姆林宫墙外的广场上。 ❑ *It took some two hours before the crowd was fully dispersed.* 用了大约两个小时才把人群完全驱散。 2 N-COUNT A particular **crowd** is a group of friends, or a set of people who share the same interests or job. 一帮 (朋友)；一群 (志趣相投的人) [INFORMAL] ❑ *All the old crowd have come out for this occasion.* 所有老朋友都前来参加了这次活动。 3 V-I When people **crowd around** someone or something, they gather closely together around them. 聚集 ❑ *The hungry refugees crowded around the tractors.* 饥饿的难民们围在拖拉机旁。 ❑ *Police blocked off the road as hotel staff and guests crowded around.* 旅馆员工和房客围聚过来时警察封锁了道路。 4 V-T/V-I If people **crowd into** a place or **are crowded into** a place, large numbers of them enter it so that it becomes very full. 挤满；挤进 ❑ *Hundreds of thousands of people have crowded into the center of the Lithuanian capital, Vilnius.* 几十万人涌进了立陶宛首都维尔纽斯的中心。 ❑ *One group of journalists were crowded into a minibus.* 一群记者挤满了一辆面包车。 5 V-T If a group of people **crowd** a place, there are so many of them there that it is full. 挤满 ❑ *Thousands of demonstrators crowded the streets shouting slogans.* 数千名示威者喊着口号，挤满了街道。

> **Word Partnership** *crowd* 的常用搭配：
>
> V. **attract a** crowd, **avoid the** crowd, crowd **gathers** 1
> ADJ. **enthusiastic** crowd, **small** crowd 1
> PREP. crowd **around** *something* 3
> crowd **into** *something* 4

crowd·ed /kraʊdɪd/ 1 ADJ If a place is **crowded**, it is full of people. 拥挤的 ❑ *He peered slowly around the small crowded room.* 他慢慢地仔细打量着那间拥挤的小房间的每个角落。 2 ADJ If a place is **crowded**, a lot of people live there. 人口密集的 ❑ *...a crowded city of 2 million.* …一个有200万人口的拥挤的城市。 3 ADJ If your schedule, your life, or your mind is **crowded**, it is full of events, activities, or thoughts. 排满的 ❑ *Never before has a summit had such a crowded agenda.* 从来没有一个高峰会议把议程安排得这样满。

crown ◆◇◇ /kraʊn/ (**crowns, crowning, crowned**) 1 N-COUNT A **crown** is a circular ornament, usually made of gold and jewels, which a king or queen wears on their head at official ceremonies. You can also use **crown** to refer to anything circular that is worn on someone's head. 王冠；冠 ❑ *...a crown of flowers.* …一个花冠。 2 N-COUNT Your **crown** is the top part of your head, at the back. 头顶后部 ❑ *He laid his hand gently on the crown of her head.* 他把手轻轻地放在她的头顶后部。 3 N-COUNT A **crown** is an artificial top piece fixed over a broken or decayed tooth. 齿冠 ❑ *How long does it take to have crowns fitted?* 镶齿冠需要多长时间？ 4 N-PROPER The government of a country that has a king or queen is sometimes referred to as **the Crown**. 王国政府 ❑ *She says the sovereignty of the Crown must be preserved.* 她说君主政权必须予以保留。 ❑ *...a minister of the Crown.* …王国政府的一位大臣。 5 V-T When a king or queen **is crowned**, a crown is placed on their head as part of a ceremony in which they are officially made king or queen. 为…加冕 [usu passive] ❑ *Two days later, Juan Carlos was crowned king.* 两天后，胡安・卡洛斯被加冕为国王。
→ see **teeth**

★ **crown·ing** /kraʊnɪŋ/ (**crownings**) 1 N-COUNT A **crowning** is a ceremony at which someone is made a king or queen by having a crown put on their head. 加冕 ❑ *This compelling story begins with the crowning of Queen Victoria in 1837.* 这个吸引人的故事开始于1837年维多利亚女王的加冕。 2 ADJ A **crowning** moment or achievement is the greatest one in a series. 最伟大的 [ADJ n] ❑ *The successful mission marked the crowning moment for the space program.* 这个成功使命标志了

太空计划的最伟大时刻。❑ *Taking the country into the euro was the crowning glory of his political career.* 将这个国家带入欧元区是他政治生涯的无比荣耀。

Word Link *cruc ≈ cross : crucial, crucifixion, crucify*

cru·cial ♦◇◇ /kruʃᵊl/ ADJ If you describe something as **crucial**, you mean it is extremely important. 至关重要的 ❑ *He had administrators under him but made the crucial decisions himself.* 尽管他手下有许多官员，但重要的决定还是他自己做。● **cru·cial·ly** ADV 至关重要地 ❑ *Chewing properly is crucially important.* 正确地咀嚼是至关重要的。

Word Partnership *crucial* 的常用搭配：
N. crucial **decision**, crucial **development**, crucial **role**, crucial **skill**, crucial **stage**, crucial **to** *something*

cru·ci·fix·ion /krusɪfɪkʃᵊn/ (**crucifixions**) 1 N-VAR **Crucifixion** is a way of killing people which was common in the Roman Empire, in which they were tied or nailed to a cross and left to die. 被钉死在十字架上 ❑ *...her historical novel about the crucifixion of Christians in Rome.* …她的关于基督徒在罗马被钉死在十字架上的历史小说。2 N-PROPER **The Crucifixion** is the crucifixion of Christ. 耶稣受难 ❑ *...the central message of the Crucifixion.* …耶稣受难的重要启示。

cru·ci·fy /krusɪfaɪ/ (**crucifies, crucifying, crucified**) 1 V-T If someone **is crucified**, they are killed by being tied or nailed to a cross and left to die. 把…钉死在十字架上 [usu passive] ❑ *...the day that Christ was crucified.* …耶稣被钉死在十字架上的那天。2 V-T To **crucify** someone means to criticize or punish them severely. 狠批；恶整 [INFORMAL] ❑ *She'll crucify me if she finds you still here.* 要是她发现你还在这里，她会狠整我的。

crude /krud/ (**cruder, crudest**) 1 ADJ A **crude** method or measurement is not exact or detailed, but may be useful or correct in a rough, general way. 粗略的 ❑ *Standard measurements of blood pressure are an important but crude way of assessing the risk of heart disease or strokes.* 标准的血压测量是评估心脏病或中风风险的一种重要却粗略的方法。● **crude·ly** ADV 粗略地 ❑ *The donors can be split – a little crudely – into two groups.* 捐献者们可以分成——大致地——两个组。2 ADJ If you describe an object that someone has made as **crude**, you mean that it has been made in a very simple way or from very simple parts. 粗制的 ❑ *...crude wooden boxes.* …粗制的木盒子。● **crude·ly** ADV 粗糙地 ❑ *...a crudely carved wooden form.* …一件粗糙的木头雕刻。3 ADJ If you describe someone as **crude**, you disapprove of them because they speak or behave in a rude, offensive, or unsophisticated way. 粗鲁的 [DISAPPROVAL] ❑ *Must you be quite so crude?* 你一定要这样粗鲁吗？● **crude·ly** ADV 粗鲁地 ❑ *He hated it when she spoke so crudely.* 他讨厌她说话那么粗鲁。4 ADJ **Crude** substances are in a natural or unrefined state, and have not yet been used in manufacturing processes. 未加工的 [ADJ n] 5 N-MASS **Crude** is the same as **crude oil**. 原油
→ see **oil**

crude oil N-UNCOUNT **Crude oil** is oil in its natural state before it has been processed or refined. 原油 ❑ *A thousand tons of crude oil has spilled into the sea from an oil tanker.* 1000吨原油从油轮泄漏到了海里。

cru·el /kruəl/ (**crueler** or **crueller, cruelest** or **cruellest**) 1 ADJ Someone who is **cruel** deliberately causes pain or distress to people or animals. 残忍的 ❑ *Children can be so cruel.* 孩子也会这么残忍。● **cru·el·ly** ADV 残忍地 [ADV with v] ❑ *Douglas was often cruelly tormented by jealous siblings.* 道格拉斯过去常遭到嫉妒他的兄弟姐妹们的残忍折磨。2 ADJ A situation or event that is **cruel** is very harsh and causes people distress. 严酷的 ❑ *...struggling to survive in a cruel world with which they cannot cope.* …在一个他们不能承受的严酷世界中挣扎着求生。● **cru·el·ly** ADV 严酷地 ❑ *His life has been cruelly shattered by an event not of his own making.* 他的生活由于一个非他自身因素造成的事件被无情地破坏了。

Thesaurus *cruel* 另参见：
ADJ. harsh, heartless, mean, nasty, unkind; *(ant.)* gentle, kind 1
grim, severe 2

cru·el·ty /kruəlti/ (**cruelties**) N-VAR **Cruelty** is behavior that deliberately causes pain or distress to people or animals. 残忍 ❑ *Britain had laws against cruelty to animals but none to protect children.* 英国曾有反对虐待动物的法律，却没有一部保护儿童的法律。

cruise ♦◇◇ /kruz/ (**cruises, cruising, cruised**) 1 N-COUNT A **cruise** is a vacation during which you travel on a ship or boat and visit a number of places. 海上航游 ❑ *He and his wife were planning to go on a world cruise.* 他和妻子那时正计划进行一次环球海上航游。2 V-T/V-I If you **cruise** an ocean, river, or canal, you travel around it or along it on a cruise. 巡航；巡航于 ❑ *She wants to cruise the canals of France in a barge.* 她想坐驳船游览法国的运河。❑ *...a vacation cruising around the Caribbean.* …环游加勒比海的度假航行。3 V-I If a car, ship, or aircraft **cruises** somewhere, it moves there at a steady comfortable speed. (车辆、船只、飞机等) 漫游 ❑ *A black and white police car cruised past.* 一辆黑白相间的警车平稳驶过。
→ see **ship**

▲ **cruis·er** /kruzər/ (**cruisers**) 1 N-COUNT A **cruiser** is a motorboat which has an area for people to live or sleep. 游艇 ❑ *...a three-hour journey in a small cruiser with indoor and outdoor seating.* …一次乘坐里外皆设有座椅的小游艇的3小时旅行。2 N-COUNT A **cruiser** is a large fast warship. 巡洋舰 ❑ *Italy had lost three cruisers and two destroyers.* 意大利损失了3艘巡洋舰和2艘驱逐舰。3 N-COUNT A **cruiser** is a police car. 警车 [AM] ❑ *Police cruisers surrounded the bank throughout the day.* 警车把这家银行包围了一整天。

▲ **crumb** /krʌm/ (**crumbs**) N-COUNT **Crumbs** are tiny pieces that fall from bread, cookies, or cake when you cut it or eat it. (面包、饼干、蛋糕等的) 碎屑 ❑ *I stood up, brushing crumbs from my pants.* 我站起来，掸去裤子上的食物碎屑。

★ **crum·ble** /krʌmbᵊl/ (**crumbles, crumbling, crumbled**) 1 V-T/V-I If something **crumbles**, or if you **crumble** it, it breaks into a lot of small pieces. 碎裂；弄碎 ❑ *Under the pressure, the flint crumbled into fragments.* 在压力作用下，燧石裂成了碎片。2 V-I If an old building or piece of land **is crumbling**, parts of it keep breaking off. 崩塌 ❑ *The high- and low-rise apartment blocks built in the 1960s are crumbling.* 建于20世纪60年代的高、低层公寓楼正摇摇欲坠。● PHRASAL VERB **Crumble away** means the same as **crumble**. 崩塌 ❑ *Much of the coastline is crumbling away.* 多处海岸线正在垮塌。3 V-I If something such as a system, relationship, or hope **crumbles**, it comes to an end. (制度、关系或希望) 崩溃 ❑ *Their economy crumbled under the weight of United Nations sanctions.* 在联合国制裁的重压之下，他们的经济崩溃了。● PHRASAL VERB **Crumble away** means the same as **crumble**. (制度、关系或希望) 崩溃 ❑ *Opposition more or less crumbled away.* 反对党差不多崩溃了。

crum·bly /krʌmbli/ (**crumblier, crumbliest**) ADJ Something that is **crumbly** is easily broken into a lot of little pieces. 易碎的；脆的 ❑ *...crumbly cheese.* …酥脆的奶酪。

▲ **crum·ple** /krʌmpᵊl/ (**crumples, crumpling, crumpled**) V-T/V-I If you **crumple** something such as paper or cloth, or if it **crumples**, it is squashed and becomes full of untidy creases and folds. 弄皱；起皱 ❑ *She crumpled the paper in her hand.* 她把手中的纸揉成了一团。● PHRASAL VERB **Crumple up** means the same as **crumple**. 弄皱 ❑ *She crumpled up her coffee cup.* 她挤瘪了咖啡杯。● **crum·pled** ADJ 褶皱的 ❑ *His uniform was crumpled and untidy.* 他的制服有很多褶皱，而且不整洁。

▲ **crunch** /krʌntʃ/ (**crunches, crunching, crunched**) 1 V-T/V-I If you **crunch** something hard, such as a piece of candy, or if it **crunches**, you crush it noisily between your teeth. 嘎吱嘎吱地咬嚼(某物)；发出嘎吱声 ❑ *She sucked an ice cube into her mouth, and crunched it loudly.* 她把一冰块儿含在嘴里，并嘎吱嘎吱地大声嚼起来。2 V-T/V-I If something **crunches** or if you **crunch** it, it makes a breaking or crushing noise, for example, when you step on it. 嘎吱嘎吱地碾或踩 (某物)；发出嘎吱声 ❑ *A piece of china crunched under my foot.* 一块瓷片在我的脚下发出嘎吱的响声。● N-COUNT **Crunch** is also a noun. 嘎吱嘎吱的声音 ❑ *She heard the crunch of tires on the gravel driveway.* 她听到车胎碾在碎石铺成的私家车道上发出的嘎吱声。3 V-I If you **crunch** across a surface made of very small stones, you move across it causing it to make a crunching noise. 嘎吱嘎吱地踩 ❑ *I crunched across the gravel.* 我从石子上嘎吱嘎吱地踩过。4 V-T To **crunch** numbers means to do a lot of calculations using a calculator or computer. (用计算器或电脑) 运算 ❑ *I pored over the books with great enthusiasm, often crunching the numbers until 1:00 a.m.* 我饶有兴趣地细读这些书，常常运算到凌晨1：00。5 N-SING You can refer to an important time or event, for example, when an important decision has to be made, as **the crunch**. 关键时刻 ❑ *He can rely on my support when the crunch comes.* 在关键时刻他会得到我的支持的。6 N-COUNT A situation in which a business or economy has very little money can be referred to as a **crunch**. 财政困难 [BUSINESS] ❑ *The U.N. is facing a cash crunch.* 联合国正面临着资金短缺。

Word Web cry

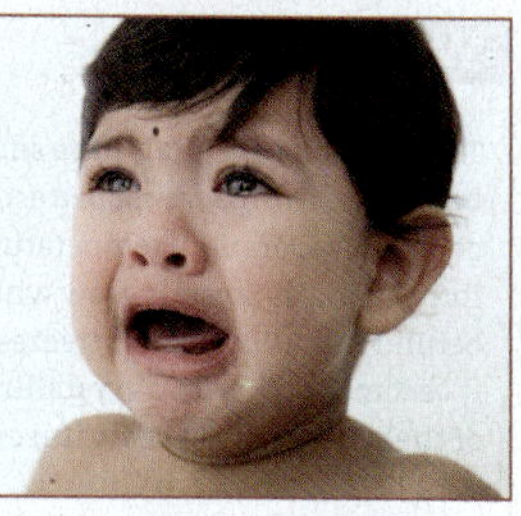

Have you ever seen someone **burst into tears** when something wonderful happened to them? We expect people to **cry** when they are **sad** or upset. But why do people sometimes **weep** when they are happy? Scientists have found there are three different types of **tears**. Basal tears lubricate the **eyes**. Reflex tears clear the eyes of dirt or smoke. The third type, emotional tears, contain high levels of manganese and prolactin. Decreasing the amount of these chemicals in the body helps us feel better. When people experience strong feelings, negative or positive, **shedding tears** may help restore emotional balance.

crunchy /krʌntʃi/ (**crunchier, crunchiest**) ADJ Food that is **crunchy** is pleasantly hard or crisp so that it makes a noise when you eat it. 脆的 [APPROVAL] ❑ *...fresh, crunchy vegetables.* …鲜脆的蔬菜。

cru·sade /kruseɪd/ (**crusades, crusading, crusaded**) 1 N-COUNT A **crusade** is a long and determined attempt to achieve something for a cause that you feel strongly about. (长期而坚定的)努力奋斗 ❑ *He made it his crusade to teach children to love books.* 他把教育孩子热爱书籍作为自己的奋斗目标。 2 V-I If you **crusade** for a particular cause, you make a long and determined effort to achieve something for it. (为推进某一事业而) 奋斗 ❑ *...a newspaper that has crusaded against the country's cocaine traffickers.* …一份致力于打击本国可卡因走私犯的报纸。

cru·sad·er /kruseɪdər/ (**crusaders**) N-COUNT A **crusader for a** cause is someone who does a lot in support of it. (支持某项事业的)斗士 ❑ *He has set himself up as a crusader for higher press and broadcasting standards.* 他成了为取得更高的新闻和广播原则而奋战的斗士。

crush /krʌʃ/ (**crushes, crushing, crushed**) 1 V-T To **crush** something means to press it very hard so that its shape is destroyed or so that it breaks into pieces. 压扁; 压碎 ❑ *Andrew crushed his empty can.* 安德鲁压扁了他的空罐子。 ❑ *...crushed ice.* …碎冰。 2 V-T To **crush** a protest or movement, or a group of opponents, means to defeat it completely, usually by force. 镇压 ❑ *The military operation was the first step in a plan to crush the uprising.* 这次军事行动是镇压暴动计划的第一步。 ● **crush·ing** N-UNCOUNT 镇压 ❑ *...the violent crushing of anti-government demonstrations.* …对反政府示威运动的武力镇压。 3 V-T If you **are crushed** by something, it upsets you a great deal. 使精神崩溃 [usu passive] ❑ *Listen to criticism but don't be crushed by it.* 听批评意见，但不要被它击垮。 4 V-T If you **are crushed** against someone or something, you are pushed or pressed against them. (与某人或某物) 挤在一起 [usu passive] ❑ *We were at the front, crushed against the stage.* 我们在前面，被挤得紧挨着舞台。 5 N-COUNT A **crush** is a crowd of people close together, in which it is difficult to move. 拥挤的人群 ❑ *His thirteen-year-old son somehow got separated in the crush.* 他13岁的儿子不知怎么在拥挤的人群里走散了。 6 N-COUNT If you have a **crush on** someone, you are in love with them but do not have a relationship with them. 暗恋 [INFORMAL] ❑ *She had a crush on you, you know.* 你知道吧，她曾暗恋过你。
→ see **crash**

crush·ing /krʌʃɪŋ/ ADJ A **crushing** defeat, burden, or disappointment is a very great or severe one. 毁灭性的 [ADJ n] [EMPHASIS] ❑ *...since their crushing defeat in the local elections.* …自从他们在地方选举中遭到毁灭性的挫败以来。

crust /krʌst/ (**crusts**) 1 N-COUNT The **crust** on a loaf of bread is the outside part. 面包皮 ❑ *Cut the crusts off the bread and soak the bread in the milk.* 切掉面包皮，将面包浸在牛奶中。 2 N-COUNT A pie's **crust** is its cooked pastry. 馅饼皮 ❑ *The Key lime pie was bursting with flavor. Good crust, too.* "基"牌酸橙派味道很浓，外皮也很好。 3 N-COUNT A **crust** is a hard layer of something, especially on top of a softer or wetter substance. 硬外壳 ❑ *As the water evaporates, a crust of salt is left on the surface of the soil.* 水蒸发后，土壤表面留下一层盐。 4 N-COUNT The Earth's **crust** is its outer layer. 地壳 ❑ *Earthquakes leave scars in the Earth's crust.* 地震会在地壳上留下痕迹。
→ see **continent, core, earthquake**

crusty /krʌsti/ (**crustier, crustiest**) ADJ **Crusty** bread has a hard, crisp outside. 有硬而脆外皮的 ❑ *...crusty French loaves.* …表皮硬而脆的法式面包。

▲ **crutch** /krʌtʃ/ (**crutches**) 1 N-COUNT A **crutch** is a stick whose top fits around or under the user's arm, which someone with an injured foot or leg uses to support their weight when walking. 拐杖 ❑ *I can walk without the aid of crutches.* 我能够不借助拐杖走路。 2 N-SING If you refer to someone or something as a **crutch**, you mean that they give you help or support. (提供帮助、支持的) 人或物 ❑ *He gave up the crutch of alcohol.* 他不再依赖酒精。

crux /krʌks/ N-SING **The crux of** a problem or argument is the most important or difficult part of it which affects everything else. 症结 ❑ *He said the crux of the matter was economic policy.* 他说该问题的症结在于经济政策。

cry ◆◆◇ /kraɪ/ (**cries, crying, cried**) 1 V-I When you **cry**, tears come from your eyes, usually because you are unhappy or hurt. 哭 ❑ *I hung up the phone and started to cry.* 我挂掉电话，开始哭了起来。 ❑ *He cried with anger and frustration.* 他愤怒而失望地哭了。 ● N-SING **Cry** is also a noun. 哭 ❑ *A nurse patted me on the shoulder and said, "You have a good cry, dear."* 一个护士拍着我的肩膀，说道："亲爱的，你就痛痛快快地哭吧。" ● **cry·ing** N-UNCOUNT 啼哭 ❑ *She had been unable to sleep for three days because of her 13-week-old son's crying.* 由于她13周大的儿子的啼哭，她3天没睡着觉了。 2 V-T If you **cry** something, you shout it or say it loudly. 大声叫喊 ❑ *"Nancy Drew," she cried, "you're under arrest!"* "南茜·德鲁，"她喊道："你被捕了！" ● PHRASAL VERB **Cry out** means the same as **cry**. 大叫 ❑ *"You're wrong, quite wrong!" Henry cried out, suddenly excited.* "你错了，大错特错！"亨利突然激动起来，大声叫道。 3 N-COUNT A **cry** is a loud, high sound that you make when you feel a strong emotion such as fear, pain, or pleasure. 尖叫 ❑ *A cry of horror broke from me.* 我发出的一声惊恐的尖叫。 4 N-COUNT A **cry** is a shouted word or phrase, usually one that is intended to attract someone's attention. 喊叫声 ❑ *Thousands of Ukrainians burst into cries of "bravo."* 数千名乌克兰人放声高呼"好！" 5 N-COUNT You can refer to a public protest about something or an appeal for something as a **cry** of some kind. (抗议某事、为某事请愿的) 公众呼声 [JOURNALISM] ❑ *There have been cries of outrage about this expenditure.* 公众对这项开支发出了愤怒的呼声。 6 N-COUNT A bird's or an animal's **cry** is the loud, high sound that it makes. (鸟的) 啼叫声; (动物的) 嚎叫声 ❑ *...the cry of a seagull.* …一只海鸥的鸣叫声。 7 → see also **crying** 8 **to cry your eyes out** → see **eye** 9 **a shoulder to cry on** → see **shoulder**
→ see Word Web: **cry**

▸ **cry out** 1 PHRASAL VERB If you **cry out**, you call out loudly because you are frightened, unhappy, or in pain. (因受惊、不快、痛苦等) 大声叫喊 ❑ *He was crying out in pain when the ambulance arrived.* 救护车到的时候，他在痛苦地大叫着。 2 → see also **cry 2**

▸ **cry out for** PHRASAL VERB If you say that something **cries out for** a particular thing or action, you mean that it needs that thing or action very much. 迫切需要 ❑ *This is a disgraceful state of affairs and cries out for a thorough investigation.* 这是一件不光彩的事情，急需进行彻底的调查。

Thesaurus *cry* 另参见：

V. sob, weep 1
call, shout, yell 2
N. howl, moan, shriek 3

Word Partnership *cry* 的常用搭配：

V. **begin to** cry, **start to** cry 1
N. cry **with anger** 2 4
cry **for help**, cry **with joy** 2
cry **of horror**, cry **of pain** 3

cry·ing /kraɪɪŋ/ 1 PHRASE If you say that there is **a crying need** for something, you mean that there is a very great need for it. 急需 ❑ *There is a crying need for more magistrates from the ethnic minority communities.* 迫切需要更多来自少数民族社区的官员。 2 → see also **cry**

cryp·tic /krɪptɪk/ ADJ A **cryptic** remark or message contains a hidden meaning or is difficult to understand. 隐晦的 ❑ *He has*

C

Word Web crystal

The outsides of **crystals** have smooth flat planes. These surfaces form because of the repeating patterns of atoms, molecules, or ions inside the crystal. Evaporation, temperature changes, and pressure can all help to form crystals. Crystals grow when sea water evaporates and leaves behind **salt**. When water freezes, **ice** crystals form. When magma cools, it becomes **rock** with a crystalline structure. Pressure can also create one of the hardest, most beautiful crystals—the **diamond**.

issued a short, cryptic statement denying the spying charges. 他发表了一个简短、令人捉摸不透的声明，否认对他从事间谍活动的指控。

● **cryp·ti·cal·ly** ADV 神秘莫测地 [ADV with V] ❑ *"Not necessarily," she says cryptically.* "不一定，"她神秘地说道。

crys·tal ♦◇◇ /krɪstᵊl/ (**crystals**) **1** N-COUNT A **crystal** is a small piece of a substance that has formed naturally into a regular symmetrical shape. 结晶体 ❑ *...salt crystals.* …盐的结晶体。❑ *...ice crystals.* …冰晶。**2** N-VAR **Crystal** is a transparent rock that is used to make jewelry and ornaments. 水晶 ❑ *She was wearing a strand of crystal beads.* 她戴着一串水晶珠子。**3** N-UNCOUNT **Crystal** is a high quality glass, usually with patterns cut into its surface. 晶质玻璃 ❑ *Some of the finest drinking glasses are made from lead crystal.* 一些最精致的酒杯是用铅晶质玻璃制成的。

→ see Word Web: **crystal**

→ see **rock, sugar**

crys·tal clear **1** ADJ Water that is **crystal clear** is absolutely clear and transparent like glass. 明澈的 ❑ *The cliffs, lapped by a crystal-clear sea, remind her of Capri.* 清澈透明的大海拍打着峭壁，让她想起卡普里岛。**2** ADJ If you say that a message or statement is **crystal clear**, you are emphasizing that it is very easy to understand. 清楚易懂的 [EMPHASIS] ❑ *The message is crystal clear – if you lose weight, you will have a happier, healthier, better life.* 这意思很清楚——如果你减肥的话，你会过上更快乐、更健康、更美好的生活。

crys·tal·lise /krɪstᵊlaɪz/ [BRIT] → see **crystallize**

crys·tal·lize /krɪstᵊlaɪz/ (**crystallizes, crystallizing, crystallized**)

in BRIT, also use **crystallise**

1 V-T/V-I If you **crystallize** an opinion or idea, or if it **crystallizes**, it becomes fixed and definite in someone's mind. 使成形；具体化 ❑ *He has managed to crystallize the feelings of millions of ordinary Russians.* 他成功地阐明了数百万普通俄国人的感情。**2** V-T/V-I If a substance **crystallizes**, or something **crystallizes** it, it turns into crystals. 使结晶；结成晶体 ❑ *Don't stir or the sugar will crystallize.* 不要搅，否则糖会结晶的。

▲ **cub** /kʌb/ (**cubs**) N-COUNT A **cub** is a young wild animal such as a lion, wolf, or bear. (狮子、狼、熊等的) 幼仔 ❑ *...three five-week-old lion cubs.* …3只5周大的幼狮。

cube /kyub/ (**cubes, cubing, cubed**) **1** N-COUNT A **cube** is a solid object with six square surfaces which are all the same size. 立方体 ❑ *...cold water with ice cubes in it.* …加冰块的冷水。❑ *...a box of sugar cubes.* …一盒方糖。**2** N-COUNT **The cube of** a number is another number that is produced by multiplying the first number by itself twice. For example, the cube of 2 is 8. 立方 **3** V-T When you **cube** food, you cut it into cube-shaped pieces. 将…切成方块 ❑ *Remove the seeds and stones and cube the flesh.* 去除籽和核，然后把果肉切成方块。

→ see **solid, volume**

★ **cu·bic** /kyubɪk/ ADJ **Cubic** is used in front of units of length to form units of volume such as "cubic meter" and "cubic foot." 立方的 [ADJ n] ❑ *...3 billion cubic meters of soil.* …30亿立方米的土。

Word Link *cle ≈ small : article, cubicle, particle*

cu·bi·cle /kyubɪkᵊl/ (**cubicles**) **1** N-COUNT A **cubicle** is a very small enclosed area, for example, one where you can take a shower or change your clothes. (用于淋浴、更衣等的) 小单间 ❑ *...a separate shower cubicle.* …一个独立的淋浴间。**2** N-COUNT A **cubicle** is an area in an office that is separated from the rest of the room by thin walls. (办公室内的) 格子间 ❑ *I'm not the kind of person to sit in a cubicle behind a desk.* 我不是那种能在格子间办公桌后坐得住的人。

→ see **office**

cuckoo /kuku, kʊku/ (**cuckoos**) N-COUNT A **cuckoo** is a bird that has a call of two quick notes, and lays its eggs in other birds' nests. 杜鹃；布谷鸟

★ **cu·cum·ber** /kyukʌmbər/ (**cucumbers**) N-VAR A **cucumber** is a long thin vegetable with a hard green skin and wet transparent flesh. It is eaten raw in salads. 黄瓜 ❑ *...a cheese and cucumber sandwich.* …一个奶酪黄瓜三明治。

cud·dle /kʌdᵊl/ (**cuddles, cuddling, cuddled**) V-T If you **cuddle** someone, you put your arms around them and hold them close as a way of showing your affection. 搂抱；拥抱；怀抱 ❑ *He cuddled the newborn girl.* 他怀抱着新生的女婴。● N-COUNT **Cuddle** is also a noun. 拥抱 ❑ *It would have been nice to give him a cuddle and a kiss but there wasn't time.* 当时要是拥抱他并吻他一下就好了，可惜时间来不及。

cud·dly /kʌdli/ (**cuddlier, cuddliest**) **1** ADJ A **cuddly** person or animal makes you want to cuddle them. 令人想拥抱的 [APPROVAL] ❑ *He is a small, cuddly man with spectacles.* 他是一个令人想拥抱的戴眼镜的小个子男人。**2** ADJ **Cuddly** toys are soft toys that look like animals. (做成动物形状的玩具) 柔软可爱的 [ADJ n]

cue ♦◇◇ /kyu/ (**cues, cueing, cued**) **1** N-COUNT In the theater or in a musical performance, a performer's **cue** is something another performer says or does that is a signal for them to begin speaking, playing, or doing something. (在戏剧或音乐表演中提示表演者说话、演奏或动作的) 提示 ❑ *The actors not performing sit at the side of the stage in full view, waiting for their cues.* 未表演的男演员们坐在舞台边，对舞台一览无余，他们等待着上场的提示。**2** N-COUNT If you say that something that happens is a **cue for** an action, you mean that people start doing that action when it happens. 触发事件 ❑ *That was the cue for several months of intense bargaining.* 此事触发了此后数月激烈的讨价还价。**3** N-COUNT A **cue** is a long, thin wooden stick that is used to hit the ball in games such as billiards, pool, and snooker. (台球等所用的) 球杆 **4** V-T If one performer **cues** another, they say or do something which is a signal for the second performer to begin speaking, playing, or doing something. (为下一位演员) 提示 ❑ *He read the scene, with Seaton cueing him.* 在西顿提示下，他朗诵了这一场的台词。

▲ **cuff** /kʌf/ (**cuffs**) **1** N-COUNT The **cuffs** of a shirt or dress are the parts at the ends of the sleeves, which are thicker than the rest of the sleeve. 袖口 ❑ *...a pale blue shirt with white collar and cuffs.* …一件白领和白袖口的淡蓝色衬衫。**2** N-COUNT The **cuffs** on a pair of pants are the parts at the ends of the legs, which are folded up. (裤脚的) 翻边 [usu pl] [AM]

in BRIT, use **turn-up**

3 PHRASE An **off-the-cuff** remark is made without being prepared or thought about in advance. 即兴的 ❑ *I didn't mean any offense. It was a flippant, off-the-cuff remark.* 我无意冒犯，那只是贸然随口而说的。

→ see **diagnosis**

▲ **cui·sine** /kwɪzin/ (**cuisines**) N-VAR The **cuisine** of a country or district is the style of cooking that is characteristic of that place. 烹调风格 ❑ *The cuisine of Japan is low in fat.* 日式烹调脂肪含量低。

→ see **restaurant**

culi·nary /kyulənɛri, kʌlə-/ ADJ **Culinary** means concerned with cooking. 烹调的 [ADJ n] [FORMAL] ❑ *...advanced culinary skills.* …高超的烹调技艺。

cull /kʌl/ (**culls, culling, culled**) **1** V-T If items or ideas **are culled from** a particular source or number of sources, they are taken and gathered together. 采集 [usu passive] ❑ *All this, needless to say, had been culled second-hand from radio reports.* 不必说，这一切都是从无线电广播报道中搜集来的第二手信息。**2** V-T To **cull** animals means to kill the weaker animals in a group in order to reduce their numbers. 宰杀 (病弱动物以减少其数目) ❑ *To save remaining herds and* *habitat, the national parks department is planning to cull 2000 elephants.* 为挽救余下的兽群及其栖息地，国家公园管理部门正计划杀掉2000头大象。● N-COUNT **Cull** is also a noun. (对病弱动物的) 宰杀 ❑ *In the reserves of Zimbabwe and South Africa, annual culls are already routine.* 在津巴布韦和南非的自然保护区，对病弱动物每年所进行的宰杀剔除已成惯例。● **cull·ing** N-UNCOUNT 杀死 ❑ *The culling of seal cubs has led to an outcry from environmental groups.* 宰杀海豹幼仔的行为已引起了环保团体的强烈抗议。

cul·mi·nate /kʌlmɪneɪt/ (**culminates, culminating, culminated**) V-I If you say that an activity, process, or series of events **culminates in** or **with** a particular event, you mean that event happens at the end of it. 以…告终；结果成为 ❑ *They had an argument, which culminated in Tom getting drunk.* 他们发生了争论，结果导致汤姆喝醉了酒。

cul·mi·na·tion /kʌlmɪneɪʃᵊn/ N-SING Something, especially something important, that is **the culmination of** an activity, process, or series of events happens at the end of it. 结局 ❑ *Their arrest was the culmination of an operation in which 120 other people were detained.* 那次行动以他们的被捕以及另外120个人的被拘留而告结束。

▲ **cul·prit** /kʌlprɪt/ (**culprits**) 1 N-COUNT When you are talking about a crime or something wrong that has been done, you can refer to the person who did it as **the culprit**. 犯罪者；犯错者 ❑ *All the men were being deported even though the real culprits in the fight have not been identified.* 尽管那次斗殴事件的真凶未被确认，但那些男人都在被驱逐出境。2 N-COUNT When you are talking about a problem or bad situation, you can refer to its cause as **the culprit**. (造成问题或麻烦的) 原因 ❑ *About 10% of Japanese teenagers are overweight. Nutritionists say the main culprit is increasing reliance on Western fast food.* 约10%的日本青少年都超重。营养学家们称主要的原因是他们越来越依赖西方快餐。

▲ **cult** /kʌlt/ (**cults**) 1 N-COUNT A **cult** is a fairly small religious group, especially one which is considered strange. 异教团体 ❑ *The teenager may have been abducted by a religious cult.* 这位少年可能被某个异教团体绑架了。2 N-COUNT The **cult** of something is a situation in which people regard that thing as very important or special. 狂热崇拜 [DISAPPROVAL] ❑ *...the cult of youth that recently gripped publishing.* …近期吸引了出版界的年青人的狂热。3 ADJ **Cult** is used to describe things that are very popular or fashionable among a particular group of people. 受到狂热崇拜的 [ADJ n] ❑ *Since her death, she has become a cult figure.* 她死后已成为人们顶礼膜拜的人物。4 N-SING Someone or something that is a **cult** has become very popular or fashionable among a particular group of people. 时尚 ❑ *Violence has become a cult among some young men.* 暴力已成为一些年轻人追逐的时尚。

cul·ti·vate /kʌltɪveɪt/ (**cultivates, cultivating, cultivated**) 1 V-T If you **cultivate** land or crops, you prepare land and grow crops on it. 开垦；种植 ❑ *She also cultivated a small garden of her own.* 她还开垦了一个自己的小花园。● ★ **cul·ti·va·tion** /kʌltɪveɪʃᵊn/ N-UNCOUNT 开垦；种植 ❑ *...the cultivation of fruits and vegetables.* …水果蔬菜的种植。2 V-T If you **cultivate** an attitude, image, or skill, you try hard to develop it and make it stronger or better. 培养 (态度、技巧等)；树立 (形象、观念等) ❑ *He has written eight books and has cultivated the image of an elder statesman.* 他已写了8本书，并树立了一个政界元老的形象。● **cul·ti·va·tion** N-UNCOUNT 培养；树立 ❑ *...the cultivation of a positive approach to life and health.* …积极的生活和健康观的树立。3 V-T If you **cultivate** someone or **cultivate** a friendship with them, you try hard to develop a friendship with them. 建立 (友谊) ❑ *Howe carefully cultivated Daniel C. Roper, the Assistant Postmaster General.* 豪精心与邮政助理部长丹尼尔·C·罗珀拉关系。

→ see farm, grain

> **Thesaurus** *cultivate* 另参见：
> V. farm, grow, tend 1
> develop, refine 2

cul·ti·vat·ed /kʌltɪveɪtɪd/ 1 ADJ If you describe someone as **cultivated**, you mean they are well educated and have good manners. 有教养的 [FORMAL] ❑ *His mother was an elegant, cultivated woman.* 他的母亲是个优雅而有教养的女人。2 ADJ **Cultivated** plants have been developed for growing on farms or in gardens. 人工栽培的 [ADJ n] ❑ *...a mixture of wild and cultivated varieties.* …野生品种与人工栽培品种的混杂。

cul·tur·al ♦◇◇ /kʌltʃərəl/ 1 ADJ **Cultural** means relating to a particular society and its ideas, customs, and art. 文化的 ❑ *...a deep sense of personal honor which was part of his cultural heritage.* …成为他文化遗产中一部分的强烈的个人荣誉感。● **cul·tur·al·ly** ADV 文化上地 ❑ *...an informed guide to culturally and historically significant sites.* …一份介绍文化和历史名胜内容丰富的指南。2 ADJ **Cultural** means involving or concerning the arts. 文化艺术的 [ADJ n] ❑ *...the sponsorship of sports and cultural events by tobacco companies.* …烟草公司对体育和文艺活动的赞助。● **cul·tur·al·ly** ADV 文化艺术上地 ❑ *...one of our better-governed, culturally active regional centers.* …管理较好、文化艺术活动活跃的地区中心之一。

cul·ture ♦♦◇ /kʌltʃər/ (**cultures**) 1 N-UNCOUNT **Culture** consists of activities such as the arts and philosophy, which are considered to be important for the development of civilization and of people's minds. 文化 ❑ *There is just not enough fun and frivolity in culture today.* 当今文化中太缺少乐趣和轻松。❑ *...aspects of popular culture.* …大众文化的方方面面。2 N-COUNT A **culture** is a particular society or civilization, especially considered in relation to its beliefs, way of life, or art. (与某种特定信仰、生活方式或艺术相连的) 社会或文明 ❑ *...people from different cultures.* …来自不同文化的人们。3 N-COUNT The **culture** of a particular organization or group consists of the habits of the people in it and the way they generally behave. (组织或团体的) 习惯和行为方式 ❑ *But social workers say that this has created a culture of dependency, particularly in urban areas.* 但是社会工作者说，这造成了一种依赖习惯，在城区尤其如此。4 N-COUNT In science, a **culture** is a group of bacteria or cells which are grown, usually in a laboratory as part of an experiment. 一组培养菌；一组培养细胞 [TECHNICAL] ❑ *...a culture of human cells.* …一组人类培养细胞。

→ see myth
→ see Word Web: culture

> **Word Partnership** *culture* 的常用搭配：
> ADJ. **ancient** culture, **popular** culture 1
> N. culture **and religion**, **society and** culture 1
> culture **shock**, **richness of** culture 1 2

cul·tured /kʌltʃərd/ ADJ If you describe someone as **cultured**, you mean that they have good manners, are well educated, and know a lot about the arts. 有修养的 ❑ *He is a cultured man with a wide circle of friends.* 他是一个有修养的、交友甚广的人。

-cum- /-kʌm-/ COMB IN N-COUNT **-cum-** is put between two nouns to form a noun referring to something or someone that is partly one thing and partly another. 兼作 ❑ *...a dining-room-cum-study.* …餐厅兼书房。

Word Web culture

Each **society** has its own **culture** which influence show people live their lives. Culture includes **customs, language, art,** and other shared **traits.** When people move from one culture to another, the result is often cultural **diffusion.** For example, European artists first saw Japanese art about 150 years ago. This caused a change in their painting style. That new approach was called Impressionism. **Assimilation** also occurs when people enter a new culture. For instance, **immigrants** may adopt American customs when they move to the U.S. People whose ideas differ from **mainstream** society may also form **subcultures** within the society.

C

▲ **cum·ber·some** /kʌmbərsəm/ 1 ADJ Something that is **cumbersome** is large and heavy and therefore difficult to carry, wear, or handle. 笨重的 ❏ *Although the machine looks cumbersome, it is actually easy to use.* 这机器虽然看起来笨重，其实使用起来很方便。 2 ADJ A **cumbersome** system or process is very complicated and inefficient. 不方便的；缺乏效率的 ❏ *...an old and cumbersome computer system.* …陈旧而效率低下的计算机系统。

★ **cu·mu·la·tive** /kyumyələtɪv/ ADJ If a series of events have a **cumulative** effect, each event makes the effect greater. 累积的 ❏ *It is simple pleasures, such as a walk on a sunny day, which have a cumulative effect on our mood.* 诸如在晴朗的日子散步这样简朴的乐趣对我们的情绪有累积性益处。

▲ **cun·ning** /kʌnɪŋ/ 1 ADJ Someone who is **cunning** has the ability to achieve things in a clever way, often by deceiving other people. 狡猾的 ❏ *These disturbed kids can be cunning.* 这些心理失常的小孩可能会很狡猾。 ● **cun·ning·ly** ADV 狡猾地 ❏ *They were cunningly disguised in golf clothes.* 他们狡猾地穿上高尔夫球服把自己伪装起来。 2 N-UNCOUNT **Cunning** is the ability to achieve things in a clever way, often by deceiving other people. 狡猾 ❏ *...one more example of the cunning of today's art thieves.* …又一个关于当今艺术品大盗狡猾伎俩的例子。

cup ♦♦♦ /kʌp/ (**cups, cupping, cupped**) 1 N-COUNT A **cup** is a small round container that you drink from. Cups usually have handles and are made from china or plastic. (有把手的陶瓷或塑料)杯子 ❏ *...cups and saucers.* …茶杯和茶碟。 2 N-COUNT You can use **cup** to refer to the cup and its contents, or to the contents only. 一杯… ❏ *...a cup of coffee.* …一杯咖啡。 3 N-COUNT A **cup** is a unit of measurement used in cooking. It is equal to 16 tablespoons or 8 fluid ounces. 量杯（等于16大汤匙或8液盎司） ❏ *Gradually add 1 cup of milk, stirring until the liquid is absorbed.* 逐渐加入一量杯牛奶，一边搅动直到液体被吸收。 ❏ *...half a cup of sugar.* …半量杯糖。 4 N-COUNT Things, or parts of things, that are small, round, and hollow in shape can be referred to as **cups**. 杯状物 ❏ *...the brass cups of the small chandelier.* …小枝形吊灯上的黄铜杯状灯罩。 5 N-COUNT A **cup** is a large metal cup with two handles that is given to the winner of a game or competition. 奖杯 ❏ *The Stars won the Stanley Cup in 1999.* 明星队赢得了1999年的斯坦利杯。 6 N-IN-NAMES **Cup** is used in the names of some sports competitions in which the prize is a cup. …杯赛 ❏ *Sri Lanka's cricket team will play India in the final of the Asia Cup.* 斯里兰卡板球队将在亚洲杯决赛中与印度队交锋。 7 V-T If you **cup** your **hands**, you make them into a curved shape like a cup. 把（手等）窝成杯状 ❏ *He cupped his hands around his mouth and called out for Diane.* 他两手窝成杯状围在嘴边，大声地呼唤黛安。 ❏ *David knelt, cupped his hands and splashed river water on to his face.* 大卫跪下去，双手成杯状，捧起河水泼到他的脸上。 8 V-T If you **cup** something in your hands, you make your hands into a curved dish-like shape and support it or hold it gently. 窝起手掌托住 ❏ *He cupped her chin in the palm of his hand.* 他窝起手掌托住她的下巴。

→ see **dish, tea**

cup·board /kʌbərd/ (**cupboards**) N-COUNT A **cupboard** is a piece of furniture that has one or two doors, usually contains shelves, and is used to store things. 橱柜 ❏ *The kitchen cupboard was stocked with cans of soup and food.* 厨房食橱里储存着一罐罐的汤和食物。

cur·able /kyʊərəbᵊl/ ADJ If a disease or illness is **curable**, it can be cured. 能治愈的 ❏ *Most skin cancers are completely curable if detected in the early stages.* 大部分的皮肤癌若在早期发现都能完全治愈。

Word Link *cur ≈ caring : curate, curator, manicure*

cu·rate (**curates, curating, curated**)

The noun is pronounced /kyʊərɪt/. The verb is pronounced /kyʊreɪt/.

名词读作 /kyʊərɪt/。动词读作 /kyʊreɪt/。

1 N-COUNT A **curate** is a clergyman in the Anglican Church who helps the priest. (英国国教的) 助理牧师 2 V-T If an exhibition is **curated** by someone, they organize it. 组织 [usu passive] ❏ *The Hayward exhibition has been curated by the artist Bernard Luthi.* 海沃德展览会是由艺术家伯纳德·卢西组织的。

cu·ra·tor /kyʊreɪtər, kyʊəreɪtər/ (**curators**) N-COUNT A **curator** is someone who is in charge of the objects or works of art in a museum or art gallery. (博物馆、美术馆的) 馆长 ❏ *Peter Forey is curator of fossil fishes at the Natural History Museum.* 彼得·富里是自然历史博物馆鱼化石的负责人。

curb /kɜrb/ (**curbs, curbing, curbed**) 1 V-T If you **curb** something, you control it and keep it within limits. 抑制 ❏ *...advertisements aimed at curbing the spread of AIDS.* …旨在抑制爱滋病蔓延的广告。 ● N-COUNT **Curb** is also a noun. 控制；限制 ❏ *He called for much stricter curbs on immigration.* 他呼吁对移民实行更为严格的限制。 2 V-T If you **curb** an emotion or your behavior, you keep it under control. 控制（脾气、行为等） ❏ *He curbed his temper.* 他控制住了自己的脾气。 3 N-COUNT **The curb** is the raised edge of a sidewalk which separates it from the road. 路边 [AM]

in BRIT, use **kerb**

❏ *I pulled over to the curb.* 我把车靠路边停下了。

cure ♦◇◇ /kyʊər/ (**cures, curing, cured**) 1 V-T If doctors or medical treatments **cure** an illness or injury, they cause it to end or disappear. 治愈（疾病、损伤） ❏ *An operation finally cured his shin injury.* 手术最终治愈了他的胫骨损伤。 2 V-T If doctors or medical treatments **cure** a person, they make the person well again after an illness or injury. 治愈（病人） ❏ *It is an effective treatment and could cure all the leprosy sufferers worldwide.* 那是一种有效的疗法，可以治愈全世界的麻疯病患者。 ❏ *Almost overnight I was cured.* 几乎在一夜之间我被治愈了。 3 V-T If someone or something **cures** a problem, they bring it to an end. 解决 ❏ *Private firms are willing to make large scale investments to help cure Russia's economic troubles.* 私有公司愿意进行大规模投资来帮助解决俄罗斯的经济困难。 4 V-T When food, tobacco, or animal skin **is cured**, it is dried, smoked, or salted so that it will last for a long time. 加工处理（食物、烟草、动物皮等） [usu passive] ❏ *Legs of pork were cured and smoked over the fire.* 猪腿在火上经过了烟熏处理。 5 N-COUNT A **cure** for an illness is a medicine or other treatment that cures the illness. (有治愈效果的) 药物、疗法 ❏ *There is still no cure for a cold.* 治感冒仍然没有特效药。 6 N-COUNT A **cure for** a problem is something that will bring it to an end. 解决方法 ❏ *The magic cure for inflation does not exist.* 解决通货膨胀的神奇方法并不存在。

★ **cur·few** /kɜrfyu/ (**curfews**) 1 N-VAR A **curfew** is a law stating that people must stay inside their houses after a particular time at night, for example, during a war. 宵禁 ❏ *The village was placed under curfew.* 该村处于宵禁之中。 2 N-VAR **Curfew** or **a curfew** is the time after which a child or student will be punished if they are found outside their home or dormitory. 熄灯令 ❏ *They raced back to the dormitory before the nine o'clock curfew.* 他们在9点熄灯之前拼命跑回了宿舍。

cu·ri·os·ity /kyʊəriɒsɪti/ (**curiosities**) 1 N-UNCOUNT **Curiosity** is a desire to know about something. 好奇心 ❏ *Ryle accepted more out of curiosity than anything else.* 赖尔接受更多是出于好奇心而不是别的原因。 ❏ *...enthusiasm and genuine curiosity about the past.* …对过去的热情和真正的好奇。 2 N-COUNT A **curiosity** is something that is unusual, interesting, and fairly rare. 奇珍异宝 ❏ *There is much to see in the way of castles, curiosities, and museums.* 那里有许多可看的城堡、奇珍异宝和博物馆。

cu·ri·ous ♦◇◇ /kyʊəriəs/ 1 ADJ If you are **curious about** something, you are interested in it and want to know more about it. 好奇的 ❏ *Steve was intensely curious about the world I came from.* 史蒂夫对我是从哪里来的有强烈的好奇心。 ● **cu·ri·ous·ly** ADV 好奇地 [ADV after v] ❏ *The woman in the shop had looked at them curiously.* 商店里的那个女人好奇地看着他们。 2 ADJ If you describe something as **curious**, you mean that it is unusual or difficult to understand. 不寻常的；难以理解的 ❏ *The pageant promises to be a curious mixture of the ancient and modern.* 这次旅行可望是一次古典与现代风格的不寻常的组合。 ● **cu·ri·ous·ly** ADV 令人不解的地 ❏ *Harry was curiously silent through all this.* 哈利自始至终都令人不解地保持着沉默。

Word Partnership *curious* 的常用搭配：

N. curious **expression**, curious **gaze**, curious **glance** 1 2
curious **mixture of** *something* 2

curl /kɜrl/ (**curls, curling, curled**) 1 N-COUNT If you have **curls**, your hair is in the form of tight curves and spirals. 卷发 ❏ *...the little girl with blonde curls.* …长着金黄色卷发的小女孩。 2 N-COUNT A **curl of** something is a piece or quantity of it that is curved or spiral in shape. 卷曲状或螺旋状 ❏ *A thin curl of smoke rose from a rusty stove.* 一缕薄薄的青烟从生锈的炉子里冉冉升起。 3 N-UNCOUNT If your hair has **curl**, it is full of curls. 卷曲 ❏ *Dry curly hair naturally for maximum curl and shine.* 让卷发自然地风干以最大限度地增加头发的卷曲

和光泽。 **4** V-T/V-I If your hair **curls** or if you **curl** it, it is full of curls. 卷曲；使卷曲 ❑ *She has hair that refuses to curl.* 她的头发怎么也不卷。 ❑ *Maria had curled her hair for the event.* 玛丽亚为这次活动卷了头发。 **5** V-T/V-I If your toes, fingers, or other parts of your body **curl**, or if you **curl** them, they form a curved or round shape. 弯曲；使弯曲 ❑ *His fingers curled gently around her wrist.* 他的手指轻握住她的手腕。 ❑ *Raise one foot, curl the toes and point the foot downwards.* 抬起一只脚，将脚趾弯曲，将脚向下指。 **6** V-T/V-I If something **curls** somewhere, or if you **curl** it there, it moves there in a spiral or curve. 缭绕；使缭绕 ❑ *Smoke was curling up the chimney.* 烟顺着烟囱缭绕升起。 **7** V-I If a person or animal **curls into** a ball, they move into a position in which their body makes a rounded shape. 蜷作一团 ❑ *He wanted to curl into a tiny ball.* 他想把自己蜷成一个小团。 ● PHRASAL VERB **Curl up** means the same as **curl**. 蜷作一团 ❑ *In colder weather, your cat will curl up into a tight, heat-conserving ball.* 在更冷的天气里，你的猫会蜷缩成紧紧的一团来保暖。 ❑ *She curled up next to him.* 她蜷卧在他身边。 **8** V-I When a leaf, a piece of paper, or another flat object **curls**, its edges bend toward the center. 卷边 ❑ *The rose leaves have curled because of an attack by grubs.* 玫瑰的叶子因虫子的侵袭打了卷。 ● PHRASAL VERB **Curl up** means the same as **curl**. 卷起 ❑ *The corners of the rug were curling up.* 地毯的各角卷起来了。

▸ **curl up** → see **curl 7, 8**

curly /kɜrli/ (**curlier, curliest**) **1** ADJ **Curly** hair is full of curls. (头发) 卷的 ❑ *I've got naturally curly hair.* 我长着天生的卷发。 **2** ADJ **Curly** is sometimes used to describe things that are curved or spiral in shape. 卷曲的 ❑ *...cauliflowers with extra-long curly leaves.* …长着特别长卷叶的花椰菜。

curly brackets [BRIT] → see **brace**

cur·ren·cy ◆◇◇ /kɜrənsi/ (**currencies**) N-VAR The money used in a particular country is referred to as its **currency**. 货币 ❑ *Tourism is the country's top earner of foreign currency.* 旅游业是该国外汇收入最高的行业。 ❑ *More people favor a single European currency than oppose it.* 支持欧洲单一货币的人比反对的多。

→ see **money**

Word Link	*curr, curs ≈ running, flowing : concurrent, current, cursor*

cur·rent ◆◆◆ /kɜrənt/ (**currents**) **1** N-COUNT A **current** is a steady and continuous flowing movement of some of the water in a river, lake, or ocean. 水流 ❑ *Under normal conditions, the ocean currents of the tropical Pacific travel from east to west.* 在正常情况下，太平洋热带洋流自东流向西。 **2** N-COUNT A **current** is a steady flowing movement of air. 气流 ❑ *I felt a current of cool air blowing in my face.* 我感到一股凉气吹在脸上。 **3** N-COUNT An electric **current** is a flow of electricity through a wire or circuit. 电流 ❑ *A powerful electric current is passed through a piece of graphite.* 一股强大的电流被传导经过一块石墨。 **4** N-COUNT A particular **current** is a particular feeling, idea, or quality that exists within a group of people. 倾向 ❑ *Each party represents a distinct current of thought.* 每个党派都代表一种独特的思想倾向。 **5** ADJ **Current** means happening, being used, or being done at the present time. 当前的 ❑ *The current situation is very different to that in 1990.* 当前的形势与1990年大不相同。 ● **cur·rent·ly** ADV 目前 [ADV before v] ❑ *Twelve potential vaccines are currently being tested on human volunteers.* 12种潜在疫苗目前正在人体志愿者身上测试。 **6** ADJ Ideas and customs that are **current** are generally accepted and used by most people. 流行的 ❑ *Current thinking suggests that toxins only have a small part to play in the build-up of cellulite.* 流行的观点认为毒素只对脂肪团形成起很小的作用。

→ see **beach, erosion, ocean, tide**

cur·rent ac·count (**current accounts**) N-COUNT A **current account** is a personal bank account which you can take money out of at any time using your checkbook or ATM card. 活期存款账户 [BRIT]

in AM, use **checking account**

cur·rent af·fairs or **current events** N-PLURAL If you refer to **current affairs**, you are referring to political events and problems in society which are discussed in newspapers, and on television and radio. 时事 ❑ *I am ill-informed on current affairs.* 我对时事不是太了解。

cur·ricu·lum /kərɪkyələm/ (**curriculums** or **curricula** /kərɪkyələ/) **1** N-COUNT A **curriculum** is all the different courses of study that are taught in a school, college, or university. 总课程 ❑ *Teachers incorporated business skills into the regular school curriculum.* 教师们将商业技能纳入学校常规课程。 **2** N-COUNT A particular **curriculum** is one particular course of study that is taught in a school, college, or university. 课程 ❑ *...the history curriculum.* …历史课程。

> Outside of the required school classes in the **curriculum**, students may participate in a variety of **extracurricular** (non-compulsory) activities that develop their interests and skills. In North American high schools there are sports clubs and teams, newspapers, future scientists' clubs and drama or music groups to name a few. Students who participate in these groups use their experience as an advantage when they apply for university. Such activities are also found on college campuses.

cur·ricu·lum vitae /kərɪkyələm vaɪti/ N-SING A **curriculum vitae** is the same as a **CV**. 简历

cur·ry /kɜri/ (**curries, currying, curried**) **1** N-VAR **Curry** is a dish composed of meat and vegetables, or just vegetables, in a sauce containing hot spices. It is usually eaten with rice and is one of the main dishes of India. 咖喱 ❑ *...vegetable curry.* …蔬菜咖喱。 **2** PHRASE If one person tries to **curry favor with** another, they do things in order to try to gain their support or cooperation. 讨好某人 ❑ *Politicians are eager to promote their "happy family" image to curry favor with voters.* 政客们积极推广其"幸福家庭"的形象以讨好选民。

curse /kɜrs/ (**curses, cursing, cursed**) **1** V-I If you **curse**, you use very impolite or offensive language, usually because you are angry about something. 诅咒 [WRITTEN] ❑ *I cursed and hobbled to my feet.* 我诅咒着，蹒跚着站起来。 ● N-COUNT **Curse** is also a noun. 诅咒 ❑ *He shot her an angry look and a curse.* 他投给她愤怒的一瞥和一句诅咒。 **2** V-T If you **curse** someone, you say insulting things to them because you are angry with them. 咒骂 (某人) ❑ *Grandma protested, but he cursed her and rudely pushed her aside.* 奶奶反对，但他咒骂她，还粗暴地把她推到一边。 **3** V-T If you **curse** something, you complain angrily about it, especially using very impolite language. 诅咒 (某事) ❑ *So we set off again, cursing the delay, toward the west.* 于是我们再次出发，诅咒着延误，向西走。 **4** N-COUNT If you say that there is a **curse on** someone, you mean that there seems to be a supernatural power causing unpleasant things to happen to them. (对某人的) 诅咒 ❑ *Maybe there is a curse on my family.* 也许存在对我的家族的诅咒。 **5** N-COUNT You can refer to something that causes a great deal of trouble or harm as a **curse**. 祸根 ❑ *Apathy is the long-standing curse of democracy.* 冷漠是民主的长期祸根。

cur·sor /kɜrsər/ (**cursors**) N-COUNT On a computer screen, the **cursor** is a small shape that indicates where anything that is typed by the user will appear. 光标 [COMPUTING] ❑ *He moves the cursor, clicks the mouse.* 他移动光标，点击鼠标。

→ see **computer**

curt /kɜrt/ ADJ If you describe someone as **curt**, you mean that they speak or reply in a brief and rather rude way. 简短无理的 ❑ *Her tone of voice was curt.* 她的语气是简短无理的。 ● **curt·ly** ADV 简短无理地 [ADV with v] ❑ *"I'm leaving," she said curtly.* "我要走了，" 她唐突地说。

▲ **cur·tail** /kɜrteɪl/ (**curtails, curtailing, curtailed**) V-T If you **curtail** something, you reduce or limit it. 缩减 [FORMAL] ❑ *NATO plans to curtail the number of troops being sent to the region.* 北大西洋公约组织计划缩减派往该地的部队数量。

cur·tain ◆◇◇ /kɜrtᵊn/ (**curtains**) **1** N-COUNT **Curtains** are pieces of material which you hang from the top of a window. 窗帘 ❑ *Her bedroom curtains were drawn.* 她卧室的窗帘拉上了。 **2** N-SING In a theater, **the curtain** is the large piece of material that hangs in front of the stage until a performance begins. 幕布 ❑ *The curtain rises toward the end of the Prelude.* 前奏接近尾声时幕布升起。

curve /kɜrv/ (**curves, curving, curved**) **1** N-COUNT A **curve** is a smooth, gradually bending line, for example, part of the edge of a circle. 曲线 ❑ *...the curve of his lips.* …他嘴唇的曲线。 **2** N-COUNT You can refer to a change in something as a particular **curve**, especially when it is represented on a graph. (图表中的) 曲线 ❑ *Youth crime overall is on a slow but steady downward curve.* 青年犯罪总体上呈一个缓慢但持续下降的曲线。 **3** → see also **learning curve** **4** V-T/V-I If something **curves**, or if someone or something **curves** it, it has the shape of a curve. 使弯曲；变弯 ❑ *Her spine curved.* 她的脊柱弯了。 ❑ *...a knife with a slightly curving blade.* …一把刀刃略弯的刀。 **5** V-I If something **curves**, it moves in a curve, for

C

example, through the air. 沿曲线运动 ❑ *The ball curved strangely in the air.* 球在空中划出奇怪的弧线。 **6** PHRASE If someone **throws** you **a curve** or **throws** you **a curve ball**, they surprise you by doing something that you do not expect. 给某人惊喜 [mainly AM] ❑ *At the last minute, I threw them a curve ball by saying, "We're going to bring spouses."* 在最后一刻，我给了他们一个惊喜，说："我们会带配偶。"

C

curved /kɜrvd/ ADJ A **curved** object has the shape of a curve or has a smoothly bending surface. 弧形的 ❑ *...the curved lines of the chairs.* …那些椅子的弧形线条。
→ see **flight**

cush·ion /kʊʃᵊn/ (**cushions, cushioning, cushioned**) **1** N-COUNT A **cushion** is a fabric case filled with soft material, which you put on a seat to make it more comfortable. 坐垫 ❑ *...a velvet cushion.* …一个天鹅绒坐垫。 **2** N-COUNT A **cushion** is a soft pad or barrier, especially one that protects something. 软垫 ❑ *The company provides a styrofoam cushion to protect the tablets during shipping.* 该公司提供一种聚苯乙烯泡沫塑料垫层用来在装运时保护牌匾。 **3** N-COUNT Something that is a **cushion against** something unpleasant reduces its effect. 缓解物 ❑ *Welfare provides a cushion against hardship.* 福利给困苦提供了一个缓解。 **4** V-T Something that **cushions** an object when it hits something protects it by reducing the force of the impact. 缓冲 ❑ *There is also a new steering wheel with an energy-absorbing rim to cushion the driver's head in the worst impacts.* 还有新式方向盘，其边缘具有减震功能在最严重的冲击中缓冲保护司机的头部。 **5** V-T To **cushion** the effect of something unpleasant means to reduce it. 缓解 ❑ *They said Western aid was needed to cushion the blows of vital reform.* 他们说需要西方国家的援助以缓解重大变革的冲击。

cus·tard /kʌstərd/ (**custards**) **1** N-VAR **Custard** is a baked dessert made of milk, eggs, and sugar. 蛋奶糕 ❑ *...a custard with a caramel sauce.* …一份配有焦糖汁的蛋奶糕。 **2** N-MASS **Custard** is a sweet yellow sauce made from milk and eggs or from milk and a powder. It is eaten with fruit and puddings. 蛋奶沙司 ❑ *...bananas and custard.* …香蕉和蛋奶沙司。
→ see **dessert**

Word Link *custod ≈ guarding : custodial, custodian, custody*

cus·to·dial /kʌstoʊdiəl/ **1** ADJ If a child's parents are divorced or separated, the **custodial** parent is the parent who has custody of the child. 有监护权的 [ADJ n] [LEGAL] ❑ *...all the general expenses that come with being the custodial parent.* …作为监护人的家长而发生的所有一般开销。 **2** ADJ **Custodial care** is help with basic personal needs, for example washing, dressing, and eating. 照管的 [usu ADJ n] ❑ *In the event that you are mentally or physically disabled, who will provide custodial care and who will pay for it?* 一旦你精神或身体残疾了，谁会为你提供看护？又有谁会承担看护费用呢？

cus·to·dian /kʌstoʊdiən/ (**custodians**) **1** N-COUNT The **custodian** of an official building, a company's assets, or something else valuable is the person who is officially in charge of it. 管理员 ❑ *...the custodian of the holy shrines in Mecca and Medina.* …在麦加和麦地那的圣地的管理员。 **2** N-COUNT The **custodian** of a large building such as an office or a school is responsible for cleaning and maintaining it. 看管人 [AM] ❑ *Augustine Hancock served as an elementary-school custodian for 20 years.* 奥古斯丁・汉考克当小学看管人20年了。

▲ **cus·to·dy** /kʌstədi/ **1** N-UNCOUNT **Custody** is the legal right to keep and take care of a child, especially the right given to a child's mother or father when they get divorced. 监护权 ❑ *I'm going to go to court to get custody of the children.* 我要打官司以争取对孩子们的监护权。 ❑ *Child custody is normally granted to the mother.* 孩子的监护权一般判给母亲。 **2** N-UNCOUNT If someone is being held in a particular type of **custody**, they are being kept in a place that is similar to a prison. 拘留 ❑ *The youngster got nine months' youth custody.* 那个小伙子被判少年拘留9个月。 **3** PHRASE Someone who is **in custody** or has been taken **into custody** has been arrested and is being kept in prison until they can be tried in a court. 在押候审 ❑ *Three people appeared in court and two of them were remanded in custody.* 3个人出庭，其中2人被还押候审。

cus·tom /kʌstəm/ (**customs**) **1** N-VAR A **custom** is an activity, a way of behaving, or an event which is usual or traditional in a particular society or in particular circumstances. 风俗 ❑ *The custom of lighting the Olympic flame goes back centuries.* 点燃奥运圣火的风俗可追溯到几个世纪前。 **2** N-SING If it is your **custom to** do something, you usually do it in particular circumstances. 习惯 ❑ *It was his custom to approach every problem cautiously.* 谨慎地处理每个问题是他的习惯。 **3** → see also **customs**
→ see **culture, society**

★ **cus·tom·ary** /kʌstəmɛri/ **1** ADJ **Customary** is used to describe things that people usually do in a particular society or in particular circumstances. 通常的 [FORMAL] ❑ *It is customary to offer a drink or a snack to guests.* 通常用饮料或小吃招待客人。 **2** ADJ **Customary** is used to describe something that a particular person usually does or has. 习惯上的 [ADJ n] ❑ *Yvonne took her customary seat behind her desk.* 伊冯娜坐在了她的书桌后面惯坐的位子上。

cus·tom·er ♦♦◊ /kʌstəmər/ (**customers**) N-COUNT A **customer** is someone who buys goods or services, especially from a store. 顾客 ❑ *...a satisfied customer.* …一位满意的顾客。 ❑ *The quality of customer service is extremely important.* 客户服务质量极其重要。

> When you buy goods from a particular shop or company, you are one of its **customers**. If you use the professional services of someone such as a lawyer or an accountant, you are one of their **clients**. Doctors and hospitals have **patients**, while hotels have **guests**. People who travel on public transportation are referred to as **passengers**.

Word Partnership *customer* 的常用搭配：

N. customer **account**, customer **loyalty**, customer **satisfaction**
V. **greet** customers, **satisfy** a customer

cus·tom·ise /kʌstəmaɪz/ [BRIT] → see **customize**

cus·tom·ize /kʌstəmaɪz/ (**customizes, customizing, customized**)

in BRIT, also use **customise**

V-T If you **customize** something, you change its appearance or features to suit your tastes or needs. 个性化设置 ❑ *...a control that allows photographers to customize the camera's basic settings.* …一种允许摄影师个性化设定相机基本设置的控制装置。

cus·toms /kʌstəmz/ **1** N-PROPER **Customs** is the official organization responsible for collecting taxes on goods coming into a country and preventing illegal goods from being brought in. 海关部门 ❑ *What right does Customs have to search my car?* 海关有什么权力搜查我的车？ **2** N-UNCOUNT **Customs** is the place where people arriving from a foreign country have to declare goods that they bring with them. 海关 ❑ *He walked through customs.* 他步行通过了海关。 **3** ADJ **Customs** duties are taxes that people pay for importing and exporting goods. 海关的 [ADJ n] ❑ *Personal property which is to be re-exported at the end of your visit is not subject to customs duties.* 停留结束时要再次带出境的个人物品免收关税。 **4** → see also **custom**

cut
❶ PHYSICAL ACTION
❷ SHORTEN OR REDUCE AMOUNT
❸ OTHER USES
❹ PHRASAL VERBS

❶ **cut** ♦♦♦ /kʌt/ (**cuts, cutting**)

> The form **cut** is used in the present tense and is the past tense and past participle.

1 V-T/V-I If you **cut** something, you use a knife or a similar tool to divide it into pieces, or to mark it or damage it. If you **cut** a shape or a hole in something, you make the shape or hole by using a knife or similar tool. 切；剪 ❑ *Mrs. Haines stood nearby, holding scissors to cut a ribbon.* 海恩斯太太站在旁边，拿着剪刀剪缎带。 ❑ *Cut the tomatoes in half vertically.* 把西红柿竖着切成两半。 ❑ *The thieves cut a hole in the fence.* 小偷在把篱笆割出了个洞。 ❑ *This little knife cuts really well.* 这把小刀切东西很好用。 ● N-COUNT **Cut** is also a noun. 切口 ❑ *Carefully make a cut in the shell with a small serrated knife.* 用有锯齿的小刀小心地在壳上切个口。 **2** V-T If you **cut yourself** or **cut** a part of your body, you accidentally injure yourself on a sharp object so that you bleed. 割破 ❑ *Johnson cut himself shaving.* 约翰逊刮胡子时割伤了自己。 ❑ *I started to cry because I cut my finger.* 因为割破了自己的手指，我哭了起来。 ● N-COUNT **Cut** is also a noun. 伤口 ❑ *He had sustained a cut on his left eyebrow.* 他的左眉留下了一处刀伤。 **3** V-T If you **cut** something such as grass, your hair, or your fingernails,

Picture Dictionary cut

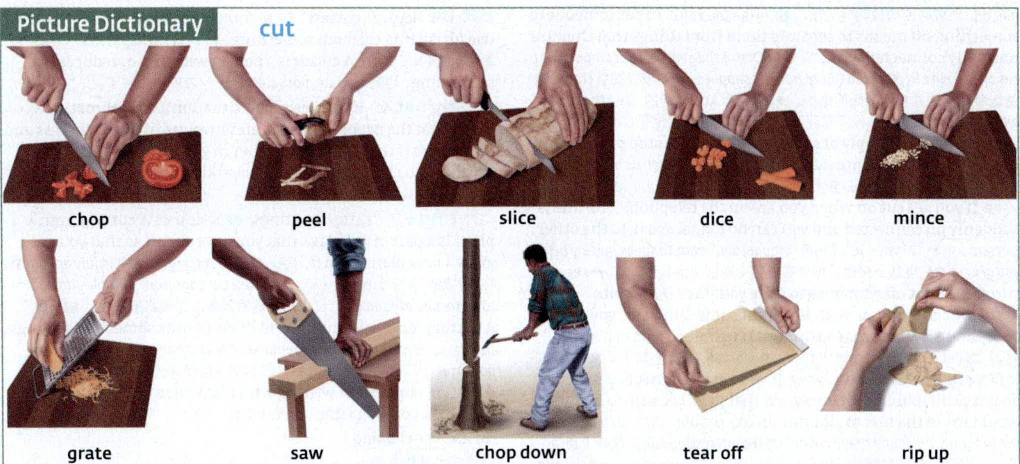

you shorten them using scissors or another tool. 修剪 ❑ *The most recent tenants hadn't even cut the grass.* 最新来的房客竟然草坪都还没修剪。❑ *You've had your hair cut, it looks great.* 你理发了，很好看。● N-SING **Cut** is also a noun. 修剪 ❑ *Prices vary from salon to salon, starting at $30 for a cut and blow-dry.* 各家美发店价格不一，剪吹起价$30。 4 V-T The way that clothes **are cut** is the way they are designed and made. 裁剪 [usu passive] ❑ *...badly cut blue suits.* …裁剪得很糟的蓝色套装。

→ see Picture Dictionary: **cut**

❷ **cut** ♦♦♦ /kʌt/ (**cuts, cutting**)

The form **cut** is used in the present tense and is the past tense and past participle.

➪ **Please look at meanings 7 and 8 to see if the expression you are looking for is shown under another headword.** 1 V-T If you **cut** something, you reduce it. 削减 ❑ *The first priority is to cut costs.* 首要任务是削减费用。❑ *The U.N. force is to be cut by 90%.* 联合国部队将被裁减90%。● N-COUNT **Cut** is also a noun. 削减 [with supp, oft N "in" n] ❑ *The economy needs an immediate 2 percent cut in interest rates.* 经济需要一个利率2%的即刻下调。 2 V-T If you **cut** a text, broadcast, or performance, you shorten it. If you **cut** a part of a text, broadcast, or performance, you do not publish, broadcast, or perform that part. 删节 ❑ *Branagh has cut the play judiciously.* 布拉纳格已经审慎地删节了那个剧作。● N-COUNT **Cut** is also a noun. 删节 ❑ *It has been found necessary to make some cuts in the text.* 已发现有必要对文章作些删节。 3 V-I If you **cut across** or **through** a place, you go through it because it is the shortest route to another place. 抄近路 ❑ *Jesse cut across the parking lot and strolled through the main entrance.* 杰西抄近道穿过停车场，漫步通过大门。 4 → see also **shortcut** 5 V-I If you **cut** in front of someone, you move in front of them and take their place. 插(队) ❑ *Somebody tried to cut in line and a fight broke out.* 有人想插队，引发了一场打斗。 6 V-T To **cut** a supply of something means to stop providing it or stop it from being provided. 中断(供给) ❑ *Winds have knocked down power lines, cutting electricity to thousands of people.* 风刮断了电线，中断了数千人的电力供应。● N-COUNT **Cut** is also a noun. (供给的) 中断 [with supp, usu N "in" n] ❑ *The strike had already led to cuts in electricity and water supplies in many areas.* 这次罢工已经导致很多地区供电和供水中断。 7 to cut something **to the bone** → see **bone** 8 to **cut corners** → see **corner**

Thesaurus *cut* 另参见：

N. incision, slit ❶ 1
gash, nick, wound ❶ 2
V. carve, slice, trim ❶ 1
graze, nick, stab ❶ 2
mow, shave, trim ❶ 3
decrease, reduce, lower; (*ant.*) increase ❷ 1

❸ **cut** ♦♦♦ /kʌt/ (**cuts, cutting**)

The form **cut** is used in the present tense and is the past tense and past participle.

➪ **Please look at meaning 8 to see if the expression you are looking for is shown under another headword.** 1 V-T If you **cut** a deck of playing cards, you divide it into two. 切(牌) ❑ *Place the cards face down on the table and cut them.* 把扑克牌正面朝下放在桌上，然后切牌。 2 V-T If you tell someone to **cut** something, you are telling them in an irritated way to stop it. (急躁地要某人) 停止 [mainly AM, INFORMAL, FEELINGS] ❑ *"Cut the euphemisms, Daniel," Brenda snapped.* "别绕弯子了，丹尼尔，"布伦达厉声说到。 3 CONVENTION When the director of a movie says "**cut**," they want the actors and the camera crew to stop filming. 停拍 4 N-COUNT A **cut** of meat is a piece or type of meat which is cut in a particular way from the animal, or from a particular part of it. 切下的肉 ❑ *Use a cheap cut such as spare rib chops.* 用一块便宜的肉，比如用剩下的排骨块。 5 N-SING Someone's **cut** of the profits or winnings from something, especially ones that have been obtained dishonestly, is their share. (不正当得来的) 份额 [INFORMAL] ❑ *The agency is expected to take a cut of the money awarded to its client.* 这家代理商理应从奖给其客户的钱中抽取它的一份。 6 N-COUNT A **cut** is a narrow valley which has been cut through a hill so that a road or railroad track can pass through. (山中开出的) 峡窄通道 [AM]

in BRIT, use **cutting**

7 → see also **cutting** 8 to **cut the mustard** → see **mustard**

❹ **cut** ♦♦♦ /kʌt/ (**cuts, cutting**)

The form **cut** is used in the present tense and is the past tense and past participle.

▸ **cut across** PHRASAL VERB If an issue or problem **cuts across** the division between two or more groups of people, it affects or matters to people in all the groups. 超越(界限) ❑ *The problem cuts across all socioeconomic lines and affects all age groups.* 这个问题超越社会经济的所有界限，影响各个年龄段的人。

▸ **cut back** 1 PHRASAL VERB If you **cut back** something such as expenditure or **cut back on** it, you reduce it. 削减 ❑ *Customers have cut back spending because of the economic slowdown.* 由于经济放缓，顾客们已经减少了花销。❑ *The Government has cut back on defense spending.* 政府已削减了国防开支。 2 → see also **cutback**

▸ **cut down** 1 PHRASAL VERB If you **cut down on** something or **cut down** something, you use or do less of it. 减少 ❑ *He cut down on coffee and cigarettes, and ate a balanced diet.* 他少喝咖啡，少抽烟，饮食均衡。❑ *Car owners were asked to cut down travel.* 车主们被要求减少出行。 2 PHRASAL VERB If you **cut down** a tree, you cut through its trunk so that it falls to the ground. 砍倒 ❑ *A vandal with a chainsaw cut down a tree.* 一个蓄意破坏公物者用链锯锯倒了一棵树。

▸ **cut in** PHRASAL VERB If you **cut in on** someone, you interrupt them when they are speaking. 打断 ❑ *Immediately, Daniel cut in on Joanne's attempts at reassurance.* 马上，丹尼尔打断了乔安妮要说的安慰的话。❑ *"Not true," the Duchess cut in.* "不是真的，"公爵夫人插话道。

▸ **cut off** 1 PHRASAL VERB If you **cut** something **off**, you remove it with a knife or a similar tool. 切掉 ❑ *Mrs. Johnson cut off a generous piece of the meat.* 约翰逊太太切下一大块肉。❑ *He threatened to cut my* *hair off.* 他威胁要剪掉我的头发。 2 PHRASAL VERB To **cut** someone or something **off** means to separate them from things that they are normally connected with. 隔离 ❑ *One of the goals of the campaign is to cut off the elite Republican Guard from its supplies.* 那场战役的目标之一就是切断精锐的共和国卫队的供给。 ● **cut off** ADJ 隔绝的 ❑ *Without a car we still felt very cut off.* 没有车我们还是觉得与外界隔绝了。 3 PHRASAL VERB To **cut off** a supply of something means to stop providing it or stop it from being provided. 切断(供给) ❑ *The rebels have cut off electricity from the capital.* 叛乱者已经切断了首都的电力。 4 PHRASAL VERB If you get **cut off** when you are on the telephone, the line is suddenly disconnected and you can no longer speak to the other person. 中断 ❑ *When you do get through, you've got to speak quickly before you get cut off.* 电话一接通，你得在通话中断前快点儿说。 5 → see also **cutoff** 6 to **cut off** your **nose to spite** your **face** → see **spite**

▸ **cut out** 1 PHRASAL VERB If you **cut** something **out**, you remove or separate it from what surrounds it using scissors or a knife. 剪下 ❑ *I cut it out and pinned it to my studio wall.* 我把它剪了下来，钉在我工作室的墙上。 2 PHRASAL VERB If you **cut out** a part of a text, you do not print, publish, or broadcast that part, because to include it would make the text too long or unacceptable. 删掉 ❑ *I listened to the program and found they'd cut out all the interesting stuff.* 我听了那个节目，发现他们已经删掉了所有有趣的内容。 3 PHRASAL VERB To **cut out** something unnecessary or unwanted means to remove it completely from a situation. For example, if you **cut out** a particular type of food, you stop eating it, usually because it is bad for you. 戒除 ❑ *I've simply cut egg yolks out entirely.* 我已经根本不吃蛋黄了。 4 PHRASAL VERB If an object **cuts out** the light, it is between you and the light so that you are in the dark. 遮挡 ❑ *The curtains were half drawn to cut out the sunlight.* 窗帘拉上了一半以遮挡阳光。 5 PHRASAL VERB If an engine **cuts out**, it suddenly stops working. 突然熄火 ❑ *The helicopter crash landed when one of its two engines cut out.* 直升飞机两个发动机中的一个突然熄火时，直升机撞地着陆。 6 → see also **cut out**

▸ **cut up** PHRASAL VERB If you **cut** something **up**, you cut it into several pieces. 切碎 ❑ *Halve the tomatoes, then cut them up coarsely.* 把西红柿切成两半，然后再把它们粗略切一下。

cut·back /kʌtbæk/ (**cutbacks**) N-COUNT A **cutback** is a reduction that is made in something. 削减 ❑ *The region has also been hit hard by cutbacks in defense spending, which has left thousands out of work.* 该地区也深受造成数千人失业的国防开支缩减的打击。

cute /kyut/ (**cuter, cutest**) 1 ADJ Something or someone that is **cute** is very pretty or attractive, or is intended to appear pretty or attractive. 可爱的 [INFORMAL] ❑ *Oh, look at that dog! He's so cute.* 哦，看那条狗！它真可爱。 2 ADJ If you describe someone as **cute**, you think they are sexually attractive. 性感的 [mainly AM, INFORMAL] ❑ *There was this girl, and I thought she was really cute.* 就是这个女孩，我觉得她真的很性感。 3 ADJ If you describe someone as **cute**, you mean that they deal with things cleverly. 聪明的 [AM] ❑ *That's a cute trick.* 那是个聪明的把戏。

Thesaurus	*cute* 另参见：
ADJ.	adorable, charming, pretty; *(ant.)* homely, ugly 1

▲ **cut·lery** /kʌtləri/ 1 N-UNCOUNT You can refer to knives and tools used for cutting as **cutlery**. 刀具 [AM] ❑ *The first catalog featured specialty shavers, accessories, and cutlery.* 第一份目录主要介绍专业剃须刀、配件和刀具。 2 N-UNCOUNT **Cutlery** consists of the knives, forks, and spoons that you eat your food with. 餐具 [mainly BRIT]

in AM, usually use **silverware, flatware**

cut·off /kʌtɔf/ (**cutoffs**) 1 N-COUNT A **cutoff** or a **cutoff** point is the level or limit at which you decide that something should stop happening. 截点 ❑ *The cutoff date for registering is yet to be announced.* 注册的截止日期尚未公布。 2 N-COUNT The **cutoff of** a supply or service is the complete stopping of the supply or service. 终止(供应或服务) ❑ *A total cutoff of supplies would cripple the country's economy.* 全面终止供给将使该国经济瘫痪。

cut out ADJ If you are not **cut out for** a particular type of work, you do not have the qualities that are needed to be able to do it well. 合适的 ❑ *I left medicine anyway. I wasn't really cut out for it.* 我还是不再从医。我不太合适干那个。

cut-price [BRIT] → see **cut-rate**

cut-rate ADJ **Cut-rate** goods or services are cheaper than usual. 降价的 [ADJ n] ❑ *...cut-rate auto insurance.* …降价的汽车保险。

in BRIT, usually use **cut-price**

cut·ter /kʌtər/ (**cutters**) 1 N-COUNT A **cutter** is a tool that you use for cutting through something. 切刀 ❑ *...wire cutters.* …电线切割刀。 2 N-COUNT A **cutter** is a person who cuts or reduces something. 切割工 ❑ *...a glass cutter.* …一名玻璃切割工。

cut-throat ADJ If you describe a situation as **cut-throat**, you mean that the people or companies involved all want success and do not care if they harm each other in getting it. 残酷的 [DISAPPROVAL] ❑ *...the cut-throat competition in personal computers.* …个人计算机领域残酷的竞争。

cut·ting ♦◇◇ /kʌtɪŋ/ (**cuttings**) 1 N-COUNT A **cutting** from a plant is a part of the plant that you have cut off so that you can grow a new plant from it. 插枝 ❑ *Take cuttings from it in July or August.* 在7月或8月从它上面剪下插枝。 ❑ *Take cuttings from suitable garden tomatoes in late summer.* 夏末从合适的园栽西红柿剪下插枝。 2 ADJ A **cutting** remark is unkind and likely to hurt someone's feelings. 尖刻的 ❑ *People make cutting remarks to help themselves feel superior or powerful.* 人们说尖刻的话来帮自己感觉优越或强势。 3 N-COUNT A **cutting** is a piece of writing which has been cut from a newspaper or magazine. 剪报 [BRIT]

in AM, use **clipping**

cut·ting edge

The spelling **cutting-edge** is used for meaning 2.

1 N-SING If you are **at the cutting edge of** a particular field of activity, you are involved in its most important or most exciting developments. 前沿 ❑ *This shipyard is at the cutting edge of world shipbuilding technology.* 这家造船厂位于世界造船技术的前沿。 2 ADJ **Cutting-edge** techniques or equipment are the most advanced that there are in a particular field. 尖端的 ❑ *What we are planning is cutting-edge technology never seen in Australia before.* 我们正在筹划的是澳大利亚前所未见的尖端技术。

→ see **technology**

CV /si vi/ (**CVs**) N-COUNT Your **CV** is a written account of your personal details, your education, and the jobs you have had. **CV** is an abbreviation for "curriculum vitae." 简历 [mainly BRIT]

in AM, usually use **résumé**

CYA **CYA** is the written abbreviation for "see you," mainly used in text messages and e-mails. 再见 (主要用于短信或邮件) [COMPUTING]

cya·nide /saɪənaɪd/ N-UNCOUNT **Cyanide** is a highly poisonous substance. 氰化物 ❑ *His death has all the signs of cyanide poisoning.* 他的死亡具有氰化物中毒的所有迹象。

cy·ber·café /saɪbərkæfeɪ/ (**cybercafés**) N-COUNT A **cybercafé** is a café where people can pay to use the Internet. 网吧

cy·ber·sex /saɪbərsɛks/ N-UNCOUNT **Cybersex** involves using the Internet for sexual purposes, especially by exchanging sexual messages with another person. 网络性关系 ❑ *It's a place where you can role-play and have cybersex.* 这是一个你可以扮演角色，进行网络性爱的地方。

▲ **cy·ber·space** /saɪbərspeɪs/ N-UNCOUNT In computer technology, **cyberspace** refers to data banks and networks, considered as a place. 网络空间 [COMPUTING] ❑ *...a report circulating in cyberspace.* …一则在网络空间里传播的报道。

Word Link	*cycl ≈ circle : bicycle, cycle, cyclical*

cy·cle ♦◇◇ /saɪkəl/ (**cycles, cycling, cycled**) 1 N-COUNT A **cycle** is a series of events or processes that is repeated again and again, always in the same order. 周期 ❑ *...the life cycle of the plant.* …植物的生命周期。 2 N-COUNT A **cycle** is a single complete series of movements in an electrical, electronic, or mechanical process. 圈 ❑ *...10 cycles per second.* …每秒10圈。 3 N-COUNT A **cycle** is a bicycle. 自行车 ❑ *We supply the travel ticket for you and your cycle.* 我们为您和您的自行车提供旅行票。 4 V-I If you **cycle**, you ride a bicycle. 骑自行车 ❑ *He cycled to Ingwold.* 他骑车去了英格沃尔德。 ● **cy·cling** N-UNCOUNT 骑自行车 ❑ *The quiet country roads are ideal for cycling.* 安静的乡村道路很适合骑自行车。

cy·cli·cal /sɪklɪkəl, saɪk-/ ADJ A **cyclical** process is one in which a series of events happens again and again in the same order. 周期的 ❑ *...the cyclical nature of the airline business.* …航空业的周期性。

cy·clist /saɪklɪst/ (**cyclists**) N-COUNT A **cyclist** is someone who rides a bicycle, or is riding a bicycle. 骑自行车者 ❑ *...better protection for pedestrians and cyclists.* …对行人和骑自行车的人的更好保护。

→ see **park**

cy·clone /saɪkloʊn/ (**cyclones**) N-COUNT A **cyclone** is a violent tropical storm in which the air goes around and around. 旋风 ❑ *The race was called off as a cyclone struck.* 由于旋风袭击，比赛被取消了。
→ see **hurricane**

★ **cyl·in·der** /sɪlɪndər/ (**cylinders**) 1 N-COUNT A **cylinder** is an object with flat circular ends and long straight sides. 圆柱 ❑ *It was recorded on a wax cylinder.* 它被刻录在了蜡柱上。 2 N-COUNT A gas **cylinder** is a cylinder-shaped container in which gas is kept under pressure. (气) 罐 ❑ *...oxygen cylinders.* …氧气瓶。 3 N-COUNT In an engine, a **cylinder** is a cylinder-shaped part in which a piston moves backward and forward. 汽缸 ❑ *...a four-cylinder engine.* …四缸发动机。
→ see **engine, solid, volume**

cyn·ic /sɪnɪk/ (**cynics**) N-COUNT A **cynic** is someone who believes that people always act selfishly. 人皆自私论者 ❑ *I have come to be very much of a cynic in these matters.* 我在这些事情上已经成了一个颇为愤世嫉俗的人。

cyni·cal /sɪnɪkᵊl/ 1 ADJ If you describe someone as **cynical**, you mean they believe that people always act selfishly. 持人皆自私论的 ❑ *...his cynical view of the world.* …他愤世嫉俗的世界观。 ● **cyni·cal·ly** ADV 持人皆自私论地 [ADV with v] ❑ *The fast-food industry cynically continues to target children.* 快餐业继续自私地把儿童当成目标。 2 ADJ If you are **cynical about** something, you do not believe that it can be successful or that the people involved are honest. (对事情的成功或人的诚信) 怀疑的 ❑ *It's hard not to be cynical about reform.* 很难对改革不持怀疑态度。

cyni·cism /sɪnɪsɪzəm/ 1 N-UNCOUNT **Cynicism** is the belief that people always act selfishly. 人皆自私论；愤世嫉俗论 ❑ *I found Ben's cynicism wearing at times.* 我觉得本的愤世嫉俗论有时让人烦。 2 N-UNCOUNT **Cynicism about** something is the belief that it cannot be successful or that the people involved are not honorable. (对事情的成功或人的诚信的) 怀疑 ❑ *In an era of growing cynicism about politicians, Mr. Mandela is a model of dignity and integrity.* 在一个对政治家越来越不信任的时代，曼德拉先生是高尚和正直的榜样。

cyst /sɪst/ (**cysts**) N-COUNT A **cyst** is a growth containing liquid that appears inside your body or under your skin. 囊肿 ❑ *He had a minor operation to remove a cyst.* 他做了一个切除了囊肿的小手术。

Dd

D

D also **d** /di/ (**D's, d's**) N-VAR **D** is the fourth letter of the English alphabet. 英文字母表中的第4个字母

dab /dæb/ (**dabs, dabbing, dabbed**) 1 V-T/V-I If you **dab** something, you touch it several times using quick, light movements. If you **dab** a substance onto a surface, you put it there using quick, light movements. 轻擦；轻敷 ❑ *She arrived weeping, dabbing her eyes with a tissue.* 她哭着来了，用纸巾轻擦着眼睛。❑ *She dabbed iodine on the cuts on her forehead.* 她在她额头的伤口处搽了碘酒。 2 N-COUNT A **dab of** something is a small amount of it that is put onto a surface. 少量 [INFORMAL] ❑ *...a dab of glue.* …一点胶水。

dab·ble /dæbᵊl/ (**dabbles, dabbling, dabbled**) V-I If you **dabble in** something, you take part in it but not very seriously. 涉猎 ❑ *He dabbled in business.* 他曾涉足商界。

dad ♦◇◇ /dæd/ (**dads**) N-FAMILY Your **dad** is your father. 爸爸 [INFORMAL] ❑ *How do you feel, Dad?* 你感觉怎么样，爸爸？ ❑ *He's living with his mom and dad.* 他跟他的爸爸妈妈住在一起。

dad·dy /dædi/ (**daddies**) N-FAMILY Children often call their father **daddy**. 爸爸 [INFORMAL] ❑ *Look at me, Daddy!* 看看我，爸爸！

daf·fo·dil /dæfədɪl/ (**daffodils**) N-COUNT A **daffodil** is a yellow spring flower with a central part shaped like a tube and a long stem. 水仙花

▲ **dag·ger** /dægər/ (**daggers**) N-COUNT A **dagger** is a weapon like a knife with two sharp edges. 匕首

dai·ly ♦♦◇ /deɪli/ 1 ADV If something happens **daily**, it happens every day. 每天地 [ADV after v] ❑ *Cathay Pacific flies daily nonstop to Hong Kong.* 国泰航空的航班每天直飞香港。● ADJ **Daily** is also an adjective. 每天的 [ADJ n] ❑ *They held daily press briefings.* 他们召开了每日例行的新闻发布会。 2 ADJ **Daily** quantities or rates relate to a period of one day. 一天的 [ADJ n] ❑ *...a diet containing adequate daily amounts of fresh fruit.* …包含一天足量新鲜水果的饮食。 3 PHRASE Your **daily life** is the things that you do every day as part of your normal life. 日常生活 ❑ *All of us in our daily life react favorably to people who take us and our views seriously.* 日常生活中，对于那些认真对待我们和我们的意见的人，我们都会与之交好。

dain·ty /deɪnti/ (**daintier, daintiest**) ADJ If you describe a movement, person, or object as **dainty**, you mean that they are small, delicate, and pretty. 娇小漂亮的 ❑ *The girls were dainty and feminine.* 这些女子们娇美而又温柔。● **dain·ti·ly** ADV 娇小漂亮地 ❑ *She walked daintily down the steps.* 她优雅轻盈地走下台阶。

dairy /dɛəri/ (**dairies**) 1 N-COUNT A **dairy** is a company that sells milk and food made from milk, such as butter, cream, and cheese. 乳品公司 ❑ *In my childhood, local dairies bought milk from local farmers.* 在我小时候，本地的乳品公司向当地农场主收购牛奶。 2 ADJ **Dairy** is used to refer to foods such as butter and cheese that are made from milk. 奶制的 [ADJ n] ❑ *He avoids all meat and dairy products.* 他不吃任何肉类和奶制品。 3 ADJ **Dairy** is used to refer to the use of cattle to produce milk rather than meat. 产乳的 [ADJ n] ❑ *...a small vegetable and dairy farm.* …一个种菜、养奶牛的小农场。
→ see Word Web: **dairy**

dai·sy /deɪzi/ (**daisies**) N-COUNT A **daisy** is a small wildflower with a yellow center and white petals. 雏菊
→ see **plant**

dam /dæm/ (**dams**) N-COUNT A **dam** is a wall that is built across a river in order to stop the water from flowing and to make a lake. 水坝 ❑ *Before the dam was built, Campbell River used to flood in the spring.* 大坝建好之前，坎贝尔河常在春季发大水。
→ see Word Web: **dam**

dam·age ♦♦◇ /dæmɪdʒ/ (**damages, damaging, damaged**) 1 V-T To **damage** an object means to break it, spoil it physically, or stop it from working properly. 破坏；损坏 ❑ *He maliciously damaged a car with a baseball bat.* 他用棒球棍恶意地损坏了一辆汽车。 2 V-T To **damage** something means to cause it to become less good, pleasant, or successful. 损害；伤害 ❑ *...the electoral chaos that damaged Florida's reputation.* …损害佛罗里达州声誉的选举骚乱。● **dam·ag·ing** ADJ 有损害性的 ❑ *The weakened currency could have damaging effects for the economy.* 货币贬值可能会对经济造成破坏性的影响。 3 N-UNCOUNT **Damage** is physical harm that is caused to an object. 破坏；损坏 ❑ *The blast had serious effects with quite extensive damage to the house.* 爆炸影响严重，对房屋造成了大面积破坏。 4 N-UNCOUNT **Damage** consists of the unpleasant effects that something has on a person, situation, or type of activity. 伤害 ❑ *Incidents of this type cause irreparable damage to relations with the community.* 此类事件对与该团体的关系造成不可挽回的伤害。 5 N-PLURAL If a court of law awards **damages** to someone, it orders money to be paid to them by a person who has damaged their reputation or property, or who has injured them. 赔偿金 ❑ *She is seeking more than $75,000 in damages.* 她要求$75000以上的赔偿金。
→ see **disaster**

Thesaurus *damage* 另参见：

V.	break, harm, hurt 1
	ruin, wreck 2
N.	harm, loss 3

Word Partnership *damage* 的常用搭配：

V.	damage **caused by/to** ***something*** 3 4
ADJ.	**extensive** damage, **permanent** damage 3 4
N.	damage **to** ***someone's*** **reputation** 4
	damage **to** ***someone's*** **health**, damage **to the environment** 3 4

dam·age con·trol N-UNCOUNT **Damage control** is action that is taken to make the bad results of something as small as possible, when it is impossible to avoid bad results completely. 损失控制 [AM]
in BRIT, use **damage limitation**
❑ *But Broomfield argues that the long-running case is now an exercise in damage control for the Los Angeles police.* 但布洛姆菲尔德争辩说，目前这一持续性事件正是对洛杉矶警察在损失控制方面的一次演习。

dam·age limi·ta·tion [BRIT] → see **damage control**

damn /dæm/ (**damns, damning, damned**) 1 EXCLAM **Damn**, **damn it**, and **dammit** are used by some people to express anger or

Word Web dairy

Gone are the days when the farmer **milked** one **cow** at a time. Today most dairy **farms** use machinery. The **milk** is taken from the cow by a vacuum-powered **milking machine**. Then it goes by pipeline directly to a **refrigerated** storage tank. From there it goes straight to the factory for pasteurization and packaging. The largest such dairy farm in the world is the Al Safi Dairy Farm in Saudi Arabia. It has 24,000 head of **cattle** and produces about 33 million gallons of milk a year.

Word Web dam

The Egyptians built the world's first **dam** in about 2900 BC. It directed water into a **reservoir** near the capital city of Memphis*. Later they constructed another dam to prevent **flooding** just south of Cairo*. Today, dams are used with **irrigation** systems to prevent **droughts**. Modern hydroelectric dams also provide over 20% of the world's electricity. Brazil and Paraguay built the largest hydroelectric power station in the world—the Itaipu Dam. It took 18 years to build and cost 18 billion dollars! Hydroelectric power is non-polluting. However, the dams endanger some species of fish and sometimes destroy valuable forest lands.

Memphis: an ancient city in Egypt.
Cairo: the capital of Egypt.

impatience. 该死；讨厌(口语中表达愤怒、厌烦等) [INFORMAL, VULGAR, FEELINGS] ❑ *Don't be flippant, damn it! This is serious.* 别吊儿郎当的，该死！这是很严肃的。 2 ADJ **Damn** is used by some people to emphasize what they are saying. 非常(用以加强语气) [ADJ n] [INFORMAL, VULGAR, EMPHASIS] ❑ *There's not a damn thing you can do about it now.* 在这件事上你现在根本什么都做不了。 ● ADV **Damn** is also an adverb. 非常地 [ADV adj/adv] ❑ *As it turned out, I was damn right.* 事实证明，我的判断完全正确。 3 V-T If you say that a person or a news report **damns** something such as a policy or action, you mean that they are very critical of it. 谴责 ❑ *...a sensational book in which she damns the ultraright party.* …她谴责极右党派的一本耸人听闻的书。 4 → see also **damned, damning** 5 PHRASE If you say that someone **does not give a damn** about something, you are emphasizing that they do not care about it at all. 毫不在乎 [INFORMAL, VULGAR, EMPHASIS] ❑ *I don't give a damn about the money, Nicole.* 我根本不是在乎钱，尼科尔。

damned /dæmd/ 1 ADJ **Damned** is used by some people to emphasize what they are saying, especially when they are angry or frustrated. 该死的 [ADJ n] [INFORMAL, VULGAR, EMPHASIS] ❑ *They're a damned nuisance most of the time.* 他们多数时候是该死的烦人的家伙。 ● ADV **Damned** is also an adverb. 非常地 [ADV adj/adv] ❑ *We are making a damned good profit, I tell you that.* 告诉你，我们获利极丰。 2 PHRASE If someone says **"I'm damned if I'm** going to do it" or **"I'll be damned if I'll** do it," they are emphasizing that they do not intend to do something and think it is unreasonable for anyone to expect them to do it. 要是…我就不是人。 [INFORMAL, VULGAR, EMPHASIS] ❑ *I was damned if I was going to ask for an explanation and beg to keep my job.* 要是我曾想要去讨个说法并乞求留住工作的话，我就不是人。

Word Link damn, demn ≈ harm, loss : con**demn**, **damn**ing, in**demn**ify

damn·ing /dæmɪŋ/ ADJ If you describe evidence or a report as **damning**, you mean that it suggests very strongly that someone is guilty of a crime or has made a serious mistake. (罪证等) 确凿的；导致定罪的 ❑ *...a damning report on safety standards at US space agency NASA.* …对美国国家航空航天局的安全标准罪证确凿的报道。

damp /dæmp/ (**damper, dampest, damps, damping, damped**) 1 ADJ Something that is **damp** is slightly wet. 潮湿的 ❑ *Her hair was still damp.* 她的头发还有点湿。 ❑ *...the damp, cold air.* …又潮又冷的空气。 2 N-UNCOUNT **Damp** is moisture on the inside walls of a house or in the air. 潮气 ❑ *There was damp everywhere and the entire building was in need of rewiring.* 到处是潮气，整座建筑需要安装新电线。 → see **weather**

▸ **damp down** PHRASAL VERB To **damp down** something such as a strong emotion, an argument, or a crisis means to make it calmer or less intense. 使平静；使减弱 ❑ *His hand moved to his mouth as he tried to damp down the panic.* 他用手捂住了嘴，试图使惊恐的情绪平静下来。

damp·en /dæmpən/ (**dampens, dampening, dampened**) V-T To **dampen** something such as someone's enthusiasm or excitement means to make it less lively or intense. 抑制；减少 ❑ *Nothing seems to dampen his perpetual enthusiasm.* 似乎没有什么能减弱他持久的热情。 ● PHRASAL VERB To **dampen** something **down** means the same as to **dampen** it. 抑制；减少 ❑ *The new penalties were aimed at dampening down consumer spending.* 新的惩罚措施旨在抑制消费者支出。

damp·ness /dæmpnɪs/ N-UNCOUNT **Dampness** is moisture in the air, or on the surface of something. 潮气 ❑ *It was cooler here, and there was dampness in the air.* 以前这儿更凉爽，而且空气中有潮气。

dance ♦♦◊ /dæns/ (**dances, dancing, danced**) 1 V-I When you **dance**, you move your body and feet in a way which follows a rhythm, usually in time to music. 跳舞 ❑ *Polly had never learned to dance.* 波莉从未学过跳舞。 2 V-T If you **dance** a particular kind of dance, you do it or perform it. 跳…舞 ❑ *Then we put the music on, and we all danced the Charleston.* 然后我们放起音乐，一块跳起了查尔斯顿舞。 3 V-I If you **dance** somewhere, you move there lightly and quickly, usually because you are happy or excited. 跳跃；雀跃 [LITERARY] ❑ *He danced off down the road.* 他沿着马路蹦蹦跳跳地走了。 4 V-I If you say that something **dances**, you mean that it moves around, or seems to move around, lightly and quickly. (轻快地)跳动 [LITERARY] ❑ *Patterns of light, reflected by the river, dance along the base of the cliffs.* 被河水倒映出的光影沿着悬崖底部轻快地跳动。 5 N-COUNT A **dance** is a particular series of graceful movements of your body and feet, which you usually do in time to music. 舞蹈 ❑ *Sometimes the people doing this dance hold brightly colored scarves.* 有时候跳这种舞的人拿着色彩鲜艳的围巾。 6 N-COUNT A **dance** is a social event where people dance with each other. 舞会 ❑ *At the school dance he sat and talked to her all evening.* 在学校的舞会上，他整晚坐着和她聊天。 7 V-RECIP When you **dance with** someone, the two of you take part in a dance together, as partners. You can also say that two people **dance**. 和…共舞 ❑ *It's a terrible thing when nobody wants to dance with you.* 没有人想和你跳舞是件糟糕的事。 ❑ *Shall we dance?* 我们跳舞吧？ ● N-COUNT **Dance** is also a noun. 一支舞 ❑ *Come and have a dance with me.* 来和我跳支舞。 8 N-UNCOUNT **Dance** is the activity of performing dances, as a public entertainment or an art form. 舞蹈艺术 ❑ *Their contribution to international dance, drama and music is inestimable.* 他们对国际舞蹈、戏剧和音乐的贡献是不可估量的。

Word Partnership *dance* 的常用搭配：

V. **learn to** dance 1
let's dance 1 7
choreograph a dance 5
N. dance **music**, dance **partner** 5
dance **class**, dance **moves** 5 8

dance floor (**dance floors**) N-COUNT In a restaurant or night club, the **dance floor** is the area where people can dance. 舞池 ❑ *Everybody is on the dance floor with the men forming a circle around the women.* 大家都在舞池里，男士绕着女士围成一个圈。

danc·er /dænsər/ (**dancers**) 1 N-COUNT A **dancer** is a person who earns money by dancing, or a person who is dancing. 舞蹈演员；舞者 ❑ *His girlfriend was a dancer with the New York City Ballet.* 他的女朋友曾是纽约市芭蕾舞团的舞蹈演员。 2 N-COUNT If you say that someone is a good **dancer** or a bad **dancer**, you are saying how well or badly they can dance. 舞跳得…的人 ❑ *He was the best dancer in LA.* 他曾是洛杉矶舞跳得最好的人。

danc·ing ♦◊◊ /dænsɪŋ/ N-UNCOUNT When people dance for enjoyment or to entertain others, you can refer to this activity as **dancing**. 跳舞 ❑ *All the schools have music and dancing as part of the curriculum.* 每个学校都设有音乐课和舞蹈课。 ❑ *Let's go dancing tonight.* 我们今晚去跳舞吧。

d

D

dan·de·lion /dændɪlaɪən/ (**dandelions**) N-COUNT A **dandelion** is a wild plant which has yellow flowers with lots of thin petals. When the petals of each flower drop off, a fluffy white ball of seeds grows. 蒲公英

dan·druff /dændrəf/ N-UNCOUNT **Dandruff** is small white pieces of dead skin in someone's hair, or fallen from someone's hair. 头皮屑 ❑ *He has very bad dandruff.* 他的头皮屑很多。

dan·ger ♦♦◇ /deɪndʒər/ (**dangers**) 1 N-UNCOUNT **Danger** is the possibility that someone may be harmed or killed. 危险 ❑ *My friends endured tremendous danger in order to help me.* 为了帮助我，我的朋友们经历了巨大的危险。 2 N-COUNT A **danger** is something or someone that can hurt or harm you. 威胁；危害 ❑ *...the dangers of smoking.* …吸烟的危害。 3 N-SING If there is a **danger that** something unpleasant will happen, it is possible that it will happen. 危险；风险 ❑ *There is a real danger that some people will no longer be able to afford insurance.* 一个真正的风险是有些人将再也负担不起保险费。 ❑ *There was no danger that any of these groups would be elected to power.* 丝毫不存在这些团体胜选掌权的危险。 4 PHRASE If someone who has been seriously ill is **out of danger**, they are still ill, but they are not expected to die. 脱离危险期 ❑ *There is some risk of the lung collapsing again, but he is out of danger.* 肺部的确存在再次衰竭的危险，但他脱离危险期了。

→ see **hero**

Word Link *ous ≈ having the qualities of : dangerous, fabulous, glamorous*

dan·ger·ous ♦♦◇ /deɪndʒərəs, deɪndʒrəs/ ADJ If something is **dangerous**, it is able or likely to hurt or harm you. 危险的 ❑ *It's a dangerous stretch of road.* 这是一截危险路段。 ❑ *...dangerous drugs.* …危险的药品。 ● **dan·ger·ous·ly** ADV 危险地 ❑ *He is dangerously ill.* 他病得很重。

Thesaurus *dangerous* 另参见：

ADJ. risky, threatening, unsafe

Word Partnership *dangerous* 的常用搭配：

N. dangerous **area**, dangerous **criminal**, dangerous **driving**, dangerous **man**, dangerous **situation**

ADV. **potentially** dangerous

dan·gle /dæŋgəl/ (**dangles, dangling, dangled**) 1 V-T/V-I If something **dangles from** somewhere or if you **dangle** it somewhere, it hangs or swings loosely. 悬挂；悬摆 ❑ *A gold bracelet dangled from his left wrist.* 一只金手镯在他左腕上晃来晃去。 2 V-T If you say that someone **is dangling** something attractive **before** you, you mean they are offering it to you in order to try to influence you in some way. 炫示 ❑ *They dangle hope in front of our eyes, then snatch it clear away.* 他们在我们眼前炫示希望，然后将它一把夺走。

dare ♦◇◇ /dɛər/ (**dares, daring, dared**)

> **Dare** sometimes behaves like an ordinary verb, for example, "He dared to speak" and "He doesn't dare to speak" and sometimes like a modal, for example, "He dare not speak."

1 V-T If you do not **dare to** do something, you do not have enough courage to do it, or you do not want to do it because you fear the consequences. If you **dare to** do something, you do something which requires a lot of courage. 敢于 ❑ *Most people hate Harry but they don't dare to say so.* 多数人都讨厌哈里，但他们不敢说出来。 ● MODAL **Dare** is also a modal. 敢；竟敢 ❑ *Dare she risk staying where she was?* 她敢冒险呆在原地不动吗？ ❑ *The yen is weakening. But Tokyo dare not raise its interest rates again.* 日元在贬值。但东京不敢再次上调利率。

> You can leave out the word **to** after **dare**. ❑ *Nobody dared complain.* The form **dares** is never used in a question or in a negative statement. You use **dare** instead. ❑ *Dare she tell him?... He dare not enter.*

2 V-T If you **dare** someone **to** do something, you challenge them to prove that they are not frightened of doing it. 向…挑战 ❑ *Over coffee, she lit a cigarette, her eyes daring him to comment.* 她一边喝着咖啡，一边点了支烟，用目光激他作出评价。 3 N-COUNT A **dare** is a challenge which one person gives to another to do something dangerous or frightening. 挑战 ❑ *Jones broke into a military base on a dare.* 约翰接受了挑战，冲进一个军事基地。 4 PHRASE If you say to someone "**don't you dare**" do something, you are telling them not to do it and letting them know that you are angry. 看你敢… [SPOKEN, FEELINGS] ❑ *Allen, don't you dare go anywhere else, you hear?* 艾伦，你哪儿都不许去，听见了吗？ 5 PHRASE You say "**how dare you**" when you are very shocked and angry about something that someone has done. 你竟敢… [SPOKEN, FEELINGS] ❑ *How dare you pick up the phone and listen in on my conversations!* 你竟敢拿起电话偷听我的谈话！ 6 PHRASE You can use "**I daresay**" or "**I dare say**" before or after a statement to indicate that you believe it is probably true. 我相信 ❑ *I daresay that the computer would provide a clear answer to that.* 我相信电脑会对此给出明确的答案。

★ **dar·ing** /dɛərɪŋ/ 1 ADJ People who are **daring** are willing to do or say things which are new or which might shock or anger other people. 大胆的 ❑ *Bergit was probably more daring than I was.* 伯杰特可能比我胆子还大。 2 ADJ A **daring** person is willing to do things that might be dangerous. 勇敢的 ❑ *His daring rescue saved the lives of the youngsters.* 他英勇的救援行动挽救了那些少年的生命。 3 N-UNCOUNT **Daring** is the courage to do things which might be dangerous or which might shock or anger other people. 胆量；鲁莽 ❑ *His daring may have cost him his life.* 他的鲁莽差点要了他的命。

dark ♦♦◇ /dɑrk/ (**darker, darkest**) 1 ADJ When it is **dark**, there is not enough light to see properly, for example, because it is night. 黑暗的 ❑ *It was too dark inside to see much.* 里面太黑，看不见什么东西。 ❑ *People usually draw the curtains once it gets dark.* 天一黑，人们通常就会拉上窗帘。 ● **dark·ness** N-UNCOUNT 黑暗 ❑ *The light went out, and the room was plunged into darkness.* 灯灭了，房间陷入了黑暗之中。 ● **dark·ly** ADV 昏暗地 [ADV -ed] ❑ *In a darkly lit, seedy dance hall, hundreds of men lounge around small tables.* 在一个灯光昏暗、破旧的舞厅里，成百上千的人围坐在小桌旁打发时间。 2 ADJ If you describe something as **dark**, you mean that it is black in color, or a shade that is close to black. 黑色的；暗色的 ❑ *He wore a dark suit and carried a black attaché case.* 他穿着深色套装，手提黑色公文包。 ● **dark·ly** ADV 呈黑色地 ❑ *The freckles on Joanne's face suddenly stood out darkly against her pale skin.* 在苍白的肤色映衬下，乔安脸上的雀斑一下子更明显了。 3 ADJ If someone has **dark** hair, eyes, or skin, they have brown or black hair, eyes, or skin. (头发、皮肤等) 棕色或黑色的 ❑ *He had dark, curly hair.* 他有一头黑色卷发。 4 ADJ A **dark** period of time is unpleasant or frightening. 黯淡的 ❑ *Once again there's talk of very dark days ahead.* 人们又一次提到了极其黯淡的前途。 5 ADJ A **dark** place or area is mysterious and not fully known about. 神秘的 [ADJ n] ❑ *The spacecraft will enable scientists to study some dark corners of the solar system.* 太空船使得科学家可以研究太阳系中一些不为人知的角落。 6 ADJ **Dark** thoughts are sad, and show that you are expecting something unpleasant to happen. 悲观的 [LITERARY] ❑ *Troy's endless happy chatter kept me from thinking dark thoughts.* 特洛伊兴高采烈地说个不停，使我忘记了悲观的想法。 ● **dark·ly** ADV 悲观地 [ADV with v] ❑ *She hinted darkly that she might have to resign.* 她悲观地暗示她可能得辞职。 7 ADJ If you describe something as **dark**, you mean that it is related to things that are serious or unpleasant, rather than lighthearted. 沉重的 ❑ *There's plenty of dark humor in the movie.* 这部电影充满了黑色幽默。 ● **dark·ly** ADV 沉重地 [ADV adj] ❑ *The atmosphere after Wednesday's debut was as darkly comic as the movie itself.* 周三首映式之后的气氛和电影本身一样像是沉重的喜剧。 8 N-SING **The dark** is the lack of light in a place. 黑暗 ❑ *I've always been afraid of the dark.* 我一直惧怕黑暗。 9 COMB IN COLOR When you use **dark** to describe a color, you are referring to a shade of that color which is close to black, or seems to have some black in it. 深色的 ❑ *She was wearing a dark blue dress.* 她穿着深蓝色的连衣裙。 10 PHRASE If you do something **after dark**, you do it when the sun has set and night has begun. 黄昏以后 ❑ *They avoid going out alone after dark.* 他们避免黄昏后独自出门。 11 PHRASE If you do something **before dark**, you do it before the sun sets and night begins. 黄昏以前 ❑ *They'll be back well before dark.* 他们会在天黑以前回来。 12 PHRASE If you are **in the dark about** something, you do not know anything about it. 一无所知 ❑ *The investigators admit that they are completely in the dark about the killing.* 调查人员承认他们对这起凶杀案一无所知。

Word Partnership *dark* 的常用搭配：

V. **get** dark 1
afraid of the dark, **scared of the** dark 8

N. dark **clouds**, dark **suit** 2

dark·en /dɑrkən/ (**darkens, darkening, darkened**) 1 V-T/V-I If something **darkens** or if a person or thing **darkens** it, it becomes darker. 变暗 使变暗 ❑ *The sky darkened abruptly.* 天突然变暗了。

2 V-T/V-I If someone's mood **darkens** or if something **darkens** their mood, they suddenly become unhappy. 黯淡 使黯淡 [LITERARY] ❑ *My sunny mood suddenly darkened.* 我快乐的情绪突然黯淡下来。

dark·room /dɑrkrum/ (**darkrooms**) N-COUNT A **darkroom** is a room which can be sealed off from natural light and is lit only by red light. It is used for developing photographs. (冲洗底片的) 暗房

dar·ling /dɑrlɪŋ/ (**darlings**) 1 N-VOC You call someone **darling** if you love them or like them very much. 亲爱的 [FEELINGS] ❑ *Thank you, darling.* 谢谢你，亲爱的。 2 ADJ Some people use **darling** to describe someone or something that they love or like very much. 心爱的 [ADJ n] [INFORMAL] ❑ *To have a darling baby boy was the greatest gift I could imagine.* 拥有一个心爱的小男孩是我所能想像的最好的礼物。 3 N-COUNT If you describe someone as a **darling**, you are fond of them and think that they are nice. 心爱的人 [INFORMAL] ❑ *He's such a darling.* 他真是个宝贝。

darn /dɑrn/ (**darns, darning, darned**) 1 V-T If you **darn** something knitted or made of cloth, you repair a hole in it by sewing stitches across the hole and then weaving stitches in and out of them. 织补 ❑ *Aunt Emilie darned old socks.* 埃米莉阿姨把旧袜子补好了。 2 ADJ People sometimes use **darn** or **darned** to emphasize what they are saying, often when they are annoyed. 该死的；可恶的 (表示厌恶) [ADJ n] [INFORMAL, EMPHASIS] ❑ *There's not a darn thing he can do about it.* 在这件事上你根本什么都做不了。 ● ADV **Darn** is also an adverb. 非常地 [ADV adj/adv] ❑ *...the desire to be free to do just as we darn well please.* …自由地做我们真正想做的事情的渴望。 3 PHRASE You can say **I'll be darned** to show that you are very surprised about something. 我太惊奇了 [AM, INFORMAL, FEELINGS] ❑ *"A talking pig!" he exclaimed. "Well, I'll be darned."* "一头会说话的猪！"他惊叫到，"啊，我太惊奇了"。

★ **dart** /dɑrt/ (**darts, darting, darted**) 1 V-I If a person or animal **darts** somewhere, they move there suddenly and quickly. 飞奔；猛冲 [WRITTEN] ❑ *Ingrid darted across the deserted street.* 英格里德飞奔过空无一人的街道。 2 V-T/V-I If you **dart** a look **at** someone or something, or if your eyes **dart to** them, you look at them very quickly. 投射 (目光) [LITERARY] ❑ *She darted a sly sideways glance at Bramwell.* 她狡猾地斜瞟了布莱威尔一眼。 3 N-COUNT A **dart** is a small, narrow object with a sharp point which can be thrown or shot. 飞镖 ❑ *Markov died after being struck by a poison dart.* 马尔科夫被毒镖击中后身亡。 4 N-UNCOUNT **Darts** is a game in which you throw darts at a round board which has numbers on it. 掷镖游戏 ❑ *I started playing darts at 15.* 我从15岁开始玩掷镖游戏。

dash /dæʃ/ (**dashes, dashing, dashed**) 1 V-I If you **dash** somewhere, you run or go there quickly and suddenly. 猛冲 ❑ *Suddenly she dashed down to the cellar.* 她猛地朝地窖冲过去。 ● N-SING **Dash** is also a noun. 猛冲 ❑ *...a 160-mile dash to the hospital.* …飞奔160英里赶向医院。 2 V-I If you say that you have to **dash**, you mean that you are in a hurry and have to leave immediately. 赶紧离开 [no cont] [INFORMAL] ❑ *Oh, Tim! I'm sorry but I have to dash.* 噢，蒂姆！很抱歉，但我得赶紧走了。 3 V-T If you **dash** something **against** a wall or other surface, you throw or push it violently, often so hard that it breaks. 猛撞；猛摔 [LITERARY] ❑ *She seized the doll and dashed it against the stone wall with tremendous force.* 她抓起洋娃娃，使劲往石墙上摔。 4 V-T If an event or person **dashes** someone's hopes or expectations, it destroys them by making it impossible that the thing that is hoped for or expected will ever happen. 使破灭 [LITERARY, JOURNALISM] ❑ *Renewed fighting has dashed hopes for a United Nations-organized interim government.* 重燃的战火粉碎了在联合国的组织下建立临时政府的希望。 5 N-COUNT A **dash of** something is a small quantity of it which you add when you are preparing food or mixing a drink. 少量 ❑ *Pour over olive oil and a dash of balsamic vinegar to accentuate the sweetness.* 倒入橄榄油和少量香醋以使甜味更浓些。 6 N-COUNT A **dash of** a quality is a small amount of it that is found in something and often makes it more interesting or distinctive. 一点 (趣味或特色) ❑ *...a story with a dash of mystery thrown in.* …加入了一抹神秘色彩的故事。 7 N-COUNT A **dash** is a straight, horizontal line used in writing, for example, to separate two main clauses whose meanings are closely connected. 破折号 ❑ *...the dash between the birth date and death date.* …生卒日期之间的破折号。 8 N-COUNT The **dash** of a car is its **dashboard**. 仪表板 9 PHRASE If you **make a dash for** a place, you run there very quickly, for example, to escape from someone or something. 冲 ❑ *I made a dash for the front door but he got there before me.* 我向前门冲去，但他却已先我而到。

▸ **dash off** 1 PHRASAL VERB If you **dash off to** a place, you go there very quickly. 迅速去做 ❑ *He dashed off to lunch at the Hard Rock Cafe.* 他急匆匆地到硬石餐馆去吃午饭。 2 PHRASAL VERB If you **dash off** a piece of writing, you write or compose it very quickly, without thinking about it very much. 匆匆地写 ❑ *He dashed off a couple of novels.* 他匆匆地完成了几本小说。

dash·board /dæʃbɔrd/ (**dashboards**) N-COUNT The **dashboard** in a car is the panel facing the driver's seat where most of the instruments and switches are. (机动车辆的) 仪表板 ❑ *The clock on the dashboard said it was five to two.* 汽车仪表板上的时钟显示当时1：55。

dash·ing /dæʃɪŋ/ ADJ A **dashing** person or thing is very stylish and attractive. 时髦的 [OLD-FASHIONED] ❑ *He was the very model of the dashing Air Force pilot.* 他当时是英俊潇洒的空军飞行员的典范。

da·ta ♦♦◇ /deɪtə, dætə/ 1 N-PLURAL N-UNCOUNT You can refer to information as **data**, especially when it is in the form of facts or statistics that you can analyze. 资料 ❑ *The study was based on data from 2,100 women.* 此项研究以从2100位女性身上获得的资料为依据。 2 N-UNCOUNT **Data** is information that can be stored and used by a computer program. 数据 [COMPUTING] ❑ *This system uses powerful microchips to compress huge amounts of data onto a CD-ROM.* 这一系统使用功能强大的微芯片来把大量数据压缩到CD-ROM上。

→ see **forecast**

Thesaurus	*data* 另参见：
N.	facts, figures, information, results, statistics 1

da·ta bank (**data banks**) also **databank** N-COUNT A **data bank** is the same as a **database**. 数据库

data·base /deɪtəbeɪs, dætə-/ (**databases**) also **data base** N-COUNT A **database** is a collection of data that is stored in a computer and that can easily be used and added to. 数据库 ❑ *The state maintains a database of names of people allowed to vote.* 该州有一个可以投票的人的姓名数据库。

da·ta pro·cess·ing N-UNCOUNT **Data processing** is the series of operations that are carried out on data, especially by computers, in order to present, interpret, or obtain information. 数据处理 ❑ *Taylor's company makes data-processing systems.* 泰勒的公司研发数据处理系统。

date ♦♦◇ /deɪt/ (**dates, dating, dated**) 1 N-COUNT A **date** is a specific time that can be named, for example, a particular day or a particular year. 日期 ❑ *What's the date today?* 今天是几号？ 2 N-COUNT A **date** is an appointment to meet someone or go out with them, especially someone with whom you are having, or may soon have, a romantic relationship. 约会 ❑ *I have a date with Bob.* 我和鲍勃有个约会。 3 V-RECIP If you **are dating** someone, you go out with them regularly because you are having, or may soon have, a romantic relationship with them. You can also say that two people **are dating**. (恋爱中) 约会 ❑ *For a year I dated a woman who was a research assistant.* 有一年的时间，我一直和一个女助理研究员约会。 4 N-COUNT If you have a date with someone with whom you are having, or may soon have, a romantic relationship, you can refer to that person as your **date**. (恋爱中的) 约会对象 ❑ *He lied to Essie, saying his date was one of the girls in the show.* 他对埃西撒谎说他约会的对象是参加演出的女孩儿其中的一个。 5 N-COUNT A **date** is a small, dark-brown, sticky fruit with a stone inside. Dates grow on palm trees in hot countries. 椰枣 6 V-T If you **date** something, you give or discover the date when it was made or when it began. 推断…的年代 ❑ *I think we can date the decline of Western Civilization quite precisely.* 我认为我们可以非常准确的推断出西方文明衰落的年代。 7 V-T When you **date** something such as a letter or a check, you write that day's date on it. 给…标注日期 ❑ *Once the decision is reached, he can date and sign the sheet.* 一旦做出决定，他就可以在那张表上签上日期和名字。 8 V-I If something **dates**, it goes out of fashion and becomes unacceptable to modern tastes. 过时 ❑ *Blue and white is the classic color combination for bathrooms. It always looks smart and will never date.* 蓝色和白色是浴室的经典色彩搭配，看起来总是很时髦，永远不会过时。 9 → see also **dated, out of date** 10 PHRASE **To date** means up until the present time. 至今为止 ❑ *"Dottie" is by far his best novel to date.* 《小多特》是他至今最为出色的小说。

▸ **date back** PHRASAL VERB If something **dates back to** a particular time, it started or was made at that time. 追溯 ❑ *The issue is not a new one. It dates back to the 1930s at least.* 这杂志不是新的，它至少可以追溯到20世纪30年代。

d

Word Partnership *date* 的常用搭配：
N. **birth** date, **cut-off** date, **due** date, **expiration** date 1
V. **set a** date 1 2
date **and sign** 7

dat·ed /deɪtɪd/ ADJ **Dated** things or ideas seem old-fashioned, although they may once have been fashionable or modern. 过时的 ❑ *Many of his ideas have value, but some are dated and others are plain wrong.* 他的许多想法都有价值，但也有一些不合时宜，还有一些很明显是错误的。

date of birth (**dates of birth**) N-COUNT Your **date of birth** is the exact date on which you were born, including the year. 出生日期 ❑ *The registration form showed his date of birth as August 2, 1979.* 登记表上显示他的出生日期是1979年8月2日。

daub /dɔb/ (**daubs, daubing, daubed**) V-T When you **daub** a substance such as mud or paint on something, you spread it on that thing in a rough or careless way. 涂抹 ❑ *The makeup woman had been daubing mock blood on Jeremy Fox when last he'd seen her.* 他上次见到那位女化妆师的时候，她正不停地往杰里米·福克斯身上涂抹假血。

daugh·ter ♦♦♦ /dɔtər/ (**daughters**) N-COUNT Someone's **daughter** is their female child. 女儿 ❑ *...Flora and her daughter Catherine.* …弗洛拉和她的女儿凯瑟琳。 ❑ *...the daughter of a university professor.* …一位大学教授的女儿。
→ see **child**

daughter-in-law (**daughters-in-law**) N-COUNT Someone's **daughter-in-law** is the wife of their son. 儿媳

▲ **daunt** /dɔnt/ (**daunts, daunting, daunted**) V-T If something **daunts** you, it makes you feel slightly afraid or worried about dealing with it. 使胆怯 ❑ *...a grueling trip that would have daunted a woman half her age.* …即使是只有她一半年纪的女人都会感到胆怯的一次痛苦旅行。 ● **daunt·ed** ADJ 胆怯的 [v-link ADJ] ❑ *It is hard to pick up such a book and not to feel a little daunted.* 读这样的一本书是很难不略微感到胆怯的。

daunt·ing /dɔntɪŋ/ ADJ Something that is **daunting** makes you feel slightly afraid or worried about dealing with it. 使人畏缩的 ❑ *He and his wife Jane were faced with the daunting task of restoring the gardens to their former splendor.* 他和他的妻子简当时面临着恢复花园昔日风采的艰巨任务。

dawn /dɔn/ (**dawns, dawning, dawned**) 1 N-VAR **Dawn** is the time of day when light first appears in the sky, just before the sun rises. 黎明 ❑ *Nancy woke at dawn.* 天刚亮南希就醒了。 2 N-SING **The dawn of** a period of time or a situation is the beginning of it. 开端 [LITERARY] ❑ *...the dawn of the radio age.* …无线通讯时代的开端。 3 V-I If something **is dawning**, it is beginning to develop or come into existence. 开始 [WRITTEN] ❑ *A new century was dawning.* 一个新的世纪开始了。 ● **dawn·ing** N-SING 开端 ❑ *...the dawning of the space age.* …太空时代的开始。
▸ **dawn on** or **dawn upon** PHRASAL VERB If a fact or idea **dawns on** you, you realize it. 使开始明白 ❑ *It gradually dawned on me that I still had talent and ought to run again.* 我渐渐明白我还有能力，应该再参加一次。

dawn raid (**dawn raids**) N-COUNT If police officers carry out a **dawn raid**, they go to someone's house very early in the morning to search it or arrest them. 凌晨突袭（尤指警方为搜捕罪犯而展开的）❑ *The dawn raids Tuesday were carried out by about 170 policemen.* 周二的凌晨突袭有大约一百七十名警察参加。

day ♦♦♦ /deɪ/ (**days**) 1 N-COUNT A **day** is one of the seven twenty-four hour periods of time in a week. （一周中的）一天 ❑ *And it has snowed almost every day for the past week.* 而且过去的一周几乎每天都在下雪。 2 N-COUNT You can refer to a particular period in history as a particular **day** or as particular **days**. 时期 ❑ *He began to talk about the Ukraine of his uncle's day.* 他开始谈论他叔叔那个年代的乌克兰。 ❑ *...his early days of struggle and deep poverty.* …他早年的奋斗和极度穷困时期。 3 **it is early days** → see **early** 4 **at the end of the day** → see **end** 5 **the good old days** → see **old** 6 N-VAR **Day** is the time when it is light, or the time when you are up and doing things. 白天 ❑ *Twenty-seven million working days are lost each year due to work accidents and sickness.* 由于工伤事故和疾病，每年损失掉2700万个工作日。 ❑ *She gives herself one day a week off, on Thursdays.* 她每周放自己一天假，在星期四。 7 PHRASE If something happens **day after day**, it happens every day without stopping. 日复一日 ❑ *The newspaper job had me doing the same thing day after day.* 这份报业的工作让我日复一日地做同一件事情。 8 PHRASE If you say that something happens **day in, day out** or **day in and day out**, you mean that it happens regularly over a long period of time. 天天 [V PHR] ❑ *I used to drink coffee day in, day out.* 过去我每天喝咖啡。 9 PHRASE **In this day and age** means in modern times. 在现代 ❑ *Even in this day and age the old attitudes persist.* 即使在今天，一些陈旧的观念仍然存在。 10 PHRASE If you say that something **has seen better days**, you mean that it is old and in poor condition. 破旧 ❑ *The tweed jacket she wore had seen better days.* 她穿的那件斜纹软呢夹克衫已经十分破旧了。 11 PHRASE If you **call it a day**, you decide to stop what you are doing because you are tired of it or because it is not successful. 结束工作；收工 ❑ *Faced with mounting debts, the decision to call it a day was inevitable.* 面对不断增加的债务，停工的决定是不可避免的。 12 PHRASE If something **makes** your **day**, it makes you feel very happy. 使某人非常高兴 [INFORMAL] ❑ *Come on, Bill. Send Tom a card and make his day.* 来，比尔，给汤姆寄张卡片让他高兴一下。 13 PHRASE **One day** or **some day** or **one of these days** means at some time in the future. 有朝一日 ❑ *I too dreamed of living in Dallas one day.* 我也曾梦想有朝一日能住在达拉斯。 ❑ *I hope some day you will find the woman who will make you happy.* 我希望有一天你会找到能让你幸福的女人。 14 PHRASE If you say that something happened **the other day**, you mean that it happened a few days ago. 几天前 ❑ *I phoned your office the other day.* 几天前，我往你的办公室打过电话。 15 PHRASE If someone or something **saves the day** in a situation which seems likely to fail, they manage to make it successful. 扭转败局 ❑ *...this story about how he saved the day at his daughter's birthday party.* …关于他如何在女儿的生日聚会上扭转局面的故事。 16 PHRASE If something happens **from day to day** or **day by day**, it happens each day. 每天 ❑ *Your needs can differ from day to day.* 你的需要可能每天都在变化。 17 PHRASE If it is a month or a year **to the day** since a particular thing happened, it is exactly a month or a year since it happened. （日期）正好 ❑ *It was January 19, a year to the day since he had arrived in Singapore.* 那是1月19日，他到新加坡正好满1年。 18 PHRASE **To this day** means up until and including the present time. 至今 ❑ *The controversy continues to this day.* 这场争论直到今天仍在继续。 19 PHRASE If you say that a task is **all in a day's work** for someone, you mean that they do not mind doing it although it may be difficult, because it is part of their job or because they often do it. 家常便饭 ❑ *For war reporters, dodging snipers' bullets is all in a day's work.* 对于战地记者来说，躲避狙击手的子弹是家常便饭。 20 **your day in court** → see **court**
→ see **year**

day·break /deɪbreɪk/ N-UNCOUNT **Daybreak** is the time in the morning when light first appears. 黎明 ❑ *Pedro got up every morning before daybreak.* 佩德罗每天早上在黎明前起床。

day care also **daycare** N-UNCOUNT **Day care** is care that is provided during the day for people who cannot take care of themselves, such as small children, old people, or people who are ill. Day care is provided by paid workers. 日托 ❑ *She had to contend with day care for her 2-year-old twins being canceled.* 她不得不就她两岁大的双胞胎日托被取消一事进行交涉。 ❑ *...a daycare center for elderly people.* …老年人日托中心。

day·dream /deɪdrim/ (**daydreams, daydreaming, daydreamed**) 1 V-I If you **daydream**, you think about pleasant things for a period of time, usually about things that you would like to happen. 做白日梦 ❑ *Do you work hard for success rather than daydream about it?* 你在努力争取成功而非做白日梦吗？ ❑ *He daydreams of being a famous journalist.* 他梦想成为一个有名的记者。 2 N-COUNT A **daydream** is a series of pleasant thoughts, usually about things that you would like to happen. 白日梦；幻想 ❑ *He learned to escape into daydreams of handsome men and beautiful women.* 他学会了躲进对俊男靓女的幻想中。

Word Link *light ≈ shining : daylight, enlighten, light*

day·light /deɪlaɪt/ 1 N-UNCOUNT **Daylight** is the natural light that there is during the day, before it gets dark. 日光 ❑ *Lack of daylight can make people feel depressed.* 缺乏日光的照射会让人情绪低落。 2 N-UNCOUNT **Daylight** is the time of day when it begins to get light. 拂晓 ❑ *Quinn returned shortly after daylight yesterday morning.* 奎因昨天天刚亮就回来了。 3 PHRASE If you say that a crime is committed **in broad daylight**, you are expressing your surprise that it is done during the day when people can see it, rather than at night. 光天化日之下 [EMPHASIS] ❑ *A girl was attacked on a train in broad daylight.* 光天化日之下，一个女孩在火车上遭袭。

Clocks are set one hour fast in the spring and in the fall returned to the standard time so that residents have more convenient use of daylight hours. The saying "spring ahead, fall back" is used to remember which way to turn the clocks. This is not practiced uniformly across the United States. Some local areas have decided not to participate, often out of economic consideration for neighboring communities.

day off (**days off**) N-COUNT A **day off** is a day when you do not go to work, even though it is usually a working day. 休息日 ❑ *It was Mrs. Dearden's day off, and Paul was on duty in her place.* 那天是迪尔登夫人休息日，保尔替她上班。

day school (**day schools**) N-COUNT A **day school** is a school where the students go home every evening and do not live at the school. Compare **boarding school**. 日校；走读学校

day·time /deɪtaɪm/ **1** N-SING **The daytime** is the part of a day between the time when it gets light and the time when it gets dark. 白天 ["the" N, also no det] ❑ *In the daytime he stayed up in his room, sleeping, or listening to music.* 白天，他呆在自己的屋子里睡觉或者听音乐。 **2** ADJ **Daytime** television and radio is broadcast during the morning and afternoon on weekdays. 日间的 [ADJ n] ❑ *She took on the role as host of a daytime TV show.* 她主持一个日间电视节目。

day-to-day ADJ **Day-to-day** things or activities exist or happen every day as part of ordinary life. 日常的 [ADJ n] ❑ *I am a vegetarian and use a lot of lentils in my day-to-day cooking.* 我是个素食者，日常烹调中使用许多兵豆。

day trad·er (**day traders**) N-COUNT In the stock market, **day traders** are traders who buy and sell particular securities on the same day. (股市中的) 当日交易者 [BUSINESS] ❑ *Unlike the day traders, they tended to hold on to stocks for days and weeks, sometimes even months.* 和当日交易者不同，他们倾向于持股几天、几周有时甚至几个月。

daze /deɪz/ N-SING If someone is **in a daze**, they are feeling confused and unable to think clearly, often because they have had a shock or surprise. 迷惑 ❑ *For an hour I was walking around in a daze.* 我茫然地走了一个小时。

dazed /deɪzd/ ADJ If someone is **dazed**, they are confused and unable to think clearly, often because of shock or a blow to the head. 头昏眼花的 ❑ *At the end of the interview I was dazed and exhausted.* 采访结束的时候，我感到头昏眼花、精疲力竭。

★ **daz·zle** /dæzᵊl/ (**dazzles, dazzling, dazzled**) **1** V-T If someone or something **dazzles** you, you are extremely impressed by their skill, qualities, or beauty. 使倾倒 ❑ *George dazzled her with his knowledge of the world.* 乔治对世界的了解令她倾倒。 **2** V-T If a bright light **dazzles** you, it makes you unable to see properly for a short time. 使目眩 ❑ *The sun, glinting from the pool, dazzled me.* 池水折射的阳光使我目眩。 **3** N-SING **The dazzle of** something is a quality it has, such as beauty or skill, which is impressive and attractive. 绚烂；辉煌 ❑ *The dazzle of stardom and status attracts them.* 明星和身份的耀眼光环吸引着他们。

dazz·ling /dæzlɪŋ/ **1** ADJ Something that is **dazzling** is very impressive or beautiful. 令人印象深刻的；惊人的 ❑ *He gave Alberg a dazzling smile.* 他向艾尔伯格粲然一笑。 ● **dazz·ling·ly** ADV 令人印象深刻地；惊人地 ❑ *The view was dazzlingly beautiful.* 景色美得令人目眩神迷。 **2** ADJ A **dazzling** light is very bright and makes you unable to see properly for a short time. 刺眼的 ❑ *He shielded his eyes against the dazzling declining sun.* 他遮着眼睛以挡住刺眼的夕阳。 ● **dazz·ling·ly** ADV 刺眼地 [ADV adj] ❑ *The loading bay seemed dazzlingly bright.* 这个进料台看起来亮得刺眼。

dead ♦♦◇ /dɛd/ **1** ADJ A person, animal, or plant that is **dead** is no longer living. 死的 ❑ *"You're a widow?"—"Yes. My husband's been dead a year now."* "你是个寡妇？" —— "是的，我丈夫去世1年了。" ❑ *The group had shot dead another hostage.* 这伙人又打死了一名人质。 ● N-PLURAL **The dead** are people who are dead. 死者 ❑ *Two American soldiers were among the dead.* 死者中有两名美军士兵。

Do not confuse **dead** with **died**. **Died** is the past tense and past participle of the verb **die**, and thus indicates the action of dying. ❑ *She died in 1934... Two men have died since the rioting broke out.* You do not use **died** as an adjective. You use **dead** instead. ❑ *More than 2,200 dead birds have been found.*

2 ADJ If you describe a place or a period of time as **dead**, you do not like it because there is very little activity taking place in it. 无生气的 [DISAPPROVAL] ❑ *...some dead little town where the liveliest thing is the flies.* …最有活力的东西是苍蝇的死气沉沉的某个小镇。 **3** ADJ Something that is **dead** is no longer being used or is finished. 用尽的；结束的 ❑ *The dead cigarette was still between his fingers.* 燃尽的香烟还夹在他指缝间。 **4** ADJ If you say that an idea, plan, or subject is **dead**, you mean that people are no longer interested in it or willing to develop it any further. 过时的；不再重要的 ❑ *It's a dead issue, Baxter.* 这件事已经不重要了，巴克斯特。 **5** ADJ A telephone or piece of electrical equipment that is **dead** is no longer functioning, for example, because it no longer has any electrical power. 不运转的 ❑ *On another occasion I answered the phone and the line went dead.* 还有一次我接了电话，但紧接着就断线了。 **6** ADJ **Dead** is used to mean "complete" or "absolute," especially before the words "center," "silence," and "stop." 全然的；绝对的 [ADJ n] [EMPHASIS] ❑ *They hurried about in dead silence, with anxious faces.* 他们四下忙乱，人人一言不发，面有忧色。 **7** ADV **Dead** means "precisely" or "exactly." 精确地 [ADV prep/adv/adj] [EMPHASIS] ❑ *Mars was visible, dead in the center of the telescope.* 火星清晰可辨，正好就在望远镜的中心。 **8** CONVENTION If you reply "**Over my dead body**" when a plan or action has been suggested, you are emphasizing that you dislike it, and will do everything you can to prevent it. 除非我死了 (表示强烈反对) [INFORMAL, EMPHASIS] ❑ *"Let's invite her to dinner."—"Over my dead body!"* "我们请她共进晚餐吧。" —— "除非我死了！" **9** PHRASE If you say that a person or animal **dropped dead** or **dropped down dead**, you mean that they died very suddenly and unexpectedly. 猝死 ❑ *He dropped dead of a heart attack.* 他心脏病突发而猝死。 **10** PHRASE If you say that you **feel dead** or **are half dead**, you mean that you feel very tired or ill and very weak. 累得半死的 [INFORMAL, EMPHASIS] ❑ *I thought you looked half dead at dinner, and who could blame you after that trip.* 我觉得你晚饭的时候看上去累得要命，但在那次旅行之后谁会怪你呢。 **11** PHRASE If something happens **in the dead of night, at dead of night**, or **in the dead of winter**, it happens in the middle part of the night or the winter, when it is darkest or coldest. 在深夜；在严冬 [LITERARY] ❑ *All three incidents occurred in the dead of night.* 3起事件都发生在深夜。 **12** PHRASE If you say that you wouldn't **be seen dead** or **be caught dead** in particular clothes, places, or situations, you are expressing strong dislike or disapproval of them. 决不 [INFORMAL, EMPHASIS] ❑ *I wouldn't be seen dead in a straw hat.* 我决不戴草帽。 **13** PHRASE To **stop dead** means to suddenly stop happening or moving. To **stop** someone or something **dead** means to cause them to suddenly stop happening or moving. 突然停止 ❑ *We all stopped dead and looked at it.* 我们都突然停下来看着它。 **14** to **stop dead in** your **tracks** → see **track**
→ see **funeral**

Thesaurus *dead* 另参见:
ADJ. deceased, lifeless; (*ant.*) alive, living **1**

dead end (**dead ends**) **1** N-COUNT If a street is a **dead end**, there is no way out at one end of it. 死胡同 ❑ *There was another alleyway which came to a dead end just behind the house.* 还有一个小巷，就在这房子后面形成了死胡同。 **2** N-COUNT A **dead-end** job or course of action is one that you think is bad because it does not lead to further developments or progress. 无前途的 ❑ *Waitressing was a dead-end job.* 服务员这一工作没什么前途。

dead·line ♦◇◇ /dɛdlaɪn/ (**deadlines**) N-COUNT A **deadline** is a time or date before which a particular task must be finished or a particular thing must be done. 最后期限 ❑ *We were not able to meet the deadline because of manufacturing delays.* 由于生产延误，我们没能在截止日期前完成工作。

▲ **dead·lock** /dɛdlɒk/ (**deadlocks**) N-VAR If a dispute or series of negotiations reaches **deadlock**, neither side is willing to give in at all and no agreement can be made. 僵局 ❑ *They called for a compromise on all sides to break the deadlock in the world trade talks.* 他们呼吁各方作出让步以打破世界贸易谈判中的僵局。

dead·ly /dɛdli/ (**deadlier, deadliest**) **1** ADJ If something is **deadly**, it is likely or able to cause someone's death, or has already caused someone's death. 致命的；致死的 ❑ *He was acquitted on charges of assault with a deadly weapon.* 他用凶器伤人的罪名不成立。 ❑ *...a deadly disease currently affecting dolphins.* …目前影响海豚的一种致命疾病。 **2** ADJ If you describe a person or their behavior as **deadly**, you mean that they will do or say anything to get what they want, without caring about other people. 不择手段的；肆无忌

d

D

悼的 [DISAPPROVAL] ❑ *The Duchess leveled a deadly look at Nikko.* 公爵夫人无所顾忌地瞪了尼克一眼。 3 ADJ A **deadly** situation has unpleasant or dangerous consequences. 极有害的 ❑ *...the deadly combination of low expectations and low achievement.* …低期望值和低成就的不良结合。 4 ADV You can use **deadly** to emphasize that something has a particular quality, especially an unpleasant or undesirable quality. 极度地 [ADV adj] [EMPHASIS] ❑ *Broadcast news was accurate and reliable but deadly dull.* 新闻广播准确、可靠，但极其枯燥。

deaf /dɛf/ (**deafer, deafest**) 1 ADJ Someone who is **deaf** is unable to hear anything or is unable to hear very well. 聋的；听不清的 ❑ *She is now profoundly deaf.* 她现在几乎一点声音都听不到了。 ● N-PLURAL **The deaf** are people who are deaf. 失聪者 ❑ *Many regular TV programs are captioned for the deaf.* 许多固定的电视节目都为失聪者提供字幕。 ● **deaf·ness** N-UNCOUNT 失聪 ❑ *Because of her deafness she was hard to make conversation with.* 由于她失聪，和她交流很困难。 2 **to fall on deaf ears** → see **ear** 3 **to turn a deaf ear** → see **ear** → see **disability**

deaf·en /dɛfən/ (**deafens, deafening, deafened**) 1 V-T If a noise **deafens** you, it is so loud that you cannot hear anything else at the same time. 使…震聋 ❑ *The noise of the typewriters deafened her.* 打字机的噪音震得她都要聋了。 2 V-T If you **are deafened by** something, you are made deaf by it, or are unable to hear for some time. 使聋 [usu passive] ❑ *He was deafened by the noise from the gun.* 枪声把他震聋了。 3 → see also **deafening**

deaf·en·ing /dɛfənɪŋ/ 1 ADJ A **deafening** noise is a very loud noise. 震耳欲聋的 ❑ *...the deafening roar of fighter jets taking off.* …战机起飞时震耳欲聋的轰鸣声。 2 ADJ If you say there was a **deafening silence**, you are emphasizing that there was no reaction or response to something that was said or done. 死一般的 [EMPHASIS] ❑ *What was truly despicable was the deafening silence maintained by the candidates concerning the riots.* 真正可鄙的是这些侯选人对暴乱所持的缄默态度。

deal
1 QUANTIFIER USES
2 VERB AND NOUN USES

1 **deal** ♦◇◇ /dil/ QUANT If you say that you need or have **a great deal of** or **a good deal of** a particular thing, you are emphasizing that you need or have a lot of it. 数量 [EMPHASIS] ❑ *...a great deal of money.* …许多钱。 ● ADV **Deal** is also an adverb. 非常 ❑ *As a relationship becomes more established, it also becomes a good deal more complex.* 当一段关系固定下来以后，它也会变得复杂得多。 ● PRON **Deal** is also a pronoun. 量 ❑ *Although he had never met Geoffrey Hardcastle, he knew a good deal about him.* 尽管他从未见过杰弗里·哈德卡斯尔，他还是十分了解他。

2 **deal** ♦♦♦ /dil/ (**deals, dealing, dealt**)
➪ **Please look at meaning 6 to see if the expression you are looking for is shown under another headword.** 1 N-COUNT If you **make a deal, do a deal,** or **cut a deal,** you complete an agreement or an arrangement with someone, especially in business. 达成协议；达成交易 [BUSINESS] ❑ *He made a deal to testify against the others and wasn't charged.* 他达成了协议出庭指证别人，因而未获指控。 ❑ *Japan will have to do a deal with the U.S. on rice imports.* 日本将不得不就水稻进口问题和美国达成协议。 2 N-COUNT If someone has had a **bad deal,** they have been unfortunate or have been treated unfairly. 不公的待遇 ❑ *The people of Hartford have had a bad deal for many, many years.* 许多年来，哈特福德地区的人们遭受着不幸。 3 V-I If a person, company, or store **deals in** a particular type of goods, their business involves buying or selling those goods. 经营 [BUSINESS] ❑ *They deal in antiques.* 他们经营古董生意。 4 V-T If someone **deals** illegal drugs, they sell them. 贩卖 (毒品) ❑ *I certainly don't deal drugs.* 我当然不做毒品生意。 5 V-T If you **deal** playing cards, you give them out to the players in a game of cards. (纸牌游戏中) 发 (牌) ❑ *The croupier dealt each player a card, face down.* 赌局主持人给每个玩牌者发了一张牌，牌面向下。 ● PHRASAL VERB **Deal out** means the same as **deal.** (纸牌游戏中) 发 (牌) ❑ *Dalton dealt out five cards to each player.* 多尔顿给每个玩牌的人发了5张牌。 6 → see also **dealings, wheel and deal**

▸ **deal out** 1 PHRASAL VERB If someone **deals out** a punishment or harmful action, they punish or harm someone. 给予 (惩罚)；使受 (伤害) [WRITTEN] ❑ *...a failure by the governments of established states to deal out effective punishment to aggressors.* …已建立起来的各州政府未能对入侵者进行有力的惩罚。 2 → see also **deal** 2 5

▸ **deal with** 1 PHRASAL VERB When you **deal with** something or someone that needs attention, you give your attention to them, and often solve a problem or make a decision concerning them. 处理 ❑ *...the way that banks deal with complaints.* …银行处理投诉的方式。 2 PHRASAL VERB If you **deal with** an unpleasant emotion or an emotionally difficult situation, you recognize it, and remain calm and in control of yourself in spite of it. 克服 (坏情绪) ❑ *She saw a psychiatrist who used hypnotism to help her deal with her fear.* 她去看了精神病医师，医生用催眠治疗帮助她克服恐惧心理。 3 PHRASAL VERB If a book, speech, or movie **deals with** a particular thing, it has that thing as its subject or is concerned with it. 以…作为内容；讨论 ❑ *...the parts of his book which deal with contemporary Paris.* …他书中讨论当代巴黎的部分。 4 PHRASAL VERB If you **deal with** a particular person or organization, you have business relations with them. 与…有商业关系；打交道 ❑ *When I worked in Florida I dealt with tourists all the time.* 我在佛罗里达州工作时一直和游客打交道。

Word Partnership *deal* 的常用搭配：

ADJ.	**better** deal, **big** deal 2 1
V.	**close** a deal, **seal** a deal, **strike** a deal 2 1
N.	**business** deal, **peace** deal 2 1
	deal **drugs** 2 4

▲ **deal·er** ♦◇◇ /dilər/ (**dealers**) 1 N-COUNT A **dealer** is a person whose business involves buying and selling things. 商人 [BUSINESS] ❑ *...an antique dealer.* …一位古董商。 2 N-COUNT A **dealer** is someone who buys and sells illegal drugs. 毒品贩子 ❑ *They will stay on the job for as long as it takes to clear every dealer from the street.* 他们将坚持工作，直到街道上所有的毒品贩子都被清除。

deal·er·ship /dilərʃɪp/ (**dealerships**) N-COUNT A **dealership** is a company that sells cars, usually for one car company. 汽车销售公司 [BUSINESS] ❑ *...a car dealership.* …一家汽车销售公司。

deal·ings /dilɪŋz/ N-PLURAL Someone's **dealings with** a person or organization are the relations that they have with them or the business that they do with them. 交往；生意往来 ❑ *He has learned little in his dealings with the international community.* 他在和国际社会的往来中所学不多。

dealt /dɛlt/ **Dealt** is the past tense and past participle of **deal** 2. **deal**的过去式和过去分词

dean /din/ (**deans**) 1 N-COUNT A **dean** is an important official at a university or college. (大学的) 学院院长；系主任 ❑ *She was dean of the University of Washington's Graduate School.* 她曾任华盛顿大学研究生院的院长。 2 N-COUNT A **dean** is a priest who is the main administrator of a large church. 教长 ❑ *...Bob Gregg, dean of the Chapel, Stanford Memorial Church.* 斯坦福纪念教堂小教堂教长，鲍勃·格雷格。

dear ♦◇◇ /dɪər/ (**dearer, dearest, dears**) 1 ADJ You use **dear** to describe someone or something that you feel affection for. 亲爱的 [ADJ n] ❑ *Mrs. Cavendish is a dear friend of mine.* 卡文迪什夫人是我的一位亲密的朋友。 2 ADJ If something is **dear to** you or **dear to** your **heart,** you care deeply about it. 宝贵的；珍视的 [v-link ADJ "to" n] ❑ *This is a subject very dear to the hearts of academics up and down the country.* 这是全国学者都极为重视的话题。 3 ADJ **Dear** is written at the beginning of a letter, followed by the name or title of the person you are writing to. 亲爱的 (写在信首，位于收信人的姓名或称呼前) [ADJ n] ❑ *Dear Peter, I have been thinking about you so much during the past few days.* 亲爱的彼得，在过去的几天中我一直深深思念着你。 4 CONVENTION You begin formal letters with **"Dear Sir"** or **"Dear Madam."** You can also begin them with "Sir" or "Madam." 尊敬的 [WRITTEN] ❑ *"Dear Sir," she began.* "尊敬的先生"，她开始写到。 5 N-VOC You can call someone **dear** as a sign of affection. 亲爱的 [FEELINGS] ❑ *You're a lot like me, dear.* 你和我太像了，亲爱的。 6 EXCLAM You can use **dear** in expressions such as **"oh dear," "dear me,"** and **"dear, dear"** when you are sad, disappointed, or surprised about something. 啊呀 [FEELINGS] ❑ *"Oh dear, oh dear." McKinnon sighed. "You, too."* "啊，天哪，"麦金农叹息道，"你也一样。"

dear·est /dɪərɪst/ ADJ When you are writing to someone you are very fond of, you can use **dearest** at the beginning of the letter before the person's name or the word you are using to address them. 最亲爱的 [ADJ n] ❑ *Dearest Maria, Aren't I terrible, not coming back like I promised?* 我至爱的玛丽亚，未能如约返回，我是不是很糟糕？

dear·ly /dɪərli/ 1 ADV If you love someone **dearly**, you love them very much. 深深地 [ADV with v] [FORMAL, EMPHASIS] ❑ *She loved her father dearly.* 她深深地爱着她的父亲。 2 ADV If you would **dearly** like to do or have something, you would very much like to do it or have it. 热切地 [ADV before v] [FORMAL, EMPHASIS] ❑ *I would dearly love to marry.* 我热切地想结婚。 3 PHRASE If you **pay dearly for** doing something or if it **costs** you **dearly**, you suffer a lot as a result. 付出很高的代价 [FORMAL] ❑ *He drank too much and is paying dearly for the pleasure.* 他饮酒过度，正为一时之乐付出极大的代价。

death ◆◆◇ /dɛθ/ (**deaths**) 1 N-VAR **Death** is the permanent end of the life of a person or animal. 死亡 ❑ *1.5 million people are in immediate danger of death from starvation.* 150万人正因饥饿而即将面临死亡的危险。 ❑ *...the thirtieth anniversary of Judy Garland's death.* …朱迪·嘉兰逝世30周年。 2 N-SING **The death of** something is the permanent end of it. 终止 ❑ *It meant the death of everything he had ever been or ever hoped to be.* 这意味着他曾拥有或希望拥有的一切的结束。 3 PHRASE If you say that someone is **at death's door**, you mean they are very ill and likely to die. 病危 [INFORMAL] ❑ *He told his boss a tale about his mother being at death's door.* 他给老板讲述了自己母亲病危的情况。 4 PHRASE If you say that you will **fight to the death** for something, you are emphasizing that you will do anything to achieve or protect it, even if you suffer as a consequence. 拼死搏斗 [EMPHASIS] ❑ *She'd have fought to the death for that child.* 她原想为那个孩子拼尽全力的。 5 PHRASE If you say that something is a matter **of life and death**, you are emphasizing that it is extremely important, often because someone may die or suffer great harm if people do not act immediately. 生死攸关 [EMPHASIS] ❑ *Well, never mind, John, it's not a matter of life and death.* 好了，别介意，约翰，这不是多么了不起的事情。 6 PHRASE If someone **is put to death**, they are executed. 处死某人 [FORMAL] ❑ *Those put to death by firing squad included three generals.* 被行刑队处死的人里有3位将军。 7 PHRASE You use **to death** after an adjective or a verb to emphasize the action, state, or feeling mentioned. For example, if you are **frightened to death** or **bored to death**, you are extremely frightened or bored. 极度 [EMPHASIS] ❑ *He scares teams to death with his pace and power.* 他的速度和力量把其他队吓破了胆。

Word Partnership *death* 的常用搭配：

N.	**brush with** death, **cause of** death, death **threat**, *someone's* death 1
ADJ.	**accidental** death, **violent** death 1 **sudden** death 1 2

death·ly /dɛθli/ 1 ADV If you say that someone is **deathly** pale or **deathly** still, you are emphasizing that they are very pale or still, like a dead person. 死一般地 [ADV adj] [LITERARY, EMPHASIS] ❑ *Bernadette turned deathly pale.* 贝尔纳黛特变得如死般地惨白。 2 ADJ If you say that there is a **deathly** silence or a **deathly** hush, you are emphasizing that it is very quiet. 死一般的 [ADJ n] [LITERARY, EMPHASIS] ❑ *A deathly silence hung over the square.* 死一般的静寂笼罩着广场。

death pen·al·ty N-SING **The death penalty** is the punishment of death used in some countries for people who have committed very serious crimes. 死刑 ❑ *If convicted for murder, both men could face the death penalty.* 如果被判谋杀罪，两人可能都会面临死刑。

death rate (**death rates**) N-COUNT The **death rate** is the number of people per thousand who die in a particular area during a particular period of time. 死亡率 ❑ *By the turn of the century, Pittsburgh had the highest death rate in the United States.* 到了世纪交替时，匹兹堡的死亡率居全美之首。

→ see **population**

death row /dɛθ roʊ/ N-UNCOUNT If someone is **on death row**, they are in the part of a prison which contains the cells for criminals who have been sentenced to death. 死囚区 [AM] ❑ *He has been on death row for 11 years.* 他在死囚区已经11年了。

death sen·tence (**death sentences**) N-COUNT A **death sentence** is a punishment of death given by a judge to someone who has been found guilty of a serious crime such as murder. 死刑 ❑ *His original death sentence was commuted to life in prison.* 他原本的死刑被减成终身监禁。

death toll (**death tolls**) also **death-toll** N-COUNT The **death toll** of an accident, disaster, or war is the number of people who die in it. 死亡人数 ❑ *The death toll continues to rise from yesterday's earthquake.* 昨天地震的死亡人数继续攀升。

death·trap /dɛθtræp/ (**deathtraps**) N-COUNT If you say that a place or vehicle is a **deathtrap**, you mean it is in such bad condition that it might cause someone's death. (指地方或交通工具)致死的危险 [INFORMAL] ❑ *Badly built cars can be deathtraps.* 劣制汽车会成为致死的危险。

de·ba·cle /dɪbɑkəl, -bækəl/ (**debacles**)

in BRIT, also use **débâcle**

N-COUNT A **debacle** is an event or attempt that is a complete failure. 彻底失败 ❑ *People believed it was a privilege to die for your country, but after the debacle of the war they never felt the same again.* 人们曾相信为国捐躯是一种荣幸，但是经过战争的彻底失败，他们再也不这样想了。

de·bat·able /dɪbeɪtəbəl/ ADJ If you say that something is **debatable**, you mean that it is not certain. 有争议的 ❑ *It is debatable whether or not the shareholders were ever properly compensated.* 股东们是否曾被合理补偿还存在争议。

de·bate ◆◆◇ /dɪbeɪt/ (**debates, debating, debated**) 1 N-VAR A **debate** is a discussion about a subject on which people have different views. 辩论 ❑ *An intense debate is going on within the Israeli government.* 一场激烈的争论正在以色列政府内部进行。 ❑ *There has been a lot of debate among scholars about this.* 在学者中有很多关于此问题的辩论。 2 N-COUNT A **debate** is a formal discussion, for example, in a parliament or institution, in which people express different opinions about a particular subject and then vote on it. (议会投票前的) 正式讨论 ❑ *He is expected to force a debate in Congress on his immigration reform.* 他预期会推动一个关于他的移民改革的正式讨论。 3 V-RECIP If people **debate** a topic, they discuss it fairly formally, putting forward different views. You can also say that one person **debates** a topic **with** another person. 辩论 ❑ *The United Nations Security Council will debate the issue today.* 联合国安理会今天将辩论该问题。 ❑ *Scientists were debating whether an asteroid was about to hit the Earth.* 科学家们在争论一颗小行星是否要撞上地球。 4 V-T If you **debate** whether to do something or what to do, you think or talk about possible courses of action before deciding exactly what you are going to do. 考虑 ❑ *Taggart debated whether to have yet another double vodka.* 塔格特考虑着是否再来一杯双份伏特加。

→ see **election**

Word Partnership *debate* 的常用搭配：

V.	**open to** debate 1 2
ADJ.	**major** debate, **ongoing** debate, **televised** debate 1 2 **political** debate, **presidential** debate 2
N.	debate **over** *something*, debate **the issue** 3 4

de·ben·ture /dɪbɛntʃər/ (**debentures**) N-COUNT A **debenture** is a type of savings bond which offers a fixed rate of interest over a long period. Debentures are usually issued by a company or a government agency. 债券 [BUSINESS]

deb·it /dɛbɪt/ (**debits, debiting, debited**) 1 V-T When your bank **debits** your account, money is taken from it and paid to someone else. 记入…的借方账户 ❑ *We will always confirm the revised amount to you in writing before debiting your account.* 在记入你的借方账户前，我们每次都会以书面形式向你确认修改过的数额。 2 N-COUNT A **debit** is a record of the money taken from your bank account, for example, when you write a check. 借方 ❑ *The total of debits must balance the total of credits.* 借方总额必须和贷款总方相抵。

deb·it card (**debit cards**) N-COUNT A **debit card** is a bank card that you can use to pay for things. When you use it the money is taken out of your bank account immediately. 借记卡

★ **de·bris** /dəɪbri/ N-UNCOUNT **Debris** is pieces from something that has been destroyed or pieces of trash or unwanted material that are spread around. 碎片；散乱的垃圾 ❑ *A number of people were killed by flying debris.* 一些人遭飞溅的碎片致死。

debt ◆◆◇ /dɛt/ (**debts**) 1 N-VAR A **debt** is a sum of money that you owe someone. 债 ❑ *Three years later, he is still paying off his debts.* 三年后，他仍旧在还他的债务。 2 → see also **bad debt** 3 N-UNCOUNT **Debt** is the state of owing money. 负债 ❑ *...a monthly report on the amount of debt owed by consumers.* …一份消费者欠款数额月报。 ● PHRASE If you are **in debt** or **get into debt**, you owe money. If you are **out of debt** or **get out of debt**, you succeed in paying all the money that you owe. 负债；还清债务 ❑ *He was already deeply in debt through gambling losses.* 赌博输的钱让他已经负债累累。 4 N-COUNT You use **debt** in expressions such as **I owe you a debt** or **I am in your debt** when you are expressing gratitude for something that someone has done for you. 人情债 [FORMAL, FEELINGS] ❑ *He was so good to me that I can never repay the debt I owe him.* 那时他对我太好了，我永远都还不清欠他的人情债。 ❑ *I owe a debt of thanks to Joyce Thompson, whose careful and able research was of great help.* 我欠乔伊斯・汤普森一份感谢之情，他谨慎杰出的研究是极大的帮助。

Word Partnership *debt* 的常用搭配：

V. **incur** debt, **pay off** a debt, **reduce** debt, **repay** a debt **1**
ADV. **deeply** in debt **2**

D

debt bur·den (**debt burdens**) N-COUNT A **debt burden** is a large amount of money that one country or organization owes to another and which they find very difficult to repay. 巨额债务负担 ❑ *The massive debt burden of the Third World has become a crucial issue for many leaders of poorer countries.* 第三世界国家的巨额债务负担成了许多较贫困国家领导人的核心问题。

debt·or /dɛtər/ (**debtors**) N-COUNT A **debtor** is a country, organization, or person who owes money. 债务人 ❑ *...important improvements in the situation of debtor countries.* …债务国境况的重大改善。

de·bug /dibʌg/ (**debugs, debugging, debugged**) V-T When someone **debugs** a computer program, they look for the problems in it and correct them so that it will run properly. (计算机程序)纠错 [COMPUTING] ❑ *The production lines ground to a halt for hours while technicians tried to debug software.* 生产线陷入停顿数小时，与此同时，技术人员尽力排除软件故障。

▲ **de·but** ♦◇◇ /deɪbyu/ (**debuts**) N-COUNT The **debut** of a performer or sports player is their first public performance, appearance, or recording. 首次登台 ❑ *She made her debut in a 1937 production of "Hamlet."* 她在1937年《哈姆雷特》的演出中首次登台。

Dec. **Dec.** is a written abbreviation for **December**. 12月

Word Link *dec ≈ ten : decade, decathlon, decimal*

dec·ade ♦♦◇ /dɛkeɪd/ (**decades**) N-COUNT A **decade** is a period of ten years, especially one that begins with a year ending in 0, for example, 1980 to 1989. 10年(尤指起始年末尾为0) ❑ *...the last decade of the nineteenth century.* …19世纪的最后10年。

deca·dent /dɛkədənt/ ADJ If you say that a person or society is **decadent**, you think that they have low moral standards and are interested mainly in pleasure. 堕落的 [DISAPPROVAL] ❑ *...the excesses and stresses of their decadent rock 'n' roll lifestyles.* …他们颓废的摇滚生活方式中的种种无度与压力。 ● **deca·dence** N-UNCOUNT 堕落 ❑ *The empire had for years been falling into decadence.* 这个帝国多年来已渐渐走向堕落。

de·caf·fein·at·ed /dikæfɪneɪtɪd, -kæfiə-/ ADJ **Decaffeinated** coffee or tea has had most of the caffeine removed from it. 脱咖啡因的
→ see **coffee**

de·capi·tate /dɪkæpɪteɪt/ (**decapitates, decapitating, decapitated**) V-T If someone **is decapitated**, their head is cut off. 斩首 [FORMAL] ❑ *There were nine corpses. Two of them had been decapitated.* 有9具尸体，其中2具是被斩首的。

de·cath·lon /dɪkæθlɒn/ (**decathlons**) N-COUNT The **decathlon** is a competition in which athletes compete in 10 different sports events. 十项全能比赛

de·cay /dɪkeɪ/ (**decays, decaying, decayed**) **1** V-I When something such as a dead body, a dead plant, or a tooth **decays**, it is gradually destroyed by a natural process. 腐坏 ❑ *The bodies buried in the fine ash slowly decayed.* 埋在细灰里的尸体慢慢腐烂了。 ● N-UNCOUNT **Decay** is also a noun. 腐坏 ❑ *When not removed, plaque causes tooth decay and gum disease.* 牙斑没有清除就会导致蛀牙和牙龈疾病。 ● **de·cayed** ADJ 腐坏的 ❑ *Even young children have teeth so decayed they need to be pulled.* 连幼儿也有这么严重的龋齿，需要拔掉。 **2** V-I If something such as a society, system, or institution **decays**, it gradually becomes weaker or its condition gets worse. (社会、制度或机构) 衰败 ❑ *In practice, the agency system has decayed. Most "agents" now sell only to themselves or their immediate family.* 实际上，这种代理制已经衰退。现在，大多数"代理人"都只把产品卖给自己或亲近的家人。 ● N-UNCOUNT **Decay** is also a noun. 衰败 ❑ *There are problems of urban decay and gang violence.* 存在都市衰败和黑帮暴力问题。
→ see **teeth**

de·ceased /dɪsist/ (**deceased**)

Deceased is both the singular and the plural form.

1 N-COUNT **The deceased** is used to refer to a particular person or to particular people who have recently died. 死者 [LEGAL] ❑ *The navy is notifying next of kin now that the identities of the deceased have been determined.* 死者的身份已得到确认，海军正在通知其最近的家属。 **2** ADJ A **deceased** person is one who has recently died. 去世的 [FORMAL] ❑ *...his recently deceased mother.* …他刚刚去世的母亲。
→ see **funeral**

▲ **de·ceit** /dɪsit/ (**deceits**) N-VAR **Deceit** is behavior that is deliberately intended to make people believe something which is not true. 欺骗 ❑ *He was living a secret life of deceit and unfaithfulness.* 他过着欺骗和不忠的隐瞒生活。

de·ceit·ful /dɪsitfəl/ ADJ If you say that someone is **deceitful**, you mean that they behave in a dishonest way by making other people believe something that is not true. 欺骗的 ❑ *The ambassador called the report deceitful and misleading.* 大使称该报导是不实的和误导的。

de·ceive /dɪsiv/ (**deceives, deceiving, deceived**) **1** V-T If you **deceive** someone, you make them believe something that is not true, usually in order to get some advantage for yourself. 欺骗 ❑ *He has deceived and disillusioned us all.* 他欺骗了我们所有人，令我们所有人失望至极。 **2** V-T If something **deceives** you, it gives you a wrong impression and makes you believe something that is not true. 误导 ❑ *Do not be deceived by claims on food labels like "light" or "low fat."* 不要被食品标签上像"少脂"或"低脂"的字样误导。

De·cem·ber ♦♦♦ /dɪsɛmbər/ (**Decembers**) N-VAR **December** is the twelfth and last month of the year in the Western calendar. 12月 ❑ *...a bright morning in mid-December.* …12月中旬一个晴朗的早晨。

de·cen·cy /disənsi/ **1** N-UNCOUNT **Decency** is the quality of following accepted moral standards. 正派 ❑ *His sense of decency forced him to resign.* 他的正派作风迫使他辞职。 **2** PHRASE If you say that someone **did not have the decency to** do something, you are criticizing them because there was a particular action which they did not do but which you believe they ought to have done. 不得体 [DISAPPROVAL] ❑ *He didn't even have the decency to tell them in person.* 他很没礼节，居然没亲自告诉他们。

de·cent /disənt/ **1** ADJ **Decent** is used to describe something which is considered to be of an acceptable standard or quality. 像样的 ❑ *He didn't get a decent explanation.* 他没有得到一个合理的解释。 ● **de·cent·ly** ADV 像样地 ❑ *The allies say they will treat their prisoners decently.* 同盟国家称他们将有分寸地对待战俘。 **2** ADJ **Decent** is used to describe something which is morally correct or acceptable. 合宜的 ❑ *But, after a decent interval, trade relations began to return to normal.* 但是在一段适当的间断之后，贸易关系开始恢复正常。 ● **de·cent·ly** ADV 合宜地 ❑ *And can't you dress more decently – people will think you're a tramp.* 而且你不能穿得再体面些吗？人们会以为你是个流浪汉。 **3** ADJ **Decent** people are honest and behave in a way that most people approve of. 正直的 ❑ *The majority of people around here are decent people.* 这儿的大多数人都是正派人。

Thesaurus *decent* 另参见：

ADJ. acceptable, adequate, passable, reasonable; (*ant.*) satisfactory **1**
honorable, respectable **2** **3**

★ **de·cen·tral·ise** /disɛntrəlaɪz/ [BRIT] → see **decentralize**

Word Link *centr ≈ middle : central, concentrated, decentralized*

★ **de·cen·tral·ize** /disɛntrəlaɪz/ (**decentralizes, decentralizing, decentralized**)

in BRIT, also use **decentralise**

V-T/V-I To **decentralize** government or a large organization means to move some departments away from the main administrative area, or to give more power to local departments. 分权 ❑ *...the need to decentralize and devolve power to regional governments.* …分权并把权力下放到地方政府的必要性。 ● **de·cen·trali·za·tion** /disɛntrəlɪzeɪʃən/ N-UNCOUNT 分权 ❑ *He seems set against the idea of increased decentralization and greater powers for regional authorities.* 他似乎坚决反对扩大分权、赋予地方当局更大权利的想法。

de·cep·tion /dɪsɛpʃən/ (**deceptions**) N-VAR **Deception** is the act of deceiving someone or the state of being deceived by someone. 欺骗；受骗 ❑ *He admitted conspiring to obtain property by deception.* 他承认曾密谋通过欺骗获取财产。

▲ **de·cep·tive** /dɪsɛptɪv/ ADJ If something is **deceptive**, it encourages you to believe something which is not true. 骗人的

❑ *Johnston isn't tired of Las Vegas yet, it seems, but appearances can be deceptive.* 似乎，约翰斯顿还没有厌倦拉斯韦加斯，但表象可能是骗人的。● **de·cep·tive·ly** ADV 骗人地 ❑ *The storyline is deceptively simple.* 故事情节看似简单。

deci·bel /dɛsɪbɛl/ (**decibels**) N-COUNT A **decibel** is a unit of measurement which is used to indicate how loud a sound is. 分贝 ❑ *Continuous exposure to sound above 80 decibels could be harmful.* 持续曝露于超过80分贝的声音可能有害。

de·cide ♦♦♦ /dɪsaɪd/ (**decides, deciding, decided**) 1 V-T/V-I If you **decide** to do something, you choose to do it, usually after you have thought carefully about the other possibilities. 决定 ❑ *She decided to take a course in philosophy.* 她决定修一门哲学课。❑ *Think about it very carefully before you decide.* 在你决定之前慎重地考虑。2 V-T If a person or group of people **decides** something, they choose what something should be like or how a particular problem should be solved. 裁定 ❑ *She was still young, he said, and that would be taken into account when deciding her sentence.* 她还年轻，他说，这一点对裁定关于她的判决时要考虑进去。3 V-T If an event or fact **decides** something, it makes it certain that a particular choice will be made or that there will be a particular result. 决定 ❑ *What happens next could decide their destiny.* 接下来发生的事可能会决定他们的命运。❑ *The election will decide if either party controls both houses of Congress.* 这次选举将决定是否由任一党控制国会两院。4 V-T If you **decide** that something is true, you form that opinion about it after considering the facts. 断定 ❑ *He decided Franklin must be suffering from a bad cold.* 他断定富兰克林肯定是得了重感冒。

▶ **decide on** PHRASAL VERB If you **decide on** something or **decide upon** something, you choose it from two or more possibilities. 作出决定 ❑ *Denikin held a staff meeting to decide on the next strategic objective.* 德尼金召开了员工大会为下一步的战略目标作出决定。

Thesaurus *decide* 另参见：
V. choose, elect, pick, select 1 2

Word Partnership *decide* 的常用搭配：
V. **try to** decide 1 2
help (to) decide, **let** *someone* decide 1 – 3
ADJ. **unable to** decide 1 2 4

de·cid·ed /dɪsaɪdɪd/ ADJ **Decided** means clear and definite. 明确的 [ADJ n] ❑ *They got involved in a long and exhausting struggle and were at a decided disadvantage in the afternoon.* 他们卷入了一场长时间的令人疲惫的斗争，下午他们处于明显的劣势。

★ **de·cid·ed·ly** /dɪsaɪdɪdli/ ADV **Decidedly** means to a great extent and in a way that is very obvious. 明确地 [ADV group] ❑ *He admits there will be moments when he's decidedly uncomfortable at what he sees on the screen.* 他承认有时候看到屏幕上的内容他感到明显不舒服。

★ **deci·mal** /dɛsɪm^əl/ (**decimals**) 1 ADJ A **decimal** system involves counting in units of ten. 十进制的 [ADJ n] ❑ *The mathematics of ancient Egypt were based on a decimal system.* 古埃及数学以十进制为基础。2 N-COUNT A **decimal** is a fraction that is written in the form of a dot followed by one or more numbers which represent tenths, hundredths, and so on: for example, .5, .51, .517. 小数 ❑ *...simple math concepts, such as decimals and fractions.* …简单的数学概念，如小数和分数。

deci·mal point (**decimal points**) N-COUNT A **decimal point** is the dot in front of a decimal fraction. 小数点 ❑ *A waiter omitted the decimal point in the $13.09 bill.* 一个侍者漏掉了那份$13.09的账单上的小数点。

deci·mate /dɛsɪmeɪt/ (**decimates, decimating, decimated**) 1 V-T To **decimate** something such as a group of people or animals means to destroy a very large number of them. 大量毁灭 ❑ *The pollution could decimate the river's thriving population of kingfishers.* 污染可能大量毁灭在这条河茁壮成长的翠鸟群。2 V-T To **decimate** a system or organization means to reduce its size and effectiveness greatly. 严重削弱 ❑ *...a recession which decimated the nation's manufacturing industry.* …严重削弱了该国制造业的一次经济衰退。

de·ci·pher /dɪsaɪfər/ (**deciphers, deciphering, deciphered**) V-T If you **decipher** a piece of writing or a message, you work out what it says, even though it is very difficult to read or understand. 破译 ❑ *I'm still no closer to deciphering the code.* 破译这个密码我还是没有进展。

de·ci·sion ♦♦♦ /dɪsɪʒ^ən/ (**decisions**) 1 N-COUNT When you make a **decision**, you choose what should be done or which is the best of various possible actions. 决定 ❑ *I don't want to make the wrong decision and regret it later.* 我不想作出错误的决定，以后后悔。2 N-UNCOUNT **Decision** is the act of deciding something or the need to decide something. 作决定 ❑ *The growing pressures of the crisis may mean that the moment of decision can't be too long delayed.* 这次危机不断增长的压力可能意味着作决定的时刻不会拖延很久。3 N-UNCOUNT **Decision** is the ability to decide quickly and definitely what to do. 果断 ❑ *He is very quick-thinking and very much a man of decision.* 他思维很敏捷，是个很果断的人。

Word Partnership *decision* 的常用搭配：
V. **arrive at a** decision, **make a** decision, **postpone a** decision, **reach a** decision 1
ADJ. **difficult** decision, **final** decision, **important** decision, **right** decision, **wise** decision, **wrong** decision 1

★ **de·ci·sive** /dɪsaɪsɪv/ 1 ADJ If a fact, action, or event is **decisive**, it makes certain a particular result. 决定性的 ❑ *...his decisive victory in the presidential elections.* …他在这次总统选举中的决定性胜利。● **de·ci·sive·ly** ADV 决定性地 ❑ *The plan was decisively rejected by Congress three weeks ago.* 这个计划三周前被国会关键性地否决了。2 ADJ If someone is **decisive**, they have or show an ability to make quick decisions in a difficult or complicated situation. 果断的 ❑ *He should give way to a younger, more decisive leader.* 他应该让位给一位更年轻、更果断的领导者。● **de·ci·sive·ly** ADV 果断地 ❑ *"I'll call for you at ten," she said decisively.* "我10点来接你，"她果断地说。● **de·ci·sive·ness** N-UNCOUNT 果断 ❑ *His supporters admire his decisiveness.* 他的支持者们佩服他的果断。

deck ♦◇◇ /dɛk/ (**decks**) 1 N-COUNT A **deck** on a vehicle such as a bus or ship is a lower or upper area of it. (公共汽车或船的) 层 ❑ *...a luxury liner with five passenger decks.* …一艘有5层舱位楼层的豪华游轮。2 N-COUNT The **deck** of a ship is the top part of it that forms a floor in the open air which you can walk on. 甲板 [also "on" N] ❑ *She stood on the deck and waved her hand to them as the steamer moved off.* 汽船驶离时，她站在甲板上和他们挥手。3 N-COUNT A **deck** is a flat wooden area next to a house, where people can sit and relax or eat. (屋边供休息的木制) 平台 ❑ *A natural timber deck leads into the main room of the home.* 一个天然木头平台通向家里的主室。4 N-COUNT A **deck** of cards is a complete set of playing cards. (纸牌) 付 [mainly AM]

in BRIT, usually use **pack**

❑ *Matt picked up the cards and shuffled the deck.* 马特收齐纸牌，洗了这付牌。

→ see **ship**

deck chair (**deck chairs**) N-COUNT A **deck chair** is a simple chair with a folding frame, and a piece of canvas as the seat and back. Deck chairs are usually used on the beach, on a ship, or in the yard. 帆布折叠躺椅

dec·la·ra·tion ♦◇◇ /dɛkləreɪʃ^ən/ (**declarations**) 1 N-COUNT A **declaration** is an official announcement or statement. 官方声明 ❑ *The opening speeches sounded more like declarations of war than offerings of peace.* 那些开幕辞听起来更像宣战书而不是和平倡议。2 N-COUNT A **declaration** is a firm, emphatic statement which shows that you have no doubts about what you are saying. 宣言 ❑ *...declarations of undying love.* …永恒爱情的宣言。3 N-COUNT A **declaration** is a written statement about something which you have signed and which can be used as evidence in a court of law. 书面声明 ❑ *On the customs declaration, the sender labeled the freight as agricultural machinery.* 在报关单上，发货方将货物列为农业机械。

Word Link *clar ≈ clear* : *clarify, clarity, declare*

de·clare ♦♦◇ /dɪklɛər/ (**declares, declaring, declared**) 1 V-T If you **declare** that something is true, you say that it is true in a firm, deliberate way. You can also **declare** an attitude or intention. 声明；表明 [WRITTEN] ❑ *He declared he would not run for a second term as president.* 他声明不再竞选连任总统。❑ *He declared his intention to become the best golfer in the world.* 他表明了要成为世界上最佳高尔夫球手的意愿。2 V-T If you **declare** something, you state officially and formally that it exists or is the case. 宣告 ❑ *The government is ready to declare a permanent ceasefire.* 政府已经准备好宣布永久停火。❑ *His lawyers are confident that the judges will declare Mr. Stevens innocent.* 他的律师们确信法官们会宣布史蒂文斯先生无罪。3 V-T If you **declare** goods that you have bought in another country or money that you have earned, you say how much you have bought or earned so that you can pay tax on it. 申报(在国外所购之物或收入等) ❑ *Declaring the wrong income by mistake will no longer lead to an automatic fine.* 由于失误申报收入不符的不再予以自动罚款。→ see **war**

Word Link *clin ≈ leaning : decline, incline, recline*

de·cline ♦♦◇ /dɪklaɪn/ (**declines, declining, declined**) 1 V-I If something **declines**, it becomes less in quantity, importance, or strength. 下降 ❑ *The number of staff has declined from 217,000 to 114,000.* 员工人数已从217000人减少到114000人。❑ *Hourly output by workers declined 1.3% in the first quarter.* 工人每小时的产量在第1季度下降了1.3%。 2 V-T/V-I If you **decline** something or **decline to** do something, you politely refuse to accept it or do it. 谢绝 [FORMAL] ❑ *He declined their invitation.* 他谢绝了他们的邀请。❑ *He offered the boys some coffee. They declined politely.* 他要给男孩们来些咖啡。他们礼貌地拒绝了。 3 N-VAR If there is a **decline in** something, it becomes less in quantity, importance, or quality. 下降 ❑ *Official figures show a sharp decline in the number of foreign tourists.* 官方数字显示外国游客数量骤降。 4 PHRASE If something is **in decline** or **on the decline**, it is gradually decreasing in importance, quality, or power. 在下降 ❑ *Thankfully the smoking of cigarettes is on the decline.* 感谢的是吸烟正在减少。 5 PHRASE If something **goes** or **falls into decline**, it begins to gradually decrease in importance, quality, or power. 开始下降 ❑ *Libraries are an investment for the future and they should not be allowed to fall into decline.* 图书馆是对未来的一种投资，不应该让图书馆衰落。

Word Partnership *decline* 的常用搭配：
ADJ. **economic** decline, **gradual** decline, **rapid** decline, **steady** decline 3

Word Link *cod ≈ writing : code, decode, encode*

▲ **de·code** /diːkoʊd/ (**decodes, decoding, decoded**) 1 V-T If you **decode** a message that has been written or spoken in a code, you change it into ordinary language. 解码 ❑ *All he had to do was decode it and pass it over.* 他所要做的就是解译它，然后把它发过去。 2 V-T A device that **decodes** a broadcast signal changes it into a form that can be displayed on a television screen. 转换(信号) ❑ *About 60,000 subscribers have special adapters to receive and decode the signals.* 大约60000用户有专用适配器来接收和转换信号。

de·com·pose /diːkəmpoʊz/ (**decomposes, decomposing, decomposed**) V-T/V-I When things such as dead plants or animals **decompose**, or when something **decomposes** them, they change chemically and begin to decay. 使分解；分解 ❑ *...a dead body found decomposing in the woods.* …在树林里发现的正在腐烂的一具死尸。❑ *The debris slowly decomposes into compost.* 这堆碎屑慢慢地分解变成了堆肥。

de·cor /deɪkɔr/ N-UNCOUNT The **decor** of a house or room is its style of furnishing and decoration. 装饰风格 ❑ *The decor is simple – black lacquer panels on white walls.* 这种装修风格简约——白色的墙上装饰着漆成黑色的板。

deco·rate ♦◇◇ /dɛkəreɪt/ (**decorates, decorating, decorated**) 1 V-T If you **decorate** something, you make it more attractive by adding things to it. 装饰 ❑ *He decorated his room with pictures of all his favorite sports figures.* 他用他所喜爱的所有运动员的照片装饰自己的房间。 2 V-T/V-I If you **decorate** a room or the inside of a building, you put new paint or wallpaper on the walls and ceiling, and paint the woodwork. 装修 ❑ *When they came to decorate the rear bedroom, it was Jemma who had the final say.* 他们开始装修后卧室时，说了算的人是杰马。❑ *The boys are planning to decorate when they get the time.* 男孩们正计划在他们有时间的时候装修。● **deco·rat·ing** N-UNCOUNT 装修 ❑ *I did a lot of the decorating myself.* 我自己干了很多装修的活儿。● **deco·ra·tion** N-UNCOUNT 装修 ❑ *The renovation and decoration took four months.* 翻新和装修花了4个月。

deco·ra·tion /dɛkəreɪʃən/ (**decorations**) 1 N-UNCOUNT The **decoration** of a room is its furniture, wallpaper, and ornaments. 装饰 ❑ *The decoration and furnishings had to be practical enough for a family home.* 装修和家具陈设必须对一个家庭住房来说够实用。 2 N-VAR **Decorations** are features that are added to something in order to make it look more attractive. 装饰品 ❑ *The only wall decorations are candles and a single mirror.* 墙上仅有的装饰品就是一些蜡烛和一面镜子。 3 N-COUNT **Decorations** are brightly colored objects such as pieces of paper and balloons, which you put up in a room on special occasions to make it look more attractive. 颜色鲜艳的饰品 ❑ *Colorful streamers and paper decorations had been hung from the ceiling.* 五颜六色的飘带和彩纸饰品被挂在天花板上。 4 → see also **decorate**

deco·ra·tive /dɛkərətɪv, -əreɪtɪv/ ADJ Something that is **decorative** is intended to look pretty or attractive. 装饰性的 ❑ *The curtains are for purely decorative purposes and do not open or close.* 那些窗帘纯粹用于装饰目的，不能开合。

deco·ra·tor /dɛkəreɪtər/ (**decorators**) 1 N-COUNT A **decorator** is a person who is employed to design and decorate the inside of people's houses. 室内装修设计师 [AM] ❑ *...Bloomberg's private palace, with its intricate interior design by decorator Jamie Drake.* …布隆伯格的私人宫殿，其精细的室内设计出自装修设计师杰米·德雷克之手。 2 → see also **interior decorator**

de·coy /diːkɔɪ/ (**decoys**) N-COUNT If you refer to something or someone as a **decoy**, you mean that they are intended to attract people's attention and deceive them, for example, by leading them into a trap or away from a particular place. 诱饵 ❑ *A plane was waiting at the airport with its engines running but this was just one of the decoys.* 一架飞机等在机场，引擎已发动，而这只是诱饵中的一个而已。

Word Link *cresc, creas ≈ growing : crescent, decrease, increase*

de·crease (**decreases, decreasing, decreased**)

The verb is pronounced /dɪkris/. The noun is pronounced /dikris/ or /dɪkris/.

动词读作 /dɪkris/。名词读作 /dikris/或 /dɪkris/。

1 V-T/V-I When something **decreases** or when you **decrease** it, it becomes less in quantity, size, or intensity. 使降低；降低 ❑ *Population growth is decreasing by 1.4% each year.* 人口增长每年下降1.4%。❑ *The number of independent firms decreased from 198 to 96.* 独立公司的数量从198家减到了96家。❑ *Since 1945 air forces have decreased in size.* 1945年以来，空军的规模已经缩小。 2 N-COUNT A **decrease in** the quantity, size, or intensity of something is a reduction in it. 减少；降低 ❑ *In Spain and Portugal there has been a decrease in the number of young people out of work.* 在西班牙和葡萄牙，失业青年人数已经有所下降。

Thesaurus *decrease* 另参见：
V. decline, diminish, go down; (*ant.*) increase 1

★ **de·cree** /dɪkri/ (**decrees, decreeing, decreed**) 1 N-COUNT A **decree** is an official order or decision, especially one made by the ruler of a country. 法令 [also "by" N] ❑ *In July he issued a decree ordering all unofficial armed groups in the country to disband.* 7月份，他颁布了一项法令，命令解散该国所有非官方武装团体。 2 N-COUNT A **decree** is a judgment made by a law court. 判决 [mainly AM] ❑ *...court decrees.* …法院的判决。 3 V-T If someone in authority **decrees** that something must happen, they decide or state this officially. 发布命令 ❑ *The government decreed that all who wanted to live and work in Kenya must hold Kenyan passports.* 政府下令要求所有想在肯尼亚居住和工作的人必须持有肯尼亚护照。

★ **dedi·cate** /dɛdɪkeɪt/ (**dedicates, dedicating, dedicated**) 1 V-T If you say that someone **has dedicated** themselves **to** something, you approve of the fact that they have decided to give a lot of time and effort to it because they think that it is important. 投身 [APPROVAL] ❑ *For the next few years, she dedicated herself to her work.* 随后的几年里，她全身心地投入工作。● **dedi·cat·ed** ADJ 投身于…的 ❑ *He's quite dedicated to his students.* 他奉献很多给他的学生们。● **dedi·ca·tion** ★ N-UNCOUNT 投身 ❑ *We admire her courage, compassion, and dedication to the cause of humanity, justice, and peace.* 我们敬佩她的勇气、同情心以及她对人道、正义与和平的献身。 2 V-T If someone **dedicates** something such as a book, play, or piece of music **to** you, they mention your name, for example, in the front of a book or when a piece of music is performed, as a way of showing affection or respect for you. (把创作品) 献给 ❑ *She dedicated her first album to Woody Allen, who she says understands her obsession.* 她把她的第一张唱片献给伍迪·艾伦，她说艾伦理解她的痴迷。

dedi·cat·ed /dɛdɪkeɪtɪd/ 1 ADJ You use **dedicated** to describe someone who enjoys a particular activity very much and spends a lot of time doing it. 投入的 ❑ *Her great-grandfather had clearly been a dedicated and stoical traveler.* 她的曾祖父显然曾是一个很投入的、坚忍的旅行者。 2 ADJ You use **dedicated** to describe something that is made, built, or designed for one particular purpose or thing. 专用的 ❑ *Such areas should also be served by dedicated cycle routes.* 这些地区也应该可由自行车专用路线到达。 ❑ *...the world's first museum dedicated to ecology.* …世界上第一家专门的生态博物馆。 3 → see also **dedicate**

★ **ded·i·ca·tion** /dɛdɪkeɪʃən/ (**dedications**) 1 N-COUNT A **dedication** is a message which is written at the beginning of a book, or a short announcement which is sometimes made before a play or piece of music is performed, as a sign of affection or respect for someone. 献辞 2 → see also **dedicate**

★ **de·duce** /dɪdus/ (**deduces, deducing, deduced**) V-T If you **deduce** something or **deduce** that something is true, you reach that conclusion because of other things that you know to be true. 演绎; 推断 ❑ *Alison cleverly deduced that I was the author of the letter.* 艾莉森聪明地推断出我是这封信的作者。 ❑ *The date of the document can be deduced from references to the Civil War.* 该文件的日期可以从其对内战的提及处推算出来。

de·duct /dɪdʌkt/ (**deducts, deducting, deducted**) V-T When you **deduct** an amount from a total, you subtract it from the total. 扣除 ❑ *The company deducted this payment from his compensation.* 公司从他的补偿金中扣除了这笔款项。

★ **de·duc·tion** /dɪdʌkʃən/ (**deductions**) 1 N-COUNT A **deduction** is an amount that has been subtracted from a total. 扣除额 ❑ *Most homeowners can get a federal income tax deduction on interest payments to a home equity loan.* 在支付房屋净值贷款利息方面，大多数房主可以享受联邦所得税减免待遇。 2 N-COUNT A **deduction** is a conclusion that you have reached about something because of other things that you know to be true. 推演出来的结论 ❑ *It was a pretty astute deduction.* 那是个非常精明的结论。 3 N-UNCOUNT **Deduction** is the process of reaching a conclusion about something because of other things that you know to be true. 演绎; 推论 ❑ *Miss Allan beamed at him. "You are clever to guess. I'm sure I don't know how you did it."—"Deduction," James said.* 阿伦小姐对他笑道："你很会猜， 我确实不知道你怎么办到的。"——杰姆斯说："推论。"
→ see **science**

★ **de·duc·tive** /dɪdʌktɪv/ ADJ **Deductive** reasoning involves drawing conclusions logically from other things that are already known. 演绎的 [usu ADJ n] [FORMAL]

deed /did/ (**deeds**) 1 N-COUNT A **deed** is something that is done, especially something that is very good or very bad. 行为 [LITERARY] ❑ *The perpetrators of this evil deed must be brought to justice.* 这件恶行的凶手必须接受法律的制裁。 2 N-COUNT A **deed** is a document containing the terms of an agreement, especially an agreement concerning the ownership of land or a building. 契约; 证书 [LEGAL] ❑ *He asked if I had the deeds to his father's property.* 他问我是否有他父亲财产的各种证书。

★ **deem** /dim/ (**deems, deeming, deemed**) V-T If something **is deemed to** have a particular quality or **to** do a particular thing, it is considered to have that quality or do that thing. 认为; 相信 [FORMAL] ❑ *French and German were deemed essential.* 法语和德语被认为是必需的。 ❑ *He says he would support the use of force if the UN deemed it necessary.* 他说如果联合国认为有必要，他就支持动用武力。

deep ♦♦◇ /dip/ (**deeper, deepest**) 1 ADJ If something is **deep**, it extends a long way down from the ground or from the top surface of something. 深的 ❑ *The water is very deep and mysterious looking.* 水很深，而且看起来很神秘。 ❑ *Den had dug a deep hole in the center of the garden.* 登在花园中间挖了一个深洞。 ● ADV **Deep** is also an adverb. 深地 ❑ *Gingerly, she put her hand in deeper, to the bottom.* 她小心翼翼地把手伸得更深，直到底部。 ● **deep·ly** ADV 深地 ❑ *There isn't time to dig deeply and put in manure or compost.* 没有时间挖得再深些，并放入粪肥或堆肥。 2 ADJ A **deep** container, such as a closet, extends or measures a long distance from front to back. 纵深的 ❑ *The wardrobe was very deep.* 橱柜很深。 3 ADJ You use **deep** to emphasize the seriousness, strength, importance, or degree of something. 深切的 [EMPHASIS] ❑ *I had a deep admiration for Sartre.* 我对萨特怀有深深的敬意。 ❑ *He wants to express his deep sympathy to the family.* 他想对那家人表示自己深切的同情。 ● **deep·ly** ADV 深深地 ❑ *He loved his brother deeply.* 他深爱自己的哥哥。 4 ADJ If you are in a **deep** sleep, you are sleeping peacefully and it is difficult to wake you. (睡) 熟的 [ADJ n] ❑ *Una soon fell into a deep sleep.* 尤纳很快就睡熟了。 ● **deep·ly** ADV (睡) 熟地 [ADV after v] ❑ *She slept deeply but woke early.* 她睡得很熟，但醒得也早。 5 ADJ If you are **deep in** thought or **deep in** conversation, you are concentrating very hard on what you are thinking or saying and are not aware of the things that are happening around you. 深入的 [v-link ADJ "in" n] ❑ *Before long, we were deep in conversation.* 我们很快就进入深谈。 6 ADJ A **deep** breath or sigh uses or fills the whole of your lungs. (指呼吸、叹息) 深长的 [ADJ n] ❑ *Cal took a long, deep breath, struggling to control his own emotions.* 卡尔深吸了一口气，努力控制住自己的情绪。 ● **deep·ly** ADV (指呼吸、叹息) 深长地 [ADV after v] ❑ *She sighed deeply and covered her face with her hands.* 她长长地叹了口气，用手捂住了脸。 7 ADJ A **deep** sound is low in pitch. 低沉的 ❑ *His voice was deep and mellow.* 他的声音低沉而柔和。 8 ADJ If you describe something such as a problem or a piece of writing as **deep**, you mean that it is important, serious, or complicated. 重要的; 严肃的; 复杂的 ❑ *They're written as adventure stories. They're not intended to be deep.* 这些内容被写成了历险故事，不想太严肃。 9 ADV **Deep** in an area means a long way inside it. 深入地 ❑ *Picking up his bag the giant strode off deep into the forest.* 巨人拿起袋子，大步走入森林深处。 10 ADV If you experience or feel something **deep inside** you or **deep down**, you feel it very strongly even though you do not necessarily show it. 在内心深处 ❑ *Deep down, she supported her husband's involvement in the organization.* 她从内心深处支持丈夫介入这个组织。 11 ADV If you are **deep in** debt, you have a lot of debts. 深陷地 [ADV "in/into" n] ❑ *He is so deep in debt and desperate for money that he's apparently willing to say anything.* 他债台高筑，急需钱，因此他显然什么都愿意说。 ● **deep·ly** ADV 深陷地 [ADV "in/into" n] ❑ *Because of her medical and her legal bills, she is now penniless and deeply in debt.* 由于医疗费和律师费，她现在身无分文，深陷负债。 12 COMB IN COLOR You use **deep** to describe colors that are strong and fairly dark. 深色的 ❑ *The sky was peach colored in the east, deep blue and starry in the west.* 东方的天空色泽桃红，西方的天空深蓝并星光灿烂。 ● ADJ **Deep** is also an adjective. 深的 (颜色) ❑ *These Amish cushions in traditional deep colors are available in two sizes.* 这些传统的深色阿米希垫子有两种尺寸现货供应。 13 PHRASE If you say that something **goes deep** or **runs deep**, you mean that it is very serious or strong and is hard to change. 非常严重 ❑ *His anger and anguish clearly went deep.* 很明显，他的愤怒和痛苦已根深蒂固。 14 **in at the deep end** → see **end** 15 **in deep water** → see **water**

deep·en /dipən/ (**deepens, deepening, deepened**) 1 V-T/V-I If a situation or emotion **deepens** or if something **deepens** it, it becomes stronger and more intense. 使加剧; 加剧 ❑ *If this is not stopped, the financial crisis will deepen.* 如果不加以阻止，金融危机将加剧。 2 V-T If you **deepen** your knowledge or understanding of a subject, you learn more about it and become more interested in it. 使加深 ❑ *The course is an exciting opportunity for anyone wishing to deepen their understanding of themselves and other people.* 这门课程对于希望加深了解自己和他人的人们来说，是个令人兴奋的机会。 3 V-T/V-I When a sound **deepens** or **is deepened**, it becomes lower in tone. 使变低沉; 变低沉 ❑ *The music room had been made to reflect and deepen sounds.* 音乐室被打造成可以产生回音并使声音变得低沉。 4 V-T If people **deepen** something, they increase its depth by digging out its lower surface. 加深 ❑ *The project would deepen the river from 40 to 45 feet, to allow for larger ships.* 这一工程将把河从40英尺加深到45英尺，以通过更大型的船只。

deep-seated ADJ A **deep-seated** problem, feeling, or belief is difficult to change because its causes have been there for a long time. 根深蒂固的 ❑ *The country is still suffering from deep-seated economic problems.* 该国仍为根深蒂固的经济问题所困扰。

deer /dɪər/ (**deer**)

Deer is both the singular and the plural form.

N-COUNT A **deer** is a large wild animal that eats grass and leaves. A male deer usually has large, branching horns. 鹿

de·face /dɪfeɪs/ (**defaces, defacing, defaced**) V-T If someone **defaces** something such as a wall or a notice, they spoil it by writing or drawing things on it. 胡乱涂写于…的外观 ❑ *It's illegal to deface property.* 在房子上乱涂乱画是非法的。

★ **de·fault** /dɪfɔlt/ (**defaults, defaulting, defaulted**) 1 V-I If a person, company, or country **defaults on** something that they have legally agreed to do, such as paying some money or doing a piece of work before a particular time, they fail to do it. 不履行 (义务); 违约 [LEGAL] ❑ *The credit card business is down, and more borrowers are defaulting on loans.* 信用卡生意正在走下坡路，更多的借贷人不履行还贷责任。 ● N-UNCOUNT **Default** is also a noun. 不履行; 违约 ❑ *The corporation may be charged with default on its contract with the government.* 该公司可能会被指控违反了与政府签订的合同。 2 ADJ

A **default** situation is what exists or happens unless someone or something changes it. 原样的 [ADJ n] ❑ *He appeared unimpressed; but then, unimpressed was his default state.* 他看似不为所动，但是，不为所动就是他的原样。 **3** N-UNCOUNT In computing, the **default** is a particular set of instructions which the computer always uses unless the person using the computer gives other instructions. 默认值 [COMPUTING] ❑ *The default setting on Windows Explorer will not show these files.* 视窗浏览器上的默认系统设定不显示这些文档。 **4** PHRASE If something happens **by default**, it happens only because something else which might have prevented it or changed it has not happened. 在另外的可能性没有发生的情况下 [FORMAL] ❑ *I would rather pay the individuals than let the money go to the State by default.* 我宁可把钱付给个人，也不会毫无选择就把钱交给国家。

D

de·feat ♦♦◇ /dɪfiːt/ **(defeats, defeating, defeated)** **1** V-T If you **defeat** someone, you win a victory over them in a battle, game, or contest. 击败 ❑ *His guerrillas defeated the colonial army in 1954.* 他的游击队在1954年打败了殖民军。 **2** V-T If a proposal or motion in a debate **is defeated**, more people vote against it than for it. (以多数票)挫败 [usu passive] ❑ *The bill was defeated with support from only two congressmen.* 由于只得到两位议员的支持，那个议案被否决了。 **3** V-T If a task or a problem **defeats** you, it is so difficult that you cannot do it or solve it. 难倒 ❑ *The book he most wanted to write was the one which nearly defeated him.* 他最想写的书恰恰是几乎难倒他的那一本。 **4** V-T To **defeat** an action or plan means to cause it to fail. 使受挫 ❑ *The navy played a limited but significant role in defeating the rebellion.* 在平息叛乱中海军起了有限但却重要的作用。 **5** N-VAR **Defeat** is the experience of being beaten in a battle, game, or contest, or of failing to achieve what you wanted to. 失败 ❑ *The most important thing is not to admit defeat until you really have to.* 最重要的事就是非到不得已不要认输。 ❑ *...the Sonics' 31-point defeat at Sacramento on Sunday.* …超音速队周日在萨克拉门托31分的挫败。

de·fect **(defects, defecting, defected)**

The noun is pronounced /diːfɛkt/. The verb is pronounced /dɪfɛkt/.

名词读作 /diːfɛkt/，动词读作 /dɪfɛkt/。

1 N-COUNT A **defect** is a fault or imperfection in a person or thing. 缺陷 ❑ *He was born with a hearing defect.* 他天生听力就有缺陷。 ❑ *A report has pointed out the defects of the present system.* 一份报告指出了现有体制的缺陷。 **2** V-I If you **defect**, you leave your country, political party, or other group, and join an opposing country, party, or group. 背叛 ❑ *...a KGB officer who defected in 1963.* …一个1963年叛变的克格勃官员。 ● **de·fec·tion ★** /dɪfɛkʃᵊn/ N-VAR **(defections)** 背叛 ❑ *...the defection of at least sixteen parliamentary deputies.* …至少16位国会议员的背叛。

★ de·fec·tive /dɪfɛktɪv/ ADJ If something is **defective**, there is something wrong with it and it does not work properly. 有缺陷的 ❑ *Retailers can return defective merchandise.* 零售商可以退回有瑕疵的商品。

de·fence /dɪfɛns/ [BRIT] → see **defense**

de·fence·less /dɪfɛnslɪs/ [BRIT] → see **defenseless**

Word Link *fend ≈ striking : defend, fender, offend*

de·fend ♦♦◇ /dɪfɛnd/ **(defends, defending, defended)** **1** V-T If you **defend** someone or something, you take action in order to protect them. 保护 ❑ *His courage in defending religious and civil rights inspired many outside the church.* 他捍卫宗教权和公民权的勇气鼓舞了许多非教会人士。 **2** V-T If you **defend** someone or something when they have been criticized, you argue in support of them. 为…争辩 ❑ *He defended his administration's response to the disaster against critics who charge the federal government is moving too slowly.* 他为他的行政部门对灾难的反应做了争辩，反驳批评人士指控联邦政府行动过于迟缓。 **3** V-T When a lawyer **defends** a person who has been accused of something, the lawyer argues on their behalf in a court of law that the charges are not true. 为…辩护 ❑ *...a lawyer who defended political prisoners during the military regime.* …一位在军权时期为政治犯进行辩护的律师。 ❑ *He has hired a lawyer to defend him against the allegation.* 他已聘请一位律师为他所受的指控辩护。 **4** V-T When a sports player plays in the tournament which they won the previous time it was held, you can say that they **are defending** their title. 卫冕 [JOURNALISM] ❑ *Torrence expects to defend her title successfully in the next Olympics.* 托伦斯希望下届奥运会能成功卫冕。

→ see **hero**

Thesaurus *defend* 另参见：

v. protect **1**
back, support **2**

Word Link *ant ≈ one who does, has : defendant, deodorant, occupant*

★ de·fend·ant /dɪfɛndənt/ **(defendants)** N-COUNT A **defendant** is a person who has been accused of breaking the law and is being tried in court. 被告 ❑ *The defendant pleaded guilty and was fined $500.* 被告认罪，并被罚款$500。

→ see **trial**

de·fend·er /dɪfɛndər/ **(defenders)** **1** N-COUNT If someone is a **defender of** a particular thing or person that has been criticized, they argue or act in support of that thing or person. 捍卫者 ❑ *...the most ardent defenders of conventional family values.* …传统家庭价值最强烈的捍卫者。 **2** N-COUNT A **defender** in a game such as soccer or hockey is a player whose main task is to try and stop the other side from scoring. 防守队员 ❑ *Lewis was the NFL's top defender in the 2000 season.* 刘易斯是2000年赛季美国国家足球联盟的最佳防守球员。

de·fense ♦♦◇ /dɪfɛns/ **(defenses)**

Defense in meaning **7** is pronounced /diːfens/.

in BRIT, use **defence**

1 N-UNCOUNT **Defense** is action that is taken to protect someone or something against attack. 保护；防卫 ❑ *The land was flat, giving no scope for defense.* 土地非常平坦，无法做防卫之用。 **2** N-UNCOUNT **Defense** is the organization of a country's armies and weapons, and their use to protect the country or its interests. 国防机构 ❑ *Twenty-eight percent of the federal budget is spent on defense.* 28%的联邦预算用于国防单位。 ❑ *...U.S. Defense Secretary Donald Rumsfeld.* …美国国防部长唐纳德・拉姆斯菲尔德。 **3** N-PLURAL The **defenses** of a country or region are all its armed forces and weapons. 防卫军备 ❑ *He emphasized the need to maintain Britain's defenses at a level sufficient to deal with the unexpected.* 他强调需要将英国的防卫军备维持在足以应付突发事件的水平。 **4** N-COUNT A **defense** is something that people or animals can use or do to protect themselves. 防御物 ❑ *Despite anything the science of medicine may have achieved, the immune system is our main defense against disease.* 不管医学科学已取得了什么样的进步，免疫系统仍是我们抵抗疾病的主要防御手段。 **5** N-COUNT A **defense** is something that you say or write which supports ideas or actions that have been criticized or questioned. 辩词 [oft N "of" n, also "in" N] ❑ *Chomsky's defense of his approach goes further.* 乔姆斯基对自己方法的辩解更进了一步。 **6** N-SING **The defense** is the case that is presented by a lawyer in a trial for the person who has been accused of a crime. You can also refer to this person's lawyers as **the defense**. (被告对指控的) 答辩；被告律师 ❑ *The defense was that the records of the interviews were fabricated by the police.* 答辩词是警察捏造了访谈纪录。 **7** N-SING-COLL In games such as soccer or hockey, the **defense** is the group of players in a team who try to stop the opposing players from scoring a goal or a point. 防守队员 [oft poss N, also "in" N] ❑ *Their defense, so strong last season, has now conceded 12 goals in six games.* 上个赛季他们的防守队员很强，但现在已经在6场比赛中丢失了12个球。 **8** PHRASE If you come **to** someone's **defense**, you help them by doing or saying something to protect them. 为某人辩护 ❑ *He realized none of his schoolmates would come to his defense.* 他意识到没有一个同学会来为他辩护。

de·fense·less /dɪfɛnslɪs/

in BRIT, use **defenceless**

ADJ If someone or something is **defenseless**, they are weak and unable to defend themselves properly. 无防御的；无防卫能力的 ❑ *...a savage attack on a defenseless young girl.* …对一个毫无防卫能力的年轻女孩的野蛮袭击。

de·fen·sive /dɪfɛnsɪv/ **1** ADJ You use **defensive** to describe things that are intended to protect someone or something. 防御性的；防卫用的 ❑ *The Government hastily organized defensive measures, deploying searchlights and antiaircraft guns around the target cities.* 政府匆忙组织了防御措施，在目标城市周围部署了探照灯和高射炮。 **2** ADJ Someone who is **defensive** is behaving in a way that shows they feel unsure or threatened. 自卫的 ❑ *Like their children, parents are often defensive about their private lives.* 跟孩子们一样，家长们对他们的私生活通常也是自卫的。 ● **de·fen·sive·ly** ADV 自卫地 ❑ *"Oh, I know, I know," said Kate, defensively.* 凯特心存戒备地说道："啊，知道，知道。"

3 ADJ In sports, **defensive** play is play that is intended to prevent your opponent from scoring points against you. 防守的 ❑ *I'd always played a defensive game, waiting for my opponent to make a mistake.* 我总是打防守战，等着对手出错。 ● **de·fen·sive·ly** ADV 防守地 [ADV after v] ❑ *We didn't play well defensively in the first half.* 我们上半场防守不佳。 4 PHRASE If someone is **on the defensive**, they are trying to protect themselves or their interests because they feel unsure or threatened. 采取防卫措施 ❑ *The administration has been on the defensive about the war.* 行政部门一直在为战争辩解。

▲ **de·fer** /dɪfɜr/ (**defers, deferring, deferred**) 1 V-T If you **defer** an event or action, you arrange for it to happen at a later date, rather than immediately or at the previously planned time. 推迟 ❑ *Customers often defer payment for as long as possible.* 顾客们经常尽可能地推迟付款。 2 V-I If you **defer to** someone, you accept their opinion or do what they want you to do, even when you do not agree with it yourself, because you respect them or their authority. 听从；服从 ❑ *Doctors are encouraged to defer to experts.* 鼓励医生们听从专家的意见。

def·er·ence /dɛfərəns/ N-UNCOUNT **Deference** is a polite and respectful attitude toward someone, especially because they have an important position. 敬重 ❑ *...the older political tradition of deference to great leaders.* …敬重伟大领导人的较老的政治传统。

Word Link *ance ≈ quality, state : defiance, performance, resistance*

★ **de·fi·ance** /dɪfaɪəns/ N-UNCOUNT **Defiance** is behavior or an attitude which shows that you are not willing to obey someone. 违抗；蔑视 [oft N "of" n] ❑ *...his courageous defiance of the government.* …他对政府的大胆蔑视。

▲ **de·fi·ant** /dɪfaɪənt/ ADJ If you say that someone is **defiant**, you mean they show aggression or independence by refusing to obey someone. 挑战的；蔑视的 ❑ *The players are in a defiant mood as they prepare for tomorrow's game.* 在准备明天的比赛时，球员们态度挑衅。 ● **de·fi·ant·ly** ADV 挑战地；蔑视地 ❑ *They defiantly rejected any talk of a compromise.* 他们轻蔑地拒绝了任何妥协谈判。

de·fi·cien·cy /dɪfɪʃənsi/ (**deficiencies**) 1 N-VAR **Deficiency in** something, especially something that your body needs, is not having enough of it. 缺乏；不足 ❑ *They did blood tests on him for signs of vitamin deficiency.* 他们给他做了血检看是否有缺乏维生素的迹象。 2 N-VAR A **deficiency** that someone or something has is a weakness or imperfection in them. 缺点；缺陷 [FORMAL] ❑ *The most serious deficiency in NATO's air defense is the lack of an identification system to distinguish friend from foe.* 北约防空的最大缺陷就是缺乏能够辨认敌友的识别系统。

★ **de·fi·cient** /dɪfɪʃənt/ ADJ If someone or something is **deficient in** a particular thing, they do not have the full amount of it that they need in order to function normally or work properly. 缺乏的；不足的 [FORMAL] ❑ *...a diet deficient in vitamin B.* …缺少维生素B的饮食。

defi·cit ♦♦◊ /dɛfəsɪt/ (**deficits**) N-COUNT A **deficit** is the amount by which something is less than what is required or expected, especially the amount by which the total money received is less than the total money spent. 亏损；赤字 ❑ *They're ready to cut the federal budget deficit for the next fiscal year.* 他们已准备好在下一个财政年度削减联邦预算赤字。 ❑ *...a deficit of five billion dollars.* …50亿美元的赤字。 ● PHRASE If an account or organization is **in deficit**, more money has been spent than has been received. 亏损的

de·fine ♦◊◊ /dɪfaɪn/ (**defines, defining, defined**) V-T If you **define** something, you show, describe, or state clearly what it is and what its limits are, or what it is like. 给…下定义；解释 ❑ *The Convention Against Torture defines torture as any act that inflicts severe pain or suffering, physical or mental.* 《反酷刑条约》把酷刑定义为任何造成严重身心疼痛和受苦的行为。

defi·nite /dɛfɪnɪt/ 1 ADJ If something such as a decision or an arrangement is **definite**, it is firm and clear, and unlikely to be changed. 明确的 ❑ *It's too soon to give a definite answer.* 现在给予明确答复还为时尚早。 ❑ *She made no definite plans for her future.* 她对自己的未来没有明确的计划。 2 ADJ **Definite** evidence or information is true, rather than being someone's opinion or guess. 确切的 ❑ *We didn't have any definite proof.* 我们没有任何确凿的证据。 3 ADJ You use **definite** to emphasize the strength of your opinion or belief. 无疑的 [ADJ n] [EMPHASIS] ❑ *There has already been a definite improvement.* 已经有了显著的改善。 4 ADJ Someone who is **definite** behaves or talks in a firm, confident way. 肯定的 ❑ *Mary is very definite about this.* 玛丽对此非常肯定。

Thesaurus *definite* 另参见：
ADJ. clear-cut, distinct, precise, specific; *(ant.)* ambiguous, vague 1

defi·nite ar·ti·cle (**definite articles**) N-COUNT The word "the" is sometimes called **the definite article**. 定冠词

defi·nite·ly ♦◊◊ /dɛfɪnɪtli/ 1 ADV You use **definitely** to emphasize that something is the case, or to emphasize the strength of your intention or opinion. 一定地 [EMPHASIS] ❑ *I'm definitely going to get in touch with these people.* 我一定要联系上这些人。 2 ADV If something has been **definitely** decided, the decision will not be changed. 确定地 [ADV before v] ❑ *She had definitely decided that she wanted to continue working with women in prison.* 她打定主意要继续与监狱里的女人一起工作。

defi·ni·tion ♦◊◊ /dɛfɪnɪʃən/ (**definitions**) 1 N-COUNT A **definition** is a statement giving the meaning of a word or expression, especially in a dictionary. 定义 ❑ *There is no general agreement on a standard definition of intelligence.* 对智力的标准定义意见不统一。 ● PHRASE If you say that something has a particular quality **by definition**, you mean that it has this quality simply because of what it is. 按照释义 2 N-UNCOUNT **Definition** is the quality of being clear and distinct. 清晰度 ❑ *The first speakers at the conference criticized Prof. Johnson's new program for lack of definition.* 会上的首批发言者批评约翰逊教授的新项目没有清晰度。

★ **de·fini·tive** /dɪfɪnɪtɪv/ 1 ADJ Something that is **definitive** provides a firm conclusion that cannot be questioned. 确定的 ❑ *No one has come up with a definitive answer as to why this should be so.* 至于为什么该这样，还没有人给出明确的答复。 ● **de·fini·tive·ly** ADV 确定地 ❑ *Law enforcement officials had definitively identified Blanco as a potential suspect.* 执法官员明确认为布兰科是个可能的嫌疑犯。 2 ADJ A **definitive** book or performance is thought to be the best of its kind that has ever been done or that will ever be done. 权威性的 ❑ *...Ian Macdonald's definitive book on The Beatles.* …伊恩·麦克唐纳写的有关甲壳虫乐队的最权威的书。

Word Link *de ≈ from, down, away : deflate, descend, detach*

de·flate /dɪfleɪt/ (**deflates, deflating, deflated**) 1 V-T If you **deflate** someone or something, you take away their confidence or make them seem less important. 使泄气 ❑ *I hate to deflate your ego, but you seem to have an exaggerated idea of your importance to me.* 我不愿伤你的自尊，但是你好像高估了你对我的重要性。 ● **de·flat·ed** ADJ 泄气的 ❑ *When she refused I felt deflated.* 她拒绝时，我感到很沮丧。 2 V-I When something such as a tire or balloon **deflates**, or when you **deflate** it, all the air comes out of it. 放气；漏气 ❑ *We drove a few miles until the tire deflated and we had to stop the car.* 我们开了几英里直到轮胎漏气了，然后我们不得不停下车。

de·fla·tion /dɪfleɪʃən/ N-UNCOUNT **Deflation** is a reduction in economic activity that leads to lower levels of industrial output, employment, investment, trade, profits, and prices. 通货紧缩 [BUSINESS] ❑ *Deflation is beginning to take hold in the clothing industry.* 服装业开始出现通货紧缩。

de·fla·tion·ary /dɪfleɪʃəneri/ ADJ A **deflationary** economic policy or measure is one that is intended to or likely to cause deflation. 通货紧缩的 [BUSINESS] ❑ *...the government's refusal to implement deflationary measures.* …政府拒绝实施通货紧缩措施。

▲ **de·flect** /dɪflɛkt/ (**deflects, deflecting, deflected**) 1 V-T If you **deflect** something such as criticism or attention, you act in a way that prevents it from being directed toward you or affecting you. 转移 ❑ *Cage changed his name to deflect accusations of nepotism.* 凯奇改了名字以转移裙带关系的指责。 2 V-T To **deflect** someone **from** a course of action means to make them decide not to continue with it by putting pressure on them or by offering them something desirable. (通过施压或给予好处) 使改变 ❑ *The war did not deflect him from the path he had long ago taken.* 战争没有使他改变很久之前就选择的道路。 3 V-T If you **deflect** something that is moving, you make it go in a slightly different direction, for example, by hitting or blocking it. 使 (动作) 偏斜 ❑ *My forearm deflected the first punch.* 我的前臂挡开了第一拳。

de·for·est /difɔrɪst/ (**deforests, deforesting, deforested**) V-T If an area **is deforested**, all the trees there are cut down or destroyed. 砍伐森林 [usu passive] ❑ *...the 400,000 square kilometers*

d

of the Amazon basin that have already been deforested. …已被砍伐的亚马逊河流域40万平方公里的森林。 ●**de·for·esta·tion** /diːfɔrɪsteɪʃən/ N-UNCOUNT 森林砍伐 ❑ *One percent of Brazil's total forest cover is being lost every year to deforestation.* 由于滥伐，巴西的森林总覆盖面积正在每年减少百分之一。

→ see **greenhouse effect**

de·form /dɪfɔrm/ (**deforms, deforming, deformed**) V-T/V-I If something **deforms** a person's body or something else, it causes it to have an unnatural shape. In technical English, you can also say that the second thing **deforms** when it changes to an unnatural shape. 使成畸形 ❑ *Bad rheumatoid arthritis deforms limbs.* 严重的类风湿性关节炎会使肢体畸形。 ●**de·formed** ADJ 畸形的 ❑ *He was born with a deformed right leg.* 他天生右腿畸形。

de·form·ity /dɪfɔrmɪti/ (**deformities**) 1 N-COUNT A **deformity** is a part of someone's body which is not the normal shape because of injury or illness, or because they were born this way. 畸形 ❑ *...facial deformities in babies.* …婴儿的面部畸形。 2 N-UNCOUNT **Deformity** is the condition of having a deformity. 畸形状态 ❑ *The object of these movements is to prevent stiffness or deformity of joints.* 这些活动的目的是防止关节僵硬或变形。

de·fraud /dɪfrɔd/ (**defrauds, defrauding, defrauded**) V-T If someone **defrauds** you, they take something away from you or stop you from getting what belongs to you by means of tricks and lies. 骗取 ❑ *He pleaded guilty to charges of conspiracy to defraud the government.* 他对阴谋诈骗政府的指控供认不讳。

deft /dɛft/ (**defter, deftest**) ADJ A **deft** action is skillful and often quick. 灵巧的 [WRITTEN] ❑ *With a deft flick of his wrist, he extinguished the match.* 他的手腕灵巧地一抖，就熄灭了火柴。 ●**deft·ly** ADV 灵巧地 ❑ *One of the waiting servants deftly caught him as he fell.* 就在他要跌到时，侍候的一名佣人敏捷地扶住了他。

de·funct /dɪfʌŋkt/ ADJ If something is **defunct**, it no longer exists or has stopped functioning or operating. 不再存在的；不再起作用的 ❑ *...the leader of the now defunct Social Democratic Party.* …现已不存在的社会民主党的领袖。

de·fuse /difyuz/ (**defuses, defusing, defused**) 1 V-T If you **defuse** a dangerous or tense situation, you calm it. 缓和 ❑ *Police administrators credited the organization with helping defuse potentially violent situations.* 警方赞扬该组织帮助缓和潜在的暴力情势。 2 V-T If someone **defuses** a bomb, they remove the fuse so that it cannot explode. 拆除…的引信 ❑ *Police have defused a bomb found in a downtown building.* 警察已拆除了在市中心一幢大楼里发现的一枚炸弹的引信。

defy /dɪfaɪ/ (**defies, defying, defied**) 1 V-T If you **defy** someone or something that is trying to make you behave in a particular way, you refuse to obey them and behave in that way. 违抗 ❑ *This was the first (and last) time that I dared to defy my mother.* 这是我第一次（也是最后一次）胆敢违抗我母亲。 2 V-T If you **defy** someone **to** do something, you challenge them to do it when you think that they will be unable to do it or too frightened to do it. 向…挑战；惹 ❑ *I defy you to come up with one major accomplishment of the current president.* 我倒要看看你能否举出现任董事长的一件主要成绩。 3 V-T If something **defies** description or understanding, it is so strange, extreme, or surprising that it is almost impossible to understand or explain. 使不可能（理解或解释）[no passive, no cont] ❑ *It's a devastating and barbaric act that defies all comprehension.* 这是毁灭性的野蛮行径，完全没有方法可理解。

★ **de·gen·er·ate** (**degenerates, degenerating, degenerated**)

> The verb is pronounced /dɪdʒɛnəreɪt/. The adjective is pronounced /dɪdʒɛnərɪt/.

> 动词读作 /dɪdʒɛnəreɪt/。形容词读作 /dɪdʒɛnərɪt/。

1 V-I If you say that someone or something **degenerates**, you mean that they become worse in some way, for example, weaker, lower in quality, or more dangerous. 退化；恶化；堕落 ❑ *Inactivity can make your joints stiff, and the bones may begin to degenerate.* 不活动会使关节僵硬，骨骼因此可能会开始退化。 ●**de·gen·era·tion** /dɪdʒɛnəreɪʃən/ N-UNCOUNT 退化；恶化；堕落 ❑ *...various forms of physical and mental degeneration.* …各种形式的身心退化。 2 ADJ If you describe a person or their behavior as **degenerate**, you disapprove of them because you think they have low standards of behavior or morality. 堕落的 [DISAPPROVAL] ❑ *...a group of degenerate computer hackers.* …一群堕落的计算机黑客。

deg·ra·da·tion /dɛgrədeɪʃən/ (**degradations**) 1 N-VAR You use **degradation** to refer to a situation, condition, or experience which you consider shameful and disgusting, especially one which involves poverty or immorality. 堕落 [DISAPPROVAL] ❑ *They were sickened by the scenes of misery and degradation they found.* 他们对所看到的凄惨和堕落景象感到恶心。 2 N-UNCOUNT **Degradation** is the process of something becoming worse or weaker, or being made worse or weaker. 恶化；衰退 ❑ *...air pollution, traffic congestion, and the steady degradation of our quality of life.* …空气污染、交通阻塞以及我们生活质量的持续恶化。

★ **de·grade** /dɪgreɪd/ (**degrades, degrading, degraded**) 1 V-T Something that **degrades** someone causes people to have less respect for them. 使贬低身份；使有辱人格 ❑ *...the notion that pornography degrades women.* …色情作品贬低妇女的这种看法。 ●**de·grad·ing** ADJ 贬低身份的；有辱人格的 ❑ *Mr. Porter was subjected to a degrading strip search.* 波特先生受到了有辱人格的脱衣搜身。 2 V-T To **degrade** something means to cause it to get worse. 使恶化 [FORMAL] ❑ *...the ability to meet human needs indefinitely without degrading the environment.* …满足人类无限需求但又不会使环境恶化的能力。

de·gree ♦♦◊ /dɪgri/ (**degrees**) 1 N-COUNT You use **degree** to indicate the extent to which something happens or is the case, or the amount which something is felt. 程度 ❑ *These man-made barriers will ensure a very high degree of protection for several hundred years.* 这些人造屏障将会确保几百年的高度保护。 ❑ *Recent presidents have used television, as well as radio, with varying degrees of success.* 新近的总统们已经利用了电视和收音机，取得了不同程度的成功。 ● PHRASE If something has **a degree of** a particular quality, it has a small but significant amount of that quality. 一定程度的 2 N-COUNT A **degree** is a unit of measurement that is used to measure temperatures. It is often written as °, for example, 23°. (指温度) 度 ❑ *It's over 80 degrees outside.* 外面超过80度。 3 N-COUNT A **degree** is a unit of measurement that is used to measure angles, and also longitude and latitude. It is often written as °, for example, 23°. (指角度、经纬度) 度 ❑ *It was pointing outward at an angle of 45 degrees.* 它以45度角指向外侧。 4 N-COUNT A **degree** is a title or rank given by a university or college when you have completed a course of study there. It can also be given as an honorary title. 学位 ❑ *...an engineering degree.* …工程学学位。 5 PHRASE You use expressions such as **to some degree, to a large degree**, or **to a certain degree** in order to indicate that something is partly true, but not entirely true. 在某种程度上 [VAGUENESS] ❑ *These statements are, to some degree, all correct.* 这些陈述在某种程度上都正确。

Word Partnership *degree* 的常用搭配：

N.	degree **of certainty**, degree **of difficulty** 1
	45/90 degree **angle** 3
	bachelor's/master's degree, **college** degree, degree **program** 4
ADJ.	**high** degree 1
	honorary degree 4

Word Link *hydr ≈ water : dehydrate, hydraulic, hydrologic cycle*

de·hy·drate /dihaɪdreɪt/ (**dehydrates, dehydrating, dehydrated**) 1 V-T When something such as food **is dehydrated**, all the water is removed from it, often in order to preserve it. 使脱水 [usu passive] ❑ *Normally specimens have to be dehydrated.* 通常标本必须得脱水。 2 V-T/V-I If you **dehydrate** or if something **dehydrates** you, you lose too much water from your body so that you feel weak or ill. 使脱水；(指人) 脱水 ❑ *People can dehydrate in weather like this.* 人在这样的天气里会脱水。 ●**de·hy·dra·tion** /dihaɪdreɪʃən/ N-UNCOUNT 脱水 ❑ *...a child who's got diarrhea and is suffering from dehydration.* …一个得了腹泻并患脱水的孩子。

→ see **sweat**

de·ity /diɪti/ (**deities**) N-COUNT A **deity** is a god or goddess. 神；女神 [FORMAL] ❑ *...a deity revered by thousands of Hindus and Buddhists.* …一个受到成千上万印度教教徒和佛教徒敬仰的神。

→ see **religion**

de·lay ♦♦◊ /dɪleɪ/ (**delays, delaying, delayed**) 1 V-T/V-I If you **delay** doing something, you do not do it immediately or at the planned or expected time, but you leave it until later. 推迟 ❑ *For sentimental reasons I wanted to delay my departure until June 1980.* 由于感情上的原因，我想把启程时间推迟到1980年6月。 ❑ *They had delayed having children, for the usual reason, to establish their careers.* 他们推迟了要孩子，为了要建立事业这个通常的理由。

If you **cancel** or **call off** an arrangement or an appointment, you stop it from happening. ❑ *His failing health forced him to cancel the meeting... The European Community has threatened to call off peace talks.* If you **postpone** or **put off** an arrangement or an appointment, you make another arrangement for it to happen at a later time. ❑ *Elections have been postponed until next year... The senate put off a vote on the nomination for one week.* If you **delay** something that has been arranged, you make it happen later than planned. ❑ *Space agency managers decided to delay the launch of the space shuttle.* If something **delays** you or **holds** you **up**, you start or finish what you are doing later than you planned. ❑ *He was delayed in traffic... Delivery of equipment had been held up by delays and disputes.*

2 V-T To **delay** someone or something means to make them late or to slow them down. 延误；耽搁 ❑ *Can you delay him in some way?* 你能用什么办法耽搁他一下吗？ ❑ *Various setbacks and problems delayed production.* 各种各样的挫折和问题延误了生产。 3 V-I If you **delay**, you deliberately take longer than necessary to do something. 拖延 ❑ *If he delayed any longer, the sun would be up.* 如果他再拖延下去，太阳就要升起来了。 4 N-VAR If there is a **delay**, something does not happen until later than planned or expected. 耽搁 ❑ *They claimed that such a delay wouldn't hurt anyone.* 他们声称这样的耽搁不会伤害任何人。 5 N-UNCOUNT **Delay** is a failure to do something immediately or in the required or usual time. 延误 ❑ *We'll send you a quote without delay.* 我们会立即向你方报价。

Thesaurus *delay* 另参见：
V. hold up, postpone, stall; *(ant.)* hurry, rush 1 2
N. interruption, lag; *(ant.)* rush 4

de·lay·er·ing /diːleɪərɪŋ/ N-UNCOUNT **Delayering** is the process of simplifying the administrative structure of a large organization in order to make it more efficient. 管理层削减 [BUSINESS] ❑ *...downsizing, delayering, and other cost cutting measures.* …裁员、管理层削减及其他削减成本的措施。

de·lec·table /dɪlɛktəbəl/ ADJ If you describe something, especially food or drink, as **delectable**, you mean that it is very pleasant. (食物、饮料) 美味可口的 ❑ *...delectable wine.* …醇香的酒。

del·egate ♦◇◇ (**delegates, delegating, delegated**)

The noun is pronounced /dɛlɪgɪt/. The verb is pronounced /dɛlɪgeɪt/.

名词读作 /dɛlɪgɪt/。动词读作 /dɛlɪgeɪt/。

1 N-COUNT A **delegate** is a person who is chosen to vote or make decisions on behalf of a group of other people, especially at a conference or a meeting. 代表 ❑ *The Canadian delegate offered no reply.* 那位加拿大代表没给答复。 2 V-T/V-I If you **delegate** duties, responsibilities, or power **to** someone, you give them those duties, those responsibilities, or that power so that they can act on your behalf. 委托；授权 ❑ *He talks of traveling less, and delegating more authority to his deputies.* 他说要减少旅行，还有要授予他的副手们更多的权力。 ● **del·ega·tion** N-UNCOUNT 委托；授权 ❑ *A key factor in running a business is the delegation of responsibility.* 经商的一个关键因素是责任委托。 3 V-T If you **are delegated to** do something, you are given the duty of acting on someone else's behalf by making decisions, voting, or doing some particular work. 委派 [usu passive] ❑ *Officials have now been delegated to start work on a draft settlement.* 官员们现已被委派开始准备一份拟定协议。

del·ega·tion ♦◇◇ /dɛlɪgeɪʃən/ (**delegations**) 1 N-COUNT A **delegation** is a group of people who have been sent somewhere to have talks with other people on behalf of a larger group of people. 代表团 ❑ *...the Chinese delegation to the UN talks in New York.* …在纽约参加联合国谈判的中国代表团。 2 → see also **delegate**

de·lete /dɪliːt/ (**deletes, deleting, deleted**) V-T If you **delete** something that has been written down or stored in a computer, you cross it out or remove it. 删除 ❑ *He also deleted files from the computer system.* 他也从计算机系统中删除了文件。

Thesaurus *delete* 另参见：
V. cut out, erase, remove

deli /dɛli/ (**delis**) N-COUNT A **deli** is a **delicatessen**. 熟食店 [INFORMAL]

de·lib·er·ate ♦◇◇ (**deliberates, deliberating, deliberated**)

The adjective is pronounced /dɪlɪbərɪt/. The verb is pronounced /dɪlɪbəreɪt/.

形容词读作 /dɪlɪbərɪt/。动词读作 /dɪlɪbəreɪt/。

1 ADJ If you do something that is **deliberate**, you planned or decided to do it beforehand, and so it happens on purpose rather than by chance. 故意的 ❑ *Witnesses say the firing was deliberate and sustained.* 目击者说这次射击是蓄意的，而且还持续了一段时间。 ● **de·lib·er·ate·ly** ADV 故意地 ❑ *It looks as if the blaze was started deliberately.* 看来那场火是有人故意放的。 2 ADJ If a movement or action is **deliberate**, it is done slowly and carefully. 从容谨慎的 ❑ *...stepping with deliberate slowness up the steep paths.* …小心翼翼地缓步走上陡峭的小径。 ● **de·lib·er·ate·ly** ADV 从容谨慎地 [ADV after v] ❑ *The Japanese have acted calmly and deliberately.* 那些日本人表现得镇定且从容。 3 V-T/V-I If you **deliberate**, you think about something carefully, especially before making a very important decision. 仔细考虑 ❑ *She deliberated over the decision for a good few years before she finally made up her mind.* 在她最终下定决心之前，她仔细考虑了这个决定多年。

→ see **trial**

▲ **de·lib·era·tion** /dɪlɪbəreɪʃən/ (**deliberations**) 1 N-UNCOUNT **Deliberation** is the long and careful consideration of a subject. 仔细的考虑 ❑ *In this house nothing is there by chance: it is always the result of great deliberation.* 在这房子里，没有什么东西是偶然的——总是非常仔细考虑后的结果。 2 N-PLURAL **Deliberations** are formal discussions where an issue is considered carefully. 审议 ❑ *Their deliberations were rather inconclusive.* 他们的审议没有什么结论。

★ **deli·ca·cy** /dɛlɪkəsi/ (**delicacies**) 1 N-UNCOUNT **Delicacy** is the quality of being easy to break or harm, and refers especially to people or things that are attractive or graceful. 娇弱；精致 ❑ *...the delicacy of a rose.* …玫瑰花的娇嫩。 2 N-UNCOUNT If you say that a situation or problem is **of** some **delicacy**, you mean that it is difficult to handle and needs careful and sensitive treatment. 微妙；棘手 ❑ *There was a matter of some delicacy on which he would be grateful for her advice.* 有一件棘手的事，若能得到她的指点，他会感激不尽。 3 N-UNCOUNT If someone handles a difficult situation **with delicacy**, they handle it very carefully, making sure that nobody is offended. 考虑周到；体谅 ❑ *Both countries are behaving with rare delicacy.* 两个国家都表现出难得的体谅周到。 4 N-COUNT A **delicacy** is a rare or expensive food that is considered especially nice to eat. 美味佳肴 ❑ *Smoked salmon was considered an expensive delicacy.* 熏三文鱼被认为是一道昂贵的佳肴。

deli·cate /dɛlɪkɪt/ 1 ADJ Something that is **delicate** is small and beautifully shaped. 精巧的；精美的 ❑ *He had delicate hands.* 他有一双纤细的手。 ● **deli·cate·ly** ADV 精巧地；精美地 [ADV adj/-ed] ❑ *She was a shy, delicately pretty girl with enormous blue eyes.* 她是个羞怯纤美的姑娘，长着一双蓝色的大眼睛。 2 ADJ Something that is **delicate** has a color, taste, or smell which is pleasant and not strong or intense. 柔和的 (颜色)；清淡可口的 (味道) ❑ *Young haricot beans have a tender texture and a delicate, subtle flavor.* 嫩扁豆肉质细嫩，味道清淡可口。 ● **deli·cate·ly** ADV 清淡可口地 [ADV -ed/adj] ❑ *...a soup delicately flavored with nutmeg.* …以肉桂清淡地调味的一道汤。 3 ADJ If something is **delicate**, it is easy to harm, damage, or break, and needs to be handled or treated carefully. 易碎的；脆弱的 ❑ *Although the coral looks hard, it is very delicate.* 虽然那珊瑚看起来坚硬，它其实非常易碎。 4 ADJ Someone who is **delicate** is not healthy and strong, and becomes ill easily. 病弱的 ❑ *She was physically delicate and psychologically unstable.* 她身体纤弱，而且心理也不稳定。 5 ADJ You use **delicate** to describe a situation, problem, matter, or discussion that needs to be dealt with carefully and sensitively in order to avoid upsetting things or offending people. 微妙的 ❑ *Ottawa and Washington have to find a delicate balance between the free flow of commerce and legitimate security concerns.* 渥太华和华盛顿必须在自由贸易流通和司法安全事务之间找到一个微妙的平衡。 ● **deli·cate·ly** ADV 微妙地 [ADV with v] ❑ *Clearly, the situation remains delicately poised.* 显而易见，形势仍然保持着微妙的平衡。 6 ADJ A **delicate** task, movement, action, or product needs or shows great skill and attention to detail. 棘手的；需要小心处理的 ❑ *...a long and delicate operation carried out at a hospital in Pittsburgh.* …匹兹堡市一家医院里进行的一项耗时且棘手的手术。 ● **deli·cate·ly** ADV 棘手地 [ADV with v] ❑ *...the delicately embroidered sheets.* …那些刺绣繁复的床单。

d

D

de·li·ca·tes·sen /dɛlɪkətɛsᵊn/ (delicatessens) N-COUNT A **delicatessen** is a store that sells cold cuts, cheeses, salads, and often a selection of imported foods. 熟食店

de·li·cious /dɪlɪʃəs/ ADJ Food that is **delicious** has a very pleasant taste. 美味的 ❑ *There's always a wide selection of delicious meals to choose from.* 总有很多种美味佳肴可供选择。● **de·li·cious·ly** ADV 美味地 [ADV adj/-ed] ❑ *This yogurt has a deliciously creamy flavor.* 这种酸奶有可口的奶油味道。

> **Thesaurus** *delicious* 另参见：
> ADJ. scrumptious, tasty

de·light ♦◇◇ /dɪlaɪt/ (delights, delighting, delighted) 1 N-UNCOUNT **Delight** is a feeling of very great pleasure. 高兴；欣喜 ❑ *Throughout the house, the views are a constant source of surprise and delight.* 整个房子，目之所及不停带来惊奇和欣喜。❑ *Andrew roared with delight when he heard Rachel's nickname for the baby.* 安德鲁听到雷切尔给那个婴儿起的爱称时，高兴地叫起来。2 PHRASE If someone **takes delight** or **takes a delight in** something, they get a lot of pleasure from it. 以…为乐 ❑ *Haig took obvious delight in proving his critics wrong.* 海格显然以证明他的批评者是错误的为乐。3 N-COUNT You can refer to someone or something that gives you great pleasure or enjoyment as a **delight**. 乐事；乐趣 [APPROVAL] ❑ *The aircraft was a delight to fly.* 驾乘这种飞机是一件乐事。4 V-T If something **delights** you, it gives you a lot of pleasure. 使高兴；使欣喜 ❑ *She has created a style of music that has delighted audiences all over the world.* 她创立了一种为全世界听众所喜爱的音乐风格。

de·light·ed ♦◇◇ /dɪlaɪtɪd/ 1 ADJ If you are **delighted**, you are extremely pleased and excited about something. 高兴的 ❑ *I know Frank will be delighted to see you.* 我知道弗兰克见到你会非常高兴。● **de·light·ed·ly** ADV 高兴地 [ADV with v] ❑ *"There!" Jackson exclaimed delightedly.* "在那儿！"杰克逊高兴地大喊起来。2 ADJ If someone invites or asks you to do something, you can say that you would be **delighted** to do it, as a way of showing that you are very willing to do it. 乐意的 [FEELINGS] ❑ *"You have to come to Todd's graduation party."—"I'd be delighted."* "你一定要来参加托德的毕业派对。"——"非常乐意。"

de·light·ful /dɪlaɪtfəl/ ADJ If you describe something or someone as **delightful**, you mean they are very pleasant. 令人愉快的 ❑ *It was the most delightful garden I had ever seen.* 这是我见过的最讨人喜欢的花园。● **de·light·ful·ly** ADV 令人愉快地 [ADV adj/-ed] ❑ *This delightfully refreshing cologne can be splashed on liberally.* 这种清爽怡人的古龙香水可以尽情喷洒。

de·lin·quen·cy /dɪlɪŋkwənsi/ (delinquencies) N-UNCOUNT **Delinquency** is criminal behavior, especially that of young people. 违法行为；少年犯罪 ❑ *He had no history of delinquency.* 他没有犯罪记录。

de·lin·quent /dɪlɪŋkwənt/ (delinquents) 1 ADJ Someone, usually a young person, who is **delinquent** repeatedly commits minor crimes. (尤指青少年) 累犯的 ❑ *...homes for delinquent children.* …少管所。● N-COUNT **Delinquent** is also a noun. 少年犯 ❑ *...a nine-year-old delinquent.* …一名9岁的少年犯。2 ADJ A **delinquent** borrower or taxpayer is someone who has failed to pay their debts or taxes. (债款、税款等) 拖欠的 [AM] ❑ *...a legal shortcut to take homes from delinquent borrowers.* …一个取得拖欠贷款者房产的法律捷径。

de·liri·ous /dɪlɪəriəs/ 1 ADJ Someone who is **delirious** is unable to think or speak in a sensible and reasonable way, usually because they are very ill and have a fever. 神智昏迷的 ❑ *I was delirious and blacked out several times.* 我当时神志不清，几次昏过去。2 ADJ Someone who is **delirious** is extremely excited and happy. 极度兴奋的 ❑ *A raucous crowd of 25,000 delirious fans greeted the team at Grand Central Station.* 一群喧闹的25000名狂热球迷在格兰德中心车站欢迎球队。● **de·liri·ous·ly** ADV 极度兴奋地 ❑ *Dora returned from her honeymoon deliriously happy.* 多拉度蜜月回来，无比幸福。

de·list /dilɪst/ (delists, delisting, delisted) V-T If a company **delists** or if its shares **are delisted**, its shares are removed from the official list of shares that can be traded on the stock market. (证券、股票等) 被…摘牌 [BUSINESS] ❑ *The company's stock was delisted from the Nasdaq market in July 2000.* 2000年7月，这家公司的股票被美国纳斯达克市场摘牌。

de·liv·er ♦♦◇ /dɪlɪvər/ (delivers, delivering, delivered) 1 V-T If you **deliver** something somewhere, you take it there. 递送 ❑ *The Canadians plan to deliver more food to southern Somalia.* 加拿大人计划向索马里南部运送更多的食物。2 V-T/V-I If you **deliver** something that you have promised to do, make, or produce, you do, make, or produce it. 实现；履行 ❑ *They have yet to show that they can really deliver working technologies.* 他们仍需证明他们确实能够实现可用的技术。❑ *The question is, can he deliver?* 问题是他能履行吗？3 V-T If you **deliver** a lecture or speech, you give it in public. 发表 [FORMAL] ❑ *The president will deliver a speech about schools.* 校长将发表关于学校的演讲。4 V-T When someone **delivers** a baby, they help the woman who is giving birth to the baby. 给 (产妇) 接生 ❑ *Although we'd planned to have our baby at home, we never expected to deliver her ourselves!* 尽管我们是打算在家生孩子，可我们从未想过要自己给她接生！5 V-T If someone **delivers** a blow to someone else, they hit them. 给予 (打击) [WRITTEN] ❑ *Those blows to the head could have been delivered by a woman.* 头上挨的那些打可能是一个女人所为。

> **Thesaurus** *deliver* 另参见：
> V. bring, give, hand over, transfer; *(ant.)* hold, keep, retain 1

> **Word Partnership** *deliver* 的常用搭配：
> N. deliver **a letter**, deliver **mail**, deliver **a message**, deliver **news**, deliver **a package** 1
> deliver **a service** 2
> deliver **a lecture**, deliver **a speech** 3
> deliver **a baby** 4
> deliver **a blow** 5

de·liv·ery ♦◇◇ /dɪlɪvəri/ (deliveries) 1 N-VAR **Delivery** or a **delivery** is the bringing of letters, packages, or other goods to someone's house or to another place where they want them. 递送 ❑ *Please allow 28 days for delivery.* 请留出28天的递送时间。❑ *The uprising is threatening the delivery of humanitarian supplies of food and medicine.* 这场暴乱正威胁到食物和药品等人道主义物资的运送。2 N-VAR **Delivery** is the process of giving birth to a baby. 分娩 ❑ *In the end, it was an easy delivery: a fine baby boy.* 最终，分娩顺利——一个健康的男婴。3 N-COUNT A **delivery** of something is the goods that are delivered. 递送的货物 ❑ *I got a delivery of fresh eggs this morning.* 今天早上我收到了一批新鲜鸡蛋。4 ADJ A **delivery** person or service delivers things to a place. 送货的 [ADJ n] ❑ *...a pizza delivery man.* …一个送比萨饼的男子。5 N-UNCOUNT You talk about someone's **delivery** when you are referring to the way in which they give a speech or lecture. 演讲方式 ❑ *His speeches were magnificently written but his delivery was hopeless.* 他的演讲辞写得很好，但他的演讲却不可救药。

de·liv·ery charge (delivery charges) N-COUNT A **delivery charge** is the cost of transporting or delivering goods. 运输费用 [AM, FORMAL] ❑ *Again, buyers need to check if delivery charges are included in the price.* 此外，买主需要核实售价中是否包含运费。

> in BRIT, usually use **carriage**

del·ta /dɛltə/ (deltas) N-COUNT A **delta** is an area of low, flat land shaped like a triangle, where a river splits and spreads out into several branches before entering the sea. (河流的) 三角洲 ❑ *...the Mississippi delta.* …密西西比河三角洲。
→ see **river**

de·lude /dɪlud/ (deludes, deluding, deluded) 1 V-T If you **delude yourself**, you let yourself believe that something is true, even though it is not true. 欺骗 ❑ *The president was deluding himself if he thought he was safe from such action.* 如果总统认为他能从这次行动中安然脱身，那就是自欺欺人。❑ *We delude ourselves that we are in control.* 我们欺骗自己一切都在我们的控制之下。2 V-T To **delude** someone **into** thinking something means to make them believe what is not true. 哄骗 ❑ *Television deludes you into thinking you have experienced reality, when you haven't.* 电视诱使你相信你体验到了你实际上并没有体验过的真情实景。

del·uge /dɛlyudʒ/ (deluges, deluging, deluged) 1 N-COUNT A **deluge of** things is a large number of them which arrive or happen at the same time. 泛滥 ❑ *There was a deluge of requests for interviews and statements.* 对接受访谈和发表声明的要求铺天盖地地涌来。2 V-T If a place or person **is deluged with** things, a large number of them arrive or happen at the same time. 使充斥 [usu passive] ❑ *During 1933, Papen's office was deluged with complaints.* 在1933年间，巴本的办公室接到的投诉案件层出不穷。

▲ **de·lu·sion** /dɪluʒᵊn/ (delusions) 1 N-COUNT A **delusion** is a false idea. 错觉 ❑ *I was under the delusion that he intended to marry me.* 我有一种错觉，他要娶我。2 N-UNCOUNT **Delusion** is the state of believing things that are not true. 妄想 ❑ *Insinuations about her* mental state, about her capacity for delusion, were being made. 当时有对她的精神状态的影射——说她有妄想症的影射。

deluxe /dɪlʌks/
in BRIT, also use **de luxe**
ADJ **Deluxe** goods or services are better in quality and more expensive than ordinary ones. 高级的；奢华的 [ADJ n, n ADJ] ❑ *...a rare, highly prized deluxe wine.* …一瓶罕见的名贵葡萄酒。

delve /dɛlv/ (**delves, delving, delved**) V-I If you **delve into** something, you try to discover new information about it. 探索 ❑ *Tormented by her ignorance, Jenny delves into her mother's past.* 珍妮为自己不了解真相而痛苦，她开始深入调查母亲的过去。

de·mand ♦♦♦ /dɪmænd/ (**demands, demanding, demanded**) 1 V-T If you **demand** something such as information or action, you ask for it in a very forceful way. 强烈要求 ❑ *Human rights groups are demanding an investigation into the shooting.* 人权组织正强烈要求对这一枪击案进行调查。❑ *Russia demanded that UNITA send a delegation to the peace talks.* 俄罗斯强烈要求安哥拉彻底独立全国同盟派遣一个代表团参加和谈。 2 V-T If one thing **demands** another, the first needs the second in order to happen or be dealt with successfully. 需要 ❑ *He said the task of reconstruction would demand much patience, hard work, and sacrifice.* 他说重建工作会需要高度坚韧、勤劳和奉献。 3 N-COUNT A **demand** is a firm request for something. 坚决的要求 ❑ *There have been demands for services from tenants up there.* 那边的房客们有服务的明确要求。 4 N-UNCOUNT If you refer to **demand**, or to the **demand for** something, you are referring to how many people want to have it, do it, or buy it. 需求量 ❑ *Another flight would be arranged on Saturday if sufficient demand arose.* 如果有足够的需求量，周六就会安排另一个航班。 5 N-PLURAL **The demands of** something or its **demands on** you are the things which it needs or the things which you have to do for it. 要求 ❑ *...the demands and challenges of a new job.* …一份新工作的要求和挑战。 6 PHRASE If someone or something is **in demand** or **in great demand**, they are very popular and a lot of people want them. 受欢迎的 ❑ *He was much in demand as a lecturer in the U.S., as well as at universities all over Europe.* 他在美国是个非常受欢迎的演讲者，在全欧洲的大学中也是。 7 PHRASE If something is available or happens **on demand**, you can have it or it happens whenever you want it or ask for it. 一经要求 ❑ *...a new entertainment system that offers 25 movies on demand.* …一经要求，即可播放25部电影的新的娱乐系统。
→ see **economics**

Thesaurus *demand* 另参见：
v. command, insist on, order; *(ant.)* give, grant, offer 1
necessitate, need, require; *(ant.)* give, supply 2

de·mand·ing /dɪmændɪŋ/ 1 ADJ A **demanding** job or task requires a lot of your time, energy, or attention. 费力的；费时的 ❑ *He tried to return to work, but found he could no longer cope with his demanding job.* 他试图回去工作，但发现自己不再能适应这项费时的工作。 2 ADJ People who are **demanding** are not easily satisfied or pleased. 苛求的 ❑ *Ricky was a very demanding child.* 里基是个非常苛求的孩子。

de·mean /dɪmiːn/ (**demeans, demeaning, demeaned**) V-T To **demean** someone or something means to make people have less respect for them. 降低…的身份；贬损 ❑ *Some groups say that pornography demeans women and incites rape.* 一些组织声称色情作品贬低妇女，并引发强奸案。

de·mean·ing /dɪmiːnɪŋ/ ADJ Something that is **demeaning** makes people have less respect for the person who is treated in that way, or who does that thing. 降低身份的；耻辱的 ❑ *...making demeaning sexist comments.* …发表可耻的性别歧视言论。

de·mean·or /dɪmiːnər/
in BRIT, use **demeanour**
N-UNCOUNT Your **demeanor** is the way you behave, which gives people an impression of your character and feelings. 行为；态度 [FORMAL] ❑ *...her calm and cheerful demeanor.* …她那冷静乐观的态度。

de·mean·our /dɪmiːnəʳ/ [BRIT] → see **demeanor**

Word Link *ment ≈ mind : dementia, mental, mentality*

de·men·tia /dɪmɛnʃə/ (**dementias**) N-VAR **Dementia** is a serious illness of the mind. 痴呆 [MEDICAL] ❑ *...a treatment for mental conditions such as dementia and Alzheimer's disease.* …对诸如痴呆和阿尔茨海默氏病等精神疾病的一种疗法。

de·mili·ta·rise /diːmɪlɪtəraɪz/ [BRIT] → see **demilitarize**

Word Link *milit ≈ soldier : demilitarize, military, militia*

de·mili·ta·rize /diːmɪlɪtəraɪz/ (**demilitarizes, demilitarizing, demilitarized**)
in BRIT, also use **demilitarise**
V-T To **demilitarize** an area means to ensure that all military forces are removed from it. 使非军事化 ❑ *He said the UN had made remarkable progress in demilitarizing the region.* 他说联合国在实现这一地区非军事化上取得了惊人的进展。

de·mise /dɪmaɪz/ N-SING The **demise** of something or someone is their end or death. 终止；死亡 [FORMAL] ❑ *...the demise of the reform movement.* …改良运动的告终。

demo /dɛmoʊ/ (**demos**) 1 N-COUNT A **demo** is a CD or tape with a sample of someone's music recorded on it. 试样唱片 [INFORMAL] ❑ *He arranged for Reba to record her first demo tape.* 他安排里巴录制了她的首张样带。 2 N-COUNT A **demo** is a demonstration of something. 演示物 [INFORMAL] ❑ *Download free demos of our newest products and upgrades.* 下载我们最新产品的免费演示版和升级版。

▲ **de·mo·bi·lise** /diːmoʊbɪlaɪz/ [BRIT] → see **demobilize**

▲ **de·mo·bi·lize** /diːmoʊbɪlaɪz/ (**demobilizes, demobilizing, demobilized**)
in BRIT, also use **demobilise**
V-T/V-I If a country or armed force **demobilizes** its troops, or if its troops **demobilize**, its troops are released from service and allowed to go home. 遣散(军队等) ❑ *Dos Santos has demanded that UNITA sign a cease-fire and demobilize its troops.* 多斯·桑托斯强烈要求安哥拉彻底独立全国同盟签订停火协议并遣散它的军队。
● **de·mo·bi·li·za·tion** /diːmoʊbɪlɪzeɪʃən/ N-UNCOUNT 遣散军队；实行复员 ❑ *The government had previously been opposed to the demobilization of its 100,000 strong army.* 该政府以前曾反对将其10万人的强大部队遣散。

Word Link *cracy ≈ rule by : aristocracy, bureaucracy, democracy*

Word Link *demo ≈ people : democracy, demographic, undemocratic*

de·moc·ra·cy ♦♦◇ /dɪmɒkrəsi/ (**democracies**) 1 N-UNCOUNT **Democracy** is a system of government in which people choose their rulers by voting for them in elections. 民主政体 ❑ *The spread of democracy in Eastern Europe appears to have had negative as well as positive consequences.* 东欧民主政体的蔓延看来既有消极也有积极的影响。 2 N-COUNT A **democracy** is a country in which the people choose their government by voting for it. 民主国家 ❑ *The new democracies face tough challenges.* 新生的民主国家面临严峻的挑战。
→ see **vote**

Word Link *crat ≈ power : aristocrat, bureaucrat, democrat*

▲ **demo·crat** ♦♦◇ /dɛməkræt/ (**democrats**) 1 N-COUNT A **Democrat** is a member or supporter of a particular political party which has the word "democrat" or "democratic" in its title, for example, the Democratic Party in the United States. 民主党人 ❑ *Murray has joined other Senate Democrats in blocking the legislation.* 默里已经加入其他民主党参议员反对这项立法了。 2 N-COUNT A **democrat** is a person who believes in the ideals of democracy, personal freedom, and equality. 民主主义者 ❑ *This is the time for democrats and not dictators.* 这是民主主义者而不是独裁者的时代。

demo·crat·ic ♦♦◇ /dɛməkrætɪk/ 1 ADJ A **democratic** country, government, or political system is governed by representatives who are elected by the people. 民主的 ❑ *Bolivia returned to democratic rule in 1982, after a series of military governments.* 玻利维亚经历了一系列军事政府统治后于1982年恢复了民主统治。 ● **demo·crati·cal·ly** /dɛməkrætɪkli/ ADV 民主地 ❑ *That June, Yeltsin became Russia's first democratically elected president.* 那年6月，叶利钦成为俄罗斯第一位通过民主选举产生的总统。 2 ADJ Something that is **democratic** is based on the idea that everyone should have equal rights and should be involved in making important decisions. 民主精神的 ❑ *Education is the basis of a democratic society.* 教育是民主社会的基础。 ● **demo·crati·cal·ly** ADV 民主精神地 ❑ *This committee will enable decisions to be made democratically.* 这个委员会将保证决策是民主地产生的。

de·mo·graph·ic /dɛməgræfɪk/ (**demographics**) 1 N-PLURAL The **demographics** of a place or society are the statistics relating to the people who live there. 人口统计数据 ❑ *...the changing demographics of the United States.* …变化的美国人口统计数据。 **2** N-SING In business, a **demographic** is a group of people in a society, especially people in a particular age group. 特定年龄段的人口 [BUSINESS] ❑ *The station has won more listeners in the 25-39 demographic.* 这个电台吸引了更多25-39岁年龄段的听众。

▲ de·mol·ish /dɪmɒlɪʃ/ (**demolishes, demolishing, demolished**) **1** V-T To **demolish** something such as a building means to destroy it completely. 彻底摧毁 ❑ *A storm moved directly over the island, demolishing buildings and flooding streets.* 一场暴风雨直扫这个岛屿，彻底摧毁了房屋，淹没了街道。 **2** V-T If you **demolish** someone's ideas or arguments, you prove that they are completely wrong or unreasonable. 驳倒 ❑ *Our intention was quite the opposite – to demolish rumors that have surrounded him since he took office.* 我们的意图恰恰相反——要粉碎自他就职以来就纠缠着他的谣言。

demo·li·tion /dɛməlɪʃᵊn/ (**demolitions**) N-VAR The **demolition** of a structure, for example, a building, is the act of deliberately destroying it, often in order to build something else in its place. 拆毁 ❑ *The project required the total demolition of the old bridge.* 这项工程要求那座旧桥的彻底拆除。

de·mon /dimən/ (**demons**) also **daemon** **1** N-COUNT A **demon** is an evil spirit. 魔鬼 ❑ *...a woman possessed by demons.* …一个被魔鬼附身的女人。 **2** N-COUNT If you approve of someone because they are very skilled at what they do or because they do it energetically, you can say that they do it like a **demon**. 精力过人的人；技艺出众的人 [APPROVAL] ❑ *She worked like a demon and expected everybody else to do the same.* 她工作起来精力过人，而且希望每个人都这么做。 ❑ *He is a demon organizer.* 他是一位高超的组织者。

de·mon·ic /dɪmɒnɪk/ ADJ **Demonic** means coming from or belonging to a demon or being like a demon. 恶魔的；恶魔似的 ❑ *...a demonic grin.* …恶魔般的狞笑。

dem·on·strate ♦◇◇ /dɛmənstreɪt/ (**demonstrates, demonstrating, demonstrated**) **1** V-T To **demonstrate** a fact means to make it clear to people. 证明 ❑ *The study also demonstrated a direct link between obesity and mortality.* 这项研究也证明了肥胖和死亡率之间的直接关系。 ❑ *They are anxious to demonstrate to the voters that they have practical policies.* 他们急于向选民证明他们有切实可行的政策。 **2** V-T If you **demonstrate** a particular skill, quality, or feeling, you show by your actions that you have it. 展现 (才能、品质、感情) ❑ *Have they, for example, demonstrated a commitment to democracy?* 例如，他们展现了对民主的奉献吗？ **3** V-I When people **demonstrate**, they march or gather somewhere to show their opposition to something or their support for something. 游行示威 ❑ *Some 30,000 angry farmers arrived in Brussels yesterday to demonstrate against possible cuts in subsidies.* 昨天大约三万名愤怒的农民到布鲁塞尔游行示威，反对可能的补贴削减。 ❑ *In the cities vast crowds have been demonstrating for change.* 在各城市，已经有大量的群众举行示威游行要求变革。 **4** V-T If you **demonstrate** something, you show people how it works or how to do it. 展示 ❑ *A selection of cosmetic companies will be there to demonstrate their new products.* 一些化妆品公司会在那里展示他们的新产品。

Thesaurus *demonstrate* 另参见：
V. describe, illustrate, prove, show **1** **4**
march, picket, protest **3**

dem·on·stra·tion ♦◇◇ /dɛmənstreɪʃᵊn/ (**demonstrations**) **1** N-COUNT A **demonstration** is a march or gathering which people take part in to show their opposition to something or their support for something. 示威游行；示威集会 ❑ *Riot police used tear gas to break up the demonstration.* 防暴警察使用了催泪瓦斯驱散示威游行。 **2** N-COUNT A **demonstration** of something is a talk by someone who shows you how to do it or how it works. 展示 ❑ *...a cooking demonstration.* …一次烹调展示。 **3** N-COUNT A **demonstration of** a fact or situation is a clear proof of it. 证明 ❑ *It was an unprecedented demonstration of people power by the citizens of Moscow.* 这是莫斯科市民对人民力量史无前例的证明。 **4** N-COUNT A **demonstration of** a quality or feeling is an expression of it. (品质、感情的) 展现 ❑ *There's been no public demonstration of opposition to the president.* 还没有反对总统的公开展现。

de·mon·stra·tor ♦◇◇ /dɛmənstreɪtər/ (**demonstrators**) **1** N-COUNT **Demonstrators** are people who are marching or gathering somewhere to show their opposition to something or their support for something. 游行者；集会示威者 ❑ *I saw the police using tear gas to try and break up a crowd of demonstrators.* 我看到警察使用催泪瓦斯试图驱散示威人群。 **2** N-COUNT A **demonstrator** is a person who shows people how something works or how to do something. 展示者 ❑ *...a demonstrator in a department store.* …一名百货商场的产品展示员。

de·mor·al·ise /dɪmɒrəlaɪz/ [BRIT] → see **demoralize**

de·mor·al·is·ing /dɪmɒrəlaɪzɪŋ/ [BRIT] → see **demoralizing**

de·mor·al·ize /dɪmɔrəlaɪz/ (**demoralizes, demoralizing, demoralized**)

in BRIT, also use **demoralise**

V-T If something **demoralizes** someone, it makes them lose so much confidence in what they are doing that they want to give up. 使泄气 ❑ *Clearly, one of the objectives is to demoralize the enemy troops in any way they can.* 很清楚，目的之一是他们想尽一切办法瓦解敌军的士气。 ● **de·mor·al·ized** ADJ 失去信心的 ❑ *The Bismarck could now move only at a crawl and her crew were exhausted, hopeless, and utterly demoralized.* 俾斯麦号现在只能慢速前进，而全体船员也早已筋疲力尽，悲观失望，完全失去信心。

de·mor·al·iz·ing /dɪmɔrəlaɪzɪŋ/

in BRIT, also use **demoralising**

ADJ If something is **demoralizing**, it makes you lose so much confidence in what you are doing that you want to give up. 使人泄气的 ❑ *Losing their star player was another demoralizing blow for the team.* 对球队来说，失去一名主力球员是又一个挫伤锐气的打击。

de·mote /dɪmoʊt/ (**demotes, demoting, demoted**) V-T If someone **demotes** you, they give you a lower rank or a less important position than you already have, often as a punishment. 使降级；使降职 ❑ *It's very difficult to demote somebody who has been filling in during maternity leave.* 给替代歇产假的人降职是很难的。 ● **de·mo·tion** /dɪmoʊʃᵊn/ N-VAR (**demotions**) 降级；降职 ❑ *He is seeking redress for what he alleges was an unfair demotion.* 他正在为他所声称不公正的降职寻求赔偿。

de·mu·tu·alise /diːmjuːtʃuəlaɪz/ [BRIT] → see **demutualize**

de·mu·tu·alize /dimyutʃuəlaɪz/ (**demutualizes, demutualizing, demutualized**)

in BRIT, also use **demutualise**

V-I If a savings and loan association or an insurance company **demutualizes**, it abandons its mutual status and becomes a different kind of company. 非互助化 [BUSINESS] ❑ *The group won the support of 97 percent of its members for plans to demutualize.* 这家公司非互助化的计划获得了97%的成员的支持。 ● **de·mu·tu·ali·za·tion** /dimyutʃuəlɪzeɪʃᵊn/ N-UNCOUNT 非互助化 ❑ *The 503,000 policyholders who voted for demutualization should be represented.* 应该有人代表这些赞同改变非互助化计划的503000名保险客户。

▲ den /dɛn/ (**dens**) **1** N-COUNT A **den** is the home of certain types of wild animals such as lions or foxes. 兽窝 **2** N-COUNT Your **den** is a quiet room in your house where you can go to study, work, or relax without being disturbed. (学习、工作或放松的)私室 [AM] ❑ *The silver-haired retiree sits in his den surrounded by photos of sailing boats.* 这位银发退休者坐在他的四壁挂满了航船照片的私室里。 **3** N-COUNT A **den** is a secret place where people meet, usually for a dishonest purpose. 进行秘密活动的场所 ❑ *I could provide you with the addresses of at least three illegal drinking dens.* 我能向你提供至少3个秘密非法酒馆的地址。 **4** N-COUNT If you describe a place as a **den of** a particular type of bad or illegal behavior, you mean that a lot of that type of behavior goes on there. (干坏事或违法活动的) 聚集地 ❑ *...this den of iniquity called New York City.* …这个称作纽约市的罪恶之地。 → see **house**

de·ni·al /dɪnaɪəl/ (**denials**) **1** N-VAR A **denial** of something is a statement that it is not true, does not exist, or did not happen. 否认 ❑ *It seems clear that despite official denials, differences of opinion lay behind the ambassador's decision to quit.* 很清楚，尽管官方否认，人们对大使决定辞职还是有不同看法。 **2** N-UNCOUNT The **denial of** something to someone is the act of refusing to let them have it. 拒绝给予 [FORMAL] ❑ *...the denial of visas to international relief workers.* …对国际救济工作人员拒发签证。 **3** N-UNCOUNT In psychology, **denial** is when a person cannot or will not accept an unpleasant truth. (不愉快事实的) 拒绝接受 ❑ *With major life traumas, like losing a loved one, for instance, the mind's first reaction is denial.* 面对人生的重大创痛，例如失去深爱的人，心理的第一反应就是拒绝接受。

den·im /dɛnɪm/ N-UNCOUNT **Denim** is a thick cotton cloth, usually blue, which is used to make clothes. Jeans are made from

denim. 粗斜棉布 ❏ *...a light blue denim jacket.* …一件淡蓝色粗斜棉布夹克衫。
→ see cotton

Word Link *nom ≈ name : denomination, nominal, nominee*

▲ **de·nomi·na·tion** /dɪnɒmɪneɪʃ°n/ (**denominations**) 1 N-COUNT A particular **denomination** is a particular religious group which has slightly different beliefs from other groups within the same faith. 教派 ❏ *Acceptance of women preachers varies greatly from denomination to denomination.* 对于女性牧师的接受，各教派差异很大。 2 N-COUNT The **denomination** of a banknote or coin is its official value. (货币的) 面额 ❏ *She paid in cash, in bills of large denominations.* 她用大面额钞票的现金支付。

★ **de·note** /dɪnoʊt/ (**denotes, denoting, denoted**) 1 V-T If one thing **denotes** another, it is a sign or indication of it. 显示 [FORMAL] ❏ *Red eyes denote strain and fatigue.* 眼睛发红显示紧张和疲劳。 2 V-T What a symbol **denotes** is what it represents. 代表 [FORMAL] ❏ *X denotes those not voting.* X表示那些没有投票的。

Word Link *nounce ≈ reporting : announce, denounce, pronounce*

★ **de·nounce** /dɪnaʊns/ (**denounces, denouncing, denounced**) 1 V-T If you **denounce** a person or an action, you criticize them severely and publicly because you feel strongly that they are wrong or evil. 谴责 ❏ *German leaders all took the opportunity to denounce the attacks and plead for tolerance.* 德国领导人们都藉此机会谴责这些攻击，并且恳请宽容。 2 V-T If you **denounce** someone who has broken a rule or law, you report them to the authorities. 告发 ❏ *They were at the mercy of informers who might at any moment denounce them.* 他们完全受那些随时可能告发他们的告密者的支配。

dense /dɛns/ (**denser, densest**) 1 ADJ Something that is **dense** contains a lot of things or people in a small area. 稠密的 ❏ *Where Bucharest now stands, there once was a large, dense forest.* 现在的布加勒斯特所在地曾经是一片茂密的大森林。 ● **dense·ly** ADV 稠密地 ❏ *Java is a densely populated island.* 爪哇是一个人口稠密的岛屿。 2 ADJ **Dense** fog or smoke is difficult to see through because it is very heavy and dark. (烟、雾等) 浓重的 ❏ *A dense column of smoke rose several miles into the air.* 一柱浓烟升上几英里高的天空。 3 ADJ In science, a **dense** substance is very heavy in relation to its volume. (物质) 密度大的 [TECHNICAL] ❏ *...a small dense star.* …一颗密度大的小恒星。

den·sity /dɛnsɪti/ (**densities**) 1 N-VAR **Density** is the extent to which something is filled or covered with people or things. 密度 ❏ *The region has a very high population density.* 这一地区人口密度很高。 2 N-VAR In science, the **density** of a substance or object is the relation of its mass or weight to its volume. 密度 [TECHNICAL] ❏ *Jupiter's moon Io, whose density is 3.5 grams per cubic centimeter, is all rock.* 木星的卫星木卫一全是岩石，其密度为每立方厘米3.5克。

dent /dɛnt/ (**dents, denting, dented**) 1 V-T If you **dent** the surface of something, you make a hollow area in it by hitting or pressing it. 使产生凹痕 ❏ *Its brass feet dented the carpet's thick pile.* 它的铜支脚在厚厚的地毯绒面上压出了印痕。 2 V-T If something **dents** your confidence or your pride, it makes you realize that you are not as good or successful as you thought. 挫伤 (信心等) ❏ *Record oil prices have dented consumer confidence.* 前所未有的高油价已经挫伤消费者信心。 3 N-COUNT A **dent** is a hollow in the surface of something which has been caused by hitting or pressing it. 凹痕 ❏ *I was convinced there was a dent in the hood which hadn't been there before.* 我确信车盖上有一个以前没有的凹痕。

Word Link *dent ≈ tooth : dental, dentist, dentures*

den·tal /dɛnt°l/ ADJ **Dental** is used to describe things that relate to teeth or to the care and treatment of teeth. 牙齿的；牙科的 [ADJ n] ❏ *Good oral hygiene and regular dental care are important, whatever your age.* 无论年龄大小，良好的口腔卫生和定期的牙齿保健都非常重要。

den·tist /dɛntɪst/ (**dentists**) N-COUNT A **dentist** is a medical practitioner who is qualified to examine and treat people's teeth. 牙科医生 ❏ *Visit your dentist twice a year for a checkup.* 每年看两次牙医做检查。 ● N-SING **The dentist** or **the dentist's** is used to refer to the office or clinic where a dentist works. 牙医诊所 ❏ *It's worse than being at the dentist's.* 这比在牙医诊所还要糟。
→ see teeth

den·tist's of·fice (**dentist's offices**) N-COUNT A **dentist's office** is the room or house where a dentist works. 牙医诊所 [AM]

in BRIT, use **dentist's surgery**

den·tist's sur·gery [BRIT] → see **dentist's office**

den·tures /dɛntʃərz/

The form **denture** is used as a modifier.

N-PLURAL **Dentures** are artificial teeth worn by people who no longer have all their own teeth. 假牙 ❏ *People who wear dentures may sleep better if they leave them in overnight.* 戴假牙的人如果晚上睡觉也戴着假牙，睡眠可能更好。
→ see teeth

de·nun·cia·tion /dɪnʌnsieɪʃ°n/ (**denunciations**) 1 N-VAR **Denunciation of** someone or something is severe public criticism of them. 谴责 ❏ *On September 24, he wrote a stinging denunciation of his critics.* 9月24号，他写了一篇针对他的批评者的言辞犀利的谴责书。 2 N-VAR **Denunciation** is the act of reporting someone who has broken a rule or law to the authorities. 告发 ❏ *...memories of the denunciation of French Jews to the Nazis during the Second World War.* …二战期间向纳粹告发法国犹太人的回忆。

Den·ver boot /dɛnvər but/ (**Denver boots**) N-COUNT A **Denver boot** is a large metal device which is attached to the wheel of an illegally parked car or other vehicle in order to prevent it from being driven away. The driver has to pay to have the device removed. 丹佛钳扣 (用来钳锁违章停车的汽车轮子) [AM]

in BRIT, use **clamp, wheel clamp**

❏ *I watched a couple of cops clap a Denver boot on a green Mercedes.* 我看到几个警察给一辆绿色奔驰车加上丹佛钳扣。

deny ◆◆◇ /dɪnaɪ/ (**denies, denying, denied**) 1 V-T When you **deny** something, you state that it is not true. 否认 ❏ *She denied both accusations.* 她否认对她的两项指控。 ❏ *The government has denied that the authorities have uncovered a plot to assassinate the president.* 政府否认当局已经发现一个暗杀总统的阴谋。 2 V-T If you **deny** someone something that they need or want, you refuse to let them have it. 拒绝给予 ❏ *Two federal courts ruled that the military cannot deny prisoners access to lawyers.* 两联邦法院裁定军方不能拒绝让囚犯聘请律师。

Do not confuse **deny** and **refuse**. If you **deny** something, you say that it is not true. ❏ *The allegation was denied by government spokesmen.* If someone **denies** you something, they do not allow you to have it. ❏ *I never denied her anything.* If you **refuse** to do something, you deliberately do not do it, or you say firmly that you will not do it. ❏ *...people who refuse to change their opinions... He refused to condemn them.* You can **refuse** something that someone offers you. ❏ *The patient has the right to refuse treatment.* If someone does not allow you to have something you ask for, or to do something you have asked to do, you can say that they **refuse** you. ❏ *He can run to Dad for money if I refuse him.*

Word Partnership *deny* 的常用搭配：

V. **confirm** or deny 1
N. deny **a charge, officials** deny 1
deny **access**, deny **entry**, deny **a request** 2

Word Link *ant ≈ one who does, has : defendant, deodorant, occupant*

de·odor·ant /dioʊdərənt/ (**deodorants**) N-MASS **Deodorant** is a substance that you can use on your body to hide or prevent the smell of sweat. 除臭剂

de·part /dɪpɑrt/ (**departs, departing, departed**) 1 V-T/V-I When something or someone **departs from** a place, they leave it and start a trip to another place. You can also say that someone **departs** a place. 离开；起程 ❏ *Flight 43 will depart from Denver at 11:45 a.m. and arrive in Honolulu at 4:12 p.m.* 43号航班将于上午11:45从丹佛起飞，并于下午4:12到达檀香山。 ❏ *In the morning Mr. McDonald departed for Sydney.* 麦克唐纳先生早上起程去了悉尼。 2 V-I If you **depart from** a traditional, accepted, or agreed way of doing something, you do it in a different or unexpected way. 偏离；违背 ❏ *Why is it in this country that we have departed from good educational sense?* 为什么我们这个国家偏离了良好的教育观念？

de·part·ment ◆◆◆ /dɪpɑrtmənt/ (**departments**) N-COUNT A **department** is one of the sections in an organization such as a government, business, or university. A department is also one of the sections in a large store. (政府、企业等机构的) 部；(大学的) 系；(大型商店的) 部门 ❏ *...the U.S. Department of Health and Human Services.* …美国健康和公共事业部。 ❏ *He moved to the sales department.* 他调到了销售部。

de·part·men·tal /dɪpɑrtmɛntᵊl/ ADJ **Departmental** is used to describe the activities, responsibilities, or possessions of a department in a government, company, or other organization. 部门的 [ADJ n] ❑ *The Secretary of Education is right to seek a bigger departmental budget.* 教育部长寻求更多的部门预算是对的。

de·part·ment store (**department stores**) N-COUNT A **department store** is a large store which sells many different kinds of goods. 百货公司 ❑ *...the dazzling window displays of world-famous department stores such as Macy's and Bloomingdales.* …像梅西和布鲁明戴尔那样举世闻名的百货公司的光彩炫目的橱窗陈设。

D

de·par·ture ♦◇◇ /dɪpɑrtʃər/ (**departures**) 1 N-VAR **Departure** or a **departure** is the act of going away from somewhere. 离开 ❑ *...the president's departure for Helsinki.* …总统前往赫尔辛基。 ❑ *They hoped this would lead to the departure of all foreign forces from the country.* 他们希望这会导致所有外国军队从该国的撤离。 2 N-COUNT If someone does something different or unusual, you can refer to their action as a **departure**. 背离 ❑ *Such a move would have been a startling departure from tradition.* 这一举措原本会是对传统习俗惊人的背离。

de·par·ture lounge (**departure lounges**) N-COUNT In an airport, the **departure lounge** is the place where passengers wait before they get onto their plane. 候机厅

Word Link *pend ≈ hanging : appendix, depend, pendant*

de·pend ♦♦◇ /dɪpɛnd/ (**depends, depending, depended**) 1 V-I If you say that one thing **depends on** another, you mean that the first thing will be affected or determined by the second. 根据…而定 ❑ *The cooking time needed depends on the size of the potato.* 烹饪时间长短取决于土豆的大小。 2 V-I If you **depend on** someone or something, you need them in order to be able to survive physically, financially, or emotionally. 依靠 ❑ *He depended on his writing for his income.* 他靠写作谋生。 3 V-I If you can **depend on** a person, organization, or law, you know that they will support you or help you when you need them. 信任 ❑ *"You can depend on me," Cross assured him.* "你可以信任我，"克罗斯向他保证。 4 V-I You use **depend** in expressions such as **it depends** to indicate that you cannot give a clear answer to a question because the answer will be affected or determined by other factors. 视情况而定 ❑ *"But how long can you stay in the house?"—"I don't know. It depends."* "但你能在这屋里待多久？"——"不知道，这要看情况而定。" 5 PHRASE You use **depending on** when you are saying that something varies according to the circumstances mentioned. 根据…而定 ❑ *I tend to have a different answer, depending on the family.* 我倾向根据不同的家庭给出一个不同的答案。

Word Partnership *depend* 的常用搭配：

N. depend **on circumstances**, **outcome will** depend, **survival may/will** depend, depend **on the weather** 1
ADV. depend **largely** 1
PREP. depend **on *someone/something*** 1 – 3

de·pend·able /dɪpɛndəbᵊl/ ADJ If you say that someone or something is **dependable**, you approve of them because you feel that you can be sure that they will always act consistently or sensibly, or do what you need them to do. 可靠的 [APPROVAL] ❑ *He was a good friend, a dependable companion.* 他是个好朋友，一个可以信赖的同伴。

de·pend·ant /dɪpɛndənt/ → see **dependent**

Word Link *ence ≈ state, condition : dependence, excellence, independence*

de·pend·ence /dɪpɛndəns/ 1 N-UNCOUNT Your **dependence on** something or someone is your need for them in order to succeed or be able to survive. 依靠 ❑ *...the city's traditional dependence on tourism.* …这个城市对旅游业的传统依赖。 2 N-UNCOUNT If you talk about drug **dependence** or alcohol **dependence**, you are referring to a situation where someone is addicted to drugs or is an alcoholic. (毒、酒) 瘾 ❑ *French doctors tend to regard drug dependence as a form of deep-rooted psychological disorder.* 法国医生倾向于将毒瘾看作是一种根深蒂固的心理疾病。 3 N-UNCOUNT You talk about the **dependence** of one thing **on** another when the first thing will be affected or determined by the second. 依赖 ❑ *...the dependence of politicians on rich donors to fund their increasingly expensive campaigns.* …政客们为资助他们日益昂贵的竞选活动而对富有的捐赠人的依赖。

▲ **de·pend·en·cy** /dɪpɛndənsi/ (**dependencies**) 1 N-COUNT A **dependency** is a country which is controlled by another country. 附属国 ❑ *...the tiny British dependency of Montserrat in the eastern Caribbean.* …东加勒比地区英国的小附属国蒙特塞拉特岛。 2 N-UNCOUNT You talk about someone's **dependency** when they have a deep emotional, physical, or financial need for a particular person or thing, especially one that you consider excessive or undesirable. 依赖 ❑ *We saw his dependency on his mother and worried that he might not survive long if anything happened to her.* 我们看到他对母亲的依赖，担心万一她有个闪失，他也会活不长。 3 N-VAR If you talk about alcohol **dependency** or chemical **dependency**, you are referring to a situation where someone is an alcoholic or is addicted to drugs. (毒、酒) 瘾 [mainly AM] ❑ *In 1985, he began to show signs of alcohol and drug dependency.* 1985年，他开始表现出酗酒和吸毒成瘾的迹象。

Word Link *ent ≈ one who does, has : dependent, resident, superintendent*

de·pend·ent /dɪpɛndənt/ (**dependents**) also **dependant**

in BRIT, also use **dependant** for meaning 3

1 ADJ To be **dependent on** something or someone means to need them in order to succeed or be able to survive. 依靠的 ❑ *The local economy is overwhelmingly dependent on oil and gas extraction.* 当地经济严重依赖石油和天然气提炼。 2 ADJ If one thing is **dependent on** another, the first thing will be affected or determined by the second. 取决于…的 [v-link ADJ "on/upon" n] ❑ *...companies whose earnings are largely dependent on the performance of the Chinese economy.* …盈利很大程度上取决于中国经济表现的公司。 3 N-COUNT Your **dependents** are the people you support financially, such as your children. 受扶养者 [FORMAL] ❑ *Companies with 200 or more workers must offer health benefits to employees and their dependents.* 拥有200名或200名以上工人的公司必须为其雇员和家属提供医疗福利。

Word Link *pict ≈ painting : depict, picture, picturesque*

de·pict /dɪpɪkt/ (**depicts, depicting, depicted**) V-T To **depict** someone or something means to show or represent them in a work of art such as a drawing or painting. 描绘 ❑ *...a gallery of pictures depicting Lee's most famous battles.* …一批描绘李的最著名战役的图画。

Word Link *ple ≈ filling : complement, complete, deplete*

▲ **de·plete** /dɪplit/ (**depletes, depleting, depleted**) V-T To **deplete** a stock or amount of something means to reduce it. 消耗 [FORMAL] ❑ *...substances that deplete the ozone layer.* …消耗臭氧层的物质。 ● **de·plet·ed** ADJ 耗尽的 ❑ *...Lee's worn and depleted army.* …李的精疲力竭的军队。 ● **de·ple·tion** /dɪpliʃᵊn/ N-UNCOUNT 消耗 ❑ *...the depletion of underground water supplies.* …地下水资源的消耗。

de·plor·able /dɪplɔrəbᵊl/ ADJ If you say that something is **deplorable**, you think that it is very bad and unacceptable. 悲惨的 [FORMAL] ❑ *Many of them live under deplorable conditions.* 他们中的许多人生活在悲惨的条件下。

★ **de·plore** /dɪplɔr/ (**deplores, deploring, deplored**) V-T If you say that you **deplore** something, you think it is very wrong or immoral. 谴责 [FORMAL] ❑ *Muslim and Jewish leaders have issued statements deploring the violence and urging the United Nations to take action.* 伊斯兰教和犹太教领袖已经发表声明谴责该暴力行为，并敦促联合国采取行动。

★ **de·ploy** /dɪplɔɪ/ (**deploys, deploying, deployed**) V-T To **deploy** troops or military resources means to organize or position them so that they are ready to be used. 部署 ❑ *The president said he had no intention of deploying ground troops.* 总统说他无意调遣地面部队。 → see **army**

▲ **de·ploy·ment** /dɪplɔɪmənt/ (**deployments**) N-VAR The **deployment** of troops, resources, or equipment is the organization and positioning of them so that they are ready for quick action. 部署 ❑ *...the deployment of troops into townships.* …把军队移向城镇的部署。

★ **de·port** /dɪpɔrt/ (**deports, deporting, deported**) V-T If a government **deports** someone, usually someone who is not a citizen of that country, it sends them out of the country because they have committed a crime or because it believes they do not have the right to be there. 把…驱逐出境 ❑ *...a government decision earlier this month to deport all illegal immigrants.* …本月早些时候政府一项驱逐所有非法移民的决定。 ● **de·por·ta·tion** /dipɔrteɪʃᵊn/ N-VAR (**deportations**) 驱逐出境 ❑ *...thousands of migrants facing deportation.* …面临被驱逐出境的数以千计的移民。

de·pose /dɪpoʊz/ (**deposes, deposing, deposed**) V-T If a ruler or political leader **is deposed**, they are forced to give up their position. 罢免 [usu passive] ❑ *Mr. Ben Bella was deposed in a coup in 1965.* 本・贝拉先生在1965年的一次政变中被罢免了。

Word Link *pos ≈ placing : deposit, preposition, repository*

de·pos·it ♦◇◇ /dɪpɒzɪt/ (**deposits, depositing, deposited**) 1 N-COUNT A **deposit** is a sum of money which is part of the full price of something, and which you pay when you agree to buy it. 保证金 ❑ *The initial deposit required to open an account is a minimum 100 dollars.* 开户需要的首笔存入额是至少100美元。 2 N-COUNT A **deposit** is a sum of money which is in a bank account or savings account, especially a sum which will be left there for some time. 存款 3 N-COUNT A **deposit** is an amount of a substance that has been left somewhere as a result of a chemical or geological process. 沉积物; 矿床 ❑ *...underground deposits of gold and diamonds.* …黄金和钻石的地下矿床。 4 N-COUNT A **deposit** is a sum of money which you pay when you start renting something. The money is returned to you if you do not damage what you have rented. 押金 [usu sing] ❑ *I put down a $500 security deposit for another apartment.* 我为另一套公寓支付了$500押金。 5 N-COUNT A **deposit** is a sum of money which you put into a bank account. 银行存款 ❑ *She told me I should make a deposit every week and they'd stamp my book.* 她告诉我我每周都要存一次钱，而他们会在我的存折上盖印。 6 V-T If you **deposit** a sum of money, you put it into a bank account or savings account. 存储 ❑ *The customer has to deposit a minimum of $100 monthly.* 顾客每月必须至少存入$100。 7 V-T To **deposit** someone or something somewhere means to put them or leave them there. 放置 ❑ *Mr. Crenshaw deposited the boys and their suitcases on Mr. Peck's lawn.* 克伦肖先生把男孩子和他们的手提箱留在了派克先生的草坪上。 8 V-T If you **deposit** something somewhere, you put it where it will be safe until it is needed again. 寄存 ❑ *You are advised to deposit valuables in the hotel safe.* 建议您将贵重物品寄存在旅馆的保险柜里。
→ see **bank**

de·pos·it ac·count (**deposit accounts**) N-COUNT A **deposit account** is the same as a **savings account**. 定期存款账户 [BRIT]

depo·si·tion /dɛpəzɪʃən/ (**depositions**) N-COUNT A **deposition** is a formal written statement, made for example, by a witness to a crime, which can be used in a court of law if the witness cannot be present. 证词 ❑ *The material would be checked against the depositions from other witnesses.* 这份材料会与其他证人的证词对照加以核对。

▲ **de·pot** /dipoʊ/ (**depots**) 1 N-COUNT A **depot** is a bus station or train station. 公共汽车站; 火车站 [AM] ❑ *She was reunited with her boyfriend in the bus depot of Ozark, Alabama.* 她和她的男朋友在亚拉巴马州的奥扎克汽车站重新团聚了。 2 N-COUNT A **depot** is a place where large amounts of raw materials, equipment, arms, or other supplies are kept until they are needed. 仓库; 库房 ❑ *...food depots.* …食物储藏室。

de·pre·ci·ate /dɪpriʃieɪt/ (**depreciates, depreciating, depreciated**) V-T/V-I If something such as a currency **depreciates** or if something **depreciates** it, it loses some of its original value. 使贬值; 贬值 ❑ *Inflation is rising rapidly; the yuan is depreciating.* 通货膨胀正在迅速上升；人民币正在贬值。 ❑ *The demand for foreign currency depreciates the real value of local currencies.* 对外币的需求降低了当地货币的实际价值。 ● **de·pre·cia·tion** ▲ /dɪpriʃieɪʃən/ N-VAR (**depreciations**) 贬值 ❑ *...miscellaneous costs, including machinery depreciation and wages.* …包括机器折旧和工资在内的杂费。

de·press /dɪprɛs/ (**depresses, depressing, depressed**) 1 V-T If someone or something **depresses** you, they make you feel sad and disappointed. 使沮丧 ❑ *I must admit the state of the country depresses me.* 我必须承认国家的形势令我沮丧。 2 V-T If something **depresses** prices, wages, or figures, it causes them to become less. 使降低 ❑ *The stronger U.S. dollar depressed sales.* 更坚挺的美元使销售量下降。

de·pressed /dɪprɛst/ 1 ADJ If you are **depressed**, you are sad and feel that you cannot enjoy anything, because your situation is so difficult and unpleasant. 沮丧的 ❑ *She's been very depressed and upset about this whole situation.* 整个境况使她感到心烦意乱，意志消沉。 2 ADJ A **depressed** place or industry does not have enough business or employment to be successful. 萧条的 ❑ *Many states already have enterprise zones and legislation that encourage investment in depressed areas.* 许多州都已经有鼓励在萧条地区投资的工业区和立法。

de·press·ing /dɪprɛsɪŋ/ ADJ Something that is **depressing** makes you feel sad and disappointed. 令人沮丧的 ❑ *Yesterday's unemployment figures were as depressing as those of the previous 22 months.* 昨天的失业数字和前22个月的一样令人沮丧。 ● **de·press·ing·ly** ADV 令人沮丧地 ❑ *It all sounded depressingly familiar to Janet.* 这在珍妮特听来熟悉得令人沮丧。

de·pres·sion ♦◇◇ /dɪprɛʃən/ (**depressions**) 1 N-VAR **Depression** is a mental state in which you are sad and feel that you cannot enjoy anything, because your situation is so difficult and unpleasant. 抑郁 ❑ *Mr. Thomas was suffering from depression.* 托马斯先生当时正受抑郁症折磨。 2 N-COUNT A **depression** is a time when there is very little economic activity, which causes a lot of unemployment and poverty. 萧条期 ❑ *He never forgot the hardships he witnessed during the Great Depression of the 1930s.* 他从未忘记20世纪30年代经济大萧条时期他所目睹的艰辛。 3 N-COUNT A **depression** in a surface is an area which is lower than the parts surrounding it. 洼地 ❑ *...an area pockmarked by rain-filled depressions.* …一个到处都是积满雨水的洼坑的地带。 4 N-COUNT A **depression** is a mass of air that has a low pressure and that often causes rain. 低气压 ❑ *To the northwest lies a depression with clouds and rain.* 西北方向有一个云雨密布的低气压。
→ see **hurricane**

dep·ri·va·tion /dɛprɪveɪʃən/ (**deprivations**) N-VAR If you suffer **deprivation**, you do not have or are prevented from having something that you want or need. 剥夺; 匮乏 ❑ *Millions more suffer from serious sleep deprivation caused by long work hours.* 还有数百万人由于工作时数长导致他们严重睡眠不足。

★ **de·prive** /dɪpraɪv/ (**deprives, depriving, deprived**) V-T If you **deprive** someone **of** something that they want or need, you take it away from them, or you prevent them from having it. 剥夺; 使不能有 ❑ *They've been deprived of the fuel necessary to heat their homes.* 他们无法得到住房取暖必需的燃料。

de·prived /dɪpraɪvd/ ADJ **Deprived** people or people from **deprived** areas do not have the things that people consider to be essential in life, for example, acceptable living conditions or education. 贫困的 ❑ *...probably the most severely deprived children in the country.* …可能是该国最贫困的儿童们。

dept. (**depts.**) **Dept.** is used as a written abbreviation for **department**, usually in the name of a particular department. **department**的缩写，常用于名称当中

in BRIT, use **dept**

❑ *...the Philadelphia Police Dept.* …费城警察局。

depth ♦◇◇ /dɛpθ/ (**depths**) 1 N-VAR The **depth** of something such as a river or hole is the distance downward from its top surface, or between its upper and lower surfaces. 深度 ❑ *The depth of the shaft is 520 yards.* 这个通道的深度是520码。 ❑ *The smaller lake ranges from five to fourteen feet in depth.* 这个较小的湖的深度在5至14英尺之间。 ❑ *The depth of a standard straight valance is usually about 12 inches.* 标准直边床幔的高度通常是12英寸左右。 2 N-VAR The **depth** of something such as a closet or drawer is the distance between its front surface and its back. 厚度 3 N-VAR If an emotion is very strongly or intensely felt, you can talk about its **depth.** (感情的) 深厚 ❑ *I am well aware of the depth of feeling that exists in Ontario.* 我深知安大略人情感的深厚。 4 N-UNCOUNT The **depth** of a situation is its extent and seriousness. 强烈程度 ❑ *The country's leadership had underestimated the depth of the crisis.* 这个国家的领导层低估了这次危机的严重程度。 5 N-UNCOUNT The **depth** of someone's knowledge is the great amount that they know. (知识的) 渊博 ❑ *We felt at home with her and were impressed with the depth of her knowledge.* 我们和她一见如故，并且被她知识的渊博所折服。 6 N-PLURAL **The depths** are places that are a long way below the surface of the sea or earth. (指远离表面) 深处 [LITERARY] ❑ *Leaves, brown with long immersion, rose to the surface and vanished back into the depths.* 长时间浸泡而成褐色的叶子浮上了水面，又消失在了水的深处。 7 N-PLURAL If you talk about **the depths of** an area, you mean the parts of it which are very far from the edge. (指距地区边缘) 深处 ❑ *...the depths of the countryside.* …乡村深处。 8 N-PLURAL If you are **in the depths of** an unpleasant emotion, you feel that emotion very strongly. (不快情绪的) 深重 ❑ *I was in the depths of despair when the baby was terribly sick every day, and was losing weight.* 宝宝每天都病得很重并且体重在下降的时候，我陷入绝望的深处。 9 PHRASE If you deal with a subject **in depth**, you deal with it very thoroughly and consider all the aspects of it.

全面透彻地 ❑ *We will discuss these three areas in depth.* 我们将全面透彻地讨论这3个领域。 **10** → see also **in-depth** **11** PHRASE If you say that someone is **out of** their **depth**, you mean that they are in a situation that is much too difficult for them to be able to cope with it. 力所不及 ❑ *Mr. Gibson is clearly intellectually out of his depth.* 吉布森先生显然在智能上有所不及。 **12** PHRASE If you are **out of** your **depth**, you are in water that is deeper than you are tall, with the result that you cannot stand up with your head above water. 在没顶的水中 ❑ *Somehow I got out of my depth in the pool.* 不知什么原因我在池子里没了顶。

dep·u·ty ◆◆◇ /dɛpyəti/ (**deputies**) **1** N-COUNT A **deputy** is the second most important person in an organization such as a business or government department. Someone's deputy often acts on their behalf when they are not there. 副手 ❑ *...Jack Lang, France's minister for culture, and his deputy, Catherine Tasca.* …法国文化部长杰克·朗和他的副手凯瑟琳·塔斯卡。 **2** N-COUNT In some legislatures, the elected members are called **deputies**. 议员 ❑ *The president appealed to deputies to approve the plan quickly.* 总统呼吁议员们迅速通过该方案。 **3** N-COUNT A **deputy** is a police officer. 警官 [AM] ❑ *Robyn asked the deputy on duty if she could speak with Sheriff Adkins.* 萝宾问值班警官她能否跟县治安官阿德金斯谈话。 **4** N-COUNT A **deputy** is a person appointed to act on another person's behalf. 代理人 ❑ *His brother was acting as his deputy in America.* 他的兄弟充当他在美洲的代理人。

★ **de·rail** /direɪl/ (**derails, derailing, derailed**) **1** V-T To **derail** something such as a plan or a series of negotiations means to prevent it from continuing as planned. 打乱(原定计划) [JOURNALISM] ❑ *The present wave of political killings is the work of people trying to derail peace talks.* 现在的政治谋杀浪潮是那些试图破坏和平谈判进程的人所为。 **2** V-T/V-I If a train **is derailed** or if it **derails**, it comes off the track on which it is running. 脱轨 ❑ *At least six people were killed and about twenty injured when a train was derailed in an isolated mountain region.* 火车在一片偏僻的山区脱轨，导致至少六人死亡，约二十人受伤。

de·ranged /direɪndʒd/ ADJ Someone who is **deranged** behaves in a wild and uncontrolled way, often as a result of mental illness. 精神错乱的 ❑ *Three years ago today a deranged man shot and killed 14 people in the main square.* 3年前的今天，一个精神错乱者在主广场上开枪打死了14个人。

de·regu·late /diregyəleɪt/ (**deregulates, deregulating, deregulated**) V-T To **deregulate** something means to remove controls and regulations from it. 解除管制 ❑ *...the need to deregulate the U.S. airline industry.* …解除对美国航空业管制的需要。

★ **de·regu·la·tion** /diregyəleɪʃən/ N-UNCOUNT **Deregulation** is the removal of controls and restrictions in a particular area of business or trade. (在商贸领域) 解除管制 [BUSINESS] ❑ *Since deregulation, banks are permitted to set their own interest rates.* 解除管制后，银行获准自定利率。

der·elict /dɛrɪlɪkt/ (**derelicts**) **1** ADJ A place or building that is **derelict** is empty and in a bad state of repair because it has not been used or lived in for a long time. 废弃的 ❑ *Her body was found dumped in a derelict warehouse less than a mile from her home.* 她的尸体被发现丢在离她家不到一英里的一座废弃的仓库里。 **2** N-COUNT A **derelict** is a person who has no home or job and who has to live on the streets. 无家可归者; 无业游民 [FORMAL] ❑ *I had never seen so many derelicts in one place.* 我从未在一个地方见到过这么多无家可归的人。

Word Link	*rid, ris ≈ laughing : deride, derision, ridicule*

de·ride /dɪraɪd/ (**derides, deriding, derided**) V-T If you **deride** someone or something, you say that they are stupid or have no value. 嘲笑 [FORMAL] ❑ *Critics derided the move as too little, too late.* 批评家们嘲笑这一行动规模太小，来得太迟。

de·ri·sion /dɪrɪʒən/ N-UNCOUNT If you treat someone or something with **derision**, you express contempt for them. 嘲弄 ❑ *He tried to calm them, but was greeted with shouts of derision.* 他试图使他们安静下来，却遭到他们大呼小叫的嘲弄。

de·ri·sive /dɪraɪsɪv/ ADJ A **derisive** noise, expression, or remark expresses contempt. 嘲弄的 ❑ *There was a short, derisive laugh.* 响起一阵短促的嘲笑声。

▲ **de·riva·tive** /dɪrɪvətɪv/ (**derivatives**) N-COUNT A **derivative** is something which has been developed or obtained from something else. 衍生物 ❑ *...a poppy-seed derivative similar to heroin.* …一种类似于海洛因的罂粟种子衍生物。

de·rive /dɪraɪv/ (**derives, deriving, derived**) **1** V-T If you **derive** something such as pleasure or benefit **from** a person or from something, you get it from them. 获得 [FORMAL] ❑ *Mr. Ying is one of those happy people who derive pleasure from helping others.* 英先生是那种助人为乐的快活人。 **2** V-T/V-I If you say that something such as a word or feeling **derives** or **is derived from** something else, you mean that it comes from that thing. 衍生 ❑ *The name Anastasia is derived from a Greek word meaning "of the resurrection."* 阿纳斯塔西娅这个名字是从一个意为"复活"的希腊词语衍生而来的。

de·roga·tory /dɪrɒgətɔri/ ADJ If you make a **derogatory** remark or comment about someone or something, you express your low opinion of them. 贬低的 ❑ *He refused to withdraw derogatory remarks made about his boss.* 他拒绝收回对自己老板的贬抑之言。

Word Link	*de ≈ from, down, away : deflate, descend, detach*

Word Link	*scend ≈ climbing : ascend, condescend, descend*

de·scend /dɪsɛnd/ (**descends, descending, descended**) **1** V-T/V-I If you **descend** or if you **descend** a staircase, you move downward from a higher to a lower level. 下(楼梯等); 下来 [FORMAL] ❑ *Things are cooler and more damp as we descend to the cellar.* 我们往地窖中下得越深，里面就越冷、越潮湿。 **2** V-I If a large group of people arrive to see you, especially if their visit is unexpected or causes you a lot of work, you can say that they **have descended on** you. 突然到访 ❑ *Some 3,000 city officials will descend on Capitol Hill on Tuesday to lobby for more money.* 大约三千名市政官员将于周二突访美国国会山，为争取更多经费游说。 **3** V-I When you want to emphasize that the situation that someone is entering is very bad, you can say that they **are descending into** that situation. 陷入 [EMPHASIS] ❑ *He was ultimately overthrown and the country descended into chaos.* 他最终被推翻，国家陷入了混乱。 **4** V-I If you say that someone **descends to** behavior which you consider unacceptable, you are expressing your disapproval of the fact that they do it. 堕落 [DISAPPROVAL] ❑ *We're not going to descend to such methods.* 我们不会堕落到使用这些方式的份上。

★ **de·scend·ant** /dɪsɛndənt/ (**descendants**) also **descendent** **1** N-COUNT Someone's **descendants** are the people in later generations who are related to them. 后代 ❑ *They are descendants of the original English and Scottish settlers.* 他们是最初的英格兰和苏格兰移民的后裔。 **2** N-COUNT Something modern which developed from an older thing can be called a **descendant of** it. 衍生物 ❑ *His design was a descendant of a 1956 device.* 他的设计是1956年一个装置的衍生物。

de·scend·ed /dɪsɛndɪd/ ADJ A person who is **descended from** someone who lived a long time ago is directly related to them. 后裔的 [v-link ADJ "from" n] ❑ *Anna is descended from pioneers who settled in Colorado in 1898.* 安娜是1898年在科罗拉多州定居的先驱们的后裔。

de·scend·ent /dɪsɛndənt/ → see **descendant**

★ **de·scent** /dɪsɛnt/ (**descents**) **1** N-VAR A **descent** is a movement from a higher to a lower level or position. 下降 ❑ *Sixteen of the youngsters set off for help, but during the descent three collapsed in the cold and rain.* 那些年轻人中有16人出发寻求帮助，但在下山过程中有3人在寒冷和阴雨中倒下了。 **2** N-COUNT A **descent** is a surface that slopes downward, for example, the side of a steep hill. 下坡 ❑ *On the descents, cyclists spin past cars, freewheeling downhill at tremendous speed.* 在下坡道上，自行车手们飞快地掠过汽车，靠惯性极速冲下山去。 **3** N-SING When you want to emphasize that a situation becomes very bad, you can talk about someone's or something's **descent** into that situation. 沉沦; 没落 [EMPHASIS] ❑ *...his swift descent from respected academic to struggling small businessman.* …他从受人尊敬的学者到挣扎求存的小商人的迅速沦落。 **4** N-UNCOUNT You use **descent** to talk about a person's family background, for example, their nationality or social status. 出身 [FORMAL] ❑ *All the contributors were of African descent.* 所有捐助者都是非洲血统。

de·scribe ◆◆◆ /dɪskraɪb/ (**describes, describing, described**) **1** V-T If you **describe** a person, object, event, or situation, you say what they are like or what happened. 描述 ❑ *We asked her to describe what kind of things she did in her spare time.* 我们请她描述她在闲暇时做些什么。 ❑ *She read a poem by Carver which describes their life together.* 她读了一首卡弗描写他们在一起生活的诗。 **2** V-T If a person

describes someone or something **as** a particular thing, he or she believes that they are that thing and says so. 讲成；称作 ❑ *He described it as an extraordinarily tangled and complicated tale.* 他把它讲成了一个格外错综复杂的故事。 ❑ *Even his closest allies describe him as forceful, aggressive, and determined.* 甚至他最亲密的同盟者们都说他强势、好斗且坚决。

> When you use **describe** with an indirect object, you must put **to** in front of the indirect object. ❑ *He later described to me what he had found... Could you describe the man to the police?* You do not say, for example, "He described me what he had found."

de·scrip·tion ♦◇◇ /dɪskrɪpʃ^ə^n/ **(descriptions)** 1 N-VAR A **description** of someone or something is an account which explains what they are or what they look like. 描述 ❑ *Police have issued a description of the man who was aged between fifty and sixty.* 警方已已公布了这一年龄在50至60之间的男子的相貌特征。 ❑ *The paper provides a detailed description of how to create human embryos by cloning.* 这篇论文对如何通过克隆制造人类胚胎提供详细的描述。 2 N-SING If something is **of** a particular **description**, it belongs to the general class of items that are mentioned. 属…种类 ❑ *Events of this description occurred daily.* 这类事件每天都有发生。 3 N-UNCOUNT You can say that something is **beyond description**, or that it **defies description**, to emphasize that it is very unusual, impressive, terrible, or extreme. 无法形容 [EMPHASIS] ❑ *His face is weary beyond description.* 他脸上的疲惫无法形容。

Thesaurus *description* 另参见：
N. account, characterization, summary 1
category, class, kind, type 2

Word Partnership *description* 的常用搭配：
ADJ. **accurate** description, **brief** description, **detailed** description, **physical** description, **vague** description 1
V. **fit a** description, **give a** description, **match a** description 1

de·scrip·tive /dɪskrɪptɪv/ ADJ **Descriptive** language or writing indicates what someone or something is like. 描述的 ❑ *The group adopted the simpler, more descriptive title of Angina Support Group.* 该组织采用了更简单、更具描述性的名称——心绞痛支持组织。

des·ecrate /dɛsɪkreɪt/ **(desecrates, desecrating, desecrated)** V-T If someone **desecrates** something which is considered to be holy or very special, they deliberately damage or insult it. 亵渎 ❑ *She shouldn't have desecrated the picture of a religious leader.* 她不该亵渎宗教领袖的肖像。 ●**des·ecra·tion** /dɛsɪkreɪʃ^ə^n/ N-UNCOUNT 亵渎 ❑ *The whole area has been shocked by the desecration of the cemetery.* 整个地区都被对公墓的亵渎震惊了。

d

des·ert ♦◇◇ **(deserts, deserting, deserted)**

> The noun is usually pronounced /dɛzərt/. The verb and the noun in meaning 6 are pronounced /dɪzɜrt/ and are hyphenated de·sert.

> 名词通常读作 /dɛzərt/。义项6的名词和动词均读作 /dɪzɜrt/ 且音节划分为**de·sert**。

1 N-VAR A **desert** is a large area of land, usually in a hot region, where there is almost no water, rain, trees, or plants. 沙漠 ❑ *...the Sahara Desert.* …撒哈拉沙漠。 2 V-T If people or animals **desert** a place, they leave it and it becomes empty. 遗弃 ❑ *Poor farmers are deserting their parched farm fields and coming here looking for jobs.* 贫穷的农民丢下干旱的农田，来这里寻找工作。 ●**de·sert·ed** ADJ 被遗弃的 ❑ *She led them into a deserted sidestreet.* 她领他们来到一条废弃的小巷。 3 V-T If someone **deserts** you, they go away and leave you, and no longer help or support you. 抛弃 ❑ *Mrs. Roding's husband deserted her years ago.* 罗丁太太的丈夫数年前抛弃了她。 ●**de·ser·tion** /dɪzɜrʃ^ə^n/ **(desertions)** N-VAR 遗弃 ❑ *It was a long time since she'd referred to her father's desertion.* 自从她谈到被父亲遗弃已经很长时间了。 4 V-T/V-I If you **desert** something that you support, use, or are involved with, you stop supporting it, using it, or being involved with it. 放弃 ❑ *The sport is being written off as boring and predictable and the fans are deserting in droves.* 这项运动因为枯燥且易于预测而不再吸引人，爱好者们正成批地退出。 ❑ *He was pained to see many youngsters deserting kibbutz life.* 他痛心地看到许多年轻人放弃集体农场生活。 ●**de·ser·tion** N-VAR 放弃 ❑ *They blamed his proposal for much of the mass desertion by the Republican electorate.* 他们把共和党选民的大批离弃

Picture Dictionary desert

主要原因归咎于他的提议。**5** V-T/V-I If someone **deserts**, or **deserts** a job, especially a job in the armed forces, they leave that job without permission. 开小差 ❑ *He was a second lieutenant in the army until he deserted.* 他在开小差之前是个少尉。 ❑ *He deserted from army intelligence last month.* 他上个月从军队情报部门开了小差。 **6** PHRASE If you say that someone got their **just deserts**, you mean that they deserved the unpleasant things that happened to them, because they did something bad. 应受的惩罚 [FEELINGS] ❑ *At the end of the book the child's true identity is discovered, and the bad guys get their just deserts.* 在书的结尾，这孩子的真实身份被揭开了，那些坏人也受到了应有的惩罚。

→ see Picture Dictionary: **desert**

de·sert·er /dɪzɜːrtər/ (**deserters**) N-COUNT A **deserter** is someone who leaves their job in the armed forces without permission. 逃兵 ❑ *Peters had two deserters followed and shot.* 彼得斯派人追赶并开枪打死了那两个逃兵。

de·serve ♦◇◇ /dɪzɜːrv/ (**deserves, deserving, deserved**) V-T If you say that a person or thing **deserves** something, you mean that they should have it or receive it because of their actions or qualities. 应得 ❑ *Government officials clearly deserve some of the blame as well.* 政府官员们显然也应受到某些谴责。 ❑ *These people deserve to make more than the minimum wage.* 这些人应该得到高于最低工资的报酬。

Word Partnership	*deserve* 的常用搭配:
N.	deserve **a chance**, deserve **credit**, deserve **recognition**, deserve **respect**
V.	**don't** deserve, deserve **to know**

de·serv·ing /dɪzɜːrvɪŋ/ ADJ If you describe a person, organization, or cause as **deserving**, you mean that you think they should be helped. 值得帮助的 ❑ *The money saved could be used for more deserving causes.* 省下的钱可以用于更需要帮助的事业。

de·sign ♦♦♦ /dɪzaɪn/ (**designs, designing, designed**) **1** V-T When someone **designs** a garment, building, machine, or other object, they plan it and make a detailed drawing of it from which it can be built or made. 设计 ❑ *They wanted to design a machine that was both attractive and practical.* 他们想设计一台既美观又实用的机器。 **2** V-T When someone **designs** a survey, policy, or system, they plan and prepare it, and decide on all the details of it. 策划 ❑ *We may be able to design a course to suit your particular needs.* 我们也许能策划一个课程来满足你的特定需求。 **3** N-UNCOUNT **Design** is the process and art of planning and making detailed drawings of something. 设计 ❑ *He was a born mechanic with a flair for design.* 他天生是个有设计才华的机械师。 **4** N-UNCOUNT The **design** of something is the way in which it has been planned and made. 设计 ❑ *...a new design of clock.* …一种新款时钟。 **5** N-COUNT A **design** is a drawing which someone produces to show how they would like something to be built or made. 设计图 ❑ *When Bernardello asked them to build him a home, they drew up the design in a week.* 伯纳德罗请他们给他建一所房子，他们在一周内画出了设计图。 **6** N-COUNT A **design** is a pattern of lines, flowers, or shapes which is used to decorate something. 图案 ❑ *Many pictures have been based on simple geometric designs.* 许多图画是以简单的几何图案为基础的。 **7** V-T PASSIVE If something **is designed** for a particular purpose, it is intended for that purpose. 旨在 ❑ *This project is designed to help homeless people.* 这个项目旨在帮助无家可归的人。

→ see **architecture, quilt**

★ **des·ig·nate** (**designates, designating, designated**)

> The verb is pronounced /dɛzɪgneɪt/. The adjective is pronounced /dɛzɪgnɪt/.

> 动词读作 /dɛzɪgneɪt/。形容词读作 /dɛzɪgnɪt/。

1 V-T When you **designate** someone or something **as** a particular thing, you formally give them that description or name. 命名 ❑ *...a man interviewed in one of our studies whom we shall designate as E.* …一个我们在一项研究中采访过并会将其命名为E的男人。 ❑ *There are efforts under way to designate the bridge a historic landmark.* 在努力把这座桥定为历史地标。 **2** V-T If something **is designated for** a particular purpose, it is set aside for that purpose. 指定 [usu passive] ❑ *Some of the rooms were designated as offices.* 其中一些房间是被指定用作办公室的。 **3** V-T When you **designate** someone **as** something, you formally choose them to do that particular job. 指派 ❑ *Designate someone as the spokesperson.* 指派某人为发言人。 **4** ADJ **Designate** is used to describe someone who has been formally chosen to do a particular job, but has not yet started doing it. 已任命但未就职的 [n ADJ] ❑ *Japan's prime minister-designate is completing his cabinet today.* 日本即将上任的首相今天将完成他的内阁组建。

de·sign·er ♦◇◇ /dɪzaɪnər/ (**designers**) **1** N-COUNT A **designer** is a person whose job is to design things by making drawings of them. 设计师 ❑ *Carolyne is a fashion designer.* 卡罗琳是位时装设计师。 **2** ADJ **Designer** clothes or **designer** labels are expensive, fashionable clothes made by a famous designer, rather than being made in large quantities in a factory. 名师设计的 [ADJ n] ❑ *He wears designer clothes and drives an antique car.* 他穿着名师设计的服装，开着一辆老爷车。 **3** ADJ You can use **designer** to describe things that are worn or bought because they are fashionable. 时尚的 [ADJ n] [INFORMAL] ❑ *She sat up and removed her designer sunglasses.* 她坐起来，摘掉她的时尚墨镜。

de·sign·er baby (**designer babies**) also **designer child** N-COUNT People sometimes refer to a baby that has developed from an embryo with certain desired characteristics as a **designer baby**. (由已具备某些想要的特征的胚胎发育而来的) 特设婴儿 [mainly JOURNALISM] ❑ *A couple with a terminally ill child want to create a designer baby that could save the boy's life.* 一对有个绝症患儿的父母想创造一个特设婴儿来挽救这男孩儿的生命。

de·sir·able /dɪzaɪərəbᵊl/ **1** ADJ Something that is **desirable** is worth having or doing because it is useful, necessary, or popular. 值得拥有的；值得做的 ❑ *Prolonged negotiation was not desirable.* 拖得很长的谈判是不受欢迎的。 ● ★ **de·sir·abil·ity** /dɪzaɪərəbɪlɪti/ N-UNCOUNT 可取性 ❑ *...the desirability of democratic reform.* …民主改革的可取性。 **2** ADJ Someone who is **desirable** is considered to be sexually attractive. 性感的 ❑ *...the young women of his own age whom his classmates thought most desirable.* …与他同龄的、在他的同学们看来最性感的年轻女子。 ● **de·sir·abil·ity** N-UNCOUNT 性感 ❑ *He had not at all overrated Veronica's desirability.* 他丝毫没有高估韦罗妮卡的性感。

de·sire ♦♦◇ /dɪzaɪər/ (**desires, desiring, desired**) **1** N-COUNT A **desire** is a strong wish to do or have something. 愿望 ❑ *I had a strong desire to help and care for people.* 我有一股强烈的帮助和关心别人的愿望。 **2** V-T If you **desire** something, you want it. 想要 [no cont] [FORMAL] ❑ *She had remarried and desired a child with her new husband.* 她再婚了，想跟新任丈夫生一个孩子。 ● **de·sired** ADJ 想要的；渴望的 [ADJ n] ❑ *You may find that just threatening this course of action will produce the desired effect.* 你会发现仅仅是威胁要采取这个行动就能产生想要的效果。 **3** N-UNCOUNT **Desire** for someone is a strong feeling of wanting to have sex with them. 性欲 ❑ *It's common to lose your sexual desire when you have your first child.* 有了第一个孩子后，丧失性欲是常见的事。

Word Partnership	*desire* 的常用搭配:
N.	**heart's** desire **1**
V.	**have no** desire, **satisfy a** desire **1**
	desire **to change** **1** **2**
	express desire **1** **3**
ADJ.	**strong** desire **1**
	sexual desire **3**

★ **de·sir·ous** /dɪzaɪərəs/ ADJ If you are **desirous of** doing something or **desirous of** something, you want to do it very much or want it very much. 渴望的 [v-link ADJ "of" -ing/n] [FORMAL] ❑ *The enemy is so desirous of peace that he will agree to any terms.* 敌人如此渴望和平，他会同意任何条件。

desk ♦♦◇ /dɛsk/ (**desks**) **1** N-COUNT A **desk** is a table, often with drawers, which you sit at to write or work. 书桌；办公桌 **2** N-SING The place in a hotel, hospital, airport, or other building where you check in or obtain information is referred to as a particular **desk**. (接待、咨询) 台 ❑ *I told the girl at the reception desk that I was terribly sorry, but I was half an hour late.* 我对接待服务台的女孩说我很抱歉，迟到了半小时。 **3** N-SING A particular department of a broadcasting company, or of a newspaper or magazine company, can be referred to as a particular **desk**. …部 ❑ *Let our news desk know as quickly as possible.* 尽快通知我们的新闻部。

→ see **office**

desk clerk (**desk clerks**) N-COUNT A **desk clerk** is someone who works at the main desk in a hotel. (旅馆总台) 接待员 [AM]

> in BRIT, use **receptionist**

de·skill /diskɪl/ (**deskills, deskilling, deskilled**) V-T If workers **are deskilled**, they no longer need special skills to do their work, especially because of modern methods of production. (因先进生产方式) 使不再需要专业技能 [oft passive] ❑ *Administrative staff may be deskilled through increased automation and efficiency.* 随着自动化程度和效率提高，行政人员可能不再需要专业技能。

desk·top /dɛsktɒp/ (**desktops**) also **desk-top** 1 ADJ **Desktop** computers are a convenient size for using on a desk or table, but are not designed to be portable. 台式的 (电脑) [ADJ n] ❑ *When launched, the Macintosh was the smallest desktop computer ever produced.* 麦金塔电脑在投放市场时，是当时最小的台式电脑。 2 N-COUNT A **desktop** is a desktop computer. 台式电脑 ❑ *We have stopped making desktops because no one is making money from them.* 我们已经停止生产台式电脑了，因为不赚钱。 3 N-COUNT The **desktop** of a computer is the display of icons that you see on the screen when the computer is ready to use. (电脑) 桌面 ❑ *A dramatic full-sized lightning bolt will then fill your screen's desktop.* 然后一道突如其来的巨大霹雳会充满你的整个电脑桌面。

desk·top pub·lish·ing N-UNCOUNT **Desktop publishing** is the production of printed materials such as newspapers and magazines using a desktop computer and a laser printer, rather than using conventional printing methods. The abbreviation **DTP** is also used. 桌面出版

▲ **deso·late** /dɛsəlɪt/ 1 ADJ A **desolate** place is empty of people and lacking in comfort. 荒凉的 ❑ *...a desolate landscape of flat green fields.* …一片荒凉平坦的绿地景观。 2 ADJ If someone is **desolate**, they feel very sad, alone, and without hope. 感到凄凉的 [LITERARY] ❑ *He was desolate without her.* 没有她，他感到很凄凉。

deso·la·tion /dɛsəleɪʃᵊn/ 1 N-UNCOUNT **Desolation** is a feeling of great unhappiness and hopelessness. 凄凉 ❑ *Kozelek expresses his sense of desolation absolutely without self-pity.* 科泽来克毫不自怜地表达了他内心的凄凉。 2 N-UNCOUNT If you refer to **desolation** in a place, you mean that it is empty and frightening, for example, because it has been destroyed by a violent force or army. 荒凉 [DISAPPROVAL] ❑ *We looked out upon a scene of desolation and ruin.* 我们向外望着一片荒凉、破败的景象。

des·pair /dɪspɛər/ (**despairs, despairing, despaired**) 1 N-UNCOUNT **Despair** is the feeling that everything is wrong and that nothing will improve. 绝望 ❑ *I looked at my wife in despair.* 我绝望地看着妻子。 2 V-I If you **despair**, you feel that everything is wrong and that nothing will improve. 绝望 ❑ *"Oh, I despair sometimes," he says in mock sorrow.* "哦，我有时会绝望。" 他假装悲伤地说。 3 V-I If you **despair of** something, you feel that there is no hope that it will happen or improve. If you **despair of** someone, you feel that there is no hope that they will improve. 对…绝望 ❑ *He wished to earn a living through writing but despaired of doing so.* 他原想通过写作谋生，但却对此绝望了。

★ **des·patch** /dɪspætʃ/ [BRIT] → see **dispatch**

Word Link *sper ≈ hope : desperate, exasperate, prosperity*

des·per·ate ♦◇◇ /dɛspərɪt/ 1 ADJ If you are **desperate**, you are in such a bad situation that you are willing to try anything to change it. 不顾一切的 ❑ *Troops are needed to help get food into Kosovo where people are in desperate need.* 需要军队协助将食物运进科索沃，那里的人们迫切需要食物。 ● **des·per·ate·ly** ADV 不顾一切地 [ADV with v] ❑ *Thousands are desperately trying to leave their battered homes and villages.* 成千上万的人们正不顾一切地试图逃离他们满目疮痍的家园和村庄。 2 ADJ If you are **desperate for** something or **desperate to** do something, you want or need it very much indeed. 极度渴望的 [v-link ADJ] ❑ *They'd been married nearly four years and June was desperate to start a family.* 他们结婚快4年了，琼非常想生个孩子。 ● **des·per·ate·ly** ADV 极其 [ADV with v] ❑ *He was a boy who desperately needed affection.* 他是个极度需要关爱的孩子。 3 ADJ A **desperate** situation is very difficult, serious, or dangerous. 危急的 ❑ *India's United Nations ambassador said the situation is desperate.* 印度驻联合国大使说局势危急。

Word Partnership *desperate* 的常用搭配:

V.	**sound** desperate 1 **grow** desperate 1–3
N.	desperate **act**, desperate **attempt**, desperate **measures**, desperate **need**, desperate **struggle** 1 desperate **situation** 3

des·pera·tion /dɛspəreɪʃᵊn/ N-UNCOUNT **Desperation** is the feeling that you have when you are in such a bad situation that you will try anything to change it. 不顾一切 ❑ *This feeling of desperation and helplessness was common to most of the refugees.* 这种不顾一切和无助的感觉在大多数难民中很常见。

des·pic·able /dɛspɪkəbᵊl/ ADJ If you say that a person or action is **despicable**, you are emphasizing that they are extremely nasty, cruel, or evil. 可鄙的 [EMPHASIS] ❑ *The minister, who visited the scene a few hours after the explosion, said it was a despicable crime.* 部长在爆炸发生后几小时视察现场后说，这是一桩可鄙的罪行。

★ **des·pise** /dɪspaɪz/ (**despises, despising, despised**) V-T If you **despise** something or someone, you dislike them and have a very low opinion of them. 鄙视 ❑ *I can never, ever forgive him. I despise him.* 我永远，永远都不会原谅他。我鄙视他。

de·spite ♦♦◇ /dɪspaɪt/ 1 PREP You use **despite** to introduce a fact which makes the other part of the sentence surprising. 尽管 [PREP n/-ing] ❑ *She has been under house arrest for most of the past decade, despite efforts by the United Nations to have her released.* 她在过去10年里大部分时间都被软禁，尽管联合国为她的释放一直在做努力。 2 PREP You use **despite** to introduce an idea that appears to contradict your main statement, without suggesting that this idea is true or that you believe it. 尽管 ❑ *She told friends she will stand by husband, despite reports that he sent another woman love notes.* 她告诉朋友说，她将支持丈夫，尽管有报道说他在给别的女人递情书。

de·spond·ent /dɪspɒndənt/ ADJ If you are **despondent**, you are very unhappy because you have been experiencing difficulties that you think you will not be able to overcome. 沮丧的 ❑ *He was despondent over the breakup of his marriage.* 他为婚姻破裂而沮丧。

des·sert /dɪzɜrt/ (**desserts**) N-MASS **Dessert** is something sweet, such as fruit, pastry, or ice cream, that you eat at the end of a meal. 餐后甜点 ❑ *She had homemade ice cream for dessert.* 她吃了些自制冰淇淋当餐后甜点。

→ see Picture Dictionary: **dessert**

de·sta·bi·lise /diːsteɪbəlaɪz/ [BRIT] → see **destabilize**

Word Link *stab ≈ steady : destabilize, establish, instability*

de·sta·bi·lize /disteɪbəlaɪz/ (**destabilizes, destabilizing, destabilized**)

in BRIT, also use **destabilise**

V-T To **destabilize** something such as a country or government means to create a situation which reduces its power or influence. 使不稳定 ❑ *Their sole aim is to destabilize the Indian government.* 他们惟一的目的就是破坏印度政府的稳定。

des·ti·na·tion /dɛstɪneɪʃᵊn/ (**destinations**) N-COUNT The **destination** of someone or something is the place to which they are going or being sent. 目的地 ❑ *Ellis Island has become one of America's most popular tourist destinations.* 埃利斯岛已经成为美国最受欢迎的游览地之一。

★ **des·tined** /dɛstɪnd/ 1 ADJ If something is **destined to** happen or if someone is **destined to** behave in a particular way, that thing seems certain to happen or be done. 注定的 ❑ *Any economic strategy based on a weak dollar is destined to fail.* 任何基于疲软的美元之上的经济策略都注定会失败。 2 ADJ If someone is **destined for** a particular place, or if goods are **destined for** a particular place, they are traveling toward that place or will be sent to that place. 去往某地的 [v-link ADJ "for" n] ❑ *...products destined for Saudi Arabia.* …运往沙特阿拉伯的产品。

★ **des·ti·ny** /dɛstɪni/ (**destinies**) 1 N-COUNT A person's **destiny** is everything that happens to them during their life, including what will happen in the future, especially when it is considered to be controlled by someone or something else. 命运 ❑ *We are masters of our own destiny.* 我们是自己命运的主人。 2 N-UNCOUNT **Destiny** is the force which some people believe controls the things that happen to you in your life. 天数；定数 ❑ *Is it destiny that brings people together, or is it accident?* 是定数，还是偶然，将人们带到一起？

des·ti·tute /dɛstɪtut/ ADJ Someone who is **destitute** has no money or possessions. 赤贫的 [FORMAL] ❑ *...destitute children who live on the streets.* …露宿街头的穷孩子们。

de·stroy ♦♦◇ /dɪstrɔɪ/ (**destroys, destroying, destroyed**) 1 V-T To **destroy** something means to cause so much damage to it that it is completely ruined or does not exist any more. 摧毁 ❑ *That's a sure recipe for destroying the economy and creating chaos.* 那是一个摧毁经济、制造混乱的注定因素。 2 V-T To **destroy** someone means to

d

D

ruin their life or to make their situation impossible to bear. 毁掉 ❑ *If I was younger or more naive, the criticism would have destroyed me.* 要是我年轻点儿或幼稚点儿，这批评可能已经把我毁了。 3 V-T If an animal **is destroyed**, it is killed, either because it is ill or because it is dangerous. 宰杀 [usu passive] ❑ *Lindsay was unhurt but the horse had to be destroyed.* 林赛没被伤着，但那匹马不得不被宰掉。

Thesaurus *destroy* 另参见：
V. annihilate, crush, demolish, eradicate, ruin, wipe out; (*ant.*) build, construct, create, repair 1

de·struc·tion ♦◇◇ /dɪstrʌkʃən/ N-UNCOUNT **Destruction** is the act of destroying something, or the state of being destroyed. 毁灭 ❑ *...an international agreement aimed at halting the destruction of the ozone layer.* …一项旨在停止对臭氧层的破坏的国际协议。

Word Link *struct ≈ building : construct, destructive, instruct*

de·struc·tive /dɪstrʌktɪv/ ADJ Something that is **destructive** causes or is capable of causing great damage, harm, or injury. 毁坏性的 ❑ *...the awesome destructive power of nuclear weapons.* …核武器可怕的毁坏性力量。

Word Link *de ≈ from, down, away : deflate, descend, detach*

★ **de·tach** /dɪtætʃ/ (**detaches, detaching, detached**) 1 V-T/V-I If you **detach** one thing **from** another that it is attached to, you remove it. If one thing **detaches from** another, it becomes separated from it. 拆卸；分离 [FORMAL] ❑ *Detach the white part of the application form and keep it for reference only.* 取下申请表的白色部分，仅备参考。 ❑ *They clambered back under the falls to detach the raft from a jagged rock.* 他们爬回到瀑布下面以便将卡在锯齿状岩石间的小艇拉出来。 2 V-T If you **detach yourself from** something, you become less involved in it or less concerned about it than you used to be. 超脱 ❑ *It helps them detach themselves from their problems and become more objective.* 这帮助他们从自己的问题中超脱出来，变得更加客观。

de·tached /dɪtætʃt/ 1 ADJ Someone who is **detached** is not personally involved in something or has no emotional interest in it. 超然的 ❑ *He tries to remain emotionally detached from the prisoners, but fails.* 他想尽力保持对囚犯们不掺杂个人感情，却做不到。 2 ADJ A **detached** building is one that is not joined to any other building. (房屋) 独立的 ❑ *...a house on the corner with a detached garage.* …拐角处一幢带独立车库的房子。

de·tach·ment /dɪtætʃmənt/ N-UNCOUNT **Detachment** is the feeling that you have of not being personally involved in something or of having no emotional interest in it. 客观；超然 ❑ *She did not care for the idea of socializing with her clients. It would detract from her professional detachment.* 她不喜欢跟客户们有社交往来。这会影响她的职业客观性。

de·tail ♦♦◇ /diteɪl/ (**details, detailing, detailed**)

The pronunciation /dɪteɪl/ is also used for the noun.
名词也可读作 /dɪteɪl/。

1 N-COUNT The **details of** something are its individual features or elements. 细节 ❑ *The details of the plan are still being worked out.* 计划的细节还在制定中。 ❑ *No details of the discussions have been given.* 会谈的细节尚未透露。 2 N-COUNT A **detail** is a minor point or aspect of something, as opposed to the central ones. 枝节 ❑ *Only minor details now remain to be settled.* 只有细枝末节还没确定。 3 N-PLURAL **Details** about someone or something are facts or pieces of information about them. 详情 ❑ *See the bottom of this page for details of how to apply for this exciting offer.* 关于如何申请这个令人激动的机会，详情请参看本页末。 4 N-UNCOUNT You can refer to the small features of something which are often not noticed as **detail**. 细微处 ❑ *We like his attention to detail and his enthusiasm.* 我们喜欢他对细微之处的关注，以及他的热情。 5 V-T If you **detail** things, you list them or give information about them. 详细列举；详细说明 ❑ *The report detailed the human rights abuses committed during the war.* 这份报告详述了战时进行的人权践踏。 6 N-COUNT A **detail** of people such as soldiers or prisoners is a small group of them who have been given a special task to carry out. 分遣队 [oft N "of" n] ❑ *...a sergeant with a detail of four men.* …1个带4人分遣队的中士。 7 PHRASE If someone does not **go into detail** about a subject, or does not **go into the details**, they mention it without explaining it fully or properly. 详细叙述 ❑ *He doesn't wish to go into detail about all the events of those days.* 他不想详述那些天发生的所有事情。 8 PHRASE If you examine or discuss something **in detail**, you do it thoroughly and carefully. 详细地 ❑ *We examine the wording in detail before deciding on the final text.* 我们详细检查了措辞，才确定了最终文本。

Thesaurus *detail* 另参见：
N. component, element, feature, point 1 3
fact, information 3
V. depict, describe, specify; (*ant.*) approximate, generalize 5

de·tailed ♦◇◇ /dɪteɪld/ ADJ A **detailed** report or plan contains a lot of details. 详细的 ❑ *Yesterday's letter contains a detailed account of the decisions.* 昨天的信里有对那些决定的详细说明。

Word Partnership *detailed* 的常用搭配：
N. detailed **account**, detailed **analysis**, detailed **description**, detailed **instructions**, detailed **plan**, detailed **record**

★ **de·tain** /dɪteɪn/ (**detains, detaining, detained**) 1 V-T When people such as the police **detain** someone, they keep them in a place under their control. 拘留 [FORMAL] ❑ *Police have detained two suspects in connection with the attack.* 警方拘留了2名与该袭击事件有关的嫌疑人。 2 V-T To **detain** someone means to delay them, for example, by talking to them. 耽搁 [FORMAL] ❑ *Millson stood up.*

"Thank you. We won't detain you any further, Mrs. Stebbing." 米尔森站起来。"谢谢您。我们不再耽搁您了，斯特宾太太。"

de·tainee /diteɪni/ (**detainees**) N-COUNT A **detainee** is someone who is held prisoner by a government because of his or her political views or activities. (因政治原因) 被拘留者 ❑ *Earlier this year, Amnesty International called for the release of more than 100 political detainees.* 今年早些时候，大赦国际呼吁释放100多名被拘留的政治犯。

Word Link *tect ≈ covering : detect, protect, protective*

de·tect /dɪtɛkt/ (**detects, detecting, detected**) **1** V-T To **detect** something means to find it or discover that it is present somewhere by using equipment or making an investigation. 探测 ❑ *...a sensitive piece of equipment used to detect radiation.* …一台探测辐射的敏感仪器。 **2** V-T If you **detect** something, you notice it or sense it, even though it is not very obvious. 察觉 ❑ *Arnold could detect a certain sadness in the old man's face.* 阿诺德能察觉到老人脸上的某种悲伤。

de·tec·tion /dɪtɛkʃᵊn/ N-UNCOUNT **Detection** is the act of noticing or sensing something. 察觉；发现 ❑ *...the early detection of breast cancer.* …乳腺癌的早期发现。

de·tec·tive ♦◇◇ /dɪtɛktɪv/ (**detectives**) **1** N-COUNT A **detective** is someone whose job is to discover what has happened in a crime or other situation and to find the people involved. Some detectives work in the police force and others work privately. 侦探 ❑ *Now detectives are appealing for witnesses who may have seen anything suspicious last night.* 现在侦探们正在呼吁昨晚可能看到任何可疑情况的人出来作证。 **2** ADJ A **detective** novel or story is one in which a detective tries to solve a crime. 侦探的 [ADJ n] ❑ *...Arthur Conan Doyle's classic detective novel.* …阿瑟·柯南·道尔的经典侦探小说。

de·tec·tor /dɪtɛktər/ (**detectors**) N-COUNT A **detector** is an instrument which is used to discover that something is present somewhere, or to measure how much of something there is. 探测器 ❑ *...a metal detector.* …一架金属探测器。

★ **de·ten·tion** /dɪtɛnʃᵊn/ (**detentions**) **1** N-UNCOUNT **Detention** is when someone is arrested or put into prison. 拘留；监禁 [also N in pl] ❑ *...the detention without trial of government critics.* …对政府批评者未经审判而进行的关押。 **2** N-VAR **Detention** is a punishment for students who misbehave, who are made to stay at school after the other students have gone home. (为惩罚学生的) 课后留校 ❑ *The teacher kept the boys in detention after school.* 老师在放学后罚男孩们留了下来。

▲ **de·ter** /dɪtɜr/ (**deters, deterring, deterred**) V-T To **deter** someone **from** doing something means to make them not want to do it or continue doing it. 阻止 ❑ *Supporters of the death penalty argue that it would deter criminals from carrying guns.* 死刑的支持者辩称，死刑可以阻止罪犯携带枪支。

▲ **de·ter·gent** /dɪtɜrdʒᵊnt/ (**detergents**) N-MASS **Detergent** is a chemical substance, usually in the form of a powder or liquid, which is used for washing things such as clothes or dishes. 清洁剂 ❑ *...a brand of detergent.* …一种品牌的清洁剂。
→ see **soap**

★ **de·terio·rate** /dɪtɪəriəreɪt/ (**deteriorates, deteriorating, deteriorated**) V-I If something **deteriorates**, it becomes worse in some way. 恶化 ❑ *There are fears that the situation might deteriorate into full-scale war.* 人们担心局势会恶化为全面战争。 ● **de·terio·ra·tion** ★ /dɪtɪəriəreɪʃᵊn/ N-UNCOUNT 恶化 ❑ *...concern about the rapid deterioration in relations between the two countries.* …对两国关系迅速恶化的担忧。

de·ter·mi·na·tion /dɪtɜrmɪneɪʃᵊn/ **1** N-UNCOUNT **Determination** is the quality that you show when you have decided to do something and you will not let anything stop you. 决心 ❑ *Everyone concerned acted with great courage and determination.* 每个相关的人都以巨大的勇气和决心行动了。 **2** → see also **determine**

Word Partnership *determination* 的常用搭配：

N. **courage and** determination, **strength and** determination **1**
ADJ. **fierce** determination **1**

Word Link *term, termin ≈ limit, end : determine, terminal, terminate*

de·ter·mine ♦♦◇ /dɪtɜrmɪn/ (**determines, determining, determined**) **1** V-T If a particular factor **determines** the nature of a thing or event, it causes it to be of a particular kind. 决定 [FORMAL] ❑ *The size of the chicken pieces will determine the cooking time.* 鸡块的大小决定烹饪时间。 ● **de·ter·mi·na·tion** N-UNCOUNT 决定 ❑ *...the gene which is responsible for male sex determination.* …决定男性性别的基因。 **2** V-T To **determine** a fact means to discover it as a result of investigation. 查明 [FORMAL] ❑ *The investigation will determine what really happened.* 该调查将查明真相。 ❑ *Experts say testing needs to be done on each contaminant to determine the long-term effects on humans.* 专家说需要对每种污染物进行测试，以查明对人类的长期影响。 **3** V-T If you **determine** something, you decide about it or settle it. 决定 ❑ *The Baltic people have a right to determine their own future.* 波罗的海人民有权决定他们自己的未来。 ● **de·ter·mi·na·tion** N-COUNT (**determinations**) 决定 ❑ *We must take into our own hands the determination of our future.* 我们必须将我们未来的决定权掌握在自己手中。 **4** V-T If you **determine to** do something, you make a firm decision to do it. 决心 [FORMAL] ❑ *He determined to rescue his two countrymen.* 他决心要援救他的两位同胞。

de·ter·mined ♦◇◇ /dɪtɜrmɪnd/ ADJ If you are **determined to** do something, you have made a firm decision to do it and will not let anything stop you. 坚决的 ❑ *His enemies are determined to ruin him.* 他的敌人决意要毁了他。 ● **de·ter·mined·ly** ADV 坚决地 ❑ *She shook her head, determinedly.* 她坚决地摇摇头。

de·ter·min·er /dɪtɜrmɪnər/ (**determiners**) N-COUNT In grammar, a **determiner** is a word which is used at the beginning of a noun group to indicate, for example, which thing you are referring to or whether you are referring to one thing or several. Common English determiners are "a," "the," "some," "this," and "each." 限定词

de·ter·rence /dɪtɜrəns/ N-UNCOUNT **Deterrence** is the prevention of something, especially war or crime, by having something such as weapons or punishment to use as a threat. 威慑 ❑ *...policies of nuclear deterrence.* …核威慑政策。

▲ **de·ter·rent** /dɪtɜrənt/ (**deterrents**) **1** N-COUNT A **deterrent** is something that prevents people from doing something by making them afraid of what will happen to them if they do it. 威慑物 ❑ *They seriously believe that capital punishment is a deterrent.* 他们坚信死刑是一种威慑手段。 **2** N-COUNT A **deterrent** is a weapon or set of weapons designed to prevent enemies from attacking by making them afraid to do so. 威慑性武器 ❑ *The idea of building a nuclear deterrent is completely off the political agenda.* 制造核威慑武器的意见完全不在政治议程中。

de·test /dɪtɛst/ (**detests, detesting, detested**) V-T If you **detest** someone or something, you dislike them very much. 憎恶 ❑ *My mother detested him.* 我母亲憎恶他。

▲ **deto·nate** /dɛtᵊneɪt/ (**detonates, detonating, detonated**) V-T/V-I If someone **detonates** a device such as a bomb, or if it **detonates**, it explodes. 引爆；爆炸 ❑ *France is expected to detonate its first nuclear device in the next few days.* 预计法国将在未来几天内引爆它的第一个核装置。

▲ **de·tour** /ditʊər/ (**detours**) **1** N-COUNT If you make a **detour** on a trip, you go by a route which is not the shortest way, because you want to avoid something such as a traffic jam, or because there is something you want to do on the way. 绕行 ❑ *He did not take the direct route to his home, but made a detour around the outskirts of the city.* 他没有直接回家，而是在市郊绕了一段路。 **2** N-COUNT A **detour** is a special route for traffic to follow when the normal route is blocked, for example, because it is being repaired. 绕行道 [AM]

in BRIT, use **diversion**

❑ *A slight detour in the road is causing major headaches for businesses along El Camino Real.* 马路上的一小段绕行道让国王大道沿街的商家十分头疼。

de·tract /dɪtrækt/ (**detracts, detracting, detracted**) V-T/V-I If one thing **detracts from** another, it makes it seem less good or impressive. 减损 ❑ *They feared that the publicity surrounding him would detract from their own election campaigns.* 他们担心围绕他的宣传会有损他们自己的竞选活动。

det·ri·ment /dɛtrɪmənt/ **1** PHRASE If something happens **to the detriment of** something or **to** a person's **detriment**, it causes harm or damage to them. 有损于 [FORMAL] ❑ *These tests will give too much importance to written exams to the detriment of other skills.* 这些测试会太侧重于书面考核而有损于其他技能。 **2** PHRASE If something happens **without detriment to** a person or thing, it does not harm or damage them. 无损于 [FORMAL] ❑ *These difficulties have been overcome without detriment to performance.* 这些困难已经被克服了，且没有损害到表演。

▲ **det·ri·men·tal** /dɛtrɪmɛntᵊl/ ADJ Something that is **detrimental to** something else has a harmful or damaging effect on it. 有害的 ❑ *Many foods are suspected of being detrimental to health because of the chemicals and additives they contain.* 许多食物因所含的化学成分和添加剂被怀疑有害健康。

D

de·value /diˈvælyu/ (**devalues, devaluing, devalued**) 1 V-T To **devalue** something means to cause it to be thought less impressive or less deserving of respect. 贬低 ❑ *They spread tales about her in an attempt to devalue her work.* 他们散布关于她的传闻，企图贬低她的工作。 2 V-T To **devalue** the currency of a country means to reduce its value in relation to other currencies. 使贬值 ❑ *India has devalued the rupee by about eleven percent.* 印度已经使卢比贬值约11%。 ● **de·valua·tion** /divælyueɪʃᵊn/ N-VAR (**devaluations**) 贬值 ❑ *It will lead to devaluation of a number of currencies.* 这将导致多种货币的贬值。

▲ **dev·as·tate** /dɛvəsteɪt/ (**devastates, devastating, devastated**) V-T If something **devastates** an area or a place, it damages it very badly or destroys it totally. 严重破坏；彻底摧毁 ❑ *The tsunami devastated parts of Indonesia and other countries in the region.* 这次海啸严重破坏了印度尼西亚和该区域其他国家的部分地区。

dev·as·tat·ed /dɛvəsteɪtɪd/ ADJ If you are **devastated** by something, you are very shocked and upset by it. 十分震惊的 [V-link ADJ] ❑ *Teresa was devastated, her dreams shattered.* 特雷莎非常震惊，她的梦想破灭了。

▲ **dev·as·tat·ing** /dɛvəsteɪtɪŋ/ 1 ADJ If you describe something as **devastating**, you are emphasizing that it is very harmful or damaging. 破坏性极强的 [EMPHASIS] ❑ *Affairs do have a devastating effect on marriages.* 外遇着实对婚姻有极具破坏性的影响。 2 ADJ You can use **devastating** to emphasize that something is very shocking, upsetting, or terrible. 令人震惊的 [EMPHASIS] ❑ *The diagnosis was devastating. She had cancer.* 诊断结果令人震惊。她得了癌症。 3 ADJ You can use **devastating** to emphasize that something or someone is very impressive. 给人印象深刻的 [EMPHASIS] ❑ *He returned to his best with a devastating display of galloping and jumping.* 他骑马飞驰和跳跃的精彩展示，说明他恢复到了最佳状态。

dev·as·ta·tion /dɛvəsteɪʃᵊn/ N-UNCOUNT **Devastation** is severe and widespread destruction or damage. 毁坏 ❑ *The war brought massive devastation and loss of life to the region.* 战争给该地区造成巨大的破坏以及生命的丧失。

de·vel·op ♦♦♦ /dɪvɛləp/ (**develops, developing, developed**) 1 V-I When something **develops**, it grows or changes over a period of time and usually becomes more advanced, complete, or severe. 发展 ❑ *It's hard to say at this stage how the market will develop.* 在现阶段很难说市场会如何发展。 ❑ *These clashes could develop into open warfare.* 这些冲突可能会发展成公开的战争。 ● **de·vel·oped** ADJ 发展的；发育的 ❑ *Their bodies were well developed and super fit.* 他们的身体发育良好，极其健康。 2 V-I If a problem or difficulty **develops**, it begins to occur. 产生 ❑ *The space agency says a problem has developed with an experiment aboard the space shuttle.* 航天局说在航天飞机上做的一项实验出了问题。 3 V-I If you say that a country **develops**, you mean that it changes from being a poor agricultural country to being a rich industrial country. 发达 ❑ *All countries, it was predicted, would develop and develop fast.* 据预测，所有的国家都会发达起来，并且很迅速。 4 → see also **developed, developing** 5 V-T/V-I If you **develop** a business or industry, or if it **develops**, it becomes bigger and more successful. 扩展 [BUSINESS] ❑ *An amateur hatmaker has won a scholarship to pursue her dreams of developing her own business.* 一位业余制帽匠赢得了一笔奖学金，来实现她扩展自己企业的梦想。 ● **de·vel·oped** ADJ 发达的 ❑ *...the countries that have suffered the most from the absence of more developed financial systems.* …因缺乏更发达的金融体系而受损最严重的国家。 6 V-T To **develop** land or property means to make it more profitable, by building houses or factories or by improving the existing buildings. 开发（房地产） ❑ *Local entrepreneurs developed fashionable restaurants, bars and discotheques in the area.* 当地的企业家在这个地区开办了时尚的餐馆、酒吧和迪斯科舞厅。 ● **de·vel·oped** ADJ 已开发的 ❑ *Developed land was to grow from 5.3% to 6.9%.* 已开发的土地将从5.3%增长到6.9%。 7 V-T If you **develop** a habit, reputation, or belief, you start to have it and it then becomes stronger or more noticeable. 获得；形成 ❑ *Mr. Robinson has developed the reputation of a ruthless cost-cutter.* 鲁宾逊先生已经有了毫不留情的成本削减者的名声。 8 V-T/V-I If you **develop** a skill, quality, or relationship, or if it **develops**, it becomes better or stronger. 增长；增进 ❑ *Now you have a good opportunity to develop a greater understanding of each other.* 现在你们有了一个好机会来增进彼此的了解。 ● **de·vel·oped** ADJ 增长的；增进的 ❑ *...a highly developed instinct for self-preservation.* …一种高度增长了的自卫本能。 9 V-T If a piece of equipment **develops** a fault, it starts to have the fault. 发生 ❑ *The aircraft made an unscheduled landing at Logan after developing an electrical fault.* 飞机发生电气故障后，临时在洛根着陆。 10 V-T If someone **develops** a new product, they design it and produce it. 开发（产品） ❑ *He claims that several countries have developed nuclear weapons secretly.* 他声称几个国家已经秘密开发了核武器。 11 V-T/V-I If you **develop** an idea, theory, story, or theme, or if it **develops**, it gradually becomes more detailed, advanced, or complex. 展开 ❑ *I would like to thank them for allowing me to develop their original idea.* 我想感谢他们允许我展开他们最初的观点。 12 V-T To **develop** photographs means to make negatives or prints from a photographic film. 冲洗 ❑ *...after developing one roll of film.* …冲洗了一卷胶卷后。

→ see **photography**

de·vel·oped /dɪvɛləpt/ ADJ If you talk about **developed** countries or the **developed** world, you mean the countries or the parts of the world that are wealthy and have many industries. 发达的 ❑ *This scarcity is inevitable in less developed countries.* 在欠发达国家这种匮乏是不可避免的。

de·vel·op·er /dɪvɛləpər/ (**developers**) 1 N-COUNT A **developer** is a person or a company that buys land and builds houses, offices, stores, or factories on it, or buys existing buildings and makes them more modern. （房地产）开发商 [BUSINESS] ❑ *...common land which would have a high commercial value if sold to developers.* …卖给开发商便有很高商业价值的普通地皮。 2 N-COUNT A **developer** is someone who develops something such as an idea, a design, or a product. 开发者 ❑ *John Bardeen was also co-developer of the theory of superconductivity.* 约翰·巴丁也是超导理论的共同发展人。

→ see **skyscraper**

de·vel·op·ing /dɪvɛləpɪŋ/ ADJ If you talk about **developing** countries or the **developing** world, you mean the countries or the parts of the world that are poor and have few industries. 发展中的 [ADJ n] ❑ *In the developing world cigarette consumption is increasing.* 在发展中国家香烟消费正在增长。

de·vel·op·ment ♦♦♦ /dɪvɛləpmənt/ (**developments**) 1 N-UNCOUNT **Development** is the gradual growth or formation of something. 发育；逐渐形成 ❑ *...an ideal system for studying the development of the embryo.* …研究胚胎发育的理想系统。 2 N-UNCOUNT **Development** is the growth of something such as a business or an industry. 发展 [BUSINESS] ❑ *He firmly believes that education and a country's economic development are key factors to progress.* 他坚信教育和一个国家的经济发展是通向进步的关键因素。 3 N-UNCOUNT **Development** is the process of making an area of land or water more useful or profitable. 开发 ❑ *The talks will focus on economic development of the region.* 会谈将聚焦于该地区的经济开发。 4 N-VAR **Development** is the process or result of making a basic design gradually better and more advanced. 改良 ❑ *It is spending $850M on research and development to get to the market place as soon as possible with faster microprocessors.* 研发上投入了$8.5亿，以期尽快将更快速的微处理器投放市场。 5 N-COUNT A **development** is an event or incident which has recently happened and is likely to have an effect on the present situation. 进展 ❑ *The police spokesman said: "We believe there has been a significant development in the case."* 警方发言人说："我们认为此案已有重大进展。" 6 N-COUNT A **development** is an area of houses or buildings which have been built by property developers. 开发区 ❑ *...a 16-house development planned by Everlast Enterprises.* …Everlast公司规划的一个拥有16幢房子的住宅区。

de·vel·op·ment bank (**development banks**) N-COUNT A **development bank** is a bank that provides money for projects in poor countries or areas. （为贫困国家或地区提供资金的）开发银行

de·vi·ant /diviənt/ ADJ **Deviant** behavior or thinking is different from what people normally consider to be acceptable. （行为或思想）反常的 ❑ *...the social reactions to deviant and criminal behavior.* 反常的犯罪行为的社会反应。 ● **de·vi·ance** /diviəns/ N-UNCOUNT 反常 ❑ *...sexual deviance, including the abuse of children.* …性反常，包括虐待儿童。

★ **de·vi·ate** /diviet/ (**deviates, deviating, deviated**) V-I To **deviate from** something means to start doing something different or not planned, especially in a way that causes problems for others. 偏离 ❑ *They stopped you as soon as you deviated from the script.* 你一偏离剧本，他们就会叫停。

de·via·tion /diviеɪʃən/ **(deviations)** N-VAR **Deviation** means doing something that is different from what people consider to be normal or acceptable. 偏离；越轨 ❑ *Deviation from the norm is not tolerated.* 偏离规范是不能容忍的。

de·vice ♦◇◇ /dɪvaɪs/ **(devices)** N-COUNT A **device** is an object that has been invented for a particular purpose, for example, for recording or measuring something. 仪器 ❑ *...the electronic device that tells the starter when an athlete has moved from his blocks prematurely.* …能在运动员抢跑时通知发令员的电子仪器。

→ see **computer**

dev·il /dɛvəl/ **(devils)** 1 N-PROPER In Judaism, Christianity, and Islam, **the Devil** is the most powerful evil spirit. 魔鬼 2 N-COUNT A **devil** is an evil spirit. (犹太教、基督教、伊斯兰教中的) 魔王 ❑ *...the idea of angels with wings and devils with horns and hoofs.* …天使长翅膀、魔鬼长角生蹄的观念。

▲ **de·vi·ous** /diviəs/ ADJ If you describe someone as **devious** you do not like them because you think they are dishonest and like to keep things secret, often in a complicated way. 狡诈的 [DISAPPROVAL] ❑ *Newman was certainly devious, prepared to say one thing in print and something quite different in private.* 纽曼确实狡诈，随时都能当众说一套，私下说一套。

de·vise /dɪvaɪz/ **(devises, devising, devised)** V-T If you **devise** a plan, system, or machine, you have the idea for it and design it. 构思；设计 ❑ *We devised a scheme to help him.* 我们想出了一个计划来帮助他。

Word Partnership *devise* 的常用搭配:
N. devise **new ways**, devise **a plan**, devise **a strategy**, devise **a system**

de·void /dɪvɔɪd/ ADJ If you say that someone or something is **devoid** of a quality or thing, you are emphasizing that they have none of it. 全无的 [v-link ADJ "of" n] [FORMAL, EMPHASIS] ❑ *I have never looked on a face that was so devoid of feeling.* 我从未见过这样一张完全没有感情的脸。

de·vo·lu·tion /dɪvəluʃən, dɛv-/ N-UNCOUNT **Devolution** is the transfer of some authority or power from a central organization or government to smaller organizations or government departments. (中央机构或政府权力的) 下放 ❑ *...the devolution of power to the regions.* …权力下放到地方。

de·volve /dɪvɒlv/ **(devolves, devolving, devolved)** V-T/V-I If you **devolve** power, authority, or responsibility **to** a less powerful person or group, or if it **devolves upon** them, it is transferred to them. (权力、责任) 下放 ❑ *...the need to decentralize and devolve power to regional governments.* …把权力分散下放到地方政府的需要。 ❑ *The best companies are those that devolve responsibility as far as they can.* 最好的公司是那些尽可能把责任下放的公司。

de·vote /dɪvoʊt/ **(devotes, devoting, devoted)** 1 V-T If you **devote** yourself, your time, or your energy **to** something, you spend all or most of your time or energy on it. 把…奉献给 ❑ *He decided to devote the rest of his life to scientific investigation.* 他决定把余生奉献给科学研究。 ❑ *Considerable resources have been devoted to proving him a liar.* 大量的资源已被用来证明他是个撒谎者。 2 V-T If you **devote** a particular proportion of a piece of writing or a speech **to** a particular subject, you deal with the subject in that amount of space or time. 作…专用 ❑ *He devoted a major section of his massive report to an analysis of U.S. aircraft design.* 他在那份厚重的报告中用一个主要章节分析了美国的飞机设计。

de·vot·ed /dɪvoʊtɪd/ 1 ADJ Someone who is **devoted to a** person loves that person very much. 挚爱的 [ADJ n, v-link ADJ "to" n] ❑ *...a loving and devoted husband.* …一个忠爱的丈夫。 2 ADJ If you are **devoted to** something, you care about it a lot and are very enthusiastic about it. 热衷于…的 [v-link ADJ "to" n, ADJ n] ❑ *I have personally been devoted to this cause for many years.* 我个人多年来一直热衷于这项事业。 3 ADJ Something that is **devoted to a** particular thing deals only with that thing or contains only that thing. 专用于…的 [v-link ADJ "to" n] ❑ *A large part of the Internet is now devoted to weblogs.* 因特网的很大一部分如今都专用于网络博客。

de·vo·tion /dɪvoʊʃən/ 1 N-UNCOUNT **Devotion** is great love, affection, or admiration for someone. 热爱 ❑ *At first she was flattered by his devotion.* 最初他的挚爱使她感到受宠若惊。 2 N-UNCOUNT **Devotion** is commitment to a particular activity. 献身 ❑ *...devotion to the cause of the people and to socialism.* …对于人民的事业和社会主义的献身。

▲ **de·vour** /dɪvaʊər/ **(devours, devouring, devoured)** 1 V-T If a person or animal **devours** something, they eat it quickly and eagerly. 狼吞虎咽地吃 ❑ *A medium-sized dog will devour at least one can of food plus biscuits per day.* 一只中等大小的狗每天至少要干掉一罐食物外加饼干。 2 V-T If you **devour** a book or magazine, for example, you read it quickly and with great enthusiasm. 急切地读 ❑ *She began buying and devouring newspapers when she was only 12.* 她才12岁时，就开始买报纸并如饥似渴地阅读。

de·vout /dɪvaʊt/ 1 ADJ A **devout** person has deep religious beliefs. 虔诚的 ❑ *She was a devout Christian.* 她是个虔诚的基督徒。 ● N-PLURAL **The devout** are people who are devout. 虔诚者 ❑ *...priests instructing the devout.* …教导虔诚信徒的牧师们。 2 ADJ If you describe someone as a **devout** supporter or a **devout** opponent of something, you mean that they support it enthusiastically or oppose it strongly. 坚定的 [ADJ n] ❑ *Devout Marxists believed fascism was the "last stand of the bourgeoisie."* 坚定的马克思主义者曾相信法西斯主义是资产阶级的"最后阵地"。

▲ **dew** /du/ N-UNCOUNT **Dew** is small drops of water that form on the ground and other surfaces outdoors during the night. 露水 ❑ *The dew gathered on the leaves.* 露水在叶片上聚集。

▲ **dia·be·tes** /daɪəbitɪs, -tiz/ N-UNCOUNT **Diabetes** is a medical condition in which someone has too much sugar in their blood. 糖尿病

→ see **sugar**

dia·bet·ic /daɪəbɛtɪk/ **(diabetics)** 1 N-COUNT A **diabetic** is a person who suffers from diabetes. 糖尿病人 ❑ *...an insulin-dependent diabetic.* …一个依赖胰岛素的糖尿病人。 ● ADJ **Diabetic** is also an adjective. 患糖尿病的 ❑ *...diabetic patients.* …糖尿病患者。 2 ADJ **Diabetic** means relating to diabetes. 与糖尿病有关的 [ADJ n] ❑ *He found her in a diabetic coma.* 他发现她因糖尿病而昏迷。

Word Link *dia ≈ across, through : diagnose, diagonal, dialogue*

di·ag·nose /daɪəgnoʊs/ **(diagnoses, diagnosing, diagnosed)** V-T If someone or something **is diagnosed as** having a particular illness or problem, their illness or problem is identified. If an illness or problem **is diagnosed**, it is identified. 诊断 ❑ *The soldiers were diagnosed as having flu.* 这些士兵被诊断为患了流感。 ❑ *Susan had a mental breakdown and was diagnosed with schizophrenia.* 苏珊精神崩溃，被诊断为精神分裂。

→ see **diagnosis, illness**

★ **di·ag·no·sis** /daɪəgnoʊsɪs/ **(diagnoses)** N-VAR **Diagnosis** is the discovery and naming of what is wrong with someone who is ill or with something that is not working properly. 诊断 ❑ *I need to have a second test to confirm the diagnosis.* 我需要复查来确诊。

→ see Word Web: **diagnosis**

di·ag·nos·tic /daɪəgnɒstɪk/ ADJ **Diagnostic** equipment, methods, or systems are used for discovering what is wrong with

Word Web **diagnosis**

Many doctors recommend that their **patients** get a routine **physical examination** once a year—even if they're feeling perfectly well. This enables the **physician** to detect **symptoms** and **diagnose** possible **diseases** at an early stage. The doctor may begin by using a tongue depressor to look down the patient's throat for possible **infections**. Then he or she may use a stethoscope to listen to subtle sounds in the heart, lungs, and stomach. A **blood pressure** reading is always part of the exam and involves the use of a **blood pressure cuff**.

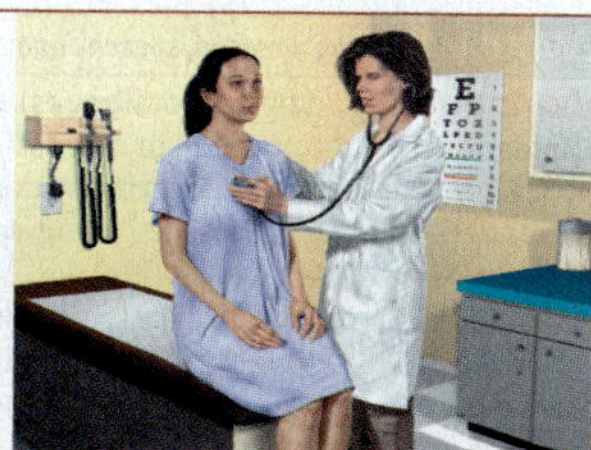

Word Web diamond

Diamonds are made of pure **carbon**. They are the hardest **mineral** to form and develop deep inside the earth. To create a diamond, the pressure must reach almost half a million pounds per square inch. The temperature must be at least 400°C*. Many of today's diamonds formed millions of years ago. They reach the surface of the earth through a process similar to a volcanic eruption. Then the diamonds are **mined**. A diamond is not beautiful until someone cuts it and exposes its many **facets**. **Jewelers** give the weight of a diamond in **carats**. One carat is about 200 milligrams.

400°C=about 752°F.

D

people who are ill or with things that do not work properly. 诊断的 [ADJ n] ❑ *...X-rays and other diagnostic tools.* …X光和其他诊断工具。

di·ago·nal /daɪæɡənᵊl, -æɡnᵊl/ ADJ A **diagonal** line or movement goes in a sloping direction, for example, from one corner of a square across to the opposite corner. 对角线的; 斜的 ❑ *...a pattern of diagonal lines.* …一个由斜线组成的图案。

● **di·ago·nal·ly** ADV 对角线地; 斜地 ❑ *Vaulting the stile, he headed diagonally across the paddock.* 他跃过梯台，从围场里斜穿过去。

Word Link *gram ≈ writing : diagram, program, telegram*

dia·gram /daɪəɡræm/ (**diagrams**) N-COUNT A **diagram** is a simple drawing which consists mainly of lines and is used, for example, to explain how a machine works. 示意图 ❑ *...a circuit diagram.* …电路图。

Thesaurus *diagram* 另参见:
N. blueprint, chart, design, illustration, plan

dial /daɪəl/ (**dials, dialing, dialed**)
in BRIT, sometimes AM use **dialling, dialled**

1 N-COUNT A **dial** is the part of a machine or instrument such as a clock or watch which shows you the time or a measurement that has been recorded. 刻度盘 ❑ *The luminous dial on the clock showed five minutes to seven.* 发光的表盘上显示6：55。 **2** N-COUNT A **dial** is a control on a device or piece of equipment which you can move in order to adjust the setting, for example, to select or change the frequency on a radio or the temperature of a heater. (收音机、加热器等的) 调谐钮 ❑ *He turned the dial on the radio.* 他转动着收音机的调谐钮。 **3** V-T/V-I If you **dial** or if you **dial** a number, you turn the dial or press the buttons on a telephone in order to phone someone. 拨号 ❑ *He lifted the phone and dialed her number.* 他拿起电话，拨她的号码。

dia·lect /daɪəlɛkt/ (**dialects**) N-COUNT A **dialect** is a form of a language that is spoken in a particular area. 方言 [also "in" N] ❑ *It is often appropriate to use the local dialect to communicate your message.* 用方言来交流信息往往很合适。

→ see **English**

dial·ling code (**dialling codes**) N-COUNT A **dialling code** for a particular city or region is the series of numbers that you have to dial before a particular telephone number if you are making a call to that place from a different area. (电话) 区号 [mainly BRIT]
in AM, use **area code**

dial·ling tone (**dialling tones**) N-COUNT The **dialling tone** is the same as the **dial tone**. 拨号音 [BRIT]

dia·log box (**dialog boxes**) N-COUNT A **dialog box** is a small area containing information or questions that appears on a computer screen when you are performing particular operations. 对话框 [COMPUTING] ❑ *You should now see a dialog box listing all of the print queues on your network.* 你现在会看到一个对话框，上面列出了你的网络上所有的打印任务。

Word Link *log ≈ reason, speech : apology, dialogue, logic*

dia·logue ♦◇◇ /daɪəlɔɡ/ (**dialogues**) also **dialog** **1** N-VAR **Dialogue** is communication or discussion between people or groups of people such as governments or political parties. 对话 ❑ *People of all social standings should be given equal opportunities for dialogue.* 社会各阶层的人都应该被给予平等对话的机会。 **2** N-VAR A **dialogue** is a conversation between two people in a book, film, or play. (书籍、影视、戏剧中的) 对白 ❑ *Although the dialogue is sharp, the actors move too awkwardly around the stage.* 尽管对白很清晰，但演员们在舞台上的动作却太不自然。

dial tone (**dial tones**) N-COUNT The **dial tone** is the noise which you hear when you pick up a telephone receiver and which means that you can dial the number you want. 拨号音
in BRIT, also use **dialling tone**
❑ *It was only as she tried for the second time that she realized that there was no dial tone.* 当她第二次拨号时，才意识到没有拨号音。

di·am·eter /daɪæmɪtər/ (**diameters**) N-COUNT The **diameter** of a round object is the length of a straight line that can be drawn across it, passing through the middle of it. 直径 [also "in" N] ❑ *...a tube less than a fifth of the diameter of a human hair.* …一根直径不到头发五分之一的微管。

→ see **area, circle**

dia·mond /daɪmənd, daɪə-/ (**diamonds**) **1** N-VAR A **diamond** is a hard, bright, precious stone which is clear and colorless. Diamonds are used in jewelry and for cutting very hard substances. 钻石 ❑ *...a pair of diamond earrings.* …一对钻石耳环。 **2** N-COUNT A **diamond** is a shape with four straight sides of equal length where the opposite angles are the same, but none of the angles is equal to 90°: ♦. 菱形 ❑ *...forming his hands into the shape of a diamond.* …用他的双手比划出一个菱形。 **3** N-UNCOUNT-COLL **Diamonds** is one of the four suits of cards in a pack of playing cards. Each card in the suit is marked with one or more red symbols in the shape of a diamond. 方块 (扑克牌中的4个花色之一) ❑ *He drew the seven of diamonds.* 他抽了方块7。 ● N-COUNT A **diamond** is a playing card of this suit. (扑克牌中的) 方块牌 ❑ *...win the ace of clubs and play a diamond.* …赢了梅花A，打出一张方块。 **4** N-COUNT In baseball, the **diamond** is the square formed by the four bases, or the whole of the playing area. (棒球) 内野; 棒球场 [usu "the" N] ❑ *He would be the best ever to walk out onto the diamond.* 他将是棒球场上最出色的球员。

→ see Word Web: **diamond**

→ see **baseball, crystal**

dia·per /daɪpər, daɪə-/ (**diapers**) N-COUNT A **diaper** is a piece of soft towel or paper, which you fasten around a baby's bottom in order to contain its urine and feces. 尿布; 纸尿片 [AM]
in BRIT, use **nappy**
❑ *He never changed her diapers, never bathed her.* 他从不给她换尿布，也不给她洗澡。

dia·phragm /daɪəfræm/ (**diaphragms**) **1** N-COUNT Your **diaphragm** is a muscle between your lungs and your stomach. It is used when you breathe. 横膈膜 (位于肺和胃之间的肌肉，呼吸时起作用) ❑ *...the skill of breathing from the diaphragm.* …从横膈膜进行呼吸的技巧。 **2** N-COUNT A **diaphragm** is a circular rubber contraceptive device that a woman places inside her vagina. (避孕用的) 子宫帽

→ see **respiratory**

di·ar·rhea /daɪəriə/
in BRIT, use **diarrhoea**

N-UNCOUNT If someone has **diarrhea**, a lot of liquid feces comes out of their body because they are ill. 腹泻 ❑ *But the food itself was barely digestible, and many team members suffered from diarrhea or constipation.* 但食物本身难以消化，许多队员患了腹泻或便秘。

di·ar·rhoea /daɪəriːə/ [BRIT] → see **diarrhea**

dia·ry ♦◇◇ /daɪəri/ (**diaries**) N-COUNT A **diary** is a book which has a separate space for each day of the year. You use a diary to write down things you plan to do, or to record what happens in your life day by day. 日记 ❑ *I had earlier read the entry from Harold Nicholson's diary for July 10, 1940.* 我早就在哈罗德·尼科尔森1940年7月10日的日记里读到过那则记录。

→ see Word Web: **diary**

→ see **history**

Word Web diary

A **diary** is an informal daily written **record** of the events in someone's life. Most diaries are private **documents**. But sometimes an important diary is published. One such example is *The Diary of a Young Girl*. This is Anne Frank's World War II **chronicle** of her family's unsuccessful attempt to hide from the Nazis. They were eventually arrested, and later Anne died in a concentration camp. This **primary source** document offers us a personal view. It is full of rich details that are often missing from other historical **texts**. The book is now available in 60 different languages.

d

▲ **dice** /daɪs/ (**dices, dicing, diced**) **1** N-COUNT A **dice** is a small cube which has between one and six spots or numbers on its sides, and which is used in games to provide random numbers. In old-fashioned English, "dice" was used only as a plural form, and the singular was **die**, but now "dice" is used as both the singular and the plural form. 骰子(古英语中，**dice**仅用作复数，单数为**die**；现在，**dice**既作单数，又作复数) ❑ *I throw both dice and get double 6.* 我掷出2个骰子，开了2个6点。 **2** V-T If you **dice** food, you cut it into small cubes. 把…切成小块 ❑ *Dice the onion and boil in the water for about fifteen minutes.* 把洋葱切成小块，在水里煮15分钟左右。 **3** PHRASE If you are trying to achieve something and you say that it's **no dice**, you mean that you are having no success or luck with it. If someone asks you for something and you reply **no dice**, you are refusing to do what they ask. 徒劳；没运气；不行(用于拒绝要求) ❑ *If there'd been a halfway decent house for rent on this island, I would have taken it. But it was no dice.* 如果这座岛上有稍微像样的房子出租，我就租下来了。但连那样的房子都租不到。 ❑ *If the Republicans were to say "no dice," the Democrats would think they have a campaign issue.* 如果共和党说"不行"，民主党就会认为这正好可以在竞选上大做文章。
→ see **cut**

Word Link *dict ≈ speaking : contradict, dictate, predict*

dic·tate (**dictates, dictating, dictated**)

The verb is pronounced /dɪkteɪt, dɪkteɪt/. The noun is pronounced /dɪkteɪt/.

动词读作 /dɪkteɪt, dɪkteɪt/。名词读作 /dɪkteɪt/。

1 V-T If you **dictate** something, you say or read it aloud for someone else to write down. 口授；使听写 ❑ *Sheldon writes every day of the week, dictating his novels in the morning.* 谢尔登每天都进行创作，在上午口述他的小说。 **2** V-T If someone **dictates to** someone else, they tell them what they should do or can do. 指示；命令 ❑ *What right has one country to dictate the environmental standards of another?* 一个国家有什么权利规定另一个国家的环境标准？ ❑ *What gives them the right to dictate to us what we should eat?* 是什么给他们权利来规定我们该吃什么？ **3** V-T If one thing **dictates** another, the first thing causes or influences the second thing. 导致；影响 ❑ *The film's budget dictated a tough schedule.* 该影片的预算决定了紧张的拍摄进度。 ❑ *Of course, a number of factors will dictate how long an apple tree can survive.* 当然，一棵苹果树能存活多久是由许多因素决定的。 **4** V-T You say that logic or common sense **dictates that** a particular thing is the case when you believe strongly that it is the case and that logic or common sense will cause other people to agree. (逻辑或常识)使人相信 ❑ *Logic dictates that our ancestors could not have held a yearly festival until they figured what a year was.* 依照逻辑推论，我们的祖先在弄清1年是什么意思之前，不可能举行过每年一度的节庆。 **5** N-COUNT **Dictates** are principles or rules which you consider to be extremely important. 原则；规定 ❑ *We have followed the dictates of our consciences and have done our duty.* 我们凭良心做事，尽了我们的职责。

Word Partnership *dictate* 的常用搭配：

N. dictate **terms** **2**
circumstances dictate, **factors** dictate, **rules** dictate **3**

dic·ta·tion /dɪkteɪʃən/ N-UNCOUNT **Dictation** is the speaking or reading aloud of words for someone else to write down. 口授；听写 ❑ *...taking dictation from the dean of the graduate school.* …记录研究生院院长的口述。

★ **dic·ta·tor** /dɪkteɪtər/ (**dictators**) N-COUNT A **dictator** is a ruler who has complete power in a country, especially power which was obtained by force and is used unfairly or cruelly. 独裁者 ❑ *...foreign dictators who contravene humanitarian conventions.* …违反人道主义公约的外国独裁者们。

dic·ta·tor·ial /dɪktətɔriəl/ ADJ If you describe someone's behavior as **dictatorial**, you do not like the fact that they tell people what to do in a forceful and unfair way. 独裁的 [DISAPPROVAL] ❑ *...his dictatorial management style.* …他专横的管理作风。

dic·ta·tor·ship /dɪkteɪtərʃɪp/ (**dictatorships**) **1** N-VAR **Dictatorship** is government by a dictator. 专政 ❑ *...a new era of democracy after a long period of military dictatorship in the country.* …该国长期军事独裁统治结束后到来的民主新纪元。 **2** N-COUNT A **dictatorship** is a country which is ruled by a dictator or by a very strict and harsh government. 独裁国家 ❑ *Every country in the region was a military dictatorship.* 这个地区的每个国家都是军事独裁国。

dic·tion·ary /dɪkʃənɛri/ (**dictionaries**) N-COUNT A **dictionary** is a book in which the words and phrases of a language are listed alphabetically, together with their meanings or their translations in another language. 词典 ❑ *...a Spanish-English dictionary.* …一本西班牙语–英语词典。

did /dɪd/ **Did** is the past tense of **do**. **do**的过去式

didn't ♦♦♦ /dɪdənt/ **Didn't** is the usual spoken form of "did not." **did not**的常用口语形式

die ♦♦♦ /daɪ/ (**dies, dying, died**) **1** V-T/V-I When people, animals, and plants **die**, they stop living. 死亡 [no passive] ❑ *A year later my dog died.* 1年后，我的狗死了。 ❑ *Sadly, both he and my mother died of cancer.* 令人悲伤的是，他和我母亲都死于癌症。 ❑ *I would die a very happy person if I could stay in music my whole life.* 如果我这一生都能生活在音乐之中，就是死，我也会死得快乐。

Do not confuse **dead** with **died**. **Died** is the past tense and past participle of the verb **die**, and thus indicates the action of dying. ❑ *She died in 1934... Two men have died since the rioting broke out.* You do not use **died** as an adjective. You use **dead** instead. ❑ *More than 2,200 dead birds have been found.*

2 V-I If a machine or device **dies**, it stops completely, especially after a period of working more and more slowly or inefficiently. 停止运转 [WRITTEN] ❑ *Then suddenly, the engine coughed, spluttered, and died.* 突然，发动机发出咯咯声、噼啪声，然后就熄火了。 **3** V-I You can say that you **are dying of** thirst, hunger, boredom, or curiosity to emphasize that you are very thirsty, hungry, bored, or curious. (饥渴、厌倦、好奇得)要命 [only cont] [INFORMAL, EMPHASIS] ❑ *Order me a soda, I'm dying of thirst.* 给我要杯汽水，我快渴死了。 **4** V-T/V-I You can say that you **are dying for** something or **are dying to** do something to emphasize that you very much want to have it or do it. 渴望 [only cont] [INFORMAL, EMPHASIS] ❑ *I'm dying for a breath of fresh air.* 我真想呼吸点新鲜空气。 **5** V-T/V-I You can use **die** in expressions such as "**I almost died**" or "**I'd die if anything happened**" where you are emphasizing your feelings about a situation, for example, to say that it is very shocking, upsetting, embarrassing, or amusing. (差点)死去 [INFORMAL, mainly SPOKEN, EMPHASIS] ❑ *I nearly died when I read what she'd written about me.* 看到她对我的描述，我差点没死。 ❑ *I nearly died of shame.* 我羞愧得要命。 ❑ *I thought I'd die laughing.* 我以为我要笑死了。 **6** → see also **dying** **7** PHRASE If you say that something is **to die for**, you mean that you want it or like it very much. 令人非常想要；令人非常喜欢 [INFORMAL] ❑ *It may be that your property has a stunning view, or perhaps it has a kitchen or bathroom to die for.* 也许是你的房子有极漂亮的景色，也许它的厨房和卫生间太令人向往。 **8** PHRASE If you say that habits or attitudes **die hard**, you mean that they take a very long time to disappear or change, so that it may not be possible to get rid of them completely. (习惯、观念等)难以消除；难以改变 ❑ *Old habits die hard.* 旧习难改。

▸ **die out** **1** PHRASAL VERB If something **dies out**, it becomes less and less common and eventually disappears completely. 逐渐消亡

D

❑ *We used to believe that capitalism would soon die out.* 我们曾以为资本主义很快会消亡。 2 PHRASAL VERB If something such as a fire or wind **dies out**, it gradually stops burning or blowing. (风) 平息; (火) 熄灭 [AM] ❑ *Once the fire has died out, the salvage team will move in.* 火一旦熄灭，抢救队就会进去。

Thesaurus *die* 另参见:
V. pass away; (*ant.*) live 1
break down, fail 2

Word Partnership *die* 的常用搭配:
V. **deserve to** die, **going to** die, **live or** die, **sentenced to** die, **want to** die, **would rather** die 1
N. **right to** die 1

▲ **die·sel** /diːzᵊl/ **(diesels)** 1 N-MASS **Diesel** or **diesel oil** is the heavy fuel used in a diesel engine. 柴油 2 N-COUNT A **diesel** is a vehicle which has a diesel engine. 柴油车 ❑ *I keep hearing that diesels are better now than ever before.* 我总听说现在的柴油车比以往的都好。

die·sel en·gine **(diesel engines)** N-COUNT A **diesel engine** is an internal combustion engine in which oil is burned by very hot air. Diesel engines are used in buses and trucks, and in some trains and cars. 柴油机

diet ◆◆◇ /daɪɪt/ **(diets, dieting, dieted)** 1 N-VAR Your **diet** is the type and variety of food that you regularly eat. 日常饮食 ❑ *It's never too late to improve your diet.* 改善饮食什么时候都不嫌晚。 2 N-VAR If you are on a **diet**, you eat special kinds of food or you eat less food than usual because you are trying to lose weight. (因减肥而吃的) 规定饮食 ❑ *Have you been on a diet? You've lost a lot of weight.* 你在节食吗？你瘦了很多。 3 N-COUNT If a doctor puts someone on a **diet**, he or she makes them eat a special type or variety of foods in order to improve their health. (医生为病人规定的) 特种饮食 ❑ *Certain chronic conditions, such as diabetes, require special diets that should be monitored by your physician.* 一些慢性病，如糖尿病，要求病人食用由医生指导的特定食物。 4 N-COUNT If you are fed on a **diet of** something, especially something unpleasant or of poor quality, you receive or experience a very large amount of it. 大量 (不愉快的事或质量差的东西) ❑ *The radio had fed him a diet of pop songs.* 收音机没完没了地向他播放流行音乐。 5 V-I If you **are dieting**, you eat special kinds of food or you eat less food than usual because you are trying to lose weight. 节食 ❑ *I've been dieting ever since the birth of my fourth child.* 自从我第4个孩子出生以后，我就一直在节食。 6 ADJ **Diet** drinks or foods have been specially produced so that they do not contain many calories. (饮食) 低热量的 [ADJ n] ❑ *...sugar-free diet drinks.* …无糖的低热量饮料。
→ see Word Web: **diet**
→ see **vegetarian**

Word Partnership *diet* 的常用搭配:
ADJ. **balanced** diet, **healthy** diet, **proper** diet, **vegetarian** diet 1
strict diet 3
N. diet **and exercise** 1 – 3
diet **pills**, diet **supplements** 2
diet **soda** 6
PREP. **on a** diet 2

★ **di·etary** /daɪətɛri/ ADJ You can use **dietary** to describe anything that concerns a person's diet. 饮食的 ❑ *Dr. Susan Hankinson has studied the dietary habits of more than 50,000 women.* 苏珊·汉金森博士研究了五万多名妇女的饮食习惯。

dif·fer /dɪfər/ **(differs, differing, differed)** 1 V-RECIP If two or more things **differ**, they are unlike each other in some way. 不同 ❑ *The story he told police differed from the one he told his mother.* 他给警察讲的事情的经过与给他母亲讲的不一样。 2 V-RECIP If people **differ** about something, they do not agree with each other about it. 有异议 ❑ *The two leaders had differed on the issue of sanctions.* 就制裁问题两位领导持不同意见。 ❑ *That is where we differ.* 那就是我们的分歧所在。
3 **to agree to differ** → see **agree**

dif·fer·ence ◆◆◇ /dɪfərəns, dɪfrəns/ **(differences)** 1 N-COUNT The **difference** between two things is the way in which they are unlike each other. 差异 ❑ *That is the fundamental difference between the two societies.* 那是两个社会之间的根本差别。 ❑ *...the vast difference in size.* …在大小方面的巨大差别。 2 N-COUNT If people have their **differences** about something, they disagree about it. 分歧 ❑ *The two communities are learning how to resolve their differences.* 这两个团体正在学会如何消除它们之间的分歧。 3 N-SING A **difference** between two quantities is the amount by which one quantity is less than the other. 差额 ❑ *The difference is 8532.* 差额是8532。 4 PHRASE If something **makes a difference** or **makes** a lot of **difference**, it affects you and helps you in what you are doing. If something **makes** no **difference**, it does not have any effect on what you are doing. 有 (某程度的) 影响/毫无影响 ❑ *Where you live can make such a difference to the way you feel.* 你居住的位置会对你的感觉产生很大的影响。 5 PHRASE If there is a **difference of opinion** between two or more people or groups, they disagree about something. 意见分歧 ❑ *Was there a difference of opinion over what to do with the Nobel Prize money?* 对于怎么使用诺贝尔奖金有不同的意见吗？

Word Partnership *difference* 的常用搭配:
ADJ. **big/major** difference 1
V. **know the** difference, **notice a** difference, **tell the** difference 1
settle a difference 2
pay the difference 3
make a difference 4
N. difference **in age**, difference **in price** 3
difference **of opinion** 5

dif·fer·ent ◆◆◆ /dɪfərənt, dɪfrənt/ 1 ADJ If two people or things are **different**, they are not like each other in one or more ways. 不同的 ❑ *London was different from most European capitals.* 伦敦与大多数的欧洲首都城市不同。 ❑ *If he'd attended music school, how might things have been different?* 如果他上的是音乐学校，一切会怎样地不同呢？ 2 ADJ People sometimes say that one thing is **different than** another. This use is acceptable in American English, but is often considered incorrect in British English. 与…不同的 (美式英语中可用，英式英语常认为是错的) [v-link ADJ "than" n/cl] ❑ *We're not really any different than they are.* 我们与他们其实没有什么不同。
● **dif·fer·ent·ly** ADV 不同地 ❑ *Every individual learns differently.* 每个人的学习方式都不一样。 3 ADJ You use **different** to indicate that you are talking about two or more separate and distinct things of the same kind. 各不相同的 [ADJ n] ❑ *Different countries specialized in different products.* 不同的国家专门生产各不相同的产品。 4 ADJ You can describe something as **different** when it is unusual and not like others of the same kind. 不寻常的; 与众不同的 [v-link ADJ] ❑ *The result is interesting and different, but do not attempt the recipe if time is short.* 结果有趣且非同寻常，但如果时间紧张就不要尝试这个食谱。

Thesaurus *different* 另参见:
ADJ. dissimilar, mismatched, unalike 1
distinct, odd, offbeat, peculiar, unique 3

dif·fer·en·tial /dɪfərɛnʃᵊl/ **(differentials)** N-COUNT In mathematics and economics, a **differential** is a difference between two values in a scale. (数学) 微分; (经济) 差价 ❑ *...the wage differential between blue-collar and white-collar workers.* …蓝领与白领工作人员之间的工资差别。

Word Web diet

Recent U.S. government reports show that about 64% of American adults are **overweight** or **obese**. The number of people on **weight loss diets** is at an all-time high. And **fad** diets are everywhere. One diet advises people to eat mostly **protein**—meat, fish, and cheese—and very few **carbohydrates**. However, another diet recommends eating at least 40% carbohydrates. But when a weight-loss diet works, it's for one simple reason. When you burn more **calories** than you take in, you lose weight. Most doctors agree that a balanced diet with plenty of exercise is best.

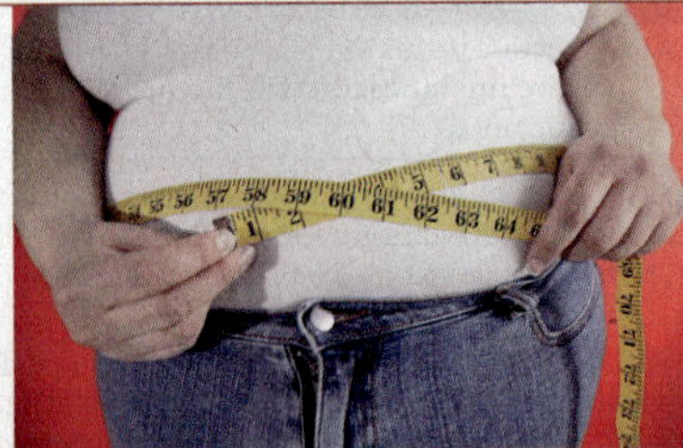

★ **dif·fer·en·ti·ate** /dɪfərɛnʃieɪt/ (**differentiates, differentiating, differentiated**) 1 V-T/V-I If you **differentiate between** things or if you **differentiate** one thing **from** another, you recognize or show the difference between them. 区分 ❑ *A child may not differentiate between his imagination and the real world.* 孩子也许无法区分想像与真实世界的差别。 2 V-T A quality or feature that **differentiates** one thing **from** another makes the two things different. 使有差别 ❑ *...distinctive policies that differentiate them from the other parties.* …使他们与其他政党区别开来的独特政策。

● **dif·fer·en·tia·tion** /dɪfərɛnʃieɪʃ^{ə}n/ N-UNCOUNT 差别 ❑ *For about six or seven weeks after conception, there is no differentiation between male and female.* 在受精后大约六七个星期时，男性和女性胚胎之间没有什么差别。

dif·fi·cult ♦♦♦ /dɪfɪkʌlt, -kəlt/ 1 ADJ Something that is **difficult** is not easy to do, understand, or deal with. 困难的 ❑ *The lack of childcare provisions made it difficult for single mothers to get jobs.* 儿童保育服务的缺乏使得单身妈妈们很难找到工作。 ❑ *It was a very difficult decision to make.* 这是个非常难作的决定。 2 ADJ Someone who is **difficult** behaves in an unreasonable and unhelpful way. 难相处的 ❑ *I had a feeling you were going to be difficult about this.* 我有种感觉，在这件事情上你将很难对付。

Thesaurus *difficult* 另参见：

ADJ. challenging, demanding, hard, tough; *(ant.)* easy, simple, uncomplicated 1
disagreeable, irritable, uncooperative; *(ant.)* accommodating, cooperative 2

dif·fi·cul·ty ♦♦◊ /dɪfɪkʌlti, -kəlti/ (**difficulties**) 1 N-COUNT A **difficulty** is a problem. 难题 ❑ *...the difficulty of getting accurate information.* …获得准确信息的困难。 2 N-UNCOUNT If you have **difficulty** doing something, you are not able to do it easily. 困难 ❑ *Do you have difficulty getting up?* 你起床有困难吗？ 3 PHRASE If someone or something is **in difficulty**, they are having a lot of problems. 在困境中 ❑ *The city's film industry is in difficulty.* 该市的电影业举步维艰。

Thesaurus *difficulty* 另参见：

N. dilemma, problem, trouble 1

dif·fi·dent /dɪfɪdənt/ ADJ Someone who is **diffident** is rather shy and does not enjoy talking about themselves or being noticed by other people. 羞怯的 ❑ *John was as bouncy and ebullient as Helen was diffident and reserved.* 约翰活泼、热情；而海伦却羞怯、矜持。

● **dif·fi·dence** /dɪfɪdəns/ N-UNCOUNT 羞怯 ❑ *He tapped on the door, opened it, and entered with a certain diffidence.* 他敲了敲门，打开了门，带着一些羞怯走了进去。

★ **dif·fuse** /dɪfyuz/ (**diffuses, diffusing, diffused**) 1 V-T/V-I If something such as knowledge or information **is diffused**, or if it **diffuses** somewhere, it is made known over a wide area or to a lot of people. 传播(知识、消息等)；散布 [WRITTEN] ❑ *Over time, however, the technology is diffused and adopted by other countries.* 然而，随着时间的推移，这项技术在其它国家得以传播并使用。 ❑ *...to diffuse new ideas obtained from elsewhere.* …传播从别处获得的新思想。 ● **dif·fu·sion** /dɪfyuʒ^{ə}n/ N-UNCOUNT (对知识、消息等的) 传播；散布 ❑ *...the development and diffusion of ideas.* …思想的发展和传播。 2 V-T To **diffuse** a feeling, especially an undesirable one, means to cause it to weaken and lose its power to affect people. 缓解；消除 ❑ *The presidents will meet to try and diffuse the tensions that threaten to reignite the conflict.* 总统们将举行会晤以试图缓解可能重新引发冲突的紧张局面。 3 V-T If something **diffuses** light, it causes the light to spread weakly in different directions. 使(光线) 漫射 ❑ *Diffusing a light also reduces its power.* 使光线漫射也会减弱其能量。 4 V-I To **diffuse** or **be diffused** through something means to move and spread through it. 扩散 ❑ *It allows nicotine to diffuse slowly and steadily into the bloodstream.* 它使尼古丁缓慢、稳步地扩散到血液当中。

● **dif·fu·sion** N-UNCOUNT 扩散 ❑ *There are data on the rates of diffusion of molecules.* 有一些关于分子的扩散速率的数据。

→ see **culture**

dig ♦◊◊ /dɪg/ (**digs, digging, dug**) 1 V-T/V-I If people or animals **dig**, they make a hole in the ground or in a pile of earth, stones, or trash. 挖掘 ❑ *I grabbed the spade and started digging.* 我抓起铁锹开始挖了起来。 ❑ *Dig a large hole and drive the stake in first.* 先挖个大洞，把桩子打进去。 2 V-I If you **dig into** something such as a deep container, you put your hand in it to search for something. 将手伸入…(以探寻某物) ❑ *He dug into his coat pocket for his keys.* 他把手伸进大衣口袋里找钥匙。 3 V-T/V-I If you **dig** one thing **into** another or if one thing **digs into** another, the first thing is pushed hard into the second, or presses hard into it. 刺入；戳进 ❑ *She digs the serving spoon into the moussaka.* 她把分菜匙插进茄合里。 4 V-I If you **dig into** a subject or a store of information, you study it very carefully in order to discover or check facts. 钻研 ❑ *...as a special congressional enquiry digs deeper into the alleged financial misdeeds of his government.* …随着一项国会特别调查行动对其政府所谓的不当财政行为的深入调查。 ❑ *He has been digging into the local archives.* 他一直在仔细研究当地的档案。 5 V-T If you **dig yourself out of** a difficult or unpleasant situation, especially one which you caused yourself, you manage to get out of it. 摆脱(困境) ❑ *He's taken these measures to try and dig himself out of a hole.* 他采取了这些措施，力图摆脱困境。 6 N-COUNT If you have a **dig at** someone, you say something which is intended to make fun of them or upset them. 挖苦；嘲弄 ❑ *She couldn't resist a dig at Dave after his unfortunate performance.* 戴夫演出失败之后，她忍不住给了他一顿嘲弄。 7 N-COUNT If you give someone a **dig** in a part of their body, you push them with your finger or your elbow, usually as a warning or as a joke. (出于警告或开玩笑而用手指或肘进行的) 戳 ❑ *Cassandra silenced him with a sharp dig in the small of the back.* 卡桑德拉在他腰背上狠狠地戳了一下让他闭上了嘴。 8 **to dig** one's **heels in** → see **heel**

→ see **tunnel**

▶ **dig out** 1 PHRASAL VERB If you **dig** someone or something **out of** a place, you get them out by digging or by forcing them from the things surrounding them. 挖掘出 ❑ *...digging minerals out of the Earth.* …开采地球上的矿物。 2 PHRASAL VERB If you **dig** something **out**, you find it after it has been stored, hidden, or forgotten for a long time. 找出 [INFORMAL] ❑ *Recently, I dug out Barstow's novel and read it again.* 最近，我翻出了巴斯托的小说，又看了一遍。

di·gest (**digests, digesting, digested**)

The verb is pronounced /dɪdʒɛst/. The noun is pronounced /daɪdʒɛst/.

动词读作 /dɪdʒɛst/。名词读作 /daɪdʒɛst/。

1 V-T/V-I When food **digests** or when you **digest** it, it passes through your body to your stomach. Your stomach removes the substances that your body needs and gets rid of the rest. 消化 ❑ *Do not undertake strenuous exercise for a few hours after a meal to allow food to digest.* 饭后几小时内不要做剧烈运动，以让食物消化。 ❑ *She couldn't digest food properly.* 她无法正常消化食物。 2 V-T If you **digest** information, you think about it carefully so that you understand it. 领会 ❑ *They learn well but seem to need time to digest information.* 他们学得很好，但似乎需要时间来吃透这些知识。 3 V-T If you **digest** some unpleasant news, you think about it until you are able to accept it and know how to deal with it. 承受(坏消息) ❑ *All this has upset me. I need time to digest it all.* 这一切让我心烦意乱。我需要时间来承受。 4 N-COUNT A **digest** is a collection of pieces of writing. They are published together in a shorter form than they were originally published. 文摘 ❑ *...the Middle East Economic Digest.* …中东经济文摘。

→ see **cooking**

di·ges·tion /daɪdʒɛstʃən/ (**digestions**) 1 N-UNCOUNT **Digestion** is the process of digesting food. 消化 ❑ *No liquids are served with meals because they interfere with digestion.* 上菜时不提供饮料，因为会妨碍消化。 2 N-COUNT Your **digestion** is the system in your body which digests your food. 消化系统 ❑ *Keep your digestion working well by eating plenty of fiber.* 吃大量的食物纤维来保持消化系统正常工作。

★ **di·ges·tive** /daɪdʒɛstɪv/ ADJ You can describe things that are related to the digestion of food as **digestive**. 消化的 [ADJ n] ❑ *...digestive juices that normally work on breaking down our food.* …通常用于分解食物的消化液。

digi·cam /dɪdʒɪkæm/ (**digicams**) N-COUNT A **digicam** is the same as a **digital camera**. 数码相机 ❑ *Filmmaking was transformed by digital editing, digital f/x, and digicams.* 电影制作被数码编辑技术、数码特技效果和数码相机改变了。

▲ **dig·it** /dɪdʒɪt/ (**digits**) N-COUNT A **digit** is a written symbol for any of the ten numbers from 0 to 9. (0到9的任一) 数字 ❑ *Her telephone number differs from mine by one digit.* 她的电话号码跟我的差一个数字。

D

digi·tal ♦♦◇ /dɪdʒɪtᵊl/ **1** ADJ **Digital** systems record or transmit information in the form of thousands of very small signals. 数码的 ❑ *The new digital technology would allow a rapid expansion in the number of TV channels.* 新的数码技术可使电视频道的数量得以快速增多。 **2** ADJ **Digital** devices such as watches or clocks give information by displaying numbers rather than by having a pointer which moves round a dial. Compare **analog**. 数字的 [ADJ n] ❑ *...a digital display.* …数字显示。 **3** PHRASE People sometimes refer to poorer people's lack of access to the latest computer technology as **the digital divide**. 数字鸿沟 ["the/a" PHR] [mainly JOURNALISM] ❑ *...an attempt to reduce the "digital divide" between poor students who have no computers and those from well-off families who do.* …缩小没有电脑的贫困生和有电脑的富裕家庭学生之间的"数字鸿沟"的努力。
→ see **DVD, technology, television**

digi·tal cam·era (**digital cameras**) N-COUNT A **digital camera** is a camera that produces digital images that can be stored on a computer, displayed on a screen, and printed. 数码相机 ❑ *The speed with which digital cameras can take, process, and transmit an image is phenomenal.* 数码相机拍摄、处理、传输图像的速度惊人。

digi·tal ra·dio (**digital radios**) **1** N-UNCOUNT **Digital radio** is radio in which the signals are transmitted in digital form and decoded by the radio receiver. 数字广播 ❑ *...those with access to digital radio, satellite TV, or the Internet.* …能够接收数字广播、卫星电视或连接互联网的人。 **2** N-COUNT A **digital radio** is a radio that can receive digital signals. 数码收音机 ❑ *Manufacturers are working on a new generation of cheaper digital radios.* 厂家正在生产新一代更便宜的数码收音机。

digi·tal tele·vi·sion (**digital televisions**) **1** N-UNCOUNT **Digital television** is television in which the signals are transmitted in digital form and decoded by the television receiver. 数字电视 ❑ *At present only 31 percent of the population has access to digital television.* 目前仅有31%的人可以收看数字电视。 **2** N-COUNT A **digital television** is a television that can receive digital signals. 数字电视机 ❑ *Other new technology products are also doing well, such as digital cameras and wide screen digital televisions.* 其它的新技术产品也发展良好，如数码照相机和宽屏数字电视机。

digi·tal TV (**digital TVs**) **1** N-UNCOUNT **Digital TV** is the same as **digital television**. 数字电视 **2** N-COUNT A **digital TV** is the same as a **digital television**. 数字电视机

Word Link *dign ≈ proper, worthy : dignified, dignitary, indignant*

dig·ni·fied /dɪgnɪfaɪd/ ADJ If you say that someone or something is **dignified**, you mean they are calm, impressive, and deserve respect. 有尊严的; 高贵的 ❑ *He seemed a very dignified and charming man.* 他似乎是个高贵而又有魅力的男士。

dig·ni·tary /dɪgnɪtɛri/ (**dignitaries**) N-COUNT **Dignitaries** are people who are considered to be important because they have a high rank in government or in a church. (政府或教会的) 显要人物 ❑ *...an office fund used to entertain visiting dignitaries.* …一笔用于招待来访要员的办公资金。

dig·nity /dɪgnɪti/ **1** N-UNCOUNT If someone behaves or moves with **dignity**, they are calm, controlled, and admirable. 尊贵 ❑ *...her extraordinary dignity and composure.* …她无与伦比的高贵与冷静。 **2** N-UNCOUNT If you talk about the **dignity** of people or their lives or activities, you mean that they are valuable and worthy of respect. 尊严 ❑ *...the sense of human dignity.* …人的尊严感。 ❑ *...the integrity and dignity of our lives and feelings.* …我们的生活与感受的正直和尊严。 **3** N-UNCOUNT Your **dignity** is the sense that you have of your own importance and value, and other people's respect for you. 自尊 ❑ *She still has her dignity.* 她还有自尊。

dike /daɪk/ (**dikes**) **1** N-COUNT A **dike** is a thick wall that is built to stop water flooding onto very low-lying land from a river or from the ocean. 堤坝 **2** → see **dyke 1**

di·lapi·da·ted /dɪlæpɪdeɪtɪd/ ADJ A building that is **dilapidated** is old and in a generally bad condition. 破旧的 ❑ *...an old dilapidated barn.* …一座破旧的谷仓。

di·late /daɪleɪt/ (**dilates, dilating, dilated**) V-T/V-I When things such as blood vessels or the pupils of your eyes **dilate** or when something **dilates** them, they become wider or bigger. 使扩大; 扩大 ❑ *At night, the pupils dilate to allow in more light.* 晚上，瞳孔放大以便让更多的光线射入。 • **di·lat·ed** ADJ 扩大的 ❑ *His eyes seemed slightly dilated.* 他的双眼瞳孔似乎稍微扩大了些。

Word Link *di ≈ two : dilemma, diverge, division*

di·lem·ma /dɪlɛmə/ (**dilemmas**) N-COUNT A **dilemma** is a difficult situation in which you have to choose between two or more alternatives. 进退两难的局面 ❑ *He was faced with the dilemma of whether or not to return to his country.* 他面临着是否回国的艰难选择。

★ **dili·gent** /dɪlɪdʒᵊnt/ ADJ Someone who is **diligent** works hard in a careful and thorough way. 勤奋的 ❑ *Meyers is a diligent and prolific worker.* 迈耶斯是个勤奋而且出活多的工人。 • **dili·gence** /dɪlɪdʒᵊns/ N-UNCOUNT 勤奋 ❑ *The police are pursuing their inquiries with great diligence.* 警察正以不懈的努力进行着调查。 • **dili·gent·ly** ADV 勤奋地 [ADV with v] ❑ *The two sides are now working diligently to resolve their differences.* 双方正为消除他们的分歧努力着。

★ **di·lute** /daɪlut/ (**dilutes, diluting, diluted**) **1** V-T/V-I If a liquid **is diluted** or **dilutes**, it is added to or mixes with water or another liquid, and becomes weaker. 稀释; 变淡 ❑ *If you give your baby juice, dilute it well with cooled, boiled water.* 喂婴儿果汁要用凉开水充分稀释。 ❑ *The liquid is then diluted.* 然后液体就变稀了。 **2** V-T If someone or something **dilutes** a belief, quality, or value, they make it weaker and less effective. 削弱 ❑ *There was a clear intention to dilute black voting power.* 削弱黑人选举权的意图是显而易见的。 **3** ADJ A **dilute** liquid is very thin and weak, usually because it has had water added to it. 稀释的 ❑ *...a dilute solution of bleach.* …稀释了的漂白液。

dim /dɪm/ (**dimmer, dimmest, dims, dimming, dimmed**) **1** ADJ **Dim** light is not bright. 昏暗的 ❑ *She stood waiting in the dim light.* 她站在昏暗的灯光下等待着。 • **dim·ly** ADV 昏暗地 ❑ *Two lamps burned dimly.* 两盏油灯昏暗地燃烧着。 **2** ADJ A **dim** place is rather dark because there is not much light in it. 黑暗的 ❑ *The room was dim and cool and quiet.* 这房间昏暗、阴冷且安静。 **3** ADJ A **dim** figure or object is not very easy to see, either because it is in shadow or darkness, or because it is far away. 蒙胧的 ❑ *Pete's flashlight picked out the dim figures of Bob and Chang.* 皮特的手电筒照射出鲍勃和常的蒙胧身影。 • **dim·ly** ADV 蒙胧地 ❑ *The shoreline could be dimly seen.* 海岸线隐约可见。 **4** ADJ If you have a **dim** memory or understanding of something, it is difficult to remember or is unclear in your mind. 模糊的 ❑ *It seems that the '60s era of social activism is all but a dim memory.* 60年代的社会激进主义时代似乎只剩下模糊的记忆。 • **dim·ly** ADV 模糊地 ❑ *Christina dimly recalled the procedure.* 克里斯蒂娜隐约地记起了那个步骤。 **5** ADJ If the future of something is **dim**, you have no reason to feel hopeful or positive about it. 悲观的 ❑ *The prospects for a peaceful solution are dim.* 找到和平解决方案的前景渺茫。 **6** ADJ If you describe someone as **dim**, you think that they are stupid. 愚蠢的 [INFORMAL] ❑ *Sometimes he thought George was a bit dim.* 有时他觉得乔治有点儿笨。 **7** V-T/V-I If you **dim** a light or if it **dims**, it becomes less bright. 使变暗; 变暗 ❑ *Dim the lighting – it is unpleasant to lie with a bright light shining in your eyes.* 把灯光调暗——在刺眼的灯光下躺着不舒服。 **8** V-T/V-I If your future, hopes, or emotions **dim** or if something **dims** them, they become less good or less strong. 使变暗淡; 变暗淡 ❑ *Their economic prospects have dimmed.* 他们的经济前景变得暗淡了。 **9** V-T/V-I If your memories **dim** or if something **dims** them, they become less clear in your mind. 使变模糊; 变模糊 ❑ *Their memory of what happened has dimmed.* 他们对所发生的事的记忆变得模糊了。

▲ **dime** /daɪm/ (**dimes**) N-COUNT A **dime** is a U.S. coin worth ten cents. 10美分硬币 ❑ *The penny meters are slowly being replaced by electronic ones that take nickels, dimes, and quarters.* 接受1美分硬币的收费表正逐渐被接受5美分、10美分和25美分的电子收费计所取代。

di·men·sion /dɪmɛnʃᵊn, daɪ-/ (**dimensions**) **1** N-COUNT A particular **dimension** of something is a particular aspect of it. 方面 ❑ *There is a political dimension to the accusations.* 这些指控含有政治因素。 **2** N-COUNT A **dimension** is a measurement such as length, width, or height. If you talk about the **dimensions** of an object or place, you are referring to its size and proportions. (单数) 尺寸; (复数) 比例大小 ❑ *Drilling will continue on the site to assess the dimensions of the new oilfield.* 钻探还将继续在现场进行以估测新油田的大小。 **3** N-PLURAL If you talk about the **dimensions** of a situation or problem, you are talking about its extent and size. 规模 ❑ *The dimensions of the market collapse, in terms of turnover and price, were certainly not anticipated.* 股市崩盘的规模，无论从成交量还是价格来看，都是出乎意料的。

Word Partnership *dimension 的常用搭配:*
ADJ. **different** dimension, **important** dimension, **new** dimension, **spiritual** dimension **1**

Word Link *min ≈ small, lessen : diminish, minus, minute*

★ **di·min·ish** /dɪmɪnɪʃ/ (**diminishes, diminishing, diminished**) **1** V-T/V-I When something **diminishes**, or when something **diminishes** it, it becomes reduced in size, importance, or intensity. 使减少；变少 ❑ *The threat of nuclear war has diminished.* 核战的威胁变小了。❑ *Federalism is intended to diminish the power of the central state.* 联邦制度旨在削弱中央政府的权力。 **2** V-T If you **diminish** someone or something, you talk about them or treat them in a way that makes them appear less important than they really are. 贬低 ❑ *He never put her down or diminished her.* 他从未轻视过她或贬低过她。

di·minu·tive /dɪmɪnyətɪv/ ADJ A **diminutive** person or object is very small. 微小的 ❑ *Her eyes scanned the room until they came to rest on a diminutive figure standing at the entrance.* 她的目光扫视着房间，最后停留在一个站在入口的小小的身影上。

din /dɪn/ N-SING A **din** is a very loud and unpleasant noise that lasts for some time. 喧嚣 ❑ *They tried to make themselves heard over the din of the crowd.* 他们竭力让自己的声音盖过人群的喧闹声。

dine /daɪn/ (**dines, dining, dined**) V-I When you **dine**, you have dinner. 吃饭 [no passive] [FORMAL] ❑ *He dines alone most nights.* 大多数晚上他都独自进餐。

din·er /daɪnər/ (**diners**) **1** N-COUNT A **diner** is a small cheap restaurant that is often open all day. (全天营业、价格便宜的) 小餐馆 [AM] **2** N-COUNT The people who are having dinner in a restaurant can be referred to as **diners**. 用餐者 ❑ *They sat in a corner, away from other diners.* 他们坐在一个远离其他用餐者的角落里。

din·ghy /dɪŋgi/ (**dinghies**) N-COUNT A **dinghy** is a small open boat that you sail or row. 小舢板；小划艇 ❑ *...a rubber dinghy.* ⋯一条橡皮艇。

din·gy /dɪndʒi/ (**dingier, dingiest**) **1** ADJ A **dingy** building or place is dark and depressing, and perhaps dirty. (建筑物或处所) 阴暗肮脏的 ❑ *Shaw took me to his dingy office.* 肖把我带到他那又暗又脏的办公室。 **2** ADJ **Dingy** clothes, curtains, or furnishings look dirty or dull. 邋遢的；暗淡的 ❑ *...wallpaper with stripes of dingy yellow.* ⋯有暗淡的黄色条纹的墙纸。

din·ing room (**dining rooms**) N-COUNT The **dining room** is the room in a house where people have their meals, or a room in a hotel where meals are served. 餐厅
→ see **house**

din·ner ◆◆◇ /dɪnər/ (**dinners**) **1** N-VAR **Dinner** is the main meal of the day, usually served in the early part of the evening. 正餐 (常指晚餐) ❑ *She invited us to her house for dinner.* 她请我们到她家吃晚饭。❑ *Would you like to stay and have dinner?* 你愿意留下来吃晚餐吗？ **2** N-VAR Any meal you eat in the middle of the day can be referred to as **dinner**. 午餐 **3** N-COUNT A **dinner** is a formal social event at which a meal is served. It is held in the evening. 晚宴 ❑ *...a series of official lunches and dinners.* ⋯一系列正式的午餐和晚宴。
→ see **dish, meal**

din·ner jack·et (**dinner jackets**) also **dinner-jacket** N-COUNT A **dinner jacket** is a jacket, usually black, worn by men for formal social events. (男子在正式社交聚会时穿的) 无尾礼服

▲ **di·no·saur** /daɪnəsɔr/ (**dinosaurs**) **1** N-COUNT **Dinosaurs** were large reptiles which lived in prehistoric times. 恐龙 **2** N-COUNT If you refer to an organization as a **dinosaur**, you mean that it is large, inefficient, and out of date. 庞大、低效且落后的机构 [DISAPPROVAL] ❑ *...industrial dinosaurs.* ⋯庞大臃肿的工业企业。

★ **di·ox·ide** /daɪɒksaɪd/ → see **carbon dioxide**

dip /dɪp/ (**dips, dipping, dipped**) **1** V-T If you **dip** something **in** a liquid, you put it into the liquid for a short time, so that only part of it is covered, and take it out again. 蘸 ❑ *Dip each apple in the syrup until thickly coated.* 把每个苹果在糖浆里蘸一下，直到被厚厚地裹上糖浆。● N-COUNT **Dip** is also a noun. 蘸 ❑ *...a quick dip of his toe into the water.* ⋯他的脚趾头在水里快速的一蘸。 **2** V-T/V-I If you **dip** your hand **into** a container or **dip into** the container, you put your hand into it in order to take something out of it. (将手) 伸入 ❑ *She dipped a hand into the jar of candies and pulled one out.* 她把手伸进糖罐里掏出一颗糖来。❑ *Nancy dipped into the bowl of popcorn that Hannah had made for them.* 南希把手伸进盛着汉娜给她们做的爆米花的碗里。 **3** V-I If something **dips**, it makes a downward movement, usually quickly. (突然) 下沉 ❑ *Blake jumped in expertly; the boat dipped slightly under his weight.* 布莱克熟练地跳了进来；船由于他的体重微微沉了一下。● N-COUNT **Dip** is also a noun. (突然的) 下沉 ❑ *I noticed little things, a dip of the head, a twitch in the shoulder.* 我注意到一些小动作，脑袋向下的一沉、肩膀的一抽动。 **4** V-I If an area of land, a road, or a path **dips**, it goes down quite suddenly to a lower level. (土地、地段、道路等) 突陷 ❑ *The road dipped and rose again as it neared the top of Parker Mountain.* 快到帕克山山顶的时候，山路突降，继而又突升。● N-COUNT **Dip** is also a noun. (土地、地段、道路等的) 突陷 ❑ *Where the road makes a dip, soon after a small vineyard on the right, turn right.* 过了右边的小葡萄园不久，在路面陡降的地方朝右转。 **5** V-I If the amount or level of something **dips**, it becomes smaller or lower, usually only for a short period of time. (暂时) 下降 ❑ *Unemployment dipped to 6.9 percent last month.* 上个月，失业率降到了6.9%。● N-COUNT **Dip** is also a noun. (暂时的) 下降 ❑ *...the current dip in farm spending.* ⋯农场开支目前的暂时下降。 **6** V-I If you **dip into** a book, you take a brief look at it without reading or studying it seriously. 浏览 ❑ *...a chance to dip into a wide selection of books on Tibetan Buddhism.* ⋯一次浏览有关藏传佛教的各种各样书籍的机会。 **7** V-I If you **dip into** a sum of money that you had intended to save, you use some of it to buy something or pay for something. 动用 (积蓄) ❑ *Just when she was ready to dip into her savings, Greg hastened to her rescue.* 就在她准备动用积蓄时，格雷格赶来救了她的急。 **8** N-COUNT If you have or take a **dip**, you go for a quick swim in the ocean, a lake, a river, or a swimming pool. 快游 ❑ *She flicked through a romantic paperback between occasional dips in the pool.* 她在泳池里偶尔的快游的间歇之中快速翻完了一本平装本的爱情小说。

★ **di·plo·ma** /dɪploʊmə/ (**diplomas**) N-COUNT A **diploma** is a document which may be awarded to a student who has completed a course of study by a university or college, or by a high school in the United States. 文凭 ❑ *...a new two-year course leading to a diploma in social work.* ⋯一门可以获得社会工作文凭的2年制的新课程。
→ see **graduation**

di·plo·ma·cy /dɪploʊməsi/ **1** N-UNCOUNT **Diplomacy** is the activity or profession of managing relations between the governments of different countries. 外交 ❑ *Today's Security Council resolution will be a significant success for American diplomacy.* 今天的安理会决议将成为美国外交的一次重大胜利。 **2** N-UNCOUNT **Diplomacy** is the skill of being careful to say or do things which will not offend people. 交际手腕 ❑ *He stormed off in a fury, and it took all Minnelli's powers of diplomacy to get him to return.* 他愤然离去，明内利使尽一切交际手腕才让他回来。

dip·lo·mat ◆◇◇ /dɪpləmæt/ (**diplomats**) N-COUNT A **diplomat** is a senior official who discusses affairs with another country on behalf of his or her own country, usually working as a member of an embassy. 外交官 ❑ *...a Western diplomat with long experience in Asia.* ⋯一名在亚洲有长期经验的西方外交官。

dip·lo·mat·ic ◆◇◇ /dɪpləmætɪk/ **1** ADJ **Diplomatic** means relating to diplomacy and diplomats. 外交的 ❑ *...before the two countries resume full diplomatic relations.* ⋯在两国全面恢复外交关系之前。● **dip·lo·mati·cal·ly** /dɪpləmætɪkli/ ADV 外交地 ❑ *...a growing sense of doubt that the conflict can be resolved diplomatically.* ⋯对该冲突能用外交手段得以解决的不断增加的怀疑。 **2** ADJ Someone who is **diplomatic** is careful to say or do things without offending people. 圆通得体的 ❑ *She is very direct. I tend to be more diplomatic, I suppose.* 她很直率。我觉得我更圆通些。● **dip·lo·mati·cal·ly** ADV 圆通得体地 [ADV with v] ❑ *"I really like their sound, although I'm not crazy about their lyrics," he says, diplomatically.* "我非常喜欢他们的声音，但不太喜欢他们的歌词，"他很圆滑地说。

Word Partnership *diplomatic* 的常用搭配：
N. diplomatic **activity**, diplomatic **immunity**, diplomatic **mission**, diplomatic **relations**, diplomatic **skills**, diplomatic **solution**, diplomatic **ties** **1**

dip·lo·mat·ic corps (**diplomatic corps**)

Diplomatic corps is both the singular and the plural form.

N-COUNT-COLL **The diplomatic corps** is the group of all the diplomats who work in one city or country. 外交使节团

dire /daɪər/ **1** ADJ **Dire** is used to emphasize how serious or terrible a situation or event is. 严重的；可怕的 [EMPHASIS] ❑ *The government looked as if it would split apart, with dire consequences for domestic peace.* 政府看似就要分崩离析，给国内和平带来可怕的后果。 **2** ADJ If you describe something as **dire**, you are emphasizing that it is of very low quality. 质量低劣的 [INFORMAL, EMPHASIS] ❑ *...a book of children's verse, which ranged from the barely tolerable to the*

d

utterly dire. …一本儿童诗集，所选诗篇有的勉强可读，有的糟糕透顶。

di·rect ♦♦♦ /dɪrɛkt, daɪ-/ (**directs, directing, directed**) 1 ADJ **Direct** means moving toward a place or object, without changing direction and without stopping, for example, in a trip. 直达的 ❑ *They'd come on a direct flight from Athens.* 他们是从雅典乘坐直达航班来的。● ADV **Direct** is also an adverb. 直达地 [ADV after v] ❑ *You can fly direct from Seattle to Europe.* 你可以从西雅图直飞欧洲。● **di·rect·ly** ADV 直达地 [ADV after v] ❑ *On arriving in New York, Dylan went directly to Greenwich Village.* 迪伦一到纽约就直接去了格林威治村。 2 ADJ If something is in **direct** heat or light, it is strongly affected by the heat or light, because there is nothing between it and the source of heat or light to protect it. 直接（受热）的；（光）直射的 [ADJ n] ❑ *All medicines should be stored away from moisture, direct sunlight, and heat.* 所有药物应避免储存在潮湿、阳光直射或者高温的地方。 3 ADJ You use **direct** to describe an experience, activity, or system which only involves the people, actions, or things that are necessary to make it happen. （经历、行动、体制等）直接的 ❑ *He has direct experience of the process of privatization.* 他有参与私有化过程的直接经验。● ADV **Direct** is also an adverb. 直接地 [ADV after v] ❑ *More farms are selling direct to consumers.* 更多的农场在直接向消费者销售产品。● **di·rect·ly** ADV 直接地 [ADV with v] ❑ *We cannot measure pain directly. It can only be estimated.* 我们无法直接测量疼痛的程度，只能估计。 4 ADJ You use **direct** to emphasize the closeness of a connection between two things. 直接相关的 [EMPHASIS] ❑ *They were unable to prove that the unfortunate lady had died as a direct result of his injection.* 他们不能证明那名不幸女士的死亡是由于他的注射直接造成的。 5 ADJ If you describe a person or their behavior as **direct**, you mean that they are honest and open, and say exactly what they mean. 直率的 ❑ *He avoided giving a direct answer.* 他回避作出直截了当的回答。● **di·rect·ly** ADV 直率地 [ADV after v] ❑ *At your first meeting, explain simply and directly what you hope to achieve.* 第一次会面时，简明扼要、直截了当地说明你希望达到什么目标。● **di·rect·ness** N-UNCOUNT 直率 ❑ *Using "I" ensures clarity and directness, and it adds warmth to a piece of writing.* 使用第一人称"我"确保文章的清晰性和直接性，还给文章增添亲切感。 6 → see also **direction, directly** 7 V-T If you **direct** something **at** a particular thing, you aim or point it at that thing. 瞄准 ❑ *I reached the cockpit and directed the extinguisher at the fire without effect.* 我进入驾驶舱，把灭火器对准火焰喷射，但没有效果。 8 V-T If your attention, emotions, or actions **are directed at** a particular person or thing, you are focusing them on that person or thing. （把注意力、感情或者行动）集中于… ❑ *The learner's attention needs to be directed to the significant features.* 学习者的注意力需要集中在重要特征上。 9 V-T If a remark or look **is directed at** you, someone says something to you or looks at you. 针对；（目光）投向 ❑ *She could hardly believe the question was directed toward her.* 她几乎不相信这个问题是针对她的。 ❑ *The abuse was directed at the TV crews.* 辱骂是针对电视台工作人员的。 10 V-T If you **direct** someone somewhere, you tell them how to get there. 指路 ❑ *Could you direct them to Dr. Lamont's office, please?* 你能告诉他们去拉蒙特医生的办公室怎么走吗？ 11 V-T When someone **directs** a project or a group of people, they are responsible for organizing the people and activities that are involved. 指挥 ❑ *Christopher will direct day-to-day operations.* 克里斯托弗将指挥日常工作。● **di·rec·tion** /dɪrɛkʃᵊn, daɪ-/ N-UNCOUNT 指挥 ❑ *Organizations need clear direction, set priorities and performance standards, and clear controls.* 组织需要明确的指挥、即定的主次顺序、绩效标准，以及正确的管理。 12 V-T/V-I When someone **directs** a movie, play, or television program, they are responsible for the way in which it is performed and for telling the actors and assistants what to do. 导演 ❑ *He directed various TV shows.* 他导演过各种电视节目。

Thesaurus *direct* 另参见：

ADJ. nonstop, straight 1
firsthand, personal 3
candid, frank, plain 5

di·rect dis·course N-UNCOUNT In grammar, **direct discourse** is speech which is reported by using the exact words that the speaker used. 直接引语 [mainly AM]

in BRIT, usually use **direct speech**

di·rec·tion ♦♦◊ /dɪrɛkʃᵊn, daɪ-/ (**directions**) 1 N-VAR A **direction** is the general line that someone or something is moving or pointing in. 方向 ❑ *St. Andrews was ten miles in the opposite direction.* 圣安德鲁斯在相反方向的10英里处。 ❑ *He got into Margie's car and swung out onto the road in the direction of Larry's shop.* 他钻进玛吉的汽车，摇晃着开上马路，朝拉里商店的方向驶去。 2 N-VAR A **direction** is the general way in which something develops or progresses. 发展方向 ❑ *They threatened to lead a mass walk-out if the party did not sharply change direction.* 他们威胁说，如果该党对其发展方向不作大的调整，他们就发动大家集体退党。 3 N-PLURAL **Directions** are instructions that tell you what to do, how to do something, or how to get somewhere. 说明书；（指示路线的）说明 ❑ *I should know by now not to throw away the directions until we've finished cooking.* 我现在应该明白，饭没做完之前，不要把食谱扔掉。 4 → see also **direct**

Word Partnership *direction* 的常用搭配：

N. **sense of** direction 1
ADJ. **opposite** direction, **right** direction, **wrong** direction 1
general direction 1 2
V. **change** direction, **move in a** direction 1 2
lack direction, **take** direction 2

di·rec·tive /dɪrɛktɪv, daɪ-/ (**directives**) N-COUNT A **directive** is an official instruction that is given by someone in authority. 官方指示 ❑ *Thanks to a new directive, food labeling will be more specific.* 由于官方的一项新指令，食品标签将会更明确具体。

di·rect·ly /dɪrɛktli, daɪ-/ 1 ADV If something is **directly** above, below, or in front of something, it is in exactly that position. 正好地 [ADV prep/adv] ❑ *The second rainbow will be bigger than the first, and directly above it.* 第二道彩虹将比第一道更大，并位于第一道的正上方。 2 ADV If you do one action **directly after** another, you do the second action as soon as the first one is finished. 立即 [ADV prep/adv] ❑ *Most guests left directly after the wake.* 守灵仪式一结束，大部分客人就立刻走了。 3 → see also **direct**

di·rect mail N-UNCOUNT **Direct mail** is a method of marketing which involves companies sending advertising material directly to people who they think may be interested in their products. 广告直邮（指给潜在的顾客直接邮寄广告资料）[BUSINESS] ❑ *...efforts to solicit new customers by direct mail and television advertising.* …通过广告直邮和电视广告争取新客户的努力。

di·rect mar·ket·ing N-UNCOUNT **Direct marketing** is the same as **direct mail.** 广告直邮 [BUSINESS] ❑ *The direct marketing industry has become adept at packaging special offers.* 广告直邮业已经很会为特价销售做包装宣传了。

di·rect ob·ject (**direct objects**) N-COUNT In grammar, the **direct object** of a transitive verb is the noun group which refers to someone or something directly affected by or involved in the action performed by the subject. For example, in "I saw him yesterday," "him" is the direct object. Compare **indirect object.** 直接宾语

di·rec·tor ♦♦♦ /dɪrɛktər, daɪ-/ (**directors**) 1 N-COUNT The **director** of a play, movie, or television program is the person who decides how it will appear on stage or screen, and who tells the actors and technical staff what to do. 导演 ❑ *"Cut!" the director yelled. "That was perfect."* "停！"导演叫道。"太好了！" 2 N-COUNT In some organizations and public authorities, the person in charge is referred to as **the director**. 主任；主管 ❑ *...the director of the intensive care unit at Buffalo General Hospital.* …布法罗总医院重症监护室的主任。 3 N-COUNT The **directors** of a company are its most senior managers, who meet regularly to make important decisions about how it will be run. 董事 [BUSINESS] ❑ *He served on the board of directors of a local bank.* 他在当地一家银行的董事会担任董事。 4 N-COUNT The **director** of a choir is the person who is conducting it. （合唱团的）指挥 [AM]

in BRIT, use **conductor**

di·rec·to·rate /dɪrɛktərɪt, daɪ-/ (**directorates**) 1 N-COUNT A **directorate** is a board of directors in a company or organization. 董事会 [BUSINESS] ❑ *The bank will be managed by a directorate of around five professional bankers.* 该银行将由五名左右的职业银行家组成的董事会管理。 2 N-COUNT A **directorate** is a part of a government department which is responsible for one particular thing. （政府的）专门部门 ❑ *...the CIA's intelligence directorate.* …中情局情报处。

di·rec·tor gen·er·al (**directors general**) N-COUNT The **director general** of a large organization is the person who is in charge of it. （大型组织的）总负责人 [BUSINESS]

di·rec·tor·ship /dɪrɛktərʃɪp, daɪ-/ (**directorships**) N-COUNT A **directorship** is the job or position of a company director. 董事之职位；管理者之职位 [BUSINESS] ❑ *Barry resigned his directorship in December 1973.* 巴里于1973年12月辞去了董事一职。

★ **di·rec·tory** /dɪrɛktəri, daɪ-/ (**directories**) 1 N-COUNT A **directory** is a book which gives lists of facts, for example, people's names, addresses, and telephone numbers, or the names and addresses of business companies, usually arranged in alphabetical order. (通常按字母顺序记录姓名、地址、电话、公司通讯录等的) 簿 ❑ *...a telephone directory.* …电话簿。 2 N-COUNT A **directory** is an area of a computer disk which contains one or more files or other directories. (计算机磁盘中包含一个或多个文件的) 目录 [COMPUTING] ❑ *This option lets you search your current directory for files by date, contents, and document summary.* 这一选项让你按日期、内容和文件摘要在当前目录中查找文件。 3 N-COUNT On the World Wide Web, a **directory** is a list of the subjects that you can find information on. (万维网上的) 主题目录 [COMPUTING] ❑ *Yahoo is the oldest and best-known Web directory service.* 雅虎是提供网上目录检索服务最早、最知名的网站。

di·rec·tory as·sis·tance N-UNCOUNT **Directory assistance** is a service which you can telephone to find out someone's telephone number. 电话查号服务 [AM]

in BRIT, use **directory enquiries**

❑ *He dialed directory assistance.* 他拨了查号台的电话。

di·rec·tory en·quiries [BRIT] → see **information**

di·rect speech N-UNCOUNT In grammar, **direct speech** is speech which is reported by using the exact words that the speaker used. 直接引语 [mainly BRIT]

in AM, also use **direct discourse**

di·rect tax (**direct taxes**) N-COUNT A **direct tax** is a tax which a person or organization pays directly to the government, for example, income tax. 直接税 (个人或组织直接付给政府的税，如所得税) [BUSINESS] ❑ *What people had to pay in direct and indirect taxes had not gone up since 1979.* 人们须缴纳的直接税和间接税从1979年开始没涨过。

dirt /dɜrt/ 1 N-UNCOUNT If there is **dirt** on something, there is dust, mud, or a stain on it. 灰尘; 污垢 ❑ *I started to scrub off the dirt.* 我开始擦除灰尘。 2 N-UNCOUNT You can refer to the earth on the ground as **dirt**, especially when it is dusty. 泥土 ❑ *They all sit on the dirt in the dappled shade of a tree.* 他们都坐在斑驳的树荫下的地上。 3 ADJ A **dirt** road or track is made from hard earth. A **dirt** floor is made from earth without any cement, stone, or wood laid on it. 泥土的 [ADJ n] ❑ *I drove along the dirt road.* 我行驶在一条土路上。 4 N-SING If you say that you have **the dirt on** someone, you mean that you have information that could harm their reputation or career. 流言蜚语 [INFORMAL] ❑ *...a sleazy reporter assigned to dig up dirt on Jack.* …一名受人指使去挖掘有关杰克的流言蜚语的低级庸俗的记者。 5 PHRASE If you say that someone **treats** you **like dirt**, you are angry with them because you think that they treat you unfairly and with no respect. 把…看得一钱不值 [DISAPPROVAL] ❑ *People think they can treat me like dirt!* 人们竟然认为可以把我完全不当一回事！ → see **erosion**

dirty ♦◇◇ /dɜrti/ (**dirtier, dirtiest, dirties, dirtying, dirtied**) 1 ADJ If something is **dirty**, it is marked or covered with stains, spots, or mud, and needs to be cleaned. 肮脏的 ❑ *She still did not like the woman who had dirty fingernails.* 她仍然不喜欢那个手指甲很脏的女人。 2 ADJ If you describe an action as **dirty**, you disapprove of it and consider it unfair, immoral, or dishonest. 卑鄙的 [DISAPPROVAL] ❑ *The gunman had been hired by a rival Mafia family to do the dirty deed.* 该杀手被敌对的黑手党家族雇来干这件卑鄙的勾当。 ● ADV **Dirty** is also an adverb. 卑鄙地 [ADV after v] ❑ *Jim Browne is the kind of fellow who can fight dirty, but make you like it.* 吉姆・布朗是那种可以卑鄙地和人争斗，却又能让你喜欢他的那种人。 3 ADJ If you describe something such as a joke, a book, or someone's language as **dirty**, you mean that it refers to sex in a way that some people find offensive. 下流的 ❑ *He laughed at their dirty jokes and sang their raucous ballads.* 他听了他们的黄色笑话而发笑，又唱着他们吵闹的民谣。 ● ADV **Dirty** is also an adverb. 下流地 [ADV after v] ❑ *I'm often asked whether the men talk dirty to me. The answer is no.* 经常有人问我那些男人是否跟我说过下流话，我的回答是没有。 4 V-T To **dirty** something means to cause it to become dirty. 把…弄脏 ❑ *He was afraid the dog's hairs might dirty the seats.* 他担心狗毛会把座椅弄脏。 5 PHRASE If someone gives you a **dirty look**, they look at you in a way which shows that they are angry with you. 怒视 [INFORMAL] ❑ *Jack was being a real pain. Michael gave him a dirty look and walked out.* 杰克真是个讨厌的人。迈克尔厌恶地看了他一眼，然后走了出去。 6 PHRASE To **do** someone's **dirty work** means to do a task for them that is dishonest or unpleasant and which they do not want to do themselves. 替…干卑鄙的勾当; 为…干难对付的活 ❑ *As a member of an elite army hit squad, the army would send us out to do their dirty work for them.* 身为精锐突击队的成员，部队会派我们去执行艰难的任务。 7 PHRASE If you say that an expression is **a dirty word** in a particular group of people, you mean it refers to an idea that they strongly dislike or disagree with. 非常难听的词; 禁忌字眼 ❑ *Marketing became a dirty word at the company.* "营销"成了该公司的禁忌字眼。 8 PHRASE If you say that someone **airs** their **dirty laundry in public**, you disapprove of their discussing or arguing about unpleasant or private things in front of other people. There are several other forms of this expression, for example **wash** your **dirty linen in public**, or **wash** your **dirty laundry in public**. 家丑外扬 [DISAPPROVAL] ❑ *The captain refuses to air the team's dirty laundry in public.* 队长拒绝把球队的丑事暴露在公众面前。

Word Partnership *dirty* 的常用搭配:

V. **get** dirty 1
talk dirty 3

N. dirty **diapers**, dirty **dishes**, dirty **laundry** 1
dirty **job** 2
dirty **joke** 3
dirty ***your* hands** 4
dirty **look** 5
dirty **word** 7

▲ **dis·abil·ity** /dɪsəbɪlɪti/ (**disabilities**) 1 N-COUNT A **disability** is a permanent injury, illness, or physical or mental condition that tends to restrict the way that someone can live their life. (身体或精神方面的) 残疾 ❑ *Facilities for people with disabilities are still insufficient.* 供残疾人使用的设施仍然不足。 2 N-UNCOUNT **Disability** is the state of being disabled. 残疾状态 ❑ *Disability can make extra demands on financial resources because the disabled need extra care.* 残疾会增加额外经济需求，因为残疾人需要特别护理。 → see Word Web: **disability**

★ **dis·able** /dɪseɪbᵊl/ (**disables, disabling, disabled**) 1 V-T If an injury or illness **disables** someone, it affects them so badly that it restricts the way that they can live their life. 使伤残 ❑ *She did all this tendon damage and it really disabled her.* 她肌腱受了这么多损伤，这真地使她致残了。 2 V-T If someone or something **disables** a system or mechanism, they stop it from working, usually temporarily. 使 (系统、机制等) 瘫痪 ❑ *...if you need to disable a car alarm.* …如果你要使汽车警报器失灵。

dis·abled /dɪseɪbᵊld/ ADJ Someone who is **disabled** has an illness, injury, or condition that tends to restrict the way that they can live their life, especially by making it difficult for them to move about. 残疾的 ❑ *...an insight into the practical problems encountered by disabled people in the workplace.* …对残疾人在工作场所遇

Word Web disability

Careful planning is making public places more **accessible** for people with **disabilities**. For hundreds of years **wheelchairs** have helped **paralyzed** people move around their homes. Today, **ramps** help these people cross the street, enter buildings, and get to work. Extra-wide doorways allow them to use public restrooms. **Blind** people are also more active and independent. **Seeing Eye dogs, canes**, and beeping crosswalks all help them get around town safely. Some movie theaters rent headsets for the **hearing-impaired**. **Hearing dogs** help **deaf** people stay connected. And sign language allows people who are deaf or **dumb** to communicate.

到的实际困难的深入了解。● N-PLURAL People who are disabled are sometimes referred to as **the disabled**. 残疾人 ❏ *There are toilet facilities for the disabled.* 有供残疾人使用的盥洗设施。

> In the United States there are many laws giving **disabled** people the same rights and benefits as other people. The adjectives **disabled, physically challenged** and **differently abled** are terms more in favor now than **handicapped**. The most sensitive ways of referring to people with a restricting physical condition are to call them **people with disabilities** or **people with special needs**.

D

dis·ad·vant·age /dɪsədvæntɪdʒ/ (**disadvantages**) **1** N-COUNT A **disadvantage** is a factor which makes someone or something less useful, acceptable, or successful than other people or things. 不利条件 ❏ *His two main rivals suffer the disadvantage of having been long-term political exiles.* 他的两名主要竞争对手由于长期被政治流放而处于不利地位。 **2** PHRASE If you are **at a disadvantage**, you have a problem or difficulty that many other people do not have, which makes it harder for you to be successful. 处于劣势 ❏ *The children from poor families were at a distinct disadvantage.* 贫困家庭的孩子明显处于劣势。 **3** PHRASE If something is **to your disadvantage** or works **to** your **disadvantage**, it creates difficulties for you. 对（某人）不利 ❏ *We need a rethink of the present law which works so greatly to the disadvantage of women.* 我们需要重新思考一下现行的法律，它使妇女处于非常不利的地位。

dis·ad·van·taged /dɪsədvæntɪd3d/ ADJ People who are **disadvantaged** or live in **disadvantaged** areas live in bad conditions and tend not to get a good education or have a reasonable standard of living. 条件差的 ❏ *...the educational problems of disadvantaged children.* …贫困儿童的教育问题。

dis·af·fect·ed /dɪsəfɛktɪd/ ADJ **Disaffected** people no longer fully support something such as an organization or political ideal which they previously supported. （对曾经支持的组织、政治理想等）不再完全支持的 ❏ *He attracts disaffected voters.* 他吸引了心生不满的投票人。

Word Link *dis ≈ negative, not : disagree, discomfort, disrespect*

dis·agree /dɪsəgri/ (**disagrees, disagreeing, disagreed**) **1** V-RECIP If you **disagree with** someone or **disagree with** what they say, you do not accept that what they say is true or correct. You can also say that two people **disagree**. 不同意；有分歧 ❏ *You must continue to see them no matter how much you may disagree with them.* 不管你与他们有多大分歧，都必须一如既往地去看他们。 ❏ *They can communicate even when they strongly disagree.* 他们即使是在有较大分歧时也能相互交流。 **2** V-I If you **disagree with** a particular action or proposal, you disapprove of it and believe that it is wrong. 不赞成 ❏ *I respect the president but I disagree with his decision.* 我尊重总统，但我不赞成他的决定。

dis·agree·ment /dɪsəgrimənt/ (**disagreements**) **1** N-UNCOUNT **Disagreement** means objecting to something such as a proposal. 反对 ❏ *Britain and France have expressed some disagreement with the proposal.* 英、法两国已表示了对这项提议的一些反对意见。 **2** N-VAR When there is **disagreement** about something, people disagree or argue about what should be done. 争执 ❏ *The United States Congress and the president are still locked in disagreement over proposals to reduce the massive budget deficit.* 美国国会与总统对减少巨额预算赤字的提议各持己见，僵持不下。

dis·al·low /dɪsəlaʊ/ (**disallows, disallowing, disallowed**) V-T If something **is disallowed**, it is not allowed or accepted officially, because it has not been done correctly. 不准许；否决 ❏ *The goal was disallowed.* 那一次进球得分被判无效。

dis·ap·pear ♦◇◇ /dɪsəpɪər/ (**disappears, disappearing, disappeared**) **1** V-I If you say that someone or something **disappears**, you mean that you can no longer see them, usually because you or they have changed position. 消失 ❏ *The black car drove away from them and disappeared.* 黑色的小汽车驶离了他们便消失了。 **2** V-I If someone or something **disappears**, they go away or are taken away somewhere where nobody can find them. 失踪 ❏ *...a Japanese woman who disappeared thirteen years ago.* …一位13年前失踪的日本妇女。 **3** V-I If something **disappears**, it stops existing or happening. 灭绝 ❏ *The immediate threat of the past has disappeared and the security situation in Europe has significantly improved.* 过去的直接威胁不复存在了，欧洲的安全状况有重大改善。

Word Partnership *disappear* 的常用搭配：

V.	**make** *someone/something* disappear **1**–**3**
ADV.	disappear **completely, quickly** disappear **1**–**3**
	mysteriously disappear **2**
	disappear **forever** **2** **3**

dis·ap·pear·ance /dɪsəpɪərəns/ (**disappearances**) **1** N-VAR If you refer to someone's **disappearance**, you are referring to the fact that nobody knows where they have gone. 失踪 ❏ *Her disappearance has baffled police.* 她的失踪令警方大为困惑。 **2** N-COUNT If you refer to the **disappearance** of an object, you are referring to the fact that it has been lost or stolen. 丢失 ❏ *Police are investigating the disappearance of key files on the killers.* 警方正在调查杀人凶手关键档案丢失一事。 **3** N-UNCOUNT The **disappearance** of a type of thing, person, or animal is a process in which it becomes less common and finally no longer exists. 绝迹 ❏ *...the virtual disappearance of common dolphins from the western Mediterranean in recent years.* …普通海豚近年来在地中海西部真正的绝迹。

dis·ap·point /dɪsəpɔɪnt/ (**disappoints, disappointing, disappointed**) V-T If things or people **disappoint** you, they are not as good as you had hoped, or do not do what you hoped they would do. 使失望 ❏ *She would do anything she could to please him, but she knew that she was fated to disappoint him.* 她愿意做任何事情来讨好他，但她知道她注定会让他失望。

dis·ap·point·ed ♦◇◇ /dɪsəpɔɪntɪd/ **1** ADJ If you are **disappointed**, you are sad because something has not happened or because something is not as good as you had hoped. 失望的 ❏ *Adamski says he was very disappointed with the mayor's decision.* 阿达姆斯基说他对市长的决定非常失望。 ❏ *I was disappointed that John was not there.* 我很失望约翰不在那儿。 **2** ADJ If you are **disappointed in** someone, you are sad because they have not behaved as well as you expected them to. 对（某人）失望的 [v-link ADJ "in" n] ❏ *You should have accepted that. I'm disappointed in you.* 你本该接受的。我对你感到失望。

dis·ap·point·ing /dɪsəpɔɪntɪŋ/ ADJ Something that is **disappointing** is not as good or as large as you hoped it would be. 令人失望的 ❏ *The wine was excellent, but the meat was overdone and the vegetables disappointing.* 酒好极了，但是肉老了，蔬菜也令人失望。 ● **dis·ap·point·ing·ly** ADV 令人失望地 ❏ *Progress is disappointingly slow.* 进展慢得令人失望。

dis·ap·point·ment /dɪsəpɔɪntmənt/ (**disappointments**) **1** N-UNCOUNT **Disappointment** is the state of feeling disappointed. 失望 ❏ *Despite winning the title, their last campaign ended in great disappointment.* 尽管得了冠军，他们最后一场比赛却在极度失望中完结。 **2** N-COUNT Something or someone that is a **disappointment** is not as good as you had hoped. 令人失望的人；令人失望的物 ❏ *For many, their long-awaited homecoming was a bitter disappointment.* 对很多人来说，他们期盼已久的返乡成了一件令人伤心失望的事。

dis·ap·prov·al /dɪsəpruvᵊl/ N-UNCOUNT If you feel or show **disapproval** of something or someone, you feel or show that you do not approve of them. 不赞成 ❏ *His action had been greeted with almost universal disapproval.* 他的行动遭到了几乎一致的反对。

dis·ap·prove /dɪsəpruv/ (**disapproves, disapproving, disapproved**) V-I If you **disapprove of** something or someone, you feel or show that you do not like them or do not approve of them. 不赞同；不喜欢 ❏ *Most people disapprove of such violent tactics.* 多数人不赞同这类暴力手段。

dis·ap·prov·ing /dɪsəpruvɪŋ/ ADJ A **disapproving** action or expression shows that you do not approve of something or someone. 不赞同的；不喜欢的 ❏ *Janet gave him a disapproving look.* 珍妮特给了他一个不赞同的眼神。 ● **dis·ap·prov·ing·ly** ADV 不赞同地；不喜欢地 [ADV after v] ❏ *Antonio looked at him disapprovingly.* 安东尼奥不赞同地看着他。

dis·arm /dɪsɑrm/ (**disarms, disarming, disarmed**) **1** V-T To **disarm** a person or group means to take away all their weapons. 解除（某人、某组织的）武装 ❏ *We will agree to disarming troops and leaving their weapons at military positions.* 我们将同意解除部队的武装，并把他们的武器留在军事阵地上。 **2** V-I If a country or group **disarms**, it gives up the use of weapons, especially nuclear weapons. 解除武装（尤指核武器） ❏ *There has also been a suggestion that the forces in Lebanon should disarm.* 也曾有一项提议说在黎巴嫩的部队应

解除武装。 3 V-T If a person or their behavior **disarms** you, they cause you to feel less angry, hostile, or critical toward them. 消除(怒气、敌意或非议) ❑ *His unease disarmed her.* 他的不安化解了她的怒气。

dis·arma·ment /dɪsɑrməmənt/ N-UNCOUNT **Disarmament** is the act of reducing the number of weapons, especially nuclear weapons, that a country has. 裁减军备(尤指核武器) ❑ *The goal would be to increase political stability in the region and accelerate the pace of nuclear disarmament.* 目标会是促进区内政局的稳定并加快核武器裁减的步伐。

dis·arm·ing /dɪsɑrmɪŋ/ ADJ If someone or something is **disarming**, they make you feel less angry or hostile. 消气的; 消除敌意的 ❑ *Leonard approached with a disarming smile.* 伦纳德带着令人消除怒气的微笑走近了。 ● **dis·arm·ing·ly** ADV 消气地; 消除敌意地 ❑ *He is, as ever, business-like, and disarmingly honest.* 他像往常一样，一副公事公办的样子，有着化解恶意的诚实。

dis·ar·ray /dɪsəreɪ/ 1 N-UNCOUNT If people or things are **in disarray**, they are disorganized and confused. 混乱 ❑ *The nation is in disarray following rioting led by the military.* 该国发生由军队发动的暴乱后，陷入一片混乱。 2 N-UNCOUNT If things or places are **in disarray**, they are in a very disorganized state. 凌乱 ❑ *She was left lying on her side and her clothes were in disarray.* 她被扔在那儿侧躺着，衣衫不整。

dis·as·ter ♦◇◇ /dɪzæstər/ (**disasters**) 1 N-COUNT A **disaster** is a very bad accident such as an earthquake or a plane crash, especially one in which a lot of people are killed. 灾难 ❑ *It was the second air disaster in the region in less than two months.* 这是不到两个月内该地区内的第2起空难。 2 N-COUNT If you refer to something as a **disaster**, you are emphasizing that you think it is extremely bad or unacceptable. 极为糟糕的事; 不能接受的事 [EMPHASIS] ❑ *The whole production was just a disaster!* 整部作品简直是一团糟! 3 N-UNCOUNT **Disaster** is something which has very bad consequences for you. 灾祸 ❑ *The government brought itself to the brink of fiscal disaster.* 该政府把自己带到了财政灾难的边缘。 4 PHRASE If you say that something is **a recipe for disaster**, you mean that it is very likely to have unpleasant consequences. 祸端 ❑ *You give them a gun, and it's a recipe for disaster.* 你给他们一把枪，那就是祸端。
→ see Word Web: **disaster**

★ **dis·as·trous** /dɪzæstrəs/ 1 ADJ A **disastrous** event has extremely bad consequences and effects. 灾难性的 ❑ *...the recent, disastrous earthquake.* …那场最近发生的、灾难性的地震。 ● **dis·as·trous·ly** ADV 灾难性地 ❑ *The vegetable harvest is disastrously behind schedule.* 蔬菜收割灾难性地滞后于计划。 2 ADJ If you describe something as **disastrous**, you mean that it was very unsuccessful. 非常失败的 ❑ *...after their disastrous performance in the election.* …继他们在竞选中非常失败的表现之后。 ● **dis·as·trous·ly** ADV 非常失败地 ❑ *...debts resulting from the company's disastrously timed venture into property development.* …该公司不合时宜地冒险投资房地产开发而导致的债务。

dis·band /dɪsbænd/ (**disbands, disbanding, disbanded**) V-T/V-I If someone **disbands** a group of people, or if the group **disbands**, it stops operating as a single unit. 解散 ❑ *All the armed groups will be disbanded.* 所有武装团体将被解散。

dis·be·lief /dɪsbɪlif/ N-UNCOUNT **Disbelief** is not believing that something is true or real. 怀疑 ❑ *She looked at him in disbelief.* 她怀疑地看着他。

disc /dɪsk/ → see **disk**
→ see **DVD**

dis·card /dɪskɑrd/ (**discards, discarding, discarded**) V-T If you **discard** something, you get rid of it because you no longer want it or need it. 丢弃 ❑ *Read the manufacturer's guidelines before discarding the box.* 先阅读制造商的说明书再把盒子丢掉。

disc drive [BRIT] → see **disk drive**

★ **dis·cern** /dɪsɜrn/ (**discerns, discerning, discerned**) 1 V-T If you can **discern** something, you are aware of it and know what it is. 认识; 了解 [FORMAL] ❑ *You need a long series of data to be able to discern such a trend.* 你需要一大串数据才能认清这一趋势。 2 V-T If you can **discern** something, you can just see it, but not clearly. 隐约看见 [FORMAL] ❑ *Below the bridge we could just discern a narrow, weedy ditch.* 在桥下我们仅可隐约看见一条狭窄的、杂草丛生的沟壑。

dis·cern·ible /dɪsɜrnəbəl/ ADJ If something is **discernible**, you can see it or recognize that it exists. 看得见的; 辨认得出的 [FORMAL] ❑ *Far away the outline of the island is just discernible.* 远远的，那岛的轮廓依稀可见。

dis·cern·ing /dɪsɜrnɪŋ/ ADJ If you describe someone as **discerning**, you mean that they are able to judge which things of a particular kind are good and which are bad. 有辨别力的 [APPROVAL] ❑ *Even the most accomplished writers show their work-in-progress to discerning readers.* 即使最有造诣的作家们都会展示他们创作中的作品给有鉴赏力的读者们看。

dis·charge (**discharges, discharging, discharged**)

The verb is pronounced /dɪstʃɑrdʒ/. The noun is pronounced /dɪstʃɑrdʒ/.

动词读作 /dɪstʃɑrdʒ/。名词读作 /dɪstʃɑrdʒ/。

1 V-T When someone **is discharged from** a hospital, prison, or one of the armed services, they are officially allowed to leave, or told that they must leave. 批准离开; 命令离开 ❑ *He has a broken nose but may be discharged today.* 他鼻梁断了，但今天可能获准出院。 ● N-VAR **Discharge** is also a noun. 释放 ❑ *He was given a conditional discharge and ordered to pay Miss Smith $500 compensation.* 他被判有条件释放，并被命令向史密斯小姐支付$500的赔偿金。 2 V-T If someone **discharges** their duties or responsibilities, they do everything that needs to be done in order to complete them. 履行(职责或义务) [FORMAL] ❑ *...the quiet competence with which he discharged his many duties.* …他履行他的诸多职责所用的平静的办事能力。 3 V-T If something **is discharged** from inside a place, it comes out. 排出 [FORMAL] ❑ *The resulting salty water will be discharged at sea.* 产生的咸水将被排放到海里。 4 N-VAR When there is a **discharge** of a substance, the substance comes out from inside somewhere. 排出 [FORMAL] ❑ *They develop a fever and a watery discharge from their eyes.* 他们开始发烧，且有一种水状分泌物从他们的眼睛里流出。
→ see **lightning**

dis·ci·ple /dɪsaɪpəl/ (**disciples**) N-COUNT If you are someone's **disciple**, you are influenced by their teachings and try to follow their example. 信徒 ❑ *...a major intellectual figure with disciples throughout Europe.* …一位信徒遍布欧洲的重要知识分子。

★ **dis·ci·pli·nary** /dɪsɪplɪnɛri/ ADJ **Disciplinary** bodies or actions are concerned with making sure that people obey rules or regulations and that they are punished if they do not. 纪律性的 [ADJ n] ❑ *He will now face a disciplinary hearing for having an affair.* 他将因一起风流韵事而面对一场纪律听证会。

dis·ci·pline ♦◇◇ /dɪsɪplɪn/ (**disciplines, disciplining, disciplined**) 1 N-UNCOUNT **Discipline** is the practice of making people obey rules or standards of behavior, and punishing them when they do not. 纪律 ❑ *Order and discipline have been placed in the hands of governing bodies.* 秩序与纪律已交由管控机构负责。 2 N-UNCOUNT **Discipline** is the quality of being able to behave and work in a controlled way which involves obeying particular rules or standards. 自律 ❑ *It was that image of calm, control, and discipline that appealed to millions of voters.* 正是那冷静、克制和自律的形象吸引了数以百万计的选民。 3 N-VAR If you refer to an activity or situation as a

Word Web disaster

We are learning more about nature's cycles. But natural **disasters** remain a big challenge. Some, such as **hurricanes** and **floods**, are predictable. However, we still can't avoid the **damage** they do. Each year **monsoons** strike southern Asia. Monsoons are a combination of **typhoons**, **tropical storms**, and heavy **rains**. In addition to the damage caused by flooding, **landslides** and mudslides add to the problem. In 2005 more than 90 million people were affected in China alone. Over 700 people died there and millions of acres of crops were destroyed. The **economic loss** totaled nearly 6 billion dollars.

d

discipline, you mean that, in order to be successful in it, you need to behave in a strictly controlled way and obey particular rules or standards. 训练；磨练 ❑ *The discipline of studying music can help children develop good work habits and improve self-esteem.* 学习音乐的规范训练能帮助孩子们养成良好的做事习惯和增强自尊心。 4 V-T If someone **is disciplined** for something that they have done wrong, they are punished for it. 处罚 ❑ *The workman was disciplined by his company but not dismissed.* 这名工人被他的公司处罚了，但没有被开除。 5 V-T If you **discipline yourself** to do something, you train yourself to behave and work in a strictly controlled and regular way. 训练 ❑ *Discipline yourself to check your messages once a day or every couple of days.* 训练你自己每天或每两天查看一次你的留言。 6 N-COUNT A **discipline** is a particular area of study, especially a subject of study in a college or university. (尤指大学里的) 学科 [FORMAL] ❑ *We're looking for people from a wide range of disciplines.* 我们正在寻找各类学科的人才。

D

★ **dis·ci·plined** /dɪsɪplɪnd/ ADJ Someone who is **disciplined** behaves or works in a controlled way. 有纪律的 ❑ *For me it meant being very disciplined about how I run my life.* 对我而言，它意味着要以非常有纪律的方式生活。

disc jock·ey (**disc jockeys**) also **disk jockey** N-COUNT A **disc jockey** is someone who plays and introduces music on the radio or at a disco. (电台) 音乐节目主持人；(迪斯科舞厅的) 唱片播放员

dis·claim·er /dɪskl̲eɪmər/ (**disclaimers**) N-COUNT A **disclaimer** is a statement in which a person says that they did not know about something or that they are not responsible for something. 免责声明 [FORMAL] ❑ *The company asserts in a disclaimer that it won't be held responsible for the accuracy of information.* 该公司在一项免责声明里宣称它不会对信息的准确性负责。

★ **dis·close** /dɪskl̲oʊz/ (**discloses, disclosing, disclosed**) V-T If you **disclose** new or secret information, you tell people about it. 透露 ❑ *Neither side would disclose details of the transaction.* 双方都不会透露交易的细节。

★ **dis·clo·sure** /dɪskl̲oʊʒər/ (**disclosures**) N-VAR **Disclosure** is the act of giving people new or secret information. 公开 ❑ *...insufficient disclosure of negative information about the company.* …有关该公司负面信息的不充分公开。

dis·co /dɪskoʊ/ (**discos**) N-COUNT A **disco** is a place or event at which people dance to pop music. 迪斯科舞厅；迪斯科舞会 ❑ *Fridays and Saturdays are regular disco nights.* 星期五和星期六是固定的迪斯科之夜。

Word Link *dis ≈ negative, not : disagree, discomfort, disrespect*

dis·com·fort /dɪsk̲ʌmfərt/ (**discomforts**) 1 N-UNCOUNT **Discomfort** is a painful feeling in part of your body when you have been hurt slightly or when you have been uncomfortable for a long time. 不舒服 ❑ *Steve had some discomfort, but no real pain.* 史蒂夫有些不舒服，但不真疼。 2 N-UNCOUNT **Discomfort** is a feeling of worry caused by shame or embarrassment. 不安 ❑ *She hears the discomfort in his voice.* 她听出他声音里的不安。 3 N-COUNT **Discomforts** are conditions which cause you to feel physically uncomfortable. 不舒适的情况 ❑ *...the discomforts of camping.* …野营不舒适的种种情况。

dis·con·cert·ing /dɪskəns̲ɜrtɪŋ/ ADJ If you say that something is **disconcerting**, you mean that it makes you feel anxious, confused, or embarrassed. 令人不安的；令人困惑的；令人尴尬的 ❑ *The reception desk is not at street level, which is a little disconcerting.* 该接待台不在临街那一层，这有点令人困惑。 ● **dis·con·cert·ing·ly** ADV 令人不安地；令人困惑地；令人尴尬地 ❑ *She looks disconcertingly like a familiar aunt or grandmother.* 她像一位熟悉的阿姨或奶奶，令人感到困惑。

dis·con·nect /dɪskən̲ɛkt/ (**disconnects, disconnecting, disconnected**) 1 V-T To **disconnect** a piece of equipment means to separate it from its source of power or to break a connection that it needs in order to work. 断开 ❑ *The device automatically disconnects the ignition when the engine is switched off.* 该设备在引擎被关闭时会自动断开点火装置。 2 V-T If you **are disconnected** by a gas, electricity, water, or telephone company, they turn off the connection to your house, usually because you have not paid the bill. 切断 (煤气、电、水、电话等的) 供应 [usu passive] ❑ *You are likely to be given almost three months – until the time of your next bill – before you are disconnected.* 你很可能会得到将近3个月的时间——即直到你下一张账单寄发为止——才会被切断供应。 3 V-T If you **disconnect** something **from** something else, you separate the two things. 使分离 ❑ *He disconnected the IV bottle from the overhead hook and carried it beside the moving cart.* 他从头顶的钩子上取下输液瓶，并在移动的手推车旁提着它。

dis·con·nect·ed /dɪskən̲ɛktɪd/ ADJ **Disconnected** things are not linked in any way. 分离的 ❑ *...sequences of utterly disconnected events.* …一连串完全无关联的事件。

dis·con·nec·tion /dɪskən̲ɛkʃ³n/ (**disconnections**) N-VAR The **disconnection** of a gas, water, or electricity supply, or of a telephone, is the act of disconnecting it so that it cannot be used. 切断 (煤气、水、电的供应或电话通讯) [oft "the" N "of" n]

★ **dis·con·tent** /dɪskənt̲ɛnt/ (**discontents**) N-UNCOUNT **Discontent** is the feeling that you have when you are not satisfied with your situation. 不满 [also N in pl] ❑ *There are reports of widespread discontent in the capital.* 有关于首都内普遍不满的多篇报道。

dis·con·tent·ed /dɪskənt̲ɛntɪd/ ADJ If you are **discontented**, you are not satisfied with your situation. 不满的 [oft ADJ "with" n] ❑ *The black freedom struggle should be the model for all discontented Americans.* 黑人争取自由的斗争应该作为所有不满的美国人的典范。

dis·con·tinue /dɪskənt̲ɪnyu/ (**discontinues, discontinuing, discontinued**) 1 V-T If you **discontinue** something that you have been doing regularly, you stop doing it. 中断 [FORMAL] ❑ *Do not discontinue the treatment without consulting your doctor.* 不要不咨询你的医生就中断治疗。 2 V-T If a product **is discontinued**, the manufacturer stops making it. 停产 [usu passive] ❑ *The Leica M2 was discontinued in 1967.* 徕卡M2型照相机于1967年停产。

▲ **dis·cord** /d̲ɪskɔrd/ N-UNCOUNT **Discord** is disagreement and argument between people. 不和 [LITERARY]

dis·count ♦◇◇ (**discounts, discounting, discounted**)

Pronounced /d̲ɪskaʊnt/ for meanings 1 and 2, and /dɪsk̲aʊnt/ for meaning 3.

义项1和2读作 /d̲ɪskaʊnt/，义项3读作 /dɪsk̲aʊnt/。

1 N-COUNT A **discount** is a reduction in the usual price of something. 折扣 ❑ *They are often available at a discount.* 它们经常可以以折扣价买到。 ❑ *All full-time staff get a 20 percent discount.* 所有全职员工都可以享受8折优惠。 2 V-T If a store or company **discounts** an amount or percentage from something that they are selling, they take the amount or percentage off the usual price. 对…打折 ❑ *This has forced airlines to discount fares heavily in order to spur demand.* 这已经迫使多家航空公司对机票大幅打折以刺激需求。 3 V-T If you **discount** an idea, fact, or theory, you consider that it is not true, not important, or not relevant. 不理会 ❑ *However, traders tended to discount the rumor.* 但是，商人们倾向于不理会这个传闻。

dis·cour·age /dɪsk̲ɜrɪdʒ/ (**discourages, discouraging, discouraged**) 1 V-T If someone or something **discourages** you, they cause you to lose your enthusiasm about your actions. 使气馁 ❑ *It may be difficult to do at first. Don't let this discourage you.* 开始时做起来也许比较困难。不要让这个泄你的气。 ● **dis·cour·aged** ADJ 气馁的 ❑ *She was determined not to be too discouraged.* 她下了决心不要太气馁。 ● **dis·cour·ag·ing** ADJ 令人气馁的 ❑ *Today's report is extremely discouraging for the economy.* 今天的报告令人对经济更加没有信心。 2 V-T To **discourage** an action or to **discourage** someone **from** doing it means to make them not want to do it. 阻拦 ❑ *...typhoons that discouraged shopping and leisure activities.* …打消购物和休闲活动的念头的数起台风。

dis·cour·age·ment /dɪsk̲ɜrɪdʒmənt/ N-UNCOUNT **Discouragement** is the act of trying to make someone not want to do something. (对某想法的) 打击 ❑ *He persevered in the face of active discouragement from those around him.* 面对周围人们的打击，他锲而不舍。

▲ **dis·course** /d̲ɪskɔrs/ (**discourses**) 1 N-UNCOUNT **Discourse** is spoken or written communication between people, especially serious discussion of a particular subject. (某专题的) 会话 ❑ *...a tradition of political discourse.* …一个政治对话的传统。 2 → see also **direct discourse, indirect discourse**

dis·cov·er ♦♦◇ /dɪsk̲ʌvər/ (**discovers, discovering, discovered**) 1 V-T If you **discover** something that you did not know about before, you become aware of it or learn of it. 发觉 ❑ *She discovered that they'd escaped.* 她发觉他们已经逃走了。 ❑ *It was difficult for the inspectors to discover which documents were important and which were not.* 检查员们难以发现哪些文件重要，哪些不重要。

You can use **discover**, **find**, or **find out** to talk about learning that something is the case. ❑ *He discovered the whole school knew about it... The young child finds that noise attracts attention... We found out that she was wrong.* **Discover** is a slightly more formal word than **find**, and is often used to talk about scientific research or formal investigations. For example, you can **discover** a cure for a particular disease. You can also use **discover** when you find something by accident. ❑ *This well-known flower was discovered in 1903.* If you cannot see something you are looking for, you say that you cannot **find** it. You do not use "discover" or "find out" in this way. ❑ *I'm lost–I can't find the bridge.* You can say that someone **finds out** facts when this is easy to do, but you cannot use "discover" or "find" in this way. ❑ *I found out the train times.*

2 V-T If a person or thing **is discovered**, someone finds them, either by accident or because they have been looking for them. 发现；找到 ❑ *A few days later his badly beaten body was discovered on a roadside outside the city.* 几天之后，他曾被毒打的尸体在城外一个路边被发现了。 3 V-T When someone **discovers** a new place, substance, scientific fact, or scientific technique, they are the first person to find it or become aware of it. (首次) 发现 ❑ *...the first European to discover America.* …第1个发现美洲的欧洲人。 4 V-T When an actor, musician, or other performer who is not well known **is discovered**, someone recognizes that they have talent and helps them in their career. 发现 (人才) [usu passive] ❑ *The Beatles were discovered in the early 1960s.* 披头士乐队是在20世纪60年代初期被发现的。

Thesaurus *discover* 另参见：
v. come upon, detect, find out, learn, uncover; (ant.) ignore, miss, overlook 1

dis·cov·ery ♦◇◇ /dɪskʌvəri/ (**discoveries**) 1 N-VAR If someone makes a **discovery**, they become aware of something that they did not know about before. 发现 ❑ *I felt I'd made an incredible discovery.* 我感到自己有了一个惊人的发现。 2 N-VAR If someone makes a **discovery**, they are the first person to find or become aware of a place, substance, or scientific fact that no one knew about before. 新发现 ❑ *In that year, two momentous discoveries were made.* 那年有2项重大的新发现。 3 N-VAR When the **discovery** of people or objects happens, someone finds them, either by accident or as a result of looking for them. 发现 ❑ *...the discovery and destruction by soldiers of millions of marijuana plants.* …士兵们对数百万株大麻的发现和摧毁。

▲ **dis·cred·it** /dɪskrɛdɪt/ (**discredits, discrediting, discredited**) V-T To **discredit** someone or something means to cause them to lose people's respect or trust. 使…丧失信誉 ❑ *...a secret unit within the company that had been set up to discredit its major rival.* …为破坏其主要竞争对手声誉而设的一个公司内秘密单位。 ● **dis·cred·it·ed** ADJ 名誉扫地的 ❑ *The previous government is, by now, thoroughly discredited.* 上届政府至今彻底名誉扫地。

★ **dis·creet** /dɪskrit/ 1 ADJ If you are **discreet**, you are polite and careful in what you do or say, because you want to avoid embarrassing or offending someone. (言行) 谨慎的 ❑ *They were gossipy and not always discreet.* 他们爱说闲话，而且不总是言语谨慎。 ● **dis·creet·ly** ADV 谨慎地 ❑ *I took the phone, and she went discreetly into the living room.* 我拿了电话，她就谨慎地到客厅去了。 2 ADJ If you are **discreet about** something you are doing, you do not tell other people about it, in order to avoid being embarrassed or to gain an advantage. 谨慎保密的 ❑ *We were very discreet about the romance.* 我们对这一段罗曼史守口如瓶。 ● **dis·creet·ly** ADV 谨慎保密地 ❑ *Everyone worked to make him welcome, and, more discreetly, to find out about him.* 大家都尽力使他受欢迎，且更为小心地去了解他。 3 ADJ If you describe something as **discreet**, you approve of it because it is small in size or degree, or not easily noticed. 小巧的；不显眼的 [APPROVAL] ❑ *She is wearing a noticeably stylish, feminine dress, plus discreet jewellery.* 她穿着一条非常时髦、有女人味的连衣裙，配以小巧的首饰。 ● **dis·creet·ly** ADV 小巧地；不显眼地 [ADV -ed/adj] ❑ *...stately houses, discreetly hidden behind great avenues of sturdy trees.* …那些豪宅，隐隐约约掩藏在茂密的林荫大道后面。

★ **dis·crep·an·cy** /dɪskrɛpənsi/ (**discrepancies**) N-VAR If there is a **discrepancy between** two things that ought to be the same, there is a noticeable difference between them. 差异 ❑ *...the discrepancy between press and radio reports.* …报刊报道与广播报道之间的差异。

★ **dis·crete** /dɪskrit/ ADJ **Discrete** ideas or things are separate and distinct from each other. 分立的 [usu ADJ n] [FORMAL] ❑ *...instruction manuals that break down jobs into scores of discrete steps.* …将这些工作分解为多个分立步骤的说明书。

dis·cre·tion /dɪskrɛʃ॰n/ 1 N-UNCOUNT **Discretion** is the quality of behaving in a quiet and controlled way without drawing attention to yourself or giving away personal or private information. 审慎 [FORMAL] ❑ *Larsson sometimes joined in the fun, but with more discretion.* 拉森有时也会跟着玩闹，但多带几分审慎。 2 N-UNCOUNT If someone in a position of authority uses their **discretion** or has **the discretion** to do something in a particular situation, they have the freedom and authority to decide what to do. 酌情决定权 [FORMAL] ❑ *This committee may want to exercise its discretion to look into those charges.* 这个委员会可能想行使其酌情决定权来调查那些指控。 3 PHRASE If something happens **at** someone's **discretion**, it can happen only if they decide to do it or give their permission. 由 (某人) 斟酌决定 [FORMAL] ❑ *We may vary the limit at our discretion and will notify you of any change.* 我们可酌情决定更改限制，并会将任何变更通知你。

dis·cre·tion·ary /dɪskrɛʃəneri/ ADJ **Discretionary** things are not fixed by rules but are decided on by people in authority, who consider each individual case. 酌情决定的 ❑ *Magistrates were given wider discretionary powers.* 地方法官们被赋予了更广泛的酌情决定权。

★ **dis·crimi·nate** /dɪskrɪmɪneɪt/ (**discriminates, discriminating, discriminated**) 1 V-I If you can **discriminate between** two things, you can recognize that they are different. 区分 ❑ *He is incapable of discriminating between a good idea and a terrible one.* 他没能力在一个好主意和一个坏主意之间进行区分。 2 V-I To **discriminate against** a group of people or **in favor of** a group of people means to unfairly treat them worse or better than other groups. 不公平对待 ❑ *They believe the law discriminates against women.* 他们认为这项法律歧视妇女。 ❑ *...legislation which would discriminate in favor of racial minorities.* …会偏向少数民族的法规。

▲ **dis·crimi·na·tion** /dɪskrɪmɪneɪʃ॰n/ 1 N-UNCOUNT **Discrimination** is the practice of treating one person or group of people less fairly or less well than other people or groups. 歧视 ❑ *She is exempt from sex discrimination laws.* 她不用遵守性别歧视法规。 2 N-UNCOUNT **Discrimination** is knowing what is good or of high quality. 鉴赏力 ❑ *They cooked without skill and ate without discrimination.* 他们做饭没厨艺，吃饭没品味。 3 N-UNCOUNT **Discrimination** is the ability to recognize and understand the differences between two things. 辨别力 ❑ *We will then have an objective measure of how color discrimination and visual acuity develop at the level of the brain.* 我们随后将进行一项客观的测量，看色彩辨别力和视觉敏锐度如何在大脑的层面形成。

▲ **dis·crimi·na·tory** /dɪskrɪmɪnətɔri/ ADJ **Discriminatory** laws or practices are unfair because they treat one group of people worse than other groups. 歧视性的 ❑ *These reforms will abolish racially discriminatory laws.* 这些改革将废除种族歧视法律。

dis·cur·sive /dɪskɜrsɪv/ ADJ If a style of writing is **discursive**, it includes a lot of facts or opinions that are not necessarily relevant. 散漫的 [FORMAL] ❑ *...a livelier, more candid and more discursive treatment of the subject.* …对这一主题更加生动、率直和散漫的论述。

dis·cuss ♦♦◇ /dɪskʌs/ (**discusses, discussing, discussed**) 1 V-T If people **discuss** something, they talk about it, often in order to reach a decision. 讨论 ❑ *I will be discussing the situation with colleagues tomorrow.* 我将于明天和同事们讨论这个情况。 2 V-T If you **discuss** something, you write or talk about it in detail. 详述 ❑ *I will discuss the role of diet in cancer prevention in Chapter 7.* 我将在第7章详述饮食在癌症预防中的作用。

Note that **discuss** is never used as an intransitive verb. You cannot say, for example, "They discussed," "I discussed with him," or "They discussed about politics." Instead, you can say that you **have a discussion** with someone about something. ❑ *I had a long discussion about all this with Stephen.* You can also add an object and say that you **discuss** something **with** someone. If the discussion is less formal, you can simply use the verb **talk**. ❑ *They come here and sit for hours talking about politics... We talked all night long.*

Word Partnership *discuss* 的常用搭配:
V. **meet to** discuss, **refuse to** discuss 1
N. discuss **options**, discuss **problems** 1
discuss **an issue**, discuss **a matter**, discuss **plans** 1 2

dis·cus·sion ♦♦◊ /dɪskʌʃᵊn/ (**discussions**) 1 N-VAR If there is **discussion** about something, people talk about it, often in order to reach a decision. 讨论 ❑ *There was a lot of discussion about the wording of the report.* 有很多关于该份报告措词的讨论。❑ *Board members are due to have informal discussions later on today.* 董事会成员们预定在今天稍后进行非正式讨论。● PHRASE If something is **under discussion**, it is still being talked about and a final decision has not yet been reached. 在讨论中 2 N-COUNT A **discussion of a** subject is a piece of writing or a lecture in which someone talks about it in detail. 详述 ❑ *For a discussion of biology and sexual politics, see chapter 4.* 欲获得一个生物学与性别政治学的论述，请看第4章。 3 ADJ A **discussion** document or paper is one that contains information and usually proposals for people to discuss. 供讨论的 [ADJ n] ❑ *...a NASA discussion paper on long-duration ballooning.* …一份美国国家航空航天局关于长时间气球飞行的讨论文件。

Thesaurus *discussion* 另参见:
N. conference, conversation, debate, talk 1

▲ **dis·dain** /dɪsdeɪn/ (**disdains, disdaining, disdained**) 1 N-UNCOUNT If you feel **disdain for** someone or something, you dislike them because you think that they are inferior or unimportant. 轻蔑 ❑ *Janet looked at him with disdain.* 珍妮特轻蔑地看着他。 2 V-T If you **disdain** someone or something, you regard them with disdain. 蔑视 ❑ *Jackie disdained the servants that her millions could buy.* 杰姬蔑视那些她的数百万财富可以买到的仆人们。

dis·ease ♦♦◊ /dɪziz/ (**diseases**) N-VAR A **disease** is an illness which affects people, animals, or plants, for example, one which is caused by bacteria or infection. 疾病 ❑ *...the rapid spread of disease in the area.* …疾病在这一地区的迅速传播。
→ see **diagnosis, medicine**

Word Partnership *disease* 的常用搭配:
V. **cause** disease, **cure a** disease, **spread** disease, **treat a** disease
ADJ. **contagious** disease, **fatal** disease, **infectious** disease, **rare** disease, **sexually transmitted** disease
N. **death and** disease, **gum** disease, **heart** disease, **symptoms of** disease

dis·eased /dɪzizd/ ADJ Something that is **diseased** is affected by a disease. 患病的 ❑ *The arteries are diseased and a transplant is the only hope.* 动脉发生了病变，移植是惟一的希望。

dis·en·chant·ed /dɪsɪntʃæntɪd/ ADJ If you are **disenchanted with** something, you are disappointed with it and no longer believe that it is good or worthwhile. 不再抱幻想的 ❑ *The electorate had grown disenchanted with politics.* 选民已变得对政治不再抱幻想。

dis·en·chant·ment /dɪsɪntʃæntmənt/ N-UNCOUNT **Disenchantment** is the feeling of being disappointed with something, and no longer believing that it is good or worthwhile. 希望幻灭 ❑ *There is growing public disenchantment with the educational system.* 公众对教育制度越来越感到希望幻灭。

dis·en·fran·chise /dɪsɪnfræntʃaɪz/ (**disenfranchises, disenfranchising, disenfranchised**) V-T To **disenfranchise** a group of people means to take away their right to vote or other rights that most other people have. 剥夺(某人群的) 权利 ❑ *...fears of an organized attempt to disenfranchise supporters of Father Aristide.* …对剥夺阿里斯蒂德神父支持者选举权的一次有组织企图的担心。
→ see **vote**

dis·en·gage /dɪsɪngeɪdʒ/ (**disengages, disengaging, disengaged**) V-T/V-I If you **disengage** something, or if it **disengages**, it becomes separate from something which it has been attached to. 使脱离; 脱离 ❑ *She disengaged the film advance mechanism on the camera.* 她卸下了照相机上的胶卷推进机械装置。❑ *John gently disengaged himself from his sister's tearful embrace.* 约翰轻轻地从含泪的姐姐的怀抱中脱出身来。

Word Link *fig ≈ form, shape : configure, disfigure, figurative*

dis·fig·ure /dɪsfɪgyər/ (**disfigures, disfiguring, disfigured**) V-T If someone **is disfigured**, their appearance is spoiled. 将(某人) 毁容 [usu passive] ❑ *Many of the wounded had been badly disfigured.* 受伤者中很多被严重毁容。● **dis·fig·ured** ADJ 容貌受损的 ❑ *She tried not to look at the scarred, disfigured face.* 她尽量不去看那张带着疤痕、被毁容的脸。

Word Link *grac ≈ pleasing : disgrace, grace, graceful*

▲ **dis·grace** /dɪsgreɪs/ (**disgraces, disgracing, disgraced**) 1 N-UNCOUNT If you say that someone is **in disgrace**, you are emphasizing that other people disapprove of them and do not respect them because of something that they have done. 耻辱 [EMPHASIS] ❑ *His vice president also had to resign in disgrace.* 他的副总统也只得不光彩地辞职。 2 N-SING If you say that something is **a disgrace**, you are emphasizing that it is very bad or wrong, and that you find it completely unacceptable. 丢脸的事 [EMPHASIS] ❑ *The way the sales were handled was a complete disgrace.* 所采取的销售方式丢尽了人。 3 N-SING You say that someone is **a disgrace to** someone else when you want to emphasize that their behavior causes the other person to feel ashamed. (给某人) 带来耻辱的人 [EMPHASIS] ❑ *Republican leaders called him a disgrace to the party.* 共和党领导人们称他为该党的耻辱。 4 V-T If you say that someone **disgraces** someone else, you are emphasizing that their behavior causes the other person to feel ashamed. 使(某人) 丢脸 [EMPHASIS] ❑ *I have disgraced my family's name.* 我玷污了家族的名声。

dis·graced /dɪsgreɪst/ ADJ You use **disgraced** to describe someone whose bad behavior has caused them to lose the approval and respect of the public or of people in authority. 被人唾弃的 ❑ *...the disgraced leader of the coup.* …被人唾弃的政变领导人。

dis·grace·ful /dɪsgreɪsfəl/ ADJ If you say that something such as behavior or a situation is **disgraceful**, you disapprove of it strongly, and feel that the person or people responsible should be ashamed of it. 可耻的; 丢脸的 [DISAPPROVAL] ❑ *It's disgraceful that they have detained him for so long.* 真是可耻，他们扣押了他这么久。● **dis·grace·ful·ly** ADV 可耻地 ❑ *He felt that his brother had behaved disgracefully.* 他觉得他兄弟表现得丢人现眼。

dis·grun·tled /dɪsgrʌntᵊld/ ADJ If you are **disgruntled**, you are angry and dissatisfied because things have not happened the way that you wanted them to happen. 生气的; 不满的 ❑ *Disgruntled employees recently called for his resignation.* 不满的雇员们最近要求他辞职。

dis·guise /dɪsgaɪz/ (**disguises, disguising, disguised**) 1 N-VAR If you are **in disguise**, you are not wearing your usual clothes or you have altered your appearance in other ways, so that people will not recognize you. 伪装 ❑ *You'll have to travel in disguise.* 你将不得不乔装出行。 2 V-T If you **disguise yourself**, you put on clothes which make you look like someone else or alter your appearance in other ways, so that people will not recognize you. 乔装 ❑ *She disguised herself as a man so she could fight on the battlefield.* 她女扮男装以便能上战场打仗。● **dis·guised** ADJ 乔装的 ❑ *The extremists entered the building disguised as medical workers.* 极端分子们假扮成医务人员，进入了大楼。 3 V-T To **disguise** something means to hide it or make it appear different so that people will not know about it or will not recognize it. 掩饰 ❑ *He made no attempt to disguise his agitation.* 他无意掩饰他的不安。● **dis·guised** ADJ 掩饰的 ❑ *The proposal is a thinly disguised effort to revive the price controls of the 1970s.* 这项提议是恢复20世纪70年代物价控制的一种几乎不加掩饰的努力。

dis·gust /dɪsgʌst/ (**disgusts, disgusting, disgusted**) 1 N-UNCOUNT **Disgust** is a feeling of very strong dislike or disapproval. 厌恶 ❑ *He spoke of his disgust at the incident.* 他谈到了对此事的厌恶。 2 V-T To **disgust** someone means to make them feel a strong sense of dislike and disapproval. 使厌恶 ❑ *He disgusted many with his boorish behavior.* 他以其粗鲁的行为使许多人感到厌恶。

dis·gust·ed /dɪsgʌstɪd/ ADJ If you are **disgusted**, you feel a strong sense of dislike and disapproval at something. 厌恶的 ❑ *I'm disgusted with the way that he was treated.* 我对他受到这样的对待感到厌恶。● **dis·gust·ed·ly** ADV 厌恶地 [ADV with v] ❑ *"It's a little late for that," Ritter said disgustedly.* "对那来说有点迟了。"里特厌恶地说。

dis·gust·ing /dɪsgʌstɪŋ/ 1 ADJ If you say that something is **disgusting**, you are criticizing it because it is extremely unpleasant. 令人厌恶的 ❑ *It tasted disgusting.* 它尝起来令人极为不快。 2 ADJ If you say that something is **disgusting**, you mean that you find it completely unacceptable. 令人极不能接受的 ❑ *It's disgusting that all this damage has been caused by mindless vandalism.* 令人无法接受的是，所有这些损坏都是由无所顾忌的肆意破坏造成的。

dish ♦◊◊ /dɪʃ/ (**dishes, dishing, dished**) 1 N-COUNT A **dish** is a shallow container with a wide uncovered top. You eat and serve

Picture Dictionary dish

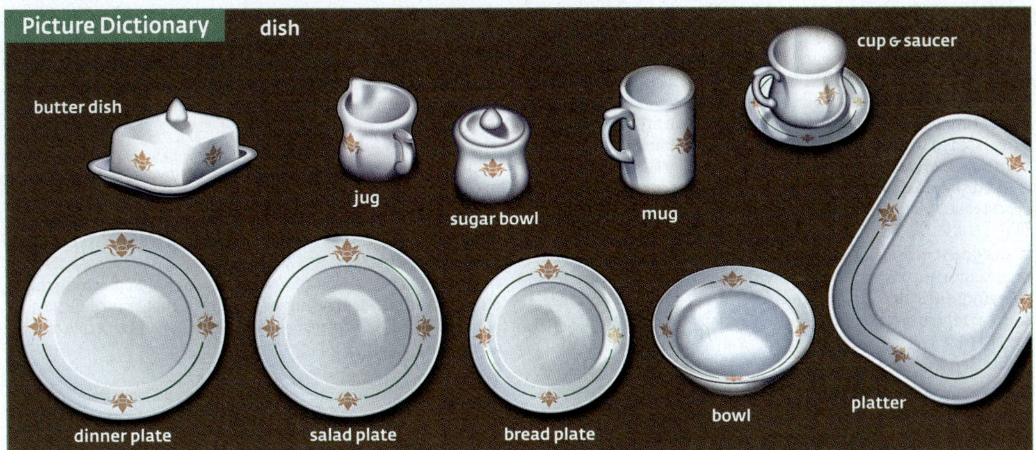

food from dishes and cook food in them. 盘子 ❑ *...plastic bowls and dishes.* …塑料碗和盘子。 **2** N-COUNT Food that is prepared in a particular style or combination can be referred to as a **dish**. (一道) 菜 ❑ *There are plenty of vegetarian dishes to choose from.* 有许多道素菜可供选择。 **3** N-COUNT You can use **dish** to refer to anything that is round and hollow in shape with a wide uncovered top. 盘形物 ❑ *...a dish used to receive satellite broadcasts.* …一个用于接收卫星广播的圆盘天线。 **4** N-PLURAL All the objects that have been used to cook, serve, and eat a meal can be referred to as **the dishes**. 餐具 ❑ *He'd cooked dinner and washed the dishes.* 他做了晚餐，洗了餐具。 **5** → see also **satellite dish** **6** PHRASE If you **do the dishes**, you wash the dishes. 洗碗 ❑ *I hate doing the dishes.* 我讨厌洗碗。

→ see Picture Dictionary: **dish**

→ see **pottery**

▶ **dish out** **1** PHRASAL VERB If you **dish out** something, you distribute it among a number of people. 分发 [INFORMAL] ❑ *Doctors, not pharmacists, are responsible for dishing out drugs.* 医生们而不是药剂师们负责分发药物。 **2** PHRASAL VERB If someone **dishes out** criticism or punishment, they give it to someone. 给予 (批评或惩罚) [INFORMAL] ❑ *Do you usually dish out criticism to someone who's doing you a favor?* 你经常会对帮你的人指指点点吗？ **3** PHRASAL VERB If you **dish out** food, you serve it to people at the beginning of each course of a meal. 分 (菜) [INFORMAL] ❑ *Here the cooks dish out sweet and sour pork.* 在这儿厨师们把咕咾肉分份儿。

▶ **dish up** PHRASAL VERB If you **dish up** food, you serve it. 上 (菜) [INFORMAL] ❑ *They dished up a superb meal.* 他们上了一桌很棒的饭菜。

dis·heart·ened /dɪshɑrtᵊnd/ ADJ If you are **disheartened**, you feel disappointed about something and have less confidence or less hope about it than you did before. 灰心的 ❑ *He was disheartened by their hostile reaction.* 他被他们敌意的反应弄得灰心了。

dis·heart·en·ing /dɪshɑrtᵊnɪŋ/ ADJ If something is **disheartening**, it makes you feel disappointed and less confident or less hopeful. 令人灰心的 ❑ *The news was disheartening for investors.* 这条消息对投资者来说是令人灰心的。

di·shev·eled /dɪʃɛvᵊld/

in BRIT, sometimes AM use **dishevelled**

ADJ If you describe someone's hair, clothes, or appearance as **disheveled**, you mean that it is very untidy. (头发、衣服或外表) 凌乱的 ❑ *She arrived flushed and disheveled.* 她面红耳赤、衣冠不整地来了。

di·shev·elled /dɪʃɛvᵊld/ [BRIT] → see **disheveled**

dis·hon·est /dɪsɒnɪst/ ADJ If you say that a person or their behavior is **dishonest**, you mean that they are not truthful or honest and that you cannot trust them. 不诚实的 ❑ *It would be dishonest to mislead people and not to present the data as fairly as possible.* 误导人们、不尽可能公正地提供数据是不诚实的。 ● **dis·hon·est·ly** ADV 不诚实地 ❑ *The key issue was whether the four defendants acted dishonestly.* 关键问题在于这4名被告是不是做事不诚实。

dis·hon·es·ty /dɪsɒnɪsti/ N-UNCOUNT **Dishonesty** is dishonest behavior. 不诚实行为 ❑ *She accused the government of dishonesty and incompetence.* 她指责政府不诚实和无能。

dish·washer /dɪʃwɒʃər/ (**dishwashers**) **1** N-COUNT A **dishwasher** is an electrically operated machine that washes and dries dishes, pans and flatware. 洗碗机 **2** N-COUNT A **dishwasher** is a person who is employed to wash dishes, for example at a restaurant, or who usually washes the dishes at home. 洗碗工 ❑ *I was a short-order cook and a dishwasher.* 我曾是一名快餐厨师兼洗碗工。

▲ **dis·il·lu·sion** /dɪsɪluʒᵊn/ (**disillusions, disillusioning, disillusioned**) **1** V-T If a person or thing **disillusions** you, they make you realize that something is not as good as you thought. 使醒悟 ❑ *I'd hate to be the one to disillusion him.* 我不愿做打破他梦想的人。 **2** N-UNCOUNT **Disillusion** is the same as **disillusionment**. 幻灭 ❑ *There is disillusion with established political parties.* 对各个确立的政党有幻灭感。

dis·il·lu·sioned /dɪsɪluʒᵊnd/ ADJ If you are **disillusioned with** something, you are disappointed, because it is not as good as you had expected or thought. 幻灭的 ❑ *I've become very disillusioned with politics.* 我变得对政治非常失望。

dis·il·lu·sion·ment /dɪsɪluʒᵊnmənt/ N-UNCOUNT **Disillusionment** is the disappointment that you feel when you discover that something is not as good as you had expected or thought. 幻灭 ❑ *Polls have charted growing disillusionment with the campaign.* 民意调查显示人们对这场运动越来越失望。

dis·in·fect /dɪsɪnfɛkt/ (**disinfects, disinfecting, disinfected**) V-T If you **disinfect** something, you clean it using a substance that kills germs. 给…消毒 ❑ *Chlorine is used to disinfect water.* 氯用来给水消毒。

dis·in·fect·ant /dɪsɪnfɛktənt/ (**disinfectants**) N-MASS **Disinfectant** is a substance that kills germs. It is used, for example, for cleaning kitchens and bathrooms. 消毒剂 ❑ *Effluent from the sedimentation tank is dosed with disinfectant to kill any harmful organisms.* 从沉降池流出的废水被加入消毒剂以杀死一切有害生物。

dis·in·fla·tion /dɪsɪnfleɪʃᵊn/ N-UNCOUNT **Disinflation** is a reduction in the rate of inflation, especially as a result of government policies. 通货紧缩 ❑ *The 1990s was a period of disinflation, when companies lost much of their power to raise prices.* 20世纪90年代是一段通货紧缩期，当时各公司大大丧失了他们的提价能力。

▲ **dis·in·te·grate** /dɪsɪntɪgreɪt/ (**disintegrates, disintegrating, disintegrated**) **1** V-I If something **disintegrates**, it becomes seriously weakened, and is divided or destroyed. 瓦解 ❑ *During October 1918 the Austro-Hungarian Empire began to disintegrate.* 1918年10月期间奥匈帝国开始瓦解。 ● **dis·in·te·gra·tion** /dɪsɪntɪgreɪʃᵊn/ N-UNCOUNT 解体 ❑ *...the violent disintegration of Yugoslavia.* …南斯拉夫的猛烈解体。 **2** V-I If an object or substance **disintegrates**, it breaks into many small pieces or parts and is destroyed. 破碎 ❑ *At 420 mph the windshield disintegrated.* 每小时420英里时，挡风玻璃碎了。 ● **dis·in·te·gra·tion** N-UNCOUNT 破碎 ❑ *The report describes the catastrophic disintegration of the aircraft after the explosion.* 该报道描述了爆炸后飞机的灾难性崩解。

dis·in·ter·est /dɪsɪntərɪst, -ɪntrɪst/ N-UNCOUNT If there is **disinterest in** something, people are not interested in it. 无兴趣 ❑ *The fact that Liberia has no oil seems to explain foreign disinterest in its internal affairs.* 利比里亚没有石油的事实似乎可以解释外国对该国内政漠不关心的原因。

D

dis·in·ter·est·ed /dɪsɪntərəstɪd, -ɪntrɪstɪd/ 1 ADJ Someone who is **disinterested** is not involved in a particular situation or not likely to benefit from it and is therefore able to act in a fair and unselfish way. 不涉己利的 ❑ *The current sole superpower is far from being a disinterested observer.* 当前惟一的超级大国远非一个公正的观察者。 2 ADJ If you are **disinterested in** something, you are not interested in it. Some users of English believe that it is not correct to use **disinterested** with this meaning. 不感兴趣的 (有些英语使用者认为**disinterested**用作此意是不正确的) ❑ *Lili had clearly regained her appetite but Doran was disinterested in food.* 莉莉已经明显恢复了食欲，但多兰对食物还是不感兴趣。

★ **dis·joint·ed** /dɪsdʒɔɪntɪd/ ADJ **Disjointed** words, thoughts, or ideas are not presented in a smooth or logical way and are therefore difficult to understand. (言语或想法等) 支离破碎 ❑ *Sally was used to hearing his complaints, usually in the form of disjointed, drunken ramblings.* 萨莉已经习惯了听他的抱怨，通常都是些语无伦次、醉后的胡言乱语。

disk /dɪsk/ (**disks**) also **disc** 1 N-COUNT A **disk** is a flat, circular shape or object. 盘状物 ❑ *The food processor has thin, medium, and thick slicing disks.* 这个食品加工机有薄、中、厚的切片盘。 2 N-COUNT A **disk** is one of the thin, circular pieces of cartilage which separates the bones in your back. 椎间盘 ❑ *I had slipped a disk and was frozen in a spasm of pain.* 我的一块椎间盘脱臼了，突然一阵疼痛使我动弹不得。 3 N-COUNT In a computer, the **disk** is the part where information is stored. (电脑) 磁盘 ❑ *The program takes up 2.5 megabytes of disk space and can be run on a standard personal computer.* 这个程序占用2.5 兆字节的磁盘空间，可以在标准个人电脑上运行。 4 N-COUNT A disk is the same as a **compact disk**. 光盘 5 → see also **disk drive, floppy disk, hard disk**

disk drive (**disk drives**)

in BRIT, also use **disc drive**

N-COUNT The **disk drive** on a computer is the part that contains the disk or into which a disk can be inserted. The disk drive allows you to read information from the disk and store information on the disk. 磁盘驱动器

Word Link *ette ≈ small : cigarette, diskette, rosette*

disk·ette /dɪskɛt/ (**diskettes**) N-COUNT A **diskette** is the same as a **floppy disk**. 软盘

dis·like /dɪslaɪk/ (**dislikes, disliking, disliked**) 1 V-T If you **dislike** someone or something, you consider them to be unpleasant and do not like them. 不喜爱 ❑ *Liver is a great favorite of his and we don't serve it often because so many people dislike it.* 肝脏是他的一种最爱，但我们不常供应这道菜，因为有那么多人不爱吃。 2 N-UNCOUNT **Dislike** is the feeling that you do not like someone or something. 厌恶 ❑ *My dislike of thunder and even small earthquakes was due to Mother.* 我对雷声甚至于轻微地震的厌恶都归因于我的母亲。 3 N-COUNT Your **dislikes** are the things that you do not like. 不喜欢的事物 ❑ *Consider what your likes and dislikes are about your job.* 考虑一下，对于你的工作哪些是你喜欢的，哪些是不喜欢的。 4 PHRASE If you **take a dislike to** someone or something, you decide that you do not like them. 讨厌 ❑ *He may suddenly take a dislike to foods that he's previously enjoyed.* 他也许会突然讨厌他以前喜欢吃的食物。

Thesaurus *dislike* 另参见：
V. disapprove of, object to 1
N. aversion to 2

dis·lo·cate /dɪsloʊkeɪt, dɪsloʊkeɪt/ (**dislocates, dislocating, dislocated**) 1 V-T If you **dislocate** a bone or joint in your body, or in someone else's body, it moves out of its proper position in relation to other bones, usually in an accident. 使脱臼 ❑ *Harrison dislocated a finger.* 哈里森让一根手指脱臼了。 2 V-T To **dislocate** something such as a system, process, or way of life means to disturb it greatly or prevent it from continuing as normal. 扰乱 ❑ *It would help to end illiteracy and disease, but it would also dislocate a traditional way of life.* 它该会有助于消除文盲和疾病，但也会打乱一种传统的生活方式。

dis·lodge /dɪslɒdʒ/ (**dislodges, dislodging, dislodged**) 1 V-T To **dislodge** something means to remove it from where it was fixed or held. 拿开 (固定在某处的某物) ❑ *Rainfall from a tropical storm dislodged the debris from the slopes of the volcano.* 一场热带风暴带来的降雨把岩屑从火山坡上冲走了。 2 V-T To **dislodge** a person from a position or job means to remove them from it. 解除 (职务) ❑ *Congress had sought to dislodge him from the post.* 国会曾试图解除他的职务。

dis·loy·al /dɪslɔɪəl/ ADJ Someone who is **disloyal to** their friends, family, or country does not support them or does things that could harm them. 不忠诚的 ❑ *She was so disloyal to her deputy she made his position untenable.* 她对她的副手如此不忠诚，以至于弄得他的职位岌岌可危。

dis·loy·al·ty /dɪslɔɪəlti/ N-UNCOUNT **Disloyalty** is disloyal behavior. 不忠 ❑ *Charges had already been made against certain officials suspected of disloyalty.* 已对某些被怀疑有不忠行为的官员提出指控。

▲ **dis·mal** /dɪzməl/ 1 ADJ Something that is **dismal** is bad in a sad or depressing way. 惨淡不良的 ❑ *...Israel's dismal record in the Olympics.* …以色列在奥运会上的惨淡纪录。 2 ADJ Something that is **dismal** is sad and depressing, especially in appearance. (尤指外表) 沉闷的 ❑ *The main part of the hospital is pretty dismal but the children's ward is really lively.* 这家医院的主要地方颇为沉闷，但是儿科病房却很有生气。

▲ **dis·man·tle** /dɪsmæntəl/ (**dismantles, dismantling, dismantled**) 1 V-T If you **dismantle** a machine or structure, you carefully separate it into its different parts. 拆除 ❑ *He asked for immediate help from the United States to dismantle the warheads.* 他向美国请求即时援助，拆除弹头。 2 V-T To **dismantle** an organization or system means to cause it to stop functioning by gradually reducing its power or purpose. 逐步废除 ❑ *Public services of all kinds are being dismantled.* 各种公共服务正被逐步废除。

★ **dis·may** /dɪsmeɪ/ (**dismays, dismaying, dismayed**) 1 N-UNCOUNT **Dismay** is a strong feeling of fear, worry, or sadness that is caused by something unpleasant and unexpected. 恐慌；悲伤 [FORMAL] ❑ *Local politicians have reacted with dismay and indignation.* 当地政客们作出了恐慌和愤慨的反应。 2 V-T If you **are dismayed** by something, it makes you feel afraid, worried, or sad. 使恐慌；使悲伤 [FORMAL] ❑ *The committee was dismayed by what it had been told.* 该委员会被所告知的情况搞得焦虑不安。 ● **dis·mayed** ADJ 恐慌的；悲伤的 ❑ *He was dismayed at the cynicism of the youngsters.* 他对年轻人们的愤世嫉俗感到伤心焦虑。

Word Link *miss ≈ sending : dismiss, missile, missionary*

dis·miss ♦◇◇ /dɪsmɪs/ (**dismisses, dismissing, dismissed**) 1 V-T If you **dismiss** something, you decide or say that it is not important enough for you to think about or consider. 不予理会 ❑ *Mr. Wakeham dismissed the reports as speculation.* 韦克厄姆先生把这些报道当作臆测而不予理会。 2 V-T If you **dismiss** something **from** your mind, you stop thinking about it. 不再考虑 ❑ *I dismissed the problem from my mind.* 我从心中摒除了这个问题。 3 V-T When an employer **dismisses** an employee, the employer tells the employee that they are no longer needed to do the job that they have been doing. 解雇 ❑ *...the power to dismiss civil servants who refuse to work.* …解雇拒绝工作的公务员们的权力。 4 V-T If you **are dismissed** by someone in authority, they tell you that you can go away from them. 准予…离去 ❑ *Two more witnesses were called, heard, and dismissed.* 又有两名证人被传讯后获准离开了。 5 V-T When a judge **dismisses** a case against someone, he or she formally states that there is no need for a trial, usually because there is not enough evidence for the case to continue. 不受理 ❑ *A federal judge dismissed the charges against the doctor yesterday.* 一名联邦法官昨天驳回了对该医生的指控。

Word Partnership *dismiss* 的常用搭配：
ADJ. easy to dismiss 1
N. dismiss **an idea**, dismiss **a possibility** 1
dismiss **an employee** 3
dismiss **a case**, dismiss **charges** 5

★ **dis·mis·sal** /dɪsmɪsəl/ (**dismissals**) 1 N-VAR When an employee is dismissed from their job, you can refer to their **dismissal**. 免职 ❑ *...Mr. Low's dismissal from his post at the head of the commission.* …洛先生被免去委员会主任的职务。 2 N-UNCOUNT **Dismissal of** something means deciding or saying that it is not important. 轻视 ❑ *...bureaucratic indifference to people's rights and needs, and high-handed dismissal of public opinion.* …官僚主义对民众权利和需求的冷漠，以及对公众意见的不懈一顾。

dis·miss·ive /dɪsmɪsɪv/ ADJ If you are **dismissive of** someone or something, you say or show that you think they are not important or have no value. 不屑一顾的 ❑ *Mr. Jones was dismissive* *of the report, saying it was riddled with inaccuracies.* 琼斯先生对那份报告不屑一顾，说那里面充斥着不准确的信息。● **dis·miss·ive·ly** ADV 不屑一顾地 ❑ *"Critical acclaim from people who don't know what they're talking about is meaningless," he claims dismissively.* "来自不懂自己在说什么的评论者们的赞扬是没意义的，"他轻蔑地说。

dis·obedi·ence /dɪsəbiːdiəns/ N-UNCOUNT **Disobedience** is deliberately not doing what someone tells you to do, or what a rule or law says that you should do. 不服从；不顺从 ❑ *A single act of rebellion or disobedience was often enough to seal a woman's fate.* 仅一次反抗或不服从的行为在以前就往往足以决定一个女人的命运。

dis·obey /dɪsəbeɪ/ (**disobeys, disobeying, disobeyed**) V-T/V-I When someone **disobeys** a person or an order, they deliberately do not do what they have been told to do. 不服从；不顺从 ❑ *...a naughty boy who often disobeyed his mother and father.* …一个经常不顺从母亲和父亲的淘气男孩。

dis·or·der /dɪsɔrdər/ (**disorders**) **1** N-VAR A **disorder** is a problem or illness which affects someone's mind or body. 紊乱 ❑ *...a rare nerve disorder that can cause paralysis of the arms.* …一种罕见的能导致手臂瘫痪的神经紊乱疾病。 **2** N-VAR **Disorder** is violence or rioting in public. 动乱 ❑ *Six months ago America's worst civil disorder in more than 100 years erupted in the city of Los Angeles.* 6个月前，美国100多年来最严重的市民骚乱在洛杉矶市爆发了。 **3** N-UNCOUNT **Disorder** is a state of being untidy, badly prepared, or badly organized. 混乱 ❑ *The emergency room was in disorder.* 急救室一片混乱。

dis·or·der·ly /dɪsɔrdərli/ **1** ADJ If you describe something as **disorderly**, you mean that it is messy, irregular, or disorganized. 混乱的 [FORMAL] ❑ *There were young men and women working away at tables all over the large and disorderly room.* 那间宽敞而又凌乱的房间里到处都是伏案工作的青年男女。 **2** ADJ If you describe someone as **disorderly**, you mean that they are behaving in a noisy, rude, or violent way in public. You can also describe a place or event as **disorderly** if the people there behave in this way. (某人) 不守秩序的; (某地) 混乱无序的 [FORMAL] ❑ *She was jailed for being drunk and disorderly.* 她因酗酒和扰乱治安而被监禁。

dis·or·gani·sa·tion /dɪsɔːʳgənaɪzeɪʃən/ [BRIT] → see **disorganization**

dis·or·gan·ised /dɪsɔːʳgənaɪzd/ [BRIT] → see **disorganized**

dis·or·gani·za·tion /dɪsɔrgənɪzeɪʃən/

in BRIT, also use **disorganisation**

N-UNCOUNT If something is in a state of **disorganization**, it is disorganized. 动乱 ❑ *The military, he says, is now in a state of disorganization.* 他说军队现在处于动乱状态。

dis·or·gan·ized /dɪsɔrgənaɪzd/

in BRIT, also use **disorganised**

1 ADJ Something that is **disorganized** is in a confused state or is badly planned or managed. 混乱无序的；缺乏组织的 ❑ *A report by the state prosecutor described the police action as confused and disorganized.* 州检察官的报告将警方的行动描述成混乱和缺乏组织的。 **2** ADJ Someone who is **disorganized** is very bad at organizing things in their life. 没有条理的 ❑ *My boss is completely disorganized and leaves the most important items until very late.* 我的老板完全没有条理，并把最重要的事项拖得很久。

dis·ori·ent /dɪsɔriɛnt/ (**disorients, disorienting, disoriented**)

in BRIT, also use **disorientate**

V-T If something **disorients** you, you lose your sense of direction, or you generally feel lost and uncertain, for example, because you are in an unfamiliar environment. 使迷失方向；使糊涂 ❑ *An overnight stay at a friend's house disorients me.* 在朋友家过夜让我感到迷糊。 ● **dis·ori·ent·ed** ADJ 迷失方向的；感到糊涂的 ❑ *I feel dizzy and disoriented.* 我感觉头晕、迷糊。 ● **dis·ori·en·ta·tion** /dɪsɔrienteɪʃən/ N-UNCOUNT 迷失方向；糊涂 ❑ *Morris was so stunned by this that he experienced a moment of total disorientation.* 莫里斯对此非常震惊，以致他感到一时间的彻底茫然。

dis·ori·en·tate /dɪsɔrienteɪt/ (**disorientates, disorientating, disorientated**) [mainly BRIT] → see **disorient**

dis·own /dɪsoʊn/ (**disowns, disowning, disowned**) V-T If you **disown** someone or something, you say or show that you no longer want to have any connection with them or any responsibility for them. 声明与…脱离关系 ❑ *The man who murdered the girl is no son of mine. I disown him.* 谋杀那个女孩的人不配做我的儿子，我和他脱离关系。

dis·par·age /dɪspærɪdʒ/ (**disparages, disparaging, disparaged**) V-T If you **disparage** someone or something, you speak about them in a way which shows that you do not have a good opinion of them. 诋毁 [FORMAL] ❑ *...Larkin's tendency to disparage literature.* …拉金诋毁文学的倾向。

dis·par·ag·ing /dɪspærɪdʒɪŋ/ ADJ If you are **disparaging** about someone or something, or make **disparaging** comments about them, you say things which show that you do not have a good opinion of them. 贬低的 ❑ *He was critical of the people, disparaging of their crude manners.* 他批评那些人，贬低他们粗鲁的举止。

Word Link *par ≈ equal : compare, disparate, part*

dis·par·ate /dɪspərɪt/ **1** ADJ **Disparate** things are clearly different from each other in quality or type. 迥然不同的 [FORMAL] ❑ *Scientists are trying to pull together disparate ideas in astronomy.* 科学家正试图把天文学界各种迥然不同的观点汇集起来。 **2** ADJ A **disparate** thing is made up of very different elements. 多元的 [FORMAL] ❑ *...a very disparate nation, with enormous regional differences.* …一个有着巨大地区差异、多元化的国家。

dis·par·ity /dɪspærɪti/ (**disparities**) N-VAR If there is a **disparity between** two or more things, there is a noticeable difference between them. 明显差异 [FORMAL] ❑ *...the health disparities between ethnic and socio-economic groups in the U.S.* …美国各种族和社会经济群体之间明显的健康差异。

★ **dis·patch** /dɪspætʃ/ (**dispatches, dispatching, dispatched**)

in BRIT, also use **despatch**

1 V-T If you **dispatch** someone to a place, you send them there for a particular reason. 派遣 [FORMAL] ❑ *He had been continually dispatching scouts ahead.* 他一直不断地派遣侦察员到前面去。 ● N-UNCOUNT **Dispatch** is also a noun. 派遣 ❑ *The dispatch of the task force is purely a contingency measure.* 派遣特遣队纯粹是应急措施。 **2** V-T If you **dispatch** a message, letter, or parcel, you send it to a particular person or destination. 发送 [FORMAL] ❑ *The victory inspired him to dispatch a gleeful telegram to Roosevelt.* 胜利鼓舞了他发喜电给罗斯福。 ● N-UNCOUNT **Dispatch** is also a noun. 发送 ❑ *We have 125 cases ready for dispatch.* 我们有125个待发的箱子。

dis·pel /dɪspɛl/ (**dispels, dispelling, dispelled**) V-T To **dispel** an idea or feeling that people have means to stop them having it. 消除 (想法或感觉) ❑ *The president is attempting to dispel the notion that he has neglected the economy.* 总统正试图消除他忽视了经济这一想法。

dis·pen·sable /dɪspɛnsəbəl/ ADJ If someone or something is **dispensable** they are not really needed. 可有可无的 ❑ *All those people in the middle are dispensable.* 那些在中间的人都是可有可无的。

★ **dis·pense** /dɪspɛns/ (**dispenses, dispensing, dispensed**) **1** V-T If someone **dispenses** something that they own or control, they give or provide it to a number of people. 分发 [FORMAL] ❑ *The union had already dispensed $60000 in grants.* 工会已经分发了6万美元的补助金。 **2** V-T If you obtain a product by getting it out of a machine, you can say that the machine **dispenses** the product. (机器) 售出 (商品) ❑ *For two weeks, the cash machine spewed out receipts apologizing for its inability to dispense money.* 两周了，自动取款机就输出了一些因其无法提款而致歉的凭条。 **3** V-T When a pharmacist **dispenses** medicine, he or she prepares it, and gives or sells it to the patient or customer. 配发；配售 (药) ❑ *Health officials hope to begin dispensing anti-retroviral drugs on a wide scale at the beginning of next year.* 卫生官员们希望在明年年初开始大规模配发抗逆转录病毒药物。

▸ **dispense with** PHRASAL VERB If you **dispense with** something, you stop using it or get rid of it completely, especially because you no longer need it. 放弃使用 ❑ *More modern heating systems dispense with the need for a tank.* 更现代化的取暖系统不再需要水箱。

dis·pens·er /dɪspɛnsər/ (**dispensers**) N-COUNT A **dispenser** is a machine or container designed so that you can get an item or quantity of something from it in an easy and convenient way. 自动售货机；自动分发器 ❑ *...cash dispensers.* …自动取款机。

★ **dis·perse** /dɪspɜrs/ (**disperses, dispersing, dispersed**) **1** V-T/V-I When something **disperses** or when you **disperse** it, it spreads over a wide area. 使分散；扩散 ❑ *The oil appeared to be dispersing.* 油看上去正在扩散。 **2** V-T/V-I When a group of people **disperses** or when someone **disperses** them, the group splits up and the people leave in different directions. 驱散；散开 ❑ *Police fired shots and used tear gas to disperse the demonstrators.* 警察开枪并使用了催泪瓦斯来驱散示威人群。

d

D

★ dis·place /dɪspleɪs/ (**displaces, displacing, displaced**) 1 V-T If one thing **displaces** another, it forces the other thing out of its place, position, or role, and then occupies that place, position, or role itself. 取代 ❑ *These factories have displaced tourism as the country's largest source of foreign exchange.* 这些工厂已经取代了旅游业而成为该国最大的外汇来源。 2 V-T If a person or group of people **is displaced**, they are forced to move away from the area where they live. 使背井离乡 [usu passive] ❑ *More than 600,000 people were displaced by the tsunami.* 超过60万人被海啸搞得背井离乡。

dis·placed per·son (**displaced people, displaced persons**) N-COUNT A **displaced person** is someone who has been forced to leave the place where they live, especially because of a war. 难民 ❑ *There is an urgent need for food and shelter for these displaced people.* 急需为这些难民提供食物和住处。

dis·place·ment /dɪspleɪsmənt/ 1 N-UNCOUNT **Displacement** is the removal of something from its usual place or position by something which then occupies that place or position. 替代 [FORMAL] ❑ *...the displacement of traditional agriculture by industrial crops.* …经济作物对传统农业的替代。 2 N-UNCOUNT **Displacement** is the forcing of people away from the area or country where they live. 逐出家园 ❑ *...the gradual displacement of the American Indian.* …对美洲印第安人的逐步强制迁移。

dis·play ♦♦◊ /dɪspleɪ/ (**displays, displaying, displayed**) 1 V-T If you **display** something that you want people to see, you put it in a particular place, so that people can see it easily. 陈列；展出 ❑ *Among the protesters and war veterans proudly displaying their medals was Aubrey Rose.* 在抗议人群和自豪地展示勋章的退伍军人中的是奥布里・罗斯。 ● N-UNCOUNT **Display** is also a noun. 陈列；展出 ❑ *Most of the other artists whose work is on display were his pupils or colleagues.* 其他有作品展出的艺术家大多数是他的学生或同事。 2 V-T If you **display** something, you show it to people. 展示 ❑ *She displayed her wound to the twelve gentlemen of the jury.* 她向陪审团的12位男士展示她的伤痕。 3 V-T If you **display** a characteristic, quality, or emotion, you behave in a way which shows that you have it. 表露(特点、素质、情感) ❑ *It was unlike Gordon to display his feelings.* 表露自己的感情这点可不像戈登。 ● N-VAR **Display** is also a noun. 表露 ❑ *Normally, such an outward display of affection is reserved for his mother.* 通常，他只在他母亲前才情感外露。 4 V-T When a computer **displays** information, it shows it on a screen. (在计算机屏幕上) 显示 ❑ *They started out by looking at the computer screens which display the images.* 他们从观看显示图像的计算机屏幕开始。 5 N-COUNT A **display** is an arrangement of things that have been put in a particular place, so that people can see them easily. 陈列 ❑ *...a display of your work.* …你作品的陈列。 6 N-COUNT A **display** is a public performance or other event which is intended to entertain people. 表演 ❑ *...the fireworks display.* …烟火表演。 7 N-COUNT The **display** on a computer screen is the information that is shown there. The screen itself can also be referred to as the **display**. (屏幕) 显示内容；(计算机) 屏幕 ❑ *A hard copy of the screen display can also be obtained from a printer.* 屏幕显示的硬拷贝也可从打印机那里获得。

dis·pleas·ure /dɪsplɛʒər/ N-UNCOUNT Someone's **displeasure** is a feeling of annoyance that they have about something that has happened. 不悦 ❑ *The population has already begun to show its displeasure at the slow pace of change.* 人民已经开始对变化的缓慢速度表示不悦。

dis·pos·able /dɪspoʊzəbəl/ (**disposables**) 1 ADJ A **disposable** product is designed to be thrown away after it has been used. 一次性的 ❑ *...disposable diapers suitable for babies up to 8lbs.* …适合重至8磅的婴儿使用的一次性尿布。 ● N-COUNT Disposable products can be referred to as **disposables**. 一次性物品 ❑ *Currently, disposables account for about 80% to 85% of the $3 billion-plus annual diaper market.* 目前，一次性尿布占年销售额30多亿美元的尿布市场的80%至85%左右。 2 ADJ Your **disposable** income is the amount of income you have left after you have paid bills and taxes. 可自由支配的 (收入) [ADJ n] ❑ *Gerald had little disposable income.* 杰拉尔德没有多少可自由支配的收入。

dis·pos·al /dɪspoʊzəl/ 1 PHRASE If you have something **at** your **disposal**, you are able to use it whenever you want, and for whatever purpose you want. If you say that you are **at** someone's **disposal**, you mean that you are willing to help them in any way you can. 任某人支配；尽力为某人提供帮助 ❑ *Do you have this information at your disposal?* 这个资料你能随意使用吗？ 2 N-UNCOUNT **Disposal** is the act of getting rid of something that is no longer wanted or needed. 清除 ❑ *...methods for the permanent disposal of radioactive wastes.* …放射性废料的永久清除方法。

dis·pose /dɪspoʊz/ (**disposes, disposing, disposed**)
▶ **dispose of** PHRASAL VERB If you **dispose of** something that you no longer want or need, you throw it away. 丢弃 ❑ *...the safest means of disposing of nuclear waste.* …丢弃核废料最安全的方法。

dis·posed /dɪspoʊzd/ 1 ADJ If you are **disposed to** do something, you are willing or eager to do it. 愿意的 [v-link ADJ to-inf] [FORMAL] ❑ *We passed one or two dwellings, but were not disposed to stop.* 我们经过一两处住所，却无意停下。 2 ADJ You can use **disposed** when you are talking about someone's general attitude or opinion. For example, if you are well or favorably **disposed to** or **toward** someone or something, you like them or approve of them. 持…态度的；有…看法的 [FORMAL] ❑ *I saw that the publishers were well disposed toward my book.* 我看出版商对我的书有好感。

★ dis·po·si·tion /dɪspəzɪʃən/ (**dispositions**) N-COUNT Someone's **disposition** is the way that they tend to behave or feel. 性情 ❑ *The rides are unsuitable for people of a nervous disposition.* 这种骑乘不适合紧张型性格的人。

dis·pro·por·tion·ate /dɪsprəpɔrʃənɪt/ ADJ Something that is **disproportionate** is surprising or unreasonable in amount or size, compared with something else. 不成比例的 ❑ *A disproportionate amount of time was devoted to one topic.* 不成比例的时间被用在一个话题上。 ● **dis·pro·por·tion·ate·ly** ADV 不成比例地 ❑ *There is a disproportionately high suicide rate among prisoners facing very long sentences.* 特长刑期的犯人中自杀率高得不成比例。

dis·prove /dɪspruv/ (**disproves, disproving, disproved, disproven**) V-T To **disprove** an idea, belief, or theory means to show that it is not true. 证明(想法、信念或理论) 为误 ❑ *The statistics to prove or disprove his hypothesis will take years to collect.* 要花数年来收集证实或推翻他的假设的数据。
→ see **science**

Word Link *put ≈ thinking : computer, dispute, indisputable*

dis·pute ♦♦◊ /dɪspyut/ (**disputes, disputing, disputed**) 1 N-VAR A **dispute** is an argument or disagreement between people or groups. 争论 ❑ *They have won previous pay disputes with the government.* 他们曾赢过前几起与政府的工资纠纷。

> Do not confuse **dispute** and **argument**. A **dispute** is a serious argument that can last for a long time. **Disputes** generally occur between organizations, political parties, or countries. ❑ *...a 10-year-old dispute over crude oil.* An **argument** is a disagreement between people who may or may not know each other. ❑ *She had an argument with her father about practicing the piano... Travis got in an argument with another motorist.*

2 V-T If you **dispute** a fact, statement, or theory, you say that it is incorrect or untrue. 反驳 ❑ *He disputed the allegations.* 他驳斥了这些无根据的指控。 ❑ *Nobody disputed that Davey was clever.* 没有人反驳戴维是聪明的。 3 V-RECIP When people **dispute** something, they fight for control or ownership of it. You can also say that one group of people **dispute** something with another group. 争夺(控制权、所有权) ❑ *Russia and Ukraine have been disputing the ownership of the fleet.* 俄罗斯和乌克兰一直在争夺该舰队的所有权。 4 PHRASE If two or more people or groups are **in dispute**, they are arguing or disagreeing about something. (人或组织) 有争议的 ❑ *The two countries are in dispute over the boundaries of their coastal waters.* 两国对它们沿海海域的边界是有争议的。 5 PHRASE If something is **in dispute**, people are questioning it or arguing about it. (某事物) 有争议的 ❑ *The schedule for the talks has been agreed, but the location is still in dispute.* 会谈的时间表已经达成一致，但地点尚有争议。

dis·quali·fy /dɪskwɒlɪfaɪ/ (**disqualifies, disqualifying, disqualified**) V-T When someone **is disqualified**, they are officially stopped from taking part in a particular event, activity, or competition, usually because they have done something wrong. 使丧失资格 ❑ *Thomson was disqualified from the 400 meter freestyle.* 汤姆森被取消了400米自由泳的参赛资格。 ● **dis·quali·fi·ca·tion** /dɪskwɒlɪfɪkeɪʃən/ N-VAR (**disqualifications**) 资格的丧失 ❑ *Livingston faces a four-year disqualification from athletics.* 利文斯顿面临着为期4年的体育禁赛。

dis·qui·et /dɪskwaɪɪt/ N-UNCOUNT **Disquiet** is a feeling of worry or anxiety. 忧虑不安 [FORMAL] ❑ *There is growing public disquiet about the cost of such policing.* 对这样的警务开支公众忧虑不断增长。

★ **dis·re·gard** /dɪsrɪgɑrd/ (**disregards, disregarding, disregarded**) V-T If you **disregard** something, you ignore it or do not take account of it. 对…置之不理 ❑ *He disregarded the advice of his executives.* 他对主管们的建议置之不理。 ● N-UNCOUNT **Disregard** is also a noun. 忽视 ❑ *Whoever planted the bomb showed a total disregard for the safety of the public.* 不论谁安置了炸弹都显示出对公众安全的全然漠视。

dis·re·pute /dɪsrɪpyut/ PHRASE If something **is brought into disrepute** or **falls into disrepute**, it loses its good reputation, because it is connected with activities that people do not approve of. 丧失名誉 ❑ *It is a disgrace that such people should bring our profession into disrepute.* 这样一些人会让我们的职业名誉扫地，真是一种耻辱。

Word Link *dis ≈ negative, not : disagree, discomfort, disrespect*

dis·re·spect /dɪsrɪspɛkt/ N-UNCOUNT If someone shows **disrespect**, they speak or behave in a way that shows lack of respect for a person, law, or custom. 不敬 ❑ *...young people with attitudes and complete disrespect for authority.* …好斗并且对权威全然不敬的年轻人。

Word Link *rupt ≈ breaking : disrupt, erupt, interrupt*

★ **dis·rupt** /dɪsrʌpt/ (**disrupts, disrupting, disrupted**) V-T If someone or something **disrupts** an event, system, or process, they cause difficulties that prevent it from continuing or operating in a normal way. 妨碍; 扰乱 ❑ *Anti-war protesters disrupted the debate.* 反战示威者们扰乱了辩论。

dis·rup·tion /dɪsrʌpʃᵊn/ (**disruptions**) N-VAR When there is **disruption** of an event, system, or process, it is prevented from continuing or operating in a normal way. 妨碍; 扰乱 ❑ *The plan was designed to ensure disruption to business was kept to a minimum.* 该计划旨在确保对业务的妨碍保持在最低限度。

dis·rup·tive /dɪsrʌptɪv/ ADJ To be **disruptive** means to prevent something from continuing or operating in a normal way. 妨碍的; 扰乱的 ❑ *Alcohol can produce violent, disruptive behavior.* 酒能促成暴力的和破坏性的行为。

Word Link *sat, satis ≈ enough : dissatisfaction, insatiable, satisfy*

dis·sat·is·fac·tion /dɪssætɪsfækʃᵊn/ (**dissatisfactions**) N-VAR If you feel **dissatisfaction with** something, you are not contented or pleased with it. 不满 ❑ *She has already expressed her dissatisfaction with this aspect of the policy.* 她已对政策的这方面表示了不满。

dis·sat·is·fied /dɪssætɪsfaɪd/ ADJ If you are **dissatisfied with** something, you are not contented or pleased with it. (对某事)不满的 ❑ *Eighty-two percent of voters are dissatisfied with the way their country is being governed.* 82%的投票者对他们国家的管理方式不满意。

Word Link *sect ≈ cutting : dissect, intersect, section*

dis·sect /dɪsɛkt, daɪ-/ (**dissects, dissecting, dissected**) **1** V-T If someone **dissects** the body of a dead person or animal, they carefully cut it up in order to examine it scientifically. 解剖 ❑ *We dissected a frog in biology class.* 我们在生物课上解剖了一只青蛙。 ● **dis·sec·tion** /dɪsɛkʃᵊn, daɪ-/ N-VAR (**dissections**) 解剖 ❑ *Researchers need a growing supply of corpses for dissection.* 研究者们为了解剖需要越来越多的尸体。 **2** V-T If someone **dissects** something such as a theory, a situation, or a piece of writing, they consider and talk about each detail of it. 剖析 ❑ *People want to dissect his work and question his motives.* 人们想剖析他的作品，质疑他的动机。 ● **dis·sec·tion** N-VAR (**dissections**) 剖析 ❑ *...her calm, condescending dissection of my proposals.* …她对我的提案冷静、居高临下的剖析。

▲ **dis·semi·nate** /dɪsɛmɪneɪt/ (**disseminates, disseminating, disseminated**) V-T To **disseminate** information or knowledge means to distribute it so that it reaches many people or organizations. 散布; 传播 [FORMAL] ❑ *They disseminated anti-French propaganda.* 他们散布了反法宣传资料。 ● **dis·semi·na·tion** /dɪsɛmɪneɪʃᵊn/ N-UNCOUNT 散布; 传播 ❑ *He actively promoted the dissemination of scientific ideas about matters such as morality.* 他积极地推动诸如道德之类的科学观念的传播。

▲ **dis·sent** /dɪsɛnt/ (**dissents, dissenting, dissented**) **1** N-UNCOUNT **Dissent** is strong disagreement or dissatisfaction with a decision or opinion, especially one that is supported by most people or by people in authority. 异议 ❑ *He is the toughest military ruler yet and has responded harshly to any dissent.* 他是迄今最苛刻的军事统治者，残酷地回应任何异议。 **2** V-I If you **dissent**, you express disagreement with a decision or opinion, especially one that is supported by most people or by people in authority. 持有异议 [FORMAL] ❑ *Just one of the 10 members dissented.* 10个成员中只有1个人持有异议。 ❑ *No one dissents from the decision to unify.* 无人对统一的决议持有异议。

dis·sent·er /dɪsɛntər/ (**dissenters**) N-COUNT **Dissenters** are people who say that they do not agree with something that other people agree with or that is official policy. 持异议者 ❑ *The party does not tolerate dissenters in its ranks.* 该党不允许党内出现持不同政见者。

▲ **dis·ser·ta·tion** /dɪsərteɪʃᵊn/ (**dissertations**) N-COUNT A **dissertation** is a long formal piece of writing on a particular subject, especially for an advanced university degree. (学位) 论文 ❑ *He is currently writing a dissertation on the Somali civil war.* 他正在写一篇关于索马里内战的论文。

d

▲ **dis·si·dent** /dɪsɪdənt/ (**dissidents**) **1** N-COUNT **Dissidents** are people who disagree with and criticize their government, especially because it is undemocratic. 异议分子 ❑ *...political dissidents.* …政治异议分子。 **2** ADJ **Dissident** people disagree with or criticize their government or a powerful organization they belong to. 持不同政见的 [ADJ n] ❑ *...a dissident Russian novelist.* …一位与政府意见相左的俄罗斯小说家。

Word Link *simil ≈ similar : assimilate, dissimilar, similarity*

dis·simi·lar /dɪsɪmɪlər/ ADJ If one thing is **dissimilar to** another, or if two things are **dissimilar**, they are very different from each other. 不同的 ❑ *His methods were not dissimilar to those used by Freud.* 他用的方法和弗洛伊德用的没有什么不同。 ❑ *It would be difficult to find two men who were more dissimilar.* 要找出两个更不同的人来可不容易。

▲ **dis·si·pate** /dɪsɪpeɪt/ (**dissipates, dissipating, dissipated**) **1** V-T/V-I When something **dissipates** or when you **dissipate** it, it becomes less or becomes less strong until it disappears or goes away completely. 驱散; 消散 [FORMAL] ❑ *The tension in the room had dissipated.* 房间里的紧张气氛已经消散了。 **2** V-T When someone **dissipates** money, time, or effort, they waste it in a foolish way. 浪费(金钱、时间、努力等) [FORMAL] ❑ *He needs someone who can keep him from dissipating his time and energy on too many different things.* 他需要有人来阻止他浪费时间和精力做太多不同的事情。

dis·so·ci·ate /dɪsoʊʃieɪt, -sieɪt/ (**dissociates, dissociating, dissociated**) **1** V-T If you **dissociate yourself from** something or someone, you say or show that you are not connected with them, usually in order to avoid trouble or blame. 使分离; 使脱离 ❑ *It seems harder and harder for the president to dissociate himself from the scandals that surround Mr. Galdos.* 看来总统越来越难以从缠绕盖尔多斯先生的丑闻中脱身。 **2** V-T If you **dissociate** one thing **from** another, you consider the two things as separate from each other, or you separate them. 把…分开 [FORMAL] ❑ *Almost the first lesson they learn is how to dissociate emotion from reason.* 第一堂课上他们学的几乎就是如何将情感和理智分开。

dis·so·lu·tion /dɪsəluʃᵊn/ **1** N-UNCOUNT **Dissolution** is the act of breaking up officially an organization or institution, or of formally ending a parliament. (组织、议会等的) 解散 [also "a" N, oft N "of" n] [FORMAL] ❑ *He stayed on until the dissolution of the firm in 1948.* 他一直呆到1948年公司解散。 **2** N-UNCOUNT **Dissolution** is the act of officially ending a formal agreement, for example, a marriage or a business arrangement. (婚姻关系或契约的) 解除 [FORMAL] ❑ *...the statutory requirement for granting dissolution of a marriage.* …允许婚姻解除的法定要求。

dis·solve /dɪzɒlv/ (**dissolves, dissolving, dissolved**) **1** V-T/V-I If a substance **dissolves** in liquid or if you **dissolve** it, it becomes mixed with the liquid and disappears. 使溶解; 溶解 ❑ *Heat gently until the sugar dissolves.* 微微加热直到糖溶解。 **2** V-T When an organization or institution **is dissolved**, it is officially ended or broken up. 解散(组织或机构) ❑ *The committee has been dissolved.* 委员会被解散了。 **3** V-T When a parliament **is dissolved**, it is formally ended, so that elections for a new parliament can be held. 解散(议会) ❑ *The present assembly will be dissolved on April 30th.* 本届议会将于4月30日解散。 **4** V-T When a marriage or business arrangement **is dissolved**, it is officially ended. 解除(婚姻关系或业务协议) [usu passive] ❑ *The marriage was dissolved in 1976.* 那桩婚姻在1976年被解除了。 **5** V-T/V-I If something such as a problem or feeling **dissolves** or **is dissolved**, it becomes weaker and disappears. 使消失; 消失 ❑ *His new-found optimism dissolved.* 他刚刚建立的乐观情绪消失了。

Word Link *suad, suas ≈ urging : dissuade, persuade, persuasive*

dis·suade /dɪsweɪd/ **(dissuades, dissuading, dissuaded)** V-T If you **dissuade** someone **from** doing or believing something, you persuade them not to do or believe it. 劝阻 [FORMAL] ❑ *Doctors had tried to dissuade patients from smoking.* 医生曾试图说服病人不要抽烟。❑ *She steadfastly maintained that her grandsons were innocent, and nothing could dissuade her from that belief.* 她始终坚持她的孙子们是无辜的，没有什么能改变她的这一信念。

D

dis·tance ♦♦◊ /dɪstəns/ **(distances, distancing, distanced)** 1 N-VAR The **distance between** two points or places is the amount of space between them. 距离 ❑ *...the distance between the island and the nearby shore.* …岛屿和附近海岸之间的距离。
2 N-UNCOUNT When two things are very far apart, you talk about the **distance** between them. 远离 ❑ *The distance wouldn't be a problem.* 距离遥远不是问题。 3 N-UNCOUNT When you want to emphasize that two people or things do not have a close relationship or are not the same, you can refer to the **distance between** them. 差距 [EMPHASIS] ❑ *There was a vast distance between psychological clues and concrete proof.* 心理线索和现实证据之间存在着巨大差距。 4 N-UNCOUNT **Distance** is coolness or unfriendliness in the way that someone behaves toward you. 疏远；冷淡 [FORMAL] ❑ *There were periods of sulking, of pronounced distance, of coldness.* 出现阶段性的愠怒、明显的疏远和冷淡。 5 ADJ **Distance** learning or **distance** education involves studying at home and sending your work to a college or university, rather than attending the college or university in person. 远程的 [ADJ n] ❑ *The Internet is often used as a resource and as a tool for distance learning.* 互联网通常被用作远程学习的资源和工具。 6 N-SING If you can see something **in the distance**, you can see it, far away from you. 在远处 ["in/into the" N] ❑ *We suddenly saw her in the distance.* 我们突然看见远处的她。 7 V-T If you **distance yourself from** a person or thing, or if something **distances** you **from** them, you feel less friendly or positive toward them, or become less involved with them. 疏远 ❑ *The author distanced himself from some of the comments in his book.* 作者在他的书里对某些评论淡然处之。● **dis·tanced** ADJ 疏远的；有距离的 [v-link ADJ] ❑ *Clough felt he'd become too distanced from his fans.* 克拉夫觉得他变得太疏远他的仰慕者们。 8 PHRASE If you are **at a distance** from something, or if you see it or remember it **from a distance**, you are a long way away from it in space or time. 在/从远处；在/从很久以前 ❑ *The only way I can cope with my mother is at a distance.* 我应付我妈妈的惟一方法就是与她保持距离。 9 PHRASE If you **keep** your **distance** from someone or something or **keep** them **at a distance**, you do not become involved with them. 保持距离 ❑ *Jay had always tended to keep his girlfriends at a distance.* 杰伊一直倾向于同他的女朋友们保持一定的距离。

Word Partnership *distance* 的常用搭配:

- ADJ. **safe** distance, **short** distance 1
- PREP. **within walking** distance 1
- distance **between** 1–3
- **in the** distance 6
- **at a** distance, **from a** distance 8

dis·tant /dɪstənt/ 1 ADJ **Distant** means very far away. 遥远的 ❑ *The mountains rolled away to a distant horizon.* 群山绵延至遥远的天边。 2 ADJ You use **distant** to describe a time or event that is very far away in the future or in the past. 久远的 ❑ *There is little doubt, however, that things will improve in the not too distant future.* 然而毋庸置疑的是，事情在不远的将来会有改观。 3 ADJ A **distant** relative is one who you are not closely related to. 远房的 ❑ *He's a distant relative of the mayor.* 他是市长的远房亲戚。● **dis·tant·ly** ADV 远亲地 ❑ *The O'Shea girls are distantly related to our family.* 奥谢家的姑娘们和我们家沾点儿亲。 4 ADJ If you describe someone as **distant**, you mean that you find them cold and unfriendly. 冷淡的；不友好的 [v-link ADJ] ❑ *He found her cold, icelike, and distant.* 他发现她冷若冰霜，不易接近。 5 ADJ If you describe someone as **distant**, you mean that they are not concentrating on what they are doing because they are thinking about other things. 恍惚的；茫然的 ❑ *There was a distant look in her eyes from time to time, her thoughts elsewhere.* 她的眼中时而出现恍惚的神情，她的思绪飘到别处。

Thesaurus *distant* 另参见:

ADJ. faraway, remote; *(ant.)* close, near 1
aloof, cool, unfriendly 4

dis·tant·ly /dɪstəntli/ 1 ADV **Distantly** means very far away. 遥远地 [LITERARY] ❑ *Distantly, to her right, she could make out the town of Chiffa.* 在右边远远的地方，她能认出那是希法镇。 2 ADV If you are **distantly** aware of something or if you **distantly** remember it, you are aware of it or remember it, but not very strongly. 模糊地 ❑ *She became distantly aware that the light had grown strangely brighter and was flickering gently.* 她模糊地意识到光线奇怪地变得明亮起来，轻轻摇曳着。 3 → see also **distant**

dis·taste /dɪsteɪst/ N-UNCOUNT If you feel **distaste for** someone or something, you dislike them and consider them to be unpleasant, disgusting, or immoral. 厌恶；反感 ❑ *He professed a violent distaste for everything related to commerce, production, and money.* 他对一切与商业、生产和金钱相关的东西表示了强烈的厌恶。

dis·taste·ful /dɪsteɪstfʊl/ ADJ If something is **distasteful to** you, you think it is unpleasant, disgusting, or immoral. 令人厌恶的；令人反感的 ❑ *He found it distasteful to be offered a cold buffet and drinks before witnessing the execution.* 他觉得观看死刑处决之前被招待吃冷盘自助餐、喝饮料很倒胃口。

★ **dis·til** /dɪstɪl/ [BRIT] → see **distill**

★ **dis·till** /dɪstɪl/ **(distills, distilling, distilled)**

in BRIT, use **distil**

1 V-I If a liquid such as whiskey or water **is distilled**, it is heated until it changes into steam or vapor and then cooled until it becomes liquid again. This is usually done in order to make it pure. 蒸馏 ❑ *The whiskey had been distilled in 1926 and sat quietly maturing until 1987.* 这瓶威士忌是1926年被蒸馏的，存放至1987年酿造成熟。● **dis·til·la·tion** /dɪstɪleɪʃən/ N-UNCOUNT 蒸馏 ❑ *Any faults in the original cider stood out sharply after distillation.* 苹果酒原浆中的任何瑕疵蒸馏后就会突现出来。 2 V-T If an oil or liquid **is distilled from** a plant, it is produced by a process which extracts the most essential part of the plant. To **distill** a plant means to produce an oil or liquid from it by this process. 提炼 ❑ *The oil is distilled from the berries of this small tree.* 这种油是从这种小树的浆果中提炼的。● **dis·til·la·tion** N-UNCOUNT 提炼 ❑ *The distillation of rose petals to produce rosewater almost certainly originated in Ancient Persia.* 用玫瑰花瓣提炼制造玫瑰水几乎可以肯定是起源于古波斯。 3 V-T If a thought or idea **is distilled from** previous thoughts, ideas, or experiences, it comes from them. If it **is distilled into** something, it becomes part of that thing. 萃取…的精华；将精华融入… ❑ *Reviews are distilled from articles previously published in the main column.* 评论文章荟萃了发表于各大专栏文章的精华。 ❑ *Eventually passion was distilled into the natural beauty of a balmy night.* 激情最终融入了芬芳夜晚的自然美之中。● **dis·til·la·tion** N-SING 精萃 ❑ *The material below is a distillation of his work.* 下面的材料是他著作的精萃。

dis·tinct /dɪstɪŋkt/ 1 ADJ If something is **distinct from** something else of the same type, it is different or separate from it. 有区别的 ❑ *Engineering and technology are disciplines distinct from one another and from science.* 工程学和工艺学是互不相同的学科，也不同于理科。● **dis·tinct·ly** ADV 不同地 [ADV adj] ❑ *...a banking industry with two distinctly different sectors.* …有两个截然不同部门的银行业。 2 ADJ If something is **distinct**, you can hear, see, or taste it clearly. 清楚的 ❑ *...to impart a distinct flavor with a minimum of cooking fat.* …加入最少量的烹调油脂做出独特的风味。● **dis·tinct·ly** ADV 清楚地 [ADV with v] ❑ *I distinctly heard the loudspeaker calling passengers for the Washington-Miami flight.* 我清楚地听到扩音器在呼叫由华盛顿飞往迈阿密的旅客。 3 ADJ If an idea, thought, or intention is **distinct**, it is clear and definite. 明显的；确切的 ❑ *Now that Tony was no longer present, there was a distinct change in her attitude.* 现在托尼不在场了，她的态度就发生了明显变化。● **dis·tinct·ly** ADV 明显地；确切地 [ADV with v] ❑ *I distinctly remember wishing I had not gotten involved.* 我清楚地记得我巴不得自己没有参与进去。 4 ADJ You can use **distinct** to emphasize that something is great enough in amount or degree to be noticeable or important. 显著的 [ADJ n] [EMPHASIS] ❑ *Being 6ft 3in tall has some distinct disadvantages!* 身高6英尺3英寸有明显的劣势！● **dis·tinct·ly** ADV 显著地 [ADV adj/-ed] ❑ *His government is looking distinctly shaky.* 他的政府看起来显然岌岌可危。 5 PHRASE If you say that you are talking about one thing **as distinct from** another, you are indicating exactly which thing you mean. 与…有区别的 ❑ *There's a lot of evidence that oily fish, as distinct from fatty meat, has a beneficial effect.* 大量证据显示，含油的鱼与肥肉不同，具有益处。

dis·tinc·tion /dɪstɪŋkʃən/ **(distinctions)** 1 N-COUNT A **distinction between** similar things is a difference. 区别 ❑ *There are obvious distinctions between the two wine-making areas.* 这两个酿酒区之

间有明显的不同。 ❑ *The distinction between craft and fine art is more controversial.* 工艺和美术之间的区别更有争议。 ● PHRASE If you **draw a distinction** or **make a distinction**, you say that two things are different. 区分 2 N-COUNT A **distinction** is a special award or honor that is given to someone because of their very high level of achievement. 荣誉 ❑ *The award was established in 1902 as a special distinction for eminent men and women.* 该奖设立于1902年，作为特别荣誉颁给杰出的男士和女士。 3 N-UNCOUNT **Distinction** is the quality of being very good or better than other things of the same type. 卓越 [FORMAL] ❑ *Lewis emerges as a composer of distinction and sensitivity.* 刘易斯脱颖而出，成为一位有卓越能力和敏锐度的作曲家。 4 N-SING If you say that someone or something has **the distinction of** being something, you are drawing attention to the fact that they have the special quality of being that thing. **Distinction** is normally used to refer to good qualities, but can sometimes also be used to refer to bad qualities. 特质 ❑ *He has the distinction of being regarded as the Federal Republic's greatest living writer.* 他有一种特质，因此被认为是联邦共和国在世的最伟大的作家。

dis·tinc·tive /dɪstɪŋktɪv/ ADJ Something that is **distinctive** has a special quality or feature which makes it easily recognizable and different from other things of the same type. 与众不同的; 有特色的 ❑ *...the distinctive odor of chlorine.* …氯气的特殊气味。 ● **dis·tinc·tive·ly** ADV 特别地; 有特色地 [ADV adj/-ed] ❑ *...the distinctively fragrant taste of elderflowers.* …接骨木花奇特的香味。

dis·tin·guish /dɪstɪŋgwɪʃ/ (**distinguishes, distinguishing, distinguished**) 1 V-T/V-I If you can **distinguish** one thing **from** another or **distinguish between** two things, you can see or understand how they are different. 辨别; 区分 ❑ *Could he distinguish right from wrong?* 他能辨别是非吗？ ❑ *Research suggests that babies learn to see by distinguishing between areas of light and dark.* 研究显示婴儿是通过区分明亮区域和黑暗区域来学会观看的。 2 V-T A feature or quality that **distinguishes** one thing **from** another causes the two things to be regarded as different, because only the first thing has the feature or quality. 有别于 ❑ *There is something about music that distinguishes it from all other art forms.* 音乐中一些因素使之有别于其他艺术形式。 3 V-T If you can **distinguish** something, you can see, hear, or taste it although it is very difficult to detect. 辨别出 [FORMAL] ❑ *There were cries, calls. He could distinguish voices.* 有各种各样的哭声和叫喊声。他能从中分辨出声音。 4 V-T If you **distinguish yourself**, you do something that makes you famous or important. 使著名 ❑ *Over the next few years he distinguished himself as a leading constitutional scholar.* 在随后的几年中，他作为宪法学的权威学者而享有盛誉。

★ **dis·tin·guish·able** /dɪstɪŋgwɪʃəᵇl/ 1 ADJ If something is **distinguishable from** other things, it has a quality or feature which makes it possible for you to recognize it and see that it is different. 可区分的 ❑ *...features that make their products distinguishable from those of their rivals.* …将他们的产品与其竞争对手们的产品区别开来的一些特色。 2 ADJ If something is **distinguishable**, you can see or hear it in conditions when it is difficult to see or hear anything. 隐约可辨的 [V-link ADJ] ❑ *It was getting light and shapes were more distinguishable.* 天亮了起来，物形可以看得更清楚了。

dis·tin·guished /dɪstɪŋgwɪʃt/ 1 ADJ If you describe a person or their work as **distinguished**, you mean that they have been very successful in their career and have a good reputation. 卓著的 ❑ *...a distinguished academic family.* …一个卓越的学术之家。 2 ADJ If you describe someone as **distinguished**, you mean that they look very noble and respectable. 高贵的 ❑ *His suit was immaculately cut and he looked very distinguished.* 他的西服剪裁完美，人显得十分高贵。

★ **dis·tort** /dɪstɔrt/ (**distorts, distorting, distorted**) 1 V-T If you **distort** a statement, fact, or idea, you report or represent it in an untrue way. 歪曲; 曲解 ❑ *The media distorts reality; it categorizes people as all good or all bad.* 媒体歪曲事实，将人分为十足的好人和坏蛋。 ● **dis·tort·ed** ADJ 扭曲的 ❑ *These figures give a distorted view of the significance for the local economy.* 这些数据对当地经济的重要性给出了歪曲的看法。 2 V-T/V-I If something you can see or hear **is distorted** or **distorts**, its appearance or sound is changed so that it seems unclear. 扭曲; 失真 ❑ *A painter may exaggerate or distort shapes and forms.* 画家可能会夸大或扭曲形状与形式。 ● **dis·tort·ed** ADJ 扭曲的; 失真的 ❑ *Sound was becoming more and more distorted through the use of hearing aids.* 由于使用助听器，声音变得越来越失真。

dis·tor·tion /dɪstɔrʃᵊn/ (**distortions**) 1 N-VAR **Distortion** is the changing of something into something that is not true or not acceptable. 歪曲; 曲解 [DISAPPROVAL] ❑ *I think it would be a gross distortion of reality to say that they were motivated by self-interest.* 我认为说他们被自身利益所驱使是对事实的公然扭曲。 2 N-VAR **Distortion** is the changing of the appearance or sound of something in a way that makes it seem strange or unclear. 变形; 失真 ❑ *He demonstrated how audio signals could be transmitted along cables without distortion.* 他演示了音频信号如何通过电缆传输而不失真。

dis·tract /dɪstrækt/ (**distracts, distracting, distracted**) V-T If something **distracts** you or your attention **from** something, it takes your attention away from it. 分散(注意力); 使分心 ❑ *Tom admits that playing video games sometimes distracts him from his homework.* 汤姆承认玩电子游戏有时让他做家庭作业时分心。 ❑ *Don't let yourself be distracted by fashionable theories.* 别让自己被新潮的理论给分心了。

★ **dis·tract·ed** /dɪstræktɪd/ ADJ If you are **distracted**, you are not concentrating on something because you are worried or are thinking about something else. 分心的; 心烦意乱的 ❑ *She had seemed curiously distracted.* 她不知为什么显得心不在焉。 ● **dis·tract·ed·ly** ADV 心不在焉地; 心烦意乱地 [ADV with v] ❑ *He looked up distractedly. "Be with you in a second."* 他心不在焉地抬头说："马上就来。"

dis·tract·ing /dɪstræktɪŋ/ ADJ If you say that something is **distracting**, you mean that it makes it difficult for you to concentrate properly on what you are doing. 使人分心的 ❑ *I find it slightly distracting to have someone watching me while I work.* 我发现，我工作时被人观看就会有些走神儿。

dis·trac·tion /dɪstrækʃᵊn/ (**distractions**) N-VAR A **distraction** is something that turns your attention away from something you want to concentrate on. 分心的事物 ❑ *Total concentration is required with no distractions.* 需要全神贯注，不可有分心之事。

dis·traught /dɪstrɔt/ ADJ If someone is **distraught**, they are so upset and worried that they cannot think clearly. 心烦意乱的 ❑ *Mr. Barker's distraught parents were last night being comforted by relatives.* 巴克先生烦躁不安的父母昨晚被亲戚们安抚了。

dis·tress /dɪstrɛs/ (**distresses, distressing, distressed**) 1 N-UNCOUNT **Distress** is a state of extreme sorrow, suffering, or pain. 悲痛; 疼痛 ❑ *Jealousy causes distress and painful emotions.* 嫉妒会引发悲伤和痛苦的情绪。 2 N-UNCOUNT **Distress** is the state of being in extreme danger and needing urgent help. 危难; 危急 ❑ *He expressed concern that the ship might be in distress.* 他对船可能处在危急状态表示忧虑。 3 V-T If someone or something **distresses** you, they cause you to be upset or worried. 使心烦; 使忧虑 ❑ *The idea of Toni being in danger distresses him enormously.* 想到托尼仍处在危险当中就使他忧心忡忡。

dis·tressed /dɪstrɛst/ ADJ If someone is **distressed**, they are upset or worried. 心烦的; 忧虑的 ❑ *I feel very alone and distressed about my problem.* 我对我的问题感到孤单无依，苦恼不已。

dis·tress·ing /dɪstrɛsɪŋ/ ADJ If something is **distressing**, it upsets you or worries you. 使人心烦的; 使人忧虑的 ❑ *It is very distressing to see your baby attached to tubes and monitors.* 看到你的孩子插着管子，连着监控器，真是令人担忧。 ● **dis·tress·ing·ly** ADV 使人心烦地; 使人忧虑地 ❑ *A distressingly large number of firms have been breaking the rules.* 违规经营的公司数目之大，令人担忧。

Word Link	*tribute ≈ giving : attribute, contribute, distribute*

dis·trib·ute /dɪstrɪbyut/ (**distributes, distributing, distributed**) 1 V-T If you **distribute** things, you hand them or deliver them to a number of people. 分发 ❑ *Students shouted slogans and distributed leaflets.* 学生们高呼口号，散发传单。 2 V-T When a company **distributes** goods, it supplies them to the stores or businesses that sell them. 配销 [BUSINESS] ❑ *We didn't understand how difficult it was to distribute a national paper.* 我们不明白配销一份全国性的报纸有多么困难。 3 V-T To **distribute** a substance **over** something means to scatter it over it. 散布 [FORMAL] ❑ *Distribute the topping evenly over the fruit.* 将浇头均匀地浇在水果上。

dis·tri·bu·tion ♦◇◇ /dɪstrɪbyuʃᵊn/ (**distributions**) 1 N-UNCOUNT The **distribution** of things involves giving or delivering them to a number of people or places. 分发 ❑ *...the council which controls the distribution of foreign aid.* …掌管分发国外援助的委员会。 2 N-VAR The **distribution** of something is how much of it there is in each place or at each time, or how much of it each person has. 分配; 分布 ❑ *Mr. Roh's economic planners sought to achieve a more equitable distribution of wealth.* 罗欧先生的经济规划者们努力实现更公平的财富分配。

dis·tribu·tor /dɪstrɪbyətər/ (**distributors**) N-COUNT A **distributor** is a company that supplies goods to stores or other businesses. 配销商；批发商 [BUSINESS] ❏ *...Spain's largest distributor of petroleum products.* …西班牙最大的石油产品经销商。

dis·tribu·tor·ship /dɪstrɪbyətərʃɪp/ (**distributorships**) N-COUNT A **distributorship** is a company that supplies goods to stores or other businesses, or the right to supply goods to stores and businesses. 配销商；配销权 [BUSINESS] ❏ *...the general manager of an automobile distributorship.* …一家汽车经销公司的总经理。

D

dis·trict ♦♦◇ /dɪstrɪkt/ (**districts**) N-COUNT A **district** is a particular area of a town or country. 地区 ❏ *I drove around the business district.* 我绕着商业区行驶。

dis·trust /dɪstrʌst/ (**distrusts, distrusting, distrusted**) 1 V-T If you **distrust** someone or something, you think they are not honest, reliable, or safe. 不信任 ❏ *I don't have any particular reason to distrust them.* 我没有任何特殊的理由不信任他们。 2 N-UNCOUNT **Distrust** is the feeling of doubt that you have toward someone or something you distrust. 怀疑 [also "a" N, oft N "of" n] ❏ *What he saw there left him with a profound distrust of all political authority.* 他在那个地方之所见让他对所有政治权威产生了极度怀疑。

dis·turb /dɪstɜrb/ (**disturbs, disturbing, disturbed**) 1 V-T If you **disturb** someone, you interrupt what they are doing and upset them. 打扰 ❏ *Did you sleep well? I didn't want to disturb you. You looked so peaceful.* 你睡得好吗？我不想打扰你。你看起来如此平静。 2 V-T If something **disturbs** you, it makes you feel upset or worried. 使不安；使烦恼 ❏ *I dream about him, dreams so vivid that they disturb me for days.* 我梦到他了，梦是那么栩栩如生以至于困扰了我好几天。 3 V-T If something **is disturbed**, its position or shape is changed. 使紊乱 ❏ *He'd placed his notes in the brown envelope. They hadn't been disturbed.* 他已把票据放在那个棕色信封里了。票据没有被动过。 4 V-T If something **disturbs** a situation or atmosphere, it spoils it or causes trouble. 使混乱 ❏ *What could possibly disturb such tranquility?* 有什么能破坏这种宁静？

Word Partnership *disturb* 的常用搭配：

V. **do not** disturb 1
be careful not to disturb 1 – 3
be sorry to disturb 1 2 4
N. disturb **the neighbors** 1 2
disturb **the peace** 4

★ **dis·turb·ance** /dɪstɜrbəns/ (**disturbances**) 1 N-COUNT A **disturbance** is an incident in which people behave violently in public. 骚乱 ❏ *During the disturbance which followed, three Englishmen were hurt.* 在随后的骚乱中，3个英国人受伤了。 2 N-UNCOUNT **Disturbance** means upsetting or disorganizing something which was previously in a calm and well-ordered state. 烦乱；扰乱 ❏ *Successful breeding requires quiet, peaceful conditions with as little disturbance as possible.* 成功繁殖需要安宁的环境，干扰越少越好。 3 N-VAR You can use **disturbance** to refer to a medical or psychological problem, when someone's body or mind is not working in the normal way. (身体) 不适；心神不安 ❏ *Poor educational performance is related to emotional disturbance.* 学习表现不好与情绪不稳定有关。

dis·turbed /dɪstɜrbd/ 1 ADJ A **disturbed** person is very upset emotionally, and often needs special care or treatment. 心理不正常的 ❏ *...working with severely emotionally disturbed children.* …照料严重心理疾患的孩子们。 2 ADJ You can say that someone is **disturbed** when they are very worried or anxious. 不安的；焦虑的 ❏ *Doctors were disturbed that less than 30 percent of the patients were women.* 医生们对女性病人占不到30%深感不安。 3 ADJ If you describe a situation or period of time as **disturbed**, you mean that it is unhappy and full of problems. 不愉快的；动荡不安的 ❏ *...women from disturbed backgrounds.* …出身凄苦的妇女们。

dis·turb·ing /dɪstɜrbɪŋ/ ADJ Something that is **disturbing** makes you feel worried or upset. 使人不安的；使人苦恼的 ❏ *There was something about him she found disturbing.* 她发现他身上有些东西让她觉得不安。 ● **dis·turb·ing·ly** ADV 使人不安地；使人苦恼地 ❏ *The government has itself recognized the disturbingly high frequency of racial attacks.* 政府本身已经认识到种族袭击事件的发案率之高令人深感不安。

dis·used /dɪsyuzd/ ADJ A **disused** place or building is empty and is no longer used. 废弃的 ❏ *...a disused air field near the village of Ive.* …伊夫村附近的一个废弃的机场。

ditch /dɪtʃ/ (**ditches, ditching, ditched**) 1 N-COUNT A **ditch** is a long narrow channel cut into the ground at the side of a road or field. 道沟；沟渠 ❏ *Both vehicles ended up in a ditch.* 两辆车都掉进了沟里。 2 V-T If you **ditch** something that you have or are responsible for, you abandon it or get rid of it, because you no longer want it. 丢弃 [INFORMAL] ❏ *I decided to ditch the sofa bed.* 我决定把沙发床扔掉。 3 V-T If someone **ditches** someone, they end a relationship with that person. 抛弃 [INFORMAL] ❏ *I can't bring myself to ditch him and start again.* 我不能说服自己抛弃他，又重新开始。 4 V-T/V-I If a pilot **ditches** an aircraft or if it **ditches**, the pilot makes an emergency landing. (飞机) 紧急迫降 ❏ *One American pilot was forced to ditch his jet in the Gulf.* 一个美国飞行员被迫在海湾紧急迫降其喷气式飞机。 5 V-T If someone **ditches** school or work, they decide not to go to school or work, although they are supposed to go there. 逃学；旷工 [AM, INFORMAL] ❏ *What do you say we ditch school and go to the mall?* 我们逃学去商场，你觉得怎样？ 6 → see also **last-ditch**

dith·er /dɪðər/ (**dithers, dithering, dithered**) V-I When someone **dithers**, they hesitate because they are unable to make a quick decision about something. 犹豫 ❏ *We have been living together for five years, and we're still dithering over whether to marry.* 我们同居了5年，但还是犹豫是否该结婚。

dit·to /dɪtoʊ/ In informal English, you can use **ditto** to represent a word or phrase that you have just used in order to avoid repeating it. In written lists, **ditto** can be represented by ditto marks - the symbol " - underneath the word that you want to repeat. 同上 (可用同上符号（ " ）表示) ❏ *Lister's dead. Ditto three Miami drug dealers and a lady.* 利斯特死了，3个迈阿密毒品贩子和1位女士也死了。

dive /daɪv/ (**dives, diving, dived, dove, dived**) 1 V-I If you **dive into** some water, you jump in head first with your arms held straight above your head. 跳水 ❏ *He tried to escape by diving into a river.* 他企图跳入河中逃走。 ❏ *She was standing by a pool, about to dive in.* 她正站在池边，准备跳进去。 ● N-COUNT **Dive** is also a noun. 跳水 ❏ *Pat had earlier made a dive of 80 feet from the Chasm Bridge.* 早些时，帕特曾从卡泽姆大桥进行过80英尺高的跳水。 2 V-I If you **dive**, you go under the surface of the sea or a lake, using special breathing equipment. 潜水 ❏ *Bezanik is diving to collect marine organisms.* 贝赞尼克正在潜水采集海洋生物。 ● N-COUNT **Dive** is also a noun. 潜水 ❏ *This sighting occurred during my dive to a sunken wreck off Sardinia.* 这次亲眼所见发生在我向撒丁岛外一艘沉船潜水的期间。 3 V-I When birds and animals **dive**, they go quickly downward, head first, through the air or through water. (鸟等动物) 俯冲 ❏ *...a pelican which had just dived for a fish.* …一只刚刚下潜捕鱼的鹈鹕。 4 V-I If you **dive** in a particular direction or into a particular place, you jump or move there quickly. 跃向；冲向 ❏ *They dived into a taxi.* 他们冲进了出租车。 ● N-COUNT **Dive** is also a noun. 冲；扑 ❏ *He made a sudden dive for Uncle Jim's legs to try to trip him up.* 他猛地扑向吉姆大叔的双腿，试图绊倒他。 5 V-I If shares, profits, or figures **dive**, their value falls suddenly and by a large amount. (股票、利润、数字等) 突然暴跌 [JOURNALISM] ❏ *They feared the stock could dive after its first day of trading.* 他们担心这支股票在其第一个交易日后会暴跌。 ❏ *Profits have dived from $7.7m to $7.1m.* 利润从770万美元骤跌至710万美元。 ● N-COUNT **Dive** is also a noun. (股票、利润、数字等) 骤降 ❏ *Stock prices took a dive.* 股票价格暴跌。 6 N-COUNT If you describe a bar or club as a **dive**, you mean it is dirty and dark, and not very respectable. 低级酒吧；低级夜总会 [INFORMAL, DISAPPROVAL] ❏ *We've played in all the little clubs and dives around Philadelphia.* 我们玩遍了费城所有的小酒吧和低级夜总会。

div·er /daɪvər/ (**divers**) N-COUNT A **diver** is a person who swims under water using special breathing equipment. 潜水员 ❏ *Police divers have recovered the body of a sixteen year old boy.* 警方潜水员已经发现了一个16岁男孩的尸体。
→ see **scuba diving**

Word Link *di ≈ two : dilemma, diverge, division*

Word Link *verg, vert ≈ turning : converge, diverge, subvert*

di·verge /dɪvɜrdʒ/ (**diverges, diverging, diverged**) 1 V-RECIP If one thing **diverges from** another similar thing, the first thing becomes different from the second or develops differently from it. You can also say that two things **diverge**. 相异 ❏ *His interests increasingly diverged from those of his colleagues.* 他和同事们的兴趣越来越不同。 2 V-RECIP If one opinion or idea **diverges from** another, they contradict each other or are different. You can also say that two opinions or ideas **diverge.** 有分歧 [no cont] ❑ *The view of the Estonian government does not diverge that far from Lipmaa's thinking.* 爱沙尼亚政府的观点和李普马的想法并无太大分歧。

di·ver·gence /dɪvɜrdʒ^əns/ (**divergences**) N-VAR A **divergence** is a difference between two or more things, attitudes, or opinions. 分歧；差异 [FORMAL] ❑ *There's a substantial divergence of opinion within the party.* 党内意见严重分歧。

di·ver·gent /dɪvɜrdʒ^ənt/ ADJ **Divergent** things are different from each other. 不同的；有分歧的 [FORMAL] ❑ *Two people who have divergent views on this question are George Watt and Bob Marr.* 在这个问题上意见相左的两个人是乔治·瓦特和鲍勃·马尔。

di·verse /dɪvɜrs/ 1 ADJ If a group of things is **diverse**, it is made up of a wide variety of things. 各种各样的 ❑ *The building houses a wide and diverse variety of antiques.* 这栋楼里摆放着大量各式各样的古董。 2 ADJ **Diverse** people or things are very different from each other. 不同的 ❑ *Albert Jones' new style will inevitably put him in touch with a much more diverse and perhaps younger audience.* 艾伯特·琼斯的新风格无疑将使他接触更多形形色色的、或许更年轻的观众。

Word Link *ify ≈ making : clarify, diversify, intensify*

▲ **di·ver·si·fy** /dɪvɜrsɪfaɪ/ (**diversifies, diversifying, diversified**) V-T/V-I When an organization or person **diversifies** into other things, or **diversifies** their product line, they increase the variety of things that they do or make. 使多样化 ❑ *The company's troubles started only when it diversified into new products.* 该公司的麻烦从实现产品多样化时才开始。 ❑ *As demand has increased, so manufacturers have been encouraged to diversify and improve quality.* 制造商们受需求增加的刺激而扩大生产品种，提高产品质量。 ● **di·ver·si·fi·ca·tion** /dɪvɜrsɪfɪkeɪʃ^ən/ N-VAR (**diversifications**) 多样化 ❑ *The seminar was to discuss diversification of agriculture.* 该研讨会讨论的是农业多种经营。

★ **di·ver·sion** /dɪvɜrʒ^ən/ (**diversions**) 1 N-COUNT A **diversion** is an action or event that attracts your attention away from what you are doing or concentrating on. 令人分心的事物 ❑ *...armed robbers who escaped after throwing smoke bombs to create a diversion.* …在扔出烟雾弹造成注意力分散之后逃跑的武装抢劫犯们。 2 N-COUNT A **diversion** is a special route arranged for traffic to follow when the normal route cannot be used. 改道路线 [BRIT]

in AM, use **detour**

3 N-UNCOUNT **The diversion of** something involves changing its course or destination. 转移；转向 ❑ *...the illegal diversion of profits from secret arms sales.* …销售秘密武器所得收益的非法转移。

di·ver·sion·ary /dɪvɜrʒənɛri/ ADJ A **diversionary** activity is one intended to attract people's attention away from something which you do not want them to think about, know about, or deal with. 转移注意力的；使人分心的 ❑ *It's thought the fires were started by the prisoners as a diversionary tactic.* 人们认为火是囚犯们放的，是一种使人分心的策略。

di·ver·sity /dɪvɜrsɪti/ (**diversities**) 1 N-VAR The **diversity** of something is the fact that it contains many very different elements. 多样性 ❑ *...the cultural diversity of Latin America.* …拉丁美洲文化的多样性。 2 N-SING A **diversity of** things is a range of things which are very different from each other. 各种各样 ❑ *Forslan's object is to gather as great a diversity of genetic material as possible.* 福斯兰的目标是尽可能收集各种不同的基因物质。
→ see **zoo**

★ **di·vert** /dɪvɜrt, daɪ-/ (**diverts, diverting, diverted**) 1 V-T/V-I To **divert** vehicles or travelers means to make them follow a different route or go to a different destination than they originally intended. You can also say that someone or something **diverts from** a particular route or **to** a particular place. 使改道；改道 ❑ *We diverted a plane to rescue 100 passengers.* 我们改变飞机航线以拯救100名乘客。 ❑ *Abington Memorial Hospital has been diverting trauma patients to other hospitals because it does not have enough surgeons.* 由于缺乏足够的外科医生，阿宾顿纪念医院一直在将外伤病人转到其他医院。 2 V-T To **divert** money or resources means to cause them to be used for a different purpose. 转移 ❑ *A wave of deadly bombings has forced the United States to divert funds from reconstruction to security.* 一系列致命的炸弹袭击迫使美国将资金从重建转向安全防御。 3 V-T To **divert** a phone call means to send it to a different number or place from the one that was dialed by the person making the call. 转接（电话） ❑ *He instructed the switchboard staff to divert all Laura's calls to him.* 他通知接线员把劳拉打来的所有电话都转给他。 4 V-T If you say that someone **diverts** your attention from something important or serious, you disapprove of them behaving or talking in a way that stops you thinking about it. 转移…的注意力 [DISAPPROVAL] ❑ *They want to divert the attention of the people from the real issues.* 他们想把人民的注意力从真正的问题上转移开。

di·vide ♦♦◇ /dɪvaɪd/ (**divides, dividing, divided**) 1 V-T/V-I When people or things **are divided** or **divide into** smaller groups or parts, they become separated into smaller parts. 分割；分离 ❑ *The physical benefits of exercise can be divided into three factors.* 锻炼对身体的好处可以分成3个方面。 ❑ *Divide the pastry in half and roll out each piece.* 把面团一分为二，把每块都擀平。 2 V-T If you **divide** something **among** people or things, you separate it into several parts or quantities which you distribute to the people or things. 分配 ❑ *Divide the sauce among 4 bowls.* 把调味汁分到4个碗里。 3 V-T If you **divide** a larger number **by** a smaller number or **divide** a smaller number **into** a larger number, you calculate how many times the smaller number can fit exactly into the larger number. 除；除尽 ❑ *Measure the floor area of the greenhouse and divide it by six.* 测量温室的地表面积，再除以6。 4 V-T If a border or line **divides** two areas or **divides** an area into two, it keeps the two areas separate from each other. 分隔 ❑ *...remote border areas dividing Tamil and Muslim settlements.* …把泰米尔人和穆斯林居住地分隔开的偏僻边界地区。 5 V-T/V-I If people **divide** over something or if something **divides** them, it causes strong disagreement between them. 使不和；不和 ❑ *...the major issues that divided the country.* …造成国家分裂的重大问题。 6 N-COUNT A **divide** is a significant distinction between two groups, often one that causes conflict. （引发冲突的）重大差异 ❑ *...a deliberate attempt to create a Hindu-Muslim divide in India.* …蓄意在印度制造印度教徒和穆斯林教徒之间差异的企图。

▶ **divide up** 1 PHRASAL VERB If you **divide** something **up**, you separate it into smaller or more useful groups. 分割 ❑ *The idea is to divide up the country into four sectors.* 该观点是将国家一分为四。 2 PHRASAL VERB If you **divide** something **up**, you share it out among a number of people or groups in approximately equal parts. 均分 ❑ *The aim was to divide up the business, give everyone an equal stake in its future.* 目的是将生意均分，让每个人在未来都有相等的股份。

Thesaurus *divide* 另参见：

V.	categorize, group, segregate, separate, split 1 part, separate, split; *(ant.)* unite 5

Word Partnership *divide* 的常用搭配：

N.	divide **in half**, divide *your* **time** 1
PREP.	divide **into** 1 divide **among** 2 divide **between**, divide **by** 3

di·vid·ed high·way (**divided highways**) N-COUNT A **divided highway** is a road which has two lanes of traffic traveling in each direction with a strip of grass or concrete down the middle to separate the traffic. （中间有分隔带的）双车道公路 [AM]

in BRIT, use **dual carriageway**

★ **divi·dend** ♦◇◇ /dɪvɪdɛnd/ (**dividends**) 1 N-COUNT A **dividend** is the part of a company's profits which is paid to people who own shares in the company. 股息 [BUSINESS] ❑ *The first quarter dividend has been increased by nearly 4 percent.* 第一季度的股息增加了近4%。 2 PHRASE If something **pays dividends**, it brings advantages at a later date. 有回报；可获益 ❑ *Steps taken now to maximize your health will pay dividends later on.* 现在采取措施充分重视你的健康将来就会有回报。
→ see **company**

★ **di·vine** /dɪvaɪn/ 1 ADJ You use **divine** to describe something that is provided by or relates to a god or goddess. 神的；神圣的 ❑ *He suggested that the civil war had been a divine punishment.* 他暗示此次内战是上天的惩罚。 ● **di·vine·ly** ADV 如神般地；神圣地 ❑ *The law was divinely ordained.* 此法律为神授。 2 ADJ People use **divine** to express their pleasure or enjoyment of something. 极好的；绝妙的 ❑ *Her carrot cake is divine.* 她的胡萝卜饼好吃极了。
→ see **religion**

div·ing /daɪvɪŋ/ 1 N-UNCOUNT **Diving** is the activity of working or looking around underwater, using special breathing equipment. 潜水 ❑ *...equipment and accessories for diving.* …用于潜水的设备和附件。 2 N-UNCOUNT **Diving** is the sport or activity in which you jump into water head first with your arms held straight above your head, usually from a diving board. 跳水

❑ *Weight is crucial in diving because the aim is to cause the smallest splash possible.* 体重对于跳水运动至关重要，因为跳水的目标是尽可能不激起水花。

Word Link *di ≈ two : dilemma, diverge, division*

di·vi·sion ♦♦◇ /dɪvɪʒᵊn/ (**divisions**) 1 N-UNCOUNT The **division** of a large unit **into** two or more distinct parts is the act of separating it into these parts. 分割；分裂 ❑ *...the unification of Germany, after its division into two states at the end of World War Two.* …德国在二战结束时分裂成两个国家，之后又统一了。 2 N-UNCOUNT The **division of** something among people or things is its separation into parts which are distributed among the people or things. 分配 ❑ *The current division of labor between workers and management will alter.* 劳资双方目前的劳动分配将会改变。 3 N-UNCOUNT **Division** is the arithmetical process of dividing one number into another number. 除法 ❑ *I taught my daughter how to do division at the age of six.* 我女儿6岁时，我就教她怎样做除法。 4 N-VAR A **division** is a significant distinction or argument between two groups, which causes the two groups to be considered as very different and separate. 分歧；不和 ❑ *The division between the prosperous west and the impoverished east remains.* 富裕的西部和贫穷的东部之间的对立依然存在。 5 N-COUNT In a large organization, a **division** is a group of departments whose work is done in the same place or is connected with similar tasks. 部门 ❑ *...the bank's Latin American division.* …该银行的拉丁美洲部。 6 N-COUNT A **division** is a group of military units which fight as a single unit. 师(军队的作战单位) ❑ *Several armoured divisions are being moved from Germany.* 几个装甲师正从德国调来。 7 N-COUNT In some sports, such as soccer, baseball, and basketball, a **division** is one of the groups of teams which make up a league. The teams in each division are of the same level, and they all play against each other during the season. (球队的) 分级 ❑ *Chico State reached the NCAA Division II national finals last season.* 奇科加州大学上个赛季进入了全国大学体育协会乙级全国决赛。
→ see **mathematics**

Word Partnership *division* 的常用搭配：

N.	division **of labor** 2
	multiplication and division 3
	division **head** 5
	infantry division 6
ADJ.	**armored** division 6

di·vi·sive /dɪvaɪsɪv/ ADJ Something that is **divisive** causes unfriendliness and argument between people. 造成不和的；引起纷争的 ❑ *Abortion has always been a divisive issue.* 堕胎一直是个有争议的问题。

di·vorce ♦◇◇ /dɪvɔrs/ (**divorces, divorcing, divorced**) 1 N-VAR A **divorce** is the formal ending of a marriage by law. 离婚 ❑ *Numerous marriages now end in divorce.* 现在许多婚姻都以离婚而告终。 2 V-RECIP If a man and woman **divorce** or if one of them **divorces** the other, their marriage is legally ended. 离婚 ❑ *He and Lillian had got divorced.* 他和莉莲离婚了。 ❑ *I am absolutely furious that he divorced me to marry her.* 我实在很生气他和我离婚娶了她。 3 N-SING A **divorce of** one thing **from** another, or a divorce **between** two things is a separation between them which is permanent or is likely to be permanent. 分离；脱离 ❑ *...this divorce of Christian culture from the roots of faith.* …基督教文化与信仰根源的分离。 4 V-T If you say that one thing cannot **be divorced from** another, you mean that the two things cannot be considered as different and separate things. 使分离；使脱离 ❑ *Good management in the police cannot be divorced from accountability.* 警政的良好管理离不开问责制。 ❑ *Democracy cannot be divorced from social and economic progress.* 民主离不开社会和经济的进步。

Word Partnership *divorce* 的常用搭配：

N.	divorce **court**, divorce **lawyer**, divorce **papers**, divorce **rate**, divorce **settlement** 1
V.	**file for** divorce, **get a** divorce, **want a** divorce 1

di·vorced /dɪvɔrst/ 1 ADJ Someone who **is divorced** from their former husband or wife has separated from them and is no longer legally married to them. 离婚的 ❑ *He is divorced, with a young son.* 他离婚了，带着一个年幼的儿子。 2 ADJ If you say that one thing **is divorced from** another, you mean that the two things are very different and separate from each other. 分离的；脱离的 [v-link ADJ "from" n] ❑ *...speculative theories divorced from political reality.* …脱离政治现实的投机理论。

di·vor·cee /dɪvɔrseɪ, -si/ (**divorcees**) N-COUNT A **divorcee** is a person, especially a woman, who is divorced. 离婚者(尤指女人) [mainly BRIT] ❑ *In 1939 he married Clare Hollway, a divorcee 13 years his senior.* 1939年他娶了克莱尔·霍尔韦，一个比他大13岁的离婚女人。

di·vulge /dɪvʌldʒ/ (**divulges, divulging, divulged**) V-T If you **divulge** a piece of secret or private information, you tell it to someone. 泄露 [FORMAL] ❑ *Officials refuse to divulge details of the negotiations.* 官员们拒绝透露谈判的细节。

DIY /di aɪ waɪ/ N-UNCOUNT **DIY** is the activity of making or repairing things yourself, especially in your home. **DIY** is an abbreviation for **do-it-yourself**. 自己动手 [mainly BRIT] ❑ *He's useless at DIY. He won't even put up a shelf.* 他的动手能力很差，甚至连搭个架子都不会。

diz·zy /dɪzi/ (**dizzier, dizziest**) 1 ADJ If you feel **dizzy**, you feel that you are losing your balance and are about to fall. 眩晕的 ❑ *Her head still hurt, and she felt slightly dizzy and disoriented.* 她的头还在痛，感觉有些眩晕，分不清方向。 ● **diz·zi·ness** N-UNCOUNT 眩晕 ❑ *His head injury causes dizziness and nausea.* 他头部受伤引起眩晕和呕吐。 2 ADJ You can use **dizzy** to describe a woman who is careless and forgets things, but is easy to like. (女人) 没头脑但招人喜爱的 ❑ *She is famed for playing dizzy blondes.* 她以扮演没头脑但招人喜爱的金发美女而闻名。 3 PHRASE If you say that someone has reached **the dizzy heights of** something, you are emphasizing that they have reached a very high level by achieving it. 显赫的地位 [HUMOROUS, EMPHASIS] ❑ *I escalated to the dizzy heights of director's secretary.* 我逐渐升到了主任秘书这样的职位。

DJ /di dʒeɪ/ (**DJs**) also **D.J., dj** N-COUNT A **DJ** is the same as a **disc jockey**. 流行音乐节目主持人

DNA /di ɛn eɪ/ N-UNCOUNT **DNA** is an acid in the chromosomes in the center of the cells of living things. DNA determines the particular structure and functions of every cell and is responsible for characteristics being passed on from parents to their children. **DNA** is an abbreviation for "deoxyribonucleic acid." 脱氧核糖核酸 ❑ *A routine DNA sample was taken.* 采集了一份常规的脱氧核糖核酸样本。
→ see **clone, gene**

do
1 AUXILIARY VERB USES
2 OTHER VERB USES
3 NOUN USES

1 **do** ♦♦♦ /də, STRONG du/ (**does, doing, did, done**)

> **Do** is used as an auxiliary with the simple present tense. **Did** is used as an auxiliary with the simple past tense. In spoken English, negative forms of **do** are often shortened, for example, **do not** is shortened to **don't** and **did not** is shortened to **didn't**.

1 AUX **Do** is used to form the negative of main verbs, by putting "not" after "do" and before the main verb in its infinitive form, that is the form without "to." 用于构成动词的否定式，即由"**do** + **not** + 不带**to**的动词不定式"构成 ❑ *They don't want to work.* 他们不想工作。 ❑ *I did not know Jamie had a knife.* 我不知道杰米有把刀。 2 AUX **Do** is used to form questions, by putting the subject after "do" and before the main verb in its infinitive form, that is the form without "to." 用于构成疑问句，即由"**do** + 主语 + 不带**to**的动词不定式"构成 ❑ *Do you like music?* 你喜欢音乐吗？ ❑ *What did he say?* 他说了什么？ 3 AUX **Do** is used in question tags. 用于附加疑问句中 ❑ *You know about Andy, don't you?* 你了解安迪，不是吗？ 4 AUX You use **do** when you are confirming or contradicting a statement containing "do," or giving a negative or positive answer to a question. 用于肯定或否定回答 ❑ *"Did he think there was anything suspicious going on?"—"Yes, he did."* "他认为有什么可疑的事情发生吗？"——"是的，他是这样认为的。" 5 V-T/V-I **Do** can be used to refer back to another verb group when you are comparing or contrasting two things, or saying that they are the same. 比较两事物时用于代替前面出现的动词，表示同一概念 ❑ *I make more money than he does.* 我挣的钱比他多。 ❑ *I had fantasies, as do all mothers, about how life would be when my girls were grown.* 和所有母亲一样，我也有幻想，想像我的女儿们长大成人后生活会是怎样。 6 V-T You use **do** after "so" and "nor" to say that the same statement is true for two people or groups. 用在**so**和**nor**之后，表示同一陈述适用于两个或两组人 ❑ *You know that's true, and so do I.* 你知道那是真的，我也知道。

❷ **do** ◆◆◆ /duː/ (**does, doing, did, done**)

Do is used in a large number of expressions which are explained under other words in the dictionary. For example, the expression "easier said than done" is explained at "easy."

1 V-T When you **do** something, you take some action or perform an activity or task. **Do** is often used instead of a more specific verb, to talk about a common action involving a particular thing. For example you can say "do your hair" instead of "brush your hair." 表示从事某种活动或工作，常用来替代有具体含义的动词 ❑ *I was trying to do some work.* 我正试图做些工作。 ❑ *After lunch Elizabeth and I did the dishes.* 午餐后，我和伊丽莎白洗了碗。 2 V-T **Do** can be used to stand for any verb group, or to refer back to another verb group, including one that was in a previous sentence. 用于代表任何动词或代替前面出现过的动词 ❑ *What are you doing?* 你在干什么？ 3 V-T You can use **do** in a clause at the beginning of a sentence after words like "what" and "all," to give special emphasis to the information that comes at the end of the sentence. 用于以**what**或**all**开头的句中，强调句子后面所说的事情 [EMPHASIS] ❑ *All she does is complain.* 她只顾抱怨。 4 V-T If you **do** a particular thing **with** something, you use it in that particular way. 做；干 ❑ *I was allowed to do whatever I wanted with my life.* 我被允许自由安排我的生活。 5 V-T If you **do** something **about** a problem, you take action to try to solve it. (为解决问题而) 采取行动 ❑ *They refuse to do anything about the real cause of crime: poverty.* 他们拒绝采取任何行动解决引发犯罪的真正原因：贫困。 6 V-T If an action or event **does** a particular thing, such as harm or good, it has that result or effect. 造成 ❑ *A few bombs can do a lot of damage.* 几颗炸弹足以造成严重破坏。 7 V-T If you ask someone what they **do**, you want to know what their job or profession is. 从事 (某种职业) ❑ *"What does your father do?"—"Well, he's a civil servant."* "你父亲是做什么工作的？"——"哦，他是个公务员。" 8 V-T If you **are doing** something, you are busy or active in some way, or have planned an activity for some time in the future. 忙于；准备做 ❑ *Are you doing anything tomorrow night?* 明晚你有事吗？ 9 V-I If you say that someone or something **does** well or badly, you are talking about how successful or unsuccessful they are. 表现；进展 ❑ *Connie did well at school and graduated with honors.* 康妮在学校表现很好，以优等成绩毕业。 10 V-T You can use **do** when referring to the speed or rate that something or someone achieves or is able to achieve. 达到 (某种速度) ❑ *They were doing 70 miles an hour.* 他们每小时达到70英里。 11 V-T If someone **does** drugs, they take illegal drugs. 吸食 (毒品) ❑ *I don't do drugs.* 我不吸毒。 12 V-T/V-I If you say that something **will do** or **will do** you, you mean that there is enough of it or that it is of good enough quality to meet your requirements or to satisfy you. 够用；满足需要 ❑ *Anything to create a scene and attract attention will do.* 只要能当众大闹，吸引人们的注意，做什么都行。 13 V-T If you **do** a subject, author, or book, you study them at school or college. 攻读；研究 [mainly BRIT, SPOKEN] ❑ *She planned to do math at night school.* 她打算上夜校学数学。 14 PHRASE If you say that you **could do with** something, you mean that you need it or would benefit from it. 需要；从…中获益 ❑ *I could do with a cup of tea.* 我需要一杯茶。 15 PHRASE You can ask someone **what** they **did with** something as another way of asking them where they put it. 把…放在何处 ❑ *What did you do with that notebook?* 你把那本笔记本放哪儿去了？ 16 PHRASE If you ask **what** someone or something **is doing** in a particular place, you are asking why they are there. 为何出现在此处 ❑ *"Dr. Campbell," he said, clearly surprised. "What are you doing here?"* "坎贝尔医生，"他一脸惊讶地说道，"你怎么会在这儿？" 17 PHRASE If you say that one thing **has** something **to do with** or **is** something **to do with** another thing, you mean that the two things are connected or that the first thing is about the second thing. 与…有关 ❑ *Mr. Butterfield denies having anything to do with the episode.* 巴特菲尔德先生否认他和这一事件有关。

▸ **do away with** 1 PHRASAL VERB To **do away with** something means to remove it completely or put an end to it. 消除；终结 ❑ *The long-range goal must be to do away with nuclear weapons altogether.* 长远目标一定是销毁所有的核武器。 2 PHRASAL VERB If one person **does away with** another, the first murders the second. If you **do away with yourself**, you kill yourself. 谋杀 [INFORMAL] ❑ *...a woman whose husband had made several attempts to do away with her.* …一位丈夫数次试图将其谋杀的女人。

▸ **do in** PHRASAL VERB To **do** someone **in** means to kill them. 杀害 [INFORMAL] ❑ *Whoever did him in removed a man who was brave as well as ruthless.* 无论是谁杀了他，都是除掉了一个既大胆又无情的人。

▸ **do up** 1 PHRASAL VERB If you **do** something **up**, you fasten it. 扣；系 ❑ *Mari did up the buttons.* 玛丽扣好了扣子。 2 PHRASAL VERB If you say that a person or room **is done up** in a particular way, you mean they are dressed or decorated in that way, often a way that is rather ridiculous or extreme. (可笑的、极端的) 打扮；(荒谬的、极端的) 装饰 ❑ *...a small salon done up in saffron silks and plum velvet cushions.* …一个用藏红色的丝织品和暗紫色的天鹅绒坐垫装饰起来的小沙龙。

▸ **do without** 1 PHRASAL VERB If you **do without** something you need, want, or usually have, you are able to survive, continue, or succeed although you do not have it. 没有…也行 ❑ *We can't do without the help of your organization.* 我们不能没有你们机构的帮助。 2 PHRASAL VERB If you say that you could **do without** something, you mean that you would prefer not to have it or it is of no benefit to you. 宁愿不要；没有好处 [INFORMAL] ❑ *He could do without her rhetorical questions at five o'clock in the morning.* 他不愿她早晨5点就问他那些无须回答的问题。

❸ **do** /duː/ (**dos**) PHRASE If someone tells you the **dos and don'ts** of a particular situation, they advise you what you should and should not do in that situation. 该做的和不该做的；行为准则；注意事项 ❑ *Please advise me on the most suitable color print film and some dos and don'ts.* 请就最适用的彩照胶卷及其使用须知给我建议。

★ **dock** /dɒk/ (**docks, docking, docked**) 1 N-COUNT A **dock** is an enclosed area in a harbor where ships go to be loaded, unloaded, and repaired. 码头 [also "in/into" N] ❑ *She headed for the docks, thinking that Ricardo might be hiding in one of the boats.* 她朝着码头走去，心想里卡多可能藏在其中的一条船上。 2 N-COUNT A **dock** is a platform for loading vehicles or trains. 装车平台 [AM] ❑ *The truck left the loading dock with hoses still attached.* 卡车离开了装货平台，软管还连着。 3 N-COUNT A **dock** is a small structure at the edge of water where boats can tie up, especially one that is privately owned. (尤指私家) 泊位 [AM] ❑ *He had a house there and a dock and a little aluminum boat.* 他在那儿有一幢房、一个泊位和一条铝制小船。 4 V-T/V-I When a ship **docks** or **is docked**, it is brought into a dock. 停靠码头 ❑ *The crash happened as the ferry attempted to dock on Staten Island.* 这次碰撞发生于渡船试图停靠在斯塔滕岛时。 5 V-T If you **dock** someone's pay or money, you take some of the money away. 扣 (钱) ❑ *He threatens to dock her fee.* 他威胁要扣她的酬金。 6 V-T If you **dock** someone points in a contest, you take away some of the points that they have. 扣 (分) 7 V-RECIP When one spacecraft **docks** or **is docked with** another, the two crafts join together in space. (宇宙飞船) 对接 ❑ *The space shuttle Atlantis is scheduled to dock with Russia's Mir space station.* 亚特兰蒂斯号航天飞机计划与俄罗斯的米尔号空间站对接。 8 N-SING In a law court, **the dock** is where the person accused of a crime stands or sits. 被告席 ❑ *What about the odd chance that you do put an innocent man in the dock?* 万一你真的将一个无辜的人送上了被告席可怎么办呢？

doc·tor ◆◆◇ /dɒktər/ (**doctors, doctoring, doctored**) 1 N-COUNT; N-TITLE; N-VOC A **doctor** is someone who has a degree in medicine and treats people who are sick or injured. 医生 ❑ *Do not discontinue the treatment without consulting your doctor.* 不要不征求医生的意见就中断治疗。 2 N-COUNT; N-TITLE; N-VOC A **dentist** or **veterinarian** can also be called **doctor**. (牙医、兽医) 医生 [AM] 3 N-COUNT **The doctor's** is used to refer to the office where a doctor works. 诊所 ❑ *I have an appointment at the doctor's.* 我在诊所有个预约。 4 N-COUNT; N-TITLE A **doctor** is someone who has been awarded the highest academic or honorary degree by a university. 博士 ❑ *He is a doctor of philosophy.* 他是一位哲学博士。 5 V-T If someone **doctors** something, they change it in order to deceive people. 窜改 ❑ *They doctored the prints, deepening the lines to make her look as awful as possible.* 他们窜改了照片，加深皱纹使她尽可能地难看。

▲ **doc·tor·ate** /dɒktərɪt/ (**doctorates**) N-COUNT A **doctorate** is the highest degree awarded by a university. 博士学位 ❑ *Professor Lanphier obtained his doctorate in social psychology from the University of Michigan.* 兰菲尔教授从密歇根大学获得了社会心理学博士学位。

doc·tor's of·fice (**doctor's offices**) N-COUNT A **doctor's office** is the room or clinic where a doctor works. 诊室；诊所 [AM] ❑ *Some people made it as far as a doctor's office, only to pass out and die within minutes.* 有些人已经到了诊所，但是在几分钟内却昏倒并死去。

doc·tor's sur·gery (**doctor's surgeries**) N-COUNT A **doctor's surgery** is the same as a **doctor's office**. 诊室；诊所 [BRIT]

d

doc·tri·nal /dɒktrɪnᵊl/ ADJ **Doctrinal** means relating to doctrines. 教义的 [FORMAL] ❑ *Doctrinal differences were vigorously debated among religious leaders.* 宗教领袖们就教义上的区别展开了激烈的辩论。

★ **doc·trine** /dɒktrɪn/ (**doctrines**) N-VAR A **doctrine** is a set of principles or beliefs, especially religious ones. (尤指宗教的) 信条; 学说 ❑ *...the Marxist doctrine of perpetual revolution.* …马克思主义不断革命的学说。

docu·ment ♦♦◊ (**documents, documenting, documented**)

The noun is pronounced /dɒkyəmənt/. The verb is pronounced /dɒkyəmɛnt/.

名词读作 /dɒkyəmənt/, 动词读作 /dɒkyəmɛnt/。

1 N-COUNT A **document** is one or more official pieces of paper with writing on them. 文件; 公文 ❑ *She produces legal documents for a downtown Seattle law firm.* 她为西雅图市区的一家法律事务所撰写法律文件。 2 N-COUNT A **document** is a piece of text or graphics, for example, a letter, that is stored as a file on a computer and that you can access in order to read it or change it. 文档 [COMPUTING] ❑ *When you are finished typing, remember to save your document.* 输入完毕后, 要记着保存文档。 3 V-T If you **document** something, you make a detailed record of it in writing or on film or tape. 记录 ❑ *He wrote a book documenting his prison experiences.* 他写了一本书, 记录他的牢狱经历。

→ see **copy, diary, history, printing**

▲ **docu·men·tary** /dɒkyəmɛntəri, -tri/ (**documentaries**) 1 N-COUNT A **documentary** is a television or radio program, or a movie, which shows real events or provides information about a particular subject. 记录片 ❑ *...a TV documentary on homelessness.* …一部关于无家可归现象的电视记录片。 2 ADJ **Documentary** evidence consists of things that are written down. 书面的 (证据) [ADJ n] ❑ *The government says it has documentary evidence that the two countries were planning military action.* 该政府宣称, 它拥有这两个国家正在策划军事行动的书面证据。

docu·men·ta·tion /dɒkyəmɛnteɪʃᵊn/ N-UNCOUNT **Documentation** consists of documents which provide proof or evidence of something, or are a record of something. 文件证据 ❑ *Passengers must carry proper documentation.* 旅客必须携带适当的证明材料。

★ **dodge** /dɒdʒ/ (**dodges, dodging, dodged**) 1 V-I If you **dodge**, you move suddenly, often to avoid being hit, caught, or seen. 躲闪 ❑ *I dodged back into the alley and waited a minute.* 我往后一闪, 躲进胡同里等了一会儿。 2 V-T If you **dodge** something, you avoid it by quickly moving aside or out of reach so that it cannot hit or reach you. 闪开 ❑ *He desperately dodged a speeding car trying to run him down.* 他拼命地闪身躲开一辆高速撞向自己的汽车。 3 V-T If you **dodge** something, you deliberately avoid thinking about it or dealing with it, often by being deceitful. 逃避 ❑ *He boasts of dodging military service by feigning illness.* 他吹嘘说自己装病逃过了兵役。 ● N-COUNT **Dodge** is also a noun. 逃避 ❑ *This was not just a tax dodge.* 这不仅仅是逃税的问题。

does /dəz, STRONG dʌz/ **Does** is the third person singular in the present tense of **do**. **do**的第三人称单数现在式

doesn't ♦♦♦ /dʌzᵊnt/ **Doesn't** is the usual spoken form of "does not." **does not**的常用口语形式

dog ♦♦◊ /dɔg/ (**dogs, dogging, dogged**) 1 N-COUNT A **dog** is a very common four-legged animal that is often kept by people as a pet or to guard or hunt. There are many different breeds of dog. 狗 ❑ *The British are renowned as a nation of dog lovers.* 英国人以爱狗著称。 2 N-COUNT People use **dog** to refer to something that they consider unsatisfactory or of poor quality. 蹩脚货 [AM, INFORMAL, DISAPPROVAL] ❑ *It's a real dog.* 这是个不折不扣的蹩脚货。 3 V-T If problems or injuries **dog** you, they are with you all the time. (问题、伤病等) 长期困扰 ❑ *His career has been dogged by bad luck.* 他的职业生涯厄运不断。 4 → see also **dogged** 5 PHRASE You use **dog eat dog** to express your disapproval of a situation where everyone wants to succeed and is willing to harm other people in order to do so. 相互倾轧 [DISAPPROVAL] ❑ *It is very much dog eat dog out there.* 那简直就是自相倾轧。 6 PHRASE If you say that something **is going to the dogs**, you mean that it is becoming weaker and worse in quality. 衰落 [INFORMAL, DISAPPROVAL] ❑ *They sit doing nothing while the country goes to the dogs.* 他们坐视整个国家衰落下去。

→ see **pet**

★ **dog·ged** /dɔgɪd/ ADJ If you describe someone's actions as **dogged**, you mean that they are determined to continue with something even if it becomes difficult or dangerous. 顽强的 [ADJ n] ❑ *They have, through sheer dogged determination, slowly gained respect for their efforts.* 他们凭借顽强的毅力慢慢地为自己的努力赢得了尊重。 ● **dog·ged·ly** ADV 顽强地 ❑ *She would fight doggedly for her rights as the children's mother.* 她会顽强地为她作为孩子们母亲的权利而斗争。 ● **dog·ged·ness** N-UNCOUNT 顽强 ❑ *Most of my accomplishments came as the result of sheer doggedness rather than talent.* 我的成就大都源于我绝对的顽强, 而非聪明才智。

dog·house /dɔghaʊs/ (**doghouses**) 1 N-COUNT A **doghouse** is a small building made especially for a dog to sleep in. 狗舍 [AM]

in BRIT, use **kennel**

2 PHRASE If you are **in the doghouse**, people are annoyed or angry with you. 招人恨的 [INFORMAL] ❑ *Her husband was in the doghouse for leaving her to cope on her own.* 她的丈夫因弃她于不顾而引起公愤。

★ **dog·ma** /dɔgmə/ (**dogmas**) N-VAR If you refer to a belief or a system of beliefs as a **dogma**, you disapprove of it because people are expected to accept that it is true, without questioning it. 教条 [DISAPPROVAL] ❑ *Their political dogma has blinded them to the real needs of the country.* 他们的政治教条使他们对国家的真正需求视而不见。

dog·mat·ic /dɔgmætɪk/ ADJ If you say that someone is **dogmatic**, you are critical of them because they are convinced that they are right, and refuse to consider that other opinions might also be justified. 自以为是的 [DISAPPROVAL] ❑ *Many writers at this time held rigidly dogmatic views.* 许多作家这一时期刻板地固守教条主义的观点。 ● **dog·mati·cal·ly** /dɔgmætɪkli/ ADV 自以为是地 [ADV with v] ❑ *Bennett had wanted this list of books to be dogmatically imposed on the nation's universities.* 贝内特曾想过要将这个书单武断地强行在全国的大学推广。

dog·ma·tism /dɔgmətɪzəm/ N-UNCOUNT If you refer to an opinion as **dogmatism**, you are criticizing it for being strongly stated without considering all the relevant facts or other people's opinions. 教条主义 [DISAPPROVAL] ❑ *We cannot allow dogmatism to stand in the way of progress.* 我们不能让教条主义阻碍前进的步伐。

do-it-yourself N-UNCOUNT **Do-it-yourself** is the same as **DIY**. 自己动手做

dol·drums /doʊldrəmz/ PHRASE If an activity or situation is **in the doldrums**, it is very quiet and nothing new or exciting is happening. 无生气的 ❑ *The economy is in the doldrums.* 经济毫无生气。

★ **dole** /doʊl/ 1 N-UNCOUNT **The dole** or **dole** is money that is given regularly by the government to people who are unemployed. 失业救济金 [mainly BRIT]

in AM, usually use **welfare**

2 PHRASE Someone who is **on the dole** is registered as unemployed and receives money from the government. 登记为失业者并从政府领取救济金的 [mainly BRIT]

in AM, usually use **on welfare**

doll /dɒl/ (**dolls**) N-COUNT A **doll** is a child's toy which looks like a small person or baby. 玩具娃娃

dol·lar ♦♦♦ /dɒlər/ (**dollars**) N-COUNT The **dollar** is the unit of money used in the U.S., Canada, Australia, and some other countries. It is represented by the symbol $, the dollar sign. A dollar is divided into one hundred smaller units called cents. 元 (美国、加拿大、澳大利亚以及其他一些国家的货币单位) ❑ *She gets paid seven dollars an hour.* 她的报酬是每小时7元。 ● N-SING **The dollar** is also used to refer to the American currency system. 美元 ❑ *In early trading in Tokyo, the dollar fell sharply against the yen.* 在东京的早盘交易中, 美元对日元的汇率急剧下跌。

dol·phin /dɒlfɪn/ (**dolphins**) N-COUNT A **dolphin** is a mammal which lives in the sea and looks like a large fish with a pointed mouth. 海豚

→ see **whale**

★ **do·main** /doʊmeɪn/ (**domains**) 1 N-COUNT A **domain** is a particular field of thought, activity, or interest, especially one over which someone has control, influence, or rights. 领域 [FORMAL] ❑ *...the great experimenters in the domain of art.* …艺术领域里伟大的实验者们。 2 N-COUNT On the Internet, a **domain** is a set of addresses that shows, for example, the category or geographical area that an Internet address belongs to. (网络) 域 [COMPUTING] ❑ *An Internet society spokeswoman said .org domain users will not experience any disruptions during the transition.* 一位互联网协会的女发言

人说，在这次过渡中，域名为.org的用户不会受到任何影响。

do·main name (**domain names**) N-COUNT A **domain name** is the name of a person's or an organization's website on the Internet, for example, "collins.co.uk." 域名 [COMPUTING] ❏ *Users need to find out if a domain name is already registered or is still available.* 用户需要查明某个域名是已经被注册过还是仍然可用。

★ **dome** /doʊm/ (**domes**) 1 N-COUNT A **dome** is a round roof. 穹顶 ❏ *...the dome of the Capitol.* …国会大厦的穹顶。 2 N-COUNT A **dome** is any object that has a similar shape to a dome. 圆顶状物 ❏ *...the dome of the hill.* …山包。

do·mes·tic ♦♦◇ /dəmɛstɪk/ 1 ADJ **Domestic** political activities, events, and situations happen or exist within one particular country. 国内的 ❏ *...over 100 domestic flights a day to 30 leading U.S. destinations.* …每天飞往美国30个主要目的地的100多个国内航班。 2 → see also **gross domestic product** 3 ADJ **Domestic** duties and activities are concerned with the running of a home and family. 家务的 [ADJ n] ❏ *...a plan for sharing domestic chores.* …一份分担家务的计划。 4 ADJ **Domestic** items and services are intended to be used in people's homes rather than in factories or offices. 家用的 [ADJ n] ❏ *...domestic appliances.* …家用电器。 5 ADJ A **domestic** situation or atmosphere is one which involves a family and their home. 家庭的 ❏ *It was a scene of such domestic bliss.* 这是一幕家庭美满的场景。 6 ADJ A **domestic** animal is one that is not wild and is kept either on a farm to produce food or in someone's home as a pet. 家养的；饲养的 ❏ *...a domestic cat.* …一只家猫。

★ **domi·nance** /dɒmɪnəns/ N-UNCOUNT The **dominance** of a particular person or thing is the fact that they are more powerful, successful, or important than other people or things. 优势；统治地位 ❏ *The latest fighting appears to be an attempt by each group to establish dominance over the other.* 最近的战斗似乎是冲突各方在试图争夺控制权。

Thesaurus *dominance* 另参见：

N. authority, control, supremacy, upper hand

domi·nant /dɒmɪnənt/ ADJ Someone or something that is **dominant** is more powerful, successful, influential, or noticeable than other people or things. 处于支配地位的 ❏ *...a change which would maintain his party's dominant position in Scotland.* …巩固他的政党在苏格兰支配地位的一场变革。

→ see **gene**

Word Link *domin ≈ rule, master : dominate, dominion, predominant*

domi·nate ♦♦◇ /dɒmɪneɪt/ (**dominates, dominating, dominated**) 1 V-T/V-I To **dominate** a situation means to be the most powerful or important person or thing in it. 占据支配地位 ❏ *The book is expected to dominate the best-seller lists.* 这本书预期将占据畅销书榜首的位置。 ❏ *...countries where life is dominated by war.* …饱受战乱的国家。 ❏ *Selling could continue to dominate as investors play it safe.*
● ★ **domi·na·tion** /dɒmɪneɪʃən/ N-UNCOUNT 支配 ❏ *...the domination of the market by a small number of organizations.* …少数机构对市场的支配。 2 V-T If one country or person **dominates** another, they have power over them. 控制 ❏ *He denied that his country wants to dominate Europe.* 他否认他的国家想称霸欧洲。 ❏ *Women are no longer dominated by the men in their relationships.* 在两性的相互关系中，女性已不再受制于男性。 ● **domi·na·tion** N-UNCOUNT 统治 ❏ *They had five centuries of domination by the Romans.* 他们被罗马人统治了5个世纪。 3 V-T If a building, mountain, or other object **dominates** an area, it is so large or impressive that you cannot avoid seeing it. 俯视；高出 ❏ *It's one of the biggest buildings in this area, and it really dominates this whole place.* 这是该地区最大的建筑物之一，俯视着整个地区。

domi·nat·ing /dɒmɪneɪtɪŋ/ ADJ A **dominating** person has a very strong personality and influences the people around them. 有影响力的 ❏ *She certainly was a dominating figure, a leader who gave her name to a political philosophy.* 她的确是个很有影响力的人物，是一位能使一派政治哲学以她而命名的领袖。

▲ **do·min·ion** /dəmɪnyən/ (**dominions**) N-COUNT A **dominion** is an area of land that is controlled by a ruler. 领土 ❏ *The republic is a dominion of the Brazilian people.* 该共和国的领土属于全体巴西人民。

domi·no /dɒmɪnoʊ/ (**dominoes**) 1 N-COUNT **Dominoes** are small rectangular blocks marked with two groups of spots on one side. They are used for playing various games. 多米诺骨牌 2 N-UNCOUNT **Dominoes** is a game in which players put dominoes onto a table in turn. 多米诺骨牌游戏 ❏ *I used to play dominoes there.* 我过去常在那里玩多米诺骨牌游戏。

domi·no ef·fect N-SING If one event causes another similar event, which in turn causes another event, and so on, you can refer to this as a **domino effect.** 多米诺效应 ❏ *The timetable for trains is so tight that if one is a bit late, the domino effect is enormous.* 列车时刻表安排得很紧凑，所以，如果一列火车晚点一会儿，就会引起巨大的多米诺效应。

Word Link *don ≈ giving : donate, donor, pardon*

★ **do·nate** /doʊneɪt/ (**donates, donating, donated**) 1 V-T If you **donate** something **to** a charity or other organization, you give it to them. 捐赠 ❏ *He frequently donates large sums to charity.* 他经常向慈善机构大笔捐款。 ● **do·na·tion** /doʊneɪʃən/ N-UNCOUNT 捐赠 ❏ *...the donation of his collection to the art gallery.* …他向艺术馆所做的收藏品捐赠。 2 V-T If you **donate** your blood or a part of your body, you allow doctors to use it to help someone who is ill. 捐献 ❏ *...people who are willing to donate their organs for use after death.* …愿意在死后捐献器官的人。 ● **do·na·tion** N-UNCOUNT 捐献 ❏ *...measures aimed at encouraging organ donation.* …旨在鼓励器官捐献的措施。

do·na·tion /doʊneɪʃən/ (**donations**) 1 N-COUNT A **donation** is something which someone gives to a charity or other organization. 捐赠物 ❏ *Employees make regular donations to charity.* 员工们定期向慈善机构捐赠物品。 2 → see also **donate**

→ see **donor**

Word Partnership *donation* 的常用搭配：

V.	**accept a** donation, **make a** donation, **receive a** donation 1
ADJ.	**charitable** donation, **generous** donation, **suggested** donation 1

done ♦◇◇ /dʌn/ 1 **Done** is the past participle of **do**. do的过去分词 2 ADJ A task or activity that is **done** has been completed successfully. 完成的 [v-link ADJ] ❏ *When her deal is done, the client emerges with her purchase.* 交易完成后，顾客拿着购买的东西出来了。 3 ADJ When something that you are cooking is **done**, it has been cooked long enough and is ready. (饭菜) 做好了的 [v-link ADJ] ❏ *As soon as the cake is done, remove it from the oven.* 蛋糕一烤好，就把它从烤箱里拿出来。 4 CONVENTION You say **"Done"** when you are accepting a deal, arrangement, or bet that someone has offered to make with you. 行；好 (表示接受建议或条件) [SPOKEN, FORMULAE] ❏ *"You lead and we'll look for it."—"Done."* "你带路，我们来找！" —— "好的！"

don·key /dɒŋki/ (**donkeys**) N-COUNT A **donkey** is an animal which is like a horse but which is smaller and has longer ears. 驴

do·nor /doʊnər/ (**donors**) 1 N-COUNT A **donor** is someone who gives a part of their body or some of their blood to be used by doctors to help a person who is ill. 器官捐献者；献血者 ❏ *Doctors removed the healthy kidney from the donor.* 医生从捐献者体内取出了健康的肾脏。 2 N-COUNT A **donor** is a person or organization who

Word Web donor

Many people **give donations.** They like to **help** others. They **donate money,** clothes, food, or their time. Some people even give parts of themselves. Doctors performed the first successful human **organ transplants** in the 1950s. Today this type of operation is a relatively routine procedure. The problem now is finding enough **donors** to meet the needs of potential **recipients.** Organs such as the **kidney** often come from a living donor. **Hearts, lungs,** and other vital organs come from deceased donors. Of course our health care system relies on **blood** donors. They help save lives every day.

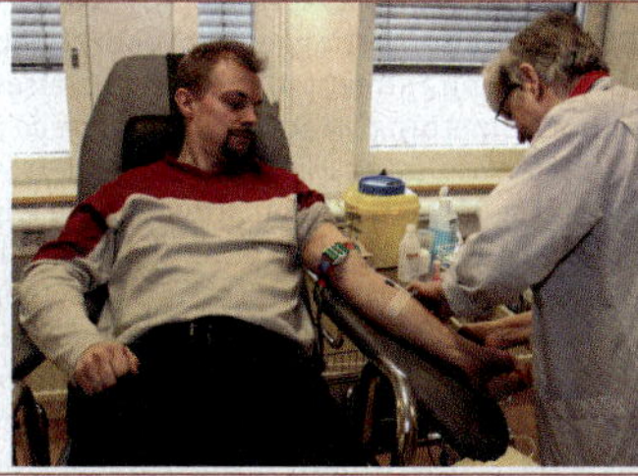

gives something, especially money, to a charity, organization, or country that needs it. 捐赠者 ❑ *Donor countries are becoming more choosy about which countries they are prepared to help.* 捐赠国对受赠国的选择变得更加慎重了。 **3** ADJ **Donor** organs or parts are organs or parts of the body which people allow doctors to use to help people who are ill. 捐献的 [ADJ n] ❑ *...the severe shortage of donor organs.* …捐献器官的严重匮乏。
→ see Word Web: **donor**

don't /doʊnt/ **Don't** is the usual spoken form of "do not." **do not** 的常用口语形式

D

do·nut /doʊnʌt, -nət/ **(donuts)** → see **doughnut**

doo·dle /duːdᵊl/ **(doodles, doodling, doodled)** **1** N-COUNT A **doodle** is a pattern or picture that you draw when you are bored or thinking about something else. 信手涂鸦之物 ❑ *Dillworthy was staring into space, with a scrawl of doodles on the pad in front of him.* 迪尔沃西凝望着天空，面前的纸上满是涂鸦。 **2** V-I When someone **doodles**, they draw doodles. 信手涂鸦 ❑ *He looked across at Jackson, doodling on his notebook.* 他一边看着对面的杰克逊，一边在笔记本上信手涂鸦。

★ **doom** /duːm/ **(dooms, dooming, doomed)** **1** N-UNCOUNT **Doom** is a terrible future state or event which you cannot prevent. 厄运 ❑ *...his warnings of impending doom.* …他对即将到来的厄运发出的警告。 **2** N-UNCOUNT If you have a sense or feeling of **doom**, you feel that things are going very badly and are likely to get even worse. 悲观 ❑ *Why are people so full of gloom and doom?* 人们的心里为什么满是悲观失望？ **3** V-T If a fact or event **dooms** someone or something **to** a particular fate, it makes certain that they are going to suffer in some way. 注定 ❑ *That argument was the turning point for their marriage, and the one which doomed it to failure.* 那次争吵是他们婚姻的一个转折点，它注定了他们婚姻的失败。

doomed /duːmd/ **1** ADJ If something **is doomed to** happen, or if you **are doomed to** a particular state, something unpleasant is certain to happen, and you can do nothing to prevent it. 注定的 [v-link ADJ] ❑ *Their plans seemed doomed to failure.* 看起来，他们的计划注定要失败。 **2** ADJ Someone or something that is **doomed** is certain to fail or be destroyed. 注定要失败的 ❑ *I used to pour time and energy into projects that were doomed from the start.* 过去我总是将时间和精力投入到一些从一开始就注定要失败的项目上。

door ♦♦♦ /dɔr/ **(doors)** **1** N-COUNT A **door** is a piece of wood, glass, or metal, which is moved to open and close the entrance to a building, room, closet, or vehicle. 门 ❑ *I was knocking at the front door but there was no answer.* 我敲了敲前门，但无人应答。 **2** N-COUNT A **door** is the space in a wall when a door is open. 门口 ❑ *She looked through the door of the kitchen. Her daughter was at the stove.* 透过厨房开着的门，她看到女儿正在炉子旁边。 **3** N-PLURAL **Doors** is used in expressions such as **a few doors down** or **three doors up** to refer to a place that is a particular number of buildings away from where you are. 建筑物 (表示两个地点之间的距离) [amount N "down/up"] [INFORMAL] ❑ *Mrs. Cade's house was only a few doors down from her daughter's apartment.* 从凯德夫人的房子到她女儿的公寓只隔了几座房屋。 **4** → see also **next door** **5** PHRASE When you **answer the door**, you go and open the door because a visitor has knocked on it or rung the bell. 应门 ❑ *Carol answered the door as soon as I knocked.* 我刚敲过门，卡罗尔就把门打开了。 **6** PHRASE If you say that someone gets or does something **by the back door** or **through the back door**, you are criticizing them for doing it secretly and unofficially. 走后门地 [DISAPPROVAL] ❑ *The government would not allow anyone to sneak in by the back door and seize power by force.* 政府不允许任何人用不正当的手段混进来，然后通过武力夺权。 **7** PHRASE If people have talks and discussions **behind closed doors**, they have them in private because they want them to be kept secret. 秘密地 ❑ *...decisions taken in secret behind closed doors.* …秘密做出的决定。 **8** PHRASE If someone goes **from door to door** or goes **door to door**, they go along a street calling at each house in turn, for example, selling something. 挨家挨户地 ❑ *They are going from door to door collecting money from civilians.* 他们挨家挨户地从老百姓那里收钱。 **9** PHRASE If you talk about a distance or trip **from door to door** or **door to door**, you are talking about the distance from the place where the trip starts to the place where it finishes. 全程的 ❑ *...tickets covering the whole trip from door to door.* …全程票。 **10** PHRASE If you say that something helps someone to get their **foot in the door**, you mean that it gives them an opportunity to start doing something new, usually in an area that is difficult to succeed in. 获得 (从事某项艰巨事业的) 机会 ❑ *If we can get our foot in the door, that can help us build our market.* 如果能获得这个机会，对我们开拓市场就会有所帮助。 **11** PHRASE If someone **shuts the door in** your **face** or **slams the door in** your **face**, they refuse to talk to you or give you any information. 拒之门外 ❑ *Did you say anything to him or just shut the door in his face?* 你对他说了什么还是直接将他拒于门外？ **12** PHRASE If you **lay** something **at** someone's **door**, you blame them for an unpleasant event or situation. 把…归咎于 ❑ *Much of the blame for the long delay could be laid at the door of the manufacturer.* 拖延了这么久，大部分的责任在于生产商。 **13** PHRASE When you are **out of doors**, you are not inside a building, but in the open air. 在户外 ❑ *The weather was fine enough for working out of doors.* 天气这么好，很适合户外工作。 **14** PHRASE If you **see** someone **to the door**, you go to the door with a visitor when they leave. 送至门口 ❑ *Politely he saw her to the door and opened it for her.* 他礼貌地将她送至门口，并为她打开了门。 **15** PHRASE If someone **shows** you **the door**, they ask you to leave because they are angry with you. 逐出 ❑ *Would they forgive and forget – or show him the door?* 他们会原谅并忘记他的过失——还是会将他赶出门去？ **16** **at death's door** → see **death**

door·man /dɔrmæn, -mən/ **(doormen)** **1** N-COUNT A **doorman** is a person, usually a uniformed employee, who stands at the door of a building such as a hotel or apartment and helps people who are going in or out. 门卫

in BRIT, also use **doorkeeper**

2 N-COUNT A **doorman** is the same as a **bouncer**. 门口保镖 [BRIT]

door·step /dɔrstɛp/ **(doorsteps)** **1** N-COUNT A **doorstep** is a step in front of a door on the outside of a building. 门前台阶 ❑ *...a youth who was sitting on a doorstep, drinking.* …一个坐在门前台阶上喝酒的年轻人。 **2** PHRASE If a place is **on** your **doorstep**, it is very near to where you live. If something happens **on** your **doorstep**, it happens very close to where you live. 在住所附近 ❑ *It is easy to lose sight of what is happening on our own doorstep.* 家门口发生的事反而容易被我们忽视。

door·way /dɔrweɪ/ **(doorways)** **1** N-COUNT A **doorway** is a space in a wall where a door opens and closes. 门口 ❑ *Hannah looked up to see David and another man standing in the doorway.* 汉纳抬起头，看到戴维和另一个男人站在门口。 **2** N-COUNT A **doorway** is a covered space just outside the door of a building. 门廊 ❑ *...homeless people sleeping in doorways.* …睡在门廊里的无家可归者。

dope /doʊp/ **(dopes, doping, doped)** **1** N-UNCOUNT **Dope** is a drug, usually an illegal drug such as marijuana or cocaine. 毒品 (通常指大麻或可卡因之类的违禁药品) [INFORMAL] ❑ *A man asked them if they wanted to buy some dope.* 一个男人问他们要不要买些毒品。 **2** V-T If someone **dopes** a person or animal or **dopes** their food, they put drugs into their food or force them to take drugs. 给…服用毒品; 强迫…吸毒 ❑ *Anyone could have got in and doped the wine.* 任何人都可能进去在酒里下毒。 ❑ *I'd been doped with Somnolin.* 有人给我下了嗜睡药。 **3** N-COUNT If someone calls a person a **dope**, they think that the person is stupid. 傻瓜 [INFORMAL, DISAPPROVAL] ❑ *I'm more comfortable with them. I don't feel I'm such a dope.* 和他们在一起我更自在些，因为我不会觉得自己像个傻瓜。

dor·mant /dɔrmənt/ ADJ Something that is **dormant** is not active, growing, or being used at the present time but is capable of becoming active later on. 休眠的 ❑ *...when the long dormant volcano of Mount St. Helens erupted in 1980.* …当长期处于休眠状态的圣海伦斯火山在1980年爆发的时候。
→ see **plant**

dor·mi·tory /dɔrmɪtɔri/ **(dormitories)** **1** N-COUNT A **dormitory** is a building at a college or university where students live. 宿舍楼 [AM]

in BRIT, use **hall of residence**

❑ *She lived in a college dormitory.* 她住在一幢大学宿舍楼里。 **2** N-COUNT A **dormitory** is a large bedroom where several people sleep, for example, in a boarding school. 宿舍 ❑ *...the boys' dormitory.* …男生宿舍。

A college **dormitory** usually provides both a place to sleep and meals, called **room and board**. Some students choose to live in privately rented accommodation outside the college, which is owned by a **landlord**. A landlord only provides the room(s) and the renter must supply his or her own food.

DOS /dɒs/ N-UNCOUNT **DOS** is the part of a computer operating system that controls and manages files and programs stored on disk. **DOS** is an abbreviation for "disk operating system." 磁盘操作系统 [COMPUTING, TRADEMARK] ❑ *Where do I find the instructions to load DOS programs from Windows 98?* 我在哪里可以找到在视窗98系统下加载磁盘操作系统的说明？

dos·age /doʊsɪdʒ/ (**dosages**) N-COUNT A **dosage** is the amount of a medicine or drug that someone takes or should take. 剂量 ❑ *He was put on a high dosage of vitamin C.* 他在大剂量服用维生素C。

dose /doʊs/ (**doses, dosing, dosed**) **1** N-COUNT A **dose of** medicine or a drug is a measured amount of it which is intended to be taken at one time. 一次用量 ❑ *One dose of penicillin can wipe out the infection.* 一剂青霉素即可消除感染。 **2** V-T If you **dose** a person or animal **with** medicine, you give them an amount of it. 给（药） ❑ *The doctor fixed the rib, dosed him heavily with drugs, and said he would probably get better.* 医生给他固定好肋骨后，又给他服了大剂量的药，说他可能会好起来。 ● PHRASAL VERB **Dose up** means the same as **dose**. 给（药） ❑ *I dosed him up with Valium.* 我给他服了安定。

dos·si·er /dɒsieɪ/ (**dossiers**) N-COUNT A **dossier** is a collection of papers containing information on a particular event, or on a person such as a criminal or a spy. 卷宗 ❑ *The company is compiling a dossier of evidence to back its allegations.* 公司正在搜集证明材料来支持自己的指控。

dot /dɒt/ (**dots, dotting, dotted**) **1** N-COUNT A **dot** is a very small round mark, for example, one that is used as the top part of the letter "i," as a period, or in the names of websites. 点 ❑ *...a system of painting using small dots of color.* …一套运用小色点作画的方法。 **2** V-T When things **dot** a place or an area, they are scattered or spread all over it. 遍布于 ❑ *Small coastal towns dot the landscape.* 海滨小镇到处都是。 **3** → see also **dotted** **4** PHRASE If you arrive somewhere or do something **on the dot**, you arrive there or do it at exactly the time that you were supposed to. 准时地 ❑ *They appeared on the dot of 9:50 p.m. as always.* 他们同往常一样在晚上9点50分准时出现了。

dot-com (**dot-coms**) also **dotcom** N-COUNT A **dot-com** is a company that does all or most of its business on the Internet. 网上公司 ❑ *In 1999, dot-coms spent more than $1 billion on TV spots.* 1999年，网上公司花在电视播播广告上的费用超过10亿 。

dote /doʊt/ (**dotes, doting, doted**) V-I If you say that someone **dotes on** a person or a thing, you mean that they love or care about them very much and ignore any faults they may have. 溺爱 ❑ *He dotes on his nine-year-old son.* 他对自己9岁的儿子十分溺爱。

dot·ing /doʊtɪŋ/ ADJ If you say that someone is, for example, a **doting** mother, husband, or friend, you mean that they show a lot of love for someone. 溺爱的 ❑ *His doting parents bought him his first racing bike at 13.* 溺爱他的父母在他13岁时给他买了第一辆自行车跑车。

dot·ted /dɒtɪd/ **1** ADJ A **dotted** line is a line which is made of a row of dots. 由点构成的 ❑ *Cut along the dotted line.* 沿虚线剪开。 ● PHRASE If you **sign on the dotted line**, you formally agree to something by signing an official document. 正式签约接受 **2** ADJ If a place or object is **dotted with** things, it has many of those things scattered over its surface. 布满的 [v-link ADJ "with" n] ❑ *The maps were dotted with the names of small towns.* 地图上标满了各个小镇的名字。 **3** ADJ If things are **dotted around** a place, they can be found in many different parts of that place. 分散的 [v-link ADJ prep] ❑ *Many pieces of sculpture are dotted around the house.* 雕塑作品在房子里四处可见。 **4** → see also **dot**

dou·ble ◆◆◇ /dʌbᵊl/ (**doubles, doubling, doubled**) **1** ADJ You use **double** to indicate that something includes or is made of two things of the same kind. 双的 [ADJ n] ❑ *...a pair of double doors into the room from the new entrance hall.* …一道从新门廊进入房间的双扇门。 **2** ADJ You use **double** before a singular noun to refer to two things of the same type that occur together, or that are connected in some way. 成对的 [ADJ n] ❑ *...an extremely nasty double murder.* …一起极残忍的双人谋杀案。 **3** ADJ You use **double** to describe something which is twice the normal size or can hold twice the normal quantity of something. 双倍的 ❑ *...a double helping of ice cream.* …双份冰激凌。 **4** ADJ A **double** room is a room intended for two people, usually a couple, to stay or live in. 双人的 ❑ *...bed and breakfast for $180 for two people in a double room.* …给两个人共用一个双人间的价格为$180的住宿加早餐。 ● N-COUNT **Double** is also a noun. 双人房间 ❑ *The Great Western Hotel is ideal, costing around 90 a night for a double.* 大西酒店是理想的，双人房间每晚约90。 **5** ADJ A **double** bed is a bed that is wide enough for two people to sleep in. 双人的 [ADJ n] ❑ *One bedroom had a double bed and the other had single beds for the boys.* 一间卧室里摆放了一张双人床，另一间则放着男孩们的几张单人床。 **6** ADJ You use **double** to describe a drink that is twice the normal measure. （酒类饮料）双份的 [ADJ n] ❑ *He was drinking his double whiskey too fast and scowling.* 他大口喝着双份威士忌，双眉紧皱。 ● N-COUNT **Double** is also a noun. 双份酒类饮料 ❑ *"Give me a whiskey," Debilly said to Francis. "Make it a double."* "给我来杯威士忌，"德比利对弗朗西斯说。"要双份的。" **7** PREDET If something is **double the** amount or size of another thing, it is twice as large. 双倍的 [PREDET "the" n] ❑ *The offer was to start a new research laboratory at double the salary he was then getting.* 提议当时是他创办一个新实验室拿双倍工资。 ● PRON **Double** is also a pronoun. 两倍 ❑ *On average doctors write just over seven prescriptions each year per patient; in Germany it is double.* 一个医生平均一年仅为每个病人开大约七个处方；而德国是这个数字的两倍。 **8** V-T/V-I When something **doubles** or when you **double** it, it becomes twice as great in number, amount, or size. 使加倍；翻倍 ❑ *The number of managers must double to 100 within 3 years.* 3年之内管理人员的数量要翻倍，达到100名。 **9** V-I If a person or thing **doubles as** someone or something else, they have a second job or purpose as well as their main one. 兼职；兼作 ❑ *Lots of homes in town double as businesses.* 许多市区的住房还兼作商铺。 ● PHRASAL VERB **Double up** means the same as **double**. 兼职；兼作（同**double**） ❑ *The lids of the casserole dishes are designed to double up as baking dishes.* 这些砂锅盖子的设计使它们可以兼作烤盘。 **10** N-COUNT If you refer to someone as a person's **double**, you mean that they look exactly like them. 一模一样的人 ❑ *Your mother sees you as her double.* 你母亲把你看成是她的翻版。 **11** N-UNCOUNT In tennis or badminton, when people play **doubles**, two teams consisting of two players on each team play against each other on the same court. 双打 ❑ *In the doubles, the pair beat Hungary's Renata Csay and Kornelia Szanda.* 在双打比赛中，那对选手战胜了匈牙利的雷纳塔・赛伊和科尼利娅・萨恩达。 **12** PHRASE If you do something **on the double**, you do it very quickly or immediately. 快速地 [INFORMAL] ❑ *I need a copy of the police report on the double.* 我急需一份警方报告。 **13** PHRASE If you are **bent double**, the top half of your body is bent downward so that your head is close to your knees. 弯腰的 ❑ *I was bent double in agony.* 我痛苦地弯下了腰。 **14** PHRASE If you **are seeing double**, there is something wrong with your eyes, and you can see two images instead of one. 看到重影 ❑ *For 35 minutes I was walking around in a daze. I was dizzy, seeing double.* 长达35分钟我茫然地走着。我头晕目眩，看东西有重影。 **15** **in double figures** → see **figure** → see **hotel, tennis**

▸ **double up** PHRASAL VERB If something **doubles** you **up**, or if you **double up**, you bend your body quickly or violently, for example, because you are laughing a lot or because you are feeling a lot of pain. 使猛地弯下腰去；猛地弯下腰去 ❑ *...a savage blow which doubled him up.* …使他猛地弯下腰去的重重一击。 ● PHRASAL VERB **Double over** means the same as **double up**. 使猛地弯下腰去；猛地弯下腰去（同**double up**） ❑ *Everyone was doubled over in laughter.* 所有的人都笑弯了腰。

dou·ble bass /dʌbᵊl beɪs/ (**double basses**) also **double-bass** N-VAR A **double bass** is the largest instrument in the violin family. 低音提琴
→ see **orchestra, string**

double-check (**double-checks, double-checking, double-checked**) V-T/V-I If you **double-check** something, you examine or test it a second time to make sure that it is completely correct or safe. 复核 ❑ *Check and double-check spelling and punctuation.* 对拼写和标点进行检查和复核。 ❑ *Double-check that the ladder is secure.* 再检查一下梯子是否安全。

double-click (**double-clicks, double-clicking, double-clicked**) V-T If you **double-click on** an area of a computer screen, you point the cursor at that area and press one of the buttons on the mouse twice quickly in order to make something happen. 双击 [no passive] [COMPUTING] ❑ *Go to Control Panel and double-click on Sounds for a list of sounds.* 到控制面板然后双击"声音"项，可以得到一个不同声音的列表。

★ **double-decker** (**double-deckers**) N-COUNT A **double-decker** or a **double-decker bus** is a bus that has two levels, so that passengers can sit upstairs or downstairs. 双层公共汽车

double-edged **1** ADJ If you say that a comment is **double-edged**, you mean that it has two meanings, so that you are not sure whether the person who said it is being critical or is giving praise. 模棱两可的 ❑ *Even his praise is double-edged.* 即使他的赞扬也是可以有两种解释的。 **2** ADJ If you say that something is **double-edged**, you mean that its positive effects are balanced by its negative effects, or that its negative effects are greater. 有利有弊的；利少弊多的 ❑ *But tourism is double-edged, for although it's boosting the country's economy, the Reef could be damaged.* 但旅游业是有利有弊的，因为尽管它能繁荣国家经济，海礁却会被破坏。 **3** **a double-edged sword → see sword**

dou·bly /dʌbli/ **1** ADV You use **doubly** to indicate that there are two aspects or features that are having an influence on a particular situation. 双重地 ❑ *Employees choosing to move with a relocating company benefit doubly from employer-related housing assistance and lower house prices.* 选择和公司一同搬迁的员工既可以得到雇主的住房补助又可以享受较低房价。 **2** ADV You use **doubly** to emphasize that something exists or happens to a greater degree than usual. 加倍地 [ADV adj/adv] [EMPHASIS] ❑ *In pregnancy a high fiber diet is doubly important.* 怀孕期间高纤维饮食倍加重要。

doubt ♦♦◊ /daʊt/ (**doubts, doubting, doubted**) **1** N-VAR If you have **doubt** or **doubts** about something, you feel uncertain about it and do not know whether it is true or possible. If you say you have **no doubt about** it, you mean that you are certain it is true. 怀疑 ❑ *This raises doubts about the point of advertising.* 这引起了人们对于广告作用的怀疑。 ❑ *There is little doubt that man has had an impact on the Earth's climate.* 毫无疑问人类对地球上的气候造成了影响。 **2** V-T If you **doubt** whether something is true or possible, you believe that it is probably not true or possible. 怀疑 ❑ *Others doubted whether that would happen.* 其他人都怀疑那会不会发生。 ❑ *He doubted if he would learn anything new from Marie.* 他怀疑自己是否能从玛丽那里学到什么新东西。 **3** V-T If you **doubt** something, you believe that it might not be true or genuine. 怀疑 ❑ *No one doubted his ability.* 没有人怀疑他的能力。 **4** V-T If you **doubt** someone or **doubt** their word, you think that they may not be telling the truth. 不信 ❑ *No one directly involved with the case doubted him.* 直接涉及此案的人都没有怀疑他。 **5** PHRASE You say that something is **beyond doubt** or **beyond reasonable doubt** when you are certain that it is true and it cannot be contradicted or disproved. 无疑 [EMPHASIS] ❑ *A referendum showed beyond doubt that voters wanted independence.* 全民公决毫无疑问地显示，选民要求独立。 **6** PHRASE If you are **in doubt** about something, you feel unsure or uncertain about it. 不肯定的 ❑ *He is in no doubt as to what is needed.* 他对需要些什么心中有数。 **7** PHRASE If you say that something is **in doubt** or **open to doubt**, you consider it to be uncertain or unreliable. 不确定的 ❑ *The outcome was still in doubt.* 结果仍不确定。 **8** PHRASE You use **no doubt** to emphasize that something seems certain or very likely to you. 毫无疑问地 [EMPHASIS] ❑ *The contract for this will no doubt be widely advertised.* 就此达成的协议无疑会被广泛宣传。 **9** PHRASE You use **no doubt** to indicate that you accept the truth of a particular point, but that you do not think it is important or contradicts the rest of what you are saying. 的确 ❑ *No doubt many will regard these as harsh words, but regrettably they are true.* 的确很多人会觉得这些话刺耳，可惜它们却是事实。 **10** PHRASE If you say that something is true **without doubt** or **without a doubt**, you are emphasizing that it is definitely true. 毋庸置疑地 [EMPHASIS] ❑ *This was without doubt the most interesting situation that Amanda had ever found herself in.* 这无疑是阿曼达遇到过的最有趣的情况。 **11** CONVENTION You say **I doubt it** as a response to a question or statement about something that you think is untrue or unlikely. 我不信 ❑ *"Somebody would have seen her."—"I doubt it, not on Monday."* "有人可能见过她。"——"我不信，不可能在星期一。" **12** **the benefit of the doubt → see benefit** **13** **a shadow of a doubt → see shadow**

Thesaurus doubt 另参见：
- N. misgivings, reservations, uncertainty **1**
- V. discredit, distrust **2**–**4**

Word Partnership doubt 的常用搭配：
- V. **cast** doubt, **express** doubt, **have** doubt, **raise** doubt **1**
- ADJ. **little** doubt, **reasonable** doubt **1**

doubt·ful /daʊtfəl/ **1** ADJ If it is **doubtful that** something will happen, it seems unlikely to happen or you are uncertain whether it will happen. 不大可能的 ❑ *For a time it seemed doubtful that he would move at all.* 短期内他似乎不大可能搬走。 **2** ADJ If you are **doubtful about** something, you feel unsure or uncertain about it. 不能肯定的 ❑ *I was still very doubtful about the chances for success.* 我仍然不能肯定成功的可能性有多大。 ● **doubt·ful·ly** ADV 不能肯定地 [ADV after v] ❑ *Keeton shook his head doubtfully.* 基顿将信将疑地摇了摇头。 **3** ADJ If you say that something is **of doubtful** quality or value, you mean that it is of low quality or value. 有问题的 [DISAPPROVAL] ❑ *...selling something that is overpriced or of doubtful quality.* …销售价格过高或质量有问题的东西。 **4** ADJ If a sports player is **doubtful for** a match or event, he or she seems unlikely to play, usually because of injury. 不太可能的 [JOURNALISM] ❑ *Forsyth is doubtful for tonight's game with a badly bruised leg.* 福赛斯因为严重的腿伤不太可能参加今晚的比赛。

Do not confuse **doubtful, dubious,** and **suspicious.** If you feel **doubtful** about something, you are unsure about it or about whether it will happen or be successful. ❑ *Do you feel insecure and doubtful about your ability?... It was doubtful he would ever see her again.* If you are **dubious** about something, you are not sure whether it is the right thing to do. ❑ *Alison sounded very dubious... The men in charge were a bit dubious about taking him on.* If you describe something as **dubious,** you think it is not completely honest, safe, or reliable. ❑ *...his dubious abilities as a teacher.* If you are **suspicious** of a person, you do not trust them and think they might be involved in something dishonest or illegal. ❑ *I am suspicious of his intentions... Miss Lenaut had grown suspicious.* If you describe something as **suspicious,** it suggests behavior that is dishonest, illegal, or dangerous. ❑ *He listened for any suspicious sounds.*

★ **doubt·less** /daʊtlɪs/ ADV If you say that something is **doubtless** the case, you mean that you think it is probably or almost certainly the case. 大概；近乎无疑地 [ADV with cl/group] ❑ *He will doubtless try and persuade his colleagues to change their minds.* 他大概会尽力说服他的同事们改变主意。

▲ **dough** /doʊ/ (**doughs**) **1** N-MASS **Dough** is a fairly firm mixture of flour, water, and sometimes also fat and sugar. It can be cooked to make bread or pastry. 面团 ❑ *Roll out the dough into one large circle.* 将面团擀成一个大圆形。 **2** N-UNCOUNT You can refer to money as **dough.** 钱 [INFORMAL] ❑ *He worked hard for his dough.* 他为了赚钱而努力工作。

dough·nut /doʊnʌt, -nət/ (**doughnuts**) also **donut** N-COUNT A **doughnut** is a breadlike cake, often in the shape of a ring, made from sweet dough that has been cooked in hot fat. 甜面圈

dour /dʊər, daʊər/ ADJ If you describe someone as **dour,** you mean that they are very serious and unfriendly. 阴沉的 ❑ *...a dour, taciturn man.* …一个阴沉、寡言的男人。

douse /daʊs/ (**douses, dousing, doused**) also **dowse** **1** V-T If you **douse** a fire, you stop it from burning by pouring a lot of water over it. 浇灭 ❑ *The pumps were started and the crew began to douse the fire with water.* 抽水机启动了，船员们开始用水将火浇灭。 **2** V-T If you **douse** someone or something **with** a liquid, you throw a lot of that liquid over them. 浇 ❑ *They hurled abuse at their victim as they doused him with gasoline.* 他们边骂边往受害者身上浇汽油。

▲ **dove** (**doves**)

Pronounced /dʌv/ for meanings **1** and **2**, and /doʊv/ for meaning **3**.

义项**1**和**2**读作 /dʌv/，义项**3**读作 /doʊv/。

1 N-COUNT A **dove** is a bird that looks like a pigeon but is smaller and lighter in color. Doves are often used as a symbol of peace. 和平鸽 **2** N-COUNT In politics, you can refer to people who support the use of peaceful methods to solve difficult situations as **doves.** Compare **hawk.** 鸽派人物 ❑ *A clear split over tactics appears to be emerging between doves and hawks in the party.* 一个明显的战术上的分歧似乎正出现在党内主和派和主战派之间。 **3** **Dove** is sometimes used as the past tense of **dive.** dive的过去式

down
1. PREPOSITION AND ADVERB USES
2. ADJECTIVE USES
3. VERB USES
4. NOUN USES

❶ down ♦♦♦ /daʊn/

Down is often used with verbs of movement, such as "fall" and "pull," and also in phrasal verbs such as "bring down" and "calm down."

➪ **Please look at meaning 13 to see if the expression you are looking for is shown under another headword.** **1** PREP To go **down** something such as a slope or a pipe means to go toward the ground or to a lower level. 沿…而下 ❑ *We're going down a mountain.* 我们向山下走去。 ❑ *A man came down the stairs to meet them.* 一个男人走下台阶迎接他们。 ● ADV **Down** is also an adverb. 向下地 [ADV after v] ❑ *She went down to the kitchen again.* 她又下到厨房去了。 **2** PREP If you are a particular distance **down** something, you are that distance below the top or surface of it. 在…下方 [amount PREP n] ❑ *He managed to cling on to a ledge 40 feet down the rock face.* 他设法抓住了岩面下方40英尺处的岩脊。 ● ADV **Down** is also an adverb. 在下方地 [amount ADV] ❑ *At the bottom of the pit, some 1,300 feet down, are huge heaps of ore.* 在距地面大约一千三百英尺的坑底，有大堆的矿石。 **3** PREP If you go or look **down** something such as a road or river, you go or look along it. If you are **down** a road or river, you are somewhere along it. 沿着 ❑ *They set off at a jog up one street and down another.* 他们跑步出发，沿着一条街跑过来又沿另外一条街跑过去。 **4** ADV You use **down** to say that you are looking or facing in a direction that is toward the ground or toward a lower level. 向下 [ADV after v] ❑ *She was still looking down at her papers.* 她还在低头看着那些纸。 **5** ADV If you put something **down**, you put it onto a surface. (放) 到平面上 [ADV after v] ❑ *Danny put down his glass.* 丹尼放下他的玻璃杯。 **6** ADV If an amount of something goes **down**, it decreases. If an amount of something is **down**, it has decreased and is at a lower level than it was. 下降 ❑ *Interest rates came down today.* 利率今天下降了。 ❑ *Inflation will be down to three percent.* 通货膨胀将下降到3%。 **7** PHRASE **Down to** a particular detail means including everything, even that detail. **Down to** a particular person means including everyone, even that person. 甚至包括 ❑ *The bedroom was an exact replica of the original, perfect right down to the patterns on the wallpaper and the hairbrushes on the dressing table.* 这间卧室精确地复制了原来的房间，模仿之细甚至连墙纸的图案和梳妆台上的发刷都一模一样。 **8** PHRASE If you are **down to** a certain amount of something, you have only that amount left. 只剩下 ❑ *The poor man's down to his last $5.* 那个可怜的男人只剩下最后的5美元了。 **9** PHRASE If someone or something is **down for** a particular thing, it has been arranged that they will do that thing, or that thing will happen. 被安排做 ❑ *Mark had told me that he was down for an interview.* 马克已经告诉我他有个采访。 **10** PHRASE If you pay money **down** on something, you pay part of the money you owe for it. 部分支付 [mainly AM] ❑ *He had a simple, conventional deal and paid 20 percent down at settlement.* 他做了一笔简单而常规的交易，在结算时预付了20%的定金。 **11** → see also **put down** **12** PHRASE If people shout "**down with**" something or someone, they are saying that they dislike them and want to get rid of them. 打倒 [SPOKEN, DISAPPROVAL] ❑ *Demonstrators chanted "down with the rebels."* 游行的人群高呼"打倒叛乱分子！" **13** **up and down** → see **up**

❷ down /daʊn/ **1** ADJ If you are feeling **down**, you are feeling unhappy or depressed. 情绪不高的 [v-link ADJ] [INFORMAL] ❑ *The old man sounded really down.* 那位老人听起来情绪真的不高。 **2** ADJ If something is **down on** paper, it has been written on the paper. 记在纸上的 [v-link ADJ] ❑ *That date wasn't down on our news sheet.* 该日期没有写在我们的报导里。 **3** ADJ If a piece of equipment, especially a computer system, is **down**, it is temporarily not working. Compare **up**. 出故障的; 死机的 [v-link ADJ] ❑ *The computer's down again.* 那台电脑又死机了。

❸ down /daʊn/ (**downs, downing, downed**) **1** V-T If you say that someone **downs** food or a drink, you mean that they eat or drink it. 吃下; 喝下 ❑ *We downed bottles of local wine.* 我们喝了好几瓶本地酒。 **2** V-T If something or someone **is downed**, they fall to the ground because they have been hurt or damaged in some way. 击落 [JOURNALISM] ❑ *A couple of jet fighters were downed during the five-week rebellion.* 在为期5周的叛乱期间，有两三架喷气式战斗机被击落。

❹ down /daʊn/ **1** N-UNCOUNT **Down** consists of the small, soft feathers on young birds. **Down** is used to make bed-covers and pillows. 羽绒 ❑ *...goose down.* …鹅绒。 **2** N-UNCOUNT **Down** is very fine hair. 绒毛 ❑ *The whole plant is covered with fine down.* 整株植物上长满了绒毛。

down-and-out ADJ If you describe someone as **down-and-out**, you mean that they have no job and nowhere to live, and they have no real hope of improving their situation. 穷困潦倒的 ❑ *...a short story about a down-and-out advertising copywriter.* …一篇关于一个穷困潦倒的广告撰稿人的短篇小说。

Word Link	*down ≈ below, lower : downfall, downhill, downstairs*

▲ **down·fall** /daʊnfɔl/ (**downfalls**) **1** N-COUNT The **downfall** of a successful or powerful person or institution is their loss of success or power. 垮台 ❑ *His lack of experience had led to his downfall.* 他的缺乏经验导致了他的垮台。 **2** N-COUNT The thing that was a person's **downfall** caused them to fail or lose power. 败落的原因 ❑ *Jeremy's honesty had been his downfall.* 诚实是杰里米失败的原因。

▲ **down·grade** /daʊngreɪd/ (**downgrades, downgrading, downgraded**) **1** V-T If something **is downgraded**, it is given less importance than it used to have or than you think it should have. 降级 [usu passive] ❑ *The boy's condition has been downgraded from critical to serious.* 那个男孩的病情得到了缓解，从危急降为重症。 **2** V-T If someone **is downgraded**, their job or status is changed so that they become less important or receive less money. 降职 ❑ *There was no criticism of her work until after she was downgraded.* 直到她被降职之后，才有人开始对她的工作说三道四。

down·hill /daʊnhɪl/ **1** ADV If something or someone is moving **downhill** or is **downhill**, they are moving down a slope or are located toward the bottom of a hill. 下坡地 ❑ *He headed downhill toward the river.* 他朝山脚下的小河走去。 ● ADJ **Downhill** is also an adjective. 下坡的 [ADJ n] ❑ *...downhill ski runs.* …向下的滑雪坡道。 **2** ADV If you say that something **is going downhill**, you mean that it is becoming worse or less successful. (走) 下坡路地 ❑ *Since I started to work longer hours things have gone steadily downhill.* 自从我延长了工作时间以后，情况不断恶化。 **3** ADJ If you say that a task or situation is **downhill** after a particular stage or time, you mean that it is easy to deal with after that stage or time. 顺利的 [v-link ADJ] ❑ *Well, I guess it's all downhill from here.* 好，我想从现在起该一帆风顺了。

down·load /daʊnloʊd/ (**downloads, downloading, downloaded**) V-T To **download** data means to transfer it to or from a computer along a line such as a telephone line, a radio link, or a computer network. 下载 ❑ *Users can download their material to a desktop PC back in the office.* 用户们可以将他们的资料下载到办公室的台式计算机上。

down·load·able /daʊnloʊdəᵊl/ ADJ If a computer file or program is **downloadable**, it can be downloaded to another computer. 可下载的 [usu ADJ n] [COMPUTING] ❑ *...downloadable computer games.* …可下载的电脑游戏。

down·market /daʊnmɑrkɪt/ also **down-market** ADJ **Downmarket** means the same as **downscale**. 面向大众的 [BRIT]

down pay·ment (**down payments**) also **downpayment** N-COUNT If you make a **down payment on** something, you pay only a percentage of the total cost when you buy it. You then finish paying for it later, usually by paying a certain amount every month. 首付款 ❑ *Celeste asked for the money as a down payment on an old farmhouse.* 西莱斯特索要那笔钱用作一座旧农舍的首付款。

▲ **down·play** /daʊnpleɪ/ (**downplays, downplaying, downplayed**) V-T If you **downplay** a fact or feature, you try to make people think that it is less important or serious than it really is. 轻描淡写 ❑ *Police sources yesterday downplayed the significance of the security breach.* 警方昨天的消息对这次安全缺口的重要性轻描淡写。

down·pour /daʊnpɔr/ (**downpours**) N-COUNT A **downpour** is a sudden and unexpected heavy fall of rain. 瓢泼大雨 ❑ *...sheltering from a sudden downpour of rain.* …躲避一场突如其来的瓢泼大雨。

down·right /daʊnraɪt/ ADV You use **downright** to emphasize unpleasant or bad qualities or behavior. (强调不快或负面事物) 彻头彻尾地 [ADV adj] [EMPHASIS] ❑ *...ideas that would have been downright dangerous if put into practice.* …那些如果付诸实施会十足危险的想法。 ● ADJ **Downright** is also an adjective. 彻头彻尾的 [ADJ n] ❑ *...downright bad manners.* …彻头彻尾的无礼行为。

★ **down·side** /daʊnsaɪd/ N-SING The **downside of** a situation is the aspect of it which is less positive, pleasant, or useful than its other aspects. 不利的一面 ❑ *The downside of this approach is a lack of clear leadership.* 这种方式的不足之处是缺乏明确的指挥。

down·size /daʊnsaɪz/ (**downsizes, downsizing, downsized**) V-T/V-I To **downsize** something such as a business or industry means to make it smaller. 使缩小规模 [BUSINESS] ❑ *American manufacturing organizations have been downsizing their factories.* 美国制造商们一直在缩小他们工厂的规模。 ❑ *...today's downsized economy.* … 今天萎缩了的经济。 ● **down·siz·ing** N-UNCOUNT 缩小规模 ❑ *...a trend toward downsizing in the personal computer market.* …个人电脑市场规模缩小的趋势。

down·stairs /daʊnstɛərz/ **1** ADV If you go **downstairs** in a building, you go down a staircase toward the ground floor. 往楼下

[ADV after v] ❑ *Denise went downstairs and made some tea.* 丹尼丝下楼沏茶。 **2** ADV If something or someone is **downstairs** in a building, they are on the ground floor or on a lower floor than you. 在楼下 ❑ *The telephone was downstairs in the entrance hall.* 电话在楼下的门厅里。 **3** ADJ **Downstairs** means situated on the ground floor of a building or on a lower floor than you are. 在楼下的 [ADJ n] ❑ *She repainted the downstairs rooms and closed off the second floor.* 她重新粉刷了楼下的房间，并把二楼封上了。 **4** N-SING **The downstairs** of a building is its lower floor or floors. 下面的楼层 ❑ *The downstairs of the two little houses had been entirely refashioned.* 两座小房子的底层已彻底翻新过了。

D

down·stream /daʊnstrim/ ADV Something that is moving **downstream** is moving toward the mouth of a river, from a point further up the river. Something that is **downstream** is further toward the mouth of a river than where you are. 朝下游方向; 在下游 ❑ *We had drifted downstream.* 我们向下游漂去。 ● ADJ **Downstream** is also an adjective. 下游的 [ADJ n] ❑ *Breaking the dam could submerge downstream cities such as Wuhan.* 毁坏大坝可能会淹没武汉这样的下游城市。

down·swing /daʊnswɪŋ/ (**downswings**) N-COUNT A **downswing** is a sudden downward movement in something such as an economy, that had previously been improving. 突然下滑 ❑ *Industry may disappear if the manufacturing economy remains on a downswing.* 如果制造业持续下滑，工业可能会不复存在。

down·time /daʊntaɪm/ **1** N-UNCOUNT In industry, **downtime** is the time during which machinery or equipment is not operating. (机器、设备的) 停止运行期 ❑ *On the production line, downtime has been reduced from 55% to 26%.* 生产线的停工期已经从55%下降到了26%。 **2** N-UNCOUNT In computing, **downtime** is time when a computer is not working. (计算机的) 停机时间 ❑ *Downtime due to worm removal from networks cost close to $450 million.* 由于停机查杀网络病毒而造成的耗费接近4.5亿美元。 **3** N-UNCOUNT **Downtime** is time when people are relaxing or not working. 工间休息时间 [mainly AM] ❑ *Downtime in Hollywood can cost a lot of money.* 好莱坞的工间休息会耗费不少钱。

down-to-earth ADJ If you say that someone is **down-to-earth**, you approve of the fact that they concern themselves with practical things and actions, rather than with abstract theories. 脚踏实地的 [APPROVAL] ❑ *Gloria is probably the most down-to-earth person I've ever met.* 格洛丽亚可能是我见过的最脚踏实地的人。

down·town ♦♦◇ /daʊntaʊn/ ADJ **Downtown** places are in or toward the center of a large town or city, where the stores and places of business are. 市中心的 [ADJ n] [mainly AM] ❑ *...an office in downtown Chicago.* …芝加哥市中心的一间办公室。 ● ADV **Downtown** is also an adverb. 在市中心 ❑ *By day he worked downtown for American Standard.* 白天，他在市中心为美国标准公司工作。 ● N-UNCOUNT **Downtown** is also a noun. 市中心 [oft "the" N] ❑ *...in a large vacant area of the downtown.* …在市中心的一大块空地上。

down·trend /daʊntrɛnd/ N-SING A **downtrend** is a general downward movement in something such as a company's profits or the economy. 下滑 ❑ *The increase slowed to 0.4 percent, possibly indicating the start of a downtrend.* 增长减缓到了0.4%，可能预示着下滑的开始。

down·turn /daʊntɜrn/ (**downturns**) N-COUNT If there is a **downturn** in the economy or in a company or industry, it becomes worse or less successful than it had been. 衰退 ❑ *They predicted a severe economic downturn.* 他们预言将会有一次严重的经济衰退。

down un·der PHRASE People sometimes refer to Australia and New Zealand as **down under**. 澳大利亚和新西兰 [INFORMAL] ❑ *For summer skiing down under, there is no better place than New Zealand.* 夏天要去澳大利亚和新西兰滑雪，没有比新西兰更好的地方了。

down·ward /daʊnwərd/

> The form **downwards** is also used for the adverb.

1 ADJ A **downward** movement or look is directed toward a lower place or a lower level. 向下的 [ADJ n] ❑ *...a firm downward movement of the hands.* …一个坚定有力的双手向下的动作。 **2** ADJ If you refer to a **downward** trend, you mean that something is decreasing or that a situation is getting worse. 逐渐下降的; 日趋恶化的 [ADJ n] ❑ *The downward trend in home ownership is likely to continue.* 住房拥有率的下降趋势有可能还要延续。 **3** ADV If you move or look **downward**, you move or look toward the ground or a lower level. 朝下地 ❑ *Benedict pointed downward again with his stick.* 贝内迪克特又用他的拐杖向下指了指。 **4** ADV If an amount or rate moves **downward**, it decreases. 下降地 [ADV after v] ❑ *Inflation is moving firmly downward.* 通货膨胀在稳步下降。 **5** ADV If you want to emphasize that a statement applies to everyone in an organization, you can say that it applies from its leader **downward**. 往下地 ["from" n ADV] [EMPHASIS] ❑ *...from the president downward.* …自总经理而下。

dowse /daʊs/ (**dowses, dowsing, dowsed**) → see **douse**

▲ **doze** /doʊz/ (**dozes, dozing, dozed**) V-I When you **doze**, you sleep lightly or for a short period, especially during the daytime. 打盹儿 ❑ *For a while she dozed fitfully.* 她断断续续地小睡了片刻。
→ see **sleep**

▸ **doze off** PHRASAL VERB If you **doze off**, you fall into a light sleep, especially during the daytime. 打瞌睡 (尤指在白天) ❑ *I closed my eyes for a minute and must have dozed off.* 我闭了会儿眼，后来一定是睡着了。

doz·en ♦♦◇ /dʌzᵊn/ (**dozens**)

> The plural form is **dozen** after a number, or after a word or expression referring to a number, such as "several" or "a few."

1 NUM If you have **a dozen** things, you have twelve of them. 12 ❑ *You will be able to take ten dozen bottles free of duty through customs.* 你可以携带120瓶免税通过海关。 **2** NUM You can refer to a group of approximately twelve things or people as **a dozen**. You can refer to a group of approximately six things or people as **half a dozen**. 大约一打 ❑ *In half a dozen words, he had explained the bond that linked them.* 他用五六个字解释了将他们联系在一起的那种关系。 **3** QUANT If you refer to **dozens of** things or people, you are emphasizing that there are very many of them. 许多 [QUANT "of" pl-n] [EMPHASIS] ❑ *...a storm which destroyed dozens of homes and buildings.* …一场毁坏了许多房屋和建筑物的暴风雨。 ● PRON You can also use **dozens** as a pronoun. 许多东西 ❑ *Just as revealing are Mr. Johnson's portraits, of which there are dozens.* 透过约翰逊先生的许多肖像画同样也可以了解其人。

Dr. ♦♦◇ (**Drs.**) **Dr.** is a written abbreviation for **Doctor**. 医生; 博士

> in BRIT, use **Dr**

❑ *...Dr. John Hardy of St. Mary's Medical School.* …圣玛丽医学院的约翰・哈迪医生。

drab /dræb/ (**drabber, drabbest**) ADJ If you describe something as **drab**, you think that it is dull and boring to look at or experience. 单调乏味的 ❑ *...his drab little office.* …他那狭小、乏味的办公室。 ● **drab·ness** N-UNCOUNT 单调乏味 ❑ *...the dusty drabness of nearby villages.* …附近村庄尘土飞扬，死气沉沉。

dra·co·nian /dreɪkoʊniən, drə-/ ADJ **Draconian** laws or measures are extremely harsh and severe. 严酷的 (法令或措施) [FORMAL] ❑ *...indications that there would be no draconian measures to lower U.S. health care costs.* …迹象表明将不会有严厉的措施来降低美国的医疗成本。

draft ♦◇◇ /dræft/ (**drafts, drafting, drafted**) **1** N-COUNT A **draft** is an early version of a letter, book, or speech. 草稿; 初稿 ❑ *I rewrote his rough draft, which was published under my name.* 我改写了他那篇以我的名义发表了的初稿。 ❑ *I faxed a first draft of this article to him.* 我把这篇文章的初稿传真给他。 **2** N-COUNT A **draft** is a written order for payment of money by a bank, especially from one bank to another. 汇票 ❑ *Payments must be made in U.S. dollars by a bank draft drawn to the order of the United Nations Postal Administration.* 付款必须用开给联合国邮政管理处的银行汇票，并以美元支付。 **3** N-COUNT A **draft** is a current of air that comes into a place in an undesirable way. (钻进某处的) 风 [AM]

> in BRIT, use **draught**

❑ *Block drafts around doors and windows.* 挡住门窗周围的风。 **4** V-T When you **draft** a letter, book, or speech, you write the first version of it. 起草 ❑ *He drafted a letter to the editors.* 他草拟了一封给编辑的信。 **5** V-T If you **are drafted**, you are ordered to serve in the armed forces, usually for a limited period of time. 征兵 [usu passive] [mainly AM] ❑ *During the Second World War, he was drafted into the U.S. Army.* 第二次世界大战期间，他应征加入美国陆军。 **6** V-T If people **are drafted** to do something, they are asked to do a particular job. 选派 ❑ *She hoped that Fox could be drafted to run the organization.* 她希望福克斯能够被选派来掌管这个组织。 **7** N-SING **The draft** is the practice of ordering people to serve in the armed forces, usually for a limited period of time. 征兵 [mainly AM] ❑ *...his effort to avoid the draft.* …他逃避兵役的努力。

Word Partnership *draft* 的常用搭配:

ADJ. **final** draft, **rough** draft 1
V. **revise a** draft, **write a** draft 1
feel a draft 3
dodge the draft 7
N. **bank** draft 2
draft **a letter,** draft **a speech** 4

drag ♦◇◇ /dræg/ (**drags, dragging, dragged**) 1 V-T If you **drag** something, you pull it along the ground, often with difficulty. (费力地) 拖 ❑ *He got up and dragged his chair toward the table.* 他站起来，把椅子拖向桌子。 2 V-T To **drag** a computer image means to use the mouse to move the position of the image on the screen, or to change its size or shape. (用鼠标) 拖 [COMPUTING] ❑ *Use your mouse to drag the pictures to their new size.* 用鼠标拖拽图片到新尺寸。 3 V-T If someone **drags** you somewhere, they pull you there, or force you to go there by physically threatening you. 硬拉; 硬拽 ❑ *The vigilantes dragged the men out of the vehicles.* 治安联防员将这些人从车里拽了出来。 4 V-T If someone **drags** you somewhere you do not want to go, they make you go there. 强迫 ❑ *When you can drag him away from his work, he can also be a devoted father.* 当你能强迫他远离工作的时候，他也可以是个充满爱心的父亲。 5 V-T If you say that you **drag yourself** somewhere, you are emphasizing that you have to make a very great effort to go there. 勉强 [EMPHASIS] ❑ *I find it really hard to drag myself out and exercise regularly.* 我发现实在很难强迫自己定期出来锻炼。 6 V-T If you **drag** your foot or your leg behind you, you walk with great difficulty because your foot or leg is injured in some way. 拖着 (受伤的脚或腿) 行走 ❑ *He was barely able to drag his poisoned leg behind him.* 他勉强拖着中了毒的腿向前走。 7 V-T If the police **drag** a river or lake, they pull nets or hooks across the bottom of it in order to look for something. (用网或钩) 在水中搜寻 ❑ *Police are planning to drag the pond later this morning.* 警方正计划今天上午晚些时候在池塘里进行打捞搜寻。 8 V-I If a period of time or an event **drags**, it is very boring and seems to last a long time. (时间或事件) 拖沓 ❑ *The minutes dragged past.* 时间一分一分地过去了。 9 N-SING If something is **a drag on** the development or progress of something, it slows it down or makes it more difficult. 阻碍 ❑ *The satellite acts as a drag on the shuttle.* 卫星是对航天飞机发展的阻碍。 10 N-SING If you say that something is **a drag**, you mean that it is unpleasant or very dull. 讨厌的事; 很没意思的事 [INFORMAL, DISAPPROVAL] ❑ *As far as shopping for clothes goes, it's a drag.* 买衣服在某种程度上是个挺没意思的事。 11 N-COUNT If you take a **drag on** a cigarette or pipe that you are smoking, you take in air through it. (抽烟时的) 一嘬 [INFORMAL] ❑ *He took a drag on his cigarette, and exhaled the smoke.* 他嘬了口烟，然后吐出烟雾。 12 N-UNCOUNT **Drag** is the wearing of women's clothes by a male entertainer. (喜剧演员) 男扮女装 ❑ *Drag has been with us since the birth of comedy, because it's funny to see a man pretending to be a woman.* 自喜剧诞生时就有男演员反串的表演，因为看男人假扮女人很有趣。 ● PHRASE If a man is **in drag**, he is wearing women's clothes. (男子) 穿着女装 13 PHRASE If you **drag** your **feet** or **drag** your **heels**, you delay doing something or do it very slowly because you do not want to do it. 拖延 ❑ *The government was dragging its feet, and this was threatening moves toward peace.* 政府一拖再拖，这是有碍和平的行径。
→ see **flight**

▶ **drag out** 1 PHRASAL VERB If you **drag** something **out**, you make it last for longer than is necessary. 拖延 ❑ *...a company that was willing and able to drag out the proceedings for years.* …一家愿意并能够把进程拖延多年的公司。 2 PHRASAL VERB If you **drag** something **out of** a person, you persuade them to tell you something that they do not want to tell you. (从某人口里) 套出 (某事) ❑ *The families soon discovered that every piece of information had to be dragged out of the authorities.* 这些家庭很快发现，每条消息都必须从官方那里套出来。

drag·on /drægən/ (**dragons**) N-COUNT In stories and legends, a **dragon** is an animal like a big lizard. It has wings and claws, and breathes out fire. 龙
→ see **fantasy**

dragon·fly /drægənflaɪ/ (**dragonflies**) N-COUNT **Dragonflies** are brightly colored insects with long, thin bodies and two sets of wings. Dragonflies are often found near slow-moving water. 蜻蜓

drain ♦◇◇ /dreɪn/ (**drains, draining, drained**) 1 V-T/V-I If you **drain** a liquid from a place or object, you remove the liquid by causing it to flow somewhere else. If a liquid **drains** somewhere, it flows there. 使流走; 流走 ❑ *Miners built the tunnel to drain water out of the mines.* 矿工们开掘了隧道以将水排出矿井。 ❑ *Now the focus is on draining the water.* 现在的焦点是排水。 2 V-T/V-I If you **drain** a place or object, you dry it by causing water to flow out of it. If a place or object **drains**, water flows out of it until it is dry. 排干; 沥干 ❑ *The authorities have mobilized vast numbers of people to drain flooded land and build or repair dikes.* 当局动员了大批民众为遭受洪灾的地区排涝并修建或修复堤坝。 3 V-T/V-I If you **drain** food or if food **drains**, you remove the liquid that it has been in, especially after it has been cooked or soaked in water. 使沥干; 沥干 ❑ *Drain the pasta well, arrange on four plates and pour over the sauce.* 把意大利面条沥干水，摆放在4个盘子里，倒上调味品。 4 V-T/V-I If the color or the blood **drains** or **is drained from** someone's face, they become very pale. You can also say that someone's face **drains** or **is drained of** color. 使 (色泽) 消退; (色泽) 消退 [LITERARY] ❑ *Harry felt the color drain from his face.* 亨利感到脸上没有了血色。 5 V-T If something **drains** you, it leaves you feeling physically and emotionally exhausted. 使心力交瘁 ❑ *My emotional turmoil had drained me.* 困惑焦灼的情绪使我心力交瘁。 ● **drained** ADJ 使心力交瘁的 ❑ *I began to suffer from headaches, which left me feeling completely drained.* 我开始感到头痛，它使我感到精疲力竭。 ● **drain·ing** ADJ 使心力交瘁的 ❑ *This work is physically exhausting and emotionally draining.* 这项工作是极度耗费体力和劳累心力的。 6 V-T If you say that a country's or a company's resources or finances **are drained**, you mean that they are used or spent completely. 耗尽 (资源、资金) ❑ *The state's finances have been drained by drought and civil disorder.* 国家财政已经被旱灾和内乱消耗殆尽了。 7 N-COUNT A **drain** is a pipe that carries water or sewage away from a place, or an opening in a surface that leads to the pipe. 排水管; 下水道; 排水沟 ❑ *Tony built his own house and laid his own drains.* 托尼盖了自己的房子，铺设了自己的排水管道。 8 N-SING If you say that something is **a drain on** an organization's finances or resources, you mean that it costs the organization a large amount of money, and you do not think that it is worth it. (资源、资金的) 外流; 消耗 ❑ *...an ultramodern printing plant, which has been a big drain on resources.* …一个消耗大量资源的超级现代化印刷厂。 9 PHRASE If you say that something **is going down the drain**, you mean that it is being destroyed or wasted. 被破坏掉; 被浪费掉 [INFORMAL] ❑ *They were aware that their public image was rapidly going down the drain.* 他们意识到自己的公众形象正被迅速地破坏掉。
→ see **plumbing**

★ **drain·age** /dreɪnɪdʒ/ N-UNCOUNT **Drainage** is the system or process by which water or other liquids are drained from a place. 排水; 排水系统 ❑ *Line the pots with pebbles to ensure good drainage.* 在这些花盆里铺上一层卵石以确保良好的排水性。
→ see **farm**

dra·ma ♦◇◇ /drɑmə, dræmə/ (**dramas**) 1 N-COUNT A **drama** is a serious play for the theater, television, or radio, or a serious movie. 戏剧 ❑ *He acted in radio dramas.* 他演过广播剧。 ❑ *The movie is a drama about a woman searching for her children.* 这部电影是关于一个女人寻找她孩子的戏。 2 N-UNCOUNT You use **drama** to refer to plays in general or to work that is connected with plays and the theater, such as acting or producing. 戏剧; 戏剧工作 ❑ *He knew nothing of Greek drama.* 他对希腊戏剧一无所知。 3 N-VAR You can refer to a real situation which is exciting or distressing as **drama**. 戏剧性场面 ❑ *There was none of the drama and relief of a hostage release.* 丝毫没有人质释放的戏剧性场面和放松。
→ see **genre**

dra·mat·ic ♦♦◇ /drəmætɪk/ 1 ADJ A **dramatic** change or event happens suddenly and is very noticeable and surprising. 突然引人注目的 ❑ *A fifth year of drought is expected to have dramatic effects on the California economy.* 预计连续干旱的第五个年头将对加利福尼亚州的经济产生引人注目的影响。 ● **dra·mati·cal·ly** /drəmætɪkli/ ADV 突然引人注目地 ❑ *At speeds above 50 mph, serious injuries dramatically increase.* 时速超过50英里时，重伤机率急剧上升。 2 ADJ A **dramatic** action, event, or situation is exciting and impressive. 紧张刺激的; 扣人心弦的 ❑ *He witnessed many dramatic escapes as people jumped from as high as the fourth floor.* 当人们从4层楼那么高的地方跳下来的时候，他目睹了许多惊心动魄的逃生情景。 ● **dra·mati·cal·ly** ADV 戏剧性地 ❑ *He tipped his head to one side and sighed dramatically.* 他把头偏向一侧，戏剧性地叹了口气。 3 ADJ You use **dramatic** to describe things connected with or relating to the theater, drama, or plays. 戏剧的; 有关戏剧的 [ADJ n] ❑ *...a dramatic arts major in college.* …一个在学院主修戏剧艺术专业的学生。

drama·tise /dræmətaɪz/ [BRIT] → see **dramatize**

drama·tist /dræmətɪst/ (**dramatists**) N-COUNT A **dramatist** is someone who writes plays. 剧作家

drama·tize /dræmətaɪz/ (**dramatizes, dramatizing, dramatized**)

in BRIT, also use **dramatise**

1 V-T If a book or story **is dramatized**, it is written or presented as a play, movie, or television drama. 把（小说、故事等）改编为剧本 [usu passive] ❑ *...an incident later dramatized in the movie "The Right Stuff."* …一个事件后来被改编成了电影《太空先锋》。

● **drama·ti·za·tion** /dræmətɪzeɪʃən/ N-COUNT (**dramatizations**) 改编成的戏剧；改编成的剧本 ❑ *...a dramatization of D. H. Lawrence's novel, "Lady Chatterley's Lover."* …根据D. H. 劳伦斯的小说《查泰莱夫人的情人》改编的剧本。 2 V-T If you say that someone **dramatizes** a situation or event, you mean that they try to make it seem more serious, more important, or more exciting than it really is. 使戏剧化；渲染 [DISAPPROVAL] ❑ *They have a tendency to show off, to dramatize almost every situation.* 他们有一种炫耀的倾向，几乎任何情况都要大肆渲染一番。

drank /dræŋk/ **Drank** is the past tense of **drink**. **drink**的过去式

drape /dreɪp/ (**drapes, draping, draped**) 1 V-T If you **drape** a piece of cloth somewhere, you place it there so that it hangs down in a casual and graceful way. 将…披挂于 ❑ *Natasha took the coat and draped it over her shoulders.* 娜塔莎拿起外套，披在肩上。 2 V-T If someone or something **is draped in** a piece of cloth, they are loosely covered by it. 覆盖 ❑ *...a casket draped in the Virginia flag.* …一口覆盖着弗吉尼亚州旗的棺材。 3 N-COUNT **Drapes** are long heavy curtains. （长且重的）帘子 [AM]

in BRIT, use **curtains**

❑ *He pulled the drapes shut, locked the door behind him.* 他拉上长帘，锁上了身后的门。

★ **dras·tic** /dræstɪk/ 1 ADJ If you have to take **drastic** action in order to solve a problem, you have to do something extreme to solve it. 极端的 ❑ *Drastic measures are needed to clean up the profession.* 需要采取极端的措施来整顿这个行业。 2 ADJ A **drastic** change is a very great change. 剧烈的 ❑ *Foreign food aid has led to a drastic reduction in the numbers of people dying of starvation.* 外国的食品援助使得因饥饿而死亡的人数大幅下降。 ● **dras·ti·cal·ly** ADV 剧烈地 [ADV with V] ❑ *As a result, services have been drastically reduced.* 结果，服务被大大减少了。

draught /drɑːft, dræft/ [BRIT] → see **draft**

draughts /dræfts/ N-UNCOUNT **Draughts** is the same as **checkers**. 国际跳棋 [BRIT]

draw

1 MAKE A PICTURE
2 MOVE, PULL, OR TAKE
3 OTHER USES AND PHRASAL VERBS

1 draw ◆◆◆ /drɔ/ (**draws, drawing, drew, drawn**)

➪ **Please look at meaning 2 to see if the expression you are looking for is shown under another headword.** 1 V-T/V-I When you **draw**, or when you **draw** something, you use a pencil or pen to produce a picture, pattern, or diagram. 画 ❑ *She would sit there drawing with the pencil stub.* 她会坐在那儿用铅笔头画画。 ● **draw·ing** N-UNCOUNT 画画 ❑ *I like dancing, singing, and drawing.* 我喜欢跳舞、唱歌和画画。 2 to **draw the line** → see **line**

→ see **animation, drawing**

2 draw ◆◆◆ /drɔ/ (**draws, drawing, drew, drawn**)

➪ **Please look at meaning 15 to see if the expression you are looking for is shown under another headword.** 1 V-I If you **draw** somewhere, you move there slowly. 缓慢移动 [WRITTEN] ❑ *She drew away and did not smile.* 她慢步走开，面无笑容。 2 V-T If you **draw** something or someone in a particular direction, you move them in that direction, usually by pulling them gently. 轻拖；轻拉 [WRITTEN] ❑ *He drew his chair nearer the fire.* 他把椅子轻轻拉近火边。 ❑ *He put his arm around Caroline's shoulders and drew her close to him.* 他把手臂搂在卡罗琳的肩膀上并且把她轻轻拉近自己。 3 V-T When you **draw** a curtain or blind, you pull it across a window, either to cover or to uncover it. 拉（窗帘等） ❑ *After drawing the curtains, she lit a candle.* 拉上窗帘后，她点了一根蜡烛。 4 V-T If someone **draws** a gun, knife, or other weapon, they pull it out of its container and threaten you with it. 拔出（武器） ❑ *He drew his dagger and turned to face his pursuers.* 他拔出匕首并且转过身去面对追他的人。 5 V-I When a vehicle **draws** somewhere, it moves there smoothly and steadily. 平稳地前进 ❑ *Claire had seen the taxi drawing away.* 克莱尔看着出租车缓缓驶走。 6 V-T If you **draw** a deep breath, you breathe in deeply once. 吸入 ❑ *He paused, drawing a deep breath.* 他停下，深吸了一口气。 7 V-I If you **draw on** a cigarette, you breathe the smoke from it into your mouth or lungs. 吸烟 ❑ *He drew on an American cigarette.* 他吸了一口美国香烟。 8 V-T To **draw** something such as water or energy **from** a particular source means to take it from that source. 汲取（水、能源等）；提取（水、能源等） ❑ *Villagers still have to draw their water from wells.* 村民仍然要从井里打水。 9 V-T If something that hits you or presses part of your body **draws** blood, it cuts your skin so that it bleeds. 抽（血） ❑ *Any practice that draws blood could increase the risk of getting the virus.* 任何形式抽血都能增加感染病毒的危险。 10 V-T If you **draw** money out of a bank account, you get it from the account so that you can use it. 提取（钱款） ❑ *She was drawing ou cash from an ATM.* 她那时正在从自动取款机上取钱。 11 V-T To **draw** something means to choose it or to be given it, as part of a competition, game, or lottery. 抽（奖）；抽（签） ❑ *He put the pile of chips in the center of the table and drew a card.* 他把一堆筹码放在桌子中央，抽了一张牌。 ● N-COUNT **Draw** is also a noun. 抽奖；抽签 ❑ *...the final draw for all prize winners takes place on March 17.* …最后一轮所有获奖者的抽签在3月17日举行。 12 V-T To **draw** something **from** a particular thing or place means to take or get it from that thing or place. 取得 ❑ *I draw strength from the millions of women who have faced this challenge successfully.* 我从许许多多成功面对这种挑战的妇女身上获得了力量。 13 V-T If something such as a movie or an event **draws** a lot of people, it is so interesting or entertaining that a lot of people go to it. 吸引 ❑ *The game is currently drawing huge crowds.* 这项比赛目前正吸引着大批群众。 14 V-T If someone or something **draws** you, it attracts you very strongly. 强烈吸引 ❑ *In no sense did he draw and enthral her as Alex had done.* 他远不如亚历克斯那么强烈地吸引她，让她着迷。 15 to **draw lots** → see **lot**

3 draw ◆◆◆ /drɔ/ (**draws, drawing, drew, drawn**) 1 V-T If you **draw** a particular conclusion, you decide that that conclusion is true. 得出（结论） ❑ *He draws two conclusions from this.* 他由此得出两个结论。 2 V-T If you **draw** a comparison, parallel, or distinction, you compare or contrast two different ideas, systems, or other things. 作出（比较）；加以（区别） ❑ *...literary critics drawing comparisons between George Sand and George Eliot.* …把乔治·桑和乔治·艾略特进行比较的文学评论家。 3 V-T If you **draw** someone's attention to something, you make them aware of it or make them think about it. 使注意 ❑ *He was waving his arms to draw their attention.* 他正挥动手臂吸引他们的注意力。 4 V-T If someone or something **draw** a particular reaction, people react to it in that way. 引起（某种反 ❑ *Such a policy would inevitably draw fierce resistance from farmers.* 这样的政策将不可避免地引起农民的激烈抵制。 5 V-RECIP In a game or competition, if one person or team **draws with** another one, or if two people or teams **draw**, they have the same number of points or goals at the end of the game. （在游戏或竞赛中）打平 [mainly BRI

in AM, usually use **tie**

❑ *Holland and the Republic of Ireland drew one-one.* 荷兰队与爱尔兰队一一平。 ❑ *We drew with Ireland in the first game.* 我们同爱尔兰队在第一局打成平局。 ● N-COUNT **Draw** is also a noun. 平局 6 → see also **drawi** 7 PHRASE When an event or period of time **draws to a close** or **draw to an end**, it finishes. 结束 ❑ *Another celebration had drawn to its close.* 另一个庆典已经结束了。 8 PHRASE If an event or period of time **is drawing closer** or **is drawing nearer**, it is approaching. 来临；临近 ❑ *Next spring's elections are drawing closer.* 下一个春季选举即将来临。

▸ **draw in** PHRASAL VERB If you **draw** someone **in** or **draw** them **into** something you are involved with, you cause them to become involved with it. 使参与 ❑ *It won't be easy for you to draw him in.* 你要把他拉进来可不容易。

▸ **draw on** PHRASAL VERB If you **draw on** or **draw upon** something such as your skill or experience, you make use of it in order to do something. 利用 ❑ *He drew on his experience as a yachtsman to make a documentary program.* 他利用当过游艇驾驶员的经历来制作纪录片。

▸ **draw up** PHRASAL VERB If you **draw up** a document, list, or plan, you prepare it and write it out. 起草 ❑ *They agreed to establish a working party to draw up a formal agreement.* 他们同意成立一个工作组来起草一份正式协议。

▸ **draw upon** → see **draw on**

Word Web drawing

The first thing **art** students must learn is how to **draw**. They often carry sketchbooks and soft **graphite pencils** around with them. You'll see them sitting and **sketching** everyday objects and **scenes**. Many famous **works of art** began as simple **pen and ink drawings**. For example, Leonardo da Vinci* did several **sketches** before he started painting "The Last Supper"*. Other sketching materials include **charcoal sticks** and **pastels**. They allow greater shading. However, they require fixative to prevent **smudging**.

Leonardo da Vinci (1452-1519): an Italian artist.
"The Last Supper": a famous painting.

Thesaurus *draw* 另参见:

v. illustrate, sketch, trace ❶ 1
bring out, pull out, take out ❷ 4
inhale ❷ 6 7
extract, take ❷ 8 12
conclude, decide, make a decision, settle on ❸ 1

draw·back /drɔbæk/ (**drawbacks**) N-COUNT A **drawback** is an aspect of something or someone that makes them less acceptable than they would otherwise be. 缺点；障碍 ❑ *He felt the apartment's only drawback was that it was too small.* 他感觉这个公寓惟一的缺点就是太小。

drawer /drɔr/ (**drawers**) N-COUNT A **drawer** is part of a desk, chest, or other piece of furniture that is shaped like a box and is designed for putting things in. You pull it toward you to open it. 抽屉 ❑ *She opened her desk drawer and took out the manual.* 她打开书桌抽屉，拿出手册。

draw·ing /drɔɪŋ/ (**drawings**) 1 N-COUNT A **drawing** is a picture made with a pencil or pen. 素描 ❑ *She did a drawing of me.* 她为我画了素描。 2 → see also **draw 1**
→ see Word Web: **drawing**

draw·ing pin (**drawing pins**) also **drawing-pin** N-COUNT A **drawing pin** is the same as a **thumbtack**. 图钉 [BRIT]

draw·ing room (**drawing rooms**) N-COUNT A **drawing room** is a room, especially a large room in a large house, where people sit and relax, or entertain guests. 客厅 [mainly BRIT, OLD-FASHIONED]

drawl /drɔl/ (**drawls, drawling, drawled**) V-T/V-I If someone **drawls**, they speak slowly and not very clearly, with long vowel sounds. 拉长声调说话 ❑ *"I guess you guys don't mind if I smoke?" he drawled.* "我想大家不会介意我抽烟吧？"他拉长声调说。 ● N-COUNT **Drawl** is also a noun. 拉长声调说出的话 ❑ *Jack's southern drawl had become more pronounced as they'd traveled southward.* 随着他们愈往南行，杰克拖腔拉调的南方口音就愈发明显了。

drawn /drɔn/ 1 **Drawn** is the past participle of **draw**. draw的过去式 2 ADJ If someone or their face looks **drawn**, their face is thin and they look very tired, ill, worried, or unhappy. 憔悴的 ❑ *She looked drawn and tired when she turned toward me.* 她转向我时，看上去既憔悴又疲惫。

drawn-out ADJ You can describe something as **drawn-out** when it lasts or takes longer than you would like it to. 拖延的 ❑ *The road to peace will be long and drawn-out.* 通向和平的路将是漫长而延宕的。

★ **dread** /drɛd/ (**dreads, dreading, dreaded**) 1 V-T If you **dread** something which may happen, you feel very anxious and unhappy about it because you think it will be unpleasant or upsetting. 害怕；担忧 ❑ *I'm dreading Christmas this year.* 我害怕今年的圣诞节。 ❑ *I dreaded coming back, to be honest.* 老实说，我很害怕回来。 2 N-UNCOUNT **Dread** is a feeling of great anxiety and fear about something that may happen. 忧虑；恐惧 ❑ *She thought with dread of the cold winters to come.* 想到寒冬即将到来，她就感到恐惧。 3 → see also **dreaded** 4 PHRASE If you say that you **dread to think** what might happen, you mean that you are anxious about it because it is likely to be very unpleasant. 不敢想 ❑ *I dread to think what will happen in the case of a major emergency.* 我不敢想像万一出现重大紧急情况会怎么样。

dread·ed /drɛdɪd/ 1 ADJ **Dreaded** means terrible and greatly feared. 可怕的；令人畏惧的 [ADJ n] ❑ *No one knew how to treat this dreaded disease.* 没人知道如何治疗这种可怕的疾病。 2 ADJ You can use **the dreaded** to describe something that you, or a particular group of people, find annoying, inconvenient, or undesirable. 讨厌的；令人不快的 [ADJ n] [INFORMAL, FEELINGS] ❑ *She's a victim of the dreaded hay fever.* 她患了讨厌的花粉热。

Word Link *ful ≈ filled with : beautiful, careful, dreadful*

★ **dread·ful** /drɛdfəl/ 1 ADJ If you say that something is **dreadful**, you mean that it is very bad or unpleasant, or very poor in quality. 糟糕透顶的 ❑ *They told us the dreadful news.* 他们告诉了我们这个坏消息。 ● **dread·fully** ADV 糟糕透顶地 [ADV with v] ❑ *You behaved dreadfully.* 你表现得糟透了。 2 ADJ **Dreadful** is used to emphasize the degree or extent of something bad. 非常的；极度的 [ADJ n] [EMPHASIS] ❑ *We've made a dreadful mistake.* 我们犯了一个很大的错误。 ● **dread·fully** ADV 非常地；极度地 ❑ *He looks dreadfully ill.* 他看上去病得非常严重。

dream ◆◆◇ /drim/ (**dreams, dreaming, dreamed** or **dreamt**) 1 N-COUNT A **dream** is a series of events that you experience only in your mind while you are asleep. 梦 ❑ *He had a dream about Claire.* 他做了一个关于克莱尔的梦。 2 N-COUNT You can refer to a situation or event as a **dream** if you often think about it because you would like it to happen. 梦想；愿望 ❑ *He had finally accomplished his dream of becoming a pilot.* 他最终实现了成为了一名飞行员的梦想。 3 N-COUNT You can refer to a situation or event that does not seem real as a **dream**, especially if it is very strange or unpleasant. 梦境般的事 ❑ *When the right woman comes along, this bad dream will be over.* 当合适的女人出现时，这场噩梦就会结束了。 4 V-T/V-I When you **dream**, you experience events in your mind while you are asleep. 梦见；做梦 ❑ *Ivor dreamed that he was on a bus.* 艾弗梦见了他在公共汽车上。 ❑ *She dreamed about her baby.* 她梦见了她的小宝贝。 5 V-T/V-I If you often think about something that you would very much like to happen or have, you can say that you **dream of** it. 梦想；渴望 ❑ *As a schoolgirl, she had dreamed of becoming an actress.* 当她是一名女学生的时候，她曾梦想过成为一名女演员。 ❑ *For most of us, a brand new designer kitchen is something we can only dream about.* 对我们大部分人来说，一个崭新的名师设计的厨房是我们只能梦想的东西。 ❑ *I dream that my son will attend college.* 我梦想着我的儿子将来能上大学。 6 V-I If you say that you **would not dream of** doing something, you are emphasizing that you would never do it because you think it is wrong or is not possible or suitable for you. 决不；不愿 [with neg] [EMPHASIS] ❑ *I wouldn't dream of making fun of you.* 我决不会拿你取乐。 7 V-T/V-I If you say that you **never dreamed that** something would happen, you are emphasizing that you did not think that it would happen because it seemed very unlikely. 没有想到 [with brd-neg] [EMPHASIS] ❑ *I never dreamed that I would be able to afford a home here.* 我从未想到我能买得起这里的房子。 8 ADJ You can use **dream** to describe something that you think is ideal or perfect, especially if it is something that you thought you would never be able to have or experience. 理想的；完美的 [ADJ n] ❑ *...a dream holiday to Jamaica.* …一个去牙买加的理想假期。 9 N-SING If you describe something as **a particular person's dream**, you think that it would be ideal for that person and that he or she would like it very much. 梦想；梦寐以求的事物 ❑ *Greece is said to be a botanist's dream.* 希腊被称作植物学家的理想圣地。 10 PHRASE If you say that someone does something **like a dream**, you think that they do it very well. If you say that something happens **like a dream**, you mean that it happens successfully without any problems. 完美地；美妙地 ❑ *She cooked like a dream.* 她的烹饪技术棒极了。 11 PHRASE If you describe someone or something as the person or thing **of your dreams**, you mean that you

D

Word Web dream

Dreams appear to happen most frequently during REM **sleep**. During these periods, the eyes move around quickly, the heart rate goes up, and respiration becomes more rapid. Seventy percent to 90 percent of people **awakened** during REM sleep report dreams. Only 10 percent to 15 percent of people **roused** during non-REM sleep remember dreaming. One of the most common dreams reported is of the person flying. Some people look for meaning in their dreams. They try to **interpret** the sights, sounds, and sensations of the dream. Some psychoanalysts say dreams show us the **unconscious** mind. Some later researchers argue that dreams are just random electrical impulses in the brain.

consider them to be ideal or perfect. (某人) 理想中的 ❑ *This could be the man of my dreams.* 这可能是我理想的男人。 12 PHRASE If you say that you could not imagine a particular thing **in your wildest dreams**, you are emphasizing that you think it is extremely strange or unlikely. 异想天开地 [EMPHASIS] ❑ *"Never in my wildest dreams did I think I'd ever accomplish this," said Toni.* "即便在我异想天开的时候，也从来没有想到过我能实现它，" 托尼说。 13 PHRASE If you describe something as being **beyond** your **wildest dreams**, you are emphasizing that it is better than you could have imagined or hoped for. 做梦也想不到的; 出乎意料的 [EMPHASIS] ❑ *She had already achieved success beyond her wildest dreams.* 她已经获得了做梦也没想到的成功。

→ see Word Web: **dream**

▸ **dream up** PHRASAL VERB If you **dream up** a plan or idea, you work it out or create it in your mind. 虚构出; 凭空设想出 ❑ *I dreamed up a plan to solve both problems at once.* 我想出了一个可以立刻解决这两个问题的计划。

Thesaurus *dream* 另参见:

N. nightmare, reverie, vision 1
ambition, aspiration, design, hope, wish 2
V. hope, long for, wish 5

Word Partnership *dream* 的常用搭配:

N. dream **interpretation** 1
dream **home**, dream **vacation** 8
V. **have** a dream 1 2
fulfill a dream, **pursue** a dream, **realize** a dream 2

dream·er /driːmər/ (**dreamers**) N-COUNT If you describe someone as a **dreamer**, you mean that they spend a lot of time thinking about and planning for things that they would like to happen but which are improbable or impractical. 空想家; 不切实际的人 ❑ *Far from being a dreamer, she's a level-headed pragmatist.* 她是个冷静理智的实用主义者，远非一个空想家。

★ **dreamy** /driːmi/ (**dreamier, dreamiest**) 1 ADJ If you say that someone has a **dreamy** expression, you mean that they are not paying attention to things around them and look as if they are thinking about something pleasant. 恍惚的; 出神的 ❑ *His face assumed a sort of dreamy expression.* 他的脸上现出一种神情恍惚的表情。 2 ADJ If you describe something as **dreamy**, you mean that you like it and that it seems gentle and soft, like something in a dream. 如梦般轻柔的 [APPROVAL] ❑ *...dreamy shots of beautiful sunsets.* …梦幻般美丽的日落照片。

▲ **dreary** /drɪəri/ (**drearier, dreariest**) ADJ If you describe something as **dreary**, you mean that it is dull and depressing. 沉闷的; 枯燥无味的 ❑ *...a dreary little town in the Midwest.* …中西部一个沉闷的小镇。

dredge /drɛdʒ/ (**dredges, dredging, dredged**) V-T When people **dredge** a harbor, river, or other area of water, they remove mud and unwanted material from the bottom with a special machine in order to make it deeper or to look for something. 清淤; 挖掘 ❑ *Police have spent weeks dredging the lake but have not found his body.* 警察已经花了几周时间挖掘湖底，但是仍未发现他的尸体。

▸ **dredge up** 1 PHRASAL VERB If someone **dredges up** a piece of information they learned a long time ago, or if they **dredge up** a distant memory, they manage to remember it. 使劲回忆起 ❑ *...an American trying to dredge up some French or German learned in high school.* …一个试图回忆起高中所学的法语或德语的美国人。 2 PHRASAL VERB If someone **dredges up** a damaging or upsetting fact about your past, they remind you of it or tell other people about it. 重提 (不快往事) ❑ *She dredges up a minor misdemeanor: "You didn't give me money for the school trip."* 她重提那件小事："那次学校旅游，你没给我钱。"

drench /drɛntʃ/ (**drenches, drenching, drenched**) V-T To **drench** something or someone means to make them completely wet. 使湿透 ❑ *They turned fire hoses on the people and drenched them.* 他们打开消防水龙头朝人群喷去，把他们浇湿。 ❑ *...the idea of spending two whole days hanging on to a raft and getting drenched by icy water.* …在筏子上飘流整整两天并让冰冷的水湿透的想法。

dress ♦♦◇ /drɛs/ (**dresses, dressing, dressed**) 1 N-COUNT A **dress** is a piece of clothing worn by a woman or girl. It covers her body and part of her legs. 连衣裙 ❑ *She was wearing a black dress.* 她穿着一套黑色连衣裙。 2 N-UNCOUNT You can refer to clothes worn by men or women as **dress**. 服装 ❑ *He wore formal evening dress.* 他穿了正式的晚礼服。 3 V-T/V-I When you **dress** or **dress yourself**, you put on clothes. 穿衣服 ❑ *He told Sarah to wait while he dressed.* 他让莎拉等着他穿好衣服。 4 V-T If you **dress** someone, for example, a child, you put clothes on them. 给…穿衣 ❑ *She bathed her and dressed her in clean clothes.* 她给她洗了澡并穿上干净衣服。 5 V-I If someone **dresses** in a particular way, they wear clothes of a particular style or color. 打扮; 穿着 ❑ *He dresses in a way that lets everyone know he's got authority.* 他着装的式样让每个人都知道他已掌有权力。 6 V-I If you **dress for** something, you put on special clothes for it. 穿礼服 ❑ *We don't dress for dinner here.* 我们这儿参加晚宴不穿礼服。 7 V-T When someone **dresses** a wound, they clean it and cover it. 清理包扎 (伤口) ❑ *The poor child never cried or protested when I was dressing her wounds.* 在我为那个可怜的女孩清理包扎伤口时，她不哭不闹。 8 → see also **dressing, dressed**

▸ **dress down** PHRASAL VERB If you **dress down**, you wear clothes that are less formal than usual. 穿便装 ❑ *She dresses down in dark glasses and baggy clothes to avoid hordes of admirers.* 她着装随意，戴墨镜，穿宽松的衣服，以避开大群的仰慕者。

▸ **dress up** 1 PHRASAL VERB If you **dress up** or **dress** yourself **up**, you put on different clothes, in order to make yourself look more formal than usual or to disguise yourself. 盛装打扮 ❑ *You do not need to dress up for dinner.* 你不必为了晚宴盛装打扮。 ❑ *I just love the fun of dressing up in another era's clothing.* 我就是喜欢穿另一个时代的服装，很好玩。 2 PHRASAL VERB If you **dress** someone **up**, you give them special clothes to wear, in order to make them look more formal or to disguise them. 装扮 ❑ *Mother loved to dress me up.* 妈妈喜欢装扮我。 3 PHRASAL VERB If you **dress** something **up**, you try to make it seem more attractive, acceptable, or interesting than it really is. 装饰; 修饰 ❑ *Politicians are happier to dress up their ruthless ambition as a necessary pursuit of the public good.* 政客们更乐于把自己的狼子野心粉饰成对公众利益的一种必要追求。

Word Partnership *dress* 的常用搭配:

V. **put on** a dress, **wear** a dress 1
ADJ. **casual** dress, **formal** dress, **traditional** dress 2
ADV. dress **appropriately**, dress **casually**, dress **well** 5

dressed ♦◇◇ /drɛst/ 1 ADJ If you are **dressed**, you are wearing clothes rather than being naked or wearing your nightclothes. If you **get dressed**, you put on your clothes. 穿上衣服的 ❑ *He was fully* *dressed, including shoes.* 他已穿戴好了，包括鞋子。 **2** ADJ If you are **dressed** in a particular way, you are wearing clothes of a particular color or kind. 穿着…衣服的 [v-link ADJ] ❑ *...a tall thin woman dressed in black.* …一个穿着黑色衣服，高高瘦瘦的女人。 **3** → see also **well-dressed** **4** **dressed to the nines** → see **nine**

dress·er /drɛ̲sər/ (**dressers**) **1** N-COUNT A **dresser** is a chest of drawers, sometimes with a mirror on the top. 梳妆台 [mainly AM] **2** N-COUNT You can use **dresser** to refer to the kind of clothes that a person wears. For example, if you say that someone is a **casual dresser**, you mean that they wear casual clothes. 穿着…衣服的人 ❑ *Mr. Jorgensen was an immaculate dresser.* 乔根森先生是个衣着考究的人。

▲ **dress·ing** /drɛ̲sɪŋ/ (**dressings**) **1** N-MASS A salad **dressing** is a mixture of oil, vinegar, and herbs or flavorings, which you pour over salad. 色拉调料 ❑ *Mix the ingredients for the dressing in a bowl.* 在碗里把这些配料搅拌成调味品。 **2** N-COUNT A **dressing** is a covering that is put on a wound to protect it while it heals. 敷料 ❑ *Miss Finkelstein will put a dressing on your thumb.* 芬克尔斯坦小姐将在你的大拇指上包一层敷料。 **3** N-MASS **Dressing** is a mixture of food that is cooked and then put inside a bird such as a turkey before it is eaten. (烹调时塞入火鸡等中的) 填料 [AM] ❑ *...cornbread dressing for the first Thanksgiving she cooked at home.* …她在家为第一个感恩节烹制的玉米饼填料。

dress·ing gown (**dressing gowns**) also **dressing-gown** N-COUNT A **dressing gown** is a long, loose garment which you wear over your nightclothes when you are not in bed. 睡袍

dress re·hears·al (**dress rehearsals**) **1** N-COUNT The **dress rehearsal** of a play, opera, or show is the final rehearsal before it is performed, in which the performers wear their costumes and the lights and scenery are all used as they will be in the performance. 彩排 ❑ *We went to all the dress rehearsals together.* 我们一起去了所有的彩排。 **2** N-COUNT You can describe an event as a **dress rehearsal** for a later, more important event when it indicates how the later event will be. (稍后更重大事件的) 预演 ❑ *Yesterday's NEA event looked like a dress rehearsal for the Democratic convention.* 昨天的全国教育协会活动看上去像是一次民主党大会的预演。

drew /dru̲/ **Drew** is the past tense of **draw**. **draw**的过去式

drib·ble /drɪ̲bᵊl/ (**dribbles, dribbling, dribbled**) **1** V-T/V-I If a liquid **dribbles** somewhere, or if you **dribble** it, it drops down slowly or flows in a thin stream. 使滴下；滴下 ❑ *Sweat dribbled down Hart's face.* 汗顺着哈特的脸往下淌。 **2** V-T/V-I When players **dribble** the ball in a game such as basketball or soccer, they keep kicking or tapping it quickly in order to keep it moving. 运球；带球 ❑ *He dribbled the ball toward Ferris.* 他运球传向费里斯。 ❑ *He dribbled past four defenders.* 他带球突破了4名防守球员。 **3** V-I If a person **dribbles**, saliva drops slowly from their mouth. 流口水 ❑ *...to protect sheets when the baby dribbles.* …在婴儿流口水时保护布单。

dried /dra̲ɪd/ **1** ADJ **Dried** food or milk has had all the water removed from it so that it will last for a long time. (食物或牛奶) 脱水的 [ADJ n] ❑ *...an infusion which may be prepared from the fresh plant or the dried herb.* …可以用新鲜植物或干的草本植物制备的一种泡剂。 **2** → see also **dry**

dri·er /dra̲ɪər/ → see **dry, dryer**

drift ♦◇◇ /drɪ̲ft/ (**drifts, drifting, drifted**) **1** V-I When something **drifts** somewhere, it is carried there by the movement of wind or water. 漂流 ❑ *We proceeded to drift on up the river.* 我们继续在河上漂流着。 **2** V-I If someone or something **drifts into** a situation, they get into that situation in a way that is not planned or controlled. 脱离正途；偏离 ❑ *We need to offer young people drifting into crime an alternative set of values.* 我们需要给误入犯罪歧途的年轻人提供另一套价值观。 **3** V-I If you say that someone **drifts** around, you mean that they travel from place to place without a plan or settled way of life. 漂泊；流浪 [DISAPPROVAL] ❑ *You've been drifting from job to job without any real commitment.* 你频频换工作，全无恒心。 **4** V-I To **drift** somewhere means to move there slowly or gradually. 缓慢地移动 ❑ *As rural factories lay off workers, people drift toward the cities.* 随着乡镇企业裁员，人们陆续移向城市。 **5** V-I If sounds **drift** somewhere, they can be heard but they are not very loud. (声音) 隐约传出 ❑ *Cool summer dance sounds are drifting from the stereo indoors.* 屋内立体声音响飘出美妙的夏季舞曲。 **6** V-I If snow **drifts**, it builds up into piles as a result of the movement of the wind. 吹积 ❑ *The snow, except where it drifted, was only calf-deep.* 除了被风吹积起来的地方外，积雪只深及小腿。 **7** N-COUNT A **drift** is a movement away from somewhere or something, or a movement toward somewhere or something different. 移向；移动 ❑ *...the drift toward the cities.* …向城市的流动。 **8** N-COUNT A **drift** is a mass of snow that has built up into a pile as a result of the movement of wind. (吹积成的) 雪堆 ❑ *A nine-year-old boy was trapped in a snow drift.* 一个9岁的男孩陷在雪堆里了。 **9** N-SING **The drift of** an argument or speech is the general point that is being made in it. (辩论、演说等的) 主旨 ❑ *Grace was beginning to get his drift.* 格雷斯开始抓住他的主旨了。
→ see **continent**

▸ **drift off** PHRASAL VERB If you **drift off** to sleep, you gradually fall asleep. 慢慢地睡去 ❑ *It was only when he finally drifted off to sleep that the headaches eased.* 当他最终慢慢睡着时，头疼才减轻了。

drill /drɪ̲l/ (**drills, drilling, drilled**) **1** N-COUNT A **drill** is a tool or machine that you use for making holes. 钻孔机 ❑ *...a dentist's drill.* …一把牙钻。 **2** N-COUNT A **drill** is a routine exercise or activity, in which people practice what they should do in dangerous situations. 演习 ❑ *...a fire drill.* …一场消防演习。 **3** V-T/V-I When you **drill into** something or **drill** a hole in something, you make a hole in it using a drill. 钻(孔)；打(眼) ❑ *He drilled into the wall of Lili's bedroom.* 他在丽莉卧室的墙上打孔。 **4** V-I When people **drill for** oil or water, they search for it by drilling deep holes in the ground or in the bottom of the sea. 钻探(石油或地下水源) ❑ *There have been proposals to drill for more oil.* 有人提出了钻探更多石油的建议。 **5** N-VAR A **drill** is repeated training for a group of people, especially soldiers, so that they can do something quickly and efficiently. 军事训练；操练 ❑ *The Marines carried out landing exercises in a drill that includes 18 ships and 90 aircraft.* 海军陆战队在一场军事训练中进行了登陆练习，共有18艘军舰和90架飞机。
→ see **oil, tool**

drink ♦♦◇ /drɪ̲ŋk/ (**drinks, drinking, drank, drunk**) **1** V-T/V-I When you **drink** a liquid, you take it into your mouth and swallow it. 喝 ❑ *He drank his cup of tea.* 他喝了他那杯茶。 ❑ *He drank thirstily.* 他迫不及待地喝了。 **2** V-I To **drink** means to drink alcohol. 喝酒 ❑ *By his own admission, he was smoking and drinking too much.* 他自己承认抽烟饮酒过度。 ● **drink·ing** N-UNCOUNT 喝酒 ❑ *She had left him because of his drinking.* 她离开了他，因为他酗酒。 **3** N-COUNT A **drink** is an amount of a liquid which you drink. 一杯 (饮料) ❑ *I'll get you a drink of water.* 我去给你弄杯水来。 **4** N-COUNT A **drink** is an alcoholic drink. (一杯) 酒 ❑ *She felt like a drink after a hard day.* 劳累一天后，她想喝杯酒。 **5** N-UNCOUNT **Drink** is alcohol, such as beer, wine, or whiskey. 酒 (如啤酒、葡萄酒、威士忌等) [mainly BRIT] ❑ *Too much drink is bad for your health.* 饮酒过度对你的身体有害。

▸ **drink to** PHRASAL VERB When people **drink to** someone or something, they wish them success, good luck, or good health before having an alcoholic drink. 举杯祝愿；为…干杯 ❑ *Let's drink to his memory, eh?* 让我们为纪念他而干杯，怎样？

Thesaurus	*drink* 另参见：
V.	gulp, sip **1**
N.	beer, liquor, spirit, wine **4**

drink-driving N-UNCOUNT **Drink-driving** is the same as **drunk driving**. 酒后驾车 [BRIT]

drink·er /drɪ̲ŋkər/ (**drinkers**) **1** N-COUNT If someone is a tea **drinker** or a beer **drinker**, for example, they regularly drink tea or beer. 常饮 (某种饮料) 的人 ❑ *Sherry drinkers far outnumber wine drinkers or whiskey drinkers.* 喝雪利酒的人数远远超过喝葡萄酒或威士忌的人数。 **2** N-COUNT If you describe someone as a **drinker**, you mean that they drink alcohol, especially in large quantities. 酒徒 ❑ *I'm not a heavy drinker.* 我不是贪杯之人。

drip /drɪ̲p/ (**drips, dripping, dripped**) **1** V-T/V-I When liquid **drips** somewhere, or you **drip** it somewhere, it falls in individual small drops. 使滴下；滴下 ❑ *Blood dripped from the corner of his mouth.* 血从他嘴角滴下来。 ❑ *Amid the trees the sea mist was dripping and moisture formed on Tom's glasses.* 树林中海雾正滴着，水气蒙上了汤姆的眼镜片。 **2** V-I When something **drips**, drops of liquid fall from it. 滴下 ❑ *A faucet in the kitchen was dripping.* 厨房的水龙头在滴水。 ❑ *Lou was dripping with perspiration.* 卢汗流浃背。 **3** V-I If you say that something **is dripping with** a particular thing, you mean that it contains a lot of that thing. 充满；布满 [usu cont] [LITERARY] ❑ *They were dazed by window displays dripping with diamonds and furs.* 他们被布满钻石和毛皮的橱窗展示弄得眼花缭乱。 **4** N-COUNT A **drip** is a small individual drop of a liquid. 滴 ❑ *Drips of water rolled down the trousers of his uniform.* 水珠从他的制服裤子上滚下来。 **5** N-COUNT A **drip** is a piece of medical equipment by which a liquid is slowly passed through a tube into a patient's blood. 滴注器 ❑ *He was put on intravenous drip to treat his dehydration.* 他打点滴来治疗脱水。

drive ♦♦♦ /draɪv/ (**drives, driving, drove, driven**) 1 V-T/V-I When you **drive** somewhere, you operate a car or other vehicle and control its movement and direction. 驾驶 ❑ *I drove into town and went to a restaurant for dinner.* 我开车进城到一家餐馆用餐。 ❑ *She never learned to drive.* 她从未学过开车。 ❑ *We drove the car down to Richmond for the weekend.* 我们开车南下到里士满度周末。 ● **driv·ing** N-UNCOUNT 驾驶 ❑ *...a qualified driving instructor.* …一名合格的驾驶教练。 2 V-T If you **drive** someone somewhere, you take them there in a car or other vehicle. 开车送 (某人去某处) ❑ *His daughter Carly drove him to the train station.* 她的女儿卡莉开车送他去火车站。 3 V-T If something **drives** a machine, it supplies the power that makes it work. 驱动 ❑ *The current flows into electric motors that drive the wheels.* 电流流入驱动轮子的电动机。 4 V-T If you **drive** something such as a nail **into** something else, you push it in or hammer it in using a lot of effort. (把钉子等) 钉进 ❑ *I had to use our sledgehammer to drive the pegs into the side of the path.* 我不得不用我们的大锤把桩子砸进路边。 5 V-I If the wind, rain, or snow **drives** in a particular direction, it moves with great force in that direction. (向某个方向猛烈地) 吹打 ❑ *Rain drove against the window.* 雨打着窗户。 ● **driv·ing** ADJ (向某个方向猛烈) 吹打的 [ADJ n] ❑ *He crashed into a tree in driving rain.* 在暴雨中他撞上了树。 6 V-T If you **drive** people or animals somewhere, you make them go to or from that place. 驱赶 ❑ *The last offensive drove thousands of people into Thailand.* 最近的一次进攻把成千上万的人驱赶到了泰国。 7 V-T To **drive** someone **into** a particular state or situation means to force them into that state or situation. 强迫；迫使 ❑ *The recession and hospital bills drove them into bankruptcy.* 经济萧条和医院的账单逼得他们破产了。 8 V-T The desire or feeling that **drives** a person **to** do something, especially something extreme, is the desire or feeling that causes them to do it. 驱使 ❑ *More than once, depression drove him to attempt suicide.* 不止一次，抑郁驱使他试图自杀。 ❑ *Jealousy drives people to murder.* 忌妒心驱使人谋杀。 9 N-COUNT A **drive** is a trip in a car or other vehicle. 驾车旅行；乘车兜风 ❑ *I thought we might go for a drive on Sunday.* 我想周日我们可以去开车兜风。 10 N-COUNT A **drive** is a wide piece of hard ground, or sometimes a private road, that leads from the road to a person's house. (将私人住宅和大路连接起来的) 车道 ❑ *The boys followed Eleanor up the drive to the house.* 男孩们跟着埃莉诺上了通向房子的车道。 11 N-COUNT You use **drive** to refer to the mechanical part of a computer which reads the data on disks and tapes, or writes data onto them. 驱动装置 ❑ *The firm specialized in supplying pieces of equipment, such as terminals, tape drives, or printers.* 这家公司专营各种设备配件，比如终端机、磁带机、打印机。 12 → see also **disk drive** 13 N-COUNT A **drive** is a very strong need or desire in human beings that makes them act in particular ways. 欲望 ❑ *...compelling, dynamic sex drives.* …不可扼制的强烈性欲。 14 N-UNCOUNT If you say that someone has **drive**, you mean they have energy and determination. 干劲儿 ❑ *John will be best remembered for his drive and enthusiasm.* 约翰将因其干劲和热情被人们牢记。 15 N-SING A **drive** is a special effort made by a group of people for a particular purpose. 运动 ❑ *The ANC is about to launch a nationwide recruitment drive.* 南非非洲人国民大会打算发动一次全国征兵运动。 16 N-IN-NAMES **Drive** is used in the names of some streets. …道；…街 ❑ *...3091 North Beverly Hills Drive, Beverly Hills, CA.* …加利福尼亚州贝弗利山，北贝弗利山庄街3091号。 17 → see also **driving**

▸ **drive away** PHRASAL VERB To **drive** people **away** means to make them want to go away or stay away. 赶走 ❑ *Patrick's rudeness soon drove Monica's friends away.* 帕特里克的粗鲁态度很快就把莫妮卡的朋友们赶走了。

drive-by ADJ A **drive-by** shooting or a **drive-by** murder involves shooting someone from a moving car. 行车间进行的 (射击或谋杀) [ADJ n] ❑ *He was killed by three shots to the head in a drive-by shooting.* 在一场飞车枪战中，他头中3枪而死。

drive-in (**drive-ins**) N-COUNT A **drive-in** is a restaurant, movie theater, or other commercial place which is specially designed so that customers can use the services provided while staying in their cars. 汽车餐厅、影院等商业场所 ❑ *...a small neat town, uncluttered by stores, gas stations, or fast food drive-ins.* …一个整洁的小镇，没有过多的商店、加油站或汽车快餐店。

driv·en /drɪvᵊn/ **Driven** is the past participle of **drive**. **drive**的过去分词

driv·er ♦♦◊ /draɪvər/ (**drivers**) 1 N-COUNT The **driver** of a vehicle is the person who is driving it. 驾驶员 ❑ *The driver got out of his van.* 司机从货车里下来。 2 N-COUNT A **driver** is a computer program that controls a device such as a printer. 驱动程序 [COMPUTING] ❑ *Printer driver software includes standard features such as print layout and fit-to-page printing.* 打印机驱动程序软件包含标准功能，比如打印版面设定和符合纸张大小的打印。

driv·er's li·cense (**driver's licenses**) N-COUNT A **driver's license** is a card showing that you are qualified to drive because you have passed a driving test. 驾驶执照 [AM]

in BRIT, use **driving licence**

drive-through (**drive-throughs**) also **drive-thru** ADJ A **drive-through** store, bank, or restaurant is one where you can be served without leaving your car. 免下车的 (餐馆、银行或饭馆) [ADJ n] ❑ *...a drive-through burger bar.* …一家汽车汉堡店。 ● N-COUNT **Drive-through** is also a noun. 免下车餐馆、银行或饭馆 ❑ *I got some dinner at a drive-through and headed home.* 我在一个汽车餐馆买了晚餐就奔家去了。

drive-thru (**drive-thrus**) [INFORMAL] → see **drive-through**

★ **drive·way** /draɪvweɪ/ (**driveways**) N-COUNT A **driveway** is a piece of hard ground that leads from the road to the front of a house, garage, or other building. 私人车道 ❑ *I was running down the driveway to the car and I lost my balance.* 我正沿着车道向车子跑去，然后我失去了平衡。

driv·ing /draɪvɪŋ/ 1 ADJ The **driving** force or idea behind something that happens or is done is the main thing that has a strong effect on it and makes it happen or be done in a particular way. 起推动作用的 [ADJ n] ❑ *Consumer spending was the driving force behind the economic growth in the summer.* 消费者支出是夏季经济增长背后的推动力。 2 → see also **drive**

→ see **car**

driv·ing li·cence (**driving licences**) [BRIT] → see **driver's license**

driv·ing li·cense (**driving licenses**) N-COUNT A **driving license** is the same as a **driver's license**. 驾驶执照

▲ **driz·zle** /drɪzᵊl/ (**drizzles, drizzling, drizzled**) 1 N-UNCOUNT **Drizzle** is light rain falling in fine drops. 毛毛雨 [also "a" N] ❑ *The drizzle had now stopped and the sun was breaking through.* 细雨已经停了，太阳露出了脸。 2 V-I If it **is drizzling**, it is raining very lightly. 下毛毛雨 ❑ *Clouds had come down and it was starting to drizzle.* 云压了下来，开始下起了毛毛雨。

drone /droʊn/ (**drones, droning, droned**) 1 V-I If something **drones**, it makes a low, continuous, dull noise. 发出单调连续的低声 ❑ *Above him an invisible plane droned through the night sky.* 在他头顶上空一架隐形飞机飞过夜空，不断发出低沉单调的声音。 ● N-SING **Drone** is also a noun. 连续单调的低声 ❑ *I hear the drone of an airplane as it banks across the bay.* 飞机倾斜飞过海湾时，我听到它低沉单调的声音。 2 V-I If you say that someone **drones**, you mean that they keep talking about something in a boring way. 唠叨 [DISAPPROVAL] ❑ *Chambers' voice droned, maddening as an insect around his head.* 钱伯斯唠叨叨，那声音像一只飞虫绕着他的头打转般令人发狂。 ● N-SING **Drone** is also a noun. 唠叨 ❑ *The minister's voice was a relentless drone.* 牧师的声音是无休止的絮叨。 ● PHRASAL VERB **Drone on** means the same as **drone**. 唠叨 ❑ *Aunt Maimie's voice droned on.* 麦科伊婶婶的声音唠叨个不休。

drool /druːl/ (**drools, drooling, drooled**) 1 V-I To **drool over** someone or something means to look at them with great pleasure, perhaps in an exaggerated or ridiculous way. 忘情地注视 [DISAPPROVAL] ❑ *Fashion editors drooled over every item.* 时尚编辑们忘情地观看了每样东西。 2 V-I If a person or animal **drools**, saliva drops slowly from their mouth. 流口水 ❑ *My dog Jacques is drooling on my shoulder.* 我的狗雅克趴在我的肩头流口水。

droop /druːp/ (**droops, drooping, drooped**) V-I If something **droops**, it hangs or leans downward with no strength or firmness. 下垂 ❑ *Crook's eyelids drooped and he yawned.* 克鲁克的眼睑垂了下来，打起了呵欠。 ● N-SING **Droop** is also a noun. 下垂 ❑ *...the droop of his shoulders.* …他肩膀的耷拉像。

drop ♦♦◊ /drɒp/ (**drops, dropping, dropped**) 1 V-T/V-I If a level or amount **drops** or if someone or something **drops** it, it quickly becomes less. 使迅速下降；迅速下降 ❑ *Temperatures can drop to freezing at night.* 晚上气温能陡降到零度以下。 ❑ *His blood pressure had dropped severely.* 他的血压严重地迅速下降。 ● N-COUNT **Drop** is also a noun. 迅速下降 ❑ *He was prepared to take a drop in wages.* 他准备好了接受一次工资的快速下调。 2 V-T If you **drop** something, you accidentally let it fall. 失手掉下 ❑ *I dropped my glasses and broke them.* 我不小心掉了

眼镜，把它摔破了。3 V-I If something **drops onto** something else, it falls onto that thing. If something **drops from** somewhere, it falls from that place. 掉 ❑ *He felt hot tears dropping onto his fingers.* 他感到热泪滴在他的手指上。4 V-T/V-I If you **drop** something somewhere or if it **drops** there, you deliberately let it fall there. 投下 ❑ *Drop the noodles into the water.* 把面条下到水里。❑ *...television footage of bombs dropping on the city.* …多枚炸弹投向该城市的电视片段。● **drop·ping** N-UNCOUNT 下投 [usu N "of" n] ❑ *...the dropping of the first atomic bomb.* …第一枚原子弹的投掷。5 V-T/V-I If a person or a part of their body **drops** to a lower position, or if they **drop** a part of their body to a lower position, they move to that position, often in a tired and lifeless way. (人) 瘫下；(身体部位无力地) 垂下 ❑ *Nancy dropped into a nearby chair.* 南希在旁边的椅子上瘫坐了下去。❑ *She let her head drop.* 她把头垂了下来。6 V-I To **drop** is used in expressions such as **to be about to drop** and **to dance until you drop** to emphasize that you are exhausted and can no longer continue doing something. (由于精疲力竭而) 放弃 [no cont] [EMPHASIS] ❑ *She looked about to drop.* 她看上去要放弃了。7 V-T/V-I If your voice **drops** or if you **drop** your voice, you speak more quietly. 使(声音) 变小；(声音) 变小 ❑ *Her voice will drop to a dismissive whisper.* 她的声音将要降低成轻视性的低语。8 V-T If you **drop** someone or something somewhere, you take them somewhere and leave them there, usually in a car or other vehicle. 将…送到并放下 ❑ *He dropped me outside the hotel.* 他让我在旅店外下了车。● PHRASAL VERB **Drop off** means the same as **drop**. 将…送到并放下 ❑ *Just drop me off at the airport.* 把我送到飞机场下车就行。9 V-T If you **drop** an idea, course of action, or habit, you do not continue with it. 放弃 (想法、行动、习惯等) ❑ *He was told to drop the idea.* 他被告知放弃这个想法。● **drop·ping** N-UNCOUNT 放弃 ❑ *This was one of the factors that led to President Suharto's dropping of his previous objections.* 这是导致苏哈托总统放弃他先前反对意见的因素之一。10 V-T If someone **is dropped** by a sports team or organization, they are no longer included in that team or employed by that organization. 把…除名；把…解职 [usu passive] ❑ *Alexander has been dropped from his multimillion-dollar-a-year job as spokesman for the company.* 亚历山大已经被拿掉了年薪数百万的发言人的工作。11 V-I If you **drop** to a lower position in a sports competition, you move to that position. (在比赛中) 名次下降 ❑ *She has dropped to third in the world ranking.* 她已跌至世界排名第三。12 N-COUNT A **drop of** a liquid is a very small amount of it shaped like a little ball. In informal English, you can also use **drop** when you are referring to a very small amount of something such as a drink. 滴；(如酒) 少量 ❑ *...a drop of blue ink.* …一滴蓝墨水。13 N-COUNT You use **drop** to talk about vertical distances. For example, a thirty-foot **drop** is a distance of thirty feet between the top of a cliff or wall and the bottom of it. 垂直距离 ❑ *There was a sheer drop just outside my window.* 我的窗外就是一个绝对垂直的落差。14 N-PLURAL **Drops** are a kind of medicine which you put drop by drop into your ears, eyes, or nose. (滴入的) 药水 ❑ *And he had to have these drops in his eyes as well.* 而且他还必须把这些药水滴进眼睛里。

> Do not confuse **drop** and **fall**. Although things can **drop** or **fall** by accident, note that **fall** is not followed by an object, so you cannot say that someone "falls" something. However, you can say that they **drop** something, or that something **drops**. ❑ *Leaves were falling to the ground... He dropped his cigar... Plate after plate dropped from his fingers.* You say that a person **drops** when they jump straight down from something, for example, when someone jumps from a plane using a parachute. If someone **falls**, it is usually because of an accident. ❑ *He stumbled and fell.* **Drop** and **fall** are also nouns. A **drop** is the height of something when you imagine falling off it. ❑ *Sixteen hundred feet is a considerable drop.* A **fall** is what happens when someone has an accident. ❑ *I had been badly bruised by the fall.*

15 PHRASE If you **drop a hint**, you give a hint or say something in a casual way. 露口风 ❑ *Jerry dropped hints that he and Julie were talking about getting married.* 杰里露出口风说他同朱莉已谈婚论嫁了。16 PHRASE If you want someone to **drop the subject, drop it**, or **let it drop**, you want them to stop talking about something, often because you are annoyed that they keep talking about it. 别再讨论某事 ❑ *MaryAnn wished he would just drop it.* 玛丽安希望他不要再谈这事。17 **to drop dead** → see **dead** 18 **at the drop of a hat** → see **hat** 19 **a drop in the ocean** → see **ocean**

▶ **drop by** PHRASAL VERB If you **drop by**, you visit someone informally. 非正式地拜访 ❑ *She and Danny will drop by later.* 她和丹尼待会儿会过来坐一下。

▶ **drop in** PHRASAL VERB If you **drop in on** someone, you visit them informally, usually without having arranged it. 顺道拜访 ❑ *Why not drop in for a chat?* 为何不顺道过来聊聊？

▶ **drop off** 1 → see **drop 8** 2 PHRASAL VERB If you **drop off** to sleep, you go to sleep. 睡着 [INFORMAL] ❑ *I must have dropped off to sleep.* 我一定是睡着了。3 PHRASAL VERB If the level of something **drops off**, it becomes less. 下降 ❑ *Two years later, earnings from the stocks had dropped off by nearly 50%.* 2年后，股票收益已下降了近50%。

▶ **drop out** 1 PHRASAL VERB If someone **drops out of** college or a race, for example, they leave it without finishing what they started. 辍学 ❑ *He'd dropped out of high school at the age of 16.* 他16岁时就从高中退学了。2 → see also **dropout**

Word Partnership *drop* 的常用搭配：

N.	drop **in sales** 1
	drop **a ball** 2
	drop **a bomb** 4
	drop **of blood, tear** drop, drop **of water** 12
	drop **a hint** 15
ADJ.	**sudden** drop 1
	steep drop 13

drop-down menu (**drop-down menus**) N-COUNT On a computer screen, a **drop-down menu** is a list of choices that appears when you give the computer a command. 下拉菜单 ❑ *In the drop-down menu with all your Favorites, right-click on any individual item.* 在你所有收藏的下拉菜单上，用鼠标右侧点击任一项。

Word Link *let = little : booklet, droplet, pamphlet*

drop·let /drɒplɪt/ (**droplets**) N-COUNT A **droplet** is a very small drop of liquid. 小滴 ❑ *Droplets of sweat were welling up on his forehead.* 一颗颗小汗珠从他额头上不断冒出来。

drop·out /drɒpaʊt/ (**dropouts**) also **drop-out** 1 N-COUNT If you describe someone as a **dropout**, you disapprove of the fact that they have rejected the accepted ways of society, for example, by not having a regular job. 离经叛道者 [DISAPPROVAL] ❑ *...long-haired, dope-smoking dropouts.* …蓄着长发，吸着大麻的离经叛道之人。2 N-COUNT A **dropout** is someone who has left school or college before they have finished their studies. 辍学者 ❑ *...high-school dropouts.* …中学辍学生。3 ADJ If you refer to the **dropout** rate, you are referring to the number of people who leave a school or college early, or leave a course or other activity before they have finished it. 辍学的 (比率)；中途退出的 [ADJ n] ❑ *The dropout rate among students is currently one in three.* 学生的辍学率目前是1/3。

★ **drought** /draʊt/ (**droughts**) N-VAR A **drought** is a long period of time during which no rain falls. 干旱 ❑ *...a country where drought and famines have killed up to two million people during the last eighteen years.* …过去18年来干旱和饥荒致死达两百万人的一个国家。→ see **dam**

drove /droʊv/ **Drove** is the past tense of **drive**. **drive**的过去式

drown /draʊn/ (**drowns, drowning, drowned**) 1 V-T/V-I When someone **drowns** or **is drowned**, they die because they have gone or been pushed under water and cannot breathe. 溺死 ❑ *A child can drown in only a few inches of water.* 儿童在仅仅几英寸深的水中就能溺死。❑ *Last night a boy was drowned in the river.* 昨晚一名男孩在那条河里溺水身亡。2 V-I If you say that a person or thing **is drowning in** something, you are emphasizing that they have a very large amount of it, or are completely covered in it. 淹没于 [EMPHASIS] ❑ *...people who gradually find themselves drowning in debt.* …逐渐发现自己深陷债务的人们。3 V-T If something **drowns** a sound, it is so loud that you cannot hear that sound properly. (一声音) 盖过 (另一声音) ❑ *Clapping drowned the speaker's words for a moment.* 掌声盖过了发言人的说话声有一阵儿。● PHRASAL VERB **Drown out** means the same as **drown**. 淹没 (同drown) ❑ *Their cheers drowned out the protests of demonstrators.* 他们的欢呼声淹没了示威者的抗议。4 PHRASE If you say that someone **is drowning** their **sorrows**, you mean that they are drinking alcohol in order to forget something sad or upsetting that has happened to them. 借酒浇愁 ❑ *Carly drowned her sorrows in vodka cocktails at a South Beach nightclub.* 卡莉在一家南海滩夜总会喝伏特加鸡尾酒借以消愁。

drowsy /draʊzi/ (**drowsier, drowsiest**) ADJ If you feel **drowsy**, you feel sleepy and cannot think clearly. 昏昏欲睡的 ❑ *He felt pleasantly drowsy and had to fight off the urge to sleep.* 他感觉舒适地昏昏欲睡，不得不击退睡意。● **drowsi·ness** N-UNCOUNT 睡意 ❑ *Big meals during the day cause drowsiness.* 白天的大餐会让人犯困。

d

D

Word Web drum

The "talking **drum**" has been common in central Africa for centuries. People use it to communicate between villages up to five miles apart. **Drummers** can **beat** a wide variety of sounds and **rhythms** on these **percussion instruments**. The languages in this part of the world are tonal. This means that different parts of a sentence are spoken at higher or lower pitches. The **tone** and the **beat** of the drum duplicate the sounds of the language very closely. This allows listeners to interpret a drummer's playing almost as if it were spoken language.

drug ♦♦♦ /drʌg/ (**drugs, drugging, drugged**) 1 N-COUNT A **drug** is a chemical which is given to people in order to treat or prevent an illness or disease. 药物 ❑ *The drug will be useful to hundreds of thousands of infected people.* 这种药物将会对成千上万感染者有用。 2 N-COUNT **Drugs** are substances that some people take because of their pleasant effects, but which are usually illegal. 毒品 ❑ *His mother was on drugs, on cocaine.* 他的母亲吸毒，吸可卡因。 ❑ *She was sure Leo was taking drugs.* 她肯定利奥在吸毒。 ❑ *...the problem of drug abuse.* …药物滥用的问题。 3 V-T If you **drug** a person or animal, you give them a chemical substance in order to make them sleepy or unconscious. 用药麻醉 ❑ *She was drugged and robbed.* 她被下了迷药，遭到抢劫。 4 V-T If food or drink **is drugged**, a chemical substance is added to it in order to make someone sleepy or unconscious when they eat or drink it. 下麻醉药于（食物或饮料）❑ *I wonder now if that drink had been drugged.* 我现在怀疑那饮料是否已被人下了麻醉药。

Word Partnership *drug* 的常用搭配：

ADJ. **generic** drug 1
dangerous drug, **experimental** drug 1 2
illegal drug 2

N. drug **abuse**, **effect of a** drug 1 2
drug **dealer**, drug **money**, drug **overdose**, drug **problem**, drug **smuggling**, drug **test**, drug **use** 2

drug ad·dict (**drug addicts**) N-COUNT A **drug addict** is someone who is addicted to illegal drugs. 吸毒成瘾者

drug·gist /drʌgɪst/ (**druggists**) 1 N-COUNT A **druggist** is the same as a **pharmacist**. 药剂师 [AM]

in BRIT, usually use **chemist**

2 N-COUNT A **druggist** or a **druggist's** is the same as a **pharmacy**. 药房 [oft "the" N] [AM]

in BRIT, usually use **chemist**

drug·store /drʌgstɔr/ (**drugstores**) N-COUNT A **drugstore** is a store where drugs and medicines are sold, and where you can buy cosmetics, some household goods, and also drinks and snacks. （兼营杂货、小吃的）药店 [AM]

In American English, the usual way of referring to a store where medicines are sold is a **drugstore**. ❑ *She went into a drugstore and bought some aspirin.* **Pharmacy** refers specifically to a part of the drugstore where you get prescription medicines. Pharmacies are often located in stores that mainly sell other merchandise, such as supermarkets and discount centers. In Britain, the nearest equivalent of a drugstore is a **chemist's**.

drum ♦◇◇ /drʌm/ (**drums, drumming, drummed**) 1 N-COUNT A **drum** is a musical instrument consisting of a skin stretched tightly over a round frame. You play a drum by beating it with sticks or with your hands. 鼓 ❑ *...a worker who died after collapsing while beating a drum during a demonstration.* …一个在游行时因击鼓过度劳累而倒毙的工人。 2 N-COUNT A **drum** is a large cylindrical container which is used to store fuel or other substances. 鼓状容器 ❑ *...an oil drum.* …一只油桶。 3 V-T/V-I If something **drums on** a surface, or if you **drum** something **on** a surface, it hits it regularly, making a continuous beating sound. 连续敲击 ❑ *He drummed his fingers on the leather top of his desk.* 他用手指不停地敲击皮桌面。

→ see Word Web: **drum**

▸ **drum into** PHRASAL VERB If you **drum** something **into** someone, you keep saying it to them until they understand it or remember it. 反复灌输 ❑ *Standard examples were drummed into students' heads.* 标准的例子被反复灌输到了学生的脑中。

▸ **drum up** PHRASAL VERB If you **drum up** support or business, you try to get it. 竭力争取 ❑ *It is to be hoped that he is merely drumming up business.* 希望他只是在招揽生意。

drum·mer /drʌmər/ (**drummers**) N-COUNT A **drummer** is a person who plays a drum or drums in a band or group. 鼓手 ❑ *He was a drummer in a rock band.* 他是一支摇滚乐队的鼓手。

→ see **drum**

drunk /drʌŋk/ (**drunks**) 1 ADJ Someone who is **drunk** has drunk so much alcohol that they cannot speak clearly or behave sensibly. 醉了的 ❑ *I got drunk and had to be carried home.* 我喝醉了，只得被搀扶回家。 2 N-COUNT A **drunk** is someone who is drunk or frequently gets drunk. 醉酒者；酗酒者 ❑ *A drunk lay in the alley.* 一个醉汉倒在巷子里。 3 **Drunk** is the past participle of **drink**. **drink**的过去分词

drunk driv·ing N-UNCOUNT **Drunk driving** is the offense of driving a vehicle after you have drunk more than the amount of alcohol that is legally allowed. 醉酒驾车 [mainly AM]

in BRIT, usually use **drink-driving**

❑ *He was arrested for drunk driving.* 他因为醉酒驾车被拘留了。 ● **drunk driv·er** N-UNCOUNT (**drunk drivers**) 醉酒驾车的司机 ❑ *...a car accident caused by a drunk driver.* …一名醉酒驾车的司机引发的车祸。

drunk·en /drʌŋkən/ 1 ADJ **Drunken** is used to describe events and situations that involve people who are drunk. 醉酒的 [ADJ n] ❑ *The pain roused him from his drunken stupor.* 疼痛让他从醉酒昏迷中醒过来。 2 ADJ A **drunken** person is drunk or is frequently drunk. 醉酒的；常醉的 [ADJ n] ❑ *Groups of drunken hooligans smashed windows and threw stones.* 成群醉酒的小流氓打碎了窗户，乱扔石头。 ● **drunk·en·ly** ADV 醉酒地；常醉地 [ADV with v] ❑ *Once Bob stormed drunkenly into her house and smashed some chairs.* 有一次，鲍勃醉醺醺地冲进她的房间，砸坏了几把椅子。 ● **drunk·en·ness** N-UNCOUNT 醉酒；酗酒 ❑ *He was arrested for drunkenness.* 他因酗酒而被拘留了。

dry ♦♦◇ /draɪ/ (**drier** or **dryer, driest, dries, drying, dried**) 1 ADJ If something is **dry**, there is no water or moisture on it or in it. 干的；干燥的 ❑ *Clean the metal with a soft dry cloth.* 用柔软的干布把这金属擦干净。 ❑ *Pat it dry with a soft towel.* 用柔软的毛巾将它轻轻拍干。 ● **dry·ness** N-UNCOUNT 干燥 ❑ *...the parched dryness of the air.* …空气的炎热干燥。 2 ADJ If you say that your skin or hair is **dry**, you mean that it is less oily than, or not as soft as, normal. （皮肤、头发）干枯的 ❑ *Nothing looks worse than dry, cracked lips.* 没有什么比干裂的嘴唇看上去更糟糕了。 ● **dry·ness** N-UNCOUNT 干枯 ❑ *Dryness of the skin can also be caused by living in centrally heated homes and offices.* 皮肤干燥还会因呆在有中央供暖的居室或办公室而引起。 3 ADJ If the weather or a period of time is **dry**, there is no rain or there is much less rain than average. 干旱的 ❑ *Exceptionally dry weather over the past year had cut agricultural production.* 过去一年里异常干旱的气候降低了农业产量。 4 ADJ A **dry** place or climate is one that gets very little rainfall. 干旱的；干燥的 ❑ *It was one of the driest and dustiest places in Africa.* 这里是非洲最干旱、灰尘最多的地方之一。 ● **dry·ness** N-UNCOUNT 干燥；干旱 ❑ *He was advised to spend time in the warmth and dryness of Italy.* 他被建议在意大利的温暖和干燥中过些日子。 5 ADJ If a river, lake, or well is **dry**, it is empty of water, usually because of hot weather and lack of rain. 干涸的 ❑ *The aquifer which had once fed the wells was pronounced dry.* 曾经给这些井提供水源的蓄水层已被宣告枯竭。 6 ADJ If an oil well is **dry**, it is no longer producing any oil. （油井）不再产油的 ❑ *To harvest oil and gas profitably from the North Sea, we must focus on the exploitation of small reserves as the big wells run dry.* 由于大油井的枯竭，要想从北海有利地获取石油和天然气，我们必须集中精力于小储量油井的开采。 7 ADJ If your mouth or throat is **dry**, it has little or no saliva in it, and so feels very unpleasant, perhaps because you are tense or ill. （口、咽）干的 ❑ *His mouth was still dry, he would certainly be glad of a drink.* 他的口还是干，他当然会乐于喝点什么。 ● **dry·ness** N-UNCOUNT （口、咽）干 ❑ *Symptoms included frequent dryness in the mouth.* 症状包括经常口干。 8 ADJ If someone has **dry** eyes, there are no tears in their eyes; often used with negatives or in contexts where you are expressing surprise that they are not crying. 无泪的 ❑ *There were few dry eyes in the house when I finished.* 当我结束时，屋里几乎没有人不掉眼泪的。 9 ADJ **Dry** humor is very amusing, but in a subtle and clever way. 冷面的 (幽默) [APPROVAL] ❑ *Though the pressure Fulton is under must be considerable, he has retained his dry humor.* 虽然富尔顿承受的压力一定是相当大的，但他还保持着冷面幽默。 ● **dry·ness** N-UNCOUNT 冷嘲 ❑ *It has a wry dryness you won't recognize.* 有一种你听不出来的讽刺。 10 ADJ If you describe something such as a book, play, or activity as **dry**, you mean that it is dull and uninteresting. 枯燥乏味的 [DISAPPROVAL] ❑ *My eyelids were drooping over the dry, academic phrases.* 这些枯燥乏味的学术用语让我的眼皮直向下耷拉。 11 ADJ **Dry** sherry or wine does not have a sweet taste. 无甜味的 (酒) ❑ *...a glass of chilled, dry white wine.* …一杯冰冻干白葡萄酒。 12 V-T/V-I When something **dries** or when you **dry** it, it becomes dry. 使…变干；变干 ❑ *Let your hair dry naturally whenever possible.* 无论何时尽可能让你的头发自然干。 13 V-T When you **dry** the dishes after a meal, you wipe the water off the plates, cups, knives, pans, and other things when they have been washed, using a cloth. 擦干 ❑ *Mrs. Madrigal picked up a towel and began drying dishes next to her daughter.* 马德里格夫人拿起一条毛巾，开始擦干她女儿旁边的盘子。 14 **high and dry** → see **high** 15 **home and dry** → see **home**

▸ **dry out** 1 PHRASAL VERB If something **dries out** or **is dried out**, it loses all the moisture that was in it and becomes hard. 使…干硬；干硬 ❑ *If the soil is allowed to dry out the tree could die.* 如果让土壤干硬，树就会死掉。 2 PHRASAL VERB If someone **dries out** or **is dried out**, they stop drinking alcohol. 使…戒酒；戒酒 [INFORMAL] ❑ *He checked into Cedars Sinai Hospital to dry out.* 他住进了雪松西奈医院去戒酒。

▸ **dry up** 1 PHRASAL VERB If something **dries up** or if something **dries it up**, it loses all its moisture and becomes completely dry and shriveled or hard. 使…干枯；干枯 ❑ *As the day goes on, the pollen dries up and becomes hard.* 随着日子一天天过去，花粉变得又干又硬。 2 PHRASAL VERB If a river, lake, or well **dries up**, it becomes empty of water, usually because of hot weather and a lack of rain. 干涸 ❑ *Reservoirs are drying up and farmers have begun to leave their land in search of water.* 水库正在干涸，农民开始离开田地去寻找水源。 3 PHRASAL VERB If a supply of something **dries up**, it stops. (供应) 停止 ❑ *The main source of income, tourism, is expected to dry up completely this summer.* 作为主要收入来源的旅游业预计将在今年夏天彻底枯竭。 4 PHRASAL VERB If you **dry up** when you are speaking, you stop in the middle of what you were saying, because you cannot think what to say next. (讲话时) 语塞 ❑ *When he turned around and saw her, his conversation dried up.* 他转过身来看见她时，他的谈话就出不来词儿了。 → see **weather**

dry-clean (**dry-cleans, dry-cleaning, dry-cleaned**) V-T When things such as clothes **are dry-cleaned**, they are cleaned with a liquid chemical rather than with water. 干洗 [usu passive] ❑ *Natural-filled duvets must be dry-cleaned by a professional.* 天然材料填充的羽绒被必须由专业人士干洗。 → see Word Web: **dry-cleaning**

dry·er /draɪər/ (**dryers**) also **drier** 1 N-COUNT A **dryer** is a machine for drying things. There are different kinds of dryers, for example, ones designed for drying clothes, crops, or people's hair or hands. 干燥器 ❑ *...hot air electric hand dryers.* …热风电动干手机。 2 → see also **dry, tumble dryer**

dry run (**dry runs**) N-COUNT If you have a **dry run**, you practice something to make sure that you are ready to do it properly. 演习；排练 ❑ *The competition is planned as a dry run for the World Cup finals.* 此次比赛是计划作为世界杯决赛的预演。

DTP /di ti pi/ **DTP** is an abbreviation for **desktop publishing**. 桌面出版

Word Link du ≈ two : dual, duopoly, duplicate

★ **dual** /duəl/ ADJ **Dual** means having two parts, functions, or aspects. 双重的 [ADJ n] ❑ *...his dual role as head of the party and head of state.* …他作为政党领袖和国家首脑的双重角色。

★ **dub** /dʌb/ (**dubs, dubbing, dubbed**) 1 V-T If someone or something **is dubbed** a particular thing, they are given that description or name. 把…称为 [JOURNALISM] ❑ *Today's session has been widely dubbed as a "make or break" meeting.* 今天的会议被大众称为"不成则散"的会议。 2 V-T If a movie or soundtrack in a foreign language **is dubbed**, a new soundtrack is added with actors giving a translation. 为 (影片等) 配音 [usu passive] ❑ *It was dubbed into Spanish for Mexican audiences.* 它已被配成西班牙语给墨西哥观众。

★ **du·bi·ous** /dubiəs/ 1 ADJ If you describe something as **dubious**, you mean that you do not consider it to be completely honest, safe, or reliable. 可疑的；不太可靠的 ❑ *This claim seems to us to be rather dubious.* 这项声明在我们看来相当不可信。 ● **du·bi·ous·ly** ADV 可疑地；不太可靠地 ❑ *Carter was dubiously convicted of shooting three white men in a bar.* 卡特很有嫌疑地被宣叛在一家酒吧射杀了3名白人。 2 ADJ If you are **dubious about** something, you are not completely sure about it and have not yet made up your mind about it. 有疑虑的 [V-link ADJ] ❑ *My parents were a bit dubious about it all at first but we soon convinced them.* 起初我父母亲对此尚心存疑虑，但很快我们便说服了他们。 ● **du·bi·ous·ly** ADV 迟疑地 ❑ *He eyed Coyne dubiously.* 他怀疑地注视着科因。

> Do not confuse **dubious**, **doubtful**, and **suspicious**. If you are **dubious** about something, you are not sure whether it is the right thing to do. ❑ *Alison sounded very dubious... The men in charge were a bit dubious about taking him on.* If you describe something as **dubious**, you think it is not completely honest, safe, or reliable. ❑ *...his dubious abilities as a teacher.* If you feel **doubtful** about something, you are unsure about it or about whether it will happen or be successful. ❑ *Do you feel insecure and doubtful about your ability?... It was doubtful he would ever see her again.* If you are **suspicious** of a person, you do not trust them and think they might be involved in something dishonest or illegal. ❑ *I am suspicious of his intentions... Miss Lenaut had grown suspicious.* If you describe something as **suspicious**, it suggests behavior that is dishonest, illegal, or dangerous. ❑ *He listened for any suspicious sounds.*

duch·ess /dʌtʃɪs/ (**duchesses**) N-COUNT A **duchess** is a woman who has the same rank as a duke, or who is a duke's wife or widow. 女公爵；公爵夫人 ❑ *...the Duchess of Kent.* …肯特公爵夫人。

duck /dʌk/ (**ducks, ducking, ducked**) 1 N-VAR A **duck** is a common water bird with short legs, a short neck, and a large flat beak. 鸭 ❑ *Chickens and ducks scratch around the outbuildings.* 鸡鸭在外屋四周挖扒。 ● N-UNCOUNT **Duck** is the flesh of this bird when it is eaten as food. 鸭肉 ❑ *...honey roasted duck.* …蜜汁烤鸭。 2 V-I If you **duck**, you move your head or the top half of your body quickly downward to avoid something that might hit you, to avoid being seen, or to hide the expression on your face. 迅速低头；猛然俯身 ❑ *He ducked in time to save his head from a blow from the poker.* 他猛地低下头，及时地躲过了一棍。 3 V-T If you **duck** something such as a blow, you avoid it by moving your head or body quickly downward. 闪避 ❑ *Hans deftly ducked their blows.* 汉斯灵活地躲过了他们的猛击。 4 V-T If you **duck** your head, you move it quickly downward to hide the expression on your face. 迅速低下 (头) ❑ *He ducked his head to hide his admiration.* 他赶忙低下头以掩饰他的羡慕。 5 V-T You say that someone **ducks** a duty or responsibility when you disapprove of the fact that they avoid it. 逃避 (责任) [INFORMAL, DISAPPROVAL] ❑ *The defense secretary ducked the question of whether the United States was winning the war.* 国防部长回避了美国是否

Word Web dry-cleaning

Dry-cleaning is not actually dry at all. It **cleans clothes** with liquid **chemicals** instead of water. The first dry-cleaning **solvent** was **kerosene**. A Frenchman named Jolly discovered dry-cleaning by accident in 1855. He had spilled kerosene from a lamp on a tablecloth. He noticed the **stains** came out when the kerosene **washed** over them. Soon Jolly opened the first dry-cleaning **service**. Since then, cleaners have also used **gasoline** and other dangerous chemicals. Recently, a company developed a safer dry-cleaning system using **carbon dioxide**. The washer is pressurized, which turns the CO_2 gas into a liquid.

在打赢这场战争的问题。 6 PHRASE You say that criticism is **like water off a duck's back** or **water off a duck's back** to emphasize that it is not having any effect on the person being criticized. (批评) 毫无效果 [EMPHASIS] ❏ *All the criticism is water off a duck's back to me.* 所有的批评对我都不起丝毫作用。 7 PHRASE If you **take to** something **like a duck to water**, you discover that you are naturally good at it or that you find it very easy to do. (尤指天生地) 轻而易举 ❏ *Some mothers take to breastfeeding like a duck to water, while others find they need some help to get started.* 有些母亲自然就会母乳喂养，而有些则觉得他们需要帮助才能开始。

D

▸ **duck out** PHRASAL VERB If you **duck out of** something that you are supposed to do, you avoid doing it. 逃避; 推托 [INFORMAL] ❏ *George ducked out of his forced marriage to a cousin.* 乔治逃避了与一个表妹的强迫婚姻。

duct /dʌkt/ (**ducts**) N-COUNT A **duct** is a pipe, tube, or channel which carries a liquid or gas. 输送管道 ❏ *...a big air duct in the ceiling.* …天花板上一根粗大的导风管。

dud /dʌd/ (**duds**) ADJ **Dud** means not working properly or not successful. 无用的; 不成功的 [ADJ n] [INFORMAL] ❏ *He replaced a dud valve.* 他换掉了一个无用的电子管。 ● N-COUNT **Dud** is also a noun. 无用的人; 废物 ❏ *The mine was a dud.* 这颗雷是颗哑雷。

dude /dud/ (**dudes**) N-COUNT A **dude** is a man. In very informal situations, **dude** is sometimes used as a greeting or form of address to a man. 男人; 伙计 [AM, INFORMAL] ❏ *My doctor is a real cool dude.* 我的医生真是个酷男人。

due ◆◆◇ /du/ 1 PHRASE If an event is **due to** something, it happens or exists as a direct result of that thing. 是…的结果 ❏ *The country's economic problems are largely due to the weakness of the recovery.* 该国的经济问题很大程度上是复苏乏力的结果。 2 PHRASE You can say **due to** to introduce the reason for something happening. Some speakers of English believe that it is not correct to use **due to** in this way. 由于 ❏ *Due to the large volume of letters he receives Dave regrets he is unable to answer queries personally.* 由于收到的来信数量太多，戴夫很遗憾不能亲自回复各种询问。 3 PHRASE If you say that something will happen or take place **in due course**, you mean that you cannot make it happen any quicker and it will happen when the time is right for it. 在适当的时候 ❏ *In due course the baby was born.* 婴儿如期降生了。 4 PHRASE You can say "**to give him his due**," or "**giving him his due**," when you are admitting that there are some good things about someone, even though there are things that you do not like about them. 给某人应得的评价 ❏ *To give Linda her due, she had tried to encourage John in his school work.* 为琳达说句公道话，她曾尽力在学习方面鼓励约翰。 5 PHRASE You can say "**with due respect**" when you are about to disagree politely with someone. 请恕冒昧; 斗胆 [POLITENESS] ❏ *With all due respect I submit to you that you're asking the wrong question.* 恕我斗胆直言，我认为您在问错误的问题。 6 ADJ If something is **due** at a particular time, it is expected to happen, be done, or arrive at that time. 预期的 ❏ *The results are due at the end of the month.* 结果预期于月底揭晓。 ❏ *Mr. Carter is due in Washington on Monday.* 卡特先生预计周一到达华盛顿。 7 ADJ **Due** attention or consideration is the proper, reasonable, or deserved amount of it under the circumstances. 适当的; 应有的 [ADJ n] ❏ *After due consideration it was decided to send him away to live with foster parents.* 经过充分考虑，决定将他送去与养父母生活。 8 ADJ Something that is **due**, or that is **due to** someone, is owed to them, either as a debt or because they have a right to it. 应得的 [v-link ADJ] ❏ *I was sent a check and advised that no further pension was due.* 我收到了一张支票并被告知不再有应领的养老金了。 9 ADJ If someone is **due for** something, that thing is planned to happen or be given to them now, or very soon, often after they have been waiting for it for a long time. (经长久等待后) 预期发生的 [v-link ADJ "for" n] ❏ *Although not due for release until 2001, he was let out of his low-security prison to spend a weekend with his wife.* 虽然要等到2001年才能获释，他却被允许离开看守宽松的监狱去和妻子共度一个周末。

duel /duəl/ (**duels**) N-COUNT A **duel** is a formal fight between two people in which they use guns or swords in order to settle a quarrel. 双人决斗 ❏ *He killed a man in one duel and was himself wounded in another.* 在一次双人决斗中他杀了人，还有一次他自己受了伤。

duet /duɛt/ (**duets**) N-COUNT A **duet** is a piece of music sung or played by two people. 二重唱; 二重奏 ❏ *Tonight she sings a duet with first husband Maurice Gibb.* 今晚她与第一任丈夫莫里斯·吉布表演了二重唱。

dug /dʌg/ **Dug** is the past tense and past participle of **dig**. dig的过去式和过去分词

→ see **tunnel**

▲ **duke** /duk/ (**dukes**) N-COUNT A **duke** is a man with a very high social rank in the nobility of some countries. 公爵 ❏ *...the Queen and the Duke of Edinburgh.* …女王和爱丁堡公爵。

dull /dʌl/ (**duller, dullest, dulls, dulling, dulled**) 1 ADJ If you describe someone or something as **dull**, you mean they are not interesting or exciting. 沉闷的; 乏味的 [DISAPPROVAL] ❏ *I felt she found me boring and dull.* 我觉得她认为我令人厌烦而又乏味。 ● **dull·ness** N-UNCOUNT 沉闷; 乏味 ❏ *They enjoy anything that breaks the dullness of their routine life.* 他们喜爱能打破他们规律生活的沉闷的任何事情。 2 ADJ Someone or something that is **dull** is not very lively or energetic. 无精打采的; 无生气的 ❏ *The body's natural rhythms mean we all feel dull and sleepy between 1 and 3 pm.* 身体的自然节律造成我们在下午1点至3点间都会感到无精打采、昏昏欲睡。 ● **dul·ly** ADV 无精打采地; 了无生气地 [ADV after v] ❏ *His giant face had a rough growth of stubble, his eyes looked dully ahead.* 他宽大的脸庞上长着粗硬的胡子茬，眼睛黯然无神地看着前方。 ● **dull·ness** N-UNCOUNT 无精打采; 了无生气 ❏ *Did you notice any unusual depression or dullness of mind?* 你注意到不同寻常的情绪消沉或心智愚钝了吗? 3 ADJ A **dull** color or light is not bright. 黯淡的 ❏ *The stamp was a dark, dull blue color with a heavy black postmark.* 这枚邮票是模糊的暗蓝色的，上面盖着一个粗黑色的邮戳。 ● **dul·ly** ADV 黯淡地 [ADV with v] ❏ *The street lamps gleamed dully through the night's mist.* 街灯透过夜的薄雾隐约地闪现。 4 ADJ You say the weather is **dull** when it is very cloudy. (天气) 阴沉的 ❏ *It's always dull and raining.* 天老是阴沉沉的，下着雨。 5 ADJ **Dull** sounds are not very clear or loud. 低沉而模糊的 ❏ *The coffin closed with a dull thud.* 随着一声沉闷地撞击声，棺材合上了。 ● **dul·ly** ADV 低沉而模糊地 [ADV after v] ❏ *He heard his heart thump dully but more quickly.* 他听见他的心跳低沉但却更急速。 6 ADJ **Dull** feelings are weak and not intense. 微弱的 [ADJ n] ❏ *The pain, usually a dull ache, gets worse with exercise.* 这种疼痛，通常是隐隐作痛，运动时会加剧。 ● **dul·ly** ADV 微弱地 ❏ *His arm throbbed dully.* 他的手臂微微地颤动。 7 V-T/V-I If something **dulls** or if it is **dulled**, it becomes less intense, bright, or lively. 使…变弱/变暗/变得无生气; 变弱/变暗/变得无生气 ❏ *Her eyes dulled and she gazed blankly.* 她双目变得黯然无神，茫然凝神。

Thesaurus *dull* 另参见:
ADJ. dingy, drab, faded, plain 3

duly /duli/ 1 ADV If you say that something **duly** happened or was done, you mean that it was expected to happen or was requested, and it did happen or it was done. 如期地 [ADV before v] ❏ *Westcott appealed to Waite for an apology, which he duly received.* 韦斯科特向韦特要求一个道歉，然后他如期得到了。 2 ADV If something is **duly** done, it is done in the correct way. 适当地 [ADV before v] [FORMAL] ❏ *He is a duly elected president of the country and we're going to be giving him all the support we can.* 他是这个国家正式选出的总统，我们将给他我们所能给的一切支持。

dumb /dʌm/ (**dumber, dumbest, dumbs, dumbing, dumbed**) 1 ADJ Someone who is **dumb** is completely unable to speak. 哑的 ❏ *...a young deaf and dumb man.* …一名年轻的聋哑人。 2 ADJ If someone is **dumb** on a particular occasion, they cannot speak because they are angry, shocked, or surprised. 说不出话的 [v-link ADJ] [LITERARY] ❏ *We were all struck dumb for a minute.* 我们一时个个都哑口无言。 3 ADJ If you call a person **dumb**, you mean that they are stupid or foolish. 蠢的 [INFORMAL, DISAPPROVAL] ❏ *The questions were set up to make her look dumb.* 这些问题是安排好让她显得蠢的。 4 ADJ If you say that something is **dumb**, you think that it is silly and annoying. 愚蠢而恼人的 [AM, INFORMAL, DISAPPROVAL] ❏ *I came up with this dumb idea.* 我想出了这个愚蠢而恼人的主意。

→ see **disability**

▸ **dumb down** PHRASAL VERB If you **dumb down** something, you make it easier for people to understand, especially when this spoils it. 通俗化 ❏ *This sounded like a case for dumbing down the magazine, which no one favored.* 这听起来像是一桩使杂志通俗化的事，没人赞成。

dum·my /dʌmi/ (**dummies**) 1 N-COUNT A **dummy** is the same as a **mannequin**. 人体模型 2 N-COUNT You can use **dummy** to refer to things that are not real, but have been made to look or behave as if they are real. 仿真品 ❏ *Dummy patrol cars will be set up beside highways to frighten speeding motorists.* 仿真巡逻车将被安置在公路旁以威慑超速行驶的驾驶员。 3 N-COUNT If you call a person a **dummy**,

Word Web dump

Most communities used to dispose of **solid waste** in **dumps**. However, more **environmentally friendly** methods are common today. There are alternatives to dumping **refuse** in a **landfill**. **Reduction** means creating less waste. For example, using washable napkins instead of paper napkins. Reuse involves finding a second use for something without processing it. For instance, giving old clothing to a charity. **Recycling** and **composting** involve finding a new use for something by processing it—using food scraps to fertilize a garden. **Incineration** involves burning solid waste and using the heat for another useful purpose.

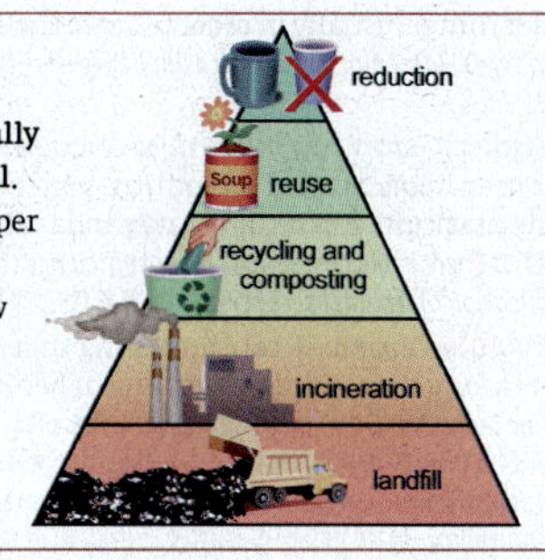

you mean that they are stupid or foolish. 笨蛋；傻瓜 [AM, INFORMAL, DISAPPROVAL] 4 N-COUNT A baby's **dummy** is the same as a **pacifier**. 抚慰奶嘴 [BRIT]

dump ♦◇◇ /dʌmp/ (**dumps, dumping, dumped**) 1 V-T If you **dump** something somewhere, you put it or unload it there quickly and carelessly. 扔下；倾倒 [INFORMAL] ❑ *We dumped our bags at the nearby Grand Hotel and hurried toward the market.* 我们把包扔在附近的格兰德旅馆，急匆匆地向市场赶去。 2 V-T If something **is dumped** somewhere, it is put or left there because it is no longer wanted or needed. 丢弃 [INFORMAL] ❑ *The getaway car was dumped near the freeway.* 那辆逃亡用的小汽车被丢弃在高速公路附近。 ● **dump·ing** N-UNCOUNT 倾倒；丢弃 ❑ *German law forbids the dumping of hazardous waste on German soil.* 德国法律禁止德国国土上危险废弃物的倾倒。 3 V-T To **dump** something such as an idea, policy, or practice means to stop supporting or using it. 抛弃（念头、政策或惯例）[INFORMAL] ❑ *The party dumped the policy of nationalization in favor of the free market.* 该党抛弃了国有化政策，转而支持自由市场政策。 4 V-T If a firm or company **dumps** goods, it sells large quantities of them at prices far below their real value, usually in another country, in order to gain a bigger market share or to keep prices high in the home market. 倾销 [BUSINESS] ❑ *It produces more than it needs, then dumps its surplus onto the world market.* 它出产过剩，于是就将过剩的产品倾销到全球市场。 5 V-T If you **dump** someone, you end your relationship with them. 抛弃（某人）[INFORMAL] ❑ *My heart sank because I thought he was going to dump me for another girl.* 想到他将抛弃我去追求另一个女孩，我的心沉了。 6 V-T To **dump** computer data or memory means to copy it from one storage system onto another, such as from disk to magnetic tape. 转储 [COMPUTING] ❑ *All the data is then dumped into the main computer.* 然后所有的资料被转储到主计算机中。 7 N-COUNT A **dump** is a place where garbage and waste material are left, for example, on open ground outside a town. 垃圾场 ❑ *...companies that bring their trash straight to the dump.* …将其废物直接运到垃圾场的公司。 8 N-COUNT If you say that a place is a **dump**, you think it is ugly and unpleasant to live in or visit. 肮脏不堪的地方 [INFORMAL, DISAPPROVAL] ❑ *"What a dump!" Christabel said, standing in the doorway of the youth hostel.* 克丽丝特布尔站在青年旅舍的门口说道："真是个肮脏的地方！" 9 N-COUNT A **dump** is a list of the data that is stored in a computer's memory at a particular time. **Dumps** are often used by computer programmers to find out what is causing a problem with a program. (常用来发现程序问题) 数据转储 [COMPUTING] ❑ *...print it out and it'll do a screen dump of what's there.* 把它打印出来，它会将所在的信息进行屏幕转储。
→ see Word Web: **dump**

dump·ling /dʌmplɪŋ/ (**dumplings**) N-VAR **Dumplings** are small lumps of dough that are cooked and eaten, either with meat and vegetables or as a fruit-filled dessert. 饺子；水果布丁

Dump·ster /dʌmpstər/ (**Dumpsters**) N-COUNT A **Dumpster** is a large metal container for holding trash. 大型金属制垃圾桶 [AM, TRADEMARK]

in BRIT, usually use **skip**

dune /dun/ (**dunes**) N-COUNT A **dune** is a hill of sand near the ocean or in a desert. 沙丘 ❑ *Large dunes make access to the beach difficult in places.* 在有些地方大沙丘使得靠近海滩很难。
→ see **beach, desert**

dung /dʌŋ/ N-UNCOUNT **Dung** is feces from animals, especially from large animals such as cattle and horses. (大型动物如牛、马的) 粪 ❑ *Workers at Sydney's harborside Taronga zoo are refusing to collect animal dung in a protest over wages.* 悉尼海港塔龙加动物园的工人因对工资的抗议而拒绝收拾动物粪便。

dun·ga·rees /dʌŋgəriz/ 1 N-PLURAL **Dungarees** are the same as **jeans**. 牛仔裤 (同 jeans) [also "a pair of" N] [AM] 2 N-PLURAL **Dungarees** are a one-piece garment consisting of pants, a piece of cloth which covers your chest, and straps which go over your shoulders. 背带裤 [also "a pair of" N] [BRIT]

in AM, use **overalls**

dun·geon /dʌndʒᵊn/ (**dungeons**) N-COUNT A **dungeon** is a dark underground prison in a castle. 地牢

dun·no /dənou/ **Dunno** is sometimes used in written English to represent an informal way of saying "don't know." 不知道 (有时用于书面语表示非正式说法) ❑ *"How on earth did she get it?"—"I dunno."* "她究竟是如何弄到它的？"——"我不知道。"

duo /duou/ (**duos**) 1 N-COUNT A **duo** is two musicians, singers, or other performers who perform together as a pair. 二重奏演奏者；二重唱演唱者；二人组合表演者 ❑ *...a famous dancing and singing duo.* …一个著名的歌舞表演二人组。 2 N-COUNT You can refer to two people together as a **duo**, especially when they have something in common. (有共同点的) 一对人 [mainly JOURNALISM] ❑ *The Giants are led by the scoring duo of Adam Courchaine and Gilbert Brule.* 巨人队由得分二人搭档亚当・库彻恩和吉尔伯特・布鲁尔领队。

Word Link *du ≈ two : dual, duopoly, duplicate*

duo·po·ly /duɒpəli/ (**duopolies**) 1 N-VAR If two companies or people have a **duopoly on** something such as an industry, they share complete control over it and it is impossible for others to become involved in it. 两强霸权 [BUSINESS] ❑ *...they are no longer part of a duopoly on overseas routes.* …他们不再是控制海外通道的两强霸权的一部分。 2 N-COUNT A **duopoly** is a group of two companies which are the only ones which provide a particular product or service, and which therefore have complete control over an industry. 两家寡头集团 [BUSINESS] ❑ *Their smaller rival is battling to end their duopoly.* 比他们小的竞争对手正在为结束他们两家寡头集团而斗争。

dupe /dup/ (**dupes, duping, duped**) 1 V-T If a person **dupes** you, they trick you into doing something or into believing something which is not true. 欺骗 ❑ *...a plot to dupe stamp collectors into buying fake rarities.* …一个欺骗集邮爱好者购买假冒珍品的阴谋。 2 N-COUNT A **dupe** is someone who is tricked by someone else. 受骗者

★ **du·pli·cate** (**duplicates, duplicating, duplicated**)

The verb is pronounced /duplɪkeɪt/. The noun and adjective are pronounced /duplɪkɪt/.

动词读作 /duplɪkeɪt/。名词和形容词读作 /duplɪkɪt/。

1 V-T If you **duplicate** something that has already been done, you repeat or copy it. 复制 ❑ *His task will be to duplicate his success overseas here at home.* 他的任务将是在国内复制他在海外的成功。 ● N-COUNT **Duplicate** is also a noun. 复制；复制品 ❑ *The tight race is almost a duplicate of the elections in Georgia and South Dakota last month that pitted a Republican challenger against a Democratic incumbent.* 这次紧张的竞选几乎是上个月在佐治亚州和南达科他州选举的翻版，由一个共和党的挑战者竞争一个现任的民主党人。 2 V-T To **duplicate** something which has been written, drawn, or recorded onto tape means to make exact copies of it. 复印；复制 ❑ *...a business which duplicates video tapes for the movie makers.* …一家为电影制片人复制录像带的企业。 ● N-COUNT **Duplicate** is also a noun. 复本 [also "in" N] ❑ *I'm on my way to Switzerland, but I've lost my card. I've got to get a duplicate.* 我在去瑞士的路上，但是我的卡丢了。我得弄张补发卡。 3 ADJ **Duplicate** is used to describe things that have been made as an exact copy of

d

other things, usually in order to serve the same purpose. 复制的 [ADJ n] ❑ *He let himself in with a duplicate key.* 他用一把另配的钥匙打开门进去了。

du·pli·ca·tion /duplɪkeɪʃ^{ə}n/ N-UNCOUNT If you say that there has been **duplication** of something, you mean that someone has done a task unnecessarily because it has already been done before. 重复 ❑ *There could be a serious loss of efficiency through unnecessary duplication of resources.* 不必要的资源重复会导致严重的效率损耗。

D

du·rable /dʊərəb^{ə}l/ ADJ Something that is **durable** is strong and lasts a long time without breaking or becoming weaker. 耐用的 ❑ *Fine bone china is eminently practical, since it is strong and durable.* 精细骨瓷是非同一般地实用，因为它坚固耐用。 ● **du·rabil·ity** /dʊərəbɪlɪti/ N-UNCOUNT 耐用性 ❑ *Airlines recommend hard-sided cases for durability.* 航空公司推荐使用硬边的提箱以求耐用。

du·rable goods also **durables** N-PLURAL **Durable goods** or **durables** are goods such as televisions or cars which are expected to last a long time, and are bought infrequently. 耐用品 [mainly AM]

in BRIT, usually use **consumer durables**

❑ *...a 2.6% rise in orders for durable goods in January.* …1月份耐用品定单2.6%的涨幅。

du·ra·tion /dʊəreɪʃ^{ə}n/ **1** N-UNCOUNT The **duration of** an event or state is the time during which it happens or exists. 持续期间 ❑ *He was given the task of protecting her for the duration of the trial.* 他被委以在审判期间保护她的任务。 **2** PHRASE If you say that something will happen **for the duration**, you mean that it will happen for as long as a particular situation continues. 在整个时间段 ❑ *His wounds knocked him out of combat for the duration.* 在整个战斗中，他的伤一直令他无法参战。

dur·ing ♦♦♦ /dʊərɪŋ/ **1** PREP If something happens **during** a period of time or an event, it happens continuously, or happens several times between the beginning and end of that period or event. 在…期间内（不断发生）❑ *Sandstorms are common during the Saudi Arabian winter.* 在沙特阿拉伯的冬季期间内沙暴很常见。 **2** PREP If something develops **during** a period of time, it develops gradually from the beginning to the end of that period. 在…期间（逐步发展）❑ *Wages have fallen by more than twenty percent during the past two months.* 在过去的两个月期间工资已下降了二十多个百分点。 **3** PREP An event that happens **during** a period of time happens at some point or moment in that period. 在…期间的某一刻（发生）❑ *During his visit, the Pope will also bless the new hospital.* 在他访问期间，教皇也将为新医院祈福。

You do not use **during** to say how long something lasts. You use **for**. You do not say, for example, "I went to Florida during two weeks." You say "**I went to Florida for two weeks.**"

dusk /dʌsk/ N-UNCOUNT **Dusk** is the time just before night when the daylight has almost gone but when it is not completely dark. 黄昏 ❑ *We arrived home at dusk.* 我们于黄昏时分到家了。

dust ♦◇◇ /dʌst/ (**dusts, dusting, dusted**) **1** N-UNCOUNT **Dust** is very small dry particles of earth or sand. 沙尘 ❑ *Tanks raise huge trails of dust when they move.* 坦克移动时掀起滚滚的尘土。 **2** N-UNCOUNT **Dust** is the very small pieces of dirt which you find inside buildings, for example, on furniture, floors, or lights. 灰尘 ❑ *I could see a thick layer of dust on the stairs.* 我能看见楼梯上厚厚的一层灰尘。 **3** N-UNCOUNT **Dust** is a fine powder which consists of very small particles of a substance such as gold, wood, or coal. 粉末 ❑ *The air is so black with diesel fumes and coal dust, I can barely see.* 天空由于充满柴油机的浓烟和煤灰而如此黑，我几乎看不见。 **4** V-T/V-I When you **dust** something such as furniture, you remove dust from it, usually using a cloth. 去除灰尘 ❑ *I vacuumed and dusted and polished the living room.* 我把起居室吸了尘、掸了灰并且擦亮了。 **5** V-T/V-I If you **dust** something **with** a fine substance such as powder or if you **dust** a fine substance **onto** something, you cover it lightly with that substance. 用（粉状物）擦涂；把（粉状物）撒于 ❑ *Lightly dust the fish with flour.* 轻轻地把鱼撒上面粉。 **6** PHRASE If you say that something **has bitten the dust**, you are emphasizing that it no longer exists or that it has failed. 不复存在；失败 [HUMOROUS, INFORMAL, EMPHASIS] ❑ *In the last 30 years many cherished values have bitten the dust.* 过去30年里许多值得珍惜的价值观已经不复存在。 **7** PHRASE If you say that something will happen when **the dust settles**, you mean that a situation will be clearer after it has calmed down. If you let **the dust settle** before doing something, you let a situation calm down before you try to do anything else. 尘埃落定 [INFORMAL] ❑ *Once the dust had settled Beck defended his decision.* 一旦尘埃落定，贝克就为自己的决定进行了辩护。 **8** PHRASE If you say that something **is gathering dust**, you mean that it has been left somewhere and nobody is using it or doing anything with it. 闲置 ❑ *Many of the machines are gathering dust in basements.* 很多的机器闲置在地下室里。

dust·bin /dʌstbɪn/ (**dustbins**) N-COUNT A **dustbin** is the same as a **garbage can.** 垃圾箱 [BRIT]

dusty /dʌsti/ (**dustier, dustiest**) **1** ADJ If places, roads, or other things outside are **dusty**, they are covered with tiny bits of earth or sand, usually because it has not rained for a long time. 覆有尘土的 ❑ *They started strolling down the dusty road in the moonlight.* 他们开始在月光下满是尘土的道路上漫步。 **2** ADJ If a room, house, or object is **dusty**, it is covered with very small pieces of dirt. 布满灰尘的 ❑ *...a dusty attic.* …一个布满灰尘的阁楼。

du·ti·ful /dutɪfəl/ ADJ If you say that someone is **dutiful**, you mean that they do everything that they are expected to do. 顺从的；尽职的 ❑ *The days of the dutiful wife, who sacrifices her career for her husband, are over.* 顺从的妻子为了丈夫而牺牲自己事业的时代已经结束了。 ● **du·ti·ful·ly** ADV 顺从地；尽职地 [ADV with v] ❑ *The inspector dutifully recorded the date in a large red book.* 巡视员尽职地在一本红色的大工作簿上记录下了日期。

duty ♦♦◇ /duti/ (**duties**) **1** N-UNCOUNT **Duty** is work that you have to do for your job. 工作 ❑ *Staff must report for duty at their normal place of work.* 职员必须到他们平常的岗位报到上班。 **2** N-PLURAL Your **duties** are tasks which you have to do because they are part of your job. 职责 ❑ *I carried out my duties conscientiously.* 我认真执行了我的各项职责。 **3** N-SING If you say that something is your **duty**, you believe that you ought to do it because it is your responsibility. 责任 ❑ *I consider it my duty to write to you and thank you.* 我觉得我有责任给你写信表示感谢。 **4** N-VAR **Duties** are taxes which you pay to the government on goods that you buy. 税 ❑ *Import duties still average 30%.* 进口关税平均仍为30%。 **5** PHRASE If someone such as a police officer or a nurse is **off duty**, they are not working. If someone is **on duty**, they are working. 下班；上班 ❑ *I'm off duty.* 我下班了。

Thesaurus *duty* 另参见：

N. assignment, responsibility, task **1**
obligation **3**

Word Partnership *duty* 的常用搭配：

N. **guard** duty, **jury** duty **1**
sense of duty **3**
ADJ. **civic** duty, **military** duty, **patriotic** duty **3**
PREP. **off** duty, **on** duty **5**

Word Link *free* ≈ *without* : *carefree, duty-free, tax-free*

duty-free ADJ **Duty-free** goods are sold at airports or on planes or ships at a cheaper price than usual because you do not have to pay import tax on them. 免关税的 ❑ *...duty-free cigarettes.* …免税香烟。

duty-free shop (**duty-free shops**) N-COUNT A **duty-free shop** is a shop, for example, at an airport, where you can buy goods at a cheaper price than usual, because no tax is paid on them. 免税商店

du·vet /duveɪ/ (**duvets**) N-COUNT A **duvet** is the same as a **comforter.** 羽绒被 [mainly BRIT]

DVD /di vi di/ (**DVDs**) N-COUNT A **DVD** is a disk on which a movie or music is recorded. DVD disks are similar to compact disks but hold a lot more information. **DVD** is an abbreviation for "digital video disk" or "digital versatile disk." 数字视频光盘 ❑ *...a DVD player.* …一个数字视频光盘播放器。

→ see Word Web: DVD

→ see **laser**

DVT /di vi ti/ (**DVTs**) N-VAR **DVT** is a serious medical condition caused by blood clots in the legs moving up to the lungs. **DVT** is an abbreviation for **deep vein thrombosis.** 深静脉血栓症 [MEDICAL]

dwarf /dwɔrf/ (**dwarves, dwarfs, dwarfing, dwarfed**)

The spellings **dwarves** or **dwarfs** are used for the plural form of the noun.

1 V-T If one person or thing **is dwarfed** by another, the second is so much bigger than the first that it makes them look very small. 使…显得过于矮小 ❑ *His figure is dwarfed by the huge red McDonald's sign.*

Word Web DVD

DVDs aren't just for **movies** anymore. New DVDs **(digital video discs)** provide even better sound quality than audio CDs **(compact discs)**. Since the 1980s, CDs have provided high fidelity sound reproduction. Both CDs and DVDs **sample** the **music**, but DVDs are able to store more information and they have more samples per second. The information is also more accurate. Many people think that when you **play** a DVD, it sounds more like live music.

d

他的个子被巨大的红色麦当劳招牌衬得格外矮小。 **2** ADJ **Dwarf** is used to describe varieties or species of plants and animals which are much smaller than the usual size for their kind. (植物或动物) 过于矮小的 [ADJ n] ❑ *...dwarf shrubs.* …过于矮小的灌木丛。 **3** N-COUNT In children's stories, a **dwarf** is an imaginary creature that is like a small man. Dwarfs often have magical powers. (童话中的) 小矮人 **4** N-COUNT In former times, people who were much smaller than normal were called **dwarves**. 侏儒 [OFFENSIVE, OLD-FASHIONED]

★ **dwell** /dwɛl/ (**dwells, dwelling, dwelt** or **dwelled**) **1** V-I If you **dwell on** something, especially something unpleasant, you think, speak, or write about it a lot or for quite a long time. 细想; 详述 ❑ *"I'd rather not dwell on the past," he told me.* "我宁愿不多想过去," 他告诉我。 **2** → see also **dwelling**

★ **dwell·er** /dwɛlər/ (**dwellers**) N-COUNT A city **dweller** or slum **dweller**, for example, is a person who lives in the kind of place or house indicated. 居住者 ❑ *The number of city dwellers is growing.* 城市居民的数量日渐增长。

dwell·ing /dwɛlɪŋ/ (**dwellings**) N-COUNT A **dwelling** or a **dwelling place** is a place where someone lives. 住所; 居住地 [FORMAL] ❑ *Some 3,500 new dwellings are planned for the area.* 大约三千五百套新住宅计划在这个地区新建。

dwelt /dwɛlt/ **Dwelt** is the past tense and past participle of **dwell**. **dwell**的过去式和过去分词

▲ **dwin·dle** /dwɪndᵊl/ (**dwindles, dwindling, dwindled**) V-I If something **dwindles**, it becomes smaller, weaker, or less in number. 缩小; 减少 ❑ *The factory's workforce has dwindled from over 4,000 to a few hundred.* 该厂的工人总数已从4000多减少到了几百人。

dye /daɪ/ (**dyes, dyeing, dyed**) **1** V-T If you **dye** something such as hair or cloth, you change its color by soaking it in a special liquid. 染色 ❑ *The women prepared, spun, and dyed the wool.* 妇女们将羊毛预备、纺线并染色。 **2** N-MASS **Dye** is a substance made from plants or chemicals which is mixed into a liquid and used to change the color of something such as cloth or hair. 染料 ❑ *...bottles of hair dye.* …一瓶瓶的染发剂。
→ see **hair**

dy·ing /daɪɪŋ/ **1** **Dying** is the present participle of **die**. **die**的现在分词 **2** ADJ A **dying** person or animal is very ill and likely to die soon. 垂死的 [ADJ n] ❑ *...a dying man.* …一个垂死之人。 ● N-PLURAL **The dying** are people who are dying. 垂死的人们 ❑ *By the time our officers arrived, the dead and the dying were everywhere.* 当我们的警官到达的时候已是遍地尸首和垂死的人。 **3** ADJ You use **dying** to describe something which happens at the time when someone dies, or is connected with that time. 临终的 [ADJ n] ❑ *It'll stay in my mind till my dying day.* 它将长存我心，直到生命的最后一天。 **4** ADJ The **dying** days or **dying** minutes of a state of affairs or an activity are its last days or minutes. 濒临消亡的 (日子); 即将结束的 (时刻) [ADJ n] ❑ *...a story of love and war in the dying days of the Ottoman Empire.* …奥特曼帝国濒临灭亡时的一个爱情与战争的故事。 **5** ADJ A **dying** tradition or industry is becoming less important and is likely to disappear completely. 没落的; 快要消亡的 [ADJ n] ❑ *Shipbuilding is a dying business.* 造船业是一个没落行业。

dyke /daɪk/ (**dykes**) **1** N-COUNT A **dyke** is a lesbian. 女同性恋者 [INFORMAL, OFFENSIVE] **2** → see **dike 1**

Word Link *dyn ≈ power : dynamic, dynamite, dynamo*

dy·nam·ic /daɪnæmɪk/ (**dynamics**) **1** ADJ If you describe someone as **dynamic**, you approve of them because they are full of energy or full of new and exciting ideas. (人) 有活力的; 有创新思维的 [APPROVAL] ❑ *He seemed a dynamic and energetic leader.* 他看来是个富有创新力与活力的领导。 ● **dy·nami·cal·ly** /daɪnæmɪkli/ ADV 有活力地; 有创新思维地 ❑ *He's one of the most dynamically imaginative jazz pianists of our time.* 他是我们这个时代最具活跃想像力的爵士乐钢琴演奏家之一。 **2** ADJ If you describe something as **dynamic**, you approve of it because it is very active and energetic. (事物) 有活力的 [APPROVAL] ❑ *South Asia continues to be the most dynamic economic region in the world.* 南亚仍然是世界上最具活力的经济区。 **3** ADJ A **dynamic** process is one that constantly changes and progresses. 动态的 ❑ *...a dynamic, evolving worldwide epidemic.* …一次不断变化发展的、世界范围内的疾疫流行。 **4** N-COUNT The **dynamic** of a system or process is the force that causes it to change or progress. 动力 ❑ *The dynamic of the market demands constant change and adjustment.* 市场的动力要求有不断的变化和调整。 **5** N-PLURAL The **dynamics** of a situation or group of people are the opposing forces within it that cause it to change. (引发变革的) 反动力 ❑ *What is needed is insight into the dynamics of the social system.* 所需要的就是对社会制度反动力的洞悉。

dy·na·mism /daɪnəmɪzəm/ **1** N-UNCOUNT If you say that someone or something has **dynamism**, you are expressing approval of the fact that they are full of energy or full of new and exciting ideas. 活力; 创新思维 [APPROVAL] ❑ *...a situation that calls for dynamism and new thinking.* …一种需要活力和新思维的局势。 **2** N-UNCOUNT If you refer to the **dynamism** of a situation or system, you are referring to the fact that it is changing in an exciting and dramatic way. 活跃 [APPROVAL] ❑ *Such changes are also indicators of economic dynamism and demographic expansion.* 这些变化也是经济活跃和人口膨胀的指示器。

▲ **dy·na·mite** /daɪnəmaɪt/ **1** N-UNCOUNT **Dynamite** is a type of explosive that contains nitroglycerin. 炸药 ❑ *Fifty yards of track was blown up with dynamite.* 50码长的轨道被炸药炸毁了。 **2** N-UNCOUNT If you describe a piece of information as **dynamite**, you think that people will react strongly to it. 引发爆炸效应事物 [INFORMAL] ❑ *The book is dynamite, and if she publishes it, there will be no hiding place for her.* 这本书是颗"炸弹", 如果她将其出版, 必无藏身之所。 **3** N-UNCOUNT If you describe someone or something as **dynamite**, you think that they are exciting. 引发轰动效应的人或物 [INFORMAL, APPROVAL] ❑ *The first kiss is dynamite.* 初吻是激动人心的。

dy·na·mo /daɪnəmoʊ/ (**dynamos**) **1** N-COUNT A **dynamo** is a device that uses the movement of a machine or vehicle to produce electricity. 发电机 ❑ *...a bicycle with a dynamo.* …一辆电动自行车。 **2** N-COUNT If you describe someone as a **dynamo**, you mean that they are very energetic and are always busy and active. 精力旺盛的人 ❑ *Myles is a human dynamo.* 迈尔斯是一个精力特别旺盛的人。

▲ **dyn·as·ty** /daɪnəsti/ (**dynasties**) **1** N-COUNT A **dynasty** is a series of rulers of a country who all belong to the same family. 王朝 ❑ *The Seljuk dynasty of Syria was founded in 1094.* 叙利亚的塞尔柱王朝建立于1094年。 **2** N-COUNT A **dynasty** is a period of time during which a country is ruled by members of the same family. 朝代 ❑ *...carvings dating back to the Ming dynasty.* …可以追溯到明朝的雕刻。 **3** N-COUNT A **dynasty** is a family which has members from two or more generations who are important in a particular field of activity, for example, in business or politics. 世家 ❑ *This is a family-owned company – the current president is the fourth in this dynasty.* 这是一个家族企业——现任总裁是该世家的第4代。

dys·lexia /dɪslɛksiə/ N-UNCOUNT If someone suffers from **dyslexia**, they have difficulty with reading because of a slight disorder of their brain. 诵读困难 [TECHNICAL]

Ee

E

E also **e** /iː/ (**E's, e's**) N-VAR **E** is the fifth letter of the English alphabet. 英语字母表中第5个字母

each ♦♦♦ /iːtʃ/ **1** DET If you refer to **each** thing or **each** person in a group, you are referring to every member of the group and considering them as individuals. 每 ❑ *Each book is beautifully illustrated.* 每本书都配有精美的插图。 ❑ *Each year, hundreds of animals are killed in this way.* 每年，数百只动物就是这样被杀死的。 ● PRON **Each** is also a pronoun. 每 ❑ *...two bedrooms, each with three beds.* …两间卧室，每间有3张床。 ● PRON-EMPH **Each** is also an emphasizing pronoun. 每个 ❑ *We each have different needs and interests.* 我们每人有不同的需要和兴趣。 ● ADV **Each** is also an adverb. 每个地 [amount ADV] ❑ *The children were given one each, handed to them or placed on their plates.* 孩子们每人给一个，递给他们或者放在他们的盘子里。 ● QUANT **Each** is also a quantifier. 每个 [QUANT "of" def-pl-n] ❑ *He handed each of them a page of photos.* 他递给他们每人一张照片。 ❑ *Each of these exercises takes one or two minutes to do.* 这些练习题每一道要花一两分钟做完。 **2** QUANT If you refer to **each one of** the members of a group, you are emphasizing that something applies to every one of them. 每个 [QUANT "of" def-pl-n] [EMPHASIS] ❑ *He picked up forty of these publications and read each one of them.* 他从这些出版物中挑了40本，每本都读了。 **3** PHRASE You can refer to **each and every** member **of** a group to emphasize that you mean all the members of that group. 每一个 [EMPHASIS] ❑ *My goal was that each and every person responsible for Yankel's murder be brought to justice.* 我的目标是，让每一个对扬克尔被谋杀负有责任的人都受到惩处。 **4** PRON-RECIP You use **each other** when you are saying that each member of a group does something to the others or has a particular connection with the others. 相互 [V PRON, prep PRON] ❑ *We looked at each other in silence, each equally shocked.* 我们无言地相互对视，每个人都同样地震惊。 ❑ *Both sides are willing to make allowances for each other's political sensitivities.* 双方都愿意顾及相互的政治敏感性。

> You use **each** to refer to every person or thing in a group when you are thinking about them as individuals. You use **every** to refer to all the members of a group that has more than two members. ❑ *He listened to every news bulletin. ...an equal chance for every child.* Note that **each** can be used to refer to both members of a pair. ❑ *Each apartment has two bedrooms... We each carried a suitcase.* Note that **each** and **every** are only used with singular nouns.

eager ♦◇◇ /iːgər/ **1** ADJ If you are **eager to** do or have something, you want to do or have it very much. 渴望的 ❑ *Robert was eager to talk about life in the Army.* 罗伯特渴望谈论军旅生活。 ❑ *When my own son was five years old, I became eager for another baby.* 当我儿子5岁的时候，我开始渴望要另一个宝宝。 ● **eager·ness** N-UNCOUNT 渴望 ❑ *...an eagerness to learn.* …一种学习的渴望。 **2** ADJ If you look or sound **eager**, you look or sound as if you expect something interesting or enjoyable to happen. 热切的 ❑ *Arty sneered at the crowd of eager faces around him.* 阿蒂对周围满脸热切的人们报以冷笑。 ● **eager·ly** ADV 热切地 ❑ *"So what do you think will happen?" he asked eagerly.* "那么你认为会发生什么事呢？" 他热切地问道。 ● **eager·ness** N-UNCOUNT 热切 ❑ *It was the voice of a woman speaking with breathless eagerness.* 那是一个女人气喘吁吁、急不可待的说话声。

eagle /iːgᵊl/ (**eagles**) N-COUNT An **eagle** is a large bird that lives by eating small animals. 鹰

ear ♦◇◇ /ɪər/ (**ears**) **1** N-COUNT Your **ears** are the two parts of your body, one on each side of your head, with which you hear sounds. 耳朵 ❑ *He whispered something in her ear.* 他在她耳边低声说了些什么。 **2** N-SING If you have **an ear for** music or language, you are able to hear its sounds accurately and to interpret them or reproduce them well. 听觉分辨力 ❑ *Moby certainly has a fine ear for a tune.* 莫比对音调的分辨能力一定很强。 **3** N-COUNT **Ear** is often used to refer to people's willingness to listen to what someone is saying. 听的意愿 ❑ *What would cause the masses to give him a far more sympathetic ear?* 什么能使大众更富同情心地听他诉说呢？ **4** N-COUNT The **ears** of a cereal plant such as corn or barley are the parts at the top of the stem that contain the seeds or grains. 穗 ❑ *American farmers use machines to pick the ears of corn from the plants.* 美国农民使用机器收割谷穗。 **5** PHRASE If a request **falls on deaf ears** or if the person to whom the request is made **turns a deaf ear to** it, they take no notice of it. 不理会 ❑ *I hope that our appeals will not fall on deaf ears.* 我希望我们的请求不会被当作耳边风。 **6** PHRASE If you **play by ear** or **play** a piece of music **by ear**, you play music by relying on your memory rather than by reading printed music. 凭记忆演奏 ❑ *Neil sat at the piano and began playing, by ear, the music he'd heard his older sister practicing.* 尼尔坐在钢琴边，凭着记忆开始演奏曾听他姐姐练习过的曲子。 **7** PHRASE If you say that someone **has a tin ear** for something, you mean that they do not have any natural ability for it and cannot appreciate or understand it fully. 无鉴赏力 [usu PHR "for" n] ❑ *Worst of all, for a playwright specializing in characters who use the vernacular, he has a tin ear for dialogue.* 最糟的是，作为一个专门刻画使用方言人物的剧作家，他在对话方面没有鉴赏力。 **8** **music to** your **ears** → see **music**

→ see Word Web: **ear**

→ see **face**

ear·ache /ɪəreɪk/ (**earaches**) N-COUNT An **earache** is a pain in the inside part of your ear. 耳痛 ❑ *He had an earache and a fever.* 他耳痛，发烧。

ear·drum /ɪərdrʌm/ (**eardrums**) also **ear drum** N-COUNT Your **eardrums** are the thin pieces of tightly stretched skin inside each ear that vibrate when sound waves reach them. 耳鼓 ❑ *The blast burst Ollie Williams' eardrum.* 爆炸声震破了奥利·威廉斯的耳鼓。

→ see **ear**

earl /ɜrl/ (**earls**) N-COUNT An **earl** is a British nobleman. 伯爵 ❑ *...the first Earl of Birkenhead.* …第一位伯肯黑德伯爵。

ear·li·er ♦♦◇ /ɜrliər/ **1** **Earlier** is the comparative of **early**. **early**的比较级 **2** ADV **Earlier** is used to refer to a point or period in time before the present or before the one you are talking about. 早些时候地 ❑ *As mentioned earlier, the university supplements this information with an interview.* 正如早些时候提到的，该大学用一次采访来补充这个资料。 ❑ *...political reforms announced by the president earlier this year.* …今年早些时候总统宣布的政治改革。 ● ADJ **Earlier** is also an adjective. 早些时候的 [ADJ n] ❑ *Earlier reports of gunshots have not been substantiated.* 早先关于枪击的报道还没有被证实。

Word Web ear

The **ear** collects **sound waves** and sends them to the brain. First the **external ear** picks up sound waves. Then these sound **vibrations** travel along the **ear canal** and strike the **eardrum**. The eardrum pushes against a series of tiny bones. These bones carry the vibrations into the **inner ear**. There they are picked up by the hair cells in the cochlea. At that point, the vibrations turn into electronic impulses. The cochlea is connected to the hearing **nerve**. It sends the electronic impulses to the brain.

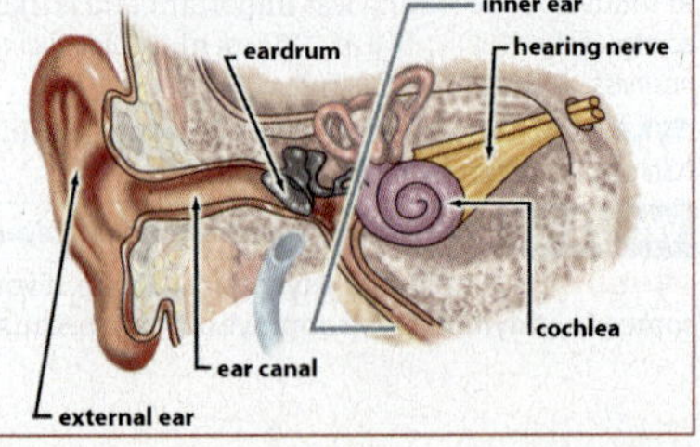

ear·li·est /ɜrliɪst/ **1** **Earliest** is the superlative of **early**. early 的最高级 **2** PHRASE **At the earliest** means not before the date or time mentioned. 最早 ❑ *The first official results are not expected until Tuesday at the earliest.* 第一批正式结果最早也要等到周二才能出来。

ear·lobe /ɪərloʊb/ (**earlobes**) also **ear lobe** N-COUNT Your **earlobes** are the soft parts at the bottom of your ears. 耳垂 ❑ *...the holes in her earlobes.* …她双耳耳垂上的那些孔。

ear·ly ♦♦♦ /ɜrli/ (**earlier, earliest**) **1** ADV **Early** means before the usual time that a particular event or activity happens. 早 [ADV after v] ❑ *I knew I had to get up early.* 我知道我得早起。 ● ADJ **Early** is also an adjective. 早的 [ADJ n] ❑ *I decided that I was going to take early retirement.* 我决定了我将提早退休。 **2** ADJ **Early** means near the beginning of a day, week, year, or other period of time. 早期的 [ADJ n] ❑ *...in the 1970s and the early 1980s.* …在20世纪70年代和20世纪80年代初期。 ❑ *She was in her early teens.* 她有十三四岁了。 ● ADV **Early** is also an adverb. 在早期 ❑ *We'll hope to see you some time early next week.* 我们希望在下周初的某个时候见你。 **3** ADV **Early** means before the time that was arranged or expected. 提前 [ADV after v] ❑ *She arrived early to get a place at the front.* 她提前到达，好在前排找个位置。 ● ADJ **Early** is also an adjective. 提前的 ❑ *I'm always early.* 我总是提早。 **4** ADJ **Early** means near the beginning of a period in history, or in the history of something such as the world, a society, or an activity. 早期的; 初期的 [ADJ n] ❑ *...the early stages of pregnancy.* …怀孕初期。 ❑ *...Fassbinder's early films.* …法斯宾德的早期电影。 **5** ADJ **Early** means near the beginning of something such as a piece of work or a process. 开始的 [ADJ n] ❑ *...the book's early chapters.* …该书开头几章。 ● ADV **Early** is also an adverb. 在开始阶段 ❑ *...an incident that occurred much earlier in the game.* …一个在比赛刚开始时发生的事件。 **6** ADJ **Early** refers to plants that flower or crop before or at the beginning of the main season. 早开花的; 早熟的 [ADJ n] ❑ *...these early cabbages and cauliflowers.* …这些早熟的卷心菜和花椰菜。 ● ADV **Early** is also an adverb. 早开花地 [ADV with v] ❑ *This early flowering gladiolus is not very hardy.* 这株开花早的剑兰不是很耐寒。 **7** ADJ **Early** reports or indications of something are the first reports or indications about it. 初期的 [ADJ n] [FORMAL] ❑ *The early indications look encouraging.* 初期的迹象看起来鼓舞人心。 **8** PHRASE You can use **as early as** to emphasize that a particular time or period is surprisingly early. 早在 [EMPHASIS] ❑ *Inflation could fall back into single figures as early as this month.* 通货膨胀最早在本月就能回落到一位数。

ear·ly bird (**early birds**) **1** N-COUNT An **early bird** is someone who does something or goes somewhere very early, especially very early in the morning. 早起者; 早到者 ❑ *We've always been early birds, getting up at 5:30 or 6 a.m.* 我们总是早起，在早上5:30或6:00起床。 **2** ADJ An **early bird** deal or special is one that is available at a reduced price, but that you must buy earlier than you would normally. 早到优惠的 [ADJ n] ❑ *Early bird discounts are usually available at the beginning of the season.* 早到早得的折扣通常在季初有。

ear·mark /ɪərmɑrk/ (**earmarks, earmarking, earmarked**) **1** V-T If resources such as money **are earmarked for** a particular purpose, they are reserved for that purpose. 留出 ❑ *...the extra money being earmarked for the new projects.* …留给新项目的额外款项。 ❑ *China has earmarked more than $20 billion for oil exploration.* 中国已留出二百多亿美元用于石油勘探。 **2** V-T If something **has been earmarked for** closure or disposal, for example, people have decided that it will be closed or got rid of. 确定 (关闭或放弃) [usu passive] ❑ *Their support meant that he was not forced to sell the business which was earmarked for disposal last year.* 他们的支持意味着他不必卖掉去年确定要出售的公司。 **3** N-COUNT The **earmark** of something or someone is their most typical quality or feature. 标记; 特征 [with poss] [AM] ❑ *Davis's solo work exhibits all the earmarks of his style: it is hesitant, tentative, spare.* 戴维斯的独奏曲尽展其风格特征：犹豫、迟疑、俭朴。

earn ♦♦◊ /ɜrn/ (**earns, earning, earned**) **1** V-T If you **earn** money, you receive money in return for work that you do. 挣 (钱) ❑ *What a lovely way to earn a living.* 一个多好的谋生方式啊！ **2** V-T If something **earns** money, it produces money as profit or interest. 赢 (利) ❑ *...a bank account that earns little or no interest.* …一个很少或不生利息的银行账户。 **3** V-T If you **earn** something such as praise, you get it because you deserve it. 赢得 ❑ *Companies must earn a reputation for honesty.* 公司必须赢得诚信。

Thesaurus *earn* 另参见:
v. bring in, make, take in **1**

ear·nest /ɜrnɪst/ **1** PHRASE If something is done or happens **in earnest**, it happens to a much greater extent and more seriously than before. 严肃地; 正式地 ❑ *Campaigning will begin in earnest tomorrow.* 活动明天正式开始。 **2** ADJ **Earnest** people are very serious and sincere in what they say or do, because they think that their actions and beliefs are important. 真挚的 ❑ *Catherine was a pious, earnest woman.* 凯瑟琳是位虔诚、真挚的女子。

ear·nest·ly /ɜrnɪstli/ **1** ADV If you say something **earnestly**, you say it very seriously, often because you believe that it is important or you are trying to persuade someone else to believe it. 严肃地 [ADV with v] ❑ *"Did you?" she asked earnestly.* "你呢？" 她严肃地问。 **2** ADV If you do something **earnestly**, you do it in a thorough and serious way, intending to succeed. 认真地 ❑ *She always listened earnestly as if this might help her to understand.* 她总是认真地听，好像这样会帮她听懂一样。

earn·ings ♦◊◊ /ɜrnɪŋz/ N-PLURAL Your **earnings** are the sums of money that you earn by working. 薪金 ❑ *Average weekly earnings rose by 1.5% in July.* 平均周薪7月份上涨了1.5%。

ear·phone /ɪərfoʊn/ (**earphones**) N-COUNT **Earphones** are a small piece of equipment that you wear over or inside your ears so that you can listen to a radio or recorded music without anyone else hearing. 耳机

▲ **ear·ring** /ɪərɪŋ/ (**earrings**) N-COUNT **Earrings** are pieces of jewelry that you attach to your ears. 耳饰 ❑ *...a pair of diamond earrings.* …一副钻石耳坠儿。
→ see **jewelry**

ear·shot /ɪərʃɒt/ PHRASE If you are **within earshot of** someone or something, you are close enough to be able to hear them. If you are **out of earshot**, you are too far away to hear them. 在能听到…的范围内 (外) ❑ *It is within earshot of a main road.* 离一条主路不远，能听到那里的动静。

earth ♦♦◊ /ɜrθ/ **1** N-PROPER **Earth** or **the Earth** is the planet on which we live. People usually say **Earth** when they are referring to the planet as part of the universe, and **the Earth** when they are talking about the planet as the place where we live. 地球 ❑ *The space shuttle Atlantis returned safely to Earth today.* 亚特兰蒂斯号航天飞机今天安全返回地球。 **2** N-SING **The earth** is the land surface on which we live and move around. 陆地; 地面 ❑ *The earth shook and swayed and the walls of neighboring houses fell around them.* 地面晃动起来，附近房子的墙壁在他们周围坍塌了。 **3** N-UNCOUNT **Earth** is the substance on the land surface of the earth, for example clay or sand, in which plants grow. 土壤; 土地 ❑ *The road winds for miles through parched earth, scrub and cactus.* 那条路蜿蜒数英里，穿过干热的土地、灌木丛和仙人掌。 **4** N-SING The **earth** in an electric plug or piece of electrical equipment is the same as the **ground**. 地线 [BRIT] **5** → see also **down-to-earth** **6** PHRASE **On earth** is used for emphasis in questions that begin with words such as "how," "why," "what," or "where." It is often used to suggest that there is no obvious or easy answer to the question being asked. 到底; 究竟 [EMPHASIS] ❑ *How on earth did that happen?* 那到底是怎么发生的？ **7** PHRASE **On earth** is used for emphasis

Word Web earth

The **earth** is made of material left over when the **sun** formed. In the beginning, about 4 billion years ago, the earth was liquid **rock**. During its first million years, it cooled into solid rock. **Life**, in the form of bacteria, began in the **oceans** about 3.5 billion years ago. During the next billion years, the **continents** formed. At the same time, the level of **oxygen** in the **atmosphere** increased. **Life forms evolved**, and some of them began to use oxygen. **Evolution** allowed **plants** and **animals** to move from the oceans onto the **land**.

E

after some negative noun groups, for example "no reason." 根本(常用在否定句中) [EMPHASIS] ❑ *There was no reason on earth why she couldn't have moved in with us.* 她不能跟我们一起搬进来根本没有道理。 8 PHRASE If you come **down to earth** or **back to earth**, you have to face the reality of everyday life after a period of great excitement. 回到现实 ❑ *When he came down to earth after his win he admitted: "It was an amazing feeling."* 当在胜利之后回来面对现实时他承认："当时感觉太棒了。"
→ see Word Web: **earth**
→ see **core, eclipse, erosion**

earth·ly /ɜrθli/ 1 ADJ **Earthly** means happening in the material world of our life on earth and not in any spiritual life or life after death. 尘世的 [ADJ n] ❑ *...the need to confront evil during the earthly life.* …尘世生活中对抗罪恶的需要。 2 ADJ **Earthly** is used for emphasis in phrases such as **no earthly reason**. If you say that there is **no earthly reason why** something should happen, you are emphasizing that there is no reason at all why it should happen. 根本 [ADJ n] [EMPHASIS] ❑ *There is no earthly reason why they should ever change.* 他们毫无理由改变。

earth·quake /ɜrθkweɪk/ (**earthquakes**) N-COUNT An **earthquake** is a shaking of the ground caused by movement of the Earth's crust. 地震 ❑ *...the San Francisco earthquake of 1906.* …1906年的旧金山地震。
→ see Word Web: **earthquake**

earthy /ɜrθi/ (**earthier, earthiest**) 1 ADJ If you describe someone as **earthy**, you mean that they are open and direct, and talk about subjects that other people avoid or feel ashamed about. 率直的 [APPROVAL] ❑ *...his extremely earthy humor.* …他极其率直的幽默。 2 ADJ If you describe something as **earthy**, you mean it looks, smells, or feels like earth. 泥土似的 ❑ *I'm attracted to warm, earthy colors.* 我被温暖的土色吸引住了。

ear·wig /ɪərwɪg/ (**earwigs**) N-COUNT An **earwig** is a small, thin, brown insect that has a pair of claws at the back end of its body. 蠼螋

ease ♦◇◇ /iz/ (**eases, easing, eased**) 1 PHRASE If you do something **with ease**, you do it easily, without difficulty or effort. 轻易地 ❑ *Anne was intelligent and capable of passing her exams with ease.* 安妮很聪明，能够轻易地通过考试。 2 N-UNCOUNT If you talk about the **ease of** a particular activity, you are referring to the way that it has been made easier to do, or to the fact that it is already easy to do. 简便 ❑ *For ease of reference, only the relevant extracts of the regulations are included.* 为便于参阅，只收录了相关条例的摘录。 3 N-UNCOUNT **Ease** is the state of being very comfortable and able to live as you want, without any worries or problems. 舒适；悠闲 ❑ *She lived a life of ease.* 她过着悠闲自在的生活。 4 V-T/V-I If something unpleasant **eases** or if you **ease** it, it is reduced in degree, speed, or intensity. 减轻；减缓 ❑ *Tensions had eased.* 紧张缓解了。 ❑ *I gave him some brandy to ease the pain.* 我给了他一些白兰地以减轻疼痛。 5 V-T/V-I If you **ease** your **way** somewhere or **ease** somewhere, you move there slowly, carefully, and gently. If you **ease** something somewhere, you move it there slowly, carefully, and gently. 小心缓慢地移动 ❑ *I eased my way toward the door.* 我缓慢地向门口走去。 ❑ *He eased his foot off the accelerator.* 他慢慢地把脚从油门上挪开。 6 PHRASE If you are **at ease**, you are feeling confident and relaxed, and are able to talk to people without feeling nervous or anxious. If you put someone **at ease**, you make them feel at ease. 放松的；自在的 ❑ *It is essential to feel at ease with your therapist.* 与治疗师在一起时，关键是放松心情。 7 PHRASE If you are **ill at ease**, you feel somewhat uncomfortable, anxious, or worried. 不舒适；不自在 ❑ *He appeared embarrassed and ill at ease with the sustained applause that greeted him.* 他对持久的掌声显得尴尬、不自在。
▸ **ease up** 1 PHRASAL VERB If something **eases up**, it is reduced in degree, speed, or intensity. 减缓；减慢；放松 ❑ *The rain had eased up.* 雨势减缓了。 2 PHRASAL VERB If you **ease up**, you start to make less effort. 松劲 ❑ *He told supporters not to ease up even though he's leading in the presidential race.* 他告诉支持者们即使他在总统竞选中处于优势也不要松劲。

easel /izᵊl/ (**easels**) N-COUNT An **easel** is a frame that supports a picture which an artist is painting or drawing. 画架
→ see **painting**

easi·ly ♦◇◇ /izɪli/ 1 ADV You use **easily** to emphasize that something is very likely to happen, or is very likely to be true. 很可能 [EMPHASIS] ❑ *It could easily be another year before the economy starts to show some improvement.* 很可能再过一年经济才会开始有所好转。 2 ADV You use **easily** to say that something happens more quickly or more often than is usual or normal. 动不动地 [ADV after v] ❑ *He had always cried very easily.* 他总是动不动就哭。 3 → see also **easy**

Thesaurus	*easily* 另参见：
ADV.	quickly, readily 2

east ♦♦♦ /ist/ also **East** 1 N-UNCOUNT **The east** is the direction where the sun rises. 东方 [also "the" N] ❑ *...the vast swamps that lie to the east of the River Nile.* …位于尼罗河以东的大片沼泽。 2 N-SING **The east of** a place, country, or region is the part which is in the east. 东部 ❑ *...a village in the east of the country.* …该国东部的一个村庄。 3 ADV If you go **east**, you travel toward the east. 向东地 [ADV after v] ❑ *To drive, go east on Route 9.* 开车的话，向东上9号路。 4 ADV Something that is **east of** a place is positioned to the east of it. 以东地 ❑ *...just east of the center of town.* …就在城中心以东。 5 ADJ The **east** edge, corner, or part of a place or country is the part toward the east. 在东边的 [ADJ n] ❑ *...a low line of hills running along the east coast.* …沿着东海岸延伸的一排小山丘。 6 ADJ **East** is used in the names of some countries, states, and regions in the east of a larger area. 东部的 [ADJ n] ❑ *He had been on safari in East Africa with his son.* 他和他的儿子曾在东非狩猎旅行。 7 ADJ An **east** wind is a wind that blows from the east. 从东而来的 ❑ *...a bitter east wind.* …一阵刺骨的东风。 8 N-SING **The East** is used to refer to the southern and eastern part of Asia, including India, China, and Japan. 东南亚地区 ❑ *Every so often, a new martial art arrives from the East.* 时不时地，一种新武术从东南亚到达至此。 9 → see also **Middle East, Far East**

★ **East·er** /istər/ (**Easters**) N-VAR **Easter** is a Christian festival when Jesus Christ's return to life is celebrated. It is celebrated on a Sunday in March or April. 复活节 [oft N n] ❑ *"Happy Easter," he yelled.* "复活节快乐，"他喊道。

east·er·ly /istərli/ 1 ADJ An **easterly** point, area, or direction is to the east or toward the east. 向东的 ❑ *He progressed slowly along the coast in an easterly direction.* 他沿着海岸向东缓慢行进。 2 ADJ An **easterly** wind is a wind that blows from the east. 从东而来的 ❑ *It was a beautiful September day, with stiff easterly winds.* 那是9月的一个晴天，刮着强劲的东风。

Word Web earthquake

Earthquakes occur when two tectonic **plates** meet and start to slide past each other. This meeting point is called the focus. It may be located anywhere from a few hundred meters to a few hundred kilometers below the surface. The resulting pressure causes a split in the earth's **crust** called a **fault**. Vibrations travel out from the focus in all directions. These **seismic waves** cause little damage until they reach the surface. The epicenter, directly above the focus, receives the greatest damage. Seismologists use seismographs to measure the amount of ground movement during an earthquake.

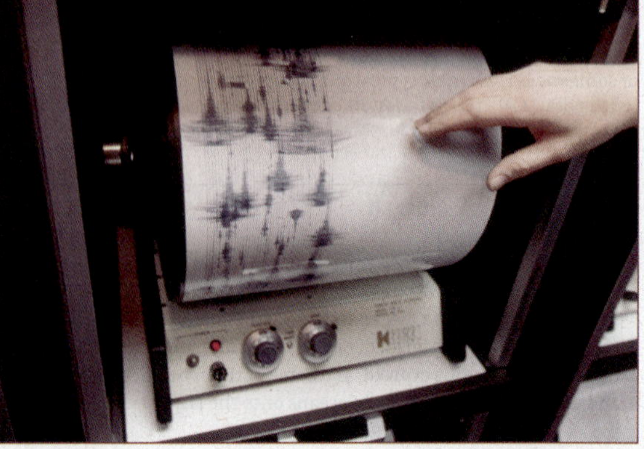

A seismograph recording a major earthquake.

east·ern ♦♦◇ /i̱stərn/ **1** ADJ **Eastern** means in or from the east of a region, state, or country. 东部的 [ADJ n] ❑ *...Eastern Europe.* …东欧。 **2** ADJ **Eastern** means coming from or associated with the people or countries of the East, such as India, China, or Japan. 东方国家的 [ADJ n] ❑ *In many Eastern countries massage was and is a part of everyday life.* 在许多东方国家，按摩过去和现在都是日常生活的一部分。

east·ward /i̱stwərd/

The form **eastwards** is also used.

ADV **Eastward** or **eastwards** means toward the east. 向东地 [ADV after v] ❑ *A powerful snow storm is moving eastward.* 一场猛烈的暴风雪正向东转移。 ● ADJ **Eastward** is also an adjective. 向东的 ❑ *...the eastward expansion of the city.* …该市的东扩。

easy ♦♦♦ /i̱zi/ (**easier, easiest**) **1** ADJ If a job or action is **easy**, you can do it without difficulty or effort, because it is not complicated and causes no problems. 容易的 ❑ *The shower is easy to install.* 淋浴器易于安装。 ❑ *This is not an easy task.* 这不是项容易的任务。 ● **easi·ly** ADV 容易地 ❑ *Dress your child in layers of clothes you can remove easily.* 给你的孩子穿几层你能容易地脱掉的衣服。 **2** ADJ If you describe an action or activity as **easy**, you mean that it is done in a confident, relaxed way. If someone is **easy about** something, they feel relaxed and confident about it. 轻松自如的 ❑ *He was an easy person to talk to.* 他是个可以与之轻松交谈的人。 ● **easi·ly** ADV 轻松自如地 [ADV with v] ❑ *They talked amiably and easily about a range of topics.* 他们亲切而又轻松地谈着一系列的话题。 **3** ADJ If you say that someone has an **easy** life, you mean that they live comfortably without any problems or worries. 舒适的 ❑ *She has not had an easy life.* 她不曾有过舒适的生活。 **4** ADJ If you say that something is **easy** or too **easy**, you are criticizing someone because they have done the most obvious or least difficult thing, and have not considered the situation carefully enough. 容易的 [DISAPPROVAL] ❑ *That's easy for you to say.* 你说得容易。 **5** PHRASE If you tell someone to **go easy on** something, you are telling them to use only a small amount of it. 省着点 [INFORMAL] ❑ *Go easy on the alcohol.* 少喝点儿酒。 **6** PHRASE If you tell someone to **go easy on**, or **be easy on**, a particular person, you are telling them not to punish or treat that person very severely. 对某人温和点儿 [INFORMAL] ❑ *"Go easy on him," Sam repeated, opening the door.* "对他温和点儿，"萨姆开门时又重复了一遍。 **7** PHRASE If someone tells you to **take it easy** or **take things easy**, they mean that you should relax and not do very much at all. 悠着点 [INFORMAL] ❑ *It is best to take things easy for a week or two.* 最好放松一两个星期。 **8** → see also **easily**

Thesaurus *easy* 另参见：
ADJ. basic, elementary, simple, uncomplicated; (*ant.*) complicated, difficult, hard **1**

easy·going /i̱zigo͟ʊɪŋ/

in BRIT, use **easy-going**

ADJ If you describe someone as **easygoing**, you mean that they are not easily annoyed, worried, or upset, and you think this is a good quality. 随和的 [APPROVAL] ❑ *He was easygoing and good-natured.* 他随和且脾气好。

eat ♦♦◇ /i̱t/ (**eats, eating, ate, eaten**) **1** V-T/V-I When you **eat** something, you put it into your mouth, chew it, and swallow it. 吃 ❑ *She was eating a sandwich.* 她正在吃一个三明治。 ❑ *I ate slowly and without speaking.* 我慢慢地吃着，没讲话。 **2** V-I If you **eat** sensibly or healthily, you eat food that is good for you. 饮食 ❑ *...a campaign to persuade people to eat more healthily.* …一场劝说人们健康饮食的运动。 **3** V-T/V-I If you **eat**, you have a meal. 吃饭 ❑ *Let's go out to eat.* 我们出去吃饭吧。 ❑ *We ate lunch together every day.* 我们每天一起吃午餐。 **4** V-T If something **is eating** you, it is annoying or worrying you. 烦扰 [only cont] [INFORMAL] ❑ *"What the hell's eating you?" he demanded.* "到底是什么在烦你？"他问道。 **5** **dog eat dog** → see **dog** **6** **to eat crow** → see **crow**
→ see **cooking, food**

▸ **eat away** PHRASAL VERB If one thing **eats away** another or **eats away at** another, it gradually destroys or uses it up. 侵蚀；逐渐用完 ❑ *Water pours through the roof, encouraging rot to eat away the interior of the house.* 水从屋顶倾泻下来，加速了对房屋内部的侵蚀。

▸ **eat into** **1** PHRASAL VERB If something **eats into** your time or your resources, it uses them, when they should be used for other things. 耗费 ❑ *Responsibilities at home and work eat into his time.* 家庭和工作的责任耗费着他的时间。 **2** PHRASAL VERB If a substance such as acid or rust **eats into** something, it destroys or damages its surface. 腐蚀 ❑ *Ulcers occur when the stomach's natural acids eat into the lining of the stomach.* 胃酸腐蚀胃壁时，就出现了溃疡。

Thesaurus *eat* 另参见：
V. chew, consume, munch, nibble, taste **1**
dine, feast **3**
bother, trouble, worry **4**

Word Partnership *eat* 的常用搭配：
V. **want** *something* **to** eat **1**
eat **and drink**, eat **and sleep** **1** **3**
ADV. eat **too much** **1**
eat **properly**, eat **well** **2**
eat **alone**, eat **together** **3**

eat·er /i̱tər/ (**eaters**) N-COUNT You use **eater** to refer to someone who eats in a particular way or who eats particular kinds of food. 吃饭…的人；吃…的人 ❑ *I've never been a fussy eater.* 我从不是一个吃饭挑剔的人。

eaves /i̱vz/ N-PLURAL The **eaves** of a house are the lower edges of its roof. 屋檐 ❑ *There were icicles hanging from the eaves.* 屋檐下挂着冰柱。

eaves·drop /i̱vzdrɒp/ (**eavesdrops, eavesdropping, eavesdropped**) V-I If you **eavesdrop on** someone, you listen secretly to what they are saying. 窃听 ❑ *The government illegally eavesdropped on his telephone conversations.* 政府非法窃听了他在电话里的通话。

e·Bay /i̱beɪ/ N-UNCOUNT **eBay** is a website that people and companies can use to buy or sell goods. Items may be bought for a fixed price, or sold to the buyer who offers the highest price. 亿贝网 [oft "on" N] ❑ *I sold my car on eBay to a man in Wisconsin.* 我在亿贝网上把我的小汽车卖给了威斯康星的一位男士。

▲ **ebb** /ɛ̱b/ (**ebbs, ebbing, ebbed**) **1** V-I When the tide or the sea **ebbs**, its level gradually falls. 退潮 ❑ *When the tide ebbs, you can paddle out for a mile and barely get your ankles wet.* 退潮时，你可以蹚水走出1英里远而几乎湿不到脚踝。 **2** N-COUNT **The ebb** or the **ebb** tide is one of the regular periods, usually two per day, when the sea gradually falls to a lower level as the tide moves away from the land. 退潮 ❑ *...the spring ebb tide.* …春季的退潮。 **3** V-I If someone's life, support, or feeling **ebbs**, it becomes weaker and gradually disappears. 衰退 [FORMAL] ❑ *Were there occasions when enthusiasm ebbed?* 热情会有衰退的时候吗？ ● PHRASAL VERB **Ebb away** means the same as **ebb**. 衰退 ❑ *His little girl's life ebbed away.* 他小女儿的生命衰竭了。 **4** PHRASE If someone or something is **at a low ebb** or **at their lowest ebb**, they are not very successful or profitable. 处于低潮 ❑ *...a time when everyone is tired and at a low ebb.* …一个每人都处于疲惫状态和低潮的时刻。
→ see **ocean, tide**

Word Link *e ≈ electronic : e-book, e-commerce, e-mail*

e-book (**e-books**) N-COUNT An **e-book** is a book which is produced for reading on a computer screen. **E-book** is an abbreviation for **electronic book**. 电子图书 ❑ *In addition to the classics, the new e-books will include a host of Rough Guide titles.* 除了经典著作，新的电子图书将包括大量**Rough Guide**出版社的图书品种。
→ see **book**

ebul·lient /ɪbʌ̱liənt, -bʊ̱l-/ ADJ If you describe someone as **ebullient**, you mean that they are lively and full of enthusiasm or excitement about something. 精力充沛的；热情洋溢的 [FORMAL] ❑ *...the ebullient Russian president.* …精力充沛的俄罗斯总统。 ● **ebul·lience** /ɪbʌ̱liəns, -bʊ̱l-/ N-UNCOUNT 精力充沛；热情洋溢 ❑ *His natural ebullience began to return.* 他天生的热情开始恢复了。

e-business (**e-businesses**) **1** N-COUNT An **e-business** is a business that uses the Internet to sell goods or services, especially one that does not also have stores or offices that people can visit or phone. 电子商务公司 [BUSINESS] ❑ *...JSL Trading, an e-business in Vancouver.* …JSL贸易公司，一家温哥华的电子商务公司。 **2** N-UNCOUNT **E-business** is the buying, selling, and ordering of goods and services using the Internet. 电子商务 [BUSINESS] ❑ *...proven e-business solutions.* …经过验证的电子商务解决方案。

Word Link *ec ≈ away, from, out : eccentric, eclectic, ecstatic*

★ **ec·cen·tric** /ɪksɛ̱ntrɪk/ (**eccentrics**) ADJ If you say that someone is **eccentric**, you mean that they behave in a strange

Word Web echo

We can learn a lot from studying **echoes**. Geologists use **sound reflection** to predict how earthquake waves will travel through the earth. They also use echolocation to find underground oil reservoirs. Oceanographers use sonar to explore the ocean. Marine mammals, bats, and humans also use sonar for navigation. Architects study building materials and surfaces to understand how they absorb or **reflect** sound **waves**. They may use hard reflective surfaces to help create a noisy, exciting atmosphere in a restaurant. They may suggest soft drapes and carpeting to create a quiet, calm library.

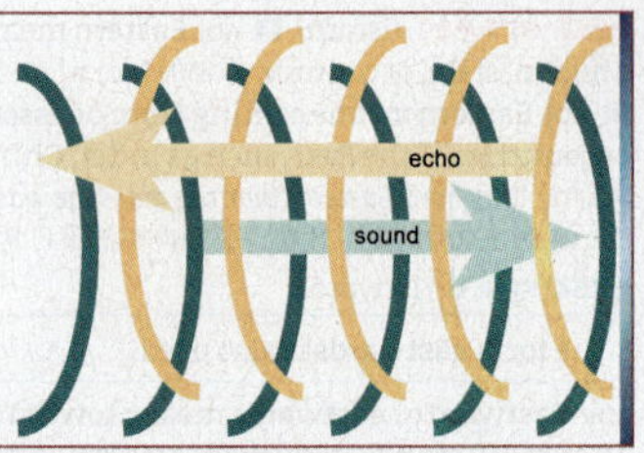

E

way, and have habits or opinions that are different from those of most people. 古怪的；异乎寻常的 ❑ *He is an eccentric character who likes wearing a beret and dark glasses.* 他是个怪人，喜欢戴贝雷帽和墨镜。 ● N-COUNT An **eccentric** is an eccentric person. 古怪的人 ❑ *Askew used several names, and had a reputation as an eccentric.* 艾斯丘用过几个名字，并以"怪人"著称。

ec·cen·tri·city /ɛ̲ksɛntrɪ̲sɪti/ (**eccentricities**) **1** N-UNCOUNT **Eccentricity** is unusual behavior that other people consider strange. 古怪 ❑ *She is unusual to the point of eccentricity.* 她与众不同到了古怪的地步。 **2** N-COUNT **Eccentricities** are ways of behaving that people think are strange, or habits or opinions that are different from those of most people. 怪癖 ❑ *We all have our eccentricities.* 我们都有自己的怪癖。

ec·cle·si·as·ti·cal /ɪkli̲ziæ̲stɪkᵊl/ ADJ **Ecclesiastical** means belonging to or connected with the Christian Church. 基督教教会的 ❑ *My ambition was to travel upwards in the ecclesiastical hierarchy.* 我的雄心是在基督教会体系内步步高升。

eche·lon /ɛ̲ʃəlɒn/ (**echelons**) N-COUNT An **echelon** in an organization or society is a level or rank in it. 等级；阶层 [FORMAL] ❑ *...the lower echelons of society.* …社会的底层。

echo ♦◇◇ /ɛ̲koʊ/ (**echoes, echoing, echoed**) **1** N-COUNT An **echo** is a sound caused by a noise being reflected off a surface such as a wall. 回声 ❑ *He listened and heard nothing but the echoes of his own voice in the cave.* 他听了听，除了自己声音在山洞里的回响什么都没听见。 **2** V-I If a sound **echoes**, it is reflected off a surface and can be heard again after the original sound has stopped. 回响 ❑ *His feet echoed on the hardwood floor.* 他的脚步声在硬木地板上回响着。 **3** V-I In a place that **echoes**, a sound is reflected off a surface, and is repeated after the original sound has stopped. 发出回声 ❑ *The room echoed.* 房间发出了回声。 ❑ *The corridor echoed with the barking of a dozen dogs.* 走廊里回荡着十几条狗的吠声。 **4** V-T If you **echo** someone's words, you repeat them or express agreement with their attitude or opinion. 附和 ❑ *Their views often echo each other.* 他们的见解常常彼此附和。 **5** N-COUNT A detail or feature that reminds you of something else can be referred to as an **echo**. 启示 ❑ *The accident has echoes of past disasters.* 该事故让人想到过去的那些灾难。 **6** V-T If one thing **echoes** another, the first is a copy of a particular detail or feature of the other. 反映 ❑ *Pinks and beiges were chosen to echo the colors of the ceiling.* 粉色和米色被选来反映天花板的那些颜色。 **7** V-I If something **echoes**, it continues to be discussed and remains important or influential in a particular situation or among a particular group of people. 流传 ❑ *The old fable continues to echo down the centuries.* 这一古老的寓言流传了数个世纪。
→ see Word Web: **echo**
→ see **sound**

ec·lec·tic /ɪklɛ̲ktɪk/ ADJ An **eclectic** collection of objects, ideas, or beliefs is wide-ranging and comes from many different sources. 兼收并蓄的 [FORMAL] ❑ *...an eclectic collection of paintings, drawings, and prints.* …一批油画、素描、版画兼有的藏品。

★ **eclipse** /ɪklɪ̲ps/ (**eclipses, eclipsing, eclipsed**) **1** N-COUNT An **eclipse of** the sun is an occasion when the moon is between the earth and the sun, so that for a short time you cannot see part or all of the sun. An **eclipse of** the moon is an occasion when the earth is between the sun and the moon, so that for a short time you cannot see part or all of the moon. （日、月）食 ❑ *...an eclipse of the sun.* …一次日食。 ❑ *...the solar eclipse on May 21.* …5月21日的日食。 **2** V-T If one thing **is eclipsed by** a second thing that is bigger, newer, or more important than it, the first thing is no longer noticed because the second thing gets all the attention. 使黯然失色 ❑ *...the space program has been eclipsed by other pressing needs.* …这项太空计划和其他的紧迫需要相比已经黯然失色了。
→ see Word Web: **eclipse**

eco-friendly ADJ **Eco-friendly** products or services are less harmful to the environment than other similar products or services. 环保的 ❑ *...eco-friendly laundry detergent.* …环保洗衣剂。

★ **eco·logi·cal** /ɛ̲kəlɒ̲dʒɪkᵊl, i̲k-/ **1** ADJ **Ecological** means involved with or concerning ecology. 生态的 [ADJ n] ❑ *Large dams have harmed Siberia's delicate ecological balance.* 大坝损害了西伯利亚脆弱的生态平衡。 ● **eco·logi·cal·ly** /ɛ̲kəlɒ̲dʒɪkli, i̲k-/ ADV 生态地 ❑ *It is economical to run and ecologically sound.* 它运行高效且有益生态。

ecolo·gist /ɪkɒ̲lədʒɪst/ (**ecologists**) N-COUNT An **ecologist** is a person who studies ecology. 生态学家 ❑ *Ecologists argue that the benefits of treating sewage with disinfectants are doubtful.* 生态学家们认为用消毒剂处理污水的好处是值得怀疑的。

★ **ecol·ogy** /ɪkɒ̲lədʒi/ (**ecologies**) **1** N-UNCOUNT **Ecology** is the study of the relationships between plants, animals, people, and their environment, and the balances between these relationships. 生态学 ❑ *...a professor in ecology.* …一位生态学教授。 **2** N-VAR When you talk about the **ecology** of a place, you are referring to the pattern and balance of relationships between plants, animals, people, and the environment in that place. 生态 ❑ *...the ecology of the rocky Negev desert in Israel.* …以色列内盖夫的多岩石沙漠生态。

e-commerce N-UNCOUNT **E-commerce** is the same as **e-business**. 电子商务 [BUSINESS] ❑ *...the anticipated explosion of e-commerce.* …预期中电子商务的激增。

eco·nom·ic ♦♦♦ /ɛ̲kənɒ̲mɪk, i̲k-/ **1** ADJ **Economic** means concerned with the organization of the money, industry, and trade of a country, region, or society. 经济的 ❑ *...Poland's radical economic reforms.* …波兰激进的经济改革。 ● **eco·nomi·cal·ly** /ɛ̲kənɒ̲mɪkli, i̲k-/ ADV 经济地 ❑ *...an economically depressed area.* …一个经济萧条地区。 **2** ADJ If something is **economic**, it produces a profit. 盈利的 ❑ *Critics say that the new system may be more economic but will lead to a decline in program quality.* 批评家们说该新系统也许更有利可图，却会导致项目质量的下降。
→ see **disaster**

eco·nomi·cal /ɛ̲kənɒ̲mɪkᵊl, i̲k-/ **1** ADJ Something that is **economical** does not require a lot of money to operate. For example, a car that only uses a small amount of gasoline is **economical**. 经济的；节省的 ❑ *...plans to trade in their car for something smaller and more economical.* …用他们的车抵价购买更小且更经济型轿车的计划。

Word Web eclipse

When the **earth** passes between the **sun** and the **moon**, we see a **lunar eclipse**. When the moon passes between the sun and the earth, we see a solar eclipse. A total eclipse of the sun happens when the moon covers it completely. In the past, people were frightened of eclipses. Leaders of some civilizations understood eclipses. They pretended to control the sun in order to gain the respect of their people. On July 22, 2009, a total eclipse of the sun will be visible in North America.

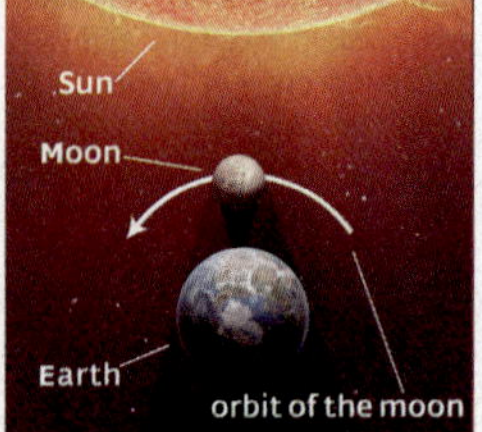

● **eco·nomi·cal·ly** ADV 经济地；节省地 [ADV after v] ❑ *Services could be operated more efficiently and economically.* 可以更有效、更经济地提供服务。 **2** ADJ Someone who is **economical** spends money sensibly and does not want to waste it on things that are unnecessary. A way of life that is **economical** does not require a lot of money. 节俭的 ❑ *...ideas for economical housekeeping.* …节俭持家的一些想法。 **3** ADJ **Economical** means using the minimum amount of time, effort, or language that is necessary. 简练的 ❑ *His gestures were economical, his words generally mild.* 他的手势简练，言语通常是温和的。

Thesaurus *economical* 另参见：
ADJ. cost-effective, inexpensive **1**
careful, frugal, practical, thrifty **2**

Word Link *ics ≈ system, knowledge : economics, electronics, ethics*

eco·nom·ics ♦◇◇ /ɛkənɒmɪks, ɪk-/ N-UNCOUNT **Economics** is the study of the way in which money, industry, and commerce are organized in a society. 经济学 ❑ *His younger sister is studying economics.* 他的妹妹在学经济学。
→ see Word Web: **economics**

eco̲no·mies of sca̲le N-PLURAL **Economies of scale** are the financial advantages that a company gains when it produces large quantities of products. 规模经济 [BUSINESS] ❑ *Some companies are simply trying to get bigger to achieve economies of scale.* 一些公司只是试图靠扩张获得规模经济。

econo·mise /ɪkɒnəmaɪz/ [BRIT] → see **economize**

econo·mist ♦◇◇ /ɪkɒnəmɪst/ (**economists**) N-COUNT An **economist** is a person who studies, teaches, or writes about economics. 经济学家

econo·mize /ɪkɒnəmaɪz/ (**economizes, economizing, economized**)
in BRIT, also use **economise**
V-I If you **economize**, you save money by spending it very carefully. 节省开支 ❑ *We're going to have to economize from now on.* 我们得从现在起节省开支。

econo·my ♦♦♦ /ɪkɒnəmi/ (**economies**) **1** N-COUNT An **economy** is the system according to which the money, industry, and commerce of a country or region are organized. 经济体制 ❑ *Zimbabwe boasts Africa's most industrialized economy.* 津巴布韦自夸有着非洲最为工业化的经济体制。 **2** N-COUNT A country's **economy** is the wealth that it gets from business and industry. 经济状况 ❑ *The Japanese economy grew at an annual rate of more than 10 percent.* 日本的经济以每年10%以上的速度增长。 **3** N-UNCOUNT **Economy** is the use of the minimum amount of money, time, or other resources needed to achieve something, so that nothing is wasted. 节省 ❑ *...improvements in the fuel economy of cars.* …在节省汽车燃料方面的一些改进。 **4** ADJ **Economy** services such as travel are cheap and have no luxuries or extras. 经济的；便宜的 [ADJ n] ❑ *...the limitations that come with economy travel.* …伴随经济舱的一些限制。 **5** → see **economy class** **6** ADJ **Economy** is used to describe large packs of products that are cheaper than normal sized packs. 经济装的 [ADJ n] ❑ *...an economy pack containing 150 assorted screws.* …内有150枚各式螺钉的一个经济装。 **7** PHRASE If you describe an attempt to save money as **a false economy**, you mean that you have not saved any money as you will have to spend a lot more later. 貌似省钱，长远上却费钱 ❑ *A cheap bed can be a false economy, so spend as much as you can afford.* 一张廉价的床长远上并不省钱，所以要尽你所能买贵的。

eco̲no·my class ADJ On an airplane, an **economy class** ticket or seat is the cheapest available. 经济舱的 [ADJ n] ❑ *The price includes two economy class airfares from Brisbane to Los Angeles.* 费用包括两张从布里斯班到洛杉矶的经济舱机票。

★ **eco·sys·tem** /ɛkoʊsɪstəm, ɪk-/ (**ecosystems**) N-COUNT An **ecosystem** is all the plants and animals that live in a particular area together with the complex relationship that exists between them and their environment. 生态系统 [TECHNICAL] ❑ *...the forest ecosystem.* …森林生态系统。

eco·tour·ism /ɛkoʊtʊərɪzəm, ɪk-/
in BRIT, use **eco-tourism**
N-UNCOUNT **Ecotourism** is the business of providing vacations and related services that are not harmful to the environment of the area. 生态旅游 ● **eco·tour·ist** /ɛkoʊtʊərɪst, ɪk-/ N-COUNT (**ecotourists**) 生态旅游者 [BUSINESS] ❑ *...an environmentally sensitive project to cater to ecotourists.* …一项迎合生态旅游者的环境敏感项目。

▲ **ec·sta·sy** /ɛkstəsi/ (**ecstasies**) **1** N-VAR **Ecstasy** is a feeling of very great happiness. 狂喜 ❑ *...a state of almost religious ecstasy.* …一种近乎宗教极乐的状态。 **2** N-UNCOUNT **Ecstasy** is an illegal drug that makes people feel happy and energetic. 摇头丸 ❑ *The teenager died after taking ecstasy on her birthday.* 那个少女在她生日当天服用摇头丸后丧生。

Word Link *ec ≈ away, from, out : eccentric, eclectic, ecstatic*

ec·stat·ic /ɛkstætɪk/ **1** ADJ If you are **ecstatic**, you feel very happy and full of excitement. 欣喜若狂的 ❑ *His wife gave birth to their first child, and he was ecstatic about it.* 他的妻子生下了他们的第一个孩子，他对此欣喜若狂。 ● **ec·stati·cal·ly** /ɛkstætɪkli/ ADV 欣喜若狂地 ❑ *We are both ecstatically happy.* 我们俩都欣喜若狂。 **2** ADJ You can use **ecstatic** to describe reactions that are very enthusiastic and excited. For example, if someone receives an **ecstatic** reception or an **ecstatic** welcome, they are greeted with great enthusiasm and excitement. 热烈的 [ADJ n] ❑ *They gave an ecstatic reception to the speech.* 他们给该演讲以热烈的欢迎。

ec·ze·ma /ɛksəmə, ɛgzə-, ɪgzi-/ N-UNCOUNT **Eczema** is a skin condition that makes your skin itch and become sore, rough, and broken. 湿疹

edge ♦♦◇ /ɛdʒ/ (**edges, edging, edged**) **1** N-COUNT The **edge** of something is the place or line where it stops, or the part of it that is farthest from the middle. 边缘；边际 ❑ *We were on a hill, right on the edge of town.* 我们在一座小山上，正好位于城镇边缘。 ❑ *She was standing at the water's edge.* 她正站在水边。 **2** N-COUNT The **edge** of something sharp such as a knife or an ax is its sharp or narrow side. 刃 ❑ *...the sharp edge of the sword.* …锋利的剑刃。 **3** V-I If someone or something **edges** somewhere, they move very slowly in that direction. 慢慢移动 ❑ *He edged closer to the telephone, ready to grab it.* 他慢慢地移近电话，准备抓起它。 **4** N-SING **The edge of** something, especially something bad, is the point at which it may start to happen. 边缘 ❑ *They have driven the rhino to the edge of extinction.* 他们已经把犀牛逼到了灭绝的边缘。 **5** N-SING If someone or something has an **edge**, they have an advantage that makes them stronger or more likely to be successful than another thing or person. 优势 ❑ *The three days Uruguay have to prepare could give them the edge over Brazil.* 3天的准备时间也许能使乌拉圭比巴西略胜一筹。 **6** N-SING If you say that someone or something has **an edge**, you mean that they have a powerful quality. 锐气 ❑ *Featuring new bands gives the show an edge.* 突出新乐队的特色给该演出一种锐气。 **7** N-SING If someone's voice has an **edge to** it, it has a sharp, bitter, or emotional quality. 尖锐；尖刻 ❑ *But underneath the humor is an edge of bitterness.* 在幽默的背后却是一种怨恨的尖刻。 **8** → see also **cutting edge, leading edge** **9** PHRASE If you or your nerves are **on edge**,

Word Web economics

The study of **economics** explores how a society distributes its **wealth**. This subject is divided into two main areas: macroeconomics and microeconomics. Macroeconomics looks at how a society as a whole handles money, **capital**, and **commodities**. Microeconomics focuses on individuals and businesses. A key microeconomic principle is the law of **supply and demand**. This theory says that prices of **goods** and **services** are based on a balance between two factors. The first is how much of something is available (supply). The second is how much people are willing to pay for it (demand).

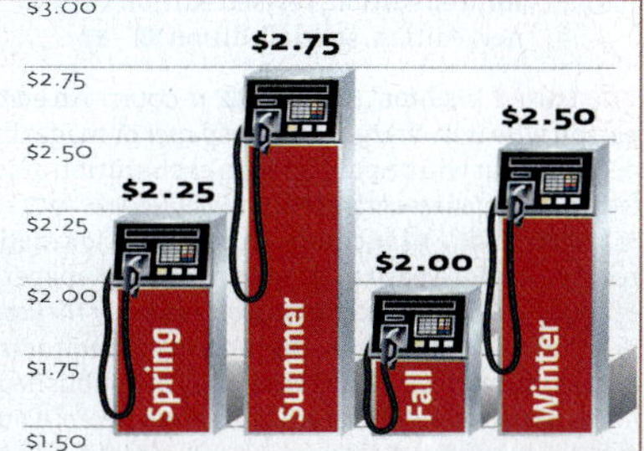

you are tense, nervous, and unable to relax. 紧张不安的 ❑ *My nerves were constantly on edge.* 我的神经处于不断紧张中。 10 PHRASE If something **takes the edge off** an unpleasant situation, it weakens its effect or intensity. 减弱 ❑ *Poor health took the edge off her performance.* 健康不佳使她的表演减色。

▸ **edge out** PHRASAL VERB If someone **edges out** someone else, they just manage to beat them or get in front of them in a game, race, or contest. 胜出 ❑ *In the second race, the American competitor edged out the Ethiopian runner by less than a second.* 在第二场赛跑中，美国选手比埃塞俄比亚选手快不到1秒钟。

Thesaurus *edge* 另参见：
N. border, boundary, rim; (*ant.*) center, middle 1
advantage 5

E

edged /ɛdʒd/ ADJ If something is **edged with** a particular thing, that thing forms a border around it. 环绕着的 [v-link ADJ "with/in" n] ❑ *...a large lawn edged with flowers and shrubs.* …一个环绕着花卉和灌木的大草坪。 ● COMB IN ADJ **Edged** is also a combining form. …边的 ❑ *...clutching a lace-edged handkerchief.* …紧攥着一块花边手帕。

edgy /ɛdʒi/ (**edgier, edgiest**) ADJ If someone is **edgy**, they are nervous and anxious, and seem likely to lose control of themselves. 急躁不安的 [INFORMAL] ❑ *She was nervous and edgy, still chain-smoking.* 她紧张，急躁不安，还在一支接一支地抽烟。

★ **ed·ible** ♦◊◊ /ɛdɪbᵊl/ ADJ If something is **edible**, it is safe to eat and not poisonous. 可食用的 ❑ *...edible fungi.* …食用菌。

edict /idɪkt/ (**edicts**) N-COUNT An **edict** is a command or instruction given by someone in authority. 命令；指令 [FORMAL] ❑ *He issued an edict that none of his writings be destroyed.* 他下了一道命令：他写的所有东西都不得毁掉。

edi·fice /ɛdɪfɪs/ (**edifices**) N-COUNT An **edifice** is a large and impressive building. 大厦 [FORMAL] ❑ *The taxi driver reeled off a list of historic edifices they must not fail to visit.* 出租车司机一口气说出了一串他们不应错过参观的历史建筑。

edit ♦◊◊ /ɛdɪt/ (**edits, editing, edited**) 1 V-T If you **edit** a text such as an article or a book, you correct and adapt it so that it is suitable for publishing. 编辑 ❑ *The majority of contracts give the publisher the right to edit a book after it's done.* 大多数合同都会赋予出版商在书稿完成后进行编辑的权利。 2 V-T If you **edit** a book or a series of books, you collect several pieces of writing by different authors and prepare them for publishing. 编选 ❑ *This collection of essays is edited by Ellen Knight.* 这本散文集是由埃伦·奈特编选的。 ❑ *He edits the literary journal, Murmur.* 他编辑了《私语》这本文学杂志。 3 V-T If you **edit** a movie or a television or radio program, you choose some of what has been filmed or recorded and arrange it in a particular order. 剪辑 ❑ *He taught me to edit and splice film.* 他教我剪辑合成影片。 4 V-T Someone who **edits** a newspaper, magazine, or journal is in charge of it. 主编 ❑ *I used to edit the college paper in the old days.* 我过去曾主编过大学校报。

edi·tion ♦♦◊ /ɪdɪʃᵊn/ (**editions**) 1 N-COUNT An **edition** is a particular version of a book, magazine, or newspaper that is printed at one time. 版本 2 N-COUNT An **edition** is the total number of copies of a particular book or newspaper that are printed at one time. 版次 ❑ *The second edition was published only in Canada.* 第2版只在加拿大出版。 3 N-COUNT An **edition** is a single television or radio program that is one of a series about a particular subject. 集 ❑ *...an interview featured on last week's edition of "60 Minutes."* …一次以上周那集《60分钟》节目为主的访谈。

Word Partnership *edition* 的常用搭配：
N. **collector's** edition, **paperback** edition 1 2
ADJ. **limited** edition, **revised** edition 1 2
new edition, **special** edition 1 – 3

edi·tor ♦♦◊ /ɛdɪtər/ (**editors**) 1 N-COUNT An **editor** is the person who is in charge of a newspaper or magazine and who decides what will be published in each edition of it. 主编 ❑ *Her father was the former editor of the Saturday Review.* 她的父亲是《星期六评论》的前任主编。 2 N-COUNT An **editor** is a journalist who is responsible for a particular section of a newspaper or magazine. 栏目编辑 ❑ *Mike later became the sports editor for The Beacon.* 迈克后来成为《烽火》的体育栏目编辑。 3 N-COUNT An **editor** is a person who checks and corrects texts before they are published. 编辑 ❑ *Your role as editor is important, for you can look at a piece of writing objectively.* 你作为编辑的角色是重要的，因为你可以客观地看一篇文字。 4 N-COUNT An **editor** is a radio or television journalist who reports on a particular type of news. 广播或电视记者 ❑ *...our economics editor, Tom Goldberg.* …我们的经济节目记者，汤姆·戈德堡。 5 N-COUNT An **editor** is a person who prepares a movie, or a radio or television program, by selecting some of what has been filmed or recorded and putting it in a particular order. 剪辑师 ❑ *A few years earlier, she had worked at 20th Century Fox as a film editor.* 几年前，她曾是20世纪福克斯公司的一名电影剪辑师。 6 N-COUNT An **editor** is a person who collects pieces of writing by different authors and prepares them for publication in a book or a series of books. (书籍、丛书) 主编 ❑ *Michael Rosen is the editor of the anthology.* 迈克尔·罗森是该文集的主编。 7 N-COUNT An **editor** is a computer program that enables you to change and correct stored data. 编辑程序 [COMPUTING] ❑ *To edit it, you need to run the built-in Windows Registry editor.* 要编辑，就需要启动内置的视窗注册编辑程序。

edi·to·rial ♦◊◊ /ɛdɪtɔriᵊl/ (**editorials**) 1 ADJ **Editorial** means involved in preparing a newspaper, magazine, or book for publication. 编辑的 [ADJ n] ❑ *I went to the editorial board meetings when I had the time.* 我当时有空儿就去参加编辑委员会的会议。 2 ADJ **Editorial** means involving the attitudes, opinions, and contents of something such as a newspaper, magazine, or television program. 社论的 [ADJ n] ❑ *We are not about to change our editorial policy.* 我们不打算改变我们的社论方针。 3 N-COUNT An **editorial** is an article in a newspaper that gives the opinion of the editor or owner on a topic or item of news. 社论 ❑ *In an editorial, The New York Times suggests the victory could turn nasty.* 在一篇社论中，《纽约时报》认为该胜利会转成恶梦。
→ see **newspaper**

edu·cate /ɛdʒʊkeɪt/ (**educates, educating, educated**) 1 V-T When someone, especially a child, **is educated**, he or she is taught at a school or college. 教育 [usu passive] ❑ *He was educated at Yale and Stanford.* 他是在耶鲁和斯坦福接受的教育。 2 V-T To **educate** people means to teach them better ways of doing something or a better way of living. 教育 ❑ *...World AIDS Day, an event designed to educate people about AIDS.* …世界艾滋病日，一项旨在教育人们了解艾滋病的活动。

Note that you do not use **educate** or **education** to talk about the way parents look after their children and teach them about good behavior and life in general. Instead, you should use the verb **bring up** or the noun **upbringing**. ❑ *His parents brought him up to be polite and courteous.*

Thesaurus *educate* 另参见：
V. coach, instruct, teach, train 2

edu·cat·ed /ɛdʒʊkeɪtɪd/ ADJ Someone who is **educated** has a high standard of learning. 受过良好教育的 ❑ *The new CEO is an educated, amiable, and decent man.* 新的首席执行官是一位受过良好教育、亲切、正派的人。

edu·ca·tion ♦♦◊ /ɛdʒʊkeɪʃᵊn/ (**educations**) 1 N-VAR **Education** involves teaching people various subjects, usually at a school or college, or being taught. 教育 ❑ *They're cutting funds for education.* 他们正在削减教育经费。 2 N-UNCOUNT **Education** of a particular kind involves teaching the public about a particular issue. 教育 ❑ *...better health education.* …更好的健康教育。 3 → see also **further education, higher education**

edu·ca·tion·al ♦◊◊ /ɛdʒʊkeɪʃənᵊl/ 1 ADJ **Educational** matters or institutions are concerned with or relate to education. 教育的 ❑ *...the Japanese educational system.* …日本教育体制。 2 ADJ An **educational** experience teaches you something. 有教育意义的 ❑ *The staff should make sure the kids have an enjoyable and educational day.* 教职员要确保孩子们度过愉快的、有教育意义的一天。

eel /il/ (**eels**) N-VAR An **eel** is a long, thin fish that looks like a snake. 鳗鱼 ● N-UNCOUNT **Eel** is the flesh of this fish eaten as food. 鳗肉 ❑ *...smoked eel.* …熏鳗。

eerie /ɪəri/ (**eerier, eeriest**) ADJ If you describe something as **eerie**, you mean that it seems strange and frightening, and makes you feel nervous. 怪异的；可怕的 ❑ *I walked down the eerie dark path.* 我沿着漆黑吓人的小路走着。 ● **eeri·ly** /ɪərɪli/ ADV 怪异地；可怕地 ❑ *Monrovia after the fighting is eerily quiet.* 战斗之后，蒙罗维亚可怕地安静。

ef·fect ♦♦♦ /ɪfɛkt/ (**effects, effecting, effected**) 1 N-VAR The **effect of** one thing **on** another is the change that the first thing causes in the second thing. 影响 ❑ *Parents worry about the effect of music on their adolescent's behavior.* 家长们担心音乐对于其青少年子女行为的影响。 2 N-COUNT An **effect** is an impression that someone creates deliberately, for example in a place or in a piece of writing. 印象 ❑ *The whole effect is cool, light, and airy.* 整体印象是凉爽、明亮和通风。 **3** N-PLURAL A person's **effects** are the things that they have with them at a particular time, for example when they are arrested or admitted to a hospital, or the things that they owned when they died. 个人财物 [FORMAL] ❑ *His daughters were collecting his effects.* 他的女儿们正在收集他的个人物品。 **4** N-PLURAL The **effects** in a movie are the specially created sounds and scenery. (影片中音响或布景的) 特殊效果 ❑ *It's got a gripping story, great acting, superb sets, and stunning effects.* 电影有扣人心弦的故事情节、精湛的表演、绝妙的布景和惊人的特效。 **5** V-T If you **effect** something that you are trying to achieve, you succeed in causing it to happen. 实现 [FORMAL] ❑ *Prospects for effecting real political change seemed to have taken a major step backwards.* 实现真正政治变革的前景似乎暗淡了许多。 **6** → see also **greenhouse effect, side-effect, special effect**

> Note that the verb **affect** is connected with the noun **effect**. You can say that something **affects** you. ❑ *Noise affects different people in different ways.* You can also say that something has an **effect** on you ❑ *...the effect that noise has on people in factories.*

7 PHRASE If you say that someone is doing something **for effect**, you mean that they are doing it in order to impress people and to draw attention to themselves. 为了加深印象; 为了引人注目 ❑ *The southern accent was put on for effect.* 假操南方口音以引人注意。 **8** PHRASE You add **in effect** to a statement or opinion that is not precisely accurate, but that you feel is a reasonable description or summary of a particular situation. 实际上 [VAGUENESS] ❑ *That deal would create, in effect, the world's biggest airline.* 那笔交易实际上将造就世界最大的航空公司。 **9** PHRASE If you **put, bring,** or **carry** a plan or idea **into effect**, you cause it to happen in practice. 实施 ❑ *These and other such measures ought to have been put into effect in 1985.* 这些及其他此类措施本应于1985年付诸实施。 **10** PHRASE If a law or policy **takes effect** or **comes into effect** at a particular time, it officially begins to apply or be valid from that time. If it **remains in effect**, it still applies or is still valid. 实施; 生效 ❑ *...the ban on new logging permits which will take effect in July.* …将于7月生效的新伐木许可证禁止令。 **11** PHRASE You can say that something **takes effect** when it starts to produce the results that are intended. 见效 ❑ *The second injection should only have been given once the first drug had taken effect.* 第2针本应只在第1针见效后才能注射。 **12** PHRASE You use **effect** in expressions such as **to good effect** and **to no effect** in order to indicate how successful or impressive an action is. 有(无) 效地 ❑ *Mr. Morris feels the museum is using advertising to good effect.* 莫里斯先生感到博物馆正在有效地利用广告。 **13** PHRASE You use **to this effect, to that effect,** or **to the effect that** to indicate that you have given or are giving a summary of something that was said or written, and not the actual words used. 大意是 ❑ *I understand that a circular to this effect will be issued in the next few weeks.* 我得知，接下来的几星期内将发布大意如此的传阅文件。

> **Word Partnership** *effect* 的常用搭配:
>
> ADJ. **adverse** effect, **negative/positive** effect **1**
> **desired** effect, **immediate** effect, **lasting** effect **1** **2**
> V. **have an** effect **1**
> **produce an** effect **2**
> **take** effect **11**
> N. effect **a change** **5**

ef·fec·tive ♦♦◊ /ɪfɛktɪv/ **1** ADJ Something that is **effective** works well and produces the results that were intended. 有效的 ❑ *The project looks at how we could be more effective in encouraging students to enter teacher training.* 该项目研究如何更有效地鼓励学生参加教师培训。 ❑ *Simple antibiotics are effective against this organism.* 普通的抗生素就能够有效地抑制这种微生物。 ● **ef·fec·tive·ly** ADV 有效地 ❑ *Services need to be organized more effectively than they are at present.* 服务需要比现在更有效地被组织起来。 ● **ef·fec·tive·ness** N-UNCOUNT 有效性 ❑ *...the effectiveness of computers as an educational tool.* …计算机作为一种教育工具的有效性。 **2** ADJ **Effective** means having a particular role or result in practice, though not officially or in theory. 实际的 [ADJ n] ❑ *They have had effective control of the area since the security forces left.* 自从安全部队离开后，他们实际控制了这一地区。 **3** ADJ When something such as a law or an agreement becomes **effective**, it begins officially to apply or be valid. (法律、协议等) 生效的 [v-link ADJ] ❑ *The new rules will become effective in the next few days.* 这些新条例将在接下来的几天内生效。

> **Word Partnership** *effective* 的常用搭配:
>
> N. effective **means**, effective **method**, effective **treatment**, effective **use** **1**
> ADV. **highly** effective **1**
> effective **immediately** **3**

ef·fec·tive·ly /ɪfɛktɪvli/ ADV You use **effectively** with a statement or opinion to indicate that it is not accurate in every detail, but that you feel it is a reasonable description or summary of a particular situation. 实际上地 ❑ *The region was effectively independent.* 该地区实际上是独立的。

ef·fi·ca·cy /ɛfɪkəsi/ N-UNCOUNT If you talk about the **efficacy** of something, you are talking about its effectiveness and its ability to do what it is supposed to. 功效 [FORMAL] ❑ *Recent medical studies confirm the efficacy of a healthier lifestyle.* 近来的医学研究证实了更健康的生活方式的功效。

ef·fi·cien·cy /ɪfɪʃᵊnsi/ N-UNCOUNT **Efficiency** is the quality of being able to do a task successfully, without wasting time or energy. 效率 ❑ *There are many ways to increase agricultural efficiency in the poorer areas of the world.* 有许多提高世界较贫困地区农业效能的方法。

ef·fi·cient ♦◊◊ /ɪfɪʃᵊnt/ ADJ If something or someone is **efficient**, they are able to do tasks successfully, without wasting time or energy. 高效的 ❑ *With today's more efficient contraception women can plan their families and careers.* 有了当今更为高效的避孕方法妇女们能够规划好自己的家庭和事业。 ● **ef·fi·cient·ly** ADV 高效地 ❑ *I work very efficiently and am decisive, and accurate in my judgment.* 我工作高效、决策果断而且判断准确。

> **Word Partnership** *efficient* 的常用搭配:
>
> N. **energy** efficient, **fuel** efficient, efficient **method**, efficient **system**, efficient **use of** *something*
> ADV. **highly** efficient

ef·fort ♦♦♦ /ɛfərt/ (**efforts**) **1** N-VAR If you make an **effort to** do something, you try very hard to do it. 努力 ❑ *He made no effort to hide his disappointment.* 他不试图隐瞒自己的失望。 ❑ *Finding a cure requires considerable time and effort.* 找到一种治愈方法需要相当的时间和努力。 **2** N-UNCOUNT If you say that someone did something **with effort** or **with an effort**, you mean it was difficult for them to do. 吃力 [usu "with" N, also "a" N] [WRITTEN] ❑ *She took a deep breath and sat up slowly and with great effort.* 她深吸一口气，慢慢地、吃力地坐了起来。 **3** N-COUNT An **effort** is a particular series of activities that is organized by a group of people in order to achieve something. 有组织的活动 ❑ *...a famine relief effort in Angola.* …一个在安哥拉的饥荒救援活动。 **4** N-SING If you say that something is **an effort**, you mean that an unusual amount of physical or mental energy is needed to do it. 极艰难的事 ❑ *Even carrying the camcorder while hiking in the forest was an effort.* 在森林徒步旅行时，即使背着摄像机也是件极难的事。 **5** PHRASE If you **make the effort to** do something, you do it, even though you need extra energy to do it or you do not really want to. 尽力 ❑ *I don't get lonely now because I make the effort to see people.* 我现在不寂寞了，因为我尽力与人接触。

> **Thesaurus** *effort* 另参见:
>
> N. attempt **1**
> exertion, labor, work **4**

ef·fort·less /ɛfərtlɪs/ **1** ADJ Something that is **effortless** is done easily and well. 不费力的 ❑ *...effortless and elegant Italian cooking.* …省力且优雅的意大利式烹调。 ● **ef·fort·less·ly** ADV 不费力地 ❑ *Her son Peter adapted effortlessly to his new surroundings.* 她的儿子彼得不费力地就适应了新环境。 **2** ADJ You use **effortless** to describe a quality that someone has naturally and does not have to learn. 天生的 ❑ *She liked him above all for his effortless charm.* 她尤其喜欢他天生的魅力。

EFL /i ɛf ɛl/ N-UNCOUNT **EFL** is the teaching of English to people whose first language is not English. **EFL** is an abbreviation for "English as a Foreign Language." 英语作为外语的教学 [oft N n] ❑ *...an EFL teacher.* …一位英语作为外语教学的老师。

e.g. /i dʒi/ **e.g.** is an abbreviation that means "for example." It is used before a noun, or to introduce another sentence. 例如 ❑ *We need helpers of all types, e.g., geologists and teachers.* 我们需要各种类型的协助者，例如地质学者和教师。

egg ♦♦◊ /ɛg/ (**eggs, egging, egged**) **1** N-COUNT An **egg** is an oval object that is produced by a female bird and contains a baby bird.

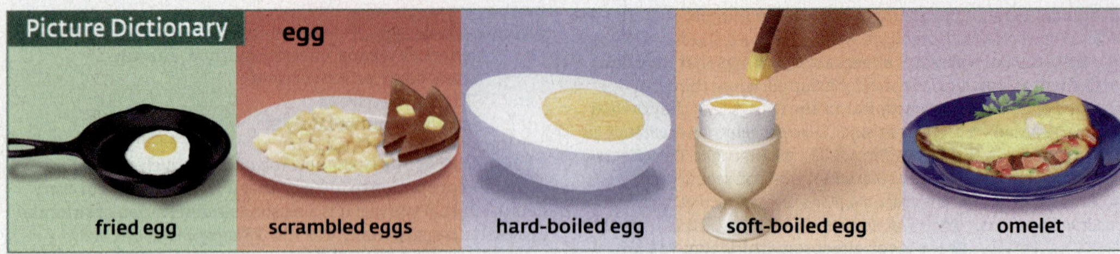

E

Other animals such as reptiles and fish also lay eggs. 蛋；卵 ❑ *...a baby bird hatching from its egg.* …一只从蛋壳里孵出来的雏鸟。 2 N-VAR In many countries, **eggs** often means hen's eggs, eaten as food. 鸡蛋 ❑ *Break the eggs into a shallow bowl and beat them lightly.* 把鸡蛋打在一个浅碗里并且稍微搅打。 3 N-COUNT **Egg** is used to refer to an object in the shape of a hen's egg. 卵状物 ❑ *...a chocolate egg.* …一个巧克力蛋。 4 N-COUNT An **egg** is a cell that is produced in the bodies of female animals and humans. If it is fertilized by a sperm, a baby develops from it. 卵子 ❑ *It only takes one sperm to fertilize an egg.* 只需一个精子就可以使卵受精。 5 PHRASE If someone puts **all** their **eggs in one basket**, they put all their effort or resources into doing one thing so that, if it fails, they have no alternatives left. 孤注一掷 ❑ *The key word here is diversify; don't put all your eggs in one basket.* 这里的关键词是多样化投资，不要孤注一掷。 6 PHRASE If someone has **egg on** their **face** or has **egg all over** their **face**, they have been made to look foolish. 出洋相 ❑ *If they take this game lightly they could end up with egg on their faces.* 如果他们轻率地对待这场比赛，他们可能会以出洋相收场。

→ see Picture Dictionary: **egg**

→ see **bird**

▸ **egg on** PHRASAL VERB If you **egg** a person **on**, you encourage them to do something, especially something dangerous or foolish. 怂恿 ❑ *He was lifting up handfuls of leaves and throwing them at her. She was laughing and egging him on.* 他正抓起把把树叶朝她扔去。她笑着，怂恿他继续扔。

egg·plant /ɛgplænt/ (**eggplants**) N-VAR An **eggplant** is a vegetable with a smooth, dark purple skin. 茄子 [AM]

in BRIT, use **aubergine**

ego /igoʊ, ɛgoʊ/ (**egos**) N-VAR Someone's **ego** is their sense of their own worth. For example, if someone has a large **ego**, they think they are very important and valuable. 自我价值感 ❑ *He had a massive ego, never would he admit he was wrong.* 他有极强的自我价值感，从来不会承认他错了。

Word Partnership *ego* 的常用搭配：

ADJ. **big** ego
V. **boost** *someone's* ego

▲ **ego·cen·tric** /igoʊsɛntrɪk, ɛg-/ ADJ Someone who is **egocentric** thinks only of themselves and their own wants, and does not consider other people. 自我中心的 [DISAPPROVAL] ❑ *He was egocentric, a man of impulse who expected those around him to serve him.* 他自我中心，易冲动，希望周围的人为他服务。

eh /eɪ/ CONVENTION **Eh** is used in writing to represent a noise that people make as a response in conversation, for example to express agreement or to ask for something to be explained or repeated. 嗯(表示同意、要求解释或重复等) ❑ *Let's talk all about it outside, eh?* 让我们到外面好好谈这事，嗯？

eight ♦♦♦ /eɪt/ (**eights**) NUM **Eight** is the number 8. 8 ❑ *So far eight workers have been killed.* 到目前为止已有8名员工遇难。

Word Link *teen ≈ plus ten, from 13-19 : eighteen, seventeen, teenager*

eight·een ♦♦♦ /eɪtin/ NUM **Eighteen** is the number 18. 18 ❑ *He was employed by them for eighteen years.* 他被他们雇佣了18年。

eight·eenth ♦♦◊ /eɪtinθ/ ORD The **eighteenth** item in a series is the one that you count as number eighteen. 第18 ❑ *The siege is now in its eighteenth day.* 围困现在是第18天了。

eighth ♦♦◊ /eɪtθ/ (**eighths**) 1 ORD The **eighth** item in a series is the one that you count as number eight. 第8 ❑ *...the eighth prime minister of India.* …印度的第8任总理。 2 FRACTION An **eighth** is one of eight equal parts of something. 1/8 ❑ *The Kuban produces an eighth of Russia's grain, meat, and milk.* 库班河流域出产俄罗斯1/8的谷物、肉类和牛奶。

eighti·eth ♦♦◊ /eɪtiəθ/ ORD The **eightieth** item in a series is the one that you count as number eighty. 第80 ❑ *Mr. Stevens recently celebrated his eightieth birthday.* 最近史蒂文斯先生庆祝了他80大寿。

eighty ♦♦♦ /eɪti/ (**eighties**) 1 NUM **Eighty** is the number 80. 80 ❑ *Eighty horses trotted up.* 80匹马小跑上来。 2 N-PLURAL When you talk about the **eighties**, you are referring to numbers between 80 and 89. For example, if you are **in your eighties**, you are aged between 80 and 89. If the temperature is **in the eighties**, the temperature is between 80 and 89 degrees. 八十几 ❑ *He was in his late eighties and had become the country's most respected elder statesman.* 那时他年近九十，并且已经成为该国最受尊敬的政界元老。 3 N-PLURAL **The eighties** is the decade between 1980 and 1989. 80年代 ❑ *He ran a property development business in the eighties.* 他在80年代经营一家房地产开发公司。

either ♦♦♦ /iðər, aɪðər/ 1 CONJ You use **either** in front of the first of two or more alternatives, when you are stating the only possibilities or choices that there are. The other alternatives are introduced by "or." 与**or**连用，表示几个可选项中只能选其一 ❑ *Sightseeing is best done either by tour bus or by bicycles.* 观光最好要么乘游览巴士，要么骑自行车。 ❑ *The former president was demanding that he should be either put on trial or set free.* 前总统一直要求要么对他进行审判，要么就无罪释放。 2 CONJ You use **either** in a negative statement in front of the first of two alternatives to indicate that the negative statement refers to both the alternatives. 用于否定句中，表示“两者都不” ❑ *There had been no indication of either breathlessness or any loss of mental faculties right until his death.* 直到去世，他既没有出现呼吸困难也没有脑功能丧失的迹象。 3 PRON You can use **either** to refer to one of two things, people, or situations, when you want to say that they are both possible and it does not matter which one is chosen or considered. 用于表示“两者中的任一个” ❑ *There were glasses of iced champagne and cigars. Unfortunately not many of either were consumed.* 有很多杯冰镇香槟和雪茄。可惜两样东西中哪一样都没被受用多少。 ● QUANT **Either** is also a quantifier. 用于表示“两者中任一…” [QUANT "of" def-pl-n] ❑ *Do either of you smoke or drink heavily?* 你们俩当中有谁抽烟、喝酒凶吗？ ● DET **Either** is also a determiner. 用于表示“两者中任一…” ❑ *...a special Indian drug police that would have the authority to pursue suspects into either country.* …有权到这两国中任意一国追捕嫌犯的一位印度缉毒特警。 4 PRON You use **either** in a negative statement to refer to each of two things, people, or situations to indicate that the negative statement includes both of them. 用于否定句中，表示“两者中任何一个都不” [with brd-neg] ❑ *She warned me that I'd never marry or have children.—"I don't want either."* 她警告我说我永远不会结婚、生孩子。——“我哪一样都不想要。” ● QUANT **Either** is also a quantifier. 用于否定句，表示“两者中任何一个…都不” ❑ *There are no simple answers to either of those questions.* 对那两个问题哪一个都没有简单的答案。 ● DET **Either** is also a determiner. 用于否定句，表示“两者中任一…都不” ❑ *He sometimes couldn't remember either man's name.* 他有时候这两个男人谁的名字都记不起来。 5 ADV You use **either** by itself in negative statements to indicate that there is a similarity or connection with a person or thing that you have just mentioned. 用于否定句，表示“也不”，与刚提过的人或事物类似或有关联 [ADV after v, with brd-neg] ❑ *He did not even say anything to her, and she did not speak to him either.* 他甚至什么都没跟她说，而她也没跟他说话。 6 ADV When one negative statement follows another, you can use **either** at the end of the second one to indicate that you are adding an extra piece of information, and to emphasize that both are equally important. 用于否定句中提供附加信息，表示“也不” [ADV after v] ❑ *Don't agree, but don't argue either.* 不要赞同，但是也不要争辩。 7 DET You can use **either** to introduce a noun that refers to each of two things when you are talking about both of them. 用于引出名词，表示“两者中每一个” ❑ *The basketball nets hung down from the ceiling at either end of the gymnasium.* 篮球网垂悬于体育馆天花板的两头。

Word Link *e ≈ away, out : eject, emigrate, emit*

★ **eject** /ɪdʒɛkt/ (**ejects, ejecting, ejected**) 1 V-T If you **eject** someone **from** a place, you force them to leave. 逐出 ❑ *Officials used guard dogs to eject the protesters.* 官员们用护卫犬驱走抗议者。 ● **ejec·tion** /ɪdʒɛkʃ°n/ N-VAR (**ejections**) 逐出 ❑ *...the ejection and manhandling of hecklers at the meeting.* …对会上起哄者的驱逐和推搡。 2 V-T To **eject** something means to remove it or push it out forcefully. 用力排出；用力推出 ❑ *He aimed his rifle, fired a single shot, then ejected the spent cartridge.* 他用步枪瞄准，开了一枪，接着排出了空弹壳。 3 V-I When a pilot **ejects from** an aircraft, he or she leaves the aircraft quickly using an ejector seat, usually because the plane is about to crash. (从飞机里) 弹射出来 ❑ *The pilot ejected from the plane and escaped injury.* 飞行员从飞机里弹出，没有受伤。

Word Link *labor ≈ working : collaborate, elaborate, laboratory*

elabo·rate (**elaborates, elaborating, elaborated**)

The adjective is pronounced /ɪlæbərɪt/. The verb is pronounced /ɪlæbəreɪt/.

形容词读作 /ɪlæbərɪt/。动词读作 /ɪlæbəreɪt/。

1 ADJ You use **elaborate** to describe something that is very complex because it has a lot of different parts. 复杂的 ❑ *...an elaborate research project.* …一项复杂的研究项目。 2 ADJ **Elaborate** plans, systems, and procedures are complicated because they have been planned in very great detail, sometimes too much detail. (有时过于) 周密的 ❑ *...elaborate efforts at the highest level to conceal the problem.* …最高层企图掩饰这个问题的百般努力。 ● **elabo·rate·ly** ADV 周密地 ❑ *It was clearly an elaborately planned operation.* 这显然是一次经过周密策划的行动。 3 ADJ **Elaborate** clothing or material is made with a lot of detailed artistic designs. 设计繁丽的 ❑ *He is known for his elaborate costumes.* 他以其繁丽的服装著称。 4 V-T If you **elaborate** a plan or theory, you develop it by making it more complicated and more effective. 周密制定；周密发展 ❑ *His task was to elaborate policies that would make a market economy compatible with a clean environment.* 他的任务是周密地制定能够让市场经济适合于无污染的环境的政策。 ● **elabo·ra·tion** /ɪlæbəreɪʃ°n/ N-UNCOUNT 周密的制定；周密的发展 ❑ *...the elaboration of specific policies and mechanisms.* …对具体政策和机制的周密制定。 5 V-I If you **elaborate on** something that has been said, you say more about it, or give more details. 作详细阐述 ❑ *A spokesman declined to elaborate on a statement released late yesterday.* 发言人拒绝对昨天晚些时候发表的一份声明作出更多说明。

Word Link *lapse ≈ falling : collapse, elapse, lapse*

★ **elapse** /ɪlæps/ (**elapses, elapsing, elapsed**) V-I When time **elapses**, it passes. (时间) 流逝 [FORMAL] ❑ *Forty-eight hours have elapsed since his arrest.* 他被捕后48小时已经过去了。

★ **elas·tic** /ɪlæstɪk/ 1 N-UNCOUNT **Elastic** is a rubber material that stretches when you pull it and returns to its original size and shape when you let it go. Elastic is often used in clothes to make them fit tightly, for example, around the waist. 松紧带 ❑ *Make a mask with long ears and attach a piece of elastic to go around the back of the head.* 做一个带长耳朵的面具，安上一条松紧带绕过后脑。 2 ADJ Something that is **elastic** is able to stretch easily and then return to its original size and shape. 有弹性的 ❑ *Beat it until the dough is slightly elastic.* 反复捶打，直到面团略有弹性。

elas·tic band (**elastic bands**) N-COUNT An **elastic band** is a thin circle of very stretchy rubber that you can put around things in order to hold them together. 橡皮筋 [mainly BRIT]

in AM, use **rubber band**

★ **elas·tici·ty** /ɪlæstɪsɪti, ɪlæst-/ N-UNCOUNT The **elasticity** of a material or substance is its ability to return to its original shape, size, and condition after it has been stretched. 弹性 ❑ *Daily facial exercises help to retain the skin's elasticity.* 每日的面部运动有助于保持皮肤弹性。

elat·ed /ɪleɪtɪd/ ADJ If you are **elated**, you are extremely happy and excited because of something that has happened. 兴高采烈的 ❑ *I was elated that my recent second bypass had been successful.* 令我高兴不已的是我最近的第二次搭桥手术成功了。

ela·tion /ɪleɪʃ°n/ N-UNCOUNT **Elation** is a feeling of great happiness and excitement about something that has happened. 兴高采烈 ❑ *His supporters have reacted to the news with elation.* 他的支持者们听到这个消息后兴高采烈。
→ see **emotion**

el·bow /ɛlboʊ/ (**elbows, elbowing, elbowed**) 1 N-COUNT Your **elbow** is the part of your arm where the upper and lower halves are joined. 肘 ❑ *He slipped and fell, badly bruising an elbow.* 他滑倒了，严重挫伤了一只胳膊肘。 2 V-T If you **elbow** people **aside** or **elbow your way** somewhere, you push people with your elbows in order to move somewhere. (用肘部) 推 ❑ *They also claim that the security team elbowed aside a steward.* 他们还声称治安队把一名乘务员推到了一边。 ❑ *Mr Smith elbowed me in the face.* 史密斯先生用肘推开我的脸。 ❑ *Brand elbowed his way to the center of the group of bystanders.* 布兰德用肘开路来到了一群旁观者的中间。 3 V-T If someone or something **elbows their way** somewhere, or **elbows** other people or things **out of the way**, they achieve success by being aggressive and determined. (用肘部) 挤 ❑ *Non-state firms gradually elbow aside the inefficient state-owned ones.* 非国有企业逐渐排挤掉了那些低效率的国有企业。 ❑ *Environmental concerns will elbow their way right to the top of the agenda.* 对环境问题的关注将挤到议程的首位。 4 to **rub elbows with** → see **rub**
→ see **body**

el·der /ɛldər/ (**elders**) 1 ADJ **The elder of** two people is the one who was born first. 年长的 [ADJ n, "the" ADJ, "the" ADJ "of" n] ❑ *...his elder brother.* …他的哥哥。 2 N-COUNT A person's **elder** is someone who is older than them, especially someone quite a lot older. 长辈 [FORMAL] ❑ *They have no respect for their elders.* 他们对长辈毫无敬意。 3 N-COUNT In some societies, an **elder** is one of the respected older people who have influence and authority. 长老 ❑ *...a meeting of political figures and tribal elders.* …政界要人和部族长老的一次会晤。

The adjective **elder** means "older" when it is followed by brother, sister, son, daughter, or other terms for relatives that are in your generation or younger. You use **older** to talk about the age of other people or things. **Elder** cannot be followed by "than" but **older** can be. ❑ *I've got a sister who is older than me.* Do not confuse **elder** and **elderly**. If you describe someone as **elderly**, you mean that they are old, but this is a slightly more polite word than **old**. **The elderly** are elderly people.

el·der·ly ♦◇◇ /ɛldərli/ ADJ You use **elderly** as a polite way of saying that someone is old. 上年纪的 [POLITENESS] ❑ *There was an elderly couple on the terrace.* 露台上有一对上年纪的老人。 ● N-PLURAL **The elderly** are people who are old. 老年人 ❑ *The elderly are a formidable force in any election.* 老年人在任何选举中都是一股强大的力量。
→ see **age**

eld·est /ɛldɪst/ ADJ The **eldest** person in a group is the one who was born before all the others. 年龄最大的 ❑ *The eldest child was a daughter called Fatiha.* 最大的孩子是个女儿叫法蒂哈。 ❑ *David was the eldest of three boys.* 大卫是3个男孩中年龄最大的一个。

elect ♦♦◇ /ɪlɛkt/ (**elects, electing, elected**) 1 V-T When people **elect** someone, they choose that person to represent them, by voting for them. 选举 ❑ *The people of the Philippines have voted to elect a new president.* 菲律宾人民已经投票选举出一位新总统。 ❑ *The University of Washington elected him dean in 1956.* 华盛顿大学在1956年选他为院长。 2 V-T If you **elect to** do something, you choose to do it. 选择 [FORMAL] ❑ *Those electing to smoke will be seated at the rear.* 选择抽烟的人将坐在后面。 3 ADJ **Elect** is added after words such as "president" or "governor" to indicate that a person has been elected to the post but has not officially started to carry out the duties involved. 当选而尚未就职的 [n ADJ] [FORMAL] ❑ *...the date when the president-elect takes office.* …总统当选人的就职日。
→ see **election**

elec·tion ♦♦♦ /ɪlɛkʃ°n/ (**elections**) 1 N-VAR An **election** is a process in which people vote to choose a person or group of people to hold an official position. 选举 ❑ *...Poland's first fully free elections for more than fifty years.* …五十多年来波兰首次完全自由选举。 ❑ *During his election campaign he promised to put the economy back on its feet.* 在竞选活动期间他承诺要重振经济。 2 N-UNCOUNT **The election** of a particular person or group of people is their success in winning an election. 当选 [usu with poss] ❑ *...the election of the Democrat candidate last year.* …去年民主党候选人的当选。 ❑ *...Vaclav Havel's election as president of Czechoslovakia.* …瓦茨拉夫・哈维尔当选捷克斯洛伐克总统。
→ see Word Web: **election**

Word Web election

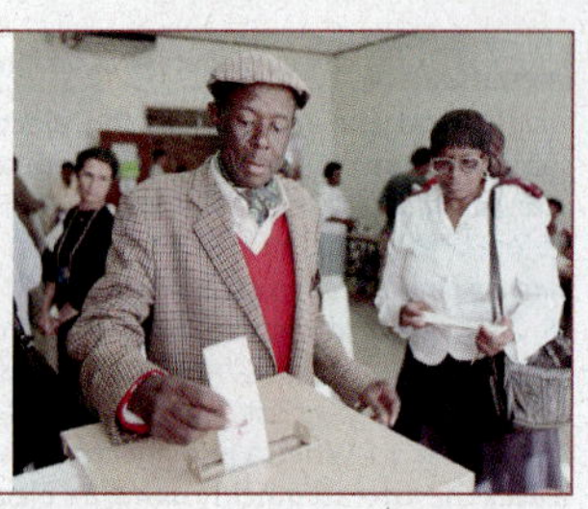

Presidential candidates spend millions of dollars on their **campaigns**. They give **speeches**, appear on TV, and **debate** each other. On election day, **voters cast** their **votes** at local **polling places**. **Citizens** living outside of the US mail in **absentee ballots**. But voters don't directly **elect** their **president**. States send representatives to the electoral college. There, representatives from all but two states must cast all their votes for one candidate—even if 49% of the people wanted the other candidate. Four times a candidate has **won** the popular vote and lost the election. This happened when George W. Bush won in 2000.

E

Word Partnership *election* 的常用搭配：

N. election **campaign**, election **day**, election **official**, election **results** 1

V. **hold an** election, **lose an** election, **vote in an** election, **win an** election 1

elec·tor /ɪlɛktər/ (**electors**) N-COUNT An **elector** is a person who has the right to vote in an election. 有选举权的人；选举人 ❑ *There are now 117 cardinals who can be cardinal electors, that is, eligible to enter the secret conclave that will choose the next pope.* 现在有117位红衣主教可以做教宗选举人，也就是说，有资格参与选举下届教皇的秘密会议。

★ **elec·tor·al** ♦◇◇ /ɪlɛktərəl/ ADJ **Electoral** is used to describe things that are connected with elections. 与选举有关的 [ADJ n] ❑ *The Mongolian Democratic Party is campaigning for electoral reform.* 蒙古民主党正在正在发起选举改革的运动。 ● **elec·tor·al·ly** ADV 与选举有关地 ❑ *He believed that the policies were both wrong and electorally disastrous.* 他认为这些政策既是错误的、又是选举上的灾难。

▲ **elec·tor·ate** /ɪlɛktərɪt/ (**electorates**) N-COUNT-COLL The **electorate** of a country or area is all the people in it who have the right to vote in an election. 全体选民 ❑ *He has the backing of almost a quarter of the electorate.* 他有将近四分之一的选民的支持。

elec·tric ♦◇◇ /ɪlɛktrɪk/ 1 ADJ An **electric** device or machine works by means of electricity, rather than using some other source of power. 电动的 ❑ *...her electric guitar.* …她的电吉他。 2 ADJ An **electric** current, voltage, or charge is one that is produced by electricity. 由电产生的 [ADJ n] 3 ADJ **Electric** plugs, sockets, or power lines are designed to carry electricity. 带电的 [ADJ n] ❑ *More people are deciding that electric power lines could present a health risk.* 更多的人在认为电线可能会带来健康隐患。 4 ADJ **Electric** is used to refer to the supply of electricity. 供电的 [ADJ n] [INFORMAL] ❑ *An average electric bill might go up $2 or $3 per month.* 一张普通电费单可能每月上涨$2或$3。 5 ADJ If you describe the atmosphere of a place or event as **electric**, you mean that people are in a state of great excitement. (气氛) 火爆的 ❑ *The mood in the hall was electric.* 礼堂里的气氛极为热烈。

→ see **keyboard**

elec·tri·cal /ɪlɛktrɪkᵊl/ 1 ADJ **Electrical** goods, equipment, or appliances work by means of electricity. 电力的 ❑ *...shipments of electrical equipment.* …电器设备的运输。 ● **elec·tri·cal·ly** /ɪlɛktrɪkli/ ADV 电力地 [ADV -ed] ❑ *...electrically powered vehicles.* …电动车。 2 ADJ **Electrical** systems or parts supply or use electricity. 电的 ❑ *...lighting and other electrical systems on the new runway.* …新跑道上的照明和其他电力系统。 3 ADJ **Electrical** energy is energy in the form of electricity. 电的 ❑ *...brief pulses of electrical energy.* …短暂的电能脉冲。 ● **elec·tri·cal·ly** ADV 电地 ❑ *...electrically charged particles.* …带电的粒子。 4 ADJ **Electrical** industries, engineers, or workers are involved in the production and supply of electricity or electrical products. 与电有关的 [ADJ n] ❑ *...company representatives from the electrical industry.* …来自电力行业的公司代表。

→ see **electricity**

elec·tric chair (**electric chairs**) N-COUNT **The electric chair** is a rarely-used method for killing criminals, in which a person is strapped to a special chair and killed by a powerful electric current. 电椅死刑 ❑ *Murderer Walter Kemmler was the first man to die in the electric chair.* 谋杀犯沃尔特·科姆勒是第一个死于电椅死刑的人。

Word Link *ician ≈ person who works at : electrician, musician, physician*

★ **elec·tri·cian** /ɪlɛktrɪʃᵊn, iːlɛk-/ (**electricians**) N-COUNT An **electrician** is a person whose job is to install and repair electrical equipment. 电工

elec·tric·ity ♦◇◇ /ɪlɛktrɪsɪti, iːlɛk-/ N-UNCOUNT **Electricity** is a form of energy that can be carried by wires and is used for heating and lighting, and to provide power for machines. 电 ❑ *We moved into a cabin with electricity but no running water.* 我们搬进了一间有电但是没有自来水的小木屋。

→ see Word Web: **electricity**

→ see **energy, light**

elec·tric shock (**electric shocks**) N-COUNT If you get an **electric shock**, you get a sudden painful feeling when you touch something connected to a supply of electricity. 电击

elec·tri·fi·ca·tion /ɪlɛktrɪfɪkeɪʃᵊn/ N-UNCOUNT The **electrification** of a house, town, or area is the connecting of that place to a supply of electricity. 电气化 ❑ *...rural electrification.* …乡村电气化。

elec·tri·fy /ɪlɛktrɪfaɪ/ (**electrifies, electrifying, electrified**) 1 V-T If people **are electrified by** an event or experience, it makes them feel very excited and surprised. 使…振奋 [usu passive] ❑ *The world was electrified by his courage and resistance.* 全世界为他的勇气和反抗所振奋。 ● **elec·tri·fy·ing** ADJ 令人振奋的 ❑ *He gave an electrifying performance.* 他做了一场令人振奋的表演。 2 V-T When a rail system or rail line **is electrified**, electric cables are put over the tracks, or electric rails are put beside them, so that the trains can be powered by electricity. 使电气化 [usu passive] ❑ *The railroad line was electrified as long ago as 1974.* 早在1974年铁路就电气化了。

elec·tro·cute /ɪlɛktrəkyut/ (**electrocutes, electrocuting, electrocuted**) 1 V-T If someone **is electrocuted**, they are accidentally killed or badly injured when they touch something connected to a source of electricity. 使…触电 (死亡或受伤) ❑ *Three people were electrocuted by falling power lines.* 三人被落下来的电线电死了。 2 V-T If a criminal **is electrocuted**, he or she is executed using electricity. 电刑处死 [usu passive] ❑ *He was electrocuted for a murder committed when he was 17.* 他因为17岁时犯下的谋杀罪而被电刑处死。 ● **elec·tro·cu·tion** /ɪlɛktrəkyuʃᵊn/ N-VAR (**electrocutions**) 电刑处死 ❑ *The court pronounced him guilty and sentenced him to death by electrocution.* 法庭宣判他有罪，并判他电刑处死。

elec·trode /ɪlɛktroud/ (**electrodes**) N-COUNT An **electrode** is a small piece of metal or other substance that is used to take an electric current to or from a source of power, a piece of equipment, or a living body. 电极 ❑ *Two electrodes that measure*

Word Web electricity

Demand for **electrical** power in the U.S. will likely rise by 35 percent over the next 20 years. **Power companies** are moving quickly to meet this need. At the heart of every **power station** are electrical **generators**. Traditionally, they ran on hydroelectric power or **fossil fuel**. However, today new sources of **energy** are available. On **wind farms**, wind **turbines** use the power of moving air to run generators. Seaside tidal power stations make use of rising and falling tides to turn turbines. And in sunny climates, **photovoltaic cells** produce electrical power from the sun's rays.

changes in the body's surface moisture are attached to the palms of your hands. 测量体表湿度变化的两个电极被连接到你的双掌上。

Word Link *electr ≈ electric : electrician, electricity, electron*

elec·tron /ɪlɛktrɒn/ (**electrons**) N-COUNT An **electron** is a tiny particle of matter that is smaller than an atom and has a negative electrical charge. 电子 [TECHNICAL] ❑ *Most things are balanced - with equal numbers of electrons and protons.* 大部分物体都是电荷平衡的——含等量的电子和质子。

→ see **television**

elec·tron·ic ♦◇◇ /ɪlɛktrɒnɪk, i-/ 1 ADJ An **electronic** device has transistors or silicon chips that control and change the electric current passing through the device. 电子的 [ADJ n] ❑ *...expensive electronic equipment.* …昂贵的电子设备。 2 ADJ An **electronic** process or activity involves the use of electronic devices. 电子的 ❑ *...electronic music.* …电子音乐。 ● **elec·troni·cal·ly** ADV 电子地 [ADV with v] ❑ *Data is transmitted electronically.* 数据是电子传输。

elec·tron·ic book (**electronic books**) N-COUNT An **electronic book** is the same as an **e-book**. 电子书 [COMPUTING]

elec·tron·ic mail N-SING **Electronic mail** is the same as **e-mail**. 电子邮件

elec·tron·ic pub·lish·ing N-UNCOUNT **Electronic publishing** is the publishing of documents in a form that can be read on a computer, for example, as a CD-ROM. 电子出版

Word Link *ics ≈ system, knowledge : economics, electronics, ethics*

elec·tron·ics /ɪlɛktrɒnɪks, i-/ N-UNCOUNT **Electronics** is the technology of using transistors and silicon chips, especially in devices such as radios, televisions, and computers. 电子技术 ❑ *...Ohio's three main electronics companies.* …俄亥俄州三大电子技术公司。

el·egant ♦◇◇ /ɛlɪgənt/ 1 ADJ If you describe a person or thing as **elegant**, you mean that they are pleasing and graceful in appearance or style. 优雅的 ❑ *Patricia looked beautiful and elegant as always.* 帕特丽夏看上去跟往常一样美丽优雅。 ● **el·egance** N-UNCOUNT 优雅 ❑ *The furniture managed to combine practicality with elegance.* 这家具结合了实用与优雅。 ● **el·egant·ly** ADV 优雅地 ❑ *...a tall, elegantly dressed man with a mustache.* …一个穿着优雅、留着胡子的高个男子。 2 ADJ If you describe a piece of writing, an idea, or a plan as **elegant**, you mean that it is simple, clear, and clever. 精妙的 ❑ *The document impressed me with its elegant simplicity.* 这份文件以其精妙的简约给我留下了深刻的印象。 ● **el·egant·ly** ADV 精妙地 ❑ *...an elegantly simple idea.* …一个精妙地简单的主意。

Thesaurus *elegant* 另参见：

ADJ. chic, exquisite, luxurious, stylish; *(ant.)* inelegant, unsophisticated 1

el·ement ♦♦◇ /ɛlɪmənt/ (**elements**) 1 N-COUNT The different **elements** of something are the different parts it contains. 组成部分 ❑ *The exchange of prisoners of war was one of the key elements of the UN's peace plan.* 交换战俘是联合国和平计划的主要内容之一。 2 N-COUNT A particular **element** of a situation, activity, or process is an important quality or feature that it has or needs. 要素；特点 ❑ *Physical fitness has now become an important element in our lives.* 身体健康现已成为我们生活中的重要元素。 3 N-COUNT When you talk about **elements** within a society or organization, you are referring to groups of people who have similar aims, beliefs, or habits. (具有相似目标、信仰或者习惯的) 群体；分子 ❑ *The government must weed out criminal elements from within the security forces.* 政府必须剔除保安队伍内部的犯罪分子。 4 N-COUNT If something has an **element of** a particular quality or emotion, it has a certain amount of this quality or emotion. 成分 ❑ *These reports clearly contain elements of propaganda.* 这些报告明显带有宣传的成分。 5 N-COUNT An **element** is a substance such as gold, oxygen, or carbon that consists of only one type of atom. 元素 6 N-COUNT The **element** in an electric or water heater is the metal part that changes the electric current into heat. 电阻丝 7 N-PLURAL You can refer to the weather, especially wind and rain, as **the elements**. 天气 (尤指风雨) ❑ *The area where most refugees are waiting is exposed to the elements.* 大部分难民滞留的地区暴露在风雨之中。 8 PHRASE If you say that someone is **in their element**, you mean that they are in a situation they enjoy. 如鱼得水 ❑ *My stepmother was in her element, organizing everything.* 我继母那时如鱼得水，安排着所有一切。

→ see Word Web: **element**

→ see **rock**

el·emen·ta·ry /ɛlɪmɛntəri, -tri/ ADJ Something that is **elementary** is very simple and basic. 基本的 ❑ *Literacy now includes elementary computer skills.* 有文化现在包括基本的计算机技能。

el·emen·ta·ry school (**elementary schools**) N-VAR An **elementary school** is a school where children are taught for the first six or sometimes seven years of their education. 小学 [mainly AM] ❑ *The move from elementary school to middle school or junior high can be difficult.* 从小学进入中学或者初中的这种变动可能会有困难。

el·ephant /ɛlɪfənt/ (**elephants**) N-COUNT An **elephant** is a very large animal with a long, flexible nose called a trunk, which it uses to pick up things. Elephants live in India and Africa. 大象

★ **el·evate** /ɛlɪveɪt/ (**elevates, elevating, elevated**) 1 V-T When someone or something achieves a more important rank or status, you can say that they **are elevated to** it. 提拔 [usu passive] [FORMAL] ❑ *He was elevated to the post of president.* 他被提拔到总裁的职位。 ● **el·eva·tion** /ɛlɪveɪʃ°n/ N-UNCOUNT 提拔 ❑ *The elevation of the assistant coach to the head coaching position within only 9 months was a surprise.* 这位助理教练仅仅在9个月内就被提拔到总教练的位置是件令人惊讶的事。 2 V-T If you **elevate** something **to** a higher status, you consider it to be better or more important than it really is. 抬高 (地位) ❑ *Don't elevate your superiors to superstar status.* 不要把你的上级抬高到超级明星的地位。 3 V-T To **elevate** something means to increase it in amount or intensity. 提高 [FORMAL] ❑ *Emotional stress can elevate blood pressure.* 情绪紧张会使血压升高。 4 V-T If you **elevate** something, you raise it higher. 举起；抬高 ❑ *A few times a day, elevate feet above heart level.* 一天几次把脚抬到高过心脏的位置。 ❑ *I built a platform to elevate the bed.* 我搭了一个台子把床抬高了。

Word Link *ation ≈ state of : celebration, elevation, relaxation*

el·eva·tion /ɛlɪveɪʃ°n/ (**elevations**) 1 N-COUNT The **elevation** of a place is its height above sea level. 海拔 ❑ *We're probably at an elevation of about 13,000 feet above sea level.* 我们很可能在海拔13000英尺的高度。 2 N-COUNT An **elevation** is a piece of ground that is higher than the area around it. 高地 ❑ *...the monument was on an elevation, which could be seen from the church.* …这座纪念碑在一块高地上，从教堂能看到。

el·eva·tor /ɛlɪveɪtər/ (**elevators**) N-COUNT An **elevator** is a device that carries people or goods up and down inside tall buildings. 电梯 [AM]

in BRIT, use **lift**

❑ *We took the elevator to the fourteenth floor.* 我们乘电梯到了第14层。

→ see **skyscraper**

Word Web element

Elements—like copper, sodium, and oxygen—are made from only one type of **atom**. Each element has its own unique **properties**. For instance, oxygen is a gas at room temperature and copper is a solid. Often elements come together with other types of elements to make **compounds**. When the atoms in a compound bind together, they form a **molecule**. One of the best known molecules is H2O. It is made up of two hydrogen atoms and one oxygen atom. This molecule is also known as water. The periodic table is a complete listing of all the elements.

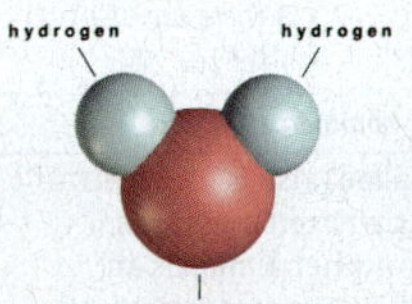

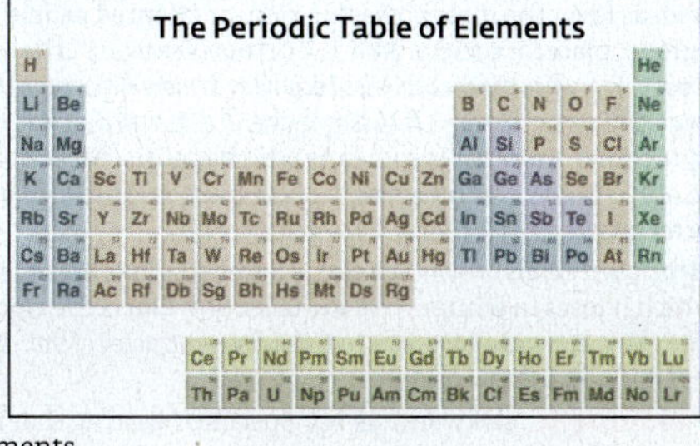

E

elev·en ♦♦♦ /ɪlɛvᵊn/ (**elevens**) NUM **Eleven** is the number 11. 11 ❑ *...the Princess and her eleven friends.* …公主和她的11个朋友。

elev·enth ♦♦◊ /ɪlɛvᵊnθ/ ORD The **eleventh** item in a series is the one that you count as number eleven. 第11 ❑ *We were working on the eleventh floor.* 我们在第11层工作。

★ **elic·it** /ɪlɪsɪt/ (**elicits, eliciting, elicited**) 1 V-T If you **elicit** a response or a reaction, you do or say something that makes other people respond or react. 引起（反应）❑ *Mr. Norris said he was hopeful that his request would elicit a positive response.* 诺里斯先生说他希望他的要求会引起积极的回应。 2 V-T If you **elicit** a piece of information, you get it by asking the right questions. 探得（信息）[FORMAL] ❑ *My letters to her have elicited no response.* 我写给她的信没有得到回应。

★ **eli·gible** /ɛlɪdʒɪbᵊl/ 1 ADJ Someone who is **eligible to** do something is qualified or able to do it, for example, because they are old enough. 有资格的 ❑ *Almost half the population are eligible to vote in today's election.* 将近一半的居民有资格在今天的选举中投票。 ● **eli·gibil·ity** ▲ /ɛlɪdʒəbɪlɪti/ N-UNCOUNT 资格；合格 ❑ *The rules covering eligibility for benefits changed in the 1980s.* 关于社会救济金合格条件的规定在20世纪80年代发生了变化。 2 ADJ An **eligible** man or woman is not yet married and is thought by many people to be a suitable partner. （指结婚对象）令人中意的 ❑ *He's the most eligible bachelor in Japan.* 他是日本最令人中意的单身汉。

elimi·nate ♦◊◊ /ɪlɪmɪneɪt/ (**eliminates, eliminating, eliminated**) 1 V-T To **eliminate** something, especially something you do not want or need, means to remove it completely. 根除 [FORMAL] ❑ *Recent measures have not eliminated discrimination in employment.* 最近的举措还未能根除就业歧视。 ● **elimi·na·tion** N-UNCOUNT 根除 ❑ *...the prohibition and elimination of chemical weapons.* …对化学武器的禁止和销毁。 2 V-T PASSIVE When a person or team **is eliminated from** a competition, they are defeated and so stop participating in the competition. 淘汰 ❑ *I was eliminated from the 400 meters in the semi-finals.* 我在400米半决赛中被淘汰了。 3 V-T If someone says that they **have eliminated** an enemy, they mean that they have killed them. By using the word "eliminate," they are trying to make the action sound more positive than if they used the word "kill." 消灭 ❑ *He declared war on the government and urged right-wingers to eliminate their opponents.* 他向政府宣战并且力劝右翼分子们消灭他们的对手。

Thesaurus *eliminate* 另参见：
v. dispose of, erase, expel, knock out; *(ant.)* choose, include 1

elimi·na·tion /ɪlɪmɪneɪʃᵊn/ 1 N-UNCOUNT **Elimination** is the process of getting rid of waste products from your body by going to the bathroom. 排泄 [FORMAL] ❑ *Breast-feeding is as natural as sex or elimination or any other bodily function.* 母乳哺养是天生的，就像性交、排泄或者其他任何身体功能一样。 2 → see **eliminate 1**

★ **elite** /ɪlit, eɪ-/ (**elites**) 1 N-COUNT You can refer to the most powerful, rich, or talented people within a particular group, place, or society as the **elite**. 精英 ❑ *...a government comprised mainly of the elite.* …主要由精英组成的政府。 2 ADJ **Elite** people or organizations are considered to be the best of their kind. 精英的 [ADJ n] ❑ *...the elite troops of the president's bodyguard.* …总统卫队中的精英部队。

elit·ism /ɪlitɪzəm, eɪ-/ N-UNCOUNT **Elitism** is the quality or practice of being elitist. 精英主义 ❑ *It became difficult to promote conventional ideas of excellence without being instantly accused of elitism.* 倡议传统优秀价值观，很难不立刻招来精英主义的指责。

elit·ist /ɪlitɪst, eɪ-/ (**elitists**) 1 ADJ **Elitist** systems, practices, or ideas favor the most powerful, rich, or talented people within a group, place, or society. 精英主义的 [DISAPPROVAL] ❑ *He worries about a time when college athletics become even more elitist than they are now.* 他担心有一天大学体育运动会变得比现在更加精英主义化。 2 N-COUNT An **elitist** is someone who has elitist ideas or is part of an elite. 精英主义者 [DISAPPROVAL] ❑ *He was an elitist who had no time for the masses.* 他是个精英主义者，没时间给民众。

elm /ɛlm/ (**elms**) N-VAR An **elm** is a tree that has broad leaves which it loses in winter. 榆树 ● N-UNCOUNT **Elm** is the wood of this tree. 榆木 ❑ *It was a good table too, sturdily constructed of elm.* 这也是一张好桌子，榆木做的，很结实。

★ **elo·quent** /ɛləkwənt/ 1 ADJ Speech or writing that is **eloquent** is well expressed and effective in persuading people. 雄辩的；有说服力的 ❑ *I heard him make a very eloquent speech at that dinner.* 我听他在那次晚餐上做了一次很有说服力的演说。 ● **elo·quence** N-UNCOUNT 雄辩力；说服力 ❑ *...the eloquence of his prose.* …他散文的说服力。 ● **elo·quent·ly** ADV 雄辩地；有说服力地 ❑ *Juanita speaks eloquently about her art.* 朱安妮塔有说服力地讲她的艺术。 2 ADJ A person who is **eloquent** is good at speaking and able to persuade people. 能言善辩的 [APPROVAL] ❑ *He was eloquent about his love of books.* 他善于谈论他对书籍的热爱。 ● **elo·quence** N-UNCOUNT 能言善辩 ❑ *She can speak with an eloquence that is almost inspirational.* 她能用一种近乎激发灵感的口才发言。

else ♦♦♦ /ɛls/ 1 ADJ You use **else** after words such as "anywhere," "someone," and "what" to refer in a vague way to another person, place, or thing. （不确指人、处、事）别的 ❑ *If I can't make a living at painting, at least I can teach someone else to paint.* 如果我不能以画画谋生的话，至少我能教别人画画。 ❑ *We had nothing else to do on those long trips.* 在那些漫长的旅途中我们别无他事可做。 ● ADV **Else** is also an adverb. 其他地 [adv ADV] ❑ *I never wanted to live anywhere else.* 我从未想要到其他任何地方去住。 2 ADJ You use **else** after words such as "everyone," "everything," and "everywhere" to refer in a vague way to all the other people, things, or places except the one you are talking about. 其他的 [pron-indef ADJ] ❑ *As I try to be truthful, I expect everyone else to be truthful.* 因为我努力做到诚实，所以我期望每个其他也都诚实。 ● ADV **Else** is also an adverb. 其他地 [adv ADV] ❑ *Cleveland seems so much dirtier than everywhere else.* 克利夫兰似乎比其他任何地方都脏得多。 3 PHRASE You use **or else** after stating a logical conclusion, to indicate that what you are about to say is evidence for that conclusion. 否则（用于给出推断的理由）❑ *Evidently no lessons have been learned or else the government would not have handled the problem so badly.* 显然没有吸取教训，否则政府不会把这个问题处理得如此糟糕。 4 PHRASE You use **or else** to introduce a statement that indicates the unpleasant results that will occur if someone does or does not do something. 否则 ❑ *This time we really need to succeed or else people will start giving us funny looks.* 这次我们真地得要成功，否则人们会开始用奇怪的眼光看我们。 5 PHRASE You use **or else** to introduce the second of two possibilities when you do not know which one is true. 要不然 ❑ *You are either a total genius or else you must be totally crazy.* 你要么是个纯粹的天才，要不然你准是完全疯了。 6 PHRASE **Above all else** is used to emphasize that a particular thing is more important than other things. 最重要地 [EMPHASIS] ❑ *Above all else I hate the cold.* 我最讨厌寒冷。 7 PHRASE You can say **"if nothing else"** to indicate that what you are mentioning is, in your opinion, the only good thing in a particular situation. 至少 ❑ *If nothing else, you'll really enjoy meeting them.* 至少，你会真地喜欢见到他们。 8 PHRASE You say **"or else"** after a command to warn someone that if they do not obey, you will be angry and may harm or punish them. 否则不客气了 [SPOKEN] ❑ *Behave, or else!* 守规矩，否则不客气了！

else·where ♦◊◊ /ɛlswɛər/ ADV **Elsewhere** means in other places or to another place. 在别处地；去别处地 ❑ *Almost 80 percent of the state's residents were born elsewhere.* 这个州几乎百分之八十的居民是在其他地方出生的。 ❑ *They were living well, in comparison with people elsewhere in the world.* 和世界上其他地方的人们比起来，他们过着舒适的生活。

elude /ɪlud/ (**eludes, eluding, eluded**) 1 V-T If something that you want **eludes** you, you fail to obtain it. 不为…所获得 [no passive] ❑ *Sleep eluded her.* 她失眠了。 2 V-T If you **elude** someone or something, you avoid them or escape from them. 躲避 ❑ *He eluded the police for 13 years.* 他躲了警察13年。 3 V-T If a fact or idea **eludes** you, you do not succeed in understanding it, realizing it, or remembering it. 把…难住 [no passive] ❑ *The appropriate word eluded him.* 他想不起来那个合适的词。

▲ **elu·sive** /ɪlusɪv/ ADJ Something or someone that is **elusive** is difficult to find, describe, remember, or achieve. 难（找、形容、记、取得）的 ❑ *In Denver late-night taxis are elusive and far from cheap.* 在丹佛，深夜出租车很难找，而且绝不便宜。

'em /əm, STRONG ɛm/ PRON **'em** is an informal way of saying or writing **them**. 他们（them的非正式的表达方式）❑ *There was also two other men there with 'em too.* 另外还有两个男人也和他们在一起。

Word Link *e ≈ electronic : e-book, e-commerce, e-mail*

e-mail ♦♦◊ (**e-mails, e-mailing, e-mailed**) also **E-mail, email** 1 N-VAR **E-mail** is a system of sending written messages electronically from one computer to another. **E-mail** is an abbreviation of **electronic mail**. 电子邮件 ❑ *You can contact us by e-mail.* 你可以通过电子邮件跟我们联系。 ❑ *Do you want to send an*

E-mail? 你想发一封电子邮件吗? **2** V-T If you **e-mail** someone, you send them an e-mail. 给…发电子邮件 ❑ *Jamie e-mailed me to say he couldn't come.* 杰米给我发了一封电子邮件说他不能来了。
→ see **Internet**

ema·nate /ɛməneɪt/ (**emanates, emanating, emanated**) **1** V-T/V-I If a quality **emanates from** you, or if you **emanate** a quality, you give people a strong sense that you have that quality. 发散出 (品质) [FORMAL] ❑ *Intelligence and cunning emanated from him.* 聪明和机灵从他身上散发出来。 **2** V-I If something **emanates from** somewhere, it comes from there. 散发 [FORMAL] ❑ *The heady aroma of wood smoke emanated from the stove.* 木头燃烧的浓郁香味从炉子里散发出来。

Word Link *man ≈ hand : emancipate, manicure, manipulate*

★ **eman·ci·pate** /ɪmænsɪpeɪt/ (**emancipates, emancipating, emancipated**) V-T If people **are emancipated**, they are freed from unpleasant or unfair social, political, or legal restrictions. 解放 [FORMAL] ❑ *Catholics were emancipated in 1792.* 天主教徒在1792年获得了解放。 ❑ *That war preserved the Union and emancipated the slaves.* 那场战争保住了联邦政府，解放了奴隶。 ● **eman·ci·pa·tion** /ɪmænsɪpeɪʃ^{ə}n/ N-UNCOUNT 解放 [oft N "of" n] ❑ *...the emancipation of women.* …妇女的解放。

em·bank·ment /ɪmbæŋkmənt/ (**embankments**) N-COUNT An **embankment** is a thick wall of earth that is built to carry a road or railroad track over an area of low ground, or to prevent water from a river or the sea from flooding the area. 堤 ❑ *They climbed a steep embankment.* 他们爬上了一个陡峭的堤岸。 ❑ *...a railroad embankment.* …一条铁路路堤。

▲ **em·bar·go** /ɪmbɑrgoʊ/ (**embargoes, embargoing, embargoed**) **1** N-COUNT If one country or group of countries imposes an **embargo** against another, it forbids trade with that country. 贸易禁运 ❑ *The United Nations imposed an arms embargo against the country.* 联合国对该国施行了武器贸易禁运。 **2** V-T If goods of a particular kind **are embargoed**, people are not allowed to import them from a particular country or export them to a particular country. 禁止贸易 ❑ *The fruit was embargoed.* 水果被禁运了。 ❑ *They embargoed oil shipments to the U.S.* 他们禁止了对美国石油船运。

★ **em·bark** /ɪmbɑrk/ (**embarks, embarking, embarked**) **1** V-I If you **embark on** something new, difficult, or exciting, you start doing it. 开始从事 ❑ *He's embarking on a new career as a writer.* 他正开始一个当作家的新生涯。 **2** V-I When someone **embarks on** a ship, they go on board before the start of a journey. 登上 (船) ❑ *They embarked on a ship bound for Europe.* 他们登上了一艘去欧洲的船。

em·bar·rass /ɪmbærəs/ (**embarrasses, embarrassing, embarrassed**) **1** V-T If something or someone **embarrasses** you, they make you feel shy or ashamed. 使…尴尬 ❑ *His clumsiness embarrassed him.* 他的笨拙令他尴尬。 **2** V-T If something **embarrasses** a public figure such as a politician or an organization such as a political party, it causes problems for them. 使…陷入麻烦 ❑ *Aides spoke of disposing of records that would embarrass the governor.* 助手们谈到了要处理掉那些会给州长找麻烦的记录。

em·bar·rassed /ɪmbærəst/ ADJ A person who is **embarrassed** feels shy, ashamed, or guilty about something. 尴尬的 ❑ *He looked a bit embarrassed.* 他看上去有点尴尬。

em·bar·rass·ing /ɪmbærəsɪŋ/ **1** ADJ Something that is **embarrassing** makes you feel shy or ashamed. 令人尴尬的 ❑ *That was an embarrassing situation for me.* 对我来说，那是个令人尴尬的场面。 ● **em·bar·rass·ing·ly** ADV 令人尴尬地 ❑ *The lyrics of the song are embarrassingly banal.* 那首歌的歌词庸俗得让人尴尬。 **2** ADJ Something that is **embarrassing to** a public figure such as a politician or an organization such as a political party causes problems for them. 为难的 ❑ *He has put the administration in an embarrassing position.* 他已把政府置于了一个为难的境地。

em·bar·rass·ment /ɪmbærəsmənt/ (**embarrassments**) **1** N-VAR **Embarrassment** is the feeling you have when you are embarrassed. 尴尬; 难堪 ❑ *I think I would have died of embarrassment.* 我觉得我一定会尴尬得要死。 ❑ *We apologize for any embarrassment this may have caused.* 我们为可能会带来的任何尴尬而道歉。 **2** N-COUNT An **embarrassment** is an action, event, or situation that causes problems for a politician, political party, government, or other public group. 难堪的事 ❑ *The poverty figures were undoubtedly an embarrassment to the president.* 这些贫困数字无疑是令总统难堪的一件事。 **3** N-SING If you refer to a person as **an embarrassment**, you mean that you disapprove of them but cannot avoid your connection with them. 丢脸的人 [DISAPPROVAL] ❑ *You have been an embarrassment to us from the day Doug married you.* 自从你和道格结婚的那天起你对我们来讲一直是个丢脸的人。

em·bas·sy ◆◇◇ /ɛmbəsi/ (**embassies**) N-COUNT An **embassy** is a group of government officials, headed by an ambassador, who represent their government in a foreign country. The building in which they work is also called an **embassy**. 大使及其随员; 大使馆 ❑ *The American embassy has already complained.* 美国使馆已经提出抗议。

Word Link *em ≈ making, putting : embed, embellish, empower*

★ **em·bed** /ɪmbɛd/ (**embeds, embedding, embedded**) **1** V-T If an object **embeds itself** in a substance or thing, it becomes fixed there firmly and deeply. 嵌入 ❑ *One of the bullets passed through Andrea's chest before embedding itself in a wall.* 其中一颗子弹穿过安德烈亚的胸膛然后嵌入一面墙中。 ● **em·bed·ded** ADJ 嵌入的 ❑ *The fossils at Dinosaur Cove are embedded in hard sandstone.* 恐龙湾中的化石嵌在坚硬的砂岩中。 **2** V-T If something such as an attitude or feeling **is embedded in** a society or system, or in someone's personality, it becomes a permanent and noticeable feature of it. 使根深蒂固 [usu passive] ❑ *This agreement will be embedded in a state treaty to be signed soon.* 这项协议将被纳入到一份即将被签署的国家条约中。 ● **em·bed·ded** ADJ 根深蒂固的 ❑ *I think that hatred of the other is deeply embedded in our society.* 我觉得对异己的憎恨在我们的社会中根深蒂固。

em·bel·lish /ɪmbɛlɪʃ/ (**embellishes, embellishing, embellished**) **1** V-T If something **is embellished with** decorative features or patterns, it has those features or patterns on it and they make it look more attractive. 装饰 ❑ *The boat was embellished with carvings in red and blue.* 这艘船饰有红、蓝雕刻。 ❑ *Ivy leaves embellish the front of the dresser.* 长春藤树叶装饰着梳妆台的正面。 **2** V-T If you **embellish** a story, you make it more interesting by adding details that may be untrue. 添油加醋 ❑ *I launched into the parable, embellishing the story with invented dialogue and extra details.* 我开始投入地讲这个寓言，编了些对话和额外细节为故事添油加醋。

em·bez·zle /ɪmbɛz^{ə}l/ (**embezzles, embezzling, embezzled**) V-T If someone **embezzles** money that their organization or company has placed in their care, they take it and use it illegally for their own purposes. 挪用 (钱款) ❑ *One former director embezzled $34 million in company funds.* 一位前任主管挪用了3400万美元的公司资金。

em·bez·zle·ment /ɪmbɛz^{ə}lmənt/ N-UNCOUNT **Embezzlement** is the crime of embezzling money. 挪用公款 ❑ *He was later charged with embezzlement.* 他后来被指控挪用公款。

em·blem /ɛmbləm/ (**emblems**) **1** N-COUNT An **emblem** is a design representing a country or organization. 徽章 ❑ *...the emblem of the Soviet Union.* …苏联的国徽。 **2** N-COUNT An **emblem** is something that represents a quality or idea. 象征; 标志 ❑ *The eagle was an emblem of strength and courage.* 鹰是力量和勇气的象征。

em·bodi·ment /ɪmbɒdimənt/ N-SING If you say that someone or something is **the embodiment of** a quality or idea, you mean that that is their most noticeable characteristic or the basis of all they do. 集中体现; 化身 [FORMAL] ❑ *A baby is the embodiment of vulnerability.* 婴儿是脆弱的化身。

★ **em·body** /ɪmbɒdi/ (**embodies, embodying, embodied**) **1** V-T To **embody** an idea or quality means to be a symbol or expression of that idea or quality. 体现; 具体象征 ❑ *Jack Kennedy embodied all the hopes of the 1960s.* 杰克•肯尼迪体现了20世纪60年代的全部希望。 ❑ *For twenty-nine years, Checkpoint Charlie embodied the Cold War.* 29年来，查理检查站具体象征了冷战。 **2** V-T If something **is embodied in** a particular thing, the second thing contains or consists of the first. 包含; 收录 ❑ *The proposal has been embodied in a draft resolution.* 这项提议已经被包含在一份决议草案中。

em·brace /ɪmbreɪs/ (**embraces, embracing, embraced**) **1** V-RECIP If you **embrace** someone, you put your arms around them and hold them tightly, usually in order to show your love or affection for them. You can also say that two people **embrace**. 拥抱 ❑ *Penelope came forward and embraced her sister.* 佩内洛普走上前来拥抱了她的妹妹。 ❑ *At first people were sort of crying for joy and embracing each other.* 开始时人们有点喜极而泣，互相拥抱。 ● N-COUNT **Embrace** is also a noun. 拥抱 ❑ *...a young couple locked in an embrace.* …紧紧相拥的年轻一对。 **2** V-T If you **embrace** a change, political system, or idea, you accept it and start supporting it or believing in it. 欣然接受; 信奉 [FORMAL] ❑ *He embraces the new* *information age.* 他欢迎新的信息时代。● N-SING **Embrace** is also a noun. 欣然接受；信奉 ❑ *The marriage signaled James's embrace of the Catholic faith.* 这场婚姻标志着詹姆士对天主教的信奉。 3 V-T If something **embraces** a group of people, things, or ideas, it includes them in a larger group or category. 囊括 [FORMAL] ❑ *...a theory that would embrace the whole field of human endeavor.* …一个会囊括整个人类奋斗领域的理论。

em·broi·der /ɪmbrɔɪdər/ (**embroiders, embroidering, embroidered**) 1 V-T/V-I If something such as clothing or cloth **is embroidered with** a design, the design is stitched into it. 绣 ❑ *The collar was embroidered with very small red strawberries.* 这衣领上绣了非常小的红色草莓。 ❑ *I have a pillow with my name embroidered on it.* 我有一个绣着我名字的枕头。 2 V-T/V-I If you **embroider** a story or account of something, or if you **embroider on** it, you try to make it more interesting by adding details that may be untrue. 渲染 ❑ *He told some lies and sometimes just embroidered the truth.* 他说了些谎话，有时候只不过是渲染了一下事实。

▲ **em·broi·dery** /ɪmbrɔɪdəri/ (**embroideries**) 1 N-VAR **Embroidery** consists of designs stitched into cloth. 刺绣 ❑ *The shorts had blue embroidery over the pockets.* 这条短裤口袋上有蓝色的刺绣。 2 N-UNCOUNT **Embroidery** is the activity of stitching designs onto cloth. 刺绣 ❑ *She learned sewing, knitting, and embroidery.* 她学过缝纫、编织和刺绣。

→ see **quilt**

em·broiled /ɪmbrɔɪld/ ADJ If you become **embroiled in** a fight or argument, you become deeply involved in it. 使卷入的 [V-LINK ADJ] ❑ *The government insisted that troops would not become embroiled in battles in Bosnia.* 政府坚持主张军队将不会卷入到波斯尼亚的战争中去。

▲ **em·bryo** /ɛmbrioʊ/ (**embryos**) 1 N-COUNT An **embryo** is an unborn animal or human being in the very early stages of development. 胚胎 ❑ *There are 24,000 frozen embryos in clinics across the country.* 全国各地的诊所里有24000个冷冻胚胎。 2 ADJ An **embryo** idea, system, or organization is in the very early stages of development, but is expected to grow stronger. 萌芽阶段的 [ADJ n] ❑ *They are an embryo party of government.* 他们是一个处于萌芽阶段的政体。

em·bry·on·ic /ɛmbriɒnɪk/ ADJ An **embryonic** process, idea, organization, or organism is one at a very early stage in its development. 萌芽阶段的；非常初期的 [FORMAL] ❑ *...Romania's embryonic democracy.* …罗马尼亚非常初期民主。 ❑ *At the time, he was trying to recruit members for his embryonic resistance group.* 那时候他正在为他那萌芽中的抵抗组织招兵买马。

em·er·ald /ɛmərəld, ɛmrəld/ (**emeralds**) 1 N-COUNT An **emerald** is a precious stone that is clear and bright green. 翡翠 2 COLOR Something that is **emerald** is bright green in color. 翠绿色的 ❑ *...an emerald valley.* …一个翠绿的山谷。

> **Word Link** *merg ≈ sinking : emerge, merge, submerge*

emerge ♦♦◊ /ɪmɜrdʒ/ (**emerges, emerging, emerged**) 1 V-I To **emerge** means to come out from an enclosed or dark space such as a room or a vehicle, or from a position where you could not be seen. (从视线以外的地方) 出现；出来 ❑ *Richard was waiting outside the door as she emerged.* 当她出现的时候，理查德正等候在门外。 ❑ *She then emerged from the courthouse to thank her supporters.* 于是她从法院大楼出来向支持者们表示感谢。 2 V-I If you **emerge from** a difficult or bad experience, you come to the end of it. 摆脱 ❑ *There is growing evidence that the economy is at last emerging from recession.* 有越来越多的迹象表明经济将最终摆脱萧条。 3 V-T/V-I If a fact or result **emerges** from a period of thought, discussion, or investigation, it becomes known as a result of it. 显露(事实、结果) ❑ *...the growing corruption that has emerged in the past few years.* …过去几年中暴露出来的日趋严重的腐败。 ❑ *It soon emerged that neither the July nor August mortgage payment had been collected.* 很快显示的是7月和8月的抵押款都没有被收取。 4 V-I If someone or something **emerges as** a particular thing, they become recognized as that thing. 立足成为 [JOURNALISM] ❑ *Vietnam has emerged as the world's third-biggest rice exporter.* 越南已立足成为世界第三大稻米出口国。 5 V-I When something such as an organization or an industry **emerges**, it comes into existence. 兴起 [JOURNALISM] ❑ *...the new republic that emerged in October 1917.* …1917年10月成立的新共和国。

> **Thesaurus** *emerge* 另参见：
> V. appear, come out; (*ant.*) disappear 1

emer·gence /ɪmɜrdʒəns/ N-UNCOUNT The **emergence of** something is the process or event of its coming into existence. 兴起 ❑ *...the emergence of new democracies in Latin America.* …拉丁美洲新民主国家的兴起。

emer·gen·cy ♦♦◊ /ɪmɜrdʒənsi/ (**emergencies**) 1 N-COUNT An **emergency** is an unexpected and difficult or dangerous situation, especially an accident, that happens suddenly and that requires quick action to deal with it. 突发事件；紧急情况 ❑ *He deals with emergencies promptly.* 他迅速地应对突发事件。 2 ADJ An **emergency** action is one that is done or arranged quickly and not in the normal way, because an emergency has occurred. 紧急的 [ADJ n] ❑ *Yesterday, the center's board held an emergency meeting.* 昨天，中心的董事会召开了一次紧急会议。 3 ADJ **Emergency** equipment or supplies are those intended for use in an emergency. 应急的 [ADJ n] ❑ *The plane is carrying emergency supplies for refugees.* 这架飞机载着给难民的应急物资。

→ see **hospital**

> **Word Partnership** *emergency* 的常用搭配：
> ADJ. **major** emergency, **medical** emergency, **minor** emergency 1
> N. **state of** emergency 1
> emergency **care**, emergency **surgery** 2
> emergency **supplies**, emergency **vehicle** 3

emer·gen·cy brake (**emergency brakes**) N-COUNT In a vehicle, the **emergency brake** is a brake that the driver operates with his or her hand or foot, and uses, for example, in emergencies or when parking. 急刹车闸 [mainly AM] ❑ *He stopped just as his truck tilted down the steep incline, put on the emergency brake, and stepped out.* 就在他的卡车沿陡峭的斜坡向下滑的时候，他停了下来，踩了急刹车，然后下了车。

emer·gen·cy room (**emergency rooms**) N-COUNT The **emergency room** is the room or department in a hospital where people who have severe injuries or sudden illnesses are taken for emergency treatment. The abbreviation **ER** is often used. 急诊室 [mainly AM] ❑ *She began hyperventilating and was rushed to the emergency room.* 她开始过度呼吸，被急忙送到急诊室。

emer·gen·cy ser·vices N-PLURAL **The emergency services** are the public organizations whose job is to take quick action to deal with emergencies when they occur, especially the fire department, the police, and the ambulance service. 应急服务机构 ❑ *...members of the emergency services.* …应急服务机构的成员。

> **Word Link** *migr ≈ moving, changing : emigrant, immigrant, migrant*

★ **emi·grant** /ɛmɪgrənt/ (**emigrants**) N-COUNT An **emigrant** is a person who has left their own country to live in another country. Compare **immigrant**. 移居国外者 ❑ *...Irish emigrants to America.* …移居美国的爱尔兰移民。

> **Word Link** *e ≈ away, out : eject, emigrate, emit*

emi·grate /ɛmɪgreɪt/ (**emigrates, emigrating, emigrated**) V-I If you **emigrate**, you leave your own country to live in another country. 移居外国 ❑ *He emigrated to Belgium.* 他移民去了比利时。 ● **emi·gra·tion** /ɛmɪgreɪʃən/ N-UNCOUNT 移居外国 ❑ *...the huge emigration of workers to the West.* …工人们的大规模向西方移居。

emi·nence /ɛmɪnəns/ N-UNCOUNT **Eminence** is the quality of being very well-known and highly respected. 显赫声名 ❑ *Many of the pilots were to achieve eminence in the aeronautical world.* 其中的很多飞行员后来在航空界都取得了显赫的声名。

▲ **emi·nent** /ɛmɪnənt/ ADJ An **eminent** person is well-known and respected, especially because they are good at their profession. 卓越的；有名望的 ❑ *...an eminent scientist.* …一位卓越的科学家。

emi·nent·ly /ɛmɪnəntli/ ADV You use **eminently** in front of an adjective describing a positive quality in order to emphasize the quality expressed by that adjective. 显著地；突出地 [ADV adj/-ed] [EMPHASIS] ❑ *His books on diplomatic history were eminently readable.* 他的研究外交史的著作特别值得一读。

★ **emis·sion** /ɪmɪʃən/ (**emissions**) N-VAR An **emission of** something such as gas or radiation is the release of it into the atmosphere. 排放 [FORMAL] ❑ *The emission of gases such as carbon dioxide should be stabilized at their present level.* 二氧化碳之类气体的排放应该被控制在目前的水平上。

→ see **pollution**

emit /ɪmɪt/ (**emits, emitting, emitted**) **1** V-T If something **emits** heat, light, gas, or a smell, it produces it and sends it out by means of a physical or chemical process. 发出；散发（热、光、气体或气味）[FORMAL] ❑ *The new device emits a powerful circular column of light.* 这个新装置发出一束强烈的环形光柱。 **2** V-T To **emit** a sound or noise means to produce it. 发出（声音或噪音）[FORMAL] ❑ *Whitney blinked and emitted a long, low whistle.* 惠特尼眨了眨眼，吹出了一声长而低沉的口哨。
→ see **light**

emo·ti·con /ɪmoʊtɪkɒn/ (**emoticons**) N-COUNT An **emoticon** is a symbol used in e-mail to show how someone is feeling. :-) is an emoticon showing happiness. 表情符号（用于电子邮件中表示感情）[COMPUTING]

emo·tion ♦◇◇ /ɪmoʊʃᵊn/ (**emotions**) **1** N-VAR An **emotion** is a feeling such as happiness, love, fear, anger, or hatred, which can be caused by the situation that you are in or the people you are with. 感情 ❑ *Happiness was an emotion that Jerry was having to relearn.* 幸福是一种杰瑞当时不得不再学习的感情。 **2** N-UNCOUNT **Emotion** is the part of a person's character that consists of their feelings, as opposed to their thoughts. （与思想相对的）情感 ❑ *...the split between reason and emotion.* …理智与情感间的分离。
→ see Word Web: **emotion**

emo·tion·al ♦◇◇ /ɪmoʊʃənᵊl/ **1** ADJ **Emotional** means concerned with emotions and feelings. 情感上的 ❑ *I needed this man's love, and the emotional support he was giving me.* 我那时需要这个男人的爱，以及他当时给予我的情感支持。 ● **emo·tion·al·ly** ADV 情感上地 [ADV adj/-ed] ❑ *Are you saying that you're becoming emotionally involved with me?* 你是说你对我产生感情了吗？ **2** ADJ An **emotional** situation or issue is one that causes people to have strong feelings. 引起情绪激动的 ❑ *Abortion is a very emotional issue.* 堕胎是个令人情绪十分激动的问题。 ● **emo·tion·al·ly** ADV 引起情绪激动地 [ADV adj/-ed] ❑ *In an emotionally charged speech, he said he was resigning.* 在一次情绪激动的发言中，他说他要辞职。 **3** ADJ If someone is or becomes **emotional**, they show their feelings very openly, especially because they are upset. 易情绪激动的；易动情的 ❑ *He is a very emotional man.* 他是个易动情的人。

emo·tive /ɪmoʊtɪv/ ADJ An **emotive** situation or issue is likely to make people feel strong emotions. 使人情绪激动的 ❑ *Embryo research is an emotive issue.* 胚胎研究是个让人情绪激动的问题。

Word Link *path ≈ feeling : apathy, empathy, sympathy*

em·pa·thy /ɛmpəθi/ N-UNCOUNT **Empathy** is the ability to share another person's feelings and emotions as if they were your own. 同感能力 ❑ *Having begun my life in a children's home, I have great empathy with the little ones.* 在一家儿童福利院长大使我对这些小孩子们怀有深深的同感。

em·per·or /ɛmpərər/ (**emperors**) N-COUNT; N-TITLE An **emperor** is a man who rules an empire or is the head of state in an empire. 皇帝 ❑ *...the emperor of Japan.* …日本天皇。
→ see **empire**

em·pha·sise ♦◇◇ /ɛmfəsaɪz/ [BRIT] → see **emphasize**

em·pha·sis ♦◇◇ /ɛmfəsɪs/ (**emphases** /ɛmfəsiz/) **1** N-VAR **Emphasis** is special or extra importance that is given to an activity or to a part or aspect of something. 重点 ❑ *Too much emphasis is placed on research.* 把重点过多地放在研究上。 **2** N-VAR **Emphasis** is extra force that you put on a syllable, word, or phrase when you are speaking in order to make it seem more important. 重音 ❑ *The emphasis is on the first syllable of the last word.* 重音是在最末一个单词的第一个音节上。

em·pha·size ♦◇◇ /ɛmfəsaɪz/ (**emphasizes, emphasizing, emphasized**)

in BRIT, also use **emphasise**

V-T To **emphasize** something means to indicate that it is particularly important or true, or to draw special attention to it. 强调 ❑ *But it's also been emphasized that no major policy changes can be expected to come out of the meeting.* 但是也强调，这次会议预期不会做出重大政策改变。

▲ **em·phat·ic** /ɪmfætɪk/ **1** ADJ An **emphatic** response or statement is one made in a forceful way, because the speaker feels very strongly about what they are saying. 断然的 ❑ *His response was immediate and emphatic.* 他的回答迅速且断然。 **2** ADJ If you are **emphatic about** something, you use forceful language that shows you feel very strongly about what you are saying. 坚决强调的 [v-link ADJ] ❑ *The rebels are emphatic that this is not a surrender.* 叛乱者坚称这不是投降。 **3** ADJ An **emphatic** win or victory is one in which the winner has won by a large amount or distance. 大比分的 ❑ *Yesterday's emphatic victory was their fifth in succession.* 昨天的大比分胜利是他们第5次的接连胜利。

em·phati·cal·ly /ɪmfætɪkli/ **1** ADV If you say something **emphatically**, you say it in a forceful way that shows you feel very strongly about what you are saying. 断然地 [ADV with v] ❑ *"No fast food," she said emphatically.* "不吃快餐，"她断然道。 **2** ADV You use **emphatically** to emphasize the statement you are making. 绝对地 [ADV with cl/group] [EMPHASIS] ❑ *Making people feel foolish is emphatically not my strategy.* 使人民感到无知绝不是我的策略。

em·pire ♦◇◇ /ɛmpaɪər/ (**empires**) **1** N-COUNT An **empire** is a number of individual nations that are all controlled by the government or ruler of one particular country. 帝国 ❑ *...the Roman Empire.* …罗马帝国。 **2** N-COUNT You can refer to a group of companies controlled by one person as an **empire**. 企业帝国 ❑ *...the global Murdoch media empire.* …默多克环球媒体帝国。
→ see Word Web: **empire**
→ see **history**

★ **em·piri·cal** /ɪmpɪrɪkᵊl/ ADJ **Empirical** evidence or study relies on practical experience rather than theories. 实证的 ❑ *There is no empirical evidence to support his thesis.* 没有实证根据来支持他的论点。 ● **em·piri·cal·ly** ADV 实证地 ❑ *They approached this part of their task empirically.* 他们实证地处理这部分任务。
→ see **science**

em·ploy ♦◇◇ /ɪmplɔɪ/ (**employs, employing, employed**) **1** V-T If a person or company **employs** you, they pay you to work for them. 雇用 ❑ *The company employs 18 workers.* 该公司雇用18位职工。 ❑ *More than 3,000 local workers are employed in the tourism industry.* 超过3000名本地工人受雇于旅游业。 **2** V-T If you **employ** certain methods, materials, or expressions, you use them. 使用 ❑ *The group will employ a mix of tactics to achieve its aim.* 该团体将运用混合策略来实现其目标。 **3** V-T If your time **is employed in** doing something, you are using the time you have to do that thing. 利用 [usu passive] ❑ *Your time could be usefully employed in attending night classes.* 你的时间可以被有效地利用来上夜课。

Word Link *ee ≈ one who receives : employee, payee, refugee*

em·ployee ♦♦◇ /ɪmplɔɪi/ (**employees**) N-COUNT An **employee** is a person who is paid to work for an organization or for another person. 雇员 ❑ *He is an employee of Fuji Bank.* 他是富士银行的一位雇员。
→ see **factory, union**

em·ploy·er ♦◇◇ /ɪmplɔɪər/ (**employers**) N-COUNT Your **employer** is the person or organization that you work for. 雇主 ❑ *He had been sent to Rome by his employer.* 他被雇主派到罗马去了。

Word Web **emotion**

Scientists believe that animals experience **emotions** such as **happiness** and **sadness** just like humans do. Research shows animals also feel **anger, fear, love,** and **hate**. Biochemical changes in mammals' brains trigger these emotions. When an elephant gives birth, a **hormone** floods her bloodstream. This causes feelings of **adoration** for her baby. The same thing happens to human mothers. When a dog chews on a bone, levels of a chemical increase in its brain. This produces feelings of **joy**. The same chemical produces **elation** in humans. Scientists aren't sure whether animals experience **shame**. However, they do know that animals experience **stress**.

E

Word Web empire

An **empire** is formed when a strong nation-state **conquers** other states and creates a larger **political union**. An early example is the Roman Empire which began in 31 BC. The Roman **emperor** Augustus Caesar* ruled a vast area from the Mediterranean Sea* to Western Europe. Later, the British Empire flourished from about 1600 to 1900 AD. Queen Victoria's* empire spread across oceans and continents. One of her many titles was **Empress** of India. Both of these empires spread their political influence as well as their language and culture over large areas.

British Empire (1900 AD)
Roman Empire (117 AD)
British and Roman Empires

Augustus Caesar: the first emperor of Rome.
Mediterranean Sea: between Europe and Africa.
Queen Victoria (1819-1901): queen of Great Britain and Ireland.

em·ploy·ment ♦◇◇ /ɪmplɔɪmənt/ 1 N-UNCOUNT **Employment** is the fact of having a paid job. 工作 ❑ *She was unable to find employment.* 她没能找到工作。 2 N-UNCOUNT **Employment** is the fact of employing someone. 雇用 ❑ *...the employment of children under nine.* …9岁以下儿童的雇用。 3 N-UNCOUNT **Employment** is the work that is available in a country or area. 就业 ❑ *...economic policies designed to secure full employment.* …为确保充分就业而制定的经济政策。

em·ploy·ment agen·cy (**employment agencies**) N-COUNT An **employment agency** is a company whose business is to help people to find work and help employers to find the workers they need. 职业介绍所 [BUSINESS]

Word Link *em ≈ making, putting : embed, embellish, empower*

▲ **em·power** /ɪmpaʊər/ (**empowers, empowering, empowered**) 1 V-T If someone **is empowered to** do something, they have the authority or power to do it. 授权 [FORMAL] ❑ *The army is now empowered to operate on a shoot-to-kill basis.* 军队现在被授权依据"杀无赦"原则行动。 2 V-T To **empower** someone means to give them the means to achieve something, for example, to become stronger or more successful. 使能够 ❑ *You must delegate effectively and empower people to carry out their roles with your full support.* 你们必须有效地下放权力，使人们能够在你们的全力支持下履行他们的职责。

em·pow·er·ment /ɪmpaʊərmənt/ N-UNCOUNT The **empowerment of** a person or group of people is the process of giving them power and status in a particular situation. 权利赋予 ❑ *This government believes very strongly in the empowerment of women.* 这届政府坚信赋权于妇女。

em·press /ɛmprɪs/ (**empresses**) N-COUNT; N-TITLE An **empress** is a woman who rules an empire or who is the wife of an emperor. 女皇；皇后 ❑ *...Catherine II, Empress of Russia.* …俄罗斯女皇叶卡特琳娜二世。
→ see **empire**

emp·ti·ness /ɛmptinɪs/ 1 N-UNCOUNT A feeling of **emptiness** is an unhappy or frightening feeling that nothing is worthwhile, especially when you are very tired or have just experienced something upsetting. 空虚 ❑ *The result later in life may be feelings of emptiness and depression.* 结果是往后的生活可能会感到空虚和沮丧。 2 N-UNCOUNT The **emptiness** of a place is the fact that there is nothing in it. 空旷 ❑ *...the emptiness of the desert.* …沙漠的空旷。

emp·ty ♦◇◇ /ɛmpti/ (**emptier, emptiest, empties, emptying, emptied**) 1 ADJ An **empty** place, vehicle, or container is one that has no people or things in it. 空的 ❑ *The room was bare and empty.* 房间空荡荡的。 ❑ *...empty cans of beer.* …空啤酒罐。 2 ADJ An **empty** gesture, threat, or relationship has no real value or meaning. 无实在意义的 ❑ *His father had threatened disinheritance, but both men had known it was an empty threat.* 他父亲威胁要剥夺他的继承权，但是两人都知道这是虚张声势。 3 ADJ If you describe a person's life or a period of time as **empty**, you mean that nothing interesting or valuable happens in it. 空虚的 ❑ *My life was very hectic but empty before I met him.* 我的生活在遇见他之前忙碌却空虚。 4 ADJ If you **feel empty**, you feel unhappy and have no energy, usually because you are very tired or have just experienced something upsetting. 消沉的 ❑ *I feel so empty, my life just doesn't seem worth living any more.* 我感到非常消沉，我的生活简直好像不值得再过下去了。 5 V-T If you **empty** a container, or **empty** something out of it, you remove its contents, especially by tipping it up. 倒空 ❑ *I emptied the ashtray.* 我倒空了烟灰缸。 ❑ *Empty the noodles and liquid into a serving bowl.* 将面条和汤全部倒入一个上菜的碗中。 6 V-T/V-I If someone **empties** a room or place, or if it **empties**, everyone in it goes away. 清场 ❑ *The stadium emptied at the end of the first day of games.* 体育馆在第一天比赛结束的时候清场了。 7 V-I A river or canal that **empties into** a lake, river, or sea flows into it. 流入 ❑ *The Milwaukee River empties into Lake Michigan near that pipe.* 密尔沃基河在那条管道附近流入密歇根湖。 8 N-COUNT **Empties** are bottles or containers that no longer have anything in them. 空容器 ❑ *After breakfast we'll take the empties down in the sack.* 早餐后我们要用袋子把空瓶子拿下去。

Thesaurus *empty* 另参见:

ADJ.	uninhabited, unoccupied, vacant; (*ant.*) full, occupied 1 meaningless, without substance 2 3
V.	drain out, pour out 5 evacuate, go out, leave 6

Word Partnership *empty* 的常用搭配:

N.	empty **bottle**, empty **box**, empty **building**, empty **room**, empty **seat**, empty **space**, empty **stomach** 1 empty **promise**, empty **threat** 2 empty **the trash** 5
V.	**feel** empty 4

empty-handed ADJ If you come away from somewhere **empty-handed**, you have failed to get what you wanted. 一无所获的 [ADJ after V] ❑ *Delegates from the warring sides held a new round of peace talks but went away empty-handed.* 交战各方代表举行了新一轮的和谈，但却空手离去。

empty-headed ADJ If you describe someone as **empty-headed**, you mean that they are not very intelligent and often do silly things. 愚蠢的

▲ **emu·late** /ɛmyʊleɪt/ (**emulates, emulating, emulated**) V-T If you **emulate** something or someone, you imitate them because you admire them a great deal. 效仿 [FORMAL] ❑ *Sons are traditionally expected to emulate their fathers.* 传统上认为儿子应该效仿他们的父亲。

Word Link *en ≈ making, putting : enable, enact, encode*

en·able ♦◇◇ /ɪneɪbᵊl/ (**enables, enabling, enabled**) 1 V-T If someone or something **enables** you **to** do a particular thing, they give you the opportunity to do it. 使能够 ❑ *The new test should enable doctors to detect the disease early.* 新的检验使医生能在早期发现该种疾病。 2 V-T To **enable** something **to** happen means to make it possible for it to happen. 使成为可能 ❑ *The hot sun enables the grapes to reach optimum ripeness.* 炙热的阳光使葡萄能达到最佳成熟状态。 3 V-T To **enable** someone **to** do something means to give them permission or the right to do it. 允许 ❑ *...legislation which enables young people to do a form of alternative service.* …允许年轻人通过一种替代性服务来服刑的立法。

Thesaurus *enable* 另参见:

v. facilitate, permit; *(ant.)* prevent 1–3
allow, approve, authorize; *(ant.)* block, disallow, forbid 3

▲ **en·act** /ɪnækt/ (**enacts, enacting, enacted**) 1 V-T When a government or authority **enacts** a proposal, they make it into a law. 通过 [TECHNICAL] ❑ *The authorities have failed so far to enact a law allowing unrestricted emigration.* 当局到目前为止还未能通过一项允许自由移民出境的法律。 2 V-T If people **enact** a story or play, they perform it by acting. 表演. ❑ *She often enacted the stories told to her by her father.* 她经常把父亲讲给她的故事表演出来。 3 V-T If a particular event or situation **is enacted**, it happens; used especially to talk about something that has happened before. 发生(尤指过去已发生的事件或情况) [usu passive] [JOURNALISM] ❑ *It was a scene enacted month after month for eight years.* 这是8年来月复一月出现的场景。

en·act·ment /ɪnæktmənt/ (**enactments**) N-VAR The **enactment of** a law is the process in a legislature by which the law is agreed upon and made official. 法律制定 [TECHNICAL] ❑ *We support the call for the enactment of a Bill of Rights.* 我们支持《权利法案》制定的呼吁。

▲ **enam·el** /ɪnæm^əl/ (**enamels**) 1 N-MASS **Enamel** is a substance like glass that can be heated and put onto metal, glass, or pottery in order to decorate or protect it. 搪瓷 ❑ *...a white enamel saucepan.* ···一个白色搪瓷煮锅。 2 N-MASS **Enamel** is a hard, shiny paint that is used especially for painting metal and wood. 瓷漆; 亮漆 ❑ *...enamel polymer paints.* ···聚合瓷漆。 3 N-UNCOUNT **Enamel** is the hard white substance that forms the outer part of a tooth. 珐琅质

en·am·ored /ɪnæmərd/ ADJ If you are **enamored of** something, you like or admire it a lot. If you are not **enamored of** something, you dislike or disapprove of it. 倾心的 [LITERARY] ❑ *I became totally enamored of the wildflowers there.* 我完全被那儿的野花儿迷住了。

en·cap·su·late /ɪnkæpsəleɪt, -syʊ-/ (**encapsulates, encapsulating, encapsulated**) V-T To **encapsulate** particular facts or ideas means to represent all their most important aspects in a very small space or in a single object or event. 概括 ❑ *A Wall Street Journal editorial encapsulated the views of many conservatives.* 《华尔街日报》的一篇社论概括了很多保守派人士的观点。

Word Link *cas ≈ box, hold : case, encase, suitcase*

en·case /ɪnkeɪs/ (**encases, encasing, encased**) V-T If a person or an object **is encased in** something, they are completely covered or surrounded by it. 包; 围 ❑ *When nuclear fuel is manufactured it is encased in metal cans.* 核燃料生产出来时被装在金属罐中。 ❑ *These weapons also had a heavy brass guard which encased almost the whole hand.* 这些武器还有一层厚厚的黄铜防护，几乎把整个手柄包了起来。

▲ **en·chant** /ɪntʃænt/ (**enchants, enchanting, enchanted**) 1 V-T If you **are enchanted by** someone or something, they cause you to have feelings of great delight or pleasure. 使陶醉 ❑ *Dena was enchanted by the house.* 蒂纳被这幢房子给迷住了。 2 V-T In fairy tales and legends, to **enchant** someone or something means to put a magic spell on them. 施魔法于 ❑ *...Celtic stories of cauldrons and enchanted vessels.* ···凯尔特人关于神锅和魔法器皿的故事。

en·chant·ing /ɪntʃæntɪŋ/ ADJ If you describe someone or something as **enchanting**, you mean that they are very attractive or charming. 迷人的 ❑ *She's an absolutely enchanting child.* 她是个顶招人喜爱的孩子。

en·cir·cle /ɪnsɜrk^əl/ (**encircles, encircling, encircled**) V-T To **encircle** something or someone means to surround or enclose them, or to go around them. 环绕 ❑ *A forty-foot-high concrete wall encircles the jail.* 一道40英尺高的水泥墙环绕着该监狱。

en·clave /ɛnkleɪv, ɒn-/ (**enclaves**) N-COUNT An **enclave** is an area within a country or a city where people live who have a different nationality or culture from the people living in the surrounding country or city. 飞地

en·close /ɪnkloʊz/ (**encloses, enclosing, enclosed**) 1 V-T If a place or object **is enclosed** by something, the place or object is inside that thing or completely surrounded by it. 包围; 装 ❑ *The rules state that samples must be enclosed in two watertight containers.* 条例规定样品必须用两个不漏水的容器封装起来。 ❑ *Enclose the flower in a small muslin bag.* 把这花用一个小棉袋包起来。 2 V-T If you **enclose** something with a letter, you put it in the same envelope as the letter. (随信) 附上 ❑ *I have enclosed a check for $100.* 我信里附上了一张$100的支票。

★ **en·clo·sure** /ɪnkloʊʒər/ (**enclosures**) N-COUNT An **enclosure** is an area of land that is surrounded by a wall or fence and that is used for a particular purpose. 围场 ❑ *This enclosure was so vast that the outermost wall could hardly be seen.* 这块圈地大得几乎看不见它最外面的围墙。

Word Link *cod ≈ writing : code, decode, encode*

en·code /ɪnkoʊd/ (**encodes, encoding, encoded**) V-T If you **encode** a message or some information, you put it into a code or express it in a different form or system of language. 将···写为密码 ❑ *The two parties encode confidential data in a form that is not directly readable by the other party.* 双方把机密数据写成一种不能被对方直接读懂的密码。

▲ **en·com·pass** /ɪnkʌmpəs/ (**encompasses, encompassing, encompassed**) 1 V-T If something **encompasses** particular things, it includes them. 包含 ❑ *His repertoire encompassed everything from Bach to Schoenberg.* 他的表演曲目从巴赫到勋伯格，样样俱全。 2 V-T To **encompass** a place means to completely surround or cover it. 围住; 覆盖 ❑ *The map shows the rest of the western region, encompassing nine states.* 这地图显示了其余西部区域，覆盖了9个州。

en·core /ɒŋkɔr, -kɔr/ (**encores**) N-COUNT An **encore** is a short extra performance at the end of a longer one, that an entertainer gives because the audience asks for it. 返场加演节目 ❑ *Lang's final encore last night was "Barefoot."* 兰昨晚最后的返场加唱曲目是《赤脚》。

en·coun·ter ♦◇◇ /ɪnkaʊntər/ (**encounters, encountering, encountered**) 1 V-T If you **encounter** problems or difficulties, you experience them. 遭遇 ❑ *Every day of our lives we encounter major and minor stresses of one kind or another.* 生活中的每一天，我们会遇到或大或小的这样那样的压力。 2 V-T If you **encounter** someone, you meet them, usually unexpectedly. 邂逅 [FORMAL] ❑ *Did you encounter anyone in the building?* 你在那栋大楼里偶然遇到什么人了吗？ 3 N-COUNT An **encounter with** someone is a meeting with them, particularly one that is unexpected or significant. 邂逅 ❑ *The author tells of a remarkable encounter with a group of South Vietnamese soldiers.* 作者讲述了他与一群南越士兵的惊人邂逅。 4 N-COUNT An **encounter** is a particular type of experience. 特殊经历 ❑ *...a sexual encounter.* ···一次性经历。

Thesaurus *encounter* 另参见:

v. bump into, come across, run into; *(ant.)* avoid, miss 1 2

en·cour·age ♦♦◇ /ɪnkɜrɪdʒ/ (**encourages, encouraging, encouraged**) 1 V-T If you **encourage** someone, you give them confidence, for example by letting them know that what they are doing is good and telling them that they should continue to do it. 鼓励 ❑ *When things aren't going well, he encourages me, telling me not to give up.* 当事情不顺利的时候，他鼓励我，告诉我不要放弃。 2 V-T If someone **is encouraged by** something that happens, it gives them hope or confidence. 鼓舞 [usu passive] ❑ *Investors were encouraged by the news.* 投资者被这条消息所鼓舞。 ● **en·cour·aged** ADJ 受到鼓舞的 [v-link ADJ] ❑ *We were very encouraged after over 17,000 pictures were submitted.* 我们深受鼓舞，17000多张照片已被提交了。 3 V-T If you **encourage** someone **to** do something, you try to persuade them to do it, for example, by telling them that it would be a pleasant thing to do, or by trying to make it easier for them to do it. You can also **encourage** an activity. 激励 ❑ *Herbie Hancock was encouraged by his family to learn music at a young age.* 赫比・汉考克小时候受到家人鼓励去学音乐。 4 V-T If something **encourages** a particular activity or state, it causes it to happen or increase. 促使. ❑ *...a natural substance that encourages cell growth.* ···促使细胞生长的一种天然物质。

en·cour·age·ment /ɪnkɜrɪdʒmənt/ (**encouragements**) N-VAR **Encouragement** is the activity of encouraging someone, or something that is said or done in order to encourage them. 鼓励; 起鼓励作用的事物 ❑ *Friends gave me a great deal of encouragement.* 朋友们给了我极大的鼓励。

en·cour·ag·ing /ɪnkɜrɪdʒɪŋ/ ADJ Something that is **encouraging** gives people hope or confidence. 鼓舞人心的 ❑ *There are encouraging signs of an artistic revival.* 有了鼓舞人心的艺术复兴的迹象。 ❑ *The results have been encouraging.* 这些结果是鼓舞人心的。 ● **en·cour·ag·ing·ly** ADV 鼓舞人心地 ❑ *The people at the next table watched me eat and smiled encouragingly.* 邻桌的人们看着我吃，鼓励地微笑着。

en·croach /ɪnkroʊtʃ/ (**encroaches, encroaching, encroached**) 1 V-I If one thing **encroaches on** another, the first thing spreads or becomes stronger, and slowly begins to restrict the power, range, or effectiveness of the second thing. 逐步侵犯 [FORMAL, DISAPPROVAL] ❑ *The new institutions do not encroach on political power.* 这些新机构没有侵犯到政治权力。 2 V-I If something **encroaches on** a place, it spreads and takes over more and more of that place. 蚕食 [FORMAL] ❑ *The shrubs encroached ever more on the twisting drive.* 灌木丛蚕食了越来越多蜿蜒的车道。

en·croach·ment /ɪnkroʊtʃmənt/ (**encroachments**) N-VAR You can describe the action or process of encroaching on something as **encroachment**. 侵犯；蚕食 [FORMAL, DISAPPROVAL] ❑ *It's a sign of the encroachment of commercialism in medicine.* 这是营利主义入侵医学界的一种迹象。

E

▲ **en·cy·clo·pedia** /ɪnsaɪkləpidiə/ (**encyclopedias**) also **encyclopaedia** N-COUNT An **encyclopedia** is a book or set of books in which facts about many different subjects or about one particular subject are arranged for reference, usually in alphabetical order. 百科全书

end
1. NOUN USES
2. VERB USES
3. PHRASAL VERBS

❶ **end** ◆◆◆ /ɛnd/ (**ends**)
➪ **Please look at meanings 20 – 23 to see if the expression you are looking for is shown under another headword.** 1 N-SING **The end of** something such as a period of time, an event, a book, or a movie is the last part of it or the final point in it. 结尾 ❑ *The report is expected by the end of the year.* 这份报告预期年底前出台。 ❑ *...families who settled in the region at the end of the 17th century.* …于17世纪末定居该地区的家庭。 2 N-COUNT An **end to** something or the **end of** it is the act or result of stopping it so that it does not continue any longer. 结束 ❑ *The government today called for an end to the violence.* 政府今天呼吁结束暴力。 ❑ *I was worried she would walk out or bring the interview to an end.* 我担心她会突然退席或者终止采访。 3 N-COUNT The two **ends** of something long and narrow are the two points or parts of it that are farthest away from each other. 末端 ❑ *The company is planning to place surveillance equipment at both ends of the tunnel.* 该公司计划在隧道的两端安装监视设备。 4 N-COUNT **The end of** a long, narrow object such as a finger or a pencil is the tip or smallest edge of it, usually the part that is furthest away from you. 末梢 ❑ *He tapped the ends of his fingers together.* 他用手指尖相互轻叩。 5 N-COUNT **End** is used to refer to either of the two extreme points of a scale, or of something that you are considering as a scale. (天平等的) 任一端 ❑ *At the other end of the social scale was the grocer.* 处于社会阶层另一端的是杂货商。 6 N-COUNT **The other end** is one of two places that are connected because people are communicating with each other by telephone or writing, or are traveling from one place to the other. 两地之一 ❑ *When he answered the phone, Fred was at the other end.* 当他接起电话，电话那头是弗雷德。 7 N-COUNT If you refer to a particular **end** of a project or piece of work, you mean a part or aspect of it, such as a part of it that is done by a particular person or in a particular place. (项目、工作的) 部分 [SPOKEN] ❑ *You take care of your end, kid, I'll take care of mine.* 你管好你那块儿，年轻人，我会管好我这块儿。 8 N-COUNT **An end** is the purpose for which something is done or toward which you are working. 目的 ❑ *The police force is being manipulated for political ends.* 警察机关正被操控用以达到政治目的。 9 PHRASE If something is **at an end**, it has finished and will not continue. 结束了 ❑ *The recession is definitely at an end.* 萧条期肯定是要结束了。 10 PHRASE If something **comes to an end**, it stops. 终止 ❑ *The cold war came to an end.* 冷战终止。 11 PHRASE You say **at the end of the day** when you are talking about what happens after a long series of events or what appears to be the case after you have considered the relevant facts. 最终；到头来 [INFORMAL] ❑ *At the end of the day it's up to them to decide.* 到头来，还得由他们决定。 12 PHRASE You say **in the end** when you are saying what is the final result of a series of events, or what is your final conclusion after considering all the relevant facts. 最终 ❑ *I toyed with the idea of calling the police, but in the end I didn't.* 我不经意地想过要报警，但最终没有。 13 PHRASE If you find it difficult to **make ends meet**, you cannot manage very well financially because you hardly have enough money for the things you need. 糊口 ❑ *With Betty's salary they barely made ends meet.* 靠贝蒂的工资，他们简直无法糊口。 14 PHRASE **No end** means a lot. 许多 [INFORMAL] ❑ *Teachers inform me that Todd's behavior has improved no end.* 老师们告诉我托德的行为改善了许多。 15 PHRASE When something happens for hours, days, weeks, or years **on end**, it happens continuously and without stopping for the amount of time that is mentioned. 连续地 ❑ *He is a wonderful companion and we can talk for hours on end.* 他是个极好的伙伴，我们可以连续谈上几个小时。 16 PHRASE Something that is **on end** is upright, instead of in its normal or natural position, for example, lying down, flat, or on its longest side. 竖着 ❑ *Wet books should be placed on end with their pages kept apart.* 弄湿的书应该竖着放置，书页分开。 17 PHRASE **To put an end to** something means to cause it to stop. 使某事终止 ❑ *Only a political solution could put an end to the violence.* 只有一个政治的解决方式才能终止暴力。 18 PHRASE If a process or person has reached **the end of the road**, they are unable to progress any further. 穷途末路 ❑ *Given the results of the vote, is this the end of the road for the hardliners in Congress?* 就投票的结果来看，国会里的强硬派是不是已经走到尽头了？ 19 PHRASE If you say that something bad is **not the end of the world**, you are trying to stop yourself or someone else being so upset by it, by suggesting that it is not the worst thing that could happen. 天塌不下来 ❑ *Obviously I'd be disappointed if we don't make it, but it wouldn't be the end of the world.* 显然，如果我们不能成功我会失望的，但天不会塌下来。 20 **the end of your tether** → see **tether** 21 **to make your hair stand on end** → see **hair** 22 **to be on the receiving end** → see **receive** 23 **to get the wrong end of the stick** → see **stick**

❷ **end** ◆◆◆ /ɛnd/ (**ends, ending, ended**) 1 V-T/V-I When a situation, process, or activity **ends**, or when something or someone **ends** it, it reaches its final point and stops. 结束 ❑ *The meeting quickly ended and Steve and I left the room.* 会议很快结束了，之后史蒂夫和我离开了房间。 ● **end·ing** N-SING 终止 ❑ *The ending of a marriage by death is different in many ways from an ending caused by divorce.* 死亡造成的婚姻终止同离婚造成的婚姻终止在很多方面是不同的。 2 V-T/V-I If you say that someone or something **ends** a period of time in a particular way, you are indicating what the final situation was like. You can also say that a period of time **ends** in a particular way. 以…终止 ❑ *The markets ended the week on a quiet note.* 市场本周在平静气氛中收市。 3 V-I If a period of time **ends**, it reaches its final point. (时间) 结束 ❑ *Reports usually come out about three weeks after each month ends.* 报告通常在每月结束后大约三周发布。 4 V-T/V-I If something such as a book, speech, or performance **ends with** a particular thing or the writer or performer **ends** it **with** that thing, its final part consists of the thing mentioned. 以…收尾 ❑ *His statement ended with the words: "Pray for me."* 他的声明以一句"为我祈祷"收尾。 ❑ *The book ends on a lengthy description of Hawaii.* 这本书以一段对夏威夷的冗长描述作结。 5 V-I If a situation or event **ends** in a particular way, it has that particular result. 以…告终 ❑ *The incident could have ended in tragedy.* 这个事件原本可能以悲剧告终。 ❑ *Our conversations ended with him saying he would try to be more understanding.* 我们的谈话结束的时候，他说他会试着更为通情达理。 6 V-I If an object **ends with** or **in** a particular thing, it has that thing on its tip or point, or as its last part. 以…为末端 ❑ *It has three pairs of legs, each ending in a large claw.* 它有3对腿，每条腿的末端都有一个大爪子。 7 V-I A journey, road, or river that **ends** at a particular place stops there and goes no further. (旅程、道路、河流等) 终止 ❑ *The highway ended at an intersection.* 这条公路止于一个十字路口。 8 V-I If you say that something **ends** at a particular point, you mean that it is applied or exists up to that point, and no further. 局限于 ❑ *Heather is also 25 and from Boston, but the similarity ends there.* 希瑟也是25岁，也是波士顿人，但是他们的相似之处仅限于此。 9 V-I If you **end by** doing something or **end** in a particular state, you do that thing or get into that state even though you did not originally intend to. 到头来 ❑ *They ended by making themselves miserable.* 他们到头来把自己弄惨了。 10 PHRASE If someone **ends it all**, they kill themselves. 自杀 ❑ *He grew suicidal, thinking up ways to end it all.* 他变得想自杀，想出了多种自杀方式。

Thesaurus *end* 另参见：

N.	close, conclusion, finale, finish, stop; (*ant.*) beginning ❶ 1 2
V.	conclude, finish, wrap up ❷ 1

❸ **end** ◆◆◆ /ɛnd/ (**ends, ending, ended**)
▸ **end up** ■1 PHRASAL VERB If someone or something **ends up** somewhere, they eventually arrive there, usually by accident. 最后来到 ❑ *She fled with her children, moving from neighbor to neighbor and ending up in a friend's basement.* 她和她的孩子们逃走了，从一家邻居转到另一家，最终来到一个朋友家的地下室。 ■2 PHRASAL VERB If you **end up** doing something or **end up** in a particular state, you do that thing or get into that state even though you did not originally intend to. 到头来 ❑ *If you don't know what you want, you might end up getting something you don't want.* 如果你不知道自己想要什么，你可能会到头来得到自己不想要的东西。 ❑ *Every time they went dancing, they ended up in a bad mood.* 每次他们去跳舞，到头来总是扫兴而归。

★ **en·dan·ger** /ɪndeɪndʒər/ (**endangers, endangering, endangered**) V-T To **endanger** something or someone means to put them in a situation where they might be harmed or destroyed completely. 危害 ❑ *The debate could endanger the proposed Mideast peace talks.* 这场争论可能会危害中东和谈的倡议。

en·dear /ɪndɪər/ (**endears, endearing, endeared**) V-T If something **endears** you **to** someone or if you **endear yourself to** them, you become popular with them and well liked by them. 使受欢迎；使人喜爱 ❑ *Their taste for gambling has endeared them to Las Vegas casino owners.* 他们对赌博的爱好使其受到了拉斯韦加斯赌场老板们的欢迎。

en·dear·ing /ɪndɪərɪŋ/ ADJ If you describe someone's behavior as **endearing**, you mean that it causes you to feel very fond of them. 惹人喜爱的 [v-link ADJ] ❑ *She has such an endearing personality.* 她有个如此招人喜爱的个性。

★ **en·deav·or** /ɪndɛvər/ (**endeavors, endeavoring, endeavored**)
in BRIT, use **endeavour**
■1 V-T If you **endeavor to** do something, you try very hard to do it. 努力 [FORMAL] ❑ *They are endeavoring to protect labor union rights.* 他们正在努力保护工会权利。 ■2 N-VAR An **endeavor** is an attempt to do something, especially something new or original. 尝试 [FORMAL] ❑ *The company's creative endeavors are thriving.* 该公司的创新尝试蓬勃兴旺。 ❑ *Extracting information about the large-scale composition of a planet from a sample weighing a millionth of a gram was a fascinating example of scientific endeavor.* 从重量为百万分之一克的样品中提取有关行星宏观组成的信息是一个极为有趣的科学尝试实例。

★ **en·deav·our** /ɪndɛvər/ [BRIT] → see **endeavor**

en·dem·ic /ɛndɛmɪk/ ■1 ADJ If a disease or illness is **endemic** in a place, it is frequently found among the people who live there. 常见的 [TECHNICAL] ❑ *Polio was then endemic among children my age.* 小儿麻痹症在当时是在我这个年纪的儿童中常见的疾病。 ■2 ADJ If you say that a condition or problem is **endemic**, you mean that it is very common and strong, and cannot be dealt with easily. (情况、问题) 极为普遍的 [WRITTEN] ❑ *Discrimination against Catholics is endemic in Northern Ireland's institutions.* 对天主教徒的歧视在北爱尔兰的公共机构中极为普遍。

end·ing /ɛndɪŋ/ (**endings**) ■1 N-COUNT You can refer to the last part of a book, story, play, or movie as the **ending**, especially when you are considering the way that the story ends. 结局 ❑ *The film has a Hollywood happy ending.* 这部电影具有好莱坞式的美满结局。 ■2 N-COUNT The **ending** of a word is the last part of it. 词尾 ❑ *...common word endings, like "ing" in walking.* …常见词尾，比如**walking**中的**-ing**。 ■3 → see also **end**

end·less /ɛndlɪs/ ADJ If you say that something is **endless**, you mean that it is very large or lasts for a very long time, and it seems as if it will never stop. 无休止的 ❑ *...the endless hours I spent on homework.* …我花在家庭作业上的无数小时。 ● **end·less·ly** ADV 无休止地 ❑ *They talk about it endlessly.* 他们无休止地谈论这件事情。

★ **en·dorse** /ɪndɔrs/ (**endorses, endorsing, endorsed**) ■1 V-T If you **endorse** someone or something, you say publicly that you support or approve of them. 公开支持；赞同 ❑ *I can endorse their opinion wholeheartedly.* 我可以全心全意地支持他们的观点。 ■2 V-T If you **endorse** a product or company, you appear in advertisements for it. 代言 ❑ *The twins endorsed a line of household cleaning products.* 这对双胞胎为一系列的家庭清洁产品代言过。

en·dorse·ment /ɪndɔrsmənt/ (**endorsements**) ■1 N-COUNT An **endorsement** is a statement or action that shows you support or approve of something or someone. 认可 ❑ *This is a powerful endorsement for his softer style of government.* 这是对他的更温和的执政风格的强有力认可。 ■2 N-COUNT An **endorsement for** a product or company involves appearing in advertisements for it or showing support for it. 代言 ❑ *His commercial endorsements for everything from running shoes to breakfast cereals will take his earnings to more than ten million dollars a year.* 他的商业代言从跑鞋到早餐麦片一应俱全，令其年收入达到一千多万美元。

★ **en·dow** /ɪndaʊ/ (**endows, endowing, endowed**) ■1 V-T You say that someone **is endowed with** a particular desirable ability, characteristic, or possession when they have it by chance or by birth. 天生赋予 [usu passive] ❑ *You are endowed with wealth, good health and a lively intellect.* 你天生赋有财富、健康，和敏锐的智力。 ■2 V-T If you **endow** something **with** a particular feature or quality, you provide it with that feature or quality. 赋予 (某种特征或品质) ❑ *Herbs have been used for centuries to endow a whole range of foods with subtle flavors.* 香草几个世纪以来一直被用来赋予各种食品细腻的味道。 ■3 V-T If someone **endows** an institution, scholarship, or project, they provide a large amount of money that will produce the income needed to pay for it. 资助 ❑ *The ambassador has endowed a $1 million public-service fellowships program.* 大使资助了一个100万美元的公共服务奖学金项目。

en·dow·ment /ɪndaʊmənt/ (**endowments**) N-COUNT An **endowment** is a gift of money that is made to an institution or community in order to provide it with an annual income. 捐赠基金 ❑ *...the National Endowment for the Arts.* …美国艺术基金会。

end prod·uct (**end products**) N-COUNT The **end product of** something is the thing that is produced or achieved by means of it. 最终产品 [oft N "of" n] ❑ *It is the end product of exhaustive research and development.* 这是经过充分研究和开发的最终产品。

end re·sult (**end results**) N-COUNT The **end result of** an activity or a process is the final result that it produces. 最终结果 ❑ *The end result is very good and very successful.* 最终结果很好、很成功。

en·dur·ance /ɪndʊərəns/ N-UNCOUNT **Endurance** is the ability to continue with an unpleasant or difficult situation, experience, or activity over a long period of time. 耐力 ❑ *The exercise obviously will improve strength and endurance.* 这项练习将明显增强力量和耐力。

en·dure /ɪndʊər/ (**endures, enduring, endured**) ■1 V-T If you **endure** a painful or difficult situation, you experience it and do not avoid it or give up, usually because you cannot. 承受 ❑ *The company endured heavy financial losses.* 公司承受了沉重的财务损失。 ■2 V-I If something **endures**, it continues to exist without any loss in quality or importance. 延续 ❑ *Somehow the language endures and continues to survive.* 由于某种原因，这种语言持续生存下来了。 ● **en·dur·ing** ADJ 持久的 ❑ *This chance meeting was the start of an enduring friendship.* 这次偶然的相遇是一段持久友情的开始。

end user (**end users**) N-COUNT The **end user** of a piece of equipment is the user that it has been designed for, rather than the person who installs or maintains it. 最终用户 [COMPUTING] ❑ *You have to be able to describe things in a form that the end user can understand.* 你必须能以最终用户能够理解的方式描述产品。

en·emy ◆◇◇ /ɛnəmi/ (**enemies**) ■1 N-COUNT If someone is your **enemy**, they hate you or want to harm you. 仇敌 ❑ *Imagine loving your enemy and doing good to those who hated you.* 想像着爱你的敌人，为仇人做好事。 ■2 N-COUNT If someone is your **enemy**, they are opposed to you and to what you think or do. 反对者 ❑ *Her political enemies were quick to pick up on this series of disasters.* 她的政敌很快注意到这一系列的灾难。 ■3 N-SING-COLL **The enemy** is an army or other force that is opposed to you in a war, or a country with which your country is at war. 敌军 ["the" N, N n] ❑ *The enemy were pursued for two miles.* 敌军被追赶了两英里。 ■4 N-COUNT If one thing is the **enemy of** another thing, the second thing cannot happen or succeed because of the first thing. 敌对面 [FORMAL] ❑ *Reform, as we know, is the enemy of revolution.* 革新，如我们所知，是革命的敌对面。

Word Partnership *enemy* 的常用搭配：
V. make an enemy ■1
defeat an enemy ■3
N. enemy **attack**, enemy **position**, enemy **territory**, enemy **troops** ■3

en·er·get·ic /ɛnərdʒɛtɪk/ ■1 ADJ If you are **energetic** in what you do, you have a lot of enthusiasm and determination. 精力充沛的 ❑ *Ibrahim is 59, strong looking, enormously energetic and accomplished.* 伊卜拉希姆59岁，健壮的样子，精力极其充沛且富有才华。
● **en·er·geti·cal·ly** /ɛnərdʒɛtɪkli/ ADV 精力充沛地 [ADV with v] ❑ *He had worked energetically all day on his new book.* 他一整天干劲十足地

Word Web energy

Wood was the primary **energy** source for American settlers. Then, as industry developed, factories began to use **coal**. Coal was also used to **generate** most of the **electrical power** in the early 1900s. However, wide spread automobile use soon made **petroleum** the most important **fuel**. **Natural gas** remains popular for home heating and industrial use. Hydroelectric power isn't a major source of energy in the U.S. It requires too much land and water to produce. Some companies built **nuclear** power plants to make **electricity** in the 1970s. Today **solar** panels convert sunlight and giant wind farms convert wind into electricity.

E

写他的新书。 2 ADJ An **energetic** person is very active and does not feel at all tired. An **energetic** activity involves a lot of physical movement and power. 精力旺盛的；剧烈的 ❑ *Ten year-olds are incredibly energetic.* 10岁的孩子精力非常旺盛。 ● **en·er·geti·cal·ly** ADV 干劲十足地 [ADV with v] ❑ *David chewed energetically on the gristly steak.* 大卫干劲十足地嚼着尽是软骨的牛排。

en·er·gy ♦♦◊ /ɛnərdʒi/ (**energies**) 1 N-UNCOUNT **Energy** is the ability and strength to do active physical things and the feeling that you are full of physical power and life. 精力 ❑ *He was saving his energy for next week's race in Tuscon.* 他正为下周在特斯康举行的比赛养精蓄锐。 2 N-UNCOUNT **Energy** is determination and enthusiasm about doing things. 干劲 [APPROVAL] ❑ *You have drive and energy for those things you are interested in.* 你对那些你感兴趣的事情有动力、有干劲。 3 N-COUNT Your **energies** are the efforts and attention that you can direct toward a particular aim. 精力 ❑ *She had started to devote her energies to teaching rather than performing.* 她已经开始将精力投入到教学而不是表演中。 4 N-UNCOUNT **Energy** is the power from sources such as electricity and coal that makes machines work or provides heat. 能 ❑ *...those who favor nuclear energy.* …那些拥护核能的人们。
→ see Word Web: **energy**
→ see **calorie, electricity, food, solar system**

Word Partnership *energy* 的常用搭配：

ADJ. **physical** energy, **sexual** energy 1
full of energy 1 2
atomic energy, **nuclear** energy, **solar** energy 4
V. **focus** energy 1 2
conserve/save energy 4

en·force /ɪnfɔrs/ (**enforces, enforcing, enforced**) 1 V-T If people in authority **enforce** a law or a rule, they make sure that it is obeyed, usually by punishing people who do not obey it. 施行 ❑ *Boulder was one of the first cities in the nation to enforce a ban on smoking.* 博尔德是该国率先施行禁烟令的城市之一。 2 V-T To **enforce** something means to force or cause it to be done or to happen. 强制执行 ❑ *They struggled to limit the cost by enforcing a low-tech specification.* 他们通过强制执行一种低技术规范来竭力限制成本。

★ **en·force·ment** ♦♦◊ /ɪnfɔrsmənt/ N-UNCOUNT If someone carries out the **enforcement of** an act or rule, they enforce it. 执行 ❑ *The doctors want stricter enforcement of existing laws.* 医生们希望现行法律的执行能更严格。

en·gage ♦◊◊ /ɪngeɪdʒ/ (**engages, engaging, engaged**) 1 V-I If you **engage in** an activity, you do it or are actively involved with it. 从事 [FORMAL] ❑ *I have never engaged in drug trafficking.* 我从来没有从事过贩毒。 2 V-T If something **engages** you or your attention or interest, it keeps you interested in it and thinking about it. 吸引 ❑ *They never learned skills to engage the attention of the others.* 他们从来没有学过吸引别人注意的技巧。 3 V-T If you **engage** someone **in** conversation, you have a conversation with them. 使加入 ❑ *They tried to engage him in conversation.* 他们试图使他加入谈话。 4 V-I If you **engage with** something or **with** a group of people, you get involved with that thing or group and feel that you are connected with it or have real contact with it. 使融入 ❑ *She found it hard to engage with office life.* 她发现难以融入办公室生活。 ● **en·gage·ment** N-UNCOUNT 密切关系 ❑ *...the candidate's apparent lack of engagement with younger voters.* …该候选人明显缺乏与年轻选民的接触。 5 V-T If you **engage** someone to do a particular job, you appoint them to do it. 聘 [FORMAL] ❑ *We engaged the services of a famous engineer.* 我们聘了一位有名的工程师来帮忙。 6 → see also **engaged, engaging**

en·gaged /ɪngeɪdʒd/ 1 ADJ Someone who is **engaged in** a particular activity is doing that thing. 正从事的 [v-link ADJ "in/on" n] [FORMAL] ❑ *...the various projects he was engaged in.* …他从事过的不同项目。 2 ADJ When two people are **engaged**, they have agreed to marry each other. 已订婚的 ❑ *We got engaged on my eighteenth birthday.* 我们在我18岁生日那天订婚了。 3 ADJ If a telephone or a telephone line is **engaged**, it is already being used by someone else so that you are unable to speak to the person you are phoning. 占线的 [BRIT]

in AM, use **busy**

4 ADJ If a public toilet is **engaged**, it is already being used by someone else. 使用中的 [mainly BRIT]

in AM, usually use **occupied**

en·gaged tone [BRIT] → see **busy signal**

en·gage·ment /ɪngeɪdʒmənt/ (**engagements**) 1 N-COUNT An **engagement** is an arrangement that you have made to do something at a particular time. 约会 [FORMAL] ❑ *He had an engagement at a restaurant at eight.* 他8点钟在一家餐馆有一个约会。 2 N-COUNT An **engagement** is an agreement that two people have made with each other to get married. 订婚约定 ❑ *I've broken off my engagement to Arthur.* 我已经解除了于阿瑟的订婚约定。 3 N-COUNT You can refer to the period of time during which two people are engaged as their **engagement**. 订婚时期 ❑ *We spoke every night during our engagement.* 我们订婚期间每晚都交谈。 4 N-VAR A military **engagement** is an armed conflict between two enemies. 交战 ❑ *The constitution prohibits them from military engagement on foreign soil.* 宪法禁止他们在外国领土上的军事交战。 5 → see also **engage**

en·gag·ing /ɪngeɪdʒɪŋ/ ADJ An **engaging** person or thing is pleasant, interesting, and entertaining. 迷人的 ❑ *...one of her most engaging and least known novels.* …她最迷人却最鲜为人知的小说之一。

en·gen·der /ɪndʒɛndər/ (**engenders, engendering, engendered**) V-T If someone or something **engenders** a particular feeling, atmosphere, or situation, they cause it to occur. 引起 [FORMAL] ❑ *It helps engender a sense of common humanity.* 它有助于引发一种共同的人道主义精神。

en·gine ♦♦◊ /ɛndʒɪn/ (**engines**) 1 N-COUNT The **engine** of a car or other vehicle is the part that produces the power which makes the vehicle move. 引擎 ❑ *He got into the driving seat and started the engine.* 他坐上驾驶座椅，发动了引擎。 2 N-COUNT An **engine** is also the large vehicle that pulls a train. 机车 ❑ *In 1941, the train would have been pulled by a steam engine.* 1941年，火车可能已由蒸汽机车来牵引了。
→ see Word Web: **engine**
→ see **car**

en·gi·neer ♦◊◊ /ɛndʒɪnɪər/ (**engineers, engineering, engineered**) 1 N-COUNT An **engineer** is a person who uses scientific knowledge to design, construct, and maintain engines and machines or structures such as roads, railroads, and bridges. 工程师 2 N-COUNT An **engineer** is a person who repairs mechanical or electrical devices. 维修师 ❑ *They send a service engineer to fix the disk drive.* 他们派一位维修师来修理磁盘驱动器。 3 N-COUNT An **engineer** is a person who is responsible for maintaining the engine of a ship while it is at sea. 轮机师 4 V-T When a vehicle, bridge, or building **is engineered**, it is planned and constructed using scientific methods. 设计制造 [usu passive] ❑ *Its spaceship was engineered by Bert Rutan, renowned for designing the Voyager.* 它的飞船由伯特・鲁坦设计建造，此人因设计"旅行者"飞船而闻名。 5 V-T If you **engineer** an event or situation, you arrange for it to happen, in a clever or indirect way. 策划

Thesaurus *engineer* 另参见：

V. arrange, concoct, create, devise, originate, plan; (*ant.*) set up 5

Word Web engine

In the **internal combustion engine** found in most cars, there are four, six, or eight **cylinders**. To produce an engine stroke, the **intake valve** opens and a small amount of **fuel** enters the **combustion** chamber of the cylinder. A **spark plug** ignites the fuel and air mixture, causing it to explode. This **combustion** moves the **cylinder head**, which causes the crankshaft to turn. Next, the **exhaust valve** opens and the burned gases are drawn out. As the cylinder head returns to its original position, it compresses the new gas and air mixture and the process repeats itself.

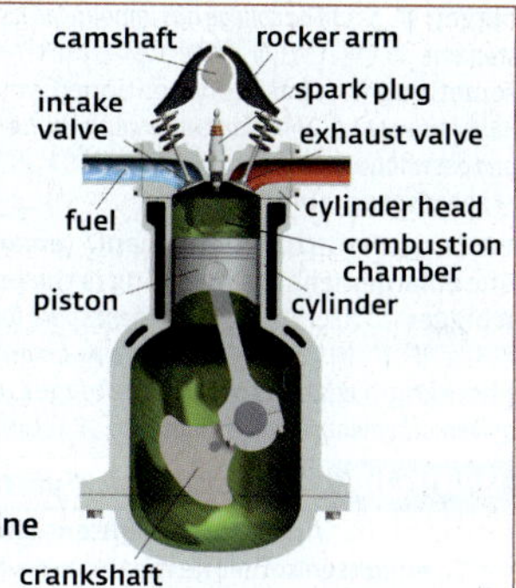

internal combustion engine

en·gi·neer·ing ♦◇◇ /ɛndʒɪnɪərɪŋ/ **1** N-UNCOUNT **Engineering** is the work involved in designing and constructing engines and machinery or structures such as roads and bridges. **Engineering** is also the subject studied by people who want to do this work. 工程；工程学 ❑ *...graduates with degrees in engineering.* …获得工程学学位的毕业生。 **2** → see also **genetic engineering**

Eng·lish ♦♦◇ /ɪŋglɪʃ/ **1** N-UNCOUNT **English** is the language spoken by people who live in Great Britain and Ireland, the United States, Canada, Australia, and many other countries. 英语 **2** ADJ **English** means belonging or relating to England, or to its people or language. It is also often used to mean belonging or relating to Great Britain, although many people object to this. 英格兰（人）的；英国（人）的；英语的 ❑ *...the English way of life.* …英格兰人的生活方式。 ● N-PLURAL **The English** are English people. 英格兰人 ❑ *It is often said that the English are reserved.* 人们常说英格兰人保守。
→ see Word Web: **English**

▲ **en·grave** /ɪngreɪv/ (**engraves, engraving, engraved**) V-T If you **engrave** something **with** a design or words, or if you **engrave** a design or words **on** it, you cut the design or words into its surface. 刻上 ❑ *Your wedding ring can be engraved with a personal inscription at no extra cost.* 你的结婚戒指可以刻上个人题字不另收费。 ❑ *The store will also engrave your child's name on the side.* 商店也将在一侧刻上你孩子的名字。 ❑ *...a bottle engraved with her name.* …一个刻有她名字的瓶子。

en·graved /ɪngreɪvd/ ADJ If you say that something is **engraved on** your mind or memory or **on** your heart, you are emphasizing that you will never forget it, because it has made a very strong impression on you. 铭刻于心的 [v-link ADJ "in/on/upon" n] [EMPHASIS] ❑ *Her image is engraved upon my heart.* 她的形象铭刻在我的心中。

en·grossed /ɪngroʊst/ ADJ If you are **engrossed in** something, it holds your attention completely. 全神贯注的 ❑ *Tony didn't notice because he was too engrossed in his work.* 托尼因过于全神贯注于工作而没有注意到。

en·gulf /ɪngʌlf/ (**engulfs, engulfing, engulfed**) **1** V-T If one thing **engulfs** another, it completely covers or hides it, often in a sudden and unexpected way. 吞没 ❑ *A seven-year-old boy was found dead after a landslide engulfed an apartment block.* 山崩掩埋了一座公寓楼之后，一名7岁的男孩被发现遇难。 **2** V-T If a feeling or emotion **engulfs** you, you are strongly affected by it. 使陷于 ❑ *...the pain that engulfed him.* …他所陷入的痛苦。

en·hance ♦◇◇ /ɪnhæns/ (**enhances, enhancing, enhanced**) V-T To **enhance** something means to improve its value, quality, or attractiveness. 提高 ❑ *The White House is eager to protect and enhance that reputation.* 白宫急于保护并提高那声望。

Thesaurus *enhance* 另参见：
V. boost, complement, improve; *(ant.)* decrease, diminish

▲ **en·hance·ment** /ɪnhænsmənt/ (**enhancements**) N-VAR The **enhancement of** something is the improvement of it in relation to its value, quality, or attractiveness. 提高 [FORMAL] ❑ *Music is merely an enhancement to the power of her words.* 音乐只不过是对她文字力量的一个提升。

enig·ma /ɪnɪgmə/ (**enigmas**) N-COUNT If you describe something or someone as an **enigma**, you mean they are mysterious or difficult to understand. 难解之谜 [usu sing] ❑ *Iran remains an enigma for the outside world.* 伊朗对外部世界而言依然是个谜。

en·ig·mat·ic /ɛnɪgmætɪk/ ADJ Someone or something that is **enigmatic** is mysterious and difficult to understand. 神秘难解的 ❑ *She starred in one of Welles's most enigmatic films.* 她主演了威尔斯最神秘的电影当中的一部。 ● **en·ig·mati·cal·ly** ADV 神秘难解地 ❑ *"Corbiere didn't deserve this," she said enigmatically.* "科比埃尔不应获得这个，"她高深莫测地说。

Word Link *joy ≈ being glad : enjoy, joyful, joyous*

en·joy ♦♦◇ /ɪndʒɔɪ/ (**enjoys, enjoying, enjoyed**) **1** V-T If you **enjoy** something, you find pleasure and satisfaction in doing it or experiencing it. 享受…的乐趣 ❑ *Ross had always enjoyed the company of women.* 罗斯一直都很享受女人的陪伴。 ❑ *He was a guy who enjoyed life to the full.* 他是个尽情享受生活乐趣的人。 **2** V-T If you **enjoy yourself**, you do something that you like doing or you take pleasure in the situation that you are in. (自) 得其乐 ❑ *I am really enjoying myself at the moment.* 我此刻很是自得其乐。 **3** V-T If you **enjoy** something such as a right, benefit, or privilege, you have it. 享有 [FORMAL] ❑ *The average German will enjoy 40 days' paid holiday this year.* 德国人今年平均将享有40天带薪假期。

Word Partnership *enjoy* 的常用搭配：
N. enjoy ***someone's*** **company**, enjoy **life**, enjoy **a meal** **1**
enjoy **privileges**, enjoy **success** **3**

en·joy·able /ɪndʒɔɪəbəl/ ADJ Something that is **enjoyable** gives you pleasure. 令人愉快的 ❑ *It was much more enjoyable than I had expected.* 它比我原先想的要令人愉快得多。

en·joy·ment /ɪndʒɔɪmənt/ N-UNCOUNT **Enjoyment** is the feeling of pleasure and satisfaction that you have when you do or experience something that you like. 愉快 ❑ *I apologize if your enjoyment of the movie was spoiled.* 我感到抱歉，如果打扰了你们对电影的欣赏。

en·large /ɪnlɑrdʒ/ (**enlarges, enlarging, enlarged**) **1** V-T/V-I When you **enlarge** something or when it **enlarges**, it becomes

Word Web English

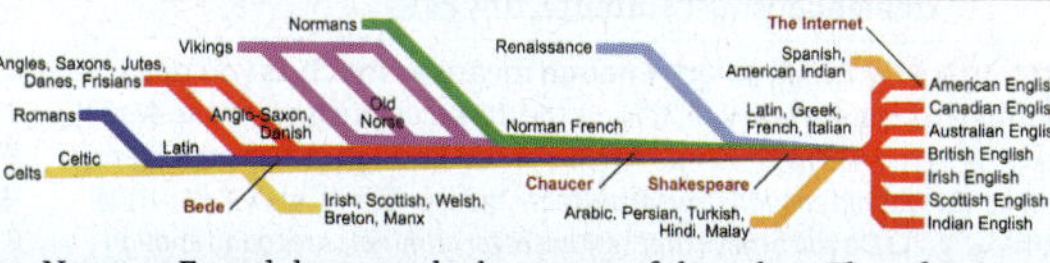

The **English language** has more **words** than any other language. Early English grew out of a Germanic language. Much of its **grammar** and basic **vocabulary** came from that language. But in 1066, England was conquered by the Normans. Norman French became the language of the rulers. Therefore many French and **Latin** words came into the English language. The playwright Shakespeare* **coined** over 1,600 new words in his plays. English has become an international language with many regional **dialects**.

William Shakespeare (1564-1616): an English playwright and poet.

e

bigger. 扩大 ❑ *The college has announced its intention to enlarge its stadium.* 该学院已宣布了扩建其体育馆的打算。 2 V-I If you **enlarge on** something that has been mentioned, you give more details about it. 详述 [FORMAL] ❑ *He didn't enlarge on the form that the interim government and assembly would take.* 他未详述临时政府和议会将会采取的形式。
→ see **photography**

en·large·ment /ɪnlɑrdʒmənt/ (**enlargements**) 1 N-UNCOUNT The **enlargement of** something is the process or result of making it bigger. 扩大 ❑ *There is insufficient space for enlargement of the buildings.* 没有足够的空间扩建这些大楼。 2 N-COUNT An **enlargement** is a photograph that has been made bigger. 放大的照片 ❑ *Ordering reprints and enlargements is easier than ever.* 按需加洗和放大照片比以前要容易。

E

Word Link *light ≈ shining : daylight, enlighten, light*

en·light·en /ɪnlaɪtᵊn/ (**enlightens, enlightening, enlightened**) V-T To **enlighten** someone means to give them more knowledge and greater understanding about something. 启迪 [no cont] [FORMAL] ❑ *A few dedicated doctors have fought for years to enlighten the profession.* 少数富有献身精神的医生为启蒙这一行业而奋斗多年。 ● **en·light·en·ing** ADJ 具有启发性的 ❑ *...an enlightening talk on the work done at the zoo.* …一段关于动物园工作的具有启发性的讲话。

en·light·ened /ɪnlaɪtᵊnd/ ADJ If you describe someone or their attitudes as **enlightened**, you mean that they have sensible, modern attitudes and ways of dealing with things. 开明的 [APPROVAL] ❑ *...an enlightened policy.* …一条开明的政策。

▲ **en·list** /ɪnlɪst/ (**enlists, enlisting, enlisted**) 1 V-T/V-I If someone **enlists** or **is enlisted**, they join the army, navy, marines, or air force. 使入伍；入伍 ❑ *He enlisted in the 82nd Airborne 20 years ago.* 他20年前加入了第82空降师。 ❑ *He enlisted as a private in the Mexican War.* 他以列兵身份参加了墨西哥战争。 2 V-T If you **enlist** the help of someone, you persuade them to help or support you in doing something. 赢得 ❑ *I had to cut down a tree and enlist the help of seven neighbors to get it out of the yard!* 我不得不砍了一棵树，然后找了7位邻居帮忙把它从院子里弄出去。

en·liv·en /ɪnlaɪvᵊn/ (**enlivens, enlivening, enlivened**) V-T To **enliven** events, situations, or people means to make them more lively or cheerful. 使更活跃；使更兴高采烈 ❑ *Even the most boring meeting was enlivened by Dan's presence.* 即使是最乏味的会议，也会因为丹在场而活跃起来。

en masse /ɒn mæs/ ADV If a group of people do something **en masse**, they do it all together and at the same time. 全体一起地 ❑ *The people marched en masse.* 人们一起齐步向前行。

en·mity /ɛnmɪti/ (**enmities**) N-VAR **Enmity** is a feeling of hatred toward someone that lasts for a long time. 敌意 ❑ *I think there is an historic enmity between them.* 我认为他们之间存在着宿怨。

enor·mity /ɪnɔrmɪti/ 1 N-UNCOUNT If you refer to **the enormity of** something that you consider to be a problem or difficulty, you are referring to its very great size, extent, or seriousness. 艰巨性；严重性 ❑ *I was numbed by the enormity of the responsibility.* 我对责任的艰巨性感到不知所措。 2 N-UNCOUNT If you refer to **the enormity of** an event, you are emphasizing that it is terrible and frightening. 深重 [EMPHASIS] ❑ *...the enormity of the disaster.* …灾难的深重。

enor·mous ♦◇◇ /ɪnɔrməs/ 1 ADJ Something that is **enormous** is extremely large in size or amount. 巨大的 ❑ *The main bedroom is enormous.* 主卧室大极了。 2 ADJ You can use **enormous** to emphasize the great degree or extent of something. （程度、范围）极大的 [EMPHASIS] ❑ *It was an enormous disappointment.* 这是件令人极为失望的事。 ● **enor·mous·ly** ADV 极其地 ❑ *This book was enormously influential.* 这本书影响极大。

Thesaurus *enormous* 另参见：
ADJ. colossal, gigantic, huge, immense, massive, tremendous; (*ant.*) minute, tiny 1 2

enough ♦♦♦ /ɪnʌf/ 1 DET **Enough** means as much as you need or as much as is necessary. 足够的 ❑ *They had enough cash for a one-way ticket.* 他们有足够的现金买一张单程票。 ● ADV **Enough** is also an adverb. 足够地 ❑ *I was old enough to work and earn money.* 我到了可以工作、挣钱的年龄了。 ❑ *Do you believe that sentences for criminals are tough enough at present?* 你认为对犯罪分子目前的刑罚足够严厉吗？ ● PRON **Enough** is also a pronoun. 足够的人或事 ❑ *Although the police say efforts are being made, they are not doing enough.* 尽管警方说他们正在努力，但是他们做得还不够。 ● QUANT **Enough** is also a quantifier. 足够的量 [QUANT "of" def-n] ❑ *All parents worry about whether their child is getting enough of the right foods.* 所有父母都担心他们的孩子是否得到足够量的恰当的食物。 ● ADJ **Enough** is also an adjective. 足够量的 [n ADJ] ❑ *Her disappearance and death would give proof enough of Charles' guilt.* 她的失踪和死亡将提供足够的证据证明查尔斯有罪。 2 PRON If you say that something is **enough**, you mean that you do not want it to continue any longer or get any worse. 够了 ❑ *I met him only the once, and that was enough.* 我只见过他一次，那就够了。 ❑ *I think I have said enough.* 我想我已经说得够多了。 ● QUANT **Enough** is also a quantifier. 足够的量 [QUANT "of" def-n] ❑ *Ann had heard enough of this.* 安这种话已经听够了。 ● DET **Enough** is also a determiner. 足够量的 ❑ *Would you shut up, please! I'm having enough trouble with these children!* 请住口！我和这帮孩子之间的麻烦已经够多了。 ● ADV **Enough** is also an adverb. 足够量地 [adj ADV] ❑ *I'm serious, things are difficult enough as they are.* 我是认真的，事情照现在这样已经够困难的了。 3 ADV You can use **enough** to say that something is the case to a moderate or fairly large degree. 相当地 [adj/adv ADV] ❑ *Winters is a common enough surname.* 温特斯是一个相当普通的姓。 4 ADV You use **enough** in expressions such as **strangely enough** and **interestingly enough** to indicate that you think a fact is strange or interesting. 真… ❑ *Strangely enough, the last thing he thought of was his beloved Tanya.* 真奇怪，他最后想到的是他心爱的坦尼娅。 5 PHRASE If you say that you **have had enough**, you mean that you are unhappy with a situation and you want it to stop. 受够了 ❑ *I had had enough of other people for one night.* 一个晚上我就受够其他人了。 6 **fair enough** → see **fair** 7 **sure enough** → see **sure**

Thesaurus *enough* 另参见：
ADJ. adequate, complete, satisfactory, sufficient; (*ant.*) deficient, inadequate, insufficient 1

en·quire /ɪnkwaɪər/ → see **inquire**

en·quiry /ɪnkwaɪəri/ → see **inquiry**

en·rage /ɪnreɪdʒ/ (**enrages, enraging, enraged**) V-T If you **are enraged** by something, it makes you extremely angry. 使狂怒 ❑ *Many were enraged by the discriminatory practice.* 很多人被这种歧视性的做法激怒了。

en·rich /ɪnrɪtʃ/ (**enriches, enriching, enriched**) 1 V-T To **enrich** something means to improve its quality, usually by adding something to it. 充实；丰富 ❑ *It is important to enrich the soil prior to planting.* 栽种之前给土壤施肥很重要。 2 V-T To **enrich** someone means to increase the amount of money that they have. 使富裕 ❑ *He will drain, rather than enrich, the country.* 他将耗尽而不是增加国家的财富。

en·rich·ment /ɪnrɪtʃmənt/ N-UNCOUNT **Enrichment** is the act of enriching someone or something or the state of being enriched. 充实；丰富 ❑ *...the enrichment of society.* …社会的富足。

en·rol /ɪnroʊl/ [BRIT] → see **enroll**

en·roll /ɪnroʊl/ (**enrolls, enrolling, enrolled**)
in BRIT, use **enrol**
V-T/V-I If you **enroll** or **are enrolled** at an institution or in a class, you officially join it. 注册 ❑ *Cherny was enrolled at the University in 1945.* 彻尼是1945年注册上大学的。 ❑ *Her mother enrolled her in acting classes.* 她母亲给她报了表演班。

★ **en·roll·ment** /ɪnroʊlmənt/ 1 N-UNCOUNT **Enrollment** is the act of enrolling at an institution or in a class. 注册 ❑ *A fee is charged for each year of study and is payable at enrollment.* 学费按年收取，可在注册时交纳。 2 N-UNCOUNT **Enrollment** is the total number of students enrolled. 注册入学人数 ❑ *The district's enrollment is expected to stabilize in 2006-07 at 10,200 students.* 本地区的注册入学人数有望在2006至2007年稳定在10200名学生。

en route /ɒn rut/ → see **route**

▲ **en·sem·ble** /ɒnsɒmbᵊl/ (**ensembles**) N-COUNT An **ensemble** is a group of musicians, actors, or dancers who regularly perform together. 表演团体 ❑ *...an ensemble of young musicians.* …一个由年轻音乐家组成的乐团。

★ **en·sue** /ɪnsu/ (**ensues, ensuing, ensued**) V-I If something **ensues**, it happens immediately after another event, usually as a result of it. 随即发生 [no cont] ❑ *If the Europeans did not reduce subsidies, a trade war would ensue.* 如果欧洲不减少补贴，贸易战将随即爆发。

en·su·ing /ɪnsuɪŋ/ 1 ADJ **Ensuing** events happen immediately after other events. 随后发生的 [ADJ n] ❑ *The ensuing argument had been bitter.* 随后的争论是激烈的。 2 ADJ **Ensuing** hours, months, or years follow the time you are talking about. 随后的（时间）[det ADJ] ❑ *The two companies grew tenfold in the ensuing ten years.* 这两家公司在随后10年里增长了10倍。

en suite /ɒn swit/ ADJ An **en suite** bathroom is next to a bedroom and can only be reached by a door in the bedroom. An **en suite** bedroom has an en suite bathroom. 卧室内的（浴室）；带浴室的（卧室） [ADJ n] [BRIT]

in AM, use **private bathroom**

en·sure ♦♦◊ /ɪnʃʊər/ (**ensures, ensuring, ensured**) V-T To **ensure** something, or to **ensure that** something happens, means to make certain that it happens. 确保 [FORMAL] ❑ *We must ensure that all patients have access to high quality care.* 我们必须确保所有的病人都能够得到高质量的护理。

★ **en·tail** /ɪnteɪl/ (**entails, entailing, entailed**) V-T If one thing **entails** another, it involves it or causes it. 牵连；导致 [FORMAL] ❑ *Such a decision would entail a huge political risk in the midst of the presidential campaign.* 这样的决定会在总统大选之际导致一个巨大的政治风险。

Word Link *tang ≈ touching : entangle, intangible, tangible*

en·tan·gle /ɪntæŋgəl/ (**entangles, entangling, entangled**) 1 V-T If one thing **entangles itself with** another, the two things become caught together very tightly. 紧紧缠住 ❑ *The blade of the oar had entangled itself with the strap of her bag.* 桨叶和她包的带子紧紧缠在了一起。 2 V-T If something **entangles** you **in** problems or difficulties, it causes you to become involved in problems or difficulties from which it is hard to escape. 使陷入；使卷入 ❑ *Bureaucracy can entangle applications for months.* 官僚主义会使申请耽搁数月之久。

en·tan·gled /ɪntæŋgəld/ 1 ADJ If something is **entangled in** something such as a rope, wire, or net, it is caught in it very firmly. 紧紧缠住的 ❑ *Divers battled for hours to try to free a whale entangled in crab nets.* 潜水员们奋战了几个小时，试图解救一条被捕蟹网缠住的鲸鱼。 2 ADJ If you become **entangled in** problems or difficulties, you become involved in problems or difficulties from which it is hard to escape. 被卷入的 [v-link ADJ] ❑ *This case was bound to get entangled in international politics.* 这个案件注定要卷入国际政治之中。

en·tan·gle·ment /ɪntæŋgəlmənt/ (**entanglements**) 1 N-COUNT An **entanglement** is a complicated or difficult relationship or situation. 纠葛 ❑ *...a military and political entanglement the president probably doesn't want.* …一个总统很可能不想要的军事政治纠葛。 2 N-VAR If things become entangled, you can refer to this as **entanglement**. 缠绕 ❑ *Many dolphins are accidentally killed through entanglement with fishing equipment.* 很多海豚因捕鱼设备的缠绕而意外死亡。

en·ter ♦♦◊ /ɛntər/ (**enters, entering, entered**) 1 V-T/V-I When you **enter** a place such as a room or building, you go into it or come into it. 进入 [FORMAL] ❑ *He entered the room briskly and stood near the door.* 他轻快地进入房间，靠近门站着。 ❑ *When Spinks entered they all turned to look at him.* 当斯平克斯进来的时候，他们都转过来看着他。 2 V-T If you **enter** an organization or institution, you start to work there or become a member of it. 加入 ❑ *He entered the firm as a junior associate.* 他作为一名初级职员进入了该公司。 3 V-T If something new **enters** your mind, you suddenly think about it. 突然出现于 ❑ *Dreadful doubts began to enter my mind.* 可怕的疑虑开始突然出现在我的脑子里。 4 V-T If it does not **enter** your head **to** do, think, or say something, you do not think of doing that thing although you should have. 想过 [with brd-neg] ❑ *It never enters his mind that anyone is better than him.* 他从来没有想过有人比他更出色。 5 V-T If someone or something **enters** a particular situation or period of time, they start to be in it or part of it. 开始进入 ❑ *The war has entered its second month.* 战争已进入了第二个月。 ❑ *A million young people enter the labor market each year.* 100万年轻人每年进入劳动力市场。 6 V-T If you **enter** a competition, race, or examination, you officially state that you will compete or take part in it. 参加 ❑ *I run so well I'm planning to enter some races.* 我跑得如此快，正计划参加一些比赛。 ❑ *As a boy soprano he entered many competitions, winning several gold medals.* 作为一位童声高音歌手，他参加过很多比赛，获得过好几枚金牌。 7 V-T If you **enter** someone **for** a race or competition, you officially state that they will compete or take part in it. 使报名参加竞赛 ❑ *His wife Marie secretly entered him for the championship.* 他的妻子玛丽偷偷给他报名参加锦标赛。 8 V-T If you **enter** something in a notebook, register, or financial account, you write it down. 记下 ❑ *Each week she meticulously entered in her notebooks all sums received.* 每周她在笔记本上一丝不苟地记下所收到的一切款项。 9 V-T To **enter** information **into** a computer or database means to record it there by typing it on a keyboard. 输入 ❑ *When a baby is born, they enter that baby's name into the computer.* 当一个婴儿出生时，他们将那个婴儿的名字输入电脑。

▶ **enter into** PHRASAL VERB If you **enter into** something such as an agreement, discussion, or relationship, you become involved in it. You can also say that two people **enter into** something. 达成（协议）；参与（讨论）；结成（关系）[FORMAL] ❑ *I have not entered into any financial agreements with them.* 我还没有和他们达成任何财务协议。 ❑ *The United States and Canada may enter into an agreement that would allow easier access to jobs across the border.* 美国和加拿大可能达成协议，简化跨国工作程序。

Thesaurus *enter* 另参见：
V. come in 1
join 2 5

en·ter·prise ♦◊◊ /ɛntərpraɪz/ (**enterprises**) 1 N-COUNT An **enterprise** is a company or business. 公司；企业 [BUSINESS] ❑ *There are plenty of small industrial enterprises.* 有很多小型的工业企业。 2 N-COUNT An **enterprise** is something new, difficult, or important that you do or try to do. 事业 ❑ *Horse breeding is indeed a risky enterprise.* 养马的确是一项有风险的事业。 3 N-UNCOUNT **Enterprise** is the activity of managing companies and businesses and starting new ones. 创业 [BUSINESS] ❑ *He is still involved in voluntary work promoting local enterprise.* 他仍从事志愿工作推动当地创业。 4 N-UNCOUNT **Enterprise** is the ability to think of new and effective things to do, together with an eagerness to do them. 开创力；开拓精神 [APPROVAL] ❑ *...the spirit of enterprise worthy of a free and industrious people.* …与一个自由勤劳的民族相称的开拓精神。

en·ter·pris·ing /ɛntərpraɪzɪŋ/ ADJ An **enterprising** person is willing to try out new, unusual ways of doing or achieving something. 有开拓精神的；有创新精神的 ❑ *Some enterprising members found ways of reducing their expenses or raising their incomes.* 一些有开拓精神的成员找到了减少开支或增加收入的方法。

en·ter·tain ♦◊◊ /ɛntərteɪn/ (**entertains, entertaining, entertained**) 1 V-T/V-I If a performer, performance, or activity **entertains** you, it amuses you, interests you, or gives you pleasure. 使娱乐；娱乐 ❑ *They were entertained by top singers, dancers and celebrities.* 他们饶有兴趣地看了顶级歌手、舞蹈演员和名流们的演出。 ● **en·ter·tain·ing** ADJ 娱乐的 ❑ *To generate new money the sport needs to be more entertaining.* 想生更多的财，这项运动得更有娱乐性。 2 V-T/V-I If you **entertain**, or **entertain** people, you provide food and drink for them, for example, when you have invited them to your house. 招待；宴客 ❑ *I don't like to entertain guests anymore.* 我不再喜欢招待客人。 ❑ *He loves to entertain.* 他喜欢宴客。 ● **en·ter·tain·ing** N-UNCOUNT 招待；宴客 ❑ *...a cozy area for entertaining and relaxing.* …一个宴客与休闲的舒适场所。 3 V-T If you **entertain** an idea or suggestion, you allow yourself to consider it as possible or as worth thinking about seriously. 心存 [FORMAL] ❑ *How foolish I am to entertain doubts.* 我心存疑虑是多么愚蠢啊。

en·ter·tain·er /ɛntərteɪnər/ (**entertainers**) N-COUNT An **entertainer** is a person whose job is to entertain audiences, for example, by telling jokes, singing, or dancing. 表演艺人 ❑ *Some have called him the greatest entertainer of the twentieth century.* 有人称他为20世纪最伟大的表演艺术家。

en·ter·tain·ment ♦◊◊ /ɛntərteɪnmənt/ (**entertainments**) N-VAR **Entertainment** consists of performances of plays and movies, and activities such as reading and watching television, that give people pleasure. 娱乐 ❑ *...the world of entertainment and international stardom.* …国际娱乐界及明星界。
→ see **radio**

en·thrall /ɪnθrɔl/ (**enthralls, enthralling, enthralled**) V-T If you **are enthralled by** something, you enjoy it and give it your complete attention and interest. 迷住 ❑ *The passengers were enthralled by the scenery.* 乘客们被这景色迷住了。

en·thuse /ɪnθuz/ (**enthuses, enthusing, enthused**) 1 V-I If you **enthuse about** something, you talk about it in a way that shows how excited you are about it. 兴奋地谈论 ❑ *Elizabeth David enthuses about the taste, fragrance and character of Provencal cuisine.* 伊丽莎白·戴维兴奋地谈论普罗旺斯菜的口味、香气和特色。 2 V-T If you **are enthused** by something, it makes you feel excited and enthusiastic. 使兴奋；使…热衷 ❑ *I was immediately enthused.* 我立刻兴奋起来了。

e

en·thu·si·asm ♦◇◇ /ɪnθuziæzəm/ (**enthusiasms**) 1 N-VAR **Enthusiasm** is great eagerness to be involved in a particular activity that you like and enjoy or that you think is important. 热情 ❑ *Their skill and enthusiasm has gotten them on the team.* 他们的技术和热情使他们进了那支团队。 2 N-COUNT An **enthusiasm** is an activity or subject that interests you very much and that you spend a lot of time on. 热衷的活动; 喜爱的科目 ❑ *Draw him out about his current enthusiasms and future plans.* 让他畅谈一下他当前喜爱的科目和将来的打算。

Thesaurus *enthusiasm* 另参见:
N. eagerness, energy, excitement, passion, zest; (*ant.*) apathy, indifference 1

E

en·thu·si·ast /ɪnθuziæst/ (**enthusiasts**) N-COUNT An **enthusiast** is a person who is very interested in a particular activity or subject and who spends a lot of time on it. 爱好者 ❑ *He is a great sports enthusiast.* 他是个真正的体育爱好者。

★ **en·thu·si·as·tic** /ɪnθuziæstɪk/ ADJ If you are **enthusiastic about** something, you show how much you like or enjoy it by the way that you behave and talk. 热衷的; 热烈的 ❑ *Tom was very enthusiastic about the place.* 汤姆曾非常热衷于那个地方。

● **en·thu·si·as·ti·cal·ly** /ɪnθuziæstɪkli/ ADV 热衷地; 热烈地 ❑ *The announcement was greeted enthusiastically.* 这则通告受到了热烈的欢迎。

en·tice /ɪntaɪs/ (**entices, enticing, enticed**) V-T To **entice** someone **to** go somewhere or **to** do something means to try to persuade them to go to that place or to do that thing. 怂恿 ❑ *They'll entice thousands of doctors to move from the cities to the rural areas by paying them better salaries.* 他们将通过支付更高的薪水怂恿成千上万的医生从城市迁往农村。 ❑ *Retailers have tried almost everything, from cheap credit to free flights, to entice shoppers through their doors.* 从低价信贷到免费航班，零售商们几乎用尽一切办法说服购物者惠顾。

en·tic·ing /ɪntaɪsɪŋ/ ADJ Something that is **enticing** is extremely attractive and makes you want to get it or to become involved with it. 诱人的 ❑ *A prospective premium of about 30 percent on their initial investment is enticing.* 初始投资30%左右的预期收益是诱人的。

en·tire ♦♦◇ /ɪntaɪər/ ADJ You use **entire** when you want to emphasize that you are referring to the whole of something, for example, the whole of a place, time, or population. 全部的; 整个的 [det ADJ] [EMPHASIS] ❑ *He had spent his entire life in China as a doctor.* 他整个一生都在中国做医生。 ❑ *There are only 60 swimming pools in the entire country.* 整个国家仅有60个游泳池。

Thesaurus *entire* 另参见:
ADJ. absolute, complete, total, whole; (*ant.*) incomplete, limited, partial

en·tire·ly ♦◇◇ /ɪntaɪərli/ 1 ADV **Entirely** means completely and not just partly. 完全地 ❑ *...an entirely new approach.* …一种全新的方法。 ❑ *Their price depended almost entirely on their scarcity.* 他们的价格几乎完全靠他们的供不应求。 ❑ *This administration is not entirely free of suspicion.* 这届政府并不是完全没有疑点。 2 ADV **Entirely** is also used to emphasize what you are saying. 完全地 [EMPHASIS] ❑ *I agree entirely.* 我完全赞同。

en·tirety /ɪntaɪərti, -taɪrɪti/ PHRASE If something is used or affected **in** its **entirety**, the whole of it is used or affected. 全部 ❑ *The peace plan has not been accepted in its entirety by all parties.* 该和平计划还没有被各方全部接受。

en·ti·tle ♦◇◇ /ɪntaɪtᵊl/ (**entitles, entitling, entitled**) 1 V-T If you **are entitled to** something, you have the right to have it or do it. 使有权 ❑ *If the warranty is limited, the terms may entitle you to a replacement or refund.* 如果保修单有限制，这些条款可让你有权换货或退款。 ❑ *They are entitled to first class travel.* 他们有权享受头等舱旅行。 2 V-T If the title of something such as a book, movie, or painting is, for example, "Sunrise," you can say that it **is entitled** "Sunrise." 给（书、电影、画作等）命名 [usu passive] ❑ *...a performance entitled "United States."* …一场名为"合众国"的演出。

en·ti·tle·ment /ɪntaɪtᵊlmənt/ (**entitlements**) N-VAR An **entitlement to** something is the right to have it or do it. 权利 [FORMAL] ❑ *They lose their entitlement to welfare when they start work.* 他们开始工作时就丧失了享受福利的权利。

★ **en·tity** /ɛntɪti/ (**entities**) N-COUNT An **entity** is something that exists separately from other things and has a clear identity of its own. 实体 [FORMAL] ❑ *...the earth as a living entity.* …作为一个生命实体的地球。

en·tou·rage /ɒnturɑʒ/ (**entourages**) N-COUNT A famous or important person's **entourage** is the group of assistants, servants, or other people who travel with them. 随从 ❑ *Rachel was quickly whisked away by her entourage.* 雷切尔很快被她的随从带走了。

entrance
❶ NOUN USES
❷ VERB USE

❶ **en·trance** ♦◇◇ /ɛntrəns/ (**entrances**) 1 N-COUNT The **entrance to** a place is the way into it, for example, a door or gate. 入口 ❑ *Beside the entrance to the church, turn right.* 在教堂入口边向右转。 ❑ *He was driven out of a side entrance with his hand covering his face.* 他被从边门赶了出来，一只手还捂着脸。 2 N-COUNT You can refer to someone's arrival in a place as their **entrance**, especially when you think that they are trying to be noticed and admired. 登场; 莅临 ❑ *If she had noticed her father's entrance, she gave no indication.* 关于她是否曾注意到她父亲的莅临，她未作表示。 3 N-COUNT When a performer makes his or her **entrance** onto the stage, he or she comes onto the stage. 出场 ❑ *When he made his entrance on stage there was uproar.* 他出场时哗然。 4 N-UNCOUNT If you gain **entrance to** a particular place, you manage to get in there. 进入许可 [FORMAL] ❑ *Hewitt had gained entrance to the Hall by pretending to be a heating engineer.* 休伊特曾假装成供暖技师得到进入那个大厅的许可。 5 N-UNCOUNT If you gain **entrance to** a particular profession, society, or institution, you are accepted as a member of it. 入（行、会、学）许可 ❑ *Many students have insufficient science and mathematics background to gain entrance to engineering school.* 许多学生没有足够的科学和数学知识背景得到进入工程学院的许可。 6 N-SING If you make an **entrance into** a particular activity or system, you succeed in becoming involved in it. 进入 ❑ *The acquisition helped BCCI make its initial entrance into the U.S. market.* 这次接管帮助国际信贷银行首次进入了美国市场。

Thesaurus *entrance* 另参见:
N. doorway, entry; (*ant.*) exit ❶ 1
appearance, approach, debut ❶ 2 3

❷ **en·trance** /ɪntræns/ (**entrances, entrancing, entranced**) V-T If something or someone **entrances** you, they cause you to feel delight and wonder, often so that all your attention is taken up and you cannot think about anything else. 使着迷 ❑ *As soon as I met Dick, he entranced me because he has a lovely voice.* 我一见到迪克，他就使我着迷，因为他有好听的嗓音。 ● **en·tranced** ADJ 着迷的 ❑ *He is entranced by the kindness of her smile.* 她善意的微笑令他着迷。

en·trance hall (**entrance halls**) N-COUNT The **entrance hall** of a large house, hotel, or other large building, is the area just inside the main door. 门厅

en·trant /ɛntrənt/ (**entrants**) 1 N-COUNT An **entrant** is a person who is taking part in a competition. 参赛者 ❑ *All items entered for the competition must be the entrant's own work.* 所有参赛作品必须是参赛者自己的作品。 2 N-COUNT An **entrant** is a person or company who has recently become a member of an institution or market. 新成员 ❑ *...the company that made a name for itself as an early entrant in the digital video-recorder market.* …这个以数码录像机市场的早期进入者而享有名气的公司。

en·trench /ɪntrɛntʃ/ (**entrenches, entrenching, entrenched**) V-T If something such as power, a custom, or an idea **is entrenched**, it is firmly established, so that it would be difficult to change it. 巩固 ❑ *...a series of measures designed to entrench democracy and the rule of law.* …一系列旨在巩固民主和法制的举措。 ● **en·trenched** ADJ 巩固的 ❑ *The recession remains deeply entrenched.* 经济衰退仍然根深蒂固。

Word Link *eur ≈ one who does : amateur, chauffeur, entrepreneur*

★ **en·tre·pre·neur** /ɒntrəprənɜr, -nʊər/ (**entrepreneurs**) N-COUNT An **entrepreneur** is a person who sets up businesses and business deals. 创业者 [BUSINESS]

en·tre·pre·neur·ial /ɒntrəprənɜriəl, -nʊər-/ ADJ **Entrepreneurial** means having the qualities that are needed to succeed as an entrepreneur. 具有创业素质的 [BUSINESS] ❑ *...her prodigious entrepreneurial flair.* …她惊人的创业天赋。

★ **en·trust** /ɪntrʌst/ (**entrusts, entrusting, entrusted**) V-T If you **entrust** something important **to** someone or **entrust** them **with** it, you make them responsible for looking after it or dealing with it. 委托 ❑ *He entrusted his cash to a business partner for investment in a series of projects.* 他把现款委托给一个生意合伙人投资一系列项目。 ❑ *They can be entrusted to solve major national problems.* 他们能受托解决重大国家问题。

en·try ♦♦◇ /ɛntri/ (**entries**) 1 N-UNCOUNT If you gain **entry to** a particular place, you are able to go in. 进入许可 ❑ *You can gain entry to the club only through a member.* 你只有通过一位会员才能进入该俱乐部。 ❑ *Entry to the museum is free.* 这座博物馆免费参观。 ● PHRASE **No Entry** is used on signs to indicate that you are not allowed to go into a particular area or go through a particular door or gate. 禁止入内 2 N-COUNT You can refer to someone's arrival in a place as their **entry**, especially when you think that they are trying to be noticed and admired. 驾到；莅临 ❑ *He made his triumphal entry into Mexico City.* 他胜利进入了墨西哥城。 3 N-UNCOUNT Someone's **entry into** a particular society or group is their joining of it. 加入 ❑ *...China's entry into the World Trade Organization.* …中国的入世。 4 N-COUNT An **entry** in a diary, account book, computer file, or reference book is a short piece of writing in it. (日记中的) 简短记录；(账簿中的) 账目；(计算机文档或参考书中的) 条目 ❑ *Violet's diary entry for April 20, 1917 records Brigit admitting to the affair.* 维奥莉特1917年4月20日的日记简短记录着布里吉特承认此事。 5 N-COUNT An **entry for** a competition is a piece of work, a story or drawing, or the answers to a set of questions, which you complete in order to take part in the competition. 参赛作品；参赛答卷 ❑ *The closing date for entries is December 31.* 参赛作品提交的截止日期是12月31日。 6 N-SING Journalists sometimes use **entry** to refer to the total number of people taking part in an event or competition. For example, if a competition has an **entry** of twenty people, twenty people take part in it. 参加总人数 ❑ *Our competition has attracted a huge entry.* 我们的比赛已吸引了大量参赛者。 7 N-UNCOUNT **Entry** in a competition is the act of taking part in it. 参加 ❑ *Entry to this competition is by invitation only.* 此次竞赛的参赛只凭邀请函。 8 N-COUNT The **entry to** a place is the way into it, for example a door or gate. 入口 ❑ *...the towering marble archway that marked the entry to the Pelican Point development.* …标志着鹈鹕顶开发区入口的、高耸的大理石拱门。
→ see **blog**

entry-level 1 ADJ **Entry-level** is used to describe basic low-cost versions of products such as cars or computers that are suitable for people who have no previous experience or knowledge of them. 初级入门的 (产品) [BUSINESS] ❑ *Several companies are offering new, entry-level models in hopes of attracting more buyers.* 数家公司正提供初级入门新款，希望吸引更多买家。 2 ADJ **Entry-level** jobs are suitable for people who do not have previous experience or qualifications in a particular area of work. 初级水平的 (工作) [BUSINESS] ❑ *Many entry-level jobs were filled by high school grads.* 许多初级水平的工作被中学毕业生占满了。

en·vel·op /ɪnvɛləp/ (**envelops, enveloping, enveloped**) V-T If one thing **envelops** another, it covers or surrounds it completely. 包裹住 ❑ *That lovely, rich fragrant smell of the forest enveloped us.* 森林那种美妙、馥郁的香气笼罩了我们。

en·velope /ɛnvəloʊp, ɒn-/ (**envelopes**) 1 N-COUNT An **envelope** is the rectangular paper cover in which you send a letter to someone through the mail. 信封 2 PHRASE If someone **pushes the envelope**, they do something to a greater degree or in a more extreme way than it has ever been done before. 挑战极限；突破常规 ❑ *There's a valuable place for fashion and design that pushes the envelope a bit.* 突破点儿常规的时尚和设计有其宝贵地位。
→ see **office**

en·vi·able /ɛnviəbᵊl/ ADJ You describe something such as a quality as **enviable** when someone else has it and you wish that you had it too. 令人羡慕的 ❑ *Japan, unlike other big economies, is in the enviable position of having a budget surplus.* 不像其他经济大国，日本有着令人羡慕的预算盈余。

en·vi·ous /ɛnviəs/ ADJ If you are **envious of** someone, you want something that they have. 羡慕的 ❑ *I don't think I'm envious of your success.* 我不认为我羡慕你的成功。 ❑ *Do I sound envious? I pity them, actually.* 我听起来像是羡慕吗？其实，我可怜他们。 ● **en·vi·ous·ly** ADV 羡慕地 [ADV with v] ❑ *"You haven't changed," I am often enviously told.* "你没变，"我常被羡慕地告知。

en·vi·ron·ment ♦♦◇ /ɪnvaɪrənmənt, -vaɪərn-/ (**environments**) 1 N-VAR Someone's **environment** is all the circumstances, people, things, and events around them that influence their life. 环境 ❑ *Students in our schools are taught in a safe, secure environment.* 我校学生在安全无忧的环境中接受教育。 ❑ *The moral characters of men are formed not by heredity but by environment.* 人的品德不是由遗传而是由环境形成的。 2 N-COUNT Your **environment** consists of the particular natural surroundings in which you live or exist, considered in relation to their physical characteristics or weather conditions. 生存环境 ❑ *...a safe environment for marine mammals.* …一个适合海洋哺乳动物的安全环境。 3 N-SING **The environment** is the natural world of land, sea, air, plants, and animals. 自然环境 ❑ *...persuading people to respect the environment.* …劝人们重视自然环境。
→ see **pollution**

Word Partnership *environment* 的常用搭配：

ADJ. **hostile** environment, **safe** environment, **supportive** environment, **unhealthy** environment 1
natural environment 2
V. **damage the** environment, **protect the** environment 3

en·vi·ron·men·tal ♦♦◇ /ɪnvaɪrənmɛntᵊl, -vaɪərn-/ 1 ADJ **Environmental** means concerned with the protection of the natural world of land, sea, air, plants, and animals. 环保的 [ADJ n] ❑ *Environmental groups plan to stage public protests during the conference.* 各环保组织计划在会议期间举行一些公众抗议行动。 ● **en·vi·ron·men·tal·ly** ADV 环保地 [ADV adj] ❑ *...the high price of environmentally friendly goods.* …环保商品的高昂价格。 2 ADJ **Environmental** means relating to or caused by the surroundings in which someone lives or something exists. 生存环境的 [ADJ n] ❑ *It protects against environmental hazards such as wind and sun.* 它防范诸如狂风和烈日等环境危害。

en·vi·ron·men·tal·ist /ɪnvaɪrənmɛntəlɪst, -vaɪərn-/ (**environmentalists**) N-COUNT An **environmentalist** is a person who is concerned with protecting and preserving the natural environment, for example, by preventing pollution. 环保主义者

★ **en·vis·age** /ɪnvɪzɪdʒ/ (**envisages, envisaging, envisaged**) V-T If you **envisage** something, you imagine that it is true, real, or likely to happen. 设想 ❑ *He envisages the possibility of establishing direct diplomatic relations in the future.* 他设想将来建立直接外交关系的可能性。

en·vi·sion /ɪnvɪʒᵊn/ (**envisions, envisioning, envisioned**) V-T If you **envision** something, you envisage it. 设想 [AM] ❑ *In the future we envision a federation of companies.* 我们设想将来会有公司联盟。 ❑ *Alana never envisioned her college career ending like this.* 阿兰娜从未想到她的大学生涯会如此结束。

▲ **en·voy** /ɛnvɔɪ, ɒn-/ (**envoys**) 1 N-COUNT An **envoy** is someone who is sent as a representative from one government or political group to another. 使者；代表 ❑ *A U.S. envoy is expected in the region this month to collect responses to the proposal.* 一位美国的代表本月将在这个地区收集对该提议的反馈意见。 2 N-COUNT An **envoy** is a diplomat in an embassy who is immediately below the ambassador in rank. 公使

envy /ɛnvi/ (**envies, envying, envied**) 1 N-UNCOUNT **Envy** is the feeling you have when you wish you could have the same thing or quality that someone else has. 羡慕 ❑ *Gradually he began to acknowledge his feelings of envy towards his mother.* 渐渐地他开始承认自己对母亲的羡慕。 2 V-T If you **envy** someone, you wish that you had the same things or qualities that they have. 羡慕 ❑ *I don't envy the young ones who've become TV superstars and know no other world.* 我不羡慕那些成为电视超级明星而对其他世界一无所知的年轻人。 3 N-SING If a thing or quality is **the envy of** someone, they wish very much that they could have or achieve it. 羡慕之处 ❑ *Their economy is the envy of the developing world.* 他们的经济令发展中国家羡慕。

en·zyme /ɛnzaɪm/ (**enzymes**) N-COUNT An **enzyme** is a chemical substance found in living creatures that produces changes in other substances without being changed itself. 酶 [TECHNICAL]

▲ **epic** /ɛpɪk/ (**epics**) 1 N-COUNT An **epic** is a long book, poem, or movie whose story extends over a long period of time or tells of great events. 史诗；史诗般的作品 ❑ *...the Middle High German epic, "Nibelungenlied," written about 1200.* …大约写于1200年的中古高地德语史诗《尼贝龙根之歌》。 ● ADJ **Epic** is also an adjective. 史诗般的 ❑ *...epic narrative poems.* …那些史诗般的叙事诗。 2 ADJ Something that is **epic** is very large and impressive. 伟大的；宏大的 ❑ *...Columbus's epic voyage of discovery.* …哥伦布的伟大发现之旅。
→ see **hero**

epi·dem·ic /ɛpɪdɛmɪk/ (**epidemics**) **1** N-COUNT If there is an **epidemic of** a particular disease somewhere, it affects a very large number of people there and spreads quickly to other areas. (疾病的) 流行 ❑ *A flu epidemic is sweeping through Moscow.* 一场流感正席卷莫斯科。 **2** N-COUNT If an activity that you disapprove of is increasing or spreading rapidly, you can refer to this as an **epidemic of** that activity. (坏事的) 盛行 [DISAPPROVAL] ❑ *...an epidemic of serial killings.* …连环谋杀的盛行。
→ see **illness**

epi·lep·sy /ɛpɪlɛpsi/ N-UNCOUNT **Epilepsy** is a brain condition that causes a person to suddenly lose consciousness and sometimes to have seizures. 癫痫 ❑ *Shawna suffers from epilepsy.* 肖娜患有癫痫。

E

epi·lep·tic /ɛpɪlɛptɪk/ (**epileptics**) **1** ADJ Someone who is **epileptic** suffers from epilepsy. 患癫痫的 ❑ *He was epileptic and refused to take medication for his condition.* 他患有癫痫，却拒绝药物治疗。 ● N-COUNT An **epileptic** is someone who is epileptic. 癫痫患者 ❑ *His wife is an epileptic.* 他的妻子是癫痫患者。 **2** ADJ An **epileptic** seizure is caused by epilepsy. 由癫痫引起的 [ADJ n] ❑ *He suffered an epileptic seizure.* 他经受了一次癫痫病发作。

epi·sode /ɛpɪsoʊd/ (**episodes**) **1** N-COUNT You can refer to an event or a short period of time as an **episode** if you want to suggest that it is important or unusual, or has some particular quality. 事件；经历 ❑ *This episode is bound to be a deep embarrassment for Washington.* 这一事件必然使华盛顿大为尴尬。 **2** N-COUNT An **episode** of something such as a series on television or a story in a magazine is one of the separate parts in which it is broadcast or published. (电视连续剧的) 集；(连载小说的) 节 ❑ *The final episode will be shown next Sunday.* 最后一集将于下周日播放。
→ see **animation**

epito·me /ɪpɪtəmi/ N-SING If you say that a person or thing is **the epitome of** something, you are emphasizing that they are the best possible example of it. 典型 [FORMAL, EMPHASIS] ❑ *Maureen was the epitome of sophistication.* 莫琳曾是老于世故的典型。

epito·mize /ɪpɪtəmaɪz/ (**epitomizes, epitomizing, epitomized**) V-T If you say that something or someone **epitomizes** a particular thing, you mean that they are a perfect example of it. 为…的典型；为…的代表 ❑ *Seafood is a regional specialty epitomized by Captain Anderson's Restaurant.* 海鲜是个当地特色，安德森船长餐厅是其典型代表。

★ **epoch** /ɛpək/ (**epochs**) N-COUNT If you refer to a long period of time as an **epoch**, you mean that important events or great changes took place during it. 时代 ❑ *The birth of Christ was the beginning of a major epoch of world history.* 基督的诞生是世界历史一个重要时代的开始。

equal ♦◇◇ /ikwəl/ (**equals, equaling, equaled**)
in BRIT, and sometimes in AM, use **equalling, equalled**

1 ADJ If two things are **equal** or if one thing is **equal to** another, they are the same in size, number, standard, or value. 相等的 ❑ *Investors can borrow an amount equal to the property's purchase price.* 投资者可以借与房地产购买价相等数额的款项。 ❑ *...in a population having equal numbers of men and women.* …男女人数相等的人口中。 **2** ADJ If different groups of people have **equal** rights or are given **equal** treatment, they have the same rights or are treated the same as each other, however different they are. 平等的 (权利、待遇等) ❑ *We will be demanding equal rights at work.* 我们将要求工作中的平等权利。 ❑ *...the commitment to equal opportunities.* …平等机会的承诺。 **3** ADJ If you say that people are **equal**, you mean that they have or should have the same rights and opportunities as each other. (权利、机会等) 平等的 [v-link ADJ] ❑ *We are equal in every way.* 我们在各方面都是平等的。 **4** N-COUNT Someone who is your **equal** has the same ability, status, or rights as you have. (能力、地位或权利等) 同等的人 ❑ *She was one of the boys, their equal.* 她是男孩们中的一员，和他们平起平坐。 **5** ADJ If someone is **equal to** a particular job or situation, they have the necessary ability, strength, or courage to deal successfully with it. 能成功应付 (某工作、某情形等) 的 [v-link ADJ "to" n] ❑ *She was determined that she would be equal to any test the corporation put to them.* 她决意要成功应对该公司对他们的任何考验。 **6** V-LINK If something **equals** a particular number or amount, it is the same as that amount or the equivalent of that amount. (数量上) 等于 ❑ *9 percent interest less 7 percent inflation equals 2 percent.* 9%的利息减去7%的通货膨胀等于2%。 **7** V-T To **equal** something or someone means to be as good or as great as them. 比得上 ❑ *The victory equaled the team's best in history.* 这次胜利平了该队历史上的最佳。 **8** PHRASE If you say "**other things being equal**" or "**all things being equal**" when talking about a possible situation, you mean if nothing unexpected happens or if there are no other factors that affect the situation. 同等条件下；如无意外情况发生 ❑ *It appears reasonable to assume that, other things being equal, most hostel tenants would prefer single to shared rooms.* 似乎有理由这样想：同等条件下，大多数旅店房客更喜欢住单人间而不愿意与人合住。

Word Partnership *equal* 的常用搭配：
N. equal **importance**, equal **number**, equal **parts**, equal **pay**, equal **share** **1**
equal **rights**, equal **treatment** **2**

equal·ity /ɪkwɒlɪti/ N-UNCOUNT **Equality** is the same status, rights, and responsibilities for all the members of a society, group, or family. 平等 ❑ *...equality of the sexes.* …性别平等。

equal·ize /ikwəlaɪz/ (**equalizes, equalizing, equalized**) V-T To **equalize** a situation means to give everyone the same rights or opportunities, for example, in education, wealth, or social status. 使…平等；使…均等 ❑ *Such measures are needed to equalize wage rates between countries.* 要使各国的工资水平平均等，这些措施是必要的。 ● **equali·za·tion** /ikwəlɪzeɪʃən/ N-UNCOUNT 平等化；均等化 ❑ *...the equalization of parenting responsibilities between men and women.* …男女之间养育责任的平等化。

equal·ly ♦◇◇ /ikwəli/ **1** ADV **Equally** means in sections, amounts, or spaces that are the same size as each other. 相等地 ❑ *Try to get into the habit of eating at least three small meals a day, at equally spaced intervals.* 试着养成每天隔相等的时间吃至少3小餐的习惯。 **2** ADV **Equally** means to the same degree or extent. 相等程度地 ❑ *All these techniques are equally effective.* 所有这些方法都同等有效。 **3** ADV **Equally** is used to introduce another comment on the same topic, that balances or contrasts with the previous comment. 同样地 (用于引出同一话题的另议) ❑ *Subscribers should be allowed call-blocking services, but equally, they should be able to choose whether to accept calls from blocked numbers.* 用户应当被允许使用拒收来电服务，但同样地，他们也应能够选择是否接听被阻拦号码的来电。

equal op·por·tu·nity em·ploy·er (**equal opportunity employers**) N-COUNT An **equal opportunity employer** is an employer who gives people the same opportunities for employment, pay, and promotion, without discrimination against anyone. 提供均等机会的雇主 [BUSINESS] ❑ *The police force is committed to being an equal opportunity employer.* 警察机构致力于成为提供均等机会的雇主。

equal sign (**equal signs**) N-COUNT An **equal sign** is the sign =, which is used in arithmetic to indicate that two numbers or sets of numbers are equal. 等号 (=)

▲ **equate** /ɪkweɪt/ (**equates, equating, equated**) V-T/V-I If you **equate** one thing **with** another, or if you say that one thing **equates with** another, you believe that they are strongly connected. 将…等同于；等同于 ❑ *I'm always wary of men wearing suits, as I equate this with power and authority.* 我总是提防着穿制服的人，因为我将其等同于权力及权威。 ❑ *The author doesn't equate liberalism and conservatism.* 该作者没有将自由主义等同于保守主义。 ● **equa·tion** N-UNCOUNT 等同 ❑ *The equation of gangsterism with business in general in Coppola's film was intended to be subversive.* 柯波拉电影中黑帮文化与普通事务的等同旨在具有颠覆性。

equa·tion /ɪkweɪʒən/ (**equations**) **1** N-COUNT An **equation** is a mathematical statement saying that two amounts or values are the same, for example 6x4=12x2. 等式 **2** N-COUNT An **equation** is a situation in which two or more parts have to be considered together so that the whole situation can be understood or explained. 制衡局面 ❑ *The equation is simple: research breeds new products.* 这个情况是简单的：研究孕育新产品。 ❑ *The party fears the equation between higher spending and higher taxes.* 该党害怕增加开支和增高税收之间的相互制衡。

★ **equa·tor** /ɪkweɪtər/ N-SING **The equator** is an imaginary line around the middle of the earth at an equal distance from the North Pole and the South Pole. 赤道
→ see **globe**

eques·trian /ɪkwɛstriən/ ADJ **Equestrian** means connected with the activity of riding horses. 骑马的 ❑ *...his equestrian skills.* …他的骑马术。

Word Link *equi ≈ equal : equilibrium, equitable, equivalent*

equi·lib·rium /ikwɪlɪbriəm/ (**equilibria**) **1** N-VAR **Equilibrium** is a balance between several different influences or aspects of a situation. 平衡 [FORMAL] ❑ *Stocks seesawed ever lower until prices found some new level of equilibrium.* 股票进一步震荡下跌，直到找到某个新的平衡。 **2** N-UNCOUNT Someone's **equilibrium** is their normal calm state of mind. 平静 ❑ *I paused in the hall to take three deep breaths to restore my equilibrium.* 我在那个大厅停下，深吸了3口气以恢复平静。

equip /ɪkwɪp/ (**equips, equipping, equipped**) **1** V-T If you **equip** a person or thing **with** something, you give them the tools or equipment that are needed. 装备；配备 ❑ *They try to equip their vehicles with gadgets to deal with every possible contingency.* 他们尽量给他们的车辆配备各种小装置以应付任何可能的突发状况。 ❑ *Owners of restaurants have to equip them to admit disabled people.* 餐馆老板们必须给餐馆配备接纳残疾人的设施。 **2** V-T If something **equips** you **for** a particular task or experience, it gives you the skills and attitudes you need for it, especially by educating you in a particular way. 训练 ❑ *Relative poverty, however, did not prevent Martin from equipping himself with an excellent education.* 然而相对的贫穷并没有妨碍马丁接受良好教育。

Thesaurus *equip* 另参见：
V. prepare, provide with, stock, supply **1**

equip·ment ♦♦◇ /ɪkwɪpmənt/ N-UNCOUNT **Equipment** consists of the things that are used for a particular purpose, such as a hobby or job. 设备；装备 ❑ *...computers, electronic equipment and machine tools.* …电脑、电子设备和机床。

Thesaurus *equipment* 另参见：
N. accessories, facilities, gear, machinery, supplies; *(ant.)* tools, utensils

equi·table /ɛkwɪtəbᵊl/ ADJ Something that is **equitable** is fair and reasonable in a way that gives equal treatment to everyone. 公平合理的 ❑ *He has urged them to come to an equitable compromise that gives Hughes his proper due.* 他已敦促他们达成公平合理的妥协，给休斯应得的权益。

equi·ties /ɛkwɪtiz/ **1** N-PLURAL **Equities** are shares in a company that are owned by people who have a right to vote at the company's meetings and to receive part of the company's profits after the holders of preference shares have been paid. 普通股 [BUSINESS] ❑ *Investors have poured money into U.S. equities.* 投资者们已注入大量资金购买美国普通股。 **2** → see also **preference shares**

▲ **equi·ty** ♦◇◇ /ɛkwɪti/ N-UNCOUNT In finance, your **equity** is the sum of your assets, for example the value of your house, once your debts have been subtracted from it. 资产净值 [BUSINESS] ❑ *To capture his equity, Murphy must either sell or refinance.* 要获取他的资产净值，墨菲必须出售或重新融资。

equiva·lent ♦◇◇ /ɪkwɪvələnt/ (**equivalents**) **1** N-SING If one amount or value is **the equivalent of** another, they are the same. 等量物；等价物 ❑ *Mr. Li's pay is the equivalent of about $80 a month.* 李先生的报酬大约等于每月80美元。 ● ADJ **Equivalent** is also an adjective. 等量的；等值的 ❑ *If they want to change an item in the budget, they will have to propose equivalent cuts elsewhere.* 如果他们想要改变预算中的一个款项，必须得提出其他等值的削减。 **2** N-COUNT The **equivalent** of someone or something is a person or thing that has the same function in a different place, time, or system. 等效对象 ❑ *...the Red Cross emblem, and its equivalent in Muslim countries, the Red Crescent.* …红十字徽章、及其在穆斯林国家对应物的红新月。 ● ADJ **Equivalent** is also an adjective. 等效的 ❑ *...a decrease of 10% in property investment compared with the equivalent period in 1991.* …房产投资相比1991年同期10%的降幅。 **3** N-SING You can use **equivalent** to emphasize the great or severe effect of something. 等效对象 [EMPHASIS] ❑ *His party has just suffered the equivalent of a near-fatal heart attack.* 他的政党刚经受了相当于一次几乎致命的心脏病发作的打击。

Thesaurus *equivalent* 另参见：
N. counterpart, match, parallel, peer, substitute **2**
ADJ. equal, similar; *(ant.)* different, dissimilar, unequal **2**

er /ɜr/ **Er** is used in writing to represent the sound that people make when they hesitate, especially while they decide what to say next. 呃（表示说话时的犹豫）❑ *People that are addicted to drugs get, er, help from the government one way or another.* 那些吸毒上瘾的人，呃，通过某种方式获得政府的帮助。

ER /i ɑr/ (**ERs**) N-COUNT The **ER** is the part of a hospital where people who have severe injuries or sudden illnesses are taken for emergency treatment. **ER** is an abbreviation for **emergency room**. 急诊室 [AM] ❑ *...people who come to the ER thinking they're having heart attacks.* …认为自己心脏病发作而来急诊室的人们。

era ♦◇◇ /ɪərə/ (**eras**) N-COUNT You can refer to a period of history or a long period of time as an **era** when you want to draw attention to a particular feature or quality that it has. 时代 ❑ *...the nuclear era.* …核时代。 ❑ *...the Reagan-Bush era.* …里根一布什时期。

★ **eradi·cate** /ɪrædɪkeɪt/ (**eradicates, eradicating, eradicated**) V-T To **eradicate** something means to get rid of it completely. 根除 [FORMAL] ❑ *They are already battling to eradicate illnesses such as malaria and tetanus.* 他们已经在为根除疟疾、破伤风等疾病而斗争。 ● **eradi·ca·tion** /ɪrædɪkeɪʃᵊn/ N-UNCOUNT 根除 ❑ *...a significant contribution toward the eradication of corruption.* …一个为根除腐败而做出的重要贡献。

★ **erase** /ɪreɪs/ (**erases, erasing, erased**) **1** V-T If you **erase** a thought or feeling, you destroy it completely so that you can no longer remember something or no longer feel a particular emotion. 抹去；消除 ❑ *They are desperate to erase the memory of that last defeat.* 他们急于抹去上次失败的记忆。 **2** V-T If you **erase** sound that has been recorded on a tape or information which has been stored in a computer, you completely remove or destroy it. 抹掉；删除 ❑ *An intruder broke into the campaign headquarters and managed to erase 17,000 names from computer files.* 一名入侵者闯入作战指挥部，设法删除了电脑文件中的17000个名字。 **3** V-T If you **erase** something such as writing or a mark, you remove it, usually by rubbing it with a cloth. 擦掉（字迹）❑ *It was unfortunate that she had erased the message.* 不幸的是她已擦掉了那条信息。

eras·er /ɪreɪsər/ (**erasers**) N-COUNT An **eraser** is an object, for example, a piece of rubber or a felt pad, that is used for removing something that has been written using a pencil or chalk. 橡皮擦；板擦 [AM]

erect /ɪrɛkt/ (**erects, erecting, erected**) **1** V-T If people **erect** something such as a building, bridge, or barrier, they build it or create it. 建造 [FORMAL] ❑ *Opposition demonstrators have erected barricades in roads leading to the parliament building.* 反对派示威者在通往议会大厦的路上设置了路障。 ❑ *The building was erected in 1900-1901.* 该建筑建于1900-1901年间。 **2** V-T If you **erect** a system, a theory, or an institution, you create it. 创建 ❑ *Japanese proprietors are erecting a complex infrastructure of political influence throughout America.* 日本业主们正在全美国构建复杂的政治影响力网络。 **3** ADJ People or things that are **erect** are straight and upright. 直立的；竖直的 ❑ *Stand reasonably erect, your arms hanging naturally.* 尽可能站直，双臂自然下垂。

erec·tion /ɪrɛkʃᵊn/ (**erections**) **1** N-COUNT If a man has an **erection**, his penis is stiff, swollen, and sticking up because he is sexually aroused. （阴茎的）勃起 **2** N-UNCOUNT The **erection of** something is the act of building it or placing it in an upright position. 建造；竖立 ❑ *...the erection of temporary fencing to protect hedges.* …为保护树篱的临时栅栏的搭建。

erode /ɪroʊd/ (**erodes, eroding, eroded**) **1** V-T/V-I If rock or soil **erodes** or **is eroded** by the weather, sea, or wind, it cracks and breaks so that it is gradually destroyed. 侵蚀 ❑ *The storm washed away buildings and roads and eroded beaches.* 暴风雨冲走了建筑物和道路，侵蚀了沙滩。 **2** V-T/V-I If someone's authority, right, or confidence **erodes** or **is eroded**, it is gradually destroyed or removed. 削弱 [FORMAL] ❑ *His critics say his fumbling on the issue of reform has eroded his authority.* 他的批评者们说他在改革问题上的拙劣做法已削弱了他的权威。 **3** V-T/V-I If the value of something **erodes** or **is eroded** by something such as inflation or age, its value decreases. 降低 ❑ *Competition in the financial marketplace has eroded profits.* 金融市场的竞争降低了利润。
→ see **beach, rock**

ero·sion /ɪroʊʒᵊn/ **1** N-UNCOUNT **Erosion** is the gradual destruction and removal of rock or soil in a particular area by rivers, the sea, or the weather. 侵蚀 ❑ *...erosion of the river valleys.* …河谷的侵蚀。 **2** N-UNCOUNT The **erosion of** a person's authority, rights, or confidence is the gradual destruction or removal of them. 削弱 ❑ *...the erosion of confidence in world financial markets.* …对世界金融市场信心的削弱。 **3** N-UNCOUNT The **erosion of** support, values, or money is a gradual decrease in its level or standard. 逐渐降低 ❑ *...the erosion of moral standards.* …道德水准的逐渐降低。
→ see Word Web: **erosion**
→ see **beach**

e

Word Web erosion

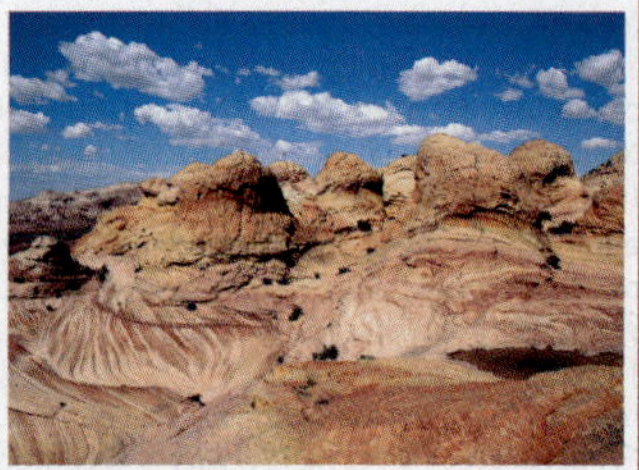

There are two main causes of **soil erosion**—**water** and **wind**. **Rainfall**, especially heavy **thunderstorms**, breaks down **dirt**. Small particles of **earth**, **sand**, and **silt** are then carried away by the water. The runoff may form **gullies** on hillsides. Heavy rain sometimes even causes a large, flat soil surface to wash away all at once. This is called sheet erosion. When the soil contains too much water, mudslides occur. Strong **currents** of **air** cause wind erosion. There are two major ways to prevent this damage. Permanent **vegetation** anchors the soil and windbreaks reduce the force of the wind.

E

Word Link *otic ≈ affecting, causing : erotic, neurotic, patriotic*

erot·ic /ɪrɒtɪk/ ADJ If you describe something as **erotic**, you mean that it involves sexual feelings or arouses sexual desire. 性爱的; 引起性欲的 ❑ *It might sound like a fantasy, but it wasn't an erotic experience at all.* 这听起来像一场梦幻，但绝不是一次性爱体验。

▲ **err** /ɜr, ɛr/ (**errs, erring, erred**) **1** V-I If you **err**, you make a mistake. 犯错 [FORMAL] ❑ *It criticizes the main contractor for seriously erring in its estimates.* 它批评主承包商在估算中严重出错。 **2** PHRASE If you **err on the side of** caution, for example, you decide to act in a cautious way, rather than take risks. 宁可失之过于… ❑ *They may be wise to err on the side of caution.* 他们宁可失之过于谨慎也不冒风险也许是明智的。

▲ **er·rand** /ɛrənd/ (**errands**) **1** N-COUNT An **errand** is a short trip that you make in order to do a job, for example, when you go to a store to buy something. (短程) 差使 ❑ *She went off on some errand.* 她出去办事了。 **2** PHRASE If you **run an errand for** someone, you do or get something for them, usually by making a short trip somewhere. 跑腿 ❑ *Run an errand for me, will you? Go find Roger for me.* 替我跑跑腿好吗？帮我去找一下罗杰。

▲ **er·rat·ic** /ɪrætɪk/ ADJ Something that is **erratic** does not follow a regular pattern, but happens at unexpected times or moves along in an irregular way. 不规则的; 不稳定的 ❑ *Argentina's erratic inflation rate threatens to upset the plans.* 阿根廷动荡不定的通货膨胀率有打乱这些计划的危险。 ● **er·rati·cal·ly** /ɪrætɪkli/ ADV 不规则地; 不稳定地 ❑ *Police stopped him for driving erratically.* 警察因其驾驶不循规则而把他拦下了。

★ **er·ro·neous** /ɪroʊniəs/ ADJ Beliefs, opinions, or methods that are **erroneous** are incorrect or only partly correct. 错误的 ❑ *Some people have the erroneous notion that one can contract AIDS by giving blood.* 有些人有这样一种错误的观念：认为献血会染上艾滋病。 ● **er·ro·neous·ly** ADV 错误地 [ADV with V] ❑ *It had been widely and erroneously reported that Armstrong had refused to give evidence.* 曾经错误地大规模报道过阿姆斯特朗拒绝提供证据。

er·ror ♦◇◇ /ɛrər/ (**errors**) **1** N-VAR An **error** is something you have done that is considered to be incorrect or wrong, or that should not have been done. 错误 ❑ *NASA discovered a mathematical error in its calculations.* 美国国家航空航天局发现了其计算中的一个数学错误。 **2** PHRASE If you do something **in error** or if it happens **in error**, you do it or it happens because you have made a mistake, especially in your judgment. 错误地 ❑ *The plane was shot down in error by a NATO missile.* 那架飞机被北大西洋公约组织的一颗导弹错误地击落了。 **3** PHRASE If someone sees **the error of** their **ways**, they realize or admit that they have made a mistake or behaved badly. 认识到自身错误 ❑ *I wanted an opportunity to talk some sense into him and try to make him see the error of his ways.* 我想找个机会给他讲讲道理，尽量让他认识到自身的错误。

Word Partnership *error* 的常用搭配：

ADJ. **clerical** error, **common** error, **fatal** error, **human** error **1**
V. **commit an** error, **correct an** error, **make an** error **1**

Word Link *rupt ≈ breaking : disrupt, erupt, interrupt*

★ **erupt** /ɪrʌpt/ (**erupts, erupting, erupted**) **1** V-I When a volcano **erupts**, it throws out a lot of hot, melted rock called lava, as well as ash and steam. 喷发 ❑ *The volcano erupted in 1980, devastating a large area of Washington state.* 这座火山1980年喷发，摧毁了华盛顿州的大片地区。 ● **erup·tion** /ɪrʌpʃ^ən/ N-VAR (**eruptions**) 喷发 ❑ *...the volcanic eruption of Tambora in 1815.* …1815年坦布拉火山的喷发。 **2** V-I If violence or fighting **erupts**, it suddenly begins or gets worse in an unexpected, violent way. 爆发 [JOURNALISM] ❑ *Heavy fighting erupted there today after a two-day cease-fire.* 激烈的战斗在两天的停火之后今天在那里爆发了。 ● **erup·tion** N-COUNT 爆发 ❑ *...this sudden eruption of violence.* …这起暴力事件的突然爆发。 **3** V-I When people in a place suddenly become angry or violent, you can say that they **erupt** or that the place **erupts**. 爆发骚乱 [JOURNALISM] ❑ *In Los Angeles, the neighborhood known as Watts erupted into riots.* 在洛杉矶，一个叫做沃茨的街区爆发了骚乱。 **4** V-I You say that someone **erupts** when they suddenly have a change in mood, usually becoming quite noisy. 爆发 (某种情绪) ❑ *Then, without warning, she erupts into laughter.* 然后，突如其来地，她爆发出笑声。 ● **erup·tion** N-COUNT (某种情绪的) 爆发 ❑ *...an eruption of despair.* …一阵突然的绝望。
→ see **rock, volcano**

Word Link *scal, scala ≈ ladder, stairs : escalate, escalator, scale*

▲ **es·ca·late** /ɛskəleɪt/ (**escalates, escalating, escalated**) V-T/V-I If a bad situation **escalates** or if someone or something **escalates** it, it becomes greater in size, seriousness, or intensity. 使…加剧; 加剧 [JOURNALISM] ❑ *Both unions and management fear the dispute could escalate.* 各工会与资方都害怕争端会加剧。 ❑ *The protests escalated into five days of rioting.* 抗议逐渐升级为5天的暴乱。 ● **es·ca·la·tion** /ɛskəleɪʃ^ən/ N-VAR (**escalations**) 加剧 ❑ *The threat of nuclear escalation remains.* 核升级的威胁依然存在。

es·ca·la·tor /ɛskəleɪtər/ (**escalators**) N-COUNT An **escalator** is a moving staircase on which people can go from one level of a building to another. 电梯 ❑ *Take the escalator to the third floor and it's the last office on the left.* 乘电梯到4楼，左边最后的那个办公室就是。

es·cape ♦♦◇ /ɪskeɪp/ (**escapes, escaping, escaped**) **1** V-I If you **escape from** a place, you succeed in getting away from it. 逃走 [no passive] ❑ *A prisoner has escaped from a jail in northern Texas.* 一名囚犯已经从北德克萨斯州的一个监狱逃走。 ❑ *They are reported to have escaped to the other side of the border.* 据报道他们已经逃过了边境。 **2** N-COUNT Someone's **escape** is the act of escaping from a particular place or situation. 逃脱 ❑ *The man made his escape.* 那个人逃走了。 **3** V-T/V-I You can say that you **escape** when you survive something such as an accident. 逃脱 ❑ *The two officers were extremely lucky to escape serious injury.* 那两名官员非常幸运地逃过了严重伤害。 ❑ *The man's girlfriend managed to escape unhurt.* 那人的女友成功逃脱了，没有受伤。 ● N-COUNT **Escape** is also a noun. 逃脱 ❑ *I hear you had a very narrow escape on the bridge.* 我听说你在桥上勉强逃过一难。 **4** N-COUNT If something is an **escape**, it is a way of avoiding difficulties or responsibilities. 逃避现实的方法 ❑ *But for me television is an escape.* 但对我而言，电视是个逃避现实的方法。 **5** ADJ You can use **escape** to describe things that allow you to avoid difficulties or problems. For example, an **escape route** is an activity or opportunity that lets you improve your situation. An **escape clause** is part of an agreement that allows you to avoid having to do something that you do not want to do. 逃避的 [ADJ n] ❑ *We all need the occasional escape route from the boring, routine aspects of our lives.* 我们都需要偶尔地逃避生活中的无聊和平淡。 **6** V-T If something **escapes** you or **escapes** your attention, you do not know about it, do not remember it, or do not notice it. 被忘掉; 被忽视 ❑ *It was an actor whose name escapes me for the moment.* 那是个我一时想不起名字的演员。

7 V-I When gas, liquid, or heat **escapes**, it comes out from a pipe, container, or place. 漏出；逸出 ❑ *Leave a vent open to let some moist air escape.* 让一个排气口开着以便让一些湿气逸出。 8 → see also **fire escape**

Thesaurus *escape* 另参见：
V. break out, flee, run away 1
N. breakout, flight, getaway 2

Word Partnership *escape* 的常用搭配：
N. **chance to** escape, escape **from prison** 1
escape **route** 5
V. **try to** escape 1
manage to escape 1 3
make an escape 2

es·cap·ism /ɪskeɪpɪzəm/ N-UNCOUNT If you describe an activity or type of entertainment as **escapism**, you mean that it makes people think about pleasant things instead of the uninteresting or unpleasant aspects of their life. 让人逃避现实的消遣方式 ❑ *Horoscopes are merely harmless escapism.* 占星术只是无害的、让人逃避现实的消遣方式。

es·cap·ist /ɪskeɪpɪst/ ADJ **Escapist** ideas, activities, or types of entertainment make people think about pleasant or unlikely things instead of the uninteresting or unpleasant aspects of their life. 逃避现实的 ❑ *...a little escapist fantasy.* …一个小小的、逃避现实的幻想。

★ **es·cort** (**escorts, escorting, escorted**)

The noun is pronounced /ɛskɔrt/. The verb is pronounced /ɪskɔrt/.

名词读作 /ɛskɔrt/，动词读作 /ɪskɔrt/。

1 V-T If you **escort** someone somewhere, you accompany them there, usually in order to make sure that they leave a place or get to their destination. 护送 ❑ *I escorted him to the door.* 我护送他到门口。 2 N-COUNT An **escort** is a person who travels with someone in order to protect or guard them. 护送者 ❑ *He arrived with a police escort shortly before half past nine.* 快到9点半时，他由警察护送到达了。 ● PHRASE If someone is taken somewhere **under escort**, they are accompanied by guards, either because they have been arrested or because they need to be protected. 在押送下；在护送下 3 N-COUNT An **escort** is a person who accompanies another person of the opposite sex to a social event. Sometimes people are paid to be escorts. (异性的) 社交陪同 ❑ *My sister needed an escort for a company dinner.* 我妹为了一个公司晚宴而需要一个社交陪同。

ESL /i ɛs ɛl/ **ESL** is taught to people whose native language is not English but who live in a society in which English is the main language or one of the main languages. **ESL** is an abbreviation for "English as a second language." 作为第二语言的英语

eso·ter·ic /ɛsətɛrɪk/ ADJ If you describe something as **esoteric**, you mean it is known, understood, or appreciated by only a small number of people. 深奥难懂的 [FORMAL] ❑ *...esoteric knowledge.* …深奥难懂的知识。

es·pe·cial·ly ♦♦◇ /ɪspɛʃəli/ 1 ADV You use **especially** to emphasize that what you are saying applies more to one person, thing, time, or area than to any others. 特别是 (用于强调所指内容更适合) [ADV with cl/group] [EMPHASIS] ❑ *Millions of wild flowers color the valleys, especially in April and May.* 成千上万的野花使峡谷五彩斑斓，特别是在四五月份。 2 ADV You use **especially** to emphasize a characteristic or quality. 尤其 (用于强调某种特质) [ADV adj/adv] [EMPHASIS] ❑ *Babies lose heat much faster than adults, and are especially vulnerable to the cold in their first month.* 婴儿比成人散热快得多，在出生第一个月里尤其易受寒。

▲ **es·pio·nage** /ɛspiənɑʒ/ N-UNCOUNT **Espionage** is the activity of finding out the political, military, or industrial secrets of your enemies or rivals by using spies. 间谍活动 [FORMAL] ❑ *The authorities have arrested several people suspected of espionage.* 当局已经逮捕了几个涉嫌从事间谍活动的人。

es·pouse /ɪspaʊz/ (**espouses, espousing, espoused**) V-T If you **espouse** a particular policy, cause, or belief, you become very interested in it and give your support to it. 拥护；支持 [FORMAL] ❑ *She ran away with him to Mexico and espoused the revolutionary cause.* 她与他一起逃到了墨西哥，支持革命事业。

es·say /ɛseɪ/ (**essays**) 1 N-COUNT An **essay** is a short piece of writing on a particular subject written by a student. (学生写的) 短文 ❑ *We asked Jason to write an essay about his hometown.* 我们让杰森写一篇关于他家乡的短文。 2 N-COUNT An **essay** is a short piece of writing on a particular subject that is written by a writer for publication. (作家写的) 文章 ❑ *...Thomas Malthus's essay on population.* …托马斯・马尔萨斯关于人口的文章。

★ **es·sence** /ɛsᵊns/ (**essences**) 1 N-UNCOUNT The **essence of** something is its basic and most important characteristic that gives it its individual identity. 本质 ❑ *The essence of consultation is to listen to, and take account of, the views of those consulted.* 咨询的本质是倾听并把那些被咨询者的观点考虑进来。 ● PHRASE You use **in essence** to emphasize that you are talking about the most important or central aspect of an idea, situation, or event. 本质上 [FORMAL, EMPHASIS] ❑ *Though complicated in detail, local taxes are in essence simple.* 虽然细节复杂，地方税本质上是简单的。 ● PHRASE If you say that something **is of the essence**, you mean that it is absolutely necessary in order for a particular action to be successful. 至关重要 [FORMAL] ❑ *Speed was of the essence in a project of this type.* 速度在一个这种类型的项目中至关重要。 2 N-MASS **Essence** is a very concentrated liquid that is used for flavoring food or for its smell. 精油 ❑ *...a few drops of vanilla essence.* …几滴香草精油。

es·sen·tial ♦♦◇ /ɪsɛnʃᵊl/ (**essentials**) 1 ADJ Something that is **essential** is extremely important or absolutely necessary to a particular subject, situation, or activity. 至关重要的 ❑ *It was absolutely essential to separate crops from the areas that animals used as pasture.* 把庄稼与牲畜的放牧区分开至关重要。 ❑ *As they must also sprint over short distances, speed is essential.* 由于他们还必须疾速短跑，因此速度是至关重要的。 2 N-COUNT The **essentials** are the things that are absolutely necessary for the situation you are in or for the task you are doing. 必需品 ❑ *The apartment contained the basic essentials for bachelor life.* 这套公寓配有单身生活的基本必需品。 3 ADJ The **essential** aspects of something are its most basic or important aspects. 基本的；重要的 ❑ *Most authorities agree that play is an essential part of a child's development.* 大多数权威人士认为玩耍是孩子成长的一个重要部分。 4 N-PLURAL The **essentials** are the most important principles, ideas, or facts of a particular subject. 要素；要点 ❑ *...the essentials of everyday life, such as eating and exercise.* …饮食、运动等日常生活要素。

Word Partnership *essential* 的常用搭配：
N. essential **personnel**, essential **services** 1
essential **information**, essential **ingredients** 1 3
essential **element**, essential **function**, essential **nutrients**, essential **oils** 3

es·sen·tial·ly ♦◇◇ /ɪsɛnʃəli/ 1 ADV You use **essentially** to emphasize a quality that someone or something has, and to say that it is their most important or basic quality. 本质上 [ADV with cl/group] [FORMAL, EMPHASIS] ❑ *It's been believed for centuries that great writers, composers, and scientists are essentially quite different from ordinary people.* 几个世纪以来人们都认为伟大的作家、作曲家和科学家本质上与常人大不相同。 2 ADV You use **essentially** to indicate that what you are saying is mainly true, although some parts of it are wrong or more complicated than has been stated. 基本上 [FORMAL, VAGUENESS] ❑ *His analysis of urban use of agricultural land has been proved essentially correct.* 他的城市对农用土地使用的分析已经被证明基本上正确。

Word Link *stab ≈ steady : destabilize, establish, instability*

es·tab·lish ♦♦◇ /ɪstæblɪʃ/ (**establishes, establishing, established**) 1 V-T If someone **establishes** something such as an organization, a type of activity, or a set of rules, they create it or introduce it in such a way that it is likely to last for a long time. 建立；确立 ❑ *The UN has established detailed criteria for who should be allowed to vote.* 联合国就谁应当被允许投票确立了详细标准。 2 V-RECIP If you **establish** contact with someone, you start to have contact with them. You can also say that two people, groups, or countries **establish** contact. 建立 (联系) [FORMAL] ❑ *We had already established contact with the museum.* 我们已经与那个博物馆建立了联系。 3 V-T If you **establish that** something is true, you discover facts that show that it is definitely true. 证实 [FORMAL] ❑ *Medical tests established that she was not their own child.* 医学检测证实她不是他们的亲生孩子。 ❑ *It will be essential to establish how the money is being spent.* 搞清这笔钱是如何被花费的将至关重要。 ● **es·tab·lished** ADJ 被证实了的 ❑ *That link is an established medical fact.* 那种联系是被证实了的医学事实。

e

E

4 V-T If you **establish yourself**, your reputation, or a good quality that you have, you succeed in doing something, and achieve respect or a secure position as a result of this. 确立(地位) ❑ *This is going to be the show where up-and-coming comedians will establish themselves.* 这会是一场很有前途的喜剧演员们将在此确立他们地位的演出。 ❑ *He has established himself as a pivotal figure in state politics.* 他作为国家政治中的一位轴心人物的地位已经确立。

Word Partnership *establish* 的常用搭配：

N. establish **control**, establish **independence**, establish **rules** 1
establish **contact**, establish **relations** 2
establish ***someone's* identity** 3
establish **credibility**, establish **a reputation** 4

es·tab·lished /ɪstæblɪʃt/ ADJ If you use **established** to describe something such as an organization, you mean that it is well known because it has existed for a long time. 老牌的 ❑ *These range from established companies to start-ups.* 这些包括老牌公司和新兴公司。

es·tab·lish·ment ♦◇◇ /ɪstæblɪʃmənt/ (**establishments**) 1 N-SING The **establishment of** an organization or system is the act of creating it or beginning it. 建立；创立 [FORMAL] ❑ *The establishment of the regional government in 1980 did not end terrorism.* 1980年地区政府的成立并没有结束恐怖主义。 2 N-COUNT An **establishment** is a store, business, or organization occupying a particular building or place. 商店；企业；机构 [FORMAL] ❑ *...a scientific research establishment.* …一个科研机构。 3 N-SING You refer to the people who have power and influence in the running of a country, society, or organization as **the establishment**. 当权者 ❑ *While scientists were once considered cranks and outsiders to the system, we are now part of the establishment.* 虽然科学家曾被认为是怪人、是该体制的局外人，而如今我们已经是权力集团的一部分。

es·tate ♦♦◇ /ɪsteɪt/ (**estates**) 1 N-COUNT An **estate** is a large area of land in the country which is owned by a person, family, or organization. 庄园 ❑ *He spent holidays at the 300-acre estate of his aunt and uncle.* 他在叔叔和婶婶的300英亩庄园里度过许多假日。 2 N-COUNT Someone's **estate** is all the money and property that they leave behind when they die. 遗产 [LEGAL] ❑ *His estate was valued at $150,000.* 他的遗产价值为15万美元。 3 → see also **real estate**

es·tate agen·cy (**estate agencies**) N-COUNT An **estate agency** is a company that sells houses and land for people. 房地产公司 [BRIT]

in AM, use **real estate agency**

es·tate agent (**estate agents**) N-COUNT An **estate agent** is someone who works for a company that sells houses and land for people. 房地产经纪人 [BRIT]

in AM, use **Realtor, real estate agent**

es·tate car (**estate cars**) N-COUNT An **estate car** is a car with a long body, a door at the rear, and space behind the back seats. 旅行小轿车 [BRIT]

in AM, use **station wagon**

★ **es·teem** /ɪstim/ 1 N-UNCOUNT **Esteem** is the admiration and respect that you feel toward another person. 敬重 [FORMAL] ❑ *He is held in high esteem by colleagues in the construction industry.* 他深受建筑业的同事们的敬重。 2 → see also **self-esteem**

★ **es·thet·ic** /ɛsθɛtɪk/ → see **aesthetic**

es·ti·mate ♦♦◇ (**estimates, estimating, estimated**)

The verb is pronounced /ɛstɪmeɪt/. The noun is pronounced /ɛstɪmɪt/.

动词读作 /ɛstɪmeɪt/。名词读作 /ɛstɪmɪt/。

1 V-T If you **estimate** a quantity or value, you make an approximate judgment or calculation of it. 估计 ❑ *Try to estimate how many steps it will take to get to a close object.* 估计一下需要多少步才能到达一个近距目标。 ❑ *I estimate that total cost for treatment will go from $9,000 to $12,500.* 我估计治疗费总额将在9千美元到1.25万美元之间。 ● **es·ti·mat·ed** ADJ 估计的 ❑ *There are an estimated 90,000 gangsters in the country.* 这个国家估计有9万名歹徒。 2 N-COUNT An **estimate** is an approximate calculation of a quantity or value. 估计 ❑ *...the official estimate of the election result.* …选举结果的官方估计。 3 N-COUNT An **estimate** is a judgment about a person or situation that you make based on the available evidence. 判断 ❑ *I hadn't been far wrong in my estimate of his grandson's capabilities.* 我对他孙子能力的判断没有太大离谱。 4 N-COUNT An **estimate** from someone who you employ to do a job for you, such as a builder or a plumber, is a written statement of how much the job is likely to cost. 估价 ❑ *Quotes and estimates can be prepared by computer on the spot.* 报价和估价可以当场用电脑做出来。

Thesaurus *estimate* 另参见：

V. appraise, gauge, guess, judge; (*ant.*) calculate 1
N. appraisal, guess, valuation 2
appraisal, evaluation 3
appraisal, valuation 4

Word Partnership *estimate* 的常用搭配：

ADJ. **best** estimate, **conservative** estimate, **rough** estimate 2
original estimate 2 4
V. **make an** estimate 2 4

es·ti·ma·tion /ɛstɪmeɪʃən/ (**estimations**) 1 N-SING Your **estimation** of a person or situation is the opinion or impression that you have formed about them. 评价；印象 [FORMAL] ❑ *He has gone down considerably in my estimation.* 我对他的评价已经大大降低了。 2 N-COUNT An **estimation** is an approximate calculation of a quantity or value. 估算；估价 ❑ *...estimations of pre-tax profits of 12.25 million.* …1225万的税前利润估算。

es·tranged /ɪstreɪndʒd/ 1 ADJ An **estranged** wife or husband is no longer living with their husband or wife. 分居的 ❑ *...his estranged wife.* …与他分居的妻子。 2 ADJ If you are **estranged from** your family or friends, you have quarreled with them and are not communicating with them. (与家人、朋友) 疏远的 [FORMAL] ❑ *Joanna spent most of her twenties virtually estranged from her father.* 乔安娜在20多岁的大部分时间和她爸爸几乎不来往。 3 ADJ If you describe someone as **estranged from** something such as society or their profession, you mean that they no longer seem involved in it. 脱离的 [v-link ADJ] [FORMAL] ❑ *Arran became increasingly estranged from the mainstream of Hollywood.* 阿伦变得越来越脱离好莱坞主流了。

es·tu·ary /ɛstʃuɛri/ (**estuaries**) N-COUNT; N-IN-NAMES An **estuary** is the wide part of a river where it joins the sea. 河口 ❑ *Sturgeon fishing has been pretty good in the estuary.* 鲟鱼捕捞在这个河口一直很好。

e-tailer /iteɪlər/ (**e-tailers**) also **etailer** N-COUNT An **e-tailer** is a person or company that sells products on the Internet. 网上零售商 [COMPUTING] ❑ *This company is the biggest wine e-tailer in California.* 这家公司是加利福尼亚州最大的网上酒业零售商。

e-tailing /iteɪlɪŋ/ also **etailing** N-UNCOUNT **E-tailing** is the business of selling products on the Internet. 网上零售业 [COMPUTING] ❑ *Electronic retailing has predictably become known as e-tailing.* 网上零售业正如所料地以**e-tailing**变得为人所知了。

et al. /ɛt æl, -ɑl/ **et al.** is used after a name or a list of names to indicate that other people are also involved. It is used especially when referring to books or articles that were written by more than two people. (用于人名后) …等 ❑ *...Blough et al.* …布劳等。

etc. ♦◇◇ /ɛt sɛtərə, -sɛtrə/ **etc.** is used at the end of a list to indicate that you have mentioned only some of the items involved and have not given a full list. **etc.** is a written abbreviation for "etcetera." 等等 ❑ *She knew all about my schoolwork, my hospital work, etc.* 她知道所有有关我的学业、医院工作等情况。

etch /ɛtʃ/ (**etches, etching, etched**) 1 V-T If a line or pattern **is etched into** a surface, it is cut into the surface by means of acid or a sharp tool. You can also say that a surface **is etched with** a line or pattern. 蚀刻；凿刻 ❑ *Crosses were etched into the walls.* 十字架被凿刻在了墙上。 ❑ *Windows are etched with the vehicle identification number.* 窗户被凿刻上了车辆识别号码。 2 V-T PASSIVE If something **is etched on** your memory, you remember it very clearly, usually because it has some special importance for you. 铭刻(在记忆中) [LITERARY] ❑ *The ugly scene in the study was still etched on her mind.* 书房中丑陋的一幕仍然铭刻在她的脑海中。

etch·ing /ɛtʃɪŋ/ (**etchings**) N-COUNT An **etching** is a picture printed from a metal plate that has had a design cut into it with acid. 蚀刻版画

eter·nal /ɪtɜrnəl/ 1 ADJ Something that is **eternal** lasts forever. 永恒的 ❑ *...the quest for eternal youth.* …对永远年轻的追求。 ● **eter·nal·ly** ADV 永恒地 ❑ *She is eternally grateful to her family for their* *support.* 她因家人的支持对他们永存感激之心。 **2** ADJ If you describe something as **eternal**, you mean that it seems to last forever, often because you think it is boring or annoying. 无休止的 ❑ *In the background was that eternal hum.* 背景里是那没完没了的哼哼声。

eter·nity /ɪtɜrnɪti/ **1** N-UNCOUNT **Eternity** is time without an end or a state of existence outside time, especially the state that some people believe they will pass into after they have died. 永恒; 永存 ❑ *I have always found the thought of eternity terrifying.* 我总觉得永生的想法很可怕。 **2** N-SING If you say that a situation lasted for **an eternity**, you mean that it seemed to last an extremely long time, usually because it was boring or unpleasant. 极长的时间 ❑ *The war continued for an eternity.* 那场战争持续了极长的时间。

ethe·real /ɪθɪəriəl/ ADJ Someone or something that is **ethereal** has a delicate beauty. 优雅的 [FORMAL] ❑ *She's the prettiest, most ethereal romantic heroine in the movies.* 她是那些电影中最美丽、最优雅浪漫的女主角。

Word Link *ics ≈ system, knowledge : economics, electronics, ethics*

▲ **eth·ic** /ɛθɪk/ (**ethics**) **1** N-PLURAL **Ethics** are moral beliefs and rules about right and wrong. 道德 ❑ *Refugee workers said such action was a violation of medical ethics.* 难民工作者称这种行为为违背了医学道德。 **2** N-PLURAL Someone's **ethics** are the moral principles about right and wrong behavior that they believe in. 行为准则 ❑ *He told the police that he had thought honestly about the ethics of what he was doing.* 他告诉警察他曾真诚地考虑过他所作所为依据的行为准则。 **3** N-UNCOUNT **Ethics** is the study of questions about what is morally right and wrong. 伦理学 ❑ *...the teaching of ethics and moral philosophy.* …伦理学和道德哲学的教学。 **4** N-SING An **ethic** of a particular kind is an idea or moral belief that influences the behavior, attitudes, and philosophy of a group of people. 道德观念 ❑ *...the ethic of public service.* …公共服务的道德观念。

ethi·cal /ɛθɪkᵊl/ **1** ADJ **Ethical** means relating to beliefs about right and wrong. 道德上的 ❑ *...the medical, nursing and ethical issues surrounding terminally-ill people.* …关于患绝症病人们的医学、护理和道德问题。 ● **ethi·cal·ly** /ɛθɪkli/ ADV 道德上地 ❑ *Attorneys are ethically and legally bound to absolute confidentiality.* 律师在道德上和法律上都得绝对保守机密。 **2** ADJ If you describe something as **ethical**, you mean that it is morally right or morally acceptable. 合乎道德的 ❑ *The trade association promotes ethical business practices.* 这个贸易协会提倡合乎道德标准的商业行为。 ● **ethi·cal·ly** ADV 合乎道德地 [ADV after v] ❑ *Mayors want local companies to behave ethically.* 市长们希望当地公司按道德行事。

eth·nic ♦◇◇ /ɛθnɪk/ **1** ADJ **Ethnic** means connected with or relating to different racial or cultural groups of people. 种族的 ❑ *...a survey of Britain's ethnic minorities.* …对英国少数民族的一项调查。 ● **eth·ni·cal·ly** /ɛθnɪkli/ ADV 种族上地 ❑ *...a predominantly young, ethnically mixed audience.* …一群大部分为年轻的、包含不同种族的观众。 **2** ADJ You can use **ethnic** to describe people who belong to a particular racial or cultural group but who, usually, do not live in the country where most members of that group live. 少数民族的 [ADJ n] ❑ *There are still several million ethnic Germans in Russia.* 在俄罗斯仍有几百万德国族裔。 ● **eth·ni·cal·ly** ADV 少数民族地 [ADV adj] ❑ *...a large ethnically Albanian population.* …大量阿尔巴尼亚族人口。 **3** ADJ **Ethnic** clothing, music, or food is characteristic of the traditions of a particular ethnic group, and different from what is usually found in modern Western culture. 具有民族特色的 ❑ *...a magnificent range of ethnic fabrics.* …各色各样具有民族特色的织物。

eth·nic cleans·ing N-UNCOUNT **Ethnic cleansing** is the process of using violent methods to force certain groups of people out of a particular area or country. 种族清洗 [DISAPPROVAL] ❑ *In late May, government forces began the "ethnic cleansing" of the area around the town.* 5月下旬，政府军队开始了对该镇周边地区的"种族清洗"。

ethos /iθɒs/ N-SING An **ethos** is the set of ideas and attitudes that is associated with a particular group of people or a particular type of activity. (某一团体或某类活动的) 理念 [FORMAL] ❑ *The whole ethos of the hotel is effortless service.* 该宾馆的整体理念是轻松服务。

▲ **eti·quette** /ɛtɪkɪt, -kɛt/ N-UNCOUNT **Etiquette** is a set of customs and rules for polite behavior, especially among a particular class of people or in a particular profession. (尤指特定阶层的) 礼仪; (尤指特定行业的) 规矩 ❑ *This was such a great breach of etiquette, he hardly knew what to do.* 这是一起规矩的严重违反，他几乎不知所措了。

EU /i yu/ N-PROPER **The EU** is an organization of European countries that have joint policies on matters such as trade, agriculture, and finance. **EU** is an abbreviation for **European Union**. 欧盟 ❑ *...the ten new EU members.* …10个新的欧盟成员国。

euphemism /yufəmɪzəm/ (**euphemisms**) N-COUNT A **euphemism** is a polite word or expression that is used to refer to things that people may find upsetting or embarrassing to talk about, for example sex, the human body, or death. 委婉语 ❑ *The term "early retirement" is nearly always a euphemism for layoffs nowadays.* 如今"提前退休"这个词几乎总是下岗的委婉语。

euphemis·tic /yufəmɪstɪk/ ADJ **Euphemistic** language uses polite, pleasant, or neutral words and expressions to refer to things that people may find unpleasant, upsetting, or embarrassing to talk about, for example, sex, the human body, or death. 委婉的 ❑ *...a euphemistic way of saying that someone has been lying.* …说某人一直在撒谎的委婉说法。 ● **euphemis·ti·cal·ly** /yufəmɪstɪkli/ ADV 委婉地 [ADV with v] ❑ *...political prisons, called euphemistically "reeducation camps."* …被委婉地称为"再教育营"的政治监狱。

eupho·ria /yufɔriə/ N-UNCOUNT **Euphoria** is a feeling of intense happiness and excitement. 狂喜 ❑ *There was euphoria after the election.* 选举之后是一片狂喜。

euphor·ic /yufɔrɪk/ ADJ If you are **euphoric**, you feel intense happiness and excitement. 狂喜的 ❑ *The war had received euphoric support from the public.* 这场战争得到了公众狂热的支持。

euro /yʊəroʊ/ (**euros**) N-COUNT The **euro** is a unit of currency that is used by several member countries of the European Union. 欧元 ❑ *Millions of words have been written about the introduction of the euro.* 已有上百万的文字论及欧元的引入。

Euro·pean ♦♦◇ /yʊərəpiən/ (**Europeans**) **1** ADJ **European** means belonging or relating to, or coming from Europe. 欧洲的 ❑ *...in some other European countries.* …在其他一些欧洲国家。 **2** N-COUNT A **European** is a person who comes from Europe. 欧洲人 ❑ *Three-quarters of working-age Americans work, compared with roughly 60% of Europeans.* 3/4处于工作年龄的美国人在工作，相比之下欧洲约为60%。

Euro·pean Un·ion N-PROPER **The European Union** is an organization of European countries that have joint policies on matters such as commerce, agriculture, and finance. 欧洲联盟

eutha·na·sia /yuθəneɪʒə/ N-UNCOUNT **Euthanasia** is the practice of killing someone who is very ill and will never get better in order to end their suffering, usually done at their request or with their consent. 安乐死 ❑ *...those in favor of voluntary euthanasia.* …那些支持自愿安乐死的。

Word Link *vac ≈ empty : evacuate, vacant, vacate*

★ **evacu·ate** /ɪvækyueɪt/ (**evacuates, evacuating, evacuated**) **1** V-T To **evacuate** someone means to send them to a place of safety, away from a dangerous building, town, or area. 疏散; 使…撤离 ❑ *They were planning to evacuate the seventy American officials still in the country.* 他们当时在计划将仍在那个国家的70位美国官员撤离。 ● **evacu·ation** ▲ /ɪvækyueɪʃᵊn/ N-VAR (**evacuations**) 疏散; 撤离 ❑ *...the evacuation of the sick and wounded.* …伤病员的撤离。 ❑ *An evacuation of the city's four-million inhabitants is planned for later this week.* 该市400万居民的撤离计划本周晚些时候进行。 **2** V-T If people **evacuate** a place, they move out of it for a period of time, especially because it is dangerous. (尤指因为危险而) 撤离 ❑ *The fire is threatening about sixty homes, and residents have evacuated the area.* 这场大火威胁着约六十个家庭，居民已经撤离了该地区。 ● **evacu·ation** N-VAR (**evacuations**) 撤离 ❑ *...the mass evacuation of the Bosnian town of Srebrenica.* …波斯尼亚的斯雷布雷尼察镇大撤离。

evac·uee /ɪvækyui/ (**evacuees**) N-COUNT An **evacuee** is someone who has been sent away from a dangerous place to somewhere safe, especially during a war. (尤指战争时期) 撤离者

▲ **evade** /ɪveɪd/ (**evades, evading, evaded**) **1** V-T If you **evade** something, you find a way of not doing something that you really ought to do. 逃避 ❑ *By his own admission, he evaded paying taxes as a Florida real-estate speculator.* 据他自己承认，他作为佛罗里达房地产投机商时逃过税。 **2** V-T If you **evade** a question or a topic, you avoid talking about it or dealing with it. 回避 (问题、话题) ❑ *Too many companies, she says, are evading the issue.* 她说太多公司都在回避这个问题。 **3** V-T If you **evade** someone or something, you move so that you can avoid meeting them or avoid being touched or hit. 避开 ❑ *She turned and gazed at the river, evading his eyes.* 她转身注视着那条河，避开了他的目光。

e

evalu·ate /ɪvæ̲lyueɪt/ (**evaluates, evaluating, evaluated**) V-T If you **evaluate** something or someone, you consider them in order to make a judgment about them, for example about how good or bad they are. 评价；评估 ❑ *The market situation is difficult to evaluate.* 市场形势难以评估。 ● **evalu·ation** /ɪvæ̲lyueɪʃᵊn/ N-VAR (**evaluations**) 评价；评估 ❑ *...the opinions and evaluations of college supervisors.* …学院督导们的意见和评价。

★ **evapo·rate** /ɪvæ̲pəreɪt/ (**evaporates, evaporating, evaporated**) 1 V-T/V-I When a liquid **evaporates**, or **is evaporated**, it changes from a liquid state to a gas, because its temperature has increased. 使…蒸发；蒸发 ❑ *Moisture is drawn to the surface of the fabric so that it evaporates.* 湿气被吸到织物表面而蒸发。 ❑ *The water is evaporated by the sun.* 水被太阳照射而蒸发。 ● **evapo·ra·tion** /ɪvæ̲pəreɪʃᵊn/ N-UNCOUNT 蒸发 ❑ *The soothing, cooling effect is caused by the evaporation of the sweat on the skin.* 凉爽怡人的效果是由皮肤上汗液挥发所致。 2 V-I If a feeling, plan, or activity **evaporates**, it gradually becomes weaker and eventually disappears completely. (情绪、计划、活动) 逐渐消逝 ❑ *My anger evaporated and I wanted to cry.* 我的怒气渐渐消了，就想哭了。

→ see **matter, sweat, water**

eva·sion /ɪveɪ̲ʒᵊn/ (**evasions**) 1 N-VAR **Evasion** means deliberately avoiding something that you are supposed to do or deal with. 逃避 ❑ *He was arrested for tax evasion.* 他因逃税被捕。 2 N-VAR If you accuse someone of **evasion** when they have been asked a question, you mean that they are deliberately avoiding giving a clear direct answer. 避而不谈 ❑ *We want straight answers. No evasions.* 我们要直接的答复。不要绕弯。

eva·sive /ɪveɪ̲sɪv/ 1 ADJ If you describe someone as **evasive**, you mean that they deliberately avoid giving clear direct answers to questions. 避而不谈的 ❑ *He was evasive about the circumstances of his first meeting with Stanley Dean.* 他对与斯坦利·迪安第一次见面的情形避而不谈。 ● **eva·sive·ly** ADV 避而不谈地 [ADV with V] ❑ *"Until I can speak to your husband I can't come to any conclusion about that," Manuel said evasively.* "关于那件事情我要跟你丈夫谈了之后才能作出结论，" 曼纽尔托辞说。 2 PHRASE If you **take evasive action**, you deliberately move away from someone or something in order to avoid meeting them or being hit by them. 采取退避行动 ❑ *At least four high-flying warplanes had to take evasive action.* 至少有4架高空飞行战机不得不采取退避行动。

eve /i̲v/ (**eves**) 1 N-COUNT **The eve of** a particular event or occasion is the day before it, or the period of time just before it. 前一天；前夕 ❑ *...on the eve of his 27th birthday.* …在他27岁生日的前夕。 2 → see also **Christmas Eve, New Year's Eve**

even
❶ DISCOURSE USES
❷ ADJECTIVE USES
❸ PHRASAL VERB USE

❶ **even** ♦♦♦ /i̲vᵊn/ 1 ADV You use **even** to suggest that what comes just after or just before it in the sentence is rather surprising. 甚至；连 ❑ *He kept calling me for years, even after he got married.* 他多年来不断给我打电话，甚至到他结婚以后。 ❑ *Even dark-skinned women should use sunscreens.* 就连肤色黑的女性也应该用防晒油。 2 ADV You use **even** with comparative adjectives and adverbs to emphasize a quality that someone or something has. (与比较级连用) 更加 [ADV compar] [EMPHASIS] ❑ *On television he made an even stronger impact as an interviewer.* 他作为采访者在电视上造成了更大的影响。 3 PHRASE You use **even if** or **even though** to indicate that a particular fact does not make the rest of your statement untrue. 即使 ❑ *Cynthia is not ashamed of what she does, even if she ends up doing something wrong.* 辛西娅并不为她所做的事感到惭愧，即使她最终把事情做错。 4 PHRASE You use **even so** to introduce a surprising fact that relates to what you have just said. 即便如此；尽管这样 [SPOKEN] ❑ *The bus was only half full. Even so, a young man asked Nina if the seat next to her was taken.* 公共汽车上只坐满了一半，即便如此，一个小伙子还问尼娜她旁边的座位有没有人坐。 5 PHRASE You use **even then** to say that something is the case in spite of what has just been stated or whatever the circumstances may be. 即便那样 ❑ *Peace could come only gradually, in carefully measured steps. Even then, it sounds almost impossible to achieve.* 和平只能以谨慎的步伐逐步到来。即便那样，它听起来还是几乎不可能实现。

❷ **even** ♦♦♦ /i̲vᵊn/
➪ **Please look at meaning 8 to see if the expression you are looking for is shown under another headword.** 1 ADJ An **even** measurement or rate stays at about the same level. 保持不变的 ❑ *How important is it to have an even temperature when you're working?* 工作时保持恒温有多重要？ ● ★ **even·ly** ADV 保持不变地 ❑ *He looked at Ellen, breathing evenly in her sleep.* 他看着在睡梦中呼吸均匀的埃伦。 2 ADJ An **even** surface is smooth and flat. 平滑的 ❑ *The tables are fitted with a glass top to provide an even surface.* 那些桌子都装有玻璃台面以提供平滑的表面。 3 ADJ If there is an **even** distribution or division of something, each person, group, or area involved has an equal amount. 均等的 ❑ *Divide the dough into 12 even pieces and shape each piece into a ball.* 把面团分为12等份并把每一块面团揉成球形。 ● **even·ly** ADV 均等地 ❑ *The meat is divided evenly and boiled in a stew.* 肉被均等地切开并在锅里炖。 4 ADJ An **even** contest or competition is equally balanced between the two sides who are taking part. 实力相当的 ❑ *It was an even game.* 这是一场势均力敌的比赛。 ● **even·ly** ADV 实力相当地 [ADV -ed] ❑ *They must choose between two evenly matched candidates for governor.* 他们必须从两个不相上下的候选人中选出州长。 5 ADJ An **even** number can be divided exactly by the number two. 偶数的 6 ADJ If there is an **even** chance that something will happen, the chances that it will or will not happen are equal. (机会) 各半的 [ADJ n] ❑ *They have a more than even chance of winning the next election.* 他们在下次竞选中有过半的胜机。 7 PHRASE When a company or a person running a business **breaks even**, they make neither a profit nor a loss. 盈亏平衡 [BUSINESS] ❑ *The airline hopes to break even next year and return to profit the following year.* 该航空公司希望来年盈亏平衡，并在随后一年重新开始盈利。 8 **to be on an even keel** → see **keel**

❸ **even** /i̲vᵊn/ (**evens, evening, evened**)
▸ **even out** PHRASAL VERB If something **evens out**, or if you **even** it **out**, the differences between the different parts of it are reduced. 使…持平；持平 ❑ *The power-balance has evened out in the interim government.* 临时政府内的权力平衡已持平。

eve·ning ♦♦◊ /i̲vnɪŋ/ (**evenings**) N-VAR The **evening** is the part of each day between the end of the afternoon and the time when you go to bed. 傍晚；晚上 ❑ *All he did that evening was sit around the house.* 那天晚上他所做的就是闲坐在家里。 ❑ *Supper is from 5:00 to 6:00 in the evening.* 晚餐是在傍晚5至6点间。

eve·ning class (**evening classes**) N-COUNT An **evening class** is a class for adults that is taught in the evening rather than during the day. 夜校 ❑ *He's trying to learn English fast with evening classes twice a week.* 他在努力通过一周上两次夜校来快速学习英语。

event ♦♦♦ /ɪve̲nt/ (**events**) 1 N-COUNT An **event** is something that happens, especially when it is unusual or important. You can use **events** to describe all the things that are happening in a particular situation. (尤指特殊、重大) 事件 ❑ *A new inquiry into the events of the day was opened in 2002.* 对那天发生的事件的新一轮调查于2002年开始。 2 N-COUNT An **event** is a planned and organized occasion, for example a social gathering or a sports tournament. (有计划、有组织的) 活动 ❑ *...major sporting events.* …重大体育赛事。 3 N-COUNT An **event** is one of the races or competitions that are part of an organized occasion such as a sports tournament. 比赛项目 ❑ *The main events start at 1 p.m.* 主赛项目下午1点开始。 4 PHRASE You use **in the event of, in the event that,** and **in that event** when you are talking about a possible future situation, especially when you are planning what to do if it occurs. 倘若发生… ❑ *The bank has agreed to give an immediate refund in the unlikely event of an error being made.* 银行已同意倘若出现不太可能的错误便立即退款。 5 PHRASE You say **in any event** after you have been discussing a situation, in order to indicate that what you are saying is true or possible, in spite of anything that has happened or may happen. 不管怎样 ❑ *In any event, the bowling alley restaurant proved quite acceptable.* 不管怎样，那家保龄球馆的餐厅证明是很受欢迎的。

→ see **history**

Thesaurus	*event* 另参见：
N.	happening, occasion, occurrence 1 competition, contest, game, meet, tournament 3

event·ful /ɪve̲ntfəl/ ADJ If you describe an event or a period of time as **eventful**, you mean that a lot of interesting, exciting, or important things have happened during it. 充满 (有趣、重要)

事件的 ❑ *This has been an eventful year for Tom, both professionally and personally.* 不论在事业方面还是在个人方面，对汤姆来说这一年都是有着许多重大变化的一年。

even·tual /ɪvɛntʃuəl/ ADJ You use **eventual** to indicate that something happens or is the case at the end of a process or period of time. 最终的 [ADJ n] ❑ *There are many who believe that civil war will be the eventual outcome of the racial tension in the country.* 有许多人认为内战将是该国种族关系紧张的最终结果。

even·tu·al·ity /ɪvɛntʃuælɪti/ (**eventualities**) N-COUNT An **eventuality** is a possible future event or result, especially one that is unpleasant or surprising. 可能发生的(尤指不测)事件；可能的后果 [FORMAL] ❑ *Every eventuality is covered, from running out of gas to needing water.* 从耗尽汽油到缺水，所有可能的后果都考虑到了。

even·tu·al·ly ♦♦◊ /ɪvɛntʃuəli/ **1** ADV **Eventually** means in the end, especially after a lot of delays, problems, or arguments. 终于 ❑ *Eventually, the army caught up with him in Latvia.* 部队终于在拉脱维亚追上了他。 **2** ADV **Eventually** means at the end of a situation or process or as the final result of it. 最终 ❑ *Eventually your child will leave home to lead her own life as a fully independent adult.* 你的孩子最终会离开家，作为完全独立的成年人过她自己的日子。

> Do not confuse **eventually** and **finally**. When something happens after a lot of delays or complications, you can say that it **eventually** happens. ❑ *Eventually they got to the hospital... I found Victoria Avenue eventually.* You can also use **eventually** to talk about what happens at the end of a series of events, often as a result of them. ❑ *Eventually, they were forced to return to Chicago.* You say that something **finally** happens after you have been waiting for it or expecting it for a long time. ❑ *Finally I went to bed... The heat of the sun finally became too much for me.* You can also use **finally** to show that something happens last in a series of events. ❑ *The sky turned red, then purple, and finally black.*

ever ♦♦♦ /ɛvər/

> **Ever** is an adverb that you use to add emphasis in negative sentences, commands, questions, and conditional structures.

1 ADV **Ever** means at any time. It is used in questions and negative statements. 在任何时候(用于否定句和疑问句) ❑ *I'm not sure I'll ever trust people again.* 我不确定我会不会再相信人。 ❑ *Neither of us had ever skied.* 我们俩谁也没有滑过雪。 **2** ADV You use **ever** in expressions such as "**did you ever**" and "**have you ever**" to express surprise or shock at something you have just seen, heard, or experienced, especially when you expect people to agree with you. 曾经(表示惊讶) [EMPHASIS] ❑ *Have you ever seen anything like it?* 你可曾见过像这样的东西？ **3** ADV You use **ever** after comparatives and superlatives to emphasize the degree to which something is true or when you are comparing a present situation with the past or the future. 以往任何时候(用于形容词或副词的比较级和最高级之后) [EMPHASIS] ❑ *She's got a great voice and is singing better than ever.* 她有一副好嗓音，比以往任何时候都唱得好。 ❑ *Japan is wealthier and more powerful than ever before.* 日本现在比以往任何时候都富有和强大。

> Do not confuse **ever** and **always**. You use **ever**, for example in negative sentences, questions, and with superlatives, to talk about any time at all when referring to the past, present, or future. ❑ *No one ever came... Will I ever see France? ...the nicest thing anyone's ever said to me.* If something **always** happens, it happens regularly or on every occasion. ❑ *I would always ask for the radio to be turned down... He's always been an active person.* If something **is always** the case, it is true at all times. ❑ *No matter what she did, she would always be forgiven.*

4 ADV You use **ever** to say that something happens more all the time. 愈发 [ADV adj/adv] ❑ *They grew ever further apart.* 他们愈发疏远了。 **5** ADV You can use **ever** for emphasis after "never." 绝不(用于"**never**"后，表示强调) [ADV before v] [INFORMAL, EMPHASIS] ❑ *I can never, ever, forgive myself.* 我绝不能原谅自己。 **6** ADV You use **ever** in questions beginning with words such as "why," "when," and "who" when you want to emphasize your surprise or shock. 究竟(用于特殊疑问句以强调语气) [quest ADV] [EMPHASIS] ❑ *Why ever didn't you tell me?* 你究竟为何不告诉我？ **7** PHRASE If something has been the case **ever since** a particular time, it has been the case all the time from then until now. 自从 ❑ *He's been there ever since you left!* 自从你离开，他一直都在那儿！ ● ADV **Ever** is also an adverb. 从此 ❑ *I simply gave in to him, and I've regretted it ever since.* 我当时完全向他屈服了，从此我为此事后悔不迭。 **8** → see also **forever** **9** PHRASE You use the expression **all** someone **ever does** when you want to emphasize that they do the same thing all the time, and this annoys you. (某人)只会… [EMPHASIS] ❑ *All she ever does is complain.* 她就会抱怨。 **10** PHRASE You say **as ever** in order to indicate that something or someone's behavior is not unusual because it is like that all the time or very often. 一如既往 ❑ *As ever, the meals are primarily fish-based.* 像往常那样，餐餐以鱼类为主。 **11** **hardly ever** → see **hardly**

> **Word Partnership** *ever* 的常用搭配：
>
> V. ever **forget**, ever **known**, ever **made**, ever **seen** **1**
> **have you** ever **2**
> ADV. ever **again** **1**
> **better than** ever, ever **more**, **more than** ever **3**
> **never** ever **5**
> **hardly** ever **11**
> ADJ. **best** ever **3**

ever- /ɛvər-/ COMB IN ADJ You use **ever** in adjectives such as **ever-increasing** and **ever-present**, to show that something exists or continues all the time. 一直(用于构成形容词，表示持续的状态) ❑ *...the ever-increasing traffic on our roads.* …道路上不断增长的交通量。

▲ **ever·green** /ɛvərgrin/ (**evergreens**) N-COUNT An **evergreen** is a tree or bush that has green leaves all year long. 常青树；常绿植物 ❑ *Holly, like ivy and mistletoe, is an evergreen.* 冬青与常春藤和槲寄生一样，也是一种常绿植物。 ● ADJ **Evergreen** is also an adjective. 常绿的 ❑ *Plant evergreen shrubs around the end of the month.* 大约在月末种植常绿灌木。

every ♦♦♦ /ɛvri/ **1** DET You use **every** to indicate that you are referring to all the members of a group or all the parts of something and not only some of them. 每个 ❑ *Every room has a window facing the ocean.* 每个房间都有一扇面对大海的窗。 ❑ *Record every expenditure you make.* 记下你的每笔花销。 ● ADJ **Every** is also an adjective. 每个的 [poss ADJ n] ❑ *His every utterance will be scrutinized.* 他说的每句话都会被细查。 **2** DET You use **every** in order to say how often something happens or to indicate that something happens at regular intervals. (时间段)每隔…的 ❑ *We were made to attend meetings every day.* 我们每天都被迫参加会议。 ❑ *A burglary occurs every three minutes in London.* 入室盗窃案在伦敦每3分钟就发生一起。 **3** DET You use **every** in front of a number when you are saying what proportion of people or things something happens to or applies to. (一定数目中)每…之中的 ❑ *Two out of every three people have a cell phone.* 每3人中有2人有一部手机。 **4** DET You can use **every** before some nouns, for example "sign," "effort," "reason," and "intention" in order to emphasize what you are saying. 全部的(用于某些名词前，表示强调) [EMPHASIS] ❑ *The Congressional Budget Office says the federal deficit shows every sign of getting larger.* 国会预算办公室称联邦赤字显示出种种增加的迹象。 ❑ *I think that there is every chance that you will succeed.* 我认为你完全有机会成功。 **5** ADJ If you say that someone's **every** whim, wish, or desire will be satisfied, you are emphasizing that everything they want will happen or be provided. (幻想、愿望)所有可能的 [poss ADJ n] [EMPHASIS] ❑ *Dozens of servants had catered to his every whim.* 几十个仆人曾迎合他所有离奇的想法。

> You use **every** to refer to all the members of a group that has more than two members. ❑ *He listened to every news bulletin. ...an equal chance for every child.* You use **each** to refer to every person or thing in a group when you are thinking about them as individuals. Note that **each** can be used to refer to both members of a pair. ❑ *Each apartment has two bedrooms... We each carried a suitcase.* Note that **each** and **every** are only used with singular nouns.

6 PHRASE You use **every** in the expressions **every now and then**, **every now and again**, **every once in a while**, and **every so often** in order to indicate that something happens occasionally. 不时；间或 ❑ *Stir the batter every now and then to keep it from separating.* 不时地搅拌面糊以防止其成分相分离。 **7** PHRASE If something happens **every other day** or **every second day**, for example, it happens one day, then does not happen the next day, then happens the day after that, and so on. You can also say that something happens **every third week**, **every fourth year**, and so on. 每隔(一天、一周等) ❑ *I went home every other week.* 我每隔一周回一次家。 **8** **every bit as good as** → see **bit**

every·body ♦♦◇ /ɛvribɒdi, -bʌdi/ **Everybody** means the same as **everyone**. 每人

every·day /ɛvrideɪ/ ADJ You use **everyday** to describe something that happens or is used every day, or forms a regular and basic part of your life, so it is not especially interesting or unusual. 日常的 ❑ *In the course of my everyday life, I had very little contact with teenagers.* 在我的日常生活中，我与青少年少有接触。

every·one ♦♦◇ /ɛvriwʌn/

The form **everybody** is also used.

1 PRON-INDEF You use **everyone** or **everybody** to refer to all the people in a particular group. (某群体中的) 所有人 ❑ *Everyone on the street was shocked when they heard the news.* 听到这个消息，街上所有人都感到震惊。 ❑ *Not everyone thinks that the government is being particularly generous.* 并不是所有人都认为政府是在特别慷慨。 2 PRON-INDEF You use **everyone** or **everybody** to refer to all people. 人人 ❑ *Everyone wrestles with self-doubt and feels like a failure at times.* 人人都会有与不自信作斗争、感觉自己是个失败者的时候。 ❑ *Everyone needs some free time for rest and relaxation.* 人人都需要一些休息和放松的空闲时间。

Do not confuse **everyone** with **every one**. **Everyone** always refers to people. In the phrase **every one**, "one" is a pronoun that can refer to any person or thing, depending on the context. It is often followed by the word **of**. ❑ *We've saved seeds from every one of our plants... Every one of them phoned me.* In these examples, **every one** is a more emphatic way of saying **all**.

every·place /ɛvripleɪs/ → see **everywhere**

every·thing ♦♦♦ /ɛvriθɪŋ/ 1 PRON-INDEF You use **everything** to refer to all the objects, actions, activities, or facts in a particular situation. (某种情形中的) 每件事物 ❑ *He'd gone to Seattle long after everything else in his life had changed.* 他生活中其他方面都改变了很久之后他去了西雅图。 2 PRON-INDEF You use **everything** to refer to all possible or likely actions, activities, or situations. 所有事物 ❑ *"This should have been decided long before now."—"We can't think of everything."* "这在此前早该定下了。"——"我们不可能事事都考虑。" ❑ *Najib and I do everything together.* 纳吉布和我什么事情都一起做。 3 PRON-INDEF You use **everything** to refer to a whole situation or to life in general. 一切情况；整体生活 ❑ *She says everything is going smoothly.* 她说一切进展顺利。 ❑ *Is everything all right?* 一切都好吗？ 4 PRON-INDEF If you say that someone or something is **everything**, you mean you consider them to be the most important thing in your life, or the most important thing that there is. 至关重要的事物 ❑ *I love him. He is everything to me.* 我爱他。他对我来说比什么都重要。 5 PRON-INDEF If you say that someone or something has **everything**, you mean they have all the things or qualities that most people consider to be desirable. 一切 (值得要的东西) ❑ *This man had everything. He had the house, the sailboat and a full life with friends and family.* 这个男人拥有一切。他有房子、帆船以及亲朋相伴的圆满生活。

every·where ♦◇◇ /ɛvriwɛər/ or **everyplace** 1 ADV You use **everywhere** to refer to a whole area or to all the places in a particular area. (某区域内的) 所有地方；各地 ❑ *Working people everywhere object to paying taxes.* 各地劳动人民都反对纳税。 ❑ *We went everywhere together.* 我们到哪里都一起去。 2 ADV You use **everywhere** to refer to all the places that someone goes to. 所到之处 ❑ *Mary Jo is still accustomed to traveling everywhere in style.* 玛丽·乔仍然习惯于很有气派地到处旅行。 3 ADV You use **everywhere** to emphasize that you are talking about a large number of places, or all possible places. 到处 (强调地方之多或所有可能的地方) [EMPHASIS] ❑ *I saw her picture everywhere.* 我到处看到她的照片。 4 ADV If you say that someone or something is **everywhere**, you mean that they are present in a place in very large numbers. 遍地 (强调在某地数量之多)；到处 ❑ *There were cartons of cigarettes everywhere.* 到处都是香烟盒。

evict /ɪvɪkt/ (**evicts, evicting, evicted**) V-T If someone **is evicted from** the place where they are living, they are forced to leave it, usually because they have broken a law or contract. 驱逐 ❑ *They were evicted from their apartment after their mother became addicted to drugs.* 他们的母亲染上毒瘾后，他们就被逐出了他们的公寓。 ❑ *In the first week, the city police evicted ten families.* 在第1周里，该市警方驱逐了10户家庭。

evic·tion /ɪvɪkʃən/ (**evictions**) N-VAR **Eviction** is the act or process of officially forcing someone to leave a house or piece of land. 驱逐 ❑ *He was facing eviction, along with his wife and family.* 他及其妻儿正面临着被驱逐。

evi·dence ♦♦◇ /ɛvɪdəns/ 1 N-UNCOUNT **Evidence** is anything that you see, experience, read, or are told that causes you to believe that something is true or has really happened. 证据；依据 ❑ *Ganley said he'd seen no evidence of widespread fraud.* 甘利说他没有看见欺骗行为泛滥的证据。 2 N-UNCOUNT **Evidence** is the information that is used in a court of law to try to prove something. Evidence is obtained from documents, objects, or witnesses. (法律上的) 证据 [LEGAL] ❑ *The evidence against him was purely circumstantial.* 不利于他的证据纯粹是间接证据。 3 PHRASE If you **give evidence** in a court of law or an official inquiry, you officially say what you know about people or events, or describe an occasion at which you were present. (在法庭上或官方调查中) 作证 ❑ *The forensic scientists who carried out the original tests will be called to give evidence.* 那些进行了原始化验的法医学家们将被叫去作证。 4 PHRASE If someone or something **is in evidence**, they are present and can be clearly seen. 显然可见 ❑ *Few soldiers were in evidence.* 几乎看不见有士兵。 → see **experiment, trial**

Word Partnership *evidence* 的常用搭配：

V. **find** evidence, **gather** evidence, **present** evidence, **produce** evidence, evidence **to support** ***something*** 1 2

ADJ. **new** evidence, **physical** evidence, **scientific** evidence 1 2 **circumstantial** evidence 2

evi·dent /ɛvɪdənt/ 1 ADJ If something is **evident**, you notice it easily and clearly. 清晰易见的 ❑ *His footprints were clearly evident in the heavy dust.* 他的脚印在厚厚的灰尘中清晰可见。 ❑ *The threat of inflation is already evident in bond prices.* 通货膨胀的威胁在证券价格上已经是明显可见的。 2 ADJ You use **evident** to show that you are certain about a situation or fact and your interpretation of it. 显然的 [EMPHASIS] ❑ *It was evident that she had once been a beauty.* 很显然的，她曾经是个美人。 3 → see also **self-evident**

evi·dent·ly /ɛvɪdəntli, -dɛnt-/ 1 ADV You use **evidently** to say that something is obviously true, for example, because you have seen evidence of it yourself. 毫无疑问地；显然 ❑ *The man wore a bathrobe and had evidently just come from the bathroom.* 那人穿着浴袍，显然刚从浴室出来。 2 ADV You use **evidently** to show that you think something is true or have been told something is true, but that you are not sure, because you do not have enough information or proof. 明显地 (但没有足够证据支持) ❑ *From childhood, he was evidently at once rebellious and precocious.* 他从小就明显地又叛逆又早熟。 3 ADV You can use **evidently** to introduce a statement or opinion and to emphasize that you feel that it is true or correct. 显然 (用以引出陈述或观点，强调主观感觉的正确性) [ADV with cl] [FORMAL, EMPHASIS] ❑ *Evidently, it has nothing to do with social background.* 显然，这与社会背景毫无关系。

evil ♦◇◇ /ivəl/ (**evils**) 1 N-UNCOUNT **Evil** is a powerful force that some people believe to exist, and that causes wicked and bad things to happen. 恶；邪恶 ❑ *There's always a conflict between good and evil in his plays.* 他的戏剧中总是有善与恶的冲突。 2 N-UNCOUNT **Evil** is used to refer to all the wicked and bad things that happen in the world. 恶行 ❑ *He could not, after all, stop all the evil in the world.* 他毕竟不能阻止世上所有的恶行。 3 N-COUNT If you refer to an **evil**, you mean a very unpleasant or harmful situation or activity. 不愉快的事；有害的事 ❑ *Higher taxes may be a necessary evil.* 提高税率虽不是件令人愉快的事，但可能是必要的。 4 ADJ If you describe someone as **evil**, you mean that they are very wicked by nature and take pleasure in doing things that harm other people. 邪恶的；凶恶的 ❑ *...the country's most evil terrorists.* …该国最凶恶的恐怖分子。 5 ADJ If you describe something as **evil**, you mean that you think it causes a great deal of harm to people and is morally bad. 伤天害理的 ❑ *A judge yesterday condemned heroin as evil.* 一名法官昨天谴责海洛因伤天害理。 6 ADJ If you describe something as **evil**, you mean that you think it is influenced by the devil. 受恶魔影响的 ❑ *I think this is an evil spirit at work.* 我想这是恶魔在作祟。 7 PHRASE If you have two choices, but think that they are both bad, you can describe the less bad one as **the lesser of two evils**, or **the lesser evil**. 两害之中的轻者 ❑ *People voted for him as the lesser of two evils.* 人们投票选他只是出于两害相权取其轻罢了。

evoca·tive /ɪvɒkətɪv/ ADJ If you describe something as **evocative**, you mean that it is good or interesting because it produces pleasant memories, ideas, emotions, and responses in people. 唤起回忆的；引起共鸣的 [FORMAL] ❑ *Her story is sharply evocative of Italian provincial life.* 她的故事鲜明地唤起意大利乡村生活的回忆。

★ **evoke** /ɪvoʊk/ (**evokes, evoking, evoked**) V-T To **evoke** a particular memory, idea, emotion, or response means to cause it to occur. 唤起（记忆）；引起（想法、情感、反应）[FORMAL] ❑ *...the scene evoking memories of those old movies.* …唤起对那些老电影的记忆的场景。

evo·lu·tion /ivəluʃən, ɛv-/ (**evolutions**) 1 N-UNCOUNT **Evolution** is a process of gradual change that takes place over many generations, during which species of animals, plants, or insects slowly change some of their physical characteristics. 进化 ❑ *...the evolution of plants and animals.* …动植物的进化。 2 N-VAR **Evolution** is a process of gradual development in a particular situation or thing over a period of time. 演化；发展 [FORMAL] ❑ *...a crucial period in the evolution of modern physics.* …现代物理学发展过程中的一个关键时期。

→ see **earth**

evo·lu·tion·ary /ivəluʃənɛri/ ADJ **Evolutionary** means relating to a process of gradual change and development. 进化的 ❑ *...an evolutionary process.* …一个进化过程。

evolve /ɪvɒlv/ (**evolves, evolving, evolved**) 1 V-I When animals or plants **evolve**, they gradually change and develop into different forms. 进化 ❑ *The bright plumage of many male birds was thought to have evolved to attract females.* 许多雄鸟的鲜艳羽毛被认为是为吸引雌鸟而进化来的。 ❑ *Birds are widely believed to have evolved from dinosaurs.* 鸟类普遍被认为是从恐龙进化而来的。 2 V-T/V-I If something **evolves** or you **evolve** it, it gradually develops over a period of time into something different and usually more advanced. 使…逐步发展；逐步发展 ❑ *...a tiny airline which eventually evolved into Pakistan International Airlines.* …最终发展成为巴基斯坦国际航空公司的一家小型航空公司。 ❑ *Popular music evolved from folk songs.* 流行音乐由民歌演变而来。

→ see **earth**

ewe /yu/ (**ewes**) N-COUNT A **ewe** is an adult female sheep. 母羊

ex·ac·er·bate /ɪgzæsərbeɪt/ (**exacerbates, exacerbating, exacerbated**) V-T If something **exacerbates** a problem or bad situation, it makes it worse. 使…恶化 [FORMAL] ❑ *Longstanding poverty has been exacerbated by racial divisions.* 由来已久的贫穷因种族分裂而更加恶化了。 ● **ex·ac·er·ba·tion** /ɪgzæsərbeɪʃən/ N-UNCOUNT 恶化 ❑ *...the exacerbation of global problems.* …全球问题的恶化。

ex·act ♦♦◊ /ɪgzækt/ (**exacts, exacting, exacted**) 1 ADJ **Exact** means correct in every detail. For example, an **exact** copy is the same in every detail as the thing it is copied from. 精确的；确切的 ❑ *I don't remember the exact words.* 我不记得确切的话了。 ❑ *The exact number of protest calls has not been revealed.* 抗议电话的确切次数尚未披露。 ● **ex·act·ly** ADV 精确地；确切地 ❑ *Try to locate exactly where the smells are entering the room.* 设法确定气味是从哪里进入房间的。 ❑ *Both drugs will be exactly the same.* 两种药将会完全一样。 2 ADJ You use **exact** before a noun to emphasize that you are referring to that particular thing and no other, especially something that has a particular significance. 正好的（用于名词前表示强调）[ADJ n] [EMPHASIS] ❑ *I hadn't really thought about it until this exact moment.* 一直到此时此刻我才真正考虑它。 ● **ex·act·ly** ADV 正好 [ADV n/wh] ❑ *These are exactly the people who do not vote.* 这些正好是那些不投票的人。 3 V-T When someone **exacts** something, they demand and obtain it from another person, especially because they are in a superior or more powerful position. （尤指因处于上级地位而）强行要求并获得 [FORMAL] ❑ *Already he has exacted a written apology from the chairman of the commission.* 他已经通过强行要求得到了委员会主席的书面道歉。 4 V-T If someone **exacts** revenge **on** a person, they have their revenge on them. 实施 ❑ *She uses the media to help her exact a terrible revenge.* 她利用媒体帮助她实施一次可怕的报复。 5 V-T If something **exacts** a high price, it has a bad effect on a person or situation. 使…付出（代价）❑ *The sheer physical effort had exacted a heavy price.* 纯粹的体力支出已付出了沉重的代价。 6 → see also **exactly** 7 PHRASE You say **to be exact** to indicate that you are slightly correcting or giving more detailed information about what you have been saying. 确切地说 ❑ *A small number – five, to be exact – have been bad.* 一个小数目——确切地说是5——已经很糟了。

Thesaurus *exact* 另参见：

ADJ. accurate, clear, precise, true; *(ant.)* inexact, wrong 1

Word Partnership *exact* 的常用搭配：

N. exact **change**, exact **duplicate**, exact **number**, exact **opposite**, exact **replica**, exact **science**, exact **words** 1
exact **cause**, exact **location**, exact **moment** 2
exact **revenge** 4

ex·act·ing /ɪgzæktɪŋ/ ADJ You use **exacting** to describe something or someone that demands hard work and a great deal of care. 费劲的；难办的 ❑ *She didn't think that he was well enough to carry out such an exacting task.* 她认为他身体不是很好，不能执行如此艰巨的任务。

ex·act·ly ♦◊◊ /ɪgzæktli/ 1 ADV You use **exactly** before an amount, number, or position to emphasize that it is no more, no less, or no different from what you are stating. 恰好 [EMPHASIS] ❑ *Each corner had a guard tower, each of which was exactly ten meters in height.* 每个角都有1个警戒塔，每个塔刚好10米高。 2 ADV If you say "**Exactly**," you are agreeing with someone or emphasizing the truth of what they say. If you say "**Not exactly**," you are telling them politely that they are wrong in part of what they are saying. 正是如此 [ADV as reply] ❑ *Eve nodded, almost approvingly. "Exactly."* 伊夫几近赞许地点点头。"正是如此。" 3 ADV You use **not exactly** to indicate that a meaning or situation is slightly different from what people think or expect. 不完全是 [VAGUENESS] ❑ *He's not exactly homeless, he just hangs out in this park.* 他不完全是无家可归，他只是常住在这个公园里。 4 ADV You can use **not exactly** to show that you mean the opposite of what you are saying. 根本不；并非 [EMPHASIS] ❑ *This was not exactly what I wanted to hear.* 这根本不是我想听的。 5 ADV You use **exactly** with a question to show that you disapprove of what the person you are talking to is doing or saying. 到底（用于质问）[ADV with quest] [DISAPPROVAL] ❑ *What exactly do you mean?* 你到底什么意思？ 6 → see also **exact**

ex·ag·ger·ate /ɪgzædʒəreɪt/ (**exaggerates, exaggerating, exaggerated**) 1 V-T/V-I If you **exaggerate**, you indicate that something is, for example, worse or more important than it really is. 夸大 ❑ *He thinks I'm exaggerating.* 他认为我在夸大其词。 ● **ex·ag·gera·tion** /ɪgzædʒəreɪʃən/ N-VAR (**exaggerations**) 夸大 ❑ *Like many stories about him, it smacks of exaggeration.* 像很多有关他的故事一样，这个也有点儿夸大的意味。 2 V-T If something **exaggerates** a situation, quality, or feature, it makes the situation, quality, or feature appear greater, more obvious, or more important than it really is. 夸大 ❑ *These figures exaggerate the loss of competitiveness.* 这些数字夸大了竞争力的下降。

ex·ag·ger·at·ed /ɪgzædʒəreɪtɪd/ ADJ Something that is **exaggerated** is or seems larger, better, worse, or more important than it actually needs to be. 夸大了的 ❑ *Western fears, he insists, are greatly exaggerated.* 他坚持认为西方的担忧被高度夸大了。

Word Link *alt* ≈ *high* : *altar, altitude, exalted*

ex·alt·ed /ɪgzɔltɪd/ ADJ Someone or something that is at an **exalted** level is at a very high level, especially with regard to rank or importance. （地位、重要性）很高的 [FORMAL] ❑ *You must decide how to make the best use of your exalted position.* 你必须决定如何充分利用你的显赫地位。

exam /ɪgzæm/ (**exams**) 1 N-COUNT An **exam** is a formal test that you take to show your knowledge or ability in a particular subject, or to obtain a qualification. 考试 ❑ *I don't want to take any more exams.* 我不想再参加任何考试。 2 N-COUNT If you have a medical **exam**, a doctor looks at your body, feels it, or does simple tests in order to check how healthy you are. （健康状况）检查 [mainly AM] ❑ *These medical exams have shown I am in perfect physical condition.* 这些体检已表明我健康状况非常好。

ex·ami·na·tion ♦◊◊ /ɪgzæmɪneɪʃən/ (**examinations**) 1 N-COUNT An **examination** is a formal test that you take to show your knowledge or ability in a particular subject, or to obtain a qualification. 考试 [FORMAL] ❑ *...college examination results.* …大学考试成绩。 2 → see also **examine** 3 N-COUNT If you have a medical **examination**, a doctor looks at your body, feels it, or does simple tests in order to check how healthy you are. （健康状况）检查 ❑ *You must see your doctor for a thorough examination.* 你必须去看医生，做个全面体检。

→ see **diagnosis**

ex·am·ine ♦♦◊ /ɪgzæmɪn/ (**examines, examining, examined**) 1 V-T If you **examine** something, you look at it carefully. 仔细检查 ❑ *He examined her passport and stamped it.* 他仔细检查了她的护照，

然后在上面盖了章。● **ex·ami·na·tion** /ɪgzæmɪneɪʃ ͤn/ N-VAR (**examinations**) 仔细检查 ❑ *The navy is to carry out an examination of the wreck tomorrow.* 海军明天将会对失事船只作仔细检查。 **2** V-T If a doctor **examines** you, he or she looks at your body, feels it, or does simple tests in order to check how healthy you are. 诊察 ❑ *Another doctor examined her and could still find nothing wrong.* 另一个医生对她进行了检查，仍然找不出任何毛病。● **ex·ami·na·tion** N-VAR 诊察 ❑ *He was later discharged after an examination at the hospital.* 后来他在医院做过检查后就出院了。 **3** V-T If an idea, proposal, or plan **is examined**, it is considered very carefully. 审查 ❑ *The plans will be examined by officials.* 这些计划将由官员们审查。● **ex·ami·na·tion** N-VAR 审查 ❑ *The government said it was studying the implications, which "required very careful examination and consideration."* 政府称正在对可能的影响进行研究，而这"需要仔细的审查和考虑"。 **4** V-T If you **are examined**, you are given a formal test in order to show your knowledge of a subject. 考试 [usu passive] ❑ *...learning to cope with the pressures of being judged and examined by our teachers.* …学会应付被老师们评价和考试所带来的压力。

Thesaurus *examine* 另参见：
V. analyze, go over, inspect, investigate, research, scrutinize **1**

ex·am·in·er /ɪgzæmɪnər/ (**examiners**) **1** N-COUNT An **examiner** is a person who conducts an examination. 检查员；考官 ❑ *...FBI senior fingerprint examiner Terry Green.* …联邦调查局高级指纹检验官特里·格林。 **2** → see also **medical examiner**

ex·am·ple ♦♦♦ /ɪgzæmp ͤl/ (**examples**) **1** N-COUNT An **example of** something is a particular situation, object, or person that shows that what is being claimed is true. 例子 ❑ *The doctors gave numerous examples of patients being expelled from the hospital.* 医生给出了大量病人被逐出医院的实例。 **2** N-COUNT An **example of** a particular class of objects or styles is something that has many of the typical features of such a class or style, and that you consider clearly represents it. 范例 ❑ *Symphonies 103 and 104 stand as perfect examples of early symphonic construction.* 第103和104号交响曲是早期交响乐谱曲的完美范本。 **3** N-COUNT If you refer to a person or their behavior as an **example to** other people, you mean that he or she behaves in a good or correct way that other people should copy. 榜样 [APPROVAL] ❑ *He is a model professional and an example to the younger boys.* 他是个模范的专业人员，是年轻人的榜样。 **4** PHRASE You use **for example** to introduce and emphasize something that shows that something is true. 例如 ❑ *Take, for example, the simple sentence: "The man climbed up the hill."* 以这个简单句为例："那个人爬上了山坡。" **5** PHRASE If you **follow** someone's **example**, you behave in the same way as they did in the past, or in a similar way, especially because you admire them. 以(某人)为榜样 ❑ *Following the example set by her father, she has fulfilled her role and done her duty.* 她以父亲为榜样，履行了她的职责，完成了她的使命 **6** PHRASE To **make an example of** someone who has done something wrong means to punish them severely as a warning to other people not to do the same thing. 严惩(某人)以警告他人 ❑ *Let us at least see our courts make an example of these despicable criminals.* 让我们至少看到我们的法庭严惩卑鄙的罪犯们以示儆戒。 **7** PHRASE If you **set an example**, you encourage or inspire people by your behavior to behave or act in a similar way. 树立榜样 ❑ *An officer's job was to set an example.* 一个官员的任务就是树立榜样。

Thesaurus *example* 另参见：
N. model, representation, sample **1** **2**
ideal, role model, standard **3**

Word Partnership *example* 的常用搭配：
ADJ. **classic** example, **obvious** example, **perfect** example, **typical** example **1** **2**
good example **1**–**3**
V. **give an** example **1** **2**
follow an example **5**

Word Link *sper ≈ hope : desperate, exasperate, prosperity*

ex·as·per·ate /ɪgzæspəreɪt/ (**exasperates, exasperating, exasperated**) V-T If someone or something **exasperates** you, they annoy you and make you feel frustrated or upset. 触怒；激怒 ❑ *The sheer futility of it all exasperates her.* 它的完全无效使她很恼火。● **ex·as·pera·tion** /ɪgzæspəreɪʃ ͤn/ N-UNCOUNT 恼怒 ❑ *Mahoney clenched his fist in exasperation.* 马奥尼恼怒地攥紧拳头。

ex·as·per·at·ed /ɪgzæspəreɪtɪd/ ADJ If you describe a person as **exasperated**, you mean that they are frustrated or angry because of something that is happening or something that another person is doing. 恼怒的 ❑ *The president was clearly exasperated by the whole saga.* 校长很显然被这整个事件激怒了。

ex·as·per·at·ing /ɪgzæspəreɪtɪŋ/ ADJ If you describe someone or something as **exasperating**, you mean that you feel angry or frustrated by them or by what they do. 使人生气的；使人沮丧的 [usu v-link ADJ] ❑ *Herrera could be exasperating to his colleagues.* 海莱拉可以让他的同事们很生气。

Word Link *cav ≈ hollow : cave, cavity, excavate*

ex·ca·vate /ɛkskəveɪt/ (**excavates, excavating, excavated**) **1** V-T When archaeologists or other people **excavate** a piece of land, they remove earth carefully from it and look for things such as pots, bones, or buildings that are buried there, in order to discover information about the past. 挖掘(古物) ❑ *A new Danish expedition is again excavating the site in annual summer digs.* 一支新的丹麦考察队又在对那个地方进行年度的夏季挖掘。● **ex·ca·va·tion** /ɛkskəveɪʃ ͤn/ N-VAR (**excavations**) 挖掘 ❑ *She worked on the excavation of a Mayan archeological site.* 她那时从事一个玛雅考古遗址的挖掘工作。❑ *...the excavation of a bronze-aged boat.* …对一艘青铜器时代的船的挖掘。 **2** V-T To **excavate** means to dig a hole in the ground, for example, in order to build there. 挖；开凿 ❑ *A contractor was hired to drain the reservoir and to excavate soil from one area for replacement with clay.* 一个承包商被雇来排干蓄水池里的水，然后挖出其中一块地方的泥土，换上粘土。● **ex·ca·va·tion** N-VAR 挖；开凿 ❑ *...the excavation of canals.* …运河的开凿。

Word Link *ex ≈ away, from, out : exceed, exit, explode*

ex·ceed /ɪksid/ (**exceeds, exceeding, exceeded**) **1** V-T If something **exceeds** a particular amount or number, it is greater or larger than that amount or number. 超过(某数量) [FORMAL] ❑ *Its research budget exceeds $700 million a year.* 其研究预算每年超过7亿美元。 **2** V-T If you **exceed** a limit or rule, you go beyond it, even though you are not supposed to or it is against the law. 超越(限制、规定) [FORMAL] ❑ *He accepts that he was exceeding the speed limit.* 他承认他当时超过了速限。

ex·ceed·ing·ly /ɪksidɪŋli/ ADV **Exceedingly** means very or very much. 极其 [OLD-FASHIONED] ❑ *We had an exceedingly good lunch.* 我们吃了一顿极其丰盛的午餐。

▲ **ex·cel** /ɪksɛl/ (**excels, excelling, excelled**) V-T/V-I If someone **excels in** something or **excels at** it, they are very good at doing it. (在某方面)擅长 ❑ *Mary was a better rider than either of them and she excelled at outdoor sports.* 玛丽比他们俩骑得都好，她擅长户外运动。❑ *Academically he began to excel.* 他开始在学术上脱颖而出。

Word Link *ence ≈ state, condition : dependence, excellence, independence*

ex·cel·lence /ɛksələns/ N-UNCOUNT If someone or something has the quality of **excellence**, they are extremely good in some way. 优秀；卓越 ❑ *...the top award for excellence in journalism and the arts.* …新闻与艺术界的最高杰出奖。

ex·cel·lent ♦♦◊ /ɛksələnt/ **1** ADJ Something that is **excellent** is extremely good. 极好的；优秀的 ❑ *The recording quality is excellent.* 录制质量极好。● **ex·cel·lent·ly** ADV 极好地；优秀地 ❑ *They're both playing excellently.* 他们演奏得都很棒。 **2** EXCLAM Some people say "**Excellent!**" to show that they approve of something. 太棒了；太好了 [FEELINGS] ❑ *"Excellent!" he shouted, yelping happily at the rain. "Now we'll see how this boat really performs!"* "太好了！"他冲着雨高兴地喊着，"这下我们可以看看这艘船真正如何表现了！"

ex·cept ♦♦◊ /ɪksɛpt/ **1** PREP You use **except** to introduce the only thing or person that a statement does not apply to, or a fact that prevents a statement from being completely true. 除…之外 ❑ *I wouldn't have accepted anything except a job in New York.* 我当时是不会接受一份除纽约以外任何其他地方的工作的。● CONJ **Except** is also a conjunction. 除了… ❑ *Freddie would tell me nothing about what he was writing, except that it was to be a Christmas play.* 弗雷迪不愿告诉我他在写什么，只说会是个圣诞剧本。 **2** PHRASE You use **except** or **except for** to introduce the only thing or person that prevents a statement from being completely true. 除了… ❑ *He hadn't eaten a thing except for one forkful of salad.* 除了一口沙拉，他什么都没吃。

Do not confuse **except**, **except for**, **besides**, and **unless**. You use **except** to introduce the only things, situations, people, or ideas that a statement does not apply to. ❑ *All of his body relaxed except his right hand... Traveling was impossible, except in the cool of the morning.* You use **except for** before something that prevents a statement from being completely true. ❑ *The classrooms were silent, except for the scratching of pens on paper... I had absolutely no friends except for Tom.* You use **besides** to introduce extra things in addition to the ones you are mentioning already. ❑ *Fruit will give you, besides enjoyment, a source of vitamins.* However, note that if you talk about "the only thing" or "the only person" **besides** a particular person or thing, **besides** means the same as "apart from." ❑ *He was the only person besides Gertrude who talked to Guy.* **Unless** is used to introduce the only situation in which something will take place or be true. ❑ *In the 1940s, unless she wore gloves a woman was not properly dressed... You must not give compliments unless you mean them.*

ex·cept·ed /ɪksɛptɪd/ ADV You use **excepted** after you have mentioned a person or thing to show that you do not include them in the statement you are making. 除…外 [n ADV] [FORMAL] ❑ *Jeremy excepted, the men seemed personable.* 除了杰里米，那些男人都显得风度翩翩。

ex·cept·ing /ɪksɛptɪŋ/ PREP You use **excepting** to introduce the only thing that prevents a statement from being completely true. 除…外 [FORMAL] ❑ *The source of meat for much of this region (excepting Japan) has traditionally been the pig.* 该区域大部分地区（除日本外）的食肉传统上都是猪肉。

ex·cep·tion ♦◊◊ /ɪksɛpʃən/ (**exceptions**) **1** N-COUNT An **exception** is a particular thing, person, or situation that is not included in a general statement, judgment, or rule. 例外 ❑ *Few guitarists can sing as well as they can play; Eddie, however, is an exception.* 很少有吉他手唱歌能唱得跟弹得一样好，而艾迪是个例外。❑ *The law makes no exceptions.* 法律不搞例外。 **2** PHRASE If you make a general statement, and then say that something or someone is **no exception**, you are emphasizing that they are included in that statement. 不例外；无例外 [EMPHASIS] ❑ *Marketing is applied to everything these days, and books are no exception.* 现在市场营销用于任何事物，图书也不例外。 **3** PHRASE If you **take exception to** something, you feel offended or annoyed by it, usually with the result that you complain about it. 厌恶；反感 ❑ *He also took exception to having been spied on.* 他也厌恶被暗中监视。 **4** PHRASE You use **with the exception of** to introduce a thing or person that is not included in a general statement that you are making. 除外 ❑ *Yesterday was a day off for everybody, with the exception of Lorenzo.* 昨天每个人休一天假，洛伦佐除外。 **5** PHRASE You use **without exception** to emphasize that the statement you are making is true in all cases. 无例外地 [EMPHASIS] ❑ *The vehicles are without exception old, rusty and dented.* 这些车辆无一例外地破旧、锈迹斑斑且有撞痕。

★ **ex·cep·tion·al** /ɪksɛpʃənəl/ **1** ADJ You use **exceptional** to describe someone or something that has a particular quality, usually a good quality, to an unusually high degree. 非凡的 [APPROVAL] ❑ *...children with exceptional ability.* …能力非凡的孩子们。 ● **ex·cep·tion·al·ly** ADV 非凡地 [ADV adj/adv] ❑ *He's an exceptionally talented dancer and needs to practice several hours every day.* 他是位非凡有天赋的的舞蹈家，每天需要练几小时。 **2** ADJ **Exceptional** situations and incidents are unusual and only likely to happen infrequently. 例外的 [FORMAL] ❑ *A review panel concluded that there were no exceptional circumstances that would warrant a lesser penalty for him.* 一个评估小组作出结论：没有什么例外情况可使他获得从轻惩罚。 ● **ex·cep·tion·al·ly** ADV 例外地 [ADV with cl] ❑ *Exceptionally, in times of emergency, we may send a team of experts.* 紧急情况下我们可以破例派遣一个专家队。

★ **ex·cerpt** ♦◊◊ /ɛksɜrpt/ (**excerpts**) N-COUNT An **excerpt** is a short piece of writing or music taken from a larger piece. 摘录；节选 ❑ *...an excerpt from Tchaikovsky's Nutcracker.* …柴可夫斯基的《胡桃夹子》选段。

ex·cess ♦◊◊ (**excesses**)

The noun is pronounced /ɪksɛs/ or /ɛksɛs/. The adjective is pronounced /ɛksɛs/.

名词读作 /ɪksɛs/ 或 /ɛksɛs/。形容词读作 /ɛksɛs/。

1 N-VAR An **excess of** something is a larger amount than is needed, allowed, or usual. 过量 ❑ *An excess of house plants in a small apartment can be oppressive.* 在一套狭小公寓里放过多的室内植物会给人压抑感。 **2** ADJ **Excess** is used to describe amounts that are greater than what is needed, allowed, or usual. 过量的 [ADJ n] ❑ *After cooking the fish, pour off any excess fat.* 烹调完鱼后，倒掉多余的油。 **3** ADJ **Excess** is used to refer to additional amounts of money that need to be paid for services and activities that were not originally planned or taken into account. 额外的 [ADJ n] [FORMAL] ❑ *Make sure that you don't have to pay expensive excess charges.* 确保你不需要支付昂贵的额外费用。 **4** PHRASE **In excess of** means more than a particular amount. 超过 [FORMAL] ❑ *The value of the company is well in excess of $2 billion.* 该公司的价值远超过20亿美元。 **5** PHRASE If you do something **to excess**, you do it too much. 过度地；过多地 [DISAPPROVAL] ❑ *I was reasonably fit, played a lot of tennis, and didn't smoke or drink to excess.* 我那时很健康，常打网球，不过度抽烟或喝酒。

ex·ces·sive /ɪksɛsɪv/ ADJ If you describe the amount or level of something as **excessive**, you disapprove of it because it is more or higher than is necessary or reasonable. 过多的；过度的 [DISAPPROVAL] ❑ *Their spending on research is excessive and is slowing developments of new treatments.* 他们在研究上的花销过多，正在减慢新疗法的开发。 ● **ex·ces·sive·ly** ADV 过多地；过度地 ❑ *Managers are also accused of paying themselves excessively high salaries.* 经理们还被指责给自己发过高的工资。

ex·change ♦♦◊ /ɪkstʃeɪndʒ/ (**exchanges, exchanging, exchanged**) **1** V-RECIP If two or more people **exchange** things of a particular kind, they give them to each other at the same time. 交换 ❑ *We exchanged addresses.* 我们交换了地址。 ❑ *The two men exchanged glances.* 那两个人交换了眼神。 ● N-COUNT **Exchange** is also a noun. 交换 ❑ *He ruled out any exchange of prisoners with the militants.* 他拒绝考虑与好战分子交换囚犯。 **2** V-T If you **exchange** something, you replace it with a different thing, especially something that is better or more satisfactory. 调换；更换 ❑ *...the chance to sell back or exchange goods.* …回售或调换货物的机会。 **3** N-COUNT An **exchange** is a brief conversation, usually an angry one. 短暂的交谈；争吵 [FORMAL] ❑ *There've been some bitter exchanges between the two groups.* 两组之间有过些激烈的争吵。 **4** N-COUNT An **exchange of** fire, for example, is an incident in which people use guns or missiles against each other. 交火 ❑ *There was an exchange of fire during which the gunman was wounded.* 发生了一场交火，其间那名枪手受伤了。 **5** N-COUNT An **exchange** is an arrangement in which people from two different countries visit each other's country, to strengthen links between them. 交流 ❑ *...a series of sporting and cultural exchanges with Seoul.* …与首尔的一系列体育和文化交流。 **6** → see also **foreign exchange, stock exchange** **7** PHRASE If you do or give something **in exchange for** something else, you do it or give it in order to get that thing. 作为交换 ❑ *It is illegal for public officials to solicit gifts or money in exchange for favors.* 公务员以提供便利来索取礼物或金钱作为交换是非法的。
→ see **stock market**

Word Partnership *exchange* 的常用搭配：

N.	exchange **gifts**, exchange **greetings** 1
	exchange **student** 5
ADJ.	**brief** exchange 3
	cultural exchange 5

ex·change rate ♦◊◊ (**exchange rates**) N-COUNT The **exchange rate** of a country's unit of currency is the amount of another country's currency that you get in exchange for it. 汇率 ❑ *...a high exchange rate for the Canadian dollar.* …加拿大元的高汇率。

ex·cise /ɛksaɪz/ (**excises**) N-VAR **Excise** is a tax that the government of a country puts on particular goods, such as cigarettes and alcoholic drinks, which are produced for sale in its own country. 消费税；国内货物税 ❑ *...this year's rise in excise duties.* …今年消费税的增长。 ❑ *...an excise tax on wine and tobacco.* …烟酒的消费税。

ex·cit·able /ɪksaɪtəbəl/ ADJ If you describe someone as **excitable**, you mean that they behave in a nervous way and become excited very easily. 易激动的 ❑ *Mary sat beside Elaine, who today seemed excitable.* 玛丽坐在了伊莱恩旁边，伊莱恩今天似乎容易激动。

ex·cite /ɪksaɪt/ (**excites, exciting, excited**) **1** V-T If something **excites** you, it makes you feel very happy, eager, or enthusiastic. 使…激动；使…兴奋 ❑ *I only take on work that excites me, even if it means*

e

turning down lots of money. 我只承接让我感兴趣的工作，即使这意味着损失很多钱。 **2** V-T If something **excites** a particular feeling, emotion, or reaction in someone, it causes them to experience it. 激起 ❑ *Daniel's early exposure to motor racing did not excite his interest.* 丹尼尔早期对赛车运动的接触并没有激起他的兴趣。

ex·cit·ed /ɪksaɪtɪd/ **1** ADJ If you are **excited**, you are so happy that you cannot relax, especially because you are thinking about something pleasant that is going to happen to you. 兴奋的 ❑ *I was excited about the possibility of playing football again.* 想到有可能再次踢足球，我很兴奋。 ● **ex·cit·ed·ly** ADV 兴奋地 [ADV with v] ❑ *"You're coming?" he said excitedly. "That's fantastic! That's incredible!"* "你要来？" 他兴奋地说，"太棒了！简直难以置信！" **2** ADJ If you are **excited**, you are worried or angry about something, and so you are very alert and cannot relax. 焦躁不安的；激愤的 ❑ *I don't think there's any reason to get excited about inflation.* 我认为没理由因通货膨胀而焦虑。 ● **ex·cit·ed·ly** ADV 焦躁不安地；激愤地 [ADV with v] ❑ *Larry rose excitedly to the edge of his seat, shook a fist at us and spat.* 拉里激愤地从座位上站了起来，向我们又晃拳头又啐唾沫。

ex·cite·ment /ɪksaɪtmənt/ (**excitements**) N-VAR You use **excitement** to refer to the state of being excited, or to something that excites you. 兴奋；令人兴奋的事物 ❑ *Everyone is in a state of great excitement.* 人人都处于极度兴奋之中。

ex·cit·ing ♦◇◇ /ɪksaɪtɪŋ/ ADJ If something is **exciting**, it makes you feel very happy or enthusiastic. 令人兴奋的 ❑ *The race itself is very exciting.* 比赛本身就令人非常兴奋。

Word Link *claim, clam ≈ shouting : acclaim, clamor, exclaim*

ex·claim /ɪkskleɪm/ (**exclaims, exclaiming, exclaimed**) V-T Writers sometimes use **exclaim** to show that someone is speaking suddenly, loudly, or emphatically, often because they are excited, shocked, or angry. (因兴奋、震惊、愤怒等) 突然呼喊；惊叫 ❑ *"He went back to the lab," Inez exclaimed impatiently.* "他回实验室了，" 伊内兹不耐烦地叫道。

ex·cla·ma·tion /ɛkskləmeɪʃ°n/ (**exclamations**) N-COUNT An **exclamation** is a sound, word, or sentence that is spoken suddenly, loudly, or emphatically and that expresses excitement, admiration, shock, or anger. 惊叫；感叹 ❑ *Sue gave an exclamation as we got a clear sight of the house.* 我们清晰地看到房子时，苏发出了一声惊叹。

ex·cla·ma·tion point (**exclamation points**) or **exclamation mark** N-COUNT An **exclamation point** is the sign ! which is used in writing to show that a word, phrase, or sentence is an exclamation. 感叹号 (!)

ex·clude /ɪksklud/ (**excludes, excluding, excluded**) **1** V-T If you **exclude** someone **from** a place or activity, you prevent them from entering it or taking part in it. 拒 (某人) 于 (某地、活动) 之外；不包括 ❑ *Many of the youngsters feel excluded.* 很多年轻人感觉受排挤。 **2** V-T If you **exclude** something that has some connection with what you are doing, you deliberately do not use it or consider it. 故意不用；故意不考虑 ❑ *In some schools, Christmas carols are being modified to exclude any reference to Christ.* 在有些学校，圣诞颂歌正在被修改以去掉任何涉及基督的内容。 **3** V-T To **exclude** a possibility means to decide or prove that it is wrong and not worth considering. 排除 (某种可能性) [usu with brd-neg] ❑ *I cannot entirely exclude the possibility that some form of pressure was applied to the neck.* 我不能完全排除有些压力作用到了颈部的可能性。 **4** V-T To **exclude** something such as the sun's rays or harmful germs means to prevent them physically from reaching or entering a particular place. 阻挡 ❑ *This was intended to exclude the direct rays of the sun.* 这是用来阻挡太阳直射光线的。

ex·clud·ing /ɪkskludɪŋ/ PREP You use **excluding** before mentioning a person or thing to show that you are not including them in your statement. 除…之外 ❑ *Excluding water, half of the body's weight is protein.* 除水之外，体重的一半是蛋白质。

ex·clu·sion /ɪkskluʒ°n/ (**exclusions**) **1** N-VAR The **exclusion of** something is the act of deliberately not using, allowing, or considering it. 故意不用；故意不考虑 ❑ *It calls for the exclusion of all commercial lending institutions from the college loan program.* 这要求大学贷款项目不考虑所有商业贷款机构。 **2** N-UNCOUNT **Exclusion** is the act of preventing someone from entering a place or taking part in an activity. 排斥 ❑ *...women's exclusion from political power.* …政治权力对妇女的排斥。 **3** PHRASE If you do one thing **to the exclusion of** something else, you only do the first thing and do not do the second thing at all. 抛开… ❑ *Diane had dedicated her life to caring for him to the exclusion of all else.* 黛安娜曾抛开其他一切，来一心一意地照顾他。

ex·clu·sive /ɪksklusɪv/ (**exclusives**) **1** ADJ If you describe something as **exclusive**, you mean that it is limited to people who have a lot of money or who are privileged, and is therefore not available to everyone. 仅限富贵人士的 ❑ *It used to be a private, exclusive club, and now it's open to all New Yorkers.* 它曾是一家高档的私人俱乐部，而现在它对所有纽约人开放。 **2** ADJ Something that is **exclusive** is used or owned by only one person or group, and not shared with anyone else. 专用的；独有的 ❑ *Our group will have exclusive use of a 60-foot boat.* 我们组将有一条专用的60英尺的船。 **3** ADJ If a newspaper, magazine, or broadcasting organization describes one of its reports as **exclusive**, they mean it is a special report that does not appear in any other publication or on any other channel. 独家的 (新闻报道) ❑ *He told the magazine in an exclusive interview: "All my problems stem from drinking."* 他在一次独家采访中告知那家杂志："我所有的问题源于饮酒。" ● N-COUNT An **exclusive** is an exclusive article or report. 独家文章；独家报道 ❑ *Some papers thought they had an exclusive.* 一些报社以为他们有一条独家报道。 **4** ADJ If a company states that its prices, goods, or services are **exclusive of** something, that thing is not included in the stated price, although it usually still has to be paid for. 不包括…的 ❑ *...the average cost of a three-course dinner exclusive of tax, tip and beverage.* …不含税、小费和酒水费用的3道菜晚餐的平均花费。 **5** PHRASE If two things are **mutually exclusive**, they are separate and very different from each other, so that it is impossible for them to exist or happen together. 互相排斥的；不兼容的 ❑ *They both have learned that ambition and successful fatherhood can be mutually exclusive.* 他们都明白了事业心与做个成功的父亲是互相排斥的。

ex·clu·sive·ly /ɪksklusɪvli/ ADV **Exclusively** is used to refer to situations or activities that involve only the thing or things mentioned, and nothing else. 排他地；独占地 ❑ *...an exclusively male domain.* …一个由男性独占的领域。

ex·crete /ɪkskrit/ (**excretes, excreting, excreted**) V-T When a person or animal **excretes** waste matter from their body, they get rid of it in feces, urine, or sweat. 排泄；分泌 [FORMAL] ❑ *Your open pores excrete sweat and dirt.* 你张开的毛孔排出汗液与污垢。

ex·cru·ci·at·ing /ɪkskruʃieɪtɪŋ/ ADJ If you describe something as **excruciating**, you are emphasizing that it is extremely painful, either physically or emotionally. 极痛苦的 [EMPHASIS] ❑ *I was in excruciating pain and one leg wouldn't move.* 我处于极度痛苦之中，一条腿动弹不了了。

ex·cur·sion /ɪkskɜrʒ°n/ (**excursions**) **1** N-COUNT You can refer to a short trip as an **excursion**, especially if it is taken for pleasure or enjoyment. 短途旅行 ❑ *In Bermuda, Sam's father took him on an excursion to a coral barrier.* 在百慕大，萨姆的父亲带他去了一趟到珊瑚堤的短途旅行。 **2** N-COUNT An **excursion** is a trip or visit to an interesting place, especially one that is arranged or recommended by a travel agency or tourist organization. (尤指旅行社安排的) 短程旅游 ❑ *Another pleasant excursion is Matamoros, 18 miles away.* 另一个怡人的短程旅游是18英里外的马塔莫罗斯。

ex·cuse ♦◇◇ (**excuses, excusing, excused**)

The noun is pronounced /ɪkskyus/. The verb is pronounced /ɪkskyuz/.

名词读作 /ɪkskyus/。动词读作 /ɪkskyuz/。

1 N-COUNT An **excuse** is a reason that you give in order to explain why something has been done or has not been done, or in order to avoid doing something. 借口 ❑ *It is easy to find excuses for his indecisiveness.* 为他的优柔寡断寻找借口是件容易的事。 ❑ *If you stop making excuses and do it, you'll wonder what took you so long.* 如果你停止辩解而开始行动，你就会惊讶是什么让你耗费了这么长的时间。 ● PHRASE If you say that there is **no excuse for** something, you are emphasizing that it should not happen, or expressing disapproval that it has happened. 没有理由 [DISAPPROVAL] ❑ *There's no excuse for behavior like that.* 像那样的行为毫无道理。 **2** V-T To **excuse** someone or **excuse** their behavior means to provide reasons for their actions, especially when other people disapprove of these actions. 为…开脱 ❑ *He excused himself by saying he was "forced to rob to maintain my wife and cat."* 他为自己开脱，说是"为养活妻子和猫才迫不得已去抢劫的"。 **3** V-T If you **excuse** someone **for** something wrong that they have done, you forgive them for it. 原谅 ❑ *Many people might have excused them for shirking some of their responsibilities.* 很多人也许已经原谅他们逃避一些责任的行为了。

4 V-T If someone **is excused from** a duty or responsibility, they are told that they do not have to carry it out. 免除…的责任 [usu passive] ❑ *She is usually excused from her duties during summer vacation.* 在暑期她一般不必担负责任。 5 V-T If you **excuse yourself**, you use a phrase such as "Excuse me" as a polite way of saying that you are about to leave. 准许…离开 ❑ *He excused himself and went up to his room.* 他礼貌地告辞后便上楼去了自己的房间。 6 CONVENTION You say "**Excuse me**" when you want to politely get someone's attention, especially when you are about to ask them a question. 打扰一下 (用于礼貌地引起某人的注意) [FORMULAE] ❑ *Excuse me, but are you Mr. Honig?* 打扰一下，请问您就是霍尼格先生吗？ 7 CONVENTION You use **excuse me** to apologize to someone when you have disturbed or interrupted them. 对不起 (用于因打扰或打断某人而表示歉意) [FORMULAE] ❑ *Excuse me interrupting, but there's something I need to say.* 恕我打断一下，但有件事我需要说。 8 CONVENTION You use **excuse me** or a phrase such as **if you'll excuse me** as a polite way of indicating that you are about to leave or that you are about to stop talking to someone. 失陪 (用于礼貌地表示要离开或中断谈话) [POLITENESS] ❑ *"Excuse me," she said to José, and left the room.* "失陪了，"她对乔赛说，然后离开了那个房间。 9 CONVENTION You use **excuse me, but** to indicate that you are about to disagree with someone. 抱歉，不过 (用于礼貌地表示不赞成) ❑ *Excuse me, but I want to know what all this has to do with us.* 抱歉，不过我想知道这一切和我们有什么关系。 10 PHRASE You say **excuse me** to apologize when you have bumped into someone, or when you need to move past someone in a crowd. 抱歉；借过 (用于因撞上别人或需要从人群中挤过表示歉意) [FORMULAE] ❑ *Saying excuse me, Seaton pushed his way into the crowded living room.* 西顿一边嘴里说着"借过"，一边奋力挤进了拥挤的客厅。 11 CONVENTION You say **excuse me** to apologize when you have done something slightly embarrassing or impolite, such as burping, hiccuping, or sneezing. 不好意思 (用于因打嗝、打喷嚏等尴尬失礼行为而表示歉意) [FORMULAE] 12 CONVENTION You say "**Excuse me?**" to show that you want someone to repeat what they have just said. 请再说一遍 [AM, FORMULAE] ❑ *"Excuse me?" Kate said, not sure she'd heard correctly.* "能再说一遍吗？"凯特说道，不确信自己有没有听对。

Thesaurus *excuse* 另参见：

N.	apology, explanation, reason 1
V.	forgive, pardon, spare; *(ant.)* accuse, blame, punish 3

ex-directory ADJ If a person or their telephone number is **ex-directory**, the number is not listed in the telephone directory, and the telephone company will not give it to people who ask for it. (电话号码) 未登记在电话簿里的 [BRIT]

in AM, use **unlisted**

exec /ɪgzɛk/ (**execs**) N-COUNT **Exec** is an abbreviation for **executive**. 主管 [INFORMAL]

ex·ecute ♦◇◇ /ɛksɪkyut/ (**executes, executing, executed**) 1 V-T To **execute** someone means to kill them as a punishment for a serious crime. 处死 ❑ *He said nobody had been executed as a direct result of the events.* 他说没有人作为这几起事件的直接后果被处死。 ❑ *One group claimed to have executed the hostage.* 一个组织声称他们已处死了那名人质。 ● **ex·ecu·tion** ★ /ɛksɪkyuʃᵊn/ N-VAR (**executions**) 处死 ❑ *Execution by lethal injection is scheduled for July 30th.* 注射死刑定于7月30日执行。 2 V-T If you **execute** a plan, you carry it out. 执行 (计划等) [FORMAL] ❑ *We are going to execute our campaign plan to the letter.* 我们将严格执行我们的竞选方案。 ● **ex·ecu·tion** ★ N-UNCOUNT 执行 ❑ *U.S. forces are fully prepared for the execution of any action once the order is given by the president.* 美国军队做好了充分准备，一旦总统下令就采取行动。 3 V-T If you **execute** a difficult action or movement, you successfully perform it. 完成 (高难动作) ❑ *The landing was skillfully executed.* 着陆熟练地完成了。

ex·ecu·tive ♦♦◇ /ɪgzɛkyətɪv/ (**executives**) 1 N-COUNT An **executive** is someone who is employed by a business at a senior level. Executives decide what the business should do, and ensure that it is done. 执行总监 ❑ *...an advertising executive.* …一位广告执行总监。 2 ADJ The **executive** sections and tasks of an organization are concerned with the making of decisions and with ensuring that decisions are carried out. 执行的 [ADJ n] ❑ *A successful job search needs to be as well organized as any other executive task.* 一次成功的寻职要像任何其他执行任务一样精心安排。 3 ADJ **Executive** goods are expensive products designed or intended for executives and other people at a similar social or economic level. 高级的 [ADJ n] ❑ *...an executive briefcase.* …一个高级公文包。 4 N-SING The **executive** committee or board of an organization is a committee within that organization that has the authority to make decisions and ensures that these decisions are carried out. 执行委员会 ["the" N, N n] ❑ *They opted to put an executive committee in charge of the project rather than a single person.* 他们选择由一个执行委员会而非个人来负责这个项目。 5 N-SING **The executive** is the part of the government of a country that is concerned with carrying out decisions or orders, as opposed to the part that makes laws or the part that deals with criminals. (政府的) 行政部门 ["the" N, N n] ❑ *The government, the executive and the judiciary are supposed to be separate.* 政府、行政和司法应该彼此分立。

e

★ **ex·em·pla·ry** /ɪgzɛmpləri/ ADJ If you describe someone or something as **exemplary**, you think they are extremely good. 堪称典范的 ❑ *Underpinning this success has been an exemplary record of innovation.* 支持这一成功的基础是一次堪称典范的革新记录。

ex·em·pli·fy /ɪgzɛmplɪfaɪ/ (**exemplifies, exemplifying, exemplified**) V-T If a person or thing **exemplifies** something such as a situation, quality, or class of things, they are a typical example of it. 是…的典范 [FORMAL] ❑ *The room's style exemplifies their ideal of "beauty and practicality."* 这个房间的风格是他们"美观实用"理想的典范。

★ **ex·empt** /ɪgzɛmpt/ (**exempts, exempting, exempted**) 1 ADJ If someone or something is **exempt from** a particular rule, duty, or obligation, they do not have to follow it or do it. 免除 (规则、职责、义务等) 的 ❑ *Men in college were exempt from military service.* 在校男大学生免服兵役。 2 V-T To **exempt** a person or thing **from** a particular rule, duty, or obligation means to state officially that they are not bound or affected by it. 免除 ❑ *South Carolina claimed the power to exempt its citizens from the obligation to obey federal law.* 南卡罗来纳州宣称有权使其公民免除遵守联邦法律的义务。 ● **ex·emp·tion** /ɪgzɛmpʃᵊn/ N-VAR (**exemptions**) 免除 [oft N "from" n] ❑ *...the exemption of employer-provided health insurance from taxation.* …雇主提供的医疗保险的税项免除。

ex·er·cise ♦♦◇ /ɛksərsaɪz/ (**exercises, exercising, exercised**) 1 V-T If you **exercise** something such as your authority, your rights, or a good quality, you use it or put it into effect. 行使；运用 [FORMAL] ❑ *They are merely exercising their right to free speech.* 他们仅仅是在行使言论自由的权利。 ● N-SING **Exercise** is also a noun. 行使；运用 ❑ *Social structures are maintained through the exercise of political and economic power.* 社会结构是通过政治和经济权力的运用来维护的。 2 V-I When you **exercise**, you move your body energetically in order to get in shape and to remain healthy. 锻炼 ❑ *She exercises two or three times a week.* 她一周锻炼两三次。 ● N-UNCOUNT **Exercise** is also a noun. 锻炼 ❑ *Lack of exercise can lead to feelings of depression and exhaustion.* 锻炼的缺乏会导致抑郁和疲倦感。 3 V-T If a movement or activity **exercises** a part of your body, it keeps it strong, healthy, or in good condition. 锻炼 (身体某一部位) ❑ *They call rowing the perfect sport. It exercises every major muscle group.* 他们把划船称之为完美的运动。它锻炼身体的各主要肌肉群。 4 N-COUNT **Exercises** are a series of movements or actions that you do in order to get in shape, remain healthy, or practice for a particular physical activity. 锻炼 ❑ *I do special neck and shoulder exercises.* 我做专门针对颈部与肩部的锻炼。 5 N-COUNT **Exercises** are military activities and operations that are not part of a real war, but that allow the armed forces to practice for a real war. (军事) 演习 [usu pl, also "on" N] ❑ *General Powell predicted that in the future it might even be possible to stage joint military exercises.* 鲍威尔将军预言将来甚至可能举行联合军事演习。 6 N-COUNT An **exercise** is a short activity or piece of work that you do, in school for example, which is designed to help you learn a particular skill. 练习 ❑ *Try working through the opening exercises in this chapter.* 努力完成本章开头部分的各个练习。
→ see **muscle**

Thesaurus *exercise* 另参见：

V.	practice, use 1 work out 2

ex·ert /ɪgzɜrt/ (**exerts, exerting, exerted**) 1 V-T If someone or something **exerts** influence, authority, or pressure, they use it in a strong or determined way, especially in order to produce a particular effect. 施加 (影响、压力)；运用 (权威) [FORMAL] ❑ *He exerted considerable influence on the thinking of the scientific community on these issues.* 他对科学界在这些问题上的思考施加了相当大的影响。

2 V-T If you **exert yourself**, you make a great physical or mental effort, or work hard to do something. 耗费(自己的精力) ❑ *Do not exert yourself unnecessarily.* 不要无谓地耗费自己的精力。

● **ex·er·tion** ▲ N-UNCOUNT (**exertions**) 耗费 [also N in pl] ❑ *He clearly found the physical exertion exhilarating.* 他明显发现体力消耗令人愉悦。

→ see **motion**

ex·hale /ɛksheɪl/ (**exhales, exhaling, exhaled**) V-T/V-I When you **exhale**, you breathe out the air that is in your lungs. 呼气 [FORMAL] ❑ *Hold your breath for a moment and exhale.* 屏息一会儿，然后呼气。

→ see **respiratory**

ex·haust ♦◊◊ /ɪgzɔst/ (**exhausts, exhausting, exhausted**) 1 V-T If something **exhausts** you, it makes you so tired, either physically or mentally, that you have no energy left. 使精疲力竭 ❑ *Don't exhaust him.* 别让他精疲力竭了。 ● **ex·haust·ed** ADJ 精疲力竭的 ❑ *She was too exhausted and distressed to talk about the tragedy.* 她太疲惫和忧伤了，不想谈论那场悲剧。 ● **ex·haust·ing** ADJ 使人精疲力竭的 ❑ *It was an exhausting schedule she had set herself.* 这是她自己制订的一个让自己精疲力竭的行事计划。 2 V-T If you **exhaust** something such as money or food, you use or finish it all. 用完 ❑ *We have exhausted all our material resources.* 我们已用完了所有的物资。 3 V-T If you **have exhausted** a subject or topic, you have talked about it so much that there is nothing more to say about it. 说尽 ❑ *She and Chantal must have exhausted the subject of clothes.* 她和钱特尔肯定说尽了服装这个主题。 4 N-UNCOUNT **Exhaust** is the gas or steam that is produced when the engine of a vehicle is running. 废气 [also N in pl] ❑ *...the exhaust from a car engine.* …从汽车引擎排出的废气。 ❑ *The city's streets are filthy and choked with exhaust fumes.* 这座城市的街道肮脏不堪，充满了废气。 5 N-COUNT The **exhaust** is the same as the **exhaust pipe**. 排气管 [BRIT]

→ see **engine, pollution**

★ **ex·haus·tion** /ɪgzɔstʃᵊn/ N-UNCOUNT **Exhaustion** is the state of being so tired that you have no energy left. 精疲力竭 ❑ *He is suffering from exhaustion.* 他精疲力竭。

ex·haus·tive /ɪgzɔstɪv/ ADJ If you describe a study, search, or list as **exhaustive**, you mean that it is very thorough and complete. 详尽无遗的 ❑ *This is by no means an exhaustive list but it gives an indication of the many projects taking place.* 这绝不是份详尽无遗的清单，但它显示出很多正在进行的项目。 ● **ex·haust·ive·ly** ADV 详尽无遗地 ❑ *Martin said these costs were scrutinized exhaustively by independent accountants.* 马丁称这些费用由独立会计师们彻底核查过。

ex·hib·it /ɪgzɪbɪt/ (**exhibits, exhibiting, exhibited**) 1 V-T If someone or something shows a particular quality, feeling, or type of behavior, you can say that they **exhibit** it. 表现出 [FORMAL] ❑ *He has exhibited symptoms of anxiety and overwhelming worry.* 他已表现出焦虑和忧心如焚的症状。 2 V-T When a painting, sculpture, or object of interest **is exhibited**, it is put in a public place such as a museum or art gallery so that people can come to look at it. You can also say that animals **are exhibited** in a zoo. 展览 [usu passive] ❑ *His work was exhibited in the best galleries in America, Europe and Asia.* 他的作品在美国、欧洲和亚洲最好的美术馆展览过。 ● **ex·hi·bi·tion** N-UNCOUNT 展览 ❑ *Five large pieces of the wall are currently on exhibition.* 那堵墙的五块大碎片目前在展览。 3 V-I When artists **exhibit**, they show their work in public. 展出作品 ❑ *He has also exhibited at galleries and museums in New York and Washington.* 他还在纽约和华盛顿的美术馆及博物馆展出过作品。 4 N-COUNT An **exhibit** is a painting, sculpture, or object of interest that is displayed to the public in a museum or art gallery. 展览品 ❑ *Shona showed me around the exhibits.* 肖纳带我参观了展品。 5 N-COUNT An **exhibit** is a public display of paintings, sculpture, or objects of interest in a museum or art gallery. 展览 [AM] ❑ *...an exhibit at the Metropolitan Museum of Art.* …大都会艺术博物馆的一场展览。 6 N-COUNT An **exhibit** is an object that a lawyer shows in court as evidence in a legal case. (法庭上出示的) 证物 ❑ *The jur has already asked to see more than 40 exhibits from the trial.* 陪审团已经要求查看了审判中超过40件的证物。

ex·hi·bi·tion ♦◊◊ /ɛksɪbɪʃᵊn/ (**exhibitions**) 1 N-COUNT An **exhibition** is a public event at which pictures, sculptures, or other objects of interest are displayed, for example at a museum or art gallery. 展览会 ❑ *...an exhibition of expressionist art.* …一场印象主义艺术展览会。 2 N-SING An **exhibition of** a particular skillful activity is a display or example of it that people notice or admire. (技能的)展示 ❑ *He responded in champion's style by treating the fans to an exhibition of power and speed.* 他回报以冠军的风格，为仰慕者们呈现了一次力量与速度的展示。 3 → see also **exhibit 2**

ex·hi·bi·tion game (**exhibition games**) N-COUNT In sports, an **exhibition game** is a game that is not part of a competition, and is played for entertainment or practice, often without any serious effort to win. 表演赛 [AM]

ex·hibi·tor /ɪgzɪbɪtər/ (**exhibitors**) N-COUNT An **exhibitor** is a person or company whose work or products are being shown in an exhibition. 参展者 ❑ *Schedules will be sent out to all exhibitors.* 日程安排将会发送给所有的参展者。

ex·hil·arat·ing /ɪgzɪləreɪtɪŋ/ ADJ If you describe an experience or feeling as **exhilarating**, you mean that it makes you feel very happy and excited. 令人欢欣的 ❑ *It was exhilarating to be on the road again and his spirits rose.* 重新上路非常令人欢欣，他的兴致高涨了起来。

ex·hila·ra·tion /ɪgzɪləreɪʃᵊn/ N-UNCOUNT **Exhilaration** is a strong feeling of excitement and happiness. 欢欣 ❑ *The exhilaration of winning such a famous event has stayed with him.* 赢得一场如此著名赛事的欢欣始终萦绕着他。

ex·ile ♦◊◊ /ɛksaɪl, ɛgz-/ (**exiles, exiling, exiled**) 1 N-UNCOUNT If someone is living **in exile**, they are living in a foreign country because they cannot live in their own country, usually for political reasons. (通常出于政治原因的) 流亡他国 ❑ *He is now living in exile in Egypt.* 他现在流亡在埃及。 ❑ *He returned from exile earlier this year.* 今年年初他流亡归国。 2 V-T If someone **is exiled**, they are living in a foreign country because they cannot live in their own country, usually for political reasons. (通常出于政治原因而) 放逐他国 ❑ *His second wife, Hilary, had been widowed, then exiled from South Africa.* 他的第二任妻子希拉里曾一度孀居，之后被逐出南非。 ❑ *They threatened to exile her in southern Spain.* 他们威胁要把她放逐到西班牙南部。 3 N-COUNT An **exile** is someone who has been exiled. 流亡者 ❑ *He is also an exile, a native of Palestine who has long given up the idea of going home.* 他也是个流亡者，一个早已放弃回家念头的巴勒斯坦人。 4 V-T If you say that someone **has been exiled from** a particular place or situation, you mean that they have been sent away from it or removed from it against their will. 逐出 [usu passive] ❑ *He served less than a year of a five-year prison sentence, but was permanently exiled from the sport.* 他5年刑期只服了1年不到，但被永远逐出了体育界。 ● N-UNCOUNT **Exile** is also a noun. 逐出 ❑ *...the Left's long exile from power from 1958 to 1981.* …左派从1958至1981年的长期失权。

Word Partnership *exile* 的常用搭配：

V.	**force into** exile, **go into** exile, **live in** exile, **return from** exile, **send into** exile 1
ADJ.	**self-imposed** exile 1 **political** exile 1 3

ex·ist ♦♦◊ /ɪgzɪst/ (**exists, existing, existed**) 1 V-I If something **exists**, it is present in the world as a real thing. 存在 [no cont] ❑ *He thought that if he couldn't see something, it didn't exist.* 他认为如果他看不见某种东西，它就不存在。 ❑ *Research opportunities exist in a wide range of areas.* 研究机会存在于广泛的领域中。 2 V-I To **exist** means to live, especially under difficult conditions or with very little food or money. (尤指在困境中) 生存 ❑ *I was barely existing.* 我几乎活不下去了。 ❑ *Some people exist on melons or coconuts for weeks at a time.* 有些人一度数周靠各种瓜与椰子生存。

ex·ist·ence ♦◊◊ /ɪgzɪstəns/ (**existences**) 1 N-UNCOUNT The **existence** of something is the fact that it is present in the world as a real thing. 存在 ❑ *...the existence of other galaxies.* …其他星系的存在。 ❑ *Public worries about accidents are threatening the very existence of the nuclear power industry.* 公众对事故的担心正威胁着核电工业的生存。 2 N-COUNT You can refer to someone's way of life as an **existence**, especially when they live under difficult conditions. (尤指困境中的) 生活方式 ❑ *You may be stuck with a miserable existence for the rest of your life.* 你的余生可能会陷入悲惨的生活。

Word Partnership *existence* 的常用搭配：

V.	**come into** existence, **deny the** existence 1
ADJ.	**continued** existence, **daily** existence, **everyday** existence 1 2

ex·ist·ing ♦◊◊ /ɪgzɪstɪŋ/ ADJ **Existing** is used to describe something that is now present, available, or in operation, especially when you are contrasting it with something that is planned for the future. 现有的; 现存的 [ADJ n] ❑ *...the need to improve existing products and develop new lines.* …改进现有产品和开发新生产线的需要。 ❑ *Existing timbers are replaced or renewed.* 现有的木材在被替换或更新。

Word Link *ex ≈ away, from, out : exceed, exit, explode*

exit /ɛgzɪt, ɛksɪt/ (**exits, exiting, exited**) **1** N-COUNT The **exit** is the door through which you can leave a public building. 出口 ❑ *He picked up the case and walked toward the exit.* 他提起箱子朝出口走去。 **2** N-COUNT An **exit** on a highway is a place where traffic can leave it. (公路的) 出口 ❑ *She continued to the next exit, got off the highway and pulled into a parking lot.* 她继续开到下个出口，出了公路，驶入一个停车场。 **3** N-COUNT If you refer to someone's **exit**, you are referring to the way that they left a room or building, or the fact that they left it. 离场 [FORMAL] ❑ *I made a hasty exit and managed to open the gate.* 我匆忙离场，设法打开了大门。 **4** N-COUNT If you refer to someone's **exit**, you are referring to the way that they left a situation or activity, or the fact that they left it. 退场；退出 [FORMAL] ❑ *It's her earliest exit from Wimbledon since going out in the opening round in 1997.* 这是她自1997年首轮出局以来最早一次从温布尔顿网球赛出局。 **5** V-T/V-I If you **exit** from a room or building, you leave it. 离开 [FORMAL] ❑ *She exits into the tropical storm.* 她走出去，进入热带风暴。 ❑ *As I exited the final display, I entered a hexagonal room.* 走出最后一个展览我便进入了一间六角形的房间。 **6** V-T If you **exit** a computer program or system, you stop running it. 退出 [COMPUTING] ❑ *I can open other applications without having to exit WordPerfect.* 我可以在不退出**WordPerfect**的情况下打开其他应用程序。 ● N-SING **Exit** is also a noun. 退出 ❑ *Press Exit to return to your document.* 按"退出"键返回到你的文档。

exit visa (**exit visas**) N-COUNT An **exit visa** is an official stamp in someone's passport, or an official document, which allows them to leave the country that they are visiting or living in. 出境签证

exo·dus /ɛksədəs/ N-SING If there is an **exodus of** people **from** a place, a lot of people leave that place at the same time. 大批离开 ❑ *The medical system is facing collapse because of an exodus of doctors.* 由于医生大批离去，该医疗体系正面临崩溃。

ex·or·bi·tant /ɪgzɔrbɪtənt/ ADJ If you describe something such as a price or fee as **exorbitant**, you are emphasizing that it is much higher than it should be. (价格、费用) 过高的 [EMPHASIS] ❑ *Exorbitant housing prices have created an acute shortage of affordable housing for the poor.* 过高的房价使穷人负担得起的房源严重短缺。

★ **ex·ot·ic** /ɪgzɒtɪk/ ADJ Something that is **exotic** is unusual and interesting, usually because it comes from or is related to a distant country. (常因来自遥远的他国而显得) 奇异的 ❑ ...*brilliantly colored, exotic flowers.* …色彩绚丽的奇异花卉。 ● **ex·oti·cal·ly** ADV 奇异地 ❑ ...*exotically beautiful scenery.* …奇异美景。

ex·pand ♦◇◇ /ɪkspænd/ (**expands, expanding, expanded**) **1** V-T/V-I If something **expands** or **is expanded**, it becomes larger. 扩大；膨胀 ❑ *Engineers noticed that the pipes were not expanding as expected.* 工程师们注意到管子并未像预期的那样膨胀。 ❑ *We have to expand the size of the image.* 我们不得不扩大图像的尺寸。 **2** V-T/V-I If something such as a business, organization, or service **expands**, or if you **expand** it, it becomes bigger and includes more people, goods, or activities. 使…发展；发展 [BUSINESS] ❑ *The popular ceramics industry expanded toward the middle of the 19th century.* 大众陶瓷业在19世纪中叶得到了发展。

▸ **expand on** or **expand upon** PHRASAL VERB If you **expand on** or **expand upon** something, you give more information or details about it when you write or talk about it. 更充分讲述；进一步论述 ❑ *The president used today's speech to expand on remarks he made last month.* 总统利用今天的演讲进一步阐述了他上个月的讲话内容。

ex·panse /ɪkspæns/ (**expanses**) N-COUNT An **expanse of** something, usually sea, sky, or land, is a very large amount of it. 一大片 (海洋、天空、土地等) ❑ ...*a vast expanse of grassland.* …一大片草地。

ex·pan·sion ♦◇◇ /ɪkspænʃᵊn/ (**expansions**) N-VAR **Expansion** is the process of becoming greater in size, number, or amount. 扩张；发展 ❑ ...*the rapid expansion of private health insurance.* …私人健康保险的快速发展。

ex·pan·sive /ɪkspænsɪv/ ADJ If you are **expansive**, you talk a lot, or are friendly or generous, because you are feeling happy and relaxed. (因高兴或放松而) 健谈的；友好的；大方的 ❑ *He was becoming more expansive as he relaxed.* 他放松时变得更健谈。

Word Link *pater, patr ≈ father : expatriate, paternal, patronize*

ex·pat·ri·ate /ɛkspeɪtriət, -pæt-/ (**expatriates**) N-COUNT An **expatriate** is someone who is living in a country that is not their own. 侨居者 ❑ ...*British expatriates in Spain.* …侨居西班牙的英国人。 ● ADJ **Expatriate** is also an adjective. 侨居的 [ADJ n] ❑ *The expatriate vote could help determine who wins in November.* 侨居者们的投票有助于决定谁在11月获胜。

ex·pect ♦♦♦ /ɪkspɛkt/ (**expects, expecting, expected**) **1** V-T If you **expect** something **to** happen, you believe that it will happen. 预料 ❑ ...*a workman who expects to lose his job in the next few weeks.* …一个预料会在接下来几周里失业的工人。 ❑ *The talks are expected to continue until tomorrow.* 会谈预料将持续到明天。 **2** V-T If you **are expecting** something or someone, you believe that they will be delivered to you or come to you soon, often because this has been arranged earlier. (常指因已安排而) 预期 [usu cont] ❑ *I wasn't expecting a visitor.* 我没有预期会有访客。

> Do not confuse **expect, wait for,** and **look forward to.** When you are **expecting** someone or something, you think that the person or thing is going to arrive or that the thing is going to happen. ❑ *I sent a postcard so they were expecting me... We are expecting rain.* When you **wait for** someone or something, you stay in the same place until the person arrives or the thing happens. ❑ *Whiskey was served while we waited for him... We got off the plane and waited for our luggage.* When you **look forward to** something that is going to happen, you feel happy because you think you will enjoy it. ❑ *I'll bet you're looking forward to your holidays... I always looked forward to seeing her.*

3 V-T If you **expect** something, or **expect** a person **to** do something, you believe that it is your right to have that thing, or the person's duty to do it for you. 期待 ❑ *He wasn't expecting our hospitality.* 他没有期待我们的热情款待。 ❑ *I do expect to have some time to myself in the evenings.* 我真期待晚上能有点儿自己的时间。 **4** V-T If you tell someone not to **expect** something, you mean that the thing is unlikely to happen as they have planned or imagined, and they should not hope that it will. 指望 [with brd-neg] ❑ *Don't expect an instant cure.* 别指望会有立竿见影的疗效。 ❑ *You cannot expect to like all the people you will work with.* 你不能指望喜欢所有和你一起工作的人。 **5** V-T/V-I If you say that a woman **is expecting** a baby, or that she **is expecting**, you mean that she is pregnant. 怀上；怀孕 [only cont] ❑ *She was expecting another baby.* 她怀上又一个孩子了。 **6** PHRASE You say "**I expect**" to suggest that a statement is probably correct, or a natural consequence of the present situation, although you have no definite knowledge. 我想 [SPOKEN] ❑ *I expect you can guess what follows.* 我想你能猜出下面会发生什么。 ❑ *I expect you're tired.* 我想你是累了。

★ **ex·pec·tan·cy** /ɪkspɛktənsi/ N-UNCOUNT **Expectancy** is the feeling or hope that something exciting, interesting, or good is about to happen. 期待 ❑ *The supporters had a tremendous air of expectancy.* 支持者满怀期待。

ex·pec·tant /ɪkspɛktənt/ **1** ADJ If someone is **expectant**, they are excited because they think something interesting is about to happen. 期待的 ❑ *An expectant crowd gathered.* 满怀期待的一群人聚在了一起。 ● **ex·pect·ant·ly** ADV 期待地 [ADV after v] ❑ *The others waited, looking at him expectantly.* 其他人等待着，期待地看着他。 **2** ADJ An **expectant** mother or father is someone whose baby is going to be born soon. 即将做父母的 [ADJ n] ❑ ...*a magazine for expectant mothers.* …一本适合孕妇的杂志。

ex·pec·ta·tion ♦◇◇ /ɛkspɛkteɪʃᵊn/ (**expectations**) **1** N-UNCOUNT Your **expectations** are your strong hopes or beliefs that something will happen or that you will get something that you want. 期盼 [also N in pl] ❑ *Their hope, and their expectation, was that she was going to be found safe and that she would be returned to her family.* 他们的希望和期盼是她被找到时安全无恙并被送回她家。 **2** N-COUNT A person's **expectations** are strong beliefs they have about the proper way someone should behave or something should happen. 期望 ❑ *Stephen Chase had determined to live up to the expectations of the company.* 斯蒂芬·蔡斯已决心不辜负公司的期望。

Word Partnership *expectation* 的常用搭配：

N.	expectation **of privacy**, **sense of** expectation **1**
ADJ.	**realistic** expectation, **reasonable** expectation **1 2**

ex·pedi·en·cy /ɪkspidiənsi/ N-UNCOUNT **Expediency** means doing what is convenient rather than what is morally right. 权宜之计 [FORMAL] ❑ *This was a matter less of morals than of expediency.* 此举主要是权宜之计，而非道德问题。

e

ex·pedi·ent /ɪkspidiənt/ (**expedients**) 1 N-COUNT An **expedient** is an action that achieves a particular purpose, but may not be morally right. 权宜之举 ❑ *The curfew regulation is a temporary expedient made necessary by a sudden emergency.* 宵禁令是应对突发事件时必要的临时权宜之举。 2 ADJ If it is **expedient to** do something, it is useful or convenient to do it, even though it may not be morally right. 权宜的 ❑ *Governments frequently ignore human rights abuses in other countries if it is politically expedient to do so.* 如果在政治上对自己有利，政府经常忽视其他国家侵犯人权的行为。

★ **ex·pedi·tion** /ɛkspɪdɪʃən/ (**expeditions**) 1 N-COUNT An **expedition** is an organized trip made for a particular purpose such as exploration. (以探险等为目的的) 有组织的旅行 ❑ *...Byrd's 1928 expedition to Antarctica.* …伯德1982年到南极洲的探险之旅。 2 N-COUNT You can refer to a group of people who are going on an expedition as an **expedition**. (以探险等为目的的) 旅行队 ❑ *Forty-three members of the expedition were killed.* 探险队中43名成员丧生。 3 N-COUNT An **expedition** is a short trip that you make for pleasure. 短程旅行 ❑ *...Officer Goss was on a fishing expedition.* …戈斯军官正在进行一次垂钓之旅。

Word Link *pel ≈ driving, forcing : compel, expel, propel*

ex·pel /ɪkspɛl/ (**expels, expelling, expelled**) 1 V-T If someone **is expelled from** a school or organization, they are officially told to leave because they have behaved badly. 开除 [usu passive] ❑ *More than five-thousand high school students have been expelled for cheating.* 五千多名中学生因考试作弊而被开除。 2 V-T If people **are expelled from** a place, they are made to leave it, often by force. 逐出 ❑ *An American academic was expelled from the country yesterday.* 一名美国学者昨天被逐出该国。 ❑ *They were told that they should expel the refugees.* 他们被告知应该逐出那些难民。 3 V-T To **expel** something means to force it out from a container or from your body. 排出 ❑ *As the lungs exhale this waste, gas is expelled into the atmosphere.* 当肺呼出这股废气，气体就被排到空气中。

★ **ex·pend** /ɪkspɛnd/ (**expends, expending, expended**) V-T To **expend** something, especially energy, time, or money, means to use it or spend it. 花费；消耗 [FORMAL] ❑ *Children expend a lot of energy and may need more high-energy food than adults.* 孩子们耗能多，可能比成人需要更多高能量的食物。

★ **ex·pendi·ture** /ɪkspɛndɪtʃər/ (**expenditures**) N-VAR **Expenditure** is the spending of money on something, or the money that is spent on something. 花销；支出 [FORMAL] ❑ *Policies of tax reduction must lead to reduced public expenditure.* 减税政策必然导致公共开支减少。

ex·pense ♦◇◇ /ɪkspɛns/ (**expenses**) 1 N-VAR **Expense** is the money that something costs you or that you need to spend in order to do something. 花费 ❑ *He's bought a big TV at vast expense so that everyone can see properly.* 他花了很多钱买了台大电视，这样人人都可以看清楚了。 2 N-PLURAL **Expenses** are amounts of money that you spend while doing something in the course of your work, which will be paid back to you afterwards. (由雇主报销的工作) 开支 [BUSINESS] ❑ *Her airfare and hotel expenses were paid by the committee.* 她乘飞机及住酒店的费用由该委员会支付了。 3 PHRASE If you do something **at** someone's **expense**, they provide the money for it. 由…付费 ❑ *Should architects continue to be trained for five years at public expense?* 建筑师继续受训5年应由公众付费吗？ 4 PHRASE If someone laughs or makes a joke **at** your **expense**, they do it to make you seem foolish. 捉弄 (某人) ❑ *I think he's having fun at our expense.* 我看他是在拿咱们寻开心。 5 PHRASE If you achieve something **at the expense of** someone, you do it in a way that might cause them some harm or disadvantage. 以牺牲 (某人的利益) 为代价 ❑ *According to this study, women have made notable gains at the expense of men.* 根据这项研究，女性以牺牲男性的利益为代价而取得了显著收益。 6 PHRASE If you say that someone does something **at the expense of** another thing, you are expressing concern that they are not doing the second thing, because the first thing uses all their resources. 以牺牲 (某物) 为代价 [DISAPPROVAL] ❑ *The orchestra has more discipline now, but at the expense of spirit.* 该管弦乐队现在更有纪律了，但却牺牲了士气。 7 PHRASE If you **go to the expense of** doing something, you do something that costs a lot of money. If you **go to** great **expense to** do something, you spend a lot of money in order to achieve it. 花大钱 (做某事) ❑ *Why go to the expense of buying an electric saw when you can borrow one?* 你能借到电锯，却为何去花钱买呢？

Word Partnership *expense* 的常用搭配：

ADJ. **additional** expense, **extra** expense, **medical** expense 1
N. **business** expense 1 2

ex·pense ac·count (**expense accounts**) N-COUNT An **expense account** is an arrangement between an employer and an employee that allows the employee to spend the company's money on things relating to their job, such as traveling or dealing with clients. (由公司报销的) 费用账户 [BUSINESS] ❑ *He put Elizabeth's motel bill and airfare on his expense account.* 他把伊丽莎白住汽车旅馆的费用和机票费用记在了他的报销账户上。

ex·pen·sive ♦♦◇ /ɪkspɛnsɪv/ ADJ If something is **expensive**, it costs a lot of money. 昂贵的 ❑ *Broadband is still more expensive than dial-up services.* 宽带还是要比拨号服务费钱得多。 ● **ex·pen·sive·ly** ADV 昂贵地 ❑ *She was expensively dressed, with fine furs and jewels.* 她衣饰奢华，穿戴着上好的毛皮和珠宝。

Thesaurus *expensive* 另参见：

ADJ. costly, pricey, upscale; *(ant.)* cheap, economical, inexpensive

ex·peri·ence ♦♦♦ /ɪkspɪəriəns/ (**experiences, experiencing, experienced**) 1 N-UNCOUNT **Experience** is knowledge or skill in a particular job or activity that you have gained because you have done that job or activity for a long time. 经验 ❑ *He has also had managerial experience on every level.* 他还具备各层次的管理经验。 2 N-UNCOUNT **Experience** is used to refer to the past events, knowledge, and feelings that make up someone's life or character. 阅历 ❑ *I should not be in any danger here, but experience has taught me caution.* 我在这里应该没有任何危险，但阅历已教会我谨慎。 3 N-COUNT An **experience** is something that you do or that happens to you, especially something important that affects you. 经历 ❑ *His only experience of gardening so far proved immensely satisfying.* 他仅有的园艺经历到目前为止非常令人满意。 4 V-T If you **experience** a particular situation, you are in that situation or it happens to you. 经历 ❑ *We had never experienced this kind of vacation before and had no idea what to expect.* 我们以前从未经历过这种假期，不知道有什么可期待的。 5 V-T If you **experience** a feeling, you feel it or are affected by it. 感受 ❑ *Widows seem to experience more distress than widowers.* 寡妇似乎比鳏夫感受更多痛苦。 ● N-SING **Experience** is also a noun. 感受 ❑ *...the experience of pain.* …痛苦的感受。

Thesaurus *experience* 另参见：

N. know-how, knowledge, wisdom; *(ant.)* inexperience 1

Word Partnership *experience* 的常用搭配：

ADJ. **professional** experience 1
valuable experience 1 – 3
past experience, **shared** experience 2 3
learning experience, **religious** experience, **traumatic** experience 3
N. **work** experience 1
life experience 2
experience **a loss** 4
experience **symptoms** 5

ex·pe·ri·enced /ɪkspɪəriənst/ ADJ If you describe someone as **experienced**, you mean that they have been doing a particular job or activity for a long time, and therefore know a lot about it or are very skillful at it. 有经验的 ❑ *...lawyers who are experienced in these matters.* …在这些事情上有经验的律师们。 ❑ *It's a team packed with experienced and mature professionals.* 这是一支经验丰富的，成熟的专家队伍。

ex·peri·ment ♦◇◇ (**experiments, experimenting, experimented**)

The noun is pronounced /ɪkspɛrɪmənt/. The verb is pronounced /ɪkspɛrɪmɛnt/.

名词读作 /ɪkspɛrɪmənt/。动词读作 /ɪkspɛrɪmɛnt/。

1 N-VAR An **experiment** is a scientific test done in order to discover what happens to something in particular conditions. 实验 ❑ *The astronauts are conducting a series of experiments to learn more about how the body adapts to weightlessness.* 那些宇航员正在进行一系列实验，以便更多地了解人体如何适应失重状态。 2 V-I If you **experiment**

Word Web

Scientists learn much of what they know through **controlled experiments**. The scientific method provides a dependable way to understand natural **phenomena**. The first step in any experiment is **observation**. During this stage researchers examine the situation and ask a question about it. They may also read what others have discovered about it. Next, they state a **hypothesis**. Then they use the hypothesis to design an experiment and **predict** what will happen. Next comes the **testing** phase. Often researchers do several experiments using different **variables**. If all of the **evidence** supports the hypothesis, it becomes a new **theory**.

with something or **experiment on** it, you do a scientific test on it in order to discover what happens to it in particular conditions. 做实验 ❑ *In 1857 Mendel started experimenting with peas in his monastery garden.* 1857年孟德尔开始在其修道院菜园里用豌豆做实验。 ❑ *The scientists have experimented on the tiny neck arteries of rats.* 那些科学家已在老鼠细小的颈动脉上做了实验。 ●

/ɪkspɛrɪmɛnteɪʃᵊn/ N-UNCOUNT 实验 ❑ *...the ethical aspects of animal experimentation.* …动物实验的伦理视角。 N-VAR An **experiment** is the trying out of a new idea or method in order to see what it is like and what effects it has. 尝试 ❑ *As an experiment, we bought Ted a watch.* 作为尝试，我们给特德买了块手表。 V-I To **experiment** means to try out a new idea or method to see what it is like and what effects it has. 尝试 ❑ *...if you like cooking and have the time to experiment.* …如果你喜欢烹饪并且有时间尝试的话。

● N-UNCOUNT 尝试 ❑ *Decentralization and experimentation must be encouraged.* 权力下放和尝试必须予以鼓励。

→ see Word Web: **experiment**

→ see **laboratory, science**

Word Partnership

conduct an experiment
perform an experiment, **try an** experiment
scientific experiment
simple experiment

/ɪkspɛrɪmɛntᵊl/ ADJ Something that is **experimental** is new or uses new ideas or methods, and might be modified later if it is unsuccessful. 试验性的 ❑ *...an experimental air-conditioning system.* …一种试验性的空调系统。 ADJ **Experimental** means using, used in, or resulting from scientific experiments. 实验的 [ADJ n] ❑ *...the main techniques of experimental science.* …实验科学的主要技术。 ● ADV 实验地 [ADV with v] ❑ *...an ecology laboratory, where communities of species can be studied experimentally under controlled conditions.* …一个可在受控条件下对物种群落进行实验研究的生态实验室。 ADJ An **experimental** action is done in order to see what it is like, or what effects it has. 试验性的 ❑ *The senator is ready to argue for an experimental lifting of the ban.* 该参议员已准备好争取那条禁令的试验性解除。

● ADV 试验性地 [ADV with v] ❑ *This system is being tried out experimentally at many universities.* 该系统正在很多大学试用。

/ɛkspɜrt/ (**experts**) N-COUNT An **expert** is a person who is very skilled at doing something or who knows a lot about a particular subject. 专家；行家 ❑ *...a yoga expert.* …一位瑜伽专家。 ADJ Someone who is **expert at** doing something is very skilled at it. 在行的 ❑ *The Japanese are expert at lowering manufacturing costs.* 日本人在降低生产成本方面很在行。 ● ADV 在行地 [ADV with v] ❑ *Shopkeepers expertly rolled spices up in bay leaves.* 店主在行地把各种香料卷进了月桂叶中。 ADJ If you say that someone has **expert** hands or an **expert** eye, you mean that they are very skillful or experienced in using their hands or eyes for a particular purpose. 行家的 [ADJ n] ❑ *Harvey cured the pain with his own expert hands.* 哈维用他那行家之手治愈了那病痛。 ADJ **Expert** advice or help is given by someone who has studied a subject thoroughly or who is very skilled at a particular job. 专家的 [ADJ n] ❑ *We'll need an expert opinion.* 我们将需要专家的意见。

Word Partnership

leading expert
expert **advice**, expert **opinion**, expert **witness**

/ɛkspɜrtiz/ N-UNCOUNT **Expertise** is special skill or knowledge that is acquired by training, study, or practice. 专业技能；专业知识 ❑ *She was not an accountant and didn't have the expertise to verify all of the financial details.* 她不是会计，不具有核查所有这些财政细目的专业知识。

(**expiration dates**) N-COUNT The **expiration date** on a food container is the date by which the food should be sold or eaten before it starts to decay. 保质期 [AM] ❑ *But soda past its expiration date goes flat and loses much of its taste.* 但是过期的苏打水跑气，味道也会大打折扣。

/ɪkspaɪər/ (**expires, expiring, expired**) V-I When something such as a contract, deadline, or visa **expires**, it comes to an end or is no longer valid. 到期；失效 ❑ *He had lived illegally in the United States for five years after his visitor's visa expired.* 访问签证到期后他在美国非法居住了5年。

/ɪkspleɪn/ (**explains, explaining, explained**) V-T/V-I If you **explain** something, you give details about it or describe it so that it can be understood. 解释（意思） ❑ *Not every judge, however, has the ability to explain the law in simple terms.* 然而，并非每个法官都能用浅易的话来解释法律。 ❑ *Don't sign anything until your lawyer has explained the contract to you.* 在你的律师向你解释该合同之前什么也别签。 ❑ *Professor Griffiths explained how the drug appears to work.* 格里菲斯教授解释了该药似乎是怎样起作用的。 V-T/V-I If you **explain**, or **explain** something that has happened, you give people reasons for it, especially in an attempt to justify it. 解释（原因） ❑ *"Let me explain, sir."—"Don't tell me about it. I don't want to know."* "让我来解释，先生。"——"别跟我说那事。我不想知道。" ❑ *Before she ran away, she left a note explaining her actions.* 逃走之前，她留下了张便条为她的行为作了解释。 ❑ *Explain why you didn't telephone.* 解释一下你为什么不打电话。

PHRASAL VERB If someone **explains away** a mistake or a bad situation they are responsible for, they try to indicate that it is unimportant or that it is not really their fault. 为…辩解 ❑ *He evaded her questions about the war and tried to explain away the atrocities.* 他回避了她关于战争的提问，试图为其暴行辩解。

Thesaurus

describe, tell
account for, justify

/ɛkspləneɪʃᵊn/ (**explanations**) N-COUNT If you give an **explanation** of something that has happened, you give people reasons for it, especially in an attempt to justify it. 解释（原因） [also "of/in" N] ❑ *She told the court she would give a full explanation of the prosecution's decision on Monday.* 她告诉法庭她将在星期一就控方的决定做出详尽的解释。 N-COUNT If you say there is an **explanation for** something, you mean that there is a reason for it. 原因 ❑ *The deputy airport manager said there was no apparent explanation for the crash.* 机场副经理称那次飞机坠毁没有明显的原因。 N-COUNT If you give an **explanation of** something, you give details about it or describe it so that it can be understood. 详细说明 ❑ *He has given a very clear explanation of his remarks and the context in which they were made.* 他对他的评论以及作出那些评论的情境已经作了非常清楚详细的说明。

Word Partnership

only explanation, **possible** explanation
brief explanation, **detailed** explanation, **logical** explanation
give an explanation, **offer an** explanation, **provide an** explanation

/ɪksplænətɔri/ ADJ **Explanatory** statements or theories are intended to make people understand something by describing it or giving the reasons for it. 解释性的 [FORMAL]

❑ *These statements are accompanied by a series of explanatory notes.* 这些声明附有一系列的解释性注释。

ex·plic·it /ɪksplɪsɪt/ **1** ADJ Something that is **explicit** is expressed or shown clearly and openly, without any attempt to hide anything. 明确表达的；公开显露的 ❑ *Sexually explicit scenes in movies and books were taboo under the old regime.* 电影和书籍中露骨的性爱场景在旧体制下是禁忌的。● **ex·plic·it·ly** ADV 明确表达地；公开显露地 ❑ *The play was the first commercially successful work dealing explicitly with homosexuality.* 该剧是首部在商业上获得成功的公然描写同性恋的作品。 **2** ADJ If you are **explicit about** something, you speak about it very openly and clearly. 直言不讳的 [v-link ADJ, oft ADJ "about" n] ❑ *He was explicit about his intention to overhaul the party's internal voting system.* 他对自己彻底革新该党内投票体制的意图直言不讳。● **ex·plic·it·ly** ADV 直言不讳地 [ADV with v] ❑ *She has been talking very explicitly about AIDS to these groups.* 她一直在毫不避讳地与这些群体谈论艾滋病。

Word Link *ex ≈ away, from, out : exceed, exit, explode*

ex·plode ♦◇◇ /ɪksploʊd/ (**explodes, exploding, exploded**) **1** V-T/V-I If an object such as a bomb **explodes** or if someone or something **explodes** it, it bursts loudly and with great force, often causing damage or injury. 使爆炸；爆炸 ❑ *They were clearing up when the second bomb exploded.* 他们在清理时第二颗炸弹爆炸了。 **2** V-I If someone **explodes**, they express strong feelings suddenly and violently. (情感) 迸发 ❑ *Do you fear that you'll burst into tears or explode with anger in front of her?* 你害怕在她面前突然大哭或勃然大怒吗？❑ *"What happened!" I exploded.* "出什么事了！"我情绪爆发了。 **3** V-I If something **explodes**, it increases suddenly and rapidly in number or intensity. 暴涨 ❑ *The population explodes to 40,000 during the tourist season.* 旅游季节人数暴涨至4万。 **4** V-T If someone **explodes** a theory or myth, they prove that it is wrong or impossible. 推翻 (理论等) ❑ *Electricity privatization has exploded the myth of cheap nuclear power.* 电力私有化打破了廉价核电力的神话。
→ see **firework**

Thesaurus *explode* 另参见：

V. blow up, erupt, go off **1**
discredit, disprove, shoot down **4**

Word Partnership *explode* 的常用搭配：

N. **bombs** explode, **missiles** explode **1**
populations explode **3**
ADJ. **ready to** explode **1** **2**
PREP. **about to** explode **1** – **3**

ex·ploit ♦◇◇ (**exploits, exploiting, exploited**)

The verb is pronounced /ɪksplɔɪt/. The noun is pronounced /ɛksplɔɪt/.

动词读作 /ɪksplɔɪt/。名词读作 /ɛksplɔɪt/。

1 V-T If you say that someone **is exploiting** you, you think that they are treating you unfairly by using your work or ideas and giving you very little in return. 利用；剥削 ❑ *Critics claim he exploited black musicians for personal gain.* 批评家们声称他为私利利用了黑人音乐家们。● **ex·ploi·ta·tion** /ɛksplɔɪteɪʃᵊn/ N-UNCOUNT 利用；剥削 ❑ *Extra payments should be made to protect the interests of the staff and prevent exploitation.* 额外报酬应被支付以维护员工的利益和防止剥削。 **2** V-T If you say that someone **is exploiting** a situation, you disapprove of them because they are using it to gain an advantage for themselves, rather than trying to help other people or do what is right. 利用 (某种情势) [DISAPPROVAL] ❑ *The government and its opponents compete to exploit the troubles to their advantage.* 政府及其反对者们竞相利用这些动乱来取得利益。● **ex·ploi·ta·tion** N-SING (对某种情势的) 利用 ❑ *...the exploitation of the famine by local politicians.* …当地政客对饥荒的利用。 **3** V-T If you **exploit** something, you use it well, and achieve something or gain an advantage from it. 充分利用 ❑ *You'll need a good antenna to exploit the radio's performance.* 你需要一根好的天线来充分利用该电台的节目。 **4** V-T To **exploit** resources or raw materials means to develop them and use them for industry or commercial activities. 开发利用 (资源、原材料) ❑ *I think we're being very short-sighted in not exploiting our own coal.* 我想我们不开采利用自己的煤矿实在是目光短浅。● **ex·ploi·ta·tion** N-UNCOUNT (对资源、原材料的) 开发利用 ❑ *...the planned exploitation of its potential oil and natural gas reserves.* …对其潜在石油和天然气储备的有计划的开采利用。 **5** N-COUNT If you refer to someone's **exploits**, you mean the brave, interesting, or amusing things that they have done. 英勇事迹 ❑ *His wartime exploits were later made into a film and a television series.* 他战时的英勇事迹后来被改编成了电影和电视剧。

ex·plora·tory /ɪksplɔrətɔri/ ADJ **Exploratory** actions are done in order to discover something or to learn the truth about something. 探索性的；探查的 ❑ *Exploratory surgery revealed her liver cancer.* 探查手术发现了她的肝癌。

ex·plore ♦◇◇ /ɪksplɔr/ (**explores, exploring, explored**) **1** V-T/V-I If you **explore**, or **explore** a place, you travel around it to find out what it is like. 考察 ❑ *I just wanted to explore on my own.* 我只是想独自考察一下。 ❑ *After exploring the old part of town there is a guided tour of the cathedral.* 考察老城区之后，有到大教堂的导览之旅。● **ex·plo·ra·tion** /ɛkspləreɪʃᵊn/ N-VAR (**explorations**) 考察 ❑ *We devote several days to the exploration of the magnificent Maya sites of Copan.* 我们投入了几天时间在科潘宏伟的玛雅遗址考察。 **2** V-T If you **explore** an idea or suggestion, you think about it or comment on it in detail, in order to assess it carefully. 探讨 ❑ *The movie is eloquent as it explores the relationship between artist and instrument.* 这部影片探讨艺术家与乐器之间的关系，意味深长。● **ex·plo·ra·tion** N-VAR 探讨 ❑ *I looked forward to the exploration of their theories.* 我期待着对他们的理论进行探讨。 **3** V-I If people **explore for** a substance such as oil or minerals, they study an area and do tests on the land to see whether they can find it. 勘探 ❑ *Central to the operation is a mile-deep well, dug originally to explore for oil.* 那次行动的重点是一口原本为勘探石油而挖的一英里深的井。● **ex·plo·ra·tion** N-UNCOUNT 勘探 ❑ *Oryx is a Dallas-based oil and gas exploration and production concern.* 奥瑞克斯公司是一家以达拉斯为基地的石油和天然气勘探及生产公司。 **4** V-T If you **explore** something with your hands or fingers, you touch it to find out what it feels like. 摸索 ❑ *He explored the wound with his finger, trying to establish its extent.* 他用手指探查伤口，试图确定受伤的程度。

ex·plor·er /ɪksplɔrər/ (**explorers**) N-COUNT An **explorer** is someone who travels to places about which very little is known, in order to discover what is there. 探险者 ❑ *...the travels of Columbus, Magellan, and many other explorers.* …哥伦布、麦哲伦和许多其他探险家的旅行。

ex·plo·sion ♦◇◇ /ɪksploʊʒᵊn/ (**explosions**) **1** N-COUNT An **explosion** is a sudden, violent burst of energy, such as one caused by a bomb. 爆炸 ❑ *After the second explosion, all of London's main train and subway stations were shut down.* 第二次爆炸后，伦敦所有的主要火车站及地铁站都被关闭了。 **2** N-VAR **Explosion** is the act of deliberately causing a bomb or similar device to explode. 引爆 ❑ *Bomb disposal experts blew up the bag in a controlled explosion.* 拆弹专家在一次控制爆破中炸掉了那个袋子。 **3** N-COUNT An **explosion** is a large rapid increase in the number or amount of something. 暴增；暴涨 ❑ *The study also forecast an explosion in the diet soft-drink market.* 这项研究还预测了低糖软饮料市场的暴增。 **4** N-COUNT An **explosion** is a sudden violent expression of someone's feelings, especially anger. (情感、尤指愤怒的) 暴发 ❑ *Every time they met, Myra anticipated an explosion.* 每次他们相见，迈拉都预期会有一场怒火暴发。 **5** N-COUNT An **explosion** is a sudden and serious political protest or violence. (抗议、暴力行为的) 爆发 ❑ *...the explosion of protest and violence sparked off by the killing of seven workers.* …由7名工人被杀引起的抗议及暴力行为的爆发。

ex·plo·sive /ɪksploʊsɪv/ (**explosives**) **1** N-VAR An **explosive** is a substance or device that can cause an explosion. 炸药；爆炸物 ❑ *...one-hundred-and-fifty pounds of Semtex explosive.* …150磅的塞姆汀塑料炸药。 **2** ADJ Something that is **explosive** is capable of causing an explosion. 能引起爆炸的 ❑ *The explosive device was timed to go off at the rush hour.* 该爆炸装置定在交通高峰时间爆炸。 **3** ADJ An **explosive** growth is a sudden, rapid increase in the size or quantity of something. 暴涨的 ❑ *The explosive growth in casinos is one of the most conspicuous signs of Westernization.* 赌场数量的暴涨是最明显的西化标志之一。 **4** ADJ An **explosive** situation is likely to have difficult, serious, or dangerous effects. 爆炸性的 (局势) ❑ *He appeared to be treating the potentially explosive situation with some sensitivity.* 他似乎正在有些敏感地处理潜在的爆炸性局面。 **5** ADJ If you describe someone as **explosive**, you mean that they tend to express sudden violent anger. 脾气暴躁的 ❑ *He's inherited his father's explosive temper.* 他遗传了他父亲的火暴性子。
→ see **tunnel**

expo /ɛkspoʊ/ (**expos**) also **Expo** N-COUNT An **expo** is a large event where goods, especially industrial goods, are displayed. 博览会 ❑ *...the 1995 Queensland Computer Expo.* …1995年昆士兰计算机博览会。

▲ **ex·po·nent** /ɪkspoʊnənt/ (**exponents**) **1** N-COUNT An **exponent of** an idea, theory, or plan is a person who supports and explains it, and who tries to persuade other people that it is a good idea. 倡导者 [FORMAL] ❑ *...a leading exponent of test-tube baby techniques.* …一位试管婴儿技术的主要倡导者。 **2** N-COUNT An **exponent of** a particular skill or activity is a person who is good at it. 擅长者；典范 ❑ *The Alvin Ailey American Dance Theater was formed in the 1950s and quickly established itself as a leading exponent of progressive choreography and contemporary dance.* 阿尔文·艾利美国舞蹈剧形成于20世纪50年代，并很快树立自己为激进舞蹈艺术和现代舞蹈的最主要的典范。

Word Link *port ≈ carrying : export, import, portable*

ex·port ♦♦◊ (**exports, exporting, exported**)

The verb is pronounced /ɪkspɔrt/. The noun is pronounced /ɛksport/.

动词读作 /ɪkspɔrt/。名词读作 /ɛksport/。

1 V-T/V-I To **export** products or raw materials means to sell them to another country. 出口 ❑ *The nation also exports beef.* 该国也出口牛肉。❑ *They expect the antibiotic products to be exported to Southeast Asia and Africa.* 他们期望抗生素产品出口到东南亚和非洲。 ❑ *The company now exports to Japan.* 该公司现在对日本出口。 ● N-UNCOUNT **Export** is also a noun. 出口 [also N in pl] ❑ *...the production and export of cheap casual wear.* …廉价休闲服的生产与出口。 ❑ *A lot of our land is used to grow crops for export.* 我们很多的土地用来种植出口作物。 **2** N-COUNT **Exports** are goods sold to another country and sent there. 出口品 ❑ *Ghana's main export is cocoa.* 加纳的主要出口产品是可可。 **3** V-T To **export** something means to introduce it into another country or make it happen there. 引入他国 ❑ *It has exported inflation at times.* 它有时将通货膨胀引入他国。 **4** V-T In computing, if you **export** files or information from one type of software into another type, you change their format so that they can be used in the new software. 导出（文件、信息）❑ *Files can be exported in ASCII or PCX formats.* 文件可用ASCII或PCX格式导出。

ex·port·able /ɪkspɔrtəbᵊl/ ADJ **Exportable** products are suitable for being exported. 可出口的 ❑ *They are reliant on a very limited number of exportable products.* 他们依赖于数量非常有限的可出口产品。

ex·port·er /ɛkspɔrtər, ɪkspɔrtər/ (**exporters**) N-COUNT An **exporter** is a country, company, or person that sells and sends goods to another country. 出口国；出口公司；出口商 ❑ *France is the world's second-biggest exporter of agricultural products.* 法国是世界第二大农产品出口国。

ex·pose ♦◊◊ /ɪkspoʊz/ (**exposes, exposing, exposed**) **1** V-T To **expose** something that is usually hidden means to uncover it so that it can be seen. 使显露 ❑ *Lowered sea levels exposed the shallow continental shelf beneath the Bering Sea.* 下降了的海平面使白令海底的浅大陆架露了出来。 **2** V-T To **expose** a person or situation means to reveal that they are bad or immoral in some way. 揭露 ❑ *...the story of how the press helped expose the truth about the Nixon administration.* …关于新闻界如何协助揭露尼克松政府真相的报道。 **3** V-T If someone **is exposed to** something dangerous or unpleasant, they are put in a situation in which it might affect them. 使暴露于（危险或令人不快的境地）❑ *They had not been exposed to most diseases common to urban populations.* 他们未曾遭遇城市人口常得的大多数疾病。 ❑ *A wise mother never exposes her children to the slightest possibility of danger.* 一个明智的母亲从不会置其孩子于丝毫可能的危险中。 **4** V-T If someone **is exposed to** an idea or feeling, usually a new one, they are given experience of it, or introduced to it. 使体验（观念、情感）；引入（观念、情感）❑ *...local people who've not been exposed to glimpses of Western life before.* …以前从未领略过西方生活方式的当地人。

★ **ex·po·si·tion** /ɛkspəzɪʃᵊn/ (**expositions**) **1** N-COUNT An **exposition of** an idea or theory is a detailed explanation or account of it. 阐述 [oft N "of" n] [FORMAL] ❑ *Aristotle was valued because of his clear exposition of rational thought.* 亚里士多德因其对理性思维的清晰阐述而被重视。 **2** N-COUNT An **exposition** is an exhibition in which something such as goods or works of art are shown to the public. 展览 ❑ *...an art exposition.* …一个艺术展览。

ex·po·sure ♦◊◊ /ɪkspoʊʒər/ (**exposures**) **1** N-UNCOUNT **Exposure to** something dangerous means being in a situation where it might affect you. 暴露 ❑ *Exposure to lead is known to damage the brains of young children.* 已知接触铅会损害幼童的大脑。 **2** N-UNCOUNT **Exposure** is the harmful effect on your body caused by very cold weather. 受冻 ❑ *He was suffering from exposure and shock but his condition was said to be stable.* 他受冻休克，但他的状态据说很稳定。 **3** N-UNCOUNT The **exposure** of a well-known person is the revealing of the fact that they are bad or immoral in some way. 揭发 ❑ *He undertook increasingly dangerous assignments until his exposure as a spy.* 在间谍身份暴露之前他一直从事日益危险的任务。 **4** N-UNCOUNT **Exposure** is publicity that a person, company, or product receives. 宣传 ❑ *All the candidates have been getting an enormous amount of exposure on television and in the press.* 所有候选人都在争取大量的电视和新闻媒体宣传。 **5** N-COUNT In photography, an **exposure** is a single photograph. 底片 [TECHNICAL] ❑ *Larger drawings tend to require two or three exposures to cover them.* 较大的图画需要两到三张底片来覆盖。

▲ **ex·pound** /ɪkspaʊnd/ (**expounds, expounding, expounded**) V-T If you **expound** an idea or opinion, you give a clear and detailed explanation of it. 阐释 [FORMAL] ❑ *Schmidt continued to expound his views on economics and politics.* 施密特继续阐释他关于经济与政治的观点。 ● PHRASAL VERB **Expound on** means the same as **expound**. 阐释 ❑ *Lawrence expounded on the military aspects of guerrilla warfare.* 劳伦斯详细阐释了游击战的军事情况。

ex·press ♦♦◊ /ɪksprɛs/ (**expresses, expressing, expressed**) **1** V-T When you **express** an idea or feeling, or **express yourself**, you show what you think or feel. 表达 ❑ *He expressed grave concern at American attitudes.* 他对美国的态度表达了严肃关注。 **2** V-T If an idea or feeling **expresses itself** in some way, it can be clearly seen in someone's actions or in its effects on a situation. （想法、情感）流露；呈现 ❑ *The anxiety of the separation often expresses itself as anger toward the child for getting lost.* 对失散的焦虑常常表现成对孩子走失的愤怒。 **3** ADJ An **express** command or order is one that is clearly and deliberately stated. 明确陈述的（命令、指令）[ADJ n] [FORMAL] ❑ *This mighty electricity-generating power station was built on the express orders of the president.* 这一大型电力发电站是按照总统的明确指令修建的。 ● **ex·press·ly** ADV 明确陈述地 [ADV before v] ❑ *He has expressly forbidden her to go out on her own.* 他已明确禁止她独自外出。 **4** ADJ If you refer to an **express** intention or purpose, you are emphasizing that it is a deliberate and specific one that you have before you do something. 特定的（意图、目的）[ADJ n] [EMPHASIS] ❑ *The express purpose of the flights was to get Americans out of the danger zone.* 这些航班的特定目的是让美国人离开该险区。 ● **ex·press·ly** ADV 特定地 ❑ *...projects expressly designed to support cattle farmers.* …为扶持养牛户而特定规划的项目。 **5** ADJ **Express** is used to describe special services provided by companies or organizations such as the U.S. Postal Service, in which things are sent or done faster than usual for a higher price. 快递的 [ADJ n] ❑ *A special express service is available by fax.* 一项特快服务通过传真可以实现。 ● ADV **Express** is also an adverb. 快递地 ❑ *Send it express.* 用快递把它送出。 **6** N-COUNT An **express** or an **express** train is a fast train that stops at very few stations. 快速列车 ❑ *Punctually at 7:45, the express to Kuala Lumpur left Singapore station.* 开往吉隆坡的特快列车7：45准时从新加坡站驶出。

Word Partnership *express* 的常用搭配：

N. express **appreciation**, express **your emotions**, express **gratitude**, express **sympathy**, **words to** express ***something*** **1**
express **purpose** **4**
express **mail**, express **service** **5**

ex·pres·sion ♦◊◊ /ɪksprɛʃᵊn/ (**expressions**) **1** N-VAR The **expression of** ideas or feelings is the showing of them through words, actions, or artistic activities. 表达 ❑ *Laughter is one of the most infectious expressions of emotion.* 笑是最具感染力的感情表达方式之一。 ❑ *...the rights of the individual to freedom of expression.* …个人表达自由权。 **2** N-VAR Your **expression** is the way that your face looks at a particular moment. It shows what you are thinking or feeling. 神情 ❑ *Levin sat there, an expression of sadness on his face.* 莱文坐在那里，神情忧伤。 **3** N-UNCOUNT **Expression** is the showing of feeling when you are acting, singing, or playing a musical instrument. （艺术表演中的）情感表现 ❑ *I think I put more expression into my lyrics than a lot of other singers do.* 我认为我比许多其他歌手在歌词中注入了更多的情感表达。 **4** N-COUNT An **expression** is a word or phrase. 字词；言辞 ❑ *She spoke in a quiet voice but used remarkably coarse expressions.* 她说话声音很轻，但使用了非常粗俗的言辞。

ex·pres·sive /ɪksprɛsɪv/ ADJ If you describe a person or their behavior as **expressive**, you mean that their behavior clearly indicates their feelings or intentions. 富于表现力的 ❑ *You can train people to be more expressive.* 你可以培训人们使其更富于表现力。❑ *...the present fashion for intuitive, expressive painting.* …当前凭直觉的、富于表现力的绘画风尚。● ADV 富于表现力地 [ADV with V] ❑ *He moved his hands expressively.* 他很有表现力地移动了双手。

/ɪksprɛsweɪ/ (**expressways**) N-COUNT An **expressway** is a wide road that is specially designed to carry a lot of traffic moving quickly. It has no stop signs or signals, and traffic traveling in one direction is separated from the traffic traveling in the opposite direction. 高速公路

Word Link	*puls ≈ driving, pushing : com ion, ex ion, im e*

/ɪkspʌlʃ°n/ (**expulsions**) N-VAR **Expulsion** is when someone is forced to leave a school, university, or organization. 被开除 ❑ *Her hatred of authority led to her expulsion from high school.* 她对权威的憎恨导致了她从高中被开除。 N-VAR **Expulsion** is when someone is forced to leave a place. 被逐出 [FORMAL] ❑ *...the expulsion of Yemeni workers.* …也门工人的被逐出。

/ɪkskwɪzɪt, ɛkskwɪzɪt/ ADJ Something that is **exquisite** is extremely beautiful or pleasant, especially in a delicate way. 精美的 ❑ *The Indians brought in exquisite beadwork to sell.* 印地安人带了精美的珠饰来销售。● ADV 精美地 ❑ *...exquisitely crafted dollshouses.* …制作精美的玩具小屋。

N-VAR **Ext.** is the written abbreviation for **extension** when it is used to refer to a particular telephone number. 分机号 [N num] ❑ *For a full festival program, call 206-555-7115, ext. 239.* 需要详尽的节日活动安排，请拨打电话206-555-7115，分机号239。

/ɪkstɛnd/ (**extends, extending, extended**)

V-I If you say that something, usually something large, **extends for** a particular distance or **extends from** one place **to** another, you are indicating its size or position. 延伸 ❑ *The caves extend for some 12 miles.* 这些洞穴延伸约12英里。 ❑ *The main stem will extend to around 12 ft, if left to develop naturally.* 如果让其自然生长，主干会延伸到12英尺左右。 V-I If an object **extends from** a surface or place, it sticks out from it. 伸出；凸出 ❑ *A table extended from the front of her desk to create a T-shaped seating arrangement.* 一张桌子从她的办公桌前端伸出，形成T型的座位排列。 V-I If an event or activity **extends over** a period of time, it continues for that time. 持续 ❑ *The normal cyclone season extends from December to April.* 正常的飓风季节从12月持续到4月。 V-I If something **extends to** a group of people, things, or activities, it includes or affects them. 包括；涉及 ❑ *The service also extends to wrapping and delivering gifts.* 这项服务还包括包装及递送礼物。 ❑ *The talks will extend to the church, human rights groups, and other social organizations.* 这些会谈将涉及教会、人权组织和其他的社会组织。 V-T If you **extend** something, you make it longer or bigger. 延长；扩大 ❑ *This year they have introduced three new products to extend their range.* 今年他们已引入了3种新产品以扩大他们的范围。 ❑ *The building was extended in 1500.* 该建筑于1500年扩建。

V-I If a piece of equipment or furniture **extends**, its length can be increased. 能伸展 ❑ *...a table that extends to accommodate extra guests.* …一张能伸展以容纳更多客人的桌子。 V-T If you **extend** something, you make it last longer than before or end at a later date. 延长期限 ❑ *They have extended the deadline by twenty-four hours.* 他们已经将最后期限延长了24小时。 V-T If you **extend** something **to** other people or things, you make it include or affect more people or things. 扩延（到其他人或物）❑ *It might be possible to extend the technique to other crop plants.* 把该技术扩延到其它农作物上也许是可能的。

V-T If someone **extends** their hand, they stretch out their arm and hand to shake hands with someone. 伸出 ❑ *The man extended his hand: "I'm Chuck."* 这位男士伸出了他的手："我是查克。"

/ɪkstɛnʃ°n/ (**extensions**) N-COUNT An **extension** is a new room or building that is added to an existing building or group of buildings. （已有建筑或建筑群的）延伸建筑 ❑ *We are thinking of having an extension built, as we now require an extra bedroom.* 我们正在考虑扩建房屋，因为我们现在需要多一间卧室。 N-COUNT An **extension** is a new section of a road or railroad that is added to an existing road or railroad. （已有公路、铁路的）延长路段 ❑ *...a proposed extension to the No. 7 subway line.* …提议的地铁7号线的一段延长路段。 N-COUNT An **extension** is an extra period of time for which something lasts or is valid, usually as a result of official permission. 延长的期限 ❑ *He first entered the country on a six-month visa, and was given a further extension of six months.* 他最初凭有效期为6个月的签证进入这个国家，之后又得到了6个月的续签。 N-COUNT Something that is an **extension of** something else is a development of it that includes or affects more people, things, or activities. 延展 ❑ *Many Filipinos see the bases as an extension of American colonial rule.* 许多菲律宾人把这些基地看作是美国殖民统治的延展。

N-COUNT An **extension** is a telephone line that is connected to the switchboard of a company or institution, and that has its own number. The written abbreviation **ext.** is also used. （电话的）分机 [also N num] ❑ *She can get me on extension 308.* 她可以通过分机308找到我。 N-COUNT An **extension** is a part connected to a piece of equipment in order to make it reach something further away. （设备的）延伸部分 ❑ *...a 30-foot extension cord.* …一条30英尺的延长线。

/ɪkstɛnsɪv/ ADJ Something that is **extensive** covers or includes a large physical area. 广阔的 ❑ *...an extensive tour of Latin America.* …在拉丁美洲的一次大范围的观光。● ADV 广阔地 [ADV after V] ❑ *Mark, however, needs to travel extensively with his varied business interests.* 然而，马克因各种各样的商业利益而需要四处旅行。 ADJ Something that is **extensive** covers a wide range of details, ideas, or items. 广泛的 ❑ *She recently completed an extensive study of elected officials who began their political careers before the age of 35.* 她最近完成了一项对35岁前开始政治生涯的当选的官员的广泛研究。● ADV 广泛地 ❑ *All these issues have been extensively researched in recent years.* 所有这些问题近年来都得到广泛地研究。 ADJ If something is **extensive**, it is very great. 巨大的 ❑ *The security forces have extensive powers of search and arrest.* 安全部队有很大的搜查和逮捕的权力。● ADV 巨大地 ❑ *Hydrogen is used extensively in industry for the production of ammonia.* 氢气大量地在工业中被用于氨的生产。

/ɪkstɛnt/ N-SING If you are talking about how great, important, or serious a difficulty or situation is, you can refer to **the extent of** it. 程度 ❑ *The government itself has little information on the extent of industrial pollution.* 政府本身对工业污染的程度知之甚少。

N-SING **The extent of** something is its length, area, or size. 长度；广度；范围 ❑ *Industry representatives made it clear that their commitment was only to maintain the extent of forests, not their biodiversity.* 业界代表们申明他们只承诺维持森林的规模而不是其生物多样性。

PHRASE You use expressions such as **to a large extent, to some extent,** or **to a certain extent** in order to indicate that something is partly true, but not entirely true. 在很大/某种/一定程度上 [VAGUENESS] ❑ *It was and, to a large extent, still is a good show.* 它曾是而且在很大程度上仍是一个好节目。 ❑ *To some extent this was the truth.* 在某种程度上这是事实。 PHRASE You use expressions such as **to what extent, to that extent,** or **to the extent that** when you are discussing how true a statement is, or in what ways it is true. 在何种/那种/这种/程度上 [VAGUENESS] ❑ *It's still not clear to what extent this criticism is originating from within the ruling party.* 现在还不清楚这个批判在多大程度上源自执政党内部。 PHRASE You use expressions such as **to the extent of, to the extent that,** or **to such an extent that** in order to emphasize that a situation has reached a difficult, dangerous, or surprising stage. 到…/那种/如此地步 [EMPHASIS] ❑ *Ford kept his suspicions to himself, even to the extent of going to jail for a murder he obviously didn't commit.* 福特把自己的怀疑藏在心里，即使到了要为他显然没有犯的谋杀罪而入狱的地步他也不说。

Word Partnership

extent **of the damage**
determine the extent, **know the** extent
lesser extent
full extent
a certain extent

/ɪkstɪəriər/ (**exteriors**) N-COUNT The **exterior** of something is its outside surface. 外部 ❑ *The exterior of the building was a masterpiece of architecture, elegant and graceful.* 该建筑物在外观上是一项建筑杰作，精美雅致。 N-COUNT You can refer to someone's usual appearance or behavior as their **exterior**, especially when it is very different from their real character. 外表 ❑ *According to Mandy, Pat's tough exterior hides a shy and sensitive soul.* 据曼迪说，帕特坚强的外表下藏着一个害羞、敏感的灵魂。

ADJ You use **exterior** to refer to the outside parts of something or things that are outside something. 外面的 [ADJ n] ❑ *The exterior walls were made of preformed concrete.* 外墙是用预制混凝土建造的。

Thesaurus

coating, cover, shell, skin
external, outer, outermost, surface

/ɪkstɜrmɪneɪt/ (**exterminates, exterminating, exterminated**) V-T To **exterminate** a group of people or animals means to kill all of them. 消灭 ❑ *A huge effort was made to exterminate the rats.* 花了大气力来消灭这些老鼠。● /ɪkstɜrmɪneɪʃᵊn/ N-UNCOUNT 消灭 ❑ *...the extermination of hundreds of thousands of their brethren.* …他们几十万同胞的灭绝。

/ɪkstɜrnᵊl/ ADJ **External** is used to indicate that something is on the outside of a surface or body, or that it exists, happens, or comes from outside. 外部的; 外来的; 外在的 ❑ *...a much reduced heat loss through external walls.* …透过外墙的大大减少的热量损失。● ADV 外部地; 外来地; 外在地 ❑ *Vitamins can be applied externally to the skin.* 维他命可以外用于皮肤上。 ADJ **External** means involving or intended for foreign countries. 涉外的; 对外的 [ADJ n] ❑ *...the commissioner for external affairs.* …外事专员。 ❑ *...Jamaica's external debt.* …牙买加的外债。● ADV 涉外地; 对外地 ❑ *...protecting the value of the dollar both internally and externally.* …保护美元在国内外的价值。 ADJ **External** means happening or existing in the world in general and affecting you in some way. 外界的 [ADJ n] ❑ *Such events occur only when the external conditions are favorable.* 此类事件只有当外界条件有利时才会发生。
→ see **ear**

/ɪkstɪŋkt/ ADJ A species of animal or plant that is **extinct** no longer has any living members, either in the world or in a particular place. 绝种的 ❑ *At the current rate of decline, many of the rainforest animals could become extinct in less than 10 years.* 按照目前的下降速度，许多雨林动物不到十年就会绝种。 ADJ If a particular kind of worker, way of life, or type of activity is **extinct**, it no longer exists, because of changes in society. 不复存在的 ❑ *Herbalism had become an all but extinct skill in the Western world.* 草药医术在西方世界几乎已成了一项绝迹的技术。 ADJ An **extinct** volcano is one that does not erupt or is not expected to erupt anymore. 死的 (火山) ❑ *Its tallest volcano, long extinct, is Olympus Mons.* 它最高的火山是已死很久的奥林匹斯山。

/ɪkstɪŋkʃᵊn/ N-UNCOUNT The **extinction** of a species of animal or plant is the death of all its remaining living members. (物种的) 灭绝 ❑ *An operation is beginning to try to save a species of crocodile from extinction.* 一项行动正在展开来拯救一个鳄鱼种类使其免遭灭绝。 N-UNCOUNT If someone refers to the **extinction** of a way of life or type of activity, they mean that the way of life or activity stops existing. (生活方式、活动的) 消亡 ❑ *The loggers say their jobs are faced with extinction because of declining timber sales.* 樵夫们说他们的工作因不断下降的木材销售而面临消亡。

/ɪkstɪŋgwɪʃ/ (**extinguishes, extinguishing, extinguished**) V-T If you **extinguish** a fire or a light, you stop it from burning or shining. 使熄灭 [FORMAL] ❑ *It took about 50 minutes to extinguish the fire.* 扑灭那场大火花了约五十分钟。 V-T If something **extinguishes** a feeling or idea, it destroys it. 使破灭; 消除 ❑ *The message extinguished her hopes of Richard's return.* 这消息使她对理查德返回的希望破灭了。

/ɪkstoʊl/ (**extols, extolling, extolled**) also V-T If you **extol** something or someone, you praise them enthusiastically. 颂扬 ❑ *Now experts are extolling the virtues of the humble potato.* 现在专家们在颂扬粗陋的马铃薯的种种好处。

/ɪkstɔrʃᵊnɪt/ ADJ If you describe something such as a price as **extortionate**, you are emphasizing that it is much greater than it should be. (价格) 离谱的 [EMPHASIS] ❑ *...a specially prepared menu on which basic dishes are charged at extortionate prices.* …一份特别准备的菜单，上面的普通菜肴定价离谱。

/ɛkstrə/ (**extras**) ADJ You use **extra** to describe an amount, person, or thing that is added to others of the same kind, or that can be added to others of the same kind. 多加的; 可另加的 [ADJ n] ❑ *Police warned motorists to allow extra time to get to work.* 警察告诫驾车者留出富余的时间去上班。 ❑ *There's an extra blanket in the bottom drawer of the cupboard.* 衣橱的底柜有一条备用毯。 ADJ If something is **extra**, you have to pay more money for it in addition to what you are already paying for something. (费用) 另计的 [V-link ADJ] ❑ *For foreign orders postage is extra.* 对于国外订单，邮资是另计的。● PRON **Extra** is also a pronoun. 额外费用 ❑ *She won't pay any extra.* 她不会支付任何额外费用。● ADV **Extra** is also an adverb. 额外地 ❑ *You may be charged 10% extra for this service.* 你可能会因此项服务而被额外收取10%的费用。 N-COUNT **Extras** are additional amounts of money that are added to the price that you have to pay for something. 额外费用 ❑ *There are no hidden extras.* 没有任何隐蔽的额外费用。 N-COUNT **Extras** are things that are not necessary in a situation, activity, or object, but that make it more comfortable, useful, or enjoyable. 额外之物 ❑ *Optional extras include cooking classes at a top restaurant.* 可选的额外之物包括一家高级餐馆的烹饪课程。

N-COUNT The **extras** in a movie are the people who play unimportant parts, for example, as members of a crowd. 临时演员 ❑ *In 1944, Kendall entered films as an extra.* 1944年，肯德尔作为一名临时演员进入电影界。 ADV You can use **extra** in front of adjectives and adverbs to emphasize the quality that they are describing. 格外地 [ADV adj/adv] [INFORMAL, EMPHASIS] ❑ *I said you'd have to be extra careful.* 我说过你必须格外小心。

Word Link *extra ≈ outside of : ct, dite, ordinary*

(**extracts, extracting, extracted**)

The verb is pronounced /ɪkstrækt/. The noun is pronounced /ɛkstrækt/.

动词读作 /ɪkstrækt/。名词读作 /ɛkstrækt/。

V-T To **extract** a substance means to obtain it from something else, for example, by using industrial or chemical processes. 提炼; 提取 ❑ *...the traditional method of pick and shovel to extract coal.* …用锄和铲采煤的传统方法。 ❑ *Citric acid can be extracted from the juice of oranges, lemons, limes or grapefruit.* 柠檬酸可以从橙汁、柠檬汁、酸橙汁或柚子汁中提取。● N-UNCOUNT 提炼; 提取 ❑ *Petroleum engineers plan and manage the extraction of oil.* 石油工程师们规划并管理石油的提炼。

V-T If you **extract** something **from** a place, you take it out or pull it out. 取出 ❑ *He extracted a small notebook from his hip pocket.* 他从臀后口袋拿出了一本小笔记簿。 V-T When a dentist **extracts** a tooth, they remove it from the patient's mouth. 拔 (牙) ❑ *A dentist may decide to extract the tooth to prevent recurrent trouble.* 牙医可能会决定拔掉这颗牙，以防复发。● N-VAR (**extractions**) 拔牙 ❑ *In those days, dentistry was basic. Extractions were carried out without anesthetic.* 那时牙科学刚起步，拔牙是在没有麻药的情况下进行的。

V-T If you say that someone **extracts** something, you disapprove of them because they take it for themselves to gain an advantage. 谋取 [DISAPPROVAL] ❑ *He sought to extract the maximum political advantage from the cut in interest rates.* 他力图从利息削减中谋取最大的政治利益。 V-T If you **extract** information or a response **from** someone, you get it from them with difficulty, because they are unwilling to say or do what you want. 探取 (消息、反映) ❑ *He made the mistake of trying to extract further information from our director.* 他犯了想从我们主任那里探取进一步信息的错误。 V-T If you **extract** a particular piece of information, you obtain it from a larger amount or source of information. 摘取 (信息) ❑ *I've simply extracted a few figures.* 我只是摘取了一些数据。 ❑ *Britain's trade figures can no longer be extracted from export-and-import documentation at ports.* 英国的贸易数字再也不能从各港口的进出口文件中摘取了。 V-T PASSIVE If part of a book or text **is extracted from** a particular book, it is printed or published. (从书中) 摘录 [JOURNALISM] ❑ *This material has been extracted from "Collins Good Wood Handbook."* 该资料摘自《柯林斯良木手册》。 N-COUNT An **extract from** a book or piece of writing is a small part of it that is printed or published separately. 摘录; 选段 ❑ *Read this extract from an information booklet about the work of an airline cabin crew.* 阅读这个航空公司机务员工作信息手册的选段。 N-MASS **Extract** is a very concentrated liquid that is used for flavoring food or for its smell. 高浓缩汁液 ❑ *Blend in the vanilla extract, lemon peel, and walnuts.* 调和香草精、柠檬皮和核桃。
→ see **industry, mineral**

/ɛkstrədaɪt/ (**extradites, extraditing, extradited**) V-T If someone **is extradited**, they are officially sent back to their own or another country or state to be tried for a crime that they have been accused of. 引渡 [FORMAL] ❑ *A judge agreed to extradite him to Texas.* 一位法官同意将他引渡到德克萨斯州。● /ɛkstrədɪʃᵊn/ N-VAR (**extraditions**) 引渡 ❑ *A New York court turned down the British government's request for his extradition.* 一个纽约法院拒绝了英国政府对他的引渡请求。

/ɪkstrɔrdᵊnɛri/ ADJ If you describe something or someone as **extraordinary**, you mean that they have some extremely good or special quality. 非凡的 [APPROVAL]

❑ *We've made extraordinary progress as a society in that regard.* 我们社会在那方面已经取得了巨大进步。❑ *The task requires extraordinary patience and endurance.* 这项工作需要非凡的耐心和毅力。● **extraor·di·nari·ly** /ɪkstrɔrdənɛrɪli/ ADV 非凡地 [ADV adj] ❑ *She's extraordinarily disciplined.* 她特别遵守纪律。 2 ADJ If you describe something as **extraordinary**, you mean that it is very unusual or surprising. 非同寻常的 [EMPHASIS] ❑ *What an extraordinary thing to happen!* 发生了多么非同寻常的事啊！● **extraor·di·nari·ly** ADV 非同寻常地 ❑ *Apart from the hair, he looked extraordinarily unchanged.* 除了头发，他看上去真是一点也没变。 3 ADJ An **extraordinary** meeting is arranged to deal with a particular situation or problem, rather than happening regularly. 特别的(会议) [ADJ n] [FORMAL] ❑ *The U.S. has called for an extraordinary emergency meeting of the UN Human Rights Commission to examine the crisis.* 美国已要求召开一次联合国人权委员特别紧急会议来调查这次危机。

E

ex·trapo·late /ɪkstræpəleɪt/ (**extrapolates, extrapolating, extrapolated**) V-I If you **extrapolate from** known facts, you use them as a basis for general statements about a situation or about what is likely to happen in the future. 推断 [FORMAL] ❑ *Extrapolating from his latest findings, he reckons about 80% of these deaths might be attributed to smoking.* 从他最近的发现推断，他估计大约80%的这类死亡可能归因于吸烟。● **ex·trapo·la·tion** /ɪkstræpəleɪʃən/ N-VAR (**extrapolations**) 推断 ❑ *His estimate of half a million HIV-positive cases was based on an extrapolation of the known incidence of the virus.* 他的50万HIV阳性病例的估计是基于对已知病毒发病率的推断。

ex·trava·gance /ɪkstrævəgəns/ (**extravagances**) 1 N-UNCOUNT **Extravagance** is the spending of more money than is reasonable or than you can afford. 奢侈 ❑ *When the company went under, tales of his extravagance surged through the industry.* 这家公司破产时，有关他的奢靡的传言传遍了整个业界。 2 N-COUNT An **extravagance** is something that you spend money on but cannot really afford. 奢侈品 ❑ *Why waste money on such extravagances?* 为什么在这样的奢侈品上浪费钱？

★ **ex·trava·gant** /ɪkstrævəgənt/ 1 ADJ Someone who is **extravagant** spends more money than they can afford or uses more of something than is reasonable. 奢侈的；浪费的 ❑ *We are not extravagant; restaurant meals are a luxury and designer clothes are out.* 我们并不浪费：餐馆用餐是一种奢侈，品牌服装也与我们无缘。● **ex·trava·gant·ly** ADV 奢侈地；浪费地 [ADV with v] ❑ *The day before they left Jeff had shopped extravagantly for presents for the whole family.* 他们离开的前一天杰夫已奢侈地为全家人采购了礼物。 2 ADJ Something that is **extravagant** costs more money than you can afford or uses more of something than is reasonable. 贵不可及的；耗费过多的 ❑ *Her aunt gave her an uncharacteristically extravagant gift.* 她的姑妈给了她一件贵得离谱的礼物。❑ *Baking a whole cheese in pastry may seem extravagant.* 烤糕饼时加一整块奶酪可能显得过于浪费。● **ex·trava·gant·ly** ADV 贵不可及地；耗费过多地 [ADV adj/-ed] ❑ *By supercar standards, though, it is not extravagantly priced for a beautifully engineered machine.* 不过以超级车的标准来看，这样一台设计精美的机车定价并不过高。 3 ADJ **Extravagant** behavior is extreme behavior that is often done for a particular effect. 过分的(行为) ❑ *He was extravagant in his admiration of Hellas.* 他对希腊的崇拜过了头。● **ex·trava·gant·ly** ADV 过分地 ❑ *She had on occasion praised him extravagantly.* 她有时曾过分地表扬他。 4 ADJ **Extravagant** claims or ideas are unrealistic or impractical. 不切实际的 [DISAPPROVAL] ❑ *Don't be afraid to consider apparently extravagant ideas.* 别怕考虑那些明显不切实际的主意。

ex·trava·gan·za /ɪkstrævəgænzə/ (**extravaganzas**) N-COUNT An **extravaganza** is a very elaborate and expensive show or performance. 盛大展示；盛大表演 ❑ *...a magnificent fireworks extravaganza.* …一场壮观的焰火表演。

ex·treme ♦◇◇ /ɪkstrim/ (**extremes**) 1 ADJ **Extreme** means very great in degree or intensity. 极大的 ❑ *The girls were afraid of snakes and picked their way along with extreme caution.* 那些女孩们害怕蛇，一路极其谨慎地看好每一步走。❑ *...people living in extreme poverty.* …活在极度贫穷中的人们。 2 ADJ You use **extreme** to describe situations and behavior that are much more severe or unusual than you would expect, especially when you disapprove of them because of this. 过激的 [DISAPPROVAL] ❑ *The extreme case was Poland, where 29 parties won seats.* 过激的案例是波兰，那里有29个政党获得席位。❑ *It is hard to imagine Jesse capable of anything so extreme.* 很难想像杰西能做这样过激的事情。 3 ADJ You use **extreme** to describe opinions, beliefs, or political movements that you disapprove of because they are very different from those that most people would accept as reasonable or normal. 偏激的 [DISAPPROVAL] ❑ *This extreme view hasn't captured popular opinion.* 这种偏激的观点还没有赢得大众的认同。 4 N-COUNT You can use **extremes** to refer to situations or types of behavior that have opposite qualities to each other, especially when each situation or type of behavior has such a quality to the greatest degree possible. 极端 ❑ *...a "middle way" between the extremes of success and failure, wealth and poverty.* …成功与失败、富裕与贫穷两个极端之间的“中道”。 5 ADJ The **extreme** end or edge of something is its farthest end or edge. 极远的(端、边缘) [ADJ n] ❑ *...the room at the extreme end of the corridor.* …走廊最尽头的房间。 6 PHRASE If a person **goes to extremes** or **takes** something **to extremes**, they do or say something in a way that people consider to be unacceptable, unreasonable, or foolish. (行动、说话) 走极端 ❑ *The police went to the extremes of installing the most advanced safety devices in the man's house.* 警察走了极端，在这个人的房屋里安装了最先进的安全设备。

Word Partnership *extreme* 的常用搭配：

N.	extreme **caution**, extreme **difficulty** 1 extreme **case**, extreme **sports** 2 extreme **left**, extreme **right**, extreme **views** 3
ADJ.	**the opposite** extreme 4

ex·treme·ly ♦♦◇ /ɪkstrimli/ ADV You use **extremely** in front of adjectives and adverbs to emphasize that the specified quality is present to a very great degree. 极端地；极度地 [ADV adj/adv] [EMPHASIS] ❑ *My cellphone is extremely useful.* 我的手机极为有用。❑ *Three of them are working extremely well.* 他们中的3个人工作极其出色。

Thesaurus *extremely* 另参见：

ADV.	awfully, exceedingly, greatly, highly, terribly, very; (*ant.*) mildly, moderately

ex·trem·ism /ɪkstrimɪzəm/ N-UNCOUNT **Extremism** is the behavior or beliefs of extremists. 极端主义 ❑ *Greater demands were being placed on the police by growing violence and left- and right-wing extremism.* 不断增加的暴行和左翼右翼极端主义使得需要更多警力。

ex·trem·ist /ɪkstrimɪst/ (**extremists**) 1 N-COUNT If you describe someone as an **extremist**, you disapprove of them because they try to bring about political change by using violent or extreme methods. 极端分子 [DISAPPROVAL] ❑ *He said the country needed a strong intelligence service to counter espionage, terrorism, and foreign extremists.* 他说该国需要一个强大的情报机构来反击间谍、恐怖主义以及外国极端分子。❑ *A previously unknown extremist group has said it carried out Friday's bomb attack.* 一个先前未知的极端分子组织声称其实施了周五的炸弹袭击。 2 ADJ If you say that someone has **extremist** views, you disapprove of them because they believe in bringing about change by using violent or extreme methods. 极端主义的 [DISAPPROVAL] ❑ *...his determination to purge the party of extremist views.* …他的清除具有极端主义观点的政党的决心。

extro·vert /ɛkstrəvɜrt/ (**extroverts**) ADJ Someone who is **extrovert** is very active, lively, and friendly. 外向的 [mainly BRIT] in AM, usually use **extroverted** ❑ *His footballing skills and extrovert personality won the hearts of the public.* 他的足球技巧和外向的个性赢得了公众的心。● N-COUNT An **extrovert** is someone who is extrovert. 性格外向者

extro·vert·ed /ɛkstrəvɜrtɪd/ ADJ Someone who is **extroverted** is very active, lively, and friendly. 外向的 [mainly AM] ❑ *Some young people who were easy-going and extroverted as children become self-conscious in early adolescence.* 一些在孩提时候随和且外向的年轻人在青春期初期变得害羞了。

▲ **exu·ber·ance** /ɪgzubərəns/ N-UNCOUNT **Exuberance** is behavior that is energetic, excited, and cheerful. 快乐有活力的行为 ❑ *Her burst of exuberance and her brightness overwhelmed me.* 她的活力勃发和她的聪明智慧征服了我。

exu·ber·ant /ɪgzubərənt/ ADJ If you are **exuberant**, you are full of energy, excitement, and cheerfulness. 充满活力的 ❑ *So the exuberant young girl with dark hair and blue eyes decided to become a screen actress.* 因此，这个充满活力的年轻黑发碧眼女孩决定成为一名荧屏演员。● **exu·ber·ant·ly** ADV 充满活力地 ❑ *They both laughed exuberantly.* 他俩都活力四射地大笑起来。

ex·ude /ɪgzud, ɪksud/ (**exudes, exuding, exuded**) 1 V-T/V-I If someone **exudes** a quality or feeling, or if it **exudes**, they show that they have it to a great extent. 充分显露；洋溢 [FORMAL] ❑ *The guerrillas exude confidence. Every town, they say, is under their control.* 这些游击队员们洋溢着自信。他们说每一座城镇都在他们的控制之下。❑ *She exudes an air of relaxed calm.* 她洋溢着一副从容平静的神情。 **2** V-T/V-I If something **exudes** a liquid or smell or if a liquid or smell **exudes from** it, the liquid or smell comes out of it slowly and steadily. 渗出；散发出 [FORMAL] ❑ *Nearby was a factory which exuded a pungent smell.* 附近是一家散发出一种刺鼻气味的工厂。

eye
❶ PART OF THE BODY, ABILITY TO SEE
❷ PART OF AN OBJECT

❶ **eye** ◆◆◆ /aɪ/ (**eyes, eyeing** or **eying, eyed**)
➪ **Please look at meanings 24 – 26 to see if the expression you are looking for is shown under another headword.** **1** N-COUNT Your **eyes** are the parts of your body with which you see. 眼睛 ❑ *I opened my eyes and looked.* 我睁开眼睛看了看。❑ *...a tall, thin white-haired lady with piercing dark brown eyes.* …一位有一双深邃的深棕色眼睛的瘦高个白发女士。

Eye contact is an important aspect of North American culture. If someone does not look at the person with whom he or she is speaking, the speaker is thought to be rude or even dishonest. An honest person is praised for **looking you straight in the eye**. Take care not to look for too long, or you'll be guilty of **staring**, which is considered bad manners.

2 V-T If you **eye** someone or something in a particular way, you look at them carefully in that way. 注视 ❑ *Sally eyed Claire with interest.* 萨莉饶有兴味地注视着克莱尔。❑ *We eyed each other thoughtfully.* 我们若有所思地看了看彼此。 **3** N-COUNT You use **eye** when you are talking about a person's ability to judge things or about the way in which they are considering or dealing with things. 眼光 ❑ *William was a man of discernment, with an eye for quality.* 威廉是个有鉴赏力的人，对于品质的优劣很有眼力。❑ *He first learned to fish under the watchful eye of his grandmother.* 他最初在祖母留心的眼光下学习钓鱼。 **4** → see also **black eye** **5** PHRASE If you say that something happens **before** your **eyes**, **in front of** your **eyes**, or **under** your **eyes**, you are emphasizing that it happens where you can see it clearly and often implying that it is surprising or unpleasant. 在…眼前/下 [EMPHASIS] ❑ *A lot of them died in front of our eyes.* 他们中很多人死在我们眼前。 **6** PHRASE If you **cast** your **eye** or **run** your **eye** over something, you look at it or read it quickly. 投以一瞥 ❑ *I would be grateful if he could cast an expert eye over it and tell me what he thought of it.* 如果他能以专家的眼光看一下它并告诉我他的想法，我将不胜感激。 **7** PHRASE If something **catches** your **eye**, you suddenly notice it. 突然使某人注意到 ❑ *As she turned back, a movement across the lawn caught her eye.* 当她转身时，草地那头的一个动静引起了她的注意。 **8** → see also **eye-catching** **9** PHRASE If you **catch** someone's **eye**, you do something to attract their attention, so that you can speak to them. 吸引某人的注意 ❑ *He tried to catch Annie's eye as he walked by her seat.* 从安妮座位旁走过时，他设法吸引她的注意。 **10** PHRASE If you **close** your **eyes to** something bad or if you **shut** your **eyes to** it, you ignore it. 不理会某事物 ❑ *Most governments must simply be shutting their eyes to the problem.* 大多数政府定会干脆不理会这个问题。 **11** PHRASE If you **cry** your **eyes out**, you cry very hard. 痛哭 [INFORMAL] ❑ *He didn't mean to be cruel but I cried my eyes out.* 他并非有意苛刻，但我还是大哭了一场。 **12** PHRASE If there is something **as far as the eye can see**, there is a lot of it and you cannot see anything else beyond it. 就视线所能及 ❑ *There are pine trees as far as the eye can see.* 极目望去只见松林。 **13** PHRASE If you say that someone **has an eye for** something, you mean that they are good at noticing it or making judgments about it. 对…有眼力；对…有判别力 ❑ *Susan has a keen eye for detail, so each dress is beautifully finished.* 苏珊对细节有敏锐的眼力，所以每件衣服都完成得相当漂亮。 **14** PHRASE You use expressions such as **in his eyes** or **to her eyes** to indicate that you are reporting someone's opinion and that other people might think differently. 在某人看来 ❑ *The other serious problem in the eyes of the new government is communalism.* 在新政府看来，另外一个严峻的问题是地方自治主义。 **15** PHRASE If you **keep** your **eyes open** or **keep an eye out for** someone or something, you watch for them carefully. 密切注意 [INFORMAL] ❑ *I ask the mounted patrol to keep their eyes open.* 我要求巡逻骑警密切注意。 **16** PHRASE If you **keep an eye on** something or someone, you watch them carefully, for example to make sure that they are satisfactory or safe, or not causing trouble. 照看；留意 ❑ *I went for a run there, keeping an eye on the children the whole time.* 我去那里跑步，其间始终留意着孩子们。 **17** PHRASE If you say that **all eyes are on** something or that the **eyes of the world are on** something, you mean that everyone is paying careful attention to it and what will happen. 众目关注 [JOURNALISM] ❑ *All eyes will be on tomorrow's vote.* 明天的投票将是众目所注。 **18** PHRASE If someone **has** their **eye on** you, they are watching you carefully to see what you do. 密切注意某人 ❑ *A spokesman for the store said: "He comes here quite a lot. We've had our eye on him before."* 一位该商店发言人说："他常常光顾这里。我们以前就注意他了。" **19** PHRASE If you **have** your **eye on** something, you want to have it. 看中 [INFORMAL] ❑ *If you're saving up for a new outfit you've had your eye on, cheap dinners for a month might let you buy it.* 如果你想省钱买一套你看中的新套装，吃一个月的廉价晚餐也许会让你买得起。 **20** PHRASE If you say that you did something **with** your **eyes open** or **with** your **eyes wide open**, you mean that you knew about the problems and difficulties that you were likely to have. 明知有问题和困难地 ❑ *We want all our members to undertake this trip responsibly, with their eyes open.* 我们希望我们所有的成员都明白其中的困难、负责任地进行这次旅行。 **21** PHRASE If something **opens** your **eyes**, it makes you aware that something is different from the way that you thought it was. 使你看到不同的一面 ❑ *Watching your child explore the world about her can open your eyes to delights long forgotten.* 看着你的孩子探索她周围的世界能使你看到遗忘很久的快乐。 **22** PHRASE If you **see eye to eye with** someone, you agree with them and have the same opinions and views. (与某人)看法一致 ❑ *Yuriko saw eye to eye with Yul on almost every aspect of the production.* 百合子和尤尔几乎在产品的每一个方面都意见一致。 **23** PHRASE When you **take** your **eyes off** the thing you have been watching or looking at, you stop looking at it. 把目光移开某事物 ❑ *She took her eyes off the road to glance at me.* 她把目光移开马路，瞥了我一眼。 **24** to **turn a blind eye** → see **blind** **25** to **feast** your **eyes** → see **feast** **26** in your **mind's eye** → see **mind**
→ see Word Web: **eye**
→ see **cry, face**

❷ **eye** /aɪ/ (**eyes**) **1** N-COUNT An **eye** is a small metal loop that a hook fits into, as a fastening on a piece of clothing. (衣服搭扣之)环扣 ❑ *There were lots of hooks and eyes in Victorian costumes!* 维多利亚时代的服装上有很多钩扣和环扣！ **2** N-COUNT The **eye** of a needle is the small hole at one end that the thread passes through. (针) 眼 ❑ *The only difficult part was threading the cotton through the eye of the needle!* 惟一困难的部分是将棉线穿过针眼！ **3** N-SING **The eye of** a storm, tornado, or hurricane is the center of it. (暴风雨的) 中心；(龙卷风、飓风的) 眼 ❑ *The eye of the hurricane hit Florida just south of Miami.* 飓风眼袭击了迈阿密正南面的佛罗里达州。
→ see **hurricane**

eye·ball /aɪbɔl/ (**eyeballs, eyeballing, eyeballed**) **1** N-COUNT Your **eyeballs** are your whole eyes, rather than just the part

Word Web eye

Light enters the **eye** through the cornea. The cornea bends the light and directs it through the **pupil**. The colored **iris** opens and closes the **lens**. This helps focus the **image** clearly on the **retina**. Nerve cells in the retina change the light into electrical signals. The **optic nerve** then carries these signals to the brain. In a **nearsighted** person the light rays focus in front of the lens. The image comes on to focus in back of the lens in a **farsighted** person. An irregularity in the cornea can cause astigmatism. Glasses or **contact lenses** can correct all three problems.

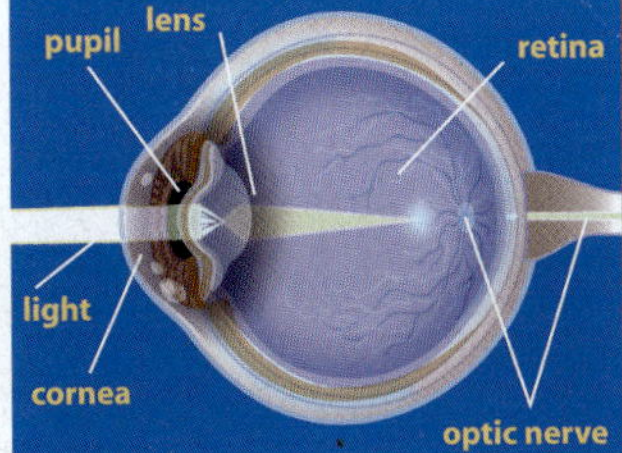

which can be seen between your eyelids. 眼球 V-T If you **eyeball** someone or something, you stare at them. 盯着看 [INFORMAL] ❑ *"Can you handle that?" Savage asked, eyeballing Cameron.* "你能对付吗？" 萨维奇盯着卡梅伦问。 PHRASE You use **up to** the **eyeballs** to emphasize that someone is in an undesirable state to a very great degree. 深陷困境 [INFORMAL, EMPHASIS] ❑ *He is out of a job and up to his eyeballs in debt.* 他失业了并且债台高筑。

/aɪbraʊ/ (**eyebrows**) N-COUNT Your **eyebrows** are the lines of hair that grow above your eyes. 眉 PHRASE If something causes you to **raise an eyebrow** or to **raise** your **eyebrows**, it causes you to feel surprised or disapproving. 扬起眉毛(表示惊讶、不赞成) ❑ *An intriguing item on the news pages caused me to raise an eyebrow over my morning coffee.* 喝早咖啡时，新闻页面上的一条趣闻让我惊讶。 ❑ *He raised his eyebrows over some of the suggestions.* 他不赞成其中的一些建议。
→ see **face**

ADJ Something that is **eye-catching** is very noticeable. 引人注目的 ❑ *...a series of eye-catching ads.* …一系列引人注目的广告。

/aɪglæsɪz/ N-PLURAL **Eyeglasses** are two lenses in a frame that some people wear in front of their eyes in order to help them see better. 眼镜 [AM, FORMAL] ❑ *...the 140 million Americans who wear eyeglasses or contact lenses.* …1.4亿戴眼镜或者隐性眼镜的美国人。

/aɪlæʃ/ (**eyelashes**) N-COUNT Your **eyelashes** are the hairs that grow on the edges of your eyelids. 睫毛
→ see **face**

/aɪlɪd/ (**eyelids**) N-COUNT Your **eyelids** are the two pieces of skin that cover your eyes when they are closed. 眼皮
→ see **face**

(**eye-openers**) N-COUNT If you describe something as an **eye-opener**, you mean that it surprises you and that you learn something new from it. 大开眼界的事物 [INFORMAL] ❑ *Writing these scripts has been quite an eye-opener for me. It proves that you can do anything if the need is urgent.* 写这些脚本对我来讲是大开眼界的事。它证明如果需求紧迫，人能做任何事情。

/aɪsaɪt/ N-UNCOUNT Your **eyesight** is your ability to see. 视力 ❑ *He suffered from poor eyesight and could no longer read properly.* 他视力不好了，再也不能正常地阅读。

/aɪsɔr/ (**eyesores**) N-COUNT You describe a building or place as an **eyesore** when it is extremely ugly and you dislike it or disapprove of it. 让人看了难受的事物 [usu sing] [DISAPPROVAL] ❑ *Poverty leads to slums, which are an eyesore and a health hazard.* 贫穷产生贫民窟，那是个让人看了难受、对健康有害的地方。

/aɪwɪtnɪs/ (**eyewitnesses**) N-COUNT An **eyewitness** is a person who was present at an event and can therefore describe it, for example in a law court. 目击者 ❑ *Eyewitnesses say the police then opened fire on the crowd.* 目击者说警察随即向人群开了火。

/izin/ (**e-zines**) N-COUNT An **e-zine** is a website which contains the kind of articles, pictures, and advertisements that you would find in a magazine. 电子杂志

also /ɛf/ (**F's, f's**) N-VAR **F** is the sixth letter of the English alphabet. 英文字母表中的第6个字母

/feɪbᵊl/ (**fables**) N-VAR A **fable** is a story which teaches a moral lesson. Fables sometimes have animals as the main characters. 寓言 ❑ *...the fable of the tortoise and the hare.* …乌龟和兔子的寓言。 N-VAR You can describe a statement or explanation that is untrue but that many people believe as **fable**. 谣传 ❑ *Is reincarnation fact or fable?* 转世投胎是事实还是谣传？

/fæbrɪk/ (**fabrics**) N-MASS **Fabric** is cloth or other material produced by weaving together cotton, nylon, wool, silk, or other threads. Fabrics are used for making things such as clothes, curtains, and sheets. 织物 ❑ *...small squares of red cotton fabric.* …几小块方形红棉布。 N-SING The **fabric** of a society or system is its basic structure, with all the customs and beliefs that make it work successfully. (社会或系统的) 结构 ❑ *The fabric of society has been deeply damaged by the previous regime.* 社会结构已被上届执政者严重地破坏了。

→ see **cotton, quilt**

/fæbrɪkeɪt/ (**fabricates, fabricating, fabricated**) V-T If someone **fabricates** information, they invent it in order to deceive people. 伪造 ❑ *All four claim that officers fabricated evidence against them.* 4人全部声称官员们伪造了不利于他们的证据。

● /fæbrɪkeɪʃᵊn/ N-VAR (**fabrications**) 伪造 ❑ *She described the interview as a "complete fabrication."* 她把这次采访描述为"纯属虚构"。

Word Link *ous ≈ having the qualities of : danger , fabul , glamor*

/fæbyələs/ ADJ If you describe something as **fabulous**, you are emphasizing that you like it a lot or think that it is very good. 极好的 [INFORMAL, EMPHASIS] ❑ *This is a fabulous album. It's fresh, varied, fun.* 这是个极好的专辑。它是新颖的、多样的、有趣的。

/fəsɑd/ (**facades**) also N-COUNT The **facade** of a building, especially a large one, is its front wall or the wall that faces the street. (建筑物的) 正面 ❑ *...the repairs to the building's facade.* …该建筑物正面墙的维修。 N-SING A **facade** is an outward appearance which is deliberately false and gives you a wrong impression about someone or something. 假象 ❑ *They hid the troubles plaguing their marriage behind a facade of family togetherness.* 他们把困扰他们婚姻的问题掩藏在家人亲密无间的假象背后。

NOUN USES
VERB AND PHRASAL VERB USES

/feɪs/ (**faces**)

➪ **Please look at meanings and to see if the expression you are looking for is shown under another headword.** N-COUNT Your **face** is the front part of your head from your chin to the top of your forehead, where your mouth, eyes, nose, and other features are. 脸 ❑ *He rolled down his window and stuck his face out.* 他摇下窗户，探出脸来。 ❑ *He was going red in the face and breathing with difficulty.* 他脸面发红，费力地喘着气。 ❑ *She had a beautiful face.* 她有张漂亮的脸。 N-COUNT If your **face** is happy, sad, or serious, for example, the expression on your face shows that you are happy, sad, or serious. 面部表情 ❑ *He was walking around with a sad face.* 他四处走着，面带哀伤。 N-COUNT The **face** of a cliff, mountain, or building is a vertical surface or side of it. (悬崖、山、建筑物的) 侧面 ❑ *Harrer was one of the first to climb the north face of the Eiger.* 哈勒是第一批登上艾格尔山北坡的人之一。 N-COUNT The **face** of a clock or watch is the surface with the numbers or hands on it, which shows the time. 钟面；表盘 ❑ *It was too dark to see the face of my watch.* 天太黑了，以致看不见我表盘上的时间。 N-SING If you say that **the face of** an area, institution, or field of activity is changing, you mean its appearance or nature is changing. (地方、机构或活动区域的) 外观特征 ❑ *...the changing face of the countryside.* …该乡村变化着的面貌。 N-SING If you refer to something as **the** particular **face of** an activity, belief, or system, you mean that it is one particular aspect of it, in contrast to other aspects. (活动、信仰或制度的) 方面 ❑ *Brothels, she insists, are the acceptable face of prostitution.* 妓院，她坚持说，是卖淫可接受的方面。 N-UNCOUNT If you lose **face**, you do something which makes you appear weak and makes people respect or admire you less. If you do something in order to save

Picture Dictionary

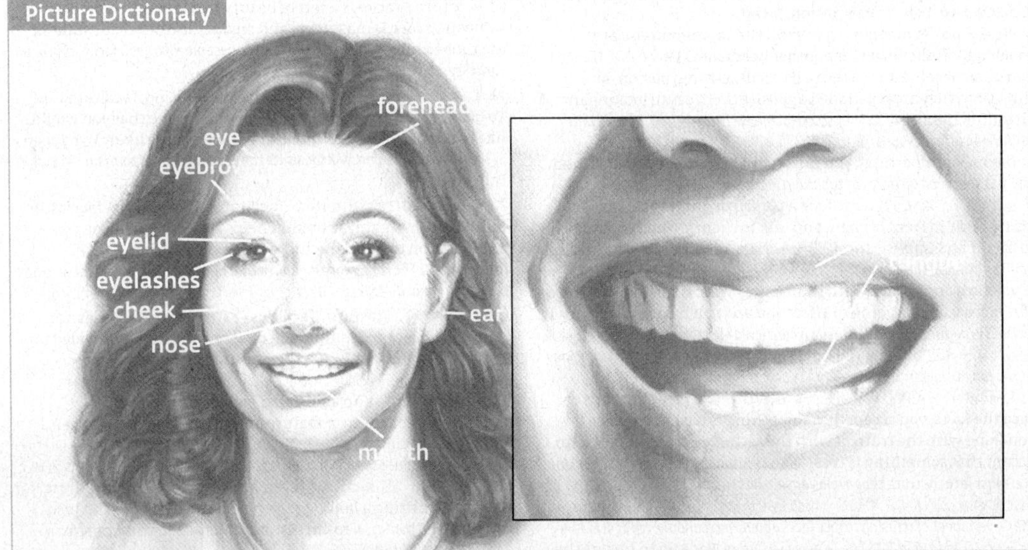

face, you do it in order to avoid appearing weak and losing people's respect or admiration. 脸面 ❑ *They don't want a war, but they don't want to lose face.* 他们不想要战争，但他们也不想丢脸面。 ❑ *To cancel the airport would mean a loss of face for the present governor.* 取消这个机场对现任州长会意味着丢面子。 8 → see also **face value** 9 PHRASE If someone or something is **face down**, their face or front points downward. If they are **face up**, their face or front points upward. 面朝下/朝上 ❑ *All the time Stephen was lying face down and unconscious in the bathtub.* 斯蒂芬始终面朝下趴在浴缸里，不省人事。 10 PHRASE If you come **face to face** with someone, you meet them and can talk to them or look at them directly. 面对面 ❑ *We were strolling into the town when we came face to face with Jacques Dubois.* 我们溜达进城时，迎面碰上了雅克·杜波依斯。 11 PHRASE If you come **face to face with** a difficulty or reality, you cannot avoid it and have to deal with it. 正视 (困难或现实) ❑ *Eventually, he came face to face with discrimination again.* 最后，他再次直面歧视。 12 PHRASE If an action or belief **flies in the face of** accepted ideas or rules, it seems to completely oppose or contradict them. 完全违背 ❑ *...scientific principles that seem to fly in the face of common sense.* …一些看似完全有悖常识的科学原理。 13 PHRASE If you take a particular action or attitude **in the face of** a problem or difficulty, you respond to that problem or difficulty in that way. 面对 ❑ *The president has called for national unity in the face of the violent anti-government protests.* 总统面对激烈的反政府抗议呼吁全国团结一致。 14 PHRASE If you **make a face**, you show a feeling such as dislike or disgust by putting an exaggerated expression on your face, for example, by sticking out your tongue. 做鬼脸 ❑ *Opening the door, she made a face at the musty smell.* 打开门，她对霉味做了个鬼脸。 15 PHRASE You say **on the face of it** when you are describing how something seems when it is first considered, in order to suggest that people's opinion may change when they know or think more about the subject. 乍看起来 ❑ *On the face of it that seems to make sense. But the figures don't add up.* 乍一看，那好像讲得通。但是数字对不上。 16 PHRASE If you **show** your **face** somewhere, you go there and see people, although you are not welcome, are somewhat unwilling to go, or have not been there for some time. 露面 ❑ *If she shows her face again back in Massachusetts she'll find a warrant for her arrest waiting.* 如果她回马萨诸塞州再次露面的话，她会发现一张拘捕令正等着她。 17 PHRASE If you manage to keep **a straight face**, you manage to look serious, although you want to laugh. 绷着的脸 ❑ *What went through Tom's mind I can't imagine, but he did manage to keep a straight face.* 汤姆心里在想什么我想像不出来，但是他确实装着一脸严肃。 18 PHRASE If you say something **to** someone's **face**, you say it openly in their presence. 当着某人的面 ❑ *Her opponent called her a liar to her face.* 她的对手当着她的面叫她骗子。 19 **to shut the door in** someone's **face** → see **door** 20 **to have egg on** your **face** → see **egg**
→ see Picture Dictionary: face
→ see **makeup**

❷ **face** ♦♦♦ /feɪs/ (**faces, facing, faced**)
⇨ **Please look at meaning 8 to see if the expression you are looking for is shown under another headword.** 1 V-T/V-I If someone or something **faces** a particular thing, person, or direction, they are positioned opposite them or are looking in that direction. 面向 ❑ *They stood facing each other.* 他们面对面站着。 ❑ *Our house faces south.* 我们的房子面朝南。 2 V-T If you **face** someone or something, you turn so that you are looking at them. 面向 ❑ *She stood up from the table and faced him.* 她从桌前站起来，面向着他。 3 V-T If you have to **face** a person or group, you have to stand or sit in front of them and talk to them, although it may be difficult and unpleasant. (不得不) 面对 ❑ *Christie looked relaxed and calm as he faced the press.* 克里斯蒂面对媒体时显得轻松而镇静。 4 V-T If you **face** or **are faced** with something difficult or unpleasant, or if it **faces** you, it is going to affect you and you have to deal with it. 面临 ❑ *Williams faces life in prison if convicted of attempted murder.* 威廉斯如被判谋杀未遂罪，将面临终身监禁。 ❑ *The immense difficulties facing European businessmen in Russia were only too evident.* 摆在俄罗斯的欧洲商人面前的巨大困难是极其明显的。 5 V-T If you **face** the truth or **face** the facts, you accept that something is true. If you **face** someone with the truth or with the facts, you try to make them accept that something is true. 正视 ❑ *Although your heart is breaking, you must face the truth that a relationship has ended.* 尽管你的心碎了，但是你必须正视事实，那就是一段恋爱关系已经结束了。 ❑ *He accused the Government of refusing to face facts about the economy.* 他指责政府拒绝正视有关经济的现实情况。 ● PHRASAL VERB **Face up to** means the same as **face**. 正视 ❑ *I have grown up now and I have to face up to my responsibilities.* 我现在已经长大了，所以必须要正视自己的责任。 6 V-T If you **cannot face** something, you do not feel able to do it because it seems so difficult or unpleasant. 对付 [with neg] ❑ *I couldn't face the prospect of spending a Saturday night there, so I decided to press on.* 我感到无法在那里过周六晚上，所以我决定继续赶路。 ❑ *My children want me with them for Christmas Day, but I can't face it.* 我的孩子们想让我和他们一起过圣诞节，但是我感到无法做到。 7 PHRASE You use the expression **"let's face it"** when you are stating a fact or making a comment about something which you think the person you are talking to may find unpleasant or be unwilling to admit. 面对事实吧 ❑ *She was always attracted to younger men. But, let's face it, who is not?* 她过去总是被比她年轻的男性吸引。不过，面对现实吧，谁不是呢？ 8 **face the music** → see **music**
▸ **face up to** → see **face** ❷ 5

face·cloth /feɪsklɔθ/ (**facecloths**) also **face cloth** N-COUNT A **facecloth** is the same as a **washcloth**. 洗脸毛巾

face·less /feɪslɪs/ ADJ If you describe someone or something as **faceless**, you dislike them because they are uninteresting and have no character. 没有个性的 [DISAPPROVAL] ❑ *Ordinary people are at the mercy of faceless bureaucrats.* 普通人任由千人一面的官僚们摆布。

face·lift /feɪslɪft/ (**facelifts**) also **face-lift** 1 N-COUNT If you give a place or thing **a facelift**, you do something to make it look better or more attractive. 翻新 ❑ *Nothing gives a room a faster facelift than a coat of paint.* 没有什么比一层油漆能更快地使房间面貌一新。 2 N-COUNT A **facelift** is an operation in which a surgeon tightens the skin on someone's face in order to make them look younger. 面部拉皮手术 ❑ *I had a facelift in 1995, which went wrong.* 我在1995年做了一次失败的面部拉皮手术。

★ **fac·et** /fæsɪt/ (**facets**) 1 N-COUNT A **facet of** something is a single part or aspect of it. 方面 ❑ *The caste system shapes nearly every facet of Indian life.* 种姓制度几乎决定了印度生活的各个方面。 2 N-COUNT The **facets** of a diamond or other precious stone are the flat surfaces that have been cut on its outside. (钻石等的) 刻面 → see **diamond**

face value 1 N-SING The **face value** of things such as coins, paper money, investment documents, or tickets is the amount of money that they are worth, and that is written on them. 面值 ❑ *Tickets were selling at twice their face value.* 这些票以其面值的两倍价格出售。 2 PHRASE If you take something **at face value**, you accept it and believe it without thinking about it very much, even though it might untrue. (相信) 表面 ❑ *Public statements from the various groups involved should not necessarily be taken at face value.* 不必轻信各有关团体的公开声明。

fa·cial /feɪʃəl/ (**facials**) 1 ADJ **Facial** means appearing on or being part of your face. 面部的 [ADJ n] ❑ *Cross didn't answer; his facial expression didn't change.* 克罗斯没有回答；他的面部表情没有改变。 2 N-COUNT A **facial** is a sort of beauty treatment in which someone's face is massaged, and creams and other substances are rubbed into it. 美容 ❑ *Where's the best place to get a facial in New York City?* 在纽约做美容最好的地方在哪儿？

fa·cili·tate /fəsɪlɪteɪt/ (**facilitates, facilitating, facilitated**) V-T To **facilitate** an action or process, especially one that you would like to happen, means to make it easier or more likely to happen. 促进 ❑ *The new airport will facilitate the development of tourism.* 新机场将促进旅游业的发展。

fa·cili·ta·tor /fəsɪlɪteɪtər/ (**facilitators**) N-COUNT A **facilitator** is a person or organization that helps another person or organization to do or to achieve a particular thing. 协调者 [FORMAL] ❑ *The conference is chaired by a highly skilled facilitator who has been fully trained.* 会议由一位受过充分训练、技巧娴熟的协调人主持。

fa·cil·ity ♦♦◊ /fəsɪlɪti/ (**facilities**) 1 N-COUNT **Facilities** are buildings, pieces of equipment, or services that are provided for a particular purpose. 设施 ❑ *What recreational facilities are now available?* 什么娱乐设施现在是可用的？ 2 N-COUNT A **facility** is something such as an additional service provided by an organization or an extra feature on a machine which is useful but not essential. 附加服务；附加功能 ❑ *One of the new models has the facility to reproduce speech as well as text.* 新款型中的一款有复制言语和文本的附加功能。 3 N-COUNT If you have a **facility** for something, for example learning a language, you find it easy to do. 天赋 [usu sing, usu N "for" n, N to-inf] ❑ *He and Marcia shared a facility for languages.* 他和马西娅都具有语言天赋。

fact ◆◆◆ /fækt/ (**facts**) **1** N-COUNT **Facts** are pieces of information that can be discovered. 实例 ❑ *There is so much information you can almost effortlessly find the facts for yourself.* 有这么多信息，你几乎能毫不费力地为自己找到实例。 ❑ *His opponent swamped him with facts and figures.* 他的对手用实例和数字让他难以招架。 **2** PHRASE You use **the fact that** after some verbs or prepositions, especially in expressions such as **in view of the fact that**, **apart from the fact that**, and **despite the fact that**, to link the verb or preposition with a clause. …这一事实 ❑ *His chances do not seem good in view of the fact that the Chief Prosecutor has already voiced his public disapproval.* 鉴于首席检察官已公开表示反对这一事实，他的机会看起来不好。 ❑ *Despite the fact that the disease is so prevalent, treatment is still far from satisfactory.* 尽管事实上这种疾病非常普遍，治疗却远不尽如人意。 **3** PHRASE You use **the fact that** instead of a simple that-clause either for emphasis or because the clause is the subject of your sentence. …这一事实 ❑ *My family now accepts the fact that I don't eat sugar or bread.* 我的家人现在接受了我不吃糖或面包这一事实。 **4** PHRASE You use **in fact**, **in actual fact**, or **in point of fact** to indicate that you are giving more detailed information about what you have just said. 确切地说 ❑ *We've had a pretty bad time while you were away. In fact, we very nearly split up this time.* 我们在你走的那段时间过得非常糟糕。确切地说，我们这次几乎分道扬镳了。 ❑ *He apologized as soon as he realized what he had done. In actual fact he wrote a nice little note to me.* 他一意识到他所做的一切就道歉了。确切地说，他给我写了一张友善的小便条。 **5** PHRASE You use **in fact**, **in actual fact**, or **in point of fact** to introduce or draw attention to a comment that modifies, contradicts, or contrasts with a previous statement. 实际上 ❑ *That sounds rather simple, but in fact it's very difficult.* 那听起来很简单，但实际上非常难。 ❑ *They complained that they had been trapped inside the police station, but in fact most were seen escaping over the adjacent roofs to safety in nearby buildings.* 他们抱怨说他们被困在警察局，但实际上大部分人被看见通过毗邻的屋顶逃往附近建筑物内的安全地带。 **6** PHRASE You use **as a matter of fact** to introduce a statement that gives more details about what has just been said, or an explanation of it, or something that contrasts with it. 确切地讲；事实上 ❑ *The local people saw the suffering to which these deportees were subjected. And, as a matter of fact, the local people helped the victims.* 当地人目睹了这些被放逐的人遭受的苦难。而且，确切地讲，当地人帮助了这些受害者。 **7** PHRASE If you say that you know something **for a fact**, you are emphasizing that you are completely certain that it is true. 确实 [EMPHASIS] ❑ *I know for a fact that baby corn is very expensive in Europe.* 我确实知道玉米笋在欧洲是非常昂贵的。 **8** PHRASE You use **the fact is** or **the fact of the matter is** to introduce and draw attention to a summary or statement of the most important point about what you have been saying. 总而言之 ❑ *The fact is blindness hadn't stopped the children from doing many of the things that sighted children enjoy.* 总而言之，失明并没有阻止这些孩子做有视力儿童喜爱做的许多事情。 **9** N-VAR When you refer to something as **a fact** or as **fact**, you mean that you think it is true or correct. 事实 ❑ *...a statement of verifiable historical fact.* …一个对可考证的历史事实的说明。

→ see **history**

Word Partnership *fact* 的常用搭配：

ADJ. **hard** fact, **historical** fact, **important** fact, **obvious** fact, **random** fact, **simple** fact **1**
N. fact **and fiction** **1**
as a matter of fact **6**
V. **accept a** fact, **check the** facts, **face a** fact **1**
know for a fact **7**

▲**fac·tion** ◆◇◇ /fækʃ^{ə}n/ (**factions**) N-COUNT A **faction** is an organized group of people within a larger group, which opposes some of the ideas of the larger group and fights for its own ideas. 派系 ❑ *A peace agreement will be signed by the leaders of the country's warring factions.* 一项和平协议将由该国交战各派领导们签署。

fac·tion·al /fækʃən^{ə}l/ ADJ **Factional** arguments or disputes involve two or more small groups from within a larger group. 派系的 ❑ *...factional disputes between the various groups that make up the leadership.* …构成领导层的不同团体之间的派系斗争。

Word Link *fact, fic ≈ making : artifact, artificial, factor*

fac·tor ◆◆◇ /fæktər/ (**factors, factoring, factored**) **1** N-COUNT A **factor** is one of the things that affects an event, decision, or situation. 因素 ❑ *Physical activity is an important factor in maintaining fitness.* 体育活动是保持健康的一个重要因素。 **2** N-COUNT If an amount increases by **a factor of** two, for example, or by **a factor of** eight, then it becomes two times bigger or eight times bigger. 倍数 ❑ *The cost of butter quadrupled and bread prices increased by a factor of five.* 黄油的价格是原来的4倍，面包的价格上涨了5倍。 **3** N-SING You can use **factor** to refer to a particular level on a scale of measurement. 系数 ❑ *A sunscreen with a protection factor of 30 allows you to stay in the sun without burning.* 一种防护系数为30的防晒霜使你能够待在太阳底下而不被晒伤。

▸ **factor in** or **factor into** PHRASAL VERB If you **factor** a particular cost or element **into** a calculation you are making, or if you **factor** it **in**, you include it. 将…因素包括进来 ❑ *You'd better consider this and factor this into your decision making.* 你最好考虑这一因素并在决策时将其包括进来。

Word Partnership *factor* 的常用搭配：

ADJ. **contributing** factor, **crucial** factor, **deciding** factor, **important** factor, **key** factor **1**
N. **risk** factor **1** **3**

Word Link *ory ≈ place where something happens : conservatory, factory, observatory*

fac·to·ry ◆◆◇ /fæktəri, -tri/ (**factories**) N-COUNT A **factory** is a large building where machines are used to make large quantities of goods. 工厂

→ see Word Web: **factory**
→ see **mass production**

fact sheet (**fact sheets**) N-COUNT A **fact sheet** is a short, printed document with information about a particular subject, especially a summary of information that has been given on a radio or television program. 简报 ❑ *...the institute's free fact sheet, Driving Abroad.* …该学院的免费简报《国外驾驶》。

▲**fac·tual** /fæktʃuəl/ ADJ Something that is **factual** is concerned with facts or contains facts, rather than giving theories or personal interpretations. 事实的 ❑ *The editorial contained several factual errors.* 这篇社论有几处事实性错误。

fac·ul·ty /fæk^{ə}lti/ (**faculties**) **1** N-COUNT Your **faculties** are your physical and mental abilities. 机能 ❑ *He was drunk and not in control of his faculties.* 他喝醉了，控制不了他的各项机能。 **2** N-VAR A **faculty** is all the teaching staff of a university or college, or of one department. 全体教员 [AM] ❑ *The faculty agreed on a change in the requirements.* 全体教员同意改变要求。 ❑ *How can faculty improve their teaching so as to encourage creativity?* 全体教员怎样才能改进教学以便激发创造力？

fad /fæd/ (**fads**) N-COUNT You use **fad** to refer to an activity or topic of interest that is very popular for a short time, but which people become bored with very quickly. 一时的狂热 ❑ *Hamnett does*

Word Web factory

Life in a 19th-century **factory** was extremely difficult. **Employees** often **worked** twelve hours a day, six days a week. **Wages** were low and **child labor** was common. Many **workers** were not allowed to take **breaks**. Some even had to eat while continuing to work. As early as 1832, doctors started warning about the dangers of **air pollution**. The 20th century brought some big changes. Workers began to join **unions**. During World War I, **government regulations** set standards for **minimum wages** and improved **working conditions**. In addition, **automation** took over some of the most difficult and dangerous jobs.

not believe environmental concern is a passing fad. 哈姆内特不相信对环境的关注是一时的狂热。
→ see **diet**

/feɪd/ (**fades, fading, faded**) V-T/V-I When a colored object **fades** or when the light **fades** it, it gradually becomes paler. 使褪色；褪色 ❑ *All color fades – especially under the impact of direct sunlight.* 所有颜色都会褪色——尤其是在直射阳光的影响下。 ❑ *No matter how soft the light is, it still fades carpets and curtains in every room.* 不论光线多么柔和，它仍然会使每个房间的地毯和窗帘褪色。 ● ADJ 褪色的 ❑ *...a girl in a faded dress.* …一个穿褪色连衣裙的女孩。 V-I When light **fades**, it slowly becomes less bright. When a sound **fades**, it slowly becomes less loud. 逐渐变暗；逐渐变弱 ❑ *Seaton lay on his bed and gazed at the ceiling as the light faded.* 西顿躺在床上凝视着天花板，那时光线逐渐变暗。 V-I If memories, feelings, or possibilities **fade**, they slowly become less intense or less strong. 逐渐变弱 ❑ *Sympathy for the rebels, the government claims, is beginning to fade.* 政府声称对造反者的同情在开始减弱。 ❑ *Prospects for peace had already started to fade.* 和平的前景已开始变得暗淡。

Word Partnership

colors fade, **images** fade
memories fade
begin to fade
fade **quickly**

/fisiz/ [BRIT] → see **feces**

/færənhaɪt/ ADJ **Fahrenheit** is a scale for measuring temperature, in which water freezes at 32 degrees and boils at 212 degrees. It is represented by the symbol °F. 华氏的 [n/num ADJ] ❑ *By mid-morning, the temperature was already above 100 degrees Fahrenheit.* 到上午10点左右，气温已超过华氏100度了。 ● N-UNCOUNT **Fahrenheit** is also a noun. 华氏温标 ❑ *He was asked for the boiling point of water in Fahrenheit.* 有人问他华氏温标下水的沸点。
→ see **climate**

/feɪl/ (**fails, failing, failed**) V-T/V-I If you **fail** to do something that you were trying to do, you are unable to do it or do not succeed in doing it. 未能 ❑ *The party failed to win the election.* 该政党未能赢得选举。 ❑ *He failed in his attempt to take control of the company.* 他的掌控这家公司的企图失败了。 V-I If an activity, attempt, or plan **fails**, it is not successful. 失败 ❑ *We tried to develop plans for them to get along, which all failed miserably.* 我们设法制定出让他们相处融洽的计划，但都惨败了。 ❑ *He was afraid the revolution they had started would fail.* 他担心他们发起的革命会失败。 ❑ *...a failed military coup.* …一次失败的军事政变。 V-T If someone or something **fails** to do a particular thing that they should have done, they do not do it. 未做 [FORMAL] ❑ *Some schools fail to require any homework.* 有些学校没有布置任何家庭作业。 ❑ *He failed to file tax returns for 1982.* 他没有填报1982年的纳税申报单。 V-I If something **fails**, it stops working properly, or does not do what it is supposed to do. 失灵 ❑ *The lights mysteriously failed, and we stumbled around in complete darkness.* 灯神秘地熄灭了，我们在完全的黑暗中跌跌撞撞。 V-I If a business, organization, or system **fails**, it becomes unable to continue in operation or in existence. 倒闭 [BUSINESS] ❑ *So far this year, 104 banks have failed.* 到今年为止，104家银行已倒闭。 ❑ *...a failed hotel business.* …一家倒闭的酒店。 V-I If something such as your health or a physical quality **is failing**, it is becoming gradually weaker or less effective. 衰退 ❑ *He was 58, and his health was failing rapidly.* 他58岁，健康状况每况愈下。 ❑ *Here in the hills, the light failed more quickly.* 在这儿的山里，光线减弱得更快了。 V-T If someone **fails** you, they do not do what you had expected or trusted them to do. 辜负 ❑ *We waited twenty-one years, don't fail us now.* 我们等了21年，如今不要辜负我们。 V-T If someone **fails** a test, examination, or course, they perform badly in it and do not reach the standard that is required. 使不及格 ❑ *I lived in fear of failing my final exams.* 我生活在期末考试不及格的担忧中。 ● N-COUNT **Fail** is also a noun. 不及格 ❑ *It's the difference between a pass and a fail.* 这是及格和不及格的区别。 V-T If someone **fails** you in a test, examination, or course, they judge that you have not reached a high enough standard in it. 使不及格 ❑ *...the two professors who had failed him during his first year of law school.* …他上法学院第一年时使他不及格的两位教授。 PHRASE You say **if all else fails** to suggest what could be done in a certain situation if all the other things you have tried are unsuccessful. 迫不得已的话 ❑ *If all else fails, I could always drive a truck.* 迫不得已的话，我总可以开卡车。 PHRASE You use **without fail** to emphasize that something always happens. 必定 [EMPHASIS] ❑ *He attended every meeting without fail.* 他逢会必参加。 PHRASE You use **without fail** to emphasize an order or a promise. 务必 [EMPHASIS] ❑ *On the 30th you must without fail hand in some money for Alex.* 在30号你务必亲手交给亚历克斯一些钱。

/feɪlɪŋ/ (**failings**) N-COUNT The **failings** of someone or something are their faults or unsatisfactory features. 错误；缺点 ❑ *Like many in Russia, she blamed the country's failings on futile attempts to catch up with the West.* 像在俄罗斯的许多人一样，她把这个国家的错误归咎于想赶上西方的徒劳。 PHRASE You say **failing that** to introduce an alternative, in case what you have just said is not possible. 如果不能的话 ❑ *Find someone who will let you talk things through, or failing that, write down your thoughts.* 找个能让你畅所欲言的人，如果不能的话，就把你的想法写下来。

/feɪlyər/ (**failures**) N-UNCOUNT **Failure** is a lack of success in doing or achieving something, especially in relation to a particular activity. 失败 ❑ *This policy is doomed to failure.* 这项政策注定要失败。 ❑ *Three attempts on the 200-meter record ended in failure.* 3次向200米纪录的冲击以失败告终。 N-UNCOUNT Your **failure to** do a particular thing is the fact that you do not do it, even though you were expected to do it. 未成 ❑ *They see their failure to produce an heir as a curse from God.* 他们将自己未能生育一个后嗣看作是来自上帝的一个诅咒。 N-COUNT If something is **a failure**, it is not a success. 失败 ❑ *The marriage was a failure and they both wanted to be free of it.* 这段婚姻是个失败，他们俩都想从中解放出来。 N-COUNT If you say that someone is **a failure**, you mean that they have not succeeded in a particular activity, or that they are unsuccessful at everything they do. 失败者 ❑ *Elgar received many honors and much acclaim and yet he often considered himself a failure.* 埃尔加获得了很多荣誉和欢呼，但是他常常把自己看成一个失败者。 N-VAR If there is a **failure** of something, for example, a machine or part of the body, it goes wrong and stops working or developing properly. 故障 ❑ *There were also several accidents mainly caused by engine failures on take-off.* 还有一些事故主要是由起飞时引擎故障导致的。 N-VAR If there is a **failure** of a business or bank, it is no longer able to continue operating. 倒闭 [BUSINESS] ❑ *Business failures rose 16% last month.* 上个月公司倒闭上升了16%。

Word Partnership

afraid of failure, **doomed to** failure
complete failure
dismal failure
feelings of failure, **risk of** failure, **success or** failure
engine failure, **heart** failure, **kidney** failure, **liver** failure
business failure
failure **to communicate**

/feɪnt/ (**fainter, faintest, faints, fainting, fainted**) ADJ A **faint** sound, color, mark, feeling, or quality has very little strength or intensity. 微弱的 ❑ *He became aware of the soft, faint sounds of water dripping.* 他开始觉察到水滴下来的轻柔、微弱的声音。 ❑ *There was still the faint hope deep within him that she might never need to know.* 他内心深处仍然存一线希望，希望她会永远都不想知道。 ● ADV 微弱地 ❑ *He was already asleep in the bed, which smelled faintly of mildew.* 他已经在微带霉味的床上睡着了。 ADJ A **faint** attempt at something is one that is made without proper effort and with little enthusiasm. 勉强的 [ADJ n] ❑ *Caroline made a faint attempt at a laugh.* 卡罗琳勉强地笑了一下。 ❑ *A faint smile crossed the Monsignor's face and faded quickly.* 一丝勉强的微笑从莫斯格诺脸上掠过，很快就消退了。 ● ADV 勉强地 [ADV after v] ❑ *John smiled faintly and shook his head.* 约翰勉强地微笑了一下，然后摇了摇头。 ADJ Someone who is **faint** feels weak and unsteady as if they are about to lose consciousness. 虚弱晕眩的 [v-link ADJ] ❑ *Other signs of angina are nausea, sweating, feeling faint and shortness of breath.* 心绞痛的其他征兆是恶心、出汗、感觉虚弱晕眩和气短。 V-I If you **faint**, you lose consciousness for a short time, especially because you are hungry, or because of pain, heat, or shock. 晕厥 ❑ *She suddenly fell forward on to the table and fainted.* 她突然向前栽倒在桌上，晕了过去。 ● N-COUNT **Faint** is also a noun. 晕厥 ❑ *She slumped to the ground in a faint.* 她跌倒在地上不醒人事。

/feɪntɪst/ ADJ You can use **faintest** for emphasis in negative statements. For example, if you say that someone hasn't the **faintest** idea what to do, you are emphasizing that they do not know what to do. 丝毫的 [ADJ n, with neg] [EMPHASIS] ❑ *I haven't the faintest idea how to care for a snake.* 我对于怎样养一条蛇没有一点儿主意。

/fɛər/ (**fairer, fairest, fairs**) ADJ Something or someone that is **fair** is reasonable, right, and just. 公平的 ❑ *It didn't seem fair to leave out her father.* 将她的父亲排除在外似乎不公平。 ❑ *Do you feel they're paying their fair share?* 你觉得他们正支付自己应分担的那一份吗？ ❑ *I wanted them to get a fair deal.* 我希望他们得到一个公平的交易。 ● ADV 公平地 ❑ *...demonstrating concern for employees and solving their problems quickly and fairly.* …证实对雇员的关注以及迅速公平地解决他们的问题。 ADJ A **fair** amount, degree, size, or distance is quite a large amount, degree, size, or distance. 相当大的；相当远的 [ADJ n] ❑ *My neighbors across the street travel a fair amount.* 我街对面的邻居们去过相当多的地方。 ADJ A **fair** guess or idea about something is one that is likely to be correct. 合理的 [ADJ n] ❑ *It's a fair guess to say that the damage will be extensive.* 说破坏将很严重是合理的猜测。 ADJ If you describe someone or something as **fair**, you mean that they are average in standard or quality, neither very good nor very bad. 一般的 ❑ *Reimar had a fair command of English.* 赖马尔具备一般的英语水平。 ADJ Someone who is **fair**, or who has **fair** hair, has light-colored hair. 浅色头发的 ❑ *Both children were very like Robina, but were much fairer than she was.* 两个孩子都很像罗比娜，但是头发颜色比她的浅得多。 ● COMB IN ADJ **Fair** is also a combining form. 金发的 ❑ *...a tall, fair-haired man.* …一个金发的高个男人。 ADJ **Fair** skin is very pale and usually burns easily. 白皙的 ❑ *It's important to protect my fair skin from the sun.* 保护我白皙的皮肤不受日晒是很重要的。 ● COMB IN ADJ **Fair** is also a combining form. 白皙的 ❑ *Fair-skinned people who spend a great deal of time in the sun have the greatest risk of skin cancer.* 皮肤白皙的人长时间待在太阳底下患皮肤癌的危险最大。 ADJ When the weather is **fair**, it is quite sunny and not raining. 晴的 [FORMAL] ❑ *Weather conditions were fair.* 天气状况晴好。 N-COUNT A county, state, or country **fair** is an event where there are, for example, displays of goods and animals, and amusements, games, and competitions. 集市 ❑ *Every fall I go to the county fair.* 每个秋季我都去县里的集市。

N-COUNT A **fair** is an event at which people display and sell goods, especially goods of a particular type. 商品展销会 ❑ *...an antiques fair.* …一个古董展销会。 → see also **trade fair** PHRASE You use **fair enough** when you want to say that a statement, decision, or action seems reasonable to a certain extent, but that perhaps there is more to be said or done. 说得过去 [mainly SPOKEN] ❑ *If you don't like it, fair enough, but that's hardly a justification to attack the whole thing.* 如果你不喜欢它，可以，但把它说得一无是处就没什么道理了。 PHRASE If you say that someone won a competition **fair and square**, you mean that they won honestly and without cheating. 正大光明地 ❑ *There are no excuses. We were beaten fair and square.* 没有什么借口，我们被正大光明地打败了。

Word Partnership

fair **and balanced**
fair **chance**, fare **deal**, fair **fight**, fair **game**, fair **play**, fair **price**, fair **share**, fair **trade**, fair **treatment**, fair **trial**
fair **amount**
fair **hair**
fair **skin**
craft fair

/fɛərgraʊnd/ (**fairgrounds**) N-COUNT A **fairground** is an area of land where a fair is held. 展销会场地

/fɛərli/ ADV **Fairly** means to quite a large degree. For example, if you say that something is **fairly** old, you mean that it is old but not very old. 在很大程度上 [ADV adj/adv] ❑ *We did fairly well but only fairly well.* 我们做得尚可，但仅仅是尚可。 ADV You use **fairly** instead of "very" to add emphasis to an adjective or adverb without making it sound too forceful. 相当 [ADV adj/adv] [VAGUENESS] ❑ *Were you always fairly bright at school?* 你上学时一直挺聪明吧？ ❑ *You've got to be fairly single-minded about it.* 你必须对此事专心一些。 → see also **fair**

/fɛərnɪs/ N-UNCOUNT **Fairness** is the quality of being reasonable, right, and just. 合理；公正 ❑ *...concern about the fairness of the election campaign.* …对竞选活动公正性的关注。

N-UNCOUNT **Fair trade** is the practice of buying goods directly from producers in developing countries at a fair price. 互惠贸易（从发展中国家的生产商那里直接购买货物） ❑ *...fair trade coffee.* …互惠贸易咖啡。

/fɛəri/ (**fairies**) N-COUNT A **fairy** is an imaginary creature with magical powers. Fairies are often represented as small people with wings. 仙女
→ see **fantasy**

(**fairy tales**) also N-COUNT A **fairy tale** is a story for children involving magical events and imaginary creatures. 童话 ❑ *She was like a princess in a fairy tale.* 她像童话故事里的一位公主。

/feɪθ/ (**faiths**) N-UNCOUNT If you have **faith in** someone or something, you feel confident about their ability or goodness. 信心 ❑ *People have lost faith in the government.* 人们已失去了对政府的信心。 N-UNCOUNT **Faith** is strong religious belief in a particular God. 宗教信仰 ❑ *Umberto Eco's loss of his own religious faith is reflected in his novels.* 翁贝托·埃科宗教信仰的丧失在他的小说当中得到了反映。 N-COUNT A **faith** is a particular religion, for example, Christianity, Buddhism, or Islam. 宗教 ❑ *England shifted officially from a Catholic to a Protestant faith in the 16th century.* 英格兰在16世纪正式从信仰天主教改信新教。 PHRASE If you do something **in good faith**, you seriously believe that what you are doing is right, honest, or legal, even though this may not be the case. 真心实意地 ❑ *This report was published in good faith but we regret any confusion which may have been caused.* 发表这份报告出自诚意，但是我们对可能引发的任何混乱而感到遗憾。

Word Partnership

blind faith, **little** faith
religious faith
have faith, **lose** faith
practice *your* faith
faith **in God**

/feɪθfəl/ ADJ Someone who is **faithful to** a person, organization, idea, or activity remains firm in their belief in them or support for them. 忠实的 ❑ *She had been faithful to her promise to guard this secret.* 她一直信守诺言保守着这个秘密。 ● N-PLURAL **The faithful** are people who are faithful to someone or something. 忠实的人 ❑ *He spends his time making speeches at factories or gatherings of the Party faithful.* 他花时间在工厂或者在该党忠实拥护者的集会上发表演讲。 ● ADV 忠实地 [ADV with v] ❑ *He has since 1965 faithfully followed and supported every twist and turn of government policy.* 他从1965年起忠实地追随并支持政府政策的每一次重大转变。 ADJ Someone who is **faithful to** their husband, wife, or lover does not have a sexual relationship with anyone else. 忠贞的 ❑ *I'm very faithful when I love someone.* 当我爱一个人时我是非常忠贞的。

ADJ A **faithful** account, translation, or copy of something represents or reproduces the original accurately. 忠实于原文的 ❑ *Colin Welland's screenplay is faithful to the novel.* 科林·韦兰的电影剧本是忠实于小说原文的。 ● ADV 忠实于原文地 [ADV with v] ❑ *When I adapt something I translate from one meaning to another as faithfully as I can.* 我在改编的时候，我用尽量忠实于原文的方式把一种含义翻译为另一种。

/feɪθfəli/ CONVENTION When you start a formal or business letter with "Dear Sir" or "Dear Madam," you write **Yours faithfully** before your signature at the end. 您忠实的（正式信函或商务信函末尾署名前的套语） → see also **faithful**

/feɪk/ (**fakes, faking, faked**) ADJ A **fake** fur or a **fake** painting, for example, is a fur or painting that has been made to look valuable or genuine, usually in order to deceive people. 伪造的 ❑ *The bank manager is said to have issued fake certificates.* 据说这个银行经理曾出具过伪造的假凭证。 ● N-COUNT A **fake** is something that is fake. 赝品 ❑ *The gallery is filled with famous works of art, and every one of them is a fake.* 画廊里满是极好的艺术名品，每一件都是赝品。

V-T If someone **fakes** something, they try to make it look valuable or genuine, although in fact it is not. 伪造 ❑ *It's safer to fake a tan with make-up rather than subject your complexion to the harsh rays of the sun.* 用化妆来伪造棕褐色的皮肤比让皮肤暴露于强烈的太阳光线更安全。 ❑ *...faked evidence.* …伪造的证据。 V-T If you **fake** a feeling, emotion, or reaction, you pretend that you are experiencing it when you are not. 假装 ❑ *He tried to fake sincerity as he smiled at them.* 当他朝他们笑的时候，他设法假装真诚。 N-COUNT Someone who is a **fake** is not what they claim to be, for example, because they do not have the qualifications that they claim to have. 骗子 ❑ *I think Jack is a good man. He isn't a fake.* 我认为杰克是个好人。他不是一个骗子。

Thesaurus *fake* 另参见：
ADJ. artificial, counterfeit, imitation 1
V. falsify, pretend 2

fall ♦♦♦ /fɔːl/ (**falls, falling, fell, fallen**) 1 V-I If someone or something **falls**, they move quickly downward onto or toward the ground, by accident or because of a natural force. 落下 ❑ *He has again fallen from his horse.* 他又一次从马上落下来。 ❑ *Bombs fell in the town.* 炸弹落在了城里。 ● N-COUNT **Fall** is also a noun. 落下 ❑ *The helmets are designed to withstand impacts equivalent to a fall from a bicycle.* 头盔设计成能承受相当于从自行车上摔下来的力度。 2 V-I If a person or structure that is standing somewhere **falls**, they move from their upright position, so that they are then lying on the ground. 跌倒 ❑ *The woman gripped the shoulders of her man to stop herself from falling.* 这个女人紧紧抓住了她男人的肩膀以防自己跌倒。 ❑ *He lost his balance and fell backwards.* 他失去了平衡，往后跌倒了。 ● N-COUNT **Fall** is also a noun. 跌倒 ❑ *She broke her right leg in a bad fall.* 她在一次严重的跌倒中右腿骨折了。 ● PHRASAL VERB **Fall down** means the same as **fall**. 跌倒 ❑ *I hit him so hard he fell down.* 我使劲地打他，他摔倒了。 ● **fall·en** ADJ 倒下的 [ADJ n] ❑ *A number of roads have been blocked by fallen trees.* 一些道路被倒下的树堵住了。

F

Note that you can use **fall down** to talk about people and objects, but for things like prices you should use the verb **fall** by itself. ❑ *Suddenly she just fell down beside me... Share prices fell sharply during the day.* Do not confuse **fall** and **drop**. Although things can **drop** or **fall** by accident, note that **fall** is not followed by an object, so you cannot say that someone "falls" something. However, you can say that they **drop** something, or that something **drops**. ❑ *Leaves were falling to the ground... He dropped his cigar... Plate after plate dropped from his fingers.* You say that a person **drops** when they jump straight down from something, for example, when someone jumps from a plane using a parachute. If someone **falls** it is usually because of an accident. ❑ *He stumbled and fell.* **Drop** and **fall** are also nouns. A **drop** is the height of something when you imagine falling off it. ❑ *Sixteen hundred feet is a considerable drop.* A **fall** is what happens when someone has an accident. ❑ *I had been badly bruised by the fall.*

3 V-I When rain or snow **falls**, it comes down from the sky. (雨或雪) 降落 ❑ *Winds reached up to 100 mph in some places with an inch of rain falling within 15 minutes.* 风在有些地方达到每小时100英里，伴有15分钟内1英寸的降雨量。 ● N-COUNT **Fall** is also a noun. 降落 ❑ *One night there was a heavy fall of snow.* 一天晚上天降大雪。 4 → see also **rainfall** 5 V-I If you **fall** somewhere, you allow yourself to drop there in a hurried or disorganized way, often because you are very tired. 一头倒下 ❑ *Totally exhausted, he tore his clothes off and fell into bed.* 他疲惫极了，胡乱地脱下衣服便一头倒在了床上。 6 V-I If something **falls**, it decreases in amount, value, or strength. (总数、价值、强度或实力等) 下降 ❑ *Output will fall by 6%.* 产量将下降6%。 ❑ *The rate of convictions has fallen.* 有罪判决率已经下降。 ● N-COUNT **Fall** is also a noun. 下降 ❑ *There was a sharp fall in the value of the dollar.* 美元的价值有大幅下降。 7 V-I If a powerful or successful person **falls**, they suddenly lose their power or position. 垮台 ❑ *Regimes fall, revolutions come and go, but places never really change.* 政权垮台了，革命起起伏伏，但各个地方从未真正改变。 ● N-SING **Fall** is also a noun. 垮台 ❑ *Following the fall of the military dictator in March, the country has had a civilian government.* 军事独裁者3月垮台之后，该国已有了一个平民政府。 8 V-I If a place **falls** in a war or election, an enemy army or a different political party takes control of it. 失守 ❑ *Croatian army troops retreated from northern Bosnia and the area fell to the Serbs.* 克罗地亚军队从波斯尼亚北部撤退，随后该地区失守了，落入塞尔维亚人之手。 ● N-SING **Fall** is also a noun. 失守 ❑ *...the fall of Rome.* …罗马的失守。 9 V-I If you say that something or someone **falls into** a particular group or category, you mean that they belong in that group or category. 属于 ❑ *The problems generally fall into two categories.* 这些问题一般属于两种类别。 10 V-I If a celebration or other special event **falls on** a particular day or date, it happens to be on that day or date. 适逢 (某日) ❑ *...the oddly named Quasimodo Sunday which falls on the first Sunday after Easter.* …被古怪地命名为"卸白衣主日"是复活节后的第一个星期天。 11 V-I When light or shadow **falls** on something, it covers it. (光线或影子) 落在 ❑ *Nancy, out of the corner of her eye, saw the shadow that suddenly fell across the doorway.* 南希从眼角余光看到那突然落在门道上的影子。 12 V-I If you say that someone's eyes **fell on** something, you mean they suddenly noticed it. 突然注意到 [WRITTEN] ❑ *As he laid the flowers on the table, his eye fell upon a note in Grace's handwriting.* 他把花放在桌上时，突然注意到一张有格雷斯笔迹的便条。 13 V-I When night or darkness **falls**, night begins and it becomes dark. (夜色或黑暗) 降临 ❑ *As darkness fell outside, they sat down to eat at long tables.* 当外面黑暗降临时，他们坐在长条桌子旁吃饭。 14 V-LINK You can use **fall** to show that someone or something passes into another state. For example, if someone **falls ill**, they become ill, and if something **falls into disrepair**, it is then in a state of disrepair. 进入 (某种状态) ❑ *It is almost impossible to visit Florida without falling in love with the state.* 参观佛罗里达州却不爱上这个州，这几乎是不可能的。 ❑ *Almost without exception these women fall victim to exploitation.* 几乎毫无例外这些女人都成为了剥削的牺牲品。 15 N-PLURAL; N-IN-NAMES You can refer to a **waterfall** as **the falls**. 瀑布 ❑ *The falls have always been an insurmountable obstacle for salmon and sea trout.* 这些瀑布始终是鲑鱼和海鳟鱼不可逾越的障碍。 16 N-VAR **Fall** is the season between summer and winter when the weather becomes cooler. 秋季 [AM] ❑ *He was elected judge in the fall of 1991.* 他于1991年秋被选为法官。 17 → see also **fallen** 18 PHRASE To **fall to pieces** means the same as to **fall apart**. 同**fall apart** ❑ *At that point the radio handset fell to pieces.* 就在那一刻收音机的遥控器摔碎了。 19 to **fall on** your **feet** → see **foot** 20 to **fall foul of** → see **foul** 21 to **fall flat** → see **flat** 22 to **fall into place** → see **place** 23 to **fall short** → see **short**

▶ **fall apart** 1 PHRASAL VERB If something **falls apart**, it breaks into pieces because it is old or badly made. 破碎 ❑ *The work was never finished and bit by bit the building fell apart.* 这项工程从来没有完工，该建筑一点一点地坍塌了。 2 PHRASAL VERB If an organization or system **falls apart**, it becomes disorganized or unable to work effectively, or breaks up into its different parts. 瓦解 ❑ *Europe's monetary system is falling apart.* 欧洲的货币体制正在瓦解。 3 PHRASAL VERB If you say that someone **is falling apart**, you mean that they are becoming emotionally disturbed and are unable to think calmly or to deal with the difficult or unpleasant situation that they are in. 精神崩溃 [INFORMAL] ❑ *I was falling apart. I wasn't getting any sleep.* 我要崩溃了。我根本睡不着觉。

▶ **fall back on** PHRASAL VERB If you **fall back on** something, you do it or use it after other things have failed. 转而使用 ❑ *When necessary, instinct is the most reliable resource you can fall back on.* 必要时，本能是你可使用的最可靠的资源。

▶ **fall behind** 1 PHRASAL VERB If you **fall behind**, you do not make progress or move forward as fast as other people. 落后于 ❑ *Boris is falling behind all the top players.* 鲍里斯正落后于所有的顶尖选手。 2 PHRASAL VERB If you **fall behind** with something or let it **fall behind**, you do not do it or produce it when you should, according to an agreement or schedule. 拖后 ❑ *He faces losing his home after falling behind with the payments.* 他拖欠还款后面临失去住房的问题。 ❑ *Thousands of people could die because the relief effort has fallen so far behind.* 成千上万的人可能会因救援跟不上而死去。

▶ **fall for** 1 PHRASAL VERB If you **fall for** someone, you are strongly attracted to them and start loving them. 爱上 ❑ *He was fantastically handsome – I just fell for him right away.* 他帅极了——我对他简直就是一见钟情。 2 PHRASAL VERB If you **fall for** a lie or trick, you believe it or are deceived by it. 被骗 ❑ *It was just a line to get you out here, and you fell for it!* 那只是一个让你到这儿来的谎言，你被骗了！

▶ **fall off** 1 PHRASAL VERB If something **falls off**, it separates from the thing to which it was attached and moves toward the ground. 脱落 ❑ *When your exhaust pipe falls off, you have to replace it.* 当你的排气管脱落时，你只能更换它。 2 PHRASAL VERB If the degree, amount, or size of something **falls off**, it decreases. 降低；减小 ❑ *Unemployment is rising again and retail buying has fallen off.* 失业率又在上升，而零售购买量已经减少。

▶ **fall out** 1 PHRASAL VERB If something such as a person's hair or a tooth **falls out**, it comes out. 脱落 ❑ *Her hair started falling out as a result of radiation treatment.* 她的头发因放射治疗而开始脱落。 2 PHRASAL VERB If you **fall out** with someone, you have an argument and stop being friendly with them. You can also say that two people **fall out**. 闹翻 ❑ *She fell out with her husband.* 她与丈夫闹翻了。 3 → see also **fallout**

▶ **fall over** PHRASAL VERB If a person or object that is standing **falls over**, they accidentally move from their upright position so that they are then lying on the ground or on the surface supporting them. 倒下 ❑ *If he drinks more than two glasses of wine he falls over.* 如果他喝酒超过两杯就会倒下。

▸ **fall through** PHRASAL VERB If an arrangement, plan, or deal **falls through**, it fails to happen. 落空 ❑ *They wanted to turn the estate into a private golf course and offered $20 million, but the deal fell through.* 他们想把这个庄园变成一个私人的高尔夫球场并出价2千万美元，但是这笔交易落空了。

▸ **fall to** PHRASAL VERB If a responsibility, duty, or opportunity **falls to** someone, it becomes their responsibility, duty, or opportunity. (责任、机会等) 落到…身上 ❑ *He's been very unlucky that no chances have fallen to him.* 他很不走运，没有任何机会落到他身上。

Thesaurus *fall* 另参见：
V. fall down, plunge, topple over 1 2
come down 3
drop, plunge; *(ant.)* increase, rise 6

fal·la·cy /fæləsi/ (**fallacies**) N-VAR A **fallacy** is an idea which many people believe to be true, but which is in fact false because it is based on incorrect information or reasoning. 谬见 ❑ *It's a fallacy that the affluent give relatively more to charity than the less prosperous.* 富人比不太有钱的人给慈善机构相对更多捐赠是一种谬见。

fall·en /fɔlən/ **Fallen** is the past participle of **fall**. **fall**的过去分词

fall·out /fɔlaʊt/ 1 N-UNCOUNT **Fallout** is the radiation that affects a particular place or area after a nuclear explosion has taken place. 核辐射 ❑ *They were exposed to radioactive fallout during nuclear weapons tests.* 他们在核武器试验过程中暴露于放射性核辐射。 2 N-UNCOUNT If you refer to the **fallout from** something that has happened, you mean the unpleasant consequences that follow it. 后果 ❑ *Grundy lost his job in the fallout from the incident.* 格伦迪因该事故丢了工作。

false ♦◇◇ /fɔls/ 1 ADJ If something is **false**, it is incorrect, untrue, or mistaken. 错误的 ❑ *It was quite clear the president was being given false information by those around him.* 很明显，总统身边的那些人正给总统提供着错误信息。 ❑ *You do not know whether what you're told is true or false.* 你不知道别人告诉你的是真的还是假的。 ● **false·ly** ADV 错误地 [ADV with v] ❑ *...a man who is falsely accused of a crime.* …一名被错误地指控犯有一个罪行的男子。 2 ADJ You use **false** to describe objects which are artificial but which are intended to look like the real thing or to be used instead of the real thing. 假的 ❑ *...a set of false teeth.* …一副假牙。 3 ADJ If you describe a person or their behavior as **false**, you are criticizing them for being insincere or for hiding their real feelings. 不真诚的 [DISAPPROVAL] ❑ *"Thank you," she said with false enthusiasm.* "谢谢你，" 她故作热情地说。 ● **false·ly** ADV 不真诚地 ❑ *They smiled at one another, somewhat falsely.* 他们相互微笑，有点假惺惺地。

false alarm (**false alarms**) N-COUNT When you think something dangerous is about to happen, but then discover that you were mistaken, you can say that it was a **false alarm**. 虚惊 ❑ *...a bomb threat that turned out to be a false alarm.* …最终证实是虚惊一场的炸弹恐吓。

★ **false·hood** /fɔlshʊd/ (**falsehoods**) 1 N-UNCOUNT **Falsehood** is the quality or fact of being untrue or of being a lie. 虚假 ❑ *She called the verdict a victory of truth over falsehood.* 她称该裁定是一个真实对虚假的胜利。 2 N-COUNT A **falsehood** is a lie. 谎言 [FORMAL] ❑ *He accused them of knowingly spreading falsehoods about him.* 他指控他们蓄意散步有关他的谎言。

false start (**false starts**) 1 N-COUNT A **false start** is an attempt to start something, such as a speech, project, or plan, which fails because you were not properly prepared or ready to begin. 失败的开端 ❑ *Any economic reform, he said, faced false starts and mistakes.* 他说任何经济改革都面临过一些不成功的开始和错误。 2 N-COUNT If there is a **false start** at the beginning of a race, one of the competitors moves before the person who starts the race has given the signal. 起跑犯规 ❑ *He powered away after two false starts to win comfortably.* 他在两次起跑犯规后奋力猛冲而轻松获胜。

fal·si·fy /fɔlsɪfaɪ/ (**falsifies, falsifying, falsified**) V-T If someone **falsifies** something, they change it or add untrue details to it in order to deceive people. 篡改 ❑ *The charges against him include fraud, bribery, and falsifying business records.* 对他的指控包括诈骗、贿赂和篡改业务记录。

▲ **fal·ter** /fɔltər/ (**falters, faltering, faltered**) 1 V-I If something **falters**, it loses power or strength in an uneven way, or no longer makes much progress. 衰退 ❑ *Normal life is at a standstill, and the economy is faltering.* 正常生活陷入停滞，经济正在衰退。 2 V-I If you **falter**, you lose your confidence and stop doing something or start making mistakes. 犹豫 ❑ *I have not faltered in my quest for a new future.* 我对崭新未来的追求未曾犹豫过。

fame /feɪm/ N-UNCOUNT If you achieve **fame**, you become very well-known. 声誉 ❑ *At the height of his fame, his every word was valued.* 在他声名鼎盛时，他的每一句话都受到了重视。 ❑ *The film earned him international fame.* 这部影片为他赢得了国际声誉。

Word Partnership *fame* 的常用搭配：
V. **bring** fame, **gain** fame, **rise to** fame
N. **claim to** fame, fame **and fortune**, **hall of** fame
ADJ. **international** fame

famed /feɪmd/ ADJ If people, places, or things are **famed for** a particular thing, they are very well known for it. 闻名的 ❑ *The city is famed for its outdoor restaurants.* 这座城市因其露天餐馆而闻名。

fa·mil·iar ♦◇◇ /fəmɪlyər/ 1 ADJ If someone or something is **familiar** to you, you recognize them or know them well. 熟悉的 ❑ *He talked of other cultures as if they were more familiar to him than his own.* 他谈起其他文化就像它们对于他比他自己的文化还熟悉。 ❑ *They are already familiar faces on our TV screens.* 他们已经是我们电视屏幕上熟悉的面孔了。 ● **fa·mil·iar·ity** /fəmɪliærɪti/ N-UNCOUNT 熟悉 ❑ *Tony was unnerved by the uncanny familiarity of her face.* 托尼被她不寻常的熟悉面孔弄得心烦意乱。 2 ADJ If you are **familiar with** something, you know or understand it well. 对…是熟悉的 [v-link ADJ "with" n] ❑ *Most people are familiar with this figure from Wagner's opera.* 多数人对瓦格纳歌剧中的这个人物是熟悉的。 ● **fa·mil·iar·ity** N-UNCOUNT 熟悉 ❑ *The enemy would always have the advantage of familiarity with the rugged terrain.* 敌人会一直在对崎岖地形的熟悉上占有优势。 3 ADJ If someone you do not know well behaves in a **familiar** way toward you, they treat you very informally in a way that you might find offensive. 随便的 [DISAPPROVAL] ❑ *It isn't appropriate for an officer to be overly familiar with an enlisted man.* 军官对入伍士兵过分随便是不合适的。 ● **fa·mil·iar·ity** N-UNCOUNT 随便 ❑ *She needed to control her surprise at the easy familiarity with which her host greeted the head waiter.* 她需要在看到主人对领班打招呼的亲热随便时控制自己的惊讶。 ● **fa·mil·iar·ly** ADV 随便地 ❑ *"Gerald, isn't it?" I began familiarly.* "杰拉尔德，是吧？" 我随便地开口问道。

Thesaurus *familiar* 另参见：
ADJ. accustomed to 1
aware of, informed about 2

Word Partnership *familiar* 的常用搭配：
N. familiar **face** 1
V. **look** familiar, **seem** familiar, **sound** familiar 1
become familiar 2
PREP. familiar **to** ***someone*** 1
familiar **with** ***someone/something*** 2

fa·mil·iar·ize /fəmɪlyəraɪz/ (**familiarizes, familiarizing, familiarized**) V-T If you **familiarize** yourself **with** something, or if someone **familiarizes** you **with** it, you learn about it and start to understand it. 使熟悉 ❑ *The goal of the experiment was to familiarize the people with the new laws.* 该实验的目的是使人们熟悉新的规则。

fami·ly ♦♦♦ /fæmɪli, fæmli/ (**families**) 1 N-COUNT-COLL A **family** is a group of people who are related to each other, especially parents and their children. 家人 ❑ *There's room in there for a family of five.* 那儿能住得下一家5口。 ❑ *Does he have any family?* 他有什么家人吗？ 2 N-COUNT-COLL When people talk about a **family**, they sometimes mean children. 孩子 ❑ *They decided to start a family.* 他们决定了要孩子。 3 N-COUNT-COLL When people talk about their **family**, they sometimes mean their ancestors. 祖先 ❑ *Her family came to Los Angeles at the turn of the century.* 她的祖先在世纪之交时来到了洛杉矶。 4 ADJ You can use **family** to describe things that belong to a particular family. 家庭的 [ADJ n] ❑ *He returned to the family home.* 他回到了自己家。 5 ADJ You can use **family** to describe things that are designed to be used or enjoyed by both parents and children. 全家用的 [ADJ n] ❑ *It had been designed as a family house.* 它已被设计成一幢适合全家人居住的房子。 6 N-COUNT A **family** of animals or plants is a group of related species. (动植物的) 科 ❑ *...foods in the cabbage family, such as Brussels sprouts.* …十字花科食物，如抱子甘蓝。

→ see Picture Dictionary: **family**

f

Picture Dictionary

N-UNCOUNT **Family planning** is the practice of using contraception to control the number of children you have. 计划生育 ❑ *...a family planning clinic.* …一个计划生育门诊部。

/fæmɪn/ (**famines**) N-VAR **Famine** is a situation in which large numbers of people have little or no food, and many of them die. 饥荒 ❑ *Thousands of refugees are trapped by war, drought and famine.* 成千上万的难民陷于战争、干旱和饥荒的困境。

/fe̲ɪməs/ ADJ Someone or something that is **famous** is very well known. 有名的 ❑ *...one of Kentucky's most famous landmarks.* …肯塔基州最有名的标志之一。

A **famous** person or thing is known to more people than a **well-known** one. A **notorious** person or thing is famous because they are connected with something bad or undesirable. **Infamous** is not the opposite of **famous**. It has a similar meaning to **notorious**, but is a stronger word. Someone or something that is **notable** is important or interesting.

Thesaurus

acclaimed, celebrated, prominent, renowned; *(ant.)* anonymous, obscure, unknown

/fe̲ɪməsli/ ADV You use **famously** to refer to a fact that is well known, usually because it is remarkable or extreme. 出了名地 ❑ *Authors are famously ignorant about the realities of publishing.* 作者们对出版业的实际情况出了名地无知。

/fæn/ (**fans, fanning, fanned**) N-COUNT If you are a **fan** of someone or something, especially a famous person or a sport, you like them very much and are very interested in them. 狂热爱好者 ❑ *If you're a Billy Crystal fan, you'll love this movie.* 如果你是比利·克里斯特尔的影迷，你就会喜欢这部电影。 ❑ *I am a great fan of rave music.* 我是个狂欢音乐的狂热乐迷。 N-COUNT **A fan** is a piece of electrical or mechanical equipment with blades that go around and around. It keeps a room or machine cool or gets rid of unpleasant smells. 风扇 ❑ *He cools himself in front of an electric fan.* 他在一个电扇前面吹凉。 N-COUNT **A fan** is a flat object that you hold in your hand and wave in order to move the air and make yourself feel cooler. 扇子 ❑ *...hundreds of dancing girls waving peacock fans.* …数百名挥动着孔雀扇的舞女。 V-T If you **fan** yourself or your face when you are hot, you wave a fan or other flat object in order to make yourself feel cooler. 给…扇风 ❑ *She would have to wait in the truck, fanning herself with a piece of cardboard.* 她只得在卡车里等候，用一块纸板给自己扇风。

→ see **concert**

PHRASAL VERB If a group of people or things **fan out**, they move forward away from a particular point in different directions. 散开 ❑ *The main body of British, American, and French troops had fanned out to the west.* 英、美、法军队的主力向西面散开。

/fənæ̲tɪk/ (**fanatics**) N-COUNT If you describe someone as a **fanatic**, you disapprove of them because you consider their behavior or opinions to be very extreme, for example, in the way they support particular religious or political ideas. 狂热分子 [DISAPPROVAL] ❑ *I am not a religious fanatic but I am a Christian.* 我不是个宗教狂热分子，但我是个基督徒。 N-COUNT If you say that someone is a **fanatic**, you mean that they are very enthusiastic about a particular activity, sport, or way of life. 入迷者 ❑ *Both Rod and Phil are football fanatics.* 罗德和菲尔两人都是足球迷。 ADJ **Fanatic** means the same as **fanatical**. 狂热的

/fənæ̲tɪkᵊl/ ADJ If you describe someone as **fanatical**, you disapprove of them because you consider their behavior or opinions to be very extreme. 狂热的 [DISAPPROVAL] ❑ *He is a fanatical fan of Mozart.* 他是一名莫扎特音乐的狂热爱好者。

/fæ̲nsɪfəl/ ADJ If you describe an idea as **fanciful**, you disapprove of it because you think it comes from someone's imagination, and is therefore unrealistic or unlikely to be true. 异想天开的 [DISAPPROVAL] ❑ *...fanciful ideas about Martian life.* …关于火星生命的异想天开。

ELABORATE OR EXPENSIVE
WANTING, LIKING, OR THINKING

/fæ̲nsi/ (**fancier, fanciest**) ADJ If you describe something as **fancy**, you mean that it is special, unusual, or elaborate, for example because it has a lot of decoration. 别致的 ❑ *The magazine was packaged in a fancy plastic case with attractive graphics.* 这本杂志装在一个带有漂亮图纹的别致塑料盒子里。 ADJ If you describe something as **fancy**, you mean that it is very expensive or of very high quality, and you often dislike it because of this. 阔气的 [INFORMAL] ❑ *My parents sent me to a fancy private school.* 我父母把我送到了一所阔气的私立学校。

Thesaurus

elegant, lavish, showy; (*ant.*) plain, simple

/fænsi/ (**fancies, fancying, fancied**) V-T If you **fancy yourself as** a particular kind of person or fancy **yourself** doing a particular thing, you like the idea of being that kind of person or doing that thing. 认为（自己）[mainly BRIT] ❑ *So you fancy yourself as the boss someday?* 那么你认为自己有一天会成老板？ V-T If you say that someone **fancies themselves as** a particular kind of person, you mean that they think, often wrongly, that they have the good qualities which that kind of person has. （自）认为是 ❑ *She fancies herself a bohemian.* 她自命为一个放荡不羁的艺术家。

V-T If you **fancy** something, you want to have it or to do it. 想要 [mainly BRIT, INFORMAL] ❑ *I just fancied a drink.* 我只是想要杯饮料。

V-T If you **fancy** someone, you feel attracted to them, especially in a sexual way. 爱慕 [BRIT, INFORMAL] EXCLAM You say "**fancy**" or "**fancy that**" when you want to express surprise or disapproval. （表示惊讶或反对）真没想到 [FEELINGS] ❑ *"Fancy that!" smiled Conti.* "真没想到！" 康蒂笑着说。 PHRASE If you **take a fancy to** someone or something, you start liking them, usually for no understandable reason. （通常指没有道理的）爱上 ❑ *Sylvia took quite a fancy to him.* 西尔维娅完全爱上了他。 PHRASE If something **takes** your **fancy** or **tickles** your **fancy**, you like it a lot when you see it or think of it. 中某人的意 ❑ *She makes most of her own clothes, copying any fashion which takes her fancy.* 她大部分的衣服是模仿中意的时装自己做的。

/fænfɛər/ (**fanfares**) N-COUNT A **fanfare** is a short, loud tune played on trumpets or other similar instruments to announce a special event. （特别仪式上的）嘹亮短曲 ❑ *The ceremony opened with a fanfare of trumpets.* 典礼以一段号角的奏鸣开始了。

N-VAR If something happens with a **fanfare**, it happens or is announced with a lot of publicity. If something happens without a **fanfare**, it happens without a lot of fuss or publicity. 大张旗鼓的宣传 [oft N "of" n] ❑ *...a fanfare of publicity.* …一次大张旗鼓的宣传。

/fæŋ/ (**fangs**) N-COUNT **Fangs** are the two long, sharp, upper teeth that some animals have. （动物的）尖牙 ❑ *The cobra sank its venomous fangs into his hand.* 眼镜蛇将毒牙咬进他的手。

/fæntəsaɪz/ (**fantasizes, fantasizing, fantasized**) V-T/V-I If you **fantasize** about an event or situation that you would like to happen, you give yourself pleasure by imagining that it is happening, although it is untrue or unlikely to happen. 幻想 ❑ *I fantasized about writing music.* 我曾幻想作曲。

/fæntæstɪk/ ADJ If you say that something is **fantastic**, you are emphasizing that you think it is very good or that you like it a lot. 极好的 [INFORMAL, EMPHASIS] ❑ *I have a fantastic social life.* 我有着极好的社交生活。 ADJ A **fantastic** amount or quantity is an extremely large one. 极大的（量）[ADJ n] ❑ *...fantastic amounts of money.* …几笔巨款。 ●
/fæntæstɪkli/ ADV 极其 [ADV adj/adv] ❑ *...a fantastically expensive restaurant.* …一家极其昂贵的餐馆。

/fæntəsi/ (**fantasies**) N-COUNT A **fantasy** is a pleasant situation or event that you think about and that you want to happen, especially one that is unlikely to happen. 幻想 ❑ *...fantasies of romance and true love.* …对浪漫和真爱的幻想。 N-VAR You can refer to a story or situation that someone creates from their imagination and that is not based on reality as **fantasy**. 虚幻的故事；幻想的情境 ❑ *The film is more of an ironic fantasy than a horror story.* 这部电影比较像是讽刺的幻想故事，而不是恐怖片。

N-UNCOUNT **Fantasy** is the activity of imagining things. 幻想 ❑ *...a world of imagination, passion, fantasy, reflection.* …一个想像、激情、幻想和反思的世界。 ADJ **Fantasy** football, baseball, or another sport is a game in which players choose an imaginary team and score points based on the actual performances of the members of their team in real games. 梦幻的（运动类电子游戏）[ADJ n] ❑ *Haskins said he has been playing fantasy baseball for the past five years.* 哈斯金斯说他在过去的 5 年里一直在打梦幻棒球游戏。
→ see Word Web: **fantasy**

You use **FAO** when addressing a letter or parcel to a particular person. **FAO** is a written abbreviation for "for the attention of." （用于寄信或包裹时）…收 [BRIT]
in AM, use **Attn.**

/fæk/ (**FAQs**) N-PLURAL **FAQ** is used especially on websites to refer to questions about a particular topic. **FAQ** is an abbreviation for "frequently asked questions." 常见问题

DISTANT IN SPACE OR TIME
THE EXTENT TO WHICH SOMETHING HAPPENS
EMPHATIC USES

/fɑr/

➪ **Please look at meaning to see if the expression you are looking for is shown under another headword.** ADV If one place, thing, or person is **far** away from another, there is a great distance between them. 很远地 ❑ *I know a nice little Italian restaurant not far from here.* 我知道一家很好的意大利小餐馆离这儿不远。 ❑ *Both of my sisters moved even farther away from home.* 我的两个姐妹都搬得离家更远了。 ADV If you ask **how far** a place is, you are asking what distance it is from you or from another place. If you ask **how far** someone went, you are asking what distance they traveled, or what place they reached. （距离）远至 ❑ *How far is Pawtucket from Providence?* 波塔基特离普罗维登斯有多远？ ❑ *How far is it to Malcy?* 这里到马尔锡有多远？ ❑ *She followed the tracks as far as the road.* 她沿着小径一直走到公路边。

Far is used in negative sentences and questions about distance, but not usually in affirmative sentences. ❑ *We stood by a stream not far from our house.* If you want to state the distance of a particular place from where you are, you can say that it is that distance **away**. ❑ *...Omaha, which is over 300 miles away.* If a place is very distant, you can say that it is **a long way away**, or that it is **a long way from** another place. ❑ *It is a long way from Atlanta... Anna was still a long way away.*

ADV A time or event that is **far** away in the future or the past is a long time from the present or from a particular point in time. 久远地 ❑ *...hidden conflicts whose roots lie far back in time.* …根源久远的

Word Web

All **fictional** writing involves the use of **imaginary** situations and characters. However, **fantasy** goes a few steps further. This **genre** leaves **reality** behind and moves into the area of **imagination**. It involves creating new creatures, **myths**, and **legends**. A **novelist** usually incorporates **realistic** people and settings. But a fantasy writer is free to create a whole different world where earthly laws no longer apply. Contemporary movies have found a rich source of stories in the genre. Today you can see a wide variety of films about **fairies**, **wizards**, and **dragons**.

各种隐藏的冲突。❑ *I can't see any farther than the next six months.* 我无法预见比6个月更往后的事。 **4** ADJ When there are two things of the same kind in a place, **the far** one is the one that is a greater distance from you. 较远一端的 [ADJ n] ❑ *He had wandered to the far end of the room.* 他已漫步走到房间的那一头。 **5** ADJ You can use **far** to refer to the part of an area or object that is the greatest distance from the center in a particular direction. For example, **the far** north **of** a country is the part of it that is the greatest distance to the north. (离中心) 最大距离的 [ADJ n] ❑ *A storm was brewing off Port Angeles in the far north of Washington State.* 一场暴风雨正在华盛顿州最北端的安吉利斯港外酝酿。 **6** **near and far** → see **near**

> **Far** has two comparatives, **farther** and **further**, and two superlatives, **farthest** and **furthest**. **Farther** and **farthest** are used mainly in sense **1**, and are dealt with here. **Further** and **furthest** are dealt with in separate entries.

F

❷far ♦♦♦ /f<u>ɑ</u>r/ **1** ADV You can use **far** to talk about the extent or degree to which something happens or is true. 到…程度 ❑ *How far did the film tell the truth about Barnes Wallis?* 这部电影对巴恩斯・沃利斯的讲述有多大程度的真实性? **2** ADV You can talk about how **far** someone or something gets to describe the progress that they make. (进展) 到…程度 ❑ *Discussions never progressed very far.* 讨论从未有太大进展。 ❑ *Think of how far we have come in a little time.* 想一想我们在短时间内已经有了多么大的进展。 **3** ADV You can talk about how **far** a person or action goes to describe the degree to which someone's behavior or actions are extreme. (人或行为) 极端到…程度 [ADV with v] ❑ *It's still not clear how far the Russian parliament will go to implement its own plans.* 现在还不清楚俄罗斯议会在实施其计划方面会极端到何种程度。 ❑ *Competition can be healthy, but if it is pushed too far it can result in bullying.* 竞争可以是良性的，但如果被推向极端，就会导致恃强凌弱。 **4** ADV You can use **far** in expressions like "**as far as I know**" and "**so far as I remember**" to indicate that you are not absolutely sure of the statement you are about to make or have just made, and you may be wrong. 用于**as far as I know**和**so far as I remember**中，意为"据我所知"和"就我记忆所及" ["as/so" ADV "as"] [VAGUENESS] ❑ *It only lasted a couple of years, as far as I know.* 据我所知，它仅维持了几年。 **5** PHRASE If you say that someone **will go far**, you mean that they will be very successful in their career. 大有前途 ❑ *I was very impressed with the talent of Michael Ball. He will go far.* 我对迈克尔・鲍尔的天赋印象极为深刻。他将前途无量。 **6** PHRASE Someone or something that is **far gone** is in such a bad state or condition that not much can be done to help or improve them. 无药可救的; 回天无力的 ❑ *In his last few days the pain seemed to have stopped, but by then he was so far gone that it was no longer any comfort.* 在他最后的几天里疼痛似乎已经停止，但那时他已病入膏肓，这已不再是什么安慰了。 **7** PHRASE You can use the expression "**as far as I can see**" when you are about to state your opinion of a situation, or have just stated it, to indicate that it is your personal opinion. 在我看来 ❑ *That's the problem as far as I can see.* 在我看来，那就是问题所在。 **8** PHRASE If you say that something only goes **so far** or can only go **so far**, you mean that its extent, effect, or influence is limited. (程度、作用、影响) 仅能如此 ❑ *Their loyalty only went so far.* 他们的忠诚只能到这个程度。 **9** PHRASE If you tell or ask someone what has happened **so far**, you are telling or asking them what has happened up until the present point in a situation or story, and often implying that something different might happen later. 到目前为止 ❑ *It's been quiet so far.* 到目前为止还是安静的。 ❑ *So far, they have met with no success.* 到目前为止，他们还没有成功过。 **10** PHRASE You can say **so far so good** to express satisfaction with the way that a situation or activity is progressing, developing, or happening. 到目前为止还算良好 [FEELINGS] ❑ *Of course, it's a case of so far, so good, but it's only one step.* 当然，到目前为止一切都还顺利，但它只是一步而已。

❸far ♦♦♦ /f<u>ɑ</u>r/ **1** ADV You can use **far** to mean "very much" when you are comparing two things and emphasizing the difference between them. For example, you can say that something is **far better** or **far worse** than something else to indicate that it is very much better or worse. You can also say that something is, for example, **far too big** to indicate that it is very much too big. (作比较时用于强调) …得多 [EMPHASIS] ❑ *Women who eat plenty of fresh vegetables are far less likely to suffer anxiety or depression.* 吃大量新鲜蔬菜的女人患焦虑症或抑郁症的几率要少得多。 ❑ *The police say the response has been far better than expected.* 警方说反应比预料的好得多。 **2** ADJ You can describe people with extreme left-wing or right-wing political views as the **far** left or the **far** right. (政治观点) 极端的 [ADJ n] ❑ *The far right is now a greater threat than the extreme left.* 极右派现在是一个比极左派更大的威胁。 **3** PHRASE You use the expression **by far** when you are comparing something or someone with others of the same kind, in order to emphasize how great the difference is between them. For example, you can say that something is **by far the best** or **the best by far** to indicate that it is definitely the best. (比较时强调差异巨大) 显然 [EMPHASIS] ❑ *By far the most important issue for them is unemployment.* 显然对他们来说最重要的问题是失业。 **4** PHRASE If you say that something is **far from** a particular thing or **far from** being the case, you are emphasizing that it is not that particular thing or not at all the case, especially when people expect or assume that it is. 绝非 [EMPHASIS] ❑ *It was obvious that much of what they recorded was far from the truth.* 很显然，他们所记录的很多内容绝非事实。 ❑ *Far from being relaxed, we both felt so uncomfortable we hardly spoke.* 我们俩非但没有放松，反而觉得很不舒服，我们几乎没说话。 **5** PHRASE You can use the expression "**far from it**" to emphasize a negative statement that you have just made. (用于强调否定陈述) 绝非如此 [EMPHASIS] ❑ *Being dyslexic does not mean that one is unintelligent. Far from it.* 诵读困难并不意味着人不聪明。绝非如此。

far·away /f<u>ɑ</u>rəweɪ/ ADJ A **faraway** place is a long distance from you or from a particular place. 遥远的 [ADJ n] ❑ *They have just returned from faraway places with wonderful stories to tell.* 他们刚从一些遥远的地方回来，有很多精彩的故事要讲。

farce /f<u>ɑ</u>rs/ (**farces**) **1** N-COUNT A **farce** is a humorous play in which the characters become involved in complicated and unlikely situations. 滑稽戏 ❑ *...an off-Broadway farce called "Lucky Stiff."* …一场名为"幸运的家伙"的外百老汇滑稽戏。 **2** N-UNCOUNT **Farce** is the style of acting and writing that is typical of farces. 滑稽风格 ❑ *The plot often borders on farce.* 那种情节常常近乎滑稽。 **3** N-SING If you describe a situation or event as a **farce**, you mean that it is so disorganized or ridiculous that you cannot take it seriously. 闹剧; 荒唐事 [also no det] [DISAPPROVAL] ❑ *The elections have been reduced to a farce.* 那些选举已经沦为一场闹剧。

far·ci·cal /f<u>ɑ</u>rsɪkᵊl/ ADJ If you describe a situation or event as **farcical**, you mean that it is so silly or extreme that you are unable to take it seriously. 荒唐的 [DISAPPROVAL] ❑ *...a farcical nine months' jail sentence imposed yesterday on a killer.* …昨天一个监禁杀人犯9个月的荒唐判决。

fare ♦◇◇ /f<u>ɛə</u>r/ (**fares, faring, fared**) **1** N-COUNT A **fare** is the money that you pay for a trip that you make, for example, in a bus, train, or taxi. 车费 ❑ *He could barely afford the fare.* 他几乎付不起车费。 **2** V-I If you say that someone or something **fares** well or badly, you are referring to the degree of success they achieve in a particular situation or activity. 进展 ❑ *It is unlikely that the marine industry will fare any better in September.* 海运业不大可能在9月份有所好转。

F<u>a</u>r E<u>a</u>st N-PROPER **The Far East** is used to refer to all the countries of Eastern Asia, including China, Japan, the Democratic People's Republic of Korea, the Republic of Korea, and Indonesia. 远东 (指所有东亚国家，包括中国，日本，朝鲜，韩国及印尼)

fare·well /f<u>ɛə</u>rwɛl/ (**farewells**) CONVENTION **Farewell** means the same as **goodbye**. 别了 (同**goodbye**) ● N-COUNT **Farewell** is also a noun. 告别 [LITERARY, OLD-FASHIONED] ❑ *They said their farewells there at the cafe.* 他们在咖啡馆那儿道了别。

f<u>a</u>r-f<u>e</u>tched ADJ If you describe a story or idea as **far-fetched**, you are criticizing it because you think it is unlikely to be true or practical. 牵强的 [DISAPPROVAL] ❑ *The storyline was too far-fetched and none of the actors was particularly good.* 故事情节太牵强，而且没有一个演员特别出色。

farm ♦♦◇ /f<u>ɑ</u>rm/ (**farms, farming, farmed**) **1** N-COUNT A **farm** is an area of land, together with the buildings on it, that is used for growing crops or raising animals, usually in order to sell them. 农场 ❑ *Farms in France are much smaller than those in the United States or even Britain.* 法国的农场比美国甚至英国的都小得多。 **2** N-COUNT A mink **farm** or a fish **farm**, for example, is a place where a particular kind of animal or fish is bred and kept in large quantities in order to be sold. 养殖场 ❑ *...trout fresh from a local trout farm.* …来自当地一家鲑鱼养殖场的新鲜鲑鱼。 **3** V-T/V-I If you **farm** an area of land, you grow crops or keep animals on it. 耕种; 养殖 ❑ *They farmed some of the best land in the country.* 他们耕种着该国最好的一些土地。 ❑ *Bease has been farming for 30 years.* 比斯经营农场已有30年。
→ see Word Web: **farm**
→ see **dairy**

Word Web farm

Gone are the days of simply planting a **crop** and **harvesting** it. Today's **farmer** relies on engineering and technology to make a living. Careful **irrigation** and **drainage** control the amount of water **plants** receive. **Insecticides** protect plants from insect damage. **Fertilizers** guarantee maximum growth. Another high-tech **agricultural** approach promises to increase the world's **food** supply. Employing hydroponic methods, farmers use **chemical** solutions to **cultivate** plants. This has several advantages. **Soil** can contain **pests** and diseases not present in water alone. Growing plants hydroponically also requires less water and less labor than conventional growing methods.

▸ **farm out** PHRASAL VERB If you **farm out** something that is your responsibility, you send it to other people for them to deal with or look after. 外包（工作、活计等）；寄养（孩子） ❑ *Scores of U.S. companies farm out software development.* 许多美国公司外包软件开发。 ❑ *She may have farmed the child out in order to remarry.* 她为了再婚可能已经把孩子寄养出去了。

farm·er ♦♦◇ /fɑrmər/ (**farmers**) N-COUNT A **farmer** is a person who owns or manages a farm. 农场主
→ see **farm**

farm·house /fɑrmhaʊs/ (**farmhouses**) N-COUNT A **farmhouse** is the main house on a farm, usually where the farmer lives. 农场住宅

farm·ing /fɑrmɪŋ/ N-UNCOUNT **Farming** is the activity of growing crops or keeping animals on a farm. 耕种；养殖 ❑ *...a career in farming.* …务农生涯。

farm·land /fɑrmlænd/ (**farmlands**) N-UNCOUNT **Farmland** is land which is farmed, or which is suitable for farming. 农田；耕地 [also N in pl] ❑ *It is surrounded by 62 acres of farmland.* 它被62英亩的农田环绕着。

farm·yard /fɑrmyɑrd/ (**farmyards**) N-COUNT On a farm, the **farmyard** is an area of land near the farmhouse which is enclosed by walls or buildings. 农家场院 ❑ *...farmyard animals including chickens, geese and rabbits.* …包括鸡、鹅和兔子在内的农家场院里的动物。

far off (**further off, furthest off**) **1** ADJ If you describe a moment in time as **far off**, you mean that it is a long time from the present, either in the past or the future. 久远的 ❑ *In those far off days it never entered anyone's mind that a woman could be prime minister.* 在那些久远的日子里，绝没有人会想到一个女人可以当上首相。 **2** ADJ If you describe something as **far off**, you mean that it is a long distance from you or from a particular place. （距离）遥远的 ❑ *...stars in far-off galaxies.* …遥远星系里的恒星。 ● ADV **Far off** is also an adverb. 遥远地 [ADV after v] ❑ *The band was playing far off in their blue and yellow uniforms.* 这个乐队身着蓝黄相间的制服正在远处演奏。

far-reaching ADJ If you describe actions, events, or changes as **far-reaching**, you mean that they have a very great influence and affect a great number of things. 影响深远的 ❑ *The economy is in danger of collapse unless far-reaching reforms are implemented.* 除非实施影响深远的改革，否则经济就有崩溃的危险。

far·sighted /fɑrsaɪtɪd/ also **far-sighted** **1** ADJ If you describe someone as **farsighted**, you admire them because they understand what is likely to happen in the future, and therefore make wise decisions and plans. 有远见的 [APPROVAL] ❑ *Haven't farsighted economists been telling us that in the future we will work less, not more?* 有远见的经济学家们不是一直在告诉我们，将来我们会工作得更少而不是更多吗？ **2** ADJ **Farsighted** people cannot see things clearly that are close to them, and therefore need to wear glasses. 远视的
→ see **eye**

far·ther /fɑrðər/ **Farther** is a comparative form of **far**. **far**的比较级

far·thest /fɑrðɪst/ **Farthest** is a superlative form of **far**. **far**的最高级

fas·ci·nate /fæsɪneɪt/ (**fascinates, fascinating, fascinated**) V-T If something **fascinates** you, it interests and delights you so much that your thoughts tend to concentrate on it. 使着迷 ❑ *Politics fascinated Franklin's father.* 政治让富兰克林的父亲着迷。

fas·ci·nat·ed /fæsɪneɪtɪd/ ADJ If you are **fascinated by** something, you find it very interesting and attractive, and your thoughts tend to concentrate on it. 入迷的 ❑ *I sat on the stairs and watched, fascinated.* 我坐在楼梯上看得入了迷。

fas·ci·nat·ing /fæsɪneɪtɪŋ/ ADJ If you describe something as **fascinating**, you find it very interesting and attractive, and your thoughts tend to concentrate on it. 迷人的 ❑ *Madagascar is the most fascinating place I have ever been to.* 马达加斯加是我去过的最迷人的地方。

fas·ci·na·tion /fæsɪneɪʃən/ N-UNCOUNT **Fascination** is the state of being greatly interested in or delighted by something. 着迷 ❑ *I've had a lifelong fascination with the sea and with small boats.* 我毕生都对海和小船有一份沉迷。

fas·cism /fæʃɪzəm/ N-UNCOUNT **Fascism** is a set of right-wing political beliefs that includes strong control of society and the economy by the state, a powerful role for the armed forces, and the stopping of political opposition. 法西斯主义 ❑ *...the rise of fascism in the 1930s.* …20世纪30年代法西斯主义的兴起。

★ **fas·cist** /fæʃɪst/ (**fascists**) ADJ You use **fascist** to describe organizations, ideas, or systems which follow the principles of fascism. 法西斯主义的 ❑ *...an upsurge of support for extreme rightist, nationalist and fascist organizations.* …支持极右组织、民族主义组织和法西斯组织的狂潮。 ● N-COUNT A **fascist** is someone who has fascist views. 法西斯分子 ❑ *...a reluctant supporter of Mussolini's Fascists.* …一个不情愿支持墨索里尼法西斯分子的人。

fash·ion ♦♦◇ /fæʃən/ (**fashions**) **1** N-UNCOUNT **Fashion** is the area of activity that involves styles of clothing and appearance. 时尚界 ❑ *There are 20 full-color pages of fashion for men.* 有20张男士时尚动态的全彩页。 **2** N-COUNT A **fashion** is a style of clothing or a way of behaving that is popular at a particular time. 时尚 ❑ *In the early seventies I wore false eyelashes, as was the fashion.* 70年代初我戴假睫毛，那是当时的时尚。 ❑ *The demand for perfume resulted in a fashion for fancy scent bottles.* 对香水的需求使别致的香水瓶成为一种时尚。 **3** N-SING If you do something **in** a particular **fashion** or **after** a particular **fashion**, you do it in that way. 方式 ❑ *There is another drug called DHE that works in a similar fashion.* 另有一种叫作二氢埃托啡的药作用相似。 **4** → see also **old-fashioned** **5** PHRASE If something is **in fashion**, it is popular and approved of at a particular time. If it is **out of fashion**, it is not popular or approved of. 流行/过时 ❑ *That sort of house is back in fashion.* 那种房子又时兴起来了。

fash·ion·able /fæʃənəbəl/ ADJ Something or someone that is **fashionable** is popular or approved of at a particular time. 时髦的 ❑ *It became fashionable to eat certain kinds of fish.* 吃某些种类的鱼变得时髦了。 ● **fash·ion·ably** ADV 时髦地 ❑ *...women who are perfectly made up and fashionably dressed.* …化妆完美、穿着入时的女人们。

fast ♦♦◇ /fæst/ (**faster, fastest, fasts, fasting, fasted**) **1** ADJ **Fast** means happening, moving, or doing something at great speed. You also use **fast** in questions or statements about speed. 迅速的 ❑ *...fast cars with flashing lights and sirens.* …闪灯、鸣笛、快速行驶的汽车。 ❑ *The only question is how fast the process will be.* 惟一的问题是这个过程会有多快。 ● ADV **Fast** is also an adverb. 迅速地 [ADV with v] ❑ *They work terrifically fast.* 他们工作极快。 ❑ *It would be nice to go faster and break the world record.* 再快一些，打破世界纪录就好了。 ❑ *How fast would the disease develop?* 这种疾病发展有多快？ **2** ADJ If a watch or clock is **fast**, it is showing a time that is later than the real time. （钟表）快于准确时间的 [v-link ADJ] ❑ *That clock's an hour fast.* 那个钟快了一个小时。 **3** ADJ If colors or dyes are **fast**, they do not come out of the fabrics they are used on when they get wet. 不褪色的 ❑ *The fabric was ironed to make the colors fast.* 这布被熨烫过以使其不褪色。 **4** ADV You use **fast** to say that something happens without any delay. 毫不耽搁地 [ADV after v] ❑ *When you've got a crisis like this you need professional help – fast!* 在遇到这样的危机时，你需要专业的救助——丝毫不能耽搁！ ● ADJ **Fast** is also an adjective. 毫不耽搁的 [ADJ n] ❑ *That* *would be an astonishingly fast action on the part of the Congress.* 那将是国会方面一次快得惊人的行动。 ADV If you hold something **fast**, you hold it tightly and firmly. If something is stuck **fast**, it is stuck very firmly and cannot move. 紧紧地 [ADV after v] ❑ *She climbed the staircase cautiously, holding fast to the rail.* 她紧握扶手，小心翼翼地爬上楼梯。 ADV If you hold **fast** to a principle or idea, or if you stand **fast**, you do not change your mind about it, even though people are trying to persuade you to. 坚定地 [ADV after v] ❑ *We can only try to hold fast to the age-old values of honesty, decency and concern for others.* 我们只能努力坚守那些古老的价值观：诚实、正派、关心他人。 V-I If you **fast**, you eat no food for a period of time, usually for either religious or medical reasons, or as a protest. (因宗教、医疗或抗议等原因) 禁食 ❑ *I fasted for a day and a half and asked God to help me.* 我禁食了一天半，请求上帝帮助我。 ● N-COUNT **Fast** is also a noun. 禁食 ❑ *The fast is broken at sunset, traditionally with dates and water.* 日落时开斋，按传统会吃海枣、喝水。 ● N-UNCOUNT 禁食 ❑ *...the Muslim holy month of fasting and prayer.* …穆斯林斋戒和祈祷的圣月。 PHRASE Someone who is **fast asleep** is completely asleep. 熟睡 ❑ *When he went upstairs five minutes later, she was fast asleep.* 他5分钟后上楼时，她已熟睡。 to **make a fast buck** → see **buck**

Thesaurus

hasty, quick, rapid, speedy, swift; *(ant.)* leisurely, slow
quickly, rapidly, soon, swiftly; *(ant.)* leisurely, slowly
firmly, tightly; *(ant.)* loosely, unsteadily

/fæsᵊn/ (**fastens, fastening, fastened**) V-T/V-I When you **fasten** something, you close it by means of buttons or a strap, or some other device. If something **fastens** with buttons or straps, you can close it in this way. 扣紧；系牢 ❑ *She got quickly into her Mini and fastened the seat-belt.* 她迅速钻进她的迷你车并系好安全带。 ❑ *Her long fair hair was fastened at the nape of her neck by an elastic band.* 她长长的金发用一根橡皮筋扎在了脖子后面。 V-T If you **fasten** one thing **to** another, you attach the first thing to the second, for example, with a piece of string or tape. 把…系在 ❑ *There were no instructions on how to fasten the carrying strap to the box.* 没有如何把背带系在箱子上的说明。 → see also **fastening**

/fæsənɪŋ/ (**fastenings**) N-COUNT A **fastening** is something such as a clasp or zipper that you use to fasten something and keep it shut. (扣钩、拉链等) 紧固件 ❑ *The sundress has a neat back zipper fastening.* 这件太阳裙背后有根灵巧的拉链。

N-UNCOUNT **Fast food** is hot food, such as hamburgers and French fries, that you obtain from particular types of restaurants, and which is served quickly after you order it. 快餐 ❑ *James works at a fast food restaurant.* 詹姆斯在一家快餐店工作。 → see **meal**

(**fast forwards, fast forwarding, fast forwarded**) also V-T/V-I When you **fast forward** the tape in a video or tape recorder or when you **fast forward**, you make the tape go forward. Compare **rewind**. 使快进；快进 ❑ *Just fast forward the video.* 让录像带快进就行了。 ❑ *He fast-forwarded the tape past the explosion.* 他让磁带快进，跳过了爆炸部分。

/fæstɪdiəs, fə-/ ADJ If you say that someone is **fastidious**, you mean that they pay great attention to detail because they like everything to be very neat, accurate, and in good order. 极其注重细节的 ❑ *...her fastidious attention to historical detail.* …她对历史细节极为细致的关注。

(**fast lanes**) N-COUNT On a highway, **the fast lane** is the part of the road where the vehicles that are traveling fastest go. 快车道 ❑ *I cut across the expressway and took the fast lane back to Miami.* 我穿过高速公路，驶入回迈阿密的快车道。 N-SING If someone is living **in the fast lane**, they have a very busy, exciting life, although they sometimes seem to take a lot of risks. 忙碌而刺激的生活 ❑ *...a tale of life in the fast lane.* …一个忙碌而刺激的生活故事。

(**fast tracks, fast tracking, fast tracked**) also N-SING The **fast track to** a particular goal, especially in politics or in your career, is the quickest route to achieving it. 捷径 ❑ *Many Croats and Slovenes saw independence as the fast track to democracy.* 很多克罗地亚人和斯洛文尼亚人把独立看作通往民主的捷径。 V-T To **fast track** something means to make it happen or progress faster or earlier than normal. 加快；提前 ❑ *A Federal Court case had been fast tracked to Wednesday.* 联邦法院的一起案件已被提前到星期三审理。

/fæt/ (**fatter, fattest, fats**) ADJ If you say that a person or animal is **fat**, you mean that they have a lot of flesh on their body and that they weigh too much. You usually use the word **fat** when you think that this is a bad thing. 肥胖的 [DISAPPROVAL] ❑ *I could eat what I liked without getting fat.* 我可以吃我喜欢的东西而不发胖。

If you describe someone as **fat**, you are speaking in a very direct way, and this may be considered rude. If you want to say more politely that someone is rather fat, it is better to describe them as **plump**, or more informally, as **chubby**. **Overweight** and **obese** are used to describe someone who may have health problems because of their size or weight. **Obese** is also a medical term used to describe someone who is extremely fat or overweight. In general you should avoid using any of these words in the presence of the person you are describing.

N-MASS **Fat** is a substance contained in foods such as meat, cheese, and butter which forms an energy store in your body. (食物中的) 脂肪 ❑ *An easy way to cut the amount of fat in your diet is to avoid eating red meats.* 减少你饮食中脂肪含量的一个简易方法就是避免吃红色肉类。 N-MASS **Fat** is a solid or liquid substance obtained from animals or vegetables, which is used in cooking. 食用油 ❑ *When you use oil or fat for cooking, use as little as possible.* 当你用油烹饪时，要尽可能少放。 ADJ A **fat** object, especially a book, is very thick or wide. (尤指书) 厚的；宽的 ❑ *..."Europe in Figures," a fat book published on September 22nd.* …《数说欧洲》，9月22日出版的一本厚书。 ADJ A **fat** profit or fee is a large one. (利润、费用) 丰厚的 [ADJ n] [INFORMAL] ❑ *They are set to make a big fat profit.* 他们决心努力大赚一笔。 N-UNCOUNT **Fat** is the extra flesh that animals and humans have under their skin, which is used to store energy and to help keep them warm. (动物或人的) 脂肪 ❑ *Because you're not burning calories, everything you eat turns to fat.* 因为你没有消耗卡路里，所以你吃的每样东西都会变成脂肪。 PHRASE If you say that there is **fat chance of** something happening, you mean that you do not believe that it will happen. 没门儿 [INFORMAL, mainly SPOKEN, FEELINGS] ❑ *"Would your car be easy to steal?"—"Fat chance. I've got a device that shuts down the gas and ignition."* "你的车容易被偷吗？"——"不可能。我有一个可以关闭油门和点火开关的装置。" → see **calorie**

Thesaurus

big, chunky, heavy, obese, overweight, stout, thick; *(ant.)* lean, skinny, slim, thin

Word Partnership

big and fat, **short and** fat
high/low in fat, **saturated** fat
excess fat
get fat
burn fat, **lose** fat

/feɪtᵊl/ ADJ A **fatal** action has very undesirable effects. 后果严重的 ❑ *It would be fatal for the nation to overlook the urgency of the situation.* 国家若忽视这一局势的紧迫性，后果将会非常严重。 ❑ *He made the fatal mistake of compromising early.* 他犯了妥协早了的致命错误。 ● ADV 后果严重地 [ADV with v] ❑ *Failure now could fatally damage his chances in the future.* 现在的失败能严重地毁掉他将来的机会。 ADJ A **fatal** accident or illness causes someone's death. (事故、疾病) 致命的 ❑ *...the fatal stabbing of a police sergeant.* …对一名警官的致命一刺。 ● ADV (事故、疾病) 致命地 ❑ *The dead soldier is reported to have been fatally wounded in the chest.* 报道说死去的那名士兵胸部受到了致命伤。

/fətælɪti/ (**fatalities**) N-COUNT A **fatality** is a death caused by an accident or by violence. (事故或暴力导致的) 死亡 [FORMAL] ❑ *Drunk driving fatalities have declined more than 10 percent over the past 10 years.* 醉酒驾车死亡事故在过去的10年里已下降了10%以上。

(**fat cats**) N-COUNT If you refer to a businessman or politician as a **fat cat**, you are indicating that you disapprove of the way they use their wealth and power. 大亨 [INFORMAL, BUSINESS, DISAPPROVAL] ❑ *...the fat cats who run the bank.* …经营这家银行的大亨们。

/feɪt/ (**fates**) N-UNCOUNT **Fate** is a power that some people believe controls and decides everything that happens, in a way that cannot be prevented or changed. You can also refer to

the fates. 命运 [also N in pl] ❑ *I see no use arguing with fate.* 我认为与命运抗争没有什么用。 ❑ *...the fickleness of fate.* …命运的变化无常。 N-COUNT A person's or thing's **fate** is what happens to them. 命运；遭遇 ❑ *The Russian Parliament will hold a special session later this month to decide his fate.* 俄罗斯议会本月晚些时候将举行一次特别会议来决定他的命运。 ❑ *He seems for a moment to be again holding the fate of the country in his hands.* 有那么一刻他似乎又把国家的命运掌握在自己手中。

/feɪtfəl/ ADJ If an action or a time when something happened is described as **fateful**, it is considered to have an important, and often very bad, effect on future events. 有重大影响的 (尤指产生负面结果的) ❑ *It was a fateful decision, one which was to break the Government.* 那是一项重大的决定，一个将使政府垮台的决定。

/fɑðər/ (**fathers, fathering, fathered**) N-FAMILY Your **father** is your male parent. You can also call someone your **father** if he brings you up as if he were this man. 父亲 ❑ *His father was a painter.* 他父亲是一位画家。 ❑ *He would be a good father to my children.* 他会成为我孩子们的好父亲。 V-T When a man **fathers** a child, he makes a woman pregnant and their child is born. 是…的父亲 ❑ *She claims Mark fathered her child.* 她声称马克是她孩子的父亲。 N-COUNT The man who invented or started something is sometimes referred to as the **father of** that thing. 发明者；创始人 ❑ *...Max Dupain, regarded as the father of modern photography.* …被认为是现代摄影之父的马科斯·杜庞。

→ see **family**

Father's Day is a special day on which children give cards and presents to their fathers as a sign of their love for them. Grown-up children often try to visit, and perhaps take their father out for the day or for a special meal. "Father's Day" is the third Sunday in June.

/fɑðərhʊd/ N-UNCOUNT **Fatherhood** is the state of being a father. 父亲的身份 ❑ *...the joys of fatherhood.* …为人父的喜悦。

(**fathers-in-law**) N-COUNT Someone's **father-in-law** is the father of their husband or wife. 公公；岳父

→ see **family**

/fæðəm/ (**fathoms, fathoming, fathomed**) N-COUNT A **fathom** is a measurement of 6 feet or 1.8 meters, used when referring to the depth of water. 英寻 ❑ *We sailed into the bay and dropped anchor in five fathoms of water.* 我们航行进入海湾，在水深5英寻处抛锚。 V-T If you cannot **fathom** something, you are unable to understand it, although you think carefully about it. 理解 [no cont, oft with brd-neg] ❑ *I really couldn't fathom what Steiner was talking about.* 我真的不明白斯坦纳在说什么。 ● PHRASAL VERB **Fathom out** means the same as **fathom**. 理解 ❑ *We're trying to fathom out what's going on.* 我们正在努力弄清楚发生了什么事。

/fətiɡ/ (**fatigues**) N-UNCOUNT **Fatigue** is a feeling of extreme physical or mental tiredness. 疲惫 ❑ *She continued to have severe stomach cramps, aches, fatigue, and depression.* 她仍有严重的胃痉挛、疼痛、疲惫和抑郁症状。 N-UNCOUNT You can say that people are suffering from a particular kind of **fatigue** when they have been doing something for a long time and feel they can no longer continue to do it. 疲乏 ❑ *...compassion fatigue caused by endless TV and celebrity appeals.* …电视和名人无休止的呼吁所引起的怜悯疲劳。 N-UNCOUNT **Fatigue** in metal or wood is a weakness in it that is caused by repeated stress. Fatigue can cause the metal or wood to break. (金属、木材的) 疲劳 ❑ *The problem turned out to be metal fatigue in the fuselage.* 问题原来出在机身的金属疲劳。 N-PLURAL **Fatigues** are clothes that soldiers wear when they are fighting or when they are doing routine jobs. 军服 ❑ *He never expected to return home wearing combat fatigues.* 他从未想到会穿着作战服回家。

/fætᵊn/ (**fattens, fattening, fattened**) V-T If you say that someone **is fattening** something such as a business or its profits, you mean that they are increasing the value of the business or its profits, in a way that you disapprove of. 养肥 [BUSINESS, DISAPPROVAL] ❑ *They have kept the price of sugar artificially high and so fattened the company's profits.* 他们一直人为地使糖价居高不下，以此为公司牟利。 ● PHRASAL VERB **Fatten up** means the same as **fatten**. 养肥 ❑ *The Government is making the taxpayer pay to fatten up a public sector business for private sale.* 政府正在让纳税人付钱来养肥一项公共服务事业，再卖给私人。

/fætᵊnɪŋ/ ADJ Food that is **fattening** is considered to make people fat easily. (食物) 易使人长胖的 ❑ *Some foods are more fattening than others.* 有些食物比较容易使人发胖。

/fæti/ (**fattier, fattiest**) ADJ **Fatty** food contains a lot of fat. (食物) 多脂肪的 ❑ *Don't eat fatty food or chocolates.* 不要吃高脂肪的食物或巧克力。 ADJ **Fatty** acids or **fatty** tissues, for example, contain or consist of fat. 含脂肪的；由脂肪组成的 [ADJ n] ❑ *...fatty acids.* …多种脂肪酸。

/fɔsɪt/ (**faucets**) N-COUNT A **faucet** is a device that controls the flow of a liquid or gas from a pipe or container. Sinks and baths have faucets attached to them. 龙头；阀门；旋塞 [mainly AM] ❑ *She turned off the faucet and dried her hands.* 她关上水龙头，把手擦干。

/fɔlt/ (**faults, faulting, faulted**) N-SING If a bad or undesirable situation is your **fault**, you caused it or are responsible for it. 过错；过失 ❑ *There was no escaping the fact: it was all his fault.* 无法逃避这一事实：这都是他的错。 N-COUNT A **fault** is a mistake in what someone is doing or in what they have done. 错误 ❑ *It is a big fault to think that you can learn how to manage people in business school.* 认为你能在商学院学会如何管理人是一大错误。 N-COUNT A **fault** in someone or something is a weakness in them or something that is not perfect. 缺点 ❑ *His manners had always made her blind to his faults.* 他的彬彬有礼总使她看不见他的缺点。 N-COUNT A **fault** is a large crack in the surface of the earth. 断层 ❑ *...the San Andreas Fault.* …圣安德烈亚斯断层。 N-COUNT A **fault** in tennis is a service that is wrong according to the rules. (网球的) 发球失误 ❑ *He caught the ball on his first toss and then served a fault.* 他击中了第一次抛起的球，随后发球失误。 V-T If you **cannot fault** someone, you cannot find any reason for criticizing them or the things that they are doing. 批评 [with brd-neg] ❑ *You can't fault them for lack of invention.* 你不能因为他们没有发明而加以批评他们。 PHRASE If someone or something is **at fault**, they are to blame or are responsible for a particular situation that has gone wrong. 有过错 ❑ *He could never accept that he had been at fault.* 他永远也无法接受他犯了过错。 PHRASE If you **find fault with** something or someone, you look for mistakes and complain about them. 挑剔；指责 ❑ *I was disappointed whenever the cook found fault with my work.* 每当厨师挑我工作上的毛病时，我都很失望。

→ see **earthquake**

Thesaurus

blunder, error, mistake, wrongdoing
defect, flaw, imperfection, weakness

Word Partnership

generous to a fault
to a fault
at fault
find fault

/fɔltlɪs/ ADJ Something that is **faultless** is perfect and has no mistakes at all. 完美无缺的 ❑ *...Mary Thomson's faultless and impressive performance on the show.* …玛丽·汤姆森在演出中完美无缺、令人印象深刻的表演。

/fɔlti/ ADJ A **faulty** piece of equipment has something wrong with it and is not working properly. 出故障的 ❑ *The money will be used to repair faulty equipment.* 这笔钱将被用来修理出故障的设备。 ADJ If you describe someone's argument or reasoning as **faulty**, you mean that it is wrong or contains mistakes, usually because they have not been thinking in a logical way. (常指未按逻辑思考而) 错误的 ❑ *Their interpretation was faulty – they had misinterpreted things.* 他们的解释是错误的——他们曲解了事物。

/fɔnə/ (**faunas**) N-COUNT-COLL Animals, especially the animals in a particular area, can be referred to as **fauna**. (尤指某区域的) 动物群 [TECHNICAL] ❑ *...the flora and fauna of the African jungle.* …非洲丛林的植物群和动物群。

/feɪvər/ (**favors, favoring, favored**)

in BRIT, use **favour**

N-UNCOUNT If you regard something or someone with **favor**, you like or support them. 喜爱；支持 ❑ *It remains to be seen if the show will find favor with an audience.* 这场演出是否将获得观众喜爱还要拭目以待。 ❑ *No one would look with favor on the continuing military rule.* 没有人会支持继续的军事统治。 N-COUNT If you **do** someone **a favor**, you do something for them even though you do not have to. 恩惠 ❑ *I've come to ask you to do me a favor.* 我是来请你帮我一个忙的。 V-T If you **favor** something, you prefer it to the other choices available. 更喜欢 ❑ *The French say they favor a transition to democracy.*

法国人说他们更喜欢向民主的过渡。 4 V-T If you **favor** someone, you treat them better or in a kinder way than you treat other people. 偏袒 ❑ *The company has no rules about favoring U.S. citizens during layoffs.* 该公司没有在裁员期间偏袒美国公民的规定。 5 PHRASE If you are **in favor of** something, you support it and think that it is a good thing. 支持 ❑ *I wouldn't be in favor of income tax cuts.* 我不会支持削减所得税。 ❑ *Yet this is a Government which proclaims that it is all in favor of openness.* 然而这是一个宣称全力支持开放的政府。 6 PHRASE If someone makes a judgment **in your favor**, they say that you are right about something. 认为…正确 ❑ *The Supreme Court ruled in Fitzgerald's favor.* 最高法院判定菲茨杰拉德胜诉。 7 PHRASE If something is **in your favor**, it helps you or gives you an advantage. 有助于; 有利于 ❑ *The protection that farmers have enjoyed amounts to a bias in favor of the countryside.* 农民们享受到的保护几乎就是对农村有利的一种偏袒。 8 PHRASE If one thing is rejected **in favor of** another, the second thing is done or chosen instead of the first. (两物相比之下) 宁愿选择 ❑ *The policy was rejected in favor of a more cautious approach.* 这一政策未被采纳，而是选择了一个更谨慎的方法。 9 PHRASE If someone or something is **in favor**, people like or support them. If they are **out of favor**, people no longer like or support them. 得宠/失宠; 得到/失去…的支持 ❑ *Governments and party leaders can only hope to remain in favor with the public for so long.* 政府和政党领导人们只能希望一直得到公众的支持。

Word Partnership *favor* 的常用搭配:

PREP.	**with favor** 1
	in *someone's* favor 6 7
	out of favor 9
V.	**ask for a favor, do *someone* a favor, need a favor, return a favor** 2
ADJ.	**big favor** 2

fa·vor·able /feɪvərəbᵊl/

in BRIT, use **favourable**

1 ADJ If your opinion or your reaction is **favorable** to something, you agree with it and approve of it. 赞成的 [ADJ n, v-link ADJ "to" n] ❑ *The president's convention speech received favorable reviews.* 总统的大会发言受到了好评。 2 ADJ **Favorable** conditions make something more likely to succeed or seem more attractive. 有利的 ❑ *It's believed the conditions in which the elections are being held are too favorable to the government.* 人们认为正在进行选举的条件对政府过于有利。 3 ADJ If you make a **favorable** comparison between two things, you say that the first is better than or as good as the second. 更优的; 不逊色的 ❑ *The film bears favorable technical comparison with Hollywood productions costing 10 times as much.* 这部电影与耗资为其10倍的好莱坞作品相比在技术上毫不逊色。

fa·vor·ite ♦♦◊ /feɪvərɪt, feɪvrɪt/ (**favorites**)

in BRIT, use **favourite**

1 ADJ Your **favorite** thing or person of a particular type is the one you like most. 最喜欢的 [ADJ n] ❑ *He celebrated by opening a bottle of his favorite champagne.* 他开了一瓶他最喜欢的香槟来庆祝。 ● N-COUNT **Favorite** is also a noun. 最喜欢的人或物 ❑ *The Metropole is my favorite. I love those huge, anonymous hotels.* 京都酒店是我最喜欢的酒店。我喜爱那些没名气的大酒店。 ● PHRASE If you refer to something as an **old favorite**, you mean that it has been in existence for a long time and everyone knows it or likes it. 名牌老产品 ❑ *This recipe is an adaptation of an old favorite.* 这个食谱是一个传统名食谱的改编。 2 N-COUNT The **favorite** in a race or contest is the competitor that is expected to win. In a team game, the team that is expected to win is referred to as the **favorites**. 夺冠热门 ❑ *The U.S. team is considered one of the favorites in next month's games.* 美国队被认为是下月比赛的夺冠热门之一。

fa·vor·it·ism /feɪvərɪtɪzəm, feɪvrɪt-/

in BRIT, use **favouritism**

N-UNCOUNT If you accuse someone of **favoritism**, you disapprove of them because they unfairly help or favor one person or group much more than another. 偏袒 [DISAPPROVAL] ❑ *Maria loved both the children. There was never a hint of favoritism.* 这两个孩子玛丽亚都爱，从未有过一丝偏袒。

fa·vour ♦♦◊ /feɪvər/ [BRIT] → see **favor**

fa·vour·able /feɪvərəbᵊl/ [BRIT] → see **favorable**

fa·vour·ite ♦♦◊ /feɪvərɪt, feɪvrɪt/ [BRIT] → see **favorite**

fa·vour·it·ism /feɪvərɪtɪzəm, feɪvrɪt-/ [BRIT] → see **favoritism**

fawn /fɔn/ (**fawns**) 1 N-COUNT A **fawn** is a very young deer. 幼鹿 ❑ *The fawn ran to the top of the ridge.* 那只小鹿跑上山脊。 2 COLOR **Fawn** is a pale yellowish-brown color. 浅黄褐色的 ❑ *Tania was standing there in her light fawn coat.* 塔妮娅穿着她那件浅黄褐色的外套站在那里。

fax /fæks/ (**faxes, faxing, faxed**) 1 N-COUNT A **fax** or a **fax machine** is a piece of equipment used to copy documents by sending information electronically along a telephone line, and to receive copies that are sent in this way. 传真机 [also "by" N] ❑ *...a modern reception desk with telephone and fax.* …一个有电话和传真机的现代化接待台。 2 N-COUNT You can refer to a copy of a document that is transmitted by a fax machine as a **fax**. 传真件 ❑ *I sent him a long fax, saying I didn't need a maid.* 我发给他一份长长的传真，说我不需要女佣。 3 V-T If you **fax** a document to someone, you send it from one fax machine to another. 发传真 ❑ *I faxed a copy of the agreement to each of the investors.* 我给每位投资者都传真了一份协议副本。 ❑ *Did you fax him a reply?* 你发传真给他答复了吗？

fear ♦♦♦ /fɪər/ (**fears, fearing, feared**) 1 N-VAR **Fear** is the unpleasant feeling you have when you think that you are in danger. 害怕 ❑ *I was sitting on the floor shivering with fear because a bullet had been fired through a window.* 我坐在地板上吓得浑身发抖，因为有一颗子弹射穿窗户打了进来。 2 N-VAR A **fear** is a thought that something unpleasant might happen or might have happened. 担忧 ❑ *These youngsters are motivated by fear of failure.* 这些年轻人因担心失败而被激发。 ❑ *Then one day his worst fears were confirmed.* 后来有一天，他最大的担心被证实了。 3 N-VAR If you say that there is a **fear that** something unpleasant or undesirable will happen, you mean that you think it is possible or likely. (发生坏事的) 可能性 ❑ *There is a fear that the freeze on bank accounts could prove a lasting deterrent to investors.* 冻结银行帐户很可能对投资者是一个长期的威慑因素。 4 N-VAR If you have **fears for** someone or something, you are very worried because you think that they might be in danger. 担忧 ❑ *He also spoke of his fears for the future of his country's culture.* 他也谈及了他对祖国文化前景的担忧。 5 V-T If you **fear** someone or something, you are frightened because you think that they will harm you. 害怕 ❑ *It seems to me that if people fear you they respect you.* 在我看来，如果人们怕你，那他们就尊重你。 6 V-T If you **fear** something unpleasant or undesirable, you are worried that it might happen or might have happened. 担心 ❑ *She had feared she was coming down with pneumonia or bronchitis.* 她担心自己会得肺炎或支气管炎。 7 V-I If you **fear for** someone or something, you are very worried because you think that they might be in danger. 担心 ❑ *Carla fears for her son.* 卡拉为她的儿子担心。 8 PHRASE If you are **in fear of** doing or experiencing something unpleasant or undesirable, you are very worried that you might have to do it or experience it. 在对…的担心中; 在对…的恐惧中 ❑ *The elderly live in fear of assault and murder.* 老年人生活在对袭击和谋杀的恐惧中。 9 PHRASE If you take a particular course of action **for fear of** something, you take the action in order to prevent that thing happening. 惟恐; 以免 ❑ *She was afraid to say anything to them for fear of hurting their feelings.* 她不敢对他们说什么，惟恐伤害他们的感情。

→ see **emotion**

Thesaurus *fear* 另参见:

N.	alarm, dread, panic, terror 1
	concern, worry 2

Word Partnership *fear* 的常用搭配:

ADJ.	**constant fear** 1
	irrational fear 1 2
	worst fear 2
V.	**face *your* fear, hide *your* fear, live in fear, overcome *your* fear** 1 2
N.	**fear of failure, fear of rejection, fear of the unknown** 2
	nothing to fear, fear the worst 5
	fear change 6

fear·ful /fɪərfəl/ 1 ADJ If you are **fearful of** something, you are afraid of it. 害怕的 [FORMAL] ❑ *Bankers were fearful of a world banking crisis.* 银行家们害怕会有一场世界性的银行业危机。 2 ADJ You use **fearful** to emphasize how serious or bad a situation is. 极严重的; 极糟糕的 [ADJ n] [FORMAL, EMPHASIS] ❑ *The region is in a fearful recession.* 该地区处于极严重的经济衰退中。

fear·less /fɪərlɪs/ ADJ If you say that someone is **fearless**, you mean that they are not afraid at all, and you admire them for this. 无畏的 [APPROVAL] ❑ *...his fearless campaigning for racial justice.* …他为种族公正所做的无畏的斗争。

Word Link *some ≈ causing : awesome, fearsome, troublesome*

fear·some /fɪərsəm/ ADJ **Fearsome** is used to describe things that are frightening, for example, because of their large size or extreme nature. 可怕的 ❑ *He had developed a fearsome reputation for intimidating people.* 他因恐吓他人而得了一个可怕的名声。

fea·sible /fizəbᵊl/ ADJ If something is **feasible**, it can be done, made, or achieved. 可行的 ❑ *She questioned whether it was feasible to stimulate investment in these regions.* 她质问在这些地区刺激投资是否可行。 ●**fea·sibil·ity** ★ /fizəbɪlɪti/ N-UNCOUNT 可行性 ❑ *The committee will study the feasibility of setting up a national computer network.* 委员会将研究建立一个国家计算机网络的可行性。

★ **feast** /fist/ (**feasts, feasting, feasted**) **1** N-COUNT A **feast** is a large and special meal. 盛宴 ❑ *Lunch was a feast of meat and vegetables, cheese, yogurt and fruit, with unlimited wine.* 午餐是一场盛宴，有肉、蔬菜、奶酪、酸奶和水果，以及不限量的葡萄酒。 ❑ *The fruit was often served at wedding feasts.* 婚宴上常有水果供应。 **2** N-COUNT A **feast** is a day or time of the year when a special religious celebration takes place. 宗教节日; 宗教节庆时期 ❑ *The Jewish feast of Passover began last night.* 犹太人的宗教节日逾越节昨晚开始了。 **3** V-I If you **feast on** a particular food, you eat a large amount of it with great enjoyment. 尽情地吃 ❑ *They feasted well into the afternoon on mutton and corn stew.* 他们尽情享用玉米炖羊肉，一直吃到下午。 **4** V-I If you **feast**, you take part in a feast. 赴宴 ❑ *Only a few feet away, their captors feasted in the castle's banqueting hall.* 仅仅几英尺外，俘获他们的人在城堡的宴会厅里大吃大喝。 ●**feast·ing** N-UNCOUNT 赴宴 ❑ *The feasting, drinking, dancing and revelry continued for several days.* 宴会、畅饮、跳舞和狂欢持续了几天。 **5** PHRASE If you **feast** your **eyes on** something, you look at it for a long time with great attention because you find it very attractive. 尽情欣赏 ❑ *She stood feasting her eyes on the view.* 她站着尽情欣赏着那片景色。

★ **feat** /fit/ (**feats**) N-COUNT If you refer to an action, or the result of an action, as a **feat**, you admire it because it is an impressive and difficult achievement. 功绩 [APPROVAL] ❑ *A racing car is an extraordinary feat of engineering.* 赛车是工程学的一项非凡业绩。

feath·er /fɛðər/ (**feathers**) **1** N-COUNT A bird's **feathers** are the soft covering on its body. Each **feather** consists of a lot of smooth hairs on each side of a thin stiff center. 羽毛 ❑ *...a hat that she had made herself from black ostrich feathers.* …她用黑色鸵鸟羽毛为自己做的一顶帽子。 **2** → see also **feathered** **3** to **ruffle** someone's **feathers**
→ see **ruffle**
→ see **bird**

feath·ered /fɛðərd/ ADJ If you describe something as **feathered**, you mean that it has feathers on it. 有羽毛的 ❑ *Her mother was the proud lady in the feathered hat.* 她母亲就是那位带着羽毛帽子的傲慢女士。

fea·ture ♦♦◇ /fitʃər/ (**features, featuring, featured**) **1** N-COUNT A **feature of** something is an interesting or important part or characteristic of it. 特点 ❑ *Patriotic songs have long been a feature of Kuwaiti life.* 爱国歌曲长期以来一直是科威特人生活的一个特点。 ❑ *The spacious gardens are a special feature of this property.* 宽敞的花园是这处房产的一大特色。 **2** N-COUNT A **feature** is a special article in a newspaper or magazine, or a special program on radio or television. (报纸、杂志的) 特写; (广播、电视的) 特别节目 ❑ *We are delighted to see the Sunday Times running a long feature on breast cancer.* 我们高兴地看到《星期日泰晤士报》刊登了关于乳腺癌的一篇长长的特写。 **3** N-COUNT A **feature** or a **feature** film or movie is a full-length film about a fictional situation, as opposed to a short film or a documentary. 正片; 故事片 ❑ *...the first feature-length cartoon, Snow White and the Seven Dwarfs.* …第一部故事片长度的卡通片《白雪公主和七个小矮人》。 **4** N-COUNT A geographical **feature** is something noticeable in a particular area of country, for example, a hill, river, or valley. (地理) 特征 ❑ *...one of the area's oddest geographical features - an eight-mile bank of pebbles shelving abruptly into the sea.* …这个地区最奇怪的地理特征之一，一条8英里长的鹅卵石堤岸陡然倾斜伸到海里。 **5** N-PLURAL Your **features** are your eyes, nose, mouth, and other parts of your face. 容貌 ❑ *His features seemed to change.* 他的容貌似乎变了。 **6** V-T When something such as a movie or exhibition **features** a particular person or thing, they are an important part of it. (电影等) 由…主演; (展览会等) 以…为重点 ❑ *It's a great movie and it features a Spanish actor who is going to be a world star within a year.* 那是一部精彩的电影，它由一位西班牙演员主演，他一年之内就会成为国际明星。 ❑ *The hour-long program will be updated each week and feature highlights from recent games.* 这个一小时的节目将每周更新，重点介绍近期比赛的精彩部分。 **7** V-I If someone or something **features in** something such as a show, exhibition, or magazine, they are an important part of it. 担任主演; 是(展览、杂志等) 的重要内容 ❑ *Jon featured in one of the show's most thrilling episodes.* 乔恩主演了该剧中最惊悚的几集之一。

Word Partnership *feature* 的常用搭配:

ADJ. **key** feature **1**
special feature **1** **2**
best feature, **striking** feature **1** **5**
animated feature, **double** feature, **full-length** feature **3**
facial feature **5**

Feb. **Feb.** is a written abbreviation for **February**. 2月

Feb·ru·ary ♦♦♦ /fɛbyuɛri, fɛbru-/ (**Februaries**) N-VAR **February** is the second month of the year in the Western calendar. 2月 ❑ *He joined the Army in February 1943.* 他1943年2月参军。 ❑ *His exhibition opens on February 5.* 他的展览2月5日开幕。

fe·ces /fisiz/ N-UNCOUNT **Feces** is the solid waste substance that people and animals get rid of from their body by passing it through the anus. 粪便 [FORMAL] ❑ *...grass contaminated by feces from infected dogs.* …被受到传染的狗的粪便污染了的草地。

fed /fɛd/ **1** **Fed** is the past tense and past participle of **feed**. See also **fed up**. **feed**的过去式和过去分词 **2** N-SING The **Fed** is the **Federal Reserve**. 联邦储备 ["the" N] [INFORMAL] ❑ *The Fed has already eased rates three times since late October.* 美联储自10月底以来已3次降低利率。

fed·er·al ♦♦◇ /fɛdərəl/ **1** ADJ A **federal** country or system of government is one in which the different states or provinces of the country have important powers to make their own laws and decisions. 联邦制的 [ADJ n] ❑ *Five of the six provinces are to become autonomous regions in a new federal system of government.* 在新的联邦政府体制下，6个省中的5个将成为自治区。 **2** ADJ **Federal** also means belonging or relating to the national government of a federal country rather than to one of the states within it. 联邦政府的 [ADJ n] ❑ *The federal government controls just 6% of the education budget.* 联邦政府只掌控教育预算的6%。 ●**fed·er·al·ly** ADV 联邦政府地 [ADV -ed] ❑ *...residents of public housing and federally subsidized apartments.* …公共住房的住户和享受联邦政府补贴的公寓住户。

fed·er·al·ist /fɛdərəlɪst/ (**federalists**) ADJ Someone or something that is **federalist** believes in, supports, or follows a federal system of government. 联邦主义的 ❑ *The new constitution includes federalist principles.* 新宪法包括联邦主义的原则。 ● N-COUNT **Federalist** is also a noun. 联邦主义者 ❑ *Many Quebeckers are federalists.* 很多魁北克人是联邦主义者。

★ **fed·era·tion** ♦◇◇ /fɛdəreɪʃᵊn/ (**federations**) **1** N-COUNT A **federation** is a federal country. 联邦制国家 ❑ *...the Russian Federation.* …俄罗斯联邦。 **2** N-COUNT A **federation** is a group of societies or other organizations which have joined together, usually because they share a common interest. 联合会 ❑ *...the American Federation of Government Employees.* …美国政府雇员联合会。

fed up ADJ If you are **fed up**, you are unhappy, bored, or tired of something, especially something that you have been experiencing for a long time. 厌倦的 [v-link ADJ] [INFORMAL] ❑ *I am fed up with reading how women should dress to please men.* 关于女人该如何着装以取悦男人我都看腻了。 ❑ *He had become fed up with city life.* 他已厌倦了城市生活。

fee ♦♦◇ /fi/ (**fees**) **1** N-COUNT A **fee** is a sum of money that you pay to be allowed to do something. 费用 ❑ *He paid his license fee, and walked out with a brand-new driver's license.* 他付了执照费，然后拿着一本崭新的驾驶执照走了出去。 **2** N-COUNT A **fee** is the amount of money that a person or organization is paid for a particular job or service that they provide. 酬金 ❑ *Lawyer's fees can be substantial.* 律师的酬金可以很丰厚。

★ **fee·ble** /fibᵊl/ (**feebler, feeblest**) **1** ADJ If you describe someone or something as **feeble**, you mean that they are weak. 虚弱的 ❑ *He told them he was old and feeble and was not able to walk so far.*

f

他告诉他们自己年老体弱，不能走那么远。● ADV 虚弱地 [ADV with v] ❑ *His left hand moved feebly at his side.* 他的左手在身边无力地动了一下。 ADJ If you describe something that someone says as **feeble**, you mean that it is not very good or convincing. 不可信的 ❑ *This is a particularly feeble argument.* 这是个特别站不住脚的论点。● ADV 薄弱地 [ADV with v] ❑ *I said "Sorry," very feebly, feeling rather embarrassed.* 我很微弱地说了句"对不起"，感到特别尴尬。

/fid/ (**feeds, feeding, fed**) V-T If you **feed** a person or animal, you give them food to eat and sometimes actually put it in their mouths. 喂养 ❑ *We brought along pieces of old bread and fed the birds.* 我们带了几片陈面包来喂鸟。● N-UNCOUNT 喂食 ❑ *The feeding of dairy cows has undergone a revolution.* 奶牛的喂食已经历了一场革命。 V-T To **feed** a family or a community means to supply food for them. 为…提供食物 ❑ *Feeding a hungry family can be expensive.* 为一家子饥饿的人张罗食物要花不少钱。 V-I When an animal **feeds**, it eats or drinks something. (动物) 进食 ❑ *After a few days the caterpillars stopped feeding.* 几天后毛虫停止了进食。 V-T/V-I When a baby **feeds**, or when you **feed** it, it drinks breast milk or milk from a bottle. 给 (婴儿) 喂奶; (婴儿) 吃奶 ❑ *When a baby is thirsty, it feeds more often.* 婴儿口渴时，吃奶更频繁。 V-T To **feed** something to a place, means to supply it to that place in a steady flow. 供给 ❑ *...blood vessels that feed blood to the brain.* …给大脑供血的血管。 V-T If you **feed** something **into** a container or piece of equipment, you put it into it. 把…放入 (容器或装置中) ❑ *He took the compact disc from her, then fed it into the player.* 他从她那儿拿过光盘，然后把它放进播放机里。 V-T If you **feed** a plant, you add substances to it to make it grow well. 给 (植物) 施肥 ❑ *Feed plants to encourage steady growth.* 给植物施肥以促进其不断生长。 V-I If one thing **feeds on** another, it becomes stronger as a result of the other thing's existence. 因…而强壮 ❑ *The drinking and the guilt fed on each other.* 喝酒和犯罪互相滋长。 V-T To **feed** information **into** a computer means to gradually put it into it. 将 (讯息) 输入 ❑ *An automatic weather station feeds information on wind direction to the computer.* 一个自动化气象站把风向信息输入电脑。 N-MASS Animal **feed** is food given to animals, especially farm animals. 饲料 [usu n N] ❑ *The grain just rotted and all they could use it for was animal feed.* 这些谷物都腐烂了，他们只能将它用作动物饲料。 to **bite the hand that feeds** you → see **bite**
mouths to feed → see **mouth**

Word Partnership

feed **the baby**, feed **the cat**, feed **the children**
feed *your* **family**, feed **the hungry**
bird feed
feed **and clothe**

/fidbæk/ N-UNCOUNT If you get **feedback on** your work or progress, someone tells you how well or badly you are doing, and how you could improve. If you get good feedback you have worked or performed well. 反馈 ❑ *Continue to ask for feedback on your work.* 继续征求对你工作的反馈。 N-UNCOUNT **Feedback** is the unpleasant high-pitched sound produced by a piece of electrical equipment when part of the signal that comes out goes back into it. (电子信号产生的) 尖厉噪声 ❑ *The microphone screeched with feedback.* 麦克风发出了尖厉的噪声。

/fil/ (**feels, feeling, felt**) V-LINK If you **feel** a particular emotion or physical sensation, you experience it. 感觉 ❑ *I am feeling very depressed.* 我感到很沮丧。 ❑ *Suddenly I felt a sharp pain in my shoulder.* 我突然感到肩部一阵剧痛。 ❑ *I felt as if all my strength had gone.* 我觉得好象自己的力气已经全没了。 ❑ *I felt like I was being kicked in the teeth every day.* 我感觉我好像每天都在经受挫折。 V-LINK If you talk about how an experience or event **feels**, you talk about the emotions and sensations connected with it. 使人感觉 [no cont] ❑ *It feels good to have finished a piece of work.* 完成一项工作让人感觉很好。 ❑ *The speed at which everything moved felt strange.* 一切进展的速度让人感觉怪异。 ❑ *Within five minutes of arriving back from vacation, it feels as if I've never been away.* 度假回来还没过5分钟，就感觉好像我从未离开过。 V-LINK If you talk about how an object **feels**, you talk about the physical quality that you notice when you touch or hold it. For example, if something **feels** soft, you notice that it is soft when you touch it. 摸上去…; 拿起来… [no cont] ❑ *The metal felt smooth and cold.* 这种金属摸上去光滑而冰冷。 ❑ *The ten-foot oars felt heavy and awkward.* 这些10英尺长的船桨拿起来又重又不方便。● N-SING **Feel** is also a noun. 手感 ❑ *He remembered the feel of her skin.* 他记得她的皮肤摸上去的那种感觉。 V-LINK If you talk about how the weather **feels**, you describe the weather, especially the temperature or whether or not you think it is going to rain or snow. (天气，尤指气温) 感觉起来 [no cont] ❑ *It felt wintry cold that day.* 那天感觉像冬天一样寒冷。 V-T/V-I If you **feel** an object, you touch it deliberately with your hand, so that you learn what it is like, for example, what shape it is or whether it is rough or smooth. 触摸 ❑ *The doctor felt his head.* 医生摸了摸他的头。 ❑ *Feel how soft the skin is in the small of the back.* 摸一摸腰背部的皮肤有多么柔软。 V-T If you can **feel** something, you are aware of it because it is touching you. (由于碰触) 感觉到 [no cont] ❑ *Through several layers of clothes I could feel his muscles.* 透过好几层衣服，我可以感觉到他的肌肉。 V-T If you **feel** something happening, you become aware of it because of the effect it has on your body. (身体) 感觉到 ❑ *She felt something being pressed into her hands.* 她感觉到有什么东西正塞进她的双手。 ❑ *He felt something move beside him.* 他感觉到身边有东西在移动。 V-T If you **feel yourself** doing something or being in a particular state, you are aware that something is happening to you which you are unable to control. 感觉到 (不禁做某事) ❑ *I felt myself blush.* 我感到自己脸红了。 ❑ *If at any point you feel yourself becoming tense, make a conscious effort to relax.* 如果什么时候你感到自己变得紧张了，就有意识地努力去放松。 V-T If you **feel** the presence of someone or something, you become aware of them, even though you cannot see or hear them. 感觉到 (某人或某物的存在) [no cont] ❑ *He felt her eyes on him.* 他感觉到她的眼睛正盯着他。 ❑ *I could feel that a man was watching me very intensely.* 我能感觉到一个男人正紧盯着我看。 V-T If you **feel** that something is the case, you have a strong idea in your mind that it is the case. 觉得 [no cont] ❑ *I feel that not enough is being done to protect the local animal life.* 我觉得在保护当地动物方面做得还不够。 ❑ *I feel certain that it will all turn out well.* 我觉得最后肯定一切都会很好 V-T If you **feel** that you should do something, you think that you should do it. 认为 [no cont] ❑ *I feel I should resign.* 我认为我应该辞职。 ❑ *You need not feel obliged to contribute.* 你不必认为你非得捐款。 V-T/V-I If you talk about how you **feel about** something, you talk about your opinion, attitude, or reaction to it. 对…表示看法 [no cont] ❑ *We'd like to know what you feel about abortion.* 我们想知道你对堕胎有什么看法。 ❑ *She feels guilty about spending less time lately with her two kids.* 她为最近和自己的两个孩子在一起的时间少了而感到内疚。 V-I If you **feel like** doing something or having something, you want to do it or have it because you are in the right mood for it and think you would enjoy it. 想要 ❑ *Neither of them felt like going back to sleep.* 他们俩都不想回去睡觉。 → see also **feeling, felt** **feel free** → see **free**

PHRASAL VERB If you **feel for** something, for example, in the dark, you try to find it by moving your hand around until you touch it. 摸索着寻找 ❑ *I felt for my wallet and papers in my inside pocket.* 我在里面的口袋里摸索着找钱包和证件。 PHRASAL VERB If you **feel for** someone, you have sympathy for them. 同情 ❑ *She cried on the phone and I really felt for her.* 她在电话里大哭，我真同情她。

Thesaurus

experience, perceive, sense

/filgʊd/ also ADJ A **feelgood** movie is a movie which presents people and life in a way which makes the people who watch it feel happy and optimistic. 令人愉悦的 (电影) [ADJ n] ❑ *This could be the feelgood movie of the season.* 这可能是本季最佳令人愉悦电影。 PHRASE When journalists refer to **the feelgood factor**, they mean that people are feeling hopeful and optimistic about the future. 乐观因素 [BRIT]

/filɪŋ/ (**feelings**) N-COUNT A **feeling** is an emotion, such as anger or happiness. 情绪 ❑ *It gave me a feeling of satisfaction.* 它给了我一种满足感。 ❑ *He was unable to contain his own destructive feelings.* 他无法克制自己的消极情绪。 N-COUNT If you have a **feeling** of hunger, tiredness, or other physical sensation, you experience it. 感觉 ❑ *I also had a strange feeling in my neck.* 我的脖子也有一种奇怪的感觉。 ❑ *Focus on the feeling of relaxation.* 专注于放松的感觉。 N-COUNT If you have **a feeling that** something is the case or **that** something is going to happen, you think that is probably the case or that it is probably going to happen. 预感 ❑ *I have a feeling that everything will be all right.* 我有种预感一切都会好起来的。 N-PLURAL Your **feelings** about something are the things that you think and feel about it, or your attitude toward it. 看法; 态度 ❑ *She has strong feelings about the alleged growth in violence against female officers.* 她对据称的女性军官遭遇暴力事件的增多有强烈的看法。 ❑ *I think that sums up the feelings of most discerning and intelligent Indians.*

我认为那综合了最有眼力和智慧的印第安人的观点。 N-PLURAL When you refer to someone's **feelings**, you are talking about the things that might embarrass, offend, or upset them. For example, if you hurt someone's **feelings**, you upset them by something that you say or do. 感情 ❑ *He was afraid of hurting my feelings.* 他害怕伤我的感情。 N-UNCOUNT **Feeling** is a way of thinking and reacting to things which is emotional and not planned rather than logical and practical. 感情用事 ❑ *He was prompted to a rare outburst of feeling.* 他被激发而感情用事，这很少见。

N-UNCOUNT **Feeling** for someone is love, affection, sympathy, or concern for them. (爱、关切、同情等) 感情 ❑ *Thomas never lost his feeling for Harriet.* 托马斯从未失去对哈丽雅特的感情。 N-UNCOUNT **Feeling** in part of your body is the ability to experience the sense of touch in this part of the body. 知觉 ❑ *After the accident he had no feeling in his legs.* 事故之后他的双腿失去了知觉。 N-UNCOUNT **Feeling** is used to refer to a general opinion that a group of people has about something. (一群人的) 观点 ❑ *There is still some feeling in the art world that the market for such works may be declining.* 艺术界仍存在一种看法，认为这种作品的市场前景暗淡。 N-SING If you have a **feeling of** being in a particular situation, you feel that you are in that situation. (处于某种处境的) 感觉 ❑ *I had the terrible feeling of being left behind to bring up the baby while he had fun.* 我有种可怕的感觉，觉得自己被扔下抚养孩子，而他却在享乐。 N-SING If something such as a place or book creates a particular kind of **feeling**, it creates a particular kind of atmosphere. 气氛 ❑ *That's what we tried to portray in the book, this feeling of opulence and grandeur.* 那正是我们想要在这本书里所要营造的，那种繁荣且伟大的气氛。 → see also **feel**

PHRASE **Bad feeling** or **ill feeling** is bitterness or anger which exists between people, for example, after they have had an argument. 敌意 ❑ *There's been some bad feeling between the two families.* 这两个家族之间互有敌意。 PHRASE **Hard feelings** are feelings of anger or bitterness toward someone who you have had an argument with or who has upset you. If you say "**no hard feelings**," you are making an agreement with someone not to be angry or bitter about something. 芥蒂 ❑ *I don't want any hard feelings between our companies.* 我不希望我们两家公司之间有任何芥蒂。

Word Partnership

express a feeling
get a feeling
have a feeling
sinking feeling
funny feeling, **strange** feeling
strong feeling
good feeling
bad feeling
feeling **of inadequacy**, feeling **of satisfaction**
depth of feeling

/fit/ **Feet** is the plural of **foot**. **foot**的复数形式

/feɪn/ (**feigns, feigning, feigned**) V-T If someone **feigns** a particular feeling, attitude, or physical condition, they try to make other people think that they have it or are experiencing it, although this is not true. 佯作 [FORMAL] ❑ *One morning, I didn't want to go to school, and decided to feign illness.* 一天早上，我不愿去上学，就决定装病。

/fɛl/ (**fells, felling, felled**) **Fell** is the past tense of **fall**. **fall**的过去式 V-T If trees **are felled**, they are cut down. 砍伐 [usu passive] **in one fell swoop** → see **swoop**

/fɛloʊ/ (**fellows**) ADJ You use **fellow** to describe people who are in the same situation as you, or people you feel you have something in common with. 同种情况的; 同类的 [ADJ n] ❑ *She discovered to her pleasure, a talent for making her fellow guests laugh.* 她高兴地发现一个把她同来的客人逗笑的本事。 N-COUNT A **fellow** is a man or boy. 家伙; 小伙儿 [INFORMAL, OLD-FASHIONED] ❑ *By all accounts, Rodger would appear to be a fine fellow.* 根据大家的说法，罗杰应该是个好小伙儿。 N-COUNT A **fellow of** an academic or professional association is someone who is a specially elected member of it, usually because of their work or achievements or as a mark of honor. 特别会员 ❑ *...the fellows of the Zoological Society.* …动物协会的特别会员们。 N-PLURAL Your **fellows** are the people who you work with, do things with, or who are like you in some way. 同事; 同伴 [POSS N] [FORMAL] ❑ *He stood out in terms of competence from all his fellows.* 他在能力方面比他所有同事都突出。
→ see **hospital**

/fɛloʊʃɪp/ (**fellowships**) N-COUNT A **fellowship** is a group of people that join together for a common purpose or interest. 团体 ❑ *...the National Schizophrenia Fellowship.* …全国精神分裂协会。 N-COUNT A **fellowship** at a university is a post which involves research work. 研究员职位 ❑ *He was offered a research fellowship at Yale.* 他得到了一个耶鲁大学的研究员职位。

N-UNCOUNT **Fellowship** is a feeling of friendship that people have when they are talking or doing something together and sharing their experiences. 交情 ❑ *...a sense of community and fellowship.* …一种社群归属感和友谊感。

/fɛləni/ (**felonies**) N-COUNT In countries where the legal system distinguishes between very serious crimes and less serious ones, a **felony** is a very serious crime such as armed robbery. 重罪 [LEGAL] ❑ *He pleaded guilty to six felonies.* 他承认犯了6项重罪。

/fɛlt/ **Felt** is the past tense and past participle of **feel**. **feel**的过去式和过去分词 N-UNCOUNT **Felt** is a thick cloth made from wool or other fibers packed tightly together. 毛毡 [oft N n] ❑ *She had on an old felt hat.* 她戴着一顶旧毡帽。

(**felt-tips**) N-COUNT A **felt-tip** or a **felt-tip pen** is a pen which has a piece of fiber at the end that the ink comes through. 毡头笔

Word Link ***fem, femin ≈ woman :*** ***ale,*** ***ine,*** ***inity***

/fimeɪl/ (**females**) ADJ Someone who is **female** is a woman or a girl. 女性的 ❑ *...a sixteen-piece dance band with a female singer.* …一支有一名女歌手的16人伴舞乐队。 ADJ **Female** matters and things relate to, belong to, or affect women rather than men. 女性的 [ADJ n] ❑ *...female infertility.* …女性不孕症。 N-COUNT Women and girls are sometimes referred to as **females** when they are being considered as a type. 女性 ❑ *Hay fever affects males more than females.* 男性感染花粉热多于女性。 N-COUNT You can refer to any creature that can lay eggs or produce babies from its body as a **female**. 雌性生物 ❑ *Each female will lay just one egg in April or May.* 每只雌性在4月或5月份将只产一颗卵。 ● ADJ **Female** is also an adjective. 雌性的 ❑ *...the scent given off by the female aphid to attract the male.* …雌性蚜虫为吸引雄性而发出的香味。

/fɛmɪnɪn/ ADJ **Feminine** qualities and things relate to or are considered typical of women, in contrast to men. 女性的 ❑ *...male leaders worrying about their women abandoning traditional feminine roles.* …担心他们的女人会抛弃传统女性角色的男性领导人。 ADJ Someone or something that is **feminine** has qualities that are considered typical of women, especially being pretty or gentle. 女人味的 [APPROVAL] ❑ *I've always been attracted to very feminine women who are not overpowering.* 我总是被那些不强悍的女人味十足的女人所吸引。 ADJ In some languages, a **feminine** noun, pronoun, or adjective has a different form from a masculine or neuter one, or behaves in a different way. 阴性的

/fɛmɪnɪnɪti/ N-UNCOUNT A woman's **femininity** is the fact that she is a woman. 女性 ❑ *...the drudgery behind the ideology of motherhood and femininity.* …母性和女性理念背后的苦差。

N-UNCOUNT **Femininity** means the qualities that are considered to be typical of women. 女性气质 ❑ *I wonder if there isn't a streak of femininity in him, a kind of sweetness.* 我想知道他身上是否没有一丝女性气质，一种温柔。

/fɛmɪnɪzəm/ N-UNCOUNT **Feminism** is the belief and aim that women should have the same rights, power, and opportunities as men. 女权主义 ❑ *...Barbara Johnson, that champion of radical feminism.* …芭芭拉・约翰逊，激进女权主义的拥护者。
→ see **society**

/fɛmɪnɪst/ (**feminists**) N-COUNT A **feminist** is a person who believes in and supports feminism. 女权主义者 ❑ *Only 16 percent of young women in a 1990 survey considered themselves feminists.* 只有16%的年轻女性在1990年的一次调查中认为自己是女权主义者。

ADJ **Feminist** groups, ideas, and activities are involved in feminism. 女权主义的 [ADJ n]

/fɛns/ (**fences, fencing, fenced**) N-COUNT A **fence** is a barrier between two areas of land, made of wood or wire supported by posts. 栅栏 ❑ *Villagers say the fence would restrict public access to the hills.* 村民们说栅栏将限制公众进入山区。 N-COUNT A **fence** in show jumping or horse racing is an obstacle or barrier that horses have to jump over. 障碍物 ❑ *The horse fell at the last fence.*

这匹马在最后一道障碍那里跌倒了。 3 V-T If you **fence** an area of land, you surround it with a fence. 圈起 ❑ *The first task was to fence the wood to exclude sheep.* 第一项任务是要把小树林圈起来使羊进入。 4 PHRASE If you **sit on the fence**, you avoid supporting a particular side in a discussion or argument. 保持中立 ❑ *They are sitting on the fence and refusing to commit themselves.* 他们保持中立，拒绝明确表态。

▲ **fenc·ing** /fɛnsɪŋ/ 1 N-UNCOUNT **Fencing** is a sport in which two competitors fight each other using very thin swords. The ends of the swords are covered and the competitors wear protective clothes, so that they do not hurt each other. 击剑 ❑ *...the amateur fencing champion.* …业余击剑冠军。 2 N-UNCOUNT Materials such as wood or wire that are used to make fences are called **fencing**. 筑栅栏的材料 ❑ *...old wooden fencing.* …筑栅栏的旧木料。

F

▲ **fend** /fɛnd/ (**fends, fending, fended**) V-I If you have to **fend for** yourself, you have to look after yourself without relying on help from anyone else. 照料（自己）❑ *The woman and her young baby had been thrown out and left to fend for themselves.* 这个女人和她年幼的婴儿被逐出家门，只得自谋生路。

▸ **fend off** 1 PHRASAL VERB If you **fend off** unwanted questions, problems, or people, you stop them from affecting you or defend yourself from them, but often only for a short time and without dealing with them completely. 避开 ❑ *He looked relaxed and determined as he fended off questions from the world's Press.* 他在回避世界媒体的问题时显得气定神闲。 2 PHRASAL VERB If you **fend off** someone who is attacking you, you use your arms or something such as a stick to defend yourself from their blows. 挡住（攻击）❑ *He raised his hand to fend off the blow.* 他抬起手挡住了那一击。

Word Link *fend ≈ striking : defend, fender, offend*

fend·er /fɛndər/ (**fenders**) N-COUNT The **fenders** of a car are the parts of the body over the wheels. 挡泥板 [AM] ❑ *Todd sat on the front fender, his legs dangling toward the ground.* 托德坐在前挡泥板上，双腿耷拉晃荡着。

fer·ment (**ferments, fermenting, fermented**)

The noun is pronounced /fɜrmɛnt/. The verb is pronounced /fərmɛnt/.

名词读作 /fɜrmɛnt/，动词读作 /fərmɛnt/。

1 N-UNCOUNT **Ferment** is excitement and trouble caused by change or uncertainty. 骚动 ❑ *The whole country has been in a state of political ferment for some months.* 整个国家几个月来一直处在政治骚动的状态中。 2 V-T/V-I If a food, drink, or other natural substance **ferments**, or if it **is fermented**, a chemical change takes place in it so that alcohol is produced. This process forms part of the production of alcoholic drinks such as wine and beer. 使发酵；发酵 ❑ *The dried grapes are allowed to ferment until there is no sugar left and the wine is dry.* 干葡萄要经过发酵，直到没有糖分存留，葡萄酒才不会有甜味。 ● **fer·men·ta·tion** /fɜrmɛnteɪʃən/ N-UNCOUNT 发酵 ❑ *Yeast is essential for the fermentation that produces alcohol.* 酵母对酿酒的发酵是必要的。

→ see **fungus**

fern /fɜrn/ (**ferns**) N-VAR A **fern** is a plant that has long stems with feathery leaves and no flowers. There are many types of fern. 蕨类植物

▲ **fe·ro·cious** /fəroʊʃəs/ 1 ADJ A **ferocious** animal, person, or action is very fierce and violent. 凶残的 ❑ *By its very nature a lion is ferocious.* 狮子本性凶残。 2 ADJ A **ferocious** war, argument, or other form of conflict involves a great deal of anger, bitterness, and determination. 激烈的 ❑ *Fighting has been ferocious.* 战斗一直很激烈。

fe·roc·ity /fərɒsɪti/ N-UNCOUNT The **ferocity** of something is its fierce or violent nature. 凶残；猛烈 ❑ *The armed forces seem to have been taken by surprise by the ferocity of the attack.* 武装部队好像被猛烈的进攻给镇住了。

★ **fer·ry** /fɛri/ (**ferries, ferrying, ferried**) 1 N-COUNT A **ferry** is a boat that transports passengers and sometimes also vehicles, usually across rivers or short stretches of sea. 渡船；渡轮 [also "by" N] ❑ *They had recrossed the River Gambia by ferry.* 他们乘船又一次渡过了冈比亚河。 2 V-T If a vehicle **ferries** people or goods, it transports them, usually by means of regular trips between the same two places. 运送 ❑ *Every day, a plane arrives to ferry guests to and from Bird Island Lodge.* 每天，一架飞机到达以运送进出鸟岛宾馆的客人。

→ see **ship**

fer·tile /fɜrtᵊl/ 1 ADJ Land or soil that is **fertile** is able to support the growth of a large number of strong healthy plants. 肥沃的 ❑ *...fertile soil.* …肥沃的土壤。 ● **fer·til·ity** /fɜrtɪlɪti/ N-UNCOUNT 肥沃 ❑ *He was able to bring large sterile acreages back to fertility.* 他能把大片不毛之地变回沃土。 2 ADJ A **fertile** mind or imagination is able to produce a lot of good, original ideas. 丰富的 ❑ *...a product of Flynn's fertile imagination.* …弗林极富想像力的一个作品。 3 ADJ A situation or environment that is **fertile** in relation to a particular activity or feeling encourages the activity or feeling. 促进的 [ADJ n] ❑ *...a fertile breeding ground for this kind of violent racism.* …一个培养这种暴力种族主义的温床。 4 ADJ A person or animal that is **fertile** is able to reproduce and have babies or young. 能生育的 ❑ *The operation cannot be reversed to make her fertile again.* 手术不可逆转，无法使她重获生育能力。 ● **fer·til·ity** N-UNCOUNT 生育能力 ❑ *Doctors will tell you that pregnancy is the only sure test for fertility.* 医生们会告诉你怀孕是测试生育能力的惟一准确的方法。

fer·ti·lize /fɜrtᵊlaɪz/ (**fertilizes, fertilizing, fertilized**) 1 V-T When an egg from the ovary of a woman or female animal **is fertilized**, a sperm from the male joins with the egg, causing a baby or young animal to begin forming. A female plant **is fertilized** when its reproductive parts come into contact with pollen from the male plant. 使受精；使授粉 ❑ *Certain varieties cannot be fertilized with their own pollen.* 某些品种不能自花授粉。 ❑ *...the normal sperm levels needed to fertilize the egg.* …使卵子受精所需的正常精子水平。 ● **fer·ti·li·za·tion** /fɜrtᵊlɪzeɪʃᵊn/ N-UNCOUNT 受精；授粉 ❑ *From fertilization until birth is about 266 days.* 从受精到出生大约是266天。 2 V-T To **fertilize** land means to improve its quality in order to make plants grow well on it, by spreading solid animal waste or a chemical mixture on it. 使肥沃 ❑ *The feces contain nitrogen which fertilizes the soil.* 排泄物含有肥沃土壤的氮。

→ see **flower**

fer·ti·liz·er /fɜrtᵊlaɪzər/ (**fertilizers**) N-MASS **Fertilizer** is a substance such as solid animal waste or a chemical mixture that you spread on the ground in order to make plants grow more successfully. 肥料 ❑ *...farming without any purchased chemical, fertilizer or pesticide.* …不使用任何购买的化学品、肥料或杀虫剂的耕作。

→ see **farm, pollution**

fer·vent /fɜrvᵊnt/ ADJ A **fervent** person has or shows strong feelings about something, and is very sincere and enthusiastic about it. 热情的；热诚的 ❑ *...a fervent admirer of Morisot's work.* …一名莫里索特作品的热诚崇拜者。 ● **fer·vent·ly** ADV 热情地；热诚地 ❑ *Their claims will be fervently denied.* 他们的索赔将被严词拒绝。

fer·vor /fɜrvər/ N-UNCOUNT **Fervor** for something is a very strong feeling for or belief in it. 热情；热诚 [FORMAL] ❑ *They were concerned only with their own religious fervor.* 他们只关心自己的宗教热诚。

fes·ter /fɛstər/ (**festers, festering, festered**) 1 V-I If you say that a situation, problem, or feeling **is festering**, you disapprove of the fact that it is being allowed to grow more unpleasant or full of anger, because it is not being properly recognized or dealt with. 恶化 [DISAPPROVAL] ❑ *Resentments are starting to fester.* 仇恨正开始逐步加深。 2 V-I If a wound **festers**, it becomes infected, making it worse. 化脓 ❑ *The wound is festering, and gangrene has set in.* 伤口在化脓，继而发生了坏疽。

fes·ti·val ◆◆◇ /fɛstɪvᵊl/ (**festivals**) 1 N-COUNT A **festival** is an organized series of events such as musical concerts or drama productions. 节 ❑ *Many towns hold their own summer festivals of music, theater, and dance.* 很多城市都举办自己的夏季音乐、戏剧和舞蹈节。 2 N-COUNT A **festival** is a day or time of the year when people do not go to work or school and celebrate some special event, often a religious event. 节日 ❑ *Shavuot is a two-day festival for Orthodox Jews.* 五旬节是正统犹太教教民为期两天的节日。

fes·tive /fɛstɪv/ 1 ADJ Something that is **festive** is special, colorful, or exciting, especially because of a holiday or celebration. 喜庆的 ❑ *The town has a festive holiday atmosphere.* 这个城市充满了喜庆的节日气氛。 2 ADJ **Festive** means relating to a holiday or celebration, especially Christmas. 节日庆典的 [ADJ n] ❑ *With Christmas just around the corner, you should start your festive cooking now.* 圣诞节就快到了，你现在该着手烹饪过节的食物了。

Thesaurus *festive* 另参见：

ADJ. happy, joyous, merry; (ant.) gloomy, somber 1

fes·tiv·ity /fɛstɪvɪti/ (**festivities**) **1** N-UNCOUNT **Festivity** is the celebration of something in a happy way. 欢庆 ❑ *There was a general air of festivity and abandon.* 那里弥漫着纵情欢庆的气氛。 **2** N-COUNT **Festivities** are events that are organized in order to celebrate something. 庆典 ❑ *The festivities included a huge display of fireworks.* 庆典包括大规模的烟花燃放。

fetch /fɛtʃ/ (**fetches, fetching, fetched**) **1** V-T If you **fetch** something or someone, you go and get them from the place where they are. 去拿 ❑ *Sylvia fetched a towel from the bathroom.* 西尔维娅从浴室拿来一条毛巾。 ❑ *Fetch me a glass of water.* 给我拿杯水来。 **2** V-T If something **fetches** a particular sum of money, it is sold for that amount. 卖得 ❑ *The painting is expected to fetch between two and three million dollars.* 这幅画预计能卖到200至300万美元。 **3** → see also **far-fetched**

fete /feɪt, fɛt/ (**fetes, feting, feted**) also **fête** **1** N-COUNT A **fete** is a fancy party or celebration. 游园会; 庆祝会 [AM] ❑ *The pop star flew 100 friends in from London and Paris for a two-day fete.* 这名歌星从伦敦和巴黎把100位朋友空运过来参加一个两天的游园会。 **2** V-T If someone **is feted**, they are celebrated, welcomed, or admired by the public. 欢迎; 款待 [usu passive] ❑ *Vera Wang was feted in New York this week at a spectacular dinner.* 维拉 • 王本周在纽约的一次盛大的晚宴上受到了款待。

fe·tus /fitəs/ (**fetuses**) N-COUNT A **fetus** is an animal or human being in its later stages of development before it is born. 胎儿 ❑ *Pregnant women who are heavy drinkers risk damaging the unborn fetus.* 酗酒的孕妇冒有伤害胎儿的危险。

feud /fyud/ (**feuds, feuding, feuded**) **1** N-COUNT A **feud** is a quarrel in which two people or groups remain angry with each other for a long time, although they are not always fighting or arguing. 积怨 ❑ *...a long and bitter feud between the state government and the villagers.* …州政府和村民们之间的长期积怨。 **2** V-RECIP If one person or group **feuds with** another, they have a quarrel that lasts a long time. You can also say that two people or groups **feud**. 争吵不休 ❑ *He feuded with his ex-wife.* 他与前妻争吵不休。

▲**feu·dal** /fyudᵊl/ ADJ **Feudal** means relating to the system or the time of feudalism. 封建制度的; 封建时期的 [ADJ n] ❑ *...the emperor and his feudal barons.* …皇帝和他的封建贵族们。

▲**feu·dal·ism** /fyudᵊlɪzəm/ N-UNCOUNT **Feudalism** was a system in which people were given land and protection by people of higher rank, and worked and fought for them in return. 封建制度 ❑ *As feudalism decayed in the West it gave rise to a mercantile class.* 随着西方封建制度解体，商业阶层应运而生。

▲**feu·dal·ist** /fyudəlɪst/ (**feudalists**) N-COUNT A **feudalist** was someone who believed in and supported the system of feudalism. 封建主义者 ❑ *In Rwanda the Hutus rose up and overthrew the feudalists.* 在卢旺达胡图族起来推翻了封建主义者们。

fe·ver /fivər/ (**fevers**) **1** N-VAR If you have a **fever** when you are ill, your body temperature is higher than usual. 发烧 ❑ *My Uncle Jim had a high fever.* 我的叔叔吉姆发高烧了。 **2** → see also **hay fever** → see **illness**

fe·ver·ish /fivərɪʃ/ **1** ADJ **Feverish** activity is done extremely quickly, often in a state of nervousness or excitement because you want to finish it as soon as possible. 紧张忙乱的 ❑ *Hours of feverish activity lay ahead. The tents had to be erected, the stalls set up.* 长达数小时紧张忙乱的活动就在前面，帐篷要支起来，摊位要搭起来。 **2** ADJ If you are **feverish**, you are suffering from a fever. 发烧的 ❑ *A feverish child refuses to eat and asks only for cold drinks.* 一个发烧的孩子不吃东西，只要喝冷饮。 ● **fe·ver·ish·ly** ADV 发烧地 ❑ *He slept feverishly all afternoon and into the night.* 他发着烧睡了整整一个下午，一直睡到晚上。

few ◆◆◆ /fyu/ (**fewer, fewest**) **1** DET You use **a few** to indicate that you are talking about a small number of people or things. You can also say **a very few**. 几个 ❑ *I gave a dinner party for a few close friends.* 我为几个密友举办了一个晚餐聚会。 ❑ *Here are a few more ideas to consider.* 这儿还有几点建议可以考虑。 ● PRON **Few** is also a pronoun. 几个 ❑ *Doctors work an average of 90 hours a week, while a few are on call for up to 120 hours.* 医生们平均每周工作90个小时，而有些出诊长达120个小时。 ● QUANT **Few** is also a quantifier. 几个 [QUANT "of" def-pl-n] ❑ *There are many ways eggs can be prepared; here are a few of them.* 烹调鸡蛋的方法有很多；这里是其中的几个。 **2** DET You use **few** to indicate that you are talking about a small number of people or things. You can use "so," "too," and "very" in front of **few**. 很少 ❑ *She had few friends, and was generally not functioning up to her potential.* 她很少有什么朋友，总体来看没有发挥她的潜能。 ❑ *Few members planned to vote for him.* 很少有成员计划投他的票。 ● PRON **Few** is also a pronoun. 很少 ❑ *Few can survive more than a week without water.* 很少有人没有水能活过一周。 ● QUANT **Few** is also a quantifier. 很少 [QUANT "of" def-pl-n] ❑ *Few of the beach houses still had lights on.* 岸边的房屋很少还亮着灯。 ● ADJ **Few** is also an adjective. 很少的 ❑ *...spending her few waking hours in front of the TV.* …把她清醒的个把钟头花在电视机前。 **3** ADJ You use **few** after adjectives and determiners to indicate that you are talking about a small number of things or people. 少数的 [adj/det ADJ n] ❑ *The past few weeks of her life had been the most pleasant she could remember.* 过去的寥寥几星期是她生命中所能记起的最快乐的时光。 ❑ *...in the last few chapters.* …在最后几章里。 **4** N-SING **The few** means a small set of people considered as separate from the majority, especially because they share a particular opportunity or quality that the others do not have. 少数人 ❑ *This should not be an experience for the few.* 这应该不只是少数人的经历。

> **Few** and **a few** are both used in front of the plural of count nouns, but they do not have the same meaning. For example, if you say **I have a few friends**, this is a positive statement and you are saying that you have some friends. However, if you say **I have few friends**, this is a negative statement and you are saying that you have almost no friends. You use **fewer** to talk about things that can be counted. ❑ *...fewer potatoes.* When you are talking about amounts that cannot be counted, you should use **less**. ❑ *...less meat.*

5 PHRASE You use **as few as** before a number to suggest that it is surprisingly small. 少到只有 [EMPHASIS] ❑ *One study showed that even as few as ten cigarettes a day can damage fertility.* 一项研究表明，每天哪怕只抽10支烟也会损害生育能力。 **6** PHRASE Things that are **few and far between** are very rare or do not happen very often. 稀少的; 罕见的 [EMPHASIS] ❑ *Successful women politicians are few and far between.* 成功的女政治家少之又少。 **7** PHRASE You use **no fewer than** to emphasize that a number is surprisingly large. 不少于 [EMPHASIS] ❑ *No fewer than thirteen foreign ministers attended the session.* 不少于13个国家的外长参加了会议。

fi·as·co /fiæskoʊ/ (**fiascos**) N-COUNT If you describe an event or attempt to do something as a **fiasco**, you are emphasizing that it fails completely. 彻底的失败 [EMPHASIS] ❑ *The blame for the Charleston fiasco did not lie with him.* 查尔斯顿惨败不归咎于他。

fi·ber /faɪbər/ (**fibers**)

> in BRIT, use **fibre**

1 N-COUNT A **fiber** is a thin thread of a natural or artificial substance, especially one that is used to make cloth or rope. 纤维 ❑ *If you look at the paper under a microscope you will see the fibers.* 如果你在显微镜下观察这张纸，你就会看到纤维。 **2** N-COUNT A **fiber** is a thin piece of flesh like a thread which connects nerve cells in your body or which muscles are made of. 纤维组织 ❑ *...the nerve fibers.* …神经纤维。 **3** N-VAR A particular **fiber** is a type of cloth or other material that is made from or consists of threads. 纤维制品 ❑ *The ball is made of rattan – a natural fiber.* 这个球是用藤——一种天然纤维制成的。 **4** N-UNCOUNT **Fiber** consists of the parts of plants or seeds that your body cannot digest. Fiber is useful because it makes food pass quickly through your body. (植物) 纤维 ❑ *Most vegetables contain fiber.* 大多数蔬菜含有纤维。 → see **laser, paper, rope, vegetable**

fi·ber op·tics

> The form **fiber optic** is used as a modifier.

1 N-UNCOUNT **Fiber optics** is the use of long thin threads of glass to carry information in the form of light. 光纤 ❑ *Thanks to fiber optics, it is now possible to illuminate many of the body's remotest organs and darkest orifices.* 多亏有了光纤，如今才能够照见人体中许多最微小的器官和最暗的腔体。 **2** ADJ **Fiber optic** means relating to or involved in fiber optics. 光纤的 [ADJ n] ❑ *...fiber optic cables.* …光纤电缆。

fi·bre /faɪbə/ [BRIT] → see **fiber**

fick·le /fɪkᵊl/ **1** ADJ If you describe someone as **fickle**, you disapprove of them because they keep changing their mind about what they like or want. 善变的 [DISAPPROVAL] ❑ *The group has been notoriously fickle in the past.* 这个团体在过去是出了名的善变。 **2** ADJ If you say that something is **fickle**, you mean that it often changes and is unreliable. 变幻莫测的; 靠不住的 ❑ *New England's weather can be fickle.* 新英格兰的天气变幻莫测。

/fɪkʃᵊn/ (**fictions**) N-UNCOUNT **Fiction** refers to books and stories about imaginary people and events, rather than books about real people or events. 小说 ❑ *Immigrant tales have always been popular themes in fiction.* 移民故事一直是小说的流行主题。 → see also **science fiction** N-UNCOUNT A statement or account that is **fiction** is not true. 虚构 ❑ *The truth or fiction of this story has never been truly determined.* 这个故事是真实还是虚构，一直没有定论。 N-COUNT If something is a **fiction**, it is not true, although people sometimes pretend that it is true. 假象 ❑ *Total recycling is a fiction.* 完全回收利用是假象。
→ see **genre, library**

/fɪkʃənᵊl/ ADJ **Fictional** characters or events occur only in stories, plays, or movies and never actually existed or happened. 虚构的 ❑ *It is drama featuring fictional characters.* 虚构的人物是戏剧的特点。
→ see **fantasy**

/fɪktɪʃəs/ ADJ **Fictitious** is used to describe something that is false or does not exist, although some people claim that it is true or exists. 虚假的；虚幻的 ❑ *We're interested in the source of these fictitious rumors.* 我们对这些子虚乌有的谣言的来源感兴趣。 ADJ A **fictitious** character, thing, or event occurs in a story, play, or film but never really existed or happened. 虚构的 ❑ *The persons and events portrayed in this production are fictitious.* 这部作品描绘的那些人物和事件是虚构的。

/fɪdᵊl/ (**fiddles, fiddling, fiddled**) V-I If you **fiddle with** an object, you keep moving it or touching it with your fingers. 不停摆弄 ❑ *Harriet fiddled with a pen on the desk.* 哈丽雅特不停地摆弄桌上的一支钢笔。 V-I If you **fiddle with** something, you change it in minor ways. 略微改动 ❑ *She told Whistler that his portrait of her was finished and to stop fiddling with it.* 她告诉惠斯勒他为她画的肖像已经完成了，不要再改来改去了。 V-I If you **fiddle with** a machine, you adjust it. 调试 ❑ *He turned on the radio and fiddled with the knob until he got a talk show.* 他打开收音机，调动旋钮，直到他收到了一个谈话节目。 N-VAR Some people call violins **fiddles**, especially when they are used to play folk music. 小提琴 ❑ *Hardy played the fiddle at local dances.* 哈迪在当地的舞会上拉了小提琴。

/fɪdɛlɪti/ N-UNCOUNT **Fidelity** is loyalty to a person, organization, or set of beliefs. 忠诚 [FORMAL] ❑ *People have failed to act in fidelity to their vows.* 人们没能忠诚地履行自己的誓言。 N-UNCOUNT **Fidelity** is being loyal to your husband, wife, or partner by not having a sexual relationship with anyone else. 忠贞 ❑ *Women expect fidelity from their men.* 女人期望来自她们男人的忠贞。

/fɪdʒɪt/ (**fidgets, fidgeting, fidgeted**) V-I If you **fidget**, you keep moving your hands or feet slightly or changing your position slightly, for example, because you are nervous, bored, or excited. 动来动去 ❑ *Brenda fidgeted in her seat.* 布伦达在椅子上坐不住。 ● PHRASAL VERB **Fidget around** and **fidget about** mean the same as **fidget**. 动来动去 (同**fidget**) ❑ *There were two new arrivals, fidgeting around, waiting to ask questions.* 有两个新来的人，坐立不定，等着提问。 V-I If you **fidget with** something, you keep moving it or touching it with your fingers with small movements, for example, because you are nervous or bored. 不停摆弄 ❑ *He fidgeted with his tie.* 他不停摆弄他的领带。

/fild/ (**fields, fielding, fielded**) N-COUNT A **field** is an area of grass, for example, in a park or on a farm. A **field** is also an area of land on which a crop is grown. 草地；田地 ❑ *...a field of wheat.* …一片麦田。 N-COUNT A sports **field** is an area of grass where sports are played. 运动场 ❑ *...a football field.* …一个足球场。 ❑ *He was the fastest thing I ever saw on a baseball field.* 他是我见过的在棒球场上跑得最快的家伙。 N-COUNT A **field** is an area of land or sea bed under which large amounts of a particular mineral have been found. 矿田 ❑ *...an extensive natural gas field in Alaska.* …阿拉斯加的一个巨大的天然气田。 N-COUNT A magnetic, gravitational, or electric **field** is the area in which that particular force is strong enough to have an effect. 场 ❑ *Some people are worried that electromagnetic fields from electric power lines could increase the risk of cancer.* 一些人担心电源线的电磁场可能增加患癌症的风险。 N-COUNT A particular **field** is a particular subject of study or type of activity. 领域 ❑ *Each of the authors of the tapes is an expert in his field.* 这些磁带的每一位作者都是其领域内的专家。 N-COUNT A **field** is an area of a computer's memory or a program where data can be entered, edited, or stored. 字段 [COMPUTING] ❑ *Go to a site like Yahoo! Finance and enter "AOL" in the Get Quotes field.* 登录雅虎财经那样的一个网站，在报价栏输入"AOL"。 N-COUNT Your **field** of vision or your visual **field** is the area that you can see without turning your head. 视野 ❑ *Our field of vision is surprisingly wide.* 我们的视野令人惊奇地广阔。 N-COUNT-COLL **The field** is a way of referring to all the competitors taking part in a particular race or sports contest. 所有参赛者 ❑ *Going into the fourth lap, the two most broadly experienced riders led the field.* 进入第4圈时，那两名经验最丰富的骑手领先。 ADJ You use **field** to describe work or study that is done in a real, natural environment rather than in a theoretical way or in controlled conditions. 现场的；实地的 [ADJ n] ❑ *I also conducted a field study among the boys about their attitude to relationships.* 我也在男生中进行了一项有关他们对人际关系态度的实地调查。 V-I In a game of baseball or cricket, the team that **is fielding** is trying to catch the ball, while the other team is trying to hit it. 防守 [usu cont] ❑ *When we are fielding, the umpires keep looking at the ball.* 当我们在防守时，裁判们都盯紧了球。 V-T If you say that someone **fields** a question, you mean that they answer it or deal with it, usually successfully. 成功应对 [JOURNALISM] ❑ *He was later shown on television, fielding questions.* 他后来在电视上露了面，答复那些问题。 V-T If a sports team **fields** a particular number or type of players, the players are chosen to play for the team on a particular occasion. 使参赛 ❑ *We're going to field an exciting and younger team.* 我们将选派一支令人振奋的较年轻队伍上场。 V-T If a candidate in an election is representing a political party, you can say that the party **is fielding** that candidate. 使参加竞选 [JOURNALISM] ❑ *There are signs that the new party aims to field candidates in elections scheduled for February next year.* 有迹象表明，该新党计划为明年2月的选举提名候选人。 → see also **minefield, playing field**
→ see **oil**

Word Partnership

open field
magnetic field
ball field, field **hockey**, **track and** field
oil field
expert in a field
field **of vision**
field **questions**
work in a field

/fɪldər/ (**fielders**) N-COUNT A **fielder** is a player in baseball or cricket who is fielding or one who has a particular skill at fielding. 守场员；外野手 ❑ *He hit 10 home runs in the Coast League and he's also a good fielder.* 他在海岸联赛中击出了10次全垒打，而且他还是个很好的守场员。

N-UNCOUNT **Field hockey** is an outdoor game played on a grass field between two teams of 11 players who use long curved sticks to hit a small ball and try to score goals. 曲棍球 [oft N n] [AM]

/fɪərs/ (**fiercer, fiercest**) ADJ A **fierce** animal or person is very aggressive or angry. 凶猛的；狂怒的 ❑ *They look like the teeth of some fierce animal.* 它们看上去像是某种猛兽的牙齿。 ● ADV 凶猛地；狂怒地 ❑ *"I don't know," she said fiercely.* "我不知道。" 她非常愤怒地说。 ADJ **Fierce** feelings or actions are very intense or enthusiastic, or involve great activity. 激烈的；狂热的 ❑ *Consumers have a wide array of choices and price competition is fierce.* 消费者的选择面很广，价格竞争也很激烈。 ❑ *The town was captured after a fierce battle with rebels.* 与叛军的一场激战后，这个城市被占领了。 ● ADV 激烈地；狂热地 ❑ *He has always been ambitious and fiercely competitive.* 他一直都野心勃勃，极其争强好斗。

/faɪəri/ (**fieriest**) ADJ If you describe something as **fiery**, you mean that it is burning strongly or contains fire. 雄雄燃烧的 [LITERARY] ❑ *A helicopter crashed in a fiery explosion in Vallejo.* 一架直升机在瓦列霍起火爆炸后坠毁了。 ADJ You can use **fiery** for emphasis when you are referring to bright colors such as red or orange. 火一般的 (颜色) [LITERARY, EMPHASIS] ❑ *The sky turned from fiery orange to lemon yellow.* 天空由火红色变成了柠檬黄。

/fɪftin/ (**fifteens**) NUM **Fifteen** is the number 15. 15 ❑ *In India, there are fifteen official languages.* 在印度，有15种官方语言。

/fɪftinθ/ ORD The **fifteenth** item in a series is the one that you count as number fifteen. 第15 ❑ *...the invention of the printing press in the fifteenth century.* …15世纪印刷机的发明。

/fɪfθ/ (**fifths**) ORD The **fifth** item in a series is the one that you count as number five. 第5 ❑ *Joe has recently returned from his fifth trip to Australia.* 乔最近从他第5次澳大利亚之旅返回。

FRACTION A **fifth** is one of five equal parts of something. 1/5 ❑ *India spends over a fifth of its budget on defense.* 印度在国防上支出预算的五分之一以上。 N-SING If you **take** or **plead** the **fifth**, you take the **Fifth Amendment**. 《美国宪法修正案》第五条

/fɪftiəθ/ ORD The **fiftieth** item in a series is the one that you count as number fifty. 第50 ❑ *He retired in 1970, on his fiftieth birthday.* 他在1970年50岁生日时退休。

/fɪfti/ (**fifties**) NUM **Fifty** is the number 50. 50 N-PLURAL When you talk about the **fifties**, you are referring to numbers between 50 and 59. For example, if you are **in your fifties**, you are aged between 50 and 59. If the temperature is **in the fifties**, the temperature is between 50 and 59 degrees. 五十多 ❑ *I probably look as if I'm in my fifties rather than my seventies.* 我可能看起来像五十多岁，而不像七十多岁。 N-PLURAL **The fifties** is the decade between 1950 and 1959. 50年代 ❑ *He began performing in the early fifties, singing and playing guitar.* 他于50年代早期开始表演唱歌和弹吉他。

ADV If something such as money or property is divided or shared **fifty-fifty** between two people, each person gets half of it. 对半地 [ADV after V] [INFORMAL] ❑ *The proceeds of the sale are split fifty-fifty.* 销售收入对半分了。 ● ADJ **Fifty-fifty** is also an adjective. 对半的 ❑ *The new firm was owned on a fifty-fifty basis by the two parent companies.* 新公司的所有权两家母公司各占一半。

/fɪg/ (**figs**) N-COUNT A **fig** is a soft sweet fruit that grows in hot areas. It is full of tiny seeds and is often eaten dried. 无花果 N-COUNT A **fig** or a **fig tree** is a tree on which figs grow. 无花果树

In books and magazines, **fig.** is used as an abbreviation for **figure** in order to tell the reader which picture or diagram is being referred to. 图 ❑ *Draw the basic outlines in black felt-tip pen (see fig. 4).* 用黑色毡头笔画出基本轮廓（见图4）。

/faɪt/ (**fights, fighting, fought**) V-T/V-I If you **fight** something unpleasant, you try in a determined way to prevent it or stop it from happening. 与…作斗争 ❑ *More units to fight forest fires are planned.* 已经计划增派部队来扑灭森林大火。 ❑ *I've spent a lifetime fighting against racism and prejudice.* 我花了毕生的时间与种族歧视和偏见作斗争。 ● N-COUNT **Fight** is also a noun. 斗争 ❑ *...the fight against drug addiction.* …与毒品上瘾的斗争。 V-I If you **fight** for something, you try in a determined way to get it or achieve it. 奋斗 ❑ *Lee had to fight hard for his place on the expedition.* 李必须为他在考察队的一席之地而努力奋斗。 ❑ *I told him how we had fought to hold on to the company.* 我告诉他我们是如何为保住公司而奋斗的。 ● N-COUNT **Fight** is also a noun. 奋斗 ❑ *I too am committing myself to continue the fight for justice.* 我也正致力于继续正义之战。 V-T/V-I If a person or army **fights** in a battle or a war, they take part in it. 参战 ❑ *He fought in the war and was taken prisoner by the Americans.* 他参加了战争，后来被美军俘虏。 ❑ *If I were a young man I would sooner go to prison than fight for this country.* 如果我还是个年轻人，我宁可坐牢也不愿为这个国家去打仗。 ● N-UNCOUNT 战斗 ❑ *More than nine hundred people have died in the fighting.* 九百多人在这场战斗中死去。 V-T If you **fight** your way to a place, you move toward it with great difficulty, for example, because there are a lot of people or obstacles in your way. 挤 ❑ *I fought my way into a carriage just before the doors closed.* 我正好在车门关闭之前挤进了一节车厢。 V-T/V-I To **fight** means to take part in a boxing match. 参加拳击赛 ❑ *In a few hours' time one of the world's most famous boxers will be fighting here for the first time.* 再过几个小时，世界最著名的拳击手之一将首次在这里参加比赛。 ❑ *I'd like to fight him because he's undefeated and I want to be the first man to beat him.* 我想跟他比赛拳击，因为他从未被打败过，而我想成为第一个战胜他的人。 V-T If you **fight** an election, you are a candidate in the election and try to win it. 参加（竞选）❑ *He helped raise almost $40 million to fight the election campaign.* 他帮忙募集了将近四千万美元来参加竞选活动。 V-T If you **fight** a case or a court action, you make a legal case against someone in a very determined way, or you put forward a defense when a legal case is made against you. 打（官司）❑ *Watkins sued the Army and fought his case in various courts for 10 years.* 沃特金斯起诉了军队并用10年在不同的法庭打他的官司。 V-T/V-I If you **fight** an emotion or desire, you try very hard not to feel it, show it, or act on it, but do not always succeed. 克制 ❑ *I desperately fought the urge to giggle.* 我拼命地忍着不笑。 ❑ *He fought with the urge to smoke one of the cigars he'd given up a while ago.* 他克制自己的烟瘾，不去想刚才没吸的那支雪茄。 V-RECIP If an army or group **fights** a battle with another army or group, they oppose each other with weapons. You can also say that two armies or groups **fight** a battle. 打（仗）❑ *Police fought a gun battle with a gang which used hand grenades against them.* 警察与使用手榴弹的一个团伙进行了枪战。 V-RECIP If one person **fights** with another, or **fights** them, the two people hit or kick each other because they want to hurt each other. You can also say that two people **fight**. 打架 ❑ *As a child she fought with her younger sister.* 小时候她跟她的妹妹打过架。 ❑ *I did fight him, I punched him but it was like hitting a wall.* 我确实打了他，我用拳头打他，却像打在一面墙上。 ● N-COUNT **Fight** is also a noun. 打架 [oft N "with" n] ❑ *He had a fight with Smith and bloodied his nose.* 他跟史密斯打了一架，把他的鼻子打出了血。 V-RECIP If one person **fights** with another, or **fights** them, they have an angry disagreement or quarrel. You can also say that two people **fight**. 吵架 [INFORMAL] ❑ *She was always arguing with him and fighting with him.* 她总是跟他争论和吵架。 ❑ *Gwendolen started fighting her teachers.* 格温德琳开始和她的老师们争吵。 ● N-COUNT **Fight** is also a noun. 吵架 ❑ *We think maybe he took off because he had a big fight with his dad the night before.* 我们认为或许他离开是因为他和他父亲在前天晚上大吵了一架。 N-COUNT A **fight** is a boxing match. 拳击赛 ❑ *The referee stopped the fight.* 裁判叫停了那场拳击赛。 N-COUNT You can use **fight** to refer to a contest such as an election or a sports competition. 角逐 [JOURNALISM] ❑ *...the fight for power between the two parties.* …两党之间权力的角逐。 N-UNCOUNT **Fight** is the desire or ability to keep fighting. 斗志 ❑ *I thought that we had a lot of fight in us.* 我认为我们斗志昂扬。 PHRASE Someone who **is fighting for** their **life** is making a great effort to stay alive, either when they are being physically attacked or when they are very ill. 与死神作斗争 ❑ *He is still fighting for his life in the hospital.* 他还在医院里与死神作斗争。
→ see **army**

PHRASAL VERB If you **fight back** against someone or something that is attacking or harming you, you resist them actively or attack them. 还击 ❑ *We should take some comfort from the ability of the judicial system to fight back against corruption.* 我们应从司法制度打击腐败的能力方面获得一些安慰。 PHRASAL VERB If you **fight back** an emotion or a desire, you try very hard not to feel it, show it, or act on it. 抑制 ❑ *She fought back the tears.* 她强忍住眼泪。

PHRASAL VERB If you **fight off** something, for example, an illness or an unpleasant feeling, you succeed in getting rid of it and in not letting it overcome you. 摆脱；抵抗 ❑ *Unfortunately these drugs are quite toxic and hinder the body's ability to fight off infection.* 不幸的是，这些药毒性很大，妨碍身体抗感染的能力。 PHRASAL VERB If you **fight off** someone who has attacked you, you fight with them, and succeed in making them go away or stop attacking you. 击退 ❑ *She fought off three armed robbers.* 她击退了3个持枪抢劫犯。

Thesaurus

scuffle, squabble, tussle
argue, bicker, quarrel
fist fight
argument, disagreement, squabble, tiff

Word Partnership

fight **crime**, fight **fire**
fight **a battle/war**, fight **an enemy**
join a fight
lose a fight, **win a** fight
stay and fight
have a fight, **pick a** fight, **start a** fight

/faɪtər/ (**fighters**) N-COUNT A **fighter** or a **fighter plane** is a fast military aircraft that is used for destroying other aircraft. 战斗机 ❑ *...a fighter pilot.* …一名战斗机飞行员。 N-COUNT If you describe someone as a **fighter**, you approve of them because they continue trying to achieve things in spite of great difficulties or opposition. 斗士 [APPROVAL] ❑ *From the start it was clear this tiny girl was a real fighter.* 从一开始，这个小女孩就显然是一名真正的斗士。 N-COUNT A **fighter** is a person who physically fights another person, especially a professional boxer. 拳手 ❑ *He was a real street fighter who'd do anything to win.* 他是一名真正的街头拳手，为了能赢会不择手段。 → see also **firefighter**

Word Link *fig ≈ form, shape : con ure, dis ure, urative*

/fɪgyərətɪv/ ADJ If you use a word or expression in a **figurative** sense, you use it with a more abstract or imaginative meaning than its ordinary literal one. 比喻的 ❑ *...an event that will* change your route – in both the literal and figurative sense. …一件将改变你路线的大事——既在原义上也在喻义上。● **fig·ura·tive·ly** ADV 比喻地 ❑ *I saw that she was, both literally and figuratively, up against a wall.* 我都看到她，既是事实上也是比喻地，面临一道墙。 **2** ADJ **Figurative** art is a style of art in which people and things are shown in a realistic way. 形象(艺术) ❑ *His career spanned some 50 years and encompassed both abstract and figurative painting.* 他的艺术生涯跨越了大约五十个年头，抽象和形象油画两者都有所造诣。

fig·ure ♦♦♦ /fɪgyər/ (**figures, figuring, figured**) **1** N-COUNT A **figure** is a particular amount expressed as a number, especially a statistic. 数字 ❑ *It would be very nice if we had a true figure of how many people in this country haven't got a job.* 要是我们有一个确切的数字反映这个国家到底有多少人没有工作就好了。❑ *It will not be long before the inflation figure starts to fall.* 过不了多久，通货膨胀的数字就会开始下降。 **2** N-COUNT A **figure** is any of the ten written symbols from 0 to 9 that are used to represent a number. 个位数字 ❑ *...the glowing red figures on the radio alarm clock which read 4:22 a.m.* …收音机闹钟上闪闪发光的红色数字显示凌晨4点22分。 **3** N-COUNT You refer to someone that you can see as a **figure** when you cannot see them clearly or when you are describing them. 身影 ❑ *Ernie saw the dim figure of Rose in the chair.* 厄尼看到了罗斯坐在椅子里的模糊身影。 **4** N-COUNT In art, a **figure** is a person in a drawing or a painting, or a statue of a person. 人像 ❑ *...a life-size bronze figure of a brooding, hooded woman.* …一个真人大小、戴着头巾、正在沉思的女铜像。 **5** N-COUNT Your **figure** is the shape of your body. 身材 ❑ *Take pride in your health and your figure.* 为你的健康和身材感到骄傲。 **6** N-COUNT Someone who is referred to as a **figure** of a particular kind is a person who is well-known and important in some way. 重要人物 ❑ *The movement is supported by key figures in the three main political parties.* 这场运动由3个主要政党的重要人物支持。 **7** N-COUNT If you say that someone is, for example, a mother **figure** or a hero **figure**, you mean that other people regard them as the type of person stated or suggested. 代表 ❑ *Daniel Boone, the great hero figure of the frontier.* 丹尼尔・布恩是伟大的前线英雄的代表。 **8** N-COUNT In books and magazines, the diagrams which help to show or explain information are referred to as **figures**. 图表 [also N num] ❑ *If you look at a world map (see Figure 1) you can identify the major wine-producing regions.* 如果你看看世界地图（见图1），你就能辨认出主要的葡萄酒生产地区。 **9** N-COUNT In geometry, a **figure** is a shape, especially a regular shape. 几何图形 [TECHNICAL] ❑ *Draw a pentagon, a regular five-sided figure.* 画一个五边形，一个规则的五边图形。 **10** N-PLURAL An amount or number that is in single **figures** is between zero and nine. An amount or number that is in double **figures** is between ten and ninety-nine. You can also say, for example, that an amount or number is in three **figures** when it is between one hundred and nine hundred and ninety-nine. 数字 ❑ *Inflation, which has usually been in single figures, is running at more than 12%.* 通货膨胀率通常都是一位数字，正飙升至12%以上。 **11** V-T If you **figure** that something is the case, you think or guess that it is the case. 想 [INFORMAL] ❑ *She figured that both she and Ned had learned a lot from the experience.* 她想她和内德都从这次经历中学到了很多。 **12** V-I If you say "**That figures**" or "**It figures**," you mean that the fact referred to is not surprising. 意料之中 [INFORMAL] ❑ *When I finished, he said, "Yeah. That figures."* 我做完时，他说："嗯，正如所料。" **13** V-I If a person or thing **figures in** something, they appear in or are included in it. 出现 [no passive] ❑ *Human rights violations figured prominently in the report.* 侵犯人权出现在报告中的显要位置。

▶ **figure out** PHRASAL VERB If you **figure out** a solution to a problem or the reason for something, you succeed in solving it or understanding it. 想出；弄明白 [INFORMAL] ❑ *It took them about one month to figure out how to start the equipment.* 他们用了大约一个月的时间才弄明白如何启动这台设备。❑ *They're trying to figure out the politics of this whole situation.* 他们正试图弄明白整个形势的利害关系。

figure·head /fɪgyərhɛd/ (**figureheads**) **1** N-COUNT If someone is the **figurehead** of an organization or movement, they are recognized as being its leader, although they have little real power. 傀儡 ❑ *The president will be little more than a figurehead.* 主席将只不过是个傀儡而已。 **2** N-COUNT A **figurehead** is a large wooden model of a person that was put just under the pointed front of a sailing ship in former times. 艏饰像

file ♦♦◇ /faɪl/ (**files, filing, filed**) **1** N-COUNT A **file** is a box or a folded piece of heavy paper or plastic in which letters or documents are kept. 文件盒；文件夹 ❑ *...a file of insurance papers.* …一个保险单文件夹。 **2** N-COUNT A **file** is a collection of information about a particular person or thing. 卷宗 ❑ *We already have files on people's tax details.* 我们已经有了人们付税详情的卷宗。 **3** N-COUNT In computing, a **file** is a set of related data that has its own name. 文件 ❑ *Be sure to save the revised version of the file under a new filename.* 确保将改过的文件版本另存在一个新的文件名下。 **4** N-COUNT A **file** is a hand tool which is used for rubbing hard objects to make them smooth, shape them, or cut through them. 锉刀 **5** V-T If you **file** a document, you put it in the correct file. 使归档 ❑ *They are all filed alphabetically under author.* 它们都是在作者一栏下面按字母顺序来归档的。 **6** V-T/V-I If you **file** a formal or legal accusation, complaint, or request, you make it officially. 提起 ❑ *I filed for divorce on the grounds of adultery a few months later.* ，我几个月后以通奸为由提起了离婚。 **7** V-T When someone **files** a report or a news story, they send or give it to their employer. 提交 ❑ *He had to rush back to the office and file a housing story before the secretaries went home.* 他不得不赶回办公室、在秘书们回家之前提交一份有关住房的报道。 **8** V-T If you **file** an object, you smooth it, shape it, or cut it with a file. 锉 ❑ *Manicurists are skilled at shaping and filing nails.* 美甲师对修剪、锉光指甲很在行。 **9** → see also **rank and file** **10** PHRASE A group of people who are walking or standing **in single file** or **single file** are in a line, one behind the other. 成单行 ❑ *We were walking in single file to the lake.* 我们排成单行走向湖边。

→ see **office, tool**

fil·ing cabi·net (**filing cabinets**) N-COUNT A **filing cabinet** is a piece of office furniture, usually made of metal, which has drawers in which files are kept. 文件柜

→ see **office**

fill ♦♦◇ /fɪl/ (**fills, filling, filled**) **1** V-T/V-I If you **fill** a container or area, or if it **fills**, an amount of something enters it that is enough to make it full. 装满 ❑ *She went to the bathroom, filled a glass with water, returned to the bed.* 她去了盥洗室，灌满了一杯水，回到床前。❑ *The boy's eyes filled with tears.* 那男孩的眼里充满了泪水。● PHRASAL VERB **Fill up** means the same as **fill**. 装满 ❑ *Warehouses at the frontier between the two countries fill up with sacks of rice and flour.* 两国交界处的仓库里装满了一袋袋大米和面粉。 **2** V-T If something **fills** a space, it is so big, or there are such large quantities of it, that there is very little room left. 占满 ❑ *He cast his eyes at the rows of cabinets that filled the enormous work area.* 他把目光投向了一排排占满了庞大工作区的柜子。● PHRASAL VERB **Fill up** means the same as **fill**. 占满 (同**fill**) ❑ *...the complicated machines that fill up today's laboratories.* …占满了现今实验室的复杂机器。● **filled** ADJ 占满的 [v-link ADJ "with" n] ❑ *...four museum buildings filled with historical objects.* …满是历史文物的4幢博物馆大楼。 **3** V-T If you **fill** a crack or hole, you put a substance into it in order to make the surface smooth again. 填平 ❑ *Fill small holes with wood filler in a matching color.* 用颜色相配的木质填充料填平小洞。● PHRASAL VERB **Fill in** means the same as **fill**. 填平 (同**fill**) ❑ *Start by filling in any cracks and gaps between window and door frames and the wall.* 先把门窗框架和墙壁之间的所有裂缝和空隙填平。 **4** V-T If a sound, smell, or light **fills** a space, or the air, it is very strong or noticeable. 充满 ❑ *In the parking lot of the school, the siren filled the air.* 学校的停车场上，警报响彻天空。 **5** V-T If something **fills** you **with** an emotion, or if an emotion **fills** you, you experience this emotion strongly. 使充满 (感情) ❑ *I admired my father, and his work filled me with awe and curiosity.* 我崇拜我的父亲，他的工作使我充满了敬畏和好奇。 **6** V-T If you **fill** a period of time with a particular activity, you spend the time in this way. 打发 ❑ *If she wants a routine to fill her day, let her do community work.* 如果她想用例行事物来打发日子，就让她做社区工作吧。● PHRASAL VERB **Fill up** means the same as **fill**. 打发 (同**fill**) ❑ *On Thursday night she went to her yoga class, glad to have something to fill up the evening.* 星期四晚上她去上了瑜珈课，很高兴有事可做来打发晚上的时间。 **7** V-T If something **fills** a need or a gap, it puts an end to this need or gap by existing or being active. 满足；填补 ❑ *She brought him a sense of fun, of gaiety that filled a gap in his life.* 她带给他一种快乐、欢愉的感觉，填补了他生命中的空白。 **8** V-T If something **fills** a role, position, or function, they have that role or position, or perform that function, often successfully. 担任 ❑ *Dena was filling the role of diplomat's wife with the skill she had learned over the years.* 德娜凭借多年来学到的技巧担任着外交家妻子的角色。 **9** V-T If a company or organization **fills** a job vacancy, they choose someone to do the job. If someone **fills** a job vacancy, they accept a job that they have been offered. 选人接任；接任 ❑ *A vacancy has arisen which I intend to fill.* 我想接任的职位已经空出来了。 **10** V-T When a dentist **fills** someone's tooth, he or she puts a filling in it. 补 ❑ *Dentists fill teeth and repair broken ones.* 牙医补牙并修理坏牙。 **11** V-T If you **fill** an order or a prescription, you provide the things that are asked for. 供应(订货或处方上的药) [mainly AM] ❑ *A pharmacist can fill any prescription if, in his or her judgment, the prescription is valid.* 一名药剂师可以供应任何处方上的药，如果他或她认为药方有效的话。 **12** to **fill the bill** → see **bill**

▸ **fill in** **1** PHRASAL VERB If you **fill in** a form or other document requesting information, you write information in the spaces on it. 填写 ❑ *Fill in the coupon and send it first class to the address shown.* 填写好赠券，用一类邮件寄到所显示的地址。 **2** PHRASAL VERB If you **fill in** a shape, you cover the area inside the lines with color or shapes so that none of the background is showing. 涂满 ❑ *With a lip pencil, outline lips and fill them in.* 用一支唇线笔画出唇线，然后涂上口红。 **3** PHRASAL VERB If you **fill** someone **in**, you give them more details about something that you know about. 提供详情 [INFORMAL] ❑ *He filled her in on Wilbur Kantor's visit.* 他告诉了她威尔伯・坎特造访的详情。 **4** PHRASAL VERB If you **fill in** for someone, you do the work or task that they normally do because they are unable to do it. 临时顶替 ❑ *Vice-presidents' wives would fill in for first ladies.* 副总统们的妻子会临时顶替第一夫人们。 **5** → see also **fill 3**

▸ **fill out** **1** PHRASAL VERB If you **fill out** a form or other document requesting information, you write information in the spaces on it. 填写 [mainly AM] ❑ *Fill out the application carefully, and keep copies of it.* 仔细填写申请表，并保留备份。 **2** PHRASAL VERB If someone or something **fills out**, they become fuller, thicker, or rounder. 变胖；变厚；变圆 ❑ *A girl may fill out before she reaches her full height.* 女孩子长足个头之前可能会变胖。

▸ **fill up** **1** PHRASAL VERB If you **fill up** or **fill** yourself **up** with food, you eat so much that you do not feel hungry. 吃饱 ❑ *Fill up on potatoes, bread and pasta, which are high in carbohydrate and low in fat.* 用高碳低脂的土豆、面包和面食填饱肚子。 **2** PHRASAL VERB A type of food that **fills** you **up** makes you feel that you have eaten a lot, even though you have only eaten a small amount. 易饱的 ❑ *Potatoes fill us up without overloading us with calories.* 土豆容易使我们产生饱腹感，使我们不摄入过多的卡路里。 **3** → see also **fill 1, 2, 6**

Thesaurus *fill* 另参见：

v. inflate, load, pour into, put into; (*ant.*) empty, pour out **1**
crowd, take up **2**
block, close, plug, seal **3**

fil·let /fɪleɪ/ (**fillets, filleting, filleted**) **1** N-VAR **Fillet** is a strip of meat, especially beef, that has no bones in it. 无骨肉片 ❑ *...fillet of beef with shallots.* …洋葱牛肉片。 ❑ *...chicken breast fillets.* …鸡脯肉。 **2** N-COUNT A **fillet** of fish is the side of a fish with the bones removed. 去骨鱼片 ❑ *...anchovy fillets.* …无骨鳀鱼片。 **3** V-T When you **fillet** fish or meat, you prepare it by taking the bones out. 使去骨 ❑ *Fillet the fish and roll the fillets in flour.* 剔出鱼骨，把鱼片在面粉里滚一下。

★ **fill·ing** /fɪlɪŋ/ (**fillings**) **1** N-COUNT A **filling** is a small amount of metal or plastic that a dentist puts in a hole in a tooth to prevent further decay. (补牙用的) 填料 ❑ *The longer your child can go without needing a filling, the better.* 你的孩子不需要补牙的时间越长越好。 **2** N-MASS The **filling** in something such as a cake, pie, or sandwich is a substance or mixture that is put inside it. (糕点里的) 馅 ❑ *Spread some of the filling over each cold pancake and then either roll or fold.* 先将一些馅摊在每个凉煎饼上，再卷起来或叠起来。 **3** N-MASS The **filling** in a piece of soft furniture or in a cushion is the soft substance inside it. (软家具或垫子的) 芯 ❑ *...second-hand sofas with old-style foam fillings.* …旧式海绵芯的二手沙发。 **4** ADJ Food that is **filling** makes you feel full when you have eaten it. (食物) 易使人饱的 ❑ *Although it is tasty, crab is very filling.* 螃蟹虽然好吃，但很容易让人饱。

→ see **teeth**

film ♦♦♦ /fɪlm/ (**films, filming, filmed**) **1** N-COUNT A **film** consists of moving pictures that have been recorded so that they can be shown in a theater or on television. A film tells a story, or shows a real situation. 电影 ❑ *Everything about the film was good. Good acting, good story, good fun.* 这部电影样样都好：演技好，故事好，非常有趣。 **2** N-COUNT A **film of** powder, liquid, or oil is a very thin layer of it. 薄层 ❑ *The sea is coated with a film of raw sewage.* 海上覆盖着薄薄一层未经处理的污水。 **3** V-T If you **film** something, you use a camera to take moving pictures which can be shown on a screen or on television. 把…拍摄成影片 ❑ *He had filmed her life story.* 他已经把她的人生故事拍成了电影。 **4** N-UNCOUNT **Film** of something is moving pictures of a real event that are shown on television or on a screen. 记实影片 ❑ *He likes to look at film of old-time players.* 他喜欢看那些以前运动员的影片。 **5** N-UNCOUNT The making of films, considered as a form of art or a business, can be referred to as **film** or **films**. 电影艺术；电影业 [also N in pl] ❑ *Film is a business with limited opportunities for actresses.* 电影业对女演员来说机会有限。 **6** N-UNCOUNT Plastic **film** is a very thin sheet of plastic used to wrap and cover things. (塑料) 薄膜 [BRIT]

in AM, use **plastic wrap, Saran wrap**

7 N-VAR A **film** is the narrow roll of plastic that is used in a camera to take photographs. 胶卷 ❑ *The photographers had already shot a dozen rolls of film.* 摄影师们已经拍了一打胶卷。

→ see **photography**

Word Partnership *film* 的常用搭配：

N. film **critic**, film **director**, film **festival**, film **producer** **1**
film **clip** **1** **4**
film **studio** **1** **5**
roll of film **7**
V. **direct** a film, **watch** a film **1**
edit film **4**
develop film **7**

film-goer [BRIT] → see **moviegoer**

film·ing /fɪlmɪŋ/ N-UNCOUNT **Filming** is the activity of making a film including the acting, directing, and camera shots. 影片摄制 ❑ *Filming was due to start next month.* 影片摄制预计下个月开始。

film·maker /fɪlmmeɪkər/ (**filmmakers**) N-COUNT A **filmmaker** is someone involved in making films, in particular a director or producer. 电影制作人

film star (**film stars**) N-COUNT A **film star** is a famous actor who appears in films. 影星

fil·ter /fɪltər/ (**filters, filtering, filtered**) **1** V-T To **filter** a substance means to pass it through a device which is designed to remove certain particles contained in it. 过滤 ❑ *The best prevention for cholera is to boil or filter water, and eat only well-cooked food.* 预防霍乱最好的方法是把水煮沸或过滤，并且只吃煮熟的食物。 **2** V-I If light or sound **filters into** a place, it comes in weakly or slowly, either through a partly covered opening, or from a long distance away. (光、声) 透入 ❑ *Light filtered into my kitchen through the soft, green shade of the honey locust tree.* 光线透过皂荚树柔和的绿荫照进了我的厨房。 **3** V-I When news or information **filters** through to people, it gradually reaches them. (新闻、信息等) 逐渐传开 ❑ *It took months before the findings began to filter through to the politicians.* 几个月后调查结果才开始逐渐传到政治家们那里。 ❑ *News of the attack quickly filtered through the college.* 袭击的消息很快就在这所大学传开了。 **4** N-COUNT A **filter** is a device through which a substance is passed when it is being filtered. 过滤器 ❑ *...a paper coffee filter.* …一张咖啡滤纸。 **5** N-COUNT A **filter** is a device through which sound or light is passed and which blocks or reduces particular sound or light frequencies. 滤声器；滤光器 ❑ *You might use a yellow filter to improve the clarity of a hazy horizon.* 你可以用一个黄色滤光器来提高模糊的地平线的清晰度。

→ see **coffee**

▸ **filter out** PHRASAL VERB To **filter out** something from a substance or from light means to remove it by passing the substance or light through something acting as a filter. 滤除 ❑ *Children should have glasses which filter out UV rays.* 孩子们应该佩戴可以滤除紫外线的眼镜。 ❑ *Plants and trees filter carbon dioxide out of the air and produce oxygen.* 植物和树木能滤除空气中的二氧化碳并制造出氧气。

▲ **filth** /fɪlθ/ **1** N-UNCOUNT **Filth** is a disgusting amount of dirt. 污物 ❑ *Thousands of tons of filth and sewage pour into the Ganges every day.* 每天都有成千上万吨的污物和污水排入恒河。 **2** N-UNCOUNT People refer to words or pictures, usually ones relating to sex, as **filth** when they think they are very disgusting and rude. 下流话；淫秽图片 [DISAPPROVAL] ❑ *The dialogue was all filth and innuendo.* 这段对话全是下流的言辞和影射。

filthy /fɪlθi/ (**filthier, filthiest**) **1** ADJ Something that is **filthy** is very dirty. 污秽的 ❑ *He never washed, and always wore a filthy old jacket.* 他从不洗澡，而且总是穿着一件极脏的旧夹克。 **2** ADJ If you describe something as **filthy**, you mean that you think it is morally very unpleasant and disgusting, sometimes in a sexual way. 淫秽的 [DISAPPROVAL] ❑ *Apparently, well known actors were at these filthy parties.* 很明显，著名的演员们参加过这些下流的聚会。

/fɪn/ (fins) N-COUNT A fish's **fins** are the flat parts which stick out of its body and help it to swim and keep its balance. 鳍 N-COUNT A **fin** on something such as an airplane, rocket, or bomb is a flat part which sticks out and which is intended to help control its movement. (飞机、火箭、炸弹等的) 翼

Word Link *fin ≈ end : al, ale, ish*

/faɪnᵊl/ (**finals**) ADJ In a series of events, things, or people, the **final** one is the last one. 最后的 [det ADJ] ❑ *Astronauts will make a final attempt today to rescue a communications satellite from its useless orbit.* 宇航员们今天将做最后一次尝试，把一颗通讯卫星从它无用的轨道上拯救出来。 ❑ *This is the fifth and probably final day of testimony before the Senate Judiciary Committee.* 这是第5天，也可能是最后一天在参议院司法委员会面前作证。 ADJ **Final** means happening at the end of an event or series of events. 最终的 [ADJ n] ❑ *You must have been on stage until the final curtain.* 你肯定是在台上一直呆到终场。 ADJ If a decision or someone's authority is **final**, it cannot be changed or questioned. 不可更改的 ❑ *The judges' decision is final.* 该法官的判决是不可更改的。 N-COUNT The **final** is the last game or contest in a series and decides who is the winner. 决赛 ❑ *...the Gold Cup final.* …金杯决赛。 → see also **quarterfinal, semifinal** N-PLURAL **The finals** of a sports tournament consist of a smaller tournament that includes only players or teams that have won earlier games. The finals decide the winner of the whole tournament. (锦标赛的) 决赛阶段的比赛 ❑ *Poland knows it has a chance of qualifying for the World Cup Finals.* 波兰队知道自己有机会获得参加世界杯决赛阶段比赛的资格。

Thesaurus

last, ultimate
absolute, decisive, definite, settled

/fɪnɑli, -næli/ (**finales**) N-COUNT **The finale** of a show, piece of music, or series of shows is the last part of it or the last one of them, especially when this is exciting or impressive. (演出的) 终场; (音乐的) 终曲 ❑ *...the finale of Shostakovich's Fifth Symphony.* …肖斯塔克维奇第五交响曲的终曲。

/faɪnᵊlɪst/ (**finalists**) N-COUNT A **finalist** is someone who reaches the last stages of a competition or tournament by doing well or winning in its earlier stages. 参加决赛者 ❑ *The twelve finalists will be listed in the Sunday Times.* 这12位决赛者的名单将刊登在《星期日泰晤士报》上。

Word Link *ize ≈ making : final , memor , normal*

/faɪnᵊlaɪz/ (**finalizes, finalizing, finalized**) V-T If you **finalize** something such as a plan or an agreement, you complete the arrangements for it, especially by discussing it with other people. 最终确定 (计划、协议等) ❑ *Negotiators from the three countries finalized the agreement in August.* 3个国家的谈判代表在8月最终确定了协议。 ❑ *We are saying nothing until all the details have been finalized.* 在所有细节最终确定之前我们无可奉告。

/faɪnᵊli/ ADV You use **finally** to suggest that something happens after a long period of time, usually later than you wanted or expected it to happen. 终于 ❑ *The food finally arrived at the end of last week and distribution began.* 食物终于在上周末抵达并开始分发。 ADV You use **finally** to indicate that something is last in a series of actions or events. 最后 [ADV with cl/group] ❑ *The action slips from comedy to melodrama and finally to tragedy.* 剧情由喜剧慢慢发展成闹剧，最后又演变为悲剧。

Do not confuse **finally** and **eventually**. You say that something **finally** happens after you have been waiting for it or expecting it for a long time. ❑ *Finally I went to bed... The heat of the sun finally became too much for me.* You can also use **finally** to show that something happens last in a series of events. ❑ *The sky turned red, then purple, and finally black.* When something happens after a lot of delays or complications, you can say that it **eventually** happens. ❑ *Eventually they got to the hospital... I found Victoria Avenue eventually.* You can also use **eventually** to talk about what happens at the end of a series of events, often as a result of them. ❑ *Eventually, they were forced to return to Chicago.*

/faɪnæns, fɪnæns/ (**finances, financing, financed**) V-T When someone **finances** something such as a project or a purchase, they provide the money that is needed to pay for them. 资助 ❑ *The fund has been used largely to finance the construction of federal prisons.* 该基金大部分已用于资助联邦监狱的建造。 ● N-UNCOUNT **Finance** is also a noun. 资助 ❑ *A United States delegation is in Japan seeking finance for a major scientific project.* 1个美国代表团正在日本为一个重大科研项目寻求资助。 N-UNCOUNT **Finance** is the commercial or government activity of managing money, debt, credit, and investment. 金融; 财政 [also N in pl] ❑ *...a major player in the world of high finance.* …高层金融界的大腕。 ❑ *The report recommends an overhaul of public finances.* 这份报告建议对公共财政进行彻底检视。 N-UNCOUNT You can refer to the amount of money that you have and how well it is organized as your **finances.** 财务状况 [also N in pl] ❑ *Be prepared for unexpected news concerning your finances.* 对关于你财务状况的意外消息要做好准备。

(**finance companies**) N-COUNT A **finance company** is a business which lends money to people and charges them interest while they pay it back. 信贷公司 [BUSINESS]

/faɪnænʃᵊl, fɪn-/ ADJ **Financial** means relating to or involving money. 金融的; 财政的 ❑ *The company is in financial difficulties.* 这个公司处于财务困难之中。 ● ADV 金融上; 财政上 ❑ *She would like to be more financially independent.* 她想要在财政上更加独立。

/fɪnənsɪər, faɪn-/ (**financiers**) N-COUNT A **financier** is a person, company, or government that provides money for projects or businesses. (为项目或企业) 提供资金者 [BUSINESS] ❑ *The Connells were leading financiers of the Democratic Party in Congress.* 康奈尔家族是民主党在国会中的主要出资方。

/faɪnd/ (**finds, finding, found**) V-T If you **find** someone or something, you see them or learn where they are. 发现; 找到 ❑ *The police also found a pistol.* 警察还发现了一把手枪。 ❑ *They have spent ages looking at the map and can't find a trace of anywhere called Darrowby.* 他们已花了很长时间察看地图，却怎么也找不到一个叫“达罗比”的地方。 V-T If you **find** something that you need or want, you succeed in achieving or obtaining it. 得到 ❑ *Many people here cannot find work.* 这里很多人找不到工作。 ❑ *He has to apply for a permit and we have to find him a job.* 他得申请一个许可证，而我们得给他找一份工作。 V-T If you **find** someone or something in a particular situation, they are in that situation when you see them or come into contact with them. 发现 (某人或某物处于某种状态) ❑ *They found her walking alone and depressed on the beach.* 他们发现她独自一人、神情沮丧地走在海滩上。 ❑ *She returned to her home to find her back door forced open.* 她回到家中，发现后门被强行打开了。 V-T If you **find yourself** doing something, you are doing it without deciding or intending to do it. 意识到 (自己无意中的动作) ❑ *It's not the first time that you've found yourself in this situation.* 这已经不是你第一次意识到自己处于这种情形了。 ❑ *I found myself having more fun than I had had in years.* 我发现自己多年来从未玩得这样开心过。 V-T If you **find** that something is the case, you become aware of it or realize that it is the case. 发觉 ❑ *The two biologists found, to their surprise, that both groups of birds survived equally well.* 这两位生物学家惊奇地发觉，两组鸟都同样很好地活了下来。 ❑ *At my age I would find it hard to get another job.* 在我这个年纪，我觉得很难再找到另一份工作。 V-T When a court or jury decides that a person on trial is guilty or innocent, you say that the person **has been found** guilty or not guilty. 判决 ❑ *She was found guilty of manslaughter and put on probation for two years.* 她被判过失杀人罪，缓刑两年。 V-T You can use **find** to express your reaction to someone or something. 觉得 ❑ *I find most of the young men of my own age so boring.* 我觉得大多数和我同龄的年轻人都很无趣。 ❑ *I find it ludicrous that nothing has been done to protect passengers from fire.* 我认为没有采取任何措施来保护乘客免受火患是荒唐的。 V-T If you **find** a feeling such as pleasure or comfort **in** a particular thing or activity, you experience the feeling mentioned as a result of this thing or activity. 体会到 ❑ *How could anyone find pleasure in hunting and killing this beautiful creature?* 怎么会有人在猎杀这种美丽的动物中体会到快乐呢? V-T If you **find** the time or money **to** do something, you succeed in making or obtaining enough time or money to do it. 找得出 (时间、金钱) ❑ *I was just finding more time to write music.* 我刚好抽得出更多的时间来作曲。 V-T PASSIVE If something **is found** in a particular place or thing, it exists in that place. 发现 (某物的存在) ❑ *Two thousand of France's 4,200 species of flowering plants are found in the park.* 法国的4200种开花植物中有2000种可以在这个公园里找到。 N-COUNT If you describe someone or something that has been discovered as a **find**, you mean that they are valuable, interesting, good, or useful. (有价值的) 发现 ❑ *Another of his lucky finds was a pair of candleholders.* 他另一个幸运的发现是一对烛台。 → see also **finding, found**

You can use **find**, **find out**, or **discover** to talk about learning that something is the case. ❑ *The young child finds that noise attracts attention... He discovered the whole school knew about it... We found out that she was wrong.* **Discover** is a slightly more formal word than **find**, and is often used to talk about scientific research or formal investigations. For example, you can **discover** a cure for a particular disease. You can also use **discover** when you find something by accident. ❑ *This well-known flower was discovered in 1903.* Note that if you cannot see something you are looking for, you say that you cannot **find** it. You do not use "discover" or "find out" in this way. ❑ *I'm lost–I can't find the bridge.* You can also say that someone **finds out** facts when this is easy to do, but you cannot use "discover" or "find" in this way. ❑ *I found out the train times.*

13 PHRASE If you **find** your **way** somewhere, you successfully get there by choosing the right way to go. 找到(去某地的路) ❑ *He was an expert at finding his way, even in strange surroundings.* 他是个找路的高手，即使在陌生的环境中也一样。 14 PHRASE If something **finds** its **way** somewhere, it comes to that place, especially by chance. (尤指偶然地) 来到 ❑ *It is one of the very few Michelangelos that have found their way out of Italy.* 它是流传到意大利境外的少数几幅米开朗基罗的作品之一。 15 **to find fault with** → see **fault** 16 **to find** one's **feet** → see **foot**

▶ **find out** 1 PHRASAL VERB If you **find** something **out**, you learn something that you did not already know, especially by making a deliberate effort to do so. 弄清 ❑ *It makes you want to watch the next episode to find out what's going to happen.* 这使你想看下一集，以弄清接下来要发生什么。 ❑ *I was relieved to find out that my problems were due to a genuine disorder.* 查明我的问题的确是失调造成的，我就放心了。 2 PHRASAL VERB If you **find** someone **out**, you discover that they have been doing something dishonest. 识破 ❑ *Her face was so grave, I wondered for a moment if she'd found me out.* 她表情非常严肃，我一时怀疑她是不是已经识破了我。

find·ing /faɪndɪŋ/ (**findings**) 1 N-COUNT Someone's **findings** are the information they get or the conclusions they come to as the result of an investigation or some research. 调查结果；研究结论 ❑ *One of the main findings of the survey was the confusion about the facilities already in place.* 该调查的主要发现之一是对已安装到位的设备的混淆。 2 N-COUNT The **findings** of a court are the decisions that it reaches after a trial or an investigation. 判决 ❑ *The government hopes the court will announce its findings before the end of the month.* 政府希望该法院能在月底前宣布判决。
→ see **laboratory, science**

fine
❶ ADJECTIVE USES
❷ PUNISHMENT

❶ **fine** ♦♦◇ /faɪn/ (**finer, finest**) 1 ADJ You use **fine** to describe something that you admire and think is very good. 美好的 ❑ *There is a fine view of the countryside.* 有一幅美丽的乡村景色。 ❑ *This is a fine book.* 这是一本好书。 ● **fine·ly** ADV 美好地 [ADV -ed] ❑ *They are finely engineered boats.* 它们是设计精美的船只。 2 ADJ If you say that you are **fine**, you mean that you are in good health or reasonably happy. 健康的；开心的 [v-link ADJ] ❑ *Lina is fine and sends you her love and best wishes.* 莉娜很好，她向你问候并祝福你。 3 ADJ If you say that something is **fine**, you mean that it is satisfactory or acceptable. 令人满意的 ❑ *The skiing is fine.* 滑雪挺好的。 ❑ *Everything was going to be just fine.* 一切都会好起来的。 ● ADV **Fine** is also an adverb. 令人满意地 ❑ *All the instruments are working fine.* 所有的仪器都运转良好。 4 ADJ Something that is **fine** is very delicate, narrow, or small. 精致的；纤细的 ❑ *The heat scorched the fine hairs on her arms.* 炙热烤焦了她胳膊上的细毛。 ● **fine·ly** ADV 精致地；纤细地 [ADV with v] ❑ *Chop the ingredients finely and mix them together.* 把这些原料剁得很细然后和在一起。 5 ADJ **Fine** objects or clothing are of good quality, delicate, and expensive. 精致的；华贵的 ❑ *We waited in our fine clothes.* 我们身着华丽的服装等待。 6 ADJ A **fine** detail or distinction is very delicate, small, or exact. 精确的；细微的 ❑ *Johnson likes the broad outline but is reserving judgment on the fine detail.* 约翰逊喜欢这个大框架，但对小细节则保留看法。 ● **fine·ly** ADV 精确地；细微地 ❑ *They had to take the finely balanced decision to let the visit proceed.* 他们不得不做出仔细权衡后的决定，让访问继续下去。 7 ADJ A **fine** person is someone you consider good, moral, and worth admiring. 品德高尚的；值得钦佩的 [APPROVAL] ❑ *He was an excellent journalist and a very fine man.* 他是名优秀的记者，也是个品德很高尚的人。 8 ADJ When the weather is **fine**, the sun is shining and it is not raining. 晴朗的 ❑ *He might be doing some gardening if the weather is fine.* 如果天气晴朗，他也许会干点儿园艺活。 9 CONVENTION You say "**fine**" or "**that's fine**" to show that you do not object to an arrangement, action, or situation that has been suggested. 好的 (表示同意) [FORMULAE] ❑ *If competition is the best way to achieve it, then, fine.* 如果竞争是实现它的最佳方式，那么，好吧。
→ see **coffee**

❷ **fine** ♦◇◇ /faɪn/ (**fines, fining, fined**) 1 N-COUNT A **fine** is a punishment in which a person is ordered to pay a sum of money because they have done something illegal or broken a rule. 罚款 2 V-T If someone **is fined**, they are punished by being ordered to pay a sum of money because they have done something illegal or broken a rule. 罚款 ❑ *She was fined $300 and banned from driving for one month.* 她被罚款$300，并被禁止驾车1个月。

Word Partnership *fine* 的常用搭配:

N. fine **example**, fine **time** ❶ 1
fine **grain**, fine **hair**, fine **line**, fine **powder** ❶ 4
fine **clothes**, fine **dining**, fine **wine** ❶ 5
V. **look** fine ❶ 1 – 3
seem fine ❶ 2 3
do fine, **feel** fine ❶ 3
charge a fine, **impose** a fine, **pay** a fine, **receive** a fine ❷ 1

fine art (**fine arts**) 1 N-UNCOUNT Painting and sculpture, in which objects are produced that are beautiful rather than useful, can be referred to as **fine art** or as the **fine arts**. 美术品 [also N in pl] ❑ *He deals in antiques and fine art.* 他经营古董和美术品。 2 PHRASE If you **have** something **down to a fine art**, you are able to do it in a very skillful or efficient way because you have had a lot of experience of doing it. 精于…之道 ❑ *They've got fruit retailing down to a fine art. You can be sure that your pears will ripen in day.* 他们精于水果零售之道。你可以放心，你那些梨一天之内就会熟。

fine print N-UNCOUNT In a contract or agreement, the **fine print** is the same as the **small print**. (合同、协议的) 附属细则

fi·nesse /fɪnɛs/ N-UNCOUNT If you do something with **finesse**, you do it with great skill and style. 技巧；策略 ❑ *...handling momentous diplomatic challenges with tact and finesse.* …以机智和策略处理重大的外交难题。

fine-tune (**fine-tunes, fine-tuning, fine-tuned**) V-T If you **fine-tune** something, you make very small and precise changes to it in order to make it as successful or effective as it possibly can be. 微调 ❑ *We do not try to fine-tune the economy on the basis of short-term predictions.* 我们不会根据短期预测而试图对经济作微调。

fin·ger ♦♦◇ /fɪŋgər/ (**fingers, fingering, fingered**) 1 N-COUNT Your **fingers** are the long thin parts at the end of each hand, sometimes also including the thumb. 手指 ❑ *She suddenly held up a small, bony finger and pointed across the room.* 她突然举起一根瘦小的手指指向房间的另一头。 ❑ *She ran her fingers through her hair.* 她用手指捋了捋头发。 2 N-COUNT The **fingers** of a glove are the parts that a person's fingers fit into. (手套的) 指套 ❑ *He bit the fingers of his right glove and pulled it off.* 他咬住右手手套的指套，把它扯了下来。 3 N-COUNT A **finger of** something such as smoke or land is an amount of it that is shaped rather like a finger. 指状物 ❑ *...a thin finger of land that separates Pakistan from the former Soviet Union.* …一片分隔巴基斯坦和前苏联的狭长地带。 4 V-T If you **finger** something, you touch or feel it with your fingers. 用手指触摸 ❑ *He fingered the few coins in his pocket.* 他用手指摸了摸他兜里的几枚硬币。 5 PHRASE If you **cross** your **fingers**, you put one finger on top of another and hope for good luck. If you say that someone **is keeping their fingers crossed**, you mean they are hoping for good luck. (交叉手指以) 祈求好运 ❑ *He crossed his fingers, asking for luck for the first time in his life.* 他把手指交叉起来，平生第一次祈求好运。 6 PHRASE If you say that someone did not **lay a finger on** a particular person or thing, you are emphasizing that they did not touch or harm them at all. 动…一个指头 [EMPHASIS] ❑ *I must make it clear I never laid a finger on her.* 我必须说清楚，我从未动过她一个指头。 7 PHRASE If you say that a person does not **lift a finger** or **raise a finger** to do something, especially to help someone, you are critical of them because they do nothing. 尽举手之劳 [DISAPPROVAL] ❑ *She never* lifted a finger around the house. 她在家里从来没有帮过忙。 8 PHRASE If you **point the finger at** someone or **point an accusing finger at** someone, you blame them or accuse them of doing wrong. 指责 ❑ *He said he wasn't pointing an accusing finger at anyone in the government or the army.* 他说他并不是在指责政府或军队里的任何人。 9 PHRASE If you **put** your **finger on** something, for example, a reason or problem, you see and identify exactly what it is. 确切地指出 ❑ *Midge couldn't quite put her finger on the reason.* 米吉不能非常确切地指出原因所在。

Word Partnership *finger* 的常用搭配:
V. **poke** a finger, **run** a finger 1
point a finger 8

finger·nail /fɪŋgərneɪl/ (**fingernails**) N-COUNT Your **fingernails** are the thin hard areas at the end of each of your fingers. 手指甲 → see **hand**

finger·print /fɪŋgərprɪnt/ (**fingerprints, fingerprinting, fingerprinted**) 1 N-COUNT **Fingerprints** are marks made by a person's fingers which show the lines on the skin. Everyone's fingerprints are different, so they can be used to identify criminals. 指纹 ❑ *The detective discovered no fewer than 35 fingerprints.* 这名侦探发现了不下35个指纹。 ❑ *...his fingerprint on the murder weapon.* …他留在凶器上的指纹。 ● PHRASE If the police **take** someone's **fingerprints**, they make that person press their fingers onto a pad covered with ink, and then onto paper, so that they know what that person's fingerprints look like. 让某人按手印 2 V-T If someone **is fingerprinted**, the police take their fingerprints. 提取指纹 [usu passive] ❑ *He took her to jail, where she was fingerprinted and booked.* 他将她带到监狱，她在那里被提取了指纹并登记在册。

finger·tip /fɪŋgərtɪp/ (**fingertips**) also **finger-tip** 1 N-COUNT Your **fingertips** are the ends of your fingers. 指尖 ❑ *The butter and flour are rubbed together with the fingertips.* 黄油和面粉被指尖给搓在一起。 2 PHRASE If you say that something is **at** your **fingertips**, you approve of the fact that you can reach it easily or that it is easily available to you. 近在手边；唾手可得 [APPROVAL] ❑ *I had the information at my fingertips and hadn't used it.* 我手头就有这种信息，而且我还没用到。

Word Link *fin = end : final, finale, finish*

fin·ish ♦♦◇ /fɪnɪʃ/ (**finishes, finishing, finished**) 1 V-T When you **finish** doing or dealing with something, you do or deal with the last part of it, so that there is no more for you to do or deal with. 结束 ❑ *As soon as he'd finished eating, he excused himself.* 他一吃完就借口离开了。 ❑ *Mr. Gould was given a standing ovation and loud cheers when he finished his speech.* 古尔德先生结束他的演讲时观众起立为他鼓掌并大声欢呼。 ● PHRASAL VERB **Finish up** means the same as **finish**. 结束 [AM] ❑ *We waited a few minutes outside his office while he finished up his meeting.* 我们在他办公室外面等了几分钟，这时他结束了他的会议。 2 V-T When you **finish** something that you are making or producing, you reach the end of making or producing it, so that it is complete. 完成 ❑ *The consultants had been working to finish a report this week.* 顾问们一直在争取于本周完成一份报告。 ● PHRASAL VERB **Finish off** and **finish up** mean the same as **finish**. 完成 ❑ *Now she is busy finishing off a biography of Queen Caroline.* 现在她正忙于完成卡罗琳女王的传记。 3 V-T/V-I When something such as a course, show, or sale **finishes**, especially at a planned time, it ends. (尤指按计划) 结束 ❑ *The teaching day finishes at around 4 p.m.* 教学日在下午4点左右结束。 4 V-T/V-I You say that someone or something **finishes** a period of time or an event in a particular way to indicate what the final situation was like. You can also say that a period of time or an event **finishes** in a particular way. (以某种方式) 结束 ❑ *The two of them finished by kissing each other goodbye.* 他们两人以互相吻别结束。 ❑ *The evening finished with the welcoming of three new members.* 这个晚会以欢迎3位新成员结束。 5 V-I If someone **finishes** second, for example, in a race or competition, they are in second place at the end of the race or competition. 最后得到 (比赛名次) ❑ *He finished second in the championship four years in a row.* 他连续4年获得锦标赛亚军。 6 V-I To **finish** means to reach the end of saying something. 说完 ❑ *Her eyes flashed, but he held up a hand. "Let me finish."* 她的眼睛一闪，但是他举起一只手说："让我说完。" 7 N-SING **The finish** of something is the end of it or the last part of it. 结尾；最后部分 ["the" N, with poss] ❑ *I intend to continue it and see the job through to the finish.* 我打算继续做下去，帮助把这项工作做到最后。 8 N-COUNT The **finish** of a race is the end of it. (比赛的) 最后阶段 ❑ *Win a trip to see the finish of the Tour de France!* 赢取一次去看环法自行车赛最后阶段比赛的旅行吧！ 9 N-COUNT If the surface of something that has been made has a particular kind of **finish**, it has the appearance or texture mentioned. (物体表面的) 抛光；修饰 ❑ *The finish and workmanship of the woodwork were excellent.* 这件木制品的抛光和做工都是极好的。 10 → see also **finished** 11 PHRASE If you add **the finishing touches** to something, you add or do the last things that are necessary to complete it. (完成某事前所必需的) 最后修饰 ❑ *Right up until the last minute, workers were still putting the finishing touches on the pavilions.* 直到最后一刻，工人们还在给那些亭子作最后的修饰。

▸ **finish off** 1 PHRASAL VERB If you **finish off** something that you have been eating or drinking, you eat or drink the last part of it with the result that there is none left. 吃光；喝光 ❑ *Kelly finished off his coffee.* 凯利喝光了他的咖啡。 2 PHRASAL VERB If someone **finishes off** a person or thing that is already badly injured or damaged, they kill or destroy them. 杀死 (已严重受伤的人)；毁灭 (已严重受损的物) ❑ *They meant to finish her off, swiftly and without mercy.* 他们打算毫不留情地迅速杀死她。 3 → see also **finish 2**

▸ **finish up** 1 PHRASAL VERB If you **finish up** something that you have been eating or drinking, you eat or drink the last part of it. 吃完；喝完 ❑ *Finish up your drinks now, please.* 请现在把你的饮料喝完。 2 → see also **finish 1, 2**

▸ **finish with** PHRASAL VERB If you **finish with** someone or something, you stop dealing with them or being involved with them. 与…断绝关系 ❑ *My boyfriend was threatening to finish with me.* 我的男朋友威胁说要跟我断绝关系。

Thesaurus *finish* 另参见:
V. conclude, end, wrap up; *(ant.)* begin, start 1 2

Word Partnership *finish* 的常用搭配:
N. finish **a conversation**, finish **school**, finish **work** 1
finish **a job**, **time to** finish 1 2
finish **line** 8
ADV. finish **first**, finish **last** 5

fin·ished /fɪnɪʃt/ 1 ADJ Someone who is **finished with** something is no longer doing it or dealing with it or is no longer interested in it. 不再做某事的；对某事不再感兴趣的 [v-link ADJ "with" n] ❑ *One suspects he will be finished with boxing.* 有人猜想他将对拳击不再感兴趣了。 2 ADJ Something that is **finished** no longer exists or is no longer happening. 不再存在的；不再发生的 [v-link ADJ] ❑ *After each game is finished, a message flashes on the screen.* 每场比赛结束以后，一条信息就会闪现在屏幕上。 3 ADJ Someone or something that is **finished** is no longer important, powerful, or effective. 失势的；失效的 [v-link ADJ] ❑ *Her power over me is finished.* 她对我的控制失效了。

★ **fi·nite** /faɪnaɪt/ ADJ Something that is **finite** has a definite fixed size or extent. 有限的 [FORMAL] ❑ *...a finite set of elements.* …有限的一组元素。 ❑ *Only a finite number of situations can arise.* 只有有限的几种情况可能会出现。

fir /fɜr/ (**firs**) N-VAR A **fir** or a **fir tree** is a tall evergreen tree that has thin needle-like leaves. 枞树；冷杉

fire
1 BURNING, HEAT, OR ENTHUSIASM
2 SHOOTING OR ATTACKING
3 DISMISSAL

1 **fire** ♦♦◇ /faɪər/ (**fires, firing, fired**)
➪ **Please look at meanings 11 – 13 to see if the expression you are looking for is shown under another headword.** 1 N-UNCOUNT **Fire** is the hot, bright flames produced by things that are burning. 火 ❑ *They saw a big flash and a huge ball of fire reaching hundreds of feet into the sky.* 他们看到一道强光和一个巨大的火球直冲天空达几百英尺。 2 N-VAR **Fire** or **a fire** is an occurrence of uncontrolled burning which destroys buildings, forests, or other things. 火灾 ❑ *87 people died in a fire at the Happy Land Social Club.* 87人死于乐土社交俱乐部的火灾中。 ❑ *A forest fire is sweeping across portions of north Maine this evening.* 今天傍晚一场森林大火正席卷着缅因州北部的部分地区。 3 N-COUNT A **fire** is a burning pile of wood, coal, or other fuel that you make, for example, to use for heat, light, or cooking. 炉火 ❑ *There was a fire in the grate.* 壁炉里烧着火。 4 N-COUNT A **fire** is a

Word Web fire

A single **match**, a campfire, or even a bolt of lightning can **spark** a **wildfire**. Wildfires race across grasslands and **burn down** forests. Huge firestorms can **burn** out of control for days. They cause death and destruction. However, some ecosystems depend on fire. Once the fire passes, the **smoke** clears, the **smoldering embers** cool, and the **ash** settles. Then the cycle of life begins again. Humans have learned to use fire. The **heat** cooks our food. People build fires in **fireplaces** and **wood** stoves. The **flames** warm our hands. And before electricity, the **glow** of candlelight lit our homes.

device that uses electricity or gas to give out heat and warm a room. 电炉；煤气炉 [BRIT]

in AM, use **heater**

5 V-T When a pot or clay object **is fired**, it is heated at a high temperature in a special oven, as part of the process of making it. 烧制 ❑ *After the pot is dipped in this mixture, it is fired.* 这个壶在混合料里浸过之后，就进行烧制。 6 V-I When the engine of a motor vehicle **fires**, an electrical spark is produced which causes the fuel to burn and the engine to work. (引擎等) 点火 ❑ *The engine fired and we moved off.* 引擎点火后我们就开走了。 7 V-T If you **fire** someone **with** enthusiasm, you make them feel very enthusiastic. If you **fire** someone's imagination, you make them feel interested and excited. 激发 ❑ *...the potential to fire the imagination of an entire generation.* …激发整整一代人的想像力的潜能。 ❑ *It was Allen who fired this rivalry with real passion.* 是艾伦满怀激情地激发了这次对抗。 8 PHRASE If an object or substance **catches fire**, it starts burning. 起火 ❑ *The blast caused several buildings to catch fire.* 爆炸导致了几个建筑物起火。 9 PHRASE If something is **on fire**, it is burning and being damaged or destroyed by an uncontrolled fire. 着火；在燃烧 ❑ *The captain radioed that the ship was on fire.* 船长发无线电报说船着火了。 10 PHRASE If you **set fire to** something or if you **set it on fire**, you start it burning in order to damage or destroy it. 放火烧 ❑ *They set fire to vehicles outside that building.* 他们放火烧了那幢楼外的车辆。 11 **to have irons on the fire** → see **iron** 12 **like a house on fire** → see **house** 13 **there's no smoke without fire** → see **smoke**

→ see **pottery**

→ see Word Web: **fire**

▸ **fire up** 1 PHRASAL VERB If you **fire up** a machine, you switch it on. 发动 (机器等) ❑ *Fire up your engine and head out.* 发动你的引擎，开出去。 2 PHRASAL VERB If you **fire** someone **up**, you make them feel very enthusiastic or motivated. 激励；鼓舞 ❑ *The president knows his task is to fire up the delegates.* 这位主席知道自己的任务就是激励代表们。

❷ **fire** ♦♦◇ /faɪər/ (**fires, firing, fired**) 1 V-T/V-I If someone **fires** a gun or a bullet, or if they **fire**, a bullet is sent from a gun that they are using. 开 (枪)；(枪) 开火 ❑ *Seven people were wounded when soldiers fired rubber bullets to disperse crowds.* 有7人在士兵们发射橡皮子弹驱散人群时受了伤。 ● **fir·ing** N-UNCOUNT 射击 ❑ *The firing continued even while the protestors were fleeing.* 即使在抗议者逃离时，枪击仍在继续。 2 V-T If you **fire** an arrow, you send it from a bow. 射 (箭) ❑ *He fired an arrow into a clearing in the forest.* 他把箭射进森林中的一片空地。 3 V-T If you **fire** questions at someone, you ask them a lot of questions very quickly, one after another. 连珠炮似地提出 (问题) ❑ *They were bombarded by more than 100 representatives firing questions on pollution.* 他们遭到了一百多位代表就污染问题连珠炮似的发问。 4 N-UNCOUNT You can use **fire** to refer to the shots fired from a gun or guns. 枪击；炮火 ❑ *His car was raked with fire from automatic weapons.* 他的汽车遭到了自动武器炮火的扫射。 5 PHRASE If someone **holds** their **fire** or **holds fire**, they stop shooting or they wait before they start shooting. 停止射击；等待射击 ❑ *Devereux ordered his men to hold their fire until the ships got closer.* 德弗罗命令他的士兵等船驶近了再开火。 6 PHRASE If you are in the **line of fire**, you are in a position where someone is aiming their gun at you. If you move into their **line of fire**, you move into a position between them and the thing they were aiming at. (枪炮的) 发射线 ❑ *He cheerfully blows away any bad guy stupid enough to get in his line of fire.* 他兴高采烈地将那些蠢得跑进他发射线内的任何坏蛋炸死。 7 PHRASE If you **open fire on** someone, you start shooting at them. 开火 ❑ *Then without warning, the troops opened fire on the crowd.* 接着，在没有警告的情况下，军队向人群开了火。 8 PHRASE If you **return fire** or you **return** someone's **fire**, you shoot back at someone who has shot at you. 还击 ❑ *The soldiers returned fire after being attacked.* 士兵们在受到攻击之后进行了还击。 9 PHRASE If you come **under fire** or are **under fire**, someone starts shooting at you. 遭到炮火袭击 ❑ *The Belgians fell back as the infantry came under fire.* 比利时人在步兵部队遭到炮火袭击时撤退了。 10 PHRASE If you come **under fire from** someone or are **under fire**, they criticize you strongly. 受到严厉批评 ❑ *The president's plan first came under fire from critics who said he hadn't included enough spending cuts.* 总统的计划首先受到了反对者们的猛烈抨击，他们说他没有把足够的费用削减包含在内。

❸ **fire** /faɪər/ (**fires, firing, fired**) V-T If an employer **fires** you, they dismiss you from your job. 解雇 ❑ *If he hadn't been so good at the rest of his job, I probably would have fired him.* 如果他不是在工作的其他方面做得这么好，我可能已经把他解雇了。 ● **fir·ing** N-COUNT 解雇 ❑ *There was yet another round of firings.* 还有另一轮的解雇。

fire alarm (**fire alarms**) N-COUNT A **fire alarm** is a device that makes a noise, for example, with a bell, to warn people when there is a fire. 火警报警器 ❑ *The smoke sets off the fire alarm.* 烟雾触发了火警报警器。

fire·arm /faɪərɑrm/ (**firearms**) N-COUNT **Firearms** are guns. 枪；炮 [FORMAL] ❑ *He was also charged with illegal possession of firearms.* 他还被控告非法拥有枪支。

→ see **war**

fire de·part·ment (**fire departments**) N-COUNT-COLL **The fire department** is an organization which has the job of putting out fires. 消防部门 [usu "the" N] [AM]

fire en·gine (**fire engines**) N-COUNT A **fire engine** is a large vehicle which carries firefighters and equipment for putting out fires. 消防车

fire es·cape (**fire escapes**) also **fire-escape** N-COUNT A **fire escape** is a metal staircase on the outside of a building, which can be used to escape from the building if there is a fire. 太平梯

fire ex·tin·guish·er (**fire extinguishers**) also **fire-extinguisher** N-COUNT A **fire extinguisher** is a metal cylinder which contains water or chemicals at high pressure which can put out fires. 灭火器

fire·fighter /faɪərfaɪtər/ (**firefighters**) N-COUNT **Firefighters** are people whose job is to put out fires. 消防员 [usu pl]

fire·man /faɪərmən/ (**firemen**) N-COUNT A **fireman** is a person, usually a man, whose job is to put out fires. 消防员

▲ **fire·place** /faɪərpleɪs/ (**fireplaces**) N-COUNT In a room, the **fireplace** is the place where a fire can be lit and the area on the wall and floor surrounding this place. 壁炉 ❑ *In the evenings, we gathered around the fireplace and talked in hushed whispers.* 晚上，我们聚集在壁炉周围轻声交谈。

→ see **fire**

fire·power /faɪərpaʊər/ N-UNCOUNT The **firepower** of an army, ship, tank, or aircraft is the amount of ammunition it can fire. 火力 ❑ *The U.S. also had superior firepower.* 美国还有更胜一筹的火力。

fire truck (**fire trucks**) N-COUNT A **fire truck** is a large vehicle which carries firefighters and equipment for putting out fires. 消防车 [mainly AM, AUSTRALIAN]

fire·wall /faɪərwɔl/ (**firewalls**) N-COUNT A **firewall** is a computer system or program that automatically prevents an unauthorized person from gaining access to a computer when it is connected to a network such as the Internet. (网络) 防火墙 [COMPUTING] ❑ *New technology should provide a secure firewall against hackers.* 新技术应该提供一个安全的防火墙以防御黑客。

→ see **Internet**

fire·wood /faɪərwʊd/ N-UNCOUNT **Firewood** is wood that has been cut into pieces so that it can be burned on a fire. 木柴 ❑ *Young Geoffrey made money by chopping and selling firewood.* 年轻的杰弗里靠砍柴卖柴挣钱。

Word Web fireworks

Fireworks originated in China over a thousand years ago. Historians believe that the discovery was made by alchemists who were looking for the elixir of life. They heated **sulfur,** potassium **nitrate, charcoal,** and arsenic together and the mixture **exploded.** It produced an extremely hot, bright fire. Later they mixed these **chemicals** in a hollow bamboo tube and threw it in the fire. Thus the firecracker was born. Marco Polo brought firecrackers to Europe from the Orient in 1292. Soon the Italians began experimenting with ways of producing elaborate, colorful fireworks displays. This launched the era of modern pyrotechnics.

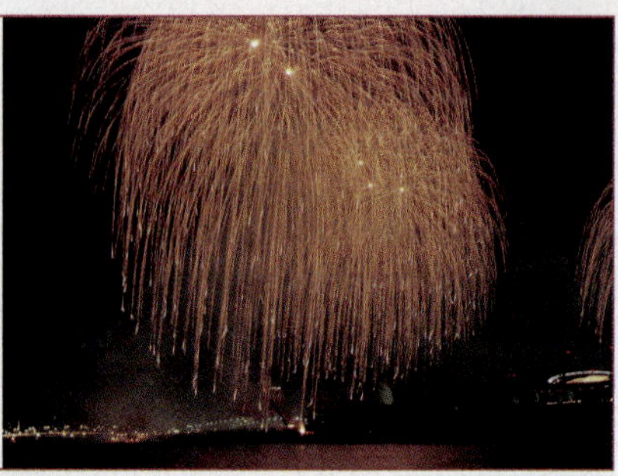

F

▲ **fire·work** /faɪərwɜrk/ (**fireworks**) N-COUNT **Fireworks** are small objects that are lit to entertain people on special occasions. They contain chemicals and burn brightly or attractively, often with a loud noise, when you light them. 烟花 ❑ *They drank champagne, set off fireworks and tooted their car horns.* 他们喝香槟、放烟花，还按他们的车喇叭。

→ see Word Web: **fireworks**

firm ♦♦♦ /fɜrm/ (**firms, firmer, firmest**) **1** N-COUNT A **firm** is an organization which sells or produces something or which provides a service which people pay for. 公司 ❑ *The firm's employees were expecting large bonuses.* 这家公司的雇员们正期待着大笔的奖金。❑ *...a legal assistant at a Chicago law firm.* …一家芝加哥律师事务所的一名法律助理。 **2** ADJ If something is **firm**, it does not change much in shape when it is pressed but is not completely hard. 结实的 ❑ *Fruit should be firm and in excellent condition.* 水果应该硬实且完好无损。 **3** ADJ If someone's grip is **firm** or if they perform a physical action in a **firm** way, they do it with quite a lot of force or pressure but also in a controlled way. 强有力的 ❑ *The quick handshake was firm and cool.* 那次迅速的握手有力而冷静。 ● **firm·ly** ADV 强有力地 [ADV after v] ❑ *She held me firmly by the elbow and led me to my aisle seat.* 她使劲抓着我的胳膊肘，把我领到靠过道的座位上。 **4** ADJ If you describe someone as **firm**, you mean they behave in a way that shows that they are not going to change their mind, or that they are the person who is in control. 坚定的 ❑ *She had to be firm with him. "I don't want to see you again."* 她不得不坚定地对他说："我再也不想见到你。" ● **firm·ly** ADV 坚定地 [ADV with v] ❑ *"A good night's sleep is what you want," he said firmly.* "好好睡上一晚才是你需要的，"他坚定地说。 **5** ADJ A **firm** decision or opinion is definite and unlikely to change. 确定的 ❑ *He made a firm decision to leave Fort Multry by boat.* 他作出了明确的决定，要乘船离开穆尔特里堡。 ● **firm·ly** ADV 确定地 ❑ *Political values and opinions are firmly held, and can be slow to change.* 政治价值观和主张是根深蒂固的，要改变可能会很慢。 **6** ADJ **Firm** evidence or information is based on facts and so is likely to be true. 确凿的；确切的 [ADJ n] ❑ *This man may have killed others but unfortunately we have no firm evidence.* 这名男子可能还杀过别的人，只可惜我们没有确凿的证据。 **7** ADJ You use **firm** to describe control or a basis or position when it is strong and unlikely to be ended or removed. (控制) 牢固的；(根基等) 稳固的 ❑ *Although the Yakutians are a minority, they have firm control of the territory.* 虽然雅库特人是少数，但他们却牢牢地控制着这个地区。 ● **firm·ly** ADV 牢固地；稳固地 ❑ *This tradition is also firmly rooted in the past.* 这个传统也牢固地植根于过去。 **8** ADJ If something is **firm**, it does not shake or move when you put weight or pressure on it, because it is strongly made or securely fastened. 稳固的 ❑ *If you have to climb up, use a firm platform or a sturdy ladder.* 如果你必须爬上去，就用一个稳固的平台或者一个结实的梯子。 ● **firm·ly** ADV 稳固地 ❑ *The front door is locked and all the windows are firmly shut.* 前门被锁，所有的窗户都关得牢牢地。 **9** PHRASE If someone **stands firm**, they refuse to change their mind about something. 立场坚定 ❑ *The council is standing firm against the protest.* 市政会对抗议毫不让步。

▸ **firm up** **1** PHRASAL VERB If you **firm up** something or if it **firms up**, it becomes firmer and more solid. 使变结实；变结实 ❑ *This treatment helps tone the body, firm up muscles and tighten the skin.* 这种治疗可以帮助保持体态，使肌肉变结实、皮肤紧致。 **2** PHRASAL VERB If you **firm** something **up** or if it **firms up**, it becomes clearer, stronger, or more definite. 使变明确；变明确 ❑ *We can give you more detail as our plans firm up.* 等我们的计划明确时，我们可以给你更多细节。

Thesaurus *firm* 另参见：

N. business, company, enterprise, organization **1**
ADJ. dense, hard, sturdy, unyielding; *(ant.)* yielding **2**

first ♦♦♦ /fɜrst/ **1** ORD The **first** thing, person, event, or period of time is the one that happens or comes before all the others of the same kind. 第一(个) 的 ❑ *She lost 16 pounds in the first month of her diet.* 她节食的第一个月减掉了16磅。❑ *...the first few flakes of snow.* …最初的几片雪花。 ● PRON **First** is also a pronoun. 第一(个) ❑ *The second paragraph startled me even more than the first.* 第二段甚至比第一段更让我吃惊。 **2** ORD When something happens or is done for the **first** time, it has never happened or been done before. 第一次的 ❑ *This is the first time she has experienced disappointment.* 这是她第一次感受到失望。 ● ADV **First** is also an adverb. 第一次 [ADV with v] ❑ *Anne and Steve got engaged two years after they had first started going out.* 安妮和史蒂夫在他们第一次约会的两年后订婚。 **3** ORD The **first** thing, person, or place in a line is the one that is nearest to you or nearest to the front. (列队中) 最前面的；(距离自己) 最近的 ❑ *Before him, in the first row, sat the president.* 在他前面第一排坐着总统。 **4** ORD You use **first** to refer to the best or most important thing or person of a particular kind. 最好的；首要的 ❑ *The first duty of any government must be to protect the interests of the taxpayers.* 任何政府的首要职责都必须是保护纳税人的利益。 **5** ADV If you do something **first**, you do it before anyone else does, or before you do anything else. 首先 ❑ *I do not remember who spoke first, but we all expressed the same opinion.* 我不记得谁先发了言，但是我们都表达了同样的观点。❑ *First, tell me what you think of my products.* 首先，告诉我你对我的产品有什么看法。 **6** ADV You use **first** when you are talking about what happens in the early part of an event or experience, in contrast to what happens later. 最初 [ADV before v] ❑ *When he first came home he wouldn't say anything about what he'd been doing.* 刚回到家时，他对自己一直在做的事只字也不愿提。 ● ORD **First** is also an ordinal. 第一 ❑ *She told him that her first reaction was disgust.* 她告诉他她的第一反应是厌恶。 **7** ADV In order to emphasize your determination not to do a particular thing, you can say that rather than do it, you would do something else **first**. 宁愿 [ADV after v] [EMPHASIS] ❑ *I'll die first, before I let you have all my money!* 我宁愿死，也不会让你得到我所有的钱！ **8** N-SING An event that is described as **a first** has never happened before and is important or exciting. 首次发生的事 ❑ *It is a first for New York. An outdoor exhibition of Fernando Botero's sculpture on Park Avenue.* 在公园大道上举办费尔南多·博特罗的雕塑户外展览，这在纽约可是第一次！ **9** PRON **The first** you hear of something or **the first** you know about it is the time when you first become aware of it. 第一次 ["the" PRON that] ❑ *We heard it on the TV last night – that was the first we heard of it.* 我们是昨晚从电视上听到的——那是我们第一次听到这件事。 **10** PHRASE You use **first of all** to introduce the first of a number of things that you want to say. 首先；第一 ❑ *The cut in the interest rates has not had very much impact in California for two reasons. First of all, banks are still afraid to loan.* 降低利率在加利福尼亚州没造成很大影响的原因有二。第一，银行仍然害怕放贷。 **11** PHRASE You use **at first** when you are talking about what happens in the early stages of an event or experience, or just after something else has happened, in contrast to what happens later. 起初 ❑ *At first, he seemed surprised by my questions.* 起初，他似乎对我的问题感到意外。 **12** PHRASE If you say that someone or something **comes first** for a particular person, you mean they treat or consider that person or thing as more important than anything else. 居于首要地位 ❑ *There's no time for boyfriends, my career comes first.* 我没有时间交男朋友，我的事业是第一位的。 **13** PHRASE If you learn or experience something **at first**

hand, you experience it yourself or learn it directly rather than being told about it by other people. 亲自地；直接地 ❑ *He arrived in Natal to see at first hand the effects of the recent heavy fighting.* 他到纳塔尔亲自察看最近的激战所造成的影响。 **14** PHRASE If you say that you **do not know the first thing about** something, you are emphasizing that you know absolutely nothing about it. 对某事一无所知 [EMPHASIS] ❑ *You don't know the first thing about farming.* 你对耕种一无所知。 **15** PHRASE If you **put** someone or something **first**, you treat or consider them as more important than anything else. 把某人或某事放在首要地位 ❑ *Somebody has to think for the child and put him first.* 得有人替这个孩子着想，把他放在第一位。 **16** **first and foremost** → see **foremost**

first aid N-UNCOUNT **First aid** is simple medical treatment given as soon as possible to a person who is injured or who suddenly becomes ill. 急救 ❑ *There are many emergencies which need prompt first aid treatment.* 有很多紧急情况需要迅速的急救治疗。

first-class also **first class** **1** ADJ If you describe something or someone as **first-class**, you mean that they are extremely good and of the highest quality. 一流的 ❑ *The food was first-class.* 这些食物是一流的。 **2** ADJ You use **first-class** to describe something that is in the group that is considered to be of the highest standard. 优等的 [ADJ n] ❑ *They always stayed in first-class hotels.* 他们总是下榻于最高级的宾馆。 **3** ADJ **First-class** accommodations on a train, airplane, or ship are the best and most expensive type of accommodations. (车厢、机舱、船舱座位) 头等的 [ADJ n] ❑ *He won himself two first-class tickets to fly to Dublin.* 他为自己赢得了两张飞往都柏林的头等舱机票。 ● ADV **First-class** is also an adverb. 坐头等车厢；坐头等舱 [ADV after v] ❑ *She had never flown first class before.* 她以前从未坐过飞机的头等舱。 ● N-UNCOUNT **First-class** is the first-class accommodations on a train, airplane, or ship. 头等车厢；头等舱 ❑ *He paid for and was assigned a cabin in first class.* 他付了钱，被安排到了头等舱。 **4** ADJ In the United States, **first-class** postage is the type of postage that is used for sending letters and postcards. 投送第一类邮件的 (邮资) [ADJ n] ❑ *Two first-class stamps, please.* 请拿两张第一类邮件的邮票。

first floor (first floors) **1** N-COUNT **The first floor** of a building is the one at ground level. 一楼 [AM] **2** N-COUNT **The first floor** of a building is the floor immediately above the one at ground level. 二楼 [BRIT]

in AM, use **second floor**

first hand also **first-hand, firsthand** **1** ADJ **First hand** information or experience is gained or learned directly, rather than from other people or from books. 直接的；第一手的 [ADJ n] ❑ *School trips give children firsthand experience not available in the classroom.* 学校组织的旅行可以给孩子们提供教室里学不到的亲身体验。 ● ADV **First-hand** is also an adverb. 直接地；第一手地 [ADV after v] ❑ *We've been through Germany and seen first-hand what's happening there.* 我们曾走遍德国，亲眼目睹了那里发生的事。 **2** **at first hand** → see **first**

first·ly /fɜrstli/ ADV You use **firstly** in speech or writing when you want to give a reason, make a point, or mention an item that will be followed by others connected with it. 第一 (演讲、文章中用于列举条目)；首先 [ADV with cl/group] ❑ *The program is now seven years behind schedule as a result, firstly of increased costs, then of technical problems.* 该计划现在比预定的计划晚了7年，首先是因为费用增加，其次是由于技术问题。

first name (first names) N-COUNT Your **first name** is the first of the names that were given to you when you were born. 名 ❑ *Her first name was Mary. I don't know what her surname was.* 她的名字叫玛丽，我不知道她的姓是什么。

first-rate also **first rate** ADJ If you say that something or someone is **first-rate**, you mean that they are extremely good and of the highest quality. 第一流的 [APPROVAL] ❑ *People who used his service knew they were dealing with a first-rate professional.* 享受过他服务的人们都知道他们是在与一位一流的专家打交道。

▲ **fis·cal** ♦◇◇ /fɪskᵊl/ ADJ **Fiscal** is used to describe something that relates to government money or public money, especially taxes. 财政的 [ADJ n] ❑ *...in 1987, when the government tightened fiscal policy.* …1987年，当该政府紧缩财政政策时。

fis·cal year (fiscal years) N-COUNT A **fiscal year** is a period of twelve months, used by government, business, and other organizations in order to calculate their budgets, profits, and losses. 财政年度 [BUSINESS] ❑ *...the budget for the coming fiscal year.* …下一个财政年度的预算。

fish ♦♦◇ /fɪʃ/ (fish or fishes, fishes, fishing, fished)

The form **fish** is usually used for the plural, but **fishes** can also be used.

1 N-COUNT A **fish** is a creature that lives in water and has a tail and fins. There are many different kinds of fish. 鱼 ❑ *An expert angler was casting his line and catching a fish every time.* 一名垂钓高手每次抛出鱼线都能钓到一条鱼。 **2** N-UNCOUNT **Fish** is the flesh of a fish eaten as food. 鱼肉 ❑ *Does dry white wine go best with fish?* 干白葡萄酒和鱼肉是最佳搭配吗？ **3** V-I If you **fish**, you try to catch fish, either for food or as a form of sport or recreation. 钓鱼 ❑ *Brian remembers learning to fish in the Colorado River.* 布莱恩记得在科罗拉多河学过钓鱼。 **4** V-I If you say that someone is **fishing for** information or praise, you disapprove of the fact that they are trying to get it from someone in an indirect way. 拐弯抹角地获取 [DISAPPROVAL] ❑ *He didn't want to create the impression that he was fishing for information.* 他不想给人留下拐弯抹角打探消息的印象。
5 → see also **fishing**
→ see Word Web: **fish**
→ see **pet, shark**

fisher·man /fɪʃərmən/ (fishermen) N-COUNT A **fisherman** is a person who catches fish as a job or for sport. 渔民；垂钓者 ❑ *The Algarve is a paradise for fishermen whether river anglers or deep-sea fishermen.* 阿尔加维对河边的垂钓者或深海的渔民都是一个天堂。

Word Link *ery ≈ place where something happens : bakery, fishery, refinery*

fish·ery /fɪʃəri/ (fisheries) **1** N-COUNT **Fisheries** are areas of the sea where fish are caught in large quantities for commercial purposes. 渔场 ❑ *...the fisheries off Newfoundland.* …纽芬兰附近的那些渔场。 **2** N-COUNT A **fishery** is a place where fish are bred and reared. 养鱼场

fish·ing ♦◇◇ /fɪʃɪŋ/ N-UNCOUNT **Fishing** is the sport, hobby, or business of catching fish. 钓鱼；捕鱼 ❑ *Despite the poor weather the fishing has been pretty good.* 尽管天气不好，捕鱼却一直收获颇丰。

fist /fɪst/ (fists) N-COUNT Your hand is referred to as your **fist** when you have bent your fingers in toward the palm in order to

Word Web fish

Commercial **fishing** has become very efficient. Fishing **trawlers** pull huge **nets** behind them and harvest thousands of fish at once. Some boats **trawl** with hundreds of meters of **fishing line** and **hooks**. Overfishing is a major problem for many countries. Some popular species of fish are disappearing from **fishing grounds**. Each year there is a smaller supply of **cod** and **sole**. So companies are changing the names of some fish to make them sound more appetizing. For example, "slimehead" is now "orange roughy." Hawaiian "dolphin fish" is now "mahi mahi." No one wants to eat a dolphin.

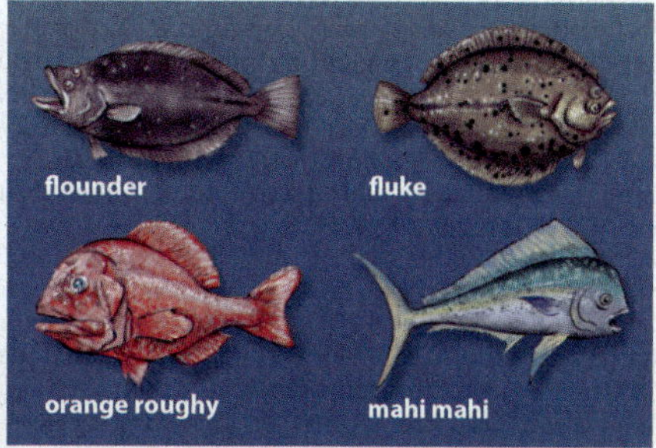

hit someone, to make an angry gesture, or to hold something. 拳头 ❑ *Angry protestors with clenched fists shouted their defiance.* 愤怒的抗议者们紧握拳头高声抗议。

fit
❶ BEING RIGHT OR GOING IN THE RIGHT PLACE
❷ HEALTHY
❸ UNCONTROLLABLE MOVEMENTS OR EMOTIONS

❶ **fit** ♦♦◇ /fɪt/ (**fits, fitting, fitted** or **fit**)
➪ **Please look at meanings 14 – 16 to see if the expression you are looking for is shown under another headword.** 1 V-T/V-I If something **fits**, it is the right size and shape to go onto a person's body or onto a particular object. 合身; 合适 ❑ *The sash, kimono, and other garments were made to fit a child.* 腰带、和服和其他衣服都做得适合孩子穿。 ❑ *She has to go to the men's department to find trousers that fit at the waist.* 她得去男装部才能找到腰围合适的裤子。

You do not use the verb **fit** to say that something looks attractive on a person or in a place. The verb you need is **suit**. ❑ *It is really feminine and pretty and it certainly suits you.* You use the verb **fit** to say that clothes are the right size for you. ❑ *The size 12 gown is gorgeous and fits perfectly... The gloves didn't fit.* You cannot usually say that one color, pattern, or object **suits** another. The verb you need is **match**. ❑ *She wears a straw hat with a yellow ribbon to match her yellow cotton dress... His clothes don't quite match.*

2 V-T If you **are fitted for** a particular piece of clothing, you try it on so that the person who is making it can see where it needs to be altered. 试穿 [usu passive] ❑ *She was being fitted for her wedding dress.* 她正在试穿她的结婚礼服。 3 V-I If something **fits** somewhere, it can be put there or is designed to be put there. 合适于(某地) ❑ *...a pocket computer which is small enough to fit into your pocket.* …一台小得足以放进你口袋里的袖珍电脑。 ❑ *He folded his long legs to fit under the table.* 他把腿弯起来伸到桌下。 4 V-T If you **fit** something into a particular space or place, you put it there. 放置 ❑ *...she fitted her key in the lock.* …她把钥匙插进锁孔。 ❑ *Who could cut the millions of stone blocks and fit them together?* 谁能切割这数百万的巨石块并将它们垒在一起呢? 5 V-T If you **fit** something somewhere, you attach it there, or put it there carefully and securely. 安装; 小心放置 ❑ *Fit hinge bolts to give extra support to the door lock.* 装上铰链螺栓，使门锁更牢固。 ❑ *Peter had built the overhead ladders, and the next day he fitted them to the wall.* 彼得已经造好了悬挂梯，第二天他就把它们装在了墙上。 6 V-T/V-I If something **fits** something else or **fits** into it, it goes together well with that thing or is able to be part of it. 相配; 符合 ❑ *Her daughter doesn't fit the current feminine ideal.* 她女儿不符合当今女性的完美典范。 ❑ *Fostering is a full-time job and you should carefully consider how it will fit into your career.* 养育孩子是一份全职工作，你应该仔细考虑如何把它跟你的事业协调起来。 7 V-T You can say that something **fits** a particular person or thing when it is appropriate or suitable for them or it. 适合 ❑ *The punishment must always fit the crime.* 刑罚必须总是适罪行而定。 8 V-T If something **fits** someone for a particular task or role, it makes them good enough or suitable for it. 使某人胜任(任务、角色) [FORMAL] ❑ *...a man whose past experience fits him for the top job in education.* …其过去的经历使之胜任教育界最高职位的一名男子。 9 N-SING If something is a good **fit**, it fits well. 适合 ❑ *Eventually he was happy that the sills and doors were a reasonably good fit.* 最后他高兴了，窗台和门配得相当合适。 10 ADJ If something is **fit** for a particular purpose, it is suitable for that purpose. 适合的 ❑ *Of the seven bicycles we had, only two were fit for the road.* 我们的7辆自行车中只有2辆适合这种路。 11 ADJ If someone is **fit** to do something, they have the appropriate qualities or skills that will allow them to do it. 胜任的 ❑ *You're not fit to be a mother!* 你不配作母亲! ❑ *In a word, this government isn't fit to rule.* 总之，这届政府不胜任统治之任。 ● **fit·ness** N-UNCOUNT 胜任 ❑ *There is a debate about his fitness for the highest office.* 关于他担任最高职务的胜任与否发生了一场争论。 12 PHRASE If you say that someone **sees fit to** do something, you mean that they are entitled to do it, but that you disapprove of their decision to do it. 执意 [FORMAL, DISAPPROVAL] ❑ *He's not a friend, you say, yet you saw fit to lend him money.* 你说他不是你的朋友，你却执意借钱给他。 13 → see also **fitted, fitting** 14 **fit the bill** → see **bill** 15 **to fit like a glove** → see **glove** 16 **not in a fit state** → see **state**

▸ **fit in** 1 PHRASAL VERB If you manage to **fit** a person or task **in**, you manage to find time to deal with them. 安排时间处理 ❑ *We work long hours both outside and inside the home and we rush around trying to fit everything in.* 我们在家在外都长时间地工作，我们到处奔波，尽力安排时间做每一件事。 2 PHRASAL VERB If you **fit in** as part of a group, you seem to belong there because you are similar to the other people in it. 相处融洽 ❑ *She was great with the children and fit in beautifully.* 她对孩子们很有一手，相处得非常融洽。 3 PHRASAL VERB If you say that someone or something **fits in**, you understand how they form part of a particular situation or system. (在某情形、体系中) 发挥作用 ❑ *He knew where I fitted in and what he had to do to get the best out of me.* 他知道我在哪里能发挥作用，以及他怎样做才能发挥我的最佳水平。

▸ **fit out** PHRASAL VERB If you **fit** someone or something **out**, or you **fit** them **up**, you provide them with equipment and other things that they need. 为…提供配备 ❑ *We helped to fit him out for a trip to the Baltic.* 我们帮他准备了去波罗的海旅行所需的物品。 ❑ *I suggest we fit you up with an office suite.* 我建议我们为你配备一间办公套房。

❷ **fit** ♦◇◇ /fɪt/ (**fitter, fittest**) ADJ Someone who is **fit** is healthy and physically strong. 健康的; 强健的 ❑ *An averagely fit person can master easy ski runs within a few days.* 中等健康的人几天内就能驾驭初级的滑雪道。 ● **fit·ness** N-UNCOUNT 健康 ❑ *Squash was once thought to offer all-round fitness.* 壁球曾一度被认为可以提供全面的健康。

❸ **fit** /fɪt/ (**fits**) 1 N-COUNT If you have a **fit of** coughing or laughter, you suddenly start coughing or laughing in an uncontrollable way. 一阵(咳嗽、大笑) ❑ *Halfway down the cigarette she had a fit of coughing.* 烟抽到一半时，她一阵咳嗽。 2 N-COUNT If you do something in a **fit of** anger or panic, you are very angry or afraid when you do it. 一阵(愤怒、恐慌等) ❑ *Pattie shot Tom in a fit of jealous rage.* 帕蒂在一阵嫉妒的愤怒中开枪打了汤姆。 3 N-COUNT If someone has a **fit** they suddenly lose consciousness and their body makes uncontrollable movements. 昏厥; 痉挛 ❑ *About two in every five epileptic fits occur during sleep.* 每5例癫痫昏厥中约有2例是在睡眠中发作的。 4 N-COUNT If someone **has a fit** or **throws a fit**, they suddenly become very agitated because they are angry or worried about something. 大发脾气; 狂躁不安 [INFORMAL] ❑ *When my landlady said she wanted to keep $380 of my deposit to paint the walls, I threw a fit.* 当女房东说她要用我的$380押金来粉刷墙壁时，我大发脾气。 ❑ *"Cathy will have a fit when she finds out you bought all that fishing gear," Harrington said.* "凯茜发现你买了那整套渔具一定会发火的。"哈林顿说。

fit·ted /fɪtɪd/ 1 ADJ A **fitted** piece of clothing is designed so that it is the same size and shape as your body rather than being loose. 合身的; 紧身的 ❑ *...baggy trousers with fitted jackets.* …宽松的裤子配紧身夹克。 2 ADJ A **fitted** sheet has the corners sewn so that they fit over the corners of the mattress and do not have to be folded. (床单)合尺寸的 [ADJ n]
→ see **bed**

★ **fit·ting** /fɪtɪŋ/ (**fittings**) 1 N-COUNT A **fitting** is one of the smaller parts on the outside of a piece of equipment or furniture, for example, a handle or a faucet. (设备、家具等的) 配件 ❑ *...brass light fittings.* …黄铜灯具配件。 ❑ *...industrial fittings for kitchen and bathroom.* …工业化生产的厨卫配件。 2 N-COUNT If someone has a **fitting**, they try on a piece of clothing that is being made for them to see if it fits. 试穿 ❑ *She lunched and shopped and went for fittings for clothes she didn't need.* 她吃过午饭就去购物，还试穿那些她根本不需要的衣服。 3 N-PLURAL **Fittings** are things such as ovens or heaters, that are fitted inside a building, but can be removed if necessary. 可拆除装置(如烤炉、暖器等) ❑ *...a detailed list of what fixtures and fittings are included in the purchase price.* …哪些固定装置和可拆除装置包含在购价中的一份详细清单。 4 ADJ Something that is **fitting** is right or suitable. 恰当的; 合适的 ❑ *A solitary man, it was perhaps fitting that he should have died alone.* 他是个独居的人，或许他本应该孤独地死去才合适。 ● **fit·ting·ly** ADV 恰当地; 合适地 ❑ *He closed out his career, fittingly, by hitting a home run.* 他以一记本垒打恰当地结束了自己的棒球生涯。

five ♦♦♦ /faɪv/ (**fives**) NUM **Five** is the number 5. 5 ❑ *I spent five years there and had a really good time.* 我在那里呆了5年，过得很愉快。

fiv·er /faɪvər/ (**fivers**) N-COUNT A **fiver** is a five dollar bill. 5美元钞票 [INFORMAL]

fix ♦◇◇ /fɪks/ (**fixes, fixing, fixed**) 1 V-T If you **fix** something which is damaged or which does not work properly, you repair it. 修理 ❑ *He cannot fix the electricity.* 他不会修理电路。 2 V-T If you **fix** a problem or a bad situation, you deal with it and make it satisfactory. 处理 ❑ *It's not too late to fix the problem, although time is clearly getting short.* 现在处理这个问题还不算太晚，尽管时间明显地变紧了。 **3** V-T If you **fix** some food or a drink for someone, you make it or prepare it for them. 准备（食物、饮料等）❑ *Sarah fixed some food for us.* 萨拉为我们准备了一些食物。 ❑ *Let me fix you a drink.* 让我给你弄一杯饮料吧。 ❑ *Scotty stayed behind to fix lunch.* 司各迪留了下来准备午饭。 **4** V-T If you **fix** your hair, clothes, or makeup, you arrange or adjust them so you look neat and tidy, showing you have taken care with your appearance. 整理 [no passive] [INFORMAL] ❑ *"I've got to fix my hair," I said and retreated to my bedroom.* "我得整理一下头发，"我说着便回到了我的卧室。 **5** V-T If you **fix** something, for example, a date, price, or policy, you decide and say exactly what it will be. 确定 ❑ *He's going to fix a time when I can see him.* 他将确定一个我可以见他的时间。 ❑ *The date of the election was fixed.* 选举的日期定下来了。 **6** V-T If you **fix** something for someone, you arrange for it to happen or you organize it for them. 安排 ❑ *I've fixed it for you to see Bonnie Lachlan.* 我已经给你安排了去见邦尼·拉克伦。 ❑ *It's fixed. He's going to meet us at the airport.* 已经安排好了，他将去机场接我们。 ❑ *He vanished after you fixed him with a job.* 你给他安排了一个工作后他就消失了。 **7** V-T If something **is fixed** somewhere, it is attached there firmly or securely. 固定 ❑ *It is fixed on the wall.* 它是固定在墙上的。 ❑ *Most blinds can be fixed directly to the top of the window-frame.* 大多数百叶窗可以直接固定在窗框的顶端。 **8** V-T/V-I If you **fix** your eyes **on** someone or something or if your eyes **fix on** them, you look at them with complete attention. 凝视 ❑ *She fixes her steel-blue eyes on an unsuspecting local official.* 她用那双铁青色的眼睛紧盯着一名毫无猜疑心的地方官员。 ❑ *Her soft brown eyes fixed on Kelly.* 她温柔的棕色眼睛凝视着凯利。 **9** V-T If someone or something **is fixed in** your mind, you remember them well, for example, because they are very important, interesting, or unusual. 牢记 ❑ *Leonard was now fixed in his mind.* 伦纳德现已铭刻在他的心中。 **10** V-T If someone **fixes** a gun, camera, or radar **on** something, they point it at that thing. 瞄准 ❑ *The U.S. crew fixed its radar on the Turkish ship.* 美国船员将雷达对准了那艘土耳其船。 **11** V-T If someone **fixes** a race, election, contest, or other event, they make unfair or illegal arrangements or use deception to affect the result. 用不正当手段操纵（比赛、选举、竞赛等）[DISAPPROVAL] ❑ *They offered opposing players bribes to fix a decisive game.* 他们向对方球员行贿以操纵一场决定性的比赛。 ● N-COUNT **Fix** is also a noun. 不正当的操纵 ❑ *It's all a fix, a deal they've made.* 这完全是一场非法的操纵，是他们作的一笔交易。 **12** V-T If you accuse someone of **fixing** prices, you accuse them of making unfair arrangements to charge a particular price for something, rather than allowing market forces to decide it. 操纵（价格）[BUSINESS, DISAPPROVAL] ❑ *...a suspected cartel that had fixed the price of steel for the construction market.* …一个涉嫌操纵建筑市场钢材价格的卡特尔垄断同盟。 **13** N-COUNT You can refer to a solution to a problem as a **fix**. 解决办法 [INFORMAL] ❑ *Many of those changes could just be a temporary fix.* 那些改变中有很多可能只是暂时的解决方法。 **14** → see also **quick fix** **15** N-SING If you get **a fix on** someone or something, you have a clear idea or understanding of them. 清楚了解 [INFORMAL] ❑ *It's been hard to get a steady fix on what's going on.* 一直很难对正在发生的事情有一个清楚可靠的了解。 **16** → see also **fixed**

→ see **interest rate**

▸ **fix up** **1** PHRASAL VERB If you **fix** something **up**, you do work that is necessary in order to make it more suitable or attractive. 修整 ❑ *I've fixed up Matthew's old room.* 我已经把马修的旧房间修缮好了。 **2** PHRASAL VERB If you **fix** someone **up with** something they need, you provide it for them. 为…准备 ❑ *We'll fix him up with a tie.* 我们会为他准备一条领带。 **3** PHRASAL VERB If you **fix** something **up**, you arrange it. 安排 [BRIT]

Thesaurus *fix* 另参见：

v. adjust, correct, repair, restore **1**
agree on, decide, establish, work out **2** **5**
arrange, plan **5**
fasten, nail, secure **7**

fixed ♦◇◇ /fɪkst/ **1** ADJ You use **fixed** to describe something which stays the same and does not or cannot vary. 固定的 ❑ *They issue a fixed number of shares that trade publicly.* 他们发行了固定数量可公开交易的股票。 ❑ *Many restaurants offer fixed-price menus.* 很多餐馆提供固定价格的菜单。 **2** ADJ If you say that someone has **fixed** ideas or opinions, you mean that they do not often change their ideas and opinions, although perhaps they should. 固执的 ❑ *...people who have fixed ideas about things.* …固执己见的人。 **3** ADJ If someone has a **fixed** smile on their face, they are smiling even though they do not feel happy or pleased. （笑容）僵硬的 ❑ *I had to go through the rest of the evening with a fixed smile on my face.* 我不得不带着一脸僵硬的笑容度过那晚余下的时间。 **4** PHRASE Someone who is of **no fixed address** does not have a permanent place to live. 居无定所的 [FORMAL] ❑ *They are not able to get a job interview because they have no fixed address.* 他们无法获得工作面试的机会，因为他们居无定所。 **5** → see also **fix**

→ see **interest rate**

★ **fix·ture** /fɪkstʃər/ (**fixtures**) N-COUNT **Fixtures** are fittings or furniture which belong to a building and are legally part of it, for example, a bathtub or a toilet. （房屋内如浴缸、马桶等的）固定装置 ❑ *...a detailed list of what fixtures and fittings are included in the purchase price.* …详细列出的室内设施与装备包括在购买价格中。

fizz /fɪz/ (**fizzes, fizzing, fizzed**) V-I If a drink **fizzes**, it produces a lot of little bubbles of gas and makes a sound like a long "s." （饮料）嘶嘶地冒泡 ❑ *After a while their mother was back, holding a tray of glasses that fizzed.* 过了一会儿他们的母亲回来了，端着一托盘嘶嘶冒泡的玻璃杯。 ● N-UNCOUNT **Fizz** is also a noun. 气泡 ❑ *I wonder if there's any fizz left in the lemonade.* 我想知道这柠檬汽水中还有没有气泡。

fizzy /fɪzi/ (**fizzier, fizziest**) ADJ **Fizzy** liquids contain small bubbles of carbon dioxide. They make a sound like a long "s" when you pour them. （饮料等）嘶嘶冒气泡的 ❑ *...fizzy water.* …汽水。

flag ♦◇◇ /flæg/ (**flags, flagging, flagged**) **1** N-COUNT A **flag** is a piece of cloth which can be attached to a pole and which is used as a sign, signal, or symbol of something, especially of a particular country. 旗（尤指国旗）❑ *The Marines climbed to the roof of the embassy building to raise the American flag.* 海军陆战队士兵爬上使馆大楼的楼顶去升美国国旗。 **2** N-COUNT Journalists sometimes refer to the **flag** of a particular country or organization as a way of referring to the country or organization itself and its values or power. 国家或组织（新闻用语）❑ *Every person who serves under the American flag will answer to his or her own superiors and to military law.* 每一个在美军服役的人都必须服从自己的上级和军法。 **3** V-I If you **flag** or if your spirits **flag**, you begin to lose enthusiasm or energy. （热情、精力等）衰退 ❑ *His enthusiasm was in no way flagging.* 他的热情丝毫没有衰退。

→ see Word Web: **flag**

fla·grant /fleɪgrənt/ ADJ You can use **flagrant** to describe an action, situation, or someone's behavior that you find extremely bad or shocking in a very obvious way. 明目张胆的 [ADJ n] [DISAPPROVAL] ❑ *The judge called the decision "a flagrant violation of international law."* 法官称这个决定是"对国际法的公然违反"。

flag·ship /flægʃɪp/ (**flagships**) **1** N-COUNT The **flagship** of a group of things that are owned or produced by a particular organization is the most important one. 王牌产品 ❑ *The company plans to open a flagship store in New York this month.* 该公司计划本月在纽

Word Web **flag**

Flags are **symbols**. Some flags **symbolize** countries. At the Olympics, each group of athletes proudly carries their country's standard. The Olympics even has its own flag. It **flies** at all Olympic games. Flags can also send messages. Most people understand that a white flag means "we **surrender**." Before radios, people used semaphore to communicate between ships. They used different colored flags. They hoisted them in special positions to spell out words. Flags can also signal danger. When people carry long pieces of wood on their cars, they use a red flag to warn other drivers.

约开一家旗舰店。 **2** N-COUNT A **flagship** is the most important ship in a fleet of ships, especially the one on which the commander of the fleet is sailing. 旗舰 [mainly BRIT]

flail /fleɪl/ (**flails, flailing, flailed**) V-T/V-I If your arms or legs **flail** or if you **flail** them about, they wave about in an energetic but uncontrolled way. 用力地胡乱挥动；用力地胡乱摆动 ❑ *His arms were flailing in all directions.* 他的双臂使劲地胡乱挥舞着。 ● PHRASAL VERB **Flail around** means the same as **flail.** 用力地胡乱挥动 ❑ *He started flailing around and hitting Vincent in the chest.* 他开始胡乱挥舞双拳，打到了文森特的胸口。

flair /fleər/ **1** N-SING If you have **a flair for** a particular thing, you have a natural ability to do it well. 天赋 ❑ *...a friend who has a flair for languages.* …一位有语言天赋的朋友。 **2** N-UNCOUNT If you have **flair**, you do things in an original, interesting, and stylish way. 才华 [APPROVAL] ❑ *Their work has all the usual punch, panache and flair you'd expect.* 如你所料，他们的作品像往常一样拥有活力、神韵和才华。

flak /flæk/ N-UNCOUNT If you get a lot of **flak** from someone, they criticize you severely. If you take **flak**, you get the blame for something. 抨击 [INFORMAL] ❑ *The president is getting a lot of flak for that.* 总统因为那件事正在遭受猛烈抨击。

▲ **flake** /fleɪk/ (**flakes, flaking, flaked**) **1** N-COUNT A **flake** is a small thin piece of something, especially one that has broken off a larger piece. 小薄片（尤指碎片）❑ *...flakes of paint.* …油漆碎片。 ❑ *Large flakes of snow began swiftly to fall.* 大片大片的雪花开始飞快地落下。 **2** V-I If something such as paint **flakes**, small thin pieces of it come off. （油漆等）剥落 ❑ *They can see how its colors have faded and where paint has flaked.* 他们可以看到其颜色褪去的情况和油漆剥落的地方。 ● PHRASAL VERB **Flake off** means the same as **flake.** 剥落 ❑ *The surface corrosion was worst where the paint had flaked off.* 油漆已经剥落的地方，表面的腐蚀最严重。 **3** N-COUNT If you refer to someone as a **flake**, you mean that you think they are very unreliable. 不可靠的人 [INFORMAL] ❑ *Sophie turned out to be such a flake. She said she'd meet me here and instead I'm just lying around this hotel room and I'm totally bored.* 索菲原来是这么不可靠。她说过要在这里见我，可现在我只能躺在这间旅馆的房间里，感到百无聊赖。

flam·boy·ant /flæmbɔɪənt/ ADJ If you say that someone or something is **flamboyant**, you mean that they are very noticeable, stylish, and exciting. 耀眼的；派头十足的 ❑ *Freddie Mercury was a flamboyant star of the hard rock scene.* 弗雷迪·默丘里曾是硬摇滚乐舞台上一颗耀眼的明星。 ● **flam·boy·ance** N-UNCOUNT 耀眼；派头十足 ❑ *Campese was his usual mixture of flamboyance and flair.* 坎皮斯仍像平时那样，既有派，又有才。

Word Link	*flam ≈ burning : **flame**, **flam**mable, in**flame***

flame /fleɪm/ (**flames, flaming, flamed**) **1** N-VAR A **flame** is a hot bright stream of burning gas that comes from something that is burning. 火焰 ❑ *The heat from the flames was so intense that roads melted.* 火焰的热度如此高以至于路面融化了。 **2** N-COUNT A **flame** is an e-mail message which severely criticizes or attacks someone. 攻击性电子邮件 [INFORMAL, COMPUTING] ❑ *The best way to respond to a flame is to ignore it.* 回应攻击性电子邮件的最好方式就是置之不理。 ● V-T **Flame** is also a verb. 发送攻击性电子邮件 ❑ *Ever been flamed?* 收到过攻击性电子邮件吗？ **3** → see also **flaming** **4** PHRASE If something **bursts into flames** or **bursts into flame**, it suddenly starts burning strongly. 突然猛烈燃烧起来 ❑ *She managed to scramble out of the vehicle as it burst into flames.* 她设法从突然起火的车里爬了出来。 **5** PHRASE Something that is **in flames** is on fire. 着火 ❑ *I woke to a city in flames.* 我醒来时看到一座燃烧着的城市。
→ see **fire**

flam·ing /fleɪmɪŋ/ ADJ **Flaming** is used to describe something that is burning and producing a lot of flames. 燃烧的 ❑ *The plane, which was full of fuel, scattered flaming fragments over a large area.* 满载燃料的飞机燃烧的碎片散落在一大片区域里。

flam·mable /flæməbᵊl/ ADJ **Flammable** chemicals, gases, cloth, or other things catch fire and burn easily. 易燃的 ❑ *...flammable liquids such as gasoline or kerosene.* …像汽油或煤油这样的易燃液体。

★ **flank** /flæŋk/ (**flanks, flanking, flanked**) **1** N-COUNT An animal's **flank** is its side, between the ribs and the hip. （动物肋骨和臀部间的）胁腹 ❑ *He put his hand on the dog's flank.* 他把手放在狗的胁腹上。 **2** N-COUNT A **flank** of an army or navy force is one side of it when it is organized for battle. （军队的）侧翼 ❑ *The assault element, led by Captain Ramirez, opened up from their right flank.* 拉米雷斯上尉率领的突击队从他们的右翼开火。 **3** N-COUNT The side of anything large can be referred to as its **flank**. （大型物体的）侧面 ❑ *They continued along the flank of the mountain.* 他们沿着山的侧面继续前进。 **4** V-T If something **is flanked by** things, it has them on both sides of it, or sometimes on one side of it. 两侧有 ❑ *The altar was flanked by two Christmas trees.* 圣坛的两侧有两棵圣诞树。

flan·nel /flænᵊl/ (**flannels**) **1** N-UNCOUNT **Flannel** is a soft cloth, usually made of cotton or wool, that is used for making clothes. 法兰绒 [oft N n] ❑ *He wore a faded red flannel shirt.* 他穿着一件褪了色的红色法兰绒衬衫。 **2** N-COUNT A **flannel** is a small cloth that you use for washing yourself. （洗澡擦身用的）法兰绒布块 [BRIT]

in AM, use **washcloth**

★ **flap** /flæp/ (**flaps, flapping, flapped**) **1** V-T/V-I If something such as a piece of cloth or paper **flaps** or if you **flap** it, it moves quickly up and down or from side to side. 使快速摆动；快速摆动 ❑ *Gray sheets flapped on the clothes line.* 灰色的床单在晾衣绳上飘动。 **2** V-T/V-I If a bird or insect **flaps** its wings or if its wings **flap**, the wings move quickly up and down. 快速振动（翅膀）❑ *The bird flapped its wings furiously.* 那只鸟儿使劲地拍打着翅膀。 **3** V-T If you **flap** your arms, you move them quickly up and down as if they were the wings of a bird. （双臂像小鸟般）扇动 ❑ *...a kid running and flapping her arms.* …一个边跑边像小鸟一样上下扇动着双臂的小女孩。 **4** N-COUNT A **flap** of cloth or skin, for example, is a flat piece of it that can move freely up and down or from side to side because it is held or attached by only one edge. （一端固定、可自由掀动的布或皮的）垂悬平片 ❑ *He drew back the tent flap and strode out into the blizzard.* 他拉开帐篷的门帘，大步走进了暴风雪中。 **5** N-COUNT A **flap** on the wing of an aircraft is an area along the edge of the wing that can be raised or lowered to control the movement of the aircraft. （飞机的）副翼 ❑ *...the sudden slowing as the flaps were lowered.* …副翼降下时的突然减速。

★ **flare** /fleər/ (**flares, flaring, flared**) **1** N-COUNT A **flare** is a small device that produces a bright flame. Flares are used as signals, for example, on ships. 信号弹 ❑ *...a ship which had fired a distress flare.* …一艘发出了遇险信号弹的船。 **2** V-I If a fire **flares**, the flames suddenly become larger. （火）突然烧旺 ❑ *Camp fires flared like beacons in the dark.* 篝火突然熊熊燃烧起来，像黑暗中的灯塔。 ● PHRASAL VERB **Flare up** means the same as **flare.** 突然烧旺 ❑ *Don't spill too much fat on the barbecue as it could flare up.* 不要在烤肉上浇太多的油，因为它可能会突然烧起来。 **3** V-I If something such as trouble, violence, or conflict **flares**, it starts or becomes more violent. 爆发；激化 ❑ *Even as the president appealed for calm, trouble flared in several American cities.* 即使在总统呼吁大家保持冷静时，美国几座城市里仍在爆发骚乱。 ● PHRASAL VERB **Flare up** means the same as **flare.** 爆发；激化 ❑ *Dozens of people were injured as fighting flared up.* 数十人由于战斗激化而负伤。 **4** V-I If people's tempers **flare**, they get angry. 发怒 ❑ *Tempers flared and harsh words were exchanged.* 人们大动肝火，对骂起来。

flare-up (**flare-ups**) N-COUNT If there is a **flare-up** of violence or of an illness, it suddenly starts or gets worse. 突发；恶化 ❑ *There's been a flare-up of violence in South Africa.* 南非的暴力冲突曾一度升级。

flash ♦◇◇ /flæʃ/ (**flashes, flashing, flashed**) **1** N-COUNT A **flash** is a sudden burst of light or of something shiny or bright. 闪光 ❑ *A sudden flash of lightning lit everything up for a second.* 突然的一道闪电刹那间把一切照亮了。 ❑ *The wire snapped at the wall plug with a blue flash.* 随着一道蓝色的闪光，墙上插座处的电线啪地一声断了。 **2** V-T/V-I If a light **flashes** or if you **flash** a light, it shines with a sudden bright light, especially as quick, regular flashes of light. 闪光 ❑ *Lightning flashed among the distant dark clouds.* 远处的乌云中电光闪闪。 ❑ *He lost his temper after a driver flashed her headlights as he overtook.* 他因为在超车时一个女司机闪车头灯而大为光火。 **3** V-I If something **flashes** past or by, it moves past you so fast that you cannot see it properly. 飞驰 ❑ *It was a busy road, cars flashed by every few minutes.* 这是条繁忙的公路，每隔几分钟就有一些汽车飞驰而过。 **4** V-I If something **flashes through** or **into** your mind, you suddenly think about it. 闪现 ❑ *A ludicrous thought flashed through Harry's mind.* 一个可笑的想法在哈里的脑子里闪过。 **5** V-T If you **flash** something such as an identification card, you show it to people quickly and then put it away again. 快速亮一下（证件等）[INFORMAL] ❑ *Halim flashed his official card, and managed to get hold of a soldier to guard the Land Rover.* 哈利姆亮了他的证件，并设法找来一名士兵守卫那辆路虎越野车。 **6** V-T/V-I If a picture or message **flashes up on** a screen, or if you **flash it onto** a screen, it is displayed there briefly or suddenly, and often repeatedly. 使闪现；闪现 ❑ *The figures flash up on the scoreboard.* 数字闪现在记分牌上。 ❑ *The words "Good Luck" were* *flashing on the screen.* "祝你好运"的字样正在屏幕上闪现。 7 V-T If you **flash** a look or a smile at someone, you suddenly look at them or smile at them. 突然投去(一瞥或一笑) [WRITTEN] ❑ *I flashed a look at Sue.* 我突然瞥了休一眼。 8 N-UNCOUNT **Flash** is the use of special bulbs to give more light when taking a photograph. 闪光灯 ❑ *He was one of the first people to use high speed flash in bird photography.* 他是鸟类摄影中最先使用高速闪光灯的人之一。 9 N-COUNT A **flash** is the same as a **flashlight**. 手电筒 [AM, INFORMAL] ❑ *Stopping to rest, Pete shut off the flash.* 停下来休息的时候，皮特关掉了手电筒。 10 PHRASE If you say that something happens **in a flash**, you mean that it happens suddenly and lasts only a very short time. 转瞬间 ❑ *The answer had come to him in a flash.* 他一下子就有了答案。 11 PHRASE If you say that someone reacts to something **quick as a flash**, you mean that they react to it extremely quickly. 反应神速地 ❑ *Quick as a flash, the man said, "I have to, don't I?"* 那人反应神速地说："我不得不这么做，是不是？"

flash·back /flæʃbæk/ (**flashbacks**) 1 N-COUNT In a movie, novel, or play, a **flashback** is a scene that returns to events in the past. (电影、戏剧中的) 闪回镜头；(小说中的) 倒叙 ❑ *There is even a flashback to the murder itself.* 甚至有一个谋杀本身的闪回镜头。 2 N-COUNT If you have a **flashback** to a past experience, you have a sudden and very clear memory of it. (往事在记忆中的) 突然重现 ❑ *He has recurring flashbacks to the night his friends died.* 他脑海中反复重现他的朋友们死去的那个夜晚。

flash·light /flæʃlaɪt/ (**flashlights**) N-COUNT A **flashlight** is a small electric light which gets its power from batteries and which you can carry in your hand. 手电筒 [also "by" N] [mainly AM] ❑ *Len studied it a moment in the beam of his flashlight.* 莱恩借着手电筒的光把它仔细察看了一会儿。

flashy /flæʃi/ (**flashier, flashiest**) ADJ If you describe a person or thing as **flashy**, you mean they are fashionable and noticeable, but in a somewhat vulgar way. 华而不实的 [INFORMAL, DISAPPROVAL] ❑ *He was much less flashy than his brother.* 他远没有他哥哥那么华而不实。

▲ **flask** /flæsk/ (**flasks**) 1 N-COUNT A **flask** is a bottle which you use for carrying drinks around with you. (可随身携带饮料的) 瓶子 ❑ *He took out a metal flask from a canvas bag.* 他从帆布袋里拿出了一个金属水瓶。 ● N-COUNT A **flask** of liquid is the flask and the liquid which it contains. 一瓶 (液体) ❑ *There are some sandwiches here and a flask of coffee.* 这儿有一些三明治和一瓶咖啡。 2 N-COUNT A **flask** is a bottle or other container which is used in science laboratories and industry for holding liquids. 烧瓶；(试验或工业用) 容器 ❑ *Flasks for the transport of spent fuel are extremely strong containers made of steel or steel and lead.* 运送废燃料的容器极为坚固，是用钢或钢铅合金制成的。

flat

❶ SURFACES, SHAPES, AND POSITIONS
❷ OTHER USES
❸ AN APARTMENT

❶ **flat** ◆◆◇ /flæt/ (**flats, flatter, flattest**) 1 ADJ Something that is **flat** is level, smooth, or even, rather than sloping, curved, or uneven. 平的 ❑ *Tiles can be fixed to any surface as long as it's flat, firm and dry.* 瓷砖可以固定在任何表面上，只要这些表面是平整、坚固、干燥的。 ❑ *...windows which a thief can reach from a drainpipe or flat roof.* …小偷从排水管或平屋顶可以够得到的窗户。 2 ADJ **Flat** means horizontal and not upright. 水平的 ❑ *Two men near him threw themselves flat.* 他旁边的两个人一下子平趴在了地上。 3 PHRASE If you **fall flat** on your face, you fall over. 脸朝下摔倒 ❑ *A man walked in off the street and fell flat on his face, unconscious.* 一个男人从街上走进来，脸朝下摔倒在地上，昏了过去。 4 ADJ A **flat** object is not very tall or deep in relation to its length and width. 扁平的 ❑ *Ellen is walking down the drive with a square flat box balanced on one hand.* 埃伦正沿着车道走着，一只手上托着一个扁平的方盒子。 5 ADJ **Flat** land is level, with no high hills or other raised parts. (地势) 平坦的 ❑ *To the north lie the flat and fertile farmlands of Nebraska.* 北面是内布拉斯加州平坦肥沃的农田。 6 ADJ **Flat** shoes have no heels or very low heels. 平底的 ❑ *People wear slacks, sweaters, flat shoes, and all manner of casual attire for travel.* 人们旅行时穿宽松长裤、运动衫、平底鞋和各式休闲服装。 ● N-PLURAL **Flats** are flat shoes. 平底鞋 [AM] ❑ *His mother looked ten years younger in jeans and flats.* 他的母亲穿着牛仔裤和平底鞋，看上去年轻了10岁。 7 ADJ A **flat** tire, ball, or balloon does not have enough air in it. 瘪的 ❑ *One vehicle with a flat tire can bring the highway to a standstill.* 一辆轮胎瘪掉的汽车就能导致公路交通的停顿。 8 N-COUNT You can refer to one of the broad flat surfaces of an object as **the flat of** that object. 平面 ❑ *He slammed the counter with the flat of his hand.* 他用手掌猛击柜台。 9 N-COUNT A **flat** is a tire that does not have enough air in it. 瘪胎 ❑ *Then, after I finally got back on the highway, I developed a flat.* 后来，等我终于回到公路上时，我有一个轮胎瘪了。 10 N-COUNT A low flat area of uncultivated land, especially an area where the ground is soft and wet, can be referred to as **flats** or a **flat**. 低洼沼泽地 ❑ *The salt marshes and mud flats attract large numbers of waterfowl.* 盐碱地和淤泥滩吸引来大量水鸟。 11 ADJ If you have **flat** feet, the arches of your feet are too low. 平足的 ❑ *The condition of flat feet runs in families.* 平足会在家族中遗传。
→ see **wetland**

Thesaurus *flat* 另参见：
ADJ. even, horizontal, level, smooth ❶ 1 2

❷ **flat** ◆◆◇ /flæt/ (**flatter, flattest**) 1 ADJ A drink that is **flat** has lost its fizz. (饮料) 走了汽的 ❑ *Could this really stop the champagne from going flat?* 这真的能使香槟酒不走汽了吗？ 2 ADJ A **flat** battery has lost some or all of its electrical charge. (电池) 电力不足的；(电池) 电力耗尽的 [BRIT]

in AM, use **dead**

3 ADJ If you say that something happened, for example, in ten seconds **flat** or ten minutes **flat**, you are emphasizing that it happened surprisingly quickly and only took ten seconds or ten minutes. 仅仅 [num n ADJ] [EMPHASIS] ❑ *You're sitting behind an engine that'll move you from 0 to 60mph in six seconds flat.* 你现在坐的这辆车的引擎只需6秒钟就能从0加速到每小时60英里。 4 ADJ A **flat** rate, price, or percentage is one that is fixed and which applies in every situation. (费率、价格或百分比) 固定的 [ADJ n] ❑ *Fees are charged at a flat rate, rather than on a percentage basis.* 费用按固定的费率收取，不是按百分比。 5 ADJ If trade or business is **flat**, it is slow and inactive, rather than busy and improving or increasing. (贸易或商业) 不景气的 ❑ *During the first eight months of this year, sales of big pickups were up 14% while car sales stayed flat.* 今年的头8个月，大货车的销售量增长了14%，而轿车的销售仍不景气。 6 ADJ **Flat** is used after a letter representing a musical note to show that the note should be played or sung half a tone lower than the note which otherwise matches that letter. **Flat** is often represented by the symbol ♭ after the letter. (用在表示音符的字母后) 降半音的 [n ADJ] ❑ *...Schubert's B flat Piano Trio (Opus 99).* …舒伯特的降B调钢琴三重奏 (作品第99号)。 7 ADV If someone sings **flat** or if a musical instrument is **flat**, their singing or the instrument is slightly lower in pitch than it should be. (演唱或乐器) 比标准音低地 [ADV after v] ❑ *She had a tendency to sing flat.* 她的唱音倾向于偏低。 ● ADJ **Flat** is also an adjective. (演唱或乐器) 比标准音低的 ❑ *He had been fired because his singing was flat.* 他因为唱音偏低已被解雇。 8 ADJ A **flat** denial or refusal is definite and firm, and is unlikely to be changed. (否认或拒绝) 断然的 [ADJ n] ❑ *The Foreign Ministry has issued a flat denial of any involvement.* 外交部已断然否认与此有任何牵连。 ● **flat·ly** ADV 断然地 ❑ *He flatly refused to discuss it.* 他断然拒绝讨论此事。 9 ADJ If you describe something as **flat**, you mean that it is dull and not exciting or interesting. 平淡无趣的 ❑ *The past few days have seemed comparatively flat and empty.* 过去的几天似乎比较平淡和无聊。 10 PHRASE If an event or attempt **falls flat** or **falls flat on** its **face**, it is unsuccessful. 失败 ❑ *Liz meant it as a joke but it fell flat.* 莉兹的本意是把它当作笑话来讲的，但没成功。 11 PHRASE If you do something **flat out**, you do it as fast or as hard as you can. 竭尽全力地；全速地 ❑ *Everyone is working flat out to try to trap those responsible.* 每个人都在竭尽全力地工作，试图捉住那些应负责任的人。 ❑ *...a flat-out sprint.* …一次全速冲刺。 12 PHRASE You use **flat out** to emphasize that something is completely the case. 彻底的 [mainly AM, INFORMAL, EMPHASIS] ❑ *That allegation is a flat-out lie.* 那一个指控是彻底的谎言。

❸ **flat** /flæt/ (**flats**) N-COUNT A **flat** is a set of rooms for living in, usually on one floor and part of a larger building. A flat usually includes a kitchen and bathroom. 公寓套房 [BRIT]

in AM, use **apartment**

flat·mate /flætmeɪt/ (**flatmates**) also **flat-mate** N-COUNT Someone's **flatmate** is a person who shares a flat with them. 合住一套公寓房的人 [BRIT]

in AM, use **roommate**

flat·ten /flætᵊn/ (**flattens, flattening, flattened**) 1 V-T/V-I If you **flatten** something or if it **flattens**, it becomes flat or flatter. 使变平；

变平 ❑ *He carefully flattened the wrappers and put them between the leaves of his book.* 他小心翼翼地弄平包装纸，把它们夹在书页里。 ❑ *The dog's ears flattened slightly as Cook spoke his name.* 当库克叫狗的名字时，狗的耳朵稍稍耷拉了下来。 ● PHRASAL VERB **Flatten out** means the same as **flatten**. 使变平；变平 ❑ *The hills flattened out just south of the mountain.* 在山的南边丘陵就变得平坦起来。 **2** V-T To **flatten** something such as a building, town, or plant means to destroy it by knocking it down or crushing it. 夷平 (建筑物、城镇或植物) ❑ *...explosives capable of flattening a five-story building.* …足以把一幢5层建筑夷为平地的炸药。 ❑ *...bombing raids flattened much of the area.* …空袭把该地区的许多地方夷为平地。 **3** V-T If you **flatten yourself against** something, you press yourself flat against it, for example, to avoid getting in the way or being seen. 使自己贴着 (以免挡道或被看见) ❑ *He flattened himself against a brick wall as I passed.* 我经过的时候，他紧贴着一堵砖墙站着。 **4** V-T If you **flatten** someone, you make them fall over by hitting them violently. 击倒 ❑ *"I've never seen a woman flatten someone like that," said a crew member. "She knocked him out cold."* "我从没见过一个女人像那样把人击倒"，一名机组人员说，"她把他打昏过去了。"

F

★ **flat·ter** /flætər/ (**flatters, flattering, flattered**) **1** V-T If someone **flatters** you, they praise you in an exaggerated way that is not sincere, because they want to please you or to persuade you to do something. 奉承 [DISAPPROVAL] ❑ *I knew she was just flattering me.* 我知道她只是在奉承我。 **2** V-T If you **flatter yourself that** something good is the case, you believe that it is true, although others may disagree. If someone says to you "**you're flattering yourself**" or "**don't flatter yourself**," they mean that they disagree with your good opinion of yourself. 自以为 (有好的情况存在)；高看自己 ❑ *I flatter myself that this campaign will put an end to the war.* 我自以为这次战役将结束这场战争。 **3** → see also **flat**, **flattered**, **flattering**

flat·tered /flætərd/ ADJ If you are **flattered** by something that has happened, you are pleased about it because it makes you feel important or special. 感到荣幸的 [v-link ADJ] ❑ *She was flattered by Roberto's long letter.* 罗伯托的长信让她感到荣幸。

flat·ter·ing /flætərɪŋ/ **1** ADJ If something is **flattering**, it makes you appear more attractive. 使更漂亮的 ❑ *It wasn't a very flattering photograph.* 这张照片照得不如本人好看。 **2** ADJ If someone's remarks are **flattering**, they praise you and say nice things about you. 恭维的 ❑ *Most of his colleagues had positive, even flattering things to say.* 他的大多数同事都有一些正面的、甚至奉承的话要说。

flat·ware /flætwɛər/ N-UNCOUNT You can refer to the knives, forks, and spoons that you eat your food with as **flatware**. 餐具 (如刀、叉、匙等) [AM] ❑ *An assortment of pots, pans, plates, cups, and flatware is provided.* 提供了一套煮锅、平底锅、盘子、杯子和刀、叉、匙等餐具。

flaunt /flɔnt/ (**flaunts, flaunting, flaunted**) V-T If you say that someone **flaunts** their possessions, abilities, or qualities, you mean that they display them in a very obvious way, especially in order to try to obtain other people's admiration. 炫耀 [DISAPPROVAL] ❑ *They drove around in Rolls-Royces, openly flaunting their wealth.* 他们开着劳斯莱斯车四处转，公开炫耀他们的财富。

fla·vor ♦◇◇ /fleɪvər/ (**flavors, flavoring, flavored**)

in BRIT, use **flavour**

1 N-VAR The **flavor** of a food or drink is its taste. 味道 ❑ *I always add some paprika for extra flavor.* 我总是加一些辣椒粉来提味。 **2** N-COUNT If something is orange **flavor** or beef **flavor**, it is made to taste of orange or beef. (某种) 味道 ❑ *It has an orange flavor and smooth texture.* 它有一种桔子的味道，质地光滑。 **3** V-T If you **flavor** food or drink, you add something to it to give it a particular taste. 给 (食物或饮料) 调味 ❑ *Lime preserved in salt is a North African specialty which is used to flavor chicken dishes.* 用盐腌的酸橙是用来给鸡肉调味的一种北非特产。

-flavored /-fleɪvərd/

in BRIT, use **-flavoured**

COMB IN ADJ **-flavored** is used after nouns such as strawberry and chocolate to indicate that a food or drink is flavored with strawberry or chocolate. (用于表示食品或饮料的名词之后) …味道的 ❑ *...strawberry-flavored candies.* …草莓味的糖果。

fla·vor·ing /fleɪvərɪŋ/ (**flavorings**)

in BRIT, use **flavouring**

N-VAR **Flavorings** are substances that are added to food or drink to give it a particular taste. 调味品 ❑ *...lemon flavoring.* …柠檬调味品。

fla·vour /fleɪvəʳ/ [BRIT] → see **flavor**

-flavoured /-fleɪvəʳd/ [BRIT] → see **-flavored**

fla·vour·ing /fleɪvərɪŋ/ [BRIT] → see **flavoring**

★ **flaw** /flɔ/ (**flaws**) **1** N-COUNT A **flaw in** something such as a theory or argument is a mistake in it, which causes it to be less effective or valid. (理论或论点中的) 错误 ❑ *There were, however, a number of crucial flaws in his monetary theory.* 然而，他的货币理论中有很多关键性的错误。 **2** N-COUNT A **flaw in** someone's character is an undesirable quality that they have. (性格中的) 缺点 ❑ *The only flaw in his character seems to be a short temper.* 他性格中惟一的缺点似乎就是脾气急躁。 **3** N-COUNT A **flaw in** something such as a pattern or material is a fault in it that should not be there. 瑕疵 ❑ *It's like having a flaw in a piece of material - the longer you leave it, the weaker it gets.* 这就像一块料子上有瑕疵一样——你把它放得越久，它就变得越不结实。

flawed /flɔd/ ADJ Something that is **flawed** has a mark, fault, or mistake in it. 有缺陷的 ❑ *These tests were so seriously flawed as to render the results meaningless.* 这些测试存在着如此严重的缺陷，以至于使得结果毫无意义。

flaw·less /flɔlɪs/ ADJ If you say that something or someone is **flawless**, you mean that they are extremely good and that there are no faults or problems with them. 完美的 ❑ *Discovery's takeoff this morning from Cape Canaveral was flawless.* "发现号"今晨从卡纳维拉尔角的发射是完美的。 ● **flaw·less·ly** ADV 完美地 ❑ *Each stage of the battle was carried off flawlessly.* 战斗的每个阶段都都进行得很完美。

flea /fli/ (**fleas**) N-COUNT A **flea** is a very small jumping insect that has no wings and feeds on the blood of humans or animals. 跳蚤

fleck /flɛk/ (**flecks**) N-COUNT **Flecks** are small marks on a surface, or objects that look like small marks. 斑点；(像斑点的) 微粒 ❑ *He went to the men's room to wash flecks of blood from his shirt.* 他去男洗手间清洗衬衫上的斑斑血迹。

fled /flɛd/ **Fled** is the past tense and past participle of **flee**. **flee**的过去式和过去分词

fledg·ling /flɛdʒlɪŋ/ (**fledglings**) **1** N-COUNT A **fledgling** is a young bird that has its feathers and is learning to fly. 刚长出羽毛的雏鸟 ❑ *...when fledglings are almost ready to leave the nests.* …当刚长出羽毛的雏鸟差不多可以离开鸟巢的时候。 **2** ADJ You use **fledgling** to describe a person, organization, or system that is new or without experience. 新的；无经验的 (人、组织、系统) [ADJ n] ❑ *...Russia's fledgling democracy.* …俄罗斯新的民主。

flee ♦◇◇ /fli/ (**flees, fleeing, fled**) V-T/V-I If you **flee from** something or someone, or **flee** a person or thing, you escape from them. 逃离 [no passive] [WRITTEN] ❑ *He slammed the bedroom door behind him and fled.* 他砰地关上卧室的门就逃走了。 ❑ *...refugees fleeing persecution or torture.* …逃避迫害或折磨的难民们。

fleece /flis/ (**fleeces, fleecing, fleeced**) **1** N-COUNT A sheep's **fleece** is the coat of wool that covers it. 羊毛 ❑ *...a special protein which triggers the animal to shed its fleece.* …一种能够促使这种动物脱毛的特殊蛋白质。 **2** N-COUNT A **fleece** is the wool that is cut off one sheep in a single piece. (从一只羊身上剪下连在一起的) 羊毛 ❑ *Wool can be spun from fleeces.* 羊毛可以纺成毛线。 **3** V-T If you **fleece** someone, you get a lot of money from them by tricking them or charging them too much. 诈骗 [INFORMAL] ❑ *She claims he fleeced her out of thousands of dollars.* 她声称他诈骗了她几千美元。 **4** N-VAR **Fleece** is a soft warm artificial fabric. A **fleece** is also a jacket or other garment made from this fabric. 仿毛织物；绒毛衣物 ❑ *...white leather slippers with fleece lining.* …带有绒毛衬里的白色皮拖鞋。

fleet ♦◇◇ /flit/ (**fleets**) **1** N-COUNT A **fleet** is a group of ships organized to do something together, for example, to fight battles or to catch fish. 舰队；船队 ❑ *A fleet sailed for New South Wales to establish the first European settlement in Australia.* 一支舰队驶向新南威尔士去建立欧洲在澳大利亚的第一个殖民地。 **2** N-COUNT A **fleet of** vehicles is a group of them, especially when they all belong to a particular organization or business, or when they are all going somewhere together. 车队 ❑ *With its own fleet of trucks, the company delivers most orders overnight.* 因为有自己的运输车队，该公司的大部分订货可以第2天就送到。

fleet·ing /flitɪŋ/ ADJ **Fleeting** is used to describe something which lasts only for a very short time. 短暂的 ❑ *The girls caught only a fleeting glimpse of the driver.* 姑娘们只是匆匆瞥了那个司机一眼。 ● **fleet·ing·ly** ADV 短暂地 ❑ *A smile passed fleetingly across his face.* 笑容从他的脸上一闪即逝。

flesh /flɛʃ/ (**fleshes, fleshing, fleshed**) 1 N-UNCOUNT **Flesh** is the soft part of a person's or animal's body between the bones and the skin. 肉 ❑ *...the pale pink flesh of trout and salmon.* …鳟鱼和鲑鱼粉白色的肉。 2 N-UNCOUNT You can use **flesh** to refer to human skin and the human body, especially when you are considering it in a sexual way. 肌肤；肉体 ❑ *...the warmth of her flesh.* …她肌肤的温暖。 3 N-UNCOUNT The **flesh** of a fruit or vegetable is the soft inside part of it. 果肉；蔬菜的可食部分 ❑ *Cut the flesh from the olives and discard the stones.* 切下橄榄的果肉，扔掉果核。 4 PHRASE You use **flesh and blood** to emphasize that someone has human feelings or weaknesses, often when contrasting them with machines. 血肉之躯 [EMPHASIS] ❑ *I'm only flesh and blood, like anyone else.* 我只是血肉之躯，跟其他人一样。 5 PHRASE If you say that someone is your **own flesh and blood**, you are emphasizing that they are a member of your family. 亲骨肉 [EMPHASIS] ❑ *The kid, after all, was his own flesh and blood. He deserved a second chance.* 这个孩子毕竟是他的亲骨肉，他应该得到再一次机会。 6 PHRASE If something **makes** your **flesh creep** or **makes** your **flesh crawl**, it makes you feel disgusted, shocked or frightened. 使厌恶；使心惊肉跳 ❑ *It makes my flesh creep to think of it.* 一想起它我就心惊肉跳。 7 PHRASE If you meet or see someone **in the flesh**, you actually meet or see them, rather than, for example, seeing them in a movie or on television. 本人 ❑ *The first thing viewers usually say when they see me in the flesh is "You're smaller than you look on TV."* 观众见到我本人时常说的第一句话往往是"你比在电视上看上去矮小一些"。
→ see **fruit**

▶ **flesh out** PHRASAL VERB If you **flesh out** something such as a story or plan, you add details and more information to it. 充实（故事或计划等） ❑ *Permission for a warehouse development has already been granted and the developers are merely fleshing out the details.* 货仓开发的许可证已获批准，开发商只是在充实细节。

flew /flu/ **Flew** is the past tense of **fly**. **fly**的过去式

Word Link *flex ≈ bending : flex, flexible, reflex*

flex /flɛks/ (**flexes, flexing, flexed**) 1 V-T If you **flex** your muscles or parts of your body, you bend, move, or stretch them for a short time in order to exercise them. 屈伸（肌肉或身体某部分） ❑ *He slowly flexed his muscles and tried to stand.* 他缓慢地活动了一下肌肉，想站起来。 2 N-VAR A **flex** is an electric cable containing two or more wires that is connected to an electrical appliance. （电器用的）花线 [mainly BRIT]
in AM, use **cord**
3 to **flex** your **muscles** → see **muscle**

Word Link *ible ≈ able to be : audible, flexible, possible*

flex·ible ♦◇◇ /flɛksɪbᵊl/ 1 ADJ A **flexible** object or material can be bent easily without breaking. 柔韧的 ❑ *...brushes with long, flexible bristles.* …毛长而柔韧的刷子。 ● **flexi·bil·ity** /flɛksɪbɪlɪti/ N-UNCOUNT 柔韧性 ❑ *The flexibility of the lens decreases with age; it is therefore common for our sight to worsen as we get older.* 眼球晶状体的柔韧性随着年龄的增长而降低；因此普遍的情况是随着我们年纪变老，我们的视力就会变差。 2 ADJ Something or someone that is **flexible** is able to change easily and adapt to different conditions and circumstances as they occur. 灵活的 [APPROVAL] ❑ *...flexible working hours.* …弹性工作时间。 ● **flexi·bil·ity** N-UNCOUNT 灵活性 ❑ *The flexibility of distance learning would be particularly suited to busy managers.* 远程学习的灵活性尤其会适合忙碌的经理们。

flex·time /flɛkstaɪm/ also **flexitime** N-UNCOUNT **Flextime** is a system that allows employees to vary the time that they start or finish work, provided that an agreed total number of hours are spent at work. 弹性工作时间制 [BUSINESS] ❑ *I have recently introduced flextime for all my staff.* 我最近已对所有的员工采用弹性工作时间制。

▲ **flick** /flɪk/ (**flicks, flicking, flicked**) 1 V-T/V-I If something **flicks** in a particular direction, or if someone **flicks** it, it moves with a short, sudden movement. 轻快地移动 ❑ *His tongue flicked across his lips.* 他的舌头在双唇间快速移动。 ❑ *He flicked his cigarette out of the window.* 他倏地一下把香烟弹出了窗外。 ● N-COUNT **Flick** is also a noun. 快速的移动 ❑ *...a flick of a paintbrush.* …画笔的快速移动。 2 V-T If you **flick** something away, or off something else, you remove it with a quick movement of your hand or finger. （用手或手指）弹掉 ❑ *Shirley flicked a piece of lint from the sleeve of her black suit.* 雪莉轻轻弹掉了黑色套装袖子上的一块棉绒。 3 V-T If you **flick** something such as a whip or a towel, or **flick** something with it, you hold one end of it and move your hand quickly up and then forward, so that the other end moves. 抽打 ❑ *She sighed and flicked a dishcloth at the counter.* 她叹了口气，用一块洗碗布在柜台上抽打了一下。 ● N-COUNT **Flick** is also a noun. 抽打 ❑ *...a flick of the whip.* …鞭子的一下轻抽。 4 V-T If you **flick** a switch, or **flick** an electrical appliance on or off, you press the switch sharply so that it moves into a different position and works the equipment. 啪地打开或关掉（开关或电器） ❑ *Sam was flicking a flashlight on and off.* 萨姆在啪啪不停地开关着手电筒。 5 V-I If you **flick through** a book or magazine, you turn its pages quickly, for example, to get a general idea of its contents or to look for a particular item. If you **flick through** television channels, you continually change channels very quickly, usually using a remote control. 快速翻看 ❑ *She was flicking through some magazines on a table.* 她正在快速翻阅桌子上的一些杂志。 ● N-SING **Flick** is also a noun. 快速翻看 ❑ *I thought I'd have a quick flick through some recent issues.* 我想我要快速浏览一下最近的几期杂志了。

▲ **flick·er** /flɪkər/ (**flickers, flickering, flickered**) V-I If a light or flame **flickers**, it shines unsteadily. 闪烁不定 ❑ *Fluorescent lights flickered, and then the room was blindingly bright.* 荧光灯闪了闪，接着房间里就亮得令人目眩了。 ● N-COUNT **Flicker** is also a noun. 闪烁 ❑ *Looking through the window I saw the flicker of flames.* 透过窗子望出去，我看到了闪烁的火光。

flight ♦♦◇ /flaɪt/ (**flights**) 1 N-COUNT A **flight** is a trip made by flying, usually in an airplane. 飞行 ❑ *The flight will take four hours.* 此次飞行将需要4个小时。 2 N-COUNT You can refer to an airplane carrying passengers on a particular trip as a particular **flight**. 航班 [also N num] ❑ *BA flight 286 was two hours late.* 英国航空286次航班晚点2个小时。 3 N-COUNT A **flight of** steps or stairs is a set of steps or stairs that lead from one level to another without changing direction. 一段（台阶或楼梯） ❑ *We walked in silence up a flight of stairs and down a long corridor.* 我们默默地走上一段楼梯，穿过一道长长的走廊。 4 N-UNCOUNT **Flight** is the action of flying, or the ability to fly. 行；飞行能力 ❑ *Supersonic flight could become a routine form of travel in the 21st century.* 搭乘超音速飞机飞行会成为21世纪常见的旅行方式。 5 N-UNCOUNT **Flight** is the act of running away from a dangerous or unpleasant situation or place. 逃跑 ❑ *The family was often in flight, hiding out in friends' houses.* 这一家人经常逃来逃去，躲藏在朋友们的家里。
→ see **fly**
→ see Word Web: **flight**

flight at·tend·ant (**flight attendants**) N-COUNT On an airplane, the **flight attendants** are the people whose job is to take care of the passengers and serve their meals. 乘务人员

flim·sy /flɪmzi/ (**flimsier, flimsiest**) 1 ADJ A **flimsy** object is weak because it is made of a weak material, or is badly made. 脆弱的；劣质的 ❑ *...a flimsy wooden door.* …劣质的木门。 2 ADJ **Flimsy** cloth or clothing is thin and does not give much protection. （布料或衣服）薄的 ❑ *...a very flimsy pink chiffon nightgown.* …一件很薄的粉红色雪纺绸睡衣。 3 ADJ If you describe something such as evidence or an excuse as **flimsy**, you mean that it is not very good or convincing. 站不住脚的 ❑ *The charges were based on very flimsy evidence.* 这些指控基于非常站不住脚的证据。

flinch /flɪntʃ/ (**flinches, flinching, flinched**) 1 V-I If you **flinch**, you make a small sudden movement, especially when something

Word Web **flight**

In order for an airplane to **fly**, it must overcome the force of **gravity** and also move forward through the air. The **propellers** or **jet engines** provide the **thrust** that helps the plane move ahead. This force is opposed by the **drag** on the wings as they encounter **air resistance**. The upper part of the wing is **curved**, which reduces the **air pressure** over it. This airflow over the wing provides the lift that allows the plane to rise from the ground.

f

surprises you or hurts you. 畏缩 [usu neg] ❑ *Leo stared back at him without flinching.* 利奥毫不畏缩地回瞪着他。 **2** V-I If you **flinch from** something unpleasant, you are unwilling to do it or think about it, or you avoid doing it. 退缩 ❑ *The world community should not flinch in the face of this challenge.* 国际社会不应该在这一挑战面前退缩。

fling /flɪŋ/ (**flings, flinging, flung**) **1** V-T If you **fling** something somewhere, you throw it there using a lot of force. 猛掷 ❑ *The woman flung the cup at him.* 那女人使劲把杯子朝他扔过去。 **2** V-T If you **fling yourself** somewhere, you move or jump there suddenly and with a lot of force. 突然移向；突然跳到 ❑ *He flung himself to the floor.* 他突然跳到了地板上。 **3** V-T If you **fling** a part of your body in a particular direction, especially your arms or head, you move it there suddenly. 猛然移动（臂、头等身体部位）❑ *She flung her arms around my neck and kissed me.* 她猛地搂住我的脖子吻了我。 **4** V-T If you **fling** someone to the ground, you push them very roughly so that they fall over. 推倒 ❑ *The youth got him by the front of his shirt and flung him to the ground.* 那个年轻人抓住他的衬衫前襟把他推倒在地。 **5** V-T If you **fling** something into a particular place or position, you put it there in a quick or angry way. 扔 ❑ *Peter flung his shoes into the corner.* 彼得把他的鞋扔到了角落里。 **6** V-T If you **fling yourself into** a particular activity, you do it with a lot of enthusiasm and energy. 投身于 ❑ *She flung herself into her career.* 她投身于自己的事业中。 **7** **Fling** can be used instead of "throw" in many expressions that usually contain "throw." 在许多短语中可以替代**throw** **8** N-COUNT If two people have **a fling**, they have a brief sexual relationship. 短暂的风流韵事 [INFORMAL] ❑ *She claims she had a brief fling with him 30 years ago.* 她声称30年前曾跟他有过一段短暂的风流韵事。

★ **flip** /flɪp/ (**flips, flipping, flipped**) **1** V-T If you **flip** a device on or off, or if you **flip** a switch, you turn it on or off by pressing the switch quickly. 快速地拨动（装置或开关）❑ *He didn't flip on the headlights until he was two blocks away.* 直到过了两个街区后，他才打开前灯。 ❑ *Then he walked out, flipping the lights off.* 接着他走了出去，随手把灯关掉。 **2** V-I If you **flip** through the pages of a book, for example, you quickly turn over the pages in order to find a particular one or to get an idea of the contents. 快速翻阅 ❑ *He was flipping through a magazine in the living room.* 他在起居室里快速翻阅一本杂志。 **3** V-T/V-I If something **flips** over, or if you **flip** it over or into a different position, it moves or is moved into a different position. 翻动 ❑ *The plane then flipped over and burst into flames.* 这时飞机翻了个个儿，接着就燃烧了起来。 **4** V-T If you **flip** something, especially a coin, you use your thumb to make it turn over and over, as it goes through the air. 投掷（尤指硬币）❑ *I pulled a coin from my pocket and flipped it.* 我从口袋里掏出一枚硬币，把它投掷出去。

flip·chart /flɪptʃɑrt/ (**flipcharts**) N-COUNT A **flipchart** is a stand with large sheets of paper which is used when presenting information at a meeting. （做展示用）挂纸白板 ❑ *There are three conference rooms each of which is equipped with a screen, flipchart and audio visual equipment.* 有3间会议室，每间都装有屏幕、挂纸白板和视听设备。

▲ **flirt** /flɜrt/ (**flirts, flirting, flirted**) **1** V-RECIP If you **flirt with** someone, you behave as if you are sexually attracted to them, in a playful or not very serious way. 跟…调情 ❑ *Dad's flirting with all the ladies, or they're all flirting with him, as usual.* 爸爸在和所有的女士打情骂俏，或者说她们都在和他调情，跟平常一样。 ● **flir·ta·tion** /flɜrteɪʃən/ N-VAR (**flirtations**) 调情 [oft N "with" n] ❑ *She was aware of his attempts at flirtation.* 她知道他想跟她调情。 **2** N-COUNT Someone who is a **flirt** likes to flirt a lot. 喜欢调情的人 ❑ *I've always been a real flirt, I had a different boyfriend every week.* 我是个不折不扣的调情老手，每个星期的男朋友都不一样。 **3** V-I If you **flirt with** the idea of something, you consider it but do not do anything about it. 有…的想法 ❑ *My mother used to flirt with Anarchism.* 我的母亲过去有过无政府主义的想法。 ● **flir·ta·tion** N-VAR 不经意的考虑 ❑ *...the party's brief flirtation with economic liberalism.* …该党一度考虑过的经济自由主义。

▲ **flit** /flɪt/ (**flits, flitting, flitted**) **1** V-I If you **flit** around or **flit** between one place and another, you go to lots of places without staying for very long in any of them. 不停地移动 ❑ *Laura flits about New York hailing taxis at every opportunity.* 劳拉在纽约到处跑来跑去，一有机会就打出租车。 **2** V-I If someone **flits from** one thing or situation **to** another, they move or turn their attention from one to the other very quickly. 很快转变 ❑ *He's prone to flit between subjects with amazing ease.* 他能轻而易举地在各学科之间换来换去。 **3** V-I If something such as a bird or a bat **flits** about, it flies quickly from one place to another. 轻快地飞过 ❑ *...the parrot that flits from tree to tree.* …从一棵树轻快地飞到另一棵树上的鹦鹉。

float ♦◇◇ /flout/ (**floats, floating, floated**) **1** V-T/V-I If something or someone **is floating** in a liquid, they are in the liquid, on or just below the surface, and are being supported by it. You can also **float** something on a liquid. 漂浮 ❑ *They noticed fifty and twenty dollar bills floating in the water.* 他们注意到水中漂浮着一些50和20美元的纸币。 ❑ *It's below freezing and small icebergs are floating by.* 气温在冰点以下，一座座小冰山正漂过。 **2** V-I Something that **floats** lies on or just below the surface of a liquid when it is put in it and does not sink. （在水面或水中）漂浮 ❑ *They will also float if you drop them in the water.* 如果你把它们丢进水里，它们也会浮起来。 **3** V-I Something that **floats** in or through the air hangs in it or moves slowly and gently through it. （在空中）飘浮 ❑ *The white cloud of smoke floated away.* 那团白色的烟雾飘走了。 **4** V-T If you **float** a project, plan, or idea, you suggest it for others to think about. 提出 ❑ *The French had floated the idea of placing the diplomatic work in the hands of the UN.* 法国人提出了将外交工作交由联合国处理的意见。 **5** V-T If a company director **floats** their company, they start to sell shares in it to the public. 使（公司）上市 [BUSINESS] ❑ *He floated his firm on the stock market.* 他让自己的公司上市了。 **6** V-T/V-I If a government **floats** its country's currency or allows it to **float**, it allows the currency's value to change freely in relation to other currencies. 使（货币）自由浮动 [BUSINESS] ❑ *On January 15th Brazil was forced to float its currency.* 1月15日巴西被迫让其货币自由浮动。 **7** N-COUNT A **float** is a light object that is used to help someone or something float. 救生圈 ❑ *Floats will provide confidence in the water.* 救生圈可以增强在水中的信心。 **8** N-COUNT A **float** is a small object attached to a fishing line which floats on the water and moves when a fish has been caught. 浮子；鱼漂 **9** N-COUNT A **float** is a truck on which displays and people in special costumes are carried in a parade. 游行彩车 ❑ *...a procession of makeshift floats bearing loudspeakers and banners.* …临时代用的装有高音喇叭、挂有横幅的游行彩车队列。

flock /flɒk/ (**flocks, flocking, flocked**) **1** N-COUNT-COLL A **flock of** birds, sheep, or goats is a group of them. 一群（鸟、羊等）❑ *They kept a small flock of sheep.* 他们养了一小群绵羊。 **2** N-COUNT-COLL You can refer to a group of people or things as a **flock of** them to emphasize that there are a lot of them. 一群；一批（人、物）[EMPHASIS] ❑ *These cases all attracted flocks of famous writers.* 这些案例均吸引了大批知名作家。 **3** V-I If people **flock to** a particular place or event, a very large number of them go there, usually because it is pleasant or interesting. 群集于 ❑ *The public has flocked to the show.* 公众蜂拥着去看那场演出。 ❑ *The criticisms will not stop people flocking to see the film.* 这些批评不会阻止人们蜂拥着去看这部影片。

flog /flɒg/ (**flogs, flogging, flogged**) V-T If someone **is flogged**, they are hit very hard with a whip or stick as a punishment. 鞭打；棒打 ❑ *In these places people starved, were flogged, were clubbed to death.* 在这些地方，人们忍饥挨饿、遭受毒打、丧命于棍棒之下。 ● **flog·ging** N-VAR (**floggings**) 鞭打；棒打 ❑ *He gets dragged off to court and sentenced to a flogging and life imprisonment.* 他被拖至法庭，被判鞭刑和终身监禁。

flood ♦◇◇ /flʌd/ (**floods, flooding, flooded**) **1** N-VAR If there is a **flood**, a large amount of water covers an area which is usually dry, for example, when a river flows over its banks or a pipe bursts. 洪水 ❑ *More than 70 people were killed in the floods, caused when a dam burst.* 大坝决堤引发的洪水灾吞噬了七十多人的生命。 ❑ *This is the type of flood dreaded by cavers.* 这正是探察洞穴者惧怕的那种洪水。 **2** V-T/V-I If something such as a river or a burst pipe **floods** an area that is usually dry or if the area **floods**, it becomes covered with water. 为水所淹；淹没 ❑ *The kitchen flooded.* 厨房被水淹了。 **3** V-I If a river **floods**, it overflows, especially after very heavy rain. 泛滥 ❑ *...the relentless rain that caused twenty rivers to flood.* …导致20条河流泛滥的那场持续不断的雨。 **4** V-I If you say that people or things **flood** into a place, you are emphasizing that they arrive there in large numbers. 涌入 [EMPHASIS] ❑ *Large numbers of immigrants flooded into the area.* 大批移民涌入了这个地区。 ❑ *Inquiries flooded in from all over the world.* 问询从世界各地如潮水般涌来。 **5** V-T If you **flood** a place **with** a particular type of thing, or if a particular type of thing **floods** a place, the place becomes full of so many of them that it cannot hold or deal with any more. 使充满；充斥 ❑ *Manufacturers are destroying American jobs by flooding the market with cheap imports.* 制造商们在以廉价进口货充斥市场，破坏了美国人的就业机会。 **6** N-COUNT If you say that a **flood of** people or things arrive somewhere, you

are emphasizing that a very large number of them arrive there. 一大批 [EMPHASIS] ❑ *The administration is trying to stem the flood of refugees out of Haiti and into Florida.* 政府正设法阻止大批逃离海地的难民涌入佛罗里达。
→ see **disaster**

flood·ing /flʌdɪŋ/ N-UNCOUNT If **flooding** occurs, an area of land that is usually dry is covered with water after heavy rain or after a river or lake flows over its banks. 洪水泛滥 ❑ *The flooding, caused by three days of torrential rain, is the worst in sixty-five years.* 由3天暴雨引发的这场洪水泛滥是65年来最为严重的。
→ see **dam, storm**

flood·light /flʌdlaɪt/ (**floodlights, floodlighting, floodlit**) **1** N-COUNT **Floodlights** are very powerful lamps that are used outside to light public buildings, sports grounds, and other places at night. 泛光灯 ❑ *A group of men were playing soccer under the glare of floodlights.* 一群男人正在泛光灯的强光下踢足球。 **2** V-T If a building or place **is floodlit**, it is lit by floodlights. 用泛光灯照明 ❑ *In the evening the facade is floodlit.* 晚上，建筑物的正面是用泛光灯照明的。

floor ♦♦◊ /flɔr/ (**floors, flooring, floored**) **1** N-COUNT **The floor** of a room is the part of it that you walk on. 地板 ❑ *Jack's sitting on the floor watching TV.* 杰克正坐在地板上看电视。 **2** N-COUNT **A floor** of a building is all the rooms that are on a particular level. 楼层 ❑ *The café was on the top floor of the hospital.* 咖啡馆在医院的顶层。

> In North America, the **floor** at street level is the first floor and the next floor up is the second floor. In Britain, the floor at street level is the ground floor and the first floor is one floor up.

3 N-COUNT **The** ocean **floor** is the ground at the bottom of an ocean. **The** valley **floor** is the ground at the bottom of a valley. (海洋、山谷等的) 底 ❑ *They spend hours feeding on the ocean floor.* 它们花几个小时在海底进食。 **4** N-COUNT The place where official debates and discussions are held, especially between members of a legislature, is referred to as **the floor**. 议政厅 ❑ *The issues were debated on the floor of the House.* 这些问题在众议院议政厅进行了辩论。 **5** N-SING-COLL In a debate or discussion, **the floor** is the people who are listening to the arguments being put forward but who are not among the main speakers. 与会者 ❑ *The president is taking questions from the floor.* 会议主席正在回答与会者提出的问题。 **6** V-T If you **are floored by** something, you are unable to respond to it because you are so surprised by it. (因惊讶而) 不知所措 [usu passive] ❑ *He was floored by the announcement.* 他被这个通告震惊得不知所措。 **7** → see also **flooring, dance floor, first floor, ground floor, shop floor** **8** PHRASE If someone **has the floor**, they are the person who is speaking in a debate or discussion. 发言 ❑ *Since I have the floor for the moment, I want to go back to a previous point.* 借此发言的机会，我想回到前面的一个问题。 **9** PHRASE If you **take to the floor**, you start dancing at a dance or disco. 开始跳舞 ❑ *The happy couple and their respective parents took to the floor.* 那幸福的一对和他们各自的父母开始跳起舞来。 **10** PHRASE If you **wipe the floor with** someone, you defeat them completely in a competition or discussion. 彻底击败 [INFORMAL] ❑ *He could wipe the floor with the opposition.* 他能彻底击败反对派。

Word Partnership *floor* 的常用搭配：
V. **fall on the** floor, **sit on the** floor, **sweep the** floor **1**
N. floor **to ceiling**, floor **space** **1**
floor **plan** **2**
forest floor, **ocean** floor **3**

floor·board /flɔrbɔrd/ (**floorboards**) N-COUNT **Floorboards** are the long pieces of wood that a wooden floor is made up of. 地板板材

floor·ing /flɔrɪŋ/ (**floorings**) N-MASS **Flooring** is a material that is used to make the floor of a room. 室内地面材料 ❑ *Quarry tiles are a popular kitchen flooring.* 缸砖是一种流行的厨房地面材料。

flop /flɒp/ (**flops, flopping, flopped**) **1** V-I If you **flop** into a chair, for example, you sit down suddenly and heavily because you are so tired. (因疲惫) 一下子重重地坐下 ❑ *Bunbury flopped down upon the bed and rested his tired feet.* 邦伯里扑通一声躺倒在床上，休息一下疲惫的双脚。 **2** V-I If something **flops** onto something else, it falls there heavily or untidily. 沉重地摔落 ❑ *The briefcase flopped onto the desk.* 公文包重重地落在桌上。 **3** V-I If something **flops**, it is completely unsuccessful. 彻底失败 [INFORMAL] ❑ *The film flopped badly at the box office.* 这部电影在票房上遭到惨败。 **4** N-COUNT If something is a **flop**, it is completely unsuccessful. 惨败 [INFORMAL] ❑ *It is the public who decide whether a film is a hit or a flop.* 决定一部电影是成功还是失败的是公众。

flop·py /flɒpi/ ADJ Something that is **floppy** is loose rather than stiff, and tends to hang downward. 软的 ❑ *...the girl with the floppy hat and glasses.* …戴着软帽和眼镜的女孩。

flop·py disk (**floppy disks**) N-COUNT A **floppy disk** is a small magnetic disk that is used for storing computer data and programs. Floppy disks are used especially with personal computers. 软盘

Word Link *flor* ≈ *flower* : *flora, floral, florist*

flo·ra /flɔrə/ N-UNCOUNT-COLL You can refer to plants as **flora**, especially the plants growing in a particular area. (尤指某个地区的) 植物群 [FORMAL] ❑ *...the variety of food crops and flora which now exists in Dominica.* …目前存在于多米尼加的各种粮食作物和植物群。

▲ **flo·ral** /flɔrəl/ **1** ADJ A **floral** fabric or design has flowers on it. 有花卉图案的 ❑ *...a bright yellow floral fabric.* …有亮黄色花卉图案的织物。 **2** ADJ You can use **floral** to describe something that contains flowers or is made of flowers. 有花的; 由花组成的 [ADJ n] ❑ *...eye-catching floral arrangements.* …夺人眼目的插花。

flo·rist /flɔrɪst/ (**florists**) **1** N-COUNT A **florist** is a storekeeper who arranges and sells flowers and sells houseplants. 花商 **2** N-COUNT A **florist** or a **florist's** is a store where flowers and houseplants are sold. 花店 ❑ *He bought her some roses at the florist's in the mall.* 他在购物中心的花店里为她买了一些玫瑰。

flo·ta·tion /floʊteɪʃən/ (**flotations**) N-VAR The **flotation** of a company is the selling of shares in it to the public. 股票发行 [BUSINESS] ❑ *Prudential's flotation will be the third largest this year, behind Kraft Foods and Agere Systems.* 保诚公司的股票发行量今年将排名第3，仅次于卡夫食品和杰尔系统。

floun·der /flaʊndər/ (**flounders, floundering, floundered**) **1** V-I If something **is floundering**, it has many problems and may soon fail completely. 陷入困境 ❑ *What a pity that his career was left to flounder.* 真遗憾，他的事业陷入了困境。 **2** V-I If you say that someone **is floundering**, you are criticizing them for not making decisions or for not knowing what to say or do. 不知所措 [DISAPPROVAL] ❑ *Right now, you've got a president who's floundering, trying to find some way to get his campaign jump-started.* 此时此刻你们的总统不知所措，尽力想办法推动他的竞选。 **3** V-I If you **flounder** in water or mud, you move in an uncontrolled way, trying not to sink. (在水或泥浆中) 挣扎 ❑ *Three men were floundering about in the water.* 3名男子正在水中挣扎。

flour /flaʊər/ (**flours**) N-MASS **Flour** is a white or brown powder that is made by grinding grain. It is used to make bread, cakes, and pastry. 面粉
→ see **grain**

flour·ish /flɜrɪʃ/ (**flourishes, flourishing, flourished**) **1** V-I If something **flourishes**, it is successful, active, or common, and developing quickly and strongly. 繁荣; 兴旺 ❑ *Business flourished and within six months they were earning 18,000 roubles a day.* 生意兴隆，6个月中他们每天挣18000卢布。 ● **flour·ish·ing** ADJ 繁荣的; 兴旺的 ❑ *Boston quickly became a flourishing port.* 波斯顿迅速成为一个繁荣的港口。 **2** V-I If a plant or animal **flourishes**, it grows well or is healthy because the conditions are right for it. (动植物因环境适宜而) 旺盛 ❑ *The plant flourishes particularly well in slightly harsher climes.* 这种植物在较为恶劣一点的气候中长得特别茂盛。 ● **flour·ish·ing** ADJ 繁盛的 ❑ *...a flourishing fox population.* …不断繁衍的狐狸群。 **3** V-T If you **flourish** an object, you wave it about in a way that makes people notice it. 挥舞 ❑ *He flourished the glass to emphasize the point.* 他挥舞着杯子来强调这一点。 ● N-COUNT **Flourish** is also a noun. 挥动 ❑ *He took his cap from under his arm with a flourish and pulled it low over his eyes.* 他挥手从腋下取出帽子，拉低帽檐盖住眼睛。

flout /flaʊt/ (**flouts, flouting, flouted**) V-T If you **flout** something such as a law, an order, or an accepted way of behaving, you deliberately do not obey it or follow it. 无视 ❑ *...illegal campers who persist in flouting the law.* …一向无视法律的非法露营者。

flow ♦♦◊ /floʊ/ (**flows, flowing, flowed**) **1** V-I If a liquid, gas, or electrical current **flows** somewhere, it moves there steadily and continuously. 流动 ❑ *A stream flowed gently down into the valley.* 一条小溪缓缓地流进山谷。 ❑ *The current flows into electric motors that drive the*

f

Word Web flower

People love **flowers** because they are **colorful** and they smell good. But the **color** and **scent** of flowers are also important in **reproduction**. Sometimes the wind helps pollinate a plant. However, most plants must attract **insects**, hummingbirds, or **bats** to guarantee **fertilization**. If this doesn't happen, no **seeds** form. As one of these creatures lands on a flower, **grains** of pollen stick to its body. It carries these to another flower. Different colors attract different insects and animals. Yellow and blue flowers seem to draw **bees** and **butterflies**. Red flowers attract hummingbirds. At night, **bats** seek out white flowers.

F

wheels. 电流流进电机，驱动轮子。● N-VAR **Flow** is also a noun. 流动 ❑ *It works only in the veins, where the blood flow is slower.* 它只在血液流动较缓的静脉中起作用。 2 V-I If a number of people or things **flow** from one place to another, they move there steadily in large groups, usually without stopping. (大量人或物) 流动 ❑ *Large numbers of refugees continue to flow from the troubled region into the no-man's land.* 大批的难民持续从骚乱地区涌进无人区。● N-VAR **Flow** is also a noun. 流动 ❑ *She watched the frantic flow of cars and buses along the street.* 她注视着街道上川流不息的小车和巴士。 3 V-I If information or money **flows** somewhere, it moves freely between people or organizations. (信息) 传播; (资金) 流通 ❑ *A lot of this information flowed through other police departments.* 该信息大批地传到了其他警务部门。● N-VAR **Flow** is also a noun. 传播; 流通 ❑ *...the opportunity to control the flow of information.* …控制信息传播的机会。 4 → see also **cash flow** 5 PHRASE If you say that an activity, or the person who is performing the activity, is **in full flow**, you mean that the activity has started and is being carried out with a great deal of energy and enthusiasm. 热火朝天的 ❑ *Lunch at Harry's Bar was in full flow when Irene made a splendid entrance.* 艾琳光彩夺目地进门时，哈里酒吧的午餐已进行得热火朝天了。
→ see **ocean, traffic**

flow chart (**flow charts**) N-COUNT A **flow chart** or a **flow diagram** is a diagram which represents the sequence of actions in a particular process or activity. 流程图 ❑ *This flow chart, shown below, summarizes the overall costing process.* 这张流程图如下所示，概括了成本计算的全程。

flow·er ♦♦◇ /flaʊər/ (**flowers, flowering, flowered**) 1 N-COUNT A **flower** is the part of a plant which is often brightly colored, grows at the end of a stem, and only survives for a short time. 花 (朵) ❑ *Each individual flower is tiny.* 每一朵花都很小。 2 N-COUNT A **flower** is a stem of a plant that has one or more flowers on it and has been picked, usually with others, for example, to give as a present or to put in a vase. 花 (株) ❑ *...a bunch of flowers sent by a new admirer.* …一位新崇拜者送来的一束花。 3 N-COUNT **Flowers** are small plants that are grown for their flowers as opposed to trees, shrubs, and vegetables. 花卉 ❑ *...a lawned area surrounded by screening plants and flowers.* …四周环绕着屏障植物和花卉的一块草地。 4 V-I When a plant or tree **flowers**, its flowers appear and open. 开花 ❑ *Several of these rhododendrons will flower this year for the first time.* 这些杜鹃花中有好几株今年将第一次开花。 5 V-I When something **flowers**, for example, a political movement or a relationship, it gets stronger and more successful. (政治运动等) 壮大; (关系等) 变得更好 ❑ *Their relationship flowered.* 他们的关系变得更好了。
→ see Word Web: **flower**

Word Partnership *flower* 的常用搭配:

V.	**pick** a flower 2
N.	flower **arrangement**, flower **garden**, flower **shop**, flower **show** 2 3
ADJ.	**dried** flower, **fresh** flower 2 3

flow·er·ing /flaʊərɪŋ/ 1 N-UNCOUNT **The flowering of** something such as an idea or artistic style is the development of its popularity and success. (思想或艺术风格的) 盛行 ❑ *He may be happy with the flowering of new thinking, but he has yet to contribute much to it himself.* 他也许对新思想的盛行感到高兴，但他自己还没有为此作出多大贡献。 2 ADJ **Flowering** shrubs, trees, or plants are those which produce noticeable flowers. 开花的 [ADJ n] ❑ *...a late summer flowering plant like an aster.* …像紫菀一样在夏末开花的植物。

flown /floʊn/ **Flown** is the past participle of **fly**. **fly**的过去分词

▲ **flu** /flu/ N-UNCOUNT **Flu** is an illness which is similar to a bad cold but more serious. It often makes you feel very weak and makes your muscles hurt. 流感 [also "the" N] ❑ *I got the flu.* 我得了流感。

fluc·tu·ate /flʌktʃueɪt/ (**fluctuates, fluctuating, fluctuated**) V-I If something **fluctuates**, it changes a lot in an irregular way. 波动 ❑ *Body temperature can fluctuate if you are ill.* 如果你病了，体温会波动。● **fluc·tua·tion** /flʌktʃueɪʃən/ N-VAR (**fluctuations**) 波动 ❑ *Don't worry about tiny fluctuations in your weight.* 不用担心你体重的轻微波动。

flu·ent /fluənt/ 1 ADJ Someone who is **fluent in** a particular language can speak the language easily and correctly. You can also say that someone speaks **fluent** French, Chinese, or some other language. 流利的 ❑ *She studied eight foreign languages but is fluent in only six of them.* 她学了8种外语，但流利的只有其中的6种。● **flu·en·cy** N-UNCOUNT 流利 ❑ *To work as a translator, you need fluency in at least one foreign language.* 要做一名译员，你至少要一门外语流利。● **flu·ent·ly** ADV 流利地 ❑ *He spoke three languages fluently.* 他可以流利地说3种语言。 2 ADJ If your speech, reading, or writing is **fluent**, you speak, read, or write easily, smoothly, and clearly with no mistakes. 流畅的 ❑ *He had emerged from being a hesitant and unsure candidate into a fluent debater.* 他从一个吞吞吐吐、毫不自信的候选人成长为一位流畅的辩手。● **flu·en·cy** N-UNCOUNT 流畅 ❑ *His son was praised for speeches of remarkable fluency.* 他的儿子非常流利的发言受到了表扬。● **flu·ent·ly** ADV 流畅地 [ADV with v] ❑ *Alex didn't read fluently till he was nearly seven.* 亚历克斯快到7岁时才能顺畅地阅读。

fluff /flʌf/ (**fluffs, fluffing, fluffed**) 1 N-UNCOUNT **Fluff** consists of soft threads or fibers in the form of small, light balls or lumps. For example, you can refer to the fur of a small animal as **fluff**. 绒毛 ❑ *The nest contained two chicks: just small gray balls of fluff.* 窝里有2只小鸡：还只是两个灰色的小毛球。 2 V-T If you **fluff** something that you are trying to do, you are unsuccessful or you do it badly. 把…搞糟 [INFORMAL] ❑ *She fluffed her interview at Harvard.* 她把哈佛的面试搞糟了。

fluffy /flʌfi/ (**fluffier, fluffiest**) 1 ADJ If you describe something such as a towel or a toy animal as **fluffy**, you mean that it is very soft. 柔软的 ❑ *...fluffy white towels.* …柔软的白毛巾。 2 ADJ A cake or other food that is **fluffy** is very light because it has a lot of air in it. (蛋糕或其它食品) 松软的 ❑ *Cream together the margarine and sugar with a wooden spoon until light and fluffy.* 用一只木勺将人造黄油和食糖搅拌为稀松的糊状。

flu·id /fluɪd/ (**fluids**) 1 N-MASS A **fluid** is a liquid. 液体 [FORMAL] ❑ *The blood vessels may leak fluid, which distorts vision.* 血管可能渗漏出液体，扰乱视觉。 ❑ *Make sure that you drink plenty of fluids.* 一定要饮用大量流质。 2 ADJ **Fluid** movements or lines or designs are smooth and graceful. 优雅流畅的 ❑ *His painting became less illustrational and more fluid.* 他的画变得更为流畅，没那么生硬了。

fluke /fluk/ (**flukes**) N-COUNT If you say that something good is a **fluke**, you mean that it happened accidentally rather than by being planned or arranged. 侥幸 [usu sing, also "by" N] [INFORMAL] ❑ *The discovery was something of a fluke.* 这项发现多少有点侥幸。

flung /flʌŋ/ **Flung** is the past tense and past participle of **fling**. **fling**的过去式和过去分词

flunk /flʌŋk/ (**flunks, flunking, flunked**) V-T If you **flunk** an exam or a course, you fail to reach the required standard. 未通过 (考试或课程) [mainly AM, INFORMAL] ❑ *Your son is upset because he flunked a history exam.* 你儿子很沮丧是因为他没通过历史考试。
▶ **flunk out** PHRASAL VERB If you **flunk out**, you are dismissed from a school or college because your grades are not satisfactory. (因成绩太差) 被退学 [mainly AM, INFORMAL] ❑ *He flunked out, a school official told CNN.* 一位校方官员告诉美国有线电视新闻网说，他被退学了。 ❑ *If he doesn't find a solution to his problem soon, he'll surely flunk out of college.* 如果他不能很快找到解决问题的办法，他肯定要被学院退学。

▲ **fluo·res·cent** /flʊrɛsᵊnt/ **1** ADJ A **fluorescent** surface, substance, or color has a very bright appearance when light is directed onto it, as if it is actually shining itself. 荧光的 ❑ *...a piece of fluorescent tape.* …一段荧光带。 **2** ADJ A **fluorescent** light shines with a very hard, bright light and is usually in the form of a long strip. 发荧光的 ❑ *Fluorescent lights flickered, and then the room was brilliantly, blindingly bright.* 荧光灯闪烁了几下，然后房间就亮得刺眼。
→ see **light**

fluo·ride /flʊəraɪd/ N-UNCOUNT **Fluoride** is a mixture of chemicals that is sometimes added to drinking water and toothpaste because it is considered to be good for people's teeth. 氟化物
→ see **teeth**

flur·ry /flɜri/ (**flurries**) **1** N-COUNT A **flurry** of something such as activity or excitement is a short intense period of it. 一段短暂的紧张期 ❑ *...a flurry of diplomatic activity aimed at ending the war.* …一阵紧张的外交活动，旨在结束战争。 **2** N-COUNT A **flurry** of something such as snow is a small amount of it that suddenly appears for a short time and moves in a quick, swirling way. (雪等的) 一阵 ❑ *The Alps expect heavy cloud over the weekend with light snow flurries and strong winds.* 阿尔卑斯山预计周末是多云，有小阵雪和强风。

★ **flush** /flʌʃ/ (**flushes, flushing, flushed**) **1** V-I If you **flush**, your face gets red because you are hot or ill, or because you are feeling a strong emotion such as embarrassment or anger. 脸红 ❑ *Do you sweat a lot or flush a lot?* 你常出汗或是常脸红吗？ ● N-COUNT **Flush** is also a noun. 脸红 ❑ *There was a slight flush on his cheeks.* 他的面颊上有淡淡的红晕。 ● **flushed** ADJ 脸红的 ❑ *Her face was flushed with anger.* 她气得满脸通红。 **2** V-T/V-I When someone **flushes** a toilet after using it, they fill the toilet bowl with water in order to clean it, usually by pressing a handle or pulling a chain. You can also say that a toilet **flushes**. 冲 (马桶) ❑ *She flushed the toilet and went back in the bedroom.* 她冲了马桶，然后回到卧室。 ● N-COUNT **Flush** is also a noun. 冲水 ❑ *He heard the flush of a toilet.* 他听到马桶的冲水声。 **3** V-T If you **flush** something **down** the toilet, you get rid of it by putting it into the toilet bowl and flushing the toilet. (从马桶里) 冲掉 ❑ *He was found trying to flush the pills down the toilet.* 他被发现试图从马桶冲掉药丸。 **4** V-T If you **flush** a part of your body, you clean it or make it healthier by using a large amount of liquid to get rid of dirt or harmful substances. 冲洗 (身体某部位) ❑ *Flush the eye with clean cold water for at least 15 minutes.* 用干净的冷水冲洗眼睛至少15分钟。 ● PHRASAL VERB **Flush out** means the same as **flush**. 冲洗 (同 **flush**) ❑ *...an "alternative" therapy that gently flushes out the colon to remove toxins.* …一种"替代"疗法，通过温和冲洗大肠排毒。 **5** V-T If you **flush** dirt or a harmful substance **out** of a place, you get rid of it by using a large amount of liquid. 用水冲 ❑ *That won't flush out all the sewage, but it should unclog some stinking drains.* 那样做不会冲走全部的污水，但应该能疏通一下发臭的下水道。 **6** V-T If you **flush** people or animals **out** of a place where they are hiding, you find or capture them by forcing them to come out of that place. 把…赶出 ❑ *They flushed them out of their hiding places.* 他们将其赶出了藏身之地。
→ see **plumbing**

Word Partnership *flush* 的常用搭配:

ADJ. **slight** flush **1**
N. ***someone's* face** flushes, flush **of embarrassment** **1**
flush **a toilet** **2**

flushed /flʌʃt/ ADJ If you say that someone is **flushed with** success or pride you mean that they are very excited by their success or pride. (因成功或自豪而) 兴奋的 [v-link ADJ "with" n] ❑ *Grace was flushed with the success of the venture.* 格雷斯为这次成功冒险感到兴奋。

flus·ter /flʌstər/ (**flusters, flustering, flustered**) V-T If you **fluster** someone, you make them feel nervous and confused by rushing them and preventing them from concentrating on what they are doing. 使慌张 ❑ *The General refused to be flustered.* 将军没有被搅得慌乱不安。 ● **flus·tered** ADJ 慌张的 ❑ *She was so flustered that she forgot her reply.* 她慌得忘了回答。

▲ **flute** /flut/ (**flutes**) N-VAR A **flute** is a musical instrument of the woodwind family. You play it by blowing over a hole near one end while holding it sideways to your mouth. 长笛
→ see **orchestra**

★ **flut·ter** /flʌtər/ (**flutters, fluttering, fluttered**) **1** V-T/V-I If something thin or light **flutters**, or if you **flutter** it, it moves up and down or from side to side with a lot of quick, light movements. 拍动；飘动 ❑ *Her chiffon skirt was fluttering in the night breeze.* 她的薄绸裙在晚风中飘动。 ❑ *...a butterfly fluttering its wings.* …一只拍动着翅膀的蝴蝶。 ● N-COUNT **Flutter** is also a noun. 飘动；拍动 ❑ *...a flutter of white cloth.* …白布的飘动。 **2** V-I If something light such as a small bird or a piece of paper **flutters** somewhere, it moves through the air with small quick movements. 飘舞；振翅

▲ **flux** /flʌks/ N-UNCOUNT If something is in a state **of flux**, it is constantly changing. 不断的变动 ❑ *Education remains in a state of flux which will take some time to settle down.* 教育处于不断的变化中，需要一段时间才能稳定下来。

fly ◆◆◆ /flaɪ/ (**flies, flying, flew, flown**) **1** N-COUNT A **fly** is a small insect with two wings. There are many kinds of flies, and the most common are black in color. 苍蝇 ❑ *Flies buzzed at the animals' swishing tails.* 苍蝇在动物甩动的尾巴边嗡嗡叫。 **2** N-COUNT The front opening on a pair of pants is referred to as the **fly**. It usually consists of a zipper or row of buttons behind a band of cloth. 裤子的前开口 ❑ *I'm the kind of person who checks to see if my fly is undone.* 我是那种会检查裤子开口是否拉上的人。 **3** V-I When something such as a bird, insect, or aircraft **flies**, it moves through the air. 飞 ❑ *The planes flew through the clouds.* 飞机穿越云层。 **4** V-I If you **fly** somewhere, you travel there in an aircraft. 乘飞机 ❑ *He flew to Los Angeles.* 他乘飞机去洛杉矶。 ❑ *He flew back to London.* 他乘飞机回到伦敦。 **5** V-T/V-I When someone **flies** an aircraft, they control its movement in the air. 驾驶 (飞机)；驾驶飞机 ❑ *Parker had successfully flown both aircraft.* 帕克成功地驾驶过这两架飞机。 ❑ *He flew a small plane to Cuba.* 他驾驶一架小飞机去古巴。 ❑ *I learned to fly in Vietnam.* 我在越南学会了驾驶飞机。 ● **fly·ing** N-UNCOUNT 飞行 ❑ *...a flying instructor.* …一名飞行教练。 **6** V-T To **fly** someone or something somewhere means to take or send them there in an aircraft. 空运 ❑ *It may be possible to fly the women and children out on Thursday.* 周四有可能将这些妇女和儿童空运出去。 **7** V-I If something such as your hair **is flying** about, it is moving about freely and loosely in the air. 飞舞 ❑ *His long, uncovered hair flew back in the wind.* 他那无遮盖的长发随风向后飞舞。 **8** V-T/V-I If you **fly** a flag or if it **is flying**, you display it at the top of a pole. 升 (旗)；飘扬 ❑ *They flew the flag of the African National Congress.* 他们挥动着非洲国民大会的旗帜。 **9** V-I If you say that someone or something **flies** in a particular direction, you are emphasizing that they move there with a lot of speed or force. 飞奔 [EMPHASIS] ❑ *She flew to their bedsides when they were ill.* 她在他们生病时飞奔到他们的床边。 **10** → see also **flying** **11** PHRASE If you say that someone wouldn't **hurt a fly** or wouldn't **harm a fly**, you are emphasizing that they are very kind and gentle. (不会) 踩死一只蚂蚁 (指温柔善良) [EMPHASIS] ❑ *Ray wouldn't hurt a fly.* 雷很温柔善良。 **12** PHRASE If you **let fly**, you attack someone, either physically by hitting them, or with words by insulting them. 攻击 ❑ *A simmering dispute ended with her letting fly with a stream of obscenities.* 激烈的争吵以她那一连串污言秽语的攻击告终。 **13** PHRASE

Word Web fly

About 500 years ago, Leonardo da Vinci* designed some simple flying machines. His sketches look a lot like modern **parachutes** and **helicopters**. About 300 years later, the Montgolfier Brothers amazed the king of France with **hot-air balloon** flights. Soon inventors in many countries began experimenting with blimps, hang gliders, and human-powered **aircraft**. Most inventors tried to imitate the **flight** of birds. Then in 1903, the Wright brothers invented the first true **airplane**. Their gasoline-powered **craft** carried one **passenger**. The trip lasted 59 seconds. And amazingly, 70 years later **jumbo jets** carrying 400 passengers became an everyday occurrence.

Leonardo da Vinci (1452-1519): an Italian inventor and artist.

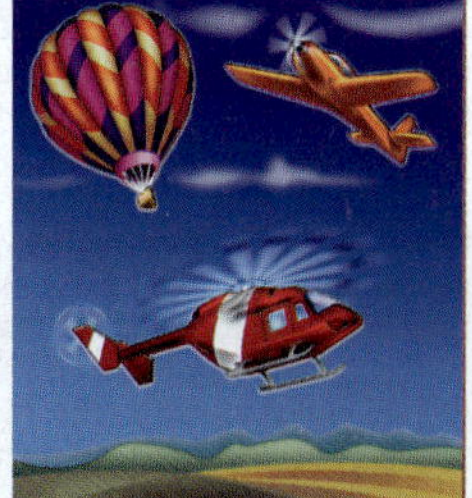

f

If you **send** someone or something **flying** or if they **go flying**, they move through the air and fall down with a lot of force. 把(某人/某物)打翻在地 ❑ *The blow sent the young man flying.* 那一击将那年轻人打翻在地。 **14** PHRASE If you do something **on the fly**, you do it quickly or automatically, without planning it in advance. 立刻;飞快 [V PHR] [mainly AM] ❑ *You've got to be able to make decisions on the fly as deadlines loom.* 你必须能够立刻作出决定，因为最后期限迫在眉睫。 **15** to **fly in the face of** → see **face** **16** to **fly off the handle** → see **handle** **17** a **fly in the ointment** → see **ointment** **18** when **pigs fly** → see **pig** **19** **sparks fly** → see **spark** **20** **time flies** → see **time**
→ see Word Web: **fly**
→ see **flag, flight**

▶ **fly into** PHRASAL VERB If you **fly into** a bad temper or a panic, you suddenly become very angry or anxious and show this in your behavior. 突然进发 ❑ *Losing a game would cause him to fly into a rage.* 输掉比赛会使他大发雷霆。

F

fly·er /flaɪər/ (**flyers**) also **flier** **1** N-COUNT A **flyer** is a pilot of an aircraft. 飞行员 ❑ *The American flyers sprinted for their planes and got into the cockpit.* 美国飞行员疾速跑向他们的飞机，进入驾驶舱。 **2** N-COUNT You can refer to someone who travels by airplane as a **flyer**. 飞机乘客 ❑ *...regular business flyers.* …经常乘飞机的商务旅客。 **3** N-COUNT A **flyer** is a small printed notice which is used to advertise a particular company, service, or event. 宣传单 ❑ *Thousands of flyers advertising the tour were handed out during the festival.* 节日期间散发了数千份推广这项旅游的宣传单。
→ see **advertising**

fly·ing /flaɪɪŋ/ **1** ADJ A **flying** animal has wings and is able to fly. 会飞的 [ADJ n] ❑ *...species of flying insects.* …飞行昆虫的种类。 **2** PHRASE If someone or something **gets off to a flying start**, or **makes a flying start**, they start very well, for example, in a race or a new job. 开端良好 ❑ *Advertising revenue in the new financial year has got off to a flying start.* 广告收入在新的财政年度开端良好。

fly·over /flaɪoʊvər/ (**flyovers**) N-COUNT A **flyover** is a structure which carries one road over the top of another road. 立交桥 [BRIT]

in AM, use **overpass**

FM /ɛf ɛm/ **FM** is a method of transmitting radio waves that can be used to broadcast high quality sound. **FM** is an abbreviation for "frequency modulation." 调频

foal /foʊl/ (**foals, foaling, foaled**) **1** N-COUNT A **foal** is a very young horse. 马驹 **2** V-I When a female horse **foals**, it gives birth. 产驹 ❑ *The mare is due to foal today.* 母马今天要下崽了。

★ **foam** /foʊm/ (**foams**) **1** N-UNCOUNT **Foam** consists of a mass of small bubbles that are formed when air and a liquid are mixed together. 泡沫(橡胶);海绵 ❑ *The water curved round the rocks in great bursts of foam.* 水流卷绕着岩石产生大量的泡沫。 **2** N-MASS **Foam** is used to refer to various kinds of manufactured products which have a soft, light texture like a thick liquid. 泡沫 ❑ *...shaving foam.* …剃须泡沫。 **3** N-MASS **Foam** or **foam rubber** is soft rubber full of small holes which is used, for example, to make mattresses and cushions. 泡沫(橡胶);海绵 ❑ *...modern three-piece suites filled with foam rubber.* …塞满海绵的现代3件套。

fo·cal point /foʊkəl pɔɪnt/ (**focal points**) N-COUNT The **focal point** of something is the thing that people concentrate on or pay most attention to. 关注点 ❑ *The focal point for the town's many visitors is the museum.* 许多到该城的游客关注的重点是这座博物馆。

fo·cus ♦♦◇ /foʊkəs/ (**focuses, focusing** or **focussing, focused** or **focussed**)

The plural of the noun can be either **focuses** or **foci** /foʊsaɪ/.

1 V-T/V-I If you **focus on** a particular topic or if your attention **is focused on** it, you concentrate on it and think about it, discuss it, or deal with it, rather than dealing with other topics. 关注 ❑ *The research effort has focused on tracing the effects of growing levels of five compounds.* 研究集中跟踪5种化合物水平上升带来的影响。 ❑ *Today he was able to focus his message exclusively on the economy.* 今天他能够将重点聚焦在经济方面。 **2** V-T/V-I If you **focus** your eyes or if your eyes **focus**, your eyes adjust so that you can clearly see the thing that you want to look at. If you **focus** a camera, telescope, or other instrument, you adjust it so that you can see clearly through it. 使(眼睛、相机、望远镜或其它仪器)对焦;聚焦 ❑ *Kelly couldn't focus his eyes well enough to tell if the figure was male or female.* 凯利无法看清那个人影是男的还是女的。 ❑ *His eyes slowly began to focus on what looked like a small dark ball.* 他的眼睛开始慢慢聚焦到那个小黑球似的东西上。

3 V-T If you **focus** rays of light on a particular point, you pass them through a lens or reflect them from a mirror so that they meet at that point. 把(光线)聚焦 ❑ *Magnetic coils focus the electron beams into fine spots.* 磁线圈将电子束聚焦成细小的点。 **4** N-COUNT **The focus** of something is the main topic or main thing that it is concerned with. 焦点 ❑ *The UN's role in promoting peace is increasingly the focus of international attention.* 联合国在促进和平方面的作用越来越成为国际关注的焦点。 ❑ *The new system is the focus of controversy.* 新系统是争议的焦点。 **5** N-COUNT Your **focus** on something is the special attention that you pay it. 关注 ❑ *He said his sudden focus on foreign policy was not motivated by presidential politics.* 他说他突然关注外交政策并不是受总统政治的驱使。 **6** N-UNCOUNT If you say that something has a **focus**, you mean that you can see a purpose in it. 诉求点 ❑ *Somehow, though, their latest CD has a focus that the others have lacked.* 但是，不管怎么说，他们的最新激光唱片具备别人没有的诉求点。 **7** N-UNCOUNT You use **focus** to refer to the fact of adjusting your eyes or a camera, telescope, or other instrument, and to the degree to which you can see clearly. 焦点;对焦 ❑ *His focus switched to the little white ball.* 他的焦点转移到了那个小白球上。 **8** PHRASE If an image or a camera, telescope, or other instrument is **in focus**, the edges of what you see are clear and sharp. (图像)清晰;(相机、望远镜或其他仪器)对准焦点 ❑ *Pictures should be in focus, with realistic colors and well composed groups.* 照片应该成像清晰，色彩逼真，构图合理。 **9** PHRASE If something is **in focus**, it is being discussed or its purpose and nature are clear. 受关注 ❑ *We want to keep the real issues in focus.* 我们要让真正的问题受到关注。 **10** PHRASE If an image or a camera, telescope, or other instrument is **out of focus**, the edges of what you see are unclear. (图像)模糊;(相机、望远镜或其他仪器)对焦不准 ❑ *In some of the pictures the subjects are out of focus while the background is sharp.* 在一些照片中，主体对焦不准，背景反而很清晰。
→ see **photography, telescope**

Word Partnership *focus* 的常用搭配:

N.	focus **attention** 1
	focus *your* **eyes**, focus **a camera** 2
V.	**shift** *your* focus 4 5 7
	come into focus 7

fo·cus group (**focus groups**) N-COUNT A **focus group** is a specially selected group of people who are intended to represent the general public. Focus groups have discussions in which their opinions are recorded as a form of market research. (代表公众的)焦点小组 ❑ *The market research company BMRB conducted 12 focus groups for the project.* 市场调研公司BMRB为此项目采用了12个焦点组。

fod·der /fɒdər/ **1** N-UNCOUNT **Fodder** is food that is given to cows, horses, and other animals. 饲料 ❑ *...fodder for horses.* …马的饲料。 **2** N-UNCOUNT If you say that something is **fodder** for a particular purpose, you mean that it is useful for that purpose and perhaps nothing else. (供某种用途的)素材 [DISAPPROVAL] ❑ *The press conference simply provided more fodder for another attack on his character.* 记者招待会只是提供更多的素材，来对他人格进行另一轮攻击。

▲ **foe** /foʊ/ (**foes**) N-COUNT Someone's **foe** is their enemy. 敌人 [WRITTEN] ❑ *But he soon discovers that his old foe may be leading him into a trap.* 但他不久发现他的老对头也许正把他引入圈套。

foe·tus /fitəs/ [BRIT] → see **fetus**

fog /fɒg/ (**fogs**) **1** N-VAR When there is **fog**, there are tiny drops of water in the air which form a thick cloud and make it difficult to see things. 雾 ❑ *The crash happened in thick fog.* 这次撞车发生在浓雾中。 **2** N-SING A **fog** is an unpleasant cloud of something such as smoke inside a building or room. 一团(烟雾) ❑ *...a fog of stale cigarette smoke.* …一团难闻的香烟烟雾。

fog·gy /fɒgi/ (**foggier, foggiest**) **1** ADJ When it is **foggy**, there is fog. 有雾的 ❑ *It's quite foggy now.* 现在雾很大。 **2** PHRASE If you say that you **haven't the foggiest** or you **haven't the foggiest idea**, you are emphasizing that you do not know something. 压根儿不知道 [INFORMAL, EMPHASIS] ❑ *I did not have the foggiest idea what he meant.* 我压根儿不知道他是什么意思。

★ **foil** /fɔɪl/ (**foils, foiling, foiled**) **1** N-UNCOUNT **Foil** consists of sheets of metal as thin as paper. It is used to wrap food in. (用于包裹食物的)箔纸 ❑ *Pour cider around the meat and cover with foil.* 在肉的四周倒上苹果酒，然后盖上箔纸。 **2** V-T If you **foil** someone's plan or attempt to do something, for example, to commit a crime, you succeed in stopping them from doing what they want. 挫败 [JOURNALISM] ❑ *A brave police chief foiled an armed robbery by grabbing the* *raider's shotgun.* 一个勇敢的警长夺过歹徒的猎枪，挫败了一起武装抢劫。

fold ♦◇◇ /fo̲ʊld/ (**folds, folding, folded**) 1 V-T If you **fold** something such as a piece of paper or cloth, you bend it so that one part covers another part, often pressing the edge so that it stays in place. 折叠 ❑ *He folded the paper carefully.* 他小心地把那张纸折起来。 ❑ *Fold the omelette in half.* 把煎蛋对折。 2 V-T/V-I If a piece of furniture or equipment **folds** or if you can **fold** it, you can make it smaller by bending or closing parts of it. 翻折 ❑ *The back of the bench folds forward to make a table.* 长椅的靠背可向前翻折成一张桌子。 ❑ *This portable seat folds flat for easy storage.* 这张便携式座椅可折平，便于存放。 ● PHRASAL VERB **Fold up** means the same as **fold**. 折叠 ❑ *When not in use it folds up out of the way.* 不用的时候，它折起来不会挡路。 3 V-T If you **fold** your arms or hands, you bring them together and cross or link them, for example, over your chest. 交叠 (双臂或双手) ❑ *Meer folded his arms over his chest and turned his head away.* 米尔把双臂交叠在胸前，扭开头去。 4 N-COUNT A **fold** in a piece of paper or cloth is a bend that you make in it when you put one part of it over another part and press the edge. 折痕 ❑ *Make another fold and turn the ends together.* 再折一次，然后把两端叠在一起。 5 N-COUNT The **folds** in a piece of cloth are the curved shapes which are formed when it is not hanging or lying flat. 褶皱 ❑ *The priest fumbled in the folds of his gown.* 这位牧师胡乱地整了整长袍上的褶皱。

▶ **fold up** 1 PHRASAL VERB If you **fold** something **up**, you make it into a smaller, neater shape by folding it, usually several times. 将…折起来 ❑ *She folded it up, and tucked it into her purse.* 她将它折起来，塞进钱包里。 2 → see also **fold 2**

Word Partnership *fold* 的常用搭配：

ADV. fold **carefully**, fold **gently**, fold **neatly** 1
N. fold **clothes**, fold **paper** 1
fold ***your* arms/hands** 3

fold·er /fo̲ʊldər/ (**folders**) 1 N-COUNT A **folder** is a thin piece of cardboard in which you can keep loose papers. 活页夹 2 N-COUNT A **folder** is a group of files that are stored together on a computer. (电脑上储存文件的) 文件夹
→ see **office**

▲ **fo·li·age** /fo̲ʊliɪdʒ/ N-UNCOUNT The leaves of a plant are referred to as its **foliage**. 叶子 ❑ *...shrubs with gray or silver foliage.* …灰叶或银叶灌木丛。

folk ♦◇◇ /fo̲ʊk/ (**folks**)

Folk can also be used as the plural form for meaning 1.

1 N-PLURAL You can refer to people as **folk** or **folks**. 人 ❑ *Country folk can tell you that there are certain places which animals avoid.* 乡下人会告诉你有些地方动物是不去的。 ❑ *These are the folks from the local TV station.* 这些是从当地电视台来的人。 2 N-PLURAL You can refer to your close family, especially your mother and father, as your **folks**. 家人 [INFORMAL] ❑ *I've been avoiding my folks lately.* 我最近一直在避开家人。 3 N-VOC You can use **folks** as a term of address when you are talking to several people. 各位 [INFORMAL] ❑ *"It's a question of money, folks," I said.* "这是钱的问题，各位。"我说道。 4 ADJ **Folk** art and customs are traditional or typical of a particular community or nation. 民间的 [ADJ n] ❑ *...South American folk art.* …南美民间艺术。 5 ADJ **Folk** music is music which is traditional or typical of a particular community or nation. 民间的 (音乐) ● N-UNCOUNT **Folk** is also a noun. 民间 (音乐) [ADJ n] ❑ *...a variety of music including classical and folk.* …包括古典音乐和民间音乐在内的各种音乐。

folk·lore /fo̲ʊklɔr/ N-UNCOUNT **Folklore** is the traditional stories, customs, and habits of a particular community or nation. 民间传说；民俗 ❑ *In Chinese folklore the bat is a symbol of good fortune.* 在中国民间传说中，蝙蝠是好运的象征。

follow

❶ GO OR COME AFTER
❷ ACT ACCORDING TO SOMETHING, OBSERVE SOMETHING
❸ UNDERSTAND
❹ PHRASAL VERBS

❶ **fol·low** ♦♦♦ /fɒloʊ/ (**follows, following, followed**)
➪ **Please look at meanings 16 – 18 to see if the expression you are looking for is shown under another headword.** 1 V-T/V-I If you **follow** someone who is going somewhere, you move along behind them because you want to go to the same place. 跟随 ❑ *We followed him up the steps into a large hall.* 我们跟他上了台阶，进入一个大厅。 ❑ *Please follow me, madam.* 夫人，请跟我来。 ❑ *They took him into a small room and I followed.* 他们把他带进一间小屋，我跟了过去。 2 V-T If you **follow** someone who is going somewhere, you move along behind them without their knowledge, in order to catch them or find out where they are going. 跟踪 ❑ *She realized that the Mercedes was following her.* 她意识到那辆奔驰在跟踪她。 3 V-T If you **follow** someone to a place where they have recently gone and where they are now, you go to join them there. 跟随 ❑ *He followed Janice to New York, where she was preparing an exhibition.* 他跟随贾妮丝去了纽约，她正在那儿准备一个展览。 4 V-T/V-I An event, activity, or period of time that **follows** a particular thing happens or comes after that thing, at a later time. 在…后到来；接着…发生 ❑ *...the rioting and looting that followed the verdict.* …判决之后发生的暴乱和抢劫。 ❑ *Other problems may follow.* 其它问题也许会随之而来。 5 V-T If you **follow** one thing **with** another, you do or say the second thing after you have done or said the first thing. 随后做 ❑ *Her first major role was in Martin Scorsese's "Goodfellas" and she followed this with a part in Spike Lee's "Jungle Fever."* 她首先在马丁・斯柯席斯的《好家伙》中演了重要角色，随后又演了斯派克・李的《丛林热》。 ● PHRASAL VERB **Follow up** means the same as **follow**. 随后做 ❑ *The book proved such a success that the authors followed it up with "The Messianic Legacy."* 该书获得了如此大的成功，以至作者随后又出了一本《天主的遗产》。 6 V-T/V-I If it **follows** that a particular thing is the case, that thing is a logical result of something else being true or being the case. 理所当然 ❑ *Just because a bird does not breed one year, it does not follow that it will fail the next.* 不能仅仅因为鸟一年没有繁殖就推断它下一年也不会繁殖。 ❑ *If the explanation is right, two things follow.* 如果该解释正确，那么就有两种情形。 7 V-T/V-I If you refer to the words that **follow** or **followed**, you are referring to the words that come next or came next in a piece of writing or speech. 接下来 ❑ *What follows is an eye-witness account.* 接下来是目击者的陈述。 ❑ *There followed a list of places where Hans intended to visit.* 接下来是一张汉斯打算参观的地点列表。 8 V-T If you **follow** a path, route, or set of signs, you go somewhere using the path, route, or signs to direct you. 沿着…走 ❑ *If they followed the road, they would be certain to reach a village.* 如果他们沿着这条路走，一定会抵达一个村庄。 ❑ *All we had to do was follow the map.* 所有我们要做的是按照地图走。 9 V-T If something such as a path or river **follows** a particular route or line, it goes along that route or line. 沿着 ❑ *Our route follows the Pacific coast through densely populated neighborhoods.* 我们一路沿着太平洋海岸，穿过人口稠密的街区。 10 V-T If you **follow** something with your eyes, or if your eyes **follow** it, you watch it as it moves or you look along its route or course. (视线) 随…而移动 ❑ *Ann's eyes followed a police car as it drove slowly past.* 安的眼睛注视着一辆缓缓开过的警车。 11 V-T Something that **follows** a particular course of development happens or develops in that way. 按照…方式发展 ❑ *His release turned out to follow the pattern set by that of the other six hostages.* 他的获释方式结果和其他6位人质相同。 12 V-T If you **follow** someone in what you do, you do the same thing or job as they did previously. 沿袭 ❑ *He followed his father and became a surgeon.* 他沿袭了他父亲，成了一名外科医生。 13 PHRASE You use **as follows** in writing or speech to introduce something such as a list, description, or an explanation. 如下 ❑ *The winners are as follows: E. Walker; R. Foster; R. Gates; A. Mackintosh.* 获胜者如下：E.沃克、R.福斯特、R.盖茨和A.麦金托什。 14 PHRASE You use **followed by** to say what comes after something else in a list or ordered set of things. 由…紧接着 ❑ *Potatoes are still the most popular food, followed by white bread.* 土豆仍然是最受欢迎的食品，其次为白面包。 15 → see also **following** 16 to **follow in** someone's **footsteps** → see **footstep** 17 to **follow** your **nose** → see **nose** 18 to **follow suit** → see **suit**

Thesaurus *follow* 另参见：

V. pursue, shadow, trail ❶ 2
succeed ❶ 12

❷ **fol·low** ♦♦♦ /fɒloʊ/ (**follows, following, followed**) 1 V-T If you **follow** advice, an instruction, or a recipe, you act or do something in the way that it indicates. 听从 (建议、指示或药法) ❑ *Take care to follow the instructions carefully.* 注意严格遵循说明。 2 V-T/V-I If you **follow** what someone else has done, you do it too because you think it is a good thing or because you want to copy them. 仿效 ❑ *His admiration for the athlete did not extend to the point where he would*

f

follow his example in taking drugs. 他对这名运动员的崇拜还不至于到效仿他吸毒的程度。 **3** V-T If you **follow** something, you take an interest in it and keep informed about what happens. 随时关注 ❑ *...the millions of people who follow football because they genuinely love it.* …数百万人随时关注足球是因为真正热爱足球。 **4** V-T If you **follow** a particular religion or political belief, you have that religion or belief. 信奉（宗教或政治主张）❑ *"Do you follow any particular religion?"—"Yes, we're all Hindus."* "你们信什么教吗？"——"信，我们都是印度教教徒。"

❸ fol·low ◆◆◆ /fɒloʊ/ (**follows, following, followed**) **1** V-T/V-I If you are able to **follow** something such as an explanation or the story of a movie, you understand it as it continues and develops. 理解 ❑ *Can you follow the plot so far?* 你到目前能理解这个情节吗？ ❑ *I'm sorry, I don't follow.* 对不起，我不理解。 **2** → see also **following**

Word Partnership *follow* 的常用搭配：

ADV. **closely** follow ❶ **1 2 4**
blindly follow ❷ **1 2 4**
N. follow **a road**, follow **signs**, follow **a trail** ❶ **8**
follow **a pattern** ❶ **11**
follow **advice**, follow **directions**, follow **instructions**, follow **orders**, follow **rules** ❷ **1**
follow **a story** ❸ **1**

❹ fol·low ◆◆◆ /fɒloʊ/ (**follows, following, followed**)

▶ **follow through** PHRASAL VERB If you **follow through** an action, plan, or idea or **follow through** with it, you continue doing or thinking about it until you have done everything possible. 坚持完成 ❑ *The leadership has been unwilling to follow through the implications of these ideas.* 领导层一直不愿意弄清楚这些想法的含意。 ❑ *I was trained to be an actress but I didn't follow it through.* 我接受过演员的训练，但没有坚持下去。

▶ **follow up** **1** PHRASAL VERB If you **follow up** something that has been said, suggested, or discovered, you try to find out more about it or take action about it. 追查 ❑ *State police are following up several leads.* 州警察局正在追查几条线索。 **2** → see also **follow** ❶ **5**, **follow-up**

fol·low·er /fɒloʊər/ (**followers**) N-COUNT A **follower** of a particular person, group, or belief is someone who supports or admires this person, group, or belief. 追随者 ❑ *...followers of the Zulu Inkatha movement.* …祖鲁印卡加运动的追随者。

fol·low·ing ◆◆◇ /fɒloʊɪŋ/ (**followings**) **1** PREP **Following** a particular event means after that event. 在…之后 ❑ *In the centuries following Christ's death, Christians genuinely believed the world was about to end.* 在耶稣死后的几个世纪里，基督徒们真地认为世界将要消亡。 **2** ADJ The **following** day, week, or year is the day, week, or year after the one you have just mentioned. 其后的（日、月、年等）[det ADJ] ❑ *The following day the picture appeared on the front pages of every newspaper in the world.* 次日，照片出现在世界各地报纸的头版。 ❑ *We went to dinner the following Monday evening.* 在接下来的那个周一晚上我们一起共进晚餐。 **3** ADJ You use **following** to refer to something that you are about to mention. 以下的 [det ADJ] ❑ *Write down the following information: name of product, type, date purchased and price.* 写下以下信息：产品名称、型号、购买日期和价格。 ● PRON **The following** refers to the thing or things that you are about to mention. 以下的事或物 ["the" PRON] ❑ *The following is a paraphrase of what was said.* 以下是对所说内容的解释。 **4** N-COUNT A person or organization that has a **following** has a group of people who support or admire their beliefs or actions. 支持者 ❑ *Australian rugby league enjoys a huge following in New Zealand.* 澳大利亚橄榄球队在新西兰有一大批支持者。

follow-up (**follow-ups**) N-VAR A **follow-up** is something that is done to continue or add to something done previously. 后续的事或物 ❑ *They are recording a follow-up to their successful 1989 album.* 他们正在为1989年那张成功专辑录制一张续辑。

fol·ly /fɒli/ (**follies**) N-VAR If you say that a particular action or way of behaving is **folly** or a **folly**, you mean that it is foolish. 愚蠢的事 ❑ *It's sheer folly to build nuclear power stations in a country that has dozens of earthquakes every year.* 在一个每年发生几十起地震的国家建立核电站实在愚蠢。

fond /fɒnd/ (**fonder, fondest**) **1** ADJ If you are **fond of** someone, you feel affection for them. 喜爱的 [v-link ADJ "of" n] ❑ *I am very fond of Michael.* 我很喜欢迈克尔。 ● **fond·ness** N-UNCOUNT 喜爱 ❑ *...a great fondness for children.* …对孩子们的深深喜爱。 **2** ADJ You use **fond** to describe people or their behavior when they show affection. 慈爱的 [ADJ n] ❑ *...a fond father.* …一个慈爱的父亲。 ● **fond·ly** ADV 慈爱地 [ADV after v] ❑ *Liz saw their eyes meet fondly across the table.* 利兹看到他们隔着桌子深情地对视着。 **3** ADJ If you are **fond of** something, you like it or you like doing it very much. 很喜欢 [v-link ADJ "of" n/-ing] ❑ *He was fond of marmalade.* 他很喜欢橘子酱。 ● **fond·ness** N-UNCOUNT 钟爱 ❑ *I've always had a fondness for chocolate cake.* 我一直对巧克力蛋糕情有独钟。 **4** ADJ If you have **fond** memories of someone or something, you remember them with pleasure. （回忆）美好的 [ADJ n] ❑ *I have very fond memories of living in our village.* 我对在我们村的生活有着美好的回忆。 ● **fond·ly** ADV 愉快地 [ADV with v] ❑ *My dad took us there when I was about four and I remembered it fondly.* 我爸爸在我四岁左右时带我去过那里，想起来很愉悦。 **5** ADJ You use **fond** to describe hopes, wishes, or beliefs which you think are foolish because they seem unlikely to be fulfilled. （希望、想法等）不切实际的 [ADJ n] ❑ *My fond hope is that we will be ready by Christmastime.* 我的不切实际的愿望就是我们能在圣诞节假期前准备好。 ● **fond·ly** ADV 不切实际地 [ADV with v] ❑ *I fondly imagined that surgery meant a few stitches and an overnight stay in the hospital.* 我不切实际地以为外科手术就是缝几针并在医院呆上一夜。

font /fɒnt/ (**fonts**) N-COUNT In printing, a **font** is a set of characters of the same style and size. 字体 ❑ *...the immense variety of fonts available in Microsoft Word and Publisher.* …微软的文字处理软件和排版软件中提供的种类繁多的字体。

food ◆◆◆ /fuːd/ (**foods**) **1** N-MASS **Food** is what people and animals eat. 食物 ❑ *Enjoy your food.* 用餐愉快。 ❑ *...frozen foods.* …冷冻食品。 **2** → see also **fast food, junk food** **3** PHRASE If you give someone **food for thought**, you make them think carefully about something. 发人深思的事 ❑ *Her speech offers much food for thought.* 她的演讲有许多发人深思的内容。

→ see Word Web: **food**

→ see **can, farm, rice, sugar, vegetarian**

food·stuff /fuːdstʌf/ (**foodstuffs**) N-VAR **Foodstuffs** are substances which people eat. 食品 ❑ *...basic foodstuffs such as sugar, cooking oil and cheese.* …糖、烹饪油、奶酪等基本食品。

fool ◆◇◇ /fuːl/ (**fools, fooling, fooled**) **1** N-COUNT If you call someone a **fool**, you are indicating that you think they are not at all sensible and show a lack of good judgment. 笨蛋 [DISAPPROVAL] ❑ *"You fool!" she shouted.* "你这个笨蛋！"她叫道。 **2** ADJ **Fool** is used to describe an action or person that is not at all sensible and shows a lack of good judgment. 愚蠢的 [ADJ n] [mainly AM, INFORMAL, DISAPPROVAL] ❑ *What a damn fool thing to do!* 这样做真是愚蠢得要死！ **3** V-T If someone **fools** you, they deceive or trick you. 欺骗；愚弄 ❑ *Art dealers fool a lot of people.* 艺术品经销商会愚弄许多人。 ❑ *Don't be fooled by his appearance.* 不要被他的外表所蒙蔽。 **4** V-I If you say that a person **is fooling with** something or someone, you mean that the way they are behaving is likely to cause problems. 瞎弄 ❑ *What are you doing fooling with such a*

Word Web food

The food chain begins with sunlight. Green **plants** absorb and store **energy** from the sun through photosynthesis. This energy is passed on to an herbivore (such as a mouse) that **eats** these plants. The mouse is then eaten by a carnivore (such as a snake). The snake may be eaten by a **top predator** (such as a hawk). When the hawk dies, its body is broken down by bacteria. Soon its **nutrients** become food for plants and the cycle begins again.

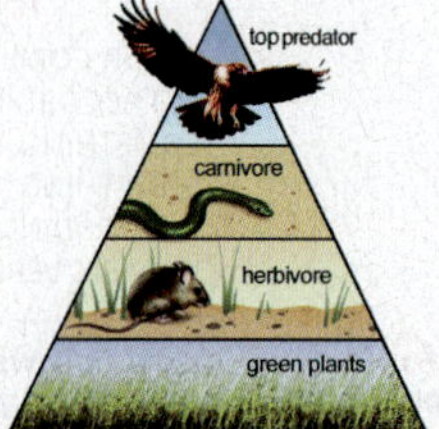

Food chain

staggering sum of money? 你拿这么惊人的一大笔钱瞎折腾什么？ 5 PHRASE If you **make a fool of** someone, you make them seem silly by telling people about something stupid that they have done, or by tricking them. 戏弄(某人) ❑ *Your brother is making a fool of you.* 你哥哥在戏弄你呢。 6 PHRASE If you **make a fool of** yourself, you behave in a way that makes other people think that you are silly or lacking in good judgment. 让(自己)出丑 ❑ *He was drinking and making a fool of himself.* 他喝酒的时候洋相百出。 7 PHRASE If you **play the fool** or **act the fool**, you behave in a playful, childish, and foolish way, usually in order to make other people laugh. 胡闹逗乐 ❑ *They used to play the fool together, calling each other silly names and giggling.* 他们过去常常一起胡闹，互相起绰号取笑。

▸ **fool around** PHRASAL VERB If you **fool around**, you behave in a silly, dangerous, or irresponsible way. 闲荡 ❑ *They were fooling around on an Army firing range.* 他们在一个部队射击场闲荡。

fool·ish /fuːlɪʃ/ 1 ADJ If someone's behavior or action is **foolish**, it is not sensible and shows a lack of good judgment. 愚蠢的 ❑ *It would be foolish to raise hopes unnecessarily.* 无缘无故地寄托希望是愚蠢的。 ●**fool·ish·ly** ADV 愚蠢地 ❑ *He admitted that he had acted foolishly.* 他承认自己做得很愚蠢。 ●**fool·ish·ness** N-UNCOUNT 愚蠢 ❑ *They don't accept any foolishness when it comes to spending money.* 他们在花钱的问题上不会接受任何愚蠢之举。 2 ADJ If you look or feel **foolish**, you look or feel so silly or ridiculous that people are likely to laugh at you. 傻乎乎的 ❑ *I just stood there feeling foolish and watching him.* 我就傻乎乎地站在那儿看着他。 ●**fool·ish·ly** ADV 傻乎乎地 [ADV after v] ❑ *He saw me standing there, grinning foolishly at him.* 他看到我站在那儿咧着嘴朝他傻乎乎地笑。

fool·proof /fulpruf/ ADJ Something such as a plan or a machine that is **foolproof** is so well designed, easy to understand, or easy to use that it cannot go wrong or be used wrongly. 不出问题的；不会弄错的 ❑ *The system is not 100 per cent foolproof.* 该系统不是百分之百不出毛病的。

foot
1 PART OF BODY
2 UNIT OF MEASUREMENT
3 LOWER END OF SOMETHING

❶ **foot** ♦♦♦ /fʊt/ (feet)
➪ **Please look at meanings 21 – 23 to see if the expression you are looking for is shown under another headword.** 1 N-COUNT Your **feet** are the parts of your body that are at the ends of your legs, and that you stand on. 脚 ❑ *She stamped her foot again.* 她又跺了跺脚。 ❑ *...a foot injury.* …脚伤。 2 ADJ A **foot** brake or **foot** pump is operated by your foot rather than by your hand. 脚踏的 [ADJ n] ❑ *I tried to reach the foot brakes but I couldn't.* 我试着去踩脚刹，但够不着。 3 ADJ A **foot** patrol or **foot** soldiers walk rather than traveling in vehicles or on horseback. 步行的 [ADJ n] ❑ *Paratroopers and foot-soldiers entered the building on the government's behalf.* 伞兵和步兵代表政府进入了大楼。 4 → see also **footing** 5 PHRASE If you get **cold feet about** something, you become nervous or frightened about it because you think it will fail. 紧张；害怕 ❑ *The Government is getting cold feet about the reforms.* 政府在改革上变得紧张胆小。 6 PHRASE If you say that someone **is finding** their **feet** in a new situation, you mean that they are starting to feel confident and to deal with things successfully. (在新环境) 站住脚 ❑ *I don't know anyone here but I am sure I will manage when I find my feet.* 我在这儿什么人都不认识，但我确信一旦站住脚就会应付过来。 7 PHRASE If you say that someone has their **feet on the ground**, you approve of the fact that they have a sensible and practical attitude toward life, and do not have unrealistic ideas. 脚踏实地 [APPROVAL] ❑ *In that respect he needs to keep his feet on the ground and not get carried away.* 就那方面看来，他需要脚踏实地而不能飘飘然。 8 PHRASE If you go somewhere **on foot**, you walk, rather than using any form of transport. 步行 ❑ *We rowed ashore, then explored the island on foot for the rest of the day.* 我们将船靠岸，然后在这天余下的时间里徒步上岛探险。 9 PHRASE If you are **on** your **feet**, you are standing up. 站着 ❑ *Everyone was on their feet applauding wildly.* 每个人都站起来热烈鼓掌。 10 PHRASE If you say that someone or something is **on** their **feet** again after an illness or difficult period, you mean that they have recovered and are back to normal. 恢复 ❑ *You need someone to take the pressure off and help you get back on your feet.* 你需要有人为你减减压，帮你恢复。 11 PHRASE If you say that someone always **lands on** their **feet**, you mean that they are always successful or lucky, although they do not seem to achieve this by their own efforts. 走运 ❑ *He has good looks and charm, and always lands on his feet.* 他长相好、有魅力，总走好运。 12 PHRASE If someone **puts** their **foot down**, they use their authority in order to stop something from happening. 坚决反对 ❑ *He had planned to go skiing on his own in March but his wife had decided to put her foot down.* 他原计划在3月独自去滑雪，但他的妻子坚决反对。 13 PHRASE If someone **puts** their **foot down** when they are driving, they drive as fast as they can. 开快车 [BRIT] 14 PHRASE If someone **puts** their **foot in it** or **puts** their **foot in** their **mouth**, they accidentally do or say something which embarrasses or offends people. (不经意间) 犯错误 [INFORMAL] ❑ *Our chairman has really put his foot in it, poor man, though he doesn't know it.* 我们的主席确实错了，可怜的人，尽管他还不知道。 15 PHRASE If you **put** your **feet up**, you relax or have a rest, especially by sitting or lying with your feet supported off the ground. 放松休息 (尤指坐着或躺着把脚抬高) ❑ *After supper he'd put his feet up and read.* 晚餐后他会放松休息一下，读点什么。 16 PHRASE If you never **put a**

f

Picture Dictionary foot

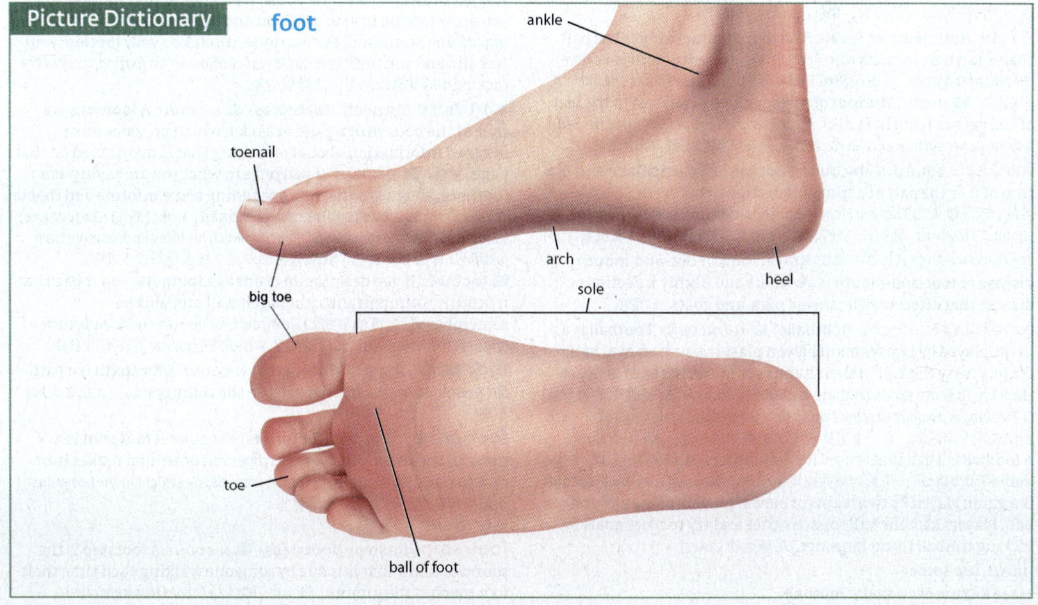

Picture Dictionary football

goalpost
yard line
sideline
fifty-yard line
goal line
end zone
player
football
referee
helmet
uniform
face mask

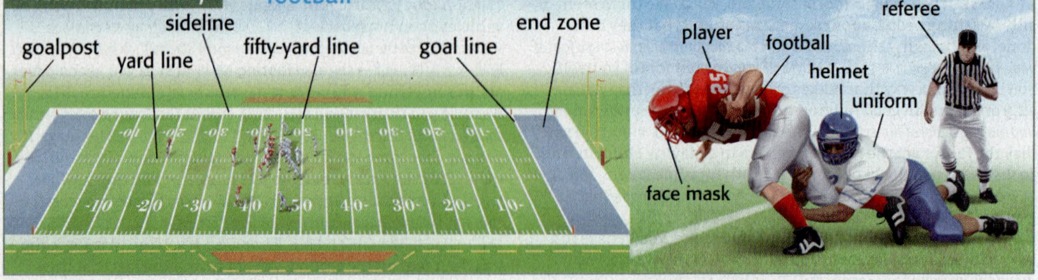

F

foot wrong, you never make any mistakes. 不出错 [mainly BRIT] ❑ *When he's around, we never put a foot wrong.* 他在的时候，我们从不出错。 **17** PHRASE If you say that someone **sets foot** in a place, you mean that they enter it or reach it, and you are emphasizing the significance of their action. If you say that someone **never sets foot** in a place, you are emphasizing that they never go there. 涉足；介入 [EMPHASIS] ❑ *...the day the first man set foot on the moon.* …人类首次踏上月球的那一天。 **18** PHRASE If someone has to **stand on** their **own two feet**, they have to be independent and manage their life without help from other people. 自立 ❑ *My father didn't mind whom I married, so long as I could stand on my own two feet and wasn't dependent on my husband.* 我父亲并不介意我跟谁结婚，只要我能够自立、不靠丈夫就行。 **19** PHRASE If you get or rise **to** your **feet**, you stand up. 站起来 ❑ *Malone got to his feet and followed his superior out of the suite.* 马隆站起来跟着他的上司走出套房。 ❑ *The delegates cheered and rose to their feet.* 代表们欢呼着站起来。 **20** PHRASE If someone **gets off on the wrong foot** in a new situation, they make a bad start by doing something in completely the wrong way. 出师不利 ❑ *Even though they called the election and had been preparing for it for some time, they got off on the wrong foot.* 虽然他们召集了这次选举，也为此准备了一段时间，他们还是出师不利。 **21** **foot in the door** → see **door** **22** to **drag** your **feet** → see **drag** **23** to **vote with** your **feet** → see **vote**
→ see Picture Dictionary: **foot**
→ see **body**

❷ foot ♦♦♦ /fʊt/ (**feet**) N-COUNT A **foot** is a unit for measuring length, height, or depth, and is equal to 12 inches or 30.48 centimeters. When you are giving measurements, the form "foot" is often used as the plural instead of the plural form "feet." 英尺（常用单数形式表示复数）❑ *This beautiful and curiously shaped lake lies at around fifteen thousand feet.* 这座形状奇特的美丽湖泊周长约一万五千英尺。 ❑ *He occupies a cell 10 foot long, 6 foot wide and 10 foot high.* 他住在一个10英尺长、6英尺宽、10英尺高的小房间里。

❸ foot /fʊt/ (**feet**) **1** N-SING **The foot of** something is the part that is farthest from its top. 底部 ❑ *David called to the children from the foot of the stairs.* 大卫在楼梯下喊孩子们。 ❑ *...the foot of the hill.* …山脚。 **2** N-SING **The foot of** a bed is the end nearest to the feet of the person lying in it. (床) 尾 ❑ *Friends stood at the foot of the bed, looking at her with serious faces.* 朋友们站在床尾，表情严肃地看着她。

foot·age /fʊtɪdʒ/ N-UNCOUNT **Footage** of a particular event is a film of it or the part of a film which shows this event. (描述某一事件的) 片段镜头 ❑ *They are planning to show exclusive footage from this summer's festivals.* 他们计划独家播放今年夏季节日活动的片断镜头。

foot-and-mouth dis·ease N-UNCOUNT **Foot-and-mouth disease** or **foot-and-mouth** is a serious and highly infectious disease that affects cattle, sheep, pigs, and goats. 口蹄疫

foot·ball ♦♦◊ /fʊtbɔl/ (**footballs**) **1** N-UNCOUNT **Football** is a game played by two teams of eleven players using an oval ball. Players carry the ball in their hands or throw it to each other as they try to score goals that are called touchdowns. 橄榄球运动 [AM] ❑ *Two blocks beyond our school was a field where boys played football.* 离我们学校两个街区远，有一个男孩子们玩橄榄球的场地。 **2** N-COUNT A **football** is a ball that is used for playing football. 橄榄球 ❑ *...a heavy leather football.* …一个沉甸甸的皮质橄榄球。 **3** N-UNCOUNT **Football** is a game played by two teams of eleven players using a round ball. Players kick the ball to each other and try to score goals by kicking the ball into a large net. 足球运动 [BRIT]

in AM, use **soccer**

→ see Picture Dictionary: **football**

foot·ball·er /fʊtbɔlər/ (**footballers**) N-COUNT A **footballer** is a person who plays football (soccer), especially as a profession. (尤指职业) 足球运动员 [BRIT]

in AM, use **soccer player**

foot·er /fʊtər/ (**footers**) **1** N-COUNT A **footer** is text such as a name or page number that can be automatically displayed at the bottom of each page of a printed document. 页脚 [COMPUTING] ❑ *Page Mode shows headers, footers, footnotes and page numbers.* 页面模式显示页眉、页脚、脚注和页码。 **2** → see also **header**

foot·hills /fʊthɪlz/ N-PLURAL **The foothills** of a mountain or a range of mountains are the lower hills or mountains around its base. 丘陵 ❑ *Pasadena lies in the foothills of the San Gabriel mountains.* 帕萨迪纳位于圣加布里埃尔山的丘陵地带。

foot·hold /fʊthoʊld/ (**footholds**) **1** N-COUNT A **foothold** is a strong or favorable position from which further advances or progress may be made. 立足点 ❑ *Businesses are investing millions of dollars to gain a foothold in this new market.* 商家们正投资数百万美元以求在新市场中赢得立足点。 **2** N-COUNT A **foothold** is a place such as a small hole or area of rock where you can safely put your foot when climbing. (攀登时的) 立足处 ❑ *He lowered his legs until he felt he had a solid foothold on the rockface beneath him.* 他往下探腿，直到感觉双脚稳稳地踩住了岩石。

foot·ing /fʊtɪŋ/ **1** N-UNCOUNT If something is put **on** a particular **footing**, it is defined, established, or changed in a particular way, often so that it is able to develop or exist successfully. 基础 ❑ *The new law will put official corruption on the same legal footing as treason.* 新法律将把职务腐败视同叛国罪。 **2** N-UNCOUNT If you are **on** a particular kind of **footing** with someone, you have that kind of relationship with them. 关系 ❑ *They decided to put their relationship on a more formal footing.* 他们决定建立更正式的关系。 **3** N-UNCOUNT You refer to your **footing** when you are referring to your position and how securely your feet are placed on the ground. For example, if you lose your **footing**, your feet slip and you fall. 站稳 ❑ *He was cautious of his footing, wary of the edge.* 他小心翼翼地站稳，注意着边缘。

foot·note /fʊtnoʊt/ (**footnotes**) **1** N-COUNT A **footnote** is a note at the bottom of a page in a book which provides more detailed information about something that is mentioned on that page. 脚注 **2** N-COUNT If you refer to what you are saying as a **footnote**, you mean that you are adding some information that is related to what has just been mentioned. 补充说明 ❑ *As a footnote, I should add that there was one point on which his bravado was more than justified.* 作为补充说明，我应该再加一点，他表现得过于逞强。 **3** N-COUNT If you describe an event as a **footnote**, you mean that it is fairly unimportant although it will probably be remembered. 次要的事物 ❑ *I'm afraid that his name will now become a footnote in history.* 我认为，他的名字在历史中恐怕将变得不再重要。

foot·path /fʊtpæθ/ (**footpaths**) N-COUNT A **footpath** is a path for people to walk on, especially in the countryside. (尤指乡间的) 小路

foot·print /fʊtprɪnt/ (**footprints**) N-COUNT A **footprint** is a mark in the shape of a foot that a person or animal makes in or on a surface. 脚印 ❑ *His footprints were clearly evident in the heavy dust.* 他的脚印在厚厚的尘土上清晰可见。
→ see **fossil**

foot·step /fʊtstɛp/ (**footsteps**) **1** N-COUNT A **footstep** is the sound or mark that is made by someone walking each time their foot touches the ground. 脚步声；脚步 ❑ *I heard footsteps outside.*

我听到外面的脚步声。 **2** PHRASE If you **follow in** someone's **footsteps**, you do the same things as they did earlier. 仿效（某人） ❑ *My father is extremely proud that I followed in his footsteps and became a doctor.* 我父亲感到非常自豪，因为我继承父业，成了医生。

foot·wear /fʊtwɛər/ N-UNCOUNT **Footwear** refers to things that people wear on their feet, for example, shoes and boots. 鞋类 ❑ *Some football players get paid millions for endorsing footwear.* 有些足球运动员因做鞋类广告得到数百万的报酬。

for

1. SAYING WHO OR WHAT SOMETHING RELATES TO, OR WHO BENEFITS
2. MENTIONING A PURPOSE, REASON, OR DESTINATION
3. BEFORE NUMBERS, AMOUNTS, AND TIMES
4. WANTING OR SUPPORTING

❶ for ♦♦♦ /fər, STRONG fɔr/
➪ **Please look at meanings 17 – 19 to see if the expression you are looking for is shown under another headword.** **1** PREP If something is **for** someone, they are intended to have it or benefit from it. 为；给 ❑ *Isn't that enough for you?* 那对你来说不够吗？ ❑ *...a table for two.* …一张双人桌。 ❑ *He wanted all the running of the business for himself.* 他想要自己管理整个企业。 **2** PREP If you work or do a job **for** someone, you are employed by them. 为…（工作） ❑ *I knew he worked for a security firm.* 我知道他为一家保安公司工作。 ❑ *Have you had any experience writing for radio?* 你有为电台撰稿的经验吗？ **3** PREP If you speak or act **for** a particular group or organization, you represent them. 代表（某团体或机构） ❑ *She appears nightly on the television news, speaking for the State Department.* 她每晚出现在电视新闻上，代表国务院发言。 **4** PREP If someone does something **for** you, they do it so that you do not have to do it. 替…（做事） ❑ *If your pharmacy doesn't stock the product you want, have them order it for you.* 如果药房没有你所要的产品，让他们替你订货。 ❑ *I hold a door open for an old person.* 我替一位老人把门开开。 **5** PREP If you feel a particular emotion **for** someone, you feel it on their behalf. 替…（感到） [adj/n PREP] ❑ *This is the best thing you've ever done – I am so happy for you!* 这是你做过的最好的事——我真为你高兴！ **6** PREP If you feel a particular emotion **for** someone or something, they are the object of that emotion, and you feel it when you think about them. 对…（常怀有某种感情） [adj/n PREP] ❑ *John, I'm sorry for Steve, but I think you've made the right decisions.* 约翰，我为史蒂夫感到难过，但我想你作出了正确的决定。 **7** PREP You use **for** after words such as "time," "space," "money," or "energy" when you say how much there is or whether there is enough of it in order to be able to do or use a particular thing. 供…使用 ❑ *Many new trains have space for wheelchair users.* 许多新火车都为坐轮椅者留有空间。 ❑ *...a huge room with plenty of room for books.* …可存放大量书籍的一间大屋子。 **8** PREP You use **for** when you make a statement about something in order to say how it affects or relates to someone, or what their attitude to it is. 对…来说 ❑ *What matters for most scientists is money and facilities.* 对大多数科学家来说，重要的是经费和设备。 ❑ *For her, books were as necessary to life as bread.* 对她来说，书就像面包一样是生活的必需。 **9** PREP After some adjective, noun, and verb phrases, you use **for** to introduce the subject of the action indicated by the following infinitive verb. 用于某些形容词、名词或动词词组之后，引出动词不定式的执行主语 [PREP n to-inf] ❑ *It might be possible for a single woman to be accepted as a foster parent.* 有可能接受单身女子做养母。 ❑ *I had made arrangements for my affairs to be dealt with by one of my children.* 我安排了自己的一个孩子处理我的事务。 **10** PREP If you say that something is **not for** you, you mean that you do not enjoy it or that it is not suitable for you. 不被…喜欢；不适合 [with neg] [INFORMAL] ❑ *Wendy decided the sport was not for her.* 温迪认定这项运动不适合她。 **11** PREP If it is **for** you **to** do something, it is your responsibility or right to do it. 由…（负责） [PREP n to-inf] ❑ *I wish you would come back to Washington with us, but that's for you to decide.* 我希望你和我们一起回华盛顿，但由你自己决定。 **12** PREP **For** is the preposition that is used after some nouns, adjectives, or verbs in order to introduce more information or to indicate what a quality, thing, or action relates to. 用于某些名词、形容词或动词之后，引出更多信息或指出相关的性质、事物、行为等 ❑ *Reduced-calorie cheese is a great substitute for cream cheese.* 低卡路里干酪是奶油干酪的极好替代品。 ❑ *Parking lot owners should be legally responsible for protecting vehicles.* 停车场场主应该依法负责保护车辆。 **13** PREP If a word or expression has the same meaning as another word or expression, you can say that the first one is another word or expression **for** the second one. 相当于（意思） ❑ *The technical term for sunburn is erythema.* 晒斑的专业术语是红斑病。 **14** PREP To be named **for** someone means to be given the same name as them. 以…（命名） [AM] ❑ *The Brady Bill is named for former White House Press Secretary James Brady.* 布雷迪法案是以前白宫新闻秘书詹姆斯·布雷迪命名的。 **15** PREP You use **for** in a piece of writing when you mention information which will be found somewhere else. 至于…（用于指可以在文中其它地方找到的信息） ❑ *For further information on the life of William James Sidis, see Amy Wallace, "The Prodigy."* 要了解更多关于威廉·詹姆斯·西迪斯的生平，参阅艾米·华莱士的《神童》。 **16** PREP **For** is used in conditional sentences, in expressions such as **"if not for"** and **"were it not for,"** to introduce the only thing which prevents the main part of the sentence from being true. （用于条件句如**if not for**或**were it not for**句式中）要不是 ❑ *If not for John, Brian wouldn't have learned the truth.* 要不是约翰，布莱恩不会了解真相。 ❑ *The earth would be a frozen ball if it were not for the radiant heat of the sun.* 要是没有太阳的辐射热，地球将会是一个冰冻的球体。 **17** **as for** → see **as** **18** **but for** → see **but** **19** **for all** → see **all**

❷ for ♦♦♦ /fər, STRONG fɔr/ **1** PREP You use **for** when you state or explain the purpose of an object, action, or activity. 为了（表示目的、用途） [PREP n/-ing] ❑ *...drug users who use unsterile equipment for injections of drugs.* …用未消过毒的器具注射毒品的吸毒者们。 ❑ *The knife for cutting sausage was sitting in the sink.* 用于切香肠的刀在水槽里。 **2** PREP You use **for** after nouns expressing reason or cause. 因为（作介词，用于表示原因的名词后） [n PREP n/-ing] ❑ *He's soon to make a speech explaining his reasons for going.* 他很快将会发表讲话说明去的原因。 ❑ *The county hospital could find no physical cause for Sumner's problems.* 县医院查不出萨姆纳的问题的生理原因。 **3** PREP If something is **for** sale, hire, or use, it is available to be sold, hired, or used. 供（销售、租用、使用） ❑ *Freshwater fish for sale.* 供出售的淡水鱼。 ❑ *...a room for rent.* …一间供租用的房间。 **4** PREP If you do something **for** a particular occasion, you do it on that occasion or to celebrate that occasion. 为（某场合） ❑ *He asked his daughter what she would like for her birthday.* 他问他女儿想要如何过她的生日。 **5** PREP If you leave **for** a particular place or if you take a bus, train, plane, or boat **for** a place, you are going there. 前往（某地） ❑ *They would be leaving for Rio early the next morning.* 他们次日一早将前往里约。

❸ for ♦♦♦ /fər, STRONG fɔr/ **1** PREP You use **for** to say how long something lasts or continues. 用于表示持续的时间 [PREP amount] ❑ *The toaster was on for more than an hour.* 烤箱开了一个多小时。 ❑ *They talked for a bit.* 他们谈了会儿。 **2** PREP You use **for** to say how far something extends. 用于表示延伸的距离 [PREP amount] ❑ *We drove on for a few miles.* 我们继续开了几英里。 **3** PREP If something is bought, sold, or done **for** a particular amount of money, that amount of money is its price. 以（某数量的钱） [PREP amount] ❑ *We got the bus back to Tange for 30 cents.* 我们以30美分乘公共汽车回到了坦格。 ❑ *The Martins sold their house for about 1.4 million dollars.* 马丁一家以约一百四十万美元把他们的房子卖了。 **4** PREP If something is planned **for** a particular time, it is planned to happen then. 于（某时间） ❑ *...the Baltimore Boat Show, planned for January 21–29.* …计划于1月21至29日举行的巴尔的摩船展。 ❑ *The designer will be unveiling her latest fashions for fall and winter.* 该设计师将公布她的最新款秋冬时装。 **5** PHRASE You use expressions such as **for the first time** and **for the last time** when you are talking about how often something has happened before. 首次/最后一次 ❑ *He was married for the second time.* 他第二次结婚了。 **6** PREP You use **for** when you say that an aspect of something or someone is surprising in relation to other aspects of them. 对…来说 ❑ *He was tall for an eight-year-old.* 对一个8岁的孩子来说他长得很高。 **7** PREP You use **for** with "every" when you are stating a ratio, to introduce one of the things in the ratio. 对于（与every连用，用于引出比率中之一） ❑ *For every farm job that is lost, two or three other jobs in the area are put at risk.* 对于失去的每份农场工作，该地区的其它两三个工作就会被置于危险中。 **8** PREP You can use **for** in expressions such as **dollar for dollar** or **mile for mile** when you are making comparisons between the values or qualities of different things. 对应（用于比较不同事物间的价值或品质） [n PREP n] ❑ *...the Antarctic, mile for mile one of the planet's most lifeless areas.* …每英里都是地球上最无生命的地区之一的南极洲。

❹ for ♦♦♦ /fər, STRONG fɔr/ **1** PREP If you say that you are **for** a particular activity, you mean that this is what you want or intend to do. 想要 ❑ *Right, who's for a toasted sandwich then?* 好了，那谁想要一

个吐司三明治呢？ **2** PREP If you are **for** something, you agree with it or support it. 赞成；支持 ❑ *Are you for or against public transportation?* 你是支持还是反对公共交通？ **3** PREP You use **for** after words such as "argue," "case," "evidence," or "vote" in order to introduce the thing that is being supported or proved. 支持 [n/v PREP n] ❑ *Another union has voted for industrial action in support of a pay claim.* 又一个工会已投票赞成支持加薪要求的劳工行动。 ❑ *The case for nuclear power is impressive.* 支持核能的论据令人印象深刻。 ● ADV **For** is also an adverb. 支持地 [ADV after v] ❑ *833 delegates voted for, and only 432 against.* 833名代表投票支持，只有432人反对。 **4** PHRASE If you say that you are **all for** doing something, you agree or strongly believe that it should be done, but you are also often suggesting that other people disagree with you or that there are practical difficulties. 完全赞成；极力支持 ❑ *He is all for players earning what they can while they are in the game.* 他完全赞成运动员在役期间能赚多少钱就赚多少。

F

In addition to the uses shown below, **for** is used after some verbs, nouns, and adjectives in order to introduce extra information, and in phrasal verbs such as "account for" and "make up for." It is also used with some verbs that have two objects in order to introduce the second object.

for·age /fɔrɪdʒ/ (**forages, foraging, foraged**) **1** V-I If someone **forages for** something, they search for it in a busy way. 匆忙搜寻 ❑ *They were forced to forage for clothing and fuel.* 他们被迫匆忙搜寻衣物和燃料。 **2** V-I When animals **forage**, they search for food. (动物)觅食 ❑ *We disturbed a wild boar that had been foraging by the roadside.* 我们惊动了一只在路边觅食的野公猪。

for·ay /fɔreɪ/ (**forays**) **1** N-COUNT If you make a **foray into** a new or unfamiliar type of activity, you start to become involved in it. 涉足 ❑ *Emporio Armani, the Italian fashion house, has made a discreet foray into furnishings.* 意大利时装公司恩波利·阿玛尼已谨慎地涉足室内装饰业。 **2** N-COUNT You can refer to a short trip that you make as a **foray** if it seems to involve excitement or risk, for example, because it is to an unfamiliar place or because you are looking for a particular thing. (带有刺激性或冒险性的) 短程旅行 ❑ *Most guests make at least one foray into the town.* 大多数客人至少去过一次城里。 **3** N-COUNT If a group of soldiers make a **foray into** enemy territory, they make a quick attack there, and then return to their own territory. 突袭 ❑ *These base camps were used by the PKK guerrillas to make forays into Turkey.* 这些基地营被库尔德工人党游击队用来对土耳其进行突袭。

for·bid /fərbɪd, fɔr-/ (**forbids, forbidding, forbade, forbidden**) **1** V-T If you **forbid** someone **to** do something, or if you **forbid** an activity, you order that it must not be done. 禁止 ❑ *They'll forbid you to marry.* 他们会不许你结婚。 ❑ *She was shut away and forbidden to read.* 她被关起来不许读书。 **2** V-T If something **forbids** a particular course of action or state of affairs, it makes it impossible for the course of action or state of affairs to happen. 使…不可能 ❑ *His own pride forbids him to ask Arthur's help.* 他自己的傲慢使他不可能寻求亚瑟的帮助。

for·bid·den /fərbɪdᵊn, fɔr-/ **1** ADJ If something is **forbidden**, you are not allowed to do it or have it. 被禁止的 ❑ *Smoking was forbidden everywhere.* 吸烟到处都是被禁止的。 **2** ADJ A **forbidden** place is one that you are not allowed to visit or enter. 禁止入内的 (地方) ❑ *This was a forbidden area for foreigners.* 这是一个禁止外国人入内的地区。 **3** ADJ **Forbidden** is used to describe things that people strongly disapprove of or feel guilty about, and that are not often mentioned or talked about. 被忌讳的 ❑ *The war was a forbidden subject.* 这场战争是一个被忌讳的话题。 ❑ *Men fantasize as a substitute for acting out forbidden desires.* 人们以幻想来作为宣泄禁欲的替代方式。

force
1 VERB USES
2 NOUN USES: POWER OR STRENGTH
3 THE ARMY, POLICE, ETC.

1 force ◆◆◆ /fɔrs/ (**forces, forcing, forced**) **1** V-T If someone **forces** you **to** do something, they make you do it even though you do not want to, for example, by threatening you. 强迫 ❑ *He took two women hostage and forced them to drive away from the area.* 他劫持了两名女人质并强迫她们开车离开这个地区。 ❑ *They were grabbed by three men who appeared to force them into a car.* 他们被3名男子抓住，这些人看上去强使他们进入了一辆汽车。 **2** V-T If a situation or event **forces** you to do something, it makes it necessary for you to do something that you would not otherwise have done. 迫使 ❑ *A back injury forced her to withdraw from Wimbledon.* 一处背伤迫使她退出了温布尔登网球赛。 ❑ *He turned right, down a dirt road that forced him into four-wheel drive.* 他向右转弯，开上了一条土路，这迫使他开始四轮驱动行驶。 **3** V-T If someone **forces** something **on** or **upon** you, they make you accept or use it when you would prefer not to. 强加 (某事物于…上) ❑ *To force this agreement on the nation is wrong.* 把这项协议强加于这个国家是错误的。 **4** V-T If you **force** something into a particular position, you use a lot of strength to make it move there. 用力使…移 (至某处) ❑ *They were forcing her head under the icy waters, drowning her.* 他们在用力把她的头按到冰冷的水中，淹死她。 **5** V-T If someone **forces** a lock, a door, or a window, they break the lock or fastening in order to get into a building without using a key. 强行打开 (锁、门、窗等) ❑ *That evening police forced the door of the apartment and arrested Mr. Roberts.* 那晚警察强行打开那公寓的门逮捕了罗伯茨先生。 **6** PHRASE If you **force** your **way through** or **into** somewhere, you have to push or break things that are in your way in order to get there. 强行到某地 ❑ *The miners forced their way through a police cordon.* 那些矿工们冲破了警察的封锁线。

2 force ◆◆◆ /fɔrs/ (**forces**) **1** N-UNCOUNT If someone uses **force** to do something, or if it is done by **force**, strong and violent physical action is taken in order to achieve it. 武力 ❑ *The government decided against using force to break up the demonstrations.* 政府决定不使用武力来驱散示威游行。 **2** N-UNCOUNT **Force** is the power or strength which something has. 力量 ❑ *The force of the explosion shattered the windows of several buildings.* 那次爆炸的力量震碎了几栋建筑的窗子。 **3** N-UNCOUNT The **force of** something is the powerful effect or quality that it has. 强大的效力；有很强影响力的品质 ❑ *He changed our world through the force of his ideas.* 他以其思想的强大影响力改变了我们的世界。 **4** N-UNCOUNT **Force** is used before a number to indicate a wind of a particular speed or strength, especially a very strong wind. 风力 ❑ *The airlift was conducted in force ten winds.* 空运是在10级大风中进行的。 **5** N-COUNT If you refer to someone or something as a **force** in a particular type of activity, you mean that they have a strong influence on it. 势力；有强大影响力的人或事物 ❑ *For years the army was the most powerful political force in the country.* 多年来军队都是该国最强大的政治势力。 ❑ *The band is still an innovative force in music.* 该乐队仍是音乐界的一支创新力量。 **6** N-COUNT You can use **forces** to refer to processes and events that do not appear to be caused by human beings, and are therefore difficult to understand or control. (非人为的、非人类所能理解或控制的) 力量 ❑ *...the protection of mankind against the forces of nature: epidemics, predators, floods, hurricanes.* …使人类免受流行病、食肉动物、洪水和飓风等自然力伤害的保护。 ❑ *The principle of market forces was applied to some of the country's most revered institutions.* 市场力量的原理被应用在了该国一些最受尊崇的机构。 **7** N-VAR In physics, a **force** is the pulling or pushing effect that something has on something else. (物理学中的) 力 ❑ *...the Earth's gravitational force.* …地球的引力。 **8** PHRASE If you do something **from force of habit**, you do it because you have always done it in the past, rather than because you have thought carefully about it. 习惯的力量 ❑ *He looked around from force of habit, but nobody paid any attention to him.* 他出于习惯环顾四周，但没人注意他。 **9** PHRASE A law, rule, or system that is **in force** exists or is being used. 在实施中 ❑ *Although the new tax is already in force, you have until November to lodge an appeal.* 尽管新税制已经实行，但你在11月之前仍可以提起上诉。 **10** PHRASE When people do something **in force**, they do it in large numbers. 大批地 ❑ *Voters turned out in force for their first taste of multiparty elections.* 选民大批到场初次体验多党选举。 **11** PHRASE If you **join forces with** someone, you work together in order to achieve a common aim or purpose. (与…) 联手 ❑ *Both groups joined forces to persuade voters to approve a tax break for the industry.* 两集团合力游说选民们同意给予这个行业减税。

→ see **motion**

Thesaurus *force* 另参见：

V.	coerce, make 1 1 2
	push, thrust 1 4
	break in, break open 1 5
N.	energy, pressure, strength 2 2

3 force ◆◆◆ /fɔrs/ (**forces**) **1** N-COUNT **Forces** are groups of soldiers or military vehicles that are organized for a particular purpose. 军事力量 ❑ *...the deployment of American forces in the region.* …美国军事力量在该地区的部署。 **2** N-PLURAL **The forces** means the

Word Web forecast

Meteorologists depend on good information. They make **observations**. They gather **data** about **barometric pressure**, **temperature**, and **humidity**. They track **storms** with **radar** and **satellites**. They track cold **fronts** and warm fronts. They put all of this information into their computers and **model** possible **weather** patterns. Today scientists are trying to make better weather **forecasts**. They are installing thousands of small, inexpensive **radar** units on rooftops and cell phone towers. They will gather information near the Earth's surface and high in the sky. This will give meteorologists more information to help them **predict** tomorrow's weather.

army, the navy, or the air force, or all three. 军队 ❑ *The more senior you become in the forces, the more likely you are to end up in a desk job.* 你在军队中的级别升得越高，你就越有可能落得个坐办公室的职位。 3 N-SING **The force** is sometimes used to mean the police force. 警察部门 ❑ *It was hard for a police officer to make friends outside the force.* 一名警官在警察部门之外交朋友很难。 4 → see also **air force, armed forces, labor force, workforce**

Word Partnership *force* 的常用搭配：

V.	force **to resign** ① 1 2
N.	force **a smile** ① 2
	use of force ② 1 2
	force **of gravity** ② 7
ADJ.	**excessive** force, **necessary** force ② 1
	driving force, **powerful** force ② 3 5
	full force ② 10
	enemy forces, **military** forces ③ 1 2

forced /fɔrst/ 1 ADJ A **forced** action is something that you do because someone else makes you do it. 受迫的 [ADJ n] ❑ *A system of forced labor was used on the cocoa plantations.* 一种受迫劳动制曾用于可可种植园。 2 ADJ A **forced** action is something that you do because circumstances make it necessary. 迫不得已的 [ADJ n] ❑ *He made a forced landing on a highway.* 他迫降在了一条高速公路上。 3 ADJ If you describe something as **forced**, you mean it does not happen naturally and easily. 勉强的 ❑ *...a forced smile.* …一个勉强的微笑。

force·ful /fɔrsfəl/ 1 ADJ If you describe someone as **forceful**, you approve of them because they express their opinions and wishes in a strong, emphatic, and confident way. 有魄力的 [APPROVAL] ❑ *He was a man of forceful character, with considerable insight and diplomatic skills.* 他是个有魄力的人，具有相当的洞察力和外交技能。 ● **force·ful·ly** ADV 有魄力地 [ADV with v] ❑ *Mrs. Dambar was talking very rapidly and somewhat forcefully.* 达姆巴夫人在很快、颇有魄力地谈话。 2 ADJ Something that is **forceful** has a very powerful effect and causes you to think or feel something very strongly. 强有力的 ❑ *It made a very forceful impression on me.* 它给我留下了非常深刻的印象。 ● **force·ful·ly** ADV 强有力地 [ADV with v] ❑ *Daytime television tended to remind her too forcefully of her own situation.* 白天的电视往往太过强烈地使她想到自己的处境。 3 ADJ A **forceful** point or argument in a discussion is one that is good, valid, and convincing. 有说服力的（观点、论据等）❑ *You may need to be armed with some forceful arguments to persuade a partner into seeing things your way.* 你也许需要备一些有说服力的论据来说服一个合伙人以你的方式看问题。

for·cible /fɔrsɪbᵊl/ ADJ **Forcible** action involves physical force or violence. 强行的 ❑ *Reports are coming in of the forcible resettlement of villagers from the countryside into towns.* 有报道称村民要从农村被强行地迁居到城镇。 ● **for·ci·bly** ★ ADV 强行地 ❑ *Four protestors had to be forcibly removed by police.* 4名抗议者不得不被警察强行拖走。

▲ **ford** /fɔrd/ (**fords, fording, forded**) 1 N-COUNT A **ford** is a shallow place in a river or stream where it is possible to cross safely without using a boat. 河流水浅处 2 V-T If you **ford** a river or stream, you cross it without using a boat, usually at a shallow point. 涉过 ❑ *They were guarding the bridge, so we forded the river.* 他们当时守着那座桥，我们就涉水过了那条河。

▲ **fore** /fɔr/ 1 PHRASE If someone or something comes **to the fore** in a particular situation or group, they become important or popular. 崭露头角；令人瞩目 ❑ *A number of low-budget independent films brought new directors and actors to the fore.* 许多低预算的独立电影使一些新的导演和演员们崭露头角。 2 ADJ **Fore** is used to refer to parts at the front of an animal, ship, or aircraft. 前部的 [ADJ n] ❑ *There had been no direct damage in the fore part of the ship.* 没有对船的前部的直接损坏。

fore·arm /fɔrarm/ (**forearms**) N-COUNT Your **forearm** is the part of your arm between your elbow and your wrist. 前臂 ❑ *...the tattoo on his forearm.* …他前臂上的刺青。

Word Link *fore ≈ before : forecast, foresight, foreword*

fore·cast ♦◇◇ /fɔrkæst/ (**forecasts, forecasting, forecasted**)

The forms **forecast** and **forecasted** can both be used for the past tense and past participle.

1 N-COUNT A **forecast** is a statement of what is expected to happen in the future, especially in relation to a particular event or situation. 预报 ❑ *...a forecast of a 2.25 percent growth in the economy.* …2.25%经济增长的预报。 ❑ *He delivered his election forecast.* 他作了他的选举预报。 2 V-T If you **forecast** future events, you say what you think is going to happen in the future. 预言 ❑ *They forecast a humiliating defeat for the president.* 他们预言总统蒙受羞辱的一次失败。 3 → see also **weather forecast**

→ see Word Web: **forecast**

fore·close /fɔrkloʊz/ (**forecloses, foreclosing, foreclosed**) V-I If the person or organization that lent someone money **forecloses**, they take possession of a property that was bought with the borrowed money, for example, because regular repayments have not been made. 取消（抵押品的）赎回权 [BUSINESS] ❑ *The bank foreclosed on the mortgage for his previous home.* 银行取消了他先前住房的抵押赎回权。

fore·clo·sure /fɔrkloʊʒər/ (**foreclosures**) N-VAR **Foreclosure** is when someone who has lent money to a person or organization so that they can buy property takes possession of the property because the money has not been repaid. （抵押品）赎回权取消 [BUSINESS] ❑ *If homeowners can't keep up the payments, they face foreclosure.* 如果房主不能继续还贷，他们就面临抵押品赎回权被取消的危险。

fore·court /fɔrkɔrt/ (**forecourts**) 1 N-COUNT In sports such as tennis and badminton, the **forecourt** is the section of each side of the court that is nearest to the net. （网球、羽毛球等球场的）前场 [usu "the"] 2 N-COUNT The **forecourt** of a large building or gas station is the open area at the front of it. （大楼的）前院；（加油站的）加油处

→ see **tennis**

fore·finger /fɔrfɪŋgər/ (**forefingers**) N-COUNT Your **forefinger** is the finger that is next to your thumb. 食指 ❑ *He took the pen between his thumb and forefinger.* 他用拇指和食指夹起笔。

▲ **fore·front** /fɔrfrʌnt/ 1 N-SING If you are at **the forefront** of a campaign or other activity, you have a leading and influential position in it. （运动、活动的）前沿 ❑ *They have been at the forefront of the campaign for political change.* 他们一直处于政治变革运动的前沿。 2 N-SING If something is **at the forefront of** people's minds or attention, they think about it a lot because it is particularly important to them. （思考、关注的）重心 ❑ *The pension issue was not at the forefront of his mind in the spring of 1985.* 养老金问题在1985年春不是他思考的重心。

fore·go /fɔrgoʊ/ (**foregoes, foregoing, forewent, foregone**) also **forgo** V-T If you **forego** something, you decide to do without it, although you would like it. 放弃 [FORMAL] ❑ *Many skiers are happy to forego a summer vacation to go skiing.* 许多滑雪者乐于放弃暑假去滑雪。

fore·gone /fɔ̲rgɔn/ **1** **Foregone** is the past participle of **forego**. forego的过去分词 **2** PHRASE If you say that a particular result is a **foregone conclusion**, you mean you are certain that it will happen. 预料中的必然结局 ❑ *Most voters believe the result is a foregone conclusion.* 多数投票人认为结果是早成定局的事。

▲ **fore·ground** /fɔ̲rgraʊnd/ (**foregrounds**) **1** N-VAR The **foreground** of a picture or scene you are looking at is the part or area of it that appears nearest to you. (图画、场景等的) 前景 ❑ *He is the bowler-hatted figure in the foreground of Orpen's famous painting.* 他就是奥彭名画的前景中那个戴圆顶礼帽的人物。 **2** N-SING If something or someone is **in the foreground**, or comes **to the foreground**, they receive a lot of attention. 关注重心 ❑ *This is another worry that has come to the foreground in recent years.* 这是近年来已变成关注重心的又一件令人担忧的事。

F

fore·head /fɔ̲rhɛd, fɔ̲rɪd/ (**foreheads**) N-COUNT Your **forehead** is the area at the front of your head between your eyebrows and your hair. 前额 ❑ *...the lines on her forehead.* …她前额上的皱纹。
→ see **face**

for·eign ♦♦♦ /fɔ̲rɪn/ **1** ADJ Something or someone that is **foreign** comes from or relates to a country that is not your own. 外国的 ❑ *She was on her first foreign vacation without her parents.* 她首次不在父母的陪同下到国外度假。 ❑ *...a foreign language.* …一门外语。 ❑ *...in Frankfurt, where a quarter of the population is foreign.* …在法兰克福，1/4的人口是外国人。 **2** ADJ In politics and journalism, **foreign** is used to describe people, jobs, and activities relating to countries that are not the country of the person or government concerned. 涉外的 [ADJ n] ❑ *...the German foreign minister.* …德国外交部长。 ❑ *I am the foreign correspondent in Washington of La Tribuna newspaper of Honduras.* 我是洪都拉斯《论坛报》驻华盛顿的记者。 **3** ADJ A **foreign** object is something that has got into something else, usually by accident, and should not be there. 异质的 [FORMAL] ❑ *The patient's immune system would reject the transplanted organ as a foreign object.* 该病人的免疫系统会将移植器官作为异物加以排斥。

Thesaurus *foreign* 另参见：
ADJ. alien, exotic, strange; (*ant.*) domestic, native **1**

for·eign·er ♦◇◇ /fɔ̲rɪnər/ (**foreigners**) N-COUNT A **foreigner** is someone who belongs to a country that is not your own. 外国人 ❑ *They are discouraged from becoming close friends with foreigners.* 他们被劝不要同外国人成为密友。

for·eign ex·change (**foreign exchanges**) **1** N-PLURAL **Foreign exchanges** are the institutions or systems involved with changing one currency into another. 外汇交易所；外汇交易 ❑ *On the foreign exchanges, the U.S. dollar is up point forty-five.* 在外汇交易所，美元上涨了0.45个百分点。 **2** N-UNCOUNT **Foreign exchange** is used to refer to foreign currency that is obtained through the foreign exchange system. 外汇 ❑ *...an important source of foreign exchange.* …一个外汇的重要来源。 **3** N-COUNT A **foreign exchange** is an arrangement in which people from two different countries visit each other's country, to strengthen links between them. 外籍互换 [oft N n] ❑ *He recently hosted a foreign exchange student from Argentina.* 他最近招待了一名来自阿根廷的外籍互换生。

Word Link *man ≈ human being : foreman, humane, woman*

fore·man /fɔ̲rmən/ (**foremen**) **1** N-COUNT A **foreman** is a person, especially a man, in charge of a group of workers. (尤指男性) 工头 ❑ *He still visited the dairy daily, but left most of the business details to his manager and foreman.* 他仍然每天去牛奶公司，但将多数生意上的细节留给了经理和工头。 **2** N-COUNT The **foreman** of a jury is the person who is chosen as their leader. 陪审团团长 ❑ *There was applause as the foreman of the jury announced the verdict.* 陪审团团长宣布裁定结果时响起了一片掌声。

★ **fore·most** /fɔ̲rmoʊst/ **1** ADJ The **foremost** thing or person in a group is the most important or best. 最重要的；最好的 ❑ *He was one of the world's foremost scholars of ancient Indian culture.* 他是世界上最优秀的古印度文化学者之一。 **2** PHRASE You use **first and foremost** to emphasize the most important quality of something or someone. 首先 [EMPHASIS] ❑ *It is first and foremost a trade agreement.* 它首先是一项贸易协定。

fore·name /fɔ̲rneɪm/ (**forenames**) N-COUNT Your **forename** is your first name. Your **forenames** are your names other than your surname. (姓前的) 名字 [FORMAL] ❑ *...the unusual spelling of his forename.* …他的名的不常见的拼法。

fo·ren·sic /fərɛ̲nsɪk/ (**forensics**) **1** ADJ **Forensic** is used to describe the work of scientists who examine evidence in order to help the police solve crimes. 法庭科学取证的 [ADJ n] ❑ *They were convicted on forensic evidence alone.* 他们被仅凭法庭科学证据定了罪。 ❑ *Forensic experts searched the area for clues.* 法庭科学取证专家们为寻找线索而搜查了这个地区。 **2** N-UNCOUNT **Forensics** is the use of scientific techniques to solve crimes. 法庭科学取证 ❑ *...the newest advances in forensics.* …法庭科学取证的最新进展。

★ **fore·run·ner** /fɔ̲rrʌnər/ (**forerunners**) N-COUNT If you describe a person or thing as the **forerunner of** someone or something similar, you mean they existed before them and either influenced their development or were a sign of what was going to happen. 先驱；前身；前兆 ❑ *...a machine which, in some respects, was the forerunner of the modern helicopter.* …一台在某些方面是现代直升飞机的前身的机器。

fore·see /fɔrsi̲/ (**foresees, foreseeing, foresaw, foreseen**) V-T If you **foresee** something, you expect and believe that it will happen. 预见 ❑ *He did not foresee any problems.* 他没有预见到任何问题。

fore·see·able /fɔrsi̲əbᵊl/ **1** ADJ If a future event is **foreseeable**, you know that it will happen or that it can happen, because it is a natural or obvious consequence of something else that you know. 可预见的 ❑ *It seems to me that this crime was foreseeable and this death preventable.* 在我看来这罪行是可预见的且这起死亡是可避免的。 **2** PHRASE If you say that something will happen **for the foreseeable future**, you think that it will continue to happen for a long time. 在可预见的将来 ❑ *Profit and dividend growth looks above average for the foreseeable future.* 利润和股息的增长看上去在可预见的将来会高于平均水平。

Word Link *fore ≈ before : forecast, foresight, foreword*

★ **fore·sight** /fɔ̲rsaɪt/ N-UNCOUNT Someone's **foresight** is their ability to see what is likely to happen in the future and to take appropriate action. 先见之明 [APPROVAL] ❑ *They had the foresight to invest in new technology.* 他们有投资新技术的先见之明。

for·est ♦◇◇ /fɔ̲rɪst/ (**forests**) N-VAR A **forest** is a large area where trees grow close together. 森林 ❑ *Parts of the forest are still dense and inaccessible.* 森林的一些地方仍然茂密不可进入。
→ see Word Web: **forest**

fore·stall /fɔrstɔ̲l/ (**forestalls, forestalling, forestalled**) V-T If you **forestall** someone, you realize what they are likely to do and prevent them from doing it. 预先阻止 ❑ *Large numbers of police were in the square to forestall any demonstrations.* 大批警察在广场上以预先阻止任何游行示威。

for·est·ry /fɔ̲rɪstri/ N-UNCOUNT **Forestry** is the science or skill of growing and taking care of trees in forests, especially in order to obtain wood. 林业学 ❑ *...his great interest in forestry.* …他对林业学的浓厚兴趣。
→ see **industry**

★ **fore·tell** /fɔrtɛ̲l/ (**foretells, foretelling, foretold**) V-T If you **foretell** a future event, you predict that it will happen. 预言

Word Web forest

Four hundred years ago, newly arrived colonists in North America encountered endless **forests**. This abundant supply of **wood** helped them get started. They used **timber** to build homes and make furniture. They burned wood for cooking and heating. They cut down the **woods** to create farmland. By the late 1800s, most of the old growth forests on the East Coast had disappeared. The **lumber** industry has also destroyed millions of trees. Reforestation has replaced some of them. However, logging companies usually plant single species forests. Some people say these are not really forests at all—just **tree** farms.

[LITERARY] ❑ *...prophets who have foretold the end of the world.* …预言了世界末日的先知们。

for·ever /fɔrɛvər, fər-/ 1 ADV If you say that something will happen or continue **forever**, you mean that it will always happen or continue. 永远地 [ADV with v] ❑ *I think that we will live together forever.* 我想我们会永远生活在一起。 2 ADV If something has gone or changed **forever**, it has gone or changed completely and permanently. 永久地；彻底地 [ADV after v] ❑ *The old social order was gone forever.* 旧的社会秩序一去不复返了。 3 ADV If you say that something takes **forever** or lasts **forever**, you are emphasizing that it takes or lasts a very long time, or that it seems to. 很长久地；似乎没完没了地 [ADV after v] [INFORMAL, EMPHASIS] ❑ *The drive seemed to take forever.* 这车好像永远也开不到头似的。

Thesaurus *forever* 另参见：
ADV. always, endlessly, eternally 1
permanently 2

fore·went /fɔrwɛnt/ **Forewent** is the past tense of **forego**. **forego**的过去式

fore·word /fɔrwɜrd/ (**forewords**) N-COUNT The **foreword** to a book is an introduction by the author or by someone else. 前言 ❑ *She has written the foreword to a book of recipes.* 她为一本食谱写了前言。

forex /fɔrɛks/ N-UNCOUNT **Forex** is an abbreviation for **foreign exchange**. 外汇交易 ❑ *...the forex market.* 外汇市场

▲ **for·feit** /fɔrfɪt/ (**forfeits, forfeiting, forfeited**) 1 V-T If you **forfeit** something, you lose it or are forced to give it up because you have broken a rule or done something wrong. (因违规或做错事而) 失去；被迫放弃 ❑ *He was ordered to forfeit more than $1.5m.* 他被令放弃了一百五十多万美元。 2 V-T If you **forfeit** something, you give it up willingly, especially so that you can achieve something else. (尤指为获得别物而) 自愿放弃 ❑ *Do you think that they would forfeit profit in the name of safety?* 你认为他们会为了安全而自愿放弃利润吗？ 3 N-COUNT A **forfeit** is something that you have to give up because you have done something wrong. (因做错事而) 被迫放弃之物 ❑ *That is the forfeit he must pay.* 那是他必须付的罚金。

for·gave /fərgeɪv/ **Forgave** is the past tense of **forgive**. **forgive**的过去式

forge /fɔrdʒ/ (**forges, forging, forged**) 1 V-RECIP If one person or institution **forges** an agreement or relationship with another, they create it with a lot of hard work, hoping that it will be strong or lasting. 费力地缔造 ❑ *The prime minister is determined to forge a good relationship with the country's new leader.* 首相决心与该国的新领袖建立良好的关系。 ❑ *They agreed to forge closer economic ties.* 他们同意建立更密切的经济联系。 2 V-T If someone **forges** something such as paper money, a document, or a painting, they copy it or make it so that it looks genuine, in order to deceive people. 伪造(纸币、文件、画作等) ❑ *He admitted seven charges including forging passports.* 他承认了包括伪造护照在内的7项罪名。 ❑ *They used forged documents to leave the country.* 他们利用伪造的文件离开了这个国家。 ● **forg·er** N-COUNT (**forgers**) 伪造者 ❑ *...the most prolific art forger in the country.* …该国最大的艺术品伪造者。

▶ **forge ahead** PHRASAL VERB If you **forge ahead** with something, you continue with it and make a lot of progress with it. 继续推进 ❑ *He again pledged to forge ahead with his plans for reform.* 他再次发誓要继续推进他的改革计划。

Word Partnership *forge* 的常用搭配：
N. forge **a bond**, forge **a friendship**, forge **links**, forge **a relationship**, forge **ties** 1
forge **documents**, forge **an identity**, forge **a signature** 2

▲ **for·gery** /fɔrdʒəri/ (**forgeries**) 1 N-UNCOUNT **Forgery** is the crime of forging money, documents, or paintings. 伪造罪 ❑ *He was found guilty of forgery.* 他被判有伪造罪。 2 N-COUNT You can refer to a forged document, bill, or painting as a **forgery**. 伪造品 ❑ *The letter was a forgery.* 这封信是伪造品。

for·get ◆◆◇ /fərgɛt/ (**forgets, forgetting, forgot, forgotten**) 1 V-T If you **forget** something or **forget** how to do something, you cannot think of it or think how to do it, although you knew it or knew how to do it in the past. 忘了(某事物、如何做某事) ❑ *She forgot where she left the car and it took us two days to find it.* 她忘了把车停在了哪里，我们花了两天时间才找到它。 2 V-T/V-I If you **forget** something or **forget** to do it, you fail to think about it or fail to remember to do it, for example, because you are thinking about other things. 忘记(某事物、做某事) ❑ *She never forgets her daddy's birthday.* 她从不忘记她爸爸的生日。 ❑ *She forgot to lock her door one day and two men got in.* 她有一天忘了锁门，结果两名男子进去了。 ❑ *When I close my eyes, I forget about everything.* 我闭上眼睛就忘记一切。 3 V-T If you **forget** something that you had intended to bring with you, you do not bring it because you did not think about it at the right time. 忘记带(某物) ❑ *Once when we were going to Paris, I forgot my passport.* 有一次我们去巴黎时，我忘了带护照。

Note that you cannot use the verb **forget** to say that you have put something somewhere and left it there. Instead you use the verb **leave**. ❑ *I left my bag on the bus.*

4 V-T/V-I If you **forget** something or someone, you deliberately put them out of your mind and do not think about them any more. 忘掉(某事物、某人) ❑ *I hope you will forget the bad experience you had today.* 我希望你会忘掉你今天的这次不愉快经历。 ❑ *I found it very easy to forget about Sumner.* 我发现要忘掉萨姆纳很容易。 5 CONVENTION You say "**Forget it**" in reply to someone as a way of telling them not to worry or bother about something, or as an emphatic way of saying no to a suggestion. 没关系；休想 [SPOKEN, FORMULAE] ❑ *"Sorry, Liz. I think I was a bit rude to you."—"Forget it, but don't do it again!"* "对不起，莉兹。我想我刚才对你有点粗鲁。"——"没关系，不过以后别再这样做了！" 6 PHRASE You say **not forgetting** a particular thing or person when you want to include them in something that you have already talked about. 别忘了(某物或人) ❑ *Leave a message, not forgetting your name and address.* 留张条，别忘了留下你的姓名和地址。

Thesaurus *forget* 另参见：
V. disregard, ignore, neglect, overlook 2

Word Partnership *forget* 的常用搭配：
ADV. **never** forget, **quickly** forget, **soon** forget 1
almost forget 1 – 3
ADJ. **easy/hard to** forget 1 – 4

for·get·ful /fərgɛtfəl/ ADJ Someone who is **forgetful** often forgets things. 健忘的 ❑ *My mother has become very forgetful and confused.* 我母亲已变得很健忘很糊涂了。

for·give /fərgɪv/ (**forgives, forgiving, forgave, forgiven**) 1 V-T If you **forgive** someone who has done something bad or wrong, you stop being angry with them and no longer want to punish them. 原谅 ❑ *Hopefully Jane will understand and forgive you, if she really loves you.* 如果简真的爱你，希望她会理解并原谅你。 ❑ *Irene forgave Terry for stealing her money.* 艾琳原谅了特丽偷了她的钱。 ❑ *He could forgive Petal anything if the children were safe.* 只要孩子们安然无恙他什么都可以原谅佩特尔。 2 V-T **Forgive** is used in polite expressions and apologies like "**forgive me**" and "**forgive my ignorance**" when you are saying or doing something that might seem rude, silly, or complicated. 请原谅 [POLITENESS] ❑ *Forgive me, I don't mean to insult you.* 请原谅我，我不是有意侮辱你。 ❑ *I do hope you'll forgive me but I've got to leave.* 我真的希望你能原谅我，不过我得走了。 3 V-T PASSIVE If you say that someone could **be forgiven for** doing something, you mean that they were wrong or mistaken, but not seriously, because many people would have done the same thing in those circumstances. 谅解 ❑ *Looking at the figures, you could be forgiven for thinking the recession is already over.* 看着这些数字，你认为经济衰退已经结束是情有可原的。

for·give·ness /fərgɪvnɪs/ N-UNCOUNT If you ask for **forgiveness**, you ask to be forgiven for something wrong that you have done. 宽恕 ❑ *...a spirit of forgiveness and national reconciliation.* …一种宽恕与民族和解的精神。

for·giv·ing /fərgɪvɪŋ/ ADJ Someone who is **forgiving** is willing to forgive. 宽容的 ❑ *Voters can be remarkably forgiving of presidents who fail to keep their campaign promises.* 选民们对于未能实现其竞选诺言的总统们能做到极其宽容。

for·go /fɔrgoʊ/ → see **forego**

for·got /fərgɒt/ **Forgot** is the past tense of **forget**. **forget**的过去式

for·got·ten /fərgɒtən/ **Forgotten** is the past participle of **forget**. **forget**的过去分词
→ see **memory**

fork /fɔrk/ (**forks, forking, forked**) 1 N-COUNT A **fork** is a tool used for eating food which has a row of three or four long metal points at the end. 餐叉 ❑ *...knives and forks.* …餐刀及餐叉。 **2** N-COUNT A **fork** in a road, path, or river is a point at which it divides into two parts and forms a "Y" shape. (道路、河流等的) 岔口 ❑ *We arrived at a fork in the road.* 我们来到了该路的一个岔口。 ❑ *The road divides; you should take the right fork.* 路分岔了；你应该走右岔路。 **3** V-T If you **fork** food **into** your mouth or **onto** a plate, you put it there using a fork. 叉起 ❑ *He forked an egg onto a piece of bread and folded it into a sandwich.* 他叉起一个鸡蛋放到一片面包上并将其折成了一个三明治。 **4** V-I If a road, path, or river **forks**, it forms a fork. (公路、路径、河流等) 分岔 [no cont] ❑ *Beyond the village the road forked.* 过了那个村子公路就分岔了。 **5** N-COUNT A garden **fork** is a tool used for breaking up soil which has a row of three or four long metal points at the end. 耙 [mainly BRIT]

in AM, usually use **pitchfork**

→ see **lightning, silverware**

▶ **fork out** PHRASAL VERB If you **fork out for** something, you spend a lot of money on it. (为某事物) 大把掏钱 [INFORMAL] ❑ *Visitors to the castle had to fork out for a guidebook.* 参观城堡的游客得为一本旅游指南掏很多钱。

▶ **fork over** PHRASAL VERB If you fork something over to someone, for example money, you give it to them. 将 (某事物) 交给 (某人) [INFORMAL] ❑ *Nonresidents who work in Philadelphia fork over 3.88 percent of their pay to the city.* 在费城工作的非本地居民将其收入的3.88%交给该市。

for·lorn /fɔrlɔrn/ **1** ADJ If someone is **forlorn**, they feel alone and unhappy. 孤苦伶仃的 [LITERARY] ❑ *One of the demonstrators, a young woman, sat forlorn on the sidewalk.* 其中一名示威者，一个年轻的女子，孤独无助地坐在人行道上。 **2** ADJ A **forlorn** hope or attempt is one that you think has no chance of success. 不可能成功的 ❑ *Peasants have left the land in the forlorn hope of finding a better life in cities.* 农民们带着在城市里寻求更好生活的遥不可及的希望离开了那块土地。

form ◆◆◆ /fɔrm/ (**forms, forming, formed**) **1** N-COUNT A **form of** something is a type or kind of it. 种类 ❑ *He contracted a rare form of cancer.* 他患上了一种罕见的癌症。 ❑ *I am against hunting in any form.* 我反对任何形式的狩猎。 **2** N-COUNT When something can exist or happen in several possible ways, you can use **form** to refer to one particular way in which it exists or happens. 方式 ❑ *They received a benefit in the form of a tax reduction.* 他们以减税的方式获得了收益。 **3** N-COUNT The **form** of something is its shape. 形状 ❑ *...the form of the body.* …体型。 **4** N-COUNT You can refer to something that you can see as a **form** if you cannot see it clearly, or if its outline is the clearest or most striking aspect of it. 外形 ❑ *His form lay still under the blankets.* 他的身形一动不动地躺在毯子下面。 **5** N-COUNT A **form** is a paper with questions on it and spaces marked where you should write the answers. Forms usually ask you to give details about yourself, for example, when you are applying for a job or joining an organization. 表格 ❑ *You will be asked to fill in a form with details of your birth and occupation.* 你会被要求填写一张有关你的出生和职业详情的表格。 **6** V-T/V-I When a particular shape **forms** or **is formed**, people or things move or are arranged so that this shape is made. 编排成 (某形状)；(某形状) 编排成 ❑ *A line formed to use the bathroom.* 排成了一条队来使用这个洗手间。 ❑ *They formed a circle and sang "Auld Lang Syne."* 他们围成一圈，唱起了《友谊地久天长》。 **7** V-T If something is arranged or changed so that it becomes similar to a thing with a particular structure or function, you can say that it **forms** that thing. (某物) 改变而形成 (另一物) ❑ *These panels folded up to form a screen some five feet tall.* 这些嵌板折起来形成了一个高约五英尺的屏风。 **8** V-T If something consists of particular things, people, or features, you can say that they **form** that thing. 构成 ❑ *...the articles that formed the basis of Randolph's book.* …构成伦道夫的书的基础的那些文章。 **9** V-T If you **form** an organization, group, or company, you start it. 组建 ❑ *They tried to form a study group on human rights.* 他们试图组建一个人权研究小组。 **10** V-T/V-I When something natural **forms** or **is formed**, it begins to exist and develop. 形成 (某自然物)；(某自然物) 形成 ❑ *The stars must have formed 10 to 15 billion years ago.* 这些恒星一定形成于100亿至150亿年前。 **11** V-T/V-I If you **form** a relationship, a habit, or an idea, or if it **forms**, it begins to exist and develop. 形成 (某关系、习惯、想法)；(某关系、习惯、想法) 形成 ❑ *She had formed the habit of giving herself freely to men.* 她已养成了随意委身于男人的习惯。 ❑ *An idea formed in his mind.* 一个想法在他的脑子里形成了。 **12** V-T If you say that something **forms** a person's character or personality, you mean that it has a strong influence on them and causes them to develop in a particular way. 塑造 ❑ *Anger at injustice formed his character.* 对不公正行为的愤怒塑造了他的性格。 **13** N-UNCOUNT In sports, **form** refers to the ability or success of a person or animal over a period of time. 竞技状态 ❑ *His form this season has been brilliant.* 他在本赛季的竞技状态一直很好。

Thesaurus *form* 另参见：

N. class, description, kind **1**
body, figure, frame, shape **3**
application, document, sheet **5**
V. construct, create, develop, establish **7**–**11**

for·mal ◆◆◇ /fɔrm^əl/ (**formals**) **1** ADJ **Formal** speech or behavior is very correct and serious rather than relaxed and friendly, and is used especially in official situations. 正式的 (演讲、行为) ❑ *He wrote a very formal letter of apology to Douglas.* 他写了一封非常正式的道歉信给道格拉斯。 ● **for·mal·ly** ADV 正式地 [ADV with v] ❑ *He took her back to Vincent Square in a taxi, saying goodnight formally on the doorstep.* 他打出租车将她送回文森特广场，在门阶上客气地道了晚安。 ● **for·mal·ity** ★ N-UNCOUNT 正式 ❑ *Lillith's formality and seriousness amused him.* 莉莉斯的正式和严肃让他觉得逗。 **2** ADJ A **formal** action, statement, or request is an official one. 官方的；正式的 (行为、陈述、要求等) [ADJ n] ❑ *UN officials said a formal request was passed to American authorities.* 联合国官员们称一份正式的要求已转给了美国当局。 ❑ *No formal announcement had been made.* 尚无官方声明。 ● **for·mal·ly** ADV 官方地；正式地 [ADV with v] ❑ *Diplomats haven't formally agreed to Anderson's plan.* 外交官们还没有正式同意安德森的计划。 **3** ADJ **Formal** occasions are special occasions at which people wear elegant clothes and behave according to a set of accepted rules. 正式的 (场合) ❑ *One evening the company arranged a formal dinner after the play.* 一天晚上该公司在演出后安排了一场正式的晚宴。 ● N-COUNT **Formal** is also a noun. 正式的社交活动 ❑ *...a wide array of events, including school formals and speech nights, weddings, and balls.* …一系列丰富多样的活动，包括学校舞会、演讲之夜、婚礼和大型舞会等。 **4** ADJ **Formal** clothes are very elegant clothes that are suitable for formal occasions. 适合正式场合的 (服装) [ADJ n] ❑ *They wore ordinary ties instead of the more formal high collar and cravat.* 他们打着普通的领带而不是更为正式的高领领结。 ● **for·mal·ly** ADV 正式地 ❑ *It was really too warm for her to dress so formally.* 她穿得这么正式真的太热了。 **5** ADJ **Formal** education or training is given officially, usually in a school, college, or university. 正规的 (教育、培训等) [ADJ n] ❑ *Wendy didn't have any formal dance training.* 温迪没受过任何正规的舞蹈训练。 ● **for·mal·ly** ADV 正规地 [ADV -ed] ❑ *Usually only formally-trained artists from established schools are chosen.* 通常只有在知名学校受过正规训练的艺术家才能被选中。 **6** → see also **formality**

★ **for·mal·ity** /fɔrmælɪti/ (**formalities**) **1** N-COUNT If you say that an action or procedure is just a **formality**, you mean that it is done only because it is normally done, and that it will not have any real effect on the situation. 走形式 ❑ *Some contracts are a mere formality.* 有些合同纯属走形式。 **2** N-COUNT **Formalities** are formal actions or procedures that are carried out as part of a particular activity or event. 正规程序 ❑ *They are whisked through the immigration and customs formalities in a matter of minutes.* 他们在短短的几分钟内就很快走完了移民与海关手续。 **3** → see also **formal**

for·mal·ize /fɔrməlaɪz/ (**formalizes, formalizing, formalized**) V-T If you **formalize** a plan, idea, arrangement, or system, you make it formal and official. 使正式化；使官方化 ❑ *A recent treaty signed by Russia, Canada and Japan formalized an agreement to work together to stop the pirates.* 最近由俄罗斯、加拿大和日本签署的一项条约使共同阻止盗版者的协议正式生效。

for·mat /fɔrmæt/ (**formats, formatting, formatted**) **1** N-COUNT The **format** of something is the way or order in which it is arranged and presented. 程式 ❑ *I had met with him to explain the format of the program and what we had in mind.* 我已经同他见过面，解释了这个节目的程式和我们的想法。 **2** N-COUNT The **format** of a piece of computer software, a movie or a musical recording is the type of equipment on which it is designed to be used or played. For example, possible formats for a movie are DVD and video cassette. (计算机软件、电影、音乐录制品等的) 格式 ❑ *His latest album is available on all formats.* 他的最新专辑有各种格式可以买到。 **3** V-T To **format** a computer disk means to run a program so that the disk can be written on. 将 (电脑磁盘) 格式化 [COMPUTING] ❑ *...a menu that includes the choice to format a disk.* …一个包括格式化磁盘选项的菜单。 **4** V-T To **format** a piece of computer text or graphics means to arrange the way in which it appears when it is printed or is displayed on a screen. 设置(电脑文本或图形的) 版式 [COMPUTING] ❑ *When text is saved from a Web page, it is often very badly formatted with many short lines.* 文本从网页上另存时版式通常会变乱，出现很多短行。

for·ma·tion /fɔrmeɪʃən/ (**formations**) 1 N-UNCOUNT **The formation of** something is the starting or creation of it. 始创 ❑ *Time is running out for the formation of a new government.* 组建新政府所剩的时间不多了。 2 N-UNCOUNT **The formation of** an idea, habit, relationship, or character is the process of developing and establishing it. (观念、习惯、关系、性格等的) 形成 ❑ *My profession had an important influence in the formation of my character and temperament.* 我的职业对我的性格和性情的形成有重要的影响。 3 N-COUNT If people or things are **in formation**, they are arranged in a particular pattern as they move. 编队 ❑ *He was flying in formation with seven other jets.* 他和另外7架喷气式飞机编队飞行。 4 N-COUNT A rock or cloud **formation** is rock or cloud of a particular shape or structure. (岩石或云的) 形成物 ❑ *...a vast rock formation shaped like a pillar.* …形状如柱子的一块巨大岩层。

forma·tive /fɔrmətɪv/ ADJ A **formative** period of time or experience is one that has an important and lasting influence on a person's character and attitudes. 形成的(时期、经历) ❑ *She was born in Barbados but spent her formative years growing up in Miami.* 她出生于巴巴多斯，但他的成长期是在迈阿密度过的。

for·mer ♦♦♦ /fɔrmər/ 1 ADJ **Former** is used to describe someone who used to have a particular job, position, or role, but no longer has it. 前任的 [ADJ n] ❑ *The unemployed executives include former sales managers, directors and accountants.* 失业的管理人员包括前销售经理、主管和会计。 ❑ *...former president Richard Nixon.* …前总统理查德·尼克松。 2 ADJ **Former** is used to refer to countries which no longer exist or whose boundaries have changed. (国家) 已不存在的; 疆界已变的 [ADJ n] ❑ *...the former Soviet Union.* …前苏联。 3 ADJ **Former** is used to describe something which used to belong to someone or which used to be a particular thing. 昔日的 [ADJ n] ❑ *...the former home of Robert E. Lee.* …罗伯特·E·李的故居。 4 PRON When two people, things, or groups have just been mentioned, you can refer to the first of them as **the former.** 前者 ["the" PRON] ❑ *They grappled with the problem of connecting the electricity and water supplies. The former proved simple compared with the latter.* 他们设法解决供电和供水的连接问题。前者与后者相比证明很简单。

> **The latter** should only be used to refer to the second of two items which have already been mentioned: ❑ *Given the choice between working for someone else and being on call day and night for the family business, she'd prefer the latter.* The last of three or more items can be referred to as **the last-named.** Compare this with **the former** which is used to talk about the first of two things already mentioned.

Thesaurus *former* 另参见:
ADJ. prior 1
past, previous 1 3

for·mer·ly /fɔrmərli/ ADV If something happened or was true **formerly**, it happened or was true in the past. 以前 ❑ *He had formerly been in the navy.* 他以前在海军服役。

★ **for·mi·dable** /fɔrmɪdəbəl, fərmɪd-/ ADJ If you describe something or someone as **formidable**, you mean that you feel slightly frightened by them because they are very great or impressive. 可怕的; 令人敬畏的 ❑ *We have a formidable task ahead of us.* 我们面前有一项艰巨的任务。

for·mu·la ♦◇◇ /fɔrmyələ/ (**formulae** /fɔrmyəli/ or **formulas**) 1 N-COUNT A **formula** is a plan that is invented in order to deal with a particular problem. 方案 ❑ *...a peace formula.* …一项和平方案。 2 N-COUNT A **formula** is a group of letters, numbers, or other symbols which represents a scientific or mathematical rule. 公式 ❑ *He developed a mathematical formula describing the distances of the planets from the Sun.* 他提出了一个描述各行星与太阳之间距离的数学公式。 3 N-COUNT In science, the **formula** for a substance is a list of the amounts of various substances which make up that substance, or an indication of the atoms that it is composed of. 分子式 ❑ *Glucose and fructose have the same chemical formula but have very different properties.* 葡萄糖和果糖具有相同的化学分子式但有很不同的特性。 4 N-SING A **formula for** a particular situation, usually a good one, is a course of action or a combination of actions that is certain or likely to result in that situation. (达成通常为好的结局的) 行动方案 ❑ *After he was officially pronounced the world's oldest man, he offered this simple formula for a long and happy life.* 在他被正式宣布为世界上最老的人之后，他提供了这一长寿和幸福生活的简单方法。

★ **for·mu·late** /fɔrmyəleɪt/ (**formulates, formulating, formulated**) 1 V-T If you **formulate** something such as a plan or proposal, you invent it, thinking about the details carefully. 构想出(计划或提案) ❑ *Little by little, he formulated his plan for escape.* 他一点一点地构想出了他的逃跑计划。 2 V-T If you **formulate** a thought, opinion, or idea, you express it or describe it using particular words. 用独特的词语表述 ❑ *I was impressed by the way he could formulate his ideas.* 我对他表述自己想法的独特用词印象深刻。

for·mu·la·tion /fɔrmyəleɪʃən/ (**formulations**) 1 N-VAR A **formulation** is the way in which you express your thoughts and ideas. 表述方式 ❑ *This is a far weaker formulation than is in the draft resolution which is being proposed.* 这是相对于正在被提议的草拟决议要弱得多的一种表述方式。 2 N-UNCOUNT The **formulation** of something such as a policy or plan is the process of creating or inventing it. 制订 ❑ *...the process of policy formulation and implementation.* …政策制订及执行过程。 3 N-VAR The **formulation** of something such as a medicine or a beauty product is the way in which different ingredients are combined to make it. You can also say that the finished product is a **formulation.** (药品或化妆品的) 配方; 配方产品 [mainly BRIT]

▲ **for·sake** /fərseɪk/ (**forsakes, forsaking, forsook** /fɔrsʊk/, **forsaken**) 1 V-T If you **forsake** someone, you leave them when you should have stayed, or you stop helping them or looking after them. 离弃 [LITERARY, DISAPPROVAL] ❑ *I still love him and I would never forsake him.* 我仍然爱他，我永远不会离弃他。 2 V-T If you **forsake** something, you stop doing it, using it, or having it. 放弃 [LITERARY] ❑ *He doubted their claim to have forsaken military solutions to the civil war.* 他对他们声称已经放弃以军事手段解决内战的说法有怀疑。

★ **fort** /fɔrt/ (**forts**) 1 N-COUNT; N-IN-NAMES A **fort** is a strong building or a place with a wall or fence around it where soldiers can stay and be safe from the enemy. 堡垒; 碉堡 2 PHRASE If you **hold the fort** for someone or if you **hold down the fort**, you take care of things for them while they are somewhere else or are busy doing something else. 代为处理事务 ❑ *His business partner is holding the fort while he is away.* 他的生意伙伴在他不在的时候代他处理事务。 ❑ *"I'll hold down the fort until he's back," Clark said.* "在他回来之前我会代他处理事务，"克拉克说。

forth ♦◇◇ /fɔrθ/

> In addition to the uses shown below, **forth** is also used in the phrasal verbs "put forth" and "set forth."

1 ADV When someone goes **forth** from a place, they leave it. 离开 [ADV after v] [LITERARY] ❑ *Go forth into the desert.* 去进入沙漠 2 ADV If one thing brings **forth** another, the first thing produces the second. (得) 出来 [ADV after v] [LITERARY] ❑ *My reflections brought forth no conclusion.* 我的思考没有得出任何结论。 3 ADV When someone or something is brought **forth**, they are brought to a place or moved into a position where people can see them. (带) 出来 [ADV after v] [LITERARY] ❑ *Pilate ordered Jesus to be brought forth.* 彼拉多命令将耶稣带上来。 4 **back and forth** → see **back** 5 **to hold forth** → see **hold**

★ **forth·com·ing** /fɔrθkʌmɪŋ/ 1 ADJ A **forthcoming** event is planned to happen soon. 即将到来的 [ADJ n] ❑ *...his opponents in the forthcoming elections.* …他在即将到来的选举中的对手们。 2 ADJ If something that you want, need, or expect is **forthcoming**, it is given to you or it happens. 实现的 [v-link ADJ] [FORMAL] ❑ *They promised that the money would be forthcoming.* 他们承诺说钱会到位的。 ❑ *One source predicts no major shift in policy will be forthcoming at the committee hearings.* 有一消息预言在委员会听证会上不会有政策上的重大变动。 3 ADJ If you say that someone is **forthcoming**, you mean that they willingly give information when you ask them. 愿意提供信息的 ❑ *William, sadly, was not very forthcoming about any other names he might have, where he lived or what his phone number was.* 很遗憾，威廉在有关他可能有的其它名字、他的住处或者电话号码等方面不太愿意提供信息。

▲ **forth·right** /fɔrθraɪt/ ADJ If you describe someone as **forthright**, you admire them because they show clearly and strongly what they think and feel. 直率的 [APPROVAL] ❑ *...a deeply religious man with forthright opinions.* …一个有直率见解、非常虔诚的宗教信徒。

f

for·ti·eth ♦♦◇ /fɔ̲rtiəθ/ ORD The **fortieth** item in a series is the one that you count as number forty. 第四十 ❑ *It was the fortieth anniversary of the death of the composer.* 那是那个作曲家逝世40周年纪念日。

▲ **for·ti·fy** /fɔ̲rtɪfaɪ/ (**fortifies, fortifying, fortified**) **1** V-T To **fortify** a place means to make it stronger and more difficult to attack, often by building a wall or ditch round it. (常通过筑墙、挖沟等) 巩固 (某地) ❑ *...soldiers working to fortify an airbase in Bahrain.* …在巩固一个在巴林的空军基地的士兵们。 **2** V-T If food or drink **is fortified**, another substance is added to it to make it healthier or stronger. (通过添加另一种物质而) 强化 (食品或饮料) [usu passive] ❑ *Choose margarine or butter fortified with vitamin D.* 选择人造黄油或用维生素D强化了的黄油。 ❑ *All sherry is made from wine fortified with brandy.* 所有雪利酒都是由用白兰地强化了的葡萄酒制成的。

fort·night /fɔ̲rtnaɪt/ (**fortnights**) N-COUNT A **fortnight** is a period of two weeks. 两周 [mainly BRIT] ❑ *I hope to be back in a fortnight.* 我希望到两周后回来。

F

fort·night·ly /fɔ̲rtnaɪtli/ ADJ A **fortnightly** event or publication happens or appears once every two weeks. 每两周一次的 [BRIT] in AM, use **biweekly**
● ADV **Fortnightly** is also an adverb. 每两周一次地

▲ **for·tress** /fɔ̲rtrɪs/ (**fortresses**) N-COUNT A **fortress** is a castle or other large strong building, or a well-protected place, which is intended to be difficult for enemies to enter. 城堡; 大堡垒; 要塞 ❑ *...a 13th-century fortress.* …一座13世纪的城堡。

for·tu·nate /fɔ̲rtʃənɪt/ ADJ If you say that someone or something is **fortunate**, you mean that they are lucky. 幸运的 ❑ *He was extremely fortunate to survive.* 他极为幸运地活了下来。 ❑ *She is in the fortunate position of having plenty of choice.* 她处在一个可有很多选择的幸运位置上。

for·tu·nate·ly /fɔ̲rtʃənɪtli/ ADV **Fortunately** is used to introduce or indicate a statement about an event or situation that is good. 幸好 ❑ *Fortunately, the weather that winter was reasonably mild.* 幸好那个冬季的天气颇暖和。

for·tune ♦◇◇ /fɔ̲rtʃən/ (**fortunes**) **1** N-COUNT You can refer to a large sum of money as **a fortune** or **a small fortune** to emphasize how large it is. 大笔钱 [EMPHASIS] ❑ *He made a small fortune in the property boom.* 他在房地产繁荣期发了一小笔财。 **2** N-COUNT Someone who has a **fortune** has a very large amount of money. 很大数额的钱 ❑ *He made his fortune in car sales.* 他在汽车销售中发了财。 **3** N-UNCOUNT **Fortune** or good **fortune** is good luck. Ill **fortune** is bad luck. 好运; 运气 ❑ *Investors are starting to wonder how long their good fortune can last.* 投资者们开始怀疑他们的好运还能持续多久。 **4** N-PLURAL If you talk about someone's **fortunes** or the **fortunes** of something, you are talking about the extent to which they are doing well or being successful. 运势 ❑ *The company had to do something to reverse its sliding fortunes.* 该公司不得不采取措施来逆转其下滑的运势。 **5** PHRASE When someone **tells** your **fortune**, they tell you what they think will happen to you in the future, which they say is shown, for example, by the lines on your hand. 算命 ❑ *I was just going to have my fortune told by a gypsy.* 我正要去找一个吉普赛人给我算命。

for·ty ♦♦♦ /fɔ̲rti/ (**forties**) **1** NUM **Forty** is the number 40. 四十; 40 **2** N-PLURAL When you talk about the **forties**, you are referring to numbers between 40 and 49. For example, if you are **in** your **forties**, you are aged between 40 and 49. If the temperature is **in the forties**, the temperature is between 40 and 49 degrees. 四十几 (指40至49之间的数字) ❑ *He was a big man in his forties, smartly dressed in a suit and tie.* 他是一个四十几岁的高大男子，穿着西服打着领带，很精神。 **3** N-PLURAL **The forties** is the decade between 1940 and 1949. 40年代 (指某世纪40到49年) ❑ *Steel cans were introduced sometime during the forties.* 钢罐是在40年代的某个时候开始使用的。

fo·rum /fɔ̲rəm/ (**forums**) N-COUNT A **forum** is a place, situation, or group in which people exchange ideas and discuss issues, especially important public issues. 论坛 ❑ *Members of the council agreed that was an important forum for discussion.* 理事会成员们一致认为那是一个用于讨论的重要论坛。

Word Link *ward ≈ in the direction of : backward, forward, inward*

for·ward ♦♦◇ /fɔ̲rwərd/ (**forwards, forwarding, forwarded**) **1** ADV If you move or look **forward**, you move or look in a direction that is in front of you. 向前 (移动、看) [ADV after v] ❑ *He came forward with his hand out. "Mr. and Mrs. Selby?" he said.* 他伸着手走上前来，"塞尔比先生和夫人吧？" 他说。 ❑ *She fell forward on to her face.* 她脸着地向前摔倒了。 **2** ADV **Forward** means in a position near the front of something such as a building or a vehicle. 靠前地 ❑ *The best seats are in the aisle and as far forward as possible.* 最好的座位在过道处尽可能靠前的地方。 ● ADJ **Forward** is also an adjective. 靠前的 [ADJ n] ❑ *Reinforcements were needed to allow more troops to move to forward positions.* 需要增援以便让更多的部队推进至前沿阵地。 **3** ADV If you say that someone looks **forward**, you approve of them because they think about what will happen in the future and plan for it. (看) 向前地 [APPROVAL] ❑ *Now the leadership wants to look forward, and to outline a strategy for the rest of the century.* 现在领导层想要向前看，为本世纪余下的时间勾画一个战略框架。 ❑ *People should forget and look forward.* 人们应当忘记过去向前看。 ● ADJ **Forward** is also an adjective. 向前的 [ADJ n] ❑ *The university system requires more forward planning.* 大学体制要求更具前瞻性的规划。 **4** ADV If you move a clock or watch **forward**, you change the time shown on it so that it shows a later time, for example, when the time changes to daylight saving time. (拨钟表) 向前地 [ADV after v] ❑ *When we put the clocks forward in March we go into daylight saving time.* 当我们在3月份把钟向前拨以后，我们就进入了夏令时。 **5** ADV When you are referring to a particular time, if you say that something was true **from** that time **forward**, you mean that it became true at that time, and continued to be true afterward. (从某时刻) 起 ["from" n ADV] ❑ *Velzquez's work from that time forward was confined largely to portraits of the royal family.* 从那以后，委拉斯开兹的作品就很大程度上仅限于王室的肖像画了。 **6** ADV You use **forward** to indicate that something progresses or improves. 向前 (进展、进步) ❑ *And by boosting economic prosperity in Mexico, Canada and the United States, it will help us move forward on issues that concern all of us.* 而且通过推动墨西哥、加拿大和美国的经济繁荣，它将会帮助我们在解决与我们大家有关的问题上取得进展。 ❑ *They just couldn't see any way forward.* 他们就是看不到任何前进之路。 **7** ADV If something or someone is put **forward**, or comes **forward**, they are suggested or offered as suitable for a particular purpose. (呈、走) 上前; (提) 出来 [ADV after v] ❑ *Over the years several similar theories have been put forward.* 多年来几种类似理论被提了出来。 ❑ *Investigations have ground to a standstill because no witnesses have come forward.* 调查已陷入一种停滞状态，因为没有证人出来作证。 **8** V-T If a letter or message **is forwarded to** someone, it is sent to the place where they are, after having been sent to a different place earlier. 转发 ❑ *When he's out on the road, office calls are forwarded to the cellular phone in his truck.* 当他外出在路上时，打到办公室的电话便被转到他卡车中的移动电话上。 **9** N-COUNT In basketball, soccer, or hockey, a **forward** is a player whose usual position is in the opponents' half of the field, and whose usual job is to attack or score goals. (篮球、足球、曲棍球等运动的) 前锋 ❑ *Junior forward Sam McCracken added 14 points for the home team.* 前锋小萨姆・麦克拉肯为主队添了14分。 **10** **backward and forward** → see **backward**

Word Web **fossil**

There are two types of animal **fossils**—body fossils and **trace** fossils. Body fossils help us understand how the animal looked when it was alive. Trace fossils, such as **tracks** and **footprints**, show us how the animal moved. Since we don't find tracks of dinosaurs' tails, we know they lifted them up as they walked. Footprints tell us about the weight of the dinosaur and how fast it moved. Scientists use two methods to calculate the date of a fossil. They sometimes count the number of **rock** layers covering it. They also use carbon dating.

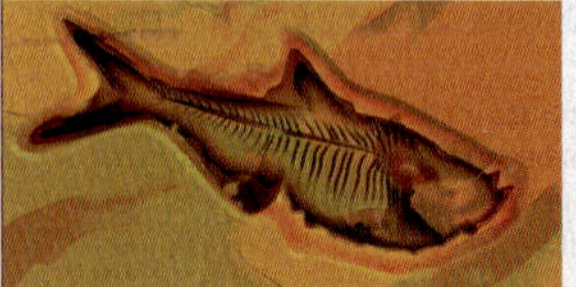

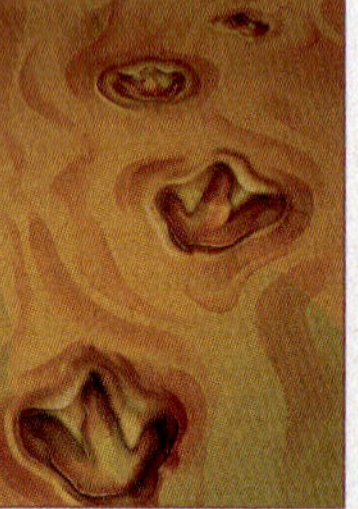

fos·sil /fɒsᵊl/ (**fossils**) N-COUNT **A fossil** is the hard remains of a prehistoric animal or plant that are found inside a rock. 化石
→ see Word Web: **fossil**

fos·sil fuel (**fossil fuels**) also **fossil-fuel** N-MASS **Fossil fuel** is fuel such as coal or oil that is formed from the decayed remains of plants or animals. 化石燃料 ❑ *Burning fossil fuels uses oxygen and produces carbon dioxide.* 燃烧化石燃料消耗氧气并产生二氧化碳。
→ see **greenhouse effect, solar system**

★ **fos·ter** /fɒstər/ (**fosters, fostering, fostered**) 1 ADJ **Foster** parents are people who officially take a child into their family for a period of time, without becoming the child's legal parents. The child is referred to as their **foster** child. 收养的 [ADJ n] ❑ *Little Jack was placed with foster parents.* 小杰克被安置在养父母家。 2 V-T If you **foster** a child, you take it into your family for a period of time, without becoming its legal parent. 收养 ❑ *She has since gone on to find happiness by fostering more than 100 children.* 她此后又通过收养一百多个孩子找到了快乐。 3 V-T To **foster** something such as an activity or idea means to help it to develop. 促进 ❑ *He said that developed countries had a responsibility to foster global economic growth to help new democracies.* 他说发达国家有一种促进全球经济增长以帮助新兴民主国家的责任。

fought /fɔt/ **Fought** is the past tense and past participle of **fight**. **fight**的过去式和过去分词

★ **foul** /faʊl/ (**fouler, foulest, fouls, fouling, fouled**) 1 ADJ If you describe something as **foul**, you mean it is dirty and smells or tastes unpleasant. 又脏又臭的; 味道不好的 ❑ *...foul polluted water.* …污染了的、又脏又臭的水。 2 ADJ **Foul** language is offensive and contains swear words or rude words. 粗俗的 (语言) ❑ *The teachers had to deal with her foul language, disruptive behavior, and low academic performance.* 老师们不得不应付她粗俗的语言、捣乱的行为和不良的学业成绩。 3 ADJ If someone has a **foul** temper or is in a **foul** mood, they become angry or violent very suddenly and easily. 暴躁的 ❑ *Collins was in a foul mood even before the interviews began.* 柯林斯甚至在面试开始之前就处于暴躁情绪。 4 ADJ **Foul** weather is unpleasant, windy, and stormy. 恶劣的 (天气) ❑ *No amount of foul weather, whether hail, wind, rain or snow, seems to deter them.* 不管天气有多恶劣，哪怕是冰雹、大风、雨还是雪，似乎都阻止不了他们。 5 V-T If an animal **fouls** a place, it drops feces onto the ground. 在 (某地上) 拉屎 ❑ *It is an offense to let your dog foul a footpath.* 让你的狗在人行道上拉屎是一种违法行为。 6 V-T In a game or sport, if a player **fouls** another player, they touch them or block them in a way which is not allowed according to the rules. 对 (某人) 犯规 ❑ *Nowitzki fouled Mitchell early in the third quarter.* 在第三节早些时候，诺维斯基就对米切尔犯了规。 ❑ *Middlesborough's Jimmy Phillips was sent off for fouling Steve Tilson.* 米德尔斯比堡队的基米·菲利普斯因为对史蒂夫·特尔逊犯规而被罚出场。 7 N-COUNT **A foul** is an act in a game or sport that is not allowed according to the rules. (体育比赛中的) 犯规 ❑ *Harridge was charged with a flagrant foul and ejected from the game.* 哈里基被指恶意犯规并被逐出了比赛。 ● ADJ **Foul** is also an adjective. 犯规的 [ADJ n] ❑ *...a foul tackle.* …一次犯规的阻截。 8 PHRASE If you **run foul of** someone or **fall foul of** them, you do something which gets you into trouble with them. 惹恼 ❑ *He had fallen foul of the FBI.* 他已惹恼了联邦调查局。

▸ **foul up** PHRASAL VERB If someone or something **fouls up**, or if they **foul** something **up**, they make a serious mistake that causes things to go badly wrong. 弄砸 ❑ *A computer software glitch fouled up their presentation.* 一个电脑软件故障弄砸了他们的展示会。

found ♦◇◇ /faʊnd/ (**founds, founding, founded**) 1 **Found** is the past tense and past participle of **find**. **find**的过去时与过去分词 2 V-T When an institution, company, or organization **is founded** by someone or by a group of people, they get it started, often by providing the necessary money. 成立 ❑ *The New York Free-Loan Society was founded in 1892.* 纽约无息贷款协会成立于1892年。 ❑ *His father founded the American Socialist Party.* 他的父亲创建了美国社会党。 ● **foun·da·tion** /faʊndeɪʃᵊn/ N-SING 成立 [with poss] ❑ *...the foundation of the National Association of Evangelicals in 1942.* …1942年全国福音协会的成立。 ● **found·ing** N-SING 成立 ❑ *The firm has never had an unprofitable year since its founding 65 years ago.* 该公司自65年前成立以来从没有过不盈利的年度。 3 V-T When a town, important building, or other place **is founded** by someone or by a group of people, they cause it to be built. 兴建 [usu passive] ❑ *The town was founded in 1610.* 该城镇兴建于1610年。 4 → see also **founded, founding**

Word Link *found ≈ base : foundation, founded, founder*

foun·da·tion ♦◇◇ /faʊndeɪʃᵊn/ (**foundations**) 1 N-COUNT **The foundation of** something such as a belief or way of life is the things on which it is based. 基础 ❑ *Best friends are the foundation of my life.* 良友们是我生活的基础。 ❑ *The issue strikes at the very foundation of our community.* 这个问题严重影响到我们社会的基础。 2 N-COUNT **A foundation** is an organization which provides money for a special purpose such as research or charity. 基金会 ❑ *...the National Foundation for Educational Research.* …全国教育研究基金会。 3 N-PLURAL **The foundations** of a building or other structure are the layer of bricks or concrete below the ground that it is built on. 地基 4 N-UNCOUNT If a story, idea, or argument has **no foundation**, there are no facts to prove that it is true. 根据 ❑ *The allegations were without foundation.* 这些指控没有根据。 5 N-MASS **Foundation** is a skin-colored cream that you put on your face before putting on the rest of your makeup. 粉底霜 ❑ *Use foundation and/or face powder afterwards for an even skin tone.* 随后使用粉底霜和（或）粉饼以使皮肤色调均匀。 6 → see also **found**
→ see **makeup**

Word Partnership *foundation* 的常用搭配:

V.	**establish a** foundation 1 2
	build a foundation, **lay a** foundation 3
	apply foundation 5
ADJ.	**firm** foundation, **solid** foundation 1 3
	charitable foundation 2

found·ed /faʊndɪd/ 1 ADJ If something **is founded on** a particular thing, it is based on it. 以…为基础 [v-link ADJ "on" n] ❑ *The criticisms are founded on facts as well as on convictions.* 这些批评是以事实和信念为基础的。 2 → see also **found**

found·er ♦◇◇ /faʊndər/ (**founders, foundering, foundered**) 1 N-COUNT **The founder** of an institution, organization, or building is the person who got it started or caused it to be built, often by providing the necessary money. 创建人 2 V-I If something such as a plan or project **founders**, it fails because of a particular point, difficulty, or problem. 失败 ❑ *The talks have foundered, largely because of the reluctance of some members of the government to do a deal with criminals.* 会谈已经失败了，主要是因为一些政府成员不愿意和罪犯们达成协议。

found·ing /faʊndɪŋ/ 1 ADJ **Founding** means relating to the starting of a particular institution or organization. 成立的 [ADJ n] ❑ *The committee held its founding congress in the capital, Riga.* 委员会在首都里加举行了成立大会。 2 → see also **found**

foun·tain /faʊntɪn/ (**fountains**) 1 N-COUNT **A fountain** is an ornamental feature in a pool or lake which consists of a long narrow stream of water that is forced up into the air by a pump. 喷泉 ❑ *...the fountains on the 16th Street Mall.* …第16街商业区的喷泉。 2 N-COUNT **A fountain of** a liquid is an amount of it which is sent up into the air and falls back. 喷射 [LITERARY] ❑ *The volcano spewed a fountain of molten rock 650 feet in the air.* 这座火山喷射出的熔岩高达650英尺。

four ♦♦♦ /fɔr/ (**fours**) 1 NUM **Four** is the number 4. 4 ❑ *Judith is married with four children.* 朱迪斯已经结婚，有4个孩子。 2 PHRASE If you are **on all fours**, your knees, feet, and hands are on the ground. 趴

four·some /fɔrsəm/ (**foursomes**) N-COUNT-COLL **A foursome** is a group of four people or things. 四个一组 ❑ *The foursome released their second CD this month.* 这个四人组合本月推出了他们的第二张激光唱片。

four·teen ♦♦♦ /fɔrtin/ (**fourteens**) NUM **Fourteen** is the number 14. 14 ❑ *I'm fourteen years old.* 我14岁。

four·teenth ♦♦◇ /fɔrtinθ/ ORD **The fourteenth** item in a series is the one that you count as number fourteen. 第14 ❑ *The Festival, now in its fourteenth year, has become a major international jazz event.* 该音乐节现在进入了第14个年头，已成为国际爵士乐的一大盛事。

fourth ♦♦◇ /fɔrθ/ (**fourths**) 1 ORD **The fourth** item in a series is the one that you count as number four. 第4 ❑ *Last year's winner Greg Lemond of the United States is in fourth place.* 去年的获胜者美国的格雷格·莱蒙德现在排名第4。 2 FRACTION **A fourth** is one of four equal parts of something. 1/4 [AM] ❑ *Three-fourths of the public say they favor a national referendum on the issue.* 3/4的公众说他们赞成就此问题举行全民公投。

four-wheel drive (**four-wheel drives**) N-COUNT **A four-wheel drive** is a vehicle in which all four wheels receive power from the engine to help with steering. This makes the vehicle easier to drive on rough roads or surfaces such as sand or snow. 四轮驱动车

fowl /faul/ (**fowls**)

> **Fowl** can also be used as the plural form.

N-COUNT A **fowl** is a bird, especially one that can be eaten as food, such as a duck or a chicken. 家禽 ❑ *Carve the fowl into 8 pieces.* 将这只家禽切成8块。

fox /fɒks/ (**foxes**) N-COUNT A **fox** is a wild animal which looks like a dog and has reddish-brown fur, a pointed face and ears, and a thick tail. Foxes eat smaller animals. 狐狸

→ see **arctic**

foy·er /fɔɪər, fɔɪeɪ, fwɑyeɪ/ (**foyers**) N-COUNT **The foyer** is the large area where people meet or wait just inside the main doors of a building such as a theater or hotel. (剧场、旅馆等的) 门厅 ❑ *I went and waited in the foyer.* 我去了，在门厅里等着。

F

> **Word Link** *fract, frag ≈ breaking : fraction, fracture, fragile*

frac·tion /frækʃən/ (**fractions**) 1 N-COUNT A **fraction of** something is a tiny amount or proportion of it. 少量 ❑ *She hesitated for a fraction of a second before responding.* 她犹豫了一下才回应。❑ *Here's how to eat like the stars, at a fraction of the cost.* 这就是如何花少量钱却能像明星一样吃喝的方法。 2 N-COUNT A **fraction** is a number that can be expressed as a proportion of two whole numbers. For example, ½ and ⅓ are both fractions. 分数 ❑ *The students had a grasp of decimals, percentages and fractions.* 学生们掌握了小数、百分数和分数。

★ **frac·ture** /fræktʃər/ (**fractures, fracturing, fractured**) 1 N-COUNT A **fracture** is a crack or break in something, especially a bone. (尤指骨头) 断裂 ❑ *At least one-third of all women over ninety have sustained a hip fracture.* 90岁以上的妇女中至少有1/3遭受过髋骨骨折。 2 V-T/V-I If something such as a bone **is fractured** or **fractures**, it gets a crack or break in it. 折断 ❑ *You've fractured a rib, maybe more than one.* 你断了一根肋骨，也许不止一根。❑ *One strut had fractured and been crudely repaired in several places.* 一根支柱断裂了，好几处已做了粗略修补。 3 V-T/V-I If something such as an organization or society **is fractured** or **fractures**, it splits into several parts or stops existing. 分裂 [FORMAL] ❑ *His policy risks fracturing the coalition.* 他的政策有分裂联盟的危险。

★ **frag·ile** /frædʒəl/ 1 ADJ If you describe a situation as **fragile**, you mean that it is weak or uncertain, and unlikely to be able to resist strong pressure or attack. 脆弱的 [JOURNALISM] ❑ *The fragile economies of several southern African nations could be irreparably damaged.* 几个南部非洲国家脆弱的经济可能会无可挽救地被摧垮。● **fra·gil·ity** /frədʒɪlɪti/ N-UNCOUNT 脆弱 ❑ *By mid-1988 there were clear indications of the extreme fragility of the Right-wing coalition.* 到1988年年中有明显的迹象表明右翼联盟极度脆弱。 2 ADJ Something that is **fragile** is easily broken or damaged. 易碎的 ❑ *He leaned back in his fragile chair.* 他向后靠在他那把不结实的椅子上。● **fra·gil·ity** N-UNCOUNT 易碎性 ❑ *Older drivers are more likely to be seriously injured because of the fragility of their bones.* 年纪较大的司机因骨骼易碎而更可能会受重伤。

> **Thesaurus** *fragile* 另参见：
> ADJ. unstable, weak 1
> breakable, delicate; (*ant.*) sturdy 2

frag·ment (**fragments, fragmenting, fragmented**)

> The noun is pronounced /frægmənt/. The verb is pronounced /frægmɛnt/.

> 名词读作 /frægmənt/，动词读作 /frægmɛnt/。

1 N-COUNT A **fragment of** something is a small piece or part of it. 碎片；片段 ❑ *The only reminder of the shooting is a few fragments of metal in my shoulder.* 惟一使我记起那次枪击的，是我肩膀里的一些金属碎片。❑ *She read everything, digesting every fragment of news.* 她什么都读，对新闻的每一个片段都细细品味。 2 V-T/V-I If something **fragments** or **is fragmented**, it breaks or separates into small pieces or parts. 碎裂 ❑ *The clouds fragmented and out came the sun.* 云开日出。

● **frag·men·ta·tion** /frægmɛnteɪʃən/ N-UNCOUNT 分裂 ❑ *...the extraordinary fragmentation of styles on the music scene.* …音乐界各种风格的不寻常分化。

★ **fra·grance** /freɪgrəns/ (**fragrances**) 1 N-VAR A **fragrance** is a pleasant or sweet smell. 香味 ❑ *...a shrubby plant with a strong characteristic fragrance.* …一种有独特浓郁香味的灌木。 2 N-MASS **Fragrance** is a pleasant-smelling liquid which people put on their bodies to make themselves smell nice. 香水 ❑ *The advertisement is for a men's fragrance.* 这则广告介绍一款男士香水。

★ **fra·grant** /freɪgrənt/ ADJ Something that is **fragrant** has a pleasant, sweet smell. 芳香的 ❑ *...fragrant oils and perfumes.* …香精油和香水。

▲ **frail** /freɪl/ (**frailer, frailest**) 1 ADJ Someone who is **frail** is not very strong or healthy. 虚弱的 ❑ *She lay in bed looking frail.* 她躺在床上，看上去很虚弱。 2 ADJ Something that is **frail** is easily broken or damaged. 易碎的；易坏的 ❑ *The frail boat rocked as he clambered in.* 他爬进去的时候，那条破船摇晃起来。

frail·ty /freɪlti, freɪəl-/ (**frailties**) 1 N-VAR If you refer to the **frailties** or **frailty** of people, you are referring to their weaknesses. 弱点 ❑ *...the frailties of human nature.* …人性的弱点。 2 N-UNCOUNT **Frailty** is the condition of having poor health. 虚弱 ❑ *She died after a long period of increasing frailty.* 她日益虚弱，经过一段长时间后去世了。

frame ♦◇◇ /freɪm/ (**frames, framing, framed**) 1 N-COUNT The **frame** of a picture or mirror is the wood, metal, or plastic that is fitted around it, especially when it is displayed or hung on a wall. 框架 ❑ *Estelle kept a photograph of her mother in a silver frame on the kitchen mantelpiece.* 埃丝特尔把她母亲的一张照片放在厨房壁炉架上的银质相框里。 2 N-COUNT The **frame** of an object such as a building, chair, or window is the arrangement of wooden, metal, or plastic bars between which other material is fitted, and which give the object its strength and shape. 构架 ❑ *He supplied housebuilders with modern timber frames.* 他为建房者提供了现代化的木制构架。❑ *With difficulty he released the mattress from the metal frame, and groped beneath it.* 他费了很大劲把床垫从金属架上卸下来，然后在下面摸索一番。 3 N-COUNT The **frames** of a pair of glasses are all the metal or plastic parts of it, but not the lenses. 眼镜框 ❑ *He was wearing new glasses with gold wire frames.* 他戴着一副新的金丝框眼镜。 4 N-COUNT A **frame** of movie film is one of the many separate photographs that it consists of. 画面 ❑ *Standard 8mm projects at 16 frames per second.* 标准的8毫米电影每秒放映16帧画面。 5 V-T When a picture or photograph **is framed**, it is put in a frame. 给 (图画或照片) 配框 [usu passive] ❑ *The picture is now ready to be mounted and framed.* 这幅画现在可以装裱、配框了。 6 V-T If an object **is framed** by a particular thing, it is surrounded by that thing in a way that makes the object more striking or attractive to look at. 环绕 [usu passive] ❑ *The swimming pool is framed by tropical gardens.* 游泳池四周环绕着热带花园。 7 V-T If someone **frames** an innocent person, they make other people think that that person is guilty of a crime, by lying or inventing evidence. 诬陷 [INFORMAL] ❑ *I need to find out who tried to frame me.* 我需要查出谁试图诬陷我。 8 N-COUNT You can refer to someone's body as their **frame**, especially when you are describing the general shape of their body. 身躯 ❑ *Their belts are pulled tight against their bony frames.* 他们的腰带紧裹着瘦骨嶙峋的躯体。

→ see **animation, bed, painting**

frame of mind (**frames of mind**) N-COUNT Your **frame of mind** is the mood that you are in, which causes you to have a particular attitude to something. 心情 ❑ *Lewis was not in the right frame of mind to continue.* 刘易斯当时心情不佳，不适合继续下去。

frame·work /freɪmwɜrk/ (**frameworks**) 1 N-COUNT A **framework** is a particular set of rules, ideas, or beliefs which you use in order to deal with problems or to decide what to do. 体系 ❑ *...within the framework of federal regulations.* …在联邦法规的体系内。 2 N-COUNT A **framework** is a structure that forms a support or frame for something. 构架 ❑ *...wooden shelves on a steel framework.* …在钢架上的木搁板。

franc /fræŋk/ (**francs**) N-COUNT **The franc** was the unit of currency that was used in France and Belgium, before it was replaced by the euro. It is also the unit of currency in some other countries where French is spoken. 法郎 [num N] ❑ *The price of grapes had shot up to 32 francs a kilo.* 葡萄的价格暴涨到了每公斤32法郎。● N-SING **The franc** was used to refer to the currency systems of France and Belgium, before it was replaced by the euro. It is also used to refer to the currency systems of some other countries where French is spoken. 法郎体系 ["the" N] ❑ *The Swiss franc has remained surprisingly strong.* 瑞士法郎保持了出人意料的强势。

▲ **fran·chise** /fræntʃaɪz/ (**franchises, franchising, franchised**) 1 N-COUNT A **franchise** is an authority that is given by an organization to someone, allowing them to sell its goods or services or to take part in an activity which the organization controls. (公司授予某人的) 特许经营权 [BUSINESS] ❑ *...fast-food* franchises. …快餐特许经营权。 ❑ ...*the franchise to build and operate the tunnel.* …建造、运营隧道的特许权。 **2** V-T If a company **franchises** its business, it sells franchises to other companies, allowing them to sell its goods or services. 出售…的特许经营权 [BUSINESS] ❑ *She has recently franchised her business.* 她最近已出售了其公司的特许经营权。 **3** N-UNCOUNT **Franchise** is the right to vote in an election. 选举权 [also "the" N] ❑ ...*the introduction of universal franchise.* …普选权的采用。

fran·chi·see /fræntʃaɪzi/ (**franchisees**) N-COUNT A **franchisee** is a person or group of people who buy a particular franchise. 特许经营者 [BUSINESS] ❑ ...*National Restaurants, a New York franchisee for Pizza Hut.* …全美餐厅，一家纽约必胜客特许经营餐厅。

fran·chi·ser /fræntʃaɪzər/ (**franchisers**) N-COUNT A **franchiser** is an organization which sells franchises. 出售特许经营权的组织 [BUSINESS] ❑ *Coca-Cola, Pepsi and Cadbury use franchisers to manufacture, bottle and distribute their products within geographical areas.* 可口可乐、百事可乐和吉百利公司利用特许经销商在一定的地区内生产、罐装和销售其产品。

frank /fræŋk/ (**franker, frankest**) ADJ If someone is **frank**, they state or express things in an open and honest way. 坦率的 ❑ *"It is clear that my client has been less than frank with me," said his lawyer.* "显然我的委托人对我不够坦率，" 他的律师说。 ● **frank·ly** ADV 坦率地 [ADV with v] ❑ *You can talk frankly to me.* 你可以坦率地对我谈。 ● **frank·ness** N-UNCOUNT 坦率 ❑ *The reaction to his frankness was hostile.* 他的坦率遭到敌意的回应。

frank·ly /fræŋkli/ **1** ADV You use **frankly** when you are expressing an opinion or feeling to emphasize that you mean what you are saying, especially when the person you are speaking to may not like it. 坦率地说 [EMPHASIS] ❑ *"You don't give a damn about my feelings, do you."—"Quite frankly, I don't."* "你一点也不在乎我的感情，是吧。"——"坦率地说，是的。" ❑ *Frankly, Thomas, this question of your loan is beginning to worry me.* 坦率地说，托马斯，你贷款的问题开始让我担忧。 **2** → see also **frank**

★ **fran·tic** /fræntɪk/ **1** ADJ If you are **frantic**, you are behaving in a wild and uncontrolled way because you are frightened or worried. (因恐惧或忧虑而) 发狂似的 ❑ *A bird had been locked in and was by now quite frantic.* 一只鸟被关了起来，到现在它都非常狂躁。 ● **fran·ti·cal·ly** /fræntɪkli/ ADV 发狂似地 [ADV with v] ❑ *She clutched frantically at Emily's arm.* 她发狂似地紧紧抓着艾米莉的胳膊。 **2** ADJ If an activity is **frantic**, things are done quickly and in an energetic but disorganized way, because there is very little time. 忙乱的 ❑ *A busy night in the restaurant can be frantic in the kitchen.* 晚上餐馆生意繁忙，厨房可能就会忙作一团了。 ● **fran·ti·cal·ly** ADV 忙乱地 [ADV with v] ❑ *We have been frantically trying to save her life.* 我们一直在手忙脚乱地设法挽救她的生命。

▲ **fra·ter·nity** /frətɜrnɪti/ (**fraternities**) **1** N-COUNT You can refer to people who have the same profession or the same interests as a particular **fraternity**. 同业者；志趣相投者 ❑ ...*the spread of stolen guns among the criminal fraternity.* …被盗枪支在犯罪同伙间的传散。 **2** N-UNCOUNT **Fraternity** refers to friendship and support between people who feel they are closely linked to each other. 友爱 [FORMAL] ❑ *Bob needs the fraternity of others who share his mission.* 鲍勃需要共负使命的同志们的友爱。 **3** N-COUNT In the United States, a **fraternity** is a society of male university or college students. 美国大学男生联谊会 ❑ *He must have been the most popular guy at the most popular fraternity in college.* 他一定曾是大学里最受欢迎的男生联谊会中最红的人。

fraud ♦◇◇ /frɔd/ (**frauds**) **1** N-VAR **Fraud** is the crime of gaining money or financial benefits by a trick or by lying. 诈骗罪 ❑ *He was jailed for two years for fraud and deception.* 他因诈骗与欺诈被监禁了两年。 **2** N-COUNT A **fraud** is something or someone that deceives people in a way that is illegal or dishonest. 骗人的东西；骗子 ❑ *He's a fraud and a cheat.* 他是一个骗子。

Word Link *ulent ≈ full of : fraudulent, opulent, virulent*

fraudu·lent /frɔdʒələnt/ ADJ A **fraudulent** activity is deliberately deceitful, dishonest, or untrue. 欺骗性的 ❑ ...*fraudulent claims about being a nurse.* …谎称自己是护士。 ● **fraudu·lent·ly** ADV 欺骗性地 [ADV with v] ❑ *All 5,000 of the homes were fraudulently obtained.* 5000所房子全都是骗取的。

▲ **fraught** /frɔt/ **1** ADJ If a situation or action is **fraught with** problems or risks, it is filled with them. 充满 (问题或风险) 的 [v-link ADJ "with" n] ❑ *The earliest operations employing this technique were fraught with dangers.* 最早采用这一技术的手术充满了危险。 **2** ADJ If you say that a situation or action is **fraught**, you mean that it is worrisome or difficult. 令人担忧的 ❑ *It has been a somewhat fraught day.* 这是令人颇为担忧的一天。

fray /freɪ/ (**frays, fraying, frayed**) **1** V-T/V-I If something such as cloth or rope **frays**, or if something **frays** it, its threads or fibers start to come apart from each other and spoil its appearance. 磨损 ❑ *The fabric is very fine or frays easily.* 这种布料很细，或者说是容易磨损。 ❑ *The stitching had begun to fray at the edges.* 边缘处的针脚已经开始磨损了。 **2** V-T/V-I If your nerves or your temper **fray**, or if something **frays** them, you become nervous or easily annoyed because of mental strain and anxiety. 烦躁 ❑ *Tempers began to fray as the two teams failed to score.* 两队都没有得分，人们开始烦躁起来。

freak /frik/ (**freaks**) **1** ADJ A **freak** event or action is one that is a very unusual or extreme example of its type. 不寻常的 [ADJ n] ❑ *Weir broke his leg in a freak accident playing golf.* 韦尔打高尔夫球时因一次不寻常的事故而摔断了腿。 **2** N-COUNT If you describe someone as a particular kind of **freak**, you are emphasizing that they are very enthusiastic about a thing or activity, and often seem to think about nothing else. 狂热爱好者 [INFORMAL] ❑ *Diaz is a fitness freak who's trained in martial arts.* 迪亚斯是个受过武术训练的健身迷。 **3** N-COUNT People are sometimes referred to as **freaks** when their behavior or attitude is very different from that of the majority of people. 怪人 [DISAPPROVAL] ❑ *Not so long ago, transsexuals were regarded as freaks.* 不久前，变性者还被认为是怪人。

freck·le /frɛkᵊl/ (**freckles**) N-COUNT **Freckles** are small light brown spots on someone's skin, especially on their face. 雀斑 ❑ *He had short ginger-colored hair and freckles.* 他一头姜黄色的短发，脸上有些雀斑。

free ♦♦♦ /fri/ (**freer, freest, frees, freeing, freed**) **1** ADJ If something is **free**, you can have it or use it without paying for it. 免费的 ❑ *The seminars are free, with lunch provided.* 研讨会是免费的，还提供午餐。 **2** **free of charge** → see **charge** **3** ADJ Someone or something that is **free** is not restricted, controlled, or limited, for example, by rules, customs, or other people. 自由的；不受限制的 ❑ *The government will be free to pursue its economic policies.* 政府将自由实行其经济政策。 ❑ *The elections were free and fair.* 选举是自由公正的。 ● **free·ly** ADV 自由地 [ADV with v] ❑ *They cast their votes freely and without coercion on election day.* 他们在选举日自由地投票，不受强迫。 **4** ADJ Someone who is **free** is no longer a prisoner or a slave. 自由的 ❑ *He walked from the court house a free man.* 他走出法庭，重获自由。 **5** ADJ If someone or something is **free of** or **free from** an unpleasant thing, they do not have it or they are not affected by it. 没有…的 [v-link ADJ "of/from" n] ❑ ...*a future far more free of fear.* …远无恐惧的未来。 ❑ *She retains her slim figure and is free of wrinkles.* 她保持着苗条的身材，而且没有皱纹。 **6** ADJ A sum of money or type of goods that is **free of** tax or duty is one that you do not have to pay tax on. 免去…的 [v-link ADJ "of" n] ❑ *This benefit is free of tax under current legislation.* 按照现行法律此项收益是免税的。 **7** → see also **duty-free, interest-free, tax-free** **8** ADJ If you have a **free** period of time or are **free** at a particular time, you are not working or occupied then. 空闲的 ❑ *She spent her free time shopping.* 她将空闲时间花在购物上。 ❑ *I used to write during my free periods at school.* 我过去上学时常在空闲时间写作。 **9** ADJ If something such as a table or seat is **free**, it is not being used or occupied by anyone, or is not reserved for anyone to use. (桌子或座位) 空着的 ❑ *There was only one seat free on the train.* 火车上只有一个空座。 **10** ADJ If you get something **free** or if it gets **free**, it is no longer trapped by anything or attached to anything. 不受束缚的 ❑ *He pulled his arm free, and strode for the door.* 他抽出他的胳膊摆脱束缚，大步朝门走去。 **11** ADJ When someone is using one hand or arm to hold or move something, their other hand or arm is referred to as their **free** one. 空闲的 (手或胳膊) [ADJ n] ❑ *He snatched up the receiver and his free hand groped for the switch on the bedside lamp.* 他一把抓起听筒，空着的手则摸索着找床头灯的开关。 **12** V-T If you **free** someone of something that is unpleasant or restricting, you remove it from them. 使免除 ❑ *It will free us of a whole lot of debt.* 这将免除我们一大笔债务。 **13** V-T To **free** a prisoner or a slave means to let them go or release them from prison. 释放 ❑ *Israel is set to free more Lebanese prisoners.* 以色列准备释放更多黎巴嫩犯人。 **14** V-T To **free** someone or something means to make them available for a task or function that they were previously not available for. 解放 ❑ *Toolbelts free both hands and lessen the risk of dropping hammers.* 工具带解放了双手，

并减少了锤子掉落的危险。❏ *His deal with Disney will run out shortly, freeing him to pursue his own project.* 他同迪斯尼的协议不久就将结束，这可以使他腾出手来从事自己的项目。● PHRASAL VERB **Free up** means the same as **free**. 使解放 ❏ *It can handle even the most complex graphic jobs, freeing up your computer for other tasks.* 它甚至能处理最复杂的绘图事宜，使你的计算机腾出来完成其他任务。15 V-T If you **free** someone or something, you remove them from the place in which they have been trapped or become fixed. 解救 ❏ *Rescue workers tried to free him by cutting away part of the car.* 救援人员设法通过切除部分车体将他解救出来。16 PHRASE You say "**feel free**" when you want to give someone permission to do something, in a very willing way. 随意 [INFORMAL, FORMULAE] ❏ *If you have any questions at all, please feel free to ask me.* 如果你有什么问题，请随意问我好了。17 PHRASE If you do something or get something **for free**, you do it without being paid or get it without having to pay for it. 无偿地；免费地 [INFORMAL] ❏ *I wasn't expecting you to do it for free.* 我并没指望你无偿地做这个。18 to **give** someone **a free hand** → see **hand** 19 to **give** someone **free rein** → see **rein**

▸ **free up** 1 PHRASAL VERB To **free up** a market, economy, or system means to make it operate with fewer restrictions and controls. 开放（市场、经济或体制）[BUSINESS] ❏ *...policies for freeing up markets and extending competition.* …开放市场和扩大竞争的政策。
2 → see **free 14**

Thesaurus	*free* 另参见：
ADJ.	complimentary 1 independent, unattached, unrestricted 3 available, unoccupied, vacant 9
V.	emancipate, let go, liberate 13 disentangle, unshackle 15

Word Link *dom ≈ state of being : boredom, freedom, wisdom*

free·dom ♦♦◇ /friːdəm/ (**freedoms**) 1 N-UNCOUNT **Freedom** is the state of being allowed to do what you want to do. **Freedoms** are instances of this. 自由 [also N in pl] ❏ *...freedom of speech.* …言论自由。❏ *The United Nations Secretary-General has spoken of the need for individual freedoms and human rights.* 联合国秘书长谈到了个人自由和人权的必要性。2 N-UNCOUNT When prisoners or slaves are set free or escape, they gain their **freedom**. 人身自由 ❏ *...the agreement worked out by the UN, under which all hostages and detainees would gain their freedom.* …联合国制定的协议，据此所有人质和被扣押者应获得自由。3 N-UNCOUNT **Freedom from** something you do not want means not being affected by it. 免除 ❏ *...all the freedom from pain that medicine could provide.* …药物所能免除的所有痛苦。

Word Partnership	*freedom* 的常用搭配：
ADJ.	**artistic** freedom, **political** freedom, **religious** freedom 1
N.	freedom **of choice**, **feeling/sense of** freedom, freedom **of the press**, freedom **of speech** 1 **struggle for** freedom 1 2

free en·ter·prise N-UNCOUNT **Free enterprise** is an economic system in which businesses compete for profit without much government control. 自由企业制度 [BUSINESS] ❏ *...a believer in democracy and free enterprise.* …一个民主和自由企业制度的信徒。

▲ **free·lance** /friːlæns/ ADJ Someone who does **freelance** work or who is, for example, a **freelance** journalist or photographer is not employed by one organization, but is paid for each piece of work they do by the organization they do it for. 自由职业的 [BUSINESS] ❏ *Michael Cross is a freelance journalist.* 迈克尔·克罗斯是一个自由新闻工作者。● ADV **Freelance** is also an adverb. 作为自由职业者 [ADV after v] ❏ *He is now working freelance from his home in New Hampshire.* 他目前在新罕布什尔州的家里从事自由职业。

freely /friːli/ 1 ADV **Freely** means many times or in large quantities. 大量地 ❏ *We have referred freely to his ideas.* 我们大量地参考他的想法。❏ *George was spending very freely.* 乔治花钱大手大脚。2 ADV If you can talk **freely**, you can talk without needing to be careful about what you say. 无所顾忌地 [ADV after v] ❏ *She wondered whether he had someone to whom he could talk freely.* 她不知道他是否有个可以畅谈的知音。3 ADV If someone gives or does something **freely**, they give or do it willingly, without being ordered or forced to do it. 自愿地 [ADV with v] ❏ *Danny shared his knowledge freely with anyone interested.* 丹尼自愿与任何感兴趣者共享他的知识。4 ADV If something or someone moves **freely**, they move easily and smoothly, without any obstacles or resistance. 顺畅地 [ADV after v] ❏ *The clay court was slippery and he was unable to move freely.* 这个红土网球场很滑，他无法自如地移动。5 → see also **free**

free mar·ket (**free markets**) N-COUNT A **free market** is an economic system in which business organizations decide things such as prices and wages, and are not controlled by the government. 自由市场 [BUSINESS] ❏ *...the creation of a free market.* …一个自由市场的创建。

free pass (**free passes**) N-COUNT A **free pass** is an official document that allows a person to travel or to enter a particular building without having to pay. 免费通行证；免费入场券

free-range ADJ **Free-range** means relating to a system of keeping animals in which they can move and feed freely on an area of open ground. 放养的（动物）❏ *...free-range eggs.* …放养的鸡下的蛋。

free·ware /friːweər/ N-UNCOUNT **Freeware** is computer software that you can use without payment. 免费软件 [COMPUTING] ❏ *Is there a freeware program that I can use to produce my own clip art?* 有没有免费软件程序让我用来制作自己的剪贴画？

free·way /friːweɪ/ (**freeways**) N-COUNT A **freeway** is a major road that has been specially built for fast travel over long distances. Freeways have several lanes and special places where traffic gets on and leaves. 高速公路 [AM] ❏ *The speed limit on the freeway is 55mph.* 这条高速公路的限速为每小时55英里。

free will 1 N-UNCOUNT If you believe in **free will**, you believe that people have a choice in what they do and that their actions have not been decided in advance by God or by any other power. 自由意志 ❏ *...the free will of the individual.* …个人的自由意志。2 PHRASE If you do something **of your own free will**, you do it by choice and not because you are forced to do it. 自愿地 ❏ *Would Bethany return of her own free will, as she had promised?* 贝萨妮会像她承诺的那样自愿回来吗？

freeze ♦◇◇ /friːz/ (**freezes, freezing, froze, frozen**) 1 V-T/V-I If a liquid or a substance containing a liquid **freezes**, or if something **freezes** it, it becomes solid because of low temperatures. 结冰 ❏ *If the temperature drops below 0°C, water freezes.* 如果温度降到摄氏零度以下，水就会结冰。❏ *The ground froze solid.* 地面冻硬了。2 V-T/V-I If you **freeze** something such as food, you preserve it by storing it at a temperature below freezing point. You can also talk about how well food **freezes**. 冷藏 ❏ *You can freeze the soup at this stage.* 你此时可以把汤冷藏。3 V-I When **it freezes** outside, the temperature falls below freezing point. 结冰 ❏ *What if it rained and then froze all through those months?* 如果那几个月一直下雨然后又结冰该怎么办？● N-COUNT **Freeze** is also a noun. 冰冻 ❏ *The trees were damaged by a freeze in December.* 那些树被12月的一次冰冻冻坏了。4 V-I If you **freeze**, you feel extremely cold. 感到极冷 ❏ *The windows didn't fit at the bottom so for a while we froze even in the middle of summer.* 那些窗子的底部关不严，所以有段时间我们甚至在仲夏时节也感到极冷。5 V-I If someone who is moving **freezes**, they suddenly stop and become completely still and quiet. 呆住不动 [WRITTEN] ❏ *She froze when the beam of the flashlight struck her.* 当手电筒的光柱照到她时，她呆住了。6 V-T If the government or a company **freeze** things such as prices or wages, they state officially that they will not allow them to increase for a fixed period of time. 冻结（物价或工资）[BUSINESS] ❏ *They want the government to freeze prices.* 他们要政府冻结物价。● N-COUNT **Freeze** is also a noun. 冻结 ❏ *A wage freeze was imposed on all staff earlier this month.* 本月早些时候，所有员工的工资都被冻结了。7 V-T If someone in authority **freezes** something such as a bank account, fund, or property, they obtain a legal order which states that it cannot be used or sold for a particular period of time. 冻结（银行账户、基金或财产）[BUSINESS] ❏ *The governor's action freezes 300,000 accounts.* 州长采取行动冻结了30万个账户。● N-COUNT **Freeze** is also a noun. 冻结 [with supp] ❏ *...a freeze on private savings.* …对私人储蓄的冻结。8 → see also **freezing, frozen**
→ see **refrigerator, water**

freez·er /friːzər/ (**freezers**) N-COUNT A **freezer** is a large container like a refrigerator in which the temperature is kept below freezing point so that you can store food inside it for long periods. 冷柜
→ see **refrigerator**

freez·ing /friːzɪŋ/ 1 ADJ If you say that something is **freezing** or **freezing cold**, you are emphasizing that it is very cold. 冰冷的 [EMPHASIS] ❏ *The movie theater was freezing.* 电影院里冰冷冰冷的。

If you want to emphasize how cold the weather is, you can say that it is **freezing**, especially in winter when there is ice or frost. In summer, if the temperature is below average, you can say that it is **cool**. In general, **cold** suggests a lower temperature than **cool**, and **cool** things may be pleasant or refreshing. ❑ *A cool breeze swept off the ocean; it was pleasant out there.* If it is very **cool** or too **cool**, you can also say that it is **chilly**.

2 ADJ If you say that you are **freezing** or **freezing cold**, you are emphasizing that you feel very cold. 感觉受冻的 [v-link ADJ] [EMPHASIS] ❑ *"You must be freezing," she said.* "你一定冻坏了吧，"她说。 3 N-UNCOUNT **Freezing** means the same as **freezing point**. 冰点 ❑ *It's 15 degrees below freezing.* 温度是零下15度。 4 → see also **freeze**

freez·ing point (**freezing points**) also **freezing-point** 1 N-UNCOUNT **Freezing point** is 32° Fahrenheit or 0° Celsius, the temperature at which water freezes. Freezing point is often used when talking about the weather. 冰点 ❑ *The temperature remained below freezing point throughout the day.* 全天气温一直在冰点以下。 2 N-COUNT The **freezing point** of a particular substance is the temperature at which it freezes. (特定物质的) 凝固点 ❑ *It was the seventeenth century before Newton determined the freezing point of water.* 那是17世纪，牛顿确定水的凝固点之前。

freight /freɪt/ 1 N-UNCOUNT **Freight** is the movement of goods by trucks, trains, ships, or airplanes. 货运 ❑ *France derives 16% of revenue from air freight.* 法国国家税收的16%来自于航空货运。 2 N-UNCOUNT **Freight** is goods that are transported by trucks, trains, ships, or airplanes. 货物 ❑ *...26 tons of freight.* …26吨货物。 → see **train**

freight car (**freight cars**) N-COUNT On a train, a **freight car** is a large container in which goods are transported. (火车的) 货运车厢 [mainly AM]

freight·er /freɪtər/ (**freighters**) N-COUNT A **freighter** is a large ship or airplane that is designed for carrying freight. 货轮；货机

French fries N-PLURAL **French fries** are long, thin pieces of potato fried in oil or fat. 炸薯条

fre·net·ic /frɪnɛtɪk/ ADJ If you describe an activity as **frenetic**, you mean that it is fast and energetic, but rather uncontrolled. 迅捷狂乱的 ❑ *...the frenetic pace of life in New York.* …纽约迅捷狂乱的生活节奏。

fren·zied /frɛnzid/ ADJ **Frenzied** activities or actions are wild, excited, and uncontrolled. 疯狂的 ❑ *...the frenzied activity of the election.* …选举中的疯狂行为。

▲ **fren·zy** /frɛnzi/ (**frenzies**) N-VAR **Frenzy** or a **frenzy** is great excitement or wild behavior that often results from losing control of your feelings. 疯狂 ❑ *"Get out!" she ordered in a frenzy.* "滚出去！"她发疯似地命令道。

fre·quen·cy /frikwənsi/ (**frequencies**) 1 N-UNCOUNT The **frequency** of an event is the number of times it happens during a particular period. 频率 ❑ *The frequency of Kara's phone calls increased rapidly.* 卡拉打电话的频率迅速增加。 2 N-VAR In physics, the **frequency** of a sound wave or a radio wave is the number of times it vibrates within a specified period of time. (物理学) 频率 ❑ *You can't hear waves of such a high frequency.* 你听不到这么高频率的声波。 ❑ *...a frequency of 24 kilohertz.* …24千赫的频率。 → see **sound**, **wave**

fre·quent ◆◆◇ /frikwənt/ ADJ If something is **frequent**, it happens often. 频繁的 ❑ *Bordeaux is on the main Paris-Madrid line so there are frequent trains.* 波尔多位于巴黎至马德里的铁路主干线上，因此有频繁的列车。 ● **fre·quent·ly** ADV 经常地 ❑ *Iron and folic acid supplements are frequently given to pregnant women.* 铁和叶酸补充剂常给孕妇服用。

Thesaurus *frequent* 另参见：
ADJ. common, everyday, habitual; (*ant.*) occasional, rare

fresh ◆◆◇ /frɛʃ/ (**fresher**, **freshest**) 1 ADJ A **fresh** thing or amount replaces or is added to a previous thing or amount. 新加的 [ADJ n] ❑ *He asked the police, who carried out the original investigation, to make fresh inquiries.* 他要求原先进行调查的警方做一轮新的调查。 2 ADJ Something that is **fresh** has been done, made, or experienced recently. 新近的 ❑ *There were no fresh car tracks or footprints in the snow.* 雪地里没有新的车辙或脚印。 ❑ *A puppy stepped in the fresh cement.* 一只小狗走到新铺的水泥路面上。 3 ADJ **Fresh** food has been picked or produced recently, and has not been preserved, for example, by being frozen or put in a can. 新鲜的 ❑ *...locally caught fresh fish.* …当地捕获的鲜鱼。 4 ADJ If you describe something as **fresh**, you like it because it is new and exciting. 新颖的 ❑ *These designers are full of fresh ideas.* 这些设计师满是新颖的想法。 5 ADJ If you describe something as **fresh**, you mean that it is pleasant, bright, and clean in appearance. 鲜艳的 ❑ *Gingham fabrics always look fresh and pretty.* 方格花布看起来总是鲜艳而美丽。 6 ADJ If something smells, tastes, or feels **fresh**, it is clean or cool. 清新的 ❑ *The air was fresh and for a moment she felt revived.* 空气清新，一会儿她就感到精力恢复了。 7 ADJ If you feel **fresh**, you feel full of energy and enthusiasm. 精力充沛的 ❑ *It's vital we are as fresh as possible for those games.* 至关重要的是，我们要尽可能精力充沛地去打那些比赛。 8 ADJ **Fresh** paint is not yet dry. (油漆) 未干的 [AM] ❑ *There was fresh paint on the walls.* 墙上有未干的油漆。 9 ADJ If you are **fresh from** a particular place or experience, you have just come from that place or you have just had that experience. You can also say that someone is **fresh out of** a place. 刚从…来的；刚经历过…的 [v-link ADJ "from/out of" n] ❑ *I returned to the office, fresh from the airport.* 我刚从机场回到办公室。 → see **vegetable**

fresh air N-UNCOUNT You can describe the air outside as **fresh air**, especially when you mean that it is good for you because it does not contain dirt or dangerous substances. 新鲜空气 [also "the" N] ❑ *"Let's take the baby outside," I suggested. "We all need some fresh air."* "我们把宝宝带出去吧，"我建议道。"我们都需要一些新鲜空气。"

fresh·ly /frɛʃli/ ADV If something is **freshly** made or done, it has been recently made or done. 刚 [ADV -ed] ❑ *...freshly baked bread.* …刚烤出的面包。

fresh·water /frɛʃwɔtər/ ADJ A **freshwater** lake contains water that is not salty, usually in contrast to the sea. **Freshwater** creatures live in water that is not salty. 淡水的 [ADJ n] ❑ *...Lake Balaton, the largest freshwater lake in Europe.* …巴拉顿湖，欧洲最大的淡水湖。 → see **wetland**

▲ **fret** /frɛt/ (**frets**, **fretting**, **fretted**) 1 V-T/V-I If you **fret** about something, you worry about it. 担心 ❑ *I was working all hours and constantly fretting about everyone else's problems.* 我一刻不停地工作着，还一直担心着其他人的问题。 ❑ *But congressional staffers fret that the project will eventually cost billions more.* 但国会的工作人员们担心这个方案最终会多花几十亿。 2 N-COUNT The **frets** on a musical instrument such as a guitar are the raised lines across its neck. (吉他等弦乐器指板上定音的) 音品

Fri. **Fri.** is a written abbreviation for **Friday**. 星期五

★ **fric·tion** /frɪkʃᵊn/ (**frictions**) 1 N-UNCOUNT If there is **friction** between people, there is disagreement and argument between them. (人与人之间的) 摩擦 [also N in pl] ❑ *Sara sensed that there had been friction between her children.* 萨拉感觉到她的孩子们中间出现了摩擦。 2 N-UNCOUNT **Friction** is the force that makes it difficult for things to move freely when they are touching each other. 摩擦力 ❑ *The pistons are graphite-coated to reduce friction.* 活塞表面涂有石墨以减少摩擦。

Fri·day ◆◆◆ /fraɪdeɪ, -di/ (**Fridays**) N-VAR **Friday** is the day after Thursday and before Saturday. 星期五 ❑ *Mr. Cook is intending to go to the Middle East on Friday.* 库克先生正打算星期五去中东。 ❑ *...Friday November 6.* …11月6日星期五。

fridge /frɪdʒ/ (**fridges**) N-COUNT A **fridge** is the same as a **refrigerator**. 冰箱 [INFORMAL]

friend ◆◆◆ /frɛnd/ (**friends**) 1 N-COUNT A **friend** is someone who you know well and like, but who is not related to you. 朋友 ❑ *I had a long talk about this with my best friend.* 我和我最好的朋友就此进行了长谈。 ❑ *She never was a close friend of mine.* 她从来就不是我的密友。 2 N-COUNT If one country refers to another as a **friend**, they mean that the other country is not an enemy of theirs. 盟国 ❑ *The president said that Japan is now a friend and international partner.* 总统说日本现在是盟国和国际伙伴。 3 N-PLURAL If you are **friends with** someone, you are their friend and they are yours. (与…是) 朋友 ❑ *I still wanted to be friends with Alison.* 我仍然希望同艾莉森做朋友。 ❑ *We remained good friends.* 我们一直是好朋友。 4 N-PLURAL; N-IN-NAMES The **friends of** a country, cause, organization, or a famous politician are the people and organizations who help and support them. 支持者 ❑ *...the friends of Israel.* …以色列的支持者。 5 PHRASE If you **make friends with** someone, you begin a friendship with them. You can also say that two people **make friends**. 同…交朋友 ❑ *He has made friends with the kids on the street.* 他同街上的孩子们交上了朋友。 ❑ *Dennis made friends easily.* 丹尼斯容易交上朋友。

Word Partnership *friend* 的常用搭配：

- ADJ. **best** friend, **close** friend, **dear** friend, **faithful** friend, **former** friend, **good** friend, **loyal** friend, **mutual** friend, **old** friend, **personal** friend, **trusted** friend **1**
- N. **childhood** friend, friend **of the family**, friend **or relative** **1**
  friend **or foe** **1** **2**
- V. **tell a** friend **1**
  make a friend **1** **5**

friend·ly ♦◇◇ /frɛ̲ndli/ (**friendlier, friendliest, friendlies**) **1** ADJ If someone is **friendly**, they behave in a pleasant, kind way, and like to be with other people. 友好的 ❑ *Godfrey had been friendly to me.* 戈弗雷过去曾经对我是友好的。 ❑ *...a man with a pleasant, friendly face.* …一个和颜悦色的男子。 ● **friend·li·ness** N-UNCOUNT 友善 ❑ *She also loves the friendliness of the people.* 她也喜爱人们的友善。 **2** ADJ If you are **friendly with** someone, you like each other and enjoy spending time together. 与…要好的 [v-link ADJ] ❑ *I'm friendly with his mother.* 我和他的母亲很要好。 **3** ADJ You can describe another country or their government as **friendly** when they have good relations with your own country rather than being an enemy. (国家或政府) 友好的 ❑ *...a worsening in relations between the two previously friendly countries.* …两个先前友好的国家之间关系的恶化。

Do not confuse **friendly** and **sympathetic**. A person who is **friendly** or has a **friendly** attitude is kind and pleasant and behaves the way a friend would. ❑ *...a friendly woman who offered me a coffee. ...a pleasant, friendly smile.* If you have a problem and someone is **sympathetic** or shows a **sympathetic** attitude, they show that they care and would like to help you. ❑ *My boyfriend was very sympathetic.* Note that people sometimes refer to characters in a play or novel who are easy to like as **sympathetic**. ❑ *There were no sympathetic characters in my book.* You usually say that real people are "nice" or "likable."

4 N-COUNT In sports, a **friendly** is a game which is not part of a competition, and is played for entertainment or practice, often without any serious effort to win. 友谊赛 [ADJ n] [BRIT]

in AM, use **exhibition game**

● ADJ **Friendly** is also an adjective. 友谊赛的

Word Partnership *friendly* 的常用搭配：

- N. friendly **atmosphere**, friendly **face**, friendly **neighbors**, friendly **service**, friendly **voice** **1**
  friendly **relationship** **2**
  friendly **game**, friendly **match** **4**
- V. **become** friendly **2**

-friendly /-frɛ̲ndli/ **1** COMB IN ADJ **-friendly** combines with nouns to form adjectives which describe things that are not harmful to the specified part of the natural world. 对…无害的 (和名词连用构成形容词) ❑ *Palm oil is environment-friendly.* 棕榈油对环境无害。 **2** COMB IN ADJ **-friendly** combines with nouns to form adjectives which describe things which are intended for or suitable for the specified person, especially things that are easy for them to understand, appreciate, or use. 便于理解或使用的 (和名词连用构成形容词) ❑ *...customer-friendly banking facilities.* …方便客户的银行设施。 **3** → see also **user-friendly**
→ see **dump**

Word Link *ship ≈ condition or state : censorship, citizenship, friendship*

friend·ship ♦◇◇ /frɛ̲ndʃɪp/ (**friendships**) **1** N-VAR **A friendship** is a relationship between two or more friends. 友谊 ❑ *Giving advice when it's not called for is the quickest way to end a good friendship.* 在不需要时给予建议是了结一段友谊的最快方式。 ❑ *She struck up a close friendship with Desiree during the week of rehearsals.* 她在那一周的排练中和德西蕾建立起亲密的友谊。 **2** N-VAR **Friendship** is a relationship between two countries in which they help and support each other. 友好关系 ❑ *The president set the targets for the future to promote friendship with East Europe.* 总统确定了与东欧增进友好关系的未来目标。 **3** N-UNCOUNT You use **friendship** to refer in a general way to the state of being friends, or the feelings that friends have for each other. 友情 ❑ *...a hobby which led to a whole new world of friendship and adventure.* …一个通向友情和冒险的一个全新世界的爱好。

frig·ate /frɪ̲gət/ (**frigates**) N-COUNT **A frigate** is a fairly small ship owned by the navy that can move at fast speeds. Frigates are often used to protect other ships. 护卫舰

★ **fright** /fra̲ɪt/ (**frights**) **1** N-UNCOUNT **Fright** is a sudden feeling of fear, especially the fear that you feel when something unpleasant surprises you. 惊吓 ❑ *The steam pipes rattled suddenly, and Franklin jumped with fright.* 蒸汽管突然发出咯咯的声音，弗兰克林吓得跳了起来。 ❑ *The birds smashed into the top of their cages in fright.* 鸟儿们吓得猛撞笼顶。 **2** N-COUNT **A fright** is an experience which makes you suddenly afraid. 惊吓 ❑ *The snake picked up its head and stuck out its tongue which gave everyone a fright.* 那条蛇昂起头，吐出信子，把每个人都吓了一大跳。

fright·en /fra̲ɪtᵊn/ (**frightens, frightening, frightened**) **1** V-T If something or someone **frightens** you, they cause you to suddenly feel afraid, anxious, or nervous. 使惊恐 ❑ *He knew that Soli was trying to frighten him, so he smiled to hide his fear.* 他知道索利想吓唬他，因此微笑着掩饰自己的恐惧。 **2** PHRASE If something **frightens the life out of** you, **frightens the wits out of** you, or **frightens** you **out of your wits**, it causes you to feel suddenly afraid or gives you a very unpleasant shock. 使吓得魂不附体 [EMPHASIS] ❑ *Fairground rides are intended to frighten the life out of you.* 露天游乐场的飞车就是要把你们吓得魂不附体。

▸ **frighten away** or **frighten off** **1** PHRASAL VERB If you **frighten away** a person or animal or **frighten** them **off**, you make them afraid so that they run away or stay some distance away from you. 吓跑 ❑ *The fishermen said the company's seismic survey was frightening away fish.* 渔民们说这家公司的地震勘测吓跑了鱼儿。 **2** PHRASAL VERB To **frighten** someone **away** or **frighten** them **off** means to make them nervous so that they decide not to become involved with a particular person or activity. 吓走 ❑ *Repossessions have frightened buyers off.* 收回未付款商品的举动吓跑了买主们。

▸ **frighten off** → see **frighten away**

fright·ened /fra̲ɪtᵊnd/ ADJ If you are **frightened**, you are anxious or afraid, often because of something that has just happened or that you think may happen. 害怕的 ❑ *She was frightened of making a mistake.* 她害怕犯错误。

fright·en·ing /fra̲ɪtᵊnɪŋ/ ADJ If something is **frightening**, it makes you feel afraid, anxious, or nervous. 令人恐惧的 ❑ *It was a very frightening experience and they were very courageous.* 那是一次非常令人恐惧的经历，但他们非常勇敢。 ● **fright·en·ing·ly** ADV 令人恐惧地 ❑ *The country is frighteningly close to possessing nuclear weapons.* 令人恐惧的是，该国离拥有核武器为期不远。

fright·ful /fra̲ɪtfəl/ **1** ADJ **Frightful** means very bad or unpleasant. 可怕的 [OLD-FASHIONED] ❑ *My father was unable to talk about the war, it was so frightful.* 我父亲没法谈论那次战争，那太可怕了。 **2** ADJ **Frightful** is used to emphasize the extent or degree of something, usually something bad. 极度的 [ADJ n] [INFORMAL, OLD-FASHIONED, EMPHASIS] ❑ *He got himself into a frightful muddle.* 他自己陷入了极度的混乱之中。

frill /frɪ̲l/ (**frills**) **1** N-COUNT **A frill** is a long narrow strip of cloth or paper with many folds in it, which is attached to something as a decoration. 褶边 ❑ *...curtains with frills.* …带褶边的窗帘。 **2** N-COUNT If you describe something as having **no frills**, you mean that it has no extra features, but is acceptable or good if you want something simple. 装饰 [APPROVAL]

★ **fringe** /frɪ̲ndʒ/ (**fringes**) **1** N-COUNT **A fringe** is a decoration attached to clothes, or other objects such as curtains, consisting of a row of hanging strips or threads. 流苏 ❑ *The jacket had leather fringes.* 这件上衣饰有皮流苏。 **2** N-COUNT To be **on the fringe** or **the fringes of** a place means to be on the outside edge of it, or to be in one of the parts that are farthest from its center. 边缘 ❑ *...black townships located on the fringes of the city.* …位于该城市边缘的黑人居住区。 **3** N-COUNT **The fringe** or **the fringes of** an activity or organization are its less important, least typical, or most extreme parts, rather than its main and central part. 次要部分；外围 ❑ *The party remained on the fringe of the political scene until last year.* 直到去年该党还一直处于政治舞台的外围。 **4** N-COUNT **A fringe** is hair which is cut so that it hangs over your forehead. (头发的) 刘海 [BRIT]

in AM, use **bangs**

5 ADJ **Fringe** groups or events are less important or popular than other related groups or events. 次要的；边缘的 [ADJ n] ❑ *The* *monarchists are a small fringe group who quarrel fiercely among themselves.* 君主制拥护者们是个边缘性小团体，内部争吵激烈。

fringe ben·efit (**fringe benefits**) N-COUNT **Fringe benefits** are extra things that some people get from their job in addition to their salary, for example, a car. 附加福利 [BUSINESS] ❑ *...insecure, badly paid jobs without any of the fringe benefits such as healthcare.* …没有医疗保健等附加福利、毫无保障的低收入工作。

fringed /frɪndʒd/ **1** ADJ **Fringed** clothes, curtains, or lampshades are decorated with fringes. 饰有流苏的 [ADJ n] ❑ *Emma wore a fringed scarf round her neck.* 爱玛脖子上围了一条饰有流苏的披巾。 **2** ADJ If a place or object **is fringed with** something, that thing forms a border around it or is situated along its edges. 边缘有…的 [v-link ADJ "with" n] ❑ *Her eyes were large and brown and fringed with incredibly long lashes.* 她褐色的大眼睛周围有一圈特别长的睫毛。

frivo·lous /frɪvələs/ **1** ADJ If you describe someone as **frivolous**, you mean they behave in a silly or light-hearted way, rather than being serious and sensible. 轻率的 ❑ *I just decided I was a bit too frivolous to be a doctor.* 我只是认定自己有点儿太轻率，不适合当医生。 **2** ADJ If you describe an activity as **frivolous**, you disapprove of it because it is not useful and wastes time or money. 无用的 [DISAPPROVAL] ❑ *The group says it wants politicians to stop wasting public money on what it believes are frivolous projects.* 该团体说他们希望政客们停止在该团体认为无用的项目上浪费公款。

fro /froʊ/ **to and fro** → see **to**

frog /frɒg/ (**frogs**) N-COUNT A **frog** is a small creature with smooth skin, big eyes, and long back legs which it uses for jumping. Frogs usually live near water. 蛙

frol·ic /frɒlɪk/ (**frolics, frolicking, frolicked**) V-I When people or animals **frolic**, they play or move in a lively, happy way. 嬉戏 ❑ *Tourists sunbathe and frolic in the ocean.* 游客们晒日光浴，在海水中嬉戏。

from
❶ MENTIONING THE SOURCE, ORIGIN, OR STARTING POINT
❷ MENTIONING A RANGE OF TIMES, AMOUNTS, OR THINGS
❸ MENTIONING SOMETHING YOU WANT TO PREVENT OR AVOID

❶ from ♦♦♦ /frəm, STRONG frʌm/ **1** PREP If something comes **from** a particular person or thing, or if you get something **from** them, they give it to you or they are the source of it. 来自 ❑ *He appealed for information from anyone who saw the attackers.* 他呼吁来自目睹袭击者的信息。 ❑ *...an anniversary present from his wife.* …他妻子送的一件结婚纪念礼物。

> When you are talking about the person who has written you a letter or sent a message to you, you say that the letter or message is **from** that person. ❑ *He received a message from Vito Corleone.* When you are talking about an author, a composer, or a painter, you say the work is **by** that person or is written or painted **by** him or her. ❑ *...three books by Michael Moorcock. ... a collection of piano pieces by Mozart.*

2 PREP Someone who comes **from** a particular place lives in that place or originally lived there. Something that comes **from** a particular place was made in that place. 来自 ❑ *...an art dealer from Zurich.* …一名来自苏黎世的艺术品商人。 ❑ *Katy Jones is nineteen and comes from Biloxi.* 凯蒂·琼斯19岁，来自比洛克西。 **3** PREP A person **from** a particular organization works for that organization. 为…工作 ❑ *...a representative from the Israeli embassy.* …以色列大使馆的一位代表。 **4** PREP If someone or something moves or is moved **from** a place, they leave it or are removed, so that they are no longer there. 从 (某处离开) ❑ *The guests watched as she fled from the room.* 客人们看着她逃离房间。 **5** PREP If you take one thing or person **from** another, you move that thing or person so that they are no longer with the other or attached to the other. (取)自 ❑ *In many bone transplants, bone can be taken from other parts of the patient's body.* 在许多骨移植手术中，骨头可以取自病人身体的其它部分。 **6** PREP If you take something **from** an amount, you reduce the amount by that much. 从…(扣除) ❑ *The $103 is deducted from Mrs. Adams' salary.* 这$103是从亚当斯太太的薪水中扣除的。 **7** PREP **From** is used in expressions such as **away from** or **absent from** to say that someone or something is not present in a place where they are usually found. 从…(离开) ❑ *Her husband worked away from home a lot.* 她丈夫经常离家在外工作。 **8** PREP If you return **from** a place or an activity, you return after being in that place or doing that activity. 从…(回来) ❑ *My son has just returned from Amsterdam.* 我儿子刚刚从阿姆斯特丹回来。 **9** PREP If you are back **from** a place or activity, you have left it and have returned to your former place. 从…(回来) ❑ *Elaine was just back from work when he called.* 他打电话的时候，伊莱恩刚下班回来。 **10** PREP If you see or hear something **from** a particular place, you are in that place when you see it or hear it. 从…(看到或听到) ❑ *Visitors see the painting from behind a plate glass window.* 参观者可以从平板玻璃窗后面看到这幅画。 **11** PREP If something hangs or sticks out **from** an object, it is attached to it or held by it. 从…(垂下或伸出) [V PREP n] ❑ *Hanging from his right wrist is a heavy gold bracelet.* 从他的右腕上垂下的是一只沉甸甸的金手镯。 ❑ *...large fans hanging from ceilings.* …在天花板上吊着的大风扇。 **12** PREP You can use **from** when giving distances. For example, if a place is fifty miles **from** another place, the distance between the two places is fifty miles. 离… [amount PREP n] ❑ *...a small park only a few hundred yards from Zurich's main shopping center.* …一个小公园，距离苏黎世主要购物中心只有几百码。 ❑ *How far is it from here?* 离这儿有多远？ **13** PREP If a road or railroad line goes **from** one place to another, you can travel along it between the two places. 从…(到…) ❑ *...the road from St. Petersburg to Tallinn.* …从圣彼得堡到塔林的路。 **14** PREP **From** is used, especially in the expression **made from**, to say what substance has been used to make something. 由…(制成) [V PREP n] ❑ *...bread made from white flour.* …白面粉做的面包。 **15** PREP If something changes **from** one thing **to** another, it stops being the first thing and becomes the second thing. 由…(变成) ❑ *The expression on his face changed from sympathy to surprise.* 他脸上的表情由同情变成惊讶。 ❑ *Unemployment has fallen from 7.5 to 7.2%.* 失业率已从7.5%降至7.2%。 **16** PREP You use **from** after some verbs and nouns when mentioning the cause of something. 因为… [PREP n/-ing] ❑ *The problem simply resulted from a difference of opinion.* 问题仅因意见不同而引起。 ❑ *They really do get pleasure from spending money on other people.* 他们确实因把钱花在别人身上而从中得到快乐。 **17** PREP You use **from** when you are giving the reason for an opinion. 根据… ❑ *She knew from experience that Dave was about to tell her the truth.* 她根据经验得知戴夫将要告诉她实情。 ❑ *He sensed from the expression on her face that she had something to say.* 他根据她脸上的表情意识到她有话要说。

❷ from ♦♦♦ /frəm, STRONG frʌm/ **1** PREP You can use **from** when you are talking about the beginning of a period of time. 从(某时) 起 ❑ *She studied painting from 1926 and also worked as a commercial artist.* 她从1926年开始研究绘画，同时也是一名商业美术家。 ❑ *Breakfast is available to fishermen from 6 a.m.* 渔民们从早上6点起就能吃到早饭。 **2** PREP You say **from** one thing **to** another when you are stating the range of things that are possible, or when saying that the range of things includes everything in a certain category. 从…(到…) [PREP n/-ing] ❑ *There are 94 countries represented in Barcelona, from Algeria to Zimbabwe.* 巴塞罗那有从阿尔及利亚到津巴布韦94个国家的代表处。

❸ from ♦♦♦ /frəm, STRONG frʌm/ PREP **From** is used after verbs with meanings such as "protect," "free," "keep," and "prevent" to introduce the action that does not happen, or that someone does not want to happen. (免) 于… ❑ *Such laws could protect the consumer from harmful or dangerous remedies.* 这类法律能保护消费者免受有害或危险的治疗。

> In addition to the uses shown here, **from** is used in phrasal verbs such as "date from" and "grow away from."

front ♦♦♦ /frʌnt/ (**fronts**) **1** N-COUNT **The front of** something is the part of it that faces you, or that faces forward, or that you normally see or use. 前面 ❑ *One man sat in an armchair, and the other sat on the front of the desk.* 一个男人坐在扶手椅上，另一个坐在桌前。 ❑ *Stand at the front of the line.* 站在队伍的前面。 **2** N-COUNT **The front of** a building is the side or part of it that faces the street. 临街面 ❑ *Attached to the front of the house, there was a large veranda.* 连着房子的临街面有一个大阳台。 **3** N-COUNT In a war, the **front** is a line where two opposing armies are facing each other. 前线 ❑ *Sonja's husband is fighting at the front.* 索妮亚的丈夫正在前线打仗。 **4** → see also **front line** **5** N-COUNT If you say that something is happening on a particular **front**, you mean that it is happening with regard to a particular situation or field of activity. 领域 ❑ *...research across a wide academic front.* …跨多个学术领域的研究。 **6** N-COUNT If someone puts on a particular kind of **front**, they

f

pretend to have a particular quality. (装出的) 样子 ❑ *Michael kept up a brave front both to the world and in his home.* 迈克尔在家外家内都保持着一副勇敢的样子。 7 N-COUNT An organization or activity that is a **front for** one that is illegal or secret is used to hide it. (非法或秘密组织或活动的) 掩护者 ❑ *...a firm later identified by the police as a front for crime syndicates.* …后来被警方证实是为犯罪团伙做掩护的一家公司。 8 N-COUNT In relation to the weather, a **front** is a line where a mass of cold air meets a mass of warm air. (冷暖空气交汇的) 锋面 ❑ *The snow signaled the arrival of a front, and a high-pressure area seemed to be settling in.* 降雪标志了一个锋面的到来，一个高压区似乎正在进入本地。 9 N-SING A person's or animal's **front** is the part of their body between their head and their legs that is on the opposite side to their back. 身体的前部 ❑ *When baby is lying on his front, hold something so that he has to raise his head to see it.* 当宝宝趴着时，抓一样东西逗他，这样他就得抬起头来才能看到。 10 ADJ **Front** is used to refer to the side or part of something that is toward the front or nearest to the front. 前面的 [ADJ n] ❑ *I went out there on the front porch.* 我走了出来，到了前门廊。 ❑ *She was only six and still missing her front teeth.* 她只有6岁，还没有长出门牙。 11 ADJ The **front** page of a newspaper is the outside of the first page, where the main news stories are printed. 头(版) [ADJ n] ❑ *The front page carries a photograph of the two foreign ministers.* 报纸头版刊登了两位外交部长的一张合影。 12 → see also **front-page** 13 PHRASE If a person or thing is **in front**, they are ahead of others in a moving group, or further forward than someone or something else. 在前面 ❑ *Officers will crack down on lunatic motorists who speed or drive too close to the car in front.* 警官们将严惩那些超速行驶或与前面车辆追尾的疯狂驾车者。 14 PHRASE Someone who is **in front** in a competition or contest at a particular point is winning at that point. (在比赛中) 领先 ❑ *Richard Dunwoody is in front in the jockeys' title race.* 理查德・邓伍迪在职业赛马冠军赛中处于领先位置。 15 PHRASE If someone or something is **in front of** a particular thing, they are facing it, ahead of it, or close to the front part of it. 在…的前面 ❑ *She sat down in front of her dressing-table mirror to look at herself.* 她在梳妆台的镜子前面坐下来端详自己。 ❑ *Something darted out in front of my car, and my car hit it.* 有东西突然从我车前冲出来，随即我的车就撞了它。 16 PHRASE If you do or say something **in front of** someone else, you do or say it when they are present. 当着…的面 ❑ *They never argued in front of their children.* 他们从来不当着孩子们的面争吵。
→ see **forecast**

Word Partnership *front* 的常用搭配:

N. front **of the line** 1
front **door**, front **end**, front **porch**, front **room**, front **tire**, front **wheel**, front **window** 1 10
front **paws**, front **teeth** 9 10

front·al /frʌntᵊl/ ADJ **Frontal** means relating to or involving the front of something, for example, the front of an army, a vehicle, or the brain. 前部的; 正面的 [FORMAL] ❑ *Military leaders are not expecting a frontal assault by the rebels.* 军方领导人们没有料到叛乱分子的正面袭击。

front desk N-SING The **front desk** in a hotel is the desk or office that books rooms for people and answers their questions. (宾馆的) 前台 [mainly AM] ❑ *Call the hotel's front desk and cancel your early morning wake-up call.* 打电话给宾馆总台取消你的清晨电话叫醒服务。
→ see **hotel**

fron·tier /frʌntɪər, frɒn-/ (**frontiers**) 1 N-COUNT When you are talking about the western part of America before the twentieth century, you use **frontier** to refer to the area beyond the part settled by Europeans. (20世纪前美国) 西部边疆 ❑ *...a far-flung outpost on the frontier.* …远驻西部边疆的一个哨所。 2 N-COUNT **The frontiers** of something, especially knowledge, are the limits to which it extends. (尤指知识的) 前沿 ❑ *...pushing back the frontiers of science.* …推进科学前沿。 3 N-COUNT A **frontier** is a border between two countries. 国界 ❑ *It wasn't difficult then to cross the frontier.* 那时候穿越国界并不难。

front line (**front lines**) also **front-line** 1 N-COUNT **The front line** is the place where two opposing armies are facing each other and where fighting is going on. 前线 ❑ *...a massive concentration of soldiers on the front line.* …前线兵力的大集结。 2 PHRASE Someone who is **in the front line** has to play a very important part in defending or achieving something. 在前线 ❑ *Information officers are in the front line of putting across government policies.* 新闻官员们处在传达政府政策的前线。

front-page ADJ A **front-page** article or picture appears on the front page of a newspaper because it is very important or interesting. 头版的 (文章、图片等) [ADJ n] ❑ *...a front-page article in last week's paper.* …上周报纸的一篇头版文章。

front-runner (**front-runners**) N-COUNT In a competition or contest, the **front-runner** is the person who seems most likely to win it. (比赛、竞赛中的) 领先者 ❑ *Neither of the front-runners in the presidential election is a mainstream politician.* 这次总统选举中的两个领先者都不是主流政客。

frost /frɔst/ (**frosts**, **frosting**, **frosted**) 1 N-VAR When there is **frost** or a **frost**, the temperature outside falls below freezing point and the ground becomes covered in ice crystals. 霜 ❑ *There is frost on the ground and snow is forecast.* 地上有霜，预报有雪。 2 V-T If you **frost** a cake, you cover and decorate it with frosting. 给 (蛋糕) 撒糖霜 [AM] ❑ *She was frosting the cupcakes while we talked.* 我们交谈时，她在给杯形蛋糕撒糖霜。

frost·ing /frɔstɪŋ/ N-UNCOUNT **Frosting** is a sweet substance made from powdered sugar that is used to cover and decorate cakes. (用于装饰蛋糕的) 糖霜 [AM] ❑ *...a huge pastry with green frosting on it.* …一个撒有绿色糖霜的大型酥饼。

frosty /frɔsti/ (**frostier**, **frostiest**) 1 ADJ If the weather is **frosty**, the temperature is below freezing. 霜冻的 ❑ *...sharp, frosty nights.* …霜冻刺骨的夜晚。 2 ADJ You describe the ground or an object as **frosty** when it is covered with frost. (地面或物体) 有霜的 ❑ *The street was deserted except for a cat lifting its paws off the frosty stones.* 那条街上空无一人，只有一只猫走在结霜的石子路上。

froth /frɔθ/ (**froths**, **frothing**, **frothed**) 1 N-UNCOUNT **Froth** is a mass of small bubbles on the surface of a liquid. (液体表面的) 泡沫 ❑ *...the froth of bubbles on the top of a glass of beer.* …一杯啤酒顶上的泡沫。 2 V-I If a liquid **froths**, small bubbles appear on its surface. 起泡沫 ❑ *The sea froths over my feet.* 海水在我脚上泛起泡沫。

frown /fraʊn/ (**frowns**, **frowning**, **frowned**) V-I When someone **frowns**, their eyebrows become drawn together, because they are annoyed, worried, or puzzled, or because they are concentrating. 皱眉 ❑ *Nancy shook her head, frowning.* 南希摇摇头，皱着眉头。 ❑ *He frowned at her anxiously.* 他焦急地朝她皱了皱眉。 ● N-COUNT **Frown** is also a noun. 皱眉状态 ❑ *There was a deep frown on the boy's face.* 那个男孩的脸上有深皱眉的表情。

▸ **frown upon** or **frown on** PHRASAL VERB If something **is frowned upon** or **is frowned on**, people disapprove of it. 不赞成 ❑ *This practice is frowned upon as being wasteful.* 这种做法被认为是浪费而不被赞成。

froze /froʊz/ **Froze** is the past tense of **freeze**. **freeze**的过去式

fro·zen /froʊzᵊn/ 1 **Frozen** is the past participle of **freeze**. **freeze**的过去分词 2 ADJ If the ground is **frozen** it has become very hard because the weather is very cold. (地面) 冰冻的 ❑ *It was bitterly cold now and the ground was frozen hard.* 现在天气冷极了，地面冻硬了。 3 ADJ **Frozen** food has been preserved by being kept at a very low temperature. 冷冻的 (食物) ❑ *Frozen fish is a very healthy convenience food.* 冻鱼是一种非常健康的方便食品。 4 ADJ If you say that you are **frozen**, or a part of your body is **frozen**, you are emphasizing that you feel very cold. 冻僵的 [EMPHASIS] ❑ *He put one hand up to his frozen face.* 他抬起一只手放在他冻僵的脸上。 ❑ *I'm frozen out here.* 我在这儿要冻僵了。 ● PHRASE **Frozen stiff** means the same as **frozen**. 冻僵的 (同**frozen**)
→ see **glacier**

fru·gal /frugᵊl/ 1 ADJ People who are **frugal** or who live **frugal** lives do not spend much money on themselves. 俭朴的 ❑ *She lives a frugal life.* 她过着俭朴的生活。 ● **fru·gal·ity** /frugælɪti/ N-UNCOUNT 俭朴 ❑ *We must practice the strictest frugality and economy.* 我们必须奉行最严格意义上的俭朴和节约。 2 ADJ A **frugal** meal is small and not expensive. (膳食) 俭省的 ❑ *The diet was frugal: cheese and water, rice and beans.* 饮食很俭省：奶酪和水，米饭和豆类。

fruit ◆◆◇ /frut/ (**fruit**, **fruits**, **fruiting**, **fruited**)

The plural form is usually **fruit**, but can also be **fruits**.

1 N-VAR **Fruit** or a **fruit** is something which grows on a tree or bush and which contains seeds or a pit covered by a substance that you can eat. 水果 ❑ *Fresh fruit and vegetables provide fiber and vitamins.* 新鲜的水果和蔬菜提供纤维素和多种维生素。 ❑ *...bananas and other tropical fruits.* …香蕉和其他热带水果。 2 V-I If a plant **fruits**, it produces fruit. 结果实 ❑ *The scientists will study the variety of trees and*

Word Web fruit

Fruits only appear on **flowering plants.** They are fleshy and **sweet** and contain **seeds** or a **stone** or **pit.** The fruit serves the plant in two ways. First, it protects seeds from damage. Secondly, it helps make sure seeds are carried to new places. After an animal eats a seed, it passes through its body unharmed. When the animal leaves droppings in a new location, the seed may start a new plant there. Fruits contain a **sugar** called fructose—an important source of energy for animals and humans. But not all fruits are sweet. **Lemons,** for example, are **sour.**

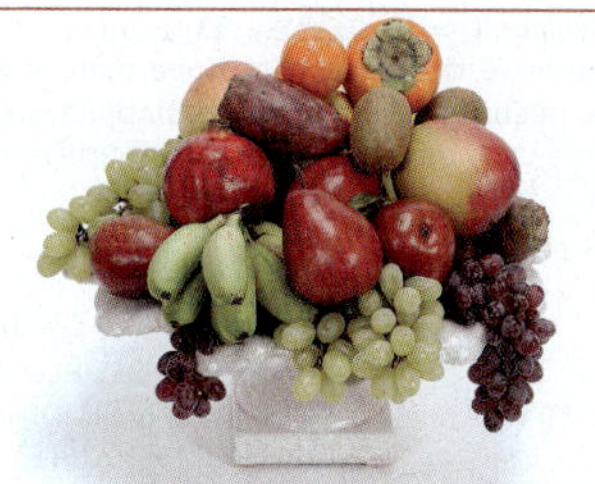

observe which are fruiting. 科学家们将研究树木的多样性并观察哪些树木结果实。 3 N-COUNT **The fruits** or **the fruit of** someone's work or activity are the good things that result from it. 成果 ❑ *The team has really worked hard and Mansell is enjoying the fruits of that labor.* 那个团队真地已很努力，而曼塞尔正在享受这一劳动的成果。 4 → see also **kiwi fruit** 5 PHRASE If the effort that you put into something or a particular way of doing something **bears fruit**, it is successful and produces good results. (付出的努力) 有成效 ❑ *Eleanor's work among the women will, I trust, bear fruit.* 埃莉诺在这些妇女中所做的工作我相信会有成效。

→ see Word Web: **fruit**

→ see **dessert, grain**

fruit·ful /fru̲tfəl/ ADJ Something that is **fruitful** produces good and useful results. 富有成效的 ❑ *We had a long, happy, fruitful relationship.* 我们曾有一段长久、愉快而富有成效的关系。

frui·tion /fruɪ̲ʃ^ən/ N-UNCOUNT If something comes **to fruition**, it starts to succeed and produce the results that were intended or hoped for. 收效 [FORMAL] ❑ *These plans take time to come to fruition.* 这些计划需要时间才会有收效。

fruit·less /fru̲tlɪs/ ADJ **Fruitless** actions, events, or efforts do not achieve anything at all. 无结果的 ❑ *It was a fruitless search.* 那是一次毫无结果的搜寻。

fruity /fru̲ti/ (**fruitier, fruitiest**) 1 ADJ Something that is **fruity** smells or tastes of fruit. 有水果味的 ❑ *This shampoo smells fruity and leaves the hair beautifully silky.* 这种洗发香波闻上去有水果味，使头发柔丽柔顺。 2 ADJ A **fruity** voice or laugh is pleasantly rich and deep. (嗓音、笑声等) 圆润的 ❑ *Jerrold laughed again, a solid, fruity laugh.* 杰罗尔德又笑了，一阵爽朗的大笑。

frus·trate ♦◇◇ /frʌ̲streɪt/ (**frustrates, frustrating, frustrated**) 1 V-T If something **frustrates** you, it upsets or angers you because you are unable to do anything about the problems it creates. 使懊丧 ❑ *These questions frustrated me.* 这些问题使我懊丧。 ● **frus·trat·ed** ADJ 懊丧的 ❑ *Roberta felt frustrated and angry.* 罗伯塔感到又懊丧又生气。 ● **frus·tra·tion** /frʌstre̲ɪʃ^ən/ N-VAR (**frustrations**) 懊丧 ❑ *The results show the level of frustration among hospital doctors.* 这些结果显示医院医生的懊丧程度。 2 V-T If someone or something **frustrates** a plan or attempt to do something, they prevent it from succeeding. 挫败 ❑ *The government has deliberately frustrated his efforts to gain work permits for his foreign staff.* 政府蓄意挫败了他为其外国员工取得工作许可证的努力。

frus·trat·ing /frʌ̲streɪtɪŋ/ ADJ Something that is **frustrating** annoys you or makes you angry because you cannot do anything about the problems it causes. 令人懊丧的 ❑ *The current situation is very frustrating for us.* 目前的局势对我们来讲是很令人懊丧的。

→ see **anger**

fry ♦◇◇ /fra̲ɪ/ (**fries, frying, fried**) 1 V-T When you **fry** food, you cook it in a pan that contains hot fat or oil. 炸 ❑ *Fry the breadcrumbs until golden brown.* 把这些面包屑炸到金褐色为止。 2 N-PLURAL **Fries** are the same as **French fries.** 炸薯条

→ see **cook, egg**

fry·ing pan (**frying pans**) N-COUNT A **frying pan** is a flat metal pan with a long handle, in which you fry food. 煎锅

→ see **pan**

ft. **ft.** is a written abbreviation for **feet** or **foot.** 英尺 ❑ *Flying at 1,000 ft., he heard a peculiar noise from the rotors.* 飞行在1000英尺的高度时，他听到了来自旋翼的一种奇怪噪音。

fuck /fʌ̲k/ (**fucks, fucking, fucked**)

> **Fuck** is a vulgar and offensive word which you should avoid using.

1 EXCLAM **Fuck** is used to express anger or annoyance. 操 (用以表达愤怒或厌烦) [OFFENSIVE, VULGAR, FEELINGS] 2 V-RECIP To **fuck** someone means to have sex with them. 操 (某人) [OFFENSIVE, VULGAR]

▸ **fuck off** PHRASAL VERB Telling someone to **fuck off** is an insulting way of telling them to go away. 滚开 [usu imper] [OFFENSIVE, VULGAR]

fuck·ing /fʌ̲kɪŋ/ ADJ **Fucking** is used by some people to emphasize a word or phrase, especially when they are feeling angry or annoyed. 形容词，用以强调某词或短语，尤在生气或愤怒时 ● ADV **Fucking** is also an adverb. 副词，用以强调某词或短语，尤在生气或愤怒时 [ADJ n] [OFFENSIVE, VULGAR, EMPHASIS] [ADV: ADV adj]

fudge /fʌ̲dʒ/ (**fudges, fudging, fudged**) 1 N-UNCOUNT **Fudge** is a soft brown candy that is made from butter, cream, and sugar. 乳脂软糖 2 V-T If you **fudge** something, you avoid making a clear and definite decision, distinction, or statement about it. 模糊处理 ❑ *Both have fudged their calculations and avoided specifics.* 双方都模糊处理了其计算结果并回避了细节。

fuel ♦♦◇ /fyu̲əl/ (**fuels, fueling** or **fuelling, fueled** or **fuelled**) 1 N-MASS **Fuel** is a substance such as coal, oil, or gasoline that is burned to provide heat or power. 燃料 ❑ *They ran out of fuel.* 他们用完了燃料。 2 V-T To **fuel** a situation means to make it become worse or more intense. 加剧 ❑ *The result will inevitably fuel speculation about the prime minister's future.* 该结果将不可避免地加剧人们对首相前途的猜测。

→ see **car, energy, engine, oil**

> **Word Partnership** *fuel* 的常用搭配:
> N. **cost of** fuel, fuel **oil**, fuel **pump**, fuel **shortage**, fuel **supply**, fuel **tank** 1
> ADJ. **unleaded** fuel 1

▲ **fu·gi·tive** /fyu̲dʒɪtɪv/ (**fugitives**) N-COUNT A **fugitive** is someone who is running away or hiding, usually in order to avoid being caught by the police. (通常为避免被警察抓住的) 逃避者 ❑ *The rebel leader was a fugitive from justice.* 叛军首领是一名逃避司法的人。

ful·fil /fʊlfɪ̲l/ [BRIT] → see **fulfill**

ful·fill ♦◇◇ /fʊlfɪ̲l/ (**fulfills, fulfilling, fulfilled**)

> in BRIT, also use **fulfil**

1 V-T If you **fulfill** something such as a promise, dream, or hope, you do what you said or hoped you would do. 实现 (承诺、梦想、希望等) ❑ *President Kaunda fulfilled his promise of announcing a date for the referendum.* 卡翁达总统实现了他的关于宣布投票公决日期的诺言。 2 V-T To **fulfill** a task, role, or requirement means to do or be what is required, necessary, or expected. 完成 (任务、角色); 达到 (要求) ❑ *Without them you will not be able to fulfill the tasks you have before you.* 没有他们你将不能完成你面前的任务。 3 V-T If something **fulfills** you, or if you **fulfill yourself**, you feel happy and satisfied with what you are doing or with what you have achieved. 使感到满足 ❑ *The war was the biggest thing in her life and nothing after that quite fulfilled her.* 那场战争是她一生中最重大的事，在那之后没有什么颇使她感到满足过。 ● **ful·filled** ADJ 感到满足的 ❑ *She has courageously continued to lead a fulfilled life.* 她已勇敢地继续过一种心满意足的生活。 ● **ful·fil·ling** ADJ 令人感到满足的 ❑ *...a fulfilling career.* …一份令人感到满足的事业。

> **Word Partnership** *fulfill* 的常用搭配:
> N. fulfill ***your* destiny**, fulfill **a dream**, fulfill **a promise** 1
> fulfill **obligations**, fulfill **a role** 2

ful·fill·ment /fʊlfɪ̲lmənt/ 1 N-UNCOUNT **Fulfillment** is a feeling of satisfaction that you get from doing or achieving something, especially something useful. 成就感 ❑ *...professional* *fulfillment.* …职业成就感。 2 N-UNCOUNT **The fulfillment of** a promise, threat, request, hope, or duty is the event or act of it happening or being made to happen. (承诺、誓言、希望、要求等的)实现 ❑ *Visiting Angkor was the fulfillment of a childhood dream.* 参观吴哥是一个儿时梦想的实现。

full

1 CONTAINING AS MANY PEOPLE/THINGS AS POSSIBLE
2 COMPLETE, INCLUDING THE MAXIMUM POSSIBLE
3 OTHER USES

F

1 full ◆◆◆ /fʊl/ (**fuller, fullest**) 1 ADJ If something is **full**, it contains as much of a substance or as many objects as it can. 装满的 ❑ *Once the container is full, it stays shut until you turn it clockwise.* 该容器一旦满了就会保持关闭，直到你将其按顺时针方向旋转。 2 ADJ If a place or thing **is full of** things or people, it contains a large number of them. 满是…的 [v-link ADJ "of" n] ❑ *The case was full of clothes.* 该箱子满是衣服。 ❑ *The streets are still full of debris from two nights of rioting.* 那些街上依然满是两夜暴乱后的狼藉。 3 ADJ You say that a place or vehicle is **full** when there is no space left in it for any more people or things. (某处、车辆) 满的 ❑ *The parking lot was full when I left about 10:45.* 停车场在我10:45左右离开时已满了。 ❑ *They stay here a few hours before being sent to refugee camps, which are now almost full.* 他们在这里呆了几个小时后被送到了难民营，难民营现在几乎满了。 4 ADJ If your hands or arms are **full**, you are carrying or holding as much as you can carry. (双手) 拿满的; (双臂) 抱满的 [v-link ADJ] ❑ *Sylvia entered, her arms full of packages.* 西尔维娅进来了，怀里抱满了包裹。 5 ADJ If you feel **full**, you have eaten or drunk so much that you do not want anything else. (感到) 饱的 [v-link ADJ] ❑ *It's healthy to eat when I'm hungry and to stop when I'm full.* 我饿了就吃、饱了就停是有益健康的。 ● **full·ness** N-UNCOUNT 饱 ❑ *High fiber diets give the feeling of fullness.* 高纤维饮食给人饱腹感。

2 full ◆◆◆ /fʊl/ (**fuller, fullest**)
➪ **Please look at meanings 12 – 14 to see if the expression you are looking for is shown under another headword.** 1 ADJ If someone or something **is full of** a particular feeling or quality, they have a lot of it. 充满(某种感情或品质) 的 [v-link ADJ "of" n] ❑ *I feel full of confidence and so open to possibilities.* 我感到充满信心且对各种可能都愿意接受。 ❑ *Mom's face was full of pain.* 妈妈的脸上充满了痛苦。 2 ADJ You use **full** before a noun to indicate that you are referring to all the details, things, or people that it can possibly include. 全部的 [ADJ n] ❑ *Full details will be sent to you once your application has been accepted.* 一旦您的申请被接受，全部的细节资料将寄给您。 ❑ *May I have your full name?* 我能知道您的全名吗？ 3 ADJ **Full** is used to describe a sound, light, or physical force which is being produced with the greatest possible power or intensity. 最大的 (音量、力); 最强的 (光) [ADJ n] ❑ *From his study came the sound of Mahler, playing at full volume.* 从他的书房里传来了马勒的音乐，以最大的音量在播放。 ❑ *Officials say the operation will be carried out in full daylight.* 官员们说此项活动将在大白天进行。 4 ADJ You use **full** to emphasize the completeness, intensity, or extent of something. 充分的 [ADJ n] [EMPHASIS] ❑ *We should conserve oil and gas by making full use of other energy sources.* 我们应该通过充分利用其他能源节约石油和天然气。 ❑ *The lane leading to the farm was in full view of the house windows.* 通往农场的那条车道从那房子的窗户可一览无余。 5 ADJ A **full** statement or report contains a lot of information and detail. 详尽的 (陈述、报告) ❑ *Mr. Primakov gave a full account of his meeting with the president.* 普里马科夫先生对他与总统的会面给予了详尽的叙述。 6 ADJ If you say that someone has or leads a **full** life, you approve of the fact that they are always busy and do a lot of different things. 充实的 (生活) [APPROVAL] ❑ *You will be successful in whatever you do and you will have a very full and interesting life.* 你在你做的任何事情中都会很成功，你会拥有非常充实而有趣的生活。 7 ADJ You use **full** to refer to something which gives you all the rights, status, or importance for a particular position or activity, rather than just some of them. (权力、地位、重要性等) 完全的 [ADJ n] ❑ *How did the meeting go, did you get your full membership?* 会议进行得如何？你得到了完全会员资格吗？ 8 ADV You use **full** to emphasize the force or directness with which someone or something is hit or looked at. 径直地 [ADV prep] [EMPHASIS] ❑ *She kissed him full on the mouth.* 她嘴正对嘴地吻了他。 9 PHRASE You say that something has been done or described **in full** when everything that was necessary has been done or described. 全部地; 全面地 ❑ *The medical experts have yet to report in full.* 医学专家们还得全面汇报。 10 PHRASE If you say that a person **knows full well** that something is true, especially something unpleasant, you are emphasizing that they are definitely aware of it, although they may behave as if they are not. 十分清楚 [EMPHASIS] ❑ *He knew full well he'd be ashamed of himself later.* 他十分清楚他以后会为自己感到羞愧。 11 PHRASE Something that is done or experienced **to the full** is done to as great an extent as is possible. 充分地 ❑ *She probably has a good mind, which should be used to the full.* 她可能有个好脑子，应该充分加以利用。 12 **full blast** → see **blast** 13 **to have your hands full** → see **hand** 14 **in full swing** → see **swing**

3 full ◆◆◆ /fʊl/ (**fuller, fullest**) 1 ADJ A **full** flavor is strong and rich. (味道) 浓郁的 [ADJ n] ❑ *Italian plum tomatoes have a full flavor, and are best for cooking.* 意大利李子形番茄有着浓郁的味道，最适合烹饪。 2 ADJ If you describe a part of someone's body as **full**, you mean that it is rounded and quite large. (身体) 丰满的 ❑ *The Juno Collection specializes in large sizes for ladies with a fuller figure.* 朱诺时装店专卖适合体型比较丰满的女士的大号女装。 3 ADJ A **full** skirt or sleeve is wide and has been made from a lot of fabric. 宽大多褶的 (裙子、袖子) ❑ *My wedding dress has a very full skirt so I need to wear a good quality slip.* 我的结婚礼服有一个非常宽大多褶的下摆，所以我需要穿一条质地好的衬裙。 ● **full·ness** N-UNCOUNT 宽大 ❑ *The coat has raglan sleeves, and is cut to give fullness at the back.* 这件外套有一对插肩袖，剪裁得使背部宽大。 4 ADJ When there is a **full** moon, the moon appears as a bright, complete circle. 圆的 (月亮) ❑ *...those nights when the moon is full.* …那些月圆之夜。

full-blown ADJ **Full-blown** means having all the characteristics of a particular type of thing or person. 具有所有特征的 [ADJ n] ❑ *Before becoming a full-blown director, he worked as the film editor on Citizen Kane.* 在成为一名完全成熟的导演之前，他曾担任影片《公民凯恩》的剪辑师。

full-fledged ADJ **Full-fledged** means complete or fully developed. 彻底的; 充分发展的 ❑ *Hungary is to have a full-fledged Stock Exchange from today.* 匈牙利从今天起将拥有一个成熟的证券交易所。

full-length 1 ADJ A **full-length** book, record, or movie is the normal length, rather than being shorter than normal. 标准长度的 (书籍、唱片、影片) [ADJ n] ❑ *...his first full-length recording in well over a decade.* …他十多年来第一张标准长度的唱片。 2 ADJ A **full-length** coat or skirt is long enough to reach the lower part of a person's leg, almost to the ankles. A full-length sleeve reaches a person's wrist. 长及小腿或脚踝的 (衣、裙); 长及手腕的 (袖子) [ADJ n] 3 ADJ **Full-length** curtains or other furnishings reach to the floor. 及地的 (窗帘等) [ADJ n] 4 ADJ A **full-length** mirror or painting shows the whole of a person. 全身的 (镜子或画像) [ADJ n] 5 ADV Someone who is lying **full-length**, is lying down flat and stretched out. 完全伸展开地 [ADV after v] ❑ *She stretched herself out full-length.* 她四肢完全伸展开。

full-scale 1 ADJ **Full-scale** means as complete, intense, or great in extent as possible. 全面的 [ADJ n] ❑ *...the possibility of a full-scale nuclear war.* …一场全面核战争的可能性。 2 ADJ A **full-scale** drawing or model is the same size as the thing that it represents. 原尺寸的 (图画、模型) [ADJ n] ❑ *...working, full-scale prototypes.* …原尺寸的工作原型。

full-size or **full-sized** ADJ A **full-size** or **full-sized** model or picture is the same size as the thing or person that it represents. 和原物或真人一样大小的 (模型或图片) [ADJ n] ❑ *I made a full-size cardboard model.* 我做了一个和原物一样大小的硬纸板模型。

full stop (**full stops**) N-COUNT A **full stop** is the punctuation mark . which you use at the end of a sentence when it is not a question or exclamation. 句号 (.) [BRIT]

in AM, use **period**

full-time also **full time** ADJ **Full-time** work or study involves working or studying for the whole of each normal working week rather than for part of it. 全职的 (工作、学习) ❑ *...a full-time job.* …一份全职工作。 ● ADV **Full-time** is also an adverb. 全职地 [ADV after v] ❑ *Deirdre works full-time.* 戴尔德丽全职工作。

full up also **full-up** 1 ADJ Something that is **full up** has no space left for any more people or things. 满的 [v-link ADJ] ❑ *The prisons are all full up.* 所有的监狱都已满。 2 ADJ If you are **full up** you have eaten or drunk so much that you do not want to eat or drink anything else. 饱的 [v-link ADJ] [INFORMAL] ❑ *He found that he was so full-up from all the liquid in his diet that he hardly had room for his evening meal.* 他发觉在喝过所有他的那些饮料后已经饱得几乎吃不下晚饭了。

ful·ly ◆◆◇ /fʊli/ **1** ADV **Fully** means to the greatest degree or extent possible. 完全地 ❑ *She was fully aware of my thoughts.* 她完全了解了我的想法。 **2** ADV You use **fully** to say that a process is completely finished. 彻底地 [ADV with v] ❑ *He had still not fully recovered.* 他还没有彻底康复。 **3** ADV If you describe, answer, or deal with something **fully**, you leave out nothing that should be mentioned or dealt with. 毫无遗漏地 [ADV with v] ❑ *Fiers promised to testify fully and truthfully.* 菲尔斯承诺毫无保留地、如实地作证。

Word Partnership *fully* 的常用搭配:

ADJ. fully **adjustable**, fully **aware**, fully **clothed**, fully **formed**, fully **functional**, fully **operational**, fully **prepared** **1**

V. fully **agree**, fully **expect**, fully **extend**, fully **understand** **1**
fully **decide**, fully **develop**, fully **heal**, fully **realize**, fully **recover** **2**
fully **explain** **3**

fully-fledged ADJ **Fully-fledged** means the same as **full-fledged**. 彻底的; 充分发展的 [BRIT]

▲ **fum·ble** /fʌmbᵊl/ (**fumbles, fumbling, fumbled**) **1** V-I If you **fumble for** something or **fumble with** something, you try to reach for it or hold it in a clumsy way. 笨拙地去够; 笨拙地把持 ❑ *She crept from the bed and fumbled for her dressing gown.* 她悄悄爬下床，笨拙地去够她的睡袍。 **2** V-I When you are trying to say something, if you **fumble** for the right words, you speak in a clumsy and unclear way. 笨拙支吾地找 (恰当的词) ❑ *I fumbled for something to say.* 我笨嘴拙舌找话讲。

▲ **fume** /fyum/ (**fumes, fuming, fumed**) **1** N-PLURAL **Fumes** are the unpleasant and often unhealthy smoke and gases that are produced by fires or by things such as chemicals, fuel, or cooking. (难闻且常有害的) 烟气 ❑ *...car exhaust fumes.* …汽车尾气。 **2** V-T/V-I If you **fume** over something, you express annoyance and anger about it. 表达气愤 ❑ *"It's monstrous!" Jackie fumed.* "这太不像话了!" 杰基表达了气愤。

fun ◆◆◇ /fʌn/ **1** N-UNCOUNT You refer to an activity or situation as **fun** if you think it is pleasant and enjoyable and it causes you to feel happy. 乐趣 ❑ *It's been a learning adventure and it's also been great fun.* 那是一次很受教育的冒险活动，也是极大的乐趣。 ❑ *It could be fun to watch them.* 看他们会是乐趣。 **2** N-UNCOUNT If you say that someone is **fun**, you mean that you enjoy being with them because they say and do interesting or amusing things. 有趣的人 [APPROVAL] ❑ *Liz was fun to be with.* 莉兹是与之相处有趣的人。 **3** ADJ If you describe something as a **fun** thing, you mean that you think it is enjoyable. If you describe someone as a **fun** person, you mean that you enjoy being with them. 令人愉快的 [ADJ n] [INFORMAL] ❑ *It was a fun evening.* 那是个令人愉快的夜晚。 **4** PHRASE If you do something **for fun** or **for the fun of it**, you do it in order to enjoy yourself rather than because it is important or necessary. 为了好玩 ❑ *We used to drive too fast, just for fun.* 我们过去常常开得太快，就为了好玩。 **5** PHRASE If you do something **in fun**, you do it as a joke or for amusement, without intending to cause any harm. 闹着玩儿地 ❑ *Don't say such things, even in fun.* 别说这样的话，即使是闹着玩儿。 **6** PHRASE If you **make fun of** someone or something or **poke fun at** them, you laugh at them, tease them, or make jokes about them in a way that causes them to seem ridiculous. 拿…开玩笑 ❑ *Don't make fun of me.* 别拿我开玩笑。

Thesaurus *fun* 另参见:

N. amusement, enjoyment, play; *(ant.)* misery **1**

ADJ. amusing, enjoyable, entertaining, happy, pleasant; *(ant.)* boring **3**

Word Partnership *fun* 的常用搭配:

N. *your* **idea of** fun, fun **part**, **sense of** fun, fun **stuff**, fun **time** **1**

V. **have** fun, **join the** fun, **ought to/should be** fun, fun **to watch** **1** **3**

func·tion ◆◆◇ /fʌŋkʃᵊn/ (**functions, functioning, functioned**) **1** N-COUNT The **function** of something or someone is the useful thing that they do or are intended to do. 作用 ❑ *The main function of the investment banks is to raise capital for industry.* 各投资银行的主要作用是为产业筹集资金。 **2** N-COUNT A **function** is a large formal dinner or party. 宴会; 社交聚会 ❑ *...a private function hosted by one of his students.* …由他的一个学生做东的一场私人宴会。 **3** V-I If a machine or system **is functioning**, it is working or operating. 运转 ❑ *The authorities say the prison is now functioning normally.* 当局称该监狱现在在正常运转。 **4** V-I If someone or something **functions as** a particular thing, they do the work or fulfill the purpose of that thing. (作为某物) 起作用 ❑ *On weekdays, one third of the room functions as workspace.* 在工作日，这个房间的三分之一充当工作场所。

Thesaurus *function* 另参见:

N. action, duty, job, responsibility **1**
celebration, gathering, occasion **2**

V. operate, perform, work **3**

func·tion·al /fʌŋkʃənᵊl/ **1** ADJ **Functional** things are useful rather than decorative. 实用的 ❑ *...modern, functional furniture.* …现代、实用的家具。 **2** ADJ **Functional** equipment works or operates in the way that it is supposed to. 起作用的 ❑ *We have fully functional smoke alarms on all staircases.* 我们在所有楼梯上都装有运转完全正常的烟雾报警器。

func·tion key (**function keys**) N-COUNT **Function keys** are the keys along the top of a computer keyboard, usually numbered from F1 to F12. Each key is designed to make a particular thing happen when you press it. (电脑的) 功能键 [COMPUTING] ❑ *Just hit the F5 function key to send and receive your e-mails.* 就按功能键F5收发你的电子邮件。

fund ◆◆◆ /fʌnd/ (**funds, funding, funded**) **1** N-PLURAL **Funds** are amounts of money that are available to be spent, especially money that is given to an organization or person for a particular purpose. (尤指为特定目的而给予某组织的) 资金 ❑ *The concert will raise funds for research into AIDS.* 这场音乐会将为艾滋病研究筹集资金。 **2** → see also **fund-raising** **3** N-COUNT A **fund** is an amount of money that is collected or saved for a particular purpose. (为特定目的而筹集或保留的) 专项资金 ❑ *...a scholarship fund for undergraduate engineering students.* …一笔用于工程学本科生的奖学金专项资金。 **4** → see also **trust fund** **5** V-T When a person or organization **funds** something, they provide money for it. 资助 ❑ *The Bush Foundation has funded a variety of faculty development programs.* 布什基金会已经资助了各种教职工发展项目。 ❑ *The airport is being privately funded by a construction group.* 该机场正由一建筑集团私家资助。

fun·da·men·tal ◆◇◇ /fʌndəmɛntᵊl/ **1** ADJ You use **fundamental** to describe things, activities, and principles that are very important or essential. They affect the basic nature of other things or are the most important element upon which other things depend. 基本的 ❑ *Our constitution embodies all the fundamental principles of democracy.* 我们的宪法体现了民主的所有基本原则。 ❑ *A fundamental human right is being withheld from these people.* 这些人的一项基本人权正被剥夺。 **2** ADJ You use **fundamental** to describe something which exists at a deep and basic level, and is therefore likely to continue. 根本的 ❑ *But on this question, the two leaders have very fundamental differences.* 但在这个问题上，这两位领导人有着极根本的分歧。 **3** ADJ If one thing **is fundamental to** another, it is absolutely necessary to it, and the second thing cannot exist, succeed, or be imagined without it. 绝对必要的 [v-link ADJ "to" n] ❑ *He believes better relations with China are fundamental to the well-being of the area.* 他相信与中国的更好关系对这个地区的福祉是绝对必要的。 **4** ADJ You can use **fundamental** to show that you are referring to what you consider to be the most important aspect of a situation, and that you are not concerned with less important details. 主要的 [ADJ n] ❑ *The fundamental problem lies in their inability to distinguish between reality and invention.* 主要问题在于他们不能区分现实和虚构。

Thesaurus *fundamental* 另参见:

ADJ. basic, essential, necessary, original, primary **1** **2**

fun·da·men·tal·ism /fʌndəmɛntᵊlɪzəm/ N-UNCOUNT **Fundamentalism** is the belief in the original form of a religion or theory, without accepting any later ideas. 原教旨主义 ❑ *Religious fundamentalism was spreading in the region.* 宗教的原教旨主义正在这一地区蔓延。 ● **fun·da·men·tal·ist** N-COUNT (**fundamentalists**) 原教旨主义者 ❑ *...fundamentalist Christians.* …原教旨主义基督徒。

fun·da·men·tal·ly /fʌndəmɛntᵊli/ **1** ADV You use **fundamentally** for emphasis when you are stating an opinion, or when you are making an important or general statement about

Word Web funeral

Many modern **funeral** practices may have their roots in ancient beliefs. Today's **wake** resembles the early custom of providing plentiful food for the departed. In some cultures the food was meant to pacify the spirits. In others, it was for the **deceased** to eat in the afterlife. In some societies **mourners** waited by the **dead** in hopes that the person would return to life. People brought flowers to please the spirit of the dead person. **Ceremonial** candles resemble the fires lit to protect the living from dangerous spirits. Wearing special clothing was also supposed to confuse the spirits.

F

something. 从根本上讲 [ADV with cl/group] [EMPHASIS] ❑ *Fundamentally, women like him for his sensitivity and charming vulnerability.* 从根本上说，女人们因他的敏感和迷人的脆弱而喜欢他。 **2** ADV You use **fundamentally** to indicate that something affects or relates to the deep, basic nature of something. 从根本上 [ADV with v] ❑ *He disagreed fundamentally with the president's judgment.* 他从根本上不同意总统的判断。 ❑ *Environmentalists say the treaty is fundamentally flawed.* 环境保护主义者称那个条约从根本上是有缺陷的。

fun·da·men·tals /fʌndəmɛntᵊlz/ N-PLURAL **The fundamentals** of something are its simplest, most important elements, ideas, or principles, in contrast to more complicated or detailed ones. 基本性的东西 ❑ *They agree on fundamentals, like the need for further political reform.* 他们在像进一步的政治改革的必要性等基本问题上意见一致。

fund·ing ♦◇◇ /fʌndɪŋ/ N-UNCOUNT **Funding** is money which a government or organization provides for a particular purpose. (政府或组织为某目的而提供的) 资金 ❑ *They hope for government funding for the program.* 他们希望得到政府为这一计划提供的资金。

fund·rais·er /fʌndreɪzər/ (**fundraisers**) also **fund-raiser** **1** N-COUNT A **fundraiser** is an event which is intended to raise money for a particular purpose, for example, for a charity. 募集资金的活动 ❑ *Organize a fundraiser for your church.* 为你们的教堂组织一次募集资金的活动吧。 **2** N-COUNT A **fundraiser** is someone who works to raise money for a particular purpose, for example, for a charity. 募集资金者 ❑ *...a fundraiser for the Democrats.* …一位民主党的募集资金者。

fund-raising also **fundraising** N-UNCOUNT **Fund-raising** is the activity of collecting money to support a charity or political campaign or organization. 资金募集 ❑ *Encourage her to get involved in fund-raising for charity.* 鼓励她参与慈善资金募集活动。

fu·ner·al /fyunərəl/ (**funerals**) N-COUNT A **funeral** is the ceremony that is held when the body of someone who has died is buried or cremated. 葬礼 ❑ *The funeral will be held in Joplin, Missouri.* 该葬礼将在密苏里州的乔普林市举行。

→ see Word Web: **funeral**

▲ **fun·gus** /fʌŋgəs/ (**fungi**) N-MASS A **fungus** is a plant that has no flowers, leaves, or green coloring, such as a mushroom or a toadstool. Other types of fungus such as mold are extremely small and look like a fine powder. 菌类

→ see Word Web: **fungus**

funky /fʌŋki/ (**funkier, funkiest**) **1** ADJ **Funky** jazz, blues, or pop music has a very strong, repeated bass part. 音低节奏强的 (爵士、布鲁斯、流行乐) ❑ *It's a funky sort of rhythm.* 这是一种音低节奏强的旋律。 **2** ADJ If you describe something or someone as **funky**, you mean that they are stylish and modern in an unconventional way. 时髦别致的 [APPROVAL] ❑ *She would love to buy her daughter funky little leopard-print skirts.* 她过去爱给女儿买时髦别致的豹纹小短裙。 ❑ *The place is quirky, funky and dazzlingly imaginative in design.* 这个地方非同凡响、时髦别致且设计极富想像力。 **3** ADJ Something that is **funky** has a strong, offensive odor. 恶臭的 ❑ *There were dirty clothes everywhere, and they all had that funky overripe smell.* 到处都有脏衣服而且它们都有那种腐烂的恶臭气味。

fun·nel /fʌnᵊl/ (**funnels, funneling** or **funnelling, funneled** or **funnelled**) **1** N-COUNT A **funnel** is an object with a wide, circular top and a narrow short tube at the bottom. Funnels are used to pour liquids into containers which have a small opening, for example, bottles. 漏斗 ❑ *Rain falls through the funnel into the jar below.* 雨水通过漏斗落进下面的罐子里。 **2** N-COUNT A **funnel** is a metal chimney on a ship or railroad engine powered by steam. (蒸汽轮船或火车机车的) 烟囱 ❑ *...a ship with three masts and two funnels.* …一艘有3根桅杆和2个烟囱的轮船。 **3** N-COUNT You can describe as a **funnel** something that is narrow, or narrow at one end, through which a substance flows and is directed. 漏斗状物 ❑ *Along the road, funnels of dark gray smoke rose from bombed villages.* 沿那条公路，暗灰色烟成漏斗状从遭到轰炸的村庄里升起。 **4** V-T/V-I If something **funnels** somewhere or **is funneled** there, it is directed through a narrow space. 使经过狭窄空间；经过狭窄空间 ❑ *The winds came from the north, across the plains, funneling down the valley.* 风从北方吹来，刮过平原，穿过山谷。 **5** V-T If you **funnel** money, goods, or information from one place or group to another, you cause it to be sent there as it becomes available. 传送 (资金、商品、信息等) ❑ *He secretly funneled credit-card information to counterfeiters.* 他秘密地将信用卡信息传送给了伪造者们。

fun·ni·ly /fʌnɪli/ PHRASE You use **funnily enough** to indicate that, although something is surprising, it is true or really happened. 说来也怪 ❑ *Funnily enough I can remember what I had for lunch on July 5th, 1956, but I've forgotten what I had for breakfast today.* 说来也怪，我能记得我1956年7月5日午餐吃的什么，却已忘了我今天早餐吃的什么。

fun·ny ♦◇◇ /fʌni/ (**funnier, funniest**) **1** ADJ Someone or something that is **funny** is amusing and likely to make you smile or laugh. 好笑的 ❑ *I'll tell you a funny story.* 我将给你讲个好笑的故事。 **2** ADJ If you describe something as **funny**, you think it is strange, surprising, or puzzling. 奇怪的 ❑ *Children get some very funny ideas sometimes!.* 孩子们有时候有一些非常奇怪的想法。 ❑ *There's something funny about him.* 他有点儿怪。 **3** ADJ If you feel **funny**, you feel slightly ill. 稍有不适的 [INFORMAL] ❑ *My head had begun to ache and my stomach felt funny.* 我的头开始疼了，我的胃也感到不对劲。

Thesaurus *funny* 另参见：

ADJ. amusing, comical, entertaining; (*ant.*) serious **1**
bizarre, odd, peculiar **2**

fur /fɜr/ (**furs**) **1** N-MASS **Fur** is the thick and usually soft hair that grows on the bodies of many mammals. (哺乳动物身上的) 毛 ❑ *This creature's fur is short, dense and silky.* 这种动物的毛短、浓密且柔顺。 **2** N-MASS **Fur** is an artificial fabric that looks like fur and is used, for example, to make clothing, soft toys, and seat covers. (用以制

Word Web fungus

Some **fungi** are destructive. For example, **mold** and mildew destroy crops, ruin clothing, cause diseases, and can even lead to death. But many fungi are useful. For instance, a single-cell fungus called **yeast** makes bread rise. Another form of yeast helps wine **ferment**. It turns the sugar in grape juice into alcohol. And **mushrooms** are a part of the diet of people all over the world. Cheese makers use a specific fungus to produce the creamy white skin on brie. A different **microorganism** gives blue cheese its characteristic color. Truffles, the most expensive fungi, cost more than $100 an ounce.

造服装、软玩具、座套等的）人造毛 **3** N-VAR **Fur** is the fur-covered skin of an animal that is used to make clothing or small carpets. (动物的）毛皮 ❑ *She had on a black coat with a fur collar.* 她穿着一件有毛皮领子的黑色外套。❑ *...the trading of furs from Canada.* …与加拿大的毛皮贸易。**4** N-COUNT A **fur** is a coat made from real or artificial fur, or a piece of fur worn around your neck. 毛皮外套；毛皮围脖 ❑ *There were women in furs and men in comfortable overcoats.* 有身穿毛皮外套的女人们和身穿舒适大衣的男人们。

★ **fu·ri·ous** /fyʊəriəs/ **1** ADJ Someone who is **furious** is extremely angry. 狂怒的 ❑ *He is furious at the way his wife has been treated.* 他因妻子所受到的对待方式而狂怒不已。● **fu·ri·ous·ly** ADV 狂怒地 ❑ *He stormed out of the apartment, slamming the door furiously behind him.* 他冲出了公寓，狂怒地把门从身后撞上。

> **Angry** is normally used to talk about someone's mood or feelings on a particular occasion. If someone is often angry, you can describe them as **bad-tempered**. ❑ *She's a bad-tempered young lady.* If someone is very angry, you can describe them as **furious**. ❑ *Senior police officers are furious at the blunder.* If they are less angry, you can describe them as **annoyed** or **irritated**. ❑ *The premier looked annoyed but calm. ...a man irritated by the barking of his neighbor's dog.* Typically, someone is **irritated** by something because it happens constantly or continually. If someone is often irritated, you can describe them as **irritable**.

2 ADJ **Furious** is also used to describe something that is done with great energy, effort, speed, or violence. 激烈的；玩命的；迅猛的 ❑ *A furious gunbattle ensued.* 接下来的一场激烈枪战。● **fu·ri·ous·ly** ADV 激烈地；玩命地；迅猛地 ❑ *Officials worked furiously to repair the center court.* 官员们玩命工作整修中央球场。

→ see **anger**

fur·long /fɜrlɔŋ/ (**furlongs**) N-COUNT A **furlong** is a unit of length that is equal to 220 yards or 201.2 meters. 浪（长度单位，等于220码或201.2米）❑ *"Although he was beaten in his first race at seven furlongs, I was thrilled with his performance," the trainer said.* "虽然他在第一场七浪比赛中被击败了，但我对他的表现无比激动，"驯马师说。

fur·lough /fɜrloʊ/ (**furloughs, furloughing, furloughed**) **1** N-VAR If workers are given **furlough**, they are told to stay away from work for a certain period because there is not enough for them to do. (因无足够工作可做而）停职（某段时间）[AM] ❑ *This could mean a massive furlough of government workers.* 这会意味着政府工作人员的一次大规模停职。**2** V-T If people who work for a particular organization **are furloughed**, they are given a furlough. 使停职 [AM] ❑ *We regret to inform you that you are being furloughed indefinitely.* 我们遗憾地通知你：你被无限期地停职了。

fur·nace /fɜrnɪs/ (**furnaces**) N-COUNT A **furnace** is a container or enclosed space in which a very hot fire is made, for example, to melt metal, burn trash, or produce heat for a building or house. 熔炉；火炉

fur·nish /fɜrnɪʃ/ (**furnishes, furnishing, furnished**) **1** V-T If you **furnish** a room or building, you put furniture and furnishings into it. 装潢；布置（房间、建筑物）❑ *Many proprietors try to furnish their hotels with antiques.* 许多企业主尽可能用古董装饰他们的旅馆。**2** V-T If you **furnish** someone **with** something, you provide or supply it. 提供 [FORMAL] ❑ *They'll be able to furnish you with the rest of the details.* 他们将能够给你提供其余的细节。

fur·nish·ings /fɜrnɪʃɪŋz/ N-PLURAL The **furnishings** of a room or house are the furniture, curtains, carpets, and decorations such as pictures. 室内陈设 ❑ *To enable rental increases, you have to have luxurious furnishings.* 为能实现租金增长，你得有豪华的室内陈设。

fur·ni·ture ♦◇◇ /fɜrnɪtʃər/ N-UNCOUNT **Furniture** consists of large objects such as tables, chairs, or beds that are used in a room for sitting or lying on or for putting things on or in. 家具 ❑ *Each piece of furniture in their home suited the style of the house.* 他们家的每件家具都与房子的风格相称。

> Note that **furniture** is only ever used as an uncount noun. You cannot say "a furniture" or "furnitures." If you want to refer in general terms to something such as a table, a chair, or a bed, you can say **a piece of furniture** or **an item of furniture**.

fu·ro·r /fyʊərɔr, -ər/ N-SING A **furor** is a very angry or excited reaction by people to something. 狂怒；狂热 ❑ *...an international furor over the plan.* …一种对这项计划的国际性狂热。

fur·row /fɜroʊ/ (**furrows**) **1** N-COUNT A **furrow** is a long, thin line in the earth which a farmer makes in order to plant seeds or to allow water to flow along. 垄沟 ❑ *...furrows of roses and corn.* …一垄一垄的玫瑰和玉米。**2** N-COUNT A **furrow** is a deep, fairly wide line in the surface of something. 沟 ❑ *I saw a dark brown fertile field in which a plow was cutting large furrows.* 我看到一块深褐色的肥沃田地，那里耕犁正犁出宽大的犁沟。**3** N-COUNT A **furrow** is a deep fold or line in the skin of someone's face. 皱纹 ❑ *He was his old self again, except for the deep furrows that marked the corners of his mouth.* 他又是他的老样子了，只是多了些深深的刻在他的嘴角的皱纹。

fur·ry /fɜri/ (**furrier, furriest**) **1** ADJ A **furry** animal is covered with thick, soft hair. 毛茸茸的（动物）❑ *People like having small furry animals to stroke, but pets can be expensive to feed.* 人们喜欢有毛茸茸的小动物以抚摸，但宠物养起来会很费钱。**2** ADJ If you describe something as **furry**, you mean that it has a soft rough texture like fur. 毛一般的 ❑ *The leaves are soft, round and rather furry.* 那些叶子软而圆，就像绒毛一般。

fur·ther ♦♦♦ /fɜrðər/ (**furthers, furthering, furthered**)

> **Further** is a comparative form of **far**. It is also a verb.

1 ADV **Further** means to a greater extent or degree. 在更大程度上 [ADV with v] ❑ *Inflation is below 5% and set to fall further.* 通货膨胀率低于5%，而且开始进一步下降。❑ *The rebellion is expected to further damage the country's image.* 该叛乱预计会进一步损害该国的形象。**2** ADV If you go or get **further with** something, or take something **further**, you make some progress. 更进一步地 [ADV with v] ❑ *They lacked the scientific personnel to develop the technical apparatus much further.* 他们缺少进一步研发这些技术设备的科技人员。**3** ADV If someone goes **further** in a discussion, they make a more extreme statement or deal with a point more thoroughly. 更深入地 [ADV after v] ❑ *To have a better comparison, we need to go further and address such issues as repairs and insurance.* 为了有一个更好的比较，我们需要更深入一步谈谈诸如维修和保险等问题。**4** ADV **Further** means a greater distance than before or than something else. 更远地 [ADV adv/prep] ❑ *People are living further away from their jobs.* 人们住得离工作地点更远了。❑ *He came to a halt at a crossroads fifty yards further on.* 他在50码远的十字路口停了下来。**5** ADV **Further** is used in expressions such as "**further back**" and "**further ahead**" to refer to a point in time that is earlier or later than the time you are talking about. (时间上往前或往后）更远地 [ADV adv/prep] ❑ *Looking still further ahead, by the end of the next century world population is expected to be about ten billion.* 再往远看，到下个世纪末，世界人口预期达到一百亿左右。**6** ADJ A **further** thing, number of things, or amount of something is an additional thing, number of things, or amount. 更多的 [ADJ n, pron-indef ADJ] ❑ *Further evidence of slowing economic growth is likely to emerge this week.* 更多有关在减慢的经济增长的证据本周可能出现。**7** V-T If you **further** something, you help it to progress, to be successful, or to be achieved. 推进 ❑ *Education needn't only be about furthering your career.* 教育不必只是与推进你的事业有关。

fur·ther edu·ca·tion N-UNCOUNT **Further education** is the education of people who have left school but who are not at a university or a college of education. 继续教育 [BRIT]

> in AM, use **continuing education, adult education**

further·more /fɜrðərmɔr/ ADV **Furthermore** is used to introduce a piece of information or opinion that adds to or supports the previous one. 此外 [ADV with cl] [FORMAL] ❑ *Furthermore, they claim that any such interference is completely ineffective.* 此外，他们声称任何此类干涉都是完全无效的。

fur·thest /fɜrðɪst/

> **Furthest** is a superlative form of **far**.

1 ADV **Furthest** means to a greater extent or degree than ever before or than anything or anyone else. 最大程度地 [ADV with v] ❑ *The south, where prices have fallen furthest, will remain the weakest market.* 价格降幅最大的南方仍将是最疲软的市场。**2** ADV **Furthest** means at a greater distance from a particular point than anyone or anything else, or for a greater distance than anyone or anything else. 最远地 ❑ *The risk of thunder is greatest in those areas furthest from the coast.* 遭雷击的危险在离海岸最远的那些地区最大。● ADJ **Furthest** is also an adjective. 最远的 [ADJ n] ❑ *...the furthest point from earth that any controlled spacecraft has ever been.* …任何受控航天器所到过的离地球最远的点。

fur·tive /fɜrtɪv/ ADJ If you describe someone's behavior as **furtive**, you disapprove of them behaving as if they want to keep something secret or hidden. 鬼鬼祟祟的 [DISAPPROVAL] ❑ *With a furtive glance over her shoulder, she unlocked the door and entered the house.* 随着越过其肩的鬼鬼祟祟的一瞥，她打开锁进了那房子。

★ **fury** /fyʊ̲əri/ N-UNCOUNT **Fury** is violent or very strong anger. 狂怒 ❑ *She screamed, her face distorted with fury and pain.* 她尖叫着，她的脸因愤怒和痛苦而扭曲了。

★ **fuse** /fyu̲z/ (**fuses, fusing, fused**)

The spelling **fuze** is also used for meaning 2.

1 N-COUNT A **fuse** is a safety device in an electric plug or circuit. It contains a piece of wire which melts when there is a fault so that the flow of electricity stops. 保险丝 ❑ *The fuse blew as he pressed the button to start the motor.* 保险丝在他按下按钮发动车子时烧断了。 2 N-COUNT A **fuse** is a device on a bomb or firework which delays the explosion so that people can move a safe distance away. 导火线 ❑ *A bomb was deactivated at the last moment, after the fuse had been lit.* 一枚炸弹在导火线已被点燃后的最后一刻被解除。 3 V-RECIP When things **fuse** or **are fused**, they join together physically or chemically, usually to become one thing. You can also say that one thing **fuses** with another. 结合；融合；熔合 ❑ *The skull bones fuse between the ages of fifteen and twenty-five.* 颅骨在15和25岁之间长合。 ❑ *Manufactured glass is made by fusing various types of sand.* 人造玻璃是通过熔合不同种类的沙子制造出来的。

fu·selage /fyu̲sɪlɑʒ, -lɪdʒ, -zɪ-/ (**fuselages**) N-COUNT The **fuselage** is the main body of an airplane, missile, or rocket. It is usually cylindrical in shape. (飞机、火箭的) 机身；(导弹的) 弹身 ❑ *The force of the impact ripped apart the plane's fuselage.* 冲击力使该飞机的机身断裂了。

★ **fu·sion** /fyu̲ʒᵊn/ (**fusions**) 1 N-COUNT A **fusion of** different qualities, ideas, or things is something new that is created by joining them together. 融合；熔合 ❑ *His previous fusions of jazz, pop and African melodies have proved highly successful.* 他先前对爵士乐、流行乐和非洲音乐旋律的融合已经证明是非常成功的。 2 N-VAR The **fusion** of two or more things involves joining them together to form one thing. 结合为一体；融为一体 ❑ *His final reform was the fusion of regular and reserve forces.* 他最后的改革是把常规军和后备军合二为一。 3 N-UNCOUNT In physics, **fusion** is the process in which atomic particles combine and produce a large amount of nuclear energy. 核聚变 ❑ *...research into nuclear fusion.* …对核聚变的研究。
→ see **sun**

fuss /fʌ̲s/ (**fusses, fussing, fussed**) 1 N-SING **Fuss** is anxious or excited behavior which serves no useful purpose. 无谓的忙乎 [also no det] ❑ *I don't know what all the fuss is about.* 我不知道这一切无谓的忙乎是怎么回事。 2 V-I If you **fuss**, you worry or behave in a nervous, anxious way about unimportant matters or rush around doing unnecessary things. 瞎紧张；瞎操心；瞎忙乎 ❑ *Carol fussed about getting me a drink.* 卡萝尔忙乎着给我弄杯饮料。 ❑ *My wife was fussing over the food and clothing we were going to take.* 我妻子在为我们要带的食物和衣服瞎操心。 ❑ *"Stop fussing," he snapped.* "别瞎忙了，"他怒斥道。 3 V-I If you **fuss over** someone, you pay them a lot of attention and do things to make them happy or comfortable. 宠爱 ❑ *Auntie Hilda and Uncle Jack couldn't fuss over them enough.* 希尔达婶婶和杰克叔叔再宠爱他们不过了。 4 PHRASE If you **make a fuss** or **kick up a fuss** about something, you become angry or excited about it and complain. 大发牢骚 [INFORMAL] ❑ *I don't know why everybody makes such a fuss about a few mosquitoes.* 我不知道为什么所有人都为几只蚊子发这么大的牢骚。

fussy /fʌ̲si/ (**fussier, fussiest**) ADJ Someone who is **fussy** is very concerned with unimportant details and is difficult to please. 爱挑剔的 [DISAPPROVAL] ❑ *She is not fussy about her food.* 她不挑食。

▲ **fu·tile** /fyu̲tᵊl/ ADJ If you say that something is **futile**, you mean there is no point in doing it, usually because it has no chance of succeeding. (常因无成功的可能而) 无谓的 ❑ *He brought his arm up in a futile attempt to ward off the blow.* 他出于挡住这一击的无谓企图抬起了他的胳膊。

fu·til·ity /fyutɪ̲lɪti/ N-UNCOUNT **Futility** is a total lack of purpose or usefulness. 无谓 ❑ *Brown's article tells of the tragedy and futility of war.* 布朗的文章讲述了战争的悲剧性和无谓性。

fu·ture ♦♦♦ /fyu̲tʃər/ (**futures**) 1 N-SING **The future** is the period of time that will come after the present, or the things that will happen then. 将来 ❑ *The spokesman said no decision on the proposal was likely in the immediate future.* 该发言人称近期不太可能有有关该提案的决议。 ❑ *He was making plans for the future.* 他正在为将来制定计划。 2 ADJ **Future** things will happen or exist after the present time. 未来的 [ADJ n] ❑ *She said if the world did not act conclusively now, it would only bequeath the problem to future generations.* 她说如果这个世界现在不采取正确的行动，那只会把问题遗留给后代。 ❑ *...the future king and queen.* …未来的国王和王后。 3 N-COUNT Someone's **future**, or **the future of** something, is what will happen to them or what they will do after the present time. (某人、某事物的) 未来 ❑ *His future depends on the outcome of the elections.* 他的未来取决于该选举的结果。 ❑ *...a proposed national conference on the country's political future.* …一次拟议的有关该国政治未来的全国会议。 4 N-PLURAL When people trade in **futures**, they buy stocks and shares, commodities such as coffee or oil, or foreign currency at a price that is agreed at the time of purchase for items which are delivered some time in the future. 期货 [BUSINESS] ❑ *This report could spur some buying in corn futures when the market opens today.* 这份报告会在今天开市时刺激玉米期货的一些购买行为。 5 PHRASE You use **in the future** when saying what will happen from now on, which will be different from what has previously happened. 在将来 ❑ *I asked her to be more careful in the future.* 我叫她将来更仔细一些。

Word Partnership *future* 的常用搭配：

V.	**discuss the** future, **plan for the** future, **predict/see the** future 1 **have a** future 3
ADJ.	**bright** future, **distant** future, **immediate** future, **near** future, **uncertain** future 1 3
N.	future **date**, future **events**, future **generations**, future **plans**, **for** future **reference** 2

fu·tur·is·tic /fyu̲tʃərɪ̲stɪk/ 1 ADJ Something that is **futuristic** looks or seems very modern and unusual, like something from the future. 未来派的 ❑ *The theater is a futuristic steel and glass structure.* 该剧院是一座未来派的钢筋玻璃结构建筑。 2 ADJ A **futuristic** movie or book tells a story that is set in the future, when things are different. 科幻性的 (影片、书) [ADJ n] ❑ *...the futuristic hit film, "Terminator 2."* …轰动一时的科幻电影《终结者2》。

fuzzy /fʌ̲zi/ (**fuzzier, fuzziest**) 1 ADJ **Fuzzy** hair sticks up in a soft, curly mass. 绒卷的 (头发) ❑ *He had fuzzy black hair and bright black eyes.* 他长着绒卷黑发和一双明亮的黑眼睛。 2 ADJ If something is **fuzzy**, it has a covering that feels soft and like fur. 绒软的 ❑ *...fuzzy material.* …绒软料子。 3 ADJ A **fuzzy** picture, image, or sound is unclear and hard to see or hear. 模糊的 (图片、图像、声音等) ❑ *A couple of fuzzy pictures have been published.* 几张模糊的图片已被刊印。 4 ADJ If you or your thoughts are **fuzzy**, you are confused and cannot think clearly. (人、思路) 糊涂 ❑ *He had little patience for fuzzy ideas.* 他对于糊涂想法没有什么耐心。

Gg

G also **g** /dʒiː/ (**G's, g's**) N-VAR **G** is the seventh letter of the English alphabet. 英语字母表中的第7个字母

★ **gadg·et** /gædʒɪt/ (**gadgets**) N-COUNT A **gadget** is a small machine or device which does something useful. You sometimes refer to something as a **gadget** when you are suggesting that it is complicated and unnecessary. 小器械（有时暗指复杂、不必要的东西） ❑ *...sales of kitchen gadgets including toasters, kettles, and percolators.* …厨房小用品的销售，包括烤面包机、水壶和咖啡渗滤壶。
→ see **technology**

Gael·ic /geɪlɪk, gælɪk/ 1 N-UNCOUNT **Gaelic** is a language spoken by people in parts of Scotland and Ireland. （在苏格兰和爱尔兰部分地区使用的）盖尔语 ❑ *We weren't allowed to speak Gaelic at school.* 我们在学校不允许说盖尔语。 ● ADJ **Gaelic** is also an adjective. 盖尔语的 ❑ *...the Gaelic language.* …盖尔语。 2 ADJ **Gaelic** means coming from or relating to Scotland and Ireland, especially the parts where Gaelic is spoken. 苏格兰或爱尔兰的（尤指盖尔语地区的） ❑ *...an evening of Gaelic music and drama.* …盖尔语地区的音乐和戏剧之夜。

gag /gæg/ (**gags, gagging, gagged**) 1 N-COUNT A **gag** is something such as a piece of cloth that is tied around or put inside someone's mouth in order to stop them from speaking. 塞口物 ❑ *His captors had put a gag of thick leather in his mouth.* 俘获他的人在他嘴里塞了一块儿厚皮革。 2 V-T If someone **gags** you, they tie a piece of cloth around your mouth in order to stop you from speaking or shouting. 堵住…的嘴 ❑ *I gagged him with a towel.* 我用一条毛巾塞住他的嘴。 3 V-T If a person **is gagged** by someone in authority, they are prevented from expressing their opinion or from publishing certain information. 压制言论自由 [DISAPPROVAL] ❑ *Judges must not be gagged.* 法官绝不能被压制言论自由。 4 V-I If you **gag**, you cannot swallow and nearly vomit. 作呕 ❑ *I knelt by the toilet and gagged.* 我跪在马桶边作呕。 5 N-COUNT A **gag** is a joke. 笑话 [INFORMAL] ❑ *The running gag is that the band never gets to play.* 那个流传的笑话说那支乐队从未演奏过。 6 N-COUNT A **gag** is a humorous trick that you play on someone. 恶作剧 [AM, INFORMAL] ❑ *Richard must have thought colleagues were playing a gag on him.* 理查德一定以为同事们在对他搞恶作剧。

▲ **gai·ety** /geɪɪti/ N-UNCOUNT **Gaiety** is a feeling, attitude, or atmosphere of liveliness and fun. 欢乐 ❑ *Music rang out, adding to the gaiety and life of the market.* 音乐响起，为市场增添了欢乐和活力。

gain ◆◆◇ /geɪn/ (**gains, gaining, gained**) 1 V-T/V-I If a person or place **gains** something such as an ability or quality, they gradually get more of it. 获得 ❑ *Students can gain valuable experience by working on the campus radio or magazine.* 学生们通过在校园广播台或校刊工作能够获得宝贵的经验。 ❑ *His reputation abroad has gained in stature.* 他在国外的声望得到了提高。 2 V-T/V-I If you **gain from** something such as an event or situation, you get some advantage or benefit from it. 受益 ❑ *The company didn't disclose how much it expects to gain from the two deals.* 该公司没有透露它期望从这两笔交易中获利多少。 ❑ *There is absolutely nothing to be gained by feeling bitter.* 忿忿不平绝对是毫无益处的。 3 V-T To **gain** something such as weight or speed means to have an increase in that particular thing. 增加 ❑ *Some people do gain weight after they stop smoking.* 有些人戒烟后的确增加体重了。 ❑ *The BMW started coming forward, passing the other cars and gaining speed as it approached.* 宝马车开始向前赶，超越了其它车，并且在接近时加速。 ● N-VAR **Gain** is also a noun. 增加 [usu with supp] ❑ *News on new home sales is brighter, showing a gain of nearly 8% in June.* 有关新房销售的新闻更加乐观，显示6月份有近8%的增长。 4 V-T If you **gain** something, you obtain it, especially after a lot of hard work or effort. （尤指经过努力）得到 ❑ *To gain a promotion, you might have to work overtime.* 为了得到晋升，你可能得加班。 5 PHRASE If something such as an idea or an ideal **gains ground**, it gradually becomes more widely known or more popular. （想法、理想等）越来越流行 ❑ *There are strong signs that his views are gaining ground.* 有明显的迹象表明他的观点正越来越深入人心。

Thesaurus	*gain* 另参见：
V.	acquire, collect, obtain; (*ant.*) lose 1
	grow, enlarge, increase 3

gait /geɪt/ (**gaits**) N-COUNT A particular kind of **gait** is a particular way of walking. 步态 [WRITTEN] ❑ *...a tubby little man in his fifties, with sparse hair and a rolling gait.* …一个矮胖的男人，五十多岁，头发稀疏，步态摇摆。

gala /geɪlə/ (**galas**) N-COUNT A **gala** is a special public celebration, entertainment, performance, or festival. 节日盛会；演出 ❑ *...a gala evening at the Metropolitan Opera House.* …大都会歌剧院的庆祝晚会。

★ **gal·axy** /gæləksi/ (**galaxies**) also **Galaxy** 1 N-COUNT A **galaxy** is an extremely large group of stars and planets that extends over many billions of light years. 星系 ❑ *Astronomers have discovered a distant galaxy.* 天文学家们发现了一个遥远的星系。 2 N-PROPER **The Galaxy** is the extremely large group of stars and planets to which the Earth and the solar system belong. 银河系 ❑ *The Galaxy consists of 100 billion stars.* 银河系由1千亿颗恒星组成。
→ see Word Web: **galaxy**
→ see **star**

▲ **gale** /geɪl/ (**gales**) 1 N-COUNT A **gale** is a very strong wind. 大风 ❑ *...forecasts of fierce gales over the next few days.* …对未来几天的强风预报。 2 N-COUNT You can refer to the loud noise made by a lot of people all laughing at the same time as a **gale of** laughter or **gales of** laughter. 一阵（大笑声） [WRITTEN] ❑ *This was greeted with gales of laughter from the audience.* 这个获得了来自观众的阵阵笑声。
→ see **wind**

gall /gɔl/ (**galls, galling, galled**) 1 N-UNCOUNT If you say that someone has **the gall to** do something, you are criticizing them for behaving in a rude or disrespectful way. 厚颜无耻 [DISAPPROVAL] ❑ *He has the gall to accuse reporters of exploiting a tragedy for their own ends.* 他竟厚颜无耻地指责记者利用一场悲剧来谋求他们的私利。 2 V-T

Word Web **galaxy**

The word **galaxy** with a small "g" refers to an extremely large group of **stars** and **planets**. It measures billions of **light years** across. There are about 100 billion galaxies in the **universe**. **Astronomers** classify galaxies into four different types. Irregular galaxies have no particular shape. Elliptical galaxies look like flattened spheres. Spiral galaxies have long curving arms. A barred spiral galaxy has straight lines of stars extending from its nucleus. Galaxy with a capital "G" refers to our own **solar system**. The name of this galaxy is the Milky Way. It is about 100,000 light years wide.

If someone's action **galls** you, it makes you feel very angry or annoyed, often because it is unfair to you and you cannot do anything about it. 激怒 ❑ *It must have galled him that Nick thwarted each of these measures.* 尼克对每一个措施都加以阻挠，这一定激怒了他。

▲ **gal·lant** /gælənt/

Pronounced /gəlænt/ or /gælənt/ for meaning 2.

义项2读作 /gəlænt/或 /gælənt/。

1 ADJ If someone is **gallant**, they behave bravely and honorably in a dangerous or difficult situation. 英勇的 [OLD-FASHIONED] ❑ *The gallant soldiers lost their lives so that peace might reign again.* 英勇的士兵为了恢复和平而牺牲了他们的生命。● **gal·lant·ly** ADV 英勇地 [ADV with V] ❑ *The town responded gallantly to the war.* 全镇居民英勇地应对这场战争。 2 ADJ If a man is **gallant**, he is kind, polite, and considerate toward women. (男人对女人) 殷勤的 [OLD-FASHIONED] ❑ *Douglas was a complex man, thoughtful, gallant, and generous.* 道格拉斯是个复杂的男人，他体贴、殷勤而且慷慨。● **gal·lant·ly** ADV 殷勤地 [ADV with V] ❑ *He gallantly kissed Marie's hand as we prepared to leave.* 我们准备离开的时候，他殷勤地吻了玛丽的手。

gall blad·der (**gall bladders**) N-COUNT Your **gall bladder** is the organ in your body which contains bile and is next to your liver. 胆囊

gal·lery ♦◇◇ /gæləri/ (**galleries**) 1 N-COUNT; N-IN-NAMES A **gallery** is a place that has permanent exhibitions of works of art in it. (艺术作品的) 陈列室; 美术馆 ❑ *...an art gallery.* …一座美术馆。 2 N-COUNT A **gallery** is a privately owned building or room where people can look at and buy works of art. 私人字画店 ❑ *The painting is in the gallery upstairs.* 那幅画在楼上的字画店里。 3 N-COUNT A **gallery** is an area high above the ground at the back or at the sides of a large room or hall. 廊台 ❑ *A crowd already filled the gallery.* 一群人已经挤满了廊台。 4 N-COUNT **The gallery** in a theater or concert hall is an area high above the ground that usually contains the cheapest seats. (剧场或音乐厅内通常票价最低的) 顶层楼座 ❑ *They had been forced to find cheap tickets in the gallery.* 他们被迫去找顶层楼座的廉价票。● PHRASE If you **play to the gallery**, you do something in public in a way which you hope will impress people. 哗众取宠 ❑ *...but I must tell you that in my opinion you're both now playing to the gallery.* …但是我必须告诉你们，在我看来你们俩现在都是在哗众取宠。

→ see Word Web: **gallery**

gal·ley /gæli/ (**galleys**) 1 N-COUNT On a ship or aircraft, the **galley** is the kitchen. (船或飞机上的) 厨房 ❑ *I awake to the smell of sizzling bacon in the galley.* 我醒来时闻到厨房里咝咝作响的熏肉的味道。 2 N-COUNT In former times, a **galley** was a ship with sails and a lot of oars, which was often rowed by slaves or prisoners. (旧时常由奴隶或犯人划桨的) 划桨帆船 ❑ *...his months pulling the oar on the galleys.* …他在帆船上划桨的几个月。

gal·lon /gælən/ (**gallons**) N-COUNT A **gallon** is a unit of measurement for liquids that is equal to eight pints or 3.785 liters. 加仑 (液体计量单位，合八品脱或3.785升) ❑ *...80 million gallons of water a day.* …一天8千万加仑水。

▲ **gal·lop** /gæləp/ (**gallops, galloping, galloped**) 1 V-T/V-I When a horse **gallops**, it runs very fast so that all four legs are off the ground at the same time. If you **gallop** a horse, you make it gallop. 使(马) 疾驰; (马) 疾驰 ❑ *The horses galloped away.* 那些马疾驰而去。 2 V-I If you **gallop**, you ride a horse that is galloping. 骑马疾驰 ❑ *Major Winston galloped into the distance.* 温斯顿少校骑马疾驰远去。 3 N-SING A **gallop** is a ride on a horse that is galloping. 骑马疾驰 ❑ *I was forced to attempt a gallop.* 我被迫尝试一次骑马疾驰。 4 V-I If something such as a process **gallops**, it develops very quickly and is often difficult to control. 飞速发展 ❑ *China's economy galloped ahead.* 中国的经济飞速向前发展。 5 PHRASE If you do something **at a gallop**, you do it very quickly. 快速地 ❑ *I read the book at a gallop.* 我迅速读完了那本书。

ga·lore /gəlɔr/ ADJ You use **galore** to emphasize that something you like exists in very large quantities. 大量的 [n ADJ] [INFORMAL, WRITTEN, EMPHASIS] ❑ *You'll be able to win prizes galore.* 你将会赢得很多奖品。

gal·va·nise /gælvənaɪz/ [BRIT] → see **galvanize**

gal·va·nize /gælvənaɪz/ (**galvanizes, galvanizing, galvanized**)

in BRIT, also use **galvanise**

V-T To **galvanize** someone means to cause them to take action, for example by making them feel very excited, afraid, or angry. 使(兴奋、害怕、愤怒等) 而采取行动 ❑ *The aid appeal has galvanized the country's business community.* 这份援助呼吁已使该国的商界采取行动。

gam·ble /gæmbᵊl/ (**gambles, gambling, gambled**) 1 N-COUNT A **gamble** is a risky action or decision that you take in the hope of gaining money, success, or an advantage over other people. 冒险 ❑ *Yesterday, he named his cabinet and took a big gamble in the process.* 昨天他冒了很大的风险任命了他的内阁。 2 V-T/V-I If you **gamble on** something, you take a risky action or decision in the hope of gaining money, success, or an advantage over other people. 冒险; 以…为赌注 ❑ *Few firms will be willing to gamble on new products.* 很少有公司愿意在新产品上冒险。 ❑ *They are not prepared to gamble their careers on this matter.* 他们没准备为此事拿自己的事业来当赌注。 3 V-T/V-I If you **gamble** an amount of money, you bet it in a game such as cards or on the result of a race or competition. People who **gamble** usually do it frequently. (纸牌、比赛等) 赌博 ❑ *Most people visit Las Vegas to gamble their hard-earned money.* 多数人去拉斯维加斯是为了用他们辛苦赚来的钱赌博。 ❑ *John gambled heavily on the horses.* 约翰在这几匹马上下了大赌注。

→ see **lottery**

gam·bler /gæmblər/ (**gamblers**) 1 N-COUNT A **gambler** is someone who gambles regularly, for example in card games or on horse racing. 赌徒 ❑ *There was a fellow in that casino tonight who's a very heavy gambler.* 今晚那家赌场有个家伙是个嗜赌成性的赌棍。 2 N-COUNT If you describe someone as a **gambler**, you mean that they are ready to take risks in order to gain advantages or success. 冒险家 ❑ *He had never been afraid of failure: he was a gambler, ready to go off somewhere else and start all over again.* 他从不害怕失败：他是个冒险家，随时准备去别的地方重新开始。

gam·bling /gæmblɪŋ/ N-UNCOUNT **Gambling** is the act or activity of betting money, for example in card games or on horse racing. 赌博 ❑ *Gambling is a form of entertainment.* 赌博是一种娱乐形式。

game ♦♦♦ /geɪm/ (**games**) 1 N-COUNT A **game** is an activity or sport usually involving skill, knowledge, or chance, in which you follow fixed rules and try to win against an opponent or to solve a puzzle. 游戏; 运动 ❑ *...the wonderful game of football.* …精彩的足球运动。 ❑ *...a playful game of hide-and-seek.* …一个有趣的捉迷藏游戏。 2 N-COUNT A **game** is one particular occasion on which a game is played. 比赛 ❑ *It was the first game of the season.* 那是本赛季的第一场比赛。 ❑ *He regularly watched our games from the stands.* 他经常从看台上观看我们的比赛。 3 N-COUNT A **game** is a part of a match, for example in tennis or bridge, consisting of a fixed number of points. (比赛中的) 一局 ❑ *She won six games to love in the second set.* 第2盘她以6-0取胜。 4 N-PLURAL **Games** are an organized event in which competitions in several sports take place. 运动会 ❑ *...the 1996 Olympic Games at Atlanta.* …1996年亚特兰大奥林匹克运动会。 5 N-COUNT You can use **game** to describe a way of behaving in which a person uses a particular plan, usually in order to gain an advantage for himself or herself. 计谋 ❑ *Until now, the Americans have been playing a very delicate political game.* 至今美国人们还在玩弄非常微妙的政治计谋。 6 N-UNCOUNT Wild animals or birds that are hunted for sport and sometimes cooked and eaten are referred to as **game**. 猎物 ❑ *As men who shot game for food, they were natural marksmen.* 作为捕捉猎

Word Web gallery

The Uffizi **Gallery** in Florence, Italy, is a world-famous art **museum**. It contains many magnificent **paintings** and **sculptures**. These include **works of art** by da Vinci, Botticelli, and Michelangelo. The building was constructed in the 1550s to house government offices. The Medici family, who ruled the area at that time, were great art **collectors**. Gradually they began to convert parts of the building into art galleries. In 1737, the Medici family gave their art collection to the people of Italy.

物当食物的人，他们是天生的射手。 7 ADJ If you are **game for** something, you are willing to do something new, unusual, or risky. 敢尝试的 [v-link ADJ] ❑ *He said he's game for a similar challenge next year.* 他说明年他敢尝试一次类似的挑战。 8 PHRASE If someone or something **gives the game away**, they reveal a secret or reveal their feelings, and this puts them at a disadvantage. 泄露秘密；露出马脚 ❑ *The faces of the two conspirators gave the game away!* 两个同谋者的表情露出了马脚。 9 PHRASE If you are **new to** a particular **game**, you have not done a particular activity or been in a particular situation before. 对…不熟悉 ❑ *Don't forget that she's new to this game and will take a while to complete the task.* 别忘了她对此没有经验，将需要一些时间来完成那项任务。 10 PHRASE If you beat someone **at** their **own game**, you use the same methods that they have used, but more successfully, so that you gain an advantage over them. 将计就计战胜某人 ❑ *He must anticipate the maneuvers of the other lawyers and beat them at their own game.* 他必须对其他律师的策略有所准备，从而将计就计战胜他们。 11 PHRASE If you say that someone is **playing games** or **playing silly games**, you mean that they are not treating a situation seriously and you are annoyed with them. 敷衍 [DISAPPROVAL] ❑ *This seemed to annoy Professor Steiner. "Don't play games with me," he thundered.* 这似乎触怒了斯坦纳教授。"别敷衍我了，"他吼道。

→ see **chess**, **mammal**

games con·sole (**games consoles**) N-COUNT A **games console** is an electronic device used for playing computer games on a television screen. 电子游戏机 [BRIT] ❑ *This Christmas sees the launch of a new games console.* 今年的圣诞节目睹了一种新电子游戏机的推出。

game show (**game shows**) N-COUNT **Game shows** are television programs on which people play games in order to win prizes. 电视竞赛节目 ❑ *Being a good game-show host means getting to know your contestants.* 做一名优秀的电视竞赛节目主持人就意味着要了解参赛者。

gam·ing /geɪmɪŋ/ N-UNCOUNT **Gaming** means the same as **gambling**. 赌博 ❑ *...offenses connected with vice, gaming, and drugs.* …与恶行、赌博、吸毒相关的犯罪行为。

gang ♦◇◇ /gæŋ/ (**gangs, ganging, ganged**) 1 N-COUNT A **gang** is a group of people, especially young people, who go around together and often deliberately cause trouble. (尤指滋事的青少年的) 团伙 ❑ *During the fight with a rival gang he lashed out with his flick knife.* 和对立帮派群殴时，他用弹簧刀猛烈攻击。 ❑ *Gang members were behind a lot of the violence.* 流氓团伙暗中策划了许多暴力行为。 2 N-COUNT A **gang** is a group of criminals who work together to commit crimes. 犯罪团伙 ❑ *Police were hunting for a gang that had allegedly stolen fifty-five cars.* 警察正在追捕一个涉嫌偷窃55辆汽车的犯罪团伙。 ❑ *...an underworld gang.* …一个地下犯罪团伙。 3 N-SING **The gang** is a group of friends who frequently meet. (经常聚会的) 一帮朋友 [INFORMAL] ❑ *Come on over, we've got lots of the old gang here.* 过来吧，我们这里有很多老朋友。 4 N-COUNT A **gang** is a group of workers who do physical work together. (一) 队 (一起干体力活的工人) ❑ *...a gang of laborers.* …一群劳工。

▸ **gang up** PHRASAL VERB If people **gang up on** someone, they unite against them for a particular reason, for example in a fight or argument. 结伙 (对付某人) [INFORMAL] ❑ *Harrison complained that his colleagues ganged up on him.* 哈里森抱怨他的同事联合起来对付他。 ❑ *All the other parties ganged up to keep them out of power.* 所有其他的党派结伙阻止他们掌权。

Thesaurus *gang* 另参见：

N.	crowd, group, pack 1 mob, ring 2

gan·grene /gæŋgrin/ N-UNCOUNT **Gangrene** is the decay that can occur in a part of a person's body if the blood stops flowing to it, for example as a result of illness or injury. 坏疽 ❑ *Once gangrene has developed, the tissue is dead, and the only hope is to contain the damage.* 一旦出现坏疽，组织就会坏死，那么惟一的希望就是抑制其损害。

Word Link *ster ≈ one who does : barrister, gangster, youngster*

▲ **gang·ster** /gæŋstər/ (**gangsters**) N-COUNT A **gangster** is a member of an organized group of violent criminals. (结成团伙的) 匪徒 ❑ *...a gangster movie.* …一部黑帮片。

gaol /dʒeɪl/ [BRIT] → see **jail**

gap ♦◇◇ /gæp/ (**gaps**) 1 N-COUNT A **gap** is a space between two things or a hole in the middle of something solid. 缺口；裂缝 ❑ *He pulled the thick curtains together, leaving just a narrow gap.* 他把厚厚的窗帘拉到一起，只留了一条窄缝。 2 N-COUNT A **gap** is a period of time when you are not busy or when you stop doing something that you normally do. 间隔期 ❑ *There followed a gap of four years, during which William joined the Army.* 之后有4年的间隔，期间威廉参军了。 3 N-COUNT If there is something missing from a situation that prevents it from being complete or satisfactory, you can say that there is a **gap**. 缺漏 ❑ *The manifesto calls for a greater effort to recruit young scientists to fill the gap left by a wave of retirements expected over the next decade.* 该声明呼吁加大力度招募年轻的科学家，以填补预期未来十年内一波退休高峰所留下的空缺。 4 N-COUNT A **gap between** two groups of people, things, or sets of ideas is a big difference between them. 差距 ❑ *...the gap between rich and poor.* …贫富差距。 ❑ *America's trade gap widened.* 美国的贸易差额加大了。

Word Partnership *gap* 的常用搭配：

ADJ.	**narrow** gap 1 2
V.	**bridge a** gap, **fill a** gap, **leave a** gap, **widen a** gap 1–4
PREP.	gap **between** *something* 1 4

gape /geɪp/ (**gapes, gaping, gaped**) 1 V-I If you **gape**, you look at someone or something in surprise, usually with an open mouth. 目瞪口呆地看 ❑ *His secretary stopped taking notes to gape at me.* 他的秘书停止了做记录，目瞪口呆地看着我。 ❑ *He was not the type to wander around gaping at everything like a tourist.* 他不是那种像个游客似的四处闲逛、惊奇地看着一切的人。 2 V-I If you say that something such as a hole or a wound **gapes**, you are emphasizing that it is big or wide. 裂开 [EMPHASIS] ❑ *The front door was missing. A hole gaped in the roof.* 前门没有了，屋顶裂开一个洞。 ● **gap·ing** ADJ 裂开的 ❑ *The aircraft took off with a gaping hole in its fuselage.* 那飞机起飞了，机身上有一个裂开的洞。

gar·age /gərɑʒ/ (**garages**) 1 N-COUNT A **garage** is a building in which you keep a car. A garage is often built next to or as part of a house. 车库 ❑ *They have turned the garage into a study.* 他们把车库改建成了书房。 2 N-COUNT; N-IN-NAMES A **garage** is a place where you can get your car repaired. 汽车修理厂 ❑ *Nancy took her car to a local garage for a check-up.* 南希把她的车开到一家当地的汽车修理厂检查。

gar·bage /gɑrbɪdʒ/ 1 N-UNCOUNT **Garbage** is waste material, especially waste from a kitchen. (尤指厨房的) 垃圾 [mainly AM] ❑ *This morning a bomb in a garbage bag exploded and injured 15 people.* 今天早上一颗放在垃圾袋中的炸弹爆炸，炸伤15人。 2 N-UNCOUNT If someone says that an idea or opinion is **garbage**, they are emphasizing that they believe it is untrue or unimportant. 废话 [INFORMAL, DISAPPROVAL] ❑ *I personally think this is complete garbage.* 我个人认为这纯属无稽之谈。

→ see **pollution**

> In American English, the words **garbage** and **trash** are most commonly used to refer to waste material that is thrown away. ❑ *...the smell of rotting garbage... She threw the bottle into the trash.* In British English, **rubbish** is the usual word. **Garbage** and **trash** are sometimes used in British English, but only informally and metaphorically. ❑ *I don't have to listen to this garbage... The book was trash.*

Thesaurus *garbage* 另参见：

N.	junk, litter, rubbish, trash 1 foolishness, nonsense 2

gar·bage can (**garbage cans**) N-COUNT A **garbage can** is a container that you put waste material into. 垃圾桶 [AM]

in BRIT, use **dustbin**

❑ *A bomb planted in a garbage can exploded early today.* 一枚安置在一个垃圾桶内的炸弹今天清早爆炸了。

gar·bage dump (**garbage dumps**) N-COUNT A **garbage dump** is a place where waste material is left. 垃圾场 [AM]

in BRIT, use **rubbish tip**

gar·bage truck (**garbage trucks**) N-COUNT A **garbage truck** is a large truck which collects the garbage from outside people's houses. 垃圾车 [AM]

in BRIT, use **dustcart**

gar·bled /gɑrbᵊld/ ADJ A **garbled** message or report contains confused or wrong details, often because it is spoken by someone who is nervous or in a hurry. (信息或报告) 混乱不清的 ❑ *The Coast*

g

Guard needs to decipher garbled messages in a few minutes. 海岸警卫队需要在几分钟内破译含混不清的讯息。

gar·den ♦♦◇ /gɑrdᵊn/ **(gardens, gardening, gardened)** 1 N-COUNT A **garden** is the part of a yard which is used for growing flowers and vegetables. 花园；菜园 ❑ *...the most beautiful garden on Earth.* …地球上最美的花园。 2 V-I If you **garden**, you do work in your garden such as weeding or planting. 干园艺活 ❑ *Jim gardened at the homes of friends on weekends.* 吉姆每逢周末在朋友们的家里干园艺活。 ● **gar·den·ing** N-UNCOUNT 园艺活 ❑ *I have taken up gardening again.* 我又开始干起了园艺活。 3 N-PLURAL **Gardens** are places like a park that have areas of plants, trees, and grass, and that people can visit and walk around. 公园 ❑ *The Gardens are open from 10:30 a.m. until 5:00 p.m.* 这些公园从上午10:30开放到下午5:00。 4 N-IN-NAMES **Gardens** is sometimes used as part of the name of a street. (用作街名) …街 ❑ *He lives at 9 Acacia Gardens.* 他住在金合欢街9号。 5 → see also **yard**

→ see **park**

G

gar·den·er /gɑrdənər/ **(gardeners)** 1 N-COUNT A **gardener** is a person who is paid to work in someone else's garden. 园丁 ❑ *She employed a gardener.* 她雇了一个园丁。 2 N-COUNT A **gardener** is someone who enjoys working in their own garden growing flowers or vegetables. 园艺爱好者 ❑ *The majority of sweet peas are still bred by enthusiastic amateur gardeners.* 大部分甜豌豆仍然是由热衷园艺的业余爱好者培育的。

gar·gle /gɑrgᵊl/ **(gargles, gargling, gargled)** V-I If you **gargle**, you wash your mouth and throat by filling your mouth with a liquid, tipping your head back and using your throat to blow bubbles through the liquid, and finally spitting it out. 漱口 ❑ *Try gargling with salt water as soon as a cough begins.* 咳嗽一开始，就试着用盐水漱口。

gar·ish /gɛərɪʃ/ ADJ You describe something as **garish** when you dislike it because it is very bright in an unattractive, showy way. 过分耀眼的 [DISAPPROVAL] ❑ *They climbed the garish, purple-carpeted stairs.* 他们登上了那些铺着耀眼紫色地毯的楼梯。

gar·land /gɑrlənd/ **(garlands)** N-COUNT A **garland** is a circular decoration made from flowers and leaves. People sometimes wear garlands of flowers on their heads or around their necks. 花环 ❑ *They wore blue silk dresses with cream sashes and garlands of summer flowers in their hair.* 她们穿着配有米色腰带的蓝色丝质连衣裙，头上戴着夏季的花儿编成的花环。

★ **gar·lic** /gɑrlɪk/ N-UNCOUNT **Garlic** is the small, white, round bulb of a plant that is related to the onion plant. Garlic has a very strong smell and taste and is used in cooking. 大蒜 ❑ *...a clove of garlic.* …一瓣大蒜。

→ see **spice**

★ **gar·ment** /gɑrmənt/ **(garments)** N-COUNT A **garment** is a piece of clothing; used especially in contexts where you are talking about the manufacture or sale of clothes. 衣服 (尤用于衣服生产和销售的领域) ❑ *Many of the garments have the customers' name tags sewn into the linings.* 这些衣服中很多都把顾客的姓名牌缝进衬里中。

gar·ner /gɑrnər/ **(garners, garnering, garnered)** V-T If someone **has garnered** something useful or valuable, they have gained it or collected it. 获得；收集 [FORMAL] ❑ *Durham had garnered three times as many votes as Carey.* 德拉姆获得的选票数是凯里的3倍。 ❑ *He has garnered extensive support for his proposals.* 他为他的提议赢得了广泛的支持。

gar·nish /gɑrnɪʃ/ **(garnishes, garnishing, garnished)** 1 N-VAR A **garnish** is a small amount of salad, herbs, or other food that is used to decorate cooked or prepared food. 装饰菜 ❑ *...a garnish of chopped raw onion, tomato, and fresh coriander.* …剁碎的生洋葱、西红柿和新鲜香菜做成的装饰菜。 2 V-T If you **garnish** cooked or prepared food, you decorate it with a garnish. 加饰菜于 ❑ *She had finished the vegetables and was garnishing the roast.* 她已经做好了蔬菜，正给烤肉配饰菜。

▲ **gar·ri·son** /gærɪsᵊn/ **(garrisons, garrisoning, garrisoned)** 1 N-COUNT-COLL A **garrison** is a group of soldiers whose task is to guard the town or building where they live. 卫戍部队 ❑ *...a five-hundred-man French army garrison.* …一支500人的法国卫戍部队。 2 N-COUNT A **garrison** is the buildings which the soldiers live in. 卫戍区 ❑ *The approaches to the garrison have been heavily mined.* 通往卫戍区的路上布满了地雷。 3 V-T To **garrison** a place means to put soldiers there in order to protect it. You can also say that soldiers **are garrisoned** in a place. 派兵驻守 ❑ *American troops still garrisoned the country.* 美军依然驻守这个国家。 ❑ *No other soldiers were garrisoned there.* 那里没有其他的士兵驻守。

gas ♦♦◇ /gæs/ **(gases, gasses, gassing, gassed)**

> The form **gases** is the plural of the noun. The form **gasses** is the third person singular of the verb.

1 N-UNCOUNT **Gas** is a substance like air that is neither liquid nor solid and burns easily. It is used as a fuel for cooking and heating. 煤气 ❑ *Coal is actually cheaper than gas.* 煤炭实际上比煤气便宜。 2 N-VAR A **gas** is any substance that is neither liquid nor solid, for example oxygen or hydrogen. 气体 ❑ *Helium is a very light gas.* 氦是一种很轻的气体。 3 N-MASS **Gas** is a poisonous gas that can be used as a weapon. 毒气 ❑ *The problem was that the exhaust gases contain many toxins.* 问题是废气含有很多毒素。 4 N-UNCOUNT **Gas** is the fuel which is used to drive motor vehicles. 汽油 [AM]

> in BRIT, use **petrol**

❑ *...a tank of gas.* …一桶汽油。 5 V-T To **gas** a person or animal means to kill them by making them breathe poisonous gas. 用毒气杀死 ❑ *Her husband ran a pipe from her car exhaust to the bedroom in an attempt to gas her.* 她丈夫将一根管子从她的汽车排气管导入卧室，试图用毒气杀死她。 6 → see also **gas mask, greenhouse gas, tear gas**

→ see **air, greenhouse effect, matter, solar**

▲ **gash** /gæʃ/ **(gashes, gashing, gashed)** 1 N-COUNT A **gash** is a long, deep cut in your skin or in the surface of something. 深长的切口 ❑ *There was an inch-long gash just above his right eye.* 有一道一英寸长的伤口就在他的右眼上方。 2 V-T If you **gash** something, you accidentally make a long and deep cut in it. 割破 ❑ *He gashed his leg while felling trees.* 他砍树的时候割破了腿。

gas mask **(gas masks)** N-COUNT A **gas mask** is a device that you wear over your face in order to protect yourself from poisonous gases. 防毒面具

gaso·line /gæsəlin/ N-UNCOUNT **Gasoline** is the fuel which is used to drive motor vehicles. 汽油 [AM]

> in BRIT, use **petrol**

→ see **dry-cleaning, oil**

★ **gasp** /gæsp/ **(gasps, gasping, gasped)** 1 N-COUNT A **gasp** is a short, quick breath of air that you take in through your mouth, especially when you are surprised, shocked, or in pain. (尤指惊讶或疼痛时的) 倒吸气 ❑ *An audible gasp went around the court as the jury announced the verdict.* 陪审团宣布判决的时候，法庭上听到倒抽了一口气的声音。 2 V-I When you **gasp**, you take a short, quick breath through your mouth, especially when you are surprised, shocked, or in pain. 倒吸气 ❑ *She gasped for air and drew in a lungful of water.* 她倒吸气，吸了一大口水。 3 PHRASE You describe something as **the last gasp** to emphasize that it is the final part of something or happens at the last possible moment. 最后时刻 [EMPHASIS] ❑ *...the last gasp of a dying system of censorship.* …行将结束的审查制度的最后时刻。

gas sta·tion **(gas stations)** N-COUNT A **gas station** is a place where you can buy fuel for your car. 加油站 [AM]

> in BRIT, use **petrol station**

gas·tric /gæstrɪk/ ADJ You use **gastric** to describe processes, pain, or illnesses that occur in someone's stomach. 胃部的 [ADJ n] [MEDICAL] ❑ *He suffered from diabetes and gastric ulcers.* 他患有糖尿病和胃溃疡。

gate ♦◇◇ /geɪt/ **(gates)** 1 N-COUNT A **gate** is a structure like a door which is used at the entrance to a field, a garden, or the grounds of a building. 大门 ❑ *He opened the gate and started walking up to the house.* 他打开大门并迈步向那房子走去。 2 N-COUNT In an airport, a **gate** is a place where passengers leave the airport and get on their airplane. 登机口 ❑ *Passengers with hand luggage can go straight to the departure gate to check in there.* 携带手提行李的乘客可以直接到登机口办理登机手续。 3 N-UNCOUNT The **gate** is the total amount of money that is paid by the people who go to a sports match or other event. 门票收入

gate·way /geɪtweɪ/ **(gateways)** 1 N-COUNT A **gateway** is an entrance where there is a gate. 大门入口 ❑ *He walked across the park and through a gateway.* 他走过那个公园，并穿过一个大门口。 2 N-COUNT A **gateway to** somewhere is a place which you go through because it leads you to a much larger place. 门户 ❑ *Denver is the gateway to some of the best skiing in the world.* 丹佛是通往世界上一些最好的滑雪场的门户。 3 N-COUNT If something is a **gateway to** a job, career, or other activity, it gives you the opportunity to make progress or get further success in that activity. 途径 ❏ *The prestigious title offered a gateway to success in the highly competitive world of modeling.* 这个有威望的头衔提供了一个在竞争非常激烈的模特圈获得成功的途径。 4 N-COUNT In computing, a **gateway** connects different computer networks so that information can be passed between them. 网关 [COMPUTING] ❏ *The network has a gateway into the hospital mainframe.* 该网络有一个网关连接医院主机。

→ see **Internet**

gath·er ♦♦◇ /gæðər/ (**gathers, gathering, gathered**) 1 V-T/V-I If people **gather** somewhere, or if someone **gathers** people somewhere, they come together in a group. 聚集 ❏ *In the evenings, we gathered around the fireplace and talked.* 晚上，我们聚在壁炉旁聊天。 2 V-T If you **gather** things, you collect them together so that you can use them. 收集 ❏ *I suggest we gather enough firewood to last the night.* 我建议我们捡拾足够的木柴来度过这个夜晚。 ● PHRASAL VERB **Gather up** means the same as **gather**. 收集 ❏ *When Steinberg had gathered up his papers, he went out.* 斯坦伯格收好文件后，走了出去。 3 V-T If you **gather** information or evidence, you collect it, especially over a period of time and after a lot of hard work. 搜集 ❏ *...a private detective using a hidden tape recorder to gather information.* …一名用一部暗藏的磁带录音机来搜集信息的私家侦探。 4 V-T If something **gathers** speed, momentum, or force, it gradually becomes faster or more powerful. 逐渐增加 ❏ *Demands for his dismissal have gathered momentum in recent weeks.* 要求把他免职的呼声最近几周越来越高。 5 V-T When you **gather** something such as your strength, courage, or thoughts, you make an effort to prepare yourself to do something. 积聚 ❏ *You must gather your strength for the journey.* 你必须为此次行程打起精神来。 ● PHRASAL VERB **Gather up** means the same as **gather**. 积聚 ❏ *She was gathering up her courage to approach him when he called to her.* 他喊她的时候，她正鼓起勇气去接近他。 6 V-T You use **gather** in expressions such as **"I gather"** and **"as far as I can gather"** to introduce information that you have found out, especially when you have found it out in an indirect way. 猜想 (用于引出间接得到的信息) ❏ *I gather his report is highly critical of the trial judge.* 我猜想他的报告毫不留情地批判了庭审法官。 ❏ *"He speaks English," she said to Graham. "I gathered that."* "他说英语，"她对格雷厄姆说。"我料到了。" 7 to **gather dust** → see **dust**

▸ **gather up** → see **gather 2, 5**

Thesaurus *gather* 另参见:
v. accumulate, collect, group; (*ant.*) scatter 1–3

gath·er·ing /gæðərɪŋ/ (**gatherings**) 1 N-COUNT A **gathering** is a group of people meeting together for a particular purpose. 聚会 ❏ *...the twenty-second annual gathering of the South Pacific Forum.* …第22届南太平洋论坛年会。 2 ADJ If there is **gathering** darkness, the light is gradually decreasing, usually because it is nearly night. 逐渐 (进入黑夜) 的 [ADJ n] ❏ *The lighthouse beam was quite distinct in the gathering dusk.* 灯塔的光柱在渐暗的黄昏中相当清楚。 3 → see also **gather**

gaudy /gɔdi/ (**gaudier, gaudiest**) ADJ If something is **gaudy**, it is very brightly colored and showy. 花哨的 [DISAPPROVAL] ❏ *...her gaudy orange-and-purple floral hat.* …她那花哨的、桔色紫色相间的花帽子。

★ **gauge** /geɪdʒ/ (**gauges, gauging, gauged**) 1 V-T If you **gauge** the speed or strength of something, or if you gauge an amount, you measure or calculate it, often by using a device of some kind. (常指用仪器) 测量 ❏ *He gauged the wind at over thirty knots.* 他测量出风速为30节以上。 2 N-COUNT A **gauge** is a device that measures the amount or quantity of something and shows the amount measured. 测量仪器 [oft n N] ❏ *...temperature gauges.* …温度计。 3 V-T If you **gauge** people's actions, feelings, or intentions in a particular situation, you carefully consider and judge them. 判定 ❏ *His mood can be gauged by his reaction to the most trivial of incidents.* 他的情绪可以通过他对最琐碎的小事的反应来判定。 4 N-SING A **gauge of** someone's feelings or a situation is a fact or event that can be used to judge them. (评价、判断的) 标准 ❏ *The index is the government's chief gauge of future economic activity.* 这个指数是政府对未来经济活动的主要判断标准。

→ see **scuba diving**

gaunt /gɔnt/ 1 ADJ If someone looks **gaunt**, they look very thin, usually because they have been very ill or worried. 憔悴的 ❏ *Looking gaunt and tired, he denied there was anything to worry about.* 他看上去憔悴而又疲劳，却否认有烦心事。 2 ADJ If you describe a building as **gaunt**, you mean it is very plain and unattractive. (建筑物) 不起眼的 [ADJ n] [LITERARY] ❏ *Above on the hillside was a large, gaunt, gray house.* 山坡上有一座巨大的、不起眼的灰房子。

gaunt·let /gɔntlɪt/ (**gauntlets**) 1 N-COUNT **Gauntlets** are long, thick, protective gloves. 长手套; 防护手套 ❏ *The smart biker also wears boots, gauntlets, and protective clothing.* 聪明的骑车人也穿上长靴、长手套和防护衣。 2 PHRASE If you **pick up the gauntlet** or **take up the gauntlet**, you accept the challenge that someone has made. 接受挑战 ❏ *She picked up the gauntlet in her incisive keynote address to the conference.* 她在其尖锐的大会主题发言中接受挑战。 3 PHRASE If you **run the gauntlet**, you go through an unpleasant experience in which a lot of people criticize or attack you. 受到猛烈攻击 ❏ *The trucks tried to drive to the American base, running the gauntlet of marauding bands of gunmen.* 受到持枪抢劫匪帮猛烈攻击的那些卡车试图开到美军基地。 4 PHRASE If you **throw down the gauntlet to** someone, you say or do something that challenges them to argue or compete with you. 向某人挑战 ❏ *Luxury car firm Jaguar has thrown down the gauntlet to competitors by giving the best guarantee on the market.* 豪华轿车生产商捷豹公司通过提供市场上最佳的保修服务向竞争对手们发出了挑战。

gave /geɪv/ **Gave** is the past tense of **give**. **give**的过去式

gay ♦♦◇ /geɪ/ (**gays**) ADJ A **gay** person is homosexual. 同性恋的 ❏ *The quality of life for gay men has improved over the last two decades.* 男同性恋者的生活质量过去20年有了改善。 ● N-PLURAL **Gays** are homosexual people, especially homosexual men. (尤指男性) 同性恋者 ❏ *More importantly, gays have proved themselves to be style leaders.* 更重要的是，同性恋们证实了他们是时尚的引导者。 ● **gay·ness** N-UNCOUNT 同性恋 ❏ *...Mike's admission of his gayness.* …迈克承认自己是同性恋。

gaze /geɪz/ (**gazes, gazing, gazed**) 1 V-I If you **gaze at** someone or something, you look steadily at them for a long time, for example because you find them attractive or interesting, or because you are thinking about something else. 凝视 ❏ *...gazing at herself in the mirror.* …凝视着镜中的她自己。 ❏ *Sitting in his wicker chair, he gazed reflectively at the fire.* 坐在他的柳条椅中，他若有所思地凝视着火焰。

The verbs **gaze** and **stare** are both used to talk about looking at something for a long time. If you **gaze at** something, it is often because you think it is marvelous or impressive. ❏ *A fresh-faced little girl gazes in wonder at the bright fairground lights.* If you **stare at** something or someone, it is often because you think they are strange or shocking. ❏ *Various families came out and stared at us.*

2 N-COUNT You can talk about someone's **gaze** as a way of describing how they are looking at something, especially when they are looking steadily at it. 凝视 [WRITTEN] ❏ *The Monsignor turned his gaze from the flames to meet the Colonel's.* 这位阁下把他凝视的目光从火焰上移开，与上校的目光相遇。 ❏ *She felt increasingly uncomfortable under the woman's steady gaze.* 她在那女人目不转睛的凝视下感到愈发不舒服。 3 PHRASE If someone or something is **in the public gaze**, they are receiving a lot of attention from the general public. 受公众关注 ❏ *You won't find a couple more in the public gaze than Michael and Lizzie.* 你找不到比迈克尔和莉齐更受公众关注的夫妻了。

ga·zette /gəzɛt/ (**gazettes**) N-IN-NAMES **Gazette** is often used in the names of newspapers. (常用于报纸名) 报 [n N] ❏ *...the Arkansas Gazette.* …阿肯色报。

G.B. /dʒi bi/ N-PROPER **G.B.** is an abbreviation for **Great Britain**. 大不列颠

GDP /dʒi di pi/ (**GDPs**) N-VAR In economics, a country's **GDP** is the total value of goods and services produced within a country in a year, not including its income from investments in other countries. **GDP** is an abbreviation for **gross domestic product**. Compare **GNP**. 国内生产总值

gear ♦◇◇ /gɪər/ (**gears, gearing, geared**) 1 N-COUNT The **gears** on a machine or vehicle are a device for changing the rate at which energy is changed into motion. 排挡 ❏ *On hills, he must use low gears.* 在山上，他必须用低速挡。 ❏ *The car was in fourth gear.* 那辆汽车处于第4挡。 2 N-UNCOUNT The **gear** involved in a particular activity is the equipment or special clothing that you use. (用于特定活动的) 设备、服装 ❏ *About 100 officers in riot gear were needed to break up the fight.* 大约需要100名配备防暴装备的警官来结束那场斗殴。 ❏ *...fishing gear.* …钓鱼用具。 3 N-UNCOUNT **Gear** means clothing. 衣服 [INFORMAL] ❏ *I used to wear trendy gear but it just looked ridiculous.* 我过去常穿时髦服装，但那看起来简直滑稽。 4 V-T PASSIVE If someone or something **is geared to** or **toward** a particular purpose, they are organized or designed in order to achieve that purpose. 使适合 ❑ *Colleges are not always geared to the needs of mature students.* 大学并不总是去适应成年学生的需要。❑ *My training was geared toward winning gold.* 我的训练是为赢得金牌去规划的。

▸ **gear up** PHRASAL VERB If someone **is gearing up for** a particular activity, they are preparing to do it. If they **are geared up to** do a particular activity, they are prepared to do it. 为…准备 ❑ *...another indication that the country is gearing up for an election.* …那个国家正为选举做准备的另一种迹象。

Word Partnership *gear* 的常用搭配：

V. **put** *something* **in** gear, **shift** gear 1
change gear 1 2
ADJ. **protective** gear 2

gear lev·er [BRIT] → see **gearshift**

gear·shift /gɪərʃɪft/ (**gearshifts**) N-COUNT In a vehicle, the **gearshift** is the lever that you use to change gear in a car or other vehicle. 变速杆

gee /dʒiː/ EXCLAM People sometimes say **gee** to emphasize a reaction or remark. (表示一种强烈的反应或意见) 哎呀 [AM, INFORMAL, EMPHASIS] ❑ *Gee, it's hot.* 哇，真热。

geese /giːs/ **Geese** is the plural of **goose**. **goose**的复数形式

gel /dʒɛl/ (**gels, gelling, gelled**)

The spelling **jell** is usually used for meanings 1 and 2.

1 V-RECIP If people **gel with** each other, or if two groups of people **gel**, they work well together because their skills and personalities fit together well. 配合融洽 ❑ *They have gelled very well with the rest of the side.* 他们和那一方的其他人配合得非常融洽。❑ *Their partnership gelled, and scriptwriting for television followed.* 他们的合作融洽，接着又一起为电视剧写剧本。 2 V-I If a vague shape, thought, or creation **gels**, it becomes clearer or more definite. (模糊的形状、思想、创造等) 变得更明确 ❑ *Even if her interpretation has not yet gelled into a satisfying whole, she displays real musicianship.* 尽管她的演绎还没有形成令人满意的整体，但她展现了真正的音乐才能。 3 N-MASS **Gel** is a thick, jelly-like substance, especially one used to keep your hair in a particular style. 凝胶 (尤指发胶)

gem /dʒɛm/ (**gems**) 1 N-COUNT A **gem** is a jewel or stone that is used in jewelry. 宝石 ❑ *The mask is formed of a gold-platinum alloy inset with emeralds and other gems.* 这张面具是由黄金和白金的合金制成，并镶嵌翡翠和其他宝石。 2 N-COUNT If you describe something or someone as a **gem**, you mean that they are especially pleasing, good, or helpful. 珍品 [INFORMAL] ❑ *...a gem of a hotel, Castel Clara.* …卡斯特尔・克拉拉酒店，酒店中的明珠。

gen·der /dʒɛndər/ (**genders**) 1 N-VAR A person's **gender** is the fact that they are male or female. 性别 ❑ *Women are sometimes denied opportunities solely because of their gender.* 女性有时仅仅因为她们的性别而被剥夺机会。 2 N-COUNT You can refer to all male people or all female people as a particular **gender**. 性 ❑ *While her observations may be true about some men, they could hardly apply to the entire gender.* 她的观察对某些男人可能是对的，但并不适用于所有男性。 3 N-VAR In grammar, the **gender** of a noun, pronoun, or adjective is whether it is masculine, feminine, or neuter. A word's gender can affect its form and behavior. In English, only personal pronouns such as "she," reflexive pronouns such as "itself," and possessive determiners such as "his" have gender. (语法上的) 性 ❑ *In both Welsh and Irish the word for "moon" is of feminine gender.* 在威尔士语和爱尔兰语中，"月亮"这个单词都是阴性。

gene ♦◇◇ /dʒiːn/ (**genes**) N-COUNT A **gene** is the part of a cell in a living thing which controls its physical characteristics, growth, and development. 基因 ❑ *The gene for asthma has been identified.* 哮喘病的基因已被识别。
→ see Word Web: **gene**

ge·neal·ogy /dʒiniælədʒi/ N-UNCOUNT **Genealogy** is the study of the history of families, especially through studying historical documents to discover the relationships between particular people and their families. 系谱学 ● **ge·nea·logi·cal** /dʒiniəlɒdʒɪkəl/ ADJ 家谱的 [ADJ n] ❑ *He had engaged in genealogical research on his family shortly before the War.* 就在战争爆发前不久，他从事过对自己家族的家谱研究。

gen·era /dʒɛnərə/ **Genera** is the plural of **genus**. **genus**的复数形式

gen·er·al ♦♦♦ /dʒɛnrəl/ (**generals**) 1 N-COUNT; N-TITLE; N-VOC A **general** is a high-ranking officer in the armed forces, usually in the army. 将军 ❑ *The General's visit to Sarajevo is part of preparations for the deployment of extra troops.* 那位将军对萨拉热窝的访问是为部署更多军队所做的准备工作的一部分。 2 ADJ If you talk about the **general** situation somewhere or talk about something in **general** terms, you are describing the situation as a whole rather than considering its details or exceptions. 大体的 [ADJ n] ❑ *The figures represent a general decline in employment.* 这些数字表明就业率的总体下降。❑ *...a general deterioration in the quality of life.* …生活质量的总体下降。● PHRASE If you describe something **in general terms**, you describe it without giving details. 笼统地说 3 ADJ You use **general** to describe several items or activities when there are too many of them or when they are not important enough to mention separately. 多种的 [ADJ n] ❑ *$2,500 for software is soon swallowed up in general costs.* 用于软件的$2500很快被各种花销耗尽了。 4 ADJ You use **general** to describe something that involves or affects most people, or most people in a particular group. 普遍的 [ADJ n] ❑ *The project should raise general awareness about bullying.* 这个项目应该引起对恃强凌弱现象的普遍注意。 5 ADJ If you describe something as **general**, you mean that it is not restricted to any one thing or area. 整体的 [ADJ n] ❑ *...a general ache radiating from the back of the neck.* …从后颈部扩散开的全身疼痛。❑ *...a general sense of well-being.* 总体上的幸福感 6 ADJ **General** is used to describe a person's job, usually as part of their title, to indicate that they have complete responsibility for the administration of an organization or business. 总管的 [ADJ n] [BUSINESS] ❑ *He joined Sanders Roe, moving on later to become general manager.* 他加入桑德斯雷奥，之后一路升任至总经理。 7 → see also **generally** 8 PHRASE You use **in general** to indicate that you are talking about something as a whole, rather than about part of it. 总体上 ❑ *I think we need to improve our educational system in general.* 我认为我们需要从总体上改进我们的教育体制。 9 PHRASE You say **in general** to indicate that you are referring to most people or things in a particular group. 总的来说 (指某一群体的大多数) ❑ *People in general will support us.* 总体而言，人们会支持我们的。

gen·er·al elec·tion ♦◇◇ (**general elections**) N-COUNT In the United States, a **general election** is a local, state, or national election where the candidates have been selected by a primary election. Compare **primary**. 大选 ❑ *Street raised $10 million during his primary and general election.* 斯特里特在他的初选和大选中筹集了1千万美元。

gen·er·ali·sa·tion /dʒɛnrəlaɪzeɪʃən/ [BRIT] → see **generalization**

★ **gen·er·al·ise** /dʒɛnrəlaɪz/ [BRIT] → see **generalize**

gen·er·al·ised /dʒɛnrəlaɪzd/ [BRIT] → see **generalized**

Word Web gene

Gregor Mendel* studied the **inheritance** of **traits** in plants. He discovered how plants pass on their physical **characteristics** from **generation** to generation. He **bred** and **cross-bred** seven varieties of pea plants. He showed that each new plant was not just a general blend of its parents. Each characteristic (for example, flower color) is inherited separately. Some characteristics are **dominant** and some are recessive. When dominant and recessive **genes** combine, there is a predictable pattern of inheritance. Today we know that genes form long strings called **DNA**.

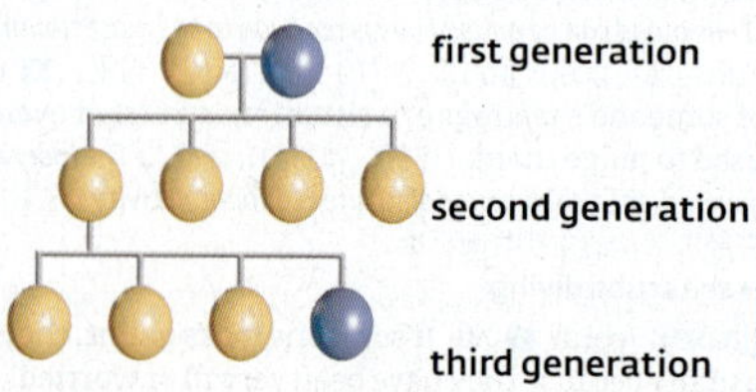

Gregor Mendel (1822-1884): a scientist.

gen·er·ali·za·tion /dʒɛnrəlaɪzeɪʃ°n/ (**generalizations**)
in BRIT, also use **generalisation**
N-VAR A **generalization** is a statement that seems to be true in most situations or for most people, but that may not be completely true in all cases. 概括 ❑ *He is making sweeping generalizations to get his point across.* 他正在进行全盘概括，好让人理解他的观点。

★ **gen·er·al·ize** /dʒɛnrəlaɪz/ (**generalizes, generalizing, generalized**)
in BRIT, also use **generalise**
1 V-I If you **generalize**, you say something that seems to be true in most situations or for most people, but that may not be completely true in all cases. 概括 ❑ *Critics love to generalize, to formulate trends into which all new work must be fitted, however contradictory.* 评论家喜欢概括，归纳出所有新作品都必须符合的趋势，不管它们是如何地不符。 2 V-T If you **generalize** something such as an idea, you apply it more widely than its original context, as if it was true in many other situations. 普及 ❑ *A child first labels the household pet cat as a "cat" and then generalizes this label to other animals that look like it.* 孩子先把家养的宠物猫称为"猫"，然后把这个称呼扩大到其他看起来像猫的动物。

gen·er·al·ized /dʒɛnrəlaɪzd/
in BRIT, also use **generalised**
1 ADJ **Generalized** means involving many different things, rather than one or two specific things. 广泛的 ❑ *...a generalized discussion about admirable singers.* …一场关于出色歌手的广泛讨论。 2 ADJ You use **generalized** to describe medical conditions or problems which affect the whole of someone's body, or the whole of a part of their body. 全身性的 [MEDICAL] ❑ *She experienced an increase in generalized aches and pains.* 她感受到了一种逐渐加剧的全身性疼痛。

gen·er·al knowl·edge N-UNCOUNT **General knowledge** is knowledge about many different things, as opposed to detailed knowledge about one particular subject. 常识 ❑ *...a general-knowledge quiz show.* …一个常识问答节目。

gen·er·al·ly ♦♦◇ /dʒɛnrəli/ 1 ADV You use **generally** to give a summary of a situation, activity, or idea without referring to the particular details of it. 笼统地 ❑ *University teachers generally have admitted a lack of enthusiasm about their subjects.* 大学教师们已大致承认对他们的学科缺乏热情。 2 ADV You use **generally** to say that something happens or is used on most occasions but not on every occasion. 通常地 ❑ *As women we generally say and feel too much about these things.* 作为女人，我们通常对这些事说得、感受得太多了。 ❑ *In the diet, it is generally true that the darker the fruit the higher its iron content.* 在饮食中，水果颜色越深，其铁含量就越高，这通常是正确的。

Thesaurus *generally* 另参见：
ADV. commonly, mainly, usually 2

gen·er·al prac·ti·tion·er (**general practitioners**) N-COUNT A **general practitioner** is the same as a **GP**. 全科医师 [FORMAL]

gen·er·al pub·lic N-SING-COLL You can refer to the people in a society as **the general public**, especially when you are contrasting people in general with a small group. 公众 ❑ *These charities depend on the compassionate feelings and generosity of the general public.* 这些慈善机构依赖于公众的同情和慷慨。

gen·er·al strike (**general strikes**) N-COUNT A **general strike** is a situation where most or all of the workers in a country are on strike and are refusing to work. 总罢工

gen·er·ate ♦◇◇ /dʒɛnəreɪt/ (**generates, generating, generated**) 1 V-T To **generate** something means to cause it to begin and develop. 造成 ❑ *The labor secretary said the reforms would generate new jobs.* 劳动部长说这些改革将带来新的工作。 2 V-T To **generate** a form of energy or power means to produce it. 产生（电等能量）❑ *The company, New England Electric, burns coal to generate power.* 新英格兰电力公司燃烧煤来发电。
→ see **energy**

gen·era·tion ♦♦◇ /dʒɛnəreɪʃ°n/ (**generations**) 1 N-COUNT A **generation** is all the people in a group or country who are of a similar age, especially when they are considered as having the same experiences or attitudes. 一代人 ❑ *...the younger generation of party members.* …较年轻一代的党员。 2 N-COUNT A **generation** is the period of time, usually considered to be about thirty years, that it takes for children to grow up and become adults and have children of their own. 代（通常约为三十年）❑ *Within a generation, flight has become the method used by many travelers.* 在不到一代的时间里，飞行已成为许多旅行者的出行方式。 3 N-COUNT You can use **generation** to refer to a stage of development in the design and manufacture of machines or equipment. （机械、设备的设计和制造的）一代 [N "of" n] ❑ *...a new generation of Apple computers.* …新一代苹果电脑。 4 ADJ **Generation** is used to indicate how long members of your family have had a particular nationality. For example, second generation means that you were born in the country you live in, but your parents were not. （指家庭成员拥有某国国籍的时间）代 [ord ADJ n] ❑ *...second-generation Jamaicans in New York.* …在纽约的第二代牙买加人。
→ see **gene**

gen·era·tor /dʒɛnəreɪtər/ (**generators**) 1 N-COUNT A **generator** is a machine which produces electricity. 发电机 ❑ *The house is far from water mains and electricity and relies on its own generators.* 这座房子远离自来水总管和供电网，依靠自备的发电机。 2 N-COUNT A **generator of** something is a person, organization, product, or situation which produces it or causes it to happen. 促使…发生的人或事物 ❑ *The company has been a very good cash generator.* 这家公司是台非常出色的赚钱机器。
→ see **electricity**

g

ge·ner·ic /dʒɪnɛrɪk/ (**generics**) 1 ADJ You use **generic** to describe something that refers or relates to a whole class of similar things. 通用的 ❑ *Parmesan is a generic term used to describe a family of hard Italian cheeses.* 巴尔马干酪是一个用来描述一类坚硬的意大利奶酪的通用名称。 2 ADJ A **generic** drug or other product is one that does not have a trademark and that is known by a general name, rather than the manufacturer's name. 非注册商标的（药等产品）❑ *Doctors sometimes prescribe cheaper generic drugs instead of more expensive brand names.* 医生有时开比较便宜的非注册商标的药品，而不开比较昂贵的品牌药。 ● N-COUNT **Generic** is also a noun. 非注册商标的药品 ❑ *The program saved $11 million in 1988 by substituting generics for brand-name drugs.* 这项计划以未注册商标的药品取代品牌药，在1988年节省了1100万美元。

★ **gen·er·os·ity** /dʒɛnərɒsɪti/ N-UNCOUNT If you refer to someone's **generosity**, you mean that they are generous, especially in doing or giving more than is usual or expected. 慷慨 ❑ *There are stories about his generosity, the massive amounts of money he gave to charities.* 关于他的慷慨有些传闻，说他向慈善机构捐献巨款。

gen·er·ous ♦◇◇ /dʒɛnərəs/ 1 ADJ A **generous** person gives more of something, especially money, than is usual or expected. 慷慨的 ❑ *Dietler is generous with his time and money.* 迪特勒在他的时间和金钱方面慷慨大方。 ● **gen·er·ous·ly** ADV 慷慨地 [ADV with v] ❑ *We would like to thank all the judges who gave so generously of their time.* 我们想感谢所有慷慨地付出时间的裁判们。 2 ADJ A **generous** person is friendly, helpful, and willing to see the good qualities in someone or something. 宽厚的 ❑ *He was always generous in sharing his enormous knowledge.* 他一直不吝分享自己丰富的知识。 ● **gen·er·ous·ly** ADV 宽厚地 [ADV with v] ❑ *The students generously gave them instruction in social responsibility.* 学生们欣然为他们讲解了社会责任。 3 ADJ A **generous** amount of something is much larger than is usual or necessary. 大量的 ❑ *He should be able to keep his room tidy with the generous amount of storage space.* 有大量的储物空间，他应该可以保持他房间的整洁。 ● **gen·er·ous·ly** ADV 大量地 ❑ *Season the steaks generously with salt and pepper.* 大量地使用盐和胡椒给牛排调味。

Thesaurus *generous* 另参见：
ADJ. charitable, kind, unselfish; *(ant.)* mean, selfish, stingy 1 2
abundant, overflowing; *(ant.)* meager 3

ge·net·ic /dʒɪnɛtɪk/ ADJ You use **genetic** to describe something that is concerned with genetics or with genes. 遗传的 ❑ *Cystic fibrosis is the most common fatal genetic disease in the United States.* 囊肿性纤维化在美国是最常见的致命性遗传疾病。 ● **ge·neti·cal·ly** /dʒɪnɛtɪkli/ ADV 遗传地 ❑ *Some people are genetically predisposed to diabetes.* 有些人因遗传因素而易患糖尿病。

ge·neti·cal·ly modi·fied ADJ **Genetically modified** plants and animals have had one or more genes changed, for example so that they resist pests and diseases better. **Genetically modified** food contains ingredients made from genetically modified plants or animals. The abbreviation **GM** is often used. 转基因的 ❑ *Top supermarkets are to ban many genetically modified foods.* 顶级的超市将禁止销售许多转基因的食品。

Word Web genre

Each of the arts includes a variety of types called **genre**. The four basic types of **literature** are **fiction**, nonfiction, **poetry**, and **drama**. In painting, some of the special areas are **realism**, expressionism, and Cubism. In music, they include **classical**, **jazz**, and **popular** forms. Each genre contains several subdivisions. For example, popular music takes in country and western, **rap music**, and **rock**. Modern movie-making has produced a wide variety of genres. These include **horror films**, **comedies**, **action movies**, film noir, and **westerns**. Some artists don't like working within just one genre.

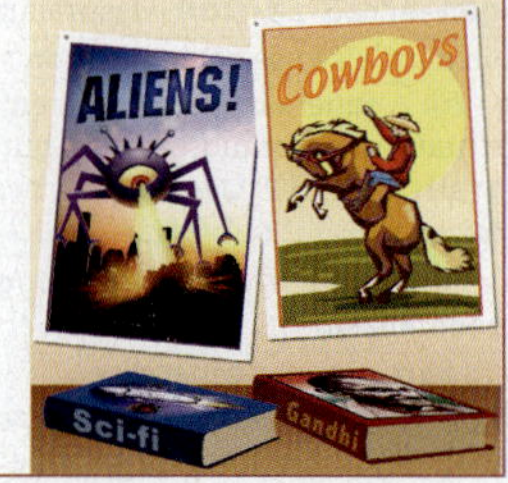

G

ge·net·ic en·gi·neer·ing N-UNCOUNT **Genetic engineering** is the science or activity of changing the genetic structure of an animal, plant, or other organism in order to make it stronger or more suitable for a particular purpose. 基因工程; 基因工程学 ❑ *Scientists have used genetic engineering to protect tomatoes against the effects of freezing.* 科学家们已利用基因工程来保护番茄不受严寒的影响。 → see **clone**

ge·neti·cist /dʒɪnɛtɪsɪst/ (**geneticists**) N-COUNT A **geneticist** is a person who studies or specializes in genetics. 基因学家

ge·net·ics /dʒɪnɛtɪks/ N-UNCOUNT **Genetics** is the study of heredity and how qualities and characteristics are passed on from one generation to another by means of genes. 遗传学 ❑ *Genetics is also bringing about dramatic changes in our understanding of cancer.* 遗传学也正使我们对癌症的理解发生巨大的变化。

gen·ial /dʒinyəl/ ADJ Someone who is **genial** is kind and friendly. 友善的 [APPROVAL] ❑ *Bob was always genial and welcoming.* 鲍勃总是和善友好。 ● **gen·ial·ly** ADV 友善地 ❑ *"If you don't mind," Mrs. Dambar said genially.* "如果你不介意的话，"达姆巴夫人友善地说。 ● **ge·ni·al·ity** /dʒiniælɪti/ N-UNCOUNT 友善 ❑ *He soon recovered his habitual geniality.* 他很快恢复了他惯常的友善。

geni·tal /dʒɛnɪtᵊl/ (**genitals**) **1** N-PLURAL Someone's **genitals** are their external sexual organs. 外生殖器 ❑ *Without thinking, Neil cupped his hands over his genitals.* 尼尔想都没想就用手捂住了他的外生殖器。 **2** ADJ **Genital** means relating to a person's external sexual organs. 外生殖器的 [ADJ n] ❑ *Wear loose clothing in the genital area.* 在外生殖器部位的衣服要宽松些。

ge·ni·us /dʒinyəs/ (**geniuses**) **1** N-UNCOUNT **Genius** is very great ability or skill in a particular subject or activity. 天赋 ❑ *This is the mark of her real genius as a designer.* 这是她作为一名设计师的真正天赋的标志。 ❑ *The man had genius and had made his mark in the aviation world.* 那位男士拥有天赋，而且在航空界已经成名。 **2** N-COUNT A **genius** is a highly talented, creative, or intelligent person. 天才 ❑ *Chaplin was not just a genius, he was among the most influential figures in film history.* 卓别林不仅是个天才，还是电影史上最有影响的人物之一。

Word Link *cide ≈ killing : genocide, homicide, pesticide*

geno·cide /dʒɛnəsaɪd/ N-UNCOUNT **Genocide** is the deliberate murder of a whole community or race. 大屠杀; 种族灭绝 ❑ *They have alleged that acts of genocide and torture were carried out.* 他们声称实施了大屠杀和酷刑。

▲ **gen·re** /ʒɒnrə/ (**genres**) N-COUNT A **genre** is a particular type of literature, painting, music, film, or other art form which people consider as a class because it has special characteristics. (文学、绘画、音乐、电影等艺术作品的) 体裁 [FORMAL] ❑ *...his love of films and novels in the horror genre.* …他对恐怖体裁电影和小说的热爱。 → see Word Web: **genre** → see **fantasy**

gent /dʒɛnt/ (**gents**) **1** N-COUNT **Gent** is an informal and old-fashioned word for **gentleman**. **gentleman**的非正式、旧式用法 ❑ *Mr. Blake was a gent. He knew how to behave.* 布莱克先生是位绅士，他知道该怎样行事。 **2** N-VOC **Gents** is used when addressing men in an informal, humorous way, especially in the expression "ladies and gents." 先生们 (非正式、诙谐用法，尤用于"**ladies and gents**.") [HUMOROUS, INFORMAL] ❑ *Don't be left standing, ladies and gents, while a bargain slips past your eyes.* 别光站着，女士们先生们，价廉的商品就要从你们眼皮底下溜走喽。

gen·teel /dʒɛntil/ **1** ADJ A **genteel** person is respectable and well-mannered, and comes or seems to come from a high social class. 有教养的 ❑ *It was a place to which genteel families came in search of health and quiet.* 这是一个上流社会家庭寻找健康和宁静的场所。 **2** ADJ A **genteel** place or area is quiet and traditional, but may also be old-fashioned and dull. 安宁而古朴的 ❑ *...the genteel towns of Winchester and Chichester.* …安宁而古朴的温切斯特和奇切斯特城。

gen·tle ♦◇◇ /dʒɛntᵊl/ (**gentler, gentlest**) **1** ADJ Someone who is **gentle** is kind, mild, and calm. 温和的 ❑ *My son was a quiet and gentle man who liked sports and enjoyed life.* 我儿子是个安静温和的男人，他喜欢运动和享受生活。 ● **gen·tly** ADV 温和地 [ADV with v] ❑ *She smiled gently at him.* 她温柔地对他微笑。 ● **gen·tle·ness** N-UNCOUNT 温和 ❑ *...the gentleness with which she treated her pregnant mother.* …她对她怀孕的母亲的温柔体贴。 **2** ADJ **Gentle** actions or movements are performed in a calm and controlled manner, with little force. (动作) 轻柔的 ❑ *...a gentle game of tennis.* …一场不很激烈的网球比赛。 ● **gen·tly** ADV 轻柔地 ❑ *Patrick took her gently by the arm and led her to a chair.* 帕特里克轻轻地扶着她的手臂，引她落座。 **3** ADJ A **gentle** slope or curve is not steep or severe. 平缓的 (斜坡或弯道) ❑ *...gentle, rolling meadows.* …平缓、起伏的草地。 ● **gen·tly** ADV 平缓地 ❑ *With its gently rolling hills it looks like Tuscany.* 它拥有平缓起伏的山丘，看起来像托斯卡纳。 **4** ADJ A **gentle** heat is a fairly low heat. 微热的 ❑ *Cook for 30 minutes over a gentle heat.* 用文火烹饪30分钟。 ● **gen·tly** ADV 微热地 [ADV with v] ❑ *Add the onion and cook gently for about 5 minutes.* 加入洋葱，文火烹饪5分钟左右。

gentle·man ♦◇◇ /dʒɛntᵊlmən/ (**gentlemen**) **1** N-COUNT If you say that a man is a **gentleman**, you mean he is polite and educated, and can be trusted. 有教养的人 ❑ *He was always such a gentleman.* 他总是这样一个彬彬有礼的人。 **2** N-COUNT A **gentleman** is a man who comes from a family of high social standing. 绅士 ❑ *...this wonderful portrait of English gentleman Joseph Greenway.* …这幅英国绅士约瑟夫·格林韦的绝妙肖像画。 **3** N-COUNT; N-VOC You can address men as **gentlemen**, or refer politely to them as **gentlemen**. 先生 (一种对人礼貌的称呼) [POLITENESS] ❑ *This way, please, ladies and gentlemen.* 请这边走，女士们先生们。 ❑ *It seems this gentleman was waiting for the doctor.* 这位先生似乎那时正在等医生。

genu·ine ♦◇◇ /dʒɛnyuɪn/ **1** ADJ **Genuine** is used to describe people and things that are exactly what they appear to be, and are not false or an imitation. 真正的 ❑ *There was a risk of genuine refugees being returned to Vietnam.* 有把真正的难民遣送回越南的风险。 ❑ *...genuine leather.* …真皮。 **2** ADJ **Genuine** refers to things such as emotions that are real and not pretended. 真诚的 ❑ *If this offer is genuine, I will gladly accept it.* 如果这份帮助是真诚的，我将愉快地接受它。 ● **genu·ine·ly** ADV 真诚地 ❑ *He was genuinely surprised.* 他真得吃了一惊。 **3** ADJ If you describe a person as **genuine**, you approve of them because they are honest, truthful, and sincere in the way they live and in their relationships with other people. 诚实可靠的 [APPROVAL] ❑ *She is very caring and very genuine.* 她很有同情心，也非常诚实可靠。

Thesaurus *genuine* 另参见:

ADJ. actual, original, real, true, valid; (*ant.*) bogus, fake **1** **2**
honest, open, sincere, true; (*ant.*) dishonest, insincere **3**

ge·nus /dʒinəs/ (**genera** /dʒɛnərə/) N-COUNT A **genus** is a class of similar things, especially a group of animals or plants that includes several closely related species. (尤指动植物的) 属 [TECHNICAL] ❑ *...a genus of plants called Sinningia.* …大岩桐属植物。

geo·graphi·cal /dʒiəgræfɪkᵊl/

The form **geographic** /dʒi̲əgræfɪk/ is also used.

ADJ **Geographical** or **geographic** means concerned with or relating to geography. 地理的 ❑ *Its geographical location stimulated overseas mercantile enterprise.* 它的地理位置激发了海外商业企业的兴趣。 ● **geo·graphi·cal·ly** /dʒiəgræfɪkli/ ADV 在地理上 ❑ *It is geographically more diverse than any other continent.* 它在地理上比其他任何大陆都更具多样性。

ge·og·ra·phy /dʒiɒgrəfi/ **1** N-UNCOUNT **Geography** is the study of the countries of the world and of such things as the land, seas, climate, towns, and population. 地理学 **2** N-UNCOUNT The **geography** of a place is the way that features such as rivers, mountains, towns, or streets are arranged within it. 地形 ❑ *...policemen who knew the local geography.* …了解当地地形的警察们。

geo·logi·cal /dʒiəlɒdʒɪkᵊl/ ADJ **Geological** means relating to geology. 地质的 ❑ *With geological maps, books, and atlases you can find out all the proven sites of precious minerals.* 有了地质地图、书籍和地图册，你就可以找到所有已探明的珍贵矿藏的位置。

Word Link *logy, ology ≈ study of : anthropology, biology, geology*

★ **ge·ol·ogy** /dʒiɒlədʒi/ **1** N-UNCOUNT **Geology** is the study of the Earth's structure, surface, and origins. 地质学 ❑ *He was visiting professor of geology at the University of Georgia.* 他曾是佐治亚大学的地质学客座教授。 ● **ge·olo·gist** N-COUNT (**geologists**) 地质学家 ❑ *Geologists have studied the way that heat flows from the earth.* 地质学家们已经研究了热量从地表流出的方式。 **2** N-UNCOUNT The **geology** of an area is the structure of its land, together with the types of rocks and minerals that exist within it. 地质状况 ❑ *...the geology of Asia.* …亚洲的地质状况。

geo·met·ric /dʒiəmɛtrɪk/

The form **geometrical** /dʒiəmɛtrɪkᵊl/ is also used.

1 ADJ **Geometric** or **geometrical** patterns or shapes consist of regular shapes or lines. 几何图形的 ❑ *Geometric designs were popular wall decorations in the 14th century.* 几何图案是14世纪流行的墙面装饰。 **2** ADJ **Geometric** or **geometrical** means relating to or involving the principles of geometry. 几何学的 ❑ *Euclid was trying to convey his idea of a geometrical point.* 欧几里德正试图表达他的一个几何学观点。

ge·om·etry /dʒiɒmɪtri/ **1** N-UNCOUNT **Geometry** is the branch of mathematics concerned with the properties and relationships of lines, angles, curves, and shapes. 几何学 ❑ *...the very ordered way in which mathematics and geometry describe nature.* …数学和几何学描述自然的条理性。 **2** N-UNCOUNT The **geometry** of an object is its shape or the relationship of its parts to each other. 几何图形；几何结构 ❑ *...the geometry of the curved roof.* …几何图形的弧形房顶。
→ see **mathematics**

Geor·gian /dʒɔrdʒᵊn/ ADJ **Georgian** means belonging to or connected with Britain in the eighteenth and early nineteenth centuries, during the reigns of King George I to King George IV. 乔治王朝时期的；(英国18至19世纪早期) 乔治一世至四世时代的 ❑ *...the restoration of his Georgian house.* …对他乔治王朝时期房屋的修复。

Word Link *iatr ≈ healing : geriatric, pediatrics, psychiatrist*

geri·at·ric /dʒɛriætrɪk/ (**geriatrics**) **1** ADJ **Geriatric** is used to describe things relating to the illnesses and medical care of old people. 老年医学的 [ADJ n] [MEDICAL] ❑ *There is a question mark over the future of geriatric care.* 老年保健医学的未来是一个问号。 **2** N-COUNT If you describe someone as a **geriatric**, you are implying that they are old and that their mental or physical condition is poor. This use could cause offense. 老家伙 (有冒犯之嫌) [DISAPPROVAL] ❑ *He will complain about having to spend time with such a boring bunch of geriatrics.* 他会抱怨不得不花费时间跟这么一帮乏味的老家伙在一起。

germ /dʒɜrm/ (**germs**) **1** N-COUNT A **germ** is a very small organism that causes disease. 病菌 ❑ *Chlorine is widely used to kill germs.* 氯广泛用于杀菌。 **2** N-SING The **germ of** something such as an idea is something which developed or might develop into that thing. (思想等的) 萌芽 ❑ *This was the germ of a book.* 这是一本书的创作萌芽。
→ see **medicine, spice**

ger·mi·nate /dʒɜrmɪneɪt/ (**germinates, germinating, germinated**) **1** V-T/V-I If a seed **germinates** or if it **is germinated**, it starts to grow. 使发芽；发芽 ❑ *Some seed varieties germinate fast, so check every day or so.* 有一些品种的种子发芽快，所以差不多每天都要察看一下。 ● **ger·mi·na·tion** /dʒɜrmɪneɪʃᵊn/ N-UNCOUNT 发芽 [usu with supp] ❑ *The poor germination of your seed could be because the soil was too cold.* 你的种子发芽不好，可能是因为土壤太冷。 **2** V-I If an idea, plan, or feeling **germinates**, it comes into existence and begins to develop. 形成 ❑ *...a big book that was germinating in his mind.* …正在他脑中酝酿的一部大作。
→ see **tree**

ger·und /dʒɛrʌnd/ (**gerunds**) N-COUNT A **gerund** is a noun formed from a verb which refers to an action, process, or state. In English, gerunds end in "-ing," for example "running" and "thinking." 动名词

ges·ture ♦◇◇ /dʒɛstʃər/ (**gestures, gesturing, gestured**) **1** N-COUNT A **gesture** is a movement that you make with a part of your body, especially your hands, to express emotion or information. 手势 ❑ *Sarah made a menacing gesture with her fist.* 萨拉用拳头做了个威胁的手势。 **2** N-COUNT A **gesture** is something that you say or do in order to express your attitude or intentions, often something that you know will not have much effect. 姿态；表示 ❑ *He questioned the government's commitment to peace and called on it to make a gesture of good will.* 他质疑政府的和平承诺，并呼吁其摆出善意姿态。 **3** V-I If you **gesture**, you use movements of your hands or head in order to tell someone something or draw their attention to something. 打手势；用动作示意 ❑ *I gestured toward the boathouse, and he looked inside.* 我朝停船小屋打手势，他在里面看了看。

get
❶ CHANGING, CAUSING, MOVING, OR REACHING
❷ OBTAINING, RECEIVING, OR CATCHING
❸ PHRASES AND PHRASAL VERBS

❶ **get** ♦♦♦ /gɛt/ (**gets, getting, got, gotten** or **got**)

In most of its uses **get** is a fairly informal word.

1 V-LINK You use **get** with adjectives to mean "become." For example, if someone **gets cold**, they become cold, and if they **get angry**, they become angry. (与形容词连用) 变得 ❑ *The boys were getting bored.* 男孩子们渐渐变得厌烦起来。 ❑ *From here on, it can only get better.* 从现在开始，情况只会变得更好。 **2** V-LINK **Get** is used with expressions referring to states or situations. For example, to **get into trouble** means to start being in trouble. 处于 ❑ *Half the pleasure of an evening out is getting ready.* 晚上外出的乐趣一半在于出门前的准备。 ❑ *Perhaps I shouldn't say that – I might get into trouble.* 也许我不该说那些——我可能会遇到麻烦。 **3** V-T To **get** someone or something into a particular state or situation means to cause them to be in it. 使…处于 ❑ *I don't know if I can get it clean.* 我不知道我能否把它清理干净。 ❑ *Brian will get them out of trouble.* 布赖恩会使他们摆脱困境。 **4** V-T If you **get** someone **to** do something, you cause them to do it by asking, persuading, or telling them to do it. 使 (某人做某事) ❑ *...a long campaign to get U.S. politicians to take the AIDS epidemic more seriously.* …一项长期运动，旨在使美国政界人士更严肃地对待艾滋病流行。 **5** V-T If you **get** something done, you cause it to be done. 使…做好 ❑ *I might benefit from getting my teeth fixed.* 把牙齿补好可能对我有好处。 **6** V-I To **get** somewhere means to move there. 移动 ❑ *I got off the bed and opened the door.* 我下床并开了门。 ❑ *How can I get past her without her seeing me?* 我怎样才能从她旁边经过而不让她看见我呢？ **7** V-I When you **get** to a place, you arrive there. 到达 ❑ *Generally I get to work at 9:30 a.m.* 我通常上午9:30上班。 **8** V-T To **get** something or someone into a place or position means to cause them to move there. 使移动到 ❑ *Mack got his wallet out.* 麦克掏出了钱包。 ❑ *Go and get your coat on.* 去把你的外套穿上。 **9** AUX **Get** is often used in place of "be" as an auxiliary verb to form passives. 常用作助动词，替代**be**构成被动语态 ❑ *A pane of glass got broken.* 一块玻璃被打碎了。 **10** V-T If you **get to** do something, you eventually or gradually reach a stage at which you do it. 最终或逐步达到 (某个阶段) ❑ *No one could figure out how he got to be so wealthy.* 没人能弄清楚他是怎样变得如此富有的。 **11** V-T If you **get to** do something, you manage to do it or have the opportunity to do it. 设法做；有机会做 ❑ *How do these people get to be the bosses of major companies?* 这些人是怎么得以成为大公司的老总的？ ❑ *Do you get to see him often?* 你能经常见到他吗？ **12** V-T You can use **get** in expressions like **get moving**, **get going**, and **get working** when you want to tell people to begin moving, going, or working quickly. 迅速开始做 ❑ *I aim to be at the lake before dawn, so let's get moving.* 我打算天亮之前到湖边，所以我们马上就动身吧。 **13** V-I If you **get to** a particular stage in your life or in something you are doing, you reach that stage. 到达 (人生等的某一阶段) ❑ *We haven't gotten to the stage of a full-scale military conflict.* 我们还没有到达全面军事冲突的阶段。 ❑ *It got to the point where I was so ill I was waiting to die.* 我已病入膏肓，到了等死的阶段。 **14** V-T/V-I You can use **get** to talk about the progress that you are making. For example, if you say that you **are getting somewhere**, you mean that you are making progress, and if you say that something

won't get you **anywhere**, you mean it will not help you to progress at all. 取得进展 ❑ *Radical factions say the talks are getting nowhere and they want to withdraw.* 激进派们说会谈没有什么进展，他们要退出。 ❑ *This bout of self-pity was getting me nowhere.* 这一阵自哀自怜对我不会有什么好处。 15 V-LINK When **it gets to be** a particular time, it is that time. If **it is getting toward** a particular time, it is approaching that time. 到/接近（…时间） ❑ *It got to be after 1 a.m. and I was exhausted.* 已到了凌晨一点多，我已筋疲力尽了。 ❑ *It was getting toward evening when we got back.* 我们回来时已将近傍晚。 16 V-I If something that has continued for some time **gets to** you, it starts causing you to suffer. 使痛苦 ❑ *That's the first time I lost my cool in 20 years in this job. This whole thing's getting to me.* 那是我干这份工作20年来头一次失去冷静。这整件事让我痛苦不堪。

❷ get ♦♦♦ /gɛt/ (**gets, getting, got, gotten** or **got**) 1 V-T If you **get** something that you want or need, you obtain it. 得到 ❑ *I got a job at the sawmill.* 我在锯木厂找到了一份工作。 2 V-T If you **get** something, you receive it or are given it. 收到 ❑ *I'm getting a bike for my birthday.* 我过生日时会得到一辆自行车。 ❑ *He gets a lot of letters from women.* 他收到很多女人的来信。 3 V-T If you **get** someone or something, you go and bring them to a particular place. 去拿来 ❑ *I came down this morning to get the newspaper.* 我今天上午下来拿了报纸。 ❑ *Go and get me a large brandy.* 去给我拿一大杯白兰地来。 4 V-T If you **get** a particular result, you obtain it from some action that you take, or from a calculation or experiment. 得出 ❑ *What do you get if you multiply six by nine?* 6乘9得几？ 5 V-T If you **get** a particular price **for** something that you sell, you obtain that amount of money by selling it. 卖得 ❑ *He can't get a good price for his crops.* 他不能把庄稼卖个好价钱。 6 V-T If you **get** the time or opportunity to do something, you have the time or opportunity to do it. 有（做…的时间或机会） ❑ *You get time to think in prison.* 你在狱中有时间思考。 7 V-T If you **get** an idea, impression, or feeling, you begin to have that idea, impression, or feeling as you learn or understand more about something. 开始有（想法、印象或感受） ❑ *I get the feeling that you're an honest man.* 我开始觉得你是个诚实的男人了。 8 V-T If you **get** a feeling or benefit from an activity or experience, the activity or experience gives you that feeling or benefit. 获得（感受或好处） ❑ *Charles got a shock when he saw him.* 查尔斯看到他时大吃一惊。 ❑ *She gets enormous pleasure out of working freelance.* 她从事自由职业感受到极大的乐趣。 9 V-T If you **get** a look, view, or glimpse of something, you manage to see it. 看到 ❑ *Young men climbed on buses and fences to get a better view.* 年轻人纷纷爬上公共汽车顶和围墙想看得更清楚些。 10 V-T If you **get** a joke or **get** the point of something that is said, you understand it. 理解 ❑ *Did you get that joke, Ann? I'll explain later.* 安，你听懂了那个笑话吗？我以后会解释的。 11 V-T If you **get** an illness or disease, you become ill with it. 患（病） ❑ *When I was five I got measles.* 我5岁时患过麻疹。 12 V-T When you **get** a train, bus, plane, or boat, you leave a place on a particular train, bus, plane, or boat. 乘坐 ❑ *It'll be a dollar to get the bus.* 乘坐公共汽车要一美元。 13 → see also **got**

Thesaurus	*get* 另参见：
v.	become ❶ 1
	bring, collect, pick up ❷ 3
	know, sense ❷ 7

❸ get ♦♦♦ /gɛt/ (**gets, getting, got, gotten** or **got**) 1 PHRASE You can say that something is, for example, **as good as you can get** to mean that it is as good as it is possible for that thing to be. …极了 ❑ *Consort has a population of 714 and is about as rural and isolated as you can get.* 康索特有居民714人，地处农村，极其偏远。 ❑ *…the diet that is as near to perfect as you can get it.* …近乎完美的饮食。 2 PHRASE If you say **you can't get away from** something or **there is no getting away from** something, you are emphasizing that it is true, even though people might prefer it not to be true. 无法否认 [INFORMAL, EMPHASIS] ❑ *There is no getting away from the fact that he is on the left of the party.* 无法否认他是该党左派的事实。 3 PHRASE If you **get away from it all**, you have a holiday in a place that is very different from where you normally live and work. 外出度假以换换环境 ❑ *…the ravishing island of Ischia, where rich Italians get away from it all.* …令人陶醉的伊斯基亚岛，有钱意大利人的消遣度假之地。 4 PHRASE You can use **you get** instead of "there is" or "there are" to say that something exists, happens, or can be experienced. 有 [SPOKEN] ❑ *That's where you get some differences of opinion.* 那是你们的观点分歧所在。

▶ **get across** PHRASAL VERB When an idea **gets across** or when you **get** it **across**, you succeed in making other people understand it. 被理解；把…讲清楚 ❑ *Officers felt their point of view was not getting across to the generals.* 军官们觉得将军们还没有理解他们的观点。

▶ **get along** PHRASAL VERB If you **get along with** someone, you have a friendly relationship with them. You can also say that two people **get along**. 与…和睦相处 ❑ *It's impossible to get along with him.* 不可能跟他和睦相处。

▶ **get around** 1 PHRASAL VERB To **get around** a problem or difficulty means to overcome it. 解决 ❑ *None of these countries has found a way yet to get around the problem of the polarization of wealth.* 这些国家均未找到一个方案来解决贫富两极分化的问题。 2 PHRASAL VERB If you **get around** a rule or law, you find a way of doing something that the rule or law is intended to prevent, without actually breaking it. 避开（规章或法律） ❑ *Although tobacco ads are prohibited, companies get around the ban by sponsoring music shows.* 虽然烟草广告是被禁止的，但各家公司却通过赞助音乐演出以避开这一禁令。 3 PHRASAL VERB If news **gets around**, it becomes well known as a result of being told to lots of people. （消息）传开 ❑ *They threw him out because word got around that he was taking drugs.* 他们解雇了他，因为有传言说他在吸毒。 4 PHRASAL VERB If you **get around** someone, you persuade them to allow you to do or have something by pleasing them or flattering them. （通过取悦或谄媚）说服 ❑ *Max could always get around her.* 麦克斯总能说服她。 5 PHRASAL VERB If you **get around**, you visit a lot of different places as part of your way of life. 四处行走 ❑ *He claimed to be a journalist, and he got around.* 他声称是记者，四处行走。 6 PHRASAL VERB The way that someone **gets around** is the way that they walk or go from one place to another. 走动 ❑ *It is difficult for Gail to get around since she broke her leg.* 盖尔行走困难，因为她摔断了腿。

▶ **get around to** PHRASAL VERB When you **get around to** doing something that you have delayed doing or have been too busy to do, you finally do it. 抽出时间做 ❑ *I said I would write to you, but as usual I never got around to it.* 我说过要写信给你，但像往常一样总是抽不出时间来。

▶ **get at** 1 PHRASAL VERB To **get at** something means to succeed in reaching it. 够得着 ❑ *A goat was standing up against a tree on its hind legs, trying to get at the leaves.* 一只山羊后腿趴在一棵树上站起来，试图去够树叶。 2 PHRASAL VERB If you **get at** the truth about something, you succeed in discovering it. 查明 ❑ *We want to get at the truth. Who killed him? And why?* 我们想查明真相。谁杀了他？为什么？ 3 PHRASAL VERB If you ask someone what they **are getting at**, you are asking them to explain what they mean, usually because you think that they are being unpleasant or are suggesting something that is untrue. 意指 ❑ *"What are you getting at now?" demanded Rick.* "你现在是什么意思？" 里克质问道。

▶ **get away** 1 PHRASAL VERB If you **get away**, you succeed in leaving a place or a person's company. 离开 ❑ *She'd gladly have gone anywhere to get away from the city.* 去任何地方她都乐意，只要能离开这座城市。 2 PHRASAL VERB If you **get away**, you go away for a period of time in order to have a vacation. 外出度假 ❑ *He is too busy to get away.* 他忙得没有时间外出度假。 3 PHRASAL VERB When someone or something **gets away**, or when you **get** them **away**, they escape. 使逃跑；逃跑 ❑ *Dr. Dunn was apparently trying to get away when he was shot.* 邓恩博士显然是在试图逃跑时被击中的。

▶ **get away with** PHRASAL VERB If you **get away with** doing something wrong or risky, you do not suffer any punishment or other bad consequences because of it. 逃脱惩罚 ❑ *The criminals know how to play the system and get away with it.* 那些罪犯知道怎样钻制度的空子并逃脱惩罚。

▶ **get back** 1 PHRASAL VERB If someone or something **gets back to** a state they were in before, they are then in that state again. 恢复 ❑ *Then life started to get back to normal.* 后来生活又开始恢复到正常状态。 2 PHRASAL VERB If you **get back to** a subject that you were talking about before, you start talking about it again. 回到（原先的话题） ❑ *It wasn't until we sat down to eat that we got back to the subject of Tom Halliday.* 我们直到坐下来吃饭时才又回到了汤姆·哈利戴这个话题上来。 3 PHRASAL VERB If you **get** something **back** after you have lost it or after it has been taken from you, you then have it again. 找回；取回 ❑ *You have 14 days in which you can cancel the contract and get your money back.* 你有14天时间，在此期间你可以取消合同并收回你的钱。

▶ **get back to** 1 PHRASAL VERB If you **get back to** an activity, you start doing it again after you have stopped doing it. 重新开始 ❑ *I think I ought to get back to work.* 我想我应该重新开始工作了。

2 PHRASAL VERB If you **get back to** someone, you contact them again after a short period of time, often by telephone. (常指通过电话) 再联系 ❑ *We'll get back to you as soon as possible.* 我们将尽快再跟你联系。

▶ **get by** PHRASAL VERB If you can **get by** with what you have, you can manage to live or do things in a satisfactory way. 勉强过活；勉强对付过去 ❑ *I'm a survivor. I'll get by.* 我是个幸存者。能勉强过活。

▶ **get down** **1** PHRASAL VERB If something **gets** you **down**, it makes you unhappy. 使沮丧 ❑ *At times when my work gets me down, I like to fantasize about being a farmer.* 当我为工作沮丧时，就爱幻想成为一个农夫。 **2** PHRASAL VERB If you **get down**, you lower your body until you are sitting, kneeling, or lying on the ground. 弯下身 (坐下、跪下、趴下) ❑ *"Get down!" she yelled. "Somebody's shooting!"* "卧倒！" 她大声喊道。"有人在开枪！"

▶ **get down to** PHRASAL VERB If you **get down to** something, especially something that requires a lot of attention, you begin doing it. 着手处理 ❑ *With the election out of the way, the government can get down to business.* 选举已结束，政府能够着手处理正事了。

▶ **get in** **1** PHRASAL VERB If a political party or a politician **gets in**, they are elected. 当选 ❑ *If the Republicans got in they might decide to change it.* 如果共和党当选，他们可能会决定改变这一状况。 **2** PHRASAL VERB If you **get** something **in**, you manage to do it at a time when you are very busy doing other things. 挤出时间做 ❑ *I plan to get a few lessons in.* 我计划挤出时间上几节课。 **3** PHRASAL VERB When a train, bus, or plane **gets in**, it arrives. (火车、公共汽车或飞机) 到达 ❑ *We would have come straight here, except our flight got in too late.* 若不是我们的航班到得太晚，我们应该直接到这里了。

▶ **get into** **1** PHRASAL VERB If you **get into** a particular kind of work or activity, you manage to become involved in it. 从事 ❑ *He was eager to get into politics.* 他渴望从政。 **2** PHRASAL VERB If you **get into** a school, college, or university, you are accepted there as a student. 被录取 ❑ *I was working hard to get into Yale.* 我为了能进入耶鲁大学而努力学习。

▶ **get off** **1** PHRASAL VERB If someone who has broken a law or rule **gets off**, they are not punished, or are given only a very small punishment. 逃脱惩罚 ❑ *He is likely to get off with a small fine.* 他可能会逃脱惩罚，只交一小笔罚金了事。 **2** PHRASAL VERB If you tell someone to **get off** a piece of land or a property, you are telling them to leave, because they have no right to be there and you do not want them there. 离开 ❑ *I told you. Get off the farm.* 我告诉过你，离开农场。 **3** PHRASAL VERB You can tell someone to **get off** when they are touching something and you do not want them to. 把手拿开 ❑ *I kept telling him to get off.* 我不停地告诉他把手拿开。

▶ **get on** PHRASAL VERB If you **get on with** something, you continue doing it or start doing it. 继续做；开始做 ❑ *Jane got on with her work.* 简继续做她的工作。

▶ **get on to** PHRASAL VERB If you **get on to** a topic when you are speaking, you start talking about it. 开始谈论 ❑ *We got on to the subject of relationships.* 我们开始谈论起男女关系这个话题。

▶ **get out** **1** PHRASAL VERB If you **get out**, you leave a place because you want to escape from it, or because you are made to leave it. 离开 ❑ *They probably wanted to get out of the country.* 他们很可能想离开这个国家。 **2** PHRASAL VERB If you **get out**, you go to places and meet people, usually in order to have a more enjoyable life. 外出 (参加社交活动等) ❑ *Get out and enjoy yourself, make new friends.* 出去玩玩，结交新朋友。 **3** PHRASAL VERB If you **get out of** an organization or a commitment, you withdraw from it. 退出 (组织等)；撤销 (承诺) ❑ *I wanted to get out of the group, but they wouldn't let me.* 我想退出这个团体，但他们不让。 **4** PHRASAL VERB If news or information **gets out**, it becomes known. (消息或信息) 泄露 ❑ *If word got out now, a scandal could be disastrous.* 如果现在泄露消息，丑闻可能会是灾难性的。

▶ **get out of** PHRASAL VERB If you **get out of** doing something that you do not want to do, you succeed in avoiding doing it. 逃避 ❑ *It's amazing what people will do to get out of paying taxes.* 人们为逃税所做之事令人吃惊。

▶ **get over** **1** PHRASAL VERB If you **get over** an unpleasant or unhappy experience or an illness, you recover from it. (从不快或疾病中) 恢复过来 ❑ *It took me a very long time to get over the shock of her death.* 我过了很长时间才从她去世的震惊中恢复过来。 **2** PHRASAL VERB If you **get over** a problem or difficulty, you overcome it. 解决 ❑ *"How would they get over that problem?" he wondered.* "他们将怎样解决那个问题呢？" 他自忖道。

▶ **get round** [BRIT] → see **get around**

▶ **get round to** [BRIT] → see **get around to**

▶ **get through** **1** PHRASAL VERB If you **get through** a task or an amount of work, especially when it is difficult, you complete it. 完成 ❑ *I think you can get through the first two chapters.* 我想你能完成前两章。 **2** PHRASAL VERB If you **get through** a difficult or unpleasant period of time, you manage to live through it. 熬过 ❑ *It is hard to see how people will get through the winter.* 很难想像人们将怎样熬过这个冬天。 **3** PHRASAL VERB If you **get through to** someone, you succeed in making them understand something that you are trying to tell them. 使…理解 ❑ *An old friend might well be able to get through to her and help her.* 一位老朋友也许能让她理解并帮助她。 **4** PHRASAL VERB If you **get through to** someone, you succeed in contacting them on the telephone. 用电话联系上 ❑ *Look, I can't get through to this number.* 哎，我打不通这个号码。 **5** PHRASAL VERB If a law or proposal **gets through**, it is officially approved by something such as a parliament or committee. (法律或提案) 被通过 ❑ *Such a radical proposal would never get through Congress.* 如此激进的提案永远不会在国会获得通过。

▶ **get together** **1** PHRASAL VERB When people **get together**, they meet in order to discuss something or to spend time together. 开会；聚会 ❑ *A whole range of people from all backgrounds can get together and enjoy themselves.* 出身经历各异的人们可以聚在一起玩得很开心。 **2** → see also **get-together** **3** PHRASAL VERB If you **get** something **together**, you organize it. 组织 ❑ *Paul and I were getting a band together, and we needed a new record deal.* 当时我和保罗正在组建一支乐队，我们需要一份新的唱片协议。 **4** PHRASAL VERB If you **get** an amount of money **together**, you succeed in getting all the money that you need in order to pay for something. 凑集 ❑ *Now you've finally got enough money together to put a down payment on your dream home.* 现在你终于凑足了钱，可以为你梦寐以求的房子交首付款了。

▶ **get up** **1** PHRASAL VERB When someone who is sitting or lying down **gets up**, they rise to a standing position. 站起来 ❑ *I got up and walked over to where he was.* 我站起来，走到他那里。 **2** PHRASAL VERB When you **get up**, you get out of bed. 起床 ❑ *They have to get up early in the morning.* 他们一大早就得起床。

get·away /gɛtəweɪ/ (**getaways**) **1** N-COUNT If someone makes a **getaway**, they leave a place quickly, especially after committing a crime or when trying to avoid someone. (尤指犯罪后或逃避某人的) 逃跑 ❑ *They made their getaway on a stolen motorcycle.* 他们骑上一辆偷来的摩托车逃掉了。 **2** N-COUNT A **getaway** is a short vacation somewhere. 短期休假 [INFORMAL] ❑ *Weekend tours are ideal for families who want a short getaway.* 周末旅行对于想要短期休假的家庭来说非常理想。

get·ting /gɛtɪŋ/ **Getting** is the present participle of **get**. **get**的现在分词

get-together (**get-togethers**) N-COUNT A **get-together** is an informal meeting or party, usually arranged for a particular purpose. (非正式的) 社交聚会 ❑ *...a get-together I had at my home.* …我在家里举行的一次聚会。

ghast·ly /gæstli/ ADJ If you describe someone or something as **ghastly**, you mean that you find them very unpleasant or shocking. 令人讨厌的 [INFORMAL] ❑ *...a mother accompanied by her ghastly, unruly child.* …一位母亲，陪着的是她那令人讨厌的、难管教的孩子。 ❑ *It was the worst week of my life. It was ghastly.* 这是我一生中最糟糕的一周。令人讨厌。

ghet·to /gɛtoʊ/ (**ghettos** or **ghettoes**) N-COUNT A **ghetto** is a part of a city in which many poor people or many people of a particular race, religion, or nationality live separately from everyone else. 贫民区；(相同种族、宗教或国籍的人的) 聚居区 ❑ *...the black ghettos of New York and Los Angeles.* …纽约和洛杉矶的黑人聚居区。

ghost /goʊst/ (**ghosts**) **1** N-COUNT A **ghost** is the spirit of a dead person that someone believes they can see or feel. 幽灵 ❑ *...the ghost of Marie Antoinette.* …玛丽·安托瓦内特的幽灵。 **2** N-COUNT The **ghost of** something, especially of something bad that has happened, is the memory of it. 阴魂 (指对坏事的记忆) ❑ *...the ghost of anti-Americanism.* …反美主义的阴魂。

ghost·ly /goʊstli/ **1** ADJ Something that is **ghostly** seems unreal or unnatural and may be frightening because of this. 怪异得令人可怕的 ❑ *...Sonia's ghostly laughter.* …索尼娅可怕的怪笑。 **2** ADJ A **ghostly** presence is the ghost or spirit of a dead person. 幽灵的 [ADJ n] ❑ *...the ghostly presences which haunt these islands.* …经常出没于这些岛屿的幽灵。

GI /dʒi aɪ/ (**GIs**) N-COUNT A **GI** is a soldier in the United States armed forces, especially the army. 美国兵 ❑ *...the GIs who came to Europe to fight the Nazis.* …来到欧洲抗击纳粹的美国士兵们。

gi·ant ♦◇◇ /dʒaɪənt/ (**giants**) **1** ADJ Something that is described as **giant** is much larger or more important than most others of its kind. 巨大的; 重大的 [ADJ n] ❑ *...America's giant car maker, General Motors.* …美国的汽车制造巨头——通用汽车公司。❑ *...a giant oak table.* …一张巨大的栎木桌。**2** N-COUNT **Giant** is often used to refer to any large, successful business organization or country. 大企业; 大国 [JOURNALISM] ❑ *...Japanese electronics giant, Sony.* …日本的电子业巨头——索尼公司。**3** N-COUNT A **giant** is an imaginary person who is very big and strong, especially one mentioned in old stories. (尤指古老故事中虚构的) 巨人 ❑ *...a Nordic saga of giants.* …一部关于巨人的北欧传奇。

> **Thesaurus** *giant* 另参见:
> ADJ. colossal, enormous, gigantic, huge, immense, mammoth; *(ant.)* miniature **1**

gibe /dʒaɪb/ [BRIT] → see **jibe**

gid·dy /gɪdi/ (**giddier, giddiest**) **1** ADJ If you feel **giddy**, you feel unsteady and think that you are about to fall over, usually because you are not well. 眩晕的 ❑ *He felt giddy and light-headed.* 他感到头晕目眩。**2** ADJ If you feel **giddy with** delight or excitement, you feel so happy or excited that you find it hard to think or act normally. (高兴或激动地) 发狂的 ❑ *Anthony was giddy with self-satisfaction.* 安东尼自鸣得意得忘乎所以了。

gift ♦◇◇ /gɪft/ (**gifts**) **1** N-COUNT A **gift** is something that you give someone as a present. 礼物 ❑ *...a gift of $50.00.* …一件$50.00的礼物。❑ *They believed the unborn child was a gift from God.* 他们相信那个尚未出生的孩子就是上帝赐予的一份礼物。**2** N-COUNT If someone has a **gift for** doing something, they have a natural ability for doing it. 天赋 ❑ *As a youth he discovered a gift for teaching.* 年轻的时候他就发现了自己教书的天赋。

> **Thesaurus** *gift* 另参见:
> N. present **1**
> ability, talent **2**

gift·ed /gɪftɪd/ **1** ADJ Someone who is **gifted** has a natural ability to do something well. 有天赋的 ❑ *...one of the most gifted players in the world.* …世界上最有天赋的运动员之一。**2** ADJ A **gifted** child is much more intelligent or talented than average. (儿童) 天资聪慧的 ❑ *...a state program for gifted children.* …一项培养天才儿童的国家计划。

gig /gɪg/ (**gigs**) N-COUNT A **gig** is a live performance by someone such as a musician or a comedian. 现场演出 [INFORMAL] ❑ *The two bands join forces for a gig at Madison Square Garden on November 28.* 这两支乐队将于11月28日在麦迪逊广场花园联合举行一场演出。

gi·ga·byte /gɪgəbaɪt/ (**gigabytes**) N-COUNT In computing, a **gigabyte** is one thousand and twenty-four megabytes. (计算机的) 千兆字节

★ **gi·gan·tic** /dʒaɪgæntɪk/ ADJ If you describe something as **gigantic**, you are emphasizing that it is extremely large in size, amount, or degree. 巨大的 [EMPHASIS] ❑ *In Red Rock Valley the road is bordered by gigantic rocks.* 在红岩谷，道路两边都是巨大的岩石。

★ **gig·gle** /gɪgᵊl/ (**giggles, giggling, giggled**) **1** V-T/V-I If someone **giggles**, they laugh in a childlike way, because they are amused, nervous, or embarrassed. 咯咯地笑 ❑ *Both girls began to giggle.* 两个女孩都咯咯地笑起来。❑ *"I beg your pardon?" she giggled.* "对不起，你说什么？" 她咯咯地笑着问。● N-COUNT **Giggle** is also a noun. 咯咯的笑 ❑ *She gave a little giggle.* 她咯咯地笑了一下。**2** N-PLURAL If you say that someone has **the giggles**, you mean they cannot stop giggling. 咯咯笑个不止 ❑ *I was so nervous I got the giggles.* 我紧张得咯咯笑个不止。
→ see **laugh**

gilt /gɪlt/ ADJ A **gilt** object is covered with a thin layer of gold or gold paint. 镀金的 ❑ *...marble columns and gilt spires.* …大理石圆柱和镀金尖顶。

gim·mick /gɪmɪk/ (**gimmicks**) N-COUNT A **gimmick** is an unusual and unnecessary feature or action whose purpose is to attract attention or publicity. 花招 [DISAPPROVAL] ❑ *It is just a public relations gimmick.* 这只是一种公关花招。

gin /dʒɪn/ (**gins**) N-MASS **Gin** is a strong, colorless, alcoholic drink made from grain and juniper berries. 杜松子酒 ● N-COUNT A gin is a glass of gin. 一杯杜松子酒 ❑ *...another gin and tonic.* …又一杯加奎宁水的杜松子酒。

▲ **gin·ger** /dʒɪndʒər/ **1** N-UNCOUNT **Ginger** is the root of a plant that is used to flavor food. It has a sweet, spicy flavor and is often sold in powdered form. 姜 **2** COLOR **Ginger** is used to describe things that are orangey brown in color. 姜黄色的 ❑ *She was a mature lady with dyed ginger hair.* 她是个成年女子，头发染成了姜黄色。

gin·ger·ly /dʒɪndʒərli/ ADV If you do something **gingerly**, you do it in a careful manner, usually because you expect it to be dangerous, unpleasant, or painful. 小心谨慎地 [ADV with v] [WRITTEN] ❑ *She was touching the dressing gingerly with both hands.* 她用双手小心翼翼地触摸着敷药。

gip·sy /dʒɪpsi/ [BRIT] → see **gypsy**

gi·raffe /dʒɪræf/ (**giraffes**) N-COUNT A **giraffe** is a large African animal with a very long neck, long legs, and dark patches on its body. 长颈鹿

girl ♦♦♦ /gɜrl/ (**girls**) **1** N-COUNT A **girl** is a female child. 女孩 ❑ *...an eleven-year-old girl.* …一个11岁的女孩。**2** N-COUNT You can refer to someone's daughter as a **girl**. 女儿 ❑ *We had a little girl.* 我们有个小女儿。**3** N-COUNT Young women are often referred to as **girls**. This use could cause offense. 妞儿 (常指年轻女人，可能有冒犯之意) ❑ *...a pretty twenty-year-old girl.* …一个20岁的漂亮妞儿。**4** N-COUNT Some people refer to a man's girlfriend as his **girl**. 女朋友 [INFORMAL] ❑ *I've been with my girl for nine years.* 我和我女友在一起已有9年了。

girl·friend /gɜrlfrend/ (**girlfriends**) **1** N-COUNT Someone's **girlfriend** is a girl or woman with whom they are having a romantic or sexual relationship. 女朋友 ❑ *He had been going out with his girlfriend for seven months.* 他已经和他的女朋友恋爱7个月了。**2** N-COUNT A **girlfriend** is a female friend. 女伴 ❑ *I met a girlfriend for lunch.* 我和一个女伴一起吃了午饭。

> A **girlfriend** is the female person in a romantic relationship. Women can also describe their female friends as their **girlfriends**, but men do not usually use this word to talk about anyone except the woman they are in a romantic relationship with.

girth /gɜrθ/ (**girths**) N-VAR The **girth** of an object, for example a person's or an animal's body, is its width or thickness, considered as the measurement around its circumference. (人或动物身体等的) 围长 [FORMAL] ❑ *A girl he knew had upset him by commenting on his increasing girth.* 他认识的一个女孩对他不断增大的腰围说长道短，这让他很不高兴。

gist /dʒɪst/ N-SING **The gist of** a speech, conversation, or piece of writing is its general meaning. 要点 ❑ *He related the gist of his conversation to Sam.* 他将他谈话的要点告诉了塞姆。

> **give**
> ❶ USED WITH NOUNS DESCRIBING ACTIONS
> ❷ TRANSFERRING
> ❸ OTHER USES, PHRASES, AND PHRASAL VERBS

❶ **give** ♦♦♦ /gɪv/ (**gives, giving, gave, given**) **1** V-T You can use **give** with nouns that refer to physical actions. The whole expression refers to the performing of the action. For example, **She gave a smile** means almost the same as "She smiled." 与表示身体动作的名词连用，表示做这一动作 [no cont] ❑ *She stretched her arms out and gave a great yawn.* 她伸开手臂，打了个大呵欠。❑ *He gave her a fond smile.* 他充满柔情地朝她微微一笑。**2** V-T You use **give** to say that a person does something for another person. For example, if you **give** someone a lift, you take them somewhere in your car. 为…做… ❑ *I gave her a lift back to her house.* 我让她搭我的车回家。❑ *He was given mouth-to-mouth resuscitation.* 对他进行了口对口的人工呼吸。**3** V-T You use **give** with nouns that refer to information, opinions, or greetings to indicate that something is communicated. For example, if you **give** someone some news, you tell it to them. 告知 ❑ *He gave no details.* 他没有提供任何细节。❑ *Would you like to give me your name?* 能告诉我你的名字吗？**4** V-T You use **give** to say how long you think something will last or how much you think something will be. 预计 ❑ *A recent poll gave Campbell a 68 percent support rating.* 最近的一次民意调查预计坎贝尔的

支持率为68%。 5 V-T People use **give** in expressions such as **I don't give a damn** to show that they do not care about something. 用于**I don't give a damn**等表达中表示"毫不在乎" [no cont, no passive, with brd-neg] [INFORMAL, FEELINGS] ❑ *They don't give a damn about the country.* 他们一点都不在乎这个国家。 6 V-T If someone or something **gives** you a particular idea or impression, it causes you to have that idea or impression. 使产生（某种想法或印象）❑ *They gave me the impression that they were doing exactly what they wanted in life.* 他们给我的印象是，他们正在做他们一生中想做的事情。 7 V-T If someone or something **gives** you a particular physical or emotional feeling, it makes you experience it. 使产生（某种情绪或感受）❑ *He gave me a shock.* 他让我大吃一惊。 8 V-T If you **give** a performance or speech, you perform or speak in public. 作（演出或演讲）❑ *Kotto gives a stupendous performance.* 科托作了一场令人惊叹的演出。 9 V-T If you **give** something thought or attention, you think about it, concentrate on it, or deal with it. 予以（考虑或关注）❑ *I've been giving it some thought.* 我一直在考虑这个问题。 10 V-T If you **give** a party or other social event, you organize it. 举行（聚会或社交活动等）❑ *That evening, I gave a dinner party for a few close friends.* 那天晚上，我设宴招待了几位密友。

❷ **give** ♦♦♦ /gɪv/ (**gives, giving, gave, given**) 1 V-T/V-I If you **give** someone something that you own or have bought, you provide them with it, so that they have it or can use it. 提供 ❑ *They gave us T-shirts and stickers.* 他们给我们提供了T恤衫和粘贴标签。❑ *He gave money to the World Health Organization to help defeat smallpox.* 他给世界卫生组织提供了资金以帮助消灭天花。 ❑ *Americans are still giving to charity despite hard times.* 尽管时世艰难，美国人依然在捐助慈善事业。 2 V-T If you **give** someone something that you are holding or that is near you, you pass it to them, so that they are then holding it. 递给 ❑ *Give me that pencil.* 请把那支铅笔递给我。 3 V-T To **give** someone or something a particular power or right means to allow them to have it. 赋予（权力或权利）❑ *The new law would give the president the power to appoint the central bank's chairman.* 新法律将赋予总统任命中央银行行长的权力。

❸ **give** ♦♦♦ /gɪv/ (**gives, giving, gave, given**)
➪ **Please look at meanings 8 – 11 to see if the expression you are looking for is shown under another headword.** 1 V-I If something **gives**, it collapses or breaks under pressure. 坍塌；断裂 ❑ *My knees gave under me.* 我的膝盖发软了。 2 V-T PASSIVE You say that you **are given to** understand or believe that something is the case when you do not want to say how you found out about it, or who told you. 获悉 [FORMAL, VAGUENESS] ❑ *We were given to understand that he was ill.* 我们获悉他生病了。 3 → see also **given** 4 PHRASE You use **give me** to say that you would rather have one thing than another, especially when you have just mentioned the thing that you do not want. 我宁愿要 ❑ *"I hate Sundays," he said. "They're endless. Give me a Saturday night any day."* "我讨厌星期日，"他说。"星期日没完没了的。我宁愿要星期六晚上，哪天都行。" 5 PHRASE If you say that something requires **give-and-take**, you mean that people must compromise or cooperate for it to be successful. 互谅互让 ❑ *...a happy relationship where there's a lot of give-and-take.* …在很多事情上互谅互让的美满情爱关系。 6 PHRASE **Give or take** is used to indicate that an amount is approximate. For example, if you say that something is fifty years old, **give or take** a few years, you mean that it is approximately fifty years old. 相差不到… ❑ *They grow to a height of 12 in. – give or take a couple of inches.* 它们能长到12英寸高——误差不超过2英寸。 7 PHRASE If an audience is asked to **give it up for** a performer, they are being asked to applaud. 为…鼓掌 [INFORMAL] ❑ *Ladies and gentlemen, give it up for Fred Durst.* 女士们先生们，为弗雷德·德斯特鼓掌吧。 8 **to give the game away** → see **game** 9 **to give notice** → see **notice** 10 **to give rise to** → see **rise** 11 **to give way** → see **way**

▸ **give away** 1 PHRASAL VERB If you **give away** something that you own, you give it to someone, rather than selling it, often because you no longer want it. 赠送 ❑ *He was giving his collection away for free.* 他正在无偿捐赠他的收藏。 2 PHRASAL VERB If someone **gives away** an advantage, they accidentally cause their opponent or enemy to have that advantage. 丧失（优势）❑ *Military advantages should not be given away.* 军事优势不应该丧失。 3 PHRASAL VERB If you **give away** information that should be kept secret, you reveal it to other people. 泄露 ❑ *She would give nothing away.* 她什么也不会泄露。 4 PHRASAL VERB To **give** someone or something **away** means to show their true nature or identity, which is not obvious. 暴露 ❑ *Although they are pretending hard to be young, gray hair and cellulite give them away.* 尽管他们尽力装出年轻的样子，但是灰白的头发和皮下脂肪团却暴露了他们的真实年龄。

▸ **give back** PHRASAL VERB If you **give** something **back**, you return it to the person who gave it to you. 归还 ❑ *I gave the textbook back to him.* 我把课本还给他了。 ❑ *You gave me back the projector.* 你把幻灯机还给我了。

▸ **give in** 1 PHRASAL VERB If you **give in**, you admit that you are defeated or that you cannot do something. 投降 ❑ *"I wasn't going to give in. I wasn't going to fall. I was going to fight like hell."* "我不会投降。我不会倒下。我将拼命战斗。" 2 PHRASAL VERB If you **give in**, you agree to do something that you do not want to do. 让步 ❑ *I pressed my parents until they finally gave in and registered me for skating classes.* 我一直催着父母，直到他们最终让步给我报了名上溜冰课。

▸ **give off** or **give out** PHRASAL VERB If something **gives off** or **gives out** a gas, heat, or a smell, it produces it and sends it out into the air. 散发出（气体、热量或气味）❑ *...natural gas, which gives off less carbon dioxide than coal.* …天然气的二氧化碳排放量少于煤。

▸ **give out** 1 PHRASAL VERB If you **give out** a number of things, you distribute them among a group of people. 分发 ❑ *There were people at the entrance giving out leaflets.* 有人在入口处分发传单。 2 PHRASAL VERB If you **give out** information, you make it known to people. 宣布 ❑ *He wouldn't give out any information.* 他不会宣布任何消息。 3 → see **give off**

▸ **give over to** or **give up to** PHRASAL VERB If something **is given over** or **given up to** a particular use, it is used entirely for that purpose. 专用于 ❑ *Much of the garden was given over to vegetables.* 花园的大部分面积专用来种蔬菜。

▸ **give up** 1 PHRASAL VERB If you **give up** something, you stop doing it or having it. 放弃 ❑ *The Coast Guard had given up all hope of finding the two divers alive.* 海岸警卫队已放弃了两名潜水员生还的全部希望。 2 PHRASAL VERB If you **give up**, you decide that you cannot do something and stop trying to do it. 放弃 ❑ *After a fruitless morning sitting at his desk he had given up.* 他在书桌前徒劳地坐了一个上午后便放弃了。 3 PHRASAL VERB If you **give up** your job, you resign from it. 辞去 ❑ *She gave up her job to join her husband's campaign.* 她辞了工作以参加丈夫的竞选活动。 4 PHRASAL VERB If you **give up** something that you have or that you are entitled to, you allow someone else to have it. 让出 ❑ *One of the men with him gave up his place on the bench.* 他的一个同伴让出了长椅上的位子。 5 PHRASAL VERB If you **give yourself up**, you let the police or other people know where you are, after you have been hiding from them. 投案自首 ❑ *A 28-year-old man later gave himself up and will appear in court today.* 后来一个28岁的男子投案自首了，他将于今天出庭。

▸ **give up on** PHRASAL VERB If you **give up on** something or someone, you decide that you will never succeed in doing what you want to with them, and you stop trying. 对…表示绝望 ❑ *He urged them not to give up on peace efforts.* 他力劝他们不要对和平努力绝望。

▸ **give up to** → see **give over to**

▲ **give·away** /gɪvəweɪ/ (**giveaways**) also **give-away** N-COUNT A **giveaway** is something that a company or organization gives to someone, usually in order to encourage people to buy a particular product. 赠品 ❑ *Free book giveaway for all who attend.* 为所有参加者准备的免费赠书。

giv·en ♦◇◇ /gɪvᵊn/ 1 **Given** is the past participle of **give**. **give**的过去分词 2 ADJ If you talk about, for example, any **given** position or a **given** time, you mean the particular position or time that you are discussing. 特定的 [det ADJ] ❑ *In chess there are typically about 36 legal moves from any given board position.* 在国际象棋中，从棋盘的任何一个特定方格通常都可以移动大致36步。 3 PREP **Given** is used when indicating a possible situation in which someone has the opportunity or ability to do something. For example, **given the chance** means "if I had the chance." 如果有（机会等）❑ *Write down the sort of thing you would like to do, given the opportunity.* 如果有机会，请写下你想做的那类事。 4 PHRASE If you say **given that** something is the case, you mean taking that fact into account. 考虑到 ❑ *Usually, I am sensible with money, as I have to be, given that I don't earn that much.* 我花钱通常是很明智的。考虑到自己挣得不多，必须这样做。 5 PREP If you say **given** something, you mean taking that thing into account. 考虑到 ❑ *Given the uncertainty over Leigh's future I was left with little other choice.* 考虑到莉前途未卜，我几乎没有选择余地。

gla·cial /gleɪʃᵊl/ 1 ADJ **Glacial** means relating to or produced by glaciers or ice. 冰河的；冰的 [TECHNICAL] ❑ *...a true glacial landscape with U-shaped valleys.* …U形山谷中真正的冰河地貌。 2 ADJ If you say that something moves or changes at a **glacial** pace, you are

emphasizing that it moves or changes very slowly. 非常缓慢的 [usu ADJ n] [EMPHASIS] ❑ *Change occurs at a glacial pace.* 变化来得极为缓慢。
→ see **lake**

▲ **glaci·er** /gleɪʃər/ (**glaciers**) N-COUNT A **glacier** is an extremely large mass of ice which moves very slowly, often down a mountain valley. 冰川 ❑ *...a guide to summer skiing on the glaciers of the Austrian alps.* …一项对于夏季在奥地利阿尔卑斯山的冰川滑雪的向导。
→ see Word Web: **glacier**
→ see **climate, mountain**

glad ♦◇◇ /glæd/ **1** ADJ If you are **glad** about something, you are happy and pleased about it. 高兴的 [v-link ADJ] ❑ *The people seem genuinely glad to see you.* 人们看到你似乎真得很高兴。 ❑ *I'd be glad if the boys slept a little longer so I could do some ironing.* 如果男孩子们多睡一会儿我就高兴了，可以熨熨衣服。 ● **glad·ly** ADV 高兴地 [ADV with v] ❑ *Malcolm gladly accepted the invitation.* 马尔科姆欣然接受了邀请。 **2** ADJ If you say that you will be **glad to** do something, usually for someone else, you mean that you are willing and eager to do it. 乐意的 [v-link ADJ to-inf] [FEELINGS] ❑ *I'll be glad to show you everything.* 我将乐意向你展示每样东西。 ● **glad·ly** ADV 乐意地 [ADV with v] ❑ *The counselors will gladly baby-sit during their free time.* 咨询员在空闲时也会乐意照看一下孩子。

glam /glæm/ **1** ADJ **Glam** is short for glamorous. 富有魅力的 [INFORMAL] ❑ *She was always glam. She looked like a star.* 她总是富有魅力。她看起来像明星。 **2** N-UNCOUNT **Glam** is short for glamour. 魅力 [INFORMAL] ❑ *...the gleam and glam of New York's Carnegie Hall.* …纽约卡内基音乐厅的光芒与魅力。

★ **glam·or** /glæmər/ N-UNCOUNT → see **glamour**

Word Link *ous ≈ having the qualities of : dangerous, fabulous, glamorous*

glam·or·ous /glæmərəs/ ADJ If you describe someone or something as **glamorous**, you mean that they are more attractive, exciting, or interesting than ordinary people or things. 富有魅力的 ❑ *...some of the world's most beautiful and glamorous women.* …世界上最美最富有魅力的一些女人。

★ **glam·our** /glæmər/ also **glamor**
in BRIT, only use **glamour**
N-UNCOUNT **Glamour** is the quality of being more attractive, exciting, or interesting than ordinary people or things. 魅力 ❑ *...the glamour of show biz.* …演艺业的诱惑力。

glance ♦◇◇ /glæns/ (**glances, glancing, glanced**) **1** V-I If you **glance at** something or someone, you look at them very quickly and then look away again immediately. 瞥 ❑ *He glanced at his watch.* 他看了一下手表。 **2** V-I If you **glance through** or **at** a newspaper, report, or book, you spend a short time looking at it without reading it very carefully. 浏览 ❑ *I picked up the phone book and glanced through it.* 我拿起电话簿浏览了一下。 **3** N-COUNT A **glance** is a quick look at someone or something. 一瞥 ❑ *Trevor and I exchanged a glance.* 特雷弗和我相互瞥了一眼。 **4** PHRASE If you see something **at a glance**, you see or recognize it immediately, and without having to think or look carefully. 一眼就 ❑ *One could tell at a glance that she was a compassionate person.* 一眼就能看出她是一个富有同情心的人。 **5** PHRASE If you say that something is true or seems to be true **at first glance**, you mean that it seems to be true when you first see it or think about it, but that your first impression may be wrong. 乍一看 ❑ *At first glance, organic farming looks much more expensive for the farmer.* 乍一看，有机耕作对农民来说似乎昂贵得多。

Word Partnership *glance* 的常用搭配:

PREP.	glance **at** *someone*, glance **over** *someone's* **shoulder** 1
	glance **at** *something*, glance **over** 1 2
	glance **through** 2
V.	**exchange a** glance, **steal a** glance 3
ADJ.	**quick** glance 3

★ **gland** /glænd/ (**glands**) N-COUNT A **gland** is an organ in the body which produces chemical substances for the body to use or get rid of. 腺 [usu supp N] ❑ *...the hormones secreted by our endocrine glands.* …我们的内分泌腺分泌的荷尔蒙。
→ see **sweat**

★ **glare** /glɛər/ (**glares, glaring, glared**) **1** V-I If you **glare at** someone, you look at them with an angry expression on your face. 怒目而视 ❑ *The old woman glared at him.* 那个老妇人怒视着他。 ❑ *Jacob glared and muttered something.* 雅各布怒目而视，嘴里嘟哝着什么。 **2** N-COUNT A **glare** is an angry, hard, and unfriendly look. 怒视 ❑ *His glasses magnified his irritable glare.* 他的眼镜使他怒视的目光显得更凶了。 **3** V-I If the sun or a light **glares**, it shines with a very bright light which is difficult to look at. 发出刺眼的光 ❑ *The sunlight glared.* 太阳光很刺眼。 **4** N-UNCOUNT **Glare** is very bright light that is difficult to look at. 刺眼的光 ❑ *...the glare of a car's headlights.* …汽车前灯刺眼的强光。 **5** N-SING If someone is in **the glare of** publicity or public attention, they are constantly being watched and talked about by a lot of people. 显眼; 张扬 ❑ *Norma is said to dislike the glare of publicity.* 据说诺尔玛不喜欢张扬。

Word Partnership *glare* 的常用搭配:

PREP.	glare **at** *someone* 1
ADJ.	**irritable** glare 2
	full glare 3 4
N.	glare **of light** 4
	glare **of publicity** 5

glar·ing /glɛərɪŋ/ **1** ADJ If you describe something bad as **glaring**, you are emphasizing that it is very obvious and easily seen or noticed. 显眼的 [EMPHASIS] ❑ *I never saw such a glaring example of misrepresentation.* 我从未见过这样一个明显歪曲事实的例子。 ● **glar·ing·ly** ADV 显眼地 ❑ *It was glaringly obvious.* 这是非常明显的。
2 → see also **glare**

glass ♦♦◇ /glɑs, glæs/ (**glasses**) **1** N-UNCOUNT **Glass** is a hard, transparent substance that is used to make things such as windows and bottles. 玻璃 ❑ *...a pane of glass.* …一块玻璃。 **2** N-COUNT A **glass** is a container made from glass, which you can drink from and which does not have a handle. 玻璃杯 ❑ *Grossman raised the glass to his lips.* 格罗斯曼把玻璃杯举到唇边。 ● N-COUNT The contents of a glass can be referred to as a **glass of** something. 一玻璃杯的量 ❑ *...a glass of milk.* …一玻璃杯牛奶。 **3** N-UNCOUNT **Glass** is used to mean objects made of glass, for example drinking containers and bowls. 玻璃制品 ❑ *There's a glittering array of glass to choose from at markets.* 市场上有大量光彩夺目的玻璃制品可供选择。 **4** N-PLURAL **Glasses** are two lenses in a frame that some people wear in front of their eyes in order to help them see better. 眼镜 ❑ *He took off his glasses.* 他摘掉了眼镜。
→ see Word Web: **glass**
→ see **light**

glass ceil·ing (**glass ceilings**) N-COUNT When people refer to a **glass ceiling**, they are talking about the attitudes and traditions in a society that prevent women from rising to the top jobs. 玻璃

Word Web glacier

Two-thirds of all **fresh water** is **frozen**. The largest **glaciers** in the world are the **polar ice caps** of Antarctica and Greenland. They cover more than six million square miles. Their average depth is almost one mile. If all the glaciers **melted**, the average **sea level** would rise by over 250 feet. Glaciologists have noted that the Antarctic is about 1º C* warmer than it was 50 years ago. Some of them are worried. Continued warming might cause floating **ice** shelves there to begin to disintegrate. This, in turn, could cause disastrous coastal flooding in low-lying areas around the world.

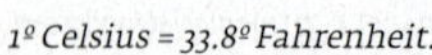
1º Celsius = 33.8º Fahrenheit.

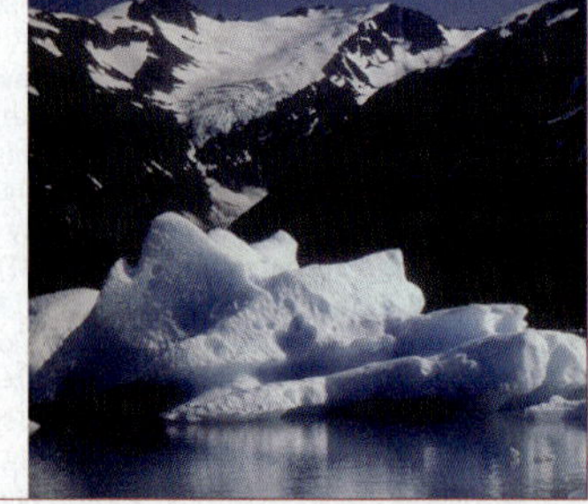

Word Web glass

The basic recipe for **glass** includes silica (found in **sand**) and **ash** (left over from burning wood). The earliest glass objects are glass **beads** made in Egypt around 3500 BC. By 14 AD, the Syrians had learned how to **blow** glass to form hollow containers. These included primitive **bottles** and **vases**. By 100 AD, the Romans were making clear glass windowpanes. Modern factories now produce **safety glass** which doesn't **shatter** when it breaks. It includes a layer of cellulose between two **sheets** of glass. **Bulletproof** glass consists of several layers of glass with a tough, **transparent** plastic between the layers.

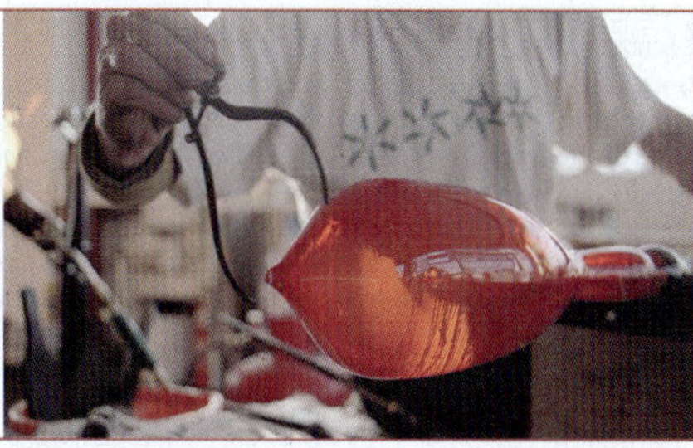

天花板(指社会上限制妇女升任高职的无形障碍) [JOURNALISM] ❑ *In her current role she broke through the glass ceiling as the first woman to reach senior management level in the company.* 在她目前的职位上，她突破了那道升迁的无形障碍，成为公司里第一位升至高级管理层的女性。

▲ **glaze** /gleɪz/ (**glazes, glazing, glazed**) **1** N-COUNT A **glaze** is a thin layer of liquid which is put on a piece of pottery and becomes hard and shiny when the pottery is heated in a very hot oven. 釉 ❑ *...hand-painted French tiles with decorative glazes.* …手工绘图的法国装饰釉瓷砖。 **2** N-COUNT A **glaze** is a thin layer of beaten egg, milk, or other liquid that you spread onto food in order to make the surface shine and look attractive. (浇在食品上使有光泽的) 浆汁 ❑ *Brush the glaze over the top and sides of the hot cake.* 在热蛋糕的顶上和周围刷上浆汁。 **3** V-T When you **glaze** food such as bread or pastry, you spread a layer of beaten egg, milk, or other liquid onto it before you cook it in order to make its surface shine and look attractive. 浇浆汁于 (食物) 表面 ❑ *Glaze the pie with beaten egg.* 把打好的蛋汁浇在馅饼上。

→ see **pottery**

▸ **glaze over** PHRASAL VERB If your eyes **glaze over**, they become dull and lose all expression, usually because you are bored or are thinking about something else. (眼睛) 变呆滞 ❑ *...movie actors whose eyes glaze over as soon as the subject wavers from themselves.* …那些电影演员一旦离开他们自己的话题目光就会呆滞。

glazed /gleɪzd/ **1** ADJ If you describe someone's eyes as **glazed**, you mean that their expression is dull or dreamy, usually because they are tired or are having difficulty concentrating on something. 呆滞的 ❑ *Doctors with glazed eyes sat chain-smoking in front of a television set.* 目光呆滞的医生们坐在电视机前一根接一根地抽着烟。 **2** ADJ **Glazed** pottery is covered with a thin layer of a hard, shiny substance. 上釉的 ❑ *...a large glazed pot.* …一只上了釉的大壶。 **3** ADJ A **glazed** window or door has glass in it. 装有玻璃的 ❑ *...the new office, with glazed windows to the corridor.* …玻璃窗面向走廊的新办公室。

★ **gleam** /gliːm/ (**gleams, gleaming, gleamed**) **1** V-I If an object or a surface **gleams**, it reflects light because it is shiny and clean. 闪光 ❑ *His black hair gleamed in the sun.* 他的黑头发在阳光下闪闪发光。 **2** N-COUNT A **gleam of** something is a faint sign of it. 一丝 ❑ *There was a gleam of hope for a peaceful settlement.* 和平解决曾有一线希望。

glean /gliːn/ (**gleans, gleaning, gleaned**) V-T If you **glean** something such as information or knowledge, you learn or collect it slowly and patiently, and perhaps indirectly. 慢慢地收集 ❑ *At present we're gleaning information from all sources.* 目前我们正从所有渠道慢慢收集信息。

glee /gliː/ N-UNCOUNT **Glee** is a feeling of happiness and excitement, often caused by someone else's misfortune. 高兴 (常指幸灾乐祸) ❑ *His victory was greeted with glee by his fellow American golfers.* 他的胜利也使他的美国高尔夫球伴们为之高兴。

glee·ful /gliːfʊl/ ADJ Someone who is **gleeful** is happy and excited, often because of someone else's bad luck. 高兴的; 幸灾乐祸的 [WRITTEN] ❑ *He took an almost gleeful delight in showing how wrong they can be.* 他感到高兴，几乎是幸灾乐祸看他们出大错。 ● **glee·ful·ly** ADV 幸灾乐祸地 [ADV with v] ❑ *I spent the rest of their visit gleefully boring them with tedious details.* 在他们造访之余，我讲些乏味琐事让他们厌烦不已，我则私下窃喜。

glib /glɪb/ ADJ If you describe what someone says as **glib**, you disapprove of it because it implies that something is simple or easy, or that there are no problems involved, when this is not the case. 油嘴滑舌的 [DISAPPROVAL] ❑ *...the glib talk of "past misery."* …对"昔日痛苦"的夸夸其谈。 ● **glib·ly** ADV 油嘴滑舌地 [ADV with v] ❑ *We talk glibly of equality of opportunity.* 我们大谈特谈机会的均等。

★ **glide** /glaɪd/ (**glides, gliding, glided**) **1** V-I If you **glide** somewhere, you move silently and in a smooth and effortless way. 滑行 ❑ *Waiters glide between tightly packed tables bearing trays of pasta.* 侍者们托着一盘盘的意大利面食在拥挤的餐桌间自如穿行。 **2** V-I When birds or airplanes **glide**, they float on air currents. 滑翔 ❑ *Our only companion is the wandering albatross, which glides effortlessly and gracefully behind the yacht.* 我们惟一的伴侣是那只漂泊信天翁，它轻快优雅地滑翔在游艇后面。

glid·er /glaɪdər/ (**gliders**) N-COUNT A **glider** is an aircraft without an engine, which flies by floating on air currents. 滑翔机

glim·mer /glɪmər/ (**glimmers, glimmering, glimmered**) **1** V-I If something **glimmers**, it produces or reflects a faint, gentle, often unsteady light. 闪烁微光 ❑ *The moon glimmered faintly through the mists.* 月亮透过薄雾闪烁着微光。 ❑ *...the glimmering ocean.* …泛着光的海洋。 **2** N-COUNT A **glimmer** is a faint, gentle, often unsteady light. 微光 ❑ *In the east there is the slightest glimmer of light.* 东方有一丝闪烁的微光。 **3** N-COUNT A **glimmer of** something is a faint sign of it. 一丝 (迹象) ❑ *Despite an occasional glimmer of hope, this campaign has not produced any results.* 尽管偶尔有一线希望，这次宣传活动并没有产生任何结果。

glimpse /glɪmps/ (**glimpses, glimpsing, glimpsed**) **1** N-COUNT If you get a **glimpse of** someone or something, you see them very briefly and not very well. 一瞥 ❑ *Some of the fans had waited 24 hours outside the hotel to catch a glimpse of their heroine.* 某些追星族为了一睹女杰的风采已在宾馆外守候了24小时。 **2** V-T If you **glimpse** someone or something, you see them very briefly and not very well. 瞥见 ❑ *She glimpsed a group of people standing on the bank of a river.* 她瞥见一群人站在河岸上。 **3** N-COUNT A **glimpse of** something is a brief experience of it or an idea about it that helps you understand or appreciate it better. 初步的感受 ❑ *As university campuses become increasingly multiethnic, they offer a glimpse of the conflicts society will face tomorrow.* 大学校园种族群体日趋多样化，使人们初步感受到未来社会面临的诸多冲突。

glint /glɪnt/ (**glints, glinting, glinted**) **1** V-I If something **glints**, it produces or reflects a quick flash of light. 闪光 [WRITTEN] ❑ *The sea glinted in the sun.* 大海在阳光下波光粼粼。 ❑ *Sunlight glinted on his glasses.* 阳光在他的眼镜上闪光。 **2** N-COUNT A **glint** is a quick flash of light. 闪光 [usu N "of" n] [WRITTEN] ❑ *...glints of sunlight.* …阳光的闪烁。

▲ **glis·ten** /glɪsᵊn/ (**glistens, glistening, glistened**) V-I If something **glistens**, it shines, usually because it is wet or oily. (因有水或有油而) 发光 ❑ *The calm sea glistened in the sunlight.* 平静的海面在阳光下闪闪发光。 ❑ *Deborah's face was white and glistening with sweat.* 德博拉面色苍白，闪着汗光。

★ **glit·ter** /glɪtər/ (**glitters, glittering, glittered**) **1** V-I If something **glitters**, light comes from or is reflected off different parts of it. 闪闪发光 ❑ *The bay glittered in the sunshine.* 海湾在阳光下闪闪发光。 **2** N-UNCOUNT **Glitter** consists of tiny, shining pieces of metal. It is glued to things for decoration. 发光小饰物 ❑ *Cut out a piece of sandpaper and sprinkle it with glitter.* 剪下一块砂纸，再在上面撒些发光小饰物。 **3** N-UNCOUNT You can use **glitter** to refer to superficial attractiveness or to the excitement connected with something. 表面光辉 ❑ *She was blinded by the glitter and the glamour of her own life.* 她被自己生活的表面光耀所蒙蔽。

gloat /gloʊt/ (**gloats, gloating, gloated**) V-I If someone **is gloating**, they are showing pleasure at their own success or at other people's failure in an arrogant and unpleasant way. (对自己的成功) 洋洋得意; (对别人的失败) 幸灾乐祸 [DISAPPROVAL] ❑ *Anti-abortionists are gloating over the court's decision.* 反堕胎主义者对法庭的裁决沾沾自喜。

g

Word Link *glob ≈ sphere : global, globe, globule*

glob·al ♦◇◇ /gloʊbᵊl/ **1** ADJ You can use **global** to describe something that happens in all parts of the world or affects all parts of the world. 全球的 ❑ *...a global ban on nuclear testing.* …一项全球性核试验禁令。● **glob·al·ly** ADV 全球地 ❑ *...a globally familiar trade name.* …一个全球熟知的商标名。 **2** ADJ A **global** view or vision of a situation is one in which all the different aspects of it are considered. 全面的 ❑ *...a global vision of contemporary societies.* …对当代社会的全面认识。
→ see **greenhouse effect**

★ **glob·al·ise** /gloʊbəlaɪz/ [BRIT] → see **globalize**

★ **glob·al·ize** /gloʊbəlaɪz/ (**globalizes, globalizing, globalized**)
in BRIT, also use **globalise**
V-T/V-I When industry **globalizes** or **is globalized**, companies from one country link with companies from another country in order to do business with them. 使全球化; 全球化 [BUSINESS] ❑ *One way to lower costs will be to forge alliances with foreign companies or to expand internationally through appropriate takeovers – in short, to "globalize."* 降低成本的途径之一将是与外国公司结成联盟或通过适当的兼并进行国际性扩张——简言之，就是"全球化"。● **glob·ali·za·tion** /gloʊbəlɪzeɪʃᵊn/ N-UNCOUNT 全球化 ❑ *Trends toward the globalization of industry have dramatically affected food production in California.* 工业全球化趋势已极大地影响了加利福尼亚的食品生产。

glob·al vil·lage N-SING People sometimes refer to the world as a **global village** when they want to emphasize that all the different parts of the world form one community linked together by electronic communications, especially the Internet. 地球村 ❑ *Now that we are all part of the global village, everyone becomes a neighbor.* 既然我们都是地球村的一部分，人人都成了邻居。

glob·al warm·ing N-UNCOUNT **Global warming** is the gradual rise in the Earth's temperature caused by high levels of carbon dioxide and other gases in the atmosphere. 全球变暖 ❑ *The threat of global warming will eventually force the U.S. to slow down its energy consumption.* 全球变暖的威胁将最终迫使美国减慢其能源消耗。
→ see **air**

globe /gloʊb/ (**globes**) **1** N-SING You can refer to the world as **the globe** when you are emphasizing how big it is or that something happens in many different parts of it. 全球 ❑ *...bottles of beer from every corner of the globe.* …一瓶瓶来自全球各个角落的啤酒。 ❑ *70% of our globe's surface is water.* 我们地球表面的70%是水。 **2** N-COUNT A **globe** is a ball-shaped object with a map of the world on it. It is usually fixed on a stand. 地球仪 ❑ *Three large globes stand on the floor.* 地板上立着三个大地球仪。 **3** N-COUNT Any ball-shaped object can be referred to as a **globe**. 球状物 ❑ *The overhead light was covered now with a white globe.* 顶灯现在被一个白色的球状物罩了起来。
→ see Picture Dictionary: **globe**

★ **gloom** /glum/ **1** N-SING **The gloom** is a state of near darkness. 昏暗 ❑ *...the gloom of a foggy November morning.* …一个雾蒙蒙的11月早晨的昏暗。 **2** N-UNCOUNT **Gloom** is a feeling of sadness and lack of hope. 忧郁 ❑ *...the deepening gloom over the economy.* …对经济日渐加深的忧虑。

gloomy /glumi/ (**gloomier, gloomiest**) **1** ADJ If a place is **gloomy**, it is almost dark so that you cannot see very well. 昏暗的 ❑ *Inside it's gloomy after all that sunshine.* 明媚的阳光过后，里面一片昏暗。 **2** ADJ If people are **gloomy**, they are unhappy and have no hope. 忧伤的 ❑ *Miller is gloomy about the fate of the serious playwright in America.* 米勒对这位严肃的美国剧作家的命运感到忧伤。● **gloomi·ly** ADV 忧伤地 [ADV with v] ❑ *He tells me gloomily that he has been called up for army service.* 他沮丧地告诉我他已经被征召入伍了。 **3** ADJ If a situation is **gloomy**, it does not give you much hope of success or happiness. 前景暗淡的 ❑ *...a gloomy picture of an economy sliding into recession.* …经济陷入衰退的一幅暗淡景象。 ❑ *Officials say the outlook for next year is gloomy.* 官员们称来年前景暗淡。
→ see **weather**

glo·ri·fied /glɔrɪfaɪd/ ADJ You use **glorified** to indicate that something is less important or impressive than its name suggests. 美化了的 [ADJ n] ❑ *Sometimes they tell me I'm just a glorified waitress.* 有时候他们告诉我说我不过是个头衔被美化了的女招待。

glo·ri·fy /glɔrɪfaɪ/ (**glorifies, glorifying, glorified**) V-T To **glorify** something means to praise it or make it seem good or special, usually when it is not. 美化 ❑ *This magazine in no way glorifies gangs.* 本杂志决不美化各种犯罪团伙。● **glo·ri·fi·ca·tion** /glɔrɪfɪkeɪʃᵊn/ N-UNCOUNT 美化 ❑ *...the glorification of violence.* …对暴力的美化。

glo·ri·ous /glɔriəs/ **1** ADJ Something that is **glorious** is very beautiful and impressive. 壮丽的 ❑ *...a glorious rainbow in the air.* …空中一道壮丽的彩虹。 ❑ *She had missed the glorious blooms of the desert spring.* 她错过了沙漠春天的繁花美景。● **glo·ri·ous·ly** ADV 壮丽地 ❑ *A tree, gloriously lit by autumn, pressed against the windowpane.* 一棵被秋色染得绚丽多彩的树压在窗玻璃上。 **2** ADJ If you describe something as **glorious**, you are emphasizing that it is wonderful

Picture Dictionary globe

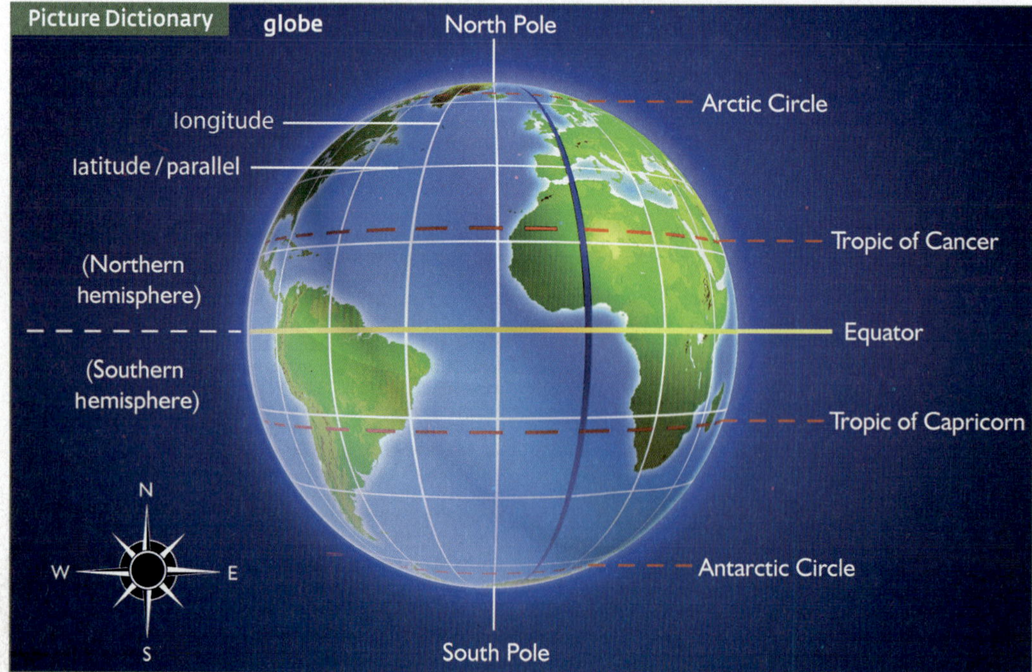

and it makes you feel very happy. 极好的 [EMPHASIS] ❑ *The win revived glorious memories of his championship-winning days.* 这次获胜勾起了他对那些夺冠岁月的美好记忆。● **glo·ri·ous·ly** ADV 极好地 ❑ *...her gloriously happy love life.* …她那极其幸福的爱情生活。 3 ADJ A **glorious** career, victory, or occasion involves great fame or success. 辉煌的 ❑ *Harrison had a glorious career spanning more than six decades.* 哈里森有过一段长达六十余年的辉煌的职业生涯。● **glo·ri·ous·ly** ADV 辉煌地 ❑ *But the mission was successful, gloriously successful.* 但这次任务很成功，辉煌地成功。

glo·ry /glɔri/ (**glories**) 1 N-UNCOUNT **Glory** is the fame and admiration that you gain by doing something impressive. 荣耀 ❑ *Walsham had his moment of glory when he won a 20km race.* 沃尔沙姆有过赢得20公里赛跑的光荣时刻。 2 N-PLURAL A person's **glories** are the occasions when they have done something people greatly admire which makes them famous. 辉煌成就 ❑ *The album sees them re-living past glories but not really breaking any new ground.* 在这张专辑中他们重温了昔日的辉煌成就，却没有任何真正新的突破。

Word Partnership *glory* 的常用搭配：

V. **bask in the** glory 1

N. **blaze of** glory, glory **days**, **hope and** glory, **moment of** glory 1

gloss /glɔs/ (**glosses, glossing, glossed**) 1 N-SING A **gloss** is a bright shine on the surface of something. 光泽 ❑ *Sheets of rain were falling and produced a black gloss on the asphalt.* 大雨倾盆而下，使沥青有了黑色的光泽。 2 N-UNCOUNT **Gloss** is an appearance of attractiveness or good quality which sometimes hides less attractive features or poor quality. 表面光 ❑ *Television commercials might seem more professional, but beware of mistaking the gloss for the content.* 电视商业广告也许看上去更加专业，但要当心别把表面光彩误当作实质。 3 N-SING If you put **a gloss on** a bad situation, you try to make it seem more attractive or acceptable by giving people a false explanation or interpretation of it. 粉饰 ❑ *He used his diary to put a fine gloss on the horrors the regime perpetrated.* 他假借日记来粉饰该政权犯下的种种恐怖行径。 4 N-MASS **Gloss** is the same as **gloss paint**. 有光涂料 5 V-T If you **gloss** a difficult word or idea, you provide an explanation of it. 注解 ❑ *"Aventure" is often glossed as simply good or bad "fortune" or "chance."* **A venture**常常被注解为简单的好或坏的**fortune**或**chance**。

▸ **gloss over** PHRASAL VERB If you **gloss over** a problem, a mistake, or an embarrassing moment, you try to make it seem unimportant by ignoring it or by dealing with it very quickly. 无视；草草了事 ❑ *Some foreign governments gloss over human rights abuses.* 一些外国政府无视对人权的践踏问题。

★ **glos·sa·ry** /glɔsəri/ (**glossaries**) N-COUNT A **glossary** of special, unusual, or technical words or expressions is an alphabetical list of them giving their meanings, for example at the end of a book on a particular subject. 词汇表 ❑ *A glossary of terms is included for the reader's convenience.* 为了方便读者，还收录了术语汇编。

gloss paint N-UNCOUNT **Gloss paint** is paint that forms a shiny surface when it dries. 有光涂料 ❑ *...a fresh coat of white gloss paint.* …新刷的一层白色有光涂料。

glossy /glɔsi/ (**glossier, glossiest**) 1 ADJ **Glossy** means smooth and shiny. 光滑的 ❑ *...glossy black hair.* …光滑的黑发。 2 ADJ You can describe something as **glossy** if you think that it has been designed to look attractive but has little practical value or may have hidden faults. 徒有其表的 ❑ *...a glossy new office.* …一个外表好看的新办公室。 3 ADJ **Glossy** magazines, leaflets, books, and photographs are produced on expensive, shiny paper. 用亮光纸印刷的 [ADJ n] ❑ *...a glossy magazine.* …一本用亮光纸印刷的杂志。

glove /glʌv/ (**gloves**) 1 N-COUNT **Gloves** are pieces of clothing which cover your hands and wrists and have individual sections for each finger. You wear gloves to keep your hands warm or dry or to protect them. 分指手套 ❑ *He stuck his gloves in his pocket.* 他把手套塞进了口袋里。 2 PHRASE If you say that something **fits like a glove**, you are emphasizing that it fits exactly. 正合适 [EMPHASIS] ❑ *I gave one of the bikinis to my sister Sara and it fit like a glove.* 我把其中一件比基尼给了妹妹萨拉，她穿正合身。

→ see **baseball**

glow /gloʊ/ (**glows, glowing, glowed**) 1 N-COUNT A **glow** is a dull, steady light, for example the light produced by a fire when there are no flames. 暗淡的光 ❑ *The cigarette's red glow danced about in the darkness.* 香烟的红色暗光在黑暗中闪烁。 2 N-SING A **glow** is a pink color on a person's face, usually because they are healthy or have been exercising. (脸上的) 红光 ❑ *The moisturizer gave my face a healthy glow that lasted all day.* 这种润肤霜给我脸上带来了持续整天的一种健康的红光。 3 N-SING If you feel a **glow of** satisfaction or achievement, you have a strong feeling of pleasure because of something that you have done or that has happened. 喜悦 ❑ *Exercise will give you a glow of satisfaction at having achieved something.* 体育锻炼会带给你一种有所成就的喜悦。 4 V-I If something **glows**, it produces a dull, steady light. 发出微弱稳定的光 ❑ *The night lantern glowed softly in the darkness.* 夜灯在黑暗中发出微弱的光。 5 V-I If someone's skin **glows**, it looks pink because they are healthy or excited, or have been doing physical exercise. (皮肤) 泛出红光 ❑ *Her freckled skin glowed with health again.* 她那有雀斑的皮肤又泛起健康的红色。 6 V-I If someone **glows with** an emotion such as pride or pleasure, the expression on their face shows how they feel. 容光焕发 ❑ *The expectant mothers that Amy had encountered positively glowed with pride.* 埃米遇见的孕妇们个个脸上都洋溢着幸福和自豪。 7 → see also **glowing**

→ see **fire, light**

Thesaurus *glow* 另参见：

N. beam, glimmer, light 1

blush, flush, radiance 2

V. gleam, radiate, shine 4 6

glow·er /glaʊər/ (**glowers, glowering, glowered**) V-I If you **glower at** someone or something, you look at them angrily. 怒视 ❑ *He glowered at me but said nothing.* 他怒视着我，却一言不发。

glow·ing /gloʊɪŋ/ 1 ADJ A **glowing** description or opinion about someone or something praises them highly or supports them strongly. 高度赞许的 ❑ *The media has been speaking in glowing terms of the relationship between the two countries.* 媒体谈及两国的关系一直给予盛赞之辞。 2 → see also **glow**

glu·cose /glukoʊs/ N-UNCOUNT **Glucose** is a type of sugar that gives you energy. 葡萄糖

glue /glu/ (**glues, glueing** or **gluing, glued**) 1 N-MASS **Glue** is a sticky substance used for joining things together, often for repairing broken things. 胶；胶水 ❑ *...a tube of glue.* …一管胶水。 2 V-T If you **glue** one object to another, you stick them together using glue. 用胶粘 ❑ *Glue the fabric around the window.* 用胶把这布粘在窗户四周。 ❑ *The material is cut and glued in place.* 材料被剪开并粘到合适的位置。 3 V-T PASSIVE If you say that someone **is glued to** something, you mean that they are giving it all their attention. 使全神贯注 ❑ *They are all glued to the Olympic Games.* 他们都全神贯注于奥运会。

glum /glʌm/ (**glummer, glummest**) ADJ Someone who is **glum** is sad and quiet because they are disappointed or unhappy about something. 闷闷不乐的 ❑ *She was very glum and was obviously missing her children.* 她十分闷闷不乐，显然在思念她的孩子们。● **glum·ly** ADV 闷闷不乐地 [ADV with v] ❑ *When Eleanor returned, I was still sitting glumly on the couch.* 埃莉诺回来时，我仍然闷闷不乐地坐在沙发上。

glut /glʌt/ (**gluts, glutting, glutted**) 1 N-COUNT If there is a **glut of** something, there is so much of it that it cannot all be sold or used. 供应过剩 [usu sing, usu with supp] ❑ *Exports have become increasingly important to wineries as they battle a global wine glut.* 出口对于各葡萄酒厂来说已变得日益重要，因为他们得应对全球性的葡萄酒供应过剩问题。 2 V-T If a market **is glutted with** something, there is a glut of that thing. 供过于求 [BUSINESS] ❑ *The region is glutted with hospitals.* 该地区的医院供过于求。

gm. (**gm.**)

> The plural can be **gm.** or **gms.**

gm. is a written abbreviation for **gram.** 克 ❑ *...450 gm. (1 lb) mixed soft summer fruits.* …450克（合1磅）拼装夏令浆果。

GM /dʒi ɛm/ ADJ **GM** crops have had one or more genes changed, for example in order to make them resist pests better. **GM** food contains ingredients made from GM crops. **GM** is an abbreviation for **genetically modified.** 转基因的 ❑ *Many of us may be eating food containing GM ingredients without realizing it.* 我们很多人可能在不知不觉地食用含转基因成分的食物。

GMO /dʒi ɛm oʊ/ (**GMOs**) N-COUNT A **GMO** is an animal, plant, or other organism whose genetic structure has been changed by genetic engineering. **GMO** is an abbreviation for "genetically modified organism." 转基因生物 ❑ ...*the presence of GMOs in many processed foods.* …许多加工食品中转基因生物的存在。

GMT /dʒi̲ ɛm ti̲/ **GMT** is the standard time in Great Britain which is used to calculate the time in the rest of the world. **GMT** is an abbreviation for **Greenwich Mean Time.** 格林尼治标准时间 ❑ *New Mexico is seven hours behind GMT.* 新墨西哥州比格林尼治标准时晚7个小时。

gnaw /nɔ̲/ (**gnaws, gnawing, gnawed**) 1 V-T/V-I If people or animals **gnaw** something or **gnaw at** it, they bite it repeatedly. 反复啃咬 ❑ *Woodlice attack living plants and gnaw at the stems.* 木虱会侵袭活体植物并不停地啃咬它们的茎。 2 V-I If a feeling or thought **gnaws at** you, it causes you to keep worrying. 困扰 [WRITTEN] ❑ ...*the nagging disquiet that had gnawed at him for days.* …困扰了他数日、令他不得安宁的忧虑。

GNP /dʒi̲ ɛn pi̲/ (**GNPs**) N-VAR In economics, a country's **GNP** is the total value of all the goods produced and services provided by that country in one year. **GNP** is an abbreviation for **gross national product.** Compare **GDP.** 国民生产总值

G

go

1 MOVING OR LEAVING
2 LINK VERB USES
3 OTHER VERB USES, NOUN USES, AND PHRASES
4 PHRASAL VERBS

1 go ♦♦♦ /goʊ̲/ (**goes, going, went, gone**)

In most cases the past participle of **go** is **gone**, but occasionally you use 'been': see **been.**

1 V-T/V-I When you **go** somewhere, you move or travel there. 去；行进 ❑ *We went to Rome.* 我们去了罗马。 ❑ *I went home for the weekend.* 我回家过周末了。 ❑ *It took us an hour to go three miles.* 行进3英里花了我们1小时。 2 V-I When you **go**, you leave the place where you are. 离开 ❑ *Let's go.* 我们走吧。 3 V-T/V-I You use **go** to say that someone leaves the place where they are and does an activity, often a leisure activity. 去（从事某活动）❑ *We went swimming very early.* 我们很早就去游泳了。 ❑ *Maybe they've just gone shopping.* 或许他们刚刚去买东西了。 ❑ *He went for a walk.* 他去散步了。 4 V-T/V-I When you **go** do something, you move to a place in order to do it and you do it. You can also **go and** do something, but you always say that someone **went and** did something. 去（做某事）❑ *I have to go see the doctor.* 我得去看病。 ❑ *I finished my beer, then went and got another.* 我喝完了自己的啤酒，然后又去拿了一瓶。 5 V-I If you **go to** school, work, or church, you attend it regularly as part of your normal life. （正常）去（上学、上班或去教堂等）❑ *She will have to go to school.* 她将不得不去上学。 6 V-I When you say where a road or path **goes**, you are saying where it begins or ends, or what places it is in. （道路）通向 ❑ *There's a mountain road that goes from Blairstown to Millbrook Village.* 有一条从布莱尔斯敦通向米尔布鲁克村的山路。 7 V-I You can use **go** with words like "further" and "beyond" to show the degree or extent of something. 与**further**、**beyond**等词连用，表示程度 ❑ *The governor went further by agreeing that all policy announcements should be made first in the House.* 州长进一步同意所有政策的宣布都应首先在议院进行。 8 V-I If you say that a period of time **goes** quickly or slowly, you mean that it seems to pass quickly or slowly. （时间）流逝 ❑ *The weeks go so quickly!* 一周周过得真快！ 9 V-I If you say where money **goes**, you are saying what it is spent on. （钱）花费在 ❑ *Most of my money goes toward bills.* 我的钱大多花在支付各种账单上。 10 V-I If you say that something **goes to** someone, you mean that it is given to them. 被给予 ❑ *A lot of credit must go to the chairman and his father.* 很大一部分赞誉必须给予主席和他的父亲。 11 V-I If someone **goes on** television or radio, they take part in a television or radio program. 出现（在电视或电台上）❑ *The president has gone on television to defend stringent new security measures.* 总统在电视上为严格的新安全措施进行了辩护。 12 V-I If something **goes**, someone gets rid of it. 被消除 ❑ *Exactly how many jobs will go remains unclear.* 具体多少个职位会被裁掉尚不清楚。 13 V-I If someone **goes**, they leave their job, usually because they are forced to. （常指被迫）离职 ❑ *He had made a humiliating tactical error and he had to go.* 他犯下了一个令他耻辱的战术错误，被迫离职。 14 V-I If something **goes into** something else, it is put in it as one of the parts or elements that form it. 加入 ❑ ...*the really interesting ingredients that go into the dishes that we all love to eat.* …我们都喜欢吃的菜肴中所加入的真正有意思的配料。 15 V-I If something **goes** in a particular place, it belongs there or should be put there, because that is where you normally keep it. （正常）应置放于 ❑ *The shoes go on the shoe shelf.* 鞋子应该放在鞋架上。 16 V-I If you say that one number **goes into** another number a particular number of times, you are dividing the second number by the first. 除 ❑ *Six goes into thirty five times.* 6除30得5。 17 V-I If one of a person's senses, such as their sight or hearing, **is going**, it is getting weak and they may soon lose it completely. （官能）衰退 [INFORMAL] ❑ *His eyes are going; he says he has glaucoma.* 他的视力在衰退；他说他得了青光眼。 18 V-I If something such as a light bulb or a part of an engine **is going**, it is no longer working properly and will soon need to be replaced. （灯泡、引擎等）不再正常工作 ❑ *I thought it looked as though the battery was going.* 我看像是电池不行了。

2 go ♦♦♦ /goʊ̲/ (**goes, going, went, gone**) V-LINK You can use **go** to say that a person or thing changes to another state or condition. For example, if someone **goes crazy**, they become crazy, and if something **goes bad**, it deteriorates. 变得 ❑ *I'm going bald.* 我在脱发。 ❑ *Sometimes food goes bad, but people don't know it, so they eat it anyway and then they get sick.* 有时食物变质了人们却不知道，所以还是食用了它，结果就病了。

3 go ♦♦♦ /goʊ̲/ (**goes, going, went, gone**) 1 V-I You use **go** to talk about the way something happens. For example, if an event or situation **goes well**, it is successful. 进展 ❑ *She says everything is going smoothly.* 她说一切进展顺利。 2 V-I If a machine or device **is going**, it is working. 运转 ❑ *What about my copier? Can you get it going again?* 我的复印机呢？你能让它重新运转起来吗？ 3 V-RECIP If something **goes with** something else, or if two things **go together**, they look or taste good together. （与…）相配 ❑ *I was searching for a pair of gray gloves to go with my new gown.* 我在找一副灰色手套来配我的新礼服。 ❑ *I can see that some colors go together and some don't.* 我能看出有些颜色相配而有些则不配。 4 V-T/V-I You use **go** to introduce something you are quoting. For example, you say **the story goes** or **the argument goes** just before you quote all or part of it. （故事、理由）是 ❑ *The story goes that she went home with him that night.* 据说那天晚上她和他一起回的家。 ❑ *The story goes like this.* 故事是这样的。 5 V-T You use **go** when indicating that something makes or produces a sound. For example, if you say that something **goes "bang,"** you mean it produces the sound "bang." 发出（某种声音）❑ *She stopped in front of a painting of a dog and she started going "woof woof."* 她在一幅狗的画像跟前停下，开始"汪汪"叫了起来。 6 V-T You can use **go** instead of "say" when you are quoting what someone has said or what you think they will say. 说（用于引出某人所说的话）[INFORMAL] ❑ *He goes to me: "Oh, what do you want?"* 他对我说："噢，你要什么？" 7 N-COUNT A **go** is an attempt at doing something. 尝试 ❑ *I always wanted to have a go at football.* 我一直都想尝试踢足球。 ❑ *She won on her first go.* 她第一次尝试就赢了。 8 N-COUNT If it is your **go** in a game, it is your turn to do something, for example to play a card or move a piece. （出牌、走棋的）轮次 [poss N] ❑ *Now whose go is it?* 现在该谁了？ 9 → see also **going, gone** 10 PHRASE If you do something **as you go along**, you do it while you are doing another thing, without preparing it beforehand. （随做其它事而）做某事 ❑ *Learning how to become a parent takes time. It's a skill you learn as you go along.* 学会为人父母需要时间，这是一种在实践中学习的技能。 11 CONVENTION If someone says **"Where do we go from here?"** they are asking what should be done next, usually because a problem has not been solved in a satisfactory way. 我们下一步该怎么办？ 12 PHRASE If you say that someone **is making a go of** something such as a business or relationship, you mean that they are having some success with it. 在…方面获得成功 ❑ *I knew we could make a go of it and be happy.* 我知道我们能做成这件事而且会很开心。 13 PHRASE If you say that someone is always **on the go**, you mean that they are always busy and active. 忙碌 [INFORMAL] ❑ *I got a new job this year where I am on the go all the time.* 我今年有了份新工作，一直在忙碌。 14 PHRASE If you say that there are a particular number of things **to go**, you mean that they still remain to be dealt with. 要做的（事情）❑ *I still had another five operations to go.* 我还有另外5个手术要做。 15 PHRASE If you say that there is a certain amount of time **to go**, you mean that there is that amount of time left before something happens or ends. 要过的（时间）❑ *There is a week to go until the elections.* 还要过1周才到选举时间。 16 PHRASE If you are in a café or restaurant and ask for an item of food **to go**, you mean that you want to take it with you and not eat it there. 要带走的（食物）[mainly AM]

in BRIT, use **to take away**

❑ *... large fries to go.* …要带走的大份炸薯条。

❹ **go** ♦♦♦ /goʊ/ (**goes, going, went, gone**)

▸ **go about** 1 PHRASAL VERB The way you **go about** a task or problem is the way you approach it and deal with it. 处理 ❑ *I want him back, but I just don't know how to go about it.* 我希望他回来，可我就是不知道怎么去做这件事。 2 PHRASAL VERB When you **are going about** your normal activities, you are doing them. 从事（常规活动）❑ *We were simply going about our business when we were pounced upon by these police officers.* 当我们被这些警官们抓住的时候，我们只是在做着正常生意。

▸ **go after** PHRASAL VERB If you **go after** something, you try to get it, catch it, or hit it. 追求；追捕；追击 ❑ *We're not going after civilian targets.* 我们不会追击平民目标。

▸ **go against** 1 PHRASAL VERB If a person or their behavior **goes against** your wishes, beliefs, or expectations, their behavior is the opposite of what you want, believe in, or expect. 违背（某人的希望、信念、期望等）❑ *Changes are being made here which go against my principles and I cannot agree with them.* 这里在被改变，这有悖我的原则，我不能同意。 2 PHRASAL VERB If a decision, vote, or result **goes against** you, you do not get the decision, vote, or result that you wanted. 对（某人）不利 ❑ *The mayor will resign if the vote goes against him.* 如果投票结果对市长不利，他将辞职。

▸ **go ahead** 1 PHRASAL VERB If someone **goes ahead with** something, they begin to do it or make it, especially after planning, promising, or asking permission to do it. 着手做 ❑ *The district board will vote today on whether to go ahead with the plan.* 区理事会将于今天就是否执行该计划投票。 2 PHRASAL VERB If a process or an organized event **goes ahead**, it takes place or is carried out. 进行 ❑ *The event will go ahead as planned in Chicago next summer.* 该活动将按计划于明年夏天在芝加哥进行。

▸ **go along with** 1 PHRASAL VERB If you **go along with** a rule, decision, or policy, you accept it and obey it. 遵从 ❑ *Whatever the majority decided I was prepared to go along with.* 不论多数人做何决定，我都准备好了遵从。 2 PHRASAL VERB If you **go along with** a person or an idea, you agree with them. 赞同 ❑ *"I don't think a government has properly done it for about the past twenty-five years."—"I'd go along with that."* "我不认为在过去约25年里有政府妥善地处理过这个问题。" ——"我赞同这一观点。"

▸ **go around** 1 PHRASAL VERB If you **go around to** someone's house, you go to visit them at their house. 造访 ❑ *I asked them to go around to the house to see if they were there.* 我叫他们去造访那所房子看他们是否在那儿。 2 PHRASAL VERB If you **go around** in a particular way, you behave or dress in that way, often as part of your normal life. （以某方式）做事；着装 ❑ *I got in the habit of going around with bare feet.* 我养成了打赤脚的习惯。 3 PHRASAL VERB If a piece of news or a joke **is going around**, it is being told by many people in the same period of time. （消息、笑话）流传 ❑ *There's a nasty sort of rumor going around about it.* 关于这件事有一种可恶的谣言正在流传。 4 PHRASAL VERB If there is enough of something **to go around**, there is enough of it to be shared among a group of people, or to do all the things for which it is needed. 满足需求 ❑ *Eventually we will not have enough water to go around.* 最终我们将没有足够的水供所有人用。

▸ **go away** 1 PHRASAL VERB If you **go away**, you leave a place or a person's company. 离开 ❑ *I think we need to go away and think about this.* 我认为我们需要离开，然后考虑这件事。 2 PHRASAL VERB If you **go away**, you leave a place and spend a period of time somewhere else, especially as a vacation. （尤指作为度假）去别地度过一段时间 ❑ *Why don't you and I go away this weekend?* 为什么这个周末咱俩不去度假呢？

▸ **go back on** PHRASAL VERB If you **go back on** a promise or agreement, you do not do what you promised or agreed to do. 背离（诺言、协议等）❑ *The budget crisis has forced the president to go back on his word.* 预算危机已迫使该总统背离了自己的承诺。

▸ **go back to** 1 PHRASAL VERB If you **go back to** a task or activity, you start doing it again after you have stopped doing it for a period of time. （停止一段时间后）回到（某任务、活动等）❑ *I now look forward to going back to work as soon as possible.* 我现在盼望尽快回到工作中。 ❑ *Amy went back to studying.* 艾美回去学习了。 2 PHRASAL VERB If you **go back to** a particular point in a lecture, discussion, or book, you start to discuss it. 回到（讲座、讨论、书等的某一点）❑ *Let me just go back to the point I was making.* 让我回到我刚才所谈的那一点上。

▸ **go before** 1 PHRASAL VERB Something that **has gone before** has happened or been discussed at an earlier time. 之前发生；之前被讨论 ❑ *This is a rejection of most of what has gone before.* 这是对先前讨论过的大部分内容的否定。 2 PHRASAL VERB To **go before** a judge, tribunal, or court of law means to be present there as part of an official or legal process. 提交给（法官、审判员、法庭等）❑ *The case went before Justice Henry on December 23 and was adjourned.* 这个案件于12月23日提交给了亨利法官，之后被延期。

▸ **go by** 1 PHRASAL VERB If you say that time **goes by**, you mean that it passes. （时间）流逝 ❑ *My grandmother was becoming more and more sad and frail as the years went by.* 随着岁月的流逝，我的祖母变得越来越伤感和虚弱。 2 PHRASAL VERB If you **go by** something, you use it as a basis for a judgment or action. 遵照 ❑ *If they prove that I was wrong, then I'll go by what they say.* 如果他们证明我错了，那么我就会照他们说的去做。

▸ **go down** 1 PHRASAL VERB If a price, level, or amount **goes down**, it becomes lower or less than it was. （价格、水平或数量等）下降 ❑ *Income from sales tax went down.* 来自销售税的收入下降了。 ❑ *Crime has gone down 70 percent.* 犯罪率已下降了70%。 2 PHRASAL VERB If you **go down on** your knees or **on** all fours, you lower your body until it is supported by your knees, or by your hands and knees. 跪下；趴下 ❑ *I went down on my knees and prayed for guidance.* 我双膝跪下，祈求得到指引。 3 PHRASAL VERB If you say that a remark, idea, or type of behavior **goes down** in a particular way, you mean that it gets a particular kind of reaction from a person or group of people. 引起…反响 ❑ *Lawyers advised their clients that a neat appearance went down well with the judges.* 律师们向其当事人们建议说，整洁的外表会赢得法官们的好感。 4 PHRASAL VERB When the sun **goes down**, it goes below the horizon. （太阳）下山 ❑ *...the glow left in the sky after the sun has gone down.* …太阳下山后留在天空中的余晖。 5 PHRASAL VERB If a ship **goes down**, it sinks. If a plane **goes down**, it crashes out of the sky. （船只）沉没；（飞机）坠毁 ❑ *Their aircraft went down during a training exercise.* 他们的飞机在一次训练演习中坠毁了。 6 PHRASAL VERB If a computer **goes down**, it stops functioning temporarily. （电脑）出故障 ❑ *The main computers went down for 30 minutes.* 这些主要计算机出了30分钟的故障。 7 PHRASAL VERB Something that **is going down** is happening. 发生 [usu cont] [INFORMAL] ❑ *The patrol can detect if something is going down or is about to go down.* 巡逻队能发现是否有情况正在发生或即将发生。

▸ **go for** 1 PHRASAL VERB If you **go for** a particular thing or way of doing something, you choose it. 选择 ❑ *People tried to persuade him to go for a more gradual reform program.* 人们试图说服他选择一个更为渐进的改革方案。 2 PHRASAL VERB If you **go for** someone, you attack them. 袭击 ❑ *Pantieri went for him, gripping him by the throat.* 潘蒂埃里扑向他，紧紧掐住了他的喉咙。 3 PHRASAL VERB If you say that a statement you have made about one person or thing also **goes for** another person or thing, you mean that the statement is also true of this other person or thing. 适用于 ❑ *It is illegal to dishonor reservations; that goes for restaurants as well as customers.* 不履行预订是违法的；这既适用于顾客，也适用于饭店。 4 PHRASAL VERB If something **goes for** a particular price, it is sold for that amount. 以（某价格）被售出 ❑ *Some old machines go for as much as 35,000 dollars.* 一些旧机器以多达3.5万美元的价格出售。

▸ **go in** PHRASAL VERB If the sun **goes in**, a cloud comes in front of it and it can no longer be seen. （太阳）被云遮蔽 ❑ *The sun went in, and the breeze became cold.* 太阳被云遮蔽，微风变冷了。

▸ **go in for** PHRASAL VERB If you **go in for** a particular activity, you decide to do it as a hobby or interest. 爱好（某活动）❑ *They go in for tennis and bowling.* 他们爱好打网球和保龄球。

▸ **go into** 1 PHRASAL VERB If you **go into** something, you describe or examine it fully or in detail. 详述；细查 ❑ *It was a private conversation and I don't want to go into details about what was said.* 那是一段私人谈话，我不想详述所谈内容。 2 PHRASAL VERB If you **go into** something, you decide to do it as your job or career. 进入（某行业）❑ *Mr. Pok has now gone into the tourism business.* 波克先生现在已进入旅游业。 3 PHRASAL VERB If an amount of time, effort, or money **goes into** something, it is spent or used to do it, get it, or make it. （时间、精力或钱等）被投入 ❑ *Is there a lot of effort and money going into this sort of research?* 有大量精力和金钱在被投入到这种研究中吗？

▸ **go off** 1 PHRASAL VERB If an explosive device or a gun **goes off**, it explodes or fires. （炸弹）爆炸；（枪）开击 ❑ *A few minutes later the bomb went off, destroying the vehicle.* 几分钟后炸弹爆炸了，摧毁了那辆车。 2 PHRASAL VERB If an alarm bell **goes off**, it makes a sudden loud noise. （警报器）突发巨响 ❑ *Then the fire alarm went off.*

I just grabbed my clothes and ran out. 之后火警响了，我只抓起衣服就跑了出去。 **3** PHRASAL VERB If an electrical device **goes off**, it stops operating. (电气设备) 停止运作 ❑ *As the water came in the windows, all the lights went off.* 随着水从窗户涌进来，所有的灯都灭了。

▶ **go off with** **1** PHRASAL VERB If someone **goes off with** another person, they leave their husband, wife, or lover and have a relationship with that person. 与…私奔 ❑ *I suppose Carolyn went off with some man she'd fallen in love with.* 我想卡罗琳跟她爱上的某个男人私奔了。 **2** PHRASAL VERB If someone **goes off with** something that belongs to another person, they leave and take it with them. 私自拿走 ❑ *He's gone off with my passport.* 他拿走了我的护照。

▶ **go on** **1** PHRASAL VERB If you **go on** doing something, or **go on with** an activity, you continue to do it. 继续 ❑ *Unemployment is likely to go on rising this year.* 失业人数今年很可能继续上升。 ❑ *I'm all right here. Go on with your work.* 我在这儿很好。继续你的工作吧。 **2** PHRASAL VERB If something **is going on**, it is happening. 发生 ❑ *While this conversation was going on, I was listening with earnest attention.* 该谈话进行时，我在聚精会神地听。 **3** PHRASAL VERB If a process or institution **goes on**, it continues to happen or exist. 继续下去；继续存在 ❑ *The population failed to understand the necessity for the war to go on.* 人们没能理解那场战争继续下去的必要性。 **4** PHRASAL VERB If you say that a period of time **goes on**, you mean that it passes. (时间) 流逝 ❑ *Renewable energy will become progressively more important as time goes on.* 随着时间的推移，可再生能源将逐渐变得更重要。 **5** PHRASAL VERB If you **go on to** do something, you do it after you have done something else. 继而 (做另一件事) ❑ *Alliss retired from golf in 1969 and went on to become a successful broadcaster.* 埃利斯1969年结束了专业高尔夫运动生涯，继而成为了一名成功的播音员。 **6** PHRASAL VERB If you **go on to** a place, you go to it from the place that you have reached. 继而去 (某地) ❑ *He goes on to New Orleans tomorrow.* 他明天继而去新奥尔良。 **7** PHRASAL VERB If you **go on**, you continue saying something or talking about something. 继续说；继续谈 ❑ *Meer cleared his throat several times before he went on.* 米尔清了几次嗓子，然后继续说下去。 **8** PHRASAL VERB If you **go on about** something, you continue talking about the same thing, often in an annoying way. 唠唠叨叨地谈 [INFORMAL] ❑ *He's always going on about his son and daughter.* 他总是没完没了地谈论他的儿子和女儿。 **9** PHRASAL VERB You say "**Go on**" to someone to persuade or encourage them to do something. 继续吧 (用以劝说或鼓励) [only imper] [INFORMAL] ❑ *Go on, it's fun.* 继续吧，很好玩。 **10** PHRASAL VERB If you talk about the information you have **to go on**, you mean the information you have available to base an opinion or judgment on. 以…为依据 ❑ *But you have to go on the facts.* 但是，你得以事实为依据。 **11** PHRASAL VERB If an electrical device **goes on**, it begins operating. (电气设备) 开始运转 ❑ *A light went on at seven every evening.* 一盏灯每晚七点钟亮。

▶ **go out** **1** PHRASAL VERB If you **go out**, you leave your home in order to do something enjoyable, for example to go to a party, a bar, or the movies. (尤指为娱乐而) 出门 ❑ *I'm going out tonight.* 我今晚要出去玩。 **2** PHRASAL VERB If you **go out with** someone, the two of you spend time together socially, and have a romantic or sexual relationship. (与某人) 恋爱 ❑ *I once went out with a French man.* 我曾与一个法国人恋爱过。 **3** PHRASAL VERB If you **go out to** do something, you make a deliberate effort to do it. 刻意去 (做某事) ❑ *You do not go out to injure opponents.* 你不会刻意去伤害对手。 **4** PHRASAL VERB If a light **goes out**, it stops shining. (灯) 熄灭 ❑ *The bedroom light went out after a moment.* 卧室的灯片刻后熄灭了。 **5** PHRASAL VERB If something that is burning **goes out**, it stops burning. (燃烧物) 熄火 ❑ *The fire seemed to be going out.* 火看来快熄灭了。 **6** PHRASAL VERB If a message **goes out**, it is announced, published, or sent out to people. (信息) 被公布 ❑ *Word went out that a column of tanks was on its way.* 有消息说一队坦克上路了。 **7** PHRASAL VERB When the tide **goes out**, the water in the sea gradually moves back to a lower level. (潮水) 退去 ❑ *The tide was going out.* 潮水正在退去。 **8** PHRASE You can say "**My heart goes out to him**" or "**My sympathy goes out to her**" to express the strong sympathy you have for someone in a difficult or unpleasant situation. 我十分同情某人 [FEELINGS] ❑ *My heart goes out to Mrs. Adams and her fatherless children.* 我十分同情亚当斯太太和她失去了父亲的孩子们。

▶ **go over** PHRASAL VERB If you **go over** a document, incident, or problem, you examine, discuss, or think about it very carefully. 仔细检查 ❑ *I won't know how successful it is until an accountant has gone over the books.* 我要等到会计仔细查看了账目后才会知道盈利状况如何。

▶ **go round** → see **go around**

▶ **go through** **1** PHRASAL VERB If you **go through** an experience or a period of time, especially an unpleasant or difficult one, you experience it. 经历 (尤为艰难时期) [BRIT] ❑ *He was going through a very difficult time.* 他在经历一段非常艰难的时期。 **2** PHRASAL VERB If you **go through** a lot of things such as papers or clothes, you look at them, usually in order to sort them into groups or to search for a particular item. 检查 ❑ *It was evident that someone had gone through my possessions.* 显然有人翻过我的物品。 **3** PHRASAL VERB If you **go through** a list, story, or plan, you read or check it from beginning to end. 通读；查阅 ❑ *Going through his list of customers is a massive job.* 查阅他的客户名单是一项繁重的工作。 **4** PHRASAL VERB If a law, agreement, or official decision **goes through**, it is approved by a legislature or committee. (法律、协议、决定) 获得通过 ❑ *The bill might have gone through if the economy was growing.* 如果经济保持增长的话，那个议案或许已经获得通过了。

▶ **go through with** PHRASAL VERB If you **go through with** an action you have decided on, you do it, even though it may be very unpleasant or difficult for you. 将 (决定的事) 做了 ❑ *Richard pleaded for Belinda to reconsider and not to go through with the divorce.* 理查德恳求贝琳达重新考虑一下而不要坚持离婚。

▶ **go under** PHRASAL VERB If a business or project **goes under**, it becomes unable to continue in operation or in existence. (商行) 倒闭；(项目) 失败 [BUSINESS] ❑ *If one firm goes under it could provoke a cascade of bankruptcies.* 如果一家公司倒闭，可能会引起一连串的破产。

▶ **go up** **1** PHRASAL VERB If a price, amount, or level **goes up**, it becomes higher or greater than it was. 上涨 ❑ *Interest rates went up.* 利率上涨了。 ❑ *The cost has gone up to $1.95 a minute.* 价格已涨到了一分钟$1.95。 **2** PHRASAL VERB When a building, wall, or other structure **goes up**, it is built or fixed in place. (建筑物、墙等) 被建造 ❑ *He noticed a new building going up near Whitaker Park.* 他注意到一幢新楼正在惠特克公园附近拔地而起。 **3** PHRASAL VERB If something **goes up**, it explodes or starts to burn, usually suddenly and with great intensity. 爆炸；着火 ❑ *The hotel went up in flames.* 那家宾馆着火了。 **4** PHRASAL VERB If a shout or cheer **goes up**, it is made by a lot of people together. (喊声、欢呼声) 响起 ❑ *A cheer went up from the other passengers.* 一阵欢呼声从其他乘客中响起。

▶ **go with** **1** PHRASAL VERB If one thing **goes with** another thing, the two things officially belong together, so that if you get one, you also get the other. 伴随…而有 ❑ *...the lucrative $250,000 salary that goes with the job.* …这份工作所提供的25万美元的丰厚薪水。 **2** PHRASAL VERB If one thing **goes with** another thing, it is usually found or experienced together with the other thing. 伴随…而存在 ❑ *For many women, the status which goes with being a wife is important.* 对许多女性来说，伴随为人妻而来的地位很重要。

▶ **go without** PHRASAL VERB If you **go without** something that you need or usually have or do, you do not get it or do it. 得不到；不做 ❑ *I have known what it is like to go without food for days.* 我已知道数日不吃东西是什么滋味了。

goad /goʊd/ (**goads, goading, goaded**) V-T If you **goad** someone, you deliberately make them feel angry or irritated, often causing them to react by doing something. 刺激 ❑ *Charles was always goading me.* 查尔斯老是刺激我。 ● N-COUNT **Goad** is also a noun. 刺激 ❑ *Her presence was just one more goad to Joanna's unraveling nerves.* 她的出现只是对乔安娜几近崩溃的神经的又一次刺激。

go-ahead **1** N-SING If you give someone or something **the go-ahead**, you give them permission to start doing something. 许可 ❑ *Chuck gave Pellman the go-ahead to speak publicly about the injury he sustained.* 查克允许佩尔曼开始公开谈论他经受的伤害。 **2** ADJ A **go-ahead** person or organization tries hard to succeed, often by using new methods. 开拓进取的 [ADJ n] ❑ *Fairview Estate is one of the oldest and the most go-ahead wine producers in South Africa.* "丽景庄园"是南非最古老、最有开拓进取精神的葡萄酒生产商之一。

goal ♦♦◇ /goʊl/ (**goals**) **1** N-COUNT In games such as soccer or hockey, the **goal** is the space into which the players try to get the ball in order to score a point for their team. 球门 ❑ *The Dragons had only one shot on goal.* 龙队只有一次射门。 **2** N-COUNT In games such as soccer or hockey, a **goal** is when a player gets the ball into the goal, or the point that is scored by doing this. 进球 ❑ *They scored five goals in the first half of the match.* 他们在上半场进了5个球。 **3** N-COUNT Something that is your **goal** is something that you hope to achieve, especially when much time and effort will be needed. 目标 ❑ *It's a matter of setting your own goals and following them.* 这是一个设定自己的目标并努力实现它们的问题。

→ see **football, soccer**

Word Partnership *goal* 的常用搭配：

V. **shoot at a goal** 1
score a goal 2
accomplish a goal, share a goal 3
ADJ. **winning goal** 2
attainable goal, main goal 3

goalie /goʊli/ (**goalies**) N-COUNT A **goalie** is the same as a **goalkeeper.** 守门员 [INFORMAL]

goal·keeper /goʊlkipər/ (**goalkeepers**) N-COUNT A **goalkeeper** is the player on a sports team whose job is to guard the goal. 守门员

goal·less /goʊlləs/ ADJ In soccer, a **goalless** draw is a game which ends without any goals having been scored. 无进球的（平局）❑ *The fixture ended in a goalless draw.* 该比赛以零比零的平局结束。

goal·post /goʊlpoʊst/ (**goalposts**) also **goal post** N-COUNT A **goalpost** is one of the two upright wooden posts that are connected by a crossbar and form the goal in games such as soccer and hockey. 球门柱
→ see **football**

goat /goʊt/ (**goats**) N-COUNT A **goat** is a farm animal or a wild animal that is about the size of a sheep. Goats have horns, and hairs on their chin which resemble a beard. 山羊

gob·ble /gɒbᵊl/ (**gobbles, gobbling, gobbled**) V-T If you **gobble** food, you eat it quickly and greedily. 狼吞虎咽地吃 ❑ *Pete gobbled all the beef stew.* 皮特狼吞虎咽地吃完了所有的炖牛肉。● PHRASAL VERB **Gobble down** and **gobble up** mean the same as **gobble.** 狼吞虎咽地吃（同**gobble**）❑ *There were dangerous beasts in the river that might gobble you up.* 那条河里曾有危险的野兽，会把你吞吃掉。

go-between (**go-betweens**) N-COUNT A **go-between** is a person who takes messages between people who are unable or unwilling to meet each other. 中间人 ❑ *He will act as a go-between to try and work out an agenda.* 他将充当中间人，尽力制订出一个日程表。

god ♦♦◇ /gɒd/ (**gods**) 1 N-PROPER The name **God** is given to the spirit or being who is worshipped as the creator and ruler of the world, especially by Jews, Christians, and Muslims. 上帝 ❑ *He believes in God.* 他信奉上帝。 2 CONVENTION People sometimes use **God** in exclamations to emphasize something that they are saying, or to express surprise, fear, or excitement. This use could cause offense. 天哪 [EMPHASIS] ❑ *Oh my God, he's shot somebody.* 噢，我的天哪，他向人开了枪。 ❑ *Good God, it's Mr. Harper!* 天哪，是哈珀先生！ 3 N-COUNT In many religions, a **god** is one of the spirits or beings that are believed to have power over a particular part of the world or nature. 神 ❑ *...Zeus, king of the gods.* …宙斯，众神之王。 4 N-COUNT Someone who is admired very much by a person or group of people, and who influences them a lot, can be referred to as a **god.** 神一般的人物 ❑ *To his followers he was a god.* 对他的追随者们来说，他是个神一般的人物。 5 PHRASE You can say **God knows, God only knows,** or **God alone knows** to emphasize that you do not know something. 天晓得（用以强调不知情）[EMPHASIS] ❑ *God alone knows what she thinks.* 天晓得她想什么。 6 PHRASE If someone says **God knows** in reply to a question, they mean that they do not know the answer. 天晓得（用以强调不知道答案）[EMPHASIS] ❑ *"Where is he now?"—"God knows."* "他现在在哪里？" —— "天晓得。" 7 PHRASE If someone uses expressions such as **what in God's name, why in God's name,** or **how in God's name,** they are emphasizing how angry, annoyed, or surprised they are. 到底（用以强调愤怒、烦恼、吃惊的程度）[INFORMAL, EMPHASIS] ❑ *What in God's name do you expect me to do?* 你到底要我做什么？ 8 PHRASE If a person thinks they are **God's gift to** someone or something, they think they are perfect or extremely good. 上帝的恩赐 [INFORMAL] ❑ *Are men God's gift to women? Some of them think they are.* 男人是上帝对女人的恩赐吗？有些男人认为他们是。 9 PHRASE If someone **plays God,** they act as if they have unlimited power and can do anything they want. 扮上帝 [DISAPPROVAL] ❑ *You have no right to play God in my life!* 你无权在我的生活中扮演上帝！ 10 PHRASE You can use **God** in expressions such as **I hope to God,** or **I wish to God,** or **I swear to God,** in order to emphasize what you are saying. 对天（希望、发誓）[EMPHASIS] ❑ *I hope to God they are paying you well.* 我真心希望他们给你好的报酬。 11 PHRASE If you say **God willing,** you are saying that something will happen if all goes well. 天公作美 ❑ *God willing, there will be a breakthrough.* 天公作美的话，会有所突破。 12 **honest to God** → see **honest** 13 **for God's sake** → see **sake** 14 **thank God** → see **thank**
→ see **religion**

god·dess /gɒdɪs/ (**goddesses**) N-COUNT In many religions, a **goddess** is a female spirit or being that is believed to have power over a particular part of the world or nature. 女神 ❑ *...Diana, the goddess of war.* …战争女神黛安娜。
→ see **religion**

going ♦♦♦ /goʊɪŋ/ 1 PHRASE If you say that something **is going to** happen, you mean that it will happen in the future, usually quite soon. 将会 ❑ *I think it's going to be successful.* 我认为它将会成功。 ❑ *You're going to enjoy this.* 你会喜欢这个的。 2 PHRASE You say that you **are going to** do something to express your intention or determination to do it. 打算（做某事）❑ *I'm going to go to bed.* 我打算上床睡觉。 ❑ *He announced that he's going to resign.* 他宣布即将辞职。 3 N-UNCOUNT You use **the going** to talk about how easy or difficult it is to do something. You can also say that something is, for example, **hard going** or **tough going.** 进展情况 ❑ *He has her support to fall back on when the going gets tough.* 当进展艰难时，他可以依赖她的支持。 4 ADJ The **going** rate or the **going** salary is the usual amount of money that you expect to pay or receive for something. 现行的（价格或工资等）[ADJ n] ❑ *That's about half the going price on world oil markets.* 那大约是世界石油市场上现行价位的一半。 5 → see also **go** 6 PHRASE If someone or something **has** a lot **going for** them, they have a lot of advantages. 具备有利条件 ❑ *This area has a lot going for it.* 该地区有许多有利条件。 7 PHRASE When you **get going,** you start doing something or start a journey, especially after a delay. （尤指耽搁后）开始 ❑ *Now what about that shopping list? I've got to get going.* 现在那张购物清单怎么样了？我得走了。 8 PHRASE If you say that someone should do something **while the going is good,** you are advising them to do it while things are going well and they still have the opportunity, because you think it will become much more difficult to do. 趁形势还好 ❑ *People are leaving in the thousands while the going is good.* 趁情况尚好，成千上万的人正在尽快撤离。 9 PHRASE If you **keep going,** you continue doing things or doing a particular thing. 继续做 ❑ *I like to keep going. I hate to sit still.* 我喜欢不停地做事。我讨厌坐着不动。 10 **going concern**
→ see **concern**

goings-on N-PLURAL If you describe events or activities as **goings-on,** you mean that they are strange, interesting, amusing, or dishonest. 诡异活动 ❑ *The Mexican girl had found out about the goings-on in the factory.* 那个墨西哥女孩已发现了工厂里的诡异活动。

gold ♦♦◇ /goʊld/ (**golds**) 1 N-UNCOUNT **Gold** is a valuable, yellow-colored metal that is used for making jewelry and ornaments, and as an international currency. 黄金 ❑ *...a sapphire set in gold.* …一颗镶嵌在金子里的蓝宝石。 ❑ *The price of gold was going up.* 黄金的价格上涨了。 2 N-UNCOUNT **Gold** is jewelry and other things that are made of gold. 金饰物；金制品 ❑ *We handed over all our gold and money.* 我们把所有的金饰物和钱都交了出来。 3 COLOR Something that is **gold** is a bright yellow color, and is often shiny. 金色的 ❑ *I'd been wearing Michel's black and gold shirt.* 我一直穿着米歇尔那件黑色和金色相间的衬衫。 4 N-VAR A **gold** is the same as a **gold medal.** 金牌 [INFORMAL] ❑ *His ambition was to win gold at the Atlanta Games in 1996.* 他的目标是在1996年的亚特兰大奥运会上夺得金牌。 5 PHRASE If you say that a child is being **as good as gold,** you are emphasizing that they are behaving very well and are not causing you any problems. （小孩）很乖的 [EMPHASIS] ❑ *The boys were as good as gold on our walk.* 这些小男孩儿在我们散步时很乖。 6 PHRASE If you say that someone has **a heart of gold,** you are emphasizing that they are very good and kind to other people. 一颗金子般的心 [EMPHASIS] ❑ *They are all good boys with hearts of gold. They would never steal.* 他们都是有着金子般心灵的好孩子。他们决不会偷窃。
→ see **metal, mineral, money**

gold card (**gold cards**) N-COUNT A **gold card** is a special type of credit card that gives you extra benefits such as a higher spending limit. （信用卡）金卡

gold·en ♦◇◇ /goʊldᵊn/ 1 ADJ Something that is **golden** is bright yellow in color. 金黄色的 ❑ *She combed and arranged her golden hair.* 她梳理好自己的金发。 2 ADJ **Golden** things are made of gold. 金制的 ❑ *...a golden chain with a golden locket.* …一条带金制盒式项链坠的金项链。 3 ADJ If you describe something as **golden,** you mean it is wonderful because it is likely to be successful and rewarding, or because it is the best of its kind. 黄金般的 [ADJ n] ❑ *He says there's a golden opportunity for peace which must be seized.* 他说必须抓住这个谋求和平的黄金时机。 4 PHRASE If you refer to a man as a **golden boy**

or a woman as a **golden girl**, you mean that they are especially popular and successful. 黄金男孩/女郎 ❑ *When the movie came out the critics went wild, hailing Tarantino as the golden boy of the 1990s.* 该影片一上映评论家们就大肆追捧，把塔兰蒂诺誉为20世纪90年代的黄金男孩。

gold·en hand·shake (**golden handshakes**) N-COUNT A **golden handshake** is a large sum of money that a company gives to an employee when he or she leaves, as a reward for long service or good work. 丰厚的离职金 [BUSINESS] ❑ *And if Mr. Pell, 49, is axed following a takeover, he would be in line to collect a golden handshake of $1 million.* 如果49岁的佩尔先生在公司被收购以后即被解雇的话，他有望获得1百万美元的丰厚离职金。

gold·en para·chute (**golden parachutes**) N-COUNT A **golden parachute** is an agreement to pay a large amount of money to a senior executive of a company if they are forced to leave. 黄金降落伞(付给被迫离职的公司高管一大笔资金的协议) [BUSINESS] ❑ *Golden parachutes entitle them to a full year's salary if they get booted out of the company.* 黄金降落伞使他们一旦被公司解雇将有权获得一整年的薪水。

G

gold·en rule (**golden rules**) N-COUNT A **golden rule** is a principle you should remember because it will help you to be successful. 黄金法则(指有助于让人成功的法则) ❑ *Hanson's golden rule is to add value to whatever business he buys.* 汉森的黄金法则是让其购买的任何企业增值。

gold·fish /gouldfɪʃ/ (**goldfish**)

> **Goldfish** is both the singular and the plural form.

N-COUNT **Goldfish** are small gold or orange fish which are often kept as pets. 金鱼

gold med·al (**gold medals**) N-COUNT A **gold medal** is a medal made of gold which is awarded as first prize in a contest or competition. 金牌 ❑ *...her ambition to win a gold medal at the Winter Olympics.* …她要在冬奥会上夺取金牌的雄心。

gold·mine /gouldmaɪn/ N-SING If you describe something such as a business or idea as a **goldmine**, you mean that it produces large profits. 宝库 ❑ *The book is a goldmine.* 这本书是个宝库。

golf ♦◇◇ /gɒlf/ N-UNCOUNT **Golf** is a game in which you use long sticks called clubs to hit a small, hard ball into holes that are spread out over a large area of grassy land. 高尔夫运动 ❑ *"Do you play golf?" he asked me suddenly.* "你打高尔夫吗？"他突然问我。
→ see Picture Dictionary: **golf**

golf club (**golf clubs**) **1** N-COUNT A **golf club** is a long, thin, metal stick with a piece of wood or metal at one end that you use to hit the ball in golf. 高尔夫球杆 **2** N-COUNT A **golf club** is a social organization which provides a golf course and a building to meet in for its members. 高尔夫俱乐部

golf course (**golf courses**) N-COUNT A **golf course** is a large area of grass which is specially designed for people to play golf on. 高尔夫球场

golf·er /gɒlfər/ (**golfers**) N-COUNT A **golfer** is a person who plays golf for pleasure or as a profession. 高尔夫球手 ❑ *...one of the world's top golfers.* …世界顶级高尔夫球手之一。
→ see **golf**

golf·ing /gɒlfɪŋ/ **1** ADJ **Golfing** is used to describe things that involve the playing of golf or that are used while playing golf. 高尔夫运动的 [ADJ n] ❑ *He was wearing a cream silk shirt and a tartan golfing cap.* 他身穿一件米黄色丝绸衬衫，头戴一顶格子呢高尔夫球帽。 **2** N-UNCOUNT **Golfing** is the activity of playing golf. 打高尔夫 ❑ *You can play tennis or go golfing.* 你可以打网球，也可以去打高尔夫。

gone ♦♦◇ /gɒn/ **1** **Gone** is the past participle of **go**. **go**的过去分词 **2** ADJ When someone is **gone**, they have left the place where you are and are no longer there. When something is **gone**, it is no longer present or no longer exists. 离开的; 不在的 [v-link ADJ] ❑ *He knows how hard it was for her while he was gone.* 他知道他不在的时候她有多难。 ❑ *He's already been gone four hours!* 他已离开4个小时了！

gong /gɒŋ/ (**gongs**) N-COUNT A **gong** is a large, flat, circular piece of metal that you hit with a hammer to make a sound like a loud bell. Gongs are sometimes used as musical instruments, or to give a signal that it is time to do something. 锣 ❑ *On the stroke of seven, a gong summons guests into the diningroom.* 7点整，一声锣响召唤客人们进餐厅。

gon·na /gɒnə/ **Gonna** is used in written English to represent the words "going to" when they are pronounced informally. 将要 (**going to**非正式发音的书面形式) ❑ *Then what am I gonna do?* 那么我将做什么呢？

> **good**
> 1 DESCRIBING QUALITY, EXPRESSING APPROVAL
> 2 BENEFICIAL
> 3 MORALLY RIGHT
> 4 OTHER USES

1 good ♦♦♦ /gʊd/ (**better, best**)
➪ **Please look at meanings 18 – 26 to see if the expression you are looking for is shown under another headword.** **1** ADJ **Good** means pleasant or enjoyable. 令人愉快的 ❑ *We had a really good time together.* 我们一起度过了非常愉快的时光。 ❑ *I know they would have a better life here.* 我知道他们在这儿会过上更好的生活。 **2** ADJ **Good** means of a high quality, standard, or level. 质量高的; 水准高的 ❑ *Exercise is just as important to health as good food.* 锻炼和好的饮食对身体健康一样重要。 ❑ *His parents wanted Raymond to have the best possible education.* 他的父母想让雷蒙德尽可能得到最好的教育。 **3** ADJ If you are **good at** something, you are skillful and successful at doing it. 擅长的 ❑ *He was very good at his work.* 他十分擅长他的工作。 ❑ *I'm not very good at singing.* 我不很擅长唱歌。 **4** ADJ If you describe a piece of news, an action, or an effect as **good**, you mean that it is likely to result in benefit or success. 很可能带来好结果的 ❑ *On balance, biotechnology should be good news for developing countries.* 总的来说，生物技术对发展中国家来说应该是好消息。 ❑ *I think the response was good.* 我认为这样的反应很有利。 **5** ADJ A **good** idea, reason, method, or decision is a sensible or valid one. 合理的; 有效的 ❑ *They thought it was a good idea to make some offenders do community service.* 他们认为让一些违法者为社区服务是个合理的意见。 ❑ *There is good reason to doubt this.* 有正当理由怀疑这件事。 **6** ADJ If you say that **it is good that** something should happen or **good to** do something, you mean it is desirable, acceptable, or right. 令人向往的; 可接受的; 对的 ❑ *I think it's good that some people are going.* 我认为

有些人要走是件好事。 7 N-UNCOUNT If someone or something is **no good** or is **not any good**, they are not satisfactory or are of a low standard. 令人不满意 [with brd-neg] ❑ *If the weather's no good then I won't take any pictures.* 如果天气不好，我就不拍照。 8 ADJ A **good** estimate or indication of something is an accurate one. 准确的 ❑ *We have a fairly good idea of what's going on.* 我们对正在发生的事情有相当准确的了解。 ❑ *This is a much better indication of what a school is really like.* 这更准确地体现了学校究竟该是什么样子。 9 ADJ If you get a **good** deal or a **good** price when you buy or sell something, you receive a lot in exchange for what you give. (买卖) 合算的 ❑ *Whether such properties are a good deal will depend on individual situations.* 这样的房产是否买得值要视具体情况而定。 10 ADJ Someone who is in a **good** mood is cheerful and pleasant to be with. 愉快的 ❑ *People were in a pretty good mood.* 那时人们心情很好。 ❑ *He exudes natural charm and good humor.* 他表现出一种与生俱来的魅力和幽默感。 11 ADJ If people are **good** friends, they get along well together and are very close. 亲密的 [ADJ n] ❑ *She and Gavin are good friends.* 她和加文是好朋友。 12 ADJ You use **good** to emphasize the great extent or degree of something. 十足的 ["a" ADJ n] [EMPHASIS] ❑ *We waited a good fifteen minutes.* 我们足足等了15分钟。 13 CONVENTION You say "**Good**" or "**Very good**" to express pleasure, satisfaction, or agreement with something that has been said or done, especially when you are in a position of authority. 很好 (用于表示高兴、满意、同意) ❑ *"Are you all right?"—"I'm fine."—"Good. So am I."* "你还好吗？"——"我很好。"——"那就好。我也很好。" ❑ *Oh good, Tom's just come in.* 嗯好，汤姆正好进来了。 14 PHRASE If you say **it's a good thing that** something is the case, you mean that it is fortunate. 庆幸的是 ❑ *It's a good thing you aren't married.* 幸好你没有结婚。 15 PHRASE If you say that something or someone is **as good as new**, you mean that they are in a very good condition or state, especially after they have been damaged or ill. 完好如新 ❑ *I only use that on special occasions, so it's as good as new.* 我只在特殊场合用，所以它完好如新。 16 PHRASE You use **good old** before the name of a person, place, or thing when you are referring to them in an affectionate way. 我亲爱的 (用以称呼某人、某地或某事物) [FEELINGS] ❑ *Good old Harry. Reliable to the end.* 我亲爱的哈里，一直那么可靠。 17 → see also **best, better** 18 **good deal** → see **deal** 19 **in good faith** → see **faith** 20 **so far so good** → see **far** 21 **good job** → see **job** 22 **the good old days** → see **old** 23 **in good shape** → see **shape** 24 **to stand** someone **in good stead** → see **stead** 25 **in good time** → see **time** 26 **too good to be true** → see **true**

Thesaurus *good* 另参见：

ADJ. agreeable, enjoyable, nice, pleasant; *(ant.)* disagreeable, unpleasant ❶ 1
able, capable, skilled; *(ant.)* unqualified, unskilled ❶ 3

❷ **good** ♦♦♦ /gʊd/ (**better, best**) 1 ADJ If something is **good for** a person or organization, it benefits them. 有益的 [v-link ADJ "for" n] ❑ *Rain water was once considered to be good for the complexion.* 雨水曾一度被认为对肤色有益。 2 N-SING If something is done for **the good** of a person or organization, it is done in order to benefit them. 利益 [with poss] ❑ *The president urged him to resign for the good of the country.* 总统敦促他为了国家利益辞职。 ❑ *Victims want to see justice done not just for themselves, but for the greater good of society.* 受害者们希望看到正义得到伸张，这不仅是为了他们自己，也是为了社会更大的利益。 3 N-UNCOUNT If you say that doing something is **no good** or does **not do any good**, you mean that doing it is not of any use or will not bring any success. 没用处 ❑ *It's no good worrying about it now.* 现在担心已没什么用处。 ❑ *We gave them water and kept them warm, but it didn't do any good.* 我们给他们水喝并让他们保持温暖，但都不管用。 4 PHRASE If you say that something will **do** someone **good**, you mean that it will benefit them or improve them. 对某人有益 ❑ *The outing will do me good.* 这次旅行将对我有益。 ❑ *It's probably done you good to get away for a few hours.* 离开了几小时也许已使你受益。 5 → see also **best, better**

❸ **good** ♦♦♦ /gʊd/ (**better, best**)
⇨ **Please look at meaning 6 to see if the expression you are looking for is shown under another headword.** 1 N-UNCOUNT **Good** is what is considered to be right according to moral standards or religious beliefs. 善 ❑ *Good and evil may co-exist within one family.* 善与恶可能共存于同一个家庭。 2 ADJ Someone who is **good** is morally correct in their attitudes and behavior. 有道德的 ❑ *The president is a good man.* 总统是个品德高尚的人。 3 ADJ Someone, especially a child, who is **good** obeys rules and instructions and behaves in a socially correct way. (尤指小孩) 听话的 ❑ *The children were very good.* 孩子们很听话。 ❑ *I'm going to be a good boy now.* 我现在要做一个听话的男孩。 4 ADJ Someone who is **good** is kind and thoughtful. 好心的 ❑ *You are good to me.* 你对我很好。 ❑ *Her good intentions were thwarted almost immediately.* 她的好意几乎立即被拒绝。 5 → see also **best, better** 6 **good as gold** → see **gold**

❹ **good** ♦♦♦ /gʊd/
⇨ **Please look at meanings 5 – 8 to see if the expression you are looking for is shown under another headword.** 1 PHRASE **As good as** can be used to mean "almost." 差不多 ❑ *His career is as good as over.* 他的事业差不多要完了。 2 PHRASE If something changes or disappears **for good**, it never changes back or comes back as it was before. 永久地 ❑ *Some of the nation's manufacturing jobs may be gone for good.* 该国制造产业中有些职业也许会永远消失。 3 PHRASE If someone **makes good** a threat or promise or **makes good on** it, they do what they have threatened or promised to do. 履行 (诺言、威胁等) [mainly AM] ❑ *He was confident the allies would make good on their pledges.* 他有信心盟国将履行他们的誓言。 4 → see also **goods** 5 **good gracious** → see **gracious** 6 **good grief** → see **grief** 7 **good heavens** → see **heaven** 8 **good lord** → see **lord**

good after·noon CONVENTION You say "**Good afternoon**" when you are greeting someone in the afternoon. 下午好 [FORMAL, FORMULAE]

good·bye /gʊdbaɪ/ (**goodbyes**) also **good-bye, good-by** 1 CONVENTION You say "**Goodbye**" to someone when you or they are leaving, or at the end of a telephone conversation. 再见 [FORMULAE] 2 N-COUNT When you say your **goodbyes**, you say something such as "Goodbye" when you leave. 告别 ❑ *He said his goodbyes knowing that a long time would pass before he would see his child again.* 他道了别，清楚要过很久才能再见到他的孩子。 ❑ *Perry and I exchanged goodbyes.* 我和佩里互相道了别。 3 PHRASE If you **say goodbye** or **wave goodbye to** something that you want or usually have, you accept that you are not going to have it. 放弃 ❑ *He has probably said goodbye to his last chance of Olympic gold.* 他或许已经放弃了夺取奥运金牌的最后机会。 4 **to kiss** something **goodbye** → see **kiss**

good eve·ning CONVENTION You say "**Good evening**" when you are greeting someone in the evening. 晚上好 [FORMAL, FORMULAE]

good-looking (**better-looking, best-looking**) ADJ Someone who is **good-looking** has an attractive face. 漂亮的 ❑ *Cassandra noticed him because he was good-looking.* 卡桑德拉注意到他是因为他长得好看。

> When you are describing someone's appearance, you generally use **pretty** and **beautiful** to describe women, girls, and babies. **Beautiful** is a much stronger word than **pretty**. The equivalent word for a man is **handsome**. **Good-looking** and **attractive** can be used to describe people of either sex. **Pretty** can also be used to modify adjectives and adverbs but is less strong than **very**. In this sense, **pretty** is informal.

good morn·ing CONVENTION You say "**Good morning**" when you are greeting someone in the morning. 早上好 [FORMAL, FORMULAE]

good-natured ADJ A **good-natured** person or animal is naturally friendly and does not get angry easily. 性情温和的 ❑ *Bates looks like a good-natured fellow.* 贝茨看上去是个性情温和的人。

good·ness /gʊdnəs/ 1 EXCLAM People sometimes say "**goodness**" or "**my goodness**" to express surprise. (表示惊讶) 天哪 [FEELINGS] ❑ *Goodness, I wonder if he knows.* 天哪，我不清楚他知不知道。 2 **for goodness sake** → see **sake** 3 **thank goodness** → see **thank** 4 N-UNCOUNT **Goodness** is the quality of being kind, helpful, and honest. 善良 ❑ *He retains a faith in human goodness.* 他依然相信人性的善。

good night also **goodnight** 1 CONVENTION You say "**Good night**" to someone late in the evening before one of you goes home or goes to sleep. 晚安 [FORMULAE] 2 PHRASE If you **say good night to** someone or **kiss** them **good night**, you say something such as "Good night" to them or kiss them before one of you goes home or goes to sleep. 道晚安，吻别道晚安 ❑ *Eleanor went upstairs to say good night to the children.* 埃莉诺走上楼去向孩子们道晚安。 ❑ *Both men rose to their feet and kissed her goodnight.* 两位男士都站起身来跟她吻别道晚安。

goods ♦♦◇ /gʊdz/ **1** N-PLURAL **Goods** are things that are made to be sold. 商品 ❑ *Money can be exchanged for goods or services.* 钱可以用来换取商品或服务。 **2** N-PLURAL Your **goods** are the things that you own and that can be moved. 私人财产；动产 ❑ *You can give your unwanted goods to charity.* 你可以把不需要的东西捐给慈善机构。
→ see **economics**

Word Partnership *goods* 的常用搭配:
V. **buy** goods, **sell** goods, **transport** goods **1**
N. **consumer** goods, **delivery of** goods, **exchange of** goods, **variety of** goods **1**
ADJ. **sporting** goods, **stolen** goods **1**

good·will /gʊdwɪl/ **1** N-UNCOUNT **Goodwill** is a friendly or helpful attitude toward other people, countries, or organizations. 友好 ❑ *I invited them to dinner, a gesture of goodwill.* 我邀请他们来吃饭以示友好。 **2** N-UNCOUNT The **goodwill** of a business is something such as its good reputation, which increases the value of the business. 商业信誉 [BUSINESS] ❑ *We do not want to lose the goodwill built up over 175 years.* 我们不想失去用175年建立起来的商业信誉。

G

goose /gus/ (**geese**) **1** N-COUNT A **goose** is a large bird that has a long neck and webbed feet. Geese are often farmed for their meat. 鹅 **2** N-UNCOUNT **Goose** is the meat from a goose that has been cooked. (熟) 鹅肉 ❑ *...roast goose.* …烤鹅。

gore /gɔr/ (**gores, goring, gored**) **1** V-T If someone **is gored** by an animal, they are badly wounded by its horns or tusks. (动物用角或獠牙) 抵伤；刺伤 [usu passive] ❑ *Carruthers had been gored by a rhinoceros.* 卡拉瑟斯被一头犀牛抵伤了。 **2** N-UNCOUNT **Gore** is blood from a wound that has become thick. (伤口流出的) 凝固的血 ❑ *There were pools of blood and gore on the pavement.* 人行道上有一滩滩鲜血和凝血。

★ **gorge** /gɔrdʒ/ (**gorges, gorging, gorged**) **1** N-COUNT A **gorge** is a deep, narrow valley with very steep sides, usually where a river passes through mountains or an area of hard rock. 峡谷 ❑ *...the deep gorge between these hills.* …山间的那个深谷。 **2** V-T/V-I If you **gorge on** something or **gorge yourself on** it, you eat lots of it in a very greedy way. 狼吞虎咽 ❑ *I could spend each day gorging on chocolate.* 我可以将每一天都花在狂吃巧克力上。
→ see **river**

★ **gor·geous** /gɔrdʒəs/ **1** ADJ If you say that something is **gorgeous**, you mean that it gives you a lot of pleasure or is very attractive. 十分宜人的；很吸引人的 [INFORMAL] ❑ *...gorgeous mountain scenery.* …壮观的山间景色。 ❑ *It's a gorgeous day.* 今天天气真棒。 **2** ADJ If you describe someone as **gorgeous**, you mean that you find them very sexually attractive. (人) 很性感的 [INFORMAL] ❑ *The cosmetics industry uses gorgeous women to sell its skincare products.* 化妆品行业用很性感的女人来推销护肤品。

▲ **go·ril·la** /gərɪlə/ (**gorillas**) N-COUNT A **gorilla** is a very large ape. It has long arms, black fur, and a black face. 大猩猩
→ see **primate**

gory /gɔri/ (**gorier, goriest**) ADJ **Gory** situations involve people being injured or dying in a horrible way. 血淋淋的 ❑ *...the gory details of Mayan human sacrifices.* …玛雅人用人祭祀的血淋淋的情节。

gosh /gɒʃ/ EXCLAM Some people say "**Gosh**" when they are surprised. (表示吃惊) 天哪 [OLD-FASHIONED] ❑ *Gosh, there's a lot of noise.* 天哪，有好多噪音呀。

go-slow (**go-slows**) N-COUNT A **go-slow** is a protest by workers in which they deliberately work slowly in order to cause problems for their employers. 怠工 [BRIT]
in AM, use **slowdown**

▲ **gos·pel** /gɒspᵊl/ (**gospels**) **1** N-COUNT; N-IN-NAMES In the New Testament of the Bible, the **Gospels** are the four books which describe the life and teachings of Jesus Christ. 福音书(《圣经·新约》中记述耶稣基督生平和教诲的头四卷) ❑ *...the parable in St. Matthew's Gospel.* …《马太福音》里的寓言故事。 **2** N-SING In the Christian religion, **the gospel** refers to the message and teachings of Jesus Christ, as explained in the New Testament. 耶稣的福音和教义 ❑ *I didn't shirk my duties. I visited the sick and I preached the gospel.* 我没有逃避责任。我探望了病人并传布了耶稣的福音和教义。 **3** N-UNCOUNT **Gospel** or **gospel music** is a style of religious music that uses strong rhythms and vocal harmony. It is especially popular among black Christians in the southern United States. (尤指在美国南部黑人基督徒中间流行的) 福音音乐 ❑ *I had to go to church, so I grew up singing gospel.* 从前我必须上教堂，所以我是唱着福音圣歌长大的。 **4** N-UNCOUNT If you take something **as gospel**, or it is **the gospel truth**, you believe that it is completely true. 绝对真理 ❑ *He wouldn't say this if it weren't the gospel truth.* 如果这不是绝对真理，他就不会这么说。

★ **gos·sip** /gɒsɪp/ (**gossips, gossiping, gossiped**) **1** N-UNCOUNT **Gossip** is informal conversation, often about other people's private affairs. (说别人的) 闲话 [also "a" N] ❑ *He spent the first hour talking gossip.* 他头一个小时尽在说人闲话。 ❑ *There has been much gossip about the possible reasons for his absence.* 关于他缺席的原因已经有多种传闻。 **2** V-RECIP If you **gossip with** someone, you talk informally, especially about other people or local events. You can also say that two people **gossip**. 闲聊 ❑ *We spoke, debated, gossiped into the night.* 我们交谈、争论、闲聊到夜间。 ❑ *Eva gossiped with Sarah.* 伊娃与萨拉闲聊。 **3** N-COUNT If you describe someone as a **gossip**, you mean that they enjoy talking informally to people about the private affairs of others. 爱讲人闲话的人 [DISAPPROVAL] ❑ *He was a vicious gossip.* 他是个可恶的饶舌者。

got ♦♦♦ /gɒt/ **1** **Got** is the past tense and sometimes the past participle of **get**. **get**的过去式和过去分词 **2** PHRASE You use **have got** to say that someone has a particular thing, or to mention a quality or characteristic that someone or something has. In informal American English, people sometimes just use "got." 拥有 [SPOKEN] ❑ *I've got a coat just like this.* 我有件外套恰好跟这件一样。 ❑ *After a pause he asked, "You got any identification?"* 他停顿了一下问道，"你们有什么身份证明吗？" **3** PHRASE You use **have got to** when you are saying that something is necessary or must happen in the way stated. In informal American English, the "have" is sometimes omitted. 必须 [SPOKEN] ❑ *I'm not happy with the situation, but I've just got to accept it.* 虽然我对这种局面并不满意，但我必须得接受它。 ❑ *You got to come clean about things.* 你必须将实情全盘交待。 **4** PHRASE People sometimes use **have got to** in order to emphasize that they are certain that something is true, because of the facts or circumstances involved. In informal American English, the "have" is sometimes omitted. 肯定 [SPOKEN, EMPHASIS] ❑ *"You've got to be joking!" he wisely replied.* "你肯定是在开玩笑！" 他机智地答道。

Goth·ic /gɒθɪk/ **1** ADJ **Gothic** architecture and religious art was produced in the Middle Ages. Its features include tall pillars, high curved ceilings, and pointed arches. 哥特式的 (建筑物或宗教艺术) ❑ *...a vast, lofty Gothic cathedral.* …一幢雄伟高耸的哥特式大教堂。 ❑ *...Gothic stained glass windows.* …哥特式彩色玻璃窗。 **2** ADJ In **Gothic** stories, strange, mysterious adventures happen in dark and lonely places such as graveyards and old castles. (以神秘、怪诞为特征的) 哥特派文学的 ❑ *This novel is not science fiction, nor is it Gothic horror.* 这部小说既非科幻故事，也非哥特式恐怖故事。

got·ta /gɒtə/ **Gotta** is used in written English to represent the words "got to" when they are pronounced informally, with the meaning "have to" or "must." 必须 ❑ *Prices are high and our kids gotta eat.* 物价很高而我们的孩子们又必须吃饭。

got·ten /gɒtᵊn/ **Gotten** is the past participle of **get** in American English. 美国英语中**get**的过去分词

gouge /gaʊdʒ/ (**gouges, gouging, gouged**) V-T If you **gouge** something, you make a hole or a long cut in it, usually with a pointed object. 凿 ❑ *He gouged her cheek with a screwdriver.* 他用螺丝起子戳她的面颊。
▸ **gouge out** PHRASAL VERB To **gouge out** a piece or part of something means to cut, dig, or force it from the surrounding surface. You can also **gouge out** a hole in the ground. 挖出 ❑ *He has accused her of threatening to gouge his eyes out.* 他控告她威胁要挖出他的眼睛。

gour·met /gʊrmeɪ/ (**gourmets**) **1** ADJ **Gourmet** food is nicer or more unusual or sophisticated than ordinary food, and is often more expensive. 菜肴精美的 [ADJ n] ❑ *Flavored coffee is sold at gourmet food stores and coffee shops.* 调味咖啡在美食店和咖啡馆出售。 ❑ *The couple share a love of gourmet cooking.* 这对夫妇都有烹饪美食的爱好。 **2** N-COUNT A **gourmet** is someone who enjoys good food, and who knows a lot about food and wine. 美食家 ❑ *The seafood here is a gourmet's delight.* 这儿的海鲜是美食家的一大享受。

gov·ern ♦◇◇ /gʌvərn/ (**governs, governing, governed**) **1** V-T To **govern** a place such as a country, or its people, means to be officially in charge of the place, and to have responsibility for making laws, managing the economy, and controlling public services. 统治 ❑ *They go to the polls on Friday to choose the people they want to govern their country.* 他们周五去投票站选出他们希望来治理国家

的人。 2 V-T If a situation or activity **is governed by** a particular factor, rule, or force, it is controlled by that factor, rule, or force. 控制 ❑ *Marine insurance is governed by a strict series of rules and regulations.* 海上保险受一系列严格的规章条例所制约。

Thesaurus *govern* 另参见：
V. administer, command, control, direct, guide, head up, lead, manage, reign, rule 1

gov·ern·ment ♦♦♦ /gʌvərnmənt/ (**governments**)
1 N-COUNT-COLL The **government** of a country is the group of people who are responsible for governing it. 政府 ❑ *The Government has insisted that confidence is needed before the economy can improve.* 政府强调需要有信心经济状况才能改善。 ❑ *...democratic governments in countries like Britain and the U.S.* …英美等国的民主政府。
2 N-UNCOUNT **Government** consists of the activities, methods, and principles involved in governing a country or other political unit. 治理 ❑ *The first four years of government were completely disastrous.* 头4年的治理彻底失败了。
→ see **country**

In the United States, the head of the government is the **President**, who appoints the members of his **administration**. Policies are debated and approved by **Congress**, which consists of the **House of Representatives** and the **Senate**. Members of the House of Representatives are known as **congressmen** and **congresswomen**, and members of the **Senate** are called **senators**. In Britain, the head of the government is the **Prime Minister**. The Prime Minister appoints the other **ministers**, who are responsible for particular areas of policy. The Prime Minister and other senior ministers together form the **Cabinet**. The policies of the government are debated and approved by **Parliament**, which consists of the **House of Commons** and the **House of Lords**. There are around 650 elected **Members of Parliament** (or **MPs**) in the House of Commons.

gov·ern·men·tal /gʌvərnmɛntᵊl/ ADJ **Governmental** means relating to a particular government, or to the practice of governing a country. 政府的；统治的 [ADJ n] ❑ *...a governmental agency for providing financial aid to developing countries.* …一个向发展中国家提供资金援助的政府机构。

gov·er·nor ♦♦◊ /gʌvərnər/ (**governors**) 1 N-COUNT; N-TITLE In some systems of government, a **governor** is a person who is in charge of the political administration of a state, colony, or region. 州长；总督 ❑ *He was governor of Iowa in the late 1970s.* 他是20世纪70年代末爱荷华州的州长。 2 N-COUNT A **governor** is a member of a committee which controls an organization such as a university or a hospital. (学校、医院等的) 董事 ❑ *Wayne Hansen was added to the board of governors at City University, Bellevue.* 韦恩•汉森已被增补为贝尔维尤城市大学的董事会成员。 3 → see also **warden**

gown /gaʊn/ (**gowns**) 1 N-COUNT A **gown** is a dress, usually a long dress, which women wear on formal occasions. (女用) 长礼服 ❑ *The new ball gown was a great success.* 那件新款长礼服非常成功。
2 N-COUNT A **gown** is a loose black garment worn on formal occasions by people such as lawyers and academics. (律师、大学教师等在正式场合穿的) 黑色礼袍 ❑ *...an old headmaster in a flowing black gown.* …一位身着飘垂黑色礼袍的老校长。

GP /dʒi pi/ (**GPs**) also **G.P.** N-COUNT A **GP** is a doctor who does not specialize in any particular area of medicine, but who has a medical practice in which he or she treats all types of illness. **GP** is an abbreviation for "general practitioner." 全科医师 ❑ *Her husband called their local GP.* 她丈夫给当地的全科医师打了电话。

grab ♦◊◊ /græb/ (**grabs, grabbing, grabbed**) 1 V-T If you **grab** something, you take it or pick it up suddenly and roughly. 抓住 ❑ *I managed to grab her hand.* 我设法抓住了她的手。 2 V-I If you **grab at** something, you try to grab it. (设法) 抓住 ❑ *He was clumsily trying to grab at Alfred's arms.* 他正笨手笨脚地试图抓住艾尔弗雷德的手臂。
● N-COUNT **Grab** is also a noun. 抓住 [usu sing, N "for/at" n] ❑ *I made a grab for the knife.* 我伸手去抓那把刀。 3 V-T If you **grab** someone who is walking past, you succeed in getting their attention. 引起…的注意 [INFORMAL] ❑ *Grab that waiter, Mary Ann.* 玛丽•安，叫住那个服务生。 4 V-T If you **grab** someone's attention, you do something in order to make them notice you. 引起 (注意) ❑ *I jumped on the wall to grab the attention of the crowd.* 我跳上墙头以引起众人的注意。 5 V-T If you **grab** something such as food, drink, or sleep, you manage to get some quickly. 匆忙地做 [INFORMAL] ❑ *Grab a beer.* 快喝杯啤酒吧。 6 **to grab hold of** → see **hold** 7 PHRASE If something is **up for grabs**, it is available to anyone who is interested. 任何人都可竞购的 [INFORMAL] ❑ *The famous Ritz hotel is up for grabs for $100 million.* 著名的里茨大饭店出价1亿美元供人竞购。

Thesaurus *grab* 另参见：
V. capture, catch, seize, snap up; (*ant.*) release 1

Word Link *grac ≈ pleasing : disgrace, grace, graceful*

grace /greɪs/ (**graces, gracing, graced**) 1 N-UNCOUNT If someone moves with **grace**, they move in a smooth, controlled, and attractive way. 优美 ❑ *He moved with the grace of a trained boxer.* 他的动作带有一个训练有素的拳击手的风采。 2 N-PLURAL The **graces** are the ways of behaving and doing things which are considered polite and well-mannered. 风度 ❑ *She didn't fit in and she had few social graces.* 她不适应而且没有什么社交风度。 3 V-T If you say that something **graces** a place or a person, you mean that it makes them more attractive. 使优美 [FORMAL] ❑ *He went to the beautiful old Shaker dresser that graced this homely room.* 他走向那个使这间陋室生辉的漂亮的夏克尔式旧橱柜。 4 N-UNCOUNT In Christianity and some other religions, **grace** is the kindness that God shows to people because He loves them. (上帝的) 恩惠 ❑ *It was only by the grace of God that no one died.* 正是承蒙上帝的恩惠才没有人死去。 5 N-VAR When someone says **grace** before or after a meal, they say a prayer in which they thank God for the food and ask Him to bless it. (饭前或饭后的) 谢恩祷告 ❑ *Leo, will you say grace?* 利奥，你要做祷告吗？

Word Partnership *grace* 的常用搭配：
N. grace **of a dancer** 1
grace **of God** 4
ADJ. **good** graces, **social** graces 2
V. **fall from** grace 4

grace·ful /greɪsfəl/ 1 ADJ Someone or something that is **graceful** moves in a smooth and controlled way that is attractive to watch. 优雅的 ❑ *His movements were so graceful they seemed effortless.* 他的动作如此优雅，看似非常从容自如。 ● **grace·ful·ly** ADV 优雅地 [ADV with v] ❑ *She stepped gracefully onto the stage.* 她步态优雅地走上舞台。 2 ADJ Something that is **graceful** is attractive because it has a pleasing shape or style. 优美的 ❑ *His handwriting, from earliest young manhood, was flowing and graceful.* 从他刚刚成年时起，他的书法就流畅而优美。 ● **grace·ful·ly** ADV 优美地 [ADV adj/-ed] ❑ *She loved the gracefully high ceiling, with its white-painted cornice.* 她喜欢那雅致的、檐口被漆成白色的高高的天花板。

★ **gra·cious** /greɪʃəs/ 1 ADJ If you describe someone as **gracious**, you mean that they are very well-mannered and pleasant. 和蔼可亲的 [FORMAL] ❑ *She is a lovely and gracious woman.* 她是个可爱而和蔼的女人。 2 ADJ If you describe the behavior of someone in a position of authority or high social standing as **gracious**, you mean that they behave in a polite and considerate way. 有礼貌的 [FORMAL] ❑ *She closed with a gracious speech of thanks.* 她以彬彬有礼的致谢辞作结。 ● **gra·cious·ly** ADV 有礼貌地 [ADV with v] ❑ *Hospitality at the presidential guest house was graciously declined.* 总统套房里的款待被婉言谢绝了。 3 ADJ You use **gracious** to describe the comfortable way of life of wealthy people. (生活) 舒适的 ❑ *He drove through the gracious suburbs with the swimming pools and tennis courts.* 他开车穿过了建有游泳池和网球场的舒适的城郊。
4 EXCLAM Some people say **good gracious** or **goodness gracious** in order to express surprise or annoyance. 天哪 (表示惊讶、不满等) [FEELINGS] ❑ *Good gracious, look at that specimen, will you?* 天哪，你看看那个家伙，好吗？

grade ♦◊◊ /greɪd/ (**grades, grading, graded**) 1 V-T If something **is graded**, its quality is judged, and it is often given a number or a name that indicates how good or bad it is. 将…分等级；给…评分 ❑ *Dust masks are graded according to the protection they offer.* 防尘面具根据其提供的防护而分级。 ❑ *Hampshire College does not grade the students' work.* 汉普郡学院不对学生们的作业评分。 2 N-COUNT The **grade** of a product is its quality, especially when this has been officially judged. 质量等级 ❑ *...a good grade of plywood.* …高品质的胶合板。
● COMB IN ADJ **Grade** is also a combining form. 也用于组合式构词 ❑ *...weapons-grade plutonium.* …武器级钚。 3 N-COUNT Your **grade** in an examination or piece of written work is the mark you get, usually in the form of a letter or number, that indicates your level

of achievement. (用字母或数字表示的) 成绩 ❑ *What grade are you hoping to get?* 你希望得到什么样的成绩？ **4** N-COUNT Your **grade** in a company or organization is your level of importance or your rank. (职员的) 等级 ❑ *Staff turnover is particularly high among junior grades.* 员工流动率在级别低的职员中特别高。 **5** N-COUNT In the United States, a **grade** is a group of classes in which all the children are of a similar age. When you are six years old you go into the first grade and you leave school after the twelfth grade. (美国学校中的) 年级 ❑ *Mr. White teaches first grade in south Georgia.* 怀特先生在佐治亚州南部教一年级。 **6** N-COUNT A **grade** is a slope. 斜坡 [AM]

in BRIT, use **gradient**

❑ *She drove up a steep grade and then began the long descent into the desert.* 她驾车爬上一个陡坡，然后开始长长的下坡进入沙漠。 **7** N-COUNT Someone's **grade** is their military rank. 军衔 [AM] ❑ *I was a naval officer, lieutenant junior grade.* 我曾是名海军军官，中尉军衔。 **8** PHRASE If someone **makes the grade**, they succeed, especially by reaching a particular standard. 成功 ❑ *She had a strong desire to be a dancer but failed to make the grade.* 她渴望成为一名舞蹈家但没有成功。

G

grade cross·ing (**grade crossings**) N-COUNT A **grade crossing** is a place where a railroad track crosses a road at the same level. (铁路与公路相交的) 平交道口 [AM]

in BRIT, use **level crossing**

grade school (**grade schools**) N-VAR In the United States, a **grade school** is the same as an **elementary school**. (美国的) 小学 ❑ *I was just in grade school at the time, but I remember it perfectly.* 我当时刚上小学，但我记得很清楚。

gra·di·ent /greɪdiənt/ (**gradients**) N-COUNT A **gradient** is a slope, or the degree to which the ground slopes. 斜坡；倾斜度 [mainly BRIT]

in AM, usually use **grade**

grad·ual /grædʒuəl/ ADJ A **gradual** change or process occurs in small stages over a long period of time, rather than suddenly. 逐渐的 ❑ *Losing weight is a slow, gradual process.* 减肥是一个缓慢而逐渐的过程。

gradu·al·ly ♦◇◇ /grædʒuəli/ ADV If something changes or is done **gradually**, it changes or is done in small stages over a long period of time, rather than suddenly. 逐渐地 [ADV with v] ❑ *Electricity lines to 30,000 homes were gradually being restored yesterday.* 通向3万户人家的电线昨日被逐步修复。

gradu·ate ♦◇◇ (**graduates, graduating, graduated**)

The noun is pronounced /grædʒuɪt/. The verb is pronounced /grædʒueɪt/.

名词读作 /grædʒuɪt/，动词读作 /grædʒueɪt/。

1 N-COUNT A **graduate** is a student who has successfully completed a course at a high school, college, or university. 毕业生 ❑ *The top one-third of all high school graduates are entitled to an education at California State University.* 全部高中毕业生当中排名前三分之一的有资格到加利福尼亚州立大学学习。 **2** V-I When a student **graduates**, they complete their studies successfully and leave their school or university. 毕业 ❑ *When the boys graduated from high school, Ann moved to a small town in Vermont.* 男孩们中学毕业后安迁到了佛蒙特州的一座小镇。 **3** V-I If you **graduate from** one thing **to** another, you go from a less important job or position to a more important one. 升迁 ❑ *Bruce graduated to chef at the Bear Hotel.* 布鲁斯晋升为大熊酒店的厨师长。

→ see **graduation**

gradu·ate school (**graduate schools**) N-VAR In the United States, a **graduate school** is a division of a university or college where graduate students are taught. 研究生院 ❑ *She was in graduate school, studying for a master's degree in social work.* 她那时在研究生院攻读社会工作硕士学位。

gradu·ate stu·dent (**graduate students**) N-COUNT In the United States, a **graduate student** is a student with a bachelor's degree from a university who is studying or doing research at a more advanced level. 研究生 [AM]

in BRIT, use **postgraduate**

gradua·tion /grædʒueɪʃ^ə^n/ (**graduations**) **1** N-UNCOUNT **Graduation** is the successful completion of a course of study at a university, college, or school, for which you receive a degree or diploma. 毕业 ❑ *They asked what his plans were after graduation.* 他们问他毕业后有何打算。 **2** N-COUNT A **graduation** is a special ceremony at a university, college, or school, at which degrees and diplomas are given to students who have successfully completed their studies. 毕业典礼 ❑ *...the graduation ceremony at Yale.* …耶鲁大学的毕业典礼。

→ see Word Web: **graduation**

graf·fi·ti /grəfiti/ N-UNCOUNT-COLL **Graffiti** is words or pictures that are written or drawn in public places, for example on walls or posters. 涂鸦 ❑ *Buildings old and new are thickly covered with graffiti.* 新旧建筑物都覆盖着密密麻麻的涂鸦。

▲ **graft** /græft/ (**grafts, grafting, grafted**) **1** N-COUNT A **graft** is a piece of healthy skin or bone, or a healthy organ, which is attached to a damaged part of your body by a medical operation in order to replace it. (皮肤、骨头等的) 移植物 ❑ *I am having a skin graft on my arm soon.* 我很快就要做手臂的植皮手术了。 **2** V-T If a piece of healthy skin or bone or a healthy organ **is grafted onto** a damaged part of your body, it is attached to that part of your body by a medical operation. 移植 [usu passive] ❑ *The top layer of skin has to be grafted onto the burns.* 表层皮肤必须移植到烧伤处。 **3** V-T If a part of one plant or tree **is grafted** onto another plant or tree, they are joined together so that they will become one plant or tree, often in order to produce a new variety. 将…嫁接 (于…) ❑ *Pear trees are grafted on quince rootstocks.* 梨树被嫁接到榅桲的根茎上。

grain ♦◇◇ /greɪn/ (**grains**) **1** N-COUNT A **grain of** wheat, rice, or other cereal crop is a seed from it. (麦、米等) 粒 ❑ *...a grain of wheat.* …一颗麦粒。 **2** N-MASS **Grain** is a cereal crop, especially wheat or corn, that has been harvested and is used for food or in trade. 谷物 ❑ *...a bag of grain.* …一袋谷物。 **3** N-COUNT A **grain of** something such as sand or salt is a tiny, hard piece of it. 细粒 ❑ *...a grain of sand.* …一粒沙子。 **4** N-SING A **grain of** a quality is a very small amount of it. 一点 [N "of" n] ❑ *There's more than a grain of truth in that.* 其中包含不少真理。 **5** N-SING **The grain** of a piece of wood is the direction of its fibers. You can also refer to the pattern of lines on the surface of the wood as **the grain**. (木材的) 纹理 ❑ *Brush the paint generously over the wood in the direction of the grain.* 顺着木材的纹理刷上厚厚的漆。 **6** PHRASE If you say that an idea or action **goes against the grain**, you mean that it is very difficult for you to accept it or do it, because it conflicts with your previous ideas, beliefs, or principles. 同…格格不入 ❑ *Privatization goes against the grain of their principle of opposition to private ownership of industry.* 私有化与他们反对产业私有制的原则相违背。

→ see Word Web: **grain**

→ see **flower, rice**

gram /græm/ (**grams**)

in BRIT, also use **gramme**

N-COUNT A **gram** is a unit of weight. One thousand grams are equal to one kilogram. 克 (重量单位) ❑ *A soccer ball weighs about 400 grams.* 一个英式足球重约400克。

Word Web graduation

High school and **college graduations** are important **rites of passage**. This **ceremony** tells the world that the **student** is an accomplished scholar. In college, **graduates** receive different types of **diplomas** depending on their subject and level of study. After four years of study, students earn a Bachelor of Arts or Bachelor of Science degree. A Master of Arts or Master of Science usually takes one or two more years. The **PhD**, or doctor of philosophy degree, may require several additional years. In addition, a PhD student must write a **thesis** and defend it in front of a group of **professors**.

Word Web grain

People first began **cultivating grain** about 10,000 years ago in Asia. Working in groups made growing and **harvesting** the **crop** easier. This probably led Stone Age people to form the first communities. Today grain is still the principal food source for humans and domestic animals. Half of all the farmland in the world is used to produce grain. The most popular are **wheat, rice, corn,** and **oats**. An individual kernel of grain is actually a dry, one-seeded **fruit**. It combines the walls of the seed and the flesh of the fruit. Grain is often **ground** into **flour** or meal.

gram·mar /græmər/ 1 N-UNCOUNT **Grammar** is the ways that words can be put together in order to make sentences. 语法 ❑ *He doesn't have mastery of the basic rules of grammar.* 他没有掌握语法的基本规则。 2 N-UNCOUNT Someone's **grammar** is the way in which they obey or do not obey the rules of grammar when they write or speak. 语法的运用 ❑ *His vocabulary was sound and his grammar excellent.* 他的词汇量丰富而且语法也很棒。
→ see **English**

gram̲mar school (**grammar schools**) N-VAR; N-IN-NAMES A **grammar school** is the same as an **elementary school**. 小学 [AM] ❑ *Jennifer hadn't been home to watch television in the afternoon since grammar school.* 自从上了小学，下午的时候詹尼弗就不在家看电视了。

gram·mati·cal /grəmætɪkᵊl/ 1 ADJ **Grammatical** is used to indicate that something relates to grammar. 语法上的 [ADJ n] ❑ *Should the teacher present grammatical rules to students?* 老师应该向学生讲解语法规则吗？ 2 ADJ If someone's language is **grammatical**, it is considered correct because it obeys the rules of grammar. 合乎语法的 ❑ *...a new test to determine whether students can write grammatical English.* …一项测定学生能否写出合乎语法的英语的新测试。

gramme /græm/ (**grammes**) [BRIT] → see **gram**

grand ♦♦◊ /grænd/ (**grander, grandest, grand**)

The form **grand** is used as the plural for meaning 6.

1 ADJ If you describe a building or a piece of scenery as **grand**, you mean that its size or appearance is very impressive. 宏伟的 ❑ *This grand building in the center of town used to be the hub of the capital's social life.* 这座位于城镇中央的宏伟建筑曾经是首都社交生活的中心。 2 ADJ **Grand** plans or actions are intended to achieve important results. (计划等) 宏大的 ❑ *Hamilton revealed his grand design for the economic future of the United States.* 汉密尔顿透露了他对美国未来经济的宏伟计划。 3 ADJ People who are **grand** think they are important or socially superior. 自视高贵的 [DISAPPROVAL] ❑ *He is grander and even richer than the Prince of Wales.* 他自视比威尔士王子还要高贵、还要富有。 4 ADJ A **grand** total is one that is the final amount or the final result of a calculation. 总计的 [ADJ n] ❑ *It came to a grand total of $220,329.* 总计$220329。 5 ADJ **Grand** is often used in the names of buildings such as hotels, especially when they are very large. 大的 (常用于大建筑物的名称前) [ADJ n] ❑ *They stayed at The Grand Hotel, Budapest.* 他们下榻在布达佩斯大饭店。 6 N-COUNT A **grand** is a thousand dollars or a thousand pounds. 一千美元；一千英镑 [INFORMAL] ❑ *They're paying you ten grand now for those adaptations of old plays.* 他们现在要付你1万美元作为那些老剧目的改编费用。

gran·dad /grændæd/ (**grandads**) → see **granddad**

grand·child /græntʃaɪld/ (**grandchildren**) N-FAMILY Someone's **grandchild** is the child of their son or daughter. 孙子；孙女；外孙子；外孙女 ❑ *Mary loves her grandchildren.* 玛丽很疼爱她的孙子孙女们。

grand·dad /grændæd/ (**granddads**) also **grandad** N-FAMILY Your **granddad** is your grandfather. 爷爷；外公 [INFORMAL] ❑ *My granddad is 85.* 我爷爷85岁。

grand·daughter /grændɔtər/ (**granddaughters**) N-FAMILY Someone's **granddaughter** is the daughter of their son or daughter. 孙女；外孙女 ❑ *...a drawing of my granddaughter Amelia.* …一幅我孙女阿梅莉亚的画像。

▲ **gran·deur** /grændʒər/ 1 N-UNCOUNT If something such as a building or a piece of scenery has **grandeur**, it is impressive because of its size, its beauty, or its power. 宏伟壮观 ❑ *Venezuela is the ideal starting point to explore the grandeur and natural beauty of South America.* 委内瑞拉是探索南美的宏伟壮观与自然美景的理想出发点。 2 N-UNCOUNT Someone's **grandeur** is the great importance and social status that they have, or think they have. 高贵；显赫 ❑ *He is wholly concerned with his own grandeur.* 他只关心他自己的显赫地位。

grand·father /grænfɑðər/ (**grandfathers**) N-FAMILY Your **grandfather** is the father of your father or mother. 祖父；外祖父 ❑ *His grandfather was a professor.* 他爷爷曾是位教授。
→ see **family**

gran·di·ose /grændioʊs/ ADJ If you describe something as **grandiose**, you mean it is bigger or more elaborate than necessary. 华而不实的 [DISAPPROVAL] ❑ *The sad truth is that not one of Tim's grandiose plans has even begun.* 可悲的是，蒂姆那些华而不实的计划没有一项付诸实施。

gra̲nd jury (**grand juries**) N-COUNT A **grand jury** is a jury, usually in the United States, which considers a criminal case in order to decide if someone should be tried in a court of law. 大陪审团 ❑ *They have already given evidence before a grand jury in Washington.* 他们在华盛顿已经向大陪审团提交了证据。

grand·ma /grænmɑ/ (**grandmas**) N-FAMILY Your **grandma** is your grandmother. 奶奶；外婆 [INFORMAL] ❑ *Grandma was from Scotland.* 奶奶来自苏格兰。

grand·mother /grænmʌðər/ (**grandmothers**) N-FAMILY Your **grandmother** is the mother of your father or mother. 祖母；外祖母 ❑ *My grandmothers are both widows.* 我的祖母和外祖母都是寡妇。
→ see **family**

grand·pa /grænpɑ/ (**grandpas**) N-FAMILY Your **grandpa** is your grandfather. 爷爷；外公 [INFORMAL] ❑ *Grandpa was not yet back from the war.* 爷爷那时还没从战场归来。

grand·parent /grænpɛrənt, -pær-/ (**grandparents**) N-FAMILY Your **grandparents** are the parents of your father or mother. 祖父(母)；外祖父(母) ❑ *Tammy was raised by her grandparents.* 塔米是由她的祖父母抚养大的。

grand·son /grænsʌn/ (**grandsons**) N-FAMILY Someone's **grandson** is the son of their son or daughter. 孙子；外孙 ❑ *My grandson's birthday was on Tuesday.* 我孙子的生日是星期二。

grand·stand /grændstænd/ (**grandstands**) N-COUNT A **grandstand** is a covered stand with rows of seats for people to sit on at sporting events. (体育赛事的) 看台

Word Link *ite ≈ mineral, rock : granite, graphite, meteorite*

▲ **gran·ite** /grænɪt/ (**granites**) N-MASS **Granite** is a very hard rock used in building. 花岗岩

gran·ny /græni/ (**grannies**) also **grannie** N-FAMILY Some people refer to their grandmother as **granny**. 奶奶；外婆 [INFORMAL] ❑ *...my old granny.* …我的老奶奶。

grant ♦♦◊ /grænt/ (**grants, granting, granted**) 1 N-COUNT A **grant** is an amount of money that a government or other institution gives to an individual or to an organization for a particular purpose such as education or home improvements. 补助金 ❑ *They'd got a special grant to encourage research.* 他们已得到了一笔用来支持研究的特别补助金。 2 V-T If someone in authority **grants** you something, or if something **is granted to** you, you are allowed to have it. 准予 [FORMAL] ❑ *France has agreed to grant him political asylum.* 法国已经同意给予他政治庇护。 ❑ *Single parents tend to grant more independence to their children than other parents do.* 单亲父母往往比其他父母给予孩子们更多的自主性。 3 V-T If you **grant that** something is true, you accept that it is true, even though your opinion about it does not change. 承认 ❑ *The magistrates granted that the charity was justified in bringing the action.* 这些地方法官承认该慈善机构提起诉讼是有正当理由的。 4 PHRASE If you say that someone **takes** you **for granted**, you are complaining that they benefit from your help, efforts, or presence without showing that they are grateful. 对某人无感激之心 ❑ *What right has the family to take me for granted, Martin?* 这一家子有什么资格认为我所做的一切都是应该的，马丁？ **5** PHRASE If you **take** something **for granted**, you believe that it is true or accept it as normal without thinking about it. 视某事为理所当然 ❑ *I was amazed that virtually all the things I took for granted up north just didn't happen in Savannah.* 令我感到惊讶的是，我在北方视为理所当然的一切事物，在南美大草原上几乎都没有发生。 **6** PHRASE If you **take it for granted that** something is the case, you believe that it is true or you accept it as normal without thinking about it. 理所当然地认为 ❑ *He seemed to take it for granted that he should speak as a representative.* 他似乎理所当然地认为他应当作为代表发言。

Word Partnership *grant* 的常用搭配：

N. grant **amnesty**, grant **equal rights**, grant **independence**, grant **membership**, grant **money**, grant **permission**, grant **a wish** **2**

V. **refuse to** grant **2**

★ **grant·ed** /grǽntɪd/ CONJ You use **granted** or **granted that** at the beginning of a clause to say that something is true, before you make a comment on it. 诚然 ❑ *Granted that the firm has not broken the law, is the law what it should be?* 诚然该公司没有违犯那条法律，那条法律就是对的吗？ ● ADV **Granted** is also an adverb. 的确 [ADV with cl] ❑ *Granted, he doesn't look too bad for his age, but I don't care for him.* 的确，就年龄来说他看上去不太差，但我不喜欢他。

grape /greɪp/ (**grapes**) **1** N-COUNT **Grapes** are small green or purple fruit which grow in bunches. Grapes can be eaten raw, used for making wine, or dried. 葡萄 ❑ *...a bunch of grapes.* …一串葡萄。 **2** PHRASE If you describe someone's attitude as **sour grapes**, you mean that they say something is worthless or undesirable because they want it themselves but cannot have it. 酸葡萄（喻指得不到而加以贬低的东西）❑ *These accusations have been going on for some time now, but it is just sour grapes.* 这些指控到现在已经持续有一段时间了，但那不过是酸葡萄心理而已。

grape·fruit /greɪpfruːt/ (**grapefruit**)

The plural can also be **grapefruits**.

N-VAR A **grapefruit** is a large, round, yellow fruit, similar to an orange, that has a sharp, slightly bitter taste. 葡萄柚

grape·vine /greɪpvaɪn/ N-SING If you hear or learn something **on** or **through the grapevine**, you hear it or learn it in casual conversation with other people. （消息、传闻等的）私下传播途径 ❑ *I had heard through the grapevine that he was quite critical of what we were doing.* 我已经私下听说他对我们的工作十分挑剔。

Word Link *graph ≈ writing : autograph, biography, graph*

graph /græf/ (**graphs**) N-COUNT A **graph** is a mathematical diagram which shows the relationship between two or more sets of numbers or measurements. 图表 ❑ *...a graph showing that breast cancer deaths rose about 20 percent from 1960 to 1985.* …一张显示1960至1985年间乳腺癌死亡人数上升了大约20%的图表。

→ see Word Web: **graph**

★ **graph·ic** /græfɪk/ (**graphics**) **1** ADJ If you say that a description or account of something unpleasant is **graphic**, you are emphasizing that it is clear and detailed. 清楚而具体的 [EMPHASIS] ❑ *The descriptions of sexual abuse are graphic.* 这些对于性虐待的描述清楚而具体。 ● **graphi·cal·ly** /græfɪkli/ ADV 清楚而具体地 [ADV with v] ❑ *Here, graphically displayed, was confirmation of the entire story.* 这里，清清楚楚地展示的，是对整件事情的证实。 **2** ADJ **Graphic** means concerned with drawing or pictures, especially in publishing, industry, or computing. 绘图的；图画的 [ADJ n] ❑ *...fine and graphic arts.* …美术与制图艺术。 **3** N-UNCOUNT **Graphics** is the activity of drawing or making pictures, especially in publishing, industry, or computing. 绘画；制图 ❑ *...a computer manufacturer that specializes in graphics.* …一家以制图为专长的电脑制造商。 **4** N-COUNT **Graphics** are drawings and pictures that are composed using simple lines and sometimes strong colors. 图形 ❑ *The Agriculture Department today released a new graphic to replace the old symbol.* 农业部今天发布了一个新的图案以取代旧的标志。

graph·ic de·sign N-UNCOUNT **Graphic design** is the art of designing advertisements, magazines, and books by combining pictures and words. 平面设计 ❑ *...the graphic design department.* …平面设计部门。

Word Link *ite ≈ mineral, rock : granite, graphite, meteorite*

graph·ite /græfaɪt/ N-UNCOUNT **Graphite** is a soft black substance that is a form of carbon. It is used in pencils and electrical equipment. 石墨

→ see **drawing**

graph pa·per N-UNCOUNT **Graph paper** is paper that has small squares printed on it so that you can use it for drawing graphs. 印有小方格的绘图纸

grap·ple /græpᵊl/ (**grapples, grappling, grappled**) **1** V-I If you **grapple with** a problem or difficulty, you try hard to solve it. 努力解决（问题）❑ *The economy is just one of several critical problems the country is grappling with.* 经济只是该国正在努力解决的几个关键问题之一。 **2** V-RECIP If you **grapple with** someone, you take hold of them and struggle with them, as part of a fight. You can also say that two people **grapple**. 与…扭打 ❑ *He was grappling with an alligator in a lagoon.* 他当时正与环礁湖里的一只鳄鱼搏斗。

grasp /græsp/ (**grasps, grasping, grasped**) **1** V-T If you **grasp** something, you take it in your hand and hold it very firmly. 抓牢 ❑ *He grasped both my hands.* 他紧紧地抓住我的双手。 **2** N-SING A **grasp** is a very firm hold or grip. 紧握 ❑ *His hand was taken in a warm, firm grasp.* 他的手被热情地、紧紧地握住了。 **3** N-SING If you say that something is **in** someone's **grasp**, you disapprove of the fact that they possess or control it. If something slips **from** your **grasp**, you lose it or lose control of it. 掌控 ❑ *The people in your grasp are not guests, they are hostages.* 在你控制之下的这些人并非宾客，而是人质。 ❑ *She allowed victory to slip from her grasp.* 她听任胜利从手中溜走。 **4** V-T If you **grasp** something that is complicated or difficult to understand, you understand it. 理解 ❑ *The government has not yet grasped the seriousness of the crisis.* 政府还不明白这场危机的严重性。 **5** N-SING A **grasp of** something is an understanding of it. 理解 ❑ *They have a good grasp of foreign languages.* 他们很好地掌握了各门外语。 **6** PHRASE If you say that something is **within** someone's **grasp**,

Word Web graph

There are three main elements in a line or **bar graph**:

- a **vertical axis** (the y-axis)
- a **horizontal axis** (the x-axis)
- at least one line or set of bars.

To understand a **graph**, do the following:

1. Read the **title** of the graph.
2. Read the **labels** and the **range** of numbers along the side (the **scale** or vertical axis).
3. Read the information along the bottom (horizontal axis) of the graph.
4. Determine what **units** the graph uses. This information can be found on the axis or in the **key**.
5. Look for patterns, groups, and differences.

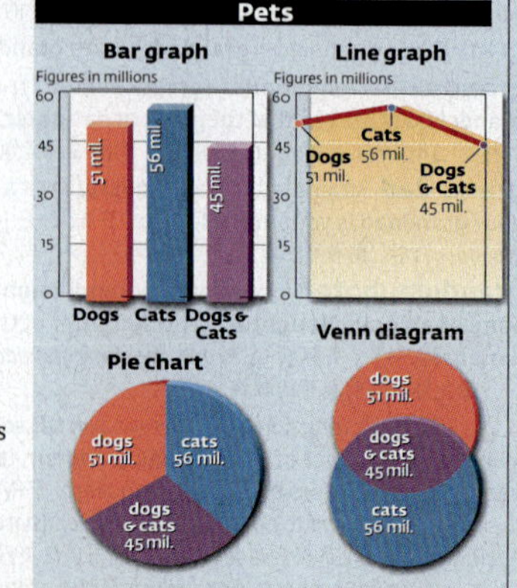

you mean that it is very likely that they will achieve it. 为某人所能及 ❑ *Peace is now within our grasp.* 我们现在和平在望。

grass ♦◇◇ /græs/ (**grasses**) 1 N-MASS **Grass** is a very common plant consisting of large numbers of thin, spiky, green leaves that cover the surface of the ground. 青草 ❑ *Small things stirred in the grass around the tent.* 帐篷周围的草丛里有小东西在动。 2 PHRASE If you say **the grass is greener** somewhere else, you mean that other people's situations always seem better or more attractive than your own, but may not really be so. 这山望着那山高 ❑ *He was very happy with us but wanted to see if the grass was greener elsewhere.* 他当时对我们感到很满意，但想看看有没有更好的。

grass·hopper /græshɒpər/ (**grasshoppers**) N-COUNT A **grasshopper** is an insect with long back legs that jumps high into the air and makes a high, vibrating sound. 蚱蜢

grass·roots /græsruts/ N-PLURAL The **grassroots** of an organization or movement are the ordinary people who form the main part of it, rather than its leaders. (组织、运动的) 基层 ❑ *You have to join the party at grassroots level from what I understand.* 据我的了解，你得由基层组织入党。

grassy /græsi/ (**grassier, grassiest**) ADJ A **grassy** area of land is covered in grass. 长满草的 ❑ *The buildings are hidden behind grassy banks.* 那些建筑掩蔽在长满草的河岸后面。

grate /greɪt/ (**grates, grating, grated**) 1 N-COUNT A **grate** is a framework of metal bars in a fireplace, which holds the wood or coal. 炉栅 ❑ *A wood fire burned in the grate.* 柴火在炉栅里燃烧。 2 V-T If you **grate** food such as cheese or carrots, you rub it over a metal tool called a grater so that the food is cut into very small pieces. 磨碎 (食物) ❑ *Grate the cheese into a mixing bowl.* 将干酪磨碎放进搅拌碗里。 3 V-I When something **grates**, it rubs against something else, making a harsh, unpleasant sound. 发出吱吱嘎嘎的摩擦声 ❑ *His chair grated as he got to his feet.* 当他站起身时，椅子发出了嘎嘎声响。 4 V-I If something such as someone's behavior **grates on** you or **grates**, it makes you feel annoyed. 使恼火 ❑ *His manner always grated on me.* 他的举止总是令我很恼火。

→ see **cut**

grate·ful /greɪtfəl/ ADJ If you are **grateful for** something that someone has given you or done for you, you have warm, friendly feelings towards them and wish to thank them. 感激的 ❑ *She was grateful to him for being so good to her.* 她很感激他对她这么好。
● **grate·ful·ly** ADV 感激地 [ADV with v] ❑ *"That's kind of you, Sally," Claire said gratefully.* "你真好，萨莉"，克莱尔感激地说。

Thesaurus *grateful* 另参见:
ADJ. appreciative, thankful; (*ant.*) ungrateful

grat·er /greɪtər/ (**graters**) N-COUNT A **grater** is a kitchen tool which has a rough surface that you use for cutting food into very small pieces. 食物磨碎器

Word Link *grat ≈ pleasing : congratulate, gratify, gratitude*

grati·fy /grætɪfaɪ/ (**gratifies, gratifying, gratified**) 1 V-T If you **are gratified** by something, it gives you pleasure or satisfaction. 使高兴；使满意 [FORMAL] ❑ *Mr. Dambar was gratified by his response.* 他的答复使丹巴尔先生感到满意。 ● **grati·fy·ing** ADJ 令人满意的 ❑ *We took a chance and we've won. It's very gratifying.* 我们碰了碰运气并且赢了。这真令人高兴。 ● **grati·fi·ca·tion** /grætɪfɪkeɪʃən/ N-UNCOUNT 满足 ❑ *He is waiting for them to recognize him and eventually they do, much to his gratification.* 他等着他们认出他来，最终，他们认出来了，这让他喜不自胜。 2 V-T If you **gratify** your own or another person's desire, you do what is necessary to please yourself or them. 满足 (愿望) [FORMAL] ❑ *We gratified our friend's curiosity.* 我们满足了朋友的好奇心。
● **grati·fi·ca·tion** N-UNCOUNT 满足 ❑ *...sexual gratification.* …性满足。

gra·tis /grætɪs, grɑ-/ ADV If something is done or provided **gratis**, it does not have to be paid for. 免费地 [ADV after v] ❑ *David gives the first consultation gratis.* 戴维免费提供第一次咨询。 ● ADJ **Gratis** is also an adjective. 免费的 ❑ *What I did for you was free, gratis, you understand?* 我为你所做的都是免费的、不收钱的，你明白吗？

grati·tude /grætɪtud/ N-UNCOUNT **Gratitude** is the state of feeling grateful. 感激 ❑ *I wish to express my gratitude to Kathy Davis for her immense practical help.* 我想向凯西•戴维斯表达谢意，因为她给了我许多实际的帮助。

gra·tui·tous /grətuɪtəs/ ADJ If you describe something as **gratuitous**, you mean that it is unnecessary, and often harmful or upsetting. 不必要的 ❑ *There's too much crime and gratuitous violence on TV.* 电视上充斥着过多的犯罪与无端的暴力。 ● **gra·tui·tous·ly** ADV 不必要地 ❑ *They wanted me to change the title to something less gratuitously offensive.* 他们想让我把标题改得不那么过于无礼。

gra·tu·ity /grətuɪti/ (**gratuities**) N-COUNT A **gratuity** is a gift of money to someone who has done something for you. 小费 [FORMAL] ❑ *The porter expects a gratuity.* 那个搬运工想要小费。

Word Link *grav ≈ heavy : grave, gravitate, gravity*

grave ♦◇◇ (**graves, graver, gravest**)

Pronounced /greɪv/, except for meaning 4, when it is pronounced /grɑv/.

义项4读作 /grɑv/，此外读作 /greɪv/。

1 N-COUNT A **grave** is a place where a dead person is buried. 坟墓 ❑ *They used to visit her grave twice a year.* 他们以前每年给她上两次坟。 2 ADJ A **grave** event or situation is very serious, important, and worrying. 严重的 ❑ *He said that the situation in his country is very grave.* 他说他的国家形势很严峻。 ● **grave·ly** ADV 严重地 ❑ *They had gravely impaired the credibility of the government.* 他们已严重地损害了政府的信用。 3 ADJ A **grave** person is quiet and serious in their appearance or behavior. 严肃的 ❑ *Anxiously, she examined his unusually grave face.* 她不安地审度着他那张异常严肃的脸。 ● **grave·ly** ADV 严肃地 ❑ *"I think I've covered that business more than adequately," he said gravely.* "我认为我已经把那件事说得够详细的了，"他一脸严肃地说。 4 ADJ In some languages, such as French, a **grave** accent is a symbol that is placed over a vowel in a word to show how the vowel is pronounced. For example, the word "mère" has a grave accent over the first "e." 抑音符号 [ADJ n] 5 PHRASE If you say that someone who is dead would **turn** or **turn over in** their **grave at** something that is happening now, you mean that they would be very shocked or upset by it, if they were alive. (让死者) 在九泉之下不得安宁 ❑ *Darwin must be turning in his grave at the thought of what is being perpetrated in his name.* 一想到冒他之名所做下的那些事，达尔文在九泉之下一定会不得安宁。

▲ **grav·el** /grævəl/ N-UNCOUNT **Gravel** consists of very small stones. It is often used to make paths. 砂砾 ❑ *...a gravel path leading to the front door.* …一条通向前门的碎石路。

grave·yard /greɪvyɑrd/ (**graveyards**) N-COUNT A **graveyard** is an area of land, sometimes near a church, where dead people are buried. 墓地 ❑ *They made their way to a graveyard to pay their traditional respects to the dead.* 他们一路前行来到墓地，以传统的方式祭奠死者。

gravi·tate /grævɪteɪt/ (**gravitates, gravitating, gravitated**) V-I If you **gravitate toward** a particular place, thing, person, or activity, you are attracted by it and go to it or get involved in it. 受吸引 ❑ *You naturally gravitate toward people with shared values.* 你自然而然地被具有共同价值观的人吸引。

gravi·ta·tion·al /grævɪteɪʃənəl/ ADJ **Gravitational** means relating to or resulting from the force of gravity. 与引力有关的；引力所致的 [ADJ n] [TECHNICAL] ❑ *If a spacecraft travels faster than 11 km a second, it escapes the Earth's gravitational pull.* 如果一架宇宙飞船飞行超过每秒11公里，它就能摆脱地球引力。

→ see **tide**

grav·ity /grævɪti/ 1 N-UNCOUNT **Gravity** is the force that causes things to drop to the ground. 地球引力；重力 ❑ *Arrows would continue to fly forward forever in a straight line were it not for gravity, which brings them down to earth.* 要不是重力使箭掉落地上，它将会一直沿直线往前飞行。 2 N-UNCOUNT The **gravity of** a situation or event is its extreme importance or seriousness. (事态、事件等的) 重要 ❑ *The president said those who grab power through violence deserve punishment which matches the gravity of their crime.* 总统说那些通过暴力攫取权力的人应当受到与其罪行严重性相一致的惩罚。 3 N-UNCOUNT The **gravity** of someone's behavior or speech is the extremely serious way in which they behave or speak. (行为、说话的) 严肃 ❑ *There was an appealing gravity to everything she said.* 她说的一切都带有一种吸引人的严肃与庄重。

→ see **flight, moon**

▲ **gra·vy** /greɪvi/ (**gravies**) N-MASS **Gravy** is a sauce made from the juices that come from meat when it cooks. 肉汁

gray ♦♦◇ /greɪ/ (**grayer, grayest**)

in BRIT, use **grey**

1 COLOR **Gray** is the color of ashes or of clouds on a rainy day. 灰色的 ❑ *...a gray suit.* …一套灰色西装。 2 ADJ If the weather is gray,

there are many clouds in the sky and the light is dull. (天气) 阴沉的 ❑ *It was a gray, wet, April Sunday.* 那是一个阴沉、潮湿、4月里的星期天。 3 ADJ If you describe a situation as **gray**, you mean that it is dull, unpleasant, or difficult. 阴郁的 ❑ *Brazilians look gloomily forward to a New Year that even the president admits will be gray and cheerless.* 巴西民众沮丧地期待着一个连总统都承认将会是阴郁而沉闷的新年。 4 ADJ If you describe someone or something as **gray**, you think that they are boring and unattractive, and very similar to other things or other people. 无特色的 [DISAPPROVAL] ❑ *Miles is one of those little gray men you find in every company.* 迈尔斯是那种你在每家公司都找得到的毫无特色的小个子男人。

Word Partnership *gray* 的常用搭配：

N. gray **eyes**, gray **hair**, **shades of** gray, gray **sky**, gray **suit** 1

V. **go** gray, **turn** gray 1

G

gray area (**gray areas**) N-COUNT If you refer to something as a **gray area**, you mean that it is unclear, for example because nobody is sure how to deal with it or who is responsible for it, or it falls between two separate categories of things. 灰色区域 (难以处理、责任不明或范畴不清的事物) ❑ *At the moment, the law on compensation is very much a gray area.* 当前，关于赔偿的法律很大程度上是一个灰色区域。

gray mar·ket (**gray markets**) 1 N-SING **Gray-market** goods are bought unofficially and then sold to customers at lower prices than usual. 灰市 (经非正式渠道购卖商品再以低于市价的价格售出) [BUSINESS] ❑ *Gray-market perfumes and toiletries are now commonly sold by mail.* 灰市的香水和化妆品现在常以邮购方式售出。 2 N-SING **Gray-market** shares are sold to investors before they have been officially issued. (股票交易的) 灰市 [BUSINESS] ❑ *An unofficial gray market in the shares has been operating for about two weeks.* 一个非官方的股票灰市已经运作了大约两个星期。

★ **graze** /greɪz/ (**grazes, grazing, grazed**) 1 V-T/V-I When animals **graze** or **are grazed**, they eat the grass or other plants that are growing in a particular place. You can also say that a field **is grazed** by animals. 放牧 (牛、羊等); (牛、羊等) 吃草 ❑ *Five cows graze serenely around a massive oak.* 5头奶牛在一棵大橡树附近安静地吃草。 ❑ *Several horses grazed the meadowland.* 几匹马在牧场上吃草。 2 V-T If you **graze** a part of your body, you injure your skin by scraping against something. 擦破皮 ❑ *I had grazed my knees a little.* 我的膝盖擦破了一点皮。 3 N-COUNT A **graze** is a small wound caused by scraping against something. 擦伤 ❑ *Although cuts and grazes are not usually very serious, they can be quite painful.* 尽管割伤和擦伤一般并无大碍，却会很疼。 4 V-T If something **grazes** another thing, it touches that thing lightly as it passes by. 擦过 ❑ *A bullet had grazed his arm.* 一颗子弹擦过他的胳膊。

GRE /dʒi ɑr i/ N-PROPER The **GRE** is the examination which you have to take to be admitted to graduate schools. **GRE** is an abbreviation for "Graduate Record Examination." 研究生入学考试

★ **grease** /gris/ (**greases, greasing, greased**) 1 N-UNCOUNT **Grease** is a thick, oily substance which is put on the moving parts of cars and other machines in order to make them work smoothly. 润滑油 ❑ *...grease-stained hands.* …沾满了油渍的手。 2 V-T If you **grease** a part of a car, machine, or device, you put grease on it in order to make it work smoothly. 给…加润滑油 ❑ *I greased front and rear hubs and adjusted the brakes.* 我把前后轮轴都加了润滑油并调试了刹车。 3 N-UNCOUNT **Grease** is an oily substance that is produced by your skin. (皮肤分泌的) 油脂 ❑ *His hair is thick with grease.* 他的头发油腻腻的。 4 N-UNCOUNT **Grease** is animal fat that is produced by cooking meat. You can use **grease** for cooking. 动物油脂 ❑ *He could smell the bacon grease.* 他闻到了一股熏肉的油脂味儿。 5 V-T If you **grease** a dish, you put a small amount of fat or oil around the inside of it in order to prevent food from sticking to it during cooking. 给…涂上油 (以避免粘锅) ❑ *Grease two sturdy baking sheets and heat the oven to 400 degrees.* 给两个坚固耐用的烘烤盘涂上油，然后把烤箱加热到400度。

greasy /grisi, -zi/ (**greasier, greasiest**) ADJ Something that is **greasy** has grease on it or in it. 有油脂的 ❑ *He propped his elbows upon a greasy counter.* 他把胳膊肘撑在油腻腻的柜台上。

great ♦♦♦ /greɪt/ (**greater, greatest, greats**) 1 ADJ You use **great** to describe something that is very large. **Great** is more formal than **big**. 大型的 [ADJ n] ❑ *The room had a great bay window.* 这个房间有个巨大的凸窗。 2 ADJ **Great** means large in amount or degree. (数量或程度) 大的 ❑ *Benjamin Britten did not live to a great age.* 本杰明•布里滕没有活到很大的岁数。 3 ADJ You use **great** to describe something that is important, famous, or exciting. 重大的 ❑ *...the great cultural achievements of the past.* …过去重大的文化成就。 ● **great·ness** N-UNCOUNT 重大 ❑ *A nation must take certain risks to achieve greatness.* 一个国家必须冒一定风险来成就伟大的事业。 4 ADJ You can describe someone who is successful and famous for their actions, knowledge, or skill as **great**. 伟大的 ❑ *He has the potential to be a great player.* 他有潜力成为一位杰出的演员。 ● **great·ness** N-UNCOUNT 伟大 ❑ *Abraham Lincoln achieved greatness.* 亚伯拉罕•林肯取得了伟大功绩。 5 N-PLURAL The **greats** in a particular subject or field of activity are the people who have been most successful or famous in it. 大人物 [JOURNALISM] ❑ *...all the greats of Hollywood.* …所有的好莱坞名人。 6 ADJ If you describe someone or something as **great**, you approve of them or admire them. 极好的 [INFORMAL, APPROVAL] ❑ *Arturo has this great place in Cozumel.* 阿图罗在科苏梅尔有这样一个很不错的住所。 ❑ *They're a great bunch of guys.* 他们是一群很棒的小伙子。 7 ADJ If you **feel great**, you feel very healthy, energetic, and enthusiastic. 精力充沛的 ["feel" ADJ] ❑ *I feel just great.* 我感觉好极了。 8 ADJ You use **great** in order to emphasize the size or degree of a characteristic or quality. 十足的 [EMPHASIS] ❑ *...a great big Italian wedding.* …一场盛大的意大利式婚礼。 9 EXCLAM You say **great** in order to emphasize that you are pleased or enthusiastic about something. 美妙的; 很棒的 [FEELINGS] ❑ *Oh great! That'll be good for Fred.* 噢，太棒了！那对弗雷德将会很有利。

Great, **big**, and **large** are all used to talk about size. In general, **great** is more formal than **large**, and **large** is more formal than **big**. You normally use **great** to emphasize the importance of someone or something. ❑ *...the great English architect, Inigo Jones.* However, you can also use **great** to suggest that something is impressive because of its size. ❑ *The great bird of prey was a dark smudge against the sun.* **Big** and **large** are normally used to describe objects, but you can also use **big** to suggest that something is important or impressive. ❑ *...his influence over the big advertisers.* You can use **large** or **great**, but not **big**, to describe amounts. ❑ *...a large amount of blood on the floor. ...the coming of tourists in great numbers.* Both **great** and **big** can be used to emphasize the intensity of something, although **great** is more formal. ❑ *It gives me great pleasure to welcome you... Most of them act like big fools.*

Thesaurus *great* 另参见：

ADJ. enormous, immense, vast, small 1 2
distinguished, famous, important, remarkable, successful 3 4

great·ly /greɪtli/ ADV You use **greatly** to emphasize the degree or extent of something. 极大地 [FORMAL, EMPHASIS] ❑ *People would benefit greatly from a pollution-free vehicle.* 人们将极大地受益于无污染汽车。

▲ **greed** /grid/ N-UNCOUNT **Greed** is the desire to have more of something, such as food or money, than is necessary or fair. 贪婪 ❑ *...an insatiable greed for personal power.* …对个人权力的贪得无厌。

greedy /gridi/ (**greedier, greediest**) ADJ If you describe someone as **greedy**, you mean that they want to have more of something such as food or money than is necessary or fair. 贪婪的 ❑ *He attacked greedy bosses for awarding themselves big raises.* 他抨击贪婪的上司们给自己大幅加薪。 ● **greedi·ly** ADV 贪婪地 [ADV with v] ❑ *Laurie ate the pastries greedily and with huge enjoyment.* 劳里十分快乐而贪婪地吃着那些糕点。

green ♦♦♦ /grin/ (**greener, greenest, greens**) 1 COLOR **Green** is the color of grass or leaves. 绿色的 ❑ *Yellow and green together make a pale green.* 黄色和绿色在一起就成了嫩绿色。 2 ADJ A place that is **green** is covered with grass, plants, and trees and not with houses or factories. 绿色植物覆盖的 ❑ *Every street ends at a park or bit of green space.* 每条街的尽头都是一个公园或一块绿地。 ● **green·ness** N-UNCOUNT 翠绿 ❑ *...the lush greenness of the river valleys.* …河谷的郁郁葱葱。 3 ADJ **Green** issues and political movements relate to or are concerned with the protection of the environment. 与环保有关的 [ADJ n] ❑ *The power of the Green movement in Germany has made that country a leader in the drive to recycle more waste materials.* 德国环保运动的力量已经使该国成了循环利用更多废料运动中的领先者。 4 ADJ If you say that someone or something is **green**, you mean they harm the environment as little as possible. 环保的 ❑ *...trying to persuade governments to adopt greener policies.* …试图说服政府通过更环

保的政策。 ● **green·ness** N-UNCOUNT 环保 ❑ *If you'd like to recognize the greenness of an individual or organization, why not nominate them for an Environmental Achievement Award.* 如果你想赞扬某个人或团体的绿色环保行为，何不将他们提名为环境成就奖的候选人？ **5** N-COUNT **Greens** are members of green political movements. 环保运动的成员 ❑ *The Greens see themselves as a radical alternative to the two major political parties.* 绿党成员们将自己视为与两大政党截然不同的选择。 **6** N-COUNT A **green** is a smooth, flat area of grass around a hole on a golf course. 果岭（高尔夫球场中靠近球洞的平整区域）❑ *...the 18th green.* …第18洞果岭。 **7** N-COUNT A **green** is an area of land covered with grass, especially in a town or in the middle of a village. （尤指城镇或村庄中心的）绿地 ❑ *...the village green.* …村子中心的绿地。 **8** ADJ If you say that someone is **green**, you mean that they have had very little experience of life or a particular job. 缺乏经验的 ❑ *He was a young fellow, very green, very immature.* 他是个年轻的家伙，没什么经验，很不成熟。 **9** PHRASE If someone has **a green thumb**, they are very good at gardening and their plants grow well. 高超的园艺技能 [AM]

in BRIT, use **green fingers**

❑ *She has an unbelievably green thumb, she can grow anything.* 她的园艺技能相当高超，什么都会种。 **10** to **give** someone **the green light**
→ see **light**
→ see **color, golf, rainbow**

green belt (**green belts**) also **greenbelt** N-VAR A **green belt** is an area of land with fields or parks around a town or city, where people are not allowed to build houses or factories by law. （城市周围的）绿化地带 ❑ *The room features a 20 feet wall of glass that overlooks a greenbelt.* 这个房间中一面20英尺高的玻璃墙很有特色，可以俯瞰绿化带。

green card (**green cards**) N-COUNT A **green card** is a document showing that someone who is not a citizen of the United States has permission to live and work there. 绿卡（允许外国公民在美国生活和工作的证件）❑ *Nicollette married Harry so she could get a green card.* 尼科莉特和哈里结婚以获得绿卡。

An alien resident may apply to stay in the U.S. through the help of his employer or family. The **green card** identifies a legal resident and permits the cardholder to apply for citizenship after 5 years (in the case of singles) or 3 years (if they are married to an American).

green·ery /griːnəri/ N-UNCOUNT Plants that make a place look attractive are referred to as **greenery**. 青葱的草木 ❑ *Adriana misses the trees and greenery of her native mountains.* 阿德里安娜想念家乡高山上的那些树和青葱的草木。

green fingers [BRIT] → see **green**

green·house /griːnhaʊs/ (**greenhouses**) **1** N-COUNT A **greenhouse** is a glass building in which you grow plants that need to be protected from bad weather. 温室 **2** ADJ **Greenhouse** means relating to or causing the greenhouse effect. 温室的；造成温室效应的 [ADJ n] ❑ *...controls on greenhouse emissions.* …对温室气体排放量的控制。
→ see **barn**

green·house ef·fect N-SING **The greenhouse effect** is the problem caused by increased quantities of gases such as carbon dioxide in the air. These gases trap the heat from the sun, and cause a gradual rise in the temperature of the Earth's atmosphere. 温室效应 ❑ *...gases that contribute to the greenhouse effect.* …导致温室效应的气体。
→ see Word Web: **greenhouse effect**

green·house gas (**greenhouse gases**) N-VAR **Greenhouse gases** are the gases which are responsible for causing the greenhouse effect. The main greenhouse gas is carbon dioxide. 温室气体

green·mail /griːnmeɪl/ N-UNCOUNT **Greenmail** is when a company buys enough shares in another company to threaten a takeover and makes a profit if the other company buys back its shares at a higher price. 绿票讹诈（指大量购买某公司的股票，迫使对方溢价回购）[mainly AM, BUSINESS] ❑ *Family control would prevent any hostile takeover or greenmail attempt.* 家族控制可以防止任何恶意收购或绿票讹诈的企图。

greet /griːt/ (**greets, greeting, greeted**) **1** V-T When you **greet** someone, you say "Hello" or shake hands with them. 向…问好；迎接 ❑ *She liked to be home to greet Steve when he came in from school.* 当史蒂夫从学校回来时她喜欢在家迎接他。 **2** V-T If something **is greeted** in a particular way, people react to it in that way. 对…作出反应 [usu passive] ❑ *His research was greeted with skepticism by advocates for children, who thought it was based on faulty data.* 他的研究遭到儿童权益拥护者们的怀疑，他们认为那是基于的错误数据。

greet·ing /griːtɪŋ/ (**greetings**) N-VAR A **greeting** is something friendly that you say or do when you meet someone. 问候 ❑ *His greeting was familiar and friendly.* 他的问候亲切而友好。 ❑ *They exchanged greetings.* 他们相互问候。

gre·nade /grɪneɪd/ (**grenades**) N-COUNT A **grenade** or a **hand grenade** is a small bomb that can be thrown by hand. 手榴弹 ❑ *A hand grenade was thrown at an army patrol.* 一颗手榴弹被扔向陆军巡逻队。

grew /gruː/ **Grew** is the past tense of **grow**. grow的过去式

grey /greɪ/ [BRIT] → see **gray**

grey·hound /greɪhaʊnd/ (**greyhounds**) **1** N-COUNT A **greyhound** is a dog with a thin body and long thin legs, which can run very fast. Greyhounds sometimes run in races and people bet on them. 灵缇犬（一种身纤细、腿瘦长、善奔跑的狗）❑ *...his love of greyhound racing.* …他对灵缇比赛的喜爱。 **2** N-COUNT In the United States, a **Greyhound** or a **Greyhound bus** is a bus that travels between towns or cities rather than within a particular town or city. 灰狗巴士（美国一种长途汽车）[AM, TRADEMARK] ❑ *I didn't fly. I took the Greyhound.* 我没有乘飞机。我乘的是灰狗巴士。

★ **grid** /grɪd/ (**grids**) **1** N-COUNT A **grid** is something which is in a pattern of straight lines that cross over each other, forming squares. On maps, the grid is used to help you find a particular thing or place. 网格；（地图上的）坐标方格 ❑ *...a grid of ironwork.* …铁格栅。 ❑ *...a grid of narrow streets.* …网格式的狭窄街道。 **2** N-COUNT A **grid** is a network of wires and cables by which sources of power, such as electricity, are distributed throughout a country or area. 系统网络（指输电网等）❑ *...breakdowns in communications and electric-power grids.* …通信与输电网故障。 **3** N-COUNT **The grid** or **the starting grid** is the starting line on a car-racing track. 赛车起跑线 ❑ *The Ferrari driver was starting second on the grid.* 那位法拉利赛车手排在起跑线的第二位。

grid·lock /grɪdlɒk/ **1** N-UNCOUNT **Gridlock** is the situation that exists when all the roads in a particular place are so full of

g

Word Web **greenhouse effect**

Over the past 100 years, the global average **temperature** has risen dramatically. Researchers believe that this **global warming** comes from added **carbon dioxide** and other **gases** in the **atmosphere**. With **water vapor**, they form a shield that holds in heat. It acts a little like the glass in a greenhouse. Scientists call this the **greenhouse effect**. Some natural causes of this warming may include increased **solar radiation** and tiny changes in the earth's orbit. However, human activities, such as **deforestation**, and the use of **fossil fuels** seem to play a much more important role.

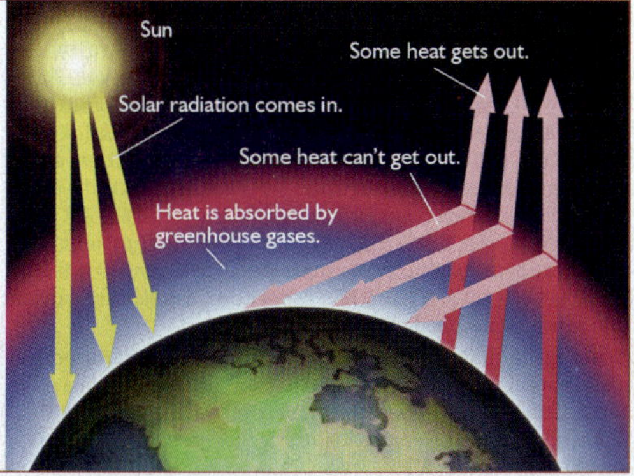
Sun
Some heat gets out.
Solar radiation comes in.
Some heat can't get out.
Heat is absorbed by greenhouse gases.

vehicles that none of them can move. 交通全面堵塞 ❑ *The streets are wedged solid with the chaos of poorly regulated parking and near-constant traffic gridlock.* 由于管理不当的乱停车以及不断的交通阻塞，街道被堵得严严实实。 **2** N-UNCOUNT You can use **gridlock** to refer to a situation in an argument or dispute when neither side is prepared to give in, so no agreement can be reached. 僵局 ❑ *He agreed that these policies will lead to gridlock in the future.* 他赞同这些政策将来会导致僵局。

→ see **traffic**

grief /gri̲f/ (**griefs**) **1** N-VAR **Grief** is a feeling of extreme sadness. 悲痛 ❑ *...a huge outpouring of national grief for the victims of the shootings.* …举国上下对枪杀案受害者们所表现出的巨大悲痛之情。 **2** PHRASE If something **comes to grief**, it fails. If someone **comes to grief**, they fail in something they are doing, and may be hurt. 失败；受伤 ❑ *So many marriages have come to grief over lack of money.* 如此多的婚姻因为缺钱而破裂。 **3** EXCLAM Some people say "**Good grief**" when they are surprised or shocked. (表示惊奇或震惊) 哎呀 [FEELINGS] ❑ *"He's been arrested for theft and burglary."—"Good grief!"* "他因为偷窃和入室盗窃被逮捕了。"——"我的天哪！"

G

Word Link *griev ≈ heavy, serious : aggrieved, grievance, grieve*

griev·ance /gri̲v^əns/ (**grievances**) N-VAR If you have a **grievance** about something that has happened or been done, you believe that it was unfair. 委屈；不满 ❑ *They had a legitimate grievance.* 他们的委屈是合乎情理的。 ❑ *The main grievance of the drivers is the imposition of higher fees for driver's licenses.* 司机们主要的不满是对驾驶执照征收了过高的费用。

★ **grieve** /gri̲v/ (**grieves, grieving, grieved**) V-I If you **grieve over** something, especially someone's death, you feel very sad about it. (尤指因某人亡故而) 感到悲痛 ❑ *He's grieving over his dead wife and son.* 他因丧妻失子而悲痛不已。 ❑ *I didn't have any time to grieve.* 我没有时间去悲伤。

griev·ous /gri̲vəs/ **1** ADJ If you describe something such as a loss as **grievous**, you mean that it is extremely serious or worrying in its effects. 极其严重的；令人担忧的 ❑ *Mr. Morris said the victims had suffered from a very grievous mistake.* 莫里斯先生说受害者们为一个非常严重的失误而受苦。 ● **griev·ous·ly** ADV 极其严重地；令人担忧地 [ADV with V] ❑ *Birds, sea life and the coastline all suffered grievously.* 鸟类、海洋生物以及海岸线都遭到重创。 **2** ADJ A **grievous** injury to your body is one that causes you great pain and suffering. (受伤) 严重的 ❑ *He survived in spite of suffering grievous injuries.* 尽管遭受重伤，他仍然活下来了。 ● **griev·ous·ly** ADV 严重地 ❑ *Nelson Piquet, three times world champion, was grievously injured.* 3度获得世界冠军的纳尔逊・皮盖受了重伤。

★ **grill** /grɪl/ (**grills, grilling, grilled**) **1** N-COUNT A **grill** is a flat frame of metal bars on which food can be cooked over a fire. (置于火上的) 烤架 ❑ *Jerry forced scrap wood through the vents in the grill to stoke the fire.* 杰里从烤架的通风孔塞一些小木片来使火更旺一些。 **2** N-COUNT A **grill** is a part of a stove which produces strong direct heat to cook food that has been placed underneath it. (烤炉内的) 烤架 [BRIT]

in AM, use **broiler**

3 V-T/V-I When you **grill** food, or when it **grills**, you cook it on metal bars above a fire or barbecue. 烧烤 ❑ *Grill the steaks over a wood or charcoal fire that is quite hot.* 在相当热的柴火或木炭火上烤牛排。 **4** V-T/V-I When you **grill** food, or when it **grills**, you cook it in a stove using very strong heat directly above it. 烘烤 [BRIT]

in AM, use **broil**

❑ *Grill the meat for 20 minutes on each side.* 把肉的两面分别烤20分钟。 ❑ *Apart from peppers and eggplant, many other vegetables grill well.* 除了甜椒和茄子，许多别的蔬菜烤起来也不错。 ● **grill·ing** N-UNCOUNT 烤 ❑ *The breast can be cut into portions for grilling.* 胸脯肉可以切成小块来烤。 **5** V-T If you **grill** someone **about** something, you ask them a lot of questions for a long period of time. 盘问 [INFORMAL] ❑ *Grill your travel agent about the facilities for families with children.* 向旅行社多问问为有孩子随行的家庭提供的设施。 ● **grill·ing** N-COUNT (**grillings**) 盘问 ❑ *He faced a hostile grilling from the committee's Republicans.* 他面临来自委员会中共和党人不怀好意的盘问。 **6** N-COUNT A **grill** is a restaurant that serves grilled food. 烤肉餐馆

grille /grɪl/ (**grilles**) also **grill** N-COUNT A **grille** is a framework of metal bars or wire which is placed in front of a window or a piece of machinery, in order to protect it or to protect people. 金属栅栏 ❑ *The single window was protected by a rusted iron grille.* 惟一的一扇窗前由一个生锈的铁栅栏所围护。

★ **grim** /grɪm/ (**grimmer, grimmest**) **1** ADJ A situation or piece of information that is **grim** is unpleasant, depressing, and difficult to accept. 严酷的；令人沮丧的 ❑ *They painted a grim picture of growing crime.* 他们描绘了一个犯罪增长的严酷局面。 ❑ *There was further grim economic news yesterday.* 昨天有更令人沮丧的经济新闻。 **2** ADJ A place that is **grim** is unattractive and depressing in appearance. (地方) 阴沉的 ❑ *The city might be grim at first, but there is a vibrancy and excitement.* 这个城市也许一开始沉闷，但它有一种活力和激情。

gri·mace /grɪməs, grɪme̲ɪs/ (**grimaces, grimacing, grimaced**) V-I If you **grimace**, you twist your face in an ugly way because you are annoyed, disgusted, or in pain. (因不快、厌恶或痛苦等) 扮怪相 [WRITTEN] ❑ *She started to sit up, grimaced, and sank back weakly against the pillow.* 她开始坐起来，痛苦地皱着脸，又虚弱地靠回到枕头上。 ● N-COUNT **Grimace** is also a noun. 怪相 ❑ *He took another drink of his coffee. "Awful," he said with a grimace.* 他又喝了一口咖啡，"太难喝了"，他边说边扮了个怪相。

grime /gra̲ɪm/ N-UNCOUNT **Grime** is dirt that has collected on the surface of something. 污垢 ❑ *Kelly got the grime off his hands before rejoining her in the kitchen.* 凯利擦干净手上的污垢，然后又回到厨房和她在一起。

grimy /gra̲ɪmi/ (**grimier, grimiest**) ADJ Something that is **grimy** is very dirty. 肮脏的 ❑ *...a grimy industrial city.* …一个肮脏的工业城市。

★ **grin** /grɪn/ (**grins, grinning, grinned**) **1** V-I When you **grin**, you smile broadly. 咧嘴笑 ❑ *He grins, delighted at the memory.* 想起往事，他咧嘴笑了。 ❑ *Sarah tried several times to catch Philip's eye, but he just grinned at her.* 萨拉几次试图吸引菲利普的注意，但他只是对她咧嘴笑笑。 **2** N-COUNT A **grin** is a broad smile. 咧嘴笑 ❑ *...a big grin on her face.* …她脸上一个大大的笑容。 **3** PHRASE If you **grin and bear it**, you accept a difficult or unpleasant situation without complaining because you know there is nothing you can do to make things better. 默默地忍受 ❑ *They cannot stand the sight of each other, but they will just have to grin and bear it.* 他们看都不想看对方一眼，但又不得不默默忍受。

grind /gra̲ɪnd/ (**grinds, grinding, ground**) **1** V-T If you **grind** a substance such as corn, you crush it between two hard surfaces or with a machine until it becomes a fine powder. 把…磨碎 ❑ *Store the peppercorns in an airtight container and grind the pepper as you need it.* 将胡椒子储藏在密封容器里，当你需要的时候把它磨成粉。 ● PHRASAL VERB **Grind up** means the same as **grind**. 磨碎 (同**grind**) ❑ *He makes his own paint, grinding up the pigment with a little oil.* 他把色料块加少许油磨碎，自己制成绘画颜料。 **2** V-T If you **grind** something **into** a surface, you press and rub it hard into the surface using small circular or sideways movements. 碾压 ❑ *"Well," I said, grinding my cigarette nervously into the granite step.* "好吧，"我边说边紧张地把香烟在花岗岩台阶上碾灭。 ● PHRASE If you **grind** your **teeth**, you rub your upper and lower teeth together as though you are chewing something. 磨牙 **3** V-T If you **grind** something, you make it smooth or sharp by rubbing it against a hard surface. 把…磨光；把…磨锋利 ❑ *It was beyond my ability to grind a blade this broad.* 把这么宽的刀刃磨锋利我做不到。 **4** V-I If a vehicle **grinds** somewhere, it moves there very slowly and noisily. (机动车) 嘎嘎作响地缓慢移动 ❑ *Tanks had crossed the border at five fifteen and were grinding south.* 坦克已在5点15分穿过边界，然后隆隆地向南开去。 **5** N-SING The **grind of** a machine is the harsh, scraping noise that it makes, usually because it is old or is working too hard. (机器因年久或过度使用而发出的) 刺耳的磨擦声 ❑ *The grind of heavy machines could get on their nerves.* 重型机器发出的嘎嘎磨擦声会让他们心烦意乱。 **6** N-SING If you refer to routine tasks or activities as **the grind**, you mean they are boring and take up a lot of time and effort. 苦差事 [INFORMAL, DISAPPROVAL] ❑ *Life continues to be a terrible grind for the ordinary person.* 对于普通人来说，生活一直是个糟糕的苦差事。 **7** PHRASE If a country's economy or something such as a process **grinds to a halt**, it gradually becomes slower or less active until it stops. (经济或进程等) 渐渐地停止 ❑ *The peace process has ground to a halt while Israel struggles to form a new government.* 当以色列力图建立新政府时，和平进程已逐渐停顿下来。 **8** PHRASE If a vehicle **grinds to a halt**, it stops slowly and noisily. (机动车) 轰隆隆地慢慢停下 ❑ *The tanks ground to a halt after a hundred yards because the fuel had been siphoned out.* 坦克在行驶100码后由于燃料被抽走而轰隆隆地慢慢停了下来。

▶ **grind down** PHRASAL VERB If you say that someone **grinds** you **down**, you mean that they treat you very harshly and cruelly, reducing your confidence or your will to resist them. 折磨 ❑ *"You see," said Hughes, "there's people who want to humiliate you and grind you down."* "你看，" 休斯说，"有人想羞辱你、折磨你。"

▸ **grind up** → see **grind 1**

grind·er /graɪndər/ (**grinders**) 1 N-COUNT In a kitchen, a **grinder** is a device for crushing food such as coffee or meat into small pieces or into a powder. 食物研磨机 ❑ *...an electric coffee grinder.* …一个电动磨咖啡机。 2 N-COUNT A **grinder** is a machine or tool for sharpening, smoothing, or polishing the surface of something. 研磨机 ❑ *The grinder is used for making precision tooling.* 这台研磨机用于制作精细工具。

grip ♦◇◇ /grɪp/ (**grips, gripping, gripped**) 1 V-T If you **grip** something, you take hold of it with your hand and continue to hold it firmly. 紧握 ❑ *She gripped the rope.* 她紧紧抓住绳子。 2 N-COUNT A **grip** is a firm, strong hold on something. 紧握 ❑ *His strong hand eased the bag from her grip.* 他强有力的手使她把紧握的包松开。 3 N-SING Someone's **grip on** something is the power and control they have over it. 掌控 ❑ *The president maintains an iron grip on his country.* 总统保持着对国家的铁腕统治。 4 V-T If something **grips** you, it affects you very strongly. 强烈地影响 ❑ *The entire community has been gripped by fear.* 整个社区已被恐惧所撼动。 5 V-T If you **are gripped by** something such as a story or a series of events, your attention is concentrated on it and held by it. 吸引 [usu passive] ❑ *The nation is gripped by the dramatic story.* 全体国民都被这个戏剧性的故事所吸引。 ●**grip·ping** ADJ 吸引人的 ❑ *The film turned out to be a gripping thriller.* 这部电影原来是一部扣人心弦的惊险片。 6 N-UNCOUNT If things such as shoes or car tires have **grip**, they do not slip. 抓力 ❑ *...a new way of reinforcing rubber which gives car tires a better grip.* …一种增强橡胶使汽车轮胎抓力加强的新方法。 7 PHRASE If you **come to grips with** a problem, you consider it seriously, and start taking action to deal with it. 认真着手处理 ❑ *The administration's first task is to come to grips with the economy.* 政府首要的任务是认真着手处理经济问题。 8 PHRASE If you **get a grip** on yourself, you make an effort to control or improve your behavior or work. 控制住（自己）；改进（行为或工作） ❑ *Part of me was very frightened and I consciously had to get a grip on myself.* 我其实非常害怕，不得不有意识地控制住自己。 9 PHRASE If a person, group, or place is **in the grip of** something, they are being severely affected by it. 在某事的强烈影响下 10 PHRASE If you **lose** your **grip**, you become less efficient and less confident, and less able to deal with things. 失去掌控 ❑ *He wondered if perhaps he was getting old and losing his grip.* 他怀疑自己或许在变老，对事情感到力不从心。 11 PHRASE If you say that someone has a **grip on reality**, you mean they recognize the true situation and do not have mistaken ideas about it. 把握现实 ❑ *Shakur loses his fragile grip on reality and starts blasting away at friends and foes alike.* 沙库尔丧失了对现实脆弱的控制力，无论对朋友还是敌人都开始猛烈抨击起来。

gripe /graɪp/ (**gripes, griping, griped**) 1 V-I If you say that someone **is griping**, you mean they are annoying you because they keep on complaining about something. 不停地抱怨 [INFORMAL, DISAPPROVAL] ❑ *Why are football players griping when the average salary is half a million dollars?* 为什么足球运动员平均薪水50万美元还总是发牢骚呢？ ●**grip·ing** N-UNCOUNT 抱怨 ❑ *Still, the griping went on.* 怨声仍旧不止。 2 N-COUNT A **gripe** is a complaint about something. 抱怨 [INFORMAL] ❑ *My only gripe is that one main course and one dessert were unavailable.* 我惟一的不满是还差一道主食和一份甜点。

gris·ly /grɪzli/ (**grislier, grisliest**) ADJ Something that is **grisly** is extremely unpleasant, and usually involves death and violence. 恐怖的 ❑ *He was insane when he carried out the grisly murders.* 他在进行那些恐怖的谋杀时已精神错乱。

grit /grɪt/ (**grits, gritting, gritted**) 1 N-UNCOUNT **Grit** is very small pieces of stone. 沙砾 ❑ *He felt tiny pieces of grit and sand peppering his knees.* 他感到细小的沙砾正打在他的膝盖上。 2 N-UNCOUNT If someone has **grit**, they have the determination and courage to continue doing something even though it is very difficult. 毅力；勇气 ❑ *If they gave gold medals for grit, Karen would be right up there on the winners' podium.* 如果他们颁发毅力金牌，卡伦应该站在领奖台上。 3 N-PLURAL **Grits** are coarsely ground grains of corn which are cooked and eaten for breakfast or as part of a meal in the southern United States. 粗玉米粉 [AM] ❑ *I want grits with my eggs instead of hash browns.* 我想要粗玉米粉加鸡蛋而不是土豆煎饼。 4 V-T If you **grit** your **teeth**, you press your upper and lower teeth tightly together, usually because you are angry about something. （通常指因愤怒而）咬紧牙关 ❑ *Gritting my teeth, I did my best to stifle one or two remarks.* 我咬紧牙关，硬是把一两句意见咽了回去。 5 PHRASE If you **grit** your **teeth**, you make up your mind to carry on even if the situation is very difficult. 下定决心 ❑ *There is going to be hardship, but we have to grit our teeth and get on with it.* 磨难会有的，但我们必须下定决心继续做下去。

grit·ty /grɪti/ (**grittier, grittiest**) 1 ADJ Something that is **gritty** contains grit, is covered with grit, or has a texture like that of grit. 覆有沙砾的；质地如沙砾般的 ❑ *The sheets fell on the gritty floor, and she just let them lie.* 床单落在满是沙砾的地板上，而她却置之不理。 2 ADJ Someone who is **gritty** is brave and determined. 坚毅的 ❑ *We have to prove how gritty we are.* 我们必须证明我们有多坚毅。 3 ADJ A **gritty** description of a tough or unpleasant situation shows it in a very realistic way. （对负面情形的描述）逼真的 ❑ *...gritty social comment.* …写实的社会评论。

★ **groan** /groʊn/ (**groans, groaning, groaned**) 1 V-I If you **groan**, you make a long, low sound because you are in pain, or because you are upset or unhappy about something. 呻吟 ❑ *Slowly, he opened his eyes. As he did so, he began to groan with pain.* 他慢慢地睁开眼睛，并开始痛苦地呻吟。 ❑ *They glanced at the man on the floor, who began to groan.* 他们扫了一眼地板上那个开始呻吟的男子。 ●N-COUNT **Groan** is also a noun. 呻吟 ❑ *She heard him let out a pitiful, muffled groan.* 她听到他发出一声可怜、压抑的呻吟。 2 V-T If you **groan** something, you say it in a low, unhappy voice. 呻吟着说 ❑ *"My leg – I think it's broken," Eric groaned.* "我的腿——我想是断了，" 埃里克呻吟着说。 3 V-I If you **groan about** something, you complain about it. 抱怨 ❑ *His parents were beginning to groan about the price of college tuition.* 他的父母开始抱怨大学的学费。 ●N-COUNT **Groan** is also a noun. 抱怨 ❑ *Listen sympathetically to your child's moans and groans about what she can't do.* 要充满同情地去倾听孩子对她不能做的事而发的牢骚和抱怨。 4 V-I If wood or something made of wood **groans**, it makes a loud sound when it moves. （木头移动时）发吱嘎声 ❑ *The timbers groan and creak and the floorboards shift.* 木料吱嘎作响，地板也跟着动。 5 V-I If you say that something such as a table **groans under** the weight of food, you are emphasizing that there is a lot of food on it. 堆满 [EMPHASIS] ❑ *The bar counter groans under the weight of huge plates of the freshest fish.* 酒吧柜台上堆满了大盘大盘最新鲜的鱼。 6 V-I If you say that someone or something **is groaning under** the weight of something, you think there is too much of that thing. 受重压 [usu cont] [DISAPPROVAL] ❑ *Consumers were groaning under the weight of high interest rates.* 消费者受着高利率的重压。

gro·cer /groʊsər/ (**grocers**) 1 N-COUNT A **grocer** is a storekeeper who sells foods such as flour, sugar, and canned foods. 食品杂货商 2 N-COUNT A **grocer** or a **grocer's** is the same as a **grocery**. 食品杂货店 [mainly BRIT]

gro·cery /groʊsəri, groʊsri/ (**groceries**) 1 N-COUNT A **grocery** or a **grocery store** is a small store that sells foods such as flour, sugar, and canned goods. 食品杂货店 [mainly AM] ❑ *They run a small grocery store.* 他们经营一家小食品杂货店。 2 → see also **supermarket** 3 N-PLURAL **Groceries** are foods you buy at a grocery or at a supermarket. 食品杂货 ❑ *...a small bag of groceries.* …一小袋食品杂货。

groin /grɔɪn/ (**groins**) N-COUNT Your **groin** is the front part of your body between your legs. 腹股沟 ❑ *I underwent an operation on my groin once.* 我的腹股沟部位曾动过一次手术。

▲ **groom** /grum/ (**grooms, grooming, groomed**) 1 N-COUNT A **groom** is the same as a **bridegroom**. 新郎 ❑ *...the bride and groom.* …新娘和新郎。 2 N-COUNT A **groom** is someone whose job is to look after the horses in a stable and to keep them clean. 马夫 3 V-T If you **groom** an animal, you clean its fur, usually by brushing it. 给（动物）梳毛刷洗 ❑ *The horses were exercised and groomed with special care.* 这些马受到特殊的训练和照料。 4 V-T If you **are groomed for** a special job, someone prepares you for it by teaching you the skills you will need. 培训 [usu passive] ❑ *George was already being groomed for the top job.* 乔治已经为担任该要职接受培训。

groomed /grumd/ ADJ You use **groomed** in expressions such as **well groomed** and **badly groomed** to say how neat and clean a person is. 穿戴（整洁、邋遢）的 ❑ *...a very well groomed man.* …一位穿戴非常整洁的男士。

groom·ing /grumɪŋ/ N-UNCOUNT **Grooming** refers to the things that people do to keep themselves clean and make their face, hair, and skin look nice. 打扮 ❑ *...a growing concern for personal grooming.* …对个人打扮越来越多的关注。

★ **groove** /gruv/ (**grooves**) N-COUNT A **groove** is a deep line cut into a surface. 凹槽 ❑ *Prior to assembly, grooves were made in the shelf, base, and sides to accommodate the back panel.* 在组装之前，隔板、底座和侧面已开槽以便与背板相嵌。

★ **grope** /group/ (**gropes, groping, groped**) 1 V-I If you **grope for** something that you cannot see, you try to find it by moving your hands around in order to feel it. 摸索 ❑ *With his left hand he groped for the knob, turned it, and pulled the door open.* 他用左手摸索到门把手，转动把手，把门拉开。 2 V-T If you **grope** your **way** to a place, you move there, holding your hands in front of you and feeling the way because you cannot see anything. 摸索而行 ❑ *I didn't turn on the light, but groped my way across the room.* 我没有开灯，而是摸索着穿过房间。 3 V-I If you **grope for** something, for example the solution to a problem, you try to think of it, when you have no real idea what it could be. 寻找 ❑ *He groped for solutions to his problems.* 他寻找问题的解决办法。

gross ♦◊◊ /grous/ (**grosser, grossest, grosses, grossing, grossed**)

The plural of the number is **gross**.

1 ADJ You use **gross** to describe something unacceptable or unpleasant to a very great amount, degree, or intensity. 严重的 [ADJ n] ❑ *The company was guilty of gross negligence.* 该公司犯了重大的失职罪。 ● **gross·ly** ADV 严重地 [ADV -ed/adj] ❑ *Funding of education had been grossly inadequate for years.* 多年来教育资金严重不足。 2 ADJ If you say that someone's speech or behavior is **gross**, you think it is very coarse, vulgar, or unacceptable. 粗俗的 [DISAPPROVAL] ❑ *He abused the Admiral in the grossest terms.* 他用最粗俗的字眼辱骂那位海军上将。 3 ADJ If you describe something as **gross**, you think it is very unpleasant. 不雅的 [INFORMAL, DISAPPROVAL] ❑ *They had a commercial on the other night for Drug Free America that was so gross I thought Dad was going to faint.* 前天晚上他们为"无毒美国"播出的一则广告如此令人恶心，我想爸爸都快晕过去了。 4 ADJ If you describe someone as **gross**, you mean that they are extremely fat and unattractive. 肥胖臃肿的 [v-link ADJ] [DISAPPROVAL] ❑ *I only resist things like chocolate if I feel really gross.* 只有当我感到自己胖得很难看时，我才会拒吃巧克力这类东西。 5 ADJ **Gross** means the total amount of something, especially money, before any has been taken away. (尤指钱) 总的; 毛的 [ADJ n] ❑ *...a fixed rate account guaranteeing 10.4% gross interest or 7.8% net until October.* …一个能保证到10月份为止获得10.4%毛利或7.8%净利的固定利率账户。 ● ADV **Gross** is also an adverb. 总地 [ADV after v] ❑ *Interest is paid gross, rather than having tax deducted.* 利息按总额来付，没有扣除税收。 6 ADJ **Gross** means the total amount of something, after all the relevant amounts have been added together. 总共的 [ADJ n] ❑ *Gross sales reached nearly $2 million a year.* 全年总销售额达到近二百万美元。 7 V-T If a person or a business **grosses** a particular amount of money, they earn that amount of money before tax has been taken away. 税前收入赚得 [BUSINESS] ❑ *The company grossed $16.8 million last year.* 该公司去年税前收入为1680万美元。 8 NUM A **gross** is a group of 144 things. 一罗(合144个) ❑ *In all honesty he could not have justified ordering more than twelve gross of the disks.* 说实话他本来就不能为定购这些超过十二罗的光碟提供正当理由。

Word Partnership *gross* 的常用搭配：

N. act of gross **injustice**, gross **mismanagement**, gross **negligence** 1
gross **income**, gross **margin** 5
V. **feel** gross 3

gross do·mes·tic prod·uct (**gross domestic products**) N-VAR A country's **gross domestic product** is the total value of all the goods it has produced and the services it has provided in a particular year, not including its income from investments in other countries. 国内生产总值 [BUSINESS]

gross na·tion·al prod·uct (**gross national products**) N-VAR A country's **gross national product** is the total value of all the goods it has produced and the services it has provided in a particular year, including its income from investments in other countries. 国民生产总值 [BUSINESS]

▲ **gro·tesque** /groutɛsk/ (**grotesques**) 1 ADJ You say that something is **grotesque** when it is so unnatural, unpleasant, and exaggerated that it upsets or shocks you. 荒唐的 ❑ *...the grotesque disparities between the wealthy few and nearly everyone else.* …少数富人和几乎所有其他人之间荒唐的差异。 ● **gro·tesque·ly** ADV 荒唐地 ❑ *He called it the most grotesquely tragic experience he's ever had.* 他称之为他所经历的最荒诞不经的悲惨经历。 2 ADJ If someone or something is **grotesque**, they are very ugly. 丑陋的 ❑ *They tried to avoid looking at his grotesque face and his crippled body.* 他们尽量不去看他那丑陋的面庞和残疾的身躯。 ● **gro·tesque·ly** ADV 丑陋地 [ADV adj/-ed] ❑ *...grotesquely deformed beggars.* …面目丑陋、身体畸形的乞丐们。 3 N-COUNT A **grotesque** is a person who is very ugly in a strange or unnatural way, especially one in a novel or painting. (尤指小说或绘画中的) 丑陋怪异的人 ❑ *Grass's novels are peopled with outlandish characters: grotesques, clowns, scarecrows, dwarfs.* 格拉斯的小说充斥着稀奇古怪的人物：丑陋的怪人、小丑、邋遢的人以及侏儒。

ground
1 NOUN USES
2 VERB AND ADJECTIVE USES
3 PHRASES

1 **ground** ♦♦♦ /graund/ (**grounds**) 1 N-SING **The ground** is the surface of the earth. 地面 ["the" N] ❑ *Forty or fifty women were sitting cross-legged on the ground.* 四五十个妇女正盘腿坐在地上。 ❑ *We slid down the roof and dropped to the ground.* 我们从屋顶滑下来，掉到地上。 ● PHRASE Something that is **below ground** is under the Earth's surface or under a building. Something that is **above ground** is on top of the earth's surface. 在地面上/在地面下 2 N-SING If you say that something takes place **on the ground**, you mean it takes place on the surface of the earth and not in the air. (发生) 在地面上 ❑ *Coordinating airline traffic on the ground is as complicated as managing the traffic in the air.* 协调飞机在地面上的交通和掌控空中交通一样复杂。 3 N-SING **The ground** is the soil and rock on the earth's surface. 岩土 ❑ *The ground had eroded.* 岩土已遭腐蚀。 4 N-UNCOUNT You can refer to land as **ground**, especially when it has very few buildings or when it is considered to be special in some way. (尤指有极少建筑物或具某种特性的) 土地 ❑ *...a stretch of waste ground.* …一大片荒地。 5 N-COUNT You can use **ground** to refer to an area of land, sea, or air which is used for a particular activity. (有特殊用途的) 场地 ❑ *The best fishing grounds are around the islands.* 最好的渔场是在岛屿周围。 6 N-PLURAL The **grounds** of a large or important building are the garden or area of land which surrounds it. (大型或重要建筑周围的) 庭院 ❑ *...the palace grounds.* …皇家庭院。 7 N-VAR You can use **ground** to refer to a place or situation in which particular methods or ideas can develop and be successful. (适于方法、思想发展的) 地方; 环境 ❑ *The company has maintained its reputation as the developing ground for new techniques.* 该公司仍保持着新技术研发地的声誉。 8 N-UNCOUNT You can use **ground** in expressions such as **on shaky ground** and **the same ground** to refer to a particular subject, area of experience, or basis for an argument. 根据 ❑ *Sensing she was on shaky ground, Marie changed the subject.* 感觉自己的根据站不住脚，玛丽于是转变了话题。 ❑ *This is the most solid ground for optimism.* 这是乐观主义最有力的根据。 9 N-UNCOUNT **Ground** is used in expressions such as **gain ground**, **lose ground**, and **give ground** in order to indicate that someone gets or loses an advantage. 优势 [JOURNALISM] ❑ *There are signs that the party is gaining ground in the latest polls.* 有迹象表明该党在最近的民意测验中正逐渐领先。 10 N-VAR If something is **grounds for** a feeling or action, it is a reason for it. If you do something **on the grounds** of a particular thing, that thing is the reason for your action. 理由 ❑ *In the interview he gave some grounds for optimism.* 采访中他给出了一些乐观的理由。 ❑ *The court overturned that decision on the grounds that the prosecution had withheld crucial evidence.* 法庭以起诉方拒绝出示关键证据为由推翻了那个判决。 11 N-COUNT The **ground** in an electric plug or piece of electrical equipment is the wire through which electricity passes into the ground and which makes the equipment safe. 地线 [usu sing] [AM]

in BRIT, use **earth**

❑ *...an insulated ground.* …一根绝缘地线。

→ see **coffee, fish, grain**

2 **ground** ♦♦♦ /graund/ (**grounds, grounding, grounded**) 1 V-T If an argument, belief, or opinion **is grounded** in something, that thing is used to justify it. 以…为根据 ❑ *Her argument was grounded in fact.* 她的论述以事实为根据。 2 V-T If an aircraft or its passengers **are grounded**, they are made to stay on the ground and are not allowed to take off. 使停飞 ❑ *The civil aviation minister ordered all the planes to be grounded.* 民航部长命令所有飞机不得起飞。 3 V-T When parents **ground** a child, they forbid them to go out and enjoy themselves for a period of time, as a punishment. 限制 (尤指父母

以限制小孩外出玩耍作为惩罚) ❑ *They grounded him for a month, and banned television.* 他们罚他一个月不能外出，并且不能看电视。 **4** V-T/V-I If a ship or boat **is grounded** or if it **grounds**, it touches the bottom of the sea, lake, or river it is on, and is unable to move off. 使搁浅；搁浅 ❑ *Residents have been told to stay away from the region where the ship was grounded.* 居民们被告知要远离轮船搁浅的区域。 ❑ *The boat finally grounded on a soft, underwater bank.* 那条船最终在一个松软的水下浅滩搁浅了。 **5** V-T If something **grounds** you, it causes you to have a sensible and practical attitude toward life and not to have unrealistic ideas. 使变得现实 ❑ *These things have grounded me and made me who I am.* 这些事使我变得很实际，造就了现在的我。 ● **ground·ed** ADJ 现实的 ❑ *She seems very grounded and down-to-earth.* 她看上去非常现实，注重实际。 **6** ADJ **Ground** meat has been cut into very small pieces in a machine. 切碎的(肉) [mainly AM]

in BRIT, usually use **minced**

❑ *...The sausages are made of coarsely ground pork.* …这些香肠是由切得很粗的猪肉绞制而成。 **7** **Ground** is the past tense and past participle of **grind**. grind过去式和过去分词 **8** → see also **grounding**

❸ ground ♦♦♦ /graʊnd/ **1** PHRASE If you **break new ground**, you do something completely different or you do something in a completely different way. 开辟新天地 [APPROVAL] ❑ *Gellhorn may have broken new ground when she filed her first report on the Spanish Civil War.* 当盖尔霍恩把她关于西班牙内战的第一份报道发送出去时，她也许已经开辟了新天地。 **2** PHRASE If you say that a town or building **is burned to the ground** or **is razed to the ground**, you are emphasizing that it has been completely destroyed by fire. 大火把某事物夷为平地 [EMPHASIS] ❑ *The town was razed to the ground after the French Revolution.* 该镇在法国大革命后被大火夷为平地。 **3** PHRASE If two people or groups find **common ground**, they agree about something, especially when they do not agree about other things. 共同立场 ❑ *The participants seem unable to find common ground on the issue of agriculture.* 这些参与者似乎无法就农业议题达成一致。 **4** PHRASE The **middle ground** between two groups, ideas, or plans involves things which do not belong to either of these groups, ideas, or plans but have elements of each, often in a less extreme form. 中间立场 ❑ *The sooner we find a middle ground between freedom of speech and protection of the young, the better for everyone.* 我们越早在言论自由和保护青年之间找到一个中间点，对大家越好。 **5** PHRASE If something such as a project gets **off the ground**, it begins or starts functioning. 开始 ❑ *We help small companies to get off the ground.* 我们帮助小公司开业。 **6** PHRASE If you **prepare the ground for** a future event, course of action, or development, you make it easier for it to happen. 打下基础 ❑ *...a political initiative which would prepare the ground for war.* …一个为战争埋下伏笔的政治倡议。 **7** PHRASE If you **shift** your **ground** or **change** your **ground**, you change the basis on which you are arguing. 改变立场 ❑ *Robert considered this, then shifted his ground slightly in line with a new thought.* 罗伯特对此进行了考虑，然后为符合新想法而稍微改变了立场。 **8** PHRASE If you **stand** your **ground** or **hold** your **ground**, you do not run away from a situation, but face it bravely. 不退却 ❑ *She had to force herself to stand her ground when she heard someone approaching.* 听到有人走近时，她得强迫自己不要退却。

ground floor (**ground floors**) **1** N-COUNT **The ground floor** of a building is the floor that is level or almost level with the ground outside. 底层

in AM, also use **first floor**

❑ *She showed him around the ground floor of the empty house.* 她带他看了那个空房子的底层。 **2** If you **get in on the ground floor**, you become involved in a business or plan in the early stages, in order to gain an advantage. 在开始阶段加入以取得优势 ❑ *A supplier wants to get in on the ground floor and grow with the business.* 一个供应商想一开始就加入并随着生意的扩大而发展。

Word Link	*ground ≈ bottom : background, grounding, groundwork*

ground·ing /graʊndɪŋ/ N-SING If you have a **grounding in** a subject, you know the basic facts or principles of that subject, especially as a result of a particular course of training or instruction. 基础训练 ❑ *The degree provides a thorough grounding in both mathematics and statistics.* 这个学位提供对数学和统计学全面的基础训练。

ground·less /graʊndlɪs/ ADJ If you say that a fear, accusation, or story is **groundless**, you mean that it is not based on evidence and is unlikely to be true or valid. 没有根据的 ❑ *Fears that the world was about to run out of fuel proved groundless.* 担心地球燃料即将用尽被证明是没有根据的。

Word Partnership	*groundless* 的常用搭配:
N.	**charges are** groundless
V.	**call** *something* groundless, **dismiss** *something* **as** groundless, **prove** groundless

ground rule (**ground rules**) N-COUNT **The ground rules for** something are the basic principles on which future action will be based. 基本原则 ❑ *The panel says the ground rules for the current talks should be maintained.* 该专门小组说应该坚持当前会谈的基本原则。

ground·work /graʊndwɜrk/ N-SING **The groundwork for** something is the early work on it which forms the basis for further work. 基础 ❑ *Yesterday's meeting was to lay the groundwork for the task ahead.* 昨天的会议为后面的任务打下了基础。

group ♦♦♦ /grup/ (**groups, grouping, grouped**) **1** N-COUNT-COLL **A group** of people or things is a number of people or things that are together in one place at one time. 群 ❑ *The trouble involved a small group of football fans.* 那次骚乱涉及到一小撮足球迷。 **2** N-COUNT A **group** is a set of people who have the same interests or aims, and who organize themselves to work or act together. 集体；团体 ❑ *Members of an environmental group are staging a protest inside a chemical plant.* 一个环保团体的成员们正在一家化工厂内进行抗议。 **3** N-COUNT A **group** is a set of people, organizations, or things which are considered together because they have something in common. (有共同之处的) 组 ❑ *She is among the most promising players in her age group.* 在她那个年龄组中她是最有前途的选手之一。 **4** N-COUNT A **group** is a number of separate commercial or industrial firms that all have the same owner. (企业) 集团 [BUSINESS] ❑ *The group made a pretax profit of $1.05 million.* 该集团赚取了105万美元的税前利润。 **5** N-COUNT A **group** is a number of musicians who perform together, especially ones who play popular music. (尤指演奏流行音乐的) 乐队 ❑ *At school he played bass in a pop group called The Urge.* 上学的时候他在一个叫"冲动"的流行乐队中担任低音电吉他手。 **6** V-T/V-I If a number of things or people **are grouped together** or **group together**, they are together in one place or within one organization or system. 把…归在一起；形成一组 ❑ *Plants are grouped into botanical "families" that have certain characteristics in common.* 具有某些共同特点的植物被归为植物学的科。 ❑ *The Species Survival Network groups together 80 international environmental organizations.* 物种生存网络把80个国际环境组织结合在一起。 **7** → see also **grouping, pressure group**

Thesaurus	*group* 另参见:
N.	collection **1**
	crowd, gang, organization, society **1** **2**
V.	arrange, categorize, class, order, rank, sort **6**

group·ing /grupɪŋ/ (**groupings**) N-COUNT A **grouping** is a set of people or things that have something in common. (有某些共同点的) 群体 ❑ *There were two main political groupings pressing for independence.* 有两个主要政治团体施压要求独立。

▲ grove /groʊv/ (**groves**) N-COUNT A **grove** is a group of trees that are close together. 树丛 [usu with supp] ❑ *...an olive grove.* …一片橄榄树丛。

grov·el /grɒvᵊl/ (**grovels, groveling, groveled**)

in BRIT, use **grovelling, grovelled**

1 V-I If you say that someone **grovels**, you think they are behaving too respectfully towards another person, for example because they are frightened or because they want something. 卑躬屈膝 [DISAPPROVAL] ❑ *I don't grovel to anybody.* 我对谁都不会卑躬屈膝。 ❑ *Speakers have been shouted down, classes disrupted, teachers made to grovel.* 发言者完全被叫嚷声压住了，教室一片混乱，老师们不得不低声下气。 **2** V-I If you **grovel**, you crawl on the ground, for example in order to find something. 爬行 (找东西等) ❑ *We groveled around the room on our knees.* 我们在房间到处爬着寻找。

grow ♦♦♦ /groʊ/ (**grows, growing, grew, grown**) **1** V-I When people, animals, and plants **grow**, they increase in size and change physically over a period of time. 成长 ❑ *We stop growing at maturity.* 我们在成熟后就停止成长了。 **2** V-I If a plant or tree **grows** in a particular place, it is alive there. 生长 ❑ *The station had roses growing at each end of the platform.* 车站月台两端生长着玫瑰。 **3** V-T If you **grow** a particular type of plant, you put seeds or young plants in the ground and take care of them as they develop. 种植

❑ *Lettuce was grown by the ancient Romans.* 莴苣是由古罗马人种植的。 **4** V-I When someone's hair **grows**, it gradually becomes longer. Your nails also **grow**. (毛发、指甲等) 逐渐变长 ❑ *Then the hair began to grow again and I felt terrific.* 接着头发又长起来了，我感觉棒极了。 **5** V-T If someone **grows** their hair, or **grows** a beard or mustache, they stop cutting their hair or shaving so that their hair becomes longer. You can also **grow** your nails. 留 (头发、胡须、指甲等) ❑ *I'd better start growing my hair.* 我最好开始留头发。 **6** V-I If someone **grows** mentally, they change and develop in character or attitude. (心理方面的) 成长 ❑ *They began to grow as individuals.* 他们开始发展独自的个性。 **7** V-LINK You use **grow** to say that someone or something gradually changes until they have a new quality, feeling, or attitude. 变得 ❑ *I grew a little afraid of the guy next door.* 我变得有点害怕隔壁那家伙。 ❑ *He's growing old.* 他正在变老。 ❑ *He grew to love his work.* 他渐渐地开始热爱他的工作了。 **8** V-I If an amount, feeling, or problem **grows**, it becomes greater or more intense. (数量) 增加; (情感) 增强; (问题) 变严重 ❑ *From 2000 to 2002, the number of uninsured grew by almost 4 million.* 从2000年到2002年，未参加保险的人数增加了差不多四百万。 ❑ *Opposition grew and the government agreed to negotiate.* 反对势力日益强烈，政府同意进行谈判。 ❑ *...a growing number of immigrants.* …越来越多的移民。 **9** V-I If one thing **grows into** another, it develops or changes until it becomes that thing. 发展为 ❑ *The boys grew into men.* 这些男孩长大成为男人了。 **10** V-I If something such as an idea or a plan **grows out of** something else, it develops from it. (观点或计划等) 产生于 ❑ *The idea for this book grew out of conversations with Philippa Brewster.* 这本书的想法产生于与菲莉帕・布鲁斯特的谈话。 **11** V-I If the economy or a business **grows**, it increases in wealth, size, or importance. (经济或企业的) 增长 [BUSINESS] ❑ *The economy continues to grow.* 经济持续增长。 ❑ *... a fast growing business.* …迅速增长的业务。 **12** V-T If someone **grows** a business, they take actions that will cause it to increase in wealth, size, or importance. 使增长 [BUSINESS] ❑ *To grow the business, he needs to develop management expertise and innovation across his team.* 为了拓展业务，他需要提高其团队的专业管理技能和创新能力。 **13** → see also **grown**
→ see **plant**

▸ **grow apart** PHRASAL VERB If people who have a close relationship **grow apart**, they gradually start to have different interests and opinions from each other, and their relationship starts to fail. (关系) 变得有隔阂 ❑ *He and his wife grew apart.* 他和妻子之间产生了隔阂。 ❑ *It sounds as if you have grown apart from Tom.* 听起来你好像跟汤姆有隔阂了。

▸ **grow into** PHRASAL VERB When a child **grows into** an item of clothing, they become taller or bigger so that it fits them properly. 长大了穿得上 (大号的衣物) ❑ *It's a little big, but she'll soon grow into it.* 这是大了点，但她很快就可以穿它了。

▸ **grow on** PHRASAL VERB If someone or something **grows on** you, you start to like them more and more. 越来越被…喜欢 ❑ *Slowly and strangely, the place began to grow on me.* 很奇怪，慢慢地这个地方越来越让我喜欢。

▸ **grow out of** **1** PHRASAL VERB If you **grow out of** a type of behavior or an interest, you stop behaving in that way or having that interest, as you develop or change. 因长大或改变而不再有 (某行为、兴趣等) ❑ *Most children who stammer grow out of it.* 大部分口吃的孩子长大后就好了。 **2** PHRASAL VERB When a child **grows out of** an item of clothing, they become so tall or big that it no longer fits them properly. 长大穿不下 (原来的衣物) ❑ *You've grown out of your shoes again.* 你又长得穿不上你的鞋了。

▸ **grow up** **1** PHRASAL VERB When someone **grows up**, they gradually change from being a child into being an adult. 长大成人 ❑ *She grew up in Tokyo.* 她在东京长大。 **2** → see also **grown-up** **3** PHRASAL VERB If you tell someone to **grow up**, you are telling them to stop behaving in a silly or childish way. 别犯傻; 别孩子气 [INFORMAL, DISAPPROVAL] ❑ *It's time you grew up.* 是时候你该去掉孩子气了。 **4** PHRASAL VERB If something **grows up**, it starts to exist and then becomes larger or more important. 兴起并发展起来 ❑ *A variety of heavy industries grew up alongside the port.* 各种重工业在港口边上兴起并发展起来。

Thesaurus *grow* 另参见:
V. develop, mature **1** **4**–**8** **11**
germinate, spring up, thrive **2**
cultivate, plant, produce **3**
heighten, intensify **10**–**13**

Word Partnership *grow* 的常用搭配:
V. **continue to grow** **1** **4**–**8** **11**
try to grow **3** **5** **12**
ADJ. grow **older** **1** **7**
grow **bored**, grow **closer**, grow **louder**, grow **silent** **7** **8**
N. grow **food** **3**

grow·er /groʊər/ (**growers**) N-COUNT A **grower** is a person who grows large quantities of a particular plant or crop in order to sell them. 种植者 ❑ *The state's apple growers are fighting an uphill battle against foreign competition.* 该州的苹果种植者们正在与外来竞争进行艰难的抗争。

▲ **growl** /graʊl/ (**growls, growling, growled**) **1** V-I When a dog or other animal **growls**, it makes a low noise in its throat, usually because it is angry. (狗或其它动物因愤怒而) 低沉地吼叫 ❑ *The dog was biting, growling, and wagging its tail.* 那条狗又咬又叫，摇着尾巴。 ● N-COUNT **Growl** is also a noun. 咆哮声 ❑ *Their noise modulated to a concerted menacing growl punctuated by sharp yaps.* 它们的喧闹声逐渐变为整齐划一的、带有威胁性的吼叫，还夹杂着刺耳的狂吠。 **2** V-T If someone **growls** something, they say something in a low, rough, and angry voice. 低吼 [WRITTEN] ❑ *His fury was so great he could hardly speak. He growled some unintelligible words at Pete.* 他的怒气大到让他几乎说不出话来。他向皮特低吼了一些莫名其妙的话。 ● N-COUNT **Growl** is also a noun. 低吼声 ❑ *...with an angry growl of contempt for her own weakness.* …带着一声对她自己的懦弱发出的轻蔑的低吼。

grown /groʊn/ ADJ A **grown** man or woman is one who is fully developed and mature, both physically and mentally. 成年的 [ADJ n] ❑ *Few women can understand a grown man's love of sports.* 很少有女人能够理解成年男人对运动的喜爱。

grown-up (**grown-ups**)

The spelling **grownup** is also used. The syllable **up** is not stressed when it is a noun.

1 N-COUNT A **grown-up** is an adult. 成年人 ❑ *Jan was almost a grown-up.* 简几乎是个大人了。 **2** ADJ Someone who is **grown-up** is physically and mentally mature and no longer depends on their parents or another adult. 长大成人的 ❑ *I seem to have everything anyone could want–a good husband, a lovely home, grown-up children who're doing well.* 我似乎拥有任何人想要的一切——好丈夫，可爱的家和已长大成人、有出息的子女。 **3** ADJ If you say that someone is **grown-up**, you mean that they behave in an adult way, often when they are in fact still a child. 似成人的 ❑ *She's very grown-up.* 她非常成人化。 **4** ADJ **Grown-up** things seem suitable for or typical of adults. 适于成人的 [INFORMAL] ❑ *Her songs tackle grown-up subjects.* 她的歌曲以成人题材为主题。

growth ♦♦◊ /groʊθ/ (**growths**) **1** N-UNCOUNT The **growth of** something such as an industry, organization, or idea is its development in size, wealth, or importance. 发展 ❑ *...the growth of nationalism.* …民族主义的高涨。 ❑ *...Japan's enormous economic growth.* …日本经济巨大的发展。 **2** N-UNCOUNT The **growth** in something is the increase in it. 增长 [also "a" N] ❑ *A steady growth in the popularity of two smaller parties may upset the polls.* 两个较小政党声誉的持续增长也许会搅乱大选。 ❑ *The area has seen a rapid population growth.* 这个地区人口快速增长。 **3** ADJ A **growth** industry, area, or market is one that is increasing in size or activity. 发展的 [ADJ n] [BUSINESS] ❑ *Computers and electronics are growth industries and need skilled technicians.* 计算机与电子属于发展中的行业，需要熟练的技术人员。 **4** N-UNCOUNT Someone's **growth** is the development and progress of their character. (性格的) 成长 ❑ *...the child's emotional and intellectual growth.* …孩子情感和智力方面的成长。 **5** N-UNCOUNT **Growth** in a person, animal, or plant is the process of increasing in physical size and development. 生长 ❑ *...hormones which control fertility and body growth.* …控制生育力和身体发育的荷尔蒙。 **6** N-VAR You can use **growth** to refer to plants that have recently developed or that developed at the same time. 植物 ❑ *This helps to ripen new growth and makes it flower profusely.* 这有助于新植物成熟并且开出繁茂的花朵。 **7** N-COUNT A **growth** is a lump that grows inside or on a person, animal, or plant, and that is caused by a disease. 肿瘤 ❑ *This type of surgery could even be used to extract cancerous growths.* 这类外科手术甚至可以用来摘除恶性肿瘤。

grub /grʌb/ (**grubs, grubbing, grubbed**) **1** N-COUNT A **grub** is a young insect which has just come out of an egg and looks like a short, fat worm. 幼虫 2 N-UNCOUNT **Grub** is food. 食物 [INFORMAL] ❑ *Get yourself some grub and come and sit down.* 自己拿一些吃的，过来坐下。 3 V-I If you **grub** around, you search for something. 搜寻 ❑ *I simply cannot face grubbing through all this paper.* 我简直受不了这样在整篇文章中搜索。

grub·by /grʌbi/ (**grubbier, grubbiest**) 1 ADJ A **grubby** person or object is rather dirty. 肮脏的 ❑ *His white coat was grubby and stained.* 他的白外套又脏又有污迹。 2 ADJ If you call an activity or someone's behavior **grubby**, you mean that it is not completely honest or respectable. 卑鄙的 [DISAPPROVAL] ❑ *...the grubby business of politics.* …政治的卑鄙勾当。

▲ **grudge** /grʌdʒ/ (**grudges**) N-COUNT If you have or bear a **grudge against** someone, you have unfriendly feelings toward them because of something they did in the past. 积怨 ❑ *He appears to have a grudge against certain players.* 他好像对某些选手有积怨。

grudg·ing /grʌdʒɪŋ/ ADJ A **grudging** feeling or action is felt or done very unwillingly. 勉强的 ❑ *He even earned his opponents' grudging respect.* 他甚至令对手也不得不尊重他。 ● **grudg·ing·ly** ADV 勉强地 [ADV with V] ❑ *The film studio grudgingly agreed to allow him to continue working.* 电影厂勉强同意让他继续工作。

★ **gru·el** /gruəl/ N-UNCOUNT **Gruel** is a food made by boiling oats with water or milk. 燕麦粥

gru·el·ing /gruəlɪŋ/

in BRIT, use **gruelling**

ADJ A **grueling** activity is extremely difficult and tiring to do. 艰难的；令人疲劳的 ❑ *He had complained of exhaustion after his grueling schedule over the past week.* 完成上星期紧张的日程安排后，他抱怨自己已筋疲力尽。

grue·some /grusəm/ ADJ Something that is **gruesome** is extremely unpleasant and shocking. 可怕的 ❑ *There has been a series of gruesome murders in the capital.* 在首都发生了一连串恐怖的谋杀案。

▲ **grum·ble** /grʌmbᵊl/ (**grumbles, grumbling, grumbled**) 1 V-T/V-I If someone **grumbles**, they complain about something in a bad-tempered way. 抱怨 ❑ *They grumble about how hard they have to work.* 他们抱怨自己工作得很辛苦。 ❑ *Taft grumbled that the law so favored the criminal that trials seemed like a game of chance.* 塔夫脱抱怨法律如此有利于罪犯，使得审判看来像是一场运气的游戏。 ● N-COUNT **Grumble** is also a noun. 抱怨 ❑ *My only grumble is that there isn't a non-smoking section.* 我惟一的抱怨是这儿没有无烟区。 2 V-I If something **grumbles**, it makes a low continuous sound. 隆隆作响 [LITERARY] ❑ *It was quiet now, the thunder had grumbled away to the west.* 现在安静了，雷声已经隆隆作响地传到西边了。 ● N-SING **Grumble** is also a noun. 隆隆响声 [usu N "of" n] ❑ *One could often hear, far to the east, the grumble of guns.* 人们经常可以听到在远远的东边有隆隆的枪炮声。

grumpy /grʌmpi/ (**grumpier, grumpiest**) ADJ If you say that someone is **grumpy**, you mean that they are bad tempered and miserable. 脾气坏的 ❑ *Some folks think I'm a grumpy old man.* 一些人认为我是个脾气很坏的老头儿。 ● **grumpi·ly** ADV 脾气坏地 [ADV with V] ❑ *"I know, I know," said Ken, grumpily, without looking up.* "我知道，我知道" 肯没好气地说着，连头也不抬。

▲ **grunt** /grʌnt/ (**grunts, grunting, grunted**) 1 V-T/V-I If you **grunt**, you make a low sound, especially because you are annoyed or not interested in something. (尤指厌烦或不感兴趣时) 嘟哝着说；嘟哝 ❑ *The driver grunted, convinced that Michael was crazy.* 司机嘟哝着，深信迈克尔疯了。 ❑ *Harvey grunted disgustedly as he tossed in his cards.* 哈维扔下了牌，厌烦地嘟哝着。 ● N-COUNT **Grunt** is also a noun. 嘟哝 [oft N "of" n] ❑ *Their replies were no more than grunts of acknowledgement.* 他们的回答不过是表示感谢的咕哝声。 2 V-I When an animal **grunts**, it makes a low, rough noise. (动物的) 咕噜声 ❑ *...the sound of a pig grunting.* …猪发出的咕噜声。 3 N-COUNT A **grunt** is a soldier of low rank in the infantry or the marines. (步兵或海军陆战队中的) 低等兵 [AM, INFORMAL] ❑ *I'm just a grunt. I have to follow everybody's orders.* 我只是个低等兵，谁的命令我都必须服从。

GSM /dʒi ɛs ɛm/ N-UNCOUNT **GSM** is a digital mobile telephone system. **GSM** is an abbreviation for "global system for mobile communication." 全球移动通信系统 ❑ *Their latest financial performance was a direct result of consistent growth in GSM cell phone subscribers.* 他们最近的财务业绩是全球移动通信系统手机用户持续增长的直接结果。

guar·an·tee ♦♦◊ /gærənti/ (**guarantees, guaranteeing, guaranteed**) 1 V-T If one thing **guarantees** another, the first is certain to cause the second thing to happen. 确保 ❑ *Surplus resources alone do not guarantee growth.* 仅有富足的资源并不能确保发展。 2 N-COUNT Something that is a **guarantee of** something else makes it certain that it will happen or that it is true. 保证 ❑ *A famous old name on a firm is not necessarily a guarantee of quality.* 公司的老字号并不一定能保证质量。 3 V-T If you **guarantee** something, you promise that it will definitely happen, or that you will do or provide it for someone. 保证…必定发生；保证…做某事或提供某物 ❑ *Most states guarantee the right to free and adequate education.* 大多数州都保证免费和适当教育的权利。 ❑ *We guarantee that you will find a community with which to socialize.* 我们保证你将找到一个可以社交的团体。 ● N-COUNT **Guarantee** is also a noun. 保证 ❑ *The editors can give no guarantee that they will fulfil their obligations.* 这些编辑不能保证他们将履行职责。 4 N-COUNT A **guarantee** is a written promise by a company to replace or repair a product free of charge if it has any faults within a particular time. 保修单 [also "under" N] ❑ *Whatever a guarantee says, when something goes wrong, you can still claim your rights from the store.* 不管保修单上怎么说，当产品出现故障时，你仍然可以去商店维护自身的权益。 5 V-T If a company **guarantees** its product or work, they provide a guarantee for it. 担保 ❑ *Some builders guarantee their work.* 一些建筑商为他们的工作担保。 ❑ *All Dreamland's electric blankets are guaranteed for three years.* 所有"梦乡"牌的电热毯都保质3年。 6 N-COUNT A **guarantee** is money or something valuable that you give to someone to show that you will do what you have promised. 担保物 ❑ *Males between 18 and 20 had to leave a deposit as a guarantee of returning to do their military service.* 18岁至20岁的男性必须留下押金作为回来服兵役的担保。

guar·an·tor /gærəntɔr/ (**guarantors**) N-COUNT A **guarantor** is a person who gives a guarantee or who is bound by one. 担保人 [LEGAL] ❑ *Someone thinking about acting as a guarantor should be clear what their obligations will be.* 想做担保的人应该清楚他们将要承担的责任。

guard ♦♦◊ /gɑrd/ (**guards, guarding, guarded**) 1 V-T If you **guard** a place, person, or object, you stand near them in order to watch and protect them. 守卫；护卫 ❑ *Gunmen guarded homes near the cemetery with shotguns.* 枪手携带猎枪守卫着公墓附近的住宅。 2 V-T If you **guard** someone, you watch them and keep them in a particular place to stop them from escaping. 看守 ❑ *Marines with rifles guarded them.* 持步枪的海军陆战队士兵看守他们。 3 N-COUNT A **guard** is someone such as a soldier, police officer, or prison officer who is guarding a particular place or person. 卫兵 ❑ *The prisoners overpowered their guards and locked them in a cell.* 囚犯们制服了卫兵，并把他们锁在一个牢房里。 4 N-SING-COLL A **guard** is a specially organized group of people, such as soldiers or police officers, who protect or watch someone or something. (一队) 卫兵 5 V-T If you **guard** some information or advantage that you have, you try to protect it or keep it for yourself. 保护；保守 ❑ *He closely guarded her identity.* 他严密地保守她的身份。 6 N-COUNT A **guard** is a protective device which covers a part of someone's body or a dangerous part of a piece of equipment. 防护装置 [usu with supp] ❑ *...the chin guard of my helmet.* …我头盔上的下巴防护罩。 7 N-COUNT On a train, a **guard** is a person whose job is to travel on the train in order to help passengers, check tickets, and make sure that the train travels safely and on time. 列车员 [BRIT]

in AM, use **conductor**

8 → see also **bodyguard, coast guard, guarded, lifeguard**
9 PHRASE If someone **catches** you **off guard**, they surprise you by doing something you do not expect. If something **catches** you **off guard**, it surprises you by happening when you are not expecting it. 乘某人不备使其大吃一惊 ❑ *Charm the audience and catch them off guard.* 让观众陶醉，然后出其不意使他们大吃一惊。 10 PHRASE If you **lower** your **guard**, **let** your **guard down** or **drop** your **guard**, you relax when you should be careful and alert, often with unpleasant consequences. 放松警惕 ❑ *The ANC could not afford to lower its guard until everything had been carried out.* 在所有任务完成之前，非洲人国民大会丝毫不敢放松警惕。 ❑ *You can't let your guard down.* 你不能掉以轻心。 11 PHRASE If you are **on** your **guard** or **on guard**, you are being very careful because you think a situation might become difficult or dangerous. 警惕 ❑ *The police have questioned him thoroughly, and he'll be on his guard.* 警察已仔细盘问了他，因此他会保持警惕。 12 PHRASE If someone **is on guard**, they are on duty and responsible for guarding a particular place or person. 值守 ❑ *Police were on guard at*

g

Barnet town hall. 警察在巴尼特市政厅值守。 13 PHRASE If you **stand guard**, you stand near a particular person or place because you are responsible for watching or protecting them. 站岗 ❑ *One young policeman stood guard outside the locked embassy gates.* 一名年轻的警察在大门紧闭的使馆外站岗。 14 PHRASE If someone is **under guard**, they are being guarded. 受到看守 ❑ *Three men were arrested and one was under guard in a hospital.* 有三人被捕，一人在医院里受到监视。
→ see **soccer**
▸ **guard against** PHRASAL VERB If you **guard against** something, you are careful to prevent it from happening, or to avoid being affected by it. 提防 ❑ *The armed forces were on high alert to guard against any retaliation.* 武装部队保持高度警惕，以防发生任何报复行为。

Word Partnership *guard* 的常用搭配：
N. guard **a door/house/prisoner** 1 2
prison guard, **security** guard 3 4
V. **catch** *someone* **off** guard 9
let your guard **down**, **be on** guard, **stand** guard 10 – 13

G

guard·ed /gɑrdɪd/ ADJ If you describe someone as **guarded**, you mean that they are careful not to show their feelings or give away information. 谨慎的 ❑ *The boy gave him a guarded look.* 这个男孩谨慎地看了他一眼。
★ **guard·ian** /gɑrdiən/ (**guardians**) 1 N-COUNT A **guardian** is someone who has been legally appointed to take charge of the affairs of another person, for example a child or someone who is mentally ill. 监护人 ❑ *Destiny's legal guardian was her grandmother.* 德斯蒂妮的法定监护人是她的祖母。 2 N-COUNT The **guardian of** something is someone who defends and protects it. 保护者 ❑ *...an institution acting as the guardian of democracy in Europe.* …一个在欧洲扮演民主捍卫者的机构。
▲ **guer·ril·la** ♦◇◇ /gərɪlə/ (**guerrillas**) also **guerilla** N-COUNT A **guerrilla** is someone who fights as part of an unofficial army, usually against an official army or police force. 游击队员 ❑ *The guerrillas threatened to kill their hostages.* 游击队员们威胁要杀死人质。
guess ♦♦◇ /gɛs/ (**guesses, guessing, guessed**) 1 V-T/V-I If you **guess** something, you give an answer or provide an opinion which may not be true because you do not have definite knowledge about the matter concerned. 猜测 ❑ *Yvonne guessed that he was a very successful publisher or a banker.* 伊冯娜猜测他是一位非常成功的出版商或银行家。 ❑ *You can only guess at what mental suffering they endure.* 你只能猜测他们忍受着什么样的精神痛苦。 ❑ *Guess what I did for the whole of the first week.* 猜猜整个第一周我都做了些什么。 2 V-T If you **guess that** something is the case, you correctly form the opinion that it is the case, although you do not have definite knowledge about it. 猜中 ❑ *By now you will have guessed that I'm back in Ohio.* 此刻，你将已经猜出我回到了俄亥俄。 ❑ *He should have guessed what would happen.* 他本应该猜出将会发生什么的。 3 N-COUNT A **guess** is an attempt to give an answer or provide an opinion which may not be true because you do not have definite knowledge about the matter concerned. 猜想 ❑ *My guess is that the chance that these vaccines will work is zero.* 我的猜想是这些疫苗将起作用的可能性为零。 ❑ *He'd taken her pulse and made a guess at her blood pressure.* 他为她把了脉，对她的血压做了估量。 4 PHRASE If you say that something is **anyone's guess** or **anybody's guess**, you mean that no one can be certain about what is really true. 谁也拿不准的事 [INFORMAL] ❑ *Just when this will happen is anyone's guess.* 谁也拿不准这件事什么时候会发生。 5 PHRASE You say **at a guess** to indicate that what you are saying is only an estimate or what you believe to be true, rather than being a definite fact. 凭猜测 [mainly BRIT, VAGUENESS] ❑ *At a guess he's been dead for two days.* 据猜测，他已经死了两天了。 6 PHRASE You say **I guess** to show that you are slightly uncertain or reluctant about what you are saying. 我想 [mainly AM, INFORMAL, VAGUENESS] ❑ *I guess he's right.* 我想他是对的。 ❑ *"I think you're being paranoid."—"Yeah. I guess so."* "我认为你是多疑了。"——"是的，我想是的。" 7 PHRASE If someone **keeps** you **guessing**, they do not tell you what you want to know. 使某人猜不透 ❑ *The author's intention is to keep everyone guessing until the bitter end.* 这位作者的意图是在最终结尾前让所有人都猜不透。 8 CONVENTION You say **guess what** to draw attention to something exciting, surprising, or interesting that you are about to say. 想不到吧 [INFORMAL] ❑ *Guess what, I just got my first part in a movie.* 想不到吧，我刚得到我的第一个电影角色。

Thesaurus *guess* 另参见：
V. estimate, predict, suspect 1
N. assumption, prediction, theory 3

Word Partnership *guess* 的常用搭配：
N. guess **a secret** 2
V. **make a** guess 3
ADJ. **educated** guess, **good** guess, **wild** guess 3

guess·ti·mate /gɛstɪmət/ (**guesstimates**) N-COUNT A **guesstimate** is an approximate calculation which is based mainly or entirely on guessing. (凭猜测得出的) 估计 [INFORMAL] ❑ *The 30 percent figure may be no more than a guesstimate.* 30%这一数字可能只是个大约的估计。
guest ♦♦◇ /gɛst/ (**guests**) 1 N-COUNT A **guest** is someone who is visiting you or is at an event because you have invited them. 客人 ❑ *She was a guest at the wedding.* 她是参加婚礼的客人。 2 N-COUNT A **guest** is someone who visits a place or organization or appears on a radio or television show because they have been invited to do so. 特邀嘉宾 ❑ *...a frequent talk show guest.* …一位经常参加访谈节目的特邀嘉宾。 ❑ *Dr. Gerald Jeffers is the guest speaker.* 杰拉尔德·杰弗斯博士是特邀演讲人。 3 N-COUNT A **guest** is someone who is staying in a hotel. (旅馆的) 客人 ❑ *I was the only hotel guest.* 我是旅馆的惟一客人。 4 CONVENTION If you say **be my guest** to someone, you are giving them permission to do something. 请便 ❑ *If anybody wants to work on this, be my guest.* 如果有人想做这件事的话，请便吧。
→ see **hotel**

Word Partnership *guest* 的常用搭配：
ADJ. **unwelcome** guest 1 2
V. **be** *someone's* guest, **entertain a** guest 1 2
accommodate a guest 1 – 3
N. guest **appearance**, guest **list**, guest **speaker** 1 2
hotel guest 3

guest house (**guest houses**) also **guesthouse** 1 N-COUNT A **guest house** is a small hotel. 小旅馆 2 N-COUNT A **guest house** is a small house in the grounds of a large house, where visitors can stay. 客房 [AM]
guid·ance /gaɪdᵊns/ N-UNCOUNT **Guidance** is help and advice. 指导 ❑ *...an opportunity for young people to improve their performance under the guidance of professional coaches.* …一个让年轻人在专业教练指导下提高成绩的机会。
guide ♦♦◇ /gaɪd/ (**guides, guiding, guided**) 1 N-COUNT; N-IN-NAMES A **guide** is a book that gives you information or instructions to help you do or understand something. 指南 ❑ *Our 10-page guide will help you to change your life for the better.* 我们这本10页的指南将会帮助改善你们的生活。 2 N-COUNT; N-IN-NAMES A **guide** is a book that gives tourists information about a town, area, or country. 旅行指南 ❑ *The Rough Guide to Paris lists accommodations for as little as $35 a night.* 《巴黎旅游简明指南》列出了价格低至每晚$35的住宿。 3 N-COUNT A **guide** is someone who shows tourists around places such as museums or cities. 导游 ❑ *We've arranged a walking tour of the city with your guide.* 我们已经和你的导游安排了一个城市步行游览。 4 V-T If you **guide** someone around a city, museum, or building, you show it to them and explain points of interest. 给…导游 ❑ *...a young Egyptologist who guided us through tombs and temples with enthusiasm.* …一位热心地领着我们参观陵墓和寺庙的年轻的埃及学家。 5 N-COUNT A **guide** is someone who shows people the way to a place in a difficult or dangerous region. 向导 ❑ *The mountain people say that, with guides, the journey can be done in fourteen days.* 山里人说，有向导的话，这趟旅行可以在14天内完成。 6 N-COUNT A **guide** is something that can be used to help you plan your actions or to form an opinion about something. 指导原则 ❑ *As a rough guide, a horse needs 2.5 percent of its body weight in food every day.* 作为一个大致的标准，一匹马每天需要相当于它体重2.5%的食物。 7 V-T If you **guide** someone somewhere, you go there with them in order to show them the way. 给…领路 ❑ *He took the bewildered Elliott by the arm and guided him out.* 他挽着晕头转向的埃利奥特的手臂，领着他出去。 8 V-T If you **guide** a vehicle somewhere, you control it carefully to make sure that it goes in the right direction. 驾驶 (车辆等) ❑ *Captain Shelton guided his plane down the runway and took off.* 谢尔顿机长驾驶飞机沿着跑道滑行起飞。 9 V-T If

something **guides** you somewhere, it gives you the information you need in order to go in the right direction. 给…指明方向 ❑ *They sailed across the Caribbean with only a compass to guide them.* 他们仅靠一只指南针来指引他们驶过了加勒比海。 10 V-T If something or someone **guides** you, they influence your actions or decisions. 指导…的行动; 影响…的决定 ❑ *He should have let his instinct guide him.* 他本该让直觉指导他的行动。 ❑ *Development has been guided by a concern for the ecology of the area.* 关注本地区的生态状况一直是发展的指导原则。 11 V-T If you **guide** someone through something that is difficult to understand or to achieve, you help them to understand it or to achieve success in it. 指导 ❑ *Gym owner David Barton will guide them through a workout.* 健身房主人戴维•巴顿将指导他们完成锻炼。

Thesaurus *guide* 另参见:

N. directory, handbook, information 1 2
V. accompany, direct, instruct, lead, navigate; *(ant.)* follow 4 7

guide·book /gaɪdbʊk/ **(guidebooks)** also **guide book** N-COUNT A **guidebook** is a book that gives tourists information about a town, area, or country. 旅行指南

guide dog **(guide dogs)** N-COUNT A **guide dog** is a dog that has been trained to lead a blind person. 导盲犬 [mainly BRIT]
in AM, usually use **seeing-eye dog**

guide·line /gaɪdlaɪn/ **(guidelines)** 1 N-COUNT If an organization issues **guidelines on** something, it issues official advice about how to do it. 指导方针 ❑ *The government should issue clear guidelines on the content of religious education.* 政府应该颁布明确的关于宗教教育内容的指导方针。 2 N-COUNT A **guideline** is something that can be used to help you plan your actions or to form an opinion about something. 参考 ❑ *A written IQ test is merely a guideline.* 书面的智商测试只是个参考。

▲ **guild** /gɪld/ **(guilds)** N-COUNT A **guild** is an organization of people who do the same job. 同业公会 ❑ *...the Writers' Guild of America.* …美国作家协会。

★ **guilt** /gɪlt/ 1 N-UNCOUNT **Guilt** is an unhappy feeling that you have because you have done something wrong or think that you have done something wrong. 内疚 ❑ *Her emotions had ranged from anger to guilt in the space of a few seconds.* 她的情绪在几秒钟内由愤怒转为内疚。 2 N-UNCOUNT **Guilt** is the fact that you have done something wrong or illegal. 罪行 ❑ *The trial is concerned only with the determination of guilt according to criminal law.* 审判只是根据刑法进行定罪。

Word Partnership *guilt* 的常用搭配:

N. **burden of** guilt, **feelings of** guilt, **sense of** guilt, guilt **trip** 1
V. **admit** guilt 2

guilty ♦◇◇ /gɪlti/ **(guiltier, guiltiest)** 1 ADJ If you feel **guilty**, you feel unhappy because you think that you have done something wrong or have failed to do something which you should have done. 内疚的 ❑ *I feel so guilty, leaving all this to you.* 把所有这一切都留给了你，我觉得很内疚。 ● **guilti·ly** ADV 内疚地 [ADV with V] ❑ *He glanced guiltily over his shoulder.* 他内疚地向后瞥了一眼。 2 ADJ **Guilty** is used of an action or fact that you feel guilty about. 罪恶的 [ADJ n] ❑ *Many may be keeping it a guilty secret.* 许多人可能将它作为一个罪恶的秘密保守着。 3 **guilty conscience** → see **conscience** 4 ADJ If someone is **guilty of** a crime or offense, they have committed that crime or offense. 犯罪的 ❑ *They were found guilty of murder.* 他们被判犯有谋杀罪。 5 ADJ If someone is **guilty of** doing something wrong, they have done that thing. 有过失的 ❑ *He claimed Mr. Brooke had been guilty of a "gross error of judgment."* 他声称布鲁克先生犯有"判决上的重大过失"。
→ see **trial**

Word Partnership *guilty* 的常用搭配:

V. **feel** guilty, **look** guilty 1
find *someone* guilty, **plead (not)** guilty, **prove** *someone* guilty 4
N. guilty **conscience**, guilty **secret** 2 3
guilty **party**, guilty **plea**, guilty **verdict** 4
PREP. guilty **of** *something* 4 5

guinea pig **(guinea pigs)** 1 N-COUNT If someone is used as a **guinea pig** in an experiment, something is tested on them that has not been tested on people before. 作为实验对象的人 ❑ *Dr. Roger Altounyan used himself as a human guinea pig.* 罗杰•奥托扬医生拿自己作为实验对象。 2 N-COUNT A **guinea pig** is a small, furry animal without a tail. Guinea pigs are often kept as pets. 豚鼠

guise /gaɪz/ **(guises)** N-COUNT You use **guise** to refer to the outward appearance or form of someone or something, which is often temporary or different from their real nature. 伪装 ❑ *He turned up at an Easter party in the guise of a white rabbit.* 他以白兔的装扮出席复活节聚会。

gui·tar ♦◇◇ /gɪtɑr/ **(guitars)** N-VAR A **guitar** is a musical instrument with six strings and a long neck. You play the guitar by plucking or strumming the strings. 吉他

gui·tar·ist /gɪtɑrɪst/ **(guitarists)** N-COUNT A **guitarist** is someone who plays the guitar. 弹奏吉他的人

gulf /gʌlf/ **(gulfs)** 1 N-COUNT A **gulf** is an important or significant difference between two people, things, or groups. 巨大的差距 ❑ *Within society, there is a growing gulf between rich and poor.* 在社会的内部，贫富之间有着一道日益加深的鸿沟。 2 N-COUNT A **gulf** is a large area of sea which extends a long way into the surrounding land. 海湾 ❑ *Hurricane Andrew was last night heading into the Gulf of Mexico.* 安德鲁飓风昨晚进入墨西哥湾。

gul·lible /gʌlɪbəl/ ADJ If you describe someone as **gullible**, you mean they are easily tricked because they are too trusting. 轻信的 ❑ *What point is there in admitting that the stories fed to the gullible public were false?* 承认向轻信的公众提供的报道不实又有什么意义呢? ● **gul·li·bil·ity** /gʌləbɪlɪti/ N-UNCOUNT 轻信 ❑ *Was she taking part of the blame for her own gullibility?* 她因为自己的轻信而承担部分责任了吗?

gul·ly /gʌli/ **(gullies)** also **gulley** N-COUNT A **gully** is a long, narrow valley with steep sides. 隘谷 ❑ *The bodies of the three climbers were located at the bottom of a steep gully.* 3名登山者的尸体在一个陡峭的隘谷谷底找到了。
→ see **erosion**

▲ **gulp** /gʌlp/ **(gulps, gulping, gulped)** 1 V-T If you **gulp** something, you eat or drink it very quickly by swallowing large quantities of it at once. 大口吞下 ❑ *She quickly gulped her soda.* 她很快地把汽水一饮而尽。 ● PHRASAL VERB **Gulp down** means the same as **gulp**. 大口吞下 (同 **gulp**) ❑ *Paige gulped down more coffee and a candy bar from the machine.* 佩奇大口饮下更多的咖啡，又一口吞下一个取自这台机器的糖块。 2 V-T/V-I If you **gulp**, you swallow air, often making a noise in your throat as you do so, because you are nervous or excited. (因担忧或兴奋) 倒吸气 [WRITTEN] ❑ *I gulped, and then proceeded to tell her the whole story.* 我倒吸了口气，接着把事情的原委都告诉了她。 3 V-T If you **gulp** air, you breathe in a large amount of air quickly through your mouth. 大口地吸 ❑ *She gulped air into her lungs.* 她大口地把空气吸入肺部。 4 N-COUNT A **gulp of** air, food, or drink, is a large amount of it that you swallow at once. 一大口 ❑ *I took in a large gulp of air.* 我吸了一大口气。

gum /gʌm/ **(gums)** 1 N-MASS **Gum** is a substance, usually tasting of mint, which you chew for a long time but do not swallow. 口香糖 ❑ *I do not chew gum in public.* 我不在公共场合嚼口香糖。 2 N-COUNT Your **gums** are the areas of firm, pink flesh inside your mouth, which your teeth grow out of. 齿龈 ❑ *The toothbrush gently removes plaque without damaging the gums or causing bleeding.* 牙刷轻轻地刷去齿菌斑，没有伤及牙床或引起出血。
→ see **teeth**

gun ♦♦◇ /gʌn/ **(guns, gunning, gunned)** 1 N-COUNT A **gun** is a weapon from which bullets or other things are fired. 枪 ❑ *He fled, pointing the gun at officers as they chased him.* 他一边逃跑，一边用枪对准追他的警察。 ❑ *He just seemed like a normal military guy who liked guns.* 他看上去就好像一个喜欢枪的普通军人。 2 N-COUNT A **gun** or a **starting gun** is an object like a gun that is used to make a noise to signal the start of a race. 发令枪 ❑ *The starting gun blasted and they were off.* 发令枪一响，他们跑了出去。 3 V-T To **gun** an engine or a vehicle means to make it start or go faster by pressing on the accelerator pedal. 把…发动起来; 给…加大油门 [mainly AM] ❑ *He gunned his engine and drove off.* 他把引擎发动起来，开车走了。 4 → see also **shotgun** 5 PHRASE If you come out **with guns blazing** or **with all guns blazing**, you put all your effort and energy into trying to achieve something. 奋力 ❑ *The company came out with guns blazing.* 这家公司尽了全力，大干了一场。 6 PHRASE If you **jump the gun**, you do something before everyone else or before the proper or right time. 过早行动 [INFORMAL] ❑ *It wasn't due to be released until September 10, but some booksellers have jumped the gun and decided to sell it early.* 应该到9月10日才发行的，但一些书商已抢先行动，

决定提早销售。 7 PHRASE If you **stick to** your **guns**, you continue to have your own opinion about something even though other people are trying to tell you that you are wrong. 固执己见 [INFORMAL] ❑ *He should have stuck to his guns and refused to meet her.* 他本该坚持立场，拒绝见她。

▸ **gun down** PHRASAL VERB If someone **is gunned down**, they are shot and severely injured or killed. 开枪打伤；枪杀 [JOURNALISM] ❑ *He had been gunned down and killed at point-blank range.* 他在近距离射程内被开枪打死。

Word Partnership *gun* 的常用搭配：

V. **aim** a gun, **carry** a gun, **fire** a gun, **load** a gun, **own** a gun, **shoot** a gun, **use** a gun 1

N. **hand** gun, **toy** gun 1
starting gun 2
gun **an engine** 3

★ **gun·fire** /gʌnfaɪr/ N-UNCOUNT **Gunfire** is the repeated shooting of guns. 炮火 ❑ *The sound of gunfire and explosions grew closer.* 枪炮声和爆炸声越来越近了。

G

gun·man /gʌnmən/ (**gunmen**) N-COUNT A **gunman** is a man who uses a gun to commit a crime such as murder or robbery. 持枪歹徒 [JOURNALISM] ❑ *Two policemen were killed when gunmen opened fire on their patrol vehicle.* 当持枪歹徒对巡逻车开枪射击时，两名警察中弹身亡。

gun·point /gʌnpɔɪnt/ PHRASE If you are held **at gunpoint**, someone is threatening to shoot and kill you if you do not obey them. 在枪口威胁下 ❑ *She and her two daughters were held at gunpoint by a gang who burst into their home.* 她和她的两个女儿被一伙闯入家中的歹徒持枪挟持。

gun·shot /gʌnʃɒt/ (**gunshots**) 1 N-UNCOUNT **Gunshot** is used to refer to bullets that are fired from a gun. 射出的子弹 ❑ *They had died of gunshot wounds.* 他们死于枪伤。 2 N-COUNT A **gunshot** is the firing of a gun or the sound of a gun being fired. 枪炮射击；枪炮声 ❑ *They heard thousands of gunshots.* 他们听见密集的枪炮声。

gur·gle /gɜrgᵊl/ (**gurgles, gurgling, gurgled**) 1 V-I If water **is gurgling**, it is making the sound that it makes when it flows quickly and unevenly through a narrow space. 作汩汩声 ❑ *...a narrow stone-edged channel along which water gurgles unseen.* …一条边沿布满石头、暗流汩汩的狭窄沟渠。 ● N-COUNT **Gurgle** is also a noun. 汩汩声 ❑ *We could hear the swish and gurgle of water against the hull.* 我们能够听见水拍击船身所发出的哗哗声和汩汩声。 2 V-I If someone, especially a baby, **is gurgling**, they are making a sound in their throat similar to the gurgling of water. (尤指婴儿) 发咯咯声 ❑ *Henry gurgles happily in his baby chair.* 亨利在婴儿椅里高兴地咯咯笑着。 ● N-COUNT **Gurgle** is also a noun. 咯咯声 ❑ *There was a gurgle of laughter on the other end of the line.* 电话线另一端传来一阵咯咯的笑声。

gur·ney /gɜrni/ (**gurneys**) N-COUNT A **gurney** is a bed on wheels that is used in hospitals for moving sick or injured people. 有轮的病床 [AM]

in BRIT, use **trolley**

❑ *A man on a gurney was being handled by an orderly.* 一个轮床上的男子正由一个护理员推送。

guru /gʊru/ (**gurus**) 1 N-COUNT A **guru** is a person who some people regard as an expert or leader. 专家 ❑ *Fashion gurus dictate crazy ideas such as squeezing oversized bodies into tight trousers.* 时装大师们常表达离奇的想法，例如把肥硕的身子塞进紧身裤中。 2 N-COUNT; N-TITLE A **guru** is a religious and spiritual leader and teacher, especially in Hinduism. (尤指印度教的) 精神领袖

▲ **gush** /gʌʃ/ (**gushes, gushing, gushed**) 1 V-T/V-I When liquid **gushes** out of something, or when something **gushes** a liquid, the liquid flows out very quickly and in large quantities. 涌出 ❑ *Piping-hot water gushed out.* 滚烫的水涌了出来。 2 N-SING A **gush of** liquid is a sudden, rapid flow of liquid, or a quantity of it that suddenly flows out. 涌流 [usu N "of" n] ❑ *I heard a gush of water.* 我听到一股流水涌出。 3 V-T/V-I If someone **gushes**, they express their admiration or pleasure in an exaggerated way. 夸张地赞扬 ❑ *"Oh, it was brilliant," he gushes.* "哦，太棒了，"他夸张地称赞道。 ● **gush·ing** ADJ 过分赞扬的 ❑ *He delivered a gushing speech.* 他发表了一场阿谀的演说。

▲ **gust** /gʌst/ (**gusts, gusting, gusted**) 1 N-COUNT A **gust** is a short, strong, sudden rush of wind. 一阵强风 ❑ *A gust of wind drove down the valley.* 一阵狂风掠过山谷。 2 V-I When the wind **gusts**, it blows with short, strong, sudden rushes. 劲吹 ❑ *The wind gusted again.* 风又猛刮起来。 3 N-COUNT If you feel a **gust of** emotion, you feel the emotion suddenly and intensely. (感情的) 迸发 [N "of" n] ❑ *...a small gust of pleasure.* …一丝愉悦的迸发。

▲ **gut** /gʌt/ (**guts, gutting, gutted**) 1 N-PLURAL A person's or animal's **guts** are all the organs inside them. 内脏 ❑ *By the time they finish, the crewmen are standing ankle-deep in fish guts.* 到他们结束时，船员们正站在齐脚踝深的鱼内脏堆里。 2 V-T When someone **guts** a dead animal or fish, they prepare it for cooking by removing all the organs from inside it. 取出…的内脏 ❑ *It is not always necessary to gut the fish prior to freezing.* 在冷冻鱼之前没有必要总是取出其内脏。 3 N-SING **The gut** is the tube inside the body of a person or animal through which food passes while it is being digested. 肠 ["the"/poss N] ❑ *Toxins can leak from the gut into the bloodstream.* 毒素能够从肠道渗透到血液里。 4 N-UNCOUNT **Guts** is the will and courage to do something that is difficult or unpleasant, or which might have unpleasant results. 胆量 [INFORMAL] ❑ *The new governor has the guts to push through unpopular tax increases.* 新任州长有胆量强制通过不得人心的增税方案通过。 5 ADJ A **gut** feeling is based on instinct or emotion rather than reason. 直觉的 ❑ *Let's have your gut reaction to the facts as we know them.* 请告诉我们你对这些我们了解的事实的直觉反应。 6 N-COUNT You can refer to someone's stomach as their **gut**, especially when it is very large and sticks out. 肚腩 [INFORMAL] ❑ *His gut sagged out over his belt.* 他的肚腩垂在腰带上。 7 V-T To **gut** a building means to destroy the inside of it so that only its outside walls remain. 损毁(建筑物) 的内部 ❑ *Over the weekend, a firebomb gutted a building where 60 people lived.* 周末，一颗燃烧弹焚毁了一座住着60人的建筑内部。 8 N-UNCOUNT **Gut** is string made from part of the stomach of an animal. Traditionally, it is used to make the strings of sports rackets or musical instruments such as violins. (用于制网球拍、琴弦等的) 肠线 ❑ *Gerald's violin strings are made of gut rather than steel.* 杰拉尔德的小提琴弦是用肠线而不是钢丝制成的。 9 PHRASE If you **hate** someone's **guts**, you dislike them very much. 对某人恨之入骨 [INFORMAL, EMPHASIS] ❑ *We hate each other's guts.* 我们对彼此恨之入骨。 10 PHRASE If you say that you **are working** your **guts out**, you are emphasizing that you are working as hard as you can. 拼命工作 [INFORMAL, EMPHASIS] ❑ *Most have worked their guts out and made sacrifices.* 大多数人都拼命工作并做出了牺牲。

▲ **gut·ter** /gʌtər/ (**gutters**) 1 N-COUNT **The gutter** is the edge of a road next to the pavement, where rainwater collects and flows away. (路边的) 排水沟 ❑ *It is supposed to be washed down the gutter and into the city's vast sewerage system.* 它应该被冲入排水沟，流入城市的巨大排污系统。 2 N-COUNT A **gutter** is a plastic or metal channel attached to the lower edge of the roof of a building, which rainwater drains into. (房檐的) 排水槽 ❑ *Did you fix the gutter?* 你修过排水槽了吗？ 3 N-SING If someone is **in the gutter**, they are very poor and live in a very bad way. 贫民窟 ❑ *Instead of ending up in jail or in the gutter he was remarkably successful.* 他最后不但没有坐牢或流落贫民窟，反而还非常成功。

gut·ter press N-SING You can refer to newspapers and magazines which print mainly stories about sex and crime as **the gutter press**. 主要刊载性与犯罪的低级趣味的报刊 [BRIT, DISAPPROVAL]

in AM, use **scandal sheets**

guy ♦♦◊ /gaɪ/ (**guys**) 1 N-COUNT A **guy** is a man. 家伙 [INFORMAL] ❑ *I was working with a guy from Milwaukee.* 我跟一个从密尔沃基来的家伙一起工作。 2 N-VOC; N-PLURAL Americans sometimes address a group of people, whether they are male or female, as **guys** or **you guys**. 伙计们 ["you" N] [INFORMAL] ❑ *Hi, guys. How are you doing?* 嗨，伙计们，你们好吗？

gym /dʒɪm/ (**gyms**) 1 N-COUNT A **gym** is a club, building, or large room, usually containing special equipment, where people go to do physical exercise and get fit. 健身房 ❑ *While the boys are golfing, I work out in the gym.* 当男孩子们在打高尔夫球时，我在健身房里锻炼。 2 N-UNCOUNT **Gym** is the activity of doing physical exercises in a gym, especially at school. (尤指学校的) 体操 ❑ *...gym classes.* …体操课。

gym·na·sium /dʒɪmneɪziəm/ (**gymnasiums** or **gymnasia**) /dʒɪmneɪziə/ N-COUNT A **gymnasium** is the same as a **gym**. 健身房 [FORMAL]

gym·nast /dʒɪmnæst/ (**gymnasts**) N-COUNT A **gymnast** is someone who is trained in gymnastics. 体操运动员

gym·nas·tics /dʒɪmnæstɪks/

> The form **gymnastic** is used as a modifier.

N-UNCOUNT **Gymnastics** consists of physical exercises that develop your strength, coordination, and ease of movement. 体操 ❑ *She competes in gymnastics, with hopes of making it to the Olympics.* 她参加体操比赛，希望能进军奥运会。

gy·nae·col·ogy /gaɪnɪkɒlədʒi/ [BRIT] → see **gynecology**

gy·ne·col·ogy /gaɪnɪkɒlədʒi/

> in BRIT, use **gynaecology**

N-UNCOUNT **Gynecology** is the branch of medical science that deals with women's diseases and medical conditions. 妇科医学

● **gy·ne·colo·gist** N-COUNT (**gynecologists**) 妇科医生 ❑ *Gynecologists at the hospital have successfully used the drug on 60 women.* 这家医院的妇科医生们已成功地在60名妇女的身上使用了该药。

● **gy·ne·co·logi·cal** /gaɪnɪkəlɒdʒɪkᵊl/ ADJ 妇科医学的 [ADJ n] ❑ *Breast examination is a part of a routine gynecological examination.* 乳房检查是妇科检查中的一项常规检查。

gyp·sy /dʒɪpsi/ (**gypsies**) also **gipsy** N-COUNT A **gypsy** is a member of a race of people who travel from place to place, usually in caravans, rather than living in one place. Some people find this word offensive. 吉卜赛人 ❑ *I'm proud of being brought up by gypsies.* 我为自己是吉卜赛人抚养长大的而感到自豪。● ADJ **Gypsy** is also an adjective. 吉卜赛人的 ❑ *...the largest gypsy community of any country.* …所有国家中最大的吉卜赛人社区。

g

Hh

H

H also **h** /eɪtʃ/ (**H's, h's** /eɪtʃɪz/) **H** is the eighth letter of the English alphabet. 英文字母表中的第8个字母

hab·it ♦◇◇ /hæbɪt/ (**habits**) **1** N-VAR A **habit** is something that you do often or regularly. 习惯 ❑ *He has an endearing habit of licking his lips when he's nervous.* 他有个紧张时舔嘴唇的可爱习惯。 ❑ *Many people add salt to their food out of habit, without even tasting it first.* 许多人出于习惯往他们的食物中加盐，甚至都不先品尝一下。 **2** N-COUNT A **habit** is an action considered bad that someone does repeatedly and finds it difficult to stop doing. 坏习惯 ❑ *A good way to break the habit of eating too quickly is to put your knife and fork down after each mouthful.* 一个改掉吃饭太快的坏习惯的好方法是每吃一口后放下刀叉。 **3** N-COUNT A drug **habit** is an addiction to a drug such as heroin or cocaine. 毒瘾 ❑ *She became a prostitute in order to pay for her cocaine habit.* 她为钱过可卡因毒瘾而成了一名妓女。 **4** PHRASE If you say that someone is **a creature of habit**, you mean that they usually do the same thing at the same time each day, rather than doing new and different things. 按习惯行事的人 ❑ *Jesse is a creature of habit and always eats breakfast.* 杰西是按习惯行事的人，每天都吃早餐。 **5** PHRASE If you are **in the habit of** doing something, you do it regularly or often. If you **get into the habit of** doing something, you begin to do it regularly or often. 习惯于…/养成…的习惯 ❑ *They were in the habit of giving two or three dinner parties a month.* 他们习惯于每月举办两三次晚宴。 **6** PHRASE If you **make a habit of** doing something, you do it regularly or often. 使成为习惯 ❑ *You can phone me at work as long as you don't make a habit of it.* 你可以在上班时给我打电话，只要你别让这成为习惯就行。

Word Partnership *habit* 的常用搭配：

N.	**force of** habit **1** **cocaine** habit, **drug** habit **3**
V.	**develop/form a** habit, **a** habit **of doing** ***something***, **do** ***something*** **out of** habit **1** **6** **break a** habit, **give up a** habit, **kick a** habit, **smoking** habit **2**
ADJ.	**bad/nasty** habit **2**

▲ **hab·i·tat** /hæbɪtæt/ (**habitats**) N-VAR The **habitat** of an animal or plant is the natural environment in which it normally lives or grows. 生长环境 ❑ *In its natural habitat, the hibiscus will grow up to 25 ft.* 在其野生环境中，木槿能长25英尺。

ha·bitu·al /həbɪtʃuəl/ **1** ADJ A **habitual** action, state, or way of behaving is one that someone usually does or has, especially one that is considered to be typical or characteristic of them. 习惯性的 ❑ *If bad posture becomes habitual, you risk long-term effects.* 如果不良姿势成为习惯，你会有遭受长期影响的危险。 ● **ha·bitu·al·ly** ADV 习惯性地 ❑ *His mother had a patient who habitually flew into rages.* 她的母亲有一个习惯性地陷入狂怒的病人。 **2** ADJ You use **habitual** to describe someone who usually or often does a particular thing. 积习难改的 [ADJ n] ❑ *Three out of four of them would become habitual criminals if actually sent to jail.* 如果真把他们投入监狱的话，他们中3/4的人会成为惯犯。

▲ **hack** /hæk/ (**hacks, hacking, hacked**) **1** V-T/V-I If you **hack** something or **hack** at it, you cut it with strong, rough strokes using a sharp tool such as an ax or a knife. 劈；砍 ❑ *An armed gang barged onto the train and began hacking and shooting anyone in sight.* 一伙武装匪徒冲上火车，开始见人就刀砍枪击。 ❑ *Matthew desperately hacked through the leather.* 马修绝望地刺穿了那块皮革。 **2** V-I If someone **hacks into** a computer system, they break into the system, especially in order to get secret information. 侵入(计算机系统) ❑ *The saboteurs had demanded money in return for revealing how they hacked into the systems.* 这些破坏分子要求以钱作交换，才会透露他们是如何侵入该系统的。 ● **hack·ing** N-UNCOUNT (计算机系统的) 侵入 ❑ *...the common and often illegal art of computer hacking.* …那种常见且常为非法的电脑入侵行径。 **3** N-COUNT If you refer to a politician as a **hack**, you disapprove of them because they are too loyal to their party and perhaps do not deserve the position they have. 唯命是从的政客 [DISAPPROVAL] ❑ *Far too many party hacks from the old days still hold influential jobs.* 太多的老一辈党仆仍然占据着有影响力的职位。 **4** N-COUNT If you refer to a professional writer, such as a journalist, as a **hack**, you disapprove of them because they write for money without worrying very much about the quality of their writing. (粗制滥造的) 职业文人 [DISAPPROVAL] ❑ *...tabloid hacks, always eager to find victims in order to sell newspapers.* …小报记者，总是为了卖掉报纸而急于找到牺牲品。 **5** N-COUNT A **hack** is the same as a **taxi**. 出租车 [AM] ❑ *I will pay for a hack. There is no need for you to return home on foot.* 我会花钱打辆出租车。你没有必要步行回家。 **6** PHRASE If you say that someone **can't hack it** or **couldn't hack it**, you mean that they do not or did not have the qualities needed to do a task or cope with a situation. 应付不了它 [INFORMAL] ❑ *You have to be strong and confident, and never give the slightest impression that you can't hack it.* 你必须坚强和自信，决不要给人留下丝毫应付不了此事的印象。

hack·er /hækər/ (**hackers**) **1** N-COUNT A computer **hacker** is someone who tries to break into computer systems, especially in order to get secret information. (电脑) 黑客 ❑ *...a hacker who steals credit card numbers.* …一个窃取信用卡号码的黑客。 **2** N-COUNT A computer **hacker** is someone who uses a computer a lot, especially so much that they have no time to do anything else. 计算机迷
→ see **Internet**

had

> The auxiliary verb is pronounced /həd, STRONG hæd/. For the main verb, and for meanings **2** to **5**, the pronunciation is /hæd/.

> 助动词读作 /həd, STRONG hæd/。主要动词以及义项**2**至**5**读作 /hæd/。

1 **Had** is the past tense and past participle of **have**. **have**的过去式和过去分词 **2** AUX **Had** is sometimes used instead of "if" to begin a clause which refers to a situation that might have happened but did not. For example, the clause "had he been elected" means the same as "if he had been elected." 代替**if**，引导一个表示虚拟假设条件的分句 ❑ *Had he succeeded, he would have acquired a monopoly.* 如果他那时成功了，他就会获得垄断地位。 **3** PHRASE If you **have been had**, someone has tricked you, for example by selling you something at too high a price. 受骗上当 [INFORMAL] ❑ *If your customer thinks he's been had, you have to make him happy.* 要是顾客觉得他受骗了，你得想法取悦他。 **4** PHRASE If you say that someone **has had it**, you mean they are in very serious trouble or have no hope of succeeding. 完蛋了 [INFORMAL] ❑ *Unless she loses some weight, she's had it.* 除非她减掉一些体重，否则她就完蛋了。 **5** PHRASE If you say that you **have had it**, you mean that you are very tired of something or very annoyed about it, and do not want to continue doing it or it to continue happening. 受够了 [INFORMAL] ❑ *I've had it. Let's call it a day.* 我受够了。我们今天就到这里吧。

had·dock /hædək/ (**haddock**) N-VAR **Haddock** is a type of edible saltwater fish found in the North Atlantic. 黑线鳕 ❑ *...fishing boats which normally catch a mix of cod, haddock, and whiting.* …一般混合捕捞鳕鱼、黑线鳕和牙鳕的渔船。

hadn't /hædᵊnt/ **Hadn't** is the usual spoken form of "had not." **had not**的常用口语形式

haemo·philia /himəfɪliə/ → see **hemophilia**

haemo·phili·ac /himəfɪliæk/ → see **hemophiliac**

haem·or·rhage /hɛmərɪdʒ/ → see **hemorrhage**

hag·gle /hægᵊl/ (**haggles, haggling, haggled**) V-RECIP If you **haggle**, you argue about something before reaching an agreement, especially about the cost of something that you are buying. 争论 (尤指讨价还价) ❑ *Ella showed her the best places to go for a good buy, and taught her how to haggle with used furniture dealers.*

埃拉告诉她买便宜货的最佳去处，还教她怎样与二手家具商讨价还价。❑ *Of course he'll still haggle over the price.* 当然他仍然要讨价还价。

● **hag·gling** N-UNCOUNT 讨价还价 ❑ *After months of haggling, they recovered only three-quarters of what they had lent.* 经过数月的讨价还价，他们仅收回了借出的3/4。

hail /heɪl/ (**hails, hailing, hailed**) **1** V-T If a person, event, or achievement **is hailed as** important or successful, they are praised publicly. 赞颂 [usu passive] ❑ *Faulkner has been hailed as the greatest American novelist of his generation.* 福克纳被赞颂为他那一代人中最伟大的美国小说家。 **2** N-UNCOUNT **Hail** consists of small balls of ice that fall like rain from the sky. 冰雹 ❑ *...a sharp short-lived storm with heavy hail.* …一场来去匆匆的大雹暴。 **3** V-I When **it hails**, hail falls like rain from the sky. 下冰雹 ❑ *It started to hail, huge great stones.* 天空开始下冰雹，巨大的雹子。 **4** N-SING A **hail of** things, usually small objects, is a large number of them that hit you at the same time and with great force. (雹子般的) 一阵 ❑ *The victim was hit by a hail of bullets.* 那名受害者被一阵弹雨击中了。 **5** V-I Someone who **hails from** a particular place was born there or lives there. 出生于；来自 [FORMAL] ❑ *He hails from Memphis.* 他出生于孟菲斯。 **6** V-T If you **hail** a taxi, you wave at it in order to stop it because you want the driver to take you somewhere. 挥手招 (出租车) ❑ *I hurried away to hail a taxi.* 我匆忙离开去挥手招了一辆出租车。
→ see **storm**

hair ♦♦◇ /hɛər/ (**hairs**) **1** N-VAR Your **hair** is the fine threads that grow in a mass on your head. 头发 ❑ *I wash my hair every night.* 我每晚洗头发。 ❑ *I get some gray hairs but I pull them out.* 我长了几根白头发，但我把它们拔掉了。 **2** N-VAR **Hair** is the short, fine threads that grow on different parts of your body. 汗毛 ❑ *The majority of men have hair on their chest.* 大多数男人长有胸毛。 **3** N-VAR **Hair** is the threads that cover the body of an animal such as a dog, or make up a horse's mane and tail. (动物的) 毛 ❑ *I am allergic to cat hair.* 我对猫毛过敏。 **4** PHRASE If you **let** your **hair down**, you relax completely and enjoy yourself. 彻底放松 ❑ *...the world-famous Oktoberfest, a time when everyone in Munich really lets their hair down.* …世界著名的啤酒节，一个让身在慕尼黑的每个人彻底放松的节日。 **5** PHRASE Something that **makes** your **hair stand on end** shocks or frightens you very much. 使毛骨悚然 ❑ *This was the kind of smile that made your hair stand on end.* 这是那种使你毛骨悚然的微笑。 **6** PHRASE If you say that someone has **not a hair out of place**, you are emphasizing that they are extremely neat and well dressed. 衣冠楚楚 [EMPHASIS] ❑ *She had a lot of makeup on and not a hair out of place.* 她浓妆艳抹，衣冠楚楚。 **7** PHRASE If you say that someone **is splitting hairs**, you mean that they are making unnecessary distinctions between things when the differences between them are so small they are not important. 做不必要的过细区分 ❑ *Don't split hairs. You know what I'm getting at.* 不要钻牛角尖。你知道我是什么意思。
→ see Word Web: **hair**

Word Partnership *hair* 的常用搭配:

ADJ.	**black/blonde/brown/gray** hair, **curly/straight/wavy** hair **1**
V.	**bleach** *your* hair, **brush/comb** *your* hair, **color** *your* hair, **cut** *your* hair, **do** *your* hair, **dry** *your* hair, **fix** *your* hair, **lose** *your* hair, **pull** *someone's* hair, **wash** *your* hair **1**
N.	**lock of** hair **1**

hair·cut /hɛərkʌt/ (**haircuts**) **1** N-COUNT If you get a **haircut**, someone cuts your hair for you. 理发 ❑ *Your hair is all right; it's just that you need a haircut.* 你的头发没问题，只是你需要理个发。 **2** N-COUNT A **haircut** is the style in which your hair has been cut. 发型 ❑ *Who's that guy with the funny haircut?* 那个发型古怪的家伙是谁？

hair·dresser /hɛərdrɛsər/ (**hairdressers**) **1** N-COUNT A **hairdresser** is a person who cuts, colors, and arranges people's hair. 理发师 **2** N-COUNT A **hairdresser** or a **hairdresser's** is a place where a hairdresser works. 理发店 ❑ *I work in this new hairdresser's.* 我在这个新开的理发店工作。

hair·dressing /hɛərdrɛsɪŋ/ N-UNCOUNT **Hairdressing** is the job or activity of cutting, coloring, and arranging people's hair. 理发 ❑ *...personal services such as hairdressing and dry cleaning.* …诸如理发、干洗之类的个人服务。

hair·grip /hɛərgrɪp/ (**hairgrips**) also **hair-grip** N-COUNT A **hairgrip** is a small piece of metal or plastic bent back on itself, which you use to hold your hair in position. 发夹 [BRIT]
in AM, use **bobby pin**

hair·style /hɛərstaɪl/ (**hairstyles**) N-COUNT Your **hairstyle** is the style in which your hair has been cut or arranged. 发型 ❑ *I think her new short hairstyle looks simply great.* 我觉得她新剪的短发看上去简直棒极了。

★ **hairy** /hɛəri/ (**hairier, hairiest**) **1** ADJ Someone or something that is **hairy** is covered with hairs. 多毛的 ❑ *He was wearing shorts which showed his long, muscular, hairy legs.* 他穿着短裤，露出修长、健壮、多毛的双腿。 **2** ADJ If you describe a situation as **hairy**, you mean that it is exciting, worrying, and somewhat frightening. 令人胆战心惊 [INFORMAL] ❑ *His driving was a bit hairy.* 他开起车来有点儿令人胆战心惊。

half ♦♦♦ /hæf/ (**halves** /hævz/) **1** FRACTION **Half of** a number, an amount, or an object is one of two equal parts that together make up the whole number, amount, or object. 一半 ❑ *She wore a diamond ring worth half a million dollars.* 她戴了一枚价值50万美元的钻戒。 ❑ *More than half of all U.S. households are heated with natural gas.* 超过半数的美国家庭用天然气供暖。 ● PREDET **Half** is also a predeterminer. 半 ❑ *We just sat and talked for half an hour or so.* 我们只是坐着谈了半小时左右。 ❑ *They had only received half the money promised.* 他们只收到了一半当初承诺的钱。 ● ADJ **Half** is also an adjective. 一半的 [ADJ n] ❑ *...a half measure of fresh lemon juice.* …半量杯的新鲜柠檬汁。 **2** ADV You use **half** to say that something is only partly the case or happens to only a limited extent. 部分地；有点儿 ❑ *His eyes were half closed.* 他的双眼半闭着。 ❑ *His refrigerator frequently looked half empty.* 他的冰箱经常看上去有点儿空。 **3** N-COUNT In games such as football, soccer, rugby, and basketball, games are divided into two equal periods of time which are called **halves**. (球赛的) 半场 ❑ *The only goal was scored by Jakobsen early in the second half.* 这惟一的进球是雅各布森在下半场开始不久打进的。 **4** ADV You use **half** to say that someone has parents of different nationalities. For example, if you are **half** German, one of your parents is German but the other is not. 一半…血统地 [ADV adj] ❑ *She was half Italian and half English.* 她是一半意大利一半英国血统。 **5** PHRASE You use **half past** to refer to a time that is thirty minutes after a particular hour. …点半 ❑ *"What time were you planning lunch?"—"Half past twelve, if that's convenient."* "你打算什么时间吃午饭?" —— "12:30，如果方便的话。" **6** ADV You can use **half** before an adjective describing an extreme quality, as a way of emphasizing and exaggerating something. 半…的 [ADV adj] [INFORMAL, EMPHASIS] ❑ *He felt half dead with tiredness.* 他感觉累得半死。 ● PREDET **Half** can also be used in this way with a noun referring to a long period of time or a large quantity. 半…的 ❑ *I thought about you half the night.* 我想了你半夜。 **7** ADV You use **not half** to emphasize a negative quality that someone has. 一点儿也不 [EMPHASIS] ❑ *You're not half the man you think you are.* 你一点儿也不是你自认为的那种男人。 **8** PHRASE If two people **go halves**, they divide the cost of something equally between them. 分摊费用 ❑ *She went halves on gas.* 她分摊了煤气费用。

half brother (**half brothers**) N-COUNT Someone's **half brother** is a boy or man who has either the same mother or the same father as they have. 同母异父兄弟；同父异母兄弟

Word Web **hair**

At any given moment, only about 90 percent of the **hair** on your **scalp** is alive. The other 10 percent is dead and getting ready to **fall out**. Each hair grows about a centimeter a month for two to six years. Then it falls out and the cycle starts all over again. It's normal to lose about 100 hairs a day from your scalp.To keep hair healthy, eat a healthy diet and use a good **shampoo** and conditioner. Gently **brush** and **comb** your hair. Avoid strong **dyes**. Using the "cool" setting on your hairdryer also helps.

h

half-day (**half-days**) also **half day** N-COUNT A **half-day** is a day when you work only in the morning or in the afternoon, but not all day. 半天 ❑ *"If I could have just what I wanted," Sharon mused, "I'd work half days."* "如果我能心想事成"，莎伦沉思自语道，"我想只工作半天。"

half·heart·ed /hæfhɑrtɪd/ ADJ If someone does something in a **halfhearted** way, they do it without any real effort, interest, or enthusiasm. 半心半意的 ❑ *...a halfhearted apology.* …一个半心半意的道歉。 ● **half·heart·ed·ly** ADV 半心半意地 [ADV with v] ❑ *I can't do anything halfheartedly. I have to do everything 100 percent.* 我做任何事情都不能半心半意。我做每件事都必须百分之百地投入。

half-price 1 ADJ If something is **half-price**, it costs only half what it usually costs. 半价的 ❑ *Main courses are half price from 12:30 p.m. to 2 p.m.* 主菜从下午12：30到2：00是半价。❑ *A half-price suit still cost $400.* 一套半价西装仍然花了$400。 2 N-UNCOUNT If something is sold **at** or **for half-price**, it is sold for only half of what it usually costs. 半价 ❑ *By yesterday she was selling off stock at half-price.* 到昨天她一直都在以半价抛售股票。

half sister (**half sisters**) N-COUNT Someone's **half sister** is a girl or woman who has either the same mother or the same father as they have. 同母异父姐妹；同父异母姐妹

half·time /hæftaɪm/ N-UNCOUNT **Halftime** is the short period of time between the two parts of a sports event such as a football, rugby, or basketball game, when the players take a short rest. (球赛的) 中场休息 ❑ *The game started in brilliant sunshine but during halftime fog closed in.* 比赛在灿烂的阳光中开始，但在中场休息时却起雾了。

half·way /hæfweɪ/ 1 ADV **Halfway** means in the middle of a place or between two points, at an equal distance from each of them. 在中途地 ❑ *He was halfway up the ladder.* 他梯子上到了一半。 2 ADV **Halfway** means in the middle of a period of time or of an event. 在中间地 [ADV prep/adv] ❑ *By then, it was October and we were more than halfway through our tour.* 那时是10月，我们的行程已经过半。 ● ADJ **Halfway** is also an adjective. 在中间的 [ADJ n] ❑ *Cleveland held a 12-point advantage at the halfway point.* 克利夫兰在半程时拥有12分的优势。 3 PHRASE If you **meet** someone **halfway**, you accept some of the points they are making so that you can come to an agreement with them. 对某人让步 ❑ *The Democrats are willing to meet the president halfway.* 民主党人愿意对总统作出让步。 4 ADV **Halfway** means fairly or reasonably. 相当地 [ADV adj] [INFORMAL] ❑ *You need hard currency to get anything halfway decent.* 你得有硬通货才能买到像样点儿的东西。

half-yearly 1 ADJ **Half-yearly** means happening in the middle of a calendar year or a financial year. 年中的 [ADJ n] [BRIT]

in AM, use **semiannual**

2 ADJ A company's **half-yearly** profits are the profits that it makes in six months. 半年的 [ADJ n] [BRIT]

in AM, use **semiannual**

hall ♦◇◇ /hɔl/ (**halls**) 1 N-COUNT The **hall** in a house or an apartment is the area just inside the front door, into which some of the other rooms open. 门厅 ❑ *The lights were on in the hall and in the bedroom.* 门厅和卧室的灯亮着。 2 N-COUNT A **hall** in a building is a long passage with doors into rooms on both sides of it. (楼里的) 过道 [mainly AM] ❑ *There are 10 rooms along each hall.* 每条过道两侧都有10个房间。 3 N-COUNT A **hall** is a large room or building which is used for public events such as concerts, exhibitions, and meetings. 大厅；礼堂 ❑ *We picked up our conference materials and filed into the lecture hall.* 我们拿了会议材料，鱼贯进入礼堂。 4 → see also **town hall**
→ see **house**

Word Partnership *hall* 的常用搭配：

PREP.	**across the** hall, **down the** hall, **in the** hall 1 2
N.	**concert** hall, **lecture** hall, **meeting** hall, **pool** hall 3

hall·mark /hɔlmɑrk/ (**hallmarks**) 1 N-COUNT The **hallmark** of something or someone is their most typical quality or feature. 标志；特征 ❑ *It's a technique that has become the hallmark of Amber Films.* 这是一项已成为安伯电影公司标志的技术。 2 N-COUNT A **hallmark** is an official mark put on things made of gold, silver, or platinum that indicates the quality of the metal, where the object was made, and who made it. (金银等制品上的) 标记 ❑ *Early pieces of Scottish silver carry the hallmarks of individual silversmiths.* 早期的苏格兰银器上都有各个银匠的标记。

hal·lo /hælou/ → see **hello**

hall of resi·dence (**halls of residence**) N-COUNT **Halls of residence** are buildings with rooms or apartments, usually built by universities or colleges, in which students live during the term. (大学或学院的) 学生宿舍 [mainly BRIT]

in AM, use **dormitory, residence hall**

hal·lowed /hæloud/ 1 ADJ **Hallowed** is used to describe something that is respected and admired, usually because it is old, important, or has a good reputation. 受尊崇的 [ADJ n] ❑ *They protested that there was no place for a school of commerce in their hallowed halls of learning.* 他们抗议说，在他们所尊崇的学术殿堂里没有商业学院的位置。 2 ADJ **Hallowed** is used to describe something that is considered to be holy. 神圣的 [ADJ n] ❑ *...hallowed ground.* …圣地。

Word Link *luc* ≈ *light* : *hallucinate, lucid, translucent*

hal·lu·ci·nate /həlusɪneɪt/ (**hallucinates, hallucinating, hallucinated**) V-I If you **hallucinate**, you see things that are not really there, either because you are ill or because you have taken a drug. 产生幻觉 ❑ *Hunger made him hallucinate.* 饥饿使他产生了幻觉。

hal·lu·ci·na·tion /həlusɪneɪʃən/ (**hallucinations**) N-VAR A **hallucination** is the experience of seeing something that is not really there because you are ill or have taken a drug. 幻觉 ❑ *The drug induces hallucinations at high doses.* 这种毒品在大剂量使用时会引发幻觉。

hall·way /hɔlweɪ/ (**hallways**) 1 N-COUNT A **hallway** in a building is a long passage with doors into rooms on both sides of it. 过道 ❑ *They took the elevator up to the third floor and walked along the quiet hallway.* 他们乘电梯到了3楼，然后走过寂静的过道。 2 N-COUNT A **hallway** in a house or an apartment is the area just inside the front door, into which some of the other rooms open. 门厅 ❑ *...the coats hanging in the hallway.* …那些挂在门厅里的上衣。

halo /heɪlou/ (**haloes** or **halos**) N-COUNT A **halo** is a circle of light that is shown in pictures around the head of a holy figure such as a saint or angel. 光环

halt ♦◇◇ /hɔlt/ (**halts, halting, halted**) 1 V-T/V-I When a person or a vehicle **halts** or when something **halts** them, they stop moving in the direction they were going and stand still. 使停住；停住 ❑ *They halted at a short distance from the house.* 他们停在了离房子不远处。 2 V-T/V-I When something such as growth, development, or activity **halts** or when you **halt** it, it stops completely. 使完全停止；完全停止 ❑ *Striking workers halted production at the auto plant yesterday.* 罢工工人昨天在汽车厂完全停止了生产。 3 PHRASE If someone **calls a halt to** something such as an activity, they decide not to continue with it or to end it immediately. 决定停止 ❑ *The Russian government had called a halt to the construction of a new project in the Rostov region.* 俄罗斯政府已经决定停止在罗斯托夫地区的一个新工程的修建。 4 PHRASE If someone or something comes **to a halt**, they stop moving. 停止移动 ❑ *The elevator creaked to a halt at the ground floor.* 电梯嘎吱一声停在了1楼。 5 PHRASE If something such as growth, development, or activity **comes** or **grinds to a halt** or **is brought to a halt**, it stops completely. 完全停止 ❑ *Her political career came to a halt in December 1988.* 她的政治生涯于1988年12月彻底结束了。

Word Partnership *halt* 的常用搭配：

V.	**call** a halt **to** *something* 3 **bring** *something* **to a** halt, **come/grind/screech to a** halt 4 5

halve /hæv/ (**halves, halving, halved**) 1 V-T/V-I When you **halve** something or when it **halves**, it is reduced to half its previous size or amount. 使减半；减为一半 ❑ *Dr. Lee believes that men who exercise can halve their risk of colon cancer.* 李医生认为，男人坚持锻炼，可以使他们患结肠癌的风险减半。 2 V-T If you **halve** something, you divide it into two equal parts. 把…对半分开 ❑ *Halve the pineapple and scoop out the inside.* 把菠萝对半切开，并取出内瓤。 3 **Halves** is the plural of **half**. half的复数形式

ham /hæm/ (**hams**) N-VAR **Ham** is meat from the top of the back leg of a pig, specially treated so that it can be kept for a long period of time. 火腿 ❑ *...ham sandwiches.* …火腿三明治。

▲ **ham·burg·er** /hæmbɜrgər/ (**hamburgers**) N-COUNT A **hamburger** is ground meat which has been shaped into a flat circle. Hamburgers are fried or grilled and then eaten, often on a bun. 汉堡包

ham·mer /hæmər/ (**hammers, hammering, hammered**) 1 N-COUNT A **hammer** is a tool that consists of a heavy piece of metal at the end of a handle. It is used, for example, to hit nails

into a piece of wood or a wall, or to break things into pieces. 锤子 ❑ *He used a hammer and chisel to chip away at the wall.* 他用锤子和凿子将墙壁一点点凿掉。 **2** V-T If you **hammer** an object such as a nail, you hit it with a hammer. 用锤击 ❑ *To avoid damaging the tree, hammer a wooden peg into the hole.* 为了避免毁坏这棵树，把一只木钉敲进那个洞里。 **3** V-I If you **hammer on** a surface, you hit it several times in order to make a noise, or to emphasize something you are saying when you are angry. 砰砰敲击 ❑ *We had to hammer and shout before they would open up.* 我们不得不砰砰敲打并大喊大叫，他们才会开门。 ❑ *A crowd of reporters was hammering on the door.* 一群记者在砰砰敲那扇门。 **4** V-T/V-I If you **hammer** something such as an idea **into** people or you **hammer at** it, you keep repeating it forcefully so that it will have an effect on people. 把…灌输给… ❑ *He hammered it into me that I had not suddenly become a rotten goalkeeper.* 他反复向我灌输，我并没有突然变成一个糟糕的守门员。 **5** V-T If you say that someone **hammers** another person, you mean that they attack, criticize, or punish the other person severely. 猛烈攻击; 严厉批评; 严厉惩罚 ❑ *Democrats insisted they will continue to hammer Bush on his tax plan.* 民主党人坚称，他们将继续抨击布什的税收计划。 **6** V-T In sports, if you say that one player or team **hammered** another, you mean that the first player or team defeated the second completely and easily. (在体育比赛中) 轻松击溃 ❑ *He hammered the young left-hander in three straight sets.* 他连胜3局，轻松击溃了这位年轻的左撇子选手。 **7** N-COUNT In track and field, a **hammer** is a heavy weight on a piece of wire, which the athlete throws as far as possible. 链球 ● N-SING **The hammer** also refers to the sport of throwing the hammer. 链球运动 ❑ *Events like the hammer and the discus are not traditional crowd-pleasers in the West.* 链球和铁饼之类的运动项目在西方通常不是很吸引观众。 **8** PHRASE If you say that someone **was going at** something **hammer and tongs**, you mean that they were doing it with great enthusiasm or energy. 劲头十足地 ❑ *He loved gardening. He went at it hammer and tongs as soon as he got back from work.* 他喜爱园艺，下班一回到家，就劲头十足地干起来。
→ see **tool**

▸ **hammer out** PHRASAL VERB If people **hammer out** an agreement or treaty, they succeed in producing it after a long or difficult discussion. (经过长时间或艰难的讨论) 制定出 ❑ *I think we can hammer out a solution.* 我想我们能够制定出一个解决方案。

★ **ham·per** /hæmpər/ (**hampers, hampering, hampered**) **1** V-T If someone or something **hampers** you, they make it difficult for you to do what you are trying to do. 妨碍 ❑ *The bad weather hampered rescue operations.* 恶劣的天气阻碍了救助行动。 **2** N-COUNT A **hamper** is a basket containing food of various kinds that is given to people as a present. 食品礼篮 ❑ *...a luxury food hamper.* …一个豪华的食品礼篮。 **3** N-COUNT A **hamper** is a large basket with a lid, used especially for carrying food. 有盖大篮 (尤装食品) ❑ *...a picnic hamper.* …一个野餐篮。 **4** N-COUNT A **hamper** is a storage container for soiled laundry. 洗衣篮 ❑ *He tossed his damp towel into the laundry hamper.* 他把湿毛巾抛入洗衣篮里。

ham·ster /hæmstər/ (**hamsters**) N-COUNT A **hamster** is a small furry animal which is similar to a mouse, and which is often kept as a pet. 仓鼠

ham·string /hæmstrɪŋ/ (**hamstrings, hamstringing, hamstrung**) **1** N-COUNT A **hamstring** is a length of tissue or tendon behind your knee which joins the muscles of your thigh to the bones of your lower leg. 腘绳肌腱 ❑ *Webster has not played since suffering a hamstring injury in the opening game.* 韦伯斯特自从首场比赛腘绳肌腱受伤以来就没有再参加比赛。 **2** V-T If you are **hamstrung** by a person, problem, or difficulty, they make it very difficult for you to take any action. 使无能为力 [usu v-link ADJ "by" n] ❑ *Rural schools were hamstrung by their inability to attract and keep experienced staff.* 农村学校因不能吸引并留住有经验的教师而难以为继。

hand
❶ NOUN USES AND PHRASES
❷ VERB USES

h

❶ **hand** ♦♦♦ /hænd/ (**hands**)
➪ **Please look at meanings 38 – 40 to see if the expression you are looking for is shown under another headword.** **1** N-COUNT Your **hands** are the parts of your body at the end of your arms. Each hand has four fingers and a thumb. 手 ❑ *I put my hand into my pocket and pulled out the letter.* 我把手伸进衣袋，掏出那封信。 **2** N-SING The **hand** of someone or something is their influence in an event or situation. 影响 ❑ *The hand of the military authorities can be seen in the entire electoral process.* 军方的影响在整个选举过程中都可以看到。 **3** N-PLURAL If you say that something is **in** a particular person's **hands**, you mean that they are taking care of it, own it, or are responsible for it. 照顾; 掌控 ❑ *I feel that possibly the majority of these dogs are in the wrong hands.* 我觉得这些狗中大多数可能没有得到适当的照顾。 ❑ *We're in safe hands.* 我们得到妥善的照顾。 **4** N-SING If you ask someone for **a hand** with something, you are asking them to help you in what you are doing. 帮助 ❑ *Come and give me a hand in the garden.* 到花园里来给我搭把手。 **5** N-SING If someone asks an audience to give someone **a hand**, they are asking the audience to clap loudly, usually before or after that person performs. 鼓掌 ❑ *Let's give 'em a big hand.* 让我们为他们热烈鼓掌。 **6** N-COUNT In a game of cards, your **hand** is the set of cards that you are holding in your hand at a particular time or the cards that are dealt to you at the beginning of the game. (纸牌游戏) 手中的牌 ❑ *He carefully*

Picture Dictionary hand

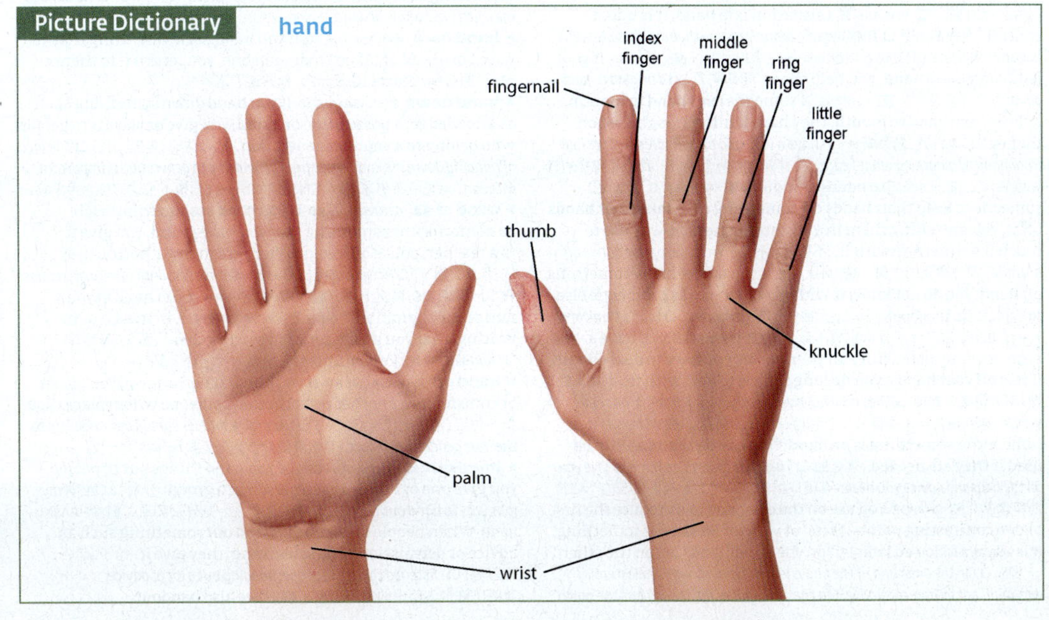

inspected his hand. 他仔细检查手中的牌。 7 N-COUNT The **hands** of a clock or watch are the thin pieces of metal or plastic that indicate what time it is. (钟表的) 指针 ❑ *The hands of the clock on the wall moved with a slight click. Half past ten.* 墙上时钟的指针伴着轻轻的嘀嗒声走着。10:30了。 8 PHRASE If something is **at hand**, **near at hand**, or **close at hand**, it is very near in place or time. 在手边；在眼前 ❑ *Having the right equipment at hand will be enormously helpful.* 有合适的工具在手边将会极为有用。 9 PHRASE If someone experiences a particular kind of treatment, especially unpleasant treatment, **at the hands of** a person or organization, they receive it from them. 在…的手中 (尤指受到不好的待遇) ❑ *The civilian population was suffering greatly at the hands of the security forces.* 这些平民在保安部队的手中吃尽了苦头。 10 PHRASE If you do something **by hand**, you do it using your hands rather than a machine. 手工 ❑ *Each pleat was stitched in place by hand.* 每个褶子都是手工缝制的。 11 PHRASE When something **changes hands**, its ownership changes, usually because it is sold to someone else. (常指某物因卖给他人) 易主 ❑ *The firm has changed hands many times over the years.* 这家公司几年来已多次易主。 12 PHRASE If you **have** your **hands full with** something, you are very busy because of it. 为…忙得不可开交 ❑ *She had her hands full with new arrivals.* 她为这些新来的忙得不可开交。 13 PHRASE If someone gives you **a free hand**, they give you the freedom to use your own judgment and to do exactly as you wish. 便宜行事 ❑ *He gave Stephanie a free hand in the decoration.* 他让斯蒂芬妮在装潢时便宜行事。 14 PHRASE If you **get** your **hands on** something or **lay** your **hands on** something, you manage to find it or obtain it, usually after some difficulty. 搞到 [INFORMAL] ❑ *Patty began reading everything she could get her hands on.* 帕蒂开始阅读她能搞到的所有东西。 15 PHRASE If two people are **hand in hand**, they are holding each other's nearest hand, usually while they are walking or sitting together. People often do this to show their affection for each other. 手拉手 ❑ *I saw them making their way, hand in hand, down the path.* 我看到他们手拉手沿着小路朝前走。 16 PHRASE If two things **go hand in hand**, they are closely connected and cannot be considered separately from each other. 密切相关 ❑ *For us, research and teaching go hand in hand.* 对于我们来说，研究与教学密切相关。 17 PHRASE If you **have a hand in** something such as an event or activity, you are involved in it. 参与某事 ❑ *He thanked all who had a hand in his release.* 他感谢了所有参与解救他的人。 18 PHRASE If two people **are holding hands**, they are holding each other's nearest hand, usually while they are walking or sitting together. People often do this to show their affection for each other. 手拉手 ❑ *She approached a young couple holding hands on a bench.* 她走近一对手拉手坐在长凳上的年轻情侣。 19 PHRASE The job or problem **in hand** is the job or problem that you are dealing with at the moment. 处理中的 ❑ *The business in hand was approaching some kind of climax.* 这件正在处理中的事情正接近某种关键时刻。 20 PHRASE If a situation is **in hand**, it is under control. 在控制之下 ❑ *The Olympic organizers say that matters are well in hand.* 奥运会组织者说各项事务完全在掌控之中。 21 PHRASE If you **lend** someone **a hand**, you help them. 帮助某人 ❑ *I'd be glad to lend a hand.* 我乐意帮忙。 22 PHRASE If someone **lives hand to mouth** or **lives from hand to mouth**, they have hardly enough food or money to live on. 勉强糊口 ❑ *I have a wife and two children and we live from hand to mouth on what I earn.* 我有妻子和两个孩子，我们靠我挣的钱勉强糊口。 23 → see also **hand-to-mouth** 24 PHRASE If you tell someone to **keep** their **hands off** something or to **take** their **hands off** it, you are telling them in a slightly aggressive way not to touch it or interfere with it. 不许碰；不许干涉 ❑ *Keep your hands off my milk.* 不许碰我的牛奶。 25 PHRASE If you do not know something **off hand**, you do not know it without having to ask someone else or look it up in a book. 马上；无需查询地 [SPOKEN] ❑ *I can't think of any off hand.* 我一下子什么也想不起来。 26 PHRASE If you have a problem or responsibility **on** your **hands**, you have to deal with it. If it is **off** your **hands**, you no longer have to deal with it. 由某人处理/不再由某人处理 ❑ *They now have yet another drug problem on their hands.* 他们现在又在处理另一个与毒品有关的问题。 27 PHRASE If someone or something is **on hand**, they are near and able to be used if they are needed. 现成的 ❑ *There are experts on hand to give you all the help and advice you need.* 有现成的专家随时为你提供所需的一切帮助和建议。 28 PHRASE You use **on the one hand** to introduce the first of two contrasting points, facts, or ways of looking at something. It is always followed later by "on the other hand" or "on the other." 一方面 ❑ *On the one hand, if the body doesn't have enough cholesterol, we would not be able to survive. On the other hand, if the body has too much cholesterol, the excess begins to line the arteries.* 一方面，如果身体没有足够的胆固醇，我们将无法生存；另一方面，如果体内胆固醇过多，多余的胆固醇就开始让动脉变厚。 29 PHRASE You use **on the other hand** to introduce the second of two contrasting points, facts, or ways of looking at something. 另一方面 ❑ *The movie lost money; reviews, on the other hand, were by and large favorable.* 这部电影赔了钱；但从另一方面来看，评论大体上是积极的。

> Do not confuse **on the other hand** with **on the contrary**. **On the other hand** is used to state a different, often contrasting aspect of the situation you are considering. **On the contrary** is used to contradict someone, to say that they are wrong. ❑ *He had no wish to hurt her. On the contrary, he thought of her with warmth and affection.*

30 PHRASE If a person or a situation gets **out of hand**, you are no longer able to control them. 失去控制 ❑ *His drinking got out of hand.* 他饮酒已失去控制。 31 PHRASE If you dismiss or reject something **out of hand**, you do so immediately and do not consider believing or accepting it. 不假思索地 ❑ *I initially dismissed the idea out of hand.* 我起初不假思索地一口否决了这个主意。 32 PHRASE If you **take** something or someone **in hand**, you take control or responsibility over them, especially in order to improve them. 对某人/某事负责 ❑ *She took the twins in hand, encouraging them to turn their thoughts to the future.* 她对这对双胞胎负起责任，鼓励他们要多想想未来。 33 PHRASE If you say that your **hands are tied**, you mean that something is preventing you from acting in the way that you want to. 受到阻碍 ❑ *Politicians are always saying that they want to help us but their hands are tied.* 政客们总说他们想帮助我们，但是却受到阻碍。 34 PHRASE If you **try** your **hand at** an activity, you attempt to do it, usually for the first time. (通常指初次) 尝试 ❑ *He tried his hand at fishing, but he wasn't really very good at it.* 他尝试过钓鱼，但他真的不在行。 35 PHRASE If you **turn** your **hand to** something such as a practical activity, you learn about it and do it for the first time. 学做某事 ❑ *...a person who can turn his hand to anything.* …一个什么事都可以学着去做的人。 36 PHRASE If you **wash** your **hands of** someone or something, you refuse to be involved with them any more or to take responsibility for them. 洗手不干；不再负责 ❑ *He seems to have washed his hands of the job.* 这种工作他似乎已洗手不干了。 37 PHRASE If you **win hands down**, you win very easily. 轻易取胜 ❑ *We have been beaten in some games which we should have won hands down.* 我们曾经在一些本应轻易取胜的比赛中落选。 38 **with** one's **bare hands** → see **bare** 39 **to shake** someone's **hand** → see **shake** 40 **to shake hands** → see **shake**
→ see Picture Dictionary: **hand**
→ see **body**

❷ **hand** ♦♦◇ /hænd/ (**hands, handing, handed**) V-T If you **hand** something **to** someone, you pass it to them. 递…给… ❑ *He handed me a little rectangle of white paper.* 他递给我一小条白纸。

▸ **hand back** PHRASAL VERB If you **hand back** something that you have borrowed or taken from someone, you return it to them. 归还 ❑ *He handed the book back.* 他归还了这本书。

▸ **hand down** PHRASAL VERB If you **hand down** something such as knowledge, a possession, or a skill, you give or leave it to people who belong to a younger generation. 把…传给 (年轻一代) ❑ *The idea of handing down his knowledge from generation to generation is important to McLean.* 对麦克莱恩来说，将自己的知识一代代传下去这一信念很重要。

▸ **hand in** 1 PHRASAL VERB If you **hand in** something such as homework or something that you have found, you give it to a teacher, police officer, or other person in authority. 上交 (作业或失物等) ❑ *I'm supposed to have handed in a first draft of my dissertation.* 我本应将论文初稿交上去。 2 PHRASAL VERB If you **hand in** your notice or resignation, you tell your employer, in speech or in writing, that you no longer wish to work there. 递交 (辞呈等) ❑ *I handed my notice in on Saturday.* 星期六我递交了辞呈。

▸ **hand on** PHRASAL VERB If you **hand** something **on**, you give it or transfer it to another person, often someone who replaces you. 把…传给 (常指取代自己的人) ❑ *Natural resources should be handed on to the next generation intact.* 自然资源应该完好无损地传给下一代。

▸ **hand out** 1 PHRASAL VERB If you **hand** things **out** to people, you give one or more to each person in a group. 分发 ❑ *One of my jobs was to hand out the prizes.* 我的工作之一是分发奖品。 2 PHRASAL VERB When people in authority **hand out** something such as advice or permission to do something, they give it. 给予 (忠告、许可等) ❑ *I listened to a lot of people handing out a lot of advice.* 我听了许多人给予的很多忠告。 3 → see also **handout**

▶ **hand over** **1** PHRASAL VERB If you **hand** something **over** to someone, you give them the responsibility for dealing with a particular situation or problem. (把某事) 交给…负责 ❑ *I wouldn't dare hand this project over to anyone else.* 我可不敢将这个项目交给其他任何人负责。 **2** PHRASAL VERB If you **hand over to** someone or hand something **over to** them, you give them the responsibility for dealing with a particular situation or problem. (把某事) 交给…负责 ❑ *The present leaders have to decide whether to hand over to a younger generation.* 现任领导者们必须决定是否把工作移交给较年轻的一代负责。

hand·bag /hændbæg/ (**handbags**) **1** N-COUNT A **handbag** is a small bag which a woman uses to carry things such as her money and keys in when she goes out. 女用手提包 **2** → see also **pocketbook, purse**

hand·book /hændbʊk/ (**handbooks**) N-COUNT A **handbook** is a book that gives you advice and instructions about a particular subject, tool, or machine. 手册; 使用说明书 ❑ *...a handbook on pool maintenance.* …一本泳池保养手册

hand·cuff /hændkʌf/ (**handcuffs, handcuffing, handcuffed**) **1** N-PLURAL **Handcuffs** are two metal rings which are joined together and can be locked around someone's wrists, usually by the police during an arrest. 手铐 [also "a pair of" N] ❑ *He was led away to jail in handcuffs.* 他戴着手铐被送进监狱。 **2** V-T If you **handcuff** someone, you put handcuffs around their wrists. 用手铐铐住 ❑ *They tried to handcuff him but, despite his injuries, he fought his way free.* 他们试图用手铐铐住他，但尽管他受了伤，还是奋力挣脱了。

hand·ful /hændfʊl/ (**handfuls**) **1** N-SING A **handful of** people or things is a small number of them. 少数 ❑ *He surveyed the handful of customers at the bar.* 他打量着吧台边仅有的几位顾客。 **2** N-COUNT A **handful of** something is the amount of it that you can hold in your hand. 一把 ❑ *She scooped up a handful of sand and let it trickle through her fingers.* 她抓了一把沙子，然后让它们从指缝间慢慢漏掉。 **3** N-SING If you say that someone, especially a child, is a **handful**, you mean that they are difficult to control. 难管的人 (尤指小孩) [INFORMAL] ❑ *Zara can be a handful sometimes.* 扎拉有时会很难管教。

hand·held /hændhɛld/ (**handhelds**) ADJ A **handheld** device such as a camera or a computer is small and light enough to be used while you are holding it. 手持式的; 掌上的 ❑ *...a handheld electric mixer.* …一个手持式电动搅拌器 ● N-COUNT **Handheld** is also a noun. 手持式装置 ❑ *Users will be able to use their handhelds to look up timetables on the net, search for a local hotel, and check their bank accounts.* 用户将能够使用掌上装置查阅网上时刻表，搜索当地旅馆并核对他们的银行账户。

★ **handi·cap** /hændikæp/ (**handicaps, handicapping, handicapped**) **1** N-COUNT A **handicap** is a physical or mental disability. 残疾 ❑ *He lost his leg when he was ten, but learned to overcome his handicap.* 他10岁时失去了一条腿，但学会了战胜自己的残疾。 **2** N-COUNT A **handicap** is an event or situation that places you at a disadvantage and makes it harder for you to do something. 不利条件 ❑ *Being a foreigner was not a handicap.* 作一名外国人并不是一个不利条件。 **3** V-T If an event or a situation **handicaps** someone or something, it places them at a disadvantage. 将…置于不利地位 ❑ *Greater levels of stress may seriously handicap some students.* 更高程度的压力可能会将一些学生置于不利地位。 **4** N-COUNT In golf, a **handicap** is an advantage given to someone who is not a good player, in order to make the players more equal. As you improve, your handicap gets lower. 差点 (高尔夫运动中给弱者增加的杆数) ❑ *I see your handicap is down from 16 to 12.* 我注意到你的差点从16降到了12。 **5** N-COUNT In horse racing, a **handicap** is a race in which some competitors are given a disadvantage of extra weight in an attempt to give everyone an equal chance of winning. (赛马中的) 让步赛 ❑ *...the Melbourne Cup, a two-mile handicap.* …墨尔本杯，一场两英里的让步赛。

handi·capped /hændikæpt/ ADJ Someone who is **handicapped** has a physical or mental disability that prevents them from living a totally normal life. 残疾的 ❑ *I'm going to work two days a week teaching handicapped kids to fish.* 我将每周工作两天教残疾儿童钓鱼。 ● N-PLURAL You can refer to people who are handicapped as **the handicapped**. 残疾人 ❑ *...measures to prevent discrimination against the handicapped.* …防止歧视残疾人的措施。

★ **handi·craft** /hændikræft/ (**handicrafts**) **1** N-COUNT **Handicrafts** are activities such as embroidery and pottery which involve making things with your hands in a skillful way. 手工艺 [usu pl] **2** N-COUNT **Handicrafts** are the objects that are produced by people doing handicrafts. 手工艺品 [usu pl] ❑ *She sells handicrafts to the tourists.* 她向游客们出售手工艺品。

hand·ker·chief /hæŋkərtʃɪf/ (**handkerchiefs**) N-COUNT A **handkerchief** is a small square piece of fabric which you use for blowing your nose. 手帕

han·dle ◆◆◇ /hænd^əl/ (**handles, handling, handled**) **1** N-COUNT A **handle** is a small round object or a lever that is attached to a door and is used for opening and closing it. 门把手 ❑ *I turned the handle and found the door was open.* 我转动把手，发现门是开着的。 **2** N-COUNT A **handle** is the part of an object such as a tool, bag, or cup that you hold in order to be able to pick up and use the object. 柄; 把 ❑ *...a broom handle.* …一个扫帚柄 **3** V-T If you say that someone can **handle** a problem or situation, you mean that they have the ability to deal with it successfully. (成功地) 处理 ❑ *To tell the truth, I don't know if I can handle the job.* 说实话，我不知道我能否做好这份工作。 **4** V-T If you talk about the way that someone **handles** a problem or situation, you mention whether or not they are successful in achieving the result they want. 应付 ❑ *I think I would handle a meeting with Mr. Siegel very badly.* 我觉得我可能应付不了与西格尔先生的会谈。 ● **han·dling** N-UNCOUNT 应付 ❑ *The family has criticized the military's handling of Robert's death.* 罗伯特的家人批评军方没有处理好罗伯特的死亡。 **5** V-T If you **handle** a particular area of work, you have responsibility for it. 负责 ❑ *She handled travel arrangements for the press corps during the presidential campaign.* 她负责安排新闻报道团在总统竞选期间的出行事宜。 **6** V-T When you **handle** something, you hold it or move it with your hands. 拿; 用手移动 ❑ *Wear rubber gloves when handling cat litter.* 捡拾猫粪时要带橡皮手套。 **7** PHRASE If you **fly off the handle**, you suddenly and completely lose your temper. 突然大发脾气 [INFORMAL] ❑ *He flew off the handle at the slightest thing.* 他为一点小事就突然大发雷霆。
→ see **silverware**

Word Partnership *handle* 的常用搭配:

N.	handle **a job/problem/situation**, handle **pressure/responsibility** 3 4
	ability to handle *something* 3 – 5
ADJ.	**difficult/easy/hard to** handle 4 6

han·dler /hændlər/ (**handlers**) **1** N-COUNT A **handler** is someone whose job is to be in charge of and control an animal. 动物训导员 ❑ *Fifty officers, including dog handlers, are searching for her.* 50名警官，包括警犬训导员，正在寻找她。 **2** N-COUNT A **handler** is someone whose job is to deal with a particular type of object. 操作工 ❑ *...baggage handlers at the airport.* …机场行李搬运工。

hand lug·gage N-UNCOUNT When you travel by air, your **hand luggage** is the luggage you have with you in the plane, rather than the luggage that is carried in the hold. (随身带上飞机的) 手提行李 ❑ *...a ban on all knives in hand luggage.* …一项禁止在手提行李内携带任何刀具的禁令。

hand·made /hændmeɪd/ also **hand-made** ADJ **Handmade** objects have been made by someone using their hands or using tools rather than by machines. 手工制作的 ❑ *Because they're handmade, each one varies slightly.* 因为它们是手工制作的，每一件都略有不同。

hand·out /hændaʊt/ (**handouts**) **1** N-COUNT A **handout** is a gift of money, clothing, or food, which is given free to poor people. 施舍物; 救济品; 救济金 ❑ *Each family is being given a cash handout of six thousand rupees.* 每个家庭都被给予6000卢比的救济金。 **2** N-COUNT If you call money that is given to someone a **handout**, you disapprove of it because you believe that the person who receives it has done nothing to earn or deserve it. 不劳而获的钱 [DISAPPROVAL] ❑ *...the tendency of politicians to use money on vote-buying handouts rather than on investment in the future.* …政客们用钱送人拉选票而不是用于未来投资的趋势。 **3** N-COUNT A **handout** is a document which contains news or information about something and which is given, for example, to journalists or members of the public. 传单; 宣传品 ❑ *Official handouts describe the Emperor as "particularly noted as a scholar."* 官方宣传品把这位皇帝描述成"尤以饱学著称"。 **4** N-COUNT A **handout** is a paper given out to students by a teacher, that contains a summary of the information or topics that will be dealt with in a lesson. (教师给学生的) 讲义 ❑ *Many teachers are opting for group discussions instead of handouts.* 许多教师选择组织小组讨论，而不是发讲义。

▲ **hand·over** /hændoʊvər/ (**handovers**) N-COUNT The **handover** of something is when possession or control of it is given by one person or group of people to another. 移交 [usu sing, oft N "of" n]

❑ *The handover is expected to be completed in the next ten years.* 移交预计在下个10年内完成。

★ **hand·set** /hændset/ (**handsets**) 1 N-COUNT The **handset** of a telephone is the part that you hold next to your face in order to speak and listen. 电话听筒 ❑ *...the cord that connects the telephone handset to the phone itself.* …那条连接听筒和电话机的电线。 2 N-COUNT You can refer to a device such as the remote control of a television or stereo as a **handset**. 遥控器 ❑ *Most VCRs can be programmed using a remote control handset.* 大多数录像机可用遥控器来设定程序。

hands-free ADJ A **hands-free** telephone or other device can be used without being held in your hand. 免提的 [ADJ n] ❑ *...legislation to ban both handheld and hands-free cellphones in moving vehicles.* …禁止在行驶车辆中使用手持式和免提式手机的法规。

hand·shake /hændʃeɪk/ (**handshakes**) 1 N-COUNT If you give someone a **handshake**, you take their right hand with your own right hand and hold it firmly or move it up and down, as a sign of greeting or to show that you have agreed about something such as a business deal. 握手 ❑ *He has a strong handshake.* 他有力地握了一下手。 2 → see also **golden handshake**

H

hand·some /hænsəm/ 1 ADJ A **handsome** man has an attractive face with regular features. 英俊的 ❑ *...a tall, dark, handsome sheep farmer.* …一位高个、皮肤黝黑、相貌英俊的牧羊人。

When you are describing someone's appearance, you generally use **pretty** and **beautiful** to describe women, girls, and babies. **Beautiful** is a much stronger word than **pretty**. The equivalent word for a man is **handsome**. **Good-looking** and **attractive** can be used to describe people of either sex. **Pretty** can also be used to modify adjectives and adverbs but is less strong than **very**. In this sense, **pretty** is informal.

2 ADJ A **handsome** sum of money is a large or generous amount. (款项) 相当大的; 可观的 [ADJ n] [FORMAL] ❑ *They will make a handsome profit on the property.* 他们将从地产中赚取一笔可观的利润。

hands-on ADJ **Hands-on** experience or work involves actually doing a particular thing, rather than just talking about it or getting someone else to do it. 亲身实践的 ❑ *This hands-on management approach often stretches his workday from 6 a.m. to 11 p.m.* 这种事必躬亲的管理方法常常使他在工作日从早晨6:00一直工作到晚上11:00。

hand-to-mouth also **hand to mouth** ADJ A **hand-to-mouth** existence is a way of life in which you have hardly enough food or money to live on. 勉强糊口的 ❑ *Unloved and uncared-for, they live a meaningless hand to mouth existence.* 没人疼爱也没人照顾，他们过着一种毫无意义、勉强糊口的日子。 ● ADV **Hand to mouth** is also an adverb. 勉强糊口地 [ADV after v] ❑ *I just can't live hand to mouth, it's too frightening.* 我就是不能过勉强糊口的日子，这太可怕了。

hand·writing /hændraɪtɪŋ/ N-UNCOUNT Your **handwriting** is your style of writing with a pen or pencil. 笔迹; 笔法 ❑ *The address was in Anna's handwriting.* 这个地址是安娜的笔迹。

hand·written /hændrɪtᵊn/ ADJ A piece of writing that is **handwritten** is one that someone has written using a pen or pencil rather than by typing it. 手写的 ❑ *...a handwritten note.* …一张手写的便条。

handy /hændi/ (**handier, handiest**) 1 ADJ Something that is **handy** is useful. 有用的 ❑ *The book gives handy hints on looking after indoor plants.* 这本书提供了关于如何照料室内植物的有用信息。 2 PHRASE If something **comes in handy**, it is useful in a particular situation. 派上用场 ❑ *The $20 check came in very handy.* 这张$20的支票正好派上用场。 3 ADJ A thing or place that is **handy** is nearby and therefore easy to get or reach. 手边的 ❑ *It would be good to have a pencil and paper handy.* 把铅笔和纸放在手边会很有好处。

hang ♦♦◇ /hæŋ/ (**hangs, hanging, hung** or **hanged**)

The form **hanged** is used as the past tense and past participle for meaning 5.

1 V-T/V-I If something **hangs** in a high place or position, or if you **hang** it there, it is attached there so it does not touch the ground. 悬挂 ❑ *Notices painted on sheets hang at every entrance.* 写在纸上的通告悬挂在每个入口处。 ❑ *...small hanging lanterns.* …几盏小吊灯。 ● PHRASAL VERB **Hang up** means the same as **hang**. 悬挂 ❑ *I found his jacket, which was hanging up in the hallway.* 我找到了他的夹克，它就挂在门厅里。 2 V-I If a piece of clothing or fabric **hangs** in a particular way or position, that is how it is worn or arranged. (衣服或织物) 披垂 ❑ *...a ragged fur coat that hung down to her calves.* …一件垂到她的小腿的破旧皮大衣。 3 V-I If something **hangs** loose or **hangs** open, it is partly fixed in position, but is not firmly held, supported, or controlled, often in such a way that it moves freely. 垂下 ❑ *...her long golden hair which hung loose about her shoulders.* …她那松散着披在肩头的金色长发。 4 V-T If something such as a wall **is hung with** pictures or other objects, they are attached to it. 悬挂着 (画等) [usu passive] ❑ *The walls were hung with huge modern paintings.* 墙上挂着一些巨幅现代油画。 5 V-T/V-I If someone **is hanged** or if they **hang**, they are killed, usually as a punishment, by having a rope tied around their neck and the support taken away from under their feet. 绞死; 吊死 ❑ *The five were expected to be hanged at 7 a.m. on Tuesday.* 这5个人将在星期二上午7:00被处以绞刑。 ❑ *He hanged himself two hours after arriving at a mental hospital.* 他到达精神病院两小时后上吊自杀了。 6 V-I If something such as someone's breath or smoke **hangs** in the air, it remains there without appearing to move or change position. 悬浮 ❑ *His breath was hanging in the air before him.* 他呼出的水汽悬浮在他面前的空气中。 7 V-I If a possibility **hangs over** you, it worries you and makes your life unpleasant or difficult because you think it might happen. 使…忧虑 ❑ *A constant threat of unemployment hangs over thousands of university researchers.* 持续的失业威胁使数千名大学研究人员感到忧虑。 8 → see also **hung** 9 PHRASE If you **get the hang of** something such as a skill or activity, you begin to understand or realize how to do it. 掌握…的窍门 [INFORMAL] ❑ *It's a bit tricky at first till you get the hang of it.* 它在一开始当你还没掌握它的窍门的时候有些棘手。 10 PHRASE If you tell someone to **hang in there** or to **hang on in there**, you are encouraging them to keep trying to do something and not to give up even though it might be difficult. 坚持下去 [INFORMAL] ❑ *Hang in there and you never know what is achievable.* 坚持下去，你永远无法知道会有什么样的收获。

▸ **hang back** 1 PHRASAL VERB If you **hang back**, you move or stay slightly behind a person or group, usually because you are shy or nervous about something. (常指因害羞或紧张) 退缩; 踌躇不前 ❑ *I saw him step forward momentarily but then hang back, nervously massaging his hands.* 我看到他向前走了片刻，然后却退缩不前，忐忑不安地搓着手。 2 PHRASAL VERB If a person or organization **hangs back**, they do not do something immediately. 拖延 ❑ *They will then hang back on closing the deal.* 他们接着会拖延成交这笔生意。

▸ **hang on** 1 PHRASAL VERB If you ask someone to **hang on**, you ask them to wait or stop what they are doing or saying for a moment. 等一会儿 [INFORMAL] ❑ *Can you hang on for a minute?* 你能等一会儿吗？ 2 PHRASAL VERB If you **hang on**, you manage to survive, achieve success, or avoid failure in spite of great difficulties or opposition. 顶住 ❑ *He hung on to finish second.* 他顶住了，得了第二名。 3 PHRASAL VERB If you **hang on to** or **hang onto** something that gives you an advantage, you succeed in keeping it for yourself, and prevent it from being taken away or given to someone else. 守住 ❑ *The driver was unable to hang on to his lead.* 这位车手没能守住自己的领先地位。 4 PHRASAL VERB If you **hang on to** or **hang onto** something, you hold it very tightly, for example to stop it from falling or to support yourself. 紧紧抓住 ❑ *She was conscious of a second man hanging on to the rail.* 她觉察到另一名男子正紧紧抓住栏杆不放。 ❑ *...a flight attendant who helped save the life of a pilot by hanging onto his legs.* …紧紧抓住飞行员的双腿而救了他一命的空服员。 5 PHRASAL VERB If you **hang on to** or **hang onto** something, you keep it for a longer time than you would normally expect. 保留 (指超出预期的时间) [INFORMAL] ❑ *You could, alternatively, hang onto it in the hope that it will be worth millions in 10 years time.* 或者，你也可以把它留着，指望它10年后值好几百万。 6 PHRASAL VERB If one thing **hangs on** another, it depends on it in order to be successful. 取决于 ❑ *Much hangs on the success of the collaboration between the Group of Seven governments and Brazil.* 很多事情都取决于七国政府集团与巴西之间合作的成功。

▸ **hang out** 1 PHRASAL VERB If you **hang out** clothes that you have washed, you hang them on a clothes line to dry. 晾出 ❑ *I was worried I wouldn't be able to hang my laundry out.* 我担心不能把洗的衣服晾到外面去。 2 PHRASAL VERB If you **hang out** in a particular place or area, you go and stay there for no particular reason, or spend a lot of time there. 闲逛 [INFORMAL] ❑ *I often used to hang out in supermarkets.* 我过去常常到超市闲逛。

▶ **hang up** 1 → see **hang** 1 2 PHRASAL VERB If you **hang up** or you **hang up** the phone, you end a phone call. If you **hang up on** someone you are speaking to on the phone, you end the phone call suddenly and unexpectedly, usually because you are angry or upset with the person you are speaking to. 挂断（电话）❑ *Mom hung up the phone.* 妈妈挂断了电话。❑ *Don't hang up!* 不要挂断电话！

Word Partnership *hang* 的常用搭配：
N. hang *up* clothes 1
ADV. hang *something* upside down 1

hang·ar /hæŋər/ (**hangars**) N-COUNT A **hangar** is a large building in which aircraft are kept. 飞机库

hang·er /hæŋər/ (**hangers**) N-COUNT A **hanger** is the same as a **coat hanger**. 衣架

hang·over /hæŋoʊvər/ (**hangovers**) 1 N-COUNT If someone wakes up with a **hangover**, they feel sick and have a headache because they drank a lot of alcohol the night before. 宿醉（过量饮酒后的恶心、头痛反应）❑ *It was a great night and I had a massive hangover.* 那是个愉快的夜晚，可第二天我出现了严重的宿醉。 2 N-COUNT Something that is a **hangover from** the past is an idea or way of behaving which people used to have in the past but which people no longer generally have. 遗留观念；遗留习俗 ❑ *As a hangover from rationing, they mixed butter and margarine.* 作为配给制的遗留习俗，他们把黄油与人造黄油混在一起吃。

hap·haz·ard /hæphæzərd/ ADJ If you describe something as **haphazard**, you are critical of it because it is not at all organized or is not arranged according to a plan. 杂乱无章的；无计划的 [DISAPPROVAL] ❑ *The investigation does seem haphazard.* 这次调查似乎的确没有计划性。● **hap·haz·ard·ly** ADV 杂乱无章地；无计划地 ❑ *She looked at the books jammed haphazardly in the shelves.* 她看了看杂乱无章地塞进书架里的书。

hap·less /hæplɪs/ ADJ A **hapless** person is unlucky. 不幸的 [ADJ n] [FORMAL] ❑ *...his hapless victim.* …他不幸的受害者。

hap·pen ♦♦♦ /hæpən/ (**happens, happening, happened**) 1 V-I Something that **happens** occurs or is done without being planned. （偶然地）发生 ❑ *We cannot say for sure what will happen.* 我们说不准将会发生些什么。 2 V-I If something **happens**, it occurs as a result of a situation or course of action. （作为结果）发生 ❑ *She wondered what would happen if her parents found her.* 她不知道如果父母发现了她会怎么样。 3 V-I When something, especially something unpleasant, **happens to** you, it takes place and affects you. （尤指不愉快的事）发生（在某人身上）❑ *If we had been spotted at that point, I don't know what would have happened to us.* 如果那时我们被发现了，我不知道我们会有什么后果。 4 V-T If you **happen to** do something, you do it by chance. If **it happens that** something is the case, it occurs by chance. 碰巧 ❑ *We happened to discover we had a friend in common.* 我们碰巧发现我们有个共同的朋友。 5 PHRASE You use **as it happens** in order to introduce a statement, especially one that is rather surprising. 碰巧（尤用以引出令人意外的内容）❑ *He called Amy to see if she knew where his son was. As it happened, Amy did know.* 他打电话给埃米，看她是否知道他儿子在哪儿。碰巧的是，埃米还真知道。

hap·pen·ing /hæpənɪŋ/ (**happenings**) N-COUNT **Happenings** are things that happen, often in a way that is unexpected or hard to explain. （常指意外或难以解释的）事件 ❑ *The Budapest office plans to hire freelance reporters to cover the latest happenings.* 布达佩斯办事处计划聘用自由职业记者来报道最近发生的事件。

hap·pi·ly /hæpɪli/ 1 ADV You can add **happily** to a statement to indicate that you are glad that something happened. 幸运的是 [ADV with cl] ❑ *Happily, his neck injuries were not serious.* 幸运的是，他脖子上的伤并不严重。 2 → see also **happy**

hap·py ♦♦◇ /hæpi/ (**happier, happiest**) 1 ADJ Someone who is **happy** has feelings of pleasure, usually because something nice has happened or because they feel satisfied with their life. 快乐的 ❑ *Marina was a confident, happy child.* 玛丽娜是个自信、快乐的孩子。● **hap·pi·ly** ADV 快乐地 ❑ *Albert leaned back happily and lit a cigarette.* 艾伯特开心地向后斜靠着并点燃一支香烟。● **hap·pi·ness** N-UNCOUNT 快乐 ❑ *I think mostly she was looking for happiness.* 我认为她大多数情况下是在寻找快乐。 2 ADJ A **happy** time, place, or relationship is full of happy feelings and pleasant experiences, or has an atmosphere in which people feel happy. 令人愉快的 ❑ *Except for her illnesses, she had a particularly happy childhood.* 除了几场病痛之外，她有个特别快乐的童年。❑ *It had always been a happy place.* 这里从前一直是个令人愉快的地方。 3 ADJ If you are **happy about** a situation or arrangement, you are satisfied with it, for example, because you think that something is being done in the right way. 对…满意的 [v-link ADJ] ❑ *If you are not happy about a repair, go back and complain.* 如果你对修理不满意，就回去投诉。❑ *He's happy that I deal with it myself.* 他对我自己处理这件事感到很满意。 4 ADJ If you say you are **happy to** do something, you mean that you are very willing to do it. 乐意的 [v-link ADJ] ❑ *I'll be happy to answer questions if there are any.* 如果有什么问题的话，我将很乐意回答。● **hap·pi·ly** ADV 乐意地 [ADV with v] ❑ *If I've caused any offense over something I have written, I will happily apologize.* 如果我所写的东西冒犯了他人，我将很乐意道歉。 5 ADJ **Happy** is used in greetings and other conventional expressions to say that you hope someone will enjoy a special occasion. （表示祝贺）快乐 [ADJ n] ❑ *Happy Birthday!* 生日快乐！
→ see **emotion**

Thesaurus *happy* 另参见：
ADJ. cheerful, content, delighted, glad, pleased, upbeat; *(ant.)* sad, unhappy 1

Word Partnership *happy* 的常用搭配：
ADV. **extremely/perfectly/very** happy 1
V. **feel** happy, **make** *someone* happy, **seem** happy 1
N. happy **ending**, happy **family**, happy **marriage** 2

h

ha·rangue /həræŋ/ (**harangues, haranguing, harangued**) V-T If someone **harangues** you, they try to persuade you to accept their opinions or ideas in a forceful way. 强有力的说教 ❑ *An argument ensued, with various band members joining in and haranguing Simpson and his girlfriend for over two hours.* 接着是一场争论，许多乐队成员加入进来，对辛普森及其女友进行长达两个多小时的强力说教。

▲ **har·ass** /həræs, hærəs/ (**harasses, harassing, harassed**) V-T If someone **harasses** you, they trouble or annoy you, for example by attacking you repeatedly or by causing you as many problems as they can. 骚扰 ❑ *A woman reporter complained one of them sexually harassed her in the locker room.* 一名女记者抱怨说，他们当中的一个在更衣室里对她进行了性骚扰。

har·assed /həræst, hærəst/ ADJ If you are **harassed**, you are anxious and tense because you have too much to do or too many problems to cope with. 疲惫不堪的 ❑ *This morning, looking harassed and drawn, Lewis tendered his resignation.* 今天早上，看上去疲惫而憔悴的刘易斯提交了辞呈。

★ **har·ass·ment** /həræsmənt, hærəs-/ N-UNCOUNT **Harassment** is behavior which is intended to trouble or annoy someone, for example repeated attacks on them or attempts to cause them problems. 骚扰 ❑ *Another survey found that 51 percent of women had experienced some form of sexual harassment in their working lives.* 另一份调查显示有51%的女性在其职业生涯中曾遭遇过某种形式的性骚扰。

har·bor ♦◇◇ /hɑrbər/ (**harbors, harboring, harbored**)
in BRIT, use **harbour**
1 N-COUNT; N-IN-NAMES A **harbor** is an area of the sea at the coast which is partly enclosed by land or strong walls, so that boats can be left there safely. 港口 ❑ *She led us to a room with a balcony overlooking the harbor.* 她领我们到一个房间，房间带一个俯瞰港口的阳台。 2 V-T If you **harbor** an emotion, thought, or secret, you have it in your mind over a long period of time. 长期怀有 ❑ *He might have been murdered by a former client or someone harboring a grudge.* 他可能是被一个前委托人或某个怀有积怨的人谋杀了。 3 V-T If a person or country **harbors** someone who is wanted by the police, they let them stay in their house or country and offer them protection. 窝藏 ❑ *Accusations of harboring suspects were raised against the former Hungarian leadership.* 匈牙利前领导人被指控窝藏疑犯。

har·bour /hɑrbə/ [BRIT] → see **harbor**

hard ♦♦♦ /hɑrd/ (**harder, hardest**) 1 ADJ Something that is **hard** is very firm and stiff to touch and is not easily bent, cut, or broken. 坚硬的 ❑ *He shuffled his feet on the hard wooden floor.* 他拖着脚走在坚硬的木地板上。● **hard·ness** N-UNCOUNT 坚硬 ❑ *He felt the hardness of the iron railing press against his spine.* 他感觉到硬梆梆的铁栏杆抵住了他的脊梁骨。 2 ADJ Something that is **hard** is very difficult to do or deal with. 困难的 ❑ *It's hard to tell what effect this latest move will have.* 很难说最近的这次行动将会有什么样的影响。❑ *That's a very hard question.* 那是个很难的问题。 3 ADV If you work **hard** doing something, you are very active or work intensely, with a lot of effort. 努力地 [ADV after v] ❑ *I'll work hard. I don't want to let him down.* 我会努力工作。我不想让他失望。● ADJ **Hard** is also an adjective. 努力的 [ADJ n] ❑ *I admired him as a true scientist and hard worker.* 我钦佩他是一名真正的科学家和勤奋的工作者。**4** ADJ **Hard** work involves a lot of activity and effort. 费劲的 ❑ *Coping with three babies is very hard work.* 照顾3个小宝宝是件很累人的活儿。❑ *...a hard day's work.* …一天累人的工作。**5** ADV If you look, listen, or think **hard**, you do it carefully and with a great deal of attention. 仔细地 [ADV after v] ❑ *He looked at me hard.* 他仔细地看着我。● ADJ **Hard** is also an adjective. 仔细的 ❑ *It might be worth taking a long hard look at your frustrations and resentments.* 也许值得对你的挫折感与愤懑做仔细的分析。**6** ADV If you strike or take hold of something **hard**, you strike or take hold of it with a lot of force. 用力地 [ADV after v] ❑ *I kicked a trash can very hard and broke my toe.* 我狠狠踢一个垃圾桶，踢破了脚趾头。● ADJ **Hard** is also an adjective. 用力的 [ADJ n] ❑ *He gave her a hard push which toppled her backwards into an armchair.* 他给了她用力的一推，将她向后推倒在一把扶手椅上。**7** ADV You can use **hard** to indicate that something happens intensely and for a long time. 厉害地 [ADV after v] ❑ *I've never seen Terry laugh so hard.* 我从没见过特里笑得如此厉害。**8** ADJ If a person or their expression is **hard**, they show no kindness or sympathy. 冷酷无情的 ❑ *His father was a hard man.* 他父亲是个冷酷无情的人。**9** ADJ If you are **hard on** someone, you treat them severely or unkindly. 严厉的 [v-link ADJ "on" n] ❑ *Don't be so hard on him.* 别对他太严厉。● ADV **Hard** is also an adverb. 严厉地 [ADV after v] ❑ *He said the security forces would continue to crack down hard on the protestors.* 他说安全部队将继续严厉镇压抗议者。**10** ADJ If you say that something is **hard on** a person or thing, you mean it affects them in a way that is likely to cause them damage or suffering. 难以忍受的 [v-link ADJ "on" n] ❑ *The gray light was hard on the eyes.* 昏暗的光线使眼睛很难受。**11** ADJ If you have a **hard** life or a **hard** period of time, your life or that period is difficult and unpleasant for you. 艰难的 ❑ *It had been a hard life for her.* 对她而言，那曾是一段艰难的日子。● **hard·ness** N-UNCOUNT 艰难 ❑ *In America, people don't normally admit to the hardness of life.* 在美国，人们通常不承认生活的艰辛。**12** ADJ **Hard** evidence or facts are definitely true and do not need to be questioned. 确凿的 [ADJ n] ❑ *He wanted more hard evidence.* 他想要更多确凿的证据。**13** ADJ **Hard** drugs are very strong illegal drugs such as heroin or cocaine. 烈性的（毒品）[ADJ n] ❑ *He then graduated from soft drugs to hard ones.* 他随后从服用软性毒品逐步发展到服用烈性毒品。**14** PHRASE If you say that something is **hard going**, you mean it is difficult and requires a lot of effort. 艰难的 ❑ *The talks had been hard going at the start.* 会谈在开始时是艰难的。**15** PHRASE To be **hard hit by** something means to be affected very severely by it. 被…严重影响 ❑ *California's been particularly hard hit by the recession.* 加利福尼亚受到经济衰退的影响尤为严重。**16** PHRASE If someone **plays hard to get**, they pretend not to be interested in another person or in what someone is trying to persuade them to do. 故意摆谱 ❑ *I wanted her and she was playing hard to get.* 我渴望她，她却摆架子。

Thesaurus *hard* 另参见：

ADJ. firm, solid, tough; *(ant.)* gentle, soft **1**
complicated, difficult, tough; *(ant.)* easy, simple **2**

hard·back /hɑrdbæk/ (**hardbacks**) N-COUNT A **hardback** is a book which has a stiff hard cover. Compare **paperback**. 精装书 [also "in" N] ❑ *The book was published in hardback last October.* 这本书去年10月以精装本出版了。

hard cash N-UNCOUNT **Hard cash** is money in the form of bills and coins as opposed to a check or a credit card. 现金 ❑ *There is no confusion about what the real dividend is since the payment comes in hard cash.* 自从用现金支付以后，对于什么是真正的股息就没有疑惑了。

hard copy (**hard copies**) N-VAR A **hard copy** of a document is a printed version of it, rather than a version that is stored on a computer. 硬拷贝 ❑ *...eight pages of hard copy.* …8页打印稿。

hard cur·ren·cy (**hard currencies**) N-VAR A **hard currency** is one which is unlikely to lose its value and so is considered to be a good one to have or to invest in. 硬通货 ❑ *The country is running short of hard currency to pay for imports.* 该国目前缺乏硬通货来支付进口货物。

hard disk (**hard disks**) N-COUNT A computer's **hard disk** is a stiff magnetic disk on which data and programs can be stored. 硬盘

hard drive (**hard drives**) also **hard-drive** N-COUNT A computer's **hard drive** is its hard disk, or the part that contains and operates the hard disk, which is used for storing and retrieving data. 硬盘 ❑ *You can store your entire CD collection on the computer's hard drive.* 你可以把你全部的激光唱片收藏存到这台电脑的硬盘里。

hard·en /hɑrdᵊn/ (**hardens, hardening, hardened**) **1** V-T/V-I When something **hardens** or when you **harden** it, it becomes stiff or firm. 使变硬；变硬 ❑ *Mold the mixture into shape while hot, before it hardens.* 在混合物变硬之前，趁热将其塑造成形。**2** V-T/V-I When an attitude or opinion **hardens** or **is hardened**, it becomes harsher, stronger, or fixed. （使）更坚定；（使）更强硬 ❑ *Their action can only serve to harden the attitude of landowners.* 他们的举动只会使土地所有者们的态度变得强硬。● **hard·en·ing** N-SING 强硬化 ❑ *...a hardening of the government's attitude toward rebellious parts of the army.* …政府对军队中反叛分子的态度的强硬化。**3** V-T/V-I When events **harden** people or when people **harden**, they become less easily affected emotionally and less sympathetic and gentle than they were before. 使变得冷酷无情；变得冷酷无情 ❑ *Her years of drunken bickering hardened my heart.* 她常年醉酒吵闹让我的心麻木了。**4** V-I If you say that someone's face or eyes **harden**, you mean that they suddenly look serious or angry. （表情或目光）突然显得严峻 ❑ *His smile died and the look in his face hardened.* 他的微笑消失了，脸上的表情突然显得严峻。

▲ **hard-line** also **hardline** ADJ If you describe someone's policy or attitude as **hard-line**, you mean that it is strict or extreme, and that they refuse to change it. 强硬的（政策或态度）❑ *The United States has taken a lot of criticism for its hard-line stance.* 美国因其强硬立场遭到众多批评。

hard·ly ♦♦◇ /hɑrdli/ **1** ADV You use **hardly** to modify a statement when you want to emphasize that it is only a small amount or detail which makes it true, and that therefore it is best to consider the opposite statement as being true. 几乎不 [EMPHASIS] ❑ *I hardly know you.* 我几乎不了解你。❑ *I've hardly slept in three days.* 我3天之中几乎没睡。**2** ADV You use **hardly** in expressions such as **hardly ever**, **hardly any**, and **hardly anyone** to mean almost never, almost none, or almost no one. （后接**ever**，**any**，**anyone**等表示）几乎从不 [ADV "ever/any"] ❑ *We hardly ever eat fish.* 我们几乎从不吃鱼。❑ *Most of the others were so young they had hardly any experience.* 其他人中的大部分都太年轻，几乎没任何经验。**3** ADV You use **hardly** before a negative statement in order to emphasize that something is usually true or usually happens. 几乎没有（后接否定，表肯定）[ADV n] [EMPHASIS] ❑ *Hardly a day goes by without a visit from someone.* 几乎没有哪一天没有来访者。**4** ADV When you say you can **hardly** do something, you are emphasizing that it is very difficult for you to do it. 很难地 ["can/could" ADV inf] [EMPHASIS] ❑ *My garden was covered with so many butterflies that I could hardly see the flowers.* 我的花园里飞满了太多的蝴蝶，我几乎看不到花了。**5** ADV You use **hardly** to mean "not" when you want to suggest that you are expecting your listener or reader to agree with your comment. 很难 ❑ *We have not seen the letter, so we can hardly comment on it.* 我们没见过那封信，所以很难对其加以评论。**6** CONVENTION You use "**hardly**" to mean "no," especially when you want to express surprise or annoyance at a statement that you disagree with. 不可能 [SPOKEN] ❑ *"They all thought you were marvelous!"—"Well, hardly."* "他们都觉得你真是太棒了！"——"喔，哪里哪里。"

hard-pressed also **hard pressed** **1** ADJ If someone is **hard-pressed**, they are under a great deal of strain and worry, usually because they do not have enough money. 窘迫的 [JOURNALISM] ❑ *The region's hard-pressed consumers are spending less on luxuries.* 该地区经济窘迫的消费者正在减少奢侈品的消费。**2** ADJ If you will be **hard-pressed to** do something, you will have great difficulty doing it. 很难的 [v-link ADJ to-inf] ❑ *This year the airline will be hard-pressed to make a profit.* 今年航空公司将很难盈利。

hard sell N-SING A **hard sell** is a method of selling in which the salesperson puts a lot of pressure on someone to make them buy something. 强行推销 ❑ *...a company whose hard sell techniques were exposed by a consumer program.* …一家被消费者节目曝光采用强行推销策略的公司。

hard·ship /hɑrdʃɪp/ (**hardships**) N-VAR **Hardship** is a situation in which your life is difficult or unpleasant, often because you do not have enough money. 困境 ❑ *Many people are suffering economic hardship.* 很多人正遭受着经济困难。

hard shoul·der (**hard shoulders**) N-COUNT **The hard shoulder** is the area at the side of a highway or other road where you are allowed to stop if your car breaks down. 硬路肩；紧急停车带 [usu "the" N in sing] [mainly BRIT]

in AM, use **shoulder**

Word Link *ware ≈ merchandise : hardware, silverware, software*

hard·ware /hɑrdwɛr/ **1** N-UNCOUNT In computer systems, **hardware** refers to the machines themselves as opposed to the programs which tell the machines what to do. Compare **software**. 硬件 ❑ *To be totally secure, you need a piece of hardware that costs about $200.* 为保证绝对安全，你需要一个花费约为两百美元的硬件。 **2** N-UNCOUNT Military **hardware** is the machinery and equipment that is used by the armed forces, such as tanks, aircraft, and missiles. 装备 ❑ *...the billions which are spent on military hardware.* …花费在军事装备上的数十亿。 **3** N-UNCOUNT **Hardware** refers to tools and equipment that are used in the home and garden, for example nuts and bolts, screwdrivers, and hinges. 五金器具 ❑ *...a shop from which an uncle had sold hardware and timber.* …一家叔叔曾经在那里卖五金器具和木材的店铺。

★ **har·dy** /hɑrdi/ (**hardier, hardiest**) ADJ Plants that are **hardy** are able to survive cold weather. (植物) 耐寒的 ❑ *The silver-leaved varieties of cyclamen are not quite as hardy.* 银色仙客来品种不是十分耐寒。

hare /hɛər/ (**hares**) N-VAR A **hare** is an animal like a rabbit but larger with long ears, long legs, and a small tail. 野兔

hark /hɑrk/ (**harks, harking, harked**)

▸ **hark back to** PHRASAL VERB If you say that one thing **harks back to** another thing in the past, you mean it is similar to it or takes it as a model. 与…类似；以…为模型 ❑ *...pitched roofs, which hark back to the Victorian era.* …与维多利亚时代风格类似的尖屋顶。

harm ♦◇◇ /hɑrm/ (**harms, harming, harmed**) **1** V-T To **harm** a person or animal means to cause them physical injury, usually on purpose. (故意地) 伤害 ❑ *The hijackers seemed anxious not to harm anyone.* 劫机犯们似乎并不急于伤害任何人。 **2** N-UNCOUNT **Harm** is physical injury to a person or an animal which is usually caused on purpose. (故意的) 伤害 ❑ *All dogs are capable of doing harm to human beings.* 所有的狗都能对人造成伤害。 **3** V-T To **harm** a thing, or sometimes a person, means to damage them or make them less effective or successful than they were. 损害 ❑ *...a warning that the product may harm the environment.* …一则该产品可能会破坏环境的警告。 **4** N-UNCOUNT **Harm** is the damage to something which is caused by a particular course of action. 损害 ❑ *The abuse of your powers does harm to all other officers who do their job properly.* 你滥用权力有损于所有其他好好工作的政府官员。 ❑ *To cut taxes would probably do the economy more harm than good.* 减税对经济的危害可能大过益处。 **5** PHRASE If you say **it does no harm to** do something or **there is no harm in** doing something, you mean that it might be worth doing, and you will not be blamed for doing it. 不妨 (做某事) ❑ *They are not always willing to take on untrained workers, but there's no harm in asking.* 他们一般不愿意雇佣没有受过训练的工人，但是问问也无妨。 **6** PHRASE If someone or something is **out of harm's way**, they are in a safe place away from danger or from the possibility of being damaged. 免于伤害 ❑ *For parents, it is an easy way of keeping their children entertained, or simply out of harm's way.* 对父母而言，这是一个保持孩子们愉悦或仅仅让他们免于伤害的简便方法。 **7** PHRASE If you say that there is **no harm done**, you are telling someone not to worry about something that has happened because it has not caused any serious injury or damage. 没有造成伤害 (或损害) ❑ *There, now, you're all right. No harm done.* 好了，现在你没事了。没出什么事。 **8** PHRASE If you say that someone or something **will come to no harm** or that **no harm will come to** them, you mean that they will not be hurt or damaged in any way. 将不受伤害；将不受损害 ❑ *There is always a lifeguard to ensure that no one comes to any harm.* 任何时候都有一名救生员以确保没有人会受到伤害。

Thesaurus *harm* 另参见：

V. abuse, damage, hurt, injure, ruin, wreck; (*ant.*) benefit **1** **3**

N. abuse, damage, hurt, injury, ruin, violence **2** **4**

Word Partnership *harm* 的常用搭配：

V. **cause** harm **2** **4**
not mean any harm **4**

N. harm **the environment** **3**

ADJ. **bodily** harm **2**

ADV. **more** harm **than good** **4**

harm·ful /hɑrmfəl/ ADJ Something that is **harmful** has a bad effect on something else, especially on a person's health. (尤指对健康) 有害的 ❑ *...the harmful effects of smoking.* …吸烟的危害。

Word Link *less ≈ without : aimless, harmless, worthless*

harm·less /hɑrmlɪs/ **1** ADJ Something that is **harmless** does not have any bad effects, especially on people's health. 无害的 ❑ *This experiment was harmless to the animals.* 这个实验对动物无害。 **2** ADJ If you describe someone or something as **harmless**, you mean that they are not important and therefore unlikely to annoy other people or cause trouble. 不会惹麻烦的 ❑ *He seemed harmless enough.* 他似乎不会惹麻烦。

har·mon·ic /hɑrmɒnɪk/ ADJ **Harmonic** means composed, played, or sung using two or more notes which sound right and pleasing together. 和声的 ❑ *I had been looking for ways to combine harmonic and rhythmic structures.* 我一直在寻求把和声与节奏结和起来的方法。

★ **har·mo·ni·ous** /hɑrmoʊniəs/ ADJ A **harmonious** relationship, agreement, or discussion is friendly and peaceful. 融洽的 ❑ *Their harmonious relationship resulted in part from their similar goals.* 他们融洽的关系部分来自于他们相似的目标。 ● **har·mo·ni·ous·ly** ADV 融洽地 [ADV after v] ❑ *To live together harmoniously as men and women is an achievement.* 作为男人和女人融洽地生活在一起是一种成就。

har·mo·nize /hɑrmənaɪz/ (**harmonizes, harmonizing, harmonized**) **1** V-RECIP If two or more things **harmonize with** each other, they fit in well with each other. 彼此协调 ❑ *How well all her garments harmonized with each other.* 她所有的衣服彼此配起来是多么地协调。 **2** V-T When governments or organizations **harmonize** laws, systems, or regulations, they agree in a friendly way to make them the same or similar. 使…统一 ❑ *The leaders have agreed to harmonize their national policies on immigration and asylum.* 领导人们已同意在移民与难民问题上将统一他们的国家政策。 **3** V-I When people **harmonize**, they sing or play notes which are different from the main tune but which sound nice with it. 和声演唱或演奏 ❑ *...a perfectly pitched gospel group that harmonized perfectly.* …一个和声完美、定调极佳的福音演唱组。

Word Link *mony ≈ resulting state : ceremony, harmony, testimony*

har·mo·ny /hɑrməni/ (**harmonies**) **1** N-UNCOUNT If people are living **in harmony with** each other, they are living together peacefully rather than fighting or arguing. 融洽 ❑ *...the notion that man should dominate nature rather than live in harmony with it.* …人类应当支配自然而并非与自然和谐相处的观点。 **2** N-VAR **Harmony** is the pleasant combination of different notes of music played at the same time. 和声 ❑ *...singing in harmony.* …和声演唱。 **3** N-UNCOUNT The **harmony** of something is the way in which its parts are combined into a pleasant arrangement. 和谐 ❑ *...the ordered harmony of the universe.* …宇宙的有序和谐。

har·ness /hɑrnɪs/ (**harnesses, harnessing, harnessed**) **1** V-T If you **harness** something such as an emotion or natural source of energy, you bring it under your control and use it. 利用 ❑ *Turkey plans to harness the waters of the Tigris and Euphrates rivers for big hydro-electric power projects.* 土耳其计划利用底格里斯河与幼发拉底河的水来建造大型水力发电工程。 **2** N-COUNT A **harness** is a set of straps which fit under a person's arms and fasten around their body in order to keep a piece of equipment in place or to prevent the person moving from a place. 背带；安全带 **3** N-COUNT A **harness** is a set of leather straps and metal links fastened around a horse's head or body so that the horse can have a carriage, cart, or plow fastened to it. 马具；挽具 **4** V-T If a horse or other animal **is harnessed**, a harness is put on it, especially so that it can pull a carriage, cart, or plow. 给…套上挽具 [usu passive] ❑ *On Sunday the horses were harnessed to a heavy wagon for a day-long ride over the border.* 星期天这些马被套在一辆沉重的货车上，踏上长达一天的旅程越过边境。

▲ **harp** /hɑrp/ (**harps, harping, harped**) N-VAR A **harp** is a large musical instrument consisting of a row of strings stretched from the top to the bottom of a frame. You play the harp by plucking the strings with your fingers. 竖琴

→ see **string**

▸ **harp on** PHRASAL VERB If you say that someone **harps on** a subject, or **harps on about** it, you mean that they keep on talking about it in a way that other people find annoying. 唠叨 ❑ *Jones harps on this theme more than on any other.* 琼斯在这个主题上比在其他任何主题上絮叨得多。

har·row·ing /hæroʊɪŋ/ ADJ A **harrowing** experience is extremely upsetting or disturbing. 折磨人的 ❑ *You've had a harrowing time this past month.* 在这过去的一个月里，你已经历了一段痛苦的日子。

h

harsh /hɑrʃ/ (**harsher, harshest**) **1** ADJ **Harsh** climates or conditions are very difficult for people, animals, and plants to live in. 严酷的 ❑ *...the harsh desert environment.* …严酷的沙漠环境。 ● **harsh·ness** N-UNCOUNT 艰苦 ❑ *...the harshness of their living conditions.* …他们生活条件之艰苦。 **2** ADJ **Harsh** actions or speech are unkind and show no understanding or sympathy. 残酷的 ❑ *He said many harsh and unkind things about his opponents.* 他说了许多关于他对手的严厉且残酷的话。 ● **harsh·ly** ADV 残酷地 [ADV with v] ❑ *She's been told that her husband is being harshly treated in prison.* 她被告知她丈夫正在监狱里遭受严酷的对待。 ● **harsh·ness** N-UNCOUNT 残酷 ❑ *...treating him with great harshness.* …以极度的苛刻对待他。 **3** ADJ Something that is **harsh** is so hard, bright, or rough that it seems unpleasant or harmful. (因过于刺激、明亮或粗糙而) 令人不快的 ❑ *Tropical colors may look rather harsh in our dull northern light.* 热带丛林的色彩在我们暗淡的北极光下也许会显得很刺眼。 ● **harsh·ness** N-UNCOUNT 不快 ❑ *As the wine ages, it loses its bitter harshness.* 随着葡萄酒变陈，酒中的苦涩味就会消失。 **4** ADJ **Harsh** voices and sounds are ones that are rough and unpleasant to listen to. 刺耳的 ❑ *It's a pity she has such a loud harsh voice.* 可惜她有这么一种响亮刺耳的声音。 ● **harsh·ly** ADV 刺耳地 [ADV with v] ❑ *Chris laughed harshly.* 克里斯大笑，声音刺耳。 ● **harsh·ness** N-UNCOUNT 刺耳 ❑ *Then in a tone of abrupt harshness, he added, "Open these trunks!"* 然后用一种粗鲁刺耳的声调，他加了一句，"打开这些箱子！" **5** ADJ If you talk about **harsh** realities or facts, or the **harsh** truth, you are emphasizing that they are true or real, although they are unpleasant and people try to avoid thinking about them. 残酷的 (事实、情况) [EMPHASIS] ❑ *The harsh truth is that luck plays a big part in who will live or die.* 残酷的现实是，运气在很大程度上决定着谁生谁死。

har·vest /hɑrvɪst/ (**harvests, harvesting, harvested**) **1** N-SING **The harvest** is the gathering of a crop. 收割 ❑ *There was about 300 million tons of grain in the fields at the start of the harvest.* 收割伊始田间大约有三亿吨的谷物。 **2** N-COUNT A **harvest** is the crop that is gathered in. 收成 ❑ *Millions of people are threatened with starvation as a result of drought and poor harvests.* 数百万人因干旱和歉收正受到饥饿的威胁。 **3** V-T When you **harvest** a crop, you gather it in. 收割 ❑ *Rice farmers here still plant and harvest their crops by hand.* 这儿的稻农仍然靠双手种植和收割庄稼。
→ see **farm, grain**

has

The auxiliary verb is pronounced /həz, STRONG hæz/. The main verb is usually pronounced /hæz/.

助动词读作 /həz, STRONG hæz/。主要动词通常读作 /hæz/。

Has is the third person singular of the present tense of **have**. **have**的第三人称单数现在式

has-been (**has-beens**) N-COUNT If you describe someone as a **has-been**, you are indicating in an unkind way that they were important or respected in the past, but they are not now. 过气的人物 [DISAPPROVAL] ❑ *...the so-called experts and various has-beens who foist opinions on us.* …那些将想法强加给我们的所谓专家和各类过气人物。

hash /hæʃ/ (**hashes, hashing, hashed**) **1** N-UNCOUNT **Hash** is a dish made from meat cut into small lumps and fried with other ingredients such as onions or potato. 回锅肉丁 ❑ *...corned beef hash.* …回锅腌牛肉丁。 **2** N-COUNT A **hash** is the sign #, found on telephone keypads and computer keyboards. 井号键 [usu sing] [mainly BRIT, SPOKEN]

in AM, usually use **pound sign**

3 PHRASE If you **make a hash of** a job or task, you do it very badly. 把…弄糟 [INFORMAL] ❑ *The government made a total hash of things and squandered a small fortune.* 政府把事情弄得一团糟，还浪费了一笔钱。

▸ **hash out** **1** PHRASAL VERB If people **hash out** something such as a plan or an agreement, they decide on it after a lot of discussion. 充分讨论后决定 [also V n P] [AM] ❑ *The House and Senate are to begin soon hashing out an agreement for sanctions legislation.* 参众两院很快将通过充分讨论就制裁立法达成一项协议。 **2** PHRASAL VERB If people **hash out** a problem or a dispute, they discuss it thoroughly until they reach an agreement. 充分协商后解决 [AM] ❑ *...while the parties try to hash out their differences in court.* …然而各党派试图在法庭上解决他们的分歧。

hasn't /hæzᵊnt/ **Hasn't** is the usual spoken form of "has not." **has not**的常用口语形式

has·sle /hæsᵊl/ (**hassles, hassling, hassled**) **1** N-VAR A **hassle** is a situation that is difficult and involves problems, effort, or arguments with people. 麻烦 [INFORMAL] ❑ *I don't think it's worth the money or the hassle.* 我认为不值得为此花钱或者费劲。 **2** V-T If someone **hassles** you, they cause problems for you, often by repeatedly telling you or asking you to do something, in an annoying way. 烦扰 [INFORMAL] ❑ *Then my husband started hassling me.* 然后我丈夫便开始不停地烦我。

haste /heɪst/ **1** N-UNCOUNT **Haste** is the quality of doing something quickly, sometimes too quickly so that you are careless and make mistakes. 仓促 ❑ *In their haste to escape the rising water, they dropped some expensive equipment.* 在仓促逃离上涨的河水时，他们丢弃了一些贵重设备。 **2** PHRASE If you do something **in haste**, you do it quickly and hurriedly, and sometimes carelessly. 匆忙地 ❑ *Don't act in haste or be hot-headed.* 别匆忙行事，也别鲁莽。

has·ten /heɪsᵊn/ (**hastens, hastening, hastened**) **1** V-T If you **hasten** an event or process, often an unpleasant one, you make it happen faster or sooner. 加速 ❑ *But if he does this, he may hasten the collapse of his own country.* 但是如果他这样做，他也许就会加速自己国家的灭亡。 **2** V-T If you **hasten to** do something, you are quick to do it. 急忙 ❑ *She more than anyone had hastened to sign the contract.* 她比任何人都急着去签那份合同。

★ **has·ty** /heɪsti/ (**hastier, hastiest**) **1** ADJ A **hasty** movement, action, or statement is sudden, and often done in reaction to something that has just happened. 匆忙的 ❑ *Donald had overturned a chair in his hasty departure.* 唐纳德仓促离开时撞翻了一把椅子。 ● **hasti·ly** /heɪstɪli/ ADV 匆忙地 [ADV with v] ❑ *The council was hastily convened after his father said he was resigning.* 在他父亲宣布他将辞职后，理事会被匆忙召集起来。 **2** ADJ If you describe a person or their behavior as **hasty**, you mean that they are acting too quickly, without thinking carefully, for example because they are angry. 草率的 [DISAPPROVAL] ❑ *A number of the United States' allies had urged him not to make a hasty decision.* 美国的一些盟友都力劝其不要作出草率的决定。 ● **hasti·ly** ADV 草率地 [ADV with v] ❑ *I decided that nothing should be done hastily, that things had to be sorted out carefully.* 我决定不草率的采取任何行动，先得认真地理清头绪。

hat ♦◇◇ /hæt/ (**hats**) **1** N-COUNT A **hat** is a head covering, often with a brim around it, which is usually worn outdoors to give protection from the weather. (常指有檐的) 帽子 ❑ *...a plump woman in a red hat.* …一个戴红帽子的丰满女人。 **2** N-COUNT If you say that someone is wearing a particular **hat**, you mean that they are performing a particular role at that time. If you say that they wear several **hats**, you mean that they have several roles or jobs. 角色；职位 ❑ *Now I'll take off my "friend hat" and put on my "therapist hat."* 现在我将从朋友的角色转为治疗专家的角色。 **3** PHRASE If you say that you are ready to do something **at the drop of a hat**, you mean that you are willing to do it immediately, without hesitating. 立刻 ❑ *India is one part of the world I would go to at the drop of a hat.* 印度是世界上我即刻就想去的一个地方。 **4** PHRASE If you tell someone to **keep** a piece of information **under** their **hat**, you are asking them not to tell anyone else about it. 保守秘密 ❑ *Look, if I tell you something, will you promise to keep it under your hat?* 喂，如果我告诉你什么事情，你能答应保守秘密吗？ **5** PHRASE If you say that you **take** your **hat off to** someone, you mean that you admire them for something that they have done. 赞赏 [APPROVAL] ❑ *I take my hat off to Mr. Clarke for taking this action.* 我很赞赏克拉克先生采取了这样的行动。 **6** PHRASE To **pull** something **out of the hat** means to do something unexpected which helps you to succeed, often when you are failing. 出乎意料地获取 ❑ *There are expectations that he'll pull a cease-fire out of a hat.* 人们期望他会意外地消弭战火。 **7** PHRASE In competitions, if you say that the winners will be drawn or picked **out of the hat**, you mean that they will be chosen randomly, so everyone has an equal chance of winning. 任意抽取 ❑ *The first 10 correct entries drawn out of the hat will win a pair of tickets, worth $30 each.* 任意抽取的前10名符合要求的入围者将赢得两张入场券，每张价值$30。

★ **hatch** /hætʃ/ (**hatches, hatching, hatched**) **1** V-T/V-I When a baby bird, insect, or other animal **hatches**, or when it **is hatched**, it comes out of its egg by breaking the shell. 使孵出；孵出 ❑ *The young disappeared soon after they were hatched.* 幼崽孵出后不久就不见了。 **2** V-T/V-I When an egg **hatches** or when a bird, insect, or other animal **hatches** an egg, the egg breaks open and a baby comes out. 孵化 ❑ *The eggs hatch after a week or ten days.* 这些蛋1周或10天后孵化。 **3** V-T If you **hatch** a plot or a scheme, you think of it and work it out. 策划 ❑ *He has accused opposition parties of hatching a plot to assassinate the pope.* 他曾指责各反对党阴谋策划暗杀教皇。 4 N-COUNT A **hatch** is an opening in the deck of a ship, through which people or cargo can go. You can also refer to the door of this opening as a **hatch**. 舱口；舱口盖 ❑ *He stuck his head up through the hatch.* 他把脑袋伸出舱口。

hatch·et /hætʃɪt/ (**hatchets**) 1 N-COUNT A **hatchet** is a small ax that you can hold in one hand. 短柄小斧 2 PHRASE If two people **bury the hatchet**, they become friendly again after a quarrel or disagreement. 言归于好 ❑ *It is time to bury the hatchet and forget about what has happened in the past.* 是言归于好并忘记过去发生的事的时候了。

hate ♦◇◇ /heɪt/ (**hates, hating, hated**) 1 V-T If you **hate** someone or something, you have an extremely strong feeling of dislike for them. 仇恨 ❑ *Most people hate him, but they don't dare to say so, because he still rules the country.* 大部分人都恨他只是不敢说出来，因为他仍统治着国家。 ● N-UNCOUNT **Hate** is also a noun. 仇恨 ❑ *I was 17 and filled with a lot of hate.* 我那时17岁，满腔仇恨。 2 V-T If you say that you **hate** something such as a particular activity, you mean that you find it very unpleasant. 讨厌 [no cont] ❑ *Ted hated parties, even gatherings of people he liked individually.* 特德讨厌聚会，即便是聚会上的每一个人他都喜欢。 ❑ *He hates to be interrupted during training.* 他讨厌训练中被打断。 ❑ *He hated coming home to the empty house.* 他讨厌回到空无一人的家里。 3 V-T You can use **hate** in expressions such as "**I hate to trouble you**" or "**I hate to bother you**" when you are apologizing to someone for interrupting them or asking them to do something. 不想 [no cont] [POLITENESS] ❑ *I hate to rush you but I have another appointment later on.* 我真不想催你，但我稍后还有一个约会。 4 V-T You can use **hate** in expressions such as "**I hate to say it**" or "**I hate to tell you**" when you want to express regret about what you are about to say, because you think it is unpleasant or should not be the case. 遗憾 [no cont] [FEELINGS] ❑ *I hate to tell you this, but tomorrow's your last day.* 我对告诉你这个很遗憾，但明天是你最后一天了。 5 to **hate** someone's **guts** → see **gut** 6 V-T You can use **hate** in expressions such as "**I hate to see**" or "**I hate to think**" when you are emphasizing that you find a situation or an idea unpleasant. 不愿 [no cont] [EMPHASIS] ❑ *I just hate to see you doing this to yourself.* 我只是不愿看到你这样对待自己。 7 V-T You can use **hate** in expressions such as "**I'd hate to think**" when you hope that something is not true or that something will not happen. 不希望 [no cont] ❑ *I'd hate to think my job would not be secure if I left it temporarily.* 我不希望一旦我暂时离开，这份工作就不保。

→ see **emotion**

Word Partnership *hate* 的常用搭配：

N. hate **the thought of** *something* 2

V. hate **to admit** *something* 4

hate **to see** *something* 6

hate **to think** *something* 6 7

ha·tred /heɪtrɪd/ N-UNCOUNT **Hatred** is an extremely strong feeling of dislike for someone or something. 憎恨 ❑ *Her hatred of them would never lead her to murder.* 她对他们的仇恨永远不会将她引向凶杀。

hat trick (**hat tricks**) also **hat-trick** N-COUNT A **hat trick** is a series of three achievements, especially in a sports event, for example three goals scored by the same person in a soccer game. 帽子戏法(指运动员连续三次取胜的好成绩) ❑ *I scored a hat-trick in my first game.* 我在第一次比赛中连进三球。

haul /hɔl/ (**hauls, hauling, hauled**) 1 V-T If you **haul** something which is heavy or difficult to move, you move it using a lot of effort. (用力地) 拉 ❑ *A crane had to be used to haul the car out of the stream.* 不得不用了一台起重机把轿车从河里拉出来。 2 V-T If someone **is hauled before** a court or someone in authority, they are made to appear before them because they are accused of having done something wrong. 传讯 [usu passive] ❑ *He was hauled before the managing director and fired.* 他被总裁叫去问话并被解雇了。 ● PHRASAL VERB **Haul up** means the same as **haul**. 传讯 ❑ *He was hauled up before the board of trustees.* 他被带到了托管委员会面前问话。 3 N-COUNT A **haul** is a quantity of things that are stolen, or a quantity of stolen or illegal goods found by police or customs. 一次偷得之量；(警察或海关) 一次查获之量 ❑ *The size of the drug haul shows that the international trade in heroin is still flourishing.* 这次的毒品缴获量说明国际性海洛因交易依然猖獗。 4 PHRASE If you say that a task or a journey is a **long haul**, you mean that it takes a long time and a lot of effort. 费时费力的工作 ❑ *Revitalizing the Romanian economy will be a long haul.* 复兴罗马尼亚经济将是一项长期艰巨的工作。 5 → see also **long-haul**

haul·er /hɔlər/ (**haulers**) N-COUNT A **hauler** is a company or a person that transports goods by road. 公路货运商；公路货运承运人 [AM]

★ **haunt** /hɔnt/ (**haunts, haunting, haunted**) 1 V-T If something unpleasant **haunts** you, you keep thinking or worrying about it over a long period of time. (令人不愉快的事) 萦绕在心头 ❑ *He would always be haunted by that scene in Well Park.* 他将不断回想起威尔公园的那一幕。 2 V-T Something that **haunts** a person or organization regularly causes them problems over a long period of time. 长期不断地纠缠 ❑ *The stigma of being a bankrupt is likely to haunt him for the rest of his life.* 作为一名破产者的耻辱很可能在他的余生不断来纠缠他。 3 N-COUNT A place that is the **haunt** of a particular person is one which they often visit because they enjoy going there. 常去之处 ❑ *The islands are a favorite summer haunt for yachtsmen.* 这片岛屿是游艇驾驶者夏天最爱去的一个地方。 4 V-T A ghost or spirit that **haunts** a place or a person regularly appears in the place, or is seen by the person and frightens them. (鬼魂等) 常出没于 ❑ *His ghost is said to haunt some of the rooms, banging a toy drum.* 据说他的鬼魂常在其中一些屋子里出现，还敲打着一个玩具鼓。

haunt·ed /hɔntɪd/ 1 ADJ A **haunted** building or other place is one where a ghost regularly appears. 闹鬼的 ❑ *Tracy said the cabin was haunted.* 特雷西说这个小木屋里闹鬼。 2 ADJ Someone who has a **haunted** expression looks very worried or troubled. 焦虑的 ❑ *She looked so haunted, I almost didn't recognize her.* 她看上去如此焦虑不安，我差点儿认不出她来了。

haunt·ing /hɔntɪŋ/ ADJ **Haunting** sounds, images, or words remain in your thoughts because they are very beautiful or sad. 令人难忘的 ❑ *...the haunting calls of wild birds in the mahogany trees.* …桃花心树林中野生鸟类令人难忘的鸣叫。 ● **haunt·ing·ly** ADV 令人难忘地 ❑ *Each one of these ancient towns is hauntingly beautiful.* 这些古镇每一座都是那样令人难忘得美丽。

hau·teur /hoʊtɜr/ N-UNCOUNT You can use **hauteur** to describe behavior which you think is proud and arrogant. 傲慢 [FORMAL, DISAPPROVAL] ❑ *Once, she had been put off by his hauteur.* 曾经有段时间，她很不喜欢他的傲慢。

have

1 AUXILIARY VERB USES
2 USED WITH NOUNS DESCRIBING ACTIONS
3 OTHER VERB USES AND PHRASES
4 MODAL PHRASES

1 **have** ♦♦♦ /həv, STRONG hæv/ (**has, having, had**)

In spoken English, forms of **have** are often shortened, for example **I have** is shortened to **I've** and **has not** is shortened to **hasn't**.

1 AUX You use the forms **have** and **has** with a past participle to form the present perfect tense of verbs. 后接过去分词，构成现在完成时态 ❑ *Alex has already gone.* 亚历克斯已经走了。 ❑ *What have you found so far?* 迄今为止，你发现了什么？ ❑ *Frankie hasn't been feeling well for a long time.* 弗朗姬感觉不舒服已经很长一段时间了。 2 AUX You use the form **had** with a past participle to form the past perfect tense of verbs. **had**后接过去分词，构成过去完成时态 ❑ *When I met her, she had just returned from a job interview.* 我遇到她时，她刚刚从一次求职面试回来。 3 AUX **Have** is used in question tags. 用于反意疑问句 ❑ *You haven't sent her away, have you?* 你还没有把她送走，是吗？ 4 AUX You use **have** when you are confirming or contradicting a statement containing "have," "has," or "had," or answering a question. 代替前一句中的**have**、**has**或**had**加上动词构成的词组，表示肯定或否定含义 ❑ *"You'd never seen the Marilyn Monroe film?"—"No I hadn't."* "你从来没看过玛丽莲·梦露的电影吗？"——"是的，从来没有。" 5 AUX The form **having** with a past participle can be used to introduce a clause in which you mention an action which had already happened before another action began. **having**后接过去分词，所引导的从句其动作先于另一有关的动作 ❑ *He arrived in San Francisco, having left New Jersey on January 19th.* 他1月19号离开新泽西后，到达了圣弗朗西斯科。

❷ have ♦♦♦ /hæv/ (**has, having, had**)

> **Have** is used in combination with a wide range of nouns, where the meaning of the combination is mostly given by the noun.

1 V-T You can use **have** followed by a noun to talk about an action or event, when it would be possible to use the same word as a verb. For example, you can say "**I had a look at the photos**" instead of "I looked at the photos." 后接描述某一动作或事件的名词，如**to have a look**同**to look**意义几乎一样 [no passive] ❑ *I went out and had a walk around.* 我出了门在附近散了散步。 ❑ *We had a laugh over that one.* 我们对此大笑。 2 V-T In normal spoken or written English, people use **have** with a wide range of nouns to talk about actions and events, often instead of a more specific verb. For example people are more likely to say "**we had ice cream**" or "**he's had a shock**" than "we ate ice cream," or "he's suffered a shock." 后接名词来描述某一动作或事件，以取代某一特定的动词 [no passive] ❑ *Come and have a meal with us tonight.* 今晚过来和我们一起吃晚饭吧。 ❑ *We will be having a meeting to decide what to do.* 我们将开会决定该做什么。

❸ have ♦♦♦ /hæv/ (**has, having, had**)

H

> For meanings 1-4, people often use **have gotten** in spoken American English or **have got** in spoken British English, instead of **have**. In this case, **have** is pronounced as an auxiliary verb. For more information and examples of the use of "have got" and "have gotten," see **got**.

➪ **Please look at meanings 17 and 18 to see if the expression you are looking for is shown under another headword.** 1 V-T You use **have** to say that someone or something owns a particular thing, or when you are mentioning one of their qualities or characteristics. 拥有 [no passive] ❑ *Oscar had a new bicycle.* 奥斯卡拥有一辆新的自行车。 ❑ *I want to have my own business.* 我想拥有自己的事业。 ❑ *She had no job and no money.* 她既没工作也没钱。 ❑ *You have beautiful eyes.* 你有美丽的眼睛。 ❑ *Do you have any brothers and sisters?* 你有什么兄弟姐妹吗？ 2 V-T If you **have** something **to** do, you are responsible for doing it or must do it. 必须（做） [no passive] ❑ *He had plenty of work to do.* 他有一大堆工作必须做。 3 V-T You can use **have** instead of "there is" to say that something exists or happens. For example, you can say "**you have no alternative**" instead of "there is no alternative," or "**he had a good view from his window**" instead of "there was a good view from his window." 有 [no passive] ❑ *He had two tenants living with him.* 他有两个房客与他同住。 4 V-T If you **have** something such as a part of your body in a particular position or state, it is in that position or state. 使处于 [no passive] ❑ *Mary had her eyes closed.* 玛丽让自己的眼睛闭着。 ❑ *They had the curtains open.* 他们把窗帘开着。 5 V-T If you **have** something done, someone does it for you or you arrange for it to be done. 让…做… [no passive] ❑ *I had your rooms cleaned and aired.* 我叫人把你的房间打扫了并通了风。 ❑ *They had him killed.* 他们找人杀了他。 6 V-T If someone **has** something unpleasant happen to them, it happens to them. 遭遇 [no passive] ❑ *We had our money stolen.* 我们的钱被偷掉了。 7 V-T If you **have** someone do something, you persuade, cause, or order them to do it. 劝说；命令 [no passive] ❑ *The bridge is not as impressive as some guides would have you believe.* 这座桥并不像有些导游试图让你相信的那样令人印象深刻。 8 V-T If someone **has** you **by** a part of your body, they are holding you there and they are trying to hurt you or force you to go somewhere. 抓住（某人身体的某部位） [no passive] ❑ *He had her by the arm and he was screaming at her.* 他抓住她的胳膊，冲着她大喊。 9 V-T If you **have** something from someone, they give it to you. 得到 [no passive] ❑ *You can have my ticket.* 你可以得到我的票。 ❑ *Can I have your name please?* 我能知道你的名字吗？ 10 V-T If you **have** an illness or disability, you suffer from it. 患 [no passive] ❑ *I had a headache.* 我头疼。 11 V-T If a woman **has** a baby, she gives birth to it. If she **is having** a baby, she is pregnant. 生 [no passive] ❑ *My wife has just had a baby boy.* 我妻子刚生了个男孩。 12 V-T You can use **have** in expressions such as "**I won't have it**" or "**I'm not having that,**" to mean that you will not allow or put up with something. 容忍 [with neg] ❑ *I'm not having any of that nonsense.* 我不要听那些废话。 13 PHRASE You can use **has it** in expressions such as "**rumor has it that**" or "**as legend has it**" when you are quoting something that you have heard, but you do not necessarily think it is true. 据谣传 [VAGUENESS] ❑ *Rumor has it that tickets were being sold for $300.* 据谣传，票价卖到了$300。 14 PHRASE If someone **has it in for** you, they do not like you and they want to make life difficult for you. 跟某人过不去 [INFORMAL] ❑ *He's always had it in for the Dawkins family.* 他总是同道金斯一家过不去。 15 PHRASE If you **have it in** you, you have abilities and skills which you do not usually use and which only show themselves in a difficult situation. 有本领 ❑ *"You were brilliant!" he said. "I didn't know you had it in you."* "你真棒！" 他说道。"我真不知道你还有这两下子。" 16 PHRASE If you **have it out** or **have things out with** someone, you discuss a problem or disagreement very openly with them, even if it means having an argument, because you think this is the best way to solve the problem. 同…讲个明白 ❑ *Why not have it out with your critic, discuss the whole thing face to face?* 为什么不同批评你的人讲个明白，面对面说说整件事情呢？ 17 **to be had** → see **had** 18 **to have had it** → see **had**

> **Thesaurus** *have* 另参见：
> v. own, possess ❸ 1
> suffer ❸ 10

❹ have ♦♦♦ /hæv, hæf/ (**has, having, had**) 1 PHRASE You use **have to** when you are saying that something is necessary or required, or must happen. If you do not **have to** do something, it is not necessary or required. 不得不 ❑ *He had to go to Germany.* 他不得不去德国。 ❑ *You have to be careful what you say on TV.* 在电视上说话时你不得不谨慎。 2 PHRASE You can use **have to** in order to say that you feel certain that something is true or will happen. 肯定 ❑ *There has to be some kind of way out.* 肯定有办法解决。

▲ **ha·ven** /heɪvᵊn/ (**havens**) 1 N-COUNT A **haven** is a place where people or animals feel safe, secure, and happy. 安全处所 2 → see also **safe haven**

haven't /hævᵊnt/ **Haven't** is the usual spoken form of "have not." **have not**的常用口语形式

▲ **hav·oc** /hævək/ 1 N-UNCOUNT **Havoc** is great disorder and confusion. 大混乱 ❑ *Rioters caused havoc in the center of the town.* 暴徒在市中心造成了极大的混乱。 2 PHRASE If one thing **plays havoc with** another or **wreaks havoc on** it, it prevents it from continuing or functioning as normal, or damages it. 打乱

★ **hawk** /hɔk/ (**hawks**) 1 N-COUNT A **hawk** is a large bird with a short, hooked beak, sharp claws, and very good eyesight. Hawks catch and eat small birds and animals. 鹰 2 N-COUNT In politics, if you refer to someone as a **hawk**, you mean that they believe in using force and violence to achieve something, rather than using more peaceful or diplomatic methods. Compare **dove**. （主张使用武力或强硬手段的）鹰派人物 ❑ *Both hawks and doves have expanded their conditions for ending the war.* 鹰派和鸽派都已详述了他们结束战争的条件。 3 PHRASE If you **watch** someone **like a hawk**, you observe them very carefully, usually to make sure that they do not make a mistake or do something you do not want them to do. 密切监视 ❑ *If we hadn't watched him like a hawk, he would have escaped.* 如果我们不是密切监视他，他早逃跑了。

hay /heɪ/ 1 N-UNCOUNT **Hay** is grass which has been cut and dried so that it can be used to feed animals. （作饲料用的）干草 ❑ *...bales of hay.* …一捆捆的干草。 2 PHRASE If you say that someone **is making hay** or **is making hay while the sun shines**, you mean that they are taking advantage of a situation that is favorable to them while they have the chance to. 晒草要趁好太阳；抓紧时机 ❑ *We knew war was coming, and were determined to make hay while we could.* 我们知道战争即将来临，所以决定尽可能抓紧时机。 → see **barn**

hay fe·ver N-UNCOUNT If someone is suffering from **hay fever**, they sneeze and their eyes itch, because they are allergic to grass or flowers. 花粉热

haz·ard /hæzərd/ (**hazards, hazarding, hazarded**) 1 N-COUNT A **hazard** is something which could be dangerous to you, your health or safety, or your plans or reputation. 危险 ❑ *A new report suggests that chewing gum may be a health hazard.* 一份新的报告指出，嚼口香糖可能给健康带来危害。 2 V-T If you **hazard** or if you **hazard a guess**, you make a suggestion about something which is only a guess and which you know might be wrong. 大胆猜测 ❑ *I would hazard a guess that they'll do fairly well in the next election.* 我大胆猜测，他们在下次选举中将会有不俗的表现。

★ **haz·ard·ous** /hæzərdəs/ ADJ Something that is **hazardous** is dangerous, especially to people's health or safety. 有危害的 ❑ *They have no way to dispose of the hazardous waste they produce.* 他们没法处理那些由他们制造出来的危害性废弃物。

▲ **haze** /heɪz/ (**hazes**) 1 N-VAR **Haze** is light mist, caused by particles of water or dust in the air, which prevents you from seeing distant objects clearly. Haze often forms in hot weather. 薄雾 ❑ *They vanished into the haze near the horizon.* 他们消失在地平线附近的薄雾中。 2 N-SING If there is a **haze of** something such as smoke or steam, you cannot see clearly through it. 烟雾 [LITERARY] ❑ *Dan smiled at him through a haze of smoke and steaming coffee.* 丹透过缭绕的烟雾和咖啡氤氲出的热气朝他微笑。

ha·zel /heɪzᵊl/ (**hazels**) 1 N-VAR A **hazel** is a small tree which produces nuts that you can eat. 榛树 2 COLOR **Hazel** eyes are greenish brown in color. 淡绿褐色(的)

hazy /heɪzi/ (**hazier, haziest**) 1 ADJ **Hazy** weather conditions are those in which things are difficult to see, because of light mist, hot air, or dust. (天气) 雾蒙蒙的 ❑ *The air was thin and crisp, filled with hazy sunshine and frost.* 空气稀薄而清新，弥漫着朦胧的阳光与霜霭。 2 ADJ If you are **hazy about** ideas or details, or if they are **hazy**, you are uncertain or confused about them. (对事物的认识等) 模糊的 ❑ *I'm a bit hazy about that.* 我对那件事不太清楚。 3 ADJ If things seem **hazy**, you cannot see things clearly, for example because you are feeling ill. (物体的外形等) 模糊不清的 ❑ *My vision has grown so hazy.* 我的视力已经变得非常模糊。

HD-DVD /eɪtʃ di di vi di/ (**HD-DVDs**) N-COUNT An **HD-DVD** is a DVD that can store at least twice as much information as a standard DVD. **HD-DVD** is an abbreviation for 'high definition DVD'. 高清晰DVD

HDTV /eɪtʃ di ti vi/ N-UNCOUNT **HDTV** is a television system that provides a clearer image than conventional television systems. **HDTV** is an abbreviation for "high-definition television." 高清电视 [oft N n] ❑ *She said the quality of digital TV is noticeably better, especially HDTV.* 她说数字电视的质量明显提高，尤其是高清电视。

he ♦♦♦ /hi, STRONG hi/

> **He** is a third person singular pronoun. **He** is used as the subject of a verb.

1 PRON-SING You use **he** to refer to a man, boy, or male animal. 他 ❑ *He could never quite remember all our names.* 他绝不可能完全记住我们所有人的名字。 2 PRON-SING In written English, **he** is sometimes used to refer to a person without saying whether that person is a man or a woman. Some people dislike this use and prefer to use "he or she" or "they." 一个人 (性别不明的情况下用；有些人不喜欢这样用，而倾向于用"**he or she**"或"**they**") ❑ *The teacher should encourage the child to proceed as far as he can, and when he is stuck, ask for help.* 老师应当鼓励孩子尽可能独立思考，自己想不出来了，再寻求帮助。

> **head**
>
> ❶ NOUN AND ADVERB USES
> ❷ VERB USES
> ❸ PHRASES

❶ **head** ♦♦♦ /hɛd/ (**heads**) 1 N-COUNT Your **head** is the top part of your body, which has your eyes, mouth, and brain in it. 头部 ❑ *She turned her head away from him.* 她扭过头，不看他。 2 N-COUNT You can use **head** to refer to your mind and your mental abilities. 头脑 ❑ *...an exceptional analyst who could do complex math in his head.* …一位能做复杂心算的杰出分析家。 3 N-SING The **head of** a line of people or vehicles is the front of it, or the first person or vehicle in the line. (人群或车辆的) 前端 ❑ *He made his way to the head of the line.* 他来到队伍的最前端。 4 N-COUNT The **head** of a company or organization is the person in charge of it and in charge of the people in it. (公司、团体的) 负责人 ❑ *Heads of government from more than 100 countries gather in Geneva tomorrow.* 来自一百多个国家的政府首脑明天将聚集在日内瓦。 5 N-COUNT The **head** of something long and thin is the end which is wider than or a different shape from the rest, and which is often considered to be the most important part. (长而细的物体的) 顶部 ❑ *There should be no exposed screw heads.* 螺钉头不应暴露在外。 6 ADV If you flip a coin and it comes down **heads**, you can see the side of the coin which has a picture of a head on it. (硬币) 有头像的一面 ❑ *"We might flip a coin for it," suggested Ted. "If it's heads, then we'll talk."* "我们来掷硬币决定这件事"，特德建议说，"如果是人头，我们就说。"
→ see **body, engine**

❷ **head** ♦♦♦ /hɛd/ (**heads, heading, headed**) 1 V-T If someone or something **heads** a line or procession, they are at the front of it. 行进在…的前头 ❑ *The parson, heading the procession, had just turned right toward the churchyard.* 走在行列最前头的那位牧师，刚朝右转走向了教堂墓地。 2 V-T If something **heads** a list or group, it is at the top of it. 居…之首 ❑ *Running a business heads the list of ambitions among the 1,000 people interviewed by Good Housekeeping magazine.* 在《好管家》杂志对1000人关于事业志向的采访中，开公司位列名单之首。 3 V-T If you **head** a department, company, or organization, you are the person in charge of it. 掌管 ❑ *...Michael Williams, who heads the department's Office of Civil Rights.* …迈克尔•威廉姆斯，他掌管着部门的民事权利办公室。 4 V-T/V-I If you **are heading** or **are headed** for a particular place, you are going toward that place. 朝着…行进 ❑ *He was headed for the bus stop.* 他朝公交车站走去。 ❑ *It is not clear how many of them will be heading back to Saudi Arabia tomorrow.* 尚不清楚他们当中有多少人明天将折回沙特阿拉伯。 5 V-T/V-I If something or someone **is heading for** or **is headed for** a particular result, the situation they are in is developing in a way that makes that result very likely. 朝…发展 ❑ *The latest talks aimed at ending the civil war appear to be heading for deadlock.* 旨在结束内战的最新谈判看来要走入僵局。 6 V-T If a piece of writing **is headed** a particular title, it has that title written at the beginning of it. 加标题于… [usu passive] ❑ *One chapter is headed, "Beating the Test."* 有一章的标题是"战胜考验。" 7 V-T If you **head** a ball in soccer, you hit it with your head in order to make it go in a particular direction. 用头顶 (球) ❑ *He headed the ball across the face of the goal.* 他用头顶球，球越过了门框。
8 → see also **heading**

> **Thesaurus** *head* 另参见：
>
> N. brain, mind ❶ 2
> beginning, front ❶ 3
> director, leader ❶ 4
> V. lead ❷ 1
> command, control, govern, manage ❷ 3

❸ **head** ♦♦♦ /hɛd/ (**heads**) 1 PHRASE You use **a head** or **per head** after stating a cost or amount in order to indicate that that cost or amount is for each person in a particular group. 每人 ❑ *This simple chicken dish costs less than $3 a head.* 吃这道简单的鸡肉菜肴，每人的花费还不到$3。 2 PHRASE If you a have **a head for** something, you can deal with it easily. For example, if you have **a head for figures**, you can do arithmetic easily, and if you have **a head for heights**, you can climb to a great height without feeling afraid. 有…的才能 ❑ *I don't have a head for business.* 我没有做生意的才能。 3 PHRASE If you **get** a fact or idea **into** your **head**, you suddenly realize or think that it is true and you usually do not change your opinion about it. 充分理解并接受 ❑ *Once they get an idea into their heads, they never give up.* 他们一旦接受了某个想法，就永远不会放弃。 4 PHRASE If you say that someone has **got** or **gotten** something **into** their **head**, you mean that they have finally understood or accepted it, and you are usually criticizing them because it has taken them a long time to do this. 终于明白 ❑ *Managers have at last got it into their heads that they can no longer rest content with inefficient operations.* 经理们最后终于明白不能再满足于低效率的运作。 5 PHRASE If alcoholic drink **goes to** your **head**, it makes you feel drunk. (酒) 使人感到醉 ❑ *That wine was strong, it went to your head.* 那种酒很烈，喝了会上头。 6 PHRASE If you say that something such as praise or success **goes to** someone's **head**, you are criticizing them because you think that it makes them too proud or confident. (成功等) 冲昏…的头脑 [DISAPPROVAL] ❑ *Ford is definitely not a man to let a little success go to his head.* 福特绝不是那种会被一点点成功冲昏头脑的人。 7 PHRASE If you are **head over heels** or **head over heels in love**, you are very much in love. 深陷情网 ❑ *I was very attracted to men and fell head over heels many times.* 我那时很容易被男性吸引，多次深陷情网。 8 PHRASE If you **keep** your **head**, you remain calm in a difficult situation. If you **lose** your **head**, you panic or do not remain calm in a difficult situation. 镇定自若；张皇失措 ❑ *She was able to keep her head and not panic.* 她当时能够镇定自若、不慌张。 9 PHRASE Phrases such as **laugh** your **head off** and **scream** your **head off** can be used to emphasize that someone is laughing or screaming a lot or very loudly. 大笑 [EMPHASIS] ❑ *He carried on telling a joke, laughing his head off.* 他不停地说笑话，大笑着。 10 PHRASE If something such as an idea, joke, or comment goes **over** someone's **head**, it is too difficult for them to understand. 超过…的理解力 ❑ *I admit that a lot of the ideas went way over my head.* 我承认有许多想法我都不能理解。 11 PHRASE If someone does something **over** another person's **head**, they do it without asking them or discussing it with them, especially when they should do so because the other person is in a position of authority. 越级 ❑ *He was reprimanded for trying to go over the heads of senior officers.* 他因试图越过上级官员而遭严斥。 12 PHRASE If you say that something unpleasant or embarrassing **rears its ugly head** or **raises its ugly head**, you mean that it occurs, often after not occurring for some time. (不好的事情) 再次出现 ❑ *There was a problem which reared its ugly head about a week after she moved back in.* 在她搬回去约一周后，有个问题又冒出来了。 13 PHRASE If you **stand on** your **head**, you balance upside down with the top of your head and your hands on the ground. 倒立 ❑ *He was photographed standing on his head doing yoga.* 他倒立着做瑜伽时被拍了下来。 14 PHRASE If you say that you cannot **make head nor tail of** something or you cannot **make heads or tails of** it, you are emphasizing that you cannot understand it at all. 理解 [INFORMAL] ❑ *I couldn't make head nor tail of the damn film.* 我压根儿看不懂这部该死的电影。 15 PHRASE If somebody **takes it into** their **head to** do something, especially something strange or foolish, they suddenly decide to do it. 突然决定 (做某事，尤指做古怪或愚蠢的事) ❑ *He suddenly took it into his head to go out to Australia to stay with his son.* 他突然心血来潮决定去澳大利亚同他儿子一起住。 16 PHRASE If a problem or disagreement **comes to a head** or **is brought to a head**, it becomes so bad that something must be done about it. 到了紧要关头 ❑ *These problems came to a head in September when five of the station's journalists were fired.* 这些问题在9月份变得十分尖锐，当时台里有5名记者被解雇。 17 PHRASE If two or more people **put** their **heads together**, they talk about a problem they have and try to solve it. 集思广益 ❑ *So everyone put their heads together and eventually an amicable arrangement was reached.* 因此大家集思广益并最终作出了妥善的安排。 18 PHRASE If you **keep** your **head above water**, you just avoid getting into difficulties; used especially to talk about business. (尤指生意上) 避免陷入困境 ❑ *We are keeping our head above water, but our cash flow position is not too good.* 我们虽然还未陷入困境，但资金流转状况不太好。 19 PHRASE If you say that **heads will roll** as a result of something bad that has happened, you mean that people will be punished for it, especially by losing their jobs. 要有许多人掉脑袋 (尤指失去工作) ❑ *The group's problems have led to speculation that heads will roll.* 该集团的问题已经引发有些人将会失业的猜测。

> **Head** is used in a large number of expressions which are explained under other words in the dictionary. For example, the expression "off the top of your head" is explained at "top."

head·ache /hɛdeɪk/ (**headaches**) 1 N-COUNT If you have a **headache**, you have a pain in your head. 头痛 ❑ *I have had a terrible headache for the last two days.* 最近两天我犯了严重的头痛病。 2 N-COUNT If you say that something is a **headache**, you mean that it causes you difficulty or worry. 棘手的事 ❑ *The airline's biggest headache is the increase in the price of aviation fuel.* 令航空公司最头疼的问题是航空燃料价格的上涨。

head count (**head counts**) N-COUNT If you do a **head count**, you count the number of people present. You can also use **head count** to talk about the number of people that are present at an event, or that an organization employs. 人数统计 ❑ *The troops rushed back onto the chopper and took off - but a head count showed one man was missing.* 士兵们迅速回到直升机上，起飞了，但清点人数后发现一人失踪。

head·er /hɛdər/ (**headers**) N-COUNT A **header** is text such as a name or a page number that can be automatically displayed at the top of each page of a printed document. Compare **footer**. 页眉 [COMPUTING] ❑ *...page formatting like headers, footers, and page numbers.* …页的版式如页眉、页脚和页码。

head·hunt /hɛdhʌnt/ (**headhunts, headhunting, headhunted**) V-T If someone who works for a particular company **is headhunted**, they leave that company because another company has approached them and offered them another job with better pay and higher status. 物色 (人才) ❑ *He was headhunted by Barkers last October to build an advertising team.* 他去年10月被巴克斯挖去组建一个广告团队。

head·hunter /hɛdhʌntər/ (**headhunters**) N-COUNT A **headhunter** is a person who tries to persuade someone to leave their job and take another job which has better pay and more status. 猎头 ❑ *...a headhunter for a bank.* …一名替银行物色人才的猎头。

head·ing /hɛdɪŋ/ (**headings**) 1 N-COUNT A **heading** is the title of a piece of writing, which is written or printed at the top of the page. 标题 ❑ *...helpful chapter headings.* …有用的章节标题。 2 → see also **head**

head·light /hɛdlaɪt/ (**headlights**) N-COUNT A vehicle's **headlights** are the large powerful lights at the front. (车辆的) 前灯 ❑ *Motorists were forced to turn on their headlights at midday.* 驾车者被强制要求在正午打开前灯。

head·line ♦◇◇ /hɛdlaɪn/ (**headlines, headlining, headlined**) 1 N-COUNT A **headline** is the title of a newspaper story, printed in large letters at the top of the story, especially on the front page. (尤指报纸头版的) 标题 ❑ *The Sydney Morning Herald carried the headline: "Sorry Ma'am, Most Australians Want a Republic."* 《悉尼先驱晨报》有这样一则头版标题："对不起，夫人，大多数澳大利亚人想要一个共和国。" 2 N-PLURAL **The headlines** are the main points of the news which are read on radio or television. 新闻提要 ❑ *I'm Claudia Polley with the news headlines.* 我是克劳迪娅·波莉，以下是新闻提要。 3 V-T If a newspaper or magazine article **is headlined** a particular thing, that is the headline that introduces it. 为…加标题 [usu passive] ❑ *The article was headlined "Tell us the truth."* 该文章题为"告诉我们真相。" 4 PHRASE Someone or something that **hits the headlines** or **grabs the headlines** gets a lot of publicity from the media. 成为新闻焦点 ❑ *El Salvador first hit the world headlines at the beginning of the 1980s.* 萨尔瓦多首度成为国际媒体的焦点是在20世纪80年代初。

head·long /hɛdlɔŋ/ 1 ADV If you move **headlong** in a particular direction, you move there very quickly. 迅猛地 [ADV after v] ❑ *He ran headlong for the open door.* 他向那扇敞开的门猛冲过去。 2 ADV If you fall or move **headlong**, you fall or move with your head furthest forward. 头朝前地 [ADV after v] ❑ *She missed her footing and fell headlong down the stairs.* 她一脚踩空了，头朝前摔下楼梯。 3 ADV If you rush **headlong into** something, you do it quickly without thinking carefully about it. 轻率地 [ADV after v] ❑ *Do not leap headlong into decisions.* 不要轻率仓促地做决定。 ● ADJ **Headlong** is also an adjective. 轻率的 [ADJ n] ❑ *...the headlong rush to independence.* …寻求独立的轻率举动。

head·master /hɛdmæstər/ (**headmasters**) N-COUNT A **headmaster** is the head teacher of a private school. 私立学校校长

head·mistress /hɛdmɪstrɪs/ (**headmistresses**) N-COUNT A **headmistress** is a woman who is the head teacher of a private school. (私立学校) 女校长 [mainly BRIT]

head of state (**heads of state**) N-COUNT A **head of state** is the leader of a country, for example a president, king, or queen. 国家首脑 ❑ *The Algerian authorities have still not named a new head of state.* 阿尔及利亚当局尚未任命新一任国家首脑。

head-on 1 ADV If two vehicles hit each other **head-on**, they hit each other with their fronts pointing toward each other. 迎面 (相撞) [ADV after v] ❑ *The car collided head-on with a van.* 小汽车迎面撞上了一辆大篷货车。 ● ADJ **Head-on** is also an adjective. 迎面的 [ADJ n] ❑ *Their car was in a head-on collision with a truck.* 他们的车同一辆卡车迎面相撞。 2 ADJ A **head-on** conflict or approach is direct, without any attempt to compromise or avoid the issue. 正面的 (冲突或争执) [ADJ n] ❑ *The only victors in a head-on clash between the president and the assembly would be the hardliners on both sides.* 总统与议会间正面冲突的惟一赢家将是双方的强硬派。 ● ADV **Head-on** is also an adverb. 正面地 [ADV after v] ❑ *Once again, I chose to confront the issue head-on.* 又一次，我选择了直面这个问题。

head·phones /hɛdfoʊnz/ N-PLURAL **Headphones** are a pair of padded speakers which you wear over your ears in order to listen to a radio, CD player, or tape recorder without other people hearing it. 耳机 [also "a pair of" N] ❑ *...while out cycling one evening and listening to your program on headphones.* …一天晚上在外面一边骑车一边戴着耳机收听你的节目时。

head·quarters ♦◇◇ /hɛdkwɔrtərz/ N-SING-COLL The **headquarters** of an organization are its main offices. 总部 ❑ *...fraud squad officers from Chicago's police headquarters.* …来自芝加哥警察局总部的诈骗侦查组的警官们。

head·rest /hɛdrɛst/ (**headrests**) N-COUNT A **headrest** is the part of the back of a seat on which you can lean your head, especially one on the front seat of a car. (尤指小汽车前座上的) 头垫

head·set /hɛdsɛt/ (**headsets**) 1 N-COUNT A **headset** is a small pair of headphones that you can use for listening to a radio or recorded music, or for using a telephone. 小型耳机 ❑ *During the race Mr. Taylor talks to the driver using a headset.* 在比赛中，泰勒先生用耳麦与车手通话。 2 N-COUNT A **headset** is a piece of equipment that you wear on your head so you can see computer images or images from a camera in front of your eyes. 头戴式视图器 ❑ *Soon the wearer* *of a virtual reality headset will be able to be "present" at sporting or theatrical events staged thousands of miles away.* 要不了多久，头戴虚拟现实视图器的人将能够"现场观看"几千英里之外举行的体育赛事或剧场演出。

head start (**head starts**) N-COUNT If you have a **head start on** other people, you have an advantage over them in something such as a competition or race. 起步前的优势 ❑ *A good education gives your child a head start in life.* 良好的教育会使你的孩子赢在人生的起跑线。

head·stone /hɛdstoʊn/ (**headstones**) N-COUNT A **headstone** is a large stone which stands at one end of a grave, usually with the name of the dead person carved on it. 墓碑

head·strong /hɛdstrɔŋ/ ADJ If you refer to someone as **headstrong**, you are slightly critical of the fact that they are determined to do what they want. 固执的 ❑ *He's young, very headstrong, but he's a good man underneath.* 他年轻、任性，但骨子里是个好人。

head teach·er (**head teachers**) also **head-teacher, headteacher** N-COUNT A **head teacher** is a teacher who is in charge of a school. 校长 [BRIT]

head·way /hɛdweɪ/ PHRASE If you **make headway**, you progress toward achieving something. 取得进展 ❑ *There was concern in the city that police were making little headway in the investigation.* 这个城市里的人们担心警方没有在调查中取得一丁点进展。

heady /hɛdi/ (**headier, headiest**) ADJ A **heady** drink, atmosphere, or experience strongly affects your senses, for example, by making you feel drunk or excited. 令人陶醉的 ❑ *...in the heady days just after their marriage.* …在他们婚后令人陶醉的日子里。

heal ♦◇◇ /hil/ (**heals, healing, healed**) **1** V-T/V-I When a broken bone or other injury **heals**, or if someone or something **heals** it, it becomes healthy and normal again. 治愈；痊愈 ❑ *Within six weeks the bruising had gone, but it was six months before it all healed.* 6周内青瘀已经消退了，可是伤在6个月后才完全愈合。 **2** V-T/V-I If you **heal** something such as a rift or a wound, or if it **heals**, the situation is put right so that people are friendly or happy again. 弥合 ❑ *We have begun to heal the wounds of war in our society.* 我们已经开始抚平战争带给这个社会的创伤。

heal·er /hilər/ (**healers**) N-COUNT A **healer** is a person who heals people, especially a person who heals through prayer and religious faith. 医治者(尤指用祈祷等方式治病的人)

health ♦♦♦ /hɛlθ/ **1** N-UNCOUNT A person's **health** is the condition of their body and the extent to which it is free from illness or is able to resist illness. 健康状况 ❑ *Tea contains caffeine. It's bad for your health.* 茶含有咖啡因，对你的健康不利。 **2** N-UNCOUNT **Health** is a state in which a person is not suffering from any illness and is feeling well. 健康 ❑ *In the hospital they nursed me back to health.* 在医院里他们精心照料我，使我恢复了健康。 **3** N-UNCOUNT The **health** of something such as an organization or a system is its success and the fact that it is working well. 兴旺 ❑ *There's no way to predict the future health of the banking industry.* 根本无法预测银行业将来的兴旺。

health care ♦♦◇ also **healthcare** N-UNCOUNT **Health care** is the various services for the prevention or treatment of illness and injuries. 医疗保健 [oft N n] ❑ *Nobody wants to pay more for health care.* 没人愿意为医疗保健花更多的钱。 ❑ *...the nation's health care system.* …国家医疗保健系统。

healthy ♦◇◇ /hɛlθi/ (**healthier, healthiest**) **1** ADJ Someone who is **healthy** is well and is not suffering from any illness. 健康的 ❑ *Most of us need to lead more balanced lives to be healthy and happy.* 我们中的多数人需要过更平衡的生活，从而达到健康和快乐。 ● **healthi·ly** /hɛlθɪli/ ADV 健康地 ❑ *What I really want is to live healthily for as long as possible.* 我真正想要的是尽可能长久、健康地活着。 **2** ADJ Something that is **healthy** is good for your health. 有益健康的 ❑ *...a healthy diet.* …一种有益健康的饮食。 **3** ADJ A **healthy** organization or system is successful. 繁荣的 ❑ *...an economically healthy socialist state.* …一个经济繁荣的社会主义国家。 **4** ADJ A **healthy** amount of something is a large amount that shows success. 可观的 ❑ *He predicts a continuation of healthy profits in the current financial year.* 他预测本财政年度能继续保持可观的利润。 **5** ADJ If you have a **healthy** attitude about something, you show good sense. 明智的 ❑ *She has a refreshingly healthy attitude to work.* 她对工作持一种爽快明智的态度。

Thesaurus *healthy* 另参见：

ADJ. fit, lively **1**
beneficial, nourishing **2**

Word Partnership *healthy* 的常用搭配：

N. healthy **baby**, healthy **glow**, healthy **skin** **1**
healthy **appetite**, healthy **diet/food**, healthy **lifestyle** **2**
healthy **attitude about** *something* **5**

heap /hip/ (**heaps, heaping, heaped**) **1** N-COUNT A **heap of** things is a pile of them, especially a pile arranged in a rather messy way. 一堆 ❑ *...a heap of bricks.* …一堆砖。

A **heap** of things is usually untidy, and often has the shape of a hill or mound. ❑ *Now, the house is a heap of rubble.* A **stack** is usually tidy, and often consists of flat objects placed directly on top of each other. ❑ *...a neat stack of dishes.* A **pile** of things can be tidy or untidy. ❑ *...a neat pile of clothes.*

2 V-T If you **heap** things in a pile, you arrange them in a large pile. 堆放 ❑ *Mrs. Madrigal heaped more carrots onto Michael's plate.* 马德里加尔太太往迈克尔的盘子里放了更多的胡萝卜。 ● PHRASAL VERB **Heap up** means the same as **heap**. 堆起 ❑ *Off to one side, the militia was heaping up wood for a bonfire.* 在一侧，民兵们正在堆起木柴，准备生起篝火。 **3** V-T If you **heap** praise or criticism **on** someone or something, you give them a lot of praise or criticism. 大量地给予(赞扬、批评等) ❑ *The head of the navy heaped scorn on both the methods and motives of the conspirators.* 这位海军首领对密谋分子的做法和动机都给予了极大的蔑视。 **4** QUANT **Heaps of** something or a **heap of** something is a large quantity of it. 许多 [INFORMAL] ❑ *You have heaps of time.* 你有很多时间。

hear ♦♦♦ /hɪər/ (**hears, hearing, heard** /hɜrd/) **1** V-T/V-I When you **hear** a sound, you become aware of it through your ears. 听见 ❑ *She heard no further sounds.* 她再也没有听见任何响声。 ❑ *They heard the protesters shout: "No more fascism!"* 他们听见抗议者在高呼："打倒法西斯主义！" ❑ *He doesn't hear very well.* 他听觉不是很好。 **2** V-T If you **hear** something such as a lecture or a piece of music, you listen to it. 听 ❑ *You can hear commentary on the game at halftime.* 你可在中场休息时听到对比赛的评论。 ❑ *I don't think you've ever heard Doris talking about her emotional life before.* 我想你以前从未听过多丽丝谈论自己的感情生活。 **3** V-T When a judge or a court of law **hears** a case, or evidence in a case, they listen to it officially in order to make a decision about it. 听审 [FORMAL] ❑ *The jury has heard evidence from defense witnesses.* 陪审团听取了被告方证人的证词。 **4** V-I If you **hear from** someone, you receive a letter or telephone call from them. 接到(信或电话) ❑ *Drop us a line, it's always great to hear from you.* 给我们写封信，能收到你的信息是让人很高兴。 **5** V-T/V-I If you **hear** some news or information about something, you find out about it by someone telling you, or from the radio or television. 听说 ❑ *My mother heard of this school through Leslie.* 我母亲从莱斯利那里听说了这所学校。 ❑ *He had heard that the trophy had been sold.* 他听说那个奖杯已经被卖掉了。 **6** V-I If you **have heard of** something or someone, you know about them, but not in great detail. 大致知道 [no cont] ❑ *Many people haven't heard of reflexology.* 很多人没有听说过反射疗法。

Do not confuse **hear** and **listen**. You use **hear** to talk about sounds that you are aware of because they reach your ears. You often use **can** with **hear**. ❑ *I can hear him yelling and swearing.* If you want to say that someone is paying attention to something they can hear, you say that they **are listening to** it. ❑ *He turned on the radio and listened to the news.* Note that **listen** is not followed directly by an object. You must always say that you listen **to** something. However, **listen** can also be used on its own without an object. ❑ *I was laughing too much to listen.*

7 PHRASE If you say that you **have heard** something **before**, you mean that you are not interested in it, or do not believe it, or are not surprised about it, because you already know about it or have experienced it. 已经知道 ❑ *Frank shrugs wearily. He has heard it all before.* 弗兰克倦怠地耸耸肩，他早已知道了这一切。 **8** PHRASE If you say that you **can't hear yourself think**, you are complaining and emphasizing that there is a lot of noise, and that it is disturbing you or preventing you from doing something. 吵得要死 [INFORMAL, EMPHASIS] ❑ *...those noisy late-night clubs where you can't even hear yourself think.* …那些开至深夜能把人吵死的夜总会。 **9** PHRASE If you say that you **won't hear of** someone doing something, you mean that you refuse to let them do it. 不同意 ❑ *I've always wanted to be an actor but Dad wouldn't hear of it.* 我一直想当演员，但爸爸总是不同意。

Thesaurus *hear* 另参见：
v. listen 2
detect, pick up 5

hear·ing ◆◇◇ /hɪərɪŋ/ (**hearings**) 1 N-UNCOUNT A person's or animal's **hearing** is the sense which makes it possible for them to be aware of sounds. 听力 ❑ *His mind still seemed clear and his hearing was excellent.* 他的头脑看来依然清醒，而且听力极好。 2 N-COUNT A **hearing** is an official meeting which is held in order to collect facts about an incident or problem. 听证会 ❑ *After more than two hours of pandemonium, the judge adjourned the hearing until next Tuesday.* 在两个多小时的混乱之后，法官暂时中止了听证会，将其延至下周二。 3 PHRASE If someone gives you **a fair hearing** or **a hearing**, they listen to you when you give your opinion about something. 发表意见的机会 ❑ *Weber gave a fair hearing to anyone who held a different opinion.* 韦伯让任何持有不同意见的人有发言的机会。 4 PHRASE If someone says something **in** your **hearing** or **within** your **hearing**, you can hear what they say because they are with you or near you. 某人听得见的范围内 ❑ *No one spoke disparagingly of her father in her hearing.* 没有人在她跟前说过她父亲的坏话。
→ see **disability**

Word Partnership *hearing* 的常用搭配：
N. hearing **impairment/loss** 1
court hearing 2
V. **hold a** hearing, **testify at/before a** hearing 2

heart
❶ NOUN USES
❷ PHRASES

❶ **heart** ◆◆◇ /hɑrt/ (**hearts**) 1 N-COUNT Your **heart** is the organ in your chest that pumps the blood around your body. People also use **heart** to refer to the area of their chest that is closest to their heart. 心脏；心口处 ❑ *The bullet had passed less than an inch from Andrea's heart.* 子弹从距安德烈亚心脏不到一英寸处穿过。 2 N-COUNT You can refer to someone's **heart** when you are talking about their deep feelings and beliefs. 内心 [LITERARY] ❑ *Alik's words filled her heart with pride.* 亚历克的话让她的内心充满骄傲。 3 N-VAR You use **heart** when you are talking about someone's character and attitude toward other people, especially when they are kind and generous. 心肠 [APPROVAL] ❑ *She loved his brilliance and his generous heart.* 她爱他的才华横溢和心地宽厚。 4 N-SING **The heart of** something is the most central and important part of it. 核心 ❑ *The heart of the problem is supply and demand.* 问题的核心是供给和需求。 5 N-SING **The heart of** a place is its center. (地方的) 中心 ❑ *...a busy dentists' practice in the heart of the city.* …位于市中心的一家忙碌的牙医诊所。 6 N-COUNT A **heart** is a shape that is used as a symbol of love: ♥. 心形 ❑ *...heart-shaped chocolates.* …心形巧克力。 7 N-UNCOUNT-COLL **Hearts** is one of the four suits in a deck of playing cards. Each card in the suit is marked with one or more symbols in the shape of a heart. 红桃牌 ● N-COUNT A **heart** is a playing card of this suit. (一张) 红桃牌 ❑ *West had to decide whether to play a heart.* 韦斯特不得不决定是否要出一张红桃牌。
→ see **donor**

❷ **heart** ◆◆◇ /hɑrt/ (**hearts**) 1 PHRASE If you feel or believe something **with all** your **heart**, you feel or believe it very strongly. 真心实意地 [EMPHASIS] ❑ *My own family I loved with all my heart.* 我真心实意地爱我的家人。 2 PHRASE If you say that someone is a particular kind of person **at heart**, you mean that that is what they are really like, even though they may seem very different. 实际上 ❑ *He was a very gentle boy at heart.* 他实际上是一个非常温和的男孩。 3 PHRASE If you say that someone has your interests or your welfare **at heart**, you mean that they are concerned about you and that is why they are doing something. 放在心上 ❑ *She told him she only had his interests at heart.* 她告诉他，她心里头只有他的利益。 4 PHRASE If someone **breaks** your **heart**, they make you very sad and unhappy, usually because they end a love affair or close relationship with you. 使某人心碎 [LITERARY] ❑ *I fell in love on vacation but the girl broke my heart.* 我在度假时坠入情网，但那个女孩却使我心碎。 5 PHRASE If something **breaks** your **heart**, it makes you feel very sad and depressed, especially because people are suffering but you can do nothing to help them. 使某人心碎 ❑ *It really breaks my heart to see them this way.* 看到他们这样确实让我心里难过。 6 PHRASE If you know something such as a poem **by heart**, you have learned it so well that you can remember it without having to read it. 靠记忆 ❑ *Mack knew this passage by heart.* 麦克会背这一段。 7 PHRASE If someone has a **change of heart**, their attitude toward something changes. 态度的改变 ❑ *Several brokers have had a change of heart about prospects for the company.* 几位代理商对于该公司前景的态度已有所改变。 8 PHRASE If something such as a subject or project is **close to** your **heart** or **near to** your **heart**, it is very important to you and you are very interested in it and concerned about it. 为某人所重视 ❑ *This is a subject very close to my heart.* 这是我十分关心的一个话题。 9 PHRASE If you can do something **to** your **heart's content**, you can do it as much as you want. 尽情地 ❑ *I was delighted to be able to eat my favorite dishes to my heart's content.* 我很高兴能够尽情地享用我最喜欢的菜肴。 10 CONVENTION You can say "**cross my heart**" when you want someone to believe that you are telling the truth. You can also ask "**cross your heart?**" when you are asking someone if they are really telling the truth. 在胸口划十字发誓 [SPOKEN] ❑ *And I won't tell any of the other girls anything you tell me about it. I promise, cross my heart.* 我不会把你告诉我的与其有关的任何事情告诉任何其他女孩。我保证，我发誓。 11 PHRASE If you say something **from the heart** or **from the bottom of** your **heart**, you sincerely mean what you say. 发自内心地 ❑ *He spoke with confidence, from the heart.* 他讲话充满自信，发自内心。 12 PHRASE If you want to do something but do **not have the heart to** do it, you do not do it because you know it will make someone unhappy or disappointed. 不忍做 ❑ *We knew all along but didn't have the heart to tell her.* 我们一直都知道，但是不忍心告诉她。 13 PHRASE If you believe or know something **in** your **heart of hearts**, that is what you really believe or think, even though it may sometimes seem that you do not. 在内心深处 ❑ *I know in my heart of hearts that I am the right man for that mission.* 我在内心深处知道，我正是完成那项使命的最合适人选。 14 PHRASE If your **heart isn't in** the thing you are doing, you have very little enthusiasm for it, usually because you are depressed or are thinking about something else. 不热衷于 ❑ *I tried to learn some lines but my heart wasn't really in it.* 我试图记住几行诗句，但我确实对此不感兴趣。 15 PHRASE If you **lose heart**, you become sad and depressed and are no longer interested in something, especially because it is not progressing as you would like. 灰心丧气 ❑ *He appealed to his countrymen not to lose heart.* 他呼吁同胞们不要灰心丧气。 16 PHRASE If your **heart is in** your **mouth**, you feel very excited, worried, or frightened. 心提到嗓子眼里 ❑ *My heart was in my mouth when I walked into her office.* 我走进她的办公室时，心提到了嗓子眼。 17 PHRASE If you **open** your **heart** or **pour out** your **heart** to someone, you tell them your most private thoughts and feelings. 对某人敞开心扉 ❑ *She opened her heart to millions yesterday and told how she came close to suicide.* 她昨天向大众敞开心扉，讲述了自己几乎要自杀的原委。 18 PHRASE If you say that someone's **heart is in the right place**, you mean that they are kind, considerate, and generous, although you may disapprove of other aspects of their character. 心地善良 ❑ *He's rich, handsome, funny, and his heart is in the right place.* 他富有、英俊、风趣，而且心地善良。 19 PHRASE If you have **set** your **heart on** something, you want it very much or want to do it very much. 一心渴望 ❑ *He had always set his heart on a career in the fine arts.* 他一心想从事一项美术方面的职业。 20 PHRASE If you **take heart from** something, you are encouraged and made to feel optimistic by it. 得到鼓舞 ❑ *Investors and dealers also took heart from the better than expected industrial production figures.* 投资者和经销商们也从高于预期的工业产值中受到鼓舞。 21 PHRASE If you **take** something **to heart**, for example someone's behavior, you are deeply affected and upset by it. 对某事物十分介意 ❑ *If someone says something critical I take it to heart.* 如果谁说一些批评的话，我就往心里去。

heart·ache /hɑrteɪk/ (**heartaches**) N-VAR **Heartache** is very great sadness and emotional suffering. 心痛 ❑ *...after suffering the heartache of her divorce from her first husband.* …经历了与第一任丈夫离婚的心痛之后。

heart at·tack (**heart attacks**) N-COUNT If someone has a **heart attack**, their heart begins to beat very irregularly or stops completely. 心脏病发作 ❑ *He died of a heart attack brought on by overwork.* 他死于劳累过度引起的一次心脏病发作。

heart·beat /hɑrtbit/ N-SING Your **heartbeat** is the regular movement of your heart as it pumps blood around your body. 心跳 ❑ *Your baby's heartbeat will be monitored continuously.* 您小宝宝的心跳将会受到持续监听。

heart·break /hɑ̲rtbreɪk/ (**heartbreaks**) N-VAR **Heartbreak** is very great sadness and emotional suffering, especially after the end of a love affair or close relationship. 心碎 ❑ *...suffering and heartbreak for those close to the victims.* …那些受害者亲人的痛苦与悲伤。

heart·breaking /hɑ̲rtbreɪkɪŋ/ ADJ Something that is **heartbreaking** makes you feel extremely sad and upset. 令人极度伤心的 ❑ *This year we won't even be able to buy presents for our grandchildren. It's heartbreaking.* 今年我们甚至不能给孙辈们买礼物，这令人极度伤心。

heart·broken /hɑ̲rtbroʊkən/ ADJ Someone who is **heartbroken** is very sad and emotionally upset. 极度伤心的 ❑ *Was your daddy heartbroken when they got a divorce?* 他们离婚时你爸爸很伤心吗？

heart·en /hɑ̲rtᵊn/ (**heartens, heartening, heartened**) V-T If someone **is heartened by** something, it encourages them and makes them cheerful. 鼓舞 ❑ *The news heartened everybody.* 这个消息鼓舞了每个人。 ● **heart·ened** ADJ 受到鼓舞的 [v-link ADJ] ❑ *I feel heartened by her progress.* 她的进步让我感到振奋。 ● **heart·en·ing** ADJ 鼓舞人心的 ❑ *This is heartening news.* 这是个鼓舞人心的消息。

heart fail·ure N-UNCOUNT **Heart failure** is a serious medical condition in which someone's heart does not work as well as it should, sometimes stopping completely so that they die. 心力衰竭 ❑ *He remained in a critical condition after suffering heart failure.* 他患心力衰竭之后一直处于危险状况。

heart·felt /hɑ̲rtfɛlt/ ADJ **Heartfelt** is used to describe a deep or sincere feeling or wish. 衷心的 ❑ *My heartfelt sympathy goes out to all the relatives.* 我对所有的亲属表示衷心的慰问。

▲ **hearth** /hɑ̲rθ/ (**hearths**) N-COUNT The **hearth** is the floor of a fireplace, which sometimes extends into the room. 壁炉地面 ❑ *It was winter and there was a huge fire roaring in the hearth.* 时值冬天，壁炉里的炉火在熊熊燃烧。

heart·land /hɑ̲rtlænd/ (**heartlands**) 1 N-COUNT Journalists use **heartland** or **heartlands** to refer to the area or region where a particular set of activities or beliefs is most significant. (某活动或信仰占优势的）中心区域 ❑ *...his six-day bus tour around the industrial heartland of America.* …他在美国工业中心地区的巴士6日游。 2 N-COUNT The most central area of a country or continent can be referred to as its **heartland** or **heartlands**. (国家或大陆的）心脏地带 [WRITTEN] ❑ *For many, the essence of French living is to be found in the rural heartlands.* 对许多人来说，法国生活方式的精髓要到心脏地带的乡村去寻找。

hearty /hɑ̲rti/ (**heartier, heartiest**) 1 ADJ **Hearty** people or actions are loud, cheerful, and energetic. 喧闹活泼的 ❑ *Wade was a hearty, athletic sort of guy.* 韦德是那种精力充沛、身体强壮的家伙。 ● **hearti·ly** ADV 喧闹活泼地 [ADV after v] ❑ *He laughed heartily.* 他开怀大笑。 2 ADJ **Hearty** feelings or opinions are strongly felt or strongly held. (感情或观点等）强烈的 ❑ *With the last sentiment, Arnold was in hearty agreement.* 对于最后一个观点，阿诺德强烈赞同。 ● **hearti·ly** ADV 强烈地 ❑ *Most Afghans are heartily sick of war.* 大多数阿富汗人极其厌恶战争。 3 ADJ A **hearty** meal is large and very satisfying. (饭菜）丰盛的 ❑ *The men ate a hearty breakfast.* 男士们吃了一顿丰盛的早餐。 ● **hearti·ly** ADV 胃口很大地 [ADV after v] ❑ *He ate heartily but would drink only beer.* 他吃饭的胃口很大，但只喝啤酒。

heat ♦♦◇ /hi̲t/ (**heats, heating, heated**) 1 V-T When you **heat** something, you raise its temperature, for example, by using a flame or a special piece of equipment. 加热 ❑ *Meanwhile, heat the tomatoes and oil in a pan.* 与此同时，将西红柿和油放在平底锅里加热。 2 N-UNCOUNT **Heat** is warmth or the quality of being hot. 热 ❑ *The seas store heat and release it gradually during cold periods.* 海洋储存热量，并在寒冷季节里逐渐将其释放。 3 N-UNCOUNT **The heat** is very hot weather. 高温天气 [also "the" N] ❑ *As an asthmatic, he cannot cope with the heat and humidity.* 身为气喘病患者，他受不了炎热与潮湿。 4 N-UNCOUNT The **heat** of something is the temperature of something that is warm or that is being heated. 热度 ❑ *Adjust the heat of the barbecue by opening and closing the air vents.* 通过开关气阀来调节烧烤架的热度。 5 N-SING You use **heat** to refer to a source of heat, for example a burner on a stove or the heating system of a house. 热源 ❑ *Immediately remove the pan from the heat.* 立即将平底锅从热源上移开。 6 N-UNCOUNT You use **heat** to refer to a state of strong emotion, especially of anger or excitement. 激动状态 ❑ *It was all done in the heat of the moment and I have certainly learned by my mistake.* 所有这一切都是在一时冲动下干的，我当然已经从我的过失中吸取了教训。 7 N-SING **The heat of** a particular activity is the point when there is the greatest activity or excitement. 最激烈的时刻 ❑ *People say all kinds of things in the heat of an argument.* 人们在争论进行到最激烈的时候口无遮拦。 8 N-COUNT A **heat** is one of a series of races or competitions. The winners of a heat take part in another race or competition, against the winners of other heats. 预赛 ❑ *...the heats of the men's 100 meter breaststroke.* …男子100米蛙泳预赛。 → see **fire, pan, weather**

▶ **heat up** 1 PHRASAL VERB When you **heat** something **up**, especially food which has already been cooked and allowed to go cold, you make it hot. 把…加热 ❑ *Freda heated up a pie for me but I couldn't eat it.* 弗雷达为我热了一块馅饼，可我不能吃。 2 PHRASAL VERB When a situation **heats up**, things start to happen much more quickly and with increased interest and excitement among the people involved. 升温 ❑ *Then in the last couple of years, the movement for democracy began to heat up.* 于是在过去几年里，民主运动开始升温。 3 PHRASAL VERB When something **heats up**, it gradually becomes hotter. 变热 ❑ *In the summer her mobile home heats up like an oven.* 在夏天，她的活动住房像个烤箱那样热起来。 → see **cooking**

heat·ed /hi̲tɪd/ 1 ADJ A **heated** discussion or quarrel is one where the people involved are angry and excited. 激烈的 ❑ *It was a very heated argument and they were shouting at each other.* 这是一场非常激烈的争论，他们彼此冲着对方大喊大叫。 2 ADJ If someone gets **heated about** something, they get angry and excited about it. 愤怒的 [v-link ADJ "about/over" n] ❑ *You will understand that people get a bit heated about issues such as these.* 你会理解人们对诸如此类的问题有些愤怒。 ● **heat·ed·ly** ADV 激烈地 [ADV with v] ❑ *The crowd continued to argue heatedly about the best way to tackle the problem.* 这群人继续激烈地争论着解决该问题的最好方式。

heat·er /hi̲tər/ (**heaters**) N-COUNT A **heater** is a piece of equipment or a machine which is used to raise the temperature of something, especially of the air inside a room or a car. 加热器

heath·er /hɛ̲ðər/ N-UNCOUNT **Heather** is a low, spreading plant with small purple, pink, or white flowers that grows wild on high land with poor soil. 石南属植物

heat·ing /hi̲tɪŋ/ 1 N-UNCOUNT **Heating** is the process of heating a building or room, considered especially from the point of view of how much this costs. 供暖 ❑ *We wanted to reduce the cost of heating and air-conditioning.* 我们想减少供暖与空调的开支。 2 N-UNCOUNT **Heating** is the system and equipment that is used to heat a building. 供暖系统和设备 ❑ *I wish I knew how to turn on the heating.* 要是我知道如何打开暖气装置就好了。 3 → see also **central heating**

heave /hi̲v/ (**heaves, heaving, heaved**) 1 V-T If you **heave** something heavy or difficult to move somewhere, you push, pull, or lift it using a lot of effort. (用力地）推；拉；举起 ❑ *It took five strong men to heave it up a ramp and lower it into place.* 用了5个壮汉把它拉上斜坡并向下放置到位。 ● N-COUNT **Heave** is also a noun. 推；拉；举 ❑ *It took only one heave to hurl him into the river.* 只是一推，就把他推进了河里。 2 V-I If something **heaves**, it moves up and down with large regular movements. (强烈而有节奏地）起伏 ❑ *His chest heaved, and he took a deep breath.* 他的胸膛上下起伏，然后他深深地吸了一口气。 3 V-I If you **heave**, or if your stomach **heaves**, you vomit or feel as if you are about to vomit. 呕吐；恶心 ❑ *He gasped and heaved again.* 他喘口气，然后又呕吐了。 ❑ *The greasy food made her stomach heave.* 油腻腻的食物让她胃里恶心。 4 V-T If you **heave a sigh**, you give a big sigh. 深深发出（叹息）❑ *Mr. Collier heaved a sigh and got to his feet.* 科利尔先生深深叹了一口气，然后站起身。 5 V-I If a place **is heaving** or if it is **heaving with** people, it is full of people. 挤满 [usu cont] [mainly BRIT, INFORMAL] ❑ *The Happy Bunny club was heaving.* 快乐兔子夜总会里挤满了人。 ❑ *Father Auberon's Academy Club positively heaved with dashing young men.* 奥伯龙神父学院俱乐部里实实在在满是风度翩翩的年轻男子。 6 to heave **a sigh of relief** → see **sigh**

heav·en ♦◇◇ /hɛ̲vən/ (**heavens**) 1 N-PROPER In some religions, **heaven** is said to be the place where God lives, where good people go when they die, and where everyone is always happy. It is usually imagined as being high up in the sky. 天堂 ❑ *I believed that when I died I would go to heaven and see God.* 我相信我死后会进入天堂，见到上帝。 2 N-UNCOUNT You can use **heaven** to refer to a place or situation that you like very much. 极好的地方（或情况）[INFORMAL] ❑ *I would go to movies in the afternoon and to ball games in the evening. It was heaven.* 我下午去看电影，晚上去看球赛，真是享受。 3 EXCLAM You say "**Good heavens!**" or "**Heavens!**" to express surprise or to

h

emphasize that you agree or disagree with someone. (表示惊奇等)天哪 [SPOKEN, FEELINGS] ❑ *Good Heavens! That explains a lot!* 天哪！那很说明问题！ **4** PHRASE You say "**Heaven help** someone" when you are worried that something bad is going to happen to them, often because you disapprove of what they are doing or the way they are behaving. (表示担心某人将有难) 老天帮帮某人吧 [SPOKEN, DISAPPROVAL] ❑ *If this makes sense to our leaders, then heaven help us all.* 如果这对我们的领导们来说是可行的，那真是老天帮助大家。 **5** PHRASE You can say "**Heaven knows**" to emphasize that you do not know something, or that you find something very surprising. 天知道 [SPOKEN, EMPHASIS] ❑ *Heaven knows what they put in it.* 天知道他们往里面放了些什么。 **6** PHRASE You can say "**Heaven knows**" to emphasize something that you feel or believe very strongly. 确实 [SPOKEN, EMPHASIS] ❑ *Heaven knows they have enough money.* 确实他们有足够的钱。 **7** PHRASE If **the heavens open**, it suddenly starts raining very heavily. 突然下起倾盆大雨 ❑ *The match had just begun when the heavens opened and play was suspended.* 比赛才刚刚开始，就突然下起倾盆大雨，于是比赛暂停。 **8** **for heaven's sake** → see **sake**
9 **thank heavens** → see **thank**

heav·en·ly /hɛvənli/ **1** ADJ **Heavenly** things are things that are connected with the religious idea of heaven. 天国的 ❑ *...heavenly beings whose function it is to serve God.* …职责为侍奉上帝的天使们。 **2** ADJ Something that is **heavenly** is very pleasant and enjoyable. 极美好的 [INFORMAL] ❑ *The idea of spending two weeks with him may seem heavenly.* 这个与他共度两周的主意似乎妙不可言。

heavy ♦♦◇ /hɛvi/ (**heavier, heaviest, heavies**) **1** ADJ Something that is **heavy** weighs a lot. 重的 ❑ *These scissors are awfully heavy.* 这些剪刀非常重。 ● **heavi·ness** N-UNCOUNT 沉重 ❑ *...a sensation of warmth and heaviness in the muscles.* …一种肌肉的温暖和沉重感。 **2** ADJ You use **heavy** to ask or talk about how much someone or something weighs. 重的 ❑ *How heavy are you?* 你有多重？ **3** ADJ **Heavy** means great in amount, degree, or intensity. 大量的；过度的；强烈的 ❑ *Heavy fighting has been going on.* 激战一直在进行。 ❑ *He worried about her heavy drinking.* 他为她的酗酒感到担忧。 ● **heavi·ly** ADV 大量地；过度地；强烈地 ❑ *It has been raining heavily all day.* 一整天雨都下得很大。 ● **heavi·ness** N-UNCOUNT 大量；过度；强烈 ❑ *...the heaviness of the blood loss.* …大量失血。 **4** ADJ A **heavy** meal is large in amount and often difficult to digest. 量大而难以消化的 ❑ *He had been feeling drowsy, the effect of an unusually heavy meal.* 他一直感到昏昏欲睡，因为吃了一顿异常量大而难以消化的饭、菜。 **5** ADJ Something that is **heavy with** things is full of them or loaded with them. 充满了…的 [v-link ADJ "with" n] [LITERARY] ❑ *The air is heavy with moisture.* 空气中充满了湿气。 **6** ADJ If a person's breathing is **heavy**, it is very loud and deep. 粗重的 (呼吸) ❑ *Her breathing became slow and heavy.* 她的呼吸变得缓慢而粗重。 ● **heavi·ly** ADV 粗重地 [ADV after v] ❑ *She sank back on the pillow and closed her eyes, breathing heavily as if asleep.* 她躺回到枕头上，闭上双眼，呼吸粗重，就像睡熟了似的。 **7** ADJ A **heavy** movement or action is done with a lot of force or pressure. 粗重的 [ADJ n] ❑ *...a heavy blow on the back of the skull.* …后脑勺上的一记重击。 ● **heavi·ly** ADV 粗重地 [ADV after v] ❑ *I sat down heavily on the ground beside the road.* 我重重地坐在路边的地上。 **8** ADJ A **heavy** machine or piece of military equipment is very large and very powerful. 重型的 [ADJ n] ❑ *...government militia backed by tanks and heavy artillery.* …有坦克和重炮支持的政府民兵组织。 **9** ADJ If you describe a period of time or a schedule as **heavy**, you mean it involves a lot of work. 繁忙的 ❑ *It's been a heavy day and I'm tired.* 这是繁忙的一天，我累坏了。 **10** ADJ **Heavy** work requires a lot of strength or energy. 繁重的 ❑ *The business is thriving and Philippa employs two full-timers for the heavy work.* 生意很兴隆，于是菲莉帕雇了两名全职员工来干重活儿。 **11** ADJ If you say that something is **heavy on** another thing, you mean that it uses a lot of that thing or too much of that thing. 耗费…的 [v-link ADJ "on" n] ❑ *Tanks are heavy on fuel, destructive to roads and difficult to park.* 坦克耗油量大，对道路有破坏性，并且难以停放。 **12** ADJ Air or weather that is **heavy** is unpleasantly still, hot, and damp. (空气或天气) 阴沉的；闷热的；潮湿的 ❑ *The outside air was heavy and moist and sultry.* 户外的空气阴沉、潮湿而闷热。 **13** ADJ A situation that is **heavy** is serious and difficult to cope with. 棘手的 [INFORMAL] ❑ *I don't want any more of that heavy stuff.* 我可再也不想碰那种麻烦事儿了。 **14** N-COUNT A **heavy** is a large strong man who is employed to protect a person or place, often by using violence. You can also use **heavy** to refer to a male character who represents such a man in a movie or play. 保镖；打手 [INFORMAL] ❑ *They had employed heavies to evict squatters from neighboring sites.* 他们雇了一些打手，以赶走来自邻近地区的私自占地者。 ❑ *In 1943, he received his first role as a heavy in "Double Indemnity."* 1943年，他接了第一个角色，在影片《双重保险》中扮演保镖。

Thesaurus	*heavy* 另参见：
ADJ.	hefty, overweight; *(ant.)* light **1**
	forceful, powerful **8**
	complex, difficult, tough **13**

Word Partnership	*heavy* 的常用搭配：
N.	heavy **competition**, heavy **drinking**, heavy **fighting** **3**

heavy-duty ADJ A **heavy-duty** piece of equipment is very strong and can be used a lot. 结实耐用的 ❑ *...a heavy-duty plastic bag.* …一个耐用的塑料袋。

heavy-handed ADJ If you say that someone's behavior is **heavy-handed**, you mean that they are too forceful or too rough. 粗暴的；暴虐的 [DISAPPROVAL] ❑ *...heavy-handed police tactics.* …警察的粗暴手段。

heavy in·dus·try (**heavy industries**) N-VAR **Heavy industry** is industry in which large machines are used to produce raw materials or to make large objects. 重工业 ❑ *...the policy of redirecting investment to heavy industries like steel and energy.* …将投资转向诸如钢铁和能源等重工业的政策。
→ see **industry**

heavy·weight /hɛviweɪt/ (**heavyweights**) **1** N-COUNT A **heavyweight** is a boxer weighing more than 175 pounds and therefore in the heaviest class. 重量级拳击手 **2** N-COUNT If you refer to a person or organization as a **heavyweight**, you mean that they have a lot of influence, experience, and importance in a particular field, subject, or activity. 极具影响力的人 (或组织) ❑ *He was a political heavyweight.* 他当时是一位政界要人。

He·brew /hibru/ **1** N-UNCOUNT **Hebrew** is a language that was spoken by Jews in former times. A modern form of Hebrew is spoken now in Israel. 希伯来语 ❑ *He is a fluent speaker of Hebrew.* 他希伯来语说得很流利。 **2** ADJ **Hebrew** means belonging to or relating to the Hebrew language or people. 希伯来语的；希伯来人的 ❑ *...the respected Hebrew newspaper Haarez.* …受敬重的希伯来语报纸《Haarez》。

heck·le /hɛkᵊl/ (**heckles, heckling, heckled**) V-T/V-I If people in an audience **heckle** public speakers or performers, they interrupt them, for example by making rude remarks. 对…起哄 ❑ *They heckled him and interrupted his address with angry questions.* 他们对他起哄，以愤怒的诘问打断他的演说。 ● N-COUNT **Heckle** is also a noun. 起哄 ❑ *The offending comment was in fact a heckle from an audience member.* 那冒犯性的评论实际上是一名观众的起哄。 ● **heck·ling** N-UNCOUNT 起哄 ❑ *The ceremony was disrupted by unprecedented heckling and slogan-chanting.* 典礼因前所未有的起哄和口号声而中断。 ● **heck·ler** /hɛklər/ N-COUNT (**hecklers**) 起哄者 ❑ *As he began his speech, a heckler called out asking for his opinion on gun control.* 当他开始演说时，一名起哄者大喊大叫起来，诘问他对枪支控制的意见。

▲ **hec·tare** /hɛktɛər/ (**hectares**) N-COUNT A **hectare** is a measurement of an area of land which is equal to 10,000 square meters, or 2.471 acres. 公顷

▲ **hec·tic** /hɛktɪk/ ADJ A **hectic** situation is one that is very busy and involves a lot of rushed activity. 紧张忙碌的 ❑ *Despite his hectic work schedule, Benny has rarely suffered poor health.* 尽管工作安排很紧张，班尼却少有健康不佳的时候。

he'd /hid, STRONG hid/ **1** **He'd** is the usual spoken form of "he had," especially when "had" is an auxiliary verb. **he had**的常用口语形式 ❑ *He'd never learned to read.* 他一直没有学会阅读。 **2** **He'd** is a spoken form of "he would." **he would**的口语形式 ❑ *He'd come into the clubhouse every day.* 他会每天到俱乐部会所来。

hedge /hɛdʒ/ (**hedges, hedging, hedged**) **1** N-COUNT A **hedge** is a row of bushes or small trees, usually along the edge of a lawn, garden, field, or road. 树篱 **2** V-I If you **hedge against** something unpleasant or unwanted that might affect you, especially losing money, you do something which will protect you from it. 防备 (尤指金钱损失) ❑ *You can hedge against illness with insurance.* 你可以买保险以备治疗患病之需。 **3** N-COUNT Something that is a **hedge against** something unpleasant will protect you from its effects. 防备手段 ❑ *Gold is traditionally a hedge against inflation.* 黄金传统上是一种防范通货膨胀的手段。 **4** PHRASE If you **hedge** your **bets**, you reduce the risk of losing a lot by supporting more than one person or thing in a situation where they are opposed to each other.

几面下注 ❑ *The company tried to hedge its bets by diversifying into other fields.* 该公司试图通过兼营其他领域几面下注。

hedge fund (**hedge funds**) N-COUNT A **hedge fund** is an investment fund that invests large amounts of money using methods that involve a lot of risk. 对冲基金 [BUSINESS]

hedge·hog /hɛdʒhɒg/ (**hedgehogs**) N-COUNT A **hedgehog** is a small brown animal with sharp spikes covering its back. 刺猬

he·don·ism /hidᵊnɪzəm/ N-UNCOUNT **Hedonism** is the belief that gaining pleasure is the most important thing in life. 享乐主义 [FORMAL] ❑ *...the life of hedonism that she embraced in her youth.* …她年轻时所奉行的享乐主义生活。

he·don·is·tic /hidᵊnɪstɪk/ ADJ **Hedonistic** means relating to hedonism. 享乐主义的 [FORMAL] ❑ *...an eccentric and flamboyant nobleman with a hedonistic lifestyle.* …一个崇尚享乐主义的生活方式、古怪而派头十足的贵族。

heed /hid/ (**heeds, heeding, heeded**) 1 V-T If you **heed** someone's advice or warning, you pay attention to it and do what they suggest. 注意；听从 [FORMAL] ❑ *But few at the conference in London last week heeded his warning.* 但几乎没有人在上周伦敦会议上注意他的警告。 2 PHRASE If you **take heed of** what someone says or if you **pay heed to** them, you pay attention to them and consider carefully what they say. 注意 [FORMAL] ❑ *But what if the government takes no heed?* 但要是政府不理会该怎么办呢？

heel /hil/ (**heels**) 1 N-COUNT Your **heel** is the back part of your foot, just below your ankle. 脚后跟 ❑ *He had an operation on his heel last week.* 他上星期脚后跟做了手术。 2 N-COUNT The **heel** of a shoe is the raised part on the bottom at the back. 鞋后跟 ❑ *...the shoes with the high heels.* …那些高跟的鞋。 3 N-PLURAL **Heels** are women's shoes that are raised very high at the back. 女高跟鞋 ❑ *She was dressed in heels and a clingy dress.* 她穿着高跟鞋和一件贴身连衣裙。 4 PHRASE If you **dig** your **heels in** or **dig in** your **heels**, you refuse to do something such as change your opinions or plans, especially when someone is trying very hard to make you do so. 固执己见 ❑ *It was really the British who, by digging their heels in, prevented any last-minute deal.* 正是英国人，因其固执己见，妨碍了最后一刻交易的达成。 5 PHRASE If you say that one event follows **hard on the heels of** another or **hot on the heels of** another, you mean that one happens very quickly or immediately after another. 接踵而至 ❑ *Unfortunately, bad news has come hard on the heels of good.* 遗憾的是，坏消息紧接着好消息而来。 6 PHRASE If you say that someone is **hot on** your **heels**, you are emphasizing that they are chasing you and are not very far behind you. 紧跟…之后 [EMPHASIS] ❑ *They sped through the southwest with the law hot on their heels.* 他们飞速穿越西南部，警察紧随其后。 7 **head over heels** → see **head** 8 **to drag** your **heels** → see **drag** → see **foot**

hefty /hɛfti/ (**heftier, heftiest**) 1 ADJ **Hefty** means large in size, weight, or amount. 庞大的；沉重的 [INFORMAL] ❑ *She was quite a hefty woman.* 她是个相当高大的女人。 2 ADJ A **hefty** movement is done with a lot of force. 有力的 [INFORMAL] ❑ *Max grabbed Sascha's hair and she retaliated by giving him a hefty push.* 马克斯抓住萨夏的头发，她回敬他猛的一推。

▲ **he·gemo·ny** /hɪdʒɛməni/ N-UNCOUNT **Hegemony** is a situation in which one country, organization, or group has more power, control, or importance than others. 霸权 [FORMAL]

height ♦◇◇ /haɪt/ (**heights**) 1 N-VAR The **height** of a person or thing is their size or length from the bottom to the top. 高度 ❑ *Her weight is about normal for her height.* 按她的身高，她的体重大体正常。 ❑ *I am 5'6" in height.* 我的身高是5英尺6英寸。 2 N-UNCOUNT **Height** is the quality of being tall. 高 ❑ *She admits that her height is intimidating for some men.* 她承认自己的高个儿对一些男人而言是吓人的。 3 N-VAR A particular **height** is the distance that something is above the ground or above something else mentioned. 高度 ❑ *At the speed and height at which he was moving, he was never more than half a second from disaster.* 以这样的速度在这么高的地方移动，他离灾难永远只有半秒之遥。 4 N-COUNT A **height** is a high position or place above the ground. 高处 ❑ *I'm not afraid of heights.* 我不恐高。 5 N-SING When an activity, situation, or organization is **at its height**, it is at its most successful, powerful, or intense. 顶点；高潮 ❑ *At its height, the antiwar movement drew supporters from nearly every political camp.* 在高潮阶段，反战运动从几乎每个政治派别那里都吸引来了支持者。 6 N-SING If you say that something is **the height of** a particular quality, you are emphasizing that it has that quality to the greatest degree possible. 顶点 [EMPHASIS] ❑ *The hip-hugging black and white polka-dot dress was the height of fashion.* 黑白圆点紧身连衣裙当时是最新潮的。 7 N-PLURAL If something reaches great **heights**, it becomes very extreme or intense. 极点 ❑ *...the mid-1980s, when prices rose to absurd heights.* …物价上升至荒谬极点的20世纪80年代中期。

→ see **area**

Thesaurus *height* 另参见：

N. altitude, elevation 3
peak 5

Word Partnership *height* 的常用搭配：

ADJ. **average** height, **medium** height, **the right** height 1
N. height **and weight**, height **and width** 1
the height **of** *someone's* **career** 5
the height **of fashion/popularity/style** 6
V. **reach a** height 1 3 5

★ **height·en** /haɪtᵊn/ (**heightens, heightening, heightened**) V-T/V-I If something **heightens** a feeling or if the feeling **heightens**, the feeling increases in degree or intensity. 加剧 ❑ *The move has heightened tension in the state.* 这一举动加剧了该州的紧张局势。 ❑ *Cross's interest heightened.* 克罗斯的兴趣增强了。

heir /ɛər/ (**heirs**) N-COUNT An **heir** is someone who has the right to inherit a person's money, property, or title when that person dies. 继承人 ❑ *...the heir to the throne.* …王位继承人。

Word Link *ess ≈ female : actress, heiress, princess*

heir·ess /ɛərɪs/ (**heiresses**) N-COUNT An **heiress** is a woman or girl who has the right to inherit property or a title, or who has inherited it, especially when this involves great wealth. (尤指大笔财产的) 女继承人 ❑ *...the heiress to a jewelry empire.* …一家大型珠宝公司的女继承人。

held /hɛld/ **Held** is the past tense and past participle of **hold**. **hold**的过去式和过去分词

heli·cop·ter ♦◇◇ /hɛlikɒptər/ (**helicopters**) N-COUNT A **helicopter** is an aircraft with long blades on top that go around very fast. It is able to stay still in the air and to move straight upward or downward. 直升机

→ see **fly**

heli·pad /hɛlipæd/ (**helipads**) N-COUNT A **helipad** is a place where helicopters can land and take off. 直升机升降坪 ❑ *Each house had a helipad for a fast evacuation.* 每所房子都有一个供快速撤离用的直升机升降坪。

hell

1 NOUN USES
2 PHRASES

1 **hell** ♦◇◇ /hɛl/ (**hells**) 1 N-PROPER; N-COUNT In some religions, **hell** is the place where the Devil lives, and where wicked people are sent to be punished when they die. Hell is usually imagined as being under the ground and full of flames. 地狱 ❑ *I've never believed. Not in heaven or hell or God or Satan until now.* 我以前一直都不信。直到现在我才相信有天堂、地狱、上帝和撒旦。 2 N-VAR If you say that a particular situation or place is **hell**, you are emphasizing that it is extremely unpleasant. 令人痛苦不堪的处境(或地方) [EMPHASIS] ❑ *...the hell of the Siberian labor camps.* …西伯利亚劳改营那个活地狱。 3 EXCLAM **Hell** is used by some people when they are angry or excited, or when they want to emphasize what they are saying. This use could cause offense. 该死 [EMPHASIS] ❑ *"Hell, no!" the doctor snapped.* "该死，不！"医生厉声说。

2 **hell** ♦◇◇ /hɛl/ 1 PHRASE You can use **as hell** after adjectives or some adverbs to emphasize the adjective or adverb. 很 [INFORMAL, EMPHASIS] ❑ *The men might be armed, but they sure as hell weren't trained.* 这些男人也许被武装了，但他们当时确确实实没受训练。 2 PHRASE If someone does something **for the hell of it**, or **just for the hell of it**, they do it for fun or for no particular reason. 只是为了好玩 [INFORMAL] ❑ *I started shouting in German, just for the hell of it.* 我当时开始用德语喊叫，只是为了好玩。 3 PHRASE You can use **from hell** after a noun when you are emphasizing that something or someone is extremely unpleasant or evil. 极坏 [INFORMAL, EMPHASIS] ❑ *He's a child from hell.* 他这个孩子坏透了。 4 PHRASE If you tell someone to **go to hell**, you are angrily telling them to go away and leave you alone. 滚开 [INFORMAL, VULGAR, FEELINGS] ❑ *"Well, you can go to hell!"*

He swept out of the room. "行了，滚开！"他大模大样地走出房间。 5 PHRASE If you say that someone can **go to hell**, you are emphasizing angrily that you do not care about them and that they will not stop you doing what you want. 见鬼去吧 [INFORMAL, VULGAR, EMPHASIS] ❑ *Peter can go to hell. It's my money and I'll leave it to who I want.* 让彼得见鬼去吧。那是我的钱，我想留给谁就留给谁。 6 PHRASE If you say that someone **is going hell for leather**, you are emphasizing that they are doing something or are moving very quickly and perhaps carelessly. 飞快地 [INFORMAL, EMPHASIS] ❑ *The first horse often goes hell for leather, hits a few fences but gets away with it.* 第一匹马往往跑得飞快，会撞落几根横杆，但一般不会被罚分。 7 PHRASE Some people say **like hell** to emphasize that they strongly disagree with you or are strongly opposed to what you say. 绝不会 [INFORMAL, EMPHASIS] ❑ *"I'll go myself."—"Like hell you will!"* "我会自己去。"——"可你绝不会！" 8 PHRASE Some people use **like hell** to emphasize how strong an action or quality is. 非常 [INFORMAL, EMPHASIS] ❑ *It hurts like hell.* 这儿非常痛。 9 PHRASE If you say that **all hell breaks loose**, you are emphasizing that a lot of arguing or fighting suddenly starts. 大乱起来 [INFORMAL, EMPHASIS] ❑ *He had an affair, I found out and then all hell broke loose.* 他有了外遇，我发现了，接着便闹翻了天。 10 PHRASE If you talk about **a hell of a lot of** something, or **one hell of a lot of** something, you mean that there is a large amount of it. 许多 [INFORMAL, EMPHASIS] ❑ *The manager took a hell of a lot of money out of the club.* 经理从夜总会拿走了许多钱。 11 PHRASE Some people use **a hell of** or **one hell of** to emphasize that something is very good, very bad, or very big. 极度的 [INFORMAL, EMPHASIS] ❑ *Whatever the outcome, it's going to be one hell of a fight.* 不管结果如何，那都将是一场恶战。 12 PHRASE Some people use **the hell out of** for emphasis after verbs such as "scare," "irritate," and "beat." 非常 (用于**scare**，**irritate**，和**beat**等动词之后表强调) [INFORMAL, EMPHASIS] ❑ *I patted the top of her head in the condescending way I knew irritated the hell out of her.* 我以降尊纡贵的姿态拍了她的头顶，知道这会让她气得七窍生烟。 13 PHRASE If you say **there'll be hell to pay**, you are emphasizing that there will be serious trouble. 会有大麻烦 [INFORMAL, EMPHASIS] ❑ *There would be hell to pay when Ferguson and Tony found out about it.* 要是弗格森和托妮发现了这事，那麻烦可就大了。 14 PHRASE To **play hell with** something means to have a bad effect on it or cause great confusion. 造成混乱 [INFORMAL] ❑ *The rain had played hell with business.* 这场雨把事情搞得一团糟。 15 PHRASE People sometimes use **the hell** for emphasis in questions, after words such as "what," "where," and "why," often in order to express anger. 究竟 [INFORMAL, VULGAR, EMPHASIS] ❑ *Where the hell have you been?* 你究竟去了哪里？ 16 PHRASE If you **go through hell**, or if someone **puts** you **through hell**, you have a very difficult or unpleasant time. 经受苦难 [INFORMAL] ❑ *All of you seem to have gone through hell making this record.* 看来在灌制这张唱片时你们经受了重重困难。 17 PHRASE If you say you **hope to hell** or **wish to hell that** something is true, you are emphasizing that you strongly hope or wish it is true. 打心底里盼望 [INFORMAL, EMPHASIS] ❑ *I hope to hell you're right.* 我打心底里希望你是对的。 18 PHRASE You can say **"what the hell"** when you decide to do something in spite of the doubts that you have about it. 不管它 [INFORMAL, FEELINGS] ❑ *What the hell, I thought, at least it will give the lazy old man some exercise.* 不管它，我想，至少这会让那个懒老头活动活动筋骨。 19 PHRASE If you say **"to hell with"** something, you are emphasizing that you do not care about something and that it will not stop you from doing what you want to do. 让…见鬼去 [INFORMAL, EMPHASIS] ❑ *To hell with this, I'm getting out of here.* 让它见鬼去吧，我要离开这里了。

he'll /hɪl, hil/ **He'll** is the usual spoken form of "he will." **he will** 的常用口语形式 ❑ *By the time he's twenty he'll know everyone worth knowing in Washington.* 到20岁时，他会认识华盛顿的每个值得认识的人。

hel·lo ♦◇◇ /hɛloʊ/ (**hellos**) also **hallo, hullo** 1 CONVENTION You say "**Hello**" to someone when you meet them. 你好 (打招呼用语) [FORMULAE] ❑ *Hello, Trish. I won't shake hands, because I'm filthy.* 你好，特里斯。我就不握手了，我的手好脏。 ● N-COUNT **Hello** is also a noun. 招呼 ❑ *The salesperson greeted me with a warm hello.* 那位推销员向我打了个热情的招呼。 2 CONVENTION You say "**Hello**" to someone at the beginning of a telephone conversation, either when you answer the phone or before you give your name or say why you are phoning. 喂 (打电话时的招呼语) [FORMULAE] ❑ *A moment later, Cohen picked up the phone. "Hello?"* 一会儿之后，科恩拿起电话。"喂？" 3 CONVENTION You can call "**hello**" to attract someone's attention. 喂 (用于唤起别人注意) ❑ *Very softly, she called out: "Hello? Who's there?"* 她很轻柔地喊道："喂？谁在那儿？"

▲ **hel·met** /hɛlmɪt/ (**helmets**) N-COUNT A **helmet** is a hat made of a strong material which you wear to protect your head. 头盔
→ see **army, football, skateboarding**

help ♦♦♦ /hɛlp/ (**helps, helping, helped**) 1 V-T/V-I If you **help** someone, you make it easier for them to do something, for example by doing part of the work for them or by giving them advice or money. 帮助 ❑ *He has helped to raise a lot of money.* 他帮着筹到了很多钱。 ❑ *You can of course help by giving them a donation directly.* 你当然可以通过直接给他们一笔捐赠来帮助他们。 ● N-UNCOUNT **Help** is also a noun. 帮助 ❑ *Thanks very much for your help.* 非常感谢你的帮助。 2 V-T/V-I If you say that something **helps**, you mean that it makes something easier to do or get, or that it improves a situation to some extent. 有助于 ❑ *The right style of swimsuit can help to hide, minimize, or emphasize what you want it to.* 款式得当的泳衣有助于按你的意愿掩饰、缩小或突出某些部位。 ❑ *Building more bypasses will help the environment by reducing pollution and traffic jams in towns and cities.* 修建更多的支路将减少城镇中的污染和交通堵塞，从而改善环境。 ❑ *If it would help, I'd be happy to take photographs.* 如果用得着，我很乐意拍照。 3 V-T If you **help** someone go somewhere or move in some way, you give them support so that they can move more easily. 扶持 ❑ *Martin helped Tanya over the rail.* 马丁扶着塔尼娅翻过栏杆。 4 N-SING If you say that someone or something has been **a help** or has been some **help**, you mean that they have helped you to solve a problem. 帮助解决困难的人 (或物) ["a" N, also no det] ❑ *Thank you. You've been a great help already.* 谢谢你。你已经帮了很大的忙。 5 N-UNCOUNT **Help** is action taken to rescue a person who is in danger. You shout "**help!**" when you are in danger in order to attract someone's attention so that they can come and rescue you. 救命 ❑ *He was screaming for help.* 他正尖声叫喊救命。 6 N-UNCOUNT In computing, **help**, or the **help** menu, is a file that gives you information and advice, for example about how to use a particular program. 帮助 [COMPUTING] ❑ *If you get stuck, click on Help.* 如果你碰到困难，请点击"帮助"。 7 V-T If you **help yourself to** something, you serve yourself or you take it for yourself. If someone tells you to **help yourself**, they are telling you politely to serve yourself anything you want or to take anything you want. 自取 ❑ *There's bread on the table. Help yourself.* 桌上有面包。你自己拿吧。 8 V-T If someone **helps themselves to** something, they steal it. 偷 [INFORMAL] ❑ *Two men forced the clerks to flee before helping themselves to the cash register.* 两名男子强迫店员跑开，然后偷走了现金出纳机里的钱。 9 PHRASE If you **can't help** the way you feel or behave, you cannot control it or stop it from happening. You can also say that you **can't help yourself**. 不禁 ❑ *I can't help feeling sorry for the poor man.* 我不禁为这个可怜的男子感到难过。 10 PHRASE If you say you **can't help** thinking something, you are expressing your opinion in an indirect way, often because you think it seems rude. (用以使唐突语气变得婉转) 不免 [VAGUENESS] ❑ *I can't help feeling that this may just be another of her schemes.* 我不免觉得这也许正是她的又一个诡计。 11 PHRASE If someone or something **is of help**, they make a situation easier or better. 有帮助 ❑ *Can I be of help to you?* 我能帮你什么忙吗？
→ see **donor**

▸ **help out** PHRASAL VERB If you **help** someone **out**, you help them by doing some work for them or by lending them some money. 帮助…做事；借钱给 ❑ *I help out with the secretarial work.* 我帮助做秘书工作。 ❑ *All these presents came to more money than I had, and my mother had to help me out.* 所有这些礼物的价钱超过了我所带的钱，母亲只好把钱借给我。

Thesaurus *help* 另参见：

V. aid, assist, support; (*ant.*) hinder 1
N. aid, assistance, guidance, support 1

Word Partnership *help* 的常用搭配：

ADJ. **financial** help, **professional** help 1
V. **ask for** help, **get** help, **need** help, **want to** help 1
try to help 1 3
cry/scream/shout for help 5
can't help **feeling/thinking** *something* 9 10

help·er /hɛlpər/ (**helpers**) N-COUNT A **helper** is a person who helps another person or group with a job they are doing. 助手 ❑ *Phyllis and her helpers provided us with refreshment.* 菲莉丝和她的助手们为我们提供了茶点。

H

help·ful /hɛ̲lpfʊl/ **1** ADJ If you describe someone as **helpful**, you mean that they help you in some way, such as doing part of your job for you or by giving you advice or information. 有帮助的 ❑ *The staff in the branch office are helpful but only have limited information.* 该分支机构的员工是帮忙的，但他们仅有有限的信息。 ● **help·ful·ly** ADV 热心地 [ADV with v] ❑ *They had helpfully provided us with instructions on how to find the house.* 他们已经热心地给我们提供了如何找到那所房子的说明。 **2** ADJ If you describe information or advice as **helpful**, you mean that it is useful for you. 有用的（信息或建议）❑ *The catalog includes helpful information on the different bike models available.* 该目录包含所销售的各种型号自行车的有用信息。 **3** ADJ Something that is **helpful** makes a situation more pleasant or more easy to tolerate. 有助益的 ❑ *It is often helpful to have your spouse in the room when major news is expected.* 在等待重大消息时，让你的配偶在场往往是很有好处的。

help·less /hɛ̲lpləs/ ADJ If you are **helpless**, you do not have the strength or power to do anything useful or to control or protect yourself. 无能为力的 ❑ *Parents often feel helpless, knowing that all the hugs in the world won't stop the tears.* 家长们常常感到无能为力，知道世上所有的拥抱也不能止住眼泪。 ● **help·less·ly** ADV 无能为力地 ❑ *Their son watched helplessly as they vanished beneath the waves.* 他们的儿子无能为力地看着他们消失在海浪之下。 ● **help·less·ness** N-UNCOUNT 无助 ❑ *I remember my feelings of helplessness.* 我记得自己那些无助的感觉。

help·line /hɛ̲lplaɪn/ (**helplines**) N-COUNT A **helpline** is a special telephone service that people can call to get advice about a particular subject. 求助热线 ❑ *...Greece's first helpline for gamblers who need counseling.* …希腊为需要心理咨询的赌徒们开设的首条求助热线。

▲ **hem** /hɛ̲m/ (**hems, hemming, hemmed**) N-COUNT A **hem** on something such as a piece of clothing is an edge that is folded over and stitched down to prevent threads coming loose. The **hem** of a skirt or dress is the bottom edge. 卷边；下摆 ❑ *She lifted the hem of her dress and brushed her knees.* 她拎起她连衣裙的下摆刷了她的两膝。

▸ **hem in** **1** PHRASAL VERB If a place **is hemmed in by** mountains or **by** other places, it is surrounded by them. 环绕 ❑ *The canyon is hemmed in by towering walls of rock.* 峡谷四周环绕着高耸的岩壁。 **2** PHRASAL VERB If someone **is hemmed in** or if someone **hems** them **in**, they are prevented from moving or changing, for example because they are surrounded by people or obstacles. 限制 ❑ *The company's competitors complain that they are hemmed in by rigid legal contracts.* 该公司的竞争对手们抱怨他们受到僵化的法律合同的限制。

Word Link *sphere ≈ ball : atmosphere, hemisphere, sphere*

★ **hemi·sphere** /hɛ̲mɪsfɪər/ (**hemispheres**) N-COUNT A **hemisphere** is one half of the earth. 半球 ❑ *...the depletion of the ozone layer in the northern hemisphere.* …北半球臭氧层的消耗。
→ see **globe, solid**

hemo·philia /hi̲məfɪ̲liə/ N-UNCOUNT **Hemophilia** is a medical condition in which a person's blood does not thicken or clot properly when they are injured, so they continue bleeding. 血友病

hemo·phili·ac /hi̲məfɪ̲liæk/ (**hemophiliacs**) N-COUNT A **hemophiliac** is a person who suffers from hemophilia. 血友病患者 ❑ *...a hemophiliac who contracted the AIDS virus through a blood transfusion.* …一位通过一次输血而感染上艾滋病毒的血友病患者。

hem·or·rhage /hɛ̲mərɪdʒ/ (**hemorrhages, hemorrhaging, hemorrhaged**) **1** N-VAR A **hemorrhage** is serious bleeding inside a person's body. 严重内出血 ❑ *Shortly after his admission into the hospital he had a massive brain hemorrhage and died.* 他住进医院不久，因脑部大量内出血而去世了。 **2** V-I If someone **is hemorrhaging**, there is serious bleeding inside their body. 内出血 ❑ *I hemorrhaged badly after the birth of all three of my sons.* 我把3个儿子都生下来之后，严重内出血。 ● **hem·or·rhag·ing** N-UNCOUNT 内出血 ❑ *A post mortem showed he died from shock and hemorrhaging.* 一份尸检表明他死于休克和内出血。

hen /hɛ̲n/ (**hens**) N-COUNT A **hen** is a female chicken. People often keep hens in order to eat or sell their eggs. 母鸡

hence /hɛ̲ns/ **1** ADV You use **hence** to indicate that the statement you are about to make is a consequence of what you have just said. 因此 [ADV cl/group] [FORMAL] ❑ *The trade imbalance is likely to rise again in 2007. Hence a new set of policy actions will be required soon.* 贸易不平衡在2007年可能会再度上扬。因此需要很快采取一系列新的政策行动。 **2** ADV You use **hence** in expressions such as "**several years hence**" or "**six months hence**" to refer to a time in the future, especially a long time in the future. 此后 [amount ADV] [FORMAL] ❑ *The gases that may be warming the planet will have their main effect many years hence.* 这些可能正在使行星变暖的气体，其重要影响将在许多年之后显现。

★ **hence·forth** /hɛ̲nsfɔ̲rθ/ ADV **Henceforth** means from this or that time onward. 从此以后 [ADV with cl] [FORMAL] ❑ *Henceforth all branches of the naval officer corps were equal to one another.* 从此以后海军军官团的各个分支都相互平等。

Word Link *itis ≈ inflammation : arthritis, hepatitis, meningitis*

hepa·ti·tis /hɛ̲pətaɪ̲tɪs/ N-UNCOUNT **Hepatitis** is a serious disease which affects the liver. 肝炎

her ♦♦♦ /hər, STRONG hɜr/

Her is a third person singular pronoun. **Her** is used as the object of a verb or a preposition. **Her** is also a possessive determiner.

1 PRON-SING You use **her** to refer to a woman, girl, or female animal. 她 [V PRON, prep PRON] ❑ *I went in the room and told her I had something to say to her.* 我走进房间，告诉她我有话要对她说。 ● DET **Her** is also a possessive determiner. 她的 ❑ *Liz traveled around the world for a year with her boyfriend James.* 莉兹跟她的男友詹姆斯到世界各地旅行了一年。 **2** PRON-SING In written English, **her** is sometimes used to refer to a person without saying whether that person is a man or a woman. Some people dislike this use and prefer to use "him or her" or "them." 她（有时在无需说明性别的情况下指人）[V PRON, prep PRON] ❑ *Talk to your baby, play games, and show her how much you enjoy her company.* 跟你的婴儿谈话，玩游戏，向她表明你是多么喜欢与她在一起。 ● DET **Her** is also a possessive determiner. 她的 ❑ *The non-drinking, non-smoking model should do nothing to risk her reputation.* 这名烟酒不沾的女模特儿不应该做任何对她的名誉不利的事情。 **3** PRON-SING **Her** is sometimes used to refer to a country or nation. 她（有时用以指国家或民族）● DET **Her** is also a possessive determiner. 她的 [V PRON, prep PRON] [FORMAL or WRITTEN] ❑ *America and her partners are helping to rebuild roads and bridges and buildings.* 美国及其伙伴正帮助重建道路、桥梁和楼房。 **4** PRON-SING People sometimes use **her** to refer to a car, machine, or ship. 她（有时用以指小汽车、机器或船）[V PRON, prep PRON] ❑ *Kemp got out of his truck. "Just fill her up, thanks."* 肯普下了卡车。“请给她加满油，谢谢。” ● DET **Her** is also a possessive determiner. 她的 ❑ *This dramatic photograph was taken from Carpathia's deck by one of her passengers.* 这张戏剧化的照片是由卡帕西亚号的一名乘客在甲板上拍下的。

▲ **her·ald** /hɛ̲rəld/ (**heralds, heralding, heralded**) **1** V-T Something that **heralds** a future event or situation is a sign that it is going to happen or appear. 预示…的来临 [FORMAL] ❑ *...the sultry evening that heralded the end of the baking hot summer.* …预示着炙热的夏天即将结束的那个闷热的夜晚。 **2** N-COUNT Something that is a **herald of** a future event or situation is a sign that it is going to happen or appear. 预兆 [FORMAL] ❑ *I welcome the report as a herald of more freedom.* 我欢迎这份报告，认为它预示着更多的自由。 **3** V-T If an important event or action **is heralded by** people, announcements are made about it so that it is publicly known and expected. 预告；宣传 [usu passive] [FORMAL] ❑ *Janet Jackson's new album has been heralded by a massive media campaign.* 珍妮特·杰克逊的新唱片已在媒体上进行了大规模的宣传。

Word Link *herb ≈ grass : herb, herbal, herbivorous*

★ **herb** /ɜrb/ (**herbs**) N-COUNT A **herb** is a plant whose leaves are used in cooking to add flavor to food, or as a medicine. （调味或药用的）香草 ❑ *...beautiful, fragrant herbs such as basil and coriander.* …罗勒和芫荽等美丽芬芳的香草。

herb·al /ɜ̲rbᵊl/ ADJ **Herbal** means made from or using herbs. 香草的；使用药草的 [ADJ n] ❑ *...herbal remedies for colds.* …感冒的草药疗法。

Word Link *vor ≈ eating : herbivorous, savory, voracious*

herbivorous /hɜrbɪ̲vərəs, ɜr-/ ADJ **Herbivorous** animals only eat plants. 食草的

herd /hɜ̲rd/ (**herds, herding, herded**) **1** N-COUNT A **herd** is a large group of animals of one kind that live together. 兽群；畜群 ❑ *Chobe is also renowned for its large herds of elephant and buffalo.* 乔贝还以其大群的大象和水牛而闻名。 **2** N-SING If you say that someone has joined **the herd** or follows **the herd**, you are criticizing them because you think that they behave just like everyone else and do not think for themselves. （缺乏独立思想的）群众 [DISAPPROVAL] ❑ *They are individuals; they will not follow the herd.* 他们是独立的个体；

h

他们不愿随大流。 **3** V-T If you **herd** people somewhere, you make them move there in a group. 把…集中赶往 ❑ *He began to herd the prisoners out.* 他开始把囚犯集中起来赶出去。 **4** V-T If you **herd** animals, you make them move along as a group. 驱赶（畜群） ❑ *Stefano used a motorcycle to herd the sheep.* 斯蒂芬诺骑一辆摩托车驱赶羊群。

here ♦♦♦ /hɪər/ **1** ADV You use **here** when you are referring to the place where you are. 在这里 ❑ *I'm here all by myself and I know I'm going to get lost.* 我独自一人在这儿，我知道我会迷路的。 ❑ *Well, I can't stand here chatting all day.* 唉，我不能一整天都站在这里闲聊。 **2** ADV You use **here** when you are pointing toward a place that is near you, in order to draw someone else's attention to it. 在（所指向的）这里 ❑ *...if you will just sign here.* …如果你愿意就在这里签字。 **3** ADV You use **here** in order to indicate that the person or thing that you are talking about is near you or is being held by you. 在身边 ❑ *My friend here writes for radio.* 我身边这位朋友为电台撰稿。 **4** ADV If you say that you are **here to** do something, that is your role or function. 来此… [“be” ADV to-inf] ❑ *I'm here to help you.* 我是来此帮助你的。 **5** ADV You use **here** in order to draw attention to something or someone who has just arrived in the place where you are, or to draw attention to the place you have just arrived at. （通报用语）…来了 ❑ *"Here's the taxi," she said politely.* “出租车来了，”她礼貌地说。 **6** ADV You use **here** to refer to a particular point or stage of a situation or subject that you have come to or that you are dealing with. 在这一点上 ❑ *It's here that we come up against the difference of approach.* 正是在这一点上我们遇到方法上的分歧。 **7** ADV You use **here** to refer to a period of time, a situation, or an event that is present or happening now. 出现了 ❑ *Economic recovery is here.* 经济复苏现在开始了。 **8** ADV You use **here** at the beginning of a sentence in order to draw attention to something or to introduce something. （用于句首以引起注意或介绍）这就是 [ADV “be” n/wh] ❑ *Now here's what I want you to do.* 听着，这就是我想让你做的事。 **9** ADV You use **here** when you are offering or giving something to someone. 给 [ADV “be” n] ❑ *Here's your coffee, just the way you like it.* 给，这是你的咖啡，按你口味调的。 ❑ *Here are some letters I want you to sign.* 给，我这有些信需要你签字。 **10** CONVENTION You say “**here we are**” when you have just found something that you have been looking for. 找到了 ❑ *I rummaged through the drawers and came up with Amanda's folder. "Here we are."* 我翻遍了抽屉，终于发现了阿曼达的活页夹。“找到了。” **11** CONVENTION You say “**here goes**” when you are about to do or say something difficult or unpleasant. 这就开始了（表示准备做或说困难或不愉快的事） ❑ *Dr. Culver nervously muttered "Here goes," and gave the little girl an injection.* 卡尔弗医生紧张地嘀咕了一句“要打了啊”，接着就给那小女孩打了一针。 **12** PHRASE You use expressions such as “**here we go**” and “**here we go again**” in order to indicate that something is happening again in the way that you expected, especially something unpleasant. 又来了 [INFORMAL] ❑ *"Police! Open up!"—"Oh well," I thought, "here we go."* “警察！开门！”——“噢，天哪，”我想，“又来了。” **13** PHRASE You use **here and now** to emphasize that something is happening at the present time, rather than in the future or past, or that you would like it to happen at the present time. 眼下 [EMPHASIS] ❑ *I'm a practicing physician trying to help people here and now.* 我眼下是一名尽力帮助别人的专业医师。 **14** PHRASE If something happens **here and there**, it happens in several different places. 在各处 ❑ *I do a bit of teaching here and there.* 我在各处教些书。 **15** CONVENTION You use expressions such as “**here's to us**” and “**here's to your new job**” before drinking a toast in order to wish someone success or happiness. （祝酒用语）为…干杯 [FORMULAE] ❑ *He raised his glass. "Here's to neighbors."* 他举起酒杯。“为邻居们干杯！”

▲**here·by** /hɪərbaɪ/ ADV You use **hereby** when officially or formally saying what you are doing. 在此 [ADV before v] [FORMAL] ❑ *I hereby consent for my son/daughter to take this personality test.* 我在此同意我儿子/女儿接受此个性测验。

▲**he·redi·tary** /hɪrɛdɪtɛri/ **1** ADJ A **hereditary** characteristic or illness is passed on to a child from its parents before it is born. 遗传（性）的 ❑ *Cystic fibrosis is the commonest fatal hereditary disease.* 囊性纤维化是最常见的致命性遗传疾病。 **2** ADJ A title or position in society that is **hereditary** is one that is passed on as a right from parent to child. 世袭的 ❑ *The position of the head of state is hereditary.* 国家元首的职位是世袭的。

her·esy /hɛrɪsi/ (**heresies**) **1** N-VAR **Heresy** is a belief or action that most people think is wrong, because it disagrees with beliefs that are generally accepted. 异端邪说 ❑ *It might be considered heresy to suggest such a notion.* 提出这样的见解可能会被认为是异端邪说。 **2** N-VAR **Heresy** is a belief or action which seriously disagrees with the principles of a particular religion. 异教 ❑ *He said it was a heresy to suggest that women should not conduct services.* 他说认为女性不应该主持礼拜仪式是一种异端邪说。

★**her·it·age** /hɛrɪtɪdʒ/ (**heritages**) N-VAR A country's **heritage** is all the qualities, traditions, or features of life there that have continued over many years and have been passed on from one generation to another. 遗产；传统 ❑ *The historic building is as much part of our heritage as the paintings.* 这座历史建筑和这些绘画作品一样也是留给我们的遗产的组成部分。

▲**her·mit** /hɜrmɪt/ (**hermits**) N-COUNT A **hermit** is a person who lives alone, away from people and society. 隐士 ❑ *I've spent the past ten years living like a hermit.* 我过去10年里过着隐士般的生活。

her·nia /hɜrniə/ (**hernias**) N-VAR A **hernia** is a medical condition which is often caused by strain or injury. It results in one of your internal organs sticking through a weak point in the surrounding tissue. （脏器的）疝

hero ♦◇◇ /hɪəroʊ/ (**heroes**) **1** N-COUNT The **hero** of a book, play, movie, or story is the main male character, who usually has good qualities. 男主人公 ❑ *The hero of Doctor Zhivago dies in 1929.* 《日瓦戈医生》的男主人公于1929年去世。 **2** N-COUNT A **hero** is someone, especially a man, who has done something brave, new, or good, and who is therefore greatly admired by a lot of people. 英雄 ❑ *He called Mr. Mandela a hero who had inspired millions.* 他称曼德拉先生是一个曾激励千百万人的英雄。 **3** N-COUNT If you describe someone as your **hero**, you mean that you admire them a great deal, usually because of a particular quality or skill that they have. 偶像 ❑ *My boyhood hero was Kit Carson.* 我孩提时的偶像是基特·卡森。
→ see Word Web: **hero**
→ see **myth**

he·ro·ic /hɪroʊɪk/ (**heroics**) **1** ADJ If you describe a person or their actions as **heroic**, you admire them because they show extreme bravery. 英勇的 ❑ *His heroic deeds were celebrated in every corner of India.* 他的英勇事迹在印度的每个角落被传颂。 ● **he·roi·cal·ly** /hɪroʊɪkli/ ADV 英勇地 [ADV with v] ❑ *He had acted heroically during the liner's evacuation.* 他在疏散客轮乘客的过程中表现得很英勇。 **2** ADJ If you describe an action or event as **heroic**, you admire it because it involves great effort or determination to succeed. 艰苦卓绝的 [APPROVAL] ❑ *The company has made heroic efforts at cost reduction.*

Word Web **hero**

Odysseus is a **hero** from Greek **mythology**. He is a warrior. He shows great courage in battle. He faces many **dangers** and temptations. However he knows he must return home after the Trojan War*. During his **epic** journey home, Odysseus faces many trials. He must survive wild storms at sea and fight a monster. He must also resist the temptations of the Sirens and outwit the goddess Circe*. At home Penelope, Odysseus' wife, **defends** their home and **protects** their son. She remains **loyal** and **brave** through many trials. She is the **heroine** of the story.

Trojan War: a legendary war between Greece and Troy.
Circe: a Greek goddess.

Odysseus saves his men from the Cyclops.

该公司在降低成本方面进行了艰苦卓绝的努力。● **he·roi·cal·ly** ADV 艰苦卓绝地 ❑ *Single parents cope heroically in doing the job of two people.* 单身父母做着两个人的工作，非常艰苦也非常有毅力。 3 ADJ **Heroic** means being or relating to the hero or heroine of a story. 主人公的 ❑ *...the book's central, heroic figure.* …书中的中心主角人物。 4 N-PLURAL **Heroics** are actions involving bravery, courage, or determination. 英雄壮举 ❑ *...the man whose aerial heroics helped save the helicopter pilot.* …那个以空中的英雄壮举拯救直升机飞行员的人。 5 N-PLURAL If you describe someone's actions or plans as **heroics**, you think that they are foolish or dangerous because they are too difficult or brave for the situation in which they occur. 逞能行为 [SPOKEN, DISAPPROVAL] ❑ *He said his advice was: "No heroics, stay within the law."* 他说他的意见是："不要有逞能行为，要依法办事。"

hero·in /hɛroʊɪn/ N-UNCOUNT **Heroin** is a powerful drug which some people take for pleasure, but which they can become addicted to. 海洛因

▲ **hero·ine** /hɛroʊɪn/ (**heroines**) 1 N-COUNT The **heroine** of a book, play, movie, or story is the main female character, who usually has good qualities. 女主人公 ❑ *The heroine is a senior TV executive.* 女主人公是一位电视台高级主管。 2 N-COUNT A **heroine** is a woman who has done something brave, new, or good, and who is therefore greatly admired by a lot of people. 女英雄 ❑ *The national heroine of the day was Xing Fen, winner of the first gold medal of the Games.* 当时的民族女英雄是在亚运会上夺得第一块金牌的邢芬。 3 N-COUNT If you describe a woman as your **heroine**, you mean that you admire her greatly, usually because of a particular quality or skill that she has. 女性偶像 ❑ *My heroine was Elizabeth Taylor.* 我崇拜的女性是伊丽莎白・泰勒。
→ see **hero**

hero·ism /hɛroʊɪzəm/ N-UNCOUNT **Heroism** is great courage and bravery. 英雄气概 ❑ *...individual acts of heroism.* …个人英雄主义行为。

her·ring /hɛrɪŋ/ (**herring, herrings**) N-VAR A **herring** is a long silver-colored fish. Herring live in large groups in the ocean. 鲱(鱼) ❑ *...a shoal of herring.* …一群鲱鱼。● N-UNCOUNT **Herring** is a piece of this fish eaten as food. 鲱鱼肉 ❑ *...a can of herring.* …鲱鱼罐头。

hers /hɜrz/

> **Hers** is a third person possessive pronoun.

1 PRON-POSS You use **hers** to indicate that something belongs or relates to a woman, girl, or female animal. 她的(东西) ❑ *His hand as it shook hers was warm and firm.* 当他握住她的手时，他的手温暖而有力。 ❑ *Professor Camm was a great friend of hers.* 卡姆教授是她的一位挚友。 2 PRON-POSS In written English, **hers** is sometimes used to refer to a person without saying whether that person is a man or a woman. Some people dislike this use and prefer to use "his or hers" or "theirs." (书面英语中泛指人) 她的；他的 ❑ *The author can report other people's results which more or less agree with hers.* 作者可以报道与自己的观点或多或少一致的别人的成果。

her·self ♦♦♦ /hərsɛlf/

> **Herself** is a third person singular reflexive pronoun. **Herself** is used when the object of a verb or preposition refers to the same person as the subject of the verb, except in meaning 3.

1 PRON-REFL You use **herself** to refer to a woman, girl, or female animal. 她自己(指女性或雌性动物) [V PRON, prep PRON] ❑ *She let herself out of the room.* 她从房间里退了出来。 ❑ *Jennifer believes she will move out on her own when she is financially able to support herself.* 珍妮弗相信，当自己能够在经济上独立的时候她就会搬出去单住。 2 PRON-REFL In written English, **herself** is sometimes used to refer to a person without saying whether that person is a man or a woman. Some people dislike this use and prefer to use "himself or herself" or "themselves." (书面英语中泛指人) 她自己；他自己 ❑ *How can anyone believe stories for which she feels herself to be in no way responsible?* 那些话连她本人都觉得是自己不负责任地瞎编的，人们怎么会相信它们呢？ 3 PRON-REFL-EMPH You use **herself** to emphasize the person or thing that you are referring to. **Herself** is sometimes used instead of "her" as the object of a verb or preposition. (用以加强语气) 她本人 [EMPHASIS] ❑ *She herself was not a keen gardener.* 她本人就不是一个热衷于园艺的人。

he's /hiz, STRONG hiz/ **He's** is the usual spoken form of "he is" or "he has," especially when "has" is an auxiliary verb. **he is**或**he has**的口语形式，尤用于**has**为助动词的情况 ❑ *He's working maybe twenty-five hours a week.* 他一星期大约工作二十五个小时。

★ **hesi·tant** /hɛzɪtᵊnt/ ADJ If you are **hesitant about** doing something, you do not do it quickly or immediately, usually because you are uncertain, embarrassed, or worried. 迟疑不决的 ❑ *She was hesitant about coming forward with her story.* 她迟迟不愿说出自己的经历。● **hesi·tan·cy** /hɛzɪtənsi/ N-UNCOUNT 迟疑 ❑ *A trace of hesitancy showed in Dr. Stockton's eyes.* 一丝迟疑出现在斯托克顿医生的双眼中。● **hesi·tant·ly** ADV 迟疑地 [ADV with v] ❑ *"Would you do me a favor?" she asked hesitantly.* "你能帮我一个忙吗？"她迟疑地问。

hesi·tate /hɛzɪteɪt/ (**hesitates, hesitating, hesitated**) 1 V-I If you **hesitate**, you do not speak or act for a short time, usually because you are uncertain, embarrassed, or worried about what you are going to say or do. 迟疑 ❑ *The telephone rang. Catherine hesitated, debating whether to answer it.* 电话响了。凯瑟琳迟疑着，考虑是否接听。● **hesi·ta·tion** /hɛzɪteɪʃᵊn/ N-VAR (**hesitations**) 迟疑 ❑ *Asked if he would go back, Mr. Searle said after some hesitation, "I'll have to think about that."* 当被问及他是否愿意回去时，瑟尔先生迟疑了一下后说："我得考虑一下。" 2 V-T If you **hesitate to** do something, you delay doing it or are unwilling to do it, usually because you are not certain it would be right. If you do not **hesitate to** do something, you do it immediately. 迟疑；不愿意 ❑ *Some parents hesitate to take these steps because they suspect that their child is exaggerating.* 一些家长迟迟不肯采取这些措施，因为他们怀疑自己的孩子在夸大其词。 3 V-T You can use **hesitate** in expressions such as "**don't hesitate to call me**" or "**don't hesitate to contact us**" when you are telling someone that they should do something as soon as it needs to be done and should not worry about disturbing other people. 迟疑 (仅用于否定祈使句) [only imper, with neg] ❑ *In the event of difficulties, please do not hesitate to contact our Customer Service Department.* 如有困难，请不要迟疑，与我们的客户服务部联系。

> **Thesaurus** *hesitate* 另参见：
> V. falter, pause, wait 1 2

hesi·ta·tion /hɛzɪteɪʃᵊn/ (**hesitations**) 1 N-VAR **Hesitation** is an unwillingness to do something, or a delay in doing it, because you are uncertain, worried, or embarrassed about it. 迟疑；不愿意 ❑ *He promised there would be no more hesitations in pursuing reforms.* 他保证在实行改革时不会再有迟疑。 2 → see also **hesitate** 3 PHRASE If you say that you **have no hesitation in** doing something, you are emphasizing that you will do it immediately or willingly because you are certain that it is the right thing to do. 毫不犹豫 [EMPHASIS] ❑ *The board said it had no hesitation in unanimously rejecting the offer.* 董事会说它毫不犹豫地一致否决了那项提议。 4 PHRASE If you say that someone does something **without hesitation**, you are emphasizing that they do it immediately and willingly. 毫不犹豫地 [EMPHASIS] ❑ *The great majority of players would, of course, sign the contract without hesitation.* 绝大多数运动员当然会毫不犹豫地签这份合同。

hetero·geneous /hɛtərədʒiniəs, -dʒinyəs/ ADJ A **heterogeneous** group consists of many different types of things or people. 由很多种类组成的 [usu ADJ n] [FORMAL] ❑ *...a rather heterogeneous collection of studies from diverse origins.* …来自各种不同渠道的一系列种类繁多的研究。

hetero·sex·ual /hɛtəroʊsɛkʃuəl/ (**heterosexuals**) 1 ADJ A **heterosexual** relationship is a sexual relationship between a man and a woman. 异性间的 ❑ *An increasing number of people are becoming infected with HIV through heterosexual sex.* 越来越多的人正通过异性间的性行为感染上艾滋病病毒。 2 ADJ Someone who is **heterosexual** is sexually attracted to people of the opposite sex. 异性恋的 ❑ *It doesn't matter whether people are heterosexual or homosexual.* 一个人是异性恋还是同性恋无关紧要。● N-COUNT **Heterosexual** is also a noun. 异性恋者 ❑ *In Denmark the age of consent is fifteen for both heterosexuals and homosexuals.* 在丹麦异性恋者和同性恋者的合法性交年龄都是15岁。
● **hetero·sexu·al·ity** /hɛtəroʊsɛkʃuælɪti/ N-UNCOUNT 异性恋 ❑ *...a challenge to the assumption that heterosexuality was "normal."* …对异性恋"是正常的"说法的挑战。

hexa·gon /hɛksəgɒn/ (**hexagons**) N-COUNT A **hexagon** is a shape that has six straight sides. 六边形
→ see **shape**

hex·ago·nal /hɛksægənᵊl/ ADJ A **hexagonal** object or shape has six straight sides. 六边形的

hey /heɪ/ 1 CONVENTION In informal situations, you say or shout "**hey**" to attract someone's attention, or to show surprise, interest, or annoyance. 嘿 (用在非正式场合以引起注意或表示惊讶、

感兴趣或恼怒等) [FEELINGS] ❑ *"Hey! Look out!" shouted Patty.* "嘿！当心！"帕蒂喊道。 **2** CONVENTION In informal situations, you can say "**hey**" to greet someone. 嘿 (非正式场合中用于打招呼) ❑ *She watched as he smiled, opened his mouth, and said, "Hey, Kate."* 她见他笑了笑，张开嘴说道："嘿，凯特。"

hey·day /heɪdeɪ/ N-SING Someone's **heyday** is the time when they are most powerful, successful, or popular. 全盛时期 ❑ *In its heyday, the studio's boast was that it had more stars than there are in heaven.* 该制片厂吹嘘，它在鼎盛时期拥有的明星比天上的星星还多。

hi ♦◇◇ /haɪ/ CONVENTION In informal situations, you say "**hi**" to greet someone. 嗨 (非正式场合中用于打招呼) [FORMULAE] ❑ *"Hi, Liz," she said shyly.* "嗨，利兹，"她羞涩地说。

★ **hi·ber·nate** /haɪbərneɪt/ (**hibernates, hibernating, hibernated**) V-I Animals that **hibernate** spend the winter in a state like a deep sleep. 冬眠 ❑ *Dormice hibernate from October to May.* 睡鼠从10月到5月冬眠。

hic·cup /hɪkʌp/ (**hiccups, hiccuping** or **hiccupping, hiccuped** or **hiccupped**) also **hiccough** **1** N-COUNT You can refer to a small problem or difficulty as a **hiccup**, especially if it does not last very long or is easily corrected. 小难题 ❑ *A recent sales hiccup is nothing to panic about.* 最近销售上出的小问题用不着惊慌。 **2** N-UNCOUNT When you have **hiccups**, you make repeated sharp sounds in your throat, often because you have been eating or drinking too quickly. 嗝 [also "the" N] ❑ *A baby may frequently get a bout of hiccups during or soon after a feeding.* 婴儿在进食时或进食后常常会打一阵嗝儿。 **3** V-I When you **hiccup**, you make repeated sharp sounds in your throat. 打嗝 ❑ *She was still hiccuping from the egg she had swallowed whole.* 她还在因为先前整个吞下鸡蛋而打嗝儿。

hid /hɪd/ **Hid** is the past tense of **hide**. **hide**的过去式

hid·den /hɪdᵊn/ **1** **Hidden** is the past participle of **hide**. **hide**的过去分词 **2** ADJ **Hidden** facts, feelings, activities, or problems are not easy to notice or discover. 隐藏的 ❑ *Under all the innocent fun, there are hidden dangers, especially for children.* 在所有无害的娱乐节目背后都有隐患，对儿童来说尤其如此。 **3** ADJ A **hidden** place is difficult to find. 隐秘的 ❑ *As you descend, suddenly you see at last the hidden waterfall.* 你往下走，最终会突然发现那个隐秘的瀑布。

hid·den agen·da (**hidden agendas**) N-COUNT If you say that someone has a **hidden agenda**, you are criticizing them because you think they are secretly trying to achieve or cause a particular thing, while they appear to be doing something else. 不可告人的目的 [DISAPPROVAL] ❑ *He accused foreign nations of having a hidden agenda to harm French influence.* 他指责一些国家怀有不可告人的目的，企图损害法国的影响力。

hide ♦◇◇ /haɪd/ (**hides, hiding, hid, hidden**) **1** V-T If you **hide** something or someone, you put them in a place where they cannot easily be seen or found. 把…藏起来 ❑ *He hid the bicycle in the hawthorn hedge.* 他把自行车藏进了山楂树树篱里。 **2** V-T/V-I If you **hide** or if you **hide yourself**, you go somewhere where you cannot easily be seen or found. 躲藏 ❑ *At their approach the little boy scurried and hid.* 当他们走近时，那个小男孩急忙跑开躲了起来。 **3** V-T If you **hide** your face, you press your face against something or cover your face with something, so that people cannot see it. 捂住；把 (脸) 埋在 ❑ *She hid her face under the collar of his jacket and started to cry.* 她把脸埋在他的外套领子下哭了起来。 **4** V-T If you **hide** what you feel or know, you keep it a secret, so that no one knows about it. 掩饰 ❑ *Lee tried to hide his excitement.* 李努力掩饰内心的激动。 **5** V-T If something **hides** an object, it covers it and prevents it from being seen. 遮盖 ❑ *The man's heavy mustache hid his upper lip completely.* 那位男士浓密的八字胡完全遮住了他的上嘴唇。 **6** N-VAR A **hide** is the skin of a large animal such as a cow, horse, or elephant, which can be used for making leather. 兽皮 ❑ *...the process of tanning animal hides.* …鞣制兽皮的过程。 **7** → see also **hidden, hiding**

Thesaurus *hide* 另参见：

V. camouflage, conceal, cover, lock up **1** **5**

Word Partnership *hide* 的常用搭配：

ADV. **nowhere to** hide **1** **2**
V. **attempt/try to** hide **1** **2** **4**
run and hide **2**
N. hide ***your* face** **3**
hide ***your* disappointment/fear/feelings/tears,**
hide **a fact/secret** **4**

▲ **hid·eous** /hɪdiəs/ **1** ADJ If you say that someone or something is **hideous**, you mean that they are very ugly or unattractive. 极丑的 ❑ *She saw a hideous face at the window and screamed.* 她在窗口看到一张奇丑无比的脸，尖叫了起来。 **2** ADJ You can describe an event, experience, or action as **hideous** when you mean that it is very unpleasant, painful, or difficult to bear. 非常可怕的；令人难以忍受的 ❑ *His family was subjected to a hideous attack by the gang.* 他一家子遭到了匪帮的可怕袭击。

hid·eous·ly /hɪdiəsli/ **1** ADV You use **hideously** to emphasize that something is very ugly or unattractive. 可怕地 [EMPHASIS] ❑ *Everything is hideously ugly.* 一切都丑陋得可怕。 **2** ADV You can use **hideously** to emphasize that something is very unpleasant or unacceptable. 令人无法接受地 [ADV adj/-ed] [EMPHASIS] ❑ *...a hideously complex program.* …一个复杂得要命的程序。

hid·ing /haɪdɪŋ/ N-UNCOUNT If someone is **in hiding**, they have secretly gone somewhere where they cannot be seen or found. 躲藏 (处) ❑ *Gray is thought to be in hiding near the France/Italy border.* 格雷被认为藏在法国和意大利的边境附近。

★ **hi·er·ar·chi·cal** /haɪərɑrkɪkᵊl/ ADJ A **hierarchical** system or organization is one in which people have different ranks or positions, depending on how important they are. 等级制度的 ❑ *...the traditional hierarchical system of military organization.* …军事组织内的传统等级制度。

Word Link *arch* ≈ *rule* : *anarchy, hierarchy, monarch*

★ **hi·er·ar·chy** /haɪərɑrki/ (**hierarchies**) **1** N-VAR A **hierarchy** is a system of organizing people into different ranks or levels of importance, for example in society or in a company. 等级制度 ❑ *Like most other American companies with a rigid hierarchy, workers and managers had strictly defined duties.* 像大多数其他等级制度森严的美国公司一样，工人和管理人员都有严格界定的职责。 **2** N-COUNT-COLL The **hierarchy** of an organization is the group of people who manage and control it. 统治集团 ❑ *The church hierarchy today feels the church should reflect the social and political realities of the country.* 教会统治集团如今感到教会应该反映国家的社会现实和政治现实。

hi-fi /haɪ faɪ/ (**hi-fis**) N-VAR A **hi-fi** is a set of equipment on which you play CDs and tapes, and which produces stereo sound of very good quality. 高保真度音响设备 [OLD-FASHIONED]

Word Link *er* ≈ *more* : *colder, higher, larger*

Word Link *est* ≈ *most* : *coldest, highest, largest*

high ♦♦♦ /haɪ/ (**higher, highest, highs**) **1** ADJ Something that is **high** extends a long way from the bottom to the top when it is upright. You do not use **high** to describe people, animals, or plants. 高的 (不用于形容人、动物或植物) ❑ *...a house with a high wall all around it.* …四周围着高墙的房子。 ❑ *Mount Marcy is the highest mountain in the Adirondacks.* 马西山是阿迪朗达克山脉中最高的山。 ● ADV **High** is also an adverb. 高高地 [ADV after V] ❑ *...wagons packed high with bureaus, bedding, and cooking pots.* …高高地堆放着衣柜、寝具和炊具的四轮运货马车。

> The word you should use to describe people, animals, or plants is **tall**, not "high". ❑ *She was rather tall for a woman.* **Tall** is also used to describe buildings such as skyscrapers, and other things whose height is much greater than their width. ❑ *...tall pine trees. ...a tall glass vase.*

2 ADJ You use **high** to talk or ask about how much something upright measures from the bottom to the top. 高度为…的 ❑ *...an elegant bronze horse only nine inches high.* …一尊高度仅为9英寸的精致的青铜马。 ❑ *The grass in the yard was a foot high.* 院子里的草有1英尺高。 **3** ADJ If something is **high**, it is a long way above the ground, above sea level, or above a person or thing. (与地面、海平面、其他人或物相比而言) 高的 ❑ *I looked down from the high window.* 我从高高的窗户往下看。 ❑ *The sun was high in the sky, blazing down on us.* 太阳高挂在空中，朝我们发出耀眼的光芒。 ● ADV **High** is also an adverb. 高高地 [ADV after V] ❑ *...being able to run faster or jump higher than other people.* …能比其他人跑得更快或跳得更高。 ● PHRASE If something is **high up**, it is a long way above the ground, above sea level, or above a person or thing. (与地面、海平面、其他人或物相比而言) 高的 ❑ *His farm was high up in the hills.* 他的农场在山上的高处。 **4** ADJ You can use **high** to indicate that something is great in amount, degree, or intensity. (数量、程度或强度) 高的 ❑ *The European country with the highest birth rate is Ireland.* 出生率最高的欧洲国家是爱尔兰。

❏ *Official reports said casualties were high.* 官方报道称人员伤亡很大。 ● ADV **High** is also an adverb. 高地 [ADV after v] ❏ *He expects the unemployment figures to rise even higher in coming months.* 他预计失业人数在未来的几个月中会继续上升。 ● PHRASE You can use phrases such as "**in the high 80s**" to indicate that a number or level is, for example, more than 85 but not as much as 90. 中间偏上 5 ADJ If a food or other substance is **high in** a particular ingredient, it contains a large amount of that ingredient. (含量) 高的 [v-link ADJ "in" n] ❏ *Don't indulge in rich sauces, fried food, and thick pastry as these are high in fat.* 不要吃太多油腻的调味汁、油炸食品和厚油酥点心，因为这些食品脂肪含量很高。 6 N-COUNT If something reaches a **high of** a particular amount or degree, that is the greatest it has ever been. 最高点 [oft N "of" amount] ❏ *Traffic from Jordan to Iraq is down to a dozen loaded trucks a day, compared with a high of 200 a day.* 从约旦到伊拉克的车辆少的时候1天有一打满载的卡车，高峰时一天则有200辆之多。 7 ADJ If you say that something is a **high** priority or is **high on** your list, you mean that you consider it to be one of the most important things you have to do or deal with. 首要的 ❏ *The party has not made the issue a high priority.* 该党还没有把这个问题列为首要考虑的事项。 8 ADJ Someone who is **high in** a particular profession or society, or has a **high** position, has a very important position and has great authority and influence. (地位) 高的 [v-link ADJ "in" n, ADJ n] ❏ *Was there anyone particularly high in the administration who was an advocate of a different policy?* 管理部门里有没有职位特别高的人支持采纳不同政策？ ❏ *...corruption in high places.* …高层的腐败。 ● PHRASE Someone who is **high up in** a profession or society has a very important position. (地位或职位) 高的 ❏ *His cousin is somebody quite high up in the navy.* 他的堂兄在海军里地位相当高。 9 ADV If you aim **high**, you try to obtain or to achieve the best that you can. 向高的目标 [ADV after v] ❏ *You should not be afraid to aim high in the quest for an improvement in your income.* 在寻求收入提高方面，你应该敢于给自己设定高的目标。 10 ADJ If someone has a **high** reputation, or people have a **high** opinion of them, people think they are very good in some way, for example at their work. (声望或评价) 高的 ❏ *People have such high expectations of you.* 人们对你抱有如此之高的期望。 11 ADJ If the quality or standard of something is **high**, it is extremely good. (品质或标准) 高的 ❏ *This is high quality stuff.* 这是高品质的东西。 12 ADJ A **high** sound or voice is close to the top of a particular range of notes. (音调) 尖声的 ❏ *Her high voice really irritated Maria.* 她的尖嗓门真的惹怒了玛丽亚。 13 ADJ If your spirits are **high**, you feel happy and excited. 兴奋的 ❏ *Her spirits were high with the hope of seeing Nick in minutes rather than hours.* 她很兴奋，因为只消等上几分钟而不是几个小时就有希望见到尼克了。 14 ADJ If someone is **high on** alcohol or drugs, they are affected by the alcoholic drink or drugs they have taken. 喝醉了的; (吸毒后) 极度兴奋的 [v-link ADJ] [INFORMAL] ❏ *He was too high on drugs and alcohol to remember them.* 他吸毒和酗酒后兴奋过度，已经记不起他们了。 15 N-COUNT A **high** is a feeling or mood of great excitement or happiness. 兴奋 [INFORMAL] ❏ *"I'm still on a high," she said after the show.* "我还兴奋着呢，"她在演出结束后说。 16 PHRASE If you say that something came from **on high**, you mean that it came from a person or place of great authority. 高层人物 ❏ *Orders had come from on high that extra care was to be taken during this week.* 上头传来话说这个星期要格外小心。 17 PHRASE If you say that you were left **high and dry**, you are emphasizing that you were left in a difficult situation and were unable to do anything about it. 陷入困境 [EMPHASIS] ❏ *Schools with better reputations will be flooded with applications while poorer schools will be left high and dry.* 声誉好些的学校将会收到大量申请，而差些的学校则将陷入困境。 18 PHRASE If you refer to the **highs and lows of** someone's life or career, you are referring to both the successful or happy times, and the unsuccessful or bad times. 快乐和痛苦; 成功和失败 ❏ *Here, she talks about the highs and lows of her life.* 此刻，她正谈论着自己生活中的酸甜苦辣。 19 PHRASE If you say that you looked **high and low** for something, you are emphasizing that you looked for it in every place that you could think of. 四处寻找 [EMPHASIS] ❏ *...and I rambled around the apartment looking high and low for an aspirin or painkiller.* …我在公寓里四处寻找阿司匹林或者止痛片。

→ see **tide**

Thesaurus *high* 另参见:

ADJ. tall 1 2
elevated, lofty, tall; *(ant.)* low 3

high·boy /haɪbɔɪ/ (**highboys**) N-COUNT A **highboy** is a high chest of drawers consisting of two sections which are placed one on top of the other. 高脚五斗橱 [AM] ❏ *She saw him methodically searching the drawers of a highboy.* 她见他正有条不紊地在高脚五斗橱的抽屉里翻找东西。

high-class ADJ If you describe something as **high-class**, you mean that it is of very good quality or of superior social status. 优质的; 上流社会的 ❏ *...a high-class jeweler.* …一流的珠宝商。

high-end ADJ **High-end** products, especially electronic products, are the most expensive of their kind. 高端的 ❏ *...high-end personal computers and computer workstations.* …高端个人电脑和电脑工作站。

high·er edu·ca·tion N-UNCOUNT **Higher education** is education at universities and colleges. 高等教育 ❏ *...students in higher education.* …接受高等教育的学生。

high-flying ADJ A **high-flying** person is successful or is likely to be successful in their career. 成功的; 有前途的 ❏ *...her high-flying newspaper-editor husband.* …她那当报社编辑的前程似锦的丈夫。

high·lands /haɪləndz/ N-PLURAL **Highlands** are mountainous areas of land. 高原地区

high·light ♦◇◇ /haɪlaɪt/ (**highlights, highlighting, highlighted**) 1 V-T If someone or something **highlights** a point or problem, they emphasize it or make you think about it. 强调; 使注意 ❏ *Last year Collins wrote a moving ballad which highlighted the plight of homeless.* 去年柯林斯写了一首感人的叙事诗，突出描写了无家可归者的苦境。 2 V-T To **highlight** a piece of text means to mark it in a different color, either with a special type of pen or on a computer screen. (用不同颜色) 标出; (在电脑屏幕上) 突出显示 ❏ *Highlight the chosen area by clicking and holding down the left mouse button.* 通过点击鼠标左键并摁住以突出显示所选区域。 3 N-COUNT The **highlights of** an event, activity, or period of time are the most interesting or exciting parts of it. 最精彩的部分 ❏ *...a match that is likely to prove one of the highlights of the tournament.* …可能是本届锦标赛最精彩的赛事之一。

Word Partnership *highlight* 的常用搭配:

N. highlight **concerns/problems**, highlight **differences** 1
highlight **of *someone's* career** 3

high·ly ♦♦◇ /haɪli/ 1 ADV **Highly** is used before some adjectives to mean "very." 非常 [ADV adj] ❏ *Mr. Singh was a highly successful salesman.* 辛格先生曾是一位非常成功的推销员。 ❏ *It seems highly unlikely that she ever existed.* 看来很有可能压根儿就没有过她这么个人。 2 ADV You use **highly** to indicate that someone has an important position in an organization or set of people. 身居高位 [ADV -ed] ❏ *...a highly placed government advisor.* …高级政府顾问。 3 ADV If someone is **highly** paid, they receive a large salary. 高水平地 [ADV -ed] ❏ *...the 30 most highly paid athletes in the world.* …世界30位薪酬最高的运动员。 4 ADV If you think **highly** of something or someone, you think they are extremely good. 极为赞许地 ❏ *Daphne and Michael thought highly of the school.* 达夫妮和迈克尔对那所学校评价很高。

Word Partnership *highly* 的常用搭配:

V. highly **recommended**, highly **respected** 1
ADJ. highly **addictive**, highly **competitive**, highly **contagious**, highly **controversial**, highly **critical**, highly **educated**, highly **intelligent**, highly **qualified**, highly **skilled**, highly **successful**, highly **technical**, highly **trained**, highly **unlikely**, highly **visible** 1
highly **paid** 3

High·ness /haɪnɪs/ (**Highnesses**) N-VOC Expressions such as "**Your Highness**" or "**His Highness**" are used to address or refer to a member of a royal family other than a king or queen. 殿下 (对除王、后以外的王室成员的尊称) [POLITENESS] ❏ *That would be best, Your Highness.* 那就再好不过了，殿下。

high-pitched ADJ A **high-pitched** sound is shrill and high in pitch. 尖声的 ❏ *A woman squealed in a high-pitched voice.* 一位女士尖声叫了起来。

high-powered 1 ADJ A **high-powered** machine or piece of equipment is very powerful and efficient. 大功率的 ❏ *...high-powered lasers.* …大功率激光器。 2 ADJ Someone who is **high-powered** or has a **high-powered** job has a very important and responsible job which requires a lot of ability. (人) 身居要职的; (职位) 要求高的 ❏ *...a high-powered lawyer.* …身居要职的律师。

high-profile ADJ A **high-profile** person or a **high-profile** event attracts a lot of attention or publicity. 引人注目的 ❏ *...high-profile* criminal defense lawyer, Gerald Shargel. …备受关注的刑事辩护律师，杰拉尔德・夏盖尔。

high-rise (high-rises) ADJ **High-rise** buildings are modern buildings which are very tall and have many levels or floors. (建筑) 高层的 [ADJ n] ❑ ...*high-rise office buildings.* …高层办公楼。 ● N-COUNT A **high-rise** is a high-rise building. 高层建筑 ❑ *That big high-rise above us is where Brian lives.* 我们头顶上那幢巨型高层建筑就是布赖恩的住处所在。

high school ◆◆◆ (high schools) N-VAR; N-IN-NAMES A **high school** is a school for children usually aged between fourteen and eighteen. (14至18岁学生就读的) 中学 ❑ ...*an 18-year-old inner-city kid who dropped out of high school.* …一名中学辍学、家住市中心贫民区的18岁的孩子。
→ see **graduation**

high-speed 1 ADJ A **high-speed** vehicle or piece of equipment moves or operates very quickly. 高速的 (车辆或设备) [ADJ n] ❑ *Japan's high-speed trains travel a long way in a short time.* 日本高速列车可以在短时间内行驶很远的路程。 2 ADJ A **high-speed** accident happens when the vehicles involved are traveling very fast. 因高速行驶导致的 (事故) [ADJ n] ❑ *They were killed in a high-speed crash in a tunnel in Paris.* 他们在一起发生在巴黎一座隧道里的高速行驶引发的撞车事故中丧生。 3 ADJ A **high-speed** Internet connection allows users to access websites very quickly. 高速的 (因特网接入) [ADJ n] ❑ *Most of our customers have now upgraded to a high-speed broadband connection.* 我们大多数的客户现已升级至高速宽带连接。

high street (high streets) N-COUNT; N-IN-NAMES The **high street** of a town is the main street where most of the stores and banks are. 主要街道 [mainly BRIT]
in AM, use **main street**

high-tech /haɪ tɛk/ also **high tech, hi tech** ADJ **High-tech** activities or equipment involve or result from the use of high technology. 高科技的 ❑ ...*such high-tech industries as computers or telecommunications.* …像计算机或电信这样的高科技行业。

high tech·nol·ogy N-UNCOUNT **High technology** is the practical use of advanced scientific research and knowledge, especially in relation to electronics and computers, and the development of new advanced machines and equipment. 高科技 ❑ ...*a limited war using high technology.* …运用高科技的有限战争。

high·way ◆◆◇ /haɪweɪ/ (highways) N-COUNT A **highway** is a main road, especially one that connects towns or cities. (尤指城市间的) 公路 [mainly AM] ❑ *I crossed the highway, dodging the traffic.* 我闪身避让着来往的车辆，穿过了公路。
→ see **traffic**

▲ **hi·jack** /haɪdʒæk/ (hijacks, hijacking, hijacked) 1 V-T If someone **hijacks** a plane or other vehicle, they illegally take control of it by force while it is traveling from one place to another. 劫持 ❑ *Two men tried to hijack a plane on a flight from Riga to Murmansk.* 两名男子试图劫持一架从里加飞往摩尔曼斯克的飞机。 ● N-COUNT **Hijack** is also a noun. 劫持 ❑ *Every minute during the hijack seemed like a week.* 劫持过程中，每一分钟都像一个星期似的。 ● **hi·jack·ing** N-COUNT (hijackings) 劫持 ❑ *Car hijackings are running at a rate of nearly 50 a day.* 平均每天发生50起劫车事件。 2 V-T If you say that someone **has hijacked** something, you disapprove of the way in which they have taken control of it when they had no right to do so. 强行控制 [DISAPPROVAL] ❑ *A peaceful demonstration had been hijacked by anarchists intent on causing trouble.* 一场和平示威已被一心想制造事端的无政府主义分子强行控制了。

hi·jack·er /haɪdʒækər/ (hijackers) N-COUNT A **hijacker** is a person who hijacks a plane or other vehicle. 劫持者

★ **hike** /haɪk/ (hikes, hiking, hiked) 1 N-COUNT A **hike** is a long walk in the country, especially one that you go on for pleasure. 远足 ❑ *The site is reached by a 30-minute hike through dense forest.* 要花30分钟徒步穿过密林才能到达那个地方。 2 V-I If you **hike**, you go for a long walk in the country. 远足 ❑ *You could hike through the Fish River Canyon – it's entirely up to you.* 你可以远足穿越菲什河大峡谷——这全由你自己决定。 ● **hik·ing** N-UNCOUNT 远足 ❑ ...*some harder, more strenuous hiking on cliff pathways.* …在悬崖峭壁的小路上进行的更艰难、更费力的长途行走。 3 N-COUNT A **hike** is a sudden or large increase in prices, rates, taxes, or quantities. 突然上涨 [INFORMAL] ❑ ...*a sudden 1.75 percent hike in interest rates.* …利率突涨1.75%。 4 V-T To **hike** prices, rates, taxes, or quantities means to increase them suddenly or by a large amount. 使大幅上升 [INFORMAL] ❑ *It has now been forced to hike its rates by 5.25 percent.* 它现在被迫将其税率提高5.25%。 ● PHRASAL VERB **Hike up** means the same as **hike**. 使大幅上升 ❑ *The insurers have started hiking up premiums by huge amounts.* 保险公司已经开始大幅度地提高保险费。

hik·er /haɪkər/ (hikers) N-COUNT A **hiker** is a person who is going for a long walk in the countryside for pleasure. 远足者

hi·lari·ous /hɪlɛəriəs/ ADJ If something is **hilarious**, it is extremely funny and makes you laugh a lot. 令人捧腹大笑的 ❑ *We thought it was hilarious when we first heard about it.* 我们第一次听说这件事的时候觉得它很可笑。 ● **hi·lari·ous·ly** ADV 令人大笑地 ❑ *She found it hilariously funny.* 她觉得这事儿滑稽极了。

hill ◆◇◇ /hɪl/ (hills) 1 N-COUNT; N-IN-NAMES A **hill** is an area of land that is higher than the land that surrounds it. 小山 ❑ ...*the shady street that led up the hill to the office building.* …通往山上的办公楼的林荫道。 2 PHRASE If you say that someone is **over the hill**, you are saying rudely that they are old and no longer fit, attractive, or capable of doing useful work. 在走下坡路 [INFORMAL, DISAPPROVAL] ❑ *He doesn't take kindly to suggestions that he is over the hill.* 他不爱听别人说他在走下坡路。

hilly /hɪli/ (hillier, hilliest) ADJ A **hilly** area has many hills. 多山丘的 ❑ *The areas where the fighting is taking place are hilly and densely wooded.* 战斗发生的地区丘陵起伏，树木茂密。

him ◆◆◆ /hɪm/

Him is a third person singular pronoun. **Him** is used as the object of a verb or a preposition.

1 PRON-SING You use **him** to refer to a man, boy, or male animal. 他；它 (指雄性动物) [V PRON, prep PRON] ❑ *John's aunt died suddenly and left him a surprisingly large sum.* 约翰的姑妈突然去世，给他留下一笔令人意想不到的巨款。 ❑ *Is Sam there? Let me talk to him.* 萨姆在吗？让我和他谈谈。 2 PRON-SING In written English, **him** is sometimes used to refer to a person without saying whether that person is a man or a woman. Some people dislike this use and prefer to use "him or her" or "them." 他 (书面英语中泛指人) [V PRON, prep PRON] ❑ *If the child encounters "hear," we should show him that this is the base word in "hearing" and "hears."* 如果孩子遇到**hear**这个单词，我们应该向他说明这个词是**hearing**和**hears**的词根。

him·self ◆◆◆ /hɪmsɛlf/

Himself is a third person singular reflexive pronoun. **Himself** is used when the object of a verb or preposition refers to the same person as the subject of the verb, except in meaning 3.

1 PRON-REFL You use **himself** to refer to a man, boy, or male animal. 他自己；它自己 (指雄性动物) [V PRON, prep PRON] ❑ *He poured himself a whiskey and sat down in the chair.* 他给自己倒了一杯威士忌，然后坐在椅子里。 ❑ *William went away muttering to himself.* 威廉喃喃自语地走了。 2 PRON-REFL In written English, **himself** is sometimes used to refer to a person without saying whether that person is a man or a woman. Some people dislike this use and prefer to use "himself or herself" or "themselves." 他自己 (书面英语里泛指人) [V PRON, prep PRON] ❑ *There is nothing more dangerous than someone who thinks of himself as a victim.* 没有比自认为是受害者的人更危险的了。 3 PRON-REFL-EMPH You use **himself** to emphasize the person or thing that you are referring to. **Himself** is sometimes used instead of "him" as the object of a verb or preposition. 他本人 (用以加强语气) [EMPHASIS] ❑ *The president himself is on a visit to Beijing.* 总统本人正在访问北京。

hind /haɪnd/ ADJ An animal's **hind** legs are at the back of its body. (动物的腿) 后面的 [ADJ n] ❑ *Suddenly the cow kicked up its hind legs.* 突然奶牛踢起了后腿。

hin·der /hɪndər/ (hinders, hindering, hindered) 1 V-T If something **hinders** you, it makes it more difficult for you to do something or make progress. 阻碍 ❑ *Further investigation was hindered by the loss of all documentation on the case.* 由于有关此案的材料全部丢失，进一步的调查受到了阻碍。 2 V-T If something **hinders** your movement, it makes it difficult for you to move forward or move around. 牵制 ❑ *A thigh injury increasingly hindered her mobility.* 大腿上的伤愈发束缚了她的活动自由。

hin·drance /hɪndrəns/ (hindrances) N-COUNT A **hindrance** is a person or thing that makes it more difficult for you to do something. 妨碍者；障碍物 ❑ *The higher rates have been a hindrance to economic recovery.* 居高不下的税率已经成为经济复苏的阻碍物。

hind·sight /haɪndsaɪt/ N-UNCOUNT **Hindsight** is the ability to understand and realize something about an event after it has happened, although you did not understand or realize it at the time. 后见之明 ❑ *With hindsight, we'd all do things differently.* 事后想来，我们可能都会以不同的方式做事。

Hin·du /hɪndu/ (**Hindus**) 1 N-COUNT A **Hindu** is a person who believes in Hinduism and follows its teachings. 印度教徒 2 ADJ **Hindu** is used to describe things that belong or relate to Hinduism. 印度教的 ❑ *...a Hindu temple.* …一座印度教寺庙。
→ see **religion**

Hin·du·ism /hɪnduɪzəm/ N-UNCOUNT **Hinduism** is an Indian religion. It has many gods and teaches that people have another life on earth after they die. 印度教

★ **hinge** /hɪndʒ/ (**hinges, hinging, hinged**) N-COUNT A **hinge** is a piece of metal, wood, or plastic that is used to join a door to its frame or to join two things together so that one of them can swing freely. 折叶 ❑ *The top swung open on well-oiled hinges.* 盖子在上好油的折叶上一下子弹开了。

▸ **hinge on** PHRASAL VERB Something that **hinges on** one thing or event depends entirely on it. 完全取决于 ❑ *The plan hinges on a deal being struck with a new company.* 该计划完全取决于正在和一家新公司谈的一笔交易。

hint ♦◇◇ /hɪnt/ (**hints, hinting, hinted**) 1 N-COUNT A **hint** is a suggestion about something that is made in an indirect way. 暗示 ❑ *I'd dropped a hint about having an exhibition of his work up here.* 我暗示要在这里举办一次他的作品展。 ● PHRASE If you **take a hint**, you understand something that is suggested to you indirectly. 领会暗示 ❑ *"I think I hear the telephone ringing."—"Okay, I can take a hint."* "我想我听见了电话在响。" "好的，我明白你的意思。" 2 V-I If you **hint at** something, you suggest it in an indirect way. 暗示 ❑ *She hinted at the possibility of a treat of some sort.* 她暗示可以找找乐子什么的。 3 N-COUNT A **hint** is a helpful piece of advice, usually about how to do something. 建议 ❑ *Here are some helpful hints to make your journey easier.* 这里是一些有用的建议，可以使你的旅途更舒适。 4 N-SING A **hint of** something is a very small amount of it. 微量 ❑ *She added only a hint of vermouth to the gin.* 她往杜松子酒里只加了一点儿苦艾酒。

Word Partnership *hint* 的常用搭配:

V. **take a hint** 1
drop a hint, give a hint 1 3
ADJ. **broad hint** 1
helpful hint 3

hip ♦◇◇ /hɪp/ (**hips**) 1 N-COUNT Your **hips** are the two areas at the sides of your body between the tops of your legs and your waist. 臀部 ❑ *Tracey put her hands on her hips and sighed.* 特蕾西把手放在自己的臀部上叹了口气。 2 N-COUNT You refer to the bones between the tops of your legs and your waist as your **hips**. 髋 ❑ *Eventually, surgeons replaced both hips and both shoulders.* 最后，外科医生把两侧的髋骨和两边的肩骨都换了。 3 ADJ If you say that someone is **hip**, you mean that they are very modern and follow all the latest fashions, for example in clothes and ideas. 时髦的 [INFORMAL] ❑ *...a hip young character with tight-cropped blond hair and stylish glasses.* …一个留着修剪得很短的金发、戴着时尚眼镜的时髦青年。 4 EXCLAM If a large group of people want to show their appreciation or approval of someone, one of them says "**Hip hip**" and they all shout "**hooray.**" 好啊 (表示欣赏或赞许的呼声) 5 PHRASE If you say that someone **shoots from the hip**, you mean that they react to situations or give their opinion very quickly, without stopping to think. 仓促行事；仓促表态 ❑ *Judges don't have to shoot from the hip. They have the leisure to think, to decide.* 法官们不必仓促作决定。他们有的是时间去思考、去裁决。

hip·pie /hɪpi/ (**hippies**) also **hippy** N-COUNT **Hippies** were young people in the 1960s and 1970s who rejected conventional ways of living, dressing, and behaving, and tried to live a life based on peace and love. Hippies often had long hair and many took drugs. 嬉皮士 (20世纪60、70年代的青年颓废派，摈弃传统的生活、衣着和行为方式，提倡和平与爱情，多蓄长发，其中有很多人吸食毒品。)

hire ♦◇◇ /haɪər/ (**hires, hiring, hired**) 1 V-T/V-I If you **hire** someone, you employ them or pay them to do a particular job for you. 雇用 ❑ *Sixteen of the contestants have hired lawyers and are suing the organizers.* 参赛者中有16人已经聘了律师，正在起诉主办方。 ❑ *He will be in charge of all hiring and firing at PHA.* 他将负责公众房产管理局里的一切人事任免事务。 2 V-T If you **hire** something, you pay money to the owner so that you can use it for a period of time. 租用 [mainly BRIT]

in AM, usually use **rent**

3 N-UNCOUNT You use **hire** to refer to the activity or business of hiring something. 租用 [mainly BRIT]

in AM, usually use **rental**

4 PHRASE If something is **for hire**, it is available for you to hire. 供出租 [mainly BRIT]

in AM, usually use **for rent**

Do not confuse **hire, rent,** and **let.** If you make a series of payments to use something for a long time, you say that you **rent** it. ❑ *...the apartment he had rented... He rented a TV..* You can say that you **rent** or **rent out** a house or room to someone when they pay you money to live there. ❑ *We rented our house to a college professor.* In British English, it is more common to say that you **let** it. ❑ *They were letting a room to a school teacher.* Americans also use **rent** when you pay a sum of money to use something for a short time. ❑ *He rented a car for the weekend.* In British English, if you pay a sum of money to use something for a short time, you usually say that you **hire** it. ❑ *He was unable to hire another car.* American English uses **hire** mainly to talk about giving jobs to people. ❑ *We hired a new waitress this week.*

▸ **hire out** PHRASAL VERB If you **hire out** a person's services, you allow them to be used in return for payment. 出租 ❑ *...employment agencies which hire out personnel to foreign companies.* …向外国公司出租人员的职业介绍所。

hire pur·chase N-UNCOUNT **Hire purchase** is a way of buying goods gradually. You make regular payments until you have paid the full price and the goods belong to you. The abbreviation **HP** is often used. 分期付款购买法 [oft N n] [BRIT]

in AM, use **installment plan**

his ♦♦♦

The determiner is pronounced /hɪz/. The pronoun is pronounced /hɪz/.

限定词读作 /hɪz/。代词读作 /hɪz/。

His is a third person singular possessive determiner. **His** is also a possessive pronoun.

DET You use **his** to indicate that something belongs or relates to a man, boy, or male animal. 他的；它的 (指雄性动物) ❑ *Brian splashed water on his face, then brushed his teeth.* 布赖恩用水拍洗了脸，然后刷了牙。 ❑ *He spent a large part of his career in Hollywood.* 他职业生涯中的大部分时间是在好莱坞度过的。 ● PRON-POSS **His** is also a possessive pronoun. 他的 (也作物主代词) ❑ *Staff say the decision was his.* 员工们说那个决定是他做出的。

His·pan·ic /hɪspænɪk/ (**Hispanics**) ADJ A **Hispanic** person is a citizen of the United States of America who originally came from Latin America, or whose family originally came from Latin America. 拉美裔美国籍的 ❑ *...a group of Hispanic doctors in Washington.* …华盛顿的一群拉美裔美国医生。 ● N-COUNT A **Hispanic** is someone who is Hispanic. 拉美裔美国人 ❑ *About 80 percent of Hispanics here are U.S. citizens.* 这里约80%的拉美裔美国人是美国公民。

▲ **hiss** /hɪs/ (**hisses, hissing, hissed**) 1 V-I To **hiss** means to make a sound like a long "s." 发嘶嘶声 ❑ *The tires of Lenny's bike hissed over the wet pavement as he slowed down.* 兰尼减速时，他自行车的两个轮胎在潮湿的路面上发出嘶嘶声。 ❑ *My cat hissed when I stepped on its tail.* 我踩在了猫的尾巴上，于是它嘶嘶地叫了起来。 ● N-COUNT **Hiss** is also a noun. 嘶嘶声 ❑ *...the hiss of water running into the burned pan.* …水流进烧红的煎锅时的嘶嘶声。 ● **hiss·ing** N-UNCOUNT 嘶嘶声 ❑ *...a silence broken only by a steady hissing from above my head.* …仅仅被我头顶上传来的持续的嘶嘶声所打破的一片寂静。 2 V-I If people **hiss at** someone such as a performer or a person making a speech, they express their disapproval or dislike of that person by making long loud "s" sounds. 发嘘声；喝倒彩 ❑ *One had to listen hard to catch the words of the president's speech as the delegates booed and hissed.* 由于代表们发嘘声、喝倒彩，得费劲儿地听才能听清总统的演讲。 ● N-COUNT **Hiss** is also a noun. 嘘声 ❑ *She was greeted with boos and hisses.* 迎接她的是一片嘘声和反对声。

★ **his·to·rian** /hɪstɔriən/ (**historians**) N-COUNT A **historian** is a person who specializes in the study of history, and who writes books and articles about it. 历史学家
→ see **history**

h

his·tor·ic ♦◇◇ /hɪstɔrɪk/ ADJ Something that is **historic** is important in history, or likely to be considered important at some time in the future. 有重大历史意义的 ❑ *...the historic changes in Eastern Europe.* …东欧有历史性意义的变化。

his·tori·cal ♦◇◇ /hɪstɔrɪkᵊl/ **1** ADJ **Historical** people, situations, or things existed in the past and are considered to be a part of history. 历史上的 [ADJ n] ❑ *...an important historical figure.* …一位重要的历史人物。 ❑ *...the historical impact of Western capitalism on the world.* …西方资本主义对全世界的历史影响。 ● **his·tori·cal·ly** ADV 在历史上 ❑ *Historically, royal marriages have been cold, calculating affairs.* 从历史上来看，王室婚姻一直都是冷酷、精心策划的结合。 **2** ADJ **Historical** books, movies, or pictures describe or represent people, situations, or things that existed in the past. 历史题材的 [ADJ n] ❑ *He is writing a historical novel about nineteenth-century France.* 他正在写一部关于19世纪的法国的历史小说。 **3** ADJ **Historical** information, research, and discussion is related to the study of history. 史学的 [ADJ n] ❑ *...historical records.* …史学记录。 ❑ *...modern historical research.* …当代史学研究。

Word Partnership *historical* 的常用搭配：

N. historical **events**, historical **figure**, historical **impact**, historical **significance** **1**
historical **detail/fact**, historical **records**, historical **research** **3**

his·to·ry ♦♦♦ /hɪstəri, -tri/ (histories) **1** N-UNCOUNT You can refer to the events of the past as **history**. You can also refer to the past events which concern a particular topic or place as its **history**. 历史 ❑ *The Catholic Church has played a prominent role throughout Polish history.* 天主教在整个波兰历史中扮演了重要的角色。 ❑ *...the most evil mass killer in history.* …历史上最邪恶的杀人狂。 ● PHRASE Someone who **makes history** does something that is considered to be important and significant in the development of the world or of a particular society. 创造历史 ❑ *Willy Brandt made history by visiting East Germany in 1970.* 威利·勃兰特1970年对东德的访问创造了历史。 ● PHRASE If someone or something **goes down in history**, people in the future remember them because of particular actions that they have done or because of particular events that have happened. 载入史册 ❑ *Bradley will go down in history as Los Angeles' longest serving mayor.* 布拉德利将作为洛杉矶任职时间最长的市长载入史册。 **2** N-UNCOUNT **History** is a subject studied in schools, colleges, and universities that deals with events that have happened in the past. 历史学 ❑ *...a lecturer in history at Birmingham University.* …伯明翰大学的一位历史讲师。 **3** N-COUNT A **history** is an account of events that have happened in the past. 历史事件纪录 ❑ *...his magnificent history of broadcasting in Canada.* …他对加拿大播音史的出色纪录。 **4** N-COUNT If a person or a place has **a history of** something, it has been very common or has happened frequently in their past. 记录 ❑ *He had a history of drinking problems.* 他有酗酒的记录。 **5** N-COUNT Someone's **history** is the set of facts that are known about their past. 履历 ❑ *He couldn't get a new job because of his medical history.* 由于他的病史，他无法找到新工作。 **6** PHRASE If you are telling someone about an event and say **the rest is history**, you mean that you do not need to tell them what happened next because everyone knows about it already. 后来发生的事情众人皆知 ❑ *We met in college, the rest is history.* 我们在大学相识，接下来的事大家都知道了。

→ see Word Web: **history**

Word Partnership *history* 的常用搭配：

N. **the course of** history, **world** history **1**
family history **1** **5**
life history **5**
V. **go down in** history, **make** history **1**
teach history **2**

hit ♦♦♦ /hɪt/ (**hits, hitting**)

The form **hit** is used in the present tense and is the past and present participle.

1 V-T If you **hit** someone or something, you deliberately touch them with a lot of force, with your hand or an object held in your hand. 打 ❑ *Find the exact grip that allows you to hit the ball hard.* 找到能让你大力击球的准确握拍方法。 **2** V-T When one thing **hits** another, it touches it with a lot of force. 猛撞 ❑ *The car had apparently hit a traffic sign before skidding out of control.* 汽车显然在失控滑出前猛地撞到了一个交通指示牌。 **3** V-T If a bomb or missile **hits** its target, it reaches it. (炸弹或导弹) 击中 ❑ *...multiple-warhead missiles that could hit many targets at a time.* …可以一次击中多个目标的多弹头导弹。 ● N-COUNT **Hit** is also a noun. 击中 ❑ *First a house took a direct hit and then the rocket exploded.* 首先一幢房子被直接击中，接着火箭弹爆炸了。 **4** V-T If something **hits** a person, place, or thing, it affects them very badly. 对…造成严重影响 [JOURNALISM] ❑ *The plan to charge motorists to use the freeway is going to hit me hard.* 向汽车驾驶员收取高速公路使用费这一方案会严重影响到我。 ❑ *About two hundred people died in the earthquake which hit northern Peru.* 大约两百人在那场袭击秘鲁北部的地震中丧生。 **5** V-T When a feeling or an idea **hits** you, it suddenly affects you or comes into your mind. 使突然意识到 ❑ *It hit me that I had a choice.* 我突然意识到我可以有所选择。 **6** V-T If you **hit** a particular high or low point on a scale of something such as success or health, you reach it. 达到 [JOURNALISM] ❑ *He admits to having hit the lowest point in his life.* 他承认自己跌到了一生中的最低谷。 **7** N-COUNT If a CD, movie, or play is a **hit**, it is very popular and successful. (唱片、电影或戏剧的) 成功 ❑ *The song became a massive hit in 1945.* 这首歌在1945年取得了巨大成功。 **8** N-COUNT A **hit** is a single visit to a website. (网站的) 点击 [COMPUTING] ❑ *Our small company has had 78,000 hits on its Internet pages.* 我们的小公司的网页已被点击了7.8万次。 **9** N-COUNT If someone who is searching for information on the Internet gets a **hit**, they find a website where there is that information. (在互联网上搜到) 所要找的网页 **10** PHRASE If two people **hit it off**, they like each other and become friendly as soon as they meet. 一见如故 [INFORMAL] ❑ *Dad and Walter hit it off straight away.* 爸爸和沃尔特一见如故。

11 to **hit the headlines** → see **headline** **12** to **hit home** → see **home**
13 to **hit the nail on the head** → see **nail** **14** to **hit the roof** → see **roof**

Word Web **history**

3800 BC The wheel is invented.

2600 BC The Pyramid of Giza is built.

31 BC Roman Empire founded.

700 AD The Great Wall of China is started.

1200 AD Incan empire is founded.

1492 Columbus sails for America.

1969 Humans land on the Moon.

Open any history textbook and you will find **timelines**. They show important dates for **ancient civilizations**—when **empires** appeared and disappeared, and when **wars** were fought. But, how much of what we read in **history** books is **fact**? **Accounts** of the **past** are often based on how archeologists interpret the **artifacts** they find. **Scholars** often rely on the **records** of the people who were in power. These **historians** included certain facts and left out others. Historians today look beyond official records. They research **primary source documents** such as **diaries**. They describe **events** from different **points of view**.

▸ **hit on** or **hit upon** 1 PHRASAL VERB If you **hit on** an idea or a solution to a problem, or **hit upon** it, you think of it. 想出 ❑ *After running through the numbers in every possible combination, we finally hit on a solution.* 将数字排列出了所有可能的组合后，我们终于找到了答案。 2 PHRASAL VERB If someone **hits on** you, they speak or behave in a way that shows they want to have a sexual relationship with you. 挑逗 [INFORMAL] ❑ *She was hitting on me and I was surprised and flattered.* 她挑逗我，这既让我吃惊又感到荣幸。

▸ **hit up** PHRASAL VERB If you **hit** somebody **up** for something, especially for money, you ask them for it. 向…索取（尤指钱财）[AM, INFORMAL] ❑ *They hit up Hector for the last $250.* 他们向赫克托索要剩下的$250。

Thesaurus *hit* 另参见：
V. bang, beat, knock, pound, slap, smack, strike 1
N. smash, success, triumph; *(ant.)* failure 7

Word Partnership *hit* 的常用搭配：
N. hit **a ball**, hit **a button**, hit **the brakes** 1
earthquakes/famine/storms hit *someplace* 4
a hit **movie/show/song** 7

hit-and-run 1 ADJ A **hit-and-run** accident is an accident in which the driver of a vehicle hits someone and then drives away without stopping. 交通肇事后逃逸的 [ADJ n] ❑ *...the victim of a hit-and-run accident.* …交通肇事逃逸事故的受害人。 2 ADJ A **hit-and-run** attack on an enemy position relies on surprise and speed for its success. 打了就跑的 [ADJ n] ❑ *The rebels appear to be making hit-and-run guerrilla style attacks on military targets.* 叛军看上去在用打了就跑的游击战术袭击军事目标。

▲ **hitch** /hɪtʃ/ (**hitches, hitching, hitched**) 1 N-COUNT A **hitch** is a slight problem or difficulty which causes a short delay. 小故障 ❑ *After some technical hitches the show finally got under way.* 几个小的技术故障后演出终于开始了。 2 V-T/V-I If you **hitch**, **hitch** a lift, or **hitch** a ride, you hitchhike. 搭便车 [INFORMAL] ❑ *There was no garage in sight, so I hitched a lift into town.* 附近没有汽车修理厂，于是我搭便车进了城。 3 V-T If you **hitch** something **to** something else, you hook it or fasten it there. 把…钩住；把…拴住 ❑ *Last night we hitched the horse to the cart and moved here.* 昨天晚上我们把马拴在马车上，搬到了这里。

hitch·hike /hɪtʃhaɪk/ (**hitchhikes, hitchhiking, hitchhiked**) V-I If you **hitchhike**, you travel by getting rides from passing vehicles without paying. 搭免费便车 ❑ *Neff hitchhiked to New York during his Christmas vacation.* 内夫在圣诞节休假期间搭免费便车去了纽约。 ● **hitch·hiker** N-COUNT (**hitchhikers**) 搭免费便车的人 ❑ *On my way to Vancouver one Friday night I picked up a hitchhiker.* 在我去温哥华的那个星期五的晚上，我载了一个搭便车的人。

hi tech → see **high-tech**

★ **hither·to** /hɪðərtu/ ADV You use **hitherto** to indicate that something was true up until the time you are talking about, although it may no longer be the case. 迄今 [FORMAL] ❑ *The ruling party is likely to be opened up to let in people hitherto excluded.* 执政党可能会放开政策，吸纳迄今被排斥在外的人士。

hit list (**hit lists**) 1 N-COUNT If someone has a **hit list of** people or things, they are intending to take action concerning those people or things. 打击名单 ❑ *Some banks also have a hit list of people whom they threaten to sue for damages.* 一些银行还有一个他们威胁要提起损坏起诉的人员名单。 2 N-COUNT A **hit list** is a list that someone makes of people they intend to have killed. 暗杀名单 ❑ *...a group of killers instructed by the deputy minister to attack people on his hit list.* …受副部长指使去袭击其暗杀名单上所列人员的一帮杀手。

HIV ♦◇◇ /eɪtʃ aɪ vi/ 1 N-UNCOUNT **HIV** is a virus which reduces people's resistance to illness and can cause AIDS. **HIV** is an abbreviation for "human immunodeficiency virus." 艾滋病病毒 2 PHRASE If someone is **HIV positive**, they are infected with the HIV virus, and may develop AIDS. If someone is **HIV negative**, they are not infected with the virus. 艾滋病病毒检测呈阳性/阴性

★ **hive** /haɪv/ (**hives**) 1 N-COUNT A **hive** is a structure in which bees are kept, which is designed so that the beekeeper can collect the honey that they produce. 蜂箱 2 N-COUNT If you describe a place as a **hive of** activity, you approve of the fact that there is a lot of activity there or that people are busy working there. 忙碌的地方 [APPROVAL] ❑ *In the morning the house was a hive of activity.* 早上，这幢房子是忙碌的地方。

▲ **hoard** /hɔrd/ (**hoards, hoarding, hoarded**) 1 V-T If you **hoard** things such as food or money, you save or store them, often in secret, because they are valuable or important to you. 贮藏 ❑ *They've begun to hoard food and gasoline and save their money.* 他们已开始贮藏食物和汽油并攒钱。 2 N-COUNT A **hoard** is a store of things that you have saved and that are valuable or important to you or you do not want other people to have. 藏品 ❑ *The case involves a hoard of silver and jewels valued at up to $40m.* 此案涉及价值高达4000万美元的白银和珠宝的收藏品。

hoard·ing /hɔrdɪŋ/ (**hoardings**) N-COUNT A **hoarding** is a very large board at the side of a road or on the side of a building, which is used for displaying advertisements and posters. 巨幅广告牌 [BRIT]

in AM, use **billboard**

▲ **hoarse** /hɔrs/ (**hoarser, hoarsest**) ADJ If your voice is **hoarse** or if you are **hoarse**, your voice sounds rough and unclear, for example because your throat is sore. 嘶哑的 ❑ *"So what do you think?" she said in a hoarse whisper.* "那么你怎么认为？"她用嘶哑的嗓音悄声说道。 ● **hoarse·ly** ADV 嘶哑地 ❑ *"Thank you," Maria said hoarsely.* "谢谢，"玛丽亚嗓音嘶哑地说道。

hoax /hoʊks/ (**hoaxes**) N-COUNT A **hoax** is a trick in which someone tells people a lie, for example that there is a bomb somewhere when there is not, or that a picture is genuine when it is not. 谎报 ❑ *He denied making the hoax call but was convicted after a short trial.* 他否认打过谎报电话，但经过一番短暂的审讯之后他被判有罪。

hob /hɒb/ (**hobs**) N-COUNT A **hob** is a surface on top of a stove or set into a work surface, which can be heated in order to cook things on it. 炉盘 [BRIT]

in AM, use **cooktop**

hob·ble /hɒbᵊl/ (**hobbles, hobbling, hobbled**) V-I If you **hobble**, you walk in an awkward way with small steps, for example because your foot is injured. 跛行 ❑ *He got up slowly and hobbled over to the coffee table.* 他慢慢地起身，一瘸一拐地走到咖啡桌边。

hob·by /hɒbi/ (**hobbies**) N-COUNT A **hobby** is an activity that you enjoy doing in your spare time. 业余爱好 ❑ *My hobbies are letter writing, music, photography, and tennis.* 我的业余爱好是写信、音乐、摄影和网球。

Thesaurus *hobby* 另参见：
N. activity, craft, interest, pastime

▲ **hock·ey** /hɒki/ 1 N-UNCOUNT **Hockey** is a game played on ice between two teams of 11 players who use long curved sticks to hit a small rubber disk, called a puck, and try to score goals. 冰球 [mainly AM] ❑ *...a new hockey arena.* …一个新的冰球场。 2 N-UNCOUNT **Hockey** is an outdoor game played between two teams of 11 players who use long curved sticks to hit a small ball and try to score goals. 曲棍球 [mainly BRIT]

in AM, usually use **field hockey**

▲ **hoe** /hoʊ/ (**hoes, hoeing, hoed**) 1 N-COUNT A **hoe** is a gardening tool with a long handle and a small square blade, which you use to remove small weeds and break up the surface of the soil. 锄头 2 V-T If you **hoe** a field or crop, you use a hoe on the weeds or soil there. 锄（以除杂草或松土）❑ *I have to feed the chickens and hoe the potatoes.* 我必须喂鸡，还得给土豆除草松土。

hog /hɒg/ (**hogs, hogging, hogged**) 1 N-COUNT A **hog** is a pig. 猪 ❑ *We picked the corn by hand and we fed it to the hogs and the cows.* 我们掰下玉米，用来喂猪和奶牛。 2 V-T If you **hog** something, you take all of it in a greedy or impolite way. 独占 [INFORMAL] ❑ *Are you done hogging the bathroom?* 你要霸占浴室到什么时候？ 3 PHRASE If you **go whole hog** or **go the whole hog**, you do something bold or extravagant in the most complete way possible. 彻底地干 [INFORMAL] ❑ *Well, I thought, I've already lost half my job, I might as well go the whole hog and lose it completely.* 嗯，我想，我已经丢了一半的工作了，我还不如彻底放弃算了。

★ **hoist** /hɔɪst/ (**hoists, hoisting, hoisted**) 1 V-T If you **hoist** something heavy somewhere, you lift it or pull it up there. 提起；拉起（重物）❑ *Hoisting my suitcase on to my shoulder, I turned and headed toward my hotel.* 我把手提箱扛到肩膀上，转身朝旅馆走去。 2 V-T If something heavy **is hoisted** somewhere, it is lifted there using a machine such as a crane. （用起重机等）吊起 ❑ *A twenty-foot steel pyramid is to be hoisted into position on top of the tower.* 一座20英尺高的钢制金字塔将被吊到塔顶该放的位置上。 3 N-COUNT A **hoist** is a

h

machine for lifting heavy things. 起重机 ❑ *He uses a hydraulic hoist to unload two empty barrels.* 他用一架液压起重机卸下两只空桶。 4 V-T If you **hoist** a flag or a sail, you pull it up to its correct position by using ropes. 升起（旗、帆等）❑ *A group forced their way through police cordons and hoisted their flag on top of the disputed monument.* 一群人强行冲破警方警戒线，把他们的旗帜升到了那座有争议的纪念碑的顶部。

hold
❶ PHYSICALLY TOUCHING, SUPPORTING, OR CONTAINING
❷ HAVING OR DOING
❸ CONTROLLING OR REMAINING
❹ PHRASES
❺ PHRASAL VERBS

❶ **hold** ◆◆◆ /hoʊld/ (**holds, holding, held**) 1 V-T When you **hold** something, you carry or support it, using your hands or your arms. 拿着；托住 ❑ *Hold the knife at an angle.* 斜握着刀。 ● N-COUNT **Hold** is also a noun. 拿；托住 ❑ *He released his hold on the camera.* 他松开了握着照相机的手。 2 N-UNCOUNT **Hold** is used in expressions such as **grab hold of, catch hold of**, and **get hold of**, to indicate that you close your hand tightly around something, for example to stop something moving or falling. 抓住 ❑ *I was woken up by someone grabbing hold of my sleeping bag.* 有人抓住我的睡袋把我弄醒了。 ❑ *A doctor and a nurse caught hold of his arms.* 一名医生和一名护士抓住了他的双臂。 3 V-T When you **hold** someone, you put your arms around them, usually because you want to show them how much you like them or because you want to comfort them. （常因想表示喜爱和安慰而）抱住 ❑ *If only he would hold her close to him.* 他要是紧紧抱住她就好了。 4 V-T If you **hold** someone in a particular position, you use force to keep them in that position and stop them from moving. 按住；使不动 ❑ *He then held the man in an armlock until police arrived.* 然后他反扭手臂将那人按住，直到警察赶来。 5 N-COUNT A **hold** is a particular way of keeping someone in a position using your own hands, arms, or legs. 按住（使某人不得动弹）❑ *The man wrestled the Indian to the ground, locked in a hold he couldn't escape.* 那人把印第安人摔倒在地，并将他死死按住，使他无法逃脱。 6 V-T When you **hold** a part of your body, you put your hand on or against it, often because it hurts. （常指因疼痛而）捂住 ❑ *Soon she was crying bitterly about the pain and was holding her throat.* 不一会儿她就疼得捂着喉咙哭了。 7 V-T When you **hold** a part of your body in a particular position, you put it into that position and keep it there. 使（自己身体某部位）保持某种姿势 ❑ *Hold your hands in front of your face.* 把双手放在面前。 8 V-T If one thing **holds** another in a particular position, it keeps it in that position. 使…保持（在某位置）不动 ❑ *...the wooden wedge which held the heavy door open.* …卡住沉重的门使之洞开着的木楔。 9 V-T If one thing is used to **hold** another, it is used to store it. 存放 ❑ *Two knife racks hold her favorite knives.* 两个刀架上放着她最喜爱的刀。 10 N-COUNT In a ship or airplane, a **hold** is a place where cargo or luggage is stored. （船、飞机等的）货舱 ❑ *A fire had been reported in the cargo hold.* 据报告货舱失火了。 11 V-T If a place **holds** something, it keeps it available for reference or for future use. 储备；储存 ❑ *The Better Business Bureau holds an enormous amount of information on any business problem.* 商业信用局存储着有关任何商务问题的大量信息。 12 V-T If something **holds** a particular amount of something, it can contain that amount. 容纳得下 [no cont] ❑ *One CD-ROM disk can hold over 100,000 pages of text.* 一张CD光盘能容纳10万多页的文字资料。

Thesaurus *hold* 另参见：
v. carry, support ❶ 1
cradle, embrace, hug ❶ 3
hang on to, pin down, restrain ❶ 4

❷ **hold** ◆◆◆ /hoʊld/ (**holds, holding, held**)

Hold is often used to indicate that someone or something has the particular thing, characteristic, or attitude that is mentioned. Therefore it takes most of its meaning from the word that follows it.

1 V-T **Hold** is used with words and expressions indicating an opinion or belief, to show that someone has a particular opinion or believes that something is true. 持有（观点或信念等）[no cont] ❑ *He held firm opinions which usually conflicted with my own.* 他持有坚定的观点，通常都与我的观点相左。 ❑ *Current thinking holds that obesity is more a medical than a psychological problem.* 现代观点认为肥胖更多是生理问题而不是心理问题。 2 V-T **Hold** is used with words such as "fear" or "mystery" to indicate someone's feelings toward something, as if those feelings were a characteristic of the thing itself. 有（可怕、神秘的）特质 [no passive] ❑ *Death doesn't hold any fear for me.* 死亡对我来说没什么可怕的。 3 V-T **Hold** is used with nouns such as "office," "power," and "responsibility" to indicate that someone has a particular position of power or authority. 担任（职务）；掌握（权力）；承担（责任）❑ *She has never held an elected office.* 她从未担任过由选举产生的职务。 4 V-T **Hold** is used with nouns such as "permit," "degree," or "ticket" to indicate that someone has a particular document that allows them to do something. 持有（许可证、学位证、票据等）❑ *Applicants should normally hold a good degree.* 申请人通常应拥有优秀学位。 ❑ *He did not hold a firearms license.* 他没有持枪许可证。 5 V-T **Hold** is used with nouns such as "party," "meeting," "talks," "election," and "trial" to indicate that people are organizing a particular activity. 举行（聚会、会议、会谈、选举和审判等）❑ *The country will hold democratic elections within a year.* 该国将在一年之内举行民主选举。 ● **hold·ing** N-UNCOUNT 举行 ❑ *They also called for the holding of multi-party general elections.* 他们还呼吁举行多党大选。 6 V-RECIP **Hold** is used with nouns such as "conversation," "interview," and "talks" to indicate that two or more people meet and discuss something. 进行（谈话、访谈等）❑ *The prime minister is holding consultations with his colleagues to finalize the deal.* 首相正和他的同僚进行磋商，以最终敲定这项协议。 ❑ *The engineer and his son held frequent meetings concerning technical problems.* 工程师和他的儿子经常就技术问题进行讨论。 7 V-T **Hold** is used with nouns such as "shares" and "stock" to indicate that someone owns a particular proportion of a business. 拥有（股份、股票等）❑ *The group said it continues to hold 1,774,687 shares in the company.* 该集团说他们继续持有这家公司1774687股的股份。 8 → see also **holding** 9 V-T **Hold** is used with nouns such as "attention" or "interest" to indicate that what you do or say keeps someone interested or listening to you. 吸引住（注意力）；保持（兴趣）❑ *If you want to hold someone's attention, look them directly in the eye but don't stare.* 如果你想吸引别人的注意力，就看着他们的眼睛，但不要死盯着看。 10 V-T If you **hold** someone responsible, liable, or accountable for something, you will blame them if anything goes wrong. 让（某人承担责任）❑ *It's impossible to hold any individual responsible.* 不可能让任何个人承担责任。

❸ **hold** ◆◆◆ /hoʊld/ (**holds, holding, held**) 1 V-T If someone **holds** you in a place, they keep you there as a prisoner and do not allow you to leave. 扣留 ❑ *The inside of a van was as good a place as any to hold a kidnap victim.* 厢式小型货车里面像其他地方一样是扣押被绑架者的好地方。 ❑ *Somebody is holding your wife hostage.* 有人在扣留你的妻子当人质。 2 V-T If people such as an army or a violent crowd **hold** a place, they control it by using force. 占据 ❑ *Demonstrators have been holding the square since Sunday.* 自星期天以来，示威者们一直占据着广场。 3 N-SING If you have a **hold over** someone, you have power or control over them, for example because you know something about them you can use to threaten them or because you are in a position of authority. 对…有控制的力量 ❑ *He had ordered his officers to keep an exceptionally firm hold over their men.* 他已经命令军官们要对他们的下属保持极为严格的控制。 4 V-T/V-I If you ask someone to **hold**, or to **hold the line**, when you are answering a telephone call, you are asking them to wait for a short time, for example so that you can find the person they want to speak to. （打电话时）不挂断 [no passive] ❑ *Could you hold the line and I'll just get my pen.* 请别挂断，我去拿支笔，好吗？ 5 V-T If you **hold** telephone calls for someone, you do not allow people who phone to speak to that person, but take messages instead. 代接（电话）并留言 ❑ *He tells his secretary to hold his calls.* 他让他的秘书代接电话。 6 V-T/V-I If something **holds** at a particular value or level, or **is held** there, it is kept at that value or level. 保持在（在一定数值或水平）❑ *OPEC production is holding at around 21.5 million barrels a day.* 石油输出国组织的石油产量目前保持在每天两千一百五十万桶左右。 7 V-T If you **hold** a sound or musical note, you continue making it. 持续发出（声音或音符）❑ *...a voice which hit and held every note with perfect ease and clarity.* …非常轻松而清晰地唱出每个音符的歌喉。 8 V-T If you **hold** something such as a train or an elevator, you delay it. 延迟；推迟 ❑ *A spokesman defended the decision to hold the train until police arrived.* 一位发言人为延迟火车发车直到警察到来的决定作了辩解。 9 V-I If an offer or invitation still **holds**, it is still available for you to accept. （报价或邀请等）有效 ❑ *Does your offer still hold?* 你的报价仍然有效吗？ 10 V-I If a good situation **holds**, it continues and does not get worse or fail. （好的状态）保持不变

❑ *Our luck couldn't hold forever.* 我们的好运不可能永远保持不变。 **11** V-I If an argument or theory **holds**, it is true or valid, even after close examination. (论点、理论等) 站得住脚 ❑ *Today, most people think that argument no longer holds.* 今天，大多数人认为这个论点不再站得住脚。 ● PHRASAL VERB **Hold up** means the same as **hold**. 站得住脚 ❑ *Democrats say arguments against the bill won't hold up.* 民主党人说，反对这项议案的论点站不住脚。 **12** V-I If part of a structure **holds**, it does not fall or break although there is a lot of force or pressure on it. (在重压下) 支撑住 ❑ *How long would the roof hold?* 这屋顶还能支撑多久？ **13** V-I If laws or rules **hold**, they exist and remain in force. (法规等) 有效 ❑ *These laws also hold for universities.* 这些法律同样适用于大学。 **14** V-I If you **hold to** a promise or to high standards of behavior, you keep that promise or continue to behave according to those standards. 遵守 (诺言或高尚的行为准则) [FORMAL] ❑ *Will the president be able to hold to this commitment?* 总统能恪守这一承诺吗？ **15** V-T If someone or something **holds** you **to** a promise or **to** high standards of behavior, they make you keep that promise or those standards. 使…恪守 (诺言或高尚的行为准则) ❑ *"I won't make you marry him." — "I'll hold you to that."* "我不会让你嫁给他的。" —— "我要你保证说话算话。"

❹ hold ♦♦♦ /hoʊld/ (holds, holding, held)

➪ **Please look at meanings 12 – 18 to see if the expression you are looking for is shown under another headword.** **1** PHRASE If you **hold forth on** a subject, you speak confidently and for a long time about it, especially to a group of people. (尤指当众) 滔滔不绝地说 ❑ *Barry was holding forth on something.* 巴里正滔滔不绝地说着什么。 **2** PHRASE If you **get hold of** an object or information, you obtain it, usually after some difficulty. (通常指克服困难后) 获得 ❑ *It is hard to get hold of guns in this country.* 在这个国家很难弄到枪。 **3** PHRASE If you **get hold of** someone, you manage to contact them. 设法与…联络 ❑ *The only electrician we could get hold of was miles away.* 我们惟一能够联络上的电工在几英里之外。 **4** CONVENTION If you say "**Hold it,**" you are telling someone to stop what they are doing and to wait. 停下 ❑ *Hold it! Don't move!* 停下！别动！ **5** PHRASE If you put something **on hold**, you decide not to do it, deal with it, or change it now, but to leave it until later. 推迟 ❑ *He put his retirement on hold to work 16 hours a day, seven days a week to find a solution.* 为了找到一个解决方案，他推迟了退休，每周工作7天，每天工作16小时。 **6** PHRASE If you **hold** your **own**, you are able to resist someone who is attacking or opposing you. (面对攻击或反对等) 顶住 ❑ *The Frenchman held his own against the challenger.* 那个法国人顶住了挑战者的攻击。 **7** PHRASE If you can do something well enough to **hold** your **own**, you do not appear foolish when you are compared with someone who is generally thought to be very good at it. 与…相匹敌 ❑ *She can hold her own against almost any player.* 她几乎能与所有选手相匹敌。 **8** PHRASE If you **hold still**, you do not move. 不动 ❑ *Can't you hold still for a second?* 你一秒钟不动都不行？ **9** PHRASE If something **takes hold**, it gains complete control or influence over a person or thing. 完全控制 (某人或某物) ❑ *She felt a strange excitement taking hold of her.* 她感到一种奇怪的兴奋感控制住了自己。 **10** PHRASE If you **hold tight**, you put your hand around or against something in order to prevent yourself from falling over. A bus driver might say "**Hold tight!**" to you if you are standing on a bus when it is about to move. 抓牢 ❑ *He held tight to the rope.* 他紧紧抓住绳子。 **11** PHRASE If you **hold tight**, you do not immediately start a course of action that you have been planning or thinking about. 不轻易行动 ❑ *The advice for individual investors is to hold tight.* 给个人投资者的建议是不要轻举妄动。 **12** to **hold** something **at bay** → see **bay** **13** to **hold** something **in check** → see **check** **14** to **hold fast** → see **fast** **15** to **hold the fort** → see **fort** **16** to **hold** your **ground** → see **ground** **17** to **hold** someone **ransom** → see **ransom** **18** to **hold sway** → see **sway**

❺ hold ♦♦♦ /hoʊld/ (holds, holding, held)

▸ **hold against** PHRASAL VERB If you **hold** something **against** someone, you let their actions in the past influence your present attitude toward them and cause you to deal severely or unfairly with them. 因…而责怪 ❑ *Bernstein lost the case, but never held it against Grundy.* 伯恩斯坦输掉了官司，但从未因此而对格伦迪有所怨恨。

▸ **hold back** **1** PHRASAL VERB If you **hold back** or if something **holds** you **back**, you hesitate before you do something because you are not sure whether it is the right thing to do. (使) 犹豫 ❑ *The Bush administration had several reasons for holding back.* 布什政府的犹豫不决有几个原因。 **2** PHRASAL VERB To **hold** someone or something **back** means to prevent someone from doing something, or to prevent something from happening. 阻止 ❑ *Stagnation in home sales is holding back economic recovery.* 住房销售的停滞正阻碍着经济的复苏。 **3** PHRASAL VERB If you **hold** something **back**, you keep it in reserve to use later. 储存 ❑ *Farmers apparently hold back produce in the hope that prices will rise.* 农场主们囤积农产品显然是希望价格会上涨。 **4** PHRASAL VERB If you **hold** something **back**, you do not include it in the information you are giving about something. 隐瞒 ❑ *You seem to be holding something back.* 你好像在隐瞒什么。 **5** PHRASAL VERB If you **hold back** something such as tears or laughter, or if you **hold back**, you make an effort to stop yourself from showing how you feel. 克制住 (泪水或笑声等) ❑ *She kept trying to hold back her tears.* 她一直在试图忍住不掉眼泪。 **6** PHRASAL VERB If a teacher **holds** a student **back**, they keep them in the same grade instead of promoting them to a higher grade, because their work is not good enough. 使…留级 ❑ *16 percent of eighth-graders were held back for poor performance.* 16%的8年级学生因为成绩差而被留级。

▸ **hold down** **1** PHRASAL VERB If you **hold down** a job or a place on a team, you manage to keep it. 保住 (工作或地位) ❑ *He never could hold down a job.* 他从来就保不住自己的工作。 **2** PHRASAL VERB If you **hold** someone **down**, you keep them under control and do not allow them to have much freedom or power or many rights. 压制 ❑ *Everyone thinks there is some vast conspiracy wanting to hold down the younger generation.* 人人都认为有个要压制年轻一代的大阴谋。

▸ **hold off** **1** PHRASAL VERB If you **hold off** doing something, you delay doing it or delay making a decision about it. 推迟 ❑ *The hospital staff held off taking Rosenbaum in for an X-ray.* 医院工作人员推迟了让罗森鲍姆做X光检查的时间。 **2** PHRASAL VERB If you **hold off** a challenge in a race or competition, you do not allow someone to pass you. (在比赛中或竞争中) 抵挡住 ❑ *Between 1987 and 1990, Steffi Graf largely held off Navratilova's challenge for the crown.* 1987到1990年期间，施特菲•格拉芙很大程度上抵挡住了纳芙拉蒂洛娃的夺冠挑战。

▸ **hold on** or **hold onto** **1** PHRASAL VERB If you **hold on**, or **hold onto** something, you keep your hand on it or around it, for example to prevent the thing from falling or to support yourself. 握住 ❑ *His right arm was extended up beside his head, still holding on to a coffee cup.* 他的右臂向头的一侧伸开，手上还紧紧握着一只咖啡杯。 ❑ *He was struggling to hold onto a rock on the face of the cliff.* 他拼命挣扎着去抓悬崖壁上的一块岩石。 **2** PHRASAL VERB If you **hold on**, you manage to achieve success or avoid failure in spite of great difficulties or opposition. 坚持不懈 ❑ *The Rams held on to defeat the Nevada Wolf Pack in Reno, 32-28.* 公羊队坚忍不拔，在雷诺市以32比28的比分击败了内华达狼群队。 **3** PHRASAL VERB If you ask someone to **hold on**, you are asking them to wait for a short time. 稍等片刻 [SPOKEN] ❑ *The manager asked him to hold on while he investigated.* 经理让他稍等一会，他去调查一下。

▸ **hold out** **1** PHRASAL VERB If you **hold out** your hand or something you have in your hand, you move your hand away from your body, for example to shake hands with someone. 伸出 (手或手里的东西) ❑ *"I'm Nancy Drew," she said, holding out her hand.* "我是南希•德鲁"，她边说边伸出手来。 **2** PHRASAL VERB If you **hold out for** something, you refuse to accept something which you do not think is good enough or large enough, and you continue to demand more. 拒绝妥协 ❑ *I should have held out for a better deal.* 我本应坚持要求更好的条件。 **3** PHRASAL VERB If you say that someone **is holding out on** you, you think that they are refusing to give you information that you want. 隐瞒 (信息) [INFORMAL] ❑ *He had always believed that kids could sense it when you held out on them.* 他一直认为，如果对孩子们有所隐瞒的话，他们能够感觉得到。 **4** PHRASAL VERB If you **hold out**, you manage to resist an enemy or opponent in difficult circumstances and refuse to give in. 坚持抵抗 ❑ *One prisoner was still holding out on the roof of the jail.* 一名囚犯仍在监狱的屋顶上拒不投降。 **5** PHRASAL VERB If you **hold out** hope of something happening, you hope that in the future something will happen as you want it to. 寄予 (希望) ❑ *He still holds out hope that they could be a family again.* 他仍然希望他们能够再次成为一家人。

▸ **hold up** **1** PHRASAL VERB If you **hold up** your hand or something you have in your hand, you move it upward into a particular position and keep it there. 举起 ❑ *She held up her hand stiffly.* 她僵硬地举起手来。 **2** PHRASAL VERB If one thing **holds up** another, it is placed under the other thing in order to support it and prevent it from falling. 支撑 ❑ *Mills have iron pillars all over the place holding up the roof.* 工厂里到处都有铁柱子支撑着屋顶。 **3** PHRASAL VERB To **hold up** a person or process means to make them late or delay them. 耽搁 ❑ *Why were you holding everyone up?* 你为什么要耽搁大家？

If you **cancel** or **call off** an arrangement or an appointment, you stop it from happening. ❑ *His failing health forced him to cancel the meeting... The European Community has threatened to call off peace talks.* If you **postpone** or **put off** an arrangement or an appointment, you make another arrangement for it to happen at a later time. ❑ *Elections have been postponed until next year... The senate put off a vote on the nomination for one week.* If you **delay** something that has been arranged, you make it happen later than planned. ❑ *Space agency managers decided to delay the launch of the space shuttle.* If something **delays** you or **holds** you **up**, you start or finish what you are doing later than you planned. ❑ *He was delayed in traffic... Delivery of equipment had been held up by delays and disputes.*

4 PHRASAL VERB If someone **holds up** a place such as a bank or a store, they point a weapon at someone there to make them give them money or valuable goods. 持械抢劫 ❑ *When his money was gone he held up a gas station with a toy gun.* 他把钱花光后，就用一把玩具枪抢劫了一家加油站。 5 PHRASAL VERB If you **hold up** something such as someone's behavior, you make it known to other people, so that they can criticize or praise it. 举出…作为褒贬的对象 ❑ *He had always been held up as an example to the younger ones.* 他总是被树立为弟妹们学习的榜样。 6 PHRASAL VERB If something such as a type of business **holds up** in difficult conditions, it stays in a reasonably good state. (在逆境中) 保持良好状况 ❑ *Children's wear is one area that is holding up well in the recession.* 在经济衰退期间，童装是持续销售良好的一个领域。 7 PHRASAL VERB If an argument or theory **holds up**, it is true or valid, even after close examination. (论据或理论等) 经受得住检验 ❑ *I'm not sure if the argument holds up, but it's stimulating.* 我不能确定这一论点能否经得住推敲，但是它却很令人兴奋。 8 → see also **holdup**

hold·all /hoʊldɔl/ (**holdalls**) also **hold-all** N-COUNT A **holdall** is a strong bag which you use to carry your clothes and other things, for example when you are traveling. 大旅行袋 [mainly BRIT]

in AM, usually use **carryall**

▲ **hold·er** ♦◇◇ /hoʊldər/ (**holders**) 1 N-COUNT A **holder** is someone who owns or has something. 持有者 ❑ *This season the club has had 73,500 season-ticket holders.* 本季该俱乐部已经有73500名季票持有者。 2 N-COUNT A **holder** is a container in which you put an object, usually in order to protect it or to keep it in place. 支持物；支架 ❑ *...a toothbrush holder.* …一只牙刷座。

Word Partnership *holder* 的常用搭配：

N. **cup** holder, **pot** holder 2

hold·ing /hoʊldɪŋ/ (**holdings**) N-COUNT If you have a **holding** in a company, you own shares in it. 持有的股份 [BUSINESS] ❑ *That would increase Olympia & York's holding to 35%.* 这将使奥林匹亚约克公司的持有股增加至35%。

hold·ing com·pa·ny (**holding companies**) N-COUNT A **holding company** is a company that has enough shares in one or more other companies to be able to control the other companies. 控股公司 [BUSINESS] ❑ *...a Montreal-based holding company with interests in telecommunications, gas, and natural resources.* …一家设在蒙特利尔，并在电信、天然气和自然资源方面有业务的控股公司。

holdup /hoʊldʌp/ (**holdups**) also **hold-up** 1 N-COUNT A **holdup** is a situation in which someone is threatened with a weapon in order to make them hand over money or valuables. 持械抢劫 ❑ *What could have happened? A hold-up? There'd been no gunshot or scream.* 发生了什么呢？持枪抢劫？没有听到枪声或尖叫声。 2 N-COUNT A **holdup** is a delay. 延搁 ❑ *...bureaucratic holdups and legal wrangles over the contract.* …围绕合同的官僚拖延和法律纠纷。 3 N-COUNT A **holdup** is the stopping or very slow movement of traffic, sometimes caused by an accident which happened earlier. 交通堵塞 ❑ *They arrived late due to a freeway holdup.* 因为高速公路上堵车，他们迟到了。

hole ♦♦◇ /hoʊl/ (**holes**) 1 N-COUNT A **hole** is a hollow space in something solid, with an opening on one side. 洞 ❑ *He took a shovel, dug a hole, and buried his once-prized possessions.* 他拿了一把铲子，挖了一个坑，埋下了他曾经珍爱的物品。 2 N-COUNT A **hole** is an opening in something that goes right through it. (贯穿的) 孔洞 ❑ *...kids with holes in the knees of their jeans.* …牛仔裤的膝盖上有破洞的孩子们。 3 N-COUNT A **hole** is the home or hiding place of a mouse, rabbit, or other small animal. (鼠、兔等小动物的) 洞穴 ❑ *...a rabbit hole.* …一个兔子窝。 4 N-COUNT A **hole in** a law, theory, or argument is a fault or weakness that it has. (法律、理论、论点等的) 漏洞 ❑ *There were some holes in that theory, some unanswered questions.* 那个理论中有些漏洞，一些没有得到解答的问题。 5 N-COUNT A **hole** is also one of the nine or eighteen sections of a golf course. (高尔夫球场上的) 球洞 ❑ *I played nine holes with Gary Carter today.* 我今天同加里・卡特打了9洞高尔夫球。 6 PHRASE If you say that you are **in a hole**, you mean that you are in a difficult or embarrassing situation. 身陷困境或窘境 [INFORMAL] ❑ *We were in a hole, but I was proud with the way we came back.* 我们虽然身陷困境，但我很为我们能像这样东山再起感到自豪。 7 PHRASE If a person or organization is **in the hole**, they owe money to someone else. 亏空 [AM, INFORMAL] ❑ *Some estimates show next year's budget could be $2.5 billion in the hole.* 一些估计显示，明年的预算将会亏空25亿美元。 8 PHRASE If you get **a hole in one** in golf, you get the golf ball into the hole with a single stroke. (高尔夫球运动中) 一杆进洞 ❑ *All they ever dream about is getting a hole in one.* 他们一直梦想着能一杆进洞。 9 PHRASE If you **pick holes** in an argument or theory, you find weak points in it so that it is no longer valid. 在 (论据或理论中) 挑毛病 [INFORMAL] ❑ *He then goes on to pick holes in the article before reaching his conclusion.* 然后，他继续挑这篇文章的毛病，最后得出了自己的结论。
→ see **golf**

Word Partnership *hole* 的常用搭配：

ADJ. **deep** hole 1
big/huge/small hole, **gaping** hole 1 2
V. **dig** a hole, **fill/plug** a hole 1
cut/punch a hole **in** *something*, **bore/drill** a hole **in** *something* 2

holi·day ♦♦◇ /hɒlɪdeɪ/ (**holidays, holidaying, holidayed**) 1 N-COUNT A **holiday** is a day when people do not go to work or school because of a religious or national celebration. 公众假日 ❑ *New Year's Day is a public holiday.* 元旦是公休日。 2 → see also **bank holiday** 3 N-COUNT A **holiday** is a period of time during which you relax and enjoy yourself away from home. People sometimes refer to their holiday as their **holidays**. (外出度过的) 假期 [BRIT]

in AM, use **vacation**

4 N-PLURAL **The holidays** are the time when children do not have to go to school. (学校的) 假期 [BRIT]

in AM, use **vacation**

5 N-UNCOUNT If you have a particular number of days' or weeks' **holiday**, you do not have to go to work for that number of days or weeks. (工作) 假期 [BRIT]

in AM, use **vacation**

6 V-I If you **are holidaying** in a place away from home, you are on holiday there. (外出) 度假 [BRIT]

in AM, use **vacation**

holi·day·maker /hɒlɪdeɪmeɪkər/ (**holidaymakers**) N-COUNT A **holidaymaker** is a person who is away from their home on holiday. 度假者 [BRIT]

in AM, use **vacationer**

ho·lism /hoʊlɪzəm/ N-UNCOUNT **Holism** is the belief that everything in nature is connected in some way. 整体主义；整体论 [FORMAL] ❑ *Nature by itself, he writes, runs on "principles of balance and holism."* 自然界本身，他写道，是按照"平衡和整体的原则"运转的。

Word Link *hol ≈ whole : holistic, holocaust, wholly*

ho·lis·tic /hoʊlɪstɪk/ ADJ **Holistic** means based on the principles of holism. 整体主义的 [FORMAL] ❑ *...practitioners of holistic medicine.* …整体医学医生。

hol·ler /hɒlər/ (**hollers, hollering, hollered**) V-T/V-I If you **holler**, you shout loudly. 喊叫 [mainly AM, INFORMAL] ❑ *The audience whooped and hollered.* 观众们欢呼着，叫喊着。 ❑ *"Watch out!" he hollered.* "小心！"他大喊一声。 ● N-COUNT **Holler** is also a noun. 喊叫 ❑ *She spun round as the man, with a holler, burst through the door.* 当那个人大喊着冲进门时，她急忙转过身去。 ● PHRASAL VERB **Holler out** means the same as **holler**. 喊叫 ❑ *I hollered out the names.* 我大声喊出这些名字。

hol·low /hɒloʊ/ (**hollows, hollowing, hollowed**) 1 ADJ Something that is **hollow** has a space inside it, as opposed to being solid all the way through. 空心的 ❑ *...a hollow tree.* …一棵空心树 2 ADJ A surface that is **hollow** curves inward. 凹陷的 ❑ *He looked young, dark and sharp-featured, with hollow cheeks.* 他看起来很年轻，肤色黝黑，面部棱角分明，双颊凹陷。 3 N-COUNT A **hollow** is an area that is lower than the surrounding surface. 凹陷处 ❑ *Below him the town lay warm in the hollow of the hill.* 在他的下面，小镇温暖地坐落在山坳里。 4 ADJ If you describe a statement, situation, or person as **hollow**, you mean they have no real value, worth, or effectiveness. 空洞的；没有价值的 ❑ *Any threat to bring in the police is a hollow one.* 任何要叫警察来的威胁都是虚张声势。 ● **hol·low·ness** N-UNCOUNT 空洞 ❑ *One month before the deadline we see the hollowness of these promises.* 截止期限前一个月我们看出了这些承诺的空洞性。 5 ADJ If someone gives a **hollow** laugh, they laugh in a way that shows that they do not really find something amusing. 虚伪的 [ADJ n] ❑ *Murray Pick's hollow laugh had no mirth in it.* 默里·皮克虚伪的笑声里没有一点快乐。 6 ADJ A **hollow** sound is dull and echoing. (声音) 空洞而沉闷的 [ADJ n] ❑ *...the hollow sound of a gunshot.* …空闷的枪声。 7 V-T If something is **hollowed**, its surface is made to curve inward or downward. 使凹陷 [usu passive] ❑ *The mule's back was hollowed by the weight of its burden.* 骡子的背被所载重物压得弯了下去。

Thesaurus *hollow* 另参见：

ADJ. empty 1
empty, meaningless 4

★ **hol·ly** /hɒli/ (**hollies**) N-VAR **Holly** is an evergreen tree or shrub which has hard, shiny leaves with sharp points, and red berries in winter. 冬青树

Word Link *hol ≈ whole : holistic, holocaust, wholly*

holo·caust /hɒləkɔst, hoʊlə-/ (**holocausts**) 1 N-VAR A **holocaust** is an event in which there is a lot of destruction and many people are killed, especially one caused by war. (尤指战争引起的) 大灾难 ❑ *A nuclear holocaust seemed a very real possibility in the '50s.* 在50年代，核灾难似乎是件很有可能发生的事。 2 N-SING **The Holocaust** is used to refer to the killing by the Nazis of millions of Jews during the Second World War. (第二次世界大战中纳粹对犹太人的) 大屠杀 ❑ *...an Israeli-based fund for survivors of the Holocaust and their families.* …设在以色列的为纳粹大屠杀的幸存者及其家属建立的基金。

holy ♦◇◇ /hoʊli/ (**holier, holiest**) ADJ If you describe something as **holy**, you mean that it is considered to be special because it is connected with God or a particular religion. 有关上帝的；神圣的 ❑ *To them, as to all Poles, this is a holy place.* 正如对所有的波兰人一样，对他们来说，这里是个神圣的地方。

▲ **hom·age** /hɒmɪdʒ, ɒm-/ N-UNCOUNT **Homage** is respect shown toward someone or something you admire, or to a person in authority. 崇敬 [usu N "to" n] ❑ *Palace has released two marvelous films that pay homage to our literary heritage.* 皇城电影公司推出了两部推崇我们文学遗产的精彩影片。

home

❶ NOUN, ADJECTIVE, AND ADVERB USES
❷ PHRASAL VERB USES

❶ **home** ♦♦♦ /hoʊm/ (**homes**) 1 N-COUNT Someone's **home** is the house or apartment where they live. 家 [oft poss N, also "at" N] ❑ *Last night they stayed at home and watched TV.* 昨天晚上他们待在家里看电视。 ❑ *The general divided his time between his shabby offices and his home in Hampstead.* 将军的时间一部分在他那破旧的办公室里度过，另一部分在他汉普斯特德的家度过。

When people move to a new **home**, they often hold a **housewarming** party. Friends and neighbors usually bring gifts for the house such as plants, soap, kitchen towels, and other non-personal items to welcome the new people to the neighborhood and make them feel welcome.

2 N-UNCOUNT You can use **home** to refer in a general way to the house, town, or country where someone lives now or where they were born, often to emphasize that they feel they belong in that place. 家乡；祖国 ❑ *She gives frequent performances of her work, both at home and abroad.* 她经常在国内外演出自己的作品。 ❑ *His father worked away from home for much of Jim's first five years.* 在吉姆5岁前的大部分时间里，他的爸爸离家在外地工作。 3 ADV **Home** means to or at the place where you live. 回家；在家 ❑ *His wife wasn't feeling too well and she wanted to go home.* 他妻子感觉有些不舒服，想要回家。 ❑ *I'll call you as soon as I get home.* 我一到家就给你打电话。 4 ADJ **Home** means made or done in the place where you live. 在家里做的或进行的 [ADJ n] ❑ *...cheap but healthy home cooking.* …便宜却健康的家常便饭。

5 ADJ **Home** means relating to your own country as opposed to foreign countries. 本国的 [ADJ n] ❑ *Europe's software companies still have a growing home market.* 欧洲的软件公司仍拥有一个不断增长的本土市场。 6 N-COUNT A **home** is a large house or institution where a number of people live and are cared for, instead of living in their own houses or apartments. They usually live there because they are too old or ill to take care of themselves or for their families to care for them. 养育院；养老院 ❑ *It's going to be a home for handicapped children.* 它将成为一家残疾儿童福利院。 7 N-COUNT You can refer to a family unit as a **home**. 家庭 ❑ *She had, at any rate, provided a peaceful and loving home for Harriet.* 她至少给哈丽雅特提供了一个宁静的、充满爱的家。 8 N-SING If you refer to the **home of** something, you mean the place where it began or where it is most typically found. 发源地 ❑ *This southwest region of France is the home of claret.* 法国西南部的这个地区是波尔多干红葡萄酒的产地。 9 N-COUNT If you find a **home for** something, you find a place where it can be kept. 适于存放…的地方 ❑ *The equipment itself is getting smaller, neater and easier to find a home for.* 该设备本身变得越来越小、越来越精巧，因而也就越来越便于存放。 10 ADV If you press, drive, or hammer something **home**, you explain it to people as forcefully as possible. 彻底地 [ADV after v] ❑ *It is now up to all of us to debate this issue and press home the argument.* 现在要靠我们大家对这个问题进行辩论，并尽可能将论点阐释清楚。 11 N-UNCOUNT When a sports team plays **at home**, they play a game on their own field, rather than on the opposing team's field. (体育比赛的) 主场 ❑ *I scored in both games; we tied at home and beat them away.* 我在两场比赛中都进了球；我们在主场打成平局，在客场击败了他们。 ● ADJ **Home** is also an adjective. 主场的 [ADJ n] ❑ *All three are fans, and attend all home games together.* 3个人都是球迷，并且都一起观看了所有主场的比赛。 12 PHRASE If you feel **at home**, you feel comfortable in the place or situation that you are in. 舒适自在 ❑ *He spoke very good English and appeared pleased to see us, and we soon felt quite at home.* 他英语说得非常好，见到我们时显得很高兴，我们很快就感到毫无拘束。 13 PHRASE To **bring** something **home to** someone means to make them understand how important or serious it is. 使…清楚地领会 (重要性或严重性) ❑ *Their sobering conversation brought home to everyone present the serious and worthwhile work the Red Cross does.* 他们的谈话发人深省，使得在场的每个人都清楚地认识到红十字会所做的严肃而有价值的工作。 14 PHRASE If you say that someone is **home free** you mean that they have been successful or that they are certain to be successful. 大功告成；稳操胜券 ❑ *Just when she thought she was home free, her father spoke from behind her.* 就在她认为已经大功告成的时候，身后传来她爸爸说话的声音。 15 PHRASE If a situation or what someone says **hits home** or **strikes home**, people accept that it is real or true, even though it may be painful for them to realize. 被深刻领会 ❑ *Did the reality of war finally hit home?* 人们最终深刻认识到战争的现实了吗？ 16 PHRASE You can say **a home away from home** to refer to a place in which you are as comfortable as in your own home. 像家一样舒适的地方 [APPROVAL] ❑ *The café seems to be her home away from home these days.* 这些天来，咖啡馆似乎成了她的第二个家。 17 CONVENTION If you say to a guest "**Make yourself at home**," you are making them feel welcome and inviting them to behave in an informal, relaxed way. 请别拘束 [POLITENESS] ❑ *Take off your jacket and make yourself at home.* 请脱下外套，随便些。 18 PHRASE If you say that something is **nothing to write home about**, you mean that it is not very interesting or exciting. 平平常常 [INFORMAL] ❑ *I see growth slightly up, but nothing to write home about.* 我看到稍有增长，但也没什么令人激动的。 19 PHRASE If something that is thrown or fired **strikes home**, it reaches its target. 打中目标 [WRITTEN] ❑ *Only two torpedoes struck home.* 只有两枚鱼雷击中目标。

Thesaurus *home* 另参见：

N. dwelling, house, residence ❶ 1
birthplace, home town ❶ 2

Word Partnership *home* 的常用搭配：

ADJ. **new** home ❶ 1 2
close to home ❶ 1 2 15

V. **bring/take** *someone/something* home, **build a** home, **buy a** home, **call/phone** home, **come** home, **drive** home, **feel at** home, **fly** home, **get** home, **go** home, **head for** home, **leave** home, **return** home, **ride** home, **sit** *at* home, **stay** *at* home, **walk** home, **work at** home ❶ 1 – 3

h

H

❷ **home** /hoʊm/ (**homes, homing, homed**)
▸ **home in** 1 PHRASAL VERB If you **home in on** one particular aspect of something, you give all your attention to it. 把全部注意力集中于… ❏ *The critics immediately homed in on the group's essential members.* 批评家们立刻就把全部注意力集中在该集团的关键成员们身上。 2 PHRASAL VERB If something such as a missile **homes in on** something else, it is aimed at that thing and moves toward it. (导弹等) 导向 ❏ *Two rockets homed in on it from behind without a sound.* 两枚火箭无声地从后面向目标射去。

home·coming /hoʊmkʌmɪŋ/ (**homecomings**) 1 N-VAR Your **homecoming** is your return to your home or your country after being away for a long time. (长期外出之后的) 回家; 回国 ❏ *Her homecoming was tinged with sadness.* 她这次回家带有一丝伤感。 2 N-UNCOUNT **Homecoming** is a day or weekend each year when former students of a particular school, college, or university go back to it to meet each other again and go to parties and sports events. (一年一度的) 校友返校节 [AM] ❏ *...a recent Penn State graduate who was back for Homecoming weekend.* …一位回来参加返校周末聚会的刚毕业的宾州州立大学毕业生。

home·grown /hoʊmgroʊn/ ADJ **Homegrown** fruit and vegetables have been grown in your garden, rather than on a farm, or in your country rather than abroad. (蔬菜、水果) 家种的; 本国产的 ❏ *Martinelli reminds visitors often that he uses 100 percent homegrown fruit from California's Bajaro Valley.* 马蒂内利经常提醒游客, 他使用100%加州巴加罗山谷产的家种水果。

home·land /hoʊmlænd/ (**homelands**) 1 N-COUNT Your **homeland** is your native country. 祖国 [mainly WRITTEN] ❏ *Many are planning to return to their homeland.* 很多人正计划回到自己的祖国去。 2 N-COUNT The **homelands** were regions within South Africa in which black South Africans had a limited form of self-government. (过去南非种族隔离制度下的)黑人家园

home·less ♦◇◇ /hoʊmlɪs/ ADJ **Homeless** people have nowhere to live. 无家可归的 ❏ *...the growing number of homeless families.* …越来越多的无家可归的家庭。 ● N-PLURAL **The homeless** are people who are homeless. 无家可归的人 ❏ *...shelters for the homeless.* …无家可归者收容所。 ● **home·less·ness** N-UNCOUNT 无家可归 ❏ *The only way to solve homelessness is to provide more homes.* 解决无家可归的惟一途径是提供更多的收容所。

home·ly /hoʊmli/ 1 ADJ If you say that someone is **homely**, you mean that they are not very attractive to look at. 相貌平平的 [AM] ❏ *The man was homely, overweight, and probably only two or three years younger than Lou.* 该男子相貌平平, 身材肥胖, 可能只比卢年轻两三岁。 2 ADJ If you describe a room or house as **homely**, you like it because you feel comfortable and relaxed there. 如在家一般; 舒适自在的 [BRIT, APPROVAL]

in AM, use **homey**

home·made /hoʊmmeɪd/ ADJ Something that is **homemade** has been made in someone's home, rather than in a store or factory. 自家做的 ❏ *The bread, pastry and mayonnaise are homemade.* 面包、糕点和蛋黄酱都是自家做的。

homeo·path /hoʊmioʊpæθ/ (**homeopaths**) N-COUNT A **homeopath** is someone who treats illness by homeopathy. 采用顺势疗法的医生 ❏ *The homeopath will test various strengths of remedies on the patient.* 采用顺势疗法的医生将对病人试验疗法的各种效力。

homeo·path·ic /hoʊmioʊpæθɪk/ ADJ **Homeopathic** means relating to or used in homeopathy. 顺势疗法的 ❏ *...homeopathic remedies.* …顺势疗法的治疗。

homeopa·thy /hoʊmiɒpəθi/ N-UNCOUNT **Homeopathy** is a way of treating an illness in which the patient is given very small amounts of a drug that produces signs of the illness in healthy people. 顺势疗法

home page (**home pages**) N-COUNT On the Internet, a person's or organization's **home page** is the main page of information about them, which often contains links to other pages about them. (因特网上的) 主页 ❏ *...the home page of a new sex education website.* …一个新的性教育网站的主页。

home shop·ping N-UNCOUNT **Home shopping** is shopping that people do by ordering goods they see in catalogs or on television channels, using the telephone or computers. (通过商品目录、电视、电话或因特网进行的) 居家购物 [oft N n] ❏ *...America's most successful home-shopping channel.* …美国最成功的电视购物频道。

home·sick /hoʊmsɪk/ ADJ If you are **homesick**, you feel unhappy because you are away from home and are missing your family, friends, and home very much. 想家的 ❏ *She's feeling a little homesick.* 她感到有些想家了。 ● **home·sick·ness** N-UNCOUNT 想家 ❏ *There were inevitable bouts of homesickness.* 难免会生出一阵阵思乡之情。

Word Link *stead ≈ place, stand : homestead, instead, steady*

home·stead /hoʊmstɛd/ (**homesteads**) 1 N-COUNT A **homestead** is a farmhouse, together with the land around it. (包括周围土地的) 农庄住宅 2 N-COUNT In United States history, a **homestead** was a piece of government land in the west, which was given to someone so they could settle there and develop a farm. (美国历史上政府按宅地法分给定居移民建农庄的) 公地 [AM]

home·work /hoʊmwɜrk/ 1 N-UNCOUNT **Homework** is schoolwork that teachers give to students to do at home in the evening or on the weekend. 家庭作业 ❏ *Have you done your homework, Gemma?* 你做完家庭作业了吗, 杰玛? 2 N-UNCOUNT If you **do** your **homework**, you find out what you need to know in preparation for something. 做必要的准备工作 ❏ *Before you go near a stockbroker, do your homework.* 在你去见股票经纪人之前, 先要做好必要的准备工作。

homey /hoʊmi/ ADJ If you describe a room or house as **homey**, you like it because you feel comfortable and relaxed there. 像家一样舒适的 [mainly AM, INFORMAL, APPROVAL] ❏ *...a large, homey dining room.* …一家宽敞而舒适的餐厅。

homi·ci·dal /hɒmɪsaɪdᵊl, hoʊmɪ-/ ADJ **Homicidal** is used to describe someone who is dangerous because they are likely to kill someone. 嗜杀成性的 ❏ *That man is a homicidal maniac.* 那人是个嗜杀成性的疯子。

Word Link *cide ≈ killing : genocide, homicide, pesticide*

homi·cide /hɒmɪsaɪd, hoʊmɪ-/ (**homicides**) N-VAR **Homicide** is the illegal killing of a person. 杀人 [mainly AM] ❏ *The police arrived at the scene of the homicide.* 警察赶到了杀人现场。

homoeo·path·ic /hoʊmiəpæθɪk/ [BRIT] → see **homeopathic**

homoeopa·thy /hoʊmiɒpəθi/ [BRIT] → see **homeopathy**

★ **homo·geneous** /hɒmədʒiniəs, hoʊ-/ also **homogenous** ADJ **Homogeneous** is used to describe a group or thing which has members or parts that are all the same. 同种类的 [FORMAL] ❏ *The unemployed are not a homogeneous group.* 失业者并不都是同一类人。

Word Link *homo ≈ same : homogenous, homophobia, homosexual*

homo·pho·bia /hɒməfoʊbiə/ N-UNCOUNT **Homophobia** is a strong and unreasonable dislike of gay people, especially gay men. 对同性恋者的憎恶 (尤指对男同性恋者)

Word Link *phob ≈ fear : homophobic, phobia, xenophobia*

ho·mo·pho·bic /hɒməfoʊbɪk/ ADJ **Homophobic** means involving or related to a strong and unreasonable dislike of gay people, especially gay men. 对同性恋者憎恶的 (尤指对男同性恋者) ❏ *I'm not homophobic in any way and certainly don't condemn gay relationships.* 我对同性恋者没有任何的憎恶, 当然也就不会谴责同性恋的关系。

★ **homo·sex·ual** ♦◇◇ /hoʊmoʊsɛkʃuəl/ (**homosexuals**) 1 ADJ A **homosexual** relationship is a sexual relationship between people of the same sex. 同性恋的 ❏ *...partners in a homosexual relationship.* …同性恋恋人。 2 ADJ Someone who is **homosexual** is sexually attracted to people of the same sex. 同性恋性向的 ❏ *...a fraud trial involving two homosexual lawyers.* …一起涉及两名同性恋律师的欺诈案的审判。 ● N-COUNT **Homosexual** is also a noun. 同性恋 ❏ *The judge said that discrimination against homosexuals is deplorable.* 法官说歧视同性恋的行为应该受到谴责。 ● **homo·sex·ual·ity** /hoʊmoʊsɛkʃuælɪti/ N-UNCOUNT 同性恋 ❏ *...a place where gays could openly discuss homosexuality.* …一个同性恋者可以公开讨论同性恋问题的场所。

hone /hoʊn/ (**hones, honing, honed**) V-T If you **hone** something, for example a skill, technique, idea, or product, you carefully develop it over a long period of time so that it is exactly right for your purpose. 磨砺 ❏ *Leading companies spend time and money on honing the skills of senior managers.* 龙头公司会花费时间和金钱提高高层管理人员的技能。

hon·est ♦◇◇ /ɒnɪst/ 1 ADJ If you describe someone as **honest**, you mean that they always tell the truth, and do not try to deceive people or break the law. 诚实的; 正直的 ❏ *I know she's honest* and reliable. 我知道她是诚实可靠的。● **hon·est·ly** ADV 诚实地；正直地 [ADV after v] ❑ *She fought honestly for a just cause and for freedom.* 她正直地为正义事业和自由而战。 2 ADJ If you are **honest** in a particular situation, you tell the complete truth or give your sincere opinion, even if this is not very pleasant. 坦诚的 ❑ *I was honest about what I was doing.* 我对我所做的一切毫不隐瞒。 ❑ *He had been honest with her and she had tricked him!* 他对她是真诚的，而她却欺骗了他。 ● **hon·est·ly** ADV 坦诚地 [ADV with v] ❑ *It came as a shock to hear an old friend speak so honestly about Ted.* 听到一位老朋友如此坦诚地谈论特德真是令人震惊。 3 ADV You say "**honest**" before or after a statement to emphasize that you are telling the truth and that you want people to believe you. 真的；不骗你 [ADV with cl] [INFORMAL, EMPHASIS] ❑ *I'm not sure, honest.* 我不能肯定，不骗你。 4 PHRASE Some people say "**honest to God**" to emphasize their feelings or to emphasize that something is really true. (表示强调) 千真万确 [INFORMAL, EMPHASIS] ❑ *I wish we weren't doing this, Lillian, honest to God, I really do.* 我希望我们没在做这件事，莉莲，真的，我确实这么想。 5 PHRASE You can say "**to be honest**" before or after a statement to indicate that you are telling the truth about your own opinions or feelings, especially if you think these will disappoint the person you are talking to. 老实说 [FEELINGS] ❑ *To be honest the house is not quite our style.* 说实话，我们不大喜欢这房子。

Thesaurus *honest* 另参见：
ADJ. fair, genuine, sincere, true, truthful, upright 1
candid, frank, straight, truthful 2

hon·est·ly /ɒnɪstli/ 1 ADV You use **honestly** to emphasize that you are referring to your, or someone else's, true beliefs or feelings. (强调信念或情感) 的确 [ADV before v] [EMPHASIS] ❑ *But did you honestly think we wouldn't notice?* 但是你真的认为我们不会注意到吗？ 2 ADV You use **honestly** to emphasize that you are telling the truth and that you want people to believe you. (强调所说的是事实) 真的 [ADV with cl] [SPOKEN, EMPHASIS] ❑ *Honestly, I don't know anything about it.* 我真的对此一无所知。 3 ADV You use **honestly** to indicate that you are annoyed or impatient. (表示恼火或不耐烦) 天哪 [ADV with cl] [SPOKEN, FEELINGS] ❑ *Honestly, Nev! Must you be so crude!.* 天哪，尼夫！你怎么能如此粗暴呢！ 4 → see also **honest**

hon·es·ty /ɒnɪsti/ N-UNCOUNT **Honesty** is the quality of being honest. 诚实 ❑ *They said the greatest virtues in a politician were integrity, correctness, and honesty.* 他们说政治家最重要的美德就是正直、得体和诚实。 ● PHRASE You say **in all honesty** when you are saying something that might be disappointing or upsetting, and you want to soften its effect by emphasizing your sincerity. 坦白地说 [EMPHASIS]

hon·ey /hʌni/ (**honeys**) 1 N-VAR **Honey** is a sweet, sticky, yellowish substance that is made by bees. 蜂蜜 2 N-VOC You call someone **honey** as a sign of affection. (用作称呼) 亲爱的 [mainly AM] ❑ *Honey, I don't really think that's a good idea.* 亲爱的，我不认为那是个好主意。

Honey is a term commonly used to express affection between two people. Other words used in a similar way include: **dear**, **darling**, **sweetheart**, or **angel**. Sometimes these words are used by adults when speaking to a child.

honey·moon /hʌnimun/ (**honeymoons, honeymooning, honeymooned**) 1 N-COUNT A **honeymoon** is a vacation taken by a man and a woman who have just gotten married. 蜜月 ❑ *The next time I went abroad was on my honeymoon.* 我接下来一次出国是去度蜜月。 2 V-I When a recently married couple **honeymoon** somewhere, they go there on their honeymoon. 度蜜月 ❑ *They honeymooned in Venice.* 他们在威尼斯度了蜜月。 3 N-COUNT You can use **honeymoon** to refer to a period of time after the start of a new job or when a newly elected official takes office when everyone is pleased with the person or people concerned and is nice to them. 蜜月期 (指新的工作开始或新当选的官员任职后的和谐工作期) ❑ *Brett is enjoying a honeymoon period with both press and public.* 布雷特正在享受同媒体和公众的蜜月期。
→ see **wedding**

honk /hɒŋk/ (**honks, honking, honked**) V-T/V-I If you **honk** the horn of a vehicle or if the horn **honks**, you make the horn produce a short loud sound. 鸣 (车辆喇叭)；(车辆喇叭) 鸣响 ❑ *Drivers honked their horns in solidarity with the peace marchers.* 司机们鸣笛，表示对和平示威者的坚决支持。 ❑ *Horns honk. An angry motorist shouts.* 喇叭鸣响。一位愤怒的司机大声叫喊着。 ● N-COUNT **Honk** is also a noun. 鸣笛；鸣响 ❑ *She pulled to the right with a honk.* 她按了声喇叭，把车开到了右边。

hon·or ♦◇◇ /ɒnər/ (**honors, honoring, honored**)
in BRIT, use **honour**
1 N-UNCOUNT **Honor** means doing what you believe to be right and being confident that you have done what is right. 道义；气节 ❑ *The officers died faithful to the honor of a soldier.* 军官们怀着对军人气节的忠诚而捐躯。 2 N-COUNT An **honor** is a special award that is given to someone, usually because they have done something good or because they are greatly respected. 荣誉 ❑ *He was showered with honors – among them an Oscar.* 他获得了很多荣誉——其中包括奥斯卡奖。 3 V-T If someone **is honored**, they are given public praise or an award for something they have done. 给…以荣誉 [usu passive] ❑ *Diego Maradona was honored with an award presented by Argentina's soccer association.* 迭戈•马拉多纳荣获阿根廷足协颁发的一个奖项。 4 N-SING If you describe doing or experiencing something as an **honor**, you mean you think it is something special and desirable. 荣幸 ❑ *Five other cities had been competing for the honor of staging the Games.* 另外五个城市一直在为赢得该运动会的举办权而相互竞争。 5 V-T PASSIVE If you say that you **would be honored to** do something, you are saying very politely and formally that you would be pleased to do it. If you say that you **are honored by** something, you are saying that you are grateful for it and pleased about it. 给予荣幸 [POLITENESS] ❑ *Ms. Payne said she was honored to accept the appointment and looked forward to its challenges.* 佩恩女士说她很荣幸接受这一任命，并期待着它所带来的挑战。 6 V-T To **honor** someone means to treat them or regard them with special attention and respect. 尊重 ❑ *They honored me with a seat at the head of the table.* 他们让我坐在桌子的上首，以示对我的尊敬。 7 V-T If you **honor** an arrangement or promise, you do what you said you would do. 执行 (安排)；履行 (诺言) ❑ *The two sides agreed to honor a new ceasefire.* 双方同意执行新的停火协议。 8 N-VOC Judges and mayors are sometimes called **your honor** or referred to as **his honor** or **her honor**. 大人 (对法官、市长等的尊称) [poss N; PRON: poss PRON] ❑ *I bring this up, your honor, because I think it is important to understand the background of the defendant.* 法官大人，我之所以提出这一点，是因为我认为了解被告的背景是很重要的。 9 PHRASE If something is arranged **in honor of** a particular event, it is arranged in order to celebrate that event. 为庆祝… ❑ *The Foundation is holding a dinner at the Museum of American Art in honor of the opening of its new show.* 基金会在美国艺术博物馆举行宴会，庆祝新展览开幕。 10 PHRASE If something is arranged or happens **in** someone's **honor**, it is done specially to show appreciation of them. 为表示对…的敬意 ❑ *Mr. Mandela will attend an outdoor concert in his honor.* 曼德拉先生将出席特地为他举办的露天音乐会。

Thesaurus *honor* 另参见：
N. award, distinction, recognition 2
V. commend, praise, recognize 3

Word Partnership *honor* 的常用搭配：
N. **code of** honor, **sense of** honor 1
honor **a ceasefire** 7
honor **the memory of** ***someone/something*** 9 10
ADJ. **great/highest** honor 2 4

hon·or·able /ɒnərəbᵊl/
in BRIT, use **honourable**
ADJ If you describe people or actions as **honorable**, you mean that they are good and deserve to be respected and admired. 值得敬仰的 ❑ *He argued that the only honorable course of action was death.* 他辩称惟一值得敬仰的行为就是牺牲生命。 ● **hon·or·ably** /ɒnərəbli/ ADV 值得敬仰地 ❑ *He also felt she had not behaved honorably in the leadership election.* 他也觉得她在这次领导选举中没有表现得令人敬仰。

★ **hon·or·ary** /ɒnərɛri/ 1 ADJ An **honorary** title or membership of a group is given to someone without their needing to have the necessary qualifications, usually because of their public achievements. (称号或成员资格) 作为荣誉的 [ADJ n] ❑ *Harvard awarded him an honorary degree.* 哈佛大学授予他荣誉学位。 2 ADJ **Honorary** is used to describe an official job that is done without payment. 名誉的但无报酬的 (职位) [ADJ n] ❑ *...the honorary secretary of the Beekeepers' Association.* …养蜂人协会的名誉秘书。

hon·our /ɒnər/ [BRIT] → see **honor**

hon·our·able /ɒnərəbᵊl/ [BRIT] → see **honorable**

▲ **hood** /hʊd/ (**hoods**) 1 N-COUNT A **hood** is a part of a coat which you can pull up to cover your head. It is in the shape of a triangular bag attached to the neck of the coat at the back. (连在外套上的) 风帽 ❑ *She threw back the hood of her cloak.* 她把风上的风帽向后甩去。 2 N-COUNT The **hood** of a car is the metal cover over the engine at the front. (汽车的) 引擎罩 [AM] ❑ *He raised the hood of McKee's truck.* 他把麦基卡车的引擎罩打开了。

hood·ed /hʊdɪd/ 1 ADJ A **hooded** piece of clothing or furniture has a hood. (衣服) 带有风帽的; (家具) 有罩的 ❑ *...a blue hooded sweatshirt.* …带有风帽的蓝色长袖运动衫。 2 ADJ A **hooded** person is wearing a hood or a piece of clothing pulled down over their face, so they are difficult to recognize. 戴头罩的; 蒙面的 [ADJ n] ❑ *The class was held hostage by a hooded gunman.* 全班学生被一名蒙面持枪歹徒挟为人质。

▲ **hoof** /hʊf, huːf/ (**hoofs** or **hooves**) N-COUNT The **hooves** of an animal such as a horse are the hard lower parts of its feet. (马等动物的) 蹄 ❑ *The horses' hooves often could not get a proper grip.* 这些马的蹄子经常踩不稳。

hoof·er /hʊfər, huː-/ (**hoofers**) N-COUNT A **hoofer** is a dancer, especially one who dances in musicals. (尤指音乐剧中的) 舞蹈演员 [INFORMAL]

H

hook ♦◇◇ /hʊk/ (**hooks, hooking, hooked**) 1 N-COUNT A **hook** is a bent piece of metal or plastic that is used for catching or holding things, or for hanging things up. 钩子 ❑ *One of his jackets hung from a hook.* 他的一件夹克衫挂在挂钩上。 2 V-T/V-I If you **hook** one thing **to** another, you attach it there using a hook. If something **hooks** somewhere, it can be hooked there. 挂; 钩 ❑ *Paul hooked his tractor to the car and pulled it to safety.* 保罗把他的拖拉机挂在那辆小汽车上，然后把它拖到安全的地方。 3 V-T If you **hook** your arm, leg, or foot round an object, you place it like a hook round the object in order to move it or hold it. 使 (臂、腿、脚等) 成钩状 ❑ *She latched on to his arm, hooking her other arm around a tree.* 她一只手抓住他的胳膊，另一只胳膊抱住一棵树。 4 V-T If you **hook** a fish, you catch it with a hook on the end of a line. 用鱼钩钓住 ❑ *At the first cast I hooked a huge fish, probably a tench.* 第一次抛竿我就钓到了一条大鱼，可能是条丁鲷。 5 N-COUNT A **hook** is a short sharp blow with your fist that you make with your elbow bent, usually in a boxing match. (拳击中的) 钩拳 ❑ *Lewis desperately needs to keep clear of Ruddock's big left hook.* 刘易斯务必要拼命躲开拉多克强有力的左钩拳。 6 V-T/V-I If you **are hooked into** something, or **hook into** something, you get involved with it. 卷入; 涉足 [mainly AM] ❑ *I'm guessing again now because I'm not hooked into the political circles.* 现在我又在猜测了，因为我没有涉足政界。 7 PHRASE If someone gets **off the hook** or is let **off the hook**, they manage to get out of the awkward or unpleasant situation that they are in. 脱身 [INFORMAL] ❑ *Officials accused of bribery and corruption get off the hook with monotonous regularity.* 被指控受贿和贪污的官员无一例外总能脱身。 8 PHRASE If you take a phone **off the hook**, you take the receiver off the part that it normally rests on, so that the phone will not ring. (电话听筒) 未挂上 ❑ *I'd taken my phone off the hook in order to get some sleep.* 我把电话听筒拿了下来，以便可以睡会儿觉。 9 PHRASE If your phone **is ringing off the hook**, so many people are trying to telephone you that it is ringing constantly. (电话) 响个不停 ❑ *Since war broke out, the phones at donation centers have been ringing off the hook.* 自从战争爆发以来，捐款中心的电话一直响个不停。

→ see **fish**

▸ **hook up** 1 PHRASAL VERB If someone **hooks up with** another person, they begin a sexual or romantic relationship with that person. You can also say that two people **hook up**. (与某人) 相恋 [INFORMAL] ❑ *I could be about to hook up with this incredibly intelligent, beautiful girl.* 我可能就要与那个聪明绝顶的美女相恋。 ❑ *We haven't exactly hooked up yet.* 我们还没有真正相恋。 2 PHRASAL VERB If you **hook up with** someone, you meet them and spend time with them. You can also say that two people **hook up**. (与某人) 结交 [mainly AM, INFORMAL] ❑ *He hooked up with fellow cycling enthusiasts and joined several clubs.* 他结交了其他自行车爱好者们，还参加了几个俱乐部。 ❑ *This afternoon Iz and Jude and Chris hooked up.* 今天下午伊兹、祖德以及克里斯待在一起。 3 PHRASAL VERB When someone **hooks up** a computer or other electronic machine, they connect it to other similar machines or to a central power supply. 把 (计算机或其他电子设备) 与 (类似机器或电源) 连接起来 ❑ *...technicians who hook up computer systems and networks.* …连接计算机系统与网络的技术员。 ❑ *He brought it down, hooked it up, and we got the generator going.* 他把它放倒，连接好，然后我们让发电机开始运转。

Word Partnership *hook* 的常用搭配:

V.	**bait a hook, hang** *something* **from a hook** 1
ADJ.	**sharp hook** 1

hooked /hʊkt/ 1 ADJ If you describe something as **hooked**, you mean that it is shaped like a hook. 钩状的 ❑ *He was thin and tall, with a hooked nose.* 他又瘦又高，长着一只鹰钩鼻。 2 ADJ If you are **hooked on** something, you enjoy it so much that it takes up a lot of your interest and attention. 被…迷住的 [v-link ADJ] [INFORMAL] ❑ *Many of the leaders have become hooked on power and money.* 很多领导人都变得迷恋权力和金钱。 3 ADJ If you are **hooked on** a drug, you are addicted to it. 上了瘾的 [v-link ADJ] [INFORMAL] ❑ *He spent a number of years hooked on cocaine, heroin, and alcohol.* 他有几年时间对可卡因、海洛因和酒上瘾。

hook·er /hʊkər/ (**hookers**) N-COUNT A **hooker** is a prostitute. 妓女 [mainly AM, INFORMAL]

hoo·li·gan /huːlɪgən/ (**hooligans**) N-COUNT If you describe people, especially young people, as **hooligans**, you are critical of them because they behave in a noisy and violent way in a public place. 小流氓 [DISAPPROVAL] ❑ *...the problem of soccer hooligans.* …足球流氓的问题。

hoo·li·gan·ism /huːlɪgənɪzəm/ N-UNCOUNT **Hooliganism** is the behavior and actions of hooligans. 流氓行为 ❑ *Officials dismiss these incidents as simple hooliganism.* 官员们把这些事件看成是一般的流氓行为而草草了事。

hoop /huːp/ (**hoops**) 1 N-COUNT A **hoop** is a ring made of wood, metal, or plastic. (木头、金属或塑料制成的) 环 ❑ *A boy came towards them, rolling an iron hoop.* 一个男孩滚着一个铁环朝他们走来。 2 N-COUNT A basketball **hoop** is the ring that players try to throw the ball into in order to score points for their team. (篮球) 篮圈 3 PHRASE If someone makes you **jump through hoops**, they make you do lots of difficult or boring things in order to please them or achieve something. 饱受折磨 ❑ *He had the receptionist almost jumping through hoops for him. But to no avail.* 他让接待员为他几乎饱经折磨，但根本没有用。

hoot /huːt/ (**hoots, hooting, hooted**) 1 V-I If you **hoot**, you make a loud high-pitched noise when you are laughing or showing disapproval. 高声大笑; (表示反对而) 尖叫 ❑ *The protesters chanted, blew whistles and hooted at the name of Governor Pete Wilson.* 抗议者们听到州长皮特・威尔逊的名字时又喊口号，又吹口哨，还大声尖叫。 ● N-COUNT **Hoot** is also a noun. 高声大笑; (表示反对的) 尖叫 ❑ *His confession was greeted with derisive hoots.* 他的坦白招来了大声嘲笑。 2 PHRASE If you say that you **don't give a hoot** or **don't care two hoots about** something, you are emphasizing that you do not care at all about it. 毫不在乎 [INFORMAL, EMPHASIS] ❑ *Alan doesn't care two hoots about politics.* 艾伦对政治根本不关心。 3 V-T/V-I If you **hoot** the horn on a vehicle or if it **hoots**, it makes a loud noise on one note. 使 (车辆喇叭) 高声鸣叫; (车辆喇叭) 高声鸣叫 [mainly BRIT]

in AM, usually use **honk, toot**

hooves /huːvz/ **Hooves** is a plural of **hoof**. **hoof**的复数形式

★ **hop** /hɒp/ (**hops, hopping, hopped**) 1 V-I If you **hop**, you move along by jumping on one foot. (人) 单脚跳行 ❑ *I hopped down three steps.* 我单脚跳下3级台阶。 ● N-COUNT **Hop** is also a noun. (人) 单脚跳行 ❑ *"This really is a catching rhythm, huh?" he added, with a few little hops.* "这节奏可真有感染力，是吧？"他补充说道，单脚小步跳了几下。 2 V-I When birds and some small animals **hop**, they move along by jumping on both or all four feet. (鸟和其他小动物) 齐足跳行 ❑ *A small brown fawn hopped across the trail in front of them.* 一只小棕鹿在他们面前蹦跳着穿过了小路。 ● N-COUNT **Hop** is also a noun. (鸟和其他小动物的) 齐足跳行 ❑ *The rabbit got up, took four hops and turned around.* 兔子直起身子，蹦跳了4下，然后转过身。 3 V-I If you **hop** somewhere, you move there quickly or suddenly. 快速移动 [INFORMAL] ❑ *My wife and I were the first to arrive and hopped on board.* 我和妻子是最先到达并跳上车的。 4 N-COUNT A **hop** is a short, quick trip, usually by plane. (通常指乘飞机的) 短途快速旅行 [INFORMAL] ❑ *It is a three-hour drive but can be reached by a 20-minute hop in a private helicopter.* 这段路程开车需要3个小时，而乘坐私人直升飞机20分钟就可以到达。 5 N-COUNT **Hops** are flowers that are dried and used for making beer. 啤酒花

hope ♦♦♦ /hoʊp/ (**hopes, hoping, hoped**) 1 V-T/V-I If you **hope** that something is true, or if you **hope** for something, you want it to be true or to happen, and you usually believe that it is possible or likely. 希望 ❑ *She had decided she must go on as usual, follow her normal routine, and hope and pray.* 她已决定自己必须一如既往地过下去，遵循自己的日常生活规律，同时心存希望并祈祷。 ❑ *He hesitates before leaving, almost as though he had been hoping for conversation.* 他离开前有些犹豫，好像希望跟人说些什么。 2 V-T/V-I If you say that you cannot **hope for** something, or if you talk about the only thing that you can **hope to** get, you mean that you are in a bad situation, and there is very little chance of improving it. 指望 [with brd-neg] ❑ *Things aren't ideal, but that's the best you can hope for.* 事情并不理想，但你只能指望这些了。 ● N-VAR **Hope** is also a noun. 指望 ❑ *The only hope for underdeveloped countries is to become, as far as possible, self-reliant.* 欠发达国家的惟一指望就是尽可能地做到自力更生。 3 N-UNCOUNT **Hope** is a feeling of desire and expectation that things will go well in the future. 期望 ❑ *Now that he has become president, many people once again have hope for genuine changes in the system.* 既然他已成为总统，许多人又一次寄期望于体制的真正改革。 ❑ *But Kevin hasn't given up hope of getting in shape.* 但是凯文仍没有放弃康复的希望。 4 N-COUNT If someone wants something to happen, and considers it likely or possible, you can refer to their **hopes of** that thing, or to their **hope that** it will happen. 希望 ❑ *They have hopes of increasing trade between the two regions.* 他们抱有增加两个地区之间贸易的希望。 ❑ *My hope is that, in the future, I will go over there and marry her.* 我的希望就是有朝一日我能去那里跟她结婚。 5 N-COUNT If you think that the help or success of a particular person or thing will cause you to be successful or to get what you want, you can refer to them as your **hope**. 被寄予希望的人(或物) ❑ *Roemer represented the best hope for a businesslike climate in Louisiana.* 罗默最有可能给路易斯安那州带来务实高效的风气。 6 PHRASE If you are in a difficult situation and do something and **hope for the best**, you hope that everything will happen in the way you want, although you know that it may not. 寄予最大希望(尤指在困境中) ❑ *Some companies are cutting costs and hoping for the best.* 一些公司在削减成本，希望能有转机。 7 PHRASE If you tell someone not to **get** their **hopes up**, or not to **build** their **hopes up**, you are warning them that they should not become too confident of progress or success. 抱太大希望 ❑ *There is no reason for people to get their hopes up over this mission.* 人们没有理由对这次任务抱有太大的希望。 8 PHRASE If you say that someone has **not got a hope in hell of** doing something, you are emphasizing that they will not be able to do it. 毫无希望(做成某事) [INFORMAL, EMPHASIS] ❑ *Everybody knows they haven't got a hope in hell of forming a government anyway.* 人人皆知他们毫无希望建成一个政府。 9 PHRASE If you have **high hopes** or **great hopes that** something will happen, you are confident that it will happen. 很大的希望 ❑ *I had high hopes that Derek Randall might play an important part.* 我对德里克・兰德尔发挥重要作用抱有很大希望。 10 PHRASE If you **hope against hope that** something will happen, you hope that it will happen, although it seems impossible. 抱一线希望 ❑ *She glanced about the hall, hoping against hope that Richard would be waiting for her.* 她扫视了一下大厅，抱一线希望理查德在等着她。 11 PHRASE You use **"I hope"** in expressions such as **"I hope you don't mind"** and **"I hope I'm not disturbing you,"** when you are being polite and want to make sure that you have not offended someone or disturbed them. 我希望(后接否定句，表示客气) [POLITENESS] ❑ *I hope you don't mind me coming to see you.* 我希望你不会介意我来看你。 12 PHRASE You say **"I hope"** when you want to warn someone not to do something foolish or dangerous. 但愿(警告某人不要做愚蠢或危险的事) ❑ *You're not trying to see him, I hope?* 但愿你不是在想方设法去见他吧？ 13 PHRASE If you do one thing **in the hope of** another thing happening, you do it because you think it might cause or help the other thing to happen, which is what you want. 怀着…的希望 ❑ *He was studying in the hope of being admitted to an engineering college.* 他在学习，希望能被某个工学院录取。 14 PHRASE If you **live in hope** that something will happen, you continue to hope that it will happen, although it seems unlikely, and you realize that you are being foolish. (在不大可能的情况下) 对…继续抱有希望 ❑ *I just live in hope that one day she'll talk to me.* 我只是希望有一天她会和我说话。 ❑ *My mother bought a ticket and lived in hope of winning the prize.* 我的母亲买了一张票，天天盼着能够中奖。

Thesaurus *hope* 另参见：
V. aspire, desire, dream, wish 1
N. ambition, aspiration, desire, dream, wish 4

Word Partnership *hope* 的常用搭配：
N. **glimmer of** hope 3
ADJ. **faint** hope, **false** hope, **little** hope 3 4
V. **give** *someone* hope, **give up** *all* hope, **hold out** hope, **lose** *all* hope 3 4

hope·ful /hoʊpfəl/ (**hopefuls**) 1 ADJ If you are **hopeful**, you are fairly confident that something that you want to happen will happen. 满怀希望的 ❑ *I am hopeful this misunderstanding will be rectified very quickly.* 我满怀希望这一误解很快就能得到澄清。 ● **hope·ful·ly** ADV 满怀希望地 [ADV with v] ❑ *"Am I welcome?" He smiled hopefully, leaning on the door.* "欢迎我吗？" 他倚着门，满怀希望地笑着问道。 2 ADJ If something such as a sign or event is **hopeful**, it makes you feel that what you want to happen will happen. (事物) 给人以希望的 ❑ *The result of the election is yet another hopeful sign that peace could come to the Middle East.* 这次选举的结果是和平有希望降临中东的又一个征兆。 3 ADJ A **hopeful** action is one that you do in the hope that you will get what you want to get. (行为) 被寄予希望的 [ADJ n] ❑ *We've chartered the aircraft in the hopeful anticipation that the government will allow them to leave.* 我们包租了那架飞机，希望政府会允许他们离开。 4 N-COUNT If you refer to someone as a **hopeful**, you mean that they are hoping and trying to achieve success in a particular career, election, or competition. 有希望成功的人 ❑ *His skills continue to be put to good use in his job as coach to young hopefuls.* 作为有望成功的年轻人的教练，他的技能继续得到充分利用。

hope·ful·ly /hoʊpfəli/ ADV You say **hopefully** when mentioning something that you hope will happen. Some careful speakers of English think that this use of **hopefully** is not correct, but it is very frequently used. 但愿 (一些严谨的说英语者认为**hopefully**如此使用不正确，但它已被普遍使用) [ADV with cl/group] ❑ *Hopefully, you won't have any problems after reading this.* 但愿你读完这个后就不会有什么问题了。

hope·less /hoʊplɪs/ 1 ADJ If you feel **hopeless**, you feel very unhappy because there seems to be no possibility of a better situation or success. 绝望的 ❑ *He had not heard her cry before in this uncontrolled, hopeless way.* 之前他从没有听过她这样失态、绝望地哭泣。 ● **hope·less·ly** ADV 绝望地 ❑ *I looked around hopelessly.* 我绝望地四下看着。 ● **hope·less·ness** N-UNCOUNT 绝望 ❑ *She had a feeling of hopelessness about the future.* 她对未来感到绝望。 2 ADJ Someone or something that is **hopeless** is certain to fail or be unsuccessful. 注定失败的 ❑ *I don't believe your situation is as hopeless as you think. If you love each other, you'll work it out.* 我不相信你的情形像你想的那样无望。如果你们相爱，你们会找到解决办法的。 3 ADJ If someone is **hopeless at** something, they are very bad at it. 不能胜任的 [INFORMAL] ❑ *I'd be hopeless at working for somebody else.* 我无法胜任为别人工作。 4 ADJ You use **hopeless** to emphasize how bad or inadequate something or someone is. 糟糕透顶的 [EMPHASIS] ❑ *Argentina's economic policies were a hopeless mess.* 阿根廷的经济政策混乱得一塌糊涂。 ● **hope·less·ly** ADV 糟糕透顶地 ❑ *Harry was hopelessly lost.* 哈里彻底迷路了。

horde /hɔrd/ (**hordes**) N-COUNT If you describe a crowd of people as a **horde**, you mean that the crowd is very large and excited and, often, rather frightening or unpleasant. (通常指熙攘纷扰的) 一大群人 ❑ *This attracts hordes of tourists to Las Vegas.* 这吸引了一群群的旅客来到拉斯维加斯。

ho·ri·zon /həraɪzᵊn/ (**horizons**) 1 N-SING **The horizon** is the line in the far distance where the sky seems to meet the land or the sea. 地平线 ❑ *In the distance, the dot of a boat appeared on the horizon.* 远处小黑点般的一条小船出现在地平线上。 2 N-COUNT Your **horizons** are the limits of what you want to do or of what you are interested or involved in. 眼界；阅历 ❑ *As your horizons expand, these new ideas can give a whole new meaning to life.* 随着你的眼界不断开阔，这些新观念将给你的生活赋予崭新的意义。 3 PHRASE If something is **on the horizon**, it is almost certainly going to happen or be done quite soon. 即将来临的 ❑ *With breast cancer, as with many common diseases, there is no obvious breakthrough on the horizon.* 就乳腺癌来说，如同许多常见病一样，目前还看不到明显的突破。

hori·zon·tal /hɔrɪzɒntᵊl/ ADJ Something that is **horizontal** is flat and level with the ground, rather than at an angle to it. 水平的；横的 ❑ *The board consists of vertical and horizontal lines.* 牌子是由纵向和横向的线条构成的。 ● N-SING **Horizontal** is also a noun. 水平线；水平面 ❑ *Do not raise your left arm above the horizontal.* 不要把你的左臂举过水平位置。 ● **hori·zon·tal·ly** ADV 水平地 ❑ *The wind was*

h

cold and drove the snow at him almost horizontally. 风很冷，裹着雪几乎是横着向他扑来。

→ see **graph**

hor·mo·nal /hɔrmoʊnəl/ ADJ **Hormonal** means relating to or involving hormones. 荷尔蒙的 ❑ *...our individual hormonal balance.* …我们个体的荷尔蒙平衡。

★ **hor·mone** /hɔrmoʊn/ (**hormones**) N-COUNT A **hormone** is a chemical, usually occurring naturally in your body, that makes an organ of your body do something. 荷尔蒙 ❑ *...the male sex hormone testosterone.* …男性性激素睾酮。

→ see **emotion**

horn /hɔrn/ (**horns**) **1** N-COUNT On a vehicle such as a car, the **horn** is the device that makes a loud noise as a signal or warning. (汽车等的) 喇叭 ❑ *He sounded the car horn.* 他按响了汽车喇叭。 **2** N-COUNT The **horns** of an animal such as a cow or deer are the hard pointed things that grow from its head. (牛、鹿等动物头上的) 角 ❑ *A mature cow has horns.* 成年母牛头上长有角。 **3** N-COUNT A **horn** is a musical instrument of the brass family. It is a long circular metal tube, wide at one end, which you play by blowing. 号 (铜管乐器) ❑ *He started playing the horn when he was eight.* 他8岁时就开始吹号。 **4** N-COUNT A **horn** is a simple musical instrument consisting of a metal tube that is wide at one end and narrow at the other. You play it by blowing into it. 号 (一种以一头宽一头窄的金属管制成的简单的吹奏乐器) ❑ *...a hunting horn.* …猎号。 **5** PHRASE If two people **lock horns**, they argue about something. 争论 ❑ *During his six years in office, Seidman has often locked horns with lawmakers.* 在任的6年里，塞德曼经常与立法者进行争论。

Word Link *scope ≈ looking : horoscope, microscope, telescope*

horo·scope /hɔrəskoʊp/ (**horoscopes**) N-COUNT Your **horoscope** is a prediction of events which some people believe will happen to you in the future. Horoscopes are based on the position of the stars when you were born. 占星 (根据星象算命) ❑ *I always read my horoscope and follow the advice.* 我总是查我的星象，然后依照其建议行事。

hor·ren·dous /hɔrɛndəs, hɒ-, hə-/ **1** ADJ Something that is **horrendous** is very unpleasant or shocking. 骇人的 ❑ *He described it as the most horrendous experience of his life.* 他把那件事形容为他生活中最恐怖的经历。 **2** ADJ Some people use **horrendous** to describe something that is so big or great that they find it extremely unpleasant. (程度大得或严重得) 极其令人不快的 [INFORMAL] ❑ *...the usually horrendous traffic jams.* …通常糟糕透顶的交通堵塞。 ● **hor·ren·dous·ly** ADV 极其令人不快地 ❑ *The man in the photo was horrendously fat.* 照片里的男人胖得惊人。

hor·ri·ble /hɔrɪbəl, hɒr-/ **1** ADJ If you describe something or someone as **horrible**, you do not like them at all. 令人讨厌的 [INFORMAL] ❑ *Her voice sounds horrible.* 她的嗓音难听死了。 ● **hor·ri·bly** /hɔrɪbli, hɒr-/ ADV 令人讨厌地 [ADV with v] ❑ *When trouble comes they behave selfishly and horribly.* 困难来临时，他们就表现得很自私，很令人厌恶。 **2** ADJ You can call something **horrible** when it causes you to feel great shock, fear, and disgust. 令人恐惧的 ❑ *Still the horrible shrieking came out of his mouth.* 吓人的尖叫声还是从他嘴里发出。 ● **hor·ri·bly** ADV 令人恐惧地 [ADV with v] ❑ *A two-year-old boy was horribly murdered.* 一个两岁的男孩惨遭杀害。 **3** ADJ **Horrible** is used to emphasize how bad something is. 糟透的 [ADJ n] [EMPHASIS] ❑ *That seems like a horrible mess that will drag on for years.* 那看来像是一个将要延续多年的糟糕困境。 ● **hor·ri·bly** ADV 糟透了地 ❑ *Our plans have gone horribly wrong.* 我们的计划已出了大问题。

hor·rid /hɔrɪd, hɒr-/ **1** ADJ If you describe something as **horrid**, you mean that it is extremely unpleasant. 极讨厌的 [INFORMAL] ❑ *What a horrid smell!* 多么难闻的气味！ **2** ADJ If you describe someone as **horrid**, you mean that they behave in a very unpleasant way toward other people. (人) 令人讨厌的 [INFORMAL] ❑ *I must have been a horrid little girl.* 我以前一定是个招人讨厌的小女孩。

▲ **hor·rif·ic** /hɔrɪfɪk, hɒ-, hə-/ **1** ADJ If you describe a physical attack, accident, or injury as **horrific**, you mean that it is very bad, so that people are shocked when they see it or think about it. 极其可怕的 ❑ *I have never seen such horrific injuries.* 我从没见过这么严重的伤。 ● **hor·rifi·cal·ly** ADV 极其可怕地 ❑ *He had been horrifically assaulted before he died.* 他死之前曾遭人毒打。 **2** ADJ If you describe something as **horrific**, you mean that it is so big that it is extremely unpleasant. 大得骇人的 ❑ *...piling up horrific extra amounts of money on top of your original debt.* …在你原有债务的基础上再加上数目骇人的几大笔钱。 ● **hor·rifi·cal·ly** ADV 大得骇人地 [ADV adj] ❑ *Opera productions are horrifically expensive.* 歌剧的演出花销大得吓人。

▲ **hor·ri·fy** /hɔrɪfaɪ, hɒr-/ (**horrifies, horrifying, horrified**) V-T If someone **is horrified**, they feel shocked or disgusted, usually because of something that they have seen or heard. 使感到惊骇 ❑ *His family was horrified by the change.* 他的家人对这一变化感到震惊。

hor·ri·fy·ing /hɔrɪfaɪɪŋ, hɒr-/ ADJ If you describe something as **horrifying**, you mean that it is shocking or disgusting. 令人震惊的 ❑ *These were horrifying experiences.* 这些都是令人震惊的经历。

hor·ror ♦◇◇ /hɔrər, hɒr-/ (**horrors**) **1** N-UNCOUNT **Horror** is a feeling of great shock, fear, and worry caused by something extremely unpleasant. 震惊；恐惧 ❑ *I felt numb with horror.* 我惊呆了。 **2** N-SING If you have a **horror of** something, you are afraid of it or dislike it very much. 恐惧；憎恶 ❑ *...his horror of death.* …他对死亡的恐惧。 **3** N-SING The **horror of** something, especially something that hurts people, is its very great unpleasantness. 恐怖性 ❑ *...the horror of this most bloody of civil wars.* …这场极其血腥的内战的惨状。 **4** N-COUNT You can refer to extremely unpleasant or frightening experiences as **horrors**. 令人恐怖的经历 ❑ *Can you possibly imagine all the horrors we have undergone since I last wrote you?* 你能想像得出自从上次我写信给你以来，我们所经历的所有恐怖的事情吗？ **5** ADJ A **horror** film or story is intended to be very frightening. (影片或故事) 内容恐怖的 [ADJ n] ❑ *...a psychological horror film.* …一部心理恐怖电影。 **6** ADJ You can refer to an account of a very unpleasant experience or event as a **horror** story. (经历或事件) 非常不愉快的 [ADJ n] ❑ *...a horror story about lost luggage while flying.* …一次关于乘飞机旅行丢失行李的糟糕经历。

→ see **genre**

horse ♦♦◇ /hɔrs/ (**horses, horsing, horsed**) **1** N-COUNT A **horse** is a large animal which people can ride. Some horses are used for pulling plows and carts. 马 ❑ *A small man on a gray horse had appeared.* 一个骑着灰马的小个子男人出现了。 **2** PHRASE If you hear something **from the horse's mouth**, you hear it from someone who knows that it is definitely true. (消息等) 来自可靠人士 ❑ *He has got to hear it from the horse's mouth. Then he can make a judgment as to whether his policy is correct or not.* 他必须获得可靠消息。然后他就能判断出他的政策是否正确。

→ see Word Web: **horse**

→ see **train, transportation**

▸ **horse around** PHRASAL VERB If you **horse around**, you play roughly and carelessly, so that you could hurt someone or damage something. 胡闹 [INFORMAL] ❑ *My friends and I would horse around and try to push each other.* 我和朋友们有时会闹着玩，互相推来搡去。

horse·back /hɔrsbæk/ **1** N-UNCOUNT If you do something **on horseback**, you do it while riding a horse. 马背 ❑ *In remote mountain areas, voters arrived on horseback.* 在偏远山区，选民们是骑着马来的。 **2** ADJ A **horseback** ride is a ride on a horse. 在马背上的 [ADJ n] ❑ *...a horseback ride into the mountains.* …骑马进山。 ● ADV **Horseback** is also an adverb. 在马背上 ❑ *Many people in this area ride horseback.* 这个地区有很多人骑马。

→ see **horse**

Word Web **horse**

The earliest use of **horses** was as a source of meat for prehistoric man. Then, around 4000 BC, groups began to carry goods on **horseback**. These people also probably milked the mares. Later on, early farmers used a primitive form of **bridle** to help guide their horses. In the Middle Ages, knights used horses in battle. Special **saddles** and stirrups helped them stay on the horse during combat. In the 1800s, **cowboys** had to move large herds of cattle thousands of miles. Some spent weeks at a time with only a horse for company.

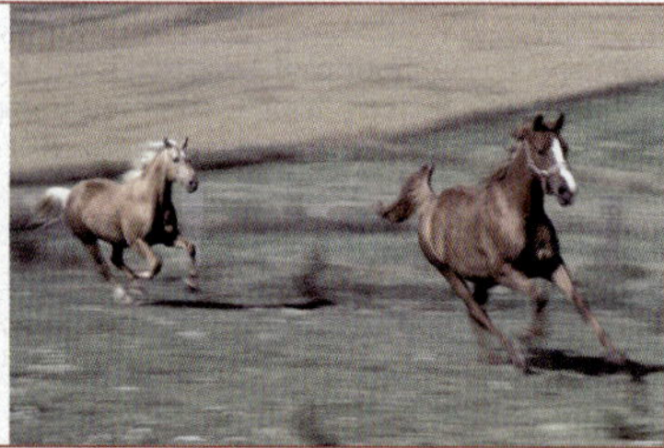

H

horse·man /hɔrsmən/ (horsemen) N-COUNT A **horseman** is a man who is riding a horse, or who rides horses well. 骑马的人；骑手 ❑ *Gerald was a fine horseman.* 杰拉尔德曾是个出色的骑手。

horse·power /hɔrspaʊər/ N-UNCOUNT **Horsepower** is a unit of power used for measuring how powerful an engine is. 马力 ❑ *...a 300-horsepower engine.* …一台300马力的发动机。

horse·shoe /hɔrsʃu/ (horseshoes) 1 N-COUNT A **horseshoe** is a piece of metal shaped like a U, which is fixed with nails to the bottom of a horse's foot in order to protect it. 马蹄铁 2 N-COUNT A **horseshoe** is an object in the shape of a horseshoe which is used as a symbol of good luck. 马蹄型吉祥物

horse-trading also **horsetrading** N-UNCOUNT When negotiation or bargaining is forceful and shows clever and careful judgment, you can describe it as **horse-trading**. 精明的交易 [AM] ❑ *...an adroit piece of political horse-trading by Senator Orrin Hatch.* …参议员奥林·哈奇一手操纵的一笔精明的政治交易。

hor·ti·cul·tur·al /hɔrtɪkʌltʃərᵊl/ ADJ **Horticultural** means concerned with horticulture. 园艺的；园艺学的 ❑ *...the John A. Sibley Horticultural Center.* …约翰A. 西布莉园艺中心。

hor·ti·cul·ture /hɔrtɪkʌltʃər/ N-UNCOUNT **Horticulture** is the study and practice of growing plants. 园艺学；园艺

★ **hose** /hoʊz/ (hoses, hosing, hosed) 1 N-COUNT A **hose** is a long, flexible pipe made of rubber or plastic. Water is directed through a hose in order to do things such as put out fires, clean cars, or water gardens. (胶皮或塑料制的) 水管 ❑ *You've left the garden hose on.* 你没有关花园的水管。 2 N-COUNT A **hose** is a pipe made of rubber or plastic, along which a liquid or gas flows, for example from one part of an engine to another. (用来输送液体或气体的) 软管 ❑ *Water in the engine compartment is sucked away by a hose.* 发动机舱里的水由一条软管吸走。 3 V-T If you **hose** something, you wash or water it using a hose. 用水管冲洗；用水管浇灌 ❑ *We wash our cars and hose our gardens without even thinking of the water that uses.* 我们冲洗汽车，浇灌花园，从没考虑过所耗费的水。
→ see **scuba diving**

hos·pice /hɒspɪs/ (hospices) 1 N-COUNT; N-IN-NAMES A **hospice** is a special hospital for people who are dying, where their practical and emotional needs are dealt with as well as their medical needs. 临终关怀医院 ❑ *...a hospice for cancer patients.* …一个癌症病人的临终关怀医院。 2 ADJ **Hospice** care is medical care that is provided for people, either in a hospice or in their own home, when they are dying. 临终护理的 [ADJ n] ❑ *Berle was diagnosed with colon cancer last year and had been under hospice care for the past few weeks.* 去年伯利被诊断患有结肠癌，在过去的几周里他一直受到临终关怀护理。 ❑ *...a hospice nurse.* …一名从事临终护理的护士。

hos·pi·table /hɒspɪtəbᵊl, hɒspɪt-/ 1 ADJ A **hospitable** person is friendly, generous, and welcoming to guests or people they have just met. 好客的；殷勤周到的 ❑ *The locals are hospitable and welcoming.* 当地人热情好客。 2 ADJ A **hospitable** climate or environment is one that encourages the existence or development of particular people or things. (气候、环境等) 适宜的 ❑ *Even in summer this place did not look exactly hospitable: in winter, conditions must have been exceedingly harsh.* 即使在夏天，这个地方看上去也并不太宜人：在冬天，条件一定非常恶劣。

Word Link *hosp, host ≈ guest : hospital, hospitality, hostage*

hos·pi·tal ♦♦♦ /hɒspɪtᵊl/ (hospitals) N-VAR A **hospital** is a place where people who are ill are cared for by nurses and doctors. 医院 ❑ *...a children's hospital with 120 beds.* …一个有120张床位的儿童医院。
→ see Word Web: **hospital**

Word Partnership *hospital* 的常用搭配：
V. **admit *someone* to a** hospital, **bring/rush/take *someone* to a** hospital, **end up in a** hospital, **go to a** hospital, **visit *someone* in a** hospital

★ **hos·pi·tal·ity** /hɒspɪtælɪti/ 1 N-UNCOUNT **Hospitality** is friendly, welcoming behavior toward guests or people you have just met. 殷勤好客 ❑ *Every visitor to Georgia is overwhelmed by the kindness, charm, and hospitality of the people.* 来到佐治亚州的每一个人都为当地人的善良、魅力和好客感动不已。 2 N-UNCOUNT **Hospitality** is the food, drink, and other privileges which some companies provide for their visitors or clients at major sports events or other public events. (在重大体育赛事或其他公共活动中，一些公司为客人提供的) 食物、饮料和其它优待 ❑ *...corporate hospitality tents.* …公司为客人提供饮料食品等招待服务的帐篷。

hos·pi·tal·ize /hɒspɪtəlaɪz/ (hospitalizes, hospitalizing, hospitalized) V-T If someone **is hospitalized**, they are sent or admitted to a hospital. 送…住院治疗 [usu passive] ❑ *Most people do not have to be hospitalized for asthma or pneumonia.* 多数人不必因哮喘或肺炎住院。 ● **hos·pi·tali·za·tion** /hɒspɪtəlɪzeɪʃᵊn/ N-UNCOUNT 住院治疗 ❑ *Occasionally hospitalization is required to combat dehydration.* 治疗脱水有时需要住院。

host ♦♦♦ /hoʊst/ (hosts, hosting, hosted) 1 N-COUNT The **host** at a party is the person who has invited the guests and provides the food, drink, or entertainment. (聚会的) 主人 ❑ *Apart from my host, I didn't know a single person there.* 除了主人，那儿的人我一个也不认识。 ❑ *Tommy Sopwith was always the perfect host.* 汤米·索普威思过去总是一个无可挑剔的主人。 2 V-T If someone **hosts** a party, dinner, or other function, they have invited the guests and provide the food, drink, or entertainment. 主办 (聚会、宴会或其他集会) ❑ *Tonight she hosts a ball for 300 guests.* 今晚她做东办一场有300名来宾参加的舞会。 ❑ *...a banquet hosted by the president of the United States.* …一场美国总统招待的宴会。 3 N-COUNT A country, city, or organization that is the **host** of an event provides the facilities for that event to take place. (举办某活动的) 东道主 ❑ *Atlanta was chosen to be host of the 1996 Olympic games.* 亚特兰大被选为1996年奥运会的东道主。 4 V-T If a country, city, or organization **hosts** an event, they provide the facilities for the event to take place. 主办 ❑ *New Bedford hosts a number of lively festivals throughout the summer months.* 新贝德福德整个夏天举办了许多个欢快有趣的艺术节。 5 PHRASE If a person or country **plays host to** an event or an important visitor, they host the event or the visit. 主办 (活动)；款待 (重要宾客) ❑ *Bush played host to Russian President Vladimir Putin.* 布什款待了俄罗斯总统弗拉基米尔·普京。 6 N-COUNT The **host** of a radio or television show is the person who introduces it and talks to the people who appear in it. (广播或电视的) 节目主持人 ❑ *I am host of a live radio program.* 我是一个直播的广播节目的主持人。 7 V-T The person who **hosts** a radio or television show introduces it and talks to the people who appear in it. 主持 (广播或电视节目) ❑ *She also hosts a show on St. Petersburg Radio.* 她还在圣彼得斯堡电台主持一个节目。 8 QUANT A **host** of things is a lot of them. 大量 ❑ *A host of problems may delay the opening of the new bridge.* 一大堆问题也许会延迟新建桥梁的开通。 9 N-COUNT A **host** or a **host computer** is the main computer in a network of computers, which controls the most important files and programs. 计算机主机 ❑ *Subscribers dial directly from their computers into the BBS host computer.* 用户直接从自己的计算机拨号接入公告版系统的主机。

★ **hos·tage** ♦♦◇ /hɒstɪdʒ/ (hostages) 1 N-COUNT A **hostage** is someone who has been captured by a person or organization and who may be killed or injured if people do not do what that person

Word Web **hospital**

Children's **Hospital** in Boston has one of the best **pediatric wards** in the country. Its Advanced Fetal Care Center can even treat babies before they are born. The hospital records about 18,000 inpatient **admissions** every year. It also has over 150 **outpatient** programs and handles more than 300,000 **emergency cases**. The staff includes 700 **residents** and **fellows**. Many of its **physicians** teach at nearby Harvard University. The hospital also employs excellent **researchers**. Their work led to the discovery of **vaccines** for **polio** and **measles**. The hospital has also led the way in liver, heart, and lung **transplants** in children.

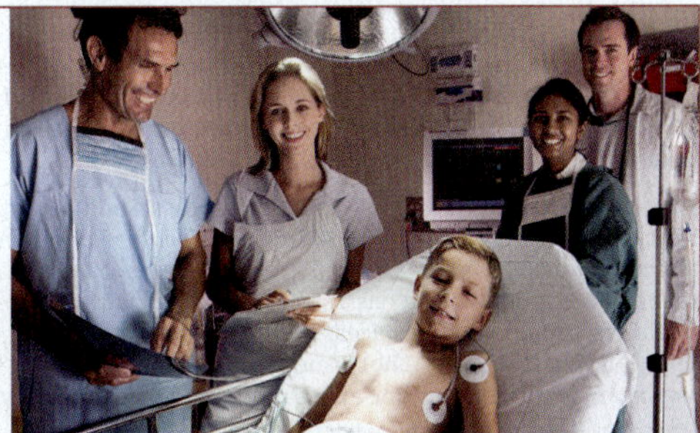

or organization demands. 人质 ❑ *It is hopeful that two hostages will be freed in the next few days.* 两名人质有望在几天后获释。 **2** PHRASE If someone **is taken hostage** or **is held hostage**, they are captured and kept as a hostage. 将某人扣作人质 ❑ *He was taken hostage while on his first foreign assignment as a television journalist.* 他第一次作为电视记者出国采访时就被扣作人质。 **3** N-VAR If you say you are **hostage to** something, you mean that your freedom to take action is restricted by things that you cannot control. 受到…的限制 ❑ *Wine growers say they've been held hostage to the interests of cereal farmers.* 葡萄酒制造商们说他们已被谷物种植者的利益所左右。

▲ **host·ess** /hoʊstɪs/ (**hostesses**) N-COUNT The **hostess** at a party is the woman who has invited the guests and provides the food, drink, or entertainment. (聚会的) 女主人 ❑ *The hostess introduced them.* 女主人介绍了他们。

hos·tile /hɒstᵊl/ **1** ADJ If you are **hostile to** another person or an idea, you disagree with them or disapprove of them, often showing this in your behavior. 反对的；敌对的 ❑ *Many people felt he would be hostile to the idea of foreign intervention.* 许多人觉得他会反对外来干预。 ❑ *The West has gradually relaxed its hostile attitude to this influential state.* 西方对这个有影响力的国家的敌对态度已趋缓和。 **2** ADJ Someone who is **hostile** is unfriendly and aggressive. 怀敌意的 ❑ *Drinking may make a person feel relaxed and happy, or it may make her hostile, violent, or depressed.* 喝酒可以使一个人感到放松和愉快，也可以让人变得不友善、粗暴或沮丧。 **3** ADJ **Hostile** situations and conditions make it difficult for you to achieve something. (环境和条件等) 不利的 ❑ *...some of the most hostile climatic conditions in the world.* …世界上最不利的一些气候条件。 **4** ADJ A **hostile** takeover bid is one that is opposed by the company that is being bid for. (收购投标) 恶意的 [BUSINESS] ❑ *Soon after he arrived, Kingfisher launched a hostile bid for Dixons.* 金费希尔到任之后不久就开始了对迪克森斯公司的恶意收购投标。 **5** ADJ In a war, you use **hostile** to describe your enemy's forces, organizations, weapons, land, and activities. (战争中) 敌方的 [ADJ n] ❑ *The city is encircled by a hostile army.* 该市被敌军包围。

Word Partnership *hostile* 的常用搭配:

N. hostile **attitude/feelings/intentions** **1**
hostile **act/action**, hostile **environment** **3**
hostile **takeover** **4**
ADV. **increasingly** hostile **1**–**3**

hos·til·ities /hɒstɪlɪtiz/ N-PLURAL You can refer to fighting between two countries or groups who are at war as **hostilities**. 战争状态 [FORMAL] ❑ *The authorities have urged people to stock up on fuel in case hostilities break out.* 当局已敦促人们储备燃料以防战争爆发。

▲ **hos·til·ity** /hɒstɪlɪti/ **1** N-UNCOUNT **Hostility** is unfriendly or aggressive behavior toward people or ideas. 敌意；敌对 ❑ *The last decade has witnessed a serious rise in the levels of racism and hostility to black and ethnic groups.* 过去的10年里，种族主义及对黑人和少数民族的敌意变得更加严重了。 **2** N-UNCOUNT Your **hostility to** something you do not approve of is your opposition to it. 反对 ❑ *There is hostility among traditionalists to this method of teaching history.* 传统主义者中有人反对这种教授历史的方法。

hot ♦♦◊ /hɒt/ (**hotter, hottest**) **1** ADJ Something that is **hot** has a high temperature. 热的 ❑ *When the oil is hot, add the sliced onion.* 油热之后，加入切好的洋葱。 ❑ *What he needed was a hot bath and a good sleep.* 他所需要的是泡个热水澡和睡个好觉。 **2** ADJ **Hot** is used to describe the weather or the air in a room or building when the temperature is high. (天气) 炎热的 ❑ *It was too hot even for a gentle stroll.* 这样的天气连慢慢散步都太热。

In informal English, if you want to emphasize how hot the weather is, you can say that it is **boiling** or **scorching**. In winter, if the temperature is above average, you can say that it is **mild**. In general, **hot** suggests a higher temperature than **warm**, and **warm** things are usually pleasant. ❑ *...a warm evening.*

3 ADJ If you are **hot**, you feel as if your body is at an unpleasantly high temperature. (人) 感到热的 ❑ *I was too hot and tired to eat more than a few mouthfuls.* 我又热又累，只能吃下几口。 **4** ADJ You can say that food is **hot** when it has a strong, burning taste caused by chilies, pepper, or other spices. (食物) 辛辣的 ❑ *...hot curries.* …辛辣的咖喱食品。 **5** ADJ A **hot** issue or topic is one that is very important at the present time and is receiving a lot of publicity. (问题或话题等) 热门的 [JOURNALISM] ❑ *The role of women in war has been a hot topic of debate since the Gulf conflict.* 自海湾冲突以来，女性在战争中的作用一直是一个热门的争论话题。 **6** ADJ **Hot** news is new, recent, and fresh. (消息) 最新的 [INFORMAL] ❑ *...eight pages of the latest movies, video releases, and the hot news from Tinseltown.* …有关最新电影、录像新片以及好莱坞最新消息的8页内容。 **7** ADJ You can use **hot** to describe something that is very exciting and that many people want to see, use, obtain, or become involved with. 火爆的；风行的 [INFORMAL] ❑ *When I was in Chicago in 1990 a friend got me a ticket for the hottest show in town: the Monet Exhibition at the Art Institute.* 1990年我在芝加哥的时候，一个朋友给我弄到了一张城里最抢手的展览门票：艺术学院的莫奈画展。 **8** ADJ A **hot** contest is one that is intense and involves a great deal of activity and determination. (比赛等) 激烈的 [INFORMAL] ❑ *It took hot competition from abroad, however, to show us just how good our product really is.* 然而，正是来自国外的激烈竞争让我们看到自己的产品有多好。 **9** ADJ If a person or team is the **hot** favorite, people think that they are the one most likely to win a race or competition. (比赛或竞争中) 最有可能获胜的 [ADJ n] ❑ *Atlantic City is the hot favorite to stage the fight.* 大西洋城最有可能赢得这次拳击赛的主办权。 **10** ADJ Someone who has a **hot** temper gets angry very quickly and easily. 暴躁的 ❑ *His hot temper was making it increasingly difficult for others to work with him.* 他暴躁的脾气使得别人越来越难与他一起工作。 **11** ADJ If you describe someone as **hot**, you mean that they are sexually attractive or sexually desirable. 性感的 [INFORMAL] ❑ *"He's great," Caroline said, "hot."* "他太棒了，"卡罗琳说道，"性感极了。" ❑ *If a hot chick comes on to you, smile and walk away.* 如果一个性感妞儿向你挑逗，你应该一笑走开。 **12** PHRASE If someone **blows hot and cold**, they keep changing their attitude toward something, sometimes being very enthusiastic and at other times expressing no interest at all. 反复无常 ❑ *The media, meanwhile, has blown hot and cold over the affair.* 同时，媒体对这件事的态度一直摇摆不定。 **13** PHRASE If you are **hot and bothered**, you are so worried and anxious that you cannot think clearly or behave sensibly. 焦虑不安的；六神无主的 ❑ *Ray was getting very hot and bothered about the idea.* 雷为这个想法感到焦虑不安。 **14** PHRASE If you say that one person **has the hots for** another, you mean that they feel a strong sexual attraction to that person. 对…有强烈的性吸引力 [INFORMAL] ❑ *I've had the hots for him ever since he arrived.* 自从他来到后，我就迷恋上他了。

→ see **weather**

Thesaurus *hot* 另参见:

ADJ. sweltering; (*ant.*) chilly, cold **2**
spicy; (*ant.*) bland, mild **4**
cool, popular; (*ant.*) unpopular **7**

hot but·ton (**hot buttons**) N-COUNT A **hot button** is a subject or problem that people have very strong feelings about. 敏感问题 [oft N n] [mainly AM, JOURNALISM] ❑ *Abortion is still one of the hot button issues of U.S. life.* 堕胎仍是美国生活中的敏感问题之一。

hot dog (**hot dogs**) N-COUNT A **hot dog** is a long bun with a hot sausage inside it. You can also use **hot dog** to refer to the sausage inside the bun. 热狗

ho·tel ♦♦◊ /hoʊtɛl/ (**hotels**) N-COUNT A **hotel** is a building where people stay, for example on vacation, paying for their rooms and meals. 旅馆

→ see Word Web: **hotel**

In addition to **hotels**, there are several other types of accommodation for travelers and tourists. A **bed and breakfast** or **B & B** is a private home that rents out rooms and serves only breakfast. A **motel** is similar in size to a hotel but particularly is designed for those traveling by car, so the parking lot is very convenient. **Youth hostels** provide dormitories for young people who want low-priced lodgings.

Word Partnership *hotel* 的常用搭配:

N. hotel **guest**, hotel **reservation**, hotel **room**
V. **check into a** hotel, **check out of a** hotel, **stay at a** hotel
ADJ. **luxury** hotel, **new** hotel

ho·tel·ier /oʊtɛlyeɪ/ (**hoteliers**) N-COUNT A **hotelier** is a person who owns or manages a hotel. 旅馆经营者

hot key (**hot keys**) N-COUNT A **hot key** is a key, or a combination of keys, on a computer keyboard that you can press in order to make something happen, without having to type the full

Word Web hotel

When making **reservations** at a **hotel**, most people request a **single** or a **double** room. Sometimes the **clerk** invites the person to **upgrade** to a **suite**. When arriving at the hotel, the first person to greet the **guest** is the bellhop. He will put the person's suitcases on a **luggage cart**. The guest then goes to the **front desk** and **checks in**. The clerk often describes **amenities** such as a **gym** or **spa**. Most hotels provide **room service** for late night snacks. There is often a concierge to help arrange dinners and other entertainment outside of the hotel.

instructions. (计算机键盘上的) 热键; 快捷键 [COMPUTING] ❑ *All macros can be set to run when a hot key is pressed.* 所有宏指令都可以被设定为按某一快捷键开始运行。

hot·line /hɒtlaɪn/ (**hotlines**) also **hot line** 1 N-COUNT A **hotline** is a telephone line that the public can use to contact an organization about a particular subject. Hotlines allow people to obtain information from an organization or to give the organization information. (供公众咨询或提供信息的) 热线 ❑ *...a telephone hotline for gardeners seeking advice.* …一条园丁们寻求咨询的电话热线。 2 N-COUNT A **hotline** is a special, direct telephone line between the heads of government in different countries. (两国首脑间的) 热线 ❑ *They have discussed setting up a military hotline between Hanoi and Bangkok.* 他们已讨论在河内和曼谷之间建立一条军事热线。

hot link (**hot links**) N-COUNT A **hot link** is a word or phrase in a hypertext document that can be selected in order to access additional information. 友情链接; 超文本链接 [COMPUTING] ❑ *Each of these pages has hot links to other documents throughout the network.* 这些网页都带有点击其他网络文献的友情链接。

★ **hot·ly** /hɒtli/ 1 ADV If people discuss, argue, or say something **hotly**, they speak in a lively or angry way, because they feel strongly. 激烈地 [ADV with v] ❑ *The bank hotly denies any wrongdoing.* 该银行强烈否认任何违规行为。 2 ADV If you are being **hotly** pursued, someone is trying hard to catch you and is close behind you. 紧随地 [ADV with v] ❑ *He'd snuck out of the U.S. hotly pursued by the CIA.* 他偷偷地溜出了美国，但已被美国中央情报局紧紧盯上。

★ **hound** /haʊnd/ (**hounds, hounding, hounded**) 1 N-COUNT A **hound** is a type of dog that is often used for hunting or racing. 猎犬; 赛犬 ❑ *Rainey's chief interest in life is hunting with hounds.* 雷尼一生中的主要嗜好是带着猎犬去打猎。 2 V-T If someone **hounds** you, they constantly disturb or speak to you in an annoying or upsetting way. (不断地) 烦扰 ❑ *Newcomers are constantly hounding them for advice.* 新来的人老是缠着他们问这问那的。 3 V-T If someone **is hounded out of** a job or place, they are forced to leave it, often because other people are constantly criticizing them. 迫使 (某人) 离开 [usu passive] ❑ *There is a general view around that he has been hounded out of office by the press.* 人们普遍认为是新闻媒体的负面报道迫使他离职的。

hour ♦♦♦ /aʊər/ (**hours**) 1 N-COUNT An **hour** is a period of sixty minutes. 小时 ❑ *They waited for about two hours.* 他们等了大约两个钟头。 ❑ *I only slept about half an hour that night.* 那天晚上我只睡了大约半个小时。 2 N-PLURAL People say that something takes or lasts **hours** to emphasize that it takes or lasts a very long time, or what seems like a very long time. 很长的一段时间 [EMPHASIS] ❑ *Getting there would take hours.* 到那儿要花很长时间。 3 N-SING A clock that strikes **the hour** strikes when it is exactly one o'clock, two o'clock, and so on. 整点 ❑ *She'd heard a clock somewhere strike the hour as she'd slipped from her room.* 她悄悄地从自己房间里溜出来时，听到某个地方的一只时钟正在整点报时。 4 N-SING You can refer to a particular time or moment as a particular **hour**. 时间; 时刻 [LITERARY] ❑ *...the hour of his execution.* …他的死刑执行时间。 5 N-COUNT If you refer, for example, to someone's **hour of** need or **hour of** happiness, you are referring to the time in their life when they are or were experiencing that condition or feeling. (人生中需要帮助、感到幸福等的) 时刻 [LITERARY] ❑ *He recalled her devotion to her husband during his hour of need.* 他回想起她在丈夫需要帮助时所做出的无私奉献。 6 N-PLURAL You can refer to the period of time during which something happens or operates each day as the **hours** during which it happens or operates. (一天中的某个) 时间段 ❑ *...the hours of darkness.* …夜间。 ❑ *Phone us on this number during office hours.* 上班时间给我们打这个电话。 7 N-PLURAL If you refer to the **hours** involved in a job, you are talking about how long you spend each week doing it and when you do it. 工作时间 ❑ *I worked quite irregular hours.* 我的工作时间很不固定。 8 → see also **rush hour** 9 PHRASE If you do something **after hours**, you do it outside normal business hours or the time when you are usually at work. 办公 (或营业) 时间之外 ❑ *...a local restaurant where steel workers unwind after hours.* …钢铁工人下班后去休息放松的一家当地餐馆。 10 PHRASE If you say that something happens **at all hours of** the day or night, you disapprove of it happening at the time that it does or as often as it does. 不分时候 [DISAPPROVAL] ❑ *She didn't want her fourteen-year-old daughter coming home at all hours of the morning.* 她不希望自己14岁的女儿在半夜凌晨才回家。 11 PHRASE If something happens **in the early hours**, **in the small hours**, or **in the wee hours**, it happens in the early morning after midnight. 在凌晨 ❑ *Gibbs was arrested in the early hours of yesterday morning.* 吉布斯在昨天凌晨被捕。 12 PHRASE If something happens **on the hour**, it happens every hour at, for example, nine o'clock, ten o'clock, and so on, and not at any number of minutes past an hour. 在整点 ❑ *During this war in the Persian Gulf, NPR will have newscasts every hour on the hour.* 在这场海湾战争期间，美国国家公共广播电台会进行整点新闻报道。

hour·ly /aʊərli/ 1 ADJ An **hourly** event happens once every hour. 每小时的 [ADJ n] ❑ *He flipped on the radio to get the hourly news broadcast.* 他把收音机打开，收听整点新闻广播。 ● ADV **Hourly** is also an adverb. 每小时地 [ADV after v] ❑ *The hospital issued press releases hourly.* 这家医院每小时发布一次新闻稿。 2 ADJ Your **hourly** earnings are the money that you earn in one hour. 按小时计算的 [ADJ n] ❑ *They have little prospect of finding new jobs with the same hourly pay.* 他们找到时薪同原来一样的新工作的机会很渺茫。

house ♦♦♦ (**houses, housing, housed**)

The noun and adjective are pronounced /haʊs/. The verb is pronounced /haʊz/. The form **houses** is pronounced /haʊzɪz/.

名词和形容词读作 /haʊs/。动词读作 /haʊz/。**houses**此词形读作 /haʊzɪz/。

1 N-COUNT A **house** is a building in which people live, usually the people belonging to one family. 房屋 ❑ *She has moved to a small house and is living off her meager savings.* 她搬进了一幢小房子，靠自己微薄的积蓄过日子。 2 N-SING You can refer to all the people who live together in a house as **the house**. 一家人; 同住一幢房子的人 ❑ *If he set his alarm clock for midnight, it would wake the whole house.* 如果他把闹钟设定在午夜，铃声会把全家人都吵醒。 3 N-COUNT **House** is used in the names of types of places where people go to eat and drink. …馆 (用于某些类型的餐馆名称中) ❑ *...a steak house.* …一家牛排馆。 4 N-COUNT **House** is used in the names of types of companies, especially ones which publish books, lend money, or design clothes. …公司 (用于某些类型的公司名称中，尤其是出版、贷款或服装设计等公司) ❑ *Many of the clothes come from the world's top fashion houses.* 这些服装中有很多来自世界顶级时装设计公司。 5 N-COUNT You can refer to one of the two bodies of the U.S. Congress as a **House**. The House of Representatives is sometimes referred to as **the House**. (美国) 众议院 ❑ *Some members of the House and Senate worked all day yesterday.* 昨天众议院和参议院的一些议员工作了一整天。 6 ADJ A restaurant's **house** wine is the cheapest wine it sells, which is not listed by name on the wine list. 店酒 (某餐馆没有列在酒水单上的最便宜的葡萄酒) [ADJ n] ❑ *Tweed ordered a carafe of the house wine.* 特威德点了一瓶店酒。 7 V-T To **house** someone means to provide a house or apartment for them to live in. 为…提供住房 ❑ *...homes that house up to nine people.* …最多可容纳9人的住处。 8 V-T A building or container that **houses** something is the place where it is located or from where it operates. 给…提供场地 [no cont] ❑ *The building is open to the public and houses a museum of motorcycles and cars.* 这座大楼对公众开放，并设有一个摩托车和汽车博物馆。 9 V-T If you say that a building **houses** a number of people,

you mean that is the place where they live or where they are staying. 供…居住 [no cont] ❑ *The building will house twelve boys and eight girls.* 这栋房子要住12个男孩和8个女孩。 10 → see also **clearinghouse, White House** 11 PHRASE If a person or their performance or speech **brings the house down**, the audience claps, laughs, or shouts loudly because the performance or speech is very impressive or amusing. 博得全场喝彩 [INFORMAL] ❑ *It's really an amazing dance. It just always brings the house down.* 这个舞蹈简直太精彩了。它总是博得全场喝彩。 12 PHRASE If two people **get on like a house on fire**, they quickly become close friends, for example because they have many interests in common. 一见如故 [INFORMAL] ❑ *I went over and struck up a conversation, and we got on like a house on fire.* 我走过去搭讪聊天，我们一见如故。 13 PHRASE If you are given something in a restaurant or bar **on the house**, you do not have to pay for it. 由店家免费提供的 ❑ *The owner knew about the engagement and brought them glasses of champagne on the house.* 店主知道了他们订婚的事，便免费请他们喝了几杯香槟酒。 14 PHRASE If someone **gets** their **house in order**, **puts** their **house in order**, or **sets** their **house in order**, they arrange their affairs and solve their problems. 把自己的事情处理妥当 ❑ *He's got his house in order and made some tremendous decisions.* 他已把自己的事情处理好，并做出了一些重大决定。

→ see Picture Dictionary: **house**

Thesaurus *house* 另参见：

N. dwelling, home, place, residence 1

Word Partnership *house* 的常用搭配：

V. **break into a** house, **build a** house, **buy a** house, **find a** house, **live in a** house, **own a** house, **rent a** house, **sell a** house 1

ADJ. **empty** house, **expensive** house, **little** house, **new/old** house 1

N. house **prices**, **a room in a** house 1

house ar·rest N-UNCOUNT If someone is **under house arrest**, they are officially ordered not to leave their home, because they are suspected of being involved in an illegal activity. (本宅) 软禁 ❑ *The main opposition leaders had been arrested or placed under house arrest.* 反对派主要领导人已被逮捕或软禁。

house·hold ♦◇◇ /haʊshoʊld/ (**households**) 1 N-COUNT A **household** is all the people in a family or group who live together in a house. 家庭；同住一所房子的人 ❑ *...growing up in a male-only household.* …在全体成员均为男性的家庭里长大。 2 N-SING The **household** is your home and everything that is connected with taking care of it. 家务 ❑ *...household chores.* …家务活。 3 ADJ Someone or something that is a **household** name or word is very well known. 家喻户晓的 [ADJ n] ❑ *Today, fashion designers are household names.* 如今，服装设计师们家喻户晓。

house·holder /haʊshoʊldər/ (**householders**) N-COUNT The **householder** is the person who owns or rents a particular house. 住户 (房主或房屋租住者) ❑ *Officials appealed to householders to open their homes to the thousands of persons made homeless by the storm.* 官员们呼吁住户们为成千上万因这次暴风雨而无家可归的人提供住宿。

house·keeper /haʊskipər/ (**housekeepers**) N-COUNT A **housekeeper** is a person whose job is to cook, clean, and take care of a house for its owner. 管家

house·keeping /haʊskipɪŋ/ N-UNCOUNT **Housekeeping** is the work and organization involved in running a home, including the shopping and cleaning. 料理家务 ❑ *I thought that cooking and housekeeping were unimportant, easy tasks.* 我曾认为做饭和料理家务是琐碎简单的工作。

House of Rep·re·senta·tives N-PROPER **The House of Representatives** is the larger of the two parts of Congress in the United States, or the equivalent part of the system of government in some other countries. (美国等的) 众议院 ❑ *The House of Representatives approved a new budget.* 众议院批准了一项新的预算方案。

house·wife /haʊswaɪf/ (**housewives**) N-COUNT A **housewife** is a married woman who does not have a paid job, but instead takes care of her home and children. 家庭主妇 ❑ *Married at nineteen, she was a traditional housewife and mother of four children.* 她19岁就结婚了，是个传统的家庭主妇和4个孩子的母亲。

Homemaker is the preferred term in the US for a woman who takes care of her home and children full time. **Housewife** is not the modern term in the US, although it is still quite common in the UK.

house·work /haʊswɜrk/ N-UNCOUNT **Housework** is the work such as cleaning, washing, and ironing that you do in your home. 家务 ❑ *Men are doing more housework nowadays.* 现今男人正在承担越来越多的家务。

hous·ing ♦♦◇ /haʊzɪŋ/ N-UNCOUNT You refer to the buildings in which people live as **housing** when you are talking about their standard, price, or availability. 住房 ❑ *...a shortage of affordable housing.* …廉价住房的短缺。

★ **hov·er** /hʌvər/ (**hovers, hovering, hovered**) 1 V-I To **hover** means to stay in the same position in the air without moving forward or backward. Many birds and insects can hover by moving their wings very quickly. (鸟、昆虫等通过快速扇动翅膀在原地) 盘旋 ❑ *Beautiful butterflies hovered above the wild flowers.* 美丽的蝴蝶在野花上方盘旋。 2 V-I If you **hover**, you stay in one place and move slightly in a nervous way, for example because you cannot decide what to do. (人) 徘徊 ❑ *Judith was hovering in the doorway.* 朱迪丝在门口徘徊。 3 V-I If you **hover**, you are in an uncertain situation or state of mind. 处于不稳定状态 ❑ *She hovered on the brink of death for three months as doctors battled to save her.* 3个月来在医生们奋力挽救她的

Picture Dictionary house

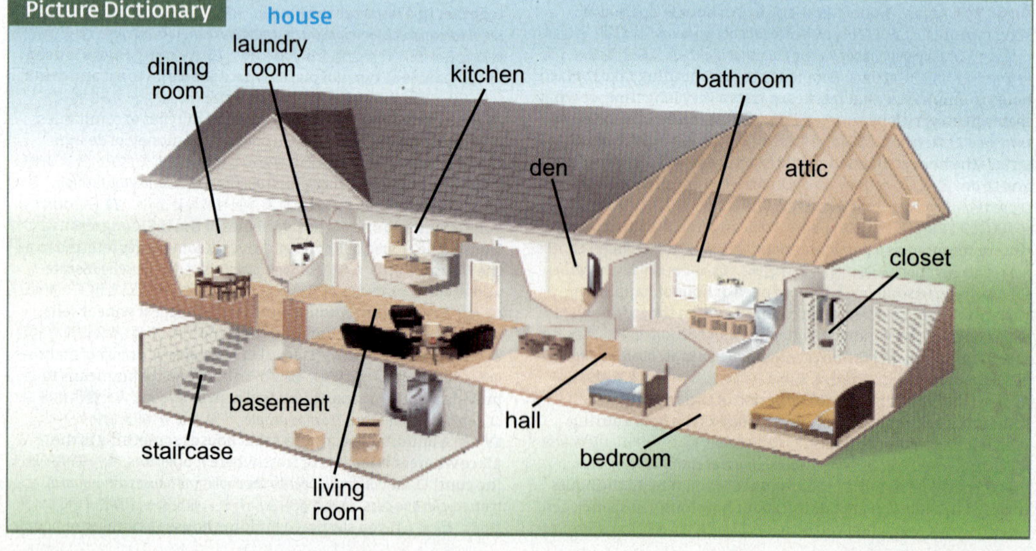

生命的过程中，她一直处在死亡的边缘。4 V-I If something such as a price, value, or score **hovers** around a particular level, it stays at more or less that level and does not change much. (价格、价值或分数等) 徘徊 (在某个水平上下) ❑ *In September 1989 the exchange rate hovered around 140 yen to the dollar.* 在1989年9月，汇率一直在140日元比1美元左右徘徊。

hover·craft /hʌvərkræft/ (**hovercraft**) N-COUNT A **hovercraft** is a vehicle that can travel across land and water. It floats above the land or water on a cushion of air. 气垫船；气垫飞行器 [also "by" N] ❑ *Traveling at speeds of up to thirty five knots, these hovercraft can easily outpace most boats.* 这些气垫船以高达每小时35海里的速度航行，很容易超过大部分船只。

how ♦♦♦ /haʊ/

The conjunction is pronounced /haʊ/.

连词读作 /haʊ/。

1 QUEST You use **how** to ask about the way in which something happens or is done. 怎样；如何 ❑ *How do I make payments into my account?* 我怎样付款到我的账户呢？ ❑ *How do you manage to keep the place so neat?* 你是怎么把这个地方保持得如此整洁的呢？ ● CONJ **How** is also a conjunction. 怎样 ❑ *I don't want to know how he died.* 我不想知道他是如何死的。 2 CONJ You use **how** after certain adjectives and verbs to introduce a statement or fact, often something that you remember or expect other people to know about. 用于某些形容词或动词后，以引出一个陈述或事实 ❑ *It's amazing how people collect so much stuff over the years.* 人们这些年下来竟能收集到这么多东西，真令人惊奇。 ❑ *It's funny how I never seem to get a thing done on my day off.* 好笑的是，在休息日里我好像从没做成一件事。 3 QUEST You use **how** to ask questions about the quantity or degree of something. (用以询问数量或程度) 多少；多么 ❑ *How much money are we talking about?* 我们所说的这笔钱有多大数目？ ❑ *How many full-time staff have we got?* 我们有多少全职员工？ ❑ *How long will you be staying?* 你要呆多长时间？ ❑ *How old is your son now?* 现在你儿子有多大？ 4 QUEST You use **how** when you are asking someone whether something was successful or enjoyable. (用以询问某人某事是否成功或愉快) 怎么样 ❑ *How was your trip down to Orlando?* 你的奥兰多之旅怎么样？ ❑ *How did your date go?* 你的约会怎么样？ 5 QUEST You use **how** to ask about someone's health or to find out someone's news. (用以询问某人健康或有关某人的消息) 怎样 ❑ *Hi! How are you doing?* 你好！最近怎么样？ ❑ *How's Rosie?* 罗茜身体好吗？

You do not use **how** to ask questions about the appearance or character of someone or something. You use an expression with **what** and **like**. For example, if you ask "**How is Susan?**," you are asking about her health. If you want to know about her appearance, you ask "**What does Susan look like?**" If you want to know about her personality, you ask "**What is Susan like?**"

6 ADV You use **how** to emphasize the degree to which something is true. (用以强调某事的真实程度) 多么 [ADV adj/adv] [EMPHASIS] ❑ *I didn't realize how heavy that bag was going to be.* 我没有想到那个包会有多重。 7 ADV You use **how** in exclamations to emphasize an adjective, adverb, or statement. (用于感叹句中以强调形容词、副词或句子) 多么 [ADV adj/adv/cl] [EMPHASIS] ❑ *How strange that something so simple as a walk on the beach could suddenly mean so much.* 在海滩上散步这么简单的事突然间变得意义如此重大，真是奇怪。 8 QUEST You use **how** in expressions such as "**How can you...**" and "**How could you...**" to indicate that you disapprove of what someone has done or that you find it hard to believe. 你怎么能… (表示不赞成或很难相信) [QUEST "can/could"] [DISAPPROVAL] ❑ *How can you drink so much beer, Luke?* 卢克，你怎么可以喝这么多啤酒？ 9 QUEST You use **how** in expressions such as "**How about...**" or "**How would you like...**" when you are making an offer or a suggestion. …怎么样 (表示提出建议) ❑ *How about a cup of coffee?* 来杯咖啡怎么样？ 10 CONVENTION If you ask someone "**How about you?**" you are asking them what they think or want. 你呢 (用以询问对方的想法或要求) ❑ *Well, I enjoyed that. How about you two?* 嗯，我很喜欢那个。你俩觉得呢？ 11 PHRASE You use **how about** to introduce a new subject which you think is relevant to the conversation you have been having. …怎么样 (用以引导一个与正在谈论的话题有关的新题目) ❑ *Are your products and services competitive? How about marketing?* 你们的产品和服务具有竞争力吗？营销怎么样？ 12 PHRASE You ask "**How come?**" or "**How so?**" when you are surprised by something and are asking why it happened or was said. 怎么会这样 (由于吃惊而询问) [INFORMAL] ❑ *"They don't say a single word to each other."—"How come?"* "他们相互不说一句话。" —— "怎么会这样？"

how·ever ♦♦♦ /haʊɛvər/ 1 ADV You use **however** when you are adding a comment which is surprising or which contrasts with what has just been said. 然而 (用以引出令人吃惊或形成对比的话语) [ADV with cl] ❑ *This was not an easy decision. It is, however, a decision that we feel is dictated by our duty.* 这可不是一个轻松的决定。不过我们觉得我们有责任做出这样的的决定。 2 ADV You use **however** before an adjective or adverb to emphasize that the degree or extent of something cannot change a situation. 不管多么 (用于形容词或副词前表强调) [EMPHASIS] ❑ *You should always strive to achieve more, however well you have done before.* 不管以前做得多么好，你应该始终争取更大的进步。 ❑ *However hard she tried, nothing seemed to work.* 无论她多么努力，好像都无济于事。 3 CONJ You use **however** when you want to say that it makes no difference how something is done. 不管用什么方法 (用以表示没有区别) ❑ *However we adopt healthcare reform, it isn't going to save major amounts of money.* 不管我们采取什么样的医疗改革措施，它都不会节省太多的钱。 4 ADV You use **however** in expressions such as **or however long it takes** and **or however many there were** to indicate that the figure you have just mentioned may not be accurate. 无论多久 (表示刚提到的数字不一定准确)；不管多少 [VAGUENESS] ❑ *Wait 30 to 60 minutes or however long it takes.* 等30到60分钟，或需要的不管多长的时间。 5 QUEST You can use **however** to ask in an emphatic way how something has happened which you are very surprised about. Some speakers of English think that this form is incorrect and prefer to use "how ever." 究竟如何 (有些说英语者更愿意用**how ever**的形式) [EMPHASIS] ❑ *However did you find this place in such weather?* 在这样的天气里你究竟是怎么找到这个地方的？

★ **howl** /haʊl/ (**howls, howling, howled**) 1 V-I If an animal such as a wolf or a dog **howls**, it makes a long, loud, crying sound. (狼、狗等动物) 嗥叫 ❑ *Somewhere a dog suddenly howled, baying at the moon.* 某个地方的一只狗突然嗥叫起来，对着月亮狂吠。 ● N-COUNT **Howl** is also a noun. 嗥叫 ❑ *The dog let out a savage howl and, wheeling round, flew at him.* 狗发出凶猛的嗥叫声，转过身向他猛扑过来。 2 V-I If a person **howls**, they make a long, loud cry expressing pain, anger, or unhappiness. (人因痛苦、愤怒、不愉快等) 嚎叫 ❑ *He howled like a wounded animal as blood spurted from the gash.* 当鲜血从伤口喷射出来时，他像受伤的动物一样嚎叫。 ● N-COUNT **Howl** is also a noun. 嚎叫 ❑ *With a howl of rage, he grabbed the neck of a broken bottle and advanced.* 他一声怒号，抓起一个破瓶子的瓶颈向前走去。 3 V-I When the wind **howls**, it blows hard and makes a loud noise. 呼啸 ❑ *The wind howled all night, but I slept a little.* 风整夜呼啸着，但我还是睡了一会儿。 4 V-T If you **howl** something, you say it in a very loud voice. 高声嚷 [INFORMAL] ❑ *"Get away, get away, get away," he howled.* "滚开，滚开，滚开，" 他高声嚷道。 5 V-I If you **howl with** laughter, you laugh very loudly. 放声大笑 ❑ *Joe, Pink, and Booker howled with delight.* 乔、平克和布克高兴地放声大笑。 ● N-COUNT **Howl** is also a noun. 大笑 ❑ *His stories caused howls of laughter.* 他的故事引起阵阵大笑。 → see **laugh**

HQ /eɪtʃ kyu/ (**HQs**) N-VAR **HQ** is an abbreviation for **headquarters.** 总部 ❑ *The regimental HQ is a tiny office manned by two retired officers.* 该团司令部是个有两个退休军官办公的小办公室。

hr (**hrs**) **hr** is a written abbreviation for **hour.** 小时 ❑ *Let this cook on low for another 1 hr 15 mins.* 让这个在小火上再烧1小时15分钟。

HR /eɪtʃ ɑr/ N-UNCOUNT In a company or other organization, the **HR** department is the department with responsibility for the recruiting, training, and welfare of the staff. **HR** is an abbreviation for **human resources.** 人力资源 [BUSINESS]

HTML /eɪtʃ ti ɛm ɛl/ N-UNCOUNT **HTML** is a system of codes for producing documents for the Internet. **HTML** is an abbreviation for "hypertext markup language." 超文本标记语言 [COMPUTING] ❑ *...HTML documents.* …超文本标记语言文件。

HTTP /eɪtʃ ti ti pi/ N-UNCOUNT **HTTP** is a way of formatting and transmitting messages on the Internet. **HTTP** is an abbreviation for "hypertext transfer protocol." 超文本传输协议 [COMPUTING]

hub /hʌb/ (**hubs**) 1 N-COUNT You can describe a place as a **hub of** an activity when it is a very important center for that activity. 活动中心 ❑ *The island's social hub is the Cafe Sport.* 该岛的社交中心是"运动咖啡馆"。 2 N-COUNT The **hub** of a wheel is the part at the center. 轮毂 3 N-COUNT A **hub** or a **hub airport** is a large airport from which you can travel to many other airports. 枢纽机场 ❑ *...a campaign to secure Heathrow's place as Europe's main international hub.*

…一场确保希思罗机场成为欧洲主要国际枢纽机场的运动。 4 N-COUNT A **hub** is a device for connecting computers in a network. 集线器 [COMPUTING]

★ **hud·dle** /hʌdᵊl/ (**huddles, huddling, huddled**) 1 V-I If you **huddle** somewhere, you sit, stand, or lie there holding your arms and legs close to your body, usually because you are cold or frightened. (由于寒冷或害怕而) 蜷缩 ❑ *Mr. Pell huddled in a corner with his notebook on his knees.* 佩尔先生缩在一个角落里，笔记本放在膝盖上。 2 V-I If people **huddle together** or **huddle around** something, they stand, sit, or lie close to each other, usually because they all feel cold or frightened. (由于寒冷或害怕) 挤成一团 ❑ *Tired and lost, we huddled together.* 又累又迷了路，我们挤在一起。 3 V-RECIP If people **huddle** in a group, they gather together to discuss something quietly or secretly. (悄悄地或秘密地) 凑在一起商讨 ❑ *Off to one side, Sticht, Macomber, Jordan, and Kreps huddled to discuss something.* 史蒂希特、麦康伯、乔丹和克雷普斯走到一边，私下商量起事情。 ❑ *The president has been huddling with his most senior aides.* 总统一直在和他的顶级高级助理们秘密地聚到一起进行商谈。 4 N-COUNT A **huddle** is a small group of people or things that are standing very close together or lying on top of each other, usually in a disorganized way. 挤在一起的一群人或东西 ❑ *We lay there: a huddle of bodies, gasping for air.* 我们躺在那儿：挤作一团，大口地喘着气。

H

▲ **hue** /hyu/ (**hues**) 1 N-COUNT A **hue** is a color. 颜色 [LITERARY] ❑ *The same hue will look different in different light.* 同一颜色在不同光线下看起来会不同。 2 PHRASE If people raise a **hue and cry** about something, they protest angrily about it. 愤怒抗议 [WRITTEN] ❑ *Just as the show ended, he heard a huge hue and cry outside.* 正当演出结束的时候，他听到外面一阵喧嚣的愤怒抗议。

huff /hʌf/ (**huffs, huffing, huffed**) 1 V-T If you **huff**, you indicate that you are annoyed or offended about something, usually by the way that you say something. 气鼓鼓地说 ❑ *"This," huffed Mr. Buthelezi, "was discrimination."* "这么做" 布特莱齐先生愤怒地说，"是歧视。" 2 PHRASE If someone is **in a huff**, they are behaving in a bad-tempered way because they are annoyed and offended. 发怒的 (地) [INFORMAL] ❑ *He was so disappointed that he drove off in a huff.* 他失望至极，愤然开车离去。

★ **hug** /hʌg/ (**hugs, hugging, hugged**) 1 V-RECIP When you **hug** someone, you put your arms around them and hold them tightly, for example because you like them or are pleased to see them. You can also say that two people **hug** each other or that they **hug**. 拥抱 ❑ *She had hugged him exuberantly and invited him to dinner the next day.* 她兴高采烈地拥抱了他，并邀请他第二天一起用晚餐。 ● N-COUNT **Hug** is also a noun. 拥抱 ❑ *She leapt out of the back seat, and gave him a hug.* 她从后座上跳了出来，给了他一个拥抱。 2 V-T If you **hug** something, you hold it close to your body with your arms tightly around it. 抱住 ❑ *Shaerl trudged toward them, hugging a large box.* 谢尔抱着一个大盒子，蹒跚地向他们走来。 3 V-T Something that **hugs** the ground or a stretch of land or water stays very close to it. 紧靠着 [WRITTEN] ❑ *The road hugs the coast for hundreds of miles.* 公路紧挨着海岸线，长达几百英里。

Thesaurus *hug* 另参见：
V. cling, embrace, hold 1

huge ♦♦◇ /hyudʒ/ (**huger, hugest**) 1 ADJ Something or someone that is **huge** is extremely large in size. (尺寸) 巨大的 ❑ *...a tiny little woman with huge black glasses.* …一位个子很小的戴着硕大黑色眼镜的女人。 2 ADJ Something that is **huge** is extremely large in amount or degree. (数量或程度) 极大的 ❑ *I have a huge number of ties because I never throw them away.* 我有非常多的领带，因为我从不扔掉它们。 ● **huge·ly** ADV (数量或程度) 极大地 ❑ *In summer this hotel is a hugely popular venue for wedding receptions.* 夏天，这家饭店是非常受欢迎的婚宴场所。 3 ADJ Something that is **huge** exists or happens on a very large scale, and involves a lot of different people or things. (规模上) 极大的 ❑ *Another team is looking at the huge problem of debts between companies.* 另一组人正在研究公司间债务这个大问题。

hull /hʌl/ (**hulls**) N-COUNT The **hull** of a boat or tank is the main body of it. 船体 ❑ *The hull had suffered extensive damage to the starboard side.* 船体右舷遭到大面积损坏。

hul·lo /hʌloʊ/ → see **hello**

★ **hum** /hʌm/ (**hums, humming, hummed**) 1 V-I If something **hums**, it makes a low continuous noise. 发出连续低沉的声音 ❑ *The birds sang, the bees hummed.* 鸟儿唱，蜂儿鸣。 ● N-SING **Hum** is also a noun. 连续低沉的声音 ❑ *...the hum of traffic.* …低沉的车流声。 2 V-T/V-I When you **hum**, or **hum** a tune, you sing a tune with your lips closed. 哼 (曲子) ❑ *She was humming a merry little tune.* 她轻轻地哼着一首欢快的小曲儿。 3 V-I If you say that a place **hums**, you mean that it is full of activity. (地方) 繁忙 ❑ *The place is really beginning to hum.* 这个地方真的开始热闹繁忙起来了。

hu·man ♦♦♦ /hyumən/ (**humans**) 1 ADJ **Human** means relating to or concerning people. 人 (类) 的 [ADJ n] ❑ *...the human body.* …人体。 2 N-COUNT You can refer to people as **humans**, especially when you are comparing them with animals or machines. 人 (类) ❑ *Like humans, cats and dogs are omnivores.* 和人类一样，猫和狗是杂食性动物。 3 ADJ **Human** feelings, weaknesses, or errors are ones that are typical of humans rather than machines. 人的 (感情、弱点)；人为的 (错误) ❑ *...an ever-growing risk of human error.* …一种日益增长的人为误差的风险。
→ see **primate**

Word Partnership *human* 的常用搭配：
N. human **behavior**, human **body**, human **brain**, human **dignity**, human **life** 1
human **error**, human **weakness** 3

hu·man be·ing (**human beings**) N-COUNT A **human being** is a man, woman, or child. 人 ❑ *The treatment will be tried out on human beings only after it has been shown to be safe and foolproof in animals.* 该疗法只有在动物身上证明安全、万无一失后才会在人体上试用。

Word Link *man ≈ human being : foreman, humane, woman*

★ **hu·mane** /hyumeɪn/ 1 ADJ **Humane** people act in a kind, sympathetic way toward other people and animals, and try to do them as little harm as possible. 人道的 ❑ *In the mid-nineteenth century, Dorothea Dix began to campaign for humane treatment of the mentally ill.* 在19世纪中叶，多罗西娅・迪克斯发起了为精神病患者争取人道待遇的运动。 ● **hu·mane·ly** ADV 人道地 [ADV with v] ❑ *Suffering animals should be humanely euthanized on the farm.* 农场上的病畜应该被人道地施与安乐死。 2 ADJ **Humane** values and societies encourage people to act in a kind and sympathetic way toward others, even toward people they do not agree with or like. 仁爱的 ❑ *...the humane values of socialism.* … 社会主义的博爱价值观。

★ **hu·man·ism** /hyumənɪzəm/ N-UNCOUNT **Humanism** is the belief that people can achieve happiness and live well without religion. 人道主义 ● **hu·man·ist** ★ N-COUNT (**humanists**) 人道主义者 ❑ *He is a practical humanist, who believes in the dignity of mankind.* 他是个真正的人道主义者，信奉人类的尊严。

Word Link *arian ≈ believing in, having : authoritarian, humanitarian, vegetarian*

★ **hu·mani·tar·ian** /hyumænɪtɛəriən/ ADJ If a person or society has **humanitarian** ideas or behavior, they try to avoid making people suffer or they help people who are suffering. 人道主义的 ❑ *Air bombardment raised criticism on the humanitarian grounds that innocent civilians might suffer.* 空袭遭到了非难，因为从人道主义的角度来看，无辜的平民可能会遭受伤害。

hu·man·ity /hyumænɪti/ (**humanities**) 1 N-UNCOUNT All the people in the world can be referred to as **humanity**. 人类 ❑ *They face charges of committing crimes against humanity.* 他们面临犯有反人类罪的指控。 2 N-UNCOUNT A person's **humanity** is their state of being a human being, rather than an animal or an object. 人性 [FORMAL] ❑ *He was under discussion and it made him feel deprived of his humanity.* 他受到议论，这使他觉得自己被剥夺了人格。 3 N-UNCOUNT **Humanity** is the quality of being kind, thoughtful, and sympathetic toward others. 仁慈；博爱 ❑ *Her speech showed great maturity and humanity.* 她的演讲表现出高度的成熟和博爱。 4 N-PLURAL **The humanities** are the subjects such as history, philosophy, and literature which are concerned with human ideas and behavior. (历史、哲学、文学等) 人文学科 ❑ *The number of students majoring in the humanities has declined by about half.* 主修人文学科的学生数量已经下降了近一半。

human·kind /hyumənkaɪnd/ N-UNCOUNT **Humankind** is the same as **mankind**. 人类

hu·man na·ture N-UNCOUNT **Human nature** is the natural qualities and ways of behavior that most people have. 人性 ❑ *It seems to be human nature to worry.* 忧虑似乎是人的天性。

hu·man race N-SING **The human race** is the same as **mankind**. 人类 ❑ *Can the human race carry on expanding and growing the same way that it is now?* 人类能够像现在这样继续发展和增长吗？

hu·man re·sources N-UNCOUNT In a company or other organization, the department of **human resources** is the department with responsibility for the recruiting, training, and welfare of the staff. The abbreviation **HR** is often used. 人力资源 [BUSINESS] ❑ *...Geoff May, the firm's head of human resources.* …杰夫·梅，公司人力资源部主任。

hu·man rights ♦◇◇ N-PLURAL **Human rights** are basic rights which many societies believe that all people should have. 人权 ❑ *In the treaty both sides pledge to respect human rights.* 双方在条约中都许诺尊重人权。

hum·ble /hʌmbəl/ (**humbler, humblest, humbles, humbling, humbled**) **1** ADJ A **humble** person is not proud and does not believe that they are better than other people. 谦卑的；谦逊的 ❑ *He gave a great performance, but he was very humble.* 他的表演很精彩，但他却很谦逊。● **hum·bly** ADV 谦卑地；谦逊地 [ADV with v] ❑ *"I'm a lucky man, undeservedly lucky," he said humbly.* "我是个幸运的人，不该这么幸运，" 他谦虚地说。**2** ADJ People with low social status are sometimes described as **humble**. (社会地位) 低下的 ❑ *Spyros Latsis started his career as a humble fisherman in the Aegean.* 斯派罗斯·拉齐斯最初的职业是爱琴海的一名地位低微的渔夫。**3** ADJ A **humble** place or thing is ordinary and not special in any way. 普通的 ❑ *There are restaurants, both humble and expensive, that specialize in noodles.* 既有普通的也有昂贵的专营面条的餐馆。**4** ADJ People use **humble** in a phrase such as **in my humble opinion** as a polite way of emphasizing what they think, even though they do not feel humble about it. 愚拙的 (用以自谦地表达想法) [POLITENESS] ❑ *It is, in my humble opinion, perhaps the best steak restaurant in the city.* 以我之拙见，它也许是该市最好的牛排馆。● **hum·bly** ADV 愚拙地 (用以自谦地表达想法) [ADV before v] ❑ *So may I humbly suggest we all do something next time.* 那么我可否愚拙地提议下次我们大家都做点什么。**5** PHRASE If you **eat humble pie**, you speak or behave in a way which tells people that you admit you were wrong about something. 赔礼道歉 ❑ *Anson was forced to eat humble pie and publicly apologize to her.* 安森被迫认错并公开向她道歉。**6** V-T If you **humble** someone who is more important or powerful than you, you defeat them easily. 轻易击败 (重要或强大对手) ❑ *Honda won fame in the 1980s as the little car company that humbled the industry giants.* 20世纪80年代，本田作为一家小型汽车公司因一举击垮行业巨头而声名鹊起。**7** V-T If something or someone **humbles** you, they make you realize that you are not as important or good as you thought you were. 使感到惭愧 ❑ *Ted's words humbled me.* 特德的一席话使我自感惭愧。● **hum·bling** ADJ 使羞辱的 ❑ *Giving up an addiction is a humbling experience.* 戒掉一种嗜好是一次令自尊心受挫的经历。

hu·mid /hyumɪd/ ADJ You use **humid** to describe an atmosphere *can expect hot and humid conditions.* 游客们会遇到炎热潮湿的天气状况。
→ see **weather**

★ **hu·mid·ity** /hyumɪdɪti/ **1** N-UNCOUNT You say there is **humidity** when the air feels very heavy and damp. 潮湿 ❑ *The heat and humidity were insufferable.* 炎热与潮湿令人难以忍受。**2** N-UNCOUNT **Humidity** is the amount of water in the air. 湿度 ❑ *The humidity is relatively low.* 湿度相对较低。
→ see **forecast**

Word Link	*ate ≈ causing to be : complicate, humiliate, motivate*

▲ **hu·mili·ate** /hyumɪlieɪt/ (**humiliates, humiliating, humiliated**) V-T To **humiliate** someone means to say or do something which makes them feel ashamed or stupid. 使蒙羞 ❑ *She had been beaten and humiliated by her husband.* 她曾被丈夫殴打和羞辱。● **hu·mili·at·ed** ADJ 感到丢脸的 ❑ *I have never felt so humiliated in my life.* 我一生中从未感到这么丢脸过。

hu·mili·at·ing /hyumɪlieɪtɪŋ/ ADJ If something is **humiliating**, it embarrasses you and makes you feel ashamed and stupid. 使蒙受耻辱的 ❑ *The Democrats have suffered a humiliating defeat.* 民主党人已经遭受了一次有失脸面的失败。

hu·milia·tion /hyumɪlieɪʃən/ (**humiliations**) **1** N-UNCOUNT **Humiliation** is the embarrassment and shame you feel when someone makes you appear stupid, or when you make a mistake in public. 耻辱 ❑ *She faced the humiliation of discussing her husband's affair.* 她面临要谈她丈夫风流韵事的耻辱。**2** N-COUNT A **humiliation** is an occasion or a situation in which you feel embarrassed and ashamed. 丢脸的事；丢脸的场合 ❑ *The result is a humiliation for the president.* 这个结果对总统而言很丢面子。

hu·mil·ity /hyumɪlɪti/ N-UNCOUNT Someone who has **humility** is not proud and does not believe they are better than other people. 谦逊 ❑ *...a deep sense of humility.* …深深的谦卑感。

hu·mor ♦◇◇ /hyumər/ (**humors, humoring, humored**)

in BRIT, use **humour**

1 N-UNCOUNT You can refer to the amusing things that people say as their **humor**. 幽默 ❑ *Her humor and determination were a source of inspiration to others.* 她的幽默与坚毅对其他人来说是一种鼓舞。**2** → see also **sense of humor** **3** N-UNCOUNT **Humor** is a quality in something that makes you laugh, for example in a situation, in someone's words or actions, or in a book or movie. 幽默性；令人发笑之处 ❑ *She felt sorry for the man but couldn't ignore the humor of the situation.* 她很同情这个男人，但面对此情此景又不禁觉得好笑。**4** N-VAR If you are **in a good humor**, you feel cheerful and happy, and are pleasant to people. If you are **in a bad humor**, you feel bad tempered and unhappy, and are unpleasant to people. 心情 ❑ *Christina was still not clear why he had been in such ill humor.* 克里斯蒂娜仍不明白为什么他的心情一直这么糟。**5** N-UNCOUNT If you do something with good **humor**, you do it cheerfully and pleasantly. 精神状态 ❑ *Hugo bore his illness with great courage and good humor.* 雨果以巨大的勇气和良好的精神状态面对疾病。**6** V-T If you **humor** someone who is behaving strangely, you try to please them or pretend to agree with them, so that they will not become upset. 迁就 ❑ *She disliked Dido but was prepared to tolerate her for a weekend in order to humor her husband.* 她讨厌黛朵，但为了迁就自己的丈夫，准备容忍她一个周末。
→ see **laugh**

Word Partnership	*humor* 的常用搭配：
N.	**brand of** humor, **sense of** humor **1**
ADJ.	**good** humor **4** **5**

hu·mor·ous /hyumərəs/ ADJ If someone or something is **humorous**, they are amusing, especially in a clever or witty way. 幽默的 ❑ *He was quite humorous, and I liked that about him.* 他很幽默，我喜欢他这一点。● **hu·mor·ous·ly** ADV 幽默地 ❑ *He looked at me humorously as he wrestled with the door.* 他一边用力地开门，一边表情滑稽地看着我。

hu·mour /hyumər/ [BRIT] → see **humor**

hump /hʌmp/ (**humps**) **1** N-COUNT A **hump** is a small hill or raised area. 小山丘 ❑ *The path goes over a large hump by a tree before running near a road.* 小道越过树旁的一个大圆丘，然后延伸至公路附近。**2** N-COUNT A camel's **hump** is the large lump on its back. 驼峰 ❑ *Camels rebuild fat stores in their hump.* 骆驼在自己的驼峰内重新贮备脂肪。**3** PHRASE If you are **over the hump** in an unpleasant or difficult situation, you are past the worst part of it. 度过最困难阶段 [V-link PHR] ❑ *It has been a traumatic week, but they are over the hump.* 这是痛苦的一周，但他们已度过最困难阶段。

hunch /hʌntʃ/ (**hunches, hunching, hunched**) **1** N-COUNT If you have a **hunch** about something, you are sure that it is correct or true, even though you do not have any proof. 直觉；预感 [INFORMAL] ❑ *I had a hunch that Susan and I would work well together.* 我凭直觉感到我和苏珊共事会很融洽。**2** V-I If you **hunch** forward, you raise your shoulders, put your head down, and lean forward, often because you are cold, ill, or unhappy. (人) 耸肩弓身 ❑ *He got out his map and hunched over it to read the small print.* 他掏出地图并俯身去看上面的小字。**3** V-T If you **hunch** your shoulders, you raise them and lean forward slightly. 耸起 (双肩) 并微微前倾 ❑ *Wes hunched his shoulders and leaned forward on the edge of the counter.* 韦斯耸起双肩，身子向前靠在柜台边。

hun·dred ♦♦♦ /hʌndrɪd/ (**hundreds**)

The plural form is **hundred** after a number, or after a word or expression referring to a number, such as "several" or "a few."

1 NUM **A hundred** or **one hundred** is the number 100. 100；百 ❑ *According to one official more than a hundred people have been arrested.* 据一名官员说，已有一百多人被捕。**2** QUANT If you refer to **hundreds of** things or people, you are emphasizing that there are very many of them. 许许多多；数百 [QUANT "of" pl-n] [EMPHASIS] ❑ *Hundreds of tree species face extinction.* 很多树种濒临灭绝。● PRON You can also use **hundreds** as a pronoun. 数百 ❑ *Hundreds have been killed in the fighting and thousands made homeless.* 数以百计的人在战斗中丧生，并有数以千计的人变得无家可归。**3** PHRASE You can use **a hundred percent** or **one hundred percent** to emphasize that you agree completely with something or that it is completely right or wrong. 百分之百 [INFORMAL, EMPHASIS] ❑ *Are you a hundred percent sure it's your neighbor?* 你百分百肯定这是你的邻居?

hun·dredth ♦♦◇ /hʌndrɪdθ/ (**hundredths**) **1** ORD The **hundredth** item in a series is the one that you count as number one hundred. 第一百 ❑ *The bank celebrates its hundredth anniversary in December.* 这家银行在12月庆祝其百年华诞。 **2** FRACTION A **hundredth of** something is one of a hundred equal parts of it. 百分之一 ❑ *Mitchell beat Lewis by three-hundredths of a second.* 米切尔以0.03秒的优势打败了刘易斯。

hung /hʌŋ/ **1** **Hung** is the past tense and past participle of most of the senses of **hang**. hang的多数义项的过去式和过去分词 **2** ADJ A **hung** jury is the situation that occurs when a jury is unable to reach a decision because there is not a clear majority of its members in favor of any one decision. (陪审团因意见不一致而)未能作出裁定的 ❑ *His first trial ended in a hung jury.* 他第一次出庭受审以陪审团未能作出裁定而告终。

hun·ger /hʌŋgər/ (**hungers, hungering, hungered**) **1** N-UNCOUNT **Hunger** is the feeling of weakness or discomfort that you get when you need something to eat. 饥饿 ❑ *Hunger is the body's signal that levels of blood sugar are too low.* 饥饿感是体内发出的血糖浓度太低的信号。 **2** N-UNCOUNT **Hunger** is a severe lack of food which causes suffering or death. 饥荒 ❑ *Three hundred people in this town are dying of hunger every day.* 该镇每天有300人因饥饿而死。 **3** N-SING If you have a **hunger for** something, you want or need it very much. 渴望 [also no det] [WRITTEN] ❑ *Geffen has a hunger for success that seems bottomless.* 格芬对成功的渴望似乎永无止境。 **4** V-I If you say that someone **hungers for** something or **hungers after** it, you are emphasizing that they want it very much. 渴望 [FORMAL, EMPHASIS] ❑ *But Jules was not eager for classroom learning, he hungered for adventure.* 但是朱尔斯并不热衷于课堂学习，他渴望冒险。

hun·ger strike (**hunger strikes**) N-VAR If someone goes **on hunger strike** or goes **on a hunger strike**, they refuse to eat as a way of protesting about something. 绝食抗议 ❑ *The protesters have been on hunger strike for 17 days.* 抗议者们已经绝食了17天。

hun·gry /hʌŋgri/ (**hungrier, hungriest**) **1** ADJ When you are **hungry**, you want some food because you have not eaten for some time and have an uncomfortable or painful feeling in your stomach. 饥饿的 ❑ *My friend was hungry, so we drove to a shopping mall to get some food.* 我朋友饿了，于是我们就驱车来到一家购物商场买些吃的。 ● **hun·gri·ly** /hʌŋgrɪli/ ADV 饥饿地 [ADV with v] ❑ *James ate hungrily.* 詹姆斯狼吞虎咽地吃了起来。 **2** PHRASE If people **go hungry**, they do not have enough food to eat. 挨饿 ❑ *They brought her meat so that she never went hungry.* 他们给她带来了肉，这样她就再也不用挨饿了。 **3** ADJ If you say that someone is **hungry** for something, you are emphasizing that they want it very much. 渴望的 [LITERARY, EMPHASIS] ❑ *I was hungry to be heard by my contemporaries.* 我渴望被同龄人所倾听。 ● COMB IN ADJ **Hungry** is also a combining form. 渴望…的(用作构词成分) ❑ *...power-hungry politicians.* …渴求权力的政客们。 ● **hun·gri·ly** ADV 热望地 [ADV with v] ❑ *He looked at her hungrily. What eyes! What skin!* 他如饥似渴地望着她。多美的眼睛啊！多好的皮肤啊！

Thesaurus *hungry* 另参见：
ADJ. famished, ravenous, starving; (*ant.*) full, stuffed **1**
eager, unsatisfied **3**

hunk /hʌŋk/ (**hunks**) **1** N-COUNT A **hunk of** something is a large piece of it. 大块 ❑ *...a thick hunk of bread.* …厚厚一大块面包。 **2** N-COUNT If you refer to a man as a **hunk**, you mean that he is big, strong, and sexually attractive. 健壮性感的男子 [INFORMAL, APPROVAL] ❑ *...a blond, blue-eyed hunk.* …一个金发碧眼的美男子。

hunt ♦◇◇ /hʌnt/ (**hunts, hunting, hunted**) **1** V-I If you **hunt for** something or someone, you try to find them by searching carefully or thoroughly. 搜寻 ❑ *A forensic team was hunting for clues.* 法医小组正在搜寻线索。 ● N-COUNT **Hunt** is also a noun. 搜寻 ❑ *The couple had helped in the hunt for the toddlers.* 这对夫妇曾帮着寻找那些蹒跚学步的孩子。 **2** V-T If you **hunt** a criminal or an enemy, you search for them in order to catch or harm them. 追捕 (罪犯、敌人等) ❑ *Detectives have been hunting him for seven months.* 7个月来警探们一直在追捕他。 ● N-COUNT **Hunt** is also a noun. 追捕 ❑ *Despite a nationwide hunt for the kidnap gang, not a trace of them was found.* 尽管已对这帮绑架团伙实行了全国范围的大搜捕，但丝毫没有发现他们的蛛丝马迹。 **3** V-T/V-I When people or animals **hunt**, or **hunt** something, they chase and kill wild animals for food or as a sport. 猎杀 (野生动物); 打猎 ❑ *As a child I learned to hunt and fish.* 我孩提时代就学会了打猎和捕鱼。 ● N-COUNT **Hunt** is also a noun. 打猎 ❑ *He set off for a nineteen-day moose hunt in Nova Scotia.* 他开始了在新斯科舍为期19天的猎驼鹿行程。 **4** PHRASE If a team or competitor is **in the hunt for** something, they still have a chance of winning it. (参赛队或竞争者) 有机会获得 ❑ *Six teams were still in the hunt for the team title.* 6支队伍仍然有机会获得团体冠军。

▸ **hunt down** PHRASAL VERB If you **hunt down** a criminal or an enemy, you find them after searching for them. 追捕到 (罪犯或敌人) ❑ *Last December they hunted down and killed one of the gangsters.* 去年12月他们追捕到其中一名歹徒并将其击毙。

hunt·er ♦◇◇ /hʌntər/ (**hunters**) **1** N-COUNT A **hunter** is a person who hunts wild animals for food or as a sport. 猎人 ❑ *The hunters stalked their prey.* 猎人们隐伏跟踪猎物。 **2** N-COUNT People who are searching for things of a particular kind are often referred to as **hunters**. 搜寻者 ❑ *...job-hunters.* …求职者。 **3** → see also **headhunter**

hunt·ing /hʌntɪŋ/ **1** N-UNCOUNT **Hunting** is the chasing and killing of wild animals by people or other animals, for food or as a sport. 狩猎; 猎食 ❑ *He'd gone deer hunting with his cousins.* 他已和堂兄弟们猎鹿去了。 **2** N-UNCOUNT **Hunting** is the activity of searching for a particular thing. 搜寻 ❑ *Job hunting should be approached as a job in itself.* 找工作本身就应当被看作是一种工作。 ● COMB IN N-UNCOUNT **Hunting** is also a combining form. 寻求… (用于构词成分) ❑ *Make job-hunting a full-time job until you find one.* 在你找到工作之前，把求职当作一项全职工作。

▲ **hur·dle** /hɜrdᵊl/ (**hurdles, hurdling, hurdled**) **1** N-COUNT A **hurdle** is a problem, difficulty, or part of a process that may prevent you from achieving something. 障碍; 困难 ❑ *Two-thirds of candidates fail at this first hurdle and are sent home.* 2/3的候选人未能通过这第一关，被打发回家了。 **2** N-COUNT-COLL **Hurdles** is a race in which people have to jump over a number of obstacles that are also called hurdles. You can use **hurdles** to refer to one or more races. 跨栏赛跑 ❑ *Davis won the 400 meter hurdles in a new Olympic time of 49.3 sec.* 戴维斯以49.3秒这一新的奥运会记录在400米跨栏赛跑中夺冠。 **3** V-T/V-I If you **hurdle**, you jump over something while you are running. (奔跑中) 跨越 ❑ *He crossed the lawn and hurdled the short fence.* 他穿过草坪，越过低矮的栅栏。

★ **hurl** /hɜrl/ (**hurls, hurling, hurled**) **1** V-T If you **hurl** something, you throw it violently and with a lot of force. 用力掷 ❑ *Groups of angry youths hurled stones at police.* 一群群愤怒的年轻人朝着警察猛掷石块。 ❑ *Simon caught the grenade and hurled it back.* 西蒙接住手榴弹，把它掷了回去。 **2** V-T If you **hurl** abuse or insults **at** someone, you shout insults at them aggressively. 大声叫骂 ❑ *How would you handle being locked in the back of a cab while the driver hurled abuse at you?* 如果你被锁在出租车后座又遭司机谩骂，你会怎么办?

★ **hur·ri·cane** /hɜrɪkeɪn, hʌr-/ (**hurricanes**) N-COUNT A **hurricane** is an extremely violent storm that begins over ocean water. 飓风
→ see Word Web: **hurricane**
→ see **disaster**

hur·ried /hɜrid, hʌr-/ **1** ADJ A **hurried** action is done quickly, because you do not have much time to do it in. 仓促完成的 ❑ *...a hurried breakfast.* …仓促吃的一顿早餐。 ● **hur·ried·ly** ADV 匆忙地 [ADV with v] ❑ *...students hurriedly taking notes.* …匆忙做着笔记的学生们。 **2** ADJ A **hurried** action is done suddenly, in reaction to something that has just happened. (行动) 突然应急采取的 ❑ *There had been a hurried overnight redrafting of the text.* 该文本被连夜做了改写。 ● **hur·ried·ly** ADV 匆忙地 [ADV with v] ❑ *The moment she saw it, she blushed and hurriedly left the room.* 她一看见它脸就红了，并慌忙地走出了房间。 **3** ADJ Someone who is **hurried** does things more quickly than they should because they do not have much time to do them. 仓促的 ❑ *Parisians on the street often looked worried, hurried, and unfriendly.* 街上的巴黎人常常看上去忧心忡忡，匆匆忙忙，还不太友好。

hur·ry /hɜri, hʌr-/ (**hurries, hurrying, hurried**) **1** V-I If you **hurry** somewhere, you go there as quickly as you can. 匆忙而行 ❑ *Claire hurried along the road.* 克莱尔匆匆地沿路而行。 **2** V-T If you **hurry to** do something, you start doing it as soon as you can, or try to do it quickly. 赶紧 (做) ❑ *Mrs. Hardie hurried to make up for her tactlessness by asking her guest about his holiday.* 哈迪太太赶紧问她的客人假期过得如何，以弥补此前不得体的言行。 **3** N-SING If you are **in a hurry to** do something, you need or want to do something quickly. If you do something **in a hurry**, you do it quickly or

Word Web hurricane

A **hurricane** is a tropical **cyclone** that develops in the Atlantic or Caribbean. When a hurricane develops in the Pacific it is known as a **typhoon**. A hurricane is a violent storm. It begins as a **tropical depression**. It becomes a **tropical storm** when its winds reach 39 miles per hour (mph). When wind speeds reach 74 mph, a distinct **eye** forms in the center. Then the storm is officially a hurricane. It has heavy rains and very high winds. When a hurricane makes landfall or moves over cool water, it loses some of its power.

suddenly. 急忙 ❑ *Kate was in a hurry to grow up, eager for knowledge and experience.* 凯特急切地想长大，渴望获得知识和经验。 4 V-T To **hurry** something means the same as to **hurry up** something. 使加快进行 ❑ *...the president's attempt to hurry the process of independence.* …总统加快独立进程的企图。 5 V-T If you **hurry** someone to a place or into a situation, you try to make them go to that place or get into that situation quickly. 催促 ❑ *They say they are not going to be hurried into any decision.* 他们说不会迫于压力而仓促做出任何决定。 6 PHRASE If you say to someone "**There's no hurry**" or "**I'm in no hurry**" you are telling them that there is no need for them to do something immediately. 不着急 ❑ *I'll need to talk with you, but there's no hurry.* 我得找你谈谈，但不着急。 7 PHRASE If you are **in no hurry to** do something, you are very unwilling to do it. 不想（做） ❑ *I love it here so I'm in no hurry to go anywhere.* 我喜欢在这里生活，所以我哪里都不想去。

▶ **hurry along** → see **hurry up 2**

▶ **hurry up** 1 PHRASAL VERB If you tell someone to **hurry up**, you are telling them to do something more quickly than they were doing it. 赶紧 ❑ *Franklin told Howe to hurry up and take his bath; otherwise, they'd miss their train.* 富兰克林催豪快点洗澡，要不然他们就赶不上火车了。 ❑ *Hurry up with that coffee, will you.* 你快点喝咖啡，好吗。 2 PHRASAL VERB If you **hurry** something **up** or **hurry** it **along**, you make it happen faster or sooner than it would otherwise have done. 使加快 ❑ *...if you're not a traditionalist and you want to hurry up the process.* …如果你不是传统主义者而是想加快这一进程。

Thesaurus *hurry* 另参见：
V. run, rush; *(ant.)* slow down, relax 1

hurt ◆◆◇ /hɜrt/ (**hurts, hurting, hurt**) 1 V-T If you **hurt yourself** or **hurt** a part of your body, you feel pain because you have injured yourself. 使受伤 ❑ *Yasin had seriously hurt himself while trying to escape from the police.* 亚辛在企图从警方手中逃脱时把自己伤得很厉害。 2 V-I If a part of your body **hurts**, you feel pain there. 感到疼痛 ❑ *His collar bone only hurt when he lifted his arm.* 他的锁骨只是在举起手臂时才感觉疼痛。 3 ADJ If you are **hurt**, you have been injured. 受了伤的 ❑ *His comrades asked him if he was hurt.* 他的伙伴们问他是否受伤了。 4 V-T/V-I If you **hurt** someone, you cause them to feel pain. 弄痛 ❑ *I didn't mean to hurt her, only to keep her still.* 我没想把她弄痛，只是想让她别动。 ❑ *That hurts!* 好痛呀！ 5 V-T/V-I If someone **hurts** you, they say or do something that makes you unhappy. 使伤心；伤心 ❑ *He is afraid of hurting Bessy's feelings.* 他是怕伤了贝西的感情。 ❑ *What hurts most is the betrayal.* 最让人伤心的是背叛。 6 ADJ If you are **hurt**, you are upset because of something that someone has said or done. (感情上) 受到伤害的 ❑ *She was deeply hurt and shocked by what Smith had said.* 史密斯的话深深地伤害了她，并使她感到吃惊。 7 V-I If you say that you **are hurting**, you mean that you are experiencing emotional pain. 感到痛苦的 [only cont] ❑ *I am lonely and I am hurting.* 我很孤独，也很痛苦。 8 V-T To **hurt** someone or something means to have a bad effect on them or prevent them from succeeding. 对…产生不良影响 ❑ *The combination of hot weather and decreased water supplies is hurting many industries.* 天气炎热和供水减少这两个因素结合在一起对很多行业造成了损害。 9 N-VAR A feeling of **hurt** is a feeling that you have when you think that you have been treated badly or judged unfairly. (感情上的) 伤心或痛苦 ❑ *I was full of jealousy and hurt.* 我内心充满了嫉妒和痛苦。 10 PHRASE If you say "**It won't hurt to** do something" or "**It never hurts to** do something," you are recommending an action which you think is helpful or useful. (做…) 不会有坏处 [INFORMAL] ❑ *It never hurts to ask.* 提问总没坏处。

Thesaurus *hurt* 另参见：
V. harm, injure, wound 1
ache, smart, sting 2
ADJ. injured, wounded 3
saddened, upset 6

Word Partnership *hurt* 的常用搭配：
ADV. **badly/seriously** hurt 1 3
V. **get** hurt 3
feel hurt 6
N. hurt ***someone's* chances**, hurt **the economy**, hurt ***someone's* feelings**, hurt **sales** 8

hurt·ful /hɜrtfəl/ ADJ If you say that someone's comments or actions are **hurtful**, you mean that they are unkind and upsetting. 引起痛苦的 ❑ *Her comments can only be very hurtful to Mrs. Green's family.* 她的话只会使格林太太一家人感到非常伤心。

hurt·le /hɜrtᵊl/ (**hurtles, hurtling, hurtled**) V-I If someone or something **hurtles** somewhere, they move there very quickly, often in a rough or violent way. 猛冲 ❑ *A pretty young girl came hurtling down the stairs.* 一个漂亮的小姑娘飞奔下楼。

hus·band ◆◆◆ /hʌzbənd/ (**husbands**) N-COUNT A woman's **husband** is the man she is married to. 丈夫 ❑ *Eva married her husband Jack in 1957.* 1957年伊娃与其丈夫杰克结婚。
→ see **family, love**

▲ **hush** /hʌʃ/ (**hushes, hushing, hushed**) 1 CONVENTION You say "**Hush!**" to someone when you are asking or telling them to be quiet. (用于告诉别人保持安静) 嘘！ ❑ *Hush, my love, it's all right.* 嘘，亲爱的，没事。 2 V-T/V-I If you **hush** someone or if they **hush**, they stop speaking or making a noise. 使安静下来；安静下来 ❑ *She tried to hush her noisy father.* 她试图让吵吵嚷嚷的父亲安静下来。 3 N-SING You say there is a **hush** in a place when everything is quiet and peaceful, or suddenly becomes quiet. 安静；(突然的) 寂静 [also no det] ❑ *A hush fell over the crowd and I knew something terrible had happened.* 人群突然一片肃静，我便知道一定发生了什么可怕的事情了。

▶ **hush up** PHRASAL VERB If someone **hushes** something **up**, they prevent other people from knowing about it. 隐瞒 ❑ *I thought it would reflect badly on me so I tried to hush the whole thing up.* 我想此事会给我的公众形象造成很坏的影响，于是我想方设法不把它声张出去。

hushed /hʌʃt/ 1 ADJ A **hushed** place is peaceful and much quieter and calmer than usual. (地方) 寂静的 ❑ *The house seemed muted, hushed as if it had been deserted.* 这房子悄无声息，好像一直没有人居住。 2 ADJ A **hushed** voice or **hushed** conversation is very quiet. (声音、谈话等) 低声的 ❑ *At first we spoke in hushed voices and crept about in order not to alarm them.* 起先我们说话时压低声音，走路蹑手蹑脚的，以免惊动他们。

▲ **hus·tle** /hʌsᵊl/ (**hustles, hustling, hustled**) 1 V-T If you **hustle** someone, you try to make them go somewhere or do something quickly, for example by pulling or pushing them along. 猛拉；猛推 ❑ *The guards hustled Harry out of the car.* 卫兵们把哈里从车子里拉了出来。 2 V-I If you **hustle**, you go somewhere or do something as quickly as you can. 快速行进；赶快做 ❑ *You'll have to hustle if you're to get home for supper.* 你想回家吃晚饭的话，得赶紧走了。 3 V-I If someone **hustles**, they try hard to earn money or to gain an advantage from a situation. 奋力争取 [mainly AM] ❑ *I like it here. It forces you to hustle and you can earn money.* 我喜欢在这里生活。这个想法迫使你拼命干活，这样可以挣到钱。 ❑ *Hustling for social contacts isn't something that just happens. You have to make it happen.* 社会关系不是说建立就建立起来的，

h

你得想尽一切办法去争取。**4** V-T If someone **hustles** you, or if they **hustle** something, they try hard to get something, often by using dishonest or illegal means. 诈取（通常用不正当或非法的手段）[mainly AM] ❑ *Two teenage boys asked us for money, saying they were forming a baseball team. Anna said they were hustling us.* 两个小男孩向我们要钱，说他们要成立棒球队。安娜说他们在骗钱。❑ *He hustled several daytime jobs and finished his education at night.* 他骗得了几份白班工作，利用晚上完成了学业。**5** N-UNCOUNT **Hustle** is busy, noisy activity. 忙碌；熙熙攘攘 ❑ *...the hustle and bustle of New York.* …纽约的熙攘喧闹。

hut /hʌt/ (**huts**) **1** N-COUNT A **hut** is a small house with only one or two rooms, especially one which is made of wood, mud, grass, or stones. （木头、泥、草或石头搭成的）小屋 **2** N-COUNT A **hut** is a small wooden building in someone's garden, or a temporary building used by builders or repair workers. （花园中的）木屋；（工人住的）临时工棚 [BRIT]

in AM, use **shed**

▲ **hy·brid** /haɪbrɪd/ (**hybrids**) **1** N-COUNT A **hybrid** is an animal or plant that has been bred from two different species of animal or plant. 杂交种 [TECHNICAL] ❑ *All these brightly colored hybrids are so lovely in the garden.* 园中所有这些色彩鲜艳的杂交植物真好看。❑ *...a hybrid of Mandarin orange and a grapefruit.* …桔子和葡萄柚的杂交品种。● ADJ **Hybrid** is also an adjective. 杂交的 [ADJ n] ❑ *...the hybrid corn seed.* …杂交玉米种子。**2** N-COUNT A **hybrid** or a **hybrid car** is a car that can be powered by either gasoline or electricity. 混合动力汽车 混合动力汽车 ❑ *Hybrids, unlike pure electric cars, never need to be plugged in.* 混合动力汽车不像纯电动汽车，它们从不需要充电。混合动力汽车，不像纯电动汽车，从不需要接电源。❑ *Hybrid cars can go almost 600 miles between refueling.* 混合动力汽车加满油能行驶将近六百英里。**3** N-COUNT You can use **hybrid** to refer to anything that is a mixture of other things, especially two other things. 混合物 ❑ *...a hybrid of solid and liquid fuel.* …固体和液体燃料的混合。● ADJ **Hybrid** is also an adjective. 混合的 [ADJ n] ❑ *...a hybrid system.* …一个混合系统。
→ see **car**

Word Link *hydr ≈ water : dehydrate, hydraulic, hydrologic cycle*

hy·drau·lic /haɪdrɔlɪk, -drɒl-/ ADJ **Hydraulic** equipment or machinery involves or is operated by a fluid that is under pressure, such as water or oil. 液压的 [ADJ n] ❑ *The boat has no fewer than five hydraulic pumps.* 这艘船有不下5个液压泵。

hydro·gen /haɪdrədʒᵊn/ N-UNCOUNT **Hydrogen** is a colorless gas that is the lightest and commonest element in the universe. 氢
→ see **sun**

hydro·log·ic cy·cle /haɪdrəlɒdʒɪk saɪkᵊl/ N-SING *The* **hydrologic cycle** is the process by which the Earth's water is circulated from the surface to the atmosphere through evaporation and back to the surface through rainfall. 水循环 ["the" N] [TECHNICAL]
→ see **water**

▲ **hy·giene** /haɪdʒin/ N-UNCOUNT **Hygiene** is the practice of keeping yourself and your surroundings clean, especially in order to prevent illness or the spread of diseases. 卫生 ❑ *Be extra careful about personal hygiene.* 要特别注意个人卫生。

▲ **hy·gien·ic** /haɪdʒɛnɪk/ ADJ Something that is **hygienic** is clean and unlikely to cause illness. 卫生的 ❑ *...a white, clinical-looking kitchen that was easy to keep clean and hygienic.* …一个白色的、诊所般的、容易保持清洁卫生的厨房。

▲ **hymn** /hɪm/ (**hymns**) **1** N-COUNT A **hymn** is a religious song that Christians sing in church. （基督教的）赞美诗 ❑ *I like singing hymns.* 我喜欢唱圣歌。**2** N-COUNT If you describe a movie, book, or speech as a **hymn to** something, you mean that it praises or celebrates that thing. 颂歌 [mainly JOURNALISM] ❑ *...a hymn to freedom and rebellion.* …自由与反叛的颂歌。

hype /haɪp/ (**hypes, hyping, hyped**) **1** N-UNCOUNT **Hype** is the use of a lot of publicity and advertising to make people interested in something such as a product. 大肆的宣传广告；炒作 [DISAPPROVAL] ❑ *We are certainly seeing a lot of hype by some companies.* 我们的确看到一些公司的天花乱坠的广告宣传。**2** V-T To **hype** a product means to advertise or praise it a lot. 大肆宣传 [DISAPPROVAL] ❑ *We had to hype the film to attract the financiers.* 我们不得不大肆炒作这部影片以吸引金融家们。● PHRASAL VERB **Hype up** means the same as **hype**. 大肆宣传 ❑ *The media seems obsessed with hyping up individuals or groups.* 传媒界似乎热衷于对某些个人或团体进行大肆炒作。

Word Link *hyper ≈ above, over : hyperactive, hyperlink, hypertext*

hyper·ac·tive /haɪpəræktɪv/ ADJ Someone who is **hyperactive** is unable to relax and is always moving around or doing things. （人）过分活跃的 ❑ *His research was used in planning treatments for hyperactive children.* 他的研究被用来为患有多动症的儿童设计治疗方案。

hyper·in·fla·tion /haɪpərɪnfleɪʃᵊn/ N-UNCOUNT **Hyperinflation** is very severe inflation. 极度通货膨胀 ❑ *In the hyperinflation of 1922-23 a dollar could be bought for 4.2 billion marks.* 在1922至1923年的极度通货膨胀期间，1美元可以兑换42亿马克。

hyper·link /haɪpərlɪŋk/ (**hyperlinks, hyperlinking, hyperlinked**) **1** N-COUNT In an HTML document, a **hyperlink** is a link to another part of the document or to another document. Hyperlinks are shown as words with a line under them. 超文本链接 [COMPUTING] ❑ *...Web pages full of hyperlinks.* …满是超文本链接的网页。**2** V-T If a document or file **is hyperlinked**, it contains hyperlinks. 将（文档、文件）进行超文本链接 [usu passive] [COMPUTING] ❑ *The database is fully hyperlinked both within the database and to thousands of external links.* 该数据库在其内部和成千上万的外部链接之间全部设置了超文本链接。

hyper·text /haɪpərtɛkst/ N-UNCOUNT In computing, **hypertext** is a way of connecting pieces of text so that you can go quickly and directly from one to another. （计算机的）超文本 [COMPUTING] ❑ *...information embroidered with colorful graphics and tied together by hypertext links.* …饰以彩色图表并用超文本链接组合在一起的信息。

▲ **hy·phen** /haɪfᵊn/ (**hyphens**) N-COUNT A **hyphen** is the punctuation sign used to join words together to make a compound, as in "left-handed." People also use a hyphen to show that the rest of a word is on the next line. 连字符

Word Link *osis ≈ state or condition : hypnosis, metamorphosis, psychosis*

hyp·no·sis /hɪpnoʊsɪs/ **1** N-UNCOUNT **Hypnosis** is a state in which a person seems to be asleep but can still see, hear, or respond to things said to them. 催眠状态 ❑ *Bevin is now an adult and has re-lived her birth experience under hypnosis.* 贝文现在已是成年人，在催眠状态下，她再次经历了出生过程。**2** N-UNCOUNT **Hypnosis** is the art or practice of hypnotizing people. 催眠术
→ see Word Web: **hypnosis**

hyp·not·ic /hɪpnɒtɪk/ **1** ADJ If someone is in a **hypnotic** state, they have been hypnotized. 被催眠了的 ❑ *The hypnotic state actually lies somewhere between being awake and being asleep.* 催眠状态实际上是介于清醒与睡眠之间。**2** ADJ Something that is **hypnotic** holds your attention or makes you feel sleepy, often because it involves repeated sounds, pictures, or movements. 有催眠作用的 ❑ *His songs are often both hypnotic and reassuringly pleasant.* 他的歌声常常在催人入眠的同时又使人放松愉悦。

hyp·no·tism /hɪpnətɪzəm/ N-UNCOUNT **Hypnotism** is the practice of hypnotizing people. 催眠术 ❑ *Dulcy also saw a psychiatrist who used hypnotism to help her deal with her fear.* 达尔茜还去看了精神科医生，那医生使用催眠术帮她消除恐惧感。● **hyp·no·tist** N-COUNT

Word Web hypnosis

Hypnosis is a **mental** state somewhere between wakefulness and sleep. When hypnotized, a person's mind is **alert** and **calm** at the same time. Scientists believe this kind of **trance** helps the **conscious** mind relax. This gives the **hypnotist** access to the **subconscious** mind. Some hypnotists are entertainers. They do things like getting **subjects** on stage to bark like dogs. Hypnotherapists, on the other hand, use the trance state to help people. For example, the therapist may suggest that smoking will make the person feel nauseous. This idea stays in the subconscious mind and helps the subject give up cigarettes.

(**hypnotists**) 催眠师 ❑ *He was put into a trance by a police hypnotist.* 他被警方的一位催眠师导入了催眠状态。

→ see **hypnosis**

hyp·no·tize /hɪpnətaɪz/ (**hypnotizes, hypnotizing, hypnotized**) **1** V-T If someone **hypnotizes** you, they put you into a state in which you seem to be asleep but can still see, hear, or respond to things said to you. 给…施催眠术 ❑ *A hypnotherapist will hypnotize you and will stop you from smoking.* 催眠疗法医生将对你进行催眠，帮你戒烟。 **2** V-T If you **are hypnotized by** someone or something, you are so fascinated by them that you cannot think of anything else. 使着迷 [usu passive] ❑ *He's hypnotized by that black hair and that white face.* 他被那乌黑的头发和白皙的脸庞迷住了。

▲ **hy·poc·ri·sy** /hɪpɒkrɪsi/ (**hypocrisies**) N-VAR If you accuse someone of **hypocrisy**, you mean that they pretend to have qualities, beliefs, or feelings that they do not really have. 虚伪 [DISAPPROVAL] ❑ *He accused newspapers of hypocrisy in their treatment of the story.* 他指责报纸在处理这篇报道时所表现出的虚伪。

hypo·crite /hɪpəkrɪt/ (**hypocrites**) N-COUNT If you accuse someone of being a **hypocrite**, you mean that they pretend to have qualities, beliefs, or feelings that they do not really have. 伪君子 [DISAPPROVAL] ❑ *The magazine wrongly suggested he was a liar and a hypocrite.* 该杂志错误地暗示他是个骗子和伪君子。

hypo·criti·cal /hɪpəkrɪtɪkᵊl/ ADJ If you accuse someone of being **hypocritical**, you mean that they pretend to have qualities, beliefs, or feelings that they do not really have. 虚伪的 [DISAPPROVAL] ❑ *It would be hypocritical to say I travel at 70 mph simply because that is the law.* 如果仅仅因为法律规定的时速是70英里我就说自己的行驶时速是70英里，那就太虚伪了。

Word Link *hypo ≈ below, under : hypodermic, hypothesis, hypothetical*

hypo·der·mic /haɪpədɜrmɪk/ (**hypodermics**) ADJ A **hypodermic** needle or syringe is a medical instrument with a hollow needle, which is used to give injections. (针头或注射器) 用于皮下注射的 ● N-COUNT **Hypodermic** is also a noun. 皮下注射器 [ADJ n] ❑ *He held up a hypodermic to check the dosage.* 他举起皮下注射器检查药剂量。

★ **hy·poth·esis** /haɪpɒθɪsɪs/ (**hypotheses**) N-VAR A **hypothesis** is an idea which is suggested as a possible explanation for a particular situation or condition, but which has not yet been proved to be correct. 假设 [FORMAL] ❑ *Work will now begin to test the hypothesis in rats.* 在老鼠身上验证这一假设的工作现在要开始了。

→ see **experiment, science**

hypo·theti·cal /haɪpəθɛtɪkᵊl/ ADJ If something is **hypothetical**, it is based on possible ideas or situations rather than actual ones. 假设的 ❑ *Let's look at a hypothetical situation in which Carol, a recovering alcoholic, gets invited to a party.* 我们来假设一下这样一个情景，卡罗尔，一个正在康复中的嗜酒者，被邀请去参加一场聚会。 ● **hypo·theti·cal·ly** /haɪpəθɛtɪkli/ ADV 以假设方式 ❑ *He was invariably willing to discuss the possibilities hypothetically.* 他总是愿意以假设方式讨论各种可能性。

hys·ter·ec·to·my /hɪstərɛktəmi/ (**hysterectomies**) N-COUNT A **hysterectomy** is a surgical operation to remove a woman's uterus. 子宫切除术 ❑ *I had to have a hysterectomy.* 我不得不做子宫切除手术。

hys·te·ria /hɪstɛriə/ N-UNCOUNT **Hysteria** among a group of people is a state of uncontrolled excitement, anger, or panic. 歇斯底里 ❑ *No one could help getting carried away by the hysteria.* 歇斯底里发作起来谁也无法控制自己。

★ **hys·teri·cal** /hɪstɛrɪkᵊl/ **1** ADJ Someone who is **hysterical** is in a state of uncontrolled excitement, anger, or panic. 歇斯底里的 ❑ *Police and bodyguards had to form a human shield around him as the almost hysterical crowds struggled to approach him.* 当近乎歇斯底里的人群奋力接近他时，警察和保镖们不得不在他周围形成一堵人墙。 ● **hys·teri·cal·ly** /hɪstɛrɪkli/ ADV 歇斯底里地 ❑ *I don't think we can go around screaming hysterically: "Ban these dogs. Muzzle all dogs."* 我认为我们不能歇斯底里地四处高喊："禁止养这些狗。给所有的狗戴上口套。" **2** ADJ **Hysterical** laughter is loud and uncontrolled. (笑) 疯狂失控的 [INFORMAL] ❑ *The young woman burst into hysterical laughter.* 那个少妇突然狂笑起来。 ● **hys·teri·cal·ly** ADV 疯狂失控地 [ADV with v] ❑ *She says she hasn't laughed as hysterically since she was 13.* 她说自己从13岁起就没有像这样狂笑过。 **3** ADJ If you describe something or someone as **hysterical**, you think that they are very funny and they make you laugh a lot. 非常滑稽的 [INFORMAL] ❑ *Paul Mazursky was Master of Ceremonies, and he was pretty hysterical.* 保罗・马祖尔斯基担任司仪，他相当诙谐风趣。 ● **hys·teri·cal·ly** ADV 滑稽地 [ADV adj] ❑ *It wasn't supposed to be a comedy but I found it hysterically funny.* 它本不是个喜剧，可我觉得它非常滑稽。

hys·ter·ics /hɪstɛrɪks/ **1** N-PLURAL If someone is **in hysterics** or is having **hysterics**, they are in a state of uncontrolled excitement, anger, or panic. 歇斯底里 [INFORMAL] ❑ *I'm sick of your having hysterics, okay?* 你歇斯底里的样子我讨厌透了，知道吗？ **2** N-PLURAL You can say that someone is **in hysterics** or is having **hysterics** when they are laughing loudly in an uncontrolled way. 狂笑 [INFORMAL] ❑ *He'd often have us all in absolute hysterics.* 他经常让我们大家狂笑不止。

h

Ii

I ◆◆◆ /aɪ/ PRON-SING A speaker or writer uses **I** to refer to himself or herself. **I** is a first person singular pronoun. **I** is used as the subject of a verb. 我(用作主格) [PRON V] ❑ *Jim and I are getting married.* 吉姆和我要结婚了。

I also **i** /aɪ/ (**I's, i's**) N-VAR **I** is the ninth letter of the English alphabet. 英文字母表中的第9个字母

ibid. CONVENTION **Ibid.** is used in books and journals to indicate that a piece of text taken from somewhere else is from the same source as the previous piece of text. (用于图书和期刊的文献注释中) 出处同上

ice ◆◆◇ /aɪs/ (**ices, icing, iced**) 1 N-UNCOUNT **Ice** is frozen water. 冰 ❑ *Glaciers are moving rivers of ice.* 冰川是流动成河的冰。 2 V-T If you **ice** a cake, you cover it with icing. 在(糕饼) 上裹糖霜 ❑ *I've made the cake. I've iced and decorated it.* 我做了蛋糕，给它裹上了糖霜并进行了装饰。 3 → see also **iced, icing** 4 PHRASE If you **break the ice** at a party or meeting, or in a new situation, you say or do something to make people feel relaxed and comfortable. 打破僵局 ❑ *That sort of approach should go a long way toward breaking the ice.* 那种方法应该对打破僵局大有帮助。 5 PHRASE If you say that something **cuts no ice with** you, you mean that you are not impressed or influenced by it. 不起作用 ❑ *That sort of romantic attitude cuts no ice with moneymen.* 那种罗曼蒂克的态度对金融家们不起作用。 6 PHRASE If someone puts a plan or project **on ice**, they delay doing it. 暂时搁置 ❑ *There would be a three-month delay while the deal would be put on ice.* 会有3个月的延误，与此同时这笔交易也将暂时搁置。 7 PHRASE If you say that someone is **on thin ice** or **is skating on thin ice**, you mean that they are doing something risky that may have serious or unpleasant consequences. 如履薄冰 ❑ *I had skated on thin ice on many assignments and somehow had gotten away with it.* 我曾在多项任务中都处于危险的境地，但不知怎么地都化险为夷了。

→ see **arctic, crystal, glacier**

ice·berg /aɪsbɜrg/ (**icebergs**) 1 N-COUNT An **iceberg** is a large tall mass of ice floating in the sea. 冰山 2 **the tip of the iceberg**

→ see **tip**

→ see **arctic**

ice cream (**ice creams**) also **ice-cream** 1 N-MASS **Ice cream** is a very cold sweet food made from frozen cream or a substance like cream and has a flavor such as vanilla, chocolate, or strawberry. 冰激凌 ❑ *I'll get you some ice cream.* 我去给你拿些冰激凌。 2 N-COUNT An **ice cream** is an amount of ice cream sold in a small container or a cone made of a thin cookie. (一客) 冰激凌；冰激凌蛋卷 ❑ *Do you want an ice cream?* 你想来个冰激凌吗？

→ see **dessert**

iced /aɪst/ 1 ADJ An **iced** drink has been made very cold, often by putting ice in it. 冰镇的 [ADJ n] ❑ *...iced tea.* …冰茶。 2 ADJ An **iced** cake is covered with a layer of icing. 裹了糖霜的蛋糕

ice hock·ey N-UNCOUNT **Ice hockey** is a game played on ice between two teams of 11 players who use long curved sticks to hit a small rubber disk, called a puck, and try to score goals. 冰上曲棍球

in AM, usually use **hockey**

ice lol·ly (**ice lollies**) N-COUNT An **ice lolly** is the same as a **Popsicle**. 冰棒 [BRIT]

ice skate (**ice skates, ice skating, ice skated**) 1 N-COUNT **Ice skates** are boots with a thin metal blade underneath that people wear to move quickly on ice. 溜冰鞋 2 V-I If you **ice skate**, you move around on ice wearing ice skates. 溜冰 ❑ *We never learned to ice skate or ski.* 我们从没学过溜冰或滑雪。 ● **ice skat·ing** N-UNCOUNT 溜冰 ❑ *I love watching ice skating on television.* 我喜欢看电视上的溜冰节目。 ❑ *We went ice skating on a frozen lake.* 我们去结冰的湖面上溜冰了。

ici·cle /aɪsɪkᵊl/ (**icicles**) N-COUNT An **icicle** is a long pointed piece of ice hanging down from a surface. It forms when water comes slowly off the surface, and freezes as it falls. 冰锥

ic·ing /aɪsɪŋ/ 1 N-UNCOUNT **Icing** is a sweet substance made from powdered sugar that is used to cover and decorate cakes. 糖霜 ❑ *Paul made five-year-old Michelle a birthday cake with yellow icing.* 保罗给5岁的米歇尔做了一个裹了黄色糖霜的生日蛋糕。 2 PHRASE If you describe something as **icing on the cake** or **the icing on the cake**, you mean that it makes a good thing even better, but it is not essential. 锦上添花之物 ❑ *Qualifying was my only goal, so winning is icing on the cake.* 取得资格是我惟一的目标，因此获胜便是锦上添花。

ic·ing sug·ar N-UNCOUNT **Icing sugar** is the same as **confectioners' sugar**. (制糖霜的) 糖粉 [BRIT]

★ **icon** /aɪkɒn/ (**icons**) also **ikon** 1 N-COUNT If you describe something or someone as an **icon**, you mean that they are important as a symbol of a particular thing. 象征物；偶像 ❑ *...only Marilyn has proved as enduring a fashion icon.* …只有玛丽莲被证明是经久不衰的时尚偶像。 2 N-COUNT An **icon** is a picture of Christ, his mother, or a saint painted on a wooden panel. (耶稣基督、圣母玛利亚等圣人的) 木制圣像 ❑ *...a painter of religious icons.* …一位宗教圣像画家。 3 N-COUNT An **icon** is a picture on a computer screen representing a particular computer function. If you want to use it, you move the cursor onto the icon using a mouse. (电脑屏幕上可用鼠标点击的) 图标 [COMPUTING] ❑ *Kate clicked on the mail icon on her computer screen.* 凯特点击了她电脑屏幕上的邮件图标。

ICT /aɪ si ti/ N-UNCOUNT **ICT** refers to activities or studies involving computers and other electronic technology. **ICT** is an abbreviation for "Information and Communications Technology". 信息技术课 [BRIT] ❑ *English, Math, ICT, and Science are compulsory subjects.* 英语、数学、信息技术和自然科学是必修课。

in AM, use **IT**

icy /aɪsi/ (**icier, iciest**) 1 ADJ If you describe something as **icy** or **icy cold**, you mean that it is extremely cold. 冰冷的 ❑ *An icy wind blew hard across the open spaces.* 一阵寒风猛烈地吹过开阔的空地。 2 ADJ An **icy** road has ice on it. 结冰的 ❑ *The roads were icy.* 道路都结冰了。 3 ADJ If you describe a person or their behavior as **icy**, you mean that they are not affectionate or friendly, and they show their dislike or anger in a quiet, controlled way. 冷漠的 [DISAPPROVAL] ❑ *His response was icy.* 他的反应很冷漠。

ID /aɪ di/ (**IDs**) N-VAR If you have **ID** or an **ID**, you are carrying a document such as an identity card or driver's license that tells who you are. 身份证件 ❑ *I had no ID on me so the police couldn't establish that I was the owner of the car.* 我没有身份证件，所以警察无法确定我就是那辆车的主人。

I'd /aɪd/ 1 **I'd** is the usual spoken form of "I had," especially when "had" is an auxiliary verb. **I had**的常用口语形式，尤其是当**had**作助动词时 ❑ *I felt absolutely certain that I'd seen her before.* 我确信自己以前曾见过她。 2 **I'd** is the usual spoken form of "I would." **I would**的常用口语形式 ❑ *There are some questions I'd like to ask.* 有些问题我想问问。

idea ◆◆◆ /aɪdiə/ (**ideas**) 1 N-COUNT An **idea** is a plan, suggestion, or possible course of action. 主意；打算 ❑ *It's a good idea to have your blood pressure checked regularly.* 定期检查你的血压是个好主意。 ❑ *I really like the idea of helping people.* 我非常喜欢帮助他人这个主意。 2 N-COUNT An **idea** is an opinion or belief about what something is like or should be like. 看法；信念 ❑ *Some of his ideas about democracy are entirely his own.* 他对民主的一些看法完全是个人的。 3 N-SING If someone gives you an **idea of** something, they give you information about it without being very exact or giving a lot of detail. 大致的信息 ❑ *This table will give you some idea of how levels of ability in a foreign language can be measured.* 这个表格将告诉你一些如何衡量外语能力级别的大致信息。 4 N-SING If you have an **idea** of something, you know about it to some extent. (对某事有) 一定的了解 ❑ *No one has any real idea how much the company will make next year.* 没有人真正知道公司明年将赚多少钱。 ❑ *We had no idea what was happening.* 我们不知道正在发生什么。 5 N-SING If you have an **idea** **that** something is the case, you think that it may be the case, although you are not certain. 猜想 [VAGUENESS] ❑ *I had an idea that he joined the army later, after college, but I may be wrong.* 我猜想他大学毕业后参了军，不过我也许错了。 **6** N-SING **The idea** of an action or activity is its aim or purpose. 目的 ❑ *The idea is to get industry to be more efficient in the way it uses energy.* 目的是使工业在使用能源的方式上效率更高。 **7** N-COUNT If you have the **idea of** doing something, you intend to do it. 意图 ❑ *He sent for a number of books he admired with the idea of rereading them.* 他订购了许多他赞赏的书，打算再读一遍。

Thesaurus *idea* 另参见：
N. plan, suggestion **1**
belief, concept, opinion, thought, viewpoint **2**

Word Partnership *idea* 的常用搭配：
ADJ. **bad** idea, **bright** idea, **brilliant** idea, **great** idea **1**
crazy idea, **different** idea, **dumb** idea, **interesting** idea, **new** idea, **original** idea **1** **2**
the main idea, **the whole** idea **1** **2** **6**
V. **get an** idea, **have an** idea **1** **3**–**5**

Word Link *ide, ideo ≈ idea : ideal, idealize, ideology*

ideal ♦◇◇ /aɪdiəl/ (**ideals**) **1** N-COUNT An **ideal** is a principle, idea, or standard that seems very good and worth trying to achieve. 理想 ❑ *Walt Disney stayed true to his ideals.* 沃尔特·迪斯尼坚持他的理想。 **2** N-SING Your **ideal of** something is the person or thing that seems to you to be the best possible example of it. 完美典范 ❑ *Her features were almost the opposite of the Japanese ideal of beauty in those days.* 她的容貌几乎和当时日本的美人典范正好相反。 **3** ADJ The **ideal** person or thing for a particular task or purpose is the best possible person or thing for it. 理想的 ❑ *She decided that I was the ideal person to take over the job.* 她认定我是接管这项工作的最佳人选。 **4** ADJ An **ideal** society or world is the best possible one that you can imagine. 完美的 [ADJ n] ❑ *We do not live in an ideal world.* 我们并非生活在一个完美的世界里。

ideal·ise /aɪdiəlaɪz/ [BRIT] → see **idealize**

ideal·ism /aɪdiəlɪzəm/ N-UNCOUNT **Idealism** is the beliefs and behavior of someone who has ideals and who tries to base their behavior on these ideals. 理想主义 ❑ *She never lost her respect for the idealism of the 1960s.* 她从未摈弃自己对20世纪60年代理想主义的崇敬。 ● **ideal·ist** N-COUNT (**idealists**) 理想主义者 ❑ *He is not such an idealist that he cannot see the problems.* 他不是一个看不见问题的理想主义者。

ideal·is·tic /aɪdiəlɪstɪk, aɪdiə-/ ADJ If you describe someone as **idealistic**, you mean that they have ideals, and base their behavior on these ideals, even though this may be impractical. 理想主义的 ❑ *Idealistic young people died for the cause.* 理想主义的年轻人为这项事业而献身。

ideal·ize /aɪdiəlaɪz/ (**idealizes, idealizing, idealized**)
in BRIT, also use **idealise**
V-T If you **idealize** something or someone, you think of them, or represent them to other people, as being perfect or much better than they really are. 把…理想化 ❑ *People idealize the past.* 人们总是把过去理想化。

ideal·ly /aɪdiəli/ **1** ADV If you say that **ideally** a particular thing should happen or be done, you mean that this is what you would like to happen or be done, but you know that this may not be possible or practical. 作为理想的做法 [ADV with cl/group] ❑ *People should, ideally, be persuaded to eat a diet with much less fat or oil.* 理想的做法是应该说服人们吃更低脂肪或更低油脂的食品。 **2** ADV If you say that someone or something is **ideally** suited, **ideally** located, or **ideally** qualified, you mean that they are as well suited, located, or qualified as they could possibly be. 完美地 ❑ *They were an extremely happy couple, ideally suited.* 他们是极其幸福、天造地设的一对。

Word Link *ident ≈ same : identical, identification, unidentified*

iden·ti·cal /aɪdɛntɪkəl/ ADJ Things that are **identical** are exactly the same. 完全相同的 ❑ *The three bombs were virtually identical.* 这3个炸弹几乎一模一样。 ● **iden·ti·cal·ly** /aɪdɛntɪkli/ ADV 完全相同地 ❑ *...nine identically dressed female dancers.* …9个着装相同的女舞蹈演员。
→ see **clone**

iden·ti·fi·able /aɪdɛntɪfaɪəbəl/ ADJ Something or someone that is **identifiable** can be recognized. 可辨认的 ❑ *In the corridor were four dirty, ragged bundles, just identifiable as human beings.* 走廊里有4堆脏兮兮、衣衫褴褛的东西，依稀可辨出人形。

iden·ti·fi·ca·tion /aɪdɛntɪfɪkeɪʃən/ (**identifications**) **1** N-VAR The **identification** of something is the recognition that it exists, is important, or is true. 确认 ❑ *Early identification of a disease can prevent death and illness.* 疾病的早期确认可避免死亡和病痛。 **2** N-VAR The **identification** of a particular person or thing is the ability to name them because you know them or recognize them. 验明 ❑ *Officials are awaiting positive identification before charging the men with war crimes.* 官员们正在等待这些人的身份得以验明，然后再以战争罪起诉他们。 **3** N-UNCOUNT If someone asks you for some **identification**, they want to see something such as a driver's license, that proves who you are. 身份证明 ❑ *He did not have any identification when he arrived at the hospital.* 他到医院的时候没有任何身份证明。 **4** N-VAR The **identification of** one person or thing **with** another is the close association of one with the other. 密切关联 ❑ *...the identification of Spain with Catholicism.* …西班牙与天主教的密切联系。 **5** N-UNCOUNT **Identification with** someone or something is the feeling of sympathy and support for them. 同情；支持 ❑ *Marilyn had an intense identification with animals.* 玛丽莲对动物有深切的同情。

iden·ti·fy ♦♦◇ /aɪdɛntɪfaɪ/ (**identifies, identifying, identified**) **1** V-T If you can **identify** someone or something, you are able to recognize them or distinguish them from others. 识别 ❑ *There are a number of distinguishing characteristics by which you can identify a Hollywood epic.* 通过其诸多与众不同的特点，你可以识别出好莱坞的史诗影片。 **2** V-T If you **identify** someone or something, you name them or say who or what they are. 确认 ❑ *Police have already identified 10 murder suspects.* 警方已经确认了10名谋杀嫌疑犯。 **3** V-T If you **identify** something, you discover or notice its existence. 发现；察觉 ❑ *Scientists claim to have identified chemicals produced by certain plants which have powerful cancer-fighting properties.* 科学家们声称已经发现某些植物产生的化学物质有强大的抗癌功能。 **4** V-T If a particular thing **identifies** someone or something, it makes them easy to recognize, by making them different in some way. 是…的标志；使易于辨认 ❑ *She wore a little nurse's hat on her head to identify her.* 她头上戴了一顶小护士帽，这使她易于辨认。 **5** V-I If you **identify with** someone or something, you feel that you understand them or their feelings and ideas. 理解；认同 ❑ *She would only play a role if she could identify with the character.* 她只愿扮演自己认同的人物角色。 **6** V-T If you **identify** one person or thing **with** another, you think that they are closely associated or involved in some way. 认为…密切相关 ❑ *Moore really hates to play the sweet, passive women that audiences have identified her with.* 穆尔非常讨厌饰演观众已将她定型的温柔可爱、逆来顺受的女性角色。

iden·tity ♦◇◇ /aɪdɛntɪti/ (**identities**) **1** N-COUNT Your **identity** is who you are. 身份 ❑ *Abu is not his real name, but it's one he uses to disguise his identity.* 阿布不是他的真名，而是一个他用来掩盖自己身份的假名。 **2** N-VAR The **identity** of a person or place is the characteristics that distinguish them from others. 特性 ❑ *I wanted a sense of my own identity.* 我需要确立自身的个性意识。

Word Partnership *identity* 的常用搭配：
N. identity **theft** **1**
identity **crisis**, **sense of** identity **2**
ADJ. **ethnic** identity, **national** identity, **personal** identity **2**

iden·tity card (**identity cards**) N-COUNT An **identity card** is a card with a person's name, photograph, date of birth, and other information on it. In some countries, people are required to carry identity cards in order to prove who they are. The abbreviation **ID card** is also used. 身份证

★ **ideo·logi·cal** /aɪdiəlɒdʒɪkəl, ɪdi-/ ADJ **Ideological** means relating to principles or beliefs. 意识形态的 ❑ *Others left the party for ideological reasons.* 其余的人因意识形态原因脱离了该党。 ● **ideo·logi·cal·ly** /aɪdiəlɒdʒɪkli, ɪdi-/ ADV 在意识形态方面 ❑ *...an ideologically sound organization.* …一个意识形态上健全的组织。

★ **ideol·ogy** /aɪdiɒlədʒi, ɪdi-/ (**ideologies**) N-VAR An **ideology** is a set of beliefs, especially the political beliefs on which people, parties, or countries base their actions. 意识形态 ❑ *...capitalist ideology.* …资本主义意识形态。

idi·om /ɪdiəm/ (**idioms**) N-COUNT An **idiom** is a group of words that have a different meaning when used together from the one they would have if you took the meaning of each word separately. 习语 [TECHNICAL] ❑ *...familiar idioms and metaphors, such as "turning over a new leaf."* …如"翻开新的一页"这样熟悉的习语和比喻。

★ **id·iot** /ɪdiət/ (**idiots**) N-COUNT If you call someone an **idiot**, you are showing that you think they are very stupid or have done something very stupid. 笨蛋 [DISAPPROVAL] ❑ *I knew I'd been an idiot to stay there.* 我知道我呆在那儿很傻。

idle /aɪdᵊl/ (**idles, idling, idled**) 1 ADJ If people who were working are **idle**, they have no jobs or work. 无事可做的 [v-link ADJ] ❑ *4,000 workers have been idle for 12 of the first 27 weeks of this year.* 4千名工人在今年最初的27个星期中有12个星期无事可干。 2 ADJ If machines or factories are **idle**, they are not working or being used. (机器或工厂) 闲置的 [v-link ADJ] ❑ *Now the machine is lying idle.* 现在这台机器正处于闲置状态。 3 ADJ If you say that someone is **idle**, you disapprove of them because they are not doing anything and you think they should be. 无所事事的 [DISAPPROVAL] ❑ *...idle bureaucrats who spent the day reading newspapers.* …整天看报纸，无所事事的官僚们。 ● **idly** ADV 无所事事地 [ADV with v] ❑ *We were not idly sitting around.* 我们并非坐着没事干。 4 ADJ **Idle** is used to describe something that you do for no particular reason, often because you have nothing better to do. 无聊的 [ADJ n] ❑ *Brian kept up the idle chatter for another five minutes.* 布赖恩又无聊地闲扯了5分钟。 ● **idly** ADV 无聊地 ❑ *We talked idly about magazines and baseball.* 我们闲聊着杂志和棒球。 5 ADJ You refer to an **idle** threat or boast when you do not think the person making it will or can do what they say. 虚张声势的 [ADJ n] ❑ *It was more of an idle threat than anything.* 那不过是虚张声势的威胁。 6 V-I If an engine or vehicle **is idling**, the engine is running slowly and quietly because it is not in gear, and the vehicle is not moving. (发动机等) 低速空转 ❑ *Beyond a stand of trees a small plane idled.* 在树丛的那一边，一架小飞机的发动机空转着。

> **Thesaurus** *idle* 另参见:
> ADJ. inactive, jobless, unemployed 1
> lazy, passive, shiftless, wasteful; *(ant.)* busy, productive 3

▲ **idol** /aɪdᵊl/ (**idols**) 1 N-COUNT If you refer to someone such as a movie, pop, or sports star as an **idol**, you mean that they are greatly admired or loved by their fans. 偶像 ❑ *A great cheer went up from the crowd as they caught sight of their idol.* 一看见他们的偶像，人群爆发出一阵热烈的欢呼声。 2 N-COUNT An **idol** is a statue or other object that is worshipped by people who believe that it is a god. 神像

idol·ise /aɪdəlaɪz/ [BRIT] → see **idolize**

idol·ize /aɪdəlaɪz/ (**idolizes, idolizing, idolized**)

in BRIT, also use **idolise**

V-T If you **idolize** someone, you admire them very much. 崇拜 ❑ *Naomi idolized her father as she was growing up.* 在成长过程中，娜奥米很崇拜她父亲。

idyl·lic /aɪdɪlɪk/ ADJ If you describe something as **idyllic**, you mean that it is extremely pleasant, simple, and peaceful without any difficulties or dangers. 闲适恬静的 ❑ *...an idyllic setting for a summer romance.* …一个适合夏季恋曲的闲适环境。

i.e. /aɪ i/ **i.e.** is used to introduce a word or sentence that makes what you have just said clearer or gives details. 即 ❑ *...an artificial intelligence system, i.e. a computer program.* …人工智能系统，即计算机程序。

if ♦♦♦ /ɪf/

Often pronounced /ɪf/ at the beginning of the sentence.

位于句首常读作 /ɪf/。

1 CONJ You use **if** in conditional sentences to introduce the circumstances in which an event or situation might happen, might be happening, or might have happened. (引导条件从句) 如果 ❑ *She gets very upset if I exclude her from anything.* 如果有什么事我将她排除在外，她就会非常难过。 ❑ *You can go if you want.* 如果你想走就走吧。 2 CONJ You use **if** in indirect questions where the answer is either "yes" or "no." (用于间接是非问句中) 是否 ❑ *He asked if I had left with you, and I said no.* 他问我是不是和你一起离开的，我说不是。 3 CONJ You use **if** to suggest that something might be slightly different from what you are stating in the main part of the sentence, for example, that there might be slightly more or less of a particular quality. (表示与主句所述事实可能有少许不同) 即使 ❑ *Sometimes that standard is quite difficult, if not impossible, to achieve.* 有时那个标准，即使并非不可能，也是很难达到的。 4 CONJ You use **if**, usually with "can," "could," "may," or "might," in a conversation when you are politely trying to make a point, change the subject, or interrupt another speaker. 常与**can**、**could**、**may**、**might**等情态动词连用，表示婉转客气 ❑ *If I could just make another small point about the weightlifters in the Olympics.* 请允许我就奥运会的举重运动员们再稍说一句。 5 CONJ You use **if** at or near the beginning of a clause when politely asking someone to do something. (用于从句句首或靠近句首的位置，表示礼貌的请求) 是否 [POLITENESS] ❑ *I wonder if you'd be kind enough to give us some information, please?* 不知能否请您向我们提供些信息? 6 PHRASE You use **if not** in front of a word or phrase to indicate that your statement does not apply to that word or phrase, but to something closely related to it that you also mention. 即便不 ❑ *She understood his meaning, if not his words, and took his advice.* 她即便不懂他的语言，也明白了他的意思，并且接受了他的建议。 7 CONJ You use **if** to introduce a subordinate clause in which you admit a fact that you regard as less important than the statement in the main clause. (引导从句，提出次要的事实) 即使 ❑ *If there was any disappointment it was probably temporary.* 即使有任何遗憾，可能也是暂时的。 8 PHRASE You use **if ever** with past tenses when you are introducing a description of a person or thing, to emphasize how appropriate it is. (与过去式连用，强调对人或事物的描述极为恰当) 如果有…的话 [EMPHASIS] ❑ *I became a distraught, worried mother, a useless role if ever there was one.* 如果有个心烦意乱、忧心忡忡的母亲，一个完全无用的角色，那就是我。 9 PHRASE You use **if only** with past tenses to introduce what you think is a fairly good reason for doing something, although you realize it may not be a very good one. 即使仅仅(与过去式连用，引出能勉强说明做某事的原因) ❑ *She always writes me once a month, if only to scold me because I haven't answered her last letter yet.* 她总是一个月写一封信给我，即使仅仅是为了责备我还没有回她的上一封信。 10 PHRASE You use **if only** to express a wish or desire, especially one that cannot be fulfilled. (尤指不能实现的愿望) 要是…多好 [FEELINGS] ❑ *If only you had told me that some time ago.* 要是你之前告诉我那件事该多好。 11 PHRASE You use **as if** when you are making a judgment about something that you see or notice. Your belief or impression might be correct, or it might be wrong. (表示判断) 好像 ❑ *It looked as if she had forgotten how to breathe.* 她看上去好像是忘了如何呼吸似的。 12 PHRASE You use **as if** to describe something or someone by comparing them with another thing or person. (表示类比) 仿佛 ❑ *He points two fingers at his head, as if he were holding a gun.* 他用两个手指对着自己的脑袋，仿佛正拿着一把枪。 13 PHRASE You use **as if** to emphasize that something is not true. (强调某事不是真的) 好像…一样 [SPOKEN, EMPHASIS] ❑ *Getting my work done! My God! As if it mattered.* 把我的活儿干完! 我的天哪! 好像这很要紧似的。

★ **ig·nite** /ɪgnaɪt/ (**ignites, igniting, ignited**) 1 V-T/V-I When you **ignite** something or when it **ignites**, it starts burning or explodes. 点燃; 着火 ❑ *The bombs ignited a fire which destroyed some 60 houses.* 炸弹引起了一场火灾，烧毁了大约六十间房屋。 2 V-T If something or someone **ignites** your feelings, they cause you to have very strong feelings about something. 激起 [LITERARY] ❑ *There was one teacher who really ignited my interest in words.* 曾经有一位老师真正激起了我对文字的兴趣。

ig·ni·tion /ɪgnɪʃᵊn/ (**ignitions**) 1 N-VAR In a car engine, the **ignition** is the part where the fuel is ignited. (汽车发动机中的) 点火装置 ❑ *The device automatically disconnects the ignition.* 那个装置自动断开了点火器。 2 N-SING Inside a car, **the ignition** is the part where you turn the key so that the engine starts. (汽车里的) 点火开关 ❑ *Abruptly he turned the ignition key and started the engine.* 他突然转动了点火开关的钥匙，发动了引擎。 3 N-UNCOUNT **Ignition** is the process of something starting to burn. 起火 ❑ *The ignition of methane gas killed eight men.* 甲烷起火造成8人死亡。

ig·no·rance /ɪgnərəns/ N-UNCOUNT **Ignorance of** something is lack of knowledge about it. 无知 ❑ *I am beginning to feel embarrassed by my complete ignorance of world history.* 我开始为自己对世界历史的一无所知感到尴尬。

ig·no·rant /ɪgnərənt/ 1 ADJ If you describe someone as **ignorant**, you mean that they do not know things they should know. If someone is **ignorant of** a fact, they do not know it. 无知的 ❑ *People don't like to ask questions for fear of appearing ignorant.* 人们不喜欢问问题，生怕显得自己无知。 2 ADJ People are sometimes described as **ignorant** when they do something that is not polite or kind. 不礼貌的 ❑ *I met some ignorant people who called me all kinds of names.* 我碰见了一些粗鲁人，他们用各种名称叫我。

ig·nore ♦♦◇ /ɪgnɔr/ (**ignores, ignoring, ignored**) 1 V-T If you **ignore** someone or something, you pay no attention to them.

不理睬 ❑ *She said her husband ignored her.* 她说她丈夫对她置之不理。
2 V-T If you say that an argument or theory **ignores** an important aspect of a situation, you are criticizing it because it fails to consider that aspect or to take it into account. (某论断或理论) 忽视 ❑ *Such arguments ignore the question of where ultimate responsibility lay.* 此类争论忽视了最终责任何在的问题。

Word Partnership *ignore* 的常用搭配:
N. ignore **advice**, ignore **a warning** **1**
V. **choose to** ignore *someone/something*, **try to** ignore *someone/something* **1**
ADJ. **hard to** ignore, **impossible to** ignore **1**

ill ♦♦◊ /ɪl/ (**ills**) **1** ADJ Someone who is **ill** is suffering from a disease or a health problem. 患病的 ❑ *In November 1941 Payne was seriously ill with pneumonia.* 1941年11月，佩恩患了严重的肺炎。● N-PLURAL People who are ill in some way can be referred to as, for example, **the** mentally **ill**. 患…病的人 ❑ *The hospice provides care for the terminally ill.* 救济院为身患绝症的人们提供护理。

The words **ill** and **sick** are very similar in meaning, but are used in slightly different ways. **Ill** is generally not used before a noun, and can be used in verbal expressions such as **fall ill** and **be taken ill**. ❑ *He fell ill shortly before Christmas... One of the jury members was taken ill.* **Sick** is often used before a noun. ❑ *...sick children.* In British English, **ill** is a slightly more polite, less direct word than **sick**. **Sick** often suggests the actual physical feeling of being ill, for example nausea or vomiting. ❑ *I spent the next 24 hours in bed, groaning and being sick.* In American English, **sick** is often used where British people would say **ill**. ❑ *Some people get hurt in accidents or get sick.*

2 N-COUNT Difficulties and problems are sometimes referred to as **ills**. 难题 [FORMAL] ❑ *His critics maintain that he's responsible for many of Algeria's ills.* 他的批评者坚持认为他对阿尔及利亚的许多问题负有责任。**3** ADJ You can use **ill** in front of some nouns to indicate that you are referring to something harmful or unpleasant. 有害的; 令人不快的 [ADJ n] [FORMAL] ❑ *She had brought ill luck into her family.* 她给家庭带来了厄运。**4** N-UNCOUNT **Ill** is evil or harm. 恶行; 伤害 [LITERARY] ❑ *They say they mean you no ill.* 他们说他们对你没有恶意。**5** ADV **Ill** means the same as "badly." 不合适地 [ADV with v] [FORMAL] ❑ *The company's conservative instincts sit ill with competition.* 该公司的保守本性不适合竞争。**6** PHRASE If you say that someone **can ill afford to** do something, or **can ill afford** something, you mean that they must prevent it from happening because it would be harmful or embarrassing to them. 难以承受 [FORMAL] ❑ *It's possible he won't play but I can ill afford to lose him.* 他有可能不会出场，但我难以承受失去他的损失。**7** PHRASE If you **fall ill** or **are taken ill**, you suddenly become ill. 突然病倒 ❑ *Shortly before Christmas, he was mysteriously taken ill.* 圣诞节前不久，他突然莫名其妙地病了。**8** to **speak ill of** someone → see **speak**

Word Partnership *ill* 的常用搭配:
V. **become** ill, **feel** ill, **look** ill **1**
ADV. **critically** ill, **mentally** ill, **physically** ill, **seriously** ill, **terminally** ill, **very** ill **1**

I'll /aɪl/ **I'll** is the usual spoken form of "I will" or "I shall." **I will**或**I shall**的常用口语形式 ❑ *I'll be leaving town in a few weeks.* 我过几个星期将出城去。

Word Link *il ≈ not : illegal, illiterate, illogical*

il·legal ♦◊◊ /ɪliɡᵊl/ (**illegals**) **1** ADJ If something is **illegal**, the law says that it is not allowed. 非法的 ❑ *It is illegal to intercept radio messages.* 窃听无线电信息是违法的。❑ *...illegal drugs.* …非法毒品。● **il·legal·ly** ADV 非法地 [ADV with v] ❑ *He was convicted of illegally using a handgun.* 他被判非法使用手枪。**2** ADJ **Illegal** immigrants or workers have traveled into a country or are working without official permission. (移民) 非法入境的; (工人) 非法务工的 ● N-COUNT Illegal immigrants or workers are sometimes referred to as **illegals**. 非法移民; 非法劳工 [ADJ n] ❑ *...a clothing factory where many other illegals also worked.* …一家允许很多其他非法劳工工作的服装厂。

il·legiti·mate /ɪlɪdʒɪtɪmɪt/ **1** ADJ A person who is **illegitimate** was born of parents who were not married to each other. 私生的 ❑ *They discovered he had an illegitimate child.* 他们发现他有一个私生子。**2** ADJ **Illegitimate** is used to describe activities and institutions that are not in accordance with the law or with accepted standards of what is right. 不合规则的; 不合法的 ❑ *He realized that, otherwise, the election would have been dismissed as illegitimate by the international community.* 他意识到，不这样的话，选举就会被国际社会以不合法为由而不予承认。

ill-fated ADJ If you describe something as **ill-fated**, you mean that it ended or will end in an unsuccessful or unfortunate way. 倒霉的; 注定以失败告终的 ❑ *...the ill-fated merger between AOL and Time Warner.* …美国在线和时代华纳的这次合并注定没有好结果。

ill health N-UNCOUNT Someone who suffers from **ill health** has an illness or keeps being ill. 健康不佳 ❑ *He was forced to retire because of ill health.* 由于健康不佳，他只得退休。

★ **il·lic·it** /ɪlɪsɪt/ ADJ An **illicit** activity or substance is not allowed by law or the social customs of a country. 违法的; 不正当的 ❑ *Dante clearly condemns illicit love.* 但丁明确地谴责不正当的恋情。

Word Link *liter ≈ letter : illiterate, literal, literature*

★ **il·lit·er·ate** /ɪlɪtərɪt/ (**illiterates**) ADJ Someone who is **illiterate** does not know how to read or write. 文盲的 ❑ *A large percentage of the population is illiterate.* 人口中文盲的比例相当高。● N-COUNT An **illiterate** is someone who is illiterate. 文盲 ❑ *...a subclass of illiterates.* …文盲阶层。

ill·ness ♦◊◊ /ɪlnɪs/ (**illnesses**) **1** N-UNCOUNT **Illness** is the fact or experience of being ill. 生病 ❑ *If your child shows any signs of illness, take her to the doctor.* 如果您的孩子出现任何生病的症兆，带她去看医生。**2** N-COUNT An **illness** is a particular disease such as measles or pneumonia. 疾病 ❑ *She returned to her family home to recover from an illness.* 她回到自己家里养病。
→ see Word Web: **illness**

Thesaurus *illness* 另参见:
N. disease, sickness; (*ant.*) health, wellness **1**
ailment, disease **2**

Word Partnership *illness* 的常用搭配:
N. **signs/symptoms of** *an* illness **1** **2**
ADJ. **mental** illness, **serious** illness, **terminal** illness **1** **2**
long/short illness, **mysterious** illness, **sudden** illness **2**
V. **suffer from** *an* illness, **treat** *an* illness **1** **2**
diagnose an illness, **have an** illness **2**

il·logi·cal /ɪlɒdʒɪkᵊl/ ADJ If you describe an action, feeling, or belief as **illogical**, you are critical of it because you think that it does not result from a logical and ordered way of thinking. 没有道理的; 不合逻辑的 [DISAPPROVAL] ❑ *It was absurd and illogical to go out into such a storm.* 在这样的暴风雨中外出简直是荒唐和莫名其妙。

★ **il·lu·mi·nate** /ɪluːmɪneɪt/ (**illuminates, illuminating, illuminated**) **1** V-T To **illuminate** something means to shine light on it and to make it brighter and more visible. 照亮 [FORMAL] ❑ *No streetlights illuminated the street.* 一盏照亮街道的路灯也没有。

Word Web illness

Most **infectious diseases** pass from person to person. However, some people have **contracted viruses** from animals. During the 2002 SARS **epidemic**, doctors discovered that the disease came from birds. SARS caused over 800 deaths in 32 countries.The disease had to be stopped quickly. Hospitals **quarantined** SARS patients. Medical workers used **symptoms** such as **fever**, **chills**, and a **cough** to help **diagnose** the disease. **Treatment** was not simple. By the time the symptoms appeared, the disease had already caused a lot of damage. **Patients** received oxygen and **physical therapy** to help clear the lungs.

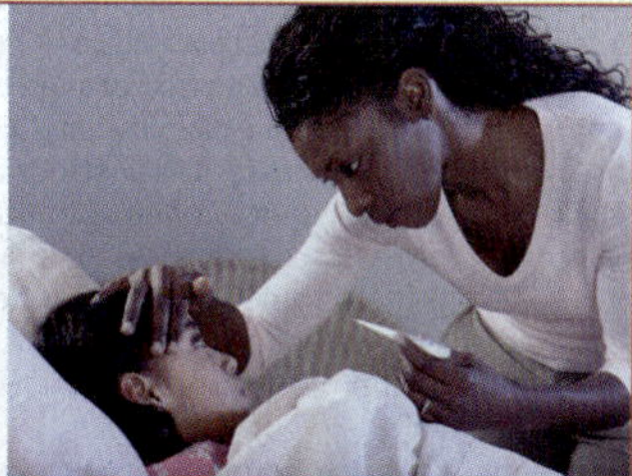

2 V-T If you **illuminate** something that is unclear or difficult to understand, you make it clearer by explaining it carefully or giving information about it. 阐明 [FORMAL] ❑ *Instead of formulas and charts, the two instructors use games and drawings to illuminate their subject.* 这两位教师用游戏和图画而不是公式和图表来阐明他们的题目。 ● **il·lu·mi·nat·ing** ADJ 富有启发性的 ❑ *It would be illuminating to hear the views of the club vice-chairman.* 听听俱乐部副主席的观点或许会有启发。

il·lu·mi·na·tion /ɪlumɪneɪʃᵊn/ N-UNCOUNT **Illumination** is the lighting that a place has. 照明 [FORMAL] ❑ *The only illumination came from a small window high in the opposite wall.* 惟一的照明来自对面墙上位于高处的一扇小窗户。

il·lu·sion /ɪluʒᵊn/ (**illusions**) 1 N-VAR An **illusion** is a false idea or belief. 幻想 ❑ *No one really has any illusions about winning the war.* 事实上没有人对打赢这场战争抱任何幻想。 2 N-COUNT An **illusion** is something that appears to exist or be a particular thing but does not actually exist or is in reality something else. 假象 ❑ *Floor-to-ceiling windows can look stunning, giving the illusion of extra height.* 从地板直抵天花板的窗户看上去非常漂亮，有增加高度的假象。

Word Partnership *illusion* 的常用搭配：

V. **be under an** illusion 1
create an illusion, **give an** illusion **about/of/that** *something* 1 2

il·lus·trate ♦◊◊ /ɪləstreɪt/ (**illustrates, illustrating, illustrated**) 1 V-T If you say that something **illustrates** a situation that you are drawing attention to, you mean that it shows that the situation exists. 表明；显示 ❑ *The example of the United States illustrates this point.* 美国的例子表明了这一点。 ❑ *The situation illustrates how vulnerable the president is.* 这个情况显示总统是多么地不堪一击。 2 V-T If you use an example, story, or diagram to **illustrate** a point, you use it to show that what you are saying is true or to make your meaning clearer. (用例子、故事或图表) 阐明 ❑ *Let me give another example to illustrate this difficult point.* 让我举另一个例子来阐明这个难点。 ● **il·lus·tra·tion** N-UNCOUNT 例证 ❑ *Here, by way of illustration, are some extracts from our new catalog.* 这里引为例证的是摘自我们新目录的部分内容。 3 V-T If you **illustrate** a book, you put pictures, photographs or diagrams into it. 给 (书) 加插图 ❑ *She went on to art school and is now illustrating a book.* 她接着上了美术学校，现在正在给一本书画插图。 ● **il·lus·tra·tion** N-UNCOUNT (书的) 插图 ❑ *...the world of children's book illustration.* …儿童书籍插图的世界。
→ see **animation**

il·lus·tra·tion ♦◊◊ /ɪləstreɪʃᵊn/ (**illustrations**) 1 N-COUNT An **illustration** is an example or a story that is used to make a point clear. 实例 ❑ *An illustration of China's dynamism is that a new company is formed in Shanghai every 11 seconds.* 说明中国活力的一个实例便是在上海每11秒钟就有一家新公司成立。 2 N-COUNT An **illustration** in a book is a picture, design, or diagram. (书中的) 插图 ❑ *She looked like a princess in a nineteenth-century illustration.* 她看上去像19世纪插图里的公主。 3 → see also **illustrate**

il·lus·tri·ous /ɪlʌstriəs/ ADJ If you describe someone as an **illustrious** person, you mean that they are extremely well known because they have a high position in society or they have done something impressive. (人) 著名的 ❑ *...the most illustrious scientists of the century.* …本世纪最著名的科学家们。

I'm /aɪm/ **I'm** is the usual spoken form of "I am." **I am**的常用口语形式 ❑ *I'm sorry.* 我很抱歉。

im·age ♦♦◊ /ɪmɪdʒ/ (**images**) 1 N-COUNT If you have an **image** of something or someone, you have a picture or idea of them in your mind. (头脑里的) 形象；概念 ❑ *The image of art theft as a gentleman's crime is outdated.* 艺术品盗窃是绅士犯罪这一观念已经过时了。 2 N-COUNT The **image** of a person, group, or organization is the way that they appear to other people. (个人、团体或组织的) 形象 ❑ *...the government's negative public image.* …政府负面的公众形象。 3 N-COUNT An **image** is a picture of someone or something. 画像 [FORMAL] ❑ *...photographic images of young children.* …小孩子们的摄影图像。 4 N-COUNT An **image** is a poetic description of something. 生动的描绘 [FORMAL] ❑ *The natural images in the poem are meant to be suggestive of realities beyond themselves.* 诗中自然景象的描写意在使人联想起那以外的现实。 5 PHRASE If you **are the image of** someone else, you look very much like them. 酷似某人 ❑ *Marianne's son was the image of his father.* 玛丽安娜的儿子酷似他的父亲。 6 **spitting image** → see **spit**
→ see **copy, eye, photography, telescope, television**

Word Partnership *image* 的常用搭配：

N. **body** image, **self-**image 1 2
image **on a screen** 3
ADJ. **corporate** image, **negative/positive** image, **public** image 2
V. **project an** image 2 3
display an image 3

im·age·ry /ɪmɪdʒri/ 1 N-UNCOUNT You can refer to the descriptions in something such as a poem or song, and the pictures they create in your mind, as its **imagery**. 形象化描述 [FORMAL] ❑ *...the nature imagery of the ballad.* …民谣中的自然意象。 2 N-UNCOUNT You can refer to pictures and representations of things as **imagery**, especially when they act as symbols. (尤指具象征意义的) 图像 [FORMAL] ❑ *This is an ambitious and intriguing movie, full of striking imagery.* 这是一部气势恢宏、引人入胜的电影，充满了惹眼的镜头。

im·agi·nable /ɪmædʒɪnəbᵊl/ 1 ADJ You use **imaginable** after a superlative such as "best" or "worst" to emphasize that something is extreme in some way. 可想像的 (常与**best**、**worst**等形容词最高级连用表示强调) [EMPHASIS] ❑ *...their imprisonment under some of the most horrible circumstances imaginable.* …他们在能想像得出的最恐怖的环境里蹲监狱。 2 ADJ You use **imaginable** after a word like "every" or "all" to emphasize that you are talking about all the possible examples of something. You use **imaginable** after "no" to emphasize that something does not have the quality mentioned. (用于**every**，**all**之后表示强调) 一切可能的；(用于**no**之后表示强调) 毫无 [ADJ n, n ADJ] [EMPHASIS] ❑ *Parents encourage every activity imaginable.* 父母鼓励一切可能的活动。 ❑ *...a place of no imaginable strategic value.* …一个毫无战略价值的地方。

im·agi·nary /ɪmædʒɪnɛri/ ADJ An **imaginary** person, place, or thing exists only in your mind or in a story, and not in real life. 假想的 ❑ *Lots of children have imaginary friends.* 许多孩子都有假想的朋友。
→ see **fantasy**

im·agi·na·tion ♦◊◊ /ɪmædʒɪneɪʃᵊn/ (**imaginations**) 1 N-VAR Your **imagination** is the ability that you have to form pictures or ideas in your mind of things that are new and exciting, or things that you have not experienced. 想像力 ❑ *Latanya is a woman with a vivid imagination.* 拉坦尼娅是一个想像力丰富的女人。 2 N-COUNT Your **imagination** is the part of your mind that allows you to form pictures or ideas of things that do not necessarily exist in real life. 想像 ❑ *Long before I ever went there, Africa was alive in my imagination.* 早在我去非洲之前，它就栩栩如生地在我的脑海中了。 3 PHRASE If you say that someone or something **captured** your **imagination**, you mean that you thought they were interesting or exciting when you saw them or heard them for the first time. 引起某人的兴趣 ❑ *Their music continues to capture the imagination of the American public.* 他们的音乐持续吸引着美国公众的兴趣。 4 **not by any stretch of the imagination** → see **stretch**
→ see **fantasy**

Word Partnership *imagination* 的常用搭配：

ADJ. **active** imagination, **lively** imagination, **vivid** imagination 1
PREP. **beyond** *(someone's)* imagination 1
N. **lack of** imagination 1

★ **im·agi·na·tive** /ɪmædʒɪnətɪv/ ADJ If you describe someone or their ideas as **imaginative**, you are praising them because they are easily able to think of or create new or exciting things. 富于想像力的 [APPROVAL] ❑ *...an imaginative writer.* …一位富有想像力的作家。 ● **im·agi·na·tive·ly** ADV 富于想像力地 [ADV with v] ❑ *The hotel is decorated imaginatively and attractively.* 这家旅馆装饰得很有想像力和吸引力。

im·ag·ine ♦♦◊ /ɪmædʒɪn/ (**imagines, imagining, imagined**) 1 V-T If you **imagine** something, you think about it and your mind forms a picture or idea of it. 想像 ❑ *He could not imagine a more peaceful scene.* 他想像不出比这更幽静的场景。 2 V-T If you **imagine** that something is the case, you think that it is the case. 猜想 ❑ *I imagine you're referring to Jean-Paul Sartre.* 我猜你指的是吉恩-保尔・萨特。 3 V-T If you **imagine** something, you think that you have seen, heard, or experienced that thing, although actually you have not. 幻想 ❑ *Looking back on it now, I realized that I must have imagined the whole thing.* 现在回想起来，我意识到这整个事情一定是我幻想出来的。

Thesaurus *imagine* 另参见：

V. picture, see, visualize 1
believe, guess, think 2

Word Partnership *imagine* 的常用搭配：

V. **can/can't/could/couldn't** imagine ***something*****, try to** imagine 1 2
ADJ. **difficult/easy/hard/impossible to** imagine 1 2

Word Link *im ≈ not : imbalance, immature, impossible*

im·bal·ance /ɪmbæləns/ (**imbalances**) N-VAR If there is an **imbalance** in a situation, the things involved are not the same size, or are not the right size in proportion to each other. 不平衡 ❑ *...the imbalance between the two sides in this war.* …这场战争中双方的不对等。

im·bue /ɪmbyu̲/ (**imbues, imbuing, imbued**) V-T If someone or something **is imbued** with an idea, feeling, or quality, they become filled with it. 灌输；使充满 [FORMAL] ❑ *The film is imbued with the star's rebellious spirit.* 这部电影充满了那位明星的反叛精神。

IMF /a̲ɪ ɛm ɛ̲f/ N-PROPER **The IMF** is an international agency that tries to promote trade and improve economic conditions in poorer countries, sometimes by lending them money. **IMF** is an abbreviation for "International Monetary Fund." 国际货币基金组织

imi·tate /ɪmɪteɪt/ (**imitates, imitating, imitated**) 1 V-T If you **imitate** someone, you copy what they do or produce. 模仿 ❑ *...a genuine German musical that does not try to imitate the American model.* …一部不试图模仿美国模式的正宗德国音乐剧。 2 V-T If you **imitate** a person or animal, you copy the way they speak or behave, usually because you are trying to be funny. (常为逗乐) 学…的样 ❑ *Clarence screws up his face and imitates the Colonel again.* 克拉伦斯又板起面孔，模仿上校的样。

★ **imi·ta·tion** /ɪmɪteɪʃən/ (**imitations**) 1 N-COUNT An **imitation** of something is a copy of it. 仿造品 ❑ *...the most accurate imitation of Chinese architecture in Europe.* …欧洲最逼真的仿中国建筑。 2 N-UNCOUNT **Imitation** means copying someone else's actions. 动作模仿 ❑ *They discussed important issues in imitation of their elders.* 他们模仿长辈的口气讨论重大问题。 3 ADJ **Imitation** things are not genuine but are made to look as if they are. 人造的；仿造的 [ADJ n] ❑ *...a complete set of Dickens bound in imitation leather.* …用人造革装帧的一整套《狄更斯全集》。 4 N-COUNT If someone does an **imitation of** another person, they copy the way they speak or behave, sometimes in order to be funny. (有时是为逗乐而) 学样 ❑ *One boy did an imitation of a soldier with a loudspeaker.* 一个男孩拿着扬声器学着士兵的样子。

im·macu·late /ɪmækyʊlɪt/ 1 ADJ If you describe something as **immaculate**, you mean that it is extremely clean, tidy, or neat. 一尘不染的 ❑ *Her kitchen was kept immaculate.* 她的厨房保持得一尘不染。 ● **im·macu·late·ly** ADV 一尘不染地 ❑ *As always he was immaculately dressed.* 他和平常一样，穿得干干净净。 2 ADJ If you say that something is **immaculate**, you are emphasizing that it is perfect, without any mistakes or bad parts at all. 完美无缺的 [EMPHASIS] ❑ *The goalie's performance was immaculate.* 守门员的表现完美无缺。 ● **im·macu·late·ly** ADV 完美无缺地 [ADV with v] ❑ *The orchestra plays immaculately.* 管弦乐队演奏得完美极了。

im·ma·teri·al /ɪmətɪ̲əriəl/ ADJ If you say that something is **immaterial**, you mean that it is not important or not relevant. 无关紧要的 [v-link ADJ] ❑ *Whether we like him or not is immaterial.* 我们喜不喜欢他都不重要。

im·ma·ture /ɪmətʃʊ̲ər, -tʊ̲ər/ 1 ADJ Something or someone that is **immature** is not yet completely grown or fully developed. 未发育完全的；不成熟的 ❑ *She is emotionally immature.* 她在情感上不成熟。 2 ADJ If you describe someone as **immature**, you are being critical of them because they do not behave in a sensible or responsible way. 冒失的 [DISAPPROVAL] ❑ *She's just being childish and immature.* 她真是小孩子气，太冒失了。

Thesaurus *immature* 另参见：

ADJ. undeveloped, unripe; *(ant.)* mature 1
childish, foolish, juvenile; *(ant.)* mature 2

▲ **im·ma·tur·ity** /ɪmətʃʊ̲ərɪti, -tʊ̲ərɪti/ 1 N-UNCOUNT **Immaturity** is the state of being not yet completely grown or fully developed. 不成熟 [DISAPPROVAL] ❑ *Photographs of the boy showed his physical immaturity.* 该男孩的那些照片显示了他生理上的不成熟。 2 N-UNCOUNT **Immaturity** is a lack of the qualities and behavior that you would expect from a sensible adult. 幼稚 ❑ *I am disgusted by the immaturity and stupidity presented in this column.* 我对这个专栏的幼稚和愚蠢感到厌恶。

im·medi·ate ♦◇◇ /ɪmi̲diɪt/ 1 ADJ An **immediate** result, action, or reaction happens or is done without any delay. 立即的 ❑ *These tragic incidents have had an immediate effect.* 这些悲惨事件已经有了立杆见影的结果。 2 ADJ **Immediate** needs and concerns exist at the present time and must be dealt with quickly. 紧急的 ❑ *Relief agencies say the immediate problem is not a lack of food, but transportation.* 救援机构称当务之急不是食品匮乏，而是交通运输不足。 3 ADJ The **immediate** person or thing comes just before or just after another person or thing in a sequence. 紧接的 [ADJ n] ❑ *In the immediate aftermath of the riots, a mood of hope and reconciliation sprang up.* 暴乱之后紧接的是一股希望与和解情绪的产生。 4 ADJ You use **immediate** to describe an area or position that is next to or very near a particular place or person. 紧邻的 [ADJ n] ❑ *Only a handful had returned to work in the immediate vicinity.* 只有少数几个人回到附近地区工作。 5 ADJ Your **immediate** family are the members of your family who are most closely related to you, such as your parents, children, brothers, and sisters. 直系的 [ADJ n] ❑ *The presence of his immediate family is obviously having a calming effect on him.* 他直系亲属的到场显然对他产生了镇定的效果。

Word Partnership *immediate* 的常用搭配：

N. immediate **action**, immediate **plans**, immediate **reaction**, immediate **response**, immediate **results** 1
immediate **future** 3
immediate **surroundings** 4
immediate **family** 5

im·medi·ate·ly ♦♦◇ /ɪmi̲diɪtli/ 1 ADV If something happens **immediately**, it happens without any delay. 立即地 [ADV with v] ❑ *He immediately flung himself to the floor.* 他立即扑倒在地。 2 ADV If something is **immediately** obvious, it can be seen or understood without any delay. 即刻地 [ADV adj] ❑ *The cause of the accident was not immediately apparent.* 这次事故的起因并非即刻可明。 3 ADV **Immediately** is used to indicate that someone or something is closely and directly involved in a situation. 直接地 [ADV adj/-ed] ❑ *The man immediately responsible for this misery is the province's governor.* 对这次惨剧负直接责任的人是该省省长。 4 ADV **Immediately** is used to emphasize that something comes next, or is next to something else. 紧接地 [ADV prep/adj] ❑ *They wish to begin immediately after dinner.* 他们希望晚饭后紧接着开始。

Thesaurus *immediately* 另参见：

ADV. at once, now, right away; *(ant.)* later 1

im·mense /ɪmɛ̲ns/ ADJ If you describe something as **immense**, you mean that it is extremely large or great. 巨大的 ❑ *...an immense cloud of smoke.* …一大片烟云。

im·mense·ly /ɪmɛ̲nsli/ ADV You use **immensely** to emphasize the degree or extent of a quality, feeling, or process. 非常 [EMPHASIS] ❑ *I enjoyed this movie immensely.* 我非常喜欢这部电影。

★ **im·merse** /ɪmɜ̲rs/ (**immerses, immersing, immersed**) 1 V-T If you **immerse** yourself in something that you are doing, you become completely involved in it. 使专心于 ❑ *Their commitments do not permit them to immerse themselves in current affairs as fully as they might wish.* 他们的职责不允许他们如其所愿地埋头于时事。 ● **im·mersed** ADJ 专心的 [v-link ADJ "in" n] ❑ *He's really becoming immersed in his work.* 他真正地变得专注于自己的工作。 2 V-T If something **is immersed** in a liquid, someone puts it into the liquid so that it is completely covered. 使浸没 [usu passive] ❑ *The electrodes are immersed in liquid.* 电极被浸没在液体中。

Word Link *migr ≈ moving, changing : emigrant, immigrant, migrant*

im·mi·grant ♦◇◇ /ɪmɪgrənt/ (**immigrants**) N-COUNT An **immigrant** is a person who has come to live in a country from some other country. Compare **emigrant**. (外来) 移民 ❑ *...illegal immigrants.* …非法移民。

→ see **culture**

im·mi·gra·tion ♦◇◇ /ɪmɪgreɪʃən/ 1 N-UNCOUNT **Immigration** is the coming of people into a country in order to live and work there. 移居 ❑ *The government has decided to tighten its immigration policy.* 政府已决定收紧其移民政策。 **2** N-UNCOUNT **Immigration** or **immigration control** is the place at a port, airport, or international border where officials check the passports of people who wish to come into the country. 移民局的检查 ❑ *First, you have to go through immigration and customs.* 首先你必须通过移民局和海关的检查。

▲ **im·mi·nent** /ɪmɪnənt/ ADJ If you say that something is **imminent**, especially something unpleasant, you mean it is almost certain to happen very soon. (尤指不好的事情) 即将发生的 ❑ *There appeared no imminent danger.* 眼前似乎没有危险。

im·mo·bi·lis·er /ɪmoʊbɪlaɪzər/ [BRIT] → see **immobilizer**

im·mo·bi·liz·er /ɪmoʊbɪlaɪzər/ (**immobilizers**) N-COUNT An **immobilizer** is a device on a car that prevents it from starting unless a special key is used, so that no one can steal the car. (汽车的) 发动机防盗锁装置

in BRIT, also use **immobiliser**

im·mor·al /ɪmɔrəl/ ADJ If you describe someone or their behavior as **immoral**, you believe that their behavior is morally wrong. 不道德的 [DISAPPROVAL] ❑ *...those who think that birth control and abortion are immoral.* …那些认为节育和堕胎是不道德的人。

Word Link *mort ≈ death : immortal, mortician, mortuary*

▲ **im·mor·tal** /ɪmɔrtəl/ (**immortals**) **1** ADJ Someone or something that is **immortal** is famous and likely to be remembered for a long time. 不朽的 ❑ *...Wuthering Heights, Emily Bronte's immortal love story.* …《呼啸山庄》，埃米莉·勃朗特不朽的爱情小说。 ● N-COUNT An **immortal** is someone who will be remembered for a long time. 不朽人物 ❑ *...the players considered to be the immortals of the game.* …被认为是该运动项目不朽人物的运动员们。 ● **im·mor·tal·ity** /ɪmɔrtælɪti/ N-UNCOUNT 不朽 ❑ *Some people want to achieve immortality through their works.* 有些人想通过他们的作品万古流芳。 **2** ADJ Someone or something that is **immortal** will live or last forever and never die or be destroyed. 不死的 ❑ *The pharaohs, after all, were considered gods and therefore immortal.* 法老毕竟被当作神，因而长生不死。 ● N-COUNT An **immortal** is an immortal being. 神仙 ❑ *...porcelain figurines of the Chinese immortals.* …中国神仙的小瓷像。 ● **im·mor·tal·ity** N-UNCOUNT 永生 ❑ *The Greeks accepted belief in the immortality of the soul.* 希腊人接受灵魂不灭的信念。 **3** ADJ If you refer to someone's **immortal** words, you mean that what they said is well-known, and you are usually about to quote it. (语句) 著名的 [ADJ n] ❑ *Everyone knows Teddy Roosevelt's immortal words, "Speak softly and carry a big stick."* 大家都知道特迪·罗斯福的名言："说话温和，手持大棒。"

im·mor·tal·ise /ɪmɔːˈtəlaɪz/ [BRIT] → see **immortalize**

im·mor·tal·ize /ɪmɔrtəlaɪz/ (**immortalizes, immortalizing, immortalized**)

in BRIT, also use **immortalise**

V-T If someone or something **is immortalized** in a story, movie, or work of art, they appear in it, and will be remembered for it. 使不朽 [WRITTEN] ❑ *His original interior design is immortalized in at least seven movies and television shows.* 他独具创意的室内设计至少在7部电影及电视节目中得到了不朽之名。

im·mune ♦◇◇ /ɪmyun/ **1** ADJ If you are **immune to** a particular disease, you cannot be affected by it. 免疫的 [v-link ADJ] ❑ *About 93 percent of U.S. residents are immune to measles either because they were vaccinated or they had the disease as a child.* 大约93%的美国居民对麻疹是免疫的，他们要么因为接种过疫苗，要么就是小时候得过麻疹。 ● **im·mun·ity** /ɪmyunɪti/ N-UNCOUNT 免疫力 ❑ *Birds in outside cages develop immunity to airborne bacteria.* 养在户外笼子里的鸟对空气传播的病毒有免疫力。 **2** ADJ If you are **immune to** something that happens or is done, you are not affected by it. 不受影响的 [v-link ADJ] ❑ *Higher education is no longer immune to state budget cuts.* 高等教育不再受州预算削减的影响。 **3** ADJ Someone or something that is **immune from** a particular process or situation is able to escape it. 免除的 [v-link ADJ] ❑ *People with diplomatic passports are immune from criminal prosecution.* 持有外交护照者享有刑事起诉豁免权。 ● **im·mun·ity** N-UNCOUNT 免除 ❑ *The police are offering immunity to witnesses who help identify the murderers.* 警方对帮助他们指认杀人凶手的证人免予起诉。

Word Partnership *immune* 的常用搭配:

N.	immune **disorder**, immune **response** **1**
	immune **from attack**, immune **from prosecution** **3**

im·mune sys·tem (**immune systems**) N-COUNT Your **immune system** consists of all the organs and processes in your body that protect you from illness and infection. 免疫系统 ❑ *His immune system completely broke down and he became very ill.* 他的免疫系统彻底崩溃了，他已病入膏肓。

★ **im·mun·ise** /ɪmyənaɪz/ [BRIT] → see **immunize**

★ **im·mun·ize** /ɪmyənaɪz/ (**immunizes, immunizing, immunized**)

in BRIT, also use **immunise**

V-T If people or animals **are immunized**, they are made immune to a particular disease, often by being given an injection. (常指通过注射疫苗) 使免疫 [usu passive] ❑ *We should require that every student is immunized against hepatitis B.* 我们应该要求每一位学生都注射乙肝疫苗。 ❑ *The monkeys used in those experiments had previously been immunized with a vaccine made from killed infected cells.* 这些实验中所用的猴子事先都已接种了由死亡的被感染细胞制成的疫苗。 ● **im·mun·iza·tion** /ɪmyənɪzeɪʃən/ N-VAR (**immunizations**) 免疫 ❑ *...universal immunization against childhood diseases.* …为预防儿童疾病的普遍接种疫苗。

im·pact ♦♦◇ (**impacts, impacting, impacted**)

The noun is pronounced /ɪmpækt/. The verb is pronounced /ɪmpækt/ or /ɪmpækt/.

名词读作 /ɪmpækt/。动词读作 /ɪmpækt/或 /ɪmpækt/。

1 N-COUNT The **impact** that something has **on** a situation, process, or person is a sudden and powerful effect that it has on them. 影响 ❑ *They say they expect the meeting to have a marked impact on the future of the country.* 他们说期望这次会议对国家的未来产生显著的影响。 **2** N-VAR An **impact** is the action of one object hitting another, or the force with which one object hits another. 撞击；撞击力 ❑ *The plane is destroyed, a complete wreck: the pilot must have died on impact.* 飞机被毁，完全成了一堆残骸：飞行员一定在撞击中丧生了。 **3** V-T/V-I To **impact** a situation, process, or person means to affect them. 对…造成影响；产生影响 ❑ *Such schemes mean little unless they impact people.* 除非能对人们造成影响，否则这样的计划意义不大。 **4** V-T/V-I If one object **impacts on** another, it hits it with great force. 撞击 [FORMAL] ❑ *...the sharp tinkle of metal impacting on stone.* …金属撞击石头的刺耳叮当声。

→ see **crash**

Word Partnership *impact* 的常用搭配:

ADJ.	**historical** impact, **important** impact **1**
V.	**have an** impact, **make an** impact **1**
	die on impact **2**
PREP.	**on** impact **2**

★ **im·pair** /ɪmpɛər/ (**impairs, impairing, impaired**) V-T If something **impairs** something such as an ability or the way something works, it damages it or makes it worse. 损害 [FORMAL] ❑ *Consumption of alcohol impairs your ability to drive a car or operate machinery.* 饮酒会削弱你驾驶汽车或操纵机器的能力。 ● **im·paired** ADJ 受损的 ❑ *The blast left him with permanently impaired hearing.* 爆炸造成了他永久性听力损伤。

im·pair·ment /ɪmpɛərmənt/ (**impairments**) N-VAR If someone has an **impairment**, they have a condition that prevents their eyes, ears, limbs or brain from working properly. (身体机能的) 损伤 ❑ *He has a visual impairment in the right eye.* 他的右眼有视力损伤。

→ see **disability**

★ **im·part** /ɪmpɑrt/ (**imparts, imparting, imparted**) **1** V-T If you **impart** information **to** people, you tell it to them. 传授；告知 [FORMAL] ❑ *The ability to impart knowledge and command respect is the essential qualification for teachers.* 传授知识并博得尊敬的能力对老师们来说是基本的条件。 **2** V-T To **impart** a particular quality to something means to give it that quality. 给予 (特定品质) [FORMAL] ❑ *She managed to impart great elegance to the unpretentious dress she was wearing.* 她努力为自己朴素的衣着增添几分优雅。

im·par·tial /ɪmpɑrʃəl/ ADJ Someone who is **impartial** is not directly involved in a particular situation, and is therefore able to give a fair opinion or decision about it. 公正的 ❑ *Career counselors offer impartial advice, guidance and information to all pupils.* 就业指导员们向所有的学生提供无偏见的建议、指导和信息。 ● **im·par·tial·ity** /ɪmpɑrʃiælɪti/ N-UNCOUNT 公正 ❑ *...a justice system lacking* *impartiality by democratic standards.* …以民主标准而言缺乏公正性的司法体系。 ● **im·par·tial·ly** ADV 公正地 [ADV with v] ❑ *He has vowed to oversee the elections impartially.* 他已宣誓公正地监督选举。

im·passe /ɪmpæs/ N-SING If people are in a difficult position in which it is impossible to make any progress, you can refer to the situation as an **impasse**. 僵局 ❑ *The company says it has reached an impasse in negotiations with the union.* 该公司称与工会的谈判已陷入僵局。

im·pas·sioned /ɪmpæʃᵊnd/ ADJ An **impassioned** speech or piece of writing is one in which someone expresses their strong feelings about an issue in a forceful way. 激昂的 [WRITTEN] ❑ *He made an impassioned appeal for peace.* 他做了一个向往和平的激昂慷慨的呼吁。

im·pas·sive /ɪmpæsɪv/ ADJ If someone is **impassive** or their face is **impassive**, they are not showing any emotion. 无动于衷的；无表情的 [WRITTEN] ❑ *He searched Hill's impassive face for some indication that he understood.* 他在希尔没有表情的脸上搜寻着一些他理解的迹象。 ● **im·pas·sive·ly** ADV 无动于衷地；无表情地 [ADV with v] ❑ *The lawyer looked impassively at him and said nothing.* 那位律师面无表情地看着他，什么也没说。

im·pa·tient /ɪmpeɪʃᵊnt/ **1** ADJ If you are **impatient**, you are annoyed because you have to wait too long for something. 不耐烦的 [v-link ADJ] ❑ *Investors are growing impatient with promises of improved earnings.* 投资者们对提高收益的承诺越来越不耐烦了。 ● **im·pa·tient·ly** ADV 不耐烦地 [ADV with v] ❑ *People have been waiting impatiently for a chance to improve the situation.* 人们一直在不耐烦地等待着改善这一状况的机会。 ● **im·pa·tience** /ɪmpeɪʃᵊns/ N-UNCOUNT 不耐烦 ❑ *There is considerable impatience with the slow pace of political change.* （人们）对于政治改革的缓慢步伐相当难以忍耐。 **2** ADJ If you are **impatient**, you are easily irritated by things. 无耐心的 ❑ *Beware of being too impatient with others.* 注意不要对别人太没有耐心。 ● **im·pa·tient·ly** ADV 无耐心地 [ADV with v] ❑ *"Come on, David," Harry said impatiently.* "戴维，快点儿！" 哈里不耐烦地说。 ● **im·pa·tience** N-UNCOUNT 无耐心 ❑ *There was a hint of impatience in his tone.* 他的语气里带有一丝不耐烦。 **3** ADJ If you are **impatient to** do something or **impatient for** something to happen, you are eager to do it or for it to happen and do not want to wait. 焦急的 [v-link ADJ] ❑ *He didn't want to tell Mr. Morrisson why he was impatient to get home.* 他不想告诉莫里森先生他为什么要着急回家。 ● **im·pa·tience** N-UNCOUNT 焦急 ❑ *She showed impatience to continue the climb.* 她表现出要继续往上爬的急切。

im·pec·cable /ɪmpɛkəbᵊl/ ADJ If you describe something such as someone's behavior or appearance as **impeccable**, you are emphasizing that it is perfect and has no faults. 无可挑剔的 [EMPHASIS] ❑ *She had impeccable taste in clothes.* 她对服装有着无可挑剔的品味。 ● **im·pec·cably** /ɪmpɛkəbli/ ADV 无可挑剔地 ❑ *He was charming, considerate and impeccably mannered.* 他富有魅力，待人体贴，举止无可挑剔。

▲ **im·pede** /ɪmpid/ (**impedes, impeding, impeded**) V-T If you **impede** someone or something, you make their movement, development, or progress difficult. 阻碍 [FORMAL] ❑ *Debris and fallen rock are impeding the progress of the rescue workers.* 瓦砾和落下的岩石正阻碍着救援人员的进程。

im·pedi·ment /ɪmpɛdɪmənt/ (**impediments**) **1** N-COUNT Something that is an **impediment to** a person or thing makes their movement, development, or progress difficult. 妨碍；障碍物 [FORMAL] ❑ *He was satisfied that there was no legal impediment to the marriage.* 他对于这场婚姻没有法律上的障碍感到很满意。 **2** N-COUNT Someone who has a speech **impediment** has a disability that makes speaking difficult. （言语）障碍 ❑ *John's slight speech impediment made it difficult for his mother to understand him.* 约翰轻微的口吃使他母亲难以听懂他。

im·pend·ing /ɪmpɛndɪŋ/ ADJ An **impending** event is one that is going to happen very soon. 即将发生的 [ADJ n] [FORMAL] ❑ *On the morning of the expedition, I awoke with a feeling of impending disaster.* 远征出发的那天早上，我醒来就有一种大难临头的感觉。

im·pen·etrable /ɪmpɛnɪtrəbᵊl/ **1** ADJ If you describe something such as a barrier or a forest as **impenetrable**, you mean that it is impossible or very difficult to get through. (障碍或森林等) 难以穿越的 ❑ *...the Caucasus range, an almost impenetrable barrier between Europe and Asia.* …高加索山脉，欧亚之间一道几乎不可逾越的屏障。 **2** ADJ If you describe something such as a book or a theory as **impenetrable**, you are emphasizing that it is impossible or very difficult to understand. 不能理解的 [EMPHASIS] ❑ *His philosophical work is notoriously impenetrable.* 他的哲学著作是出了名地令人费解。

★ **im·pera·tive** /ɪmpɛrətɪv/ (**imperatives**) **1** ADJ If it is **imperative** that something be done, that thing is extremely important and must be done. 至关重要的 [FORMAL] ❑ *It was imperative that he act as naturally as possible.* 至关重要的是他要尽可能地自然行事。 **2** N-COUNT An **imperative** is something that is extremely important and must be done. 紧迫之事 [FORMAL] ❑ *The most important political imperative is to limit the number of U.S. casualties.* 政治上的当务之急是控制美国的伤亡人数。 **3** N-SING In grammar, a clause that is in **the imperative**, or in **the imperative** mood, contains the base form of a verb and usually has no subject. Examples are "Go away" and "Please be careful." Clauses of this kind are typically used to tell someone to do something. 祈使语气 **4** N-COUNT An **imperative** is a verb in the base form that is used, usually without a subject, in an imperative clause. 祈使语气动词

Word Partnership *imperative* 的常用搭配：

ADV.	**absolutely** imperative **1**
N.	imperative **need** **1**
ADJ.	**economic/political** imperative, **moral** imperative **2**

im·per·fect /ɪmpɜrfɪkt/ ADJ Something that is **imperfect** has faults and is not exactly as you would like it to be. 不完美的 [FORMAL] ❑ *We live in an imperfect world.* 我们活在一个不完美的世界里。

im·per·fec·tion /ɪmpərfɛkʃᵊn/ (**imperfections**) **1** N-VAR An **imperfection in** someone or something is a fault, weakness, or undesirable feature that they have. 缺点 **2** N-COUNT An **imperfection in** something is a small mark or damaged area that may spoil its appearance. 瑕疵 ❑ *Optical scanners ensure that imperfections in the cloth are located and removed.* 光电扫描器能确保找出并去除布料上的瑕疵。

im·perial /ɪmpɪəriəl/ **1** ADJ **Imperial** is used to refer to things or people that are or were connected with an empire. 帝国的 [ADJ n] ❑ *...the Imperial Palace in Tokyo.* …东京的皇宫。 **2** ADJ The **imperial** system of measurement uses inches, feet, yards and miles to measure length, ounces and pounds to measure weight, and pints, quarts and gallons to measure volume. (度量衡) 英制的 [ADJ n]

★ **im·peri·al·ism** /ɪmpɪəriəlɪzəm/ N-UNCOUNT **Imperialism** is a system in which a rich and powerful country controls other countries, or a desire for control over other countries. 帝国主义 ❑ *...nations or groups which have been victims of imperialism.* …沦为帝国主义牺牲品的国家或集团。

★ **im·peri·al·ist** /ɪmpɪəriəlɪst/ (**imperialists**) ADJ **Imperialist** means relating to or based on imperialism. 帝国主义的 ❑ *The developed nations have all benefited from their imperialist exploitation.* 发达国家都从他们帝国主义的剥削中获益。 ● N-COUNT An **imperialist** is someone who has imperialist views. 帝国主义者 ❑ *He claims that imperialists are trying to re-establish colonial rule in the country.* 他声称帝国主义者正试图在该国重建殖民统治。

im·per·son·al /ɪmpɜrsənᵊl/ **1** ADJ If you describe a place, organization, or activity as **impersonal**, you mean that it is not very friendly and makes you feel unimportant because it involves or is used by a large number of people. 无人情味的 [DISAPPROVAL] ❑ *Before then many children were cared for in large impersonal orphanages.* 在那以前，许多孩子在无人情味的大孤儿院里被照料。 **2** ADJ If you describe someone's behavior as **impersonal**, you mean that they do not show any emotion about the person they are dealing with. 不受个人感情影响的 ❑ *We must be as impersonal as a surgeon with his knife.* 我们必须像拿着手术刀的外科医生一样不受个人感情影响。 **3** ADJ An **impersonal** room or statistic does not give any information about the character of the person to whom it belongs or relates. 没有个人色彩的 ❑ *The rest of the room was neat and impersonal.* 房间的其余部分整洁干净，没有个人色彩。

im·per·son·ate /ɪmpɜrsəneɪt/ (**impersonates, impersonating, impersonated**) V-T If someone **impersonates** a person, they pretend to be that person, either to deceive people or to make people laugh. 假扮；模仿 ❑ *He was returned to prison in 1977 for impersonating a police officer.* 他1977年因假扮一名警官再次入狱。 ● **im·per·sona·tion** /ɪmpɜrsəneɪʃᵊn/ N-COUNT (**impersonations**) 假扮；模仿 ❑ *She excelled at impersonations of his teachers, which provided great amusement for him.* 她擅长模仿他的老师们，这带给他许多乐趣。

im·per·ti·nent /ɪmpɜrtᵊnənt/ ADJ If someone talks or behaves in a rather impolite and disrespectful way, you can say that they are being **impertinent**. 不礼貌的 ❑ *Would it be impertinent to ask where exactly you were?* 询问一下你确切在哪里是否是不礼貌的？

★ **im·pe·tus** /ɪmpɪtəs/ N-UNCOUNT Something that gives a process **impetus** or an **impetus** makes it happen or progress more quickly. 推动力；促进因素 [also "an" N, oft N "for" n] ❑ *The impetus for change came from lawyers.* 促进转变的动力来自于律师们。

imp·ish /ɪmpɪʃ/ ADJ If you describe someone or their behavior as **impish**, you mean that they are disrespectful or naughty in a playful way. 调皮的 ❑ *Garcia is well known for his impish sense of humor.* 加西亚调皮的幽默感众所周知。

im·plac·able /ɪmplækəbᵊl/ ADJ If you say that someone is **implacable**, you mean that they have very strong feelings of hostility or disapproval that nobody can change. (敌意) 无法改变的 ❑ *...the threat of invasion by a ruthless and implacable enemy.* …一个残酷死敌的入侵威胁。● **im·plac·ably** ADV 无法改变地 ❑ *...two implacably hostile groups.* …两个不共戴天的敌对集团。

▲ **im·plant** (implants, implanting, implanted)

The verb is pronounced /ɪmplænt/. The noun is pronounced /ɪmplænt/.

动词读作 /ɪmplænt/。名词读作 /ɪmplænt/。

1 V-T To **implant** something into a person's body means to put it there, usually by means of a medical operation. 将…移植入 ❑ *Two days later, they implanted the fertilized eggs back inside me.* 两天后他们把受精卵移植回我的体内。 **2** N-COUNT An **implant** is something that is implanted into a person's body. 植入物 ❑ *They felt a woman had a right to choose to have a breast implant.* 他们认为妇女有权利选择隆胸。 **3** V-I When an egg or embryo **implants in** the womb, it becomes established there and can then develop. (受精卵或胚胎) 着床 ❑ *Non-identical twins are the result of two fertilized eggs implanting in the uterus at the same time.* 非同卵双生胎是两个受精卵同时在子宫着床的结果。 **4** V-T If you **implant** an idea or attitude **in** people, you make it become accepted or believed. 灌输 ❑ *The diagram implanted a dangerous prejudice firmly in the minds of countless economics students.* 该图表在无数经济学学生的头脑中牢牢地灌输了一种危险的偏见。

im·ple·ment ♦◇◇ (implements, implementing, implemented)

The verb is pronounced /ɪmplɪmɛnt/ or /ɪmplɪmənt/. The noun is pronounced /ɪmplɪmənt/.

动词读作 /ɪmplɪmɛnt/或 /ɪmplɪmənt/。名词读作 /ɪmplɪmənt/。

1 V-T If you **implement** something such as a plan, you ensure that what has been planned is done. 实施；执行 ❑ *The government promised to implement a new system to control financial loan institutions.* 政府许诺要实施新的制度来控制金融贷款机构。

● **im·ple·men·ta·tion** /ɪmplɪmənteɪʃᵊn, -mɛn-/ N-UNCOUNT 实施；执行 ❑ *Very little has been achieved in the implementation of the peace agreement signed last January.* 去年1月份签署的和平协议的执行几乎没有什么进展。 **2** N-COUNT An **implement** is a tool or other piece of equipment. 器具 [FORMAL] ❑ *...writing implements.* …书写用具。

Thesaurus *implement* 另参见：
V. bring about, carry out, execute, fulfill **1**

▲ **im·pli·cate** /ɪmplɪkeɪt/ (implicates, implicating, implicated) V-T To **implicate** someone means to show or claim that they were involved in something wrong or criminal. 表明(某人)与(罪行)有牵连 ❑ *He was obliged to resign when one of his own aides was implicated in a financial scandal.* 他因一名助手涉入一起金融丑闻案而被迫辞职。

● **im·pli·ca·tion** N-UNCOUNT 牵连 ❑ *Implication in a murder finally brought him to the gallows.* 与一桩谋杀案的牵连最终把他送上了绞刑架。

im·pli·ca·tion ♦◇◇ /ɪmplɪkeɪʃᵊn/ (implications) **1** N-COUNT **The implications of** something are the things that are likely to happen as a result. 可能的结果 ❑ *The Attorney General was aware of the political implications of his decision to prosecute.* 总检察长知道自己起诉的决定可能引起的政治后果。 **2** N-COUNT **The implication** of a statement, event, or situation is what it implies or suggests is the case. 含意 ❑ *The implication was obvious: vote for us or it will be very embarrassing for you.* 含意很明显：投票给我们，否则你会很难堪。

● PHRASE If you say that something is the case **by implication**, you mean that a statement, event, or situation implies that it is the case. 言下之意；暗示地 ❑ *Now his authority and, by implication, that of the whole management team are under threat as never before.* 言下之意，现在他的权力以及整个管理团队的权威正面临空前的威胁。 **3** → see also **implicate**

Word Partnership *implication* 的常用搭配：
ADJ. **clear** implication, **important** implication, **obvious** implication **2**

im·plic·it /ɪmplɪsɪt/ **1** ADJ Something that is **implicit** is expressed in an indirect way. 含蓄的 ❑ *...an implicit warning to the Moroccans not to continue or repeat the military actions they began a week ago.* …叫摩洛哥人不要继续或重复一周前开始的军事行动的含蓄警告。

● **im·plic·it·ly** ADV 含蓄地 [ADV with v] ❑ *The jury implicitly criticized the government by their verdict.* 陪审团通过他们的裁决含蓄地批评了政府。 **2** ADJ If a quality or element is **implicit in** something, it is involved in it or is shown by it. 内含的 [v-link ADJ "in" n] [FORMAL] ❑ *Trust is implicit in the system.* 信任是这种体制里内含的。 **3** ADJ If you say that someone has an **implicit** belief or faith in something, you mean that they have complete faith in it and no doubts at all. 绝对的 (信任) ❑ *He had implicit faith in the noble intentions of the Emperor.* 他对皇帝的崇高旨意笃信不疑。● **im·plic·it·ly** ADV 绝对地 [ADV after v] ❑ *I trust him implicitly.* 我绝对信任他。

im·plore /ɪmplɔr/ (implores, imploring, implored) V-T If you **implore** someone **to** do something, you ask them to do it in a forceful, emotional way. 恳求 ❑ *We will implore both parties to stay at the negotiating table.* 我们将恳求双方留在谈判桌上。

im·ply ♦◇◇ /ɪmplaɪ/ (implies, implying, implied) **1** V-T If you **imply that** something is the case, you say something that indicates that it is the case in an indirect way. 暗指 ❑ *"Are you implying that I have something to do with those attacks?" she asked coldly.* "你在暗指我和那些袭击有关吗？" 她冷冷地问道。 **2** V-T If an event or situation **implies** that something is the case, it makes you think that it is the case. 意味着 ❑ *Exports in June rose 1.5%, implying that the economy was stronger than many investors had realized.* 6月份的出口额增加了1.5%，这意味着经济比许多投资者所了解的要强劲。

Do not confuse **imply** and **infer**. If you **imply** that something is the case, you suggest that it is the case without actually saying so. ❑ *Rose's lawyer implied that he had married her for her money.* If you **infer** that something is the case, you decide that it must be the case because of what you know, but without actually being told. ❑ *From this simple statement I could infer a lot about his wife.* Note that some English speakers use **infer** with the same meaning as **imply**, but this is considered incorrect by careful speakers.

Thesaurus *imply* 另参见：
V. hint, insinuate, point to, suggest **1** **2**

Word Partnership *imply* 的常用搭配：
V. **not mean to** imply **1**
seem to imply **2**
ADV. **not necessarily** imply **1** **2**

im·po·lite /ɪmpəlaɪt/ ADJ If you say that someone is **impolite**, you mean that they are rather rude and do not have good manners. 不礼貌的 ❑ *The Count acknowledged the two newcomers as briefly as was possible without being impolite.* 伯爵尽可能简短而又不失礼节地向两位新来者打招呼。

Thesaurus *impolite* 另参见：
ADJ. ill-mannered, rude, ungracious; (*ant.*) courteous, polite

Word Link *port ≈ carrying : export, import, portable*

im·port ♦♦◇ (imports, importing, imported)

The verb is pronounced /ɪmpɔrt/ or /ɪmpɔrt/. The noun is pronounced /ɪmpɔrt/.

动词读作 /ɪmpɔrt/或 /ɪmpɔrt/。名词读作 /ɪmpɔrt/。

1 V-T/V-I To **import** products or raw materials means to buy them from another country for use in your own country. 进口 ❑ *Rich countries benefited from importing Indonesia's timber.* 富国从进口印度尼西亚木材中获利。 ❑ *To import from Russia, a Ukrainian firm needs Russian roubles.* 要从俄罗斯进口，乌克兰公司需要俄罗斯卢布。

● N-UNCOUNT **Import** is also a noun. 进口 [also N in pl] ❑ *Germany, however, insists on restrictions on the import of Polish coal.* 然而德国坚持对波兰煤炭的进口限制。● **im·por·ta·tion** /ɪmpɔrteɪʃᵊn/ N-UNCOUNT

进口 ❑ *...restrictions concerning the importation of birds.* …关于鸟类进口的种种限制。 **2** N-COUNT **Imports** are products or raw materials bought from another country for use in your own country. 进口商品 ❑ *...cheap imports from other countries.* …来自其他国家的廉价进口商品。 **3** N-UNCOUNT The **import** of something is its importance. 重要性 [FORMAL] ❑ *Such arguments are of little import.* 这种争论几乎不具重要性。 **4** V-T If you **import** files or information into one type of software from another type, you open them in a format that can be used in the new software. 导入 [COMPUTING] ❑ *Users can import files made in other packages.* 用户能够导入其他程序包里的文件。

im·por·tance ♦◇◇ /ɪmpɔrtᵊns/ **1** N-UNCOUNT The **importance** of something is its quality of being significant, valued, or necessary in a particular situation. 重要 ❑ *China has been stressing the importance of its ties with third world countries.* 中国一贯强调与第三世界国家联系的重要。 **2** N-UNCOUNT **Importance** means having influence, power, or status. 名望 ❑ *Obviously a man of his importance is going to be missed.* 显然，他这么一位重要人士将会被缅怀。

Word Partnership *importance* 的常用搭配：
ADJ. **critical** importance, **enormous** importance, **growing/increasing** importance, **utmost** importance **1**
V. **place less/more** importance **on** *something*, **recognize the** importance, **understand the** importance **1**
N. **self-**importance, **sense of** importance **2**

im·por·tant ♦♦♦ /ɪmpɔrtᵊnt/ **1** ADJ Something that is **important** is very significant, is highly valued, or is necessary. 重要的 ❑ *The most important thing in my life was my career.* 我生活中最重要的部分是我的事业。 ❑ *It's important to answer her questions as honestly as you can.* 重要的是你要尽可能如实地回答她的问题。 ● **im·por·tant·ly** ADV 重要地 ❑ *I was hungry, and, more importantly, my children were hungry.* 我饿了，更重要的是，我的孩子们饿了。 **2** ADJ Someone who is **important** has influence or power within a society or a particular group. 有势力的 ❑ *...an important figure in the media world.* …一位传媒界有势力的人物。

You do not use **important** to say that an amount or quantity is very large. Instead, you use words such as **large**, **considerable**, or **substantial**. ❑ *...a large sum of money. ...a man with considerable influence... The armed forces face substantial cuts.*

Thesaurus *important* 另参见：
ADJ. critical, essential, principal, significant; (*ant.*) unimportant **1**
distinguished, high-ranking **2**

im·port·er /ɪmpɔrtər/ (**importers**) N-COUNT An **importer** is a country, company, or person that buys goods from another country for use in their own country. 进口国；进口商 ❑ *Japan is the biggest importer of U.S. beef.* 日本是美国牛肉的最大进口国。

im·pose ♦♦◇ /ɪmpoʊz/ (**imposes, imposing, imposed**) **1** V-T If you **impose** something **on** people, you use your authority to force them to accept it. 强制实行 ❑ *Fines are imposed on retailers who sell tobacco to minors.* 向未成年人销售烟草制品的零售商要被强制罚款。 ❑ *A third of companies reviewing pay since last August have imposed a pay freeze of up to a year.* 自去年8月以来，在审检工资发放的公司中，有三分之一已经强制实行工资冻结长达1年。 ● **im·po·si·tion** ▲ /ɪmpəzɪʃᵊn/ N-UNCOUNT 强制实行 ❑ *...the imposition of sanctions against Pakistan.* …对巴基斯坦制裁的强制实行。 **2** V-T If you **impose** your opinions or beliefs **on** other people, you try and make people accept them as a rule or as a model to copy. 把（观点、信仰等）强加于 ❑ *Parents should beware of imposing their own tastes on their children.* 父母应该提防把自己的兴趣强加给孩子。 **3** V-T If something **imposes** strain, pressure, or suffering **on** someone, it causes them to experience it. 使承受（令人不快之事物） ❑ *The filming imposed an additional strain on her.* 影片拍摄使她承受了额外的压力。 **4** V-I If someone **imposes on** you, they unreasonably expect you to do something for them which you do not want to do. 不合理地要求 ❑ *I was afraid you'd feel we were imposing on you.* 我担心你会觉得我们在不合理地要求你。 ● **im·po·si·tion** N-COUNT 不合理的要求 ❑ *I know this is an imposition. But please hear me out.* 我知道这是个不合理的要求，但请听我把话说完。 **5** V-T If someone **imposes themselves on** you, they force you to accept their company although you may not want to. 使强迫接受 ❑ *I didn't want to impose myself on my married friends.* 我不想硬要我的已婚朋友们接受我。

Word Partnership *impose* 的常用搭配：
N. impose **a fine**, impose **limits**, impose **order**, impose **a penalty**, impose **restrictions**, impose **sanctions**, impose **a tax** **1**

im·pos·ing /ɪmpoʊzɪŋ/ ADJ If you describe someone or something as **imposing**, you mean that they have an impressive appearance or manner. 仪态使人印象深刻的 ❑ *He was an imposing man.* 他是个仪表堂堂的男子汉。

Word Link *im ≈ not : imbalance, immature, impossible*

im·pos·sible ♦♦◇ /ɪmpɒsɪbᵊl/ **1** ADJ Something that is **impossible** cannot be done or cannot happen. 不可能的 ❑ *It was impossible for anyone to get in because no one knew the password.* 任何人都不可能进得去，因为没人知道口令。 ❑ *He thinks the tax is impossible to administer.* 他认为治税是不可能的。 ● N-SING **The impossible** is something that is impossible. 不可能的事 ❑ *They were expected to do the impossible.* 他们被要求去做不可能的事。 ● **im·pos·sibly** ADV 不可能地 [ADV adj] ❑ *Mathematical physics is an almost impossibly difficult subject.* 数学物理学是一门难得难以想像的学科。 ● **im·pos·sibil·ity** /ɪmpɒsɪbɪlɪti/ N-VAR (**impossibilities**) 不可能性 ❑ *...the impossibility of knowing absolute truth.* …了解绝对真理的不可能性。 **2** ADJ An **impossible** situation or an **impossible** position is one that is very difficult to deal with. 极难应付的 [ADJ n] ❑ *I think he was in an impossible position.* 我想他当时处于一个极难应付的境地。 **3** ADJ If you describe someone as **impossible**, you are annoyed that their bad behavior or strong views make them difficult to deal with. 难以忍受的 [DISAPPROVAL] ❑ *The woman is impossible, thought Francesca.* 弗朗西丝卡暗自思忖，这个女人真让人受不了。

Thesaurus *impossible* 另参见：
ADJ. unreasonable, unworkable; (*ant.*) possible **2**
absurd, difficult, trying **3**

Word Partnership *impossible* 的常用搭配：
V. impossible **to describe**, impossible **to find**, impossible **to ignore**, impossible **to prove**, impossible **to say/tell**, **seem** impossible **1**
ADV. **absolutely** impossible, **almost** impossible, **nearly** impossible **1** **2**
N. **an** impossible **task** **1** **2**

im·po·tence /ɪmpətəns/ **1** N-UNCOUNT **Impotence** is a lack of power to influence people or events. 无能为力 ❑ *...a sense of impotence in the face of deplorable events.* …面对悲惨事件时无能为力的感觉。 **2** N-UNCOUNT **Impotence** is a man's sexual problem in which his penis fails to get hard or stay hard. 阳痿 ❑ *Impotence affects 10 million men in the U.S. alone.* 仅在美国，就有1千万男子患有阳痿。

Word Link *potent ≈ ability, power : impotent, potent, potential*

im·po·tent /ɪmpətənt/ **1** ADJ If someone feels **impotent**, they feel that they have no power to influence people or events. 无力的 ❑ *The aggression of a bully leaves people feeling hurt, angry and impotent.* 恶棍的挑衅让人感到受伤、愤怒而又无力。 **2** ADJ If a man is **impotent**, he is unable to have sex normally, because his penis fails to get hard or stay hard. 阳痿的 ❑ *At the age of 40, 1.9 percent of men are impotent.* 1.9%的男人在40岁时阳痿。

im·pound /ɪmpaʊnd/ (**impounds, impounding, impounded**) V-T If something **is impounded** by police officers, customs officers, or other officials, they officially take possession of it because a law or rule has been broken. 扣押 ❑ *The ship was impounded under the terms of the UN trade embargo.* 那条船因联合国贸易禁令而遭扣押。

▲ **im·pov·er·ish** /ɪmpɒvərɪʃ/ (**impoverishes, impoverishing, impoverished**) **1** V-T Something that **impoverishes** a person or a country makes them poor. 使贫困 ❑ *We need to reduce the burden of taxes that impoverish the economy.* 我们需要减少使经济贫困的租税负担。 ● **im·pov·er·ished** ADJ 贫困的 ❑ *The goal is to lure businesses into impoverished areas by offering them tax breaks.* 目的是通过提供减税优惠把企业吸引到贫困地区。 **2** V-T A person or thing that **impoverishes** something makes it worse in quality. 使质量下降 ❑ *A top dressing of fertilizer should be added to improve growth as mint impoverishes the soil quickly.* 应施顶肥以促进生长，因为薄荷会使土壤迅速变得贫瘠。

★ **im·prac·ti·cal** /ɪmpræktɪkᵊl/ **1** ADJ If you describe an object, idea, or course of action as **impractical**, you mean that it is

i

not sensible or realistic, and does not work well in practice. 不切实际的 ❑ *Once there were regularly scheduled airlines, it became impractical to make a business trip by ocean liner.* 一旦有了定期的飞机航班，乘坐远洋客轮出差就变得不切实际了。 2 ADJ If you describe someone as **impractical**, you mean that they do not have the abilities or skills to do practical work such as making, repairing, or organizing things. 缺乏实际能力的 ❑ *Geniuses are supposed to be difficult, eccentric and hopelessly impractical.* 天才被认为很难相处、行为怪僻且毫无实际能力。

im·press ♦◇◇ /ɪmprɛs/ (**impresses, impressing, impressed**) 1 V-T/V-I If something **impresses** you, you feel great admiration for it. 使钦佩 ❑ *What impressed him most was their speed.* 最令他钦佩的是他们的速度。 ● **im·pressed** ADJ 使钦佩的 [v-link ADJ] ❑ *I was very impressed by one young man at my lectures.* 来上我课的一个年轻人让我很钦佩。 2 V-T If you **impress** something **on** someone, you make them understand its importance or degree. 使明白（重要性或程度） ❑ *I had always impressed upon the children that if they worked hard they would succeed in life.* 我一直在使孩子们明白，生活中如果他们努力就会成功。 ❑ *I've impressed upon them the need for more professionalism.* 我已让他们明白更高专业性的需要。 3 V-T If something **impresses itself on** your mind, you notice and remember it. 使铭记在心 ❑ *But this change has not yet impressed itself on the minds of the public.* 但是这种变化仍没有使公众对此铭记在心。 4 V-T If someone or something **impresses** you **as** a particular thing, usually a good one, they give you the impression of being that thing. 使留下印象 ❑ *It didn't impress me as a good place to live.* 那地方没有给我留下适合居住的印象。

im·pres·sion ♦◇◇ /ɪmprɛʃn/ (**impressions**) 1 N-COUNT Your **impression** of a person or thing is what you think they are like, usually after having seen or heard them. Your **impression** of a situation is what you think is going on. 印象；认识 ❑ *What were your first impressions of college?* 你对大学的第一印象是什么？ ❑ *My impression is that they are totally out of control.* 我的认识是他们完全失去了控制。 2 N-SING If someone gives you a particular **impression**, they cause you to believe that something is the case, often when it is not. （常指错误的）印象 ❑ *I don't want to give the impression that I'm running away from the charges.* 我并不想给人留下一种我在逃避指控的印象。 3 N-COUNT An **impression** is an amusing imitation of someone's behavior or way of talking, usually someone well-known. 滑稽模仿 ❑ *I did an impression of daddy saying "do as I say, not as I do."* 我滑稽地模范爸爸说话，"照我说的做，别照我做的做。" 4 N-COUNT An **impression** of an object is a mark or outline that it has left after being pressed hard onto a surface. 压印 ❑ *...the world's oldest fossil impressions of plant life.* …世界上最古老的植物化石印痕。 5 PHRASE If someone or something **makes an impression**, they have a strong effect on people or a situation. 造成强烈影响 ❑ *The type of aid coming in makes no immediate impression on the horrific death rates.* 这种即将到来的救助不会对恐怖的死亡率造成立杆见影的强烈影响。 6 PHRASE If you are **under the impression that** something is the case, you believe that it is the case, usually when it is not actually the case. （通常是错误地）认为 ❑ *He had apparently been under the impression that a military coup was in progress.* 他显然一直认为一场军事政变正在进行。

Word Partnership *impression* 的常用搭配：

ADJ. **favorable** impression, **first** impression, **good** impression 1
strong impression 1 2
the wrong impression 2
V. **have an** impression 1 2
get the impression **that, give the** impression **that** 2

im·pres·sive ♦◇◇ /ɪmprɛsɪv/ ADJ Something that is **impressive** impresses you, for example, because it is great in size or degree, or is done with a lot of skill. 令人敬佩的；给人印象深刻的 ❑ *It is an impressive achievement.* 这是一项令人敬佩的成就。 ● **im·pres·sive·ly** ADV 令人敬佩地；给人印象深刻地 ❑ *...an impressively bright and energetic woman called Cathie Gould.* …一个聪明过人而又精力充沛、名叫凯茜·古尔德的女人。

im·print (**imprints, imprinting, imprinted**)

The noun is pronounced /ɪmprɪnt/. The verb is pronounced /ɪmprɪnt/.

名词读作 /ɪmprɪnt/，动词读作 /ɪmprɪnt/。

1 N-COUNT If something leaves an **imprint** on a place or on your mind, it has a strong and lasting effect on it. 深远影响 ❑ *World War I left an indelible imprint on the twentieth-century world.* 第一次世界大战给20世纪的世界留下了深远的影响。 2 V-T When something **is imprinted on** your memory, it is firmly fixed in your memory so that you will not forget it. 铭刻 ❑ *As I arrived, the shimmering skyline of domes and minarets was imprinted on my memory.* 当我到达时，穹顶和尖塔形成的泛着微光的空中轮廓线铭刻在我的记忆中。 3 N-COUNT An **imprint** is a mark or outline made by the pressure of one object on another. 印痕 ❑ *She could see the imprint of her fingers on his pale face.* 她可以看到自己的手指在他苍白的脸上留下的印痕。 4 V-T If a surface **is imprinted with** a mark or design, that mark or design is printed on the surface or pressed into it. 压印 [usu passive] ❑ *The company carries a variety of binders that can be imprinted with your message or logo.* 该公司经营各种可以印上客户所需信息或标识的活页夹。

★ **im·pris·on** /ɪmprɪzn/ (**imprisons, imprisoning, imprisoned**) V-T If someone **is imprisoned**, they are locked up or kept somewhere, usually in prison, as a punishment for a crime or for political opposition. 监禁 ❑ *He was imprisoned for 18 months on charges of theft.* 他因盗窃指控而被监禁了18个月。

im·pris·on·ment /ɪmprɪznmənt/ N-UNCOUNT **Imprisonment** is the state of being imprisoned. 监禁 ❑ *She was sentenced to seven years' imprisonment.* 她被判处7年监禁。

im·prob·able /ɪmprɒbəbl/ 1 ADJ Something that is **improbable** is unlikely to be true or to happen. 不大可能的 ❑ *Ordered arrangements of large groups of atoms and molecules are highly improbable.* 大的原子群和分子群的有序排列是极不可能的。 ● **im·prob·abil·ity** /ɪmprɒbəbɪlɪti/ N-VAR (**improbabilities**) 不可能性 ❑ *...the improbability of such an outcome.* …这种结果的不可能性。 2 ADJ If you describe something as **improbable**, you mean it is strange, unusual, or ridiculous. 奇异的；荒谬的 ❑ *On the face of it, their marriage seems an improbable alliance.* 从表面上看，他们的婚姻似乎是一个荒谬的结合。 ● **im·prob·ably** ADV 奇异地；荒谬地 ❑ *The sea is an improbably pale turquoise.* 那片海是不寻常的淡绿松石色。

★ **im·promp·tu** /ɪmprɒmptu/ ADJ An **impromptu** action is one that you do without planning or organizing it in advance. 无事先准备的 ❑ *This afternoon the Palestinians held an impromptu press conference.* 今天下午巴勒斯坦人召开了一场临时记者招待会。

im·prop·er /ɪmprɒpər/ 1 ADJ **Improper** activities are illegal or dishonest. 不合法的；不诚实的 [FORMAL] ❑ *25 officers were investigated following allegations of improper conduct.* 25名警官被指控行为不当而受到调查。 ● **im·prop·er·ly** ADV 不合法地；不诚实地 [ADV with v] ❑ *I acted neither fraudulently nor improperly.* 我既未欺诈又未犯法。 2 ADJ **Improper** conditions or methods of treatment are not suitable or good enough for a particular purpose. 不适当的 [ADJ n] [FORMAL] ❑ *The improper use of medicine could lead to severe adverse reactions.* 用药不当会引起严重的不良反应。 ● **im·prop·er·ly** ADV 不适当地 [ADV with v] ❑ *The study confirmed many reports that doctors were improperly trained.* 该研究证实了许多关于医生培训不足的报导。 3 ADJ If you describe someone's behavior as **improper**, you mean it is rude or shocking or in some way socially unacceptable. 不得体的 ❑ *Such improper behavior and language from a young lady left me momentarily incapable of speech.* 如此不得体的言行竟来自一位年轻女士，这让我惊愕得一时无语。 ● **im·prop·er·ly** ADV 不得体地 [ADV with v] ❑ *The company turns down people who show up at job interviews improperly dressed.* 该公司拒绝那些在面试时衣着不得体的人。

im·prove ♦♦◇ /ɪmpruv/ (**improves, improving, improved**) 1 V-T/V-I If something **improves** or if you **improve** it, it gets better. 改进 ❑ *Within a month, both the texture and condition of your hair should improve.* 不出一个月，你头发的质地和状况应该都会改善。 2 V-T/V-I If a skill you have **improves** or you **improve** a skill, you get better at it. 提高 ❑ *Their French has improved enormously.* 他们的法语水平提高了很多。 3 V-I If you **improve** after an illness or an injury, your health gets better or you get stronger. 康复 ❑ *He had improved so much the doctor had cut his dosage.* 他康复了很多，医生减少了他的用药量。 4 V-I If you **improve on** a previous achievement of your own or of someone else, you achieve a better standard or result. 提高 ❑ *We need to improve on our performance against Nabisco.* 我们需根据纳贝斯克公司标准来提高我们的业绩。

Word Partnership *improve* 的常用搭配：

ADV. **significantly** improve, improve **slightly** 1 – 4
V. **continue to** improve, **expected to** improve 1 – 4
need to improve, **try to** improve 1 2 4

im·prove·ment ♦◇◇ /ɪmpruːvmənt/ (**improvements**) 1 N-VAR If there is an **improvement in** something, it becomes better. If you make **improvements to** something, you make it better. 改进 ❑ *...the dramatic improvements in organ transplantation in recent years.* …近几年器官移植上令人瞩目的改进。 2 N-COUNT If you say that something is **an improvement on** a previous thing or situation, you mean that it is better than that thing. 改进的事物；胜过他人的人 ❑ *The new governor is an improvement on his predecessor.* 新任总督胜过他的前任。

Thesaurus *improvement* 另参见：
N. advancement, betterment, progress; *(ant.)* deterioration 1 2

Word Partnership *improvement* 的常用搭配：
N. **home** improvement, **self-improvement**, **signs of** improvement 1
ADJ. **gradual** improvement 1
big improvement, **dramatic** improvement, **marked** improvement, **significant** improvement, **slight** improvement 1 2

im·pro·vise /ɪmprəvaɪz/ (**improvises, improvising, improvised**) 1 V-T/V-I If you **improvise**, you make or do something using whatever you have or without having planned it in advance. 临时拼凑 ❑ *You need a wok with a steaming rack for this; if you don't have one, improvise.* 你需要一口带有蒸笼的锅，如果没有就临时凑合一下。 ❑ *The vet had improvised a harness.* 兽医临时凑成了一套马具。 2 V-T/V-I When performers **improvise**, they invent music or words as they play, sing, or speak. 即兴演奏；即席演说 ❑ *I asked her what the piece was and she said, "Oh, I'm just improvising."* 我问她那首乐曲是什么，她说，"哦，我只是即兴演奏。" ❑ *Uncle Richard read a chapter from the Bible and improvised a prayer.* 理查德叔叔吟诵了《圣经》中的一个章节，然后即兴说了一段祷告。

im·pu·dent /ɪmpyədənt/ ADJ If you describe someone as **impudent**, you mean they are rude or disrespectful, or do something they have no right to do. 放肆的；不恭的 [FORMAL, DISAPPROVAL] ❑ *Some of them spoke pleasantly and were well behaved, while others were impudent and insulting.* 他们当中的一些人谈吐不俗、举止得体，而另一些人则行为不恭、傲慢无礼。

Word Link *puls ≈ driving, pushing : compulsion, expulsion, impulse*

im·pulse /ɪmpʌls/ (**impulses**) 1 N-VAR An **impulse** is a sudden desire to do something. 冲动 ❑ *Unable to resist the impulse, he glanced at the sea again.* 他抑制不住冲动，又看了一眼大海。 2 N-COUNT An **impulse** is a short electrical signal that is sent along a wire or nerve or through the air, usually as one of a series. 脉冲 ❑ *It works by sending a series of electrical impulses which are picked up by hi-tech sensors.* 它通过传输由高技术传感器收集的电脉冲而起作用。 3 ADJ An **impulse** buy or **impulse** purchase is something that you decide to buy when you see it, although you had not planned to buy it. 一时心血来潮的 [ADJ n] ❑ *The curtains were an impulse buy.* 这窗帘是一时心血来潮买下的。 4 PHRASE If you do something **on impulse**, you suddenly decide to do it, without planning it. 凭一时冲动 ❑ *Sean's a fast thinker, and he acts on impulse.* 肖恩是个思维敏捷、凭一时冲动行事的人。

Word Partnership *impulse* 的常用搭配：
ADJ. **first** impulse, **strong** impulse, **sudden** impulse 1
V. **control an** impulse, **resist an** impulse 1
act on impulse 4

im·pul·sive /ɪmpʌlsɪv/ ADJ If you describe someone as **impulsive**, you mean that they do things suddenly without thinking about them carefully first. 易冲动的 ❑ *He is too impulsive to be a responsible mayor.* 他太容易冲动，无法成为一个可靠的市长。
● **im·pul·sive·ly** ADV 冲动地 [ADV with v] ❑ *He studied her face for a moment, then said impulsively: "Let's get married."* 他仔细端详了一会她的脸，然后冲动地说："我们结婚吧。"

im·pure /ɪmpyʊər/ ADJ A substance that is **impure** is not of good quality because it has other substances mixed with it. 不纯的 ❑ *...diarrhea, dysentery and other diseases borne by impure water.* …不洁的水所引起的腹泻、痢疾和其他疾病。

im·pu·rity /ɪmpyʊərɪti/ (**impurities**) N-COUNT **Impurities** are substances that are present in small quantities in another substance and make it dirty or of an unacceptable quality. 杂质 ❑ *The air in the factory is filtered to remove impurities.* 工厂里的空气经过过滤去除杂质。

in
1 POSITION OR MOVEMENT
2 INCLUSION OR INVOLVEMENT
3 TIME AND NUMBERS
4 STATES AND QUALITIES
5 OTHER USES AND PHRASES

1 in ♦♦♦

The preposition is pronounced /ɪn/. The adverb is pronounced /ɪn/.

介词读作 /ɪn/。副词读作 /ɪn/。

In addition to the uses shown below, **in** is used after some verbs, nouns, and adjectives in order to introduce extra information. **In** is also used with verbs of movement such as "walk" and "push," and in phrasal verbs such as "give in" and "dig in."

1 PREP Someone or something that is **in** something else is enclosed by it or surrounded by it. If you put something **in** a container, you move it so that it is enclosed by the container. 在…里面 ❑ *He was in his car.* 他在他的汽车里。 2 PREP If something happens **in** a place, it happens there. 在…地方 ❑ *...spending a few days in a hotel.* …在宾馆住了几天。 3 ADV If you **are in**, you are present at your home or place of work. 在家；在工作地方 ["be" ADV] ❑ *My roommate was in at the time.* 我的室友那时在房间里。 4 ADV When someone comes **in**, they enter a room or building. 进入 [ADV after v] ❑ *She looked up anxiously as he came in.* 他进来时，她焦虑地抬头看了一眼。 5 ADV If a train, boat, or plane has come **in** or is **in**, it has arrived at a station, port, or airport. (火车、轮船或飞机)抵达 ❑ *...every plane coming in from Melbourne.* …从墨尔本飞来的每一架飞机。 6 ADV When the sea or tide comes **in**, the sea moves toward the shore rather than away from it. (潮水)在上涨 ❑ *She thought of the tide rushing in, covering the wet sand.* 她想到潮水涨上来，淹没了潮湿的沙滩。 7 PREP Something that is **in** a window, especially a store window, is just behind the window so that you can see it from outside. 在(橱窗)里面 ❑ *There was a camera for sale in the window.* 橱窗里有一架待售的相机。 8 PREP When you see something **in** a mirror, the mirror shows an image of it. 在(镜子)里 ❑ *I couldn't bear to see my reflection in the mirror.* 我受不了看镜子里我的模样。 9 PREP If you are dressed **in** a piece of clothing, you are wearing it. 穿着 ❑ *He was a big man, dressed in a suit and tie.* 他是个高大的男人，穿着西服，打着领带。 10 PREP Something that is covered or wrapped **in** something else has that thing over or around its surface. 在…表面 ❑ *His legs were covered in mud.* 他的双腿沾满了泥。 11 PREP If there is something such as a crack or hole **in** something, there is a crack or hole on its surface. (裂缝、洞)在…表面 ❑ *There was a deep crack in the ceiling above him.* 他头顶上方的天花板上有一个很深的裂缝。

2 in ♦♦♦ /ɪn/ 1 PREP If something is **in** a book, movie, play, or picture, you can read it or see it there. 在(书、电影、戏剧或图片等)之中 ❑ *Don't stick too precisely to what it says in the book.* 不要过分拘泥于书本上的内容。 2 PREP If you are **in** something such as a play or a race, you are one of the people taking part. 参加(演出、比赛等) ❑ *Alfredo offered her a part in the play he was directing.* 阿尔弗雷德让她在他导演的一出戏里担任一个角色。 3 PREP Something that is **in** a group or collection is a member of it or part of it. 在(团体、收藏品)之中 ❑ *The New England team is the worst in the league.* 新英格兰队是联盟中最差劲的球队。 4 PREP You use **in** to specify a general subject or field of activity. 在(学科、活动领域)方面 ❑ *...those working in the defense industry.* …在国防工业工作的那些人。

3 in ♦♦♦ /ɪn/ 1 PREP If something happens **in** a particular year, month, or other period of time, it happens during that time. 在…期间 ❑ *...that early spring day in April 1949.* …1949年4月早春的那一天。 ❑ *Export orders improved in the last month.* 出口订单在上个月增加了。 2 PREP If something happens **in** a particular situation, it happens while that situation is going on. 在(某情形)中 ❑ *His father had been badly wounded in the last war.* 他父亲在上次战争中受了重伤。 3 PREP If you do something **in** a particular period of time, that is how long it takes you to do it. 在(一段时间) 内 [PREP amount] ❑ *He walked two hundred and sixty miles in eight days.* 他在8天里走了260英里。 4 PREP If something will happen **in** a particular length of time, it will happen after that length of time. 在(一段时间) 之后 [PREP amount] ❑ *I'll have some breakfast ready in a few minutes.* 我将在几分钟后把早餐准备好。 5 PREP You use **in** to indicate roughly how old someone is. For example, if someone is **in** their fifties, they are between 50 and 59 years old. 在…岁数 [PREP poss pl-num] ❑ *...young people in their twenties.* …二十几岁的年轻人。 6 PREP You use **in** to indicate roughly how many people or things do something. 以…的数量 ❑ *...men who came there in droves.* …成群结队到那儿的人们。 7 PREP You use **in** to express a ratio, proportion, or probability. 从…之中 (表示比率、概率、可能性) [num PREP num] ❑ *One in three fourth-graders couldn't find their state on a map of the U.S.* 4年级学生中有1/3在美国地图上找不到自己所在的州。

❹ **in** ◆◆◆ /ɪn/ 1 PREP If something or someone is **in** a particular state or situation, that is their present state or situation. 处于(状态、地位) 中 [v-link PREP n] ❑ *The economy was in trouble.* 经济陷于困境。 ❑ *Dave was in a hurry to get back to work.* 戴夫急于回去工作。 2 PREP You use **in** to indicate the feeling or desire that someone has when they do something, or which causes them to do it. 处于(某种情感等) 之中 ❑ *Simpson looked at them in surprise.* 辛普森惊异地看着他们。 3 PREP If a particular quality or ability is **in** you, you naturally have it. 在(本性) 中 ❑ *Violence is not in his nature.* 粗暴不在他的本性中。 4 PREP You use **in** when saying that someone or something has a particular quality. 具有(某种品质) ❑ *He had all the qualities I was looking for in a partner.* 他有我所要找的合伙人具有的所有品质。 5 PREP You use **in** to indicate how someone is expressing something. (表达) 以…方式 ❑ *Information is given to the patient verbally and in writing.* 病人以口头和书面方式被告知信息。 6 PREP You use **in** in expressions such as **in a row** or **in a ball** to describe the arrangement or shape of something. (排列) 以…方式 ❑ *The cards need to be laid out in two rows.* 这些卡片需摆放成两排。 7 PREP If something is **in** a particular color, it has that color. 带(某种颜色) ❑ *...white flowers edged in pink.* …带粉边的白花。 8 PREP You use **in** to specify which feature or aspect of something you are talking about. 在…方面 ❑ *The movie is nearly two hours in length.* 这部电影长达近两个小时。 ❑ *There is a big difference in the amounts that banks charge.* 各个银行在收费数额上有很大差异。

❺ **in** (ins)

> Pronounced /ɪn/ for meanings 1 and 3 to 8, and /ɪn/ for meaning 2.

> 义项1以及3至8读作 /ɪn/, 义项2读作 /ɪn/。

1 ADJ If you say that something is **in**, or is the **in** thing, you mean it is fashionable or popular. 时髦的; 流行的 [INFORMAL] ❑ *A few years ago jogging was the in thing.* 几年前慢跑是流行的事。 2 PREP You use **in** with a present participle to indicate that when you do something, something else happens as a result. (与现在分词连用) 在…过程中 [PREP -ing] ❑ *He shifted uncomfortably on his feet. In doing so he knocked over Steven's briefcase.* 他不自在地变换着站姿, 在这过程中他碰倒了史蒂文的公文包。 3 PHRASE If you say that someone **is in for** a shock or a surprise, you mean that they are going to experience it. 将要经历 ❑ *You might be in for a shock at the sheer hard work involved.* 对所涉及的这些绝对艰难的工作, 你也许会大吃一惊。 4 PHRASE If someone **has it in for** you, they dislike you and try to cause problems for you. 对某人怀有仇恨 [INFORMAL] ❑ *The other kids had it in for me.* 别的孩子对我怀有仇恨。 5 PHRASE If you are **in on** something, you are involved in it or know about it. 参与; 了解 ❑ *I don't know. I wasn't in on that particular argument.* 我不知道。我没有参与那场争论。 6 PHRASE If you **are in with** a person or group, they like you and accept you, and are likely to help you. 与…处得很好 [INFORMAL] 7 PHRASE You use **in that** to introduce an explanation of a statement you have just made. 因为 ❑ *I'm lucky in that I've got four sisters.* 我很幸运, 因为我有4个姐妹。 8 PHRASE The **ins and outs** of a situation are all the detailed points and facts about it. 详情 ❑ *...the ins and outs of high finance.* …巨额融资的来龙去脉。

> **Word Link** *in ≈ not : inability, inaccurate, inadequate*

in·abil·ity /ɪnəbɪlɪti/ N-UNCOUNT If you refer to someone's **inability to** do something, you are referring to the fact that they are unable to do it. 无力 ❑ *Her inability to concentrate could cause an accident.* 她无法集中注意力可能会导致意外。

in·ac·ces·sible /ɪnæksɛsɪbᵊl/ 1 ADJ An **inaccessible** place is very difficult or impossible to reach. 难到达的; 不可及的 ❑ *...people living in remote and inaccessible parts of China.* …居住在中国偏远难及地区的人们。 2 ADJ If something is **inaccessible**, you are unable to see, use, or buy it. 看不到的; 不可使用的; 买不到的 ❑ *Ninety-five percent of its magnificent collection will remain inaccessible to the public.* 其中95%的精美绝伦的收藏品公众仍将看不到。 3 ADJ Someone or something that is **inaccessible** is difficult or impossible to understand or appreciate. 难懂的; 无法理解的 [DISAPPROVAL] ❑ *...language that is inaccessible to working people.* …劳动人民无法理解的语言。

in·ac·cu·ra·cy /ɪnækyərəsi/ (**inaccuracies**) N-VAR The **inaccuracy** of a statement or measurement is the fact that it is not accurate or correct. 不准确 ❑ *He was disturbed by the inaccuracy of the answers.* 他为答案的不准确性而感到不安。

in·ac·cu·rate /ɪnækyərɪt/ ADJ If a statement or measurement is **inaccurate**, it is not accurate or correct. 不准确的 ❑ *The book is both inaccurate and exaggerated.* 那本书既不准确又夸大事实。

in·ac·tion /ɪnækʃᵊn/ N-UNCOUNT If you refer to someone's **inaction**, you disapprove of the fact that they are doing nothing. 不作为 [DISAPPROVAL] ❑ *He is bitter about the inaction of the other political parties.* 他为其他政党的不作为感到愤愤不平。

in·ac·tive /ɪnæktɪv/ ADJ Someone or something that is **inactive** is not doing anything or is not working. 不作为的; 不起作用的 ❑ *He certainly was not politically inactive.* 他在政治上当然不是无所作为。 ● **in·ac·tiv·ity** /ɪnæktɪvɪti/ N-UNCOUNT 不作为; 不起作用 ❑ *The players have comparatively long periods of inactivity.* 这些运动员有相当长的一段时间会无所事事。

in·ad·equa·cy /ɪnædɪkwəsi/ (**inadequacies**) 1 N-VAR The **inadequacy** of something is the fact that there is not enough of it, or that it is not good enough. 不足; 不够好 ❑ *...the inadequacy of the water supply.* …水供应不足。 2 N-UNCOUNT If someone has feelings of **inadequacy**, they feel that they do not have the qualities and abilities necessary to do something or to cope with life in general. 能力不足 ❑ *...his deep-seated sense of inadequacy.* …他根深蒂固的能力不足之感。

in·ad·equate /ɪnædɪkwɪt/ 1 ADJ If something is **inadequate**, there is not enough of it or it is not good enough. 不足的; 不够好的 ❑ *Supplies of food and medicines are inadequate.* 食品和药物的供应是不足的。 ● **in·ad·equate·ly** ADV 不足地; 不够好地 [ADV with v] ❑ *The projects were inadequately funded.* 这些项目资助不足。 2 ADJ If someone feels **inadequate**, they feel that they do not have the qualities and abilities necessary to do something or to cope with life in general. 能力不足的 ❑ *I still feel inadequate, useless and mixed up.* 我仍旧感到能力不足, 毫无用处, 混淆不清。

Word Partnership *inadequate* 的常用搭配:

N.	inadequate **funding**, inadequate **supply**, inadequate **training** 1
ADV.	**woefully** inadequate 1 2
V.	**feel** inadequate 2

in·ad·vert·ent /ɪnədvɜrtᵊnt/ ADJ An **inadvertent** action is one that you do without realizing what you are doing. 无意的 ❑ *The government has said it was an inadvertent error.* 政府声称那是无意的过失。 ● **in·ad·vert·ent·ly** ADV 无意中 [ADV with v] ❑ *You may have inadvertently pressed the wrong button.* 你也许无意中按错了按钮。

in·ap·pro·pri·ate /ɪnəproʊpriɪt/ 1 ADJ Something that is **inappropriate** is not useful or suitable for a particular situation or purpose. 没有用的; 不适合的 ❑ *There is no suggestion that clients have been sold inappropriate policies.* 没有迹象表明向客户出售过不适当的保险单。 2 ADJ If you say that someone's speech or behavior in a particular situation is **inappropriate**, you are criticizing it because you think it is not suitable for that situation. (言行举止) 不恰当的 [DISAPPROVAL] ❑ *I feel the remark was inappropriate for such a serious issue.* 我觉得对如此严肃的问题来说, 这评论是不恰当的。

in·as·much as /ɪnəzmʌtʃ æz/ PHRASE You use **inasmuch as** to introduce a statement that explains something you have just said, and adds to it. 因为 [FORMAL] ❑ *We were doubly lucky inasmuch as my friend was living on the island and spoke Greek fluently.* 我们真是幸运极了, 因为我的朋友住在岛上而且希腊语说得很流利。

▲ **in·augu·ral** /ɪnɔgyərəl/ ADJ An **inaugural** meeting or speech is the first meeting of a new organization or the first speech by the new leader of an organization or a country. 揭幕的；就职的 [ADJ n] ❑ *In his inaugural address, the president appealed for national unity.* 总统在他的就职演说中呼吁全国团结。

★ **in·augu·rate** /ɪnɔgyʊreɪt/ (**inaugurates, inaugurating, inaugurated**) 1 V-T When a new leader **is inaugurated**, they are formally given their new position at an official ceremony. 使正式就任 [usu passive] ❑ *The new president will be inaugurated on January 20th.* 新总统将在1月20日正式就任。 ● **in·augu·ra·tion** /ɪnɔgyʊreɪʃᵊn/ N-VAR (**inaugurations**) 就职典礼 ❑ *...the inauguration of the new Governor.* …新任州长的就职典礼。 2 V-T When a new building or institution **is inaugurated**, it is declared open in a formal ceremony. 为…举行开幕式；为…举行落成典礼 [usu passive] ❑ *A Mafia Museum was inaugurated in Corleone.* 一座黑手党博物馆在科莱奥内举行落成典礼。 ● **in·augu·ra·tion** N-COUNT 就职典礼；落成典礼 ❑ *They later attended the inauguration of the University.* 他们后来参加了该大学的成立典礼。 3 V-T If you **inaugurate** a new system or service, you start it. 开创 [FORMAL] ❑ *Pan Am inaugurated the first scheduled international flight.* 泛美航空开创了第一个定期的国际航班。

★ **in·born** /ɪnbɔrn/ ADJ **Inborn** qualities are natural ones that you are born with. 天生的 [usu ADJ n] ❑ *He had an inborn talent for languages.* 他有天生的语言才能。

in·box /ɪnbɒks/ (**inboxes**) also **in-box** 1 N-COUNT An **inbox** is a shallow container used in offices to put letters and documents in before they are dealt with. (办公室里存放待处理的来函及文件等的) 收文篮 [AM]

in BRIT, use **in-tray**

2 N-COUNT On a computer, your **inbox** is the part of your mailbox which stores e-mails that have arrived for you. (电子邮箱中的) 收件箱 ❑ *I returned home and checked my inbox.* 我回家后查看了收件箱。

inc. In written advertisements, **inc.** is an abbreviation for **including**. 包含 ❑ *The hotel offers a two-night stay for $210 per person, inc. breakfast and dinner.* 宾馆提供两晚的住宿，每人$210，含早晚餐。

Inc. ♦◇◇ **Inc.** is an abbreviation for **Incorporated** when it is used after a company's name. 股份有限公司 [AM, BUSINESS] ❑ *...Sun Microsystems Inc.* …太阳微系统股份有限公司。

in·ca·pable /ɪnkeɪpəbᵊl/ 1 ADJ Someone who is **incapable of** doing something is unable to do it. 无能力的 [v-link ADJ "of" -ing/n] ❑ *She seemed incapable of making the decision.* 她似乎无法做出这个决定。 2 ADJ An **incapable** person is weak or stupid. 软弱的；愚蠢的 ❑ *He lost his job for allegedly being incapable.* 据称他是因软弱愚蠢而丢掉了工作。

in·car·cer·ate /ɪnkɑrsəreɪt/ (**incarcerates, incarcerating, incarcerated**) V-T If people **are incarcerated**, they are kept in a prison or other place. 监禁 [FORMAL] ❑ *They were incarcerated for the duration of the war.* 他们在战争期间被监禁。 ● **in·car·cera·tion** N-UNCOUNT 监禁 ❑ *...her mother's incarceration in a psychiatric hospital.* …她母亲在精神病院里的监禁。

Word Link *carn ≈ flesh : carnage, incarnation, reincarnation*

in·car·na·tion /ɪnkɑrneɪʃᵊn/ (**incarnations**) 1 N-COUNT If you say that someone is the **incarnation of** a particular quality, you mean that they represent that quality or are typical of it in an extreme form. 典型 ❑ *The regime was the very incarnation of evil.* 该政权正是邪恶的典型。 2 N-COUNT An **incarnation** is an instance of being alive on earth in a particular form. Some religions believe that people have several incarnations in different forms. 化身 ❑ *She began recalling a series of previous incarnations.* 她开始回想起种种前世化身。

in·cen·di·ary /ɪnsɛndieri/ (**incendiaries**) 1 ADJ **Incendiary** weapons or attacks are ones that cause large fires. 能引起燃烧的 [ADJ n] ❑ *Five incendiary devices were found in her house.* 5个燃烧装置在她家里被发现了。 2 N-COUNT An **incendiary** is an incendiary bomb. 燃烧弹 ❑ *A shower of incendiaries struck the Opera House.* 阵雨般的燃烧弹击中了歌剧院。 3 ADJ If you accuse someone of saying or doing **incendiary** things, you mean that what they say or do is likely to make people react very angrily. 煽动性的 [DISAPPROVAL] ❑ *... incendiary slogans such as "Hospital closures kill more than car bombs."* …诸如"关闭医院比汽车炸弹杀人更多"之类的煽动性标语。

▲ **in·cense** (**incenses, incensing, incensed**)

The noun is pronounced /ɪnsɛns/. The verb is pronounced /ɪnsɛns/.

名词读作 /ɪnsɛns/，动词读作 /ɪnsɛns/。

1 N-UNCOUNT **Incense** is a substance that is burned for its sweet smell, often as part of a religious ceremony. (常指祭祀时用的) 香 2 V-T If you say that something **incenses** you, you mean that it makes you extremely angry. 使大怒 ❑ *This proposal will incense conservation campaigners.* 这项提议将激怒自然保护的倡导者。 ● **in·censed** ADJ 被激怒的 ❑ *Mom was incensed at his lack of compassion.* 妈妈对他缺乏同情心非常愤怒。

★ **in·cen·tive** /ɪnsɛntɪv/ (**incentives**) N-VAR If something is an **incentive to** do something, it encourages you to do it. 鼓励 ❑ *There is little or no incentive to adopt such measures.* 几乎或根本没有鼓励来采取这样的措施。

▲ **in·ces·sant** /ɪnsɛsᵊnt/ ADJ An **incessant** process or activity is one that continues without stopping. 持续不断的 ❑ *Incessant rain made conditions almost intolerable.* 阴雨绵绵让情况几乎无法忍受。 ● **in·ces·sant·ly** ADV 持续不断地 ❑ *Dee talked incessantly about herself.* 迪伊滔滔不绝地谈论她自己。

in·cest /ɪnsɛst/ N-UNCOUNT **Incest** is the crime of two members of the same family having sexual intercourse, such as a father and daughter, or a brother and sister. 乱伦 ❑ *Oedipus, according to ancient Greek legend, killed his father and committed incest with his mother.* 据古希腊传说，俄狄浦斯杀死了父亲并与母亲乱伦。

inch ♦◇◇ /ɪntʃ/ (**inches, inching, inched**) 1 N-COUNT An **inch** is an imperial unit of length, approximately equal to 2.54 centimeters. There are twelve inches in a foot. 英寸 ❑ *...18 inches below the surface.* …表层以下18英寸。 2 V-T/V-I To **inch** somewhere means to move there very slowly and carefully, or to make something do this. 使缓慢地移动；缓慢地移动 ❑ *...a climber inching up a vertical wall of rock.* …一个沿着陡峭的岩壁缓慢往上攀登的人。 ❑ *He inched the van forward.* 他驾着厢式货车缓缓前行。 3 PHRASE If you say that someone looks **every inch** a certain type of person, you are emphasizing that they look exactly like that kind of person. 在各方面 [EMPHASIS] ❑ *He looks every inch the businessman, with his gray suit, dark-blue shirt and blue tie.* 他身穿灰色西服、深蓝色衬衫，打着蓝色领带，在各方面俨然一副生意人的模样。

in·ci·dence /ɪnsɪdəns/ (**incidences**) N-VAR **The incidence of** something, especially something bad such as a disease, is the frequency with which it occurs, or the occasions when it occurs. (尤指坏事的) 发生率 ❑ *The incidence of breast cancer increases with age.* 乳腺癌的发病率随着年龄的增长而上升。

in·ci·dent ♦♦◇ /ɪnsɪdənt/ (**incidents**) N-COUNT An **incident** is something that happens, often something that is unpleasant. 事件；事故 [also "without" N] [FORMAL] ❑ *These incidents were the latest in a series of disputes between the two nations.* 这些事件是两国一系列争端中最近的几起。

Thesaurus *incident* 另参见：

N. episode, event, fact, happening, occasion, occurrence

in·ci·den·tal /ɪnsɪdɛntᵊl/ ADJ If one thing is **incidental** to another, it is less important than the other thing or is not a major part of it. 附带的；次要的 ❑ *The playing of music proved to be incidental to the main business of the evening.* 音乐演奏结果只是当晚主要活动的陪衬。

★ **in·ci·den·tal·ly** /ɪnsɪdɛntli/ 1 ADV You use **incidentally** to introduce a point that is not directly relevant to what you are saying, often a question or extra information that you have just thought of. 顺便说及地 [ADV with cl] ❑ *"I didn't ask you to come. Incidentally, why have you come?"* "我没有叫你来。顺便问一下，你为什么来呢？" 2 ADV If something occurs only **incidentally**, it is less important than another thing or is not a major part of it. 附带地 [ADV with v] ❑ *The letter mentioned my great-aunt and uncle only incidentally.* 信里只是附带地提到我的叔祖母和叔祖父。

in·cin·er·ate /ɪnsɪnəreɪt/ (**incinerates, incinerating, incinerated**) V-T When authorities **incinerate** garbage or waste material, they burn it completely in a special container. 把…烧成灰烬 ❑ *They were incinerating hazardous waste without a license.* 他们没有许可就把危险废弃物烧成灰烬。 ● **in·cin·era·tion** /ɪnsɪnəreɪʃᵊn/ N-UNCOUNT 焚烧 ❑ *South Pacific nations have protested against the incineration of the weapons.* 南太平洋各国抗议武器的焚烧。

→ see **dump**

in·cin·era·tor /ɪnsɪnəreɪtər/ (**incinerators**) N-COUNT An **incinerator** is a special large container for burning garbage at a very high temperature. 垃圾焚化炉

i

in·ci·sive /ɪnsaɪsɪv/ ADJ You use **incisive** to describe a person, their thoughts, or their speech when you approve of their ability to think and express their ideas clearly, briefly, and forcefully. 敏锐的；深刻的 [APPROVAL] ❑ *He is a very shrewd operator with an incisive mind.* 他是一位非常精明的经营者，有着敏锐的头脑。

▲**in·cite** /ɪnsaɪt/ (**incites, inciting, incited**) V-T If someone **incites** people **to** behave in a violent or illegal way, they encourage people to behave in that way, usually by making them excited or angry. 煽动 ❑ *He incited his fellow citizens to take their revenge.* 他煽动他的同胞们进行报复。❑ *The party agreed not to incite its supporters to violence.* 该党同意不再鼓动其支持者使用暴力。

in·cite·ment /ɪnsaɪtmənt/ (**incitements**) N-VAR If someone is accused of **incitement to** violent or illegal behavior, they are accused of encouraging people to behave in that way. 煽动 ❑ *Insults can lead to the incitement of violence.* 侮辱会导致对暴力的煽动。

incl. 1 In written advertisements, **incl.** is an abbreviation for **including** or **included**. 包含 ❑ *...blood pressure monitor with batteries, case and 1-year warranty incl.* …包括电池、套子以及一年保用期在内的血压监控器。2 In written advertisements, **incl.** is an abbreviation for **inclusive**. 首末项包括在内的 ❑ *Open July 19th - September 6th, Sun. to Thurs. incl.* 7月19日至9月6日，从周日（含）到周四（含）开放。

in·cli·na·tion /ɪnklɪneɪʃ^{ə}n/ (**inclinations**) N-VAR An **inclination** is a feeling that makes you want to act in a particular way. 意向 ❑ *He had neither the time nor the inclination to think of other things.* 他既没时间也无意考虑其他事宜。❑ *She showed no inclination to go.* 她没有表现出要走的意向。

I

Word Link *clin ≈ leaning : decline, incline, recline*

in·cline (**inclines, inclining, inclined**)

The noun is pronounced /ɪnklaɪn/. The verb is pronounced /ɪnklaɪn/.

名词读作 /ɪnklaɪn/，动词读作 /ɪnklaɪn/。

1 N-COUNT An **incline** is land that slopes at an angle. 斜坡 [FORMAL] ❑ *He came to a halt at the edge of a steep incline.* 他停步在一个陡坡的边上。2 V-T If you **incline** your head, you bend your neck so that your head is leaning forward. 点（头）[WRITTEN] ❑ *Jack inclined his head very slightly.* 杰克微微点了点头。3 V-T If you **incline to** think or act in a particular way, or if something **inclines** you **to** it, you are likely to think or act in that way. 使倾向于；使有意于 [FORMAL] ❑ *...the factors that incline us toward particular beliefs.* …使我们倾向于特定信念的种种因素。❑ *Those who fail incline to blame the world for their failure.* 那些失败者往往会将其失败归咎于社会。

in·clined /ɪnklaɪnd/ 1 ADJ If you are **inclined to** behave in a particular way, you often behave in that way, or you want to do so. 常表现出…的；有…意向的 [v-link ADJ] ❑ *Nobody felt inclined to argue with Smith.* 没人想和史密斯争论。❑ *He was inclined to self-pity.* 他总是自哀自怜。2 ADJ If you say that you are **inclined to** have a particular opinion, you mean that you hold this opinion but you are not expressing it strongly. 倾向于…的 [v-link ADJ to-inf] [VAGUENESS] ❑ *I am inclined to agree with Alan.* 我倾向于同意艾伦的看法。3 ADJ Someone who is mathematically **inclined** or artistically **inclined**, for example, has a natural talent for mathematics or art. 有…天赋的 [adv ADJ] ❑ *...the needs of academically-inclined pupils.* …有学术天赋的学生的需求。

Word Partnership *inclined* 的常用搭配：

V. inclined **to agree**, inclined **to believe** *someone/something*, inclined **to think** 2

in·clude ◆◆◆ /ɪnklud/ (**includes, including, included**) 1 V-T If one thing **includes** another thing, it has the other thing as one of its parts. 包括 ❑ *The trip has been extended to include a few other events.* 行程已经延长以包括其他几项活动。2 V-T If someone or something **is included in** a large group, system, or area, they become a part of it or are considered a part of it. 把…列为一部分 ❑ *I had worked hard to be included in a project like this.* 为了成为这样的项目的一分子，我过去一直埋头苦干。

in·clud·ed ◆◆◇ /ɪnkludɪd/ ADJ You use **included** to emphasize that a person or thing is part of the group of people or things that you are talking about. 包括在内的 [n ADJ, v-link ADJ] [EMPHASIS] ❑ *Many runners, myself included, are loners.* 包括我本人在内的许多赛跑选手都是喜欢独来独往的人。

in·clud·ing ◆◆◆ /ɪnkludɪŋ/ PREP You use **including** to introduce examples of people or things that are part of the group of people or things that you are talking about. 包括 [PREP n/-ing] ❑ *Thousands were killed, including many women and children.* 数千人被杀，包括许多妇女和儿童。

in·clu·sion /ɪnkluʒ^{ə}n/ (**inclusions**) N-VAR **Inclusion** is the act of making a person or thing part of a group or collection. 包括 ❑ *...a confident performance that justified his inclusion in the team.* …证明他入选该队是明智之举的自信表现。

★**in·clu·sive** /ɪnklusɪv/ 1 ADJ If you describe a group or organization as **inclusive**, you mean that it allows all kinds of people to belong to it, rather than just one kind of person. 兼收并蓄的 ❑ *The academy is far more inclusive now than it used to be.* 该学院如今比过去更为兼收并蓄。2 ADJ After stating the first and last item in a set of things, you can add **inclusive** to make it clear that the items stated are included in the set. 首末项包括在内的 [n ADJ] ❑ *You are also invited to join us on our prayer days (this year, June 6 to June 14 inclusive).* 你也受邀加入我们的祷告日（今年从6月6日（含）至6月14日（含））。3 ADJ If a price is **inclusive**, it includes all the charges connected with the goods or services offered. If a price is **inclusive of** shipping and handling, it includes the charge for this. 包括一切费用在内的 ❑ *...all prices are inclusive of delivery.* …所有价格包括运费。● ADV **Inclusive** is also an adverb. 包括一切费用在内地 [amount ADV] ❑ *The outpatient program costs $105 per day, all inclusive.* 门诊病人方案收费每人每天105美元，一切费用包括在内。

in·co·her·ent /ɪnkoʊhɪərənt/ 1 ADJ If someone is **incoherent**, they are talking in a confused and unclear way. 语无伦次的 ❑ *The man was almost incoherent with fear.* 那人几乎害怕得说话语无伦次。2 ADJ If you say that something such as a policy is **incoherent**, you are criticizing it because the different parts of it do not fit together properly. 不连贯的 [DISAPPROVAL]

in·come ◆◆◇ /ɪnkʌm/ (**incomes**) N-VAR A person's or organization's **income** is the money that they earn or receive, as opposed to the money that they have to spend or pay out. 收入 [BUSINESS] ❑ *Many families on low incomes will be unable to afford to buy their own home.* 许多低收入家庭根本无力购买房子。

Word Partnership *income* 的常用搭配：

ADJ. **average** income, **fixed** income, **large/small** income, **a second** income, **steady** income, **taxable** income
V. **earn** *an* income, **supplement** *your* income
N. **loss of** income, **source of** income

in·come tax (**income taxes**) N-VAR **Income tax** is a part of your income that you have to pay regularly to the government. 所得税 [BUSINESS] ❑ *You pay income tax on all your earnings, not just your salary.* 你所有的收入都得交所得税，不仅仅是工资。

in·com·ing /ɪnkʌmɪŋ/ 1 ADJ An **incoming** message or phone call is one that you receive. （短信、邮件等）进来的 [ADJ n] ❑ *We keep a tape of incoming calls.* 我们保留打进电话的录音磁带。2 ADJ An **incoming** plane or passenger is one that is arriving at a place. （飞机、旅客等）正到达的 [ADJ n] ❑ *The airport was closed for incoming flights.* 机场为正到达的飞机而关闭。3 ADJ An **incoming** official or government is one that has just been appointed or elected. 新任的 [ADJ n] ❑ *...the problems confronting the incoming government.* …新一届政府面临的难题。

in·com·pa·rable /ɪnkɒmpərəb^{ə}l/ 1 ADJ If you describe someone or something as **incomparable**, you mean that they are extremely good or impressive. 非常好的；印象非常深刻的 ❑ *...the incomparable Tony Bennet singing "It had to be you."* …技艺精湛的托尼·本内特演唱的《非你莫属》。2 ADJ You use **incomparable** to emphasize that someone or something has a good quality to a great degree. 无以伦比的 [ADJ n] [FORMAL, EMPHASIS] ❑ *...an area of incomparable beauty.* …一处美景无以伦比的地区。

★**in·com·pat·ible** /ɪnkəmpætɪb^{ə}l/ 1 ADJ If one thing or person is **incompatible with** another, they are very different in important ways, and do not suit each other or agree with each other. 不相容的；不协调的 ❑ *They feel strongly that their religion is incompatible with the political system.* 他们强烈地感到他们的宗教信仰与政治体制格格不入。● **in·com·pat·ibil·ity** /ɪnkəmpætɪbɪlɪti/ N-UNCOUNT 不相容 ❑ *Incompatibility between the mother's and the baby's blood groups may cause jaundice.* 母亲和胎儿的血型不合有可能导致黄疸。2 ADJ If one type of computer or computer system is **incompatible with** another, they cannot use the same programs or be linked up. 不兼容的 ❑ *This made its mini-computers incompatible with its mainframes.* 这使得它的微型电脑与其主机不兼容。

★ **in·com·pe·tence** /ɪnkɒmpɪtəns/ N-UNCOUNT If you refer to someone's **incompetence**, you are criticizing them because they are unable to do their job or a task properly. 无能 [DISAPPROVAL] ❑ *The incompetence of government officials is appalling.* 政府官员的无能令人吃惊。

in·com·pe·tent /ɪnkɒmpɪtənt/ (**incompetents**) ADJ If you describe someone as **incompetent**, you are criticizing them because they are unable to do their job or a task properly. 无能的; 不称职的 [DISAPPROVAL] ❑ *He wants the power to fire incompetent employees.* 他希望有权解雇不称职的雇员。● N-COUNT An **incompetent** is someone who is incompetent. 无能的人; 不称职者 ❑ *The president turned furiously on his staff. "I'm surrounded by incompetents!"* 董事长愤怒地指责其职员, "我身边全是些没用的人!"

Word Partnership *incompetent* 的常用搭配:
ADJ. **corrupt and** incompetent, **lazy and** incompetent
N. incompetent **leadership**, incompetent **management**

in·com·plete /ɪnkəmplit/ ADJ Something that is **incomplete** is not yet finished, or does not have all the parts or details that it needs. 没完成的; 不完全的 ❑ *The clearing of garbage and drains is still incomplete.* 垃圾和污水的清理工作还没有完成。

in·com·pre·hen·sible /ɪnkɒmprɪhɛnsɪbᵊl/ ADJ Something that is **incomprehensible** is impossible to understand. 无法理解的 ❑ *He spent his time devising incomprehensible mathematics puzzles.* 他把时间花在设计难以破解的数学难题上。

★ **in·com·pre·hen·sive** /ɪnkɒmprɪhɛnsɪv/ ADJ Something that is **incomprehensive** is limited because it does not include everything that is needed. 涵盖不全面的 ❑ *The report is incomprehensive; it does not provide information on how the project will be financed.* 这篇报告不全面; 它没有提供有关该项目资金来源的信息。

in·con·ceiv·able /ɪnkənsivəbᵊl/ ADJ If you describe something as **inconceivable**, you think it is very unlikely to happen or be true. 不可思议的 ❑ *It was inconceivable to me that Toby could have been my attacker.* 托比竟会是袭击我的人, 这对我来说简直是匪夷所思。

in·con·clu·sive /ɪnkənklusɪv/ **1** ADJ If research or evidence is **inconclusive**, it has not proved anything. (研究或证据) 无定论的 ❑ *Research has so far proved inconclusive.* 迄今为止研究还没有任何定论。 **2** ADJ If a contest or conflict is **inconclusive**, it is not clear who has won or who is winning. (竞赛或冲突) 胜负不明的 ❑ *The past two elections were inconclusive.* 过去的两次选举都没有结果。

in·con·gru·ous /ɪnkɒŋgruəs/ ADJ Someone or something that is **incongruous** seems strange when considered together with other aspects of a situation. 不协调的 [FORMAL] ❑ *She was small and fragile and looked incongruous in an army uniform.* 她人瘦小, 穿上军装显得很不协调。● **in·con·gru·ous·ly** ADV 不协调地 ❑ *...a town of Western-style buildings perched incongruously in a high green valley.* …一个西式建筑风格的小镇突兀地坐落在高处的绿色山谷中。

in·con·sid·er·ate /ɪnkənsɪdərɪt/ ADJ If you accuse someone of being **inconsiderate**, you mean that they do not take enough care over how their words or actions will affect other people. 不体谅人的 [DISAPPROVAL] ❑ *It's a bit inconsiderate of her not to let you know when she expects to arrive.* 她不让你知道她什么时候会到, 这样做有些不体谅人。

★ **in·con·sist·en·cy** /ɪnkənsɪstənsi/ (**inconsistencies**) **1** N-UNCOUNT If you refer to someone's **inconsistency**, you are criticizing them for not behaving in the same way every time a similar situation occurs. (行为) 反复无常 [DISAPPROVAL] ❑ *His worst fault was his inconsistency.* 他的最大缺点就是反复无常。 **2** N-VAR If there are **inconsistencies** between two statements, one cannot be true if the other is true. 不一致 ❑ *We were asked to investigate the alleged inconsistencies in his evidence.* 我们被要求调查他证词中所称的前后矛盾之处。

in·con·sist·ent /ɪnkənsɪstənt/ **1** ADJ If you describe someone as **inconsistent**, you are criticizing them for not behaving in the same way every time a similar situation occurs. 反复无常的 [DISAPPROVAL] ❑ *You are inconsistent and unpredictable.* 你反复无常, 让人捉摸不透。 **2** ADJ Someone or something that is **inconsistent** does not stay the same, being sometimes good and sometimes bad. 不稳定的; 时好时坏的 ❑ *We had a terrific start to the season, but recently we've been inconsistent.* 我们在本赛季的开头极好, 但最近时好时坏。 **3** ADJ If two statements are **inconsistent**, one cannot possibly be true if the other is true. 不一致的 ❑ *The evidence given in court was inconsistent with what he had previously told them.* 他在法庭上的证词与他当初告诉他们的不一致。 **4** ADJ If something is **inconsistent with** a set of ideas or values, it does not fit in well with them or match them. 与…不相合的 [v-link ADJ "with" n] ❑ *This legislation is inconsistent with what they call Free Trade.* 这项法规与他们所称的自由贸易是相矛盾的。

in·con·ti·nence /ɪnkɒntɪnəns/ N-UNCOUNT **Incontinence** is the inability to control urine or feces from coming out of your body. (大小便的) 失禁 ❑ *Incontinence is not just a condition of old age.* 大小便失禁不仅仅是一种老年病。

in·con·ti·nent /ɪnkɒntɪnənt/ ADJ Someone who is **incontinent** is unable to control urine or feces from coming out of their body. (大小便) 失禁的 ❑ *His diseased bladder left him incontinent.* 他患病的膀胱使得他小便失禁。

in·con·ven·ience /ɪnkənvinyəns/ (**inconveniences, inconveniencing, inconvenienced**) **1** N-VAR If someone or something causes **inconvenience**, they cause problems or difficulties. 不方便 ❑ *We apologize for any inconvenience caused during the repairs.* 我们对在修理过程中所造成的任何不便表示歉意。 **2** V-T If someone **inconveniences** you, they cause problems or difficulties for you. 给…带来不便 ❑ *He promised to be quick so as not to inconvenience them any further.* 他答应快一些, 以免给他们带来更多不便。

in·con·ven·ient /ɪnkənvinyənt/ ADJ Something that is **inconvenient** causes problems or difficulties for someone. 不方便的 ❑ *Can you come at 10:30? I know it's inconvenient, but I have to see you.* 你能10:30来吗? 我知道这不方便, 但是我必须要见你。

Word Link *corp ≈ body : corporal, corpse, incorporate*

★ **in·cor·po·rate** /ɪnkɔrpəreɪt/ (**incorporates, incorporating, incorporated**) **1** V-T If one thing **incorporates** another thing, it includes the other thing. 包含 [FORMAL] ❑ *The new cars will incorporate a number of major improvements.* 这种新型汽车将包含许多重大的改进。 **2** V-T If someone or something **is incorporated into** a large group, system, or area, they become a part of it. 使并入 [FORMAL] ❑ *The agreement would allow the rebels to be incorporated into a new national police force.* 该协议将允许叛军并入一支新的国家警察部队。

In·cor·po·rated /ɪnkɔrpəreɪtɪd/ ADJ **Incorporated** is used after a company's name to show that it is a legally established company. (公司) 股份有限的 [n ADJ] [AM, BUSINESS] ❑ *...MCA Incorporated.* …MCA股份有限公司。

in·cor·rect /ɪnkərɛkt/ **1** ADJ Something that is **incorrect** is wrong and untrue. 不正确的; 不真实的 ❑ *He denied that his evidence about the telephone call was incorrect.* 他否认他关于电话的证词是不真实的。● **in·cor·rect·ly** ADV 不正确地 [ADV with v] ❑ *The magazine suggested, incorrectly, that he was planning to announce his retirement.* 该杂志错误地暗示说他正打算宣布退休。 **2** ADJ Something that is **incorrect** is not the thing that is required or is most suitable in a particular situation. 不适当的 ❑ *...injuries caused by incorrect posture.* …由不当姿势造成的伤害。● **in·cor·rect·ly** ADV 不适当地 [ADV with v] ❑ *He was told that the doors had been installed incorrectly.* 他被告知房门安装不当。

Word Link *cresc, creas ≈ growing : crescent, decrease, increase*

in·crease ♦♦♦ (**increases, increasing, increased**)

The verb is pronounced /ɪnkris/. The noun is pronounced /ɪnkris/.

动词读作 /ɪnkris/。名词读作 /ɪnkris/。

1 V-T/V-I If something **increases** or you **increase** it, it becomes greater in number, level, or amount. 使增加; 增加 ❑ *The population continues to increase.* 人口持续增长。 ❑ *Japan's industrial output increased by 2%.* 日本的工业产量增长了2%。 **2** N-COUNT If there is an **increase in** the number, level, or amount of something, it becomes greater. 增加 ❑ *...a sharp increase in productivity.* …生产率的急速增长。 **3** PHRASE If something **is on the increase**, it is happening more often or becoming greater in number or intensity. 正在增长 ❑ *Crime is on the increase.* 犯罪活动日益猖獗。

Thesaurus *increase* 另参见:
V. expand, extend, raise; *(ant.)* decrease, reduce **1**
N. gain, hike, raise, rise; *(ant.)* decrease, reduction **2**

i

Word Partnership *increase* 的常用搭配：

ADV. increase **dramatically**, increase **rapidly** 1
N. increase **in size**, increase **in temperature**, increase **in value** 1 2
increase in crime, increase **in demand**, increase **in spending**, **population** increase, **price** increase, **salary** increase 2
ADJ. **big** increase, **marked** increase, **sharp** increase 2

in·creas·ing·ly ◆◆◇ /ɪnkriːsɪŋli/ ADV You can use **increasingly** to indicate that a situation or quality is becoming greater in intensity or more common. 渐增地 ❑ *He was finding it increasingly difficult to make decisions.* 他发现决策越来越困难了。 ❑ *The U.S. has increasingly relied on Japanese capital.* 美国越来越依赖日本资本。

Word Partnership *increasingly* 的常用搭配：

ADJ. increasingly **clear**, increasingly **common**, increasingly **complex**, increasingly **difficult**, increasingly **important**, increasingly **popular**

Word Link *cred ≈ to believe : credentials, credibility, incredible*

in·cred·ible ◆◇◇ /ɪnkrɛdɪbᵊl/ 1 ADJ If you describe something or someone as **incredible**, you like them very much or are impressed by them, because they are extremely or unusually good. 极好的 [APPROVAL] ❑ *The wildflowers will be incredible after this rain.* 这场雨过后，野花将开得非常好。 ● **in·cred·ibly** /ɪnkrɛdɪbli/ ADV 极好地 [ADV adj/adv] ❑ *Their father was incredibly good-looking.* 他们的父亲十分英俊。 2 ADJ If you say that something is **incredible**, you mean that it is very unusual or surprising, and you cannot believe it is really true, although it may be. 难以置信的 ❑ *It seemed incredible that people would still want to play football during a war.* 在战争期间人们仍然想踢足球，这似乎不可思议。 ● **in·cred·ibly** ADV 难以置信地 ❑ *Incredibly, some people don't like the name.* 令人难以置信的是，有些人不喜欢这个名字。 3 ADJ You use **incredible** to emphasize the degree, amount, or intensity of something. 非常的 [EMPHASIS] ❑ *I work an incredible amount of hours.* 我工作的时间极长。 ● **in·cred·ibly** ADV 非常地 [ADV adj/adv] ❑ *It was incredibly hard work.* 那是个非常艰辛的工作。

Word Partnership *incredible* 的常用搭配：

N. incredible **discovery**, incredible **prices** 1
incredible **experience** 1 – 3
ADV. **absolutely** incredible 1 – 3

in·credu·lous /ɪnkrɛdʒələs/ ADJ If someone is **incredulous**, they are unable to believe something because it is very surprising or shocking. 怀疑的 ❑ *"He made you do it?" Her voice was incredulous.* "他让你做的？" 她的声音是怀疑的。 ● **in·credu·lous·ly** ADV 怀疑地 [ADV with v] ❑ *"You told Pete?" Rachel said incredulously. "I can't believe it!"* "你告诉皮特了？" 雷切尔怀疑地说道。"真不敢相信！"

in·cre·ment /ɪnkrɪmənt/ (**increments**) 1 N-COUNT An **increment in** something or **in** the value of something is an amount by which it increases. 增加量 [FORMAL] ❑ *The average yearly increment in productivity was 4.5 per cent.* 生产率的年平均增长量是4.5%。 2 N-COUNT An **increment** is an amount by which your salary automatically increases after a fixed period of time. 定期加薪 [BRIT, FORMAL]

in AM, use **raise**

in·crimi·nate /ɪnkrɪmɪneɪt/ (**incriminates, incriminating, incriminated**) V-T If something **incriminates** you, it suggests that you are responsible for something bad, especially a crime. 显示…有罪 ❑ *He claimed that the drugs had been planted to incriminate him.* 他声称那些毒品是有人为了栽赃陷害他而放在那里的。 ● **in·crimi·nat·ing** ADJ 显示有罪的 ❑ *Police had reportedly searched his house and found incriminating evidence.* 据报道，警察搜查了他的房子，并且发现了罪证。

in·cu·bate /ɪnkyəbeɪt, ɪŋ/ (**incubates, incubating, incubated**) V-T/V-I When birds **incubate** their eggs, or when they **incubate**, they keep the eggs warm until the baby birds come out. 孵（卵）；孵化 ❑ *The birds returned to their nests and continued to incubate the eggs.* 那些鸟儿返巢继续孵卵。 ❑ *They lay eggs that incubate through the winter.* 它们产下卵，要孵化整个冬天。 ● **in·cu·ba·tion** ▲ /ɪnkyəbeɪʃᵊn, ɪŋ/ N-UNCOUNT 孵卵；孵化 ❑ *Male albatrosses share in the incubation of eggs.* 雄性信天翁参与孵卵。

▲ **in·cum·bent** /ɪnkʌmbənt/ (**incumbents**) 1 N-COUNT An **incumbent** is someone who holds an official post at a particular time. 在职者 [FORMAL] ❑ *In general, incumbents have a 94 percent chance of being re-elected.* 一般情况下，现任官员有94%的几率会再次当选。 ● ADJ **Incumbent** is also an adjective. 在职的 [ADJ n] ❑ *...the only candidate who defeated an incumbent senator.* …惟一击败了现任参议员的候选人。 2 ADJ If it is **incumbent on** or **upon** you to do something, it is your duty or responsibility to do it. 有责任履行的 [FORMAL] ❑ *She felt it was incumbent on herself to act immediately.* 她感到立即采取行动是她义不容辞的责任。

★ **in·cur** /ɪnkɜr/ (**incurs, incurring, incurred**) V-T If you **incur** something unpleasant, it happens to you because of something you have done. 招致；蒙受 [WRITTEN] ❑ *The government had also incurred huge debts.* 政府也已承受了大笔债务。

Word Link *able ≈ able to be : incurable, portable, unavoidable*

in·cur·able /ɪnkyʊərəbᵊl/ 1 ADJ If someone has an **incurable** disease, they cannot be cured of it. 无法治愈的 ❑ *He is suffering from an incurable skin disease.* 他身患一种无可救治的皮肤病。 ● **in·cur·ably** /ɪnkyʊərəbli/ ADV 无法治愈地 [ADV adj] ❑ *...youngsters who are disabled, or incurably ill.* …残疾或患不治之症的青少年。 2 ADJ You can use **incurable** to indicate that someone has a particular quality or attitude and will not change. 不能改变的 [ADJ n] ❑ *Poor old Willy is an incurable romantic.* 可怜的老威利是个无可救药的浪漫主义者。 ● **in·cur·ably** ADV 不能改变地 [ADV adj] ❑ *I know you think I'm incurably nosy, but the truth is I'm concerned about you.* 我知道你认为我总爱管闲事，但事实是我关心你。

▲ **in·debt·ed** /ɪndɛtɪd/ 1 ADJ If you say that you are **indebted to** someone for something, you mean that you are very grateful to them for something. 感激的 [v-link ADJ "to" n] ❑ *I am deeply indebted to him for his help.* 我对他的帮助深深感激。 2 ADJ **Indebted** countries, organizations, or people are ones that owe money to other countries, organizations, or people. 负债的 ❑ *The treasury secretary identified the most heavily indebted countries.* 财政部长明确指出了负债最多的一些国家。

in·de·cen·cy /ɪndiːsᵊnsi/ (**indecencies**) 1 N-UNCOUNT If you talk about the **indecency** of something or someone, you are indicating that you find them morally or sexually offensive. 下流 ❑ *...the indecency of their language.* …他们言语的下流。 2 N-COUNT In law, an **indecency** is an illegal sexual act. 猥亵 ❑ *...sexual indecencies.* …性猥亵。

in·de·cent /ɪndiːsᵊnt/ 1 ADJ If you describe something as **indecent**, you mean that it is shocking and offensive, usually because it relates to sex or nakedness. 下流的 ❑ *He accused Mrs. Moore of making an indecent suggestion.* 他指控穆尔太太做下流的性暗示。 ● **in·de·cent·ly** ADV 下流地 ❑ *...an indecently short skirt.* …一条有伤风化的短裙。 2 ADJ If you describe the speed or amount of something as **indecent**, you are indicating, often in a humorous way, that it is much quicker or larger than is usual or desirable. 过于（快或大）的 ❑ *She finished her first glass of wine with indecent haste.* 她忙不迭地把第一杯酒干了。 ● **in·de·cent·ly** ADV 过于 ❑ *...an indecently large office.* …过大的办公室。

in·de·ci·sion /ɪndɪsɪʒᵊn/ N-UNCOUNT If you say that someone suffers from **indecision**, you mean that they find it very difficult to make decisions. 迟疑不决 ❑ *After months of indecision, the government gave the plan the go-ahead on Monday.* 经过几个月的犹豫不决，政府在周一批准了这项计划。

in·de·ci·sive /ɪndɪsaɪsɪv/ 1 ADJ If you say that someone is **indecisive**, you mean that they find it very difficult to make decisions. 优柔寡断的 ❑ *He was criticized as a weak and indecisive leader.* 他被批评是位既懦弱又优柔寡断的领导人。 2 ADJ An **indecisive** result in a contest or election is one that is not clear or definite. 非决定性的 ❑ *The outcome of the battle was indecisive.* 此役的结局是胜负不明的。

in·deed ◆◆◇ /ɪndiːd/ 1 ADV You use **indeed** to confirm or agree with something that has just been said. （用于强调真实性）确实 [EMPHASIS] ❑ *Later, he admitted that the payments had indeed been made.* 后来，他承认说的确是付过款了。 ❑ *"Did you know him?"—"I did indeed."* "你认识他吗？"——"我确实认识他。" 2 ADV You use **indeed** to introduce a further comment or statement that strengthens the point you have already made. （表示递进语气）其实 [ADV with cl] [EMPHASIS] ❑ *We have nothing against diversity; indeed, we want more of it.* 我们并不反对多样化；其实，我们希望有更多的多样化。 3 ADV You use **indeed** at the end of a clause to give extra force to the word "very," or to emphasize a particular word. 真正地（用于句

未修饰very或强调某词以加强语气）[adj ADV] [EMPHASIS] ❑ *The results are often strange indeed.* 结果往往真是奇怪。

★ **in·defi·nite** /ɪndɛfɪnɪt/ 1 ADJ If you describe a situation or period as **indefinite**, you mean that people have not decided when it will end. 不确定的 ❑ *The trial was adjourned for an indefinite period.* 审判被无限期推迟。 2 ADJ Something that is **indefinite** is not exact or clear. 不明确的 ❑ *...at some indefinite time in the future.* …在未来不确定的某个时间。

in·defi·nite ar·ti·cle (**indefinite articles**) N-COUNT The words "a" and "an" are sometimes called **the indefinite article**. 不定冠词

in·defi·nite·ly /ɪndɛfɪnɪtli/ ADV If a situation will continue **indefinitely**, it will continue forever or until someone decides to change it or end it. 无限期地 [ADV with v] ❑ *The visit has now been postponed indefinitely.* 这次访问现在已被无限期地推迟。

Word Link *damn, demn ≈ harm, loss : condemn, damning, indemnify*

in·dem·ni·fy /ɪndɛmnɪfaɪ/ (**indemnifies, indemnifying, indemnified**) V-T To **indemnify** someone against something bad happening means to promise to protect them, especially financially, if it happens. 保障；保证赔偿 [FORMAL] ❑ *They agreed to indemnify the taxpayers against any loss.* 他们同意赔偿纳税人的任何损失。

in·dem·nity /ɪndɛmnɪti/ N-UNCOUNT If something provides **indemnity**, it provides insurance or protection against damage or loss. 保障；保证 [FORMAL] ❑ *Political exiles had not been given indemnity from prosecution.* 政治流亡者还没有被给予免于起诉的保证。

Word Link *ence ≈ state, condition : dependence, excellence, independence*

in·de·pend·ence ♦♦◇ /ɪndɪpɛndəns/ 1 N-UNCOUNT If a country has or gains **independence**, it has its own government and is not ruled by any other country. (国家的）独立 ❑ *In 1816, Argentina declared its independence from Spain.* 1816年，阿根廷宣布脱离西班牙而独立。 2 N-UNCOUNT Someone's **independence** is the fact that they do not rely on other people. (人的）自立 ❑ *He was afraid of losing his independence.* 他担心丧失自己的独立。

Word Partnership *independence* 的常用搭配：
N. **a struggle for** independence 1
V. **fight for** independence, **gain** independence 1
ADJ. **economic/financial** independence 1 2

in·de·pend·ent ♦♦♦ /ɪndɪpɛndənt/ (**independents**) 1 ADJ If one thing or person is **independent of** another, they are separate and not connected, so the first one is not affected or influenced by the second. 无关联的；相互独立的 ❑ *Your questions should be independent of each other.* 你们的问题应该是相互间毫无关联的。 ❑ *We're going independent from the university and setting up our own group.* 我们将从大学独立出去，成立我们自己的集团。 ● **in·de·pen·dent·ly** ADV 独立地 ❑ *...several people working independently in different areas of the world.* …在世界不同地区独立工作的几个人。 2 ADJ If someone is **independent**, they do not need help or money from anyone else. 不依赖的 ❑ *Phil was now much more independent of his parents.* 菲尔现在不大依赖他的父母了。 ● **in·de·pen·dent·ly** ADV 不依赖地 ❑ *...helping disabled students to live and study as independently as possible.* …帮助残疾学生尽可能不依赖地生活和学习。 3 ADJ **Independent** countries and states are not ruled by other countries but have their own government. (国家）独立的 ❑ *Papua New Guinea became independent from Australia in 1975.* 巴布亚新几内亚1975年脱离澳大利亚而独立。 4 ADJ An **independent** organization or other body is one that controls its own finances and operations, rather than being controlled by someone else. 独立的；不受他人左右的 [ADJ n] ❑ *...an independent television station.* …一家独立的电视台。 5 ADJ An **independent** inquiry or opinion is one that involves people who are not connected with a particular situation, and should therefore be fair. 客观公正的；不偏不倚的 [ADJ n] ❑ *There were calls in Congress for an independent inquiry.* 国会中有对一次独立调查的呼吁。 6 ADJ An **independent** politician is one who does not represent any political party. 无党派的 ❑ *There's been a late surge of support for an independent candidate.* 对一位独立候选人的支持最近有骤然的增多。 ● N-COUNT An **independent** is an independent politician. 无党派人士 ❑ *Mr. Vassiliou, standing as an independent, succeeded in convincing a significant number of voters of his argument.* 瓦西里欧先生以无党派人士身份成功地说服了大量选民支持他的观点。

Thesaurus *independent* 另参见：
ADJ. self-reliant, self-supporting; (*ant.*) dependent 1 2
liberated, self-governing 3

▲ **in·de·ter·mi·nate** /ɪndɪtɜrmɪnɪt/ ADJ If something is **indeterminate**, you cannot say exactly what it is. 说不清的 [usu ADJ n] ❑ *I hope to carry on for an indeterminate period.* 我希望在一段不确定的时间内这样继续下去。

in·dex ♦◇◇ /ɪndɛks/ (**indices, indexes, indexing, indexed**)

The usual plural is **indexes**, but the form **indices** can be used for meaning 1.

1 N-COUNT An **index** is a system by which changes in the value of something and the rate at which it changes can be recorded, measured, or interpreted. 指数 ❑ *...the consumer price index.* …消费价格指数。 2 N-COUNT An **index** is an alphabetical list that is printed at the back of a book and tells you on which pages important topics are referred to. 索引 ❑ *There's even a special subject index.* 甚至有一个特别的主题索引。 3 V-T If you **index** a book or a collection of information, you make an alphabetical list of the items in it. 为…编索引 ❑ *A quarter of this vast archive has been indexed and made accessible to researchers.* 这批数量巨大的档案的1/4都已编了索引，可供研究者查阅。 4 V-T If a quantity or value **is indexed to** another, a system is arranged so that it increases or decreases whenever the other one increases or decreases. 使与…挂钩 [usu passive] ❑ *Minimum benefits and wages are to be indexed to inflation.* 最低养老金和最低工资都要与通货膨胀挂钩。 5 → see also **card index**

in·di·cate ♦♦◇ /ɪndɪkeɪt/ (**indicates, indicating, indicated**) 1 V-T If one thing **indicates** another, the first thing shows that the second is true or exists. 表明 ❑ *A survey of retired people has indicated that most are independent and enjoying life.* 一项对退休人员的调查表明，他们中的大部分人生活自立而愉快。 ❑ *Our vote today indicates a change in United States policy.* 我们今天的投票表明了美国政策的变化。 2 V-T If you **indicate** an opinion, an intention, or a fact, you mention it in an indirect way. 暗示 ❑ *Mr. Rivers has indicated that he may resign.* 里弗斯先生已经暗示他可能要辞职。 3 V-T If you **indicate** something to someone, you show them where it is, especially by pointing to it. 指示 [FORMAL] ❑ *He indicated a chair. "Sit down."* 他指着一把椅子说，“坐下。” 4 V-T If one thing **indicates** something else, it is a sign of that thing. 象征；代表 ❑ *Dreams can help indicate your true feelings.* 梦能代表你的真实情感。 5 V-T If a technical instrument **indicates** something, it shows a measurement or reading. (仪器等）指示 ❑ *...an instrument used to indicate wind direction.* …一台用于指示风向的仪器。 6 V-T/V-I When drivers **indicate**, they make lights flash on one side of their vehicle to show that they are going to turn in that direction. (车辆打转向灯）指示转向 [mainly BRIT]

in AM, use **signal**

Thesaurus *indicate* 另参见：
V. demonstrate, hint, mean, reveal, show 1 2

Word Partnership *indicate* 的常用搭配：
N. **polls** indicate, **records** indicate, **reports** indicate, **results** indicate, **statistics** indicate, **studies** indicate, **surveys** indicate 1
indicate **a change in** *something* 1 2 4

in·di·ca·tion ♦◇◇ /ɪndɪkeɪʃ°n/ (**indications**) N-VAR An **indication** is a sign that suggests, for example, what people are thinking or feeling. 象征；迹象 ❑ *He gave no indication that he was ready to compromise.* 他没有流露出打算妥协的迹象。

Word Partnership *indication* 的常用搭配：
ADJ. **a clear** indication, **a strong** indication
V. **give an** indication

★ **in·dica·tive** /ɪndɪkətɪv/ ADJ If one thing is **indicative of** another, it suggests what the other thing is likely to be. 标示的；指示的 [FORMAL] ❑ *His action is indicative of growing concern about the shortage of skilled labor.* 他的行为显示对于熟练工人短缺现象的日益关注。

in·di·ca·tor /ɪndɪkeɪtər/ (**indicators**) 1 N-COUNT An **indicator** is a measurement or value that gives you an idea of what something is like. 指示物 ❑ *...vital economic indicators, such as inflation, growth and the trade gap.* …重要的经济指标，如通货膨胀，

经济增长以及贸易差额。 **2** N-COUNT A car's **indicators** are the flashing lights that tell you when it is going to turn left or right. (车辆上的) 转向指示灯 [mainly BRIT]

in AM, use **turn signals**

Word Partnership *indicator* 的常用搭配：

ADJ. **economic** indicator, **good** indicator, **important** indicator, **reliable** indicator **1**

in·di·ces /ɪndɪsiz/ **Indices** is a plural form of **index**. **index**的复数形式

▲ **in·dict** /ɪndaɪt/ (**indicts, indicting, indicted**) V-T If someone **is indicted for** a crime, they are officially charged with it. 控告 [usu passive] [mainly AM, LEGAL] ❑ *He was later indicted on corruption charges.* 他后来被控贪污。

▲ **in·dict·ment** /ɪndaɪtmənt/ (**indictments**) **1** N-COUNT If you say that one thing is **an indictment of** another thing, you mean that it shows how bad the other thing is. 控诉 ❑ *The movie is an indictment of Hollywood.* 这部电影是对好莱坞的一种谴责。 **2** N-VAR An **indictment** is a formal accusation that someone has committed a crime. 控告 [mainly AM, LEGAL] ❑ *Prosecutors may soon seek an indictment on racketeering and fraud charges.* 检察官们可能很快就会以敲诈勒索和欺骗罪进行起诉。

in·die /ɪndi/ (**indies**) **1** ADJ **Indie** music refers to rock or pop music produced by new bands working with small, independent record companies. (摇滚或流行音乐等) 独立制作的 [ADJ n] ❑ *...a multi-racial indie band.* …一个多种族的独立乐队。 ● N-COUNT An **indie** is an indie band or record company. 独立乐队；独立唱片公司 ❑ *The fact is that the indies are selling a lot more CDs than the major record labels.* 事实是独立制作的唱片公司销售的激光唱片要比大牌公司多得多。 **2** ADJ **Indie** films are produced by small independent companies rather than by major studios. (影片) 独立制作的 [ADJ n] ❑ *With a role in the indie movie "Happiness," her career is now swimming along.* 在独立制作的影片《幸福》中扮演角色之后，她的事业现在进展得非常顺利。 ● N-COUNT An **indie** is an indie film or film company. 独立制作的影片；独立制片公司 ❑ *The indies convert their digital movies to film.* 独立制片公司把他们的数字电影转为胶片电影。

in·dif·fer·ence /ɪndɪfərəns/ N-UNCOUNT If you accuse someone of **indifference to** something, you mean that they have a complete lack of interest in it. 漠不关心 ❑ *...his callous indifference to the plight of his son.* …他对儿子困境的冷漠无情。

in·dif·fer·ent /ɪndɪfərənt/ **1** ADJ If you accuse someone of being **indifferent to** something, you mean that they have a complete lack of interest in it. 漠不关心的 ❑ *People have become indifferent to the suffering of others.* 人们已经变得对别人的痛苦漠不关心。 ● **in·dif·fer·ent·ly** ADV 漠不关心地 [ADV after v] ❑ *"Not that it matters," said Trujillo indifferently.* "它倒不是那么重要"，特鲁希略漠然地说。 **2** ADJ If you describe something or someone as **indifferent**, you mean that their standard or quality is not very good, and often quite bad. 平庸的 ❑ *She had starred in several very indifferent movies.* 她领衔主演过好几部非常平庸的电影。 ● **in·dif·fer·ent·ly** ADV 平庸地 [ADV with v] ❑ *...a shoddy piece of work, poorly written, indifferently performed.* …一部粗制滥造的作品，写得差劲，演得也蹩脚。

▲ **in·dig·enous** /ɪndɪdʒɪnəs/ ADJ **Indigenous** people or things belong to the country in which they are found, rather than coming there or being brought there from another country. 本土的；当地的 [FORMAL] ❑ *...the country's indigenous population.* …该国的本土人口。

in·di·ges·tion /ɪndɪdʒɛstʃ ͤn, -daɪ-/ N-UNCOUNT If you have **indigestion**, you have pains in your stomach and chest that are caused by difficulties in digesting food. 消化不良

Word Link *dign ≈ proper, worthy : dignified, dignitary, indignant*

★ **in·dig·nant** /ɪndɪgnənt/ ADJ If you are **indignant**, you are shocked and angry, because you think that something is unjust or unfair. 愤怒不平的 ❑ *He is indignant at suggestions that they were secret agents.* 他对关于他们是特务的暗示很愤慨。 ❑ *He was indignant that his rival was offered the job.* 他对他的对手得到了那份工作感到愤愤不平。 ● **in·dig·nant·ly** ADV 愤怒地 [ADV with v] ❑ *"That is not true," Erica said indignantly.* "那不是真的，" 埃丽卡气愤地说。

★ **in·dig·na·tion** /ɪndɪgneɪʃ ͤn/ N-UNCOUNT **Indignation** is a feeling of shock and anger when you think that something is unjust or unfair. 愤怒不平 ❑ *She was filled with indignation at the conditions under which miners were forced to work.* 她为矿工们被迫工作的条件满心愤慨。

in·dig·nity /ɪndɪgnɪti/ (**indignities**) N-VAR If you talk about **the indignity of** doing something, you mean that it makes you feel embarrassed or unimportant. 侮辱 [FORMAL] ❑ *Later, he suffered the indignity of having to flee angry protesters.* 后来，他因为不得不逃离愤怒的抗议者而蒙受羞辱。

in·di·rect /ɪndaɪrɛkt, -dɪr-/ **1** ADJ An **indirect** result or effect is not caused immediately and obviously by a thing or person, but happens because of something else that they have done. 间接的 ❑ *Businesses are feeling the indirect effects from the recession that's going on elsewhere.* 企业正感受到其他地区经济不景气造成的间接影响。 ● **in·di·rect·ly** ADV 间接地 ❑ *Drugs are indirectly responsible for the violence.* 毒品间接对暴力负有责任。 **2** ADJ An **indirect** route or journey does not use the shortest or easiest way between two places. 迂回的 ❑ *He took an indirect route back home.* 他选择了一条迂回的路线回家。 **3** ADJ **Indirect** remarks and information suggest something or refer to it, without actually mentioning it or stating it clearly. 拐弯抹角的 ❑ *His remarks amounted to an indirect appeal for economic aid.* 他的话等于是一个对经济援助拐弯抹角的请求。 ● **in·di·rect·ly** ADV 拐弯抹角地 [ADV with v] ❑ *He referred indirectly to the territorial dispute.* 他拐弯抹角地提到了领土争端。

in·di·rect dis·course N-UNCOUNT **Indirect discourse** is speech that tells you what someone said, but does not use the person's actual words; for example, "They said you didn't like it.", "I asked him what his plans were.", and "Citizens complained about the smoke." 间接引语

in·di·rect ob·ject (**indirect objects**) N-COUNT An **indirect object** is an object that is used with a transitive verb to indicate who benefits from an action or gets something as a result. For example, in "She gave him her address.", "him" is the indirect object. Compare **direct object**. 间接宾语

in·di·rect speech N-UNCOUNT **Indirect speech** is the same as **indirect discourse**. 间接引语

in·dis·crimi·nate /ɪndɪskrɪmɪnɪt/ ADJ If you describe an action as **indiscriminate**, you are critical of it because it does not involve any careful thought or choice. 任意而为的 [DISAPPROVAL] ❑ *The indiscriminate use of fertilizers is damaging to the environment.* 化肥的滥用化正在损害环境。 ● **in·dis·crimi·nate·ly** ADV 任意而为地 ❑ *The men opened fire indiscriminately.* 那些男人不分青红皂白地开枪。

in·dis·pen·sable /ɪndɪspɛnsəb ͤl/ ADJ If you say that someone or something is **indispensable**, you mean that they are absolutely essential and other people or things cannot function without them. 必不可少的 ❑ *She was becoming indispensable to him.* 对他来说她正变得不可或缺。

Word Link *put ≈ thinking : computer, dispute, indisputable*

in·dis·put·able /ɪndɪspyutəb ͤl/ ADJ If you say that something is **indisputable**, you are emphasizing that it is true and cannot be shown to be untrue. 无可争辩的 [EMPHASIS] ❑ *It is indisputable that birds are harboring this illness.* 无可争辩的是，鸟类携带着这种疾病。

in·dis·tin·guish·able /ɪndɪstɪŋgwɪʃəb ͤl/ ADJ If one thing is **indistinguishable from** another, the two things are so similar that it is difficult to know which is which. 难以区别的 ❑ *Replica weapons are indistinguishable from the real thing.* 仿真武器与真武器难以辨别。

in·di·vid·ual ♦♦◊ /ɪndɪvɪdʒuəl/ (**individuals**) **1** ADJ **Individual** means relating to one person or thing, rather than to a large group. 单独的 [ADJ n] ❑ *...waiting for the group to decide rather than making individual decisions.* …等待集体作决定而不是作单独的决定。 ● **in·di·vid·ual·ly** ADV 单独地 ❑ *...individually crafted tiles.* …一块块单独制作的瓦片。 **2** N-COUNT An **individual** is a person. 个人 ❑ *...anonymous individuals who are doing good things within our community.* …一些在我们社区里做好事不留名人士。 **3** ADJ If you describe someone or something as **individual**, you mean that you admire them because they are very unusual and do not try to imitate other people or things. 独特的 [APPROVAL] ❑ *It was really all part of her very individual personality.* 那确实是她非常独特个性的全部。

Thesaurus *individual* 另参见：

N. human being, person, somebody, someone **2**
ADJ. distinctive, original, unique **3**

in·di·vidu·al·ise /ɪndɪvɪdʒuəlaɪz/ [BRIT] → see **individualize**

in·di·vidu·al·ity /ɪndɪvɪdʒuælɪti/ N-UNCOUNT The **individuality** of a person or thing consists of the qualities that make them different from other people or things. 独特性 ❑ *People should be free to express their individuality.* 人们应该自由表现自己的个性。

in·di·vidu·al·ize /ɪndɪvɪdʒuəlaɪz/ (**individualizes, individualizing, individualized**) V-T To **individualize** a thing or person means to make them different from other things or people and to give them a recognizable identity. 使表现出区别 [FORMAL]

in BRIT, also use **individualise**

❑ *You can individualize a document by adding comments in the margins.* 你可以通过在页边的空白处添加评论来使文件与众不同。 ● **in·di·vidu·al·ized** ADJ 表现出区别的 ❑ *Doctors feel that a more individualized approach to patients should now be adopted.* 医生们认为现在应该对病人们采用一种更加个人化的治疗方案。

in·door /ɪndɔr/ ADJ **Indoor** activities or things are ones that happen or are used inside a building and not outside. 室内的 [ADJ n] ❑ *No smoking in any indoor facilities.* 在任何室内场所都禁止抽烟。

in·doors /ɪndɔrz/ ADV If something happens **indoors**, it happens inside a building. 在室内 ❑ *I think perhaps we should go indoors.* 我想也许我们该进屋了。

in·duce /ɪndus/ (**induces, inducing, induced**) **1** V-T To **induce** a state or condition means to cause it. 引起 ❑ *Doctors said surgery could induce a heart attack.* 医生们说手术可能导致心脏病。 **2** V-T If you **induce** someone **to** do something, you persuade or influence them to do it. 引诱；劝说 ❑ *More than 4,000 teachers were induced to take early retirement.* 四千多名教师被劝说提前退休。

in·duce·ment /ɪndusmənt/ (**inducements**) N-COUNT If someone is offered an **inducement to** do something, they are given or promised gifts or benefits in order to persuade them to do it. 引诱物；诱因 ❑ *They offer every inducement to foreign businesses to invest in their states.* 他们提供了种种优惠条件吸引外国公司在他们州投资。

★ **in·duc·tion** /ɪndʌkʃ^ən/ (**inductions**) N-VAR **Induction** is a procedure or ceremony for introducing someone to a new job, organization, or way of life. 入门；就职仪式 ❑ *...his induction as president.* …他的总统就职仪式。

★ **in·duc·tive** /ɪndʌktɪv/ ADJ **Inductive** reasoning is based on a method in which you use individual ideas or facts to give you a general rule or conclusion. 归纳的 [FORMAL]

★ **in·dulge** /ɪndʌldʒ/ (**indulges, indulging, indulged**) **1** V-T/V-I If you **indulge in** something or if you **indulge yourself**, you allow yourself to have or do something that you know you will enjoy. 使沉溺；沉溺 ❑ *Only rarely will she indulge in a glass of wine.* 她只是偶尔才会喝上杯葡萄酒。 ❑ *He returned to Ohio so that he could indulge his passion for football.* 他重返俄亥俄以释放自己对足球的激情。 **2** V-T If you **indulge** someone, you let them have or do what they want, even if this is not good for them. 纵容 ❑ *He did not agree with indulging children.* 他不同意娇惯孩子。

Word Partnership *indulge* 的常用搭配:

ADV.	**freely** indulge **1**
PREP.	indulge **in** *something* **1**
N.	indulge **children** **2**

in·dul·gence /ɪndʌldʒ^əns/ (**indulgences**) N-VAR **Indulgence** means treating someone with special kindness, often when it is not a good thing. 纵容 ❑ *The king's indulgence toward his sons angered the business community.* 国王对孩子们的纵容激怒了商界。

in·dul·gent /ɪndʌldʒ^ənt/ ADJ If you are **indulgent**, you treat a person with special kindness, often in a way that is not good for them. 纵容的 ❑ *His indulgent mother was willing to let him do anything he wanted.* 他那宽纵的母亲任他为所欲为。 ● **in·dul·gent·ly** ADV 纵容地 ❑ *Najib smiled at him indulgently and said, "Come on over when you feel like it."* 纳吉布放任地对他笑着说，"你什么时候想来就过来。"

in·dus·trial ♦♦◊ /ɪndʌstriəl/ **1** ADJ You use **industrial** to describe things that relate to or are used in industry. 工业的 ❑ *...industrial machinery and equipment.* …工业机械及设备。 **2** ADJ An **industrial** city or country is one in which industry is important or highly developed. 工业高度发达的 ❑ *...leading western industrial countries.* …主要的西方工业发达国家。

Word Partnership *industrial* 的常用搭配:

N. industrial **machinery**, industrial **production**, industrial **products** **1**
industrial **area**, industrial **city**, industrial **country** **2**

in·dus·trial es·tate (**industrial estates**) N-COUNT An **industrial estate** is the same as an **industrial park**. 工业园区 [BRIT]

in·dus·tri·al·ise /ɪndʌstriəlaɪz/ [BRIT] → see **industrialize**

in·dus·tri·al·ist /ɪndʌstriəlɪst/ (**industrialists**) N-COUNT An **industrialist** is a powerful businessperson who owns or controls large industrial companies or factories. 工业家 ❑ *...prominent Japanese industrialists.* …杰出的日本工业家。

in·dus·tri·al·ize /ɪndʌstriəlaɪz/ (**industrializes, industrializing, industrialized**)

in BRIT, also use **industrialise**

V-T/V-I When a country **industrializes** or **is industrialized**, it develops a lot of industries. 使工业化；实现工业化 ❑ *Energy consumption rises as countries industrialize.* 能源消耗随着各国工业化而增加。

● **in·dus·tri·ali·za·tion** /ɪndʌstriəlɪzeɪʃ^ən/ N-UNCOUNT 工业化 ❑ *Industrialization began early in Spain.* 工业化很早就在西班牙开始了。

in·dus·trial park (**industrial parks**) N-COUNT An **industrial park** is an area that has been specially planned for a lot of factories. 工业园区 [AM]

in BRIT, use **industrial estate**

in·dus·trial re·la·tions N-PLURAL **Industrial relations** refers to the relationship between employers and employees in industry, and the political decisions and laws that affect it. 劳资关系 [BUSINESS] ❑ *The offer is seen as an attempt to improve industrial relations.* 这一提议被看作是改善劳资关系的一次尝试。

in·dus·try ♦♦♦ /ɪndəstri/ (**industries**) **1** N-UNCOUNT **Industry** is the work and processes involved in collecting raw materials, and making them into products in factories. 工业 ❑ *Our industry suffers through insufficient investment in research.* 我们的工业因研究投入不足而大吃苦头。 **2** N-COUNT A particular **industry** consists of all the people and activities involved in making a particular product or providing a particular service. 行业 ❑ *...the motor vehicle and textile industries.* …机动车与纺织行业。 **3** N-COUNT If you refer to a social or political activity as an **industry**, you are criticizing it because you think it involves a lot of people in unnecessary or useless work. 兴师动众 [DISAPPROVAL] ❑ *...the industry of western capitalism.* …西方资本主义的大张旗鼓。 **4** N-UNCOUNT **Industry** is the fact of working very hard. 勤奋 [FORMAL] ❑ *No one doubted his*

Word Web industry

There are three general categories of **industry**. Primary industry involves **extracting raw materials** from the environment. Examples include **agriculture, forestry,** and **mining**. Secondary industry involves **refining** raw materials to make new **products**. It also includes **assembling** parts created by other **manufacturers**. There are two types of secondary industry—**light industry** (such as **textile weaving**) and **heavy industry** (such as shipbuilding).Tertiary industry deals with **services** which don't involve a concrete product. Some examples are **banking, tourism**, and education. Recently, computers have created millions of jobs in the **information technology** field. Some researchers describe this as a fourth type of industry.

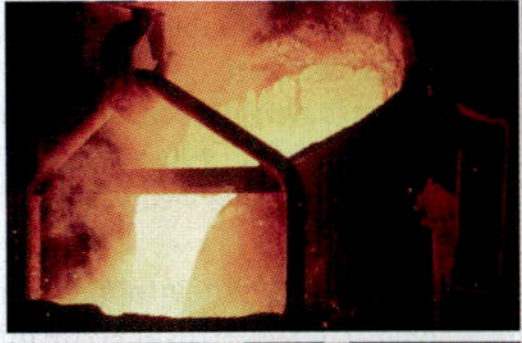

ability, his industry or his integrity. 没有人怀疑他的能力、勤奋和正直。
5 → see also **cottage industry, service industry**
→ see Word Web: **industry**
→ see **cotton**

in·ed·ible /ɪnɛdɪbᵊl/ ADJ If you say that something is **inedible**, you mean you cannot eat it, for example, because it tastes bad or is poisonous. 不可食用的 ❑ *Detainees complained of being given inedible food.* 被拘押者抱怨所给的食物不能吃。
→ see **cooking**

in·ef·fec·tive /ɪnɪfɛktɪv/ ADJ If you say that something is **ineffective**, you mean that it has no effect on a process or situation. 不起作用的 ❑ *Economic reform will continue to be painful and ineffective.* 经济改革将仍是痛苦和不见效的。

in·ef·fec·tual /ɪnɪfɛktʃuəl/ ADJ If someone or something is **ineffectual**, they fail to do what they are expected to do or are trying to do. 无能的；无效的 ❑ *The mayor had become ineffectual in the struggle to clamp down on drugs.* 该市长在打击毒品的斗争中行动不力。
●**in·ef·fec·tu·al·ly** ADV 无效地 ❑ *Her voice trailed off ineffectually.* 她的声音渐渐微弱得听不见了。

in·ef·fi·cient /ɪnɪfɪʃᵊnt/ ADJ **Inefficient** people, organizations, systems, or machines do not use time, energy, or other resources in the best way. 效率低的 ❑ *Their communication systems are inefficient in the extreme.* 他们通讯系统的效率极其低下。●**in·ef·fi·cien·cy** N-VAR (**inefficiencies**) 低效 ❑ *The inefficiency of the distribution system has led to the loss of millions of tons of food.* 分送系统的低效已经造成了数百万吨食物的损失。●**in·ef·fi·cient·ly** ADV 低效率地 [ADV with v] ❑ *Energy prices have been kept low, so energy is used inefficiently.* 能源价格一直被保持在低位，所以能源就被低效使用。

in·ept /ɪnɛpt/ ADJ If you say that someone is **inept**, you are criticizing them because they do something with a complete lack of skill. 无能的 [DISAPPROVAL] ❑ *He was inept and lacked the intelligence to govern.* 他无能而且缺乏管理才干。

in·equal·ity /ɪnɪkwɒlɪti/ (**inequalities**) N-VAR **Inequality** is the difference in social status, wealth, or opportunity between people or groups. 不平等；不公平 ❑ *People are concerned about corruption and social inequality.* 人们对腐败和社会不公感到担忧。

Word Partnership *inequality* 的常用搭配：

ADJ.	**economic** inequality, **growing/increasing** inequality, **racial** inequality, **social** inequality
N.	**gender** inequality, **income** inequality

in·ert /ɪnɜrt/ **1** ADJ Someone or something that is **inert** does not move at all. 不动的 ❑ *He covered the inert body with a blanket.* 他用一床毯子盖住那具一动不动的尸体。 **2** ADJ If you describe something as **inert**, you are criticizing it because it is not very lively or interesting. 无生气的 [DISAPPROVAL] ❑ *The novel itself remains oddly inert.* 那小说本身异常乏味。 **3** ADJ An **inert** substance is one that does not react with other substances. 惰性的 [TECHNICAL] ❑ *...inert gases like neon and argon.* …像氖和氩这样的惰性气体。

★ **in·er·tia** /ɪnɜrʃə/ **1** N-UNCOUNT If you have a feeling of **inertia**, you feel very lazy and unwilling to move or be active. 懒惰 ❑ *He resented her inertia, her lack of energy and self-direction.* 他讨厌她的懒惰、缺乏活力和自我。 **2** N-UNCOUNT **Inertia** is the tendency of a physical object to remain still or to continue moving, unless a force is applied to it. 惯性 [TECHNICAL]

in·es·cap·able /ɪnɪskeɪpəbᵊl/ ADJ If you describe a fact, situation, or activity as **inescapable**, you mean that it is difficult not to notice it or be affected by it. 不可避免的 ❑ *The inescapable conclusion is that he was trying to avenge the death of his friend.* 不可避免的结论就是他试图为他的朋友之死复仇。●**in·es·cap·ably** /ɪnɪskeɪpəbli/ ADV 不可避免地 ❑ *...the inescapably dreary hopelessness of the universe.* …宇宙不可避免地沉闷的绝望。

in·evi·tabil·ity /ɪnɛvɪtəbɪlɪti/ (**inevitabilities**) N-VAR The **inevitability** of something is the fact that it is certain to happen and cannot be prevented or avoided. 必然性 ❑ *We are all bound by the inevitability of death.* 我们都免不了一死。

in·evi·table ♦◇◇ /ɪnɛvɪtəbᵊl/ ADJ If something is **inevitable**, it is certain to happen and cannot be prevented or avoided. 必然发生的 ❑ *If the case succeeds, it is inevitable that other trials will follow.* 如果这场官司获胜，其他审判必将效法。●N-SING **The inevitable** is something that is inevitable. 必然发生的事 ❑ *"It's just delaying the inevitable," he said.* "那只是拖延该发生的事罢了，" 他说。

in·evi·tably /ɪnɛvɪtəbli/ ADV If something will **inevitably** happen, it is certain to happen and cannot be prevented or avoided. 必然发生地 ❑ *Technological changes will inevitably lead to unemployment.* 技术变革将必然导致失业。

in·exo·rable /ɪnɛksərəbᵊl/ ADJ You use **inexorable** to describe a process that cannot be prevented from continuing or progressing. 不可阻挡的 [FORMAL] ❑ *...the seemingly inexorable rise in unemployment.* …似乎不可阻挡的失业增长。●**in·exo·rably** /ɪnɛksərəbli/ ADV 不可阻挡地 [ADV with v] ❑ *Spending on health is growing inexorably.* 健康上的花费在不可阻挡地增加。

in·ex·pen·sive /ɪnɪkspɛnsɪv/ ADJ Something that is **inexpensive** does not cost very much. 便宜的 ❑ *There is a large variety of good, inexpensive restaurants.* 有多种物美价廉的餐馆。

in·ex·pe·ri·ence /ɪnɪkspɪəriəns/ N-UNCOUNT If you refer to someone's **inexperience**, you mean that they have little knowledge or experience of a particular situation or activity. 缺乏经验 ❑ *Critics attacked the youth and inexperience of his staff.* 评论家们抨击他的员工年轻且缺乏经验。

in·ex·pe·ri·enced /ɪnɪkspɪəriənst/ ADJ If you are **inexperienced**, you have little knowledge or experience of a particular situation or activity. 缺乏经验的 ❑ *Routine tasks are often delegated to inexperienced young doctors.* 例行的差事经常交给缺乏经验的年轻医生们去做。

in·ex·pli·cable /ɪnɛksplɪkəbᵊl, ɪnɪksplɪk-/ ADJ If something is **inexplicable**, you cannot explain why it happens or why it is true. 无法解释的 ❑ *His behavior was extraordinary and inexplicable.* 他的行为离奇且令人费解。●**in·ex·pli·cably** /ɪnɛksplɪkəbli, ɪnɪksplɪk-/ ADV 无法解释地 ❑ *She suddenly and inexplicably announced her retirement.* 她突然令人费解地宣布退休。

in·ex·tri·cably /ɪnɛkstrɪkəbli, ɪnɪkstrɪk-/ ADV If two or more things are **inextricably** linked, they cannot be considered separately. 密不可分地 [ADV with v] [FORMAL] ❑ *Our survival is inextricably linked to the survival of the rainforest.* 我们的生存与雨林的生存息息相关。

▲ **in·fa·mous** /ɪnfəməs/ ADJ **Infamous** people or things are well-known because of something bad. 声名狼藉的 [FORMAL] ❑ *He was infamous for his anti-feminist attitudes.* 他因为他的反女权主义姿态而臭名昭著。

> A **famous** person or thing is known to more people than a **well-known** one. A **notorious** person or thing is famous because they are connected with something bad or undesirable. **Infamous** is not the opposite of **famous**. It has a similar meaning to **notorious**, but is a stronger word. Someone or something that is **notable** is important or interesting.

in·fan·cy /ɪnfənsi/ **1** N-UNCOUNT **Infancy** is the period of your life when you are a very young child. 婴儿期 ❑ *...the development of the mind from infancy onwards.* …从婴儿期开始的智力开发。 **2** N-UNCOUNT If something is **in its infancy**, it is new and has not developed very much. 初期 ❑ *Computing science was still in its infancy.* 计算机科学仍然处于初期阶段。

in·fant /ɪnfənt/ (**infants**) **1** N-COUNT An **infant** is a baby or very young child. 婴儿；幼儿 [FORMAL] ❑ *...holding the infant in his arms.* …把婴儿抱在他手里。 ❑ *They are saying that he is tiring of playing daddy to their infant son.* 他们说他厌倦于在他们的幼儿面前装扮爸爸的角色。 **2** ADJ **Infant** means designed especially for very young children. 供幼儿用的 [ADJ n] [BRIT]

in AM, use **baby**

3 ADJ An **infant** organization or system is new and has not developed very much. 初期的 [ADJ n] ❑ *The infant company was based in Nebraska.* 这家初创的公司总部设在内布拉斯加州。
→ see **age, child**

▲ **in·fan·try** /ɪnfəntri/ N-UNCOUNT-COLL **Infantry** are soldiers who fight on foot rather than in tanks or on horses. 步兵 ❑ *...an infantry division.* …一个步兵师。

in·fect ♦◇◇ /ɪnfɛkt/ (**infects, infecting, infected**) **1** V-T To **infect** people, animals, or plants means to cause them to have a disease or illness. 传染 ❑ *A single mosquito can infect a large number of people.* 一只蚊子就能传染很多人。 ❑ *...objects used by an infected person.* …一名感染者使用过的物品。●**in·fec·tion** /ɪnfɛkʃᵊn/ N-UNCOUNT 传染 ❑ *...plants that are resistant to infection.* …抗感染的植物。 **2** V-T To **infect** a substance or area means to cause it to contain harmful germs or bacteria. 使感染有害菌 ❑ *The birds infect the milk.* 鸟使牛奶受污染。 **3** V-T When people, places, or things **are infected** by a feeling or influence, it spreads to them. 使受影响 ❑ *For an instant I was infected by her fear.* 一瞬间，我被她的恐惧所感染。 ❑ *He thought they might infect others with their bourgeois ideas.* 他认为他们可能用中产阶级思想去影响别人。 **4** V-T If a virus **infects** a computer, it damages or destroys files or programs. 使(计算机)中毒 [COMPUTING] ❑ *This virus infected thousands of computers across the U.S. and Europe within days.* 这种病毒几天之内就使美国和欧洲成千上万台电脑中毒。

Word Partnership *infect* 的常用搭配:

PRON.	infect **others** **1** **2**
N.	**bacteria** infect, infect **cells**, infect **people** **1** **2**
	viruses infect, infect **with a virus** **1** **4**

in·fec·tion ♦◇◇ /ɪnfɛkʃən/ (**infections**) **1** N-COUNT An **infection** is a disease caused by germs or bacteria. 传染病 ❑ *Ear infections are common in preschool children.* 耳朵感染在学前儿童中很常见。 **2** → see also **infect**
→ see **diagnosis**

Word Partnership *infection* 的常用搭配:

N.	**cases of** infection, **rates of** infection, **risk of** infection, **symptoms of** infection **1**
V.	**cause an** infection, **have an** infection, **prevent** infection, **spread an** infection **1**

★ **in·fec·tious** /ɪnfɛkʃəs/ **1** ADJ A disease that is **infectious** can be caught by being near a person who has it. Compare **contagious**. 传染的 ❑ *...infectious diseases such as measles.* …像麻疹这样的传染病。 **2** ADJ If a feeling is **infectious**, it spreads to other people. 有感染力的 ❑ *She radiates an infectious enthusiasm for everything she does.* 她做的每件事都散发出一种有感染力的热情。
→ see **illness**

in·fer /ɪnfɜr/ (**infers, inferring, inferred**) **1** V-T If you **infer** that something is the case, you decide that it is true on the basis of information that you already have. 推断 ❑ *I inferred from what she said that you have not been well.* 我从她的话里推断出你身体一直不大好。 ❑ *By measuring the motion of the galaxies in a cluster, astronomers can infer the cluster's mass.* 通过测量一个天体群中星系的运动，天文学家可以推测该天体群的质量。 **2** V-T Some people use **infer** to mean "imply," but this use is incorrect. 暗指(一些人用**infer**表示**imply**的意思，但这种用法是错误的) ❑ *The police inferred, though they didn't exactly say it, that they found her behavior rather suspicious.* 警方虽未明说却暗示他们发现她的行迹相当可疑。

Do not confuse **infer** and **imply**. If you **infer** that something is the case, you decide that it must be the case because of what you know, but without actually being told. ❑ *From this simple statement I could infer a lot about his wife.* If you imply that something is the case, you suggest that it is the case without actually saying so. ❑ *Rose's lawyer implied that he had married her for her money.*

in·fer·ence /ɪnfərəns/ (**inferences**) **1** N-COUNT An **inference** is a conclusion that you draw about something by using information that you already have about it. 推论 ❑ *There were two inferences to be drawn from her letter.* 从她的来信可以得到两种推论。 **2** N-UNCOUNT **Inference** is the act of drawing conclusions about something on the basis of information that you already have. 推断 ❑ *It had an extremely tiny head and, by inference, a tiny brain.* 它的头极小，可以根据推断得出，大脑也小。

in·fe·ri·or /ɪnfɪəriər/ (**inferiors**) **1** ADJ Something that is **inferior** is not as good as something else. 较差的 ❑ *The cassettes were of inferior quality.* 这些盒式磁带质量较差。 ❑ *This resulted in overpriced and often inferior products.* 这就导致产品标价过高而往往质量较次。 **2** ADJ If one person is regarded as **inferior to** another, they are regarded as less important because they have less status or ability. 低等的；次要的 ❑ *He preferred the company of those who were intellectually inferior to himself.* 他喜欢与那些智力不如他的人为伍。 ● N-COUNT **Inferior** is also a noun. (能力或地位) 低于他人者；部下 ❑ *It was a gentleman's duty always to be civil, even to his inferiors.* 一个绅士的责任是一直保持彬彬有礼，即使是对比自己地位低的人。 ● **in·fe·ri·or·ity** /ɪnfɪriɔrɪti/ N-UNCOUNT 自卑 ❑ *I found it difficult to shake off a sense of social inferiority.* 我发现很难摆脱社会地位低下的自卑感。

Thesaurus *inferior* 另参见:

ADJ.	mediocre, second-rate, substandard **1**

in·fer·tile /ɪnfɜrtəl/ **1** ADJ A person or animal that is **infertile** is unable to produce babies. (人) 不能生育的; (动物) 不能繁殖的 ❑ *According to one survey, one woman in eight is infertile.* 根据一项调查，每8个妇女中就有1个不能生育。 ● **in·fer·til·ity** /ɪnfɜrtɪlɪti/ N-UNCOUNT 不育 ❑ *Male infertility is becoming commonplace.* 男性不育越来越常见。 **2** ADJ **Infertile** soil is of poor quality because it lacks substances that plants need. 贫瘠的 ❑ *The land was barren and infertile.* 这片土地荒芜而贫瘠。

in·fest /ɪnfɛst/ (**infests, infesting, infested**) **1** V-T When creatures such as insects or rats **infest** plants or a place, they are present in large numbers and cause damage. (昆虫或老鼠等) 大批出没于 ❑ *...pests like aphids which infest cereal crops.* …像蚜虫那样大肆侵害谷类作物的害虫。 ● **in·fest·ed** ADJ 大批出没的 ❑ *The prison is infested with rats.* 那座监狱里鼠满为患。 **2** V-T If you say that people or things you disapprove of or regard as dangerous **are infesting** a place, you mean that there are large numbers of them in that place. 充斥着 [DISAPPROVAL] ❑ *Crime and drugs are infesting the inner cities.* 犯罪和毒品充斥着市中心区。 ● **in·fest·ed** ADJ 成群危害的 ❑ *The road further south was infested with bandits.* 更南边的公路盗匪猖獗。

in·fi·del·ity /ɪnfɪdɛlɪti/ (**infidelities**) N-VAR **Infidelity** occurs when a person who is married or in a steady relationship has sex with another person. 私通 ❑ *George turned a blind eye to his partner's infidelities.* 乔治对他伴侣的私通睁一只眼闭一只眼。

in·fil·trate /ɪnfɪltreɪt/ (**infiltrates, infiltrating, infiltrated**) **1** V-T/V-I If people **infiltrate** a place or organization, or **infiltrate into** it, they enter it secretly in order to spy on it or influence it. 渗入；潜入 (某地方或组织) ❑ *Activists had infiltrated the student movement.* 激进分子已经渗入学生运动。 ● **in·fil·tra·tion** /ɪnfɪltreɪʃən/ N-VAR (**infiltrations**) 渗透 ❑ *...an inquiry into alleged infiltration by the far left group.* …一项对被指称的极左团体渗入的调查。 **2** V-T To **infiltrate** people **into** a place or organization means to get them into it secretly in order to spy on it or influence it. 使…渗入 ❑ *He claimed that some countries have been trying to infiltrate their agents into the republic.* 他声称有些国家一直试图使他们的特工渗入该共和国。

in·fi·nite /ɪnfɪnɪt/ **1** ADJ If you describe something as **infinite**, you are emphasizing that it is extremely great in amount or degree. 极大的；极多的 [EMPHASIS] ❑ *...an infinite variety of landscapes.* …极其多样的地形地貌。 ❑ *With infinite care, John shifted position.* 约翰小心翼翼地换了位置。 ● **in·fi·nite·ly** ADV 极大地 [ADV adj/adv] ❑ *His design was infinitely better than anything I could have done.* 他的设计比我所能设计的不知要好上多少倍。 **2** ADJ Something that is **infinite** has no limit, end, or edge. 无穷的；无限的 ❑ *...an infinite number of atoms.* …无数个原子。 ● **in·fi·nite·ly** ADV 无穷无尽地 [ADV with v] ❑ *A centimeter can be infinitely divided into smaller units.* 一厘米能被无穷尽地分为更小的单位。

in·fini·tive /ɪnfɪnɪtɪv/ (**infinitives**) N-COUNT The **infinitive** of a verb is the basic form, for example, "do," "be," "take," and "eat." The infinitive is often used with "to" in front of it. (动词的) 不定式

★ **in·fin·ity** /ɪnfɪnɪti/ **1** N-UNCOUNT **Infinity** is a number that is larger than any other number and can never be given an exact value. 无穷大 [also "a" N "of" n] ❑ *These permutations multiply toward infinity.* 这些排列向无穷大增加。 **2** N-UNCOUNT **Infinity** is a point that is further away than any other point and can never be reached. 无限远的点 ❑ *...the darkness of a starless night stretching to infinity.* …没有星星的黑夜，向无垠延伸。

Word Link *firm ≈ making strong : affirm, confirm, infirm*

in·firm /ɪnfɜrm/ ADJ A person who is **infirm** is weak or ill, and usually old. (常指因年迈而) 体弱的 [FORMAL] ❑ *...her aging, infirm husband.* …她那年迈体弱的丈夫。 ● N-PLURAL **The infirm** are people who are infirm. 体弱者 ❑ *We are here to protect and assist the weak and infirm.* 我们来这里保护和帮助病弱者。

in·fir·ma·ry /ɪnfɜrməri/ (**infirmaries**) N-COUNT An **infirmary** is a place in a school or other institution that is used to take care of people who are sick or injured. 医务室

Word Link *flam ≈ burning : flame, flammable, inflame*

in·flame /ɪnfleɪm/ (**inflames, inflaming, inflamed**) V-T If something **inflames** a situation or **inflames** people's feelings, it makes people feel even more strongly about something. 使加剧 [JOURNALISM] ❑ *They are responsible for inflaming the situation.* 他们应该对事态激化负责。

in·flamed /ɪnfleɪmd/ ADJ If part of your body is **inflamed**, it is red or swollen, usually as a result of an infection, injury, or illness. 红肿的; 发炎的 ❑ *Symptoms include red, itchy and inflamed skin.* 症状包括皮肤红肿、瘙痒和发炎。

in·flam·mable /ɪnflæməbᵊl/ ADJ An **inflammable** material or chemical catches fire and burns easily. 易燃的 ❑ *A highly inflammable liquid escaped into the drilling equipment.* 一种高度易燃的液体漏进了钻孔设备。

in·flam·ma·tion /ɪnfləmeɪʃᵊn/ (**inflammations**) N-VAR An **inflammation** is a painful redness or swelling of a part of your body that results from an infection, injury, or illness. 炎症 ❑ *The drug can cause inflammation of the liver.* 这种药会引发肝脏炎症。

in·flam·ma·tory /ɪnflæmətɔri/ **1** ADJ If you accuse someone of saying or doing **inflammatory** things, you mean that what they say or do is likely to make people react very angrily. 使人激愤的 [DISAPPROVAL] ❑ *...nationalist policies that are too drastic and inflammatory.* …过于激烈、煽动性强的民族主义政策。 **2** ADJ An **inflammatory** condition or disease is one in which the patient suffers from inflammation. 炎症的 [ADJ n] [FORMAL] ❑ *...the inflammatory reactions that occur in asthma.* …出现于哮喘的炎症反应。

in·flat·able /ɪnfleɪtəbᵊl/ (**inflatables**) **1** ADJ An **inflatable** object is one that you fill with air when you want to use it. 可充气的 ❑ *The children were playing on the inflatable castle.* 孩子们在充气城堡上玩。 **2** N-COUNT An **inflatable** is an inflatable object, especially a small boat. 可充气物品 ❑ *...floats, tubes and other inflatables.* …救生艇、轮胎和其他可充气物品。

▲ **in·flate** /ɪnfleɪt/ (**inflates, inflating, inflated**) **1** V-T/V-I If you **inflate** something such as a balloon or tire, or if it **inflates**, it becomes bigger as it is filled with air or a gas. 使充气; 充气 ❑ *Stuart jumped into the sea and inflated the liferaft.* 斯图尔特跳进海里给救生筏充气。 **2** V-T/V-I If you say that someone **inflates** the price of something, or that the price **inflates**, you mean that the price increases. 抬高(物价); 涨高 ❑ *The promotion of a big release can inflate a film's final cost.* 一部大片的发行宣传会抬高影片的最终成本。 ● **in·flat·ed** ADJ 高涨的 ❑ *They had to buy everything at inflated prices at the ranch store.* 他们不得不以高价购买牧场商店里的各种物品。 **3** V-T If someone **inflates** the amount or effect of something, they say it is bigger, better, or more important than it really is, usually so that they can profit from it. 夸大 ❑ *They inflated their clients' medical injuries and treatment to defraud insurance companies.* 他们夸大了客户受伤及治疗的情况以欺骗保险公司。

in·fla·tion ♦♦◇ /ɪnfleɪʃᵊn/ N-UNCOUNT **Inflation** is a general increase in the prices of goods and services in a country. 通货膨胀 [BUSINESS] ❑ *...rising unemployment and high inflation.* …上涨的失业率和高通胀。

Word Partnership *inflation* 的常用搭配:

- V. **control** inflation, **reduce** inflation
- N. inflation **fears**, **increase in** inflation, inflation **rate**
- ADJ. **high/low** inflation

in·fla·tion·ary /ɪnfleɪʃəneri/ ADJ **Inflationary** means connected with inflation or causing inflation. 有关通货膨胀的; 引起通货膨胀的 [BUSINESS] ❑ *The bank is worried about mounting inflationary pressures.* 银行对日趋加大的通货膨胀压力感到担心。

in·flec·tion /ɪnflɛkʃᵊn/ (**inflections**) N-VAR An **inflection** in someone's voice is a change in its tone or pitch as they are speaking. 变音; 变调 [WRITTEN] ❑ *...the upward inflection of her voice.* …她声调的升高。

in·flex·ible /ɪnflɛksɪbᵊl/ **1** ADJ Something that is **inflexible** cannot be altered in any way, even if the situation changes. 不可改变的 ❑ *Workers insisted the new system was too inflexible.* 工人们坚持认为新制度过于僵化。 ● **in·flex·ibil·ity** /ɪnflɛksɪbɪlɪti/ N-UNCOUNT 不可改变 ❑ *The system's inflexibility was highlighted by several recent failures.* 最近的几次失败突显了这项制度的刻板。 ❑ *Marvin's father was exceptional for the inflexibility of his rules.* 马文的父亲特别对他定的规矩不容变通。 **2** ADJ If you say that someone is **inflexible**, you are criticizing them because they refuse to change their mind or alter their way of doing things. 顽固的 [DISAPPROVAL] ❑ *His opponents viewed him as stubborn, dogmatic, and inflexible.* 他的对手认为他固执、教条而且死板。 ● **in·flex·ibil·ity** N-UNCOUNT 顽固 ❑ *Joyce was irritated by the inflexibility of her colleagues.* 乔伊斯被她同事的顽固惹恼了。

Word Link *flict ≈ striking : affliction, conflict, inflict*

★ **in·flict** /ɪnflɪkt/ (**inflicts, inflicting, inflicted**) V-T To **inflict** harm or damage **on** someone or something means to make them suffer it. 使遭受(伤害或破坏等) ❑ *...the damage being inflicted on industries by the recession.* …经济衰退给工业造成的损失。

in·flu·ence ♦♦◇ /ɪnfluəns/ (**influences, influencing, influenced**) **1** N-UNCOUNT **Influence** is the power to make other people agree with your opinions or do what you want. 权势 ❑ *He used his influence to get his son into medical school.* 他利用权势把儿子弄进了医学院。 ❑ *He denies exerting any political influence over them.* 他否认曾向他们施加过政治影响。 **2** V-T If you **influence** someone, you use your power to make them agree with you or do what you want. 影响 ❑ *He is trying to improperly influence a witness.* 他正试图不适当地影响一名证人。 **3** N-COUNT To have an **influence on** people or situations means to affect what they do or what happens. 影响 ❑ *Van Gogh had a major influence on the development of modern painting.* 凡·高对现代绘画的发展有着重大的影响。 **4** V-T If someone or something **influences** a person or situation, they have an effect on that person's behavior or that situation. 影响 ❑ *We became the best of friends and he influenced me deeply.* 我们成了最好的朋友，而他深深地影响了我。 **5** N-COUNT Someone or something that is a good or bad **influence on** people has a good or bad effect on them. 有影响的人(或事物) ❑ *I thought Sonny would be a good influence on you.* 我认为桑尼对你会有好的影响。 **6** PHRASE If you are **under the influence of** someone or something, you are being affected or controlled by them. 在…影响之下 ❑ *He was arrested on suspicion of driving under the influence of alcohol.* 他因涉嫌酒后驾车而被捕。

Word Partnership *influence* 的常用搭配:

- ADJ. **political** influence **1**
  considerable influence, **important** influence, **major** influence, **powerful** influence, **strong** influence **1** **3**
  bad/good influence **5**
- N. influence **behavior**, influence **opinion**, influence **people** **2** **4**

in·flu·en·tial /ɪnfluɛnʃᵊl/ ADJ Someone or something that is **influential** has a lot of influence over people or events. 有影响力的; 有权势的 ❑ *It helps to have influential friends.* 交上几个有权势的朋友很有好处。 ❑ *He had been influential in shaping economic policy.* 他在制定经济政策方面曾起过很大作用。

in·flux /ɪnflʌks/ (**influxes**) N-COUNT An **influx of** people or things into a place is their arrival there in large numbers. (人或物的)大量涌入 ❑ *...problems caused by the influx of refugees.* …难民大量涌入所造成的问题。

info /ɪnfoʊ/ N-UNCOUNT **Info** is information. 信息 [INFORMAL] ❑ *For more info call 414-3935.* 欲知详情，请拨打电话414-3935。

in·form ♦◇◇ /ɪnfɔrm/ (**informs, informing, informed**) **1** V-T If you **inform** someone **of** something, you tell them about it. 告知 ❑ *They would inform him of any progress they had made.* 他们将把自己所取得的任何进展都告诉他。 ❑ *My daughter informed me that she was pregnant.* 我女儿告诉我她怀孕了。 **2** V-I If someone **informs on** a person, they give information about the person to the police or another authority, which causes the person to be suspected or proved guilty of doing something bad. 检举 ❑ *Thousands of American citizens have informed on these organized crime syndicates.* 成千上万的美国公民检举了这些有组织的犯罪集团。 **3** V-T If a situation or activity **is informed** by an idea or a quality, that idea or quality is very noticeable in it. 弥漫(思想或品质等) [FORMAL] ❑ *All great songs are informed by a certain sadness and tension.* 所有动听的歌曲无不弥漫着某种伤感和紧绷感。

Word Partnership *inform* 的常用搭配:

- N. inform **parents**, inform **people**, inform **the police**, inform **readers**, inform ***someone* in writing** **1**

in·for·mal /ɪnfɔrmᵊl/ **1** ADJ **Informal** speech or behavior is relaxed and friendly rather than serious, very correct, or official. 非正式的(言行) ❑ *She is refreshingly informal.* 她随和得令人耳目一新。 ● **in·for·mal·ly** ADV 非正式地(言行) [ADV after v] ❑ *She was always there at half past eight, chatting informally to the children.* 她总是八点半钟

到那儿，与孩子们随意交谈。● **in·for·mal·ity** /ɪnfɔrmælɪti/ N-UNCOUNT 非正式；随意 ❑ *He was overwhelmed by their friendly informality.* 他们的友好和随意使他无比激动。**2** ADJ An **informal** situation is one that is relaxed and friendly and not very serious or official. 轻松随意的 ❑ *The house has an informal atmosphere.* 这屋子里有一种轻松随意的气氛。● **in·for·mal·ity** N-UNCOUNT 轻松随意 ❑ *She enjoyed the relative informality of island life.* 她喜欢相对轻松随意的岛屿生活。**3** ADJ **Informal** clothes are casual and suitable for wearing when you are relaxing, but not on formal occasions. (衣服) 休闲的 ❑ *For lunch, dress is informal.* 吃午餐可以穿着休闲装。● **in·for·mal·ly** ADV (穿着) 休闲地 ❑ *Everyone dressed informally in shorts or faded jeans, and baggy sweatshirts.* 大家都穿休闲装，或短裤、或褪色牛仔裤、或宽松的运动衫。**4** ADJ You use **informal** to describe something that is done unofficially or casually without planning. 非正式的；非正规的 ❑ *The two leaders will retire to Camp David for informal discussions.* 这两位领导人将去戴维营进行非正式会谈。● **in·for·mal·ly** ADV 非正式地 ❑ *He began informally to handle Ted's tax affairs for him.* 他开始非正式地为特德管理他的税务。

Thesaurus *informal* 另参见：

ADJ. natural, relaxed; *(ant.)* formal **1** **2**
casual; *(ant.)* formal **3**
unofficial; *(ant.)* formal **4**

in·form·ant /ɪnfɔrmənt/ (**informants**) **1** N-COUNT An **informant** is someone who gives another person a piece of information. 信息提供者 [FORMAL] ❑ *On the basis of data furnished by her informants, Mead concluded that adolescents in Samoa had complete sexual freedom.* 米德根据信息提供者所给的资料，得到的结论是萨摩亚的青少年有完全的性自由。**2** N-COUNT An **informant** is the same as an **informer**. 告密者

in·for·ma·tion ♦♦♦ /ɪnfərmeɪʃən/ **1** N-UNCOUNT **Information** about someone or something consists of facts about them. 消息；资料 ❑ *Pat refused to give her any information about Sarah.* 帕特拒绝向她提供任何有关萨拉的消息。❑ *Each center would provide information on technology and training.* 每个中心都将提供有关技术与培训的资料。**2** N-UNCOUNT **Information** consists of the facts and figures that are stored and used by a computer program. (电脑中储存和使用的) 数据 [COMPUTING] ❑ *Pictures are scanned into a form of digital information that computers can recognize.* 图片被扫描成一种计算机能识别的数字化资料。**3** N-UNCOUNT **Information** is a service that you can telephone to find out someone's telephone number. 问讯处 [AM]

in BRIT, use **directory enquiries**

❑ *He called information, and they gave him the number.* 他打电话给信息台，他们便给了他电话号码。

Note that **information** is only ever used as an uncount noun. You cannot say "an information" or "informations." However, you can say a **piece of information** or an **item of information** when you are referring to a particular fact that someone has informed you of.

Word Partnership *information* 的常用搭配：

ADJ. **additional** information, **background** information, **classified** information, **important** information, **new** information, **personal** information **1**
V. **find** information, **get** information, **have** information, **need** information, **provide** information, **want** information **1**
retrieve information, **store** information **2**

in·for·ma·tion tech·nol·ogy N-UNCOUNT **Information technology** is the theory and practice of using computers to store and analyze information. The abbreviation **IT** is often used. 信息技术 ❑ *...the information technology industry.* …信息技术产业。→ see **industry**

in·forma·tive /ɪnfɔrmətɪv/ ADJ Something that is **informative** gives you useful information. 提供有用信息的；使人增进知识的 ❑ *Both men termed the meeting friendly and informative.* 他们两人都称这次会晤亲切友好，使双方增进了解。

Thesaurus *informative* 另参见：

ADJ. educational, informational, instructional

in·formed /ɪnfɔrmd/ **1** ADJ Someone who is **informed** knows about a subject or what is happening in the world. 见多识广的；了解情况的 ❑ *Informed people know the company is shaky.* 了解情况的人知道该公司状况不稳定。**2** → see also **well-informed** **3** ADJ When journalists talk about **informed** sources, they mean people who are likely to give correct information because of their private or special knowledge. 有根据的 (消息来源) [ADJ n] ❑ *According to informed sources, those taken into custody include at least one major-general.* 据可靠消息来源，被拘捕者中至少包括一名陆军少将。**4** ADJ An **informed** guess or decision is one that likely to be good, because it is based on definite knowledge or information. 明智的 (猜测或决定) [ADJ n] ❑ *Science is now enabling us to make more informed choices about how we use common drugs.* 科学现在使得我们能够对如何使用常用药品做出更明智的选择。**5** → see also **inform**

in·form·er /ɪnfɔrmər/ (**informers**) N-COUNT An **informer** is a person who tells the police that someone has done something illegal. 告密者 ❑ *...two men suspected of being police informers.* …被怀疑为警方线人的两名男子。

info·tain·ment /ɪnfoʊteɪnmənt/ N-UNCOUNT **Infotainment** is used to refer to radio or television programs that are intended both to entertain people and to give information. The word is formed from "information" and "entertainment." (广播或电视中的) 资讯娱乐节目 ❑ *Cable TV's Food Network offers a buffet of food-related infotainment.* 有线电视的食品网提供各种有关食品的资讯娱乐节目。

▲ **infra·red** /ɪnfrərɛd/ also **infra-red** **1** ADJ **Infrared** radiation is similar to light but has a longer wavelength, so we cannot see it without special equipment. 红外线的 [ADJ n] **2** ADJ **Infrared** equipment detects infrared radiation. 使用红外线的 [ADJ n] ❑ *...searching with infrared scanners for weapons and artillery.* …用红外线扫描仪搜查武器和大炮。

▲ **infra·struc·ture** /ɪnfrəstrʌktʃər/ (**infrastructures**) N-VAR The **infrastructure** of a country, society, or organization consists of the basic facilities such as transportation, communications, power supplies, and buildings, which enable it to function. (国家、社会、组织赖以行使职能的) 基础设施 ❑ *...improvements in the country's infrastructure.* …国家基础设施的改善。

★ **in·fringe** /ɪnfrɪndʒ/ (**infringes, infringing, infringed**) **1** V-T If someone **infringes** a law or a rule, they break it or do something that disobeys it. 违反 ❑ *The film exploited his image and infringed his copyright.* 该影片利用了他的肖像，侵犯了他的肖像权。**2** V-T/V-I If something **infringes** people's rights, or **infringes on** them, it interferes with these rights and does not allow people the freedom they are entitled to. 侵犯 ❑ *They rob us, they infringe our rights, they kill us.* 他们劫掠我们，他们侵犯我们的权利，他们屠杀我们。

in·fringe·ment /ɪnfrɪndʒmənt/ (**infringements**) **1** N-VAR An **infringement** is an action or situation that interferes with your rights and the freedom you are entitled to. (对他人权利或自由等的) 侵犯 ❑ *...infringement of privacy.* …对隐私的侵犯。**2** N-VAR An **infringement of** a law or rule is the act of breaking it or disobeying it. 违反 ❑ *There might have been an infringement of the rules.* 也许有违反规章制度的情况。

in·furi·ate /ɪnfyʊərieɪt/ (**infuriates, infuriating, infuriated**) V-T If something or someone **infuriates** you, they make you extremely angry. 激怒 ❑ *His manner infuriated him.* 他的举止激怒了他。

in·furi·at·ing /ɪnfyʊərieɪtɪŋ/ ADJ Something that is **infuriating** annoys you very much. 激怒人的 ❑ *A man of indecision is infuriating to watch.* 优柔寡断的男人让人一看就生气。

in·fuse /ɪnfyuz/ (**infuses, infusing, infused**) V-T To **infuse** a quality **into** someone or something, or to **infuse** them **with** a quality, means to fill them with it. 注入 (某种特性) [FORMAL] ❑ *Many of the girls seemed to be infused with excitement on seeing the snow.* 许多女孩子似乎一看到雪心里就充满了兴奋。

★ **in·gen·ious** /ɪndʒinyəs/ ADJ Something that is **ingenious** is very clever and involves new ideas, methods, or equipment. 灵巧的；新颖的 ❑ *...a truly ingenious invention.* …一项的确新颖的发明。

▲ **in·genu·ity** /ɪndʒənuɪti/ N-UNCOUNT **Ingenuity** is skill at working out how to achieve things or skill at inventing new things. 善于创新；足智多谋 ❑ *Inspecting the nest can be difficult and may require some ingenuity.* 仔细检查鸟巢可能有困难，也许需要一些巧妙的心思。

in·grained /ɪngreɪnd/ ADJ **Ingrained** habits and beliefs are difficult to change or remove. (习惯或信仰) 根深蒂固的 ❑ *Morals tend to be deeply ingrained.* 道德观念往往是根深蒂固的。

in·gre·di·ent ♦◇◇ /ɪngridiənt/ (**ingredients**) **1** N-COUNT **Ingredients** are the things that are used to make something,

i

especially all the different foods you use when you are cooking a particular dish. (尤指烹调用的) 原料 ❑ *Mix in the remaining ingredients.* 掺入剩下的原料。 2 N-COUNT An **ingredient** of a situation is one of the essential parts of it. 要素 ❑ *The meeting had all the ingredients of high political drama.* 这次会议拥有了极富戏剧性的政治紧张场面的全部要素。

Word Partnership *ingredient* 的常用搭配:
ADJ. **active** ingredient, **a common** ingredient, **secret** ingredient 1
important ingredient, **key** ingredient, **main** ingredient 1 2

★ **in·hab·it** /ɪnhæbɪt/ (**inhabits, inhabiting, inhabited**) V-T If a place or region **is inhabited** by a group of people or a species of animal, those people or animals live there. 居住于 ❑ *The valley is inhabited by the Dani tribe.* 这个山谷里居住着丹尼部落。 ❑ *...the people who inhabit these islands.* …居住于这些岛屿的人们。

in·hab·it·ant /ɪnhæbɪtənt/ (**inhabitants**) N-COUNT The **inhabitants** of a place are the people who live there. 居民 ❑ *...the inhabitants of Boise.* …博伊斯的居民。

▲ **in·hale** /ɪnheɪl/ (**inhales, inhaling, inhaled**) V-T/V-I When you **inhale**, you breathe in. When you **inhale** something such as smoke, you take it into your lungs when you breathe in. 吸入; 吸气 ❑ *He took a long slow breath, inhaling deeply.* 他缓缓地深吸了一口气。

in·her·ent /ɪnhɛrənt, -hɪər-/ ADJ The **inherent** qualities of something are the necessary and natural parts of it. 内在的 ❑ *Stress is an inherent part of dieting.* 要节食必定会经受压力。
● **in·her·ent·ly** ADV 内在地 ❑ *Man is not inherently violent.* 人类并非生来就暴力。

in·her·it /ɪnhɛrɪt/ (**inherits, inheriting, inherited**) 1 V-T If you **inherit** money or property, you receive it from someone who has died. 继承 (财产) ❑ *He has no son to inherit his land.* 他没有儿子来继承他的土地。 2 V-T If you **inherit** something such as a task, problem, or attitude, you get it from the people who used to have it, for example, because you have taken over their job or been influenced by them. 接手; 接任 ❑ *The Endara government inherited an impossibly difficult situation from its predecessors.* 恩达拉政府从其前任手里接过了一个极为困难的局面。 3 V-T If you **inherit** a characteristic or quality, you are born with it, because your parents or ancestors also had it. 经遗传而得 (特征、品质等) ❑ *We inherit from our parents many of our physical characteristics.* 我们从父母的遗传中得到许多体貌特征。 ❑ *Her children have inherited her love of sports.* 她的孩子们从她那里继承了对体育运动的爱好。

in·her·it·ance /ɪnhɛrɪtᵊns/ (**inheritances**) 1 N-VAR An **inheritance** is money or property that you receive from someone who has died. 继承物; 遗产 ❑ *She feared losing her inheritance to her stepmother.* 她担心她的遗产会落到继母的手里。 2 N-COUNT If you get something such as a job, problem, or attitude from someone who used to have it, you can refer to this as an **inheritance**. 转接物; 沿袭物 ❑ *...starvation and disease over much of Europe and Asia, which was Truman's inheritance as president.* …在欧亚大部分地区肆虐的饥馑和疾病，这是杜鲁门接任总统时面临的状况。 3 N-SING Your **inheritance** is the particular characteristics or qualities that your family or ancestors had and that you are born with. 遗传特征 ❑ *Eye color shows more than your genetic inheritance.* 眼睛的颜色显示的不只是你基因的遗传特征。
→ see **gene**

in·her·it·ance tax (**inheritance taxes**) N-COUNT An **inheritance tax** is a tax paid on the money and property of someone who has died. 遗产税

★ **in·hib·it** /ɪnhɪbɪt/ (**inhibits, inhibiting, inhibited**) 1 V-T If something **inhibits** an event or process, it prevents it or slows it down. 阻碍; 抑制 ❑ *The high cost of borrowing is inhibiting investment by industry in new equipment.* 高昂的借贷成本正抑制行业对新设备的投资。 2 V-T To **inhibit** someone **from** doing something means to prevent them from doing it, although they want to do it or should be able to do it. 禁止; 阻止 ❑ *Officers will be inhibited from doing their duty.* 官员们将被阻止履行其职责。

in·hib·it·ed /ɪnhɪbɪtɪd/ ADJ If you say that someone is **inhibited**, you mean that they find it difficult to behave naturally and show their feelings, and that you think this is a bad thing. 拘谨的; 拘束的 [DISAPPROVAL] ❑ *Men are more inhibited about touching each other than women are.* 触摸同性时男人比女人要更加拘谨。

in·hi·bi·tion /ɪnɪbɪʃᵊn/ (**inhibitions**) N-VAR **Inhibitions** are feelings of fear or embarrassment that make it difficult for you to behave naturally. 拘谨; 拘束 ❑ *The whole point about dancing is to stop thinking and lose all your inhibitions.* 跳舞的整个要点在于停止思考并丢掉所有拘束。

in-house ADJ **In-house** work or activities are done by employees of an organization or company, rather than by workers outside the organization or company. 机构内部的 ❑ *A lot of companies do in-house training.* 许多公司都进行内部人员培训。 ● ADV **In-house** is also an adverb. 在机构内部 ❑ *The magazine is still produced in-house.* 该杂志仍然在机构内部出版。

in·hu·man /ɪnhyumən/ 1 ADJ If you describe treatment or an action as **inhuman**, you mean that it is extremely cruel. 不人道的; 极其残酷的 ❑ *The detainees are often held in cruel and inhuman conditions.* 被拘留者经常被羁押在既残酷又不人道的环境里。 2 ADJ If you describe someone or something as **inhuman**, you mean that they are strange or bad because they do not seem human in some way. 非人类的; (不像人类所为而) 怪异的 ❑ *...inhuman screams and moans.* …不像人类的尖叫和呻吟。

in·hu·mane /ɪnhyumeɪn/ ADJ If you describe something as **inhumane**, you mean that it is extremely cruel. 残忍的; 不人道的 ❑ *He was kept under inhumane conditions.* 他被置于惨无人道的环境里。

ini·tial ♦◇◇ /ɪnɪʃᵊl/ (**initials, initialing, initialed**)
in BRIT, sometimes AM use **initialling, initialled**
1 ADJ You use **initial** to describe something that happens at the beginning of a process. 最初的 [ADJ n] ❑ *The initial reaction has been excellent.* 最初的反应极好。 2 N-COUNT **Initials** are the capital letters that begin each word of a name. For example, if your full name is Michael Dennis Stocks, your initials are M.D.S. (姓名的) 大写首字母 ❑ *...a silver Porsche with her initials JB on the side.* …一辆银色保时捷汽车，侧面有她的姓名首字母JB。 3 V-T If someone **initials** an official document, they write their initials on it, to show that they have seen it or that they accept or agree with it. 签姓名的首字母于 ❑ *Would you mind initialing this voucher?* 请您在这张单子上签上姓名的首字母，好吗?

Word Partnership *initial* 的常用搭配:
N. initial **diagnosis**, initial **estimate**, initial **investment**, initial **phase**, initial **reaction**, initial **results**, initial **stages** 1

ini·tial·ly ♦◇◇ /ɪnɪʃəli/ ADV **Initially** means soon after the beginning of a process or situation, rather than in the middle or at the end of it. 最初 ❑ *Forecasters say the storms may not be as bad as they initially predicted.* 预报员们说暴风雨不像他们最初预报的那样糟。

★ **ini·ti·ate** /ɪnɪʃieɪt/ (**initiates, initiating, initiated**) 1 V-T If you **initiate** something, you start it or cause it to happen. 使开始; 发起 ❑ *They wanted to initiate a discussion on economics.* 他们想发起一次关于经济学的讨论。 2 V-T If you **initiate** someone **into** something, you introduce them to a particular skill or type of knowledge and teach them about it. 使初步了解; 传授 ❑ *He initiated her into the study of other cultures.* 他引导她进入对于其他文化的研究。 3 V-T If someone **is initiated into** something such as a religion, secret society, or social group, they become a member of it by taking part in special ceremonies. (常通过特殊仪式) 使加入 ❑ *In many societies, young people are formally initiated into their adult roles.* 在很多社会，年轻人要通过正式的仪式进入成年。

ini·tia·tion /ɪnɪʃieɪʃᵊn/ (**initiations**) 1 N-UNCOUNT The **initiation** of something is the starting of it. 开始; 发起 ❑ *...the initiation of a rural development program.* …一项农村发展规划的启动 2 N-VAR Someone's **initiation into** a particular group is the act or process by which they officially become a member, often involving special ceremonies. 入会; 入会仪式 ❑ *This was my initiation into the peace movement.* 那是我加入和平运动的开始。

ini·tia·tive ♦◇◇ /ɪnɪʃiətɪv, -ʃətɪv/ (**initiatives**) 1 N-COUNT An **initiative** is an important act or statement that is intended to solve a problem. (重要的) 法案; 倡议 ❑ *Local initiatives to help young people have been inadequate.* 当地对年轻人的扶助法案一直不够完善。 2 N-SING In a fight or contest, if you have **the initiative**, you are in a better position than your opponents to decide what to do next. 主动权 ❑ *We have the initiative; we intend to keep it.* 我们拥有主动权; 我们想要保持主动权。 3 N-UNCOUNT If you have **initiative**, you have the ability to decide what to do next and to do it, without needing other people to tell you what to do. 主动性 ❑ *She was disappointed by his lack of initiative.* 她对他缺乏主动性感到失望。 **4** N-COUNT An **initiative** is a political procedure in which a group of citizens propose a new law or a change to the law, which all voters can then vote on. 公民立法提案程序 [mainly AM] ❑ *If they reject or ignore the initiative, the public will vote on it in November.* 如果他们拒绝或无视公民立法提案程序，公众将于11月对它进行投票表决。 **5** PHRASE If you **take the initiative** in a situation, you are the first person to act, and are therefore able to control the situation. 采取主动 ❑ *We are the only power willing to take the initiative in the long struggle to end the war.* 在旨在结束战争的长期斗争中，我们是惟一愿意首先采取行动的国家。

Word Partnership *initiative* 的常用搭配：
ADJ. **diplomatic** initiative, **political** initiative **1**
V. **have the** initiative, **seize the** initiative **2**
take the initiative **5**

★ **in·ject** /ɪndʒɛkt/ (**injects, injecting, injected**) **1** V-T To **inject** a substance such as a medicine into someone means to put it into their body using a device with a needle called a syringe. 给…注射 ❑ *His son was injected with strong drugs.* 他的儿子被注射了强效的药。 ❑ *The technique consists of injecting healthy cells into the weakened muscles.* 这项技术包括把健康细胞注射进衰弱的肌肉里。 **2** V-T If you **inject** a new, exciting, or interesting quality **into** a situation, you add it. 注入；增添 ❑ *She kept trying to inject a little fun into their relationship.* 她一直设法给他们的关系增添一点情趣。 **3** V-T If you **inject** money or resources **into** a business or organization, you provide more money or resources for it. 注入 (资金或资源) [BUSINESS] ❑ *The insurance fund would inject $750 into the banks.* 该保险基金将向银行投入750美元。

Word Partnership *inject* 的常用搭配：
N. inject **a drug**, inject **insulin** **1**
inject **humor**, inject **life** **2**

in·jec·tion /ɪndʒɛkʃᵊn/ (**injections**) **1** N-COUNT If you have an **injection**, a doctor or nurse puts a medicine into your body using a device with a needle called a syringe. 注射 [also "by" N] ❑ *They gave me an injection to help me sleep.* 他们给我打了一针以助我入眠。 **2** N-COUNT An **injection of** money or resources into an organization is the act of providing it with more money or resources, to help it become more efficient or profitable. (资金或资源的) 注入 [BUSINESS] ❑ *An injection of cash is needed to fund some of these projects.* 其中的一些项目需要投入现金资助。

in·junc·tion /ɪndʒʌŋkʃᵊn/ (**injunctions**) **1** N-COUNT An **injunction** is a court order, usually one telling someone not to do something. (法院的) 禁令；强制令 [LEGAL] ❑ *He took out a court injunction against the newspaper demanding the return of the document.* 他拿出法院强制令，要求这家报纸归还该文件。 **2** N-COUNT An **injunction to** do something is an order or strong request to do it. 指令 [FORMAL] ❑ *We hear endless injunctions to managers to build commitment and a sense of community among their staff.* 我们听到对经理们无休无止的训示，要他们在其员工中培养奉献精神和团队意识。

in·jure /ɪndʒər/ (**injures, injuring, injured**) V-T If you **injure** a person or animal, you damage some part of their body. 使受伤；伤害 ❑ *A number of bombs have exploded, seriously injuring at least five people.* 一些炸弹爆炸了，至少5人严重受伤。
→ see **war**

Word Partnership *injure* 的常用搭配：
V. **kill or** injure
ADV. **seriously** injure
PRON. injure ***someone***, injure ***yourself***

in·jured ♦◇◇ /ɪndʒərd/ **1** ADJ An **injured** person or animal has physical damage to part of their body, usually as a result of an accident or fighting. 受伤的 ❑ *The other injured man had a superficial stomach wound.* 另一名受伤男子是腹部表层受伤。 ● N-PLURAL **The injured** are people who are injured. 受伤者 ❑ *Army helicopters tried to evacuate the injured.* 军用直升机设法撤出伤员。 **2** ADJ If you have **injured** feelings, you feel upset because you believe someone has been unfair or unkind to you. (感情) 受伤害的 ❑ *...a look of injured pride.* …自尊心受伤的表情。

Word Partnership *injured* 的常用搭配：
N. injured **in an accident/attack**, injured **people** **1**
ADV. **badly** injured, **critically** injured, **seriously** injured **1**
ADJ. **dead/killed and** injured **1**
V. **get** injured, **rescue the** injured **1**

in·ju·ry ♦♦◇ /ɪndʒəri/ (**injuries**) **1** N-VAR An **injury** is damage done to a person's or an animal's body. 伤害；损害 ❑ *Four police officers sustained serious injuries in the explosion.* 四名警官在爆炸中受了重伤。

Note that when someone is hurt accidentally, for example, in a car crash or when they are playing sports, you do not use the word **wound**. You use **injury** instead. ❑ *A man and his baby were injured in the explosion... Many of the deaths that occur in cycling are due to head injuries.* In more formal English, **injury** can also be an uncount noun. ❑ *Two teenagers escaped serious injury when their car rolled down an embankment.* **Wound** is normally restricted to soldiers who are injured in battle, or to deliberate acts of violence against a particular person. ❑ *...stab wounds*

2 N-VAR If someone suffers **injury to** their feelings, they are badly upset by something. If they suffer **injury to** their reputation, their reputation is seriously harmed. (对感情或名誉等的) 伤害 [LEGAL] ❑ *She was awarded $3,500 for injury to her feelings.* 她获得了3500美元的精神损伤费。 **3** to **add insult to injury** → see **insult**

Word Partnership *injury* 的常用搭配：
ADJ. **bodily** injury, **internal** injury, **minor** injury, **personal** injury, **serious** injury, **severe** injury **1**
V. **escape** injury, **suffer an** injury **1**

in·jus·tice /ɪndʒʌstɪs/ (**injustices**) **1** N-VAR **Injustice** is a lack of fairness in a situation. 不公正 ❑ *They'll continue to fight injustice.* 他们将继续与不公正的现象抗争。 **2** N-COUNT An injustice is an action or statement in which someone judges you or treats you unfairly. 不公正的行为；不公平的评论 ❑ *Calling them a bunch of capricious kids with half-formed ideas does them an injustice.* 把他们称作一群懵懂无知、喜怒无常的孩子是冤枉了他们。

ink /ɪŋk/ (**inks**) N-MASS **Ink** is the colored liquid used for writing or printing. 墨水；油墨 ❑ *The letter was handwritten in black ink.* 这封信是用黑墨水手写的。
→ see **drawing**

in·laid /ɪnleɪd/ ADJ An object that is **inlaid** has a design on it that is made by putting materials such as wood, gold, or silver into the surface of the object. 镶嵌的 ❑ *...a box inlaid with little triangles.* …一个镶嵌着小三角形的盒子。

★ **in·land**

The adverb is pronounced /ɪnlænd/ or /ɪnlənd/. The adjective is pronounced /ɪnlənd/.

副词读作 /ɪnlænd/或 /ɪnlənd/。形容词读作 /ɪnlənd/。

1 ADV If something is situated **inland**, it is away from the coast, toward or near the middle of a country. If you go **inland**, you go away from the coast, toward the middle of a country. 在内地 (或内陆)；向内地 (或内陆) ❑ *The vast majority live further inland.* 大多数人居住在更远的内陆。 ❑ *It's about 15 minutes' drive inland from Pensacola.* 从彭萨科拉出发向内陆行驶，大约有15分钟的车程。 **2** ADJ **Inland** areas, lakes, and places are not on the coast, but in or near the middle of a country. 内地的；内陆的 [ADJ n] ❑ *...a rather quiet inland town.* …一个很安静的内陆城镇。

in-laws N-PLURAL Your **in-laws** are the parents and close relatives of your husband or wife. 亲家 ❑ *...meals with the in-laws.* …和亲家们一起吃饭。

★ **in·let** /ɪnlɛt, -lɪt/ (**inlets**) N-COUNT An **inlet** is a narrow strip of water that goes from a sea or lake into the land. 水湾 ❑ *A tiny fishing village by a rocky inlet.* 岩石嶙峋的水湾边上的一个小渔村。

▲ **in·mate** /ɪnmeɪt/ (**inmates**) N-COUNT The **inmates** of a prison or mental hospital are the prisoners or patients who are living there. 监犯；(精神病院的) 住院者 ❑ *...education for prison inmates.* …对囚犯们的教育。

inn /ɪn/ (**inns**) N-COUNT; N-IN-NAMES An **inn** is a hotel, bar, or restaurant, often one in the country. (常指乡村的) 小旅店；小酒馆；小餐厅 ❑ *...the Waterside Inn.* …水滨旅馆。

i

Word Link *nat ≈ being born : innate, native, prenatal*

▲ **in·nate** /ɪneɪt/ ADJ An **innate** quality or ability is one that a person is born with. 天生的；固有的 ❑ *Americans have an innate sense of fairness.* 美国人有一种天生的公平感。 ● **in·nate·ly** ADV 天生地 [ADV adj] ❑ *I believe everyone is innately psychic.* 我相信每个人都天生具有超自然能力。

in·ner ♦◇◇ /ɪnər/ 1 ADJ The **inner** parts of something are the parts contained or enclosed inside the other parts, closest to the center. 内部的；里面的 [ADJ n] ❑ *She got up and went into an inner office.* 她起身走进里间办公室。 2 ADJ Your **inner** feelings are feelings that you have but do not show to other people. 内心的 [ADJ n] ❑ *Loving relationships that a child makes will give him an inner sense of security.* 儿童所建立的友爱关系会使他的内心有一种安全感。
→ see core, ear

in·ner cir·cle (inner circles) N-COUNT An **inner circle** is a small group of people within a larger group who have a lot of power, influence, or special information. 核心集团 ❑ *...the inner circle of company executives.* …由公司行政主管人员组成的核心集团。

in·ner city (inner cities) N-COUNT You use **inner city** to refer to the areas in or near the center of a large city where people live and where there are often social and economic problems. (大城市的)市中心区 ❑ *No one could deny that problems of crime in the inner city exist.* 没人能够否认市中心区存在犯罪问题。
→ see city

in·no·cence /ɪnəsəns/ 1 N-UNCOUNT **Innocence** is the quality of having no experience or knowledge of the more complex or unpleasant aspects of life. 天真 ❑ *...the sweet innocence of youth.* …青年时代的天真可爱。 2 N-UNCOUNT If someone proves their **innocence**, they prove that they are not guilty of a crime. 清白 ❑ *He claims he has evidence which could prove his innocence.* 他声称有证据能证明自己的清白。

in·no·cent ♦◇◇ /ɪnəsənt/ (innocents) 1 ADJ If someone is **innocent**, they did not commit a crime that they have been accused of. 清白的 ❑ *He was sure that the man was innocent of any crime.* 他确信此人是清白无罪的。 2 ADJ If someone is **innocent**, they have no experience or knowledge of the more complex or unpleasant aspects of life. 阅历浅的；天真的 ❑ *They seemed so young and innocent.* 他们看上去如此少不更事。 ● N-COUNT An **innocent** is someone who is innocent. 阅历浅的人；天真的人 ❑ *She had always regarded Greg as a hopeless innocent where women were concerned.* 她过去一直认为格雷格在关于女人方面是一个不可救药的无知者。 ● **in·no·cent·ly** ADV 天真地 ❑ *The baby gurgled innocently on the bed.* 那个婴儿在床上天真地咯咯笑。 3 ADJ **Innocent** people are those who are not involved in a crime or conflict, but are injured or killed as a result of it. 无辜受害的 ❑ *All those wounded were innocent victims.* 所有受伤的人都是无辜的受害者。 4 ADJ An **innocent** question, remark, or comment is not intended to offend or upset people, even if it does so. 无恶意的 ❑ *It was probably an innocent question, but Michael got flustered anyway.* 那也许是个没有恶意的问题，但迈克尔还是变得紧张不安。

Word Partnership *innocent* 的常用搭配：

V. **plead** innocent, **presumed** innocent, **proven** innocent 1
N. innocent **man/woman** 1
innocent **children** 2
innocent **bystander**, innocent **civilians**, innocent **people**, innocent **victim** 3
ADV. **perfectly** innocent 4

in·no·cent·ly /ɪnəsəntli/ 1 ADV If you say that someone does or says something **innocently**, you mean that they are pretending not to know something about a situation. 故作无知地；故作天真地 [ADV with v] ❑ *"What do you mean?" Annie asked innocently.* "你这是什么意思？"安妮故作无知地问道。 2 → see also **innocent**

in·nocu·ous /ɪnɒkyuəs/ ADJ Something that is **innocuous** is not at all harmful or offensive. 无害的；无恶意冒犯的 [FORMAL] ❑ *Both mushrooms look innocuous but are in fact deadly.* 两个蘑菇看起来都无害，但实际上却能致命。

Word Link *nov ≈ new : innovate, novel, renovate*

in·no·vate /ɪnəveɪt/ (innovates, innovating, innovated) V-I To **innovate** means to introduce changes and new ideas in the way something is done or made. 创新；革新 ❑ *What sets Rice apart from most engineers is his constant desire to innovate and experiment.* 赖斯与大多数工程师不同之处在于他不断地渴望创新和实验。

★ **in·no·va·tion** /ɪnəveɪʃᵊn/ (innovations) 1 N-COUNT An **innovation** is a new thing or a new method of doing something. 新事物；新方法 ❑ *They produced the first vegetarian beanburger – an innovation which was rapidly exported.* 他们制造出第一个素式豆堡包——一种被迅速销往国外的新食品。 2 N-UNCOUNT **Innovation** is the introduction of new ideas, methods, or things. 创新；革新 ❑ *We must promote originality, inspire creativity and encourage innovation.* 我们必须提倡独创性，激发创造力，鼓励创新。
→ see inventor

▲ **in·no·va·tive** /ɪnəveɪtɪv/ 1 ADJ Something that is **innovative** is new and original. 创新的；革新的 ❑ *...products which are cheaper, more innovative and more reliable than those of their competitors.* …比其竞争对手更便宜、更新颖、更可靠的产品。 2 ADJ An **innovative** person introduces changes and new ideas. 富有创新精神的；采用新观念的 ❑ *He was one of the most creative and innovative engineers of his generation.* 他是同代人中最富有创造力和革新精神的工程师之一。
→ see technology

Word Link *ator ≈ one who does : creator, innovator, spectator*

in·no·va·tor /ɪnəveɪtər/ (innovators) N-COUNT An **innovator** is someone who introduces changes and new ideas. 创新者；革新者 ❑ *He is an innovator in this field.* 他是这个领域的革新者。

in·nu·en·do /ɪnyuɛndoʊ/ (innuendoes or innuendos) N-VAR **Innuendo** is indirect reference to something rude or unpleasant. 影射；暗讽 ❑ *The report was based on rumors, speculation, and innuendo.* 该报告以传言、臆测和影射为基础。

Word Link *numer ≈ number : innumerable, numerical, numerous*

★ **in·nu·mer·able** /ɪnuːmərəbᵊl/ ADJ **Innumerable** means very many, or too many to be counted. 数不清的；无数的 [FORMAL] ❑ *He has invented innumerable excuses, told endless lies.* 他编造了数不清的借口，说了无止尽的谎言。

in·or·di·nate /ɪnɔrdᵊnɪt/ ADJ If you describe something as **inordinate**, you are emphasizing that it is unusually or excessively great in amount or degree. 极度的 [FORMAL, EMPHASIS] ❑ *They spend an inordinate amount of time talking.* 他们聊天时间长得超乎想像。 ● **in·or·di·nate·ly** ADV 极度地 ❑ *He is inordinately proud of his wife's achievements.* 他对妻子的成就感到非常骄傲。

in·or·gan·ic /ɪnɔrgænɪk/ ADJ **Inorganic** substances are substances such as stone and metal that do not come from living things. 无机的 ❑ *...roofing made from organic and inorganic fibers.* …由有机和无机纤维制成的屋顶材料。

in·put /ɪnpʊt/ (inputs, inputting)

> The form **input** is used in the present tense and is the past tense and past participle.

1 N-VAR **Input** consists of information or resources that a group or project receives. 信息；资源 ❑ *It's up to the teacher to provide a variety of types of input in the classroom.* 教师负责在课堂上提供各种各样的信息资源。 ❑ *We listen to our employees and value their input.* 我们倾听员工的意见并重视他们的建议。 2 N-UNCOUNT **Input** is information that is put into a computer. (计算机的) 输入信息 [COMPUTING] ❑ *The x-ray detectors feed the input into computer programs.* X射线探测器把输入信息传入计算机程序。 3 V-T If you **input** information into a computer, you feed it in, for example, by typing it on a keyboard. 输入(信息) [COMPUTING] ❑ *The computer acts as a word processor where the text of a speech can be input at any time.* 计算机起着文字处理器的作用，一篇讲话的文本可随时输入。

in·put de·vice (input devices) N-COUNT An **input device** is a piece of computer equipment such as a keyboard that enables you to put information into a computer. (计算机的) 输入设备 [COMPUTING] ❑ *The officers use stylus pen-based input devices to write their reports onto touch-sensitive screens.* 警官们使用指示笔式输入设备在触摸屏上写报告。

input/output 1 N-UNCOUNT **Input/output** refers to the information that is passed into or out of a computer. 输入/输出信息 [COMPUTING] ❑ *...input/output delays.* …输入/输出信息延迟。 2 N-UNCOUNT **Input/output** refers to the hardware or software that controls the passing of information into or out of a computer. 输入/输出端 [COMPUTING] ❑ *...an input/output system.* …一套输入/输出系统。

in·quest /ɪnkwɛst/ (**inquests**) 1 N-COUNT When an **inquest** is held, a public official hears evidence about someone's death in order to find out the cause. (调查死因的) 讯问 ❑ *The inquest into their deaths opened yesterday in Little Rock.* 昨天在小石城展开了对他们死因的调查讯问。 2 N-COUNT You can refer to an investigation by the people involved in a defeat or failure as an **inquest**. (对失败原因的) 调查 ❑ *His plea came last night as party chiefs held an inquest into the election disaster.* 昨晚政党领袖对竞选失败进行调查时，他提出了申辩。

in·quire /ɪnkwaɪər/ (**inquires, inquiring, inquired**) also **enquire** 1 V-T/V-I If you **inquire** about something, you ask for information about it. 查询；打听 [FORMAL] ❑ *"What are you doing there?" she inquired.* "你在那里做什么？"她问道。 ❑ *He called them several times to inquire about job possibilities.* 他给他们打了几次电话打听就业的可能性。 2 V-I If you **inquire into** something, you investigate it carefully. 调查；查究 ❑ *Inspectors were appointed to inquire into the affairs of the company.* 检查员被派去调查该公司的事务。

Thesaurus *inquire* 另参见：
V. ask, question, quiz 1

in·quir·ing /ɪnkwaɪərɪŋ/ also **enquiring** 1 ADJ If you have an **inquiring** mind, you have a great interest in learning new things. 好问的；爱探索的 [ADJ n] ❑ *All this helps children to develop an inquiring attitude to learning.* 这一切都有助于孩子们养成好问爱学的态度。 2 ADJ If someone has an **inquiring** expression on their face, they are showing that they want to know something. 探询的；追根究底的 [ADJ n] [WRITTEN] ❑ *"That's right," she said in reply to his inquiring glance.* "对，"她说道，以回应他探询的一瞥。 ● **in·quir·ing·ly** ADV 探询地 ❑ *She looked at me inquiringly. "Well?"* 她以探询的目光看了看我。"噢？"

in·quiry ♦◇◇ /ɪnkwaɪəri, ɪŋkwɪri/ (**inquiries**) also **enquiry** 1 N-COUNT An **inquiry** is a question you ask in order to get some information. 询问 ❑ *He made some inquiries and discovered she had gone to Connecticut.* 他询问了一番，发现她已去了康涅狄格州。 2 N-COUNT An **inquiry** is an official investigation. (官方的) 调查 ❑ *...a shocking murder inquiry.* …一例令人震惊的谋杀案调查。 3 N-UNCOUNT **Inquiry** is the process of asking about or investigating something in order to find out more about it. 调查 ❑ *The investigation has suddenly switched to a new line of inquiry.* 调查突然改用一种新的探询方法。

Word Partnership *inquiry* 的常用搭配：
N. **board of** inquiry, **the outcome of an** inquiry 2
V. **conduct an** inquiry, **hold an** inquiry 2
ADJ. **scientific** inquiry 3

in·quisi·tive /ɪnkwɪzɪtɪv/ ADJ An **inquisitive** person likes finding out about things, especially secret things. 好奇的；爱打听的 ❑ *Barrow had an inquisitive nature.* 巴罗生性好奇。

in·roads /ɪnroʊdz/ PHRASE If one thing **makes inroads into** another, the first thing starts affecting or destroying the second. 影响；损害 ❑ *In Italy, as elsewhere, television has made deep inroads into movies.* 在意大利，如同在别国一样，电视严重影响了电影市场。

Word Link *san ≈ health : insane, sane, sanitation*

in·sane /ɪnseɪn/ 1 ADJ Someone who is **insane** is severely mentally ill. 精神病的；精神失常的 ❑ *Some people simply can't take it and they just go insane.* 一些人就是接受不了，于是便变得精神错乱。 2 ADJ If you describe a decision or action as **insane**, you think it is very foolish or excessive. 疯狂的；愚蠢的 [DISAPPROVAL] ❑ *He asked me what I thought and I said, "Listen, this is completely insane."* 他问我是怎么想的，我说，"听着，这十分愚蠢。" ● **in·sane·ly** ADV 疯狂地 ❑ *I would be insanely jealous if Bill left me for another woman.* 如果比尔为了另一个女人而离开我，我会妒忌得发疯的。

in·san·ity /ɪnsænɪti/ 1 N-UNCOUNT **Insanity** is the state of being insane. 精神错乱 ❑ *...a psychiatrist who specialized in diagnosing insanity.* …一位专门诊断精神错乱的精神病学家。 2 N-UNCOUNT If you describe a decision or an action as **insanity**, you think it is very foolish. 荒唐的决定；极端愚蠢的行为 [DISAPPROVAL] ❑ *...the final financial insanity of the 1980s.* …20世纪80年代财政上最后的荒唐举措。

Word Link *sat, satis ≈ enough : dissatisfaction, insatiable, satisfy*

in·sa·tiable /ɪnseɪʃəbəl, -ʃiə-/ ADJ If someone has an **insatiable** desire for something, they want as much of it as they can possibly get. 无法满足的；贪得无厌的 ❑ *A section of the reading public has an insatiable appetite for dirty stories about the famous.* 阅读大众中有一部分人对名人的风流韵事的欲望总是无法满足。

Word Link *scrib ≈ writing : inscribe, scribble, transcribe*

in·scribe /ɪnskraɪb/ (**inscribes, inscribing, inscribed**) 1 V-T If you **inscribe** words **on** an object, you write or carve the words on the object. 题写；刻 ❑ *Some galleries commemorate donors by inscribing their names on the walls.* 一些展览馆把捐赠者的名字刻在墙上以纪念他们。 2 V-T If you **inscribe** something in the front of a book or on a photograph, you write it there, often before giving it to someone. 题赠 ❑ *On the back I had inscribed the words: "Here's to Great Ideas! John."* 在背面我题写了这样的话："献给伟大的思想！约翰"。

▲ **in·scrip·tion** /ɪnskrɪpʃən/ (**inscriptions**) 1 N-COUNT An **inscription** is writing carved into something made of stone or metal, such as a gravestone or medal. 铭文；碑文 ❑ *The medal bears the inscription "For distinguished service."* 那块奖章上刻有"功勋卓著"的字样。 2 N-COUNT An **inscription** is something written by hand in the front of a book or on a photograph. 题词 ❑ *The inscription reads: "To Emma, with love from Harry."* 题词是："献给爱玛，爱你的哈里。"

in·sect /ɪnsɛkt/ (**insects**) N-COUNT An **insect** is a small animal that has six legs. Most insects have wings. Ants, flies, butterflies, and beetles are all insects. 昆虫
→ see **flower**

in·sec·ti·cide /ɪnsɛktɪsaɪd/ (**insecticides**) N-MASS **Insecticide** is a chemical substance that is used to kill insects. 杀虫剂 ❑ *Spray the plants with insecticide.* 给植物喷洒杀虫剂。
→ see **farm**

in·secure /ɪnsɪkyʊər/ 1 ADJ If you are **insecure**, you lack confidence because you think that you are not good enough or are not loved. 不自信的；缺乏安全感的 ❑ *Most mothers are insecure about their performance as mothers.* 大多数母亲对自己作为母亲的表现缺乏自信。 ● **in·secu·rity** /ɪnsɪkyʊərɪti/ N-VAR (**insecurities**) 不自信；缺乏安全感 ❑ *She is always assailed by self-doubt and emotional insecurity.* 她总是被自我怀疑和情感上的不安全感所困扰。 2 ADJ Something that is **insecure** is not safe or protected. 不安全的；无保障的 ❑ *...low-paid, insecure jobs.* …工资低、无保障的工作。 ● **in·secu·rity** N-UNCOUNT 不安全 ❑ *...the increase in crime, which has created feelings of insecurity in the population.* …犯罪的增加让民众感到不安全。

in·sen·si·tive /ɪnsɛnsɪtɪv/ 1 ADJ If you describe someone as **insensitive**, you are criticizing them for being unaware of or unsympathetic to other people's feelings. 不顾他人感受的；麻木不仁的 [DISAPPROVAL] ❑ *I feel my husband is very insensitive about my problem.* 我感到丈夫对我的问题麻木不仁。 ● **in·sen·si·tiv·ity** /ɪnsɛnsɪtɪvɪti/ N-UNCOUNT 麻木不仁 ❑ *I was ashamed and appalled at my clumsiness and insensitivity toward her.* 我为自己对她如此笨拙和冷漠而感到羞耻和震惊。 2 ADJ Someone who is **insensitive to** a situation or to a need does not think or care about it. 不敏感的；反应迟钝的 ❑ *...women's and Latino organizations that say he is insensitive to civil rights.* …指责他漠视民权的女性和拉丁美洲人的组织。 ● **in·sen·si·tiv·ity** N-UNCOUNT 不敏感 ❑ *...insensitivity to the environmental consequences.* …对环境后果的不敏感。 3 ADJ Someone who is **insensitive to** a physical sensation is unable to feel it. 无感觉的 ❑ *He had become insensitive to cold.* 他已经感觉不到寒冷了。

in·sepa·rable /ɪnsɛpərəbəl/ 1 ADJ If one thing is **inseparable from** another, the things are so closely connected that they cannot be considered separately. 分不开的 ❑ *He firmly believes liberty is inseparable from social justice.* 他坚信自由与社会正义是不可分开的。 ● **in·sepa·rably** ADV 分不开地 ❑ *In his mind, religion and politics were inseparably intertwined.* 在他心中，宗教和政治密不可分地交织在一起。 2 ADJ If you say that two people are **inseparable**, you are emphasizing that they are very good friends and spend a lot of time together. 形影不离的 [EMPHASIS] ❑ *She and Kristin were inseparable.* 她与克里斯廷形影不离。

in·sert (**inserts, inserting, inserted**)

The verb is pronounced /ɪnsɜrt/. The noun is pronounced /ɪnsɜrt/.

动词读作 /ɪnsɜrt/。名词读作 /ɪnsɜrt/。

1 V-T If you **insert** an object **into** something, you put the object inside it. 插入；嵌入 ❑ *He took a small key from his pocket and slowly inserted it into the lock.* 他从衣袋里掏出一把小钥匙，然后缓缓地将其插入锁孔里。 ● **in·ser·tion** /ɪnsɜrʃən/ N-VAR (**insertions**) 插入；嵌入 ❑ *...the first experiment involving the insertion of a new gene into a human*

being. …首次把新基因嵌入人体的实验。 **2** V-T If you **insert** a comment into a piece of writing or a speech, you add it. (在文件或讲话中) 插入；添加 ❑ *They joined with the monarchists to insert a clause calling for a popular vote on the issue.* 他们与君主制主义者一起添加了一个条款，要求对该问题进行全民投票表决。 ● **in·ser·tion** N-VAR 插入；添加 ❑ *...an item for insertion in the program.* …插入节目中的一则消息。 **3** N-COUNT An **insert** is something that is inserted somewhere, especially an advertisement on a piece of paper that is placed between the pages of a book or magazine. 插入物；(尤指书刊中的) 活页广告 ❑ *Sunday is the preferred day for advertising inserts in newspapers.* 星期天是添加广告插页的最佳日子。

in-service ADJ If people working in a particular profession are given **in-service** training, they attend special courses to improve their skills or to learn about new developments in their field. 在职期间进行的 [ADJ n] ❑ *...in-service courses for people such as doctors, teachers, and civil servants.* …针对医生、教师和公务员等的在职学习课程。

in·side ♦♦◇ /ɪnsaɪd/ (**insides**)

The preposition is usually pronounced /ɪnsaɪd/.

介词通常读作 /ɪnsaɪd/。

The form **inside of** can also be used as a preposition in American English.

1 PREP Something or someone that is **inside** a place, container, or object is in it or is surrounded by it. 在…里面；在…内侧 ❑ *Inside the passport was a folded slip of paper.* 护照里面是一张折叠的纸条。 ❑ *There is a telephone inside the entrance hall.* 门廊里有一部电话。 ● ADV **Inside** is also an adverb. 在里面；往里面 ❑ *The couple chatted briefly on the doorstep before going inside.* 夫妇俩进屋前在门阶上简单地聊了几句。 ❑ *Inside, clouds of cigarette smoke swirled.* 里面香烟的烟雾缭绕。 ● ADJ **Inside** is also an adjective. 里面的 [ADJ n] ❑ *...an inside wall.* …一面内墙。 **2** N-COUNT The **inside** of something is the part or area that its sides surround or contain. 里面；内部 ❑ *The doors were locked from the inside.* 门从里面锁住了。 ● ADJ **Inside** is also an adjective. 内部的 [ADJ n] ❑ *The popular papers all have photo features on their inside pages.* 通俗报纸的内页都有照片特写。 ● ADV **Inside** is also an adverb. 在内部 [adj ADV] ❑ *The potato cakes can be shallow or deep-fried until crisp outside and meltingly soft inside.* 薯饼可以微煎或熟炸，直到变得外脆内软。 **3** ADJ **Inside** information is obtained from someone who is involved in a situation and therefore knows a lot about it. (消息) 内幕的 [ADJ n] ❑ *Sloane used inside diplomatic information to make himself rich.* 斯隆利用外交内幕消息发了财。 ❑ *I cannot claim any inside knowledge of government policies.* 我不能说自己了解政府政策的内幕。 **4** PREP If you are **inside** an organization, you belong to it. 在 (组织) 的内部 ❑ *75 percent of chief executives come from inside the company.* 75%的高层主管来自公司内部。 ● ADJ **Inside** is also an adjective. 内部的 [ADJ n] ❑ *...a recent book about the inside world of pro football.* …最近的一本关于职业足球运动内幕的书。 ● N-SING **Inside** is also a noun. 内部 ❑ *McAvoy was convinced he could control things from the inside but he lost control.* 麦卡沃伊深信他能够从内部控制形势，可他却失去了控制。 **5** ADV You can say that someone is **inside** when they are in prison. 在监牢里 [INFORMAL] ❑ *They've both done prison time – he's been inside three times.* 他们俩都蹲过监狱——他蹲过3次。 **6** N-PLURAL Your **insides** are your internal organs, especially your stomach. 内脏 (尤指胃) [INFORMAL] ❑ *Every pill made my insides turn upside down.* 每片药都使我的胃翻江倒海。 **7** ADV If you say that someone has a feeling **inside**, you mean that they have it but have not expressed it. 在心里 ❑ *There is nothing left inside – no words, no anger, no tears.* 心里头空落落的啥也没留下——没有话语，没有愤怒，没有眼泪。 ● PREP **Inside** is also a preposition. 在…的心里 ❑ *He felt a great weight of sorrow inside him.* 他感到沉重的悲痛压在心口。 ● N-SING **Inside** is also a noun. 内心 ❑ *What is needed is a change from the inside, a real change in outlook and attitude.* 所需要的是来自内心深处的改变，在观点和态度上的真正改变。 **8** PREP If you do something **inside** a particular time, you do it before the end of that time. 在 (某段时间) 之内 [PREP amount] ❑ *They should have everything working inside an hour.* 他们应该在一小时之内让一切都运转起来。 **9** PHRASE If something such as a piece of clothing is **inside out**, the part that is normally inside now faces outward. 里面朝外地 ❑ *Her umbrella blew inside out.* 她的伞被吹得往外翻了。 **10** PHRASE If you say that you know something or someone **inside out**, you are emphasizing that you know them extremely well. 彻底地 [EMPHASIS] ❑ *He knew the game inside out.* 他对这个游戏了如指掌。

Thesaurus *inside* 另参见：

PREP.	in; (*ant.*) outside **1**
ADV.	indoors **1**
N.	interior, middle **2**

in·sid·er /ɪnsaɪdər/ (**insiders**) N-COUNT An **insider** is someone who is involved in a situation and who knows more about it than other people. 知情者；圈内人 ❑ *An insider said, "Katharine has told friends it is time to end her career."* 一名知情者说，“凯瑟琳告诉朋友们她该结束自己的职业生涯了。”

in·sid·er trad·ing N-UNCOUNT **Insider trading** is the illegal buying or selling of a company's stock by someone who has secret or private information about the company. 内幕交易 [BUSINESS] ❑ *...a friend of Ms. Stewart's who is accused of insider trading in shares of his own company.* …斯图尔特女士的被指控在自己公司的股票中有内幕交易的一个朋友。

in·sidi·ous /ɪnsɪdiəs/ ADJ Something that is **insidious** is unpleasant or dangerous and develops gradually without being noticed. 潜伏的；暗中为害的 ❑ *The changes are insidious, and will not produce a noticeable effect for 15 to 20 years.* 变化是悄然发生的，15到20年间不会产生明显效果。

in·sight /ɪnsaɪt/ (**insights**) **1** N-VAR If you gain **insight** or an **insight into** a complex situation or problem, you gain an accurate and deep understanding of it. 深入了解；深刻见解 ❑ *The project would give scientists new insights into what is happening to the Earth's atmosphere.* 该项目将使科学家们对地球大气层正在发生的情况有更新的了解。 **2** N-UNCOUNT If someone has **insight**, they are able to understand complex situations. 洞察力 ❑ *He was a man of forceful character, with considerable insight and diplomatic skills.* 他是个性格坚强的人，有着非凡的洞察力和交际手腕。

in·sig·nifi·cance /ɪnsɪgnɪfɪkəns/ N-UNCOUNT **Insignificance** is the quality of being insignificant. 不重要；无足轻重 ❑ *These prices pale into insignificance when compared with what was paid for two major works by the late Alfred Stieglitz.* 与购买已故的阿尔弗雷德・史蒂格利兹的两件重要作品所支付的费用相比，这些价格就变得微不足道了。

in·sig·nifi·cant /ɪnsɪgnɪfɪkənt/ ADJ Something that is **insignificant** is unimportant, especially because it is very small. 不重要的；无足轻重的 ❑ *In 1949 Bonn was a small, insignificant city.* 1949年，波恩还是个不足称道的小城市。

in·sin·cere /ɪnsɪnsɪər/ ADJ If you say that someone is **insincere**, you are being critical of them because they say things they do not really mean, usually pleasant, admiring, or encouraging things. 不诚恳的；虚伪的 [DISAPPROVAL] ❑ *Some people are so terribly insincere you can never tell if they are telling the truth.* 有些人虚伪得可怕，你绝对无法搞清楚他们是否在讲真话。

in·sist ♦♦◇ /ɪnsɪst/ (**insists, insisting, insisted**) **1** V-T/V-I If you **insist that** something should be done, you say so very firmly and refuse to give in about it. If you **insist on** something, you say firmly that it must be done or provided. 坚持认为；执意要求 ❑ *My family insisted that I should not give in, but stay and fight.* 我家人坚持认为我不应该屈服，而应该留下来斗争。 ❑ *She insisted on being present at all the interviews.* 她坚决要求出席所有的采访。 **2** V-T/V-I If you **insist** that something is the case, you say so very firmly and refuse to say otherwise, even though other people do not believe you. 坚持说 ❑ *The president insisted that he was acting out of compassion, not political opportunism.* 总统坚持说他这么做是出于同情而不是政治投机。 ❑ *"It's not that difficult," she insists.* “事情并没有像想的那么难，”她坚持说。 ❑ *He insisted on his innocence.* 他坚持说自己是清白的。

Word Partnership *insist* 的常用搭配：

V.	**continue to insist** **1** **2**
N.	**critics** insist, **leaders/officials** insist, **people** insist **1** **2**

in·sist·ence /ɪnsɪstəns/ N-UNCOUNT Someone's **insistence** on something is the fact that they insist that it should be done or insist that it is the case. 坚持；坚决要求 ❑ *...her insistence on personal privacy.* …她对个人隐私权的坚持。

in·sist·ent /ɪnsɪstənt/ **1** ADJ Someone who is **insistent** keeps insisting that a particular thing should be done or is the case. 坚持的；坚决的 ❑ *Stalin was insistent that the war would be won and lost in the machine shops.* 斯大林坚持认为，战争输赢将取决于这些机械厂。 ● **in·sist·ent·ly** ADV 坚决地 [ADV with v] ❑ *"What is it?" his wife asked* *again, gently but insistently.* “这是什么？”他妻子再次问道，语气温和但很坚决。 2 ADJ An **insistent** noise or rhythm keeps going on for a long time and holds your attention. (声音、节奏等) 持续的 ❑ *...the insistent rhythms of the Caribbean and Latin America.* …不停息的加勒比和拉丁美洲的音乐节奏。

in·so·far as /ɪnsəfɑr æz, ɪnsoʊ-/ PHRASE You use **insofar as** to introduce a statement that explains and adds to something you have just said. 到…程度; 在…范围内 [FORMAL] ❑ *Looking back helps insofar as it helps you learn from your mistakes.* 回顾往事助人进步，基于它可以帮助你从错误中学习。

in·so·lent /ɪnsələnt/ ADJ If you say that someone is being **insolent**, you mean they are being rude to someone they ought to be respectful to. 粗鲁的; 无礼的 ❑ *...her insolent stare.* …她那无礼的凝视。

in·sol·uble /ɪnsɒlyəbᵊl/ 1 ADJ An **insoluble** problem is so difficult that it is impossible to solve. 不能解决的 ❑ *I pushed the problem aside; at present it was insoluble.* 我把这个问题放到了一边；目前它是无法解决的。 2 ADJ If a substance is **insoluble**, it does not dissolve in a liquid. 不溶解的 ❑ *Carotenes are insoluble in water and soluble in oils and fats.* 胡萝卜素不溶于水，但溶于油和脂肪。

in·sol·ven·cy /ɪnsɒlvᵊnsi/ (**insolvencies**) N-VAR **Insolvency** is the state of not having enough money to pay your debts. 无清偿能力; 破产 [FORMAL, BUSINESS] ❑ *...eight mortgage companies, seven of which are on the brink of insolvency.* …8家抵押贷款公司，其中7家濒临破产。

in·sol·vent /ɪnsɒlvᵊnt/ ADJ A person or organization that is **insolvent** does not have enough money to pay their debts. 无清偿能力的; 破产的 [FORMAL, BUSINESS] ❑ *Two years later, the bank was declared insolvent.* 两年后，这家银行宣布破产。

▲ **in·som·nia** /ɪnsɒmniə/ N-UNCOUNT Someone who suffers from **insomnia** finds it difficult to sleep. 失眠
→ see **sleep**

in·spect ♦◇◇ /ɪnspɛkt/ (**inspects, inspecting, inspected**) 1 V-T If you **inspect** something, you look at every part of it carefully in order to find out about it or check that it is all right. 检查; 检验 ❑ *Elaine went outside to inspect the playing field.* 伊莱恩到外边去检查运动场。 ●**in·spec·tion** /ɪnspɛkʃᵊn/ N-VAR (**inspections**) 检查; 检验 ❑ *"Excellent work," he said when he had completed his inspection of the painted doors.* “干得好，”他在检查完刷过油漆的门之后说道。 2 V-T When an official **inspects** a place or a group of people, they visit it and check it carefully, for example, in order to find out whether regulations are being obeyed. 视察 ❑ *The Public Utilities Commission inspects us once a year.* 公用设施委员会每年到我们这里视察一次。 ●**in·spec·tion** N-VAR 视察 ❑ *Officers making a routine inspection of the vessel found fifty kilograms of cocaine.* 对船只做例行检查的警官们发现了50公斤可卡因。

Word Partnership	*inspect* 的常用搭配:
N.	inspect **damage**, inspect **records**, inspect **sites**, inspect **weapons** 1 2

in·spec·tor ♦◇◇ /ɪnspɛktər/ (**inspectors**) 1 N-COUNT An **inspector** is a person, usually employed by a government agency, whose job is to find out whether people are obeying official regulations. 检查员; 督察员 ❑ *The mill was finally shut down by state safety inspectors.* 这家工厂最终被州安全检查官关闭了。 2 N-COUNT; N-TITLE; N-VOC An **inspector** is an officer in the police who is next in rank to a superintendent or police chief. 巡官 (官阶仅次于警长或警察局长的警官) ❑ *...San Francisco police inspector Tony Camileri.* …旧金山市巡官托尼·卡米勒瑞。

in·spi·ra·tion /ɪnspɪreɪʃᵊn/ (**inspirations**) 1 N-UNCOUNT **Inspiration** is a feeling of enthusiasm you get from someone or something, that gives you new and creative ideas. 灵感 ❑ *My inspiration comes from poets like Baudelaire and Jacques Prévert.* 我的灵感来自像波德莱尔和雅克·普莱维尔这样的诗人。 2 N-SING If you describe someone or something good as **an inspiration**, you mean that they make you or other people want to do or achieve something. 鼓舞人心的人 (或事物) [APPROVAL] ❑ *Powell's unusual journey to high office is an inspiration to millions.* 鲍威尔升任高官的不寻常历程对许多人来说是一种激励。 3 N-SING If something or someone is **the inspiration for** a particular book, work of art, or action, they are the source of the ideas in it or act as a model for it. 灵感来源; 原始动力 ❑ *India's myths and songs are the inspiration for her books.* 印度的神话与歌曲是她著书的灵感源泉。 4 N-COUNT If you suddenly have an **inspiration**, you suddenly think of an idea of what to do or say. (突然想到的) 妙计 ❑ *She had an inspiration, "Could we take Janice?"* 她灵机一动，“我们可以带珍妮斯吗？”

Word Partnership	*inspiration* 的常用搭配:
N.	**source of** inspiration 1
V.	**draw** inspiration **from** *someone/something*, **find** inspiration 1
	have an inspiration 4
	provide *an* inspiration 1 – 3

Word Link	*spir ≈ breath : aspire, inspire, respiratory*

in·spire /ɪnspaɪər/ (**inspires, inspiring, inspired**) 1 V-T If someone or something **inspires** you **to** do something new or unusual, they make you want to do it. 鼓舞; 激励 ❑ *Our challenge is to motivate those voters and inspire them to join our cause.* 我们的艰巨任务是要激励那些投票者并鼓励他们加入我们的事业。 2 V-T If someone or something **inspires** you, they give you new ideas and a strong feeling of enthusiasm. 唤起; 激起 ❑ *In the 1960s, the electric guitar virtuosity of Jimi Hendrix inspired a generation.* 20世纪60年代，吉米·亨德里克斯演奏电吉他的精湛技巧激发了一代人的热情。 3 V-T If a book, work of art, or action **is inspired by** something, that thing is the source of the idea for it. 赋…以灵感; 给…以启示 [usu passive] ❑ *The book was inspired by a real person, namely Tamara de Treaux.* 这本书是受一个叫塔玛拉·德特罗的人启发而写成的。 ●**-inspired** COMB IN ADJ 受…灵感启示的 ❑ *...Mediterranean-inspired ceramics in bright yellow and blue.* …源自地中海风格灵感的明黄色和蓝色瓷器。 4 V-T Someone or something that **inspires** a particular emotion or reaction in people makes them feel that emotion or reaction. 唤起; 激起 ❑ *The car's performance is effortless and its handling is precise and quickly inspires confidence.* 这辆车开起来毫不费劲且精确到位，能很快激起驾驶员的信心。

Word Partnership	*inspire* 的常用搭配:
N.	inspire **people** 1 2
	ability to inspire 1 2 4
	inspire **affection**, inspire **confidence**, inspire **fear** 4

in·spir·ing /ɪnspaɪərɪŋ/ ADJ Something or someone that is **inspiring** is exciting and makes you feel strongly interested and enthusiastic. 鼓舞人心的; 启发灵感的 ❑ *She was a very strong, impressive character and one of the most inspiring people I've ever met.* 她性格坚强，令人钦佩，是我见过的最能鼓舞人心的人物之一。

Word Link	*stab ≈ steady : destabilize, establish, instability*

in·stabil·ity /ɪnstəbɪlɪti/ N-UNCOUNT **Instability** is the quality of being unstable. 不稳定 ❑ *...unpopular policies, which resulted in social discontent and political instability.* …导致社会不满和政治不稳定的不得人心的政策。

in·stal /ɪnstɔl/ [BRIT] → see **install**

in·stall ♦◇◇ /ɪnstɔl/ (**installs, installing, installed**)
in BRIT, also use **instal**

1 V-T If you **install** a piece of equipment, you put it somewhere so that it is ready to be used. 安装 ❑ *They had installed a new phone line in the apartment.* 他们在公寓里安装了一根新的电话线。 ●**in·stal·la·tion** N-UNCOUNT 安装 ❑ *Hundreds of lives could be saved if the installation of alarms was more widespread.* 如果警报器的安装范围更为广泛，成百上千人的生命就可能获救。 2 V-T If someone **is installed** in a new job or important position, they are officially given the job or position, often in a special ceremony. 正式任命 ❑ *A new Catholic bishop was installed in Galway yesterday.* 一名天主教新主教昨天在高威被任命。 ❑ *A temporary government was installed.* 一届临时政府被正式任命。 ❑ *Professor Sawyer was formally installed as president last Thursday.* 上星期二，索耶教授被正式任命为校长。 ●**in·stal·la·tion** N-UNCOUNT 任命仪式; 就职仪式 ❑ *He sent a letter inviting Naomi to attend his installation as chief of his tribe.* 他给娜奥米寄了封信，邀请她来参加他就任部落酋长的仪式。 3 V-T If you **install yourself** in a particular place, you settle there and make yourself comfortable. 安顿 [FORMAL] ❑ *Before her husband's death she had installed herself in a modern villa.* 在丈夫去世之前她就已经在一所现代的别墅里安顿了下来。

Word Partnership	*install* 的常用搭配:
ADJ.	**easy to** install 1
N.	install **equipment**, install **machines**, install **software** 1

in·stal·la·tion /ɪnstəleɪʃⁿn/ (**installations**) 1 N-COUNT An **installation** is a place that contains equipment and machinery that are being used for a particular purpose. 设备处 ❑ *The building was turned into a secret military installation.* 该楼被改建成一个秘密军事设施处。 2 → see also **install**

★ **in·stall·ment** /ɪnstɔːlmənt/ (**installments**)

in BRIT, use **instalment**

1 N-COUNT If you pay for something in **installments**, you pay small sums of money at regular intervals over a period of time, rather than paying the whole amount at once. 分期付款的一期 ❑ *Upper-bracket taxpayers who elected to pay their tax increase in installments must pay the third installment by April 15.* 选择分期支付增税的高额纳税人必须在4月15日之前交纳第3期税款。 2 N-COUNT An **installment** of a story or plan is one of its parts that are published or carried out separately one after the other. (报刊上连载故事的)一集；一部分 ❑ *The next installment of this four-part series deals with the impact of the war on the continent of Africa.* 这部4集系列片的下一集将探讨战争对非洲大陆的影响。

★ **in·stalment** /ɪnstɔːlmənt/ [BRIT] → see **installment**

in·stall·ment plan (**installment plans**) N-COUNT An **installment plan** is a way of buying products gradually. You make regular payments to the seller until, after some time, you have paid the full price. 分期付款购货法 [AM]

in BRIT, use **hire purchase**

in·stance ◆◆◇ /ɪnstəns/ (**instances**) 1 PHRASE You use **for instance** to introduce a particular event, situation, or person that is an example of what you are talking about. 例如 ❑ *In sub-Saharan Africa today, for instance, gross investment accounts for roughly 15% of national income.* 例如，在如今的撒哈拉以南的非洲国家，总投资大约占国民收入的15%。 2 N-COUNT An **instance** is a particular example or occurrence of something. 例子 ❑ *...an investigation into a serious instance of corruption.* …对一例严重腐败事件的调查。 3 PHRASE You say **in the first instance** to mention something that is the first step in a series of actions. 首先 [INFORMAL] ❑ *In the first instance your child will be seen by an ear, nose and throat specialist.* 你的孩子首先要由耳鼻喉专家诊查。

in·stant ◆◇◇ /ɪnstənt/ (**instants**) 1 N-COUNT An **instant** is an extremely short period of time. 瞬间；刹那 ❑ *For an instant, Barney was tempted to flee.* 那一瞬间，巴尼很想逃走。 2 N-SING If you say that something happens **at** a particular **instant**, you mean that it happens at exactly the time you have been referring to, and you are usually suggesting that it happens quickly or immediately. 时刻 ❑ *At that instant the museum was plunged into total darkness.* 在那一刻，博物馆陷入一片黑暗。 3 PHRASE To do something **the instant** something else happens means to do it immediately. 一…就… [EMPHASIS] ❑ *I bolted the door the instant I saw the bat.* 我一看到那只蝙蝠就把门闩上了。 4 ADJ You use **instant** to describe something that happens immediately. 立即的 ❑ *Mr. Porter's book was an instant hit.* 波特先生的书立刻引起了轰动。 ● **in·stant·ly** ADV 立即地 ❑ *The man was killed instantly.* 那人立即被杀死了。 5 ADJ **Instant** food is food that you can prepare very quickly, for example, by just adding water. 调制快速方便的(食品) [ADJ n] ❑ *He stirred instant coffee into a mug of hot water.* 他将速溶咖啡搅入一大杯热水中。

Thesaurus *instant* 另参见：
N. minute, second, split second 1

Word Partnership *instant* 的常用搭配：
PREP. **for an** instant, **in an** instant 1
ADJ. **the next** instant 1 2
N. instant **access**, instant **messaging**, instant **success** 4

★ **in·stan·ta·neous** /ɪnstənteɪniəs/ ADJ Something that is **instantaneous** happens immediately and very quickly. 即刻的 ❑ *Death was not instantaneous because none of the bullets hit the heart.* 因为没有一颗子弹射中心脏，所以没有即刻死亡。 ● **in·stan·ta·neous·ly** ADV 即刻地 [ADV with v] ❑ *Airbags inflate instantaneously on impact to form a cushion between the driver and the steering column.* 安全气囊在碰撞时立刻膨胀，在司机和方向盘之间形成一个缓冲。

in·stant mes·sag·ing N-UNCOUNT **Instant messaging** is the sending of written messages from one computer to another. The message appears immediately on the screen of the computer you send it to, provided the computer is using the service. The abbreviation **IM** is also used. 即时通讯 [oft N n] ❑ *...users of the instant-messaging services of Yahoo, Microsoft and other rivals.* …使用雅虎、微软和其他竞争公司即时通讯服务的用户们。

Word Link *stead ≈ place, stand : homestead, instead, steady*

in·stead ◆◆◇ /ɪnstɛd/ 1 PHRASE If you do one thing **instead of** another, you do the first thing and not the second thing, as the result of a choice or a change of behavior. 而不是… ❑ *They raised prices and cut production, instead of cutting costs.* 他们提高了价格，减少了产量，而没有削减成本。 2 ADV If you do not do something, but do something else **instead**, you do the second thing and not the first thing, as the result of a choice or a change of behavior. 而 [ADV with cl] ❑ *My husband asked why I couldn't just forget about dieting and eat normally instead.* 丈夫问我为什么就不能忘掉节食而正常吃饭。

in·sti·gate /ɪnstɪgeɪt/ (**instigates, instigating, instigated**) V-T Someone who **instigates** an event causes it to happen. 发起 ❑ *He did not instigate the coup or even know of it beforehand.* 他没有发起政变，甚至事先都不知道。 ● **in·sti·ga·tion** /ɪnstɪgeɪʃⁿn/ N-UNCOUNT 鼓动 ❑ *The talks are taking place at the instigation of Germany.* 在德国的鼓动下会谈正在进行。

in·sti·ga·tor /ɪnstɪgeɪtər/ (**instigators**) N-COUNT The **instigator** of an event is the person who causes it to happen. 唆使者 ❑ *He was accused of being the main instigator of the coup.* 他被指控为政变的主要唆使者。

in·still /ɪnstɪl/ (**instills, instilling, instilled**)

in BRIT, use **instil**

V-T If you **instill** an idea or feeling in someone, especially over a period of time, you make them think it or feel it. 逐渐灌输 ❑ *The tough thing is trying to instill a winning attitude in the kids.* 困难在于要尽力给孩子们灌输胜利的心态。

in·stinct /ɪnstɪŋkt/ (**instincts**) 1 N-VAR **Instinct** is the natural tendency that a person or animal has to behave or react in a particular way. 本能 ❑ *I didn't have as strong a maternal instinct as some other mothers.* 我不像其他一些母亲那样有那么强烈的母性本能。 2 N-COUNT If you have an **instinct for** something, you are naturally good at it or able to do it. 天分 ❑ *He seems to have an instinct for smart advertising and marketing.* 他好像在广告和营销方面有天分。 3 N-VAR If it is your **instinct to** do something, you feel that it is right to do it. 本能的反应 ❑ *I should've gone with my first instinct, which was not to do the interview.* 我应该凭我的本能反应行事，那就是，不去面试。 4 N-VAR **Instinct** is a feeling, rather than an opinion or idea based on facts, that something is the case. 直觉 ❑ *There is scientific evidence to support our instinct that being surrounded by plants is good for health.* 有科学证据表明我们的直觉是正确的，即被植物环绕着有益健康。

Word Partnership *instinct* 的常用搭配：
ADJ. **basic** instinct, **maternal** instinct, **natural** instinct 1
N. **survival** instinct 1

in·stinc·tive /ɪnstɪŋktɪv/ ADJ An **instinctive** feeling, idea, or action is one that you have or do without thinking or reasoning. 本能的 ❑ *It's an instinctive reaction – if a child falls you pick it up.* 这是一种本能的反应——如果小孩摔倒了你会扶他起来。 ● **in·stinc·tive·ly** ADV 本能地 [ADV with v] ❑ *Jane instinctively knew all was not well with her 10-month old son.* 简本能地知道她10个月大的儿子不太对劲。

in·sti·tute ◆◆◇ /ɪnstɪtuːt/ (**institutes, instituting, instituted**) 1 N-COUNT; N-IN-NAMES An **institute** is an organization set up to do a particular type of work, especially research or teaching. You can also use **institute** to refer to the building the organization occupies. 协会；研究所 ❑ *...the National Cancer Institute.* …国家癌症研究所。 2 V-T If you **institute** a system, rule, or course of action, you start it. 制定(规章、制度)；创立 [FORMAL] ❑ *We will institute a number of measures to better safeguard the public.* 我们将制定许多措施更好地保护公众。

in·sti·tu·tion ◆◆◇ /ɪnstɪtuːʃⁿn/ (**institutions**) 1 N-COUNT; N-IN-NAMES An **institution** is a large important organization such as a university, church, or bank. 机构 ❑ *...financial institutions.* …金融机构。 2 N-COUNT; N-IN-NAMES An **institution** is a building where certain people are cared for, such as people who are mentally ill or children who have no parents. 社会福利机构 ❑ *Larry has been in an institution since he was four.* 拉里从4岁起就在孤儿院生活。 3 N-COUNT An **institution** is a custom or system that is considered an important or typical feature of a particular society or group, usually because it has existed for a long time. 习俗；制度

❑ *I believe in the institution of marriage.* 我相信婚姻制度。 4 N-UNCOUNT The **institution** of a new system is the act of starting it or bringing it in. 建立 ❑ *There was never an official institution of censorship in Albania.* 阿尔巴尼亚从来就没有正式建立过审查制度。

★ **in·sti·tu·tion·al** /ɪnstɪtuʃən^əl/ 1 ADJ **Institutional** means relating to a large organization, such as a university, bank, or church. 机构的 [ADJ n] ❑ *NATO remains the United States' chief institutional anchor in Europe.* 北大西洋公约组织仍然是美国在欧洲的主要支柱机构。 2 ADJ **Institutional** means relating to a building where people are cared for or held. 社会福利机构的 [ADJ n] ❑ *Outside the protected environment of institutional care he could not survive.* 离开福利机构照顾下的这个受保护的环境，他无法生存。 3 ADJ An **institutional** value or quality is considered an important and typical feature of a particular society or group, usually because it has existed for a long time. 惯例化的 [ADJ n] ❑ *...social and institutional values.* …社会及惯例化的价值观。 4 ADJ If someone accuses an organization of **institutional** racism or sexism, they mean that the organization is deeply racist or sexist and has been so for a long time. 根深蒂固的 [usu ADJ n] ❑ *The report accused the police department of institutional racism.* 报告指责警察局的种族歧视根深蒂固。 ● **in·sti·tu·tion·al·ly** /ɪnstɪtuʃən^əli/ ADV 根深蒂固地 [ADV adj] ❑ *The government's policy still appeared to be institutionally racist.* 该政府的政策看来仍然具有根深蒂固的种族歧视。

in·sti·tu·tion·al·ise /ɪnstɪtjuːʃənəlaɪz/ [BRIT] → see **institutionalize**

in·sti·tu·tion·al·ize /ɪnstɪtuʃənəlaɪz/ (**institutionalizes, institutionalizing, institutionalized**)

in BRIT, also use **institutionalise**

1 V-T If someone such as a sick, mentally ill, or old person is **institutionalized**, they are sent to stay in a special hospital or home, usually for a long period. 把(病人、精神病人、老人等)收容在社会福利机构 [usu passive] ❑ *She became seriously ill and had to be institutionalized for a lengthy period.* 她病情严重，不得不被长期收容治疗。 2 V-T To **institutionalize** something means to establish it as part of a culture, social system, or organization. 使制度化 ❑ *The goal is to institutionalize family planning into community life.* 目标是使计划生育在社区生活中制度化。

Word Link *struct ≈ building : construct, destructive, instruct*

in·struct /ɪnstrʌkt/ (**instructs, instructing, instructed**) 1 V-T If you **instruct** someone to do something, you formally tell them to do it. 指示；吩咐 [FORMAL] ❑ *A doctor will often instruct patients to exercise.* 医生将经常嘱咐病人要锻炼身体。 ❑ *"Go and have a word with her, Ken," Wojtowicz instructed.* "去跟她谈谈，肯，"沃耶托维奇吩咐道。 2 V-T Someone who **instructs** people **in** a subject or skill teaches it to them. 教 ❑ *He instructed family members in nursing techniques.* 他教家人们护理技术。

in·struc·tion ♦◇◇ /ɪnstrʌkʃ^ən/ (**instructions**) 1 N-COUNT An **instruction** is something that someone tells you to do. 指示 ❑ *Two lawyers were told not to leave the building but no reason for this instruction was given.* 两位律师被告知不要离开这座建筑，但没被告知这一指示的原因。 2 N-UNCOUNT If someone gives you **instruction** in a subject or skill, they teach it to you. 讲授；指导 [FORMAL] ❑ *Each candidate is given instruction in safety.* 每位候选人都被给予了安全指导。 3 N-PLURAL **Instructions** are clear and detailed information on how to do something. 用法说明 ❑ *This book gives instructions for making a wide range of skin and hand creams.* 这本书给出了多种护肤霜和护手霜的制作说明。

Thesaurus *instruction* 另参见：
N. direction, order 1
education, learning 2

Word Partnership *instruction* 的常用搭配：
ADJ. **explicit** instruction 1 2
N. **classroom** instruction, instruction **manual** 2
V. **give** instruction, **provide** instruction, **receive** instruction 2

in·struc·tive /ɪnstrʌktɪv/ ADJ Something that is **instructive** gives useful information. 增长知识的；有启发性的 ❑ *...an entertaining and instructive documentary.* …一部既有趣又能增长知识的纪录片。

in·struc·tor /ɪnstrʌktər/ (**instructors**) N-COUNT An **instructor** is someone who teaches a skill such as driving or skiing. An **instructor** can also be used to refer to a schoolteacher or to a university teacher of low rank. 教练；教师 ❑ *...a fitness instructor.* …一位健身教练。

Thesaurus *instructor* 另参见：
N. educator, leader, professor, teacher

in·stru·ment ♦◇◇ /ɪnstrəmənt/ (**instruments**) 1 N-COUNT An **instrument** is a tool or device that is used to do a particular task, especially a scientific task. 器械 ❑ *...instruments for cleaning and polishing teeth.* …清洁和抛光牙齿的各种器械。 2 N-COUNT A musical **instrument** is an object such as a piano, guitar, or flute, which you play in order to produce music. 乐器 ❑ *Learning a musical instrument introduces a child to an understanding of music.* 学习一种乐器能引导孩子对音乐有所了解。 3 N-COUNT An **instrument** is a device that is used for making measurements of something such as speed, height, or sound, for example, on a ship or plane or in a car. 仪器 ❑ *The design of crucial instruments on the control panel will have to be improved.* 控制板上关键仪器的设计必须要改进。 4 N-COUNT Something that is an **instrument** for achieving a particular aim is used by people to achieve that aim. 手段 ❑ *The veto has been a traditional instrument of diplomacy for centuries.* 数世纪以来，否决已经成为一种传统的外交手段。
→ see **concert, drum, orchestra**

★ **in·stru·men·tal** /ɪnstrəmɛnt^əl/ (**instrumentals**) 1 ADJ Someone or something that is **instrumental in** a process or event helps to make it happen. 起作用的 ❑ *In his first years as chairman he was instrumental in raising the company's wider profile.* 在刚担任董事长的头几年，他在提升公司形象方面发挥了作用。 2 ADJ **Instrumental** music is performed by instruments and not by voices. 用乐器演奏的 [ADJ n] ❑ *...a CD of vocal and instrumental music.* …一张声乐和器乐光盘。 ● N-COUNT **Instrumentals** are pieces of instrumental music. 器乐曲 ❑ *After a couple of brief instrumentals, he puts his guitar down.* 演奏了几首简短的器乐曲之后，他放下了吉他。

in·suf·fi·cient /ɪnsəfɪʃ^ənt/ ADJ Something that is **insufficient** is not large enough in amount or degree for a particular purpose. 不充分的 [FORMAL] ❑ *He decided there was insufficient evidence to justify criminal proceedings.* 他判定没有充分的证据提起刑事诉讼。 ● **in·suf·fi·cient·ly** ADV 不充分地 [ADV adj/-ed] ❑ *Food that is insufficiently cooked can lead to food poisoning.* 未煮熟的食物可能造成食物中毒。

Word Link *insula ≈ island : insular, insulate, peninsula*

in·su·lar /ɪnsələr/ ADJ If you say that someone is **insular**, you are being critical of them because they are unwilling to meet new people or to consider new ideas. 与世隔绝的；保守的 [DISAPPROVAL] ❑ *They were an insular family.* 他们一家人与世隔绝。 ● **in·su·lar·ity** /ɪnsəlærɪti/ N-UNCOUNT 保守 ❑ *But at least they have started to break out of their old insularity.* 但他们至少已经开始打破以前的保守状态了。

★ **in·su·late** /ɪnsəleɪt/ (**insulates, insulating, insulated**) 1 V-T To **insulate** something such as a building means to protect it from cold, heat, or noise by placing a layer of other material around it or inside it. 使隔(冷)热；使隔音 ❑ *People should insulate their homes to conserve energy.* 人们应该使住房隔冷以保存能量。 ❑ *Is there any way we can insulate our home from the noise?* 有什么办法能使我们家隔音吗？ 2 V-T If a piece of equipment **is insulated**, it is covered with rubber or plastic to prevent electricity from passing through it and giving the person using it an electric shock. 使绝缘 ❑ *In order to make it safe, the element is electrically insulated.* 为安全起见，该元件做了绝缘处理。 3 V-T If a person or group **is insulated from** the rest of society or from outside influences, they are protected from them. 使隔离 ❑ *They wonder if their community is no longer insulated from big-city problems.* 他们想知道他们的社区是否不再与那些大城市的问题隔离。 ● **in·su·la·tion** N-UNCOUNT 隔绝 ❑ *They lived in happy insulation from brutal facts.* 他们生活在幸福中，与残酷事实相隔绝。

in·su·la·tion /ɪnsəleɪʃ^ən/ 1 N-UNCOUNT **Insulation** is a thick layer of a substance that keeps something warm, especially a building. 隔热材料 ❑ *High electricity bills point to a poor heating system or bad insulation.* 高额的电费账单表明供暖系统较差或者是隔热材料不好。 2 → see also **insulate**

in·su·lin /ɪnsəlɪn/ N-UNCOUNT **Insulin** is a substance that most people produce naturally in their body and that controls the level of sugar in their blood. 胰岛素 ❑ *Sufferers from the more severe form of diabetes have faulty insulin-producing cells.* 患有更严重类型的糖尿病患者其胰岛素分泌细胞存在问题。

in·sult (insults, insulting, insulted)

The verb is pronounced /ɪnsʌlt/. The noun is pronounced /ɪnsʌlt/.

动词读作 /ɪnsʌlt/。名词读作 /ɪnsʌlt/。

1 V-T If someone **insults** you, they say or do something that is rude or offensive. 辱骂；侮辱；冒犯 ❑ *I did not mean to insult you.* 我并非故意要冒犯你。 ● **in·sult·ed** ADJ 被侮辱的 ❑ *I mean, I was a bit insulted that they thought I needed bribing to shut up.* 我的意思是，我感到有些受侮辱的是他们认为我收受贿赂才肯闭嘴。 2 N-COUNT An **insult** is a rude remark, or something a person says or does which insults you. 侮辱；辱骂；冒犯 ❑ *Their behavior was an insult to the people they represent.* 他们的行为是对他们所代表的人们的一种侮辱。 3 PHRASE You say **to add insult to injury** when mentioning an action or fact that makes an unfair or unacceptable situation even worse. 更糟糕的是 ❑ *It is the victim who is often put on trial and, to add insult to injury, she is presumed guilty until proven innocent of provoking the rape.* 受到审问的往往是受害者，更糟糕的是，她被假定为有罪，直到证明强奸并非由她挑逗而引起。

in·sult·ing /ɪnsʌltɪŋ/ ADJ Something that is **insulting** is rude or offensive. 侮辱的 ❑ *...insulting language.* …侮辱的语言。

in·sur·ance ♦♦◊ /ɪnʃʊərəns/ (**insurances**) 1 N-VAR **Insurance** is an arrangement in which you pay money to a company, and they pay you if something unpleasant happens to you, for example, if your property is stolen or damaged, or if you get a serious illness. 保险 ❑ *The house was a total loss and the insurance company promptly paid us the policy limit.* 房屋被定为全损，保险公司按保险限额迅速赔付了我们。 2 N-VAR If you do something as **insurance against** something unpleasant happening, you do it to protect yourself in case the unpleasant thing happens. 预防措施 ❑ *Attentive proofreading is the only insurance against the kind of omissions described in this section.* 仔细校对是避免本节提到的那种遗漏问题的惟一预防措施。

Word Partnership *insurance* 的常用搭配：

V. **buy/purchase** insurance, **carry** insurance, **sell** insurance 1

N. insurance **claim**, insurance **company**, insurance **coverage**, insurance **payments**, insurance **policy** 1

in·sur·ance ad·just·er (**insurance adjusters**) N-COUNT An **insurance adjuster** is the same as a **claims adjuster**. 保险理算员 [AM, BUSINESS]

in BRIT, use **loss adjuster**

in·sure /ɪnʃʊər/ (**insures, insuring, insured**) 1 V-T/V-I If you **insure** yourself or your property, you pay money to an insurance company so that, if you become ill or if your property is damaged or stolen, the company will pay you a sum of money. 为…投保；投保 ❑ *For protection against unforeseen emergencies, you insure your house, your furnishings and your car.* 为防止发生无法预料的紧急情况，人们给房屋、家具和汽车投保。 ❑ *While many people insure against death, far fewer take precautions against long-term loss of income because of sickness.* 虽然许多人买人寿险，但很少有人采取预防措施以避免因疾病而造成的长期收入损失。 2 V-T If you **insure yourself against** something unpleasant that might happen in the future, you do something to protect yourself in case it happens, or to prevent it from happening. 使预防 ❑ *All the electronics in the world cannot insure people against accidents, though.* 不过，世界上所有的电子设备并不能预防意外的发生。 ❑ *He insured himself against failure by treating only people he was sure he could cure.* 他通过只治疗他有把握治好的病人而确保自己不会失败。

Word Partnership *insure* 的常用搭配：

N. insure ***your* car/health/house/property** 1
insure ***your* safety** 2

ADJ. **difficult to** insure, **necessary to** insure 1 2

in·sur·er /ɪnʃʊərər/ (**insurers**) N-COUNT An **insurer** is a company that sells insurance. 保险公司 [BUSINESS]

★ **in·sur·gen·cy** /ɪnsɜrdʒənsi/ (**insurgencies**) N-VAR An **insurgency** is a violent attempt to oppose a country's government carried out by citizens of that country. 暴动 [FORMAL]

★ **in·sur·gent** /ɪnsɜrdʒənt/ (**insurgents**) N-COUNT **Insurgents** are people who are fighting against the government or army of their own country. 起义者 [usu pl] [FORMAL] ❑ *By early yesterday, the insurgents had taken control of the country's main military air base.* 到昨天早些时候，那些起义者已控制了该国的主要空军基地。

in·sur·rec·tion /ɪnsərɛkʃən/ (**insurrections**) N-VAR An **insurrection** is violent action that is taken by a large group of people against the rulers of their country, usually in order to remove them from office. 叛乱 [FORMAL] ❑ *They were plotting to stage an armed insurrection if negotiations with the government should fail.* 他们正在策划如果与政府的谈判失败就发动武装叛乱。

in·tact /ɪntækt/ ADJ Something that is **intact** is complete and has not been damaged or changed. 完整无缺的 ❑ *Customs men put dynamite in the water to destroy the cargo, but most of it was left intact.* 海关人员把炸药放入水中以摧毁货物，但大部分货物却完好无损。

▲ **in·take** /ɪnteɪk/ (**intakes**) 1 N-SING Your **intake** of a particular kind of food, drink, or air is the amount that you eat, drink, or breathe in. 摄取量；吸入量；接受量 ❑ *Your intake of alcohol should not exceed two units per day.* 你每天酒精摄入量不能超过两个单位。 2 N-COUNT The people who are accepted into an organization or place at a particular time are referred to as a particular **intake**. 新纳入者 [BRIT] ❑ *...one of this year's intake of students.* …今年新招学生中的一个。

Word Partnership *intake* 的常用搭配：

ADJ. **alcohol** intake, **caloric** intake, **daily** intake, **total** intake 1

V. **increase *your*** intake, **limit *your*** intake, **reduce *your*** intake 1

Word Link *tang ≈ touching : entangle, intangible, tangible*

in·tan·gible /ɪntændʒɪbəl/ (**intangibles**) ADJ Something that is **intangible** is abstract or is hard to define or measure. 难以捉摸的；难以确定的 ❑ *...the intangible and non-material dimensions of our human and social existence.* …我们人类社会生活的那些难以捉摸的和非物质的方面。 ● N-PLURAL You can refer to intangible things as **intangibles**. 无形的东西 ❑ *That approach fails to take into consideration intangibles such as pride of workmanship, loyalty and good work habits.* 那种方法没有考虑无形的因素例如对手艺的自豪感、忠诚和良好的工作习惯。

★ **in·te·gral** /ɪntɪgrəl/ ADJ Something that is an **integral** part of something is an essential part of that thing. 构成整体所必需的 ❑ *Rituals, celebrations, and festivals form an integral part of every human society.* 仪式、庆典和节日是每个人类社会不可缺少的组成部分。

in·te·grate ♦◊◊ /ɪntɪgreɪt/ (**integrates, integrating, integrated**) 1 V-T/V-I If someone **integrates** into a social group, or **is integrated** into it, they behave in such a way that they become part of the group or are accepted into it. 使融入；结合在一起 ❑ *He didn't integrate successfully into the Italian way of life.* 他没有成功融入到意大利的生活方式中去。 ❑ *Integrating the kids with the community is essential.* 使孩子们融入这个社区是非常必要的。 ● **in·te·grat·ed** ADJ 融合的 ❑ *He thinks we are living in a fully integrated, supportive society.* 他认为我们生活在一个完全融合、互相帮助的社会。 ● **in·te·gra·tion** /ɪntɪgreɪʃən/ N-UNCOUNT 融合 ❑ *Americans overwhelmingly support the integration of disabled people into mainstream society.* 美国人极为支持残疾人融入主流社会。 2 V-T/V-I When races **integrate** or when schools and organizations **are integrated**, people who belong to ethnic minorities can join others in their schools and organizations. 使合并；成为一体 [AM] ❑ *The Marine Corps was the last service to integrate.* 美国海军陆战队是最后合并的部队。 ● **in·te·grat·ed** ADJ (种族) 融合的 [ADJ n] ❑ *...a black honor student in Chicago's integrated Lincoln Park High School.* …在芝加哥混合种族的林肯公园高中上学的一位黑人优等生。 ● **in·te·gra·tion** N-UNCOUNT (种族) 融合 ❑ *Lots of people in Chicago don't see that racial border. They see progress toward integration.* 在芝加哥，许多人并没有看到种族界限，他们看到的是种族融合取得的进步。 3 V-RECIP If you **integrate** one thing **with** another, or one thing **integrates with** another, the two things become closely linked or form part of a whole idea or system. You can also say that two things **integrate**. 结合 ❑ *Writing about a topic helps you integrate new knowledge with what you already know.* 围绕某一题目写作有助于你将新知识和已有知识结合起来。 ❑ *...historic landmarks that integrate with the community.* …与社区融为一体的历史性里程碑。 ● **in·te·grat·ed** ADJ 整体的 ❑ *There is, he said, a lack of an integrated national transportation policy.* 他说目前缺乏一个整体的全国运输政策。 ● **in·te·gra·tion** N-UNCOUNT 融合 ❑ *With Germany, France has been the prime mover behind closer European integration.* 法国同德国一起成为促进欧洲更加融合的主要推动者。

Thesaurus *integrate* 另参见：
V. assimilate, combine, consolidate, incorporate, synthesize, unite; *(ant.)* separate 3

Word Partnership *integrate* 的常用搭配：
N. integrate **schools** 2
integrate **efforts**, integrate **information/knowledge** 3

in·te·grat·ed /ɪntɪgreɪtɪd/ 1 ADJ An **integrated** institution is intended for use by all races or religious groups. 种族(或宗教)融合的 ❑ *We believe that students of integrated schools will have more tolerant attitudes.* 我们相信在种族融合的学校上学的学生将拥有更加宽容的态度。 2 → see also **integrate**

in·teg·rity /ɪntɛgrɪti/ 1 N-UNCOUNT If you have **integrity**, you are honest and firm in your moral principles. 正直；诚实 ❑ *I have always regarded him as a man of integrity.* 我一直把他当作一个正直诚实的人。 2 N-UNCOUNT The **integrity** of something such as a group of people or a text is its state of being a united whole. 完整 [FORMAL] ❑ *Separatist movements are a threat to the integrity of the nation.* 分裂活动是对国家领土完整的威胁。

Word Partnership *integrity* 的常用搭配：
N. **honesty and** integrity, **a man of** integrity, **sense of** integrity 1
ADJ. **moral** integrity, **personal** integrity 1
structural integrity, **territorial** integrity 2

★ **in·tel·lect** /ɪntɪlɛkt/ (**intellects**) 1 N-VAR **Intellect** is the ability to understand or deal with ideas and information. 智力 ❑ *Do the emotions develop in parallel with the intellect?* 情感与智力同步发展吗？ 2 N-VAR **Intellect** is the quality of being intelligent. 才智 ❑ *She is famed for her intellect.* 她因才智而出名。

in·tel·lec·tual ♦◇◇ /ɪntɪlɛktʃuəl/ (**intellectuals**) 1 ADJ **Intellectual** means involving a person's ability to think and to understand ideas and information. 智力的 [ADJ n] ❑ *High levels of lead could damage the intellectual development of children.* 高含铅量会损害儿童的智力发育。 ● **in·tel·lec·tual·ly** ADV 智力地 ❑ *...intellectually satisfying work.* …在智力上令人满意的工作。 2 N-COUNT An **intellectual** is someone who spends a lot of time studying and thinking about complicated ideas. 知识分子 ❑ *Teachers, artists and other intellectuals urged political parties to launch a united movement against the government.* 教师们、艺术家们和其他知识分子们敦促各政党发动一场反政府的联合运动。 ● ADJ **Intellectual** is also an adjective. 有高智力的 ❑ *They were very intellectual and witty.* 他们非常聪明、机智。

Word Partnership *intellectual* 的常用搭配：
N. intellectual **ability**, intellectual **activity**, intellectual **freedom**, intellectual **interests** 1

in·tel·li·gence ♦◇◇ /ɪntɛlɪdʒᵊns/ 1 N-UNCOUNT **Intelligence** is the quality of being intelligent or clever. 聪明 ❑ *She's a woman of exceptional intelligence.* 她是个格外聪明的女人。 2 N-UNCOUNT **Intelligence** is the ability to think, reason, and understand instead of doing things automatically or by instinct. 智能 ❑ *Nerve cells, after all, do not have intelligence of their own.* 神经元本身毕竟不具备智能。 3 N-UNCOUNT **Intelligence** is information that is gathered by the government or the army about their country's enemies and their activities. 情报 ❑ *Why was military intelligence so lacking?* 为什么军事情报如此缺乏？

Word Partnership *intelligence* 的常用搭配：
N. **human** intelligence 2
intelligence **agent**, intelligence **expert**, **military** intelligence, **secret** intelligence 3
N.

in·tel·li·gent ♦◇◇ /ɪntɛlɪdʒᵊnt/ 1 ADJ A person or animal that is **intelligent** has the ability to think, understand, and learn things quickly and well. 有智慧的 ❑ *Susan's a very bright and intelligent woman who knows her own mind.* 苏珊是一个非常聪明伶俐而且清楚自己想法的女人。 ● **in·tel·li·gent·ly** ADV 有头脑地 ❑ *They are incapable of thinking intelligently about politics.* 他们在考虑政治问题时缺乏头脑。 2 ADJ Something that is **intelligent** can think and understand instead of doing things automatically or by instinct. 有智能的 ❑ *Intelligent computers will soon be an indispensable diagnostic tool for every doctor.* 智能计算机很快将会成为每位医生必不可少的诊断工具。

Thesaurus *intelligent* 另参见：
ADJ. bright, clever, sharp, smart; *(ant.)* dumb, stupid 1 2

★ **in·tel·li·gi·ble** /ɪntɛlɪdʒɪbᵊl/ ADJ Something that is **intelligible** can be understood. 容易理解的 ❑ *The language of Darwin was intelligible to experts and non-experts alike.* 达尔文的语言对专家和平常人来说都容易理解。

in·tend ♦♦◇ /ɪntɛnd/ (**intends, intending, intended**) 1 V-T If you **intend** to do something, you have decided or planned to do it. 打算 ❑ *Maybe he intends to leave her.* 也许他打算离开她。 ❑ *What do you intend doing when you get to this place?* 你打算到这里干什么？ 2 V-T If something **is intended** for a particular purpose, it has been planned to fulfill that purpose. If something **is intended** for a particular person, it has been planned to be used by that person or to affect them in some way. 被用于(某目的或某人) [usu passive] ❑ *This money is intended for the development of the tourist industry.* 这笔钱是准备用于发展旅游业的。 ❑ *Columns are usually intended in architecture to add grandeur and status.* 柱子被用于建筑通常是为了增添宏伟和高贵。 3 V-T If you **intend** a particular idea or feeling in something that you say or do, you want to express it or want it to be understood. 想要 ❑ *He didn't intend any sarcasm.* 他没有任何讽刺的意思。 ❑ *Barzun's response seemed a little patronizing, though he undoubtedly hadn't intended it that way.* 巴曾的反应好像显得有点屈尊俯就，但无疑他不是想要那样。

Word Partnership *intend* 的常用搭配：
V. intend **to be**, intend **to continue**, intend **to do**, intend **to go**, intend **to leave**, intend **to make**, intend **to return**, intend **to say**, intend **to stay** 1

in·tense ♦◇◇ /ɪntɛns/ 1 ADJ **Intense** is used to describe something that is very great or extreme in strength or degree. 剧烈的；极度的 ❑ *He was sweating from the intense heat.* 由于剧烈的热量，他一直出汗。 ❑ *Stevens's murder was the result of a deep-seated and intense hatred.* 史蒂文斯凶杀案源于深仇大恨。 ● **in·tense·ly** ADV 剧烈地；极度地 ❑ *The fast-food business is intensely competitive.* 快餐业竞争非常激烈。 ● **in·ten·sity** /ɪntɛnsɪti/ N-VAR (**intensities**) 剧烈；极度 ❑ *The attack was anticipated but its intensity came as a shock.* 进攻是在预料之中的，但其激烈程度却令人震惊。 2 ADJ If you describe an activity as **intense**, you mean that it is very serious and concentrated, and often involves doing a lot in a short time. 集中的；紧张的 ❑ *The battle for third place was intense.* 竞争第3名的较量很紧张。 3 ADJ If you describe the way someone looks at you as **intense**, you mean that they look at you very directly and seem to know what you are thinking or feeling. 热切的 ❑ *I felt so self-conscious under Luke's mother's intense gaze.* 在卢克母亲热切的注视下，我感到很不自在。 ● **in·tense·ly** ADV 热切地 [ADV with v] ❑ *He sipped his drink, staring intensely at me.* 他一边小口喝着饮料，一边热切地盯着我。 4 ADJ If you describe a person as **intense**, you mean that they appear to concentrate very hard on everything that they do, and they feel their emotions very strongly. 很认真的 ❑ *I know he's an intense player, but he does enjoy what he's doing.* 我知道他是名很认真的选手，可他确实喜欢他所做的事情。 ● **in·ten·sity** N-UNCOUNT 过分认真 ❑ *His intensity and the ferocity of his feelings alarmed me.* 他的过分认真和激烈的感受令我恐慌。

Word Partnership *intense* 的常用搭配：
N. intense **concentration**, intense **feelings**, intense **pain**, intense **pressure** 1
intense **activity**, intense **competition**, intense **debate**, intense **fighting**, intense **relationship** 2
intense **scrutiny** 2 3

Word Link *ify ≈ making : clarify, diversify, intensify*

in·ten·si·fy /ɪntɛnsɪfaɪ/ (**intensifies, intensifying, intensified**) V-T/V-I If you **intensify** something or if it **intensifies**, it becomes greater in strength, amount, or degree. 加强；强化 ❑ *I jump, intensifying the pain in all my muscles.* 我跳起来，浑身的肌肉更加疼痛了。

in·ten·sive /ɪntɛnsɪv/ 1 ADJ **Intensive** activity involves concentrating a lot of effort or people on one particular task in order to try to achieve a lot in a short time. 集中的 ❑ *...after several days and nights of intensive negotiations.* …在几个日夜的集中谈判之后。 ● **in·ten·sive·ly** ADV 集中地 [ADV with v] ❑ *Caitlin's parents opted to* *educate her intensively at home.* 凯特林的父母选择在家对她进行强化教育。 2 ADJ **Intensive** farming involves producing as many crops or animals as possible from your land, usually with the aid of chemicals. 集约的 ❑ *...intensive methods of rearing poultry.* …集约饲养家禽的方法。 ● **in·ten·sive·ly** ADV 集约地 [ADV with v] ❑ *Will they farm the rest of their land less intensively?* 他们会在耕种其余土地时不这么集约吗？

Word Partnership *intensive* 的常用搭配：

N. intensive **efforts**, intensive **negotiations**, intensive **program**, intensive **study**, intensive **training**, intensive **treatment** 1

in·ten·sive care N-UNCOUNT If someone is **in intensive care**, they are being given extremely thorough care in a hospital because they are very ill or very badly injured. 重症特别护理 ❑ *She spent the night in intensive care after the operation.* 手术后的那天晚上她受到重症特别护理。

★ **in·tent** /ɪntɛnt/ (**intents**) 1 ADJ If you are **intent on** doing something, you are eager and determined to do it. 坚决的 [v-link ADJ "on/upon" -ing/n] ❑ *The rebels are obviously intent on keeping up the pressure.* 反叛分子显然决心继续施加压力。 2 ADJ If someone does something in an **intent** way, they pay great attention to what they are doing. 专注的 [WRITTEN] ❑ *She looked from one intent face to another.* 她看着一张张专注的面孔。 ● **in·tent·ly** ADV 专注地 [ADV after v] ❑ *He listened intently, then slammed down the phone.* 他专注地听着，然后猛地把电话放下。 3 N-VAR A person's **intent** is their intention to do something. 意图 [FORMAL] ❑ *The timing of this strong statement of intent on arms control is crucial.* 发表这项意图实施军备控制的强硬声明的时机至关重要。 4 PHRASE You say **to all intents and purposes** to suggest that a situation is not exactly as you describe it but the effect is the same as if it were. 实际上 ❑ *To all intents and purposes he was my father.* 他实际上可以称得上是我的父亲。

in·ten·tion ♦◇◇ /ɪntɛnʃᵊn/ (**intentions**) 1 N-VAR An **intention** is an idea or plan of what you are going to do. 意图 ❑ *The company has every intention of keeping the share price high.* 该公司有将自己的股票保持在高价的意图。 ❑ *It is my intention to remain in my position until a successor is elected.* 我的打算是我继续留任直到选出接班人。 2 PHRASE If you say that you **have no intention of** doing something, you are emphasizing that you are not going to do it. If you say that you **have every intention of** doing something, you are emphasizing that you intend to do it. 不打算/打算 [EMPHASIS] ❑ *I have no intention of allowing you to continue living here alone.* 我不打算让你继续独自生活在这里。

Word Partnership *intention* 的常用搭配：

ADJ. **clear** intention, **original** intention 1
V. **express** *your* intention, **state** *your* intention 1
have every intention of, **have no** intention of 2

in·ten·tion·al /ɪntɛnʃənᵊl/ ADJ Something that is **intentional** is deliberate. 故意的 ❑ *Women who are the victims of intentional discrimination will be able to get compensation.* 遭受故意歧视的妇女们将能得到赔偿。 ● **in·ten·tion·al·ly** ADV 故意地 ❑ *I've never intentionally hurt anyone.* 我从未故意伤害过任何人。

inter·act /ɪntərækt/ (**interacts, interacting, interacted**) 1 V-RECIP When people **interact with** each other or **interact**, they communicate as they work or spend time together. 相互交往 ❑ *While the other children interacted and played together, Ted ignored them.* 当其他孩子们相互交往、一起玩耍时，泰德却不理他们。 ● **inter·ac·tion** /ɪntərækʃᵊn/ N-VAR (**interactions**) 相互交往 ❑ *...superficial interactions with other people.* …和其他人的表面交往。 2 V-I When people **interact with** computers, or when computers **interact with** other machines, information or instructions are exchanged. 互动 ❑ *...new, simplified ways of interacting with a computer.* …与计算机互动的简化新方法。 ● **inter·ac·tion** N-VAR (**interactions**) 互动 ❑ *...experts on human-computer interaction.* …人机互动专家。 3 V-RECIP When one thing **interacts with** another or two things **interact**, the two things affect each other's behavior or condition. 相互作用 ❑ *You have to understand how cells interact.* 你必须得了解细胞之间是如何相互作用的。 ● **inter·ac·tion** N-VAR 相互作用 ❑ *...the interaction between physical and emotional illness.* …生理疾病和心理疾病之间的相互作用。

★ **inter·ac·tive** /ɪntəræktɪv/ 1 ADJ An **interactive** computer program or electronic device is one that allows direct communication between the user and the machine. 交互的 ❑ *This will make computer games more interactive than ever.* 这将使电脑游戏比以前更具交互性。 ● **inter·ac·tiv·ity** /ɪntəræktɪvɪti/ N-UNCOUNT 交互性 ❑ *...digital television, with more channels and interactivity.* …有更多频道和交互功能的数字电视。 2 ADJ If you describe a group of people or their activities as **interactive**, you mean that the people communicate with each other. 互动的 ❑ *There is little evidence that this encouraged flexible, interactive teaching in the classroom.* 几乎没有证据表明这促进灵活互动的课堂教学。

▲ **inter·cept** /ɪntərsɛpt/ (**intercepts, intercepting, intercepted**) V-T If you **intercept** someone or something that is traveling from one place to another, you stop them before they get to their destination. 拦截 ❑ *Gunmen intercepted him on his way to the airport.* 持枪人在他去机场的路上截住了他。 ● **inter·cep·tion** /ɪntərsɛpʃᵊn/ N-VAR (**interceptions**) 拦截 ❑ *...the interception of a ship off the coast of Oregon.* …对一艘驶离俄勒冈海岸的轮船的拦截。

Word Link *inter* ≈ *between* : *interchange, interconnect, internal*

inter·change (**interchanges, interchanging, interchanged**)

The noun is pronounced /ɪntərtʃeɪndʒ/. The verb is pronounced /ɪntərtʃeɪndʒ/.

名词读作 /ɪntərtʃeɪndʒ/，动词读作 /ɪntərtʃeɪndʒ/。

1 N-VAR If there is an **interchange** of ideas or information among a group of people, each person talks about his or her ideas or gives information to the others. 交换；交流 ❑ *What made the meeting exciting was the interchange of ideas from different disciplines.* 会议上令人兴奋的是来自不同学科之间的交流。 2 V-RECIP If you **interchange** one thing **with** another, or you **interchange** two things, each thing takes the place of the other or is exchanged for the other. You can also say that two things **interchange**. 互换 ❑ *You cannot interchange a "male" with a "female" electric plug.* 你不能将"凸"、"凹"插头互换。 ❑ *Your task is to interchange words so that the sentence makes sense.* 你的任务是替换单词使这句话讲得通。 ● N-VAR **Interchange** is also a noun. 互换 ❑ *...the interchange of matter and energy at atomic or sub-atomic levels.* …物质和能量在原子层或亚原子层的互换。 3 N-COUNT An **interchange** on a highway, freeway, or road is a place where it joins a main road or another highway or freeway. 道路立体交叉 ❑ *...Sudley Road in Manassas, near the interchange with Interstate 66.* …在与66号州际公路交叉处附近的马那萨斯的萨德力路。

inter·change·able /ɪntərtʃeɪndʒəbᵊl/ ADJ Things that are **interchangeable** can be exchanged with each other without it making any difference. 可互换的 ❑ *His greatest innovation was the use of interchangeable parts.* 他最伟大的创新是使用了可互换部件。 ● **inter·change·ably** ADV 可互换地 [ADV after v] ❑ *These expressions are often used interchangeably, but they do have different meanings.* 这些表达法经常可以互换使用，但它们的确有不同的含义。

inter·com /ɪntərkɒm/ (**intercoms**) N-COUNT An **intercom** is a small box with a microphone that is connected to a loudspeaker in another room. You use it to talk to the people in the other room. 对讲机 ❑ *I pushed a button on my intercom and told Viktor Ilyushin that I needed to see him.* 我按了一下对讲机上的一个按键，告诉维克多·伊留申我要见他。

inter·con·nect /ɪntərkənɛkt/ (**interconnects, interconnecting, interconnected**) V-RECIP Things that **interconnect** or **are interconnected** are connected to or with each other. You can also say that one thing **interconnects with** another. 使互相联系；互相联系 ❑ *The causes are many and may interconnect.* 原因很多，而且还可能互相关联。

inter·con·nec·tion /ɪntərkənɛkʃᵊn/ (**interconnections**) N-VAR If you say that there is an **interconnection** between two or more things, you mean that they are very closely connected. 互相关联 [FORMAL] ❑ *...the alarming interconnection of drug abuse and AIDS infection.* …吸毒与艾滋病感染之间惊人的相互关联。

inter·con·ti·nen·tal /ɪntərkɒntɪnɛntᵊl/ ADJ **Intercontinental** is used to describe something that exists or happens between continents. 洲际的 [ADJ n] ❑ *...intercontinental flights.* …洲际航班。

★ **inter·course** /ɪntərkɔrs/ 1 N-UNCOUNT **Intercourse** is the act of having sex. 性交 [FORMAL] ❑ *...sexual intercourse.* …性交。 2 N-UNCOUNT Social **intercourse** is communication between people as they spend time together. 交际 [OLD-FASHIONED] ❑ *There was social intercourse between the old and the young.* 老年人和年轻人之间有社会交往。

inter·de·pend·ence /ɪntərdɪpɛndəns/ N-UNCOUNT **Interdependence** is the condition of a group of people or things that all depend on each other. 互相依赖 ❑ *...the interdependence of nations.* …国家间的相互依赖。

inter·de·pend·ent /ɪntərdɪpɛndənt/ ADJ People or things that are **interdependent** all depend on each other. 互相依赖的 ❑ *We live in an increasingly interdependent world.* 我们生活在一个日益相互依赖的世界。

inter·dict /ɪntərdɪkt/ (**interdicts, interdicting, interdicted**) V-T If an armed force **interdicts** something or someone, they stop them and prevent them from moving. If they **interdict** a route, they block it or cut it off. 阻断；封锁 [AM, FORMAL] ❑ *Troops could be ferried in to interdict drug shipments.* 军队可以被渡运来阻断毒品运输。

in·ter·est ♦♦♦ /ɪntrɪst, -tərɪst/ (**interests, interesting, interested**) **1** N-UNCOUNT If you have an **interest in** something, you want to learn or hear more about it. 兴趣 [also "a" N] ❑ *There has been a lively interest in the elections in the last two weeks.* 过去两周人们对选举一直有强烈的兴趣。 ❑ *She'd liked him at first, but soon lost interest.* 最初她喜欢过他，但很快就失去了兴趣。 **2** N-COUNT Your **interests** are the things that you enjoy doing. 爱好 ❑ *Encourage your child in her interests and hobbies.* 鼓励你的孩子发展她的兴趣和爱好。 **3** V-T If something **interests** you, it attracts your attention so that you want to learn or hear more about it or continue doing it. 使感兴趣 ❑ *Your financial problems do not interest me.* 我对你的财务问题不感兴趣。 **4** V-T If you are trying to persuade someone to buy or do something, you can say that you are trying to **interest** them **in** it. 引起（购买或做某事）的意愿 ❑ *Can I interest you in a new car?* 我给你介绍一下新车，你感兴趣吗？ **5** N-COUNT If something is in the **interests** of a particular person or group, it will benefit them in some way. 利益 ❑ *Did those directors act in the best interests of their club?* 那些董事们是从他们俱乐部的最大利益出发而行动的吗？ **6** N-COUNT You can use **interests** to refer to groups of people who you think use their power or money to benefit themselves. 利益集团 ❑ *The government accused unnamed "foreign interests" of inciting the trouble.* 政府不点名地指责一些"外国利益集团"煽动骚乱。 **7** N-COUNT A person or organization that has an **interest** in an area, a company, a property or in a particular type of business owns stock in it. 股权 [BUSINESS] ❑ *My father had many business interests in Vietnam.* 我父亲在越南有许多公司股权。 **8** N-COUNT If a person, country, or organization has an **interest in** a possible event or situation, they want that event or situation to happen because they are likely to benefit from it. 利害关系 ❑ *The West has an interest in promoting democratic forces in Eastern Europe.* 西方国家在促使东欧民主力量壮大中有利害关系。 **9** N-UNCOUNT **Interest** is extra money that you receive if you have invested a sum of money. **Interest** is also the extra money that you pay if you have borrowed money or are buying something on credit. 利息 ❑ *Does your checking account pay interest?* 你的活期存款账户计息吗？ **10** → see also **interested, interesting, compound interest, self-interest, vested interest** **11** PHRASE If you do something **in the interests of** a particular result or situation, you do it in order to achieve that result or maintain that situation. 为了…的利益 ❑ *...a call for all businessmen to work together in the interests of national stability.* …为了国家稳定而向所有商人发出的共同合作的号召。 **12** to have someone's **interests at heart** → see **heart**
→ see **bank, interest rate**

Word Partnership *interest* 的常用搭配：

N. **level of** interest, **places of** interest, **self**-interest **1**
conflict of interest **7** **8**
interest **charges**, interest **expenses**, interest **payments** **9**
V. **attract** interest, **express** interest, **lose** interest **1**
earn interest, **pay** interest **9**
ADJ. **great** interest, **little** interest, **strong** interest **1** **8**

in·ter·est·ed ♦♦◇ /ɪntərɛstɪd, -trɪstɪd/ **1** ADJ If you are **interested in** something, you think it is important and want to learn more about it or spend time doing it. 感兴趣的 ❑ *I thought she might be interested in Paula's proposal.* 我以为她可能会对保拉的提议感兴趣。 **2** ADJ An **interested** party or group of people is affected by or involved in a particular event or situation. 有关的 [ADJ n] ❑ *The success was only possible because all the interested parties eventually agreed to the idea.* 因为有关各方最终同意了这一意见所以才有可能成功。 **3** ADJ If you say that one person is **interested in** another person, you mean that the first person would like to have a romantic or sexual relationship with the other person. 着迷的 [usu v-link ADJ "in" n] ❑ *I heard there are a lot of guys interested in her.* 我听说很多小伙子迷上了她。

Word Partnership *interested* 的常用搭配：

V. **become** interested, interested **in buying**, **get** interested, interested **in getting**, interested **in helping**, interested **in learning**, interested **in making**, **seem** interested **1**
ADV. **really** interested, **very** interested **1**

interest-free ADJ An **interest-free** loan has no interest charged on it. 无息的 ❑ *He was offered a $10,000 interest-free loan.* 他获得了一笔1万美元的无息贷款。 ● ADV **Interest-free** is also an adverb. 无息地 [ADV after v] ❑ *Customers allowed the banks to use their money interest-free.* 客户们允许银行无息使用他们的钱。

in·ter·est·ing ♦◇◇ /ɪntərɛstɪŋ, -trɪstɪŋ/ ADJ If you find something **interesting**, it attracts your attention, for example, because you think it is exciting or unusual. 有趣的 ❑ *It was interesting to be in a different environment.* 换一换环境很有趣。

Thesaurus *interesting* 另参见：

ADJ. absorbing, compelling, engrossing, unusual; *(ant.)* boring

Word Partnership *interesting* 的常用搭配：

ADV. **especially** interesting, **really** interesting, **very** interesting
N. interesting **idea**, interesting **people**, interesting **point**, interesting **question**, interesting **story**, interesting **things**

in·ter·est·ing·ly /ɪntərɛstɪŋli, -trɪstɪŋli/ ADV You use **interestingly** to introduce a piece of information that you think is interesting or unexpected. 有趣地 [ADV with cl] ❑ *Interestingly enough, a few weeks later, Benjamin remarried.* 有趣的是，几周后本杰明再婚了。

Word Web interest rate

Borrowers have several options when choosing a **mortgage** to purchase a new home. The most common home **loan** is the **fixed rate** mortgage. With this loan the **interest rate** does not change, so the borrower pays the same amount of **principal** and interest each month. The interest on an **adjustable rate** mortgage does change. With an **interest only** mortgage, the borrower pays only the interest every month and owes the **lender** the entire principal amount at the end of the period.

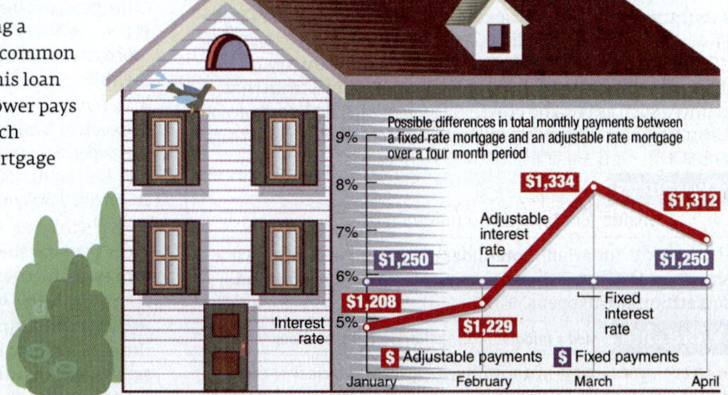

i

in·ter·est rate (**interest rates**) N-COUNT The **interest rate** is the amount of interest that must be paid. It is expressed as a percentage of the amount that is borrowed or gained as profit. 利率 [BUSINESS] ❑ *The Federal Reserve lowered interest rates by half a point.* 联邦储备委员会将利率降低了0.5个百分点。

→ see Word Web: **interest rate**

▲ **inter·face** /ɪntərfeɪs/ (**interfaces, interfacing, interfaced**) 1 N-COUNT The **interface** between two subjects or systems is the area in which they affect each other or have links with each other. 交叉区域 ❑ *...a witty exploration of that interface between bureaucracy and the working world.* …对官僚阶层和劳动大众之间的临界区域的巧妙探究。 2 N-COUNT The user **interface** of a particular piece of computer software is its presentation on the screen and how easy it is to operate. 界面 [COMPUTING] ❑ *...the development of better user interfaces.* …更好用户界面的开发。 3 V-RECIP If one thing **interfaces with** another, or if two things **interface**, they have connections with each other. If you **interface** one thing with another, you connect the two things. 相互联系；连接 [FORMAL] ❑ *...the way we interface with the environment.* …我们与环境相互联系的方式。 ❑ *He had interfaced all this machinery with a master computer.* 他已将这整台机器与一台主控计算机连接起来。

inter·fere /ɪntərfɪər/ (**interferes, interfering, interfered**) 1 V-I If you say that someone **interferes in** a situation, you mean they get involved in it although it does not concern them and their involvement is not wanted. 干涉 [DISAPPROVAL] ❑ *I wish everyone would stop interfering and just leave me alone.* 我希望所有人都不再干涉我，让我一个人静一静。 2 V-I Something that **interferes with** a situation, activity, or process has a damaging effect on it. 妨碍 ❑ *Smoking and drinking interfere with your body's ability to process oxygen.* 吸烟和喝酒妨碍身体对氧的吸收能力。

Word Partnership *interfere* 的常用搭配：

N. **ability to** interfere, **right to** interfere 1

V. **try to** interfere, **not want to** interfere 1

inter·fer·ence /ɪntərfɪərəns/ 1 N-UNCOUNT **Interference** by a person or group is their unwanted or unnecessary involvement in something. 干涉 [DISAPPROVAL] ❑ *Airlines will be able to set cheap fares without further interference from the government.* 如果不受政府更多的干预，各航空公司将能够把票价定得很低。 2 N-UNCOUNT When there is **interference**, a radio signal is affected by other radio waves or electrical activity so that it cannot be received properly. 干扰 ❑ *...electrical interference.* …电子干扰。

★ **in·ter·im** ♦◊◊ /ɪntərɪm/ 1 ADJ **Interim** is used to describe something that is intended to be used until something permanent is done or established. 临时的 [ADJ n] ❑ *She was sworn in as head of an interim government in March.* 她3月份宣誓出任临时政府首脑。 2 PHRASE **In the interim** means until a particular thing happens or until a particular thing happened. 在过渡时期 [FORMAL] ❑ *But, in the interim, we obviously have a duty to maintain law and order.* 但是，在过渡时期我们显然有责任维持法律与秩序。

in·te·ri·or ♦◊◊ /ɪntɪəriər/ (**interiors**) 1 N-COUNT The **interior** of something is the inside part of it. 内部 ❑ *The interior of the house was furnished with heavy, old-fashioned pieces.* 房内陈设着些笨重、老式的家具。 2 ADJ You use **interior** to describe something that is inside a building or vehicle. (建筑或者车辆) 内部的 [ADJ n] ❑ *The interior walls were painted green.* 内墙被漆成了绿色。 3 N-SING The **interior** of a country or continent is the central area of it. 内地 ❑ *The Yangtze River would give access to much of China's interior.* 长江使得人们能够到达中国内陆许多地方。 4 ADJ An **interior** minister, ministry, or department in some countries deals with affairs within that country, such as law and order. 内政的 [ADJ n] ❑ *The French Interior Minister has intervened in a scandal over the role of a secret police force.* 法国内务部长对一起有关秘密警察部队职责的丑闻进行了干预。

Thesaurus *interior* 另参见：

N. inside; *(ant.)* exterior, outside 1

inter·lude /ɪntərlud/ (**interludes**) N-COUNT An **interlude** is a short period of time when an activity or situation stops and something else happens. 间歇

Word Link *med ≈ middle : intermediary, media, mediate*

★ **inter·medi·ary** /ɪntərmidieri/ (**intermediaries**) N-COUNT An **intermediary** is a person who passes messages or proposals between two people or groups. 中间人 ❑ *She wanted him to act as an intermediary in the dispute with Moscow.* 她想让他在与莫斯科的争端中担当中间人。

inter·medi·ate /ɪntərmidiɪt/ (**intermediates**) 1 ADJ An **intermediate** stage, level, or position is one that occurs between two other stages, levels, or positions. 中间的 ❑ *Do you make any intermediate stops between your home and work?* 你在住所和工作地点之间停留吗？ 2 ADJ **Intermediate** learners of something have some knowledge or skill but are not yet advanced. 中级的 ❑ *Students are categorized as novice, intermediate, or advanced.* 学生分为新生、中级生或高级生。 ● N-COUNT An **intermediate** is an intermediate learner. 中级生 ❑ *The ski school coaches beginners, intermediates, and advanced skiers.* 滑雪学校训练初级、中级和高级水平的滑雪者。

in·ter·mi·nable /ɪntɜrmɪnəbəl/ ADJ If you describe something as **interminable**, you are emphasizing that it continues for a very long time and indicating that you wish it was shorter or would stop. 无休止的 [EMPHASIS] ❑ *...an interminable meeting.* …一次没完没了的会议。 ● **in·ter·mi·nably** ADV 无休止地 ❑ *He talked to me interminably about his first wife.* 他喋喋不休地给我讲他第一任妻子的事。

inter·mis·sion /ɪntərmɪʃən/ (**intermissions**) 1 N-COUNT An **intermission** is a short break between two parts of a concert, show, or movie. 幕间休息 ❑ *...during the intermission of the musical "Steppin' Out."* …在音乐剧《影舞追梦》的幕间休息期间。 2 N-COUNT You can use **intermission** to refer to a short break between two parts of a game, or say that something happens **at**, **after**, or **during** the **intermission**. 中场休息 ❑ *Fraser did not perform until after the intermission.* 弗雷泽直到中场休息之后才出场。

★ **inter·mit·tent** /ɪntərmɪtənt/ ADJ Something that is **intermittent** happens occasionally rather than continuously. 断断续续的 ❑ *After three hours of intermittent rain, the game was abandoned.* 雨断断续续地下了3个小时之后，比赛被取消了。 ● **inter·mit·tent·ly** ADV 断断续续地 ❑ *The talks went on intermittently for three years.* 会谈断断续续地进行了3年。

in·tern (**interns, interning, interned**)

The verb is pronounced /ɪntɜrn/. The noun is pronounced /ɪntɜrn/.

动词读作 /ɪntɜrn/。名词读作 /ɪntɜrn/。

1 V-T If someone **is interned**, they are put in prison or in a prison camp for political reasons. 扣押 [usu passive] ❑ *He was interned as an enemy alien at the outbreak of the Second World War.* 他在第二次世界大战爆发时被作为敌国侨民扣押了。 2 N-COUNT An **intern** is an advanced student or a recent graduate, especially in medicine, who is being given practical training under supervision. 实习生；实习医生 [AM] ❑ *...a medical intern.* …一位实习医生。

Word Link *inter ≈ between : interchange, interconnect, internal*

in·ter·nal ♦◊◊ /ɪntɜrnəl/ 1 ADJ **Internal** is used to describe things that exist or happen inside a country or organization. 国内的；组织内部的 [ADJ n] ❑ *The country stepped up internal security.* 该国加强了国内安全防卫。 ❑ *...Russia's Ministry of Internal Affairs.* …俄罗斯内务部。 ● **in·ter·nal·ly** ADV 在国内；在组织内部 ❑ *The state is not a unified and internally coherent entity.* 这个国家不是一个内部凝聚的统一体。 2 ADJ **Internal** is used to describe things that exist or happen inside a particular person, object, or place. 体内的；内部的 [ADJ n] ❑ *The doctor said the internal bleeding had been massive.* 医生说内出血的量很大。 ● **in·ter·nal·ly** ADV 在体内；在内部 ❑ *Evening primrose oil is used on the skin as well as taken internally.* 夜来香油可外用在皮肤上，也可内服。

inter·na·tion·al ♦♦♦ /ɪntərnæʃənəl/ ADJ **International** means between or involving different countries. 国际的 ❑ *...an international agreement against exporting arms to that country.* …一项禁止向那个国家出口武器的国际协议。 ● **inter·na·tion·al·ly** ADV 国际上 ❑ *...internationally agreed-upon rules.* …国际上公认的章程。

In·ter·net ♦♦♦ /ɪntərnɛt/ also **internet** N-PROPER **The Internet** is the network that allows computer users to connect with computers all over the world, and that carries e-mail. 国际互联网

→ see Word Web: **Internet**

in·tern·ship /ɪntɜrnʃɪp/ (**internships**) N-COUNT An **internship** is the position held by an intern, or the period of time when someone is an intern. 实习生的职位；实习期 [AM] ❑ *...an internship in surgery in New York.* …一个在纽约做外科实习的职位。

Word Web Internet

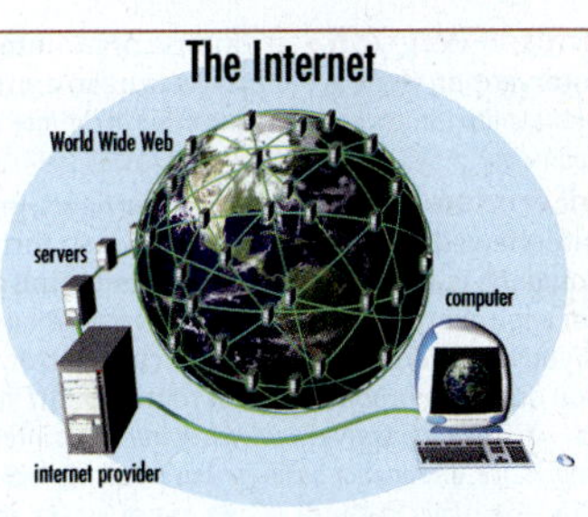

The **Internet** allows information to be shared around the world. The **World-Wide Web** allows users to access **servers** anywhere. **User names** and **passwords** give access and protect information. **E-mail** travels through **networks**. **Websites** are created by companies and individuals to share information. **Web pages** can include images, words, sound, and video. Some organizations build private **intranets**. These groups have to guard the **gateway** between their system and the larger Internet. **Hackers** can break into computer networks. They sometimes steal information or damage the system. **Webmasters** usually build **firewalls** for protection.

inter·per·son·al /ɪntərpɜrsənᵊl/ ADJ **Interpersonal** means relating to relationships between people. 人际的 [ADJ n] ❏ *Training in interpersonal skills is essential.* 各种人际交往技巧的训练是非常必要的。

in·ter·pret /ɪntɜrprɪt/ (**interprets, interpreting, interpreted**) **1** V-T If you **interpret** something in a particular way, you decide that this is its meaning or significance. 解释 ❏ *The fact that they had decided to come was interpreted as a positive sign.* 他们已经决定要来的事实可被解释为一个积极的信号。 ❏ *The judge quite rightly says that he has to interpret the law as it's been passed.* 法官很有理地说他必须按照法律被通过时的意义进行解释。 **2** V-T/V-I If you **interpret** what someone is saying, you translate it immediately into another language. 口译；作口译 ❏ *The chambermaid spoke little English, so her husband came with her to interpret.* 那个女服务员几乎不会说英语，所以她丈夫来给她作口译。
→ see **dream**

Word Partnership *interpret* 的常用搭配：
N. interpret **data**, interpret **the meaning of** *something*, interpret **results**, **ways to** interpret **1**
ADJ. **difficult to** interpret **1** **2**

in·ter·pre·ta·tion /ɪntɜrprɪteɪʃᵊn/ (**interpretations**) **1** N-VAR An **interpretation** of something is an opinion about what it means. 解释 ❏ *Professor Wolfgang gives the data a very different interpretation.* 沃尔夫冈教授对数据作出很不一样的解释。 **2** N-COUNT A performer's **interpretation** of something such as a piece of music or a role in a play is the particular way in which they choose to perform it. 演奏；表演 ❏ *...a pianist celebrated for his interpretation of Chopin.* …一位以演奏萧邦作品而闻名的钢琴家。
→ see **art**

Word Partnership *interpretation* 的常用搭配：
ADJ. **correct** interpretation, **literal** interpretation, **open to** interpretation, **strict** interpretation **1**
N. **data** interpretation, interpretation **of results** **1**

in·ter·pret·er /ɪntɜrprɪtər/ (**interpreters**) N-COUNT An **interpreter** is a person whose job is to translate what someone is saying into another language. 口译员 ❏ *Speaking through an interpreter, Aristide said that Haitians had hoped coups were behind them.* 通过口译员，亚里斯蒂德说海地人希望政变再也不发生了。

in·ter·ro·gate /ɪntɛrəgeɪt/ (**interrogates, interrogating, interrogated**) V-T If someone, especially a police officer, **interrogates** someone, they question them thoroughly for a long time in order to get some information from them. 审问 ❏ *I interrogated everyone even slightly involved.* 我审问了每个人，即便是稍有关联的人也在其中。

★ **in·ter·ro·ga·tion** /ɪntɛrəgeɪʃᵊn/ (**interrogations**) N-VAR An **interrogation** is the act of interrogating someone. 审问 ❏ *...the right to silence in police interrogations.* …在警察审问时保持沉默的权利。

Word Link *rupt ≈ breaking : disrupt, erupt, interrupt*

in·ter·rupt /ɪntərʌpt/ (**interrupts, interrupting, interrupted**) **1** V-T/V-I If you **interrupt** someone who is speaking, you say or do something that causes them to stop. 打断 ❏ *Turkin tapped him on the shoulder. "Sorry to interrupt, Colonel."* 图尔金拍了拍他肩膀说："对不起，上校，打断你一下。" ● **in·ter·rup·tion** /ɪntərʌpʃᵊn/ N-VAR (**interruptions**) 打断 ❏ *The sudden interruption stopped Justin in mid-sentence.* 贾斯廷话说到一半时被突然打断了。 **2** V-T If someone or something **interrupts** a process or activity, they stop it for a period of time. 妨碍 ❏ *People kept nosing around the place, interrupting my work.* 人们在这周围不断查看着，打断了我的工作。 ● **in·ter·rup·tion** N-VAR 中断 ❏ *...interruptions in the supply of food and fuel.* …食品和燃料供应的中断。 **3** V-T If something **interrupts** a line, surface, or view, it stops it from being continuous or makes it look irregular. 遮住 ❏ *Taller plants interrupt the views from the house.* 高的树木遮住了房子外的视线。

Word Link *sect ≈ cutting : dissect, intersect, section*

inter·sect /ɪntərsɛkt/ (**intersects, intersecting, intersected**) **1** V-RECIP If two or more lines or roads **intersect**, they meet or cross each other. You can also say that one line or road **intersects** another. 相交 ❏ *The orbit of this comet intersects the orbit of the Earth.* 这颗彗星的轨道和地球的轨道相交。 **2** V-RECIP If one thing **intersects with** another or if two things **intersect**, the two things connect at a particular point. 连结 ❏ *...the ways in which historical events intersect with individual lives.* …历史事件与个人生活相互交织的方式。

★ **inter·sec·tion** /ɪntərsɛkʃᵊn/ (**intersections**) N-COUNT An **intersection** is a place where roads or other lines meet or cross. 道路交叉口；交点 ❏ *We crossed at a busy intersection.* 我们穿过了一个繁忙的道路交叉口。

inter·spersed /ɪntərspɜrst/ ADJ If one group of things is **interspersed with** another or **interspersed among** another, the second things occur between or among the first things. 夹杂着的 [v-link ADJ prep] ❏ *...a series of bursts of gunfire, interspersed with single shots.* …一阵阵剧烈的炮火声，中间夹杂着零星射击。

inter·state /ɪntərsteɪt/ (**interstates**) **1** ADJ **Interstate** means between states, especially the states of the United States. 州际的 [ADJ n] ❏ *...interstate commerce.* …州际贸易。 **2** N-COUNT An **interstate** or **interstate highway** is a major road linking states. 州际公路 [also N num] ❏ *...the southbound lane of Interstate 75.* …75号州际公路的南行车道。

in·ter·val /ɪntərvᵊl/ (**intervals**) **1** N-COUNT An **interval** between two events or dates is the period of time between them. (时间上的) 间隔 ❏ *The process is repeated after a short interval of time.* 该程序间隔很短时间就重复一次。 **2** N-COUNT An **interval** during a concert, show, movie, or game is a short break between two of the parts. 幕间休息；中场休息 [mainly BRIT]

in AM, usually use **intermission**

3 PHRASE If something happens **at intervals**, it happens several times with gaps or pauses in between. 不时 ❏ *She woke him for his medicines at intervals throughout the night.* 整个晚上她不时叫醒他，让他吃药。 **4** PHRASE If things are placed **at particular intervals**, there are spaces of a particular size between them. 每隔 ❏ *Several red and white barriers marked the road at intervals of about a mile.* 每隔1英里左右就有一些红白相间的路障来标示道路。

★ **inter·vene** /ɪntərvin/ (**intervenes, intervening, intervened**) **1** V-I If you **intervene in** a situation, you become involved in it and try to change it. 干预 ❏ *The situation calmed down when police intervened.* 警察干预后，局势平静了下来。 **2** V-I If you **intervene**, you interrupt a conversation in order to add something to it. 插话 ❏ *Hernandez intervened and told me to stop it.* 贺尔南德兹插话，不让我再说下去。 **3** V-I If an event **intervenes**, it happens suddenly in a way that stops, delays, or prevents something from happening. 干扰 ❏ *The mailboat arrived on Friday mornings unless bad weather intervened.* 除非受到恶劣天气的干扰，邮船于星期五上午到达。

inter·ven·ing /ɪntərvinɪŋ/ **1** ADJ An **intervening** period of time is one that separates two events or points in time. 发生于其间的 [ADJ n] ❏ *During those intervening years Bridget had married her husband Robert.* 在其间的那些年里，布里奇特与罗伯特结为夫妻。 **2** ADJ An **intervening** object or area comes between two other objects or areas. 介于中间的 [ADJ n] ❏ *They had scoured the intervening miles of desert.* 他们已经搜索了那介于中间几英里宽的沙漠地带。

i

▲**inter·ven·tion** ♦◇◇ /ɪntərvɛnʃ^ə^n/ (**interventions**) N-VAR **Intervention** is the act of intervening in a situation. 干涉 ❑ *...the role of the United States and its intervention in the internal affairs of many countries.* …美国所扮演的角色及其对许多国家内政的干涉。

inter·view ♦♦◇ /ɪntərvyu/ (**interviews, interviewing, interviewed**) **1** N-VAR An **interview** is a formal meeting at which someone is asked questions in order to find out if they are suitable for a job or school. 面试 ❑ *The interview went well.* 面试很顺利。 **2** V-T If you **are interviewed** for a particular job or school, someone asks you questions about yourself to find out if you are suitable for it. 对…面试 [usu passive] ❑ *When Wardell was interviewed, he was impressive, and on that basis, he was hired.* 当沃德尔接受面试时，他给人印象深刻，因此他被雇用了。 **3** N-COUNT An **interview** is a conversation in which a journalist puts questions to someone such as a famous person or politician. 采访 ❑ *The trouble began when Allan gave an interview to the Chicago Tribune last month.* 麻烦开始于艾伦上个月接受《芝加哥论坛报》的采访。 **4** V-T When a journalist **interviews** someone such as a famous person, they ask them a series of questions. 采访 ❑ *I'd interviewed him often in the past.* 我过去经常采访他。 **5** V-T When the police **interview** someone, they ask them questions about a crime that has been committed. 询问 ❑ *The police interviewed the driver, but had no evidence to go on.* 警察询问了司机，但没有得到继续调查的证据。

I

Word Partnership *interview* 的常用搭配:

N. **job** interview **1**
(tele)phone interview **1** **3**
magazine/newspaper/radio/television interview **3**

V. **conduct an** interview, **give an** interview, **request an** interview **1** **3**

inter·viewee /ɪntərvyui/ (**interviewees**) N-COUNT An **interviewee** is a person who is being interviewed. 被面试者；被采访者；被询问者 ❑ *Is there any interviewee who stands out as memorable?* 参加面试的人中有特别值得注意的？

inter·view·er /ɪntərvyuər/ (**interviewers**) N-COUNT An **interviewer** is a person who is asking someone questions at an interview. 进行面试者；采访者；询问者 ❑ *Being a good interviewer, however, requires much preparation and skill.* 不过，好的采访者需要许多准备和技巧。

★**inter·weave** /ɪntərwiv/ (**interweaves, interweaving, interwove, interwoven**) V-RECIP If two or more things **are interwoven** or **interweave**, they are very closely connected or are combined with each other. 交织 ❑ *For these people, land is inextricably interwoven with life itself.* 对那些人来说，土地和生活本身紧密交织在一起。 ❑ *Complex family relationships interweave with a murder plot in this ambitious new novel.* 在这部构思大胆的新小说中，复杂的家庭关系与一个谋杀阴谋交织在一起。 ❑ *The program successfully interweaves words and pictures.* 该节目将文字和画面成功地交织在一起。 ❑ *Social structures are not discrete objects; they overlap and interweave.* 社会结构不是离散的客体；他们重叠并交织在一起。

in·tes·tine /ɪntɛstɪn/ (**intestines**) N-COUNT Your **intestines** are the tubes in your body through which food passes when it has left your stomach. 肠 ❑ *This area is always tender to the touch if the intestines are not functioning properly.* 如果肠功能不正常的话，这个部位总是一按就痛。

in·ti·ma·cy /ɪntɪməsi/ **1** N-UNCOUNT **Intimacy** between two people is a very close personal relationship between them. 亲密 ❑ *...a means of achieving intimacy with another person.* …和另一个人建立亲密关系的一种方法。 **2** N-UNCOUNT You sometimes use **intimacy** to refer to sex or a sexual relationship. 性关系 ❑ *He did not feel like intimacy with any woman.* 他不想和任何女人发生性关系。

in·ti·mate (**intimates, intimating, intimated**)

The adjective is pronounced /ɪntɪmɪt/. The verb is pronounced /ɪntɪmeɪt/.

形容词读作 /ɪntɪmɪt/。动词读作 /ɪntɪmeɪt/。

1 ADJ If you have an **intimate** friendship with someone, you know them very well and like them a lot. 亲密的 ❑ *I discussed with my intimate friends whether I would immediately have a baby.* 我和我的密友们商量我是不是该马上要孩子。 ●**in·ti·mate·ly** ADV 亲密地 ❑ *He did not feel he had gotten to know them intimately.* 他觉得自己不必和他们亲密熟悉。 **2** ADJ If two people are in an **intimate** relationship, they are involved with each other in a loving or sexual way. 有性关系的；有恋爱关系的 ❑ *...their intimate moments with their boyfriends.* …她们和其男友们的私密时刻。 ●**in·ti·mate·ly** ADV 在私密方面 [ADV after v] ❑ *You have to be willing to get to know yourself and your partner intimately.* 你必须乐意在私密方面逐渐了解自己和伴侣。 **3** ADJ An **intimate** conversation or detail, for example, is very personal and private. 个人的；私下的 ❑ *He wrote about the intimate details of his family life.* 他写下了家庭生活中一些私人的细节。 ●**in·ti·mate·ly** ADV 个人地；私下地 [ADV after v] ❑ *It was the first time they had attempted to talk intimately.* 这是他们第一次试图私下交谈。 **4** ADJ If you use **intimate** to describe an occasion or the atmosphere of a place, you like it because it is quiet and pleasant, and seems suitable for close conversations between friends. 宁静怡人的 [APPROVAL] ❑ *...an intimate candlelit dinner for two.* …宁静怡人的二人烛光晚餐。 **5** ADJ An **intimate** connection between ideas or organizations, for example, is a very strong link between them. 密切的 ❑ *...an intimate connection between madness and wisdom.* …疯狂和睿智之间的密切联系。 ●**in·ti·mate·ly** ADV 密切地 [ADV after v] ❑ *Scientific research and conservation are intimately connected.* 科学研究与环境保护联系密切。 **6** ADJ An **intimate** knowledge of something is a deep and detailed knowledge of it. 深刻的；精通的 ❑ *He surprised me with his intimate knowledge of Kierkegaard and Schopenhauer.* 他对克尔恺郭尔和叔本华的深刻了解令我感到惊奇。 ●**in·ti·mate·ly** ADV 深刻地；精通地 ❑ *...a golden age of musicians whose work she knew intimately.* …她熟知的那些音乐家们的黄金时代。 **7** V-T If you **intimate** something, you say it in an indirect way. 暗示 [FORMAL] ❑ *He went on to intimate that he was indeed contemplating a shake-up of the company.* 他接着暗示他确实在考虑对公司进行改组。

Word Partnership *intimate* 的常用搭配:

N. intimate **friend** **1**
intimate **relationship** **2**
intimate **details** **3**
intimate **atmosphere** **4**

in·timi·date /ɪntɪmɪdeɪt/ (**intimidates, intimidating, intimidated**) V-T If you **intimidate** someone, you deliberately make them frightened enough to do what you want them to do. 恐吓；威胁 ❑ *Jones had set out to intimidate and dominate Paul.* 琼斯曾试图威胁并控制保罗。 ●**in·timi·da·tion** /ɪntɪmɪdeɪʃ^ə^n/ N-UNCOUNT 威胁 ❑ *...an inquiry into allegations of intimidation during last week's vote.* …一项对上周选举期间恐吓指控的调查。

in·timi·dat·ed /ɪntɪmɪdeɪtɪd/ ADJ Someone who feels **intimidated** feels frightened and lacks confidence because of the people they are with or the situation they are in. 被吓倒的 ❑ *Women can come in here and not feel intimidated.* 女人们可以进到这里而不会感觉害怕。

in·timi·dat·ing /ɪntɪmɪdeɪtɪŋ/ ADJ If you describe someone or something as **intimidating**, you mean that they are frightening and make people lose confidence. 令人惊恐的 ❑ *He was a huge, intimidating figure.* 他是个身材高大、令人生畏的人。

into ♦♦♦ /ɪntu/

Pronounced /ɪntu/ or /ɪntu/, particularly before pronouns and for meaning **14**.

特别是位于代词前或用于义项**14**，读作 /ɪntu/或 /ɪntu/。

In addition to the uses shown below, **into** is used after some verbs and nouns in order to introduce extra information. **Into** is also used with verbs of movement, such as "walk" and "push," and in phrasal verbs such as "enter into" and "talk into."

1 PREP If you put one thing **into** another, you put the first thing inside the second. 放到…里面 ❑ *Combine the remaining ingredients and put them into a dish.* 把剩余的配料混起来放到一个盘子里。 **2** PREP If you go **into** a place or vehicle, you move from being outside it to being inside it. 进；上(车) ❑ *I have no idea how he got into Iraq.* 我不知道他是怎么进入伊拉克的。 **3** PREP If one thing goes **into** another, the first thing moves from the outside to the inside of the second thing, by breaking or damaging the surface of it. (通过破坏表面) 进 ❑ *The blade missed his kidney, but went into his bowel.* 刀片没刺中他的肾脏，但却扎进了他的肠子。 **4** PREP If one thing gets **into** another, the first thing enters the second and becomes part of it. 融入；渗入

❑ *Poisonous chemicals got into the water supply.* 有毒的化学药品进入了供水系统。 5 PREP If you are walking or driving a vehicle and you bump **into** something or crash **into** something, you hit it accidentally. (意外) 撞上 ❑ *A train from New Jersey plowed into the barrier at the end of the track.* 从新泽西驶来的一辆火车撞上了轨道尽头的栅栏。 6 PREP When you get **into** a piece of clothing, you put it on. (穿) 上 ❑ *She could change into a different outfit in two minutes.* 她能在两分钟内换上一套不同的衣服。 7 PREP If someone or something gets **into** a particular state, they start being in that state. 进入 (某种状态) [V PREP n, n PREP n] ❑ *I slid into a depression.* 我渐渐陷入了抑郁之中。 8 PREP If you talk someone **into** doing something, you persuade them to do it. 从事 [V n PREP n/-ing] ❑ *They sweet-talked him into selling the farm.* 他们甜言蜜语地哄骗他卖掉了那个农场。 9 PREP If something changes **into** something else, it then has a new form, shape, or nature. 成为 ❑ *...to turn a nasty episode into a joke.* …把一件不愉快的事转化成一个小玩笑。 10 PREP If something is cut or split **into** a number of pieces or sections, it is divided so that it becomes several smaller pieces or sections. 分成 ❑ *Sixteen teams are taking part, divided into four groups.* 16支队伍参加，它们被分成4组。 11 PREP An investigation **into** a subject or event is concerned with that subject or event. 关于 [n PREP n] ❑ *It would provide hundreds of millions of dollars for research into alternative energy sources.* 它可以提供数亿美元用于可替代能源的研究。 12 PREP If you move or go **into** a particular career or business, you start working in it. 进入 (某种职业或行业) ❑ *In the early 1980s, it was easy to get into the rental business.* 在20世纪80年代早期，进入租赁业是很容易的。 13 PREP If something continues **into** a period of time, it continues until after that period of time has begun. 进入 (时期) ❑ *He had three children, and lived on into his sixties.* 他有3个孩子，并活到了六十多岁。 14 PREP If you are very interested in something and like it very much, you can say that you are **into** it. 对…很感兴趣 [V-link PREP n] [INFORMAL] ❑ *I'm into electronics myself.* 我自己对电子学很感兴趣。

in·tol·er·able /ɪntɒlərəbᵊl/ ADJ If you describe something as **intolerable**, you mean that it is so bad or extreme that no one can bear it or tolerate it. 无法忍受的 ❑ *They felt this would put intolerable pressure on them.* 他们认为这会给他们带来无法承受的压力。 ● **in·tol·er·ably** /ɪntɒlərəbli/ ADV 无法忍受地 ❑ *...intolerably cramped conditions.* …拥挤不堪的环境。

★ **in·tol·er·ance** /ɪntɒlərəns/ N-UNCOUNT **Intolerance** is unwillingness to let other people act in a different way or hold different opinions from you. 不容忍 (他人的做事方式或观点) [DISAPPROVAL] ❑ *...his intolerance of any opinion other than his own.* …他对除自己以外任何观点的不容忍。

★ **in·tol·er·ant** /ɪntɒlərənt/ ADJ If you describe someone as **intolerant**, you mean that they do not accept behavior and opinions that are different from their own. 不宽容的 [DISAPPROVAL] ❑ *...intolerant attitudes toward non-Catholics.* …对非天主教徒的不宽容态度。

▲ **in·toxi·cat·ed** /ɪntɒksɪkeɪtɪd/ 1 ADJ Someone who is **intoxicated** is drunk. 喝醉的 [FORMAL] ❑ *He appeared intoxicated, police said.* 他看上去好像是喝醉了，警察说。 2 ADJ If you are **intoxicated by** or **with** something such as a feeling or an event, you are so excited by it that you find it hard to think clearly and sensibly. 陶醉的 [V-link ADJ "by/with" n] [LITERARY] ❑ *My cousins seem to have become intoxicated by their success.* 我的堂兄弟们好象已经被他们的成功陶醉了。

in·trac·table /ɪntræktəbᵊl/ 1 ADJ **Intractable** people are very difficult to control or influence. (人) 难对付的 [FORMAL] ❑ *What may be done to reduce the influence of intractable opponents?* 可以做些什么来削弱难以对付的对手们的影响呢？ 2 ADJ **Intractable** problems or situations are very difficult to deal with. 棘手的 [FORMAL] ❑ *The economy still faces intractable problems.* 经济依然面临一些棘手的问题。

in·tra·net /ɪntrənɛt/ (**intranets**) N-COUNT An **intranet** is a network of computers, similar to the Internet, within a particular company or organization. 内联网
→ see **Internet**

in·tran·si·gence /ɪntrænsɪdʒᵊns/ N-UNCOUNT If you talk about someone's **intransigence**, you mean that they refuse to behave differently or to change their attitude to something. 顽固 [FORMAL, DISAPPROVAL] ❑ *He often appeared angry and frustrated by the intransigence of both sides.* 他好像总是为双方的强硬态度而愤怒和沮丧。

in·tran·si·gent /ɪntrænsɪdʒᵊnt/ ADJ If you describe someone as **intransigent**, you mean that they refuse to behave differently or to change their attitude to something. 顽固的 [FORMAL, DISAPPROVAL] ❑ *...Sami's opinionated and intransigent father.* …萨米那武断而固执的父亲。

in·tran·si·tive /ɪntrænsɪtɪv/ ADJ An **intransitive** verb does not have an object. 不及物的

intra·venous /ɪntrəvinəs/ ADJ **Intravenous** foods or drugs are put into people's bodies through their veins, rather than their mouths. 静脉输入的 [ADJ n] [MEDICAL] ❑ *...an intravenous drip.* …一种静脉滴注。 ● **intra·venous·ly** ADV 静脉输入地 [ADV after v] ❑ *Premature babies have to be fed intravenously.* 早产儿必须通过静脉输入来喂食。

in tray (**in trays**) also **in-tray** N-COUNT An **in tray** is a shallow container used in offices to put letters and documents in before they are dealt with. Compare **out tray**. (办公室里存放待处理来函或来文的) 收文篮 (比较**out tray**) [mainly BRIT]

in AM, usually use **inbox**

in·trep·id /ɪntrɛpɪd/ ADJ An **intrepid** person acts in a brave way. 勇敢的 ❑ *...an intrepid space traveler.* …一位勇敢的太空旅行者。

in·tri·ca·cy /ɪntrɪkəsi/ N-UNCOUNT **Intricacy** is the state of being made up of many small parts or details. 复杂精细 ❑ *The price depends on the intricacy of the work.* 价格取决于工艺的精细程度。

★ **in·tri·cate** /ɪntrɪkət/ ADJ You use **intricate** to describe something that has many small parts or details. 复杂精细的 ❑ *...the production of carpets with highly intricate patterns.* …图案复杂精细的地毯的制作。 ● **in·tri·cate·ly** ADV 复杂精细地 ❑ *...intricately carved sculptures.* …一些精雕细刻的雕塑。

★ **in·trigue** (**intrigues, intriguing, intrigued**)

The noun is pronounced /ɪntrig/. The verb is pronounced /ɪntrig/.

名词读作 /ɪntrig/，动词读作 /ɪntrig/。

1 N-VAR **Intrigue** is the making of secret plans to harm or deceive people. 阴谋 ❑ *...political intrigue.* …政治阴谋。 2 V-T If something, especially something strange, **intrigues** you, it interests you and you want to know more about it. 激起…的好奇心 ❑ *The novelty of the situation intrigued him.* 那种新奇的情景激起了他的好奇心。

in·trigued /ɪntrigd/ ADJ If you are **intrigued by** something, especially something strange, it interests you and you want to know more about it. 感兴趣的 ❑ *I would be intrigued to hear others' views.* 我对倾听别人的看法会感兴趣的。

in·tri·guing /ɪntrigɪŋ/ ADJ If you describe something as **intriguing**, you mean that it is interesting or strange. 新奇的 ❑ *This intriguing book is both thoughtful and informative.* 这本引人入胜的书既有思想性又有知识性。 ● **in·tri·guing·ly** ADV 新奇地 ❑ *...the intriguingly-named newspaper Le Canard enchaîné (The Chained Duck).* …那份名字起得非常新奇的报纸**Le Canard enchaîné**（《戴锁链的鸭》）。

★ **in·trin·sic** /ɪntrɪnsɪk/ ADJ If something has **intrinsic** value or **intrinsic** interest, it is valuable or interesting because of its basic nature or character, and not because of its connection with other things. 内在的；本质的 [ADJ n] [FORMAL] ❑ *Diamonds have little intrinsic value and their price depends almost entirely on their scarcity.* 钻石没有多少内在价值，它们的价格几乎完全取决于其稀有程度。 ● **in·trin·si·cal·ly** /ɪntrɪnsɪkli/ ADV 固有地 ❑ *Sometimes I wonder if people are intrinsically evil.* 有时我怀疑人是否生来就是邪恶的。

intro·duce ◆◆◇ /ɪntrədus/ (**introduces, introducing, introduced**) 1 V-T To **introduce** something means to cause it to enter a place or exist in a system for the first time. 引进 ❑ *MGM introduced a new system for hiring writers.* 米高梅公司引进了一项新的制度来雇人写作。 ● **intro·duc·tion** N-UNCOUNT 引进 ❑ *What he is better remembered for is the introduction of the moving assembly-line in Detroit in 1913.* 他更加令人铭记在心的是曾在1913年将流动生产线引入底特律。 2 V-T If you **introduce** one person **to** another, or you **introduce** two people, you tell them each other's names, so that they can get to know each other. If you **introduce yourself** to someone, you tell them your name. 介绍 ❑ *Tim, may I introduce you to my uncle's secretary, Mary Waller?* 蒂姆，我可以把你介绍给我叔叔的秘书玛丽·沃勒吗？ ❑ *We haven't been introduced. My name is Nero Wolfe.* 我们还没有被介绍到。我叫尼罗·沃尔夫。 ● **intro·duc·tion** N-VAR (**introductions**) 介绍 ❑ *With considerable shyness, Elaine performed the introductions.* 伊莱恩十分害羞地做了介绍。 3 V-T If you **introduce** someone **to** something, you cause them to learn about it or experience it for the first time. 使初次接触 ❑ *He introduced us to the delights of natural food.* 他使我们第一次享受到了品尝天然食品的乐趣。 ● **intro·duc·tion** N-SING 初次接触 ❑ *His introduction to fieldwork was a series of expeditions.* 他初次参加的实地考察工作是一系列的探险活动。 **4** V-T The person who **introduces** a television or radio program speaks at the beginning of it, and often between the different items in it, in order to explain what the program or the items are about. 为(电视或广播节目)作开场白；主持 ❑ *...talk shows introduced by women.* …由女性主持的访谈节目。

Word Partnership *introduce* 的常用搭配：
N. introduce **a bill**, introduce **changes**, introduce **legislation**, introduce **reform** **1**
V. **allow me to** introduce, **let me** introduce, **want to** introduce **2**

intro·duc·tion /ɪntrədʌ̲kʃᵊn/ (**introductions**) **1** N-COUNT The **introduction to** a book or talk is the part that comes at the beginning and tells you what the rest of the book or talk is about. 引言；序 ❑ *Ellen Malos, in her introduction to "The Politics of Housework," provides a summary of the debates.* 埃伦·马洛斯在她的《家务政治学》一书的引言中对这些争论做了一个概述。 **2** N-COUNT If you refer to a book as an **introduction to** a particular subject, you mean that it explains the basic facts about that subject. (书) 入门 ❑ *The book is a friendly, down-to-earth introduction to physics.* 这是一本简明、实用的物理学入门书。 **3** N-COUNT You can refer to a new product as an **introduction** when it becomes available in a place for the first time. 引进品 ❑ *There are two among their recent introductions that have greatly impressed me.* 他们最新引进的产品中有两件给我留下了深刻的印象。 **4** → see also **introduce**

intro·duc·tory /ɪntrədʌ̲ktəri/ **1** ADJ An **introductory** remark, talk, or part of a book gives a small amount of general information about a particular subject, often before a more detailed explanation. 引言的 [ADJ n] ❑ *...an introductory course in religion and theology.* …一门宗教和神学的入门课程。 **2** ADJ An **introductory** offer or price on a new product is something such as a free gift or a low price that is meant to attract new customers. 试销的 [ADJ n] [BUSINESS] ❑ *...a special introductory offer.* …一次特价试销。

▲ **in·trude** /ɪntru̲d/ (**intrudes, intruding, intruded**) **1** V-I If you say that someone **is intruding into** a particular place or situation, you mean that they are not wanted or welcome there. 侵扰 ❑ *The press has been blamed for intruding into people's personal lives in an unacceptable way.* 新闻媒体因以一种令人无法接受的方式侵入人们的私生活而受到谴责。 **2** V-I If something **intrudes on** your mood or your life, it disturbs it or has an unwanted effect on it. 扰乱 ❑ *Do you feel anxious when unforeseen incidents intrude on your day?* 当无可预料的事件侵扰到你的生活时，你会感到焦虑吗？ **3** V-I If someone **intrudes into** a place, they go there even though they are not allowed to be there. 侵入 ❑ *An American officer on the scene said no one had intruded into the space he was defending.* 现场的一名美国军官说还没有人闯入过他所防卫的区域。

▲ **in·trud·er** /ɪntru̲dər/ (**intruders**) N-COUNT An **intruder** is a person who goes into a place where they are not supposed to be. 侵入者 ❑ *He owned a gun for scaring off intruders.* 他有一支枪，用来吓走入侵者。

in·tru·sion /ɪntru̲ʒᵊn/ (**intrusions**) **1** N-VAR If someone disturbs you when you are in a private place or having a private conversation, you can call this event an **intrusion**. 打扰 ❑ *I hope you don't mind this intrusion, Jon.* 乔恩，我希望你不会介意这次打扰。 **2** N-VAR An **intrusion** is something that disturbs your mood or your life in a way you do not like. 侵扰 ❑ *I felt it was a grotesque intrusion into our lives.* 我觉得它对我们的生活是一种莫名其妙的侵扰。

in·tru·sive /ɪntru̲sɪv/ ADJ Something that is **intrusive** disturbs your mood or your life in a way you do not like. 打扰的 ❑ *The cameras were not an intrusive presence.* 这些摄像机的存在不会造成干扰。

★ **in·tui·tion** /ɪntuɪ̲ʃᵊn/ (**intuitions**) N-VAR Your **intuition** or your **intuitions** are unexplained feelings that something is true even when you have no evidence or proof of it. 直觉 ❑ *Her intuition was telling her that something was wrong.* 她的直觉在告诉她事情有些不对头。

in·tui·tive /ɪntu̲ətɪv/ ADJ If you have an **intuitive** idea or feeling about something, you feel that it is true although you have no evidence or proof of it. 直觉的 ❑ *A positive pregnancy test soon confirmed her intuitive feelings.* 阳性的孕检结果很快证实了她的直觉。 ● **in·tui·tive·ly** ADV 凭直觉地 ❑ *He seemed to know intuitively that I must be missing my mother.* 他似乎凭直觉知道我一定是在思念我的母亲。

in·un·date /ɪnʌndeɪt/ (**inundates, inundating, inundated**) **1** V-T If you say that you **are inundated with** things such as letters, demands, or requests, you are emphasizing that you receive so many of them that you cannot deal with them all. 被(大量信件或请求等) 淹没 [EMPHASIS] ❑ *Her office was inundated with requests for tickets.* 她的办公室接到了铺天盖地的索票请求。 **2** V-T If an area of land **is inundated**, it becomes covered with water. 淹没 [usu passive] ❑ *Their neighborhood is being inundated by the rising waters of the Colorado River.* 他们的临近区域正被科罗拉多河不断上涨的河水所淹没。

in·vade /ɪnve̲ɪd/ (**invades, invading, invaded**) **1** V-T/V-I To **invade** a country means to enter it by force with an army. 侵入 ❑ *In autumn 1944 the Allies invaded the Italian mainland at Anzio and Salerno.* 1944年秋，盟军从安齐奥和萨莱诺侵入意大利大陆。 **2** V-T If you say that people or animals **invade** a place, you mean that they enter it in large numbers, often in a way that is unpleasant or difficult to deal with. 拥入 ❑ *People invaded the streets in victory processions almost throughout the day.* 几乎一整天，大街上挤满了欢庆胜利的游行队伍。

in·vad·er /ɪnve̲ɪdər/ (**invaders**) **1** N-COUNT **Invaders** are soldiers who are invading a country. 侵略者 ❑ *The city was destroyed by foreign invaders.* 这座城市被外国侵略者毁坏了。 **2** N-COUNT You can refer to a country or army that has invaded or is about to invade another country as an **invader**. 侵略国；侵略军 ❑ *...action against a foreign invader.* …反对外国侵略者的行动。

★ **in·va·lid** (**invalids**)

The noun is pronounced /ɪnvəlɪd/. The adjective is pronounced /ɪnvæ̲lɪd/ and is hyphenated in·val·id.

名词读作 /ɪnvəlɪd/。形容词读作 /ɪnvæ̲lɪd/且连字符添加方式为 **in·val·id**。

1 N-COUNT An **invalid** is someone who needs to be cared for because they have an illness or disability. 病人；残疾人 ❑ *I hate being treated as an invalid.* 我讨厌被当作病人对待。 **2** ADJ If an action, procedure, or document is **invalid**, it cannot be accepted, because it breaks the law or some official rule. 无效的 ❑ *The trial was stopped and the results declared invalid.* 审判被终止了，其结果被宣布无效。 **3** ADJ An **invalid** argument or conclusion is wrong because it is based on a mistake. 站不住脚的 ❑ *We think that those arguments are rendered invalid by the facts.* 我们认为那些论点在事实面前站不住脚。

in·vali·date /ɪnvæ̲lɪdeɪt/ (**invalidates, invalidating, invalidated**) V-T If something **invalidates** something such as a law, contract, or election, it causes it to be considered illegal. 使无效 ❑ *An official decree invalidated the vote in the capital.* 一项官方法令使首都的投票失去了效力。

★ **in·valu·able** /ɪnvæ̲lyuəbᵊl/ ADJ If you describe something as **invaluable**, you mean that it is extremely useful. 非常宝贵的 ❑ *I was able to gain invaluable experience over that year.* 在那一年里我获得了十分宝贵的经验。

★ **in·vari·ably** /ɪnvɛ̲əriəbli/ ADV If something **invariably** happens or is **invariably** true, it always happens or is always true. 不变地 ❑ *They almost invariably get it wrong.* 他们几乎总是将它弄错。

in·va·sion ♦◇◇ /ɪnve̲ɪʒᵊn/ (**invasions**) **1** N-VAR If there is an **invasion** of a country, a foreign army enters it by force. 入侵 ❑ *...seven years after the Roman invasion of Britain.* …罗马人入侵大不列颠岛之后的7年。 **2** N-VAR If you refer to the arrival of a large number of people or things as an **invasion**, you are emphasizing that they are unpleasant or difficult to deal with. 大群涌入 ❑ *...this year's annual invasion of flies, wasps and ants.* …今年苍蝇、黄蜂和蚂蚁像往年一样的大量涌入。 **3** N-VAR If you describe an action as an **invasion**, you disapprove of it because it affects someone or something in a way that is not wanted. 侵扰 [DISAPPROVAL] ❑ *Is reading a child's diary always a gross invasion of privacy?* 看孩子的日记在任何情况下都是严重侵犯隐私的行为吗？

in·va·sive /ɪnve̲ɪsɪv/ **1** ADJ You use **invasive** to describe something undesirable that spreads very quickly and that is very difficult to stop from spreading. (令人不快的事物) 迅速扩散的 ❑ *They found invasive cancer during a routine examination.* 他们在一次例行检查中发现了扩散的癌细胞。 **2** ADJ An **invasive** medical procedure involves operating on a patient or examining the inside of their body. 开刀的 ❑ *Many people find the idea of any kind of invasive surgery* unbearable. 许多人觉得任何一种开刀手术都是难以忍受的。

in·vent /ɪnvɛ̱nt/ (**invents, inventing, invented**) 1 V-T If you **invent** something such as a machine or process, you are the first person to think of it or make it. 发明 ❑ *He invented the first electric clock.* 他发明了第一个电动钟。 2 V-T If you **invent** a story or excuse, you try to make other people believe that it is true when in fact it is not. 虚构 ❑ *I stood still, trying to invent a plausible excuse.* 我静静地站着，努力想编出一个听上去可信的借口。

Thesaurus *invent* 另参见:
V. come up with, concoct, devise, originate 1 2
fabricate, make up 2

in·ven·tion /ɪnvɛ̱nʃ°n/ (**inventions**) 1 N-COUNT An **invention** is a machine, device, or system that has been invented by someone. 发明物 ❑ *The spinning wheel was a Chinese invention.* 纺车是中国人的一项发明。 2 N-UNCOUNT **Invention** is the act of inventing something that has never been made or used before. 发明 ❑ *...the invention of the telephone.* …电话的发明。 3 N-VAR If you refer to someone's account of something as an **invention**, you think that it is untrue and that they have made it up. 虚构 ❑ *The story was certainly a favorite one, but it was undoubtedly pure invention.* 这个故事的确是人们最喜欢的一个，但毫无疑问它纯粹是虚构的。 4 N-UNCOUNT **Invention** is the ability to invent things or to have clever and original ideas. 发明才能 ❑ *Perhaps, with such powers of invention and mathematical ability, he will be offered a job in computers.* 或许，拥有这样的创造能力和数学才能，他会得到一份计算机方面的工作。

in·ven·tive /ɪnvɛ̱ntɪv/ ADJ An **inventive** person is good at inventing things or has clever and original ideas. 有创造才能的 ❑ *It inspired me to be more inventive with my own cooking.* 它激励我在自己烹饪时更具创造力。 ●**in·ven·tive·ness** N-UNCOUNT 创造才能 ❑ *He has surprised us before with his inventiveness.* 他以前曾以创造才能令我们吃惊。

in·ven·tor /ɪnvɛ̱ntər/ (**inventors**) N-COUNT An **inventor** is a person who has invented something, or whose job is to invent things. 发明者 ❑ *...Alexander Graham Bell, the inventor of the telephone.* …亚历山大・格雷厄姆・贝尔，电话的发明者。
→ see Word Web: **inventor**

★ **in·ven·tory** /ɪnvᵊntɔri/ (**inventories**) 1 N-VAR An **inventory** is a supply or stock of something. 存货 [AM] ❑ *...one inventory of twelve sails for each yacht.* …为每艘游艇配备12张帆的存货。 2 N-COUNT An **inventory** is a written list of all the objects in a particular place such as all the merchandise in a store. 清单 ❑ *Before starting, he made an inventory of everything that was to stay.* 出发前，他把要留下的所有东西列了一份详细清单。

Word Link *vert ≈ turning : convert, invert, revert*

★ **in·vert** /ɪnvɜ̱rt/ (**inverts, inverting, inverted**) V-T If you **invert** something, you turn it upside down or inside out. 使倒置; 将里面翻到外面 [FORMAL] ❑ *Invert the cake onto a serving plate.* 把蛋糕倒扣过来放到一个盘子上。

in·vert·ed com·mas N-PLURAL **Inverted commas** are punctuation marks that are used in writing to show where speech or a quotation begins and ends. They are usually written or printed as " " or ' '. Inverted commas are also sometimes used around the titles of books, plays, or songs, or around a word or phrase that is being discussed. 引号 [BRIT]
in AM, use **quotation marks**

in·vest ◆◇◇ /ɪnvɛ̱st/ (**invests, investing, invested**) 1 V-T/V-I If you **invest in** something, or if you **invest** a sum of money, you use your money in a way that you hope will increase its value, for example, by putting it in a bank, or buying securities or property. 投(资); 投资 ❑ *Many people don't like to invest in stocks.* 许多人不喜欢投资股票。 ❑ *I'm tired of watching you invest our money in insane projects.* 我看够了你将我们的钱投到一些荒唐的项目上。 2 V-T/V-I If you **invest in** something useful, you buy it, because it will help you to do something more efficiently or more cheaply. 购买 ❑ *The company has invested a six-figure sum in an electronic order-control system which is used to keep stores stocked.* 这家公司已经耗资6位数购买了电子定单控制系统来为商店进货。 3 V-T/V-I When a government or organization **invests in** something, it gives or lends money for a purpose that it considers useful or profitable. (政府或机构) 投资 ❑ *...the need to invest in new technology.* …这种投资于新技术的需要。 ❑ *Government agencies must invest more funds in training and development programs.* 政府机构必须将更多的资金投入到培训和开发项目中。 4 V-T If you **invest** time or energy **in** something, you spend a lot of time or energy on it because you think it will be useful or successful. 投入(时间、精力) ❑ *I would rather invest time in Rebecca than in the kitchen.* 我宁愿把时间花在丽贝卡身上，也不愿花在厨房里。 5 V-T To **invest** someone **with** rights or responsibilities means to give them those rights or responsibilities legally or officially. 赋予 [FORMAL] ❑ *The constitution invested him with certain powers.* 宪法赋予了他一些权力。
→ see **stock market**

Word Partnership *invest* 的常用搭配:
N. invest **in a company**, invest **in stocks** 1
invest **funds/money** 1 – 3
invest **energy**, invest **time** 4
ADV. invest **heavily** 1 – 3

in·ves·ti·gate ◆◆◇ /ɪnvɛ̱stɪgeɪt/ (**investigates, investigating, investigated**) V-T/V-I If someone, especially an official, **investigates** an event, situation, or claim, they try to find out what happened or what is the truth. 调查 ❑ *They're still investigating the accident.* 他们还在调查这个事故。 ●**in·ves·ti·ga·tion** /ɪnvɛ̱stɪgeɪʃ°n/ N-VAR (**investigations**) 调查 ❑ *He ordered an investigation into the affair.* 他下令对此事进行调查。

Word Partnership *investigate* 的常用搭配:
N. investigate **complaints**, investigate **a crime**, **police** investigate, investigate **the possibility of** *something*
ADV. **fully** investigate, investigate **further**

in·ves·ti·gative /ɪnvɛ̱stɪgeɪtɪv/ ADJ **Investigative** work, especially journalism, involves investigating things. 调查的 ❑ *...an investigative reporter.* …一位新闻调查记者。

★ **in·ves·ti·ga·tor** /ɪnvɛ̱stɪgeɪtər/ (**investigators**) N-COUNT An **investigator** is someone who carries out investigations, especially as part of their job. 调查者 ❑ *...an undercover investigator.* …一位秘密侦探。

in·vest·ment ◆◆◇ /ɪnvɛ̱stmənt/ (**investments**) 1 N-UNCOUNT **Investment** is the activity of investing money. 投资 ❑ *He said the government must introduce tax incentives to encourage investment.* 他说，政府必须通过给予税收利益来鼓励投资。 2 N-VAR An **investment** is an amount of money that you invest, or the thing that you invest it in. 投资额 ❑ *...an investment of twenty-eight million dollars.* …2800万美元的投资额。 3 N-COUNT If you describe something you buy as an **investment**, you mean that it will be useful, especially because it will help you to do a task more cheaply or efficiently. 有益的购买物 ❑ *When selecting boots, fine, quality leather will be a wise investment.* 在挑选靴子时，买精致、质量上乘的皮靴会是明智的。 4 N-UNCOUNT

Word Web inventor

In the 1920s, Thomas Midgley, Jr.* developed two important chemical compounds. He was the **inventor** of leaded gasoline and Freon* gas. He found that a lead compound added to gasoline gave cars more power. Freon gas replaced the poisonous gases originally used in refrigerators. Both **products** were very popular when they first appeared. But over time, both **innovations** created new problems. **Research** has shown that leaded gas causes lead poisoning—particularly in children. Freon gas is harmful to the ozone layer around the earth. Scientists believe this contributes to global warming, skin cancer, and other serious problems.

Thomas Midgley, Jr. (1889-1944): an American engineer and chemist.
Freon: a trade name for a chemical compound.

Investment of time or effort is the spending of time or effort on something in order to make it a success. 投入 ❑ *I worry about this big investment of time not working.* 我担心这么多的时间投入不起作用。

Word Partnership *investment* 的常用搭配：

V. **encourage** investment, **stimulate** investment 1
make an investment 2 – 4
N. **capital** investment 1 2
investment **advisor**, investment **banker**, investment **company**, investment **fund**, investment **opportunity**, investment **plan** 2
ADJ. **long-term/short-term** investment 2

★ **in·ves·tor** ♦♦◇ /ɪnvɛstər/ (**investors**) N-COUNT An **investor** is a person or organization that buys securities or property in order to receive a profit. 投资者 ❑ *The main investor in the project is the French bank Credit National.* 该项目的主要投资方是法国国民信贷银行。

Word Link *vig ≈ awake, strong : invigorating, vigil, vigilant*

in·vig·or·at·ing /ɪnvɪgəreɪtɪŋ/ ADJ If you describe something as **invigorating**, you mean that it makes you feel more energetic. 使精力充沛的 ❑ *...the invigorating northern air.* …北方清爽宜人的空气。

Word Link *vict, vinc ≈ conquering : convict, convince, invincible*

▲ **in·vin·cible** /ɪnvɪnsɪbᵊl/ 1 ADJ If you describe an army or sports team as **invincible**, you believe that they cannot be defeated. 不可战胜的 ❑ *You couldn't help feeling the military's fire power was invincible.* 你不禁会感到这支军队的火力是无可匹敌的。 2 ADJ If someone has an **invincible** belief or attitude, it cannot be changed. 无法改变的 ❑ *He also had an invincible faith in the medicinal virtues of garlic.* 他对大蒜的药用功效深信不疑。

in·vis·ible /ɪnvɪzɪbᵊl/ 1 ADJ If you describe something as **invisible**, you mean that it cannot be seen, for example, because it is transparent, hidden, or very small. 看不见的 ❑ *The lines were so finely etched as to be invisible from a distance.* 这些线条蚀刻得如此精细，离远点都看不出来。 ● **in·vis·ibly** /ɪnvɪzɪbli/ ADV 看不见地 [ADV with v] ❑ *A thin coil of smoke rose almost invisibly into the sharp, bright sky.* 一缕轻烟几乎不见踪迹地升上了耀眼的晴空。 2 ADJ You can use **invisible** when you are talking about something that cannot be seen but has a definite effect. In this sense, **invisible** is often used before a noun that refers to something visible. 无形的 [ADJ n] ❑ *All the time you are in doubt about the cause of your illness, you are fighting against an invisible enemy.* 一直以来你都在怀疑自己的病因，你是在和一个无形的敌人斗争。 ● **in·vis·ibly** ADV 无形地 [ADV with v] ❑ *...the tradition that invisibly shapes things in the present.* …这种无形地影响着现有事物的传统。 3 ADJ If you say that you feel **invisible**, you are complaining that you are being ignored by other people. If you say that a particular problem or situation is **invisible**, you are complaining that it is not being considered or dealt with. 被忽视的 ❑ *It was strange, how invisible a clerk could feel.* 很奇怪一名职员会感到如此地受人忽视。 ● **in·vis·ibil·ity** /ɪnvɪzɪbɪlɪti/ N-UNCOUNT 被忽视 ❑ *She takes up the issue of the invisibility of women and women's concerns in society.* 她着手处理社会上对妇女及其所关注的事物的忽视问题。 4 ADJ In stories, **invisible** people or things have a magic quality that makes people unable to see them. 隐身的 ❑ *...The Invisible Man.* …《隐身人》。 5 ADJ In economics, **invisible** earnings are the money that a country makes as a result of services such as banking and tourism, rather than by producing goods. 非贸易性的 [ADJ n] [BUSINESS] ❑ *The revenue from tourism is the biggest single item in the country's invisible earnings.* 旅游收入是该国非贸易性收益中最大的单项收入。
→ see **sun**

in·vi·ta·tion ♦◇◇ /ɪnvɪteɪʃᵊn/ (**invitations**) 1 N-COUNT An **invitation** is a written or spoken request to come to an event such as a party, a meal, or a meeting. 邀请 ❑ *...an invitation to lunch.* …午餐邀请。 ❑ *The Syrians have not yet accepted an invitation to attend.* 那些叙利亚人还没有接受邀请。 2 N-COUNT An **invitation** is the card or paper on which an invitation is written or printed. 请贴 ❑ *Hundreds of invitations are being sent out this week.* 本周数百张请贴正在发出。 3 N-SING If you believe that someone's action is likely to have a particular result, especially a bad one, you can refer to the action as an **invitation to** that result. 招惹 ❑ *Don't leave your shopping on the back seat of your car – it's an open invitation to a thief.* 不要把买好的东西放在车的后座上——这很容易招惹小偷。

Word Partnership *invitation* 的常用搭配：

V. **accept an** invitation, **decline an** invitation, **extend an** invitation 1
get/receive an invitation 1 2

in·vite ♦♦◇ (**invites, inviting, invited**)

The verb is pronounced /ɪnvaɪt/. The noun is pronounced /ɪnvaɪt/.

动词读作 /ɪnvaɪt/。名词读作 /ɪnvaɪt/。

1 V-T If you **invite** someone to something such as a party or a meal, you ask them to come to it. 邀请 ❑ *She invited him to her 26th birthday party in New Jersey.* 她邀请了他参加她在新泽西举办的26岁生日聚会。 ❑ *Barron invited her to accompany him to the races.* 巴伦邀请了她陪他去看比赛。 2 V-T If you **are invited to** do something, you are formally asked or given permission to do it. 邀请；聘请 ❑ *At a future date, managers will be invited to apply for a management buy-out.* 在将来的某一天，经理们将受邀参加一项管理层控股收购。 ❑ *He invited me to go into partnership with him.* 他邀请了我与他合作。 3 V-T If something you say or do **invites** trouble or criticism, it makes trouble or criticism more likely. 招致 ❑ *Their refusal to compromise will inevitably invite more criticism from the U.N.* 他们的拒绝让步将不可避免地招致来自联合国的更多批评。 4 N-COUNT An **invite** is an invitation to something such as a party or a meal. 请贴 [INFORMAL] ❑ *She tried to wangle an invite to the party.* 她试图骗取一张聚会请柬。

Word Partnership *invite* 的常用搭配：

N. invite *someone* **to dinner**, invite **friends**, invite **people** 1
invite **criticism**, invite **questions** 3

in·vit·ing /ɪnvaɪtɪŋ/ 1 ADJ If you say that something is **inviting**, you mean that it has good qualities that attract you or make you want to experience it. 诱人的 ❑ *The February air was soft, cool, and inviting.* 2月的空气温和、清爽，而且怡人。 ● **in·vit·ing·ly** ADV 诱人地 ❑ *The waters of the tropics are invitingly clear.* 热带地区的水域清澈诱人。
2 → see also **invite**

in·voice /ɪnvɔɪs/ (**invoices, invoicing, invoiced**) 1 N-COUNT An **invoice** is a document that lists goods that have been supplied or services that have been done, and says how much money you owe for them. 费用清单；发票 ❑ *We will then send you an invoice for the total course fees.* 然后我们将寄给你一张全部课程费用的发票。 2 V-T If you **invoice** someone, you send them a bill for goods or services you have provided them with. 给…开具发票 ❑ *The agency invoices the client who then pays the full amount to the agency.* 那个代销处给客户开具发票，然后客户向代销处支付全部的款项。

▲ **in·voke** /ɪnvoʊk/ (**invokes, invoking, invoked**) 1 V-T If you **invoke** a law, you state that you are taking a particular action because that law allows or tells you to. 求助于（法律） ❑ *The judge invoked an international law that protects refugees.* 法官援用了一项保护难民的国际法律。 2 V-T If you **invoke** something such as a principle, a saying, or a famous person, you refer to them in order to support your argument. 援引 ❑ *...economists who invoke the principle of "consumer sovereignty" to support their arguments.* …援引"消费者主权"原则来支持自己论点的经济学家们。 3 V-T If something such as a piece of music **invokes** a feeling or an image, it causes someone to have the feeling or to see the image. Many people consider this use to be incorrect because **evoke** is the correct word for this. 使人想起 ❑ *"Appalachian Spring" by Aaron Copland invoked the atmosphere of the wide open spaces of the prairies.* 艾伦·科普兰的《阿帕拉契亚的春天》使人想起了那种辽阔草原的氛围。

Word Link *vol ≈ will : benevolent, involuntary, volunteer*

in·vol·un·tary /ɪnvɒlənteri/ 1 ADJ If you make an **involuntary** movement or exclamation, you make it suddenly and without intending to because you are unable to control yourself. 不由自主的 ❑ *Another surge of pain in my ankle caused me to give an involuntary shudder.* 踝关节的又一阵疼痛使我不由自主地颤抖了一下。 ● **in·vol·un·tari·ly** /ɪnvɒlənteərɪli/ ADV 不由自主地 [ADV with v] ❑ *His left eyelid twitched involuntarily.* 他的左眼皮不由自主地跳着。 2 ADJ You use **involuntary** to describe an action or situation that is forced on someone. 非自愿的 ❑ *...insurance policies that cover death, accident, sickness and involuntary unemployment.* …承保死亡、事故、疾病和非自愿性失业的保险。
→ see **muscle**

in·volve ◆◆◇ /ɪnvɒlv/ (**involves, involving, involved**) 1 V-T If a situation or activity **involves** something, that thing is a necessary part or consequence of it. 需要 ❑ *Running a kitchen involves lots of discipline and speed.* 管理厨房需要讲究纪律和速度。 2 V-T If a situation or activity **involves** someone, they are taking part in it. 涉及 ❑ *If there was a cover-up, it involved people at the very highest levels of government.* 如果有掩盖真相的行为，它就牵扯到了处于政府最高层的那些人。 3 V-T If you say that someone **involves** themselves **in** something, you mean that they take part in it, often in a way that is unnecessary or unwanted. 使卷入 ❑ *I seem to have involved myself in something I don't understand.* 我似乎已经将自己卷入了我不了解的事情当中。 4 V-T If you **involve** someone **in** something, you get them to take part in it. 使参与 ❑ *Nasser and I do everything together, he involves me in everything.* 纳萨和我做什么事都在一起，他让我参与所有的事情。 5 V-T If one thing **involves** you **in** another thing, especially something unpleasant or inconvenient, the first thing causes you to do or deal with the second. 使陷入 ❑ *I don't want to do anything that will involve me in a long-term commitment.* 我不想做任何会使自己做出长期承诺的事情。

in·volved ◆◆◇ /ɪnvɒlvd/ 1 ADJ If you are **involved in** a situation or activity, you are taking part in it or have a strong connection with it. 参与的; 涉及的 [v-link ADJ] ❑ *If she were involved in business, she would make a strong chief executive.* 如果她经商的话，将会是一位有力的首席执行官。 2 ADJ If you are **involved in** something, you give a lot of time, effort, or attention to it. 专心于…的 [v-link ADJ] ❑ *The family was deeply involved in Jewish culture.* 这家人醉心于犹太文化。 3 ADJ The things **involved in** something such as a job or system are the necessary parts or consequences of it. 必须投入的 [v-link ADJ] ❑ *We believe the time and hard work involved in completing such an assignment are worthwhile.* 我们相信为完成这项任务所需要投入的时间和付出的努力是值得的。 4 ADJ If a situation or activity is **involved**, it has a lot of different parts or aspects, often making it difficult to understand, explain, or do. 复杂难懂的 ❑ *The operations can be quite involved, requiring many procedures in order to restructure the anatomy.* 手术可能会十分复杂，需要许多步骤来重建结构。 5 ADJ If one person is **involved with** another, especially someone they are not married to, they are having a sexual or romantic relationship. 有暧昧关系的 ❑ *During a visit to Kenya in 1928 he became romantically involved with a married woman.* 在1928年到肯尼亚访问期间，他和一位已婚妇女产生了暧昧关系。

Word Partnership *involved* 的常用搭配:

N. involved **in an accident**, involved **in planning**, involved **in politics** 1
people involved, involved **in a process** 1 2
risks involved, **work** involved 3

ADJ. **actively** involved, **directly** involved, **heavily** involved, **personally** involved 1 2
deeply involved, **emotionally** involved 1 2 5
romantically involved 5

in·volve·ment ◆◇◇ /ɪnvɒlvmənt/ (**involvements**) 1 N-UNCOUNT Your **involvement** in or **with** something is the fact that you are taking part in it. 参与 ❑ *She disliked his involvement with the group and disliked his friends.* 她讨厌他加入的那个团体，也不喜欢他的那些朋友。 2 N-UNCOUNT **Involvement** is the enthusiasm that you feel when you care deeply about something. 感情投入 ❑ *Ben has always felt a deep involvement with animals.* 本一直对动物怀有很深的热爱。 3 N-VAR An **involvement** is a close relationship between two people, especially if they are not married to each other. 暧昧关系 ❑ *They were very good friends but there was no romantic involvement.* 他们是非常要好的朋友，但却没有发生过任何暧昧关系。

Word Partnership *involvement* 的常用搭配:

N. **community** involvement 1

ADJ. **active** involvement, **direct** involvement, **parental** involvement 1
romantic involvement 3

Word Link *ward ≈ in the direction of : backward, forward, inward*

in·ward /ɪnwərd/ 1 ADJ Your **inward** thoughts or feelings are the ones that you do not express or show to other people. 内心的 [ADJ n] ❑ *I sighed with inward relief.* 我内心释然地长出了一口气。 ● **in·ward·ly** ADV 内心地 ❑ *Sara was inwardly furious.* 萨拉内心异常愤怒。 2 ADJ An **inward** movement is one toward the inside or center of something. 向内的 [ADJ n] ❑ *...a sharp, inward breath like a gasp.* …像倒抽气一样急速吸入的一口气。 3 ADV If something moves or faces **inward**, it moves or faces toward the inside or center of something. 向内地 [ADV after v] ❑ *He pushed open the front door, which swung inward with a groan.* 他推开前门，门呀的一声向里开了。

iodine /aɪədaɪn/ N-UNCOUNT **Iodine** is a dark-colored substance used in medicine and photography. 碘

IOU /aɪ oʊ yu/ (**IOUs**) N-COUNT An **IOU** is a written promise that you will pay back some money that you have borrowed. **IOU** is an abbreviation for "I owe you." 欠条

iPod /aɪpɒd/ (**iPods**) N-COUNT An **iPod** is a portable MP3 player that can play music downloaded from the Internet. **iPod**音乐播放器 [COMPUTING, TRADEMARK]

IQ /aɪ kyu/ (**IQs**) N-VAR Your **IQ** is your level of intelligence, as indicated by a special test that you do. **IQ** is an abbreviation for "intelligence quotient." 智商 ❑ *His IQ is above average.* 他的智商处于中等偏上。

irate /aɪreɪt/ ADJ If someone is **irate**, they are very angry about something. 愤怒的 ❑ *The owner was so irate he almost threw me out of the place.* 主人那么生气，他差点儿把我从那个地方赶出去。

IRC /aɪ ɑr si/ N-UNCOUNT **IRC** is a way of having conversations with people who are using the Internet, especially people you do not know. **IRC** is an abbreviation for "Internet Relay Chat." 因特网中继聊天 ❑ *Not long ago, just being in IRC was enough to forge bonds between chatters.* 不久前，只需参加因特网中继聊天就足以在聊天者之间建立联系。

iris /aɪrɪs/ (**irises**) N-COUNT The **iris** is the round colored part of a person's eye. 虹膜
→ see **eye, muscle**

iron ◆◇◇ /aɪərn/ (**irons, ironing, ironed**) 1 N-UNCOUNT **Iron** is an element that usually takes the form of a hard, dark gray metal. It is used to make steel, and also forms part of many tools, buildings, and vehicles. Very small amounts of iron occur in your blood and in food. 铁 ❑ *The huge, iron gate was locked.* 那扇巨大的铁门被锁上了。 ❑ *...the highest grade iron ore deposits in the world.* …世界上最优质的铁矿床。 2 N-COUNT An **iron** is an electrical device with a flat metal base. You heat it until the base is hot, then rub it over clothes to remove creases. 熨斗 3 V-T If you **iron** clothes, you remove the creases from them using an iron. 熨 ❑ *She used to iron his shirts.* 她过去常给他熨衬衫。 ● **iron·ing** N-UNCOUNT 熨烫 ❑ *I managed to get all the ironing done this morning.* 今天上午我设法把所有的衣物都熨了。 4 ADJ You can use **iron** to describe the character or behavior of someone who is very firm in their decisions and actions, or who can control their feelings well. 坚强的 [ADJ n] ❑ *...a man of icy nerve and iron will.* …一个头脑冷静、意志坚强的男人。 5 ADJ **Iron** is used in expressions such as **an iron hand** and **iron discipline** to describe strong, harsh, or unfair methods of control that do not allow people much freedom. 强硬的 [ADJ n] ❑ *He died in 1985 after ruling Albania with an iron fist for 40 years.* 他用铁腕统治了阿尔巴尼亚40年后，于1985年去世。 6 PHRASE If someone has a lot of **irons in the fire**, they are involved in several different activities or have several different plans. 同时要做的事情 ❑ *Too many irons in the fire can sap your energy and prevent you from seeing which path to take.* 同时做太多的事情可能会消耗你的精力，使你看不清该走哪条路。
▸ **iron out** PHRASAL VERB If you **iron out** difficulties, you resolve them and bring them to an end. 解决 ❑ *"It was in the beginning, when we were still ironing out problems," a company spokesman said.* "那是在开始的时候，当时我们仍在解决问题，"公司的一位发言人说。

Word Partnership *iron* 的常用搭配:

ADJ. **cast** iron, **wrought** iron 1
a hot iron 2

N. iron **bar**, iron **gate** 1
iron **a shirt** 3
an iron **fist/hand** 5

iron·ic /aɪrɒnɪk/ or **ironical** /aɪrɒnɪkəl/ 1 ADJ When you make an **ironic** remark, you say the opposite of what you really mean, as a joke. 讽刺的 ❑ *At the most solemn moments he will flash a mocking smile or make an ironic remark.* 在最庄严的的时刻他也会露出嘲弄的微笑或是说些讽刺挖苦的话。 2 ADJ If you say that it is **ironic** that something happens, you mean that it is odd or amusing because it involves a contrast. 具有讽刺意味的 ❑ *It is ironic that so many women are* *anti-feminist.* 具有讽刺意味的是，竟然有那么多妇女是反对女权主义的。

▲ **i·roni·cal·ly** /aɪrɒnɪkli/ **1** ADV You use **ironically** to draw attention to a situation that is odd or amusing because it involves a contrast. 具有讽刺意味的是 [ADV with cl] ❑ *Ironically, for a man who hated war, he would have made a superb war cameraman.* 具有讽刺意味的是，他这样一个憎恨战争的人曾经可能成为一名优秀的战地摄影师。 **2** ADV If you say something **ironically**, you say the opposite of what you really mean, as a joke. 讽刺地 [ADV with v] ❑ *Classmates at West Point had ironically dubbed him Beauty.* 西点军校的同学们曾经讽刺地给他起了一个绰号——"美人"。

★ **iro·ny** /aɪrəni, aɪər-/ (**ironies**) **1** N-UNCOUNT **Irony** is a subtle form of humor that involves saying things that are the opposite of what you really mean. 讽刺 ❑ *His tone was tinged with irony.* 他的语气中微含讽刺。 **2** N-VAR If you talk about the **irony** of a situation, you mean that it is odd or amusing because it involves a contrast. 具有讽刺意味的事 ❑ *The irony is that many officials in Washington agree in private that their policy is inconsistent.* 具有讽刺意味的是，华盛顿的许多官员私下里承认他们的政策是前后矛盾的。

Word Partnership *irony* 的常用搭配：

ADJ. **bitter** irony **1**
ultimate irony **1** **2**
N. **hint of** irony, **sense of** irony, **trace of** irony **1**
irony **of a situation** **2**

Word Link *ir ≈ not : irrational, irregular, irresponsible*

Word Link *ratio ≈ reasoning : irrational, rational, rationale*

★ **ir·ra·tion·al** /ɪræʃənᵊl/ ADJ If you describe someone's feelings and behavior as **irrational**, you mean they are not based on logical reasons or clear thinking. 不理性的 ❑ *...an irrational fear of science.* …一种对科学毫无根据的恐惧。 ● **ir·ra·tion·al·ly** ADV 不理性地 ❑ *My husband is irrationally jealous over my past loves.* 我丈夫对我从前的几次恋爱毫无道理地妒忌。 ● **ir·ra·tion·al·ity** /ɪræʃənælɪti/ N-UNCOUNT 不理性 ❑ *...the irrationality of his behavior.* …他行为的不合情理。

ir·rec·on·cil·able /ɪrɛkənsaɪləbᵊl/ **1** ADJ If two things such as opinions or proposals are **irreconcilable**, they are so different from each other that it is not possible to believe or have both of them. 相对立的 [FORMAL] ❑ *These old concepts are irreconcilable with modern life.* 这些旧观念与现代生活是相互对立的。 **2** ADJ An **irreconcilable** disagreement or conflict is so serious that it cannot be settled. 无法消除的 [FORMAL] ❑ *...an irreconcilable clash of personalities.* …一种无法消除的个性冲突。

★ **ir·regu·lar** /ɪrɛgyələr/ (**irregulars**) **1** ADJ If events or actions occur at **irregular** intervals, the periods of time between them are of different lengths. 不规律的 ❑ *Cars passed at irregular intervals.* 汽车以不规律的时间间隔驶过。 ❑ *She was taken to a hospital suffering from an irregular heartbeat.* 她因心律不齐而被送进医院。 ● **ir·regu·lar·ly** ADV 不规律地 [ADV with v] ❑ *He was eating irregularly, steadily losing weight.* 他吃饭不规律，体重不断下降。 ● **ir·regu·lar·ity** /ɪrɛgyəlærɪti/ N-VAR (**irregularities**) 不规律 ❑ *...a dangerous irregularity in her heartbeat.* …她危险的心律不齐。 **2** ADJ Something that is **irregular** is not smooth or straight, or does not form a regular pattern. 不规则的; 不平整的 ❑ *He had bad teeth, irregular and discolored.* 他的牙齿不好，不整齐，而且变了色。 ● **ir·regu·lar·ly** ADV 不规则地; 不平整地 ❑ *Located off-center in the irregularly shaped lake was a fountain.* 在那个形状不规则的湖的中心之外，有一个喷泉。 ● **ir·regu·lar·ity** N-VAR 不规则; 不平整 ❑ *...treatment of abnormalities or irregularities of the teeth.* …对畸形或不整齐的牙齿的治疗。 **3** ADJ **Irregular** behavior is dishonest or not in accordance with the normal rules. 不正规的; 不合常规的 ❑ *...irregular business practices.* …不合常规的商务活动。 ● **ir·regu·lar·ity** N-VAR 不正当; 不合常规 ❑ *He faced charges arising from alleged financial irregularities.* 他面临涉嫌不正当财务行为的控告。 **4** ADJ An **irregular** verb, noun, or adjective has different forms from most other verbs, nouns, or adjectives in the language. For example, "break" is an irregular verb because its past form is "broke," not "breaked." 不规则的

ir·rel·evance /ɪrɛlɪvᵊns/ (**irrelevances**) **1** N-UNCOUNT If you talk about **the irrelevance of** something, you mean that it is irrelevant. 不相关 ❑ *...the utter irrelevance of the debate.* …与这一争论完全毫不相关。 **2** N-COUNT If you describe something as an **irrelevance**, you have a low opinion of it because it is not important in a situation. 无意义的事 ❑ *The Patriotic Front has been a political irrelevance since it was abandoned by its foreign backers.* "爱国阵线"自从被其外国支持者们遗弃之后就已经没有任何政治意义了。

ir·rel·evant /ɪrɛlɪvᵊnt/ **1** ADJ If you describe something such as a fact or remark as **irrelevant**, you mean that it is not connected with what you are discussing or dealing with. 不相关的 ❑ *...irrelevant details.* …一些不相关的细节。 **2** ADJ If you say that something is **irrelevant**, you mean that it is not important in a situation. 不重要的 ❑ *The choice of subject matter is irrelevant.* 主题的选择不重要。

ir·re·sist·ible /ɪrɪzɪstɪbᵊl/ **1** ADJ If you describe something such as a desire or force as **irresistible**, you mean that it is so powerful that it makes you act in a certain way, and there is nothing you can do to prevent this. 无法抑制的 ❑ *It proved an irresistible temptation to Bob to go back.* 后来证明，回去对于鲍勃来说是一种无法抑制的诱惑。 ● **ir·re·sist·ibly** /ɪrɪzɪstɪbli/ ADV 无法抑制地 [ADV with v] ❑ *I found myself irresistibly drawn to Steve's world.* 我发现自己情不自禁地被史蒂夫的世界所吸引了。 **2** ADJ If you describe something or someone as **irresistible**, you mean that they are so good or attractive that you cannot stop yourself from liking them or wanting them. 无法抵制诱惑的 [INFORMAL] ❑ *The music is irresistible.* 这段音乐非常有感染力。 ● **ir·re·sist·ibly** ADV 无法抵制诱惑地 [ADV adj] ❑ *She had a charm that men found irresistibly attractive.* 她有一种令男人无法抵制的魅力。

★ **ir·re·spec·tive** /ɪrɪspɛktɪv/ PHRASE If you say that something happens or should happen **irrespective of** a particular thing, you mean that it is not affected or should not be affected by that thing. 不考虑的 [FORMAL] ❑ *...their commitment to a society based on equality for all citizens irrespective of ethnic origin.* …他们为建设一个没有种族差别、全民平等的社会所做出的贡献。

ir·re·spon·sible /ɪrɪspɒnsɪbᵊl/ ADJ If you describe someone as **irresponsible**, you are criticizing them because they do things without properly considering their possible consequences. 不负责任的 [DISAPPROVAL] ❑ *I felt that it was irresponsible to advocate the legalization of drugs.* 我觉得主张毒品合法化是不负责任的。 ● **ir·re·spon·sibly** /ɪrɪspɒnsɪbli/ ADV 不负责任地 ❑ *They resent the implication that they have behaved irresponsibly.* 他们对那种暗示他们的行为不负责任的言论非常不满。 ● **ir·re·spon·sibil·ity** /ɪrɪspɒnsɪbɪlɪti/ N-UNCOUNT 不负责任 ❑ *I can only wonder at the irresponsibility of people who advocate such destruction to our environment.* 竟然有人主张对我们的环境进行如此的破坏，我只能对他们的不负责任感到惊讶。

Word Link *vere ≈ fear, awe : irreverent, revere, reverence*

ir·rev·er·ent /ɪrɛvərənt/ ADJ If you describe someone as **irreverent**, you mean that they do not show respect for people or things that are generally respected. 不尊敬的 [APPROVAL] ❑ *Taylor combined great knowledge with an irreverent attitude to history.* 泰勒知识渊博，但对历史却持不尊重态度。 ● **ir·rev·er·ence** N-UNCOUNT 不尊敬 ❑ *His irreverence for authority marks him out as a troublemaker.* 他对权威的蔑视表明他是个惹事的人。

ir·re·vers·ible /ɪrɪvɜrsɪbᵊl/ ADJ If a change is **irreversible**, things cannot be changed back to the way they were before. 不可逆转的 ❑ *She could suffer irreversible brain damage if she is not treated within seven days.* 如果在7天内得不到治疗，她的大脑有可能会受到不可恢复的损害。

ir·revo·cable /ɪrɛvəkəbᵊl/ ADJ If a decision, action, or change is **irrevocable**, it cannot be changed or reversed. 不可改变的 [FORMAL] ❑ *He said the decision was irrevocable.* 他说过这项决定是不可改变的。 ● **ir·revo·cably** /ɪrɛvəkəbli/ ADV 不可改变地 ❑ *My relationships with friends have been irrevocably altered by their reactions to my illness.* 由于朋友们对我的病情所做出的反应，我和他们的关系已经彻底改变了。

ir·ri·gate /ɪrɪgeɪt/ (**irrigates, irrigating, irrigated**) V-T To **irrigate** land means to supply it with water in order to help crops grow. 灌溉 ❑ *None of the water from Lake Powell is used to irrigate the area.* 鲍威尔湖的水没有被用来灌溉这一地区。 ● **ir·ri·ga·tion** /ɪrɪgeɪʃᵊn/ N-UNCOUNT 灌溉 ❑ *The agricultural land is hilly and the irrigation poor.* 这片农田多丘陵，而且灌溉条件很差。

→ see **dam, farm**

ir·ri·table /ɪrɪtəbᵊl/ ADJ If you are **irritable**, you are easily annoyed. 易怒的 ❑ *He had been waiting for over an hour and was beginning to feel irritable.* 他已经等了一个多小时，开始觉得有些烦躁了。 ● **ir·ri·tably** /ɪrɪtəbli/ ADV 易怒地 [ADV with v] ❑ *"Why are you whispering?" he asked irritably.* "你们为什么窃窃私语？"他生气地问。 ● **ir·ri·tabil·ity** /ɪrɪtəbɪlɪti/ N-UNCOUNT 易怒 ❑ *Patients usually suffer*

I

from memory loss, personality changes, and increased irritability. 病人们通常会记忆力减退，个性发生变化，而且越来越容易烦躁。

ir·ri·tant /ɪrɪtənt/ **(irritants)** **1** N-COUNT If you describe something as an **irritant**, you mean that it keeps annoying you. 让人恼火的事 [FORMAL] ❑ *He said the issue was not a major irritant.* 他说这一问题不是让他恼火的主要原因。 **2** N-COUNT An **irritant** is a substance that causes a part of your body to itch or become sore. 刺激物 [FORMAL] ❑ *Many pesticides are irritants.* 许多杀虫剂都有刺激性。

★ **ir·ri·tate** /ɪrɪteɪt/ **(irritates, irritating, irritated)** **1** V-T If something **irritates** you, it keeps annoying you. 激怒 ❑ *Their attitude irritates me.* 他们的态度激怒了我。 ● **ir·ri·tat·ed** ADJ 被激怒的 ❑ *Not surprisingly, her teacher is getting irritated with her.* 不出所料，她的老师快被她激怒了。 **2** V-T If something **irritates** a part of your body, it causes it to itch or become sore. 刺激 ❑ *Wear rubber gloves while chopping chilies as they can irritate the skin.* 剁辣椒时戴上橡皮手套，因为它们会刺激皮肤。

> **Angry** is normally used to talk about someone's mood or feelings on a particular occasion. If someone is often angry, you can describe them as **bad-tempered.** ❑ *She's a bad-tempered young lady.* If someone is very angry, you can describe them as **furious.** ❑ *Senior police officers are furious at the blunder.* If they are less angry, you can describe them as **annoyed** or **irritated.** ❑ *The premier looked annoyed but calm. ...a man irritated by the barking of his neighbor's dog.* Typically, someone is **irritated** by something because it happens constantly or continually. If someone is often irritated, you can describe them as **irritable**.

ir·ri·tat·ing /ɪrɪteɪtɪŋ/ **1** ADJ Something that is **irritating** keeps annoying you. 恼人的 ❑ *They also have the irritating habit of interrupting.* 他们也有打断别人这个令人恼火的习惯。 ● **ir·ri·tat·ing·ly** ADV 恼人地 ❑ *They can be irritatingly indecisive at times.* 他们有时会犹豫不决而令人着恼。 **2** ADJ An **irritating** substance can cause your body to itch or become sore. 刺激性的 ❑ *In heavy concentrations, ozone is irritating to the eyes, nose and throat.* 浓度极高时，臭氧对眼睛、鼻子和喉咙是有刺激的。

ir·ri·ta·tion /ɪrɪteɪʃᵊn/ **(irritations)** **1** N-UNCOUNT **Irritation** is a feeling of annoyance, especially when something is happening that you cannot easily stop or control. 恼怒 ❑ *He tried not to let his irritation show as he blinked in the glare of the television lights.* 在对着耀眼的电视光线眨眼时，他竭力不把自己的恼怒表现出来。 **2** N-COUNT An **irritation** is something that keeps annoying you. 恼人的事 ❑ *Don't allow a minor irritation in the workplace to mar your ambitions.* 不要让工作场所中一件烦人的小事把你远大的抱负破坏了。 **3** N-VAR **Irritation** in a part of your body is a feeling of slight pain and discomfort there. 刺激 ❑ *These oils may cause irritation to sensitive skins.* 这几种油可能会对敏感皮肤有刺激。

IRS /aɪ ɑr ɛs/ N-PROPER **The IRS** is the federal government authority that collects taxes. **IRS** is an abbreviation for **Internal Revenue Service.** (美国) 国内税务署

is /ɪz/ **Is** is the third person singular of the present tense of **be**. **Is** is often added to other words and shortened to **-'s**. **be**的第三人称单数现在时

ISDN /aɪ ɛs di ɛn/ N-UNCOUNT **ISDN** is a telephone network that can send voice and computer messages. **ISDN** is an abbreviation for "Integrated Service Digital Network." 综合业务数字网 ❑ *...an ISDN phone line.* …一条综合业务数字网电话线。

Is·lam ♦◇◇ /ɪslɑm/ **1** N-UNCOUNT **Islam** is the religion of the Muslims, which was started by Mohammed. 伊斯兰教 ❑ *He converted to Islam at the age of 16.* 他在16岁时皈依了伊斯兰教。 **2** N-UNCOUNT Some people use **Islam** to refer to all the countries where Islam is the main religion. 伊斯兰教国家 ❑ *...relations between Islam and the West.* …伊斯兰教国家和西方国家之间的关系。 → see **religion**

▲ **Is·lam·ic** ♦◇◇ /ɪslæmɪk, -lɑ-/ ADJ **Islamic** means belonging or relating to Islam. 伊斯兰教的 [ADJ n] ❑ *...Islamic law.* …伊斯兰教法律。 → see **religion**

is·land ♦♦◇ /aɪlənd/ **(islands)** N-COUNT; N-IN-NAMES An **island** is a piece of land that is completely surrounded by water. 岛 ❑ *...the Canary Islands.* …加那利群岛。

is·land·er /aɪləndər/ **(islanders)** N-COUNT **Islanders** are people who live on an island. 岛民 ❑ *The islanders endured centuries of exploitation.* 岛民们忍受了几个世纪的剥削。

★ **isle** /aɪl/ **(isles)** N-COUNT; N-IN-NAMES An **isle** is an island; often used as part of an island's name, or in literary English. 岛 (用于岛名或文学作品中) ❑ *...the Isle of Pines.* …派恩斯岛。

isn't /ɪzᵊnt/ **Isn't** is the usual spoken form of "is not." **is not**的常用口语形式

iso·late /aɪsəleɪt/ **(isolates, isolating, isolated)** **1** V-T To **isolate** a person or organization means to cause them to lose their friends or supporters. 孤立 ❑ *This policy could isolate the country from the other permanent members of the United Nations Security Council.* 这项政策可能会将这个国家从联合国安理会的其他常任理事国中孤立出来。 ● **iso·lat·ed** ADJ 孤立的 ❑ *They are finding themselves increasingly isolated within the teaching profession.* 他们发现自己在教育界中越来越孤立。 ● **iso·la·tion** ★ /aɪsəleɪʃᵊn/ N-UNCOUNT 孤立 ❑ *Diplomatic isolation could lead to economic disaster.* 外交孤立可能会导致经济灾难。 **2** V-T If you **isolate yourself**, or if something **isolates** you, you become physically or socially separated from other people. 使孤立 孤立 ❑ *She seemed determined to isolate herself from everyone, even him.* 她似乎决心要与每个人，甚至是他割断联系。 ❑ *His radicalism and refusal to compromise isolated him.* 他的激进和拒绝让步使他受到了孤立。 **3** V-T If you **isolate** something such as an idea or a problem, you separate it from others that it is connected with, so that you can concentrate on it or consider it on its own. 单独考虑 ❑ *Our anxieties can also be controlled by isolating thoughts, feelings and memories.* 我们的焦虑也可以通过对思想、感情和记忆分别进行考虑来加以控制。 **4** V-T To **isolate** a substance means to obtain it by separating it from other substances using scientific processes. 使离析 [TECHNICAL] ❑ *We can use genetic engineering techniques to isolate the gene that is responsible.* 我们可以用遗传工程技术将起作用的基因离析出来。 **5** V-T To **isolate** a sick person or animal means to keep them apart from other people or animals, so that their illness does not spread. 隔离 ❑ *Patients will be isolated from other people for between three days and one month after treatment.* 治疗之后，患者将被与他人隔离3天到1个月。 ● **iso·la·tion** ★ N-UNCOUNT 隔离 [oft N n] ❑ *Hayley contracted tuberculosis and had to be put in an isolation ward.* 海利感染了肺结核而不得不被送进一个隔离病房。

iso·lat·ed /aɪsəleɪtɪd/ **1** ADJ An **isolated** place is a long way away from large towns and is difficult to reach. 偏僻的 ❑ *Many of the refugee villages are in isolated areas.* 许多难民村位于偏僻的地方。 **2** ADJ If you feel **isolated**, you feel lonely and without friends or help. 孤独的 ❑ *Some patients may become very isolated and depressed.* 有些病人可能变得非常孤独和抑郁。 **3** ADJ An **isolated** example is an example of something that is not very common. 个别的 [ADJ n] ❑ *They said the allegations related to an isolated case of cheating.* 他们说这些指控与一件孤立的欺诈案有关。

★ **iso·la·tion** /aɪsəleɪʃᵊn/ **1** N-UNCOUNT **Isolation** is the state of feeling alone and without friends or help. 孤独 ❑ *Many deaf people have feelings of isolation and loneliness.* 许多失聪的人有孤独和寂寞的感觉。 **2** → see also **isolate** **3** PHRASE If something is considered **in isolation from** other things that it is connected with, it is considered separately, and those other things are not considered. 孤立 ❑ *Punishment cannot, therefore, be discussed in isolation from social and political theory.* 因此，对惩罚进行讨论不能脱离社会和政治理论。 **4** PHRASE If someone does something **in isolation**, they do it without other people present or without their help. 单独地 ❑ *Malcolm, for instance, works in isolation but I have no doubts about his abilities.* 例如，马尔科姆虽然一个人独立工作，但我丝毫不怀疑他的能力。

ISP /aɪ ɛs pi/ **(ISPs)** N-COUNT An **ISP** is a company that provides Internet and e-mail services. **ISP** is an abbreviation for "Internet service provider." 因特网服务提供商

is·sue ♦♦♦ /ɪʃu/ **(issues, issuing, issued)** **1** N-COUNT An **issue** is an important subject that people are arguing about or discussing. 议题 ❑ *Agents will raise the issue of prize-money for next year's world championships.* 代理商们会提出明年世界锦标赛的奖金问题。 ❑ *A key issue for higher education in the 1990s is the need for greater diversity of courses.* 20世纪90年代高等教育的一个关键问题是需要使课程更加多样化。 **2** N-SING If something is **the issue**, it is the thing you consider to be the most important part of a situation or discussion. 要点 ❑ *I was earning a lot of money, but that was not the issue.* 我是挣着很多钱，但那不是问题的关键。 ❑ *Do not draw it on the chart, however, as this will confuse the issue.* 但是不要把它画在图表上，因为这将使要点模糊不清。 **3** N-COUNT An **issue** of something such as a magazine or newspaper is the version of it that is published, for example, in

a particular month or on a particular day. (杂志或报刊的) 期 ❑ *The growing problem is underlined in the latest issue of the Scientific American.* 这一日益严重的问题在最新一期的《科学美国人》上得到强调。 **4** V-T If you **issue** a statement or a warning, you make it known formally or publicly. 发表 (声明); 发出 (警告) ❑ *Last night he issued a statement denying the allegations.* 昨天晚上，他发表了一项声明否认那些说法。 ❑ *The government issued a warning that the strikers should end their action or face dismissal.* 该政府发出了警告，罢工者们应停止他们的行动，否则将被免职。 **5** V-T If you **are issued with** something, it is officially given to you. 分发 [usu passive] ❑ *On your appointment you will be issued with a written statement of particulars of employment.* 你上任时会收到一份聘用细则的书面材料。 ● N-UNCOUNT **Issue** is also a noun. 分发 ❑ *...a standard army issue rifle.* …一支标准的军队配发的步枪。 **6** PHRASE The question or point **at issue** is the question or point that is being argued about or discussed. 争论中的 ❑ *The problems of immigration were not the question at issue.* 移民问题不在争论之列。 **7** PHRASE If you **make an issue of** something, you try to make other people think about it or discuss it, because you are concerned or annoyed about it. 挑起对…的争论 ❑ *It seemed the Colonel had no desire to make an issue of the affair.* 那位上校似乎不愿挑起对此事的争论。 **8** PHRASE If you **take issue with** someone or something they said, you disagree with them, and start arguing about it. 对…持异议 ❑ *I will not take issue with the fact that we have a recession.* 我不会对我们经历经济衰退这一事实表示异议。 **9** PHRASE If someone **has issues with** a particular aspect of their life, they have problems connected with it. 有…方面的问题 [oft PHR "with/about" n] ❑ *Once you have issues with food, you're going to have them for the rest of your life.* 一旦你在食物方面有问题，你以后的生活中就一直会有这样的问题。
→ see **philosophy**

Word Partnership *issue* 的常用搭配：

V.	**become an** issue, **debate an** issue, **discuss an** issue, **raise an** issue, **vote on an** issue **1**
	address an/the issue, **deal with an/the** issue **1 2**
ADJ.	**complicated** issue, **controversial** issue, **difficult** issue, **legal** issue, **political** issue, **sensitive** issue, **serious** issue, **unresolved** issue **1**
	big issue, **critical** issue, **important** issue, **major** issue **1 2**
	current issue, **recent** issue **1 3**
N.	**election** issue, **safety** issue, **security** issue **1**
	issue **an appeal**, issue **a statement**, issue **a warning** **4**

is·sue price (**issue prices**) N-COUNT The **issue price** of shares is the price at which they are offered for sale when they first become available to the public. (股票的) 发行价 [BUSINESS] ❑ *Shares in the company slipped below their issue price on their first day of trading.* 该公司的股票在第一个交易日跌破了发行价。

it ♦♦♦ /ɪt/

It is a third person singular pronoun. **It** is used as the subject or object of a verb, or as the object of a preposition.

1 PRON-SING You use **it** to refer to an object, animal, or other thing that has already been mentioned. 它 (指上文提及的某一物体、动物或其他事物) ❑ *It's a wonderful city, really. I'll show it to you if you want.* 这确实是个很棒的城市。如果你愿意的话，我带你看一下。 ❑ *My wife has become crippled by arthritis. She is embarrassed to ask the doctor about it.* 我妻子因患关节炎腿瘸了。她不好意思去向医生询问相关病情。 **2** PRON-SING You use **it** to refer to a child or baby whose sex you do not know or whose sex is not relevant to what you are saying. 它 (指小孩或婴儿) ❑ *She could compel him to support the child after it was born.* 她可以迫使他在孩子出生后抚养孩子。 **3** PRON-SING You use **it** to refer in a general way to a situation that you have just described. 它 (指刚刚说过的情况) ❑ *He was through with sports, not because he had to be but because he wanted it that way.* 他放弃体育运动了，不是因为他非放弃不可，而是因为他想要那样。 **4** PRON-SING You use **it** before certain nouns, adjectives, and verbs to introduce your feelings or point of view about a situation. 用于某些名词、形容词或动词前表达对某种情况的看法或观点 ❑ *It was nice to see Steve again.* 很高兴又见到了史蒂夫。 ❑ *It's a pity you never got married, Sarah.* 萨拉，很遗憾你从来没有结过婚。 **5** PRON-SING You use **it** in passive clauses that report a situation or event. 用于被动句表示对某一情况或事件的报道 ❑ *It has been said that stress causes cancer.* 据说压力会诱发癌症。 **6** PRON-SING You use **it** with some verbs that need a subject or object, although there is no noun that "it" refers to. 用作某些动词的形式主语或宾语 ❑ *Of course, as it turned out, three-fourths of the people in the group were psychiatrists.* 当然，结果证明这些人中3/4是精神病医生。 **7** PRON-SING You use **it** as the subject of "be" to say what the time, day, or date is. 用作动词**be**的主语，指时间、日期等 ❑ *It's three o'clock in the morning.* 现在是凌晨3点。 ❑ *It was a Monday, so she was at home.* 那是个星期一，所以她在家。 **8** PRON-SING You use **it** as the subject of a linking verb to describe the weather, the light, or the temperature. 用作系动词的主语，指天气、光线、温度等 ❑ *It was very wet and windy the day I drove over the hill to Del Norte.* 我开车越过小山去德尔诺特的那天下大雨又刮大风。 **9** PRON-SING You use **it** when you are telling someone who you are, or asking them who they are, especially at the beginning of a phone call. You also use **it** in statements and questions about the identity of other people. 通电话时用作开首语，报出身份或名字 ❑ *"Who is it?" he called.—"It's your neighbor."* "谁呀？"他喊道。——"你的邻居。" **10** PRON When you are emphasizing or drawing attention to something, you can put that thing immediately after **it** and a form of the verb "be." 与**be**动词配合起强调作用，引起对某事物的注意 [EMPHASIS] ❑ *It's really the poor countries that don't have an economic base that have the worst environmental records.* 确实是那些没有经济基础的贫穷国家的环保记录最糟糕。 **11** PHRASE You use **it** in expressions such as **it's not that** or **it's not just that** when you are giving a reason for something and are suggesting that there are several other reasons. 用于**it's not that**、**it's not just that**等表达法中，表示提出一个理由并同时暗示还有其它一些理由 ❑ *It's not that I didn't want to be with my family.* 并不是因为我不愿意和我的家人在一起。 **12** **if it wasn't for** → see **be**

IT ♦♦♦ /aɪ ti/ **IT** is an abbreviation for **information technology**. 信息技术 ❑ *...people with IT skills.* …掌握信息技术的人。

ital·ic /ɪtælɪk/ (**italics**) **1** N-PLURAL **Italics** are letters that slope to the right. Italics are often used to emphasize a particular word or sentence. The examples in this dictionary are printed in italics. 斜体字 ❑ *The title is printed in italics.* 标题被印成斜体。 **2** ADJ **Italic** letters slope to the right. 斜体的 [ADJ n] ❑ *She addressed them by hand in her beautiful italic script.* 她用她漂亮的斜体字亲笔给他们写信。

▲ **itch** /ɪtʃ/ (**itches, itching, itched**) **1** V-I When a part of your body **itches**, you have an unpleasant feeling on your skin that makes you want to scratch. 发痒 ❑ *When someone has hay fever, the eyes and nose will stream and itch.* 当一个人染上花粉热时，会流眼泪、流鼻涕，还会感到眼睛和鼻子发痒。 ● N-COUNT **Itch** is also a noun. 痒 ❑ *Scratch my back – I've got an itch.* 给我挠挠背——我痒痒。 ● **itch·ing** N-UNCOUNT 痒 ❑ *It may be that the itching is caused by contact with irritant material.* 那儿的痒也许是由于接触刺激物而引起的。 **2** V-T/V-I If you **are itching** to do something, you are very eager or impatient to do it. 渴望；渴望 [usu cont] [INFORMAL] ❑ *I was itching to get involved.* 我渴望参与。 ● N-SING **Itch** is also a noun. 渴望 ❑ *...cable TV viewers with an insatiable itch to switch from channel to channel.* …难以满足的、渴望不停变换频道的有线电视观众。

itchy /ɪtʃi/ **1** ADJ If a part of your body or something you are wearing is **itchy**, you have an unpleasant feeling on your skin that makes you want to scratch. 发痒的 [INFORMAL] ❑ *...itchy, sore eyes.* …刺痒酸痛的眼睛。 **2** PHRASE If you have **itchy feet**, you have a strong desire to leave a place and to travel. 强烈的旅行渴望 [INFORMAL] ❑ *The thought gave me really itchy feet so within a couple of months I decided to leave.* 这个想法带给我强烈的旅行渴望，所以几个月之内我就决定出发了。

it'd /ɪtəd/ **1** **It'd** is a spoken form of "it would." **it would**的口语形式 ❑ *It'd be better for a place like this to remain closed.* 这样的地方最好继续关闭。 **2** **It'd** is a spoken form of "it had," especially when "had" is an auxiliary verb. **it had**的口语形式 ❑ *Marcie was watching the news. It'd just started.* 玛西正在看新闻。新闻刚刚开始。

item ♦♦◇ /aɪtəm/ (**items**) **1** N-COUNT An **item** is one of a collection or list of objects. 一些物品中的一项 ❑ *The most valuable item on show will be a Picasso drawing.* 展览中最有价值的作品将是毕加索的一幅画。 **2** N-COUNT An **item** is one of a list of things for someone to do, deal with, or talk about. 项目 ❑ *The other item on the agenda is the tour.* 另一项议程是旅行。 **3** N-COUNT An **item** is a report or article in a newspaper or magazine, or on television or radio. (报刊、电视或广播中的) 一篇报道或文章 ❑ *There was an item in the paper about him.* 报纸上有一篇关于他的报道。 **4** N-SING If you say that two people are an **item**, you mean that they are having a romantic or sexual relationship. (在恋爱或有性关系的) 一对 [INFORMAL] ❑ *She and Gino were an item.* 她和吉诺曾是一对。

Thesaurus *item* 另参见:

N. issue, subject, task 2
article, story 3
a couple 4

Word Partnership *item* 的常用搭配:

N. **item of clothing** 1
agenda item (or item **on an agenda**) 2
newspaper item 3

item·ise /aɪtəmaɪz/ [BRIT] → see **itemize**

item·ize /aɪtəmaɪz/ (**itemizes, itemizing, itemized**)

in BRIT, also use **itemise**

V-T If you **itemize** a number of things, you make a list of them. 逐条列记 ❑ *The report will itemize the cost of various improvements.* 报告将逐条列记各种改进工作所需的费用。

itin·er·ary /aɪtɪnərɛri/ (**itineraries**) N-COUNT An **itinerary** is a plan of a trip, including the route and the places that you will visit. 旅行计划 ❑ *The next place on our itinerary was Sedona.* 我们旅行计划的下一站是塞多纳。

it'll /ɪtᵊl/ **It'll** is a spoken form of "it will." **it will**的口语形式 ❑ *It's been a while since I've seen her so it'll be nice to meet her in town on Thursday.* 我很长时间没见她了，所以星期四在镇里见到她将会很高兴。

its ♦♦♦ /ɪts/

Its is a third person singular possessive determiner.

DET You use **its** to indicate that something belongs or relates to a thing, place, or animal that has just been mentioned or whose identity is known. You can use **its** to indicate that something belongs or relates to a child or baby. 它的 ❑ *He held the knife by its blade.* 他握住了刀刃。

Do not confuse **its** and **it's**. **Its** means "belonging to it." **It's** is short for "it is" or "it has." ❑ *The horse raised its head... It's hot in here... It's stopped raining.*

it's /ɪts/ 1 **It's** is the usual spoken form of "it is." **it is**的常用口语形式 ❑ *It's the best news I've heard in a long time.* 这是我很长时间以来听到的最好消息。 2 **It's** is the usual spoken form of "it has," especially when "has" is an auxiliary verb. **it has**的常用口语形式 ❑ *It's been such a long time since I played.* 自从我上次演奏以来已经过了这么长时间了。

it·self ♦♦♦ /ɪtsɛlf/ 1 PRON-REFL **Itself** is used as the object of a verb or preposition when it refers to something that is the same thing as the subject of the verb. 它本身 [V PRON, prep PRON] ❑ *Scientists have discovered remarkable new evidence showing how the body rebuilds itself while we sleep.* 科学家们已经发现了非同寻常的新证据，证明睡眠时我们的身体如何自行恢复。 2 PRON-REFL-EMPH You use **itself** to emphasize the thing you are referring to. 本身（表示强调）[EMPHASIS] ❑ *I think life itself is a learning process.* 我认为生活本身是一个学习的过程。 3 PRON-REFL-EMPH If you say that someone is, for example, politeness **itself** or kindness **itself**, you are emphasizing that they are extremely polite or extremely kind. (加在词后表示强调) 自身 [N PRON] [EMPHASIS] ❑ *He is rarely satisfied with anything less than perfection itself.* 他对任何不十分完美的事情都极少满意。

I've /aɪv/ **I've** is the usual spoken form of "I have," especially when "have" is an auxiliary verb. **I have**的常用口语形式 ❑ *I've been invited to meet with the ambassador.* 我已经被邀请和大使会晤。

IVF /aɪ vi ɛf/ N-UNCOUNT **IVF** is a method of helping a woman to have a baby in which an egg is removed from one of her ovaries, fertilized outside her body, and then replaced in her womb. **IVF** is an abbreviation for "in vitro fertilization." 体外受精 ❑ *When she first underwent IVF it was still a relatively new procedure.* 她第一次接受体外受精时，那还是一个比较新的方法。

★ **ivo·ry** /aɪvəri/ 1 N-UNCOUNT **Ivory** is a hard cream-colored substance that forms the tusks of elephants and some other animals. It is valuable and can be used for making carved ornaments. (象或其他一些动物的) 长牙 ❑ *...the international ban on the sale of ivory.* …禁止销售象牙的国际禁令。 2 COLOR **Ivory** is a creamy-white color. 乳白色(的) ❑ *...small ivory flowers.* …乳白色的小花。

▲ **ivy** /aɪvi/ (**ivies**) N-VAR **Ivy** is an evergreen plant that grows up walls or along the ground. 常春藤

Jj

J also **j** /dʒeɪ/ (**J's, j's**) N-VAR J is the tenth letter of the English alphabet. 英语字母表中第10个字母

jab /dʒæb/ (**jabs, jabbing, jabbed**) **1** V-T/V-I If you **jab** one thing into another, you push it there with a quick, sudden movement and with a lot of force. 猛推；猛按 ❑ *He saw her jab her thumb on a red button – a panic button.* 他看见她用拇指猛按了一个红色按钮——应急按钮。❑ *Stern jabbed at me with his glasses.* 斯特恩用他的眼镜捅了我一下。**2** N-COUNT A **jab** is a sudden, sharp punch. 刺戳；快速猛击 ❑ *He was simply too powerful for his opponent, rocking him with a steady supply of left jabs.* 他对于他的对手来说简直太强大了，用一连串的左刺拳打得对手摇摇晃晃。

▲**jack** /dʒæk/ (**jacks**) **1** N-COUNT A **jack** is a device for lifting a heavy object, such as a car, off the ground. 千斤顶 **2** N-COUNT A **jack** is a playing card whose value is between a ten and a queen. A jack is usually represented by a picture of a young man. (纸牌中的) J ❑ *...the jack of spades.* …黑桃J。

jack·et ♦◇◇ /dʒækɪt/ (**jackets**) **1** N-COUNT A **jacket** is a short coat with long sleeves. 短上衣；夹克 ❑ *...a black leather jacket.* …一件黑色皮夹克。**2** N-COUNT The **jacket** of a book is the paper cover that protects the book. (书的) 护封 [mainly AM] ❑ *A beautiful girl gazes from the jacket of this book.* 一位漂亮的女孩从这本书的护封里凝视过来。**3** → see also **dinner jacket, straitjacket**
→ see **clothing**

jack·pot /dʒækpɒt/ (**jackpots**) **1** N-COUNT A **jackpot** is the most valuable prize in a game or lottery, especially when the game involves increasing the value of the prize until someone wins it. (累加奖金的游戏或彩票中的) 头奖 ❑ *A nurse who gambled $5 in a slot machine walked away with the biggest ever jackpot of more than $5 million.* 一名护士在一个老虎机上赌了$5，捧走了有史以来的最高奖五百多万美元。**2** PHRASE If you **hit the jackpot**, you have a great success, for example by winning a lot of money or having a piece of good luck. 中头彩 [INFORMAL] ❑ *Tennis player Michael Stich hit the jackpot yesterday when he won $2 million.* 网球运动员迈克尔・施蒂希昨天获胜赢了2百万美元。
→ see **lottery**

Ja·cuz·zi /dʒəkuzi/ (**Jacuzzis**) N-COUNT A **Jacuzzi** is a large circular bath fitted with a device that makes the water move around. "极可意"漩水浴缸 [TRADEMARK]

▲**jade** /dʒeɪd/ **1** N-UNCOUNT **Jade** is a hard stone, usually green in color, that is used for making jewelry and ornaments. 玉 ❑ *The Burmese jade choker in the catalog was very beautiful.* 该目录中的缅甸玉贴颈项链非常漂亮。**2** COLOR Something that is **jade** or **jade green** is bright green in color. 翠绿色 ❑ *Amy had bought a soft, jade green cashmere jacket for Helen.* 埃米给海伦买了一件柔软的、翠绿色的山羊绒短上衣。

jad·ed /dʒeɪdɪd/ ADJ If you are **jaded**, you feel bored, tired, and not enthusiastic, because you have had too much of the same thing. 厌倦的 ❑ *We had both become jaded, disinterested, and disillusioned.* 我们两人都变得厌倦、了无兴趣且心灰意冷了。

jag·ged /dʒægɪd/ ADJ Something that is **jagged** has a rough, uneven shape or edge with lots of sharp points. 锯齿状的 ❑ *...jagged black cliffs.* …嶙峋的黑色峭壁。

jail ♦◇◇ /dʒeɪl/ (**jails, jailing, jailed**)

in BRIT, also use **gaol**

1 N-VAR A **jail** is a place where criminals are kept in order to punish them, or where people waiting to be tried are kept. 监狱 ❑ *Three prisoners escaped from a jail.* 3个囚犯从一个监狱逃跑了。**2** V-T If someone **is jailed**, they are put into jail. 监禁 [usu passive] ❑ *He was jailed for twenty years.* 他被监禁了20年。

jam /dʒæm/ (**jams, jamming, jammed**) **1** V-T If you **jam** something somewhere, you push or put it there roughly. 胡乱地塞 ❑ *Pete jammed his hands into his pockets.* 皮特把他的双手胡乱塞进了他的兜里。**2** V-T/V-I If something such as a part of a machine **jams**, or if something **jams** it, the part becomes fixed in position and is unable to move freely or work properly. 卡住 ❑ *The second time he fired his gun jammed.* 他开第二枪时，枪卡壳了。❑ *A rope jammed the boat's propeller.* 一条绳子卡住了船的推进器。**3** V-T If vehicles **jam** a road, there are so many of them that they cannot move. (车辆) 堵塞 ❑ *Hundreds of departing motorists jammed roads that had been closed during the height of the storm.* 数百名要开走的驾车者堵住了在风暴最猛烈时被关闭了的那些公路。● N-COUNT **Jam** is also a noun. 堵塞 ❑ *400 trucks may sit in a jam for ten hours waiting to cross the limited number of bridges.* 400 辆卡车可能会堵上10个小时才能通过有限的几座桥。● **jammed** ADJ 堵塞了的 ❑ *Nearby roads and the dirt track to the beach were jammed with cars.* 附近的公路和通往海滩的土路都堵满了汽车。**4** V-T/V-I If a lot of people **jam** a place, or **jam into** a place, they are pressed tightly together so that they can hardly move. 挤满 ❑ *Hundreds of people jammed the boardwalk to watch.* 上百人挤在木板道上观看。● **jammed** ADJ 挤满的 ❑ *The stadium was jammed and they had to turn away hundreds of disappointed fans.* 该体育场挤满了人，他们不得不谢绝上百名失望的球迷入场。**5** V-T To **jam** a radio or electronic signal means to interfere with it and prevent it from being received or heard clearly. 干扰 (无线电、电子信号等) ❑ *They will try to jam the transmissions electronically.* 他们会设法用电子手段干扰这些发射。● **jam·ming** N-UNCOUNT 干扰 ❑ *The plane is used for electronic jamming and radar detection.* 这架飞机用于进行电子干扰和雷达探测。**6** V-T If callers **are jamming** telephone lines, there are so many callers that the people answering the telephones find it difficult to deal with them all. 堵塞 (电话线路) ❑ *Hundreds of callers jammed the switchboard for more than an hour.* 上百个来电者堵塞了总机一个多小时。**7** N-MASS **Jam** is a sweet food consisting of pieces of fruit cooked with a large amount of sugar until it is thickened. It is usually spread on bread. 果酱 [mainly BRIT]

in AM, use **jelly**

→ see **traffic**

Word Partnership *jam* 的常用搭配：

N.	**traffic** jam **3**
	jam **jar**, **strawberry** jam **7**

Jan. **Jan.** is a written abbreviation for **January**. 1月

jan·gle /dʒæŋgᵊl/ (**jangles, jangling, jangled**) V-T/V-I When objects strike against each other and make a ringing noise, you can say that they **jangle** or **are jangled**. 使发出叮当声；发出叮当声 ❑ *Her bead necklaces and bracelets jangled as she walked.* 她的珠子项链和手镯在她走路时叮当作响。

jani·tor /dʒænɪtər/ (**janitors**) N-COUNT A **janitor** is a person whose job is to take care of a building. 看门人 [mainly AM] ❑ *Ed Roberts had been a school janitor for a long time.* 埃德・罗伯茨做学校的看门人已很久了。

Janu·ary ♦♦♦ /dʒænyuɛri/ (**Januaries**) N-VAR **January** is the first month of the year in the Western calendar. 1月 ❑ *We always have snow in January.* 我们这里1月份总会下雪。

jar /dʒɑr/ (**jars, jarring, jarred**) **1** N-COUNT A **jar** is a glass container with a lid that is used for storing food. (用于存放食物的) 玻璃罐 ❑ *...cucumbers in glass jars.* …玻璃罐里的黄瓜。**2** N-COUNT You can use **jar** to refer to a jar and its contents, or to the contents only. 一罐的量或物 ❑ *She opened up a jar of plums.* 她打开了一罐李子。**3** V-T/V-I If something **jars**, or **jars** you, you find it unpleasant, disturbing, or shocking. 令人不快；产生不快影响 ❑ *...televised congressional hearings that jarred the nation's faith in the presidency.* …令国民对总统执政产生动摇的电视国会听证会。● **jar·ring** ADJ 令人不快的 ❑ *In the context of this chapter, Dore's comments strike a jarring note.* 在本章的语境中，多尔的评论显得刺耳。**4** V-T/V-I If an object **jars**, or if something **jars** it, the object moves with a fairly hard shaking movement. 震动 ❑ *The ship jarred a little.* 船轻微震了一下。❑ *The sudden movement jarred the box and it fell off the table.* 这突然一动震动了那个箱子，然后它从桌上掉了下去。
→ see **can**

▲**jar·gon** /dʒɑrgən/ N-UNCOUNT You use **jargon** to refer to words and expressions that are used in special or technical ways by particular groups of people, often making the language difficult to understand. 行话 ❑ *The manual is full of the jargon and slang of self-improvement courses.* 该手册中满是自我完善课程的行话和俚语。

jaun·ty /dʒɔnti/ (**jauntier, jauntiest**) ADJ If you describe someone or something as **jaunty**, you mean that they are full of confidence and energy. 充满信心和活力的 ❑ *...a jaunty little man.* …一个充满信心和活力的小个子男人。 ●**jaun·ti·ly** /dʒɔntɪli/ ADV 充满信心和活力地 ❑ *He walked jauntily into the café.* 他昂首阔步地走进了咖啡馆。

Java /dʒɑvə/ N-UNCOUNT **Java** is a computer programming language. It is used especially in creating websites. **Java**语言 [TRADEMARK] ❑ *...applications written in Java.* …用**Java**语言编写的应用软件。

jave·lin /dʒævlɪn/ (**javelins**) **1** N-COUNT A **javelin** is a long spear that is used in sports competitions. Competitors try to throw the javelin as far as possible. 标枪 **2** N-SING You can refer to the competition in which the javelin is thrown as **the javelin**. 标枪比赛 ❑ *...Steve Backley who won the javelin.* …赢了标枪比赛的史蒂夫・巴克里。

jaw /dʒɔ/ (**jaws**) **1** N-COUNT Your **jaw** is the lower part of your face below your mouth. The movement of your jaw is sometimes considered to express a particular emotion. For example, if your **jaw drops**, you are very surprised. 下颌 ❑ *He thought for a moment, stroking his well-defined jaw.* 他抚摸着他棱角分明的下巴想了一会儿。 **2** N-COUNT A person's or animal's **jaws** are the two bones in their head that their teeth are attached to. 颌骨 ❑ *...a forest rodent with powerful jaws.* …一种长着强劲有力的颌骨的森林啮齿动物。 **3** N-PLURAL If you talk about the **jaws of** something unpleasant such as death or hell, you are referring to a dangerous or unpleasant situation. (险恶或令人不愉快的) 关口 ❑ *A family dog rescued a newborn boy from the jaws of death.* 一只家犬把一个男婴从鬼门关救了出来。

jaw-dropping ADJ Something that is **jaw-dropping** is extremely surprising, impressive, or shocking. 令人目瞪口呆的 [INFORMAL, JOURNALISM] ❑ *One insider who has seen the report said it was pretty jaw-dropping stuff.* 一位看过那份报告的内部人士说那是相当触目惊心的。

jazz ♦◇◇ /dʒæz/ N-UNCOUNT **Jazz** is a style of music that was invented by African American musicians in the early part of the twentieth century. Jazz music has very strong rhythms and often involves improvisation. 爵士乐 ❑ *The club has live jazz on Sundays.* 该俱乐部每个星期天都有现场爵士乐演奏。
→ see **genre**

jeal·ous /dʒɛləs/ **1** ADJ If someone is **jealous**, they feel angry or bitter because they think that another person is trying to take a lover or friend, or a possession, away from them. 好猜忌的 ❑ *She got insanely jealous and there was a terrible fight.* 她变得过分地猜忌，接着是一场激烈的打斗。 ●**jeal·ous·ly** ADV 好猜忌地 [ADV with v] ❑ *The formula is jealously guarded.* 对该配方戒备森严。 **2** ADJ If you are **jealous of** another person's possessions or qualities, you feel angry or bitter because you do not have them. 嫉妒的 ❑ *She was jealous of his wealth.* 她嫉妒他的富有。 ●**jeal·ous·ly** ADV 嫉妒地 [ADV after v] ❑ *Gloria eyed them jealously.* 格洛丽亚当时嫉妒地看着他们。

★**jeal·ousy** /dʒɛləsi/ **1** N-UNCOUNT **Jealousy** is the feeling of anger or bitterness that someone has when they think that another person is trying to take a lover or friend, or a possession, away from them. 猜忌 ❑ *At first his jealousy only showed in small ways – he didn't mind me talking to other guys.* 开始时，他的猜忌只是小小地表现出来——他并不介意我和其他男孩子说话。 **2** N-UNCOUNT **Jealousy** is the feeling of anger or bitterness that someone has when they wish that they could have the qualities or possessions that another person has. 嫉妒 ❑ *Her beauty causes envy and jealousy.* 她的美丽招人妒羡。

jeans /dʒinz/ N-PLURAL **Jeans** are casual pants that are usually made of strong cotton cloth called denim. 牛仔裤 [also "a pair of" N] ❑ *...a young man in jeans and a worn T-shirt.* …一个穿着牛仔裤和破旧T恤衫的年轻人。
→ see **clothing**

▲**Jeep** /dʒip/ (**Jeeps**) N-COUNT A **Jeep** is a type of car that can travel over rough ground. 吉普车 [TRADEMARK] ❑ *...a U.S. Army Jeep.* …一辆美军吉普车。

jeer /dʒɪər/ (**jeers, jeering, jeered**) **1** V-T/V-I To **jeer at** someone means to say or shout rude and insulting things to them to show that you do not like or respect them. 嘲弄 ❑ *Marchers jeered at white passers-by, but there was no violence, nor any arrests.* 游行者们嘲弄路过的白人们，但并没有发生暴力事件，也没人被逮捕。 ❑ *Demonstrators jeered the mayor as he arrived for a week-long visit.* 示威者们在市长到达进行为期一周访问的时候嘲弄了他。 ●**jeer·ing** N-UNCOUNT 嘲弄 ❑ *There was constant jeering and interruption from the floor.* 议员席上不时有嘲笑和打岔。 **2** N-COUNT **Jeers** are rude and insulting things that people shout to show they do not like or respect someone. 奚落人的话 ❑ *...the heckling and jeers of his audience.* …观众对他的那些诘问和奚落。

Jell-O N-UNCOUNT **Jell-O** is a transparent, usually colored food that is eaten as a dessert. It is made from gelatin, fruit juice, and sugar. 果冻 [AM, TRADEMARK]
in BRIT, use **jelly**
❑ *...a bowl of Jell-O.* …一碗果冻。
→ see **dessert**

★**jel·ly** /dʒɛli/ (**jellies**) **1** N-MASS **Jelly** is a sweet food that is made by cooking fruit or fruit juice with a large amount of sugar until it is thickened. It is usually spread on bread. 果酱 ❑ *I had two peanut butter and jelly sandwiches.* 我吃了两个花生酱果酱三明治。 **2** N-VAR **Jelly** is the same as **Jell-o**. 果冻 [BRIT]

★**jeop·ard·ise** /dʒɛpərdaɪz/ [BRIT] → see **jeopardize**

★**jeop·ard·ize** /dʒɛpərdaɪz/ (**jeopardizes, jeopardizing, jeopardized**)
in BRIT, also use **jeopardise**
V-T To **jeopardize** a situation or activity means to do something that may destroy it or cause it to fail. 损害；危及 ❑ *He has jeopardized his future career.* 他损害了他的前程。

▲**jeop·ardy** /dʒɛpərdi/ PHRASE If someone or something is **in jeopardy**, they are in a dangerous situation where they might fail, be lost, or be destroyed. 处于险境 ❑ *A series of setbacks have put the whole project in jeopardy.* 一系列的挫折已经使整个项目陷入险境。

★**jerk** /dʒɜrk/ (**jerks, jerking, jerked**) **1** V-T/V-I If you **jerk** something or someone in a particular direction, or they **jerk** in a particular direction, they move a short distance very suddenly and quickly. 使…猝然一动；猝然一动 ❑ *Mr. Griffin jerked forward in his chair.* 格里芬先生在椅子上猛地向前一动。 ❑ *"This is Brady Coyne," said Sam, jerking his head in my direction.* "这是布雷迪・科因"，萨姆说，他的头朝我这边甩了一下。 ●N-COUNT **Jerk** is also a noun. 猝然一动 ❑ *He indicated the bedroom with a jerk of his head.* 他用头的猝然一动示意了卧室的方向。 **2** N-COUNT If you call someone a **jerk**, you are insulting them because you think they are stupid or you do not like them. 蠢货 [INFORMAL, OFFENSIVE, DISAPPROVAL] ❑ *The guy is such a jerk! He only cares about himself.* 这家伙真是个蠢货！他只关心他自己。

jerky /dʒɜrki/ (**jerkier, jerkiest**) ADJ **Jerky** movements are very sudden and quick, and do not flow smoothly. 急促而不流畅的 ❑ *Mr. Griffin made a jerky gesture.* 格里芬先生打了个急促而不连贯的手势。 ●**jerki·ly** /dʒɜrkɪli/ ADV 急促而不流畅地 [ADV with v] ❑ *Using his cane heavily, he moved jerkily toward the car.* 费劲地拄着拐杖，他匆忙磕绊着走向那辆车。

jer·sey ♦◇◇ /dʒɜrzi/ (**jerseys**) **1** N-COUNT A **jersey** is a knitted piece of clothing that covers the upper part of your body and your arms and does not open at the front. Jerseys are usually worn over a shirt or blouse. 针织套衫 [OLD-FASHIONED] ❑ *...a sports jersey.* …一件运动针织套衫。 **2** N-VAR **Jersey** is a knitted, slightly stretchy fabric used especially to make women's clothing. 弹性针织布料 ❑ *Sheila had come to dinner in a black jersey top.* 希拉穿着件黑色针织紧身上衣来吃饭了。 **3** N-VAR A **jersey** is a shirt that you wear when playing football, soccer, or some other sports. 运动衣

Jesus ♦◇◇ /dʒizəs/ **1** N-PROPER **Jesus** or **Jesus Christ** is the name of the man who Christians believe was the son of God, and whose teachings are the basis of Christianity. 耶稣 **2** EXCLAM **Jesus** is used by some people to express surprise, shock, or annoyance. This use could cause offense. 天哪 (用以表示惊奇、震惊或恼怒) [FEELINGS]

jet ♦◇◇ /dʒɛt/ (**jets, jetting, jetted**) **1** N-COUNT A **jet** is an aircraft that is powered by jet engines. 喷气式飞机 [also "by" N] ❑ *Her private jet landed in the republic on the way to Japan.* 她的私人喷气式飞机在去日本的途中在该共和国降落。 ❑ *He had arrived from Key West by jet.* 他已乘喷气式飞机从基韦斯特来了。 **2** V-I If you **jet** somewhere, you travel there in a fast plane. 乘喷气式飞机前往 ❑ *The president will be jetting off to Germany today.* 总统今天要乘喷气式飞机去德国。 **3** N-COUNT A **jet** of liquid or gas is a strong, fast, thin stream of it. 喷射流 ❑ *A jet of water poured through the windows.* 一股水柱从窗户喷了过来。
→ see **fly**

j

jet en·gine (jet engines) N-COUNT A **jet engine** is an engine in which hot air and gases are forced out at the back. Jet engines are used for most modern aircraft. 喷气发动机
→ see **flight**

jet lag
in BRIT, also use **jetlag**
N-UNCOUNT If you are suffering from **jet lag**, you feel tired and slightly confused after a long trip by airplane, especially after traveling between places that have a time difference of several hours. 飞行时差反应 ❑ *...the best way to avoid jet lag.* …避免时差反应的最好方法。

Jet Ski (Jet Skis) also **jet ski, jet-ski** N-COUNT A **Jet Ski** is a small machine like a motorcycle that is powered by a jet engine and can travel on the surface of water. 喷气式滑艇 [TRADEMARK] ❑ *I watched as they got on the jet ski.* 我看着他们坐上了喷气式滑艇。● **jet ski·ing** N-UNCOUNT 喷气式滑水 ❑ *I like jet skiing, being out on boats, doing stuff like that.* 我喜欢喷气式滑水、坐船出游等诸如此类的活动。

jet·ti·son /dʒɛtɪsən, -zən/ (jettisons, jettisoning, jettisoned) **1** V-T If you **jettison** something, such as an idea or a plan, you deliberately reject it or decide not to use it. 拒绝接受 ❑ *The governor seems to have jettisoned the plan.* 州长似乎已经拒绝了这个计划。 **2** V-T To **jettison** something that is not needed or wanted means to throw it away or get rid of it. 丢弃；处理掉 ❑ *The crew jettisoned excess fuel and made an emergency landing.* 机组人员丢弃了多余的燃料，紧急着陆。

jet·ty /dʒɛti/ (jetties) **1** N-COUNT A **jetty** is a wide stone wall or wooden platform where boats stop to let people get on or off, or to load or unload goods. 码头 **2** N-COUNT A **jetty** is a structure that is built at the edge of a shore in order to protect a harbor or to reduce the force of currents and waves. 防波堤

J

Jew ♦◇◇ /dʒu/ (Jews) N-COUNT A **Jew** is a person who believes in and practices the religion of Judaism. 犹太教徒

jew·el /dʒuəl/ (jewels) **1** N-COUNT A **jewel** is a precious stone used to decorate valuable things that you wear, such as rings or necklaces. 宝石 ❑ *...a golden box containing precious jewels.* …一个装着贵重宝石的金盒子。 **2** N-COUNT If you describe something or someone as a **jewel**, you mean that they are better, more beautiful, or more special than other similar things or than other people. 宝贝 (指宝贵的物或难能可贵的人) ❑ *...a small jewel of a theater.* …剧场的一个小宝贝。 **3** PHRASE If you refer to an achievement or thing as the **jewel in** someone's **crown**, you mean that it is considered to be their greatest achievement or the thing they can be most proud of. 最耀眼的成就；最得意之物 ❑ *His achievement is astonishing and this book is the jewel in his crown.* 他成就斐然，这本书是他的最得意之作。

jew·el·er /dʒuələr/ (jewelers)
in BRIT, use **jeweller**
1 N-COUNT A **jeweler** is a person who makes, sells, and repairs jewelry and watches. 珠宝钟表商 **2** N-COUNT A **jeweler** is a store where jewelry and watches are made, sold, and repaired. 珠宝钟表店 ❑ *...a jeweler on Fifth Avenue that sells Rolex.* …第五大道上卖劳力士表的一家珠宝钟表店。
→ see **diamond**

jew·el·ler /dʒuːələr/ [BRIT] → see **jeweler**

jew·el·lery /dʒuːəlri/ [BRIT] → see **jewelry**

▲**jew·el·ry** /dʒuəlri/
in BRIT, use **jewellery**
N-UNCOUNT **Jewelry** is ornaments that people wear, such as rings, bracelets, and necklaces. It is often made of a valuable metal such as gold, and sometimes decorated with precious stones. 珠宝首饰 ❑ *Discover a full selection of fine watches and jewelry at these two Upper Manhattan stores.* 在这两家上曼哈顿区的商店里找到全套精品手表和珠宝。
→ see Picture Dictionary: **jewelry**

Jew·ish ♦◇◇ /dʒuɪʃ/ ADJ **Jewish** means belonging or relating to the religion of Judaism, or to Jews as an ethnic group. 犹太教的；犹太人的 ❑ *...the Jewish festival of Passover.* …犹太逾越节。
→ see **religion**

jibe /dʒaɪb/ (jibes, jibing, jibed)
The spelling **gibe** is also used for meanings **1** and **2**.
1 N-COUNT A **jibe** is a rude or insulting remark about someone that is intended to make them look foolish. 嘲讽 ❑ *...a cheap jibe about his loss of hair.* …一个对他脱发的粗俗嘲讽。 **2** V-T To **jibe** means to say something rude or insulting that is intended to make another person look foolish. 嘲讽 [WRITTEN] ❑ *"No doubt he'll give me the chance to fight him again," he jibed.* "毫无疑问，他会给我机会与他再打一次。" 他嘲讽道。 **3** V-RECIP If numbers, statements, or events **jibe**, they are exactly the same as each other or they are consistent with each other. 相一致 [mainly AM] ❑ *The numbers don't jibe.* 这些数字不一致。

jig /dʒɪg/ (jigs, jigging, jigged) **1** N-COUNT A **jig** is a lively dance. 吉格舞 ❑ *She danced an Irish jig.* 她跳了一曲爱尔兰吉格舞。 **2** V-I To **jig** means to dance or move energetically, especially bouncing up and down. 轻快地跳舞；蹦跳 ❑ *His son, Louis, laughed and jigged around to the music.* 他儿子路易斯和着音乐又笑又蹦。

★**jig·saw** /dʒɪgsɔ/ (jigsaws) **1** N-COUNT A **jigsaw** or **jigsaw puzzle** is a picture on cardboard or wood that has been cut up into odd shapes. You have to make the picture again by putting the pieces together correctly. 拼图游戏 ❑ *Both her children did jigsaw puzzles easily.* 她的两个孩子玩拼图游戏都很轻松。 **2** N-COUNT You can describe a complicated situation as a **jigsaw**. 错综复杂的形势 ❑ *...the jigsaw of high-level diplomacy.* …高层外交的复杂形势。

jin·gle /dʒɪŋgᵊl/ (jingles, jingling, jingled) **1** V-T/V-I When something **jingles** or when you **jingle** it, it makes a gentle ringing noise, like small bells. 使发出丁零声；发出丁零声 ❑ *Brian put his hands in his pockets and jingled some change.* 布赖恩把双手伸进口袋，碰得一些硬币丁零作响。● N-SING **Jingle** is also a noun. 丁零声 ❑ *...the jingle of money in a man's pocket.* …一个男人口袋里硬币的丁零声。 **2** N-COUNT A **jingle** is a short, simple tune, often with words, that is used to advertise a product or program on radio or television. (广播、电视中用于广告的) 短歌曲 ❑ *...advertising jingles.* …广告短歌。

jit·ters /dʒɪtərz/ N-PLURAL If you have the **jitters**, you feel extremely nervous, for example because you have to do something important or because you are expecting important news. 紧张不安 [INFORMAL] ❑ *This only increased market jitters.* 这只是加重了市场的恐慌。

jit·tery /dʒɪtəri/ ADJ If someone is **jittery**, they feel nervous or are behaving nervously. 紧张不安的 [INFORMAL] ❑ *International investors have become jittery about the country's economy.* 国际投资者们已对该国的经济惴惴不安了。

job ♦♦♦ /dʒɒb/ (**jobs**) 1 N-COUNT A **job** is the work that someone does to earn money. 工作 ❑ *Once I'm in Miami I can get a job.* 一旦我到了迈阿密就能找到工作。 ❑ *Thousands have lost their jobs.* 数千人都丢了工作。 2 N-COUNT A **job** is a particular task. 任务 ❑ *He said he hoped that the job of putting together a coalition wouldn't take too much time.* 他说他希望结成联盟这项任务不会花太长时间。 3 N-COUNT The **job** of a particular person or thing is their duty or function. 职责 ❑ *Their main job is to preserve health rather than treat illness.* 他们的主要职责是保健而不是治病。 ❑ *His first job will be to try and get talks going between the two sides.* 他的首要职责将是设法让双方的谈话进行下去。 4 N-SING If you say that someone is doing a good **job**, you mean that they are doing something well. 活儿 ❑ *We could do a far better job of managing it than they have.* 我们会比他们管理得好得多。 5 N-SING If you say that you have **a job** doing something, you are emphasizing how difficult it is. 难做的事情 [EMPHASIS] ❑ *He may have a hard job selling that argument to investors.* 他要让投资者们接受那一观点可能是件难事。 6 PHRASE If someone is **on the job**, they are actually doing a particular job or task. 在职；在岗 ❑ *The top pay scale after five years on the job would reach $5.00 an hour.* 从事这一工作 5 年后最高薪金等级可达每小时$5。 7 **the job in hand → see hand**

Thesaurus *job* 另参见：
N. employment, occupation, profession, vocation, work 1
assignment, duty, obligation, task 2 3

job de·scrip·tion (**job descriptions**) N-COUNT A **job description** is a written account of all the duties and responsibilities involved in a particular job or position. 岗位职责说明 ❑ *...the job description for the position of division general manager.* …部门总经理职位的职责说明。

job·less /dʒɒblɪs/ ADJ Someone who is **jobless** does not have a job, although they would like one. 失业的 ❑ *He has turned his back on millions of jobless Americans.* 他已经不管上百万失业的美国人了。 ● N-PLURAL **The jobless** are people who are jobless. 失业者 ❑ *They joined the ranks of the jobless.* 他们加入了失业大军。

job share (**job shares, job sharing, job shared**) V-I If two people **job share**, they share the same job by working part-time, for example, one person working in the mornings and the other in the afternoons. 共做一份工作 ❑ *They both want to job share.* 他们两人都想共做一份工作。

▲**jock·ey** /dʒɒki/ (**jockeys, jockeying, jockeyed**) 1 N-COUNT A **jockey** is someone who rides a horse in a race. 赛马骑手 2 PHRASE If you say that someone **is jockeying for** something, you mean that they are using whatever methods they can in order to get it or do it before their competitors can get it or do it. 不择手段地谋取 ❑ *The rival political parties are already jockeying for power.* 各反对党已经在不择手段地谋取权势了。 ● PHRASE If someone **is jockeying for position**, they are using whatever methods they can in order to get into a better position than their rivals. 不择手段地谋取有利地位

★**jog** /dʒɒg/ (**jogs, jogging, jogged**) 1 V-I If you **jog**, you run slowly, often as a form of exercise. 慢跑 ❑ *I got up early the next morning to jog.* 我次日清晨早起去慢跑了。 ● N-COUNT **Jog** is also a noun. 慢跑 ❑ *He went for another early morning jog.* 他又去晨跑了。 ● **jog·ging** N-UNCOUNT 慢跑 ❑ *It isn't the walking and jogging that got his weight down.* 不是散步和慢跑使他体重下降了。 2 V-T If you **jog** something, you push or bump it slightly so that it moves. 轻推；轻撞 ❑ *Avoid jogging the camera.* 不要碰撞像机。 3 PHRASE If something or someone **jogs** your **memory**, they cause you to suddenly remember something that you had forgotten. 唤起某人的记忆 ❑ *Police have planned a reconstruction of the crime tomorrow in the hope that this will jog the memory of passersby.* 警方已计划明天再现犯罪过程，希望以此唤起过路人的记忆。

jog·ger /dʒɒgər/ (**joggers**) N-COUNT A **jogger** is a person who jogs as a form of exercise. 慢跑者

join ♦♦♦ /dʒɔɪn/ (**joins, joining, joined**) 1 V-T If one person **joins** another, they move or go to the same place, for example, so that both of them can do something together. 和…一道 ❑ *His wife and children moved to join him in their new home.* 他的妻子和孩子们搬来和他一起住在新家。 2 V-T If you **join** an organization, you become a member of it or start work as an employee of it. 参加（组织）❑ *He joined the Army five years ago.* 他 5 年前参了军。 3 V-T/V-I If you **join** an activity that other people are doing, you take part in it or become involved with it. 参加（活动）❑ *The United States joined the war in April 1917.* 美国于1917年4月参战。 ❑ *The pastor requested the women present to join him in prayer.* 该牧师请在场的妇女和他一起祈祷。 ❑ *Nine Republicans joined in supporting the measure.* 9 名共和党人加入支持这项举措。 4 V-T If you **join** a line, you stand at the end of it so that you are part of it. 加入（队列）❑ *It is advised that fans seeking autographs join the line before practice starts.* 建议寻求亲笔签名的影迷们在活动开始前排好队。 5 V-T To **join** two things means to attach or fasten them together. 连接；接合 ❑ *The opened link is used to join the two ends of the chain.* 这个开口环是用来连接链条两头的。 ❑ *...the conjunctiva, the skin which joins the eye to the lid.* …结膜，连接眼球和眼睑的外膜。 6 V-T If something such as a line or path **joins** two things, it connects them. （线、路等）连接（两物）❑ *...a global highway of cables joining all the continents together.* …一条连接各大洲的全球电缆主干线路。 7 V-RECIP If two roads or rivers **join**, they meet or come together at a particular point. 汇合 ❑ *Do you know the highway to Tulsa? The airport road joins it.* 你知道通往塔尔萨的公路吗？机场公路和它相连。 8 **join forces → see force**

▸ **join in** PHRASAL VERB If you **join in** an activity, you take part in it or become involved in it. 参加（活动）❑ *I hope everyone will join in the fun.* 我希望每个人都能参与这个娱乐活动。

▸ **join up** 1 PHRASAL VERB If someone **joins up**, they become a member of the army, the navy, or the air force. 参军 ❑ *When hostilities broke out he joined up.* 战争爆发后，他参了军。 2 PHRASAL VERB If one person or organization **joins up with** another, they start doing something together. 与…联手 ❑ *Dwight decided to withdraw from the committee and join up with the opposition.* 德怀特决定退出该委员会并和反对派联手。

joint ♦♦◇ /dʒɔɪnt/ (**joints**) 1 ADJ **Joint** means shared by or belonging to two or more people. 联合的；共同的 [ADJ n] ❑ *She and Frank had never gotten around to opening a joint account.* 她和弗兰克还没能抽出时间开个联名账户。 ● **joint·ly** ADV 联合地；共同地 [ADV with v] ❑ *The Port Authority is an agency jointly run by New York and New Jersey.* 该港务局是纽约和新泽西共管的机构。 2 N-COUNT A **joint** is a part of your body such as your elbow or knee where two bones meet and are able to move together. 关节 ❑ *Her joints ache if she exercises.* 她的关节一运动就疼。 3 N-COUNT A **joint** is the place where two things are fastened or joined together. 连接处 ❑ *...the joint between the inner and outer panels.* …内外嵌板的连接处。 4 N-COUNT You can refer to a cheap place where people go for some form of entertainment as a **joint**. 低档娱乐场所 [INFORMAL] ❑ *They had come to the world's most famous pick-up joint.* 他们来到了世界上最有名的声色场所。 5 N-COUNT A **joint** is a cigarette that contains cannabis or marijuana. 大麻烟卷 [INFORMAL] ❑ *He's smoking a joint.* 他在吸大麻烟。 6 PHRASE If something puts someone's **nose out of joint**, it upsets or offends them because it makes them feel less important or less valued. 使某人价值被贬低 [INFORMAL] ❑ *Barry had his nose put out of joint by Lucy's aloof sophistication.* 露西的冷漠世故让巴里显得很不重要。

Word Partnership *joint* 的常用搭配：
N. joint **account**, joint **agreement**, joint **effort**, joint **resolution**, joint **statement** 1

joint-stock com·pany (**joint-stock companies**) N-COUNT A **joint-stock company** is a company that is owned by the people who have bought shares in that company and who are responsible for its debts. 股份公司 [BUSINESS]

joke ♦◇◇ /dʒoʊk/ (**jokes, joking, joked**) 1 N-COUNT A **joke** is something that is said or done to make you laugh, such as a funny story. 笑话；玩笑 ❑ *No one told worse jokes than Claus.* 没人比克劳斯讲笑话讲得更糟。 2 V-I If you **joke**, you tell funny stories or say amusing things. 说笑话；开玩笑 ❑ *She would joke about her appearance.* 她会拿她的长相开玩笑。 ❑ *Luanne was laughing and joking with Tritt.* 露安妮边笑边和特里特开着玩笑。 3 N-COUNT A **joke** is something untrue that you tell another person in order to amuse yourself. 说着玩的把戏 ❑ *It was probably just a joke to them, but it wasn't* *funny to me.* 这对他们来说可能只是说着玩，但对我来说一点也不好笑。 **4** V-I If you **joke**, you tell someone something that is not true in order to amuse yourself. 说着玩 ❑ *Don't get defensive, Charlie. I was only joking.* 不要有戒心，查理。我只是说着玩呢。 **5** N-SING If you say that something or someone is **a joke**, you think they are ridiculous and do not deserve respect. 可笑的人或事 [INFORMAL, DISAPPROVAL] ❑ *It's ridiculous, it's pathetic, it's a joke.* 这真是荒唐、可悲、可笑。 **6** PHRASE If you **make a joke of** something, you laugh at it even though it is in fact serious or sad. 拿…当玩笑 ❑ *I wish I had your courage, Michael, to make a joke of it like that.* 我真希望能有你那般勇气，迈克尔，那样拿它当玩笑。 **7** PHRASE If you describe a situation as **no joke**, you are emphasizing that it is very difficult or unpleasant. 不是闹着玩的 [INFORMAL, EMPHASIS] ❑ *Eight hours on a bus is no joke, is it.* 坐 8 个小时的公交车可不是闹着玩儿的，对吧。 **8** PHRASE If you say that **the joke is on** a particular person, you mean that they have been made to look very foolish by something. 玩笑开在某人身上 ❑ *"For once," he said, "the joke's on me. And it's not very funny."* "只一次，"他说，"玩笑开在了我身上。而且那并不是很有趣。" **9** CONVENTION You say **you're joking** or **you must be joking** to someone when they have just told you something that is so surprising or unreasonable that you find it difficult to believe. 你是在 / 你一定是在 / 你肯定是在开玩笑 [SPOKEN, FEELINGS] ❑ *You're joking. Are you serious?* 你在开玩笑吧。你是认真的吗？

Word Partnership *joke* 的常用搭配：

- ADJ. **bad** joke, **cruel** joke, **dirty** joke, **funny** joke, **good** joke, **old** joke, **practical** joke **1**
- V. **crack** a joke, **laugh at** a joke, **make** a joke, **play** a joke, **tell** a joke **1**
  make a joke **of** *something* **6**

jok·er /dʒoʊkər/ (**jokers**) **1** N-COUNT Someone who is a **joker** likes making jokes or doing amusing things. 爱开玩笑；逗趣的人 ❑ *He is, by nature, a joker, a witty man with a sense of fun.* 他天生是个爱开玩笑的人，是个有幽默感的风趣男人。 **2** N-COUNT The **joker** in a deck of playing cards is the card that does not belong to any of the four suits. (纸牌中不属于任何一套花色的) 百搭牌 **3** N-COUNT You can call someone a **joker** if you think they are behaving in a stupid or dangerous way. 家伙 [INFORMAL, DISAPPROVAL] ❑ *Keep your eye on these jokers, you never know what they will come up with.* 盯住这些家伙，你永远不知道他们会想出什么来。

▲**jol·ly** /dʒɒli/ (**jollier, jolliest**) **1** ADJ Someone who is **jolly** is happy and cheerful in their appearance or behavior. 快乐的 ❑ *She was a jolly, kindhearted woman.* 她是一个开朗、善良的女人。 **2** ADJ A **jolly** event is lively and enjoyable. 令人愉快的 ❑ *She had a very jolly time in Korea.* 她在韩国过得很愉快。

▲**jolt** /dʒoʊlt/ (**jolts, jolting, jolted**) **1** V-T/V-I If something **jolts** or if something **jolts** it, it moves suddenly and quite violently. 使颠簸；颠簸 ❑ *The wagon jolted again.* 马车又颠簸起来。 ❑ *The train jolted into motion.* 火车颠了一下开动了。 ● N-COUNT **Jolt** is also a noun. 颠簸 ❑ *We were worried that one tiny jolt could worsen her injuries.* 我们担心一次轻微的颠簸都可能加剧她的伤情。 **2** V-T If something **jolts** someone, it gives them an unpleasant surprise or shock. 震惊 ❑ *A stinging slap across the face jolted her.* 火辣辣的一记巴掌使她惊呆了。 ● N-COUNT **Jolt** is also a noun. 震惊 ❑ *Then my husband left me. It gave me the jolt I needed.* 后来我的丈夫离开了我。这给了我那个我需要的震动。

jos·tle /dʒɒsəl/ (**jostles, jostling, jostled**) **1** V-T/V-I If people **jostle** you, they bump against you or push you in a way that annoys you, usually because you are in a crowd and they are trying to get past you. 推搡；推挤 ❑ *You get 2,000 people jostling each other and bumping into furniture.* 你令2000人互相推搡并撞倒家具。 ❑ *We spent an hour jostling with the crowds as we did our shopping.* 我们花了一个小时在人群中挤来挤去买东西。 **2** V-I If people or things **are jostling for** something such as attention or a reward, they are competing with other people or things in order to get it. 争夺 ❑ *...the contenders who have been jostling for the top job.* …一直在争夺最高职位的竞争者们。

jot /dʒɒt/ (**jots, jotting, jotted**) V-T If you **jot** something short such as an address somewhere, you write it down so that you will remember it. 简单记下 ❑ *Could you just jot his name on there?* 你能就把他的名字简单记在那儿吗？ ● PHRASAL VERB **Jot down** means the same as **jot**. 简单记下 ❑ *Christine uses her journal to jot down ideas and lists of things to do.* 克里斯蒂娜用她的日志簿简单记下自己的想法和要做的事情清单。

jour·nal ♦♦◊ /dʒɜrnəl/ (**journals**) **1** N-COUNT A **journal** is a magazine, especially one that deals with a specialized subject. 期刊 ❑ *All our results are published in scientific journals.* 我们所有的结果都发表在科学刊物上。 **2** N-COUNT A **journal** is a daily or weekly newspaper. The word journal is often used in the name of the paper. 日报；周报 ❑ *...ads in The New York Times, the Wall Street Journal and other publications.* …纽约时报、华尔街日报和其他出版物上的广告。 **3** N-COUNT A **journal** is an account that you write of your daily activities. 日记 ❑ *Sara confided to her journal.* 萨拉在日记中倾吐心事。

jour·nal·ism /dʒɜrnəlɪzəm/ N-UNCOUNT **Journalism** is the job of collecting news and writing about it for newspapers, magazines, television, or radio. 新闻工作 ❑ *He began a career in journalism, working for the Rocky Mountain News.* 他开始从事新闻事业，供职于落基山新闻报。

jour·nal·ist ♦♦◊ /dʒɜrnəlɪst/ (**journalists**) N-COUNT A **journalist** is a person whose job is to collect news and write about it for newspapers, magazines, television, or radio. 新闻工作者
→ see **newspaper**

jour·ney ♦◊◊ /dʒɜrni/ (**journeys, journeying, journeyed**) **1** N-COUNT When you make a **journey**, you travel from one place to another. 旅行 [FORMAL] ❑ *There is an express service from Paris that completes the journey to Bordeaux in under 4 hours.* 有一趟从巴黎开出的快车，到波尔多全程不到4小时。

> The noun **travel** is used to talk about the general activity of traveling. It is either uncount or plural. You cannot say "a travel," you would use the word **trip** or **journey** instead.
> ❑ *First-class rail travel to Paris or Brussels is included... We were going to go on a trip to Florida together.*

2 N-COUNT You can refer to a person's experience of changing or developing from one state of mind to another as a **journey**. (心路) 历程 ❑ *My films try to describe a journey of discovery, both for myself and the viewer.* 我的影片力图为我自己和观众描述一段自我发现的心路历程。 **3** V-I If you **journey** somewhere, you travel there. 旅行 [FORMAL] ❑ *In February 1935, Naomi journeyed to the United States for the first time.* 1935年2月，内奥米第一次踏入美国。

Thesaurus *journey* 另参见：

- N. adventure, trip, visit, voyage **1**
- V. cruise, fly, go, travel **3**

Word Partnership *journey* 的常用搭配：

- V. **begin a** journey, **complete a** journey, **make a** journey **1** **2**
- N. **end of a** journey, **first/last leg of a** journey **1** **2**
  journey **of discovery** **2**

joy ♦◊◊ /dʒɔɪ/ (**joys**) **1** N-UNCOUNT **Joy** is a feeling of great happiness. 高兴 ❑ *Salter shouted with joy.* 索尔特高兴地叫起来。 **2** N-COUNT A **joy** is something or someone that makes you feel happy or gives you great pleasure. 使人高兴的事；使人高兴的人 ❑ *Spending evenings outside is one of the joys of summer.* 在户外消磨晚间时光是夏天的乐事之一。 **3** PHRASE If you say that someone is **jumping for joy**, you mean that they are very pleased or happy about something. 兴高采烈 ❑ *He jumped for joy on being told the news.* 听到这个消息他兴高采烈。
→ see **emotion**

Word Partnership *joy* 的常用搭配：

- V. **bring** *someone* joy, **cry/weep for** joy, **feel** joy **1**
- ADJ. **filled with** joy, **great** joy, **pure** joy, **sheer** joy **1**
- N. **tears of** joy **1**

joy·ful /dʒɔɪfəl/ **1** ADJ Something that is **joyful** causes happiness and pleasure. 令人喜悦的 [FORMAL] ❑ *A wedding is a joyful celebration of love.* 婚礼是令人喜悦的爱情庆典。 **2** ADJ Someone who is **joyful** is extremely happy. 非常快乐的 [FORMAL] ❑ *We're a very joyful people; we're very musical people and we love music.* 我们是非常快乐的民族；我们是音乐之族；我们热爱音乐。 ● **joy·ful·ly** ADV 非常快乐地 ❑ *They greeted him joyfully.* 他们非常快乐地跟他打了招呼。

Word Link *joy ≈ being glad : enjoy, joyful, joyous*

joy·ous /dʒɔɪəs/ ADJ **Joyous** means extremely happy. 非常快乐的 [LITERARY] ❑ *She had made their childhood so joyous and carefree.* 她使他们的童年生活非常快乐、无忧无虑。 ● **joy·ous·ly** ADV 非常快乐地 ❑ *Sarah accepted joyously.* 萨拉非常快乐地接受了。

joy·rider /dʒɔɪraɪdər/ (**joyriders**) N-COUNT A **joyrider** is someone who steals cars in order to drive around in them at high speed. 窃车兜风的人 ❑ *...a car crash caused by joyriders.* …一场由窃车兜风的人们造成的撞车事故。

joy·stick /dʒɔɪstɪk/ (**joysticks**) N-COUNT In some computer games, the **joystick** is the lever that the player uses in order to control the direction of the things on the screen. (计算机游戏的)操纵杆

JPEG /dʒeɪpɛg/ (**JPEGs**) also **Jpeg** N-UNCOUNT **JPEG** is a standard file format for compressing pictures so they can be stored or sent by e-mail more easily. **JPEG** is an abbreviation for "Joint Photographic Experts Group." 联合图像专家组格式 [COMPUTING] ❑ *...JPEG images.* …JPEG格式的图像。 ● N-COUNT A **JPEG** is a JPEG file or picture. JPEG格式的文件; JPEG格式的图像 ❑ *You can add edge enhancement or smoothness to a Jpeg, or vary the color depth.* 你可以对JPEG格式的图像进行锐化或钝化，或改变颜色的深浅。

ju·bi·lant /dʒubɪlənt/ ADJ If you are **jubilant**, you feel extremely happy because of a success. 欢欣鼓舞的 ❑ *The team were greeted by thousands of jubilant supporters.* 该队受到了上千名欢欣鼓舞的支持者的欢迎。

ju·bi·lee /dʒubɪli/ (**jubilees**) N-COUNT A **jubilee** is a special anniversary of an event, especially the 25th or 50th anniversary. (尤指25或50周年的) 周年纪念 ❑ *...Queen Victoria's jubilee.* …维多利亚女王执政50周年纪念。

Ju·da·ism /dʒudiɪzəm, -deɪ-/ N-UNCOUNT **Judaism** is the religion of the Jewish people. It is based on the Old Testament of the Bible and the Talmud. 犹太教

judge ♦♦◇ /dʒʌdʒ/ (**judges, judging, judged**) **1** N-COUNT; N-TITLE A **judge** is the person in a court of law who decides how the law should be applied, for example how criminals should be punished. 法官 ❑ *The judge adjourned the hearing until next Tuesday.* 法官将听证延至下星期二。 **2** N-COUNT A **judge** is a person who decides who will be the winner of a competition. 裁判员 ❑ *A panel of judges is now selecting the finalists.* 裁判组现在正在选拔参加决赛的选手。 **3** V-T If you **judge** something such as a competition, you decide who or what is the winner. 评判 ❑ *He was asked to judge a literary competition.* 他被邀请评判一场文学竞赛。 **4** V-T If you **judge** something or someone, you form an opinion about them after you have examined the evidence or thought carefully about them. 判断 ❑ *It will take a few more years to judge the impact of these ideas.* 还需要再过几年才能判断这些思想的影响。 ❑ *I am ready to judge any book on its merits.* 我会根据每本书自身的性质来对其进行评判。 ❑ *It's for other people to judge how much I have improved.* 应当由别人来评判我进步的大小。 **5** V-T If you **judge** something, you guess its amount, size, or value or you guess what it is. 估计 ❑ *It is important to judge the weight of your washing load correctly.* 正确估计你的待洗衣物的量很重要。 ❑ *I judged him to be about forty.* 我估计他四十岁左右。 **6** N-COUNT If someone is a good **judge of** something, they understand it and can make sensible decisions about it. If someone is a bad **judge of** something, they cannot do this. 鉴定人 ❑ *I'm a pretty good judge of character.* 我非常善于判别性格。 **7** PHRASE You use **judging by**, **judging from**, or **to judge from** to introduce the reasons why you believe or think something. 根据…判断 ❑ *Judging by the opinion polls, he seems to be succeeding.* 根据民意调查判断，他似乎稳操胜券。 ❑ *Judging from the way he laughed as he told it, it was meant to be humorous.* 从他讲述时笑的方式看来，那是为逗人发笑。 → see **trial**

> **Word Partnership** *judge* 的常用搭配:
>
> V. judge **approves** *something*, judge **asks** *something*, judge **decides** *something*, judge **denies a motion/request**, judge **grants** *something*, judge **orders** *something*, judge **rules** *something*, judge **says** *something*, judge **sentences** *someone* **1**
>
> N. **decision by/of a** judge, **trial** judge **1**

judge·ment /dʒʌdʒmənt/ [BRIT] → see **judgment**

judg·ment ♦◇◇ /dʒʌdʒmənt/ (**judgments**)

in BRIT, also use **judgement**

1 N-VAR A **judgment** is an opinion that you have or express after thinking carefully about something. 看法 ❑ *In your judgment, what has changed over the past few years?* 依你看，过去几年里发生了哪些变化? **2** N-UNCOUNT **Judgment** is the ability to make sensible guesses about a situation or sensible decisions about what to do. 判断力 ❑ *I respect his judgment and I'll follow any advice he gives me.* 我敬重他的判断力，并将听从他给我的任何建议。 **3** N-VAR A **judgment** is a decision made by a judge or by a court of law. 判决 ❑ *We are awaiting a judgment from the Supreme Court.* 我们正等着最高法院的判决。 **4** PHRASE If something is **against** your **better judgment**, you believe that it would be more sensible or better not to do it. 明知不可取 ❑ *Against our better judgment, we buy the products of manufacturers whose claims seem too good to be true.* 明知不可取，我们还是买了那些自我宣传好得令人难以置信的厂家的产品。 **5** PHRASE If you **pass judgment** on someone or something, you give your opinion about it, especially if you are making a criticism. 对…做出评论 ❑ *They won't pass judgment on their friends or family.* 他们不愿评论他们的朋友或家庭。 **6** PHRASE If you **reserve judgment on** something, you refuse to give an opinion about it until you know more about it. 保留看法 ❑ *I think I'd have to reserve judgment on whether it'll make any difference until I see some of those key details.* 至于它是否会有影响，我想在我看到一些关键细节之前我会保留看法。

> **Word Partnership** *judgment* 的常用搭配:
>
> V. **make a** judgment, **rush to** judgment **1**
> **exercise** judgment, **trust** *someone's* judgment, **use** judgment **2**
>
> ADJ. **bad** judgment, **good** judgment, **poor** judgment **2**

judg·men·tal /dʒʌdʒmɛntᵊl/ ADJ If you say that someone is **judgmental**, you are critical of them because they form opinions of people and situations very quickly, when it would be better for them to wait until they know more about the person or situation. 妄下结论的 [DISAPPROVAL] ❑ *We tried not to seem critical or judgmental while giving advice that would protect him from ridicule.* 在提出使他免受奚落的建议时，我们尽量不表现得挑剔或妄下结论。

★**ju·di·cial** /dʒudɪʃᵊl/ ADJ **Judicial** means relating to the legal system and to judgments made in a court of law. 司法的; 审判的 [ADJ n] ❑ *...an independent judicial system.* …一个独立的司法体系。 ❑ *...efforts to manipulate the judicial process.* …操纵审判程序的努力。 ●**ju·di·cial·ly** ADV 司法地; 审判地 [ADV with v] ❑ *Even if the amendment is passed it can be defeated judicially.* 即使这项修正案获得了通过，它也有可能通过司法程序被否决。

★**ju·di·ci·ary** /dʒudɪʃieri/ N-SING **The judiciary** is the branch of authority in a country that is concerned with law and the legal system. 司法部 [FORMAL] ❑ *The judiciary must think very hard before jailing nonviolent offenders.* 司法部在把非暴力罪犯投入监狱之前一定要慎重考虑。

ju·di·cious /dʒudɪʃəs/ ADJ If you describe an action or decision as **judicious**, you approve of it because you think that it shows good judgment and sense. 明智的 [FORMAL, APPROVAL] ❑ *The president authorizes the judicious use of military force to protect our citizens.* 总统授权明智动用军队来保护我们的公民。 ●**ju·di·cious·ly** ADV 明智地 [ADV with v] ❑ *Modern fertilizers should be used judiciously.* 现代化肥应被明智地使用。

judo /dʒudoʊ/ N-UNCOUNT **Judo** is a sport in which two people fight without weapons and try to throw each other to the ground. 柔道 ❑ *He was also a black belt in judo.* 他还是一名柔道黑带。

▲**jug** /dʒʌg/ (**jugs**) **1** N-COUNT A **jug** is a cylindrical container with a handle and is used for holding and pouring liquids. 水罐 **2** N-COUNT You can use **jug** to refer to the jug and its contents, or to the contents only. 一水罐的量 ❑ *...a jug of water.* …一罐水。 → see **dish**

▲**jug·gle** /dʒʌgᵊl/ (**juggles, juggling, juggled**) **1** V-T If you **juggle** lots of different things, such as your work and your family, you try to give enough time or attention to all of them. 尽量兼顾 ❑ *The management team meets several times a week to juggle budgets and resources.* 管理团队一周开几次会，力图兼顾预算和资源。 **2** V-T/V-I If you **juggle**, you entertain people by throwing things into the air, catching each one, and throwing it up again so that there are several of them in the air at the same time. 用…玩抛接杂耍; 玩抛接杂耍 ❑ *Soon she was juggling five eggs.* 很快她就在抛接5个鸡蛋了。 ●**jug·gl·ing** N-UNCOUNT 抛接杂耍 ❑ *He can perform an astonishing variety of acts, including mime and juggling.* 他会表演的节目种类多得惊人，包括哑剧和抛接杂耍。

jug·gler /dʒʌglər/ (**jugglers**) N-COUNT A **juggler** is someone who juggles in order to entertain people. 抛接杂耍表演者

juice ♦◇◇ /dʒus/ (**juices, juicing, juiced**) **1** N-MASS **Juice** is the liquid that can be obtained from a fruit or vegetable. (果、蔬菜)汁 ❏ *...fresh orange juice.* …新鲜橙汁。 **2** N-PLURAL The **juices** of a piece of meat are the liquid that comes out of it when you cook it. (肉) 汁 ❏ *When cooked, drain off the juices and put the meat in a processor.* 肉煮熟后，把汁控干，然后放入加工机。

▸ **juice up** PHRASAL VERB If you **juice up** a place or event, you do something to make it more lively or exciting. 使增加活力 [AM, INFORMAL] ❏ *Look at the ads for Chamber of Secrets, and you'll see that the filmmakers are doing all they can to juice up the formula.* 看看《秘室》的广告，你就会发现电影制作方在想尽一切办法使老套的手法增色。

Word Partnership *juice* 的常用搭配:

N. **bottle of** juice, **fruit** juice, **glass of** juice **1**
ADJ. **fresh-squeezed** juice **1**

juicy /dʒusi/ (**juicier, juiciest**) **1** ADJ If food is **juicy**, it has a lot of juice in it and is very enjoyable to eat. 多汁的 ❏ *...a thick, juicy steak.* …一块厚而多汁的牛排。 **2** ADJ **Juicy** gossip or stories contain details about people's lives, especially details that are normally kept private. 绘声绘色的 [INFORMAL] ❏ *It provided some juicy gossip for a few days.* 这提供了些绘声绘色的、够聊几天的谈资。

Jul. **Jul.** is a written abbreviation for **July**. 7月

July ♦♦♦ /dʒʊlaɪ/ (**Julys**) N-VAR **July** is the seventh month of the year in the Western calendar. 7月 ❏ *In July 1969, Neil Armstrong walked on the moon.* 1969年7月，尼尔·阿姆斯特朗踏上了月球。

J

jum·ble /dʒʌmbᵊl/ (**jumbles, jumbling, jumbled**) **1** N-COUNT **A jumble** of things is a lot of different things that are all mixed together in a disorganized or confused way. 杂乱的一堆 ❏ *The shoreline was made up of a jumble of huge boulders.* 这海岸线由一堆杂乱的巨石构成。 **2** V-T/V-I If you **jumble** things, they become mixed together so that they are untidy or are not in the correct order. 混杂 ❏ *He's making a new film by jumbling together bits of his other movies.* 他正通过混杂自己其他电影的片段来制作一部新电影。 ● PHRASAL VERB To **jumble up** means the same as to **jumble**. 混杂 ❏ *They had jumbled it all up into a heap.* 他们已把这些都混在一起堆成一大堆。 ❏ *The bank scrambles all that money together, jumbles it all up and lends it out to hundreds and thousands of borrowers.* 该银行把那些钱集中凑在一起，然后贷给成千上万的借款人。

▲**jum·bo** /dʒʌmboʊ/ (**jumbos**) **1** ADJ **Jumbo** means very large; used mainly in advertising and in the names of products. 特大的 [ADJ n] ❏ *...a jumbo box of tissues.* …一个特大盒纸巾。 **2** N-COUNT A **jumbo** or a **jumbo jet** is a very large jet aircraft that can carry several hundred passengers. 巨型喷气式飞机

jump ♦♦◇ /dʒʌmp/ (**jumps, jumping, jumped**) **1** V-T/V-I If you **jump**, you bend your knees, push against the ground with your feet, and move quickly upward into the air. 跳 ❏ *I jumped over the fence.* 我从篱笆上跳了过去。 ❏ *I'd jumped seventeen feet six in the long jump, which was a school record.* 我跳远曾跳了17.6英尺，这是个校纪录。 ● N-COUNT **Jump** is also a noun. 跳 ❏ *The longest jumps by a man and a woman were witnessed in Sestriere, Italy, yesterday.* 男女跳远项目最远的一跳都于昨天在意大利的塞斯特雷得以见证。 **2** V-T/V-I If you **jump** from something above the ground, you deliberately push yourself into the air so that you drop toward the ground. 跳下 ❏ *I jumped the last six feet down to the deck.* 我跳下最后6英尺，到了甲板上。 ❏ *He jumped out of a third-floor window.* 他从3楼的一个窗口跳了出去。 **3** V-T If you **jump** something such as a fence, you move quickly up and through the air over or across it. 跳过 ❏ *He jumped the first fence beautifully.* 他漂亮地跃过了第一道篱笆。 **4** V-I If you **jump** somewhere, you move there quickly and suddenly. 跳起 ❏ *Adam jumped from his seat at the girl's cry.* 听到女孩的哭声，亚当从座位上跳起来。 **5** V-I If something **makes** you **jump**, it makes you make a sudden movement because you are frightened or surprised. 惊跳 ❏ *The phone shrilled, making her jump.* 电话突然响起，把她吓了一跳。 **6** V-T/V-I If an amount or level **jumps**, it suddenly increases or rises by a large amount in a short time. 猛增 ❏ *Sales jumped from $94 million to over $101 million.* 销售额从9400万美元猛增到超过1.01亿美元。 ❏ *The number of crimes jumped by ten percent last year.* 犯罪数量去年猛增了10%。 ❏ *Squibb shares jumped $2.50.* 施贵宝的股票猛涨了$2.50。 ● N-COUNT **Jump** is also a noun. 猛增 ❏ *A big jump in energy conservation could be achieved without much disruption of anyone's standard of living.* 能源节约的一个大飞跃可以在不太影响任何人生活水平的前提下得以实现。 **7** V-I If you **jump at** an offer or opportunity, you accept it quickly and eagerly. 迫不及待地接受 [no cont] ❏ *Members of the public would jump at the chance to become part owners of the corporation.* 公众成员会迫不及待地抓住机会成为该公司的部分所有人。 **8** V-I If someone **jumps on** you, they quickly criticize you for doing something that they do not approve of. 立刻斥责 ❏ *A lot of people jumped on me about that, you know.* 很多人马上就为那个指责我，你知道的。 **9** V-T If someone **jumps** you, they attack you suddenly or unexpectedly. 突然袭击 [mainly AM, INFORMAL] ❏ *Half a dozen sailors jumped him.* 6名水手突袭了他。 **10** PHRASE If you **get a jump on** something or someone or **get the jump on** them, you gain an advantage over them. 胜过 [AM] ❏ *Helicopters helped fire crews get a jump on the blaze.* 直升机帮助救火人员控制住了火势。 **11** to **jump on the bandwagon** → see **bandwagon** **12** to **jump bail** → see **bail** **13** to **jump the gun** → see **gun** **14** to **jump for joy** → see **joy**

Thesaurus *jump* 另参见:

V. bound, hop, leap, lunge **1**
dive, leap, parachute **2**
hurdle **3**
startle **5**
increase, rise, shoot up **6**

Word Partnership *jump* 的常用搭配:

ADJ. **big** jump **1** **6**
N. jump **to *your* feet** **4**
jump **in prices**, jump **in sales** **6**

jump·er /dʒʌmpər/ (**jumpers**) **1** N-COUNT If you refer to a person or a horse as a particular kind of **jumper**, you are describing how good they are at jumping or the way that they jump. 跳跃者；跳跃的动物 ❏ *He is a terrific athlete and a brilliant jumper.* 他是一名优秀的运动员和一位杰出的跳跃者。 **2** N-COUNT A **jumper** is a sleeveless dress that is worn over a blouse or sweater. (穿在衬衫或毛线衫外的) 无袖连衣裙 [AM]

in BRIT, use **pinafore**

❏ *She wore a checkered jumper and had ribbons in her hair.* 她穿了一件格子无袖连衣裙，发上系着缎带。 **3** N-COUNT A **jumper** is a warm knitted piece of clothing that covers the upper part of your body and your arms. 针织套衫 [BRIT]

in AM, use **sweater**

jump·start /dʒʌmpstɑrt/ (**jumpstarts, jumpstarting, jumpstarted**) **1** V-T To **jumpstart** a vehicle that has a dead battery means to make the engine start by getting power from the battery of another vehicle, using special cables called jumper cables. 借电启动 ❏ *He was huddled with John trying to jumpstart his car.* 他和约翰挤在一起，试图借电启动他的车。 ● N-COUNT **Jumpstart** is also a noun. 借电启动 ❏ *I drove out to give him a jumpstart because his battery was dead.* 我把车开出来帮他做借电启动，因为他的电池没电了。 **2** V-T To **jumpstart** a system or process that has stopped working or progressing means to do something that will make it start working quickly or effectively. 快速重新启动 ❏ *The EU is trying to jumpstart the peace process.* 欧盟正试图快速重新启动和平进程。 ● N-COUNT **Jumpstart** is also a noun. 快速重新启动 ❏ *...attempts to give the industry a jumpstart.* …让该行业快速重振的尝试。

Jun. **Jun.** is a written abbreviation for **June**. 6月

★**junc·tion** /dʒʌŋkʃᵊn/ (**junctions**) N-COUNT; N-IN-NAMES A **junction** is a place where roads or railroad lines join. (铁路、公路的) 汇合点 [BRIT]

in AM, usually use **intersection**

June ♦♦♦ /dʒun/ (**Junes**) N-VAR **June** is the sixth month of the year in the Western calendar. 6月 ❏ *He spent two and a half weeks with us in June 1986.* 1986年6月，他和我们呆了两个半星期。 ❏ *I am moving out on June 5th.* 我将于6月5日搬出去。

jun·gle /dʒʌŋgᵊl/ (**jungles**) **1** N-VAR A **jungle** is a forest in a tropical country where large numbers of tall trees and plants grow very close together. 丛林 ❏ *...the mountains and jungles of Papua New Guinea.* …巴布亚新几内亚的山脉和丛林。 **2** N-SING If you describe a place as **a jungle**, you are emphasizing that it is full of lots of things and very messy. 杂乱之地 [EMPHASIS] ❏ *...a jungle of stuffed sofas, stuffed birds, knick-knacks, potted plants.* …一个堆满沙发、标本鸟、小摆设、盆栽植物的杂乱之地。 **3** N-SING If you describe a situation as **a jungle**, you dislike it because it is complicated and difficult to get what you want from it. 一团糟 [DISAPPROVAL] ❏ *Social Security law and procedure remain a jungle of complex rules.* 社会保障法律和程序仍然是充满复杂规定的一团糟。

jun·ior ♦◇◇ /dʒuniər/ (**juniors**) 1 ADJ A **junior** official or employee holds a low-ranking position in an organization or profession. 低级别的（官员、职员）❑ *A handful of junior officers were made to bear responsibility for the incident.* 几名下级军官被迫对此事件负责。● N-COUNT **Junior** is also a noun. 低级别者 ❑ *He has said legal aid work is for juniors when they start out in the law.* 他曾说过，法律援助工作适合初涉法律工作的低级别律师来做。 2 N-SING If you are someone's **junior**, you are younger than they are. 较年幼者 ❑ *She now lives with actor Denis Lawson, 10 years her junior.* 她现在和比她小10岁的演员丹尼斯·劳森同居。 3 N-COUNT In the United States, a student in the third year of high school or college is called a **junior**. （美国中学、大学）三年级学生 ❑ *Their youngest daughter Amy's a junior at the University of Evansville in Indiana.* 他们最小的女儿埃米是印第安纳州埃文斯维尔大学的三年级学生。 4 N-IN-NAMES **Junior** is sometimes used after the name of the younger of two men in a family who have the same name, sometimes in order to prevent confusion. The abbreviation **Jr.** is also used. 用于家族中同名两男子中的较年幼者的姓名后 [AM] ❑ *His son, Arthur Ochs Junior, is expected to succeed him as publisher.* 他的儿子，小阿瑟·奥克斯，被期望来继承他做出版商。

Word Partnership *junior* 的常用搭配：

N. junior **executive**, junior **officer**, junior **partner**, junior **senator** 1

jun·ior high school (**junior high schools**) or **junior high** N-VAR; N-IN-NAMES A **junior high school** or a **junior high** is a school for students from 7th through 9th or 10th grade. 初级中学 [AM] ❑ *He dropped out of junior high school.* 他初中辍学了。 ❑ *...Benjamin Franklin Junior High.* …本杰明·富兰克林初级中学。

★ **junk** /dʒʌŋk/ (**junks, junking, junked**) 1 N-UNCOUNT **Junk** is old and used things that have little value and that you do not want any more. 废旧物品 ❑ *Rose finds her furniture in junk shops.* 罗丝在旧货店里找到她的家具。 2 V-T If you **junk** something, you get rid of it or stop using it. 丢掉 [INFORMAL] ❑ *Consumers will not have to junk their old cassettes to use the new format.* 消费者们将不必为了使用新制式而丢掉他们的老盒式磁带。

junk bond (**junk bonds**) N-COUNT If a company issues **junk bonds**, it borrows money from investors, usually at a high rate of interest, in order to finance a particular deal that is risky. （高利息高风险的）垃圾债券 [BUSINESS]

junk food (**junk foods**) N-MASS If you refer to food as **junk food**, you mean that it is quick and easy to prepare but is not good for your health. 垃圾食品 ❑ *Sharon fears that her love of junk food may have contributed to her cancer.* 莎伦怕她对垃圾食品的喜好可能导致了她的癌症。

junkie /dʒʌŋki/ (**junkies**) 1 N-COUNT A **junkie** is a drug addict. 吸毒成瘾者 [INFORMAL] ❑ *...those desperate junkies who have tried every known drug.* …那些试遍每一种已知毒品、不可救药的吸毒成瘾的人。 2 N-COUNT You can use **junkie** to refer to someone who is very interested in a particular activity, especially when they spend a lot of time on it. 迷 [INFORMAL] ❑ *...a computer junkie.* …一个计算机迷。

junk mail N-UNCOUNT **Junk mail** is advertisements and publicity materials in your mail that you have not asked for and that you do not want. 垃圾邮件 ❑ *We still get junk mail for the previous occupants.* 我们仍会收到给先前住户的垃圾邮件。

▲ **ju·ris·dic·tion** /dʒʊərɪsdɪkʃᵊn/ (**jurisdictions**) 1 N-UNCOUNT **Jurisdiction** is the power that a court of law or an official has to carry out legal judgments or to enforce laws. 司法权；管辖权 [FORMAL] ❑ *The British police have no jurisdiction over foreign bank accounts.* 英国警方对外国银行的账户没有司法管辖权。 2 N-COUNT A **jurisdiction** is a state or other area in which a particular court and system of laws has authority. 管辖范围 [LEGAL] ❑ *In the U.K., unlike in most other European jurisdictions, there is no right to strike.* 英国与欧洲大部分其他司法辖区不同，没有权利去罢工。

ju·ror /dʒʊərər/ (**jurors**) N-COUNT A **juror** is a member of a jury. 陪审员 ❑ *The foreman was asked by the clerk whether the jurors had reached verdicts on which they all agreed.* 书记员问陪审团主席是不是陪审员们已作出了全体一致的裁决。

jury ♦◇◇ /dʒʊəri/ (**juries**) 1 N-COUNT-COLL In a court of law, the **jury** is the group of people who have been chosen from the general public to listen to the facts about a crime and to decide whether the person accused is guilty or not. 陪审团 [also "by" N] ❑ *The jury convicted Mr. Hampson of all offenses.* 该陪审团裁定汉普森先生的全部罪名成立。 2 N-COUNT-COLL A **jury** is a group of people who choose the winner of a competition. （竞赛的）评委会 ❑ *I am not surprised that the jury chose to award this novel the prize.* 我并不惊讶于评委选择给这部小说颁奖。 3 PHRASE If you say that **the jury is out** or that **the jury is still out** on a particular subject, you mean that people in general have still not made a decision or formed an opinion about that subject. 尚无定论 ❑ *The jury is out on whether or not this is true.* 这是否属实尚无定论。

→ see **trial**

Word Partnership *jury* 的常用搭配：

N. jury **duty**, **trial by** jury 1
V. jury **convicts** 1
jury **announces** 1 2
ADJ. **hung** jury 1
unbiased jury 1 2

just
1 ADVERB USES
2 ADJECTIVE USE

1 **just** ♦♦♦ /dʒʌst/

➪ **Please look at meanings 17 – 20 to see if the expression you are looking for is shown under another headword.** 1 ADV You use **just** to say that something happened a very short time ago, or is starting to happen at the present time. For example, if you say that someone **just arrived** or **has just arrived**, you mean that they arrived a very short time ago. 刚刚 [ADV before v] ❑ *I've just bought a new house.* 我刚买了一个新房子。 ❑ *I just had the most awful dream.* 我刚做了一个最可怕的梦。 2 ADV If you say that you are **just** doing something, you mean that you are doing it now and will finish it very soon. If you say that you are **just about to** do something, or **just going to** do it, you mean that you will do it very soon. 正在；正要 ❑ *I'm just making the sauce for the cauliflower.* 我正在给花椰菜做调味汁。 ❑ *I'm just going to go mail a letter.* 我正要去寄一封信。 3 ADV You can use **just** to emphasize that something is happening at exactly the moment of speaking or at exactly the moment that you are talking about. 正（表强调）[EMPHASIS] ❑ *Randall would just now be getting the Sunday paper.* 兰德尔这个时候正应该要去取星期日的报纸。 ❑ *Just then the phone rang.* 正在那时，电话铃响了。 4 ADV You use **just** to indicate that something is no more important, interesting, or difficult, for example, than you say it is, especially when you want to correct a wrong idea that someone may get or has already gotten. 只不过 [ADV group/cl] [EMPHASIS] ❑ *It's just a suggestion.* 这只是一个建议。 ❑ *It's not just a financial matter.* 这不只是个财务问题。 5 ADV You use **just** to emphasize that you are talking about a small part, not the whole of an amount. 只是 [ADV n] [EMPHASIS] ❑ *That's just one example of the kind of experiments you can do.* 这只是你所能做的实验中的一个例子。 6 ADV You use **just** to emphasize how small an amount is or how short a length of time is. 仅仅（强调数量少或时间短）[ADV amount] [EMPHASIS] ❑ *Stephanie and David redecorated a room in just three days.* 斯蒂芬妮和戴维仅在3天之内就重新装修了一个房间。 7 ADV You can use **just** in front of a verb to indicate that the result of something is unfortunate or undesirable and is likely to make the situation worse rather than better. 只会（造成不良后果）[ADV before v] [ADV before v] ❑ *By doing what they did, they just hurt the people in their community.* 通过做他们的那些事，他们只会伤害自己社区的人们。 8 ADV You use **just** to indicate that what you are saying is the case, but only by a very small degree or amount. 勉强地 ❑ *Her hand was just visible in the dimly lit room.* 她的手在这个昏暗的房间里勉强可见。 ❑ *I arrived just in time for my flight to London.* 我勉强赶上了飞往伦敦的航班。 9 ADV You use **just** with "might," "may," and "could," when you mean that there is a small chance of something happening, even though it is not very likely. 也许（与**might**，**may**和**could**连用）[ADV with modal] ❑ *It's an old trick but it just might work.* 它是个老把戏，不过也许能管用。 10 ADV You use **just** to emphasize the following word or phrase, in order to express feelings such as annoyance, admiration, or certainty. 就是（加强表示感情的语气）[EMPHASIS] ❑ *She just won't relax.* 她就是不放松。 11 ADV You use **just** in expressions such as **just a minute** and **just a moment** to ask someone to wait for a short time. 用于**just a minute**和**just a moment**等短语中，表示稍等 [ADV n] [SPOKEN] ❑ *"Let me in, Di."—"Okay. Just a minute."* "让我进去，迪。"——"好的，稍等。" 12 ADV You can use **just** in expressions such as **just a second** and **just a moment** to interrupt someone, for example, in order to disagree with them, explain something, or calm them down. 用于**just a minute**和**just a moment**等短语中，插话时用 [ADV n] [SPOKEN] ❏ *Well, now just a second, I don't altogether agree.* 哎，等一下，我不完全同意。 13 ADV If you say that you can **just** see or hear something, you mean that it is easy for you to imagine seeing or hearing it. 简直（表示能想像出）[ADV before v] ❏ *I can just hear her telling her friends, "Well, I blame his mother!"* 我简直都能听到她对朋友们说："哎，是他母亲的错！" 14 ADV You use **just** in expressions such as **just like, just as...as**, and **just the same** when you are emphasizing the similarity between two things or two people. 用于**just like**，**just as...as**和**just the same**等短语中，强调相似性 [EMPHASIS] ❏ *Behind the facade they are just like the rest of us.* 在这种外表背后，他们同我们其他的人一样。 ❏ *He worked just as hard as anyone.* 他同每个人一样勤奋工作。 15 PHRASE You use **just about** to indicate that what you are talking about is so close to being the case that it can be regarded as being the case. 几乎可算是 ❏ *There are those who believe that Nick Price is just about the best golfer in the world.* 有些人认为尼克·普赖斯算是世界上最优秀的高尔夫球手了。 16 PHRASE You use **just about** to indicate that what you are talking about is in fact the case, but only by a very small degree or amount. 勉强 ❏ *I can just about tolerate it at the moment.* 我眼下勉强可以忍受它。 17 **just my luck** → see **luck** 18 **not just** → see **not** 19 **just now** → see **now** 20 **it just goes to show** → see **show**

Thesaurus *just* 另参见：

ADV.	now, presently ❶ 2
	only, merely ❶ 4 – 6
	barely ❶ 6 8

J

❷**just** /dʒʌst/ ADJ If you describe a situation, action, or idea as **just**, you mean that it is right or acceptable according to particular moral principles, such as respect for all human beings. 正义的 [FORMAL] ❏ *They believe that they are fighting a just war.* 他们相信他们在打一场正义的战争。 ●**just·ly** ADV 正义地 [ADV with v] ❏ *They were not treated justly in the past.* 他们过去没有被公正地对待过。

jus·tice ♦♦◊ /dʒʌstɪs/ (**justices**) 1 N-UNCOUNT **Justice** is fairness in the way that people are treated. 公正 ❏ *He has a good overall sense of justice and fairness.* 他有良好的公正和公平的整体意识。 ❏ *He only wants freedom, justice and equality.* 他只要自由、公正和平等。 2 N-UNCOUNT The **justice of** a cause, claim, or argument is its quality of being reasonable, fair, or right. 正当性 ❏ *We are a minority and must convince people of the justice of our cause.* 我们是少数，必须让人们相信我们动机的正当性。 3 N-UNCOUNT **Justice** is the legal system that a country uses in order to deal with people who break the law. 司法 ❏ *Many in Toronto's black community feel that the justice system does not treat them fairly.* 多伦多黑人社区的很多人觉得司法制度对他们不公正。 4 N-COUNT A **justice** is a judge. 法官 [AM] ❏ *Thomas will be sworn in today as a justice on the Supreme Court.* 托马斯将在今天宣誓就任最高法院法官。 5 N-TITLE **Justice** is used before the names of judges. 法官（表示头衔）❏ *A preliminary hearing was due to start today before Justice Hutchison, but was adjourned.* 预审原定由哈奇森法官今天开始审理，但延期了。 6 PHRASE If a criminal is **brought to justice**, he or she is punished for a crime by being arrested and tried in a court of law. 依法惩处 ❏ *They demanded that those responsible be brought to justice.* 他们要求那些责任人应依法予以惩处。 7 PHRASE To **do justice** to a person or thing means to reproduce them accurately and show how good they are. 准确再现优点 ❏ *The photograph I had seen didn't do her justice.* 我看到的那张照片不如她本人。 8 PHRASE If you **do justice to** someone or something, you deal with them properly and completely. 恰如其分地处理 ❏ *No one article can ever do justice to the topic of fraud.* 没有一篇文章能恰如其分地处理欺诈这一主题。 9 PHRASE If you **do yourself justice**, you do something as well as you are capable of doing it. 充分发挥某人能力 ❏ *I don't think he did himself justice in the game today.* 我认为今天他在比赛中没有充分发挥出自己的实力。

Word Partnership *justice* 的常用搭配：

V.	**seek** justice 1
ADJ.	**racial** justice, **social** justice 1
	criminal justice, **equal** justice 3
N.	**obstruction of** justice, justice **system** 3

jus·ti·fi·able /dʒʌstɪfaɪəbᵊl/ ADJ An action, situation, emotion, or idea that is **justifiable** is acceptable or correct because there is a good reason for it. 无可非议的 ❏ *The violence of the revolutionary years was justifiable on the grounds of political necessity.* 出于政治需要的立场，革命年代的暴力行为是无可非议的。 ●**jus·ti·fi·ably** /dʒʌstɪfaɪəbli/ ADV 无可非议地 ❏ *He was justifiably proud of his achievements.* 他无可非议地为自己的成就感到骄傲。

jus·ti·fi·ca·tion /dʒʌstɪfɪkeɪʃᵊn/ (**justifications**) N-VAR A **justification for** something is an acceptable reason or explanation for it. 正当的理由 ❏ *To me the only justification for a zoo is educational.* 对我来说，动物园存在的惟一正当理由就是它的教育意义。

jus·ti·fied /dʒʌstɪfaɪd/ 1 ADJ If you describe a decision, action, or idea as **justified**, you think it is reasonable and acceptable. 合理的 ❏ *In my opinion, the decision was wholly justified.* 在我看来，这个决定是完全合理的。 2 ADJ If you think that someone is **justified in** doing something, you think that their reasons for doing it are good and valid. 理所应当的 [v-link ADJ "in" -ing] ❏ *He's absolutely justified in resigning. He was treated shamefully.* 他完全有理由辞职。他受了侮辱。

jus·ti·fy ♦◊◊ /dʒʌstɪfaɪ/ (**justifies, justifying, justified**) 1 V-T To **justify** a decision, action, or idea means to show or prove that it is reasonable or necessary. 证明…有理 ❏ *No argument can justify a war.* 没有任何理由能证明一个战争有理。 2 V-T To **justify** printed text means to adjust the spaces between the words so that each line of type is exactly the same length. 使（文本）对齐 ❏ *Click on this icon to align or justify text at both the left and right margins.* 点击这个图标调整文本，使其左右两端对齐。 3 → see also **left-justify**

just·ly /dʒʌstli/ 1 ADV You use **justly** to show that you approve of someone's attitude toward something, because it seems to be based on truth or reality. 理所应当地 [APPROVAL] ❏ *Australians are justly proud of their native wildlife.* 澳大利亚人理应为他们本土的野生动植物而自豪。 2 → see also **just**

jut /dʒʌt/ (**juts, jutting, jutted**) 1 V-I If something **juts out**, it sticks out above or beyond a surface. 伸出 ❏ *The northern end of the island juts out like a long, thin finger into the sea.* 该岛的北端像一根细长的手指伸进大海。 2 V-T/V-I If you **jut** a part of your body, especially your chin, or if it **juts**, you push it forward in an aggressive or determined way. 抬起 ❏ *His jaw jutted stubbornly forward; he would not be denied.* 他的下巴倔强地向前抬起；他不会被拒绝。 ❏ *Gwen jutted her chin forward, her nose in the air, and did not bother to answer the teacher.* 格温向前扬起下巴，鼻孔朝天，懒得答复那个老师。

★**ju·venile** /dʒuvənᵊl, -naɪl/ (**juveniles**) 1 N-COUNT A **juvenile** is a child or young person who is not yet old enough to be regarded as an adult. 青少年 [FORMAL] ❏ *The number of juveniles in the general population has fallen by a fifth in the past 10 years.* 在过去的10年中，青少年在总人口中所占的比重下降了1/5。 2 ADJ **Juvenile** activity or behavior involves young people who are not yet adults. 青少年的 [ADJ n] ❏ *Juvenile crime is increasing at a terrifying rate.* 青少年犯罪在以惊人的速度增加。

ju·venile de·lin·quent (**juvenile delinquents**) N-COUNT A **juvenile delinquent** is a young person who is guilty of committing crimes, especially destruction of property or violence. 青少年罪犯

jux·ta·pose /dʒʌkstəpoʊz/ (**juxtaposes, juxtaposing, juxtaposed**) V-T If you **juxtapose** two contrasting objects, images, or ideas, you place them together or describe them together, so that the differences between them are emphasized. 把…并列 [FORMAL] ❏ *The technique Mr. Wilson uses most often is to juxtapose things for dramatic effect.* 威尔逊先生最常用的技巧是把事物并列起来以获得戏剧性效果。 ❏ *Contemporary photographs are juxtaposed with a sixteenth century, copper Portuguese mirror.* 把当代的照片与一面16世纪的葡萄牙铜镜摆放在一起。 ❏ *...art's oldest theme: the celebration of life juxtaposed with the terror of mortality.* …艺术最古老的主题：对生命的庆祝与对死亡的恐惧并存。

jux·ta·po·si·tion /dʒʌkstəpəzɪʃᵊn/ (**juxtapositions**) N-VAR The **juxtaposition of** two contrasting objects, images, or ideas is the fact that they are placed together or described together, so that the differences between them are emphasized. 并列 [FORMAL] ❏ *This juxtaposition of brutal reality and lyrical beauty runs through Park's stories.* 残酷的现实和抒情诗般的美并存贯穿于帕克的故事之中。

Kk

K also **k** /keɪ/ (**K's, k's**) N-VAR **K** is the eleventh letter of the English alphabet. 英语字母表中的第11个字母

kan·ga·roo /kæŋgəru/ (**kangaroos**) N-COUNT A **kangaroo** is a large Australian animal which moves by jumping on its back legs. Female kangaroos carry their babies in a pouch on their stomach. 袋鼠

ka·ra·te /kərɑti/ N-UNCOUNT **Karate** is a Japanese sport or way of fighting in which people fight using their hands, elbows, feet, and legs. 空手道

KB **KB** is a written abbreviation for **kilobyte** or **kilobytes**. 千字节

Kbps also **kbps** **Kbps** is a unit for measuring the speed of a modem. **Kbps** is a written abbreviation for 'kilobits per second'. 千位每秒 [COMPUTING] ❑ *...a 28.8 Kbps modem.* …一个28.8千位每秒的调制解调器。

keel /kil/ (**keels, keeling, keeled**) **1** N-COUNT The **keel** of a boat is the long, specially shaped piece of wood or steel along the bottom of it. (船的) 龙骨 ❑ *The keel hit the rock first.* 船龙骨先撞到岩石。 **2** PHRASE If you say that someone or something is **on an even keel**, you mean that they are working or progressing smoothly and steadily, without any sudden changes. 平稳地 ❑ *Jason had helped him out with a series of loans, until he could get back on an even keel.* 詹森给他提供了一连串贷款帮他摆脱困境，直到他能够重新稳定下来。

▸ **keel over** PHRASAL VERB If someone **keels over**, they collapse because they are tired or ill. (因疲倦或疾病而) 倒下 [INFORMAL] ❑ *He then keeled over and fell flat on his back.* 然后他就倒下了，仰面朝天。

keen ♦◇◇ /kin/ (**keener, keenest**) **1** ADJ If you say that someone has a **keen** mind, you mean that they are very clever and aware of what is happening around them. (头脑) 敏锐的 [ADJ n] ❑ *They described him as a man of keen intellect.* 他们把他描述成一个才思敏锐的人。 ● **keen·ly** ADV 敏锐地 ❑ *They're keenly aware that whatever they decide will set a precedent.* 他们敏锐地意识到无论他们决定怎么做，都会开创先例。 **2** ADJ If you have a **keen** eye or ear, you are able to notice things that are difficult to detect. (视觉、听觉) 灵敏的 ❑ *...an amateur artist with a keen eye for detail.* …一位对细节有敏锐洞察力的业余艺术家。 ● **keen·ly** ADV 灵敏地 [ADV with v] ❑ *Charles listened keenly.* 查尔斯竖起耳朵听着。 **3** ADJ A **keen** interest or emotion is one that is very intense. (兴趣或情感) 强烈的 [mainly BRIT] ❑ *He had retained a keen interest in the progress of the work.* 他一直对工作的进展保持着强烈的兴趣。 ● **keen·ly** ADV 强烈地 ❑ *She remained keenly interested in international affairs.* 她一直对国际事务有强烈的兴趣。 **4** ADJ If you are **keen on** doing something, you very much want to do it. 渴望的 [v-link ADJ] ❑ *You're not keen on going, are you?* 你不是很想走，对吗？ ● **keen·ness** N-UNCOUNT 渴望 ❑ *...Doyle's keenness to please.* …多伊尔的极欲讨好心态。 **5** ADJ If you are **keen on** something, you like it a lot and are very enthusiastic about it. 热衷的 [v-link ADJ "on" n] ❑ *I wasn't too keen on physics and chemistry.* 我对物理和化学并不太热衷。 **6** ADJ You use **keen** to indicate that someone has a lot of enthusiasm for a particular activity and spends a lot of time doing it. 着迷的 ❑ *She was a keen amateur photographer.* 她是一个痴迷的业余摄影师。 **7** ADJ A **keen** fight or competition is one in which the competitors are all trying very hard to win, and it is not easy to predict who will win. 激烈的 ● **keen·ly** ADV 激烈地 [mainly BRIT] ❑ *The contest should be very keenly fought.* 比赛应该争夺很激烈。

keep

1. REMAIN, STAY, OR CONTINUE TO HAVE/DO
2. STOP OR PREVENT
3. SUPPORT, PROVIDE FOR
4. NOUN USE
5. PHRASAL VERBS

❶ keep ♦♦♦ /kip/ (**keeps, keeping, kept**)

➪ **Please look at meanings 18 – 26 to see if the expression you are looking for is shown under another headword.** **1** V-LINK If someone **keeps** or **is kept** in a particular state, they remain in it. 保持 (特定状态) ❑ *The noise kept him awake.* 噪音使他一直醒着。 ❑ *People had to burn these trees to keep warm during harsh winters.* 在寒冷的冬天，人们得靠烧这些树保暖。 **2** V-T/V-I If you **keep** or you **are kept** in a particular position or place, you remain in it. 留在 ❑ *Keep away from the doors while the train is moving.* 列车运行时请远离车门。 ❑ *He kept his head down, hiding his features.* 他一直低着头藏住脸。 **3** V-I If you **keep off** something or **keep away from** it, you avoid it. If you **keep out of** something, you avoid getting involved in it. 避开 ❑ *I managed to stick to the diet and keep off sweet foods.* 我设法坚持节食，不吃甜食。 **4** V-T If you **keep** doing something, you do it repeatedly or continue to do it. 继续 ❑ *I keep forgetting it's December.* 我总是忘了现在是12月份。 ● PHRASAL VERB **Keep on** means the same as **keep**. 继续 ❑ *Did he give up or keep on trying?* 他是放弃了，还是在继续努力？ **5** V-T **Keep** is used with some nouns to indicate that someone does something for a period of time or continues to do it. For example, if you **keep a grip on** something, you continue to hold or control it. 继续 (持有或控制) ❑ *Until last year, the regime kept a tight grip on the country.* 直到去年，该政权一直牢牢地控制着这个国家。 **6** V-T If you **keep** something, you continue to have it in your possession and do not throw it away, give it away, or sell it. 保留 ❑ *We must decide what to keep and what to give away.* 我们必须决定哪些该留、哪些该扔。 **7** V-T If you **keep** something in a particular place, you always have it or store it in that place so that you can use it whenever you need it. 保存 ❑ *She kept her money under the mattress.* 她把钱存放在床垫下面。 **8** V-T When you **keep** something such as a promise or an appointment, you do what you said you would do. 信守 ❑ *I'm hoping you'll keep your promise to come for a long visit.* 我希望你会信守诺言，来这里多呆一段时间。 **9** V-T If you **keep** a record of a series of events, you write down details of it so that they can be referred to later. 记录 ❑ *Eleanor began to keep a diary.* 埃莉诺开始记日记了。 **10** V-I If food **keeps** for a certain length of time, it stays fresh and suitable to eat for that time. 保鲜 ❑ *Whatever is left over may be put into the refrigerator, where it will keep for 2-3 weeks.* 所有吃剩下的东西都可以放进冰箱，可保鲜2至3周。 **11** V-I You can say or ask how someone **is keeping** as a way of saying or asking whether they are well. 保持健康 [only cont] ❑ *She hasn't been keeping too well lately.* 她最近身体一直不太好。 **12** PHRASE If you **keep at it**, you continue doing something that you have started, even if you are tired and would prefer to stop. 坚持 ❑ *It may take a number of attempts, but it is worth keeping at it.* 可能需要多次尝试，但这件事值得坚持做下去。 **13** PHRASE If you **keep going**, you continue moving along or doing something that you have started, even if you are tired and would prefer to stop. 坚持下去 ❑ *She forced herself to keep going.* 她强迫自己坚持下去。 **14** PHRASE If one thing is **in keeping with** another, it is suitable in relation to that thing. If one thing is **out of keeping with** another, you mean that it is not suitable in relation to that thing. 与…(不)一致 ❑ *This is not in keeping with our objective of representing the community.* 这与我们代表该社区的目标不一致。 **15** PHRASE If you **keep it up**, you continue working or trying as hard as you have been in the past. 坚持不懈 ❑ *There are fears that he will not be able to keep it up when he gets to the particularly demanding third year.* 有人担心到了极其艰难的第3年他会坚持不下去的。 **16** PHRASE If you **keep** something **to yourself**, you do not tell anyone else about it. 对某事守口如瓶 ❑ *I have to tell someone. I can't keep it to myself.* 我得告诉别人。我不能对此守口如瓶。 **17** PHRASE If you **keep to yourself**, you stay on your own most of the time and do not mix socially with other people. 不与人交往 ❑ *He was a quiet man who always kept to himself.* 他不爱说话，总是独来独往。 **18** **to keep** someone **company** → see **company** **19** **to keep a straight face** → see **face** **20** **to keep your head** → see **head** **21** **to keep pace** → see **pace** **22** **to keep the peace** → see **peace** **23** **to keep quiet** → see **quiet** **24** **to keep a secret** → see **secret** **25** **to keep time** → see **time** **26** **to keep track** → see **track**

❷ **keep** ◆◆◆ /kip/ (**keeps, keeping, kept**) 1 V-T If someone or something **keeps** you **from** a particular action, they prevent you from doing it. 阻止 ❑ *Embarrassment has kept me from doing all sorts of things.* 难为情使得我什么也做不了。 2 V-T If someone or something **keeps** you, they delay you and make you late. 耽搁 ❑ *Sorry to keep you, Jack.* 抱歉耽搁你了，杰克。 ❑ *"What kept you?"–"I went in the wrong direction."* "你怎么耽搁了？"——"我走错了方向。" 3 V-T If you **keep** something **from** someone, you do not tell them about it. 隐瞒 ❑ *She knew that Gabriel was keeping something from her.* 她知道加布里埃尔正有事瞒着她。

❸ **keep** ◆◆◆ /kip/ (**keeps, keeping, kept**) 1 N-SING Someone's **keep** is the cost of food and other things that they need in their daily life. 生活费 ❑ *Ray will earn his keep on local farms while studying.* 学习期间，雷将在当地农场挣取生活费。 2 V-T If you **keep** animals, you own them and take care of them. 饲养 ❑ *I've brought you some eggs. We keep chickens.* 我给你带来了些鸡蛋。我们养着一些鸡。 3 V-T If you **keep** yourself or **keep** someone else, you support yourself or the other person by earning enough money to provide food, clothing, money, and other necessary things. 抚养 [mainly BRIT] ❑ *She could just about afford to keep her five kids.* 她勉强能抚养她的5个孩子。 ❑ *I just cannot afford to keep myself.* 我连自己也养活不了。

❹ **keep** /kip/ (**keeps**) N-COUNT A **keep** is the main tower of a medieval castle, in which people lived. 中世纪城堡主楼 ❑ *...the first stone-built castle keep in Britain.* …英国第一座石建中世纪城堡主楼。

❺ **keep** /kip/ (**keeps, keeping, kept**)

▸ **keep down** 1 PHRASAL VERB If you **keep** the number, size, or amount of something **down**, you do not let it get bigger or go higher. 抑制 ❑ *The prime aim is to keep inflation down.* 首要目标是抑制通货膨胀。 2 PHRASAL VERB If someone **keeps** a group of people **down**, they prevent them from getting power and status and being completely free. 压制 ❑ *No matter what a woman tries to do to improve her situation, there is some barrier or attitude to keep her down.* 不管女性如何试图改善自己的境遇，总有障碍或看法压制她们。 3 PHRASAL VERB If you **keep** food or drink **down**, you manage to swallow it properly and not vomit, even though you feel sick. 勉强吞下 ❑ *I tried to give her something to drink but she couldn't keep it down.* 我试图让她喝点儿什么，但她咽不下去。

▸ **keep on** 1 → see **keep** ❶ 4 2 PHRASAL VERB If you **keep** someone **on**, you continue to employ them, for example after other employees have lost their jobs. 继续雇用 ❑ *They concluded that firing him would be more damaging than keeping him on.* 他们得出结论，解雇他会比留用他的损害更大。

▸ **keep to** 1 PHRASAL VERB If you **keep to** a rule, plan, or agreement, you do exactly what you are expected or supposed to do. 遵守 ❑ *You've got to keep to the speed limit.* 你必须遵守限速的规定。 2 PHRASAL VERB If you **keep to** something such as a path or river, you do not move away from it as you go somewhere. 不偏离 ❑ *Please keep to the paths.* 请不要偏离道路。 3 PHRASAL VERB If you **keep to** a particular subject, you talk only about that subject, and do not talk about anything else. 不偏离（主题） ❑ *Let's keep to the subject, or you'll get me too confused.* 咱们不要离题，否则你会把我弄得很糊涂。 4 PHRASAL VERB If you **keep** something **to** a particular number or quantity, you limit it to that number or quantity. 把…局限于 ❑ *Keep costs to a minimum.* 把成本控制到最低。

▸ **keep up** 1 PHRASAL VERB If you **keep up with** someone or something that is moving near you, you move at the same speed. 跟上 ❑ *He lengthened his stride to keep up with his father.* 他迈开大步跟上他父亲。 ❑ *She shook her head and started to walk. He kept up with her.* 她摇了摇头，开始步行。他跟随着她。 2 PHRASAL VERB To **keep up with** something that is changing means to be able to cope with the change, usually by changing at the same rate. 跟上（变化） ❑ *The union called the strike to press for wage increases which keep up with inflation.* 工会号召罢工，要求工资增长跟上通货膨胀。 3 PHRASAL VERB If you **keep up with** your work or **with** other people, you manage to do or understand all your work, or to do or understand it as well as other people. 跟上（工作进度等） ❑ *Penny tended to work through her lunch hour in an effort to keep up with her work.* 为了努力跟上工作进度，彭妮往往午饭时间也在工作。 4 PHRASAL VERB If you **keep up with** what is happening, you make sure that you know about it. 了解 ❑ *She did not bother to keep up with the news.* 她不愿操心去了解新闻。 5 PHRASAL VERB If you **keep** something **up**, you continue to do it or provide it. 使继续下去 ❑ *I was so hungry all the time that I could not keep the diet up for longer than a month.* 我总是饿，所以我的节食一个月后就继续不下去了。 6 PHRASAL VERB If you **keep** something **up**, you prevent it from growing less in amount, level, or degree. 使不下降 ❑ *The riders had to keep their pace up.* 骑手们必须保持速度不减。 7 → see also **keep** ❶ 15

keep·er /kipər/ (**keepers**) 1 N-COUNT In football, a **keeper** is a play in which the quarterback keeps the ball. （足球运动中）守球 [AM] 2 N-COUNT A **keeper** at a zoo is a person who takes care of the animals. （动物园）饲养员 3 N-COUNT A **keeper** is something or someone that you value and that you feel is worth keeping. 值得保留的东西；值得保留的人 [AM, INFORMAL] ❑ *The show's a keeper–daring, imaginative and provocative.* 这部电影值得收藏——大胆、富于想像力和煽动性。 ❑ *His sweet nature and kindness made him a keeper, she said.* 她说他的可爱和善良使他成为值得珍视的人。

ken·nel /kɛnᵊl/ (**kennels**) 1 N-COUNT A **kennel** is a place where dogs are bred and trained, or cared for when their owners are away. 养狗场 ❑ *Once you have chosen a kennel, make a booking for your pet.* 一旦您选定了养狗场，请为您的宠物预约。 2 N-COUNT A **kennel** is a small building made especially for a dog to sleep in. 犬舍 [mainly BRIT]

in AM, usually use **doghouse**

kept /kɛpt/ **Kept** is the past tense and past participle of **keep**. **keep**的过去式和过去分词

kerb /kɜrb/ [BRIT] → see **curb** 3

kero·sene /kɛrəsin/ N-UNCOUNT **Kerosene** is a clear, strong-smelling liquid which is used as a fuel, for example in heaters and lamps. 煤油 [mainly AM]

in BRIT, usually use **paraffin**

❑ *...a kerosene lamp.* …一盏煤油灯。

→ see **dry-cleaning**

ket·tle /kɛtᵊl/ (**kettles**) 1 N-COUNT A **kettle** is a covered container that you use for boiling water. It has a handle, and a spout for the water to come out of. 水壶 ❑ *I'll put the kettle on and make us some tea.* 我来烧壶水给咱们沏点儿茶。 2 N-COUNT A **kettle of** water is the amount of water contained in a kettle. 一壶的量

in AM, also use **teakettle**

❑ *Pour a kettle of boiling water over the onions.* 往这些洋葱上倒一壶开水。 3 PHRASE If you say that something is **a different kettle of fish**, you mean that it is very different from another related thing that you are talking about. 两码事 [INFORMAL] ❑ *Banking today is a very different kettle of fish from the industry of the past.* 如今的银行业与过去的已是两码事了。

key ◆◆◇ /ki/ (**keys, keying, keyed**) 1 N-COUNT A **key** is a specially shaped piece of metal that you place in a lock and turn in order to open or lock a door, or to start or stop the engine of a vehicle. 钥匙 ❑ *They put the key in the door and entered.* 他们用钥匙开了门然后走了进去。 2 N-COUNT The **keys** on a computer keyboard or typewriter are the buttons that you press in order to operate it. 键 ❑ *Finally, press the Delete key.* 最后，按删除键。 3 N-COUNT The **keys** of a piano or organ are the long narrow pieces of wood or plastic that you press in order to play it. 琴键 ❑ *...the black and white keys on a piano keyboard.* …一个钢琴键盘上的黑白琴键。 4 N-VAR In music, a **key** is a scale of musical notes that starts on one specific note. 调 ❑ *...the key of A minor.* …A小调。 5 N-COUNT The **key** on a map or diagram or in a technical book is a list of the symbols or abbreviations used and their meanings. 图例 ❑ *You will find a key at the front of the book.* 你在书的前面会看到一个图例。 6 ADJ The **key** person or thing in a group is the most important one. 关键的 [ADJ n] ❑ *He is expected to be the key witness at the trial.* 预计他将成为审判时的关键证人。 7 N-COUNT The **key to** a desirable situation or result is the way in which it can be achieved. 关键 ❑ *The key to success is to be ready from the start.* 成功的关键是从一开始就做好准备。 8 N-COUNT A **key** is a small low island or reef, especially one in the Gulf of Mexico. （尤指墨西哥湾内的）低岛；礁 ❑ *...the Florida Keys.* …佛罗里达群岛。

→ see **graph**

▸ **key in** PHRASAL VERB If you **key** something **in**, you put information into a computer or you give the computer a particular instruction by typing the information or instruction on the keyboard. 键入 ❑ *Brian keyed in his personal code.* 布赖恩键入了他的个人密码。

Thesaurus *key* 另参见：

N.	code, explanation, guide 5
ADJ.	critical, important, major, vital 6

Word Partnership *key* 的常用搭配：

V. turn a key **1**
N. key **component**, key **decision**, key **factor**, key **figure**, key **ingredient**, key **issue**, key **official**, key **player**, key **point**, key **question**, key **role**, key **word** **6**
key **to success** **7**

key·board /kibɔrd/ (**keyboards**) **1** N-COUNT The **keyboard** of a typewriter or computer is the set of keys that you press in order to operate it. (打字机、计算机等的) 键盘 ❏ *He was in his office, battering the keyboard of his computer as if it were an old manual typewriter.* 他在办公室重重地敲打着他的计算机键盘，好像在用一部老式的手动打字机。 **2** N-COUNT The **keyboard** of a piano or organ is the set of black and white keys that you press in order to play it. (钢琴等的) 键盘 ❏ *Tanya's hands rippled over the keyboard.* 坦尼娅的双手在键盘上起伏摆动。 **3** N-COUNT People sometimes refer to musical instruments that have a keyboard as **keyboards**. 键盘乐器 ❏ *...Sean O'Hagan on keyboards.* …演奏键盘乐器的肖恩・奥黑根。
→ see Picture Dictionary: **keyboard**
→ see **computer**

key card (**key cards**) N-COUNT A **key card** is a small plastic card which you can use instead of a key to open a door or barrier, for example in some hotels and parking lots. 门卡 ❏ *The electronic key card to Julie's room would not work.* 朱莉房间的门卡不能用了。

key·note /kinoʊt/ (**keynotes**) N-COUNT The **keynote of** a policy, speech, or idea is the main theme of it or the part of it that is emphasized the most. 主题；要旨 ❏ *He would be setting out his plans for the party in a keynote speech.* 他将在一次主题发言中陈述他对该政党的规划。

key·pad /kipæd/ (**keypads**) N-COUNT The **keypad** on a telephone is the set of buttons that you press in order to operate it. Some other machines, such as ATMs, also have a keypad. (电话机等上的) 小键盘 ❏ *...an elevator's push-button keypad.* …一部电梯的按钮操纵键盘。

key·stone /kistoʊn/ (**keystones**) **1** N-COUNT A **keystone of** a policy, system, or process is an important part of it, which is the basis for later developments. 基础；根本 ❏ *The government's determination to beat inflation has so far been the keystone of its economic policy.* 政府对通货膨胀的坚决抑制迄今为止一直是其经济政策的根本。 **2** N-COUNT A **keystone** is a stone at the top of an arch, which keeps the other stones in place by its weight and position. 拱顶石 [TECHNICAL]
→ see **architecture**

key·stroke /kistroʊk/ (**keystrokes**) N-COUNT A **keystroke** is one touch of one of the keys on a computer or typewriter keyboard. 按键 ❏ *With a few keystrokes, Rebecca was connected to her computer at Liberty Air Service.* 按了几个键后，丽贝卡连接上了她在自由航空公司的电脑。

kg kg is a written abbreviation for **kilogram** or **kilograms**. 公斤

kha·ki /kæki/ **1** N-UNCOUNT **Khaki** is a strong material of a beige color, used especially to make uniforms for some soldiers. 卡其布 ❏ *On each side of me was a figure in khaki.* 我的两侧各有一个身穿卡其布衣服的人。 **2** COLOR Something that is **khaki** is beige in color. 卡其色的；土黄色的 ❏ *He was dressed in khaki trousers.* 他穿着一条卡其色的裤子。

kick ♦♦◊ /kɪk/ (**kicks, kicking, kicked**) **1** V-T/V-I If you **kick** someone or something, you hit them forcefully with your foot. 踢 ❏ *He kicked the door hard.* 他用力踢门。 ❏ *He threw me to the ground and started to kick.* 他把我摔在地上开始踢我。 ● N-COUNT **Kick** is also a noun. 踢 ❏ *He suffered a kick to the knee.* 他的膝盖被踢了一脚。 **2** V-T When you **kick** a ball or other object, you hit it with your foot so that it moves through the air. 踢 ❏ *I went to kick the ball and I completely missed it.* 我去踢球却踢空了。 ❏ *He kicked the ball away.* 他把球踢开了。 ● N-COUNT **Kick** is also a noun. 踢 ❏ *He missed an easy kick.* 他错失很容易的一脚球。 **3** V-T/V-I If you **kick** or if you **kick** your legs, you move your legs with very quick, small, and forceful movements, once or repeatedly. 踢动 ❏ *They were dragged away struggling and kicking.* 他们又挣又踢地被拖走了。 ❏ *First he kicked the left leg, then he kicked the right.* 他先踢左腿，然后踢右腿。 ● PHRASAL VERB **Kick out** means the same as **kick**. 踢动 ❏ *As its rider tried to free it, the horse kicked out and rolled over, crushing her.* 当骑手设法把它放开的时候，那匹马一阵踢，又一打滚，把她压伤了。 **4** V-T If you **kick** your legs, you lift your legs up very high one after the other, for example when you are dancing. 高高踢起 ❏ *...kicking his legs like a cancan dancer.* …像康康舞演员一样把他的腿高高踢起。 **5** V-T If you **kick** a habit, you stop doing something that is bad for you and that you find difficult to stop doing. 戒绝 (恶习) [INFORMAL] ❏ *She's kicked her drug habit and learned that her life has value.* 她已经戒掉吸毒的恶习，懂得了她的生命有价值。 **6** N-SING If something gives you **a kick**, it makes you feel very excited or very happy for a short period of time. 极大的快感；极度的兴奋 [INFORMAL] ❏ *I got a kick out of seeing my name in print.* 看到我的名字被印成铅字，我感到非常兴奋。 **7** PHRASE If you say that someone **kicks** you **when** you **are down**, you think they are behaving unfairly because they are attacking you when you are in a weak position. 落井下石 ❏ *In the end I just couldn't kick Jimmy when he was down.* 最后我就是不忍对吉米落井下石。 **8** PHRASE If you say that someone does something **for kicks**, you mean that they do it because they think it will be exciting. 为了追求刺激 [INFORMAL] ❏ *They made a few small bets for kicks.* 为了追求刺激，他们下了几个小赌注。 **9** PHRASE If you say that someone is dragged **kicking and screaming into** a particular course of action, you are emphasizing that they are very unwilling to do what they are being made to do. 极不情愿 [EMPHASIS] ❏ *He had to be dragged kicking and screaming into action.* 他非要被强迫着极不情愿地去做事。 **10** PHRASE If you describe an event as **a kick in the teeth**, you are emphasizing that it is very disappointing and upsetting. 重大打击 [INFORMAL, EMPHASIS] ❏ *We've been struggling for years and it's a real kick in the teeth to see a new band make it ahead of us.* 我们一直奋斗了很多年，看到一个新乐队在我们之前成功，这对我们是个重大打击。 **11** to **kick up a fuss** → see **fuss**

▸ **kick around** **1** PHRASAL VERB If you **kick around** ideas or

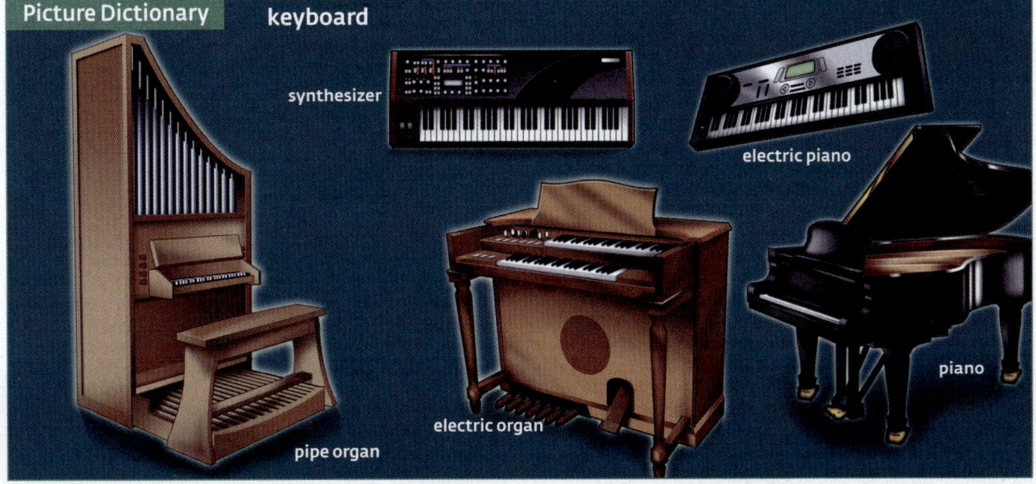

k

suggestions, you discuss them informally. 非正式讨论 ❑ *We kicked a few ideas around.* 我们随便谈了几个想法。❑ *They started to kick around the idea of going to Brazil next month.* 他们开始商量下个月去巴西。

▸ **kick off** 1 PHRASAL VERB In soccer or football, when the players **kick off**, they start a game by kicking the ball. (足球或橄榄球比赛的) 开球 ❑ *They kicked off an hour ago.* 他们是1小时前开球的。 2 PHRASAL VERB In football, when the players **kick off**, they resume a game by kicking the ball. (足球比赛中) 重新开始 3 PHRASAL VERB If an event, game, series, or discussion **kicks off**, or **is kicked off**, it begins. 开始 (事件、比赛等) ❑ *The shows kick off on October 24th.* 展览从10月24日开始。 ❑ *The mayor kicked off the party.* 市长揭开了宴会的序幕。 4 PHRASAL VERB If you **kick off** your shoes, you shake your feet so that your shoes come off. 踢掉 (鞋子) ❑ *She stretched out on the sofa and kicked off her shoes.* 她在沙发上伸了个懒腰然后踢掉鞋子。 5 PHRASAL VERB To **kick** someone **off** an area of land means to force them to leave it. 赶走 [INFORMAL] ❑ *We can't kick them off the island.* 我们不能把他们从岛上赶走。

▸ **kick out** 1 PHRASAL VERB To **kick** someone **out of** a place or an organization means to force them to leave it. 撵走；开除 [INFORMAL] ❑ *The country's leaders kicked five foreign journalists out of the country.* 该国首脑将5名外国记者驱逐出境。 ❑ *Her family kicked her out.* 她家人把她撵走了。 2 → see also **kick 3**

Thesaurus *kick* 另参见：

V.	abandon, give up, quit, stop; *(ant.)* start, take up 5
N.	enjoyment, excitement, fun, thrill 6

Word Partnership *kick* 的常用搭配：

N.	kick **a door** 1
	kick **a ball, penalty** kick 2
	kick **a habit**, kick **smoking** 5

kick·off /kɪkɔf/ (**kickoffs**)

in BRIT, use **kick-off**

1 N-VAR In football or soccer, the **kickoff** is the time at which a particular game starts. (足球比赛中的) 开球 ❑ *Hakan Sukur netted the goal just 10.8 seconds after the kickoff.* 开球后仅10.8秒，哈坎·苏克就踢球入网。 2 N-COUNT In football, a **kickoff** is the kick that begins a play, for example at the beginning of a half or after a touchdown or goal has been scored. (橄榄球比赛中的) 中线开球 [AM] ❑ *Gunn fumbled away the opening kickoff for the second straight week.* 甘恩接连两周在中线开球时失球。 3 N-SING The **kickoff** of an event or activity is its beginning. (事件或活动的) 开始 [INFORMAL] ❑ *Memorial Day weekend marks the kickoff of the summer vacation season.* 周末的阵亡将士纪念日标志着暑假的开始。

kick-start (**kick-starts, kick-starting, kick-started**) also **kickstart** 1 V-T To **kick-start** a process that has stopped working or progressing is to take a course of action that will quickly start it going again. 重振 ❑ *The president has chosen to kick-start the economy by slashing interest rates.* 总统已经决定通过大幅度降低利率重振经济。 ● N-COUNT **Kick-start** is also a noun. 重振 ❑ *The housing market needs a kick-start.* 房产市场需要重振。 2 V-T If you **kick-start** a motorcycle, you press the lever that starts it with your foot. 脚踏启动 ❑ *He lifted the bike off its stand and kick-started it.* 他把摩托车从展台上搬下来并用脚发动了它。

kid ◆◆◇ /kɪd/ (**kids, kidding, kidded**) 1 N-COUNT You can refer to a child as a **kid**. 孩子 [INFORMAL] ❑ *They've got three kids.* 他们有3个孩子。 ❑ *All the kids in my class could read.* 我班上的所有孩子都能读。 2 V-I If you **are kidding**, you are saying something that is not really true, as a joke. 开玩笑 [usu cont] [INFORMAL] ❑ *I'm not kidding, Frank. There's a cow out there, just standing around.* 我不是在开玩笑，弗兰克。那边有一头奶牛，就在那里站着呢。 ❑ *I'm just kidding.* 我只是在开玩笑。 3 V-T If you **kid** someone, you tease them. 戏弄 ❑ *He liked to kid Ingrid a lot.* 他很喜欢戏弄英格里德。 4 V-T If people **kid themselves**, they allow themselves to believe something that is not true because they wish that it was true. 欺骗 (自己) ❑ *We're kidding ourselves, Bill. We're not winning, we're not even doing well.* 我们是在欺骗自己，比尔。我们不会赢的。我们做得甚至都不好。 5 N-COUNT A **kid** is a young goat. 小山羊 6 PHRASE You can say "**you've got to be kidding**" or "**you must be kidding**" to someone if they have said something that you think is ridiculous or completely untrue. 你一定是在开玩笑 [INFORMAL, FEELINGS] ❑ *You've got to be kidding! I can't live here!* 你一定是在开玩笑！我不能住这儿！

Word Partnership *kid* 的常用搭配：

N.	kid **brother/sister, school** kid, kid **stuff** 1
ADJ.	**fat** kid, **friendly** kid, **good** kid, **little** kid, **new** kid, **nice** kid, **poor** kid, **skinny** kid, **smart** kid, **tough** kid, **young** kid 1
V.	**raise a** kid 1

★ **kid·nap** /kɪdnæp/ (**kidnaps, kidnaping** or **kidnapping, kidnaped** or **kidnapped**) 1 V-T/V-I To **kidnap** someone is to take them away illegally and by force, and usually to hold them prisoner in order to demand something from their family, employer, or government. 绑架 ❑ *Police in Brazil uncovered a plot to kidnap him.* 巴西警方侦破了一起要绑架他的阴谋。 ❑ *They were middle-class university students, intelligent and educated, yet they chose to kidnap and kill.* 他们是中产阶级大学生，聪明而且受过教育，却选择了绑架和谋杀。 ● **kid·nap·per** N-COUNT (**kidnappers**) 绑架者 ❑ *His kidnappers have threatened that they will kill him unless three militants are released from prison.* 绑架者威胁说，如果不释放3个武装分子出狱，他们就会杀了他。 ● **kid·nap·ping** N-VAR (**kidnappings**) 绑架 ❑ *Two youngsters have been arrested and charged with kidnapping.* 两个年轻人已被逮捕，并被指控犯绑架罪。 2 N-VAR **Kidnap** or **a kidnap** is the crime of taking someone away by force. 绑架 ❑ *Stewart denies attempted murder and kidnap.* 斯图尔特否认有谋杀和绑架的企图。

★ **kid·ney** /kɪdni/ (**kidneys**) 1 N-COUNT Your **kidneys** are the organs in your body that take waste matter from your blood and send it out of your body as urine. 肾脏 ❑ *...a kidney transplant.* …一次肾脏移植。 2 N-VAR **Kidneys** are the kidneys of an animal, for example a lamb, calf, or pig, that are eaten as meat. 腰子 ❑ *...lambs' kidneys.* …羊腰子。

→ see **donor**

kid·ney bean (**kidney beans**) N-COUNT **Kidney beans** are small, reddish-brown beans that are eaten as a vegetable. They are the seeds of a bean plant. 四季豆 [usu pl]

kill ◆◆◆ /kɪl/ (**kills, killing, killed**) 1 V-T/V-I If a person, animal, or other living thing **is killed**, something or someone causes them to die. 杀死 ❑ *More than 1,000 people have been killed by the armed forces.* 已经有一千多人被武装部队杀死。 ❑ *He had attempted to kill himself on several occasions.* 他好几次都企图自杀。 ❑ *Drugs can kill.* 毒品可以致死。 ● **kill·ing** N-UNCOUNT 杀害 ❑ *There is tension in the region following the killing of seven civilians.* 7名平民被杀害后，该地区的局势紧张。 2 N-COUNT The act of killing an animal after hunting it is referred to as **the kill**. 猎杀 ❑ *After the kill the men and old women collect in an open space and eat a meal of whale meat.* 猎杀结束后，男人们和年长的妇女们聚在一个空地吃了一顿鲸肉宴。 3 V-T If someone or something **kills** a project, activity, or idea, they completely destroy or end it. 使停止；扼杀 ❑ *His objective was to kill the space station project altogether.* 他的目的是使太空站计划完全停止。 ● PHRASAL VERB **Kill off** means the same as **kill**. 使停止；扼杀 ❑ *He would soon launch a second offensive, killing off the peace process.* 他将很快发起第二次攻击，扼杀和平进程。 4 V-T If something **kills** pain, it weakens it so that it is no longer as strong as it was. 缓解 (疼痛等) ❑ *He was forced to take opium to kill the pain.* 他被迫服用鸦片止痛。 5 V-T If you say that something **is killing** you, you mean that it is causing you physical or emotional pain. 使痛得要命 [only cont] [INFORMAL] ❑ *My feet are killing me.* 我的脚痛死了。 6 V-T If you say that you **kill yourself to** do something, you are emphasizing that you make a great effort to do it, even though it causes you a lot of trouble or suffering. 拼命去做 [INFORMAL, EMPHASIS] ❑ *I'm killing myself to get my work done.* 我正在拼命完成我的工作。 ❑ *To kill the hours while she waited, Ann worked in the garden.* 为了消磨等待的几个小时，安在花园里工作了。 7 V-T If you say that you will **kill** someone for something they have done, you are emphasizing that you are extremely angry with them. (因为极度愤怒而想要) 杀死 [EMPHASIS] ❑ *Tell Richard I'm going to kill him when I get hold of him.* 告诉理查德，我要抓住他就杀了他。 8 V-T If you say that something will not **kill** you, you mean that it is not really as difficult or unpleasant as it might seem. 难倒；伤害 [INFORMAL] ❑ *Three or four more weeks won't kill me!* 再多上三四个星期也难不倒我。 9 V-T If you **are killing** time, you are doing something because you have some time available, not because you really want to do it. 消磨 (时间) ❑ *I'm just killing time until I can talk to the other witnesses.* 我正在消磨时间，直到能跟其他的证人交谈。 ❑ *You shouldn't always have to kill yourself to do well.* 你不能总是非得拼命去做好。

K

There are several words which mean similar things to **kill**. To **murder** someone means to kill them deliberately. **Assassinate** is used to talk about the murder of an important person, often for political reasons. If a large number of people are murdered, the words **slaughter** or **massacre** are sometimes used. **Slaughter** can also be used to talk about killing animals for their meat.

10 PHRASE If you say that you will do something **if it kills** you, you are emphasizing that you are determined to do it even though it is extremely difficult or painful. 即使把命豁出去 [EMPHASIS] ❑ *I'll make this marriage work if it kills me.* 即使把命豁出去，我也要使这婚姻成功。 11 PHRASE If you say that you **killed yourself laughing**, you are emphasizing that you laughed a lot because you thought something was extremely funny. 笑得要死 [INFORMAL, EMPHASIS] ❑ *I eventually got to the top about an hour after everyone else, and they were all killing themselves laughing.* 我终于在所有其他人之后又用了大概1小时到了顶部，他们都笑得要死。 12 PHRASE If you **move in for the kill** or if you **close in for the kill**, you take advantage of a changed situation in order to do something that you have been preparing to do. 伺机而动 ❑ *Seeing his chance, Dennis moved in for the kill.* 看到机会来了，丹尼斯伺机而动。 13 **dressed to kill** → see **dressed** 14 **to be killed outright** → see **outright** → see **war**

▸ **kill off** 1 → see **kill** 3 2 PHRASAL VERB If you say that a group or an amount of something **has been killed off**, you mean that all of them or all of it have been killed or destroyed. 杀光；把…灭绝 ❑ *Their natural predators have been killed off.* 他们的天敌已被灭绝。 ❑ *It is an effective treatment for the bacteria and does kill it off.* 这是一种有效的灭菌方法，确实把细菌都杀光了。

Thesaurus *kill* 另参见：
V. execute, murder, put down, slay, wipe out 1

kill·er ♦◇◇ /kɪlər/ (**killers**) 1 N-COUNT A **killer** is a person who has killed someone, or who intends to kill someone. 杀人者；杀手 ❑ *The police are searching for his killers.* 警方正在缉拿杀死他的凶手。 2 N-COUNT You can refer to something that causes death or is likely to cause death as a **killer**. 致命的事物 ❑ *Heart disease is the biggest killer of men in developed countries.* 对于发达国家的人来说，心脏病是最致命的杀手。

kill·ing ♦◇◇ /kɪlɪŋ/ (**killings**) 1 N-COUNT A **killing** is an act of deliberately killing a person. 谋杀 ❑ *This is a brutal killing.* 这是一起残忍的谋杀。 2 PHRASE If you **make a killing**, you make a large profit very quickly and easily. 发大财 [INFORMAL] ❑ *They have made a killing on the deal.* 他们在这笔交易中发了大财。

kilo /kiloʊ/ (**kilos**) N-COUNT A **kilo** is the same as a **kilogram**. 公斤 ❑ *He'd lost ten kilos in weight.* 他的体重已经减了10公斤。

Word Link *kilo ≈ thousand : kilobyte, kilogram, kilometer*

kilo·byte /kɪləbaɪt/ (**kilobytes**) N-COUNT In computing, a **kilobyte** is one thousand bytes of data. 千字节

kilo·gram /kɪləgræm/ (**kilograms**)
in BRIT, also use **kilogramme**
N-COUNT A **kilogram** is a metric unit of weight. One kilogram is a thousand grams, or a thousandth of a metric ton, and is equal to 2.2 pounds. 公斤 ❑ *...a parcel weighing around 4.5 kilograms.* …一个重约4.5公斤的包裹。

kilo·gramme /kɪləgræm/ [BRIT] → see **kilogram**

kilo·hertz /kɪləhɜrts/ (**kilohertz**)
Kilohertz is both the singular and the plural form.
N-COUNT A **kilohertz** is a unit of measurement of radio waves. One kilohertz is a thousand hertz. 千赫 ❑ *Their instruments detected very faint radio waves at a frequency of 3 kilohertz.* 他们的仪器探测到了频率为3千赫的非常微弱的无线电波。

Word Link *meter ≈ measuring : kilometer, meter, perimeter*

kilo·meter ♦◇◇ /kɪləmitər, kɪlɒmɪtər/ (**kilometers**)
in BRIT, use **kilometre**
N-COUNT A **kilometer** is a metric unit of distance or length. One kilometer is a thousand meters and is equal to 0.62 miles. 公里 ❑ *...only one kilometer from the border.* …距离边境只有1公里。

kilo·metre /kɪləmiːtəʳ, kɪlɒmɪtəʳ/ [BRIT] → see **kilometer**

★ **kilo·watt** /kɪləwɒt/ (**kilowatts**) N-COUNT A **kilowatt** is a unit of power. One kilowatt is a thousand watts. 千瓦 ❑ *...a prototype system which produces 25 kilowatts of power.* …一个生产25千瓦电量的样机。

▲ **kin** /kɪn/ 1 N-PLURAL Your **kin** are your relatives. 亲戚 [DIALECT or OLD-FASHIONED] 2 → see also **next of kin**

kind
❶ NOUN USES AND PHRASES
❷ ADJECTIVE USES

❶ **kind** ♦♦♦ /kaɪnd/ (**kinds**) 1 N-COUNT If you talk about a particular **kind of** thing, you are talking about one of the types or sorts of that thing. 种类 ❑ *The party needs a different kind of leadership.* 该党需要一种不同的领导。 ❑ *Had Jamie ever been in any kind of trouble?* 杰米曾经遇到过什么样的麻烦吗？ 2 N-COUNT If you refer to someone's **kind**, you are referring to all the other people that are like them or that belong to the same class or set. 同一类的人 [DISAPPROVAL] ❑ *I can take care of your kind.* 我能对付你这类人。 3 PHRASE You can use **all kinds of** to emphasize that there are a great number and variety of particular things or people. 各种各样的 [EMPHASIS] ❑ *Adoption can fail for all kinds of reasons.* 收养可能因为各种各样的原因失败。 4 PHRASE You use **kind of** when you want to say that something or someone can be roughly described in a particular way. 有点 [SPOKEN, VAGUENESS] ❑ *It was kind of sad, really.* 这真的有点伤感。 5 PHRASE If you refer to someone or something as **one of a kind**, you mean that there is nobody or nothing else like them. 独一无二的 [APPROVAL] ❑ *She's a very unusual woman, one of a kind.* 她是个很不平常的女人，独一无二。 6 PHRASE If you refer, for example, to **two, three,** or **four of a kind**, you mean two, three, or four similar people or things that seem to go well or belong together. 两/三/四个同一类的人 ❑ *They were two of a kind, from the same sort of background.* 他们两个是一类人，来自相同的背景。 7 PHRASE If you respond **in kind**, you react to something that someone has done to you by doing the same thing to them. 以同样的方式 ❑ *They hurled defiant taunts at the riot police, who responded in kind.* 他们对着防暴警察愤然大骂，对方也以牙还牙。 8 PHRASE If you pay a debt **in kind**, you pay it in the form of goods or services and not money. 以货代款；以服务代款 ❑ *...benefits in kind.* …实物形式的收益。 9 PHRASE You can use **of a kind** to indicate that something is not as good as it might be expected to be, but that it seems to be the best that is possible or available. 差强人意的一种 [mainly BRIT] ❑ *She finds solace of a kind in alcohol.* 她在酒精里勉强找到一点安慰。

❷ **kind** /kaɪnd/ (**kinder, kindest**) 1 ADJ Someone who is **kind** behaves in a gentle, caring, and helpful way toward other people. 和蔼的；仁慈的；乐于助人的 ❑ *I must thank you for being so kind to me.* 真要感谢您对我这么好。 ● **kind·ly** ADV 和蔼地；仁慈地；乐于助人地 [ADV after v] ❑ *"You seem tired this morning, Jenny," she said kindly.* "今天早上你看起来有些疲倦，詹妮，"她和蔼地说道。 2 ADJ You can use **kind** in expressions such as **please be so kind as to** and **would you be kind enough to** in order to ask someone to do something in a firm but polite way. 用于**please be so kind as to**和**would you be kind enough to**中，表坚定而礼貌的命令 [v-link ADJ] [POLITENESS] ❑ *Please be so kind as to see to it that all the alterations are made at once!* 请注意所有变更必须马上完成！ 3 → see also **kindly, kindness**

Thesaurus *kind* 另参见：
N. sort, type ❶ 1
ADJ. affectionate, considerate, gentle ❷ 1

kinda /kaɪndə/ **Kinda** is used in written English to represent the words "kind of" when they are pronounced informally. 有点儿 ❑ *I'd kinda like to have a sheep farm in New Mexico.* 我有点想在新墨西哥城有个牧羊农场。

kin·der·gar·ten /kɪndərgɑrtᵊn/ (**kindergartens**) N-COUNT A **kindergarten** is a school or class for children aged 4 to 6 years old. It prepares them to go into the first grade. 幼儿园 [also "in/to/at" N] ❑ *She's in kindergarten now.* 她现在在上幼儿园。

kind·ly /kaɪndli/ 1 ADJ A **kindly** person is kind, caring, and sympathetic. 仁慈的；体贴的；富于同情心的 ❑ *He was a stern critic but an extremely kindly man.* 他是一位严厉的批评家，却是一个非常仁慈的人。 2 ADV If someone **kindly** does something for you, they act in a thoughtful and helpful way. 体贴地；好意地 [ADV before v] ❑ *She kindly offered to go and fetch him some beer.* 她体贴地主动去给他拿了些啤酒来。 3 ADV If someone asks you to **kindly** do something,

k

they are asking you in a way which shows that they have authority over you, or that they are angry with you. (表命令或生气的口气) 烦请 [ADV before v] [FORMAL] ❑ *Will you kindly obey the instructions I am about to give?* 烦请您依照我要发出的指令去做好吗？ 4 → see also **kind**

kind-hearted ADJ If you describe someone as **kind-hearted**, you mean that they are kind, caring, and generous. 好心的

Word Link *ness ≈ state, condition : cleanliness, consciousness, kindness*

kind·ness /kaɪndnɪs/ N-UNCOUNT **Kindness** is the quality of being gentle, caring, and helpful. 和蔼；亲切；好意 ❑ *We have been treated with such kindness by everybody.* 我们受到了大家如此亲切的对待。

king ♦♦◊ /kɪŋ/ (**kings**) 1 N-TITLE; N-COUNT A **king** is a man who is the most important member of the royal family of his country, and who is considered to be the head of state of that country. 君主；国王 ❑ *...the king and queen of Spain.* …西班牙国王和王后。 2 N-COUNT If you describe a man as **the king of** something, you mean that he is the most important person doing that thing or he is the best at doing it. 首屈一指的男性；佼佼者 ❑ *He was the king of the cowboys.* 他是牛仔之王。 3 N-COUNT A **king** is a playing card with a picture of a king on it. (扑克牌的) 老K ❑ *...the king of diamonds.* …方片K。 4 N-COUNT In chess, the **king** is the most important piece. When you are in a position to capture your opponent's king, you win the game. (国际象棋的) 王
→ see **chess**

king·dom /kɪŋdəm/ (**kingdoms**) 1 N-COUNT A **kingdom** is a country or region that is ruled by a king or queen. 王国 ❑ *The kingdom's power declined.* 王国的势力衰落了。 2 N-SING All the animals, birds, and insects in the world can be referred to together as the animal **kingdom**. All the plants can be referred to as the plant **kingdom**. (动物或植物) 界 ❑ *The animal kingdom is full of fine and glorious creatures.* 动物界有很多精巧而美妙的生物。

ki·osk /kiːɒsk/ (**kiosks**) N-COUNT A kiosk is a small structure with an open window at which people can buy things like newspapers, pay an attendant at a parking lot, or get information about something. (出售报刊、停车收费或问讯的) 亭子 ❑ *I was getting cigarettes at the kiosk.* 我正在书报亭买烟。 ❑ *...an information kiosk.* …一个问讯亭。

kiss ♦◊◊ /kɪs/ (**kisses, kissing, kissed**) 1 V-RECIP If you **kiss** someone, you touch them with your lips to show affection or sexual desire, or to greet them or say goodbye. 吻 ❑ *She leaned up and kissed him on the cheek.* 她靠过来吻了他的脸颊。 ❑ *Her parents kissed her goodbye as she set off from their home.* 当她动身离开家时，她的父母跟她吻别。 ● N-COUNT **Kiss** is also a noun. 吻 ❑ *I put my arms around her and gave her a kiss.* 我抱住她然后给了她一个吻。 2 V-T If you say that something **kisses** another thing, you mean that it touches that thing very gently. 轻触 ❑ *The wheels of the aircraft kissed the runway.* 飞机的轮子擦过跑道。 3 PHRASE If you **blow** someone **a kiss** or **blow a kiss**, you touch the palm of your hand lightly with your lips, and then blow across your hand toward the person, in order to show them your affection. 给…飞吻 ❑ *Maria blew him a kiss.* 玛丽亚给了他一个飞吻。 4 PHRASE If you say that you **kiss** something **goodbye** or **kiss goodbye to** something, you accept the fact that you are going to lose it, although you do not want to. 不舍地告别 [INFORMAL] ❑ *I felt sure I'd have to kiss my dancing career goodbye.* 我确实感到我将不得不告别自己的舞蹈生涯。
→ see Word Web: **kiss**

Word Partnership *kiss* 的常用搭配：
ADJ. **big kiss, first kiss, quick kiss** 1
N. kiss *someone* **on the cheek/lips/mouth,** kiss *(someone)* **goodbye/goodnight, hug and kiss** 1
V. **give** *someone* **a kiss, plant a kiss on** *someone*, **want to** kiss *someone* 1

kit /kɪt/ (**kits, kitting, kitted**) 1 N-COUNT A **kit** is a group of items that are kept together, often in the same container, because they are all used for similar purposes. 成套用具 ❑ *Make sure you keep a well-stocked first aid kit ready to deal with any emergency.* 确保你有一套保存良好的急救用具，随时应对任何突发情况。 2 N-COUNT A **kit** is a set of parts that can be put together in order to make something. 配套组件 ❑ *Her popular potholder is also available in do-it-yourself kits.* 在自己动手的配套组件中也有她受欢迎的防烫布垫。 3 N-UNCOUNT **Kit** is special clothing and equipment that you use when you take part in a particular activity, especially a sport. (参加活动或运动时穿用的) 装备 [mainly BRIT]

in AM, usually use **gear**

kitch·en ♦♦◊ /kɪtʃən/ (**kitchens**) N-COUNT A **kitchen** is a room that is used for cooking and for household jobs such as washing dishes. 厨房
→ see **house**

kite /kaɪt/ (**kites**) 1 N-COUNT A **kite** is an object, usually used as a toy, which is flown in the air. It consists of a light frame covered with paper or cloth and has a long string attached which you hold while the kite is flying. 风筝 ❑ *Willy asks if I've ever flown a kite before.* 威利问我以前是否放过风筝。 2 PHRASE If you say that someone is **as high as a kite**, you mean that they are very excited or that they are greatly affected by alcohol or drugs. 如痴如狂的；因饮酒或吸毒而飘飘然的 ❑ *The steroids made me feel so strange. I was as high as a kite some of the time.* 类固醇令我感觉很奇特。有时我感到飘飘然的。

kitsch /kɪtʃ/ N-UNCOUNT You can refer to a work of art or an object as **kitsch** if it is showy and thought by some people to be in bad taste. 庸俗的东西 ❑ *...a hideous ballgown verging on the kitsch.* …一件难看得近乎庸俗的晚礼服。 ● ADJ **Kitsch** is also an adjective. 庸俗的 ❑ *Blue and green eyeshadow has long been considered kitsch.* 蓝色和绿色的眼影很久以来一直被认为是庸俗的。

▲ **kit·ten** /kɪtən/ (**kittens**) N-COUNT A **kitten** is a very young cat. 小猫

kit·ty /kɪti/ (**kitties**) 1 N-COUNT A **kitty** is an amount of money gathered from several people, which is meant to be spent on things that these people will share or use together. 公共储金 ❑ *You haven't put any money in the kitty for three weeks.* 你已经3个星期不交公共储金了。 2 N-COUNT A **kitty** is the total amount of money which is bet in a gambling game, and which is taken by the winner or winners. (赌博中赢家获得的) 全部赌注 ❑ *Each month the total prize kitty is $13.5 million.* 每月全部的赌注奖金是1350万美元。 3 N-COUNT A **kitty** is a cat, especially a young cat. 小猫 [INFORMAL] ❑ *...a cute little kitty.* …一只可爱的小猫。 ❑ *...kitty litter made of wood shavings.* …刨花做的猫砂。 4 N-COUNT **Kitty** is sometimes used as an affectionate way of referring to a cat or a kitten. 猫咪 [INFORMAL] ❑ *"Gertie!" the kids were calling into the yard. "Here kitty, kitty, kitty!"* "格蒂！"孩子们冲着院子里喊，"猫咪，猫咪，猫咪过来！"

kiwi /kiwi/ (**kiwis**) A **kiwi** is the same as a **kiwi fruit**. 猕猴桃

kiwi fruit (**kiwi fruits**)

Word Web **kiss**

Some anthropologists believe mothers invented the **kiss**. They chewed a bit of food and then used their lips to place it in their child's mouth. Others believe that primates started the practice. There are many types of kisses. Kisses express affection or accompany a greeting or a goodbye. Friends and family members exchange **social kisses** on the **lips** or sometimes on the **cheek**. When people are about to kiss they pucker their lips. In European countries, friends kiss each other lightly on both cheeks. And in the Middle East, a kiss between two political figures indicates a pledge of mutual support.

Kiwi fruit can also be used as the plural form.

N-VAR A **kiwi fruit** is a fruit with a brown hairy skin and green flesh. 猕猴桃

km (**kms**) **km** is a written abbreviation for **kilometer**. 公里

knack /næk/ (**knacks**) N-COUNT A **knack** is a particularly clever or skillful way of doing something successfully, especially something which most people find difficult. 诀窍 ❑ *He's got the knack of getting people to listen.* 他有让人们倾听的诀窍。

knap·sack /næpsæk/ (**knapsacks**) or **backpack** N-COUNT A **knapsack** is a cloth or leather bag that you carry on your back or over your shoulder, for example when you are walking in the countryside. 背包

knead /nid/ (**kneads, kneading, kneaded**) **1** V-T When you **knead** dough or other food, you press and squeeze it with your hands so that it becomes smooth and ready to bake. 揉（面团等） ❑ *Lightly knead the mixture on a floured surface.* 在撒有面粉的案板上轻揉该混合物。 **2** V-T If you **knead** a part of someone's body, you press or squeeze it with your fingers. 揉捏 ❑ *She felt him knead the aching muscles.* 她感到他在揉捏那些疼痛的肌肉。

knee ♦◇◇ /ni/ (**knees, kneeing, kneed**) **1** N-COUNT Your **knee** is the place where your leg bends. 膝 ❑ *He will receive physical therapy on his damaged left knee.* 他受损的左膝将接受理疗。 **2** N-COUNT If something or someone is **on** your **knee** or **on** your **knees**, they are resting or sitting on the upper part of your legs when you are sitting down. （坐着时）大腿上部 ❑ *He sat with the package on his knees.* 他坐着，包放在大腿上。 **3** N-PLURAL If you are **on** your **knees**, your legs are bent and your knees are on the ground. 膝部 ❑ *She fell to the ground on her knees and prayed.* 她跪在地上祈祷。 **4** V-T If you **knee** someone, you hit them using your knee. 用膝盖撞击 ❑ *Ian kneed him in the groin.* 伊恩用膝盖撞击他的腹股沟。 **5** PHRASE If a country or organization **is brought to its knees**, it is almost completely destroyed by someone or something. 彻底击败；使屈服 ❑ *The country was being brought to its knees by the loss of 2.4 million manufacturing jobs.* 该国由于失去240万制造业工作机会，濒临崩溃。 **6** **on bended knee** → see **bended**
→ see **body**

Word Partnership *knee* 的常用搭配：

N.	knee **injury** 1
ADJ.	**left/right** knee, **weak-**kneed 1
V.	**bend your** knees, knees **buckle** 1
	fall on your knees 3

kneel /nil/ (**kneels, kneeling, kneeled** or **knelt**) V-I When you **kneel**, you bend your legs so that your knees are touching the ground. 跪下 ❑ *She knelt by the bed and prayed.* 她跪在床边祷告。 ❑ *Other people were kneeling, but she just sat.* 别人都跪下，但她只是坐着。 ● PHRASAL VERB **Kneel down** means the same as **kneel**. 跪下 ❑ *She kneeled down beside him.* 她在他身边跪下。

knew /nu/ **Knew** is the past tense of **know**. **know**的过去式

knick·ers /nɪkərz/

The form **knicker** is used as a modifier.

N-PLURAL **Knickers** are the same as **panties**. 短衬裤 [also "a pair of" N] [BRIT]

knife ♦◇◇ /naɪf/ (**knives, knifes, knifing, knifed**)

Knives is the plural form of the noun and **knifes** is the third person singular of the present tense of the verb.

1 N-COUNT A **knife** is a tool for cutting or a weapon and consists of a flat piece of metal with a sharp edge on the end of a handle. 刀 ❑ *...a knife and fork.* …一副刀叉。 **2** V-T To **knife** someone means to attack and injure them with a knife. 用刀砍 ❑ *Dawson takes revenge on the man by knifing him to death.* 道森向那人报仇，用刀砍死了他。 **3** PHRASE If you **twist the knife in someone's wound**, you do or say something to make an unpleasant situation they are in even more unpleasant. 在某人伤口上撒盐 ❑ *Hearing his own plans was like having a knife twisted in his wound.* 听到他自己的计划就像是有人在自己伤口上撒盐。
→ see **silverware, tool**

▲ **knight** /naɪt/ (**knights, knighting, knighted**) **1** N-COUNT In medieval times, a **knight** was a man of noble birth, who served his king or lord in battle. （中世纪的）骑士 ❑ *...King Arthur's faithful knight, Gawain.* …亚瑟王的忠实骑士高文。 **2** V-T If someone **is knighted**, they are given a knighthood. 授予爵士称号 [usu passive] ❑ *He was knighted in June 1988.* 他于1988年6月被授予爵士称号。 **3** N-COUNT In chess, a **knight** is a piece which is shaped like a horse's head. （国际象棋中的）马 **4** PHRASE If you refer to someone as a **knight in shining armor**, you mean that they are kind and brave, and likely to rescue you from a difficult situation. 困境中救助人的勇士 ❑ *The love songs tricked us all into believing in happy endings and knights in shining armor.* 那些情歌骗我们都去相信有幸福的结局和于危难中救助我们的勇士。
→ see **chess**

knight·hood /naɪthʊd/ (**knighthoods**) N-COUNT A **knighthood** is a title that is given to a man by a British king or queen for his achievements or his service to his country. A man who has been given a knighthood can put "Sir" in front of his name instead of "Mr." （英国的）爵士称号及身份 ❑ *When he finally received his knighthood in 1975 Chaplin was 85.* 当他最终在1975年得到爵士封号时，卓别林已经85岁了。

knit /nɪt/ (**knits, knitting, knitted**) **1** V-T/V-I If you **knit** something, especially an article of clothing, you make it from wool or a similar thread by using two knitting needles or a machine. 编织 ❑ *I had endless hours to knit and sew.* 我有无数的时间来缝缝织织。 ❑ *I have already started knitting baby clothes.* 我已经开始织婴儿的衣服了。 ● COMB IN ADJ **Knit** is also a combining form. 编织（用于合成词中） [ADJ n] ❑ *Ferris wore a heavy knit sweater.* 菲立斯穿着一件织得厚厚的毛衣。 **2** V-T If someone or something **knits** things or people **together**, they make them fit or work together closely and successfully. 紧密连接 ❑ *The best thing about sports is that they knit the whole family close together.* 体育运动最大的好处就是将全家紧密连接在一起。 ● COMB IN ADJ **Knit** is also a combining form. 紧密连接（用于合成词中） ❑ *...a closer-knit family.* …一个连接更为紧密的家庭。 **3** V-I When broken bones **knit**, the broken pieces grow together again. （骨头）愈合 ❑ *The bone hasn't knitted together properly.* 骨头还没有完全愈合。

Word Partnership *knit* 的常用搭配：

N.	knit **a sweater** 1
ADV.	**closely/tightly** knit, knit **together** 2

knit·ting /nɪtɪŋ/ **1** N-UNCOUNT **Knitting** is something, such as an article of clothing, that is being knitted. 编织物 ❑ *She had been sitting with her knitting at her fourth-floor window.* 她一直坐在5楼的窗户旁做编织活。 **2** N-UNCOUNT **Knitting** is the action or process of knitting. 编织 ❑ *Take up a relaxing hobby, such as knitting.* 从事一种让人放松的业余爱好，比如编织。

knives /naɪvz/ **Knives** is the plural of **knife**. **knife**的复数形式

★ **knob** /nɒb/ (**knobs**) **1** N-COUNT A **knob** is a round handle on a door or drawer which you use in order to open or close it. 球形把手 ❑ *He turned the knob and pushed against the door.* 他转动门把手，推了那扇门。 **2** N-COUNT A **knob** is a round switch on a piece of machinery or equipment. 旋钮 ❑ *...the volume knob.* …音量旋钮。

knock ♦◇◇ /nɒk/ (**knocks, knocking, knocked**) **1** V-I If you **knock on** something such as a door or window, you hit it, usually several times, to attract someone's attention. 敲 ❑ *She went directly to Simon's apartment and knocked on the door.* 她径直走到西蒙的住处，敲了敲门。 ● N-COUNT **Knock** is also a noun. 敲的声音 ❑ *They heard a knock at the front door.* 他们听到前门有一敲门声。 ● **knock·ing** N-SING 敲的声音 [also no det] ❑ *They were wakened by a loud knocking at the door.* 他们被一阵很响的敲门声吵醒。 **2** V-T If you **knock** something, you touch or hit it roughly, especially so that it falls or moves. 碰撞 ❑ *She accidentally knocked the glass off the shelf.* 她无意中把架子上的玻璃杯碰了下来。 ● N-COUNT **Knock** is also a noun. 碰撞 ❑ *The bags have tough exterior materials to protect against knocks, rain, and dust.* 这些袋子结实的外层材料有防撞、防雨、防尘的作用。 **3** V-T To **knock** someone into a particular position or condition means to hit them very hard so that they fall over or become unconscious. 重击 ❑ *The third wave was so strong it knocked me backwards.* 第3个浪头如此猛烈，把我击得往后退。 **4** V-T To **knock** a particular quality or characteristic **out of** someone means to make them lose it. 使失去 [no cont] ❑ *The school system is designed to knock passion out of people.* 学校体制是设计来抹杀人的激情的。 **5** V-T If you **knock** something or someone, you criticize them and say unpleasant things about them. 批评；指责 [INFORMAL] ❑ *I'm not knocking them: if they want to do* it, it's up to them. 我不是在说他们的坏话：如果他们打算做这件事，由他们决定。 6 N-COUNT If someone receives a **knock**, they have an unpleasant experience which prevents them from achieving something or which causes them to change their attitudes or plans. 打击

in BRIT, also use **knock about**

7 to **knock** someone or something **into shape** → see **shape**

▶ **knock about** [BRIT] → see **knock around**

▶ **knock around** 1 PHRASAL VERB If someone **knocks around** somewhere, they spend time there, experiencing different situations or just passing time. 漫游 ❑ *...reporters who knock around in troubled parts of the world.* …游历世界动乱地区的记者们。 ❑ *They knock around on weekends in grubby sweaters and pants.* 他们周末穿着邋遢的毛线衫和裤子到处闲逛。 2 PHRASAL VERB If someone **knocks** you **around**, they hit or kick you several times. 拳打脚踢 [INFORMAL] ❑ *He lied to me constantly and started knocking me around.* 他经常跟我撒谎并且开始对我拳打脚踢。

▶ **knock down** 1 PHRASAL VERB To **knock down** a building or part of a building means to demolish it. 拆掉（建筑物等） ❑ *Why doesn't he just knock the wall down?* 他为什么不索性把墙拆掉？ 2 PHRASAL VERB To **knock down** a price or amount means to decrease it. 降低（价格） [mainly AM]

in BRIT, usually use **bring down**

❑ *The market might abandon the stock, and knock down its price.* 商场可能会清理库存，降低价格。 3 PHRASAL VERB If someone **is knocked down** or **is knocked over** by a vehicle or its driver, they are hit by a car and fall to the ground, and are often injured or killed. （开车）撞倒 [mainly BRIT]

in AM, usually use **hit**

❑ *He died after being knocked down by a car.* 他被一辆汽车撞倒后死了。 ❑ *A drunk driver knocked down and killed two girls.* 一个喝醉了酒的司机撞死了两个女孩子。 ❑ *A car knocked him over.* 一辆汽车把他撞倒了。

▶ **knock off** 1 PHRASAL VERB To **knock off** an amount from a price, time, or level means to reduce it by that amount. 减去（一定数额） ❑ *We have knocked 10% off admission prices.* 我们已将入场票的价格降低了10%。 2 PHRASAL VERB When you **knock off**, you finish work at the end of the day or before a break. 歇工；下班 [INFORMAL] ❑ *If I get this report finished I'll knock off early.* 如果我完成这个报告就会早点儿下班。

▶ **knock out** 1 PHRASAL VERB To **knock** someone **out** means to cause them to become unconscious or to go to sleep. 使失去知觉；使昏昏欲睡 ❑ *The three drinks knocked him out.* 这3杯酒让他昏昏欲睡。 2 PHRASAL VERB If a person or team **is knocked out** of a competition, they are defeated in a game, so that they take no more part in the competition. 淘汰 ❑ *He got knocked out in the first inning.* 他在第1局就被淘汰了。 3 → see also **knockout** 4 PHRASAL VERB If something **is knocked out** by enemy action or bad weather, it is destroyed or stops functioning because of it. 破坏 ❑ *Our bombers have knocked out the mobile launchers.* 我们的轰炸机已经破坏了那些移动发射台。

▶ **knock over** → see **knock down 1, 4**

▶ **knock up** 1 PHRASAL VERB If you **knock** something **up**, you make it or build it very quickly, using whatever materials are available. 赶做 2 PHRASAL VERB If a woman **is knocked up** by a man, she is made pregnant by him. 搞大肚子 [BRIT, INFORMAL] [usu passive] [INFORMAL, VULGAR] ❑ *When I got knocked up, the whole town knew it.* 我肚子大起来时，全镇的人都知道了。

Thesaurus *knock* 另参见：

V. rap, tap 1
bash, hit, strike 2
belittle, criticize, denounce; (*ant.*) praise 5

Word Partnership *knock* 的常用搭配：

V. **answer a** knock, **hear a** knock 1
N. knock **at/on a door** 1
ADJ. **loud** knock 1
knock ***someone*** **out cold**, knock ***someone*** **unconscious** 3

knock·out /nɒkaʊt/ (**knockouts**) also **knock-out** 1 N-COUNT In boxing, a **knockout** is a situation in which a boxer wins the fight by making his opponent fall to the ground and be unable to stand up before the referee has counted to ten. （拳击中的）击倒获胜 [also "by" N] ❑ *Lennox Lewis ended the scheduled 12-round fight with a knockout in the eighth round.* 莱诺克斯·刘易斯在第8回合击倒对方，结束了预定12回合的比赛。 2 ADJ A **knockout** blow is an action or event that completely defeats an opponent. 彻底击败对手的 [ADJ n] ❑ *He delivered a knockout blow to all of his rivals.* 他彻底击败了所有对手。 3 ADJ A **knockout** competition is one in which the players or teams that win continue playing until there is only one winner left. 淘汰制的（比赛） [ADJ n] [mainly BRIT]

in AM, use **elimination**

4 N-SING If you describe someone as a **knockout**, you think that they are extremely attractive or impressive. 引人注目的人 [INFORMAL, APPROVAL] ❑ *Jill was a knockout with her biker leathers and t-shirt.* 吉尔穿上她的摩托车皮衣和T恤衫非常引人注目。

knot /nɒt/ (**knots, knotting, knotted**) 1 N-COUNT If you tie a **knot** in a piece of string, rope, cloth, or other material, you pass one end or part of it through a loop and pull it tight. 结 ❑ *One lace had broken and been tied in a knot.* 一根带子已经断了，被打成一个结。 2 V-T If you **knot** a piece of string, rope, cloth, or other material, you pass one end or part of it through a loop and pull it tight. 把…打成结 ❑ *He knotted the laces securely together.* 他把带子牢牢地系在一起。 ❑ *He knotted the bandanna around his neck.* 他把印花大围巾系在他的脖子上。 3 N-COUNT If you feel a **knot** in your stomach, you get an uncomfortable tight feeling in your stomach, usually because you are afraid or excited. 痉挛 ❑ *There was a knot of tension in his stomach.* 他心里一阵紧张。 4 V-T/V-I If your stomach **knots** or if something **knots** it, it feels tight because you are afraid or excited. 使（心）揪紧；揪紧 ❑ *I felt my stomach knot with apprehension.* 我感到心里因为担心而揪紧。 5 V-I If part of your face or your muscles **knot**, they become tense, usually because you are worried or angry. （脸部或肌肉）紧皱 ❑ *His forehead knotted in a frown.* 他的眉头紧皱。 6 N-COUNT A **knot** in a piece of wood is a small hard area where a branch grew. 节疤 ❑ *A carpenter often rejects half his wood because of knots or cracks.* 木匠常常因为有节疤或裂缝而把一半的木材都扔掉。 7 N-COUNT A **knot** is a unit of speed. The speed of ships, aircraft, and wind is measured in knots. 节（航速和风速单位） ❑ *They travel at speeds of up to 30 knots.* 他们以高达30节的航速行进。
→ see **rope**

know

❶ VERB USES
❷ PHRASES

❶ **know** ♦♦♦ /noʊ/ (**knows, knowing, knew, known**) 1 V-T/V-I If you **know** a fact, a piece of information, or an answer, you have it correctly in your mind. 知道 [no cont] ❑ *I don't know the name of the place.* 我不知道那个地方的名称。 ❑ *"People like doing things for nothing."—"I know they do."* "人们喜欢白忙活。"——"我知道他们是那样。" ❑ *I don't know what happened to her husband.* 我不知道她的丈夫出了什么事。 ❑ *"How did he meet your mother?"—"I don't know."* "他是怎么遇到你母亲的？"——"我不知道。" 2 V-T If you **know** someone, you are familiar with them because you have met them and talked to them before. 认识 [no cont] ❑ *Gifford was a friend. I'd known him for nine years.* 吉福德曾是个朋友。我那时认识他已有9年。 3 V-I If you say that you **know of** something, you mean that you have heard about it but you do not necessarily have a lot of information about it. 听说过 [no cont] ❑ *We know of the incident but have no further details.* 我们听说过那个事件，但不了解更多的细节。 ❑ *The president admitted that he did not know of any rebels having surrendered so far.* 总统承认迄今为止他未曾听说有任何反叛分子投降。 4 V-I If you **know about** a subject, you have studied it or taken an interest in it, and understand part or all of it. 了解 [no cont] ❑ *Hire someone with experience, someone who knows about real estate.* 用一位有经验并了解房地产的人。 ❑ *She didn't know anything about music.* 她对音乐一点都不了解。 5 V-T If you **know** a language, you have learned it and can understand it. 懂（某种语言） [no cont] ❑ *It helps to know French and Creole if you want to understand some of the lyrics.* 如果你想明白其中一些歌词，需要懂法语和克里奥尔语。 6 V-T If you **know** something such as a place, a work of art, or an idea, you have visited it, seen it, read it, or heard about it, and so you are familiar with it. 熟悉 [no cont] ❑ *No matter how well you know this city, it is easy to get lost.* 不论你多么熟悉这座城市，都容易迷路。 7 V-T If you **know how to** do something, you have the necessary skills and knowledge to do it. 知道 [no cont] ❑ *The health authorities now know how to deal with the disease.* 卫生部门现在知道如何对付这种疾病。 8 V-T You can say that someone **knows that** something is happening when they become aware of it. 意识到 [no cont] ❑ *Then I saw a gun under the hall table so I knew that something was wrong.* 当时我看到大厅的桌子下面有一支枪，就意识到出问题了。 9 V-T If you **know** something or someone, you recognize them when you see them or hear them. 辨认出 [no cont] ❑ *Would she know you if she saw you on the street?* 如果在街上见到你，她会认出你吗？ 10 V-T If someone or something **is known as** a particular name, they are called by that name. 把…称作 [no cont] ❑ *The disease is more commonly known as Mad Cow Disease.* 这种病一般更多地被称作"疯牛病"。 ❑ *...Peter and his wife Antonella (also known as Tony).* 彼得和妻子安托妮拉（亦称托妮）。 11 V-T If you **know** someone or something **as** a person or thing that has particular qualities, you consider that they have those qualities. 认为 ❑ *Lots of people know her as a very kind woman.* 很多人都认为她是一个很善良的女人。 12 → see also **knowing, known**

Thesaurus *know* 另参见：

V. comprehend, recognize, understand ❶ 1
be acquainted, be familiar with ❶ 2

❷ **know** /noʊ/ (**knows, knowing, knew, known**)
➪ **Please look at meanings 14 – 22 to see if the expression you are looking for is shown under another headword.** 1 PHRASE If you talk about a thing or system **as we know it**, you are referring to the form in which it exists now and which is familiar to most people. 如我们所知 ❑ *He planned to end the welfare system as we know it.* 正如我们所知，他曾计划废除这种福利制度。 2 PHRASE If you **get to know** someone, you find out what they are like by spending time with them. (逐渐) 了解 ❑ *The new neighbors were getting to know each other.* 新邻居们正在逐渐彼此了解。 3 PHRASE People use expressions such as **goodness knows, Heaven knows**, and **God knows** when they do not know something and want to suggest that nobody could possibly know it. 天晓得 [INFORMAL] ❑ *"Who's he?"—"God knows."* "他是谁？"——"天晓得。" 4 CONVENTION You say "**I know**" to show that you agree with what has just been said. 我知道(表示赞同) ❑ *"This country is so awful."—"I know, I know."* "这个国家真糟糕。"——"我知道，我知道。" 5 PHRASE You can use **I don't know** to indicate that you do not completely agree with something or do not really think that it is true. 我说不准(表不完全同意) ❑ *"He should quite simply resign."—"I don't know about that."* "他只要辞职就行了。"——"我说不准。" 6 PHRASE You can say "**I don't know about you**" to indicate that you are going to give your own opinion about something and you want to find out if someone else feels the same. 我不知道你怎么想 ❑ *I don't know about the rest of you, but I'm hungry.* 不知道你们怎么样，我可是饿了。 7 PHRASE You use **I don't know** in expressions which indicate criticism of someone's behavior. For example, if you say that you **do not know how** someone can do something, you mean that you cannot understand or accept them doing it. 我真想像不出 [DISAPPROVAL] ❑ *I don't know how he could do this to his own daughter.* 我真想像不出他怎么能这样对待自己的女儿。 8 PHRASE If you are **in the know** about something, especially something that is not known about or understood by many people, you have information about it. 了解内幕 ❑ *It was gratifying to be in the know about important people.* 了解重要人物的内幕令人满足。 9 CONVENTION You can use expressions such as **you know what I mean** and **if you know what I mean** to suggest that the person listening to you understands what you are trying to say, and so you do not have to explain any more. 你懂我的意思 [SPOKEN] ❑ *None of us stayed long. I mean, the atmosphere wasn't – well, you know what I mean.* 我们都没久留。我是说，气氛不是——嗯，你懂我的意思。 10 CONVENTION You say "**You never know**" or "**One never knows**" to indicate that it is not definite or certain what will happen in the future, and to suggest that there is some hope that things will turn out well. (指有希望向好的方向发展) 很难说；难以预料 [VAGUENESS] ❑ *You never know, I might get lucky.* 很难说，我也许会走运。 11 CONVENTION You say "**Not that I know of**" when someone has asked you whether or not something is true and you think the answer is "no" but you cannot be sure because you do not know all the facts. 据我所知并非如此 [VAGUENESS] ❑ *"Is he married?"—"Not that I know of."* "他结婚了吗？"——"据我所知没有。" 12 CONVENTION You use **you know** to emphasize or to draw attention to what you are saying. 你知道 [SPOKEN, EMPHASIS] ❑ *The conditions in there are awful, you know.* 你知道，那里的条件非常糟糕。 13 PHRASE You can say "**You don't know**" in order to emphasize how strongly you feel about the remark you are going to make. 你想像不出 [SPOKEN, EMPHASIS] ❑ *You don't know how good it is to speak to somebody from home.* 你不知道跟家里来的人说说话有多好！ 14 **to know best** → see **best** 15 **to know better** → see **better** 16 **to know** something **for a fact** → see **fact** 17 **as far as I know** → see **far** 18 **not to know the first thing about** something → see **first** 19 **to know full well** → see **full** 20 **to let** someone **know** → see **let** 21 **to know** your **own mind** → see **mind** 22 **to know the ropes** → see **rope**

know-all (**know-alls**) N-COUNT A **know-all** is the same as a **know-it-all**. 自以为是的人 [BRIT, INFORMAL, DISAPPROVAL]

know-how ♦◇◇ N-UNCOUNT **Know-how** is knowledge of the methods or techniques of doing something, especially something technical or practical. 专门知识；技能 [INFORMAL] ❑ *He hasn't got the know-how to run a farm.* 他没有经营一个农场的专门知识。

know·ing /noʊɪŋ/ ADJ A **knowing** gesture or remark is one that shows that you understand something, for example the way that someone is feeling or what they really mean, even though it has not been mentioned directly. 会意的 ❑ *Ron gave her a knowing smile.* 罗恩向她报以一个会意的微笑。 ● **know·ing·ly** ADV 会意地 ❑ *He smiled knowingly.* 他会意地笑了。

know·ing·ly /noʊɪŋli/ ADV If you **knowingly** do something wrong, you do it even though you know it is wrong. 故意地 [ADV before V] ❑ *He repeated that he had never knowingly taken illegal drugs.* 他反复说自己从未故意吸毒。

know-it-all (**know-it-alls**) N-COUNT If you say that someone is a **know-it-all**, you are critical of them because they think that they know a lot more than other people. 自以为是的人 [AM, INFORMAL, DISAPPROVAL]

in BRIT, use **know-all**

❑ *Don't act like a know-it-all. You listen to your mother.* 不要那样自以为是。听你妈妈的话。

knowl·edge ♦♦◇ /nɒlɪdʒ/ 1 N-UNCOUNT **Knowledge** is information and understanding about a subject which a person has, or which all people have. 知识；学识 ❑ *She disclaims any knowledge of her husband's business concerns.* 她自称不知道丈夫生意上的顾虑。 2 PHRASE If you say that something is true **to** your **knowledge** or **to the best of** your **knowledge**, you mean that you believe it to be true but it is possible that you do not know all the facts. 据某人所知 ❑ *Alec never carried a gun to my knowledge.* 亚历克据我所知从不带枪。

Thesaurus *knowledge* 另参见：

N. comprehension, consciousness, education, intelligence, wisdom; *(ant.)* ignorance 1

Word Partnership *knowledge* 的常用搭配：

V. **acquire** knowledge, **gain** knowledge, **have** knowledge, **lack** knowledge, **require** knowledge, **test *your*** knowledge, **use *your*** knowledge 1
ADJ. **background** knowledge, **common** knowledge, **general** knowledge, **prior** knowledge, **scientific** knowledge, **useful** knowledge, **vast** knowledge 1
N. knowledge **base** 1

knowl·edge·able /nɒlɪdʒəbᵊl/ also **knowledgable** ADJ Someone who is **knowledgeable** has or shows a clear understanding of many different facts about the world or about a particular subject. 知识渊博的 ❑ *Do you think you are more knowledgeable about life than your parents were at your age?* 父母在你这个年龄时，你认为你比他们更了解生活吗？

known /noʊn/ 1 **Known** is the past participle of **know**. **know**的过去分词 2 ADJ You use **known** to describe someone or something that is clearly recognized by or familiar to all people or to a particular group of people. 众所周知的；公认的 ❑ *...He was a known drug dealer.* …他是一个臭名昭著的毒品贩子。 3 ADJ If someone or something is **known for** a particular achievement or feature, they are familiar to many people because of that achievement or feature. 著名的 [v-link ADJ "for" n/-ing] ❑ *He is better known for his film and TV work.* 他更为著名的是影视作品。 4 PHRASE If you **let it be known that** something is the case, or you **let** something **be known**, you make sure that people know it or can find out about it. 明确表示 ❑ *The president has let it be known that he is against it.* 总统已经明确表示，他反对此事。

▲ **knuck·le** /nʌkᵊl/ (**knuckles**) 1 N-COUNT Your **knuckles** are the rounded pieces of bone that form lumps on your hands where

k

your fingers join your hands, and where your fingers bend. 指关节
2 **a rap on the knuckles** → see **rap**
→ see **hand**

Ko·ran /kɔrɑn/ N-PROPER **The Koran** is the sacred book on which the religion of Islam is based. 古兰经

kph /keɪ pi eɪtʃ/ **kph** is written after a number to indicate the speed of something such as a vehicle. **kph** is an abbreviation for "kilometers per hour." 千米每小时; 公里每小时

kW also **KW** **kW** is a written abbreviation for **kilowatt**. 千瓦

K

Ll

L also **l** /ɛl/ (**L's, l's**) N-VAR **L** is the twelfth letter of the English alphabet. 英语字母表中的第12个字母

L8R **L8R** is the written abbreviation for "later," mainly used in text messages and e-mails. 再见 [COMPUTING] ❑ *C U L8R!* 再见！

lab /læb/ (**labs**) N-COUNT A **lab** is the same as a **laboratory**. 实验室

la·bel ♦◇◇ /leɪbᵊl/ (**labels, labeling** or **labelling, labeled** or **labelled**) **1** N-COUNT A **label** is a piece of paper or plastic that is attached to an object in order to give information about it. 标签 ❑ *He peered at the label on the bottle.* 他注视着瓶子上的标签。 **2** V-T If something **is labeled**, a label is attached to it giving information about it. 贴标签于 [usu passive] ❑ *It requires foreign frozen-food imports to be clearly labeled.* 它要求外国进口冷冻食品要粘贴明确的标签。 ❑ *The produce was labeled "Made in China."* 该产品上贴有"中国制造"的标签。 **3** V-T If you say that someone or something **is labeled as** a particular thing, you mean that people generally describe them that way and you think that this is unfair. 把…称为 [usu passive] [DISAPPROVAL] ❑ *It won't be labeled in any way as a military expedition.* 它无论如何也称不上是一次军事远征。 ❑ *It does not matter whether these duties are labeled "duties" or "tasks."* 这些义务被称作"义务"还是"任务"都无关紧要。

→ see **graph**

Thesaurus *label* 另参见：

N. sticker, tag, ticket **1**

V. brand, characterize, classify **3**

la·bor ♦♦♦ /leɪbər/ (**labors, laboring, labored**)

in BRIT, use **labour**

1 N-UNCOUNT **Labor** is very hard work, usually physical work. 劳动 [also N in pl] ❑ *...the labor of hauling the rocks away.* …拖走这些岩石的劳动。 **2** V-I Someone who **labors** works hard using their hands. 艰苦劳动 ❑ *...he will be laboring 14 hundred meters below ground.* …他将在地下1400米处艰苦劳动。 **3** V-T/V-I If you **labor to** do something, you do it with difficulty. 艰难地工作 ❑ *Scientists labored for months to unravel the mysteries of Neptune and still remain baffled.* 科学家们为揭开海王星之谜艰难地工作了数月，但依然迷惑不解。 ❑ *We're laboring under an unfair disadvantage.* 我们在不公平的劣势下艰难地工作。 **4** N-UNCOUNT **Labor** is used to refer to the workers of a country or industry, considered as a group. (总称) 劳工 ❑ *We have a problem of skilled labor.* 我们缺少熟练工。 ❑ *Employers want cheap labor and consumers want cheap houses.* 雇主需要廉价的劳动力，消费者需要便宜的房子。 **5** N-UNCOUNT The work done by a group of workers or by a particular worker is referred to as their **labor**. 工作 ❑ *He exhibits a profound humility in the low rates he pays himself for his labor.* 他给自己工作支付的低工资展现了他极度的谦逊。 **6** N-UNCOUNT **Labor** is the last stage of pregnancy, in which the baby is gradually pushed out of the womb by the mother. 分娩 ❑ *Her labor had lasted ten hours before the doctor arranged a Cesarean section.* 她的分娩持续了10个小时后，医生才给她安排了剖腹产手术。

Thesaurus *labor* 另参见：

N. effort, employment, work; *(ant.)* leisure, rest **1**
employees, help, workforce, working people; *(ant.)* management **4**

V. exert, strain, struggle, work;, relax, rest **2**

Word Link *labor ≈ working : collaborate, elaborate, laboratory*

la·bora·tory ♦◇◇ /læbrətɔri/ (**laboratories**) **1** N-COUNT A **laboratory** is a building or a room where scientific experiments, analyses, and research are carried out. 实验室 (用于分析研究) ❑ *...a brain research laboratory at Columbia University.* …哥伦比亚大学的一个大脑研究实验室。 **2** N-COUNT A **laboratory** in a school, college, or university is a room containing scientific equipment where students are taught science subjects such as chemistry. 实验室 (用于教学) ❑ *...my old school chemistry laboratory.* …我母校的化学实验室。

→ see Word Web: **laboratory**

Word Partnership *laboratory* 的常用搭配：

N. laboratory **conditions**, **research** laboratory, laboratory **technician**, laboratory **test** **1**
laboratory **equipment**, laboratory **experiment** **1** **2**

la·bor·er /leɪbərər/ (**laborers**) N-COUNT A **laborer** is a person who does a job which involves a lot of hard physical work. 体力劳动者 ❑ *She still lives on the farm where he worked as a laborer.* 她还住在他当过工人的那个农场。

→ see **union**

la·bor force (**labor forces**) N-COUNT **The labor force** consists of all the people who are able to work in a country or area, or all the people who work for a particular company. 劳动力 [BUSINESS] ❑ *He says the reduction of the labor force could be significant.* 他说劳动力的缩减可能会有重大影响。

labor-intensive ADJ **Labor-intensive** industries or methods of making things involve a lot of workers. Compare **capital-intensive.** 劳动密集型的 [BUSINESS] ❑ *For labor-intensive businesses like garments, factory labor is cheap.* 像服装业这样的劳动密集型产业，工厂劳动力是廉价的。

la·bo·ri·ous /ləbɔriəs/ ADJ If you describe a task or job as **laborious**, you mean that it takes a lot of time and effort. 费时费力的 ❑ *Keeping the yard tidy all year round can be a laborious task.* 保持院子全年整洁会是一项费时费力的任务。 ● **la·bo·ri·ous·ly** ADV 费时费力地 [ADV with v] ❑ *...the embroidery she'd worked on so laboriously during the long winter nights.* …那件她在漫长的冬夜里辛勤制成的刺绣品。

la·bor mar·ket (**labor markets**) N-COUNT When you talk about **the labor market**, you are referring to all the people who are able to work and want jobs in a country or area, in relation to the number of jobs there are available in that country or area. 劳动力市场 [BUSINESS] ❑ *In a tight labor market, demand by employers exceeds*

Word Web laboratory

The discovery of the life-saving drug penicillin was a fortunate accident. While cleaning up his **laboratory**, a **researcher** named Alexander Fleming* noticed that the bacteria in one petri dish had been killed by some kind of **mold**. He took a **sample** and found that it was a form of penicillin. Fleming and others did further **research** and **published** their **findings** in 1928, but few people took notice. However, ten years later a team at Oxford University read Fleming's **study** and began animal and human **experiments**. Within a decade, companies were manufacturing 650 billion units of penicillin a month!

Alexander Fleming (1881-1955): a Scottish biologist and pharmacologist.

the available supply of workers. 在劳动力走俏的市场上，雇主的需求超过工人的供应。

la·bor re·la·tions N-PLURAL **Labor relations** refers to the relationship between employers and employees in industry, and the political decisions and laws that affect it. 劳资关系 ❑ *We have to balance good labor relations against the need to cut costs.* 我们必须掌握好劳资关系和降低成本的平衡。

labor-saving ADJ A **labor-saving** device or idea makes it possible for you to do something with less effort than usual. 节省人工的(仪器或想法) [usu ADJ n] ❑ *...labor-saving devices such as washing machines.* …节省人工的装置，例如洗衣机。

la·bor un·ion (**labor unions**) N-COUNT A **labor union** is an organization that represents the rights and interests of workers to their employers, for example in order to improve working conditions or wages. 工会 [AM]

in BRIT, use **trade union**

❑ *...NYSUT, the state's largest labor union.* …纽约州教师联盟，该州最大的工会。

la·bour /leɪbər/ [BRIT] → see **labor**

la·bour·er /leɪbərər/ [BRIT] → see **laborer**

lab·ra·dor /læbrədɔr/ (**labradors**) or **labrador retriever, Labrador retriever** N-COUNT A **labrador** or **labrador retriever** is a type of large dog with short, thick black or gold hair. 拉不拉多犬

▲ **laby·rinth** /læbɪrɪnθ/ (**labyrinths**) **1** N-COUNT If you describe a place as a **labyrinth**, you mean that it is made up of a complicated series of paths or passages, through which it is difficult to find your way. 迷宫 [LITERARY] ❑ *...the labyrinth of corridors.* …迷宫般的走廊。 **2** N-COUNT If you describe a situation, process, or area of knowledge as a **labyrinth**, you mean that it is very complicated. 错综复杂的事物 [FORMAL] ❑ *...a labyrinth of conflicting political and sociological interpretations.* …错综复杂的、互相矛盾的政治和社会学解释。

L

★ **lace** /leɪs/ (**laces, lacing, laced**) **1** N-UNCOUNT **Lace** is a very delicate cloth which is made with a lot of holes in it. It is made by twisting together very fine threads of cotton to form decorative patterns. 花边 ❑ *She finally found the perfect gown, a beautiful creation trimmed with lace.* 她最终找到了那件完美的大衣，款式漂亮、饰有花边。 **2** N-COUNT **Laces** are thin pieces of material that are put through special holes in some types of clothing, especially shoes. The laces are tied together in order to tighten the clothing. 系带 ❑ *Barry was sitting on the bed, tying the laces of an old pair of running shoes.* 巴里正坐在床上系一双旧跑鞋的鞋带。 **3** V-T If you **lace** something such as a pair of shoes, you tighten the shoes by pulling the laces through the holes, and usually tying them together. 系…的带子 ❑ *I have a good pair of skates, but no matter how tightly I lace them, my ankles wobble.* 我有一双很好的溜冰鞋，但是无论我把鞋带系得多么紧，我的脚踝还是在里面晃荡。 ● PHRASAL VERB **Lace up** means the same as **lace**. 系…的带子(同**lace**) ❑ *He sat on the steps, and laced up his boots.* 他坐在台阶上系好靴子。 **4** V-T To **lace** food or drink with a substance such as alcohol or a drug means to put a small amount of the substance into the food or drink. 在(食物、饮料)中添加 ❑ *She laced his food with sleeping pills.* 她在他的食物里加了安眠药。

lack ♦♦◇ /læk/ (**lacks, lacking, lacked**) **1** N-UNCOUNT If there is a **lack of** something, there is not enough of it or it does not exist at all. 缺乏；不存在 [also "a" N, usu N "of" n] ❑ *Despite his lack of experience, he got the job.* 尽管缺乏经验，他还是得到了那份工作。 ❑ *The charges were dropped for lack of evidence.* 由于缺少证据，起诉被撤销了。 **2** V-T/V-I If you say that someone or something **lacks** a particular quality or that a particular quality **is lacking** in them, you mean that they do not have any or enough of it. 缺乏；没有 ❑ *It lacked the power of the Italian cars.* 它没有意大利汽车那样的动力。 ❑ *He lacked the judgment and political acumen for the post of chairman.* 他缺少作为主席的判断力和政治敏锐性。 **3** PHRASE If you say there is **no lack of** something, you are emphasizing that there is a great deal of it. 不缺某物 [EMPHASIS] ❑ *He said there was no lack of things for them to talk about.* 他说他们不缺话题谈。

Thesaurus *lack* 另参见：

N. absence, shortage; *(ant.)* abundance **1**

V. be without, miss, need, require, want; *(ant.)* have, own **2**

Word Partnership *lack* 的常用搭配：

N. lack *of* **confidence**, lack *of* **control**, lack *of* **enthusiasm**, lack *of* **evidence**, lack *of* **exercise**, lack *of* **experience**, lack *of* **food**, lack *of* **information**, lack *of* **knowledge**, lack *of* **money**, lack *of* **progress**, lack *of* **resources**, lack *of* **skills**, lack *of* **sleep**, lack *of* **support**, lack *of* **trust**, lack *of* **understanding** **1**

lack·ing /lækɪŋ/ ADJ If something or someone **is lacking in** a particular quality, they do not have any of it or enough of it. 缺乏的；没有的 [v-link ADJ] ❑ *...if your hair is lacking in luster and feeling dry.* …如果你的头发缺乏光泽并且感觉干燥。 ❑ *She felt nervous, increasingly lacking in confidence about herself.* 她感到紧张，对自己越来越缺乏信心。

lack·luster /læklʌstər/

in BRIT, use **lacklustre**

ADJ If you describe something or someone as **lackluster**, you mean that they are not exciting or energetic. 无精打采的 ❑ *He has already been blamed for his party's lackluster performance during the election campaign.* 他已经因为自己的党在选举中的不活跃表现而受到了谴责。

lack·lustre /læklʌstəʳ/ [BRIT] → see **lackluster**

lac·quer /lækər/ (**lacquers**) N-MASS **Lacquer** is a special liquid which is painted on wood or metal in order to protect it and to make it shiny. 漆 ❑ *We put on the second coating of lacquer.* 我们刷了第二层漆。

lacy /leɪsi/ (**lacier, laciest**) ADJ **Lacy** things are made from lace or have pieces of lace attached to them. 有花边的 ❑ *...lacy nightgowns.* …有花边的睡袍。

lad ♦◇◇ /læd/ (**lads**) N-COUNT; N-VOC A **lad** is a young man or boy. 小伙子 [OLD-FASHIONED] ❑ *When I was a lad his age I would laugh at the strangest things.* 我是他那么大的小伙子时，我常嘲笑一些最奇怪的事情。

lad·der /lædər/ (**ladders**) **1** N-COUNT A **ladder** is a piece of equipment used for climbing up something or down from something. It consists of two long pieces of wood, metal, or rope with steps fixed between them. 梯子 ❑ *He climbed the ladder to the next deck.* 他登上梯子爬到了上一层甲板。 **2** N-SING You can use **the ladder** to refer to something such as a society, organization, or system which has different levels that people can progress up or drop down. 阶梯 ❑ *If they want to climb the ladder of success they should be given that opportunity.* 如果他们想攀登成功的阶梯，他们应该被给与那个机会。 **3** N-COUNT A **ladder** is a hole or torn part in a woman's stocking or pantyhose, where some of the vertical threads have broken, leaving only the horizontal threads. (长筒丝袜等的) 脱丝 [BRIT]

in AM, use **run**

▲ **lad·en** /leɪdᵊn/ **1** ADJ If someone or something is **laden with** a lot of heavy things, they are holding or carrying them. 装满的 [LITERARY] ❑ *I came home laden with cardboard boxes.* 我满载着纸箱子回了家。 ❑ *The following summer the peach tree was laden with fruit.* 第二年夏天，桃树上结满了果实。 **2** ADJ If you describe a person or thing as **laden with** something, particularly something bad, you mean that they have a lot of it. 充满的 (尤指令人不快的东西) [v-link ADJ "with" n] ❑ *We're so laden with guilt.* 我们满怀内疚。

lady ♦♦◇ /leɪdi/ (**ladies**) **1** N-COUNT You can use **lady** when you are referring to a woman, especially when you are showing politeness or respect. 女士 ❑ *She's a very sweet old lady.* 她是一位非常亲切的老太太。 ❑ *...a cream-colored lady's shoe.* …一只奶黄色的女鞋。 **2** N-VOC **"Lady"** is sometimes used by men as a form of address when they are talking to a woman that they do not know, especially in stores and on the street. 女士 (对陌生女子的称呼) [AM, INFORMAL, POLITENESS] ❑ *What seems to be the trouble, lady?* 有什么麻烦吗，女士？ **3** N-TITLE In Britain, **Lady** is a title used in front of the names of some female members of the nobility, or the wives of knights. (在英国用在女贵族成员或爵士妻子名前) 夫人；小姐

lag /læg/ (**lags, lagging, lagged**) **1** V-I If one thing or person **lags behind** another thing or person, their progress is slower than that of the other thing or person. 落后 ❑ *Western banks still lag behind financial institutions in most other regions of the country.* 西部地区的银行仍然落后于这个国家其他大部分地区的金融机构。 ❑ *The restructuring of the pattern of consumption also lagged behind.* 消费结构的调整也落后了。 **2** N-COUNT A time **lag** or a **lag** of a particular length of time is a period of time between one event and another related event. 间隔 ❑ *There's a time lag between infection with HIV and* developing AIDS. 从感染艾滋病病毒到发展成为艾滋病病人有一定的时间间隔。

la·goon /ləgun/ (**lagoons**) N-COUNT A **lagoon** is an area of calm sea water that is separated from the ocean by a line of rock or sand. 环礁湖

laid /leɪd/ **Laid** is the past tense and past participle of **lay**. **lay**的过去式和过去分词

laid-back ADJ If you describe someone as **laid-back**, you mean that they behave in a calm relaxed way as if nothing will ever worry them. 遇事泰然的 [INFORMAL] ❑ *Everyone here has a really laid-back attitude.* 这里的每个人都很放松。

lain /leɪn/ **Lain** is the past participle of **lie**. **lie**的过去分词

laissez-faire /leɪseɪ fɛər, lɛs-/ N-UNCOUNT **Laissez-faire** is the policy which is based on the idea that governments and the law should not interfere with business, finance, or the conditions of people's working lives. 自由放任的政策 [BUSINESS] ❑ *...the doctrine of laissez-faire and unbridled individualism.* …自由放任和肆无忌惮的个人主义信条。

lake ♦◇◇ /leɪk/ (**lakes**) N-COUNT A **lake** is a large area of fresh water, surrounded by land. 湖 ❑ *They can go fishing in the lake.* 他们可以去湖里钓鱼。
→ see Word Web: **lake**
→ see **river**

lake·front /leɪkfrʌnt/ also **lake front, lake-front** N-SING The **lakefront** is the area of land around the edge of a lake. 湖边的平地 [oft N n] [mainly AM] ❑ *...a cabin down on the lakefront.* …湖边的小木屋。

lamb /læm/ (**lambs**) N-COUNT A **lamb** is a young sheep. 羔羊 ● N-UNCOUNT **Lamb** is the flesh of a lamb eaten as food. 羔羊肉 ❑ *Laura was basting the leg of lamb.* 劳拉正在往烤羔羊腿上涂油。

★ **lame** /leɪm/ (**lamer, lamest**) **1** ADJ If someone is **lame**, they are unable to walk properly because of damage to one or both of their legs. 瘸的 ❑ *He was aware that she was lame in one leg.* 他知道她有一条腿是瘸的。 ● N-PLURAL **The lame** are people who are lame. 瘸子 ❑ *...the wounded and the lame of the last war.* …在上次战争中受伤的和腿瘸的人。 **2** ADJ If you describe an excuse, argument, or remark as **lame**, you mean that it is poor or weak. 站不住脚的 ❑ *He mumbled some lame excuse about having gone to sleep.* 他为刚才睡着咕哝了个站不住脚的理由。 ● **lame·ly** ADV 站不住脚地 [ADV with v] ❑ *"Lovely house," I said lamely.* "好漂亮的房子，"我勉强地说。

▲ **la·ment** /ləmɛnt/ (**laments, lamenting, lamented**) **1** V-T/V-I If you **lament** something, you express your sadness, regret, or disappointment about it. 感到悲痛；感到遗憾；感到失望 [mainly FORMAL or WRITTEN] ❑ *Ken began to lament the death of his only son.* 肯为他独生子的去世开始感到悲痛。 ❑ *He laments that people in Villa El Salvador are suspicious of the police.* 他感到遗憾的是埃尔萨尔瓦多城的人们不信任警察。 **2** N-COUNT Someone's **lament** is an expression of their sadness, regret, or disappointment about something. 哀叹 [mainly FORMAL or WRITTEN] ❑ *She spoke of the professional woman's lament that a woman's judgment is questioned more than a man's.* 她谈到职业女性的悲哀，即女性的判断会比男性的遭到更多的置疑。 **3** N-COUNT A **lament** is a poem, song, or piece of music which expresses sorrow that someone has died. 悼诗；悼歌；哀乐 ❑ *...Shelley's lament for the death of Keats.* …雪莱为济慈之死写的悼诗。

lamp /læmp/ (**lamps**) N-COUNT A **lamp** is a light that works by using electricity or by burning oil or gas. 灯 ❑ *She switched on the bedside lamp.* 她打开了床头灯。

LAN /læn/ (**LANs**) N-COUNT A **LAN** is a group of personal computers and associated equipment that are linked by cable, for example in an office building, and that share a communications line. **LAN** is an abbreviation for **local area network**. 局域网 [COMPUTING] ❑ *You can take part in multiplayer games either on a LAN network or via the Internet.* 你可以上局域网或者国际互联网参加多人游戏。

▲ **lance** /læns/ (**lances, lancing, lanced**) **1** V-T If a boil on someone's body **is lanced**, a small cut is made in it so that the liquid inside comes out. 切开 (放脓) [usu passive] [MEDICAL] ❑ *It is a painful experience having the boil lanced.* 将疖子切开是个痛苦的经历。 **2** N-COUNT A **lance** is a long spear used in former times by soldiers on horseback. 长矛 ❑ *...the clang of lances striking armor.* …长矛撞击盔甲的铿锵声。

land ♦♦♦ /lænd/ (**lands, landing, landed**) **1** N-UNCOUNT **Land** is an area of ground, especially one that is used for a particular purpose such as farming or building. 土地 ❑ *Good agricultural land is in short supply.* 肥沃的农业用地短缺。 ❑ *...160 acres of land.* …160英亩土地。 **2** N-COUNT You can refer to an area of land which someone owns as their **land** or their **lands**. 地产 ❑ *Their home is on his father's land.* 他们的家坐落在他父亲的土地上。 **3** N-SING If you talk about **the land**, you mean farming and the way of life in farming areas, in contrast to life in the cities. 农村生活 ❑ *Living off the land was hard enough at the best of times.* 即使是在最好的时期靠种地生活也是很艰难的。 **4** N-UNCOUNT **Land** is the part of the world that consists of ground, rather than sea or air. 陆地 [also "the" N] ❑ *It isn't clear whether the plane went down over land or sea.* 不清楚飞机是落在陆地上还是海里。 **5** N-COUNT You can use **land** to refer to a country in a poetic or emotional way. 国家 [LITERARY] ❑ *...America, land of opportunity.* …美国，充满机会的国度。

> **Country** is the most usual word to use when you are talking about the major political units that the world is divided into. **State** is used when you are talking about politics or government institutions. ❑ *...the new German state created by the unification process. ...Italy's state-controlled telecommunications company.* **State** can also refer to a political unit within a particular country. ❑ *...the state of California.* **Nation** is often used when you are talking about a country's inhabitants, and their cultural or ethnic background. ❑ *Wales is a proud nation with its own traditions... A senior government spokesman will address the nation.* **Land** is a less precise and more literary word, which you can use, for example, to talk about the feelings you have for a particular country. ❑ *She was fascinated to learn about this strange land at the edge of Europe.*

6 V-I When someone or something **lands**, they come down to the ground after moving through the air or falling. 降落 ❑ *He was sent flying into the air and landed 20 feet away.* 他被抛入空中，在20英尺以外落地。 **7** V-T/V-I When someone **lands** a plane, ship, or spacecraft, or when it **lands**, it arrives somewhere after a journey. 抵达 ❑ *The jet landed after a flight of just under three hours.* 这架喷气式飞机在仅仅不到三个小时的飞行后就抵达了。 ❑ *He landed his troops on the western shore.* 他的部队抵达了西海岸。 **8** V-T/V-I If you **land in** an unpleasant situation or place or if something **lands** you **in** it, something causes you to be in it. 陷入 (不愉快境地) [INFORMAL] ❑ *He landed in a psychiatric ward.* 他住进了精神病病房。 **9** V-I If something **lands** somewhere, it arrives there unexpectedly, often causing problems. 意外出现 [INFORMAL] ❑ *Two days later the book had already landed on his desk.* 两天后，这本书意外地出现在了他的桌子上。 **10** to **land on your feet** → see **foot**
→ see **continent, earth, skyscraper**

Thesaurus *land* 另参见：
N. acreage, area, country, real estate **1**
V. arrive, touch down; *(ant.)* take off **6** **7**

Word Web **lake**

Several forces create **lakes**. The movement of a glacier can carve out a deep **basin** in the soil. The Great Lakes between the U.S. and Canada are **glacial** lakes. Very deep lakes appear when large pieces of the Earth's crust suddenly shift. Lake Baikal in Russia is over a mile deep. When a volcano erupts, it creates a **crater**. Crater Lake in Oregon is the perfectly round remains of a volcanic cone. It contains **water** from melted snow and rain. Erosion also creates lakes. When the wind blows away sand, the hole left behind forms a natural lake **bed**.

Word Partnership *land* 的常用搭配：

N. **acres** of land, **area** of land, **desert** land, land **development**, land **management**, land **ownership**, **parcel** of land, **piece** of land, **plot** of land, **strip** of land, **tract** of land, land **use** 1 2

ADJ. **agricultural** land, **fertile** land, **flat** land, **grazing** land, **private** land, **public** land, **undeveloped** land, **vacant** land, **vast** land 1 2

V. **buy** land, **own** land, **sell** land 1 2

land·fill /lændfɪl/ (**landfills**) 1 N-UNCOUNT **Landfill** is a method of getting rid of very large amounts of garbage by burying it in a large deep hole. 垃圾填埋法 ❑ *...the environmental costs of landfill.* …垃圾填埋法对环境的损害。 2 N-COUNT A **landfill** is a large deep hole in which very large amounts of garbage are buried. 垃圾填埋场 ❑ *The rubbish in modern landfills does not rot.* 现代垃圾填埋场里的垃圾不会腐烂。
→ see **dump**

land·ing /lændɪŋ/ (**landings**) 1 N-COUNT In a house or other building, the **landing** is the area at the top of the staircase which has rooms leading off it. 楼梯平台 ❑ *I ran out onto the landing.* 我跑出去上了楼梯平台。 2 N-VAR A **landing** is an act of bringing an aircraft or spacecraft down to the ground. 着陆 ❑ *I had to make a controlled landing into the sea.* 我不得不在海里进行有控制的降落。 3 N-COUNT When a **landing** takes place, troops are unloaded from boats or aircraft at the beginning of a military invasion or other operation. (部队) 登陆 ❑ *American forces have begun a big landing.* 美军已经开始大规模的登陆。

land·lady /lændleɪdi/ (**landladies**) N-COUNT Someone's **landlady** is the woman who allows them to live or work in a building which she owns, in return for rent. 女房东 ❑ *There was a note under the door from my landlady.* 门下有我女房东的一张便条。

land·lord /lændlɔrd/ (**landlords**) N-COUNT Someone's **landlord** is the man who allows them to live or work in a building which he owns, in return for rent. 房东 ❑ *His landlord doubled the rent.* 他的房东把房租提高了一倍。

★ **land·mark** /lændmɑrk/ (**landmarks**) 1 N-COUNT A **landmark** is a building or feature which is easily noticed and can be used to judge your position or the position of other buildings or features. 地标 ❑ *The Menger Hotel is a San Antonio landmark.* 蒙尔饭店是圣安东尼奥的一个标志性建筑。 2 N-COUNT You can refer to an important stage in the development of something as a **landmark**. 里程碑 ❑ *...a landmark arms control treaty.* …具有里程碑意义的武器控制条约。

★ **land·mine** /lændmaɪn/ (**landmines**) also **land mine** N-COUNT A **landmine** is an explosive device which is placed on or under the ground and explodes when a person or vehicle touches it. 地雷

land·scape ♦◇◇ /lændskeɪp/ (**landscapes, landscaping, landscaped**) 1 N-VAR The **landscape** is everything you can see when you look across an area of land, including hills, rivers, buildings, trees, and plants. 风景 ❑ *...Arizona's desert landscape.* …亚利桑那州的沙漠风光。

> Do not confuse **landscape, scenery, countryside,** and **nature.** With **landscape**, the emphasis is on the physical features of the land, while **scenery** includes everything you can see when you look out over an area of land. ❑ *...the landscape of steep woods and distant mountains. ...unattractive urban scenery.* **Countryside** is land which is away from towns and cities. ❑ *...3,500 acres of mostly flat countryside.* **Nature** includes the landscape, the weather, animals, and plants. ❑ *These creatures roamed the Earth as the finest and rarest wonders of nature.*

2 N-COUNT A **landscape** is all the features that are important in a particular situation. 局面 ❑ *June's events completely altered the political landscape.* 6月的事件完全改变了政治局面。 3 N-COUNT A **landscape** is a painting which shows a scene in the countryside. 乡村风景画 ❑ *Kenna's latest series of landscapes is on show at the Zelda Cheatle Gallery.* 肯纳的乡村风景画系列正在塞尔达・奇特尔画廊展出。 4 V-T If an area of land **is landscaped**, it is changed to make it more attractive, for example, by adding streams or ponds and planting trees and bushes. 对…做景观美化 ❑ *The gravel pits have been landscaped and planted to make them attractive to wildfowl.* 这些乱石坑已经被美化，种了树来吸引野生鸟类。 ❑ *They had landscaped their property with trees, shrubs, and lawns.* 他们种了树、灌木和草坪来美化家园。 ● **land·scap·ing** N-UNCOUNT 景观美化 ❑ *The landowner insisted on a high standard of landscaping.* 土地所有人执意要求高标准的景观美化。 5 N-UNCOUNT If a sheet of paper is in **landscape** format or mode, the longer edge of the paper is horizontal and the shorter edge is vertical. 横排格式 [oft N n] ❑ *Most powerpoint presentations are prepared for screens in landscape format.* 大部分幻灯片演示在屏幕上都是横排格式。
→ see **art, painting**

land·scape archi·tect (**landscape architects**) N-COUNT A **landscape architect** is the same as a **landscape gardener**. 园艺设计者

land·scape gar·den·er (**landscape gardeners**) N-COUNT A **landscape gardener** is a person who designs gardens or parks so that they look attractive. 园艺设计者

land·slide /lændslaɪd/ (**landslides**) 1 N-COUNT A **landslide** is a victory in an election in which a person or political party gets far more votes or seats than their opponents. (选举中) 压倒性优势的胜利 ❑ *He won last month's presidential election by a landslide.* 他以绝对优势赢得了上个月的总统选举。 2 N-COUNT A **landslide** is a large amount of earth and rocks falling down a cliff or the side of a mountain. 山崩 ❑ *The storm caused landslides and flooding in Savona.* 暴风雨引发了萨沃纳的山崩和水灾。
→ see **disaster**

lane ♦◇◇ /leɪn/ (**lanes**) 1 N-COUNT A **lane** is a narrow road, especially in the country. (尤指乡间的) 小路 ❑ *...a quiet country lane.* …一条安静的乡间小路。 2 N-IN-NAMES **Lane** is also used in the names of roads, either in cities or in the country. 用于街路名 ❑ *They had a house on Spring Park Lane in East Hampton.* 他们曾在东汉普顿的春园路有一幢房子。 3 N-COUNT A **lane** is a part of a main road which is marked by the edge of the road and a painted line, or by two painted lines. 车道 ❑ *The truck was traveling at 20 mph in the slow lane.* 那辆卡车以每小时20英里的速度行驶在慢车道上。 4 N-COUNT At a swimming pool, athletics track, or bowling alley, a lane is a long narrow section which is separated from other sections, for example by lines or ropes. 泳道；跑道；保龄球道 ❑ *...after being disqualified for running out of his lane in the 200 meters.* …在200米比赛中由于冲出跑道而被取消比赛资格以后。 5 N-COUNT A **lane** is a route that is frequently used by aircraft or ships. 航线 ❑ *The collision took place in one of the busiest shipping lanes in the world.* 撞船事件发生在世界上最繁忙的一条船运航道上。
→ see **traffic**

lan·guage ♦♦◇ /læŋgwɪdʒ/ (**languages**) 1 N-COUNT A **language** is a system of communication which consists of a set of sounds and written symbols which are used by the people of a particular country or region for talking or writing. 语言 ❑ *...the English language.* …英语。 ❑ *Students are expected to master a second language.* 学生们应该掌握一门第二语言。 2 N-UNCOUNT **Language** is the use of a system of communication which consists of a set of sounds or written symbols. 语言的使用 ❑ *Students examined how children acquire language.* 学生们调查了儿童是怎样学习语言的。 3 N-UNCOUNT You can refer to the words used in connection with a particular subject as **the language of** that subject. 专门用语 ❑ *...the language of business.* …商业用语。 4 N-UNCOUNT You can refer to someone's use of rude words or swearing as **bad language** when you find it offensive. 粗话 ❑ *Television companies tend to censor bad language in feature films.* 电视公司往往把故事片中的粗话删掉。 5 N-UNCOUNT The **language** of a piece of writing or speech is the style in which it is written or spoken. 语言风格 ❑ *...a booklet summarizing it in plain language.* …用平实的语言对其进行概述的一本小册子。 ❑ *The tone of his language was diplomatic and polite.* 他说话的语调既圆滑又有礼貌。 6 N-VAR You can use **language** to refer to various means of communication involving recognizable symbols, nonverbal sounds, or actions. 交流语言 ❑ *Some sign languages are very sophisticated means of communication.* 一些手势语是非常复杂的交流方式。 ❑ *...the digital language of computers.* …计算机数码语言。
→ see **culture**

Thesaurus *language* 另参见：

N. communication, dialect, lexicon 1 2 6
jargon, slang, terminology 3 5
swear 4

Word Partnership *language* 的常用搭配:

V. **know a** language, **learn a** language, **speak a** language, **study a** language, **teach a** language, **understand a** language, **use a** language 1

ADJ. **a different** language, **foreign** language, **native** language, **official** language, **second** language, **universal** language 1
bad language, **foul** language, **vulgar** language 4
plain language, **simple** language, **technical** language 5

N. language **acquisition**, language **barrier**, **child** language, language **of children**, language **classes**, language **comprehension**, language **development**, **proficiency in a** language, language **skills** 1 2
body language, **computer** language, **programming** language, **sign** language 6

lan·guid /læŋgwɪd/ ADJ If you describe someone as **languid**, you mean that they show little energy or interest and are very slow and casual in their movements. 无精打采的 [LITERARY] ❑ *He's a large, languid man with a round and impassive face.* 他是一个无精打采的大汉，长着一张毫无表情的圆脸。 ● **lan·guid·ly** ADV 无精打采地 ❑ *We sat about languidly after dinner.* 我们饭后无精打采地坐着。

▲ **lan·guish** /læŋgwɪʃ/ (**languishes, languishing, languished**) 1 V-I If someone **languishes** somewhere, they are forced to remain and suffer in an unpleasant situation. 受折磨 ❑ *Pollard continues to languish in prison.* 波拉德继续在牢里受折磨。 2 V-I If something **languishes**, it is not successful, often because of a lack of effort or because of a lot of difficulties. (由于不努力或困难太多) 未成功 ❑ *Without the founder's drive and direction, the company gradually languished.* 由于没有创始人的干劲和指导，这家公司逐渐衰败了。

▲ **lan·tern** /læntərn/ (**lanterns**) N-COUNT A **lantern** is a lamp in a metal frame with glass sides and with a handle on top so you can carry it. 灯笼

lap ◆◇◇ /læp/ (**laps, lapping, lapped**) 1 N-COUNT If you have something on your **lap** when you are sitting down, it is on top of your legs and near to your body. (人坐着时的) 大腿部 ❑ *She waited quietly with her hands in her lap.* 她双手放在大腿上静静地等候。 2 N-COUNT In a race, a competitor completes a **lap** when they have gone around a course once. (跑道的) 一圈 ❑ *...that last lap of the race.* …比赛的最后一圈。 3 V-T In a race, if you **lap** another competitor, you go past them while they are still on the previous lap. 比…领先一圈 ❑ *He then built a 10-bike lead before lapping his first rider on lap 14.* 他领先了10辆自行车的距离，然后在第14圈又超过了前一个车手一圈。 4 N-COUNT A **lap** of a long journey is one part of it, between two points where you stop. 一段行程 ❑ *I had thought we might travel as far as Oak Valley, but we only managed the first lap of the journey.* 我原以为我们可以到达橡树谷，但是我们仅仅完成了行程的第一段。 5 V-I When water **laps** against something such as the shore or the side of a boat, it touches it gently and makes a soft sound. 轻拍 [WRITTEN] ❑ *...the water that lapped against the pillars of the boathouse.* …水轻拍着船屋的柱子。 ❑ *With a rising tide the water was lapping at his chin before rescuers arrived.* 在救生员到达之前，上涨的潮水打着了他的下巴。 ● **lap·ping** N-UNCOUNT 轻拍 ❑ *The only sound was the lapping of the waves.* 惟一的声音是浪涛的拍打声。 6 V-T When an animal **laps** a drink, it uses short quick movements of its tongue to take liquid up into its mouth. (动物) 舐食 ❑ *It lapped milk from a dish.* 它从一个盘子里舐食牛奶。 ● PHRASAL VERB **Lap up** means the same as **lap**. 舐食 ❑ *She poured some water into a plastic bowl. Faust, her Great Dane, lapped it up with relish.* 她往一个塑料碗里倒了些水，她的丹麦大狗福斯特津津有味地舐食起来。

▸ **lap up** 1 PHRASAL VERB If you say that someone **laps up** something such as information or attention, you mean that they accept it eagerly, usually when you think they are being foolish for believing that it is sincere. 照单全收 ❑ *Their audience will lap up whatever they throw at them.* 他们的观众会照单全收他们抛来的任何信息。 2 → see **lap 6**

la·pel /ləpɛl/ (**lapels**) N-COUNT The **lapels** of a jacket or coat are the two top parts at the front that are folded back on each side and join on to the collar. 翻领 ❑ *He sports a small red flower in his lapel.* 他炫耀自己衣服翻领上的一朵小红花。

Word Link *lapse ≈ falling : collapse, elapse, lapse*

▲ **lapse** /læps/ (**lapses, lapsing, lapsed**) 1 N-COUNT A **lapse** is a moment or instance of bad behavior by someone who usually behaves well. (一时的) 行为失检 ❑ *On Friday he showed neither decency nor dignity. It was an uncommon lapse.* 星期五他既不庄重也不体面。这可是他少有的失礼。 2 N-COUNT A **lapse of** something such as concentration or judgment is a temporary lack of that thing, which can often cause you to make a mistake. (一时的) 走神; 判断错误 ❑ *I had a little lapse of concentration in the middle of the race.* 我在比赛中走了一下神。 ❑ *He was a genius and because of it you could accept lapses of taste.* 他是一个天才，因此他偶失得体，人们也可以接受。 3 V-I If you **lapse into** a quiet or inactive state, you stop talking or being active. 陷入 (某种静止状态) ❑ *She muttered something unintelligible and lapsed into silence.* 她咕哝了几句难以理解的话，然后就陷入了沉默。 4 V-I If someone **lapses into** a particular way of speaking, or behaving, they start speaking or behaving in that way, usually for a short period. 开始 (以某种方式) 说话; 开始行事 ❑ *She lapsed into a little girl voice to deliver a nursery rhyme.* 她用小女孩的声音唱起了一首童谣。 ● N-COUNT **Lapse** is also a noun. 开始说; 开始做 ❑ *Her lapse into German didn't seem peculiar. After all, it was her native tongue.* 她开始说德语并不奇怪，毕竟那是她的母语。 5 N-SING A **lapse of** time is a period that is long enough for a situation to change or for people to have a different opinion about it. (时间的) 间隔 ❑ *...the restoration of diplomatic relations after a lapse of 24 years.* …间隔24年后外交关系的恢复。 6 V-I If a period of time **lapses**, it passes. 流逝 ❑ *New products and production processes are transferred to the developing countries only after a substantial amount of time has lapsed.* 只有经过很长时间以后，新产品和新生产流程才转移到发展中国家。 7 V-I If a situation or legal contract **lapses**, it is allowed to end rather than being continued, renewed, or extended. 终止 ❑ *The terms of the treaty lapsed in 1987.* 协定的条款在1987年就终止了。 8 V-I If a member of a particular religion **lapses**, they stop believing in it or stop following its rules and practices. 放弃 (宗教信仰) ❑ *I lapsed in my 20s, returned to it, then lapsed again, while writing the life of historical Jesus.* 我20来岁就放弃信教，后来又信了。到后来在写历史上的耶稣生平时又放弃了信教。

lap·top /læptɒp/ (**laptops**) N-COUNT A **laptop** or a **laptop computer** is a small portable computer. 笔记本电脑 ❑ *She used to work at her laptop until four in the morning.* 她以前经常在笔记本电脑前工作到凌晨4点钟。

Word Link *er ≈ more : colder, higher, larger*

Word Link *est ≈ most : coldest, highest, largest*

large ◆◆◆ /lɑrdʒ/ (**larger, largest**) 1 ADJ A **large** thing or person is greater in size than usual or average. 大的 ❑ *The pike lives mainly in large rivers and lakes.* 梭鱼主要生活在大的江河湖泊里。 ❑ *In the largest room about a dozen children and seven adults are sitting on the carpet.* 在最大的那个房间里，十几个孩子和七个大人正坐在地毯上。 2 ADJ A **large** amount or number of people or things is more than the average amount or number. 大量的 ❑ *The gang finally fled with a large amount of cash and jewelry.* 那帮歹徒最终带着大量的现金和珠宝逃走了。 ❑ *There are a large number of centers where you can take full-time courses.* 这里有很多你可以上全日制课程的培训中心。 3 ADJ **Large** is used to indicate that a problem or issue which is being discussed is very important or serious. 重要的; 严重的 ❑ *...the already large problem of under-age drinking.* …已颇为严重的未成年人酗酒问题。

Large, **big**, and **great** are all used to talk about size. In general, **large** is more formal than **big**, and **great** is more formal than **large**. **Large** and **big** are normally used to describe objects, but you can also use **big** to suggest that something is important or impressive. ❑ *...his influence over the big advertisers.* You normally use **great** to emphasize the importance of someone or something. ❑ *...the great English architect, Inigo Jones.* However, you can also use **great** to suggest that something is impressive because of its size. ❑ *The great bird of prey was a dark smudge against the sun.* You can use **large** or **great**, but not **big**, to describe amounts. ❑ *...a large amount of blood on the floor. ...the coming of tourists in great numbers.* Both **big** and **great** can be used to emphasize the intensity of something, although **great** is more formal. ❑ *It gives me great pleasure to welcome you... Most of them act like big fools.*

L

4 PHRASE You use **at large** to indicate that you are talking in a general way about most of the people mentioned. 大多数 ❑ *I think the chances of getting reforms accepted by the community at large remain extremely remote.* 我认为，让该团体的大部分人都接受改革的希望仍然极其渺茫。 **5** PHRASE If you say that a dangerous person, thing, or animal is **at large**, you mean that they have not been captured or made safe. 逍遥法外 ❑ *The man who tried to have her killed is still at large.* 企图谋杀她的那个男人仍然逍遥法外。 **6** **to a large extent** → see **extent**

Thesaurus *large* 另参见：
ADJ. big, sizable, spacious, substantial; *(ant.)* small **1**

large·ly ♦♦◇ /lɑrdʒli/ **1** ADV You use **largely** to say that a statement is not completely true but is mostly true. 基本上 ❑ *The fund is largely financed through government borrowing.* 这项基金基本上靠政府借款资助。 ❑ *I largely work with people who already are motivated.* 我总是与积极性高的人一起工作。 **2** ADV **Largely** is used to introduce the main reason for a particular event or situation. (用于说明原因) 主要地 [ADV prep] ❑ *Retail sales dipped 6/10ths of a percent last month, largely because Americans were buying fewer cars.* 零售额上个月下降了0.6%，主要是由于美国人汽车买得更少了。

large-scale also **large scale** **1** ADJ A **large-scale** action or event happens over a very wide area or involves a lot of people or things. 大规模的 [ADJ n] ❑ *...a large scale military operation.* …一次大规模的军事行动。 **2** ADJ A **large-scale** map or diagram represents a small area of land or a building or machine on a scale that is large enough for small details to be shown. (地图或图表) 大比例尺的 [ADJ n] ❑ *...a large-scale map of the county.* …一张该县的大比例尺地图。

lar·va /lɑrvə/ (**larvae** /lɑrvi/) N-COUNT A **larva** is an insect at the stage of its life after it has developed from an egg and before it changes into its adult form. 幼虫 ❑ *The eggs quickly hatch into larvae.* 这些卵很快孵化成幼虫。

la·ser /leɪzər/ (**lasers**) N-COUNT A **laser** is a narrow beam of concentrated light produced by a special machine. It is used for cutting very hard materials, and in many technical fields such as surgery and telecommunications. 激光 ❑ *...new laser technology.* …新的激光技术。
→ see Word Web: **laser**

la·ser print·er (**laser printers**) N-COUNT A **laser printer** is a computer printer that produces clear words and pictures by using laser beams. 激光打印机

★ **lash** /læʃ/ (**lashes, lashing, lashed**) **1** N-COUNT Your **lashes** are the hairs that grow on the edge of your upper and lower eyelids. 睫毛 ❑ *...somber gray eyes, with unusually long lashes.* …忧郁的灰眼睛，长着特长的睫毛。 **2** V-T If you **lash** two or more things together, you tie one of them firmly to the other. 捆紧 ❑ *Secure the anchor by lashing it to the rail.* 把锚紧紧地捆在横木上。 ❑ *The shelter is built by lashing poles together to form a small dome.* 该掩蔽处是把杆子捆到一起形成一个小圆顶而搭建成。 **3** V-T/V-I If wind, rain, or water **lashes** someone or something, it hits them violently. (风、雨、水等) 猛袭 [WRITTEN] ❑ *The worst winter storms of the century lashed the east coast of North America.* 本世纪最猛烈的暴风雪袭击了北美的东海岸。 **4** V-T/V-I If someone **lashes** you or **lashes into** you, they speak very angrily to you, criticizing you or saying you have done something wrong. 怒斥 ❑ *She went quiet for a moment while she summoned up the words to lash him.* 她沉默了一会儿，想了些话来怒斥他。 **5** N-COUNT A **lash** is a blow with a whip, especially a blow on someone's back as a punishment. 鞭打 ❑ *The villagers sentenced one man to five lashes for stealing a ham from his neighbor.* 村民们判一个男人5下鞭刑，因为他偷了一个邻居的火腿。

▸ **lash out** **1** PHRASAL VERB If you **lash out**, you attempt to hit someone quickly and violently with a weapon or with your hands or feet. 猛击 ❑ *Riot police fired in the air and lashed out with clubs to disperse hundreds of demonstrators.* 防暴警察向空中开了枪，并猛击警棍来驱散数百名示威者。 **2** PHRASAL VERB If you **lash out at** someone or something, you speak to them or about them very angrily or critically. 痛斥 ❑ *As a politician Jefferson frequently lashed out at the press.* 作为一名政治家，杰斐逊曾屡次痛斥新闻媒体。

lass /læs/ (**lasses**) N-COUNT; N-VOC A **lass** is a young woman or girl. 小姑娘 [OLD-FASHIONED] ❑ *Anne is a Lancashire lass from Longton, near Preston.* 安妮是兰开夏的一个小姑娘，来自普雷斯顿附近的朗顿。

last ♦♦♦ /læst/ (**lasts, lasting, lasted**) **1** DET You use **last** in expressions such as **last Friday, last night**, and **last year** to refer, for example, to the most recent Friday, night, or year. 上一个的 ❑ *I got married last July.* 我去年7月结的婚。 ❑ *He never made it home at all last night.* 他昨天晚上根本没有回家。 **2** ADJ The **last** event, person, thing, or period of time is the most recent one. 最近的 [det ADJ] ❑ *Much has changed since my last visit.* 自我上次来访后，变化很大。 ❑ *I split up with my last boyfriend three years ago.* 我和前任男友在3年前分手了。 ● PRON **Last** is also a pronoun. 最近发生的事情 ❑ *The next tide, it was announced, would be even higher than the last.* 通告说下次涨潮会比上次更高。 **3** ADV If something **last** happened on a particular occasion, that is the most recent occasion on which it happened. 最近一次 [ADV with v] ❑ *When were you there last?* 你最近一次在那里是什么时候？ ❑ *The house is a little more dilapidated than when I last saw it.* 这幢房子比我上次看到时更破一些了。 **4** ORD The **last** thing, person, event, or period of time is the one that happens or comes after all the others of the same kind. 最后的 ❑ *...the last three pages of the chapter.* …这章的最后3页。 ● PRON **Last** is also a pronoun. 最后的人或事物 ❑ *It wasn't the first time that this particular difference had divided them and it wouldn't be the last.* 这个特殊差异使他们产生分歧不是第一次，也不会是最后一次。 **5** ADV If you do something **last**, you do it after everyone else does, or after you do everything else. 最后地 [ADV after v] ❑ *I testified last.* 我最后作了证。 ❑ *I was always picked last for the football team at school.* 我在上学时总是最后一个被选入足球队。 **6** PRON If you are **the last to** do or know something, everyone else does or knows it before you. 最后的人 [PRON to-inf] ❑ *She was the last to go to bed.* 她是最后一个睡觉的人。 **7** ADJ **Last** is used to refer to the only thing, person, or part of something that remains. 仅剩的 [det ADJ] ❑ *Jed nodded, finishing off the last piece of pizza.* 杰德点了点头，吃完了仅剩的一块比萨饼。 ● N-SING **Last** is also a noun. 剩下的东西(或人) ❑ *He finished off the last of the wine.* 他喝完了剩下的酒。 **8** ADJ You can use **last** to indicate that something is extremely undesirable or unlikely. 最不想要的；最不可能的 [det ADJ] [EMPHASIS] ❑ *The last thing I wanted to do was teach.* 我最不想做的事就是教书了。 ● PRON **Last** is also a pronoun. 最不想要的事；最不可能的事 [PRON to-inf] ❑ *I would be the last to say that science has explained everything.* 我绝不可能说科学已经解释了一切。 **9** PRON **The last** you see of someone or **the last** you hear of them is the final time that you see them or talk to them. 最后一次 ["the" PRON that] ❑ *She disappeared shouting, "To the river, to the river!" And that was the last we saw of her.* 她喊着"去河边，去河边"，然后就不见了。那是我们最后一次看到她。 **10** V-T/V-I If an event, situation, or problem **lasts** for a particular length of time, it continues to exist or happen for that length of time. 持续 ❑ *The marriage had lasted for less than two years.* 这桩婚姻持续了不到两年。 ❑ *The games lasted only half the normal time.* 这场比赛只持续了正常比赛时间的一半。 **11** V-T/V-I If something **lasts** for a particular length of time, it continues to be able to be used for that time, for example, because there is some of it left or because it is in good enough condition. 够用(一段时间) ❑ *You only need a very small blob of glue, so one tube lasts for ages.* 你仅需要很小一滴胶水，所以一管胶水能用很久。 ❑ *The repaired sail lasted less than 24 hours.* 修好的帆只维持了不到二十四小时。 **12** → see also **lasting** **13** PHRASE

Word Web laser

Lasers are an amazing form of technology. Laser **beams** read **CDs** and **DVDs**. They can create three-dimensional holograms. Laser **light shows** add excitement at concerts. **Fiber optic cables** carry intense flashes of laser light. This allows a single cable to transmit thousands of e-mail and phone messages at the same time. Laser **scanners** read prices from **bar codes**. Lasers are also used as scalpels in **surgery**, and to remove hair, birthmarks, and tattoos. Dentists use them to remove cavities. Laser eye surgery has become very popular. In manufacturing, lasers make precise cuts in everything from fabric to steel.

If you say that something has happened **at last** or **at long last** you mean it has happened after you have been hoping for it for a long time. 终于 ❏ *I'm so glad that we've found you at last!* 我太高兴了，我们终于找到你了！ ❏ *Here, at long last, was the moment he had waited for.* 终于，他期待的时刻来临了。 14 PHRASE You use expressions such as **the night before last, the election before last** and **the leader before last** to refer to the period of time, event, or person that came immediately before the most recent one in a series. 再上一次；再上一个人或物 ❏ *It was the dog he'd heard the night before last.* 这是他前天夜里听见吼叫的那只狗。 15 PHRASE You can use expressions such as **the last I heard** and **the last she heard** to introduce a piece of information that is the most recent that you have on a particular subject. 某人最近获悉 ❏ *The last I heard, Joe and Irene were still happily married.* 我最近得知，乔和艾琳的婚姻依然幸福。 16 PHRASE If you **leave** something or someone **until last**, you delay using, choosing, or dealing with them until you have used, chosen, or dealt with all the others. 把…留到最后 ❏ *I have left my best wine until last.* 我把最好的酒留到最后喝。 17 **the last straw** → see **straw** 18 **last thing** → see **thing**

last-ditch ADJ A **last-ditch** action is done only because there are no other ways left to achieve something or to prevent something from happening. It is often done without much hope that it will succeed. 孤注一掷的 [ADJ n] ❏ *...a last-ditch attempt to prevent civil war.* …阻止内战发生的最后一搏。

last·ing /læstɪŋ/ 1 ADJ You can use **lasting** to describe a situation, result, or agreement that continues to exist or have an effect for a very long time. 持久的 ❏ *We are well on our way to a lasting peace.* 我们正迈向持久的和平。 2 → see also **last**

last·ly /læstli/ 1 ADV You use **lastly** when you want to make a final point, ask a final question, or mention a final item that is connected with the other ones you have already asked or mentioned. 最后 [ADV with cl/group] ❏ *Lastly, I would like to ask about your future plans.* 最后，我想问一下你们的未来计划。 2 ADV You use **lastly** when you are saying what happens after everything else in a series of actions or events. 最后 [ADV cl] ❏ *They wash their hands, arms and faces, and lastly, they wash their feet.* 他们洗了手、胳膊和脸，最后洗了脚。

last-minute → see **minute**

latch /lætʃ/ (**latches, latching, latched**) 1 N-COUNT A **latch** is a fastening on a door or gate. It consists of a metal bar which you lift in order to open the door. 门闩 ❏ *You left the latch off the gate and the dog escaped.* 你没插门闩，狗跑了。 2 N-COUNT A **latch** is a lock on a door which locks automatically when you shut the door, so that you need a key in order to open it from the outside. 弹簧锁 ❏ *...a key clicked in the latch of the front door.* …钥匙在前门的弹簧锁里发出咔哒的声响。

▸ **latch onto** or **latch on** 1 PHRASAL VERB If someone **latches onto** a person or an idea or **latches on**, they become very interested in the person or idea, often finding them so useful that they do not want to leave them. 缠住不放 [INFORMAL] ❏ *Rob had latched onto me. He followed me around and sat beside me at lunch.* 罗布缠着我不放。他到处跟着我，吃午饭时坐在我旁边。 2 PHRASAL VERB If one thing **latches onto** another, or if it **latches on**, it attaches itself to it and becomes part of it. 黏附在…上 ❏ *These are substances which specifically latch onto the protein on the cell membrane.* 这些是专门黏附在细胞膜蛋白质上的物质。

late ♦♦♦ /leɪt/ (**later, latest**) 1 ADV **Late** means near the end of a day, week, year, or other period of time. (时间) 接近终了 ❏ *It was late in the afternoon.* 那是在接近傍晚的时候。 ❏ *His autobiography was written late in life.* 他的自传是在晚年写的。 ● ADJ **Late** is also an adjective. 接近终了的 [ADJ n] ❏ *The talks eventually broke down in late spring.* 会谈最终在暮春时破裂。 ❏ *He was in his late 20s.* 他年近三十。 2 ADJ If it is **late**, it is near the end of the day or it is past the time that you feel something should have been done. 晚的；迟的 [v-link ADJ] ❏ *It was very late and the streets were deserted.* 天很晚了，街道上空无一人。 ● **late·ness** N-UNCOUNT 晚 ❏ *A large crowd had gathered despite the lateness of the hour.* 尽管时间很晚了，还有一大群人聚集在了一起。 3 ADV **Late** means after the time that was arranged or expected. (比安排或预计时间) 迟 ❏ *Steve arrived late.* 史蒂夫迟到了。 ❏ *The talks began some fifteen minutes late.* 商谈迟了约十五分钟才开始。 ● ADJ **Late** is also an adjective. 迟的 ❏ *His campaign got off to a late start.* 他的竞选活动开始较迟。 ❏ *The train was 40 minutes late.* 火车晚点了40分钟。 ● **late·ness** N-UNCOUNT 迟到 ❏ *He apologized for his lateness.* 他为自己的迟到道歉。 4 ADV **Late** means after the usual time that a particular event or activity happens. (比通常时间) 晚 [ADV after v] ❏ *We went to bed very late.* 我们很晚才睡觉。 ● ADJ **Late** is also an adjective. 晚的 [ADJ n] ❏ *They had a late lunch in a café.* 他们很晚才在一家餐馆吃了午饭。 5 ADJ You use **late** when you are talking about someone who is dead, especially someone who has died recently. 已故的 [det ADJ] ❏ *...my late husband.* …我已故的丈夫。 6 → see also **later, latest** 7 PHRASE If an action or event is **too late**, it is useless or ineffective because it occurs after the best time for it. 太迟的 ❏ *It was too late to turn back.* 要回头，为时已晚。 8 **a late night** → see **night**

Thesaurus *late* 另参见：

ADJ. belated, overdue, tardy; *(ant.)* early 3 4
deceased; *(ant.)* living 5

late·ly /leɪtli/ ADV You use **lately** to describe events in the recent past, or situations that started a short time ago. 最近 ❏ *Dad's health hasn't been too good lately.* 爸爸的身体最近一直不太好。 ❏ *"Have you talked to her lately?"—"Not lately, really."* "最近你和她谈过吗？" —— "最近没谈过，真的。"

▲ **la·tent** /leɪtᵊnt/ ADJ **Latent** is used to describe something which is hidden and not obvious at the moment, but which may develop further in the future. 潜在的 ❏ *Advertisements attempt to project a latent meaning behind an overt message.* 广告试图传达一种隐藏在公开信息里的潜在意义。

lat·er ♦♦♦ /leɪtər/ 1 **Later** is the comparative of **late**. **late**的比较级 2 ADV You use **later** to refer to a time or situation that is after the one that you have been talking about or after the present one. 以后 ❏ *He resigned ten years later.* 他10年后辞职了。 ● PHRASE You use **later on** to refer to a time or situation that is after the one that you have been talking about or after the present one. 以后 ❏ *Later on I'll be speaking to Patty Davis.* 以后我会和帕蒂・戴维斯谈谈。 3 ADJ You use **later** to refer to an event, period of time, or other thing which comes after the one that you have been talking about or after the present one. 后来的 [ADJ n, "the" ADJ, "the" ADJ "of" n] ❏ *At a later news conference, he said differences should not be dramatized.* 在后来的新闻发布会上，他说差异不应该被夸大。 ❏ *The competition should have been re-scheduled for a later date.* 本该把比赛重新安排在一个晚些的日期。 4 ADJ You use **later** to refer to the last part of someone's life or career or the last part of a period of history. 晚年的；后期的 [ADJ n] ❏ *He found happiness in later life.* 他在晚年找到了幸福。 ❏ *...the later part of the 20th century.* …20世纪后期。 5 → see also **late**

You use **after, afterward**, and **later** to talk about things that happen following the time when you are speaking, or following a particular event. Expressions such as "not long" and "shortly" can also be used with **after**. ❏ *After dinner she spoke to him... I returned to England after visiting India... Shortly after, she called me.* **Afterward** can be used when you do not need to mention the particular time or event. ❏ *Afterward we went to a night club.* You can also use words such as "soon" and "shortly" with **afterward**. ❏ *Soon afterward, he came to the clinic.* You can use **later** to refer to a time or situation that follows the time when you are speaking. ❏ *I'll go and see her later.* "A little," "much," and "not much" can also be used with **later**. ❏ *A little later, the lights went out... I learned all this much later.* You can use **after, afterward**, or **later** following a phrase that mentions a period of time, in order to say when something happens. ❏ *...five years after his death... She wrote about it six years afterward... Ten minutes later he left the house.*

lat·er·al /lætərəl/ ADJ **Lateral** means relating to the sides of something, or moving in a sideways direction. 侧面的；横向的 ❏ *McKinnon estimated the lateral movement of the bridge to be between four and six inches.* 麦金农估计大桥的横向移动范围在4到6英寸之间。

lat·est ♦♦◊ /leɪtɪst/ 1 **Latest** is the superlative of **late**. **Latest**是**late**的最高级形式 2 ADJ You use **latest** to describe something that is the most recent thing of its kind. 最近的 ❏ *...her latest book.* …她最近出版的书。 3 ADJ You can use **latest** to describe something that is very new and modern and is better than older things of a similar kind. 最新式的 ❏ *Crooks are using the latest laser photocopiers to produce millions of fake banknotes.* 骗子们用最新型的激光影印机制作出了上百万的假钞。 ❏ *I got to drive the latest model.* 我得以驾驶最新式的车。 4 → see also **late** 5 PHRASE You use **at the latest** in order to indicate that something must happen at or before a particular time and not after that time. 最晚 [EMPHASIS] ❑ *She should be back by ten o'clock at the latest.* 她最晚应该在10点钟回来。

lathe /leɪð/ **(lathes)** N-COUNT A **lathe** is a machine which is used for shaping wood or metal. 车床

Lat·in ♦◇◇ /lætɪn, -tᵊn/ **1** N-UNCOUNT **Latin** is the language which the ancient Romans used to speak. 拉丁语 **2** ADJ **Latin** countries are countries where Spanish, or perhaps Portuguese, Italian, or French, is spoken. You can also use **Latin** to refer to things and people that come from these countries. 拉丁语系的; 拉丁语国家的 ❑ *Cuba was one of the least Catholic of the Latin countries.* 古巴是拉丁语国家中最不信仰天主教的国家之一。

→ see **English**

Lat·in Ameri·can /lætɪn əmɛrɪkən/ ADJ **Latin American** means belonging or relating to the countries of South America, Central America, and Mexico. **Latin American** also means belonging or relating to the people or culture of these countries. 拉丁美洲的 ❑ *Leaders of eight Latin American countries are meeting in Caracas, Venezuela, today.* 拉丁美洲八国首脑今天正在委内瑞拉的加拉加斯会晤。

★ **lati·tude** /lætɪtud/ **(latitudes)** **1** N-VAR The **latitude** of a place is its distance from the equator. Compare **longitude**. 纬度 ❑ *In the middle to high latitudes rainfall has risen steadily over the last 20-30 years.* 中高纬度地区的降雨量在过去的20到30年间稳步上升了。 ● ADJ **Latitude** is also an adjective. 纬度的 ❑ *The army must cease military operations above 36° latitude north.* 军队必须停止在北纬36度以北地区的军事行动。 **2** N-UNCOUNT **Latitude** is freedom to choose the way in which you do something. 自由度 [FORMAL] ❑ *He would be given every latitude in forming a new government.* 他将被给予高度自由来建立一个新政府。

→ see **globe**

lat·ter ♦◇◇ /lætər/ **1** PRON When two people, things, or groups have just been mentioned, you can refer to the second of them as **the latter**. 后者 ["the" PRON] ❑ *He tracked down his cousin and uncle. The latter was sick.* 他追踪找到了他的堂兄和叔叔。后者病了。 ● ADJ **Latter** is also an adjective. 后面的 [ADJ n] ❑ *There are the people who speak after they think and the people who think while they're speaking. Mike definitely belongs in the latter category.* 有些人先想后说，有些人边想边说。迈克当然属于后一类人。 **2** ADJ You use **latter** to describe the later part of a period of time or event. 晚期的 [ADJ n] ❑ *He is getting into the latter years of his career.* 他正进入职业生涯的晚期。

> **The latter** should only be used to refer to the second of two items which have already been mentioned: ❑ *Given the choice between working for someone else and being on call day and night for the family business, she'd prefer the latter.* The last of three or more items can be referred to as **the last-named**. Compare this with **the former** which is used to talk about the first of two things already mentioned.

lat·tice /lætɪs/ **(lattices)** N-COUNT A **lattice** is a pattern or structure made of strips of wood or another material which cross over each other diagonally leaving holes in between. 格状结构 ❑ *We were crawling along the narrow steel lattice of the bridge.* 我们沿着大桥窄窄的钢制格子爬行着。

laugh ♦♦♦ /læf/ **(laughs, laughing, laughed)** **1** V-T/V-I When you **laugh**, you make a sound with your throat while smiling and show that you are happy or amused. People also sometimes laugh when they feel nervous or are being unfriendly. 笑 ❑ *He was about to offer an explanation, but she was beginning to laugh.* 他刚要加以解释，她就开始笑起来了。 ❑ *I just couldn't laugh at his jokes the way I used to.* 我就是不能像以前那样笑他讲的笑话。 ❑ *"We could do with some help from our friends," he laughed.* "如果我们朋友来帮助就好了，"他笑着说道。 ● N-COUNT **Laugh** is also a noun. 笑 ❑ *Lysenko gave a deep rumbling laugh at his own joke.* 李森科对自己讲的笑话报以朗声大笑。 **2** V-I If people **laugh at** someone or something, they mock them or make jokes about them. 嘲笑 ❑ *I thought they were laughing at me because I was ugly.* 我想他们在嘲笑我长得丑。 **3** PHRASE If you do something **for a laugh** or **for laughs**, you do it as a joke or for fun. 为了开玩笑 ❑ *They were persuaded onstage for a laugh.* 为了开开玩笑，他们被说服登上了台。 **4** PHRASE If you describe a situation as **a laugh** or **a good laugh**, you think that it is fun and do not take it too seriously. 有趣的事 [INFORMAL] ❑ *Working there's great. It's a good laugh.* 在那里工作很棒，是一件有趣的事情。 **5** to **laugh** your **head off** → see **head**

→ see Word Web: **laugh**

▸ **laugh off** PHRASAL VERB If you **laugh off** a difficult or serious situation, you try to suggest that it is amusing and unimportant, for example, by making a joke about it. 一笑置之 ❑ *Frank tried to laugh off his aunt's worry.* 弗兰克试图对他姑妈的烦恼一笑置之。

Thesaurus *laugh* 另参见：

V. chuckle, crack up, giggle, howl, snicker; *(ant.)* cry **1**

Word Partnership *laugh* 的常用搭配：

V. **begin/start to** laugh, **hear** *someone* laugh, **make** *someone* laugh, **try to** laugh **1**

ADJ. **big** laugh, **good** laugh, **hearty** laugh, **little** laugh **1**

laugh·able /læfəᵊl/ ADJ If you say that something such as an idea or suggestion is **laughable**, you mean that it is so silly or stupid as to be funny and not worth serious consideration. 可笑的 [usu v-link ADJ] ❑ *The idea that TV shows like "Dallas" or "Dynasty" represent typical American life is laughable.* 认为像《豪门恩怨》或《鹰冠庄园》那样的电视剧代表典型美国生活的想法是可笑的。 ● **laugh·ably** ADV 可笑地 [usu ADV adj] ❑ *To an outsider, the issues that we fight about would seem almost laughably petty.* 对于一个局外人，我们争执的那些问题会显得几乎可笑地微不足道。

laugh·ter ♦◇◇ /læftər/ N-UNCOUNT **Laughter** is the sound of people laughing, for example, because they are amused or happy. 笑声 ❑ *Their laughter filled the corridor.* 他们的笑声充满了走廊。 ❑ *He delivered the line perfectly, and everybody roared with laughter.* 他完美地演绎了这句台词，所有的人都哈哈大笑起来。

→ see **laugh**

Word Partnership *laughter* 的常用搭配：

V. **burst into** laughter, **hear** laughter, **roar with** laughter

N. **burst of** laughter, **sound of** laughter

ADJ. **hysterical** laughter, **loud** laughter, **nervous** laughter

launch ♦♦◇ /lɔntʃ/ **(launches, launching, launched)** **1** V-T To **launch** a rocket, missile, or satellite means to send it into the air or into space. 发射 ❑ *NASA plans to launch a satellite to study cosmic rays.* 美国国家航空航天局计划发射一颗卫星来研究宇宙射线。 ● N-VAR **Launch** is also a noun. 发射 ❑ *This morning's launch of the space shuttle Columbia has been delayed.* 定于今天上午哥伦比亚号航天飞机的发射已经被推迟了。 **2** V-T To **launch** a ship or a boat means to put it into water, often for the first time after it has been built. 使(新船等)下水 ❑ *There was no time to launch the lifeboats because the ferry capsized with such alarming speed.* 因为渡船倾斜的速度如此之快，根本没有时间把救生艇放下水。 ● N-COUNT **Launch** is also a noun. 下水 ❑ *The launch of a ship was a big occasion.* 船下水曾是一件大事。 **3** V-T To **launch** a large and important activity, for example, a military attack, means to start it. 发起 ❑ *A group of 80 attackers launched an all-out assault just before dawn.* 有80名攻击者的一个小队在黎明前发起了一次全面进攻。 ❑ *The police have launched an investigation into the*

Word Web laugh

There is an old saying, "**Laughter** is the best medicine." New scientific research supports the idea that **humor** really is good for your health. For example, laughing 100 times provides the same exercise benefits as a 15-minute bike ride. When a person **bursts out laughing**, levels of stress hormones in the bloodstream immediately drop. And laughter is more than just a sound. **Howling with laughter** gives face, stomach, leg, and back muscles a good workout. From polite **giggles** to noisy guffaws, laughter allows the release of anger, sadness, and fear. And that has to be good for you.

incident. 警察已经开始对此事件进行调查。● N-COUNT **Launch** is also a noun. 发起 ❑ *...the launch of a campaign to restore law and order.* …旨在恢复法律和秩序的运动的发起。 4 V-T If a company **launches** a new product, it makes it available to the public. 推出(新产品) ❑ *...powerful allies to help the company launch a low-cost "network computer."* …帮助公司推出一种低价"网络电脑"的强大同盟。● N-COUNT **Launch** is also a noun. 推出 ❑ *The company's spending has also risen following the launch of a new Sunday magazine.* 公司的花费也随着一份新星期日杂志的推出而增加。

→ see **satellite**

▸ **launch into** PHRASAL VERB If you **launch into** something such as a speech, task, or fight, you enthusiastically start it. (热情地)开始做 ❑ *Horrigan launched into a speech about the importance of new projects.* 霍里根就新项目的重要性进行了一番热烈的演讲。

laun·der /lɔndər/ (**launders, laundering, laundered**) 1 V-T To **launder** money that has been obtained illegally means to process it through a legitimate business or to send it abroad to a foreign bank, so that when it comes back nobody knows that it was illegally obtained. 洗(钱) ❑ *The House voted today to crack down on banks that launder drug money.* 下议院今天投票打击为贩毒洗钱的银行。● **laun·der·er** N-COUNT (**launderers**) 洗钱者 ❑ *...a businessman and self-described money launderer.* …一位自称洗钱者的商人。 2 V-T When you **launder** clothes, sheets, and towels, you wash and iron them. 洗熨 [FORMAL] ❑ *How many guests who expect clean towels every day in an hotel launder their own every day at home?* 旅店里希望每天有干净毛巾的客人中，有多少人每天在家洗自己的毛巾呢？

laun·dry /lɔndri/ (**laundries**) 1 N-UNCOUNT **Laundry** is used to refer to clothes, sheets, and towels that are about to be washed, are being washed, or have just been washed. (待洗、正在洗或刚洗过的)衣物 ❑ *I'll do your laundry.* 我会给你洗衣服的。 ❑ *...the room where I hang the laundry.* …我晾衣服的房间。 2 N-COUNT A **laundry** is a business that washes and irons clothes, sheets, and towels for people. 洗衣店 ❑ *We had to have the washing done at the laundry.* 我们不得不把衣服放在洗衣店里洗。

> A business where people go to wash their clothes for themselves is called a **Laundromat**. The machines are operated by inserting coins so another name for these is **coin laundry**. In the UK, the usual word is **launderette**.

3 N-COUNT A **laundry** or a **laundry room** is a room in a house, hotel, or institution where clothes, sheets, and towels are washed. 洗衣间 ❑ *He worked in the laundry at Oxford prison.* 他曾在牛津监狱的洗衣房工作。

→ see **house, soap**

lau·rel /lɔrᵊl/ (**laurels**) 1 N-VAR A **laurel** or a **laurel tree** is a small evergreen tree with shiny leaves. The leaves are sometimes used to make decorations such as wreaths. 月桂树 2 PHRASE If someone is **resting on** their **laurels**, they appear to be satisfied with the things they have achieved and have stopped putting effort into what they are doing. 不思进取 [DISAPPROVAL] ❑ *The committee's chairman accused NASA of resting on its laurels after making it to the moon.* 委员会主席谴责美国国家航空航天局在登月后便不思进取。

lava /lɑvə, lævə/ (**lavas**) N-MASS **Lava** is the very hot liquid rock that comes out of a volcano. 熔岩 ❑ *Mexico's Mount Colima began spewing lava and ash last night.* 墨西哥科利马山昨晚开始喷发熔岩和火山灰。

→ see **rock, volcano**

lava·tory /lævətɔri/ (**lavatories**) N-COUNT A **lavatory** is a toilet or a room with a toilet in it. 厕所 [mainly BRIT] ❑ *...the ladies' lavatory.* …女厕所。

lav·en·der /lævɪndər/ N-UNCOUNT **Lavender** is a garden plant with sweet-smelling, bluish-purple flowers. 熏衣草

▲ **lav·ish** /lævɪʃ/ (**lavishes, lavishing, lavished**) 1 ADJ If you describe something as **lavish**, you mean that it is very elaborate and impressive and a lot of money has been spent on it. 盛大奢华的 ❑ *...a lavish party to celebrate Bryan's fiftieth birthday.* …庆祝布赖恩50岁生日的盛会。 ❑ *He staged the most lavish productions of Mozart.* 他举办了最盛大的莫扎特作品演奏会。● **lav·ish·ly** ADV 盛大奢华地 [ADV with v] ❑ *The apartment building was lavishly decorated.* 这幢公寓楼装修豪华。 2 ADJ If you say that spending, praise, or the use of something is **lavish**, you mean that someone spends a lot or that something is praised or used a lot. 挥霍的 ❑ *Critics attack his lavish spending and flamboyant style.* 批评家们抨击他的挥霍无度和过分夸张的作风。 3 ADJ If you say that someone is **lavish** in the way they behave, you mean that they give, spend, or use a lot of something. 慷慨的 ❑ *Reviewers are lavish in their praise of this book.* 评论家们对于这本书大加赞赏。● **lav·ish·ly** ADV 慷慨地 [ADV with v] ❑ *Entertaining in style needn't mean spending lavishly.* 时尚娱乐并不意味着要无度地花钱。 4 V-T If you **lavish** money, affection, or praise **on** someone or something, you spend a lot of money on them or give them a lot of affection or praise. 为…花很多钱; 对…十分殷勤; 对…大加赞赏 ❑ *He lavished praise on his opponents.* 他对他的对手大加赞赏。

law ♦♦♦ /lɔ/ (**laws**) 1 N-SING **The law** is a system of rules that a society or government develops in order to deal with crime, business agreements, and social relationships. You can also use **the law** to refer to the people who work in this system. 法律; 执法者 ❑ *Obscene and threatening phone calls are against the law.* 猥亵电话和恐吓电话是违法的。 ❑ *They are beginning criminal proceedings against him for breaking the law on financing political parties.* 他们正开始对他进行刑事诉讼，因为他违反了政党资助法。 ❑ *The book analyzes why women kill and how the law treats them.* 这本书分析了妇女为什么杀人以及法律如何处置她们。 2 N-UNCOUNT **Law** is used to refer to a particular branch of the law, such as **criminal law** or **business law**. (某一类) 法律 ❑ *He was a professor of criminal law at Harvard University law school.* 他曾是哈佛大学法学院的刑法教授。 ❑ *Under international law, diplomats living in foreign countries are exempt from criminal prosecution.* 按照国际法，驻外外交官免受刑事诉讼。 3 N-COUNT A **law** is one of the rules in a system of law which deals with a particular type of agreement, relationship, or crime. (特定的)法规 ❑ *...the country's liberal political asylum law.* …该国的自由政治避难法。 4 N-PLURAL **The laws of** an organization or activity are its rules, which are used to organize and control it. 戒律; 守则 ❑ *...the laws of the Catholic Church.* …天主教会的戒律。 5 N-COUNT A **law** is a rule or set of rules for good behavior which is considered right and important by the majority of people for moral, religious, or emotional reasons. 准则 ❑ *...inflexible moral laws.* …不容更改的道德准则。 6 N-COUNT A **law** is a natural process in which a particular event or thing always leads to a particular result. 规律 ❑ *The laws of nature are absolute.* 自然规律是绝对确凿的。 7 N-COUNT A **law** is a scientific rule that someone has invented to explain a particular natural process. 定律 ❑ *...the law of gravity.* …万有引力定律。 8 N-UNCOUNT **Law** or **the law** is all the professions which deal with advising people about the law, representing people in court, or giving decisions and punishments. 法律行业 ❑ *A career in law is becoming increasingly attractive to young people.* 从事法律行业对于年轻人越来越有吸引力。 9 N-UNCOUNT **Law** is the study of systems of law and how laws work. 法学 ❑ *He studied law.* 他学习法学。 10 PHRASE If you accuse someone of thinking they are **above the law**, you criticize them for thinking that they are so clever or important that they do not need to obey the law. 凌驾于法律之上 [DISAPPROVAL] ❑ *He accuses the government of wanting to be above the law.* 他谴责政府想凌驾于法律之上。 11 PHRASE If you have to do something **by law** or if you are not allowed to do something **by law**, the law states that you have to do it or that you are not allowed to do it. 根据法律 ❑ *By law all restaurants must display their prices outside.* 根据法律所有饭店必须在外面亮出他们的价目。

law-abiding ADJ A **law-abiding** person always obeys the law and is considered to be good and honest because of this. 守法的 ❑ *We believe that the law should protect decent law-abiding citizens and their property.* 我们相信法律会保护正派守法的公民及其财产。

law and or·der N-UNCOUNT When there is **law and order** in a country, the laws are generally accepted and obeyed, so that society there functions normally. 社会秩序 ❑ *If there were a breakdown of law and order, the army might be tempted to intervene.* 如果社会秩序瘫痪，军队将会试图干预。

★ **law·ful** /lɔfəl/ ADJ If an activity, organization, or product is **lawful**, it is allowed by law. 合法的 [FORMAL] ❑ *The detention of the fugitive was lawful.* 对逃亡者的拘留是合法的。● **law·ful·ly** ADV 合法地 [ADV with v] ❑ *Amnesty International is trying to establish whether the police acted lawfully in shooting him.* 大赦国际正试图证实警察向他开枪是否合法。

law·less /lɔlɪs/ 1 ADJ **Lawless** actions break the law, especially in a wild and violent way. 非法的 ❑ *The government recognized there were problems in urban areas but these could never be an excuse for lawless behavior.* 政府认识到市区存在问题，但是这绝不能成为非法行为的借口。● **law·less·ness** N-UNCOUNT 违法 ❑ *Lawlessness is a major problem.* 违反法律是一个严重的问题。 2 ADJ A **lawless** place or time is one where people do not respect the law. 无视法律的 (地方); 不受法律约束的 (时代) ❑ *...lawless inner-city streets plagued by muggings, thefts, assaults and even murder.* …没有法纪的市中心街区，受抢劫、偷盗、袭击甚至凶杀的困扰。

lawn /lɔn/ (**lawns**) N-VAR A **lawn** is an area of grass that is kept cut short and is usually part of someone's yard, or part of a park. 草坪 ❑ *They were sitting on the lawn under a large beech tree.* 他们当时正坐在一棵大山毛榉树下的草坪上。

lawn·mow·er /lɔnmoʊər/ (**lawnmowers**) N-COUNT A **lawnmower** is a machine for cutting grass on lawns. 割草机

★ **law·suit** ◆◆◇ /lɔsut/ (**lawsuits**) N-COUNT A **lawsuit** is a case in a court of law which concerns a dispute between two people or organizations. 诉讼案 [FORMAL] ❑ *The dispute culminated last week in a lawsuit against the government.* 这场针对政府诉讼案的争论在上星期达到了高潮。

law·yer ◆◆◇ /lɔɪər, lɔyər/ (**lawyers**) N-COUNT A **lawyer** is a person who is qualified to advise people about the law and represent them in court. 律师 ❑ *Prosecution and defense lawyers are expected to deliver closing arguments next week.* 原告律师和被告律师下周将要作终结辩论。

→ see **trial**

In both British and American English, **lawyer** is a general term for someone who is qualified in law and represents people in legal matters. American **lawyers** can prepare cases and can also represent their clients in court. Another American word commonly used for **lawyer** is **attorney**. In Britain, a **solicitor** prepares legal documents such as wills and contracts, and also prepares cases that are heard in court. **Solicitors** can also represent their clients, especially in lower courts. In higher courts, the argument for each side is usually presented by a **barrister**. In Scotland, a **barrister** is usually called an **advocate**.

Word Link *lax ≈ allowing, loosening : lax, laxative, relax*

lax /læks/ (**laxer, laxest**) ADJ If you say that a person's behavior or a system is **lax**, you mean they are not careful or strict about maintaining high standards. 松懈的; 不严格的 ❑ *One of the problem areas is lax security for airport personnel.* 其中一个问题是对机场人员的安全措施不严格。 ❑ *There have been allegations from survivors that safety standards had been lax.* 幸存者们指控安全标准不严格。 ● **lax·ity** N-UNCOUNT 松懈 ❑ *The laxity of export control authorities has made a significant contribution to the problem.* 出口管理当局的松懈是导致此问题的重要因素。

laxa·tive /læksətɪv/ (**laxatives**) N-MASS A **laxative** is something you eat or drink that makes you go to the toilet. 泻药 ❑ *Foods that ferment quickly in the stomach are excellent natural laxatives.* 在胃里快速发酵的食物是极好的天然泻药。

lay

❶ VERB AND NOUN USES
❷ ADJECTIVE USES

❶ **lay** ◆◆◇ /leɪ/ (**lays, laying, laid**)

In standard English, the form **lay** is also the past tense of the verb **lie** in some meanings. In informal English, people sometimes use the word **lay** instead of **lie** in those meanings.

➪ **Please look at meanings 7 – 10 to see if the expression you are looking for is shown under another headword.**

Do not confuse the verb **lay** with the verb **lie**. Because **lay** is used to talk about putting something in a particular place or position, it is related to the verb **lie**. If someone **lays** something somewhere, it **lies** there. The past tense and past participle of **lay** are both **laid** and it is usually a transitive verb. ❑ *They laid him on the floor.* However, **lie** is an intransitive verb with the past tense **lay** and the past participle **lain**. ❑ *I lay on the floor with my legs in the air.*

1 V-T If you **lay** something somewhere, you put it there in a careful, gentle, or neat way. 放置 ❑ *Lay a sheet of newspaper on the floor.* 把一张报纸放在地板上。 ❑ *Mothers routinely lay babies on their backs to sleep.* 母亲们通常会把婴儿平躺着放下睡觉。 2 V-T If you **lay** something such as carpets, cables, or foundations, you put them into their permanent position. 铺设 ❑ *A man came to lay the carpet.* 一名男子来铺地毯。 3 V-T/V-I When a female bird **lays**, or **lays** an egg, it produces an egg by pushing it out of its body. 下 (蛋) ❑ *My canary has laid an egg.* 我的金丝雀下了一个蛋。 4 V-T **Lay** is used with some nouns to talk about making official preparations for something. For example, if you **lay the basis** for something or **lay plans** for it, you prepare it carefully. 奠定 (基础); 制定 (规划) ❑ *Diplomats meeting in Chile have laid the groundwork for far-reaching environmental regulations.* 在智利会晤的外交官们已经为长远的环境保护规则奠定了基础。 5 V-T **Lay** is used with some nouns in expressions about accusing or blaming someone. For example, if you **lay the blame** for a mistake on someone, you say it is their fault, or if the police **lay charges** against someone, they officially accuse that person of a crime. 归罪于 ❑ *She refused to lay the blame on any one party.* 她拒绝归罪于任何一方。 6 V-T If you **lay** the table or **lay** the places at a table, you arrange the knives, forks, and other things that people need on the table before a meal. 摆放 (餐具) [OLD-FASHIONED] ❑ *The butler always laid the table.* 餐具总是由管家来摆放。 7 to **lay** something **at** someone's **door** → see **door** 8 to **lay a finger on** someone → see **finger** 9 to **lay** your **hands on** something → see **hand** 10 to **lay siege to** something → see **siege**

▸ **lay aside** 1 PHRASAL VERB If you **lay aside** a feeling or belief, you reject it or give it up in order to progress with something. 放弃 ❑ *Perhaps the opposed parties will lay aside their sectional interests and rise to this challenge.* 反对党或许会放弃他们的局部利益，站起来面对这一挑战。 2 PHRASAL VERB If you **lay** something **aside**, you put it down, usually because you have finished using it or want to save it to use later. 把…搁置一边 [BRIT] ❑ *He finished the tea and laid the cup aside.* 他喝完了茶，把杯子搁在一边。

▸ **lay down** 1 PHRASAL VERB If you **lay** something **down**, you put it down, usually because you have finished using it. 放下 ❑ *Daniel finished the article and laid the newspaper down on his desk.* 丹尼尔看完了那篇文章就把报纸放在了他的桌子上。 2 PHRASAL VERB If rules or people in authority **lay down** what people should do or must do, they officially state what they should or must do. 制定 ❑ *Not all companies lay down written guidelines and rules.* 不是所有的公司都制定书面的准则和条例。 3 PHRASAL VERB If someone **lays down** their weapons, they stop fighting a battle or war and make peace. 放下 (武器) ❑ *The drug-traffickers have offered to lay down their arms.* 贩毒分子已经主动要放下武器。

▸ **lay off** 1 PHRASAL VERB If workers **are laid off**, they are told by their employers to leave their job, usually because there is no more work for them to do. 解雇 [BUSINESS] ❑ *100,000 federal workers will be laid off to reduce the deficit.* 10万名联邦工作人员将被解雇以减少赤字。 2 → see also **layoff**

▸ **lay on** PHRASAL VERB If you **lay on** something such as food, entertainment, or a service, you provide or supply it, especially in a generous or grand way. 精心安排 (食物、娱乐、服务等) [mainly BRIT] ❑ *They laid on a superb evening.* 他们精心安排了一个美好的夜晚。

▸ **lay out** 1 PHRASAL VERB If you **lay out** a group of things, you spread them out and arrange them neatly, for example, so that they can all be seen clearly. 摆放 ❑ *Grace laid out the knives and forks on the table.* 格雷丝把刀叉摆放在桌子上。 2 PHRASAL VERB To **lay out** ideas, principles, or plans means to explain or present them clearly, for example, in a document or a meeting. 清晰地表达 ❑ *Maxwell listened closely as Johnson laid out his plan.* 马克斯韦尔倾听约翰逊清晰地讲述他的计划。 3 → see also **layout**

▸ **lay up** PHRASAL VERB If someone **is laid up with** an illness, the illness makes it necessary for them to stay in bed. (因病) 卧床 [usu passive] [INFORMAL] ❑ *She was in the hospital for a week and laid up for a month after that.* 她住院一星期后又卧床一个月。 ❑ *Powell ruptured a disc in his back and was laid up for a year.* 鲍威尔背部椎间盘破裂，因此卧床一年。

❷ **lay** /leɪ/ 1 ADJ You use **lay** to describe people who are involved with a Christian church but are not members of the clergy or are not monks or nuns. 世俗的 [ADJ n] ❑ *Edwards is a Methodist lay preacher and social worker.* 爱德华兹是一位卫理公会的世俗布道者和社工。 2 ADJ You use **lay** to describe people who are not experts or professionals in a particular subject or activity. 非专业的 [ADJ n] ❑ *It is difficult for a lay person to gain access to medical libraries.* 非专业人员很难进入医学图书馆。

lay·er ◆◇◇ /leɪər/ (**layers, layering, layered**) 1 N-COUNT A **layer** of a material or substance is a quantity or piece of it that covers a

L

surface or that is between two other things. 层 ❑ *...the depletion of the ozone layer.* …臭氧层的损耗。 **2** N-COUNT If something such as a system or an idea has many **layers**, it has many different levels or parts. 层次 ❑ *Critics and the public puzzle out the layers of meaning in his photos.* 评论家和公众苦思冥想出了他照片中的层层含意。 **3** V-T If you **layer** something, you arrange it in layers. 分层放置 ❑ *Layer half the onion slices on top of the potatoes.* 把一半洋葱片一层层地放在土豆上。

Word Partnership *layer* 的常用搭配:
ADJ. **bottom/top** layer, **lower/upper** layer, **outer** layer, **protective** layer, **single** layer, **thick/thin** layer **1**
N. layer **cake**, layer **of dust**, layer **of fat**, **ozone** layer, layer **of skin**, **surface** layer **1**

★ **lay·man** /leɪmən/ (**laymen**) N-COUNT A **layman** is a person who is not trained, qualified, or experienced in a particular subject or activity. 外行人 ❑ *The mere mention of the words "heart failure" can conjure up, to the layman, the prospect of imminent death.* 一提到"心力衰竭"几个字，外行人就会想到立即死亡。

★ **lay·off** /leɪɔf/ (**layoffs**) N-COUNT When there are **layoffs** in a company, people become unemployed because there is no more work for them in the company. 解雇 [BUSINESS] ❑ *It will close more than 200 stores nationwide resulting in the layoffs of an estimated 2,000 employees.* 在全国范围内将关闭二百多家商店，造成约两千人失业。

lay·out /leɪaʊt/ (**layouts**) N-COUNT The **layout** of a park, building, or piece of writing is the way in which the parts of it are arranged. (建筑或文章的) 布局 ❑ *He tried to recall the layout of the farmhouse.* 他想回忆那农舍的布局。

lazy /leɪzi/ (**lazier, laziest**) **1** ADJ If someone is **lazy**, they do not want to work or make any effort to do anything. 懒惰的 ❑ *Lazy and incompetent police officers are letting the public down.* 懒惰无能的警官们让公众失望。 ● **la·zi·ness** N-UNCOUNT 懒惰 ❑ *Current employment laws will be changed to reward effort and punish laziness.* 现行的雇佣法将被修改以便奖勤罚懒。 **2** ADJ You can use **lazy** to describe an activity or event in which you are very relaxed and which you do or take part in without making much effort. 悠懒的 [ADJ n] ❑ *Her latest novel is perfect for a lazy summer afternoon's reading.* 她的最新小说是悠懒的夏日午后的完美读物。 ● **la·zi·ly** /leɪzɪli/ ADV 悠懒地 [ADV with v] ❑ *Liz went back into the kitchen, stretching lazily.* 莉兹回到厨房，悠懒地伸了伸腰。

lb (**lbs**) **lb** is a written abbreviation for **pound**, when it refers to weight. 磅 ❑ *The baby was born three months early at 3 lbs 5 oz.* 这个婴儿早产 3 个月，体重3磅5盎司。

LCD /ɛl si di/ (**LCDs**) N-COUNT An **LCD** is a display of information on a screen, which uses liquid crystals that become visible when electricity is passed through them. **LCD** is an abbreviation for **liquid crystal display**. 液晶显示 ❑ *...a color LCD screen.* …一台彩色液晶显示屏。

lead
❶ BEING AHEAD OR TAKING SOMEONE SOMEWHERE
❷ SUBSTANCES

❶ **lead** ♦♦♦ /lid/ (**leads, leading, led**)
➪ **Please look at meaning 18 and 19 to see if the expression you are looking for is shown under another headword.** **1** V-T If you **lead** a group of people, you walk or ride in front of them. 带领 ❑ *The president and vice president led the mourners.* 总统和副总统带领着送葬人群。 ❑ *He walks with a stick but still leads his soldiers into battle.* 尽管他拄着拐杖，但他仍带领士兵上战场。 **2** V-T If you **lead** someone to a particular place or thing, you take them there. 引领 ❑ *He took Dickon by the hand to lead him into the house.* 他拉着迪肯的手领他进了那幢房子。 ❑ *She confessed to the killing and led police to his remains.* 她承认杀了人，并且带警察找到了他的遗骸。 **3** V-I If a road, gate, or door **leads** somewhere, you can get there by following the road or going through the gate or door. 通往 ❑ *...the door that led to the yard.* …通往院子的门。 ❑ *...a hallway leading to the living room.* …通往客厅的过道。 **4** V-I If you **are leading** at a particular point in a race or competition, you are winning at that point. (在比赛中) 领先 ❑ *He's leading in the presidential race.* 他在总统竞选中领先。 ❑ *So far Fischer leads by five wins to two.* 到目前为止，菲舍尔以 5 : 2 领先。 **5** N-SING If you have **the lead** or are **in the lead** in a race or competition, you are winning. 领先地位 ❑ *Harvard took the lead and remained unperturbed by the repeated challenges.* 哈佛取得了领先地位，经过再三挑战后仍然镇定自若。 **6** V-T If one company or country **leads** others in a particular activity such as scientific research or business, it is more successful or advanced than they are in that activity. (在某领域) 领先 ❑ *In 1920, the United States led the world in iron and steel manufacturing.* 美国的钢铁制造业在1920年领先于世界。 **7** V-T If you **lead** a group of people, an organization, or an activity, you are in control or in charge of the people or the activity. 领导 ❑ *He led the country between 1949 and 1984.* 他在1949到1984年间领导着这个国家。 **8** N-COUNT If you take **the lead**, you do something new or develop new ideas or methods that other people consider to be a good example or model to follow. 领先 ❑ *The American and Japanese navies took the lead in the development of naval aviation.* 美国和日本海军在海军航空的发展方面领先。 **9** V-T You can use **lead** when you are saying what kind of life someone has. For example, if you **lead** a busy life, your life is busy. 过…的生活 ❑ *She led a normal, happy life with her sister and brother.* 她和弟弟妹妹过着平常和幸福的生活。 **10** V-I If something **leads to** a situation or event, usually an unpleasant one, it begins a process which causes that situation or event to happen. 导致 (通常为不愉快的情况) ❑ *Ethnic tensions among the republics could lead to civil war.* 各共和国之间紧张的民族关系可能导致内战。 **11** V-T If something **leads** you **to** do something, it influences or affects you in such a way that you do it. 促使 ❑ *His abhorrence of racism led him to write "The Algiers Motel Incident".* 他对种族主义的痛恨促使他写了《阿尔及尔汽车旅馆事件》。 **12** V-T You can say that one point or topic in a discussion or piece of writing **leads** you **to** another in order to introduce a new point or topic that is linked with the previous one. 引导 ❑ *Well, I think that leads me to the real point.* 嗯，我想这把我引向要点。 **13** N-COUNT A **lead** is a piece of information or an idea which may help people to discover the facts in a situation where many facts are not known, for example, in the investigation of a crime or in a scientific experiment. 线索 ❑ *The inquiry team is also following up possible leads after receiving 400 calls from the public.* 调查组正在接到的400个公众电话中追踪可能的线索。 **14** N-COUNT A dog's **lead** is a long, thin chain or piece of leather which you attach to the dog's collar so that you can control the dog. 牵狗的皮带；牵狗的链子 [BRIT]

in AM, use **leash**

15 N-COUNT A **lead** in a piece of equipment is a piece of wire covered in plastic which supplies electricity to the equipment or carries it from one part of the equipment to another. 导线 ❑ *...a lead that plugs into a socket on the camcorder.* …一根插到便携式摄影机插孔上的导线。 **16** N-COUNT **The lead** in a play, film, or show is the most important part in it. The person who plays this part can also be called the **lead**. 主角；扮演主角的演员 ❑ *Nina Ananiashvili and Alexei Fadeyechev from the Bolshoi Ballet dance the leads.* 来自莫斯科大剧院芭蕾舞团的妮娜・安娜尼雅什维莉和阿历克谢・费德耶切夫担任主角。 ❑ *Neve Campbell is the lead, playing one of the dancers.* 内芙・坎贝尔是主演，扮演其中一个舞蹈者。 **17** → see also **leading** **18** to **lead** someone **astray** → see **astray** **19** to **lead the way** → see **way**

▸ **lead up to** **1** PHRASAL VERB The events that **led up to** a particular event happened one after the other until that event occurred. 导致 ❑ *Alan Tomlinson has reconstructed the events that led up to the deaths.* 阿伦・汤姆林森再现了导致死亡的事件。 **2** PHRASAL VERB If someone **leads up to** a particular subject, they gradually guide a conversation to a point where they can introduce it. 逐渐引到 (某一个话题) ❑ *I'm leading up to something quite important.* 我正要说到很重要的事情上。

Thesaurus *lead* 另参见:
V. escort, guide, precede; (*ant.*) follow ❶ **1** **2**
govern, head, manage ❶ **7**

❷ **lead** /lɛd/ (**leads**) **1** N-UNCOUNT **Lead** is a soft, gray, heavy metal. 铅 ❑ *...drinking water supplied by old-fashioned lead pipes.* …通过老式铅管供应的饮用水。 **2** N-COUNT The **lead** in a pencil is the center part of it which makes a mark on paper. 铅笔芯 ❑ *He grabbed a pencil, and the lead immediately broke.* 他抓起一支铅笔，铅笔芯立刻就断了。
→ see **mineral, plumbing**

lead·er ♦♦♦ /lidər/ (**leaders**) **1** N-COUNT The **leader** of a group of people or an organization is the person who is in control of it or in charge of it. 领导人 ❑ *We now need a new leader of the party and a new style of leadership.* 我们现在需要一个新的政党领导人和一种新的领导风格。 **2** N-COUNT The **leader** at a particular point in a race or competition is the person who is winning at that point. 领先者 ❑ *The leaders came in two minutes clear of the field.* 领先的选手们早两分钟到达终点。

lead·er·board /liːdərbɔrd/ N-SING **The leaderboard** is a board that shows the names and positions of the leading competitors in a competition, especially a golf tournament. 排行榜（尤指高尔夫球比赛的）❑ *I'm delighted to be on top of the leaderboard in a tournament that has so many star names playing.* 我很高兴能在有这么多明星参赛的锦标赛上名列榜首。

lead·er·ship ♦♦◊ /liːdərʃɪp/ (**leaderships**) **1** N-COUNT You refer to people who are in control of a group or organization as the **leadership**. 领导人；领导层 ❑ *He is expected to hold talks with both the Croatian and Slovenian leaderships.* 人们希望他能与克罗地亚和斯洛文尼亚两国的领导人举行会谈。 **2** N-UNCOUNT Someone's **leadership** is their position or state of being in control of a group of people. 领导地位 ❑ *He praised her leadership during the crisis.* 他称赞了她在危机中的领导作用。

lead·ing ♦♦◊ /liːdɪŋ/ **1** ADJ The **leading** person or thing in a particular area is the one which is most important or successful. 主要的 [ADJ n] ❑ *...a leading member of the city's Sikh community.* …该市锡克教团体的一名主要成员。 **2** ADJ The **leading** role in a play or movie is the main role. A **leading** lady or man is an actor who plays this role. 主要的（角色）；担任主要角色的 [ADJ n] ❑ *...an offer to play the leading role in an Arthur Miller play.* …一个在亚瑟·米勒的剧目中出演主角的提议。 **3** ADJ The **leading** group, vehicle, or person in a race or procession is the one that is at the front. 在前面的 [ADJ n] ❑ *The leading car came to a halt.* 行驶在前面的车停了下来。

Word Partnership *leading* 的常用搭配：

N. leading **advocate**, leading **cause of death**, leading **expert**, leading **manufacturer** **1**
leading **candidate**, leading **contender**, leading **in the polls**, leading **in a race**, leading **runner**, leading **scorer** **3**

L

lead·ing edge N-SING **The leading edge of** a particular area of research or development is the area of it that seems most advanced or sophisticated. 前沿 ❑ *I think Israel tends to be at the leading edge of technological development.* 我认为以色列会走在技术发展的前沿。● **leading-edge** ADJ 前沿的 ❑ *...leading-edge technology.* …前沿技术。

lead time (**lead times**) **1** N-COUNT **Lead time** is the time between the original design or idea for a particular product and its actual production. 从最初设计到投产的时间 [BUSINESS] ❑ *They aim to cut production lead times to under 18 months.* 他们的目标是把产品从设计到投产的时间缩短到18个月以内。 **2** N-COUNT **Lead time** is the period of time that it takes for goods to be delivered after someone has ordered them. 从订货到交货的时间 [BUSINESS] ❑ *Lead times on new equipment orders can run as long as three years.* 新设备从订货到交货的时间可能长达3年。

leaf ♦◊◊ /liːf/ (**leaves, leafs, leafing, leafed**) **1** N-COUNT The **leaves** of a tree or plant are the parts that are flat, thin, and usually green. Many trees and plants lose their leaves in the winter and grow new leaves in the spring. 叶子 [usu pl, also "in/into" N] ❑ *In the garden, the leaves of the horse chestnut had already fallen.* 园子里的七叶树已经落叶了。 **2** N-COUNT A **leaf** is one of the pieces of paper of which a book is made. 一页 ❑ *He flattened the wrappers and put them between the leaves of his book.* 他抚平了包装纸，把它们夹在了书页中间。 **3** PHRASE If you say that you are going to **turn over a new leaf**, you mean that you are going to start to behave in a better or more acceptable way. 开始新的一页 ❑ *He realized he was in the wrong and promised to turn over a new leaf.* 他认识到自己错了，承诺要重新开始。

→ see **tea**

▸ **leaf through** PHRASAL VERB If you **leaf through** something such as a book or magazine, you turn the pages without reading or looking at them very carefully. 翻阅 ❑ *Most patients derive enjoyment from leafing through old picture albums.* 大部分病人能从翻阅旧相册中获得乐趣。

★ **leaf·let** /liːflɪt/ (**leaflets**) N-COUNT A **leaflet** is a little book or a piece of paper containing information about a particular subject. 传单 ❑ *Campaigners handed out leaflets on passive smoking.* 发起人分发了关于被动吸烟的传单。

leafy /liːfi/ **1** ADJ **Leafy** trees and plants have lots of leaves on them. 多叶的 ❑ *His two-story brick home was surrounded by tall, leafy trees.* 他那栋两层的砖楼被枝繁叶茂的大树环绕着。 **2** ADJ You say that a place is **leafy** when there are lots of trees and plants there. 树木茂密的 ❑ *...a gate leading to the narrow leafy streets at the top of the hill.* …通向山顶树木茂密的狭窄街道的一扇大门。

→ see **vegetable**

league ♦♦◊ /liːg/ (**leagues**) **1** N-COUNT A **league** is a group of people, clubs, or countries that have joined together for a particular purpose, or because they share a common interest. 联盟；协会 ❑ *...the League of Nations.* …国际联盟。 **2** N-COUNT A **league** is a group of teams that play the same sport or activity against each other. （各种运动队的）联盟 ❑ *...the American League series between the Boston Red Sox and World Champion Oakland Athletics.* …波士顿红袜队和世界冠军奥克兰运动家队之间的美国职业棒球联盟系列赛。 **3** N-COUNT You use **league** to make comparisons between different people or things, especially in terms of their quality. 级别；水平 ❑ *Her success has taken her out of my league.* 她的成功使她和我不再处于同一个等级上了。 **4** PHRASE If you say that someone is **in league with** another person to do something bad, you mean that they are working together to do that thing. （与某人）勾结 ❑ *There is no evidence that the broker was in league with the fraudulent vendor.* 没有代理人和奸商相勾结的证据。

Word Partnership *league* 的常用搭配：

N. league **leader**, league **record**, league **schedule** **2**
V. **lead the** league **2**
PREP. **out of *someone's*** league **3**
in league **with *someone*** **4**

leak ♦◊◊ /liːk/ (**leaks, leaking, leaked**) **1** V-T/V-I If a container **leaks**, there is a hole or crack in it which lets a substance such as liquid or gas escape. You can also say that a container **leaks** a substance such as liquid or gas. 渗漏（液体或气体）；（容器）渗漏 ❑ *The roof leaked.* 屋顶漏了。 ❑ *The pool's fiberglass sides had cracked and the water had leaked out.* 池子的玻璃纤维侧面裂了，水已经渗了出来。 ● N-COUNT **Leak** is also a noun. 渗漏 ❑ *It's thought a gas leak may have caused the blast.* 人们认为可能是煤气泄漏引起了爆炸。 **2** N-COUNT A **leak** is a crack, hole, or other gap that a substance such as a liquid or gas can pass through. 裂缝；漏洞 ❑ *...a leak in the radiator.* …散热器上的裂缝。 **3** V-T/V-I If a secret document or piece of information **leaks** or **is leaked**, someone lets the public know about it. 泄露 ❑ *Mr. Ashton accused police of leaking information to the press.* 艾什顿先生指控警察向媒体泄露了消息。 ❑ *We don't know how the transcript leaked.* 我们不知道抄本是怎样泄露的。 ● N-COUNT **Leak** is also a noun. 泄露 ❑ *More serious leaks, possibly involving national security, are likely to be investigated by the police.* 可能涉及国家安全的更严重泄密会受到警方的调查。 ● PHRASAL VERB **Leak out** means the same as **leak**. 泄露 ❑ *More details are now beginning to leak out.* 更多的细节现在开始泄露出来。

Thesaurus *leak* 另参见：

V. discharge, drip, ooze, seep, trickle **1**
come out, divulge, pass on **3**
N. crack, hole, opening **2**

Word Partnership *leak* 的常用搭配：

V. **cause a** leak, **spring a** leak **1**
N. **fuel** leak, **gas** leak, **oil** leak, leak **in the roof**, **water** leak **1**
leak **in the roof** **2**
leak **information**, leak **news**, leak **a story** **3**

leak·age /liːkɪdʒ/ (**leakages**) N-VAR A **leakage** is an amount of liquid or gas that is escaping from a pipe or container by means of a crack, hole, or other fault. （液体或气）泄漏 ❑ *A leakage of kerosene has polluted water supplies.* 泄漏的煤油已污染了水源。

lean ♦◊◊ /liːn/ (**leans, leaning, leaned, leaner, leanest**) **1** V-I When you **lean** in a particular direction, you bend your body in that direction. （身体）倾斜 ❑ *Eileen leaned across and opened the passenger door.* 艾琳探过身来打开了乘客门。 **2** V-T/V-I If you **lean on** or **against** someone or something, you rest against them so that they partly support your weight. If you **lean** an object **on** or **against** something, you place the object so that it is partly supported by that thing. 把…靠（在…上）；靠（在…上） ❑ *She was feeling tired and was* *glad to lean against him.* 她感到累了，乐意靠在他身上。 ❑ *Lean the plants against a wall and cover the roots with peat.* 把这些植物靠在墙上，用泥炭盖住根部。 **3** ADJ If you describe someone as **lean**, you mean that they are thin but look strong and healthy. 清瘦而且健康 [APPROVAL] ❑ *Like most athletes, she was lean and muscular.* 像大部分运动员一样，她清瘦而且肌肉强健。 **4** ADJ If meat is **lean**, it does not have very much fat. 少脂肪的 ❑ *It is a beautiful meat, very lean and tender.* 这是一块好肉，又瘦又嫩。 **5** ADJ If you describe an organization as **lean**, you mean that it has become more efficient and less wasteful by getting rid of staff, or by dropping projects which were unprofitable. 高效的 ❑ *...reforms which turned us into a lean and competitive nation.* …使我们成为高效率、竞争力强的国家的改革。 **6** ADJ If you describe periods of time as **lean**, you mean that people have less of something such as money or are less successful than they used to be. 贫乏的 ❑ *My parents lived through the lean years of the 1930s.* 我的父母经历了20世纪30年代的萧条期。

▸ **lean on** or **lean upon** PHRASAL VERB If you **lean on** someone or **lean upon** them, you depend on them for support and encouragement. 依靠（支持和鼓励）❑ *She leaned on him to help her to solve her problems.* 她依靠他帮忙解决问题。

Thesaurus *lean* 另参见：

V.	bend, incline, prop, tilt **1**
	recline, rest **2**
ADJ.	angular, lanky, slender, slim, wiry **3**

Word Partnership *lean* 的常用搭配：

ADV.	lean **heavily** **2**
ADJ.	**long and** lean, **tall and** lean **3**
N.	lean **body** **3**
	lean **beef**, lean **meat** **4**

leap ♦◇◇ /liːp/ (**leaps, leaping, leaped** or **leapt**) **1** V-T/V-I If you **leap**, you jump high in the air or jump a long distance. 跳跃 ❑ *He leaped in the air and waved his fists to the fans as he ran out of the stadium.* 他跑出体育馆，跳起来向他的崇拜者们挥舞着拳头。 ❑ *Frederick leaped 22 feet, 7-1/4 inches on his second attempt.* 弗雷德里克第2次试跳跳了22英尺7.25英寸。 ● N-COUNT **Leap** is also a noun. 跳跃 ❑ *The suspect took a leap out of a third-story window.* 那个犯罪嫌疑人从三楼的窗口跳了出去。 **2** V-I If you **leap** somewhere, you move there suddenly and quickly. 急速移动 ❑ *The two men leaped into the jeep and roared off.* 那两个人飞快地跳上吉普车呼啸而去。 **3** V-I If a vehicle **leaps** somewhere, it moves there in a short sudden movement. (车辆) 突然移动 ❑ *The car leaped forward.* 汽车突然向前冲去。 **4** N-COUNT A **leap** is a large and important change, increase, or advance. 巨变；剧增 [JOURNALISM] ❑ *The result has been a giant leap in productivity.* 其结果就是生产力的大幅度提高。 ❑ *...the leap in the unemployed from 35,000 to 75,000.* …失业人数从3.5万人猛增到7.5万人。 **5** V-I If you **leap to** a particular place or position, you make a large and important change, increase, or advance. 巨变；剧增 ❑ *Bush's approval rating leaped to an astounding 88 percent.* 布什的支持率令人吃惊地剧增到了88%。

Word Partnership *leap* 的常用搭配：

V.	**make a** leap, **take a** leap **1**
ADJ.	**big** leap, **giant** leap, **sudden** leap **1** **4**
N.	leap **to *your* feet** **2**

leap·frog /liːpfrɒg/ (**leapfrogs, leapfrogging, leapfrogged**) **1** N-UNCOUNT **Leapfrog** is a game which children play, in which a child bends over, while others jump over their back. 跳背游戏 ❑ *The kids were playing leapfrog and doing somersaults in the backyard.* 孩子们正在后院玩跳背游戏和翻筋斗。 **2** V-T/V-I If one group of people **leapfrogs** into a particular position or **leapfrogs** someone else, they use the achievements of another person or group in order to make advances of their own. (利用别人成就) 超越 ❑ *It is already obvious that all four American systems have leapfrogged over the European versions.* 显然，美国的全部4套系统已经超越了欧洲的版本。

leap year (**leap years**) N-COUNT A **leap year** is a year which has 366 days. The extra day is February 29th. There is a leap year every four years. 闰年
→ see year

learn ♦♦♦ /lɜːrn/ (**learns, learning, learned**) **1** V-T/V-I If you **learn** something, you obtain knowledge or a skill through studying or training. 学习 ❑ *Their children were going to learn English.* 他们的孩子们打算学英语。 ❑ *He is learning to play the piano.* 他正在学弹钢琴。 ❑ *It's going to be tough, but these guys learn quickly.* 这会很难，但是这些家伙们学得很快。 ● **learn·ing** N-UNCOUNT 学习 ❑ *...a bilingual approach to the learning of English.* …英语学习的双语法。 **2** V-T/V-I If you **learn** of something, you find out about it. 得知 ❑ *It was only after his death that she learned of his affair with Betty.* 是在他去世之后她才得知他和贝蒂的风流事。 ❑ *It didn't come as a shock to learn that the fuel and cooling systems are the most common causes of breakdown.* 不足为怪的是，燃料和冷却系统是故障的最常见原因。 **3** V-T If people **learn to** behave or react in a particular way, they gradually start to behave in that way as a result of a change in attitudes. 学会 ❑ *You have to learn to face your problem.* 你得学会面对自己的问题。 **4** V-T/V-I If you **learn from** an unpleasant experience, you change the way you behave so that it does not happen again or so that, if it happens again, you can deal with it better. 从…吸取教训 ❑ *I am convinced that he has learned from his mistakes.* 我确信他已经从错误中吸取了教训。 ❑ *I just hope we all learn some lessons from this.* 我只是希望我们都能以此为戒。 **5** V-T If you **learn** something such as a poem or a role in a play, you study or repeat the words so that you can remember them. 学会 ❑ *He learned this song as an inmate at a Texas prison.* 他在德克萨斯监狱服刑时学会了这首歌。 **6** → see also **learned**, **learning** **7** to **learn** something **the hard way** → see **hard** **8** **to learn the ropes** → see **rope**

Thesaurus *learn* 另参见：

V.	master, pick up, study **1**
	discover, find out, understand **2**

Word Partnership *learn* 的常用搭配：

V.	learn **to drive**, learn **to read**, learn **to speak**, learn **to swim**, learn **to use *something***, learn **to write** **1**
	have to learn, **must** learn, **need to** learn, **try to** learn, **want to** learn **1**–**5**
	learn **to cope with *someone/something*** **3**
N.	learn **a language**, learn **a secret**, learn **a skill**, learn **things**, learn **the truth** **1**
	children learn, learn **from experience**, learn **a lesson**, learn **from mistakes**, **opportunity to** learn, **people** learn, learn **in school**, **students** learn **1** **3** **4**
ADJ.	**eager to** learn **1**–**3**
	shocked to learn **2**

learn·ed /lɜːrnɪd/ ADJ A **learned** person has gained a lot of knowledge by studying. 博学的 ❑ *He is a scholar, a genuinely learned man.* 他是个学者，一个真正博学的人。

learn·er /lɜːrnər/ (**learners**) N-COUNT A **learner** is someone who is learning about a particular subject or how to do something. 学习者 ❑ *Clinton proved to be a quick learner and soon settled into serious struggles over cutting the budget.* 克林顿果然学得很快，不久就着手解决降低预算的重大问题。

learn·ing /lɜːrnɪŋ/ **1** N-UNCOUNT **Learning** is the process of gaining knowledge through studying. 学习 ❑ *The brochure described the library as the focal point of learning on the campus.* 这本小册子把图书馆描述为校园学习的中心。 **2** → see also **learn**
→ see brain

learn·ing curve (**learning curves**) N-COUNT A **learning curve** is a process where people develop a skill by learning from their mistakes. A steep learning curve involves learning very quickly. 学习曲线 [usu sing] ❑ *They are on a steep learning curve.* 他们学得很快。

lease ♦◇◇ /liːs/ (**leases, leasing, leased**) **1** N-COUNT A **lease** is a legal agreement by which the owner of a building, a piece of land, or something such as a car allows someone else to use it for a period of time in return for money. 租约 ❑ *He took up a 10-year lease on the house.* 他为这房子签了10年的租约。 **2** V-T If you **lease** property or something such as a car from someone or if they **lease** it **to** you, they allow you to use it in return for regular payments of money. 租进；租出 ❑ *He went to Toronto, where he leased an apartment.* 他去了多伦多，在那里租了一套公寓。 ❑ *She hopes to lease the building to students.* 她希望把大楼租给学生。

lease·hold /liːshoʊld/ ADJ If a building or land is described as **leasehold**, it is allowed to be used in return for payment according to the terms of a lease. 租的 ❑ *I went into a leasehold property at four hundred and fifty dollars rent per year.* 我住进了年租金450美元的房子。

leash /liːʃ/ (leashes) N-COUNT A dog's **leash** is a long thin piece of leather or a chain, which you attach to the dog's collar so that you can keep the dog under control. (牵狗的) 皮带或链条 ❑ *All dogs in public places should be on a leash.* 所有的狗在公共场所必须拴上链子。

least ♦♦♦ /liːst/

Least is often considered to be the superlative form of **little**.

1 PHRASE You use **at least** to say that a number or amount is the smallest that is possible or likely and that the actual number or amount may be greater. The forms **at the least** and **at the very least** are also used. (在数量上) 至少 ❑ *Aim to have at least half a pint of milk each day.* 目标是每天至少喝半品脱牛奶。❑ *About two-thirds of adults consult their doctor at least once a year.* 大约三分之二的成年人一年至少看一次医生。 2 PHRASE You use **at least** to say that something is the minimum that is true or possible. The forms **at the least** and **at the very least** are also used. 至少 (最小的可能性) ❑ *She could take a nice vacation at least.* 她至少能过一个美好的假期。❑ *His possession of classified documents in his home was, at the very least, a violation of navy security regulations.* 他把机密文件放在家里，这最起码是违反了海军安全条例。 3 PHRASE You use **at least** to indicate an advantage that exists in spite of the disadvantage or bad situation that has just been mentioned. 尽管如此 ❑ *We've no idea what his state of health is but at least we know he is still alive.* 我们不清楚他健康状况怎样，尽管如此我们知道他还活着。 4 PHRASE You use **at least** to indicate that you are correcting or changing something that you have just said. 至少 (修正刚说过的话) ❑ *It's not difficult to get money for research or at least it's not always difficult.* 获得研究的资金不难，至少说，不总是很难。 5 ADJ You use **the least** to mean a smaller amount than anyone or anything else, or the smallest amount possible. 最少的 ["the" ADJ n] ❑ *I try to offend the least amount of people possible.* 我尽可能少得罪人。● PRON **Least** is also a pronoun. 最少量 ["the" PRON] ❑ *On education funding, Japan performs best but spends the least per student.* 在教育资金方面，日本做得最好，但是对每个学生的投入却最少。● ADV **Least** is also an adverb. 最少地 ["the" ADV after v] ❑ *Damming the river may end up benefiting those who need it the least.* 在河上建大坝最终可能有利于那些最不需要大坝的人。 6 ADV You use **least** to indicate that someone or something has less of a particular quality than most other things of its kind. 最少地 [ADV adj/adv] ❑ *He was one of the least warm human beings I had ever met.* 他是我所见过的最不热情的人之一。 7 ADJ You use **the least** to emphasize the smallness of something, especially when it hardly exists at all. 一点儿 ["the" ADJ n] [EMPHASIS] ❑ *I don't have the least idea of what you're talking about.* 我一点儿也不明白你在说什么。 8 ADV You use **least** to indicate that something is true or happens to a smaller degree or extent than anything else or at any other time. 最低程度地 [ADV with v] ❑ *He had a way of throwing Helen off guard with his charm when she least expected it.* 他有办法用他的魅力让海伦在最意想不到的时候失去戒备。 9 ADJ You use **least** in structures where you are emphasizing that a particular situation or event is much less important or serious than other possible or actual ones. 最微不足道的 [ADJ "of" def-n] [EMPHASIS] ❑ *Having to get up at three o'clock every morning was the least of her worries.* 必须每天早晨3点起床是她烦恼中最微不足道的。 10 PRON You use **the least** in structures where you are stating the minimum that should be done in a situation, and suggesting that more should really be done. 起码 ["the" PRON cl] ❑ *Well, the least you can do, if you won't help me yourself, is to tell me where to go instead.* 哦，如果你不愿意亲自帮助我，起码应该告诉我往哪儿走吧。

Thesaurus *least* 另参见：

ADJ. fewest, lowest, minimum, smallest 5

leath·er ♦◇◇ /lɛðər/ (leathers) N-MASS **Leather** is treated animal skin, usually from cows, which is used for making shoes, clothes, bags, and furniture. 皮革 ❑ *He wore a leather jacket and dark trousers.* 他穿着皮夹克和黑裤子。

leave

1 VERB USES
2 NOUN USE
3 PHRASES AND PHRASAL VERBS

1 **leave** ♦♦♦ /liːv/ (leaves, leaving, left) 1 V-T/V-I If you **leave** a place or person, you go away from that place or person. 离开 ❑ *He would not be allowed to leave the country.* 他不准离开这个国家。❑ *My flight leaves in less than an hour.* 我的航班一小时内起飞。 2 V-T/V-I If you **leave** an institution, group, or job, you permanently stop attending that institution, being a member of that group, or doing that job. 离开 (机构、团体或工作) ❑ *He left school with no qualifications.* 他离开学校时没有拿到证书。❑ *I am leaving to concentrate on writing fiction.* 我要离开去专心写小说。 3 V-T/V-I If you **leave** your husband, wife, or some other person with whom you have had a close relationship, you stop living with them or you end the relationship. 与…脱离关系; 离开 (某人) ❑ *He'll never leave you. You needn't worry.* 他永远都不会离开你的，你不必担心。 4 V-T If you **leave** something or someone in a particular place, you let them remain there when you go away. If you **leave** something or someone with a person, you let them remain with that person so they are safe while you are away. 留下 ❑ *I left my bags in the car.* 我把包留在车里。❑ *From the moment that Philippe had left her in the bedroom at the hotel, she had heard nothing of him.* 自从菲利普把她遗弃在旅店房间的那一刻起，她就再没有他的任何消息。 5 V-T If you **leave** a message or an answer, you write it, record it, or give it to someone so that it can be found or passed on. 留下 (信息或答复) ❑ *You can leave a message on our answering machine.* 你可以在我们的电话留言机上留言。❑ *I left my phone number with several people.* 我把我的电话号码留给了几个人。 6 V-T If you **leave** someone doing something, they are doing that thing when you go away from them. 留下…继续作某事 ❑ *Salter drove off, leaving Callendar surveying the scene.* 索特尔开车走了，留下加林达继续调查现场。 7 V-T If you **leave** someone **to** do something, you go away from them so that they do it on their own. If you **leave** someone **to** himself or herself, you go away from them and allow them to be alone. 留给…自己做; 把…留下 ❑ *I'll leave you to get to know each other.* 我让你们自己互相认识一下。❑ *Diana took the hint and left them to it.* 戴安娜心领神会，让他们自己完成这件事。 8 V-T To **leave** an amount of something means to keep it available after the rest has been used or taken away. 留出 ❑ *He always left a little food for the next day.* 他总是留出一点食物第二天吃。 9 V-T To **leave** someone **with** something, especially when that thing is unpleasant or difficult to deal with, means to make them have it or make them deal with it. 给…留下 (不愉快的东西) ❑ *...a crash which left him with a broken collar-bone.* …一次给他留下锁骨骨折的车祸。 10 V-T If an event **leaves** people or things in a particular state, they are in that state when the event has finished. 致使 ❑ *...violent disturbances which have left at least ten people dead.* …致使至少十人死亡的暴力骚乱。 11 V-T If you **leave** food or drink, you do not eat or drink it, often because you do not like it. 剩下 (食物或饮料) ❑ *If you don't like the cocktail you ordered, just leave it and try a different one.* 如果你不喜欢你点的鸡尾酒，剩着吧，尝尝别的。 12 V-T If something **leaves** a mark, effect, or sign, it causes that mark, effect, or sign to remain as a result. 留下 (痕迹、影响等) ❑ *A muscle tear will leave a scar after healing.* 肌肉撕裂在治愈后会留下伤疤。 13 V-T If you **leave** something in a particular state, position, or condition, you let it remain in that state, position, or condition. 使处于 (某种状态、位置或情形) ❑ *He left the album open on the table.* 他把相册敞开着放在桌子上了。❑ *I've left the car lights on.* 我把车灯开着。 14 V-T If you **leave** a space or gap in something, you deliberately make that space or gap. 留 (空隙或空白) ❑ *Leave a gap at the top and bottom so air can circulate.* 在顶部和底部各留一点空隙，这样空气就可以流通了。 15 V-T If you **leave** a job, decision, or choice **to** someone, you give them the responsibility for dealing with it or making it. 留给…办理 ❑ *Affix the blue airmail label and leave the rest to us.* 贴上蓝色航空邮件标签，剩下的就留给我们办吧。❑ *The judge should not have left it to the jury to decide.* 法官本不应该让陪审团作决定。 16 V-T To **leave** someone **with** a particular course of action or the opportunity to do something means to let it be available to them, while restricting them in other ways. 留给 (指有限的机会) ❑ *He was left with no option but to resign.* 留给他的除了辞职别无选择。 17 V-T If you **leave** something **until** a particular time, you delay doing it or dealing with it until then. 留到…时才 ❑ *Don't leave it all until the last minute.* 不要把什么事都留到最后一分钟。● PHRASE If you **leave** something **too late**, you delay doing it so that when you eventually do it, it is useless or ineffective. 耽误 18 V-T If you **leave** a particular subject, you stop talking about it and start discussing something else. 不再谈论 ❑ *I think we'd better leave the subject of nationalism.* 我想我们最好不要再谈论民族主义这个话题了。 19 V-T If you **leave** property or money **to** someone, you arrange for it to be given to them after you have died. 把 (遗产) 留给 ❑ *He died two and a half years later, leaving everything to his wife.* 他两年半后去世，把所有的财产都留给了他的妻子。 20 V-T If you **leave** something somewhere, you forget to bring it with you. 忘拿 21 → see also **left**

L

Thesaurus *leave* 另参见：

V. abandon, depart, go away; *(ant.)* arrive, come, stay ❶ 1
give up, quit, resign; *(ant.)* remain, stay ❷ 2
abandon, desert, ditch, take off ❸ 3

❷ **leave** ♦♦♦ /liv/ N-UNCOUNT **Leave** is a period of time when you are not working at your job, because you are on vacation, or for some other reason. If you are **on leave**, you are not working at your job. 休假 ❑ *Why don't you take a few days' leave?* 你为什么不休几天假？ ❑ *...maternity leave.* …产假。

❸ **leave** ♦♦♦ /liv/ (**leaves, leaving, left**)
➪ **Please look at meaning 3 to see if the expression you are looking for is shown under another headword.** 1 PHRASE If you **leave** someone or something **alone**, or if you **leave** them **be**, you do not pay them any attention or bother them. 不管；不打扰 ❑ *Some people need to confront a traumatic past; others find it better to leave it alone.* 一些人需要面对伤痕累累的过去；另一些人认为最好不管它。 2 PHRASE If something continues **from where** it **left off**, it starts happening again at the point where it had previously stopped. 死灰复燃 ❑ *As soon as the police disappear, the violence will take up from where it left off.* 只要警察不在，暴力就会死灰复燃。 3 **take it or leave it** → see **take**

▸ **leave behind** 1 PHRASAL VERB If you **leave** someone or something **behind**, you go away permanently from them. 永远离开 ❑ *"I'd go and live there and leave Kentucky behind," says Brown.* "我要去那里生活，永远离开肯塔基州"，布朗说道。 2 PHRASAL VERB If you **leave behind** an object or a situation, it remains after you have left a place. 留下 ❑ *I don't want to leave anything behind.* 我不想留下任何东西。 3 PHRASAL VERB If a person, country, or organization **is left behind**, they remain at a lower level than others because they are not as quick at understanding things or developing. 落后 ❑ *We're going to be left behind by the rest of the world.* 我们就要落后于世界的其他地区了。 ❑ *People are concerned about getting left behind right now.* 人们现在非常担心被落下。

▸ **leave off** PHRASAL VERB If someone or something **is left off** a list, they are not included on that list. 漏掉 ❑ *She has been deliberately left off the guest list.* 她被故意从客人名单里漏掉了。

▸ **leave out** PHRASAL VERB If you **leave** someone or something **out** of an activity, collection, discussion, or group, you do not include them in it. 排除 ❑ *Some would question the wisdom of leaving her out of the team.* 有些人会问，把她排除在团队之外是否明智。 ❑ *If you prefer mild flavors, reduce or leave out the chili.* 如果你喜欢清淡口味，可以少放或不放辣椒。

leaves /livz/ **Leaves** is the plural form of **leaf**, and the third person singular form of **leave**. **leaf**的复数形式；**leave**的第三人称单数形式

lec·tern /lɛktərn/ (**lecterns**) N-COUNT A **lectern** is a high sloping desk on which someone puts their notes when they are standing up and giving a lecture. 讲台

lec·ture ♦◇◇ /lɛktʃər/ (**lectures, lecturing, lectured**) 1 N-COUNT A **lecture** is a talk someone gives in order to teach people about a particular subject, usually at a university or college. 讲座 ❑ *...a series of lectures by Professor Eric Robinson.* …埃里克·鲁滨逊教授的系列讲座。 2 V-I If you **lecture on** a particular subject, you give a lecture or a series of lectures about it. 讲授 ❑ *She then invited him to Atlanta to lecture on the history of art.* 她于是邀请他去亚特兰大讲授艺术史。 3 V-T If someone **lectures** you about something, they criticize you or tell you how they think you should behave. 批评；责备 ❑ *He used to lecture me about getting too much sun.* 他过去经常批评我太阳晒得过多。 ❑ *Chuck would lecture me, telling me to get a haircut.* 查克会责备我，叫我去理发。 ● N-COUNT **Lecture** is also a noun. 批评；责备 ❑ *Our captain gave us a stern lecture on safety.* 我们的船长在安全问题上给了我们严厉的批评。

lec·tur·er /lɛktʃərər/ (**lecturers**) 1 N-COUNT A **lecturer** is a teacher at a university or college. 讲师 ❑ *...a lecturer in law.* …法学讲师。 2 N-COUNT A **lecturer** is a person who gives lectures. 演讲人

led /lɛd/ **Led** is the past tense and past participle of **lead**. **lead**的过去式和过去分词

▲ **ledge** /lɛdʒ/ (**ledges**) 1 N-COUNT A **ledge** is a piece of rock on the side of a cliff or mountain, which is in the shape of a narrow shelf. 岩脊 ❑ *...like a wounded bird seeking refuge on a mountain ledge.* …就像一只受伤的鸟在山的岩脊上寻找藏身处一样。 2 N-COUNT A **ledge** is a narrow shelf along the bottom edge of a window. 窗台 ❑ *Dorothy had climbed onto the ledge outside his window.* 多萝西已经爬到了他窗台外面。

ledg·er /lɛdʒər/ (**ledgers**) N-COUNT A **ledger** is a book in which a company or organization writes down the amounts of money it spends and receives. 分类账 [BUSINESS]

leek /lik/ (**leeks**) N-VAR **Leeks** are long thin vegetables which smell like onions. They are white at one end, have long light green leaves, and are eaten cooked. 葱

leer /lɪər/ (**leers, leering, leered**) V-I If someone **leers** at you, they smile in an unpleasant way, usually because they are sexually interested in you. (挑逗地) 斜睇 [DISAPPROVAL] ❑ *...men standing around, swilling beer and occasionally leering at passing females.* …男人们站在周围，大口喝着啤酒，偶尔色迷迷地斜睇着过路的女性。

left
❶ REMAINING
❷ DIRECTION AND POLITICAL GROUPINGS

❶ **left** ♦◇◇ /lɛft/ 1 **Left** is the past tense and past participle of **leave**. **leave**的过去式和过去分词 2 ADJ If there is a certain amount of something **left**, or if you have a certain amount of it **left**, it remains when the rest has gone or been used. 剩下的 [v-link ADJ, v n ADJ] ❑ *Is there any gin left?* 还有杜松子酒吗？ ❑ *They still have six games left to play.* 他们还剩下6场比赛要打。 ● PHRASE If there is a certain amount of something **left over**, or if you have it **left over**, it remains when the rest has gone or been used. 剩余 ❑ *So much income is devoted to monthly mortgage payments that nothing is left over.* 这么多的收入都用来偿还每月的抵押贷款了，因此没什么剩余。

Thesaurus *left* 另参见：

ADJ. extra, leftover, remaining ❶ 2

❷ **left** ♦♦♦ /lɛft/

The spelling **Left** is also used for meanings 3 and 4.

1 N-SING The **left** is one of two opposite directions, sides, or positions. If you are facing north and you turn to the left, you will be facing west. In the word "to," the "t" is to the left of the "o." 左边 ❑ *Go back to the last fork in the road and take a left.* 回到路的上一个岔口，然后左转。 ❑ *...the brick wall to the left of the conservatory.* …温室左边的砖墙。 ● ADV **Left** is also an adverb. 向左地 [ADV after v] ❑ *Turn left at the crossroads into Clay Lane.* 在十字路口向左转到克莱路上。 2 ADJ Your **left** arm, leg, or ear, for example, is the one which is on the left side of your body. Your **left** shoe or glove is the one which is intended to be worn on your left foot or hand. 左边的 [ADJ n] ❑ *Ferdinand landed awkwardly on top of Delgado's right boot and twisted his left leg.* 费迪南笨拙地落地，踩在德尔加多的右靴上，扭伤了左腿。 3 N-SING-COLL In the U.S., **the left** refers to people who want to use legislation and the tax system to improve social conditions. In most other countries, **the left** refers to people who support the ideas of socialism. 左派 ❑ *...the traditional parties of the Left.* …传统的左派政党。 4 N-SING If you say that a person or political party has moved **to the left**, you mean that their political beliefs have become more left-wing. 左倾 ❑ *After 1979, the party moved sharply to the left.* 1979年以后，该党迅速左倾。

left-click (**left-clicks, left-clicking, left-clicked**) V-I To **left-click** or to **left-click on** something means to press the left-hand button on a computer mouse. 点击鼠标左键 [COMPUTING] ❑ *When the menu has popped up you should left-click on one of the choices to make it operate.* 菜单弹出以后，选择一项并点击鼠标左键使之运行。

left-hand ADJ If something is on the **left-hand** side of something, it is positioned on the left of it. 左边的 [ADJ n] ❑ *The Japanese drive on the left-hand side of the road.* 日本人在道路的左边开车。

left-handed ADJ Someone who is **left-handed** uses their left hand rather than their right hand for activities such as writing and sports and for picking things up. 左撇子的 ❑ *There is a store in town that supplies practically everything for left-handed people.* 镇上有一家商店，出售左撇子用品。

★ **left·ist** /lɛftɪst/ (**leftists**) N-COUNT A **leftist** is someone who supports the ideas of the political left. 左派分子 ❑ *Two of the men were leftists and two were centrists.* 这些人其中两人是左派分子，两人是中间派。

left-justify (**left-justifies, left-justifying, left-justified**) V-T If printed text is **left-justified**, each line begins at the same distance from the left-hand edge of the page or column. 把…左对齐 ❑ *The data in the cells should be left-justified.* 存储单元里的数据应该左对齐。

left·over /lɛftoʊvər/ (**leftovers**) 1 N-PLURAL You can refer to food that has not been eaten after a meal as **leftovers**. 剩余食物 ❑ *Refrigerate any leftovers.* 把剩饭冷藏起来。 2 ADJ You use **leftover** to describe an amount of something that remains after the rest of it has been used or eaten. 剩余的 [ADJ n] ❑ *...leftover pieces of wallpaper.* …剩余的壁纸。

left·ward /lɛftwərd/ also **leftwards** ADJ **Leftward** or **leftwards** means on or towards the ideals of the political left. (政治上) 左倾的 [ADJ n] ❑ *Their success does not necessarily reflect a leftward shift in politics.* 他们的成功并不一定意味着政治上转向左倾。 ● ADV **Leftward** or **leftwards** is also an adverb. (政治上) 左倾地 [ADV after v] ❑ *He seemed to move leftwards as he grew older.* 随着年龄的增长，他在政治上似乎变得越来越左倾。

left-wing also **left wing** 1 ADJ **Left-wing** people support the ideas of the political left. 左翼的 ❑ *They said they would not be voting for him because he was too left-wing.* 他们说不会选他，因为他太偏左了。 2 N-SING **The left wing** of a group of people, especially a political party, consists of the members of it whose beliefs are closer to those of the political left than are those of its other members. 左翼 ❑ *She belongs on the left wing of the Democratic Party.* 她是民主党内的左翼分子。

leg ♦♦◊ /lɛg/ (**legs**) 1 N-COUNT A person or animal's **legs** are the long parts of their body that they use to stand on. 腿 ❑ *He was tapping his walking stick against his leg.* 他用拐杖轻轻敲打着他的腿。 2 N-COUNT The **legs** of a pair of pants are the parts that cover your legs. 裤腿 ❑ *He moved on through wet grass that soaked the legs of his pants.* 他继续走在湿漉漉的草地上，弄湿了他的裤腿。 3 N-COUNT A **leg** of lamb, pork, chicken, or other meat is a piece of meat that consists of the animal's or bird's leg, especially the thigh. (羊、猪、鸡等的) 腿肉 ❑ *...a chicken leg.* …一只鸡腿。 4 N-COUNT The **legs** of a table, chair, or other piece of furniture are the parts that rest on the floor and support the furniture's weight. (桌子、椅子等家具的) 腿 ❑ *His ankles were tied to the legs of the chair.* 他的脚踝被绑在了椅腿上。 5 N-COUNT A **leg** of a long journey is one part of it, usually between two points where you stop. 一段旅程 ❑ *The first leg of the journey was by boat to Lake Naivasha in Kenya.* 第一段旅程是坐船到肯尼亚的奈瓦夏湖。 6 N-COUNT A **leg** of a sports competition is one of a series of games that are played to find an overall winner. 一段赛程 [mainly BRIT] 7 PHRASE If you **are pulling** someone's **leg**, you are teasing them by telling them something shocking or worrying as a joke. 开某人的玩笑 [INFORMAL] ❑ *Of course I won't tell them; I was only pulling your leg.* 我当然不会告诉他们；我只是和你开玩笑的。
→ see **body**

> **Word Partnership** *leg* 的常用搭配：
>
> V. **amputate a/*your*** leg, **break a/*your*** leg, **lose a/*your*** leg 1
> ADJ. **front** leg, **hind** leg, **left/right** leg, **lower** leg 1
> **broken** leg 1 4
> N. leg **bones**, leg **injury**, leg **muscles**, leg **pain** 1
> **final/first/last/second** leg **of a journey/tour/trip** 5

▲ **lega·cy** /lɛgəsi/ (**legacies**) 1 N-COUNT A **legacy** is money or property which someone leaves to you when they die. 遗产 ❑ *You could make a real difference to someone's life by leaving them a generous legacy.* 你留给某人一大笔遗产就可以真正改变他的生活。 2 N-COUNT A **legacy of** an event or period of history is something which is a direct result of it and which continues to exist after it is over. 遗留问题 ❑ *...a program to overcome the legacy of inequality and injustice created by Apartheid.* …解决种族隔离引起的不平等和不公正等遗留问题的一个计划。

le·gal ♦♦◊ /ligᵊl/ 1 ADJ **Legal** is used to describe things that relate to the law. 法律的 [ADJ n] ❑ *He vowed to take legal action.* 他发誓要诉诸法律行动。 ❑ *...the legal system.* …法律制度。 ● **le·gal·ly** ADV 在法律上 ❑ *It could be a bit problematic, legally speaking.* 从法律上说，可能是有点问题。 2 ADJ An action or situation that is **legal** is allowed or required by law. 合法的 ❑ *What I did was perfectly legal.* 我做的事情完全合法。

> **Word Partnership** *legal* 的常用搭配：
>
> N. legal **action**, legal **advice**, legal **battle**, legal **bills**, legal **costs/expenses**, legal **defense**, legal **department**, legal **documents**, legal **expert**, legal **fees**, legal **guardian**, legal **issue**, legal **liability**, legal **matters**, legal **obligation**, legal **opinion**, legal **problems/troubles**, legal **procedures/proceedings**, legal **profession**, legal **responsibility**, legal **rights**, legal **services**, legal **status**, legal **system** 1
> ADV. **perfectly** legal 2

le·gal·ise /ligəlaɪz/ [BRIT] → see **legalize**

le·gal·ity /ligælɪti/ N-UNCOUNT If you talk about **the legality of** an action or situation, you are talking about whether it is legal or not. 合法性 ❑ *The auditor has questioned the legality of the contracts.* 审计员已经质疑合同的合法性。

le·gal·ize /ligəlaɪz/ (**legalizes, legalizing, legalized**)

in BRIT, also use **legalise**

V-T If something **is legalized**, a law is passed that makes it legal. 使合法化 ❑ *Divorce was legalized in 1981.* 离婚在1981年被合法化了。 ● **le·gal·iza·tion** ★ N-UNCOUNT 合法化 ❑ *Legalization of drugs would drive the drug-dealing business off the streets.* 毒品合法化会将毒品买卖从大街上清除。

le·gal ten·der N-UNCOUNT **Legal tender** is money, especially a particular coin or banknote, which is officially part of a country's currency at a particular time. 法定货币 ❑ *The French franc was no longer legal tender after midnight last night.* 法国法郎在昨天午夜以后就不再是法定货币。

★ **leg·end** /lɛdʒᵊnd/ (**legends**) 1 N-VAR A **legend** is a very old and popular story that may be true. 传说 ❑ *...the legends of ancient Greece.* …古希腊的传说。 2 N-COUNT If you refer to someone as a **legend**, you mean that they are very famous and admired by a lot of people. 传奇人物 [APPROVAL] ❑ *...blues legends John Lee Hooker and B.B. King.* …布鲁斯音乐传奇人物约翰・李・胡克和B・B・金。
→ see **fantasy**

leg·end·ary /lɛdʒᵊndɛri/ 1 ADJ If you describe someone or something as **legendary**, you mean that they are very famous and that many stories are told about them. 大名鼎鼎的 ❑ *...the legendary Jazz singer Adelaide Hall.* …大名鼎鼎的爵士乐歌手阿德莱德・霍尔。 2 ADJ A **legendary** person, place, or event is mentioned or described in an old legend. 传说中的 ❑ *The hill is supposed to be the resting place of the legendary King Lud.* 这座山据说是传说中的路德国王休息的地方。

leg·gings /lɛgɪŋz/ N-PLURAL **Leggings** are close-fitting pants, usually made out of a stretchy fabric, that are worn by women and girls. 紧身弹力裤 [also "a pair of" N] ❑ *She is wearing tight black leggings and a baggy green jersey.* 她穿着黑色紧身裤和宽大的绿色运动上衣。

le·gion /lidʒᵊn/ (**legions**) N-COUNT A **legion** is a large group of soldiers who form one section of an army. 军团 ❑ *...the Sudan-based troops of the Libyan Islamic Legion.* …在苏丹驻扎的利比里亚伊斯兰教军团部队。

leg·is·late /lɛdʒɪsleɪt/ (**legislates, legislating, legislated**) V-T/V-I When a government or state **legislates**, it passes a new law. 通过 (法律) 立法 [FORMAL] ❑ *Most member countries have already legislated against excessive overtime.* 大部分成员国已经立法禁止过度加班。 ❑ *You cannot legislate to change attitudes.* 你不能靠立法来让人们改变态度。

leg·is·la·tion ♦◊◊ /lɛdʒɪsleɪʃᵊn/ N-UNCOUNT **Legislation** consists of a law or laws passed by a government. 立法 [FORMAL] ❑ *...a letter calling for legislation to protect women's rights.* …呼吁立法保护妇女权利的一封信。

> **Word Partnership** *legislation* 的常用搭配：
>
> V. **draft** legislation, **enact** legislation, **introduce** legislation, **oppose** legislation, **pass** legislation, **support** legislation, **veto** legislation
> ADJ. **federal** legislation, **new** legislation, **proposed** legislation

★ **leg·is·la·tive** /lɛdʒɪsleɪtɪv/ ADJ **Legislative** means involving or relating to the process of making and passing laws. 立法的 [ADJ n] [FORMAL] ❑ *Today's hearing was just the first step in the legislative process.* 今天的听证会仅仅是立法程序的第一步。

★ **leg·is·la·tor** /lɛdʒɪsleɪtər/ (**legislators**) N-COUNT A **legislator** is a person who is involved in making or passing laws. 立法者 [FORMAL] ❑ *...an attempt to get U.S. legislators to change the system.* …让美国立法者改变体制的一次努力。

leg·is·la·ture /lɛdʒɪsleɪtʃər/ (**legislatures**) N-COUNT The **legislature** of a particular state or country is the group of people in it who have the power to make and pass laws. 立法机构；议会 [FORMAL] ❑ *The proposals before the legislature include the creation of two special courts to deal exclusively with violent crimes.* 摆在议会面前的提案包括建立两个特殊法庭专门审理暴力犯罪案件。

★ **le·giti·mate** /lɪdʒɪtɪmɪt/ **1** ADJ Something that is **legitimate** is acceptable according to the law. 合法的 ❑ *The French government has condemned the coup in Haiti and has demanded the restoration of the legitimate government.* 法国政府已经谴责了海地的政变，并要求恢复合法政府。 ● **le·giti·ma·cy** ▲ /lɪdʒɪtəmɪsi/ N-UNCOUNT 合法性 ❑ *The opposition parties do not recognize the political legitimacy of his government.* 反对党不承认他的政府的政治合法性。 ● **le·giti·mate·ly** ADV 合法地 [ADV with v] ❑ *The government has been legitimately elected by the people.* 该政府是人民合法选举产生的。 **2** ADJ If you say that something such as a feeling or claim is **legitimate**, you think that it is reasonable and justified. 合理的 ❑ *That's a perfectly legitimate fear.* 那是种完全合乎逻辑的恐惧。 ● **le·giti·ma·cy** ▲ N-UNCOUNT 合理性 ❑ *Sampras beat Carl-Uwe Steeb by 6-1, 6-2, 6-1 to underline the legitimacy of his challenge for the title.* 桑普拉斯以6比1、6比2和6比1战胜了卡尔-尤韦・斯蒂布，证明了他挑战冠军头衔的合理性。 ● **le·giti·mate·ly** ADV 合理地 [ADV with v] ❑ *They could quarrel quite legitimately with some of my choices.* 他们可以合理地质疑我的几个选择。

lei·sure /liʒər, lɛʒ-/ **1** N-UNCOUNT **Leisure** is the time when you are not working and you can relax and do things that you enjoy. 空闲时间 ❑ *...a relaxing way to fill my leisure time.* …我消磨空闲时间的一种放松方式。 **2** PHRASE If someone does something **at leisure** or **at their leisure**, they enjoy themselves by doing it when they want to, without hurrying. 悠闲地 ❑ *You will be able to stroll at leisure through the gardens.* 你将能在花园里悠闲地散步。

> **Word Partnership** *leisure* 的常用搭配：
> N. leisure **activity**, leisure **class**, leisure **goods**, leisure **hours**, leisure **time** **1**

lei·sure·ly /liʒərli, lɛʒ-/ ADJ A **leisurely** action is done in a relaxed and unhurried way. 从容的 ❑ *Lunch was a leisurely affair.* 吃午餐曾是一件从容的事。 ● ADV **Leisurely** is also an adverb. 从容地 [ADV with v] ❑ *We walked leisurely into the hotel.* 我们从容地走进旅馆。

lem·on /lɛmən/ (**lemons**) N-VAR A **lemon** is a bright yellow fruit with very sour juice. Lemons grow on trees in warm countries. 柠檬 ❑ *...a slice of lemon.* …一片柠檬。 ❑ *...oranges, lemons and other citrus fruits.* …橘子、柠檬和其他的柑橘属水果。
→ see **fruit**

▲ **lem·on·ade** /lɛməneɪd/ N-UNCOUNT **Lemonade** is a drink that is made from lemons, sugar, and water. 柠檬汽水 ❑ *He was pouring ice and lemonade into tall glasses.* 他正往高脚杯中倒冰和柠檬汽水。

lend ♦◇◇ /lɛnd/ (**lends, lending, lent**) **1** V-T/V-I When people or organizations such as banks **lend** you money, they give it to you and you agree to pay it back at a future date, often with an extra amount as interest. 出借；贷款 ❑ *The bank is reassessing its criteria for lending money.* 银行正在重新评估其贷款标准。 ❑ *The government will lend you money at incredible rates, between zero percent and 3 percent.* 政府将会以0到3%的利率贷款给你，这真是不可思议。 ● **lend·ing** N-UNCOUNT 出借；贷款 ❑ *...a financial institution that specializes in the lending of money.* …一个专门贷款的金融机构。 **2** V-T If you **lend** something that you own, you allow someone to have it or use it for a period of time. 出借 ❑ *Will you lend me your jacket for a little while?* 能把你的夹克借给我一会儿吗？

> Do not confuse **lend** and **borrow**. You say that you **borrow** something **from** another person. However, if you allow someone to **borrow** something that belongs to you, you say that you **lend** it **to** them. **Lend** is often followed by two objects. ❑ *Betty lent him some blankets... He lent Tim the money.* Both **borrow** and **lend** can be used without objects. ❑ *The poor had to borrow from the rich... Banks will not lend to them.* The noun related to **lend** is **loan**. ❑ *...a government loan of $3m.* **Loan** can also be used as a verb in the same way as **lend**, especially in American English. ❑ *I'll loan you fifty dollars.*

3 V-T If you **lend** your support **to** someone or something, you help them with what they are doing or with a problem that they have. 给予(支持) ❑ *He was approached by the organizers to lend support to a benefit concert.* 组织者接洽了他，希望他能支持一场慈善音乐会。 **4** V-T If something **lends itself to** a particular activity or result, it is easy for it to be used for that activity or to achieve that result. 易于；适合于 ❑ *The room lends itself well to summer eating with its light, airy atmosphere.* 这间屋子采光和通风都好，很适合夏天在这里吃饭。 **5** → see also **lent** **6** to **lend a hand** → see **hand**
→ see **bank**, **interest rate**

> **Word Partnership** *lend* 的常用搭配：
> N. lend **money** **1**
> lend **support** **3**

lend·er /lɛndər/ (**lenders**) N-COUNT A **lender** is a person or an institution that lends money to people. 贷方 [BUSINESS] ❑ *...the six leading mortgage lenders.* …6家最大的抵押贷款机构。
→ see **interest rate**

lend·ing rate (**lending rates**) N-COUNT The **lending rate** is the rate of interest that you have to pay when you are repaying a loan. 贷款利率 [BUSINESS] ❑ *The bank left its lending rates unchanged.* 银行保持其贷款利率不变。

length ♦♦◇ /lɛŋθ/ (**lengths**) **1** N-VAR The **length** of something is the amount that it measures from one end to the other along the longest side. 长度 ❑ *It is about a meter in length.* 它大约有一米长。 ❑ *...the length of the fish.* …鱼的长度。 **2** N-VAR The **length** of something such as a piece of writing is the amount of writing that is contained in it. 篇幅 ❑ *...a book of at least 100 pages in length.* …一本至少有100页篇幅的书。 **3** N-VAR The **length** of an event, activity, or situation is the period of time from beginning to end for which something lasts or during which something happens. (事件、活动等) 持续时间 ❑ *The exact length of each period may vary.* 每一时期的确切持续时间可能有所不同。 **4** N-COUNT A **length of** rope, cloth, wood, or other material is a piece of it that is intended to be used for a particular purpose or that exists in a particular situation. 一段(绳子、布、木头等) ❑ *...a 30 feet length of rope.* …一段30英尺长的绳子。 **5** N-UNCOUNT The **length of** something is its quality of being long. 长度 ❑ *Many have been surprised at the length of time it has taken him to make up his mind.* 很多人都为他用这么长的时间才下定决心感到吃惊。 **6** → see also **full-length** **7** **at arm's length** → see **arm**
→ see **ratio**

> **Word Partnership** *length* 的常用搭配：
> N. length **and width** **1**
> length **of *your* stay**, length **of time**, length **of treatment** **3** **5**
> ADJ. **average** length, **entire** length **1**–**4**

length·en /lɛŋθən/ (**lengthens, lengthening, lengthened**) **1** V-T/V-I When something **lengthens** or when you **lengthen** it, it increases in length. 使变长；变长 ❑ *The evening shadows were lengthening.* 傍晚的影子正在变长。 **2** V-T/V-I When something **lengthens** or when you **lengthen** it, it lasts for a longer time than it did previously. 使延长；延长 ❑ *Vacations have lengthened and the work week has shortened.* 假期延长了，工作周变短了。

length·wise /lɛŋθwaɪz/ or **lengthways** /lɛŋθweɪz/ ADV **Lengthwise** or **lengthways** means in a direction or position along the length of something. 纵向地 [ADV after v] ❑ *She tore off two sections of paper towel and folded them lengthwise.* 她扯出两块纸巾，把它们纵向叠了起来。

lengthy /lɛŋθi/ (**lengthier, lengthiest**) **1** ADJ You use **lengthy** to describe an event or process which lasts for a long time. 漫长的 ❑ *The board members held a lengthy meeting to decide future policy.* 董事会成员开了一次漫长的会议来决定未来的政策。 **2** ADJ A **lengthy** report, article, book, or document contains a lot of speech, writing, or other material. 冗长的 ❑ *Friedman's lengthy report quoted an unnamed source.* 弗里德曼冗长的报告引用了一个未指明出处的资料。

> **Word Partnership** *lengthy* 的常用搭配：
> N. lengthy **period** **1**
> lengthy **description**, lengthy **discourse**, lengthy **discussion**, lengthy **report** **2**

▲**le·ni·ent** /liniənt, linyənt/ ADJ When someone in authority is **lenient**, they are not as strict or severe as expected. 宽大的 ❑ *He believes the government already is lenient with drug traffickers.* 他认为政府对贩毒分子已经很宽大了。 ●**le·ni·ent·ly** ADV 宽大地 [ADV after v] ❑ *Many people believe reckless drivers are treated too leniently.* 很多人认为对鲁莽的司机处理得太宽大了。

lens ♦◇◇ /lɛnz/ (**lenses**) 1 N-COUNT A **lens** is a thin curved piece of glass or plastic used in things such as cameras, telescopes, and pairs of glasses. You look through a lens in order to make things look larger, smaller, or clearer. 镜头 ❑ *...a camera lens.* …一个照相机镜头。 2 N-COUNT In your eye, the **lens** is the part behind the pupil that focuses light and helps you to see clearly. (眼睛的) 晶状体 ❑ *...degenerative changes in the lens of the eye.* …眼睛晶状体的退化。 3 → see also **contact lens**
→ see **eye**

lent /lɛnt/ **Lent** is the past tense and past participle of **lend**. **lend** 的过去式和过去分词

leop·ard /lɛpərd/ (**leopards**) N-COUNT A **leopard** is a type of large, wild cat. Leopards have yellow fur and black spots, and live in Africa and Asia. 豹

★**les·bian** ♦◇◇ /lɛzbiən/ (**lesbians**) ADJ **Lesbian** is used to describe homosexual women. 女同性恋的 ❑ *...a woman who had contacts in the homosexual and lesbian community.* …和男、女同性恋团体有联系的一个女人。 ●N-COUNT A **lesbian** is a woman who is lesbian. 女同性恋者 ❑ *...a youth group for lesbians, gays and bisexuals.* …一个由女同性恋者、男同性恋者和双性恋者组成的青年群体。

less ♦♦♦ /lɛs/

> **Less** is often considered to be the comparative form of **little**.

1 DET You use **less** to indicate that there is a smaller amount of something than before or than average. You can use "a little," "a lot," "a bit," "far," and "much" in front of **less**. 较少的; 更少的 ❑ *People should eat less fat to reduce the risk of heart disease.* 人们应该少吃脂肪以减少患心脏病的风险。 ❑ *...a dishwasher that uses less water and electricity than older machines.* …一台比老式机器用水用电更少的洗碗机。 ●PRON **Less** is also a pronoun. 较少 ❑ *Borrowers are striving to ease their financial position by spending less and saving more.* 借款者都在努力通过少花多存来缓解经济紧张状况。 ●QUANT **Less** is also a quantifier. 较少 ❑ *Last year less of the money went into high-technology companies.* 去年，投入到高科技公司的钱较少。 2 PHRASE You use **less than** before a number or amount to say that the actual number or amount is smaller than this. 少于 ❑ *...a country whose entire population is less than 12 million.* …一个总人口少于1200万的国家。 3 ADV You use **less** to indicate that something or someone has a smaller amount of a quality than they used to or than is average or usual. 比…少地 ❑ *I often think about those less fortunate than me.* 我经常想到那些不如我幸运的人。 ❑ *Other amenities, less commonly available, include a library and exercise room.* 其他不常有的便利设施包括一个图书馆和健身房。 4 ADV If you say that something is **less** one thing **than** another, you mean that it is like the second thing rather than the first. 不像…更像… ❑ *At first sight it looked less like a capital city than a mining camp.* 第一眼看上去它不像一座首都城市倒更像一个采矿工地。 5 ADV If you do something **less** than before or **less** than someone else, you do it to a smaller extent or not as often. 更少地 [ADV with v] ❑ *We are eating more and exercising less.* 我们吃得更多，锻炼得却更少。 6 PREP When you are referring to amounts, you use **less** in front of a number or quantity to indicate that it is to be subtracted from another number or quantity already mentioned. 减去 ❑ *You will pay between ten and twenty-five percent, less tax.* 你要付税后的10%到25%。

> You use **less** to talk about amounts that cannot be counted. ❑ *...less meat.* When you are talking about things that can be counted, you should use **fewer**. ❑ *...fewer potatoes.*

7 PHRASE You use **less than** to say that something does not have a particular quality. For example, if you describe something as **less than** perfect, you mean that it is not perfect at all. 根本不 [EMPHASIS] ❑ *Her greeting was less than enthusiastic.* 她打招呼根本不热情。 8 **couldn't care less** → see **care** 9 **more or less** → see **more**

less·en /lɛsᵊn/ (**lessens, lessening, lessened**) V-T/V-I If something **lessens** or you **lessen** it, it becomes smaller in size, amount, degree, or importance. 减少; 降低; 减轻 ❑ *He is used to a lot of attention from his wife, which will inevitably lessen when the baby is born.* 他习惯了妻子无微不至的关心，这种关心在孩子出生以后将不可避免地减少。 ●**less·en·ing** N-UNCOUNT 减轻 ❑ *...increased trade and a lessening of tension on the border.* …贸易的增加和边境紧张局势的减轻。

less·er /lɛsər/ 1 ADJ You use **lesser** in order to indicate that something is smaller in extent, degree, or amount than another thing that has been mentioned. (范围或程度) 较小的; (数量) 较少的 [ADJ n, "the" ADJ "of" n] ❑ *No medication works in isolation but is affected to a greater or lesser extent by many other factors.* 任何药都不能独立起效果，而是或多或少地受到很多其它因素的影响。 ●ADV **Lesser** is also an adverb. (范围或程度) 较小地; (数量) 较少地 [ADV -ed] ❑ *...lesser known works by famous artists.* …著名艺术家创作的名气较小的作品。 2 ADJ You can use **lesser** to refer to something or someone that is less important than other things or people of the same type. 次要的; 较轻的 [ADJ n, "the" ADJ "of" n] ❑ *They pleaded guilty to lesser charges of criminal damage.* 他们对较轻的刑事伤害罪的指控服罪。 3 **the lesser of two evils** → see **evil**

les·son ♦◇◇ /lɛsᵊn/ (**lessons**) 1 N-COUNT A **lesson** is a fixed period of time when people are taught about a particular subject or taught how to do something. 课 ❑ *It would be his last French lesson for months.* 这将是他以后几个月里的最后一次法语课。 2 N-COUNT You use **lesson** to refer to an experience which acts as a warning to you or an example from which you should learn. 教训 ❑ *There's still one lesson to be learned from the crisis – we all need to better understand the thinking of the other side.* 从危机中还要吸取一个教训——我们都需要更好地理解对方的想法。 ●PHRASE If you say that you are going to **teach** someone **a lesson**, you mean that you are going to punish them for something that they have done so that they do not do it again. 给某人一个教训

> **Thesaurus** *lesson* 另参见：
> N. class, course, instruction, session 1

> **Word Partnership** *lesson* 的常用搭配：
> ADJ. **private** lesson 1
> **hard** lesson, **important** lesson, **painful** lesson, **valuable** lesson 2
> V. **get** a lesson, **give** a lesson 1 2
> **learn** a lesson, **teach** *someone* **a** lesson 2

lest /lɛst/ CONJ If you do something **lest** something unpleasant should happen, you do it to try to prevent the unpleasant thing from happening. 以防 [FORMAL] ❑ *I was afraid to open the door lest he should follow me.* 我当时害怕打开那个门惟恐他跟踪我。 ❑ *And, lest we forget, Einstein wrote his most influential papers while working as a clerk.* 而且，为了不使我们忘记，爱因斯坦在做小职员的时候写了他最有影响的论文。

let ♦♦♦ /lɛt/ (**lets, letting**)

> The form **let** is used in the present tense and is the past tense and past participle.

1 V-T If you **let** something happen, you allow it to happen without doing anything to stop or prevent it. 任由 ❑ *People said we were interfering with nature, and that we should just let the animals die.* 人们说我们在干涉大自然，还说我们应该任由那些动物去死。 ❑ *I can't let myself be distracted by those things.* 我不能任由自己被那些东西分散注意力。 2 V-T If you **let** someone do something, you give them your permission to do it. 允许 ❑ *I love candy but Mom doesn't let me have it very often.* 我爱吃糖果，但是妈妈不允许我常吃。 3 V-T If you **let** someone into, out of, or through a place, you allow them to enter, leave, or go through it, for example, by opening a door or making room for them. 允许 (进入、离开、通过等) ❑ *I had to let them into the building because they had lost their keys.* 我不得不允许他们进楼，因为他们丢了钥匙。 4 V-T You use **let me** when you are introducing something you want to say. 让我 (引出要说的内容) [only imper] ❑ *Let me tell you what I saw last night.* 让我告诉你昨晚我见到的事。 ❑ *Let me explain why.* 让我来解释为什么。 5 V-T You use **let me** when you are offering politely to do something. 让我 (表示礼貌地提出帮忙) [only imper] [POLITENESS] ❑ *Let me take your coat.* 让我帮您拿外套吧。 6 V-T You say **let's** or, in more formal English, **let us**, to direct the attention of the people you are talking to toward the subject that you want to consider next. 让我们 (引起人们对将谈论的事物的注意) [only imper] ❑ *Let us look at these views in more detail.* 让我们更详细地看待这些观点。 7 V-T You say **let's** or, in formal English, **let us**, when you are making a suggestion that involves both you

and the person you are talking to, or when you are agreeing to a suggestion of this kind. 让我们 (表示提议或同意) [only imper] ❑ *I'm bored. Let's go home.* 我无聊着呢。让我们回家吧。 8 V-T Someone in authority, such as a teacher, can use **let's** or, in more formal English, **let us**, in order to give a polite instruction to another person or group of people. 我们…吧 (表示礼貌地下达指令) [only imper] [POLITENESS] ❑ *Let's have some quiet, please.* 我们安静点吧。 9 V-T You can use **let** when you are saying what you think someone should do, usually when they are behaving in a way that you think is unreasonable or wrong. 让 (表示批评和要求) [only imper] ❑ *Let him get his own cup of tea.* 让他自己去倒茶。 10 V-T If you **let** your house or land **to** someone, you allow them to use it in exchange for money that they pay you regularly. 出租 [mainly BRIT]

in AM, use **rent**

● PHRASAL VERB **Let out** means the same as **let**. 出租 ❑ *I couldn't sell the apartment, so I let it out.* 我不能把公寓卖掉，因此把它出租了。

> Do not confuse **let**, **rent**, and **hire**. You can say that you **rent** a house or room to someone when they pay you money to live there. ❑ *We rented our house to a college professor.* You can also say that you **let** a house or room to someone. ❑ *They were letting a room to a school teacher.* In British English, if you pay a sum of money to use something for a short time, you say that you **hire** it. In American English, it is more common to say that you **rent** it. ❑ *He was unable to hire another car... He rented a car for the weekend.* If you make a series of payments to use something for a long time, you say that you **rent** it. ❑ *...the apartment he had rented... He rented a TV.*

11 PHRASE **Let alone** is used after a statement, usually a negative one, to indicate that the statement is even more true of the person, thing, or situation that you are going to mention next. 更不用说 [EMPHASIS] ❑ *It is incredible that the 12-year-old managed to even reach the pedals, let alone drive the car.* 这个12岁的小孩能够得着踏板都令人难以置信，更不用说开汽车了。 12 PHRASE If you **let go of** someone or something, you stop holding them. 放开某人/某物 ❑ *She let go of Mona's hand and took a sip of her drink.* 她放开莫娜的手，轻轻呷了一口她的饮料。 13 PHRASE If you **let** someone or something **go**, you allow them to leave or escape. 放走某人 ❑ *They held him for three hours and they let him go.* 他们扣押了他3个小时才放走他。 14 PHRASE When someone leaves a job, either because they are told to or because they want to, the employer sometimes says that they are **letting** that person **go**. 解雇某人 [BUSINESS] ❑ *I've assured him I have no plans to let him go.* 我已经向他保证我不打算解雇他。 15 PHRASE If you say that you did not know what you were **letting yourself in for** when you decided to do something, you mean you did not realize how difficult, unpleasant, or expensive it was going to be. 给自己惹上 (麻烦) ❑ *He got the impression that Miss Hawes had no idea of what she was letting herself in for.* 他感觉霍伊斯小姐并不知道她给自己惹了多大的麻烦。 16 PHRASE If you **let** someone **know** something, you tell them about it or make sure that they know about it. 让某人知道 ❑ *They want to let them know that they are safe.* 他们想让他们知道，他们很安全。 17 to **let fly** → see **fly** 18 to **let your hair down** → see **hair** 19 to **let** someone **off the hook** → see **hook** 20 to **let it be known** → see **known**

▸ **let down** PHRASAL VERB 1 If you **let** someone **down**, you disappoint them, by not doing something that you have said you will do or that they expected you to do. 使失望 ❑ *Don't worry, Xiao, I won't let you down.* 不要担心，肖，我不会让你失望的。 ● **let down** ADJ 失望的 [v-link ADJ] ❑ *The company now has a large number of workers who feel badly let down.* 现在公司里现在有很多员工感到很失望。 2 PHRASAL VERB If something **lets** you **down**, it is the reason you are not as successful as you could have been. 使失败 ❑ *Many believe it was his shyness and insecurity which let him down.* 许多人认为是他的胆怯和缺乏安全感使他失败。

▸ **let in** PHRASAL VERB If an object **lets in** something such as air, light, or water, it allows air, light, or water to get into it, for example, because the object has a hole in it. 让 (空气、光线或水等) 进入 ❑ *...balconies shaded with lattice-work which lets in air but not light.* …用格子窗遮荫的阳台透气但不透光。

▸ **let off** 1 PHRASAL VERB If someone in authority **lets** you **off** a task or duty, they give you permission not to do it. 免除 (任务或义务) ❑ *I realized that having a new baby lets you off going to boring dinner parties.* 我意识到，生了个孩子你就可以不参加无聊的宴会了。 2 PHRASAL VERB If you **let** someone **off**, you give them a lighter punishment than they expect or no punishment at all. 宽恕 ❑ *Because he was a Christian, the judge let him off.* 因为他是一个基督徒，法官宽恕了他。 3 PHRASAL VERB If you **let off** an explosive or a gun, you explode or fire it. 放 (枪炮等); 使爆炸 ❑ *A resident of his neighborhood had let off fireworks to celebrate the revolution.* 他邻里的一个居民燃放了烟花来庆祝革命。

▸ **let out** 1 PHRASAL VERB If something or someone **lets** water, air, or breath **out**, they allow it to flow out or escape. 使 (水、空气等) 通过 ❑ *It lets sunlight in but doesn't let heat out.* 它透光但不散热。 2 PHRASAL VERB If you **let out** a particular sound, you make that sound. 发出 (声音) [WRITTEN] ❑ *When she saw him, she let out a cry of horror.* 看到他时，她发出了惊恐的叫声。 3 PHRASAL VERB If you **let out** a dress or pair of pants, you make it larger by undoing the seams and sewing closer to the edge of the material. 加宽 (衣服) ❑ *I'll have to let this dress out a bit before the wedding next week.* 我不得不在下星期的婚礼前把这条裙子加宽一点。 4 → see also **let 10**

▸ **let up** PHRASAL VERB If an unpleasant, continuous process **lets up**, it stops or becomes less intense. 停止; 减弱 ❑ *The traffic in this city never lets up, even at night.* 这座城市里的交通从不会停止，即使是在晚上。

> **Thesaurus** *let* 另参见:
> V. allow, approve, permit; (*ant.*) prevent, stop 1 2

le·thal /liθ^ə^l/ 1 ADJ A substance that is **lethal** can kill people or animals. 致命的 ❑ *...a lethal dose of sleeping pills.* …安眠药的致命剂量。 2 ADJ If you describe something as **lethal**, you mean that it is capable of causing a lot of damage. 危害极大的 ❑ *Amorality and intelligence is probably the most lethal combination to be found within one personality.* 缺乏道德却聪明智慧可能是同一人格中危害最大的组合。

le·thar·gic /lɪθɑrdʒɪk/ ADJ If you are **lethargic**, you do not have much energy or enthusiasm. 没精打采的 ❑ *He felt too miserable and lethargic to get dressed.* 他感到很难受而且有气无力，以至于穿不了衣服。

leth·ar·gy /lɛθərdʒi/ N-UNCOUNT **Lethargy** is the condition or state of being lethargic. 没精打采 ❑ *Symptoms include tiredness, paleness, and lethargy.* 症状包括疲倦、面色苍白和没精打采。

let's ◆◆◇ /lɛts/ **Let's** is the usual spoken form of "let us." **let us**的口语形式

let·ter ◆◆◆ /lɛtər/ (**letters**) 1 N-COUNT If you write a **letter** to someone, you write a message on paper and send it to them, usually through the mail. 信 [also "by" N] ❑ *I had received a letter from a very close friend.* 我收到了一位非常亲近的朋友的来信。 ❑ *...a letter of resignation.* …一封辞职信。 2 N-COUNT **Letters** are written symbols which represent one of the sounds in a language. 字母 ❑ *...the letters of the alphabet.* …字母表中的字母。 3 V-I If a student **letters** in sports or athletics by being part of the university or college team, they are entitled to wear on their jacket the initial letter of the name of their university or college. (因体育运动出色) 赢得校名首字母徽章 [AM] ❑ *Burkoth lettered in soccer.* 伯考斯在足球赛中赢得了校名首字母徽章。 4 → see also **covering letter**, **newsletter**

let·ter·box /lɛtərbɒks/ (**letterboxes**) also **letter box** 1 N-COUNT A **letterbox** is a rectangular hole in a door or a small box at the entrance to a building into which letters and small packages are delivered. 信箱 [mainly BRIT]

in AM, usually use **mailbox**

2 ADJ If something is displayed on a television or computer screen in **letterbox** format, it is displayed across the middle of the screen with dark bands at the top and bottom of the screen. (电视或电脑上的影像) 宽屏带黑边的

let·ter·ing /lɛtərɪŋ/ N-UNCOUNT **Lettering** is writing, especially when you are describing the type of letters used. 写字 ❑ *...a small blue sign with white lettering.* …一个写有白字的蓝色小标志。

▲ **let·tuce** /lɛtɪs/ (**lettuces**) N-VAR A **lettuce** is a plant with large green leaves that is the basic ingredient of many salads. 莴苣

leu·kae·mia /lukiːmiə/ [BRIT] → see **leukemia**

leu·ke·mia /lukimiə/

in BRIT, use **leukaemia**

N-UNCOUNT **Leukemia** is a disease of the blood in which the body produces too many white blood cells. 白血病

lev·el ◆◆◆ /lɛv^ə^l/ (**levels, leveling** or **levelling, leveled** or **levelled**) 1 N-COUNT A **level** is a point on a scale, for example, a scale of

l

amount, quality, or difficulty. 水平 ❑ *If you don't know your cholesterol level, it's a good idea to have it checked.* 如果你不知道自己的胆固醇水平，最好去查一下。 ❑ *We do have the lowest level of inflation for some years.* 我们几年来的确保持最低水平的通货膨胀。 2 N-SING The **level** of a river, lake, or ocean or the **level** of liquid in a container is the height of its surface. 水位 ❑ *The water level of the Mississippi River is already 6.5 feet below normal.* 密西西比河的水位已经比正常水位低6.5英尺。 3 → see also **sea level** 4 N-SING If something is at a particular **level**, it is at that height. 水平高度 ❑ *Liz sank down until the water came up to her chin and the bubbles were at eye level.* 莉兹下沉直到水漫到她的下巴，泡沫到了她眼睛的高度。 5 N-COUNT A **level** of a building is one of its different stories, which is situated above or below other stories. 层 ❑ *Thurlow and Brown's rooms were on the second level, to the rear of the building.* 瑟洛和布朗的房间都在大楼背面的第二层。 6 N-COUNT A **level** is a device for testing to see if a surface is level. It consists of a plastic, wood, or metal frame containing a glass tube of liquid with an air bubble in it. 水平仪 [AM] 7 ADJ If one thing is **level with** another thing, it is at the same height as it. 与…等高的 [v-link ADJ] ❑ *He leaned over the counter so his face was almost level with the boy's.* 他俯在柜台上，这样他的脸几乎和那男孩的脸一样高。 8 ADJ When something is **level**, it is completely flat with no part higher than any other. 平坦的 ❑ *The floor was level, but the ceiling sloped toward his head.* 地面平平坦坦，但是天花板向他的头部倾斜。 9 ADV If you draw **level** with someone or something, you get closer to them until you are by their side. 接近 [ADV after v] ❑ *Just before we drew level with the gates, he slipped out of the jeep and disappeared.* 就在我们快接近大门口时，他溜出吉普车不见了。 ● ADJ **Level** is also an adjective. 接近的 [v-link ADJ] ❑ *He waited until they were level with the door before he pivoted around sharply and punched Graham hard.* 他等他们接近门口时才一个急转身用拳头猛揍格雷厄姆。 10 V-T If someone or something such as a violent storm **levels** a building or area of land, they destroy it completely or make it completely flat. 夷平 ❑ *The storm was the most powerful to hit Hawaii this century. It leveled sugar plantations and destroyed homes.* 这是本世纪袭击夏威夷最猛烈的暴风雨。它夷平了甘蔗种植园，也摧毁了家园。 11 V-T If an accusation or criticism **is leveled at** someone, they are accused of doing wrong or they are criticized for something they have done. (指责或批评) 针对 ❑ *Allegations of corruption were leveled at him and his family.* 对腐败的指控是针对他和他的家人的。 12 **a level playing field** → see **playing field**

▸ **level off** or **level out** 1 PHRASAL VERB If a changing number or amount **levels off** or **levels out**, it stops increasing or decreasing at such a fast speed. 趋向稳定 ❑ *The figures show evidence that murders in the nation's capital are beginning to level off.* 这些数据证明该国首都的凶杀发案率正开始趋向稳定。 2 PHRASAL VERB If an aircraft **levels off** or **levels out**, it travels horizontally after having been traveling in an upward or downward direction. (飞机在爬升或俯冲后) 水平飞行 ❑ *The aircraft leveled out at about 30,000 feet.* 飞机在大约三万英尺的高度水平飞行。

Thesaurus *level* 另参见：

ADJ.	even, flat, horizontal, smooth 8

Word Partnership *level* 的常用搭配：

ADJ.	**basic** level, **increased** level, **intermediate** level, **top** level, **upper** level 1 **high/low** level 1 2 4
N.	level **of activity**, level **of awareness**, **cholesterol** level, **college** level, **comfort** level, level **of difficulty**, **energy** level, **noise** level, **reading** level, **skill** level, **stress** level, level **of violence** 1 **eye** level, **ground** level, **street** level 4

lev·el cross·ing (**level crossings**) N-COUNT A **level crossing** is a place where a railroad track crosses a road at the same level. (铁路和公路等的) 平面交叉处 [BRIT]

in AM, use **grade crossing, railroad crossing**

★ **lev·er** /lɪvər, lɛv-/ (**levers, levering, levered**) 1 N-COUNT A **lever** is a handle or bar that is attached to a piece of machinery and which you push or pull in order to operate the machinery. 控制杆 ❑ *Push the tiny lever on the lock and let the door lock itself.* 推锁上的小控制杆，让门自动锁上。 2 → see also **gear lever** 3 N-COUNT A **lever** is a long bar, one end of which is placed under a heavy object so that when you press down on the other end you can move the object. 杠杆 ❑ *He examined the machine, worked a lever that lifted the lid.* 他检查了机器，并使用杠杆打开盖子。 4 V-T If you **lever** something in a particular direction, you move it there, especially by using a lot of effort. 撬动 ❑ *Neighbors eventually levered open the door with a crowbar.* 邻居们最后用一根撬棍撬开了门。

▲ **lev·er·age** /lɛvərɪdʒ/ (**leverages, leveraging, leveraged**) 1 N-UNCOUNT **Leverage** is the ability to influence situations or people so that you can control what happens. 影响力 ❑ *His position as mayor gives him leverage to get things done.* 他的市长职位使其有影响力来办事。 2 V-T To **leverage** a company or investment means to use borrowed money in order to buy it or pay for it. 举债经营 [BUSINESS] ❑ *He might feel that leveraging the company at a time when he sees tremendous growth opportunities would be a mistake.* 他可能感觉到在看到巨大的发展机会时举债经营公司是一个错误。

★ **levy** /lɛvi/ (**levies, levying, levied**) 1 N-COUNT A **levy** is a sum of money that you have to pay, for example, as a tax to the government. 税款 ❑ *...an annual levy on all drivers.* …向所有司机征收的年税。 2 V-T If a government or organization **levies** a tax or other sum of money, it demands it from people or organizations. 征 (税) ❑ *They levied religious taxes on Christian commercial transactions.* 他们对基督教的商业交易征收宗教税。

★ **lia·bil·ity** /laɪəbɪlɪti/ (**liabilities**) 1 N-COUNT If you say that someone or something is **a liability**, you mean that they cause a lot of problems or embarrassment. 累赘 ❑ *As the president's prestige continues to fall, they're clearly beginning to consider him a liability.* 随着总统的威信持续下降，他们显然开始认为他是一个累赘。 2 N-COUNT A company's or organization's **liabilities** are the sums of money which it owes. 负债 [BUSINESS or LEGAL] ❑ *The company had assets of $138 million and liabilities of $120.5 million.* 该公司有1.38亿美元资产和1.205亿美元的负债。 3 → see also **liable**

lia·ble /laɪəbᵊl/ 1 PHRASE When something **is liable to** happen, it is very likely to happen. 很有可能的 ❑ *Only a small minority of the mentally ill are liable to harm themselves or others.* 只有极少数的精神病人很有可能伤害到自己或他人。 2 ADJ If people or things are **liable to** something unpleasant, they are likely to experience it or do it. 易于…的 [v-link ADJ "to" n] ❑ *She will grow into a woman particularly liable to depression.* 她将变成一个特别易于消沉的女人。 3 ADJ If you are **liable for** something such as a debt, you are legally responsible for it. 负法律责任的 [v-link ADJ] ❑ *The airline's insurer is liable for damages to the victims' families.* 航空公司投保的保险公司为遇难者家庭的损失负法律责任。 ● **lia·bil·ity** ★ N-UNCOUNT 责 ❑ *The company does not accept liability for fragile, valuable or perishable articles.* 公司对于易碎、贵重或易腐烂的物品不负责任。

li·aise /lieɪz/ (**liaises, liaising, liaised**) V-RECIP When organizations or people **liaise**, or when one organization **liaises with** another, they work together and keep each other informed about what is happening. 联络 [mainly BRIT] ❑ *Detectives are liaising with police following the bomb explosion early today.* 在今天早些时候炸弹爆炸之后侦探们就一直在联络警方。

★ **liai·son** /liezɒn/ 1 N-UNCOUNT **Liaison** is cooperation and the exchange of information between different organizations or between different sections of an organization. 联络 ❑ *Liaison between police forces and the art world is vital to combat art crime.* 警方和艺术界之间的联络对于打击艺术犯罪是至关重要的。 2 N-UNCOUNT If someone acts as **liaison** with a particular group, or **between** two or more groups, their job is to encourage co-operation and the exchange of information. 联络员 [also "a" N, oft N "with" n] ❑ *He is acting as liaison with the film crew.* 他担任拍摄组的联络员。 ❑ *She acts as a liaison between patients and staff.* 她担当病人和医务人员之间的联络员。

Word Link *ar, er ≈ one who acts as: buyer, liar, seller*

liar /laɪər/ (**liars**) N-COUNT If you say that someone is a **liar**, you mean that they tell lies. 说谎的人 ❑ *He was a liar and a cheat.* 他是一个说谎的人，一个骗子。

li·bel /laɪbᵊl/ (**libels, libeling** or **libelling, libeled** or **libelled**) 1 N-VAR **Libel** is a written statement which wrongly accuses someone of something, and which is therefore against the law. Compare **slander**. 诽谤 [LEGAL] ❑ *Warren sued him for libel over the remarks.* 沃伦因为他言论诽谤而起诉了他。 2 V-T To **libel** someone means to write or print something in a book, newspaper, or magazine which wrongly damages that person's reputation and is therefore against the law. 诽谤 [LEGAL] ❑ *The newspaper which libeled him had already offered compensation.* 那家诽谤他的报纸已经提出赔偿。

L

Word Link liber ≈ free : **liber**al, **liber**ate, **liber**ty

lib·er·al ♦♦◇ /lɪbərəl, lɪbrəl/ (**liberals**) 1 ADJ Someone who has **liberal** views believes people should have a lot of freedom in deciding how to behave and think. 开明的 ❑ *She is known to have liberal views on divorce and contraception.* 大家知道，她对于离婚和避孕持开明的观点。● N-COUNT **Liberal** is also a noun. 开明者 ❑ *...a nation of free-thinking liberals.* …一个思想自由的开明者的国家。 2 ADJ A **liberal** system allows people or organizations a lot of political or economic freedom. 自由的 ❑ *...a liberal democracy with a multiparty political system.* …多党政体的自由民主国家。● N-COUNT **Liberal** is also a noun. 自由主义者 ❑ *These kinds of price controls go against all the financial principles of the free market liberals.* 这些价格控制违反了支持自由市场的自由主义者的所有金融原则。 3 ADJ A **Liberal** politician or voter is a member of a Liberal Party or votes for a Liberal Party. 自由党的 [ADJ n] ❑ *She withdrew because she did not wish to split the Liberal vote.* 她退出是因为不想分散自由党的选票。● N-COUNT **Liberal** is also a noun. 自由党人 ❑ *The Liberals hold twenty-three seats.* 自由党拥有23个席位。 4 ADJ **Liberal** means giving, using, or taking a lot of something, or existing in large quantities. 慷慨的；大量的 ❑ *As always he is liberal with his jokes.* 他总有讲不完的笑话。● **lib·er·al·ly** ADV 慷慨地；大量地 [ADV with v] ❑ *Chemical products were used liberally over agricultural land.* 化学产品被大量用于农田。

lib·er·al·ise /lɪbrəlaɪz/ [BRIT] → see **liberalize**

lib·er·al·ize /lɪbərəlaɪz, lɪbrəl-/ (**liberalizes, liberalizing, liberalized**)

in BRIT, also use **liberalise**

V-T/V-I When a country or government **liberalizes**, or **liberalizes** its laws or its attitudes, it becomes less strict and allows people more freedom in their actions. 放宽(限制) ❑ *...authoritarian states that have only now begun to liberalize.* …现在刚刚开始放宽限制的独裁国家。● **lib·er·ali·za·tion** /lɪbərəlɪzeɪʃən, lɪbrəl-/ N-UNCOUNT 放宽 ❑ *...the liberalization of divorce laws in the late 1960s.* …20世纪60年代后期对离婚法规的放宽。

lib·er·ate ♦◇◇ /lɪbəreɪt/ (**liberates, liberating, liberated**) 1 V-T To **liberate** a place or the people in it means to free them from the political or military control of another country, area, or group of people. 解放 ❑ *They planned to march on and liberate the city.* 他们打算继续前进解放这座城市。● **lib·era·tion** /lɪbəreɪʃən/ N-UNCOUNT 解放 ❑ *...a mass liberation movement.* …一场大众解放运动。 2 V-T To **liberate** someone **from** something means to help them escape from it or overcome it, and lead a better way of life. 使解脱 ❑ *He asked how committed the leadership was to liberating its people from poverty.* 他问领导层让人民脱贫的态度有多么坚决。● **lib·er·at·ing** ADJ 解脱的 ❑ *If you have the chance to spill your problems out to a therapist it can be a very liberating experience.* 如果有机会向治疗专家倾诉问题，那会是一种让人非常解脱的体验。● **lib·era·tion** N-UNCOUNT 解放 ❑ *...the women's liberation movement.* …妇女解放运动。

Thesaurus *liberate* 另参见：
V. emancipate, free, let out, release; (*ant.*) confine, enslave 1

lib·er·ty ♦◇◇ /lɪbərti/ (**liberties**) 1 N-VAR **Liberty** is the freedom to live your life in the way that you want, without interference from other people or the authorities. 自由 ❑ *...the ideal of equality and the appreciation of liberty.* …对平等的向往及对自由的欣赏。 2 N-UNCOUNT **Liberty** is the freedom to go wherever you want, which you lose when you are a prisoner. 人身自由 ❑ *Why not say that three convictions before court for stealing cars means three months' loss of liberty.* 为什么不说法庭上关于盗车的3项判决就意味着失去了3个月的人身自由。 3 PHRASE If someone is **at liberty to** do something, they have been given permission to do it. 获得许可的 ❑ *The island's in the Pacific Ocean; I'm not at liberty to say exactly where, because we're still negotiating for its purchase.* 这个岛屿在太平洋上；我还不能说具体在哪里，因为我们仍然在就它的购买问题进行谈判。

Thesaurus *liberty* 另参见：
N. freedom, independence, privilege 1 2

Word Partnership *liberty* 的常用搭配：
ADJ. **human** liberty, **individual** liberty, **personal** liberty, **religious** liberty 1

li·brar·ian /laɪbrɛəriən/ (**librarians**) N-COUNT A **librarian** is a person who is in charge of a library or who has been specially trained to work in a library. 图书管理员 ❑ *The new librarian is a friend of mine.* 这位新来的图书管理员是我的朋友。
→ see **library**

li·brary ♦◇◇ /laɪbreri/ (**libraries**) 1 N-COUNT A public **library** is a building where things such as books, newspapers, videos, and music are kept for people to read, use, or borrow. 图书馆 ❑ *...the local library.* …当地的图书馆。 2 N-COUNT A private **library** is a collection of things such as books or music, that is normally only used with the permission of the owner. 收藏品 ❑ *The company owns a very diverse library of Arabic music.* 公司收藏有多种多样的阿拉伯音乐。 3 N-COUNT A **library** is a public building or a room, for example in a school or hospital, where things such as books, newspapers, videos, and music are kept for people to read, use, or borrow. 图书馆；图书室 4 N-COUNT In some large houses the **library** is the room where most of the books are kept. 书房 ❑ *Guests were rarely entertained in the library.* 很少会在书房招待客人。
→ see Word Web: **library**

lice /laɪs/ **Lice** is the plural of **louse**. **louse**的复数形式

li·cence /laɪsəns/ [BRIT] → see **license**

li·cense ♦◇◇ /laɪsəns/ (**licenses, licensing, licensed**)

in BRIT, use the spelling **licence** for the noun

1 N-COUNT A **license** is an official document which gives you permission to do, use, or own something. 许可证；执照 ❑ *The judge fined the man and suspended his license.* 法官罚了那个人的款，并且吊销了他的执照。 ❑ *The company has applied to the FDA for a license to sell the drug.* 该公司已向美国食品及药品管理局申请了销售药物的许可证。 2 N-UNCOUNT If you say that something gives someone **license** or **a license to** act in a particular way, you mean that it gives them an excuse to behave in an irresponsible or excessive way. 借口 [also "a" N, N to-inf] [DISAPPROVAL] ❑ *Partition would give license to other aggressors in other conflicts.* 分裂组织给其他侵略者提供其他冲突的借口。 3 V-T To **license** a person or activity means to give official permission for the person to do something or for the activity to take place. 准许 ❑ *...a proposal that would require the state to license guns the way it does cars.* …提案要求政府像发驾驶证一样发放枪支许可证。

Thesaurus *license* 另参见：
N. authorization, certificate, permission, permit, warrant 1

Word Partnership *license* 的常用搭配：
N. **driver's** license, license **fees**, **hunting** license, **liquor** license, **marriage** license, **pilot's** license, **software** license 1
V. **get/obtain a** license, **renew a** license, **revoke a** license 1
ADJ. **suspended** license, **valid** license 1

Word Web library

Public libraries are changing. You can still **borrow** and **return books**, **magazines**, DVDs, CDs, and other **media** free of charge. However, many new **services** are now available. Websites often allow you to search the library's **catalog** of books and **periodicals**. Many libraries have computers with Internet access for the public. Some offer literacy classes, tutoring, and homework assistance. You can still wander through the **fiction** section to find a good **novel**. You can also search the nonfiction bookshelves for an interesting **biography**. And if you need help, the **librarian** is still there to answer your questions.

li·censed /laɪsᵊnst/ **1** ADJ If you are **licensed to** do something, you have official permission from the government or from the authorities to do it. 获许的 ❑ *There were about 250 people on board, about 100 more than the ferry was licensed to carry.* 船上大约有二百五十人，超过准载人数约一百人。 **2** ADJ If something that you own or use is **licensed**, you have official permission to own it or use it. 领有许可证的 ❑ *While searching the house they discovered an unlicensed shotgun and a licensed rifle.* 搜查房子时，他们发现了一支没有许可证的猎枪和一支有许可证的步枪。

li·cense num·ber (**license numbers**) N-COUNT The **license number** of a car or other road vehicle is the series of letters and numbers shown on the back, and in many places also on the front, of a vehicle. 车牌号码 [AM]

in BRIT, use **registration number**

❑ *...a maroon 1992 Ford Taurus, license number 2YMT 804.* …一辆栗色的1992年款福特金牛星汽车，车牌号码是2YMT 804。

li·cense plate (**license plates**) N-COUNT A **license plate** is a sign on the back, and in some places also on the front, of a vehicle that shows its license number. 车牌 [AM]

in BRIT, use **number plate**

❑ *...a car with Austrian license plates.* …一辆挂着奥地利车牌的汽车。

lick /lɪk/ (**licks, licking, licked**) **1** V-T When people or animals **lick** something, they move their tongue across its surface. 舔 ❑ *She folded up her letter, licking the envelope flap with relish.* 她把信折起来，享受地舔着信封盖。 ● N-COUNT **Lick** is also a noun. 舔 ❑ *It's incredible how long a cat can go without more than a lick of milk or water.* 不可思议的是，猫不舔一口奶或一滴水能活这么久。 **2** N-COUNT A **lick of** something is a small amount of it. 少量 [usu N "of" n] [INFORMAL] ❑ *It could do with a lick of paint to brighten up its premises.* 用一点涂料就可以让房子明亮起来。 **3** to **lick into shape** → see **shape**

Word Partnership *lick* 的常用搭配：

N.	lick *someone's* **hand**, lick *your* **lips** **1**
PREP.	lick *something* **off** *something* **1**

lid /lɪd/ (**lids**) N-COUNT A **lid** is the top of a box or other container which can be removed or raised when you want to open the container. 盖子 ❑ *She lifted the lid of the box and displayed the contents.* 她把盒盖掀起，展示了里边的东西。

→ see **can**

lie

❶ POSITION OR SITUATION
❷ THINGS THAT ARE NOT TRUE

❶ **lie** ♦♦◇ /laɪ/ (**lies, lying, lay, lain**)

➪ **Please look at meanings 8 and 9 to see if the expression you are looking for is shown under another headword.** **1** V-I If you **are lying** somewhere, you are in a horizontal position and are not standing or sitting. 躺 ❑ *There was a child lying on the ground.* 地上躺着一个小孩。 **2** V-I If an object **lies** in a particular place, it is in a flat position in that place. 平放在 ❑ *...a newspaper lying on a nearby couch.* …平放在旁边沙发上的一张报纸。 **3** V-I If you say that a place **lies** in a particular position or direction, you mean that it is situated there. 位于 ❑ *The islands lie at the southern end of the Kurile chain.* 这些岛屿位于千岛群岛的南端。 **4** V-LINK You can use **lie** to say that something is or remains in a particular state or condition. For example, if something **lies forgotten**, it has been and remains forgotten. 处于（某种状态） ❑ *The picture lay hidden in the archives for over 40 years.* 这张画在档案室藏了40多年。 **5** V-I You can talk about where something such as a problem, solution, or fault **lies** to say what you think it consists of, involves, or is caused by. （问题、办法或错误）在于 ❑ *The problem lay with the family and the school system rather than with television.* 问题在于家庭和学校体制而非电视。 **6** V-I You use **lie** in expressions such as **lie ahead**, **lie in store**, and **lie in wait** when you are talking about what someone is going to experience in the future, especially when it is something unpleasant or difficult. （尤指不愉快或困难的事情）即将发生 ❑ *She'd need all her strength and bravery to cope with what lay in store.* 她需要拿出全部的力量和勇气来应对即将发生的事情。 **7** V-T/V-I You can use **lie** to say what position a competitor or team is in during a competition. （比赛中）名列 [BRIT] ❑ *I was going well and was lying fourth.* 我干得不错，名列第4。 **8** to **lie in state** → see **state** **9** to **take** something **lying down** → see **take**

Do not confuse the verb **lie** with the verb **lay**. Because **lay** is used to talk about putting something in a particular place or position, it is related to the verb **lie**. If someone **lays** something somewhere, it **lies** there. The past tense of **lie** is **lay** and the past participle is **lain**. It is an intransitive verb. ❑ *I lay on the floor with my legs in the air.* However, **lay**, whose past tense and past participle are both **laid**, is usually a transitive verb. ❑ *They laid him on the floor.*

▸ **lie around** PHRASAL VERB If things are left **lying around** or **lying about**, they are not put away but left casually somewhere where they can be seen. 到处乱放 ❑ *People should be careful about their possessions and not leave them lying around.* 人们应该看管好自己的物品，不要到处乱放。

▸ **lie behind** PHRASAL VERB If you refer to what **lies behind** a situation or event, you are referring to the reason the situation exists or the event happened. 是造成…的原因 ❑ *It seems that what lay behind the clashes was disagreement over the list of candidates.* 造成冲突的原因好像是对于候选人名单意见不一致。

▸ **lie down** PHRASAL VERB When you **lie down**, you move into a horizontal position, usually in order to rest or sleep. 躺下 ❑ *Why don't you go upstairs and lie down for a bit?* 你为什么不上楼躺一会儿？

❷ **lie** ♦◇◇ /laɪ/ (**lies, lying, lied**) **1** N-COUNT A **lie** is something that someone says or writes which they know is untrue. 谎言 ❑ *"Who else do you work for?"—"No one."—"That's a lie."* "你还为其他什么人工作吗？"——"没其他人。"——"撒谎。" ❑ *I've had enough of your lies.* 我已经听够了你的谎言。 **2** V-I If someone **is lying**, they are saying something which they know is not true. 撒谎 ❑ *I know he's lying.* 我知道他在撒谎。 ● **ly·ing** N-UNCOUNT 撒谎 ❑ *Lying is something that I will not tolerate.* 撒谎是我所不能容忍的。 **3** → see also **lying**

Thesaurus *lie* 另参见：

V.	recline, rest; (*ant.*) stand ❶ **1** **2**
	deceive, distort, fake, falsify, mislead ❷ **2**
N.	dishonesty, falsehood, fib ❷ **1**

Word Partnership *lie* 的常用搭配：

ADJ.	lie **awake** ❶ **1**
	lie **flat** ❶ **2**
	lie **hidden** ❶ **4**
N.	lie **on** *your* **back**, lie **on the beach**, lie **in/on a bed**, lie **on a couch/sofa** ❶ **1**
	lie **on the floor**, lie **on the ground** ❶ **1** **2**
	lie **in ruins** ❶ **4**
V.	**tell a** lie ❷ **1**
PREP.	lie **about** *something*, lie **to** *someone* ❷ **2**

lieu /lu/ **1** PHRASE If you do, get, or give one thing **in lieu of** another, you do, get, or give it instead of the other thing, because the two things are considered to have the same value or importance. 替代 [FORMAL] ❑ *He left what little furniture he owned to his landlord in lieu of rent.* 他把他仅有的几件家具给了房东以抵房租。 **2** PHRASE If you do, get, or give something **in lieu**, you do, get, or give it instead of something else, because the two things are considered to have the same value or importance. 替代 [FORMAL] ❑ *...an increased salary or time off in lieu.* …或者涨工资或者休假。

★ **lieu·ten·ant** /lutɛnənt/ (**lieutenants**) N-COUNT; N-TITLE A **lieutenant** is a person who holds a junior officer's rank in the army, navy, marines, or air force, or in the U.S. police force. 陆军中尉；海军上尉；（美国的）警官 ❑ *Lieutenant Campbell ordered the man at the wheel to steer for the gunboat.* 坎贝尔上尉命令舵手向炮艇驶去。

life ♦♦♦ /laɪf/ (**lives** /laɪvz/) **1** N-UNCOUNT **Life** is the quality which people, animals, and plants have when they are not dead, and which objects and substances do not have. 生命 ❑ *...a baby's first minutes of life.* …婴儿生命的头几分钟。 ❑ *Amnesty International opposes the death penalty as a violation of the right to life.* 大赦国际组织反对死刑，因其侵犯生存权。 **2** N-UNCOUNT You can use **life** to refer to things or groups of things which are alive. 生物；生命 ❑ *Is there life on Mars?* 火星上有生命吗？ **3** N-COUNT If you refer to someone's **life**, you mean their state of being alive, especially when there is a risk or danger of them dying. 生存；性命 ❑ *Your life is in danger.* 你有生命危险。 ❑ *A nurse began to try to save his life.* 一名护士开始设法抢救他。 **4** N-COUNT Someone's **life** is the period of time during which they are alive. 一生 ❑ *He spent the last fourteen years of his life in retirement.* 他生命的最后14年退休在家。 5 N-COUNT You can use **life** to refer to a period of someone's life when they are in a particular situation or job. 人生阶段；生涯 ❑ *Interior designers spend their working lives keeping up to date with the latest trends.* 室内设计者们把他们的职业生涯都花在追赶最新潮流上。 6 N-COUNT You can use **life** to refer to particular activities which people regularly do during their lives. 生活 ❑ *My personal life has had to take second place to my career.* 我的个人生活不得不放在我的事业之后。 7 N-UNCOUNT You can use **life** to refer to the things that people do and experience that are characteristic of a particular place, group, or activity. (特定的) 生活 ❑ *How did you adjust to college life?* 你是怎么适应大学生活的？ ❑ *He abhors the wheeling-and-dealing associated with conventional political life.* 他憎恶传统政治生活中的尔虞我诈。 8 N-UNCOUNT A person, place, book, or movie that is full of **life** gives an impression of excitement, energy, or cheerfulness. 活力 [APPROVAL] ❑ *The town itself was full of life and character.* 这座城镇本身就充满了活力和个性。 9 N-UNCOUNT If someone is sentenced to **life**, they are sentenced to stay in prison for the rest of their life or for a very long time. 终身监禁 [INFORMAL] ❑ *He could get life in prison, if convicted.* 他会遭终身监禁，如果罪名成立的话。 10 N-COUNT The **life** of something such as a machine, organization, or project is the period of time that it lasts for. (机器、组织或项目的) 寿命 ❑ *The repairs did not increase the value or the life of the equipment.* 这些修理没有提高设备的价值，也没有延长它的寿命。 11 PHRASE If you **bring** something **to life** or if it **comes to life**, it becomes interesting or exciting. 带来生机；使变得生动 ❑ *The cold, hard cruelty of two young men is vividly brought to life in this true story.* 两个年轻人的冷漠和残忍在这个真实的故事里被生动地表现了出来。 12 PHRASE If you say that someone **is fighting for** their **life**, you mean that they are in a very serious condition and may die as a result of an accident or illness. 挣扎在死亡线上 [JOURNALISM] ❑ *...a horrifying robbery that left a man fighting for his life.* …一场恐怖的抢劫，导致一人生命垂危。 13 PHRASE **For life** means for the rest of a person's life. 终身 ❑ *He was jailed for life in 1966 for the murder of three policemen.* 1966年，由于杀害了3名警察他被终身监禁。 ❑ *She may have been scarred for life.* 她可能已受到终身难以愈合的创伤。 14 PHRASE If someone **takes** another person's **life**, they kill them. If someone **takes** their own **life**, they kill themselves. 杀死某人 [FORMAL] ❑ *Before execution, he admitted to taking the lives of at least 35 more women.* 在赴死刑前，他承认了还杀死过另外至少35名妇女。 15 PHRASE You can use expressions such as **to come to life**, **to spring to life**, and **to roar into life** to indicate that a machine or vehicle suddenly starts working or moving. (机器或车辆) 突然开动 [LITERARY] ❑ *To his great relief the engine came to life.* 让他松一口气的是，引擎发动起来了。 16 a matter of **life and death** → see **death** → see **earth**

life·boat /laɪfbout/ (**lifeboats**) 1 N-COUNT A **lifeboat** is a medium-sized boat that is sent out from a port or harbor in order to rescue people who are in danger at sea. 救生船 2 N-COUNT A **lifeboat** is a small boat that is carried on a ship, which people on the ship use to escape when the ship is in danger of sinking. 救生艇 ❑ *The captain ordered all passengers and crew into lifeboats.* 船长命令所有的乘客和船员上救生艇。

life cy·cle (**life cycles**) 1 N-COUNT The **life cycle** of an animal or plant is the series of changes and developments that it passes through from the beginning of its life until its death. (动植物的) 生命周期 ❑ *...a plant that completes its life cycle in a single season.* …在一个季节内完成其生命周期的一种植物。 2 N-COUNT The **life cycle** of something such as an idea, product, or organization is the series of developments that take place in it from its beginning until the end of its usefulness. (思想、产品或机构等的) 使用周期 ❑ *Each new product would have a relatively long life cycle.* 每一种新产品都会有一个相对较长的使用周期。
→ see **plant**

life·guard /laɪfgɑrd/ (**lifeguards**) N-COUNT A **lifeguard** is a person who works at a beach or swimming pool and rescues people when they are in danger of drowning. 救生员

life in·sur·ance N-UNCOUNT **Life insurance** is a form of insurance in which a person makes regular payments to an insurance company, in return for a sum of money to be paid to them after a period of time, or to their family if they die. 人寿保险 ❑ *I have also taken out a life insurance policy on him just in case.* 我也给他买了一份人寿保险以防万一。

life·less /laɪflɪs/ 1 ADJ If a person or animal is **lifeless**, they are dead, or are so still that they appear to be dead. (人或动物) 无生命的；无生机的 ❑ *Their cold-blooded killers had then dragged their lifeless bodies upstairs to the bathroom.* 那些杀死他们的冷血杀手们随后把他们的尸体拖到了楼上的浴室。 2 ADJ If you describe an object or a machine as **lifeless**, you mean that they are not living things, even though they may resemble living things. (物体或机器) 无生命的 ❑ *It was made of plaster, hard and white and lifeless, bearing no resemblance to human flesh.* 它是由石膏做成的，又硬又白，没有生命，与人的皮肤毫无相似之处。 3 ADJ A **lifeless** place or area does not have anything living or growing there at all. (地方) 没有生命存在的 ❑ *Dry stone walls may appear stark and lifeless, but they provide a valuable habitat for plants and animals.* 干燥的石墙看上去荒凉而且没有生命迹象，但是它们却为动植物提供了宝贵的栖居地。

life·line /laɪflaɪn/ (**lifelines**) N-COUNT A **lifeline** is something that enables an organization or group to survive or to continue with an activity. 生命线 ❑ *Information about the job market can be a lifeline for those who are out of work.* 有关就业市场的信息可能就是失业者的生命线。

life·long /laɪflɔŋ/ ADJ **Lifelong** means existing or happening for the whole of a person's life. 终生的 [ADJ n] ❑ *...her lifelong friendship with Naomi.* …她与娜奥米的终生友谊。

life·span /laɪfspæn/ (**lifespans**) also **life span** 1 N-VAR The **lifespan** of a person, animal, or plant is the period of time for which they live or are normally expected to live. (人或动植物的) 寿命 ❑ *A 15-year lifespan is not uncommon for a dog.* 15年的寿命对狗来说并非罕见。 2 N-COUNT The **lifespan** of a product, organization, or idea is the period of time for which it is expected to work properly or to last. (产品、组织或想法的) 使用期限 ❑ *Most boilers have a lifespan of 15 to 20 years.* 大部分锅炉的使用期限是15到20年。

life·style /laɪfstaɪl/ (**lifestyles**) also **life-style, life style** 1 N-VAR The **lifestyle** of a particular person or group of people is the living conditions, behavior, and habits that are typical of them or are chosen by them. 生活方式 ❑ *They enjoyed an income and lifestyle that many people would envy.* 他们享有很多人会羡慕的收入和生活方式。 2 ADJ **Lifestyle** magazines, television programs, and products are aimed at people who wish to be associated with glamorous and successful lifestyles. 关于时尚生活的 (杂志、电视节目、产品等) [ADJ n] ❑ *This year people are going for luxury and buying lifestyle products.* 今年人们在追求奢侈品，购买时尚生活产品。 3 ADJ **Lifestyle** drugs are drugs that are intended to improve people's quality of life rather than to treat particular medical disorders. 保健的 [ADJ n] ❑ *"I see anti-depressants as a lifestyle drug," says Dr. Charlton.* "我把抗抑郁药视为一种保健药物，" 查尔顿医生说道。

life·time /laɪftaɪm/ (**lifetimes**) N-COUNT A **lifetime** is the length of time that someone is alive. 一生 ❑ *During my lifetime I haven't got around to much traveling.* 我一生中没有旅行过多少。 ❑ *...a trust fund to be administered throughout his wife's lifetime.* …在他妻子一生中都要管理的一份信托基金。

lift ♦♦◊ /lɪft/ (**lifts, lifting, lifted**) 1 V-T If you **lift** something, you move it to another position, especially upward. 举起；拿起 ❑ *The colonel lifted the phone and dialed his superior.* 上校拿起电话拨了他上司的号码。 ● PHRASAL VERB **Lift up** means the same as **lift**. 举起 ❑ *She put her arms around him and lifted him up.* 她双臂拥住他，把他举起来。

> Do not confuse **lift** and **carry**. When you **carry** something, you move it from one place to another without letting it touch the ground. When you **lift** something, you move it upwards using your hands or a machine. After you have lifted it, you may **carry** it to a different place.

2 V-T If you **lift** your eyes or your head, you look up, for example, when you have been reading and someone comes into the room. 抬起 (眼睛或头) ❑ *When he finished he lifted his eyes and looked out the window.* 他完成以后抬眼向窗外看去。 3 V-T If people in authority **lift** a law or rule that prevents people from doing something, they end it. 解除 (法令等) ❑ *The European Commission has urged France to lift its ban on imports of British beef.* 欧盟委员会已敦促法国解除对英国牛肉进口的禁令。 4 V-T/V-I If something **lifts** your spirits or your mood, or if they **lift**, you start feeling more cheerful. 鼓舞 ❑ *He used his incredible sense of humor to lift my spirits.* 他以不可思议的幽默感鼓舞了我的士气。 5 N-COUNT If you give someone a **lift** somewhere, you take them there in your car as a favor to them.

搭便车 ❑ *He had a car and often gave me a lift home.* 他有一辆汽车，经常让我搭便车回家。 **6** N-UNCOUNT **Lift** is the force that makes an aircraft leave the ground and stay in the air. 提升力 ❑ *An airplane has to reach a certain speed before there is enough lift to get it off the ground.* 飞机得在达到一定的速度以后，才能有足够的提升力从地面起飞。 **7** V-T If a government or organization **lifts** people or goods in or out of an area, it transports them there by aircraft, especially when there is a war. 空运 ❑ *The army lifted people off rooftops where they had climbed to escape the flooding.* 军队把爬到房顶躲避洪水的人们空运走。 **8** V-T To **lift** something means to increase its amount or to increase the level or the rate at which it happens. 提高 [BRIT] **9** N-COUNT A **lift** is a device that carries people or goods up and down inside tall buildings. 电梯 [BRIT]

in AM, use **elevator**

10 to **lift a finger** → see **finger**

Thesaurus *lift* 另参见：

V. boost, hoist, pick up; (*ant.*) drop, lower, put down **1**
cancel, repeal, rescind, terminate **3**
boost, enhance, raise **4**

Word Partnership *lift* 的常用搭配：

N. lift *your* **arm**, lift *your* **hand**, lift **weights** **1**
lift **a ban**, lift **a blockade**, lift **an embargo**, lift **restrictions**, lift **sanctions**, lift **a siege** **3**

liga·ment /lɪgəmənt/ (**ligaments**) N-COUNT A **ligament** is a band of strong tissue in a person's body which connects bones. 韧带 ❑ *He suffered torn ligaments in his knee.* 他的膝部韧带撕裂了。

Word Link *light ≈ shining : daylight, enlighten, light*

light
❶ BRIGHTNESS OR ILLUMINATION
❷ NOT GREAT IN WEIGHT, AMOUNT, OR INTENSITY
❸ UNIMPORTANT OR NOT SERIOUS

❶ light ♦♦◇ /laɪt/ (**lights, lighting, lit** or **lighted, lighter, lightest**) ⇨ **Please look at meaning 15 to see if the expression you are looking for is shown under another headword.** **1** N-UNCOUNT **Light** is the brightness that lets you see things. Light comes from sources such as the sun, moon, lamps, and fire. 光；光线 [also "the" N] ❑ *Cracks of light filtered through the shutters.* 一束束阳光透过百叶窗照射进来。 ❑ *...ultraviolet light.* …紫外线。 **2** N-COUNT A **light** is something such as an electric lamp which produces light. 灯 ❑ *The janitor comes around to turn the lights out.* 看门人回来把灯关掉。 **3** N-PLURAL You can use **lights** to refer to a set of traffic lights. 交通信号灯 ❑ *...the heavy city traffic with its endless delays at lights and crosswalks.* …拥挤的城市交通，以及在交通信号灯和人行横道前没完没了的耽搁。 **4** V-T If a place or object **is lit** by something, it has light shining on it. 照亮 ❑ *It was dark and a giant moon lit the road so brightly you could see the landscape clearly.* 天黑了，一轮明月照亮了道路，你都可以清楚地看到风景。 ❑ *The room was lit by only the one light.* 这个房间只有这一盏灯照明。 **5** ADJ If it is **light**, the sun is providing light at the beginning or end of the day. 天亮的 ❑ *It was still light when we arrived at Lalong Creek.* 我们到达拉隆港时，天还亮着。 **6** ADJ If a room or building is **light**, it has a lot of natural light in it, for example, because it has large windows. 明亮的 ❑ *It is a light room with tall windows.* 这是一间明亮的房间，窗户高大。 ● **light·ness** N-UNCOUNT 明亮 ❑ *The dark green spare bedroom is in total contrast to the lightness of the large main bedroom.* 深绿色的客卧与明亮宽敞的主卧形成了鲜明的对比。 **7** V-T/V-I If you **light** something such as a cigarette or fire, or if it **lights**, it starts burning. 点燃 ❑ *Stephen hunched down to light a cigarette.* 斯蒂芬弓起身子点了一支烟。 ❑ *If the charcoal does fail to light, use a special liquid spray and light it with a long taper.* 如果木炭确实点不着，喷一种专用液体喷雾剂，再用一根长蜡烛把它点燃。 **8** N-COUNT If something is presented in a particular **light**, it is presented so that you think about it in a particular way or so that it appears to be of a particular nature. 角度；状态 ❑ *He has worked hard in recent months to portray New York in a better light.* 最近几个月他一直努力工作要从一个更好的角度描绘纽约。 **9** → see also **lighter, lighting** **10** PHRASE If something **comes to light** or **is brought to light**, it becomes obvious or is made known to a lot of people. 暴露；被揭露 ❑ *Nothing about this sum has come to light.* 这个数目一点也被没揭露。 **11** PHRASE If someone in authority gives you **a green light**, they give you permission to do something. 准许 ❑ *The food industry was given a green light to extend the use of these chemicals.* 食品业获准扩大这些化学品的应用范围。 **12** PHRASE If something is possible **in the light of** particular information, it is only possible because you have this information. 根据 ❑ *In the light of this information it is now possible to identify a number of key issues.* 根据这一信息，现在有可能发现很多关键问题。 **13** PHRASE To **shed light on, throw light on,** or **cast light on** something means to make it easier to understand, because more information is known about it. 阐明某事 ❑ *A new approach offers an answer, and may shed light on an even bigger question.* 一种新方法提供一个答案，而且可能阐明更大的问题。 **14** PHRASE If you **set light to** something, you make it start burning. 点燃 [mainly BRIT]

in AM, usually use **set fire to**

15 **all sweetness and light** → see **sweetness**
→ see **color, laser, light, telescope, wave**

▸ **light up** **1** PHRASAL VERB If you **light** something **up** or if it **lights up**, it becomes bright, usually when you shine light on it. 照亮；变亮 ❑ *...a keypad that lights up when you pick up the handset.* …当你拿起听筒就变亮的拨号盘。 **2** PHRASAL VERB If your face or your eyes **light up**, you suddenly look very surprised or happy. 露出吃惊的表情；露出喜色 ❑ *Sue's face lit up with surprise.* 苏的脸上露出惊讶的表情。

❷ light ♦◇◇ /laɪt/ (**lighter, lightest**) **1** ADJ Something that is **light** does not weigh very much, or weighs less than you would expect it to. (重量) 轻的 ❑ *Modern tennis rackets are now apparently 20 per cent lighter.* 据我所知现代的网球拍轻了20%。 ❑ *...weight training with light weights.* …使用轻量负荷的举重训练。 ● **light·ness** N-UNCOUNT 轻巧 [usu with supp] ❑ *The toughness, lightness, strength, and elasticity of whalebone gave it a wide variety of uses.* 鲸须的坚韧、轻巧、结实而又有弹性赋予它广泛的用途。 **2** ADJ Something that is **light** is not very great in amount, degree, or intensity. (数量) 少的；(程度、强度等) 低的 ❑ *It's a Sunday like any other with the usual light traffic in the city.* 和以往的星期天一样，今天城里车辆稀少。 ❑ *Trading was very light ahead of yesterday's auction.* 昨天的拍卖之前交易很少。 ● **light·ly** ADV 轻地 ❑ *Put the onions in the pan and cook until lightly browned.* 把洋葱放入锅中，炒到稍微发褐色。 **3** ADJ Something that is **light** is very pale in color. 浅色的 ❑ *He is light haired with gray eyes.* 他长着浅色的头发和灰色的眼睛。 ● COMB IN COLOR **Light** is also a combining form. **Light**也是一个构词成分 ❑ *We know he has a light green van.* 我们知道他有一辆浅绿色的货车。 **4** ADJ A **light** sleep is one that is easily disturbed and in which you are often aware of the things around you. If you are a **light** sleeper, you are easily woken when you are asleep. (睡眠) 浅的；易醒的 [ADJ n] ❑ *She had drifted into a light sleep.* 她已经慢慢进入了浅睡眠。 ● **light·ly** ADV 易醒地 [ADV after v] ❑ *He was dozing lightly in his chair.* 他在椅子上浅浅地打着瞌睡。 **5** ADJ A **light** meal consists of food that is easy to digest. 易消化的 ❑ *...a light, healthy lunch.* …易消化的健康午餐。 ● **light·ly** ADV 易消化地 [ADV after v] ❑ *She found it impossible to eat lightly.* 她当时发现不可能吃到易消化的东西。 **6** ADJ **Light** work does not involve much physical effort. (工作) 轻松的 ❑ *He was on the training field for some light work yesterday.* 他昨天在训练场进行一些轻松的训练。 **7** ADJ If you describe the result of an action or a punishment as **light**, you mean that it is less serious or severe than you expected. (事情) 不严重的；(惩罚) 轻的 ❑ *She confessed her astonishment at her light sentence when her father visited her at the jail.* 她父亲去牢里探望她的时候，她承认自己对于受到从轻判决感到吃惊。 ● **light·ly** ADV 轻地 [ADV after v] ❑ *One of the accused got off lightly in exchange for pleading guilty to withholding information from Congress.* 其中一名被告获得了从轻发落，因其承认了未向国会提供情报的罪行。 **8** ADJ Movements and actions that are **light** are graceful or gentle and are done with very little force or effort. (动作、活动等) 轻盈的 ❑ *Use a light touch when applying cream or makeup.* 用面霜或化妆品时动作要轻柔。 ● **light·ly** ADV 轻轻地 [ADV with v] ❑ *He kissed her lightly on the mouth.* 他轻轻地吻了一下她的嘴。 ● **light·ness** N-UNCOUNT 轻盈 ❑ *She danced with a grace and lightness that were breathtaking.* 她以一种令人惊叹的优雅与轻盈翩翩起舞。 **9** ADJ **Light** is used to describe foods or drinks that contain few calories or low amounts of sugar, fat, or alcohol. (食品) 清淡的；(酒) 低度的；(饮料) 低热量的 ❑ *There's been a flood of low-fat and light ice creams on the market.* 市场上一直有大量低脂低热量冰淇淋。 ❑ *They refreshed themselves with cans of light beer.* 他们喝了几听低度啤酒提神。

Word Web light bulb

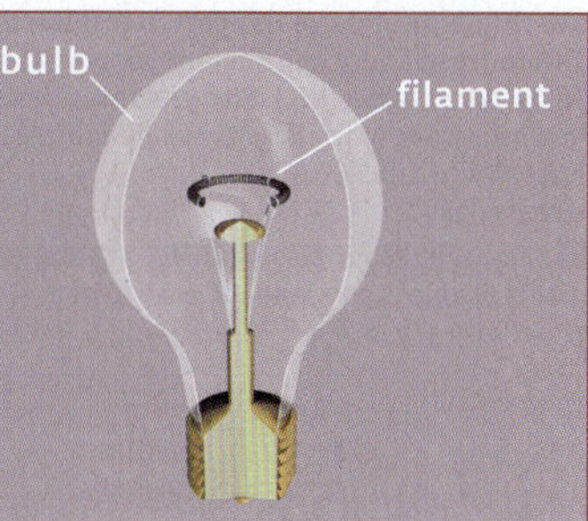

The incandescent **light bulb** has changed little since the 1870s. It consists of a **glass** globe containing an inert gas, such as argon, some wires, and a filament. **Electricity** flows through the wires and the tungsten filament. The filament heats up and **glows**. Light bulbs aren't very efficient. They give off more heat than **light**. **Fluorescent** lights are much more efficient. They contain liquid mercury and argon gas. A layer of phosphorus covers the inside of the tube. When electricity begins to flow, the mercury becomes a gas and **emits** ultraviolet light. This causes the phosphorus coating to **shine**.

Thesaurus *light* 另参见：
N. brightness, gleam, glow, radiance, shine ❶ 1
ADJ. bright, sunny ❶ 5 6
weightless; *(ant.)* heavy, solid ❷ 1

❸ **light** ♦◇◇ /laɪt/ (**lighter, lightest**) 1 ADJ If you describe things such as books, music, and movies as **light**, you mean that they entertain you without making you think very deeply. 轻松的 ❑ *He doesn't like me reading light novels.* 他不喜欢我读轻松的小说。❑ *...light classical music.* …古典轻音乐。 2 ADJ If you say something in a **light** way, you sound as if you think that something is not important or serious. 轻松的 ❑ *Talk to him in a friendly, light way about the relationship.* 以一种友好轻松的方式跟他谈谈这一关系。 ● **light·ly** ADV 轻松地 [ADV after v] ❑ *"Once a detective, always a detective," he said lightly.* 他轻松地说："一朝是侦探，终身是侦探。" ● **light·ness** N-UNCOUNT 轻松 ❑ *"I'm not an authority on them," Jessica said with forced lightness.* 杰西卡故作轻松地说："我对它们不大精通。" 3 PHRASE If you **make light of** something, you treat it as though it is not serious or important, when in fact it is. 轻视 ❑ *Roberts attempted to make light of his discomfort.* 罗伯茨试图不去在乎自己的不适。

light bulb (**light bulbs**) N-COUNT A **light bulb** or **bulb** is the round glass part of an electric light or lamp which light shines from. 灯泡
→ see Word Web: **light bulb**
→ see **light**

Word Link *light ≈ not heavy : lighten, lighthearted, lightweight*

light·en /laɪtᵊn/ (**lightens, lightening, lightened**) 1 V-T/V-I When something **lightens** or when you **lighten** it, it becomes less dark in color. 使变明亮；变得明亮 ❑ *The sky began to lighten.* 天空开始变得明亮了。 2 V-T If someone **lightens** a situation, they make it less serious or less boring. 缓和 ❑ *Anthony felt the need to lighten the atmosphere.* 安东尼觉得需要缓和一下气氛。 3 V-T/V-I If your attitude or mood **lightens**, or if someone or something **lightens** it, they make you feel more cheerful, happy, and relaxed. 使轻松；变得轻松 ❑ *As they approached the outskirts of the city, Ella's mood visibly lightened.* 随着他们越来越接近市郊，埃拉的心情明显变得轻松了。

light·er /laɪtər/ (**lighters**) N-COUNT A **lighter** is a small device that produces a flame which you can use to light cigarettes, cigars, and pipes. 打火机

light·hearted /laɪthɑrtɪd/
in BRIT, use **light-hearted**
1 ADJ Someone who is **lighthearted** is cheerful and happy. 轻松愉快的 ❑ *I was amazingly lighthearted and peaceful.* 我当时出奇地轻松和平静。 2 ADJ Something that is **lighthearted** is intended to be entertaining or amusing, and not at all serious. 轻松有趣的 ❑ *There have been many attempts, both lighthearted and serious, to locate the Loch Ness Monster.* 为寻找"尼斯湖水怪"，已经进行了很多或轻松有趣或认真的尝试。

light·house /laɪthaʊs/ (**lighthouses**) N-COUNT A **lighthouse** is a tower containing a powerful flashing lamp that is built on the coast or on a small island. Lighthouses are used to guide ships or to warn them of danger. 灯塔

light in·dus·try (**light industries**) N-VAR **Light industry** is industry in which only small items are made, for example, household goods and clothes. 轻工业 ❑ *State and local officials are hoping to bring some light industry to the site.* 国家和地方的官员正希望把一些轻工业引入该地。
→ see **industry**

light·ing /laɪtɪŋ/ N-UNCOUNT The **lighting** in a place is the way that it is lit, for example, by electric lights, by candles, or by windows, or the quality of the light in it. 照明 ❑ *...the bright fluorescent lighting of the laboratory.* …实验室明亮的荧光照明。 ❑ *The whole room is bathed in soft lighting.* 整个房间笼罩在柔和的照明中。
→ see **concert, photography**

light·ning /laɪtnɪŋ/ 1 N-UNCOUNT **Lightning** is the very bright flashes of light in the sky that happen during thunderstorms. 闪电 ❑ *One man died when he was struck by lightning.* 一个人遭雷击身亡。 ❑ *Another flash of lightning lit up the cave.* 又一道闪电照亮了那个洞穴。 2 ADJ **Lightning** describes things that happen very quickly or last for only a short time. 飞快的 [ADJ n] ❑ *Driving today demands lightning reflexes.* 如今驾车需要飞快的反应。
→ see Word Web: **lightning**
→ see **storm**

★ **light·weight** /laɪtweɪt/ (**lightweights**) also **light-weight** 1 ADJ Something that is **lightweight** weighs less than most other things of the same type. 重量轻的 ❑ *...lightweight denim.* …轻薄的粗斜纹棉布。 2 N-UNCOUNT **Lightweight** is a category in some sports, such as boxing, judo, or rowing, based on the weight of the athlete. (运动中的) 轻量级 ❑ *By the age of sixteen he was the junior lightweight champion of Poland.* 16岁时他已是波兰少年轻量级冠军。 3 N-COUNT If you describe someone as a **lightweight**, you are critical of them because you think that they are not very important or skillful in a particular area of activity. 无足轻重者 [DISAPPROVAL] ❑ *Brian considered Sam a lightweight, a real amateur.* 布赖恩认为萨姆是个无足轻重的人，是个真正的业余选手。 ● ADJ **Lightweight** is also an adjective. 无足轻重的 ❑ *Some of the discussion in the book is lightweight and unconvincing.* 书中的一些讨论无足轻重而且缺乏说服力。

light year (**light years**) 1 N-COUNT A **light year** is the distance that light travels in a year. 光年 ❑ *...a star system millions of light years away.* …数百万光年之外的一个星系。 2 N-COUNT You can say that

Word Web lightning

Lightning originates in storm clouds. Strong winds cause tiny **particles** within the clouds to rub together violently. This creates **positive charges** on some particles and **negative charges** on others. The negatively charged particles sink to the bottom of the cloud. There they are attracted by the positively charged surface of the earth. Gradually a large negative charge accumulates in a cloud. When it is large enough, a **bolt** of lightning strikes the earth. When a bolt branches out, the result is called **forked lightning**. Sheet lightning occurs when the bolt **discharges** within a cloud, instead of on the earth.

two things are **light years** apart to emphasize a very great difference or a very long distance or period of time between them. (差异) 极大; (距离、年代) 极远 [INFORMAL, EMPHASIS] ❑ *She says the French education system is light years ahead of the English one.* 她说法国的教育体制远比英国的先进。
→ see **galaxy**

lik·able /laɪkəbᵊl/ also **likeable** ADJ Someone or something that is **likable** is pleasant and easy to like. 可爱的 ❑ *He was a bright guy, a likable guy.* 他是一个聪明伶俐、讨人喜欢的家伙。

like
❶ PREPOSITION AND CONJUNCTION USES
❷ VERB USES
❸ NOUN USES AND PHRASES

❶ **like** ♦♦♦ /laɪk, laɪk/ **1** PREP If you say that one person or thing is **like** another, you mean that they share some of the same qualities or features. 像 ❑ *He looks like Father Christmas.* 他长得像圣诞老人。 ❑ *It's a bit like going to the dentist; it's never as bad as you fear.* 这有点像去看牙医，它决不像你所担心的那样糟糕。 ❑ *It's nothing like what happened in the mid-Seventies.* 那根本不像发生在七十年代中期的事情。 **2** PREP If you talk about what something or someone is **like**, you are talking about their qualities or features. (指人或事物的品质、特点) 像…样 ❑ *What was Bulgaria like?* 保加利亚情况怎么样？ ❑ *What did she look like?* 她长什么样？ **3** PREP You can use **like** to introduce an example of the set of things or people that you have just mentioned. 例如 [n PREP n/-ing] ❑ *The neglect that large cities like New York have received over the past 12 years is tremendous.* 诸如纽约这样的大城市在过去12年里所受到的忽视是巨大的。 **4** PREP You can use **like** to say that someone or something is in the same situation as another person or thing. 像…一样 ❑ *It also moved those who, like me, are too young to have lived through the war.* 它也感动了那些跟我一样、太年轻而没有经历过战争的人。 **5** PREP If you say that someone is behaving **like** something or someone else, you mean that they are behaving in a way that is typical of that kind of thing or person. **Like** is used in this way in many fixed expressions, for example, **to cry like a baby** and **to watch someone like a hawk**. 像…一样 [V PREP n] ❑ *I was shaking all over, trembling like a leaf.* 我浑身颤抖、像一片叶子似的抖动。 **6** CONJ **Like** is sometimes used as a conjunction in order to say that something appears to be the case when it is not. Some people consider this use to be incorrect. 仿佛 ❑ *His arms look like they might snap under the weight of his gloves.* 他的双臂看起来好像要在他手套的重压下突然折断似的。 **7** CONJ **Like** is sometimes used as a conjunction in order to indicate that something happens or is done in the same way as something else. Some people consider this use to be incorrect. 像…那样 ❑ *People are strolling, buying ice cream for their children, just like they do every Sunday.* 人们散着步，给孩子们买着冰淇淋，就像他们每个周日做的一样。 ❑ *He spoke exactly like I did.* 他说得跟我一模一样。 **8** PREP You can use **like** in negative expressions such as **nothing like it** and **no place like it** to emphasize that there is nothing as good as the situation, thing, or person mentioned. (用于否定式短语中) 比得上 [with neg] [EMPHASIS] ❑ *There's nothing like candlelight for creating a romantic mood.* 没有什么比烛光更能营造浪漫氛围了。 **9** PREP You can use **like** in expressions such as **nothing like** to make an emphatic negative statement. 用于固定短语中表否定强调 [with neg] [EMPHASIS] ❑ *Three hundred million dollars will be nothing like enough.* 3亿美元根本不够。

❷ **like** ♦♦♦ /laɪk/ (**likes, liking, liked**) **1** V-T If you **like** something or someone, you think they are interesting, enjoyable, or attractive. 喜欢 [no cont] ❑ *He likes baseball.* 他喜欢棒球运动。 ❑ *I just didn't like being in crowds.* 我只是不喜欢呆在人群中。 ❑ *Do you like to go swimming?* 你喜欢去游泳吗？ **2** V-T If you ask someone how they **like** something, you are asking them for their opinion of it and whether they enjoy it or find it pleasant. 觉得 [no cont, no passive] ❑ *How do you like America?* 你觉得美国怎么样？ **3** V-T If you say that you **like to** do something or that you **like** something to be done, you mean that you prefer to do it or prefer it to be done as part of your normal life or routine. 喜欢 (做某事、习惯某事) [no cont, no passive] ❑ *I like to get to airports in good time.* 我喜欢提前到机场。 **4** V-T If you say that you **would like** something or **would like** to do something, you are indicating a wish or desire that you have. 想 [no cont, no passive] ❑ *I'd like a bath.* 我想洗个澡。 **5** V-T If you ask someone if they **would like** something or **would like** to do something, you are making a polite offer or invitation. 想要 (向某人提供帮助、提出邀请) [no cont, no passive] [POLITENESS] ❑ *Here's your change. Would you like a bag?* 这是找给您的零钱。您要个袋子吗？ ❑ *Perhaps while you wait you would like a drink at the bar.* 也许你等的时候会想要去酒吧喝一杯。 **6** V-T If you say to someone that you **would like** something or you **would like** them to do something, or ask them if they **would like** to do it, you are politely telling them what you want or what you want them to do. 想要 (请别人做某事) [no cont, no passive] [POLITENESS] ❑ *I'd like an explanation.* 我想要一个解释。 ❑ *We'd like you to look around and tell us if anything is missing.* 我们想请你四处看看，并且告诉我们是否缺少什么。

Thesaurus *like* 另参见：
PREP. alike, comparable, similar ❶ **1**
V. admire, appreciate, enjoy; (*ant.*) dislike ❷ **1**

❸ **like** ♦♦♦ /laɪk/ (**likes**) **1** N-UNCOUNT You can use **like** in expressions such as **like attracts like**, when you are referring to two or more people or things that have the same or similar characteristics. 同样 (或相似) 的人或事物 ❑ *You have to make sure you're comparing like with like.* 你得确定你是在把同类事物相比较。 **2** N-PLURAL Someone's **likes** are the things that they enjoy or find pleasant. 喜好 ❑ *I thought that I knew everything about Jemma: her likes and dislikes, her political viewpoints.* 我曾以为我了解杰玛的一切：她的喜恶以及她的政治观点。 **3** → see also **liking** **4** PHRASE You say **if you like** when you are making or agreeing to an offer or suggestion in a casual way. 如果你愿意的话 ❑ *You can stay here if you like.* 如果你愿意的话，你可以呆在这里。 **5** PHRASE You say **like this**, **like that**, or **like so** when you are showing someone how something is done. 像那样；像这样 ❑ *It opens and closes, like this.* 它就像这样打开和关上。 **6** PHRASE You use **like this** or **like that** when you are drawing attention to something that you are doing or that someone else is doing. 像这样 ❑ *I'm sorry to intrude on you like this.* 很抱歉这样打扰你。 **7** PHRASE You use the expression **something like** with an amount, number, or description to indicate that it is approximately accurate. 大约 ❑ *They can get something like $3,000 a year.* 他们一年能得到大约$3000。

-like /-laɪk/ COMB IN ADJ **-like** combines with nouns to form adjectives which describe something as being similar to the thing referred to by the noun. 像…一样的 (与名词一起组成复合形容词) ❑ *...beautiful purple-red petunia-like flowers.* …矮牵牛花般美丽的紫红色花朵。 ❑ *...a tiny worm-like creature.* …一个像虫子一样的微小生物。

like·able /laɪkəbᵊl/ → see **likable**

★ **like·li·hood** /laɪklihʊd/ **1** N-UNCOUNT The **likelihood of** something happening is how likely it is to happen. 可能性 ❑ *The likelihood of infection is minimal.* 传染的可能性微乎其微。 **2** N-SING If something is a **likelihood**, it is likely to happen. 可能发生的事情 ❑ *But the likelihood is that people would be willing to pay if they were certain that their money was going to a good cause.* 但有可能的是，如果人们确信自己的钱将用于善事，他们会愿意出钱的。

like·ly ♦♦♦ /laɪkli/ (**likelier, likeliest**) **1** ADJ You use **likely** to indicate that something is probably the case or will probably happen in a particular situation. 可能的 ❑ *Experts say a "yes" vote is still the likely outcome.* 专家们表示投赞成票仍是可能的结果。 ❑ *If this is your first baby, it's far more likely that you'll get to the hospital too early.* 如果这是你的第一胎，你就非常有可能会太早到医院。 ● ADV **Likely** is also an adverb. 可能地 [ADV with cl/group] ❑ *Profit will most likely have risen by about $25 million.* 利润将极有可能增长约2500万美元。 **2** ADJ If someone or something is **likely to** do a particular thing, they will very probably do it. 很可能地 [v-link ADJ to-inf] ❑ *In the meantime the war of nerves seems likely to continue.* 同时心理战似乎很有可能要继续下去。

like-minded ADJ **Like-minded** people have similar opinions, ideas, attitudes, or interests. 想法相同的 ❑ *...the opportunity to mix with hundreds of like-minded people.* …与数百个志趣相投的人打交道的机会。

lik·en /laɪkən/ (**likens, likening, likened**) V-T If you **liken** one thing or person **to** another thing or person, you say that they are similar. 把…比作 ❑ *She likens marriage to slavery.* 她把婚姻比作奴役。

Word Link *like ≈ similar : alike, childlike, likeness*

like·ness /laɪknɪs/ (**likenesses**) **1** N-SING If two things or people have a **likeness to** each other, they are similar to each other. 相似之处 ❑ *These myths have a startling likeness to one another.* 这些神话彼此有惊人的相似之处。 **2** N-COUNT A **likeness of** someone is a picture or sculpture of them. 肖像 ❑ *The museum displays wax* *likenesses of every U.S. president.* 这个博物馆里陈列着每一位美国总统的蜡像。 3 N-COUNT If you say that a picture of someone is a good **likeness**, you mean that it looks just like them. 相像 ❏ *She says the artist's impression is an excellent likeness of her abductor.* 她说画家凭印象画出的肖像与绑架她的人极度相像。

Word Link *wise ≈ in the direction or manner of : clockwise, likewise, otherwise*

like·wise /laɪkwaɪz/ 1 ADV You use **likewise** when you are comparing two methods, states, or situations and saying that they are similar. 同样地 ❏ *What is fair for homeowners likewise should be fair to businesses.* 对私房业主公平的，同样也该对商家公平。 2 ADV If you do something and someone else does **likewise**, they do the same or a similar thing. 照样地 [ADV after v] ❏ *He lent money, made donations and encouraged others to do likewise.* 他把钱借出、捐出，并鼓励其他人这么做。

lik·ing /laɪkɪŋ/ 1 N-SING If you have **a liking for** something or someone, you like them. 爱好 ❏ *She had a liking for good clothes.* 她有种对好衣服的爱好。 ❏ *He bought me CDs to encourage my liking for music.* 他给我买了CD光盘来鼓励我对音乐的爱好。 2 PHRASE If something is, for example, too fast **for** your **liking**, you would prefer it to be slower. If it is not fast enough **for** your **liking**, you would prefer it to be faster. 对…来说 (太快或不够快) ❏ *He had become too powerful for their liking.* 对于他们来说，他已变得过于强大。 3 PHRASE If something is **to** your **liking**, it suits your interests, tastes, or wishes. 适合某人的口味 ❏ *London was more to his liking than Rome.* 伦敦比罗马更合他的口味。

li·lac /laɪlɑk, -læk, -lək/ (**lilacs**)

Lilac can also be used as the plural form.

1 N-VAR A **lilac** or a **lilac tree** is a small tree which has sweet-smelling purple, pink, or white flowers in large, cone-shaped groups. 丁香；丁香树 ❏ *Lilacs grew against the side wall.* 丁香树倚着边墙生长。 2 COLOR Something that is **lilac** is pale pinkish-purple in color. 淡紫粉色的 ❏ *All shades of mauve, lilac, lavender and purple were fashionable.* 所有紫红色、淡紫粉色、淡紫色和紫色都很流行。

▲ **lily** /lɪli/ (**lilies**) N-VAR A **lily** is a plant with large flowers that are often white. 百合

limb /lɪm/ (**limbs**) 1 N-COUNT Your **limbs** are your arms and legs. 四肢 ❏ *She would be able to stretch out her cramped limbs and rest for a few hours.* 她将可以伸开蜷缩的四肢，休息几个小时。 2 PHRASE If someone goes **out on a limb**, they do something they strongly believe in even though it is risky or extreme, and is likely to fail or be criticized by other people. (因大胆冒险而) 处于困境 ❏ *They can see themselves going out on a limb, voting for a very controversial energy bill.* 他们会发现自己由于投票赞成一个有争议的能源法案而陷入困境。

→ see **mammal**

lim·bo /lɪmboʊ/ N-UNCOUNT If you say that someone or something is **in limbo**, you mean that they are in a situation where they seem to be caught between two stages and it is unclear what will happen next. 前途未卜的境地 ❏ *The negotiations have been in limbo since mid-December.* 谈判自12月中旬已陷入了僵局。

lime /laɪm/ (**limes**) 1 N-VAR A **lime** is a green fruit that tastes like a lemon. Limes grow on trees in tropical countries. 酸橙 ❏ *...peeled slices of lime.* …去皮橙片。 2 N-UNCOUNT **Lime** is a substance containing calcium. It is found in soil and water. 石灰 ❏ *If your soil is very acidic, add lime.* 如果你的土壤酸性很强，就加点石灰。

lime·light /laɪmlaɪt/ N-UNCOUNT If someone is in the **limelight**, a lot of attention is being paid to them, because they are famous or because they have done something very unusual or exciting. 众人注意的中心 ❏ *Tony has now been thrust into the limelight, with a high-profile job.* 托尼有一份令人注目的工作，现在已成为人们关注的焦点。

lime·stone /laɪmstoʊn/ (**limestones**) N-MASS **Limestone** is a whitish-colored rock which is used for building and for making cement. 石灰岩 ❏ *...high limestone cliffs.* …高耸的石灰岩峭壁。

lim·it ♦♦◇ /lɪmɪt/ (**limits, limiting, limited**) 1 N-COUNT A **limit** is the greatest amount, extent, or degree of something that is possible. 极限 ❏ *Her love for him was being tested to its limits.* 她对他的爱正在考验着极限。 ❏ *There is no limit to how much fresh fruit you can eat in a day.* 你一天内能吃多少新鲜水果并无上限。 2 N-COUNT A **limit** of a particular kind is the largest or smallest amount of something such as time or money that is allowed because of a rule, law, or decision. 限制 ❏ *The three month time limit will be up in mid-June.* 3个月的时间限制将于6月中旬到期。 3 N-COUNT The **limit** of an area is its boundary or edge. 界限 ❏ *...the city limits of Baghdad.* …巴格达的城市边界。 4 N-PLURAL **The limits of** a situation are the facts involved in it which make only some actions or results possible. 范围 ❏ *She has to work within the limits of a fairly tight budget.* 她不得不在一个相当紧张的预算范围内工作。 5 V-T If you **limit** something, you prevent it from becoming greater than a particular amount or degree. 限制 ❏ *He limited payments on the country's foreign debt.* 他限制了国家外债的支付。 6 V-T If you **limit yourself** to something, or if someone or something **limits** you, the number of things that you have or do is reduced. 对…作出限制 ❏ *Please limit letters to 125 words or less.* 请把信函限制到125字或更少的字数内。 ● **lim·it·ing** ADJ 限制的 ❏ *The conditions laid down to me were not too limiting.* 给我定下的条件没有太大的限制性。 7 V-T If something **is limited to** a particular place or group of people, it exists only in that place, or is had or done only by that group. 仅限于(某地、某团体) [usu passive] ❏ *The protests were not limited to New York.* 抗议活动并不仅限于纽约。 8 → see also **limited** 9 PHRASE If an area or a place is **off limits**, you are not allowed to go there. 禁止入内 ❏ *A one-mile area around the wreck is still off limits.* 沉船周围一英里的地区仍然禁止入内。

Thesaurus *limit* 另参见：

N.	ceiling, maximum 1
	border, edge, extremity, perimeter 3
V.	cap, check, confine, reduce, restrict 5

Word Partnership *limit* 的常用搭配：

ADJ.	**lower** limit, **upper** limit 1 2
	legal limit 2
PREP.	**beyond the** limit, **over the** limit 2
N.	**credit** limit, **term** limit, **time** limit 2
	limit **the amount of** *something*, limit **benefits**, limit **damage**, limit **growth**, limit **the number of** *something*, limit **spending** 5

limi·ta·tion /lɪmɪteɪʃᵊn/ (**limitations**) 1 N-UNCOUNT The **limitation** of something is the act or process of controlling or reducing it. 限制 ❏ *All the talk had been about the limitation of nuclear weapons.* 整个会谈都是关于核武器的限制。 2 N-VAR A **limitation on** something is a rule or decision which prevents that thing from growing or extending beyond certain limits. 限定 ❏ *...a limitation on the tax deductions for people who make more than $100,000 a year.* …对年收入高于10万美元者在减税上的限定。 3 N-PLURAL If you talk about the **limitations** of someone or something, you mean that they can only do some things and not others, or cannot do something very well. 局限 ❏ *I realized how possible it was to overcome your limitations, to achieve well beyond what you believe yourself capable of.* 我意识到如何有可能克服自身的局限，取得自认为力不能及的成就。 4 N-VAR A **limitation** is a fact or situation that allows only some actions and makes others impossible. 限制因素 ❏ *This drug has one important limitation. Its effects only last six hours.* 这种药物有一个很大的限制因素，其药效只能持续6个小时。

lim·it·ed ♦◇◇ /lɪmɪtɪd/ 1 ADJ Something that is **limited** is not very great in amount, range, or degree. 有限的 ❏ *They may only have a limited amount of time to get their points across.* 他们可能只有有限的时间来阐述清楚他们的观点。 2 ADJ A **limited** company is one whose owners are legally responsible for only a part of any money that it may owe if it goes bankrupt. 有限责任的 (公司) [BRIT, CANADIAN, BUSINESS]

in AM, use **incorporated**

lim·it·ed edi·tion (**limited editions**) N-COUNT A **limited edition** is a work of art, such as a book which is only produced in very small numbers, so that each one will be valuable in the future. 限量版本 ❏ *The limited edition of 300 copies was edited by Rebekah Scott.* 那300册的限量版本是由丽贝卡·斯科特编辑的。

lim·it·less /lɪmɪtlɪs/ ADJ If you describe something as **limitless**, you mean that there is or appears to be so much of it that it will never be exhausted. 无限的 ❏ *...a cheap and potentially limitless supply of energy.* …一种廉价而又潜力无限的能源供给。

▲ **lim·ou·sine** /lɪməzin/ (**limousines**) N-COUNT A **limousine** is a large and very comfortable car. Limousines are usually driven by a chauffeur and often hired for important occasions. 豪华轿车

limp /lɪmp/ (**limps, limping, limped, limper, limpest**) 1 V-I If a person or animal **limps**, they walk with difficulty or in an uneven way because one of their legs or feet is hurt. 跛行 ❑ *I wasn't badly hurt, but I injured my thigh and had to limp.* 我伤得并不严重，但我伤到了大腿，不得不一瘸一拐地走路。● N-COUNT **Limp** is also a noun. 跛行 ❑ *A stiff knee following surgery forced her to walk with a limp.* 手术后僵直的膝盖迫使她瘸着走路。 2 V-I If you say that something such as an organization, process, or vehicle **limps along**, you mean that it continues slowly or with difficulty, for example because it has been weakened or damaged. (交通工具等) 缓慢或艰难地前进；(组织、进程等) 进展缓慢 ❑ *In recent years the newspaper had been limping along on limited resources.* 近年来该报一直靠有限的资源艰难地发展。 3 ADJ If you describe something as **limp**, you mean that it is soft or weak when it should be firm or strong. 无力的 ❑ *She was told to reject applicants with limp handshakes.* 有人告诉她通过无力的握手来拒绝申请者。● **limp·ly** ADV 无力地 [ADV with v] ❑ *Flags and bunting hung limply in the still, warm air.* 旗子和飘带在静止、温暖的空中无力地垂着。 4 ADJ If someone is **limp**, their body has no strength and is not moving, for example, because they are asleep or unconscious. 软弱无力的 ❑ *He carried her limp body into the room and laid her on the bed.* 他抱起她软绵绵的身体走进那房间，把她放到床上。

line
- ❶ NOUN USES
- ❷ PHRASES
- ❸ VERB USES
- ❹ PHRASAL VERB

❶ **line** ♦♦♦ /laɪn/ (**lines**) 1 N-COUNT A **line** is a long thin mark which is drawn or painted on a surface. 线 ❑ *Draw a line down that page's center.* 沿着那一页的中心向下画一条线。 ❑ *...a dotted line.* …一条虚线。 2 N-COUNT The **lines** on someone's skin, especially on their face, are long thin marks that appear there as they grow older. 皱纹 ❑ *He has a large, generous face with deep lines.* 他宽大的面庞上带着很深的皱纹。 3 N-COUNT A **line** of people or things is a number of them arranged one behind the other or side by side. (一) 排 ❑ *The sparse line of spectators noticed nothing unusual.* 稀稀疏疏的一排观众并没注意到什么特别之处。 4 N-COUNT A **line** of people or vehicles is a number of them that are waiting one behind another, for example, in order to buy something or to go in a particular direction. 队列 ❑ *Children clutching empty bowls form a line.* 抓着空碗的孩子们排成一队。 5 N-COUNT A **line** of a piece of writing is one of the rows of words, numbers, or other symbols in it. (一) 行 (文字、数字、符号) ❑ *The next line should read: Five days, 23.5 hours.* 下一行文字应是：5天，23.5小时。 6 N-COUNT A **line** of a poem, song, or play is a group of words that are spoken or sung together. If an actor **learns** his or her **lines** for a play or film, they learn what they have to say. 台词；诗行 ❑ *...a line from Shakespeare's Othello: "one that loved not wisely but too well."* …莎士比亚戏剧《奥赛罗》里的一句台词："一个在恋爱上不聪明却过于深情的人。" ❑ *Every time I sing that line, I have to compete with that darn trombone!* 每当我唱那行歌词时，我都得和那该死的长号比赛。 7 N-VAR You can refer to a long piece of wire, string, or cable as a **line** when it is used for a particular purpose. 线；绳 ❑ *She put her washing on the line.* 她把洗好的衣服晾在绳子上。 ❑ *...a piece of fishing-line.* …一根钓鱼线。 8 N-COUNT A **line** is a connection which makes it possible for two people to speak to each other on the telephone. 电话线路 ❑ *The telephone lines went dead.* 电话线路不通了。 ❑ *It's not a very good line. Shall we call you back Susan?* 线路不太好。苏珊，我们给你打回去好吗？ 9 N-COUNT You can use **line** to refer to a telephone number which you can call in order to get information or advice. 咨询电话号码 ❑ *...the 24-hour information line.* …24小时信息咨询电话号码。 10 N-COUNT A **line** is a route, especially a dangerous or secret one, along which people move or send messages or supplies. (发送信息、输送人员或物资的危险、秘密) 通道 ❑ *The North American continent's geography severely limited the lines of attack.* 北美大陆的地形严格限制了进攻通道。 ❑ *Negotiators say they're keeping communication lines open.* 谈判代表声称他们保持着沟通管道的通畅。 11 N-COUNT The **line** in which something or someone moves is the particular route that they take, especially when they keep moving straight ahead. 运动路线 ❑ *Walk in a straight line.* 走直线。 12 N-COUNT A **line** is a particular route, involving the same stations, roads, or stops along which a train or bus service regularly operates. (火车、公共汽车运行的) 路线 ❑ *They've got to ride all the way to the end of the line.* 他们得乘车直到路线的终点。 13 N-COUNT A railroad **line** consists of the pieces of metal and wood which form the track that the trains travel along. 铁轨 ❑ *Floods washed out much of the railroad line.* 洪水冲毁了很多铁轨。 14 N-COUNT A shipping, air, or bus **line** is a company which provides services for transporting people or goods by sea, air, or bus. 运输公司 [BUSINESS] ❑ *The Cunard shipping line came up with a clever slogan: "Getting there is half the fun..."* 冠达海运公司想出了一个聪明的口号："一半的乐趣来自于到达目的地…" 15 N-COUNT A state or county **line** is a boundary between two states or counties. 界限 [AM] ❑ *...the California state line.* …加利福尼亚州的州界。 16 N-COUNT You can use **lines** to refer to the set of physical defenses or the soldiers that have been established along the boundary of an area occupied by an army. 防线 ❑ *Their unit was shelling the German lines only seven miles away.* 他们的部队正炮轰仅7英里外的德国防线。 17 N-COUNT The particular **line** that a person has toward a problem is the attitude that they have toward it. For example, if someone takes a **hard line** on something, they have a firm strict policy which they refuse to change. 方针 ❑ *Forty members of the governing Conservative party rebelled, voting against the government line.* 执政的保守党中的40名成员倒戈，投票反对政府方针。 18 N-COUNT You can use **line** to refer to the way in which someone's thoughts or activities develop, particularly if it is logical. 思路 ❑ *Our discussion in the previous chapter continues this line of thinking.* 我们在前一章的讨论延续了这种思维方式。 19 N-PLURAL If you say that something happens **along** particular **lines**, or **on** particular **lines**, you are giving a general summary or approximate account of what happens, which may not be correct in every detail. 概况 ❑ *There followed an assortment of praise for the coffee along the lines of "Hey, this coffee is fantastic!"* 接着是各种各样大概就像"嘿，这咖啡真棒"一样的对咖啡的称赞。 ❑ *He'd said something on those lines already.* 他已说过内容大致类似的话。 20 N-PLURAL If something is organized **on** particular **lines**, or **along** particular **lines**, it is organized according to that method or principle. 原则；方法 ❑ *...so-called autonomous republics based on ethnic lines.* …建立在种族原则基础上的所谓自治共和国。 21 N-COUNT Your **line of** business or work is the kind of work that you do. 行业 [BUSINESS] ❑ *So what was your father's line of business?* 那么你父亲是干哪一行的？ 22 N-COUNT In a factory, a **line** is an arrangement of workers or machines where a product passes from one worker to another until it is finished. 流水线 ❑ *...a production line capable of producing three different products.* …一条能生产3种不同产品的流水线。 23 N-COUNT You can use **line** when you are referring to a number of people who are ranked according to status. 次序 ❑ *Nicholas Paul Patrick was seventh in the line of succession to the throne.* 尼古拉斯·保罗·帕特里克在王位继承顺序上排第7。 24 N-COUNT A particular **line of** people or things is a series of them that has existed over a period of time, when they have all been similar in some way, or done similar things. (某个时期有某种共同之处的人、事物的) 系列 ❑ *We were part of a long line of artists.* 我们是由古至今代代艺术家中的一代。 25 → see also **bottom line, front line, picket line**

→ see **fish, football, graph, mass production, mathematics, soccer, tennis, train**

Thesaurus *line* 另参见：
N. cable, clothes line, rope, wire ❶ 7

❷ **line** ♦♦♦ /laɪn/ (**lines**)
➪ **Please look at meaning 11 to see if the expression you are looking for is shown under another headword.** 1 PHRASE If you say that someone has **crossed the line** or has **stepped over the line**, you mean that they have behaved in a way that is considered unacceptable. 举止不当 ❑ *He has crossed the line, and it must stop.* 他言行出格，必须制止。 ❑ *Sometimes, I think the administration steps over the line when they make these kinds of accusations.* 有时候，我认为行政部门在发出这类指责时，他们已经出格了。 2 PHRASE If you **draw the line at** a particular activity, you refuse to do it, because you disapprove of it or because it is more extreme than what you normally do. 拒绝 ❑ *Letters have come from prisoners, declaring that they would draw the line at hitting an old lady.* 来自囚犯们的信件声明他们不会袭击一个老妇人。 3 PHRASE If you do something or if it happens to you **in the line of duty**, you do it or it happens as part of your regular work or as a result of it. 在执行公务中 ❑ *More than 3,000 police officers were wounded in the line of duty last year.* 去年三千多名警官在执行任务时受伤。 4 PHRASE If you refer to a method as **the first line of**, for example, defense or treatment, you mean that it is the first or most important method to be used in dealing with a problem. 首要手段 ❑ *Residents have the responsibility of being the first line of defense against*

wildfires. 居民有责任成为野火的首要防卫人员。 5 PHRASE If one object is **in line with** others, or moves **into line with** others, they are arranged in a line. You can also say that a number of objects are **in line** or move **into line.** 成一直线 ❑ *The device itself was right under the vehicle, almost in line with the gear lever.* 这个装置本身就在车子下面，几乎与换挡杆成一直线。 6 PHRASE If one thing is **in line with** another, or is brought **into line with** it, the first thing is, or becomes, similar to the second, especially in a way that has been planned or expected. 与…一致 ❑ *The structure of our schools is now broadly in line with the major countries of the world.* 目前我国学校的结构与世界主要国家的是基本一致的。 ❑ *This brings the law into line with most medical opinion.* 这使得该法律与医疗界的大多数意见一致。 7 PHRASE If you **keep** someone **in line** or **bring** them **into line**, you make them obey you, or you make them behave in the way you want them to. 守规矩 ❑ *All this was just designed to frighten me and keep me in line.* 所有这一切只是设计来吓唬我、让我守规矩。 8 PHRASE If a machine or piece of equipment comes **on line**, it starts operating. If it is **off line**, it is not operating. 在运行中 ❑ *The new machine will go on line in June 2006.* 这台新机器将在2006年6月投入使用。 9 PHRASE If you do something **on line**, you do it using a computer or a computer network. 在网上 ❑ *They can order their requirements on line.* 他们可以在网上定购所需物品。 10 → see also **online** 11 **to sign on the dotted line** → see **dotted**

❷ **line** ♦♦♦ /laɪn/ (**lines, lining, lined**) 1 V-T If people or things **line** a road, room, or other place, they are present in large numbers along its edges or sides. 沿…排列成行 ❑ *Thousands of local people lined the streets and clapped as the procession went by.* 游行队伍经过时，数以千计的当地人在街上列队并鼓掌。 2 V-T If you **line** a wall, container, or other object, you put a layer of something such as leaves or paper on the inside surface of it in order to make it stronger, warmer, or cleaner. 给…加衬 ❑ *Line the basket with a bright checkered napkin just before adding the cookies.* 放入饼干前，先往篮子里垫上一张鲜亮的方格餐巾。 3 → see also **lining**

❸ **line** ♦♦♦ /laɪn/ (**lines, lining, lined**)

▶ **line up** 1 PHRASAL VERB If people **line up** or if you **line** them **up**, they move so that they are standing in a line. 将…排成队；排队 ❑ *The senior leaders lined up behind him in orderly rows.* 高级领导人有序地排列在他身后。 ❑ *The gym teachers lined us up against the cement walls.* 体操老师们让我们靠水泥墙排成队。 2 PHRASAL VERB If you **line** things **up**, you move them into a straight row. 将…排成行 ❑ *I would line up my toys on this windowsill and play.* 我要把玩具在这个窗台上排成一行来玩。 3 PHRASAL VERB If you **line** one thing **up with** another, or one thing **lines up with** another, the first thing is moved into its correct position in relation to the second. You can also say that two things **line up**, or **are lined up**. 与…对齐；对齐 ❑ *You have to line the car up with the ones beside you.* 你必须把你的车与你旁边的车对齐。 ❑ *The plane circled twice, trying in vain to line up with the runway.* 飞机盘旋了两圈，试图对准跑道降落却没成功。 4 PHRASAL VERB If you **line up** an event or activity, you arrange for it to happen. If you **line** someone **up** for an event or activity, you arrange for them to be available for that event or activity. 安排（比赛、活动等）；组织准备（人员） ❑ *She lined up executives, politicians and educators to serve on the board of directors.* 她组织行政领导、政界人物和教育家们担任董事会成员。 5 → see also **lineup**

★ **lin·ear** /lɪniər/ 1 ADJ A **linear** process or development is one in which something changes or progresses straight from one stage to another, and has a starting point and an ending point. 线性的 ❑ *...decisions that lead the story in various directions, rather than follow traditional linear storytelling.* …引导故事向不同方向发展、而不是遵循传统的线性故事讲述的一些决定。 2 ADJ A **linear** shape or form consists of straight lines. 由直线组成的 ❑ *...the sharp, linear designs of the Seventies and Eighties.* …七、八十年代锐利的、以线条表现的设计。 3 ADJ **Linear** movement or force occurs in a straight line rather than in a curve. 直线的 ❑ *...linear movement toward a goal.* …朝着一个目标的直线运动。

line man·ag·er (**line managers**) N-COUNT Your **line manager** is the person at work who is in charge of your department, group, or project. 部门经理 [mainly BRIT, BUSINESS]

★ **lin·en** /lɪnɪn/ (**linens**) 1 N-MASS **Linen** is a kind of cloth that is made from a plant called flax. It is used for making clothes and things such as tablecloths and sheets. 亚麻布 ❑ *...a white linen suit.* …一套白色亚麻衣服。 2 N-UNCOUNT **Linen** is tablecloths, sheets, pillowcases, and similar things made of cloth that are used in the home. 亚麻织品 [also N in pl] ❑ *...embroidered bed linen.* …刺绣的亚麻布床上用品。

★ **lin·er** /laɪnər/ (**liners**) N-COUNT A **liner** is a large ship in which people travel long distances, especially on vacation. 客轮 ❑ *...luxury ocean liners.* …豪华远洋客轮。

→ see **ship**

lines·man /laɪnzmən/ (**linesmen**) N-COUNT A **linesman** is an official who assists the referee or umpire in games such as football and tennis by indicating when the ball goes over the lines around the edge of the field or court. 边线裁判员

line·up /laɪnʌp/ (**lineups**) 1 N-COUNT A **lineup** is a group of people or a series of things that have been gathered together to be part of a particular event. 阵容；阵列 ❑ *One player sure to be in the lineup is star midfielder Landon Donovan.* 肯定列入该阵容的一名球员是中场球星兰登·多诺万。 2 N-COUNT At a **lineup**, a witness to a crime tries to identify the criminal from among a line of people. （为从中识别嫌疑犯而聚集起的）队列 ❑ *He failed to identify Graham from photographs, but later picked him out of a police lineup.* 他没有从照片中认出格雷厄姆，但后来从警察安排的指认队列里把他认了出来。

★ **lin·ger** /lɪŋgər/ (**lingers, lingering, lingered**) 1 V-I When something such as an idea, feeling, or illness **lingers**, it continues to exist for a long time, often much longer than expected. （想法、感觉、疾病）继续存留 ❑ *The scent of her perfume lingered on in the room.* 她的香水味在房间里久久不散。 ❑ *He was ashamed. That feeling lingered, and he was never comfortable in church after that.* 他很惭愧。这种感觉持续着，此后他在教堂里就再没有自在过。 2 V-I If you **linger** somewhere, you stay there for a longer time than is necessary, for example, because you are enjoying yourself. 继续逗留 ❑ *Customers are welcome to linger over coffee until around midnight.* 顾客们可以慢慢品味咖啡到午夜。

lin·gerie /lɑnʒəreɪ, læn-/ N-UNCOUNT **Lingerie** is women's underwear and nightclothes. 女用内衣；女用睡衣 ❑ *...a new range of lingerie.* …一系列新式女内衣。

Word Link *lingu ≈ language : bi**lingu**al, **lingu**ist, **lingu**istic*

lin·guist /lɪŋgwɪst/ (**linguists**) 1 N-COUNT A **linguist** is someone who is good at speaking or learning foreign languages. 通晓数国外语的人；学多种外语的人 ❑ *He had a scholarly air and was an accomplished linguist.* 他有一种学者的风度，而且是个熟练掌握多国语言的人。 2 N-COUNT A **linguist** is someone who studies or teaches linguistics. 语言学家 ❑ *Many linguists have looked at language in this way.* 许多语言学家就是这样看待语言的。

▲ **lin·guis·tic** /lɪŋgwɪstɪks/ (**linguistics**) 1 ADJ **Linguistic** abilities or ideas relate to language or linguistics. 语言的；语言学的 ❑ *...linguistic skills.* …语言技能。 2 N-UNCOUNT **Linguistics** is the study of the way in which language works. 语言学 ❑ *Modern linguistics emerged as a distinct field in the nineteenth century.* 现代语言学在19世纪作为一个独立的领域出现。

lin·ing /laɪnɪŋ/ (**linings**) 1 N-VAR The **lining** of something such as a piece of clothing or a curtain is a layer of cloth attached to the inside of it in order to make it thicker or warmer, or in order to make it hang better. 内衬 ❑ *...a padded satin jacket with quilted lining.* …一件絮有棉花内衬的缎子夹克。 2 N-COUNT The **lining** of your stomach or other organ is a layer of tissue on the inside of it. （胃等器官内部的）保护层 ❑ *...a bacterium that attacks the lining of the stomach.* …一种侵袭胃粘膜的细菌。 3 → see also **line**

link ♦♦◇ /lɪŋk/ (**links, linking, linked**) 1 N-COUNT If there is a **link between** two things or situations, there is a relationship between them, for example, because one thing causes or affects the other. 关系 ❑ *...the link between smoking and lung cancer.* …吸烟和肺癌之间的关系。 2 V-T If someone or something **links** two things or situations, there is a relationship between them, for example, because one thing causes or affects the other. 使联系起来 ❑ *The U.N. Security Council has linked any lifting of sanctions to compliance with the ceasefire terms.* 联合国安全理事会将任何制裁的解除与遵守停火条款联系起来。 ❑ *The study further strengthens the evidence linking smoking with early death.* 这项研究进一步加强了联系吸烟与早亡的证据。 3 N-COUNT A **link between** two things or places is a physical connection between them. 连接物 ❑ *...the railroad link between Boston and New York.* …波士顿与纽约之间的铁路连接线。 ❑ *Drivers ran into a field of weeds at the state border, where no link with the neighboring state had yet been planned.* 司机们闯入了州界处一块杂草丛生的原野，在那里还没有计划修建连接邻州的道路。 4 V-T If two places or objects **are**

l

linked or something **links** them, there is a physical connection between them. 连接 ❏ *...the Rama Road, which links the capital, Managua, with the Caribbean coast.* …连接首都马那瓜与加勒比海岸的拉玛公路。 ❏ *Seven miles of track were installed to link the hotel to the golf course.* 七英里的轨道被铺设来连接宾馆和高尔夫球场。 **5** N-COUNT A **link** between two people, organizations, or places is a friendly or business connection between them. 关系 ❏ *Kiev hopes to cement close links with Bonn.* 基辅希望巩固与波恩之间的密切关系。 ❏ *In 1984 the long link between AC Cars and the Hurlock family was severed.* 1984年AC汽车公司与赫洛克家族间的长期关系中断了。 **6** N-COUNT A **link** to another person or organization is something that allows you to communicate with them or have contact with them. 联系 ❏ *She was my only link with the past.* 她是我和过去的惟一联系。 ❏ *The Red Cross was created to provide a link between soldiers in battle and their families at home.* 红十字会被创立来为前线士兵与其家乡的亲人之间提供联系。 **7** V-T If you **link** one person or thing to another, you claim that there is a relationship or connection between them. 认为…有关联 ❏ *Criminologist Dr. Ann Jones has linked the crime to social circumstances.* 犯罪学家安·琼斯博士认为这起犯罪与社会环境有关。 ❏ *They've linked her with various men, including magnate Donald Trump.* 他们认为她和多个男人有关系，包括巨头唐纳德·特朗普。 **8** N-COUNT In computing, a **link** is a connection between different documents, or between different parts of the same document, using hypertext. 链接 ❏ *Available in English, French, German and Italian, it has links to other relevant tourism sites.* 它有可供阅读的英文、法文、德文和意大利文版本，也有通向其它相关旅游网站的链接。 ● V-T **Link** is also a verb. 链接 ❏ *Certainly, Andreessen didn't think up using hypertext to link Internet documents.* 当然，安德森并没想到用超文本链接互联网文档。 **9** N-COUNT A **link** is one of the rings in a chain. (链的) 环 ❏ *...a chain of heavy gold links.* …一串沉重的金链环。 **10** V-T If you **link** one thing with another, you join them by putting one thing through the other. 将…套在一起 ❏ *She linked her arm through his.* 她用自己的胳膊挽住他的胳膊。 ● PHRASE If two or more people **link arms**, or if one person **links arms** with another, they stand next to each other, and each person puts their arm around the arm of the person next to them. 挽着胳膊 ❏ *It was so slippery that some of the walkers linked arms and proceeded very carefully.* 地太滑了，所以一些行人挽着胳膊小心翼翼地前行。 **11** → see also **linkup**

▶ **link up** **1** PHRASAL VERB If you **link up with** someone, you join them for a particular purpose. (与某人) 联合 ❏ *They linked up with a series of local anti-nuclear and anti-apartheid groups.* 他们与一系列反对核武器及反种族隔离的地方团体联合起来了。 **2** PHRASAL VERB If one thing **is linked up to** another, the two things are connected to each other. 相连 ❏ *The television screens of the next century will be linked up to an emerging world telecommunications grid.* 下个世纪的电视屏幕将与一种新兴的世界电信网格相连。

Word Partnership *link* 的常用搭配:

ADJ.	**direct** link, **possible** link, **vital** link **1 3 5 6**
	strong/weak link **1 5 6**
V.	**establish** a link, **find** a link **1 3 5 6**
	attempt to link **2 4 7 10**
	click on a link **8**

link·up /lɪŋkʌp/ (**linkups**) **1** N-COUNT A **linkup** is a connection between two machines or communication systems. (两台机器或两套通讯系统的) 连接 ❏ *...a live satellite linkup with Bonn.* …与波恩的直播卫星连线。 **2** N-COUNT A **linkup** is a relationship or partnership between two organizations. 合作关系 ❏ *...new linkups between school and commerce.* …学校与商业的新合作。

lion /laɪən/ (**lions**) N-COUNT A **lion** is a large wild member of the cat family that is found in Africa. Lions have yellowish fur, and male lions have long hair on their head and neck. 狮子

lion's share N-SING If a person, group, or project gets **the lion's share of** something, they get the largest part of it, leaving very little for other people. 最大的一份 ❏ *Military and nuclear research have received the lion's share of public funding.* 军事研究和核研究得到了公共资助里最大的份额。

lip ♦◇◇ /lɪp/ (**lips**) N-COUNT Your **lips** are the two outer parts of the edge of your mouth. 嘴唇 ❏ *Wade stuck the cigarette between his lips.* 韦德嘴里叼着烟。

→ see **face, kiss**

★ **lip·stick** /lɪpstɪk/ (**lipsticks**) N-MASS **Lipstick** is a colored substance in the form of a stick which women put on their lips. 唇膏 ❏ *She was wearing red lipstick.* 她涂着红色唇膏。

→ see **makeup**

li·queur /lɪkɜr, -kyʊər/ (**liqueurs**) N-MASS A **liqueur** is a strong alcoholic drink with a sweet taste. You drink it after a meal. 餐后甜酒 ❏ *...liqueurs such as Grand Marnier and Kirsch.* …诸如金万利和樱桃白兰地的甜酒。

liq·uid /lɪkwɪd/ (**liquids**) **1** N-MASS A **liquid** is a substance which is not solid but which flows and can be poured, for example, water. 液体 ❏ *Drink plenty of liquid.* 饮用大量液体。 ❏ *Boil for 20 minutes until the liquid has reduced by half.* 煮沸20分钟直到液体减少一半为止。 **2** ADJ A **liquid** substance is in the form of a liquid rather than being solid or a gas. 液体的 ❏ *Wash in warm water with liquid detergent.* 用液体清洁剂在温水中清洗。 ❏ *The tanker was carrying liquid nitrogen.* 油轮那时正在运送液态氮。 **3** ADJ **Liquid** assets are the things that a person or company owns which can be quickly turned into cash if necessary. (资金等) 流动的 [BUSINESS] ❏ *The bank had sufficient liquid assets to continue operations.* 该银行拥有足够的流动资产来继续运转。

→ see **matter**

liq·ui·date /lɪkwɪdeɪt/ (**liquidates, liquidating, liquidated**) **1** V-T To **liquidate** a company is to close it down and sell all its assets, usually because it is in debt. 清算 [BUSINESS] ❏ *A unanimous vote was taken to liquidate the company.* 投票一致通过对这家公司进行清算。 ● **liq·ui·da·tion** /lɪkwɪdeɪʃən/ N-VAR (**liquidations**) 清算 ❏ *The company went into liquidation.* 这家公司进入了停业清理阶段。 **2** V-T If a company **liquidates** its assets, its property such as buildings or machinery is sold in order to get money. 将资产换成现金 [BUSINESS] ❏ *The company closed down operations and began liquidating its assets in January.* 这家公司在1月份停止运作，开始把其资产折换成现金。

liq·ui·da·tor /lɪkwɪdeɪtər/ (**liquidators**) N-COUNT A **liquidator** is a person who is responsible for settling the affairs of a company that is being liquidated. 清算人 [BUSINESS] ❏ *...the failed company's liquidators.* …破产公司的清算人。

li·quid·ity /lɪkwɪdɪti/ N-UNCOUNT In finance, a company's **liquidity** is the amount of cash or liquid assets it has easily available. 资产折现力 [BUSINESS] ❏ *The company maintains a high degree of liquidity.* 这个公司保持着很强的资产折现力。

liq·uid·iz·er /lɪkwɪdaɪzər/ (**liquidizers**) N-COUNT A **liquidizer** is the same as a **blender**. 榨汁机 [BRIT]

liq·uor /lɪkər/ (**liquors**) N-MASS Strong alcoholic drinks such as whiskey, vodka, and gin can be referred to as **liquor**. 烈性酒 [AM]

in BRIT, use **spirits**

❏ *The room was filled with cases of liquor.* 房间里满是一箱箱的烈性酒。

liq·uor store (**liquor stores**) N-COUNT A **liquor store** is a store which sells beer, wine, and other alcoholic drinks. 卖酒的商店 [AM]

in BRIT, use **off-licence**

list ♦♦♦ /lɪst/ (**lists, listing, listed**) **1** N-COUNT A **list** of things such as names or addresses is a set of them which all belong to a particular category, written down one below the other. 清单 ❏ *We are making a list of the top ten men we would not want to be married to.* 我们正在列一个我们最不想嫁的10种男人的名单。 ❏ *There were six names on the list.* 单子上有6个名字。 **2** → see also **hit list, mailing list, waiting list** **3** N-COUNT A **list** of things is a set of them that you think of as being in a particular order. (按一定顺序排列的) 系列事项 ❏ *High on the list of public demands is to end military control of broadcasting.* 高居公众要求事项前列的是结束对广播的军事控制。 ❏ *The criminal judicial system always comes up at the top of the list of voters' concerns in focus groups.* 刑事司法制度总是出现在焦点小组中投票者关注事项之首。 **4** V-T To **list** several things such as reasons or names means to write or say them one after another, usually in a particular order. 列出 ❏ *The pupils were asked to list the sports they loved most and hated most.* 学生们被要求列出他们最喜欢的和最讨厌的运动。 **5** V-T To **list** something in a particular way means to include it in that way in a list or report. 把…列入 (表、报告) ❏ *A medical examiner has listed the deaths as homicides.* 验尸官已将这些死亡列为他杀案件。 **6** V-T/V-I If a company **is listed**, or if it **lists**, on a stock exchange, it obtains an official quotation for its shares so that people can buy and sell them. 使 (公司) 上市; (公司) 上市 [BUSINESS] ❏ *...a basket of blue chip stocks listed on the American Exchange.* …在美国证券交易所上市的一组绩优股。 **7** → see also **listed company**

L

Word Partnership *list* 的常用搭配：

ADJ. **disabled** list, **injured** list 1
complete list, **long** list, **short** list 1 3
V. **add** ***someone/something*** **to a** list, list **includes, make a** list 1 3
N. list **of candidates**, list **of demands**, **guest** list, list **of ingredients**, list **of items**, list **of names**, **price** list, list **of questions**, **reading** list, list **of things**, **wine** list, **wish** list, list **of words** 1 3

list·ed com·pa·ny (**listed companies**) N-COUNT A **listed company** is a company whose shares are quoted on a stock exchange. 上市公司 [BUSINESS] ❑ *Some of Australia's largest listed companies are expected to announce huge interim earnings this week.* 澳大利亚一些最大的上市公司预期会在本周公布高额中期盈利。

lis·ten ♦♦◇ /lɪsᵊn/ (**listens, listening, listened**) 1 V-I If you **listen to** someone who is talking or **to** a sound, you give your attention to them or it. 听 ❑ *He spent his time listening to the radio.* 他把时间花在了听收音机上。 ● **lis·ten·er** N-COUNT (**listeners**) 听者 ❑ *One or two listeners had fallen asleep while the president was speaking.* 总统讲话时，有一两个听众睡着了。 2 V-I If you **listen for** a sound, you keep alert and are ready to hear it if it occurs. 留心听 ❑ *We listen for footsteps approaching.* 我们侧耳倾听脚步声靠近。 3 V-I If you **listen to** someone, you do what they advise you to do, or you believe them. 听从 ❑ *Anne, you need to listen to me this time.* 安妮，这次你要听我的。 4 CONVENTION You say **listen** when you want someone to pay attention to you because you are going to say something important. 听我说 ❑ *Listen, I finish at one.* 听着，我一点钟结束。

Do not confuse **listen** and **hear**. If you want to say that someone is paying attention to something they can hear, you say that they **are listening to** it. ❑ *He turned on the radio and listened to the news.* Note that **listen** is not followed directly by an object. You must always say that you listen **to** something. However, **listen** can also be used on its own without an object. ❑ *I was laughing too much to listen.* You use **hear** to talk about sounds that you are aware of because they reach your ears. You often use **can** with **hear**. ❑ *I can hear him yelling and swearing.*

▸ **listen in** PHRASAL VERB If you **listen in** to a private conversation, you secretly listen to it. 偷听 ❑ *He assigned federal agents to listen in on Martin Luther King's phone calls.* 他指派联邦特工去窃听马丁・路德・金的电话。

Thesaurus *listen* 另参见：

V. catch, pick up, tune in; (*ant.*) ignore 1
heed, mind 3

Word Partnership *listen* 的常用搭配：

V. listen **to** ***someone's*** **voice** 1
sit up and listen, **willing to** listen 1 – 3
ADV. listen **carefully**, listen **closely** 1 2

lis·ten·er /lɪsᵊnər, lɪsnər/ (**listeners**) 1 N-COUNT A **listener** is a person who listens to the radio or to a particular radio program. 听众 ❑ *I'm a regular listener to her show.* 我是她节目的一名固定听众。 2 N-COUNT If you describe someone as a good **listener**, you mean that they listen carefully and sympathetically to you when you talk, for example, about your problems. 倾听者 ❑ *Dr. Brian was a good listener.* 布赖恩医生是一位不错的倾听者。 3 → see also **listen**
→ see **radio**

list·less /lɪstlɪs/ ADJ Someone who is **listless** has no energy or enthusiasm. 无精打采的 ❑ *He was listless and pale and wouldn't eat much.* 他无精打采，脸色苍白，而且食欲不振。 ● **list·less·ly** ADV 无精打采地 [ADV with v] ❑ *Usually, you would just sit listlessly, too hot to do anything else.* 通常，你只会无精打采地坐着，热得干不了别的事情。

list price (**list prices**) N-COUNT The **list price** of an item is the price which the manufacturer suggests that a store should charge for it. 标价 ❑ *...a small car with a list price of $18,000.* …一辆标价为$18000的小汽车。

lit /lɪt/ **Lit** is a past tense and past participle of **light**. **light**的过去式和过去分词

li·ter /liːtər/ (**liters**)
in BRIT, use **litre**
N-COUNT A **liter** is a metric unit of volume that is a thousand cubic centimeters. It is equal to 2.11 pints. 升（公制容量单位）❑ *...a 13-thousand liter water tank.* …一个13000升的水箱。 ❑ *It is sold to the public at eight cents a liter.* 它以每升8美分的价格出售给公众。

lit·era·cy /lɪtərəsi/ N-UNCOUNT **Literacy** is the ability to read and write. 读写能力 ❑ *Many adults have problems with literacy and numeracy.* 很多成年人有读写和计算的困难。

Word Link *liter ≈ letter : illiterate, literal, literature*

★ **lit·er·al** /lɪtərəl/ 1 ADJ The **literal** sense of a word or phrase is its most basic sense. 字面上的 ❑ *In many cases, the people there are fighting, in a literal sense, for their homes.* 多数情况下，那里的人们实际上都是在为他们的家园而战斗。 2 ADJ A **literal** translation is one in which you translate each word of the original work rather than giving the meaning of each expression or sentence using words that sound natural. 按字面意思的 ❑ *A literal translation of the name Tapies is "walls."* 名字**Tapies**的字面翻译是"墙"。

lit·er·al·ly /lɪtərəli/ 1 ADV You can use **literally** to emphasize an exaggeration. Some careful speakers of English think that this use is incorrect. 真地 [EMPHASIS] ❑ *We've got to get the economy under control or it will literally eat us up.* 我们必须控制住经济，否则它真地就会把我们困住。 2 ADV You use **literally** to emphasize that what you are saying is true, even though it seems exaggerated or surprising. 确实地 [EMPHASIS] ❑ *Putting on an opera is a tremendous enterprise involving literally hundreds of people.* 上演一台话剧是一项巨大的事业，它确实要几百个人参与。 3 ADV If a word or expression is translated **literally**, its most simple or basic meaning is translated. 字面上地 ❑ *The word "volk" translates literally as "folk."* "**volk**"这个词照字面意思翻译为"**folk**"。

lit·er·ary ♦◇◇ /lɪtərɛri/ 1 ADJ **Literary** means concerned with or connected with the writing, study, or appreciation of literature. 文学的 ❑ *Her literary criticism focuses on the way great literature suggests ideas.* 她的文学批评集中于伟大文学作品表达思想的方法。 ❑ *She's the literary editor of the "Sunday Review."* 她是《周日评论》的文学编辑。 2 ADJ **Literary** words and expressions are often unusual in some way and are used to create a special effect in a piece of writing such as a poem, speech, or novel. 书面的 ❑ *...archaic, literary words from the Tang dynasty.* …唐代的古文书面用词。
→ see **book**

▲ **lit·er·ate** /lɪtərɪt/ 1 ADJ Someone who is **literate** is able to read and write. 能读会写的 ❑ *Over one-quarter of the adult population are not fully literate.* 四分之一以上的成年人是半文盲。 2 → see also **computer-literate**

lit·era·ture ♦◇◇ /lɪtərətʃər, -tʃʊr/ (**literatures**) 1 N-VAR Novels, plays, and poetry are referred to as **literature**, especially when they are considered to be good or important. 文学 ❑ *...classic works of literature.* …古典文学作品。 ❑ *I have spent my life getting to know diverse literatures of different epochs.* 我花费一生时间来逐渐了解不同时代形形色色的文学。 2 N-UNCOUNT **The literature** on a particular subject of study is all the books and articles that have been published about it. 文献 ❑ *...the literature on immigration policy.* …关于外来移民政策的文献。 3 N-UNCOUNT **Literature** is written information produced by people who want to sell you something or give you advice. 印刷品 ❑ *I am sending you literature from two other companies that provide a similar service.* 我在给你邮寄来自另外两家提供类似服务的公司的宣传单。
→ see **genre**

▲ **liti·ga·tion** /lɪtɪgeɪʃᵊn/ N-UNCOUNT **Litigation** is the process of fighting or defending a case in a civil court of law. 诉讼 ❑ *The settlement ends more than four years of litigation on behalf of the residents.* 这次和解结束了代表居民的长达四年多的诉讼。

li·tre /liːtər/ [BRIT] → see **liter**

★ **lit·ter** /lɪtər/ (**litters, littering, littered**) 1 N-UNCOUNT **Litter** is garbage or trash that is left lying around outside. 垃圾 ❑ *If you see litter in the corridor, pick it up.* 如果你看到走廊里有垃圾，就把它捡起来。 2 V-T If a number of things **litter** a place, they are scattered around it or over it. 散放在 ❑ *Glass from broken bottles litters the sidewalk.* 碎瓶子的玻璃渣散落在人行道上。 ● **lit·tered** ADJ 散放的 [v-link ADJ prep] ❑ *The entrance hall is littered with toys.* 入口大厅里散落着玩具。 3 ADJ If something is **littered with** things, it contains many examples of it. 充满的 [v-link ADJ "with" n] ❑ *History is* littered with men and women spurred into achievement by a father's disregard. 历史上常有受父亲漠视的刺激而取得成就的男男女女。 4 N-COUNT A **litter** is a group of animals born to the same mother at the same time. 一窝 ❑ ...a litter of pups. …一窝小狗。

Thesaurus *litter* 另参见：
N. clutter, debris, garbage, trash 1
V. clutter, scatter, strew 2

little
❶ DETERMINER, QUANTIFIER, AND ADVERB USES
❷ ADJECTIVE USES

❶ **lit·tle** ♦♦♦ /lɪtᵊl/ 1 DET You use **little** to indicate that there is only a very small amount of something. You can use "so," "too," and "very" in front of **little**. 微少的 ❑ *I had little money and little free time.* 我没什么钱，也很少有空闲时间。 ❑ *I find that I need very little sleep these days.* 我觉得我现在需要的睡眠很少。 ● QUANT **Little** is also a quantifier. 一点 [QUANT "of" def-n] ❑ *Little of the existing housing is of good enough quality.* 现有的住房中少有质量够好的。 ● PRON **Little** is also a pronoun. 少量 ❑ *He ate little, and drank less.* 他吃得不多，喝得更少。 ❑ *In general, employers do little to help the single working mother.* 总的来说，雇主很少帮助那些工作的单身妈妈们。 2 ADV **Little** means not very often or to only a small extent. 不多 [ADV with v] ❑ *On their way back to Marseille they spoke very little.* 在他们回马赛的路上，他们说话不多。 3 DET **A little** of something is a small amount of it, but not very much. You can also say **a very little**. 一点儿 ❑ *Mrs. Caan needs a little help getting her groceries home.* 凯恩夫人需要一点儿帮助才能把杂货弄回家。 ❑ *A little food would do us all some good.* 吃一点儿东西会对我们大家都有些好处。 ● PRON **Little** is also a pronoun. 一点儿 ❑ *They get paid for it. Not much. Just a little.* 他们拿到工资了。不太多，就一点点。 ● QUANT **Little** is also a quantifier. 一点 ❑ *Pour a little of the sauce over the chicken.* 往鸡肉上倒一点调料。 4 ADV If you do something **a little**, you do it for a short time. 一小会儿 [ADV after v] ❑ *He walked a little by himself in the garden.* 他在花园里独自散了会儿步。 5 ADV **A little** or **a little bit** means to a small extent or degree. (程度上) 有点 ❑ *He complained a little of a nagging pain between his shoulder blades.* 他抱怨说他的肩胛之间有点持续的疼痛。 ❑ *He was a little bit afraid of his father's reaction.* 他有点害怕他父亲的反应。

You can use the adjective **little** to talk about things that are small. ❑ *...a little house. ...little children.* However, **little** is not normally used to emphasize or draw attention to the fact that something is small. For instance, you do not usually say "The town is little" or "I have a very little car," but you can say "**The town is small**" or "**I have a very small car.**" **Little** is a less precise word than **small**, and may be used to suggest the speaker's feelings or attitude toward the person or thing being described. For that reason, **little** is often used after another adjective. ❑ *What a nice little house you've got here!... Shut up, you horrible little boy!* **Little** and **a little** are both used as determiners in front of uncount nouns, but they do not have the same meaning. For example, if you say "**I have a little money**," this is a positive statement and you are saying that you have some money. However, if you say "**I have little money**," this is a negative statement and you are saying that you have almost no money.

❷ **lit·tle** ♦♦♦ /lɪtᵊl/ (littler, littlest)

The comparative **littler** and the superlative **littlest** are sometimes used in spoken English for meanings 1, 3, and 4, but otherwise the comparative and superlative forms of the adjective **little** are not used.

1 ADJ **Little** things are small in size. **Little** is slightly more informal than **small**. (尺寸) 小的 ❑ *We sat around a little table, eating and drinking wine.* 我们围坐在一张小桌子旁吃饭、喝酒。 2 ADJ You use **little** to indicate that someone or something is small, in a pleasant and attractive way. 小巧的 [ADJ n] ❑ *She's got the nicest little house not far from the library.* 她在离图书馆不远处有座最漂亮的小房子。 ❑ *...a little old lady.* …一位娇小的老太太。 3 ADJ Your **little** sister or brother is younger than you are. 年纪小的 [ADJ n] ❑ *Whenever Daniel's little sister was asked to do something she always had a naughty reply.* 每次让丹尼尔的小妹妹做点事情，她总是有调皮的回应。 4 ADJ **A little** distance, period of time, or event is short in length. (时间、距离、比赛) 短的 [ADJ n] ❑ *Just go down the road a little way, turn left, and cross the bridge.* 只沿着公路走一小段距离，向左转，然后跨过那座桥。 ❑ *Why don't we just wait a little while and see what happens.* 我们何不就等一小会儿，看看发生什么事。 5 ADJ A **little** sound or gesture is quick. (声音或动作) 迅速的 [ADJ n] ❑ *I had a little laugh to myself.* 我暗自笑了笑。 6 ADJ You use **little** to indicate that something is not serious or important. 微小的 [ADJ n] ❑ *...irritating little habits.* …恼人的小习惯。

Thesaurus *little* 另参见：
DET. bit, dab, hint, touch, trace ❶ 3
ADJ. miniature, petite, slight, small, young; (*ant.*) big ❷ 1
casual, insignificant, minor, small, unimportant; (*ant.*) important ❷ 6

live
❶ VERB USES
❷ ADJECTIVE USES

❶ **live** ♦♦♦ /lɪv/ (lives, living, lived)
➪ **Please look at meaning 8 to see if the expression you are looking for is shown under another headword.** 1 V-I If someone **lives** in a particular place or with a particular person, their home is in that place or with that person. 居住 ❑ *She has lived here for 10 years.* 她在这里住了10年了。 ❑ *Where do you live?* 你住在哪里？ 2 V-T/V-I If you say that someone **lives** in particular circumstances or that they **live** a particular kind of life, you mean that they are in those circumstances or that they have that kind of life. 生活 ❑ *We lived quite grandly.* 我们生活得相当快乐。 ❑ *Compared to people living only a few generations ago, we have greater opportunities to have a good time.* 与生活在仅仅几代之前的人相比，我们有更大的过得快乐的机会。 3 V-I If you say that someone **lives for** a particular thing, you mean that it is the most important thing in their life. (为…而) 活 ❑ *He lived for his work.* 他为了工作而活。 4 V-T/V-I To **live** means to be alive. If someone **lives to** a particular age, they stay alive until they are that age. 活着 ❑ *He's got a terrible disease and will not live long.* 他得了一种重病，活不长了。 ❑ *He lived to be 103.* 他活到了103岁。 5 V-I If people **live by** doing a particular activity, they get the money, food, or clothing they need by doing that activity. 以…为生 [no cont] ❑ *...the last indigenous people to live by hunting.* …最后一个以打猎为生的土著民族。 6 → see also **living** 7 PHRASE If you **live it up**, you have a very enjoyable and exciting time, for example by going to lots of parties or going out drinking with friends. 尽情玩乐 [INFORMAL] ❑ *There is no reason why you couldn't live it up once in a while.* 没有理由不让你偶尔尽情玩乐一下的。 8 to **live hand to mouth** → see **hand**

When you are talking about someone's home, the verb **live** has a different meaning in the continuous tenses than it does in the simple tenses. For example, if you say "**I'm living in Boston,**" this suggests that the situation is temporary and you may soon move to a different place. If you say "**I live in Boston,**" this suggests that Boston is your permanent home.

▸ **live down** PHRASAL VERB If you are unable to **live down** a mistake, failure, or bad reputation, you are unable to make people forget about it. (无法) 使人忘记 (自己的错误、失败、恶名) ❑ *It was unable to live down its reputation as the party of high taxes.* 它无法让人忘掉其高赋税政党的恶名。

▸ **live off** PHRASAL VERB If you **live off** another person, you rely on them to provide you with money. 依赖 (某人) 生活 ❑ *...a man who all his life had lived off his father.* …一个终生依赖他父亲生活的男人。

▸ **live on** or **live off** 1 PHRASAL VERB If you **live on** or **live off** a particular amount of money, you have that amount of money to buy things. 靠 (某数额的钱) 过活 ❑ *...people trying to live on $100 a week.* …设法靠每周$100过日子的人们。 2 PHRASAL VERB If you **live on** or **live off** a particular source of income, that is where you get the money that you need. 以…为收入来源 ❑ *The proportion of Americans living on welfare rose.* 靠福利生活的美国人的比例上升了。 3 PHRASAL VERB If an animal **lives on** or **lives off** a particular food, this is the kind of food that it eats. 以…为主食 ❑ *The fish live on the plankton.* 这种鱼以浮游生物为主食。

▸ **live on** PHRASAL VERB If someone **lives on**, they continue to be alive for a long time after a particular point in time or after a particular event. 继续生活 ❑ *I know my life has been cut short by this terrible virus but Daniel will live on after me.* 我知道我的寿命已被这种可怕的病毒缩短了，但是丹尼尔会在我之后继续生活下去。

▸ **live up to** PHRASAL VERB If someone or something **lives up to** what they were expected to be, they are as good as they were expected to be. 达到 ❑ *Sales have not lived up to expectations this year.* 销售额今年还没有达到预期目标。

❷ **live** ♦◇◇ /laɪv/ 1 ADJ **Live** animals or plants are alive, rather than being dead or artificial. 活的 [ADJ n] ❑ *...a protest against the company's tests on live animals.* …反对该公司对活的动物进行实验的抗议。 2 ADJ A **live** television or radio program is one in which an event or performance is broadcast at exactly the same time as it happens, rather than being recorded first. 现场直播的 ❑ *Murray was a guest on a live radio show.* 默里曾是一个无线电直播节目的嘉宾。 ❑ *They watch all the live matches.* 他们观看所有现场直播的比赛。 ● ADV **Live** is also an adverb. 现场直播地 [ADV after v] ❑ *It was broadcast live in 50 countries.* 它在50个国家进行了现场直播。 3 ADJ A **live** performance is given in front of an audience, rather than being recorded and then broadcast or shown in a movie. 现场表演的 ❑ *The Rainbow has not hosted live music since the end of 1981.* 彩虹乐队自1981年底以来还没有举办过现场音乐会。 ❑ *A live audience will pose the questions.* 一位现场观众将会提些问题。 ● ADV **Live** is also an adverb. 现场表演地 [ADV after v] ❑ *Kat Bjelland has been playing live with her new band.* 凯特・本杰拉德与她的新乐团一直在进行现场表演。 4 ADJ A **live** wire or piece of electrical equipment is directly connected to a source of electricity. 带电的 ❑ *The plug broke, exposing live wires.* 插头坏了，露出带电的电线。 5 ADJ **Live** bullets are made of metal, rather than rubber or plastic, and are intended to kill people rather than injure them. 实(弹) 的 ❑ *They trained in the jungle using live ammunition.* 他们在丛林里使用真枪实弹进行训练。

Thesaurus *live* 另参见：

V.	dwell, inhabit, occupy, reside ❶ 1
	manage, subsist, survive ❶ 2 5
	exist ❶ 4
ADJ.	active, alive, living, vigorous ❷ 1

live-in ♦◇◇ /lɪv ɪn/ 1 ADJ A **live-in** partner is someone who lives in the same house as the person they are having a sexual relationship with, but is not married to them. 未婚同居的 [ADJ n] ❑ *She shared the apartment with her live-in partner.* 她和她的同居伴侣一起住在这个公寓里。 2 ADJ A **live-in** servant or other domestic worker sleeps and eats in the house where they work. 在雇主家吃住的 [ADJ n] ❑ *I have a live-in nanny for my youngest daughter.* 我为我最小的女儿雇了一个在家吃住的保姆。

★ **live·li·hood** /laɪvlihʊd/ (**livelihoods**) N-VAR Your **livelihood** is the job or other source of income that gives you the money to buy the things you need. 生计 ❑ *...fishermen who depend on the seas for their livelihood.* …依靠大海谋生的渔夫。

live·ly /laɪvli/ (**livelier, liveliest**) 1 ADJ You can describe someone as **lively** when they behave in an enthusiastic and cheerful way. 活泼的 ❑ *She had a sweet, lively personality.* 她有着可爱活泼的性格。 ● **live·li·ness** N-UNCOUNT 活泼 ❑ *Amy could sense his liveliness even from where she stood.* 艾米甚至能从她所站的地方感受到他的勃勃生气。 2 ADJ A **lively** event or a **lively** discussion, for example, has lots of interesting and exciting things happening or being said in it. 热烈的 ❑ *It turned out to be a very interesting session with a lively debate.* 结果成了一次充满激烈辩论、非常有意思的会议。 ● **live·li·ness** N-UNCOUNT 热烈 ❑ *Some may enjoy the liveliness of such a restaurant for a few hours a day or week.* 有人每天或每周都会来这样一个餐馆，享受几小时热烈氛围。 3 ADJ Someone who has a **lively** mind is intelligent and interested in a lot of different things. 活跃的 ❑ *She was a very well educated girl with a lively mind, a girl with ambition.* 她是一个非常有教养、头脑活跃、有抱负的女孩。

Word Partnership *lively* 的常用搭配：

ADV.	very lively 1 – 3
N.	lively **atmosphere**, lively **conversation**, lively **debate**, lively **discussion**, lively **music**, lively **performance** 2 lively **imagination**, lively **interest**, lively **sense of humor** 3

liv·en /laɪvᵊn/ (**livens, livening, livened**)

▸ **liven up** 1 PHRASAL VERB If a place or event **livens up**, or if something **livens it up**, it becomes more interesting and exciting. 变得更有生气；使…更有生气 ❑ *How could we decorate the room to liven it up?* 我们怎样才能把这房间装饰得更有生气呢？ ❑ *The multicolored rag rug was chosen to liven up the gray carpet.* 挑选了多彩的碎呢毯子来使灰色地毯更有生气。 2 PHRASAL VERB If people **liven up**, or if something **livens them up**, they become more cheerful and energetic. (人) 更有生气 ❑ *Talking about her daughters livens her up.* 谈到她的女儿们使她更加神采飞扬。

liv·er /lɪvər/ (**livers**) 1 N-COUNT Your **liver** is a large organ in your body which processes your blood and helps to clean unwanted substances out of it. 肝脏 ❑ *Three weeks ago, it was discovered the cancer had spread to his liver.* 三周前，发现癌已扩散到了他的肝脏。 2 N-VAR **Liver** is the liver of some animals, especially lambs, pigs, and cows, which is cooked and eaten. (供食用的动物) 肝脏 ❑ *...grilled calves' liver.* …烤牛肝。

→ see **donor**

lives

Pronounced /laɪvz/ for meaning 1, and /lɪvz/ for meaning 2.

义项1读作 /laɪvz/，义项2读作 /lɪvz/。

1 **Lives** is the plural of **life**. **life**的复数形式 2 **Lives** is the third person singular form of **live**. **live**的第三人称单数形式

▲ **live·stock** /laɪvstɒk/ N-UNCOUNT-COLL Animals such as cattle and sheep which are kept on a farm are referred to as **livestock**. 家畜 ❑ *The heavy rains and flooding killed scores of livestock.* 大雨和洪水淹死了许多家畜。

liv·id /lɪvɪd/ ADJ Someone who is **livid** is extremely angry. 狂怒的 [INFORMAL] ❑ *I am absolutely livid about it.* 我对此恼怒至极。

liv·ing ♦◇◇ /lɪvɪŋ/ (**livings**) 1 N-COUNT The work that you do for a **living** is the work that you do in order to earn the money that you need. 生计 ❑ *Father never talked about what he did for a living.* 父亲从未谈起他是做什么来谋生的。 2 N-UNCOUNT You use **living** when you are talking about the quality of people's daily lives. 生活质量 ❑ *Olivia has always been a model of healthy living.* 奥利维亚一直是健康生活的榜样。 3 ADJ You use **living** to talk about the places where people relax when they are not working. 居住的 [ADJ n] ❑ *The spacious living quarters were on the second floor.* 宽敞的起居间在二楼。

liv·ing room (**living rooms**) also **living-room** N-COUNT The **living room** in a house is the room where people sit and relax. 起居室 ❑ *We were sitting on the couch in the living room watching TV.* 我们那时正坐在起居室的沙发上看电视。

→ see **house**

liz·ard /lɪzərd/ (**lizards**) N-COUNT A **lizard** is a reptile with short legs and a long tail. 蜥蜴

→ see **desert**

load ♦◇◇ /loʊd/ (**loads, loading, loaded**) 1 V-T If you **load** a vehicle or a container, you put a large quantity of things into it. (向车辆或容器里) 大量装入 ❑ *The three men seemed to have finished loading the truck.* 这3个人好像已经装好了那辆卡车。 ❑ *Mr. Dambar had loaded his plate with lasagne.* 丹巴先生已经往他的盘子里盛了很多意大利千层面。 2 N-COUNT A **load** is something, usually a large quantity or heavy object, which is being carried. 装载物 ❑ *He drove by with a big load of hay.* 他开着装满干草的车过去了。 3 QUANT If you refer to **a load of** people or things or **loads of** them, you are emphasizing that there are a lot of them. 许多 [INFORMAL, EMPHASIS] ❑ *I've got loads of money.* 我有许多钱。 ❑ *...a load of kids.* …许多小孩。 4 V-T When someone **loads** a weapon such as a gun, they put a bullet or missile in it so that it is ready to use. (给武器) 装弹药 ❑ *I knew how to load and handle a gun.* 我知道怎么装子弹和使用枪支。 ❑ *He carried a loaded gun.* 他带着一支装了子弹的枪。 5 V-T To **load** a camera or other piece of equipment means to put film, tape, or data into it so that it is ready to use. 装填 (胶卷、磁带或数据) ❑ *A photographer from the newspaper was loading his camera with film.* 那家报社的一个摄影师正在给他的摄像机装胶卷。 6 N-COUNT You can refer to the amount of work you have to do as a **load**. 工作量 ❑ *She's taking some of the load off the secretaries.* 她正给秘书们减少一些工作量。 7 N-COUNT The **load** of a system or piece of equipment, especially a system supplying electricity or a computer, is the extent to which it is being used at a particular time. 负荷量 ❑ *An efficient bulb may lighten the load of power stations.* 节能灯可减轻发电站的负荷。 8 N-SING The **load on** something is the amount of weight that is pressing down on it or the amount of strain that it is under. 压力 ❑ *Some of these chairs have flattened feet which spread the load on the ground.* 这些椅子中有些是平脚的，这样可分散地面所受的压力。 9 → see also **loaded** 10 **a load off** your **mind** → see **mind**

→ see **photography**

L

▸ **load down** PHRASAL VERB If you **load** someone **down** with things, especially heavy things, you give them a large number of them or put a large number of them on them. 使负重 ❑ *She loaded me down with around a dozen cassettes.* 她给我的十几个盒子加重了我的负担。❑ *They had come up from London loaded down with six suitcases.* 他们带着6个手提箱从伦敦来。

▸ **load up** PHRASAL VERB **Load up** means the same as **load**. (向车辆或容器里) 大量装入 ❑ *I've just loaded my truck up.* 我刚刚装完我的卡车。❑ *The giggling couple loaded up their red sports car and drove off.* 这对笑哈哈的夫妇装好他们的红色跑车，开走了。

Thesaurus *load* 另参见：
V. arrange, fill, pack, pile up, stack 1
N. bundle, cargo, freight, haul, shipment 2

Word Partnership *load* 的常用搭配：
N. load **a truck** 1
ADJ. **big** load, **full** load, **heavy** load 2 6
V. **carry a** load, **handle a** load, **lighten a** load, **take on a** load 2 6

load·ed /loʊdɪd/ 1 ADJ A **loaded** question or word has more meaning or purpose than it appears to have, because the person who uses it hopes it will cause people to respond in a particular way. 有深意的 ❑ *That's a loaded question.* 那是一个意味深长的问题。 2 ADJ If something is **loaded with** a particular characteristic, it has that characteristic to a very great degree. 充满 (某特性的) 的 ❑ *The president's visit is loaded with symbolic significance.* 总统的访问富有象征意义。 3 ADJ If a place or object is **loaded with** things, it has very many of them in it or it is full of them. 装满的 ❑ *...a tray loaded with cups.* …一个盛满杯子的托盘。❑ *The second store you enter is loaded with jewelry.* 你进入的第二家商店满是珠宝首饰。 4 ADJ If you say that something is **loaded in favor of** someone, you mean it works unfairly to their advantage. If you say it is **loaded against** them, you mean it works unfairly to their disadvantage. 有偏向的 [DISAPPROVAL] ❑ *The press is loaded in favor of this present government.* 新闻界倾向于现任政府。 5 ADJ If someone is **loaded**, they are intoxicated as a result of drinking alcohol or taking drugs. 喝醉的；(吸毒) 亢奋的 [INFORMAL] ❑ *We gather as a group once or twice a year, for old times' sake, and get loaded.* 为了过去的时光我们每年都会聚一两次，并喝得大醉。

loaf /loʊf/ (**loaves, loafs, loafing, loafed**) 1 N-COUNT A **loaf** of bread is bread which has been shaped and baked in one piece. It is usually large enough for more than one person and can be cut into slices. (一) 条 (面包) ❑ *...a loaf of crusty bread.* …一条硬皮面包。 2 V-I If you **loaf**, you spend time in a lazy way, doing nothing in particular, especially when you should be working. 闲着 ❑ *There were always a lot of men loafing in the shop.* 总有许多人在商店里闲逛。

loan ♦♦◊ /loʊn/ (**loans, loaning, loaned**) 1 N-COUNT A **loan** is a sum of money that you borrow. 贷款 ❑ *The country has no access to foreign loans or financial aid.* 该国得不到外国贷款或财政援助。❑ *The president wants to make it easier for small businesses to get bank loans.* 总统想使小公司能更容易地获得银行贷款。 2 → see also **bridge loan, soft loan** 3 N-SING If someone gives you a **loan of** something, you borrow it from them. 借用 ❑ *I am in need of a loan of a bike for a few weeks.* 我需要借辆自行车来用几周。 4 V-T If you **loan** something to someone, you lend it to them. 借出 ❑ *He had kindly offered to loan us all the plants required for the exhibit.* 他友好地主动提出了借给我们展览会所需的全部植物。● PHRASAL VERB **Loan out** means the same as **loan**. 借出 ❑ *It is common practice for clubs to loan out players to sides in the lower divisions.* 将球员借给下级球队是俱乐部的惯例。 5 PHRASE If something is **on loan**, it has been borrowed. 借来的 ❑ *...impressionist paintings on loan from the National Gallery.* …从国家美术馆借来的印象派画作。

→ see **bank, interest rate**

Word Partnership *loan* 的常用搭配：
N. loan **agreement**, loan **application**, **bank** loan, **home** loan, **interest on a** loan, **mortgage** loan, loan **payment/repayment**, **savings and** loan, **student** loan 1
V. **apply for a** loan, **get/receive a** loan, **make a** loan, **pay off a** loan, **repay a** loan 1

loath /loʊθ/ also **loth** ADJ If you are **loath to** do something, you do not want to do it. 不情愿的 [v-link ADJ to-inf] ❑ *Sensing he held the advantage, Mr. Danbar was loath to change the subject.* 丹巴先生觉得占有优势，不愿改变话题。

loathe /loʊð/ (**loathes, loathing, loathed**) V-T If you **loathe** something or someone, you dislike them very much. 厌恶 ❑ *The two men loathe each other.* 这两个男人相互厌恶。

loath·ing /loʊðɪŋ/ N-UNCOUNT **Loathing** is a feeling of great dislike and disgust. 憎恶 ❑ *She looked at him with loathing.* 她憎恶地看着他。

loaves /loʊvz/ **Loaves** is the plural of **loaf**. **loaf**的复数形式

lob·by ♦◊◊ /lɒbi/ (**lobbies, lobbying, lobbied**) 1 V-T/V-I If you **lobby** someone such as a member of a government or council, you try to persuade them that a particular law should be changed or that a particular thing should be done. 游说 ❑ *The Wilderness Society lobbied Congress to authorize the Endangered Species Act.* 荒野协会游说国会批准《濒危物种法》。 2 N-COUNT A **lobby** is a group of people who represent a particular organization or campaign, and try to persuade a government or council to help or support them. 游说团体 ❑ *Agricultural interests are some of the most powerful lobbies in Washington.* 农业利益集团是华盛顿最有影响力的游说团体中的一部分。 3 N-COUNT In a hotel or other large building, the **lobby** is the area near the entrance that usually has corridors and staircases leading off it. 大厅 ❑ *I met her in the lobby of the museum.* 我在博物馆大厅遇到了她。

▲ **lob·ster** /lɒbstər/ (**lobsters**) N-VAR A **lobster** is a sea creature that has a hard shell, two large claws, and eight legs. 龙虾 ❑ *She sold me a couple of live lobsters.* 她卖给了我几只活龙虾。● N-UNCOUNT **Lobster** is the flesh of a lobster eaten as food. 龙虾肉 ❑ *...lobster on a bed of fresh vegetables.* …放在一层新鲜蔬菜上的龙虾肉。

lo·cal ♦♦♦ /loʊkᵊl/ (**locals**) 1 ADJ **Local** means existing in or belonging to the area where you live, or to the area that you are talking about. 本地的；当地的 [ADJ n] ❑ *We'd better check on the game in the local paper.* 我们最好在本地报纸上查一下这场比赛。❑ *Some local residents joined the students' protest.* 一些当地居民加入了学生的抗议活动。● N-COUNT The **locals** are local people. 当地居民 ❑ *Camping is a great way to meet the locals as the Portuguese themselves are enthusiastic campers.* 野营是与当地居民接触的好途径，因为葡萄牙人本身就是热情的露营者。● **lo·cal·ly** ADV 在当地 ❑ *We've got cards which are drawn and printed and designed by someone locally.* 我们得到了由某人在当地绘制、印刷和设计的纸牌。 2 ADJ **Local** government is elected by people in one area of a country and controls aspects such as education, housing, and transportation within that area. 地方的 ❑ *Education comprises two-thirds of all local government spending.* 教育经费占地方政府所有开销的2/3。 3 ADJ A **local** anesthetic or condition affects only a small area of your body. (身体上) 局部的 [MEDICAL] ❑ *The procedure was done under local anesthetic in the physician's office.* 在医师诊所里经过局部麻醉完成了手术。

Thesaurus *local* 另参见：
ADJ. neighboring, regional 1

Word Partnership *local* 的常用搭配：
N. local **area**, local **artist**, local **business**, local ***phone* call**, local **community**, local **customs**, local **group**, local **hospital**, local **library**, local **news**, local **newspaper**, local **office**, local **people**, local **residents**, local **restaurant**, local **store** 1
local **government**, local **officials**, local **police**, local **politicians**, local **politics** 2

lo·cal area net·work (**local area networks**) N-COUNT A **local area network** is a group of computers and associated equipment that are linked by cable, for example, in an office building, and that share a communications line. The abbreviation **LAN** is also used. 局域网 [COMPUTING] ❑ *Users can easily move files between PCs connected by local area networks or the Internet.* 用户可以轻松地在局域网或互联网连接的个人电脑之间传送文件。

lo·cal author·ity ♦◊◊ (**local authorities**) N-COUNT A **local authority** is the same as a **local government**. 地方当局

lo·cal gov·ern·ment (**local governments**) 1 N-UNCOUNT **Local government** is the system of electing representatives to be responsible for the administration of public services and facilities in a particular area. 地方政府 ❑ *...careers in local government.*

L

…在地方政府的职业生涯。 **2** N-COUNT A **local government** is an organization that is officially responsible for all the public services and facilities in a particular area. 地方当局 [AM]

in BRIT, use **local authority**

★ **lo·cal·ity** /loʊkælɪti/ (**localities**) N-COUNT A **locality** is a small area of a country or city. (小片) 地区 [FORMAL] ❑ *Following the discovery of the explosives the president canceled his visit to the locality.* 发现爆炸物之后总统取消了对该地区的访问。

lo·cate /loʊkeɪt/ (**locates, locating, located**) **1** V-T If you **locate** something or someone, you find out where they are. 找到 [FORMAL] ❑ *The scientists want to locate the position of the gene on a chromosome.* 科学家们想找到该基因在染色体上的位置。 **2** V-T If you **locate** something in a particular place, you put it there or build it there. 把…建在 [FORMAL] ❑ *Atlanta was voted the best city in which to locate a business by more than 400 chief executives.* 亚特兰大被四百多位企业首席执行官投票选为建立公司的最佳城市。 **3** V-I If you **locate** in a particular place, you move there or open a business there. 定居；营业 [mainly AM, BUSINESS] ❑ *...tax breaks for businesses that locate in run-down neighborhoods.* …对在衰落地段营业的公司的减税。

lo·cat·ed /loʊkeɪtɪd/ ADJ If something is **located** in a particular place, it is present or has been built there. 位于…的 [v-link ADJ prep, adv ADJ] [FORMAL] ❑ *A boutique and beauty salon are conveniently located within the grounds.* 时装与美容店就在院内，很方便。

lo·ca·tion ♦◇◇ /loʊkeɪʃ°n/ (**locations**) **1** N-COUNT A **location** is the place where something happens or is situated. 地点 ❑ *The first thing he looked at was his office's location.* 他最先关注的是其办公室的位置。 **2** N-COUNT The **location** of someone or something is their exact position. 准确位置 ❑ *She knew the exact location of The Eagle's headquarters.* 她知道"飞鹰"总部的准确位置。 **3** N-VAR A **location** is a place away from a studio where a movie or part of a movie is made. 外景拍摄地 ❑ *...an art movie with dozens of exotic locations.* …一部含有许多异国外景的艺术电影。

Word Partnership *location* 的常用搭配:
- ADJ. **central** location, **convenient** location, **secret** location **1**
  exact location, **geographic** location, **present** location, **specific** location **2**
- V. **pinpoint a** location **1** **2**

loch /lɒx, lɒk/ (**lochs**) N-COUNT A **loch** is a large area of water in Scotland that is completely or almost completely surrounded by land. (苏格兰的) 湖泊 ❑ *...twenty miles north of Loch Ness.* …尼斯湖以北20英里。

lock ♦◇◇ /lɒk/ (**locks, locking, locked**) **1** V-T When you **lock** something such as a door, drawer, or case, you fasten it, usually with a key, so that other people cannot open it. 锁 ❑ *Are you sure you locked the front door?* 你确定锁前门了吗？ **2** N-COUNT The **lock** on something such as a door or a drawer is the device which is used to keep it shut and prevent other people from opening it. Locks are opened with a key. 锁 ❑ *At that moment he heard Gill's key turning in the lock of the door.* 那时他听到吉尔的钥匙在门锁里转动的声音。 **3** V-T If you **lock** something or someone in a place, room, or container, you put them there and fasten the lock. 将…锁起来 ❑ *Her maid locked the case in the safe.* 她的女仆把那盒子锁进了保险箱。 **4** V-T/V-I If you **lock** something in a particular position, or if it **locks** there, it is held or fitted firmly in that position. 锁定 ❑ *He leaned back in the swivel chair and locked his fingers behind his head.* 他向后靠在转椅上，两手手指交叉锁定在脑后。 **5** N-COUNT On a canal or river, a **lock** is a place where walls have been built with gates at each end so that boats can move to a higher or lower section of the canal or river, by gradually changing the water level inside the gates. 水闸 ❑ *As the lock filled, the ducklings rejoined their mother to wait for another vessel to go through.* 水闸里注满水时，小鸭子们回到它们的妈妈身旁等待另一艘船通过。 **6** N-COUNT A **lock of** hair is a small bunch of hairs on your head that grow together and curl or curve in the same direction. (一) 绺 ❑ *She brushed a lock of hair off his forehead.* 她拂开他额头的一绺头发。

▸ **lock away** **1** PHRASAL VERB If you **lock** something **away** in a place or container, you put or hide it there and fasten the lock. 把…锁藏起来 ❑ *She meticulously cleaned the gun and locked it away in its case.* 她小心翼翼地把那把枪擦干净，并把它锁藏在枪盒里。 **2** PHRASAL VERB To **lock** someone **away** means to put them in prison or a secure mental hospital. 把…关进 (监狱、精神病院等) ❑ *Locking them away is not sufficient, you have to give them treatment.* 把他们关起来是不够的，你必须给他们治疗。

▸ **lock out** **1** PHRASAL VERB If someone **locks** you **out** of a place, they prevent you entering it by locking the doors. 把…关在门外 ❑ *His wife locked him out of their bedroom after the argument.* 争吵之后妻子把他关在他们的卧室外面。 **2** PHRASAL VERB In an industrial dispute, if a company **locks** its workers **out**, it closes the factory or office in order to prevent the employees coming to work. (雇主) 不准 (员工) 进入工作场所 [BUSINESS] ❑ *The company locked out the workers, and then the rest of the work force went on strike.* 公司把那些工人拒之门外，接着其余工人举行了罢工。

▸ **lock up** **1** PHRASAL VERB If you **lock** something **up** in a place or container, you put or hide it there and fasten the lock. 把…锁藏起来 ❑ *Give away any food you have on hand, or lock it up and give the key to the neighbors.* 把你手头的食物分发送人，或锁藏起来，把钥匙交给邻居们。 **2** PHRASAL VERB To **lock** someone **up** means to put them in prison or a secure psychiatric hospital. 把…关入 (监狱、精神病院等) ❑ *Mr. Milner persuaded the federal prosecutors not to lock up his client.* 米尔纳先生说服联邦检查官不要把他的当事人关起来。 **3** PHRASAL VERB When you **lock up** a building or car or **lock up**, you make sure that all the doors and windows are locked so that nobody can get in. 锁好 (房子门窗或汽车) ❑ *Don't forget to lock up.* 别忘记锁好。

Word Partnership *lock* 的常用搭配:
- N. lock **a car**, lock **a door**, lock **a room** **1**
  combination lock, **door** lock, lock **and key**, **key in a** lock **2**
- V. **change a** lock, **open a** lock, **pick a** lock **2**

▲ **lock·er** /lɒkər/ (**lockers**) N-COUNT A **locker** is a small metal or wooden cabinet with a lock, where you can put your personal possessions, for example in a school, place of work, or sports club. 锁柜

lock·out (**lockouts**)

in BRIT, use **lock-out**

N-COUNT A **lockout** is a situation in which employers close a place of work and prevent workers from entering it until the workers accept the employer's new proposals on pay or conditions of work. (雇主为逼迫工人接受新的薪酬、工作条件而进行的) 闭厂停业 [BUSINESS] ❑ *The lockout could resume if no new contract agreement is signed.* 如果不签定新的合同协议，闭厂停业可能再次发生。

★ **lo·co·mo·tive** /loʊkəmoʊtɪv/ (**locomotives**) N-COUNT A **locomotive** is a large vehicle that pulls a train. 火车头 [FORMAL] → see **train**

★ **lo·cust** /loʊkəst/ (**locusts**) N-COUNT **Locusts** are large insects, similar to grasshoppers, that live mainly in hot areas and often cause serious damage to crops. 蝗虫 ❑ *...a swarm of locusts.* …一群蝗虫。

lodge /lɒdʒ/ (**lodges, lodging, lodged**) **1** N-COUNT A **lodge** is a house or hotel in the country or in the mountains where people stay on vacation, especially when they want to hunt or fish. (乡野中的度假) 屋舍；旅馆 ❑ *...a Victorian hunting lodge.* …一间维多利亚式的小屋。 **2** N-COUNT A **lodge** is a small house at the entrance to the grounds of a large house. 门房 ❑ *I drove out of the gates, past the keeper's lodge.* 我开车出了大门，经过看门人的门房。 **3** V-T If you **lodge** a complaint, protest, accusation, or claim, you officially make it. 正式提出 (投诉、抗议、指控、要求) ❑ *He has four weeks in which to lodge an appeal.* 他有4周时间来正式提出上诉。 **4** V-T/V-I If you **lodge** somewhere, such as in someone else's house or if you **are lodged** there, you live there, usually paying rent. 借住；租住 ❑ *...the story of the farming family she lodged with as a young teacher.* …关于她还是个年轻老师时所借住的那个农家的故事。 **5** V-I If an object **lodges** somewhere, it becomes stuck there. 卡住 ❑ *The bullet lodged in the sergeant's leg, shattering his thigh bone.* 子弹射入这个军士的腿部，击碎了他的大腿骨。 **6** → see also **lodging**

Word Partnership *lodge* 的常用搭配:
- N. **country** lodge, **hunting** lodge, **ski** lodge **1**

lodg·er /lɒdʒər/ (**lodgers**) N-COUNT A **lodger** is a person who pays money to live in someone else's house. 房客 ❑ *Jennie took in a lodger to help with the mortgage.* 詹妮招了一名房客来为她分担房屋贷款。

lodg·ing /lɒdʒɪŋ/ (**lodgings**) N-UNCOUNT If you are provided with **lodging** or **lodgings**, you are provided with a place to stay for a period of time. You can use **lodgings** to refer to one or more of these places. 寄宿处 [also N in pl] ❑ *He was given free lodging.* 他得到了免费住宿。

loft /lɔft/ (**lofts**) 1 N-COUNT A **loft** is the space inside the sloping roof of a house or other building, where things are sometimes stored. 阁楼 ❑ *A loft conversion can add considerably to the value of a house.* 阁楼改建能大大增加房屋价值。 2 N-COUNT A **loft** is an apartment in the upper part of a building, especially a building such as a warehouse or factory that has been converted for people to live in. Lofts are usually large and not divided into separate rooms. 顶楼寓所 ❑ *...Andy Warhol's New York loft.* …安迪・沃霍尔在纽约的顶楼寓所。

★ **lofty** /lɔfti/ (**loftier, loftiest**) 1 ADJ A **lofty** ideal or ambition is noble, important, and admirable. 崇高的 ❑ *It was a bank that started out with grand ideas and lofty ideals.* 那是一家创办时带着宏大理念、崇高理想的银行。 2 ADJ A **lofty** building or room is very high. 高耸的 [FORMAL] ❑ *...a light, lofty apartment in the suburbs of Salzburg.* …位于萨尔茨堡郊外的一幢光线充足、高高耸立的公寓。 3 ADJ If you say that someone behaves in a **lofty** way, you are critical of them for behaving in a proud and somewhat overbearing way, as if they think they are very important. 高傲的 [DISAPPROVAL] ❑ *...the lofty disdain he often expresses for his profession.* …他经常表露出的对其职业的轻慢。

log /lɔg/ (**logs, logging, logged**) 1 N-COUNT A **log** is a piece of a thick branch or of the trunk of a tree that has been cut so that it can be used for fuel or for making things. 木柴; 原木 ❑ *He dumped the logs on the big stone hearth.* 他把木柴扔进那个大石炉里。 2 N-COUNT A **log** is an official written account of what happens each day, for example, on board a ship. 日志 ❑ *The family made an official complaint to a ship's officer, which was recorded in the log.* 这家人向一位高级船员提出过正式投诉，此事记入了航行日志。 3 V-T If you **log** an event or fact, you record it officially in writing or on a computer. 把…载入日志 ❑ *They log everyone and everything that comes in and out of here.* 他们把在这里出入的人和发生的事都记入日志。
→ see **blog**

▸ **log in** or **log on** PHRASAL VERB When someone **logs in** or **logs on**, or **logs into** a computer system, they start using the system, usually by typing their name or identity code and a password. 登录 ❑ *Customers pay to log on and gossip with other users.* 顾客们花钱登录，与其他用户闲聊。

▸ **log out** or **log off** PHRASAL VERB When someone who is using a computer system **logs out** or **logs off**, they finish using the system by typing a particular command. 登出 ❑ *If a computer user fails to log off, the system is accessible to all.* 如果一位电脑用户没有登出，所有人都可以进入该系统。

Word Link *log ≈ reason, speech : apology, dialogue, logic*

log·ic /lɒdʒɪk/ 1 N-UNCOUNT **Logic** is a method of reasoning that involves a series of statements, each of which must be true if the statement before it is true. 逻辑(学) ❑ *Apart from criminal investigation techniques, students learn forensic medicine, philosophy and logic.* 除犯罪调查技术外，学生们还学习法医学、哲学和逻辑学。 2 N-UNCOUNT The **logic** of a conclusion or an argument is its quality of being correct and reasonable. (结论或观点的) 逻辑 ❑ *I don't follow the logic of your argument.* 我不理解你观点的逻辑。 3 N-UNCOUNT A particular kind of **logic** is the way of thinking and reasoning about things that is characteristic of a particular type of person or particular field of activity. (某种人或某行为领域的) 逻辑 ❑ *The plan was based on sound commercial logic.* 这个计划建立在合理的商业逻辑之上。
→ see **philosophy**

logi·cal /lɒdʒɪkᵊl/ 1 ADJ In a **logical** argument or method of reasoning, each step must be true if the step before it is true. 逻辑的 (观点或推理方式) ❑ *Only when each logical step has been checked by other mathematicians will the proof be accepted.* 只有在每个逻辑步骤都由其他数学家验证之后，该证明才会被接受。 ● **logi·cal·ly** /lɒdʒɪkli/ ADV 逻辑地 ❑ *My professional training has taught me to look at things logically.* 我的专业训练教会了我逻辑地看待事物。 2 ADJ The **logical** conclusion or result of a series of facts or events is the only one which can come from it, according to the rules of logic. 合乎逻辑的 (结论或结果等) ❑ *If the climate gets drier, then the logical conclusion is that even more drought will occur.* 如果气候变得更干燥，那么符合逻辑的结论就是甚至更多的旱灾将会发生。 ● **logi·cal·ly** ADV 合乎逻辑地 [ADV with v] ❑ *From that it followed logically that he would not be meeting Hildegarde.* 从那一点看来，他不会见希尔德加德是合乎逻辑的。 3 ADJ Something that is **logical** seems reasonable or sensible in the circumstances. 合理的; 明智的 ❑ *Connie suddenly struck her as a logical candidate.* 她突然想到康尼是个合适的人选。 ❑ *There was a logical explanation.* 存在一个合理的解释。 ● **logi·cal·ly** ADV 合理地; 明智地 ❑ *This was the one possibility I hadn't taken into consideration, though logically I should have.* 这是一种我没有考虑到的可能性，尽管按道理我本该考虑到的。

log·ic bomb (**logic bombs**) N-COUNT A **logic bomb** is an unauthorized program that is inserted into a computer system so that when it is started it affects the operation of the computer. 逻辑炸弹 [COMPUTING] ❑ *Viruses and logic bombs can doubtless do great damage under some circumstances.* 病毒以及逻辑炸弹无疑会在某些情况下造成巨大损失。

▲ **lo·gis·tic** /loʊdʒɪstɪk/ or **logistical** /loʊdʒɪstɪkᵊl/ ADJ **Logistic** or **logistical** means relating to the organization of something complicated. 在组织上的 [ADJ n] ❑ *Logistical problems may be causing the delay.* 组织上的一些问题可能会造成延误。 ❑ *She described the distribution of food and medical supplies as a logistical nightmare.* 她将食物和医疗供给的分发描述为一个组织上的梦魇。 ● **lo·gis·ti·cal·ly** /loʊdʒɪstɪkli/ ADV 在组织上地 ❑ *Some women find breast-feeding logistically difficult because of work.* 有些妇女因为工作感到母乳喂养在安排上是困难的。 ❑ *It is about time that the U.N. considers logistically deploying additional military resources.* 联合国到了该考虑有组织地部署额外军事资源的时候了。 ❑ *Logistically it is very difficult to value unit-linked policies.* 在组织上很难重视基金连锁政策。

lo·gis·tics /loʊdʒɪstɪks/ N-UNCOUNT-COLL If you refer to the **logistics** of doing something complicated that involves a lot of people or equipment, you are referring to the skillful organization of it so that it can be done successfully and efficiently. 后勤 ❑ *The skills and logistics of getting such a big show on the road pose enormous practical problems.* 这样的一个大型节目进行巡演在技术和后勤方面都会面临大量实际问题。

logo /loʊgoʊ/ (**logos**) N-COUNT The **logo** of a company or organization is the special design or way of writing its name that it puts on all its products, stationery, or advertisements. 标志 ❑ *...the famous MGM logo of the roaring lion.* …米高梅公司著名的怒吼狂狮标志。
→ see **advertising**

loi·ter /lɔɪtər/ (**loiters, loitering, loitered**) V-I If you **loiter** somewhere, you remain there or walk up and down without any real purpose. 闲逛 ❑ *Unemployed young men loiter at the entrance of the factory.* 失业的年轻人在工厂门口游荡。

lone /loʊn/ ADJ If you talk about a **lone** person or thing, you mean that they are alone. 孤单的 [ADJ n] ❑ *A lone woman motorist waited for six hours for help yesterday because of a name mix-up.* 一位女性独自驾车者昨日因名字弄混等待了6个小时才得到救援。

lone·li·ness /loʊnlinɪs/ N-UNCOUNT **Loneliness** is the unhappiness that is felt by someone because they do not have any friends or do not have anyone to talk to. 孤独 ❑ *I have so many friends, but deep down, underneath, I have a fear of loneliness.* 我有这么多朋友，但是内心深处我还是有一种对孤独的恐惧。

lone·ly /loʊnli/ (**lonelier, loneliest**) 1 ADJ Someone who is **lonely** is unhappy because they are alone or do not have anyone they can talk to. (人) 孤独的 ❑ *...lonely people who just want to talk.* …只想聊聊天的孤独的人。 2 ADJ A **lonely** situation or period of time is one in which you feel unhappy because you are alone or do not have anyone to talk to. 孤独的 (情形、时期) ❑ *I desperately needed something to occupy me during those long, lonely nights.* 在那些漫长而又孤独的夜晚我拼命想找点事做。 3 ADJ A **lonely** place is one where very few people come. 偏僻的 ❑ *It felt like the loneliest place in the world.* 这就像是世界上最偏僻的地方。

lon·er /loʊnər/ (**loners**) N-COUNT If you describe someone as a **loner**, you mean they prefer to be alone rather than with a group of people. 不合群的人 ❑ *I'm very much a loner – I never go out.* 我是个非常不合群的人——我从来不出门。

long
1 TIME
2 DISTANCE AND SIZE
3 PHRASES
4 VERB USES

1 **long** ◆◆◆ /lɔŋ/ (**longer** /lɔŋgər/, **longest** /lɔŋgɪst/) 1 ADV **Long** means a great amount of time or for a great amount of time. 长时

间地 ❑ *Repairs to the cable did not take too long.* 维修电缆没花太长时间。❑ *Have you known her parents long?* 你认识她的父母很久了吗？ ❑ *I learned long ago to avoid these invitations.* 我很早以前就学会了回避这些邀请。 ● PHRASE The expression **for long** is used to mean "for a great amount of time." 长久 ❑ *"Did you live there?"—"Not for long."* "你以前住在那里吗？"——"没住多久。" **2** ADJ A **long** event or period of time lasts for a great amount of time or takes a great amount of time. 长时间的 ❑ *We had a long meeting with the attorney general.* 我们和首席检察官开了一个长会。 ❑ *She is planning a long vacation in Europe.* 她正打算去欧洲度一次长假。 **3** ADV You use **long** to ask or talk about amounts of time. 长久地 ❑ *How long have you lived around here?* 你在这附近住多久了？ ❑ *He has been on a diet for as long as any of his friends can remember.* 从他的朋友能记得时开始，他就一直在节食。 ● ADJ **Long** is also an adjective. 长久的 ["how" ADJ, amount ADJ] ❑ *So how long is your commute?* 那么你上下班路程要花多长时间？ **4** ADJ A **long** speech, book, movie, or list contains a lot of information or a lot of items and takes a lot of time to listen to, read, watch, or deal with. (篇幅) 长的 ❑ *He was making quite a long speech.* 他当时正在发表一个相当长的演讲。 **5** ADJ If you describe a period of time or work as **long**, you mean it lasts for more hours or days than is usual, or seems to last for more time than it actually does. 长的 (时间) ❑ *Go to sleep. I've got a long day tomorrow.* 去睡吧。我明天要工作很长时间。 ❑ *She was a TV reporter and worked long hours.* 她曾是个电视记者，长时间工作。 **6** ADJ If someone has a **long** memory, they are able to remember things that happened far back in the past. (记性) 好的 ❑ *Mr. Assad, who has a long memory, will not have forgotten that meeting.* 好记性的阿萨德先生不会忘记那次会面的。 **7** ADV **Long** is used in expressions such as **all year long**, **the whole day long**, and **your whole life long** to say and emphasize that something happens for the whole of a particular period of time. 整个 (时间段) [n ADV] [EMPHASIS] ❑ *We played that CD all night long.* 我们整晚都在播放那张CD。

❷ long ♦♦♦ /lɔŋ/ (**longer** /lɔŋgər/, **longest** /lɔŋgɪst/) **1** ADJ Something that is **long** measures a great distance from one end to the other. (长度) 长的 ❑ *...a long table.* …一张长桌子。 ❑ *Lucy was 27, with long dark hair.* 露西27岁，留着长长的黑发。 **2** ADJ A **long** distance is a great distance. A **long** journey or route covers a great distance. (路程) 长的 ❑ *These people were a long way from home.* 这些人离家遥远。 ❑ *The long journey tired him.* 漫长的旅程使他疲倦。 **3** ADJ A **long** piece of clothing covers the whole of someone's legs or more of their legs than usual. Clothes with **long** sleeves cover the whole of someone's arms. (衣服) 长的 [ADJ n] ❑ *She is wearing a long black dress.* 她穿着一件黑色长裙。 **4** ADJ You use **long** to talk or ask about the distance something measures from one end to the other. (某长度) 长的 ❑ *An eight-week-old embryo is only an inch long.* 一个8周大的胎儿仅1英寸长。 ❑ *How long is the tunnel?* 这隧道有多长？ ● COMB IN ADJ **Long** is also a combining form. (某长度) 长的 ❑ *...a three-foot-long gash in the tanker's side.* …油轮侧面一条3英尺长的裂缝。
→ see **ratio**

❸ long ♦♦♦ /lɔŋ/ (**longer** /lɔŋgər/)
➪ **Please look at meanings 6 – 10 to see if the expression you are looking for is shown under another headword.** **1** PHRASE If you say that something is the case **as long as** or **so long as** something else is the case, you mean that it is only the case if the second thing is the case. 只要 ❑ *He said he would still support them, as long as they didn't break the rules.* 他说只要他们不违反规则，他仍然会支持他们。 **2** PHRASE If you say that someone **won't be long**, you mean that you think they will arrive or be back soon. If you say that it **won't be long** before something happens, you mean that you think it will happen soon. (某人) 很快就来; (某事) 即将发生 ❑ *"What's happened to her?"—"I'm sure she won't be long."* "她出什么事了？"——"我肯定她马上就到了。" **3** PHRASE If you say that something will happen or happened **before long**, you mean that it will happen or it happened soon. 不久 ❑ *German interest rates will come down before long.* 德国的利率不久就会降下来。 **4** PHRASE Something that is **no longer** the case used to be the case but is not the case now. You can also say that something is not the case **any longer**. 不再 ❑ *Food shortages are no longer a problem.* 食物短缺不再是个问题。 ❑ *She could no longer afford to keep him at school.* 她再也供不起他上学了。 **5** PHRASE You can say **so long** as an informal way of saying goodbye. 再见 ❑ *Well, so long, pal, see you around.* 好了，再见，伙计，回头见。 **6** **at long last** → see **last** **7** **in the long run** → see **run** **8** **a long shot** → see **shot** **9** **in the long term** → see **term** **10** **to go a long way** → see **way**

❹ long /lɔŋ/ (**longs, longing, longed**) **1** V-T/V-I If you **long for** something, you want it very much. 渴望；极想念 ❑ *Steve longed for the good old days.* 史蒂夫怀念过去的好时光。 ❑ *I'm longing to meet her.* 我正渴望着见她。 **2** → see also **longing**

long-distance **1** ADJ **Long-distance** is used to describe travel between places that are far apart. (旅行) 长途的 [ADJ n] ❑ *Trains are reliable, cheap and best for long-distance travel.* 乘火车可靠、便宜，最适合长途旅行。 **2** ADJ **Long-distance** is used to describe communication that takes place between people who are far apart. (通信) 长途的 ❑ *He received a long-distance phone call from his girlfriend in Colorado.* 他接到女朋友从科罗拉多州打来的长途电话。

▲ **lon·gev·ity** /lɒndʒɛvɪti/ N-UNCOUNT **Longevity** is long life. 长寿 [FORMAL] ❑ *Human longevity runs in families.* 人类长寿是有遗传的。 ❑ *The main characteristic of the strike has been its longevity.* 这次罢工的主要特点是持续时间长。

long-haul **1** ADJ **Long-haul** is used to describe things that involve transporting passengers or goods over long distances. Compare **short-haul**. (运输) 长途的 [ADJ n] ❑ *...learning how to avoid the unpleasant side-effects of long-haul flights.* …学会如何避免长途飞行的令人不快的副作用。 **2** → see also **haul**

long·ing /lɔŋɪŋ/ (**longings**) N-VAR If you feel **longing** or a **longing for** something, you have a rather sad feeling because you want it very much. 渴望；极想念 ❑ *He felt a longing for the familiar.* 他渴望熟悉的氛围。

★ **lon·gi·tude** /lɒndʒɪtud/ (**longitudes**) N-VAR The **longitude** of a place is its distance to the west or east of a line passing through Greenwich, England. Compare **latitude**. 经度 ❑ *He noted the latitude and longitude, then made a mark on the admiralty chart.* 他记下经度和纬度，然后在海图上作了标记。 ● ADJ **Longitude** is also an adjective. 经度的 ❑ *A similar feature is found at 13 degrees north between 230 degrees and 250 degrees longitude.* 在北纬13度、经度230度到250度之间也发现了类似的特点。
→ see **globe**

long-lost ADJ You use **long-lost** to describe someone or something that you have not seen for a long time. 很久没见的 [ADJ n] ❑ *For me it was like meeting a long-lost sister. We talked, and talked, and talked.* 对我来说就像见了久未谋面的姐妹一样。我们聊了又聊，聊个不停。

long-range **1** ADJ A **long-range** piece of military equipment or vehicle is able to hit or detect a target a long way away or to travel a long way in order to do something. 远程的 ❑ *He is eager to reach agreement with the U.S. on reducing long-range nuclear missiles.* 他渴望与美国就减少远程核导弹达成协议。 **2** ADJ A **long-range** plan or prediction relates to a period extending a long time into the future. 长期的 (规划等) ❑ *Eisenhower was intensely aware of the need for long-range planning.* 艾森豪威尔强烈地意识到长期规划的必要。

long-running (**longest-running**) ADJ Something that is **long-running** has been in existence, or has been performed, for a long time. 存在许久的 [ADJ n] ❑ *...a long-running trade dispute.* …一个存在许久的贸易争端。

long-standing ADJ A **long-standing** situation has existed for a long time. 长期存在的 ❑ *They are on the brink of resolving their long-standing dispute over money.* 他们即将要解决彼此之间为时已久的金钱争议。

long-suffering ADJ Someone who is **long-suffering** patiently puts up with a lot of trouble or unhappiness, especially when it is caused by someone else. 长期受苦的 ❑ *He went back to his loyal, long-suffering wife.* 他回到了对他忠贞不渝、长期受苦的妻子身边。

long-term ♦♦◊ (**longer-term**) **1** ADJ Something that is **long-term** has continued for a long time or will continue for a long time in the future. 长期的 ❑ *They want their parents to have access to affordable long-term care.* 他们希望他们的父母可以得到负担得起的长期看护。 **2** N-SING When you talk about what happens in **the long term**, you are talking about what happens over a long period of time, either in the future or after a particular event. 从长远来看 ❑ *In the long term the company hopes to open in Moscow and other major cities.* 从长远来看，该公司希望能在莫斯科和其它主要城市开展业务。
→ see **memory**

long-time ♦◊◊ ADJ You use **long-time** to describe something that has existed or been a particular thing for a long time. 为时甚久的 [ADJ n] ❑ *Newcomers had to pay far more in taxes than long-time land owners.* 新来者必须比久居于此的土地所有者交纳多得多的税金。

long-winded ADJ If you describe something that is written or said as **long-winded**, you are critical of it because it is longer than necessary. 冗长的 [usu v-link ADJ] [DISAPPROVAL] ❑ *The manifesto is long-winded, repetitious and often ambiguous or poorly drafted.* 该宣言冗长、重复，而且往往含糊不清或者起草得很差。 ❑ *I hope I'm not being too long-winded.* 我希望我没有太啰嗦。

look
❶ USING YOUR EYES OR YOUR MIND
❷ APPEARANCE

❶ **look** ♦♦♦ /lʊk/ (**looks, looking, looked**)
➪ **Please look at meaning 12 to see if the expression you are looking for is shown under another headword.** 1 V-I If you **look** in a particular direction, you direct your eyes in that direction, especially so that you can see what is there or see what something is like. 看 ❑ *I looked down the hallway to room number nine.* 我沿着走廊向9号房间看过去。 ❑ *If you look, you'll see what was a lake.* 如果你看一下，就会看到那个曾经是湖的地方。 ● N-SING **Look** is also a noun. 看 ❑ *Lucille took a last look in the mirror.* 露西尔往镜子里看了最后一眼。 2 V-I If you **look at** a book, newspaper, or magazine, you read it fairly quickly or read part of it. 浏览 ❑ *You've just got to look at the last bit of Act Three.* 你只须浏览一下第三幕最后一小段。 ● N-SING **Look** is also a noun. 浏览 ❑ *A quick look at Monday's newspapers shows that there's plenty of interest in foreign news.* 快速浏览一下星期一的报纸，就会发现许多有趣的国外新闻。 3 V-I If you **look at** someone in a particular way, you look at them with your expression showing what you are feeling or thinking. (带着某种神情) 看 ❑ *She looked at him earnestly. "You don't mind?"* 她诚挚地看着他说："你不介意吧？" ● N-COUNT **Look** is also a noun. 看 ❑ *He gave her a blank look, as if he had no idea who she was.* 他茫然地看了看她，好像不认识她似的。 4 V-I If you **look for** something, for example, something that you have lost, you try to find it. 寻找 ❑ *I'm looking for a child. I believe your husband can help me find her.* 我正在找一个孩子。我相信你丈夫能帮我找到她。 ❑ *I looked everywhere for ideas.* 我到处搜寻意见。 ● N-SING **Look** is also a noun. 寻找 ❑ *Go and have another look.* 再去找一找。 5 V-I If you are **looking for** something such as the solution to a problem or a new method, you want it and are trying to obtain it or think of it. 寻求 ❑ *The working group will be looking for practical solutions to the problems faced by doctors.* 工作组将会寻求切实可行的方案，以解决医生们所面临的问题。 6 V-I If you **look at** a subject, problem, or situation, you think about it or study it, so that you know all about it and can perhaps consider what should be done in relation to it. 考虑；研究 ❑ *Next term we'll be looking at the Second World War period.* 下学期我们将研究一下二战时期。 ❑ *Anne Holker looks at the pros and cons of making changes to your property.* 安妮・霍尔卡会研究对你的财产进行变更的利与弊。 ● N-SING **Look** is also a noun. 考虑；研究 ❑ *A close look at the statistics reveals a troubling picture.* 对这些统计数据的仔细研究显示情况不妙。 7 V-I If you **look at** a person, situation, or subject from a particular point of view, you judge them or consider them from that point of view. 看待 ❑ *Brian had learned to look at her with new respect.* 布赖恩已学会从新的角度看待她。 8 CONVENTION You say **look** when you want someone to pay attention to you because you are going to say something important. (用于引起注意) 喂 ❑ *Look, I'm sorry. I didn't mean it.* 喂，对不起。我不是故意的。 9 V-T/V-I You can use **look** to draw attention to a particular situation, person, or thing, for example because you find it very surprising, significant, or annoying. (表达惊奇、重要或讨厌) 瞧 [only imper] ❑ *Hey, look at the time! We'll talk about it tonight. All right?* 嘿，看看时间吧！我们今晚再谈论这个，好吗？ ❑ *I mean, look at how many people watch television and how few read books.* 我想说的是，看看有多少人看电视，又有几个人读书。 ❑ *Look what you've done!* 瞧你都干了些什么！ 10 V-I If something such as a building or window **looks** somewhere, it has a view of a particular place. (建筑物、窗户等) 面朝 ❑ *The castle looks over private parkland.* 这座城堡面朝私家绿地。 ● PHRASAL VERB **Look out** means the same as **look**. 面朝 (同 **look**) ❑ *Nine windows looked out over the sculpture gardens.* 九扇窗户面朝雕塑花园。 11 EXCLAM If you say or shout "**look out!**" to someone, you are warning them that they are in danger. 小心 ❑ *"Look out!" somebody shouted, as the truck started to roll toward the sea.* 卡车开始滚向大海时，有人大喊："小心！" 12 to **look down** your **nose at** someone → see **nose**

If you want to say that someone is paying attention to something they can see, you say that they **are looking at** it or **watching** it. In general, you **look at** something that is not moving, while you **watch** something that is moving or changing. ❑ *I asked him to look at the picture above his bed... He watched Blake run down the stairs.* **Look** is never followed directly by an object. You must always use **at** or some other preposition. ❑ *I looked toward the plane.* You use **see** to talk about things that you are aware of because a visual impression reaches your eyes. You often use **can** in this case. ❑ *I can see the fax here on the desk.*

▸ **look after** 1 PHRASAL VERB If you **look after** someone or something, you do what is necessary to keep them healthy, safe, or in good condition. 照顾；照管 ❑ *I love looking after the children.* 我喜欢照顾孩子们。 2 PHRASAL VERB If you **look after** something, you are responsible for it and deal with it or make sure it is all right, especially because it is your job to do so. 负责照管 ❑ *...the farm manager who looks after the day-to-day organization.* …负责日常组织工作的农场经营者。

▸ **look around** PHRASAL VERB If you **look around** or **look round** a building or place, you walk round it and look at the different parts of it. 游览 ❑ *She left Annie and Cooper looking around the store and headed back onto the street.* 她丢下安妮和库珀在商场游逛，自己回到了街上。

▸ **look back** PHRASAL VERB If you **look back**, you think about things that happened in the past. 回顾 ❑ *Looking back, I am staggered how easily it was all arranged.* 回顾过去，我感到惊讶的是，这一切都那么轻易地安排好了。

▸ **look down on** PHRASAL VERB To **look down on** someone means to consider that person to be inferior or unimportant, usually when this is not true. 瞧不起 ❑ *I wasn't successful, so they looked down on me.* 我并不成功，所以他们瞧不起我。

▸ **look forward to** 1 PHRASAL VERB If you **look forward to** something that is going to happen, you want it to happen because you think you will enjoy it. 期待 ❑ *He was looking forward to working with the new manager.* 他那时正期待着和新来的经理一起工作。 2 PHRASAL VERB If you say that someone **is looking forward** to something useful or positive, you mean they expect it to happen. 盼望 ❑ *He now says that he's looking forward to increased trade after the war.* 他现在说他正盼望着战后的贸易增长。

Do not confuse **look forward to, expect**, and **wait for**. When you **look forward to** something that is going to happen, you feel happy because you think you will enjoy it. ❑ *I'll bet you're looking forward to your holidays... I always looked forward to seeing her.* When you are **expecting** someone or something, you think that the person or thing is going to arrive or that the thing is going to happen. ❑ *I sent a postcard so they were expecting me... We are expecting rain.* When you **wait for** someone or something, you stay in the same place until the person arrives or the thing happens. ❑ *Soft drinks were served while we waited for him... We got off the plane and waited for our luggage.*

▸ **look in** PHRASAL VERB If you **look in on** a person, you visit that person for a short time to check on their health or safety. 顺便看望 ❑ *Could I look in on Sam?* 我可以顺便看望一下萨姆吗？ ❑ *I think I'll look in on my parents on the way home from work.* 我想我要在下班回家的路上顺便看望一下我的父母。

▸ **look into** PHRASAL VERB If a person or organization **is looking into** a possible course of action, a problem, or a situation, they are finding out about it and examining the facts relating to it. 调查 ❑ *He had once looked into buying his own island off Nova Scotia.* 他曾经考虑过在新斯科舍省沿海购买属于自己的小岛。

▸ **look on** PHRASAL VERB If you **look on** while something happens, you watch it happening without taking part yourself. 旁观 ❑ *About 150 local people looked on in silence as the two coffins were taken into the church.* 大约一百五十名当地人默默地看着那两口棺材被抬进教堂。

▸ **look on** or **look upon** PHRASAL VERB If you **look on** or **look upon** someone or something in a particular way, you think of them in that way. 把…当作 ❑ *A lot of people looked on him as a healer.* 很多人把他当作一位疗伤者。 ❑ *A lot of people look on it like that.* 许多人是那样看待这件事的。

▸ **look out** → see **look** ❶ 10

▸ **look out for** PHRASAL VERB If you **look out for** something, you pay attention to things so that you notice it if or when it occurs. 留意 ❑ *Look out for special deals.* 留意一下特殊交易。

▸ **look over** PHRASAL VERB If you **look** something **over**, you examine it in order to get an idea of what it is like. 检查 ❑ *They presented their draft to the president, who looked it over, nodded and signed it.* 他们把草案呈交给总统，总统看了看，点了点头，签了字。

▸ **look round** → see **look around**

▸ **look through** 1 PHRASAL VERB If you **look through** a group of things, you examine each one so that you can find or choose the one that you want. 逐一查看 ❑ *Peter starts looking through the mail as soon as the door shuts.* 门一关上，彼得就开始查看邮件。 2 PHRASAL VERB If you **look through** something that has been written or printed, you read it. 阅读 ❑ *He happened to be looking through the medical book "Gray's Anatomy" at the time.* 他那时碰巧在看《格雷氏解剖学》这本医学书。

▸ **look to** 1 PHRASAL VERB If you **look to** someone or something for a particular thing that you want, you expect or hope that they will provide it. 指望 ❑ *He runs the team because he commands their respect. The kids really look to him.* 他管理这个团队，因为他博得了孩了们的尊敬。孩子们确实指望他。 2 PHRASAL VERB If you **look to** something that will happen in the future, you think about it. 展望 ❑ *Looking to the future, though, we asked him what the prospects are for a vaccine to prevent infection in the first place.* 然而，展望未来时，我们首先问他一种预防传染的疫苗前景如何。

▸ **look up** 1 PHRASAL VERB If you **look up** a fact or a piece of information, you find it out by looking in something such as a reference book or a list. 查阅 ❑ *I looked your address up in the personnel file.* 我从人事档案里查到了你的地址。 2 PHRASAL VERB If you **look** someone **up**, you visit them after not having seen them for a long time. (久别后) 拜访 ❑ *I'll try to look him up, ask him a few questions.* 我想要去拜访他，问他几个问题。

▸ **look up to** PHRASAL VERB If you **look up to** someone, especially someone older than you, you respect and admire them. 仰慕 ❑ *You're a popular girl, Grace, and a lot of the younger ones look up to you.* 你是个受欢迎的女孩，格雷丝，许多比你小的女孩都仰慕你。

❷ **look** ♦♦♦ /lʊk/ (**looks, looking, looked**) 1 V-LINK You use **look** when describing the appearance of a person or thing or the impression that they give. 看上去 ❑ *Sheila was looking miserable.* 希拉当时显得痛苦。 ❑ *They look like stars to the naked eye.* 用肉眼看上去它们像星星。 ❑ *He looked as if he was going to smile.* 他看上去好像要微笑。 2 N-SING If someone or something has a particular **look**, they have a particular appearance or expression. 外表；神态 ❑ *She had the look of someone deserted and betrayed.* 她露出被抛弃、被背叛的人的神情。 ❑ *When he came to decorate the kitchen, Kenneth opted for a friendly rustic look.* 当他来装修厨房时，肯尼思选出一副友好质朴的样子。 3 N-PLURAL When you refer to someone's **looks**, you are referring to how beautiful or ugly they are, especially how beautiful they are. 外貌 ❑ *I never chose people just because of their looks.* 我从不单凭外貌取人。 4 V-LINK You use **look** when indicating what you think will happen in the future or how a situation seems to you. 看起来 ❑ *He had lots of time to think about the future, and it didn't look good.* 他有很多时间考虑未来，而未来看上去并不乐观。 ❑ *So far it looks like Warner Brothers' gamble is paying off.* 就目前情况来看，华纳兄弟公司的冒险一博似乎要赢了。 ❑ *The Europeans had hoped to win, and, indeed, had looked like they would win.* 欧洲人原本希望能赢，而且当时看起来他们的确会赢。 5 PHRASE You use expressions such as **by the look of him** and **by the looks of it** when you want to indicate that you are giving an opinion based on the appearance of someone or something. 由表象(来看) ❑ *He was not a well man by the look of him.* 他表面看来不是个健康的人。 6 PHRASE If you **don't like the look of** something or someone, you feel that they may be dangerous or cause problems. 看出…危险或麻烦 ❑ *I don't like the look of those clouds.* 我看这些乌云不对头。 7 PHRASE If you ask **what** someone or something **looks like**, you are asking for a description of them. (某人、某物的)样子是

Thesaurus *look* 另参见：

- N. gaze, glance, glimpse, stare ❶ 1
- V. gaze, glance, observe, stare, view, watch ❶ 1; examine, inspect, investigate, observe, study; (*ant.*) survey ❶ 6
- V-LINK. appear, seem ❷ 1

look·out /lʊkaʊt/ (**lookouts**) 1 N-COUNT A **lookout** is a place from which you can see clearly in all directions. 瞭望台 ❑ *Troops tried to set up a lookout post inside a refugee camp.* 军队试图在一个难民营里设一个瞭望台。 2 N-COUNT A **lookout** is someone who is watching for danger in order to warn other people about it. 望风者 ❑ *One of them, Bayer's girlfriend, helped plan the botched burglary and acted as a lookout.* 其中一个是拜尔的女朋友，她帮助策划了这次拙劣的入室盗窃并充当了望风者。 3 PHRASE If someone **keeps a lookout**, especially on a boat, they look around all the time in order to make sure there is no danger. 小心戒备 ❑ *He denied that he'd failed to keep a proper lookout that night.* 他否认那天晚上他未能小心警戒。

★ **loom** /lum/ (**looms, looming, loomed**) 1 V-I If something **looms over** you, it appears as a large or unclear shape, often in a frightening way. (常以可怕的方式) 赫然出现；隐约显现 ❑ *Vincent loomed over me, as pale and gray as a tombstone.* 文森特赫然出现在我面前，脸色苍白阴沉得像块墓碑。 2 V-I If a worrying or threatening situation or event **is looming**, it seems likely to happen soon. (令人担忧的或危险的情形或事件) 可能发生；逐渐逼近 [JOURNALISM] ❑ *Another government spending crisis is looming in the United States.* 又一次政府开支危机正在美国酝酿。 ❑ *The threat of renewed civil war looms ahead.* 新一轮内战的威胁在逼近。 3 N-COUNT A **loom** is a machine that is used for weaving thread into cloth. 织布机

loony /luni/ (**loonies**) 1 N-COUNT If you refer to someone as a **loony**, you mean that they behave in a way that seems crazy, strange, or eccentric. Some people consider this use offensive. 疯子 [INFORMAL, DISAPPROVAL] ❑ *At first they all thought I was a loony.* 起初他们都以为我是个疯子。 2 ADJ If you describe someone's behavior or ideas as **loony**, you mean that they seem mad, strange, or eccentric. Some people consider this use offensive. 发疯的 [INFORMAL] ❑ *What's she up to? She's as loony as her brother!* 她在干嘛？她和她的兄弟一样疯狂。

loop /lup/ (**loops, looping, looped**) 1 N-COUNT A **loop** is a curved or circular shape in something long, for example, in a piece of string. 圈 ❑ *Mrs. Morrell reached for a loop of garden hose.* 莫雷尔夫人伸手去拿一圈橡胶软管。 2 V-T If you **loop** something such as a piece of rope around an object, you tie a length of it in a loop around the object, for example, in order to fasten it to the object. 打环 ❑ *He looped the rope over the wood.* 他把绳子打了环系在木头上。 3 V-I If something **loops** somewhere, it goes there in a circular direction that makes the shape of a loop. 环绕 ❑ *The enemy was looping around the south side.* 敌人正包围南边。

loop·hole /luphoʊl/ (**loopholes**) N-COUNT A **loophole** in the law is a small mistake which allows people to do something that would otherwise be illegal. 漏洞 ❑ *It is estimated that 60,000 businesses are exploiting a loophole in the law to avoid prosecution.* 据估计6万家公司在钻法律的空子来逃避起诉。

loose ♦◇◇ /lus/ (**looser, loosest**) 1 ADJ Something that is **loose** is not firmly held or fixed in place. 松的 ❑ *If a tooth feels very loose, your dentist may recommend that it's taken out.* 如果有颗牙齿非常松动，你的牙医可能会建议拔掉它。 ❑ *Two wooden beams had come loose from the ceiling.* 天花板上的两根木梁松动了。 ● **loose·ly** ADV 松松地 [ADV with v] ❑ *Tim clasped his hands together and held them loosely in front of his belly.* 蒂姆十指交叉搭在腹前。 2 ADJ Something that is **loose** is not attached to anything, or held or contained in anything. 零散的 ❑ *Frank emptied a handful of loose change on the table.* 弗兰克将一把零钱全部放在了桌子上。 3 ADJ If people or animals break **loose** or are set **loose**, they are no longer held, tied, or kept somewhere and can move around freely. 自由的 ❑ *She broke loose from his embrace and crossed to the window.* 她从他的拥抱中挣脱出来，穿过房间走到窗边。 4 ADJ Clothes that are **loose** are somewhat large and do not fit closely. 宽松的 ❑ *A pistol wasn't that hard to hide under a loose shirt.* 把一支手枪藏在宽松的衬衣里面并没那么难。 ● **loose·ly** ADV 宽松地 ❑ *His shirt hung loosely over his thin shoulders.* 他的衬衣松松垮垮地挂在他瘦削的双肩上。 5 ADJ If your hair is **loose**, it hangs freely around your shoulders and is not tied back. 披散的 ❑ *She was still in her nightgown, with her hair hanging loose over her shoulders.* 她仍穿着睡衣，头发披散在肩上。 6 ADJ A **loose** grouping, arrangement, or organization is flexible rather than strictly controlled or organized. 松散的 (分组、安排、组织) ❑ *Murray and Alison came to some sort of loose arrangement before he went home.* 在他回家之前，默里和艾莉森做了些松散的安排。 ● **loose·ly** ADV 松散地 [ADV with v] ❑ *The investigation had aimed at a loosely organized group of criminals.* 该调查曾是针对一群组织松散的罪犯的。 7 PHRASE If a person or an animal is **on the loose**, they are free because they have escaped from a person or place. 在逃；行动自由 ❑ *Up to a thousand prisoners* may be on the loose inside the jail. 多达一千名的囚犯可能在监狱里行动自由。 8 a loose cannon → see cannon 9 all hell breaks loose → see hell

Do not confuse **loose** and **lose**. **Loose** is usually an adjective. If something is **loose**, it is not properly fixed or held in place. ❑ *...the loose floorboards on the landing. ...a loose tooth.* If you let an animal **loose**, you release it from where it was kept. ❑ *He brought a pair of white rats into church, and let them loose on the floor.* **Lose** is a verb. If you **lose** something, you no longer have it and cannot find it. ❑ *I've lost my wallet.* The past participle and past tense of **lose** are both **lost**.

Thesaurus *loose* 另参见:
ADJ. slack, wobbly 1
free 3
loose-fitting, baggy 4

Word Partnership *loose* 的常用搭配:
V. **break** loose, **cut** *someone/something* loose, **set** *someone/something* loose, **turn** *someone/ something* loose 1 – 3
hang loose 1 2 4 5
come loose 1 2 5
N. loose **coalition**, loose **confederation** 6

loose end (**loose ends**) 1 N-COUNT A **loose end** is part of a story, situation, or crime that has not yet been explained. (故事、情况或犯罪案件中) 尚未解释清楚的地方 ❑ *There are some annoying loose ends in the plot.* 情节中有一些令人烦恼、尚待弄清的东西。 2 PHRASE If you are **at loose ends**, you are bored because you do not have anything to do and cannot think of anything that you want to do. 闲得无聊 [INFORMAL] ❑ *She had woken feeling at loose ends.* 她醒了，感到闲得无聊。

loos·en /luːsᵊn/ (**loosens, loosening, loosened**) 1 V-T If someone **loosens** restrictions or laws, for example, they make them less strict or severe. 放宽 (限制或法律) ❑ *Many business groups have been pressing the Federal Reserve to loosen interest rates.* 许多商业团体一直在施加压力要求联邦储备局放宽利率。 • **loos·en·ing** N-SING 放宽 ❑ *Domestic conditions did not justify a loosening of monetary policy.* 国内的条件不适宜放宽货币政策。 2 V-T/V-I If someone or something **loosens** the ties between people or groups of people, or if the ties **loosen**, they become weaker. 疏远; 减弱 ❑ *The Federal Republic must loosen its ties with the United States.* 联邦共和国必须疏远同美国的关系。 ❑ *The deputy leader is cautious about loosening the links with the unions.* 副领导对疏远和工会的关系持谨慎态度。 3 V-T If you **loosen** your clothing or something that is tied or fastened, you undo it slightly so that it is less tight or less firmly held in place. 略微松开 ❑ *He reached up to loosen the scarf around his neck.* 他抬手松了松脖子上的围巾。 ❑ *Loosen the bolt so the bars can be turned.* 松开螺栓，这样那些木板就能被翻过来了。 4 V-T/V-I If you **loosen** your grip on something, or if your grip **loosens**, you hold it less tightly. 放开 ❑ *Harry loosened his grip momentarily and Anna wriggled free.* 哈里刚松了一下手，安娜就挣脱了。 5 V-T/V-I If a government or organization **loosens** its grip on a group of people or an activity, or if its grip **loosens**, it begins to have less control over it. 放松 (控制) ❑ *There is no sign that the party will loosen its grip on the country.* 没有任何迹象表明该党会放松对这个国家的控制。

▸ **loosen up** 1 PHRASAL VERB If a person or situation **loosens up**, they become more relaxed and less tense. 放松; 缓解 ❑ *Relax, smile; loosen up in mind and body.* 放松，微笑; 身心俱放松。 ❑ *Things loosened up, in politics and the economy.* 政治和经济方面的情况都有所缓解。 2 PHRASAL VERB If you **loosen up** your body, or if it **loosens up**, you do simple exercises to get your muscles ready for a difficult physical activity, such as running or playing sports. 放松 (肌肉) ❑ *Squeeze the foot with both hands to loosen up tight muscles.* 用双手捏脚以放松僵硬的肌肉。

▲ **loot** /luːt/ (**loots, looting, looted**) 1 V-T/V-I If people **loot**, or **loot** stores or houses, they steal things from them, for example, during a war or riot. (战争或暴乱时) 抢劫 (商店或房屋) ❑ *The trouble began when gangs began breaking windows and looting shops.* 骚乱起始时，歹徒们就开始砸橱窗、抢商店。 • **loot·ing** N-UNCOUNT 抢劫 ❑ *In the country's largest cities there has been rioting and looting.* 在这个国家的大城市里一直都有暴乱和抢劫事件发生。 2 V-T If someone **loots** things, they steal them, for example, during a war or riot. (战争或暴乱时) 掠夺 ❑ *The town has been plagued by armed thugs who have looted food supplies and terrorized the population.* 小镇一直受到武装暴徒的侵扰，他们掠夺食物，恐吓民众。

lop·sided /lɒpsaɪdɪd/ ADJ Something that is **lopsided** is uneven because one side is lower or heavier than the other. 两边高低不平的; 不均衡的 ❑ *His suit had shoulders that made him look lopsided.* 他西装的肩部使他看上去两肩高低不平。

lord ♦♦◇ /lɔrd/ (**lords**) 1 N-COUNT; N-TITLE A **lord** is a man who has a high rank in the nobility, for example, an earl, a viscount, or a marquis. 贵族 ❑ *She married a lord and lives in this huge house in the Cotswolds.* 她嫁给了一个贵族，现在住在科茨沃尔德的这所大房子里。 2 N-PROPER In the Christian church, people refer to God and to Jesus Christ as the **Lord**. 上帝; 耶稣 [usu "the" N; N-VOC] ❑ *I know the Lord will look after him.* 我知道上帝会照顾他的。 ❑ *She prayed now. "Lord, help me to find courage."* 这时她祈祷道: "上帝啊，赐给我勇气吧。" 3 EXCLAM **Lord** is used in exclamations such as "**good Lord!**" and "**oh Lord!**" to express surprise, shock, frustration, or annoyance about something. (表示吃惊、震惊或懊恼) 天哪 [FEELINGS] ❑ *"Good lord, that's what he is: he's a policeman."* "天哪，原来他是干这个的，他是个警察。"

★ **Lord·ship** /lɔrdʃɪp/ (**Lordships**) N-VOC; N-PROPER You use the expressions **Your Lordship, His Lordship,** or **Their Lordships** when you are addressing or referring to a judge, a bishop, or a male member of the British nobility. 大人 [det-poss N] [POLITENESS] ❑ *My name is Richard Savage, your Lordship.* 我叫理查德·萨威之，大人。 ❑ *His Lordship expressed the hope that the Law Commission might look at the subject.* 法官大人表示了法律委员会可能会对这个问题加以考虑的希望。

lor·ry /lɔri/ (**lorries**) N-COUNT A **lorry** is the same as a **truck**. 卡车 [BRIT]

lor·ry driv·er [BRIT] → see **trucker**

lose ♦♦♦ /luz/ (**loses, losing, lost**) 1 V-T/V-I If you **lose** a contest, a fight, or an argument, you do not succeed because someone does better than you and defeats you. 输掉; 失败 ❑ *The Golden Bears have lost three games this season.* 金熊队本赛季已输了3场比赛。 ❑ *The government lost the argument over the pace of reform.* 政府输掉了关于改革速度的辩论。 ❑ *No one likes to lose.* 没人愿意失败。 2 V-T If you **lose** something, you do not know where it is, for example, because you have forgotten where you put it. 丢失 ❑ *I lost my keys.* 我丢了钥匙。 3 V-T You say that you **lose** something when you no longer have it because it has been taken away from you or destroyed. 失去 ❑ *I lost my job when the company moved to another state.* 当公司迁往另一个州时我失去了工作。 ❑ *He lost his license for six months.* 他曾被吊销执照6个月。 4 V-T If someone **loses** a quality, characteristic, attitude, or belief, they no longer have it. 丧失 (品质、特征、态度或信仰等) ❑ *He lost all sense of reason.* 他完全丧失了理智。 ❑ *The government had lost all credibility.* 政府完全丧失了信誉。 5 V-T If you **lose** an ability, you stop having that ability because of something such as an accident. 失去 (能力) ❑ *They lost their ability to hear.* 他们失聪了。 6 V-T If someone or something **loses** heat, their temperature becomes lower. 降低 (温度) ❑ *Babies lose heat much faster than adults.* 幼儿散热比成人快得多。 7 V-T If you **lose** blood or fluid from your body, it leaves your body so that you have less of it. 失去 (血或体液) ❑ *The victim suffered a dreadful injury and lost a lot of blood.* 受害人伤势严重，失血很多。 8 V-T If you **lose** weight, you become less heavy, and usually look thinner. 减轻 (体重) ❑ *I have lost a lot of weight.* 我体重减轻了不少。 9 V-T If someone **loses** their life, they die. 失去 (生命) ❑ *...the ferry disaster in 1987, in which 192 people lost their lives.* …1987年的渡船灾难中有192人丧生。 10 V-T If you **lose** a close relative or friend, they die. 失去 (亲人或朋友) ❑ *My Grandma lost her brother in the war.* 我的祖母在战争中失去了弟弟。 11 V-T If things **are lost**, they are destroyed in a disaster. (在灾难中) 损毁 [usu passive] ❑ *...the famous Nankin pottery that was lost in a shipwreck off the coast of China.* …颇具名气的白底青花瓷器，在中国沿海的沉船事故中被损毁。 12 V-T If you **lose** time, something slows you down so that you do not make as much progress as you hoped. 错过 (时机) ❑ *They claim that police lost valuable time in the early part of the investigation.* 他们声称，警察在调查初期错失良机。 13 V-T If you **lose** an opportunity, you do not take advantage of it. 失去 (机会) ❑ *If you don't do it soon you're going to lose the opportunity.* 如果你不尽快做，你会失去机会的。 ❑ *They did not lose the opportunity to say what they thought of events.* 他们抓住机会说出他们对事件的看法。 14 V-T If you **lose yourself in** something or if you **are lost in** it, you give a lot of attention to it and do not think about anything else. 使专注 ❑ *Michael held on to her arm, losing himself in the music.* 迈克尔挽着她的胳膊，陶醉于音乐之中。 15 V-T If a business **loses** money, it earns less money than it spends, and is therefore in debt. 亏损 [BUSINESS] ❑ *His stores stand to lose millions of dollars.* 他的商店承受着数百万美元的损失。 16 V-T If something **loses** you a contest or **loses** you something that you had, it causes you to fail or to no longer have what you had. 使输掉; 使失去 ❑ *My own stupidity lost me the match.* 我个人的愚蠢使我输了这场比赛。 17 → see also **lost** 18 PHRASE If you **lose** your **way**, you become lost when you are trying to go somewhere. 迷路 ❑ *The men lost their way in a sandstorm.* 那些人在沙尘暴中迷路了。 19 **to lose your balance** → see **balance** 20 **to lose contact** → see **contact** 21 **to lose face** → see **face** 22 **to lose your grip** → see **grip** 23 **to lose your head** → see **head** 24 **to lose heart** → see **heart** 25 **to lose your mind** → see **mind** 26 **to lose your nerve** → see **nerve** 27 **to lose sight of** → see **sight** 28 **to lose your temper** → see **temper** 29 **to lose touch** → see **touch** 30 **to lose track of** → see **track**

> Do not confuse **lose** and **loose. Lose** is a verb. If you lose something, you no longer have it and cannot find it. ❑ *I've lost my wallet.* The past participle and past tense of **lose** are both **lost. Loose** is usually an adjective. If something is **loose**, it is not properly fixed or held in place. ❑ *...the loose floorboards on the landing. ...a loose tooth.* If you let an animal **loose**, you release it from where it was kept. ❑ *He brought a pair of white rats into church, and let them loose on the floor.*

▸ **lose out** PHRASAL VERB If you **lose out**, you suffer a loss or disadvantage because you have not succeeded in what you were doing. 损失; 失利 ❑ *We both lost out.* 我们双双失利。 ❑ *Laura lost out to Tom.* 劳拉输给了汤姆。

los·er /luːzər/ (**losers**) 1 N-COUNT The **losers** of a game, contest, or struggle are the people who are defeated or beaten. 失败者 ❑ *...the Dallas Cowboys and Buffalo Bills, the winners and losers of this year's Super Bowl.* …达拉斯牛仔队和布法罗比利队，今年超级杯赛的获胜者和失败者。 ● PHRASE If someone is a **good loser**, they accept that they have lost a game or contest without complaining. If someone is a **bad loser**, they hate losing and complain about it. 输得起的人/输不起的人 ❑ *I'm a great winner and I try to be a good loser.* 我赢得起，也要努力做一个输得起的人。 2 N-COUNT If you refer to someone as a **loser**, you have a low opinion of them because you think they are always unsuccessful. 老是失败的人 [INFORMAL, DISAPPROVAL] ❑ *They've only been trained to compete with other men, so a successful woman can make them feel like a real loser.* 他们只被训练与其他的男性竞争，所以一个成功的女性会让他们觉得自己确实是失败者。 3 N-COUNT People who are **losers** as the result of an action or event, are in a worse situation because of it or do not benefit from it. 损失者 ❑ *Some of the top business successes of the 1980s became the country's greatest losers in the recession.* 20世纪80年代的一些极其成功的商人在该国经济萧条时期沦为损失最惨重的人。

loss ♦♦◇ /lɒs/ (**losses**) 1 N-VAR **Loss** is the fact of no longer having something or having less of it than before. 丧失 ❑ *...loss of sight.* …失明。 ❑ *...hair loss.* …脱发。 2 N-VAR **Loss** of life occurs when people die. 死亡 ❑ *...a terrible loss of human life.* …人员死亡惨重。 3 N-UNCOUNT The **loss** of a relative or friend is their death. (亲人、朋友的) 亡故 ❑ *They took the time to talk about the loss of Thomas and how their grief was affecting them.* 他们花时间来谈论托马斯的去世以及悲伤给他们带来的影响。 4 N-UNCOUNT **Loss** is the feeling of sadness you experience when someone or something you like is taken away from you. 失落感 ❑ *Talk to others about your feelings of loss and grief.* 和别人说说你失落和悲伤。 5 N-COUNT A **loss** is the disadvantage you suffer when a valuable and useful person or thing leaves or is taken away. 损失 ❑ *She said his death was a great loss to herself.* 她说他的去世对于她来说是个巨大的损失。 6 N-UNCOUNT The **loss** of something such as heat, blood, or fluid is the gradual reduction of it or of its level in a system or in someone's body. (热量、血液或液体等的) 流失 ❑ *...blood loss.* …失血。 ❑ *...a rapid loss of heat from the body.* …体内热量迅速流失。 7 N-VAR If a business makes a **loss**, it earns less than it spends. 亏损 [BRIT] ❑ *In 1986 Rover made a loss of nine hundred million dollars.* 1986年，罗孚集团亏损9亿美元。 ❑ *The company said it will stop producing fertilizer in 1990 because of continued losses.* 该公司称，由于持续亏损而将于1990年停止生产化肥。 8 PHRASE If a business produces something **at a loss**, they sell it at a price which is less than it cost them to produce it or buy it. 亏本地 [BUSINESS] ❑ *Timber owners have often produced lumber at a loss and survived these down cycles in demand.* 木场主经常赔本生产木料，以便在需求低迷期挺过来。 9 PHRASE If you say that you are **at a loss**, you mean that you do not know what to do in a particular situation. 不知所措 ❑ *I was at a loss for what to do next.* 我不知道下一步该怎么办。 → see **disaster**

> **Word Partnership** *loss* 的常用搭配:
>
> N. loss **of appetite**, loss **of control**, loss **of income**, loss **of a job** 1
> **blood** loss, **hair** loss, **hearing** loss, **memory** loss, **weight** loss 1 6
>
> ADJ. **great/huge/substantial** loss 1 – 7
> **tragic** loss 2 3
> **net** loss 7

loss ad·just·er (**loss adjusters**) also **loss adjustor** 1 N-COUNT A **loss adjuster** is someone who is employed by an insurance company to decide how much money should be paid to a person making a claim. (保险公司聘请的) 定损员 [BRIT, BUSINESS] 2 → see also **claims adjuster, insurance adjuster**

loss lead·er (**loss leaders**) also **loss-leader** N-COUNT A **loss leader** is an item that is sold at such a low price that it makes a loss in the hope that customers will be attracted by it and buy other products at the same store. (为吸引顾客而) 亏本出售的商品 [BUSINESS] ❑ *Hoskins does not expect a huge profit from the cookies, viewing them more as a loss leader.* 霍斯金斯没有指望从曲奇饼上赚大钱，更多的是将其作为吸引顾客而亏本出售的商品。

lost ♦◇◇ /lɒst/ 1 **Lost** is the past tense and past participle of **lose**. lose的过去式和过去分词 2 ADJ If you are **lost** or if you get **lost**, you do not know where you are or are unable to find your way. 迷路的 ❑ *Barely had I set foot in the street when I realized I was lost.* 我刚走上那条街就发现自己迷路了。 3 ADJ If something is **lost**, or gets **lost**, you cannot find it, for example, because you have forgotten where you put it. 丢失的 ❑ *...a lost book.* …一本丢失的书。 ❑ *He was scrabbling for his pen, which had got lost somewhere under the sheets of paper.* 他当时正在翻找钢笔，那支笔在纸堆下的某个地方找不到了。 4 ADJ If you feel **lost**, you feel very uncomfortable because you are in an unfamiliar situation. 迷惘的 ❑ *Of the funeral he remembered only the cold, the waiting, and feeling very lost.* 有关那次葬礼，他只记得当时很冷，等了很长时间，而且感到很迷惘。 5 ADJ If you describe something as **lost**, you mean that you no longer have it or it no longer exists. 失去的; 不复存在的 ❑ *...their lost homeland.* …他们失去的家园。 ❑ *The sense of community is lost.* 团体意识没有了。 6 ADJ You use **lost** to refer to a period or state of affairs that existed in the past and no longer exists. (时间或事件) 逝去的 [ADJ n] ❑ *He seemed to pine for his lost youth.* 他似乎在怀念他逝去的青春。 ❑ *They are links to a lost age.* 他们是连接一个逝去年代的纽带。 7 ADJ If something is **lost**, it is not used properly and is considered wasted. 浪费的 ❑ *Smith is not bitter about the lost opportunity to compete in the games.* 史密斯没有因为错过参赛机会而痛苦。

> **Thesaurus** *lost* 另参见:
>
> ADJ. adrift, off-track 2
> missing 3

lost and found 1 N-SING **Lost and found** is the place where lost property is kept. 失物招领处 [AM]

> in BRIT, use **lost property**

❑ *Excuse me, can you tell me where the lost and found is?* 打扰一下，您能告诉我失物招领处在哪儿吗？ 2 ADJ **Lost-and-found** things are things which someone has lost and which someone else has found. 失物的 ❑ *...the shelf where they stored lost-and-found articles.* …他们存放失物的架子。

lost prop·er·ty 1 N-UNCOUNT **Lost property** consists of things that people have lost or accidentally left in a public place, for example, on a train or in a school. 丢失物品 [BRIT] ❑ *Lost property should be handed to the driver.* 丢失物品应上缴这位司机。 2 → see **lost and found**

lot ♦♦♦ /lɒt/ (**lots**) 1 QUANT **A lot of** something or **lots of** it is a large amount of it. **A lot of** people or things, or **lots of** them, is a large number of them. 大量 [QUANT "of" n] ❑ *A lot of our land is used to grow crops for export.* 我们的土地大多用来种植出口农作物。 ❑ *He drank lots of milk.* 他喝了许多奶。 ● PRON **Lot** is also a pronoun. 大量 ❑ *I personally prefer to be in a town where there's lots going on.* 我个人更喜欢呆在充满生机的小镇上。 ❑ *I learned a lot from him about how to run a band.* 我从他那里学了很多管理乐队的知识。 2 ADV **A lot** means to a great extent or degree. 非常 ❑ *Matthew's out quite a lot doing his research.* 马修经常出去做研究。 ❑ *I like you, a lot.* 我非常喜欢你。

l

3 ADV If you do something **a lot**, you do it often or for a long time. 频繁地; 长期地 [ADV after v] ❑ *They went out a lot, to restaurants and bars.* 他们经常去饭店和酒吧。 4 N-COUNT You can use **lot** to refer to a set or group of things or people. 一组 ❑ *He bought two lots of 1,000 shares in the company during August and September.* 他在8月和9月期间两次购进了这家公司的股票，每次1千股。 5 N-SING You can refer to a specific group of people as a particular **lot**. 一群人 [INFORMAL] ❑ *Future generations are going to think that we were a pretty boring lot.* 后辈们会认为我们是一群无聊的人。 6 N-SING You can use **the lot** to refer to the whole of an amount that you have just mentioned. 全部; 全体 [INFORMAL] ❑ *This may turn out to be the best football game of the lot.* 这可能会是全部足球比赛中最棒的一场。 7 N-SING Your **lot** is the kind of life you have or the things that you have or experience. 命运 ❑ *She tried to accept her marriage as her lot in life but could not.* 她试图认命接受这桩婚姻，但做不到。 8 N-COUNT A **lot** is a small area of land that belongs to a person or company. (个人或公司的) 一小块地 [AM] ❑ *If oil or gold are discovered under your lot, you can sell the mineral rights.* 如果在你的地里发现石油或金子，你可以出售开采权。 9 → see also **parking lot** 10 N-COUNT A **lot** in an auction is one of the objects or groups of objects that are being sold. 拍卖物 ❑ *The receivers are keen to sell the stores as one lot.* 接受方非常愿意把这些商店一起拍卖。 11 PHRASE If people **draw lots** to decide who will do something, they each take a piece of paper from a container. One or more pieces of paper is marked, and the people who take marked pieces are chosen. 抽签 ❑ *For the first time in the World Cup finals, lots had to be drawn to decide who would finish second and third.* 世界杯决赛中首次由抽签决定谁将获得第二名和第三名。

loth /loʊθ/ → see **loath**

▲ **lo·tion** /loʊʃᵊn/ (**lotions**) N-MASS A **lotion** is a liquid that you use to clean, improve, or protect your skin or hair. (涂在皮肤或头发以清洁或保护的) 涂剂 ❑ *...suntan lotion.* …防晒霜。

L

▲ **lot·tery** /lɒtəri/ (**lotteries**) 1 N-COUNT A **lottery** is a type of gambling game in which people buy numbered tickets. Several numbers are then chosen, and the people who have those numbers on their tickets win a prize. 彩票抽奖 ❑ *...the national lottery.* …全国性的彩票抽奖。 2 N-SING If you describe something as **a lottery**, you mean that what happens depends entirely on luck or chance. 靠运气的事 ❑ *The stockmarket is a lottery.* 股市靠的是运气。
→ see Word Web: **lottery**

▲ **lo·tus** /loʊtəs/ (**lotuses**) N-COUNT A **lotus** or a **lotus flower** is a type of water lily that grows in Africa and Asia. 莲花

loud ♦◇◇ /laʊd/ (**louder, loudest**) 1 ADJ If a noise is **loud**, the level of sound is very high and it can be easily heard. Someone or something that is **loud** produces a lot of noise. 大声的; 吵闹的 ❑ *Suddenly there was a loud bang.* 突然砰地一声响。 ❑ *His voice became harsh and loud.* 他的声音变得又尖又响。 ● ADV **Loud** is also an adverb. 大声地; 吵闹地 [ADV after v] ❑ *She wonders whether Paul's hearing is OK because he turns the television up very loud.* 她怀疑保罗的听力有问题，因为他把电视机的音量调得很大。 ● **loud·ly** ADV 大声地; 吵闹地 [ADV with v] ❑ *His footsteps echoed loudly in the tiled hall.* 他的脚步声响亮地回荡在铺着瓷砖的大厅里。 2 ADJ If you describe something, especially a piece of clothing, as **loud**, you dislike it because it has very bright colors or very large, bold patterns which look unpleasant. (尤指衣服) 花哨的 [DISAPPROVAL] ❑ *He liked to shock with his gold chains and loud clothes.* 他喜欢戴金链子，穿花哨衣服，以此制造轰动。 3 PHRASE If you say or read something **out loud**, you say it or read it so that it can be heard, rather than just thinking it. 出声地 ❑ *Even Ford, who seldom smiled, laughed out loud a few times.* 即使是平时不苟言笑的福特也好几次笑出了声。 4 **for crying out loud** → see **cry**

Thesaurus loud 另参见:

ADJ. deafening, noisy, piercing; (*ant.*) quiet, soft 1
flashy, gaudy, tasteless 2

Word Partnership loud 的常用搭配:

N. loud **bang**, loud **crash**, loud **explosion**, loud **music**, loud **noise**, loud **voice** 1
ADJ. loud **and clear** 1
V. **laugh out** loud, **read out** loud, **say** *something* **out** loud, **think out** loud 3

loud·hail·er /laʊdheɪlər/ (**loudhailers**) also **loud-hailer** N-COUNT A **loudhailer** is the same as a **bullhorn**. 手提式扩音喇叭 [BRIT]

▲ **loud·speaker** /laʊdspikər/ (**loudspeakers**) also **loud speaker** 1 N-COUNT A **loudspeaker** is a piece of electronic equipment that forms part of a public address system and transmits sound. 扬声器 ❑ *The loudspeaker announced the arrival of the train.* 广播说火车进站了。 2 N-COUNT A **loudspeaker** is a piece of equipment, for example, part of a radio or hi-fi system, through which sound comes out. 喇叭 [BRIT]

★ **lounge** /laʊndʒ/ (**lounges, lounging, lounged**) 1 N-COUNT In a hotel, club, or other public place, a **lounge** is a room where people can sit and relax. (酒店、俱乐部或其他公共场合的) 休息室 ❑ *I spoke to her in the lounge of a big Johannesburg hotel where she was attending a union meeting.* 我在约翰内斯堡一家大酒店的休息室和她说过话，当时她在那儿参加一个工会会议。 2 N-COUNT In an airport, a **lounge** is a very large room where people can sit and wait for aircraft to arrive or leave. 候机厅 ❑ *Instead of taking me to the departure lounge they took me right to my seat on the plane.* 他们没有带我去候机厅，而是直接把我带到了飞机的座位上。 3 N-COUNT In a house, a **lounge** is a room where people sit and relax. 起居室 [BRIT]
in AM, use **family room**
4 V-I If you **lounge** somewhere, you sit or lie there in a relaxed or lazy way. 懒洋洋地坐着; 懒散地躺着 ❑ *They ate and drank and lounged in the shade.* 他们在阴凉处懒洋洋地坐着，又吃又喝。

louse /laʊs/ (**lice**) N-COUNT **Lice** are small insects that live on the bodies of people or animals and bite them in order to feed off their blood. 虱子

lousy /laʊzi/ (**lousier, lousiest**) 1 ADJ If you describe something as **lousy**, you mean that it is of very bad quality or that you do not like it. 糟糕的 [INFORMAL] ❑ *He blamed Fiona for a lousy weekend.* 他指责菲奥娜让他过了一个糟糕的周末。 ❑ *At Billy's Café, the menu is limited and the food is lousy.* 比利餐馆饭菜品种有限，质量也很糟。 2 ADJ If you describe someone as **lousy**, you mean that they are very bad at something they do. 蹩脚的 [INFORMAL] ❑ *I was a lousy secretary.* 我曾是个蹩脚的秘书。 3 ADJ If you describe the number or amount of something as **lousy**, you mean it is smaller than you think it should be. 微薄的 [INFORMAL] ❑ *The pay is lousy.* 薪水少得可怜。 4 ADJ If you feel **lousy**, you feel very ill. 极不舒服的 ["feel/look" ADJ] [INFORMAL] ❑ *I wasn't actually sick but I felt lousy.* 我其实没有生病，但感觉很不舒服。

lout /laʊt/ (**louts**) N-COUNT If you describe a man or boy as a **lout**, you are critical of them because they behave in an impolite or aggressive way. 粗鲁的人 (常指男子) [DISAPPROVAL] ❑ *...a drunken lout.* …一个醉鬼。

lov·able /lʌvəbᵊl/ ADJ If you describe someone as **lovable**, you mean that they have attractive qualities, and are easy to like.

Word Web lottery

People **gamble** for many different reasons. Some want to become rich. Some find it entertaining or exciting. Others need more **money** to live. **Lotteries** have become a popular form of **betting**. Most places have a lottery. **Winners** can choose between a **lump sum** payment and annual **payouts**. Either way, they usually have to pay the government about half their **winnings** in taxes. The **odds** of **winning** a lottery are very tiny. There is often only about one chance in 20 million of winning the **jackpot**. Studies have shown that poor people are the most likely to **play** the lottery.

Word Web love

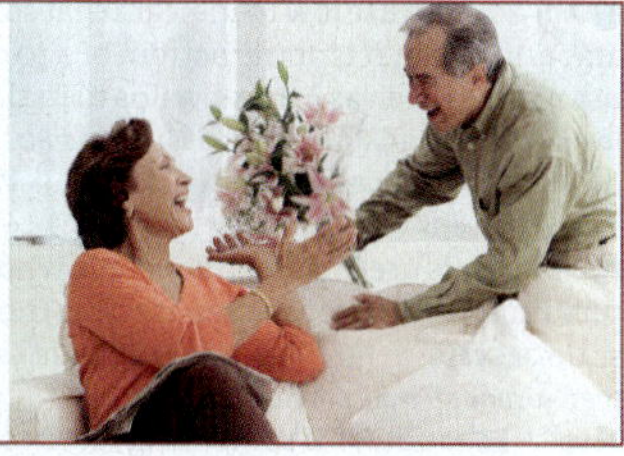

Until the Middle Ages, **romance** was not an important part of **marriage**. Parents decided who their children would marry. Often social class and political connections were the deciding factor. No one expected a couple to **fall in love**. However, during the Middle Ages, poets and musicians began to write about love in a new way. These **romantic** poems and songs describe a new type of courtship. In them, the man **woos** a woman for her **affection**. This is the basis for the modern idea of a romantic **bond** between **husband** and **wife**.

可爱的 ❑ *His vulnerability makes him even more lovable.* 他的弱点甚至使他显得更可爱。

love ♦♦♦ /lʌv/ (**loves, loving, loved**) **1** V-T If you **love** someone, you feel romantically or sexually attracted to them, and they are very important to you. 爱 ❑ *Oh, Amy, I love you.* 啊，埃米，我爱你。❑ *We love each other. We want to spend our lives together.* 我们很爱对方。我们希望共度一生。 **2** N-UNCOUNT **Love** is a very strong feeling of affection toward someone who you are romantically or sexually attracted to. 爱情 ❑ *Our love for each other has been increased by what we've been through together.* 我们对彼此的爱因我们共同经历的一切而增强。 ❑ *...an old fashioned love story.* …一个老套的爱情故事。 **3** V-T You say that you **love** someone when their happiness is very important to you, so that you behave in a kind and caring way toward them. 疼爱 ❑ *You'll never love anyone the way you love your baby.* 你永远不会像疼爱你的孩子那样爱任何人。 **4** N-UNCOUNT **Love** is the feeling that a person's happiness is very important to you, and the way you show this feeling in your behavior toward them. 疼爱 ❑ *My love for all my children is unconditional.* 我对我所有孩子的疼爱是无条件的。 **5** V-T If you **love** something, you like it very much. 非常喜欢 ❑ *We loved the food so much, especially the fish dishes.* 我们非常喜欢这些食物，尤其是那儿盘鱼。 ❑ *...one of these people that loves to be in the outdoors.* …那些喜欢户外生活的人们中的一员。 **6** V-T You can say that you **love** something when you consider that it is important and want to protect or support it. 热爱 ❑ *I love my country as you love yours.* 我热爱我的国家，就像你热爱你的国家一样。 **7** N-UNCOUNT **Love** is a strong liking for something, or a belief that it is important. 热爱 ❑ *This is no way to encourage a love of literature.* 这不可能激发对文学的热爱。 **8** N-COUNT Your **love** is someone or something that you love. 心爱之人；心爱之物 ❑ *"She is the love of my life," he said.* "她是我今生至爱，"他说道。 **9** V-T If you **would love to** have or do something, you very much want to have it or do it. 很愿意 ❑ *I would love to play for England again.* 我很愿意再次为英格兰参赛。 ❑ *I would love a hot bath and clean clothes.* 我很想洗个热水澡，换身干净衣服。 **10** NUM In tennis, **love** is a score of zero. (网球比赛中的) 零分 ❑ *He beat Thomas Muster of Austria three sets to love.* 他以3比0战胜了奥地利的托马斯·穆斯特。 **11** CONVENTION You can use expressions such as **love**, **love from**, and **all my love**, followed by your name, as an informal way of ending a letter to a friend or relative. (给亲友的书信结尾，置于写信人名前) 爱你的 ❑ *...with love from Grandma and Grandpa.* …爱你的祖父母。 **12** N-UNCOUNT If you send someone your **love**, you ask another person, who will soon be speaking or writing to them, to tell them that you are thinking about them with affection. 问候 ❑ *Please give her my love.* 请代我问候她。 **13** → see also **loving** **14** PHRASE If you **fall in love with** someone, you start to be in love with them. 爱上 (某人) ❑ *I fell in love with him because of his kind nature.* 我爱上了他，因为他天性善良。 **15** PHRASE If you **fall in love with** something, you start to like it very much. 非常喜欢 (某物) ❑ *I fell in love with the movies.* 我非常喜欢这些电影。 **16** PHRASE If you **are in love with** someone, you feel romantically or sexually attracted to them, and they are very important to you. (与某人) 恋爱 ❑ *Laura had never before been in love.* 劳拉以前从未谈过恋爱。 **17** PHRASE If you are **in love with** something, you like it very much. 迷恋 (某物) ❑ *He had always been in love with the enchanted landscape of the West.* 他一直都非常迷恋西部令人陶醉的风光。 **18** PHRASE When two people **make love**, they have sex. 做爱 ❑ *Have you ever made love to a girl before?* 你以前和女孩子做过爱吗？

→ see Word Web: **love**

→ see **emotion**

Thesaurus *love* 另参见：

V. adore, cherish, treasure; *(ant.)* dislike, hate **1** **3** **5**

N. adoration, devotion, tenderness; *(ant.)* hate **2** **4** **7**

Word Partnership *love* 的常用搭配：

N. love **a girl/guy**, love-**hate relationship**, love *your* **husband/wife**, love **a man/woman**, love **and marriage** **1** **3**
love *of* **books**, love *of* **life**, love **music**, love *of* **nature** **7**

ADJ. **passionate** love, **romantic** love, **sexual** love **2**
great love, **true** love **2** **4** **7** **8**

love af·fair (**love affairs**) **1** N-COUNT A **love affair** is a romantic and usually sexual relationship between two people who love each other but who are not married or living together. 风流韵事 ❑ *...a stressful love affair with a married man.* …和一个已婚男子的一段备受压力的风流恋情。 **2** N-SING If you refer to someone's **love affair with** something, you mean that they like it a lot and are very enthusiastic about it. (对某物的) 强烈兴趣 ❑ *...the American love affair with firearms.* …美国人对枪支的强烈兴趣。

love life (**love lives**) N-COUNT Someone's **love life** is the part of their life that consists of their romantic and sexual relationships. 爱情生活 ❑ *His love life was complicated, and involved intense relationships.* 他的爱情生活很复杂，有过一些热恋。

love·ly ♦◇◇ /lʌvli/ (**lovelier, loveliest**) **1** ADJ If you describe someone or something as **lovely**, you mean that they are very beautiful and therefore pleasing to look at or listen to. 美丽的；美妙的 ❑ *You look lovely, Marcia.* 你看起来很美，马西娅。 ❑ *He had a lovely voice.* 他嗓音甜美。 ● **love·li·ness** N-UNCOUNT 漂亮 ❑ *You are a vision of loveliness.* 你貌美如画。 **2** ADJ If you describe something as **lovely**, you mean that it gives you pleasure. 令人愉快的 [mainly SPOKEN] ❑ *Mary! How lovely to see you!* 玛丽，见到你多么愉快！ ❑ *It's a lovely day.* 天气很好。

lov·er ♦◇◇ /lʌvər/ (**lovers**) **1** N-COUNT Someone's **lover** is someone who they are having a sexual relationship with but are not married to. 情人 ❑ *Every Thursday she would meet her lover Leon.* 每个星期四她都去约会她的情人利昂。 **2** N-COUNT If you are a **lover** of something such as animals or the arts, you enjoy them very much and take great pleasure in them. 爱好者 ❑ *She is a great lover of horses and horse racing.* 她非常喜欢马，并热衷于赛马。

Word Partnership *lover* 的常用搭配：

ADJ. **former** lover, **great** lover, **jealous** lover, **married** lover **1**

N. **animal** lover, **music** lover, **nature** lover **2**

lov·ing /lʌvɪŋ/ **1** ADJ Someone who is **loving** feels or shows love to other people. 富有爱心的 ❑ *Jim was a most loving husband and father.* 吉姆是一个最富有爱心的丈夫和父亲。 ● **lov·ing·ly** ADV 充满爱心地 ❑ *Brian gazed lovingly at Mary Ann.* 布赖恩充满爱意地凝视着玛丽·安。 **2** ADJ **Loving** actions are done with great enjoyment and care. 精心呵护的 ❑ *The house has been restored with loving care.* 这房子已经被精心修复。 ● **lov·ing·ly** ADV 精心呵护地 ❑ *I lifted the box and ran my fingers lovingly over the top.* 我提起盒子，爱惜地用手指抚过盒盖。

low ♦♦♦ /loʊ/ (**lower, lowest, lows**) **1** ADJ Something that is **low** measures only a short distance from the bottom to the top, or from the ground to the top. 低矮的 ❑ *...the low garden wall that separated the front garden from next door.* …低矮的花园围墙隔开了前花园与邻院。 ❑ *The country, with its low, rolling hills was beautiful.* 这一地区山势低缓，连绵起伏，非常美丽。 **2** ADJ If something is **low**, it is close to the ground, to sea level, or to the bottom of something. 接近地面的；接近海平面的；接近底部的 ❑ *He bumped his head on the low beams.* 他的头撞到了低矮的横梁上。 ❑ *It was late afternoon and the sun was low in the sky.* 当时是傍晚时分，太阳低低地挂在天上。 **3** ADJ When a river is **low**, it contains less water than usual. 水位浅的 ❑ *...pumps that guarantee a constant depth of water even when the supplying river is low.* …那些水泵即使在供应水源的河流水位很低时仍能保持水位。

4 ADJ You can use **low** to indicate that something is small in amount or that it is at the bottom of a particular scale. You can use phrases such as **in the low 80s** to indicate that a number or level is less than 85 but not as little as 80. 数量少的；数值偏低的 ❑ *Casualties remained remarkably low.* 伤亡人数依然很少。 ❑ *They are still having to live on very low incomes.* 他们仍然不得不靠微薄的收入为生。 5 ADJ **Low** is used to describe people who are not considered to be very important because they are near the bottom of a particular scale or system. (级别等) 低微的 ❑ *She refused to promote Colin above the low rank of "legal adviser."* 她拒绝提升科林，只让他做低级别的"法律顾问"。 6 N-COUNT If something reaches a **low** of a particular amount or degree, that is the smallest it has ever been. 最低点 ❑ *Prices dropped to a low of about $1.12 in December.* 价格在12月份跌到大约$1.12的最低点。 7 ADJ If the quality or standard of something is **low**, it is very poor. (品质) 差的；(水平) 低的 ❑ *A school would not accept low-quality work from any student.* 学校不会接受任何学生的低水平作品。 ❑ *The inquiry team criticizes staff at the psychiatric hospital for the low standard of care.* 调查组批评精神病医院工作人员的低护理水平。 8 ADJ If a food or other substance is **low in** a particular ingredient, it contains only a small amount of that ingredient. 含量低的 [v-link ADJ "in" n] ❑ *They look for foods that are low in calories.* 他们寻找低热量食物。 ● COMB IN ADJ **Low** is also a combining form. 用于构成合成词 ❑ *...low-sodium tomato sauce.* …钠含量低的番茄酱。 9 ADJ If you have a **low** opinion of someone or something, you disapprove of them or dislike them. (评价) 很差的 ❑ *The majority of sex offenders have a low opinion of themselves.* 大多数性犯罪者自我评价都很低。 10 ADJ You can use **low** to describe negative feelings and attitudes. 消沉的 ❑ *We are all very tired and morale is low.* 我们都疲惫不堪，士气低落。 11 ADJ If a sound or noise is **low**, it is deep. 低沉的 ❑ *Then suddenly she gave a low, choking moan and began to tremble violently.* 然后她突然发出一声低沉的、令人窒息的呻吟，身体开始剧烈地抖动。 12 ADJ If someone's voice is **low**, it is quiet or soft. 轻声的 ❑ *Her voice was so low he had to strain to catch it.* 她的声音太小，他不得不费力地听着。 13 ADJ A light that is **low** is not bright or strong. 暗淡的 ❑ *Their eyesight is poor in low light.* 他们在昏暗的光线下看不清东西。 14 ADJ If a radio, oven, or light is on **low**, it has been adjusted so that only a small amount of sound, heat, or light is produced. (收音机、烤箱或灯光调成) 低档的 ❑ *She turned her little kitchen radio on low.* 她把厨房的小收音机声音调得很低。 ❑ *Buy a dimmer switch and keep the light on low, or switch it off altogether.* 买一个调光器，把亮度调低，或者完全关掉。 15 ADJ If you are **low on** something or if a supply of it is **low**, there is not much of it left. 不多的 [v-link ADJ] ❑ *We're a bit low on bed linen.* 我们的床上用品不多了。 16 ADJ If you are **low**, you are depressed. 情绪低落的 [INFORMAL] ❑ *"I didn't ask for this job, you know," he tells friends when he is low.* "我没有要求做这份工作，你知道的。"他在情绪低落的时候告诉朋友们。 17 → see also **lower** 18 to look **high and low** → see **high** 19 **low profile** → see **profile** 20 to **be running low** → see **run** → see **tide**

L

> **Thesaurus** *low* 另参见：
> ADJ. bottom 2
> inferior, second-rate, shoddy 7

low·er ♦◇◇ /loʊər/ (**lowers, lowering, lowered**) 1 ADJ You can use **lower** to refer to the bottom one of a pair of things. (一对物品中) 下面的 [ADJ n, "the" ADJ, "the" ADJ "of" n] ❑ *She bit her lower lip.* 她咬着下唇。 ❑ *...the lower of the two holes.* …两个洞中下面的那个。 2 ADJ You can use **lower** to refer to the bottom part of something. 底部的 [ADJ n] ❑ *Use a small cushion to help give support to the lower back.* 用一个小垫子来辅助支撑腰部。 3 ADJ You can use **lower** to refer to people or things that are less important than similar people or things. 下等的；低级的 [ADJ n, "the" ADJ] ❑ *Already the awards are causing resentment in the lower ranks of council officers.* 那些奖励已经引起了委员会下层工作人员的不满。 ❑ *The nation's highest court reversed the lower court's decision.* 该国的最高法院推翻了下级法院的判决。 4 V-T If you **lower** something, you move it slowly downward. (缓慢地) 放下；降下 ❑ *Two reporters had to help lower the coffin into the grave.* 两名记者不得不帮忙把棺材下放至墓穴中。 ❑ *Sokolowski lowered himself into the black leather chair.* 索科罗斯基缓缓地在黑皮椅里坐下。 ● **low·er·ing** N-UNCOUNT (缓慢地) 放下；降下 ❑ *...the extinguishing of the Olympic flame and the lowering of the flag.* …熄奥运圣火和降奥运旗帜。 5 V-T If you **lower** something, you make it less in amount, degree, value, or quality. 减少；降低 ❑ *The Central Bank has lowered interest rates by 2 percent.* 中央银行已经降低了2%的利率。 ● **low·er·ing** N-UNCOUNT 减少；降低 ❑ *...a package of social measures which included the lowering of the retirement age.* …包括降低退休年龄在内的一系列社会措施。 6 V-T If someone **lowers** their head or eyes, they look downward, for example, because they are sad or embarrassed. 垂下 ❑ *She lowered her head and brushed past photographers as she went back inside.* 当她走回屋里时，她垂下了头，与摄影师擦肩而过。 7 V-T If you say that you would not **lower yourself** by doing something, you mean that you would not behave in a way that would make you or other people respect you less. 贬低 (身份) [oft with brd-neg] ❑ *Don't lower yourself, don't be the way they are.* 不要贬低自己的身份，别像他们那样。 8 V-T/V-I If you **lower** your voice or if your voice **lowers**, you speak more quietly. 放低 (声音)；降低 ❑ *The man moved closer, lowering his voice.* 那个男人走近了些，同时放低了声音。 9 → see also **low**

low·er·case also **lower-case, lower case** N-UNCOUNT **Lowercase** letters are small letters, not capital letters. 小写体 ❑ *It was printed in lowercase.* 这是用小写体打印的。

low-key ADJ If you say that something is **low-key**, you mean that it is on a small scale rather than involving a lot of activity or being made to seem impressive or important. 有节制的；低调的 ❑ *The wedding will be a very low-key affair.* 这场婚礼将非常低调。

low·ly /loʊli/ (**lowlier, lowliest**) ADJ If you describe someone or something as **lowly**, you mean that they are low in rank, status, or importance. 卑微的；低级的 ❑ *...lowly bureaucrats pretending to be senators.* …假称参议员的低级官员。

low-paid ADJ If you describe someone or their job as **low-paid**, you mean that their work earns them very little money. 低薪的 ❑ *...low-paid workers.* …低薪工人。

low-tech /loʊ tɛk/ ADJ **Low-tech** machines or systems are ones that do not use modern or sophisticated technology. 技术含量低的 ❑ *...a simple form of low-tech electric propulsion.* …一种技术含量低的简单的电力牵引形式。

loy·al /lɔɪəl/ ADJ Someone who is **loyal** remains firm in their friendship or support for a person or thing. 忠诚的 [APPROVAL] ❑ *They had remained loyal to the president.* 他们一直忠于总统。 ● **loy·al·ly** ADV 忠诚地 [ADV with v] ❑ *They have loyally supported their party and their leader.* 他们忠心耿耿地支持自己的政党和领导人。 → see **hero**

loy·al·ty /lɔɪəlti/ (**loyalties**) 1 N-UNCOUNT **Loyalty** is the quality of staying firm in your friendship or support for someone or something. 忠诚 ❑ *I have sworn an oath of loyalty to the monarchy.* 我已经发誓效忠君主制。 2 N-COUNT **Loyalties** are feelings of friendship, support, or duty toward someone or something. 效忠的义务 ❑ *She had developed strong loyalties to the Manet family.* 她深深感到对马奈一家有效忠的义务。

loy·al·ty card (**loyalty cards**) N-COUNT A **loyalty card** is a plastic card that some stores give to regular customers. Each time the customer buys something from the store, points are electronically stored on their card and can be exchanged later for goods or services. (商场的) 积分卡

LPG /ɛl pi dʒi/ N-UNCOUNT **LPG** is a type of fuel consisting of hydrocarbon gases in liquid form. **LPG** is an abbreviation for "liquefied petroleum gas." 液化石油气

★ **lu·bri·cate** /lubrɪkeɪt/ (**lubricates, lubricating, lubricated**) V-T If you **lubricate** something such as a part of a machine, you put a substance such as oil on it so that it moves smoothly. 使润滑 [FORMAL] ❑ *Mineral oils are used to lubricate machinery.* 矿物油被用来润滑机器。 ● **lu·bri·ca·tion** /lubrɪkeɪʃən/ N-UNCOUNT 润滑 ❑ *Use a touch of linseed oil for lubrication.* 用一点蓖麻油来润滑一下。

> **Word Link** *luc ≈ light : hallucinate, lucid, translucent*

lu·cid /lusɪd/ 1 ADJ **Lucid** writing or speech is clear and easy to understand. 清晰简明的 ❑ *...a lucid account of the history of mankind.* …对人类历史清晰简明的介绍。 ● **lu·cid·ly** ADV 清晰简明地 [ADV with v] ❑ *Both of them had the ability to present complex matters lucidly.* 他们两个人都曾具备把复杂的事情清晰明了地表达出来的能力。 ● **lu·cid·ity** /lusɪdɪti/ N-UNCOUNT 清晰简明 ❑ *His writings were marked by an extraordinary lucidity and elegance of style.* 他的作品以非凡的清晰简明和优雅风格而著称。 2 ADJ If someone is **lucid**, they are thinking clearly again after a period of illness or confusion. (生病或头脑不清后) 神志清醒的 [FORMAL] ❑ *He wasn't very lucid, he didn't quite know where he was.* 他神志不太清醒，不大清楚自己在哪儿。 ● **lu·cid·ity** N-UNCOUNT 神志清醒 ❑ *The pain had lessened in the night, but so had his lucidity.* 晚上他疼痛减轻，但神志不那么清醒了。

luck ♦◇◇ /lʌk/ (**lucks, lucking, lucked**) 1 N-UNCOUNT **Luck** or **good luck** is success or good things that happen to you, that do not come from your own abilities or efforts. 运气 ❑ *I knew I needed a bit of luck to win.* 我知道我得靠点运气才能取胜。 ❑ *The Sri Lankans have been having no luck with the weather.* 斯里兰卡人一直没运气碰上好天。 2 N-UNCOUNT **Bad luck** is lack of success or bad things that happen to you, that have not been caused by yourself or other people. 霉运 ❑ *I had a lot of bad luck during the first half of this season.* 我在这一季节的前半季遭了很多霉运。 3 CONVENTION If you ask someone the question "**Any luck?**" or "**No luck?**," you want to know if they have been successful in something they were trying to do. 运气如何 [INFORMAL] ❑ *"Any luck?"—"No."* "运气如何？"——"不好。" 4 CONVENTION You can say "**Bad luck**" or "**Hard luck**" to someone when you want to express sympathy to them. 运气不好 (表同情) [INFORMAL, FORMULAE] ❑ *Bad luck, man, just bad luck.* 运气不好，老弟，只是运气不好。 5 CONVENTION If you say "**Good luck**" or "**Best of luck**" to someone, you are telling them that you hope they will be successful in something they are trying to do. 祝你好运 [INFORMAL, FORMULAE] ❑ *He kissed her on the cheek. "Best of luck!"* 他吻了一下她的面颊："祝你好运！" 6 PHRASE You can say someone **is in luck** when they are in a situation where they can have what they want or need. 交好运 ❑ *You're in luck. The doctor's still in.* 你运气不错，医生还在。 7 PHRASE If you say that someone **is out of luck**, you mean that they cannot have something which they can normally have. 运气不佳 ❑ *"What do you want, Roy? If it's money, you're out of luck."* "你想要什么，罗伊？如果是钱，你的运气不怎么样。"

▸ **luck out** PHRASAL VERB If you **luck out**, you get some advantage or are successful because you have good luck. 侥幸成功 ❑ *Was he born to be successful, or did he just luck out?* 他是天生注定成功，还是侥幸成功呢？

Word Partnership *luck* 的常用搭配：

ADJ.	**dumb** luck, **good** luck, **just** luck, **pure** luck, **sheer** luck 1
V.	**bring** *someone* luck, **need a little** luck, **need some** luck, **push** *your* luck, **try** *your* luck, **wish** *someone* luck 1 **have any/bad/better/good/no** luck 1 2

lucki·ly /lʌkɪli/ ADV You add **luckily** to a statement to indicate that it is good that a particular thing happened or is the case because otherwise the situation would have been difficult or unpleasant. 幸运地 [ADV with cl] ❑ *Luckily, we both love football.* 幸好我们俩都热爱足球。

lucky ♦◇◇ /lʌki/ (**luckier, luckiest**) 1 ADJ You say that someone is **lucky** when they have something that is very desirable or when they are in a very desirable situation. 幸运的 ❑ *I am luckier than most. I have a job.* 我比大多数人幸运，有份工作。 ❑ *He is incredibly lucky to be alive.* 他竟然幸运地活了下来。 2 ADJ Someone who is **lucky** seems to always have good luck. 常走运的 ❑ *Some people are born lucky, aren't they?* 一些人天生好运不断，不是吗？ 3 ADJ If you describe an action or experience as **lucky**, you mean that it was good or successful, and that it happened by chance and not as a result of planning or preparation. 侥幸的 ❑ *They admit they are now desperate for a lucky break.* 他们承认现在非常渴望交上好运。 4 ADJ A **lucky** object is something that people believe helps them to be successful. 吉祥的 ❑ *He did not have on his other lucky charm, a pair of green socks.* 他没穿另一件吉祥物：一双绿袜子。 5 PHRASE If you say that someone **will be lucky to** do or get something, you mean that they are very unlikely to do or get it, and will definitely not do or get any more than that. 某人可就走运了 (指不太可能做成) ❑ *You'll be lucky if you get any breakfast.* 如果你能弄到早餐那可就幸运了。 ❑ *Those remaining in work will be lucky to get the smallest of pay increases.* 那些仍在工作的人若能涨一点点薪水就算是幸运的了。

Word Partnership *lucky* 的常用搭配：

V.	**be** lucky, **feel** lucky, **get** lucky, lucky **to get** *something*, lucky **to have** *something* 1
ADV.	lucky **enough**, **pretty** lucky, **really** lucky, **so** lucky, **very** lucky 1
N.	lucky **break**, lucky **guess** 3

▲ **lu·cra·tive** /lukrətɪv/ ADJ A **lucrative** activity, job, or business deal is very profitable. 获利丰厚的 ❑ *Thousands of ex-army officers have found lucrative jobs in private security firms.* 成千上万的退役军官在私人保安公司找到了薪水丰厚的工作。

lu·di·crous /ludɪkrəs/ ADJ If you describe something as **ludicrous**, you are emphasizing that you think it is foolish, unreasonable, or unsuitable. 荒谬的 [EMPHASIS] ❑ *It was ludicrous to suggest that the visit could be kept secret.* 认为此次访问可以保密的想法真是荒唐可笑。 ● **lu·di·crous·ly** ADV 荒谬地 ❑ *By Western standards the prices are ludicrously low.* 按照西方的标准，价格低得近乎荒唐。

lug /lʌg/ (**lugs, lugging, lugged**) V-T If you **lug** a heavy or awkward object somewhere, you carry it there with difficulty. (费力地) 拖 [INFORMAL] ❑ *Nobody wants to lug around huge suitcases full of clothes.* 没有人愿意拖着装满衣服的大箱子到处转。

lug·gage /lʌgɪdʒ/ N-UNCOUNT **Luggage** is the suitcases and bags that you take with you when travel. 行李 ❑ *Leave your luggage in the hotel.* 把你的行李留在旅馆吧。

> **Luggage** is an uncount noun. You can have **a piece of luggage** or **some luggage** but you cannot have "a luggage" or "some luggages." In British English, people normally use **luggage** when they are talking about everything that travelers carry. **Baggage** is a more technical word and is used for example when discussing airports or travel insurance. In American English, **luggage** refers to empty bags and suitcases and **baggage** refers to bags and suitcases with their contents. Both British and American speakers can refer to everything that travelers carry as their **bags**. American speakers can also call an individual suitcase a **bag**.

lug·gage rack (**luggage racks**) 1 N-COUNT A **luggage rack** is a shelf for putting luggage on, on a vehicle such as a train or bus. (火车或公交车上的) 行李架 2 N-COUNT A **luggage rack** is a metal frame that is fixed on top of a car and used for carrying large objects. (汽车顶部的) 行李架 [AM]

in BRIT, use **roof rack**

luke·warm /lukwɔrm/ 1 ADJ Something, especially a liquid, that is **lukewarm** is only slightly warm. (尤指液体) 微温的 ❑ *Wash your face with lukewarm water.* 用温水洗脸。 2 ADJ If you describe a person or their attitude as **lukewarm**, you mean that they are not showing much enthusiasm or interest. 不热情的；不感兴趣的 ❑ *Economists have never been more than lukewarm toward him.* 经济学家们从未对他有过多少兴趣。

▲ **lull** /lʌl/ (**lulls, lulling, lulled**) 1 N-COUNT A **lull** is a period of quiet or calm in a longer period of activity or excitement. 间歇期 ❑ *There was a lull in political violence after the election of the current president.* 现任总统选举结束以后，政治暴力曾暂时平息。 2 V-T If you **are lulled into** feeling safe, someone or something causes you to feel safe at a time when you are not safe. 蒙蔽；误导 ❑ *It is easy to be lulled into a false sense of security.* 很容易因受到蒙蔽而产生错误的安全感。 ❑ *I had been lulled into thinking the publicity would be a trivial matter.* 我曾被误导相信宣传是件小事。

▲ **lum·ber** /lʌmbər/ (**lumbers, lumbering, lumbered**) 1 N-UNCOUNT **Lumber** consists of trees and large pieces of wood that have been roughly cut up. 木材 [mainly AM] ❑ *It was made of soft lumber, spruce by the look of it.* 它是软木做的，看样子是云杉。 2 V-I If someone or something **lumbers** from one place to another, they move there very slowly and clumsily. 缓慢笨拙地移动 ❑ *He lumbered back to his chair.* 他蹒跚地坐回到椅子上。

★ **lu·mi·nous** /lumɪnəs/ ADJ Something that is **luminous** shines or glows in the dark. 发亮的 ❑ *The luminous dial on the clock showed five minutes to seven.* 时钟上发光的表盘显示当时7点差5分。

lump /lʌmp/ (**lumps, lumping, lumped**) 1 N-COUNT A **lump of** something is a solid piece of it. 块 ❑ *The potter shaped and squeezed the lump of clay into a graceful shape.* 制陶工人把一块黏土塑形，压成漂亮的形状。 ❑ *...a lump of wood.* …一块木头。 2 N-COUNT A **lump** on or in someone's body is a small, hard swelling that has been caused by an injury or an illness. 肿块 ❑ *I've got a lump on my shoulder.* 我的肩膀上有个肿块。 3 N-COUNT A **lump of** sugar is a small cube of it. 一小方块 (糖) ❑ *...a nugget of rough gold about the size of a lump of sugar.* …未加工的天然金块，约一块方糖大小。 4 → see also **lump sum** 5 PHRASE If you say that you have a **lump in** your **throat**, you mean that you have a tight feeling in your throat because of a strong emotion such as sorrow or gratitude. 喉咙哽咽 ❑ *I stood there with a lump in my throat and tried to fight back tears.* 我站在那儿，喉咙哽咽，拼命忍住眼泪。

▸ **lump together** PHRASAL VERB If a number of different people or things **are lumped together**, they are considered as a group rather than separately. 把…扯到一起；把…混为一谈 ❏ *Policemen and prostitutes, bankers and butchers are all lumped together in the service sector.* 警察和妓女、银行家和屠夫都被扯到一起，归入服务业。

lump sum (**lump sums**) N-COUNT A **lump sum** is an amount of money that is paid as a large amount on a single occasion rather than as smaller amounts on several separate occasions. 一次付清的大笔钱款 ❏ *...a tax-free lump sum of $50,000.* …一整笔免税的$50000款项。
→ see **lottery**

lumpy /lʌmpi/ (**lumpier, lumpiest**) ADJ Something that is **lumpy** contains lumps or is covered with lumps. 结成块的 ❏ *When the rice isn't cooked properly it goes lumpy and gooey.* 米饭煮得不好会结块儿发粘。

★ **lu·nar** /lunər/ ADJ **Lunar** means relating to the moon. 月球的 [ADJ n] ❏ *The vast volcanic slope was eerily reminiscent of a lunar landscape.* 巨大的火山坡很奇怪地让人想起月球上的景观。
→ see **eclipse**

lu·na·tic /lunətɪk/ (**lunatics**) 1 N-COUNT If you describe someone as a **lunatic**, you think they behave in a dangerous, stupid, or annoying way. 疯子 [INFORMAL, DISAPPROVAL] ❏ *Her son thinks she's an absolute raving lunatic.* 她的儿子认为她是个十足的满口胡言的疯子。 2 ADJ If you describe someone's behavior or ideas as **lunatic**, you think they are very foolish and possibly dangerous. 极端愚蠢的；疯狂的 [DISAPPROVAL] ❏ *...the operation of the market taken to lunatic extremes.* …疯狂到极点的市场运作。 3 N-COUNT People who were mentally ill used to be called **lunatics**. 精神病患者 [OLD-FASHIONED] ❏ *...the lunatics in the Bedlam asylum.* …贝德兰疯人院的精神病人。

lunch ♦♦◇ /lʌntʃ/ (**lunches, lunching, lunched**) 1 N-VAR **Lunch** is the meal that you have in the middle of the day. 午餐 ❏ *Shall we meet somewhere for lunch?* 我们约个地方一起吃午饭好吗？ ❏ *He did not enjoy business lunches.* 他不喜欢工作午餐。 2 V-I When you **lunch**, you have lunch, especially at a restaurant. (尤指在餐馆) 进午餐 [FORMAL] ❏ *Only the extremely rich could afford to lunch at the Mirabelle.* 只有大富豪才吃得起米拉贝尔饭店的午餐。
→ see **meal**

Word Partnership *lunch* 的常用搭配：

V.	**break for** lunch, **bring *your*** lunch, **buy *someone*** lunch, **eat** lunch, **go *somewhere* for** lunch, **go to** lunch, **have** lunch, **pack a** lunch, **serve** lunch 1
ADJ.	**free** lunch, **good** lunch, **hot** lunch, **late** lunch 1

lunch·eon /lʌntʃən/ (**luncheons**) N-COUNT A **luncheon** is a formal lunch, for example, to celebrate an important event or to raise money for charity. 午宴 ❏ *Earlier this month, a luncheon for former U.N. staff was held in Vienna.* 本月早些时候在维也纳为前联合国工作人员举行了午宴。

lunch·time /lʌntʃtaɪm/ (**lunchtimes**) also **lunch time** N-VAR **Lunchtime** is the period of the day when people have their lunch. 午餐时间 ❏ *Could we meet at lunchtime?* 我们能在午餐时间见个面吗？

lung /lʌŋ/ (**lungs**) N-COUNT Your **lungs** are the two organs inside your chest which fill with air when you breathe in. 肺 ❏ *...a smoker who died of lung cancer.* …一位死于肺癌的吸烟者。
→ see **donor, respiratory**

lunge /lʌndʒ/ (**lunges, lunging, lunged**) V-I If you **lunge** in a particular direction, you move in that direction suddenly and clumsily. 猛冲 ❏ *He lunged at me, grabbing me violently.* 他向我猛冲过来，狠狠地抓住了我。 ● N-COUNT **Lunge** is also a noun. 猛冲 ❏ *The attacker knocked on their door and made a lunge for Wendy when she answered.* 袭击者敲了他们的门，并在温迪开门时，向她猛冲过去。

lurch /lɜrtʃ/ (**lurches, lurching, lurched**) 1 V-I To **lurch** means to make a sudden movement, especially forward, in an uncontrolled way. (尤指向前) 打趔趄 ❏ *As the car sped over a pothole she lurched forward.* 汽车飞速驶过路面上的一个坑洼时，她身体前倾打了个趔趄。 ❏ *Henry looked, stared, and lurched to his feet.* 亨利看了看，瞪着眼，踉踉跄跄地站了起来。 ● N-COUNT **Lurch** is also a noun. 趔趄 ❏ *The car took a lurch forward.* 汽车一个趔趄，向前冲去。 2 V-I If you say that a person or organization **lurches from** one thing **to** another, you mean they move suddenly from one course of action or attitude to another in an uncontrolled way. (行为或态度随意的) 突然改变 [DISAPPROVAL] ❏ *The state government has lurched from one budget crisis to another.* 州政府突然从一个预算危机陷入了另一个危机。 ● N-COUNT **Lurch** is also a noun. (行为或态度随意地) 突然改变 ❏ *The property sector was another casualty of the lurch toward higher interest rates.* 房地产业是利率突然提高的又一受损行业。

★ **lure** /lʊər/ (**lures, luring, lured**) 1 V-T To **lure** someone means to trick them into a particular place or to trick them into doing something that they should not do. 引诱 ❏ *He lured her to his home and shot her with his father's gun.* 他把她诱骗到家里，然后用父亲的枪把她打死。 ❏ *They did not realize that they were being lured into a trap.* 他们没有意识到正被人骗入圈套。 2 N-COUNT A **lure** is an object which is used to attract animals, especially fish, so that they can be caught. 诱饵 3 N-COUNT A **lure** is an attractive quality that something has, or something that you find attractive. 诱惑力；魅力 ❏ *The excitement of hunting big game in Africa has been a lure to Europeans for 200 years.* 在非洲捕捉大型猎物所带来的刺激，200年来一直吸引着欧洲人。

lu·rid /lʊərɪd/ 1 ADJ If you say that something is **lurid**, you are critical of it because it involves a lot of violence, sex, or shocking detail. 耸人听闻的 [DISAPPROVAL] ❏ *...lurid accounts of Claire's sexual exploits.* …对克莱尔的性行为耸人听闻的描述。 ❏ *Some reports have contained lurid accounts of death and mutilations.* 有些报告包含对死亡和残肢的骇人描述。 2 ADJ If you describe something as **lurid**, you do not like it because it is very brightly colored. 艳丽的 [DISAPPROVAL] ❏ *She took care to paint her toe nails a lurid red or orange.* 她小心翼翼地把脚趾甲涂成艳丽的红色或桔色。

lurk /lɜrk/ (**lurks, lurking, lurked**) 1 V-I If someone **lurks** somewhere, they wait there secretly so that they cannot be seen, usually because they intend to do something bad. 潜藏 ❏ *He thought he saw someone lurking above the chamber during the address.* 他以为，在演讲期间曾看见有人藏在议会厅上面。 2 V-I If something such as a danger, doubt, or fear **lurks** somewhere, it exists but is not obvious or easily recognized. 潜伏 ❏ *Hidden dangers lurk in every family home.* 每个家庭都存在潜伏的危险。

lus·cious /lʌʃəs/ 1 ADJ If you describe a woman or something about her as **luscious**, you mean that you find her or this thing sexually attractive. 性感的 ❏ *...a luscious young blonde.* …一个年轻性感的金发女郎。 2 ADJ **Luscious** food is juicy and very good to eat. 美味多汁的 ❏ *...a small apricot tree which bore luscious fruit.* …一棵小杏树，结着美味多汁的果实。

lush /lʌʃ/ (**lushes, lusher, lushest**) 1 ADJ **Lush** fields or gardens have a lot of very healthy grass or plants. 茂盛的 ❏ *...the lush green meadows bordering the river.* …河边青葱翠绿的草地。 2 ADJ If you describe a place or thing as **lush**, you mean that it is very luxurious. 豪华的 [v-link ADJ] ❏ *The Carlton-intercontinental hotel is lush, plush, and very non- backpacker.* 卡尔顿洲际酒店豪华舒适，背包徒步旅行者是绝对住不起的。 3 N-COUNT If you describe someone as a **lush**, you mean that they drink too much alcohol. 酒鬼

▲ **lust** /lʌst/ 1 N-UNCOUNT **Lust** is a feeling of strong sexual desire for someone. 淫欲 ❏ *His relationship with Angie was the first which combined lust with friendship.* 他和安吉的关系是他第一次将色欲和友谊相结合。 2 N-UNCOUNT A **lust** for something is a very strong and eager desire to have it. 欲望 ❏ *It was Fred's lust for glitz and glamour that was driving them apart.* 弗雷德对浮华和美艳的欲望使他们分手。

luxu·ri·ous /lʌɡʒʊəriəs/ 1 ADJ If you describe something as **luxurious**, you mean that it is very comfortable and expensive. 豪华的 ❏ *Our honeymoon was two days in Las Vegas at a luxurious hotel called Le Mirage.* 我们的蜜月为期两天，是在拉斯维加斯一家名为"幻影"的豪华酒店度过的。 ● **luxu·ri·ous·ly** ADV 豪华地 ❏ *The dining-room is luxuriously furnished and carpeted.* 餐厅里的家具和地毯非常豪华。 2 ADJ **Luxurious** means feeling or expressing great pleasure and comfort. 心情舒畅的 ❏ *Amy tilted her wine in her glass with a luxurious sigh.* 埃米把杯中的葡萄酒斜向一边，适意地叹了口气。 ● **luxu·ri·ous·ly** ADV 心情舒畅地 [ADV after v] ❏ *Liz laughed, stretching luxuriously.* 莉兹一边大笑，一边心情舒畅地伸了个懒腰。

luxu·ry ♦◇◇ /lʌkʃəri, lʌɡʒə-/ (**luxuries**) 1 N-UNCOUNT **Luxury** is very great comfort, especially among beautiful and expensive surroundings. 奢侈 ❏ *By all accounts he leads a life of considerable luxury.* 从方方面面来讲，他都过着极为奢侈的生活。 2 N-COUNT A **luxury** is something expensive which is not necessary but which gives you pleasure. 奢侈品 ❏ *A week by the sea is a luxury they can no longer afford.* 去海边一周成了一种奢侈，他们再也负担不起。 3 ADJ A **luxury** item is something expensive which is not necessary but which gives you pleasure. 奢侈的 (物品) [ADJ n] ❏ *He could not afford luxury food on his pay.* 凭他的薪水，他吃不起奢侈的食品。 4 N-SING A **luxury** is a pleasure which you do not often have the opportunity to enjoy. 难得的享受 ❏ *Hot baths are my favorite luxury.* 热水浴是我钟爱而难得的享受。

Thesaurus *luxury* 另参见：

N. comfort, richness, splendor 1
extra, extravagance, nonessential, treat 2 4

ly·ing /laɪɪŋ/ **Lying** is the present participle of **lie**. **lie**的现在分词

lynch /lɪntʃ/ (**lynches, lynching, lynched**) V-T If an angry crowd of people **lynch** someone, they kill that person by hanging them, without letting them have a trial, because they believe that that person has committed a crime. 对…以私刑绞死 ❑ *They were about to lynch him when reinforcements from the army burst into the room and rescued him.* 他们正要以私刑绞死他，军队就冲进房间救了他。

● **lynch·ing** N-VAR (**lynchings**) 私刑绞死 ❑ *Some towns found that lynching was the only way to drive away bands of outlaws.* 有些城镇的人们发现私刑是惟一能够驱走那一帮帮歹徒的方法。

▲ **lyr·ic** /lɪrɪk/ (**lyrics**) 1 ADJ **Lyric** poetry is written in a simple and direct style, and usually expresses personal emotions such as love. 抒情的（诗歌）[ADJ n] ❑ *...Lawrence's splendid short stories and lyric poetry.* …劳伦斯出色的短篇小说和抒情诗。 2 N-COUNT The **lyrics** of a song are its words. 歌词 ❑ *...Kurt Weill's Broadway opera with lyrics by Langston Hughes.* …由兰斯顿·休斯作词的库尔特·韦尔的百老汇歌剧。

Mm

M also **m** /ɛm/ (**M's, m's**) N-VAR **M** is the thirteenth letter of the English alphabet. 英语字母表中的第13个字母

ma'am /mæm/ N-VOC People sometimes say **ma'am** as a polite way of addressing a woman whose name they do not know, especially in the American South. 女士 (对不知其名的女子的礼貌称呼) [mainly AM, POLITENESS] ❑ *Would you repeat that please, ma'am?* 女士，请您重复一遍好吗？

ma·ca·bre /məkɑbrə/ ADJ You describe something such as an event or story as **macabre** when it is strange and horrible or upsetting, usually because it involves death or injury. 恐怖的 ❑ *Police have made a macabre discovery.* 警察有了个可怕的发现。

ma·chete /məʃɛti/ (**machetes**) N-COUNT A **machete** is a large knife with a broad blade. 宽刃大刀

ma·chine ♦♦◊ /məʃin/ (**machines, machining, machined**) **1** N-COUNT A **machine** is a piece of equipment that uses electricity or an engine in order to do a particular kind of work. 机器 [also "by" N] ❑ *I put the coin in the machine and pulled the lever.* 我把硬币投进机器，然后拉了控制杆。 **2** N-COUNT You can use **machine** to refer to a large and well-controlled system or organization. 机构 ❑ *...Nazi Germany's military machine.* …纳粹德国的军事机构。 **3** → see also **vending machine** **4** V-T If you **machine** something, you make it or work on it using a machine. 用机器制造；用机器加工 [usu passive] ❑ *The material is machined in a factory.* 该材料在一家工厂用机器加工而成。 ❑ *...machined brass zinc alloy gears.* …机器加工的黄铜锌合金齿轮。
→ see **dairy**

Thesaurus *machine* 另参见：

N. appliance, computer, gadget, mechanism **1**
organization, structure, system **2**

Word Partnership *machine* 的常用搭配：

V. **design a** machine, **invent a** machine, **use a** machine **1**
ADJ. **heavy** machine, **new** machine, machine **washable** **1**
N. machine **oil**, machine **parts**, machine **shop**, **Xerox** machine **1**

ma·chine gun (**machine guns**) N-COUNT A **machine gun** is a gun which fires a lot of bullets one after the other very quickly. 机枪 ❑ *Attackers fired machine guns at the convoy.* 袭击者们向护运车队开机枪。

ma·chin·ery /məʃinəri/ **1** N-UNCOUNT You can use **machinery** to refer to machines in general, or machines that are used in a factory or on a farm. 机器；机械 ❑ *...quality tools and machinery.* …优质工具和机械。 **2** N-SING **The machinery** of a government or organization is the system and all the procedures that it uses to deal with things. (政府或组织的) 体制 ❑ *The machinery of democracy could be created quickly.* 民主体制很快就能建立起来。

ma·chin·ist /məʃinɪst/ (**machinists**) N-COUNT A **machinist** is a person whose job is to operate a machine, especially in a factory. 机工；机械师 ❑ *His father is a machinist in an aerospace plant.* 他的父亲是一家航空工厂的机械师。

macho /mɑtʃoʊ/ ADJ You use **macho** to describe men who are very conscious and proud of their masculinity. 大男子气的 [INFORMAL] ❑ *...displays of macho bravado.* …大男子气概的展现。

macke·rel /mækərəl, mækrəl/ (**mackerel**)

Mackerel is both the singular and the plural form.

N-VAR A **mackerel** is a sea fish with a dark, patterned back. 鲭鱼 ❑ *Almiro's boat had sailed out to the middle of the bay to fish for mackerel.* 阿尔米罗的船已驶向海湾中部去捕鲭鱼。 ● N-UNCOUNT **Mackerel** is this fish eaten as food. 鲭鱼肉 ❑ *...piles of smoked mackerel.* …成堆的熏鲭鱼肉。

macro·eco·nom·ics /mækroʊɛkənɒmɪks, -ikə-/ also **macro-economics** N-UNCOUNT **Macroeconomics** is the branch of economics that is concerned with the major, general features of a country's economy, such as the level of inflation, unemployment, or interest rates. 宏观经济学 [BUSINESS] ❑ *Too many politicians forget the importance of macroeconomics.* 太多的政治家们忽视宏观经济学的重要性。 ● **ma·cro·ec·o·nom·ic** /mækroʊɛkənɒmɪk, -ikə-/ ADJ 宏观经济学的 [usu ADJ n] ❑ *...the attempt to substitute low inflation for full employment as a goal of macro-economic policy.* …用低通货膨胀取代充分就业作为宏观经济政策目标的尝试。

mad ♦◊◊ /mæd/ (**madder, maddest**) **1** ADJ If you say that someone is **mad**, you mean that they are very angry. 狂怒的 [INFORMAL] ❑ *You're just mad at me because I don't want to go.* 因为我不想去，你就冲我发火。 **2** ADJ You use **mad** to describe people or things that you think are very foolish. 蠢疯的 [DISAPPROVAL] ❑ *You'd be mad to work with him again.* 你要是再和他一起工作就是蠢疯了。 ● **mad·ness** N-UNCOUNT 蠢疯 ❑ *It is political madness.* 这是政治蠢疯。 **3** ADJ Someone who is **mad** has a mind that does not work in a normal way, with the result that their behavior is very strange. (人) 疯的 ❑ *She was afraid of going mad.* 她担心变疯。 ● **mad·ness** N-UNCOUNT 疯 ❑ *He was driven to the brink of madness.* 他被逼到了疯狂的边缘。 **4** ADJ If you are **mad about** something or someone, you like them very much. 疯迷的 [v-link ADJ "about/on" n] [INFORMAL] ❑ *He's mad about you.* 他对你疯迷。 ● COMB IN ADJ **Mad** is also a combining form. 疯迷…的 (用于构成合成词) [mainly BRIT] ❑ *...his football-mad son.* …他的疯迷足球的儿子。 **5** ADJ **Mad** behavior is wild and uncontrolled. (行为) 疯狂的 ❑ *You only have an hour to complete the game so it's a mad dash against the clock.* 你们只有一个小时完成比赛，因此这是和时间的一次疯狂角逐。 ● **mad·ly** ADV 疯狂地 [ADV with v] ❑ *Down in the streets people were waving madly.* 下面大街上，人们在疯狂地挥手。 **6** PHRASE If you say that someone or something **drives** you **mad**, you mean that you find them extremely annoying. 使某人发疯 [INFORMAL] ❑ *There are certain things he does that drive me mad.* 他干的某些事使我发疯。 **7** PHRASE If you do something **like mad**, you do it very energetically or enthusiastically. 疯了似地 [INFORMAL] ❑ *He was weight training like mad.* 他在疯了似地进行举重训练。 **8** → see also **madly**

Thesaurus *mad* 另参见：

ADJ. angry, furious **1**
crazy, foolish, senseless **2**
deranged, insane **3**

Word Partnership *mad* 的常用搭配：

V. **get** mad, **make** *someone* mad **1**
go mad **3**
N. mad **as hell** **1**
mad **dog**, mad **scientist** **3**
mad **dash**, mad **rush** **5**

mad·am /mædəm/ also **Madam** N-VOC People sometimes say **Madam** as a very formal and polite way of addressing a woman whose name they do not know. For example, a store clerk might address a woman customer as **Madam**. 女士 (对不知其名的女子的礼貌称呼) [POLITENESS] ❑ *Try them on, madam.* 试穿一下吧，女士。

mad·den /mædᵊn/ (**maddens, maddening, maddened**) V-T To **madden** a person or animal means to make them very angry. 使狂怒 ❑ *The deer were maddening farmers by eating their crops.* 那些鹿吃庄稼，让农民们狂怒。

mad·den·ing /mædᵊnɪŋ/ ADJ If you describe something as **maddening**, you mean that it makes you feel angry, irritated, or frustrated. 使人恼火的 ❑ *Shopping during sales can be maddening.* 促销期间购物会让人恼火。 ● **mad·den·ing·ly** ADV 使人恼火地 ❑ *The service is maddeningly slow.* 服务慢得让人恼火。

made /meɪd/ **1** **Made** is the past tense and past participle of **make**. make的过去式和过去分词 **2** ADJ If something is **made of** or **made out of** a particular substance, that substance was used to build it. (用某物质) 制成的 [v-link ADJ "of/out of" n] ❑ *The top of the table is made of glass.* 该桌台面由玻璃制成。 **3** PHRASE If you say that someone **has it made** or **has got it made**, you mean that they are certain to be rich or successful. 确信能成功 [INFORMAL] ❑ *When I was at school, I thought I had it made.* 在学校的时候，我以为自己一定能成功。

made-up ♦◇◇ also **made up** **1** ADJ If you are **made-up**, you are wearing makeup such as powder or eye shadow. 化过妆的 [v-link ADJ] ❑ *She was beautifully made up, beautifully groomed.* 她化着亮妆，穿戴漂亮。 **2** ADJ A **made-up** word, name, or story is invented, rather than really existing or being true. 虚构的 ❑ *It looks like a made-up word.* 这看起来像是一个杜撰的词。

mad·ly /mædli/ ADV You can use **madly** to indicate that one person loves another a great deal. 疯狂地 ❑ *She has fallen madly in love with him.* 她疯狂地爱上了他。

mag /mæg/ (**mags**) N-COUNT A **mag** is the same as a magazine. 杂志 [INFORMAL] ❑ *...a well-known glossy mag.* …一本知名的光面杂志。

maga·zine ♦♦◇ /mægəzin, -zin/ (**magazines**) **1** N-COUNT A **magazine** is a publication with a paper cover which is issued regularly, usually every week or every month, and which contains articles, stories, photographs, and advertisements. 杂志 ❑ *Her face is on the cover of a dozen or more magazines.* 她的面孔出现在10多种杂志的封面上。 **2** N-COUNT In an automatic gun, the **magazine** is the part that contains the bullets. 弹匣 ❑ *The corporal ignored him, sliding the empty magazine from his weapon and replacing it with a fresh one.* 那个下士没理睬他，把空弹匣从他的武器上卸下来并换上了一个新的。

→ see **advertising, library**

mag·got /mægət/ (**maggots**) N-COUNT **Maggots** are creatures that look like very small worms and turn into flies. 蛆

mag·ic ♦◇◇ /mædʒɪk/ **1** N-UNCOUNT **Magic** is the power to use supernatural forces to make impossible things happen, such as making people disappear or controlling events in nature. 魔力 ❑ *They believe in magic.* 他们相信魔力。 ❑ *...the use of magic to combat any adverse powers or influences.* …魔力在抗击敌对力量或有害影响中的作用。 **2** N-UNCOUNT You can use **magic** when you are referring to an event that is so wonderful, strange, or unexpected that it seems as if supernatural powers have caused it. You can also say that something happens **as if by magic** or **like magic**. 魔法 ❑ *All this was supposed to work like magic.* 这一切应该魔法般地起作用。 **3** ADJ You use **magic** to describe something that does things, or appears to do things, by magic. 有魔力的 [ADJ n] ❑ *So it's a magic potion?* 这么说它是一种魔药？ **4** N-UNCOUNT **Magic** is the art and skill of performing mysterious tricks to entertain people, for example by making things appear and disappear. 魔术 ❑ *His secret hobby: performing magic tricks.* 他的秘密嗜好：表演魔术。 **5** N-UNCOUNT If you refer to **the magic of** something, you mean that it has a special mysterious quality which makes it seem wonderful and exciting to you and which makes you feel happy. 魔力；神秘之处 ❑ *It infected them with some of the magic of a lost age.* 它使之有了逝去岁月的些许神秘。 ● ADJ **Magic** is also an adjective. 有魔力的；神秘的 ❑ *Then came those magic moments in the rose garden.* 接着就是玫瑰园里的魔力时刻。 **6** N-UNCOUNT If you refer to a person's **magic**, you mean a special talent or ability that they have, which you admire or consider very impressive. 特殊才能；神奇功能 ❑ *The 32-year-old Jamaican-born fighter believes he can still regain some of his old magic.* 那个32岁、生于牙买加的斗士相信自己仍能重拾一些昔日的神奇功能。 **7** ADJ You can use expressions such as **the magic number** and **the magic word** to indicate that a number or word is the one which is significant or desirable in a particular situation. 关键的；向往的 ["the" ADJ n] ❑ *...their quest to gain the magic number of 270 electoral votes on Election Day.* …他们渴求在大选日获得关键的270张选票。 **8** ADJ **Magic** is used in expressions such as **there is no magic formula** and **there is no magic solution** to say that someone will have to make an effort to solve a problem, because it will not solve itself. 有魔力的 (解决方案) [ADJ n, with neg] ❑ *There is no magic formula for producing winning products.* 生产受欢迎的产品并没有魔方。

Thesaurus *magic* 另参见：
N. enchantment, illusion, sorcery, witchcraft **1**

magi·cal /mædʒɪkᵊl/ **1** ADJ Something that is **magical** seems to use magic or to be able to produce magic. 魔法般的 ❑ *...the story of Sin-Sin, a little boy who has magical powers.* …一个有魔力的小男孩辛辛的故事。 ● **magi·cal·ly** /mædʒɪkli/ ADV 魔法般地 [ADV with v] ❑ *During the holiday season the town is magically transformed into a Christmas wonderland.* 在节日期间该镇魔法般地变成了圣诞仙境。 **2** ADJ You can say that a place or object is **magical** when it has a special mysterious quality that makes it seem wonderful and exciting. 神奇的 ❑ *The beautiful island of Bermuda is a magical place to get married.* 美丽的百慕大岛是缔结良缘的神奇之地。

ma·gi·cian /mədʒɪʃᵊn/ (**magicians**) N-COUNT A **magician** is a person who entertains people by doing magic tricks. 魔术师

★ **mag·is·trate** /mædʒɪstreɪt/ (**magistrates**) N-COUNT A **magistrate** is an official who acts as a judge in law courts which deal with minor crimes or disputes. 治安法官 ❑ *She will face a local magistrate on Tuesday.* 她将在星期二面见一位地方治安法官。

Word Link *magn ≈ great : magnate, magnify, magnitude*

mag·nate /mægneɪt, -nɪt/ (**magnates**) N-COUNT A **magnate** is someone who has earned a lot of money from a particular business or industry. 巨头；大亨 ❑ *...a multimillionaire shipping magnate.* …一位身价数千万的船业巨头。

mag·net /mægnɪt/ (**magnets**) **1** N-COUNT If you say that something is a **magnet** or is like a **magnet**, you mean that people are very attracted by it and want to go to it or look at it. 有吸引力的事物 ❑ *Prospect Park, with its vast lake, is a magnet for all health freaks.* 拥有大片湖区的展望公园是所有健身迷的向往之地。 **2** N-COUNT A **magnet** is a piece of iron or other material which attracts iron toward it. 磁体 ❑ *It's possible to hang a nail from a magnet and then use that nail to pick up another nail.* 把一颗钉子挂在一个磁体上再用这颗钉子去吸起另一颗钉子是可能的。

→ see Word Web: **magnet**

mag·net·ic /mægnetɪk/ **1** ADJ If something metal is **magnetic**, it acts like a magnet. 有磁性的 ❑ *...magnetic particles.* …磁性粒子。 **2** ADJ You use **magnetic** to describe something that is caused by or relates to the force of magnetism. 有磁力的 ❑ *The electrically charged gas particles are affected by magnetic forces.* 带电的气体粒子受磁力的影响。 **3** ADJ You use **magnetic** to describe tapes and other objects which have a coating of a magnetic substance and contain coded information that can be read by computers or other machines. (磁带、卡等) 有磁的 ❑ *...her magnetic-strip ID card.* …她的带磁条的身份证。 **4** ADJ If you describe something as **magnetic**, you mean that it is very attractive to people because it has unusual, powerful, and exciting qualities. 有吸引力的 ❑ *...the magnetic effect of the prosperous American economy on would-be immigrants.* …繁荣的美国经济对未来移民的吸引力。

mag·net·ism /mægnɪtɪzəm/ **1** N-UNCOUNT Someone or something that has **magnetism** has unusual, powerful, and exciting qualities which attract people to them. 魅力 ❑ *There was no doubting the animal magnetism of the man.* 那个男人的动物性魅力无可置疑。 **2** N-UNCOUNT **Magnetism** is the natural power of some objects and substances, especially iron, to attract other objects toward them. 磁性 ❑ *...his research in electricity and magnetism.* …他在电、磁领域的研究。

Word Web magnet

Magnets have a north **pole** and a south pole. One side has a **negative charge** and the other side has a **positive** charge. The negative side of a magnet **attracts** the positive side of another magnet. This is where the phrase "opposites attract" comes from. Two sides that have the same charge will **repel** each other. The earth itself is a huge magnet, with a North Pole and a South Pole. A **compass** uses a magnetized needle to indicate directions. The "north" end of the needle always points toward the earth's North Pole.

mag·ni·fi·ca·tion /mæɡnɪfɪkeɪʃ^{ə}n/ (**magnifications**) 1 N-UNCOUNT **Magnification** is the act or process of magnifying something. 放大 ❑ *The man was tall, his figure shortened by the magnification of Lenny's binoculars.* 那个男子高高的，其个头因伦尼的双筒望远镜的放大而变矮了。 2 N-VAR **Magnification** is the degree to which a lens, mirror, or other device can magnify an object, or the degree to which the object is magnified. 放大倍数；放大率 ❑ *The electron microscope uses a beam of electrons to produce images at high magnifications.* 电子显微镜利用一束电子产生高倍放大的影像。

mag·nifi·cent /mæɡnɪfɪsənt/ ADJ If you say that something or someone is **magnificent**, you mean that you think they are extremely good, beautiful, or impressive. 出色的；壮丽的 ❑ *...a magnificent country house in wooded grounds.* …林地中一座漂亮的村宅。 ● **mag·nifi·cence** N-UNCOUNT 出色；壮丽 ❑ *I shall never forget the magnificence of the Swiss mountains and the beauty of the lakes.* 我永远也不会忘记瑞士山岳的壮美和湖泊的秀丽。 ● **mag·nifi·cent·ly** ADV 出色地 ❑ *The team played magnificently throughout the competition.* 该队在整个比赛中表现出色。

Word Link *magn ≈ great : magnate, magnify, magnitude*

★ **mag·ni·fy** /mæɡnɪfaɪ/ (**magnifies, magnifying, magnified**) 1 V-T To **magnify** an object means to make it appear larger than it really is, by means of a special lens or mirror. 放大 ❑ *This version of the Digges telescope magnifies images 11 times.* 这种型号的迪格斯望远镜能将图像放大11倍。 ❑ *A lens would magnify the picture so it would be like looking at a large TV screen.* 透镜会把图像放大，这样就会像看大电视屏幕。 2 V-T To **magnify** something means to increase its effect, size, loudness, or intensity. 增大 ❑ *Poverty and human folly magnify natural disasters.* 贫穷和人类的愚蠢加剧自然灾难。 3 V-T If you **magnify** something, you make it seem more important or serious than it really is. 夸大 ❑ *They do not grasp the broad situation and spend their time magnifying ridiculous details.* 他们没有把握大局而把时间花费在夸大荒谬的细节上。

★ **mag·ni·tude** /mæɡnɪtud/ 1 N-UNCOUNT If you talk about the **magnitude** of something, you are talking about its great size, scale, or importance. (尺寸、规模、重要性等) 大的程度 ❑ *An operation of this magnitude is going to be difficult.* 一个这么大的手术会很难的。 2 PHRASE You can use **order of magnitude** when you are giving an approximate idea of the amount or importance of something. 重要级；数量级 ❑ *America and Russia do not face a problem of the same order of magnitude as Japan.* 美俄两国没有面临与日本同样的重要级别的问题。

M

mag·pie /mæɡpaɪ/ (**magpies**) N-COUNT A **magpie** is a large black and white bird with a long tail. 喜鹊

ma·hoga·ny /məhɒɡəni/ N-UNCOUNT **Mahogany** is a dark reddish brown wood that is used to make furniture. 红木 ❑ *...mahogany tables and chairs.* …红木桌椅。

maid /meɪd/ (**maids**) N-COUNT A **maid** is a woman who works as a servant in a hotel or private house. 女侍者；女仆 ❑ *A maid brought me breakfast at nine o'clock.* 一个女侍者9点钟给我送来了早餐。

▲ **maid·en** /meɪd^{ə}n/ (**maidens**) 1 N-COUNT A **maiden** is a young girl or woman. 少女 [LITERARY] ❑ *...stories of noble princes and their brave deeds on behalf of beautiful maidens.* …高贵的王子以及他们英雄救美的故事。 2 ADJ The **maiden** voyage or flight of a ship or aircraft is the first official journey that it makes. (航行、飞行) 首次的 [ADJ n] ❑ *In 1912, the Titanic sank on her maiden voyage.* 1912年，泰坦尼克号首次航行时沉没。

maid·en name (**maiden names**) N-COUNT A married woman's **maiden name** is her parents' surname, which she used before she got married and started using her husband's surname. (已婚女子的) 娘家姓 ❑ *The marriage broke up in 1997 and she took back her maiden name of Boreman.* 1997年婚姻破裂后她重新使用娘家姓博尔曼。

mail ♦◇◇ /meɪl/ (**mails, mailing, mailed**) 1 N-SING **The mail** is the public service or system by which letters and packages are collected and delivered. 邮政 ["the" N, also "by" N] ❑ *Your check is in the mail.* 你的支票在邮寄中。 2 N-UNCOUNT You can refer to letters and packages that are delivered to you as **mail**. 邮件 [also "the" N] ❑ *There was no mail except the usual junk addressed to the occupant.* 除了寄给住户的常见的垃圾邮件之外，没有其他邮件。 3 V-T If you **mail** a letter or package to someone, you send it to them by putting it in a mailbox or taking it to a post office. 邮寄 [mainly AM]

in BRIT, usually use **post**

❑ *Last year, he mailed the documents to French journalists.* 去年，他把那些文件寄给了法国记者。 ❑ *He mailed me the contract.* 他把合同寄给了我。 4 V-T To **mail** a message to someone means to send it to them by means of e-mail or a computer network. 发送 (电子邮件) ● N-COUNT **Mail** is also a noun. 电子邮件 ❑ *If you have any problems then send me a mail.* 如有任何问题就给我发邮件。 5 → see also **airmail, electronic mail, e-mail, junk mail, mailing, surface mail**

Word Partnership *mail* 的常用搭配：

PREP.	**by** mail, **in the** mail, **through the** mail 1
N.	mail **carrier**, **fan** mail 2
V.	**deliver** mail, **get** mail, **open** mail, **read** mail, **receive** mail, **send** mail 2

mail·box /meɪlbɒks/ (**mailboxes**) 1 N-COUNT A **mailbox** is a box outside your house where your letters are delivered. 信箱 [AM] ❑ *The next day there was a letter in her mailbox.* 第二天她的信箱里有封信。 2 N-COUNT A **mailbox** is a metal box in a public place, where you put letters and small packages to be collected. They are then sorted and delivered. 邮筒 [mainly AM]

in BRIT, use **post box**

❑ *And with a trembling hand, he dropped the letters into the mailbox.* 他颤抖的手把信投进了邮箱。 3 N-COUNT On a computer, your **mailbox** is the file where your e-mail is stored. 电子邮箱 ❑ *The prank crammed his mailbox with computer-delivered electronic junk mail.* 该恶作剧病毒把他的邮箱塞满计算机发送的电子垃圾邮件。

mail·ing /meɪlɪŋ/ (**mailings**) 1 N-UNCOUNT **Mailing** is the activity of sending things to people through the postal service. 邮寄 [also N in pl] ❑ *The newsletter was printed toward the end of June and ready for mailing July 1.* 该简讯接近6月底时印了出来，7月1日可以邮递。 2 N-COUNT A **mailing** is something that is sent to people through the postal service. 邮件 ❑ *Most of Mahony's expenses were for mass mailings to conservatives across the state.* 马奥尼的大部分花销都用于给全州的保守派寄送批量邮件。

mail·ing list (**mailing lists**) N-COUNT A **mailing list** is a list of names and addresses that a company or organization keeps, so that they can send people information or advertisements. 邮寄名单 ❑ *Place your name on our mailing list now.* 现在把你的名字写在我们的邮寄名单上。

mail·man /meɪlmæn/ (**mailmen**) N-COUNT A **mailman** is a man whose job is to collect and deliver letters and parcels that are sent by mail. 邮递员 [AM]

in BRIT, usually use **postman**

mail merge N-UNCOUNT **Mail merge** is a word processing procedure which enables you to combine a document with a data file, for example a list of names and addresses, so that copies of the document are different for each person it is sent to. 邮件合并 [COMPUTING] ❑ *Using mail-merge software, she makes sure each card goes out on time.* 通过使用邮件合并软件，她确保每张贺卡都准时寄出。

mail or·der (**mail orders**) 1 N-UNCOUNT **Mail order** is a system of buying and selling goods. You choose the goods you want from a company by looking at their catalog, and the company sends them to you by mail. 邮购 ❑ *The toys are available by mail order from Opi Toys.* 这些玩具可以从欧派玩具公司邮购。 2 N-COUNT **Mail orders** are goods that have been ordered by mail order. 邮购商品 [mainly AM] ❑ *I supervise the packing of all mail orders.* 我监督所有邮购商品的包装。

maim /meɪm/ (**maims, maiming, maimed**) V-T To **maim** someone means to injure them so badly that part of their body is permanently damaged. 致残 ❑ *Mines have been scattered in rice paddies and jungles, maiming and killing civilians.* 地雷散布在稻田和丛林中，致使平民伤残和死亡。

main ♦♦♦ /meɪn/ (**mains**) 1 ADJ The **main** thing is the most important one of several similar things in a particular situation. 最重要的；主要的 [det ADJ] ❑ *...one of the main tourist areas of San Francisco.* …旧金山的主要旅游区之一。 ❑ *My main concern now is to protect the children.* 我现在最关心的是保护这些孩子。 2 PHRASE If you say that something is true **in the main**, you mean that it is generally true, although there may be exceptions. 大体上 ❑ *Tourists are, in the main, sympathetic people.* 游客们大都是有同情心的人。 3 N-COUNT The **mains** are the pipes which supply gas or water to buildings, or which take sewage away from them. 总管道 ❑ *...the water supply from the mains.* …总管道的水供应。

Thesaurus *main* 另参见:
ADJ. chief, major, primary, principal 1

main·frame /meɪnfreɪm/ (**mainframes**) N-COUNT A **mainframe** or **mainframe computer** is a large, powerful computer which can be used by many people at the same time and which can do very large or complicated tasks. 主机(指可同时供多人使用的大型计算机) ❑ *I downloaded the whole thing into the hospital mainframe before I left work today.* 我今天下班前把全部内容下载到了医院的主机上。

main·land /meɪnlænd/ N-SING You can refer to the largest part of a country or continent as **the mainland** when contrasting it with the islands around it. 大陆 ❑ *She was going to Nanaimo to catch the ferry to the mainland.* 她打算到纳奈莫乘渡船去大陆。

main·ly ♦♦◊ /meɪnli/ 1 ADV You use **mainly** when mentioning the main reason or thing involved in something. 主要地 ❑ *The stock market scandal is refusing to go away, mainly because there's still no consensus over how it should be dealt with.* 此次股市丑闻历久不散，主要是因为在此事如何处理上尚无共识。 2 ADV You use **mainly** when you are referring to a group and stating something that is true of most of it. 大部分地 [ADV with group] ❑ *The African half of the audience was mainly from Senegal or Mali.* 观众中的一半非洲人主要来自塞内加尔或马里。

main road (**main roads**) N-COUNT A **main road** is an important road that leads from one town or city to another. 主干道 ❑ *Troops had barricaded the main road from the airport.* 部队已经在出机场的主干道上设了路障。

main·stream /meɪnstrim/ (**mainstreams**) N-COUNT People, activities, or ideas that are part of the **mainstream** are regarded as the most typical, normal, and conventional because they belong to the same group or system as most others of their kind. 主流 ❑ *...people outside the economic mainstream.* …经济主流之外的人们。
→ see **culture**

Main Street 1 N-PROPER In small towns in the United States, the street where most of the stores are is often called **Main Street**. (美国小城镇的) 主街 ❑ *Almost all the stores and restaurants along Main Street were shut for the season.* 几乎所有主街上的商店和饭店都因假期而关门了。 2 N-UNCOUNT **Main Street** is used by journalists to refer to ordinary Americans who live in small towns rather than big cities or are not very rich. 小市民 [AM] ❑ *This financial crisis had a much greater impact on Main Street.* 这次金融危机对小市民的影响大得多。

main·tain ♦♦◊ /meɪnteɪn/ (**maintains, maintaining, maintained**) 1 V-T If you **maintain** something, you continue to have it, and do not let it stop or grow weaker. 保持 2 V-T If you say that someone **maintains that** something is true, you mean that they have stated their opinion strongly but not everyone agrees with them or believes them. 坚持说；坚持认为 ❑ *He has maintained that the money was donated for international purposes.* 他坚持说这笔钱是出于国际目的而捐助的。 ❑ *"Not all feminism has to be like this," Jo maintains.* 乔坚持认为，“并非女权主义都得像这样。” 3 V-T If you **maintain** something **at** a particular rate or level, you keep it at that rate or level. 维持(某比率或水平) ❑ *The government was right to maintain interest rates at a high level.* 政府维持高利率是正确的。 4 V-T If you **maintain** a road, building, vehicle, or machine, you keep it in good condition by regularly checking it and repairing it when necessary. 维修；保养 ❑ *The house costs a fortune to maintain.* 这房子要花一大笔钱维修。 5 V-T If you **maintain** someone, you provide them with money and other things that they need. 供养 ❑ *...the basic costs of maintaining a child.* …供养一个孩子的基本费用。

Thesaurus *maintain* 另参见:
V. carry on, continue; *(ant.)* neglect 1
keep up, look after, protect, repair 4

Word Partnership *maintain* 的常用搭配:
N. maintain **friendship**, maintain **law**, maintain **a relationship** 1
V. **need to** maintain, **pledge to** maintain, **try to** maintain 1–5

main·te·nance /meɪntɪnəns/ 1 N-UNCOUNT The **maintenance** of a building, vehicle, road, or machine is the process of keeping it in good condition by regularly checking it and repairing it when necessary. 检修 ❑ *...maintenance work on government buildings.* …政府各大楼的检修工作。 ❑ *The window had been replaced last week during routine maintenance.* 那窗在上星期的例行检修中已被换掉了。 2 N-UNCOUNT **Maintenance** is money that someone gives regularly to another person to pay for the things that the person needs. 赡养费；抚养费 ❑ *...the government's plan to make absent fathers pay maintenance for their children.* …让那些不在孩子身边的父亲为孩子提供抚养费的政府计划。 3 N-UNCOUNT If you ensure the **maintenance** of a state or process, you make sure that it continues. 维持 ❑ *...the maintenance of peace and stability in Asia.* …亚洲和平与稳定的维持。

maize /meɪz/ N-UNCOUNT **Maize** is the same as **corn**. 玉米 [BRIT]

▲ **ma·jes·tic** /mədʒɛstɪk/ ADJ If you describe something or someone as **majestic**, you think they are very beautiful, dignified, and impressive. 壮丽的；雄伟的 ❑ *...a majestic country home that once belonged to the Astor family.* …一座曾经属于阿斯特家族的漂亮的乡村住所。 ● **ma·jes·ti·cal·ly** /mədʒɛstɪkli/ ADV 壮丽地；雄伟地 ❑ *She rose majestically to her feet.* 她端庄地站了起来。

★ **maj·es·ty** /mædʒɪsti/ (**majesties**) 1 N-VOC; PRON You use majesty in expressions such as **Your Majesty** or **Her Majesty** when you are addressing or referring to a king or queen. 陛下 [poss PRON] [POLITENESS] ❑ *His Majesty requests your presence in the royal chambers.* 国王陛下要求你在皇室受召见。 2 N-UNCOUNT **Majesty** is the quality of being beautiful, dignified, and impressive. 壮丽；雄伟 ❑ *...the majesty of the mainland mountains.* …大陆山岳的壮美。

Word Link *major ≈ larger : major, majority, major league*

ma·jor ♦♦♦ /meɪdʒər/ (**majors, majoring, majored**) 1 ADJ You use **major** when you want to describe something that is more important, serious, or significant than other things in a group or situation. 主要的；重大的 [ADJ n] ❑ *The major factor in the decision to stay or to leave was usually professional.* 决定去留的主要因素通常与职业相关。 ❑ *Drug abuse has long been a major problem for the authorities there.* 毒品滥用长期以来一直是那里的当局的一大难题。 2 N-COUNT; N-TITLE; N-VOC A **major** is an officer who is one rank above captain in the United States Army, Air Force, or Marines. 少校 ❑ *I was a major in the war, you know.* 你知道，我在那场战争期间是个少校。 3 N-COUNT At a university or college in the United States, a student's **major** is the main subject that they are studying. 专业 ❑ *English majors would be asked to explore the roots of language.* 英语专业的学生会被要求探究语言的根源。 4 N-COUNT At a university or college in the United States, if a student is, for example, a geology **major**, geology is the main subject they are studying. …专业的学生 ❑ *She was a history major at the University of Oklahoma.* 她曾是俄克拉何马大学历史专业的学生。 5 V-I If a student at a university or college in the United States **majors in** a particular subject, that subject is the main one they study. 以…为专业 ❑ *He majored in finance at Claremont Men's College in California.* 他在加利福尼亚州的克莱尔蒙特男子大学主修金融。 6 ADJ In music, a **major** scale is one in which the third note is two tones higher than the first. (音乐) 大调的 [n ADJ, ADJ n] ❑ *The orchestra played Mozart's Symphony No. 35 in D Major.* 该管弦乐队演奏了莫扎特D大调第35交响曲。 7 N-PLURAL **The majors** are groups of professional sports teams that compete against each other, especially in baseball. (尤指棒球中的) 职业总会 [mainly AM] ❑ *I knew what I could do in the minor leagues, I just wanted a chance to prove myself in the majors.* 我知道我能在小联合会中做些什么，我只是想要一个在大型职业总会中证明自己的机会。 8 N-COUNT A **major** is an important sports competition, especially in golf or tennis. (尤指高尔夫球或网球中的) 大赛 ❑ *Sarazen became the first golfer to win all four majors.* 萨拉曾成为了第一个赢得全部4场大赛的高尔夫球员。

Thesaurus *major* 另参见:
ADJ. chief, critical, crucial, key, main, principal; *(ant.)* little, minor, unimportant 1

ma·jor·ity ♦♦◊ /mədʒɔrɪti/ (**majorities**) 1 N-SING-COLL The **majority** of people or things in a group is more than half of them. 多数 ❑ *The majority of my patients come to me from out of town.* 我的多数病人来自市区外。 ● PHRASE If a group is **in a majority** or **in the majority**, they form more than half of a larger group. 占多数 ❑ *Surveys indicate that supporters of the treaty are still in the majority.* 调查显示该条约的支持者仍占多数。 2 N-COUNT A **majority** is the difference between the number of votes or seats in a legislature or parliament that the winner gets in an election, and the number of votes or seats that the next person or party gets. 多得的票数；多获得的席位 ❑ *Members of parliament approved the move by a majority of ninety-nine.* 国会议员们以99票的多数批准了该提案。 3 ADJ **Majority** is used to describe opinions, decisions, and systems of government that are supported by more than half the people involved. 多数人支持的 [ADJ n] ❑ *...her continuing disagreement with the majority view.* …她与多数人观点的持续不一致。 **4** N-UNCOUNT **Majority** is the state of legally being an adult. In most states in the United States, people reach their majority at the age of eighteen. 成年 ❑ *...a citizen of Russia who has reached the age of majority.* …一个已成年的俄罗斯公民。

Word Partnership *majority* 的常用搭配:

N. majority **leader**, majority **of people**, majority **of the population** **1**
majority **opinion**, majority **rule**, majority **vote** **3**
ADJ. **overwhelming** majority, **vast** majority **1** **2**

Word Link *major ≈ larger : major, majority, majorleague*

ma·jor league (major leagues) **1** N-PLURAL **The major leagues** are groups of professional sports teams that compete against each other, especially in baseball. (尤指棒球中的) 职业总会 ❑ *Chandler was instrumental in making Jackie Robinson the first black player in the major leagues.* 钱德勒帮助杰基・鲁宾逊成为职业总会中第一个黑人球员。 **2** ADJ **Major league** means connected with the major leagues in baseball. 职业棒球总会的 ❑ *I'm doomed to live in a town with no major league baseball.* 我注定要住在一个没有职业棒球总会的棒球队的镇子上。 **3** ADJ **Major-league** people or institutions are important or successful. 重要的; 成功的 ❑ *James Hawes's books have achieved cult status, and his first film boasts major-league stars.* 詹姆斯・霍威的书已备受推崇，而他的第一部电影也明星荟萃。 **4** PHRASE If someone **moves into the major league** or **makes it into the major league**, they become very successful in their career. 跻身成功人士行列 [JOURNALISM] ❑ *Once a model has made it into the major league every detail is mapped out by her agency.* 模特儿一朝成名后，她的一切细节将由其经纪人安排。

make
❶ CARRYING OUT AN ACTION
❷ CAUSING OR CHANGING
❸ CREATING OR PRODUCING
❹ LINK VERB USES
❺ ACHIEVING OR REACHING
❻ STATING AN AMOUNT OR TIME
❼ PHRASAL VERBS

❶ make ♦♦♦ /meɪk/ (**makes, making, made**)

> **Make** is used in a large number of expressions which are explained under other words in this dictionary. For example, the expression "to make sense" is explained at "sense."

1 V-T You can use **make** with a wide range of nouns to indicate that someone performs an action or says something. For example, if you **make** a suggestion, you suggest something. 与名词连用，表示做动作或说某事 ❑ *I'd just like to make a comment.* 我只想做一下评论。 ❑ *I made a few phone calls.* 我打了几个电话。 **2** V-T You can use **make** with certain nouns to indicate that someone does something well or badly. For example, if you **make** a success of something, you do it successfully, and if you **make** a mess of something, you do it very badly. 与某些名词连用，表示做得好或做得糟 ❑ *Apparently he made a mess of his audition.* 显然他把试演搞得一团糟。 **3** V-T/V-I If you **make as if to** do something or **make to** do something, you behave in a way that makes it seem that you are just about to do it. 摆出 (要做某事的姿态) [WRITTEN] ❑ *Mary made as if to protest, then hesitated.* 玛丽似乎要抗议，又犹豫了。 **4** PHRASE If you **make do with** something, you use or have it instead of something else that you do not have, although it is not as good. (拿…) 凑合 ❑ *Why make do with a copy if you can afford the genuine article?* 如果你买得起正品，为什么还拿复制品凑合呢？

❷ make ♦♦♦ /meɪk/ (**makes, making, made**)
➪ **Please look at meaning 10 to see if the expression you are looking for is shown under another headword.** **1** V-T If something **makes** you do something, it causes you to do it. 致使 (某人做某事) ❑ *Dirt from the highway made him cough.* 公路上的灰尘使他咳嗽起来。 ❑ *The white tips of his shirt collar made him look like a choirboy.* 他衬衣的白色领尖使他看起来像个唱诗班男童。 **2** V-T If you **make** someone do something, you force them to do it. 迫使 (某人做某事) ❑ *You can't make me do anything.* 你不能强迫我做任何事。 **3** V-T You use **make** to talk about causing someone or something to be a particular thing or to have a particular quality. For example, to **make** someone a star means to cause them to become a star, and to **make** someone angry means to cause them to become angry. 使 (某人、某事物) 变成…; 使变得… ❑ *...James Bond, the role that made him a star.* …詹姆斯・邦德，那个使他成为明星的角色。 ❑ *She made life very difficult for me.* 她使我的生活变得很艰难。 **4** V-T If you say that one thing or person **makes** another seem, for example, small, stupid, or good, you mean that they cause them to seem small, stupid, or good in comparison, even though they are not. 使 (某物、某人) 显得… ❑ *They live in fantasy worlds which make Disneyland seem uninventive.* 他们生活在幻想世界里，那些幻想使迪斯尼乐园也显得毫无创意。 **5** V-T If you **make yourself** understood, heard, or known, you succeed in getting people to understand you, hear you, or know that you are there. 使 (自己被人理解、听到、知晓等) ❑ *He learned enough Spanish to make himself understood.* 他学的西班牙语足以让别人明白他。 **6** V-T If you **make** someone something, you appoint them to a particular job, role, or position. 任命 (某人担任某职或角色) ❑ *He made her a director in his numerous companies.* 他任命她为他数家公司的主管。 **7** V-T If you **make** something **into** something else, you change it in some way so that it becomes that other thing. 把 (某物) 变成 (另一物) ❑ *We made it into a beautiful home.* 我们把它变成了一个漂亮的家。 **8** V-T To **make** a total or score a particular amount means to increase it to that amount. 使 (总数、分数) 升为 (某数) ❑ *This makes the total cost of the bulb and energy $27.* 这使得灯泡和电量的总耗费升为$27。 **9** V-T When someone **makes** a friend or an enemy, someone becomes their friend or their enemy, often because of a particular thing they have done. 结成 (朋友或敌人) ❑ *Lorenzo was a natural leader who made friends easily.* 洛伦佐是个天生的领导者，结交朋友容易。 **10** to **make friends** → see **friend**

❸ make ♦♦♦ /meɪk/ (**makes, making, made**) **1** V-T To **make** something means to produce, construct, or create it. 制作; 创作 ❑ *She made her own bread.* 她自己做了面包。 ❑ *Having curtains made professionally can be costly.* 找专业人员制作窗帘会很贵。 **2** V-T If you **make** a note or list, you write something down in that form. 写 (笔记、清单等) ❑ *Mr. Perry made a note in his book.* 佩里先生在他的书里做了批注。 **3** V-T If you **make** rules or laws, you decide what these should be. 制定 (规则、法律等) ❑ *The police don't make the laws, they merely enforce them.* 警察不制定法律，只是执行法律。 **4** V-T If you **make** money, you get it by working for it, by selling something, or by winning it. 挣; 赚; 赢 (钱) ❑ *I think every business's goal is to make money.* 我想每笔生意的目的都是赚钱。 **5** V-T If you **make** a case **for** something, you try to establish or prove that it is the best thing to do. (为某事) 做解释 ❑ *You could certainly make a case for this point of view.* 你当然可以为这种观点做解释。 **6** N-COUNT The **make** of something such as a car or radio is the name of the company that made it. (产品的) 牌子 ❑ *The only car parked outside is a black Saab – a different make.* 停在外面的惟一一辆车是黑色的萨博——一个不同的牌子。

> The **brand** of a product such as jeans, tea, or soap is its name, which can also be the name of the company that makes or sells it. The **make** of a car or electrical appliance such as a radio or washing machine is the name of the company that produces it. If you talk about what **type** of product or service you want, you are talking about its quality and what features it should have. You can also talk about **types** of people or of abstract things. ❑ *...which type of coffeemaker to choose. ...a new type of bank account. ...looking for a certain type of actor.* A **model** of car or of some other devices is a name that is given to a particular **type**, for example, a Ford Escort. Note that **type** can also be used informally to mean either **make** or **model**. For example, if someone asks what **type** of car you have got, you could reply "an SUV," "a Ford," or perhaps "an Escort."

Thesaurus *make* 另参见:

V. build, compose, create, fabricate, produce; (*ant.*) destroy ❸ **1**

❹ make ♦♦♦ /meɪk/ (**makes, making, made**) **1** V-LINK You can use **make** to say that someone or something has the right qualities for a particular task or role. For example, if you say that someone will **make** a good politician, you mean that they have the right qualities to be a good politician. 成为 ❑ *She'll make a good actress, if she gets the right training.* 如果她得到恰当训练，她会成为一名

好演员。 ❑ *You've a very good idea there. It will make a good book.* 你的那个绝妙观点会使之成为一本好书。 **2** V-LINK If people **make** a particular pattern such as a line or a circle, they arrange themselves in this way. 排成 (某图案) ❑ *A group of people made a circle around the Pentagon.* 一群人绕五角大楼围成了一个圈。 **3** V-LINK You can use **make** to say what two numbers add up to. 是 (用于加法) ❑ *Four twos make eight.* 4个2是8。

5 make ♦♦♦ /meɪk/ (**makes, making, made**) **1** V-T If someone **makes** a particular team or **makes** a particular high position, they do so well that they are put in that team or get that position. 成为 (某队成员); 得到 (某职位) ❑ *The athletes are just happy to make the team.* 那些运动员很高兴加入该队。 **2** V-T If you **make** a place in or by a particular time, you get there in or by that time, often with some difficulty. (常指艰难地) 到达 (某地) ❑ *The engine is gulping two tons of fuel an hour in order to make New Orleans by nightfall.* 引擎每小时消耗两吨燃料以便在天黑之前赶到新奥尔良。 **3** PHRASE If you **make it** somewhere, you succeed in getting there, especially in time to do something. 成功到达 (某地) ❑ *So you did make it to America, after all.* 这样你终究成功到达了美国。 ❑ *...the hostages who never made it home.* …始终没能回家的人质们。 **4** PHRASE If you **make it**, you are successful in achieving something difficult, or in surviving through a very difficult period. (历经艰难) 获得成功 ❑ *I believe I have the talent to make it.* 我相信我有获得成功的才干。 **5** PHRASE If you cannot **make it**, you are unable to attend an event that you have been invited to. 如约而至 ❑ *He hadn't been able to make it to our dinner.* 他没能如约参加我们的晚宴。

6 make ♦♦♦ /meɪk/ (**makes, making, made**) **1** V-T You use **make it** when saying what you calculate or guess an amount to be. 计算; 估计 ❑ *"How many shots has she got left?"—"I make it two."* "她还剩几颗子弹?" —— "我估计是两颗。" **2** V-T You use **make it** when saying what time your watch says it is. 看表上是 (某时间) ❑ *I make it nearly nine o'clock.* 我的表上快9:00了。

7 make ♦♦♦ /meɪk/ (**makes, making, made**)

▸ **make for** **1** PHRASAL VERB If you **make for** a place, you move toward it. 前往 ❑ *He rose from his seat and made for the door.* 他起身向门口走去。 **2** PHRASAL VERB If something **makes for** another thing, it causes or helps to cause that thing to happen or exist. 促成; 造就 [INFORMAL] ❑ *A happy parent makes for a happy child.* 幸福的家长造就幸福的孩子。

▸ **make of** PHRASAL VERB If you ask a person what they **make of** something, you want to know what their impression, opinion, or understanding of it is. 从 (某事物) 中得出 (某印象、看法、理解等) ❑ *Nancy wasn't sure what to make of Mick's apology.* 南希不确定该怎样看待米克的道歉。

▸ **make off** PHRASAL VERB If you **make off**, you leave somewhere as quickly as possible, often in order to escape. (常指为逃离而) 尽快离开 ❑ *They broke free and made off in a stolen car.* 他们挣脱后开着一辆偷来的车尽快逃离了。

▸ **make off with** PHRASAL VERB If you **make off with** something, you steal it and take it away with you. 偷走 ❑ *Otto made off with the last of the brandy.* 奥托把最后一点儿白兰地偷走了。

▸ **make out** **1** PHRASAL VERB If you **make** something **out**, you manage with difficulty to see or hear it. (费力地) 看出; 听出 ❑ *I could just make out a tall, pale, shadowy figure tramping through the undergrowth.* 我只能看出一个高高的、苍白的、朦胧的人影穿行在矮灌木丛中。 ❑ *She thought she heard a name. She couldn't make it out, though.* 她以为自己听到了一个名字，但听不清楚。 **2** PHRASAL VERB If you try to **make** something **out**, you try to understand it or decide whether or not it is true. 理解; 辨清 ❑ *I couldn't make it out at all.* 我完全不能明白它。 ❑ *It is hard to make out what criteria are used.* 难以辨清使用了什么标准。 **3** PHRASAL VERB If you **make out that** something is the case or **make** something **out to** be the case, you try to cause people to believe that it is the case. 证明; 竭力说 ❑ *They were trying to make out that I'd actually done it.* 他们在试图证明我确实做了那件事。 ❑ *I don't think it was as glorious as everybody made it out to be.* 我认为这不像大家说的那样了不起。 **4** PHRASAL VERB When you **make out** a check, receipt, or order form, you write all the necessary information on it. 填写完 ❑ *I'll make the check out to you and put it in the mail this afternoon.* 我会给你写一张支票并于今天下午邮寄给你。 **5** PHRASAL VERB If two people **are making out**, they are engaged in sexual activity. 性交 [mainly AM, INFORMAL] ❑ *...pictures of the couple making out on the beach.* …那对夫妇在海滩做爱的照片。

▸ **make up** **1** PHRASAL VERB The people or things that **make up** something are the members or parts that form that thing. 构成 ❑ *The Chinese make up the largest single ethnic group in the city's public classrooms.* 华人在该市公立学校的课堂中构成最大的一个族群。 ❑ *Women officers make up 13 percent of the police force.* 女警察构成警力的13%。 **2** PHRASAL VERB If you **make up** something such as a story or excuse, you invent it, sometimes in order to deceive people. 编造 ❑ *I think it's very unkind of you to make up stories about him.* 我认为你编造关于他的故事是很不友好的。 **3** PHRASAL VERB If you **make up** an amount, you add something to it so that it is as large as it should be. 补足 (某数量) ❑ *Less than half of the money that students receive is in the form of grants, and loans have made up the difference.* 学生们获得的有不到一半的钱是助学金形式的，贷款补上了不足的部分。 **4** PHRASAL VERB If you **make up** time or hours, you work some extra hours because you have previously taken some time off work. 加班补足 (缺工时间) ❑ *They'll have to make up time lost during the strike.* 他们将不得不补上因罢工失去的时间。 **5** PHRASAL VERB If a student **makes up** an examination or course they have failed or missed, they take the examination or course again. 补考; 补修 (某课程) [AM] ❑ *Everyone gets a chance to make up tests.* 每个人都有一次补考的机会。 **6** PHRASAL VERB If two people **make up** after a quarrel or disagreement, they become friends again. 和好 ❑ *She came back and they made up.* 她回来了，他们和好了。 **7** PHRASAL VERB If you **make up** something such as food or medicine, you prepare it by mixing or putting different things together. 配制 (食物、药等) ❑ *Prepare the soufflé dish before making up the soufflé mixture.* 在配制蛋奶酥混合料之前先准备蛋奶酥烤盘。 **8** PHRASAL VERB If you **make up** a bed, you put sheets and blankets on it so that someone can sleep there. 铺 (床) ❑ *Her mother made up a bed in her old room.* 她母亲在她的旧房间里铺了个床。

mak·er ♦♦◇ /meɪkər/ (**makers**) **1** N-COUNT The **maker** of a product is the company that manufactures it. 制造商 ❑ *...Japan's two largest car makers.* …日本两家最大的汽车制造商。 **2** N-COUNT You can refer to the person who makes something as its **maker**. 制作者 ❑ *...the makers of news and current affairs programs.* …新闻和时事节目制片人。

▲ **make·shift** /meɪkʃɪft/ ADJ **Makeshift** things are temporary and usually of poor quality, but they are used because there is nothing better available. 临时凑合的 ❑ *...the cardboard boxes and makeshift shelters of the homeless.* …无家可归者的纸板箱和临时栖身处。

★ **make·up** ♦◇◇ /meɪkʌp/ **1** N-UNCOUNT **Makeup** consists of things such as lipstick, eye shadow, and powder which some women put on their faces to make themselves look more attractive or which actors use to change or improve their appearance. 化妆品 ❑ *Normally she wore little makeup, but this evening was clearly an exception.* 通常她很少化妆，可今晚显然是个例外。 **2** N-UNCOUNT Someone's **makeup** is their nature and the various qualities in their character. 性格 ❑ *There was some fatal flaw in his makeup, and as time went on he lapsed into long silences or became off-hand.* 他性格中有某种致命的缺陷，随着时间的推移，他要么陷入长时间沉默要么行为随便。 **3** N-UNCOUNT The **makeup** of something consists of its different parts and the way these parts are arranged. 构造;

m

Word Web makeup

The women of ancient Egypt were among the first to **wear makeup**. They **applied foundation** to lighten their skin and used kohl as eye shadow to darken their eyelids. Greek women used charcoal as an eyeliner and **rouge** on their cheeks. In 14th century Europe, the most popular **cosmetic** was wheat flour. Women whitened their faces to show their social class. A light **complexion** indicated the woman didn't have to work outdoors. **Cosmetics** containing lead and arsenic sometimes caused illness and death. Makeup use increased in the early 1900s. Suddenly many women could afford mass-produced **lipstick**, **mascara**, and **face powder**.

组成 ❑ *The ideological makeup of the unions is now radically different from what it had been.* 这些协会的意识形态构成如今与过去大相径庭。
→ see Word Web: **makeup**

mak·ing /meɪkɪŋ/ **(makings)** 1 N-UNCOUNT The **making** of something is the act or process of producing or creating it. 制作; 创作 ❑ *...Salamon's book about the making of this movie.* 萨拉蒙的关于制作这部影片的书。 2 PHRASE If you describe a person or thing as something **in the making**, you mean that they are going to become known or recognized as that thing. 形成中的 ❑ *Her drama teacher is confident Julie is a star in the making.* 她的戏剧老师相信朱莉是未来的明星。 3 PHRASE If something **is the making of** a person or thing, it is the reason that they become successful or become very much better than they used to be. 是某人/某物成功的因素 ❑ *This discovery may yet be the making of him.* 这一发现也许成为他成功的因素。 4 PHRASE If you say that a person or thing **has the makings of** something, you mean it seems possible or likely that they will become that thing, as they have the necessary qualities. 有某事物的素质 ❑ *Godfrey had the makings of a successful journalist.* 戈弗雷具备一个成功记者的素质。 5 PHRASE If you say that something such as a problem you have is **of your own making**, you mean you have caused or created it yourself. (问题等) 由某人自己造成的 ❑ *Some of the university's financial troubles are of its own making.* 该大学的一些财政困难是其自身造成的。

Word Link *mal ≈ bad : malaria, malfunction, malpractice*

▲ **ma·laria** /məlɛəriə/ N-UNCOUNT **Malaria** is a serious disease carried by mosquitoes, which causes periods of fever. 疟疾

male ◆◆◇ /meɪl/ **(males)** 1 ADJ Someone who is **male** is a man or a boy. 男性的 ❑ *Many women achievers appear to pose a threat to their male colleagues.* 许多女性成功者似乎对她们的男同事造成一种威胁。 ❑ *The company has engaged two male dancers from the Bolshoi.* 该公司聘了两名来自波修瓦剧院的男舞蹈演员。 2 N-COUNT Men and boys are sometimes referred to as **males** when they are being considered as a type. 男性 ❑ *...the remains of a Caucasian male, aged 65-70.* …一个年龄在65至70岁之间的高加索男子的遗骸。 3 ADJ **Male** means relating to, belonging to, or affecting men rather than women. 男性的 [ADJ n] ❑ *Massive male unemployment has diminished the status of men in the family.* 大量男性失业已经降低了男人在家庭中的地位。 ❑ *...male violence.* …男性暴力。 4 N-COUNT You can refer to any creature that belongs to the sex that cannot lay eggs or have babies as a **male**. 雄性 ❑ *Males and females take turns brooding the eggs.* 雌雄轮流孵卵。 ● ADJ **Male** is also an adjective. 雄性的 ❑ *After mating, the male wasps tunnel through the sides of their nursery.* 交配后，雄黄蜂们从育蜂室的两侧钻过。

mal·func·tion /mælfʌŋkʃ°n/ **(malfunctions, malfunctioning, malfunctioned)** V-I If a machine or part of the body **malfunctions**, it fails to work properly. 出故障 [FORMAL] ❑ *The radiation can damage microprocessors and computer memories, causing them to malfunction.* 该辐射会破坏微处理器和计算机存储器，使之出故障。 ● N-COUNT **Malfunction** is also a noun. 出故障 ❑ *There must have been a computer malfunction.* 肯定出了电脑故障。

▲ **mal·ice** /mælɪs/ N-UNCOUNT **Malice** is behavior that is intended to harm people or their reputations, or cause them embarrassment and upset. 恶行 ❑ *There was a strong current of malice in many of his portraits.* 他的许多肖像画中都透出强烈的恶意。

★ **ma·li·cious** /məlɪʃəs/ ADJ If you describe someone's words or actions as **malicious**, you mean that they are intended to harm people or their reputation, or cause them embarrassment and upset. 恶意的 ❑ *That might merely have been malicious gossip.* 那可能只是恶意闲言。 ● **ma·li·cious·ly** ADV 恶意地 ❑ *...his maliciously accurate imitation of Hubert de Burgh.* …他对休伯特・德・伯格的恶意精确模仿。

▲ **ma·lig·nant** /məlɪgnənt/ 1 ADJ A **malignant** tumor or disease is out of control and likely to cause death. 恶性的 [MEDICAL] ❑ *She developed a malignant breast tumor.* 她得了恶性乳腺瘤。 2 ADJ If you say that someone is **malignant**, you think they are cruel and like to cause harm. 恶毒的 ❑ *He said that we were evil, malignant, and mean.* 他说我们邪恶、恶毒、卑鄙。

★ **mall** /mɔl/ **(malls)** N-COUNT A **mall** is a very large, enclosed shopping area. 大型购物区

mal·let /mælɪt/ **(mallets)** N-COUNT A **mallet** is a wooden hammer with a square head. 木槌

▲ **mal·nu·tri·tion** /mælnutrɪʃ°n/ N-UNCOUNT If someone is suffering from **malnutrition**, they are physically weak and extremely thin because they have not eaten enough food. 营养不良 ❑ *Infections are more likely in those suffering from malnutrition.* 感染更有可能发生在那些营养不良的人身上。

★ **mal·prac·tice** /mælpræktɪs/ **(malpractices)** N-VAR If you accuse someone of **malpractice**, you are accusing them of being careless or of breaking the law or the rules of their profession. 渎职; 玩忽职守 [FORMAL] ❑ *There were only one or two serious allegations of malpractice.* 只有一两起严肃的渎职指控。

malt /mɔlt/ **(malts)** 1 N-UNCOUNT **Malt** is a substance made from grain that has been soaked in water and then dried in a hot oven. Malt is used in the production of whiskey, beer, and other alcoholic drinks. 麦芽 ❑ *German beer has traditionally been made from just four ingredients – hops, malt, yeast, and water.* 德国啤酒传统上一直是只由4种原料酿造而成的——啤酒花、麦芽、酵母和水。 2 N-COUNT A **malt** is a drink made from malted milk powder, milk, ice cream, and sometimes other flavorings. 麦乳精饮料 [AM] ❑ *...a chocolate malt.* …一种巧克力麦乳精饮料。

▲ **mam·mal** /mæm°l/ **(mammals)** N-COUNT **Mammals** are animals such as humans, dogs, lions, and whales. In general, female mammals give birth to babies rather than laying eggs, and feed their young with milk. 哺乳动物
→ see Word Web: **mammal**
→ see **bat, pet, whale**

▲ **mam·moth** /mæməθ/ **(mammoths)** 1 ADJ You can use **mammoth** to emphasize that a task or change is very large and needs a lot of effort to achieve. 巨大的; 艰巨的 [EMPHASIS] ❑ *...the mammoth task of relocating the library.* …搬迁图书馆的艰巨任务。 2 N-COUNT A **mammoth** was an animal like an elephant, with very long tusks and long hair, that lived a long time ago but no longer exists. 猛犸

man ◆◆◆ /mæn/ **(men, mans, manning, manned)** 1 N-COUNT A **man** is an adult male human being. 男子; 男人 ❑ *He had not expected the young man to reappear before evening.* 他没想到那个年轻男子傍晚前会再次出现。 ❑ *I have always regarded him as a man of integrity.* 我一直把他看作个正直的男人。 2 N-VAR **Man** and **men** are sometimes used to refer to all human beings, including both males and females. Some people dislike this use. 人 (用以泛指) ❑ *The chick initially has no fear of man.* 小鸡最初不怕人。 3 N-COUNT If you say that a man is, for example, **a gambling man** or **an outdoors man**, you mean that he likes gambling or outdoor activities. (有某嗜好的) 人 ❑ *Are you a gambling man, Mr. Graham?* 你是个赌徒吗，格雷勒姆先生? 4 N-COUNT If you say that a man is, for example, **a Harvard man** or **a Yale man**, you mean that he went to that university. (属某院校的) 人 ❑ *Stewart, a Yale man, was invited to stay on and write the script.* 斯图尔特，一个耶鲁人，应邀留下来写该剧本。

Word Web **mammal**

Elephants, dogs, mice, and humans all belong to the class of animals called **mammals**. Mammals have live babies rather than laying eggs. The females also suckle their **young** with milk from their bodies. Mammals are warm-blooded and usually have hair on their bodies. Some, such as the brown bear and the raccoon, are omnivorous. Deer and zebras are herbivorous, living mostly on grass and leaves. Lions and tigers are carnivorous. They must have a supply of large **game** to survive. Mammals have a variety of different types of **limbs**. Monkeys have long arms for climbing. Seals have flippers for swimming.

M

5 N-COUNT If you refer to a particular company's or organization's **man**, you mean a man who works for or represents that company or organization. (属某公司或组织的) 人 [JOURNALISM] ❑ *...the Chicago Tribune's man in Abu Dhabi.* …驻阿布扎比的《芝加哥论坛》人。 **6** N-SING Some people refer to a woman's husband, lover, or boyfriend as her **man**. 男人 (指丈夫、情人或男友) [INFORMAL] ❑ *...if they see your man cuddle you in the kitchen or living room.* …要是他们看见你的男人在厨房或客厅拥抱你。 **7** N-VOC In very informal social situations, **man** is sometimes used as a greeting or form of address to a man. 老兄 [FORMULAE] ❑ *Hey wow, man! Where d'you get those boots?* 哇，老兄！你从哪儿弄来的那双靴子？ **8** V-T If you **man** something such as a place or machine, you operate it or are in charge of it. 操控 (机器等)；控制 (某地) ❑ *French soldiers manned roadblocks in the capital city.* 法国士兵控制了首都的路障。 ❑ *...the person manning the phone at the complaint department.* …在投诉部负责接听电话的人。 **9** → see also **manned, no-man's land** **10** PHRASE If you say that a man is **man enough** to do something, you mean that he has the necessary courage or ability to do it. 有足够的勇气或能力 (做某事) ❑ *I told him that he should be man enough to admit he had done wrong.* 我告诉过他应该有足够的勇气承认自己做错了。 **11** PHRASE If you describe a man as **a man's man**, you mean that he has qualities which make him popular with other men rather than with women. 受男人喜爱的男人 ❑ *Very much a man's man, he enjoyed drinking and jesting with his cronies.* 作为一个很受男人喜爱的男人，他喜欢和朋友喝酒开玩笑。 **12** PHRASE If you say that a man **is his own man**, you approve of the fact that he makes his decisions and his plans himself, and does not depend on other people. 自己的主人 [APPROVAL] ❑ *Be your own man. Make up your own mind.* 做自己的主人，自己做决定吧。 **13** PHRASE If you say that a group of men are, do, or think something **to a man**, you are emphasizing that every one of them is, does, or thinks that thing. 一致地 [EMPHASIS] ❑ *To a man, the survivors blamed the government.* 幸存者们一致谴责该政府。
→ see **age**

man·age ♦♦◊ /mænɪdʒ/ (**manages, managing, managed**) **1** V-T If you **manage** an organization, business, or system, or the people who work in it, you are responsible for controlling them. 管理；经营 (机构、企业、系统等) ❑ *Within two years he was managing the store.* 两年内他经营着该商店。 ❑ *There is a lack of confidence in the government's ability to manage the economy.* 对政府管理经济的能力缺乏信心。 **2** V-T If you **manage** time, money, or other resources, you deal with them carefully and do not waste them. 管理 (时间、金钱等) ❑ *In a busy world, managing your time is increasingly important.* 在一个忙碌的世界里，管理好你的时间越来越重要。 **3** V-T If you **manage to** do something, especially something difficult, you succeed in doing it. 设法 (做成某事) ❑ *Somehow, he'd managed to persuade Kay to buy one for him.* 不管怎么说，他已设法说服了凯给他买一个。 ❑ *I managed to pull myself up onto a wet, sloping ledge.* 我设法爬上了一个潮湿的倾斜岩脊。 **4** V-I If you **manage**, you succeed in coping with a difficult situation. 成功应对 ❑ *She had managed perfectly well without medication for three years.* 她3年没用药，却成功地挺了过来。 **5** V-T If you say that you can **manage** an amount of time or money for something, you mean that you can afford to spend that time or money on it. 腾出 (时间、金钱等) ❑ *I try to manage about five hours a week on my bike.* 我尽量每周抽出约五小时骑自行车。 **6** V-T If you say that someone **managed** a particular response, such as a laugh or a greeting, you mean that it was difficult for them to do it because they were feeling sad or upset. 勉强做出 (某种回应) ❑ *He looked dazed as he spoke to reporters, managing only a weak smile.* 他和记者说话时显得恍惚，只勉强做了个淡淡的微笑。 **7** CONVENTION You say "**I can manage**" or "**I'll manage**" as a way of refusing someone's offer of help and insisting on doing something by yourself. 我能应付 ❑ *I know you mean well, but I can manage by myself.* 我知道你是好意，但我自己能应付得了。

Word Partnership *manage* 的常用搭配：
- N. manage **a business/company**, manage **people** **1**; manage **expenses**, manage **money**, manage **resources**, manage **time** **2**
- ADV. manage **effectively** **1**–**4**
- V. manage **to escape**, manage **to survive** **3**

man·age·able /mænɪdʒəbᵊl/ ADJ Something that is **manageable** is of a size, quantity, or level of difficulty that people are able to deal with. 能应付的 ❑ *He will now try to cut down the task to a manageable size.* 他现在将尽力把任务缩减到能应对的程度。

Word Link *ment ≈ state, condition : agreement, management, movement*

man·age·ment ♦♦◊ /mænɪdʒmənt/ (**managements**) **1** N-UNCOUNT **Management** is the control and organizing of a business or other organization. (对企业等组织的) 管理 ❑ *The zoo needed better management rather than more money.* 动物园需要更好的管理而非更多的钱。 ❑ *The dispute is about wages, working conditions, and the management of the mining industry.* 这场争端涉及工资、工作环境和采矿业的管理。 **2** N-VAR-COLL You can refer to the people who control and organize a business or other organization as the **management**. 管理层 [BUSINESS] ❑ *The management is doing its best to improve the situation.* 管理层正在尽全力改善局面。 ❑ *We need to get more women into top management.* 我们需要让更多的女性进入高管层。 **3** N-UNCOUNT **Management** is the way people control different parts of their lives. (对生活的) 管理 ❑ *...her management of her professional life.* …她对自己职业生涯的管理。

Word Partnership *management* 的常用搭配：
- N. **business** management, management **skills**, management **style**, management **team**, management **training** **2**; **anger** management, **money** management, **crisis** management, **stress** management, **waste** management **3**
- ADJ. **new** management, **senior** management **2**

man·age·ment buy·out (**management buyouts**) N-COUNT A **management buyout** is the buying of a company by its managers. The abbreviation **MBO** is also used. 管理层收购 [BUSINESS] ❑ *Dozens of company boards are now discreetly sounding out venture capitalists to see if they will support management buyouts.* 十几家公司的董事会正在谨慎地试探风险投资者，以了解他们是否支持管理层收购。

man·ag·er ♦♦◊ /mænɪdʒər/ (**managers**) **1** N-COUNT A **manager** is a person who is responsible for running part of or the whole of a business organization. 经理 ❑ *The chef, staff, and managers are all Chinese.* 厨师、工作人员和经理都是中国人。 **2** N-COUNT The **manager** of a pop star or other entertainer is the person who takes care of their business interests. (明星等艺人的) 经纪人 ❑ *...the star's manager and agent, Anne Chudleigh.* …那位明星的经纪人兼代理人安妮・查德利。 **3** N-COUNT The **manager** of a baseball team is the person responsible for training the players and organizing the way they play. In other sports, **coach** is used instead. (棒球队) 教练
→ see **concert, restaurant**

★ **mana·gerial** /mænɪdʒɪəriəl/ ADJ **Managerial** means relating to the work of a manager. 经理的；管理上的 ❑ *...his managerial skills.* …他的管理技能。 ❑ *...a managerial career.* …管理生涯。

man·ag·ing di·rec·tor (**managing directors**) N-COUNT The **managing director** of a company is the most important working director, and is in charge of the way the company is managed. 总经理 [mainly BRIT, BUSINESS]

▲ **man·date** /mændeɪt/ (**mandates, mandating, mandated**) **1** N-COUNT If a government or other elected body has a **mandate** to carry out a particular policy or task, they have the authority to carry it out as a result of winning an election or vote. (政府或机构经选举而获得的) 授权 ❑ *The president and his supporters are almost certain to read this vote as a mandate for continued economic reform.* 总统和他的支持者们几乎肯定地认为这次投票是对继续进行经济改革的授权。 **2** N-COUNT If someone is given a **mandate** to carry out a particular policy or task, they are given the official authority to do it. (个人所获得的) 授权 ❑ *How much longer does the independent prosecutor have a mandate to pursue this investigation?* 这名独立检察官获得授权去调查这件事情的权限还有多长？ **3** N-COUNT You can refer to the fixed length of time that a country's leader or government remains in office as their **mandate**. 任期 [FORMAL] ❑ *...his intention to leave politics once his mandate ends.* …他任期一结束就将离开政界的打算。 **4** V-T When someone **is mandated to** carry out a particular policy or task, they are given the official authority to do it. 授权 [usu passive] [FORMAL] ❑ *He'd been mandated by the West African Economic Community to go in and to enforce a ceasefire.* 他受西非经济共同体授权去介入并执行停火协定。 **5** V-T To **mandate** something means to make it mandatory. 强制执行 [AM] ❑ *The proposed initiative would mandate a reduction of carbon dioxide of 40%.* 这个倡议将把二氧化

碳排放量强制降低40%。 ❑ *Sixteen years ago, Quebec mandated that all immigrants send their children to French schools.* 16年前，魁北克省规定所有移民都要送孩子上法语学校。

▲ **man·da·tory** /mændətɔri/ **1** ADJ If an action or procedure is **mandatory**, people have to do it, because it is a rule or a law. 法定的 [FORMAL] ❑ *...the mandatory retirement age of 65.* …65岁的法定退休年龄。 **2** ADJ If a crime carries a **mandatory** punishment, that punishment is fixed by law for all cases, in contrast to crimes for which the judge or magistrate has to decide the punishment for each particular case. (刑罚) 强制性的 [FORMAL] ❑ *...the mandatory life sentence for murder.* …谋杀罪的强制性终身监禁。

mane /meɪn/ (**manes**) N-COUNT The **mane** on a horse or lion is the long, thick hair that grows from its neck. (马或狮子的) 鬃毛 ❑ *The horse's mane can be washed at the same time as his body.* 马的鬃毛可以随其身体一起刷洗。

★ **ma·neu·ver** /mənuvər/ (**maneuvers, maneuvering, maneuvered**)

in BRIT, use **manoeuvre**

1 V-T/V-I If you **maneuver** something into or out of an awkward position, you skillfully move it there. (熟练地) 移动 ❑ *That will allow them to maneuver the satellite into the shuttle's cargo bay.* 那将使得他们能把人造卫星移入飞船的货物舱。 ❑ *I maneuvered my way among the tables to the back corner of the place.* 我在那些桌子间穿行，来到那地方后面的角落。 ● N-VAR **Maneuver** is also a noun. 移动 ❑ *The chopper shot upward in a maneuver matched by the other pilot.* 这架直升飞机向上冲去，另一架飞机也以相同的移动方向冲了上去。 **2** V-T/V-I If you **maneuver** a situation, you change it in a clever and skillful way so that you can benefit from it. 操控 ❑ *The president has tried to maneuver the campaign away from himself.* 总统试图操控该活动，使其远离自身。 ● N-COUNT **Maneuver** is also a noun. 操控手段 ❑ *The company announced a series of maneuvers to raise cash and reduce debt.* 这家公司宣布了一系列筹措现金、减少债务的手段。 **3** N-PLURAL Military **maneuvers** are training exercises which involve the movement of soldiers and equipment over a large area. 演习 ❑ *Allied troops begin maneuvers tomorrow to show how quickly forces could be mobilized in case of a new invasion.* 盟军部队明天开始演习，来展示一旦发生新的入侵，军队能以多快的速度集结起来。

M

man·gle /mæŋgᵊl/ (**mangles, mangling, mangled**) V-T If a physical object **is mangled**, it is crushed or twisted very forcefully, so that it is difficult to see what its original shape was. 严重损毁 [usu passive] ❑ *His body was crushed and mangled beyond recognition.* 他的身体被轧得血肉模糊而无法辨认。

man·go /mæŋgoʊ/ (**mangoes** or **mangos**) N-VAR A **mango** is a large, sweet, yellowish fruit which grows on a tree in hot areas. 芒果 ❑ *Peel, stone, and dice the mango.* 把芒果削皮、去核、切成丁。 ● N-COUNT A **mango** is the tree that this fruit grows on. 芒果树 ❑ *...orchards of lime and mango trees.* …有酸橙树和芒果树的果园。

Word Link *hood ≈ state, condition : adulthood, childhood, manhood*

★ **man·hood** /mænhʊd/ N-UNCOUNT **Manhood** is the state of being a man rather than a boy. (男子的) 成年 ❑ *They were failing lamentably to help their sons grow from boyhood to manhood.* 令人惋惜的是，他们没能帮助儿子们从少年长大成人。

man-hour (**man-hours**) N-COUNT A **man-hour** is the average amount of work that one person can do in an hour. **Man-hours** are used to estimate how long jobs take, or how many people are needed to do a job in a particular time. 工时 ❑ *The restoration took almost 4,000 man-hours over four years.* 这项修复工作大概用了4000工时，历时4年。

ma·nia /meɪniə/ (**manias**) **1** N-COUNT If you say that a person or group has a **mania for** something, you mean that they enjoy it very much or spend a lot of time on it. 狂热 ❑ *The mania for dinosaurs began in the late 1800s.* 恐龙热兴起于19世纪晚期。 **2** N-UNCOUNT **Mania** is a mental illness which causes the sufferer to become very worried or concerned about something. 狂躁症 [also N in pl] ❑ *...the treatment of mania.* …狂躁症的治疗。

ma·ni·ac /meɪniæk/ (**maniacs**) **1** N-COUNT A **maniac** is a crazy person who is violent and dangerous. 疯子 ❑ *The cabin looked as if a maniac had been let loose there.* 小屋看上去像是被放任的疯子光顾过一样。 **2** ADJ If you describe someone's behavior as **maniac**, you are emphasizing that it is extremely foolish and uncontrolled. 疯狂的 [ADJ n] [EMPHASIS] ❑ *He could not maintain his maniac speed for much longer.* 他不能太长时间地保持这种疯狂的速度。 **3** N-COUNT If you call someone, for example, a religious **maniac** or a sports **maniac**, you are critical of them because they have such a strong interest in religion or sports. 狂热分子 [DISAPPROVAL] ❑ *My mom is turning into a religious maniac.* 我妈妈正在变成一个宗教狂热分子。

man·ic /mænɪk/ **1** ADJ If you describe someone as **manic**, you mean that they do things extremely quickly or energetically, often because they are very excited or anxious about something. 狂热的 ❑ *He was really manic.* 他真的很狂热。 ● **man·ic·al·ly** /mænɪkli/ ADV 狂热地 ❑ *We cleaned the house manically over the weekend.* 我们周末热情十足地打扫了房间。 **2** ADJ If you describe someone's smile, laughter, or sense of humor as **manic**, you mean that it seems excessive or strange, as if they were insane. 发疯似的 ❑ *...a manic grin.* …傻傻的咧嘴笑。

Word Link *cur ≈ caring : curate, curator, manicure*

Word Link *man ≈ hand : emancipate, manicure, manipulate*

mani·cure /mænɪkyʊər/ (**manicures, manicuring, manicured**) V-T If you **manicure** your hands or nails, you care for them by softening your skin and cutting and polishing your nails. 护理手甲 ❑ *He was surprised to see how carefully she had manicured her broad hands.* 他很惊讶，看到她那么仔细地护理她那双大手。 ● N-COUNT **Manicure** is also a noun. 手甲护理 ❑ *I have a manicure occasionally.* 我偶尔会做一次手甲护理。

★ **mani·fest** /mænɪfɛst/ (**manifests, manifesting, manifested**) **1** ADJ If you say that something is **manifest**, you mean that it is clearly true and that nobody would disagree with it if they saw it or considered it. 明显的 [FORMAL] ❑ *...the manifest failure of the policies.* …这些政策明显的失败。 ● **mani·fest·ly** ADV 明显地 ❑ *She manifestly failed to last the mile-and-a-half of the race.* 她显然没有跑完1.5英里的比赛。 **2** V-T If you **manifest** a particular quality, feeling, or illness, or if it **manifests itself**, it becomes visible or obvious. 显现出 [FORMAL] ❑ *He manifested a pleasing personality on stage.* 他在舞台上表现出讨人喜欢的个性。 ❑ *The virus needs two weeks to manifest itself.* 这种病毒需要两周才能发作。 ● ADJ **Manifest** is also an adjective. 显现出的 ❑ *The same alarm is manifest everywhere.* 同样的恐慌在各地都已出现。

mani·fes·ta·tion /mænɪfɛsteɪʃᵊn/ (**manifestations**) N-COUNT A **manifestation of** something is one of the different ways in which it can appear. 表现 [FORMAL] ❑ *Different animals in the colony had different manifestations of the disease.* 同一群体的不同动物对同一疾病有不同的表现形式。

mani·fes·to /mænɪfɛstoʊ/ (**manifestos** or **manifestoes**) N-COUNT A **manifesto** is a statement published by a person or group of people, especially a political party, or a government, in which they say what their aims and policies are. 宣言 ❑ *The Republicans are currently drawing up their election manifesto.* 共和党人目前正在起草他们的竞选宣言。

ma·nipu·late /mənɪpyəleɪt/ (**manipulates, manipulating, manipulated**) **1** V-T If you say that someone **manipulates** people, you disapprove of them because they skillfully force or persuade people to do what they want. 控制 [DISAPPROVAL] ❑ *She's always borrowing my clothes and manipulating me to give her vast sums of money.* 她总是向我借衣服，并控制我，让我给她大笔的钱。 ● **ma·nipu·la·tion** /mənɪpyəleɪʃᵊn/ N-VAR (**manipulations**) 控制 ❑ *...repeated criticism or manipulation of our minds.* …对我们思想的反复批评或一再控制。 **2** V-T If you say that someone **manipulates** an event or situation, you disapprove of them because they use or control it for their own benefit, or cause it to develop in the way they want. 操纵 [DISAPPROVAL] ❑ *She was unable, for once, to control and manipulate events.* 她曾一度无法控制和操纵事件。 ● **ma·nipu·la·tion** N-VAR 操纵 ❑ *...accusations of political manipulation.* …对政治操纵的指控。 **3** V-T If you **manipulate** something that requires skill, such as a complicated piece of equipment or a difficult idea, you operate it or process it. 操作 ❑ *The technology uses a pen to manipulate a computer.* 这项技术使用笔来操作计算机。 ● **ma·nipu·la·tion** N-VAR 操作 ❑ *...science that requires only the simplest of mathematical manipulations.* …只要求进行最简单数学运算的科学。 **4** V-T If someone **manipulates** your bones or muscles, they skillfully move and press them with their hands in order to push the bones into their correct position or make the muscles less stiff. 使脱臼复位；用推拿术治疗 ❑ *The way he can manipulate my leg has helped my arthritis so much.* 他针对我的腿部做的推

拿治疗对我的关节炎大有帮助。● **ma·nipu·la·tion** N-VAR 推拿术 ❑ *A permanent cure will only be effected by acupuncture, chiropractic, or manipulation.* 只有针灸、按摩或推拿术才能实现永久的治愈。

ma·nipu·la·tive /mənɪpyəleɪtɪv, -lətɪv/ ADJ If you describe someone as **manipulative**, you disapprove of them because they skillfully force or persuade people to act in the way that they want. 操纵别人的 [DISAPPROVAL] ❑ *He described Mr. Long as cold, calculating, and manipulative.* 他把朗先生描述为冷漠、有心计和善于操纵别人。

man·kind /mænkaɪnd/ N-UNCOUNT You can refer to all human beings as **mankind** when considering them as a group. Some people dislike this use. 人类 ❑ *...the evolution of mankind.* …人类的进化。

man·ly /mænli/ (**manlier, manliest**) ADJ If you describe a man's behavior or appearance as **manly**, you approve of it because it shows qualities that are considered typical of a man, such as strength or courage. 有男子气概的 [APPROVAL] ❑ *He set himself manly tasks and expected others to follow his example.* 他给自己安排了体现男子气概的任务，并期待其他人去效仿他。● **man·li·ness** N-UNCOUNT 男子气概 ❑ *He has no doubts about his manliness.* 他毫不怀疑他的男子气概。

man-made also **manmade** ADJ **Man-made** things are created or caused by people, rather than occurring naturally. 人造的 ❑ *Man-made and natural disasters have disrupted the government's economic plans.* 人为和自然灾害打乱了政府的经济计划。 ❑ *...man-made lakes.* …人工湖。

manned /mænd/ 1 ADJ A **manned** vehicle such as a spacecraft has people in it who are operating its controls. 载人的 ❑ *In thirty years from now the United States should have a manned spacecraft on Mars.* 从现在开始30年内，美国会把载人航天器送上火星。 2 → see also **man 8**

man·ner ♦◇◇ /mænər/ (**manners**) 1 N-SING The **manner** in which you do something is the way that you do it. 方式 ❑ *She smiled again in a friendly manner.* 她又友好地笑了笑。 ❑ *I'm a professional and I have to conduct myself in a professional manner.* 我是专业人士，必须以专业方式行事。 2 N-SING Someone's **manner** is the way in which they behave and talk when they are with other people, for example whether they are polite, confident, or bad-tempered. 举止 ❑ *His manner was self-assured and brusque.* 他的举止自负而且粗鲁。 ● **-mannered** COMB IN ADJ …的态度 ❑ *Forrest was normally mild-mannered, affable, and untalkative.* 福里斯特通常态度温和，和蔼可亲，不善言辞。 3 N-PLURAL If someone has **good manners**, they are polite and observe social customs. If someone has **bad manners**, they are impolite and do not observe these customs. 礼貌 ❑ *He dressed well and had impeccable manners.* 他穿着得体，举止无可挑剔。 ❑ *The manners of many doctors were appalling.* 许多医生很没礼貌。

Word Partnership *manner* 的常用搭配:

ADJ. **effective** manner, **efficient** manner 1
abrasive manner, **abrupt** manner, **appropriate** manner, **businesslike** manner, **different** manner, **friendly** manner, **usual** manner 1 2

★ **ma·noeu·vre** /mənuvər/ [BRIT] → see **maneuver**

man·power /mænpaʊər/ N-UNCOUNT Workers are sometimes referred to as **manpower** when they are being considered as a part of the process of producing goods or providing services. 劳动力 ❑ *...the shortage of skilled manpower in the industry.* …这个行业技术劳动力的短缺。

★ **man·sion** /mænʃən/ (**mansions**) N-COUNT A **mansion** is a very large house. 大厦 ❑ *...an eighteenth-century mansion in New Hampshire.* …新罕布什尔州一座18世纪的大厦。

man·slaughter /mænslɔtər/ N-UNCOUNT **Manslaughter** is the illegal killing of a person by someone who did not intend to kill them. 过失杀人 [LEGAL] ❑ *A judge accepted her plea that she was guilty of manslaughter, not murder.* 法官接受了她的申诉，她犯的是过失杀人而不是蓄意谋杀。

mantel·piece /mæntəlpis/ (**mantelpieces**) also **mantlepiece** N-COUNT A **mantelpiece** is a wood or stone shelf which is the top part of a border around a fireplace. 壁炉台 ❑ *On the mantelpiece are a pair of bronze Ming vases.* 在壁炉台上的是一对明代的青铜花瓶。

man·tra /mæntrə/ (**mantras**) 1 N-COUNT A **mantra** is a word or phrase repeated by Buddhists and Hindus when they meditate, or to help them feel calm. (佛教和印度教中的) 祷语 2 N-COUNT You can use **mantra** to refer to a statement or a principle that people repeat very often because they think it is true, especially when you think that it not true or is only part of the truth. 准则 ❑ *Listening to customers is now part of the mantra of new management in public services.* 倾听顾客的要求是当今公用事业新型管理准则中的一部分。

Word Link *manu ≈ hand : manual, manufacture, manuscript*

manu·al /mænyuəl/ (**manuals**) 1 ADJ **Manual** work is work in which you use your hands or your physical strength rather than your mind. 手工的; 靠劳力的 ❑ *...skilled manual workers.* …熟练的手工工人。 2 ADJ **Manual** is used to talk about movements which are made by someone's hands. 用手的 [ADJ n] [FORMAL] ❑ *...toys designed to help develop manual dexterity.* …旨在培养手的灵活性的玩具。 3 ADJ **Manual** means operated by hand, rather than by electricity or a motor. 用手操作的 [ADJ n] ❑ *There is a manual pump to get rid of the water.* 有一台手动水泵用来排水。● **manu·al·ly** ADV 用手操作地 [ADV with v] ❑ *The device is manually operated, using a simple handle.* 这个装置利用一个简单的手柄，可以用手操作。 4 N-COUNT A **manual** is a book which tells you how to do something or how a piece of machinery works. 使用手册 ❑ *...the instruction manual.* …使用说明书。

manu·fac·ture ♦◇◇ /mænyəfæktʃər/ (**manufactures, manufacturing, manufactured**) 1 V-T To **manufacture** something means to make it in a factory, usually in large quantities. 生产 [BUSINESS] ❑ *They manufacture the class of plastics known as thermoplastic materials.* 他们生产被称为热塑材料的塑料类制品。 ❑ *The first three models are being manufactured at the factory in Dayton.* 最初的3个型号正在代顿的工厂生产。● N-UNCOUNT **Manufacture** is also a noun. 生产 ❑ *...the manufacture of nuclear weapons.* …核武器的生产。● **manu·fac·tur·ing** N-UNCOUNT 生产 ❑ *...management headquarters for manufacturing in China.* …设在中国的生产管理总部。 2 N-COUNT In economics, **manufactures** are goods or products which have been made in a factory. 工业品 [BUSINESS] ❑ *...a long-term rise in the share of manufactures in non-oil exports.* …非石油出口产品中工业品份额的长期增长。 3 V-T If you say that someone **manufactures** information, you are criticizing them because they invent information that is not true. 捏造 [DISAPPROVAL] ❑ *According to the prosecution, the officers manufactured an elaborate story.* 根据起诉，军官们精心编造了事情的经过。
→ see **mass production**

manu·fac·tur·er ♦◇◇ /mænyəfæktʃərər/ (**manufacturers**) N-COUNT A **manufacturer** is a business or company which makes goods in large quantities to sell. 生产商 [BUSINESS] ❑ *...the world's largest doll manufacturer.* …世界上最大的玩偶生产商。
→ see **industry**

ma·nure /mənʊər/ (**manures**) N-MASS **Manure** is animal feces, sometimes mixed with chemicals, that is spread on the ground in order to make plants grow healthy and strong. 肥料 ❑ *...bags of manure.* …一袋袋的肥料。

Word Link *script ≈ writing : manuscript, scripture, transcript*

★ **manu·script** /mænyəskrɪpt/ (**manuscripts**) N-COUNT A **manuscript** is a handwritten or typed document, especially a writer's first version of a book before it is published. 手稿 [also "in" N] ❑ *He had seen a manuscript of the book.* 他见过这本书的一份手稿。

many ♦♦♦ /mɛni/ 1 DET You use **many** to indicate that you are talking about a large number of people or things. 许多的 ❑ *I don't think many people would argue with that.* 我认为许多人对那都不会有争议。 ❑ *Not many films are made in Finland.* 芬兰出品的电影并不多。● PRON **Many** is also a pronoun. 许多 ❑ *We stood up, thinking through the possibilities. There weren't many.* 我们站起来，考虑着各种可能的情况，并无多少。● QUANT **Many** is also a quantifier. 许多 [QUANT "of" def-pl-n] ❑ *So, once we have cohabited, why do many of us feel the need to get married?* 那么，一旦我们同居了，为何我们中的许多人就觉得有必要结婚呢？ ❑ *It seems there are not very many of them left in the sea.* 似乎在海洋中它们所剩不多了。● ADJ **Many** is also an adjective. 许多的 ❑ *Among his many hobbies was the breeding of fine horses.* 在他的众多爱好中有饲养名马。 2 ADV You use **many** in expressions such as "not many," "not very many," and "too many" when replying to questions about numbers of things or people. 多 (用于"**not many**，" "**not very many**，" 和 "**too many**" 中回答有关数量的问题) [ADV as reply] ❑ *"How many of the songs that dealt with this theme became hit songs?"—"Not very many."* "有多少关于这个主题的歌曲成为了畅销歌曲？"——"不太多。" 3 PREDET You use **many** followed by "a" and a noun to emphasize that there are a lot of people or things involved in something. 许多(用于a+单数名词之前) [EMPHASIS] ❑ *Many a mother tries to act out her unrealized dreams through her daughter.* 许多母亲都试图通过女儿实现她们未能实现的梦想。 **4** DET You use **many** after "how" to ask questions about numbers or quantities. You use **many** after "how" in reported clauses to talk about numbers or quantities. 用于**how**之后，询问数量多少 ❑ *How many years have you been here?* 你在这儿多少年了？ ● PRON **Many** is also a pronoun. 用于**how**之后，作代词 ["how" PRON] ❑ *How many do you smoke a day?* 你一天吸多少支烟？ **5** DET You use **many** with "as" when you are comparing numbers of things or people. 和**as**连用，用于比较物或人的数量 ❑ *I've always entered as many photo competitions as I can.* 我总是尽可能多地参加摄影比赛。 ● PRON **Many** is also a pronoun. 和**as**连用，作代词 ["as" PRON] ❑ *Let the child try on as many as she likes.* 让这个孩子爱试穿多少就试多少吧。 **6** PRON You use **many** to mean "many people." 许多人 ❑ *Iris Murdoch was regarded by many as a supremely good and serious writer.* 艾里斯·默多克被许多人认为是一位极其出色而又严肃的作家。 **7** N-SING **The many** means a large group of people, especially the ordinary people in society, considered as separate from a particular small group. 多数人 ❑ *The printing press gave power to a few to change the world for the many.* 印刷机赋予了少数人为多数人改变世界的力量。

> You only use **many** to talk about things that can be counted. ❑ *They owned many cars.* You should use **much** if you want to talk about things that cannot be counted. ❑ *...too much water.*

8 PHRASE You use **as many as** before a number to suggest that it is surprisingly large. 多达 [EMPHASIS] ❑ *As many as 4 million people watched today's parade.* 多达400万的人观看了今天的游行。

map ♦◇◇ /mæp/ (**maps, mapping, mapped**) **1** N-COUNT A **map** is a drawing of a particular area such as a city, a country, or a continent, showing its main features as they would appear if you looked at them from above. 地图 ❑ *He unfolded the map and set it on the floor.* 他展开地图，把它放在了地板上。 **2** V-T To **map** an area means to make a map of it. 绘制…的地图 ❑ *...a spacecraft which is using radar to map the surface of Venus.* …一艘利用雷达绘制金星表面地图的航天器。
▸ **map out** PHRASAL VERB If you **map out** something that you are intending to do, you work out in detail how you will do it. 设计 ❑ *I went home and mapped out my strategy.* 我回到家，制定出了我的策略。 ❑ *I cannot conceive of anybody writing a play by sitting down and mapping it out.* 我无法想像有人能坐下来凭空想象就写出剧本。

M

Word Partnership	*map* 的常用搭配:
ADJ.	**detailed** map **1**
V.	**draw** a map, **look at** a map, **open** a map, **read** a map **1**

▲ **ma·ple** /meɪpᵊl/ (**maples**) N-VAR A **maple** or a **maple tree** is a tree with five-pointed leaves which turn bright red or gold in the fall. 枫树 ● N-UNCOUNT **Maple** is the wood of this tree. 枫木 ❑ *...a solid maple worktop.* …一张结实的枫木工作台。

▲ **mar** /mɑr/ (**mars, marring, marred**) V-T To **mar** something means to spoil or damage it. 破坏 ❑ *A number of problems marred the smooth running of this event.* 许多问题破坏了该事件的顺利进行。

Mar. **Mar.** is a written abbreviation for **March**. 3月

▲ **mara·thon** /mærəθɒn/ (**marathons**) **1** N-COUNT A **marathon** is a race in which people run a distance of 26 miles, which is about 42 km. 马拉松赛跑 ❑ *...running in his first marathon.* …正在跑他的第一次马拉松比赛。 **2** ADJ If you use **marathon** to describe an event or task, you are emphasizing that it takes a long time and is very tiring. 漫长而累人的 [ADJ n] [EMPHASIS] ❑ *People make marathon journeys to buy glass here.* 人们经过漫长而艰辛的旅途到这儿来买玻璃。

★ **mar·ble** /mɑrbᵊl/ (**marbles**) **1** N-UNCOUNT **Marble** is a type of very hard rock which feels cold when you touch it and which shines when it is cut and polished. Statues and parts of buildings are sometimes made of marble. 大理石 ❑ *The house has a superb staircase made from oak and marble.* 这座房子里有用栎木和大理石做成的一流的楼梯。 **2** N-COUNT **Marbles** are sculptures made of marble. 大理石雕像 ❑ *...marbles and bronzes from the Golden Age of Athens.* …雅典全盛时期的大理石雕像和青铜像。 **3** N-UNCOUNT **Marbles** is a children's game played with small balls, usually made of colored glass. You roll a ball along the ground and try to hit an opponent's ball with it. 弹子游戏 ❑ *On the far side of the street, two boys were playing marbles.* 在这条街的那一头，两个男孩子正在玩弹子游戏。 **4** N-COUNT A **marble** is one of the small balls used in the game of marbles. 弹子 ❑ *...a glass marble.* …一个玻璃弹子。

march ♦◇◇ /mɑrtʃ/ (**marches, marching, marched**) **1** V-T/V-I When soldiers **march** somewhere, or when a commanding officer **marches** them somewhere, they walk there with very regular steps, as a group. 使齐步走；行军 ❑ *A U.S. infantry battalion was marching down the street.* 一个美军步兵营沿着街道行进。 ❑ *Captain Ramirez called them to attention and marched them off to the main camp.* 拉米雷斯上校命令他们立正，然后让他们向主营地行进。 ● N-COUNT **March** is also a noun. 行军 ❑ *After a short march, the column entered the village.* 短途行军之后，队伍进入了村子。 **2** V-I When a large group of people **march** for a cause, they walk somewhere together in order to express their ideas or to protest about something. 游行 ❑ *The demonstrators then marched through the capital chanting slogans and demanding free elections.* 示威者然后穿越首都游行，反复喊着口号，要求进行自由选举。 ● N-COUNT **March** is also a noun. 游行 ❑ *Organizers expect up to 300,000 protesters to join the march.* 组织者预计多达30万的抗议者参加这次游行。 ● **march·er** N-COUNT (**marchers**) 游行者 ❑ *Fights between police and marchers lasted for three hours.* 警察和游行者之间的战斗持续了3个小时。 **3** V-I If you say that someone **marches** somewhere, you mean that they walk there quickly and in a determined way, for example because they are angry. (坚定地)快步走 ❑ *He marched into the kitchen without knocking.* 他没敲门就快步走进了厨房。 **4** V-T If you **march** someone somewhere, you force them to walk there with you, for example by holding their arm tightly. 迫使…同行 ❑ *They were marched through a crocodile-infested area and, if they slowed down, were beaten with sticks.* 他们被迫一同穿过一个鳄鱼出没的地区，如果走得慢了，就会遭到棍棒责打。 **5** N-SING **The march of** something is its steady development or progress. 进展 ❑ *It is easy to feel trampled by the relentless march of technology.* 技术日新月异的发展容易让人感到压抑。 **6** N-COUNT A **march** is a piece of music with a regular rhythm that you can march to. 进行曲 ❑ *A military band played Russian marches and folk tunes at the parade last Sunday.* 一个军乐团在上周日的游行中演奏了俄罗斯的进行曲和民乐。

March ♦♦♦ /mɑrtʃ/ (**Marches**) N-VAR **March** is the third month of the year in the Western calendar. 3月 ❑ *I flew to Milwaukee in early March.* 我3月初飞到了密尔沃基。 ❑ *She was born in Austria on March 6, 1920.* 她于1920年3月6日在奥地利出生。

▲ **mare** /mɛər/ (**mares**) N-COUNT A **mare** is an adult female horse. 母马

mar·ga·rine /mɑrdʒərɪn/ (**margarines**) N-MASS **Margarine** is a yellow substance made from vegetable oil that is similar to butter. You spread it on bread or use it for cooking. 人造黄油

mar·gin ♦◇◇ /mɑrdʒɪn/ (**margins**) **1** N-COUNT A **margin** is the difference between two amounts, especially the difference in the number of votes or points between the winner and the loser in an election or other contest. 差数 ❑ *They could end up with a 50-point winning margin.* 他们最后可能会以50点的优势获胜。 **2** N-COUNT The **margin** of a written or printed page is the empty space at the side of the page. 页边的空白 ❑ *She added her comments in the margin.* 她在页边空白处加上了她的评语。 **3** N-VAR If there is a **margin** for something in a situation, there is some freedom to choose what to do or decide how to do it. 余地 ❑ *The money is collected in a straightforward way with little margin for error.* 这笔钱是直接募集上来的，几乎没有出错的余地。 **4** N-COUNT The **margin** of a place or area is the extreme edge of it. 边缘 ❑ *...the low coastal plain along the western margin.* …沿着西部边缘地带的低洼海岸平原。 **5** N-PLURAL To be **on the margins** of a society, group, or activity means to be among the least typical or least important parts of it. 非主体部分 ❑ *Students have played an important role in the past, but for the moment, they're on the margins.* 学生们过去发挥了重要的作用，但现在，他们不再重要了。 **6** → see also **profit margin**

Word Partnership	*margin* 的常用搭配:
ADJ.	**comfortable** margin, **large** margin, **slim** margin **1**
	narrow margin, **wide** margin **1** **2**
N.	margin **for error** **3**

mar·gin·al /mɑrdʒɪnᵊl/ **1** ADJ If you describe something as **marginal**, you mean that it is small or not very important. 微小的 ❑ *This is a marginal improvement on October.* 这是对10月份的一个小小的改进。 **2** ADJ If you describe people as **marginal**, you mean that they are not involved in the main events or developments in society because they are poor or have no power. 无足轻重的 ❑ *The tribunals were established for the well-integrated members of society and not for marginal individuals.* 这个特别法庭是为社会中的主流人群设立的，而不

是为了无足轻重的小人物。 **3** ADJ **Marginal** activities, costs, or taxes are not the main part of a business or an economic system, but often make the difference between its success or failure, and are therefore important to control. 边际的 [BUSINESS] ❏ *The analysts applaud the cuts in marginal businesses, but insist the company must make deeper sacrifices.* 分析家们赞同对边际业务的削减，但坚持认为公司必须作出更大牺牲。

mar·gin·al·ly /mɑrdʒɪnəli/ ADV **Marginally** means to only a small extent. 略微地 ❏ *Sales last year were marginally higher than in 1991.* 去年的销售量比1991年略微高一点。

▲ **ma·ri·jua·na** /mærɪwɑnə/ N-UNCOUNT **Marijuana** is a drug which is made from the dried leaves and flowers of the hemp plant, and which can be smoked. 大麻

ma·ri·na /mərinə/ (**marinas**) N-COUNT A **marina** is a small harbor for small boats that are used for leisure. (停泊游艇的) 小船坞

mari·nade /mærɪneɪd/ (**marinades, marinading, marinaded**) **1** N-COUNT A **marinade** is a sauce of oil, vinegar, spices, and herbs, which you pour over meat or fish before you cook it, in order to add flavor, or to make the meat or fish softer. (调味油、醋和香料制成的) 腌汁 ❏ *Fish is already tender and moist, so a marinade is just added for flavor.* 鱼肉已经鲜嫩松软，所以加入腌汁只是提味。 **2** V-T/V-I To **marinade** means the same as to **marinate**. 腌泡 ❏ *Leave to marinade for 24 hours.* 腌制24个小时。

mari·nate /mærɪneɪt/ (**marinates, marinating, marinated**) V-T/V-I If you **marinate** meat or fish, or if it **marinates**, you keep it in a mixture of oil, vinegar, spices, and herbs before cooking it, so that it can develop a special flavor. 使受腌汁浸泡; 腌泡 ❏ *Marinate the chicken for at least 4 hours.* 把鸡肉放在腌汁里浸泡至少四个小时。

Word Link *mar ≈ sea : marine, maritime, submarine*

ma·rine ♦◇◇ /mərin/ (**marines**) **1** N-COUNT A **marine** is a member of an armed force, for example the U.S. Marine Corps or the Royal Marines, who is specially trained for military duties at sea as well as on land. 海军陆战队士兵 ❏ *A small number of Marines were wounded.* 几名海军陆战队士兵受了伤。 **2** ADJ **Marine** is used to describe things relating to the sea or to the animals and plants that live in the sea. 海洋的 [ADJ n] ❏ *...breeding grounds for marine life.* …海洋生物的繁殖地。 **3** ADJ **Marine** is used to describe things relating to ships and their movement at sea. 海事的 [ADJ n] ❏ *...a lawyer specializing in marine law.* …一名专攻海事法的律师。 → see **ship**

▲ **mari·tal** /mærɪtəl/ ADJ **Marital** is used to describe things relating to marriage. 婚姻的 [ADJ n] ❏ *Caroline was hoping to make her marital home in Pittsburgh to be near her family.* 卡罗琳希望把婚后的家安置在匹兹堡，离父母家近些。

mari·tal sta·tus N-UNCOUNT Your **marital status** is whether you are married, single, or divorced. 婚姻状况 [FORMAL] ❏ *How well off you are in old age is largely determined by race, sex, and marital status.* 你老年生活的幸福在很大程度上取决于种族、性别和婚姻状况。

▲ **mari·time** /mærɪtaɪm/ ADJ **Maritime** is used to describe things relating to the sea and to ships. 海事的 [ADJ n] ❏ *...the largest maritime museum of its kind.* …同类型海洋博物馆中最大的。

mark ♦♦◇ /mɑrk/ (**marks, marking, marked**) **1** N-COUNT A **mark** is a small area of something such as dirt that has accidentally gotten onto a surface or piece of clothing. 斑点 ❏ *The dogs are always rubbing against the wall and making dirty marks.* 这些狗总是往墙上蹭，留下了点点污斑。 **2** V-T/V-I If something **marks** a surface, or if the surface **marks**, the surface is damaged by marks or a mark. 玷污; 留下污痕 ❏ *Leather overshoes were put on the horses' hooves to stop them from marking the turf.* 皮套子被套在了马蹄上，防止它们弄脏了跑马场。 **3** N-COUNT A **mark** is a written or printed symbol, for example a letter of the alphabet. 记号 ❏ *He made marks with a pencil.* 他用铅笔作了记号。 **4** V-T If you **mark** something with a particular word or symbol, you write that word or symbol on it. 在…上作记号 ❏ *The bank marks the check "certified."* 银行在支票上标有"保付"的字样。 ❏ *Mark them with a symbol.* 用个记号把他们标出来。 **5** N-COUNT A **mark** is a point that is given for a correct answer or for doing something well in an exam or competition. A **mark** can also be a written symbol such as a letter that indicates how good a student's or competitor's work or performance is. 分数 ❏ *...a simple scoring device of marks out of 10, where "1" equates to "Very poor performance."* …一个简单的十分制评分体系，其中1分相当于表现"很差"。 **6** N-PLURAL If someone gets good or high **marks** for doing something, they have done it well. If they get poor or low **marks**, they have done it badly. 评价 ❏ *You have to give her top marks for moral guts.* 你必须给她的道德勇气最高的评价。 **7** V-T When a teacher **marks** a student's work, the teacher decides how good it is and writes a number or letter on it to indicate this opinion. 打分 ❏ *He was marking essays in his small study.* 他正在他的小书房里批阅文章。

● **mark·ing** N-UNCOUNT 打分 ❏ *For the rest of the lunch break I do my marking.* 在剩余的午休时间，我批改作业。 **8** N-COUNT A particular **mark** is a particular number, point, or stage which has been reached or might be reached, especially a significant one. (重要的) 指标 ❏ *Unemployment is rapidly approaching the one million mark.* 失业人数正迅速接近百万大关。 **9** N-COUNT The **mark of** something is the characteristic feature that enables you to recognize it. 特征 ❏ *The mark of a civilized society is that it looks after its weakest members.* 文明社会的特征是它关心最弱势群体。 **10** N-SING If you say that a type of behavior or an event is **a mark of** a particular quality, feeling, or situation, you mean it shows that that quality, feeling, or situation exists. 表示 ❏ *It was a mark of his unfamiliarity with Hollywood that he didn't understand that an agent was paid out of his client's share.* 他不知道经纪人的报酬由客户支付，这就是他对好莱坞并不熟悉的表现。 **11** V-T If something **marks** a place or position, it shows where something else is or where it used to be. 标明 (位置) ❏ *A huge crater marks the spot where the explosion happened.* 一个巨大的弹坑标明了爆炸发生的地点。 **12** V-T An event that **marks** a particular stage or point is a sign that something different is about to happen. 标志 (转折点) ❏ *The announcement marks the end of an extraordinary period in European history.* 这个声明标志着欧洲历史上一个伟大时代的终结。 **13** V-T If you do something to **mark** an event or occasion, you do it to show that you are aware of the importance of the event or occasion. 纪念 ❏ *Hundreds of thousands of people took to the streets to mark the occasion.* 数十万人走上了街头纪念这一时刻。 **14** V-T Something that **marks** someone **as** a particular type of person indicates that they are that type of person. 表明 (为某一种类的人) ❏ *Her opposition to abortion and feminism marks her as a convinced traditionalist.* 她对堕胎和女权主义的反对表明她是一个坚定的传统主义者。 **15** → see also **marked, marking, punctuation mark, question mark** **16** PHRASE If someone or something **leaves** their **mark** or **leaves a mark**, they have a lasting effect on another person or thing. 留下深远的影响 ❏ *Years of conditioning had left their mark on her, and she never felt inclined to talk to strange men.* 多年的熏陶给她留下了深远的影响，她从来不愿意和陌生男人说话。 **17** PHRASE If you **make** your **mark** or **make a mark**, you become noticed or famous by doing something impressive or unusual. 获得名望 ❏ *She made her mark in the film industry in the 1960s.* 20世纪60年代她在电影界颇有名望。 **18** PHRASE If something such as a claim or estimate is **wide of the mark**, it is incorrect or inaccurate. 离谱 ❏ *That comparison isn't as wide of the mark as it seems.* 那种比较不像看上去那么离谱。

▸ **mark down** **1** PHRASAL VERB To **mark** an item **down** or **mark** its price **down** means to reduce its price. 降低…的价格 ❏ *A toy store has marked down the latest computer games.* 一家玩具商店已经降低了最新版电脑游戏的价格。 **2** PHRASAL VERB If you **mark** something **down**, you write it down. 记下 ❏ *I tend to forget things unless I mark them down.* 我常常会忘事，除非我把它们记下来。

▸ **mark off** PHRASAL VERB If you **mark off** a piece or length of something, you make it separate, for example by putting a line on it or around it. 画线分隔出 ❏ *He used a rope to mark off the circle.* 他用一根绳子把这个圈围了起来。

▸ **mark up** **1** PHRASAL VERB If you **mark** something **up**, you increase its price. 提高…的价格 ❏ *You can sell it to them at a set wholesale price, allowing them to mark it up for retail.* 你可以按固定的批发价卖给他们，这样他们可以提高价格零售。 **2** → see also **markup**

Thesaurus *mark* 另参见：

N. dot, smudge **1**
attribute, feature, label, quality, trait **9**
V. dent, scratch **2**

marked ♦◇◇ /mɑrkt/ ADJ A **marked** change or difference is very obvious and easily noticed. 明显的 ❏ *There has been a marked increase in crimes against property.* 侵犯财产罪的数量有了明显的增加。

● **mark·ed·ly** /mɑrkɪdli/ ADV 明显地 ❏ *The current economic downturn is markedly different from previous recessions.* 目前的经济衰退和以前的经济衰退明显不同。

mark·er /mɑrkər/ (**markers**) **1** N-COUNT A **marker** is an object which is used to show the position of something, or is used to

m

help someone remember something. 标示物 ❑ *He put a marker in his book and followed her out.* 他在书里夹了一个书签，就随她出去了。
2 N-COUNT A **marker** or a **marker pen** is a pen with a thick tip made of felt, which is used for drawing and for coloring things. 毡笔 ❑ *Draw your child's outline with a heavy black marker or crayon.* 用浓黑色的毡笔或蜡笔画出你孩子的轮廓。

mar·ket ♦♦♦ /mɑrkɪt/ (**markets, marketing, marketed**)
1 N-COUNT A **market** is a place where goods are bought and sold, usually outdoors. 市场 ❑ *He sold boots at a market stall.* 他在市场的一个摊位上卖靴子。 **2** N-COUNT The **market** for a particular type of thing is the number of people who want to buy it, or the area of the world in which it is sold. 需求量; 商品行销地区 [BUSINESS] ❑ *The foreign market was increasingly crucial.* 国外的市场越来越关键了。
3 N-SING The **market** refers to the total amount of a product that is sold each year, especially when you are talking about the competition between the companies who sell that product. 年总销售量 [BUSINESS] ❑ *The two big companies control 72% of the market.* 这两家大公司控制了72%的市场份额。 **4** ADJ If you talk about a **market** economy, or the **market** price of something, you are referring to an economic system in which the prices of things depend on how many are available and how many people want to buy them, rather than prices being fixed by governments. 市场的 [ADJ n] [BUSINESS] ❑ *Their ultimate aim was a market economy for Hungary.* 他们的最终目标是为匈牙利建立市场经济。 ❑ *He must sell the house for the current market value.* 他必须按照目前的市场价格出售这套房子。
5 V-T To **market** a product means to organize its sale, by deciding on its price, where it should be sold, and how it should be advertised. 营销 [BUSINESS] ❑ *...if you marketed our music the way you market pop music.* …如果你按照营销流行音乐的方式营销我们的音乐。
6 N-SING **The job market** or **the labor market** refers to the people who are looking for work and the jobs available for them to do. 就业市场 [BUSINESS] ❑ *Every year, 250,000 people enter the job market.* 每年有250000人进入就业市场。 **7** N-SING The stock market is sometimes referred to as **the market.** 股票市场 [BUSINESS] ❑ *The market collapsed last October.* 股票市场去年10月崩盘了。 **8** → see also **black market, market forces, open market** **9** PHRASE If you say that it is **a buyer's market**, you mean that it is a good time to buy a particular thing, because there is a lot of it available, so its price is low. If you say that it is **a seller's market**, you mean that very little of it is available, so its price is high. 买方市场; 卖方市场 [BUSINESS] ❑ *Don't be afraid to haggle: for the moment, it's a buyer's market.* 别怕讨价还价：目前是买方市场。 **10** PHRASE If you are **in the market for** something, you are interested in buying it. 很想购买 ❑ *If you're in the market for a new radio, you'll see that the latest models are very different.* 如果你想买台新收音机，你会发现最新的款型很不同。
11 PHRASE If something is **on the market**, it is available for people to buy. If it comes **onto the market**, it becomes available for people to buy. 在市场上出售 [BUSINESS] ❑ *...putting more empty offices on the market.* …把更多的闲置办公间投入市场。 **12** PHRASE If you **price** yourself **out of the market**, you try to sell goods or services at a higher price than other people, with the result that no one buys them from you. 要价过高而未能成交 [BUSINESS] ❑ *At $250,000 for a season, he really is pricing himself out of the market.* 一个赛季要25万美元，他确实要价太高，让别人不敢问津了。
→ see **stock market**

Thesaurus	*market* 另参见:
N.	farmers' market, grocery store, supermarket **1**

mar·ket·able /mɑrkɪtəbᵊl/ ADJ Something that is **marketable** is able to be sold because people want to buy it. 可以出售的 [BUSINESS] ❑ *What began as an attempt at artistic creation has turned into a marketable commodity.* 原本艺术创作上的一个尝试最终变成了一个可以出售的商品。

mar·ket·eer /mɑrkɪtɪər/ (**marketeers**) **1** N-COUNT A **marketeer** is the same as a **marketer.** 商人 [BUSINESS] **2** → see also **free-marketeer**

mar·ket·er /mɑrkɪtər/ (**marketers**) N-COUNT A **marketer** is someone whose job involves marketing. 商人 [BUSINESS] ❑ *As a marketer I understood what makes people buy things.* 作为一个生意人，我知道如何让人们买东西。

mar·ket forces N-PLURAL When politicians and economists talk about **market forces**, they mean the economic factors that affect the availability of goods and the demand for them, without any help or control by governments. 市场力量 [BUSINESS] ❑ *...opening the economy to market forces and increasing the role of private enterprise.* …让市场力量在经济中发挥作用，增强私营企业的作用。

mar·ket·ing ♦◇◇ /mɑrkɪtɪŋ/ N-UNCOUNT **Marketing** is the organization of the sale of a product, for example, deciding on its price, the areas it should be supplied to, and how it should be advertised. 销售 [BUSINESS] ❑ *...expert advice on production and marketing.* …对生产和销售的专业建议。

mar·ket lead·er (**market leaders**) N-COUNT A **market leader** is a company that sells more of a particular product or service than most of its competitors do. 市场领先者 [BUSINESS] ❑ *We are becoming one of the market leaders in the fashion industry.* 我们正在成为时装行业的领军者之一。

market·place /mɑrkɪtpleɪs/ (**marketplaces**) **1** N-COUNT The **marketplace** refers to the activity of buying and selling products. 市场交易 [BUSINESS] ❑ *It's our hope that we will play an increasingly greater role in the marketplace and, therefore, supply more jobs.* 希望我们能在市场交易中扮演越来越重要的角色，从而提供更多的工作。
2 N-COUNT A **marketplace** is a small area in a town or city where goods are bought and sold, often outdoors. 集市 ❑ *The marketplace was jammed with a noisy crowd of buyers and sellers.* 集市上挤满了吵吵嚷嚷的买东西和卖东西的人。

mar·ket re·search N-UNCOUNT **Market research** is the activity of collecting and studying information about what people want, need, and buy. 市场调查 [BUSINESS] ❑ *A new all-woman market research company has been set up to find out what women think about major news and issues.* 一个新的全部由女性组成的市场调查公司成立了，以了解女性关于重要新闻和问题的看法。

mar·ket share (**market shares**) N-VAR A company's **market share** in a product is the proportion of the total sales of that product that is produced by that company. 市场份额 [BUSINESS] ❑ *Ford has been gaining market share this year at the expense of GM and some Japanese car manufacturers.* 福特公司今年一直在扩大自己的市场份额，这导致通用公司和一些日本汽车制造商市场份额减少。

mar·ket test (**market tests, market testing, market tested**)
1 N-COUNT If a company carries out a **market test**, it asks a group of people to try a new product or service and give their opinions on it. 市场测试 [BUSINESS] ❑ *Results from market tests in the U.S. and Europe show little enthusiasm for the product.* 美国和欧洲的市场测试结果显示，这种产品引不起兴趣。 **2** V-T If a new product or service is **market tested**, a group of people are asked to try it and then asked for their opinions on it. 对…进行市场试验 [BUSINESS] ❑ *These nuts have been market tested and found to be most suited to the Australian palate.* 这些干果已经过了市场试验，结果发现它们最适合澳大利亚人的口味。
• **mar·ket test·ing** N-UNCOUNT 市场测试 ❑ *They learned a lot from the initial market testing exercise.* 他们从最初的市场测试活动中学到了许多。

mark·ing /mɑrkɪŋ/ (**markings**) **1** N-COUNT **Markings** are colored lines, shapes, or patterns on the surface of something, which help to identify it. 记号 ❑ *A plane with Danish markings was over-flying his vessel.* 一架带有丹麦标志的飞机正从他的轮船上空飞过。
2 → see also **mark**

mark·up /mɑrkʌp/ (**markups**) N-COUNT A **markup** is an increase in the price of something, for example the difference between its cost and the price that it is sold for. 涨价 ❑ *We all know that most wine in restaurants is over-priced: a markup of 200 percent on cost is considered normal.* 我们都知道饭店中大部分葡萄酒标价过高：在成本价上涨200%被认为是正常的。

mar·ma·lade /mɑrməleɪd/ (**marmalades**) N-MASS **Marmalade** is a food made from oranges, lemons, or grapefruit that is similar to jam. It is eaten on bread or toast at breakfast. 橘子酱; 柠檬酱; 柚子酱

ma·roon /mərun/ (**maroons, marooning, marooned**) **1** COLOR Something that is **maroon** is dark reddish purple in color. 绛紫色的 ❑ *...maroon velvet curtains.* …绛紫色的天鹅绒窗帘。 **2** V-T If someone **is marooned** somewhere, they are left in a place that is difficult for them to escape from. 使无法逃脱 [usu passive] ❑ *He was marooned for a year in Jamaica.* 他在牙买加被困了一年。

Word Link	*age ≈ state of, related to : courage, marriage, patronage*

mar·riage ♦♦◇ /mærɪdʒ/ (**marriages**) **1** N-COUNT A **marriage** is the relationship between a husband and wife. 婚姻 ❑ *In a good marriage, both husband and wife work hard to solve any problems that arise.*

在一桩美满的婚姻中，夫妻双方共同致力于解决出现的任何问题。❑ *When I was 35 my marriage broke up.* 35岁时我的婚姻破裂了。2 N-VAR A **marriage** is the act of marrying someone, or the ceremony at which this is done. 结婚；婚礼 ❑ *I opposed her marriage to Darryl.* 我反对她嫁给达里尔。

→ see **love, wedding**

Do not confuse **marriage** and **wedding**. A **wedding** is a ceremony in which a man and woman get married. It usually includes a meal or other celebration that takes place after the ceremony itself. ❑ *It wasn't a formal wedding.* This ceremony can also be called a **marriage**. ❑ *...the day of my marriage.* **Marriage** can also be used to refer to the relationship between a husband and wife. ❑ *It has been a happy marriage.*

mar·ried ♦◇◇ /mærid/ 1 ADJ If you are **married**, you have a husband or wife. 已婚的 ❑ *We have been married for 14 years.* 我们已经结婚14年了。❑ *She is married to an Englishman.* 她嫁给了一个英国人。2 ADJ **Married** means relating to marriage or to people who are married. 婚姻的；夫妻的 [ADJ n] ❑ *For the first ten years of our married life we lived in a farmhouse.* 在结婚后的前10年，我们住在一间农舍里。3 ADJ If you say that someone is **married to** their work or another activity, you mean that they are very involved with it and have little interest in anything else. 献身的 [v-link ADJ "to" n] ❑ *"Sam was married to his job," McWhorter said.* "萨姆对工作全身心投入，"麦克沃特说。

mar·ry ♦♦◇ /mæri/ (**marries, marrying, married**) 1 V-RECIP When two people **get married** or **marry**, they legally become husband and wife in a special ceremony. **Get married** is less formal and more commonly used than **marry**. 结婚 ❑ *I thought he would change after we got married.* 我原以为他会在我们结婚后改变的。❑ *They married a month after they met.* 他们在认识一个月后就结婚了。❑ *He wants to marry her.* 他想娶她。2 V-T When a priest or official **marries** two people, he or she conducts the ceremony in which the two people legally become husband and wife. 为…主持婚礼 ❑ *The minister has agreed to marry us in the college chapel.* 这位牧师已经同意在学校的小教堂为我们主持婚礼。

marsh /mɑrʃ/ (**marshes**) N-VAR A **marsh** is a wet, muddy area of land. 沼泽

→ see **wetland**

mar·shal /mɑrʃᵊl/ (**marshals, marshaling** or **marshalling, marshaled** or **marshalled**) 1 V-T If you **marshal** people or things, you gather them together and arrange them for a particular purpose. 召集；安排 ❑ *The company turned its attention to marshaling its creditors' approval.* 这家公司把注意力转向了集结债权人的支持。2 N-COUNT A **marshal** is an official who helps to supervise a public event, especially a sports event. (尤指体育赛事的) 典礼官 ❑ *The grand prix is controlled by well-trained marshals.* 大赛由训练有素的典礼官们掌控。3 N-COUNT In the United States and some other countries, a **marshal** is a police officer, often one who is responsible for a particular area. (美国等国家的) 警察局长 ❑ *A federal marshal was killed in a shoot-out.* 一名联邦警察局长在枪战中被打死了。4 N-COUNT A **marshal** is an officer in a fire department. 消防队长 [AM] ❑ *She was ordered out of her home by a fire marshal because the house next door had an explosion from a leaking gas main.* 她被消防队长命令离开自己的家，因为隔壁房的煤气主管道泄漏发生了爆炸。

mart /mɑrt/ (**marts**) N-COUNT A **mart** is a place such as a market where things are bought and sold. 市场 [AM] ❑ *...the flower mart.* …花卉市场。

▲ **mar·tial** /mɑrʃᵊl/ 1 ADJ **Martial** is used to describe things relating to soldiers or war. 军人的；军事的 [FORMAL] ❑ *The paper was actually twice banned under the martial regime.* 这份报纸在军人统治时期确实曾两次被禁。2 → see also **court martial**

mar·tial art (**martial arts**) N-COUNT A **martial art** is one of the methods of fighting, often without weapons, that come from the Far East, for example kung fu, karate, or judo. 武术

mar·tial law N-UNCOUNT **Martial law** is control of an area by soldiers, not the police. 军事管制 ❑ *The military leadership has lifted martial law in several more towns.* 军方领导层又解除了几个城镇的军事管制。

★ **mar·tyr** /mɑrtər/ (**martyrs, martyring, martyred**) 1 N-COUNT A **martyr** is someone who is killed or made to suffer greatly because of their religious or political beliefs, and is admired and respected by people who share those beliefs. 殉教者；烈士 ❑ *...a glorious martyr to the cause of liberty.* …为自由事业光荣献身的一名烈士。2 V-T If someone **is martyred**, they are killed or made to suffer greatly because of their religious or political beliefs. 使殉难；折磨 [usu passive] ❑ *St. Pancras was martyred in 304 A.D.* 圣·潘克瑞斯在公元304年蒙难。3 N-COUNT If you refer to someone as a **martyr**, you disapprove of the fact that they pretend to suffer, or exaggerate their suffering, in order to get sympathy or praise from other people. 假装受苦者；夸大自己所受苦难的人 [DISAPPROVAL] ❑ *When are you going to quit acting like a martyr?* 什么时候你不再装得像个受苦受难的人呢？4 N-COUNT If you say that someone is a **martyr to** something, you mean that they suffer as a result of it. 受折磨的人 ❑ *Edgar was a martyr to his sense of honor and responsibility.* 埃德加深为他的荣誉感和责任感所累。

▲ **mar·vel** /mɑrvᵊl/ (**marvels, marveling** or **marvelling, marveled** or **marvelled**) 1 V-I If you **marvel** at something, you express your great surprise, wonder, or admiration. 大为赞叹 ❑ *Her fellow members marveled at her seemingly infinite energy.* 她的同事们对她那似乎无尽的精力大为赞叹。❑ *Sara and I read the story and marveled.* 我和萨拉读了这个故事后惊叹不已。2 N-COUNT You can describe something or someone as a **marvel** to indicate that you think that they are wonderful. 奇迹 ❑ *The whale, like the dolphin, has become a symbol of the marvels of creation.* 鲸，和海豚一样，已经成为造物杰作的象征。

mar·vel·lous /mɑːʳvələs/ [BRIT] → see **marvelous**

mar·vel·ous /mɑrvələs/

in BRIT, use **marvellous**

ADJ If you describe someone or something as **marvelous**, you are emphasizing that they are very good. 美妙的 ❑ *It's the most marvelous piece of music.* 这是最美妙的一篇乐曲。● **mar·vel·ous·ly** ADV 美妙地 ❑ *We want people to think he's doing marvelously.* 我们想让人们认为他做得真是很棒。

Marx·ism /mɑrksɪzəm/ N-UNCOUNT **Marxism** is a political philosophy based on the writings of Karl Marx which stresses the importance of the struggle between different social classes. 马克思主义

Marx·ist /mɑrksɪst/ (**Marxists**) 1 ADJ **Marxist** means based on Marxism or relating to Marxism. 马克思主义的 ❑ *...a Marxist state.* …一个信奉马克思主义的国家。2 N-COUNT A **Marxist** is a person who believes in Marxism or who is a member of a Marxist party. 马克思主义者；马克思主义政党成员 ❑ *...a 78-year-old former Marxist.* …一位78岁的前马克思主义者。

mas·cara /mæskærə/ (**mascaras**) N-MASS **Mascara** is a substance used as makeup to make eyelashes darker. 睫毛膏 ❑ *...water-resistant mascaras.* …防水睫毛膏。

→ see **makeup**

mas·cot /mæskɒt/ (**mascots**) N-COUNT A **mascot** is an animal, toy, or symbol which is associated with a particular organization or event, and which is thought to bring good luck. 吉祥物 ❑ *...the official mascot of the Detroit Tigers.* …官方吉祥物：底特律虎。

★ **mas·cu·line** /mæskyəlɪn/ 1 ADJ **Masculine** qualities and things relate to or are considered typical of men, in contrast to women. 男性的 ❑ *...masculine characteristics like a husky voice and facial hair.* …沙哑的嗓音和面部的胡须之类的男性特征。2 ADJ If you say that someone or something is **masculine**, you mean that they have qualities such as strength or confidence which are considered typical of men. 男子气概的 ❑ *...her aggressive, masculine image.* …她敢作敢为、男人般的形象。3 ADJ In some languages, a **masculine** noun, pronoun, or adjective has a different form from a feminine or neuter one, or behaves in a different way. (某些语言中的词) 阳性的

mas·cu·lin·ity /mæskyəlɪnɪti/ 1 N-UNCOUNT A man's **masculinity** is the fact that he is a man. 男性 ❑ *...a project on the link between masculinity and violence.* …一项关于男性和暴力之间关系的研究项目。2 N-UNCOUNT **Masculinity** means the qualities, especially sexual qualities, which are considered to be typical of men. 阳刚之气 ❑ *The old ideas of masculinity do not work for most men.* 过去对阳刚味的看法已不适用于大多数男人了。

▲ **mash** /mæʃ/ (**mashes, mashing, mashed**) V-T If you **mash** food that is solid but soft, you crush it so that it forms a soft mass. 把…捣成糊状 ❑ *Mash the bananas with a fork.* 用叉子把这些香蕉捣成糊。

mask ♦◇◇ /mæsk/ (**masks, masking, masked**) 1 N-COUNT A **mask** is a piece of cloth or other material, which you wear over

your face so that people cannot see who you are, or so that you look like someone or something else. 面具 ❑ *The gunman, whose mask had slipped, fled.* 面具滑落的持枪歹徒逃走了。 2 N-COUNT A **mask** is a piece of cloth or other material that you wear over all or part of your face to protect you from germs or harmful substances. 防护面具 ❑ *You must wear goggles and a mask that will protect you against the fumes.* 你必须带上护目镜和防护面具，以保护你不被烟熏。 3 N-COUNT If you describe someone's behavior as a **mask**, you mean that they do not show their real feelings or character. 伪装 ❑ *His mask of detachment cracked, and she saw for an instant an angry and violent man.* 他冷静超然的伪装破碎了，她一瞬间看到了一个愤怒而又狂暴的男人。 4 N-COUNT A **mask** is a thick cream or paste made of various substances, which you spread over your face and leave for some time in order to improve your skin. 面膜 ❑ *This mask leaves your complexion feeling soft and supple.* 这种面膜使你的皮肤变得柔软娇嫩。 5 V-T If you **mask** your feelings, you deliberately do not show them in your behavior, so that people cannot know what you really feel. 掩饰 ❑ *Dina lit a cigarette, trying to mask her agitation.* 黛娜点燃了一支烟，试图掩饰她的不安。 6 V-T If one thing **masks** another, it prevents people from noticing or recognizing the other thing. 遮掩 ❑ *He was squinting through the smoke that masked the enemy.* 他眯眼看着遮住敌人的那片烟雾。 7 → see also **gas mask**
→ see **football, scuba diving, theater**

masked /mæskt/ ADJ If someone is **masked**, they are wearing a mask. 戴着面具的 ❑ *Masked youths threw stones and firebombs.* 戴着面具的年轻人投掷了石头和燃烧弹。

maso·chism /mæsəkɪzəm/ 1 N-UNCOUNT **Masochism** is behavior in which someone gets sexual pleasure from their own pain or suffering. 性受虐狂 ❑ *The tendency toward masochism is however always linked with elements of sadism.* 然而性受虐狂倾向总是和一些施虐因素相关。 ● **maso·chist** N-COUNT (**masochists**) 性受虐狂者 ❑ *...consensual sexual masochists.* …两厢情愿的性受虐狂者。 2 N-UNCOUNT If you describe someone's behavior as **masochism**, you mean that they seem to be trying to get into a situation which causes them suffering or great difficulty. 自虐狂 ❑ *Once you have tasted life in southern California, it takes a peculiar kind of masochism to return to a British winter.* 一旦尝试过南加利福尼亚州的生活，只有某种怪异的自虐狂才会想要返回寒冷的英国。 ● **maso·chist** N-COUNT 乐于自我虐待的人 ❑ *Anybody who enjoys this is a masochist.* 以此为乐的人就是自虐狂。

maso·chis·tic /mæsəkɪstɪk/ 1 ADJ **Masochistic** behavior involves a person getting sexual pleasure from their own pain or suffering. 性受虐狂的 ❑ *...his masochistic tendencies.* …他性受虐狂的倾向。 2 ADJ If you describe someone's behavior as **masochistic**, you mean that they seem to be trying to get into a situation which causes them suffering or great difficulty. 受虐狂的 ❑ *It seems masochistic, somehow.* 不知道为什么，这看上去像受虐狂的样子。

ma·son /meɪsᵊn/ (**masons**) N-COUNT A **mason** is a person who is skilled at making things or building things with stone or bricks. 石匠

ma·son·ry /meɪsənri/ N-UNCOUNT **Masonry** is bricks or pieces of stone which have been stuck together with cement as part of a wall or building. 砖石建筑 ❑ *...a huge blast that sent pieces of masonry flying through the air.* …一场使砖石碎片漫天横飞的巨大爆炸。

mas·quer·ade /mæskəreɪd/ (**masquerades, masquerading, masqueraded**) 1 V-I To **masquerade as** someone or something means to pretend to be that person or thing, particularly in order to deceive other people. 冒充 ❑ *He masqueraded as a doctor and fooled everyone.* 他冒充医生，骗过了每一个人。 2 N-COUNT A **masquerade** is an attempt to deceive people about the true nature or identity of something. 伪装 ❑ *He told a news conference that the elections would be a masquerade.* 他在记者招待会上说选举将是骗人的把戏。

mass ♦♦◊ /mæs/ (**masses, massing, massed**) 1 N-SING A **mass of** things is a large number of them grouped together. 一堆 ❑ *On his desk is a mass of books and papers.* 在他书桌上有大堆的书和文件。 2 N-SING A **mass of** something is a large amount of it. 许多 ❑ *She had a mass of auburn hair.* 她有一头浓密的棕发。 3 QUANT **Masses of** something means a great deal of it. 大量 [INFORMAL] ❑ *There's masses of work for her to do.* 她有一大堆的工作去做。 4 ADJ **Mass** is used to describe something which involves or affects a very large number of people. 人数众多的 [ADJ n] ❑ *...ideas on combating mass unemployment.* …对付失业人数众多的方法。 ❑ *All the lights went off, and mass hysteria broke out.* 所有的灯都熄灭了，大家变得歇斯底里起来了。 5 N-COUNT A **mass of** a solid substance, a liquid, or a gas is an amount of it, especially a large amount which has no definite shape. 块；团；堆 ❑ *...before it cools and sets into a solid mass.* …在它冷却成为一块固体之前。 6 N-PLURAL If you talk about **the masses**, you mean the ordinary people in society, in contrast to the leaders or the highly educated people. 普通百姓 ❑ *His music is commercial. It is aimed at the masses.* 他的音乐很商业化，针对的是一般大众。 7 N-SING **The mass of** people are most of the people in a country, society, or group. 大多数 ❑ *The 1939-45 world war involved the mass of the population.* 1939至1945年间的世界大战卷入了多数民众。 8 V-T/V-I When people or things **mass**, or when you **mass** them, they gather together into a large crowd or group. 聚集 ❑ *Shortly after the workers went on strike, police began to mass at the shipyard.* 工人罢工后不久，警察开始在造船厂集结。 9 N-SING If you say that something is **a mass of** things, you mean that it is covered with them or full of them. 充满 ❑ *His body was a mass of sores.* 他浑身伤痛。 10 N-VAR In physics, the **mass** of an object is the amount of physical matter that it has. 质量 [TECHNICAL] ❑ *Astronomers know that Pluto and Triton have nearly the same size, mass, and density.* 天文学家们知道冥王星和海王卫一拥有几乎相同的体积、质量和密度。 11 N-VAR **Mass** is a Christian church ceremony, especially in a Roman Catholic or Orthodox church, during which people eat bread and drink wine in order to remember the last meal of Jesus Christ. 弥撒 ❑ *She attended a convent school and went to Mass each day.* 她上了一所女修道院设立的学校，每天都去作弥撒。 12 → see also **massed**
→ see **continent**

Word Partnership	*mass* 的常用搭配：
N.	mass **communication**, mass **destruction**, mass **evacuation**, mass **execution**, mass **exodus**, mass **grave**, mass **hysteria**, mass **killings**, mass **layoffs**, mass **mailing**, mass **migration**, mass **protest**, mass **unemployment** 4 **bone** mass, **muscle** mass 5

★ **mas·sa·cre** /mæsəkər/ (**massacres, massacring, massacred**) 1 N-VAR A **massacre** is the killing of a large number of people at the same time in a violent and cruel way. 大屠杀 ❑ *Maria lost her 62-year-old mother in the massacre.* 玛丽亚在大屠杀中失去了她62岁的母亲。 2 V-T If people **are massacred**, a large number of them are attacked and killed in a violent and cruel way. 大规模屠杀 ❑ *300 civilians are believed to have been massacred by the rebels.* 据信300名平民被叛乱分子屠杀了。

▲ **mas·sage** /məsɑʒ/ (**massages, massaging, massaged**) 1 N-VAR **Massage** is the action of squeezing and rubbing someone's body, as a way of making them relax or reducing their pain. 按摩 ❑ *Alex asked me if I wanted a massage.* 亚历克斯问我是否需要一次按摩。 2 V-T If you **massage** someone or a part of their body, you squeeze and rub their body, in order to make them relax or reduce their pain. 按摩 ❑ *She continued massaging her right foot, which was bruised and aching.* 她继续按摩她的右脚，那只脚又肿又疼。 3 V-T If you say that someone **massages** statistics, figures, or evidence, you are criticizing them for changing or presenting the facts in a way that misleads people. 窜改 [DISAPPROVAL] ❑ *Their governments have no reason to "massage" the statistics.* 他们的政府没有理由"窜改"这些数据。

masse /mæs/ → see **en masse**

massed /mæst/ ADJ **Massed** is used to describe a large number of people who have been brought together for a particular purpose. 聚集的 [ADJ n] ❑ *He could not escape the massed ranks of newsmen who spotted him crossing the lawn.* 他无法躲开那些发现他穿过草坪的成群记者。

mas·sive ♦◊◊ /mæsɪv/ 1 ADJ Something that is **massive** is very large in size, quantity, or extent. (尺寸、数量、规模) 非常大的 [EMPHASIS] ❑ *There was evidence of massive fraud.* 有证据表明是巨额欺诈。 ❑ *...massive air attacks.* …大规模的空袭。 ● **mas·sive·ly** ADV 非常大地 ❑ *...a massively popular game.* …一种非常受欢迎的游戏。 2 ADJ If you describe a medical condition as **massive**, you mean that it is extremely serious. 严重的 [ADJ n] ❑ *He died six weeks later of a massive heart attack.* 他6周后死于一次严重的心脏病发作。

mass mar·ket (**mass markets**) 1 N-COUNT **Mass market** is used to refer to the large numbers of people who want to buy a particular product. 大众市场 [BUSINESS] ❑ *They now have access to the mass markets of China, Japan and the U.K.* 他们现在有通路进入中国、

日本和英国的大众市场了。**2** ADJ **Mass-market** products are designed and produced for selling to large numbers of people. 大众市场的 [ADJ n] [BUSINESS] ❑ *...mass-market paperbacks.* …面向大众市场的平装书。

mass me·dia N-SING-COLL You can use the **mass media** to refer to the various ways, especially television, radio, newspapers, and magazines, by which information and news is given to large numbers of people. 大众传媒 ❑ *...mass media coverage of the issue.* …大众传媒对此事的全面报道。

mass-produce (**mass-produces, mass-producing, mass-produced**) V-T If someone **mass-produces** something, they make it in large quantities, usually by machine. This means that the product can be sold cheaply. 大批量生产 [BUSINESS] ❑ *...the invention of machinery to mass-produce footwear.* …大批量生产鞋的机器的发明。 ●**mass-produced** ADJ 大批量生产的 [ADJ n] ❑ *In 1981 it launched the first mass-produced mountain bike.* 在1981年，首款大批量生产的山地车投放市场。

mass pro·duc·tion N-UNCOUNT **Mass production** is the production of something in large quantities, especially by machine. 大批量生产 [BUSINESS] ❑ *...equipment that would allow the mass production of baby food.* …允许婴儿食品大批量生产的设备。

▲ **mast** /mæst/ (**masts**) **1** N-COUNT The **masts** of a boat are the tall, upright poles that support its sails. 桅杆 **2** N-COUNT A radio **mast** is a tall upright structure that is used to transmit radio or television signals. 天线杆

mas·ter ♦♦◇ /mæstər/ (**masters, mastering, mastered**) **1** N-COUNT A servant's **master** is the man that he or she works for. 主人 ❑ *My master ordered me not to deliver the message except in private.* 主人命令我不能传送信息，除非在私下里。 **2** N-COUNT If you say that someone is a **master** of a particular activity, you mean that they are extremely skilled at it. 专家 ❑ *She was a master of the English language.* 她曾是一名英语语言专家。 ● ADJ **Master** is also an adjective. 精通的 [ADJ n] ❑ *...a master craftsman.* …一名手艺高超的工匠。 **3** N-VAR If you are **master** of a situation, you have complete control over it. 控制者 ❑ *Jackson remained calm and always master of his passions.* 杰克逊保持着平静，始终是自己情感的掌控者。 **4** V-T If you **master** something, you learn how to do it properly or you succeed in understanding it completely. 掌握 ❑ *Duff soon mastered the skills of radio production.* 达夫很快掌握了广播节目制作的技能。 **5** V-T If you **master** a difficult situation, you succeed in controlling it. 掌控 ❑ *When you have mastered one situation you have to go on to the next.* 当你掌控了一种局面，你不得不继续下一个。 **6** → see also **headmaster** **7** N-COUNT A famous male painter of the past is often called a **master**. (旧时) 著名男画家 ❑ *...a portrait by the Dutch master, Vincent Van Gogh.* …一幅荷兰著名男画家文森特・凡・高所作的画像。 **8** ADJ A **master** copy of something, such as a film or a tape recording, is an original copy that can be used to produce other copies. 母带的 [ADJ n] ❑ *Keep one as a master copy for your own reference and circulate the others.* 留下一盘作为母带供你自己参考，然后分发其他的。 **9** N-SING A **master's degree** can be referred to as a **master's**. 硕士学位 ❑ *I've got a master's in economics.* 我已经获得了经济学硕士学位。

Thesaurus *master* 另参见：

N. owner; (*ant.*) servant, slave **1**
artist, expert, professional **2**
V. learn, study, understand **4**

Word Partnership *master* 的常用搭配：

N. **lord and** master, master **and slave** **1**
master **chef**, master **craftsman**, master **criminal**, master **of disguise**, master **spy**, **Zen** master **2**
master **a skill** **4**
master **drawings** **7**

★ **mas·ter·ful** /mæstərfəl/ **1** ADJ If you describe a man as **masterful**, you approve of him because he behaves in a way which shows that he is in control of a situation and can tell other people what to do. 有驾驭力的 [APPROVAL] ❑ *Big, successful moves need bold, masterful managers.* 大的成功的行动需要大胆有驾驭力的管理者。 **2** ADJ If you describe someone's behavior or actions as **masterful**, you mean that they show great skill. 技艺精湛的 ❑ *...a masterful performance of boxing and punching skills.* …一个拳术和攻击技艺的精湛表演。

★ **master·mind** /mæstərmaɪnd/ (**masterminds, masterminding, masterminded**) **1** V-T If you **mastermind** a difficult or complicated activity, you plan it in detail and then make sure that it happens successfully. 策划 ❑ *There are many theories as to who masterminded the attacks.* 关于谁策划了这些攻击，有许多的猜测。 **2** N-COUNT The **mastermind behind** a difficult or complicated plan, often a criminal one, is the person who is responsible for planning and organizing it. 幕后操纵者 ❑ *He was the mastermind behind the plan to acquire the explosives.* 他是获取炸药计划的幕后操纵者。

★ **master·piece** /mæstərpis/ (**masterpieces**) **1** N-COUNT A **masterpiece** is an extremely good painting, novel, movie, or other work of art. 杰作 ❑ *His book, I must add, is a masterpiece.* 他的书，我必须补充一点，是一部杰作。 **2** N-COUNT An artist's, writer's, or composer's **masterpiece** is the best work that they have ever produced. 代表作 ❑ *"Man's Fate," translated into sixteen languages, is probably his masterpiece.* 《人类的命运》，被翻译成16种文字，可能是他的代表作。 **3** N-COUNT A **masterpiece** is an extremely clever or skillful example of something. 典范 ❑ *The whole thing was a masterpiece of crowd management.* 整件事情是大众管理的典范。

mas·ter plan (**master plans**) N-COUNT A **master plan** is a thorough plan that is intended to help someone succeed in a very difficult or important task. 全面规划 ❑ *...the master plan for the reform of the economy.* …经济改革的全面规划。

mas·ter's de·gree (**master's degrees**) also **Master's degree** N-COUNT A **master's degree** is a university degree such as an M.A. or an M.S. which is of a higher level than a bachelor's degree and usually takes one or two years to complete. 硕士学位
→ see **graduation**

★ **mas·tery** /mæstəri/ N-UNCOUNT If you show **mastery of** a particular skill or language, you show that you have learned or understood it completely and have no difficulty using it. 掌握 ❑ *He doesn't have mastery of the basic rules of grammar.* 他没有掌握基本的语法规则。

mas·tur·bate /mæstərbeɪt/ (**masturbates, masturbating, masturbated**) V-I If someone **masturbates**, they stroke or rub their own genitals in order to get sexual pleasure. 手淫 ❑ *Do women masturbate as often as men?* 女性手淫如男人一样频繁吗？

mat /mæt/ (**mats**) **1** N-COUNT A **mat** is a small piece of something such as cloth, card, or plastic which you put on a table to protect it from plates or cups. (杯、盘的) 垫子 ❑ *The food is served on polished tables with mats.* 食物被摆放在擦得光亮的餐桌的垫子上。 **2** N-COUNT A **mat** is a small piece of carpet or other thick material which is put on the floor for protection, decoration, or comfort. 小地毯；厚垫子 ❑ *There was a letter on the mat.* 地毯上有一封信。 **3** → see also **matte**

match ♦♦♦ /mætʃ/ (**matches, matching, matched**) **1** N-COUNT A **match** is an organized game of tennis, soccer, cricket, or some other sport. 比赛 ❑ *He was watching a soccer match.* 他正在看一场英式足球比赛。 **2** N-COUNT A **match** is a small wooden stick with a substance on one end that produces a flame when you rub it along the rough side of a matchbox or a matchbook. 火柴 ❑ *...a pack of cigarettes and a book of matches.* …一包香烟和一包火柴。 **3** V-RECIP If something of a particular color or design **matches** another thing, they have the same color or design, or have a pleasing appearance when they are used together. 和…相配 ❑ *"The shoes are too tight."—"Well, they do match your dress."* "这双鞋太紧了。"——"不过，它们确实和你的裙子相配。" ❑ *All the chairs matched.* 所有的椅子都相配。 ● PHRASAL VERB **Match up** means the same as **match**. 和…相配 ❑ *The pillow cover can match up with the sheets.* 这个枕巾可以和这些被单相配。 **4** V-RECIP If something such as an amount or a quality **matches with** another amount or quality, they are both the same or equal. If you **match** two things, you make them the same or equal. 与…一样；使一样 ❑ *Their strengths in memory and spatial skills matched.* 他们的记忆力和空间技能一样。 ❑ *Our value system does not match with their value system.* 我们的价值体系与他们的价值体系不一样。 **5** V-RECIP If one thing **matches** another, they are connected or suit each other in some way. 使对应 ❑ *The students are asked to match the books with the authors.* 学生们被要求把书和作家一一对应起来。 ❑ *It can take time and effort to match buyers and sellers.* 匹配买主和卖主可能需要花费一些时间和精力。 ● PHRASAL VERB **Match up** means the same as **match**. 使对应 ❑ *The consultant seeks to match up jobless professionals with small companies in need of expertise.* 这名顾问力求使失

业的专业人员对应需要专门技术的小公司。❑ *They compared the fat intake of groups of vegetarians and meat eaters, and matched their diets up with levels of harmful blood fats.* 他们比较了素食者组和肉食者组的脂肪摄入量，并把他们的膳食和血脂危险水平对应起来。 6 N-SING If a combination of things or people is a good **match**, they have a pleasing effect when placed or used together. 相配的人或物 ❑ *Helen's choice of lipstick was a good match for her skin tone.* 海伦选择的唇膏与她的肤色是很好的搭配。 7 V-T If you **match** something, you are as good as it or equal to it, for example in speed, size, or quality. 比得上 ❑ *They played some fine offensive football, but I think we matched them in every department.* 他们踢了一些漂亮的攻势足球，但我认为我们各方面都比得上他们。 8 → see also **matched, matching**
→ see **fire**

Word Partnership *match* 的常用搭配：

N. **boxing** match, **chess** match, **tennis** match, **wrestling** match 1
V. **strike** a match 2
ADJ. **bad** match, **good** match, **perfect** match 6

matched /mætʃt/ 1 ADJ If you say that two people are well **matched**, you mean that they have qualities that will enable them to have a good relationship. 相配的 [adv ADJ] ❑ *My parents were not very well matched.* 我父母不是很般配。 2 ADJ In sports and other competitions, if the two opponents or teams are well **matched**, they are both of the same standard in strength or ability. 势均力敌的 [adv ADJ] ❑ *Two well-matched sides conjured up an entertaining game.* 势均力敌的双方魔术般地进行了一场妙趣横生的比赛。

match·ing /mætʃɪŋ/ ADJ **Matching** is used to describe things that are of the same color or design. 相匹配的 [ADJ n] ❑ *...a coat and a matching handbag.* …一件大衣和一个与之相匹配的手提包。

mate ♦◇◇ /meɪt/ (**mates, mating, mated**) 1 N-COUNT Someone's wife, husband, or sexual partner can be referred to as their **mate**. 配偶；性伴侣 ❑ *He has found his ideal mate.* 他已经找到了理想的配偶。 2 N-COUNT An animal's **mate** is its sexual partner. 交配对象 ❑ *The males guard their mates zealously.* 雄性动物热情地守护它们的交配对象。 3 V-RECIP When animals **mate**, a male and a female have sex in order to produce young. 交配 ❑ *This allows the pair to mate properly and stops the hen from staying in the nest.* 这可以使这一对正常交配同时也阻止雌禽待在窝里。 ❑ *They want the males to mate with wild females.* 他们想让这些雄性动物和野生的雌性动物交配。 4 → see also **classmate, roommate, running mate**

ma·terial ♦♦◇ /mətɪəriəl/ (**materials**) 1 N-VAR A **material** is a solid substance. 固态物质 ❑ *...electrons in a conducting material such as a metal.* …金属等导电物质中的电子。 2 N-MASS **Material** is cloth. 布料 ❑ *...the thick material of her skirt.* …她裙子的厚布料。 3 N-PLURAL **Materials** are the things that you need for a particular activity. 材料 ❑ *The builders ran out of materials.* 建筑商用完了材料。 4 N-UNCOUNT Ideas or information that are used as a basis for a book, play, or film can be referred to as **material**. 素材 ❑ *In my version of the story, I added some new material.* 在我这个版本的故事中，我添加了一些新素材。 5 ADJ **Material** things are related to possessions or money, rather than to more abstract things such as ideas or values. 物质的 ❑ *Every room must have been stuffed with material things.* 每个房间肯定已经堆满了东西。 ● **ma·teri·al·ly** ▲ ADV 物质上地 ❑ *He has tried to help this child materially and spiritually.* 他已经尽力在物质和精神上帮助这个孩子了。 6 ADJ **Material** evidence or information is directly relevant and important in a legal or academic argument. (法律或学术辩论中) 实质性的 (证据或信息) [ADJ n] [FORMAL] ❑ *The nature and availability of material evidence was not to be discussed.* 关键证据的性质和有效性将不予以讨论。
→ see **industry**

Word Partnership *material* 的常用搭配：

ADJ. **genetic** material, **hazardous** material 1
new material, **original** material 2 4
raw materials 3
classified material, **instructional** material, **sensitive** material 4

ma·teri·al·ise /mətɪəriəlaɪz/ [BRIT] → see **materialize**

ma·teri·al·ism /mətɪəriəlɪzəm/ 1 N-UNCOUNT **Materialism** is the attitude of someone who attaches a lot of importance to money and wants to possess a lot of material things. 物质主义 ❑ *...the rising consumer materialism in society at large.* …全社会范围内日益高涨的消费者物质主义。 2 N-UNCOUNT **Materialism** is the belief that only physical matter exists, and that there is no spiritual world. 唯物主义 ❑ *Scientific materialism thus triumphed over ignorance and superstition.* 科学唯物主义就这样战胜了无知和迷信。

▲ **ma·teri·al·is·tic** /mətɪəriəlɪstɪk/ ADJ If you describe a person or society as **materialistic**, you are critical of them because they attach too much importance to money and material possessions. 过分强调金钱和物质的 [DISAPPROVAL] ❑ *During the 1980s the U.S. became a very materialistic society.* 在20世纪80年代，美国成为了一个物质至上的社会。

ma·teri·al·ize /mətɪəriəlaɪz/ (**materializes, materializing, materialized**)

in BRIT, also use **materialise**

1 V-I If a possible or expected event does not **materialize**, it does not happen. 实现 [usu with brd-neg] ❑ *A rebellion by radicals failed to materialize.* 激进分子的一次叛乱未能实现。 2 V-I If a person or thing **materializes**, they suddenly appear, after they have been invisible or in another place. 突然出现 ❑ *A moment later Jane materialized, coming in the front door.* 过了一会儿，简突然出现了，从前门进来。

▲ **ma·ter·nal** /mətɜrnəl/ 1 ADJ **Maternal** is used to describe feelings or actions which are typical of those of a kind mother toward her child. 母亲般的 2 ADJ **Maternal** is used to describe things that relate to the mother of a baby. 母亲的 [ADJ n] ❑ *Maternal smoking can damage the unborn child.* 母亲吸烟可能会伤害未出生的孩子。 3 ADJ A **maternal** relative is one who is related through a person's mother rather than their father. 母系的 [ADJ n] ❑ *Her maternal grandfather was mayor of Karachi.* 她的外祖父曾是卡拉奇市的市长。

★ **ma·ter·nity** /mətɜrnɪti/ ADJ **Maternity** is used to describe things relating to the help and medical care given to a woman when she is pregnant and when she gives birth. 孕妇的；产妇的 [ADJ n] ❑ *Your job will be kept open for your return after maternity leave.* 你的工作会一直保留到你休完产假回来。

math /mæθ/ N-UNCOUNT **Math** is the same as **mathematics**. 数学 [AM]

in BRIT, use **maths**

❑ *He studied math in college.* 他在大学里学过数学。
→ see **mathematics**

math·emati·cal /mæθəmætɪkəl/ 1 ADJ Something that is **mathematical** involves numbers and calculations. 数学的 [ADJ n] ❑ *...mathematical calculations.* …数学计算。 ● **math·emati·cal·ly** /mæθəmætɪkli/ ADV 在数学上地 ❑ *...a mathematically complicated formula.* …一个在数学上复杂的公式。 2 ADJ If you have **mathematical**

Word Web mathematics

At first prehistoric people **counted** things they could see—for example, four sheep. Later they began to use **numbers** with abstract **quantities** like time—for example, two days. This led to the development of basic **arithmetic**—**addition, subtraction, multiplication,** and **division.** When people discovered how to use written **numerals**, they could do more complex **mathematical calculations**. **Mathematicians** developed new types of **math** to **measure** land and keep financial records. **Algebra** and **geometry** developed in the Middle East between 2,000 and 3,000 years ago. Algebra uses letters to represent possible quantities. Geometry deals with the relationships among **lines, angles,** and **shapes.**

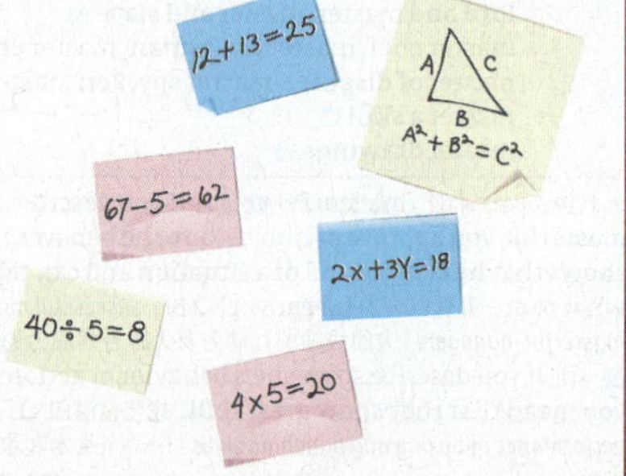

M

Word Web matter

Matter exists in three states—**solid**, **liquid**, and **gas**. When a solid becomes hot enough, it **melts** and becomes a liquid. When a liquid is hot enough, it **evaporates** into a gas. The process also works the other way around. A gas which becomes very cool will **condense** into a liquid. And a liquid that is cooled enough will freeze and become a solid. Other changes in **state** are possible. Sublimation describes what happens when a solid, dry ice, turns directly into a gas, carbon dioxide. And did you know that glass is actually a liquid, not a solid?

abilities or a **mathematical** mind, you are good at doing calculations or understanding problems that involve numbers. 具有数学头脑的 ❑ *...a mathematical genius.* …一个数学天才。 ● **math·emati·cal·ly** ADV 具有数学头脑地 [ADV -ed/adj] ❑ *Anyone can be an astrologer as long as they are mathematically minded.* 任何人都可能成为占星家，只要他们具有数学头脑。
→ see **mathematics**

math·ema·ti·cian /mæθəmətɪʃən/ (**mathematicians**) **1** N-COUNT A **mathematician** is a person who is trained in the study of numbers and calculations. 数学家 ❑ *The risks can be so complex that banks hire mathematicians to assess them.* 这类风险可以是如此复杂以至于银行雇佣数学家们去评估它们。 **2** N-COUNT A **mathematician** is a person who is good at doing calculations and using numbers. 善作数字计算的人 ❑ *I'm not a very good mathematician.* 我不是一个非常善作数字计算的人。
→ see **mathematics, ratio**

math·emat·ics /mæθəmætɪks/ **1** N-UNCOUNT **Mathematics** is the study of numbers, quantities, or shapes. 数学 ❑ *...a professor of mathematics at Boston College.* …一位波士顿大学的数学教授。 **2** N-UNCOUNT **The mathematics of** a problem is the calculations that are involved in it. 数学运算 ❑ *Once you understand the mathematics of debt you can work your way out of it.* 一旦你理解了债务的数学计算，你就能解决它。
→ see Word Web: **mathematics**

maths /mæθs/ N-UNCOUNT **Maths** is the same as **mathematics**. 数学 [BRIT]

mati·nee /mætənei/ (**matinees**) N-COUNT A **matinee** is a performance of a play or a showing of a movie which takes place in the afternoon. (戏剧、电影的) 午后场

ma·trix /meɪtrɪks/ (**matrices**) **1** N-COUNT A **matrix** is the environment or context in which something such as a society develops and grows. 发源地 [FORMAL] ❑ *...the matrix of their culture.* …他们文明的发源地。 **2** N-COUNT In mathematics, a **matrix** is an arrangement of numbers, symbols, or letters in rows and columns which is used in solving mathematical problems. 矩阵

matte /mæt/ also **matt, mat** ADJ A **matte** color, paint, or surface is dull rather than shiny. 无光泽的 ❑ *...a creamy white matte emulsion.* …奶白色亚光乳剂。

mat·ter ♦♦♦ /mætər/ (**matters, mattering, mattered**) **1** N-COUNT A **matter** is a task, situation, or event which you have to deal with or think about, especially one that involves problems. 事情 ❑ *It was clear that she wanted to discuss some private matter.* 很明显她想讨论一些私事。 ❑ *Business matters drew him to Louisville.* 生意上的事情吸引他去路易斯维尔。 **2** N-PLURAL You use **matters** to refer to the situation you are talking about, especially when something is affecting the situation in some way. 事态 [no det] ❑ *We have no objection to this change, but doubt that it will significantly improve matters.* 我们不反对这种变化，但怀疑这是否将明显地改善事态。 ❑ *If it would facilitate matters, I would be happy to come to New York.* 如果这有利于事态，我将乐意来纽约。 **3** N-SING If you say that a situation is **a matter of** a particular thing, you mean that that is the most important thing to be done or considered when you are involved in the situation or explaining it. 问题 ❑ *History is always a matter of interpretation.* 历史总是一个诠释的问题。 ❑ *Observance of the law is a matter of principle for us.* 遵守法律对于我们是一个原则问题。 **4** N-UNCOUNT Printed **matter** consists of books, newspapers, and other texts that are printed. Reading **matter** consists of things that are suitable for reading, such as books and newspapers. (印刷或阅读的) 物品 ❑ *...the government's plans to place a tax on printed matter.* …政府对印刷品征税的计划。 **5** N-UNCOUNT **Matter** is the physical part of the universe consisting of solids, liquids, and gases. 物质 ❑ *A proton is an elementary particle of matter that possesses a positive charge.* 质子是带正电荷的物质的基本粒子。 **6** N-UNCOUNT You use **matter** to refer to a particular type of substance. 物料 ❑ *...waste matter from industries.* …来自工业的废料。 **7** N-SING You use **matter** in expressions such as "**What's the matter?**" or "**Is anything the matter?**" when you think that someone has a problem and you want to know what it is. 麻烦事 ❑ *Carole, what's the matter? You don't seem happy.* 卡萝尔，你怎么啦？你好像不高兴。 **8** N-SING You use **matter** in expressions such as "**a matter of weeks**" when you are emphasizing how small an amount is or how short a period of time is. 仅仅 [EMPHASIS] ❑ *Within a matter of days she was back at work.* 仅仅几天之后，她又回来工作了。 **9** V-T/V-I If you say that something does not **matter**, you mean that it is not important to you because it does not have an effect on you or on a particular situation. 要紧 [no cont, usu with brd-neg] ❑ *A lot of the food goes on the floor but that doesn't matter.* 很多食物掉在地板上，但是那不要紧。 ❑ *As long as staff members are well-groomed, it does not matter how long their hair is.* 只要工作人员打扮整齐，他们的头发多长不要紧。 **10** → see also **subject matter** **11** PHRASE If you say that something is **another matter** or **a different matter**, you mean that it is very different from the situation that you have just discussed. 另一码事 ❑ *Being responsible for one's own health is one thing, but being responsible for another person's health is quite a different matter.* 对自己的健康负责是一码事，但对别人的健康负责完全是另一码事。 **12** PHRASE If you are going to do something **as a matter of** urgency or priority, you are going to do it as soon as possible, because it is important. 作为…的事情 ❑ *Your doctors can help a great deal and you need to talk about it with them as a matter of urgency.* 你的医生能够帮你很大的忙，你应该把此事当作紧急情况和他们谈谈。 **13** PHRASE If something is **no easy matter**, it is difficult to do it. 并非易事 ❑ *Choosing the color for the living-room walls was no easy matter.* 为起居室的墙壁选择颜色并非易事。 **14** PHRASE If someone says **that's the end of the matter** or **that's an end to the matter**, they mean that a decision that has been taken must not be changed or discussed any more. 此事已定 ❑ *"He's moving in here," Maria said. "So that's the end of the matter."* "他就要搬来住了，"玛丽亚说。"所以此事已定。" **15** PHRASE You use **the fact of the matter is** or **the truth of the matter is** to introduce a fact which supports what you are saying or which is not widely known, for example because it is a secret. 事实 ❑ *The fact of the matter is that most people consume far more protein than they actually need.* 事实是大多数人摄入的蛋白质比他们真正需要的要多。 **16** CONVENTION You say "**it doesn't matter**" to tell someone who is apologizing to you that you are not angry or upset, and that they should not worry. 没关系 ❑ *"Did I wake you?"—"Yes, but it doesn't matter."* "我把您吵醒了吗？"——"是的，不过没关系。" **17** PHRASE If you say that something **makes matters worse**, you mean that it makes a difficult situation even more difficult. 使情况变得更糟 ❑ *Don't let yourself despair; this will only make matters worse.* 别让你自己绝望；这样将只会使情况变得更糟。 **18** PHRASE You use **no matter** in expressions such as "**no matter how**" and "**no matter what**" to say that something is true or happens in all circumstances. 不管… ❑ *No matter what your age, you can lose weight by following this program.* 不管你多大年龄，你都可以通过这个方案减轻体重。 **19** **a matter of life and death** → see **death** **20** **as a matter of course** → see **course** **21** **as a matter of fact** → see **fact**
→ see Word Web: **matter**

matter-of-fact ADJ If you describe a person as **matter-of-fact**, you mean that they show no emotions such as enthusiasm, anger, or surprise, especially in a situation where you would expect them to be emotional. 面无表情的 ❑ *John was doing his best to give Francis the news in a matter-of-fact way.* 约翰尽量用不带感情的方式把这个消息告诉了弗朗西斯。● **matter-of-factly** ADV 面无表情地 [ADV after v] ❑ *"She thinks you're a spy," Scott said matter-of-factly.* "她认为你是一名间谍，"斯科特面无表情地说。

▲ **mat·tress** /mætrɪs/ (**mattresses**) N-COUNT A **mattress** is the large, flat object which is put on a bed to make it comfortable to sleep on. 床垫
→ see **bed**

ma·ture /mətyʊər, -tʊər, -tʃʊər/ (**matures, maturing, matured, maturer, maturest**) **1** V-I When a child or young animal **matures**, it becomes an adult. (小孩、幼崽) 发育成熟 ❑ *You will learn what to expect as your child matures physically.* 当你的孩子身体发育成熟时，你将知道会发生什么。 **2** V-I When something **matures**, it reaches a state of complete development. (某物) 长成 ❑ *When the trees matured they were cut.* 当这些树长成时，它们就会被砍掉。 **3** V-I If someone **matures**, they become more fully developed in their personality and emotional behavior. 成熟 ❑ *They have matured way beyond their age.* 他们已经成熟得远远超过了他们的年龄。 **4** ADJ If you describe someone as **mature**, you think that they are fully developed and balanced in their personality and emotional behavior. 成熟的 [APPROVAL] ❑ *They are emotionally mature and should behave responsibly.* 他们在情感上是成熟的，应该负责任地行事。 **5** V-T/V-I If something such as wine or cheese **matures** or **is matured**, it is left for a time to allow its full flavor or strength to develop. 使酿熟；酿成 ❑ *Unlike wine, brandy matures only in wood, not glass.* 和葡萄酒不同，白兰地只能在木质容器里酿成，玻璃容器不行。 **6** ADJ **Mature** cheese or wine has been left for a time to allow its full flavor or strength to develop. 酿熟的 ❑ *Grate some mature cheddar cheese.* 磨碎一些酿熟的切达干酪。 **7** V-I When an investment such as an insurance policy or bond **matures**, it reaches the stage when the company pays you back the money you have saved, and the interest your money has earned. (保险单、债券等) 到期 [BUSINESS] ❑ *These bonuses will be paid when your savings plan matures in ten years' time.* 当你的储蓄计划在10年后到期时，这些红利将会被支付。 **8** ADJ If you say that someone is **mature** or of **mature** years, you are saying politely that they are middle-aged or old. 成年的 (中年和老年的礼貌说法) [POLITENESS] ❑ *...a man of mature years who had been in the job for longer than most of the members could remember.* …一个成年男子，从事这项工作的时间已经长得大部分成员都记不清了。

★ **ma·tur·ity** /mətyʊərɪti, -tʊər-, -tʃʊər-/ (**maturities**) **1** N-UNCOUNT **Maturity** is the state of being fully developed or adult. 发育成熟 ❑ *Humans experience a delayed maturity; we arrive at all stages of life later than other mammals.* 人类经历着一个迟来的成熟：我们进入生命各个阶段的时间比其他哺乳动物要晚。 **2** N-UNCOUNT Someone's **maturity** is their quality of being fully developed in their personality and emotional behavior. (性格、情感) 成熟 ❑ *Her speech showed great maturity and humanity.* 她的演讲显示出十足的成熟和博爱。 **3** N-VAR When an investment such as an insurance policy or bond reaches **maturity**, it reaches the stage when the company pays you back the money you have saved, and the interest your money has earned. (保险单、债券等的) 到期 [BUSINESS] ❑ *Customers are told what their policies will be worth on maturity, not what they are worth today.* 客户们被告知的是他们的保险单到期时的价值，不是现在的价值。

> **Thesaurus** *maturity* 另参见：
> N. adulthood, manhood, womanhood; (*ant.*) immaturity **1**

maul /mɔl/ (**mauls, mauling, mauled**) V-T If you **are mauled** by an animal, you are violently attacked by it and badly injured. (动物) 袭击 ❑ *He had been mauled by a bear.* 他被一只熊抓伤过。

mav·er·ick /mævərɪk/ (**mavericks**) N-COUNT If you describe someone as a **maverick**, you mean that they are unconventional and independent, and do not think or behave in the same way as other people. 特立独行的人 ❑ *He was too much of a maverick ever to hold high office.* 他太特立独行了，永远都担当不了高级职位。● ADJ **Maverick** is also an adjective. 特立独行的 [ADJ n] ❑ *...a maverick group of scientists, who oppose the prevailing medical opinion on the disease.* …一群特立独行的科学家，他们反对关于这种疾病的医学界的盛行观点。

max. /mæks/ ADJ **Max.** is the abbreviation for **maximum**. 最大的 [num ADJ, ADJ n] ❑ *I'll give him eight out of 10, max.* 我将最多给他十分之八。

> **Word Link** *maxim ≈ greatest : maxim, maximize, maximum*

max·im /mæksɪm/ (**maxims**) N-COUNT A **maxim** is a rule for good or sensible behavior, especially one in the form of a saying. 格言 ❑ *I believe in the maxim "if it ain't broke, don't fix it."* 我相信这句格言："如果它没坏，不要去修理它。"

★ **max·im·ise** /mæksɪmaɪz/ [BRIT] → see **maximize**

★ **max·im·ize** /mæksɪmaɪz/ (**maximizes, maximizing, maximized**)

> in BRIT, also use **maximise**

1 V-T If you **maximize** something, you make it as great in amount or importance as you can. 使增加到最大限度；充分重视 ❑ *In order to maximize profit, the firm would seek to maximize output.* 为了最大限度地增加利润，这家公司将试图最大限度地增加产量。 **2** V-T If you **maximize** a window on a computer screen, you make it as large as possible. 使 (计算机屏幕上的窗口) 最大化 ❑ *Click on the square icon to maximize the window.* 点击正方形图标，使窗口最大化。

maxi·mum ♦◇◇ /mæksɪməm/ **1** ADJ You use **maximum** to describe an amount which is the largest that is possible, allowed, or required. 最大的 [ADJ n] ❑ *Under planning law the maximum height for a fence or hedge is 6 feet.* 根据规划法，栅栏或树篱的最高高度为6英尺。● N-SING **Maximum** is also a noun. 最大值 ❑ *The law provides for a maximum of two years in prison.* 法律规定监禁最长两年。 **2** ADJ You use **maximum** to indicate how great an amount is. 最大的 [ADJ n] ❑ *I need the maximum amount of information you can give me.* 我需要你所能给我的最大的信息量。 ❑ *It was achieved with minimum fuss and maximum efficiency.* 它以最少的慌乱和最高的效率被做到了。 **3** ADV If you say that something is a particular amount **maximum**, you mean that this is the greatest amount it should be or could possibly be, although a smaller amount is acceptable or very possible. 最多 [amount ADV] ❑ *We need an extra 6 grams a day maximum.* 我们一天最多还需要6克。

> **Thesaurus** *maximum* 另参见：
> ADJ. biggest, greatest, highest; (*ant.*) lowest, minimum most **1** **2**

> **Word Partnership** *maximum* 的常用搭配：
> N. maximum **benefit**, maximum **charge**, maximum **efficiency**, maximum **fine**, maximum **flexibility**, maximum **height**, maximum **penalty**, maximum **rate**, maximum **sentence**, maximum **speed** **1**

may ♦♦♦ /meɪ/

> **May** is a modal verb. It is used with the base form of a verb.

1 MODAL You use **may** to indicate that something will possibly happen or be true in the future, but you cannot be certain. (将来) 可能 [VAGUENESS] ❑ *We may have some rain today.* 今天可能会下点雨。 ❑ *I may be back next year.* 我可能明年回来。 **2** MODAL You use **may** to indicate that there is a possibility that something is true, but you cannot be certain. 可能 (是真的) [VAGUENESS] ❑ *Civil rights officials say there may be hundreds of other cases of racial violence.* 负责公民权利的官员说可能有几百起其他的种族暴力案件。 **3** MODAL You use **may** to indicate that something is sometimes true or is true in some circumstances. 可能 (有时或在某些情况下属实) ❑ *A vegetarian diet may not provide enough calories for a child's normal growth.* 素食可能无法提供一名孩子正常成长所需要的足够热量。 **4** MODAL You use **may have** with a past participle when suggesting that it is possible that something happened or was true, or when giving a possible explanation for something. 与过去分词连用，表示某事可能已经发生、属实或提供解释 [VAGUENESS] ❑ *He may have been to some of those places.* 那些地方他可能去过一些。 **5** MODAL You use **may** in statements where you are accepting the truth of a situation, but contrasting it with something that is more important. 用于承认情况属实，但同时将之与更重要的东西作比较 ❑ *I may be almost 50, but there's not much I've forgotten.* 我是快五十岁了，但我没忘记多少事情。 **6** MODAL You use **may** when you are mentioning a quality or fact about something that people can make use of if they want to. 可以 (加以利用) ❑ *The bag has narrow straps, so it may be worn over the shoulder or carried in the hand.* 这个书包有细长带子，所以它可以被肩挎，也可以用手拎。 **7** MODAL You use **may** to indicate that someone is allowed to do something, usually because of a rule or law. You use **may not** to indicate that someone is not allowed to do something. (法规)允许/不允许 ❑ *In the US, any two persons may marry provided that both persons are at least 16 years of age on the day of their marriage.* 在美国，任何两个人都可以结婚，只要在结婚日双方都至少十六岁。 **8** MODAL You use **may** when you are giving permission to someone to do something, or when asking for permission. 可以(表示许可) [FORMAL] ❑ *Mr. Hobbs? May we come in?* 霍布斯先生？我们可以进去吗？ **9** MODAL You use **may** when you are making polite requests. 可以(用于礼貌的请求) [FORMAL, POLITENESS] ❑ *I'd like the use of your living room, if I may.* 如果可以，我想用用你的起居室。 **10** MODAL You use **may** when you are mentioning the reaction or attitude that you think someone is likely to have to something you are about to say. 可能会(用于别人对自己所说的话可能会有的反应或态度) ❑ *You know, Brian, whatever you may think, I work hard for a living.* 你知道，布雷恩，不管你会怎么想，我是为了生计而努力工作。 **11** MODAL If you do something so that a particular thing **may** happen, you do it so that there is an opportunity for that thing to happen. 以便能 ❑ *...the need for an increase in the numbers of surgeons so that patients may be treated as soon as possible.* …增加外科医生人数以便让病人能尽快被救治的需要。 **12** **may as well** → see **well**

May ♦♦♦ /meɪ/ (**Mays**) N-VAR **May** is the fifth month of the year in the Western calendar. 5月 ❑ *Graduation ceremonies are held in early May.* 毕业典礼在5月初举行。

may·be ♦♦◊ /meɪbi/ **1** ADV You use **maybe** to express uncertainty, for example when you do not know that something is definitely true, or when you are mentioning something that may possibly happen in the future in the way you describe. 也许 [ADV with cl/group] [VAGUENESS] ❑ *Maybe she is in love.* 也许她是恋爱了。 ❑ *I do think about having children, maybe when I'm 40.* 我确实考虑要孩子，也许在我40岁时。 **2** ADV You use **maybe** when you are making suggestions or giving advice. **Maybe** is also used to introduce polite requests. 也许该(用于提出建议、作出礼貌的请求) [ADV with cl/group] [POLITENESS] ❑ *Maybe we can go to the movies or something.* 也许我们可以去看电影什么的。 ❑ *Maybe you'd better tell me what this is all about.* 也许你该告诉我，这到底是怎么一回事。 **3** ADV You use **maybe** to indicate that, although a comment is partly true, there is also another point of view that should be considered. 可能(用于表示某个评论部分属实，但另一观点也应该加以考虑) [ADV cl] ❑ *Maybe there is jealousy, but I think the envy is more powerful.* 可能是有嫉妒，但我想更强烈的是羡慕。 **4** ADV You can say **maybe** as a response to a question or remark, when you do not want to agree or disagree. 可能吧(用于表示未置可否) [ADV as reply] ❑ *"Is she coming back?"—"Maybe. No one hears from her."* "她快回来了吗？"——"可能吧，没有人知道她的消息。" **5** ADV You use **maybe** when you are making a rough guess at a number, quantity, or value, rather than stating it exactly. 大约 [ADV amount] [VAGUENESS] ❑ *The men were maybe a hundred feet away and coming closer.* 那些人大约有一百英尺远，正在向这里靠近。 **6** ADV People use **maybe** to mean "sometimes," particularly in a series of general statements about what someone does, or about something that regularly happens. 有时 [ADV with cl/group] ❑ *They'll come to the bar for a year, or maybe even two, then they'll find another favorite spot.* 他们将会来这个酒吧待上一年，或者有时甚至两年，然后他们会再找另外一个喜欢的地方。

may·hem /meɪhem/ N-UNCOUNT You use **mayhem** to refer to a situation that is not controlled or ordered, when people are behaving in a disorganized, confused, and often violent way. 混乱 ❑ *Their arrival caused mayhem as crowds of refugees rushed towards them.* 他们的到来引起了混乱，一群群难民冲向他们。

may·on·naise /meɪəneɪz/ N-UNCOUNT **Mayonnaise** is a thick, pale sauce made from egg yolks and oil. It is put on food such as salad and sandwiches. 蛋黄酱

mayor ♦◊◊ /meɪər, mɛər/ (**mayors**) N-COUNT The **mayor** of a town or city is the person who has been elected for a fixed period of time to run its government. 市长 ❑ *...the new mayor of New York.* …新任纽约市长。

maze /meɪz/ (**mazes**) **1** N-COUNT A **maze** is a complex system of passages or paths between walls or hedges and is designed to confuse people who try to find their way through it, often as a form of amusement. 迷宫 ❑ *The palace has extensive gardens, a maze, and tennis courts.* 这座宫殿有几个大花园，一处迷宫和几处网球场。 **2** N-COUNT A **maze of** streets, rooms, or tunnels is a large number of them that are connected in a complicated way, so that it is difficult to find your way through them. 曲径 ❑ *The children lead me through the maze of alleys to the edge of the city.* 孩子们领着我穿过曲径小巷，来到了城市边缘处。 **3** N-COUNT You can refer to a set of ideas, topics, or rules as a **maze** when a large number of them are related to each other in a complicated way that makes them difficult to understand. 错综复杂 ❑ *The book tries to steer you through the maze of alternative therapies.* 这本书试图引导你穿越替代疗法的迷雾。

M.B.A. /ɛm bi eɪ/ (**M.B.A.s**) also **MBA** N-COUNT An **M.B.A.** is a master's degree in business administration. **M.B.A.** is an abbreviation for "Master of Business Administration." 工商管理硕士

MBO /ɛm bi oʊ/ (**MBOs**) N-COUNT **MBO** is an abbreviation for **management buyout.** 管理层收购 [BUSINESS] ❑ *...the largest MBO ever undertaken by Australian financial investors.* …澳大利亚金融投资者们进行的有史以来最大的一次管理层收购。

M.D. /ɛm di/ (**M.D.s**) N-COUNT **M.D.** is an abbreviation for "medical doctor." You can also refer to a person who has this degree as an **M.D.** 医学博士

me ♦♦♦ /mi, STRONG mi/ PRON-SING A speaker or writer uses **me** to refer to himself or herself. **Me** is a first person singular pronoun. **Me** is used as the object of a verb or a preposition. 我(第一人称单数宾格代词) [V PRON, prep PRON] ❑ *I had to make important decisions that would affect me for the rest of my life.* 我不得不做出一些会影响我后半生的重要决定。 ❑ *He asked me to go to California with him.* 他邀我和他一起去加利福尼亚。

★ **mead·ow** /mɛdoʊ/ (**meadows**) N-COUNT A **meadow** is a field which has grass and flowers growing in it. 草地

mea·ger /migər/
in BRIT, use **meagre**
ADJ If you describe an amount or quantity of something as **meager**, you are critical of it because it is very small or not enough. 数量很少的 [DISAPPROVAL] ❑ *The rations that they gave us were meager and inadequate.* 他们给我们的配给量是很少的，是不够的。

mea·gre /migər/ [BRIT] → see **meager**

meal ♦◊◊ /mil/ (**meals**) **1** N-COUNT A **meal** is an occasion when people sit down and eat, usually at a regular time. 一顿饭 ❑ *She sat next to him throughout the meal.* 她在这一顿饭的时间里坐在他旁边。 **2** N-COUNT A **meal** is the food you eat during a meal. (一餐所吃的)食物 ❑ *The waiter offered him red wine or white wine with his meal.* 那位侍者为他的餐配了红葡萄酒或白葡萄酒。 **3** PHRASE If you have a **square meal**, you have a large, healthy meal. 丰盛的一餐 ❑ *The troops are very tired. They haven't had a square meal for four or five days.* 这些部队非常疲惫。他们已经四五天没有丰盛食物了。
→ see Word Web: **meal**
→ see **restaurant**

m

Word Web **meal**

Mealtime customs vary widely around the world. In the Middle East, popular **breakfast** foods include pita bread, olives and white cheese. In China, favorite **fast food** breakfast items are steamed buns and fried breadsticks. The continental **breakfast** in Europe consists of bread, butter, jam, and a hot drink. In many places **lunch** is a light **meal**, perhaps a **sandwich**. But in Germany, it is the main meal of the day. In most places, **dinner** is the name of the meal eaten in the evening. However, some people say they eat dinner at noon and supper at night.

The first meal of the day is called **breakfast**. The most common word for the midday meal is **lunch**, but in some parts of Britain, and in some contexts, **dinner** is used as well. ❑ *He seldom has lunch at all. ...school dinners. ...Christmas dinner.* However, **dinner** is used mainly to refer to a meal in the evening. ❑ *...a celebratory dinner in the evening.* In British English, it may also suggest a formal or special meal. **Supper** and **tea** are sometimes also used to refer to the evening meal, though for some people, **supper** is a snack in the late evening and **tea** is a light meal in the afternoon.

Thesaurus *meal* 另参见:
N. breakfast, dinner, lunch, supper 1

Word Partnership *meal* 的常用搭配:
V. **enjoy** a meal, **miss** a meal, **skip** a meal 1
cook a meal, **eat** a meal, **have** a meal, **order** a meal, **prepare** a meal, **serve** a meal 2
ADJ. **big** meal, **delicious** meal, **good** meal, **hot** meal, **large** meal, **simple** meal, **well-balanced** meal 2

mean
❶ VERB USES
❷ ADJECTIVE USES
❸ NOUN USE

❶ **mean** ♦♦♦ /miːn/ (**means, meaning, meant**) ⇨ **Please look at meanings 18 and 19 to see if the expression you are looking for is shown under another headword.** 1 V-T If you want to know what a word, code, signal, or gesture **means**, you want to know what it refers to or what its message is. 意思是… [no cont] ❑ *"Credible" means "believable."* **Credible**的意思是**believable**。 ❑ *What does "evidence" mean?* **evidence**是什么意思? 2 V-T If you ask someone what they **mean**, you are asking them to explain exactly what or who they are referring to or what they are intending to say. 意指 [no cont] ❑ *Do you mean me?* 你指我吗? ❑ *Let me illustrate what I mean with an old story.* 让我用一个老故事来说明我指的是什么吧。 3 V-T If something **means** something **to** you, it is important to you in some way. (对某人) 很重要 [no cont] ❑ *The idea that she witnessed this shameful incident meant nothing to him.* 他知道她目击了这可耻的一幕，但这对他来说并不重要。 4 V-T If one thing **means** another, it shows that the second thing exists or is true. 表明…的存在; 表明…属实 [no cont] ❑ *An enlarged prostate does not necessarily mean cancer.* 肿大的前列腺并不一定表明癌症的存在。 5 V-T If one thing **means** another, the first thing leads to the second thing happening. 导致 [no cont] ❑ *It would almost certainly mean the end of NATO.* 这的确几乎导致北大西洋公约组织的终结。 6 V-T If doing one thing **means** doing another, it involves doing the second thing. 意味着 ❑ *Children universally prefer to live in peace and security, even if that means living with only one parent.* 孩子们普遍愿意过平静安宁的生活，即使那意味着只能和单亲生活在一起。 7 V-T If you say that you **mean** what you are saying, you are telling someone that you are serious about it and are not joking, exaggerating, or just being polite. 对…当真 [no cont] ❑ *He says you're fired if you're not back at work on Friday. And I think he meant it.* 他说如果你周五不回来上班的话，就会被解雇。我想他是当真的。 8 V-T If you say that someone **meant to** do something, you are saying that they did it deliberately. 有意 [no cont] ❑ *I didn't mean to hurt you.* 我不是有意要伤害你。 ❑ *If that sounds harsh, it is meant to.* 如果那声音听起来是刺耳的，它就是如此。 9 V-T If you say that someone **did not mean any** harm, offense, or disrespect, you are saying that they did not intend to upset or offend people or to cause problems, even though they may in fact have done so. 本意为 [no cont, with brd-neg] ❑ *I'm sure he didn't mean any harm.* 我敢肯定他本无恶意。 10 V-T If you **mean to** do something, you intend or plan to do it. 打算 [no cont] ❑ *Summer is the perfect time to catch up on the new books you meant to read.* 夏天是补看想读的新书的最佳时间。 11 V-T If you say that something **was meant to** happen, you believe that it was made to happen by God or fate, and did not just happen by chance. 注定 [usu passive, no cont] ❑ *John was constantly reassuring me that we were meant to be together.* 约翰不停地安慰我说，我们注定在一起。 12 PHRASE You say **"I mean"** when making clearer something that you have just said. 也就是说 [SPOKEN] ❑ *It was his idea. Gordon's, I mean.* 那是他的主意。也就是说，戈登的主意。 13 PHRASE You can use **"I mean"** to introduce a statement, especially one that justifies something that you have just said. 我的意思是 (证明前述) [SPOKEN] ❑ *I'm sure he wouldn't mind. I mean, I was the one who asked him.* 我肯定他不会介意。我的意思是，我就是问他的那个人。 14 PHRASE You say **I mean** when correcting something that you have just said. 我刚才是说 [SPOKEN] ❑ *It was law or classics – I mean English or classics.* 那是法律或者古典文学——我是说，英语或者古典文学。 15 PHRASE If you **know what it means** to do something, you know everything that is involved in a particular activity or experience, especially the effect that it has on you. (亲身) 体会了解 ❑ *I know what it means to lose a child under such tragic circumstances.* 我能切身体会在那样悲惨的情况下失去孩子的感觉。 16 PHRASE If a name, word, or phrase **means something to** you, you have heard it before and you know what it refers to. 对某人来说意味着什么 ❑ *"Oh, Gairdner," he said, as if that meant something to him.* "啊，盖尔德纳，"他说道，好像这个名字对他来说意味着什么。 17 PHRASE You use **"you mean"** in a question to check that you have understood what someone has said. 你是说 (疑问句中用于核实是否理解别人所说的话) ❑ *What accident? You mean Christina's?* 什么事故? 你是说克里斯蒂娜的那次吗? 18 → see also **meaning, means, meant** 19 **if you know what I mean** → see **know**

❷ **mean** /miːn/ (**meaner, meanest**) 1 ADJ If someone is being **mean**, they are being unkind to another person, for example by not allowing them to do something. 不友好的 ❑ *The little girls had locked themselves in the room because Mack had been mean to them.* 这些小女孩们把自己锁在房间里，因为麦克对她们不友好。 2 ADJ If you describe a person or animal as **mean**, you are saying that they are very bad-tempered and cruel. 脾气极坏的; 残忍的 [mainly AM] ❑ *The state's former commissioner of prisons once called Leonard the meanest man he'd ever seen.* 这个州的前任监狱长曾经把伦纳德称为他所见过的最残忍的人。 3 ADJ If you describe someone as **mean**, you are being critical of them because they are unwilling to spend much money or to use very much of a particular thing. 吝啬的 [BRIT, DISAPPROVAL]

in AM, use **cheap, stingy**

Thesaurus *mean* 另参见:
V. aim, intend, plan ❶ 8 10
ADJ. nasty, unfriendly, unkind; *(ant.)* kind ❷ 1
miserly, penny-pinching, stingy, tight-fisted ❷ 3

❸ **mean** /miːn/ 1 N-SING **The mean** is a number that is the average of a set of numbers. 平均数 ❑ *Take a hundred and twenty values and calculate the mean.* 取120个值计算平均数。 2 → see also **means**

me·ander /miændər/ (**meanders, meandering, meandered**) 1 V-I If a river or road **meanders**, it has a lot of bends, rather than going in a straight line from one place to another. 蜿蜒而行 ❑ *We took a gravel road that meandered through farmland.* 我们走上了一条蜿蜒穿越农田的石子路。 ❑ *We crossed a small iron bridge over a meandering stream.* 我们穿过了蜿蜒小溪上的一座小铁桥。 2 V-I If you **meander** somewhere, you move slowly and not in a straight line. 漫步 ❑ *We meandered through a landscape of mountains, rivers, and vineyards.* 我们在有群山、河流和葡萄园的风景中漫步。

mean·ing ♦◇◇ /miːnɪŋ/ (**meanings**) 1 N-VAR The **meaning** of a word, expression, or gesture is the thing or idea that it refers to or represents and which can be explained using other words. 意思 ❑ *I hadn't a clue as to the meaning of "activism."* 我对**activism**的意思一无所知。 2 N-VAR The **meaning** of what someone says or of something such as a book or film is the thoughts or ideas that are intended to be expressed by it. 含义 ❑ *Unsure of the meaning of this remark, Ryle chose to remain silent.* 由于对这个评论的含义不确定，赖尔选择了保持沉默。 3 N-UNCOUNT If an activity or action has **meaning**, it has a purpose and is worthwhile. 价值 ❑ *Art has real meaning when it helps people to understand themselves.* 当艺术有助于人们了解自身时，才有真正的价值。

Word Partnership *meaning* 的常用搭配:
N. meaning **of a term**, meaning **of a word** 1
ADJ. **literal** meaning 1 2
deeper meaning, **new** meaning, **real** meaning, **true** meaning 1 – 3
V. **explain the** meaning **of** *something*, **understand the** meaning **of** *something* 1 – 3

M

mean·ing·ful /mɪnɪŋfəl/ **1** ADJ If you describe something as **meaningful**, you mean that it is serious, important, or useful in some way. 严肃的; 重要的; 有用的 ❑ *She believes these talks will be the start of a constructive and meaningful dialogue.* 她相信这些谈话将是一次建设性的、重要的对话的开始。 **2** ADJ A **meaningful** look or gesture is one that is intended to express something, usually to a particular person, without anything being said. 意味深长的 [ADJ n] ❑ *Upon the utterance of this word, Dan and Harry exchanged a quick, meaningful look.* 这个字一出口，丹和哈里马上交换了一个意味深长的眼神。 ● **mean·ing·ful·ly** ADV 意味深长地 ❑ *He glanced meaningfully at the other policeman, then he went up the stairs.* 他向另一名警察意味深长地扫了一眼，然后走上楼去。

mean·ing·less /mɪnɪŋlɪs/ **1** ADJ If something that someone says or writes is **meaningless**, it has no meaning, or appears to have no meaning. 没有含义的 ❑ *The sentence "kicked the ball the man" is meaningless.* 句子**kicked the ball the man**是没有含义的。 **2** ADJ Something that is **meaningless** in a particular situation is not important or relevant. 不重要的; 不相关的 ❑ *Fines are meaningless to guys earning millions.* 罚款对于能挣几百万的人来说是不重要的。 **3** ADJ If something that you do is **meaningless**, it has no purpose and is not at all worthwhile. 无目的的; 无价值的 ❑ *They seek strong sensations to dull their sense of a meaningless existence.* 他们追求强烈的刺激以减轻他们没有价值的存在感。

means ♦♦◇ /minz/ **1** N-COUNT A **means** of doing something is a method, instrument, or process which can be used to do it. **Means** is both the singular and the plural form for this use. 方法; 手段; 过程 ❑ *The move is a means to fight crime.* 这个行动是打击犯罪的一种手段。 ❑ *The army had perfected the use of terror as a means of controlling the population.* 军队已经能很好地利用恐怖手段来控制这里的人们。 **2** N-PLURAL You can refer to the money that someone has as their **means**. 财富 [FORMAL] ❑ *...a person of means.* …一个富有的人。 **3** PHRASE If you do something **by means of** a particular method, instrument, or process, you do it using that method, instrument, or process. 通过(方法、手段或过程) ❑ *This is a two-year course taught by means of lectures and seminars.* 这是一门通过讲座和研讨会形式讲授的两年制课程。 **4** CONVENTION You can say "**by all means**" to tell someone that you are very willing to allow them to do something. 当然可以 [FORMULAE] ❑ *"Can I come and have a look at your house?"—"Yes, by all means."* "我能过来看看你的房子吗?" —— "可以，当然可以。"

Word Partnership *means* 的常用搭配:

ADJ.	**available** means, **different** means, **diplomatic** means, **legal** means, **military** means, **necessary** means, **other** means **1**
N.	means **of communication**, means **of transportation** **1**

meant /mɛnt/ **1** **Meant** is the past tense and past participle of **mean**. **mean**的过去式和过去分词 **2** ADJ You use **meant to** to say that something or someone was intended to be or do a particular thing, especially when they have failed to be or do it. 原本 [v-link ADJ to-inf] ❑ *I can't say any more, it's meant to be a big secret.* 我再也无可奉告了，这原本是个大秘密。 ❑ *Everything is meant to be businesslike.* 所有的事情原本应该是公事公办的。 **3** ADJ If something **is meant for** particular people or for a particular situation, it is intended for those people or for that situation. 为…而做的 [v-link ADJ "for" n] ❑ *Fairy tales weren't just meant for children.* 童话故事不单单是为孩子们写的。 ❑ *The seeds were not meant for human consumption.* 这些种子并不是给人吃的。 **4** PHRASE If you say that something **is meant to** happen, you mean that it is expected to happen or that it ought to happen. 理应 ❑ *The peculiar thing about getting engaged is that you're meant to announce it to everyone.* 订婚特别要做的事是你理应该向每个人宣布你订婚了。 **5** PHRASE If you say that something **is meant to** have a particular quality or characteristic, you mean that it has a reputation for being like that. 公认 ❑ *The Spurs are meant to be one of the top teams in the league.* 马刺队被公认为是联盟中的强队之一。

mean·time /mintaɪm/ **1** PHRASE **In the meantime** or **meantime** means in the period of time between two events. 在…期间 ❑ *Eventually your child will leave home to lead her own life, but in the meantime she relies on your support.* 最终你的孩子将会离开家去过她自己的生活，不过在此期间她依赖你的支持。 **2** PHRASE **For the meantime** means for a period of time from now until something else happens. 暂时 ❑ *Some of her stuff is stored for the meantime with her children.* 她的一些东西暂时保存在她的孩子那里。

mean·while ♦♦◇ /minwaɪl/ **1** ADV **Meanwhile** means while a particular thing is happening. 同时 [ADV with cl] ❑ *Brush the eggplant with oil, add salt and pepper, and bake till soft. Meanwhile, heat the remaining oil in a heavy pan.* 给茄子刷好油，加盐和胡椒粉，烤到软。同时，加热厚底锅中剩余的油。 **2** ADV **Meanwhile** means in the period of time between two events. 在此期间 [ADV with cl] ❑ *You needn't worry; I'll be ready to greet them. Meanwhile, I'm off to discuss the Fowler's party with Felix.* 你不用担心；我会做好准备迎接他们的。在此期间，我会去和费利克斯商量在福勒家聚会的事情。 **3** ADV You use **meanwhile** to introduce a different aspect of a particular situation, especially one that is completely opposite to the one previously mentioned. 另一方面 [ADV with cl] ❑ *He had always found his wife's mother a bit annoying. The mother-daughter relationship, meanwhile, was close.* 他总是觉得他的岳母有点烦人。另一方面，她们母女之间的关系很亲近。

mea·sles /mizəlz/ N-UNCOUNT **Measles** is an infectious illness that gives you a high temperature and red spots on your skin. 麻疹 [also "the" N]
→ see **hospital**

★ **meas·ur·able** /mɛʒərəbəl/ **1** ADJ If you describe something as **measurable**, you mean that it is large enough to be noticed or to be significant. 显著的 [FORMAL] ❑ *Both leaders seemed to expect measurable progress.* 两位领导人好像都期待着显著的进展。 **2** ADJ Something that is **measurable** can be measured. 可测量的 ❑ *Economists emphasize measurable quantities – the number of jobs, the per capita income.* 经济学家们强调可以测算的量——职位数量，人均收入。

meas·ure ♦♦◇ /mɛʒər/ (**measures, measuring, measured**) **1** V-T If you **measure** the quality, value, or effect of something, you discover or judge how great it is. 估量 ❑ *I continued to measure his progress against the charts in the doctor's office.* 我继续根据医生办公室里的图表来估量他的进展。 **2** V-T If you **measure** a quantity that can be expressed in numbers, such as the length of something, you discover it using a particular instrument or device, for example a ruler. 测量 ❑ *Measure the length and width of the gap.* 测量一下这个裂口的长度和宽度。 **3** V-T If something **measures** a particular length, width, or amount, that is its size or intensity, expressed in numbers. (长度、宽度、数量的) 数值为 [no cont] ❑ *It measures 20 yards from side to side.* 从这边到那边的距离为20码。 **4** N-SING A **measure of** a particular quality, feeling, or activity is a fairly large amount of it. 一定数量; 一定程度 [FORMAL] ❑ *With the exception of Juan, each attained a measure of success.* 除了胡安，每个人都取得了一定的成功。 **5** N-SING If you say that one aspect of a situation is **a measure of** that situation, you mean that it shows that the situation is very serious or has developed to a very great extent. (严重程度的) 标准 ❑ *That is a measure of how bad things have become at the bank.* 那就是银行的局面已经糟糕到何种程度的衡量标准。 **6** N-COUNT When someone, usually a government or other authority, takes **measures** to do something, they carry out particular actions in order to achieve a particular result. 措施 [FORMAL] ❑ *The government warned that police would take tougher measures to contain the trouble.* 政府警告说警察将采取更为强硬的措施来制止这场动乱。 **7** N-COUNT A **measure of** a strong alcoholic drink such as brandy or whiskey is an amount of it in a glass. In bars, a **measure** is an official standard amount. (标准量的) 一杯 [BRIT] ❑ *He poured himself another generous measure of whiskey.* 他又给自己慷慨地倒了一杯威士忌。 **8** N-COUNT In music, a **measure** is one of the several short parts of the same length into which a piece of music is divided. (音乐的) 小节 [AM]

in BRIT, use **bar**

❑ *Malcolm wanted to mix the beginning of a sonata, then add Beethoven for a few measures, then go back to Bach.* 马尔科姆想要在开头部分加入一段奏鸣曲，然后加上几个小节的贝多芬作品，然后再回到巴赫的作品。 **9** → see also **tape measure** **10** PHRASE If you say that something has changed or that it has affected you **beyond measure**, you are emphasizing that it has done this to a great extent. 极度 [EMPHASIS] ❑ *Mankind's knowledge of the universe has increased beyond measure.* 人类关于宇宙的知识已经极大增加。
→ see **mathematics**

▸ **measure up** PHRASAL VERB If you do not **measure up to a** standard or to someone's expectations, you are not good enough to achieve the standard or fulfill the person's expectations. 符合 (标准); 达到 (期望) ❑ *It was fatiguing sometimes to try to measure up to her standard of perfection.* 力求达到她的完美标准，有时是很累人的。

Word Partnership *measure* 的常用搭配:

N. measure **intelligence**, measure **performance**, measure **progress** 1
tests measure 1 2
emergency measure, **safety** measure, **security** measure 6

V. **adopt** a measure, **approve** a measure, **support** a measure, **veto** a measure 6

ADJ. **drastic** measure, **economic** measure 6

meas·ure·ment /mɛʒərmənt/ (**measurements**) 1 N-COUNT A **measurement** is a result, usually expressed in numbers, that you obtain by measuring something. 测量的结果 ❑ *We took lots of measurements.* 我们得到了许多测量的结果。 2 N-VAR **Measurement** of something is the process of measuring it in order to obtain a result expressed in numbers. 测量 ❑ *Tests include measurement of height, weight, and blood pressure.* 检查包括对身高、体重和血压的测量。 3 N-VAR The **measurement** of the quality, value, or effect of something is the activity of deciding how great it is. 评估 ❑ *The measurement of intelligence has been the greatest achievement of twentieth-century scientific psychology.* 对智商的评估一直是20世纪科学心理学的最大成就。 4 N-PLURAL Your **measurements** are the size of your waist, chest, hips, and other parts of your body, which you need to know when you are buying clothes. (身体) 尺寸 ❑ *I know all her measurements and find it easy to buy stuff she likes.* 我知道她所有的身体尺寸，觉得买到她喜欢的东西很容易。

meat ♦◇◇ /mit/ (**meats**) N-MASS **Meat** is flesh taken from a dead animal that people cook and eat. (供食用的) 肉 ❑ *Meat and fish are relatively expensive.* 肉和鱼相对较贵。 ❑ *...imported meat products.* …进口的肉制品。
→ see Word Web: **meat**
→ see **vegetarian**

meaty /miti/ (**meatier, meatiest**) 1 ADJ Food that is **meaty** contains a lot of meat. (食物) 多肉的 ❑ *...a pleasant lasagna with a meaty sauce.* …一份美味的肉汁宽面条。 2 ADJ You can describe something such as a piece of writing or a part in a movie as **meaty** if it contains a lot of interesting or important material. 内容丰富的 ❑ *The short, meaty reports are those he likes best.* 那些简短、内容丰富的报告是他最喜欢的类型。

★ **me·chan·ic** /mɪkænɪk/ (**mechanics**) 1 N-COUNT A **mechanic** is someone whose job is to repair and maintain machines and engines, especially car engines. 机修工 ❑ *If you smell something unusual (gas fumes or burning, for instance), take the car to your mechanic.* 如果你闻到了异味（例如汽油味或燃烧味），就把车带给你的修理工。 2 N-PLURAL **The mechanics of** a process, system, or activity are the way in which it works or the way in which it is done. 运作方式 ❑ *What are the mechanics of this new process?* 这一新工序的运作方式是什么？ 3 N-UNCOUNT **Mechanics** is the part of physics that deals with the natural forces that act on moving or stationary objects. 力学 ❑ *He has not studied mechanics or engineering.* 他没有学习过力学或者工程学。

me·chani·cal /mɪkænɪkəl/ 1 ADJ A **mechanical** device has parts that move when it is working, often using power from an engine or from electricity. 机械的 ❑ *...a small mechanical device that taps out the numbers.* …一种能够敲打出数字的小型机械装置。 ❑ *This is the oldest working mechanical clock in the world.* 这是世界上最古老的还可以使用的机械钟。 ● **me·chani·cal·ly** /mɪkænɪkli/ ADV 机械地 [ADV with v] ❑ *The air was circulated mechanically.* 空气是用机械推动循环的。 2 ADJ **Mechanical** means relating to machines and engines and the way they work. 机械方面的 [ADJ n] ❑ *...mechanical engineering.* …机械工程学。 ● **me·chani·cal·ly** ADV 机械方面地 [ADV adj/-ed] ❑ *The car was mechanically sound, he decided.* 这辆车从机械的角度来说是非常可靠的，他判定道。 3 ADJ If you describe a person as **mechanical**, you mean they are naturally good at understanding how machines work. 天生对机械擅长的 ❑ *He was a very mechanical person, who knew a lot about sound.* 他是个非常精通机械的人，对声音很了解。 ● **me·chani·cal·ly** ADV 天生对机械擅长地 [ADV -ed] ❑ *I'm not mechanically minded.* 我没有机械方面的头脑。 4 ADJ If you describe someone's action as **mechanical**, you mean that they do it automatically, without thinking about it. 机械似的 ❑ *It is real prayer, and not mechanical repetition.* 这是真正的祈祷，而不是机械式的重复。 ● **me·chani·cal·ly** ADV 机械似地 [ADV with v] ❑ *He nodded mechanically, his eyes fixed on the girl.* 他机械地点点头，眼睛盯着那个女孩。

mecha·nise /mɛkənaɪz/ [BRIT] → see **mechanize**

mecha·nism ♦◇◇ /mɛkənɪzəm/ (**mechanisms**) 1 N-COUNT In a machine or piece of equipment, a **mechanism** is a part, often consisting of a set of smaller parts, which performs a particular function. 机械装置 ❑ *...the locking mechanism.* …锁定装置。 2 N-COUNT A **mechanism** is a special way of getting something done within a particular system. 机制 ❑ *There's no mechanism for punishing arms exporters who break the rules.* 对于违反规定的军火出口商还没有惩罚机制。 3 N-COUNT A **mechanism** is a part of your behavior that is automatic and that helps you to survive or to cope with a difficult situation. (行为的) 机制 ❑ *...a survival mechanism, a means of coping with intolerable stress.* …一种生存机制，一种应对无法承受的压力的方法。

mecha·nize /mɛkənaɪz/ (**mechanizes, mechanizing, mechanized**)
in BRIT, also use **mechanise**
V-T If someone **mechanizes** a process, they cause it to be done by a machine or machines, when it was previously done by people. 使机械化 ❑ *Only gradually are technologies being developed to mechanize the task.* 渐渐地科技才发展到能使这项任务机械化。 ● **mecha·ni·za·tion** /mɛkənɪzeɪʃən/ N-UNCOUNT 机械化 ❑ *Mechanization happened years ago on the farms of Islay.* 机械化数年前在艾莱的农场实现了。

med·al ♦◇◇ /mɛdəl/ (**medals**) N-COUNT A **medal** is a small metal disk which is given as an award for bravery or as a prize in a sports event. 奖章 ❑ *Dufour was awarded his country's highest medal for bravery.* 杜富尔被授予他的国家的最高英勇奖章。

med·dle /mɛdəl/ (**meddles, meddling, meddled**) V-I If you say that someone **meddles** in something, you are criticizing the fact that they try to influence or change it without being asked. 干涉 [DISAPPROVAL] ❑ *Already some people are asking whether scientists have any right to meddle in such matters.* 已经有些人在问科学家是否有权利去干涉此类事情。 ❑ *If only you hadn't felt compelled to meddle.* 只要你没有觉得是被迫去干预。

Word Link *med* ≈ *middle* : *intermediary, media, mediate*

me·dia ♦♦◇ /midiə/ 1 N-SING-COLL You can refer to television, radio, newspapers, and magazines as **the media**. 媒体 ❑ *It is hard work and not a glamorous job as portrayed by the media.* 这份工作很辛苦，并不是一份像媒体描述的那样令人向往的工作。 ❑ *They are wondering whether bias in the news media contributed to the president's defeat.* 他们正在想是否新闻媒体的偏见导致了总统的失败。 2 → see also **mass media, multimedia** 3 **Media** is a plural of **medium**. 媒体 (**medium** 的复数形式)
→ see **library**

Word Web meat

The English language has different words for animals and the **meat** that comes from them. In the year 1066 AD the Anglo-Saxons of England lost a major battle to the French-speaking Normans. As a result, the Normans became the ruling class and the Anglo-Saxons worked on farms. The Anglo-Saxons tended the animals. They tended **sheep, cows, chickens,** and **pigs** in the fields. The wealthier Normans, who purchased and ate the meat from these animals, used different words. They bought "mouton," which became the word **mutton**, "boeuf," which became **beef**, "poulet," which became **poultry**, and "porc," which became **pork**.

me·dia cir·cus (**media circuses**) N-COUNT If an event is described as a **media circus**, a large group of people from the media are there to report on it and take photographs. 媒体关注的焦点 [DISAPPROVAL] ❑ *The couple married in the Caribbean to avoid a media circus.* 这对情侣在加勒比海结了婚，为了避免成为媒体关注的焦点。

me·di·aeval /mɪdiiːvᵊl, mɪdiᵊl/ [BRIT] → see **medieval**

★ **me·di·ate** /midieɪt/ (**mediates, mediating, mediated**) V-T/V-I If someone **mediates between** two groups of people, or **mediates** an agreement **between** them, they try to settle an argument between them by talking to both groups and trying to find things that they can both agree to. 调解 ❑ *My mom was the one who mediated between Zelda and her mom.* 我妈妈是那个调解塞尔达和她妈妈的人。 ❑ *United Nations officials have mediated a series of peace meetings between the two sides.* 联合国官员们已经调解了双方的一系列和谈。

● **me·dia·tion** /midieɪʃᵊn/ N-UNCOUNT 调解 ❑ *The agreement provides for United Nations mediation between the two sides.* 该协议为联合国对双方的调解奠定了基础。 ● **me·dia·tor** ★ N-COUNT (**mediators**) 调解人 ❑ *An archbishop has been acting as mediator between the rebels and the authorities.* 一位大主教一直充当叛乱者和当局之间的调解人。

→ see **war**

medi·cal ♦♦◇ /mɛdɪkᵊl/ (**medicals**) 1 ADJ **Medical** means relating to illness and injuries and to their treatment or prevention. 医学的；医疗的 [ADJ n] ❑ *Several police officers received medical treatment for cuts and bruises.* 几位警官接受了割伤和瘀伤的治疗。 ● **medi·cal·ly** /mɛdɪkli/ ADV 医学上地；医疗上地 ❑ *Therapists cannot prescribe drugs as they are not necessarily medically qualified.* 治疗师们不能开药方，因为他们不一定具备医疗资格。 2 N-COUNT A **medical** is a thorough examination of your body by a doctor, for example before you start a new job. 全面体检 [mainly BRIT]

in AM, use **physical**

Word Partnership *medical* 的常用搭配：

N. medical **advice**, medical **attention**, medical **bills**, medical **care**, medical **center**, medical **doctor**, medical **emergency**, medical **practice**, medical **problems**, medical **research**, medical **science**, medical **supplies**, medical **tests**, medical **treatment** 1

★ **Medi·care** /mɛdɪkɛər/ N-UNCOUNT In the United States, **Medicare** is a government program that provides health insurance to cover medical costs for people aged 65 and older. (美国) 国家老年人医疗保险制度 [oft N n] ❑ *...cuts in services like Medicare.* …如国家老年人医疗保险制度的各类服务的经费缩减。

medi·ca·tion /mɛdɪkeɪʃᵊn/ (**medications**) N-VAR **Medication** is medicine that is used to treat and cure illness. 药物 ❑ *When somebody comes for treatment I always ask them if they are on any medication.* 有人来治疗时，我总是会问他们是否在服药。

me·dici·nal /mədɪsənᵊl/ ADJ **Medicinal** substances or substances with **medicinal** effects can be used to treat and cure illnesses. 药用的 ❑ *...medicinal plants.* …药用植物。

medi·cine ♦◇◇ /mɛdɪsɪn/ (**medicines**) 1 N-UNCOUNT **Medicine** is the treatment of illness and injuries by doctors and nurses. 医疗 ❑ *He pursued a career in medicine.* 他从事了医务工作。 ❑ *I was interested in alternative medicine and becoming an aromatherapist.* 我对替代疗法感兴趣，想成为一名芳香疗法治疗师。 2 N-MASS **Medicine** is a substance that you drink or swallow in order to cure an illness. 药 ❑ *People in hospitals are dying because of shortages of medicine.* 各医院的病人们因药物短缺正濒临死亡。 ❑ *...the growing popularity of herbal medicines.* …日渐流行的草药。

→ see Word Web: **medicine**

Word Partnership *medicine* 的常用搭配：

V. **practice** medicine, **study** medicine 1
give *someone* medicine, **take** medicine, **use** medicine 2

★ **me·di·eval** /mɪdiiːvᵊl, mɪdiᵊl/

in BRIT, also use **mediaeval**

ADJ Something that is **medieval** relates to or was made in the period of European history between the end of the Roman Empire in AD 476 and about AD 1500. 中世纪的 ❑ *...a medieval castle.* …一座中世纪的城堡。 ❑ *...the most famous of all medieval chroniclers.* …所有中世纪编年史作者中最有名的。

me·dio·cre /midioʊkər/ ADJ If you describe something as **mediocre**, you mean that it is of average quality but you think it should be better. 平庸的 [DISAPPROVAL] ❑ *His school record was mediocre.* 他的学业成绩一般。

me·di·oc·rity /midiɒkrɪti/ N-UNCOUNT If you refer to the **mediocrity** of something, you mean that it is of average quality but you think it should be better. 平庸 [DISAPPROVAL] ❑ *...the mediocrity of most contemporary literature.* …大多数当代文学作品的平庸。

medi·tate /mɛdɪteɪt/ (**meditates, meditating, meditated**) 1 V-I If you **meditate on** something, you think about it very carefully and deeply for a long time. 深思 ❑ *On the day her son began school, she meditated on the uncertainties of his future.* 在她儿子入学那天，她深思了有关他未来的种种不确定因素。 2 V-I If you **meditate** you remain in a silent and calm state for a period of time, as part of a religious training or so that you are more able to deal with the problems and difficulties of everyday life. 冥想 ❑ *I was meditating, and reached a higher state of consciousness.* 我正在冥想，并进入了一种更高的意识境界。

▲ **medi·ta·tion** /mɛdɪteɪʃᵊn/ N-UNCOUNT **Meditation** is the act of remaining in a silent and calm state for a period of time, as part of a religious training, or so that you are more able to deal with the problems of everyday life. 沉思 ❑ *Many busy executives have begun to practice yoga and meditation.* 许多工作繁忙的主管已开始练习瑜伽和冥想。

Medi·ter·ra·nean /mɛdɪtəreɪniən/ 1 N-PROPER **The Mediterranean** is the sea between southern Europe and North Africa. 地中海 ❑ *You have the choice of night fishing in the Mediterranean, or windsurfing on a lake in Switzerland.* 你可选择在地中海夜间垂钓，或是在瑞士的湖上玩帆板。 2 N-PROPER **The Mediterranean** refers to the southern part of Europe, which is next to the Mediterranean Sea. 地中海地区 ❑ *Barcelona has become one of the most dynamic and prosperous cities in the Mediterranean.* 巴塞罗那已经成为地中海地区最具活力、最为繁荣的城市之一。

me·dium ♦◇◇ /midiəm/ (**mediums** or **media**)

The plural of the noun can be either **mediums** or **media** for meanings 4 and 5. The form **mediums** is the plural for meaning 6.

Word Web **medicine**

Western **medicine** began in ancient Greece. The Greek philosopher Hippocrates separated medicine from religion and **disease** from supernatural explanations. He is also responsible for the Hippocratic oath which describes a **physician's** duties. During the Middle Ages, Andreas Vesalius helped to advance medicine through his **research** on **anatomy**. Another major step forward was Friedrich Henle's development of **germ** theory. An understanding of germs led to Joseph Lister's demonstrations of the effective use of **antiseptics**, and Alexander Fleming's discovery of the **antibiotic** penicillin.

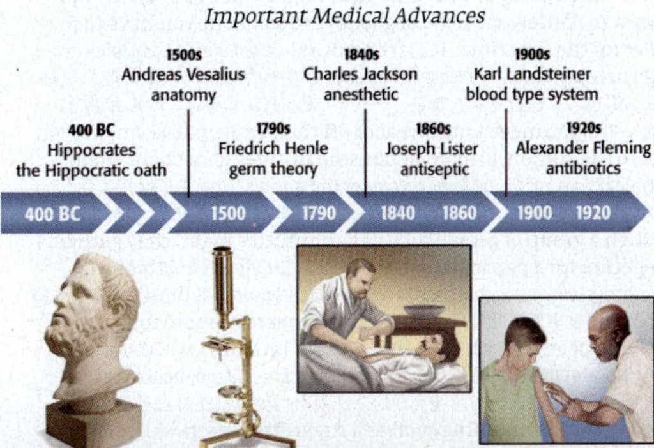

1 ADJ If something is of **medium** size, it is neither large nor small, but approximately halfway between the two. 中等的 ❑ *A medium dose produces severe nausea within hours.* 中等剂量会在几小时内引起严重的恶心。 2 ADJ You use **medium** to describe something that is average in degree or amount, or approximately halfway along a scale between two extremes. 中等程度的 ❑ *Foods that contain only medium levels of sodium are bread, cakes, milk, butter, and margarine.* 含钠量仅为中等水平的食物有面包、蛋糕、牛奶、黄油和人造黄油。 ● ADV **Medium** is also an adverb. 中等程度地 [ADV adj] ❑ *Toast by stirring in a medium-hot skillet for a few minutes.* 在中温的长柄平锅里搅拌烤焙几分钟。 3 COMB IN COLOR If something is of a **medium** color, it is neither light nor dark, but approximately halfway between the two. (颜色) 中度的 ❑ *Andrea has medium brown hair, gray eyes, and very pale skin.* 安德烈娅有着中褐色的头发、灰色的眼睛和非常苍白的皮肤。 4 N-COUNT A **medium** is a way or means of expressing your ideas or of communicating with people. 表现方式; 交流手段 ❑ *In Sierra Leone, English is used as the medium of instruction for all primary education.* 在塞拉利昂，所有基础教育都用英语授课。 5 N-COUNT A **medium** is a substance or material which is used for a particular purpose or in order to produce a particular effect. 媒介物 ❑ *Blood is the medium in which oxygen is carried to all parts of the body.* 血液是把氧气输送到身体各部分的媒介。 6 N-COUNT A **medium** is a person who claims to be able to contact and speak to people who are dead, and to pass messages between them and people who are still alive. 灵媒(自称能够在死者与生者之间传递信息的人) ❑ *Bruce Willis says he has been talking to his dead brother through a medium.* 布鲁斯・威利斯说他一直在通过一位灵媒和他死去的兄弟交谈。 7 → see also **media**

me·dium term N-SING **The medium term** is the period of time which lasts a few months or years beyond the present time, in contrast with the short term or the long term. 中期 ❑ *Economists had been arguing that the medium-term economic prospects remained poor.* 经济学家们一直认为中期经济前景仍然不好。

meek /mik/ (**meeker, meekest**) ADJ If you describe a person as **meek**, you think that they are gentle and quiet, and likely to do what other people say. 温顺的 ❑ *He was a meek, mild-mannered fellow.* 他是一个性情温顺、举止文雅的小伙子。 ● **meek·ly** ADV 温顺地 [ADV with v] ❑ *Most have meekly accepted such advice.* 大多数人都已顺从地接受了这样的建议。

M

meet ♦♦♦ /mit/ (**meets, meeting, met**) 1 V-RECIP If you **meet** someone, you happen to be in the same place as them and start talking to them. You may know the other person, but be surprised to see them, or you may not know them at all. 遇见 ❑ *I have just met the man I want to spend the rest of my life with.* 我刚刚遇到了我想与之共度余生的男人。 ❑ *He's the kindest and sincerest person I've ever met.* 他是我见过的最和善、最真诚的人。 ● PHRASAL VERB **Meet up** means the same as **meet**. 同**meet** ❑ *Last night, when he was parking my car, he met up with a buddy he had at Stanford.* 昨晚他为我泊车时，遇见了他在斯坦福时的一位朋友。 2 V-RECIP If two or more people **meet**, they go to the same place, which they have earlier arranged to do, so that they can talk or do something together. 会见 ❑ *We could meet for a drink after work.* 我们可以在下班后见面喝一杯。 ● PHRASAL VERB **Meet up** means the same as **meet**. 同**meet** ❑ *We tend to meet up for lunch once a week.* 我们往往会每周共进一次午餐。 3 V-T If you **meet** someone, you are introduced to them and begin talking to them and getting to know them. 被引见给… ❑ *Hey, Terry, come and meet my Dad.* 嗨，特里，过来见见我爸爸。 4 V-T You use **meet** in expressions such as "**Pleased to meet you**" and "**Nice to have met you**" when you want to politely say hello or goodbye to someone you have just met for the first time. 认识 [FORMULAE] ❑ *"Jennifer," Miss Mallory said, "this is Leigh Taylor."—"Pleased to meet you," Jennifer said.* "珍妮弗，"马洛里小姐说，"这位是利・泰勒。"——"很高兴认识你，" 珍妮弗说道。 5 V-T If you **meet** someone at or off their train, plane, or bus, you go to the station, airport, or bus stop in order to be there when they arrive. 迎接 ❑ *Mama met me at the station.* 妈妈在车站接了我。 ❑ *Lili and my father met me off the boat.* 莉莉和我爸爸接我下了船。 6 V-I When a group of people such as a committee **meet**, they gather together for a particular purpose. 会晤 ❑ *Officials from the two countries will meet again soon to resume negotiations.* 两国的官员们不久将再次会晤以重新开始谈判。 7 V-I If you **meet with** someone, you have a meeting with them. (与…) 会晤 [mainly AM] ❑ *Most of the lawmakers who met with the president yesterday said they backed the mission.* 大多数昨天与总统会面的立法委员们说他们支持这项使命。 8 V-T/V-I If something such as a suggestion, proposal, or new book **meets with** or **is met with** a particular reaction, it gets that reaction from people. 遇到 ❑ *The idea met with a cool response from various quarters.* 这个想法遭到了各方人士的冷遇。 ❑ *We hope today's offer will meet with your approval too.* 我们希望今天的提议也将会得到您的批准。 9 V-T If something **meets** a need, requirement, or condition, it is good enough to do what is required. 满足 ❑ *He suggested that the current arrangements for the care of severely mentally ill people are inadequate to meet their needs.* 他认为目前对患有严重精神病的人的护理安排不足以满足他们的需要。 10 V-T If you **meet** something such as a problem or challenge, you deal with it satisfactorily or do what is required. 成功应付 ❑ *Manufacturing failed to meet the crisis of the 1970s.* 制造业没能成功地应对20世纪70年代危机的考验。 11 V-T If you **meet** the cost of something, you provide the money that is needed for it. 支付 ❑ *The government said it will help meet some of the cost of the damage.* 政府说它会帮助支付一些损害造成的费用。 12 V-T If you **meet** a situation, attitude, or problem, you experience it or become aware of it. 遇到 (情况、态度、问题等) ❑ *I honestly don't know how I will react the next time I meet a potentially dangerous situation.* 老实说，下次再遇到有潜在危险的情况时，我不知道自己会如何反应。 13 V-I You can say that someone **meets with** success or failure when they are successful or unsuccessful. 获得 (成功); 遇到 (失败) ❑ *Attempts to find civilian volunteers have met with embarrassing failure.* 寻找平民志愿者的种种尝试均遭遇到了令人尴尬的失败。 14 V-RECIP When a moving object **meets** another object, it hits or touches it. 击中; 碰到 ❑ *He held the lighter so it met the tip of his cigarette.* 他举起了打火机，这样它就碰到了香烟头。 15 V-RECIP If your eyes **meet** someone else's, you both look at each other at the same time. (目光) 接触 [WRITTEN] ❑ *Nina's eyes met her sisters' across the table.* 尼娜的目光碰上了桌对面她的姐妹们的目光。 16 V-RECIP If two areas **meet**, especially two areas of land or sea, they are next to one another. (尤指两片地域或海域) 相接 ❑ *It is one of the rare places in the world where the desert meets the sea.* 那是世界上沙漠和海洋相接的少有的地方之一。 17 V-RECIP The place where two lines **meet** is the place where they join together. 相交 ❑ *Parallel lines will never meet no matter how far extended.* 相平行的线不管延伸多长，永远都不会相交。 18 **to make ends meet** → see **end** 19 **to meet** someone **halfway** → see **halfway**

▶ **meet up** → see **meet** 1, 2

Thesaurus *meet* 另参见：

V.	bump into, encounter, run into 1
	get together 2
	gather 6
	comply with, follow, fulfill 9
	accomplish, achieve, complete, make 10

meet·ing ♦♦♦ /mitɪŋ/ (**meetings**) 1 N-COUNT A **meeting** is an event in which a group of people come together to discuss things or make decisions. 会议 ❑ *Can we have a meeting to discuss that?* 我们可以开个会来讨论那件事吗？ ● N-SING You can also refer to the people at a meeting as **the meeting**. 参会人员 ❑ *The meeting decided that further efforts were needed.* 与会者认为进一步的努力是需要的。 2 N-COUNT When you meet someone, either by chance or by arrangement, you can refer to this event as a **meeting**. 碰见 ❑ *In January, 37 years after our first meeting, I was back in the studio with Dennis.* 1月份，在我们初次相遇的37年后，我和丹尼斯一起回到了工作室。

Word Partnership *meeting* 的常用搭配：

N.	meeting **agenda**, **board** meeting, **business** meeting 1
V.	**attend a** meeting, **call a** meeting, **go to a** meeting, **have a** meeting, **hold a** meeting 1
	plan a meeting, **schedule a** meeting 1 2

mega·byte /mɛgəbaɪt/ (**megabytes**) N-COUNT In computing, a **megabyte** is one million bytes of data. 兆字节 ❑ *...256 megabytes of memory.* …256兆字节的内存。

mega·phone /mɛgəfoʊn/ (**megaphones**) 1 N-COUNT A **megaphone** is a cone-shaped device for making your voice sound louder in the open air. 麦克风 2 → see also **bullhorn**

mega·pixel //mɛgəpɪksᵊl// N-COUNT A **megapixel** is one million pixels: used as a measure of the quality of the picture created by a digital camera, scanner, or other imaging device. 百万像素

▲ **mel·an·choly** /mɛlənkɒli/ ADJ You describe something that you see or hear as **melancholy** when it gives you an intense feeling of sadness. 忧郁的 ❑ *The only sounds were the distant, melancholy cries of the sheep.* 惟一的声音是远处的羊群的哀叫。

▲ **mel·low** /mɛloʊ/ (**mellower, mellowest, mellows, mellowing, mellowed**) **1** ADJ **Mellow** is used to describe things that have a pleasant, soft, rich color, usually red, orange, yellow, or brown. 柔和的 ❑ *...the softer, mellower light of evening.* …傍晚较柔和的灯光。 **2** ADJ A **mellow** sound or flavor is pleasant, smooth, and rich. (声音) 柔美的; (味道) 香醇的 ❑ *His voice was deep and mellow and his speech had a soothing and comforting quality.* 他的嗓音深沉柔美，他的演讲令人舒心宽慰。 **3** V-T/V-I If someone **mellows** or if something **mellows** them, they become kinder or less extreme in their behavior, especially as a result of growing older. 使变平和; 变平和 ❑ *He became a taciturn man, a man not easy to live with. Later, when the older children married and had children of their own, he mellowed a little.* 他变成了一个沉默寡言的人、一个不容易相处的人。后来，等大点的孩子们结了婚，也有了他们自己的孩子，他变得平和了些。● ADJ **Mellow** is also an adjective. 平和的 ❑ *Is she more mellow and tolerant?* 她更平和、更宽容了吗?

▸ **mellow out** PHRASAL VERB If someone **mellows out**, they become very relaxed. 放松的 [INFORMAL] ❑ *Until the moment everyone started telling me to mellow out, I had never been tense for a single moment in my life.* 直到每个人开始叫我放松那一刻，我一生中还从来没有一刻紧张过。

melo·dra·ma /mɛlədramə/ (**melodramas**) N-VAR A **melodrama** is a story or play in which there are a lot of exciting or sad events and in which people's emotions are very exaggerated. 惊险故事; 传奇剧

melo·dra·mat·ic /mɛlədrəmætɪk/ ADJ **Melodramatic** behavior is behavior in which someone treats a situation as much more serious than it really is. 过于夸张的 ❑ *"Don't you think you're being slightly melodramatic?" Jane asked.* "你不觉得你有点夸张吗?" 简问道。

★ **melo·dy** /mɛlədi/ (**melodies**) N-COUNT A **melody** is a tune. 旋律 [FORMAL] ❑ *I whistle melodies from Beethoven and Vivaldi and the more popular classical composers.* 我用口哨吹贝多芬、维瓦尔迪和更大众化一些的古典作曲家的曲子。

▲ **mel·on** /mɛlən/ (**melons**) N-VAR A **melon** is a large fruit which is sweet and juicy inside and has a hard green or yellow skin. 甜瓜 ❑ *...some juicy slices of melon.* …几片多汁的甜瓜。

melt /mɛlt/ (**melts, melting, melted**) **1** V-T/V-I When a solid substance **melts** or when you **melt** it, it changes to a liquid, usually because it has been heated. 使融化; 融化 ❑ *The snow had melted, but the lake was still frozen solid.* 雪已经融化了，但湖面仍然冻得结结实实。 ❑ *Meanwhile, melt the white chocolate in a bowl suspended over simmering water.* 同时，把碗架在快烧开的水上，融化碗里的白巧克力。 **2** V-I If something such as your feelings **melt**, they suddenly disappear and you no longer feel them. 消散 [LITERARY] ❑ *His anxiety about the outcome melted, only to return later.* 他对结果的焦虑消失了，但过后又来了。● PHRASAL VERB **Melt away** means the same as **melt**. 同**melt** ❑ *When he heard these words, Scot felt his inner doubts melt away.* 听到这些话，斯科特觉得内心的疑虑消失了。 **3** V-I If a person or thing **melts into** something such as darkness or a crowd of people, they become difficult to see, for example because they are moving away from you or are the same color as the background. 消失 (在黑暗、人群等中) [LITERARY] ❑ *The youths dispersed and melted into the darkness.* 年轻人们散开了，消失在夜色中。

→ see **glacier, matter**

Thesaurus *melt* 另参见:

v. dissolve, soften, thaw **1**
disappear, fade **2** **3**

melt·down /mɛltdaʊn/ (**meltdowns**) **1** N-VAR If there is **meltdown** in a nuclear reactor, the fuel rods start melting because of a failure in the system, and radiation starts to escape. (核反应堆的) 堆芯熔毁 ❑ *Scientists warned that emergency cooling systems could fail and a reactor meltdown could occur.* 科学家们警告说紧急冷却系统可能失灵，核反应堆的堆芯熔毁可能会发生。 **2** N-UNCOUNT The **meltdown** of a company, organization, or system is its sudden and complete failure. (公司、机构、系统等的) 突然崩溃 [JOURNALISM] ❑ *Urgent talks are going on to prevent the market going into financial meltdown during the summer.* 紧急谈判正在进行中，以防止市场在夏天陷入金融崩溃。

melt·ing pot (**melting pots**) N-COUNT A **melting pot** is a place or situation in which people or ideas of different kinds gradually get mixed together. 熔炉 (指不同民族或思想融合的地方或状况) ❑ *The republic is a melting pot of different nationalities.* 该共和国是一个不同民族的大熔炉。

> The term **melting pot** is used to picture the mixing of various immigrant traditions together into one American culture. In places where the cultures do not blend but exist intact side by side, this phenomenon has been described as a **mosaic.**

mem·ber ◆◆◆ /mɛmbər/ (**members**) **1** N-COUNT A **member** of a group is one of the people, animals, or things belonging to that group. (某群体的) 成员 ❑ *He refused to name the members of staff involved.* 他拒绝说出所涉职员的名字。 ❑ *Their lack of training could put members of the public at risk.* 他们训练的缺乏会使公众成员面临风险。 **2** N-COUNT A **member** of an organization such as a club or a political party is a person who has officially joined the organization. 会员; 成员 ❑ *The support of our members is of great importance to the association.* 我们会员的支持对协会来说非常重要。 **3** ADJ A **member country** or **member state** is one of the countries that has joined an international organization or group. 会员国 [ADJ n] ❑ *...the member countries of the North American Free Trade Association.* …北美自由贸易联盟的会员国。 **4** N-COUNT A **member** or **Member** is a person who has been elected to a legislature or parliament. 议员 ❑ *He was elected to Parliament as the Member for Leeds.* 他被选入国会作为利兹市的议员。

Mem·ber of Con·gress (**Members of Congress**) N-COUNT A **Member of Congress** is a person who has been elected to the United States Congress. (美国的) 国会议员 ❑ *...the party's only black member of Congress.* …该党惟一的黑人国会议员。

Mem·ber of Par·lia·ment (**Members of Parliament**) N-COUNT A **Member of Parliament** is a person who has been elected by the people in a particular area to represent them in a country's parliament. The abbreviation **MP** is often used. 国会议员 ❑ *...the Member of Parliament for Torbay.* …托贝的国会议员。

mem·ber·ship ◆◇◇ /mɛmbərʃɪp/ (**memberships**) **1** N-UNCOUNT **Membership** in an organization is the state of being a member of it. 成员身份 ❑ *...his membership in the Communist Party.* …他的共产党党员身份。 **2** N-VAR-COLL The **membership** of an organization is the people who belong to it, or the number of people who belong to it. 全体成员; 成员数 ❑ *By 1890 the organization had a membership of 409,000.* 到1890年该组织有409000名成员。

mem·brane /mɛmbreɪn/ (**membranes**) N-COUNT A **membrane** is a thin piece of skin that connects or covers parts of a person's or animal's body. 膜 ❑ *...inflammation of the thin membrane that lines the heart.* …心膜发炎。

▲ **memo** /mɛmoʊ/ (**memos**) N-COUNT A **memo** is a short official note that is sent by one person to another within the same company or organization. 简报 ❑ *He sent out a memo expressing his disagreement with their decisions.* 他发出一份简报表达他对他们的决定的不赞同。

▲ **mem·oirs** /mɛmwɑrz/ N-PLURAL A person's **memoirs** are a written account of the people who they have known and events that they remember. 回忆录 [usu with poss] ❑ *In retirement he published his memoirs.* 退休后他出版了他的回忆录。

memo·ra·bilia /mɛmərəbɪliə/ N-PLURAL **Memorabilia** are things that you collect because they are connected with a person or organization in which you are interested. 纪念品 ❑ *...the country's leading dealer in Beatles memorabilia.* …这个国家披头士乐队纪念品的最大经销商。

memo·rable /mɛmərəbᵊl/ ADJ Something that is **memorable** is worth remembering or likely to be remembered, because it is special or very enjoyable. 值得记住的; 易记住的 ❑ *...the perfect setting for a nostalgic memorable day.* …作为怀念难忘的一天的最佳景场。

★ **memo·ran·dum** /mɛmərændəm/ (**memoranda** or **memorandums**) **1** N-COUNT A **memorandum** is a written report that is prepared for a person or committee in order to provide them with information about a particular matter. 备忘录 ❑ *...a memorandum from the Department of Defense on its role.* …一份来自国防部的有关其角色的备忘录。 **2** N-COUNT A **memorandum** is a short official note that is sent by one person to another within the same company or organization. 简报 [FORMAL] ❑ *...a memorandum sent to all senior UN personnel.* …一份发给联合国所有资深人员的简报。

Word Link *memor ≈ memory : commemorate, memorial, memory*

me·mo·rial /mɪmɔriəl/ (**memorials**) **1** N-COUNT A **memorial** is a structure built in order to remind people of a famous person or event. 纪念碑 ❑ *Building a memorial to Columbus has been his lifelong*

m

dream. 建一座哥伦布纪念碑一直是他一生的梦想。 2 ADJ A **memorial** event, object, or prize is in honor of someone who has died, so that they will be remembered. 纪念性的 [ADJ n] ❑ *A memorial service is being held for her at St. Paul's Church.* 一场为她举行的纪念仪式正在圣保罗教堂举行。 3 N-COUNT If you say that something will be a **memorial to** someone who has died, you mean that it will continue to exist and remind people of them. 纪念物 ❑ *The museum will serve as a memorial to the millions who passed through Ellis Island.* 这个博物馆将成为曾经过埃利斯岛的数百万人的纪念馆。

Me·mo·rial Day N-UNCOUNT In the United States, **Memorial Day** is a public holiday when people honor the memory of Americans who have died in wars. (美国) 阵亡将士纪念日

★ **memo·rise** /mɛməraɪz/ [BRIT] → see **memorize**

Word Link *ize ≈ making : finalize, memorize, normalize*

★ **memo·rize** /mɛməraɪz/ (**memorizes, memorizing, memorized**)

in BRIT, also use **memorise**

V-T If you **memorize** something, you learn it so that you can remember it exactly. 记住 ❑ *He studied his map, trying to memorize the way to Rose's street.* 他研究了地图，努力记住去罗丝家那条街的路。

Word Link *memor ≈ memory : commemorate, memorial, memory*

memo·ry ♦♦◊ /mɛməri/ (**memories**) 1 N-VAR Your **memory** is your ability to remember things. 记忆力 ❑ *All the details of the meeting are fresh in my memory.* 会议的所有细节我都记忆犹新。 ❑ *But locals with long memories thought this was fair revenge for the injustice of 1961.* 但是记忆力好的当地人认为这是对1961年那起不公正事件的合理报复。 ❑ *He had a good memory for faces.* 他对相貌有很好的记忆力。 2 N-COUNT A **memory** is something that you remember from the past. 记忆 ❑ *She cannot bear to watch the film because of the bad memories it brings back.* 由于这部电影勾起的糟糕回忆，她不能忍受观看它。 ❑ *Her earliest memory is of singing at the age of four to wounded soldiers.* 她最早的记忆是在4岁时为受伤的士兵唱歌。 3 N-COUNT A computer's **memory** is the part of the computer where information is stored, especially for a short time before it is transferred to disks or magnetic tapes. 内存 [COMPUTING] ❑ *The data are stored in the computer's memory.* 这些数据存储在计算机的内存中。 4 N-SING If you talk about the **memory** of someone who has died, especially someone who was loved or respected, you are referring to the thoughts, actions, and ceremonies by which they are remembered. 怀念 ❑ *She remained devoted to his memory.* 她依然对他十分怀念。 5 PHRASE If you say that someone is taking a walk or trip **down memory lane**, you mean that they are talking, writing, or thinking about something that happened to them a long time ago. 沿着记忆的轨迹 [INFORMAL] ❑ *His 1998 memoir is a delightful trip down memory lane.* 他1998年的回忆录是一次愉快的怀旧之旅。 6 PHRASE If you do something **from memory**, for example speak the words of a poem or play a piece of music, you do it without looking at it, because you know it very well. 凭记忆 ❑ *Many members of the church sang from memory.* 许多教徒都是凭记忆唱颂歌。 7 PHRASE If you say that something is, for example, the best, worst, or first thing of its kind **in living memory**, you are emphasizing that it is the only thing of that kind that people can remember. 在人们的记忆里 [EMPHASIS] ❑ *The floods are the worst in living memory.* 那次洪水在人们的记忆中是最严重的。 8 PHRASE If you **lose your memory**, you forget things that you used to know. 失去记忆 ❑ *His illness caused him to lose his memory.* 他的病使他失去了记忆。 9 **to commit** something **to memory** → see **commit**
→ see Word Web: **memory**

M

Word Partnership *memory* 的常用搭配:

ADJ. **collective** memory, **conscious** memory, **failing** memory, **fresh in** *your* memory, **long-/short-term** memory, **poor** memory, **in recent** memory 1
bad memory, **good** memory 1 2
happy memory, **painful** memory, **sad** memory, **vivid** memory 2
N. **computer** memory, **random access** memory, memory **storage** 3

memo·ry card (**memory cards**) N-COUNT A **memory card** is a type of card containing computer memory that is used in digital cameras and other devices. 存储卡 [COMPUTING]

men /mɛn/ **Men** is the plural of **man**. **man**的复数形式

★ **men·ace** /mɛnɪs/ (**menaces, menacing, menaced**) 1 N-COUNT If you say that someone or something is a **menace** to other people or things, you mean that person or thing is likely to cause serious harm. 威胁 ❑ *In my view, you are a menace to the public.* 在我看来，你对公众是一个威胁。 2 N-COUNT You can refer to someone or something as a **menace** when you want to say that they cause you trouble or annoyance. 烦人之人; 烦人之物 [INFORMAL] ❑ *You're a menace to my privacy, Kenton.* 你是个侵犯我隐私的讨厌的人，肯顿。 3 N-UNCOUNT **Menace** is a quality or atmosphere that gives you the feeling that you are in danger or that someone wants to harm you. 危险性; 威胁性 ❑ *There is a pervading sense of menace.* 有一种在蔓延的危险感。 4 V-T If you say that one thing **menaces** another, you mean that the first thing is likely to cause the second thing serious harm. 威胁 ❑ *They seem determined to menace the United States and its allies.* 他们好像决心要威胁美国及其盟国。

men·ac·ing /mɛnɪsɪŋ/ ADJ If someone or something looks **menacing**, they give you a feeling that they are likely to cause you harm or put you in danger. 威胁的 ❑ *The strong, dark eyebrows give his face an oddly menacing look.* 两道又浓又黑的眉毛给他的脸一种异常吓人的神情。 ● **men·ac·ing·ly** ADV 威胁地 ❑ *A group of men suddenly emerged from a doorway and moved menacingly forward to block her way.* 一群人突然从门口冒出来，向她逼近，堵住了她的去路。

mend /mɛnd/ (**mends, mending, mended**) 1 V-T If you **mend** a tear or a hole in a piece of clothing, you repair it by sewing it. 修补 ❑ *Men say that we are only good for cooking their meals and mending their socks.* 男人们说我们只擅长给他们做饭和补袜子。 2 V-T/V-I If a person or a part of their body **mends** or **is mended**, they get better after they have been ill or have had an injury. 使 (病情、伤情) 好转; (病情、伤情) 好转 ❑ *I'm feeling a lot better. The cut aches, but it's mending.* 我感觉好多了。伤口还疼，但正在好转。 3 V-T If you try to **mend** divisions between people, you try to end the disagreements or quarrels between them. 弥合 (分歧) ❑ *He sent Evans as his personal envoy to discuss ways to mend relations between the two countries.* 他派埃文斯作为他的私人代表去商讨改善两国关系的途径。 4 V-T If you **mend** something that is broken or not working, you repair it, so that it works properly or can be used. 修理 [mainly BRIT] ❑ *They took a long time to mend the roof.* 他们花了好长时间修缮房顶。 5 PHRASE If a relationship or situation is **on the mend** after a difficult or unsuccessful period, it is improving. (关系) 在改善; (形势) 在好转 [INFORMAL] ❑ *More evidence that the economy was on the mend was needed.* 需要更多表明经济在好转的证据。 6 PHRASE If you are **on the mend** after an illness or injury, you are recovering from it. (病情、伤情) 在好转 [INFORMAL] ❑ *The baby had been ill but seemed to be on the mend.* 这婴儿生病了，但看起来病情正在好转。 7 PHRASE If someone who has been behaving badly **mends** their **ways**, they

Word Web memory

Scientists divide **memory** into three types. **Short-term** memory holds small amounts of information for a short time. The information is then **forgotten**. Short-term memory lasts from two to thirty seconds. Working memory organizes items in the short-term memory. For example, adding up several numbers in your mind involves working memory. **Long-term** memory can last for years. Several things influence long-term memory. You remember an event with meaningful **associations** better than a routine event. **Rehearsing** the information also helps preserve a long-term memory. In addition, mnemonics can help you **remember** the most important details.

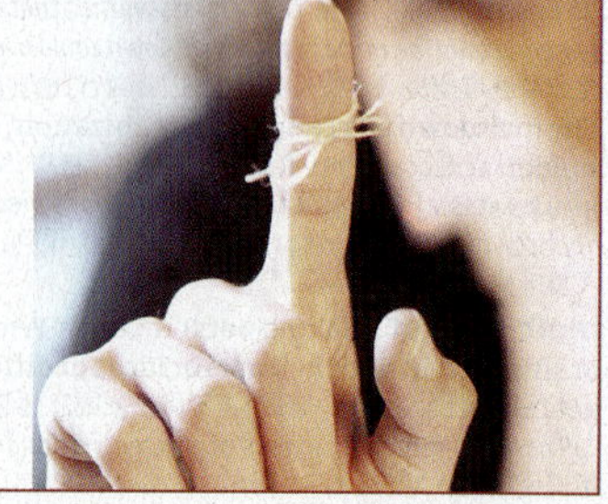

begin to behave well. 改过自新 ❏ *He has promised drastic disciplinary action if they do not mend their ways.* 如果他们不改过自新的话，他已保证会严惩不贷。

me·nial /miniəl, minyəl/ ADJ **Menial** work is very boring, and the people who do it have a low status and are usually badly paid. 卑微的 ❏ *...low-paid menial jobs, such as cleaning and domestic work.* …工钱少又卑微的工作，诸如打扫清洁或做家务。

Word Link *itis ≈ inflammation : arthritis, hepatitis, meningitis*

men·in·gi·tis /mɛnɪndʒaɪtɪs/ N-UNCOUNT **Meningitis** is a serious infectious illness which affects your brain and spinal cord. 脑膜炎

meno·pause /mɛnəpɔz/ N-SING **Menopause** is the time during which a woman gradually stops menstruating, usually when she is about fifty years old. (女性的) 更年期

in BRIT, sometimes use **the menopause**

❏ *...alternative therapies to fight the symptoms of menopause.* …对抗更年期症状的替代疗法。 ● **meno·pau·sal** ADJ 更年期的 ❏ *A menopausal woman of average build and height requires 1600–2400 calories daily.* 一位一般体形和身高的更年期女性每天需要1600——2400卡的热量。

men·strual /mɛnstruəl/ ADJ **Menstrual** means relating to menstruation. 月经的 [ADJ n] ❏ *...the menstrual cycle.* …月经周期。

men·stru·ate /mɛnstrueɪt/ (**menstruates, menstruating, menstruated**) V-I When a woman **menstruates**, a flow of blood comes from her uterus. Women menstruate once a month unless they are pregnant or have reached menopause. 行经 [FORMAL] ❏ *Lean, hard-training women athletes may menstruate less frequently or not at all.* 清瘦、训练艰苦的女运动员行经可能不那么频繁或根本没有月经。 ● **men·strua·tion** /mɛnstrueɪʃən/ N-UNCOUNT 来潮 ❏ *Menstruation may cease when a woman is anywhere between forty-five and fifty years of age.* 月经可能在女性45至50岁之间停止。

mens·wear /mɛnzwɛər/ N-UNCOUNT **Menswear** is clothing for men. 男装 ❏ *...the menswear industry.* …男装行业。

Word Link *ment ≈ mind : dementia, mental, mentality*

men·tal ♦◇◇ /mɛntəl/ **1** ADJ **Mental** means relating to the process of thinking. 智力的 [ADJ n] ❏ *The intellectual environment has a significant influence on the mental development of the children.* 知识环境对孩子智力的发展有着重大的影响。 ● **men·tal·ly** ADV 智力地 ❏ *I think you are mentally tired.* 我觉得你的头脑累了。 **2** ADJ **Mental** means relating to the state or the health of a person's mind. 心理上的 [ADJ n] ❏ *The mental state that had created her psychosis was no longer present.* 导致她精神错乱的那种心理状态已经不见了。 ● **men·tal·ly** ADV 心理上地 ❏ *...an inmate who is mentally disturbed.* …一个心理不正常的病人。 **3** ADJ A **mental** act is one that involves only thinking and not physical action. 在头脑中进行的 [ADJ n] ❏ *Practice mental arithmetic when you go out shopping.* 外出购物时练习一下心算。 ● **men·tal·ly** ADV 在头脑中进行地 [ADV with v] ❏ *This technique will help people mentally organize information.* 这个技术会帮助人们在头脑里组织信息。

→ see **hypnosis**

▲ **men·tal·ity** /mɛntælɪti/ (**mentalities**) N-COUNT Your **mentality** is your attitudes and your way of thinking. 心态 ❏ *...a criminal mentality.* …一种犯罪心态。

men·tion ♦♦◇ /mɛnʃən/ (**mentions, mentioning, mentioned**) **1** V-T If you **mention** something, you say something about it, usually briefly. 提到 ❏ *She did not mention her mother's absence.* 她没有提到她母亲的缺席。 ❏ *I may not have mentioned it to her.* 我可能没有和她提过此事。 ❏ *I had mentioned that I didn't really like contemporary music.* 我曾经说过我并不真正喜欢现代音乐。 **2** N-VAR A **mention** is a reference to something or someone. 提及 ❏ *The statement made no mention of government casualties.* 这项声明没有提及政府方面的伤亡情况。 **3** V-T If someone **is mentioned** in writing, a reference is made to them by name, often to criticize or praise something that they have done. 提及 (某人的名字) [usu passive] ❏ *I was absolutely outraged that I could be even mentioned in an article of this kind.* 我十分恼火，我的名字居然出现在这种文章里。 **4** N-VAR A special or honorable **mention** is formal praise that is given for an achievement that is very good, although not usually the best of its kind. 提名表扬 ❏ *Two of the losers deserve special mention: Caroline Swaithes, of Kingston, and Maria Pons, of Valley Stream.* 其中的两位失败者值得特别表扬：来自金斯顿的卡罗琳·斯威西斯和来自谷溪镇的玛丽亚·庞斯。 **5** CONVENTION People sometimes say **"don't mention it"** as a polite reply to someone who has just thanked them for doing something. 不必客气 [FORMULAE] ❏ *"Thank you very much."—"Don't mention it."* "非常感谢你。"——"不必客气。"

If you **mention** something, you say it, but only briefly, especially when you have not talked about it before. ❏ *He mentioned that he might go to New York.* If you **comment** on a situation, or make a **comment** about it, you give your opinion on it. ❏ *Mr. Cook has not commented on these reports... I was wondering whether you had any comments.* If you **remark** on something, or make a **remark** about it, you say what you think or what you have noticed, often in a casual way. ❏ *Visitors remark on how well the children look... General Sutton's remarks about the conflict.*

Word Partnership *mention* 的常用搭配:

V.	**fail to** mention, **forget to** mention, **neglect to** mention **1**
	make *no* mention **of** *someone/something* **2**
ADJ.	**honorable** mention, **special** mention **4**

men·tor /mɛntɔr/ (**mentors, mentoring, mentored**) **1** N-COUNT A person's **mentor** is someone who gives them help and advice over a period of time, especially help and advice related to their job. 导师 ❏ *Leon Sullivan was my mentor and my friend.* 利昂·沙利文既是我的导师，也是我的朋友。 **2** V-T To **mentor** someone means to give them help and advice over a period of time, especially help and advice related to their job. 指导 ❏ *He had mentored scores of younger doctors.* 他指导过许多更年轻的医生。

menu /mɛnyu/ (**menus**) **1** N-COUNT In a restaurant or café or at a formal meal, the **menu** is a list of the meals and drinks that are available. 菜单 ❏ *A waiter offered him the menu.* 一个侍者给他送上了菜单。 **2** N-COUNT A **menu** is the food that you serve at a meal. 饭菜 ❏ *Try out the menu on a few friends.* 请几个朋友来尝尝这道菜。 **3** N-COUNT On a computer screen, a **menu** is a list of choices. Each choice represents something that you can do using the computer. (电脑屏幕上的) 菜单 ❏ *Hold down the shift key and press F7 to display the print menu.* 按住**shift**键的同时按下**F7**键，以显示打印菜单。

m

MEP /ɛm i pi/ (**MEPs**) N-COUNT An **MEP** is a person who has been elected to the European Parliament. **MEP** is an abbreviation for "Member of the European Parliament." 欧洲议会议员 ❏ *...Tuesday's secret ballot of Europe's 626 MEPs.* …星期二进行的626位欧洲议会议员无记名投票。

mer·ce·nary /mɜrsənɛri/ (**mercenaries**) **1** N-COUNT A **mercenary** is a soldier who is paid to fight by a country or group that they do not belong to. 雇佣兵 ❏ *...the recruitment of foreign mercenaries.* …对外籍雇佣兵的招募。 **2** ADJ If you describe someone as **mercenary**, you are criticizing them because you think that they are only interested in the money that they can get from a particular person or situation. 惟利是图的 [DISAPPROVAL] ❏ *"I hate to sound mercenary," Labane said, "but am I getting paid to be in this play of yours?"* "我不愿让自己听起来惟利是图，" 拉班说："但是参与你这出戏演出我会得到报酬吗？"

Word Link *merc ≈ trading : commerce, merchandise, merchant*

▲ **mer·chan·dise** /mɜrtʃəndaɪz, -daɪs/ N-UNCOUNT **Merchandise** is products that are bought, sold, or traded. 商品 [FORMAL] ❏ *...a mail-order company that provides merchandise for people suffering from allergies.* …一家为患过敏症的人提供商品的邮购公司。

mer·chan·dis·er /mɜrtʃəndaɪzər/ (**merchandisers**) N-COUNT A **merchandiser** is a person or company that sells products to the public. 商家 [AM, BUSINESS]

in BRIT, use **retailer**

❏ *In 1979, Liquor Barn thrived as a discount merchandiser.* 1979年，作为折扣酒品专卖店的立可仓生意兴隆。

mer·chan·dis·ing /mɜrtʃəndaɪzɪŋ/ **1** N-UNCOUNT **Merchandising** is used to refer to the way stores and businesses organize the sale of their products, for example the way they are displayed and the prices that are chosen. 销售规划 [mainly AM, BUSINESS] ❏ *Company executives say revamped merchandising should help Macy's earnings to grow.* 公司主管说改进后的销售规划应该能帮助梅西公司提高收益。 **2** N-UNCOUNT **Merchandising** consists of goods such as toys and clothes that are linked with something such as a movie, sports team, or pop group. 附带商品 ❏ *We are selling the full range of World Cup merchandising.* 我们正在出售世界杯的所有附带商品。

Word Link *merc ≈ trading : commerce, merchandise, merchant*

mer·chant ♦◇◇ /mɜrtʃənt/ (merchants) 1 N-COUNT A **merchant** is a person who buys or sells goods in large quantities, especially one who imports and exports them. 商人 ❑ *Any knowledgeable wine merchant would be able to advise you.* 任何一位内行的葡萄酒商人都能为你提出建议。 2 N-COUNT A **merchant** is a person who owns or runs a store, or other business. 店主 [AM]

in BRIT, usually use **retailer, shopkeeper**

❑ *The family was forced to live on credit from local merchants.* 这家人不得不靠向当地的商家赊账过活。 3 ADJ **Merchant** seamen or ships are involved in carrying goods for trade. 商船的 [ADJ n] ❑ *There's been a big reduction in the size of the merchant fleet in recent years.* 近年来商船队的数量大为缩减。

mer·chant bank (merchant banks) N-COUNT A **merchant bank** is the same as an **investment bank**. 投资银行

mer·ci·ful·ly /mɜrsɪfəli/ ADV You can use **mercifully** to show that you are glad that something good has happened, or that something bad has not happened or has stopped. 幸运地 [FEELINGS] ❑ *Mercifully, a friend came to the rescue.* 很幸运，一个朋友赶来解救了。

mer·ci·less /mɜrsɪlɪs/ ADJ If you describe someone as **merciless**, you mean that they are very cruel or determined and do not show any concern for the effect their actions have on other people. 冷酷无情的 ❑ *...the merciless efficiency of a modern police state.* …现代警察国家冷酷无情的效率。 ● **mer·ci·less·ly** ADV 冷酷无情地 ❑ *We teased him mercilessly.* 我们毫不同情地取笑他。

★ **mer·cu·ry** /mɜrkyəri/ N-UNCOUNT **Mercury** is a silver-colored liquid metal that is used especially in thermometers and barometers. 水银

mer·cy /mɜrsi/ (mercies) 1 N-UNCOUNT If someone in authority shows **mercy**, they choose not to harm someone they have power over, or they forgive someone they have the right to punish. 仁慈；宽恕 ❑ *Neither side took prisoners or showed any mercy.* 双方都没有抓俘虏，也没有表现出丝毫的仁慈。 2 ADJ **Mercy** is used to describe a special journey to help someone in great need, such as people who are sick or made homeless by war. 善行 [ADJ n] [JOURNALISM] ❑ *She vanished nine months ago while on a mercy mission to West Africa.* 她在9个月前去西非的慈善之旅中消失不见了。 3 N-COUNT If you refer to an event or a situation as **a mercy**, you mean that it makes you feel happy or relieved, usually because it stops something unpleasant from happening. 幸运 ❑ *It really was a mercy that he'd gone so rapidly at the end.* 这真幸运，他最后走得那么快。 4 PHRASE If one person or thing is **at the mercy of** another, the first person or thing is in a situation where they cannot prevent themselves from being harmed or affected by the second. 完全由…支配 ❑ *Buildings are left to decay at the mercy of vandals and the weather.* 这些建筑物因人为的肆意破坏和日晒雨淋而破败不堪。

Word Partnership *mercy* 的常用搭配：

V.	**beg for** mercy, **call for** mercy, **have** mercy **on** *someone*, **show** mercy 1
N.	mercy **of God** 1
PREP.	**at the** mercy **of** *someone/something* 4

mere ♦◇◇ /mɪər/ (merest)

Mere does not have a comparative form. The superlative form **merest** is used to emphasize how small something is, rather than in comparisons.

1 ADJ You use **mere** to emphasize how unimportant or inadequate something is, in comparison to the general situation you are describing. 只不过 [ADJ n] [EMPHASIS] ❑ *...successful exhibitions which go beyond mere success.* …不仅仅是成功，而是大获成功的展览。 ❑ *There is more to good health than the mere absence of disease.* 健康不仅仅指不生病，还包括更多。 2 ADJ You use **mere** to indicate that a quality or action that is usually unimportant has a very important or strong effect. 单单的 (用来指某事虽小却有重要影响) [ADJ n] ❑ *The mere mention of food had triggered off hunger pangs.* 单单提到食物就引起了阵阵的饥饿感。 3 ADJ You use **mere** to emphasize how small a particular amount or number is. 只不过 (用于强调数量之少) ["a" ADJ amount] [EMPHASIS] ❑ *Sixty percent of teachers are women, but a mere five percent of women are principals.* 60%的教师是女性，但只有5%的女性是校长。

mere·ly ♦◇◇ /mɪərli/ 1 ADV You use **merely** to emphasize that something is only what you say and not better, more important, or more exciting. 只不过 (用来强调某事物不是很重要或很有价值) [EMPHASIS] ❑ *Michael is now merely a good friend.* 迈克尔现在只不过是一个好朋友而已。 ❑ *Francis Watson was far from being merely a furniture expert.* 弗兰西斯・沃森不仅仅是位家具专家。 2 ADV You use **merely** to emphasize that a particular amount or quantity is very small. 仅仅 (用来强调数量之少) [ADV amount] [EMPHASIS] ❑ *The brain accounts for merely three percent of body weight.* 大脑仅占体重的3%。 3 PHRASE You use **not merely** before the less important of two contrasting statements, as a way of emphasizing the more important statement. 不仅仅 [EMPHASIS] ❑ *The team needs players who want to play for Canada, not merely any country that will have them.* 这个队需要愿意为加拿大比赛的运动员，而不仅仅是愿意为任何一个雇用他们的国家去比赛的运动员。

Word Link *merg ≈ sinking : emerge, merge, submerge*

★ **merge** /mɜrdʒ/ (merges, merging, merged) 1 V-RECIP If one thing **merges with** another, or **is merged with** another, they combine or come together to make one whole thing. You can also say that two things **merge**, or **are merged**. 使合并；合并 ❑ *Bank of America merged with a rival bank.* 美国银行和一家竞争银行合并了。 ❑ *The rivers merge just north of a vital irrigation system.* 这些河流在一个重要的灌溉系统的北部汇合了。 ❑ *The two countries merged into one.* 这两个国家合二为一了。 2 V-RECIP If one sound, color, or object **merges** into another, the first changes so gradually into the second that you do not notice the change. 融入 ❑ *Like a chameleon, he could merge unobtrusively into the background.* 他像变色龙一样，可以不引人注意地融入背景之中。 ❑ *His features merged with the darkness.* 他的面容融入了黑暗中。

★ **mer·ger** ♦◇◇ /mɜrdʒər/ (mergers) N-COUNT A **merger** is the joining together of two separate companies or organizations so that they become one. 合并 [BUSINESS] ❑ *...a merger between two of America's biggest trade unions.* …美洲两个最大的工会的合并。

mer·it /mɛrɪt/ (merits, meriting, merited) 1 N-UNCOUNT If something has **merit**, it has good or worthwhile qualities. 优点；价值 ❑ *The argument seemed to have considerable merit.* 这个论点似乎有相当大的价值。 2 N-PLURAL The **merits** of something are its advantages or other good points. 好处 ❑ *They have been persuaded of the merits of peace.* 他们已经被说服，认识到了和平的好处。 3 V-T If someone or something **merits** a particular action or treatment, they deserve it. 应受到 [FORMAL] ❑ *He said he had done nothing wrong to merit a criminal investigation.* 他说他没有做错任何事，不应该受到刑事调查。

mer·maid /mɜrmeɪd/ (mermaids) N-COUNT In fairy tales and legends, a **mermaid** is a woman with a fish's tail instead of legs, who lives in the sea. 美人鱼

mer·ri·ly /mɛrɪli/ 1 ADV If you say that someone **merrily** does something, you are critical of the fact that they do it without realizing that there are a lot of problems which they have not thought about. 轻松地 (含有批评之意，指在做某事时没有考虑到该事有许多问题) [ADV with v] [DISAPPROVAL] ❑ *There they were, merrily describing their 16-hour working days while claiming to be happily married.* 他们一边轻松地描绘着他们16个小时的工作日，还一边声称他们的婚姻幸福。 2 ADV If you say that something is happening **merrily**, you mean that it is happening fairly quickly, and in a pleasant or satisfactory way. 轻快地 [ADV with v] ❑ *The ferry cut merrily through the water.* 这只渡船轻快地划开水面航行。

mer·ry /mɛri/ (merrier, merriest) 1 ADJ If you describe someone's character or behavior as **merry**, you mean that they are happy and cheerful. 欢快的 [OLD-FASHIONED] ❑ *From the house come bursts of merry laughter.* 从房子里传出阵阵欢快的笑声。 ● **mer·ri·ly** ADV 欢快地 [ADV after v] ❑ *Chris threw back his head and laughed merrily.* 克里斯开心地仰天大笑。 2 CONVENTION Just before Christmas and on Christmas Day, people say "**Merry Christmas**" to other people to express the hope that they will have a happy time. 祝圣诞快乐 [FORMULAE] ❑ *Merry Christmas, everyone.* 祝大家圣诞快乐。

merry-go-round (merry-go-rounds) 1 N-COUNT A **merry-go-round** is a circular platform at a carnival or amusement park on which there are model animals or vehicles for people to ride on as it turns around. 旋转木马 2 N-COUNT You can refer to a continuous series of activities as a **merry-go-round**. 一连串的繁忙

活动 [usu sing, oft N "of" n] ❑ *...a merry-go-round of parties, dances, musical events, and the like.* …一连串的晚会、舞会、音乐活动以及诸如此类的事情。

mesh /mɛʃ/ (**meshes, meshing, meshed**) **1** N-VAR **Mesh** is material like a net made from wire, thread, or plastic. 网眼织品 ❑ *The ground-floor windows are obscured by wire mesh.* 底楼的窗户被铁丝网罩着。 **2** V-RECIP If two things or ideas **mesh** or **are meshed**, they go together well or fit together closely. 使紧密配合；紧密配合 ❑ *Their senses of humor meshed perfectly.* 他们的幽默感配合得天衣无缝。 ❑ *This of course meshes with the economic philosophy of those on the right.* 这当然和那些右翼派的经济哲学相吻合。

mes·mer·ise /mɛzməraɪz/ [BRIT] → see **mesmerize**

mes·mer·ize /mɛzməraɪz/ (**mesmerizes, mesmerizing, mesmerized**)

in BRIT, also use **mesmerise**

V-T If you **are mesmerized** by something, you are so interested in it or so attracted to it that you cannot think about anything else. 迷住 ❑ *He was absolutely mesmerized by Pavarotti on television.* 他完全被电视上的帕瓦罗蒂迷住了。

mess ♦◇◇ /mɛs/ (**messes, messing, messed**) **1** N-SING If you say that something is **a mess** or **in a mess**, you think that it is not neat. 凌乱 [also no det] ❑ *The house is a mess.* 这个房间又脏又乱。 **2** N-VAR If you say that a situation is **a mess**, you mean that it is full of trouble or problems. You can also say that something is **in a mess**. 困境 ❑ *I've made such a mess of my life.* 我把自己的生活弄得一团糟。 ❑ *...the many reasons why the economy is in such a mess.* …经济陷入如此困境的诸多原因。 **3** N-VAR **A mess** is something liquid or sticky that has been accidentally dropped on something. (意外滴落的) 液体; (意外滴落的) 黏稠物 ❑ *I'll clear up the mess later.* 我过会儿会把滴落的东西擦干净。 **4** N-COUNT The **mess** at a military base or military barracks is the building in which members of the armed forces can eat or relax. (军队的) 餐厅 ❑ *...a party at the officers' mess.* …在军官餐厅里举办的晚会。

▸ **mess around**

in BRIT, also use **mess about**

1 PHRASAL VERB If you **mess around**, you spend time doing things without any particular purpose or without achieving anything. 混时间 ❑ *We were just messing around playing with paint.* 我们瞎混时间，玩玩油彩。 **2** PHRASAL VERB If you say that someone **is messing around with** something, you mean that they are interfering with it in a harmful way. 乱弄 ❑ *"Don't be stupid," Max snapped. "You don't want to go messing around with bears."* "别傻了，"马克斯厉声说。"你不会去跟熊斗着玩儿吧。" **3** PHRASAL VERB If someone **is messing around**, they are behaving in a joking or silly way. 胡闹 ❑ *I thought she was messing around.* 我想她是在胡闹。

▸ **mess up** **1** PHRASAL VERB If you **mess** something **up** or if you **mess up**, you cause something to fail or be spoiled. 把…搞糟；把…弄乱 [INFORMAL] ❑ *When politicians mess things up, it is the people who pay the price.* 政客们把事情搞砸时，承受损失的是老百姓。 ❑ *He had messed up one career.* 他已经把一份工作搞砸了。 **2** PHRASAL VERB If you **mess up** a place or a thing, you make it dirty or not neat. 弄脏；弄乱 [INFORMAL] ❑ *I hope they haven't messed up your video tapes.* 我希望他们没有弄乱你的录像带。

▸ **mess with** PHRASAL VERB If you tell someone not to **mess with** a person or thing, you are warning them not to get involved with that person or thing. 干涉 ❑ *You are messing with people's religion and they don't like that.* 你正在干涉人们的宗教信仰，他们不喜欢你这样做。

Word Partnership *mess* 的常用搭配:

V. **clean up** a mess, **leave** a mess, **make** a mess **1**–**3**
get into a mess **2**

mes·sage ♦♦◇ /mɛsɪdʒ/ (**messages, messaging, messaged**) **1** N-COUNT A **message** is a piece of information or a request that you send to someone or leave for them when you cannot speak to them directly. 留言 ❑ *I got a message you were trying to reach me.* 我得到了一条留言，说你在设法联系我。 **2** N-COUNT The **message** that someone is trying to communicate, for example in a book or play, is the idea or point that they are trying to communicate. 信息 ❑ *The report's message was unequivocal.* 报告中传达的信息相当明确。 ❑ *I no longer want to be friends with her but I don't know how to get the message across.* 我再也不想和她做朋友了，但我不知道如何告诉她。 **3** V-T/V-I If you **message** someone, you send them a message electronically using a computer or another device such as a cellphone. 发短信 ❑ *People who message a lot feel unpopular if they don't get many back.* 如果发送许多短信的人并未得到很多回复，他们会觉得自己不受欢迎。

Word Partnership *message* 的常用搭配:

V. **give** *someone* a message, **leave** a message, **read** a message, **take** a message **1**
deliver a message, **get** a message, **hear** a message, **send** a message **1** **2**
get a message **across**, **spread** a message **2**

ADJ. **clear** message, **important** message, **urgent** message **1** **2**
powerful message, **simple** message, **strong** message, **wrong** message **2**

mes·sage board (**message boards**) N-COUNT In computing, a **message board** is a system that allows users to send and receive messages of general interest. 留言板 [COMPUTING] ❑ *Have your say on our message board by clicking here.* 请点击这里在我们的留言板上发表评论。

mes·sag·ing /mɛsɪdʒɪŋ/ N-UNCOUNT **Messaging** is the sending of written or spoken messages using a computer or another electronic device such as a cellphone. 信息的发送 ❑ *Messaging allows real-time communication by keyboard with up to five people at any one time.* 信息的发送能使最多五个人同时通过键盘进行实时交流。

mes·sen·ger /mɛsɪndʒər/ (**messengers**) N-COUNT A **messenger** takes a message to someone, or takes messages regularly as their job. 信使 [also "by" N] ❑ *There will be a messenger at the airport to collect the photographs from our courier.* 机场会有一名信使从我们的快递员那儿取走照片。

messy /mɛsi/ (**messier, messiest**) **1** ADJ A **messy** person or activity makes things dirty or not neat. 邋遢的 ❑ *She was a good, if messy, cook.* 尽管有点邋遢，她还是一名好厨师。 **2** ADJ Something that is **messy** is dirty or not neat. 脏的 ❑ *Don't worry if this first coat of paint looks messy.* 如果这第一层油漆看上去有点脏的话，不用担心。 **3** ADJ If you describe a situation as **messy**, you are emphasizing that it is confused or complicated, and therefore unsatisfactory. 混乱而复杂的 ❑ *John had been through a messy divorce himself.* 约翰自己经历过一次棘手的离婚。

met /mɛt/ **Met** is the past tense and past participle of **meet**. **meet**的过去式和过去分词

meta·bol·ic /mɛtəbɒlɪk/ ADJ **Metabolic** means relating to a person's or animal's metabolism. 新陈代谢的 [ADJ n] ❑ *People who have inherited a low metabolic rate will gain weight.* 因遗传而新陈代谢速度慢的人会发胖。

Word Link *meta ≈ beyond, change : metabolism, metamorphosis, metaphor*

me·tabo·lism /mɪtæbəlɪzəm/ (**metabolisms**) N-VAR Your **metabolism** is the way that chemical processes in your body cause food to be used in an efficient way, for example to make new cells and to give you energy. 新陈代谢

met·al ♦◇◇ /mɛtᵊl/ (**metals**) N-MASS **Metal** is a hard substance such as iron, steel, gold, or lead. 金属 ❑ *...pieces of furniture in wood, metal, and glass.* …用木料、金属和玻璃制成的一件件家具。

→ see Word Web: **metal**

→ see **can, mineral**

★ **me·tal·lic** /mətælɪk/ **1** ADJ A **metallic** sound is like the sound of one piece of metal hitting another. (声音) 金属般的 ❑ *There was a metallic click and the gates swung open.* 一声金属碰撞的咔嗒声后，大门打开了。 **2** ADJ **Metallic** paint or colors shine like metal. 有金属光泽的 ❑ *He had painted all the wood with metallic silver paint.* 他把所有木料涂上了有金属光泽的银漆。 **3** ADJ Something that tastes **metallic** has a bitter, unpleasant taste. 金属腥味的 ❑ *There was a metallic taste at the back of his throat.* 他喉咙深处有一股金属的腥味。 **4** ADJ **Metallic** means consisting entirely or partly of metal. 含金属的 ❑ *Even the smallest metallic object, whether a nail file or cigarette lighter, is immediately confiscated.* 即便是最小的金属物品，不论是指甲锉刀还是打火机，都会立刻被没收。

Word Link *osis ≈ state or condition : hypnosis, metamorphosis, psychosis*

meta·mor·pho·sis /mɛtəmɔrfəsɪs/ (**metamorphoses**) N-VAR When a **metamorphosis** occurs, a person or thing develops and

Word Web metal

In their natural state, most **metals** are not pure. They are usually combined with other materials in mixtures known as **ores**. Almost all metals are **shiny**. Many metals share these special properties–they are ductile, meaning that they can be made into **wire**; they are malleable and can be formed into thin, flat sheets; they are also good **conductors** of heat and electricity. Except for **copper** and **gold**, metals are generally gray or silver in color.

changes into something completely different. 变质 [FORMAL] ❑ *...his metamorphosis from a Republican to a Democrat.* …他从共和党党员到民主党党员的转变。

Word Link *meta ≈ beyond, change : metabolism, metamorphosis, metaphor*

▲ **meta·phor** /mɛtəfɔr/ (**metaphors**) **1** N-VAR A **metaphor** is an imaginative way of describing something by referring to something else which is the same in a particular way. For example, if you want to say that someone is very shy and frightened of things, you might say that they are a mouse. 隐喻 ❑ *...the avoidance of violent expressions and metaphors like "kill two birds with one stone."* …避免使用有暴力意味的表达和隐喻，如“一石二鸟。” ❑ *...the writer's use of metaphor.* …作者对暗喻的运用。 **2** N-VAR If one thing is a **metaphor for** another, it is intended or regarded as a symbol of it. 象征 ❑ *The divided family remains a powerful metaphor for a society that continued to tear itself apart.* 破裂的家庭仍然是一个持续分裂的社会的有力象征。 **3** PHRASE If you **mix** your **metaphors**, you use two conflicting metaphors. People do this accidentally, or sometimes deliberately as a joke. 把两个矛盾的隐喻混用在一起 ❑ *To mix yet more metaphors, you were trying to run before you could walk, and I've clipped your wings.* 再混用一些隐喻，你还不会走就想跑，而我又修短了你的翅膀。

M

meta·phori·cal /mɛtəfɔrɪkᵊl/ ADJ You use the word **metaphorical** to indicate that you are not using words with their ordinary meaning, but are describing something by means of an image or symbol. 比喻意义上的 ❑ *It turns out Levy is talking in metaphorical terms.* 原来利维说的是比喻。● **meta·phori·cal·ly** ADV 比喻意义上地 ❑ *You're speaking metaphorically, I hope.* 我希望你是在打比方。

mete /mit/ (**metes, meting, meted**)
▸ **mete out** PHRASAL VERB To **mete out** a punishment means to order that someone should be punished in a certain way. 对…施以(处罚) [FORMAL] ❑ *His father meted out punishment with a slipper.* 他父亲用一只拖鞋来进行处罚。

me·teor /mitiər/ (**meteors**) N-COUNT A **meteor** is a piece of rock or metal that burns very brightly when it enters the Earth's atmosphere from space. 流星
→ see Word Web: meteor

Word Link *ite ≈ mineral, rock : granite, graphite, meteorite*

me·teor·ite /mitiəraɪt/ (**meteorites**) N-COUNT A **meteorite** is a large piece of rock or metal from space that has landed on Earth. 陨石

me·teoro·logi·cal /mitiərəlɒdʒɪkᵊl/ ADJ **Meteorological** means relating to meteorology. 气象学的 [ADJ n] ❑ *...adverse meteorological conditions.* …不利的气象条件。

me·teor·ol·ogy /mitiərɒlədʒi/ N-UNCOUNT **Meteorology** is the study of the processes in the Earth's atmosphere that cause particular weather conditions, especially in order to predict the weather. 气象学 ● **me·teor·olo·gist** /mitiərɒlədʒɪst/ N-COUNT (**meteorologists**) 气象学家 ❑ *Meteorologists have predicted mild rains for the next few days.* 气象学家们已经预测接下来的几天有小雨。

Word Link *meter ≈ measuring : kilometer, meter, perimeter*

me·ter /mitər/ (**meters, metering, metered**)
in BRIT, also use **metre**
1 N-COUNT A **meter** is a device that measures and records something such as the amount of gas or electricity that you have used. 表 ❑ *He was there to read the electricity meter.* 他在那儿读电表。 **2** V-T To **meter** something such as gas or electricity means to use a meter to measure how much of it people use, usually in order to calculate how much they have to pay. 用表测量 ❑ *Only a third of these households thought it reasonable to meter water.* 这些用户中只有1/3认为用水表计量是合理的。 **3** N-COUNT A **meter** is the same as a **parking meter**. 停车收费器 **4** N-COUNT A **meter** is a metric unit of length equal to 100 centimeters. 米
in BRIT, use **metre**
❑ *She's running the 1,500 meters here.* 她正在这儿跑1500米。

me·thane /mɛθeɪn/ N-UNCOUNT **Methane** is a colorless gas that has no smell. Natural gas consists mostly of methane. 甲烷

meth·od ♦♦◇ /mɛθəd/ (**methods**) N-COUNT A **method** is a particular way of doing something. 方法 ❑ *The pill is the most efficient method of birth control.* 避孕药是最有效的节育办法。
→ see **science**

Thesaurus *method* 另参见：
N. manner, procedure, process, system, technique

Word Partnership *method* 的常用搭配：
ADJ. **alternative/traditional** method, **best** method, **effective** method, **new** method, **preferred** method, **scientific** method
V. **develop a** method, **use a** method
N. method **of payment**, **teaching** method

▲ **me·thodi·cal** /məθɒdɪkᵊl/ ADJ If you describe someone as **methodical**, you mean that they do things carefully, thoroughly, and in order. 有条不紊的 ❑ *Da Vinci was methodical in his research, carefully recording his observations and theories.* 达·芬奇作研究非常有条理，他仔细地记录下他的观察所得和理论。● **me·thodi·cal·ly** /məθɒdɪkli/ ADV 有条不紊地 [ADV with v] ❑ *She methodically put the things into her suitcase.* 她把东西井井有条地放进了她的手提箱。

★ **meth·od·ol·ogy** /mɛθədɒlədʒi/ (**methodologies**) N-VAR A **methodology** is a system of methods and principles for doing something, for example for teaching or for carrying out research. 方法论 [FORMAL] ❑ *Teaching methodologies vary according to the topic.*

Word Web meteor

As an asteroid flies through **space**, small pieces called meteoroids sometimes break off. When a meteoroid enters the earth's **atmosphere**, we call it a **meteor**. As the earth passes through asteroid belts we see spectacular **meteor showers**. Meteors that reach the earth are called meteorites. Scientists believe a huge meteorite struck the earth about 65 million years ago. It left a pit in Mexico called the Chicxulub **Crater**. It's about 150 miles wide. The crash caused earthquakes and tsunamis. It may also have produced a change in the earth's environment. Some believe this event caused the dinosaurs to die out.

教学方法因题目而不同。● **meth·odo·logi·cal** /mɛθədəlɒdʒɪkᵊl/ ADJ 方法的 ❑ *...theoretical and methodological issues raised by the study of literary texts.* …文学文本研究提出的理论和方法方面的问题。

▲ **me·ticu·lous** /mətɪkyələs/ ADJ If you describe someone as **meticulous**, you mean that they do things very carefully and with great attention to detail. 小心谨慎的 ❑ *He was so meticulous about everything.* 他对任何事情都很小心谨慎。● **me·ticu·lous·ly** ADV 细致地 ❑ *The flat had been meticulously cleaned.* 这间公寓被仔仔细细地打扫过了。

me·tre ♦◇◇ /mitər/ [BRIT] → see **meter**

met·ric /mɛtrɪk/ ADJ **Metric** means relating to the metric system. 公制的 ❑ *Around 180,000 metric tons of food aid is required.* 大约需要十八万公吨的食品援助。

▲ **met·ro** /mɛtroʊ/ (**metros**) also **Metro** N-COUNT **The metro** is the subway system in some cities, for example in Washington or Paris. 地铁 ❑ *A new metro runs under the square, carrying hundreds of thousands who used to cycle to work.* 一条新地铁在广场下面运行，载着数以千计过去骑自行车上班的人们。

→ see **transportation**

Word Link *poli ≈ city : metropolis, police, policy*

me·tropo·lis /mətrɒpəlɪs/ (**metropolises**) N-COUNT A **metropolis** is the largest, busiest, and most important city in a country or region. 大都会

★ **met·ro·poli·tan** /mɛtrəpɒlɪtᵊn/ ADJ **Metropolitan** means belonging to or typical of a large, busy city. 大都会的 [ADJ n] ❑ *...the metropolitan district of Miami.* …迈阿密的大都会区。❑ *...a dozen major metropolitan hospitals.* …12家主要的大都会医院。

mg **mg** is a written abbreviation for **milligram** or **milligrams**. 毫克 ❑ *...300 mg of calcium.* …300毫克的钙。

mice /maɪs/ **Mice** is the plural of **mouse**. **mouse**的复数形式

Word Link *micro ≈ small : microbe, microcosm, microscope*

mi·crobe /maɪkroʊb/ (**microbes**) N-COUNT A **microbe** is a very small, living thing, which you can only see if you use a microscope. 微生物 ❑ *...a type of bacteria that include the microbes responsible for tuberculosis and leprosy.* …包括引起结核病和麻风病的微生物在内的一类细菌。

micro·chip /maɪkroʊtʃɪp/ (**microchips**) N-COUNT A **microchip** is a very small piece of silicon inside a computer. It has electronic circuits on it and can hold large quantities of information or perform mathematical and logical operations. 集成电路片

micro·com·put·er /maɪkroʊkəmpyutər/ (**microcomputers**) N-COUNT A **microcomputer** is a small computer, especially one used for writing documents. 微型计算机

micro·cosm /maɪkrəkɒzəm/ (**microcosms**) N-COUNT A **microcosm** is a small society, place, or activity which has all the typical features of a much larger one and so seems like a smaller version of it. 社会的缩影 [oft N "of" n, also "in" N] [FORMAL] ❑ *Kitchell says the city was a microcosm of all American culture during the '60s.* 基切尔说这个城市曾经是60年代所有美国文化的一个缩影。

micro·cred·it /maɪkroʊkrɛdɪt/ N-UNCOUNT **Microcredit** is credit in the form of small loans offered to local businesses, especially in developing countries. 小额信贷 [BUSINESS] ❑ *One tool to fight poverty is the use of microcredit loans.* 和贫困斗争的方法之一是利用小额贷款。

micro·ec·o·nom·ics /maɪkroʊɛkənɒmɪks, -ikə[ɛˋ]-/ also **micro-economics** N-UNCOUNT **Microeconomics** is the branch of economics that is concerned with individual areas of economic activity, such as those within a particular company or relating to a particular market. 微观经济学 [BUSINESS] ❑ *He has 250 students in his microeconomics module.* 有250名学生上他的微观经济教学课。

● **micro·eco·nom·ic** /maɪkroʊɛkənɒmɪk, -ik-/ ADJ [usu ADJ n] ❑ *...an important flaw in microeconomic theory.* …微观经济学理论中重要的缺陷。❑ *It is possible to have a microeconomic success and a macroeconomic failure, as Britain did in the late eighties.* 微观经济的成功和宏观经济的失败是可能共存的，就像80年代末的英国那样。

→ see **economics**

micro·fiber /maɪkroʊfaɪbər/ (**microfibers**)

in BRIT, use **microfibre**

N-VAR **Microfibers** are extremely light, artificial fibers that are used to make cloth. 微纤维 ❑ *...woven in great looking and durable microfiber.* …用非常好看且耐用的微纤维织成的。

micro·fibre /maɪkroʊfaɪbəʳ/ [BRIT] → see **microfiber**

micro·organism /maɪkroʊɔrgənɪzəm/ (**microorganisms**) N-COUNT A **microorganism** is a very small living thing which you can only see if you use a microscope. 微生物

→ see **fungus**

Word Link *phon ≈ sound : microphone, symphony, telephone*

micro·phone /maɪkrəfoʊn/ (**microphones**) N-COUNT A **microphone** is a device that is used to make sounds louder or to record them on a tape recorder. 麦克风

→ see **concert**

micro·proc·es·sor /maɪkroʊprɒsɛsər/ (**microprocessors**) N-COUNT In a computer, the **microprocessor** is the main microchip, which controls its most important functions. 微处理器 [COMPUTING]

Word Link *scope ≈ looking : horoscope, microscope, telescope*

micro·scope /maɪkrəskoʊp/ (**microscopes**) N-COUNT A **microscope** is a scientific instrument which makes very small objects look bigger so that more detail can be seen. 显微镜

micro·scop·ic /maɪkrəskɒpɪk/ **1** ADJ **Microscopic** objects are extremely small, and usually can be seen only through a microscope. 极小的 ❑ *Microscopic fibers of protein were visible.* 极为精密的蛋白质纤维是能被看见的。**2** ADJ A **microscopic** examination is done using a microscope. (用) 显微镜的 [ADJ n] ❑ *Microscopic examination of a cell's chromosomes can reveal the sex of the fetus.* 用显微镜检查细胞染色体可以查出胎儿的性别。

micro·wave /maɪkroʊweɪv/ (**microwaves, microwaving, microwaved**) **1** N-COUNT A **microwave** or a **microwave oven** is an oven which cooks food very quickly by electromagnetic radiation rather than by heat. 微波炉 **2** V-T To **microwave** food or drink means to cook or heat it in a microwave oven. 用微波炉 (烹调或加热) ❑ *Steam or microwave the vegetables until tender.* 蒸或用微波炉加热蔬菜，直至蔬菜变得软嫩。

→ see **cook, wave**

mid·air also **mid-air** /mɪdɛər/ N-UNCOUNT If something happens in **midair**, it happens in the air, rather than on the ground. 空中 ❑ *The bird stopped and hovered in mid-air.* 这只鸟儿停下来，在半空中盘旋。

Mid-Autumn Festival (**Mid-Autumn Festivals**) N-VAR **The Mid-Autumn Festival** is a Chinese festival that is held to celebrate the end of the summer harvest, when the crops have been gathered. It is also called the **Moon Festival**. 中秋节

mid·day /mɪddeɪ/ **1** N-UNCOUNT **Midday** is twelve o'clock in the middle of the day. 中午 ❑ *At midday everyone would go down to Reg's Café.* 中午每个人都去雷吉的小餐馆。**2** N-UNCOUNT **Midday** is the middle part of the day, from late morning to early afternoon. 中午时分 ❑ *People were beginning to tire in the midday heat.* 在中午的炎炎烈日下，人们开始感到疲劳。

mid·dle ♦♦♦ /mɪdᵊl/ (**middles**) **1** N-COUNT **The middle of** something is the part of it that is farthest from its edges, ends, or outside surface. 中间 ❑ *Howard stood in the middle of the room sipping a cup of coffee.* 霍华德站在房子中间，啜饮着一杯咖啡。❑ *They had a volleyball court in the middle of the courtyard.* 他们在院子中央有一个排球场。**2** **the middle of nowhere** → see **nowhere** **3** ADJ The **middle** object in a row of objects is the one that has an equal number of objects on each side. 当中的 [ADJ n] ❑ *The middle button of his uniform jacket was strained over his belly.* 他制服上衣中间的那个扣子在他的肚子上绷得紧紧的。**4** N-SING **The middle of** an event or period of time is the part that comes after the first part and before the last part. 中期 ❑ *I woke up in the middle of the night and could hear a tapping on the window.* 我半夜醒来，听到轻敲窗户的声音。● ADJ **Middle** is also an adjective. 中期的 [ADJ n] ❑ *Many classical violinists and pianists become conductors in their middle years.* 许多古典小提琴手和钢琴演奏者在中年时变成指挥家。**5** PHRASE If you are **in the middle of** doing something, you are busy doing it. 正忙于 ❑ *It's a bit hectic. I'm in the middle of cooking for nine people.* 有点儿忙不过来了。我正忙着给9个人做饭呢。

→ see **hand**

mid·dle age N-UNCOUNT **Middle age** is the period in your life when you are no longer young but have not yet become old. Middle age is usually considered to take place between the ages of 40 and 60. 中年 ❑ *Men tend to put on weight in middle age.* 男人到了中年体重往往会增加。

m

middle-aged 1 ADJ If you describe someone as **middle-aged**, you mean that they are neither young nor old. People between the ages of 40 and 60 are usually considered to be middle-aged. 中年的 ❑ *...middle-aged, married businessmen.* …中年的已婚商人们。 2 ADJ If you describe someone's activities or interests as **middle-aged**, you are critical of them because you think they are typical of a middle-aged person, for example by being conventional or old-fashioned. 具有中年人特点的（如保守、守旧）[DISAPPROVAL] ❑ *Her novels are middle-aged and boring.* 她的小说具有中年人的保守，而且枯燥乏味。
→ see age

mid·dle class ♦◇◇ (**middle classes**) N-COUNT-COLL **The middle class** or **middle classes** are the people in a society who are not working class or upper class. Business people, managers, doctors, lawyers, and teachers are usually regarded as middle class. 中产阶级 ❑ *...the expansion of the middle class in the late 19th century.* …19世纪后期中产阶级的扩大。● ADJ **Middle class** is also an adjective. 中产阶级的 ❑ *He is rapidly losing the support of blue-collar voters and of middle-class conservatives.* 他正在迅速失去蓝领选民和中产阶级保守人士的支持。

Mid·dle East ♦♦◇ N-PROPER **The Middle East** is the area around the eastern Mediterranean that includes Iran and all the countries in Asia to the west and southwest of Iran. 中东地区 ❑ *The two great rivers of the Middle East rise in the mountains of Turkey.* 中东地区的两大河流都发源于土耳其的山脉。

middle·man /mɪdᵊlmæn/ (**middlemen**) 1 N-COUNT A **middleman** is a person or company which buys things from the people who produce them and sells them to the people who want to buy them. 中间商 [BUSINESS] ❑ *Why don't they cut out the middleman and let us do it ourselves?* 他们为什么不取消中间商，让我们自己来做呢？ 2 N-COUNT A **middleman** is a person who helps in negotiations between people who are unwilling to meet each other directly. 中间人 ❑ *The two sides would only meet indirectly, through middlemen.* 双方只会通过中间人间接会晤。

mid·dle man·age·ment N-UNCOUNT **Middle management** refers to managers who are below the top level of management, and who are responsible for controlling and running an organization rather than making decisions about how it operates. 中层管理人员 [BUSINESS] ❑ *The proportion of women in middle management has risen to 40%.* 中层管理人员中女性的比例已经上升到了40%。

middle-of-the-road 1 ADJ If you describe someone's opinions or policies as **middle-of-the-road**, you mean that they are neither left wing nor right wing, and not at all extreme. 中立的 ❑ *Consensus need not be weak, nor need it result in middle-of-the-road policies.* 多数人的意见不一定就软弱，也不一定会导致中立的政策。 2 ADJ If you describe something or someone as **middle-of-the-road**, you mean that they are ordinary or unexciting. 平庸的 ❑ *I actually don't want to be a middle-of-the-road person, married with a mortgage.* 我真的不想作一个平庸的人，结完婚，背着抵押贷款。

Word Link *mid ≈ middle : midnight, midst, midweek*

mid·night ♦◇◇ /mɪdnaɪt/ 1 N-UNCOUNT **Midnight** is twelve o'clock in the middle of the night. 午夜 ❑ *It was well after midnight by the time Anne returned to her apartment.* 安妮回到公寓时早已过了午夜。 2 ADJ **Midnight** is used to describe something that happens or appears at midnight or in the middle of the night. 午夜时的 [ADJ n] ❑ *It is totally out of the question to postpone the midnight deadline.* 延迟午夜的最后期限是根本不可能的。 3 PHRASE If someone **is burning the midnight oil**, they are staying up very late in order to study or do some other work. 开夜车 ❑ *Chris is asleep after burning the midnight oil trying to finish his article.* 克里斯在熬夜赶完他的文章后，睡着了。

mid-range also **midrange** ADJ You can use **mid-range** to describe products or services which are neither the most expensive nor the cheapest of their type. 中档的 [ADJ n] ❑ *...the price of a mid-range family car.* …中档家用轿车的价格。

★ **midst** /mɪdst/ 1 PHRASE If you are **in the midst of** doing something, you are doing it at the moment. 正当…的时候 ❑ *We are in the midst of one of the worst recessions for many, many years.* 我们正处于许多年以来最严重的一次经济衰退。 2 PHRASE If something happens **in the midst of** an event, it happens during it. 正当…时 ❑ *Eleanor arrived in the midst of a blizzard.* 埃莉诺到达时正下着暴风雪。 3 PHRASE If someone or something is **in the midst of** a group of people or things, they are among them or surrounded by them. 在…当中 ❑ *Many were surprised to see him exposed like this in the midst of a large crowd.* 很多人看到他这样暴露在一大群人当中，都感到很意外。

mid·way /mɪdweɪ/ 1 ADV If something is **midway between** two places, it is between them and the same distance from each of them. 中间 [ADV prep] ❑ *The studio is midway between his aunt's old home and his cottage.* 那个工作室位于他姑姑的老房子和他的小屋中间。● ADJ **Midway** is also an adjective. 中间的 [ADJ n] ❑ *Fresno is close to the midway point between LA and San Francisco.* 弗雷斯诺位于接近洛杉矶和旧金山的中间点。 2 ADV If something happens **midway through** a period of time, it happens during the middle part of it. 当中 ❑ *He crashed midway through the race.* 他在赛跑中途突然摔倒。● ADJ **Midway** is also an adjective. 当中的 [ADJ n] ❑ *They were denied an obvious penalty before the midway point of the first half.* 上半场比赛还未过半，他们被否决了一次明显的罚球机会。

mid·week /mɪdwiːk/ ADJ **Midweek** describes something that happens in the middle of the week. 一周中间的 [ADJ n] ❑ *Enjoy the peace and beauty of midweek walks in the park.* 享受一周中间公园漫步的平静与美好。● ADV **Midweek** is also an adverb. 在一周的中间 ❑ *They'll be able to go up to Washington midweek.* 他们将能在一周中间去华盛顿。

Mid·west /mɪdwɛst/ N-PROPER **The Midwest** is the region in the central part of the United States and north of Texas. (美国) 中西部 [usu "the" N] ❑ *...farmers in the Midwest.* …中西部的农场主们。❑ *...the Midwest states.* …中西部各州。

★ **mid·wife** /mɪdwaɪf/ (**midwives**) N-COUNT A **midwife** is a nurse who is trained to deliver babies and to advise pregnant women. 助产士 ❑ *You don't have to call the midwife as soon as labor starts.* 你不必刚开始分娩就叫助产士。

might
❶ MODAL USES
❷ NOUN USES

❶ **might** ♦♦♦ /maɪt/

Might is a modal verb. It is used with the base form of a verb.

⇨ **Please look at meaning 11 to see if the expression you are looking for is shown under another headword.** 1 MODAL You use **might** to indicate that something will possibly happen or be true in the future, but you cannot be certain. 有可能会；也许会 [VAGUENESS] ❑ *There's a report today that smoking might be banned in most buildings.* 今日有报道说大多数建筑里有可能要禁止吸烟。❑ *I might well regret it later.* 我以后也许会对此很后悔。 2 MODAL You use **might** to indicate that there is a possibility that something is true, but you cannot be certain. 或许(是) [VAGUENESS] ❑ *She and Robert's father had not given up hope that he might be alive.* 她和罗伯特的父亲都没有放弃他可能还活着的希望。❑ *You might be right.* 你或许是对的。 3 MODAL You use **might** to indicate that something could happen or be true in particular circumstances. 可能(发生) [VAGUENESS] ❑ *America might sell more cars to the islands if they were made with the steering wheel on the right.* 如果把方向盘装在右侧，美国有可能在这些岛屿销售更多的车辆。 4 MODAL You use **might have** with a past participle to indicate that it is possible that something happened or was true, or when giving a possible explanation for something. 可能(对过去的事进行推测或提供解释) ❑ *I heard what might have been an explosion.* 我听到的可能是爆炸的声音。 5 MODAL You use **might have** with a past participle to indicate that something was a possibility in the past, although it did not actually happen. (表示与过去事实相反的虚拟语气) 本来可能 ❑ *If she had had to give up riding she might have taken up sailing competitively.* 如果当时她不得不放弃马术，她可能就已经从事帆船竞赛了。 6 MODAL You use **might** in statements where you are accepting the truth of a situation, but contrasting it with something that is more important. 也许(接受事实，但与更重要的事对比) ❑ *They might not have two cents to rub together, but at least they have a kind of lifestyle that is different.* 他们也许手里没有几个钱，但至少他们过着一种与众不同的生活方式。 7 MODAL You use **might** when you are saying emphatically that someone ought to do the thing mentioned, especially when you are annoyed because they have not done it. 应该(做但还没做) [EMPHASIS] ❑ *You might have told me that before!* 你以前就该告诉我这件事！ 8 MODAL You use **might** to make a suggestion or to give advice in a very polite way. (表示礼貌的建议) 可以 [POLITENESS] ❑ *They might be wise to stop advertising on television.* 他们可以明智些，停止在电视上做广告。 9 MODAL You use **might** as a polite way of interrupting someone, asking a question, making a request, or introducing what you are going to say next. (礼貌地打断、提问等) 可以 [FORMAL, SPOKEN, POLITENESS] ❑ *Might I make a suggestion?* 我可以提个建议么? ❑ *Might I ask what you're doing here?* 我可以问问你在这里做什么吗? **10** MODAL You use **might** in expressions such as **I might have known** and **I might have guessed** to indicate that you are not surprised at a disappointing event or fact. 早该 (表示不感到意外) ❑ *I might have known I'd find you with some little slut.* 我早该知道会发现你跟某个小荡妇在一起。 **11 might as well** → see **well**

❷ **might** /maɪt/ **1** N-UNCOUNT **Might** is power or strength. 力量 [FORMAL] ❑ *The might of the army could prove a decisive factor.* 军队的力量最终可能成为一个决定性的因素。 **2** PHRASE If you do something **with all** your **might**, you do it using all your strength and energy. 竭尽全力地 ❑ *She swung the hammer at his head with all her might.* 她用尽全力抡起锤子砸向他的脑袋。

mightn't /maɪtᵊnt/ **Mightn't** is a spoken form of "might not." **might not**的口语形式

might've /maɪtəv/ **Might've** is the usual spoken form of "might have," especially when "have" is an auxiliary verb. **might have**的口语形式

mighty /maɪti/ (**mightier, mightiest**) **1** ADJ **Mighty** is used to describe something that is very large or powerful. 强大的 [LITERARY] ❑ *There was a flash and a mighty bang.* 一道闪光伴随着一声轰然巨响。 **2** ADV **Mighty** is used in front of adjectives and adverbs to emphasize the quality that they are describing. 非常 [ADV adj/adv] [mainly AM, INFORMAL, EMPHASIS] ❑ *It's something you'll be mighty proud of.* 这是个你会非常骄傲的事。 **3** → see also **high-and-mighty**

mi·graine /maɪgreɪn/ (**migraines**) N-VAR A **migraine** is an extremely painful headache that makes you feel very ill. 偏头痛 ❑ *Her mother suffered from migraines.* 她母亲患了偏头痛。

Word Link *migr ≈ moving, changing : emigrant, immigrant, migrant*

★ **mi·grant** /maɪgrənt/ (**migrants**) **1** N-COUNT A **migrant** is a person who moves from one place to another, especially in order to find work. 移民 ❑ *The government divides asylum seekers into economic migrants and genuine refugees.* 政府将寻求政治庇护的人划分为经济移民和真正的难民。 **2** N-COUNT **Migrants** are birds, fish, or animals that migrate from one part of the world to another. 迁徙动物 ❑ *Migrant birds shelter in the reeds.* 候鸟隐蔽在芦苇丛中。

mi·grate /maɪgreɪt/ (**migrates, migrating, migrated**) **1** V-I If people **migrate**, they move from one place to another, especially in order to find work or to live somewhere for a short time. 迁移 ❑ *People migrate to cities like Jakarta in search of work.* 人们移居到雅加达这样的城市找工作。 ❑ *They have learned that they have to migrate if they want to survive.* 他们认识到如果他们想要生存只能移民。 ● **mi·gra·tion** /maɪgreɪʃᵊn/ N-VAR (**migrations**) 迁移 ❑ *...the migration of Soviet Jews to Israel.* …苏联犹太人向以色列的迁移。 **2** V-I When birds, fish, or animals **migrate**, they move at a particular season from one part of the world or from one part of a country to another, usually in order to breed or to find new feeding grounds. 迁徙 ❑ *Most birds have to fly long distances to migrate.* 大多数的鸟类不得不飞行很长的距离进行迁徙。 ● **mi·gra·tion** N-VAR 迁徙 ❑ *...the migration of animals in the Serengeti.* …塞伦盖蒂的动物迁徙。

mike /maɪk/ (**mikes**) N-COUNT A **mike** is the same as a **microphone**. 麦克风 [INFORMAL]

mil /mɪl/ NUM **Mil** means the same as **million**. 百万 [INFORMAL] ❑ *Zhamnov, 22, signed for $1.25 mil over three years.* 22岁的扎默诺夫签下了为期3年125万美元的合同。

mild ♦◇◇ /maɪld/ (**milder, mildest**) **1** ADJ **Mild** is used to describe something such as a feeling, attitude, or illness that is not very strong or severe. 轻微的 ❑ *Teddy turned to Mona with a look of mild confusion.* 特迪转向莫娜，脸上带着些许困惑。 ● **mild·ly** ADV 轻微地 ❑ *Josephine must have had the disease very mildly as she showed no symptoms.* 约瑟芬那时一定病得很轻，因为她没表现出什么症状。 **2** ADJ A **mild** person is gentle and does not get angry easily. 性情温和的 ❑ *He is a mild man, who is reasonable almost to the point of blandness.* 他是个性情温和、理智到了近乎呆板的人。 ● **mild·ly** ADV 温和地 [ADV after v] ❑ *"I'm not meddling," Ken said mildly, "I'm just curious."* "我不是在管闲事，"肯温和地说，"我只是好奇。" **3** ADJ **Mild** weather is pleasant because it is neither extremely hot nor extremely cold. 温暖的 ❑ *The area is famous for its very mild winter climate.* 这个地区以其非常温暖的冬季气候而闻名。

In informal English, if you want to emphasize how hot the weather is, you can say that it is **boiling** or **scorching**. In winter, if the temperature is above average, you can say that it is **mild**. In general, **hot** suggests a higher temperature than **warm**, and **warm** things are usually pleasant. ❑ *...a warm evening.*

4 ADJ You describe food as **mild** when it does not taste or smell strong, sharp, or bitter, especially when you like it because of this. 味淡的 ❑ *This cheese has a soft, mild flavor.* 这种奶酪有种柔和的、淡淡的味道。 **5** → see also **mildly**

Thesaurus *mild* 另参见:

ADJ. slight **1**
friendly, gentle, kind, warm **2**
comfortable, pleasant, warm; *(ant.)* harsh, severe **3**
weak; *(ant.)* spicy, strong **4**

mild·ly /maɪldli/ **1** → see **mild** **2** PHRASE You use **to put it mildly** to indicate that you are describing something in language that is much less strong, direct, or critical than what you really think. 说得委婉些 ❑ *But not all the money, to put it mildly, has been used wisely.* 但是说得委婉些，并不是所有的钱都用得很明智。

mile ♦♦◇ /maɪl/ (**miles**) **1** N-COUNT A **mile** is a unit of distance equal to 1760 yards or approximately 1.6 kilometers. 英里 ❑ *They drove 600 miles across the desert.* 他们驱车600英里横穿沙漠。 ❑ *She lives just half a mile away.* 她就住在半英里之外。 **2** N-PLURAL **Miles** is used, especially in the expression **miles away**, to refer to a long distance. 很远的距离 ❑ *If you enroll at a gym that's miles away, you won't be visiting it as often as you should.* 如果你加入的健身房离这儿很远的话，你就不会像应该地那样经常去了。 **3** N-COUNT **Miles** or **a mile** is used with the meaning "very much" in order to emphasize the difference between two things or qualities, or the difference between what you aimed to do and what you actually achieved. (相差) 远 [INFORMAL, EMPHASIS] ❑ *You're miles better than most of the performers we see nowadays.* 你比我们现今看到的大多数表演者们要好得多。 ❑ *With a Democratic candidate in place they won by a mile.* 随着一位民主党候选人的到位，他们轻松胜出。

Word Partnership *mile* 的常用搭配:

ADJ. mile **high**, mile **long**, **nautical** mile, **square** mile, mile **wide** **1**

▲ **mile·age** /maɪlɪdʒ/ **1** N-UNCOUNT **Mileage** refers to the distance that you have traveled, measured in miles. 英里里程 ❑ *While most of their mileage may be in and around town, they still want highways for longer trips.* 他们大多数的行程可能都在城里或城周围，可是他们仍然需要适合长距离旅行的高速公路。 **2** N-UNCOUNT The **mileage** of a vehicle is the number of miles that it can travel using one gallon or liter of fuel. (耗油1加仑或1升可行驶的) 英里里程 ❑ *They are willing to pay up to $500 more for cars that get better mileage.* 他们愿意多付$500来买单位汽油里程数更高的汽车。 **3** N-UNCOUNT The **mileage** in a particular course of action is its usefulness in getting you what you want. 好处 ❑ *It's obviously important to get as much mileage out of the convention as possible.* 从契约中得到尽可能多的好处显然很重要。

★ **mile·stone** /maɪlstoʊn/ (**milestones**) N-COUNT A **milestone** is an important event in the history or development of something or someone. 里程碑 ❑ *He said the launch of the party represented a milestone in Zambian history.* 他说该党的成立代表着赞比亚历史上的一个里程碑。

mi·lieu /mɪlyʊ, mil-/ (**milieux** or **milieus**) N-COUNT Your **milieu** is the group of people or activities that you live among or are familiar with. (社会) 环境 [FORMAL] ❑ *They stayed, safe and happy, within their own social milieu.* 他们呆在自己所属的社交圈里，安稳又愉快。

★ **mili·tant** ♦◇◇ /mɪlɪtənt/ (**militants**) ADJ You use **militant** to describe people who believe in something very strongly and are active in trying to bring about political or social change, often in extreme ways that other people find unacceptable. 激进的 ❑ *Militant mine workers in the Ukraine have voted for a one-day stoppage next month.* 在乌克兰，激进的煤矿工人们已经投票决定在下个月进行一天的罢工。 ● N-COUNT **Militant** is also a noun. 激进分子 ❑ *Even now we could not be sure that the militants would not find some new excuse to call a strike the following winter.* 即使到现在，我们也不能确定这些激进分子不会找到某个新的借口在下一年冬天号召一场罢工。 ● **mili·tan·cy** N-UNCOUNT 好战性 ❑ *...the rise of labor union militancy.* …工会好战情绪的高涨。

Word Link *milit ≈ soldier : demilitarize, military, militia*

mili·tary ♦♦♦ /mɪlɪteri/ (militaries) **1** ADJ **Military** means relating to the armed forces of a country. 军事的 ❑ *Military action may become necessary.* 军事行动可能会成为必要。 ❑ *The president is sending in almost 20,000 military personnel to help with the relief efforts.* 总统将派遣近20000名军事人员来协助救援行动。 ● **mili·tari·ly** /mɪltɛərɪli/ ADV 在军事上 ❑ *They remain unwilling to intervene militarily in what could be an unending war.* 他们仍然不愿意对一场可能无休止的战争进行军事干预。 **2** N-COUNT-COLL **The military** are the armed forces of a country, especially officers of high rank. 军方（尤指高级军官） ❑ *The bombing has been far more widespread than the military will admit.* 爆炸波及的范围远大于军方愿意承认的范围。 **3** ADJ **Military** means well organized, controlled, or neat, in a way that is typical of a soldier. 军人般的 ❑ *Your working day will need to be organized with military precision.* 你们的工作日需要以军人般的精确性来安排。
→ see **army**

★ **mi·li·tia** /mɪlɪʃə/ (militias) N-COUNT A **militia** is an organization that operates like an army but whose members are not professional soldiers. 民兵组织 ❑ *The troops will not attempt to disarm the warring militias.* 军队不会试图解除交战民兵组织的武装。
→ see **army**

milk ♦◊◊ /mɪlk/ (milks, milking, milked) **1** N-UNCOUNT **Milk** is the white liquid produced by cows, goats, and some other animals, which people drink and use to make butter, cheese, and yogurt. 奶 ❑ *He stepped out to buy a quart of milk.* 他出去买了一夸脱奶。 **2** V-T If someone **milks** a cow or goat, they get milk from it, using either their hands or a machine. 给…挤奶 ❑ *Farm workers milked cows by hand.* 农场工人们手工给奶牛挤奶。 **3** N-UNCOUNT **Milk** is the white liquid produced by women to feed their babies. 母乳 ❑ *Milk from the mother's breast is a perfect food for the human baby.* 母乳是婴儿的最佳食物。 **4** N-MASS Liquid products for cleaning your skin or making it softer are sometimes referred to as **milks**. 乳剂 ❑ *Sales of cleansing milks, creams, and gels have doubled over the past decade.* 在过去10年中，洁面乳、面霜以及发胶的销售已经增长了一倍。 **5** V-T If you say that someone **milks** something, you mean that they get as much benefit or profit as they can from it, without caring about the effects this has on other people. 榨取 [DISAPPROVAL] ❑ *A few people tried to milk the insurance companies.* 有些人试图榨取保险公司的钱。 **6** → see also **skim milk**
→ see **dairy**

★ **milky** /mɪlki/ (milkier, milkiest) **1** ADJ If you describe something as **milky**, you mean that it is pale white in color. You can describe other colors as **milky** when they are very pale. 乳白色的 ❑ *A milky mist filled the valley.* 乳白色的薄雾弥漫了山谷。 **2** ADJ Drinks or food that are **milky** contain a lot of milk. 加了牛奶的 ❑ *...his big cup of milky coffee.* …他那一大杯加了牛奶的咖啡。

mill ♦◊◊ /mɪl/ (mills, milling, milled) **1** N-COUNT A **mill** is a building in which grain is crushed to make flour. 磨坊 ❑ *There was an old mill that really did grind corn.* 有一个真正碾磨玉米的老磨坊。 **2** N-COUNT A **mill** is a small device used for grinding something such as coffee beans or pepper into powder. 碾磨器 ❑ *...a pepper mill.* …一个胡椒碾磨器。 **3** N-COUNT A **mill** is a factory used for making and processing materials such as steel, wool, or cotton. （加工钢材、羊毛、棉花等的）工厂 ❑ *...a steel mill.* …一家钢厂。 **4** V-T To **mill** something such as wheat or pepper means to grind it in a mill. 碾磨 ❑ *They do not have the capacity to mill the grain.* 它们没有碾磨谷物的功能。

▸ **mill around**

in BRIT, also use **mill about**

PHRASAL VERB When a crowd of people **mill around**, they move around within a particular place or area, so that the movement of the whole crowd looks very confused. 无目的地乱转 ❑ *Quite a few people were milling around, but nothing was happening.* 好些人在转来转去，但什么都没发生。

Word Link *enn ≈ year : centennial, millennium, perennial*

Word Link *mill ≈ thousand : millennium, million, millionaire*

mil·len·nium /mɪlɛniəm/ (millenniums or millennia) **1** N-COUNT A **millennium** is a period of one thousand years, especially one which begins and ends with a year ending in "000," for example the period from the year 1000 to the year 2000. 一千年 [FORMAL] ❑ *...the dawn of a new millennium.* …新千年的开始。 **2** N-SING Many people refer to the year 2000 as **the Millennium**. 2000年；千禧年 ❑ *...the eve of the Millennium.* …千禧年的前夜。

Word Link *milli ≈ thousandth : milligram, milliliter, millimeter*

mil·li·gram /mɪlɪgræm/ (milligrams)

in BRIT, also use **milligramme**

N-COUNT A **milligram** is a unit of weight that is equal to a thousandth of a gram. 毫克 ❑ *...0.5 milligrams of mercury.* …0.5毫克的汞。

mil·li·gramme /mɪlɪgræm/ [BRIT] → see **milligram**

mil·li·li·ter /mɪlɪlitər/ (milliliters)

in BRIT, use **millilitre**

N-COUNT A **milliliter** is a unit of volume for liquids and gases that is equal to a thousandth of a liter. 毫升 ❑ *...100 milliliters of blood.* …100毫升的血液。

mil·li·li·tre /mɪlɪliːtəʳ/ [BRIT] → see **milliliter**

mil·li·meter /mɪlɪmitər/ (millimeters)

in BRIT, use **millimetre**

N-COUNT A **millimeter** is a metric unit of length that is equal to a tenth of a centimeter or a thousandth of a meter. 毫米 ❑ *The creature is a tiny centipede, just 10 millimeters long.* 那个生物是一只很小的蜈蚣，只有10毫米长。

mil·li·metre /mɪlɪmiːtəʳ/ [BRIT] → see **millimeter**

mil·lion ♦♦♦ /mɪlyən/ (millions)

The plural form is **million** after a number, or after a word or expression referring to a number, such as "several" or "a few."

1 NUM A **million** or one **million** is the number 1,000,000. 百万 ❑ *Up to five million people a year visit the county.* 每年多达500万人到这个县游览。 **2** QUANT-PLURAL If you talk about **millions of** people or things, you mean that there is a very large number of them but you do not know or do not want to say exactly how many. 大量 [QUANT "of" pl-n] ❑ *The program was viewed on television in millions of homes.* 无数的家庭从电视上收看了这个节目。

mil·lion·aire /mɪlyənɛər/ (millionaires) N-COUNT A **millionaire** is a very rich person who has money or property worth at least a million dollars. 百万富翁 ❑ *By the time he died, he was a millionaire.* 到他去世的时候，他已是一位百万富翁。

mil·lionth ♦♦◊ /mɪlyənθ/ (millionths) **1** ORD The **millionth** item in a series is the one you count as number one million. 第一百万的 ❑ *Last year the millionth truck rolled off the assembly line.* 去年，第100万辆卡车驶下了装配线。 **2** FRACTION A **millionth of** something is one of a million equal parts of it. 百万分之一的 ❑ *The bomb must explode within less than a millionth of a second.* 那枚炸弹必须在百万分之一秒内爆炸。

Word Link *mim ≈ copying : mime, mimic, pantomime*

mime /maɪm/ (mimes, miming, mimed) **1** N-VAR **Mime** is the use of movements and gestures in order to express something or tell a story without using speech. 用手势语；哑剧表演 ❑ *Music, mime, and strong visual imagery play a strong part in the productions.* 音乐、哑剧动作以及强烈的视觉影像在这些作品中起重要作用。 **2** V-T/V-I If you **mime** something, you describe or express it using mime rather than speech. 用哑剧动作表现 ❑ *It featured a solo dance in which a woman mimed a lot of dainty housework.* 它展示了一段独舞，一位妇女在其中用哑剧动作表演了许多细致的家务活。 **3** V-T/V-I If you **mime**, you pretend to be singing or playing an instrument, although the music is in fact coming from a CD or cassette. 假唱；假装演奏 [BRIT]

in AM, use **lip-synch**

mim·ic /mɪmɪk/ (mimics, mimicking, mimicked) **1** V-T If you **mimic** the actions or voice of a person or animal, you imitate them, usually in a way that is meant to be amusing or entertaining. 模仿 ❑ *He could mimic anybody, and he often reduced Isabel to helpless laughter.* 他可以模仿任何人，而且经常逗得伊莎贝尔情不自禁地大笑。 **2** V-T If someone or something **mimics** another person or thing, they try to be like them. 模仿 ❑ *The computer doesn't mimic human thought; it reaches the same ends by different means.* 计算机模仿不了人类的思维；它通过不同的方式达到相同的目的。 **3** N-COUNT A **mimic** is a person who is able to mimic people or animals. 善于模仿的人 ❑ *At school I was a good mimic.* 上学时我是一个善于模仿的人。

min. **Min.** is a written abbreviation for **minimum**, or for **minutes** or **minute**. **minimum**、**minutes**或**minute**的缩写

M

mince /mɪns/ (**minces, mincing, minced**) 1 V-T If you **mince** food such as meat or vegetables, you cut or grind it up into very small pieces, usually in a machine. 铰碎 ❑ *Perhaps I'll buy lean meat and mince it myself.* 也许我会买来瘦肉然后自己把它铰碎。 2 N-UNCOUNT **Mince** is meat which has been cut or ground up into very small pieces using a machine. 肉末 [BRIT]

in AM, use **ground beef, hamburger meat**

→ see **cut**

mind
❶ NOUN USES
❷ VERB USES

❶ **mind** ♦♦♦ /maɪnd/ (**minds**)
➪ **Please look at meaning 39 to see if the expression you are looking for is shown under another headword.** 1 N-COUNT You refer to someone's **mind** when talking about their thoughts. For example, if you say that something is **in your mind**, you mean that you are thinking about it, and if you say that something is **at the back of your mind**, you mean that you are aware of it, although you are not thinking about it very much. 想法 ❑ *I'm trying to clear my mind of all this.* 我正试图把这一切都从我脑子里清理出去。 ❑ *There was no doubt in his mind that the man was serious.* 毫不怀疑在他的脑海里这个人是认真的。 2 N-COUNT Your **mind** is your ability to think and reason. 才智 ❑ *You have a good mind.* 你很有才智。 ❑ *Studying stretched my mind and got me thinking about things.* 学习扩展了我的才智，使我开始思考事情了。 3 N-COUNT If you have a particular type of **mind**, you have a particular way of thinking which is part of your character, or a result of your education or professional training. 思维方式 ❑ *Andrew, you have a very suspicious mind.* 安德鲁，你疑心太重了。 ❑ *The key to his success is his logical mind.* 他成功的关键在于他的逻辑思维。 4 N-COUNT You can refer to someone as a particular kind of **mind** as a way of saying that they are smart, intelligent, or imaginative. 有才智的人 ❑ *She moved to New York, meeting some of the best minds of her time.* 她搬到了纽约，遇到了她那个时代最具才智的一些人。 5 → see also **frame of mind, state of mind** 6 PHRASE If you tell someone to **bear** something **in mind** or to **keep** something **in mind**, you are reminding or warning them about something important which they should remember. 记住 ❑ *Bear in mind that gas stations are scarce in the more remote areas.* 记住，加油站在那些比较偏远的地区是很稀少的。 7 PHRASE If you **cast** your **mind back to** a time in the past, you think about what happened then. 回想起 ❑ *Cast your mind back to 1978, when Forest won the title.* 回想一下1978年，那时福里斯特赢得了这个头衔。 8 PHRASE If you **change** your **mind**, or if someone or something **changes** your **mind**, you change a decision you have made or an opinion that you had. 改变主意 ❑ *I was going to vote for him, but I changed my mind and voted for Reagan.* 我本打算投他的票，但后来改变了主意投了里根的票。 9 PHRASE If something **comes to mind** or **springs to mind**, you think of it without making any effort. 马上想到 ❑ *Integrity and honesty are words that spring to mind when talking of the man.* 谈到这个人时就会马上想到"正直"和"诚实"这两个词。 10 PHRASE If you say that an idea or possibility never **crossed** your **mind**, you mean that you did not think of it. 想到 ❑ *It had never crossed his mind that there might be a problem.* 他从来没想到过会有问题。 11 PHRASE If you see something **in** your **mind's eye**, you imagine it and have a clear picture of it in your mind. 在脑海中 ❑ *In his mind's eye, he can imagine the effect he's having.* 在他脑海中，他可以想像到自己正在产生的影响。 12 PHRASE If you say that you **have a good mind to** do something or **have half a mind to** do it, you are threatening or announcing that you have a strong desire to do it, although you probably will not do it. 非常想做 ❑ *He raged on about how he had a good mind to resign.* 他很恼火他怎么会那么想辞职。 13 PHRASE If you ask someone what they **have in mind**, you want to know in more detail about an idea or wish they have. 打算做某事 ❑ *"Maybe we could celebrate tonight."—"What did you have in mind?"* "或许我们今晚可以庆祝一下。"——"你有什么打算？" 14 PHRASE If you do something **with** a particular thing **in mind**, you do it with that thing as your aim or as the reason or basis for your action. 心中怀有某事 ❑ *These families need support. With this in mind a group of 35 specialists met last weekend.* 这些家庭需要资助。怀着这个想法，35人的专家组于上周末聚在了一起。 15 PHRASE If you say that something such as an illness is **all in the mind**, you mean that it relates to someone's feelings or attitude, rather than having any physical cause. 凭空想像 ❑ *It could be a virus, or it could be all in the mind.* 这可能是种病毒，或者可能全是凭空想像。 16 PHRASE If you **know** your **own mind**, you are sure about your opinions, and are not easily influenced by other people. 有主见 ❑ *She knows her own mind and won't let anyone talk her into something she doesn't want to do.* 她很有主见，不会听从任何人劝说去做自己不想做的事。 17 PHRASE If you say that someone **is losing** their **mind**, you mean that they are becoming mad. 失去理智 ❑ *Sometimes I feel like I'm losing my mind.* 有时我觉得自己好像要失去理智了。 18 PHRASE If you **make up** your **mind** or **make** your **mind up**, you decide which of a number of possible things you will have or do. 下定决心 ❑ *Once he made up his mind to do something, there was no stopping him.* 他一旦下定决心做什么事，没有什么可以阻止他。 19 PHRASE If a number of people are **of one mind, of like mind**, or **of the same mind**, they all agree about something. 意见一致 ❑ *Contact with other disabled yachtsmen of like mind would be helpful.* 联系一下其他具有同样想法的残疾帆船赛手是会有帮助的。 20 PHRASE If you say that something that happens is **a load off** your **mind** or **a weight off** your **mind**, you mean that it causes you to stop worrying, for example because it solves a problem that you had. 使不再忧虑 ❑ *Knowing that she had medical insurance took a great load off her mind.* 知道自己有医疗保险，她不再担心了。 21 PHRASE If something is **on** your **mind**, you are worried or concerned about it and think about it a lot. 惦记着 ❑ *This game has been on my mind all week.* 整整一周我一直惦记着这场比赛。 22 PHRASE If your **mind is on** something or you **have** your **mind on** something, you are thinking about that thing. 专心于某事 ❑ *At school I was always in trouble – my mind was never on my work.* 上学时我一直麻烦不断——总也无法专注于我的功课。 23 PHRASE If you have **an open mind**, you avoid forming an opinion or making a decision until you know all the facts. 开放的心态 ❑ *It's hard to see it any other way, though I'm trying to keep an open mind.* 尽管我试图保持开放的心态，可是很难换个角度去看这件事。 24 PHRASE If something **opens** your **mind to** new ideas or experiences, it makes you more willing to accept them or try them. 使愿意尝试；使愿意接受 ❑ *She also stimulated his curiosity and opened his mind to other cultures.* 她还激发了他的好奇心，使他愿意接受其他文化。 25 PHRASE If you say that someone is **out of their mind**, you mean that they are mad or very foolish. 发疯 [INFORMAL, DISAPPROVAL] ❑ *What are you doing? Are you out of your mind?* 你在干什么？你疯了吗？ 26 PHRASE If you say that someone is **out of their mind with** a feeling such as worry or fear, you are emphasizing that they are extremely worried or afraid. 极度(焦虑、害怕等) [INFORMAL, EMPHASIS] ❑ *I was out of my mind with fear. I didn't know what to do.* 我害怕极了。我不知道该怎么办。 27 PHRASE If you say that someone is, for example, **bored out of** their **mind, scared out of** their **mind**, or **stoned out of** their **mind**, you are emphasizing that they are extremely bored, scared, or affected by drugs. 感到非常无聊、害怕或受毒品的影响 [INFORMAL, EMPHASIS] ❑ *That was one of the most depressing experiences of my life. I was bored out of my mind after five minutes.* 那是我一生中最沮丧的经历之一。5分钟后我就觉得无聊透顶了。 28 PHRASE If you **put** your **mind to** something, you start making an effort to do it. 专心做某事 ❑ *You could do fine in the world if you put your mind to it.* 在这个世界上，只要你认真做事，就能做好。 29 PHRASE If you can **read** someone's **mind**, you know what they are thinking without them saying anything. 看出某人的心思 ❑ *Don't expect others to read your mind.* 不要期望别人能看出你的心思。 30 PHRASE To **put** someone's **mind at rest** or **set** their **mind at rest** means to stop them from worrying about something. 使某人安心 ❑ *It may be advisable to have a blood test to put your mind at rest.* 验一下血让你自己安心也许是明智的。 31 PHRASE If you say that nobody **in** their **right mind** would do a particular thing, you are emphasizing that it is an irrational thing to do and you would be surprised if anyone did it. 神智正常(不会做某事) [EMPHASIS] ❑ *No one in her right mind would make such a major purchase without asking questions.* 没有一个神智正常的女人会不问问题就买这么一个大件。 32 PHRASE If you **set** your **mind on** something or **have** your **mind set on** it, you are determined to do it or obtain it. 决心做某事 ❑ *When my wife sets her mind on something, she invariably finds a way to achieve it.* 当我妻子下定决心做什么事情，她总会找到办法做到。 33 PHRASE If something **slips** your **mind**, you forget it. 忘记 ❑ *I was going to mention it, but it slipped my mind.* 我正要说到它，可是想不起来了。 34 PHRASE If you **speak** your **mind**, you say firmly and honestly what you think about a situation, even if this may offend or upset people. 说出心中所想 ❑ *Martina Navratilova has never been afraid to speak her mind.* 马丁娜·纳夫拉蒂洛娃从来不怕说出自己心中的想法。 35 PHRASE If something **sticks in** your **mind**, it remains

m

firmly in your memory. 被铭记于心 ❑ *I've always been fond of poetry and one piece has always stuck in my mind.* 我一直喜欢诗歌，有一首诗一直被我铭记于心。 36 PHRASE If something **takes** your **mind off** a problem or unpleasant situation, it helps you to forget about it for a while. 转移注意力 ❑ *"How about a game of tennis?" suggested Alan. "That'll take your mind off things."* "打一场网球怎么样？"艾伦建议道，"那会转移一下你的注意力。" 37 PHRASE You say or write **to my mind** to indicate that the statement you are making is your own opinion. 依我看 ❑ *There are scenes in this play which, to my mind, are incredibly violent.* 这部戏中的一些场面依我看太过暴力了。 38 PHRASE If you are **of two minds**, you are uncertain about what to do, especially when you have to choose between two courses of action. 犹豫不决 ❑ *He was of two minds about this plan.* 他对于这个计划犹豫不决。 39 to **give** someone **a piece of** your **mind** → see **piece**

❷ **mind** ♦◇◇ /maɪnd/ (**minds, minding, minded**) 1 V-T/V-I If you do not **mind** something, you are not annoyed or bothered by it. 介意 [usu with brd-neg] ❑ *I don't mind the noise during the day.* 白天我不介意这种噪声。 ❑ *I hope you don't mind me stopping in like this, without an appointment.* 我希望你别介意我这样冒昧拜访，都没有事先约定。 ❑ *I lit a cigarette and nobody seemed to mind.* 我点了一支烟，好像并没有人介意。 2 V-T/V-I You use **mind** in the expressions "**do you mind?**" and "**would you mind?**" as a polite way of asking permission or asking someone to do something. 介意(表示礼貌地征询许可或提出请求) [POLITENESS] ❑ *Do you mind if I ask you one more thing?* 您介意我再提一个问题吗？ ❑ *Would you mind waiting outside for a moment?* 您介意在外面等一会儿吗？ 3 V-T If someone does not **mind** what happens or what something is like, they do not have a strong preference for any particular thing. 介意(用于否定句中表达"…均可"之意) [with brd-neg] ❑ *I don't mind what we play, really.* 我不介意咱们玩什么，真的。 4 V-T If you **mind** a child or something such as a store or luggage, you take care of it, usually while the person who owns it or is usually responsible for it is somewhere else. 照看 ❑ *Jim Coulters will mind the store while I'm away.* 我不在时，吉姆・库尔特斯会照看商店。 5 PHRASE People use the expression **if you don't mind** when they are rejecting an offer or saying that they do not want to do something, especially when they are annoyed. 如果你不介意(用于委婉地拒绝别人的提议和建议) [FEELINGS] ❑ *"Sit down."—"I prefer standing for a while, if you don't mind."* "坐吧。"——"如果你不介意，我想站一会儿。" 6 PHRASE You use **mind you** to emphasize a piece of information that you are adding, especially when the new information explains what you have said or contrasts with it. Some people use **mind** in a similar way. 记住；务必 [EMPHASIS] ❑ *They pay full rates. Mind you, they can afford it.* 他们是全额支付的。记住，他们能付得起。 7 CONVENTION You say **never mind** when you are emphasizing that something is not serious or important, especially when someone is upset about it or is saying they are sorry. 没什么 [EMPHASIS] ❑ *Her voice trembled. "Oh, Sylvia, I'm so sorry."—"Never mind."* 她的声音颤抖着。"哎呀，西尔维娅，我真抱歉。"——"没什么。" 8 PHRASE You use **never mind** to tell someone that they need not do something or worry about something, because it is not important or because you will do it yourself. 别担心 ❑ *"Was his name David?"—"No I don't think it was, but never mind, go on."* "他的名字是大卫吗？"——"不，我想不是，不过没关系，继续。" ❑ *Dorothy, come on. Never mind your shoes. They'll soon dry off.* 多萝西，快点。别担心你的鞋。它们很快就会干的。 9 PHRASE You use **never mind** after a statement, often a negative one, to indicate that the statement is even more true of the person, thing, or situation that you are going to mention next. 更不用说 [EMPHASIS] ❑ *I'm not going to believe it myself, never mind convince anyone else.* 我自己都不会相信它，更不用说说服其他人了。 10 PHRASE If you say that you **wouldn't mind** something, you mean that you would quite like it. 很喜欢；很愿意 ❑ *I wouldn't mind a coffee.* 我很想喝杯咖啡。 11 V-T If you tell someone to **mind** something, you are warning them to be careful not to hurt themselves or other people, or damage something. 当心 [mainly BRIT]

in AM, usually use **watch**

12 V-T You use **mind** when you are reminding someone to do something or telling them to be careful not to do something. 注意 [mainly BRIT]

in AM, usually use **make sure, take care**

mind·ful /maɪndfəl/ ADJ If you are **mindful of** something, you think about it and consider it when taking action. 留意的 [v-link ADJ] [FORMAL] ❑ *We must be mindful of the consequences of selfishness.* 我们一定要留意自私自利的后果。

mind·less /maɪndlɪs/ 1 ADJ If you describe a violent action as **mindless**, you mean that it is done without thought and will achieve nothing. 盲目的 [DISAPPROVAL] ❑ *...a plot that mixes blackmail, extortion and mindless violence.* …一个混合了敲诈、勒索和盲目暴力的阴谋。 2 ADJ If you describe a person or group as **mindless**, you mean that they are stupid or do not think about what they are doing. 没头脑的 [DISAPPROVAL] ❑ *She wasn't at all the mindless little wife so many people perceived her to be.* 她可不是那么多人所以为的没头脑的小媳妇。 ● **mind·less·ly** ADV 没头脑地 [ADV with v] ❑ *I was annoyed with myself for having so quickly and mindlessly lost thirty dollars.* 那么快愚蠢地丢了30美元，我很生自己的气。 3 ADJ If you describe an activity as **mindless**, you mean that it is so dull that people do it or take part in it without thinking. 单调乏味的 [DISAPPROVAL] ❑ *...the mindless repetitiveness of some tasks.* …一些任务的单调重复。 ● **mind·less·ly** ADV 单调乏味地 [ADV with v] ❑ *I spent many hours mindlessly banging a tennis ball against the wall.* 我花了好多个小时单调地对着墙打网球。

mine
❶ PRONOUN USE
❷ NOUN AND VERB USES

❶ **mine** ♦♦♦ /maɪn/ PRON-POSS **Mine** is the first person singular possessive pronoun. A speaker or writer uses **mine** to refer to something that belongs or relates to himself or herself. 我的 ❑ *Her right hand is inches from mine.* 她的右手离我的几英寸远。 ❑ *That wasn't his fault, it was mine.* 那不是他的错，是我的。

❷ **mine** /maɪn/ (**mines, mining, mined**) 1 N-COUNT A **mine** is a place where deep holes and tunnels are dug under the ground in order to obtain a mineral such as coal, diamonds, or gold. 矿 ❑ *...coal mines.* …煤矿。 2 V-T When a mineral such as coal, diamonds, or gold **is mined**, it is obtained from the ground by digging deep holes and tunnels. 采掘 [usu passive] ❑ *The pit is being shut down because it no longer has enough coal that can be mined economically.* 那个煤矿要关闭了，因为储量不足，难以经济开采。 3 N-COUNT A **mine** is a bomb which is hidden in the ground or in water and which explodes when people or things touch it. 地雷；水雷 4 V-T If an area of land or water **is mined**, mines are placed there which will explode when people or things touch them. 布雷 ❑ *The approaches to the garrison have been heavily mined.* 进入驻地的几条通道都已布满了雷。 5 → see also **mining**
→ see **diamond**

mine·field /maɪnfild/ (**minefields**) 1 N-COUNT A **minefield** is an area of land or water where explosive mines have been hidden. 地雷区；水雷区 2 N-COUNT If you describe a situation as a **minefield**, you are emphasizing that there are a lot of hidden dangers or problems, and people need to behave with care because things could easily go wrong. 充满隐伏危险的事物 [EMPHASIS] ❑ *The whole subject is a political minefield.* 整个话题成了一个政治雷区。

min·er ♦◇◇ /maɪnər/ (**miners**) N-COUNT A **miner** is a person who works underground in mines in order to obtain minerals such as coal, diamonds, or gold. 矿工

min·er·al /mɪnərəl/ (**minerals**) N-COUNT A **mineral** is a substance such as tin, salt, or sulfur that is formed naturally in rocks and in the earth. Minerals are also found in small quantities in food and drink. 矿物
→ see Word Web: **mineral**
→ see **diamond, rock**

min·er·al wa·ter (**mineral waters**) N-MASS **Mineral water** is water that comes out of the ground naturally and is considered healthy to drink. 矿泉水

★ **min·gle** /mɪŋgəl/ (**mingles, mingling, mingled**) 1 V-RECIP If things such as sounds, smells, or feelings **mingle**, they become mixed together but are usually still recognizable. 混合 ❑ *Now the cheers and applause mingled in a single sustained roar.* 这时欢呼声和掌声汇聚成了一阵经久不息的轰响。 2 V-RECIP At a party, if you **mingle with** the other people there, you move around and talk to them. 交际 ❑ *Go out of your way to mingle with others at the wedding.* 在婚礼上你要主动地和别人交际。 ❑ *Guests ate and mingled.* 客人们边吃边交谈。

Word Link *mini ≈ very small : miniature, minibar, minibus*

★ **minia·ture** /mɪniətʃər, -tʃʊər/ (**miniatures**) 1 ADJ **Miniature** is used to describe something that is very small, especially a

Word Web mineral

The **extraction** of **minerals** from ore is an ancient process. Neolithic man discovered **copper** around 8000 BC. Using fire and charcoal, they **reduced** the ore to its pure **metal** form. About 4,000 years later, Egyptians learned to pour molten copper into molds and metallurgy was born. **Silver** ore often contains large amounts of copper and **lead**. Silver **refineries** often use the smelting process to remove these impurities. Most **gold** does not exist as an ore. Instead, veins of gold run through the earth. Refiners use solvents such as cyanide to obtain pure gold.

smaller version of something which is normally much bigger. 微型的 [ADJ n] ❑ *Rosehill Farm has been selling miniature roses since 1979.* 自1979年起，玫瑰山农场就一直出售袖珍玫瑰。 **2** PHRASE If you describe one thing as another thing **in miniature**, you mean that it is much smaller in size or scale than the other thing, but is otherwise exactly the same. 缩影 ❑ *Ecuador provides a perfect introduction to South America; it's a continent in miniature.* 厄瓜多尔是南美的一个绝佳概览：它是整个大陆的缩影。 **3** N-COUNT A **miniature** is a very small, detailed painting, often of a person. 袖珍画像

mini·bar /mɪnibɑr/ (**minibars**) N-COUNT In a hotel room, a **minibar** is a small refrigerator containing alcoholic drinks. 迷你吧（指宾馆里放有酒类饮料的小冰箱）

★ **mini·bus** /mɪnibʌs/ (**minibuses**) also **mini-bus** N-COUNT A **minibus** is a large van which has seats in the back for passengers, and windows along its sides. 小型公共汽车 [also "by" N] ❑ *He was then taken by minibus to the military base.* 接着他被小型公共汽车带到了军事基地。

mini·disc /mɪnidɪsk/ (**minidiscs**) N-COUNT A **minidisc** is a small compact disc which you can record music or data on. 微型碟片 [TRADEMARK]

mini·dish /mɪnidɪʃ/ (**minidishes**) N-COUNT A **minidish** is a small satellite dish that can receive signals from communications satellites for media such as television programs and the Internet. 微型卫星电视接收天线

Word Link *minim ≈ smallest : minimal, minimize, minimum*

★ **mini·mal** /mɪnɪməl/ ADJ Something that is **minimal** is very small in quantity, value, or degree. 尽可能少的；最低限度的 ❑ *The cooperation between the two is minimal.* 两者之间的合作是最低程度的。

mini·mal·ism /mɪnɪməlɪzəm/ N-UNCOUNT **Minimalism** is a style in which a small number of very simple things are used to create a particular effect. 简约风格 ❑ *In her own home, she replaced austere minimalism with cosy warmth and color.* 她在自己家中用舒适温暖和色彩变化取代了极度的简约。

mini·mal·ist /mɪnɪməlɪst/ (**minimalists**) **1** N-COUNT A **minimalist** is an artist or designer who uses minimalism. 极简抽象派艺术家 ❑ *He was influenced by the minimalists in the 1970s.* 他受到了20世纪70年代那些极简抽象派艺术家们的影响。 **2** ADJ **Minimalist** is used to describe ideas, artists, or designers that are influenced by minimalism. 极简抽象派艺术家的 ❑ *The two designers settled upon a minimalist approach.* 这两位设计师决定采用极简抽象派艺术家的方法。

★ **mini·mise** /mɪnɪmaɪz/ [BRIT] → see **minimize**

★ **mini·mize** /mɪnɪmaɪz/ (**minimizes, minimizing, minimized**)

in BRIT, also use **minimise**

1 V-T If you **minimize** a risk, problem, or unpleasant situation, you reduce it to the lowest possible level, or prevent it from increasing beyond that level. 减到最低数量；降到最低程度 ❑ *Concerned people want to minimize the risk of developing cancer.* 忧心忡忡的人们想把患上癌症的风险降到最低。 **2** V-T If you **minimize** something, you make it seem smaller or less significant than it really is. 贬低…的重要性 ❑ *Some have minimized the importance of ideological factors.* 一些人已经贬低了意识形态因素的重要性。 **3** V-T If you **minimize** a window on a computer screen, you make it very small, because you do not want to use it. 使最小化 ❑ *Click the square icon again to minimize the window.* 再次点击正方形图标使那个窗口最小化。

mini·mum ♦◊◊ /mɪnɪməm/ **1** ADJ You use **minimum** to describe an amount which is the smallest that is possible, allowed, or required. 最小量的；最低限度的 [ADJ n] ❑ *He was only five feet nine, the minimum height for a policeman.* 他只有5.9英尺高，这是警察身高要求的底线。 ● N-SING **Minimum** is also a noun. 最小量；最低限度 ❑ *This will take a minimum of one hour.* 这最少要用一个小时。 **2** ADJ You use **minimum** to state how small an amount is. 很小的 [ADJ n] ❑ *The basic needs of life are available with minimum effort.* 生活的基本需求花很小的力气就能得到。 ● N-SING **Minimum** is also a noun. 很小量 ❑ *With a minimum of fuss, she produced the grandson he had so desperately wished for.* 她不声不响地生出了他翘首以待的孙子。 **3** ADV If you say that something is a particular amount **minimum**, you mean that this is the smallest amount it should be or could possibly be, although a larger amount is acceptable or very possible. 至少 [amount ADV] ❑ *You're talking over a thousand dollars minimum for one course.* 你们在讨论一门课程至少一千美元。

Word Partnership *minimum* 的常用搭配:

N. minimum **age**, minimum **balance**, minimum **payment**, minimum **purchase**, minimum **requirement**, minimum **salary** **1**

ADJ. **absolute** minimum, **bare** minimum **1** **2**

mini·mum wage N-SING **The minimum wage** is the lowest wage that an employer is allowed to pay an employee, according to a law or agreement. 最低工资 ❑ *Some of them earn below the minimum wage.* 他们中的一些人挣的钱低于最低工资。

→ see **factory**

min·ing /maɪnɪŋ/ N-UNCOUNT **Mining** is the industry and activities connected with getting valuable or useful minerals from the ground, for example coal, diamonds, or gold. 矿业 ❑ *...traditional industries such as coal mining and steel making.* …像采煤和炼钢这样的传统工业。

→ see **industry, tunnel**

min·is·ter ♦♦♦ /mɪnɪstər/ (**ministers**) **1** N-COUNT A **minister** is a member of the clergy, especially in Protestant churches. 牧师 ❑ *His father was a Baptist minister.* 他父亲是一名浸礼会牧师。 **2** N-COUNT A **minister** is a person who officially represents their government in a foreign country and has a lower rank than an ambassador. 公使 ❑ *He concluded a deal with the Danish minister in Washington.* 他在华盛顿与丹麦公使达成了一项协议。 **3** N-COUNT In some countries outside the United States, a **minister** is a person who is in charge of a particular government department. 政府部门部长 ❑ *When the government came to power, he was named minister of culture.* 这届政府上台时，他被任命为了文化部长。

★ **min·is·terial** /mɪnɪstɪəriəl/ ADJ You use **ministerial** to refer to people, events, or jobs that are connected with government ministers. 部长的 [ADJ n] ❑ *The prime minister's initial ministerial appointments haven't pleased all his supporters.* 这位首相最初的部长任命没有令他所有的支持者都满意。

min·is·try ♦♦◊ /mɪnɪstri/ (**ministries**) N-COUNT In many countries, a **ministry** is a government department which deals with a particular thing or area of activity, for example trade, defense, or transportation. （政府的）部 ❑ *...the Ministry of Justice.* …司法部。

mink /mɪŋk/ (**minks**)

Mink can also be used as the plural form.

1 N-COUNT A **mink** is a small animal with highly valued fur. 貂 ❑ *...a proposal for a ban on the hunting of foxes, mink, and hares.* …一项禁止猎杀狐狸、貂和野兔的提案。 ● N-UNCOUNT **Mink** is the fur of a mink. 貂皮 ❑ *...a mink coat.* …一件貂皮大衣。 **2** N-COUNT A **mink** is a coat or other garment made from the fur of a mink. 貂皮外衣 ❑ *Some people like to dress up in minks and diamonds.* 有些人喜欢穿貂皮、戴钻石。

m

mi·nor ♦◇◇ /maɪnər/ (**minors**) 1 ADJ You use **minor** when you want to describe something that is less important, serious, or significant than other things in a group or situation. 次要的 ❑ *She is known in Italy for a number of minor roles in films.* 她因担任电影中一些配角而闻名意大利。2 ADJ A **minor** illness or operation is not likely to be dangerous to someone's life or health. 不严重的 ❑ *Sarah had been plagued continually by a series of minor illnesses since her mid teens.* 自从十四五岁起萨拉就一直小病不断。3 N-COUNT A **minor** is a person who is still legally a child. In most states in the United States, people are minors until they reach the age of eighteen. 未成年者 ❑ *The approach has virtually ended cigarette sales to minors.* 这一作法实际上已经终止了向未成年人出售香烟。4 ADJ A **minor** scale is one in which the third note is three semitones higher than the first. 小调的 ❑ *...the unfinished sonata movement in F minor.* …未完成的F小调奏鸣曲乐章。

Thesaurus *minor* 另参见：
ADJ. insignificant, lesser, small, unimportant; (*ant.*) important, major, significant 1

Word Partnership *minor* 的常用搭配：
N. minor **adjustment**, minor **damage**, minor **detail**, minor **problem** 1
minor **illness**, minor **injury**, minor **operation**, minor **surgery** 2
ADV. **relatively** minor 1 2

mi·nor·ity ♦♦◇ /mɪnɔrɪti, maɪ-/ (**minorities**) 1 N-SING If you talk about a **minority** of people or things in a larger group, you are referring to a number of them that forms less than half of the larger group, usually much less than half. 少数 ❑ *Local authority child-care provision covers only a tiny minority of working mothers.* 地方政府提供的儿童保育服务只惠及了极少数上班族母亲们。● PHRASE If people are **in a minority** or **in the minority**, they belong to a group of people or things that form less than half of a larger group. 占少数 ❑ *Even in the 1960s, politically active students and academics were in a minority.* 即使是在20世纪60年代，政治上活跃的学生和高校教师也是占少数。2 N-COUNT A **minority** is a group of people of the same race, culture, or religion who live in a place where most of the people around them are of a different race, culture, or religion. 少数民族；信仰其他宗教的少数派 ❑ *...the region's ethnic minorities.* …这个地区的少数民族。

Word Partnership *minority* 的常用搭配：
N. minority **leader**, minority **party** 1
minority **applicants**, minority **community**, minority **group**, minority **population**, minority **students**, minority **voters**, minority **women** 2

★ **mint** /mɪnt/ (**mints, minting, minted**) 1 N-UNCOUNT **Mint** is an herb with fresh-tasting leaves. 薄荷 ❑ *Garnish with mint sprigs.* 以薄荷枝装饰。2 N-COUNT A **mint** is a candy with a peppermint flavor. Some people suck mints in order to make their breath smell fresher. 薄荷糖 ❑ *She popped a mint into her mouth.* 她往嘴里丢了块儿薄荷糖。3 N-COUNT **The mint** is the place where the official coins of a country are made. 造币厂 ❑ *In 1965 the mint stopped putting silver in dimes.* 1965年，造币厂停止在10美分铸币中加入银。4 V-T To **mint** coins or medals means to make them in a mint. 铸造 ❑ *...the right to mint coins.* …铸造硬币权。
→ see **money**

Word Link *min* ≈ *small, lessen : diminish, minus, minute*

mi·nus /maɪnəs/ (**minuses**) 1 CONJ You use **minus** to show that one number or quantity is being subtracted from another. 减 ❑ *One minus one is zero.* 一减一等于零。2 ADJ **Minus** before a number or quantity means that the number or quantity is less than zero. 负的 [ADJ amount] ❑ *The aircraft was subjected to temperatures of minus 65 degrees and plus 120 degrees.* 该飞机经受了零下65度和零上120度的温度。3 ADJ Teachers use **minus** in grading work in schools and colleges. "B minus" is not as good as "B," but is a better grade than "C." 略低的 ❑ *I'm giving him a B minus.* 我打算给他一个B–。4 PREP To be **minus** something means not to have that thing. 失去 ❑ *The film company collapsed, leaving Chris jobless and minus his life savings.* 这家电影公司垮了，使克里斯失业了，同时也失去了他的生活积蓄。5 N-COUNT A **minus** is a disadvantage. 不利因素 [INFORMAL] ❑ *The minuses far outweigh that possible gain.* 不利因素远远超过了那可能获得的收益。

Thesaurus *minus* 另参见：
PREP. without 4
N. deficiency, disadvantage, drawback 5

Word Link *cule* ≈ *small : minuscule, molecule, ridicule*

mi·nus·cule /mɪnɪskyul/ ADJ If you describe something as **minuscule**, you mean that it is very small. 极小的 ❑ *The film was shot in 17 days, a minuscule amount of time.* 这部电影用了短短的17天就拍摄完成了。

minute
❶ NOUN AND VERB USES
❷ ADJECTIVE USE

❶ **mi·nute** ♦♦♦ /mɪnɪt/ (**minutes, minuting, minuted**) 1 N-COUNT A **minute** is one of the sixty parts that an hour is divided into. People often say "**a minute**" or "**minutes**" when they mean a short length of time. 分钟；片刻 ❑ *The pizza will then take about twenty minutes to cook.* 接下来，比萨饼大约要用20分钟烤好。❑ *Bye Mom, see you in a minute.* 再见，妈妈，一会儿见。2 N-PLURAL The **minutes** of a meeting are the written records of the things that are discussed or decided at it. 会议记录 ❑ *He'd been reading the minutes of the last meeting.* 他一直在看上次会议的记录。3 V-T When someone **minutes** something that is discussed or decided at a meeting, they make a written record of it. 做会议记录 ❑ *You don't need to minute that.* 你不必记录那些。4 CONVENTION People often use expressions such as **wait a minute** or **just a minute** when they want to stop you doing or saying something. 等一下 ❑ *Wait a minute, folks, something is wrong here.* 等一下，伙计们，这地方不对劲。5 PHRASE If you say that something will or may happen **at any minute** or **any minute now**, you are emphasizing that it is likely to happen very soon. 随时 [EMPHASIS] ❑ *It looked as though it might rain at any minute.* 看起来随时都有可能下雨。6 PHRASE A **last-minute** action is one that is done at the latest time possible. 最后一刻 ❑ *He will probably wait until the last minute.* 他可能会等到最后一刻。7 PHRASE If you say that something happens **the minute** something else happens, you are emphasizing that it happens immediately after the other thing. 一…就… [EMPHASIS] ❑ *The minute you do this, you'll lose control.* 你一干这个，就会失去控制。

❷ **mi·nute** /maɪnut/ (**minutest**) ADJ If you say that something is **minute**, you mean that it is very small. 非常小的 ❑ *Only a minute amount is needed.* 只需很少的一点。

Word Partnership *minute* 的常用搭配：
V. **take** a minute ❶ 1
wait a minute ❶ 4
DET. **a** minute **or two**, **another** minute, **each** minute, **every** minute, **half a** minute ❶ 1
any minute **now**, **at any** minute ❶ 5
N. minute **detail**, minute **quantity of** *something* ❷

mira·cle /mɪrəkᵊl/ (**miracles**) 1 N-COUNT If you say that a good event is a **miracle**, you mean that it is very surprising and unexpected. 奇迹 ❑ *It is a miracle no one was killed.* 没有人死亡真是个奇迹。2 ADJ A **miracle** drug or product does something that was thought almost impossible. 神奇的 [ADJ n] [JOURNALISM] ❑ *...the miracle drugs that keep his 94-year-old mother healthy.* …使他那94岁高龄的老母亲保持健康的神奇药物。3 N-COUNT A **miracle** is a wonderful and surprising event that is believed to be caused by God. 上帝创造的奇迹 ❑ *...Jesus's ability to perform miracles.* …耶稣行神的能力。

▲ **mi·racu·lous** /mɪrækyələs/ 1 ADJ If you describe a good event as **miraculous**, you mean that it is very surprising and unexpected. 奇迹般的 ❑ *The horse made a miraculous recovery to finish a close third.* 这匹马奇迹般地缓过劲来，最终以微弱的差距获得了第三名。● **mi·racu·lous·ly** ADV 神奇地 ❑ *Miraculously, the guards escaped death or serious injury.* 警卫们奇迹般地逃脱了伤亡。2 ADJ If someone describes a wonderful event as **miraculous**, they believe that the event was caused by God. 超自然的 ❑ *...miraculous healing.* …奇迹般的治愈。

mir·ror ♦◇◇ /mɪrər/ (**mirrors, mirroring, mirrored**) 1 N-COUNT A **mirror** is a flat piece of glass which reflects light, so that when you look at it you can see yourself reflected in it. 镜子 ❑ *He went into the bathroom absent-mindedly and looked at himself in the mirror.* 他心不在焉地走进了浴室，照着镜子看了看自己。 **2** V-T If something **mirrors** something else, it has similar features to it, and therefore seems like a copy or representation of it. 反映 ❑ *Despite the fact that I have tried to be objective, the book inevitably mirrors my own interests and experiences.* 尽管我曾努力做到客观，但这本书还是不可避免地反映出了我自己的兴趣和经历。 **3** V-T If you see something reflected in water, you can say that the water **mirrors** it. (水) 映出 [LITERARY] ❑ *...the sudden glitter where a newly flooded field mirrors the sky.* …那突然的闪光，使新近被水淹没的田地映出了天空。

→ see **telescope**

Word Partnership *mirror* 的常用搭配：

V.	**glance in a** mirror, **look in a** mirror, **reflect in a** mirror, **see in a** mirror **1**
PREP.	**in front of a** mirror **1**
N.	**reflection in a** mirror **1**

mis·be·have /mɪsbɪheɪv/ (**misbehaves, misbehaving, misbehaved**) V-I If someone, especially a child, **misbehaves**, they behave in a way that is not acceptable to other people. 行为不当 ❑ *When the children misbehaved she was unable to cope.* 当孩子们捣乱时，她无能为力。

mis·cal·cu·late /mɪskælkyəleɪt/ (**miscalculates, miscalculating, miscalculated**) V-T/V-I If you **miscalculate**, you make a mistake in judging a situation or in making a calculation. 错误判断 ❑ *It's clear that he has badly miscalculated the mood of the people.* 显而易见，他严重地判断错了人们的情绪。 ● **mis·cal·cu·la·tion** /mɪskælkyəleɪʃən/ N-VAR (**miscalculations**) 判断错误 ❑ *The coup failed because of miscalculations by the plotters.* 因为策划者判断失误，那场政变失败了。

mis·car·riage /mɪskærɪdʒ, -kær-/ (**miscarriages**) N-VAR If a pregnant woman has a **miscarriage**, her baby dies and she gives birth to it before it is properly formed. 小产 ❑ *No one had any idea she had had a miscarriage.* 没有一个人会想到她曾经历过一次小产。

mis·cel·la·neous /mɪsəleɪniəs/ ADJ A **miscellaneous** group consists of many different kinds of things or people that are difficult to put into a particular category. 各式各样的 [ADJ n] ❑ *...a hoard of miscellaneous junk.* …五花八门的废旧物品的贮藏库。

▲ **mis·chief** /mɪstʃɪf/ **1** N-UNCOUNT **Mischief** is playing harmless tricks on people or doing things you are not supposed to do. It can also refer to the desire to do this. 恶作剧；捣乱 ❑ *The little boy was a real handful. He was always up to mischief.* 这个小男孩真是难管教。他总是在搞恶作剧。 **2** N-UNCOUNT **Mischief** is behavior that is intended to cause trouble for people. It can also refer to the trouble that is caused. 制造麻烦 ❑ *The more sinister explanation is that he is about to make mischief in the Middle East again.* 更为险恶的解释是他又要在中东制造事端。

mis·chie·vous /mɪstʃɪvəs/ **1** ADJ A **mischievous** person likes to have fun by playing harmless tricks on people or doing things they are not supposed to do. 调皮的 ❑ *She rocks back and forth on her chair like a mischievous child.* 她在椅子上前后晃动，像个调皮的孩子。 ● **mis·chie·vous·ly** ADV 调皮地 ❑ *Kathryn winked mischievously.* 凯瑟琳调皮地眨了眨眼。 **2** ADJ A **mischievous** act or suggestion is intended to cause trouble. 恶意的 ❑ *"I have a few mischievous plans," says Zevon.* "我有几个鬼点子。"泽冯说。 ● **mis·chie·vous·ly** ADV 恶意地 ❑ *That does not require "massive" military intervention, as some have mischievously claimed.* 那不需要"大规模"的军事干涉，一些人恶意地如此宣称。

▲ **mis·con·cep·tion** /mɪskənsɛpʃən/ (**misconceptions**) N-COUNT A **misconception** is an idea that is not correct. 错误观念 ❑ *It is a misconception that Peggy was fabulously wealthy.* 说佩吉以前极其富有，这是一个错误的看法。

mis·con·duct /mɪskɒndʌkt/ N-UNCOUNT **Misconduct** is bad or unacceptable behavior, especially by a professional person. 不端行为 ❑ *A psychologist was found guilty of serious professional misconduct yesterday.* 昨天一名心理学家被判严重的失职罪。

mis·de·mean·or /mɪsdɪminər/ (**misdemeanors**)

in BRIT, use **misdemeanour**

1 N-COUNT A **misdemeanor** is an act that some people consider to be wrong or unacceptable. 行为不端 [FORMAL] ❑ *Paul appeared before the faculty to account for his various misdemeanors.* 保罗在全体教职员面前解释了他的种种不端行为。 **2** N-COUNT In the United States and other countries where the legal system distinguishes between very serious crimes and less serious ones, a **misdemeanor** is a less serious crime. 轻罪 [LEGAL] ❑ *Under state law, it is a misdemeanor to possess a firearm on school premises.* 根据该州法律，在校园里拥有枪械是一种轻罪。

mis·de·mean·our /mɪsdɪmiːnəʳ/ [BRIT] → see **misdemeanor**

mis·er·able /mɪzərəbəl/ **1** ADJ If you are **miserable**, you are very unhappy. 痛苦的 ❑ *I took a series of badly paid secretarial jobs which made me really miserable.* 我连着干了几份工资很低的秘书工作，这让我感到真的很痛苦。 ● **mis·er·ably** /mɪzərəbli/ ADV 痛苦地 ❑ *He looked miserably down at his plate.* 他痛苦地低头看着自己的盘子。 **2** ADJ If you describe a place or situation as **miserable**, you mean that it makes you feel unhappy or depressed. 令人忧伤的 ❑ *There was nothing at all in this miserable place to distract him.* 在这个令人忧伤的地方，根本没什么东西可以转移他的注意力。 **3** ADJ If you describe the weather as **miserable**, you mean that it makes you feel depressed, because it is raining or dull. 阴冷多雨的 ❑ *On a gray, wet, miserable day our teams congregated in Port Townsend.* 在灰暗、潮湿而又阴冷的一天，我们几队人聚集在了汤森港。 **4** ADJ If you describe someone as **miserable**, you mean that you do not like them because they are bad-tempered or unfriendly. 脾气不好的；不友好的 [ADJ n] ❑ *He always was a miserable man. He never spoke to me nor anybody else, not even to pass the time of day.* 他总是不友好。他从不和我说话，也不和别人说话，那怕是为了打发时光。 **5** ADJ You can describe a quantity or quality as **miserable** when you think that it is much smaller or worse than it ought to be. 少得可怜的 [EMPHASIS] ❑ *Our speed over the ground was a miserable 2.2 knots.* 我们在地面上的速度只有区区的2.2节。 ● **mis·er·ably** ADV 少得可怜地 [ADV adj] ❑ *...the miserably inadequate supply of books now provided for schools.* …现在提供给学校的书籍少得可怜。 **6** ADJ A **miserable** failure is a very great one. 惨痛的 [ADJ n] [EMPHASIS] ❑ *The film was a miserable commercial failure both in Italy and in the United States.* 这部电影在意大利和美国票房收入都遭到了惨败。 ● **mis·er·ably** ADV 悲惨地 [ADV with v] ❑ *Some manage it. Some fail miserably.* 有人成功了。有些人败得很惨。

Thesaurus *miserable* 另参见：

ADJ.	unhappy **1**
	unfortunate, wretched **2**

★ **mis·ery** /mɪzəri/ (**miseries**) **1** N-VAR **Misery** is great unhappiness. 苦难 ❑ *All that money brought nothing but sadness and misery and tragedy.* 那些钱带来的只有悲哀、苦难和不幸。 **2** N-UNCOUNT **Misery** is the way of life and unpleasant living conditions of people who are very poor. 穷困 ❑ *A tiny, educated elite profited from the misery of their two million fellow countrymen.* 一个小小的受过教育的精英团体从他们两百万同胞的穷困中获了利。 **3** PHRASE If someone **makes** your **life a misery**, they behave in an unpleasant way towards you over a period of time and make you very unhappy. 使某人的生活非常不开心 ❑ *I would really like living here if it wasn't for the gangs of kids who make our lives a misery.* 要不是那一群群的孩子搅得我们生活不宁，我还是挺喜欢住在这里的。 **4** PHRASE If you **put** someone **out of** their **misery**, you tell them something that they are very anxious to know. 告知情况（使不再焦虑）[INFORMAL] ❑ *Please put me out of my misery. How do you do it?* 请别让我着急了。你是怎么做的呀？ **5** PHRASE If you **put** an animal **out of** its **misery**, you kill it because it is sick or injured and cannot be cured or healed. 杀死（动物）以使其摆脱痛苦 ❑ *He notes grimly that the Watsons have called the vet to put their dog out of its misery.* 他难过地记录下沃森家已经给兽医打了电话，要永远结束他们家狗的痛苦。

mis·fit /mɪsfɪt/ (**misfits**) N-COUNT A **misfit** is a person who is not easily accepted by other people, often because their behavior is very different from that of everyone else. 与别人合不来的人 ❑ *I have been made to feel a social and psychological misfit for not wanting children.* 因为不想要孩子，使我觉得自己在社交和心理上与他人格格不入。

★ **mis·for·tune** /mɪsfɔrtʃən/ (**misfortunes**) N-VAR A **misfortune** is something unpleasant or unlucky that happens to someone. 不幸 ❑ *She seemed to enjoy the misfortunes of others.* 她似乎很喜欢幸灾乐祸。

▲ **mis·giv·ing** /mɪsgɪvɪŋ/ (**misgivings**) N-VAR If you have **misgivings** about something that is being suggested or done, you feel that it is not quite right, and are worried that it may have unwanted results. 疑虑 ❑ *She had some misgivings about what she was about to do.* 她对自己要做的事有些疑虑。

m

★ **mis·guid·ed** /mɪsgaɪdɪd/ ADJ If you describe an opinion or plan as **misguided**, you are critical of it because you think it is based on an incorrect idea. You can also describe people as misguided. (观点或计划) 以错误观念为指导的; (人) 误入歧途的 [DISAPPROVAL] ❑ *In a misguided attempt to be funny, he manages only offensiveness.* 他试图使自己很风趣，可弄巧成拙地冒犯了别人。

mis·han·dle /mɪshændᵊl/ (**mishandles, mishandling, mishandled**) V-T If you say that someone **has mishandled** something, you are critical of them because you think they have dealt with it badly. 对…处理不当 [DISAPPROVAL] ❑ *She completely mishandled an important project purely through lack of attention.* 她纯粹由于不用心，把一件重要项目完全搞砸了。 ● **mis·han·dling** N-UNCOUNT 处理不当 ❑ *...the government's mishandling of the economy.* …政府对经济的不当管理。

mis·hap /mɪshæp/ (**mishaps**) N-VAR A **mishap** is an unfortunate but not very serious event that happens to someone. 小灾难 ❑ *After a number of mishaps she did manage to get back to Germany.* 发生了几次小的不幸之后，她设法回到了德国。

mis·in·for·ma·tion /mɪsɪnfərmeɪʃᵊn/ N-UNCOUNT **Misinformation** is wrong information which is given to someone, often in a deliberate attempt to make them believe something that is not true. (常指故意提供的) 虚假消息 ❑ *This was a deliberate piece of misinformation.* 这是一条故意提供的虚假消息。

Word Link *mis ≈ bad : misinterpret, misleading, mistrust*

mis·in·ter·pret /mɪsɪntɜrprɪt/ (**misinterprets, misinterpreting, misinterpreted**) V-T If you **misinterpret** something, you understand it wrongly. 误解 ❑ *He was amazed that he'd misinterpreted the situation so completely.* 他对自己完全误解了形势感到很吃惊。 ● **mis·in·ter·pre·ta·tion** /mɪsɪntɜrprɪteɪʃᵊn/ N-VAR (**misinterpretations**) 误解 ❑ *...a misinterpretation of the aims and ends of socialism.* …对社会主义目标和目的的误解。

M

mis·judge /mɪsdʒʌdʒ/ (**misjudges, misjudging, misjudged**) V-T If you say that someone **has misjudged** a person or situation, you mean that they have formed an incorrect idea or opinion about them, and often that they have made a wrong decision as a result of this. 对…判断错误 ❑ *Perhaps I had misjudged him, and he was not so predictable after all.* 也许我对他的判断是错误的，他根本就不是那么墨守成规。

mis·lead /mɪslid/ (**misleads, misleading, misled**) V-T If you say that someone or something **has misled** you, you mean that they have made you believe something that is not true, either by telling you a lie or by giving you a wrong idea or impression. 误导 ❑ *It's this legend which has misled scholars.* 正是这个传奇故事误导了学者们。

mis·lead·ing /mɪslidɪŋ/ ADJ If you describe something as **misleading**, you mean that it gives you a wrong idea or impression. 误导性的 ❑ *It would be misleading to say that we were friends.* 说我们是朋友会对别人产生误导。 ● **mis·lead·ing·ly** ADV 误导性地 ❑ *The data had been presented misleadingly.* 数据被以一种令人误解的方式表达出来。

mis·led /mɪslɛd/ **Misled** is the past tense and past participle of **mislead**. **mislead**的过去式和过去分词

mis·man·age /mɪsmænɪdʒ/ (**mismanages, mismanaging, mismanaged**) V-T To **mismanage** something means to manage it badly. 对…处置不当 ❑ *75% of voters think the president has mismanaged the economy.* 75%的选民认为总统对经济管理不当。

mis·man·age·ment /mɪsmænɪdʒmənt/ N-UNCOUNT Someone's **mismanagement** of a system or organization is the bad way they have dealt with it or organized it. 处置不当 ❑ *His gross mismanagement left the company desperately in need of restructuring.* 他处理事务的严重不当使得公司急需重组。

mis·placed /mɪspleɪst/ ADJ If you describe a feeling or action as **misplaced**, you are critical of it because you think it is inappropriate, or directed towards the wrong thing or person. (感情或行动) 不适当的; 定位不当的 [DISAPPROVAL] ❑ *A telling sign of misplaced priorities is the concentration on health, not environmental issues.* 首要问题定位不当的一个显著标志就是专注于健康而非环境问题。

mis·read /mɪsrid/ (**misreads, misreading**)

The form **misread** is used in the present tense, and is the past tense and past participle, when it is pronounced /mɪsrɛd/.

misread此词形被用于现在时，并且在读作 /mɪsrɛd/时，是过去时和过去完成时。

1 V-T If you **misread** a situation or someone's behavior, you do not understand it properly. 误解 ❑ *The administration largely misread the mood of the electorate.* 该政府大大地误解了选民的情绪。 ● **mis·read·ing** N-COUNT (**misreadings**) 误解 ❑ *...a misreading of opinion in France.* …对法国的看法的误解。 2 V-T If you **misread** something that has been written or printed, you look at it and think that it says something that it does not say. 看错 ❑ *His chauffeur misread his route and took a wrong turn.* 他的司机看错了路线，结果拐错了弯。

mis·rep·re·sent /mɪsrɛprɪzɛnt/ (**misrepresents, misrepresenting, misrepresented**) V-T If someone **misrepresents** a person or situation, they give a wrong or inaccurate account of what the person or situation is like. 曲解 ❑ *He said that the press had misrepresented him as arrogant and bullying.* 他说新闻界把他曲解成了一个傲慢霸道的人。 ❑ *Hollywood films misrepresented us as drunks, maniacs, and murderers.* 好莱坞电影把我们歪曲成了醉鬼、疯子和杀人犯。 ● **mis·rep·re·sen·ta·tion** /mɪsrɛprɪzɛnteɪʃᵊn/ N-VAR (**misrepresentations**) 曲解 ❑ *I wish to point out your misrepresentation of the facts.* 我想指出你们对事实的曲解。

miss

1 USED AS A TITLE OR A FORM OF ADDRESS
2 VERB AND NOUN USES

1 **Miss** ♦♦♦ /mɪs/ (**Misses**) N-TITLE You use **Miss** in front of the name of a girl or unmarried woman when you are speaking to her or referring to her. 小姐 (用于未婚女子的姓名前) [FORMAL] ❑ *It was nice talking to you, Miss Ellis.* 很高兴与你交谈，埃利斯小姐。

In English-speaking countries **Miss** is used in front of the name of an unmarried woman when you are speaking or referring to her. **Mrs.** is used before the name of a married woman. Some women who do not think it is important to let people know whether they are married or not, choose to call themselves **Ms.** instead. Just like **Mr.**, used for men, Ms. does not tell you whether a person is married or single.

2 **miss** ♦♦◊ /mɪs/ (**misses, missing, missed**)

➪ **Please look at meaning 11 to see if the expression you are looking for is shown under another headword.** 1 V-T/V-I If you **miss** something, you fail to hit it, for example when you have thrown something at it or you have shot a bullet at it. 未击中 ❑ *She hurled the ashtray across the room, narrowly missing my head.* 她从屋子那头儿把烟灰缸扔过来，差一点就打中我的脑袋。 ❑ *When I'd missed a few times, he suggested I rest the rifle on a rock to steady it.* 由于我几次都没打中，他就建议我把步枪放到石头上来保持稳定。 ● N-COUNT **Miss** is also a noun. 未击中 ❑ *After more misses, they finally put two arrows into the lion's chest.* 又射偏了几次后，他们终于将两只箭射进了狮子的胸膛。 2 V-T/V-I In sports, if you **miss** a shot, you fail to get the ball in the goal, net, or hole. (体育运动中) 未投中 (球) ❑ *He scored four of the baskets but missed a free throw.* 他4次投篮得分，可是有一次罚篮却没中。 ❑ *He dived for the ball and missed.* 他去扑球，却没扑到。 ● N-COUNT **Miss** is also a noun. (体育运动中) 未投中 (球) ❑ *Snow made his first basket of the game after eight misses.* 斯诺在8次投球不中后，投进了他本场比赛的第一个球。 3 V-T If you **miss** something, you fail to notice it. 未注意到 ❑ *From this vantage point he watched, his searching eye never missing a detail.* 从这个有利的位置进行观察，他那锐利的目光从未漏掉一个细节。 4 V-T If you **miss** the meaning or importance of something, you fail to understand or appreciate it. 没有领会 ❑ *One ABC correspondent had totally missed the point of the question.* 美国广播公司的一名记者完全没有领会这个问题的关键。 5 V-T If you **miss** a chance or opportunity, you fail to take advantage of it. 错过 (机会) ❑ *It was too good an opportunity to miss.* 这个机会太好了，不容错过。 6 V-T If you **miss** someone who is no longer with you or who has died, you feel sad and wish that they were still with you. 想念 ❑ *Your mama and I are going to miss you at Christmas.* 我和你妈妈在圣诞节会想你的。 7 V-T If you **miss** something, you feel sad because you no longer have it or are no longer doing or experiencing it. 留恋 ❑ *I could happily move back into an apartment if it wasn't for the fact that I'd miss my garden.* 我要不是留恋我的花园，会很高兴地搬回到一套公寓里。 8 V-T If you **miss** something such as a plane or train, you arrive too late to catch it. 没有赶上 (飞机或火车等) ❑ *He missed the last bus* home and had to stay with a friend. 他没赶上回家的末班车，只好住在一个朋友那里。 9 V-T If you **miss** something such as a meeting or an activity, you do not go to it or take part in it. 未参加（会议或活动） ❑ *It's a pity Martha and I had to miss our class last week.* 很遗憾，我和玛莎上周不得不缺课。 ❑ *You won't be missing much on TV tonight apart from the usual repeats.* 除了通常的重播节目外，今晚的电视节目你不会错过什么。 10 → see also **missing** 11 to **miss the boat** → see **boat**

▸ **miss out** 1 PHRASAL VERB If you **miss out on** something that would be enjoyable or useful to you, you are not involved in it or do not take part in it. 错失 ❑ *We're missing out on a tremendous opportunity.* 我们正在错失一个绝佳的机会。 2 PHRASAL VERB If you **miss out** something or someone, you fail to include them. 遗漏 [BRIT]

in AM, use **leave out**

Word Partnership *miss* 的常用搭配：

N. miss **the point** 2 4
miss **a chance**, miss **an opportunity** 2 5
miss **a class**, miss **school** 2 9
ADV. miss ***someone/something*** **terribly** 2 6 7

Word Link *miss ≈ sending : dismiss, missile, missionary*

mis·sile ♦◇◇ /mɪsᵊl/ (**missiles**) 1 N-COUNT A **missile** is a tube-shaped weapon that travels long distances through the air and explodes when it reaches its target. 导弹 ❑ *The authorities offered to stop firing missiles if the rebels agreed to stop attacking civilian targets.* 当局提出如果叛乱者同意停止袭击民用目标，他们就停止发射导弹。 2 N-COUNT Anything that is thrown as a weapon can be called a **missile**. （作为武器的）投掷物 ❑ *The football fans began throwing missiles, one of which hit the referee.* 足球球迷们开始扔东西，其中的一个打中了裁判。

miss·ing ♦◇◇ /mɪsɪŋ/ 1 ADJ If something is **missing** or has **gone missing**, it is not in its usual place, and you cannot find it. 找不到的 ❑ *It was only an hour or so later that I discovered that my gun was missing.* 也就是一个小时左右后，我发现自己的枪不见了。 2 ADJ If a part of something is **missing**, it has been removed or has come off, and has not been replaced. 缺失的 ❑ *Three buttons were missing from his shirt.* 他的衬衫少了3颗纽扣。 3 ADJ If you say that something is **missing**, you mean that it has not been included, and you think that it should have been. 遗漏的 ❑ *She had given me an incomplete list. One name was missing from it.* 她给了我一份不全的名单，上面漏掉了一个名字。 4 ADJ Someone who is **missing** cannot be found, and it is not known whether they are alive or dead. （人）失踪的 ❑ *Five people died in the explosion and more than one thousand were injured. One person is still missing.* 爆炸中5人丧生，一千多人受伤，还有1人失踪。 ● PHRASE If a member of the armed forces is **missing in action**, they have not returned from a battle, their body has not been found, and they are not thought to have been captured. （士兵）在战斗中失踪的

Word Partnership *missing* 的常用搭配：

N. missing **piece** 1 2
missing **information**, missing **ingredient** 3
missing **children**, missing **girl**, missing **people**, missing **soldiers** 4
ADV. **still** missing 1 – 4

mis·sion ♦♦◇ /mɪʃᵊn/ (**missions**) 1 N-COUNT A **mission** is an important task that people are given to do, especially one that involves traveling to another country. （尤指远赴他国的）使命 ❑ *Salisbury sent him on a diplomatic mission to North America.* 索尔兹伯里派他到北美执行一项外交使命。 2 N-COUNT A **mission** is a group of people who have been sent to a foreign country to carry out an official task. 驻外使团 ❑ *...a senior member of a diplomatic mission.* …外交使团中的一名高级成员。 3 N-COUNT A **mission** is a special journey made by a military airplane or spacecraft. （军用飞机或宇宙飞船的）飞行任务 ❑ *...a bomber that crashed during a training mission in the west Texas mountains.* …在德克萨斯州西部山区执行训练任务时坠毁的一架轰炸机。 4 N-SING If you say that you have a **mission**, you mean that you have a strong commitment and sense of duty to do or achieve something. 使命；天职 ❑ *He viewed his mission in life as protecting the weak from the evil.* 他把保护弱者不受坏人伤害看作自己一生的使命。 5 N-COUNT A **mission** is the activities of a group of Christians who have been sent to a place to teach people about Christianity. 传教活动 ❑ *They say God spoke to them and told them to go on a mission to the poorest country in the Western Hemisphere.* 他们说上帝向他们开口讲话，告诉他们到西半球最贫穷的国家继续进行传教活动。 6 N-COUNT A **mission** is a building or group of buildings in which missionary work is carried out. 布道所 ❑ *I reside at the mission at St. Michael's.* 我住在圣迈克尔教堂的布道所。

Word Partnership *mission* 的常用搭配：

ADJ. **dangerous** mission, **secret** mission, **successful** mission 1
N. **peacekeeping** mission 1 2
combat mission, **rescue** mission, **suicide** mission, **training** mission 1 3
V. **accomplish a** mission, **carry out a** mission 1 3 4

★ **mis·sion·ary** /mɪʃənɛri/ (**missionaries**) 1 N-COUNT A **missionary** is a Christian who has been sent to a foreign country to teach people about Christianity. 传教士 ❑ *My mother would still like me to be a missionary in Africa.* 我母亲还是想让我在非洲做一名传教士。 2 ADJ **Missionary** is used to describe the activities of missionaries. 传教的 [ADJ n] ❑ *You should be in missionary work.* 你该参加传教工作。 3 ADJ If you refer to someone's enthusiasm for an activity or belief as **missionary** zeal, you are emphasizing that they are very enthusiastic about it. 传教士般的 [ADJ n] [EMPHASIS] ❑ *She had a kind of missionary zeal about bringing culture to the masses.* 她对把文化带给大众具有一种传教士般的热情。

mis·sion state·ment (**mission statements**) N-COUNT A company's or organization's **mission statement** is a document which states what they aim to achieve and the kind of service they intend to provide. （公司或组织的）宗旨声明 [BUSINESS] ❑ *Our mission statement is to be the best design firm in the world.* 我们的宗旨是成为世界上最好的设计公司。

mis·spend /mɪsspɛnd/ (**misspends, misspending, misspent**) V-T If you say that time or money **has been misspent**, you disapprove of the way in which it has been spent. 滥用（金钱）；虚度（时间） [DISAPPROVAL] ❑ *Much of the money was grossly misspent.* 很多钱都被挥霍了。

mist /mɪst/ (**mists, misting, misted**) 1 N-VAR **Mist** consists of a large number of tiny drops of water in the air, which make it difficult to see very far. 雾 ❑ *Thick mist made flying impossible.* 浓雾使得无法飞行。 2 V-T/V-I If a piece of glass **mists** or **is misted**, it becomes covered with tiny drops of moisture, so that you cannot see through it easily. 使蒙上薄雾；蒙上薄雾 ❑ *The windows misted, blurring the stark streetlight.* 窗户蒙上了一层水汽，使得明亮的街灯模糊了。 ● PHRASAL VERB **Mist over** means the same as **mist**. 同**mist** ❑ *The front windshield was misting over.* 前挡风玻璃蒙上了一层水汽。

mis·take ♦♦◇ /mɪsteɪk/ (**mistakes, mistaking, mistook, mistaken**) 1 N-COUNT If you make a **mistake**, you do something which you did not intend to do, or which produces a result that you do not want. 错误 [oft N "of" -ing, also "by" N] ❑ *They made the big mistake of thinking they could seize its border with a relatively small force.* 他们犯了个大错，认为他们可以用相对少的军队占领边界。 ❑ *There must be some mistake.* 一定是出了什么错。 2 N-COUNT A **mistake** is something or part of something that is incorrect or not right. 错事 ❑ *Her mother sighed and rubbed out another mistake in the crossword puzzle.* 她母亲叹了口气，擦掉了拼字游戏中的另一个填错的地方。 3 V-T If you **mistake** one person or thing **for** another, you wrongly think that they are the other person or thing. 误认为 ❑ *When hay fever first occurs it is often mistaken for a summer cold.* 花粉病刚发作时，常会被误认为是热伤风。 4 V-T If you **mistake** something, you fail to recognize or understand it. 误解 ❑ *The administration completely mistook the feeling of the country.* 政府完全误解了国民的感情。 5 PHRASE You can say **there is no mistaking** something when you are emphasizing that you cannot fail to recognize or understand it. 不会弄错 [EMPHASIS] ❑ *There's no mistaking the eastern flavor of the food.* 该食物的东方口味肯定不会错的。

Word Partnership *mistake* 的常用搭配：

ADJ. **fatal** mistake, **honest** mistake, **tragic** mistake 1
big mistake, **common** mistake, **costly** mistake, **huge** mistake, **serious** mistake, **terrible** mistake 1 2
V. **admit a** mistake, **correct a** mistake, **fix a** mistake, **make a** mistake, **realize a** mistake 1 2

mis·tak·en /mɪsteɪkən/ 1 ADJ If you are **mistaken about** something, you are wrong about it. 弄错的 [v-link ADJ] ❑ *I see I was*

m

mistaken about you. 我明白我错看了你。● PHRASE You use expressions such as **if I'm not mistaken** and **unless I'm very much mistaken** as a polite way of emphasizing the statement you are making, especially when you are confident that it is correct. 如果我没搞错的话(委婉地表示强调，尤指自信为正确) [EMPHASIS] ❑ *I think Alfred wanted to marry Jennifer, if I am not mistaken.* 我想如果我没搞错的话，当时艾尔弗雷德想娶珍妮弗。 2 ADJ A **mistaken** belief or opinion is incorrect. (信念或观点) 错误的 [ADJ n] ❑ *I had a mistaken view of what was happening.* 我对于所发生事情的看法是错误的。● **mis·tak·en·ly** ADV 错误地 [ADV with v] ❑ *He says they mistakenly believed the standard licenses they held were sufficient.* 他说他们错误地以为持有标准许可证就足够了。

Word Partnership *mistaken* 的常用搭配:
V. if I'm not mistaken 1
N. mistaken **belief**, mistaken **impression**, mistaken **notion** 2

mis·ter /mɪstər/ N-VOC Men are sometimes addressed as **mister**, especially by children and especially when the person talking to them does not know their name. 先生 (对男子的称呼，尤为儿童使用或称呼不知姓名的男子) [INFORMAL] ❑ *Look, Mister, we know our job, so don't try to tell us what to do.* 哎，先生，我们了解自己的工作，所以你不必告诉我们该干什么。

mis·took /mɪstʊk/ **Mistook** is the past tense of **mistake**. **mistake**的过去式

★ **mis·tress** /mɪstrɪs/ (**mistresses**) N-COUNT A married man's **mistress** is a woman who is not his wife and with whom he is having a sexual relationship. 情妇 [OLD-FASHIONED] ❑ *Tracy was his mistress for three years.* 特蕾西给他做了3年情妇。

Word Link *mis ≈ bad : misinterpret, misleading, mistrust*

mis·trust /mɪstrʌst/ (**mistrusts, mistrusting, mistrusted**) 1 N-UNCOUNT **Mistrust** is the feeling that you have toward someone who you do not trust. 不信任 ❑ *There was mutual mistrust between the two men.* 这两人之间互不信任。 2 V-T If you **mistrust** someone or something, you do not trust them. 不信任 ❑ *It frequently appears that Bell mistrusts all journalists.* 贝尔常常表露出他不信任所有的记者。

M

misty /mɪsti/ ADJ On a **misty** day, there is a lot of mist in the air. 有雾的 ❑ *It's a little misty this morning.* 今天早晨有薄雾。

mis·under·stand /mɪsʌndərstænd/ (**misunderstands, misunderstanding, misunderstood**) 1 V-T/V-I If you **misunderstand** someone or something, you do not understand them properly. 误解 ❑ *I misunderstood you.* 我误会你了。❑ *They have simply misunderstood what rock and roll is.* 他们完全误解了摇滚乐是什么。● CONVENTION You can say **don't misunderstand me** when you want to correct a wrong impression that you think someone may have gotten about what you are saying. 别误会 (用以纠正别人对自己所说话的错误理解) 2 → see also **misunderstood**

mis·under·stand·ing /mɪsʌndərstændɪŋ/ (**misunderstandings**) 1 N-VAR A **misunderstanding** is a failure to understand something properly, for example a situation or a person's remarks. 误解 ❑ *There has been some misunderstanding of our publishing aims.* 对于我们的出版目的存在一些误解。 2 N-COUNT You can refer to a disagreement or slight quarrel as a **misunderstanding**. 分歧；争执 [FORMAL] ❑ *There was a little misunderstanding with the police and he was arrested.* 由于与警方有些小争执，他被捕了。

mis·under·stood /mɪsʌndərstʊd/ 1 **Misunderstood** is the past tense and past participle of **misunderstand**. **misunderstand** 的过去式和过去分词 2 ADJ If you describe someone or something as **misunderstood**, you mean that people do not understand them and have a wrong impression or idea of them. 被误解的 ❑ *Eric is very badly misunderstood.* 埃里克被深深地误解了。

mis·use (**misuses, misusing, misused**)

The noun is pronounced /mɪsyus/. The verb is pronounced /mɪsyuz/.

名词读作 /mɪsyus/，动词读作 /mɪsyuz/。

1 N-VAR The **misuse** of something is incorrect, careless, or dishonest use of it. 误用；滥用 ❑ *...the misuse of power and privilege.* …权力和特权的滥用。 2 V-T If someone **misuses** something, they use it incorrectly, carelessly, or dishonestly. 误用；滥用 ❑ *She misused her position in the appointment of 26,000 party supporters to government jobs.* 她滥用职权任命了26000名党派支持者从事政府工作。❑ *Tess would like a dollar for every time she had heard that word misused by television journalists.* 特丝每次听到电视台记者用错那个词，都恨不得收他们一美元。

mite /maɪt/ (**mites**) N-COUNT **Mites** are very tiny creatures that live on plants, for example, or in animals' fur. (生活在植物或动物皮毛中的) 螨 ❑ *...an itching skin disorder caused by parasitic mites.* …寄生螨虫引起的一种皮肤瘙痒病。

miti·gate /mɪtɪgeɪt/ (**mitigates, mitigating, mitigated**) V-T To **mitigate** something means to make it less unpleasant, serious, or painful. 缓解 [FORMAL] ❑ *...ways of mitigating the effects of an explosion.* …减轻爆炸后果的方法。

miti·gat·ing /mɪtɪgeɪtɪŋ/ ADJ **Mitigating** circumstances or factors make a bad action, especially a crime, easier to understand and excuse, and may result in the person responsible being punished less severely. 可减轻罪责的 (情节、因素) [ADJ n] [LEGAL] ❑ *The judge found that in her case there were mitigating circumstances.* 法官发现她的案件中有可以减轻罪责的情节。

mix ♦♦◊ /mɪks/ (**mixes, mixing, mixed**) 1 V-RECIP If two substances **mix** or if you **mix** one substance **with** another, you stir or shake them together, or combine them in some other way, so that they become a single substance. 混合 ❑ *Oil and water don't mix.* 油与水无法混合。❑ *A quick stir will mix them thoroughly.* 快速搅拌会使它们完全混合。❑ *Mix the cinnamon with the rest of the sugar.* 把肉桂与剩余的糖混合起来。 2 V-T If you **mix** something, you prepare it by mixing other things together. 调制 ❑ *He had spent several hours mixing cement.* 他用了几个小时的时间来搅拌水泥。 3 N-VAR A **mix** is a powder containing all the substances that you need in order to make something such as a cake or a sauce. When you want to use it, you add liquid. (制作蛋糕或调味汁等的) 混合干配料 ❑ *For speed we used packets of pizza dough mix.* 为了赶速度，我们用了几包做比萨饼的混合面粉。 4 N-COUNT A **mix of** different things or people is two or more of them together. 混合体 ❑ *The story is a magical mix of fantasy and reality.* 这个故事是一个幻想与现实的奇妙组合。 5 V-RECIP If two things or activities do not **mix**, it is not a good idea to have them or do them together, because the result would be unpleasant or dangerous. 相协调 [usu with brd-neg] ❑ *Politics and sports don't mix.* 政治与体育无法协调一致。❑ *Some of these pills don't mix with drink.* 有些药片不能和酒混饮。 6 V-RECIP If you **mix with** other people, you meet them and talk to them. You can also say that people **mix**. 交往 ❑ *I ventured the idea that the secret of staying young was to mix with older people.* 我大胆地提出这样一个观点，即保持年轻的秘诀是和比自己年长的人交往。❑ *People are supposed to mix, do you understand?* 人们应该多交往，明白吗？ 7 → see also **mixed** 8 **to mix your metaphors** → see **metaphor**

▸ **mix up** 1 PHRASAL VERB If you **mix up** two things or people, you confuse them, so that you think that one of them is the other one. 混淆 ❑ *People often mix me up with other actors.* 人们总是把我和其他演员弄混。❑ *Depressed people may mix up their words.* 沮丧的人可能会语无伦次。 2 PHRASAL VERB If you **mix up** a number of things, you put things of different kinds together or place things so that they are not in order. 把不同类的事物混放在一起；弄乱 ❑ *I like to mix up designer clothes.* 我喜欢把各种名牌服装混穿在一起。❑ *Take the cards and mix them up.* 拿出这些卡片，把它们打乱。 3 → see also **mixed up**

Word Partnership *mix* 的常用搭配:
N. mix **ingredients**, mix **with water** 1 2
ADV. mix **thoroughly**, mix **together** 1 2

mixed ♦◊◊ /mɪkst/ 1 ADJ If you have **mixed** feelings about something or someone, you feel uncertain about them because you can see both good and bad points about them. (感情等) 矛盾复杂的 ❑ *I came home from the meeting with mixed feelings.* 我带着复杂的心情从会场回到家。 2 ADJ A **mixed** group of people consists of people of many different types. (不同类型的人) 混合的 ❑ *I found a very mixed group of individuals, some of whom I could relate to and others with whom I had very little in common.* 我碰到了一群形形色色的人，其中一些人能和我合得来，而其他的则和我根本合不来。 3 ADJ **Mixed** is used to describe something that involves people from two or more different races. 不同种族混合的 ❑ *Sally had attended a racially mixed school.* 萨莉曾上过一所种族混合的学校。 4 ADJ **Mixed** education or accommodations are intended for both males and females. 男女混合的 (学校或住所) ❑ *Girls who have always been at a mixed school know how to stand up for themselves.* 一直在男女混合学校上学的女孩子们知道

如何自我保护。 **5** ADJ **Mixed** is used to describe something which includes or consists of different things of the same general kind. (同一类的不同物品) 混合的 [ADJ n] ❑ *...a teaspoon of mixed herbs.* …一茶匙混合草药。

mixed econo·my (**mixed economies**) N-COUNT A **mixed economy** is an economic system in which some companies are owned by the state and some are not. (国有和私营并存的) 混合型经济 [BUSINESS] ❑ *The African National Congress today dropped its doctrine of nationalizing industry in favor of a mixed economy.* 非洲国民大会今天放弃了工业国有化的信条转而赞同公私并存的混合型经济。

mixed up **1** ADJ If you are **mixed up**, you are confused, often because of emotional or social problems. (因感情或社会问题而) 迷惑不解的 ❑ *I think he's a rather mixed up kid.* 我觉得他是个内心充满困惑的孩子。 **2** ADJ To be **mixed up in** something bad, or **with** someone you disapprove of, means to be involved in it or with them. 混在…的 (指坏事或不喜欢的人) [v-link ADJ "in/with" n] ❑ *Why did I ever get mixed up with you?* 我怎么就和你混在了一起？

mix·er /mɪksər/ (**mixers**) **1** N-COUNT A **mixer** is a machine used for mixing things together. 搅拌机 ❑ *...an electric mixer.* …一台电动搅拌机。 **2** N-COUNT A **mixer** is a nonalcoholic drink such as fruit juice or soda that you mix with strong alcohol such as gin. 调酒的软饮料 ❑ *At the Tropicana you order ice and mixers from the waiters at the table.* 在"热带酒吧"，你从吧台的服务生那儿点些冰块和调酒的软饮料。 **3** N-COUNT If you say that someone is a good **mixer**, you mean that they are good at talking to people and making friends. (善于) 交际的人 ❑ *Cooper was a good mixer, he was popular.* 库珀是个善交际的人，很受欢迎。 **4** N-COUNT A **mixer** is a piece of equipment that is used to make changes to recorded music or film. 音频混合器；图像剪接器 ❑ *...a three-channel audio mixer.* …一个3声道的音频混合器。

mix·ture ♦◇◇ /mɪkstʃər/ (**mixtures**) **1** N-SING A **mixture of** things consists of several different things together. 混合 ❑ *They looked at him with a mixture of horror, envy, and awe.* 他们带着害怕、羡慕和敬畏的混合表情看着他。 **2** N-COUNT A **mixture** is a substance that consists of other substances which have been stirred or shaken together. 混合物 ❑ *...a mixture of water and sugar and salt.* …水、糖和盐的混合物。

Thesaurus *mixture* 另参见：
N. blend, collection, variety **1**
blend, compound, fusion **2**

ml **ml** is a written abbreviation for **milliliter** or **milliliters**. 毫升 ❑ *Boil the sugar and 100 ml of water.* 把糖和100毫升的水煮沸。

mm ♦◇◇ **mm** is a written abbreviation for **millimeter** or **millimeters**. 毫米 ❑ *...a 135mm lens.* …一个135毫米的透镜。

moan /moʊn/ (**moans, moaning, moaned**) **1** V-T/V-I If you **moan**, you make a low sound, usually because you are unhappy or in pain. 呻吟 ❑ *Tony moaned in his sleep and then turned over on his side.* 托尼在睡梦中呻吟了一下，然后转身侧躺。 ● N-COUNT **Moan** is also a noun. 呻吟 ❑ *Suddenly she gave a low, choking moan and began to tremble violently.* 突然她发出了一声低沉、令人窒息的呻吟，身体开始剧烈地抖动。 **2** V-I To **moan** means to complain or speak in a way which shows that you are very unhappy. 抱怨 [DISAPPROVAL] ❑ *I used to moan if I didn't get at least six hours' sleep at night.* 我过去常常抱怨晚上睡不够6小时。 ❑ *...moaning about the weather.* …抱怨天气。 **3** N-COUNT A **moan** is a complaint. 抱怨 [INFORMAL] ❑ *They have been listening to people's moans and praise.* 他们一直在倾听人民的抱怨与称赞。

★ **mob** /mɒb/ (**mobs, mobbing, mobbed**) **1** N-COUNT A **mob** is a large, disorganized, and often violent crowd of people. 一大群乱民 ❑ *The inspectors watched a growing mob of demonstrators gathering.* 这些监察员看着越来越多的粗暴的示威人群聚集在一起。 **2** N-SING You can refer to the people involved in organized crime as **the Mob**. 犯罪团伙 [INFORMAL] ❑ *He makes ends meet by working as a forger for the Mob.* 他通过为犯罪团伙造假来养家糊口。 **3** N-SING People sometimes use **the mob** to refer in a disapproving way to the majority of people in a country or place, especially when these people are behaving in a violent or uncontrolled way. 暴民 [mainly BRIT, DISAPPROVAL] ❑ *If they continue like this there is a danger of the mob taking over.* 如果他们继续如此，就有被暴民接管的危险。 **4** V-T If you say that someone **is being mobbed by** a crowd of people, you mean that the people are trying to talk to them or get near them in an enthusiastic or threatening way. 成群围住 [usu passive] ❑ *Her car was mobbed by the media.* 她的汽车被媒体团团围住。

Word Link *mobil ≈ moving : automobile, mobile, mobilize*

mo·bile ♦◇◇ /moʊbəl/ (**mobiles**) **1** ADJ You use **mobile** to describe something large that can be moved easily from place to place. 可移动的 ❑ *...the four-hundred seat mobile theater.* …拥有400个座位的活动剧场。 **2** ADJ If you are **mobile**, you can move or travel easily from place to place, for example because you are not physically disabled or because you have your own transportation. 行动方便的 ❑ *I'm still very mobile.* 我仍然行动很方便。 ● **mo·bil·ity** /moʊbɪlɪti/ N-UNCOUNT 行动方便 ❑ *Two cars gave them the freedom and mobility to go their separate ways.* 两辆汽车给了他们自由和行动的便利，使得他们能够各走各的路。 **3** ADJ In a **mobile** society, people move easily from one job, home, or social class to another. 流动性的 (指工作、住所或社会地位可变动的) ❑ *We are a very mobile society and can't resist trying to take everything with us.* 我们是个流动性很强的社会，所以忍不住想携带一切东西。 ● **mo·bil·ity** N-UNCOUNT 流动性 ❑ *Prior to the nineteenth century, there were almost no channels of social mobility.* 19世纪以前，几乎没有社会流动的渠道。 **4** N-COUNT A **mobile** is a decoration that you hang from a ceiling. It usually consists of several small objects which move as the air around them moves. (通常由几个小物件组成的可随风摆动的) 悬挂在天花板的装饰物 **5** N-COUNT A **mobile** is the same as a **mobile phone**. 移动电话 [mainly BRIT]
→ see **cellphone**

Thesaurus *mobile* 另参见：
ADJ. movable, portable **1**

mo·bile phone (**mobile phones**) N-COUNT A **mobile phone** is a telephone that you can carry with you and use to make or receive calls wherever you are. 移动电话 [BRIT]

in AM, use **cellphone, cellular phone**

★ **mo·bi·lise** /moʊbɪlaɪz/ [BRIT] → see **mobilize**

★ **mo·bi·lize** /moʊbɪlaɪz/ (**mobilizes, mobilizing, mobilized**)

in BRIT, also use **mobilise**

1 V-T/V-I If you **mobilize** support or **mobilize** people to do something, you succeed in encouraging people to take action, especially political action. If people **mobilize**, they prepare to take action. 动员；动员起来 ❑ *The best hope is that we will mobilize international support and get down to action.* 最大的希望就是我们将动员国际社会的支持，开始行动。 ● **mo·bi·li·za·tion** /moʊbɪlɪzeɪʃən/ N-UNCOUNT 动员 ❑ *...the rapid mobilization of international opinion in support of the revolution.* …对支持革命的国际舆论的迅速动员。 **2** V-T If you **mobilize** resources, you start to use them or make them available for use. 调动 ❑ *If you could mobilize the resources, you could get it done.* 如果你能调动资源，你就能完成它。 ● **mo·bi·li·za·tion** N-UNCOUNT 调动 ❑ *...the mobilization of resources for education.* …调动教育资源。 **3** V-T/V-I If a country **mobilizes**, or **mobilizes** its armed forces, or if its armed forces **mobilize**, they are given orders to prepare for a conflict. 动员 (军队)；(国家军事力量) 动员起来 [JOURNALISM or MILITARY] ❑ *Sudan even threatened to mobilize in response to the ultimatums.* 苏丹甚至威胁说要动用军事力量来回应最后通牒。 ● **mo·bi·li·za·tion** N-UNCOUNT (军事) 动员 ❑ *...a demand for full-scale mobilization to defend the republic.* …全面动员来保卫共和国的命令。

★ **mock** /mɒk/ (**mocks, mocking, mocked**) **1** V-T If someone **mocks** you, they show or pretend that they think you are foolish or inferior, for example by saying something funny about you, or by imitating your behavior. 嘲笑；(为了取笑) 模仿 ❑ *I thought you were mocking me.* 我以为你在嘲笑我。 **2** ADJ You use **mock** to describe something which is not real or genuine, but which is intended to be very similar to the real thing. 假装的 [ADJ n] ❑ *"It's tragic!" swoons Jeffrey in mock horror.* "太悲惨了！"杰弗里假装害怕得昏了过去。

mock·ery /mɒkəri/ **1** N-UNCOUNT If someone mocks you, you can refer to their behavior or attitude as **mockery**. 嘲讽 ❑ *Was there a glint of mockery in his eyes?* 他的眼里是不是有一丝嘲讽？ **2** N-SING If something makes **a mockery of** something, it makes it appear worthless and foolish. 显得无价值和愚蠢 ❑ *This action makes a mockery of the administration's continuing protestations of concern.* 这个行动使政府给予关怀的一再声明显得毫无价值和愚蠢。

mock·ing /mɒkɪŋ/ ADJ A **mocking** expression or **mocking** behavior indicates that you think someone or something is stupid or inferior. 嘲讽的 ❑ *She gave a mocking smile.* 她嘲讽地笑了笑。

mod·al /moʊdəl/ (**modals**) N-COUNT In grammar, a **modal** or a **modal auxiliary** is a word such as "can" or "would" which is used

m

with a main verb to express ideas such as possibility, intention, or necessity. 情态动词 [TECHNICAL]

Word Link *mod ≈ measure, manner : mode, model, modern*

mode /moʊd/ (**modes**) **1** N-COUNT A **mode** of life or behavior is a particular way of living or behaving. (生活或行为) 方式 [FORMAL] ❑ *...the capitalist mode of production.* …资本主义的生产方式。❑ *He switched automatically into interview mode.* 他自动转换到面试的状态。 **2** N-COUNT A **mode** is a particular style in art, literature, or dress. (文学、艺术或穿着等的) 风格 ❑ *...a slightly more elegant and formal mode of dress.* …略显雅致和正式的着装风格。 **3** N-COUNT On some cameras or electronic devices, the different **modes** available are the different programs or settings that you can choose when you use them. 模式 ❑ *...when the camera is in manual mode.* …照相机处于手动模式时。

mod·el ♦♦◇ /mɒdᵊl/ (**models, modeling, modeled**)

in BRIT, sometimes in AM, use **modelling, modelled**

1 N-COUNT A **model** of an object is a physical representation that shows what it looks like or how it works. The model is often smaller than the object it represents. 模型 ❑ *...an architect's model of a wooden house.* …一名建筑师的木屋模型。❑ *I made a model out of paper and glue.* 我用纸和胶水做了一个模型。● ADJ **Model** is also an adjective. 模型的 [ADJ n] ❑ *...a model railway.* …一个铁路模型。❑ *I had made a model airplane.* 我做了一个飞机模型。 **2** N-COUNT A **model** is a system that is being used and that people might want to copy in order to achieve similar results. 模式 [FORMAL] ❑ *...the Chinese model of economic reform.* …中国经济改革的模式。 **3** N-COUNT A **model** of a system or process is a theoretical description that can help you understand how the system or process works, or how it might work. 理论模式 [FORMAL] ❑ *Darwin eventually put forward a model of biological evolution.* 达尔文最终提出了一套生物进化的理论模式。 **4** V-T If someone such as a scientist **models** a system or process, they make an accurate theoretical description of it in order to understand or explain how it works. 建立…的理论模式 [FORMAL] ❑ *I have moved from trying to model and understand the distribution and evolution of water vapor.* 我已经不再试图构建和理解水汽的分布和演变的理论模式了。 **5** N-COUNT If you say that someone or something is **a model of** a particular quality, you are showing approval of them because they have that quality to a large degree. 典范 [APPROVAL] ❑ *A model of good manners, he has conquered any inward fury.* 作为礼貌行为的典范，他已经克服了内心的狂怒情绪。 **6** ADJ You use **model** to express approval of someone when you think that they perform their role or duties extremely well. 模范的 [ADJ n] [APPROVAL] ❑ *As a girl she had been a model student.* 还是女孩的时候她一直是模范学生。 **7** V-T If one thing **is modeled on** another, the first thing is made so that it is like the second thing in some way. 使仿造 ❑ *The quota system was modeled on those operated in America and continental Europe.* 配额制是仿照美国和欧洲大陆所施行的那些制度制定出来的。 **8** V-T If you **model** yourself **on** someone, you copy the way that they do things, because you admire them and want to be like them. 以…为榜样 ❑ *You have been modeling yourself on others all your life.* 你一辈子都在以别人为榜样。 **9** N-COUNT A particular **model** of a machine is a particular version of it. 型号 ❑ *To keep the cost down, opt for a basic model.* 为了降低成本，就选择一个基本型号吧。 **10** N-COUNT An artist's **model** is a person who stays still in a particular position so that the artist can make a picture or sculpture of them. (艺术家据以绘画或雕塑的) 模特儿 ❑ *...the model for his portrait of Mary Magdalene, the Marchesa Attavanti.* …他绘制玛丽・马格达莱妮，即阿塔凡蒂侯爵夫人肖像画的模特儿。 **11** V-I If someone **models** for an artist, they stay still in a particular position so that the artist can make a picture or sculpture of them. 当模特儿 ❑ *Tullio has been modeling for Sandra for eleven years.* 图利奥已经为桑德拉当了11年的模特儿。 **12** N-COUNT A fashion **model** is a person whose job is to display clothes by wearing them. (时装) 模特儿 ❑ *...Paris's top fashion model.* …巴黎的顶级时装模特儿。 **13** V-T/V-I If someone **models** clothes, they display them by wearing them. 当模特儿展示(服装); 当时装模特儿 ❑ *She began modeling in Paris at age 15.* 她15岁就开始在巴黎当时装模特儿。● **mod·el·ing** N-UNCOUNT 当模特儿 ❑ *She was being offered a modeling contract.* 她得到一份当模特儿的合同。 **14** V-T/V-I If you **model** shapes or figures, you make them out of a substance such as clay or wood. (用黏土或木头等) 塑造; 做模型 ❑ *There she began to model in clay.* 她开始在那儿用黏土做模型。 **15** → see also **role model**

→ see **forecast**

The **brand** of a product such as jeans, tea, or soap is its name, which can also be the name of the company that makes or sells it. The **make** of a car or electrical appliance such as a radio or washing machine is the name of the company that produces it. If you talk about what **type** of product or service you want, you are talking about its quality and what features it should have. You can also talk about **types** of people or of abstract things. ❑ *...which type of coffeemaker to choose. ...a new type of bank account. ...looking for a certain type of actor.* A **model** of car or of some other devices is a name that is given to a particular **type**, for example, a Ford Escort. Note that **type** can also be used informally to mean either **make** or **model**. For example, if someone asks what **type** of car you have got, you could reply "an SUV," "a Ford," or perhaps "an Escort."

Word Partnership *model* 的常用搭配:

V. **build** a model, **make** a model **1**
base *something* **on** a model, **follow** a model, **serve as** a model **1–3**
N. **business** model **3**
ADJ. **basic** model, **current** model, **latest** model, **new** model, **standard** model **3 9**

mo·dem /moʊdəm, -dɛm/ (**modems**) N-COUNT A **modem** is a device which uses a telephone line to connect computers or computer systems. 调制解调器 [also "by" N] [COMPUTING] ❑ *He sent his work to his publishers by modem.* 他通过调制解调器把作品发给他的出版商。

mod·er·ate ♦◇◇ (**moderates, moderating, moderated**)

The adjective and noun are pronounced /mɒdərɪt/. The verb is pronounced /mɒdəreɪt/.

形容词和名词读作 /mɒdərɪt/。动词读作 /mɒdəreɪt/。

1 ADJ **Moderate** political opinions or policies are not extreme. (政见或政策) 温和的 ❑ *He was an easygoing man of very moderate views.* 他是一个有着温和观点性情随和的人。 **2** ADJ You use **moderate** to describe people or groups who have moderate political opinions or policies. (人或团体) 温和的 ❑ *...a moderate Democrat.* …温和的民主党人。● N-COUNT A **moderate** is someone with moderate political opinions. 温和派 ❑ *If he presents himself as a radical he risks scaring off the moderates whose votes he so desperately needs.* 如果他表现出自己是个激进分子的话，他就有可能吓跑那些温和派，而他急需那些人的选票。 **3** ADJ You use **moderate** to describe something that is neither large nor small in amount or degree. (数量或程度) 适中的 ❑ *While a moderate amount of stress can be beneficial, too much stress can exhaust you.* 适当的压力可能有益，而压力过大会让你筋疲力尽。 ● **mod·er·ate·ly** ADV 适中地 ❑ *Both are moderately large insects, with a wingspan of around four centimeters.* 这两只都是中等大小的昆虫，翼幅大约为四厘米。 **4** ADJ A **moderate** change in something is a change that is not great. (变化) 不大的 ❑ *Most drugs offer either no real improvement or, at best, only moderate improvements.* 大多数药或者没有真正疗效，或者最多也就是稍有疗效。● **mod·er·ate·ly** ADV 不大地 [ADV after v] ❑ *Share prices on the Tokyo Exchange declined moderately.* 东京股票交易所的股票价格稍有下降。 **5** V-T/V-I If you **moderate** something or if it **moderates**, it becomes less extreme or violent and easier to deal with or accept. 使缓和; 变得缓和 ❑ *They are hoping that once in office he can be persuaded to moderate his views.* 他们希望他一上台后就能他说服，使他的观点变得温和些。● **mod·era·tion** /mɒdəreɪʃᵊn/ N-UNCOUNT 缓和 ❑ *A moderation in food prices helped to offset the first increase in energy prices.* 食品价格的降低有助于抵消能源价格的第一次上涨。

Word Partnership *moderate* 的常用搭配:

N. moderate **approach**, moderate **position**, moderate **view** **1**
moderate **amount**, moderate **exercise**, moderate **heat**, moderate **prices**, moderate **speed** **3**
moderate **growth**, moderate **improvement** **4**

mod·era·tion /mɒdəreɪʃᵊn/ **1** N-UNCOUNT If you say that someone's behavior shows **moderation**, you approve of them because they act in a way that you think is reasonable and not extreme. 节制 [APPROVAL] ❑ *The United Nations Secretary General called*

on all parties to show moderation. 联合国秘书长呼吁各方要克制。
● PHRASE If you say that someone does something such as eat, drink, or smoke **in moderation**, you mean that they do not eat, drink, or smoke too much or more than is reasonable. 有节制地
2 → see also **moderate**

★ **mod·era·tor** /mɒdəreɪtər/ (**moderators**) 1 N-COUNT In debates and negotiations, the **moderator** is the person who is in charge of the discussion and makes sure that it is conducted in a fair and organized way. (争论和谈判的) 主持人 [FORMAL]
2 N-COUNT In some Protestant churches, a **moderator** is a senior member of the clergy who is in charge at large and important meetings. (基督教的) 会议主席 ❑ *...a former moderator of the General Assembly of the Presbyterian Church.* …一位前基督教长老会大会主席。

mod·ern ♦♦◊ /mɒdərn/ 1 ADJ **Modern** means relating to the present time, for example the present decade or present century. 现代的 [ADJ n] ❑ *We had a long talk about the problem of materialism in modern society.* 我们就现代社会中的实利主义问题进行了一次长谈。
2 ADJ Something that is **modern** is new and involves the latest ideas or equipment. 现代化的 ❑ *In many ways, it was a very modern school for its time.* 从多方面看，这是当时很现代化的一所学校。 3 ADJ People are sometimes described as **modern** when they have opinions or ways of behaving that have not yet been accepted by most people in a society. 时髦的 ❑ *She is very modern in outlook.* 她的看法很时髦。 4 ADJ **Modern** is used to describe styles of art, dance, music, and architecture that have developed in recent times, in contrast to classical styles. (艺术、舞蹈、音乐和建筑) 现代派的 [ADJ n] ❑ *She'd been a dancer with a modern dance company in New York.* 她过去一直是纽约一家现代舞公司的舞蹈演员。

Thesaurus *modern* 另参见：
ADJ. contemporary, current, present 1 4
state-of-the-art, up-to-date 2

Word Partnership *modern* 的常用搭配：
N. modern **civilization**, modern **culture**, modern **era**, modern **life**, modern **science**, modern **society**, modern **times**, modern **warfare** 1
modern **conveniences**, modern **equipment**, modern **methods**, modern **techniques**, modern **technology** 2
modern **art**, modern **dance**, modern **literature**, modern **music** 4

mod·ern·ise /mɒdərnaɪz/ [BRIT] → see **modernize**

mod·ern·ize /mɒdərnaɪz/ (**modernizes, modernizing, modernized**)
in BRIT, also use **modernise**
V-T To **modernize** something such as a system or a factory means to change it by replacing old equipment or methods with new ones. 使现代化 ❑ *...plans to modernize the refinery.* …使精炼厂现代化的各项计划。 ● **mod·erni·za·tion** /mɒdərnɪzeɪʃən/ N-UNCOUNT 现代化 ❑ *...a five-year modernization program.* …一个为期5年的现代化规划。

mod·est ♦◊◊ /mɒdɪst/ 1 ADJ A **modest** house or other building is not large or expensive. 适度的 ❑ *They had spent the night at a modest hotel.* 他们在一家普通的旅馆过夜。 2 ADJ You use **modest** to describe something such as an amount, rate, or improvement which is fairly small. (数量、比率或改进幅度等) 较小的 ❑ *Unemployment rose to the still modest rate of 0.7%.* 失业率升高到0.7%这个还算低的水平。 ● **mod·est·ly** ADV 较小地 ❑ *The nation's balance of payments improved modestly last month.* 这个国家上个月的国际收支有了较小的改善。 3 ADJ If you say that someone is **modest**, you approve of them because they do not talk much about their abilities or achievements. 谦虚的 [APPROVAL] ❑ *He's modest, as well as being a great player.* 他是一个谦虚而且出色的运动员。 ● **mod·est·ly** ADV 谦虚地 [ADV with v] ❑ *"You really must be very good at what you do."—"I suppose I am," Kate said modestly.* "你确实非常擅长你所做的。"——"我觉得是吧。"凯特谦虚地说。

Word Partnership *modest* 的常用搭配：
N. modest **home/house** 1
modest **amount**, modest **fee**, modest **income**, modest **increase** 2

mod·es·ty /mɒdɪsti/ 1 N-UNCOUNT Someone who shows **modesty** does not talk much about their abilities or achievements. 谦虚 [APPROVAL] ❑ *His modesty does him credit, for the food he produces speaks for itself.* 他的谦虚为他赢得了信誉，他生产的食品就是最好的证明。 2 N-UNCOUNT You can refer to the **modesty** of something such as a place or amount when it is fairly small. (某地或数量等) 小 ❑ *The modesty of the town itself comes as something of a surprise.* 这个城镇的小巧挺让人吃惊。 3 N-UNCOUNT If someone, especially a woman, shows **modesty**, they are cautious about the way they dress and behave because they are aware that other people may view them in a sexual way. (尤指妇女) 端庄 ❑ *There were shrieks of embarrassment, mingled with giggles, from some of the girls as they struggled to protect their modesty.* 有些女孩子努力要保持端庄，但还是发出了尴尬的尖叫声，其中还夹杂着咯咯的笑声。

modi·fy /mɒdɪfaɪ/ (**modifies, modifying, modified**) V-T If you **modify** something, you change it slightly, usually in order to improve it. 修改 ❑ *The club members did agree to modify their recruitment policy.* 俱乐部成员确已同意修改他们的入会政策。
● **modi·fi·ca·tion** ▲ /mɒdɪfɪkeɪʃən/ N-VAR (**modifications**) 修改 ❑ *Relatively minor modifications were required.* 需要相对较小的修改。

modu·lar /mɒdʒələr/ 1 ADJ **Modular** means relating to a part of a machine, especially a computer, which performs a particular function. 组件的 (尤指电脑的一部分) ❑ *Its modular architecture allows modules to be swapped in and out depending on the processor and operating system.* 它的组件结构使得各组件可以依靠处理器和操作系统进行进出交换。 2 ADJ In building, **modular** means relating to the construction of buildings in parts called modules. (建筑) 组合式的 ❑ *They ended up buying a modular home on a two-acre lot.* 他们最终买了一所占地两英亩的组合式房屋。

★ **mod·ule** /mɒdʒul/ (**modules**) 1 N-COUNT A **module** is a part of a machine, especially a computer, which performs a particular function. (尤指计算机的) 组件 2 N-COUNT A **module** is a part of a spacecraft which can operate by itself, often away from the rest of the spacecraft. (航天器的) 舱 ❑ *A rescue plan could be achieved by sending an unmanned module to the space station.* 营救计划可以通过向空间站发送一个无人舱来完成。

moist /mɔɪst/ (**moister, moistest**) ADJ Something that is **moist** is slightly wet. 湿润的 ❑ *The soil is reasonably moist after the September rain.* 9月的雨水之后，土壤适度湿润。

mois·ten /mɔɪsən/ (**moistens, moistening, moistened**) V-T To **moisten** something means to make it slightly wet. 使湿润 ❑ *She took a sip of water to moisten her dry throat.* 她抿了一小口水，润一润自己干燥的喉咙。

mois·ture /mɔɪstʃər/ N-UNCOUNT **Moisture** is tiny drops of water in the air, on a surface, or in the ground. 潮气；水分 ❑ *When the soil is dry, more moisture is lost from the plant.* 土壤干燥时，植物就会失去更多的水分。

mois·tur·ise /mɔɪstʃəraɪz/ [BRIT] → see **moisturize**

mois·tur·ize /mɔɪstʃəraɪz/ (**moisturizes, moisturizing, moisturized**)
in BRIT, also use **moisturise**
V-T If you **moisturize** your skin, you rub cream into it to make it softer. If a cream **moisturizes** your skin, it makes it softer. 使 (皮肤) 滋润 ❑ *...products to moisturize, protect, and firm your skin.* …用于润肤、护肤和紧肤的各种产品。

mold /moʊld/ (**molds, molding, molded**)
in BRIT, use **mould**
1 N-COUNT A **mold** is a hollow container that you pour liquid into. When the liquid becomes solid, it takes the same shape as the mold. 模子 ❑ *He makes plastic reusable molds.* 他制作可再次使用的塑料模子。 2 N-COUNT If a person fits into or is cast in a **mold** of a particular kind, they have the characteristics, attitudes, behavior, or lifestyle that are typical of that type of person. (人的) 类型 ❑ *He could never be accused of fitting the mold.* 他永远都不可能被指责属于这个类型。 ● PHRASE If you say that someone **breaks the mold**, you mean that they do completely different things from what has been done before or from what is usually done. 突破固有模式 3 V-T If you **mold** a soft substance such as plastic or clay, you make it into a particular shape or into an object. 塑造 ❑ *He would dampen the clay and begin to mold it into an entirely different shape.* 他把黏土弄湿，然后着手把它塑造成一个完全不同的形状。 4 V-T To **mold** someone or something means to change or influence them over a period of time so that they develop in a particular way. 对…的形成施加影响 ❑ *It was a very safe, long childhood with Diane, and she really molded my ideas a lot.* 那是一段和黛安娜一起度过的安全而漫长的童年时光，

m

而且她确实在很大程度上影响了我思想的形成。 5 V-T/V-I When something **molds** to an object or when you **mold** it there, it fits around the object tightly so that the shape of the object can still be seen. 使与…轮廓吻合；与…轮廓吻合 ❑ *It looked as though the plastic wrap was molded to the fruit.* 看上去好像那个塑料包装与这个水果的轮廓完全吻合。 6 N-MASS **Mold** is a soft gray, green, or blue substance that sometimes forms in spots on old food or on damp walls or clothes. 霉菌 ❑ *She discovered black and green mold growing in her hall closet.* 她发现大厅的壁橱里长着黑绿色的霉菌。
→ see **fungus, laboratory**

mole /moʊl/ (**moles**) 1 N-COUNT A **mole** is a natural dark spot or small dark lump on someone's skin. 痣 ❑ *Researchers studied moles on those aged between 12 and 50.* 研究者们研究了12岁到50岁的人身上长的痣。 2 N-COUNT A **mole** is a small animal with black fur that lives underground. 鼹鼠 3 N-COUNT A **mole** is a member of a government or other organization who gives secret information to the press or to a rival organization. (政府或机构内的) 间谍 ❑ *He had been recruited by the Russians as a mole and trained in Moscow.* 他曾经被俄国人招做间谍，在莫斯科受训。

mo·lecu·lar /məlɛkyələr/ ADJ **Molecular** means relating to or involving molecules. 分子的 [ADJ n] ❑ *...the molecular structure of fuel.* …燃料的分子结构。

Word Link *cule ≈ small : minuscule, molecule, ridicule*

mol·ecule /mɒlɪkyul/ (**molecules**) N-COUNT A **molecule** is the smallest amount of a chemical substance which can exist by itself. 分子 ❑ *...the hydrogen bonds between water molecules.* …水分子之间的氢连接。
→ see **element**

mo·lest /məlɛst/ (**molests, molesting, molested**) V-T A person who **molests** someone, especially a woman or a child, interferes with them in a sexual way against their will. 对…性骚扰 (尤指妇女或孩子) ❑ *He was accused of sexually molesting a female colleague.* 他被指控对一名女同事进行性骚扰。

M

mol·ten /moʊltᵊn/ ADJ **Molten** rock, metal, or glass has been heated to a very high temperature and has become a hot, thick liquid. 熔化的 ❑ *The molten metal is poured into the mold.* 这块熔化了的金属被倒入模子。
→ see **volcano**

mom ◆◆◇ /mɒm/ (**moms**) N-FAMILY Your **mom** is your mother. 妈妈 [AM, INFORMAL]

in BRIT, use **mum**

❑ *We waited for Mom and Dad to get home.* 我们等着爸爸妈妈回家。

mo·ment ◆◆◆ /moʊmənt/ (**moments**) 1 N-COUNT You can refer to a very short period of time, for example a few seconds, as a **moment** or **moments**. 瞬间 ❑ *In a moment he was gone.* 不一会儿他就不见了。 ❑ *In moments, I was asleep once more.* 很快，我又睡着了。 2 N-COUNT A particular **moment** is the point in time at which something happens. 时刻 ❑ *At this moment a car stopped at the house.* 就在此时，一辆汽车停在那座房子前。 3 PHRASE If you say that something will or may happen **at any moment** or **any moment now**, you are emphasizing that it is likely to happen very soon. 随时 [EMPHASIS] ❑ *He'll be here to see you any moment now.* 他随时会来这里看你。 4 PHRASE You use expressions such as **at the moment, at this moment**, and **at the present moment** to indicate that a particular situation exists at the time when you are speaking. 此刻 ❑ *At the moment, no one is talking to me.* 此刻没人和我说话。 ❑ *He's touring South America at this moment in time.* 他此刻正在周游南美。 5 PHRASE You use **for the moment** to indicate that something is true now, even if it will not be true in the future. 至少目前 ❑ *For the moment, a potential crisis appears to have been averted.* 至少目前，一个潜在的危机好像已被避免了。 6 PHRASE If you say that someone or something **has** their **moments**, you are indicating that there are times when they are successful or interesting, but that this does not happen very often. 有成功或吸引人的时刻 ❑ *The film has its moments.* 这部电影有它走红的时候。 7 PHRASE If someone does something at **the last moment**, they do it at the latest time possible. 最后一刻 ❑ *They changed their minds at the last moment and refused to go.* 他们在最后一刻改变了主意，拒绝前往。 8 PHRASE You use the expression **the next moment**, or expressions such as "**one moment** he was there, **the next** he was gone," to emphasize that something happens suddenly, especially when it is very different from what was happening before. 紧接着 [EMPHASIS] ❑ *He is unpredictable, weeping one moment, laughing the next.* 他令人难以捉摸，一会儿哭，一会儿笑。 9 PHRASE You use **of the moment** to describe someone or something that is or was especially popular at a particular time, especially when you want to suggest that their popularity is unlikely to last long or did not last long. 当前红极一时的 (尤指这种受欢迎的情况不会持续很久) ❑ *He's the man of the moment, isn't he?* 他是当前的红人，对吧？ 10 PHRASE If you say that something happens **the moment** something else happens, you are emphasizing that it happens immediately after the other thing. 一…就 [EMPHASIS] ❑ *The moment I closed my eyes, I fell asleep.* 我一闭上眼睛就睡着了。 11 **spur of the moment** → see **spur**

Word Partnership *moment* 的常用搭配：

ADV.	a moment **ago**, **just** a moment 1
N.	moment **of silence**, moment **of thought** 1
V.	**stop for a** moment, **take a** moment, **think for a** moment, **wait a** moment 1
ADJ.	**an awkward** moment, **a critical** moment, **the right** moment 2

mo·men·tari·ly /moʊmənteərɪli/ 1 ADV **Momentarily** means for a short time. 短暂地 ❑ *She paused momentarily when she saw them.* 她看到他们时稍停了一会儿。 2 ADV **Momentarily** means very soon. 马上 [AM] ❑ *"My husband will be here momentarily," Sophia informed them.* "我丈夫马上就到，"索菲娅告诉他们。 ❑ *The Senate Judiciary Committee is expected to vote momentarily on his nomination to the Supreme Court.* 参议院司法委员会立刻向联邦最高法院对其提名进行表决。

★ **mo·men·tary** /moʊmənteri/ ADJ Something that is **momentary** lasts for a very short period of time, for example for a few seconds or less. 短暂的 ❑ *...a momentary lapse of concentration.* …稍一走神。

▲ **mo·men·tous** /moʊmɛntəs/ ADJ If you refer to a decision, event, or change as **momentous**, you mean that it is very important, often because of the effects that it will have in the future. 重大的 ❑ *...the momentous decision to send in the troops.* …派兵的重大决定。

★ **mo·men·tum** /moʊmɛntəm/ 1 N-UNCOUNT If a process or movement gains **momentum**, it keeps developing or happening more quickly and keeps becoming less likely to stop. 势头 ❑ *This campaign is really gaining momentum.* 这场运动确实势头正猛。 2 N-UNCOUNT In physics, **momentum** is the mass of a moving object multiplied by its speed in a particular direction. 动量 [TECHNICAL]
→ see **motion**

Word Partnership *momentum* 的常用搭配：

V.	**build** momentum, **gain** momentum, **gather** momentum, **have** momentum, **lose** momentum, **maintain** momentum 1 2

mom·my /mɒmi/ (**mommies**) N-FAMILY Some people, especially young children, call their mother **mommy**. 妈咪 (尤为儿童使用) [AM, INFORMAL]

in BRIT, use **mummy**

❑ *Be very good and very quiet and help your mommy.* 你要乖乖的，安静些，要帮妈咪。

Mon. **Mon.** is a written abbreviation for **Monday**. 星期一 ❑ *...Mon., Oct. 19.* …10月19日，星期一。

Word Link *arch ≈ rule : anarchy, hierarchy, monarch*

mon·arch /mɒnərk, -ark/ (**monarchs**) N-COUNT The **monarch** of a country is the king, queen, emperor, or empress. 君主

mon·ar·chist /mɒnərkɪst/ (**monarchists**) ADJ If someone has **monarchist** views, they believe that their country should have a monarch, such as a king or queen. 主张君主政体的 ❑ *A monarchist party is running in the forthcoming elections.* 一个主张君主政体的政党要参加即将来临的大选。 ● N-COUNT A **monarchist** is someone with monarchist views. 主张君主政体的人 ❑ *The queen's responses to Mr. Chretien will be studied by republicans and monarchists alike here.* 女王对克雷蒂安先生的回应将会同样在这儿受到共和派和君主派的关注。

▲ **mon·ar·chy** /mɒnərki/ (**monarchies**) 1 N-VAR A **monarchy** is a system in which a country has a monarch. 君主制 ❑ *...a serious debate on the future of the monarchy.* …一场有关君主制未来的重大辩论。 2 N-COUNT A **monarchy** is a country that has a monarch. 君主国 ❑ *Britain is a constitutional monarchy.* 英国是个君主立宪制国家。 3 N-COUNT The **monarchy** is used to refer to the monarch and his or her family. 王室 ❑ *The monarchy has to create a balance between its public and private lives.* 王室不得不在公众生活和私生活之间建立一种平衡。

▲ **mon·as·tery** /mɒnəstɛri/ (**monasteries**) N-COUNT A **monastery** is a building or collection of buildings in which monks live. 修道院

Mon·day ♦♦♦ /mʌndeɪ, -di/ (**Mondays**) N-VAR **Monday** is the day after Sunday and before Tuesday. 星期一 ❑ *I went back to work on Monday.* 我星期一回去上班了。❑ *The first meeting of the group took place last Monday.* 该集团的第一次会议于上周一召开。

mon·etar·ism /mɑnɪtərɪzəm/ N-UNCOUNT **Monetarism** is an economic policy that involves controlling the amount of money that is available and in use in a country at any one time. 货币控制政策 [BUSINESS]

mon·etar·ist /mɑnɪtərɪst/ (**monetarists**) ADJ **Monetarist** policies or views are based on the theory that the amount of money that is available and in use in a country at any one time should be controlled. 关于货币控制政策的 [BUSINESS] ❑ *...tough monetarist policies.* …强硬的货币控制政策。● N-COUNT A **monetarist** is someone with monetarist views. 主张实施货币控制政策的人 ❑ *Such a policy, monetarists claim, encourages steady growth and price stability.* 主张实施货币控制政策的人士宣称，这样一个政策会鼓励稳步增长和价格稳定。

★ **mon·etary** ♦◇◇ /mɑnɪtɛri/ ADJ **Monetary** means relating to money, especially the total amount of money in a country. 货币的 [ADJ n] [BUSINESS] ❑ *Some countries tighten monetary policy to avoid inflation.* 一些国家紧缩货币政策以避免通货膨胀。

mon·ey ♦♦♦ /mʌni/ (**monies** or **moneys**) **1** N-UNCOUNT **Money** is the coins or bank notes that you use to buy things, or the sum that you have in a bank account. 钱 ❑ *A lot of the money that you pay at the movies goes back to the film distributors.* 你付给电影院的钱有很多又回到了电影发行人的手里。❑ *Players should be allowed to earn money from advertising.* 应该允许运动员拍广告挣钱。**2** N-PLURAL **Monies** is used to refer to several separate sums of money that form part of a larger amount that is received or spent. 款项 [FORMAL] ❑ *We drew up a schedule of payments for the rest of the monies owed.* 我们制定了一个剩余欠款的还款计划。**3** → see also **pocket money** **4** PHRASE If you say that someone **has money to burn**, you mean that they have more money than they need, or that they spend their money on things that you think are unnecessary. 有花不完的钱；乱花钱 ❑ *He was a high-earning broker with money to burn.* 他是一个收入高得花不完的经纪人。**5** PHRASE If you are **in the money**, you have a lot of money to spend. 非常有钱的 [INFORMAL] ❑ *If you are one of the lucky callers chosen to play, you could be in the money.* 如果你是一个幸运打进电话的人，且被选中参赛，你就可能要发财了。**6** PHRASE If you **make money**, you obtain money by earning it or by making a profit. 赚钱 ❑ *...the only part of the firm that consistently made money.* …公司里惟一一个一直赚钱的部门。**7** PHRASE If you say that you want someone to **put** their **money where** their **mouth is**, you want them to spend money to improve a bad situation, instead of just talking about improving it. 说话兑现 ❑ *The government might be obliged to put its money where its mouth is to prove its commitment.* 政府可能要被迫兑现它的承诺来证明其信用。**8** PHRASE If you say that **the smart money** is on a particular person or thing, you mean that people who know a lot about it think that this person will be successful, or this thing will happen. 知情者下的注 [JOURNALISM] ❑ *With Japan not playing, the smart money was on the Canadians.* 由于日本不参加，注下在加拿大队上。**9** PHRASE If you say that **money talks**, you mean that if someone has a lot of money, they also have a lot of power. 金钱万能 ❑ *The formula in Hollywood is simple – money talks.* 好莱坞的规则很简单——金钱万能。**10** PHRASE If you say that someone is **throwing money at** a problem, you are critical of them for trying to improve it by spending money on it, instead of doing more thoughtful and practical things to improve it. (不采用合理有效的办法解决问题，而是) 对…大肆花钱 [DISAPPROVAL] ❑ *The governor's answer to the problem has been to throw money at it.* 州长对这个问题的解决就是在滥花冤枉钱。**11** PHRASE If you **get** your **money's worth**, you get something which is worth the money that it costs or the effort you have put in. 钱花得值 ❑ *The fans get their money's worth.* 星迷们的钱花得值。**12** to **give** someone **a run for** their **money** → see **run**
→ see Word Web: **money**
→ see **bank, donor, lottery, salt**

Thesaurus *money* 另参见：
N. capital, cash, currency, funds, wealth **1**

mon·ey laun·der·ing N-UNCOUNT **Money laundering** is the crime of processing stolen money through a legitimate business or sending it abroad to a foreign bank, to hide the fact that the money was illegally obtained. 洗钱 ❑ *Investigators are looking at what they believe may be the largest money-laundering scandal in history.* 调查者们正在研究他们认为可能是史上最大的一起洗钱丑闻。

money·maker /mʌnimeɪkər/ (**moneymakers**) N-COUNT If you say that a business, product, or investment is a **moneymaker**, you mean that it makes a big profit. 赚钱的生意 [BUSINESS] ❑ *The drug is a big moneymaker for them.* 毒品对他们来说是个赚钱的大买卖。

mon·ey mar·ket (**money markets**) N-COUNT A country's **money market** consists of all the banks and other organizations that deal with short-term loans, capital, and foreign exchange. 金融市场 [BUSINESS] ❑ *On the money markets the dollar was weaker against European currencies.* 货币市场上，美元较欧洲货币表现疲软。

mon·ey or·der (**money orders**) N-COUNT A **money order** is a piece of paper representing a sum of money which you can buy at a post office or a bank and send to someone as a way of sending them money by mail. 汇票；汇款单 [AM]
in BRIT, use **postal order**
❑ *I sent them a money order for $40.* 我寄给他们一张$40的汇款单。

mon·ey sup·ply N-UNCOUNT **The money supply** is the total amount of money in a country's economy at any one time. 货币供应量 [BUSINESS] ❑ *They believed that controlling the money supply would reduce inflation.* 他们相信控制货币供应量会降低通货膨胀。

moni·tor ♦◇◇ /mɒnɪtər/ (**monitors, monitoring, monitored**) **1** V-T If you **monitor** something, you regularly check its development or progress, and sometimes comment on it. 监控 ❑ *Officials had not been allowed to monitor the voting.* 官员们未曾获许监控选举。**2** V-T If someone **monitors** radio broadcasts from other countries, they record them or listen carefully to them in order to obtain information. 监听 ❑ *Peter Murray is in Washington and has been monitoring reports out of Monrovia.* 彼得·默里在华盛顿，一直监听来自蒙罗维亚的报道。**3** N-COUNT A **monitor** is a machine that is used to check or record things, for example processes or substances inside a person's body. 监控器 ❑ *The heart monitor shows low levels of consciousness.* 心脏监控器显示低意识水平。**4** N-COUNT A **monitor** is a screen which is used to display certain kinds of information, for example on a computer, in airports, or in television studios. 显示屏 ❑ *He was watching a game of tennis on a television monitor.* 他那时正在电视监控器上观看一场网球赛。**5** N-COUNT You can refer to a person

m

Word Web money

Early traders used a system of **barter** which didn't involve **money**. For example, a farmer might trade a cow for a wooden cart. In China, India, and Africa, cowrie shells* became a form of **currency**. The first **coins** were crude lumps of metal. Uniform circular coins appeared in China around 1500 BC. In 1150 AD, the Chinese started using paper bills. In 560 BC, the Lydians (living in what is now Turkey) **minted** three types of coins—a **gold** coin, a **silver** coin, and a mixed metal coin. Their use quickly spread through Asia Minor and Greece.

cowrie shell: a small, shiny, oval shell.

who checks that something is done correctly, or that it is fair, as a **monitor**. 监督员 ❑ *Government monitors will continue to accompany reporters.* 政府监督员们将继续陪同记者们。

Word Partnership *monitor* 的常用搭配:

N. monitor **activity**, monitor **elections**, monitor **performance**, monitor **progress**, monitor **a situation** 1
color monitor, **computer** monitor, **video** monitor 4

ADV. **carefully** monitor, **closely** monitor 1 2

▲ **monk** /mʌŋk/ (**monks**) N-COUNT A **monk** is a member of a male religious community that is usually separated from the outside world. 僧侣 ❑ *...saffron-robed Buddhist monks.* …身穿黄袍的和尚们。

mon·key /mʌŋki/ (**monkeys**) 1 N-COUNT A **monkey** is an animal with a long tail which lives in hot countries and climbs trees. 猴子 2 N-COUNT If you refer to a child as a **monkey**, you are saying in an affectionate way that he or she is very lively and naughty. 淘气鬼 [FEELINGS] ❑ *She's such a little monkey.* 她是这么个小淘气。

→ see **primate**

mon·key wrench (**monkey wrenches**) → see **wrench**

mono /mɒnoʊ/ ADJ **Mono** is used to describe a system of playing music in which all the sound is directed through one speaker only. Compare **stereo**. 单声道的 ❑ *This model has a mono soundtrack.* 这个型号是单声道的。

mo·noga·mous /mənɒgəməs/ 1 ADJ Someone who is **monogamous** or who has a **monogamous** relationship has a sexual relationship with only one partner. 单一性伴侣的 ❑ *Do you believe that men are not naturally monogamous?* 你相信男人天生就不是单一性伴侣的吗? 2 ADJ **Monogamous** animals have only one sexual partner during their lives or during each mating season. (动物)单一配偶的 ❑ *Only about five percent of mammals are monogamous.* 只有约百分之五的哺乳动物是单一配偶的。

M

Word Link *mono ≈ one : monogamy, monologue, monopoly*

mo·noga·my /mənɒgəmi/ 1 N-UNCOUNT **Monogamy** is used to refer to the state or custom of having a sexual relationship with only one partner. 单一配偶制 ❑ *People still opt for monogamy and marriage.* 人们还是选择单一配偶制和婚姻。 2 N-UNCOUNT **Monogamy** is the state or custom of being married to only one person at a particular time. 一夫一妻制 ❑ *In many non-Western societies, however, monogamy has never dominated.* 然而，在很多非西方社会，一夫一妻制从未占主导地位。

mono·lith·ic /mɒnəlɪθɪk/ 1 ADJ If you refer to an organization or system as **monolithic**, you are critical of it because it is very large and very slow to change, and does not seem to have different parts with different characters. 大一统的 [DISAPPROVAL] ❑ *...an authoritarian and monolithic system.* …大一统的独裁体制。 2 ADJ If you describe something such as a building as **monolithic**, you do not like it because it is very large and plain with no character. 巨大而平庸的 [DISAPPROVAL] ❑ *...a huge monolithic concrete building.* …一座巨大而平庸的混凝土建筑。

▲ **mono·logue** /mɒnəlɔg/ (**monologues**) also **monolog** 1 N-COUNT If you refer to a long speech by one person during a conversation as a **monologue**, you mean it prevents other people from talking or expressing their opinions. 长篇大论 ❑ *Morris ignored the question and continued his monologue.* 莫里斯不理会那个问题，继续他的长篇大论。 2 N-VAR A **monologue** is a long speech which is spoken by one person as an entertainment, or as part of an entertainment such as a play. 独白; 独角戏 ❑ *...a monologue based on the writing of Quentin Crisp.* …根据昆廷·克里斯普的作品改编的一段独白。

▲ **mo·nopo·lise** /mənɒpəlaɪz/ [BRIT] → see **monopolize**

▲ **mo·nopo·lize** /mənɒpəlaɪz/ (**monopolizes, monopolizing, monopolized**)

in BRIT, also use **monopolise**

1 V-T If you say that someone **monopolizes** something, you mean that they have a very large share of it and prevent other people from having a share. 垄断 ❑ *They are controlling so much cocoa that they are virtually monopolizing the market.* 控制着那么多可可粉，他们实际上是在垄断市场。 ● **mo·nopo·li·za·tion** /mənɒpəlaɪzeɪʃən/ N-UNCOUNT 垄断 ❑ *...the monopolization of a market by a single supplier.* …单一供货商对一个市场的垄断。 2 V-T If something or someone **monopolizes** you, they demand a lot of your time and attention, so that there is very little time left for anything or anyone else. 独占 ❑ *He would monopolize her totally, to the exclusion of her brothers and sisters.* 他要完全独占她，甚至排斥她的兄弟和姐妹。

★ **mo·nopo·ly** /mənɒpəli/ (**monopolies**) 1 N-VAR If a company, person, or state has a **monopoly on** something such as an industry, they have complete control over it, so that it is impossible for others to become involved in it. 垄断 [BUSINESS] ❑ *...Russian moves to end a state monopoly on land ownership.* …俄罗斯人提议结束国家对土地所有权的垄断。 2 N-COUNT A **monopoly** is a company which is the only one providing a particular product or service. 垄断企业 [BUSINESS] ❑ *...a state-owned monopoly.* …一个国有垄断企业。 3 N-SING If you say that someone does not have a **monopoly on** something, you mean that they are not the only person who has that thing. 独有 ❑ *Women do not have a monopoly on feelings of betrayal.* 背叛感并非是女人独有的。

▲ **mo·noto·nous** /mənɒtənəs/ ADJ Something that is **monotonous** is very boring because it has a regular, repeated pattern which never changes. 单调的 ❑ *It's monotonous work, like most factory jobs.* 这是个单调的工作，和大多数工厂工作一样。

mon·soon /mɒnsuːn/ (**monsoons**) 1 N-COUNT The **monsoon** is the season in Southern Asia when there is a lot of very heavy rain. (南亚地区的) 雨季 ❑ *...the end of the monsoon.* …雨季的结束。 2 N-PLURAL Monsoon rains are sometimes referred to as **the monsoons**. 雨季的降雨 ❑ *In Bangladesh, the monsoons have started.* 在孟加拉国，雨季已经开始。

→ see **disaster**

mon·ster /mɒnstər/ (**monsters**) 1 N-COUNT A **monster** is a large imaginary creature that looks very ugly and frightening. 怪物 ❑ *Both movies are about a monster in the bedroom closet.* 两部电影都是关于卧室橱柜里的一个怪物。 2 N-COUNT A **monster** is something which is extremely large, especially something that is difficult to manage or which is unpleasant. 庞然大物 (尤指棘手的事物) ❑ *...the monster which is now the Boston marathon.* …波士顿马拉松赛现在成了棘手的事。 3 ADJ **Monster** means extremely and surprisingly large. 庞大的 [ADJ n] [INFORMAL, EMPHASIS] ❑ *...a monster weapon.* …一个巨型武器。 4 N-COUNT If you describe someone as a **monster**, you mean that they are cruel, frightening, or evil. 恶魔 ❑ *Galbraith said that her husband was a depraved monster who threatened and humiliated her.* 加尔布雷思说她丈夫是个没有人性的恶魔，威胁她并羞辱她。

mon·strous /mɒnstrəs/ 1 ADJ If you describe a situation or event as **monstrous**, you mean that it is extremely shocking or unfair. 骇人听闻的; 极不公正的 ❑ *She endured the monstrous behavior for years.* 她忍受这种骇人听闻的行为多年。 ● **mon·strous·ly** ADV 骇人听闻地; 极不公正地 [ADV after v] ❑ *Your husband's family has behaved monstrously.* 你婆家人做得太不公正了。 2 ADJ If you describe an unpleasant thing as **monstrous**, you mean that it is extremely large in size or extent. (令人不悦的事物) 巨大的 [EMPHASIS] ❑ *A group of men are erecting a monstrous copper edifice.* 一群人正在建造一座巨大的铜色建筑。 ● **mon·strous·ly** ADV 巨大地 [ADV adj/-ed] ❑ *It would be monstrously unfair.* 那将太不公平了。 3 ADJ If you describe something as **monstrous**, you mean that it is extremely frightening because it appears unnatural or ugly. 恐怖的 ❑ *...the film's monstrous fantasy figure.* …电影中恐怖的魔幻形象。

month ♦♦♦ /mʌnθ/ (**months**) 1 N-COUNT A **month** is one of the twelve periods of time that a year is divided into, for example January or February. 月份 ❑ *The trial is due to begin next month.* 审判定于下个月开始。 ❑ *...an exhibition which opens this month at the Guggenheim Museum.* …本月在古根海姆博物馆开幕的展览。 2 N-COUNT A **month** is a period of about four weeks. 1个月的时间 ❑ *She was here for a month.* 她在这里呆了1个月。 ❑ *Over the next several months I met most of her family.* 在此后的几个月中，我见到了她大部分家人。

→ see **year**

month·ly ♦◊◊ /mʌnθli/ (**monthlies**) 1 ADJ A **monthly** event or publication happens or appears every month. 每月的; 每月一次的 [ADJ n] ❑ *Many people are now having trouble making their monthly house payments.* 现在许多人都有支付按月房贷的困难。 ❑ *Kidscape runs monthly workshops for teachers.* 基德思加坡为教师举行每月一次的研讨会。 ● ADV **Monthly** is also an adverb. 每月地; 每月一次地 [ADV after v] ❑ *In some areas the property price can rise monthly.* 有些地区，房价能每月都涨。 2 N-COUNT You can refer to a publication that is published monthly as a **monthly**. 月刊 ❑ *...a satirical monthly.* …一份讽刺月刊。

Word Web moon

Scientists believe the **moon** is about five billion years old. They think a large asteroid hit the earth. A big piece of the earth broke off. It went flying into **space**. However, Earth's **gravity** caught it and it began to circle the earth. This piece became our moon. The moon orbits the earth once a month. It also **rotates** on its **axis** every thirty days. The moon has no **atmosphere**, so meteoroids constantly crash into it. When a meteoroid hits the surface of the moon, it makes a **crater**. Craters cover the surface of the moon.

3 ADJ **Monthly** quantities or rates relate to a period of one month. 每月的 [ADJ n] ❑ *Consumers are charged a monthly fee above their basic cable costs.* 消费者每月被收取高于基本有线费的一笔费用。

monu·ment /mɒnyəmənt/ (**monuments**) 1 N-COUNT A **monument** is a large structure, usually made of stone, which is built to remind people of an event in history or of a famous person. 纪念碑 ❑ *...a newly restored monument commemorating a 119-year-old tragedy.* …为纪念一起有着119年历史的惨剧而新修复的一座纪念碑。 2 N-COUNT A **monument** is something such as a castle or bridge that was built a very long time ago and is regarded as an important part of a country's history. 历史遗迹 ❑ *...the ancient monuments of Mexico and Peru.* …墨西哥和秘鲁的历史古迹。 3 N-COUNT If you describe something as a **monument to** someone's qualities, you mean that it is a very good example of the results or effects of those qualities. 典范 ❑ *By his international achievements he leaves a fitting monument to his beliefs.* 他在国际上的成就恰好成为他信仰的一个例证。

monu·men·tal /mɒnyəmɛntᵊl/ 1 ADJ You can use **monumental** to emphasize the large size or extent of something. 巨大的 [EMPHASIS] ❑ *It had been a monumental blunder to give him the assignment.* 分配给他这项任务是一个巨大的错误。 2 ADJ If you describe a book or musical work as **monumental**, you are emphasizing that it is very large and impressive, and is likely to be important for a long time. 意义深远的; 不朽的 [EMPHASIS] ❑ *...his monumental work on Chinese astronomy.* …他关于中国天文学的不朽著作。 3 ADJ A **monumental** building or sculpture is very large and impressive. 宏伟的 [ADJ n] ❑ *I take no real interest in monumental sculpture.* 我对宏伟的雕塑并没有真正感兴趣。

mood ♦◇◇ /mud/ (**moods**) 1 N-COUNT Your **mood** is the way you are feeling at a particular time. If you are **in** a good **mood**, you feel cheerful. If you are **in** a bad **mood**, you feel angry and impatient. 情绪 ❑ *He is clearly in a good mood today.* 显然他今天心情不错。 ❑ *Lily was in one of her aggressive moods.* 莉莉又在咄咄逼人了。 ● PHRASE If you say that you are **in the mood for** something, you mean that you want to do it or have it. If you say that you are **in no mood to** do something, you mean that you do not want to do it or have it. 有/无心情 (做某事) ❑ *After a day of air and activity, you should be in the mood for a good meal.* 在户外活动了一天，你应该想好好吃一顿。 2 N-COUNT If someone is **in a mood**, the way they are behaving shows that they are feeling angry and impatient. 心情不好 ❑ *She was obviously in a mood.* 显然她心情不好。 3 N-SING **The mood** of a group of people is the way that they think and feel about an idea, event, or question at a particular time. (群体的) 想法 ❑ *The government seemed to be in tune with the popular mood.* 政府似乎与公众的想法一致。 4 N-COUNT The **mood** of a place is the general impression that you get of it. 气氛 ❑ *First set the mood with music.* 首先用音乐制造气氛。

Word Partnership *mood* 的常用搭配:

ADJ. **bad/good** mood, **depressed** mood, **foul** mood, **positive** mood, **tense** mood 1
N. mood **change**, mood **disorder**, mood **swings** 1
V. **create** a mood, **set** a mood 4 5

moody /mudi/ (**moodier, moodiest**) 1 ADJ If you describe someone as **moody**, you mean that their feelings and behavior change frequently, and in particular that they often become depressed or angry without any warning. 喜怒无常的; 闷闷不乐的 ❑ *David's mother was unstable and moody.* 戴维的母亲情绪不稳定，喜怒无常。 ● **moodi·ly** /mudɪli/ ADV 喜怒无常地; 闷闷不乐地 ❑ *He sat and stared moodily out the window.* 他坐在那里，闷闷不乐地盯着窗外。 ● **moodi·ness** N-UNCOUNT 喜怒无常; 闷闷不乐 ❑ *His moodiness may have been caused by his poor health.* 他的郁郁寡欢可能是由于健康状况不佳引起的。 2 ADJ If you describe a picture, movie, or piece of music as **moody**, you mean that it suggests particular emotions, especially sad ones. 令人感伤的 ❑ *...moody black and white photographs.* …令人感伤的黑白照片。

moon ♦◇◇ /mun/ (**moons**) 1 N-SING **The moon** is the object that you can often see in the sky at night. It goes around the earth once every four weeks, and as it does so its appearance changes from a circle to part of a circle. 月亮 [usu "the" N, also "full/new" N] ❑ *...the first man on the moon.* …登月第一人。 2 N-COUNT A **moon** is an object similar to a small planet that travels around a planet. 卫星 ❑ *...Neptune's large moon.* …海王星的大卫星。
→ see Word Web: **moon**
→ see **astronomer, eclipse, satellite, solar, tide**

A **blue moon** is the name given to the second full moon occurring within one calendar month. It happens at long intervals so the phrase "Once in a blue moon" means "not often."

moon·cake /munkeɪk/ also **moon cake** (**mooncakes**) N-VAR A **mooncake** is a type of cake that is eaten during the Chinese **Mid-Autumn Festival**. It is filled with a thick paste, and often has a salted egg inside it. 月饼 ❑ *Parents make mooncakes, moon masks, and lanterns with their children.* 家长们与他们的孩子们一起制作月饼、月亮形面具和灯笼。

Moon Festival (**Moon Festivals**) N-VAR In China, the **Moon Festival** is the **Mid-Autumn Festival**. 中秋节

moon·light /munlaɪt/ (**moonlights, moonlighting, moonlighted**) 1 N-UNCOUNT **Moonlight** is the light that comes from the moon at night. 月光 ❑ *They walked along the road in the moonlight.* 他们在月光下沿路散步。 2 V-I If someone **moonlights**, they have a second job in addition to their main job, often without informing their main employers or the tax office. (常指隐瞒雇主或税务机关的) 兼职 ❑ *...an engineer who was moonlighting as a taxi driver.* …一位兼职做出租车司机的工程师。

moor /mʊər/ (**moors, mooring, moored**) 1 N-VAR A **moor** is an area of open and usually high land with poor soil that is covered mainly with grass and heather. 荒野 [mainly BRIT] ❑ *Colliford is higher, right up on the moors.* 考里弗德更高，正好在荒野之上。 2 V-T/V-I If you **moor**, or **moor** a boat somewhere, you stop and tie it to the land with a rope or chain so that it cannot move away. 停泊 ❑ *She had moored her barge on the right bank of the river.* 她已经把她的驳船停泊在河的右岸。 ❑ *I decided to moor near some tourist boats.* 我决定挨着一些游船停泊。 3 N-COUNT The **Moors** were a Muslim people who established a civilization in North Africa and Spain between the 8th and the 15th centuries A.D. 摩尔人 4 → see also **mooring**

moor·ing /mʊərɪŋ/ (**moorings**) 1 N-COUNT A **mooring** is a place where a boat can be tied so that it cannot move away, or the object it is tied to. 停泊处; 系船柱 ❑ *Free moorings will be available.* 将有免费停泊处。 2 N-PLURAL **Moorings** are the ropes, chains, and other objects used to moor a boat. 系泊设备 ❑ *He cut the engine and grabbed the mooring lines.* 他关掉发动机，抓住了系船的绳索。

moor·land /mʊərlænd/ (**moorlands**) N-UNCOUNT **Moorland** is land which consists of moors. 荒原 [also N in pl] [mainly BRIT] ❑ *...rugged Yorkshire moorland.* …约克郡崎岖不平的荒原。

moose /mus/ (**moose**)

Moose is both the singular and the plural form.

N-COUNT A **moose** is a large type of deer. Moose have big flat horns called antlers and are found in Northern Europe, Asia, and North America. Some people use **moose** to refer to the North American variety of this animal, and **elk** to refer to the European and Asian

m

varieties. 驼鹿(生长在北欧、亚洲和北美，长有大而扁的鹿角。有些人用**moose**指北美的该物种，用**elk**指欧洲和亚洲的该物种)

▲ **mop** /mɒp/ (**mops, mopping, mopped**) **1** N-COUNT A **mop** is a piece of equipment for washing floors. It consists of a sponge or many pieces of string attached to a long handle. 拖把 **2** V-T If you **mop** a surface such as a floor, you clean it with a mop. 用拖把擦 ❑ *There was a woman mopping the stairs.* 有个女人正在拖楼梯。 **3** V-T If you **mop** sweat from your forehead or **mop** your forehead, you wipe it with a piece of cloth. 擦拭 ❑ *He mopped perspiration from his forehead.* 他擦去额头上的汗水。

▸ **mop up** **1** PHRASAL VERB If you **mop up** a liquid, you clean it with a cloth so that the liquid is absorbed. 擦干 ❑ *A waiter mopped up the mess as best he could.* 一位服务生尽力地擦干遗洒物。 ❑ *When the washing machine spurts out water at least we can mop it up.* 当洗衣机喷出水时，至少我们可以把它擦干。 **2** PHRASAL VERB If you **mop up** something that you think is undesirable or dangerous, you remove it or deal with it so that it is no longer a problem. 清除(不合意或危险的事物) ❑ *The infantry divisions mopped up remaining centers of resistance.* 几个步兵师肃清了残余的抵抗据点。

mope /moʊp/ (**mopes, moping, moped**) V-I If you **mope**, you feel miserable and do not feel interested in doing anything. 感到郁闷 ❑ *Get on with life and don't sit back and mope.* 继续好好生活，不要闲在那里闷闷不乐。

mo·ped /moʊpɛd/ (**mopeds**) N-COUNT A **moped** is a small motorcycle which you can also pedal like a bicycle. 电动自行车

mor·al ♦◇◇ /mɔrᵊl/ (**morals**) **1** N-PLURAL **Morals** are principles and beliefs concerning right and wrong behavior. 道德 ❑ *...Western ideas and morals.* …西方的思想和道德。 **2** ADJ **Moral** means relating to beliefs about what is right or wrong. 道德的 [ADJ n] ❑ *She describes her own moral dilemma in making the film.* 她描述了自己拍摄这部电影时面临的道德困境。 ● **mor·al·ly** ADV 道德上 ❑ *When, if ever, is it morally justifiable to allow a patient to die?* 假如可以的话，什么情况下允许病人放弃生命在道德上是正当的？ **3** ADJ **Moral** courage or duty is based on what you believe is right or acceptable, rather than on what the law says should be done. 道义上的 [ADJ n] ❑ *The government had a moral, if not a legal, duty to pay compensation.* 政府即使没有法律上的义务也有道义上的义务进行赔偿。 **4** ADJ A **moral** person behaves in a way that is believed by most people to be good and right. 有道德的 ❑ *The people who will be on the committee are moral, cultured, competent people.* 将要加入委员会的是那些有道德、有文化、有能力的人。 ● **mor·al·ly** ADV 道德上地 [ADV with v] ❑ *Art is not there to improve you morally.* 艺术不是从道德上提升你。 **5** ADJ If you give someone **moral** support, you encourage them in what they are doing by expressing approval. 道义上的(支持) [ADJ n] ❑ *Moral as well as financial support is what the West should provide.* 道义上和经济上的支持是西方国家应该提供的。 **6** N-COUNT **The moral** of a story or event is what you learn from it about how you should or should not behave. 道德寓意 ❑ *I think the moral of the story is let the buyer beware.* 我想这个故事的寓意是提醒购买者当心。 **7** **moral victory** → see **victory** → see **philosophy**

Thesaurus *moral* 另参见：

N. ideology, philosophy, principle, standard **1**
ADJ. moralistic, respectable, upright **2** **4**

Word Partnership *moral* 的常用搭配：

N. moral **dilemma**, moral **sense**, moral **values** **2**
moral **obligation**, moral **responsibility** **3**
moral **behavior**, moral **character** **4**
moral **support** **5**

▲ **mo·rale** /məræl/ N-UNCOUNT **Morale** is the amount of confidence and cheerfulness that a group of people have. 士气 ❑ *Many pilots are suffering from low morale.* 很多飞行员现在士气低落。

mo·ral·ity /məræliti/ (**moralities**) **1** N-UNCOUNT **Morality** is the belief that some behavior is right and acceptable and that other behavior is wrong. 道德观念 ❑ *...standards of morality and justice in society.* …社会中道德和正义的标准。 **2** N-COUNT A **morality** is a system of principles and values concerning people's behavior, which is generally accepted by a society or by a particular group of people. 道德规范 ❑ *...a morality that is sexist.* …性别歧视的道德规范。 **3** N-UNCOUNT **The morality of** something is how right or acceptable it is. 道德性 ❑ *...the arguments about the morality of blood sports.* …关于流血运动的道德性的争论。

mora·to·rium /mɔrətɔriəm/ (**moratoriums** or **moratoria**) N-COUNT A **moratorium on** a particular activity or process is the stopping of it for a fixed period of time, usually as a result of an official agreement. 暂停 ❑ *The House voted to impose a one-year moratorium on nuclear testing.* 议会投票要强行暂停核试验一年。

mor·bid /mɔrbɪd/ ADJ If you describe a person or their interest in something as **morbid**, you mean that they are very interested in unpleasant things, especially death, and you think this is strange. 病态的 [DISAPPROVAL] ❑ *Some people have a morbid fascination with crime.* 有些人对犯罪有种病态的迷恋。 ● **mor·bid·ly** ADV 病态地 ❑ *There's something morbidly fascinating about the thought.* 这个想法有种令人病态地痴迷的因素。

more ♦♦♦ /mɔr/

More is often considered to be the comparative form of **much** and **many**.

1 DET You use **more** to indicate that there is a greater amount of something than before or than average, or than something else. You can use "a little," "a lot," "a bit," "far," and "much" in front of **more**. 更多的 ❑ *More and more people are surviving heart attacks.* 越来越多的人在心脏病发作后存活下来。 ❑ *He spent more time perfecting his dance moves instead of gym work.* 他用更多的时间来完善他的舞蹈动作而不是健身。 ● PRON **More** is also a pronoun. 更多 ❑ *As the level of work increased from light to heavy, workers ate more.* 随着工作强度由轻转重，工人们吃得更多了。 ● QUANT **More** is also a quantifier. 更多 [QUANT "of" def-n] ❑ *Employees may face increasing pressure to take on more of their own medical costs in retirement.* 雇员们可能面临越来越大的在退休后自己负担更多医疗费用的压力。 **2** PHRASE You use **more than** before a number or amount to say that the actual number or amount is even greater. 超过 ❑ *The Afghan authorities say the airport had been closed for more than a year.* 阿富汗当局称该机场已关闭1年以上。 **3** ADV You use **more** to indicate that something or someone has a greater amount of a quality than they used to or than is average or usual. 更加 [ADV adj/adv] ❑ *Prison conditions have become more brutal.* 监狱的条件已经变得更加严酷。 **4** ADV If you say that something is **more** one thing **than** another, you mean that it is like the first thing rather than the second. 与其说…，倒不如说… ❑ *He's more like a movie star than a lifeguard, really.* 与其说他像个救生员，倒不如说他像个影星，真的。 ❑ *Sue screamed, not loudly, more in surprise than terror.* 苏尖叫起来，声音不大，与其说是害怕不如说是吃惊。 **5** ADV If you do something **more** than before or **more** than someone else, you do it to a greater extent or more often. 更大程度地；更经常地 [ADV with v] ❑ *When we are tired, tense, depressed, or unwell, we feel pain much more.* 当我们疲劳、紧张、沮丧或者身体不适时，就更觉得疼。 **6** ADV You can use **more** to indicate that something continues to happen for a further period of time. 继续 [ADV after v] ❑ *Things might have been different if I'd talked a bit more.* 如果我再多说一点，结果或许会不同。 ● PHRASE You can use **some more** to indicate that something continues to happen for a further period of time. 继续 **7** ADV You use **more** to indicate that something is repeated. For example, if you do something "once more," you do it again once. 再次 ❑ *This train would stop twice more in the suburbs before rolling southeast toward Baltimore.* 这辆火车在朝东南开往巴尔的摩前将在郊区多停两站。 **8** DET You use **more** to refer to an additional thing or amount. You can use "a little," "a lot," "a bit," "far," and "much" in front of **more**. 额外的 ❑ *They needed more time to consider whether to hold an inquiry.* 他们需要更多的时间来考虑是否进行一次调查。 ● ADJ **More** is also an adjective. 额外的 [ADJ n] ❑ *We stayed in Danville two more days.* 我们在丹维尔多呆了两天。 ● PRON **More** is also a pronoun. 更多 ❑ *Oxfam has appealed to western nations to do more to help the refugees.* 牛津饥荒救济委员会已经呼吁西方国家采取更多的措施来帮助这些难民。 **9** ADV You use **more** in conversations when you want to draw someone's attention to something interesting or important that you are about to say. 更(用来吸引听话人的注意力) [ADV adv/adj] ❑ *More seriously for him, there are members who say he is wrong on this issue.* 对他而言更严重的是，有些成员说他在这个问题上是错的。 **10** PHRASE You can use **more and more** to indicate that something is becoming greater in amount, extent, or degree all the time. 越来越 ❑ *Her life was heading more and more where she wanted it to go.* 她的生活正越来越朝着她想要的方向发展。 **11** PHRASE If something is **more or less** true, it is true in a general way, but is not completely true. 或多或少地；大致 [VAGUENESS] ❑ *The conference is more or less over.* 会议大致结束了。 **12** PHRASE If something is **more than** a particular thing, it has greater value or importance than this thing. 不只是 ❑ *He's more than a coach, he's a friend.* 他不只是个教练，还是个朋友。 13 PHRASE You use **more than** to say that something is true to a greater degree than is necessary or than average. 超出(需要或平均水平) ❑ *The company has more than enough cash available to refinance the loan.* 公司有绰绰有余的现金再为贷款提供资金。 14 PHRASE You can use **what is more** or **what's more** to introduce an extra piece of information which supports or emphasizes the point you are making. 此外 [EMPHASIS] ❑ *Many more institutions, especially banks, were allowed to lend money for mortgages, and what was more, banks could lend out more money than they actually held.* 更多机构，特别是银行，被允许做抵押贷款；此外，银行还可以借出比实际持有量更多的钱。 15 **all the more** → see **all** 16 **any more** → see **any**

more·over ♦◇◇ /mɔroʊvər/ ADV You use **moreover** to introduce a piece of information that adds to or supports the previous statement. 此外 [FORMAL] ❑ *She saw that there was indeed a man immediately behind her. Moreover, he was observing her strangely.* 她看到的确有个男人紧跟在她身后。而且，他还在怪异地观察着她。

morgue /mɔrg/ (**morgues**) N-COUNT A **morgue** is a building or a room in a hospital where dead bodies are kept before they are buried or cremated, or before they are identified or examined. 停尸房

morn·ing ♦♦♦ /mɔrnɪŋ/ (**mornings**) 1 N-VAR The **morning** is the part of each day between the time that people usually wake up and 12 o'clock noon or lunchtime. 早晨；上午 ❑ *During the morning your guide will take you around the city.* 上午导游将带你们逛逛这座城市。 ❑ *On Sunday morning Bill was woken by the telephone.* 周日早晨，比尔被电话吵醒了。 2 N-SING If you refer to a particular time in **the morning**, you mean a time between 12 o'clock midnight and 12 o'clock noon. 从子夜12:00到中午12:00之间 ❑ *I often stayed up until two or three in the morning.* 我经常熬夜到凌晨两三点钟。 3 PHRASE If you say that something will happen **in the morning**, you mean that it will happen during the morning of the following day. 次日上午 ❑ *I'll fly it to St Louis in the morning.* 我会在明天上午把它空运到圣路易斯。 4 PHRASE If you say that something happens **morning, noon and night**, you mean that it happens all the time. 从早到晚；一直 ❑ *You get fit by playing the game, day in, day out, morning, noon and night.* 每日坚持做这项运动，你就会变得健壮。

Thesaurus	*morning* 另参见：
N.	dawn, daybreak, light, sunrise 1

mo·rose /məroʊs/ ADJ Someone who is **morose** is miserable, bad-tempered, and not willing to talk very much to other people. 阴郁的；坏脾气的 ❑ *She was morose, pale, and reticent.* 她闷闷不乐，面色苍白，沉默寡言。 ● **mo·rose·ly** ADV 阴郁地；坏脾气地 ❑ *One elderly man sat morosely at the bar.* 一个上了年纪的男人郁郁寡欢地坐在吧台。

mor·phine /mɔrfin/ N-UNCOUNT **Morphine** is a drug used to relieve pain. 吗啡

mor·sel /mɔrsᵊl/ (**morsels**) N-COUNT A **morsel** is a very small amount of something, especially a very small piece of food. (尤指食物) 极少的量 ❑ *...a delicious little morsel of meat.* …一丁点儿好吃的肉。

★ **mor·tal** /mɔrtᵊl/ (**mortals**) 1 ADJ If you refer to the fact that people are **mortal**, you mean that they have to die and cannot live forever. 终有一死的 ❑ *A man is deliberately designed to be mortal. He grows, he ages, and he dies.* 人是被故意设计成终归一死的。成长，变老，然后死去。 ● **mor·tal·ity** /mɔrtælɪti/ N-UNCOUNT 终有一死 ❑ *She has suddenly come face to face with her own mortality.* 突然，她已经与死神面对面了。 2 N-COUNT You can describe someone as a **mortal** when you want to say that they are an ordinary person. 凡人 ❑ *Tickets seem unobtainable to the ordinary mortal.* 票对于普通大众来说似乎是得不到的。 3 ADJ You can use **mortal** to show that something is very serious or may cause death. 致命的 [ADJ n] ❑ *The police were defending themselves and others against mortal danger.* 警察在保卫他们自己和其他人免受致命的危险。 ● **mor·tal·ly** ADV 致命地 ❑ *He falls, mortally wounded.* 他摔了，伤得很重。 4 ADJ You can use **mortal** to emphasize that a feeling is extremely great or severe. 极度的 [ADJ n] [EMPHASIS] ❑ *When self-esteem is high, we lose our mortal fear of jealousy.* 当自尊心很强时，我们会失去对嫉妒的极度恐惧。 ● **mor·tal·ly** ADV 极度地 [ADV -ed/adj/adv] ❑ *Candace admits to having been "mortally embarrassed."* 坎达丝承认曾经"极其尴尬"。

mor·tal·ity /mɔrtælɪti/ N-UNCOUNT The **mortality** in a particular place or situation is the number of people who die. 死亡人数 ❑ *The nation's infant mortality rate has reached a record low.* 该国的婴儿死亡率已达历史最低。

mor·tar /mɔrtər/ (**mortars**) 1 N-COUNT A **mortar** is a big gun that fires missiles high into the air over a short distance. 迫击炮 ❑ *The two sides exchanged fire with mortars and small arms.* 双方以迫击炮和轻型武器交火。 2 N-UNCOUNT **Mortar** is a mixture of sand, water, and cement or lime which is put between bricks to hold them together. 灰浆 ❑ *...the mortar between the bricks.* …砖块间的灰浆。 3 N-COUNT A **mortar** is a bowl in which you can crush things such as herbs, spices, or grain using a rod called a pestle. 研钵 ❑ *Use a mortar and pestle to crush the shells and claws.* 用一个研钵和杵把壳和钳捣碎。

★ **mort·gage** ♦♦◇ /mɔrgɪdʒ/ (**mortgages, mortgaging, mortgaged**) 1 N-COUNT A **mortgage** is a loan of money which you get from a bank or savings and loan association in order to buy a house. 房屋抵押贷款 ❑ *...an increase in mortgage rates.* …房屋抵押贷款利率的上升。 2 V-T If you **mortgage** your house or land, you use it as a guarantee to a company in order to borrow money from them. 抵押 ❑ *They had to mortgage their home to pay the bills.* 他们不得不抵押他们的房子来还账。 → see **interest rate**

Word Link	*mort ≈ death : immortal, mortician, mortuary*

mor·ti·cian /mɔrtɪʃᵊn/ (**morticians**) N-COUNT A **mortician** is a person whose job is to deal with the bodies of people who have died and to arrange funerals. 殡葬承办者 [mainly AM]

mor·tu·ary /mɔrtʃuɛri/ (**mortuaries**) N-COUNT A **mortuary** is a building or a room in a hospital where dead bodies are kept before they are buried or cremated, or before they are identified or examined. 停尸房

mo·sa·ic /moʊzeɪɪk/ (**mosaics**) N-VAR A **mosaic** is a design which consists of small pieces of colored glass, pottery, or stone set in concrete or plaster. 马赛克 ❑ *...a Roman villa which once housed a fine collection of mosaics.* …一座曾藏有一批精美的马赛克收藏品的罗马别墅。

Mos·lem /mɒzləm, mʊzlɪm/ → see **Muslim**

mosque /mɒsk/ (**mosques**) N-COUNT A **mosque** is a building where Muslims go to worship. 清真寺

mos·qui·to /məskitoʊ/ (**mosquitoes** or **mosquitos**) N-COUNT **Mosquitos** are small flying insects which bite people and animals in order to suck their blood. 蚊子

▲ **moss** /mɒs/ (**mosses**) N-MASS **Moss** is a very small, soft, green plant which grows on damp soil, or on wood or stone. 青苔 ❑ *...ground covered over with moss.* …长满青苔的地面。

most ♦♦♦ /moʊst/

> **Most** is often considered to be the superlative form of **much** and **many**.

1 QUANT You use **most** to refer to the majority of a group of things or people or the largest part of something. 大多数；大部分 [QUANT "of" def-n] ❑ *Most of the houses in the capital don't have indoor plumbing.* 首都大多数房屋没有室内管道装置。 ❑ *By stopping smoking you are undoing most of the damage smoking has caused.* 通过戒烟，你就是在消除吸烟所致的大多数危害。 ● DET **Most** is also a determiner. 大多数的 ❑ *Most people think the queen has done a good job over the last 50 years.* 大多数人认为女王在过去的50年中尽职尽责。 ● PRON **Most** is also a pronoun. 大多数 ❑ *Seventeen civilians were hurt. Most are students who had been attending a twenty-first birthday party.* 17名平民受了伤，其中大多数是参加一个21岁生日聚会的学生。 2 ADJ You use **the most** to mean a larger amount than anyone or anything else, or the largest amount possible. 最多的 ["the" ADJ n] ❑ *The president himself won the most votes.* 总统本人赢得了最多的选票。 ● PRON **Most** is also a pronoun. 最多 ❑ *The most they earn in a day is fifty rubles.* 他们一天最多挣50卢布。 3 ADV You use **most** to indicate that something is true or happens to a greater degree or extent than anything else. 最 [ADV with v] ❑ *What she feared most was becoming like her mother.* 她最害怕的是变得像她母亲一样。 ❑ *...Professor Morris, the person he most hated.* …莫里斯教授，他最恨的那个人。 ● PHRASE You use **most of all** to indicate that something happens or is true to a greater extent than anything else. 最 4 ADV You use **most** to indicate that someone or something has a greater amount of a particular quality than most other things of its kind. 最 [ADV adj/adv] ❑ *Her children had the best, most elaborate birthday parties in the neighborhood.* 她孩子们的生日聚会是左邻右舍中最好、最精心策划的。 ❑ *He was one of the most influential performers of modern jazz.* 他是最有影响力的现代爵士乐表演者之一。 5 ADV If you do something **the most**, you do it to

the greatest extent possible or with the greatest frequency. 最大程度地；最频繁地 ["the" ADV after v] ❑ *What question are you asked the most?* 什么问题是你最常被问到的？ **6** ADV You use **most** in conversations when you want to draw someone's attention to something very interesting or important that you are about to say. (谈话中用于吸引注意力) 最 [ADV adv/adj] ❑ *Most surprisingly, quite a few said they don't intend to vote at all.* 最令人吃惊的是，相当一部分人说他们根本不打算投票。

Note that you can say "**Most children love candy**," but you cannot say "Most of children love candy." However, when a pronoun is used, you can say "**Most of them love candy**."

7 PHRASE You use **at most** or **at the most** to say that a number or amount is the maximum that is possible and that the actual number or amount may be smaller. 至多 ❑ *Poach the pears in apple juice or water and sugar for ten minutes at most.* 把梨放入苹果汁或水和糖中，煮最多十分钟。 **8** PHRASE If you **make the most of** something, you get the maximum use or advantage from it. 充分利用 ❑ *Happiness is the ability to make the most of what you have.* 幸福就是充分享用你所拥有的一切的能力。

most·ly ♦◇◇ /moʊstli/ ADV You use **mostly** to indicate that a statement is generally true, for example true about the majority of a group of things or people, true most of the time, or true in most respects. 主要地；大多地 [ADV with cl/group] ❑ *I am working with mostly highly motivated people.* 我正与大多都积极性很高的人们共事。 ❑ *Cars are mostly metal.* 汽车人多是金属制成的。

★ **mo·tel** /moʊtɛ̱l/ (**motels**) N-COUNT A **motel** is a hotel intended for people who are traveling by car. 汽车旅馆

▲ **moth** /mɔ̱θ/ (**moths**) N-COUNT A **moth** is an insect like a butterfly which usually flies around at night. 蛾

moth·er ♦♦♦ /mʌ̱ðər/ (**mothers, mothering, mothered**) **1** N-FAMILY Your **mother** is the woman who gave birth to you. You can also call someone your **mother** if she brings you up as if she was this woman. 母亲 ❑ *She sat on the edge of her mother's bed.* 她坐在母亲的床边。 ❑ *She's an English teacher and a mother of two children.* 她是一位英语老师，也是两个孩子的母亲。 **2** V-T If a woman **mothers** a child, she takes care of it and brings it up, usually because she is its mother. 抚养 ❑ *Colleen had dreamed of mothering a large family.* 科琳曾经梦想过要抚养一大群孩子。 **3** V-T If you **mother** someone, you treat them with great care and affection, as if they were a small child. 爱护 ❑ *Stop mothering me.* 别再像妈妈似的照顾我了。
→ see **family**

★ **moth·er·hood** /mʌ̱ðərhʊd/ N-UNCOUNT **Motherhood** is the state of being a mother. 母亲身份 ❑ *...women who try to combine work and motherhood.* …试图兼顾工作又当好母亲的女性们。

mother-in-law (**mothers-in-law**) N-COUNT Someone's **mother-in-law** is the mother of their husband or wife. 婆婆；岳母
→ see **family**

moth·er·ly /mʌ̱ðərli/ ADJ **Motherly** feelings or actions are like those of a kind mother. 慈母般的 ❑ *It was an incredible display of motherly love and forgiveness.* 那是慈母般关爱与宽容的一次令人难以置信的体现。

mo·tif /moʊti̱f/ (**motifs**) N-COUNT A **motif** is a design which is used as a decoration or as part of an artistic pattern. (用作装饰的)图案 ❑ *...a rose motif.* …一个玫瑰图案。

Word Link *mot ≈ moving : motion, motivate, promote*

mo·tion ♦◇◇ /moʊʃ°n/ (**motions, motioning, motioned**) **1** N-UNCOUNT **Motion** is the activity or process of continually changing position or moving from one place to another. 运动 ❑ *...the laws governing light, sound, and motion.* …支配光、声和运动的规律。 ❑ *One group of muscles sets the next group in motion.* 一组肌肉带动下一组肌肉运动。 **2** N-COUNT A **motion** is an action, gesture, or movement. 动作；手势 ❑ *He made a neat chopping motion with his hand.* 他用手做了一个干净利落的砍的动作。 **3** N-COUNT A **motion** is a formal proposal or statement in a meeting, debate, or trial, which is discussed and then voted on or decided on. 动议 ❑ *The conference is now debating the motion and will vote on it shortly.* 大会现在正在讨论这个动议，并将马上就此投票。 ❑ *Opposition parties are likely to bring a no-confidence motion against the government.* 反对党可能会对政府提出一项不信任议案。 **4** V-T/V-I If you **motion** to someone, you move your hand or head as a way of telling them to do something or telling them where to go. (用手势或头) 示意 ❑ *She motioned for the locked front doors to be opened.* 她打手势示意把锁着的前门打开。 ❑ *He stood aside and motioned Don to the door.* 他站在一边，示意唐到门口。 **5** → see also **slow motion** **6** PHRASE If you say that someone **is going through the motions**, you think they are only saying or doing something because it is expected of them without being interested, enthusiastic, or sympathetic. 敷衍了事 ❑ *"You really don't care, do you?" she said quietly. "You're just going through the motions."* "你真的不在意，是吗？"她平静地说。"你只是在敷衍了事。" **7** PHRASE If a process or event is **in motion**, it is happening. If it is set **in motion**, it is happening or beginning to happen. 在进行中 ❑ *The current chain of events was set in motion by that kidnapping.* 目前的一系列事件都是由那次绑架引发的。 **8** PHRASE If someone **sets the wheels in motion**, they take the necessary action to make something start happening. 开动 ❑ *I have set the wheels in motion to sell their Arizona ranch.* 我已着手出售他们在亚利桑那州的大农场。
→ see Word Web: **motion**

Word Partnership *motion* 的常用搭配：

ADJ. **constant** motion, **full** motion, **perpetual** motion **1**
circular motion, **smooth** motion **1** **2**
quick motion **2**
V. **set *something* in** motion **1** **7** **8**

mo·tion·less /moʊʃ°nlɪs/ ADJ Someone or something that is **motionless** is not moving at all. 静止的 ❑ *He has this ability of being able to remain as motionless as a statue, for hours on end.* 他有能像雕塑一样连续数小时保持静止的能力。

mo·tion pic·ture (**motion pictures**) N-COUNT A **motion picture** is a movie made for movie theaters. 电影 [mainly AM, FORMAL] ❑ *It was there that I saw my first motion picture.* 就是在那里我看了我的第一场电影。

Word Link *ate ≈ causing to be : complicate, humiliate, motivate*

mo·ti·vate ♦◇◇ /moʊtɪveɪt/ (**motivates, motivating, motivated**) **1** V-T If you **are motivated** by something, especially an emotion, it causes you to behave in a particular way. 激发…的积极性 ❑ *They are motivated by a need to achieve.* 他们被成功的需要激励着。 ● **mo·ti·vat·ed** ADJ 有积极性的 ❑ *...highly motivated employees.* …积极性很高的员工。 ● **mo·ti·va·tion** /moʊtɪveɪʃ°n/ N-UNCOUNT 积极性 ❑ *His poor performance may be attributed to lack of motivation rather than to reading difficulties.* 他糟糕的表现可能归因于积极性的缺乏而不是阅读上的困难。 **2** V-T If someone **motivates** you to do something, they make you feel determined to do it. 激起 (某行动) ❑ *How do you motivate people to work hard and efficiently?* 你是如何激励人们努力而高效地工作的？ ● **mo·ti·va·tion** N-UNCOUNT 激起行动 ❑ *Given parental motivation, we are optimistic about the ability of people to change.* 有了父母的激励，我们对于人们改变的能力很乐观。

Word Web motion

Newton's three laws of **motion** describe how **forces** affect the movement of objects. This is the first law: an object at **rest** won't move unless a force makes it move. Similarly, a moving object keeps its **momentum** unless something stops it. The second law describes **acceleration**. The **rate** of acceleration depends on two things: how strong the push on the object is, and how much the object weighs. The third law says that for every **action** there is an equal and opposite **reaction**. When one object **exerts** a force on another, the second object pushes back with an equal force.

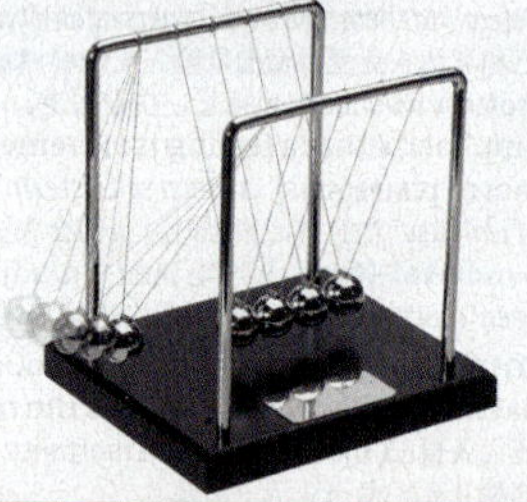

Word Partnership *motivate* 的常用搭配:
N. motivate **an audience**, motivate **consumers**, motivate **employees**, motivate **people**, motivate **students** 2

mo·ti·va·tion /moʊtɪveɪʃ^ən/ (**motivations**) N-COUNT Your **motivation** for doing something is what causes you to want to do it. 动力 ❑ *Money is my motivation.* 金钱就是我的动力。

mo·tive /moʊtɪv/ (**motives**) N-COUNT Your **motive** for doing something is your reason for doing it. 动机 ❑ *Police have ruled out robbery as a motive for the killing.* 警方已排除了抢劫是杀人的动机。

Word Partnership *motive* 的常用搭配:
PREP. motive **behind** *something*, motive **for** *something*
ADJ. **possible** motive, **primary** motive, **ulterior** motive

mo·tor ♦♦◇ /moʊtər/ (**motors**) 1 N-COUNT The **motor** in a machine, vehicle, or boat is the part that uses electricity or fuel to produce movement, so that the machine, vehicle, or boat can work. 发动机 ❑ *She got in and started the motor.* 她上了车，发动了引擎。 2 ADJ **Motor** vehicles and boats have a gasoline or diesel engine. 机动的 [ADJ n] ❑ *Theft of motor vehicles is up by 15.9%.* 机动车盗窃案增加了15.9%。 3 ADJ **Motor** is used to describe activities relating to vehicles such as cars and buses. 汽车的 [mainly BRIT]
in AM, usually use **automotive, automobile**
4 → see also **motoring**
→ see **boat**

motor·bike /moʊtərbaɪk/ (**motorbikes**) N-COUNT A **motorbike** is a lighter, less powerful motorcycle. 轻型摩托车 [AM]

▲ **motor·cycle** /moʊtərsaɪk^əl/ (**motorcycles**) N-COUNT A **motorcycle** is a vehicle with two wheels and an engine. 摩托车

motor·cyclist /moʊtərsaɪklɪst/ (**motorcyclists**) N-COUNT A **motorcyclist** is a person who rides a motorcycle. 骑摩托车的人

mo·tor·ing /moʊtərɪŋ/ ADJ **Motoring** means relating to cars and driving. 汽车的; 汽车驾驶的 [mainly BRIT]
in AM, usually use **driving, automobile**

mo·tor·ised /moʊtəraɪzd/ [BRIT] → see **motorized**

mo·tor·ist /moʊtərɪst/ (**motorists**) N-COUNT A **motorist** is a person who drives a car. 汽车驾驶员 ❑ *Police urged motorists to take extra care on the roads.* 警方敦促汽车驾驶员们在路上要格外当心。

mo·tor·ized /moʊtəraɪzd/
in BRIT, also use **motorised**
1 ADJ A **motorized** vehicle has an engine. 有发动机的 ❑ *Around 1910 motorized carriages were beginning to replace horse-drawn cabs.* 大约一九一零年，装有发动机的四轮车开始取代马车。 2 ADJ A **motorized** group of soldiers is equipped with motor vehicles. (部队) 摩托化的 ❑ *...motorized infantry and artillery.* …摩托化的步兵和炮兵。

motor·way /moʊtərweɪ/ (**motorways**) N-VAR A **motorway** is a major road that has been specially built for fast travel over long distances. Motorways have several lanes and special places where traffic gets on and leaves. 高速公路 [BRIT]
in AM, usually use **freeway** or **highway**

▲ **mot·to** /mɒtoʊ/ (**mottoes** or **mottos**) N-COUNT A **motto** is a short sentence or phrase that expresses a rule for sensible behavior, especially a way of behaving in a particular situation. 格言 ❑ *"Stay true to yourself" has always been his motto.* "忠于自己"一直是他的座右铭。

mould /moʊld/ [BRIT] → see **mold**

▲ **mound** /maʊnd/ (**mounds**) 1 N-COUNT A **mound of** something is a large, rounded pile of it. 堆 ❑ *The bulldozers piled up huge mounds of dirt.* 推土机堆起大堆大堆的土。 2 N-COUNT In baseball, the **mound** is the raised area where the pitcher stands when he or she throws the ball. (棒球运动中的) 投球区土墩 ❑ *He went to the mound to talk with a struggling pitcher who spoke only Spanish.* 他走到投球区土墩和一名只讲西班牙语、奋力拼搏的投手交谈。
→ see **baseball**

mount ♦◇◇ /maʊnt/ (**mounts, mounting, mounted**) 1 V-T If you **mount** a campaign or event, you organize it and make it take place. 组织; 发动 ❑ *The ANC announced it was mounting a major campaign of mass political protests.* 非国大宣布正在发动一场大型群众性政治抗议运动。 2 V-I If something **mounts**, it increases in intensity. 增强 ❑ *For several hours, tension mounted.* 几个小时中，紧张局势加剧了。 3 V-I If something **mounts**, it increases in quantity. 增加 ❑ *The uncollected garbage mounts in city streets.* 城市街道中未被收集的垃圾增多。 ● PHRASAL VERB To **mount up** means the same as to **mount**. 增加 ❑ *Her medical bills mounted up.* 她的医疗账单越来越多。 4 V-T If you **mount** the stairs or a platform, you go up the stairs or go up onto the platform. 登上 (楼梯或平台) [FORMAL] ❑ *Larry was mounting the stairs up into the attic.* 拉里正在拾级而上到阁楼去。 5 V-T If you **mount** a horse or motorcycle, you climb on to it so that you can ride it. 骑上 ❑ *A man in a crash helmet was mounting a motorcycle.* 一个戴着防撞头盔的男子正骑上一辆摩托车。 6 V-T If you **mount** an object **on** something, you fix it there firmly. 安装 ❑ *Her husband mounts the work on velour paper and makes the frame.* 她丈夫把作品装裱到丝绒纸上，又做了框架。 ● **-mounted** COMB IN ADJ (用于构成复合形容词) 安装在…上的 ❑ *She installed a wall-mounted electric fan.* 她装了一台安装在墙上的电扇。 7 V-T If you **mount** an exhibition or display, you organize and present it. 举办 (展览或展示) ❑ *The gallery has mounted an exhibition of art by Irish women painters.* 这家画廊已经举办过一次爱尔兰女画家们的艺术作品展。 8 N-IN-NAMES **Mount** is used as part of the name of a mountain. (冠于山名之前) 山 ❑ *...Mount Everest.* …珠穆朗玛峰。 9 → see also **mounted**

moun·tain ♦♦◇ /maʊnt^ən/ (**mountains**) 1 N-COUNT A **mountain** is a very high area of land with steep sides. 山 ❑ *Mt. McKinley, in Alaska, is the highest mountain in North America.* 位于阿拉斯加的麦金利山是北美最高的山。 2 QUANT If you talk about a **mountain of** something, or **mountains of** something, you are emphasizing that there is a large amount of it. 大堆 [INFORMAL, EMPHASIS] ❑ *They are faced with a mountain of bureaucracy.* 他们面临着一大堆的官僚制度。 3 PHRASE If you say that someone has **a mountain to climb**, you mean that it will be difficult for them to achieve what they want to achieve. 困难 [JOURNALISM] ❑ *"We had a mountain to climb after the second goal went in," said Crosby.* 克罗斯比说："第2个球进了后，我们面临着很大的困难。"
→ see Picture Dictionary: **mountain**

moun·tain bike (**mountain bikes**) N-COUNT A **mountain bike** is a type of bicycle that is suitable for riding over rough ground. It has a strong frame and thick tires. 山地车
→ see **bicycle**

m

Word Link *eer ≈ one who does : auctioneer, mountaineer, volunteer*

moun·tain·eer /maʊnt^ənɪər/ (**mountaineers**) N-COUNT A **mountaineer** is a person who is skillful at climbing the steep sides of mountains. 善于登山者

★ **moun·tain·ous** /maʊnt^ənəs/ 1 ADJ A **mountainous** place has a lot of mountains. 多山的 ❑ *...the mountainous region of New Mexico.* …新墨西哥州的多山地区。 2 ADJ You use **mountainous** to emphasize that something is great in size, quantity, or degree. 巨大的; 大量的 [ADJ n] [EMPHASIS] ❑ *The plan is designed to reduce some of the company's mountainous debt.* 制定这个计划是为了减少该公司的一部分巨额债务。

moun·tain·side /maʊnt^ənsaɪd/ (**mountainsides**) N-COUNT A **mountainside** is one of the steep sides of a mountain. 山坡 ❑ *The couple trudged up the dark mountainside.* 这对夫妇沿着黑暗的山坡向上跋涉。

mount·ed /maʊntɪd/ 1 ADJ **Mounted** police or soldiers ride horses when they are on duty. 骑马执勤的 (警察或士兵) [ADJ n] ❑ *A dozen mounted police rode into the square.* 12名骑警来到了广场。
2 → see also **mount**

★ **mourn** /mɔrn/ (**mourns, mourning, mourned**) 1 V-T/V-I If you **mourn** someone who has died or **mourn for** them, you are very sad that they have died and show your sorrow in the way that you behave. 悼念 ❑ *Joan still mourns her father.* 琼还在哀悼她的父亲。 ❑ *He mourned for his valiant men.* 他为他的勇士们悼念。 2 V-T/V-I If you **mourn** something or **mourn for** it, you regret that you no longer have it and show your regret in the way that you behave. 为 (失去) …而痛惜 ❑ *We mourned the loss of our cities.* 我们为失去我们那些城市而痛惜。

mourn·er /mɔrnər/ (**mourners**) N-COUNT A **mourner** is a person who attends a funeral, especially as a relative or friend of the dead person. 送葬者; 哀悼者 ❑ *Weeks after his death, mourners still gather outside the house.* 他死后几个星期，哀悼者仍然聚集在屋外。
→ see **funeral**

mourn·ful /mɔrnfəl/ 1 ADJ If you are **mournful**, you are very sad. 悲伤的 ❑ *He looked mournful, even near to tears.* 他看上去很悲伤，

Picture Dictionary **mountain**

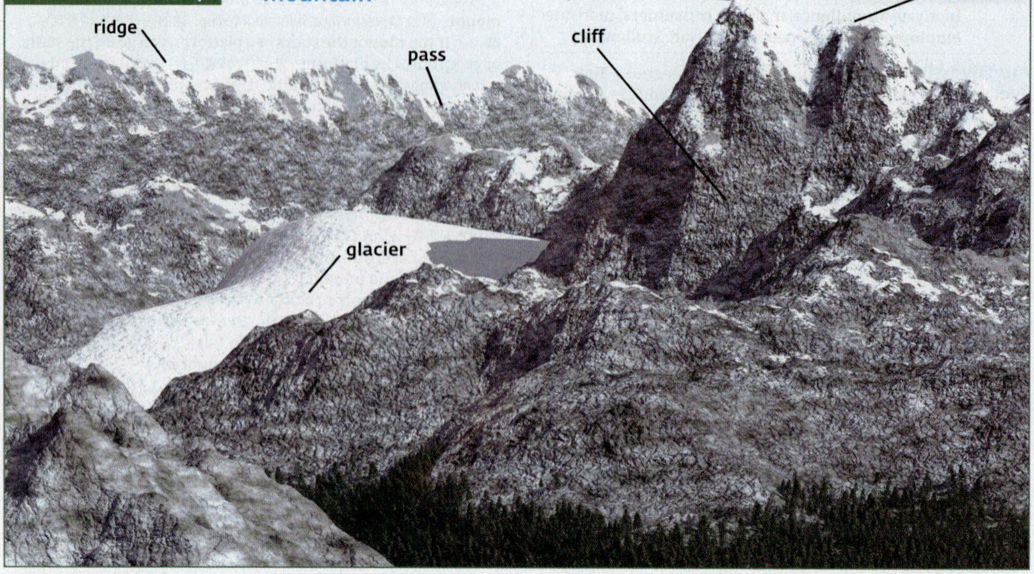

几乎要掉泪了。● **mourn·ful·ly** ADV 悲伤地 ❑ *He stood mournfully at the gate waving bye bye.* 他悲伤地站在门口，挥手说再见。 **2** ADJ A **mournful** sound seems very sad. (声音) 悲切的 ❑ *...the mournful wail of bagpipes.* …风笛的悲鸣声。

mouse /maʊ̲s/ (**mice**) **1** N-COUNT A **mouse** is a small, furry animal with a long tail. 鼠 ❑ *...a mouse running in a wheel in its cage.* …笼子里一只踩着转轮跑的老鼠。 **2** N-COUNT A **mouse** is a device that is connected to a computer. By moving it over a flat surface and pressing its buttons, you can move the cursor around the screen and do things without using the keyboard. 鼠标 ❑ *Her message had been written; all she had to do was click the mouse.* 她的信息已经写好；她要做的只是点击鼠标。

mouse mat (**mouse mats**) also **mousemat** N-COUNT A **mouse mat** is the same as a **mouse pad**. 鼠标垫 [BRIT]

mouse pad (**mouse pads**) also **mousepad** N-COUNT A **mouse pad** is a flat piece of plastic or some other material that you rest the mouse on while using a computer. 鼠标垫 [mainly AM]

in BRIT, usually use **mouse mat**

mousse /mu̲s/ (**mousses**) **1** N-VAR **Mousse** is a sweet, light food made from eggs and cream. It is often flavored with fruit or chocolate. 慕斯 (用鸡蛋和奶油制成的甜点) ❑ *...a rich chocolate mousse.* …味道十足的巧克力慕斯。 **2** N-MASS **Mousse** is a soft substance containing a lot of tiny bubbles, for example one that you can put in your hair to make it easier to shape into a particular style. 摩丝 ❑ *He had even put mousse in his hair.* 他甚至还往头发上抹了摩丝。 → see **dessert**

mous·tache /mʌ̲stæʃ/ [BRIT] → see **mustache**

mouth ♦♦◊ (**mouths, mouthing, mouthed**)

The noun is pronounced /maʊ̲θ/. The verb is pronounced /maʊ̲ð/. The plural of the noun and the third person singular of the verb are both pronounced /maʊ̲ðz/.

名词读作 /maʊ̲θ/。动词读作 /maʊ̲ð/。名词复数和动词第三人称单数时均读作 /maʊ̲ðz/。

1 N-COUNT Your **mouth** is the area of your face where your lips are, or the space behind your lips where your teeth and tongue are. 嘴 ❑ *She clamped her hand against her mouth.* 她用手紧紧捂住嘴。 ● **-mouthed** /-maʊ̲ðd/ COMB IN ADJ (用于构成复合形容词) 嘴…的 ❑ *He straightened up and looked at me, open-mouthed.* 他直起身子看着我，嘴大张着。 **2** N-COUNT You can say that someone has a particular kind of **mouth** to indicate that they speak in a particular kind of way or that they say particular kinds of things. 说话 (方式或内容) ❑ *I've always had a loud mouth, I refuse to be silenced.* 我总是有话就讲，我拒绝保持沉默。 ● **-mouthed** COMB IN ADJ (用于构成复合形容词) 说话…的 ❑ *...Sam, their smart-mouthed teenage son.* …萨姆，他们十几岁的伶牙俐齿的儿子。 **3** N-COUNT The **mouth** of a cave, hole, or bottle is its entrance or opening. (洞) 口；(瓶) 口 ❑ *By the mouth of the tunnel he bent to retie his shoelace.* 到隧道的入口处，他弯腰重新系了系鞋带。 ● **-mouthed** COMB IN ADJ (用于构成复合形容词) 口…的 ❑ *He put the flowers in a wide-mouthed blue vase.* 他把花放进一只蓝色的大口花瓶。 **4** N-COUNT The **mouth** of a river is the place where it flows into the sea. 河口 ❑ *...the town at the mouth of the River Fox.* …位于福克斯河河口的那座城镇。 **5** V-T If you **mouth** something, you form words with your lips without making any sound. 用口形不出声地说 ❑ *I mouthed a goodbye and hurried in behind Momma.* 我只张嘴不出声地说了个再见就赶紧跟在妈妈身后进去了。 **6** PHRASE If you have a number of **mouths to feed**, you have the responsibility of earning enough money to feed and take care of that number of people. 需要抚养的人 ❑ *He had to feed his family on the equivalent of seven hundred dollars a month and, with five mouths to feed, he found this very hard.* 他每月不得不用相当于700美元的钱来养家，5张嘴等着吃饭，他觉得很困难。 **7** PHRASE If you say that someone does not **open** their **mouth**, you are emphasizing that they never say anything at all. 开口说话 [EMPHASIS] ❑ *Sometimes I hardly dare open my mouth.* 有时我几乎不敢开口说话。 **8** PHRASE If you **keep** your **mouth shut** about something, you do not talk about it, especially because it is a secret. 守口如瓶 ❑ *You wouldn't be here now if she'd kept her mouth shut.* 如果她当时守口如瓶，你现在就不会在这里了。 **9** **to live hand to mouth** → see **hand** **10** **heart in your mouth** → see **heart** **11** **from the horse's mouth** → see **horse** **12** **to put your money where your mouth is** → see **money** **13** **shut your mouth** → see **shut** **14** **word of mouth** → see **word**

→ see **face, respiratory**

Word Partnership *mouth* 的常用搭配：

ADJ. **big mouth** **1** **2**
V. **close *your* mouth, keep *your* mouth closed/shut, shut *your* mouth** **1** **8**

mouth·ful /maʊ̲θfʊl/ (**mouthfuls**) **1** N-COUNT A **mouthful of** drink or food is the amount that you put or have in your mouth. 一口 (食物或饮料) ❑ *She gulped down a mouthful of coffee.* 她咽下了一大口咖啡。 **2** N-SING If you describe a long word or phrase as a **mouthful**, you mean that it is difficult to say. 长而绕嘴的字词 [INFORMAL] ❑ *It's called the Pan-Caribbean Disaster Preparedness and Prevention Project, which is quite a mouthful.* 它被称为泛加勒比海灾难准备及预防计划，挺绕嘴的一个名字。

mouth·piece /maʊ̲θpis/ (**mouthpieces**) **1** N-COUNT The **mouthpiece** of a telephone is the part that you speak into. (电话的)

话筒 ❑ *He shouted into the mouthpiece.* 他冲着电话话筒大叫。 2 N-COUNT The **mouthpiece** of a musical instrument or other device is the part that you put into your mouth. (乐器的) 吹口; (器具的) 衔口 ❑ *He showed him how to blow into the ivory mouthpiece.* 他给他演示了如何把气吹进象牙吹口。 3 N-COUNT The **mouthpiece** of an organization or person is someone who informs other people of the opinions and policies of that organization or person. 代言人 ❑ *Their mouthpiece is the vice president.* 他们的代言人是副总裁。

→ see **scuba diving**

mov·able /muvəbᵊl/ also **moveable** ADJ Something that is **movable** can be moved from one place or position to another. 可移动的 ❑ *It's a vinyl doll with movable arms and legs.* 这是个胳膊和腿都能活动的乙烯基塑料娃娃。

move
❶ VERB AND NOUN USES
❷ PHRASES
❸ PHRASAL VERBS

❶ **move** ♦♦♦ /muv/ (**moves, moving, moved**) 1 V-T/V-I When you **move** something or when it **moves**, its position changes and it does not remain still. 移动 ❑ *She moved the sheaf of papers into position.* 她把那捆纸移到了位置上。 ❑ *A traffic policeman asked him to move his car.* 一位交警让他挪动一下他的车。 ❑ *The train began to move.* 火车开动了。 2 V-I When you **move**, you change your position or go to a different place. 移动 (位置) ❑ *She waited for him to get up, but he didn't move.* 她等着他起来，可他没有动。 ❑ *He moved around the room, putting his possessions together.* 他在屋里走来走去，把他的东西都放在一起。 ● N-COUNT **Move** is also a noun. 位移 ❑ *The doctor made a move toward the door.* 医生朝门口挪了一下。 3 V-I If you **move**, you act or you begin to do something. 采取行动 ❑ *Industrialists must move fast to take advantage of new opportunities in Eastern Europe.* 实业家们必须快速采取行动，抓住东欧的新机遇。 4 N-COUNT A **move** is an action that you take in order to achieve something. 行动 ❑ *The one-point cut in interest rates was a wise move.* 利率下调1个点是明智之举。 ❑ *It may also be a good move to suggest she talks things over.* 建议她仔细讨论一下这些事情可能也是一个好的做法。 5 V-I If a person or company **moves**, they leave the building where they have been living or working, and they go to live or work in a different place, taking their possessions with them. 搬迁 ❑ *Two people in love are at home wherever they are, no matter how often they move.* 无论在哪里，不管搬多少次家，两个相爱的人都会过得舒舒服服。 ❑ *She had often considered moving to Seattle.* 她那时常常考虑搬到西雅图去。 ● N-COUNT **Move** is also a noun. 搬迁 ❑ *Modigliani announced his move to Montparnasse in 1909.* 莫迪里亚尼1909年宣布他要搬到蒙帕尔纳斯去。 6 V-T If people in authority **move** someone, they make that person go from one place or job to another one. 调动 ❑ *His superiors moved him to another parish.* 他的上级把他调到了另一个教区。 7 V-I If you **move from** one job or interest **to** another, you change to it. 变换 (职业); 改变 (兴趣) ❑ *He moved from being a part-time tutor to being a lecturer in social history.* 他从一名兼职助教转变成了一名社会史讲师。 ● N-COUNT **Move** is also a noun. (职业的) 变换; (兴趣的) 改变 ❑ *His move to the chairmanship means he will take a less active role in day-to-day management.* 他主席职务的调任意味着他将更少地参与日常管理工作。 8 V-I If you **move to** a new topic in a conversation, you start talking about something different. 改变 (话题) ❑ *Let's move to another subject, Dan.* 丹，我们换个话题吧。 9 V-T If you **move** an event or the date of an event, you change the time at which it happens. 更改 (时间) ❑ *The club has moved its meeting to Saturday, January 22nd.* 该俱乐部把会议日期改到了星期六，1月22日。 10 V-I If you **move** toward a particular state, activity, or opinion, you start to be in that state, do that activity, or have that opinion. 转变 ❑ *The Labour Party has moved to the right and become like your Democratic Party.* 工党已经转向右翼，变得像你们民主党了。 ● N-COUNT **Move** is also a noun. 转变 ❑ *His move to the left was not a sudden leap but a natural working out of ideas.* 他左倾的转变并非突然，而是思想发展的自然结果。 11 V-I If a situation or process **is moving**, it is developing or progressing, rather than staying still. 进展 [usu cont] ❑ *Events are moving fast.* 事件进展很快。 12 V-T If you say that you will not **be moved**, you mean that you have come to a decision and nothing will change your mind. 使动摇 [usu passive] ❑ *Everyone thought I was crazy to go back, but I wouldn't be moved.* 人人都认为我回去是疯了，可我是不会动摇的。 13 V-T If something **moves** you **to** do something, it influences you and causes you to do it. 促使 ❑ *It was punk that first moved him to join a band seriously.* 最初是朋克摇滚乐促使他认真地加入了一个乐队。 14 V-T If something **moves** you, it has an effect on your emotions and causes you to feel sadness or sympathy for another person. 感动 ❑ *These stories surprised and moved me.* 这些故事令我吃惊，并且感动了我。 ● **moved** ADJ 被感动的 [v-link ADJ] ❑ *Those who listened to him were deeply moved.* 听他讲话的人都被深深地感动了。 15 V-I If you say that someone **moves in** a particular society, circle, or world, you mean that they know people in a particular social class or group and spend most of their time with them. 跻身于 (某个社会、圈子或领域) ❑ *She moves in high-society circles in Palm Beach.* 她跻身于棕榈海滩的上流社会。 16 V-T/V-I At a meeting, if you **move for** something or **move that** something should happen, you formally suggest it so that everyone present can vote on it. 提议 ❑ *Somebody needs to move for an adjournment.* 需要有人提议休会。 17 N-COUNT A **move** is an act of putting a chess piece or other counter in a different position on a board when it is your turn to do so in a game. 一步棋 ❑ *With no idea of what to do for my next move, my hand hovered over the board.* 不知道我下一步棋该怎么走，我的手在棋盘上方举棋不定。

❷ **move** ♦♦♦ /muv/ (**moves, moving, moved**)

➪ **Please look at meanings 5 and 6 to see if the expression you are looking for is shown under another headword.** 1 PHRASE If you say that one **false move** will cause a disaster, you mean that you or someone else must not make any mistakes because the situation is so difficult or dangerous. 错误之举 ❑ *He knew one false move would end in death.* 他知道稍有差池就会送命。 2 PHRASE If you **make a move**, you prepare or begin to leave one place and go somewhere else. 准备出发; 出发 ❑ *He glanced at his wristwatch. "I suppose we'd better make a move."* 他看了一眼手表说："我想我们最好动身吧。" 3 PHRASE If you **make a move**, you take a course of action. 采取行动 ❑ *The week before the deal was supposed to close, fifteen Japanese banks made a move to pull out.* 该交易本应结束的前一周，15家日本银行采取行动撤出了。 4 PHRASE If you are **on the move**, you are going from one place to another. 奔波 ❑ *Jack never wanted to stay in one place for very long, so they were always on the move.* 杰克从不想在一个地方久留，所以他们总在辗转奔波。 5 to **move the goalposts** → see **goalpost** 6 to **move a muscle** → see **muscle**

❸ **move** ♦♦♦ /muv/ (**moves, moving, moved**)

▶ **move in** 1 PHRASAL VERB When you **move in** somewhere, you begin to live there as your home. 搬进 ❑ *Her house was in perfect order when she moved in.* 她搬进来的时候，房子里井井有条。 ❑ *Her husband had moved in with a younger woman.* 她丈夫已经和一个更年轻的女人同居了。 2 PHRASAL VERB If police, soldiers, or attackers **move in**, they go toward a place or person in order to deal with or attack them. (警察、士兵或袭击者) 逼近 ❑ *There were violent and chaotic scenes when police moved in to disperse the crowd.* 警察上前驱散人群时，现场出现了暴力和混乱场面。 3 PHRASAL VERB If someone **moves in on** an area of activity which was previously only done by a particular group of people, they start becoming involved with it for the first time. 介入 ❑ *I don't want another guy moving in on my territory, you know?* 我不想另一个家伙介入我的领域，你知道吗？

▶ **move off** PHRASAL VERB When you **move off**, you start moving away from a place. 离开 ❑ *Gil waved his hand and the car moved off.* 吉尔挥了挥手，汽车开走了。

▶ **move on** 1 PHRASAL VERB When you **move on** somewhere, you leave the place where you have been staying or waiting and go there. 继续前往 ❑ *Mr. Brooke moved on from LA to Phoenix.* 布鲁克先生离开洛杉矶继续前往菲尼克斯市。 2 PHRASAL VERB If someone such as a police officer **moves** you **on**, they order you to stop standing in a particular place and to go somewhere else. 命令…走开 ❑ *Eventually the police were called to move them on.* 最后叫了警察命令他们离开。 3 PHRASAL VERB If you **move on**, you finish or stop one activity and start doing something different. 罢手去做别的事 ❑ *She ran this shop for ten years before deciding to move on to fresh challenges.* 她经营这家商店10年之后，决定罢手去迎接新的挑战。

▶ **move out** PHRASAL VERB If you **move out**, you stop living in a particular house or place and go to live somewhere else. 搬走 ❑ *The harassment had become too much to tolerate and he decided to move out.* 骚扰已让他忍无可忍，他决定搬走。

▶ **move over** 1 PHRASAL VERB If you **move over to** a new system or way of doing something, you change to it. 转变 (到一种新制度或做法) ❑ *The government is having to introduce some difficult changes, particularly in moving over to a market economy.* 政府将不得不引入一些艰难的变革，特别是在转向市场经济的过程中。 2 PHRASAL VERB If

m

someone **moves over**, they leave their job or position in order to let someone else have it. 让位 ❑ *Mr. Jenkins should make balanced programs or move over and let someone else who can.* 詹金斯先生应该制定协调的计划，或者让位给其他能做的人。 **3** PHRASAL VERB If you **move over**, you change your position in order to make room for someone else. 让开 ❑ *Move over and let me drive.* 让开，让我来开车。

▸ **move up** **1** PHRASAL VERB If you **move up**, you change your position, especially in order to be nearer someone or to make room for someone else. (尤指为靠近某人或给他人腾出地方而) 挪动 ❑ *Move up, John, and let the lady sit down.* 约翰，挪一挪，让这位女士坐下。 **2** PHRASAL VERB If someone or something **moves up**, they go to a higher level, grade, or class. 上升 ❑ *Share prices moved up.* 股票价格上涨了。 ❑ *Children learn in mixed-ability classes and move up a class each year.* 孩子们在混合能力班学习而且每年升一个班级。

move·able /muvəbᵊl/ → see **movable**

Word Link *ment ≈ state, condition : agreement, management, movement*

Word Link *mov ≈ moving : movement, movie, unmoved*

move·ment ◆◆◇ /muvmənt/ (**movements**) **1** N-COUNT A **movement** is a group of people who share the same beliefs, ideas, or aims. 运动 (指具有共同信仰、思想或目标的团体) ❑ *It's part of a broader nationalist movement that's gaining strength throughout the country.* 这是一场正在全国范围内日益壮大的更为广泛的民族主义运动的一部分。 ❑ *She became a member of the women's movement in the early 1980s.* 在20世纪80年代初，她成了一名妇女运动的成员。 **2** N-VAR **Movement** involves changing position or going from one place to another. 移动 ❑ *They actually monitor the movement of the fish going up river.* 他们实际上在观测鱼向上游的迁移活动。 ❑ *There was movement behind the window in the back door.* 后门窗户的后面有动静。 ❑ *A tall, thin man was waving his arms in an effort to direct the movements of a large truck.* 一位高瘦的男子在挥舞着胳膊，试图为一辆大卡车指示移动方向。 **3** N-VAR A **movement** is a planned change in position that an army makes during a battle or military exercise. (军队作战或演习时的) 调遣 ❑ *There are reports of fresh troop movements across the border.* 有报道称新近有部队越过边境。 **4** N-VAR **Movement** is a gradual development or change of an attitude, opinion, or policy. (态度、观点、政策等的) 逐渐变化 ❑ *...the movement toward democracy in Latin America.* …拉丁美洲民主的渐进。 **5** N-PLURAL Your **movements** are everything that you do or plan to do during a period of time. (某人在某段时间内的) 行踪 ❑ *I want a full account of your movements the night Mr. Gower was killed.* 我想要了解高尔先生被杀当晚你的所有行踪。

→ see **brain**

Word Partnership *movement* 的常用搭配：

N. **freedom** movement, **labor** movement, **leader of a** movement, **peace** movement, **reform** movement **1**

ADJ. **environmental** movement, **political** movement **1** **rapid** movement, **slow** movement, **sudden** movement **2**

mov·er /muvər/ (**movers**) PHRASE The **movers and shakers** in a place or area of activity are the people who have the most power or influence. 有权势的人 ❑ *It is the movers and shakers of the record industry who will decide which bands make it.* 由唱片业的权势人物决定哪些乐队来灌制它。

movie ◆◆◇ /muvi/ (**movies**) **1** N-COUNT A **movie** is a series of moving pictures that have been recorded so that they can be shown in a theater or on television. A movie tells a story, or shows a real situation. 电影 ❑ *In the first movie Tony Curtis ever made he played a grocery clerk.* 在托尼・柯蒂斯制作的第一部影片中，他出演一名杂货店店员。 **2** N-PLURAL You can talk about **the movies** when you are talking about seeing a movie in a movie theater. 看电影 [mainly AM]

in BRIT, usually use **the cinema**

❑ *He took her to the movies.* 他带她去看电影了。

→ see **DVD**

An **Oscar** is the nickname for the golden statue given as the prize to those films considered the best each year. Also known as the **Academy Awards**, these prizes also recognize the talent of actors, writers, designers and other staff members. Not only American movies but also foreign films are included.

Word Partnership *movie* 的常用搭配：

ADJ. **bad/good** movie, **favorite** movie, **new/old** movie, **popular** movie **1**

V. **go to a** movie, **see a** movie, **watch a** movie **1**

N. **scene in a** movie, movie **screen**, movie **set**, movie **studio**, **television/TV** movie **1**

movie·goer /muvigoʊər/ (**moviegoers**) N-COUNT A **moviegoer** is a person who often goes to the movies. 常看电影的人 [AM]

in BRIT, usually use **cinema-goer, film-goer**

❑ *What is it about Tom Hanks that moviegoers find so appealing?* 汤姆・汉克斯哪点让电影观众觉得那么有吸引力？

movie star (**movie stars**) N-COUNT A **movie star** is a famous actor or actress who appears in movies. 电影明星 [mainly AM]

in BRIT, usually use **film star**

movie thea·ter (**movie theaters**) N-COUNT A **movie theater** is a place where people go to watch movies for entertainment. 电影院 [AM]

in BRIT, use **cinema**

mov·ing /muvɪŋ/ **1** ADJ If something is **moving**, it makes you feel an emotion such as sadness, pity, or sympathy very strongly. 感人的 ❑ *It is very moving to see how much strangers can care for each other.* 令人非常感动的是看到陌生人能够如此互相关心。 ● **mov·ing·ly** ADV 感人地 [ADV with v] ❑ *You write very movingly of your sister Amy's suicide.* 你把你妹妹埃米的自杀写得非常令人感伤。 **2** ADJ A **moving** model or part of a machine moves or is able to move. (模型或机器部件) 活动的；可移动的 [ADJ n] ❑ *It also means there are no moving parts to break down.* 这也意味着没有活动零部件可拆卸。

▲ **mow** /moʊ/ (**mows, mowing, mowed, mown**)

The past participle can be either **mowed** or **mown**.

V-T/V-I If you **mow** an area of grass, you cut it using a machine called a lawn mower. (用割草机) 割草 ❑ *He continued to mow the lawn and do other routine chores.* 他继续给草坪割草，并做其他日常杂务。

▸ **mow down** PHRASAL VERB If someone **is mowed down**, they are killed violently by a vehicle or gunfire. (用车辆或炮) 残杀 ❑ *She was mowed down on a pedestrian crossing.* 她被撞死在人行横道上。

mow·er /moʊər/ (**mowers**) **1** N-COUNT A **mower** is the same as a **lawnmower**. 割草机 **2** N-COUNT A **mower** is a machine that has sharp blades for cutting something such as corn or wheat. 收割机

MP3 /ɛm pi θri/ N-UNCOUNT **MP3** is a kind of technology that enables you to record and play music from the Internet. 一种使人们能够从网上录制和播放音乐的技术

MPEG /ɛmpɛg/ N-UNCOUNT **MPEG** is a standard file format for compressing video images so that they can be stored or sent by e-mail more easily. **MPEG** is an abbreviation for "Motion Picture Experts Group." 一种压缩视频图像的标准文件格式 [COMPUTING]

mph also **m.p.h.** **mph** is written after a number to indicate the speed of something such as a vehicle. **mph** is an abbreviation for "miles per hour." 英里/小时 ❑ *Inside these zones, traffic speeds are restricted to 20 mph.* 在这些区域内，交通限速为20英里/小时。

Mr. ◆◆◆ /mɪstər/

in BRIT, use **Mr**

1 N-TITLE **Mr.** is used before a man's name when you are speaking or referring to him. 先生 (用于男子姓名之前) ❑ *...Mr. Grant.* …格兰特先生。 ❑ *...Mr. Bob Price.* …鲍勃・普赖斯先生。 **2** N-VOC **Mr.** is sometimes used in front of words such as "president" and "chairman" to address the man who holds the position mentioned. 先生 (用于职务之前) ❑ *Mr. President, you're aware of the system.* 总统先生，您是了解该体制的。 **3** → see also **Messrs.**

Mrs. ◆◆◆ /mɪsɪz/

in BRIT, use **Mrs**

N-TITLE **Mrs.** is used before the name of a married woman when you are speaking or referring to her. 夫人；太太 (用于已婚女子的夫姓之前) ❑ *Hello, Mrs. Miles.* 你好，迈尔斯夫人。 ❑ *...Mrs. Anne Pritchard.* …安妮・普里查德太太。

Ms. ◆◆◆ /mɪz/

in BRIT, use **Ms**

N-TITLE **Ms.** is used, especially in written English, before a woman's name when you are speaking to her or referring to her. If you use **Ms.**, you are not specifying if the woman is married or not. 女士 (尤用于书面语，用于婚姻状况不明的女子姓名之前) ❑ ...Ms. Brown. …布朗女士。

much ♦♦♦ /mʌtʃ/ 1 ADV You use **much** to indicate the great intensity, extent, or degree of something such as an action, feeling, or change. **Much** is usually used with "so," "too," and "very," and in negative clauses with this meaning. (做得、感到得、变得等) 多地 (常与**so, too, very**连用，或用于否定句中) [ADV after v] ❑ *She laughs too much.* 她笑得太多了。 ❑ *Thank you very much.* 非常感谢您。 2 ADV If something does not happen **much**, it does not happen very often. (发生得) 多地 (常用于否定句) ❑ *He said that his father never talked much about the war.* 他说他父亲从不多谈这场战争。 ❑ *Gwen had not seen her dad all that much, because mostly he worked on the ships.* 格温见她爸爸不是很多，因为他多数时间都在船上工作。 3 ADV You use **much** in front of "too" or comparative adjectives and adverbs in order to emphasize that there is a large amount of a particular quality. 很大程度上 (用于比较级或**too**前) [EMPHASIS] ❑ *The skin is much too delicate.* 皮肤太过娇嫩了。 4 ADV If one thing is **much** the same as another thing, it is very similar to it. 很 (像…那样) ❑ *The day ended much as it began.* 这一天结束时还像开始时一样。 5 DET You use **much** to indicate that you are referring to a large amount of a substance or thing. 多的 ❑ *They are grown on the hillsides in full sun, without much water.* 它们被种在阳光充足、没有多少水分的山坡上。 ❑ *Japan has been reluctant to offer much aid to Russia.* 日本向来不愿为俄罗斯提供多少援助。 ● PRON **Much** is also a pronoun. 多 ❑ *...eating too much and drinking too much.* …暴饮暴食。 ● QUANT **Much** is also a quantifier. 多 ❑ *Much of the time we do not notice that we are solving problems.* 很多时候我们没有注意到我们正在解决问题。 6 ADV You use **much** in expressions such as **not much**, **not very much**, and **too much** when replying to questions about amounts. 多地 (用于**not much**、**not very much**、**too much**等表达中) [ADV as reply] ❑ *"Can you hear it where you live?" He shook his head. "Not much."* "在你住的地方能听到吗？" 他摇摇头："不怎么听得到。" 7 QUANT If you do not see **much of** someone, you do not see them very often. 多 (见面) [with brd-neg, QUANT "of" n-proper/pron] ❑ *I don't see much of Tony nowadays.* 我现在见托尼不多。 8 DET You use **much** in the expression **how much** to ask questions about amounts or degrees, and also in reported clauses and statements to give information about the amount or degree of something. 多少的 (用于**how much**中) ❑ *How much money can I afford?* 我能出得起多少钱？ ● ADV **Much** is also an adverb. 多少 ❑ *She knows how much this upsets me but she persists in doing it.* 她知道这让我有多烦，但她还是坚持这么做。 ● PRON **Much** is also a pronoun. 多少 ["how" PRON] ❑ *How much do you earn?* 你挣多少？ 9 DET You use **much** in the expression **as much** when you are comparing amounts. (和…一样) 多的 (用于**as much**中) ❑ *I shall try, with as much patience as is possible, to explain yet again.* 我会尽量耐心地再解释一遍。 ❑ *Their aim will be to produce as much milk as possible.* 他们的目标是尽可能多地产奶。

> You should use **much** if you want to talk about things that cannot be counted. ❑ *...too much water.* You only use **many** to talk about things that can be counted. ❑ *They owned many cars.*

10 PHRASE You use **much as** to introduce a fact which makes something else you have just said or will say rather surprising. 尽管 ❑ *Much as they hope to go home tomorrow, they're resigned to staying on until the end of the year.* 尽管他们很希望明天就回家，但不得不待到年底。 11 PHRASE You use **as much** in expressions such as **"I thought as much"** and **"I guessed as much"** after you have just been told something and you want to say that you already believed or expected it to be true. 如此 ❑ *You're waiting for a woman – I thought as much.* 你在等一个女人——这我早料到了。 12 PHRASE You use **as much as** before an amount to suggest that it is surprisingly large. 多达 [EMPHASIS] ❑ *The organizers hope to raise as much as $6M for charity.* 组织者们希望筹集到多达6百万美元的慈善款。 13 PHRASE You use **much less** after a statement, often a negative one, to indicate that the statement is more true of the person, thing, or situation that you are going to mention next. 更不用说 ❑ *They are always short of water to drink, much less to bathe in.* 他们总是缺饮用水，更不用说洗澡水了。 14 PHRASE If you say that something is not **so much** one thing **as** another, you mean that it is more like the second thing than the first. (不如…) 那么多 ❑ *I don't really think of her as a daughter so much as a very good friend.* 我其实更多地把她当做好朋友，而不是女儿。 15 PHRASE You use **so much so** to indicate that your previous statement is true to a very great extent, and therefore it has the result mentioned. 到如此程度以至于 ❑ *He himself believed in freedom, so much so that he would rather die than live without it.* 他本人如此信奉自由，以至于宁死也不愿没有自由地活着。 16 PHRASE If a situation or action is **too much for** you, it is so difficult, tiring, or upsetting that you cannot cope with it. 非…所能忍受; 非…力所能及 ❑ *His inability to stay at one job for long had finally proved too much for her.* 他干什么工作都不能长久，终于让她无法忍受。 17 PHRASE You use **very much** to emphasize that someone or something has a lot of a particular quality, or that the description you are about to give is particularly accurate. 非常 [EMPHASIS] ❑ *...a man very much in charge of himself.* …一个很能自制的人。 18 **a bit much** → see **bit**

muck /mʌk/ N-UNCOUNT **Muck** is dirt or some other unpleasant substance. 污物 [INFORMAL] ❑ *This congealed muck was interfering with the filter and causing the flooding.* 这凝固的污物堵塞着滤器，导致淹水。

mu·cus /myukəs/ N-UNCOUNT **Mucus** is a thick liquid that is produced in some parts of your body, for example the inside of your nose. (身体分泌的) 黏液 ❑ *...the thin layer of mucus that helps protect the delicate lining of the rectum.* 有助于保护娇嫩的直肠内壁的那层薄薄的黏液。

mud /mʌd/ N-UNCOUNT **Mud** is a sticky mixture of earth and water. 泥 ❑ *His uniform was crumpled, untidy, splashed with mud.* 他的制服皱皱巴巴，邋里邋遢，还溅上了泥点。

mud·dle /mʌdᵊl/ (**muddles, muddling, muddled**) 1 N-VAR If people or things are **in a muddle**, they are in a state of confusion or disorder. 混乱 ❑ *My thoughts are all in a muddle.* 我的思维一片混乱。 ❑ *We are going to get into a hopeless muddle.* 我们将陷入绝望的混乱。 2 V-T If you **muddle** things or people, you get them mixed up, so that you do not know which is which. 混淆 ❑ *Already, one or two critics have begun to muddle the two names.* 已经有一两个评论家开始混淆这两个名字了。 ● PHRASAL VERB **Muddle up** means the same as **muddle**. 混淆 ❑ *The question muddles up three separate issues.* 该问题把3件互不相干的事情混淆了。 ● **mud·dled up** ADJ 弄乱了的 ❑ *I know that I am getting my words muddled up.* 我知道我现在语无伦次了。

▸ **muddle through** PHRASAL VERB If you **muddle through**, you manage to do something even though you do not have the proper equipment or do not really know how to do it. 应付过去 ❑ *We will muddle through and just play it day by day.* 我们会混过去的，就一天天混下去。 ❑ *They may be able to muddle through the next five years like this.* 他们也许能像这样应付过未来的5年。

▸ **muddle up** → see **muddle 2**

mud·dled /mʌdᵊld/ ADJ If someone is **muddled**, they are confused about something. 糊涂的 ❑ *I'm afraid I'm a little muddled. I'm not exactly sure where to begin.* 恐怕我有点糊涂了，不太确定从哪儿开始。

★ **mud·dy** /mʌdi/ (**muddier, muddiest, muddies, muddying, muddied**) 1 ADJ Something that is **muddy** contains mud or is covered in mud. 泥泞的 ❑ *...a muddy track.* …一条泥泞的小路。 2 V-T If you **muddy** something, you cause it to be muddy. 使沾上泥巴 ❑ *The ground still smelled of rain and they muddied their shoes.* 地面仍散发着雨水的气息，他们的鞋沾上了泥巴。 3 V-T If someone or something **muddies** a situation or issue, they cause it to seem less clear and less easy to understand. 搅乱 (局势、问题等) ❑ *It's difficult enough without muddying the issue with religion.* 即使不和宗教搅在一起，这个问题也已够难的了。 ● PHRASE If someone or something **muddies the waters**, they cause a situation or issue to seem less clear and less easy to understand. 搅浑水

muf·fle /mʌfᵊl/ (**muffles, muffling, muffled**) V-T If something **muffles** a sound, it makes it quieter and more difficult to hear. 压低 (声音) ❑ *Blake held his handkerchief over the mouthpiece to muffle his voice.* 布莱克用手帕遮住话筒来压低声音。

mug /mʌg/ (**mugs, mugging, mugged**) 1 N-COUNT A **mug** is a large, deep cup with straight sides and a handle, used for hot drinks. 圆筒形有柄大杯 ❑ *He spooned instant coffee into two of the mugs.* 他用勺子把速溶咖啡舀进其中两个大杯里。 2 N-COUNT You can use **mug** to refer to the mug and its contents, or to the contents only. 一大杯; 一大杯所容物 ❑ *He had been drinking mugs of coffee to keep himself awake.* 他一直在喝大杯大杯的咖啡让自己保持清醒。 3 N-COUNT Someone's **mug** is their face. 脸 [INFORMAL] ❑ *He managed to get his ugly mug on TV.* 他设法让他那张丑脸上了电视。 4 V-T If someone **mugs** you, they attack you in order to steal your money. 袭击并抢劫 ❑ *I was walking out to my car when this guy tried to mug me.* 我出来后向自己的汽车走去，这时候这家伙企图抢劫我。 ● **mug·ging** N-VAR (**muggings**) 行凶抢劫 ❑ *Bank robberies, burglaries, and muggings are reported almost daily in the press.* 银行抢劫、入室盗窃以及行凶抢劫几乎在每天的新闻中都有报道。 → see **dish**

mug·ger /mʌgər/ (**muggers**) N-COUNT A **mugger** is a person who attacks someone violently in a street in order to steal money from them. 行凶抢劫者 ❑ *...hiding places for muggers and thieves.* …行凶抢劫犯和小偷的藏身之处。

mug·gy /mʌgi/ ADJ **Muggy** weather is unpleasantly warm and damp. (天气) 闷热而潮湿的 ❑ *It was muggy and overcast.* 那天天气闷热又潮湿，阴沉沉的。

▲ **mule** /myul/ (**mules**) 1 N-COUNT A **mule** is an animal whose parents are a horse and a donkey. 骡 2 N-COUNT A **mule** is a shoe or slipper which is open around the heel. 拖鞋式便鞋；拖鞋

mull /mʌl/ (**mulls, mulling, mulled**) V-T If you **mull** something, you think about it for a long time before deciding what to do. 斟酌 [AM] ❑ *Last month, a federal grand jury began mulling evidence in the case.* 上个月，一个联邦大陪审团开始仔细斟酌该案的证据。

▸ **mull over** PHRASAL VERB If you **mull** something **over**, you think about it for a long time before deciding what to do. 斟酌 ❑ *McLaren had been mulling over an idea to make a movie.* 麦克拉伦一直在琢磨着要拍一部电影。

Word Link *multi ≈ many : multicultural, multimedia, multinational*

★ **multi·cul·tur·al** /mʌltikʌltʃərəl/ ADJ **Multicultural** means consisting of or relating to people of many different nationalities and cultures. 多元文化的 ❑ *...children growing up in a multicultural society.* …在多元文化社会中长大的孩子们。

★ **multi·lat·er·al** /mʌltilætərᵊl/ ADJ **Multilateral** means involving at least three different groups of people or nations. 多边的；多国的 ❑ *Many want to abandon the multilateral trade talks in Geneva.* 许多国家想要放弃在日内瓦的多边贸易会谈。

multi·media /mʌltimidiə/ 1 N-UNCOUNT You use **multimedia** to refer to computer programs and products which involve sound, pictures, and film, as well as text. 多媒体 (技术) ❑ *...the case of an insurance company using multimedia to improve customer service in its branches.* …一家保险公司利用多媒体技术改善其分支机构的客户服务的实例。 2 N-UNCOUNT In education, **multimedia** is the use of television and other different media in a lesson, as well as books. 多媒体 (应用) ❑ *I am making a multimedia presentation for my science project.* 我正在为我的科学项目做多媒体演示。

★ **multi·na·tion·al** /mʌltinæʃənᵊl/ (**multinationals**) 1 ADJ A **multinational** company has branches or owns companies in many different countries. 跨国的 (公司) ● N-COUNT **Multinational** is also a noun. 跨国公司 ❑ *...multinationals such as Ford and IBM.* …像福特和IBM这样的跨国公司。 2 ADJ **Multinational** armies, organizations, or other groups involve people from several different countries. 多国的 (军队、组织等) ❑ *The U.S. troops would be part of a multinational force.* 美军将成为一支多国部队的成员。 3 ADJ **Multinational** countries or regions have a population that is made up of people of several different nationalities. 多民族的 ❑ *We live in a multinational country.* 我们生活在一个多民族的国家。

mul·ti·play·er /mʌltipleɪəʳ/ ADJ A **multiplayer** computer or video game is played by more than one player at one time. 多人玩的 [COMPUTING] ❑ *Internet multiplayer games are responsible for much of the increase in broadband use.* 多人玩的网络游戏是导致宽带使用率上升的重要因素。

multi·ple /mʌltɪpᵊl/ (**multiples**) 1 ADJ You use **multiple** to describe things that consist of many parts, involve many people, or have many uses. 多部分的；涉及多人的；多功能的 ❑ *He died of multiple injuries.* 他死于多处受伤。 2 N-COUNT If one number is a **multiple of** a smaller number, it can be exactly divided by that smaller number. 倍数 ❑ *Their numerical system, derived from the Babylonians, was based on multiples of the number six.* 他们的数制是袭用巴比伦人的，以数字6的倍数为基准。
→ see **copy**

multi·ple choice ADJ In a **multiple choice** test or question, you have to choose the answer that you think is right from several possible answers that are listed on the question paper. 多项选择的 ❑ *The multiple-choice questions must be answered within a strict time limit.* 多项选择题必须在严格的时限内回答。

multi·pli·ca·tion /mʌltɪplɪkeɪʃᵊn/ 1 N-UNCOUNT **Multiplication** is the process of calculating the total of one number multiplied by another. 乘法 ❑ *There will be simple tests in addition, subtraction, multiplication, and division.* 将会有加减乘除的简单测试。 2 N-UNCOUNT The **multiplication** of things of a particular kind is the process or fact of them increasing in number or amount. 增加 ❑ *Increasing gravity is known to speed up the multiplication of cells.* 为人所知的是，不断增加的重力会加速细胞数量的递增。
→ see **mathematics**

multi·plic·ity /mʌltɪplɪsɪti/ QUANT A **multiplicity of** things is a large number or a large variety of them. 大量；多种多样 [QUANT "of" pl-n] [FORMAL] ❑ *...a writer who uses a multiplicity of styles.* …一个运用多种风格的作家。

multi·ply /mʌltɪplaɪ/ (**multiplies, multiplying, multiplied**) 1 V-T/V-I When something **multiplies** or when you **multiply** it, it increases greatly in number or amount. 使大大增加；大大增加 ❑ *Such disputes multiplied in the eighteenth and nineteenth centuries.* 此类争论在18世纪和19世纪大大增加。 2 V-I When animals and insects **multiply**, they increase in number by giving birth to large numbers of young. 大量繁殖 ❑ *These creatures can multiply quickly.* 这些生物能迅速大量繁殖。 3 V-T If you **multiply** one number by another, you add the first number to itself as many times as is indicated by the second number. For example 2 multiplied by 3 is equal to 6. 乘 ❑ *What do you get if you multiply six by nine?* 6乘以9得多少？

multi·ra·cial /mʌltireɪʃᵊl/ ADJ **Multiracial** means consisting of or involving people of many different races. 多种族的 ❑ *We live in a multiracial society.* 我们生活在一个多种族的社会里。

multi-storey car park [BRIT] → see **parking garage**

multi·tasking /mʌltitæskɪŋ/ N-UNCOUNT **Multitasking** is a situation in which a computer or person does more than one thing at the same time. 同时处理多项任务 ❑ *Often women are so good at multitasking that it appears it's all effortless.* 通常女性很善于同时处理多项任务，而且看起来似乎完全不费力。

★ **multi·tude** /mʌltɪtud/ (**multitudes**) 1 QUANT A **multitude of** things or people is a very large number of them. 大量 [QUANT "of" pl-n] ❑ *There are a multitude of small, quiet roads to cycle along.* 有多条可以骑自行车的僻静小路。 ❑ *Addiction to drugs can bring a multitude of other problems.* 毒瘾会带来其他许多问题。 ● PHRASE If you say that something covers or hides **a multitude of sins**, you mean that it hides something unattractive or does not reveal the true nature of something. (被掩盖的) 种种丑恶 2 N-COUNT You can refer to a very large number of people as a **multitude**. 一大群人 [WRITTEN] ❑ *...surrounded by a noisy multitude.* …被吵吵嚷嚷的一大群人围着。 3 N-COUNT-COLL You can refer to the great majority of people in a particular country or situation as **the multitude** or **the multitudes**. 大多数人 ❑ *The hideous truth was hidden from the multitude.* 向大众隐瞒了丑恶的真相。

mum ◆◇◇ /mʌm/ (**mums**) N-FAMILY Your **mum** is your mother. 妈妈 [BRIT, INFORMAL]
in AM, use **mom**

▲ **mum·ble** /mʌmbᵊl/ (**mumbles, mumbling, mumbled**) V-T/V-I If you **mumble**, you speak very quietly and not at all clearly with the result that the words are difficult to understand. 咕哝 ❑ *Her grandmother mumbled in her sleep.* 她祖母睡觉时咕哝了。 ❑ *He mumbled a few words.* 他咕哝了几句。 ● N-COUNT **Mumble** is also a noun. 咕哝 ❑ *He could hear the low mumble of Navarro's voice.* 他能听到纳瓦罗的低声咕哝。

mum·my /mʌmi/ (**mummies**) 1 N-COUNT A **mummy** is a dead body which was preserved long ago by being rubbed with special oils and wrapped in cloth. 木乃伊 ❑ *...an Egyptian mummy.* …一具埃及木乃伊。 2 N-FAMILY **Mummy** is the same as **mommy**. 妈咪 (尤为儿童使用) [BRIT, INFORMAL]

munch /mʌntʃ/ (**munches, munching, munched**) V-T/V-I If you **munch** food, you eat it by chewing it slowly, thoroughly, and rather noisily. 大声咀嚼 ❑ *Luke munched the chicken sandwiches.* 卢克大声嚼着鸡肉三明治。 ❑ *Across the table, his son Benjie munched appreciatively.* 桌子对面，他儿子本吉津津有味地大声咀嚼着。

mun·dane /mʌndeɪn/ ADJ Something that is **mundane** is very ordinary and not at all interesting or unusual. 平凡的；单调的 ❑ *Be willing to do mundane tasks with good grace.* 有风度地主动做平凡的工作。 ● N-SING You can refer to mundane things as **the mundane**. 平凡的事物；单调的事物 ❑ *It's an attitude that turns the mundane into something more interesting and exciting.* 正是一种态度使单调平凡的工作变得更加有趣和刺激。

★ **mu·nici·pal** /myunɪsɪpᵊl/ ADJ **Municipal** means associated with or belonging to a city or town that has its own local government. 市政的 [ADJ n] ❑ *The municipal authorities gave the* go-ahead for the march. 市政当局批准了此次游行。 ❑ ...next month's municipal elections. …下个月的市政选举。

mu·nici·pal·ity /myunɪsɪpælɪti/ (**municipalities**) N-COUNT A **municipality** is a city or town that is incorporated and can elect its own government, which is also called a **municipality**. 自治市

mu·ni·tions /myunɪʃᵊnz/ N-PLURAL **Munitions** are military equipment and supplies, especially bombs, shells, and guns. 军火 ❑ ...*the shortage of men and munitions*. …人员和军火的短缺。

mu·ral /myʊ̲ərəl/ (**murals**) N-COUNT A **mural** is a picture painted on a wall. 壁画 ❑ ...*a mural of San Francisco Bay*. …一幅旧金山湾壁画。

mur·der ♦♦◊ /mɜ̲rdər/ (**murders, murdering, murdered**) **1** N-VAR **Murder** is the deliberate and illegal killing of a person. 谋杀 ❑ *The three accused, aged between 19 and 20, are charged with attempted murder.* 3名年龄在19到20岁之间的被告被指控蓄意谋杀。 ❑ *She refused to testify, unless the murder charge against her was dropped.* 她拒绝作证，除非取消她的谋杀指控。 **2** V-T To **murder** someone means to commit the crime of killing them deliberately. 谋杀 ❑ ...*a thriller about two men who murder a third to see if they can get away with it*. …一部惊悚电影，关于两人谋杀了第3个人并看他们是否能逃脱惩罚。 **3** PHRASE If you say that someone **gets away with murder**, you are complaining that they can do whatever they like without anyone trying to control them or punish them. 无法无天为所欲为 [INFORMAL, DISAPPROVAL] ❑ *His charm and the fact that he is so likeable often allows him to get away with murder.* 他的魅力和受宠程度常让他无法无天为所欲为。

mur·der·er /mɜ̲rdərər/ (**murderers**) N-COUNT A **murderer** is a person who has murdered someone. 谋杀者 ❑ *One of these men may have been the murderer.* 这些人中有一个可能就是谋杀者。

murky /mɜ̲rki/ (**murkier, murkiest**) **1** ADJ A **murky** place or time of day is dark and rather unpleasant because there is not enough light. 阴暗的 ❑ *The large lamplit room was murky with wood smoke.* 那亮灯的大房间因木柴烟而昏暗不明。 **2** ADJ **Murky** water or fog is so dark and dirty that you cannot see through it. 混浊的 ❑ ...*the deep, murky waters of Loch Ness*. …尼斯湖混浊的深水。 **3** ADJ If you describe something as **murky**, you mean that the details of it are not clear or that it is difficult to understand. 含糊不清的；晦涩难懂的 ❑ *The law here is a little bit murky.* 该法律此处有点含糊不清。

★ **mur·mur** /mɜ̲rmər/ (**murmurs, murmuring, murmured**) **1** V-T If you **murmur** something, you say it very quietly, so that not many people can hear what you are saying. 小声说 ❑ *He turned and murmured something to the professor.* 他转过身，小声对教授说了些什么。 ❑ *"How lovely," she murmured.* "多可爱呀，"她低声说。 **2** N-COUNT A **murmur** is something that is said but can hardly be heard. 低语 ❑ *They spoke in low murmurs.* 他们窃窃私语。 **3** N-SING A **murmur** is a continuous low sound, like the noise of a river or of voices far away. (河水、远处谈话等) 轻微连续的声音 ❑ *The piano music mixes with the murmur of conversation.* 钢琴音乐与轻轻的谈话声混合在一起。 **4** N-COUNT A **murmur of** a particular emotion is a quiet expression of it. (情感的) 默认 ❑ *The promise of some basic working rights draws murmurs of approval.* 对一些基本工作权利的承诺得到默认。 **5** N-COUNT A **murmur** is an abnormal sound which is made by the heart and which shows that there is probably something wrong with it. (心脏发出的) 杂音 ❑ *The doctor said James had now developed a heart murmur.* 医生说詹姆斯心脏现在出现了杂音。 **6** PHRASE If someone does something **without a murmur**, they do it without complaining. 毫无怨言 ❑ *Then came the bill and my friend paid up without a murmur.* 然后账单来了，我朋友毫无怨言地结了帐。

mus·cle ♦◊◊ /mʌ̲sᵊl/ (**muscles, muscling, muscled**) **1** N-VAR A **muscle** is a piece of tissue inside your body that connects two bones and which you use when you make a movement. 肌肉 ❑ *Keeping your muscles strong and in tone helps you to avoid back problems.* 保持强壮有力的肌肉有助于防范背疾。 **2** N-UNCOUNT If you say that someone has **muscle**, you mean that they have power and influence, which enables them to do difficult things. 影响力 ❑ *Eisenhower used his muscle to persuade Congress to change the law.* 艾森豪威尔施展了他的影响力来说服国会修改该法律。 **3** PHRASE If a group, organization, or country **flexes** its **muscles**, it does something to impress or frighten people, in order to show them that it has power and is considering using it. 显示实力 ❑ *The Fair Trade Commission has of late been flexing its muscles, cracking down on cases of corruption.* 公平交易委员会最近一展雄威，对腐败案件进行了严惩。 **4** PHRASE If you say that someone did not **move a muscle**, you mean that they stayed absolutely still. 动一下 ❑ *He stood without moving a muscle, unable to believe what his eyes saw so plainly.* 他一动也不动地站着，不敢相信自己的眼睛。

→ see Word Web: **muscle**

→ see **nervous system**

▸ **muscle in** PHRASAL VERB If someone **muscles in on** something, they force their way into a situation where they have no right to be and where they are not welcome, in order to gain some advantage for themselves. 强行挤入(以分享利益) [DISAPPROVAL] ❑ *Cohen complained that Kravis was muscling in on his deal.* 科恩抱怨克莱维斯正强行插足他的生意。

Word Partnership *muscle* 的常用搭配:

N. muscle **aches**, muscle **mass**, muscle **pain**, muscle **tone** **1**

V. **contract** a muscle, **flex** a muscle, **pull** a muscle **1**

★ **mus·cu·lar** /mʌ̲skyələr/ **1** ADJ **Muscular** means involving or affecting your muscles. (有关) 肌肉的 [ADJ n] ❑ *As a general rule, all muscular effort is enhanced by breathing in as the effort is made.* 一般规律是，肌肉都通过用力吸气而增强力量。 **2** ADJ If a person or their body is **muscular**, they are very fit and strong, and have firm muscles which are not covered with a lot of fat. 强壮的 ❑ *Like most female athletes, she was lean and muscular.* 像大多数女运动员一样，她精瘦而健壮。

muse /myu̲z/ (**muses, musing, mused**) V-T/V-I If you **muse** on something, you think about it, usually saying or writing what you are thinking at the same time. 揣摩 [WRITTEN] ❑ *Many of the papers muse on the fate of the president.* 许多报纸在揣测总统的命运。 ❑ *"As a whole," she muses, "the 'organized church' turns me off."* "总的来说，"她若有所思地说，"'组织严密的教会'让我厌烦。" ● **mus·ing** N-COUNT (**musings**) 沉思 ❑ *His musings were interrupted by Montagu who came and sat down next to him.* 蒙塔古来到他旁边坐下时，他的思绪被打断了。

mu·seum ♦♦◊ /myuzi̲əm/ (**museums**) N-COUNT A **museum** is a building where a large number of interesting and valuable objects, such as works of art or historical items, are kept, studied, and displayed to the public. 博物馆 ❑ *For months Malcolm had wanted to visit the New York art museums.* 马尔科姆想参观纽约的艺术博物馆有好几个月了。

→ see **gallery**

mush·room /mʌ̲ʃrum/ (**mushrooms, mushrooming, mushroomed**) **1** N-VAR **Mushrooms** are fungi that you can eat. They have short stems and round tops. 蘑菇 ❑ *There are many types of wild mushrooms.* 有许多种野生蘑菇。 **2** V-I If something such as an industry or a place **mushrooms**, it grows or comes into existence very quickly. 迅速发展 ❑ *The media training industry has mushroomed over the past decade.* 媒体培训业在过去的十年中迅速发展。

→ see **fungus**

Word Web **muscle**

There are three types of **muscles** in the body. **Voluntary** or **skeletal** muscles produce external movements. **Involuntary** or **smooth** muscles provide internal movement within the body. For example, the smooth muscles in the **iris** of the eye adjust the size of the pupil. This controls how much light enters the eye. **Cardiac** muscles are found only in the heart. They work constantly but never get tired. When we **exercise**, voluntary muscles **contract** and then **relax**. With repeated **workouts**, we can **build** these muscles and increase their **strength**. If we don't exercise, these muscles can atrophy and become **weak**.

Word Web music

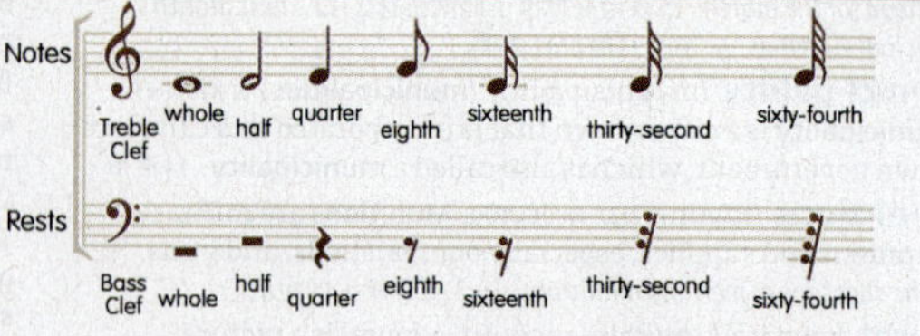

Wolfgang Amadeus Mozart lived only 35 years (1756-1791). However, he is one of the most important **musicians** in history. Mozart began playing the **piano** at the age of four. A year later he **composed** his first **song**. Since he hadn't yet learned musical notation, his father wrote out the **score** for him. Mozart's father arranged for the boy to play for royalty across Europe. Soon Mozart became known as a gifted **composer**. During his lifetime, he wrote more than 50 **symphonies**. He also composed numerous **operas**, **concertos**, arias, and other musical works.

mu·sic ♦♦♦ /myuzɪk/ **1** N-UNCOUNT **Music** is the pattern of sounds produced by people singing or playing instruments. 音乐 ❑ *...classical music.* …古典音乐。 **2** N-UNCOUNT **Music** is the art of creating or performing music. 音乐创作；音乐表演 ❑ *He went on to study music, specializing in the clarinet.* 他继续学习音乐，专攻单簧管。 **3** N-UNCOUNT **Music** is the symbols written on paper which represent musical sounds. 乐谱 ❑ *He's never been able to read music.* 他从来就不识乐谱。 **4** PHRASE If something that you hear is **music to** your **ears**, it makes you feel very happy. 佳音 [FEELINGS] ❑ *Popular support – it's music to the ears of any politician.* 公众的支持——这对任何政客都是佳音。 **5** PHRASE If you **face the music**, you put yourself in a position where you will be criticized or punished for something you have done. 承担自己行为的后果 ❑ *Sooner or later, I'm going to have to face the music.* 迟早我得自食其果。
→ see Word Web: **music**
→ see **concert**, **DVD**

Word Partnership *music* 的常用搭配：
ADJ. **live** music, **loud** music, **new** music, **pop(ular)** music **1**
N. **background** music, music **critic**, music **festival** **1**
music **business**, music **industry**, music **lesson** **2**
V. **download** music, **hear** music, **listen to** music, **play** music **1**
compose music, **study** music, **write** music **2**

M

mu·si·cal ♦◇◇ /myuzɪkᵊl/ (**musicals**) **1** ADJ You use **musical** to indicate that something is connected with playing or studying music. 关于音乐的 [ADJ n] ❑ *We have a wealth of musical talent in this region.* 我们在该地区有丰富的音乐人才。 ● **mu·si·cal·ly** /myuzɪkli/ ADV 关于音乐地 ❑ *Musically there is a lot to enjoy.* 在音乐方面有许多可欣赏。 **2** N-COUNT A **musical** is a play or movie that uses singing and dancing in the story. 音乐剧；音乐歌舞片 ❑ *...the smash hit musical, Miss Saigon.* …轰动一时的音乐剧《西贡小姐》。 **3** ADJ Someone who is **musical** has a natural ability and interest in music. 有音乐天赋的；喜爱音乐的 ❑ *I came from a musical family.* 我来自一个音乐家庭。 **4** ADJ Sounds that are **musical** are light and pleasant to hear. 悦耳的 ❑ *He had a soft, almost musical voice.* 他有着轻柔悦耳的嗓音。

mu·si·cal in·stru·ment (**musical instruments**) N-COUNT A **musical instrument** is an object such as a piano, guitar, or violin which you play in order to produce music. 乐器 ❑ *The drum is one of the oldest musical instruments.* 鼓是最古老的乐器之一。

Word Link *ician ≈ person who works at : electrician, musician, physician*

mu·si·cian ♦◇◇ /myuzɪʃᵊn/ (**musicians**) N-COUNT A **musician** is a person who plays a musical instrument as their job or hobby. 音乐家；音乐演奏者 ❑ *He was a brilliant musician.* 他曾是一位出色的音乐家。
→ see **concert**, **music**, **orchestra**

▲ **Mus·lim** ♦♦◇ /mʌzlɪm, mʊs-/ (**Muslims**) **1** N-COUNT A **Muslim** is someone who believes in Islam and lives according to its rules. 穆斯林（即伊斯兰教信徒） **2** ADJ **Muslim** means relating to Islam or Muslims. 穆斯林的；伊斯兰教的 ❑ *...Iran and other Muslim countries.* …伊朗和其他穆斯林国家。

mus·lin /mʌzlɪn/ (**muslins**) N-MASS **Muslin** is very thin, cotton cloth. 薄棉布 ❑ *...white muslin curtains.* …白色薄棉窗帘。

mus·sel /mʌsᵊl/ (**mussels**) N-COUNT **Mussels** are a kind of shellfish that you can eat from their shells. 贻贝

must ♦♦♦ /məst, STRONG mʌst/ (**musts**)

The noun is pronounced /mʌst/.
名词读作 /mʌst/。

Must is a modal verb. It is followed by the base form of a verb.

1 MODAL You use **must** to indicate that you think it is very important or necessary for something to happen. You use **must not** or **mustn't** to indicate that you think it is very important or necessary for something not to happen. 必须（表示重要或必要） ❑ *What you wear should be stylish and clean, and must definitely fit well.* 你的穿着应该时尚整洁，而且必须非常合体。 ❑ *You are going to have to take a certain amount of criticism, but you must cope with it.* 你会受到一定程度的批评，但这是你必须面对的。 **2** MODAL You use **must** to indicate that it is necessary for something to happen, usually because of a rule or law. 必要（表示依据法律或规则） ❑ *Candidates must satisfy the general conditions for admission.* 应试者必须满足录取的一般条件。 ❑ *Mr. Allen must pay Mr. Farnham's legal costs.* 艾伦先生必须支付法纳姆先生的诉讼费用。 **3** MODAL You use **must** to indicate that you are fairly sure that something is the case. 肯定（表示猜测） ❑ *At 29 Russell must be one of the youngest ever international referees.* 29岁的拉塞尔想必是迄今为止最年轻的国际裁判之一。 ❑ *Claire's car wasn't there, so she must have gone to her mother's.* 克莱尔的汽车不在那儿，想必她是去她母亲家了。 **4** MODAL You use **must**, or **must have** with a past participle, to indicate that you believe that something is the case, because of the available evidence. 必定（表示有据推断） ❑ *"You must be Emma," said the visitor.* "你一定是埃玛，"来访者说道。 ❑ *Miss Holloway had a weak heart. She must have had a heart attack.* 霍洛韦小姐心脏衰弱。她一定得过心脏病。 **5** MODAL If you say that one thing **must have** happened in order for something else to happen, you mean that it is necessary for the first thing to have happened before the second thing can happen. 肯定已经发生（表示前者为后者的前提） ❑ *In order to take that job, you must have left another job.* 为了去做那份工作，你肯定已经辞去了另一份工。 **6** MODAL You use **must** to express your intention to do something. 一定要（表示意愿） ❑ *I must be getting back.* 我该回去了。 ❑ *I must telephone my parents.* 我一定要给父母打个电话。 **7** MODAL You use **must** to make suggestions or invitations very forcefully. 务必；一定得（提出建议或邀请） ❑ *You must see a doctor, Frederick.* 弗雷德里克，你一定得看医生。 **8** MODAL You use **must** in remarks and comments where you are expressing sympathy. 想必（表示同情） ❑ *This must be a very difficult job for you.* 这对你来说肯定是一项非常艰巨的任务。 **9** MODAL You use **must** in conversation in expressions such as **"I must say"** and **"I must admit"** in order to emphasize a point that you are making. 必须（用于表示强调） [EMPHASIS] ❑ *This came as a surprise, I must say.* 我得说这发生得很突然。 ❑ *I must admit I like looking feminine.* 我得承认我喜欢看上去娇柔些。 **10** MODAL You use **must** in expressions such as **"it must be noted"** and **"it must be remembered"** in order to draw the reader's or listener's attention to what you are about to say. 一定（用于引起注意） ❑ *It must be noted, however, that not all British and American officers carried out orders.* 然而，一定要注意，并非所有英美军官都执行命令。 **11** MODAL You use **must** in questions to express your anger or irritation about something that someone has done, usually because you do not understand their behavior. 偏要（用于问句中，表示因不理解某人的行为而愤怒） [FEELINGS] ❑ *Why must she interrupt?* 她为什么偏要打断呢？ **12** MODAL You use **must** in exclamations to express surprise or shock. 一定（用于感叹句，表示惊奇或震惊） [EMPHASIS] ❑ *"Go! Please go."—"You must be joking!"* "走吧！请走吧。"——"你一定是在开玩笑！" ❑ *I really must be quite mad!* 我真的一定是气坏了！ **13** N-COUNT If you refer to something as **a must**, you mean that it is absolutely necessary. 必不可少的事物；必须要做的事 [INFORMAL] ❑ *Taking out travel insurance may seem an unnecessary expense, but it is a must.* 旅游保险费用看起来似乎是没必要的，但却是必

不可少的开支。14 PHRASE You say "**if you must**" when you know that you cannot stop someone doing something that you think is wrong or stupid. 如果你一定要(表示虽不赞同但无法阻止) ❑ *If you must be in the sunlight, use the strongest sunscreen you can get.* 如果你一定要呆在阳光下的话，就用你能买到的最有效的防晒霜。15 PHRASE You say "**if you must know**" when you tell someone something that you did not want them to know and you want to suggest that you think they were wrong to ask you about it. 如果你一定要知道的话 ❑ *It scared the hell out of her, if you must know. And me, too.* 这把她的魂都吓飞了，如果你一定要知道的话。而且我也被吓坏了。

mus·tache /mʌstæʃ/ also **mous+tache** (**mustaches**) N-COUNT A man's **mustache** is the hair that grows on his upper lip. If it is very long, it is sometimes referred to as his **mustaches**. 小胡子(嘴唇以上) ❑ *The thick beard had gone, replaced by a bushy mustache.* 浓密的络腮胡子不见了，换成了一撇密匝匝的小胡子。

▲ **mus·tard** /mʌstərd/ (**mustards**) 1 N-MASS **Mustard** is a yellow or brown paste usually eaten with meat. It tastes hot and spicy. 芥末酱 ❑ *...a jar of mustard.* …一罐芥末酱。2 COLOR **Mustard** is used to describe things that are brownish yellow in color. 褐黄色(的) ❑ *I sat in my father's chair, a mustard-colored recliner.* 我坐在父亲的椅子上，一把褐黄色的躺椅。3 PHRASE If someone does not **cut the mustard**, their work or their performance is not as good as it should be or as good as it is expected to be. 未能达到要求；不如所期待地那么好 [INFORMAL] ❑ *He just wasn't a good student. He wasn't cutting the mustard and we let him go.* 他不是什么好学生。不合格，我们就让他走了。

mus·ter /mʌstər/ (**musters, mustering, mustered**) 1 V-T If you **muster** something such as support, strength, or energy, you gather as much of it as you can in order to do something. 聚集(支持、力量、精力等) ❑ *He traveled around West Africa trying to muster support for his movement.* 他走遍西非，努力为他的运动寻求支持。2 V-T/V-I When soldiers **muster** or **are mustered**, they gather together in one place in order to take part in a military action. 召集；(军队等)集合 ❑ *The men mustered before their clan chiefs.* 男人们在他们的氏族首领前集合。

mustn't /mʌsᵊnt/ **Mustn't** is the usual spoken form of "must not." **must not**的常用口语形式

must've /mʌstəv/ **Must've** is the usual spoken form of "must have," especially when "have" is an auxiliary verb. **must have**的常用口语形式，尤用于**have**作为助动词时

mu·tant /myutᵊnt/ (**mutants**) N-COUNT A **mutant** is an animal or plant that is physically different from others of the same species because of a change in its genes. 突变体 ❑ *New species are merely mutants of earlier ones.* 新物种不过是早先物种的突变体。

Word Link *mut ≈ changing : commute, mutate, mutilate*

mu·tate /myuteɪt/ (**mutates, mutating, mutated**) 1 V-T/V-I If an animal or plant **mutates**, or something **mutates** it, it develops different characteristics as the result of a change in its genes. 使(遗传基因等)突变；经受突变 ❑ *The virus mutates in the carrier's body.* 该病毒在携带者体内发生突变。❑ *HIV has proven to possess an ability to mutate into drug-resistant forms.* 艾滋病病毒经证实能突变成抗药型病毒。● **mu·ta·tion** /myuteɪʃᵊn/ N-VAR (**mutations**) 突变 ❑ *Scientists have found a genetic mutation that appears to be the cause of Huntington's disease.* 科学家们已经发现一个似乎是亨廷顿病病因的遗传突变。2 V-I If something **mutates into** something different, it changes into that thing. 变成 ❑ *Overnight, the gossip begins to mutate into headlines.* 一夜之间，流言蜚语开始变成头条新闻了。

★ **mute** /myut/ (**mutes, muting, muted**) 1 ADJ Someone who is **mute** is silent for a particular reason and does not speak. 缄默的 ❑ *He was mute, distant, and indifferent.* 他缄默无言，对人疏远而且冷漠。● ADV **Mute** is also an adverb. 缄默地 [ADV after V] ❑ *He could watch her standing mute by the phone.* 他能看到她缄默地站在电话旁。2 ADJ Someone who is **mute** is unable to speak. 哑的 ❑ *Marianna, the duke's daughter, became mute after a shock.* 公爵的女儿玛丽安娜在一场惊吓之后失语了。3 V-T If someone **mutes** something such as their feelings or their activities, they reduce the strength or intensity of them. 抑制(感情等)；减弱(行动的力度等) ❑ *The corruption does not seem to have muted the country's prolonged economic boom.* 腐败看来没有减缓该国持续的经济繁荣。● **mut·ed** ADJ 温和的 ❑ *The threat contrasted starkly with his administration's previous muted criticism.* 这恐吓与他执政当局先前温和的批评形成了鲜明的对比。4 V-T If you **mute** a noise or sound, you lower its volume or make it less distinct. 降低(声音) ❑ *They begin to mute their voices, not be as assertive.* 他们开始放低嗓门，不再那么肯定了。● **mut·ed** ADJ (声音)降低的 ❑ *"Yes," he muttered, his voice so muted I hardly heard his reply.* "是啊，"他轻声说道，声音轻得我几乎听不到他的回答。

mut·ed /myutɪd/ ADJ **Muted** colors are soft and gentle, not bright and strong. (颜色)柔和的 ❑ *...painted in subtle, muted colors.* …涂着浅淡柔和的颜色。

mu·ti·late /myutᵊleɪt/ (**mutilates, mutilating, mutilated**) 1 V-T If a person or animal **is mutilated**, their body is severely damaged, usually by someone who physically attacks them. 使伤残 ❑ *More than 30 horses have been mutilated in the last nine months.* 三十多匹马在过去的9个月中受了重伤。❑ *He tortured and mutilated six young men.* 他折磨致残了6个年轻男人。● **mu·ti·la·tion** /myutᵊleɪʃᵊn/ N-VAR (**mutilations**) 伤残 ❑ *Amnesty International chronicles cases of torture and mutilation.* 大赦国际记载酷刑及伤残案。2 V-T If something **is mutilated**, it is deliberately damaged or spoiled. 毁坏 ❑ *Brecht's verdict was that his screenplay had been mutilated.* 布雷赫特的意见是他的电影剧本已经被删改得面目全非了。

mu·ti·ny /myutᵊni/ (**mutinies, mutinying, mutinied**) 1 N-VAR A **mutiny** is a refusal by people, usually soldiers or sailors, to continue obeying a person in authority. (常指士兵或水手的)哗变 ❑ *A series of coup attempts and mutinies within the armed forces destabilized the regime.* 武装部队内部一系列政变图谋和哗变动摇了该政权。2 V-I If a group of people, usually soldiers or sailors, **mutiny**, they refuse to continue obeying a person in authority. 反叛 ❑ *Units stationed around the capital mutinied because they had received no pay for nine months.* 驻扎在首都周边的部队反叛了，因为他们9个月没领到工资了。

★ **mut·ter** /mʌtər/ (**mutters, muttering, muttered**) V-T/V-I If you **mutter**, you speak very quietly so that you cannot easily be heard, often because you are complaining about something. 轻声说话；小声抱怨 ❑ *"God knows," she muttered, "what's happening in that madman's mind."* "天知道，"她低声抱怨，"那个疯子脑子里正在想什么。" ❑ *She can hear the old woman muttering about consideration.* 她能听见这老妇人低声说要考虑考虑。● N-COUNT **Mutter** is also a noun. 轻声低语；小声抱怨 ❑ *They make no more than a mutter of protest.* 他们不过是小声抗议了一下。● **mut·ter·ing** N-VAR (**mutterings**) 喃喃细语 ❑ *He heard muttering from the front of the crowd.* 他听到人群前面传来喃喃低语。

m

▲ **mut·ton** /mʌtᵊn/ N-UNCOUNT **Mutton** is meat from an adult sheep that is eaten as food. 羊肉 ❑ *...a leg of mutton.* …一条羊腿。→ see **meat**

mu·tu·al ♦◇◇ /myutʃuəl/ 1 ADJ You use **mutual** to describe a situation, feeling, or action that is experienced, felt, or done by both of two people mentioned. 相互的 ❑ *The East and the West can work together for their mutual benefit and progress.* 东西方可以为互惠和进步而合作。● **mu·tu·al·ly** ADV 相互地 ❑ *Attempts to reach a mutually agreed solution had been fruitless.* 想要达成一个彼此同意的解决方案，却无果而终。2 → see **exclusive** 3 ADJ You use **mutual** to describe something such as an interest which two or more people share. 共同的 ❑ *They do, however, share a mutual interest in design.* 然而，他们确实对设计有共同的兴趣。4 ADJ If an insurance company or savings bank has **mutual** status, it is not owned by shareholders but by its customers, who receive a share of the profits. (保险公司或储蓄银行)互助的 [ADJ n] [BUSINESS] ❑ *...a mutual company based in Columbus, Ohio.* …一家总部在俄亥俄州哥伦布市的互助公司。

Word Partnership *mutual* 的常用搭配：

N. **the feeling is** mutual, mutual **respect**, mutual **trust**, mutual **understanding** 1
mutual **agreement**, mutual **friend**, mutual **interest** 3

mu·tu·al fund (**mutual funds**) N-COUNT A **mutual fund** is an organization which invests money in many different kinds of business and which offers units for sale to the public as an investment. 共同基金(为客户进行不同组合的投资) [AM, BUSINESS]
in BRIT, use **unit trust**

▲ **muz·zle** /mʌzᵊl/ (**muzzles, muzzling, muzzled**) 1 N-COUNT The **muzzle** of an animal such as a dog is its nose and mouth. (动物的)口鼻部 ❑ *The mongrel presented his muzzle for scratching.* 这只杂种狗探出口鼻挠痒。2 N-COUNT A **muzzle** is an object that is put over a dog's nose and mouth so that it cannot bite people or make a noise. (动物的)口套 ❑ *...dogs like pit bulls, which have to wear a muzzle.* …像比特犬一样得戴口套的狗。3 V-T If you **muzzle** a dog or other animal, you put a muzzle over its nose and mouth. 给…戴上口套 ❑ *He was convicted of failing to muzzle a pit bull.* 他因没有给一条比特犬戴口套而被判有罪。 4 V-T If you say that someone **is muzzled**, you are complaining that they are prevented from expressing their views freely. 阻止…的言论 [DISAPPROVAL] ❑ *He complained of being muzzled by the chairman.* 他抱怨被主席阻止了发言。 5 N-COUNT The **muzzle** of a gun is the end where the bullets come out when it is fired. 枪口 ❑ *Mickey felt the muzzle of a rifle press hard against his neck.* 米奇感到一支步枪枪口紧紧地抵住他的脖子。

my ♦♦♦ /maɪ/

My is the first person singular possessive determiner.

1 DET A speaker or writer uses **my** to indicate that something belongs or relates to himself or herself. 我的 ❑ *I invited him back to my apartment for coffee.* 我请他回我的公寓喝咖啡。 2 DET In conversations or in letters, **my** is used in front of a word like "dear" or "darling" to show affection. 我的 (用在对话或信件中表示亲密) [FEELINGS] ❑ *My sweet Freda.* 我可爱的弗雷达。 3 DET **My** is used in phrases such as "**My God**" and "**My goodness**" to express surprise or shock. 用于口语中表示惊讶或震惊 [SPOKEN, FEELINGS] ❑ *My God, I've never seen you so nervous.* 我的天呀！我从没见你这么紧张过。

▲ **myr·i·ad** /mɪriəd/ 1 QUANT **A myriad** or **myriads of** people or things is a very large number or great variety of them. 大量；各种各样 [QUANT "of" pl-n] ❑ *They face a myriad of problems bringing up children.* 他们在抚养孩子上面临着各种问题。 2 ADJ **Myriad** means having a large number or great variety. 大量的；各种各样的 [ADJ n] ❑ *The magazine has been celebrating pop in all its myriad forms.* 该杂志一直在赞美各种形式的流行音乐。

my·self ♦♦◊ /maɪsɛlf/

Myself is the first person singular reflexive pronoun.

1 PRON-REFL A speaker or writer uses **myself** to refer to himself or herself. **Myself** is used as the object of a verb or preposition when the subject refers to the same person. 我自己 [V PRON, prep PRON] ❑ *I asked myself what I would have done in such a situation.* 我问过自己在这样一种情况下我会做什么。 2 PRON-REFL-EMPH You use **myself** to emphasize a first person singular subject. In more formal English, **myself** is sometimes used instead of "me" as the object of a verb or preposition, for emphasis. 我自己 (用于强调第一人称单数主语) [EMPHASIS] ❑ *I myself enjoy movies, poetry, eating out, and long walks.* 我本人喜欢电影、诗歌、外出就餐和远足。 3 PRON-REFL-EMPH If you say something such as "I did it **myself**," you are emphasizing that you did it, rather than anyone else. 我独自 [EMPHASIS] ❑ *"Where did you get that embroidery?"—"I made it myself."* "你从哪儿得到那件刺绣的？" "我自己做的。"

mys·teri·ous /mɪstɪəriəs/ 1 ADJ Someone or something that is **mysterious** is strange and is not known about or understood. 神秘的；难以理解的 ❑ *He died in mysterious circumstances.* 他死得蹊跷。 ❑ *A mysterious illness confined him to bed for over a month.* 一种怪病让他卧床一个多月。 ● **mys·teri·ous·ly** ADV 神秘地 ❑ *A couple of messages had mysteriously disappeared.* 几条信息已经神秘地消失了。 2 ADJ If someone is **mysterious** about something, they deliberately do not talk much about it, sometimes because they want to make people more interested in it. 诡秘的 [v-link ADJ] ❑ *As for his job – well, he was very mysterious about it.* 至于他的工作——嘿，他对此十分诡秘。 ● **mys·teri·ous·ly** ADV 诡秘地 [ADV after v] ❑ *Asked what she meant, she said mysteriously: "Work it out for yourself."* 当被问及她什么意思时，她诡秘地说："你自己想想吧。"

mys·tery ♦◊◊ /mɪstəri, mɪstri/ (**mysteries**) 1 N-COUNT A **mystery** is something that is not understood or known about. 迷 ❑ *The source of the gunshots still remains a mystery.* 枪弹来自何处依然是一个迷。 2 N-UNCOUNT If you talk about the **mystery** of someone or something, you are talking about how difficult they are to understand or know about, especially when this gives them a rather strange or magical quality. 神秘 (性) ❑ *She's a lady of mystery.* 她是一个神秘的女人。 3 ADJ A **mystery** person or thing is one whose identity or nature is not known. 来历不明的 [ADJ n] ❑ *The mystery hero immediately alerted police after spotting a bomb.* 那个不知名的英雄发觉炸弹后马上报了警。 4 N-COUNT A **mystery** is a story in which strange things happen that are not explained until the end. 悬疑 (推理) 故事 ❑ *His fourth novel is a murder mystery set in London.* 他的第4本小说是一个以伦敦为背景的凶杀疑案。

Word Partnership *mystery* 的常用搭配:

V.	**remain a** mystery, **unravel a** mystery 1 **solve a** mystery 1 4
N.	**murder** mystery, mystery **novel**, mystery **readers** 4

▲ **mys·tic** /mɪstɪk/ (**mystics**) 1 N-COUNT A **mystic** is a person who practices or believes in religious mysticism. 神秘主义者 ❑ *...an Indian mystic known as Bhagwan Shree Rajneesh.* …一个叫作巴格万·什里·劳伊尼希的印度神秘主义者。 2 ADJ **Mystic** means the same as **mystical**. 神秘的；难以理解的 [ADJ n] ❑ *...mystic union with God.* …与上帝的神秘结合。

mys·ti·cal /mɪstɪkəl/ ADJ Something that is **mystical** involves spiritual powers and influences that most people do not understand. 神秘的；难以理解的 ❑ *That was clearly a deep mystical experience.* 那显然是一次刻骨铭心的神秘经历。

mys·ti·cism /mɪstɪsɪzəm/ N-UNCOUNT **Mysticism** is a religious practice in which people search for truth, knowledge, and closeness to God through meditation and prayer. 神秘主义 (一种通过冥想和祷告寻求真理、知识以及与神相通的宗教行为) ❑ *As a younger man Harrison was intrigued by Indian mysticism.* 哈里森年轻时被印度神秘主义迷住了。

mys·ti·fy /mɪstɪfaɪ/ (**mystifies, mystifying, mystified**) V-T If you **are mystified** by something, you find it impossible to explain or understand. 使困惑不解 ❑ *The audience must have been totally mystified by the plot.* 观众肯定对该情节困惑不解。 ● **mys·ti·fy·ing** ADJ 令人困惑的 ❑ *I find your attitude a little mystifying, Marilyn.* 玛丽莲，我觉得你的态度有点令人困惑。

mys·tique /mɪstik/ N-SING If there is a **mystique** about someone or something, they are thought to be special and people do not know much about them. 神秘感 [also N-UNCOUNT] ❑ *His book destroyed the mystique of monarchy.* 他的书消除了君主制的神秘感。

myth ♦◊◊ /mɪθ/ (**myths**) 1 N-VAR A **myth** is a well-known story which was made up in the past to explain natural events or to justify religious beliefs or social customs. 神话 ❑ *There is a famous Greek myth in which Icarus flew too near to the Sun.* 一个著名的希腊神话中说，伊卡洛斯飞得离太阳太近了。 2 N-VAR If you describe a belief or explanation as a **myth**, you mean that many people believe it but it is actually untrue. 谬见 ❑ *Contrary to the popular myth, women*

Word Web myth

The scholar Joseph Campbell* believed that **mythologies** explain a **culture's** understanding of their world. **Stories, symbols, rituals,** and **myths** explain the **psychological**, **social**, cosmological, and **spiritual** parts of life. Campbell also believed that artists and philosophers are a culture's mythmakers. He explored **archetypal themes** in myths from many different cultures. He showed how these themes are repeated in many different cultures. For example, the **hero's** journey appeared in ancient Greece in *The Odyssey**, and the same theme appears later in England in King Arthur's* search for the Holy Grail*. A 20th-century version shows up in the film *Star Wars*.

Joseph Campbell (1904–1987): an American professor and author.
The Odyssey: an epic poem from ancient Greece.
King Arthur: a legendary king of Great Britain.
Holy Grail: a cup that legends say Jesus used.

are not reckless spendthrifts. 与盛行的谬见相反，女人们并非挥霍无度。
→ see Word Web: **myth**
→ see **fantasy**

Word Partnership *myth* 的常用搭配：

ADJ. **ancient** myth, **Greek** myth 1
popular myth 2

mythi·cal /mɪθɪkəl/ 1 ADJ Something or someone that is **mythical** exists only in myths and is therefore imaginary. 神话中的 ❑ *...the Hydra, the mythical beast that had seven or more heads.* …许德拉，神话中长着7个或者更多头的怪兽。 2 ADJ If you describe something as **mythical**, you mean that it is untrue or does not exist. 虚构的 ❑ *...the American West, not the mythical, romanticized West of cowboys and gunslingers, but the real West.* …美国西部，不是虚构的、带浪漫色彩有牛仔和枪手的西部，而是真正的西部。

▲ **my·thol·ogy** /mɪθɒlədʒi/ (**mythologies**) 1 N-VAR **Mythology** is a group of myths, especially all the myths from a particular country, religion, or culture. 神话(集体名词) ❑ *In Greek mythology, the god Zeus took the form of a swan to seduce Leda.* 在希腊神话中，主神宙斯用天鹅之形引诱勒达。 ● **mytho·logi·cal** /mɪθəlɒdʒɪkəl/ ADJ 神话中的 ❑ *...the mythological beast that was part lion and part goat.* …神话中半狮半羊的怪兽。 2 N-VAR You can use **mythology** to refer to the beliefs or opinions that people have about something, when you think that they are false or untrue. 神话 ❑ *Altman strips away the pretense and mythology to expose the film industry as a business like any other, dedicated to the pursuit of profit.* 奥尔特曼揭去电影业的伪装和神话，揭示了其与任何行业一样追逐利润的本质。
→ see **hero**

m

Nn

N also **n** /ɛn/ (**N's, n's**) N-VAR **N** is the fourteenth letter of the English alphabet. 英语字母表中的第14个字母

NA also **n/a** CONVENTION **NA** is a written abbreviation for **not applicable** or **not available**. **not applicable**或**not available**的缩写

nag /næg/ (**nags, nagging, nagged**) 1 V-T/V-I If someone **nags** you, or if they **nag**, they keep asking you to do something you have not done yet or do not want to do. 唠叨催促 [DISAPPROVAL] ❑ *The more Sarah nagged her, the more stubborn Cissie became.* 萨拉越是对她唠叨不休，茜茜就越是固执。 ❑ *My girlfriend nagged me to cut my hair.* 我女朋友唠叨着催我去理发。[JC1][JC2][JC3] ● N-COUNT A **nag** is someone who nags. 唠叨催促的人 ❑ *Aunt Molly is a nag about regular meals.* 莫莉姨妈是个对一日三餐絮絮叨叨的人。● **nag·ging** N-UNCOUNT 唠叨催促 ❑ *Her endless nagging drove him away from home.* 她无休止的唠叨催促迫使他离开了家。 2 V-T/V-I If something such as a doubt or worry **nags at** you, or **nags** you, it keeps worrying you. 烦扰 ❑ *He could be wrong about her. The feeling nagged at him.* 他可能错怪她了。这种感觉烦扰着他。 ❑ *...the anxiety that had nagged Amy all through lunch.* …烦扰了埃米整个午餐时间的焦虑情绪。

nail /neɪl/ (**nails, nailing, nailed**) 1 N-COUNT A **nail** is a thin piece of metal with one pointed end and one flat end. You hit the flat end with a hammer in order to push the nail into something such as a wall. 钉子 ❑ *A mirror hung on a nail above the sink.* 一面镜子挂在洗脸池上方的一个钉子上。 2 V-T If you **nail** something somewhere, you fasten it there using one or more nails. (用钉子)钉住 ❑ *Frank put the first plank down and nailed it in place.* 弗兰克放下第一块木板，把它钉到位。 ❑ *They nail shut the front door.* 他们将前门钉死。 3 N-COUNT Your **nails** are the thin hard parts that grow at the ends of your fingers and toes. 指甲；趾甲 ❑ *Keep your nails short and your hands clean.* 指甲要短，保持双手清洁。 4 V-T To **nail** someone means to catch them and prove that they have been breaking the law. 逮住并证明…犯法 [INFORMAL] ❑ *The prosecution still managed to nail him for robberies at the homes of leading industrialists.* 原告律师仍设法证明他因在知名实业家的家中抢劫而犯法。 5 PHRASE If you say that someone **has hit the nail on the head**, you think they are exactly right about something. 正中要害 ❑ *"I think it would civilize people a bit more if they had decent conditions."—"I think you've hit the nail on the head."* "我认为如果人们有好的条件，就会使其更有教养一点。"——"我想你说到点子上了。"

▸ **nail down** 1 PHRASAL VERB If you **nail down** something unknown or uncertain, you find out exactly what it is. 弄清 ❑ *It would be useful if you could nail down the source of this tension.* 如果你能弄清这种紧张情绪的根源，会是有用的。 2 PHRASAL VERB If you **nail down** an agreement, you manage to reach a firm agreement with a definite result. 确定(协议) ❑ *The Secretary of State and his Russian counterpart met to try to nail down the elusive accord.* 美国国务卿与俄罗斯外交部长会晤，试图确定这项表述模糊的协议。

★ **na·ive** /nɑiːv/ also **naïve** ADJ If you describe someone as **naive**, you think they lack experience and so expect things to be easy or people to be honest or kind. 幼稚的 ❑ *It's naive to think that teachers are always tolerant.* 认为老师总是很宽容是幼稚的。 ❑ *Their view was that he had been politically naive.* 他们的看法是，他在政治上曾是幼稚的。● **na·ive·ly** ADV 幼稚地 ❑ *...naively applying Western solutions to Eastern problems.* …幼稚地用西方的办法来解决东方的问题。● **na·ive·ty** /nɑiːvɪti/ N-UNCOUNT 幼稚 ❑ *I was alarmed by his naivety and ignorance of international affairs.* 他对国际事务的幼稚和无知让我感到忧虑。

na·ked /neɪkɪd/ 1 ADJ Someone who is **naked** is not wearing any clothes. 裸体的 ❑ *Her naked body was found wrapped in a sheet in a field.* 她赤裸的尸体在野外被找到了，裹在一张床单里。 ❑ *They stripped me naked.* 他们扒了我的衣服使我全身赤裸。● **na·ked·ness** N-UNCOUNT 裸体 ❑ *He had pulled the blanket over his body to hide his nakedness.* 他拽过了毯子盖在他的身体上以遮住他的裸体。 2 ADJ If an animal or part of an animal is **naked**, it has no fur or feathers on it. 没有毛的 ❑ *The nest contained eight little mice that were naked and blind.* 这窝里有8只小老鼠，没毛也看不见东西。 3 ADJ You can describe an object as **naked** when it does not have its normal covering. 无(正常)遮盖的 ❑ *...a naked bulb dangling in a bare room.* …一只没有灯罩、在一个空房间里摇荡的灯泡。 4 ADJ You can use **naked** to describe unpleasant or violent actions and behavior which are not disguised or hidden in any way. 公然的；赤裸裸的(行为等) [ADJ n] [JOURNALISM] ❑ *Naked aggression and an attempt to change frontiers by force could not go unchallenged.* 对公然侵略和企图用武力改变疆域，人们不会坐视不管。 ❑ *...violence and the naked pursuit of power.* …暴力和对权力赤裸裸的追求。

Word Partnership *naked* 的常用搭配：

ADV. **bare** naked, **completely** naked, **half** naked, **nearly** naked 1

name ♦♦♦ /neɪm/ (**names, naming, named**) 1 N-COUNT The **name** of a person, place, or thing is the word or group of words that is used to identify them. 名字 ❑ *"What's his name?"—"Peter."* "他叫什么名字？"——"彼得。" ❑ *I don't even know if Sullivan's his real name.* 我甚至不知道沙利文是不是他的真名。

> Your **first name** is the name that your parents chose for you. When you are telling someone your name, this comes first in English-speaking countries. Your **last name**, or **surname**, is the name that you share with other members of your family. In between your first name and your last name you may have a **middle name**, a second name that your parents chose for you. It is only usually used in official circumstances such as registering for a course or signing documents.

2 V-T When you **name** someone or something, you give them a name, usually at the beginning of their life. 给…取名 ❑ *My mother insisted on naming me Horace.* 我母亲执意给我取名叫霍勒斯。 ❑ *...a man named John T. Benson.* …一个叫约翰·T·本森的男子。 3 V-T If you **name** someone or something **after** another person or thing, you give them the same name as that person or thing. 以(某人或某物的名字)命名 ❑ *Why haven't you named any of your sons after yourself?* 为什么你没用你名字给你儿子中的任何一个命名？ 4 V-T If you **name** someone, you identify them by stating their name. 说出…的名称 ❑ *It's nearly thirty years since a journalist was jailed for refusing to name a source.* 一名记者因拒绝说出消息来源而入狱已近三十年了。 5 V-T If you **name** something such as a price, time, or place, you say what you want it to be. 提出(价格、时间、地点等) ❑ *Call Marty, tell him to name his price.* 给马蒂打电话，让他开个价。 6 V-T If you **name** the person for a particular job, you say who you want to have the job. 提名 ❑ *The CEO has named a new chief financial officer.* 执行总裁已经提名了一位新的财务总监。 ❑ *When the chairman of Campbell's retired, McGovern was named as his successor.* 坎贝尔公司的董事长退休时，麦戈文被提名为其继任者。 7 N-COUNT You can refer to the reputation of a person or thing as their **name**. 名声 ❑ *He had a name for good judgement.* 他以判断力强著称。 8 N-COUNT You can refer to someone as, for example, a famous **name** or a great **name** when they are well known. (名)人 [JOURNALISM] ❑ *...some of the most famous names in modeling and show business.* …模特界和演艺界的一些大人物。 9 → see also **brand name, Christian name, first name, maiden name** 10 PHRASE If something is **in** someone's **name**, it officially belongs to them or is reserved for them. 在…的名下 ❑ *The house is in my husband's name.* 这所房子在我丈夫名下。 11 PHRASE If someone does something **in the name of** a group of people, they do it as the representative of that group. 代表 ❑ *In the United States the majority governs in the name of the people.* 在美国，多数派代表民众执政。 12 PHRASE If you do something **in the name of** an ideal or an abstract thing, you do it in order to preserve or promote that thing. 为了(理想或抽象的事物) ❑ *...one of those rare occasions in history when a political leader risked his own power in the name of the greater public good.*

…政治领袖为了更大的公共利益而将自己权力置于风险之中的那些罕有历史时刻之一。 13 PHRASE When you mention someone or something **by name**, or address someone **by name**, you use their name. 用名字(提到或称呼) ❑ *When he walks down 131st street, he greets most people he sees by name.* 当他沿第131大街走着的时候，他跟他看见的大多数人用名字打着招呼。 14 PHRASE You can use **by name** or **by the name of** when you are saying what someone is called. 名叫…的 [FORMAL] ❑ *In 1911 he met up with a young Australian by the name of Harry Busteed.* 1911年，他与一个叫哈里・巴斯蒂德的年轻澳大利亚人会了面。 15 PHRASE If someone **calls** you **names**, they insult you by saying unpleasant things to you or about you. 谩骂 ❑ *At my last school they called me names because I was so slow.* 在上一所学校，他们骂过我，因为我反应太慢。 16 PHRASE If you **make a name for yourself** or **make your name as** something, you become well known for that thing. 使某人出名 ❑ *She was beginning to make a name for herself as a portrait photographer.* 她当时作为一名肖像摄影师开始出名。

→ see **Internet**

Word Partnership *name* 的常用搭配：

N. name **and address**, **company** name, name **and number** 1

ADJ. **common** name, **full** name, **real** name 1
familiar name, **famous** name, **well-known** name 8

name·ly /neɪmli/ ADV You use **namely** to introduce detailed information about the subject you are discussing, or a particular aspect of it. 即 ❑ *A district should serve its clientele, namely students, staff, and parents.* 一个学区应该服务于其主顾，即学生、教职员工和家长。

nan·ny /næni/ (**nannies**) N-COUNT A **nanny** is a woman who is paid by parents to take care of their child or children. (受雇照看小孩的) 保姆

▲ **nap** /næp/ (**naps, napping, napped**) 1 N-COUNT If you take or have a **nap**, you have a short sleep, usually during the day. (通常指白天的) 小睡 ❑ *I might take a little nap.* 我可能会打个盹儿。 2 V-I If you **nap**, you sleep for a short period of time, usually during the day. (通常指在白天) 小睡 ❑ *An elderly person may nap during the day and then sleep only five hours a night.* 上了年纪的人白天会小睡一会儿，然后晚上只睡5个小时。 3 PHRASE If someone **is caught napping**, something happens when they are not prepared for it, although they should have been. 使…措手不及 [INFORMAL] ❑ *The security services were clearly caught napping.* 安全服务人员显然被弄得措手不及。

→ see **sleep**

nap·kin /næpkɪn/ (**napkins**) N-COUNT A **napkin** is a square of cloth or paper that you use when you are eating to protect your clothes, or to wipe your mouth or hands. 餐巾；餐巾纸 ❑ *...taking tiny bites of a hot dog and daintily wiping my lips with a napkin.* …小口咬着热狗并用餐巾文雅地擦着我的嘴唇。

nap·py /næpi/ (**nappies**) N-COUNT A **nappy** is a piece of soft thick cloth or paper which is fastened around a baby's bottom in order to soak up its urine and feces. 尿布；纸尿裤 [BRIT]

in AM, use **diaper**

nar·cot·ic /nɑrkɒtɪk/ (**narcotics**) 1 N-COUNT **Narcotics** are drugs such as opium or heroin which make you sleepy and stop you from feeling pain. You can also use **narcotics** to mean any kind of illegal drugs. 麻醉剂；毒品 ❑ *He was indicted for dealing in narcotics.* 他因贩卖毒品而受到起诉。 2 ADJ If something, especially a drug, has a **narcotic** effect, it makes the person who uses it feel sleepy. 麻醉的 ❑ *...hormones that have a narcotic effect on the immune system.* …对免疫系统有麻醉作用的激素。

nar·rate /næreɪt/ (**narrates, narrating, narrated**) 1 V-T If you **narrate** a story, you tell it from your own point of view. 叙述 [FORMAL] ❑ *The three of them narrate the same events from three perspectives.* 他们3个人从3个角度叙述同样那些事件。 ● **nar·ra·tion** /nəreɪʃᵊn/ N-UNCOUNT 叙述 ❑ *Its story-within-a-story method of narration is confusing.* 它那故事里套故事的叙述方法令人迷惑。 ● **nar·ra·tor** /næreɪtər/ N-COUNT (**narrators**) 叙述人 ❑ *Jules, the story's narrator, is an actress in her late thirties.* 故事的叙述者朱尔斯是位年近四十的女演员。 2 V-T The person who **narrates** a film or program speaks the words which accompany the pictures, but does not appear in it. 给 (电影或节目) 作解说 ❑ *She also narrated a documentary about the Kirov Ballet School.* 她还为一部关于基洛夫芭蕾舞学院的记录片作过解说。 ● **nar·ra·tion** N-UNCOUNT (电影或节目的) 解说 ❑ *As soon as the crew gets back from lunch, we can put your narration on it right away.* 工作人员吃过午饭一回来，我们就能马上把你的解说加在上面。 ● **nar·ra·tor** N-COUNT (**narrators**) 解说员 ❑ *...the narrator of the documentary.* …该纪录片的解说员。

nar·ra·tive /nærətɪv/ (**narratives**) 1 N-COUNT A **narrative** is a story or an account of a series of events. 故事；叙事 ❑ *...a fast-moving narrative.* …一个快节奏的叙事。 2 N-UNCOUNT **Narrative** is the description of a series of events, usually in a novel. (尤指小说中的) 记叙 ❑ *Neither author was very strong on narrative.* 两位作者在记叙方面都不强。

nar·row ♦♦◇ /næroʊ/ (**narrower, narrowest, narrows, narrowing, narrowed**) 1 ADJ Something that is **narrow** measures a very small distance from one side to the other, especially compared to its length or height. 狭窄的 ❑ *...through the town's narrow streets.* …穿过小镇狭窄的街道。 ❑ *She had long, narrow feet.* 她有一双瘦长的脚。 ● **nar·row·ness** N-UNCOUNT 狭窄 ❑ *...the narrowness of the river mouth.* …河口的狭窄。 2 V-I If something **narrows**, it becomes less wide. 变窄 ❑ *The wide track narrows before crossing another stream.* 宽宽的路径在穿越另一条小溪前变窄了。 3 V-T/V-I If your eyes **narrow** or if you **narrow** your eyes, you almost close them, for example because you are angry or because you are trying to concentrate on something. 眯起 [WRITTEN] ❑ *Coggins' eyes narrowed angrily. "You think I'd tell you?"* 科金斯愤怒地眯起双眼说，"你以为我会告诉你？" 4 ADJ If you describe someone's ideas, attitudes, or beliefs as **narrow**, you disapprove of them because they are restricted in some way, and often ignore the more important aspects of an argument or situation. (想法、态度、信仰等) 狭隘的 [DISAPPROVAL] ❑ *...a narrow and outdated view of family life.* …对家庭生活狭隘过时的一种看法。 ● **nar·row·ly** ADV 狭隘地 ❑ *They may define their contribution too narrowly.* 他们可能把他们的贡献说得太狭隘了。 ● **nar·row·ness** N-UNCOUNT 狭隘 ❑ *...the narrowness of their mental and spiritual outlook.* …他们心理和精神境界的狭隘。 5 V-T/V-I If something **narrows** or if you **narrow** it, its extent or range becomes smaller. 使…缩小；缩小 ❑ *Most recent opinion polls suggest that the gap between the two main parties has narrowed.* 最近的民意调查表明，两个主要政党之间的分歧已经缩小。 ● **nar·row·ing** N-SING 缩小 ❑ *...a narrowing of the gap between rich members and poor.* …贫富成员间差距的缩小。 6 ADJ If you have a **narrow** victory, you succeed in winning but only by a small amount. 勉强的 ❑ *Voters approved the plan by a narrow majority.* 投票人以微弱的多数通过了这个方案。 ● **nar·row·ly** ADV 勉强地 ❑ *She narrowly failed to win enough votes.* 她差点赢得足够的选票。 ● **nar·row·ness** N-UNCOUNT 勉强 ❑ *The narrowness of the victory reflected deep division within the party.* 这次勉强获胜反映了该党内部深刻的分歧。 7 ADJ If you have a **narrow** escape, something unpleasant nearly happens to you. 很险的 (逃脱) [ADJ n] ❑ *Two police officers had a narrow escape when rioters attacked their vehicles.* 暴徒们攻击他们的车辆时，两名警官死里逃生。 ● **nar·row·ly** ADV 很险地 (逃脱) [ADV with v] ❑ *Five firemen narrowly escaped death when a staircase collapsed beneath their feet.* 一段楼梯在他们脚下坍塌时，五名消防队员险些丧命。

▸ **narrow down** PHRASAL VERB If you **narrow down** a range of things, you reduce the number of things included in it. 缩减 ❑ *What's happened is that the new results narrow down the possibilities.* 现有的情况是，新的结果缩小了可能性的范围。

Thesaurus *narrow* 另参见：

ADJ. close, cramped, restricted, tight; *(ant.)* broad, wide 1 4

Word Partnership *narrow* 的常用搭配：

ADV. **relatively** narrow, **too** narrow 1

N. narrow **band**, narrow **hallway**, narrow **opening**, narrow **path** 1
narrow **definition**, narrow **focus**, narrow **mind**, narrow **view** 4

narrow-minded ADJ If you describe someone as **narrow-minded**, you are criticizing them because they are unwilling to consider new ideas or other people's opinions. 心胸狭窄的 [DISAPPROVAL] ❑ *...a narrow-minded bigot.* …一个心胸狭窄的执拗的人。

NASA /næsə/ N-PROPER **NASA** is a U.S. government organization concerned with spacecraft and space travel. **NASA** is an abbreviation for "National Aeronautics and Space Administration." 美国国家航空航天局

na·sal /neɪzᵊl/ 1 ADJ **Nasal** is used to describe things relating to the nose and the functions it performs. 与鼻子有关的 [ADJ n]

❑ ...*inflamed nasal passages.* …发炎的鼻腔。 **2** ADJ If someone's voice is **nasal**, it sounds as if air is passing through their nose as well as their mouth while they are speaking. 带鼻音的 ❑ *Her voice was nasal and penetrating.* 她的声音是带鼻音和有穿透性的。

nas·ty /næsti/ (**nastier, nastiest**) **1** ADJ Something that is **nasty** is very unpleasant to see, experience, or feel. 可恶的 (事物) ❑ ...*an extremely nasty murder.* …一起极其令人厌恶的谋杀。 • **nas·ti·ness** N-UNCOUNT 可恶 ❑ ...*the nastiness of war.* …战争的可恶。 **2** ADJ If you describe a person or their behavior as **nasty**, you mean that they behave in an unkind and unpleasant way. 可恶的 (人或行为) ❑ *What nasty little snobs you all are.* 你们是多么可恶的势利小人！ ❑ *The guards looked really nasty.* 那些警卫看上去真可恶。 • **nas·ti·ly** ADV 厌恶地 [ADV after v] ❑ *She took the money and eyed me nastily.* 她拿了钱，厌恶地盯着我。 • **nas·ti·ness** N-UNCOUNT 可恶 ❑ *As the years went by his nastiness began to annoy his readers.* 随着岁月的推移，他的可恶开始惹恼他的读者。 **3** ADJ If you describe something as **nasty**, you mean it is unattractive, undesirable, or in bad taste. 低俗可厌的 (事物) ❑ *They should put warning labels on those nasty little devices.* 他们应该在那些讨厌的小装置上贴警示标签。 **4** ADJ A **nasty** problem or situation is very worrisome and difficult to deal with. 难对付的 (问题、情况等) ❑ *A spokesman said this firm action had defused a very nasty situation.* 一位发言人说，这次果断的行动已经缓解了僵局。 **5** ADJ If you describe an injury or a disease as **nasty**, you mean that it is serious or looks unpleasant. (伤、疾病等) 严重的 ❑ *My little granddaughter caught her heel in the spokes of her bicycle – it was a very nasty wound.* 我的小孙女把她的后脚跟卷到她的自行车辐条里了——伤得很严重。

na·tion ♦♦♦ /neɪʃᵊn/ (**nations**) **1** N-COUNT A **nation** is an individual country considered together with its social and political structures. 国家 ❑ *Such policies would require unprecedented cooperation between nations.* 这样的一些政策会要求国与国之间前所未有的合作。

> **Country** is the most usual word to use when you are talking about the major political units that the world is divided into. **State** is used when you are talking about politics or government institutions. ❑ ...*the new German state created by the unification process.* ...*Italy's state-controlled telecommunications company.* **State** can also refer to a political unit within a particular country. ❑ ...*the state of California.* **Nation** is often used when you are talking about a country's inhabitants, and their cultural or ethnic background. ❑ *Wales is a proud nation with its own traditions*... *A senior government spokesman will address the nation.* **Land** is a less precise and more literary word, which you can use, for example, to talk about the feelings you have for a particular country. ❑ *She was fascinated to learn about this strange land at the edge of Europe.*

N

2 N-SING **The nation** is sometimes used to refer to all the people who live in a particular country, or all the people who belong to a particular ethnic group. 全国国民; 民族 [JOURNALISM] ❑ *It was a story that touched the nation's heart.* 这是一个感动了全民族的故事。 ❑ ...*the former chief of the Cherokee nation.* …前任切罗基族酋长。
→ see **country**

Thesaurus *nation* 另参见:
N. country, democracy, population, republic, society **1**

na·tion·al ♦♦♦ /næʃənᵊl/ (**nationals**) **1** ADJ **National** means relating to the whole of a country or nation rather than to part of it or to other nations. 全国的 ❑ ...*major national and international issues.* …重大的国内和国际问题。 • **na·tion·al·ly** ADV 全国地 ❑ ...*a nationally televised speech.* …一个全国电视讲话。 **2** ADJ **National** means typical of the people or customs of a particular country or nation. 国民的; 民族的 [ADJ n] ❑ ...*the national characteristics and history of the country.* …该国的民族特点和历史。 **3** N-COUNT You can refer to someone who is legally a citizen of a country as a **national** of that country. 国民 ❑ ...*a Sri-Lankan national.* …一位斯里兰卡国民。

na·tion·al·ise /næʃənᵊlaɪz/ [BRIT] → see **nationalize**

★ **na·tion·al·ism** /næʃənᵊlɪzəm/ **1** N-UNCOUNT You can refer to a person's great love for their nation as **nationalism**. It is often associated with the belief that a particular nation is better than any other nation, and in this case is often used showing disapproval. 民族主义 ❑ *This kind of fierce nationalism is a powerful and potentially volatile force.* 这种强劲的民族主义势力是一股强大和潜在的不稳定的力量。 **2** N-UNCOUNT **Nationalism** is the desire for political independence of people who feel they are historically or culturally a separate group within a country. 民族独立主义 ❑ *The rising tide of Slovak nationalism may also help the party to win representation in parliament.* 斯洛伐克民族独立主义浪潮的高涨也有可能帮助该党在议会中赢得席位。

★ **na·tion·al·ist** ♦◇◇ /næʃənᵊlɪst/ (**nationalists**) **1** ADJ **Nationalist** means connected with the desire of a group of people within a country for political independence. 民族独立主义的 [ADJ n] ❑ *The crisis has set off a wave of nationalist feelings in Quebec.* 这场危机已经在魁北克掀起了一个民族独立情绪的浪潮。 • N-COUNT A **nationalist** is someone with nationalist views. 民族独立主义者 ❑ ...*demands by nationalists for an independent state.* …民族独立主义者们为一个独立国家而提出的一些要求。 **2** ADJ **Nationalist** means connected with a person's great love for their nation. It is often associated with the belief that their nation is better than any other nation, and in this case is often used showing disapproval. 民族主义的 [ADJ n] ❑ *Political life has been infected by growing nationalist sentiment.* 政治生活已经受到日渐增长的民族主义情绪的影响。 • N-COUNT A **nationalist** is someone with nationalist views. 民族主义者 ❑ *The parliament is composed mainly of extreme nationalists.* 国会主要由极端民族主义者组成。

na·tion·al·is·tic /næʃənᵊlɪstɪk/ ADJ If you describe someone as **nationalistic**, you mean they are very proud of their nation. They also often believe that their nation is better than any other nation, and in this case it is often used showing disapproval. 极端民族主义的 ❑ *Nationalistic fervor is running high.* 极端民族主义的狂热正在升温。

na·tion·al·ity /næʃənælɪti/ (**nationalities**) **1** N-VAR If you have the **nationality** of a particular country, you were born there or have the legal right to be a citizen. 国籍 ❑ *Asked his nationality, he said American.* 问到他的国籍，他说是美国人。 **2** N-COUNT You can refer to people who have the same racial origins as a **nationality**, especially when they do not have their own independent country. (尤指没有自己独立国家的) 民族 ❑ ...*the many nationalities that comprise Ethiopia.* …组成埃塞俄比亚的众多民族。

na·tion·al·ize /næʃənᵊlaɪz/ (**nationalizes, nationalizing, nationalized**)

in BRIT, also use **nationalise**

V-T If a government **nationalizes** a private company or industry, that company or industry becomes owned by the state and controlled by the government. 把…收归国有 [BUSINESS] ❑ *In 1987, Garcia introduced legislation to nationalize Peru's banking and financial systems.* 1987年，加西亚立法，将秘鲁的银行和财政系统收归国有。 • **na·tion·ali·za·tion** /næʃənᵊlɪzeɪʃᵊn/ N-UNCOUNT 国有化 ❑ ...*the campaign for the nationalization of the coal mines.* …煤矿国有化运动。

na·tion·al park (**national parks**) N-COUNT; N-IN-NAMES A **national park** is a large area of land which is protected by the government because of its natural beauty, plants, or animals, and which the public can usually visit. 国家公园 ❑ *Roads into Yosemite National Park are closed due to landslides.* 通进约塞米蒂国家公园的路因塌方而被关闭。

Word Link *wide ≈ extending throughout : nationwide, widespread, worldwide*

nation·wide /neɪʃᵊnwaɪd/ ADJ **Nationwide** activities or situations happen or exist in all parts of a country. 全国性的 ❑ *The rising number of car crimes is a nationwide problem.* 汽车犯罪不断增加是个全国性的问题。 • ADV **Nationwide** is also an adverb. 遍及全国地 ❑ *The figures show unemployment falling nationwide last month.* 数字显示，上个月失业数字正全国性地下降。

Word Link *nat ≈ being born : innate, native, prenatal*

na·tive ♦◇◇ /neɪtɪv/ (**natives**) **1** ADJ Your **native** country or area is the country or area where you were born and brought up. 出生并从小长大的 (国家或地方) [ADJ n] ❑ *It was his first visit to his native country since 1948.* 这是1948年以来他首次访问祖国。 **2** N-COUNT A **native of** a particular country or region is someone who was born in that country or region. 本国人; 本地人 ❑ *Dr. Aubin is a native of St. Louis.* 奥宾医生是圣路易斯人。 • ADJ **Native** is also an adjective. 本国的; 本地的 [ADJ n] ❑ *Joshua Halpern is a native Northern Californian.* 乔舒亚·哈尔彭是土生土长的北加州人。 **3** N-COUNT Some European people use **native** to refer to a person living in a non-Western country who belongs to the race or tribe that the majority of people there belong to. This use could cause offense. 土著 ❑ *They* used force to banish the natives from the more fertile land. 他们用武力将土著人驱逐出更加肥沃的土地。● ADJ **Native** is also an adjective. 土著的 [ADJ n] ❑ *Native people were allowed to retain some sense of their traditional culture and religion.* 土著人被允许保留一些自己的传统文化和宗教。 4 ADJ Your **native** language or tongue is the first language that you learned to speak when you were a child. 第一(语言) [ADJ n] ❑ *She spoke not only her native language, Swedish, but also English and French.* 她不仅讲她的母语瑞典语，还讲英语和法语。 5 ADJ Plants or animals that are **native to** a particular region live or grow there naturally and were not brought there. 当地土生的(动、植物) [ADJ n, v-link ADJ "to" n] ❑ *...a project to create a 50 acre forest of native Caledonian pines.* …一个营造50英亩喀里多尼亚土生松林的项目。● N-COUNT **Native** is also a noun. 土生动植物 ❑ *The coconut palm is a native of Malaysia.* 这棵椰子树是马来西亚的土生植物。

Thesaurus *native* 另参见：
N. citizen, resident 2

Word Partnership *native* 的常用搭配：
N. native **country**, native **land** 1
native **language**, native **tongue** 4

NATO ♦◇◇ /neɪtoʊ/ N-PROPER **NATO** is an international organization which consists of the U.S., Canada, Britain, and other European countries, all of whom have agreed to support one another if they are attacked. **NATO** is an abbreviation for "North Atlantic Treaty Organization." 北大西洋公约组织 ❑ *NATO says it will keep a reduced number of modern nuclear weapons to guarantee peace.* 北约称将保持削减后的现代核武器数量以确保和平。

natu·ral ♦♦◇ /nætʃərəl, nætʃrəl/ (**naturals**) 1 ADJ If you say that it is **natural** for someone to act in a particular way or for something to happen in that way, you mean that it is reasonable in the circumstances. 自然的 ❑ *It is only natural for youngsters to crave the excitement of driving a fast car.* 年轻人渴望开快车的刺激相当自然。❑ *It is only natural that he should resent you.* 他会怨恨你是很自然的。 2 ADJ **Natural** behavior is shared by all people or all animals of a particular type and has not been learned. 天生的(行为) ❑ *...the insect's natural instinct to feed.* …昆虫进食的天生本能。 3 ADJ Someone with a **natural** ability or skill was born with that ability and did not have to learn it. 天赋的(才能等) ❑ *She has a natural ability to understand the motives of others.* 她具备洞察别人动机的天赋。 4 N-COUNT If you say that someone is **a natural**, you mean that they do something very well and very easily. 天才 ❑ *He's a natural with any kind of engine.* 他是发动机方面的天才。 5 ADJ If someone's behavior is **natural**, they appear to be relaxed and are not trying to hide anything. 自然的 ❑ *Bethan's sister was as friendly and natural as the rest of the family.* 伯森的姊妹和其他家庭成员一样亲切自然。● **natu·ral·ly** ADV 自然地 [ADV after v] ❑ *For pictures of people behaving naturally, not posing for the camera, it is essential to shoot unnoticed.* 要拍摄人物表现自然、不对镜头摆姿式的照片，抓拍很关键。● **natu·ral·ness** N-UNCOUNT 自然 ❑ *The critics praised the reality of the scenery and the naturalness of the acting.* 评论家们赞扬了布景的真实及表演的自然。 6 ADJ **Natural** things exist or occur in nature and are not made or caused by people. 天然的 [ADJ n] ❑ *The gigantic natural harbor is a haven for boats.* 这个巨大的天然港是船舶的避风港。● **natu·ral·ly** ADV 天然地 ❑ *Nitrates are chemicals that occur naturally in water and the soil.* 硝酸盐是水和土壤里天然存在的化学物质。 7 PHRASE If someone dies of or **from natural causes**, they die because they are ill or old rather than because of an accident or violence. 自然原因 ❑ *Your brother died of natural causes.* 你哥哥是自然死亡。

Thesaurus *natural* 另参见：
ADJ. normal 1
inborn, innate, instinctive 2 3
genuine, sincere, unaffected 5
wild; (*ant.*) artificial 6

Word Partnership *natural* 的常用搭配：
ADV. **perfectly** natural 1 2
N. natural **reaction**, natural **tendency** 2
natural **beauty**, natural **disaster**, natural **food** 6

natu·ral·ist /nætʃərəlɪst, nætʃrəl-/ (**naturalists**) N-COUNT A **naturalist** is a person who studies plants, animals, insects, and other living things. 博物学家

natu·ral·is·tic /nætʃərəlɪstɪk, nætʃrəl-/ 1 ADJ **Naturalistic** art or writing tries to show people and things in a realistic way. (艺术或文学作品) 自然主义的 ❑ *These drawings are among his most naturalistic.* 这些绘画是他的作品之中非常自然主义的。 2 ADJ **Naturalistic** means resembling something that exists or occurs in nature. 类似自然的

natu·ral·ly ♦◇◇ /nætʃərəli, nætʃrəli/ 1 ADV You use **naturally** to indicate that you think something is very obvious and not at all surprising under the circumstances. 自然而然地 ❑ *When things go wrong, all of us naturally feel disappointed and frustrated.* 出问题时，我们自然而然都会觉得失望和沮丧。❑ *Naturally these comings and goings excited some curiosity.* 这些来来往往自然会引发一些好奇心。 2 ADV If one thing develops **naturally** from another, it develops as a normal consequence or result of it. 自然地 [ADV after v] ❑ *A study of yoga leads naturally to meditation.* 习练瑜珈自然地导致冥想。 3 ADV You can use **naturally** to talk about a characteristic of someone's personality when it is the way that they normally act. 大方地 [ADV adj] ❑ *He has a lively sense of humor and appears naturally confident.* 他有一种生动的幽默感，看起来大方自信。 4 ADV If someone is **naturally** good at something, they learn it easily and quickly and do it very well. 天生地 [ADV adj] ❑ *Some individuals are naturally good communicators.* 一些人天生善于沟通。 5 PHRASE If something **comes naturally to** you, you find it easy to do and quickly become good at it. (对…而言) 轻而易举 ❑ *Humanitarian work comes naturally to them.* 人道主义工作对他们而言轻而易举。 6 → see also **natural**

natu·ral re·sources N-PLURAL **Natural resources** are all the land, forests, energy sources and minerals existing naturally in a place that can be used by people. 天然资源 ❑ *Angola was a country rich in natural resources.* 安哥拉是个天然资源丰富的国家。

natu·ral wast·age N-UNCOUNT **Natural wastage** is the same as **attrition**. 人员缩减 [mainly BRIT, BUSINESS]

na·ture ♦♦◇ /neɪtʃər/ (**natures**) 1 N-UNCOUNT **Nature** is all the animals, plants, and other things in the world that are not made by people, and all the events and processes that are not caused by people. 大自然 ❑ *The most amazing thing about nature is its infinite variety.* 大自然最让人惊叹的地方在于它的无限多样性。❑ *...grasses that grow wild in nature.* …自然界生长的野草

> Do not confuse **nature**, **landscape**, **scenery**, and **countryside**. **Nature** includes the landscape, the weather, animals, and plants. ❑ *These creatures roamed the Earth as the finest and rarest wonders of nature.* With **landscape**, the emphasis is on the physical features of the land, while **scenery** includes everything you can see when you look out over an area of land. ❑ *...the landscape of steep woods and distant mountains. ...unattractive urban scenery.* **Countryside** is land which is away from towns and cities. ❑ *...3,500 acres of mostly flat countryside.*

2 N-SING The **nature** of something is its basic quality or character. 本质 ❑ *Mr. Sharp would not comment on the nature of the issues being investigated.* 夏普先生不愿就被调查问题的本质发表评论。❑ *The rise of a major power is both economic and military in nature.* 一个大国的崛起本质上既是经济上的，也是军事上的。 3 N-SING Someone's **nature** is their character, which they show by the way they behave. 性格 [with poss, also "by" N] ❑ *Jeya feels that her ambitious nature made her unsuitable for an arranged marriage.* 耶雅觉得她的雄心勃勃的个性使她不适合包办婚姻。❑ *She trusted people. That was her nature.* 她信任人，那是她的天性。 4 → see also **human nature** 5 PHRASE If you say that something has a particular characteristic **by** its **nature** or **by** its **very nature**, you mean that things of that type always have that characteristic. 本质上 ❑ *Peacekeeping, by its nature, makes pre-planning difficult.* 维和行动本质上很难预先计划。 6 PHRASE If you say that something is **in the nature of things**, you mean that you would expect it to happen in the circumstances mentioned. 事出必然 ❑ *Of course, in the nature of things, and with a lot of drinking going on, people failed to notice.* 当然了，事出必然，酒酣之间人们没有注意到。 7 PHRASE If you say that one thing is **in the nature of** another, you mean that it is like the other thing. 和…类似的 ❑ *There is movement toward, I think, something in the nature of a pluralistic system.* 我认为，有向类多元化体系发展的趋势。 8 PHRASE If a way of behaving is **second nature to** you, you do it almost without thinking because it is easy for you or obvious to you. 第二天性 ❑ *Planning ahead had always come as second nature to her.* 预先计划一直是她的第二天性。

Word Partnership *nature* 的常用搭配:

V. love nature, preserve nature 1

N. love of nature, wonders of nature 1
nature of life, nature of society, nature of work 2
nature and nurture 3

▲ **naugh·ty** /nɔti/ (**naughtier, naughtiest**) 1 ADJ If you say that a child is **naughty**, you mean that they behave badly or do not do what they are told. 淘气 ❑ *Girls, you're being very naughty.* 姑娘们,你们太调皮了。 2 ADJ You can describe books, pictures, or words as **naughty** when they are slightly vulgar or related to sex. 下流的 ❑ *You know what little boys are like with naughty words.* 你知道小男孩们说下流话是什么样子。

▲ **nau·sea** /nɔziə, -ʒə, -siə, -ʃə/ N-UNCOUNT **Nausea** is the condition of feeling sick and the feeling that you are going to vomit. 恶心 ❑ *I was overcome with a feeling of nausea.* 我感到一阵恶心。

nau·ti·cal /nɔtɪkᵊl/ ADJ **Nautical** means relating to ships and sailing. 航海的 ❑ *...a nautical chart of the region you sail.* …一张你们航行区域的航海图。

Word Link *nav ≈ ship : naval, navigate, navy*

na·val ♦◇◇ /neɪvᵊl/ ADJ **Naval** means belonging to, relating to, or involving a country's navy. 海军的 [ADJ n] ❑ *He was the senior serving naval officer.* 他曾是高级现役海军军官。

na·vel /neɪvᵊl/ (**navels**) N-COUNT Your **navel** is the small hollow near your waist at the front of your body. 肚脐 ❑ *...a girl with a ring in her navel.* …一个肚脐上挂环的姑娘。

navi·gate /nævɪgeɪt/ (**navigates, navigating, navigated**) 1 V-T/V-I When someone **navigates** a ship or an aircraft somewhere, they decide which course to follow and steer it there. 给(船或飞机)导航 ❑ *Captain Cook was responsible for safely navigating his ship without accident for 100 voyages.* 库克船长负责了安全导航他的船,百次航行无事故。 ❑ *The purpose of the visit was to navigate into an ice-filled fiord.* 这次访问的目的是为驶入一个冰雪覆盖的峡湾导航。 ● **navi·ga·tion** ★ /nævɪgeɪʃᵊn/ N-VAR (**navigations**) 导航 ❑ *The expedition was wrecked by bad planning and poor navigation.* 这次探险因计划不周和导航不利而失败。 2 V-T/V-I When a ship or boat **navigates** an area of water, it sails on or across it. 航行 ❑ *...a lock system to allow sea-going craft to navigate the upper reaches of the river.* 一个能使海轮航行至河流上游的船闸系统。 ❑ *Such boats can navigate on the Hudson.* 这样的船能在哈得孙河上航行。 3 V-I When someone in a car **navigates**, they decide what roads the car should be driven along in order to get somewhere. (为汽车)导航 ❑ *When traveling on fast roads at night it is impossible to drive and navigate at the same time.* 夜晚在快速路上行驶时,不可能边开车边找路。 ❑ *...the relief at successfully navigating across the Golden Gate Bridge to arrive here.* …成功指引通过金门大桥抵达这里的如释重负。 4 V-I When fish, animals, or insects **navigate** somewhere, they find the right direction to go and travel there. (鱼、动物或昆虫)找到正确的行进方向 ❑ *In tests, the bees navigate back home after being placed in a field a mile away.* 在试验中,蜜蜂们被放到一英里之外的田地中后,寻找到回家的路。 5 V-T If you **navigate** an obstacle, you move carefully in order to avoid hitting the obstacle or hurting yourself. 绕过 ❑ *He's got to learn how to navigate his way around the residence.* 他应该学会如何绕过这片住处。
→ see **star**

★ **navi·ga·tion** /nævɪgeɪʃᵊn/ 1 N-UNCOUNT You can refer to the movement of ships as **navigation**. 航行 ❑ *Pack ice around Iceland was becoming a threat to navigation.* 冰岛周围的浮冰一度成为船舶航行的威胁。 2 → see also **navigate**
→ see Word Web: **navigation**

navi·ga·tor /nævɪgeɪtər/ (**navigators**) N-COUNT The **navigator** on an aircraft or ship is the person whose job is to work out the direction in which the aircraft or ship should be traveling. 领航员 ❑ *He became a navigator during the war.* 战争期间他成了一名领航员。

navy ♦♦◇ /neɪvi/ (**navies**) 1 N-COUNT A country's **navy** consists of the people it employs to fight at sea, and the ships they use. 海军 ❑ *The operation was organized by the US Navy.* 这次行动是由美国海军组织的。 ❑ *Her own son was also in the navy.* 她自己的儿子也曾在海军里。 2 COLOR Something that is **navy** or **navy-blue** is very dark blue. 深蓝色的 ❑ *When I was a fashion editor, I mostly wore white shirts and black or navy trousers.* 当时尚编辑的时候,我大多数时间穿白衬衫和黑色或深蓝色裤子。

Nazi ♦◇◇ /nɑtsi/ (**Nazis**) 1 N-COUNT **The Nazis** were members of the right-wing political party, led by Adolf Hitler, which held power in Germany from 1933 to 1945. 纳粹 2 ADJ You use **Nazi** to say that something relates to the Nazis. 纳粹的 ❑ *...the rise of the Nazi Party.* …纳粹党的崛起。

NB /ɛn bi/ also **N.B.** You write **NB** or **N.B.** to draw someone's attention to what you are about to say or write. 注意(所说或所写内容) ❑ *NB: The opinions stated in this essay do not necessarily represent those of the Church of God Missionary Society.* 请注意:本文所述观点不一定代表上帝传教会教堂的观点。

near ♦♦♦ /nɪər/ (**nearer, nearest, nears, nearing, neared**) 1 PREP If something is **near** a place, thing, or person, it is a short distance from them. 离…近 ❑ *Don't come near me.* 别靠近我。 ❑ *He drew his chair nearer the fire.* 他把他的椅子向炉火拉近了些。 ● ADV **Near** is also an adverb. 靠近 ❑ *He crouched as near to the door as he could.* 他蜷缩在尽可能靠近门的地方。 ❑ *She took a step nearer to the barrier.* 她向路障走近了一步。 ● ADJ **Near** is also an adjective. 靠近的 [ADJ n, "the" ADJ "of" n] ❑ *He collapsed into the nearest chair.* 他瘫在最近的椅子上。 ❑ *The nearer of the two barges was perhaps a mile away.* 两条驳船中较近的一条约有一英里远。 2 PHRASE If someone or something is **near to** a particular state, they have almost reached it. 接近(某一状态) ❑ *After the war, the firm came near to bankruptcy.* 战后这家公司濒临破产。 ❑ *The repairs to the Hafner machine were near to completion.* 哈芙纳牌机器的维修工作已接近尾声。 ● PREP **Near** means the same as **near to**. 接近 ❑ *He was near tears.* 他几乎要流泪了。 ❑ *For almost a month he lay near death.* 他半死不活地躺了将近一个月。 3 PHRASE If something is similar to something else, you can say that it is **near to** it. 与…相似 ❑ *It combined with the resinous cedar smell of the logs to produce a sickening sensation that was near to nausea.* 它与那些圆木的雪松树脂气味混杂在一起,以产生一种快要呕吐的恶心感觉。 ● PREP **Near** means the same as **near to.** 与…相似 ❑ *Often her feelings were nearer hatred than love.* 她的感情往往更像是恨,而不是爱。 4 ADJ You describe the thing most similar to something as **the nearest** thing **to** it when there is no example of the thing itself. 与(某物)最相似的 ["the" ADJ n "to" n, "the" ADJ "to" n] ❑ *It would appear that the legal profession is the nearest thing to a recession-proof industry.* 看起来司法行业最接近于一种不怕经济衰退的行业。 5 ADV If a time or event draws **near**, it will happen soon. 临近 [WRITTEN] ❑ *The time for my departure from Japan was drawing nearer every day.* 我离开日本的时间一天天临近了。 6 PREP If something happens **near** a particular time, it happens just before or just after that time. 离(某一时间)近 ❑ *Performance is lowest between 3 a.m. and 5 a.m., and reaches a peak near midday.* 工作状态凌晨3点到5点最差,近中午时分达到最高点。 ❑ *"Since I retired to this place," he wrote near the end of his life, "I have never been out of these mountains."* "自从退休到这里,"他在快到生命尽头时写到,"我从没出过这些山。" 7 PREP You use **near** to say that something is a little more or less than an amount or number stated. 接近于(某数量或数字) ❑ *...to increase manufacturing from about 2.5 million cars a year to nearer*

Word Web navigation

Early explorers used the **sun** and **stars** to navigate the seas. The sextant allowed later navigators to use these celestial objects to accurately calculate their **position**. By sighting or measuring their position at noon, sailors could determine their latitude. The **compass** helped sailors determine their position at any time of night or day. It also worked in any weather. Today all sorts of travelers use the global positioning system (GPS) to guide their journeys. A GPS receiver is connected to a system of 24 **satellites** that can establish a location within a few feet.

compass

sextant

GPS

4.75 million. …把轿车年产量从250万辆左右提高到接近475万辆。
8 PREP You can say that someone will **not go near** a person or thing when you are emphasizing that they refuse to see them or go there. 拒绝与(某人或某物)接触 [with brd-neg] [EMPHASIS] ❑ *He will absolutely not go near a hospital.* 他绝不去医院。 9 ADJ **The near** one of two things is the one that is closer. (二者中)离得近些的 [det ADJ n] ❑ *...a mighty beech tree on the near side of the little clearing.* …小片林间空地近侧一棵硕大的山毛榉树。 10 ADJ You use **near** to indicate that something is almost the thing mentioned. 差不多的 [ADJ n] ❑ *She was believed to have died in near poverty.* 人们相信，她死时几乎一贫如洗。 ● ADV **Near** is also an adverb. 差不多地 [ADV adj] ❑ *...his near fatal accident two years ago.* …两年前那场险些让他丧命的事故。 11 ADJ In a contest, your **nearest** rival or challenger is the person or team that is most likely to defeat you. 最接近的(对手或挑战者) [ADJ n] ❑ *He completed the lengthy course some three seconds faster than his nearest rival, Jonathon Ford.* 他比劲敌乔纳松・福特快约三秒钟完成了漫长的赛程。 12 V-T When you **near** a place, you get quite near to it. 接近(地点) [no passive] [LITERARY] ❑ *As he neared the stable, he slowed the horse and patted it on the neck.* 接近马厩时，他让马慢下来并拍拍它的脖子。 13 V-T When someone or something **nears** a particular stage or point, they will soon reach that stage or point. 快到(某个阶段或时间) [no passive] ❑ *His age was hard to guess – he must have been nearing fifty.* 他的年龄很难猜出来——他肯定快50岁了。 ❑ *You are nearing the end of your training and you haven't attempted any assessments yet.* 你们的培训快结束了，而你们还未尝试做过任何评估。 14 V-I You say that an important time or event **nears** when it is going to occur quite soon. (重要时刻或事件等)临近 [LITERARY] ❑ *As half time neared, Hardyman almost scored twice.* 中场休息临近时，哈迪曼几乎两度得分。 15 PHRASE You use **near and far** to indicate that you are referring to a very large area or distance. 四处 ❑ *People would gather from near and far.* 人们会从四面八方聚起来。 16 PHRASE If you say that something will happen **in the near future**, you mean that it will happen quite soon. 在不久的将来 ❑ *The controversy regarding vitamin C is unlikely to be resolved in the near future.* 关于维生素C的争论近期不大可能被解决。 17 PHRASE You use **nowhere near** and **not anywhere near** to emphasize that something is not the case. 远不 [EMPHASIS] ❑ *They are nowhere near good enough.* 他们远不够好。 ❑ *It was nowhere near as painful as David had expected.* 这远远不像大卫预料的那么痛苦。

near·by ♦◇◇ /nɪərbaɪ/ ADV If something is **nearby**, it is only a short distance away. 在附近 ❑ *He might easily have been seen by someone who lived nearby.* 他可能很容易被住在附近的人看到。 ❑ *The helicopter crashed to earth nearby.* 直升机坠毁在附近的地面上。 ● ADJ **Nearby** is also an adjective. 附近的 [ADJ n] ❑ *At a nearby table a man was complaining in a loud voice.* 附近的一张餐桌旁一个男子在高声抱怨着。

near·ly ♦♦◇ /nɪərli/ 1 ADV **Nearly** is used to indicate that something is not quite the case, or not completely the case. 几乎 ❑ *Goldsworth stared at me in silence for nearly twenty seconds.* 戈兹沃斯默默盯着我有差不多20秒钟。 ❑ *Hunter knew nearly all of this already.* 亨特几乎知道这事的全部了。 ❑ *The beach was nearly empty.* 海滩几乎是空荡荡的。 2 ADV **Nearly** is used to indicate that something will soon be the case. 即将 ❑ *It was already nearly eight o'clock.* 已经快8点钟了。 ❑ *I was nearly asleep.* 我快睡着了。 ❑ *I've nearly finished the words for your song.* 我快要完成为你那首歌填词了。

Thesaurus *nearly* 另参见:
ADV. almost, approximately 1

near·sighted /nɪərsaɪtɪd/ also **near-sighted** ADJ Someone who is **nearsighted** cannot see distant things clearly. 近视的 ❑ *As you get older, you may become farsighted or near-sighted.* 随着年龄的增长，你可能变得远视或近视。
→ see **eye**

neat ♦◇◇ /nit/ (**neater, neatest**) 1 ADJ A **neat** place, thing, or person is organized and clean, and has everything in the correct place. 整洁的 ❑ *So they left her in the neat little house, alone with her memories.* 因此他们把她留在那个整洁的小房子里，独自一人回忆往事。 ❑ *Everything was neat and tidy and gleamingly clean.* 所有的东西都井然有序，洁净得闪闪发光。 ● **neat·ly** ADV 整齐地 [ADV with v] ❑ *He folded his paper neatly and sipped his coffee.* 他把报纸叠整齐，抿着他的咖啡。 ● **neat·ness** N-UNCOUNT 整齐 ❑ *The grounds were a perfect balance between neatness and natural wildness.* 这些庭园是一个整洁有序与天然随意的理想平衡。 2 ADJ Someone who is **neat** keeps their home or possessions organized and clean, with everything in the correct place. 整洁的(人) ❑ *"That's not like Alf," he said, "leaving papers muddled like that. He's always so neat."* "那可不像阿尔夫，"他说，"让文件乱成那样。他总是很整洁的。" ● **neat·ly** ADV 整洁地 [ADV with v] ❑ *I followed her into that room which her mother had maintained so neatly.* 我跟着她进了那个她母亲保持得特别整洁的房间。 ● **neat·ness** N-UNCOUNT 整洁 ❑ *...a paragon of neatness, efficiency and reliability.* …一个整洁、高效和诚信的典范。 3 ADJ A **neat** object, part of the body, or shape is quite small and has a smooth outline. 小巧秀气 ❑ *...neat handwriting.* …娟秀的字体。 4 ADJ A **neat** movement or action is done accurately and skillfully, with no unnecessary movements. 干净利索的(行动) ❑ *"Did you have any trouble?" Byron asked, driving into a small parking lot and changing the subject in the same neat maneuver.* "有什么麻烦吗？"拜伦问道，同时把车开进了一个小停车场并用同样干净利落的手法转换了话题。 ● **neat·ly** ADV 干净利索地 [ADV with v] ❑ *He watched her peel and dissect a pear neatly, no mess, no sticky fingers.* 他看着她利索地削了个梨并切成几块，整整齐齐，手指干干净净。 5 ADJ A **neat** way of organizing, achieving, explaining, or expressing something is clever and convenient. 高明而简便易行的(办法) ❑ *It had been such a neat, clever plan.* 这曾是一个如此简便易行的高明计划。 ❑ *Neat solutions are not easily found to these issues.* 对这些问题，简便巧妙的解决办法不容易被找到。 ● **neat·ly** ADV 高明而简便易行地 [ADV with v] ❑ *Real people do not fit neatly into these categories.* 真实的人们不会简便地融入这些类别。 6 ADJ If you say that something is **neat**, you mean that it is very good. 很棒的 [INFORMAL, APPROVAL] ❑ *He thought Mick was a really neat guy.* 他认为迈克是个很棒很棒的家伙。 7 ADJ When someone drinks strong alcohol **neat**, they do not add a weaker liquid such as water to it. 未经稀释的 [mainly BRIT]
in AM, usually use **straight**

Thesaurus *neat* 另参见:
ADJ. orderly, tidy, uncluttered 1 2

nec·es·sari·ly ♦◇◇ /nɛsɪsɛərɪli/ 1 ADV If you say that something is **not necessarily** the case, you mean that it may not be the case or is not always the case. 必要地 [VAGUENESS] ❑ *Anger is not necessarily the most useful or acceptable reaction to such events.* 生气未必是对待此类事件最有用或最适合的反应。 ● CONVENTION If you reply **"Not necessarily,"** you mean that what has just been said or suggested may not be true. 不一定 ❑ *"He was lying, of course."—"Not necessarily."* "他当然是在撒谎。"——"不一定。" 2 ADV If you say that something **necessarily** happens or is the case, you mean that it has to happen or be the case and cannot be any different. 必然地 ❑ *Brookman & Langdon were said to manufacture the most desirable pens and these necessarily command astonishingly high prices.* 据说布鲁克曼兰登公司制造的钢笔最令人满意，而这必然地导致高得惊人的价格。

nec·es·sary ♦♦◇ /nɛsɪsɛri/ 1 ADJ Something that is **necessary** is needed in order for something else to happen. 必要的 ❑ *I kept the engine running because it might be necessary to leave fast.* 我让发动机一直开着，因为可能需要快速离开。 ❑ *Make the necessary arrangements.* 做必要的一些安排。 2 ADJ A **necessary** consequence or connection must happen or exist, because of the nature of the things or events involved. 必然的 [ADJ n] ❑ *Scientific work is differentiated from art by its necessary connection with the idea of progress.* 科学工作不同于艺术在于它与进步的概念有必然联系。

Thesaurus *necessary* 另参见:
ADJ. essential, mandatory, obligatory, required; (*ant.*) unnecessary 1
unavoidable 2

★ **ne·ces·si·tate** /nɪsɛsɪteɪt/ (**necessitates, necessitating, necessitated**) V-T If something **necessitates** an event, action, or situation, it makes it necessary. 使成为必需 [FORMAL] ❑ *A prolonged drought had necessitated the introduction of water rationing.* 一场持续的干旱使定量供水的引进成为必需。

ne·ces·sity /nɪsɛsɪti/ (**necessities**) 1 N-UNCOUNT The **necessity** of something is the fact that it must happen or exist. 必要性 ❑ *There is agreement on the necessity of reforms.* 关于改革的必要性有一致意见。 ❑ *As soon as the necessity for action is over the troops must be withdrawn.* 一旦军事行动的必要性不复存在，部队必须撤离。 ● PHRASE If you say that something is **of necessity** the case, you mean that it is the case because nothing else is possible or practical under the circumstances. 势必 [FORMAL] ❑ *...large families where children, of necessity, shared a bed.* …孩子们必定共睡一张床的大型家庭。 2 N-COUNT A **necessity** is something that you must have in order to live properly or do something. 必需品 ❑ *Water is a basic necessity*

n

of life. 水是一种基本生活必需品。 3 N-COUNT A situation or action that is a **necessity** is necessary and cannot be avoided. 不可避免 ❑ *The president pleaded that strong rule from the center was a necessity.* 总统争辩说来自中央的强有力的统治是一种必然。

Word Partnership *necessity* 的常用搭配：

ADJ. **absolute** necessity 1 – 3
economic necessity 2 3
political necessity 3

neck ♦◇◇ /nɛk/ (**necks**) 1 N-COUNT Your **neck** is the part of your body which joins your head to the rest of your body. 颈 ❑ *She threw her arms around his neck and hugged him warmly.* 她伸出双臂搂住他的脖子，热烈地拥抱他。 2 N-COUNT The **neck** of an article of clothing such as a shirt, dress, or sweater is the part which surrounds your neck. 领口 ❑ *...the low, ruffled neck of her blouse.* …她褶边低胸的衬衫领口。 3 N-COUNT The **neck** of something such as a bottle or a guitar is the long narrow part at one end of it. (瓶子、吉他等的) 颈状部位 ❑ *Catherine gripped the broken neck of the bottle.* 凯瑟琳紧握着破裂的瓶颈。 4 PHRASE If you say that someone **is breathing down** your **neck**, you mean that they are watching you very closely and checking everything you do. 密切监视 ❑ *Most farmers have loan officers breathing down their necks.* 大多数农场主受到信贷员的密切监视。 5 PHRASE In a competition, especially an election, if two or more competitors are **neck and neck**, they are level with each other and have an equal chance of winning. 势均力敌 ❑ *The latest polls indicate that the two main parties are neck and neck.* 最新的民意测验显示两个主要政党势均力敌。 6 PHRASE If you **stick** your **neck out**, you bravely say or do something that might be criticized or might turn out to be wrong. 敢说敢干 [INFORMAL] ❑ *During my political life I've earned myself a reputation as someone who'll stick his neck out, a bit of a rebel.* 我在自己的政治生涯中得了一个敢说敢干、有点叛逆的名声。
→ see **body**

Word Partnership *neck* 的常用搭配：

N. **back/nape of the** neck, **head and** neck, neck **injury** 1
ADJ. **broken** neck, **long** neck, **stiff** neck, **thick** neck 1 3

N

▲ **neck·lace** /nɛklɪs/ (**necklaces**) N-COUNT A **necklace** is a piece of jewelry such as a chain or a string of beads which someone, usually a woman, wears around their neck. 项链 ❑ *...a diamond necklace and matching earrings.* …一条钻石项链和与之相配的耳环。
→ see **jewelry**

nec·tar·ine /nɛktərin/ (**nectarines**) N-COUNT A **nectarine** is a round, juicy fruit which is similar to a peach but has a smooth skin. 油桃

need ♦♦♦ /nid/ (**needs, needing, needed**)

> **Need** sometimes behaves like an ordinary verb, for example "She needs to know" and "She doesn't need to know" and sometimes like a modal, for example "No-one need know," "She needn't know," or, in more formal English, "She need not know."

1 V-T If you **need** something, or **need to** do something, you cannot successfully achieve what you want or live properly without it. 需要 [no cont] ❑ *He desperately needed money.* 他急需钱。 ❑ *I need to make a phone call.* 我需要打个电话。 ❑ *I need you to do something for me.* 我需要你为我做些事。 ❑ *I need you here, Wally.* 沃利，我这儿需要你。 ● N-COUNT **Need** is also a noun. 需要 ❑ *Charles has never felt the need to compete with anyone.* 查尔斯从未感觉到与人竞争的需要。 ❑ *...the child who never had his need for attention and importance satisfied.* …那个受关注和重视的需要从未得到过满足的孩子。 2 V-T If an object or place **needs** something done to it, that action should be done to improve the object or place. If a task **needs** doing, it should be done to improve a particular situation. 需要 [no cont] ❑ *The building needs quite a few repairs.* 这栋楼不少处需要修缮。 ❑ *...a garden that needs tidying.* …一个需要整理的花园。 3 N-SING If there is a **need for** something, that thing would improve a situation or something cannot happen without it. 需要；必要 ❑ *Mr. Forrest believes there is a need for other similar schools throughout the country.* 福里斯特先生相信全国上下有对其他类似学校的需要。 ❑ *"I think we should see a specialist."—"I don't think there's any need for that."* "我想我们应该看个专家。"—— "我认为没那必要。" 4 V-T If you say that someone does not **need to** do something, you are telling them not to do it, or advising or suggesting that they should not do it. 必要 (用于劝告或建议) [with neg] ❑ *Well, for Heaven's sake, you don't need to apologize.* 好啦，看在老天爷的份上，你不必道歉了。 ● MODAL **Need** is also a modal. 必要 (用于劝告或建议) [no cont, with neg] ❑ *"I'll put the key in the window."—"You needn't bother," he said gruffly.* "我将把钥匙放进窗户里去。"—— "不必麻烦，" 他粗声粗气地说。 ❑ *Look, you needn't shout.* 喂，你不必喊。 5 V-T If you tell someone that they don't **need to** do something, or that something **need** not happen, you are telling them that that thing is not necessary, in order to make them feel better. 一定 (用于劝告或建议) [no cont, with neg] ❑ *He replied, with a reassuring smile, "Oh, you don't need to worry about them."* 他面带鼓励的微笑答道："哦，你不必为他们担心。" ● MODAL **Need** is also a modal. 一定 (用于劝告或建议) [with brd-neg] ❑ *You needn't worry.* 你不必担心。 ❑ *We have learned that a market crash need not lead to economic disaster.* 我们已经认识到一次市场崩溃未必导致经济灾难。 6 V-T You use don't **need to** when you are giving someone permission not to do something. 否定词后接**need to**，表示允许不做某事 [no cont] ❑ *You don't need to wait for me.* 你不用等我。 ● MODAL **Need** is also a modal. **Need**也作情态动词 [with neg] ❑ *You needn't come again, if you don't want to.* 如果你不愿意，就不用再来了。 7 MODAL If someone **needn't have** done something, they didn't need to do it. 本不需要 [with neg] ❑ *She could have made the sandwich herself; her mother needn't have bothered to do anything.* 她本可以自己做三明治；她母亲本来不用费心做任何事。 ❑ *I was a little nervous when I announced my engagement to Grace, but I needn't have worried.* 当宣布和格雷丝订婚时我有点儿紧张，其实不用担心。 8 V-T If someone **didn't need to** do something, it wasn't necessary or useful for them to do it, although they did it. 本不需要 [no cont, with neg] ❑ *You didn't need to give me any more money you know, but thank you.* 你知道你本不需要再给我钱了，不过谢谢了。 9 MODAL You use **need** in expressions such as **I need hardly say** and **I needn't add** to emphasize that the person you are talking to already knows what you are going to say. 用于**I need hardly say**和**I needn't add**短语中，强调对方已然知晓将要说的话 [EMPHASIS] ❑ *I needn't add that if you fail to do as I ask, you will suffer the consequences.* 我不必再说了，如果你不能按我说的做，你要承担一切后果。 ● V-T **Need** is also a verb. **Need**亦为动词 [no cont] ❑ *I hardly need to say that I have never lost contact with him.* 几乎不用说，我从未和他失去联系。 10 PHRASE People **in need** do not have enough of essential things such as money, food, or good health. 需要帮助的 ❑ *The portable clinic will take doctors to children in need.* 移动诊所将为需要帮助的孩子们带去医生。 11 PHRASE If you are **in need of** something, you need it or ought to have it. 需要 ❑ *I was all right but in need of rest.* 当时我挺好的，就是需要休息。 ❑ *He was badly in need of a shave.* 当时他特别需要刮个胡子。 12 PHRASE If you say that you will do something, especially an extreme action, **if need be**, you mean that you will do it if it is necessary. 需要的话 ❑ *They will act as my legal advisers if need be.* 需要的话，他们会作我的法律顾问。

Thesaurus *need* 另参见：

V. demand, must have, require 1

nee·dle /nidᵊl/ (**needles**) 1 N-COUNT A **needle** is a small, very thin piece of polished metal which is used for sewing. It has a sharp point at one end and a hole in the other for a thread to go through. 针 ❑ *He took a needle and thread and sewed it up.* 他取来一根针和线并把它缝起来。 2 N-COUNT A **needle** is a thin hollow metal rod with a sharp point, which is part of a medical instrument called a syringe. It is used to put a drug into someone's body, or to take blood out. 注射针 ❑ *...the transmission of the AIDS virus through dirty needles.* …爱滋病病毒通过不洁注射针头的传播。 3 N-COUNT Knitting **needles** are thin sticks that are used for knitting. They are usually made of plastic or metal and have a point at one end. (编织) 针 ❑ *...a pair of knitting needles.* …一副编织针。 4 N-COUNT A **needle** is a thin metal rod with a point which is put into a patient's body during acupuncture. (针灸用的) 银针 ❑ *I gave Kevin a course of acupuncture using six needles strategically placed on the scalp.* 我给凯文进行了一个疗程的针灸治疗，把6支银针分别扎在头皮的关键穴位上。 5 N-COUNT On an instrument which measures something such as speed or weight, the **needle** is the long strip of metal or plastic on the dial that moves backward and forward, showing the measurement. (仪表上的) 指针 ❑ *She kept looking at the dial on the boiler. The needle had reached 250 degrees.* 她一直看着锅炉上的刻度盘，指针已经到达250度。 6 N-COUNT The **needles** of a fir or pine tree are its thin, hard, pointed leaves. (杉树、松树等的) 针叶 ❑ *The carpet of pine needles was soft underfoot.* 松针铺成的地毯在脚下软软的。

need·less /ni̲dlɪs/ ADJ Something that is **needless** is completely unnecessary. 不必要的 ❑ *But his death was so needless.* 然而他的死却太没有必要了。 ❑ *He never knowingly exposed patients to any needless risks.* 他从来没有故意将病人置于不必要的危险之中。● **need·less·ly** ADV 不必要地 ❑ *Half a million women die needlessly each year during childbirth.* 每年有50万妇女在分娩时不必要地死去。

needn't /ni̲dᵊnt/ **Needn't** is the usual spoken form of "need not." **Needn't**是**need not**的常用口语形式

needy /ni̲di/ (**needier, neediest**) ADJ **Needy** people do not have enough food, medicine, or clothing, or adequate houses. 贫困的 ❑ *...a multinational force aimed at ensuring that food and medicine get to needy Somalis.* …旨在确保食品和药品送到索马里贫民手中的一支多国部队。● N-PLURAL **The needy** are people who are needy. 穷人 ❑ *There will be efforts to get larger amounts of food to the needy.* 将努力把更多的食品送给穷人。

ne·gate /nɪge̲ɪt/ (**negates, negating, negated**) **1** V-T If one thing **negates** another, it causes that other thing to lose the effect or value that it had. 使无效 [FORMAL] ❑ *These weaknesses negated his otherwise progressive attitude towards the staff.* 这些缺点抹杀了他本来对工作人员的开明态度。 **2** V-T If someone **negates** something, they say that it does not exist. 否定 [FORMAL] ❑ *He warned that to negate the results of elections would only make things worse.* 他警告说否定选举结果只能使事态更加恶化。

nega·tive ♦◇◇ /nɛ̲gətɪv/ (**negatives**) **1** ADJ A fact, situation, or experience that is **negative** is unpleasant, depressing, or harmful. 负面的；消极的 ❑ *The news from overseas is overwhelmingly negative.* 来自海外的消息完全不容乐观。● **nega·tive·ly** ADV 负面地 [ADV with v] ❑ *This will negatively affect the result over the first half of the year.* 这将会给前半年的结果带来负面影响。 **2** ADJ If someone is **negative** or has a **negative** attitude, they consider only the bad aspects of a situation, rather than the good ones. 消极的；持否定态度的 ❑ *When asked for your views about your current job, on no account must you be negative about it.* 当被问及你对自己目前工作的看法时，你无论如何都不能持否定态度。● **nega·tive·ly** ADV 消极地 ❑ *A few weeks later he said that maybe he viewed all his relationships rather negatively.* 几个星期后，他说或许他把自己和他人的各种关系看得太消极了。● **nega·tiv·ity** /nɛ̲gətɪ̲vɪti/ N-UNCOUNT 消极性；否定性 ❑ *I loathe negativity. I can't stand people who moan.* 我厌恶消极。我无法忍受抱怨的人。 **3** ADJ A **negative** reply or decision indicates the answer "no." 否定的 ❑ *Dr. Velayati gave a vague but negative response.* 韦拉亚提医生做出了一个含糊但否定的答复。 ❑ *Upon a negative decision, the applicant loses the protection offered by Belgian law.* 一旦得到否定裁决，申请人就失去了比利时法律所给予的保护。● **nega·tive·ly** ADV 否定地 [ADV after v] ❑ *Sixty percent of people answered negatively.* 60%的人做出了否定回答。 **4** N-COUNT A **negative** is a word, expression, or gesture that means "no" or "not." 否定词；表示否定的动作或姿态 ❑ *In the past we have heard only negatives when it came to following a healthy diet.* 过去一谈到遵循健康饮食我们就只听到否定的意见。 **5** ADJ In grammar, a **negative** clause contains a word such as "not," "never," or "no one." (语法中) 含否定词的 **6** ADJ If a medical test or scientific test is **negative,** it shows no evidence of the medical condition or substance that you are looking for. (医检、试验等) 呈阴性的 ❑ *So far 57 have taken the test and all have been negative.* 到目前为止已有57人进行了这项检验，所有人都呈阴性反应。 **7** HIV **negative** → see **HIV** **8** N-COUNT In photography, a **negative** is an image that shows dark areas as light and light areas as dark. Negatives are made from camera film, and are used to print photographs. 底片 ❑ *...negatives of Diana's wedding dress.* …戴安娜婚纱照的底片。 **9** ADJ A **negative** charge or current has the same electrical charge as an electron. (电荷或电流) 负极的 ❑ *Stimulate the injury or site of greatest pain with a small negative current.* 用一股微弱的负电流刺激伤处或最疼的地方。● **nega·tive·ly** ADV 带负电荷地 [ADV -ed] ❑ *As these electrons are negatively charged they will attempt to repel each other.* 由于这些电子都带负电荷，它们会相互排斥。 **10** ADJ A **negative** number, quantity, or measurement is less than zero. 负数的 ❑ *Difficult texts record a positive score and simple ones score negative numbers.* 难度大的文本标为正值，简单的文本标为负值。 **11** PHRASE If an answer is **in the negative**, it is "no" or means "no." (回答等) 否定的 ❑ *The Council answered those questions in the negative.* 理事会对那些问题做出了否定回答。

→ see **lightning, magnet**

> **Word Partnership** *negative* 的常用搭配：
>
> N. negative **effect**, negative **experience**, negative **image**, negative **publicity** **1**
> negative **attitude**, negative **thoughts** **1** **2**
> negative **comment**, negative **reaction**, negative **response** **3**

ne·glect /nɪglɛ̲kt/ (**neglects, neglecting, neglected**) **1** V-T If you **neglect** someone or something, you fail to take care of them properly. 疏于照管 ❑ *The woman denied that she had neglected her child.* 那位妇女否认疏于照管她的孩子。 ❑ *Feed plants and they grow, neglect them and they suffer.* 给植物施肥，它们就生长；疏于照管，它们就遭殃。● N-UNCOUNT **Neglect** is also a noun. 疏于照管 ❑ *The town's old quayside is collapsing after years of neglect.* 这座小镇的旧码头区在多年疏于保养后快要坍塌了。 **2** V-T If you **neglect** someone or something, you fail to give them the amount of attention that they deserve. 忽视 ❑ *He'd given too much to his career, worked long hours, neglected her.* 他在事业上投入太多了，长时间地工作，冷落了她。● **ne·glect·ed** ADJ 被忽视的 ❑ *The fact that she is not coming today makes her grandmother feel lonely and neglected.* 她今天不来了，这让她的祖母感到孤单，受到冷落。 ❑ *...a neglected aspect of the city's forgotten history.* …这座城市被遗忘的历史中一个被忽视的方面。 **3** V-T If you **neglect to** do something that you ought to do or **neglect** your duty, you fail to do it. 疏忽 ❑ *We often neglect to make proper use of our bodies.* 我们经常疏忽了合理使用我们的身体。

★ **ne·glect·ful** /nɪglɛ̲ktfəl/ **1** ADJ If you describe someone as **neglectful**, you think they fail to do everything they should do to take care of someone or something properly. 失职的 ❑ *...neglectful parents.* …失职的家长们。 **2** ADJ If someone is **neglectful of** something, they do not give it the attention or consideration that it should be given. 忽视的 [oft v-link ADJ "of" n] ❑ *Have I been neglectful of my friend, taking him for granted?* 我忽视了我的朋友、没有把他当回事吗？

▲ **neg·li·gence** /nɛ̲glɪdʒᵊns/ N-UNCOUNT If someone is guilty of **negligence**, they have failed to do something which they ought to do. 渎职 [FORMAL] ❑ *The soldiers were ordered to appear before a disciplinary council on charges of negligence.* 士兵们被控玩忽职守，被要求接受纪律委员会审查。

neg·li·gent /nɛ̲glɪdʒᵊnt/ ADJ If someone in a position of responsibility is **negligent**, they do not do something which they ought to do. 渎职的 ❑ *The jury determined that the airline was negligent in training and supervising the crew.* 陪审团认定该航空公司在培训和管理其机组成员方面渎职。● **neg·li·gent·ly** ADV 渎职地 [ADV with v] ❑ *A manufacturer negligently made and marketed a car with defective brakes.* 一家制造商渎职，制造并销售了一款有制动缺陷的汽车。

★ **neg·li·gible** /nɛ̲glɪdʒɪbᵊl/ ADJ An amount or effect that is **negligible** is so small that it is not worth considering or worrying about. 微不足道的 ❑ *The pay that the soldiers received was negligible.* 士兵们得到的津贴微乎其微。

★ **ne·go·tiable** /nɪgo̲ʊʃiəbᵊl, -ʃəbᵊl/ ADJ Something that is **negotiable** can be changed or agreed upon when people discuss it. 可协商的 ❑ *He warned that his economic program for the country was not negotiable.* 他告诫说他为国家制订的经济计划是不容商榷的。

ne·go·ti·ate ♦♦◇ /nɪgo̲ʊʃieɪt/ (**negotiates, negotiating, negotiated**) **1** V-RECIP If people **negotiate with** each other or **negotiate** an agreement, they talk about a problem or a situation such as a business arrangement in order to solve the problem or complete the arrangement. 谈判 ❑ *It is not clear whether the president is willing to negotiate with the Democrats.* 尚不清楚总统是否愿意与民主党人进行谈判。 ❑ *When you have two adversaries negotiating, you need to be on neutral territory.* 在你让敌对双方谈判时，你应该采取中间立场。 ❑ *The local government and the army negotiated a truce.* 该地方政府和军方谈判达成了休战协定。 ❑ *Western governments have this week urged him to negotiate and avoid force.* 西方国家政府本周已敦促他进行谈判并且避免使用武力。 **2** V-T If you **negotiate** an area of land, a place, or an obstacle, you successfully travel across it or around it. 成功越过 ❑ *Frank Mariano negotiates the desert terrain in his battered pickup.* 弗兰克·马里亚诺驾驶他那辆破旧的敞篷小货车成功地穿越了沙漠地区。 ❑ *I negotiated the corner on my motorcycle and pulled to a stop.* 我骑着摩托车顺利地绕过弯道，停了下来。

n

Word Partnership *negotiate* 的常用搭配：
V. **agree to** negotiate, **fail to** negotiate, **refuse to** negotiate, **try to** negotiate 1
N. negotiate **an agreement**, negotiate **a contract**, negotiate **a deal**, negotiate **a settlement**, negotiate **the terms of** *something* 1

ne·go·ti·at·ing ta·ble N-SING If you say that people are at **the negotiating table**, you mean that they are having discussions in order to settle a dispute or reach an agreement. 谈判桌 ❑ *"We want to settle all matters at the negotiating table," he said.* "我们要在谈判桌上解决所有问题，"他说。

ne·go·tia·tion ♦♦◊ /nɪgoʊʃieɪʃᵊn/ (**negotiations**) N-VAR **Negotiations** are formal discussions between people who have different aims or intentions, especially in business or politics, during which they try to reach an agreement. (尤指商业或政治上的）谈判 ❑ *Warren said, "We have had meaningful negotiations and I believe we are very close to a deal."* 沃伦说："我们已经进行了富有意义的谈判，我相信我们很快就能达成协议。"

Word Partnership *negotiation* 的常用搭配：
N. **basis for** negotiation, **process of** negotiation
PREP. negotiation **between**, **under** negotiation
ADJ. **successful** negotiation

ne·go·tia·tor /nɪgoʊʃieɪtər/ (**negotiators**) N-COUNT **Negotiators** are people who take part in political or financial negotiations. 谈判人 ❑ *On Thursday night the rebels' chief negotiator at the peace talks announced that dialogue had gone as far as it could go.* 周四晚上，参加和谈的叛乱分子的首席谈判代表宣布已经尽可能深入地进行了对话。

Ne·gro /nigroʊ/ (**Negroes**) N-COUNT A **Negro** is someone with dark skin who comes from Africa or whose ancestors came from Africa. 黑鬼 [OFFENSIVE, OLD-FASHIONED]

neigh·bor ♦◊◊ /neɪbər/ (**neighbors**)
in BRIT, use **neighbour**
1 N-COUNT Your **neighbor** is someone who lives near you. 邻居 ❑ *My neighbor spies on me through a crack in the fence.* 我的邻居通过篱笆墙的缝隙窥探我。 2 N-COUNT You can refer to the person who is standing or sitting next to you as your **neighbor**. 邻近的人 ❑ *The woman prodded her neighbor and whispered urgently in his ear.* 那个女人戳了一下她旁边的人，急切地对他耳语起来。 3 N-COUNT You can refer to something which stands next to something else of the same kind as its **neighbor**. 邻近的同类物 ❑ *...its big oil-rich neighbor.* …它那幅员辽阔、石油资源丰富的邻国。

N

neigh·bor·hood ♦♦◊ /neɪbərhʊd/ (**neighborhoods**)
in BRIT, use **neighbourhood**
1 N-COUNT A **neighborhood** is one of the parts of a town where people live. 居住区 ❑ *There is no neighborhood which is really safe.* 没有一个真正安全的居住区。 2 N-COUNT The **neighborhood** of a place or person is the area or the people around them. 附近 ❑ *...a suburban Boston neighborhood close to where I live.* …离我住处较近的波士顿城郊。 3 PHRASE **In the neighborhood of** a number means approximately that number. 大约为 ❑ *The album's now sold something in the neighborhood of 2 million copies.* 该唱片目前已卖出了大约两百万张。 4 PHRASE A place that is **in the neighborhood of** another place is near it. 在…附近 ❑ *We went to visit two charming young ladies who lived in the neighborhood of our camp.* 我们去拜访了住在我们营地附近的两位年轻迷人的女士。

Word Partnership *neighborhood* 的常用搭配：
ADJ. **poor** neighborhood, **residential** neighborhood, **run-down** neighborhood 1

neigh·bor·ing /neɪbərɪŋ/
in BRIT, use **neighbouring**
ADJ **Neighboring** places or things are near other things of the same kind. 邻近的 [ADJ n] ❑ *He is on his way back to Beijing after a tour of neighboring Asian capitals.* 结束对几个亚洲邻邦首都的访问之后，他正在回北京的路上。

neigh·bour /neɪbəʳ/ [BRIT] → see **neighbor**

neigh·bour·hood /neɪbəʳhʊd/ [BRIT] → see **neighborhood**

neigh·bour·ing /neɪbərɪŋ/ [BRIT] → see **neighboring**

nei·ther ♦♦◊ /niðər, naɪ-/ 1 CONJ You use **neither** in front of the first of two or more words or expressions when you are linking two or more things which are not true or do not happen. The other thing is introduced by "nor." 既不…（也不…）❑ *Professor Hisamatsu spoke neither English nor German.* 久松教授既不讲英语，也不讲德语。 2 DET You use **neither** to refer to each of two things or people, when you are making a negative statement that includes both of them. 两者都不 ❑ *At first, neither man could speak.* 开始两个人都不能说。 ● QUANT-NEG **Neither** is also a quantifier. 两者都不 ❑ *Neither of us felt like going out.* 我们两个都不愿意出去。 ● PRON-NEG **Neither** is also a pronoun. 两者都不 ❑ *They both smiled; neither seemed likely to be aware of my absence for long.* 他们两个人都笑了，看来都没意识到我离开了很长时间。 3 CONJ If you say that one person or thing does not do something and **neither** does another, what you say is true of all the people or things that you are mentioning. 也不（用于否定句后，表示前句适用于所有提到的人或物）❑ *I never learned to swim and neither did they.* 我从没学过游泳，他们也没学过。 4 CONJ You use **neither** after a negative statement to emphasize that you are introducing another negative statement. 也不（用于否定句后，强调要引出另一否定句）[FORMAL] ❑ *I can't ever recall Dad hugging me. Neither did I sit on his knee.* 我记不得爸爸拥抱过我，也不曾在他膝上坐过。

Do not confuse **neither** and **none**. You use **neither** in negative statements to refer to two people or things. ❑ *Neither had close friends in college.* You use **neither of** in the same way, followed by a pronoun or a noun group. ❑ *Neither of them spoke... Neither of these extremes is desirable.* Note that you can also use **neither** before a singular count noun. ❑ *Neither side can win.* You use **none** in negative statements to refer to three or more people or things. ❑ *None could afford the food.* You use **none of** in the same way, followed by a pronoun or a noun group. ❑ *None of them had learned anything... None of his companions answered.*

Word Partnership *neither* 的常用搭配：
V. neither **confirm nor deny** 1
N. neither **candidate**, neither **man**, neither **party**, neither **side**, neither **team** 2

▲ **neon** /niɒn/ 1 ADJ **Neon** lights or signs are made from glass tubes filled with neon gas which produce a bright electric light. 霓虹的 [ADJ n] ❑ *In the city squares the neon lights flashed in turn.* 在城市的各个广场上，霓虹灯交替闪烁。 2 N-UNCOUNT **Neon** is a gas which occurs in very small amounts in the atmosphere. 氖 ❑ *Inert gases like neon and argon have eight electrons in their outer shell.* 像氖和氩这样的惰性气体，在它们的外电子层有8个电子。

neph·ew /nɛfyu/ (**nephews**) N-COUNT Someone's **nephew** is the son of their sister or brother. 侄子；外甥 ❑ *I am planning a 25th birthday party for my nephew.* 我正在为侄子筹划他25岁的生日聚会。

nerve ♦◊◊ /nɜrv/ (**nerves**) 1 N-COUNT **Nerves** are long thin fibers that transmit messages between your brain and other parts of your body. 神经 ❑ *...spinal nerves.* …脊椎神经。 2 N-PLURAL If you refer to someone's **nerves**, you mean their ability to cope with problems such as stress, worry, and danger. （对压力、烦恼和危险等的）精神承受力 ❑ *Jill's nerves are stretched to breaking point.* 吉尔的神经紧张得快到极点了。 3 N-PLURAL You can refer to someone's feelings of anxiety or tension as **nerves**. 神经紧张 ❑ *I just played badly. It wasn't nerves.* 我就是演得不好，不是紧张。 4 N-UNCOUNT **Nerve** is the courage that you need in order to do something difficult or dangerous. 勇气 ❑ *The brandy made him choke, but it restored his nerve.* 白兰地呛到他了，但恢复了他的勇气。 5 PHRASE If someone or something **gets on** your **nerves**, they annoy or irritate you. 惹…心烦 [INFORMAL] ❑ *Lately he hasn't done a thing and it's getting on my nerves.* 最近他什么都没做，这让我大为恼火。 6 PHRASE If you say that someone **has a nerve** or **has the nerve** to do something, you are criticizing them for doing something which you feel they had no right to do. 放肆 [INFORMAL, DISAPPROVAL] ❑ *He told his critics they had a nerve complaining about him.* 他对他的批评者说，他们对他抱怨真是放肆。 7 PHRASE If you **lose** your **nerve**, you suddenly panic and become too afraid to do something that you were about to do. 惊慌失措 ❑ *The bomber had lost his nerve and fled.* 投炸弹的人惊惶失措地逃走了。

→ see **ear, eye, nervous system, smell**

Word Partnership *nerve* 的常用搭配：

N. nerve **cells**, nerve **damage**, nerve **fibers**, nerve **impulses** 1

V. **hit a** nerve, **strike a** nerve, **touch a** nerve 1
get up the nerve, **got** *a/the* nerve, **have** *a/the* nerve 4 6

nerv·ous ♦◇◇ /nɜrvəs/ 1 ADJ If someone is **nervous**, they are frightened or worried about something that is happening or might happen, and show this in their behavior. 神经紧张的 ❑ *The party has become deeply nervous about its prospects of winning the next election.* 该党对其赢得下一届大选的前景极其紧张。 ● **nerv·ous·ly** ADV 神经紧张地 [ADV with v] ❑ *Brunhilde stood up nervously as the men came into the room.* 那些人进屋时布伦希尔德紧张地站了起来。 ● **nerv·ous·ness** N-UNCOUNT 神经紧张 ❑ *I smiled warmly so he wouldn't see my nervousness.* 我热情地微笑着，所以他看不出我的紧张。 2 ADJ A **nervous** person is very tense and easily upset. 神经质的 ❑ *She was apparently a very nervous woman, and that affected her career.* 她显然是个很神经质的女人，这影响到了她的事业。 3 ADJ A **nervous** illness or condition is one that affects your emotions and your mental state. 神经性的 [ADJ n] ❑ *The number of nervous disorders was rising in the region.* 该地区神经紊乱的病例数正在上升。

Word Partnership *nervous* 的常用搭配：

PREP. nervous **about** *something* 1

V. **become** nervous, **feel** nervous, **get** nervous, **look** nervous, **make** *someone* nervous 1

ADV. **increasingly** nervous, **a little** nervous, **too** nervous, **very** nervous 1 2

nerv·ous break·down (**nervous breakdowns**) N-COUNT If someone has a **nervous breakdown**, they become extremely depressed and cannot cope with their normal life. 神经崩溃 ❑ *His wife would not be able to cope and might suffer a nervous breakdown.* 他妻子会应付不了，也许会神经崩溃。

nerv·ous sys·tem (**nervous systems**) N-COUNT Your **nervous system** consists of all the nerves in your body together with your brain and spinal cord. 神经系统 ❑ *So it is possible that the symptoms will not finally go until your nervous system is in a better state.* 可能这些症状不会彻底消失，除非你的神经系统有所改善。
→ see Word Web: **nervous system**

nest /nɛst/ (**nests, nesting, nested**) 1 N-COUNT A bird's **nest** is the home that it makes to lay its eggs in. (鸟类的) 巢 ❑ *I can see an eagle's nest on the rocks.* 我能看到岩石上的一个鹰巢。 2 V-I When a bird **nests** somewhere, it builds a nest and settles there to lay its eggs. 筑巢 ❑ *Some species may nest in close proximity to each other.* 一些鸟类可能彼此紧挨着筑巢。 3 N-COUNT A **nest** is a home that a group of insects or other creatures make in order to live in and give birth to their young in. (昆虫或其他动物的) 巢穴 ❑ *Some solitary bees make their nests in burrows in the soil.* 一些独居的蜜蜂将它们的巢筑在土壤中的洞穴里。
→ see **bird**

nes·tle /nɛs^{ə}l/ (**nestles, nestling, nestled**) 1 V-T/V-I If you **nestle** or **are nestled** somewhere, you move into a comfortable position, usually by pressing against someone or against something soft. 舒服地靠在；依偎 ❑ *John took one child into the crook of each arm and let them nestle against him.* 约翰一手搂过一个孩子，让他们依偎着他。 2 V-I If something such as a building **nestles** somewhere, it is in that place and seems safe or sheltered. 坐落 ❑ *Nearby, nestling in the hills, was the children's home.* 附近的山岗上坐落着那些孩子们的家。

net
❶ NOUN AND VERB USES
❷ ADJECTIVE AND ADVERB USES

❶ **net** ♦◇◇ /nɛt/ (**nets, netting, netted**) 1 N-UNCOUNT **Net** is a kind of cloth that you can see through. It is made of fine threads woven together so that there are small equal spaces between them. 网 2 N-COUNT A **net** is a piece of netting which is used as a protective covering for something, for example to protect vegetables from birds. (保护性的) 网罩 ❑ *I threw aside my mosquito net, jumped out of bed and drew up the blind.* 我撩开蚊帐，跳下床，拉开百叶窗。 3 N-COUNT A **net** is a piece of netting which is used for catching fish, insects, or animals. (用于捕猎的) 罗网 ❑ *Several fishermen sat on wooden barrels, tending their nets.* 几个渔民坐在木桶上修补他们的鱼网。 4 V-T If you **net** a fish or other animal, you catch it in a net. 捕捞 ❑ *I'm quite happy to net a fish and then let it go.* 我特别喜欢捞到一条鱼后再把它放了。 5 V-T If you **net** something, you manage to get it, especially by using skill. (尤指运用技巧) 获取 ❑ *Two fourth-quarter drives netted a grand total of 21 yards.* 第4节的两次击球总计获得了21码。 6 V-T If you **net** a particular amount of money, you gain it as profit after all expenses have been paid. 净赚 ❑ *He netted profit of $1.85 billion from three large sales of stock.* 他通过3大笔股票销售，净赚了18.5亿美元。 7 N-SING **The Net** is the same as the **Internet**. 互联网 8 → see also **safety net**
→ see **fish, tennis**

❷ **net** ♦◇◇ /nɛt/

in BRIT, also use **nett**

1 ADJ A **net** amount is one which remains when everything that should be subtracted from it has been subtracted. 净数的 [ADJ n, v-link ADJ "of" n] ❑ *...a rise in sales and net profit.* …销售和纯利润的增长。 ❑ *What you actually receive is net of deductions.* 你实际上得到的是净扣除额。 ● ADV **Net** is also an adverb. 净数地 ❑ *Balances of $5,000 and above will earn 11 percent gross, 8.25 percent net.* 账户余额为$5000或以上时，会获得11%的毛利息，8.25%的净利息。 ❑ *They pay him around $2 million net.* 他们净付给他约两百万美元。 2 ADJ The **net** weight of something is its weight without its container or the material that has been used to wrap it. (重量) 净的 [ADJ n] ❑ *...350 mg net weight.* …净重350毫克。 3 ADJ A **net** result is a final result after all the details have been considered or included. 最终的 (结果) [ADJ n] ❑ *There has been a net gain in jobs in our country.* 我们国家的工作机会最终还是增多了。

Word Partnership *net* 的常用搭配：

N. **fishing** net ❶ 3

V. **access the** Net, **surf the** Net, Net **users** ❶ 7

N. net **earnings**, net **income/loss**, net **proceeds**, net **profit**, net **revenue** ❷ 1
net **gain**, net **increase**, net **result** ❷ 1 3

nett /nɛt/ [BRIT] → see **net** ❷

net·tle /nɛt^{ə}l/ (**nettles, nettling, nettled**) 1 N-COUNT **Nettles** are wild plants which have leaves covered with fine hairs that sting you when you touch them. 荨麻 ❑ *The nettles stung their legs.* 荨麻刺痛了他们的腿。 2 V-T If you **are nettled** by something, you are annoyed or offended by it. 使恼怒 ❑ *He was nettled by her manner.* 他被她的举止激怒了。

net·work ♦♦◇ /nɛtwɜrk/ (**networks, networking, networked**) 1 N-COUNT A radio or television **network** is a company or group of companies that broadcast radio or television programs throughout an area. (广播或电视) 网 ❑ *Los Angeles-based Univision is a Spanish-language broadcast television network.* 位于洛杉矶的"联合视野"是一家

Word Web **nervous system**

The body's **nervous system** is a two-way road which transmits electrochemical messages to and from various parts of the body. **Sensory neurons** carry information from both inside and outside the body to the **central nervous system** (CNS) which consists of the **brain** and the **spinal cord**. Motor neurons carry impulses from the CNS to **organs** and to **muscles** such as the muscles in the hand, telling them how to move. Sensory and motor neurons are bound together, creating **nerves** that run throughout the body.

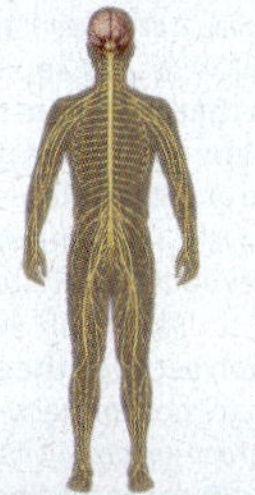

西班牙语的广播电视网。 **2** N-COUNT A **network of** people or institutions is a large number of them that have a connection with each other and work together as a system. (由许多人或机构组成的) 组织网络 ❑ *Distribution of the food is going ahead using a network of local church people and other volunteers.* 食品的分发正在通过当地教会人士和其他志愿者组织网络进行。 **3** N-COUNT A particular **network** is a system of things which are connected and which operate together. For example, a **computer network** consists of a number of computers that are part of the same system. 网络系统 ❑ *...a computer network with 154 terminals.* …一个有154台终端的计算机网络。 **4** N-COUNT A **network of** lines, roads, veins, or other long thin things is a large number of them which cross each other or meet at many points. (线路、道路、血管等的) 网状系统 ❑ *...Strasbourg, with its rambling network of medieval streets.* …斯特拉斯堡，有着修建于中世纪的不规则街网。 **5** V-I If you **network**, you try to meet new people who might be useful to you in your job. 建立关系网 [BUSINESS] ❑ *In business, it is important to network with as many people as possible on a face to face basis.* 在生意场上，与尽可能多的人建立面对面的关系网是重要的。

→ see **Internet**

Word Partnership *network* 的常用搭配：

N. **broadcast** network, **cable** network, **radio** network, **television/TV** network **1**
network **administrator**, **computer** network, network **coverage**, network **support** **3**

ADJ. **extensive** network, **nationwide** network, **vast** network, **worldwide** network **1** – **4**
wireless network **3**

net·work·ing /nɛtwɜrkɪŋ/ **1** N-UNCOUNT **Networking** is the process of trying to meet new people who might be useful to you in your job, often through social activities. 建立关系网 [BUSINESS] ❑ *If executives fail to exploit the opportunities of networking they risk being left behind.* 假如管理人员未能利用机会建立关系网，他们就有落后的危险。 **2** N-UNCOUNT You can refer to the things associated with a computer system or the process of establishing such a system as **networking**. (计算机) 网络 ❑ *Managers have learned to grapple with networking, artificial intelligence, computer-aided engineering and manufacturing.* 管理人员已经学会如何去应付网络、人工智能、计算机辅助工程和制造等问题。

N

Word Link *otic ≈ affecting, causing : erotic, neurotic, patriotic*

neu·rot·ic /nʊərɒtɪk/ (**neurotics**) ADJ If you say that someone is **neurotic**, you mean that they are always frightened or worried about things that you consider unimportant. 神经过敏的 [DISAPPROVAL] ❑ *He was almost neurotic about being followed.* 他对被人跟踪几乎神经过敏。 ● N-COUNT A **neurotic** is someone who is neurotic. 神经官能症患者 ❑ *These patients are not neurotics.* 这些病人不是神经官能症患者。

neu·tral /nutrəl/ (**neutrals**) **1** ADJ If a person or country adopts a **neutral** position or remains **neutral**, they do not support anyone in a disagreement, war, or contest. 中立的 ❑ *Let's meet on neutral territory.* 我们在中立地区会面吧。 ● N-COUNT A **neutral** is someone who is neutral. 中立者 ❑ *It was a good game to watch for the neutrals.* 对于中立观众来说，这是一场精彩的比赛。 ● ▲ **neu·tral·ity** /nutrælɪti/ N-UNCOUNT 中立 ❑ *...a reputation for political neutrality and impartiality.* …政治上中立和公正的名声。 **2** ADJ If someone speaks in a **neutral** voice or if the expression on their face is **neutral**, they do not show what they are thinking or feeling. 不动声色的 ❑ *Isabel put her magazine down and said in a neutral voice, "You're very late, darling."* 伊莎贝尔放下她的杂志，以不动声色的口吻说，"亲爱的，你太晚了"。 ● **neu·tral·ity** N-UNCOUNT 不动声色 ❑ *I noticed, behind the neutrality of his gaze, a deep weariness.* 我觉察到，在他那不动声色的凝视背后有一种深深的厌倦。 **3** ADJ If you say that something is **neutral**, you mean that it does not have any effect on other things because it lacks any significant qualities of its own, or it is an equal balance of two or more different qualities, amounts, or ideas. 不引起变化的；中和的 ❑ *Three in every five interviewed felt that the budget was neutral and they would be no better off.* 每5个受访者中有3个认为该预算不会带来什么变化，他们的境况也不会改善。 **4** N-UNCOUNT **Neutral** is the position between the gears of a vehicle such as a car, in which the gears are not connected to the engine. 空档 ❑ *Graham put the van in neutral and jumped out into the road.* 格雷厄姆把货车挂到空挡，然后跳到路上。 **5** ADJ In an electrical device or system, the **neutral** wire is one of the three wires needed to complete the circuit so that the current can flow. The other two wires are called the ground wire and the live or positive wire. (电线) 不带电的 (三股中的一股，其它两股分别叫做地线和火线) ❑ *The ground wire in the house is connected to the neutral wire.* 这所房子里的地线接在了零线上。 **6** COLOR **Neutral** is used to describe things that have a pale color such as cream or gray, or that have no color at all. 浅灰色的；无色的 ❑ *At the horizon the land mass becomes a continuous pale neutral gray, almost blending with the sky.* 在地平线上，大片陆地变成一片连绵而暗淡的浅灰色，几乎与天空交融在一起。 **7** ADJ In chemistry, **neutral** is used to describe things that are neither acid nor alkaline. (化学上) 中性的 ❑ *Pure water is neutral with a pH of 7.* 纯净水是中性的，PH值为7。

→ see **war**

★ **neu·tral·ise** /nju͟ːtrəlaɪz/ [BRIT] → see **neutralize**

★ **neu·tral·ize** /nu͟trəlaɪz/ (**neutralizes, neutralizing, neutralized**)

in BRIT, also use **neutralise**

1 V-T To **neutralize** something means to prevent it from having any effect or from working properly. 使无效；使不能正常运作 ❑ *The U.S. is trying to neutralize the resolution in the UN Security Council.* 美国试图在联合国安理会阻止该决议的通过。 **2** V-T When a chemical substance **neutralizes** an acid, it makes it less acid. 中和 ❑ *Antacids are alkaline and they relieve pain by neutralizing acid in the contents of the stomach.* 抗酸剂是碱性的，它们通过中和胃容物中的酸来缓解疼痛。

▲ **neu·tron** /nutrɒn/ (**neutrons**) N-COUNT A **neutron** is an atomic particle that has no electrical charge. 中子 ❑ *Each atomic cluster is made up of neutrons and protons.* 每个原子团簇是由中子和质子组成的。

nev·er ♦♦♦ /nɛvər/ **1** ADV **Never** means at no time in the past or at no time in the future. 从不；永不 ❑ *I have never lost the weight I put on in my teens.* 我在十几岁时增加的体重从没减下去过。 ❑ *Never had he been so free of worry.* 他从没这样无忧无虑过。 ❑ *That was a mistake. We'll never do it again.* 那是个错误，我们永远不会再犯了。 **2** ADV **Never** means "not in any circumstances at all." 决不 ❑ *I would never do anything to hurt him.* 我决不会做任何事去伤害他。 ❑ *Divorce is never easy for children.* 离婚对于孩子们来说决不轻松。 **3** PHRASE **Never ever** is an emphatic way of saying "never." **Never ever**是**never**的强调说法 [EMPHASIS] ❑ *I never, ever sit around thinking, "What shall I do next?"* 我从来就不会闲坐着想："我下一步该做什么？" **4** ADV **Never** is used to refer to the past and means "not." 没有；不 ❑ *He never achieved anything.* 他一事无成。 ❑ *I never knew him.* 我不认识他。 **5** **never mind** → see **mind**

never-ending ADJ If you describe something bad or unpleasant as **never-ending**, you are emphasizing that it seems to last a very long time. 永无休止的 [EMPHASIS] ❑ *...a never-ending series of scandals rocking the presidency.* …一连串动摇总统职位的永无休止的丑闻。

never·the·less ♦◊◊ /nɛvərðəlɛs/ ADV You use **nevertheless** when saying something that contrasts with what has just been said. 然而 [ADV with cl] [FORMAL] ❑ *Although the market has been flat, residential property costs remain high. Nevertheless, the fall-off in demand has had an impact on resale values.* 尽管市场一直疲软，房价持续偏高。然而需求的减少还是对二手房价格产生了影响。

new ♦♦♦ /nu/ (**newer, newest**) **1** ADJ Something that is **new** has been recently created, built, or invented or is in the process of being created, built, or invented. 新的 ❑ *They've just opened a new hotel in the area.* 他们刚在该地区新开了一家旅馆。 ❑ *These ideas are nothing new.* 这些想法并不新鲜。 **2** ADJ Something that is **new** has not been used or owned by anyone. 崭新的 ❑ *That afternoon she went out and bought a new dress.* 那天下午她出去买了一条新裙子。 ❑ *There are many boats, new and used, for sale.* 有许多新船和旧船出售。 **3** ADJ You use **new** to describe something which has replaced another thing, for example because you no longer have the old one, or it no longer exists, or it is no longer useful. 更新的 ❑ *Under the new rules, some factories will cut emissions by as much as 90 percent.* 根据新规定，一些工厂将要削减多达90%的排放量。 ❑ *I had to find somewhere new to live.* 我不得不找个新住处。 ❑ *Rachel has a new boyfriend.* 雷切尔交了一个新的男朋友。 **4** ADJ **New** is used to describe something that has only recently been discovered or noticed. 新发现的 ❑ *The new planet is about ten times the size of the earth.* 这个新发现的行星大约是地球大小的10倍。 **5** ADJ A **new** day or year is the beginning of the next day or year. 新开始的 (一天、一年等) [ADJ n] ❑ *The start of a new year is a good time to reflect on the many achievements of the past.* 新年伊始正是回顾过去许多成绩的好时候。 **6** ADJ **New** is used to describe someone

or something that has recently acquired a particular status or position. 新具有某一身份的 [ADJ n] ❏ *...the usual exhaustion of a new mother.* …初为人母常有的疲惫不堪。 **7** ADJ If you are **new to** a situation or place, or if the situation or place is **new to** you, you have not previously seen it or had any experience with it. 新接触的 [v-link ADJ] ❏ *She wasn't new to the company.* 她对于公司来说并非是新人。 ❏ *His name was new to me then and it stayed in my mind.* 那时他的名字对我来说是陌生的，后来我记住了它。 **8** ADJ **New** potatoes, carrots, or peas are produced early in the season for such vegetables and are usually small with a sweet flavor. 时鲜的（蔬菜）[ADJ n] ❏ *Serve with a salad and new potatoes.* 配着色拉和时鲜土豆一起吃。 **9** → see also **brand-new** **10** **as good as new**
→ see **good**

Thesaurus *new* 另参见：
ADJ. contemporary, current, latest, modern, novel; (*ant.*) existing, old, past **1**

new blood N-UNCOUNT If people talk about bringing **new blood** into an organization or onto a sports team, they are referring to new people who are likely to improve the organization or team. （组织、运动队等的）新鲜血液 ❏ *We'll get some new blood in there.* 我们将在那儿获得一些新鲜血液。

new·born /nubɔrn/ (**newborns**) ADJ A **newborn** baby or animal is one that has just been born. （婴儿或动物）新生的 ❏ *The electronic sensor has been adapted to fit on a newborn baby.* 电子传感器已被改装以适应新生儿。 ● N-PLURAL **The newborn** are babies or animals who are newborn. 新生儿；新生幼崽 ❏ *Mild jaundice in the newborn is common and often clears without treatment.* 新生儿有轻微的黄疸较为常见，通常会不治自愈。

new·comer /nukʌmər/ (**newcomers**) N-COUNT A **newcomer** is a person who has recently arrived in a place, joined an organization, or started a new activity. 新来的人 ❏ *He must be a newcomer to town and he obviously didn't understand our local customs.* 他肯定是新到小城，显然不了解我们当地习俗。

new·found /nufaʊnd/ ADJ A **newfound** quality or ability is one that you have got recently. 新得到的 [ADJ n] ❏ *His friends have a newfound sense of patriotism.* 他的朋友们有一种新萌生的爱国主义意识。

new·ly ♦◇◇ /nuli/ ADV **Newly** is used before a past participle or an adjective to indicate that a particular action is very recent, or that a particular state of affairs has very recently begun to exist. 新近地 [ADV -ed/adj] ❏ *She was young at the time, and newly married.* 那时她还年轻，刚结婚。

new me·dia N-PLURAL **New media** are new technologies such as the Internet, and digital television and radio. 新媒体 ❏ *...a company which specialises in new media.* …一家专门经营新媒体业务的公司。 ❏ *The new-media industry attracts young and creative people.* 新媒体产业吸引了年轻、有创造力的人们。

news ♦♦♦ /nuz/ **1** N-UNCOUNT **News** is information about a recently changed situation or a recent event. 消息 ❏ *We waited and waited for news of him.* 我们等啊等啊，等他的消息。 ❏ *They still haven't had any news about when they'll be able to go home.* 他们仍然没有得到任何关于他们何时才能回家的消息。 **2** N-UNCOUNT **News** is information that is published in newspapers and broadcast on radio and television about recent events in the country or world or in a particular area of activity. 新闻 [also "the" N] ❏ *Foreign News is on page 16.* 国外新闻在第16版。 ❏ *Those are some of the top stories in the news.* 那是新闻中的一些顶级报道。 **3** N-SING **The news** is a television or radio broadcast which consists of information about recent events in the country or the world. （电视、电台等的）新闻广播 ❏ *I heard all about the bombs on the news.* 我从新闻广播里听到了关于炸弹的所有消息。 **4** N-UNCOUNT If you say that someone or something is **news**, you mean that they are considered to be interesting and important at the moment, and that people want to hear about them on the radio and television and in newspapers. 新闻人物；新闻事件 [INFORMAL] ❏ *A murder was big news.* 谋杀案是大新闻。

> Note that, although **news** looks like a plural, it is often in fact an uncount noun. ❏ *Good news is always worth waiting for.* You cannot say "a news," but you can say a **piece of news** when you are referring to a particular fact or message. ❏ *One of my Dutch colleagues told me a very exciting piece of news.* When you are talking about television and radio news, or newspapers, you can refer to an individual story or report as a **news item**.

5 PHRASE If you say that something is **bad news**, you mean that it will cause you trouble or problems. If you say that something is **good news**, you mean that it will be useful or helpful to you. 坏事/好事 ❏ *The drop in travel is bad news for the airline industry.* 旅游业滑坡对航空业来说是件坏事。 **6** PHRASE If you say that something **is news to** you, you mean that you did not previously know what you have just been told, especially when you are surprised or annoyed about it. 对…来说是新闻 ❏ *I'd certainly tell you if I knew anything, but I don't. What you're saying is news to me.* 我要是知道点儿什么，我肯定告诉你，可我不知道。你现在说的对我还是新闻呢。

Word Partnership *news* 的常用搭配：
ADJ. **big** news, **grim** news, **sad** news **1**
latest news **1** **2**
V. **spread the** news, **tell *someone* the** news **1**
hear the news **1** – **3**
listen to the news, **watch the** news **3**
N. news **headlines**, news **media**, news **report**, news **update** **2**

news agen·cy ♦◇◇ (**news agencies**) N-COUNT A **news agency** is an organization that gathers news stories from a particular country or from all over the world and supplies them to journalists. 通讯社 ❏ *A correspondent for Reuters news agency says he saw a number of demonstrators being beaten.* 路透通讯社的一名记者说他看到一些示威者遭到殴打。

▲ **news·caster** ♦♦♦ /nuzkæstər/ (**newscasters**) N-COUNT A **newscaster** is a person who reads the news on the radio or on television. 新闻广播员 ❏ *...TV newscaster Barbara Walters.* …电视新闻广播员芭芭拉·沃尔特斯。

news con·fer·ence (**news conferences**) N-COUNT A **news conference** is a meeting held by a famous or important person in which they answer journalists' questions. 记者招待会 ❏ *He is due to hold a news conference in about an hour.* 他应该在大约一小时之后召开一次记者招待会。

news·group /nuzgrup/ (**newsgroups**) N-COUNT A **newsgroup** is an Internet site where people can put information and opinions about a particular subject so they can be read by everyone who looks at the site. （互联网的）新闻组 ❏ *Surfwatch allows parents to prohibit access to specific web sites, newsgroups, and bulletin boards.* 过滤器软件可以让父母禁止对特定的网站、新闻组和电子布告栏的访问。

news·letter /nuzlɛtər/ (**newsletters**) N-COUNT A **newsletter** is one or more printed sheets of paper containing information about an organization that is sent regularly to its members. （组织等定期印发给其成员的）内部通讯 ❏ *The organization now has around 18,000 members who receive a quarterly newsletter.* 该组织目前约有18000名会员收到内部通讯季刊。

news·paper ♦♦◇ /nuzpeɪpər, nus-/ (**newspapers**) **1** N-COUNT A **newspaper** is a publication consisting of a number of large sheets of folded paper, on which news, advertisements, and other information is printed. 报纸 ❏ *He was carrying a newspaper.* 他正拿着一份报纸。 ❏ *They read their daughter's allegations in the newspaper.* 他们从报纸上看到女儿的声明。 **2** N-COUNT A **newspaper** is an organization that produces a newspaper. 报社 ❏ *It is the nation's fastest growing national daily newspaper.* 这是该国发展最快的全国性日报社。 **3** N-UNCOUNT **Newspaper** consists of pieces of old newspapers, especially when they are being used for another purpose such as wrapping things up. （尤指作其他用途的）旧报纸 ❏ *He found two pots, each wrapped in newspaper.* 他找到了两只罐子，分别用旧报纸包着。
→ see Word Web: **newspaper**
→ see **advertising**

news·print /nuzprɪnt/ **1** N-UNCOUNT **Newsprint** is the cheap, fairly rough paper on which newspapers are printed. 新闻纸 ❏ *...a newsprint warehouse.* …一个新闻纸货仓。 **2** N-UNCOUNT **Newsprint** is the text that is printed in newspapers. 报纸上的文字 ❏ *...the acres of newsprint devoted to Madonna in the past seven days.* …过去7天报纸上有关麦当娜的大量的文字报道。 **3** N-UNCOUNT **Newsprint** is the ink which is used to print newspapers and magazines. 印刷油墨 ❏ *They get their hands covered in newsprint.* 他们的手上沾满了油墨。

news·read·er /nuzridər/ (**newsreaders**) N-COUNT A **newsreader** is a person who reads the news on the radio or on television. 新闻播音员 [BRIT]

in AM, use **newscaster**

Word Web newspaper

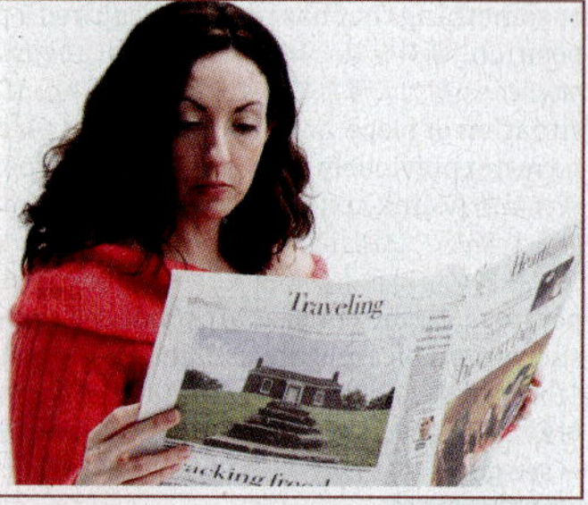

Newspapers played an important role in freeing colonial America from British rule. In 1733, John Peter Zenger* began **publishing** the *New York Weekly Journal*. Some **articles** and **editorials** in the paper were critical of the British governor. The governor accused Zenger of libel and put him in prison. At his trial, Zenger's lawyer showed that the newspaper had told the truth. The jury sided with the **journalist**. This trial helped establish freedom of the **press** in America. The U.S. Constitution, signed nearly 60 years later, contains the First Amendment. This is a clear guarantee of the freedom of the press.

John Peter Zenger (1697-1746): an American journalist and printer.

▲ **news·reel** /nuzril/ (**newsreels**) N-COUNT A **newsreel** is a short film of national or international news events. In the past newsreels were made for showing in movie theaters. 新闻影片 [oft N n]

news re·lease (**news releases**) N-COUNT A **news release** is a written statement about a matter of public interest which is given to the press by an organization concerned with the matter. 新闻稿 [mainly AM] ❑ *In a news release, the company said it had experienced severe financial problems.* 在一篇新闻稿中，该公司称他们遭遇了严重的财务问题。

in BRIT, usually use use **press release**

new wave (**new waves**) N-COUNT In the arts or in politics, a **new wave** is a group or movement that deliberately introduces new or unconventional ideas instead of using traditional ones. 新浪潮 ❑ *...the new wave of satirical comedy.* …讽刺喜剧的新浪潮。

New Year 1 N-UNCOUNT **New Year** or **the New Year** is the time when people celebrate the start of a year. 新年 [also "the" N] ❑ *Happy New Year, everyone.* 大家新年好！ ❑ *The restaurant was closed over the New Year.* 元旦期间该饭店停业。

New Year's Eve, the last day of the old year, is known as **Hogmanay** in Scotland, where the festivities are particularly important. Families and friends gather together for the chimes at midnight, and then go "first-footing" – visiting friends and neighbors, and taking along something to drink (often whisky) and a piece of coal which is supposed to bring good luck for the coming year.

N

2 N-SING **The New Year** is the first few weeks of a year. 年初 ❑ *Isabel was expecting their baby in the New Year.* 伊莎贝尔年初要生孩子。

next ♦♦♦ /nɛkst/ 1 ORD The **next** period of time, event, person, or thing is the one that comes immediately after the present one or after the previous one. 下一个的 ❑ *I got up early the next morning.* 第二天早晨我起得很早。 ❑ *...the next available flight.* …下一趟可以乘坐的航班。 ❑ *Who will be the next mayor?* 谁将是下一任市长呢？ 2 DET You use **next** in expressions such as **next Friday**, **next day** and **next year** to refer, for example, to the first Friday, day, or year that comes after the present or previous one. 下一（年、月、星期等） ❑ *Let's plan a big night next week.* 我们下周组织一次盛大的晚会吧。 ❑ *He retires next January.* 他明年1月份退休。 ● ADJ **Next** is also an adjective. 下一（年、月、星期等）的 [n ADJ] ❑ *I'll be 26 years old next Friday.* 我下周五就26岁了。 ● PRON **Next** is also a pronoun. 下一个 ❑ *He predicted that the region's economy would grow by about six percent both this year and next.* 他预测该地区的经济在今年和明年都会以约6%的速度增长。 3 ADJ **The next** place or person is the one that is nearest to you or that is the first one that you come to. 紧邻的 [det ADJ] ❑ *Grace sighed so heavily that Trish could hear it in the next room.* 格雷丝沉重地叹气，特蕾什在隔壁房间都听到了。 ❑ *The man in the next chair was asleep.* 邻座的男子睡着了。 4 ADV The thing that happens **next** is the thing that happens immediately after something else. 紧接着 ❑ *Next, close your eyes then screw them up tight.* 接着，合上双眼，再闭紧。 ❑ *I don't know what to do next.* 我不知道接着该做什么了。 5 ADV When you **next** do something, you do it for the first time since you last did it. 再次 [ADV before v] ❑ *I next saw him at his house in Vermont.* 我在他佛蒙特州的家里再次见到了他。 6 ADV You use **next** to say that something has more of a particular quality than all other things except one. For example, the thing that is **next** best is the one that is the best except for one other thing. 仅次于 [ADV adj-superl] ❑ *The one thing he didn't have was a son. I think he's felt that a grandson is the next best thing.* 有一样东西他没有，就是儿子。我觉得他有个外孙感觉也不错。 7 PHRASE You use **after next** in expressions such as **the week after next** to refer to a period of time after the next one. For example, when it is May, the month after next is July. 下下（星期、月等） ❑ *...the party's annual conference, to be held the week after next.* …在下下周举行的该党的年会。 8 PHRASE If you say that you do something or experience something as much **as the next** person, you mean that you are no different from anyone else in the respect mentioned. 跟别人一样 [EMPHASIS] ❑ *I enjoy pleasure as much as the next person.* 我享受的乐趣和别人一样多。 9 PHRASE If one thing is **next to** another thing, it is at the other side of it. 靠近 ❑ *She sat down next to him on the sofa.* 她在沙发上靠着他坐下来。 ❑ *...at the southern end of the Gaza Strip next to the Egyptian border.* …在邻近埃及边境的加沙地带的南端。 10 PHRASE You use **next to** in order to give the most important aspect of something when comparing it with another aspect. 仅次于 ❑ *Her children were the number two priority in her life next to her career.* 她的孩子们在她的生活里占第2位，仅次于她的事业。 11 PHRASE You use **next to** before a negative, or a word that suggests something negative, to mean almost, but not completely. 几乎（用于否定性词语之前） ❑ *Johnson still knew next to nothing about tobacco.* 约翰逊仍然对烟草几乎一无所知。

Word Partnership *next* 的常用搭配：

N. next **election**, next **generation**, next **level**, next **meeting**, next **move**, next **question**, next **step**, next **stop**, next **time**, next **train** 1
next **day/hour/month/week/year** 1 2
V. **come** next, **go** next, **happen** next 4

next door

The adjective is usually spelled **next-door**.

1 ADV If a room or building is **next door**, it is the next one to the right or left. 在隔壁 ❑ *I went next door to the bathroom.* 我进了隔壁的洗手间。 ❑ *...the old lady who lived next door.* …住在隔壁的老妇人。 ● ADJ **Next door** is also an adjective. 隔壁的 [ADJ n] ❑ *...a thud like a cellar door slamming shut in a next-door house.* …砰的一声，好像隔壁房子一扇地窖门被重重地关上了。 2 PHRASE If a room or building is **next door to** another one, it is the next one to the left or right. 在…的隔壁 ❑ *The kitchen is right next door to the dining room.* 厨房就在餐厅的隔壁。 3 ADV The people **next door** are the people who live in the house or apartment to the right or left of yours. 隔壁（住家） [n ADV] ❑ *The neighbors thought the family next door had moved.* 邻居们认为隔壁这家已经搬走了。 ● ADJ **Next door** is also an adjective. 隔壁的 [ADJ n] ❑ *Even your next-door neighbor didn't see through your disguise.* 甚至你隔壁的邻居都没有看透你的伪装。 4 PHRASE If you refer to someone as **the boy next door** or **the girl next door**, you mean that they are pleasant, respectable, and likeable. （友善、可敬、可爱的）邻家男孩/女孩 ❑ *He was dependable, straightforward, the boy next door.* 他是个可靠、坦率的邻家男孩儿。

next of kin N-UNCOUNT-COLL **Next of kin** is sometimes used to refer to the person who is your closest relative, especially in official or legal documents. 近亲（尤用于官方或法律文件） [FORMAL] ❑ *We have notified the next of kin.* 我们已经通知了直系亲属。

nib·ble /nɪbᵊl/ (**nibbles**, **nibbling**, **nibbled**) 1 V-T/V-I If you **nibble** food, you eat it by biting very small pieces of it, for example because you are not very hungry. 小口地吃 ❑ *Linda lay face down on a living room couch, nibbling popcorn.* 琳达趴在客厅的一张沙发上，小口吃着爆米花。 ❑ *She nibbled at a piece of dry toast.* 她小口啃着一片干面包。 ● N-COUNT **Nibble** is also a noun. 一小口 ❑ *We each took a nibble.* 我们每人吃了一小口。 2 V-T/V-I If you **nibble** something, you bite it very gently. 轻咬 ❑ *John found he was kissing and nibbling her ear.* 约翰发觉他正轻轻吻咬她的耳朵。 ❑ *Daniel nibbled on his pen.* 丹尼尔轻

轻咬着他的钢笔。 **3** V-T/V-I When an animal **nibbles** something, it takes small bites of it quickly and repeatedly. (动物) 啃啄 ❑ *A herd of goats was nibbling the turf around the base of the tower.* 一群山羊正在啃着塔基周围的草皮。 ❑ *The birds nibble at the brickwork.* 鸟儿们啄着砖墙。 ● PHRASAL VERB **Nibble away** means the same as **nibble**. 啃啄 ❑ *The rabbits nibbled away on the herbaceous plants.* 野兔把那些草本植物慢慢啃光了。 **4** V-I If one thing **nibbles at** another, it gradually affects, harms, or destroys it. 逐渐影响; 逐渐破坏 ❑ *It was all going according to plan, yet small doubts kept nibbling at the edges of his mind.* 一切都在按计划进行，只是一些小小的疑虑一直在折磨着他。 ● PHRASAL VERB **Nibble away** means the same as **nibble**. 逐步的破坏影响 ❑ *Several manufacturers are also nibbling away at Ford's traditional customer base.* 几家制造商也正在蚕食福特公司传统的客户基础。

nice ♦♦◇ /naɪs/ (**nicer, nicest**) **1** ADJ If you say that something is **nice**, you mean that you find it attractive, pleasant, or enjoyable. 好看的; 令人愉快的 ❑ *I think silk ties can be quite nice.* 我觉得真丝领带会非常好看。 ❑ *It's nice to be here together again.* 又在这儿相聚太好了。 ● **nice·ly** ADV 好看地; 令人愉快地 ❑ *He's just written a book, nicely illustrated and not too technical.* 他刚写完一本书，插图精美，专业性也不是太强。 **2** ADJ If you say that it is **nice of** someone to say or do something, you are saying that they are being kind and thoughtful. This is often used as a way of thanking someone. 体贴人的 (常表谢意) ❑ *It's awfully nice of you to come all this way to see me.* 你大老远赶来看我，真是太体贴了。 ❑ *"How are your boys?"—"How nice of you to ask."* "你的儿子们好吗？" —— "劳您惦记"。 **3** ADJ If you say that someone is **nice**, you mean that you like them because they are friendly and pleasant. 友好的; 可爱的 ❑ *I've met your father and he's rather nice.* 我见过你父亲了，他非常和蔼可亲。 **4** ADJ If you are **nice to** people, you are friendly, pleasant, or polite toward them. 对…友好的; 对…亲切的 [v-link ADJ] ❑ *She met Mr. and Mrs. Ricciardi, who were very nice to her.* 她见到了里恰尔迪先生和太太，他们对她非常友好。 ● **nice·ly** ADV 对…友好地; 对…亲切地 [ADV after v] ❑ *He treated you very nicely and acted like a decent guy.* 他待你很好，行为举止非常得体。 **5** ADJ When the weather is **nice**, it is warm and pleasant. (天气) 宜人的 ❑ *He nodded to us and said, "Nice weather we're having."* 他对我们点点头说："我们遇上好天气了。" **6** ADJ You can use **nice** to emphasize a particular quality that you like. 令人喜爱的 (用于加强语气) [EMPHASIS] ❑ *With a nice dark color, the wine is medium to full bodied.* 这种葡萄酒具有令人喜爱的深色调，从中度到高度都有。 ❑ *I'll explain it nice and simply so you can understand.* 我会把它解释得清楚简单，以便你能明白。 **7** ADJ You can use **nice** when you are greeting people. For example, you can say "**Nice to meet you,**" "**Nice to have met you,**" or "**Nice to see you.**" 很高兴的 (用于打招呼) ["it" v-link ADJ to-inf] [FORMULAE] ❑ *Good morning. Nice to meet you and thanks for being with us this weekend.* 早上好！很高兴认识大家，谢谢和我们共度这个周末。 **8** → see also **nicely**

Thesaurus *nice* 另参见：

ADJ. friendly, kind, likable, pleasant, polite; (*ant.*) mean, unpleasant **2** – **4**

Word Partnership *nice* 的常用搭配：

ADJ. nice **and clean** **1**
V. **look** nice, nice **to see** *someone/something* **1**
N. nice **clothes**, nice **guy**, nice **people**, nice **place**, nice **smile** **1** **3**
nice **day**, nice **weather** **5**

nice·ly /naɪsli/ **1** ADV If something is happening or working **nicely**, it is happening or working in a satisfactory way or in the way that you want it to. 令人满意地 [ADV with v] ❑ *She has a bit of private money, so they manage quite nicely.* 她有一些私房钱，因此他们过得还不错。 **2** → see also **nice** **3** PHRASE If someone or something **is doing nicely**, they are being successful. 成功 ❑ *...another hotel owner who is doing very nicely.* …另一个非常成功的旅店老板。

niche /nɪtʃ, niʃ/ (**niches**) **1** N-COUNT A **niche** in the market is a specific area of marketing which has its own particular requirements, customers, and products. (有特定的要求、顾客群和产品的) 专营市场 [BUSINESS] ❑ *I think we have found a niche in the toy market.* 我认为我们已经在玩具市场找到了领地。 **2** ADJ **Niche** marketing is the practice of dividing the market into specialized areas for which particular products are made. A **niche** market is one of these specialized areas. 专营市场的 [ADJ n] [BUSINESS] ❑ *Many media experts see such all-news channels as part of a general move towards niche marketing.* 许多媒体专家把这些全新闻频道看作是向专营市场营销全面发展的一部分。 **3** N-COUNT A **niche** is a hollow area in a wall which has been made to hold a statue, or a natural hollow part in a hill or cliff. 壁龛; (山坡或峭壁上) 天然凹陷处 ❑ *Above him, in a niche on the wall, sat a tiny veiled Ganesh, the elephant god.* 在他头顶上方一个壁龛里，坐着一尊极小的蒙着面纱的象神伽内什。 **4** N-COUNT Your **niche** is the job or activity which is exactly suitable for you. 合适的职位; 合适的活动 ❑ *Simon Lane quickly found his niche as a busy freelance model maker.* 西蒙・莱恩很快找到了合适的工作，成为了一名忙碌的自由职业模型工。

nick /nɪk/ (**nicks, nicking, nicked**) **1** V-T If you **nick** something or **nick** yourself, you accidentally make a small cut in the surface of the object or your skin. 划伤 ❑ *When I pulled out of the space, I nicked the rear bumper of the car in front of me.* 我把车从车位开出来时，蹭到了我前面那辆车的后保险杠。 ❑ *A sharp blade is likely to nick the skin and draw blood.* 锋利的刀刃可能会划破皮肤，引起出血。 **2** N-COUNT A **nick** is a small cut made in the surface of something, usually in someone's skin. 划痕 ❑ *The barbed wire had left only the tiniest nick just below my right eye.* 这带刺的铁丝在我右眼正下方只留下了极小的划痕。

nick·el /nɪkᵊl/ (**nickels**) **1** N-UNCOUNT **Nickel** is a silver-colored metal that is used in making steel. 镍 **2** N-COUNT In the United States and Canada, a **nickel** is a coin worth five cents. (美国和加拿大的) 五分镍币 ❑ *...a large glass jar filled with pennies, nickels, dimes, and quarters.* …一个装满1分、5分、10分和25分硬币的大玻璃罐。

★ **nick·name** /nɪkneɪm/ (**nicknames, nicknaming, nicknamed**) **1** N-COUNT A **nickname** is an informal name for someone or something. 绰号 ❑ *Red got his nickname for his red hair.* "红红"因为他的红头发而得了这个绰号。 **2** V-T If you **nickname** someone or something, you give them an informal name. 给…起绰号 ❑ *When he got older I nicknamed him Little Alf.* 他长大些后，我给他起了绰号"小阿尔夫"。

▲ **nico·tine** /nɪkɪtin/ N-UNCOUNT **Nicotine** is the substance in tobacco that people can become addicted to. 尼古丁 ❑ *Nicotine produces a feeling of well-being in the smoker.* 尼古丁能让吸烟者产生一种愉悦的感觉。

niece /nis/ (**nieces**) N-COUNT Someone's **niece** is the daughter of their sister or brother. 侄女; 外甥女 ❑ *...his niece, the daughter of his eldest sister.* …他的外甥女，他大姐的女儿。

nig·gle /nɪgᵊl/ (**niggles, niggling, niggled**) V-T/V-I If someone **niggles** you, they annoy you by continually criticizing you for what you think are small or unimportant things. 对…吹毛求疵; 吹毛求疵 ❑ *I don't react anymore when opponents try to niggle me.* 当反对者试图对我吹毛求疵时，我不再回应了。 ● N-COUNT **Niggle** is also a noun. 琐碎烦恼 ❑ *The life we have built together is more important than any minor niggle either of us might have.* 我们共同建立的生活比你我各自可能会有的任何琐碎事更重要。

night ♦♦♦ /naɪt/ (**nights**) **1** N-VAR The **night** is the part of each day when the sun has set and it is dark outside, especially the time when people are sleeping. 夜 ❑ *The fighting began in the late afternoon and continued all night.* 那场战斗傍晚开始，持续了一整夜。 ❑ *Finally night fell.* 夜幕终于降临了。 **2** N-COUNT The **night** is the period of time between the end of the afternoon and the time that you go to bed, especially the time when you relax before going to bed. 晚上 (尤指睡前) ❑ *So whose party was it last night?* 那么昨天晚上是谁的晚会？ **3** N-COUNT A particular **night** is a particular evening when a special event takes place, such as a show or a play. (演出等的) 夜场 ❑ *The first night crowd packed the building.* 首次夜场演出，观众全场爆满。 **4** PHRASE If it is a particular time **at night**, it is during the time when it is dark and is before midnight. 晚上 ❑ *It's eleven o'clock at night in Moscow.* 现在莫斯科是晚上11点。 **5** PHRASE If something happens **at night**, it happens regularly during the evening or night. 每晚 ❑ *He was going to college at night, in order to become an accountant.* 他为了当会计，每晚要去学院听课。 **6** PHRASE If something happens **day and night** or **night and day**, it happens all the time without stopping. 夜以继日地 ❑ *Dozens of doctors and nurses have been working day and night for weeks.* 很多医生和护士夜以继日地工作了几周了。 **7** PHRASE If you have **an early night**, you go to bed early. If you have **a late night**, you go to bed late. 早睡/晚睡 ❑ *I've had a hell of a day, and all I want is an early night.* 今天真是太糟糕了，我只想早早睡觉。 **8** **morning, noon, and night** → see **morning**
→ see **star**

Word Partnership *night* 的常用搭配：
ADJ. **cold** night, **cool** night, **dark** night, **rainy** night, **warm** night 1
V. **spend a/the** night 1 2
sleep at night, **stay out at** night, **stay the** night, **work at** night 1 5
N. **election** night, **wedding** night 3

night·club /naɪtklʌb/ (**nightclubs**) N-COUNT A **nightclub** is a place where people go late in the evening to drink and dance. 夜总会

night·life /naɪtlaɪf/ N-UNCOUNT **Nightlife** is all the entertainment and social activities that are available at night in cities and towns, such as nightclubs and theaters. 夜生活 ❑ *New York's energetic nightlife is second to none.* 纽约充满活力的夜生活不亚于任何地方。

night·ly /naɪtli/ ADJ A **nightly** event happens every night. 每夜的 [ADJ n] ❑ *I'm sure we watched the nightly news, and then we turned on the movie.* 我肯定我们看了晚间新闻，然后又看了电影。● ADV **Nightly** is also an adverb. 每夜地 ❑ *She appears nightly on the television news.* 她每晚都在电视新闻中出现。

night·mare ♦◇◇ /naɪtmeər/ (**nightmares**) 1 N-COUNT A **nightmare** is a very frightening dream. 恶梦 ❑ *All the victims still suffered nightmares.* 所有的受害者仍为恶梦所扰。 2 N-COUNT If you refer to a situation as a **nightmare**, you mean that it is very frightening and unpleasant. 噩梦（指可怕处境）❑ *The years in prison were a nightmare.* 数年的铁窗生涯是一场噩梦。 3 N-COUNT If you refer to a situation as a **nightmare**, you are saying in a very emphatic way that it is irritating because it causes you a lot of trouble. 噩梦（指恼人的情况）[EMPHASIS] ❑ *Taking my son Peter to a restaurant was a nightmare.* 带我儿子彼得去饭店吃饭真是一场噩梦。

Word Partnership *nightmare* 的常用搭配：
ADJ. **worst** nightmare 1 2
bureaucratic nightmare, **logistical** nightmare 3
V. **become a** nightmare, **turn into a** nightmare 2 3

★ **nil** /nɪl/ N-UNCOUNT If you say that something **is nil**, you mean that it does not exist at all. 不存在 ❑ *Their legal rights are virtually nil.* 他们的法定权利实际上不存在。

nim·ble /nɪmbəl/ (**nimbler, nimblest**) 1 ADJ Someone who is **nimble** is able to move their fingers, hands, or legs quickly and easily. 敏捷灵巧的 ❑ *Everything had been stitched by Molly's nimble fingers.* 样样都是莫利敏捷灵巧的手缝制成的。 2 ADJ If you say that someone has a **nimble** mind, you mean they are clever and can think very quickly. 机智的 ❑ *A nimble mind backed by a degree in economics gave him a firm grasp of financial matters.* 一个机智头脑加上一个经济学学位使他对金融问题能准确把握。

nine ♦♦♦ /naɪn/ (**nines**) NUM **Nine** is the number 9. 9 ❑ *We still sighted nine yachts.* 我们还是看到了9艘游艇。

911 /naɪn wʌn wʌn/ NUM **911** is the number that you call in the United States in order to contact the emergency services. 美国的紧急呼救电话号码 ❑ *The women made their first 911 call about a prowler at 12:46 a.m.* 这些妇女在午夜12：46打了第1个报警电话，报告有人在附近徘徊。

nine·teen ♦♦♦ /naɪntin/ (**nineteens**) NUM **Nineteen** is the number 19. 19 ❑ *They have nineteen days to make up their minds.* 他们有19天的时间来做出决定。

nine·teenth ♦♦◇ /naɪntinθ/ ORD The **nineteenth** item in a series is the one that you count as number nineteen. 第19 ❑ *...my nineteenth birthday.* …我的19岁生日。

nine·ti·eth ♦♦◇ /naɪntiəθ/ ORD The **ninetieth** item in a series is the one that you count as number ninety. 第90 ❑ *He celebrates his ninetieth birthday on Friday.* 他周五庆祝他的90岁生日。

nine·ty ♦♦♦ /naɪnti/ (**nineties**) 1 NUM **Ninety** is the number 90. 90 ❑ *It was decided she had to stay another ninety days.* 经决定，她必须再呆90天。 2 N-PLURAL When you talk about the **nineties**, you are referring to numbers between 90 and 99. For example, if you are **in** your **nineties**, you are aged between 90 and 99. If the temperature is **in the nineties**, the temperature is between 90 and 99 degrees. 九十几（指从90到99）❑ *By this time she was in her nineties and needed help more and more frequently.* 到这时她已经九十多岁了，越来越频繁地需要帮助。 3 N-PLURAL **The nineties** is the decade between 1990 and 1999. （二十世纪）九十年代 ❑ *These trends only got worse as we moved into the nineties.* 当我们进入了90年代，这些风气只不过变得更糟了。

ninth ♦♦◇ /naɪnθ/ (**ninths**) 1 ORD The **ninth** item in a series is the one that you count as number nine. 第9 ❑ *...January the ninth.* …1月9号。❑ *...students in the ninth grade.* …9年级的学生们。 2 FRACTION A **ninth** is one of nine equal parts of something. 1/9 ❑ *The dollar rose by a ninth of a cent.* 美元升值了1/9美分。

nip /nɪp/ (**nips, nipping, nipped**) 1 V-T If an animal or person **nips** you, they bite you lightly or squeeze a piece of your skin between their finger and thumb. 轻咬；轻捏 ❑ *I have known cases where dogs have nipped babies.* 我知道一些狗咬婴儿的事例。● N-COUNT **Nip** is also a noun. 轻咬；轻捏 ❑ *Incidents range from a nip, which fails to break the skin or draw blood, to serious injuries.* 各种情况都有，从并未咬破皮肤或出血的轻伤到重伤。 2 N-COUNT A **nip** is a small amount of a strong alcoholic drink. （烈性酒的）一小口 ❑ *She had a habit of taking an occasional nip from a flask of cognac.* 她有一个偶尔就着瓶子喝一小口法国白兰地的习惯。 3 **to nip** something **in the bud** → see **bud**

nip·ple /nɪpəl/ (**nipples**) 1 N-COUNT The **nipples** on someone's body are the two small pieces of slightly hard flesh on their chest. Babies suck milk from their mothers' breasts through their mothers' nipples. 乳头 ❑ *Sore nipples can inhibit the milk supply.* 乳头疼痛可能抑制母乳分泌。 2 N-COUNT A **nipple** is a piece of rubber or plastic which is attached to the top of a baby's bottle. （橡皮或塑料的）奶嘴 ❑ *...a white plastic bottle with a rubber nipple.* …一个带橡皮奶嘴的白色塑料奶瓶。

ni·trate /naɪtreɪt/ (**nitrates**) N-MASS **Nitrate** is a chemical compound that includes nitrogen and oxygen. Nitrates are used as fertilizers in agriculture. 硝酸盐 ❑ *High levels of nitrate occur in the Midwest because of the heavy use of fertilizers.* 因为大量使用化肥，中西部地区的硝酸盐含量很高。
→ see **firework**

ni·tro·gen /naɪtrədʒən/ N-UNCOUNT **Nitrogen** is a colorless element that has no smell and is usually found as a gas. It forms about 78 percent of the Earth's atmosphere, and is found in all living things. 氮
→ see **air**

no ♦♦♦ /noʊ/ (**noes** or **no's**) 1 CONVENTION You use **no** to give a negative response to a question. （用于否定回答）不；没有 ❑ *"Any problems?"—"No, I'm O.K."* "有问题吗？"——"没有，我挺好。" 2 CONVENTION You use **no** to say that something that someone has just said is not true. （用于否定别人的陈述）不；没有 ❑ *"We thought you'd emigrated."—"No, no."* "我们还以为你已经移民了呢。"——"不，没有。" 3 CONVENTION You use **no** to refuse an offer or a request, or to refuse permission. （用于拒绝建议、请求或许可）不用；不行 ❑ *"Here, have mine."—"No, this is fine."* "给，用我的。"——"不用，这个挺好的。" ❑ *"Can you just get the message through to Pete for me?"—"No, no I can't."* "你能帮我把这个信儿带给皮特吗？"——"不行，我不能。" 4 EXCLAM You use **no** to indicate that you do not want someone to do something. （表示禁止）不要 ❑ *No. I forbid it. You cannot.* 不，我不准。你不可以。 5 CONVENTION You use **no** to acknowledge a negative statement or to show that you accept and understand it. （表示接受或理解对方的否定陈述）对，不是 ❑ *"We're not on the main campus."—"No."* "我们不在主校园。"——"是的。" ❑ *"It's not one of my favorite forms of music."—"No."* "它不是我最喜欢的音乐形式之一。"——"对，不是。" 6 CONVENTION You use **no** before correcting what you have just said. （用于纠正刚说过的话）噢不 ❑ *I was twenty-two – no, twenty-one.* 我那时22岁。——噢不，21岁。 7 EXCLAM You use **no** to express shock or disappointment at something you have just been told. （表示对获知的事情的惊讶或失望）是吗；不会吧 [FEELINGS] ❑ *"We went with Sarah and the married man that she's currently seeing."—"Oh no."* "我们与萨拉和她最近约会的那个已婚男子一起去的。"——"不会吧。" 8 DET You use **no** to mean not any or not one person or thing. 没有 ❑ *He had no intention of paying the cash.* 他丝毫没有付现金的意思。 ❑ *No job has more influence on the future of the world.* 没有哪种工作对世界的未来具有更大的影响。 9 DET You use **no** to emphasize that someone or something is not the type of thing mentioned. 绝非 [EMPHASIS] ❑ *He is no singer.* 他绝非唱歌家。 ❑ *I make it no secret that our worst consultants earn nothing.* 我毫不隐瞒地说我们最差的顾问挣不到一分钱。 10 ADV You can use **no** to make the negative form of a comparative. （用于比较级的否定形式）不 [ADV compar] ❑ *It is to start broadcasting no later than the end of 1994.* 开始广播不会晚于1994年底。 ❑ *Yesterday no fewer than thirty climbers reached the summit.* 昨天不少于三十名登山者到达了顶峰。 11 DET You use **no**

in front of an adjective and noun to make the noun group mean its opposite. (用于名词及其修饰形容词前表示否定) 并非 ❑ *Sometimes a bit of selfishness, if it leads to greater self-knowledge, is no bad thing.* 有时候一点点的自私，如果能引发更多自知之明，也并非坏事。 **12** DET **No** is used in notices or instructions to say that a particular activity or thing is forbidden. (用于通知或指示中) 禁止 ❑ *The captain turned out the "no smoking" signs.* 机长关掉了"禁止吸烟"标志灯。 ❑ *No talking after lights out.* 熄灯后禁止说话。 **13** N-COUNT A **no** is a person who has answered "no" to a question or who has voted against something. **No** is also used to refer to their answer or vote. 作否定回答者；投反对票者；否定回答 ❑ *According to the latest opinion polls, the noes have 50 percent, the yeses 35 percent.* 根据最新的民意测验，投反对票的人占50%，投赞成票的人占35%。 **14** PHRASE If you say **there is no** doing a particular thing, you mean that it is very difficult or impossible to do that thing. 不可能(做某事) [EMPHASIS] ❑ *There is no going back to the life she had.* 不可能回到她过去的生活。 **15** **not to take no for an answer** → see **answer** **16** **no doubt** → see **doubt** **17** **no longer** → see **long** **18** **in no way** → see **way** **19** **there's no way** → see **way** **20** **no way** → see **way**

No. (Nos) **No.** is a written abbreviation for **number**. **number**的缩写 ❑ *That year he was named the nation's No. 1 college football star.* 那年他被称为国家的1号大学足球明星。

no·bil·ity /noʊbɪlɪti/ **1** N-SING-COLL **The nobility** of a society are all the people who have titles and belong to a high social class. 贵族阶层 ❑ *They married into the nobility and entered the highest ranks of state administration.* 他们与贵族阶层联姻，进入了国家行政机关的最高级别。 **2** N-UNCOUNT A person's **nobility** is their noble character and behavior. 高尚品格；高贵行为 [FORMAL] ❑ *...his nobility of character, and his devotion to his country.* …他的高尚品格和他对他国家的献身精神。

no·ble /noʊbᵊl/ (**nobler, noblest**) **1** ADJ If you say that someone is a **noble** person, you admire and respect them because they are unselfish and morally good. 高尚的 [APPROVAL] ❑ *He was an upright and noble man who was always willing to help in any way he could.* 他是一个正直、高尚的人，总是愿意尽其所能来帮忙。 ● **no·bly** ADV 高尚地 [ADV with v] ❑ *Eric's sister had nobly volunteered to help with the gardening.* 埃里克的姐姐无私地主动帮忙做些园艺工作。 **2** ADJ If you say that something is a **noble** idea, goal, or action, you admire it because it is based on high moral principles. 崇高的 [APPROVAL] ❑ *He had implicit faith in their noble intentions.* 他对他们的崇高目标深信不疑。 ❑ *We'll always justify our actions with noble sounding theories.* 我们将始终用崇高的理论思想指导我们的行动。 **3** ADJ If you describe something as **noble**, you think that its appearance or quality is very impressive, making it superior to other things of its type. 卓越的；超群的 ❑ *...the great parks with their noble trees.* …树木参天的大公园。 **4** ADJ **Noble** means belonging to a high social class and having a title. 高贵的；贵族的 ❑ *...rich and noble families.* …富有而高贵的家族。

no·body ♦♦◇ /noʊbɒdi, -bʌdi/ (**nobodies**) **1** PRON-INDEF-NEG **Nobody** means not a single person, or not a single member of a particular group or set. 没有人 ❑ *They were shut away in a little room where nobody could overhear.* 他们躲在一个小屋子里，没有人能偷听得到。 ❑ *Nobody realizes how bad things are.* 没人意识到事情有多么糟糕。 **2** N-COUNT If someone says that a person is a **nobody**, they are saying in an unkind way that the person is not at all important. 无名之辈 [DISAPPROVAL] ❑ *A man in my position has nothing to fear from a nobody like you.* 在我这样职位的一个男人没什么好怕像你这样一个无名之辈的。

> You do not use **nobody** or **no one** in front of **of** to talk about a particular group of people. The word you need is **none**.
> ❑ *None of his companions answered.*

noc·tur·nal /nɒktɜrnᵊl/ **1** ADJ **Nocturnal** means occurring at night. 夜间发生的 ❑ *The dog's main duty will be to accompany me on long nocturnal walks.* 那只狗的主要职责将是陪我走长途夜路。 **2** ADJ **Nocturnal** creatures are active mainly at night. 夜间活动的 ❑ *When there is a full moon, this nocturnal rodent is careful to stay in its burrow.* 在有满月出现的时候，这种夜间出没的啮齿类动物小心地呆在它的洞里。 → see **bat**

nod ♦◇◇ /nɒd/ (**nods, nodding, nodded**) **1** V-T/V-I If you **nod**, you move your head downward and upward to show that you are answering "yes" to a question, or to show agreement, understanding, or approval. 点头 [no passive] ❑ *"Are you okay?" I asked. She nodded and smiled.* "你还好吧？"我问道。她点点头笑了。 ❑ *Jacques tasted one and nodded his approval.* 雅克品尝了一个并点头表示赞许。 ● N-COUNT **Nod** is also a noun. 点头 ❑ *She gave a nod and said, "I see."* 她点了一下头说："我明白了。" ❑ *"Probably," agreed Hunter, with a slow nod of his head.* "可能，"亨特慢慢点了一下头赞同地说道。 **2** V-I If you **nod** in a particular direction, you bend your head once in that direction in order to indicate something or to give someone a signal. (朝某方向) 点头示意 [no passive] ❑ *"Does it work?" he asked, nodding at the piano.* "它能弹吗？"他问道，点头指向那架钢琴。 ❑ *She nodded toward the dining room. "He's in there."* 她朝餐厅点了点头说："他在那里面。" **3** V-T/V-I If you **nod**, you bend your head once, as a way of saying hello or goodbye. 点头 (以示打招呼或告别) [no passive] ❑ *All the girls nodded and said "Hi."* 所有女孩们都点头说："你好。" ❑ *Both of them smiled and nodded at friends.* 他们两个都微笑着朝朋友们点了点头。 ❑ *Tom nodded a greeting.* 汤姆点头打了个招呼。

▸ **nod off** PHRASAL VERB If you **nod off**, you fall asleep, especially when you had not intended to. 打瞌睡 [INFORMAL] ❑ *The judge appeared to nod off yesterday while a witness was being cross-examined.* 昨天当一名证人被盘问时，法官好像在打瞌睡。

Word Partnership *nod* 的常用搭配：
- N. nod **in agreement**, nod **your head** **1**
- V. **give a** nod **1**

noise ♦◇◇ /nɔɪz/ (**noises**) **1** N-UNCOUNT **Noise** is a loud or unpleasant sound. 噪音 ❑ *There was too much noise in the room and he needed peace.* 房间里有太多噪音了，他需要安静。 ❑ *The noise of bombs and guns was incessant.* 爆炸声和枪击声接连不断。 **2** N-COUNT A **noise** is a sound that someone or something makes. 声音 ❑ *Gerald made a small noise in his throat.* 杰拉尔德从他的嗓子里发出轻轻的一声。 ❑ *...birdsong and other animal noises.* …鸟鸣声和其他动物的叫声。 **3** N-PLURAL If someone **makes noises** of a particular kind about something, they say things that indicate their attitude to it in a rather indirect or vague way. (间接、含蓄地表达的) 观点 ❑ *The president took care to make encouraging noises about the future.* 那位总统小心谨慎地表达了对未来的乐观。 **4** PHRASE If you say that someone **makes the right noises** or **makes all the right noises**, you think that they are showing concern or enthusiasm about something because they feel they ought to rather than because they really want to. 故作热情地附和 ❑ *But at the annual party conference he always made the right noises.* 但在年会上他总是故作热情地随声附和。

Thesaurus *noise* 另参见：
- N. boom, crash; *(ant.)* quiet, silence **1**

Word Partnership *noise* 的常用搭配：
- N. **background** noise, noise **level**, noise **pollution**, **traffic** noise **1**
- ADJ. **loud** noise **1** **2**
- V. **hear a** noise, **make a** noise **2**

noisy /nɔɪzi/ (**noisier, noisiest**) **1** ADJ A **noisy** person or thing makes a lot of loud or unpleasant noise. 喧闹的；有噪音的 ❑ *...my noisy old typewriter.* …我的噪音大的旧打字机。 ● **noisi·ly** ADV 喧闹地；有噪音地 ❑ *The students on the grass bank cheered noisily.* 学生们在草堤上喧闹地欢呼。 **2** ADJ A **noisy** place is full of a lot of loud or unpleasant noise. 嘈杂的 ❑ *It's a noisy place with film clips showing constantly on one of the cafe's giant screens.* 这是一个嘈杂的地方，电影片断不停地在咖啡厅其中一个大屏幕上放映。 ❑ *The baggage hall was crowded and noisy.* 行李大厅拥挤而嘈杂。 **3** ADJ If you describe someone as **noisy**, you are critical of them for trying to attract attention to their views by frequently and forcefully discussing them. 过分渲染的；哗众取宠的 [DISAPPROVAL] ❑ *It might, at last, silence the small but noisy intellectual clique.* 它或许最终能让那个人数不多却哗众取宠的知识分子群体安静下来。

no·mad·ic /noʊmædɪk/ **1** ADJ **Nomadic** people travel from place to place rather than living in one place all the time. 游牧的 ❑ *...the great nomadic tribes of the Western Sahara.* …西撒哈拉的大游牧部落。 **2** ADJ If someone has a **nomadic** way of life, they travel from place to place and do not have a settled home. 流浪的 ❑ *The daughter of a railroad engineer, she at first had a somewhat nomadic childhood.* 一名铁路工程师的女儿，她起初有过一个流浪般的童年。

no-man's land **1** N-UNCOUNT **No-man's land** is an area of land that is not owned or controlled by anyone, for example the area of land between two opposing armies. 无主土地；无人管辖的地带 ❑ *In Tobruk, leading a patrol in no-man's land, he was blown up by a mortar*

n

bomb. 在图卜鲁格，他领着一支巡逻队在无人地带时，被一枚迫击炮弹击中。 **2** N-SING If you refer to a situation as a **no-man's land** between different things, you mean that it seems unclear because it does not fit into any of the categories. (介于两者之间的)中间状态 ❑ *The play is set in the dangerous no-man's land between youth and adolescence.* 该剧定位于少年和青春期之间的危险的中间年龄段。

Word Link *nom ≈ name : denomination, nominal, nominee*

★ **nomi·nal** /nɒmɪnəl/ **1** ADJ You use **nominal** to indicate that someone or something is supposed to have a particular identity or status, but in reality does not have it. 名义上的 ❑ *As he was still not allowed to run a company, his wife became its nominal head.* 由于他仍未获准管理公司，他的妻子就成了公司名义上的老板。 ● **nomi·nal·ly** ADV 在名义上 ❑ *The sultan was still nominally the chief of staff.* 苏丹在名义上仍是军队领导人。 ❑ *The road is nominally under the control of UN peacekeeping troops.* 那条路名义上是在联合国维和部队的控制之下。 **2** ADJ A **nominal** price or sum of money is very small in comparison with the real cost or value of the thing that is being bought or sold. (价格、金额) 象征性的 [ADJ n] ❑ *I am prepared to sell my shares at a nominal price.* 我准备以低价卖掉我的股票。 **3** ADJ In economics, the **nominal** value, rate, or level of something is the one expressed in terms of current prices or figures, without taking into account general changes in prices that take place over time. 票面上的 [ADJ n] ❑ *Inflation would be lower and so nominal rates would be more attractive in real terms.* 通货膨胀将要降低，所以名义汇率实际上会更有吸引力。

★ **nomi·nate** /nɒmɪneɪt/ (**nominates, nominating, nominated**) **1** V-T If someone **is nominated** for a job or position, their name is formally suggested as a candidate for it. (为工作、职位) 提名 ❑ *This week one of them will be nominated by the Democratic Party for the presidency of the United States.* 本周他们中的一人将被民主党提名为美国总统职位的候选人。 ❑ *The Security Council can nominate anyone for secretary-general.* 安全理事会可以提名任何人为秘书长。 **2** V-T If you **nominate** someone to a job or position, you formally choose them to hold that job or position. 任命 ❑ *In 1967 Johnson nominated Thurgood Marshall to the Supreme Court.* 1967年，约翰逊任命瑟古德·马歇尔为最高法院法官。 ❑ *She was nominated by the president as ambassador to Barbados.* 她被总统任命为驻巴巴多斯大使。 **3** V-T If someone or something such as an actor or a movie **is nominated** for an award, someone formally suggests that they should be given that award. (某人或某物) 被提名 (某奖项) ❑ *Practically every movie he made was nominated for an Oscar.* 他制作的每部电影几乎都获得了奥斯卡提名。

nomi·na·tion /nɒmɪneɪʃən/ (**nominations**) **1** N-COUNT A **nomination** is an official suggestion of someone as a candidate in an election or for a job. (选举、工作的) 提名 ❑ *...his candidacy for the Republican presidential nomination.* …他共和党总统提名的候选资格。 **2** N-COUNT A **nomination for** an award is an official suggestion that someone or something should be given that award. (奖项的) 提名 ❑ *They say he's certain to get a nomination for best supporting actor.* 他们说他肯定会获得最佳男配角奖的提名。 **3** N-VAR The **nomination** of someone to a particular job or position is their appointment to that job or position. 任命 ❑ *...the nomination of Texas Senator Lloyd Bentsen to be treasury secretary.* …德克萨斯州议员劳埃德·本特森作财政部长的任命。

★ **nomi·nee** /nɒmɪniː/ (**nominees**) N-COUNT A **nominee** is someone who is nominated for a job, position, or award. 候选人 ❑ *His nominee for vice president was elected only after a second ballot.* 他的副总统候选人仅在第二轮投票后就被选中。

non·cha·lant /nɒnʃələnt/ ADJ If you describe someone as **nonchalant**, you mean that they appear not to worry or care about things and that they seem very calm. 若无其事的；漠不关心的 ❑ *Clark's mother is nonchalant about her role in her son's latest work.* 克拉克的母亲对她在儿子最新作品中的角色反应平淡。 ❑ *Denis tried to look nonchalant and uninterested.* 丹尼斯尽力作出冷淡、不感兴趣的样子。 ● **non·cha·lance** /nɒnʃələns/ N-UNCOUNT 若无其事；漠不关心 ❑ *Affecting nonchalance, I handed her two hundred dollar bills.* 我假装若无其事地递给她两张百元钞票。 ● **non·cha·lant·ly** ADV 若无其事地；漠不关心地 ❑ *"Does Will intend to return with us?" Joanna asked as nonchalantly as she could.* "威尔打算和我们一起回去吗？" 乔安娜尽可能若无其事地问道。

none ♦♦◊ /nʌn/ **1** QUANT **None of** something means not even a small amount of it. **None of** a group of people or things means not even one of them. 没有任何 [QUANT "of" def-n] ❑ *None of us knew how to treat her.* 我们中没有任何人知道该如何对待她。 ● PRON-INDEF-NEG **None** is also a pronoun. 没有任何人；没有任何事物 ❑ *I searched bookstores and libraries for information, but found none.* 我查找了多家书店和图书馆，但没查到任何信息。 ❑ *No one could imagine a great woman painter. None had existed yet.* 没人能想像会有出色的女画家。还没有那样的人存在过。 **2** PHRASE If you say that someone **will have none of** something, or **is having none of** something, you mean that they refuse to accept it. 不接受 [INFORMAL] ❑ *He knew his own mind and was having none of their attempts to keep him at home.* 他知道自己想要什么，不会接受他们要把他留在家里的企图。 **3** PHRASE You use **none too** in front of an adjective or adverb in order to emphasize that the quality mentioned is not present. 毫不 [FORMAL, EMPHASIS] ❑ *He was none too thrilled to hear from me at that hour.* 他在那个时刻接到我的电话不太高兴。 **4** PHRASE You use **none the** to say that someone or something does not have any more of a particular quality than they did before. 一点也不比以前… (表示某原有特质没有增) ❑ *You could end up none the wiser about managing your finances.* 你最终可能一点儿也不会比以前更会理财。 **5** **second to none** → see **second**

> Do not confuse **none** and **neither**. You use **none** in negative statements to refer to three or more people or things. ❑ *None could afford the food.* You use **none of** in the same way, followed by a pronoun or a noun group. ❑ *None of them had learned anything... None of his companions answered.* You use **neither** in negative statements to refer to two people or things. ❑ *Neither had close friends in college.* You use **neither of** in the same way, followed by a pronoun or a noun group. ❑ *Neither of them spoke... Neither of these extremes is desirable.* Note that you can also use **neither** before a singular count noun. ❑ *Neither side can win.*

Word Partnership *none* 的常用搭配：

PRON.	none **of that/this/those**, none **of them/us** **1**
ADV.	**almost** none, **virtually** none, none **whatsoever** **1** none **too** **3**

★ **none·the·less** /nʌnðəlɛs/ ADV **Nonetheless** means the same as **nevertheless**. 然而 [ADV with cl] [FORMAL] ❑ *There was still a long way to go. Nonetheless, some progress had been made.* 仍然有很长的路要走。不过还是取得了一些进步。

non·executive /nɒnɪgzɛkyətɪv/

in BRIT, also use **non-executive**

ADJ Someone who has a **nonexecutive** position in a company or organization gives advice but is not responsible for making decisions or ensuring that decisions are carried out. 非执行的 [ADJ n] [BUSINESS] ❑ *...nonexecutive directors.* …非执行董事们。

Word Link *non ≈ not : nonexistent, nonprofit, nonstop*

non·existent /nɒnɪgzɪstənt/

in BRIT, also use **non-existent**

ADJ If you say that something is **nonexistent**, you mean that it does not exist when you feel that it should. 不存在的 ❑ *Hygiene was non-existent: no running water, no bathroom.* 卫生根本不存在：没有自来水，没有浴室。

no-nonsense **1** ADJ If you describe someone as a **no-nonsense** person, you approve of the fact that they are efficient, direct, and quite tough. 高效干练的 [APPROVAL] ❑ *She saw herself as a direct, no-nonsense, modern woman.* 她视自己为一个率直、高效干练的现代女性。 **2** ADJ If you describe something as a **no-nonsense** thing, you approve of the fact that it is plain and does not have unnecessary parts. 简单实用的 [APPROVAL] ❑ *You'll need no-nonsense boots for the jungle.* 你将需要实用的靴子穿越丛林。

non·payment /nɒnpeɪmənt/

in BRIT, also use **non-payment**

N-UNCOUNT **Nonpayment** is a failure to pay a sum of money that you owe. 未支付 ❑ *She faced an end to treatments because of nonpayment of her claim.* 由于她的索赔未付，所以她的治疗可能被终止。

★ **non·profit** /nɒnprɒfɪt/

in BRIT, also use **non-profit**

ADJ A **nonprofit** organization is one which is not run with the aim of making a profit. 非营利的 [BUSINESS] ❑ *Most of that money goes to nonprofit organizations that run programs for the poor.* 那笔钱的大部分用于从事扶贫项目的非营利性组织。

non·sense /nɒnsɛns, -səns/ **1** N-UNCOUNT If you say that something spoken or written is **nonsense**, you mean that you consider it to be untrue or silly. 胡言乱语；蠢话 [DISAPPROVAL] ❑ *Most orthodox doctors however dismiss this as complete nonsense.* 然而大多数传统的医生将此视为纯粹的胡言乱语而不予考虑。 ❑ *...all that poetic nonsense about love.* …所有关于爱情的诗一般的傻话。 **2** N-UNCOUNT You can use **nonsense** to refer to something that you think is foolish or that you disapprove of. 蠢事 [also "a" N, usu supp N] [DISAPPROVAL] ❑ *Surely it is an economic nonsense to deplete the world of natural resources.* 耗尽世界的自然资源无疑是一件经济上的愚蠢行为。 **3** N-UNCOUNT You can refer to spoken or written words that do not mean anything because they do not make sense as **nonsense**. 无意义的话 ❑ *...a children's nonsense poem by Charles E Carryl.* …查尔斯・E・卡里尔写的一首儿童打油诗。 **4** → see also **no-nonsense** **5** PHRASE To **make a nonsense of** something or to **make nonsense of** it means to make it seem ridiculous or pointless. 使…荒唐可笑；使…失去意义 ❑ *The fighting made a nonsense of peace pledges made last week.* 这场战斗使上周做出的和平承诺失去了意义。

Thesaurus *nonsense* 另参见：
N. foolishness, gibberish **1** **3**
absurdity, irrationality, rubbish **2**

Word Partnership *nonsense* 的常用搭配：
ADJ. **absolute** nonsense, **complete** nonsense, **utter** nonsense **1**–**3**
V. **talk** nonsense **1** **3**

non·smoker /nɒnsmoʊkər/ (**nonsmokers**)
in BRIT, also use **non-smoker**
N-COUNT A **nonsmoker** is someone who does not smoke. 不吸烟的人 ❑ *It could be fair to nonsmokers to allow smoking in a building with windows that open.* 允许在开着窗户的楼房里抽烟对于不抽烟的人来说可能是公平的。

non·stick /nɒnstɪk/
in BRIT, also use **non-stick**
ADJ **Nonstick** saucepans, frying pans, or baking pans have a special coating on the inside which prevents food from sticking to them. (煎锅等) 不粘食物的 ❑ *Use a shallow nonstick baking pan.* 用一个浅的不粘食物的平底烘锅。

Word Link *non ≈ not : nonexistent, nonprofit, nonstop*

non·stop /nɒnstɒp/
in BRIT, also use **non-stop**
ADJ Something that is **nonstop** continues without any pauses or interruptions. 不停的；不间断的 ❑ *Many U.S. cities now have nonstop flights to Aspen.* 很多美国城市现在都有飞往亚斯本的直飞航班。 ❑ *...80 minutes of nonstop music.* …80分钟不间断的音乐。 ● ADV **Nonstop** is also an adverb. 不停地；不间断地 [ADV after v] ❑ *Amy and her group had driven nonstop through Spain.* 艾米和她的小组成员一刻不停地开车穿过西班牙。

Thesaurus *nonstop* 另参见：
ADJ. continuous, direct, uninterrupted

noo·dle /nudəl/ (**noodles**) N-COUNT **Noodles** are long, thin strips of pasta. They are used especially in Chinese and Italian cooking. 面条

noon /nun/ **1** N-UNCOUNT **Noon** is twelve o'clock in the middle of the day. 中午 ❑ *The long day of meetings started at noon.* 漫长的会议日从中午开始了。 **2** ADJ **Noon** means happening or appearing in the middle part of the day. 中午的 [ADJ n] ❑ *The noon sun was fierce.* 中午的太阳火辣辣的。 **3** **morning, noon, and night** → see **morning**

no one ♦♦◇
in BRIT, also use **no-one**
PRON-INDEF-NEG **No one** means not a single person, or not a single member of a particular group or set. 没有人 ❑ *Everyone wants to be a hero, but no one wants to die.* 人人都想当一名英雄，但没有人想死。

noose /nus/ (**nooses**) N-COUNT A **noose** is a circular loop at the end of a piece of rope or wire. A noose is tied with a knot that allows it to be tightened, and it is usually used to trap animals or hang people. 套索；绞索 ❑ *...a horrifying videotape of a man swinging from a noose.* …一盘一名男子吊在绞索上的恐怖录像带。

nope /noʊp/ CONVENTION **Nope** is sometimes used instead of "no" as a negative response. (有时用于替代no作否定回答) 不 [INFORMAL, SPOKEN] ❑ *"Is she supposed to work today?"—"Nope, tomorrow."* "她今天应该上班吗？"——"不，明天。"

nor ♦♦◇ /nɔr/ **1** CONJ You use **nor** after "neither" in order to introduce the second alternative or the last of a number of alternatives in a negative statement. (用于**neither**后，以引出被否定的第二项或几项中的最后一项) 也不 ❑ *Neither Mr. Rose nor Mr. Woodhead was available for comment yesterday.* 罗斯先生和伍德黑德先生昨天都没有时间做出评论。 ❑ *I can give you neither an opinion nor any advice.* 我既不能给你一个意见，也不能给你任何建议。 **2** CONJ You use **nor** after a negative statement in order to introduce another negative statement which adds information to the previous one. (用于否定句后，引出另一否定句以补充前句) 也不 ❑ *Cooking up a quick dish doesn't mean you have to sacrifice flavor. Nor does fast food have to be junk food.* 做一道快餐并不意味着你就得牺牲味道。快餐也不见得非得是垃圾食品。 **3** CONJ You use **nor** after a negative statement in order to indicate that the negative statement also applies to you or to someone or something else. (用于否定句后，以表示此否定也适用于自己、他人或别的事情) 也不 ❑ *"None of us has any idea how long we're going to be here."—"Nor do I."* "我们当中没人知道我们将要在这儿呆多久。"——"我也不知道。" ❑ *"If my husband has no future," she said, "then nor do my children."* "要是我丈夫没有前途，"她说道，"那么我的孩子们也没有。"

norm /nɔrm/ (**norms**) **1** N-COUNT **Norms** are ways of behaving that are considered normal in a particular society. 准则 ❑ *The actions taken depart from what she called the commonly accepted norms of democracy.* 所采取的这些行动背离了她所谓的那些普遍接受的民主准则。 **2** N-SING If you say that a situation is **the norm**, you mean that it is usual and expected. 惯例；常规 ❑ *Families of six or seven are the norm in Borough Park.* 六七口人的家庭在菠萝园是常事儿。 **3** N-COUNT A **norm** is an official standard or level that organizations are expected to reach. 标准 ❑ *About 32 percent of students meet national norms in reading.* 大约32%的学生达到国家阅读标准。

nor·mal ♦♦◇ /nɔrməl/ **1** ADJ Something that is **normal** is usual and ordinary, and is what people expect. 正常的；平常的 ❑ *The two countries resumed normal diplomatic relations.* 这两个国家恢复了正常的外交关系。 ❑ *Her height and weight are normal for her age.* 她的身高和体重对于她的年龄来说是正常的。 **2** ADJ A **normal** person has no serious physical or mental health problems. 身心正常的 ❑ *Statistics indicate that depressed patients are more likely to become ill than are normal people.* 统计表明抑郁的患者比正常人更可能得病。

Thesaurus *normal* 另参见：
ADJ. ordinary, regular, typical, usual **1**

Word Partnership *normal* 的常用搭配：
N. normal **conditions**, normal **development**, normal **routine** **1**
V. **return to** normal **1**
ADV. **back to** normal **1**
completely normal, **perfectly** normal **1** **2**

★ **nor·mal·ise** /nɔːməlaɪz/ [BRIT] → see **normalize**

nor·mal·ity /nɔrmælɪti/ N-UNCOUNT **Normality** is a situation in which everything is normal. 正常状态 ❑ *A semblance of normality has returned with people going to work and shops reopening.* 随着人们上班、商店重新营业，表面已恢复了常态。

Word Link *ize ≈ making : finalize, memorize, normalize*

★ **nor·mal·ize** /nɔrməlaɪz/ (**normalizes, normalizing, normalized**)
in BRIT, also use **normalise**
1 V-T/V-I When you **normalize** a situation or when it **normalizes**, it becomes normal. 使(情形) 正常化；(情形) 正常化 ❑ *Meditation tends to lower or normalize blood pressure.* 静坐易于降低血压或使血压正常化。 **2** V-RECIP If people, groups, or governments **normalize** relations, or when relations **normalize**, they become normal or return to normal. 使(关系) 正常化；(关系) 正常化 ❑ *The two governments were close to normalizing relations.* 两国政府即将使关系正常化。 ❑ *The United States says they are not prepared to join in normalizing ties with their former enemy.* 美国声称他们不准备与他们的前敌建立正常化的关系。 ● **nor·mali·za·tion** /nɔrməlɪzeɪʃən/ N-UNCOUNT 正常化 ❑ *The two sides would like to see the normalization of diplomatic relations.* 双方都愿意看到外交关系的正常化。

n

nor·mal·ly ◆◇◇ /nɔrməli/ 1 ADV If you say that something **normally** happens or that you **normally** do a particular thing, you mean that it is what usually happens or what you usually do. 通常 ❑ *All airports in the country are working normally today.* 该国所有的机场今日都在正常运营。 ❑ *Social progress is normally a matter of struggles and conflicts.* 社会进步通常要经过斗争和冲突。 2 ADV If you do something **normally**, you do it in the usual or conventional way. 按常规地 [ADV after v] ❑ *...failure of the blood to clot normally.* …血液正常凝结的失败。

north ◆◆◆ /nɔrθ/ also **North** 1 N-UNCOUNT The **north** is the direction which is on your left when you are looking toward the direction where the sun rises. 北方 [also "the" N] ❑ *In the north the ground becomes very cold as the winter snow and ice covers the ground.* 在北方地面变得很冷，因为冬天的冰雪覆盖着地面。 2 N-SING **The north** of a place, country, or region is the part which is in the north. 北部 ❑ *The plan mostly benefits people in the North and Midwest.* 该计划使北部和中西部的人们最为受益。 3 ADV If you go **north**, you travel toward the north. 向北方 [ADV after v] ❑ *Anita drove north up Pacific Highway.* 安尼塔开车沿着太平洋公路向北行驶。 4 ADV Something that is **north** of a place is positioned to the north of it. 在…以北 ❑ *...a little village a few miles north of Portland.* …在波特兰以北几英里处的一个小村子。 5 ADJ The **north** edge, corner, or part of a place or country is the part which is toward the north. 北部的 [ADJ n] ❑ *...the north side of the mountain.* …山的北侧。 6 ADJ "**North**" is used in the names of some countries, states, and regions in the north of a larger area. (用于某区域北部的国名、州名或地名中) 北 [ADJ n] ❑ *There were demonstrations this weekend in cities throughout North America, Asia and Europe.* 本周末示威游行遍布了北美洲、亚洲和欧洲的多个城市。 7 ADJ A **north** wind is a wind that blows from the north. (风等) 来自北方的 [ADJ n] ❑ *...a bitterly cold north wind.* …一阵非常寒冷的北风。 8 N-SING **The North** is used to refer to the richer, more developed countries of the world. 北方发达国家 ["the" N] ❑ *Malaysia has emerged as the toughest critic of the North's environmental attitudes.* 马来西亚已成为对北方发达国家环境态度的最强硬的批评者。 → see **globe**

north·east ◆◆◇ /nɔrθist/

in BRIT, also use **north-east**

1 N-UNCOUNT The **northeast** is the direction which is halfway between north and east. 东北方 [also "the" N] ❑ *...the warm waters of Salt Springs Island to the northeast.* …流向东北方向的盐泉岛的温泉水。 2 N-SING **The northeast** of a place, country, or region is the part which is in the northeast. 东北部 ❑ *The northeast has been particularly hard hit..* 东北部受影响尤其严重。 3 ADV If you go **northeast**, you travel toward the northeast. 向东北 [ADV after v] ❑ *"We're going northeast," Paula told them, before they started.* "我们将朝东北方向走，" 葆拉在他们出发前告诉他们。 4 ADV Something that is **northeast of** a place is positioned to the northeast of it. 在…东北 [ADV "of" n] ❑ *This latest attack was at Careysburg, twenty miles northeast of the capital, Monrovia.* 最近这次袭击发生在凯里斯堡，首府蒙罗维亚东北方向20英里处。 5 ADJ The **northeast** edge, corner, or part of a place is the part which is toward the northeast. 东北部的 [ADJ n] ❑ *...a climate like that of our northeast coast.* …同我们东北部沿海气候相似的一种气候。

north·eastern /nɔrθistərn/

in BRIT, also use **north-eastern**

ADJ **Northeastern** means in or from the northeast of a region or country. 东北部的；来自东北部的 ❑ *...on the northeastern coast of Florida.* …在佛罗里达州的东北部海岸上。

nor·ther·ly /nɔrðərli/ ADJ A **northerly** point, area, or direction is to the north or toward the north. 北方的；向北的 ❑ *The storm is headed on a northerly path.* 风暴正朝着向北的路线移动。

north·ern ◆◆◇ /nɔrðərn/ also **Northern** ADJ **Northern** means in or from the north of a region, state, or country. 在北部的；来自北部的 [ADJ n] ❑ *Their two children were immigrants to Northern Ireland from Pennsylvania.* 他们的两个孩子是从宾夕法尼亚到北爱尔兰的移民。

north·ward /nɔrθwərd/ also **northwards** ADV **Northward** or **northwards** means toward the north. 向北 ❑ *Tropical storm Marco is pushing northward up Florida's coast.* 热带风暴"马可"正沿着佛罗里达海岸向北推进。 ● ADJ **Northward** is also an adjective. 向北的 [ADJ n] ❑ *The northward journey from Jalalabad was no more than 120 miles.* 从贾拉拉巴德向北的行程不超过120英里。

north·west ◆◆◇ /nɔrθwɛst/

in BRIT, also use **north-west**

1 N-UNCOUNT The **northwest** is the direction which is halfway between north and west. 西北方 [also "the" N] ❑ *...four miles to the northwest.* …西北方向4英里。 2 N-SING **The northwest** of a place, country, or region is the part which is toward the northwest. 西北部 ❑ *...in the extreme northwest of the country.* …在该国的最西北部。 3 ADV If you go **northwest**, you travel toward the northwest. 向西北 [ADV after v] ❑ *Take the narrow lane going northwest parallel with the railroad line.* 走那条与铁路线平行的通向西北的窄路。 4 ADV Something that is **northwest of** a place is positioned to the northwest of it. 在…西北 [ADV "of" n] ❑ *Just a couple of hours to the northwest of the capital is the wine-growing area of Hunter Valley.* 在首都的西北仅两三个小时的路程就是猎人谷的葡萄酒酿造区。 ❑ *The museum was situated in the northwest of the town, a short walk from the station.* 博物馆位于城镇的西北部，步行一小段就到车站。 5 ADJ The **northwest** part of a place, country, or region is the part which is toward the northwest. 西北部的 [ADJ n] ❑ *...the northwest coast of the United States.* …美国西北部海岸。

north·western /nɔrθwɛstərn/

in BRIT, also use **north-western**

ADJ **Northwestern** means in or from the northwest of a region or country. 在西北部的；来自西北部的 ❑ *Virtually every river in northwestern Oregon was near flood stage.* 俄勒冈西北部的差不多每条河都接近洪涝阶段了。

nose ◆◇◇ /noʊz/ (**noses, nosing, nosed**) 1 N-COUNT Your **nose** is the part of your face which sticks out above your mouth. You use it for smelling and breathing. 鼻子 ❑ *She wiped her nose with a tissue.* 她用一张纸巾擦了擦鼻子。 2 N-COUNT The **nose** of a vehicle such as an airplane or a boat is the front part of it. (飞机、船等的) 前部 ❑ *They went over to the airplane and stood near its nose.* 他们朝飞机走了过去并站在靠近机头的地方。 3 N-COUNT You can refer to your sense of smell as your **nose**. 嗅觉 ❑ *The river that runs through Middlesbrough became ugly on the eye and hard on the nose.* 那条流经米德尔斯伯勒的河变得丑不忍睹，臭不可闻。 4 V-T/V-I If a vehicle **noses** in a certain direction or if you **nose** it there, you move it slowly and carefully in that direction. 使缓慢行驶；缓慢行驶 ❑ *He could not see the driver as the car nosed forward.* 当那辆车缓慢向前行驶时，他看不见司机。 ❑ *A motorboat nosed out of the mist and nudged into the branches of a tree.* 一艘摩托艇缓缓地驶出薄雾，轻触上一棵树的枝条。 5 PHRASE If you **keep** your **nose clean**, you behave well and stay out of trouble. 行为规矩 [INFORMAL] ❑ *If you kept your nose clean, you had a job for life.* 你要是规规矩矩的，就一辈子会有工作。 6 PHRASE If you **follow** your **nose** to get to a place, you go straight ahead or follow the most obvious route. 直着往前走；沿最明显路线 ❑ *Just follow your nose and in about five minutes you're at the old railway.* 就直着往前走大约五分钟你会到达旧铁道。 7 PHRASE If you **follow** your **nose**, you do something in a particular way because you feel it should be done like that, rather than because you are following any plan or rules. 凭直觉行事 ❑ *You won't have to think, just follow your nose.* 你不必考虑，凭直觉行事就行。 8 PHRASE If you say that someone **has a nose for** something, you mean that they have a natural ability to find it or recognize it. 有发现…的能力；善于识别 ❑ *He had a nose for trouble and a brilliant tactical mind.* 他有发现问题的能力和一个精于谋略的头脑。 9 PHRASE If you say that someone **looks down** their **nose** at something or someone, you mean that they believe they are superior to that person or thing and treat them with disrespect. 轻视 [DISAPPROVAL] ❑ *I don't look down my nose at comedy.* 我不轻视喜剧。 10 PHRASE If you say that you **paid through the nose** for something, you are emphasizing that you had to pay what you consider too high a price for it. 花大价钱 [INFORMAL, EMPHASIS] ❑ *We don't like paying through the nose for our wine when eating out.* 我们在外面吃饭时不喜欢将大把的钱花在酒水上。 11 PHRASE If someone **pokes** their **nose into** something or **sticks** their **nose into** something, they try to interfere with it even though it does not concern them. 管闲事 [INFORMAL, DISAPPROVAL] ❑ *We don't like strangers who poke their noses into our affairs.* 我们不喜欢那些干预我们事务的陌生人。 12 PHRASE To **rub** someone's **nose in** something that they do not want to think about, such as a failing or a mistake they have made, means to remind them repeatedly about it. 揭 (某人的) 伤疤；抓住 (某人的过失等) 不放 [INFORMAL] ❑ *His enemies will attempt to rub his nose in past policy statements.* 他的对手们将试图揪住他过去政策声明中的纰漏不放。 13 PHRASE If you **turn up** your **nose at** something, you reject it because you think that it is not good enough for you. 对…不屑一顾 ❑ *I'm not in a financial position to turn up my nose at several hundred thousand dollars.* 我没有达到对几十万美元不屑一顾的经济境况。 14 PHRASE If you do something **under** someone's **nose**, you do it right in front of them, without trying to hide it from them.

当着…的面 ❑ *We've been married 25 years and this carrying on under my nose was the last straw.* 我们已经结婚25年了，而我眼皮底下发生的这事儿使我最终忍无可忍。 15 PHRASE If vehicles are **nose to tail**, the front of one vehicle is close behind the back of another. (车辆)首尾相接 [mainly BRIT]

in AM, use **bumper-to-bumper**

16 to put someone's **nose out of joint** → see **joint**
→ see **face, respiratory, smell**

▸ **nose around** PHRASAL VERB If you **nose around**, you look around a place that belongs to someone else, to see if you can find something interesting. 探查 [INFORMAL] ❑ *I wondered what else he'd taken and nosed around his bureau.* 我想知道他还拿走了什么，就探查了他的办事处。 ❑ *He had thought to just nose around, see what he could.* 他原本只想打探打探，看他能发现什么。

Word Partnership *nose* 的常用搭配：
ADJ. **big** nose, **bloody** nose, **broken** nose, **long** nose, **red** nose, **runny** nose, **straight** nose 1

nose·dive /noʊzdaɪv/ (**nosedives, nosediving, nosedived**) also **nose-dive** 1 V-I If prices, profits, or exchange rates **nosedive**, they suddenly fall by a large amount. (价格、利润或汇率) 暴跌 [JOURNALISM] ❑ *The value of other shares nosedived by $2.6 billion.* 其他股票市值暴跌了26亿美元。 ● N-SING **Nosedive** is also a noun. 暴跌 ❑ *The bank yesterday revealed a 30 percent nosedive in profits.* 该银行昨天透露了其利润暴跌30%。 2 V-I If something such as someone's reputation or career **nosedives**, it suddenly gets much worse. (声誉) 骤降; (事业) 突然下滑 [JOURNALISM] ❑ *Since the U.S. invasion the president's reputation has nosedived.* 自从美国入侵以来，这位总统的声誉一落千丈。 ● N-SING **Nosedive** is also a noun. 骤降 ❑ *He told the tribunal his career had "taken a nosedive" since his dismissal last year.* 他告诉法庭自从去年被解雇以来，他的职业生涯就遭受了一次直线下降。

nos·tal·gia /nɒstældʒə/ N-UNCOUNT **Nostalgia** is an affectionate feeling you have for the past, especially for a particularly happy time. (尤指对幸福时光的) 怀旧 ❑ *He might be influenced by nostalgia for the surroundings of his happy youth.* 他也许被他对快乐青年时代的环境的怀念影响了。

▲ **nos·tal·gic** /nɒstældʒɪk/ 1 ADJ **Nostalgic** things cause you to think affectionately about the past. 引起怀旧的 ❑ *Although we still depict nostalgic snow scenes on Christmas cards, winters are now very much warmer.* 虽然我们还在圣诞卡上描绘引人怀旧的雪景，但现在冬天温暖多了。 2 ADJ If you feel **nostalgic**, you think affectionately about experiences you had in the past. 怀旧的 ❑ *Many people were nostalgic for the good old days.* 很多人都怀念过去的好时光。 ● **nos·tal·gi·cal·ly** /nɒstældʒɪkli/ ADV 怀旧地 ❑ *People look back nostalgically on the war period, simply because everyone pulled together.* 人们怀旧地回忆战争时期，就因为当时大家齐心协力。

▲ **nos·tril** /nɒstrɪl/ (**nostrils**) N-COUNT Your **nostrils** are the two openings at the end of your nose. 鼻孔 ❑ *Keeping your mouth closed, breathe in through your nostrils.* 把嘴闭着，用鼻孔吸气。

nosy /noʊzi/ (**nosier, nosiest**) also **nosey** ADJ If you describe someone as **nosy**, you mean that they are interested in things which do not concern them. 爱管闲事的 [INFORMAL, DISAPPROVAL] ❑ *He was having to whisper in order to avoid being overheard by their nosy neighbors.* 他不得不低声耳语，以免被他们爱管闲事的邻居们听见。

not ♦♦♦ /nɒt/

Not is often shortened to **n't** in spoken English, and added to the auxiliary or modal verb. For example, "did not" is often shortened to "didn't."

1 NEG You use **not** with verbs to form negative statements. (与动词连用构成否定句) 不 ❑ *The sanctions are not working the way they were intended.* 制裁没有像他们原本打算的那样奏效。 ❑ *I don't trust my father anymore.* 我再也不相信我父亲了。 2 NEG You use **not** to form questions to which you expect the answer "yes." (用于构成期待肯定回答的疑问句) 难道不 ❑ *Haven't they got enough problems there already?* 难道他们那里的问题还不够多吗？ ❑ *Didn't I see you at the party last week?* 难道我在上周的聚会上没见到你吗？ 3 NEG You use **not**, usually in the form **n't**, in questions which imply that someone should have done something, or to express surprise that something is not the case. (常以**n't**的形式出现于问句中，用于暗示某人早该做某事或表示惊讶) 不 ❑ *Why didn't you do it months ago?* 为什么你几个月前不做呢？ ❑ *Why couldn't he listen to her?* 为什么他不能听她的话？ 4 NEG You use **not**, usually in the form **n't**, in question tags after a positive statement. (常以**n't**的形式用于反意疑问句的附加问句中) 不是吗 ❑ *It's crazy, isn't it?* 这真是疯了，不是吗？ ❑ *I've been a great husband, haven't I?* 我一直是个很不错的丈夫，不是吗？ 5 NEG You use **not**, usually in the form **n't**, in polite suggestions. (常以**n't**的形式用于礼貌的建议语中) 不 [POLITENESS] ❑ *Actually we do have a position in mind. Why don't you fill out our application?* 实际上我们确实在考虑设一个职位。你为什么不填一下我们的申请表呢？ 6 NEG You use **not** to represent the negative of a word, group, or clause that has just been used. (用于表示对前面出现过的单词、词组或从句的否定) 不 ❑ *"Have you found Paula?"—"I'm afraid not, Kate."* "你找到葆拉了吗？"——"恐怕还没有，凯特。" 7 NEG You can use **not** in front of "all" or "every" when you want to say something that applies only to some members of the group that you are talking about. (用于**all**或**every**之前，表示部分否定) 并非 (所有) ❑ *Not all the money, to put it mildly, has been used wisely.* 客气地讲，并非所有的钱都花得很明智。 8 NEG If something is **not** always the case, you mean that sometimes it is the case and sometimes it is not. 并非 (总是) ❑ *He didn't always win the arguments, but he often was right.* 他并非总是在辩论中获胜，但他常常是正确的。 ❑ *She couldn't always afford a babysitter.* 她并非总能雇得起一名临时保姆。 9 NEG You can use **not** or **not even** in front of "a" or "one" to emphasize that there is none at all of what is being mentioned. (连一个) 也不 [EMPHASIS] ❑ *...no office, no phone, not even a shelf on which to put my meager belongings.* 没有办公室，没有电话，甚至连个摆放我寥寥无几的物品的架子也没有。 ❑ *I sent report after report. But not one word was published.* 我寄了一篇又一篇报告，但一个字也没有发表。 10 NEG You can use **not** in front of a word referring to a distance, length of time, or other amount to say that the actual distance, time, or amount is less than the one mentioned. (用于表示距离、时间或其他数量的词之前) 不到 [NEG amount] ❑ *The tug crossed our stern not fifty yards away.* 那艘拖船在不到50码的地方与我们的船尾错过。 ❑ *...a large crowd not ten yards away waiting for a bus.* …不到10码远的一大群等公共汽车的人。 11 NEG You use **not** when you are contrasting something that is true with something that is untrue. You use this especially to indicate that people might think that the untrue statement is true. (用以对比真实和不真实的情况，尤用于可能会被误认为真实的陈述) 不是 ❑ *He has his place in the Asian team not because he is white but because he is good.* 他在亚洲队有一席之地，不是因为他是白人而是因为他很出色。 ❑ *Training is an investment not a cost.* 培训是一种投资而不是一种花费。 12 NEG You use **not** in expressions such as "not only," "not just," and "not simply" to emphasize that something is true, but it is not the whole truth. (用于**not only**，**not just**和**not simply**词组中) 不仅 [EMPHASIS] ❑ *These movies were not only making money; they were also perceived to be original.* 这些电影不仅赚钱，它们还被认为是有创意的。 ❑ *What's it going to cost us, not just in terms of money, but in terms of lives?* 它将让我们付出什么代价，不仅在钱的方面，而且还在生命方面？ 13 PHRASE You use **not that** to introduce a negative clause that contradicts something that the previous statement implies. (用于引出否定从句以与前句形成矛盾) 并非 ❑ *His death took me a year to get over; not that you're ever really over it.* 我用了一年的时间才从他的去世中恢复过来；不过永远也不可能真正恢复过来。 14 CONVENTION **Not at all** is an emphatic way of saying "No" or of agreeing that the answer to a question is "No." 一点不 [EMPHASIS] ❑ *"Sorry. I sound like Abby, don't I?"—"No. Not at all."* "抱歉。我听上去像阿比，是吗？"——"不，一点不像。" 15 CONVENTION **Not at all** is a polite way of acknowledging a person's thanks. 不用谢; 不客气 [FORMULAE] ❑ *"Thank you very much for speaking with us."—"Not at all."* "非常感谢您与我们交谈。"——"不客气。" 16 **not half** → see **half** 17 **if not** → see **if** 18 **more often than not** → see **often**

★ **no·table** /noʊtəbᵊl/ ADJ Someone or something that is **notable** is important or interesting. 值得注意的; 有趣的 ❑ *The proposed new structure is notable not only for its height, but for its shape.* 那座提议的新建筑值得注意，不仅因其高度，还因其外形。 ❑ *Mo did not want to be ruled by anyone and it is notable that she never allowed the men in her life to eclipse her.* 莫不想被任何人管制，很显然，她从不允许她生活中的男性使她黯然失色。

A **famous** person or thing is known to more people than a **well-known** one. A **notorious** person or thing is famous because they are connected with something bad or undesirable. **Infamous** is not the opposite of **famous**. It has a similar meaning to **notorious**, but is a stronger word. Someone or something that is **notable** is important or interesting.

no·tably /noʊtəbli/ 1 ADV You use **notably** to specify an important or typical example of something that you are talking about. 尤其 [ADV group/cl] ❏ *The divorce would be granted when more important problems, notably the fate of the children, had been decided.* 当更重要的问题，尤其是孩子们的命运被决定时，离婚就会获得批准。 2 ADV You can use **notably** to emphasize a particular quality that someone or something has. 明显地 [ADV adj/adv] [EMPHASIS] ❏ *Old established friends are notably absent, so it's a good opportunity to make new contacts.* 老朋友们显然都已不在身边，所以这是结交新朋友的一个好机会。

★ **no·ta·tion** /noʊteɪʃən/ (**notations**) N-VAR A system of **notation** is a set of written symbols that are used to represent something such as music or mathematics. 符号 [usu supp N] ❏ *Musical notation was conceived for the C major scale and each line and space represents a note in this scale.* 乐谱为C大音阶而构思，在这个音阶中的每一个线和间都代表一个音符。 ❏ *...some other abstract notation system like a computer language.* …一些如计算机语言的其它抽象符号系统。

notch /nɒtʃ/ (**notches, notching, notched**) 1 N-COUNT You can refer to a level on a scale of measurement or achievement as a **notch**. 等级 [JOURNALISM] ❏ *Average earnings in the economy moved up another notch in August.* 平均经济收入在8月份又上升了一级。 ❏ *In this country the good players are pulled down a notch or two.* 在这个国家优秀运动员们被降了一到两级。 2 V-T If you **notch** a success, especially in a sports contest, you achieve it. (尤指体育比赛) 赢得 [JOURNALISM] ❏ *"It took longer than we wanted," Clemens said after notching his first victory since June 9.* "用的时间比我们希望的要长，" 克莱门斯在6月9日以来赢得他的第一次胜利后说。 3 N-COUNT A **notch** is a small V-shaped or circular cut in the surface or edge of something. V形槽口；圆形凹口 ❏ *It is a myth that gunslingers in the American west cut notches in the handle of their pistol for each man they shot.* 有种传说，美国西部的枪手们每杀死一个人就在他们的枪柄上刻下一个V形记号。

▸ **notch up** PHRASAL VERB If you **notch up** something such as a score or total, you achieve it. 赢得；达到 [JOURNALISM] ❏ *He had notched up more than 25 victories worldwide.* 他已在世界范围内赢得了超过25次的胜利。

N

note ◆◆◇ /noʊt/ (**notes, noting, noted**) 1 N-COUNT A **note** is a short letter. 便条 ❏ *Stevens wrote him a note asking him to come to his apartment.* 史蒂文斯给他写了个便条让他到他的公寓来。 2 N-COUNT A **note** is something that you write down to remind yourself of something. 记录；笔记 ❏ *I knew that if I didn't make a note I would lose the thought so I asked to borrow a pen or pencil.* 我知道如果我不做一个记录我就会忘记这个想法，于是我要求借支钢笔或铅笔。 ❏ *She wasn't taking notes on the lecture.* 她没记讲座笔记。 3 N-COUNT In a book or article, a **note** is a short piece of additional information. 注释 ❏ *See Note 16 on p. 223.* 参见223页的注释16。 4 N-COUNT A **note** is a short document that has to be signed by someone and that gives official information about something. 证明；单据 ❏ *Since Mr. Bennett was going to need some time off work, he asked for a sick note.* 因为本内特先生需要请假一段时间，所以他要求开一张病假条。 5 N-COUNT In music, a **note** is the sound of a particular pitch, or a written symbol representing this sound. 音符 ❏ *She has a deep voice and doesn't even try for the high notes.* 她有一副低沉的嗓音，对高音她甚至试都不试。 6 N-SING You can use **note** to refer to a particular quality in someone's voice that shows how they are feeling. 声调；语气 ❏ *There is an unmistakable note of nostalgia in his voice when he looks back on the early years of the family business.* 在他回忆早年的家族企业时，他的声音里带有一种确定无疑的怀旧语气。 7 N-SING You can use **note** to refer to a particular feeling, impression, or atmosphere. (特别的) 感觉；印象；气氛 ❏ *Yesterday's testimony began on a note of passionate but civilized disagreement.* 昨天的证词是在一种激烈但文明的争执氛围中开始的。 ❏ *Somehow he tells these stories without a note of horror.* 不知为什么，他讲述这些故事时没有一丝害怕的感觉。 8 V-T If you **note** a fact, you become aware of it. 注意到 ❏ *The White House has noted his promise to support any attack that was designed to enforce the UN resolutions.* 白宫已经注意到他支持任何旨在加强联合国决议的抨击的承诺。 ❏ *Suddenly, I noted that the rain had stopped.* 突然，我注意到雨已经停了。 9 V-T If you tell someone to **note** something, you are drawing their attention to it. 注意 ❏ *Note the statue to Sallustio Bandini, a prominent Sienese.* 注意那座萨卢斯蒂奥·班迪尼的雕像，一个杰出的锡耶纳人。 10 V-T If you **note** something, you mention it in order to draw people's attention to it. 提到 ❏ *The report notes that export and import volumes picked up in leading economies.* 该报道提到主要经济大国的进出口额增加了。 11 V-T When you **note** something, you write it down as a record of what has happened. 记录 ❏ *"He has had his tonsils out and has been ill, too," she noted in her diary.* "他已经做了扁桃腺切除，又一直在生病。" 她在自己的日记中写道。 ❏ *They never noted the building's history of problems.* 他们从未记录过那座建筑的问题的历史。 12 N-COUNT You can refer to a banknote as a **note**. 钞票 [mainly BRIT]

in AM, usually use **bill**

13 → see also **noted, promissory note** 14 PHRASE Someone or something that is **of note** is important, worth mentioning, or well-known. 显要的；有名的 ❏ *...politicians of note.* …显要的政客们。 15 PHRASE If you **take note of** something, you pay attention to it because you think that it is important or significant. 注意 ❏ *Take note of the weather conditions.* 注意天气情况。

▸ **note down** PHRASAL VERB If you **note down** something, you write it down quickly, so that you have a record of it. 迅速记录 ❏ *She had noted down the names and she told me the story simply and factually.* 她迅速记录下那些名字，然后她简单如实地给我讲了那个故事。 ❏ *If you find a name that's on the list I've given you, note it down.* 如果你找到了我给你的那张清单上的名字，就把它记下来。

Word Partnership *note* 的常用搭配：

V. **leave** a note, **send** a note 1
find a note, **read** a note, **scribble** a note, **write** a note 1 2
make a note 2
sound a note, **strike** a note 5 7
take note of *something* 15

note·book /noʊtbʊk/ (**notebooks**) 1 N-COUNT A **notebook** is a small book for writing notes in. 笔记本 ❏ *He brought out a notebook and pen from his pocket.* 他从口袋里掏出了一个笔记本和一支钢笔。 2 N-COUNT A **notebook** computer is a small personal computer. 笔记本 (电脑) ❏ *...a range of notebook computers which allows all your important information to travel safely with you.* …使你的所有重要信息和你一起安全旅行的一系列笔记本电脑。
→ see **office**

not·ed ◆◇◇ /noʊtɪd/ ADJ To be **noted for** something you do or have means to be well known and admired for it. 知名的 ❏ *...a television program noted for its attacks on organized crime.* …以对有组织犯罪的抨击而知名的一档电视节目。

★ **note·worthy** /noʊtwɜrði/ ADJ A fact or event that is **noteworthy** is interesting, remarkable, or significant in some way. 值得关注的 [FORMAL] ❏ *It is noteworthy that the program has been shifted from its original August slot to July.* 该节目从最初的8月档移到7月值得关注。 ❏ *I found nothing particularly noteworthy to report.* 我没什么特别值得关注的事情可报告。 ❏ *The most noteworthy feature of the list is that there are no women on it.* 该名单最值得关注的是上面没有女性。

noth·ing ◆◆◆ /nʌθɪŋ/ (**nothings**) 1 PRON-INDEF-NEG **Nothing** means not a single thing, or not a single part of something. 没有一个；没有一点 ❏ *I've done nothing much since this morning.* 自从今天上午我什么都没做。 ❏ *There is nothing wrong with the car.* 那辆车没有一点毛病。 2 PRON-INDEF-NEG You use **nothing** to indicate that something or someone is not important or significant. 无关紧要的事；无足轻重的人 ❏ *Because he had always had money it meant nothing to him.* 因为他一直很有钱，所以钱对他来说无关紧要。 ❏ *Do our years together mean nothing?* 我们在一起的这些年一点都不重要吗？
● N-COUNT **Nothing** is also a noun. 无关紧要的事；无足轻重的人 ❏ *It is the picture itself that is the problem; so small, so dull. It's a nothing, really.* 是这张图片本身的问题，那么小，那么乏味。它没什么价值，真的。 3 PRON-INDEF-NEG If you say that something cost **nothing** or is worth **nothing**, you are indicating that it cost or is worth a surprisingly small amount of money. 极低的价格；极低的价值 ❏ *The furniture was threadbare; he'd obviously picked it up for nothing.* 那件家具破破烂烂；显然他没花什么钱就捡来了。 4 PRON-INDEF-NEG You use **nothing** before an adjective or 'to'-infinitive to say that something or someone does not have the quality indicated. (用于形容词或带**to**的不定式之前，表示事物或人不具备所说的性质) 没有什么 ❏ *Around the lake the countryside generally is nothing special.* 那片湖周围的乡村总的来说没什么特别的。 ❏ *There was nothing remarkable about him.* 他没有什么非凡之处。 5 PRON-INDEF-NEG You can use **nothing** before "so" and an adjective or adverb, or before a comparative, to emphasize how strong or great a particular quality is. (表示强调) 没有别的东西 [EMPHASIS] ❏ *Youngsters learn nothing so fast as how to beat the system.* 年轻人没有什么别的东西学得像如何钻制度的空子这样快。

❑ *I consider nothing more important in my life than songwriting.* 我认为我的生活中没有什么比歌曲创作更重要。 **6** PHRASE You can use **all or nothing** to say that either something must be done fully and completely or else it cannot be done at all. 要么彻底做完，要么彻底不做 ❑ *Either he went through with this thing or he did not; it was all or nothing.* 他要么把这件事做完，要么就不做，只有这两种选择。 **7** PHRASE If you say that something is **better than nothing**, you mean that it is not what is required, but that it is better to have that thing than to have nothing at all. 比没有强 ❑ *After all, 15 minutes of exercise is better than nothing.* 毕竟，15分钟的锻炼比没锻炼强。 **8** PHRASE You use **nothing but** in front of a noun, an infinitive without "to," or an "-ing" form to mean "only." (用于名词、不带**to**的不定式或**-ing**形式前) 仅仅 ❑ *All that money brought nothing but sadness and misery and tragedy.* 所有那些钱带来的仅仅是悲伤、痛苦和悲剧。 ❑ *It did nothing but make us ridiculous.* 它只是让我们显得可笑。 ❑ *He is focused on nothing but winning.* 他只关注胜利。 **9** CONVENTION People sometimes say "**It's nothing**" as a polite response after someone has thanked them for something they have done. 不用谢; 没什么 [FORMULAE] ❑ *"Thank you for the wonderful dinner."—"It's nothing," Sarah said.* "谢谢你这顿丰盛的晚餐。"——"没什么，"萨拉说道。 **10** PHRASE If you say about a story or report that there is **nothing to it**, you mean that it is untrue. 不真实 ❑ *It's all superstition, and there's nothing to it.* 这全是迷信，不是真的。 **11** PHRASE If you say about an activity that there is **nothing to it**, you mean that it is extremely easy. 轻而易举 ❑ *If you've shied away from making pancakes in the past, don't be put off – there's really nothing to it!* 如果你过去没有信心做烙饼的话，就别再被它吓着——真没什么难的。 **12** PHRASE **Nothing of the sort** is used when strongly contradicting something that has just been said. 绝无此事 [EMPHASIS] ❑ *"We're going to talk this over in my office."—"We're going to do nothing of the sort."* "我们将在我的办公室讨论这件事。"——"我们将绝对不会这么做。" **13** **nothing to write home about** → see **home** **14** **to stop at nothing** → see **stop** **15** **to think nothing of** → see **think**

no·tice ♦♦◇ /noʊtɪs/ (**notices, noticing, noticed**) **1** V-T/V-I If you **notice** something or someone, you become aware of them. 注意到; 察觉 ❑ *He stressed that people should not hesitate to contact the police if they've noticed any strangers recently.* 他强调人们最近如果注意到任何陌生人，要马上与警方联系。 ❑ *I noticed that most academics were writing papers during the summer.* 我注意到大部分学者那个暑期都在撰写论文。 ❑ *Luckily, I'd noticed where you left the car.* 幸好，我注意了你停车的地点。 ❑ *If he thought no one would notice, he's wrong.* 如果他认为无人察觉，那他就错了。 **2** N-COUNT A **notice** is a written announcement in a place where everyone can read it. 告示 ❑ *Notices in the waiting room requested that you neither smoke nor spit.* 等候室的告示要求人们不要吸烟也不要随地吐痰。 ❑ *A few guest houses had "No Vacancies" notices in their windows.* 几家旅社在他们的窗户上贴出了"客满"的告示。 **3** N-UNCOUNT If you give **notice** about something that is going to happen, you give a warning in advance that it is going to happen. 事先通知 ❑ *Interest is paid monthly. Three months' notice is required for withdrawals.* 利息按月给付。提款要求提前三个月通知。 ❑ *The insured must be given at least 10 days' notice of cancellation.* 取消保险必须给被保险人至少十天的事先通知。 **4** N-COUNT A **notice** is a formal announcement in a newspaper or magazine about something that has happened or is going to happen. 启事 ❑ *I spotted a notice in a local newspaper.* 我在当地一家报纸上看到了一则启事。 **5** N-COUNT A **notice** is one of a number of letters that are similar or exactly the same which an organization sends to people in order to give them information or ask them to do something. 通告 ❑ *Bonus notices were issued each year from head office to local agents.* 红利通告每年由总公司发给各地方代理商。 **6** N-COUNT A **notice** is a written article in a newspaper or magazine in which someone gives their opinion of a play, movie, or concert. (报刊上的) 评论 [BRIT]

in AM, use **review**

7 PHRASE **Notice** is used in expressions such as "**on short notice**," "**at a moment's notice**," or "**at twenty-four hours' notice**," to indicate that something can or must be done within a short period of time. 提前…时间通知 ❑ *There's no one available on such short notice to take her class.* 仅提前这么短时间通知，找不到人接她的课。 ❑ *I live just a mile away, so I can usually be available on short notice.* 我就住在一英里远，所以我通常接到通知就能到。 **8** PHRASE If a situation is said to exist **until further notice**, it will continue for an uncertain length of time until someone changes it. 直到另行通知 ❑ *The bad news was that all flights had been canceled until further notice.* 坏消息是所有航班都已被取消，何时恢复另行通知。 **9** PHRASE If an employer **gives** an employee **notice**, the employer tells the employee that he or she must leave his or her job within a short fixed period of time. 通知某人在限期内离职 [BUSINESS] ❑ *The next morning I telephoned him and gave him his notice.* 第二天早晨我给他打电话通知他在限期内离职。 **10** PHRASE If you **give notice** or **hand in notice** you tell your employer that you intend to leave your job soon, within a set period of time. You can also **hand in** your **notice**. 提出辞职 [BUSINESS] ❑ *He handed in his notice at the bank and ruined his promising career.* 他向银行提交了辞呈，毁掉了他的大好前程。 **11** PHRASE If you **take notice of** a particular fact or situation, you behave in a way that shows that you are aware of it. 提起注意 ❑ *We want the government to take notice of what we think they should do for single parents.* 我们希望政府对我们希望他们为单亲父母亲应该做的事情提起注意。 **12** PHRASE If you **take no notice of** someone or something, you do not consider them to be important enough to affect what you think or what you do. 不理会 ❑ *They took no notice of him, he did not stand out, he was in no way remarkable.* 他们对他不予理会，他不出众，一点也不优秀。

Thesaurus *notice* 另参见：

V.	note, observe, perceive, see **1**
N.	advertisement, announcement **2** **4**

Word Partnership *notice* 的常用搭配：

N.	notice **a change**, notice **a difference** **1**
V.	**begin to** notice, **fail to** notice, **pretend not to** notice **1**
	receive notice, **serve** notice **3**
	give notice **3** **9** **10**

no·tice·able /noʊtɪsəbᵊl/ ADJ Something that is **noticeable** is very obvious, so that it is easy to see, hear, or recognize. 显而易见的 ❑ *It is noticeable that women do not have the rivalry that men have.* 显而易见的是女性没有像男性那样的争强好胜。 ● **no·tice·ably** ADV 显而易见地 ❑ *Standards of living were deteriorating rather noticeably.* 生活水平相当明显地下降了。

Word Partnership *noticeable* 的常用搭配：

ADV.	**barely** noticeable, **hardly** noticeable, **less** noticeable, **more** noticeable
N.	noticeable **change**, noticeable **difference**, noticeable **improvement**

no·tice·board /noʊtɪsbɔrd/ (**noticeboards**) N-COUNT A **noticeboard** is a board which is usually attached to a wall in order to display notices giving information about something. 布告牌 [mainly BRIT]

in AM, usually use **bulletin board**

no·ti·fi·ca·tion /noʊtɪfɪkeɪʃᵊn/ (**notifications**) N-VAR If you are given **notification of** something, you are officially informed of it. 正式通知 ❑ *Names of the dead and injured are being withheld pending notification of relatives.* 伤亡者的姓名在通知亲属前不被公布。

no·ti·fy /noʊtɪfaɪ/ (**notifies, notifying, notified**) V-T If you **notify** someone of something, you officially inform them about it. 通知 [FORMAL] ❑ *The skipper notified the coastguard of the tragedy.* 船长通知了海岸警卫队这一灾难。 ❑ *Earlier this year they were notified that their homes were to be cleared away.* 今年早些时候他们被通知说他们的家将被拆除。

no·tion ♦◇◇ /noʊʃᵊn/ (**notions**) **1** N-COUNT A **notion** is an idea or belief about something. 想法 ❑ *We each have a notion of just what kind of person we'd like to be.* 我们每个人都对自己要做个什么样的人有各自的想法。 ❑ *I reject absolutely the notion that privatization of our industry is now inevitable.* 我绝不接受我们的产业私有化在当今是不可避免的这种看法。 **2** N-PLURAL **Notions** are small articles for sewing, such as buttons, zips, and thread. 缝纫用的杂物 (如扣子、拉锁、线等) [AM]

Thesaurus *notion* 另参见：

N.	concept, idea, opinion, thought **1**

no·to·ri·ety /noʊtəraɪɪti/ N-UNCOUNT To achieve **notoriety** means to become well known for something bad. 声名狼藉 ❑ *He achieved notoriety as chief counsel to President Nixon in the Watergate break-in.* 在水门事件中，他作为尼克松总统的首席辩护律师被搞得声名狼藉。

★ **no·to·ri·ous** /noʊtɔriəs/ ADJ To be **notorious** means to be well known for something bad. 声名狼藉的 ❑ *...an area notorious for* drugs, crime and violence. …一个因毒品、犯罪和暴力而声名狼藉的地区。 ● **no·to·ri·ous·ly** ADV 声名狼藉地 ❑ *The train company is overstaffed and notoriously inefficient.* 这家铁路公司人员超编，且出了名地没有效率。 ❑ *He worked mainly in New York City where living space is notoriously at a premium.* 他主要在纽约市工作，那里的生存空间出了名地昂贵。

> A **famous** person or thing is known to more people than a **well-known** one. A **notorious** person or thing is famous because they are connected with something bad or undesirable. **Infamous** is not the opposite of **famous**. It has a similar meaning to **notorious**, but is a stronger word. Someone or something that is **notable** is important or interesting.

★ **not·with·stand·ing** /nɒtwɪθstændɪŋ, -wɪð-/ PREP If something is true **notwithstanding** something else, it is true in spite of that other thing. 尽管 [FORMAL] ❑ *He despised William Pitt, notwithstanding the similar views they both held.* 他瞧不起威廉·皮特，尽管他们俩所持有的观点相似。 ● ADV **Notwithstanding** is also an adverb. 尽管 [n ADV] ❑ *His relations with colleagues, differences of opinion notwithstanding, were unfailingly friendly.* 他与同事们尽管有意见分歧，但关系一直很融洽。

nought /nɔt/ (**noughts**) NUM **Nought** is the number 0. 零 [mainly BRIT]

in AM, usually use **zero**

Nought·ies also **noughties** /nɔtiz/ N-PLURAL The **Noughties** is the decade from 2000 to 2009. 21世纪的头10年 [INFORMAL] ❑ *...the economic realities of the noughties.* …21世纪头10年的经济现实。

noun /naʊn/ (**nouns**) 1 N-COUNT A **noun** is a word such as "car," "love," or "Anne" which is used to refer to a person or thing. 名词 2 → see also **count noun, proper noun**

nour·ish /nɜrɪʃ/ (**nourishes, nourishing, nourished**) V-T To **nourish** a person, animal, or plant means to provide them with the food that is necessary for life, growth, and good health. 为…提供营养 ❑ *The food she eats nourishes both her and the baby.* 她吃的食物为她和婴儿提供营养。 ● **nour·ish·ing** ADJ 有营养的 ❑ *Most of these nourishing substances are in the yolk of the egg.* 这些营养物质大部分在蛋黄里。

N

nour·ish·ment /nɜrɪʃmənt/ 1 N-UNCOUNT If something provides a person, animal, or plant with **nourishment**, it provides them with the food that is necessary for life, growth, and good health. 营养 ❑ *The mother provides the embryo with nourishment and a place to grow.* 母亲为胎儿提供营养和一个生长的地方。 2 N-UNCOUNT The action of nourishing someone or something, or the experience of being nourished, can be referred to as **nourishment**. 营养的供给; 营养的吸收 ❑ *Sugar gives quick relief to hunger but provides no lasting nourishment.* 糖能快速缓解饥饿感，但不提供持久的营养。

Nov. **Nov.** is a written abbreviation for **November**. 11月 ❑ *The first ballot is on Tuesday Nov. 20.* 第一轮投票是在11月20日，星期二。

Word Link *nov ≈ new : innovate, novel, renovate*

nov·el ♦♦◇ /nɒvᵊl/ (**novels**) 1 N-COUNT A **novel** is a long written story about imaginary people and events. 长篇小说 ❑ *...a novel by Herman Hesse.* …一部赫尔曼·赫西写的长篇小说。 2 ADJ **Novel** things are new and different from anything that has been done, experienced, or made before. 新奇的 ❑ *Protesters found a novel way of demonstrating against steeply rising oil prices.* 抗议者们找到一种新奇的示威方式来反对石油价格飙升。
→ see **library**

nov·el·ist /nɒvəlɪst/ (**novelists**) N-COUNT A **novelist** is a person who writes novels. 小说家 ❑ *The key to success as a romantic novelist is absolute belief in your story.* 一个浪漫派小说家成功的关键在于对自己故事的绝对信念。
→ see **fantasy**

★ **nov·el·ty** /nɒvᵊlti/ (**novelties**) 1 N-UNCOUNT **Novelty** is the quality of being different, new, and unusual. 新奇 ❑ *In the contemporary western world, rapidly changing styles cater to a desire for novelty and individualism.* 在当代西方世界，快速变换着的款式迎合了人们对新奇和独特性的追求。 2 N-COUNT A **novelty** is something that is new and therefore interesting. 新奇的事物 ❑ *Stores really like orange cauliflower because it's a novelty, it's something different.* 商店真地喜欢橘黄色花椰菜，因为它是一种新奇的东西，与众不同。 3 N-COUNT **Novelties** are cheap toys, ornaments, or other objects that are sold as presents or souvenirs. 新奇的小玩意儿 ❑ *At Easter, we give them plastic eggs filled with small toys, novelties, and coins.* 在复活节，我们送给他们装有小玩具、新奇的小玩意儿和硬币的塑料蛋。

No·vem·ber ♦♦♦ /noʊvɛmbər/ (**Novembers**) N-VAR **November** is the eleventh month of the year in the Western calendar. 11月 ❑ *He arrived in London in November 1939.* 他于1939年11月到达伦敦。

nov·ice /nɒvɪs/ (**novices**) 1 N-COUNT A **novice** is someone who has been doing a job or other activity for only a short time and so is not experienced at it. 新手 ❑ *I'm a novice at these things, Lieutenant. You're the professional.* 在这些事情上我是一名新手，中尉。你是行家。 2 N-COUNT In a monastery or convent, a **novice** is a person who is preparing to become a monk or nun. 见习修士; 见习修女

now ♦♦♦ /naʊ/ 1 ADV You use **now** to refer to the present time, often in contrast to a time in the past or the future. 现在 ❑ *She's a widow now.* 她现在是一个寡妇。 ❑ *But we are now a much more fragmented society.* 但是我们现在是一个更加四分五裂的社会。 ● PRON **Now** is also a pronoun. 现在 ❑ *Now is the time when we must all live as economically as possible.* 现在是我们都必须尽可能节俭度日的时候了。 2 ADV If you do something **now**, you do it immediately. 马上 [ADV after v] ❑ *I'm sorry, but I must go now.* 对不起，但是我得马上走。 ● PRON **Now** is also a pronoun. 马上 ❑ *Now is your chance to talk to him.* 马上就是你和他谈话的机会了。 3 CONJ You use **now** or **now that** to indicate that an event has occurred and as a result something else may or will happen. 既然 ❑ *Now you're settled, why don't you take up some serious study?* 既然你安顿下来了，为什么不做些认真的研究呢？ 4 ADV You use **now** to indicate that a particular situation is the result of something that has recently happened. 这样一来 ❑ *Mrs. Chandra has received one sweater for each of her five children and says that the winter will not be so hard now.* 钱德拉太太已经收到了发给她5个孩子每人一件的毛衫，并且说这样一来冬天就不会那么难过了。 ❑ *She told me not to repeat it, but now I don't suppose it matters.* 她告诉我不要重复它，但是这样一来我认为它不重要了。 5 ADV In stories and accounts of past events, **now** is used to refer to the particular time that is being written or spoken about. 这会儿; 那时候 ❑ *She felt a little better now.* 这会儿她觉得好点儿了。 ❑ *It was too late now for Blake to lock his room door.* 布莱克那时锁他的房门已经太晚了。 6 ADV You use **now** in statements which specify the length of time up to the present that something has lasted. 到现在 ❑ *They've been married now for 30 years.* 他们结婚至今已30年。 ❑ *They have been missing for a long time now.* 到现在他们已经失踪很长时间了。 7 ADV You say "**Now**" or "**Now then**" to indicate to the person or people you are with that you want their attention, or that you are about to change the subject. (用于引起注意或用于转换话题) 好了 [ADV cl] [SPOKEN] ❑ *"Now then," Max said, "to get back to the point."* "好了，"马克斯说："回到正题。" ❑ *Now then, what's the trouble?* 好了，出什么问题了？ 8 ADV You use **now** to give a slight emphasis to a request or command. (用于婉转地强调请求或命令) 好了 [ADV with cl] [SPOKEN] ❑ *Come on now. You know you must be hungry.* 好了。你看你一定是饿了。 ❑ *Come and sit down here, now.* 好了，来坐在这里吧。 9 ADV You can say "**Now**" to introduce information which is relevant to the part of a story or account that you have reached, and which needs to be known before you can continue. 你要知道 (用于信息承上启下) [ADV cl] [SPOKEN] ❑ *My son went to Aspen, in Colorado. Now he and his wife are people who love a quiet vacation.* 我儿子去了科罗拉多的阿斯彭。你要知道，他和他妻子是喜欢安静假期的人。 10 ADV You say "**Now**" to introduce something which contrasts with what you have just said. 然而 [ADV cl] [SPOKEN] ❑ *Now, if it was me, I'd want to do more than just change the locks.* 然而，如果是我，我要做的远不只是换换锁。 11 PHRASE If you say that something happens **now and then** or **every now and again**, you mean that it happens sometimes but not very often or regularly. 偶尔 ❑ *My father has a collection of magazines to which I return every now and then.* 我父亲收藏杂志，我偶尔会翻阅一下。 12 PHRASE If you say that something will happen **any day now**, **any moment now**, or **any time now**, you mean that it will happen very soon. 不久 ❑ *Jim expects to be sent to Europe any day now.* 吉姆期待不久就被派往欧洲。 13 PHRASE **Just now** means a very short time ago. 刚才 [SPOKEN] ❑ *You looked pretty upset just now.* 你刚才看上去很沮丧。 ❑ *I spoke just now of being in love.* 我刚才说到恋爱了。 14 PHRASE You use **just now** when you want to say that a particular situation exists at the time when you are speaking, although it may change in the future. 此刻 [SPOKEN] ❑ *I'm pretty busy just now.* 我此刻很忙。 15 PHRASE People such as television hosts sometimes use **now for** when they are going to start talking about a different subject or start presenting a new activity. 现在转到 (另一个话题或活动)

[SPOKEN] ❑ *And now for something completely different.* 现在谈点完全不同的事情。

nowa·days /naʊədeɪz/ ADV **Nowadays** means at the present time, in contrast with the past. 如今 [ADV with cl] ❑ *Nowadays it's acceptable for women to be ambitious. But it wasn't then.* 如今女人有雄心是可以接受的。但在那时候不行。

no·where ♦◇◇ /noʊweər/ **1** ADV You use **nowhere** to emphasize that a place has more of a particular quality than any other place, or that it is the only place where something happens or exists. 任何其他地方都不 [EMPHASIS] ❑ *Nowhere is language a more serious issue than in Hawaii.* 语言在任何地方都不像在夏威夷那样是个严重的问题。 ❑ *This kind of forest exists nowhere else in the world.* 这种森林在世界任何其他地方都没有。 **2** ADV You use **nowhere** when making negative statements to say that a suitable place of the specified kind does not exist. 没有任何地方 ❑ *There was nowhere to hide and nowhere to run.* 没有任何地方可藏，也没有任何地方可逃。 ❑ *I have nowhere else to go, nowhere in the world.* 我无别处可去，在这个世界没有任何可去的地方。 **3** ADV You use **nowhere** to indicate that something or someone cannot be seen or found. 任何地方都没有 ❑ *Michael glanced anxiously down the corridor, but Wilfred was nowhere to be seen.* 迈克尔焦虑地顺着走廊扫视，但任何地方都没有威尔弗雷德的身影。 ❑ *The escaped prisoner was nowhere in sight.* 那个越狱的囚犯已无踪影。 **4** ADV You can use **nowhere** to refer in a general way to small, unimportant, or uninteresting places. 无名的小地方 ❑ *...endless paths that led nowhere in particular.* …不特别通往什么名胜的无尽头的小路。 **5** ADV If you say that something or someone appears **from nowhere** or **out of nowhere**, you mean that they appear suddenly and unexpectedly. 无故突然出现 ["from/out of" ADV] ❑ *A car came from nowhere, and I had to jump back into the hedge just in time.* 一辆轿车不知从哪里突然开了过来，我不得不赶紧向后跳进篱笆，险些来不及。 **6** ADV You use **nowhere** to mean not in any part of a text, speech, or argument. (在文本、演讲或争论中) 任何地方都没有 [EMPHASIS] ❑ *He nowhere offers concrete historical background to support his arguments.* 他在任何地方都没有给出具体的历史背景来支持他的论点。 ❑ *Point taken, but nowhere did we suggest that this yacht's features were unique.* 你说的是，但是我们在任何地方都没有表示这艘游艇的特点是独一无二的。 **7** PHRASE If you say that a place is **in the middle of nowhere**, you mean that it is a long way from other places. 在遥远偏僻处 ❑ *At dusk we pitched camp in the middle of nowhere.* 黄昏时我们在遥远偏僻的地方搭起了帐篷。 **8** PHRASE If you use **nowhere near** in front of a word or expression, you are emphasizing that the real situation is very different from, or has not yet reached, the state which that word or expression suggests. 远非 [EMPHASIS] ❑ *He's nowhere near recovered yet from his experiences.* 他远未从他的经历中恢复过来。

Word Partnership *nowhere* 的常用搭配：
v. nowhere **to be found**, nowhere **to be seen**, ***have*** nowhere **to go**, ***have*** nowhere **to hide**, ***have*** nowhere **to run** **2** **3**
go nowhere **4**

no-win situ·ation (**no-win situations**) N-COUNT If you are in a **no-win situation**, any action you take will fail to benefit you in any way. 只输无赢的情况 ❑ *It was a no-win situation. Either she pretended she hated Ned and felt awful or admitted she loved him and felt even worse!* 这是一个只输无赢的情形。如果她假装讨厌内德，她会觉得痛苦；而如果她承认喜欢他，她会感觉更难受！

▲ **nu·ance** /nuɑns/ (**nuances**) N-VAR A **nuance** is a small difference in sound, feeling, appearance, or meaning. (声音、感觉、外貌或意义等方面的) 细微差别 ❑ *We can use our eyes and facial expressions to communicate virtually every subtle nuance of emotion there is.* 我们可以用眼睛和面部表情来如实地传达情感上的每一丝细微差别。

nu·clear ♦♦◇ /nukliər/ **1** ADJ **Nuclear** means relating to the nuclei of atoms, or to the energy released when these nuclei are split or combined. 核的 [ADJ n] ❑ *...a nuclear power station.* …一座核电站。 ❑ *...nuclear energy.* …核能。 **2** ADJ **Nuclear** means relating to weapons that explode by using the energy released when the nuclei of atoms are split or combined. 核武器的 [ADJ n] ❑ *They rejected a demand for the removal of all nuclear weapons.* 他们拒绝了清除所有核武器的要求。
→ see **energy**

nu·clear re·ac·tor (**nuclear reactors**) N-COUNT A **nuclear reactor** is a machine which is used to produce nuclear energy or the place where this machine and other related machinery and equipment is kept. 核反应堆 ❑ *The nuclear reactor was not damaged in the lightning storm that struck late last night.* 核反应堆在昨晚后半夜的雷雨中没有受损。

nu·cleus /nukliəs/ (**nuclei** /nukliaɪ/) **1** N-COUNT The **nucleus** of an atom or cell is the central part of it. (原子或细胞) 核 ❑ *Neutrons and protons are bound together in the nucleus of an atom.* 在一个原子的核内，中子和质子聚合在一起。 **2** N-COUNT **The nucleus of** a group of people or things is the small number of members which form the most important part of the group. 核心 ❑ *Matt Cummings and Liko Soules-Ono form the nucleus of the team.* 马特・卡明斯和莱克・索尔斯-奥诺形成了这个团队的核心。

▲ **nude** /nud/ (**nudes**) **1** ADJ A **nude** person is not wearing any clothes. 裸体的 ❑ *The occasional nude bather comes here.* 偶尔裸浴的那个人来到这里。 ● PHRASE If you do something **in the nude**, you are not wearing any clothes. If you paint or draw someone **in the nude**, they are not wearing any clothes. 裸体中 ❑ *Sleeping in the nude, if it suits you, is not a bad idea.* 如果适合你的话，光着身子睡觉并不是一个坏主意。 **2** N-COUNT A **nude** is a picture or statue of a person who is not wearing any clothes. A **nude** is also a person in a picture who is not wearing any clothes. 裸体画; 裸体雕像; 画像中裸体的人 ❑ *He was one of Australia's most distinguished artists, renowned for his portraits, landscapes, and nudes.* 他是澳大利亚最杰出的艺术家之一，以肖像画、风景画和裸体画而闻名。

nudge /nʌdʒ/ (**nudges, nudging, nudged**) **1** V-T If you **nudge** someone, you push them gently, usually with your elbow, in order to draw their attention to something. (常用肘为引起注意) 轻推 ❑ *I nudged Stan and pointed again.* 我轻推了推斯坦，又指了一下。 ● N-COUNT **Nudge** is also a noun. (用肘) 轻推 ❑ *She slipped her arm under his and gave him a nudge.* 她迅速地把胳膊放在他的胳膊下面，给了他轻轻一推。 **2** V-T If you **nudge** someone or something into a place or position, you gently push them there. 把…轻轻地推动 ❑ *Edna Swinson nudged him into the sitting room.* 埃德娜・斯温森把他轻轻地推进了起居室。 ● N-COUNT **Nudge** is also a noun. 轻轻的推动 ❑ *McKinnon gave the wheel another slight nudge to starboard.* 麦金农把轮子向船的右舷又轻推了一下。 **3** V-T If you **nudge** someone into doing something, you gently persuade them to do it. 好言说服 ❑ *Bit by bit Bob had nudged Fritz into selling his controlling interest.* 鲍勃一点一点地说服弗里茨卖掉自己的控股权。 ❑ *Foreigners must use their power not simply to punish the country but to nudge it toward greater tolerance.* 外国人动用他们的力量，不应仅仅是为了惩罚这个国家而是要说服该国使之变得更宽容。 ● N-COUNT **Nudge** is also a noun. 说服 ❑ *I had a feeling that the challenge appealed to him. All he needed was a nudge.* 我有一种感觉这个挑战吸引了他。他所需要的只是一点说服。

nu·dity /nudɪti/ N-UNCOUNT **Nudity** is the state of wearing no clothes. 裸体 ❑ *...constant nudity and bad language on TV.* …电视上不断出现的裸体画面和脏话。

nui·sance /nusᵊns/ (**nuisances**) N-COUNT If you say that someone or something is a **nuisance**, you mean that they annoy you or cause you a lot of problems. 令人讨厌的人或事物; 麻烦的人或事情 ❑ *He could be a bit of a nuisance when he was drunk.* 他喝醉时会是一个有点令人讨厌的人。 ❑ *Sorry to be a nuisance.* 对不起，麻烦一下。 ● PHRASE If someone **makes a nuisance of** themselves, they behave in a way that annoys other people. 惹人讨厌。

null /nʌl/ PHRASE If an agreement, a declaration, or the result of an election is **null and void**, it is not legally valid. 无法律效力的 ❑ *A spokeswoman said the agreement had been declared null and void.* 一位女发言人说那个协议已被宣布为无效的。
→ see **zero**

▲ **numb** /nʌm/ (**numbs, numbing, numbed**) **1** ADJ If a part of your body is **numb**, you cannot feel anything there. 麻木的 ❑ *He could feel his fingers growing numb at their tips.* 他能感觉到他的手指尖正在变得麻木。 ● **numb·ness** N-UNCOUNT 麻木 ❑ *I have recently been suffering from pain and numbness in my hands.* 近来我双手一直疼痛、麻木。 **2** ADJ If you are **numb with** shock, fear, or grief, you are so shocked, frightened, or upset that you cannot think clearly or feel any emotion. 木然的 ❑ *The mother, numb with grief, has trouble speaking.* 那位母亲，由于悲伤而木然，说不出话来。 ● **numb·ness** N-UNCOUNT 木然 ❑ *Many men become more aware of emotional numbness in their 40s.* 很多男性四十多岁时愈发意识到自己情感上的麻木。 **3** V-T If an event or experience **numbs** you, you can no longer think clearly or feel any emotion. 使木呆 ❑ *For a while the shock of Philippe's letter numbed her.* 收到菲利普来信的惊愕让她木呆了好一会儿。

n

• **numbed** ADJ 惊呆的 ❑ *I'm so numbed with shock that I can hardly think.* 我被惊呆了，以致几乎无法思考。 **4** V-T If cold weather, a drug, or a blow **numbs** a part of your body, you can no longer feel anything in it. 使失去知觉 ❑ *The cold numbed my fingers.* 寒冷使我的手指失去了知觉。 ❑ *An injection of local anesthetic is usually given first to numb the area.* 通常先局部麻药注射使这一部位失去知觉。

num·ber ♦♦♦ /nʌmbər/ (**numbers, numbering, numbered**) **1** N-COUNT A **number** is a word such as "two," "nine," or "twelve," or a symbol such as 1, 3, or 47. You use numbers to say how many things you are referring to or where something comes in a series. 数字；号码 ❑ *No, I don't know the room number.* 不，我不知道房间号。 ❑ *Stan Laurel was born at number 3, Argyll Street.* 斯坦・劳雷尔出生于阿盖尔街3号。 **2** N-COUNT You use **number** with words such as "large" or "small" to say approximately how many things or people there are. 数量 ❑ *Quite a considerable number of interviews are going on.* 许许多多的面试正在进行。 ❑ *I have had an enormous number of letters from single parents.* 我收到了大量单亲家长的来信。 **3** N-SING If there are **a number of** things or people, there are several of them. If there are **any number of** things or people, there is a large quantity of them. 几个；许多 ❑ *I seem to remember that Sam told a number of lies.* 我记得好像萨姆撒过一些谎。 **4** N-UNCOUNT You can refer to someone's or something's position in a list of the most successful or most popular of a particular type of thing as, for example, **number** one or **number** two. (排名) 第…号 ❑ *Martin now faces the world number one, Jansher Khan of Pakistan.* 马丁现在面对的是世界头号选手，巴基斯坦的詹舍尔汉。 ❑ *Before you knew it, the single was at number 90 in the U.S. singles charts.* 转眼间这张单曲唱片在美国单曲唱片排行榜上排第90位了。 **5** V-T If a group of people or things **numbers** a particular total, that is how many there are. 总计 ❑ *They told me that their village numbered 100.* 他们告诉我他们村共有100人。 **6** N-COUNT A **number** is the series of numbers that you dial when you are making a telephone call. 电话号码 ❑ *...a list of names and telephone numbers.* …一张姓名和电话号码单子。 ❑ *My number is 414-3925.* 我的电话号码是414-3925。 **7** N-COUNT You can refer to a short piece of music, a song, or a dance as a **number**. 一首（歌曲、乐曲）；一段（舞蹈） ❑ *..."Unforgettable," a number that was written and performed in 1951.* …《难以忘怀》，一首在1951年创作并演唱的歌曲。 **8** V-T If someone or something **is numbered among** a particular group, they are believed to belong in that group. 把…列入 [FORMAL] ❑ *Lech Walesa and Nelson Mandela are numbered among my personal heroes.* 莱奇・维尔萨和纳尔逊・曼德拉被列入了我心目中的英雄。 **9** V-T If you **number** something, you mark it with a number, usually starting at 1. 把…编号 ❑ *He cut his paper up into tiny squares, and he numbered each one.* 他把纸裁成小方块并给每个方块编号。 **10** → see also **serial number**
→ see **mathematics, zero**

num·ber one (**number ones**) **1** ADJ **Number one** means better, more important, or more popular than anything else or anyone else of its kind. 头等的 [ADJ n] [INFORMAL] ❑ *The economy is the number one issue by far.* 到目前为止经济是头等大事。 **2** N-COUNT In popular music, the **number one** is the best-selling recording in any one week, or the group or person who has made that recording. 最畅销的唱片；最畅销的歌手 [INFORMAL] ❑ *Paula is the only artist to achieve four number ones from a debut album.* 葆拉是惟一一位首发专辑获得4个畅销榜冠军的音乐家。

num·ber plate (**number plates**) also **numberplate** N-COUNT A **number plate** is the same as a **license plate.** 车号牌 [BRIT]

Word Link *numer ≈ number : innumerable, numerical, numerous*

★ **nu·meri·cal** /numɛrɪkᵊl/ ADJ **Numerical** means expressed in numbers or relating to numbers. 用数字表达的；数字的 ❑ *Your job is to group them by letter and put them in numerical order.* 你的工作是把它们按字母编组，再把它们按数字顺序排序。 • **nu·meri·cal·ly** ADV 用数字表达地；数字地 ❑ *...a numerically coded color chart.* …一张用数字编码的比色表。

nu·mer·ous ♦◇◇ /numərəs/ ADJ If people or things are **numerous**, they exist or are present in large numbers. 许多的 ❑ *Sex crimes were just as numerous as they are today.* 当时的性犯罪与现在一样多。

Word Partnership *numerous* 的常用搭配:
N. numerous **attempts**, numerous **examples**, numerous **occasions**, numerous **problems**, numerous **times**

▲ **nun** /nʌn/ (**nuns**) N-COUNT A **nun** is a member of a female religious community. 尼姑；修女 ❑ *Mr. Thomas was taught by the Catholic nuns whose school he attended to work and study hard.* 托马斯先生受教于天主教修女，在修女开办的学校里他专心工作，刻苦学习。

nurse ♦◇◇ /nɜrs/ (**nurses, nursing, nursed**) **1** N-COUNT; N-TITLE; N-VOC A **nurse** is a person whose job is to care for people who are ill. 护士 ❑ *She had spent 29 years as a nurse.* 她已当了29年护士。 **2** V-T If you **nurse** someone, you care for them when they are ill. 护理 ❑ *All the years he was sick my mother had nursed him.* 在他有病的那些年里，我母亲一直照顾他。 **3** V-T If you **nurse** an illness or injury, you allow it to get better by resting as much as possible. 调治 ❑ *We're going to go home and nurse our colds.* 我们打算回家调治感冒。 **4** V-T If you **nurse** an emotion or desire, you feel it strongly for a long time. 怀有 ❑ *Jane still nurses the pain of rejection.* 简依然怀着被拒绝的痛苦。

Word Partnership *nurse* 的常用搭配:
N. nurse's **aide, visiting** nurse **1**

nurse·ry /nɜrsəri/ (**nurseries**) **1** N-COUNT A **nursery** is a room in a family home in which the young children of the family sleep or play. 育儿室 ❑ *He has painted murals in his children's nursery.* 他在他家的育儿室画上了壁画。 **2** N-COUNT A **nursery** is a place where children who are not old enough to go to school are cared for. 托儿所 [also "at/from/to" N] ❑ *She puts her baby in this nursery and then goes back to work.* 她把孩子送到这家托儿所然后回去上班。 **3** N-VAR **Nursery** is a school for very young children. 幼儿园 [BRIT]

in AM, use **nursery school, preschool**

4 N-COUNT A **nursery** is a place where plants are grown in order to be sold. 苗圃 ❑ *The garden, developed over the past 35 years, includes a nursery.* 这个有35年历史的园子里有一个苗圃。

nurse·ry school (**nursery schools**) N-VAR A **nursery school** is a school for very young children. 幼儿园 ❑ *She began her professional career as a nursery school teacher.* 她从一名幼儿园教师开始了职业生涯。

nurs·ing /nɜrsɪŋ/ N-UNCOUNT **Nursing** is the profession of caring for people who are ill. 护理工作 ❑ *She had no aptitude for nursing.* 她没有从事护理工作的能力。

nurs·ing home (**nursing homes**) N-COUNT A **nursing home** is a residence for old or sick people. 养老院；疗养院 ❑ *Isaac Binger has died in a nursing home in Florida at the age of 87.* 艾萨克・班热在佛罗里达的一家养老院里去世了，享年87岁。

★ **nur·ture** /nɜrtʃər/ (**nurtures, nurturing, nurtured**) **1** V-T If you **nurture** something such as a young child or a young plant, you care for it while it is growing and developing. 养育 [FORMAL] ❑ *Parents want to know the best way to nurture and raise their child to adulthood.* 父母们想了解把他们的孩子养育成人的最好方法。 **2** V-T If you **nurture** plans, ideas, or people, you encourage them or help them to develop. 培养 [FORMAL] ❑ *She had always nurtured great ambitions for her son.* 她一直在培养她儿子的雄心大志。 ❑ *...parents whose political views were nurtured in the sixties.* …政治观点形成于60年代的父母们。 **3** N-UNCOUNT **Nurture** is care and encouragement that is given to someone while they are growing and developing. 培育 ❑ *The human organism learns partly by nature, partly by nurture.* 人的学习能力部分是先天的，部分是后天培育的。

nut /nʌt/ (**nuts**) **1** N-COUNT The firm shelled fruit of some trees and bushes are called **nuts.** Some nuts can be eaten. 坚果 ❑ *Nuts and seeds are good sources of vitamin E.* 坚果和种子是维生素E的良好来源。 **2** → see also **peanut** **3** N-COUNT A **nut** is a thick metal ring which you screw onto a metal rod called a bolt. Nuts and bolts are used to hold things such as pieces of machinery together. 螺母 ❑ *If you want to repair the wheels you just undo the four nuts.* 如果你要修理轮子，只拧下那4个螺母就行了。 **4** N-COUNT If you describe someone as, for example, a baseball **nut** or a health **nut**, you mean that they are extremely enthusiastic about the thing mentioned. 狂热者 [INFORMAL] ❑ *...Annie, the girlfriend who was a true baseball nut.* …女朋友安妮，一个十足的棒球迷。 **5** ADJ If you are **nuts about** something or someone, you like them very much. 狂热于…的 [v-link ADJ "about" n] [INFORMAL, FEELINGS] ❑ *They're nuts about the car.* 他们酷爱那辆车。 **6** ADJ If you say that someone goes **nuts** or is **nuts**, you mean that they go crazy or are very foolish. 发疯的；愚蠢的 [v-link ADJ] [INFORMAL] ❑ *You guys are nuts.* 你们这些家伙疯了。 **7** PHRASE If someone **goes nuts**, they become extremely angry. 大发雷霆 [INFORMAL] ❑ *My father would go nuts if he saw bruises on me.* 要是我父亲看见我身上的淤伤，他会大发雷霆的。
→ see **peanut**

N

▲ **nu·tri·ent** /nu̲triənt/ (**nutrients**) N-COUNT **Nutrients** are substances that help plants and animals to grow. 营养物 ❑ *In her first book she explained the role of vegetable fibers, vitamins, minerals, and other essential nutrients.* 在她第一本书中，她解释了植物纤维、维生素、矿物质和其他重要营养物质的作用。
→ see **food**

★ **nu·tri·tion** /nu̲trɪʃᵊn/ N-UNCOUNT **Nutrition** is the process of taking food into the body and absorbing the nutrients in those foods. 吸收营养 ❑ *There are alternative sources of nutrition to animal meat.* 有能替代动物肉类的其他营养来源。

nu·tri·tion·al /nu̲trɪʃənᵊl/ ADJ The **nutritional** content of food is all the substances that are in it which help you to remain healthy. 营养的 ❑ *It does sometimes help to know the nutritional content of foods.* 了解食物的营养成份有时的确有用。● **nu·tri·tion·al·ly** ADV 营养地 ❑ *...a nutritionally balanced diet.* …营养均衡的饮食。

nu·tri·tious /nutrɪ̲ʃəs/ ADJ **Nutritious** food contains substances which help your body to be healthy. 有营养的 ❑ *It is always important to choose enjoyable, nutritious foods.* 选择好吃的、有营养的食品总是很重要的。

ny·lon /na̲ɪlɒn/ (**nylons**) **1** N-UNCOUNT **Nylon** is a strong, flexible artificial fiber. 尼龙 ❑ *The chair is made of lightweight nylon.* 那把椅子是由轻质尼龙制作的。 **2** N-PLURAL **Nylons** are stockings made of nylon. 尼龙袜 [OLD-FASHIONED] ❑ *She wore a long skirt with pink pumps and black nylons.* 她穿了一条长裙，配粉色轻软舞鞋和黑色尼龙袜。
→ see **rope**

Oo

O also **o** /oʊ/ (**O's, o's**) N-VAR **O** is the fifteenth letter of the English alphabet. 英语字母表中的第15个字母

oak /oʊk/ (**oaks**) N-VAR An **oak** or an **oak tree** is a large tree that often grows in forests and has strong, hard wood. 橡树 ❑ *Many large oaks were felled during the war.* 许多大橡树在那场战争期间被砍伏了。 ❑ *...forests of chestnut, beech, and oak.* …栗树、山毛榉和橡树组成的森林。 ● N-UNCOUNT **Oak** is the wood of this tree. 橡木 ❑ *The cabinet was made of oak and was hand-carved.* 这个柜子是橡木做的，并且经手工雕刻而成。
→ see **plant**

▲ **oar** /ɔr/ (**oars**) N-COUNT **Oars** are long poles with a wide, flat blade at one end which are used for rowing a boat. 桨
→ see **boat**

oasis /oʊeɪsɪs/ (**oases** /oʊeɪsiz/) **1** N-COUNT An **oasis** is a small area in a desert where water and plants are found. (沙漠中的) 绿洲 **2** N-COUNT You can refer to a pleasant place or situation as an **oasis** when it is surrounded by unpleasant ones. 绿洲般的地方 ❑ *The immaculately tended gardens are an oasis in the midst of Cairo's urban sprawl.* 那些打理得非常整洁的花园是杂乱扩张的开罗市区中的一片绿洲。
→ see **desert**

★ **oath** /oʊθ/ (**oaths**) **1** N-COUNT An **oath** is a formal promise, especially a promise to be loyal to a person or country. (尤指忠于某人或国家的) 誓言；宣誓 ❑ *He took an oath of loyalty to the government.* 他做了效忠于政府的宣誓。 **2** N-SING In a court of law, when someone takes **the oath**, they make a formal promise to tell the truth. You can say that someone is **under oath** when they have made this promise. (在法庭上的) 宣誓 ["the" N, also "on/under" N] ❑ *His girlfriend had gone into the witness box and taken the oath.* 他的女朋友已进了证人席并宣了誓。 ❑ *Under oath, Andy finally admitted that he had lied.* 宣誓之后，安迪终于承认他曾撒了谎。

O

oat·meal /oʊtmil/ **1** N-UNCOUNT **Oatmeal** is a kind of flour made by crushing oats. 燕麦粉 [oft N n] ❑ *...oatmeal cookies.* …燕麦小甜饼。 **2** N-UNCOUNT **Oatmeal** is a thick sticky food made from oats cooked in water or milk and eaten hot, especially for breakfast. 燕麦糊 [mainly AM]

> in BRIT, usually use **porridge**

oats /oʊts/

> The form **oat** is used as a modifier.

N-PLURAL **Oats** are a cereal crop or its grains, used for making cookies or a food called oatmeal, or for feeding animals. 燕麦 ❑ *Oats provide good, nutritious food for horses.* 燕麦为马提供营养丰富的好饲料。 ❑ *...oat bran.* …燕麦麸。
→ see **grain**

★ **obedi·ent** /oʊbidiənt/ ADJ A person or animal who is **obedient** does what they are told to do. 顺从的；服从的 ❑ *He was very respectful at home and obedient to his parents.* 他在家里很尊重人而且顺从父母。 ● **obedi·ence** ★ N-UNCOUNT 顺从；服从 ❑ *...unquestioning obedience to the law.* …对法律的绝对服从。 ● **obedi·ent·ly** ADV 顺从地；服从地 [ADV with v] ❑ *He was looking obediently at Keith, waiting for orders.* 他顺从地看着基思，等待吩咐。

★ **obese** /oʊbis/ ADJ If someone is **obese**, they are extremely fat. 肥胖的 ❑ *Obese people tend to have higher blood pressure than lean people.* 肥胖的人往往比瘦人血压高。 ● **obesity** ★ /oʊbisɪti/ N-UNCOUNT 肥胖 ❑ *...the excessive consumption of sugar that leads to problems of obesity.* …导致肥胖问题的过量糖分摄入。
→ see **diet**, **sugar**

obey /oʊbeɪ/ (**obeys, obeying, obeyed**) V-T/V-I If you **obey** a person, a command, or an instruction, you do what you are told to do. 顺服；遵守 ❑ *Cissie obeyed her mother without question.* 茜茜绝对服从她的母亲。 ❑ *Most people obey the law.* 大多数人遵守法律。 ❑ *It was his duty to obey.* 服从是他的职责。

> **Word Partnership** *obey* 的常用搭配：
> N. obey **a command**, obey **God**, obey **the law**, obey **orders**, obey **the rules**
> V. **refuse to** obey

obi·tu·ary /oʊbɪtʃuɛri/ (**obituaries**) N-COUNT Someone's **obituary** is an account of their life and character which is presented in a newspaper or broadcast soon after they die. 讣文 ❑ *His obituary was published in one edition of his own newspaper before it was discovered that he was alive.* 他的讣文刊登在他自己的报纸版面上之后，才发现他还活着。

ob·ject ♦♦◊ (**objects, objecting, objected**)

> The noun is pronounced /ɒbdʒɪkt/. The verb is pronounced /əbdʒɛkt/.

> 名词读作 /ɒbdʒɪkt/。动词读作 /əbdʒɛkt/。

1 N-COUNT An **object** is anything that has a fixed shape or form, that you can touch or see, and that is not alive. 物体 ❑ *He squinted his eyes as though he were studying an object on the horizon.* 他眯着眼睛，好像在研究地平线上的某个物体。 ❑ *...an object the shape of a coconut.* …一个椰子状的物体。 **2** N-COUNT The **object** of what someone is doing is their aim or purpose. 目的 ❑ *The object of the exercise is to raise money for the charity.* 此项活动的目的是为慈善筹款。 **3** N-COUNT The **object of** a particular feeling or reaction is the person or thing it is directed toward or that causes it. (某情感或反应的) 对象 ❑ *The object of her hatred was 24-year-old model Ros French.* 她憎恨的对象是24岁的模特罗斯·弗伦奇。 ❑ *The object of great interest at the temple was a large marble tower built in memory of Buddha.* 那庙里使人极感兴趣的东西是一座为纪念佛陀而修建的大理石巨塔。 **4** N-COUNT In grammar, the **object** of a verb or a preposition is the word or phrase which completes the structure begun by the verb or preposition. 宾语 **5** → see also **direct object**, **indirect object** **6** V-T If you **object** to something, you express your dislike or disapproval of it. 反对 ❑ *A lot of people will object to the book.* 很多人会反对这本书。 ❑ *Cullen objected that his small staff would be unable to handle the added work.* 卡伦反对说，他职员少，将无法应付增多的工作。 **7** PHRASE If you say that **money is no object** or **distance is no object**, you are emphasizing that you are willing or able to spend as much money as necessary or travel whatever distance is required. …不成问题 [EMPHASIS] ❑ *This was a very impressive program in which money seems to have been no object.* 这是一项颇具影响的计划，钱似乎从来不成问题。

> **Thesaurus** *object* 另参见：
> N. item, thing **1**
> aim, goal, intent **2**
> V. argue, disagree, oppose, protest against **6**

> **Word Partnership** *object* 的常用搭配：
> ADJ. **foreign** object, **inanimate** object, **moving** object, **solid** object **1**
> PREP. object **to** *someone/something* **6**

ob·jec·tion /əbdʒɛkʃən/ (**objections**) **1** N-VAR If you express or raise an **objection to** something, you say that you do not like it or agree with it. 反对 ❑ *Despite objections by the White House, the Senate voted today to cut off aid.* 尽管白宫反对，参议院今天投票中断援助。 **2** N-UNCOUNT If you say that you have **no objection to** something, you mean that you are not annoyed or bothered by it. 反对意见 ❑ *I have no objection to banks making money.* 我对银行赚钱没有反对意见。

Word Partnership *objection* 的常用搭配：
V. **make an** objection, **raise an** objection, **sustain an** objection 1
have no objection 2

ob·jec·tive ♦◇◇ /əbdʒɛktɪv/ (**objectives**) 1 N-COUNT Your **objective** is what you are trying to achieve. 目标 ❑ *Our main objective was the recovery of the child safe and well.* 我们的主要目标是让这个孩子安然无恙地恢复健康。 2 ADJ **Objective** information is based on facts. 客观的 [ADJ n] ❑ *He had no objective evidence that anything extraordinary was happening.* 他没有客观证据证明有什么非同寻常的事情发生。 ● **ob·jec·tive·ly** ADV 客观地 ❑ *We simply want to inform people objectively about events.* 我们只想客观地把事件告之于众。 ● **ob·jec·tiv·ity** /ɒbdʒɛktɪvɪti/ N-UNCOUNT 客观性 ❑ *The poll, whose objectivity is open to question, gave the party a 39% share of the vote.* 这次投票使该党获得了39%的选票，其客观性有可疑之处。 3 ADJ If someone is **objective**, they base their opinions on facts rather than on their personal feelings. 客观的 ❑ *I believe that a journalist should be completely objective.* 我认为一名记者应该完全客观。 ● **ob·jec·tive·ly** ADV 客观地 ❑ *Try to view situations more objectively, especially with regard to work.* 尽量更客观地看待情况，尤其对于工作。 ● **ob·jec·tiv·ity** N-UNCOUNT 客观性 ❑ *The psychiatrist must learn to maintain an unusual degree of objectivity.* 精神病学家必须学会保持非凡的客观性。

Word Partnership *objective* 的常用搭配：
V. **achieve an** objective 1
ADJ. **important** objective, **main** objective, **primary** objective 1

ob·li·ga·tion /ɒblɪgeɪʃən/ (**obligations**) 1 N-VAR If you have an **obligation to** do something, it is your duty to do that thing. 义务 ❑ *When teachers assign homework, students usually feel an obligation to do it.* 老师布置家庭作业时，学生们通常感觉做作业是一种义务。 2 N-VAR If you have an **obligation to** a person, it is your duty to take care of them or protect their interests. 义务；责任 ❑ *The United States will do that which is necessary to meet its obligations to its own citizens.* 美国会尽其对国民应尽的义务。 3 PHRASE In advertisements, if a product or a service is available **without obligation**, you do not have to pay for that product or service until you have tried it and are satisfied with it. 无义务地 ❑ *If you are selling your property, why not call us for a free valuation without obligation.* 如果你打算出售房产，为什么不打电话让我们做个免费的评估呢。

Thesaurus *obligation* 另参见：
N. duty, responsibility 1 2

Word Partnership *obligation* 的常用搭配：
V. obligation **to pay** 1
feel an obligation, **fulfill an** obligation, **meet an** obligation 1 2
ADJ. **legal** obligation, **moral** obligation 1 2
N. **sense of** obligation 1 2

ob·liga·tory /əblɪgətɔri/ ADJ If something is **obligatory**, you must do it because of a rule or a law. 规定性的 ❑ *Most women will be offered an ultrasound scan during pregnancy, although it's not obligatory.* 大部分妇女怀孕期间都将进行超声波检查，尽管不是规定性的。

oblige /əblaɪdʒ/ (**obliges, obliging, obliged**) 1 V-T If you are **obliged to** do something, a situation, rule, or law makes it necessary for you to do that thing. 迫使 ❑ *The storm got worse and worse. Finally, I was obliged to abandon the car and continue on foot.* 暴风雨越来越猛烈。最终，我被迫弃车徒步前行。 2 V-T/V-I To **oblige** someone means to be helpful to them by doing what they have asked you to do. (通过满足要求而) 帮助 ❑ *Mr. Oakley has always been ready to oblige journalists with information.* 奥克利先生一直乐于提供信息帮助记者们。 ❑ *We called up three economists to ask how to eliminate the deficit and they obliged with very straightforward answers.* 我们致电3位经济学家咨询消除赤字的方法，他们满足了我们的要求，给出了非常直接的答复。 3 CONVENTION If you tell someone that you **would be obliged** or **should be obliged** if they would do something, you are telling them in a polite but firm way that you want them to do it. (如蒙…) 将不胜感激 [FORMAL, POLITENESS] ❑ *I would be obliged if you could read it to us.* 如果你能把它读给我们听，我将不胜感激。

oblig·ing /əblaɪdʒɪŋ/ ADJ If you describe someone as **obliging**, you think that they are willing and eager to be helpful. 乐于助人的 [OLD-FASHIONED or WRITTEN, APPROVAL] ❑ *He is an extremely pleasant and obliging man.* 他这人非常和蔼可亲，且乐于助人。 ● **oblig·ing·ly** ADV 乐于助人地 [ADV with v] ❑ *Benedict obligingly held the door open.* 贝内迪克主动帮忙将门打开。

oblique /oʊblik/ ADJ If you describe a statement as **oblique**, you mean that is not expressed directly or openly, making it difficult to understand. 隐晦的 ❑ *It was an oblique reference to his mother.* 这是对他母亲的隐射。 ● **oblique·ly** ADV 隐晦地 [ADV with v] ❑ *He obliquely referred to the U.S., Britain and Saudi Arabia.* 他隐晦提到美国、英国和沙特阿拉伯。

oblit·erate /əblɪtəreɪt/ (**obliterates, obliterating, obliterated**) 1 V-T If something **obliterates** an object or place, it destroys it completely. 摧毁 ❑ *Their warheads are enough to obliterate the world several times over.* 他们的弹头足以摧毁这个世界好几次。 ● **oblit·era·tion** /əblɪtəreɪʃən/ N-UNCOUNT 摧毁 ❑ *...the obliteration of three isolated rainforests.* …3处孤立雨林的毁灭。 2 V-T If you **obliterate** something such as a memory, emotion, or thought, you remove it completely from your mind. (从头脑中) 抹掉 ❑ *There was time enough to obliterate memories of how things once were for him.* 有足够的时间来抹掉他对过去的记忆。

oblivi·on /əblɪviən/ 1 N-UNCOUNT **Oblivion** is the state of not being aware of what is happening around you, for example, because you are asleep or unconscious. 神志不清 ❑ *He just drank himself jovially into oblivion.* 他一味痛饮直到自己神志不清。 2 N-UNCOUNT **Oblivion** is the state of having been forgotten or of no longer being considered important. 被淡忘状态 ❑ *It seems that the so-called new theory is likely to sink into oblivion.* 那所谓的新理论似乎可能被淡忘。 3 N-UNCOUNT If you say that something is bombed or blasted **into oblivion**, you are emphasizing that it is completely destroyed. 被彻底摧毁 [EMPHASIS] ❑ *An entire poor section of town was bombed into oblivion.* 城镇的整个贫民区被彻底炸毁了。

oblivi·ous /əblɪviəs/ ADJ If you are **oblivious** to something or **oblivious** of it, you are not aware of it. 没意识到的 ❑ *She lay motionless where she was, oblivious to pain.* 她一动不动地躺在原地，感觉不到疼痛。

ob·nox·ious /əbnɒkʃəs/ ADJ If you describe someone or their behavior as **obnoxious**, you think that they are very unpleasant because of being aggressive, loud, or offensive. 令人讨厌的 [DISAPPROVAL] ❑ *The people at my table were so obnoxious I had to change my seat.* 我那桌的人非常讨厌，我只好换了座位。

obo In advertisements, **obo** is used after a price to indicate that the person who is selling something is willing to accept slightly less money than the sum they have mentioned. **obo** is a written abbreviation for "or best offer." 价格可议 (在广告中标在价格后表示卖主愿意还价) [mainly AM] ❑ *Family boat. $6,000 obo.* 家用船。$6000，价格可议。

→ see **orchestra**

★ **ob·scene** /əbsin/ 1 ADJ If you describe something as **obscene**, you mean it offends you because it relates to sex or violence in a way that you think is unpleasant and shocking. 淫秽下流的 ❑ *I'm not prudish but I think these photographs are obscene.* 我不是假正经，不过我认为这些照片淫秽下流。 2 ADJ In legal contexts, books, pictures, or movies which are judged **obscene** are illegal because they deal with sex or violence in a way that is offensive to the general public. (书籍、图片、电影等) 淫秽非法的 ❑ *A city magistrate ruled that the novel was obscene and copies should be destroyed.* 一位市治安官裁定该小说是淫秽非法作品，应予以销毁。 3 ADJ If you describe something as **obscene**, you disapprove of it very strongly and consider it to be offensive or immoral. 令人憎恶的 [DISAPPROVAL] ❑ *It was obscene to spend millions producing unwanted food.* 耗资数百万生产无用的食品令人憎恶。

ob·scen·ity /əbsɛnɪti/ (**obscenities**) 1 N-UNCOUNT **Obscenity** is behavior, art, or language that is sexual and offends or shocks people. 猥亵(行为、语言等)；❑ *He insisted these photographs were not art but obscenity.* 他坚持认为这些照片不是艺术而是淫秽品。 2 N-VAR An **obscenity** is a very offensive word or expression. 猥亵言辞 ❑ *They shouted obscenities at us and smashed bottles on the floor.* 他们冲我们骂脏话，还往地板上砸瓶子。

★ **ob·scure** /əbskyʊər/ (**obscurer, obscurest, obscures, obscuring, obscured**) 1 ADJ If something or someone is **obscure**, they are unknown, or are known by only a few people. 鲜为人知的 ❑ *The origin of the custom is obscure.* 该习俗的起源鲜为人知。 2 ADJ Something that is **obscure** is difficult to understand or deal with, usually because it involves so many parts or details. 复杂难懂的；

难处理的 ❑ *The contracts are written in obscure language.* 那些合同是用复杂难懂的语言写的。 **3** V-T If one thing **obscures** another, it prevents it from being seen or heard properly. 遮掩 ❑ *Trees obscured his vision; he couldn't see much of the square's southern half.* 树木遮住了他的视线，他不怎么看得见广场南半部。 **4** V-T To **obscure** something means to make it difficult to understand. 使…难懂 ❑ *...the jargon that frequently obscures educational writing.* …常使教学行文变得复杂难懂的术语。

ob·scu·rity /əbskyʊərɪti/ (**obscurities**) **1** N-UNCOUNT **Obscurity** is the state of being known by only a few people. 鲜为人知的状态 ❑ *For the lucky few, there's the chance of being plucked from obscurity and thrown into the glamorous world of modelling.* 极少数幸运者有机会从默默无闻中脱颖而出，跻身多彩的模特儿世界。 **2** N-VAR **Obscurity** is the quality of being difficult to understand. An **obscurity** is something that is difficult to understand. 难懂性；难懂之物 ❑ *"How can that be?" asked Hunt, irritated by the obscurity of Henry's reply.* "怎么会那样？"亨特问道，亨利费解的回答让他气馁。

ob·ser·vance /əbzɜrvᵊns/ (**observances**) N-VAR The **observance** of something such as a law or custom is the practice of obeying or following it. (对法律、习俗等的) 遵守 ❑ *County governments should use their powers to ensure strict observance of laws.* 县政府应该利用他们的权力确保法律的严格遵守。

ob·ser·vant /əbzɜrvᵊnt/ ADJ Someone who is **observant** pays a lot of attention to things and notices more about them than most people do. 善于观察的 ❑ *That's a good description, Mrs. Drummond. You're very observant.* 描述得很好，德拉蒙德太太。你很善于观察。

ob·ser·va·tion /ɒbzərveɪʃᵊn/ (**observations**) **1** N-UNCOUNT **Observation** is the action or process of carefully watching someone or something. 观察 ❑ *...careful observation of the movement of the planets.* …对行星运行的仔细观测。 **2** N-COUNT An **observation** is something that you have learned by seeing or watching something and thinking about it. 观察结果 ❑ *This book contains observations about the causes of addictions.* 这本书包含关于上瘾原因的观察结果。 **3** N-COUNT If a person makes an **observation**, they make a comment about something or someone, usually as a result of watching how they behave. 观察评论 ❑ *Is that a criticism or just an observation?* 那是一种批评呢，还是一种观察评论而已？ **4** N-UNCOUNT **Observation** is the ability to pay a lot of attention to things and to notice more about them than most people do. 观察力 ❑ *She has good powers of observation.* 她有很强的观察力。

→ see **experiment, forecast, science**

> **Word Partnership** *observation* 的常用搭配：
> PREP. **by** observation, **through** observation, **under** observation **1**
> ADJ. **careful** observation **1**
> **direct** observation **1** – **3**
> V. **make an** observation **3**

> **Word Link** *ory ≈ place where something happens : conservatory, factory, observatory*

▲ **ob·ser·va·tory** /əbzɜrvətɔri/ (**observatories**) N-COUNT An **observatory** is a building with a large telescope from which scientists study things such as the planets by watching them. 天文台

> **Word Link** *serv ≈ keeping : conserve, observe, preserve*

ob·serve ♦◊◊ /əbzɜrv/ (**observes, observing, observed**) **1** V-T If you **observe** a person or thing, you watch them carefully, especially in order to learn something about them. 观察 ❑ *Olson also studies and observes the behavior of babies.* 奥尔森还研究并观察婴儿的行为。 ❑ *Are there any classes I could observe?* 有我可以观摩的课吗？ **2** V-T If you **observe** someone or something, you see or notice them. 观察到 [FORMAL] ❑ *In 1664 Hooke observed a reddish spot on the surface of the planet.* 1664年，胡克观察到了那颗行星表面的一个微红的斑点。 **3** V-T If you **observe** that something is the case, you make a remark or comment about it, especially when it is something you have noticed and thought about a lot. 评述 [FORMAL] ❑ *We observe that the first calls for radical transformation did not begin until the period of the industrial revolution.* 我们认为，首次要求彻底改革的呼声直到工业革命时期才出现。 **4** V-T If you **observe** something such as a law or custom, you obey it or follow it. 遵从 ❑ *Imposing speed restrictions is easy, but forcing drivers to observe them is trickier.* 实行速度限制容易，而迫使司机遵守较难。 ❑ *The army was observing a ceasefire.* 军队当时在遵守一项停火协议。 **5** V-T If you **observe** an important day such as a holiday or anniversary, you do something special in order to honor or celebrate it. 庆祝 ❑ *...where he will observe Thanksgiving with family members.* …在那里他将与家人一起庆祝感恩节。

> **Thesaurus** *observe* 另参见：
> V. study, watch **1**
> detect, notice, spot **2**
> celebrate **5**

> **Word Partnership** *observe* 的常用搭配：
> N. observe **behavior**, **opportunity to** observe **1** **2**
> observe **guidelines**, observe **rules** **4**
> observe **an anniversary** **5**

ob·serv·er ♦◊◊ /əbzɜrvər/ (**observers**) **1** N-COUNT You can refer to someone who sees or notices something as an **observer**. 目击者 ❑ *A casual observer would have taken them to be three men out for an evening stroll.* 一位不经意的目击者会认为他们是晚上出来闲逛的3个男人。 **2** N-COUNT An **observer** is someone who studies current events and situations, especially in order to comment on them and predict what will happen next. 观察家 [JOURNALISM] ❑ *Observers say the events of the weekend seem to have increased support for the opposition.* 观察家们说周末事件似乎增加了对反对派的支持。 **3** N-COUNT An **observer** is a person who is sent to observe an important event or situation, especially in order to make sure it happens as it should, or to tell other people about it. 观察员 ❑ *The president suggested that a UN observer should attend the conference.* 大会主席建议应该有一名联合国观察员参加该会议。

> **Word Partnership** *observer* 的常用搭配：
> ADJ. **casual** observer **1**
> **independent** observer, **outside** observer **1** – **3**

ob·sess /əbsɛs/ (**obsesses, obsessing, obsessed**) V-T/V-I If something **obsesses** you or if you **obsess about** something, you keep thinking about it and find it difficult to think about anything else. 困扰；心神不宁 ❑ *A string of scandals is obsessing America.* 一系列丑闻在困扰着美国。 ❑ *She stopped drinking but began obsessing about her weight.* 她戒了酒，但开始不停地担心她的体重。

ob·sessed /əbsɛst/ ADJ If someone is **obsessed with** a person or thing, they keep thinking about them and find it difficult to think about anything else. 受困扰的；对…痴迷的 ❑ *He was obsessed with gangster movies.* 他那时迷上了警匪片。

▲ **ob·ses·sion** /əbsɛʃᵊn/ (**obsessions**) N-VAR If you say that someone has an **obsession** with a person or thing, you think they are spending too much time thinking about them. 迷恋 ❑ *She would try to forget her obsession with Christopher.* 她会试图忘掉她对克里斯托弗的迷恋。

ob·ses·sive /əbsɛsɪv/ (**obsessives**) **1** ADJ If someone's behavior is **obsessive**, they cannot stop doing a particular thing or behaving in a particular way. 痴迷的 ❑ *Williams is obsessive about motor racing.* 威廉斯痴迷于赛车。 ● **ob·ses·sive·ly** ADV 痴迷地 ❑ *He couldn't help worrying obsessively about what would happen.* 他禁不住着魔般地担忧将会发生的事情。 **2** N-COUNT An **obsessive** is someone who is obsessive about something or who behaves in an obsessive way. 痴迷者 ❑ *Obsessives, in any area, are invariably as boring as their hobbies.* 任何领域的痴迷者们无一例外地和他们的癖好一样令人厌烦。

obsessive-compulsive dis·or·der N-UNCOUNT If someone suffers from **obsessive-compulsive disorder**, they cannot stop doing a particular thing, for example, washing their hands. The abbreviation **OCD** is also used. 强迫性神经官能症 ❑ *We aim to bring the facts about obsessive compulsive disorder to the public and to support those who suffer from this often debilitating anxiety disorder.* 我们旨在向公众呈现有关强迫性神经官能症的事实并且支持患此经常让人虚弱的焦虑性病症的患者。

ob·so·lete /ɒbsəliːt/ ADJ Something that is **obsolete** is no longer needed because something better has been invented. 被淘汰的 ❑ *So much equipment becomes obsolete almost as soon as it's made.* 很多设备几乎刚制造出来就过时了。

ob·sta·cle /ɒbstəkᵊl/ (**obstacles**) **1** N-COUNT An **obstacle** is an object that makes it difficult for you to go where you want to go, because it is in your way. 障碍物 ❑ *Most competition cars will only roll over if they hit an obstacle.* 多数赛车在撞到障碍物时都会翻车。 **2** N-COUNT You can refer to anything that makes it difficult for you to do something as an **obstacle**. 障碍 ❑ *Overcrowding remains a large obstacle to improving conditions.* 过度拥挤仍然是改善条件的一大障碍。

Word Partnership *obstacle* 的常用搭配:

N. obstacle **course** 1
obstacle **to peace** 2
V. **be an** obstacle, **hit an** obstacle, **overcome an** obstacle 1 2
ADJ. **big/biggest** obstacle, **main** obstacle, **major** obstacle, **serious** obstacle 1 2

ob·ste·tri·cian /ɒbstətrɪʃ°n/ (**obstetricians**) N-COUNT An **obstetrician** is a doctor who is specially trained to deal with pregnancy and birth. 产科医生 [MEDICAL] → see **gynecologist**

ob·sti·nate /ɒbstɪnɪt/ 1 ADJ If you describe someone as **obstinate**, you are being critical of them because they are very determined to do what they want, and refuse to change their mind or be persuaded to do something else. 固执的 [DISAPPROVAL] ❑ *He is obstinate and determined and will not give up.* 他固执、坚决，不会放弃。 ● **ob·sti·nate·ly** ADV 固执地 [ADV with v] ❑ *I stayed obstinately in my room, sitting by the telephone.* 我执意呆在自己的房间里，坐在电话旁。 ● **ob·sti·na·cy** N-UNCOUNT 固执 ❑ *I might have become a dangerous man with all that stubbornness and obstinacy built into me.* 我或许已变成一个集固执和顽固于一身的危险人物了。 2 ADJ You can describe things as **obstinate** when they are difficult to move, change, or destroy. 难以消除的 ❑ *...rusted farm equipment strewn among the obstinate weeds.* …散落在丛生的杂草中生了锈的农具。 ● **ob·sti·nate·ly** ADV 顽固地 [ADV with v] ❑ *...the door of the shop which obstinately stayed closed when he tried to push it open.* …那扇他尽力想推开可又推不开的店门。

▲ **ob·struct** /əbstrʌkt/ (**obstructs, obstructing, obstructed**) 1 V-T If something **obstructs** a road or path, it blocks it, stopping people or vehicles getting past. 阻塞 ❑ *A knot of black and white cars obstructed the intersection.* 挤作一团的黑白轿车阻塞了那个十字路口。 2 V-T To **obstruct** someone or something means to make it difficult for them to move forward by blocking their path. 阻拦 ❑ *A number of local people have been arrested for trying to obstruct trucks loaded with logs.* 许多当地人因试图阻拦装有原木的卡车被逮捕了。 3 V-T To **obstruct** progress or a process means to prevent it from happening properly. 阻挠 ❑ *The authorities are obstructing a United Nations investigation.* 当局在阻挠一次联合国调查。 4 V-T If someone or something **obstructs** your view, they are positioned between you and the thing you are trying to look at, stopping you from seeing it completely. 阻挡 ❑ *Claire positioned herself so as not to obstruct David's line of sight.* 克莱尔让自己就位以便不挡住戴维的视线。

ob·struc·tion /əbstrʌkʃ°n/ (**obstructions**) 1 N-COUNT An **obstruction** is something that blocks a road or path. 障碍 ❑ *John was irritated by drivers parking near his house and causing an obstruction.* 约翰被众司机在他房子附近停车而造成阻塞所激怒。 2 N-VAR An **obstruction** is something that blocks a passage in your body. 梗阻 ❑ *The boy was suffering from a bowel obstruction.* 那男孩当时在受肠梗阻之苦。 3 N-UNCOUNT **Obstruction** is the act of deliberately delaying something or preventing something from happening, usually in business, law, or government. 故意妨碍 ❑ *Mr. Anderson refused to let them in and now faces a criminal charge of obstruction.* 安德森先生当时拒绝让他们进入，现在面临一项故意妨碍罪的指控。

ob·tain ♦◇◇ /əbteɪn/ (**obtains, obtaining, obtained**) V-T To **obtain** something means to get it or achieve it. 获得 [FORMAL] ❑ *Evans was trying to obtain a false passport and other documents.* 埃文斯当时正试图获取假护照和其他文件。

Word Partnership *obtain* 的常用搭配:

ADJ. **able to** obtain, **difficult to** obtain, **easy to** obtain, **unable to** obtain
N. obtain **approval**, obtain **a copy**, obtain **financing**, obtain **help**, obtain **information**, obtain **insurance**, obtain **permission**, obtain **weapons**

ob·tuse /əbtus/ 1 ADJ An **obtuse** angle is between 90° and 180°. Compare **acute** angle. (角) 钝的 [TECHNICAL] 2 ADJ Someone who is **obtuse** has difficulty understanding things, or makes no effort to understand them. 迟钝的 ❑ *I've been waiting for you to ask me the question yourself, and you're being obtuse and slow about it.* 我一直在等你亲自问我这个问题，而你对此一直迟钝缓慢。

ob·vi·ous ♦♦◇ /ɒbviəs/ 1 ADJ If something is **obvious**, it is easy to see or understand. 明显的 ❑ *...the need to rectify what is an obvious injustice.* …纠正明显不公行为的必要性。 2 ADJ If you describe something that someone says as **obvious**, you are being critical of it because you think it is unnecessary or shows lack of imagination. 无新意的 [DISAPPROVAL] ❑ *Such an explanation seems too simple, and too obvious.* 这样的一个解释似乎太简单而且太没新意。 ● PHRASE If you say that someone **is stating the obvious**, you mean that they are saying something that everyone already knows and understands. 说人人皆知的事

Thesaurus *obvious* 另参见:

ADJ. noticeable, plain, unmistakable 1

Word Partnership *obvious* 的常用搭配:

N. obvious **answer**, obvious **choice**, obvious **differences**, obvious **example**, obvious **question**, obvious **reasons**, obvious **solution** 1 2
ADV. **fairly** obvious, **immediately** obvious, **less** obvious, **most** obvious, **painfully** obvious, **quite** obvious, **so** obvious 1 2

ob·vi·ous·ly ♦♦◇ /ɒbviəsli/ 1 ADV You use **obviously** when you are stating something that you expect the person who is listening to know already. 显然地 [ADV with cl] [EMPHASIS] ❑ *Obviously, they've had sponsorship from some big companies.* 显然，他们已有一些大公司赞助。 2 ADV You use **obviously** to indicate that something is easily noticed, seen, or recognized. 明显地 [ADV with cl/group] ❑ *They obviously appreciate you very much.* 他们明显很欣赏你。

oc·ca·sion ♦♦◇ /əkeɪʒ°n/ (**occasions**) 1 N-COUNT An **occasion** is a time when something happens, or a case of it happening. (某事发生的) 时候; 场景 ❑ *I often think fondly of an occasion some years ago in New Orleans.* 我经常深情地想起一些年前在新奥尔良所发生的一幕。 2 N-COUNT An **occasion** is an important event, ceremony, or celebration. 重大场合 ❑ *Taking her with me on official occasions has been a challenge.* 在正式场合带上她对我而言是一种挑战。 3 N-COUNT An **occasion for** doing something is an opportunity for doing it. 机会 [FORMAL] ❑ *It is an occasion for all the family to celebrate.* 那是个全家庆祝的机会。 4 PHRASE If you **have occasion to** do something, you have the opportunity to do it or have a need to do it. 有机会; 有必要 ❑ *Over the next few years many people had occasion to reflect on the truth of his warnings.* 在随后的几年里许多人有机会反思他那些警告的真相。 5 PHRASE If you say that someone **rose to the occasion**, you mean that they did what was necessary to successfully overcome a difficult situation. 应付自如 ❑ *Colorado rose to the occasion with four players scoring 16 points or more.* 科罗拉多队从容应对，4个队员赢得16分或更多得分。

Word Partnership *occasion* 的常用搭配:

ADJ. **festive** occasion, **historic** occasion, **rare** occasion, **solemn** occasion, **special** occasion 1 2
V. **mark an** occasion 2
rise to the occasion 5

oc·ca·sion·al ♦◇◇ /əkeɪʒən°l/ ADJ **Occasional** means happening sometimes, but not regularly or often. 偶尔的 ❑ *I've had occasional mild headaches all my life.* 我此生一直有偶尔的轻微头疼。 ● **oc·ca·sion·al·ly** ADV 偶尔地 ❑ *He still misbehaves occasionally.* 他仍偶尔行为不乖。

oc·cult /əkʌlt, ɒkʌlt/ N-SING **The occult** is the knowledge and study of supernatural or magical forces. 神秘学 ❑ *Interest in the occult tended toward ceremonial magic rather than witchcraft.* 对神秘学的兴趣趋向于仪式性魔术而非巫术。 ● ADJ **Occult** is also an adjective. 神秘的 [ADJ n] ❑ *...paganism and occult practice.* …异教和神秘习俗。

▲ **oc·cu·pan·cy** /ɒkyəpənsi/ N-UNCOUNT **Occupancy** is the act of using a room, building, or area of land, usually for a fixed period of time. 占用 [FORMAL] ❑ *Hotel occupancy has been as low as 40%.* 酒店入住率已低至40%。

Word Link *ant ≈ one who does, has : defendant, deodorant, occupant*

▲ **oc·cu·pant** /ɒkyəpənt/ (**occupants**) 1 N-COUNT The **occupants** of a building or room are the people who live or work there. (建筑、房间的) 居用者 ❑ *Most of the occupants had left before the fire broke out.* 大多数人在火灾发生之前已经离开。 2 N-PLURAL You can refer to the people who are in a place such as a room, vehicle, or bed at a particular time as the **occupants**. (房间、车辆、床的) 占用者 ❑ *He wanted the occupants of the vehicle to get out.* 他想让车里的人出来。

O

oc·cu·pa·tion ♦◇◇ /ɒkyəpeɪʃən/ (**occupations**) 1 N-COUNT Your **occupation** is your job or profession. 职业 ❑ *I suppose I was looking for an occupation which was going to be an adventure.* 我想我那时在寻找一份冒险型职业。 2 N-COUNT An **occupation** is something that you spend time doing, either for pleasure or because it needs to be done. 消遣 ❑ *Parachuting is a dangerous occupation.* 跳伞是一种危险的消遣。 3 N-UNCOUNT The **occupation** of a country happens when it is entered and controlled by a foreign army. 占领 ❑ *...the occupation of Poland.* …对波兰的占领。

★ **oc·cu·pa·tion·al** /ɒkyəpeɪʃənəl/ ADJ **Occupational** means relating to a person's job or profession. 职业的 ❑ *Some received substantial occupational assistance in the form of low-interest loans.* 一些人得到了大量的低息贷款形式的职业援助。

oc·cu·pi·er /ɒkyəpaɪər/ (**occupiers**) N-COUNT The **occupier** of a house, apartment, or piece of land is the person who lives or works there. (房屋、公寓、土地等的) 占用者 [BRIT, FORMAL]

in AM, use **occupant**

oc·cu·py ♦♦◇ /ɒkyəpaɪ/ (**occupies, occupying, occupied**) 1 V-T The people who **occupy** a building or a place are the people who live or work there. 占用 (某建筑、某地) ❑ *There were over 40 tenants, all occupying one wing of the building.* 有40多位房客，都住在该大楼的一翼。 2 V-T PASSIVE If a room or something such as a seat **is occupied**, someone is using it, so that it is not available for anyone else. 占用 (座位等) ❑ *The hospital bed is occupied by his wife.* 那张病床由他妻子占用。 3 V-T If a group of people or an army **occupies** a place or country, they move into it, using force in order to gain control of it. 占领 ❑ *U.S. forces now occupy a part of the country.* 美国军队现在占领着该国的一部分地区。 4 V-T If someone or something **occupies** a particular place in a system, process, or plan, they have that place. 占有 (某位置) ❑ *Many men still occupy more positions of power than women.* 许多男性仍比女性占有更多的权力职位。 5 V-T If something **occupies** you, or if you **occupy** yourself, your time, or your mind with it, you are busy doing that thing or thinking about it. (某事物) 占据 (某人); 使 (自己、自己的时间、自己的思维) 被 (某事物) 占据 ❑ *Her career occupies all of her time.* 她的事业占用了她所有的时间。 ❑ *He occupied himself with packing the car.* 他忙于装那辆车。 ● **oc·cu·pied** ADJ 占用的 [v-link ADJ] ❑ *Keep the brain occupied.* 不让脑子闲下来。 6 V-T If something **occupies** you, it requires your efforts, attention, or time. (某事物) 占用 (某人) ❑ *I had other matters to occupy me, during the day at least.* 我有别的事要做，至少白天要被占用。 7 V-T If something **occupies** a particular area or place, it fills or covers it, or exists there. (某事物) 占据 (某区域、某地) ❑ *Even small aircraft occupy a lot of space.* 即便小飞机也占很多空间。

Word Partnership *occupy* 的常用搭配：

N. occupy **a house**, occupy **land** 1
occupy **a place** 1 3 4 7
occupy **a position** 3 4
occupy **an area**, **forces** occupy ***someplace***, occupy **space**, **troops** occupy ***someplace*** 3 7

oc·cur ♦♦◇ /əkɜr/ (**occurs, occurring, occurred**) 1 V-I When something **occurs**, it happens. 发生 ❑ *If headaches only occur at night, lack of fresh air and oxygen is often the cause.* 如果头痛只发生在晚上，缺少新鲜空气和氧气常常是其原因。 ❑ *The crash occurred when the crew shut down the wrong engine.* 机组人员关错发动机后就坠毁了。 2 V-I When something **occurs** in a particular place, it exists or is present there. (某事物在某地) 出现 ❑ *These snails do not occur on low-lying coral islands.* 这些蜗牛不会出现在低洼的珊瑚岛上。 3 V-I If a thought or idea **occurs to** you, you suddenly think of it or realize it. (想法、主意在某人脑海中) 突然出现 [no passive, no cont] ❑ *It did not occur to me to check my insurance policy.* 我没想到要核对我的保险单。

Thesaurus *occur* 另参见：

V. come about, develop, happen 1
dawn on, strike 3

Word Partnership *occur* 的常用搭配：

N. **accidents** occur, **changes** occur, **deaths** occur, **diseases** occur, **events** occur, **injuries** occur, **problems** occur 1
ADV. **frequently** occur, **naturally** occur, **normally** occur, **often** occur, **usually** occur 1 – 3

oc·cur·rence /əkɜrəns/ (**occurrences**) 1 N-COUNT An **occurrence** is something that happens. 发生的事情 [FORMAL] ❑ *Complaints seemed to be an everyday occurrence.* 投诉似乎成了天天发生的事。 2 N-COUNT **The occurrence of** something is the fact that it happens or is present. (某事物的) 发生；存在 ❑ *The greatest occurrence of coronary heart disease is in those over 65.* 冠心病的最高发病率在65岁以上的人群中。

Word Partnership *occurrence* 的常用搭配：

ADJ. **common** occurrence, **daily** occurrence, **everyday** occurrence, **frequent** occurrence, **rare** occurrence, **unusual** occurrence 1 2

ocean ♦◇◇ /oʊʃən/ (**oceans**) 1 N-SING **The ocean** is the sea. 大海 ❑ *There were few sights as beautiful as the calm ocean on a warm night.* 很少有景色像温暖夜晚的平静大海那样美丽。 2 N-COUNT An **ocean** is one of the five very large areas of sea on the Earth's surface. 洋 ❑ *They spent many days cruising the northern Pacific Ocean.* 他们花了很多天巡游北太平洋。 3 N-COUNT If you say that there is an **ocean of** something, you are emphasizing that there is a very large amount of it. 极大量 [INFORMAL, EMPHASIS] ❑ *I had cried oceans of tears.* 我已哭得泪流成河。 4 PHRASE If you say that something is **a drop in the ocean**, you mean that it is a very small amount which is unimportant compared to the cost of other things or is so small that it has very little effect on something. 沧海一粟 [EMPHASIS] ❑ *His fee is a drop in the ocean compared with the real cost of broadcasting.* 他的费用与广播的实际成本相比是沧海一粟。

→ see Word Web: **ocean**
→ see **beach, earth, river, ship, tide, whale**

o'clock ♦♦◇ /əklɒk/ ADV You use **o'clock** after numbers from one to twelve to say what time it is. For example, if you say that it is 9 o'clock, you mean that it is nine hours after midnight or nine hours after noon. …点钟 [num ADV] ❑ *The trouble began just after ten o'clock last night.* 麻烦在昨晚刚过10点时开始了。

Oct. **Oct.** is a written abbreviation for **October**. 10月 ❑ *...Tuesday Oct. 25th.* …10月25日，星期二。

Oc·to·ber ♦♦♦ /ɒktoʊbər/ (**Octobers**) N-VAR **October** is the tenth month of the year in the Western calendar. 10月 ❑ *Most*

Word Web ocean

Oceans cover over seventy-five percent of the earth's surface. These huge bodies of **salt water** are constantly in motion. On the surface, the wind pushes the water into **waves**. At the same time, **currents** under the surface flow like rivers through the oceans. These currents are affected by the earth's rotation. It shifts them to the right in the northern hemisphere and to the left in the southern hemisphere. Other forces affect the oceans as well. For example, the gravitational pull of the moon and sun cause the **ebb** and **flow** of ocean **tides**.

O

seasonal hiring is done in early October. 多数季节性招聘是在10月初进行。❑ *The first plane is due to leave on October 2.* 第一架飞机定于10月2日起飞。

oc·to·pus /ɒktəpəs/ (octopuses) N-VAR An **octopus** is a soft sea creature with eight long arms called tentacles which it uses to catch food. 章鱼 ● N-UNCOUNT **Octopus** is this creature eaten as food. 章鱼肉 ❑ *...plates of octopus.* …一盘盘章鱼肉。

OD /oʊ di/ (OD's, OD'ing, OD'd) V-I To **OD** means the same as to **overdose**. 用药过量 [INFORMAL] ❑ *His son was a junkie; the kid OD'd a year ago.* 他儿子是个瘾君子。那孩子一年前吸毒过量。● N-COUNT **OD** is also a noun. 用药过量 ❑ *"I had a friend who died of an OD," she said.* "我有个朋友死于用药过量。"她说。

odd ♦♦◊ /ɒd/ (odder, oddest) 1 ADJ If you describe someone or something as **odd**, you think that they are strange or unusual. 古怪的；不寻常的 ❑ *He'd always been odd, but not to this extent.* 他曾一直很古怪，但没到这种程度。❑ *What an odd coincidence that he should have known your family.* 他已认识你的家人，多么不寻常的巧合。● **odd·ly** ADV 古怪地；不寻常地 [ADV with v] ❑ *...an oddly shaped hill.* …一座形状奇怪的小山。2 ADJ You use **odd** before a noun to indicate that you are not mentioning the type, size, or quality of something because it is not important. (用于名词前) 任意的 [det ADJ] ❑ *...moving from place to place where she could find the odd bit of work.* …在她能找到点事做的地方搬来搬去。❑ *He had various odd cleaning jobs around the place.* 他在该地附近做过各种不同的清洁工作。3 ADV You use **odd** after a number to indicate that it is only approximate. …左右 (用于数字后) [num ADV] [INFORMAL] ❑ *How many pages was it, 500 odd?* 它多少页，500左右？❑ *He has now appeared in sixty odd films.* 他如今已在六十部左右的电影中露过面。4 ADJ **Odd** numbers, such as 3 and 17, are those which cannot be divided exactly by the number two. 奇数的 ❑ *The odd numbers are on the left as you walk up the street.* 你沿这条街走时，单号在左边。5 ADJ You say that two things are **odd** when they do not belong to the same set or pair. 单的 ❑ *I'm wearing odd socks today by the way.* 顺便说一下，我今天穿着两只不成对儿的袜子。6 PHRASE **The odd man out, the odd woman out**, or **the odd one out** in a particular situation is a person who is different from the other people in it. 与众不同者 ❑ *Azerbaijan has been the odd man out, the one republic not to hold democratic elections.* 阿塞拜疆一直是个与众不同者，一个不举行民主选举的共和国。7 → see also **odds**

Thesaurus *odd* 另参见：

ADJ. bizarre, different, eccentric, peculiar, strange, unusual, weird; *(ant.)* normal, regular 1

Word Partnership *odd* 的常用搭配：

V. **feel** odd, **look** odd, **seem** odd, **sound** odd, **strike** *someone* **as** odd, **think** *something* odd 1
N. odd **combination**, odd **thing** 1
odd **job** 2
ADJ. odd **numbered** 4

odd·ity /ɒdɪti/ (oddities) N-COUNT An **oddity** is someone or something that is very strange. 怪人；怪事 ❑ *Losing my hair made me feel an oddity.* 脱发使我觉得自己是个怪人。

odd·ly /ɒdli/ 1 ADV You use **oddly** to indicate that what you are saying is true, but that it is not what you expected. 奇怪地 ❑ *He said no and seemed oddly reluctant to talk about it.* 他说了不，而且很奇怪他似乎不愿谈论这件事。❑ *Oddly, Emma says she never considered her face to be attractive.* 奇怪，埃玛说她从来都不认为她的脸蛋吸引人。2 → see also **odd**

odds /ɒdz/ 1 N-PLURAL You refer to how likely something is to happen as the **odds** that it will happen. 可能性 ❑ *What are the odds of finding a parking space right outside the door?* 就在门外找到一个停车位的可能性有多大？2 N-PLURAL In betting, **odds** are expressions with numbers such as "10 to 1" and "7 to 2" that show how likely something is thought to be, for example, how likely a particular horse is to lose or win a race. (赌博中的) 赔率 ❑ *We are offering odds of 6-1 on the fight ending in a knockout.* 我们以6比1的赔率赌该拳击赛以击倒告终。3 PHRASE If someone is **at odds** with someone else, or if two people are **at odds**, they are disagreeing or arguing with each other. (与某人) 不合 ❑ *He was at odds with the boss.* 他与老板不合。4 PHRASE If you say that **the odds are against** something or someone, you mean that they are unlikely to succeed. (某人、某事物) 不大可能成功 ❑ *He reckons the odds are against the plan going ahead.* 他认为该计划不太可能进行下去。5 PHRASE If something happens **against all odds**, it happens or succeeds although it seemed impossible or very unlikely. 貌似不可能 (却发生或成功) ❑ *...families in terrible circumstances, who have stayed together against all odds.* …状况糟糕的家庭，似乎不可能维持下去，却仍然住在一起。6 PHRASE If you say that **the odds are in** someone's **favor**, you mean that they are likely to succeed in what they are doing. (某人) 可能会成功 ❑ *The troops will only engage in a ground battle when all the odds are in their favor.* 该部队只会在完全可能取胜的情况下进行一场地面战斗。

→ see **lottery**

Word Partnership *odds* 的常用搭配：

V. **beat the** odds 1 2
PREP. **the** odds **of** *something* 1 2
at odds **(with** *someone***)** 3
odds **against** *something* 4
against all odds 5
N. odds **of winning** 1 2
odds **in** *someone's/something's* **favor** 6

★ **odor** /oʊdər/ (odors)

in BRIT, use **odour**

N-VAR An **odor** is a particular and distinctive smell. 独特气味 ❑ *...the lingering odor of automobile exhaust.* …挥之不去的汽车尾气的独特气味。

→ see **smell, taste**

★ **odour** /oʊdər/ [BRIT] → see **odor**

of ♦♦♦ /əv, STRONG ʌv/

In addition to the uses shown below, **of** is used after some verbs, nouns, and adjectives in order to introduce extra information. **Of** is also used in phrasal prepositions such as "because of," "instead of," and "in spite of," and in phrasal verbs such as "make of" and "dispose of."

1 PREP You use **of** to combine two nouns when the first noun identifies the feature of the second noun that you want to talk about. 用以连接2个名词，其中第1个名词指明第2个名词的特征 [n PREP n] ❑ *The average age of the women interviewed was only 21.5.* 受访女性的平均年龄只有21.5岁。❑ *...the population of this town.* …这个城镇的人口。2 PREP You use **of** to combine two nouns, or a noun and a present participle, when the second noun or present participle defines or gives more information about the first noun. 用以连接2个名词或1个名词和1个现在分词，其中第2个名词或现在分词限定第1个名词或给出有关第1个名词的更多信息 [n PREP n/-ing] ❑ *She let out a little cry of pain.* 她疼得轻轻叫了一声。❑ *...the problem of having a national shortage of teachers.* …一个全国性教师短缺问题。3 PREP You use **of** after nouns referring to actions to specify the person or thing that is affected by the action or that performs the action. For example, "the kidnapping of the child" refers to an action affecting a child; "the arrival of the next train" refers to an action performed by a train. 用于动作名词后以说明此动作的受影响者或执行者 [n PREP n] ❑ *It sets targets for reduction of greenhouse-gas emissions.* 它为减少温室气体排放设立了目标。4 PREP You use **of** after words and phrases referring to quantities or groups of things to indicate the substance or thing that is being measured. 用于指数量或物群的词或短语后以表示受量的物质或事物 ❑ *...dozens of people.* …几十人。❑ *...a collection of short stories.* …一部短篇小说集。5 PREP You use **of** after the name of someone or something to introduce the institution or place they belong to or are connected with. 用于人或事物名称后以引入其所属或所关联的机构或地点 [n PREP n] ❑ *...the governor of Missouri.* …密苏里州州长。6 PREP You use **of** after a noun referring to a container to form an expression referring to the container and its contents. 用于指容器的名词后以构成指该容器及其所容之物的表达 [n PREP n] ❑ *...a box of tissues.* …一盒纸巾。❑ *...a roomful of people.* …一屋子人。7 PREP You use **of** after a countable noun and before an uncountable noun when you want to talk about an individual piece or item. 用于可数名词后或不可数名词前以谈论一单片或一项 [n PREP n] ❑ *...a blade of grass.* …一片草叶 ❑ *Marina ate only one slice of bread.* 玛丽娜只吃了一片面包。8 PREP You use **of** to indicate the materials or things that form something. 用以表示构成某物的材料或物体 [n PREP n] ❑ *...local decorations of wood and straw.* …用木头和草做的本地饰品。❑ *...loose-fitting garments of linen.* …宽松的亚麻衣服。9 PREP You use **of** after a noun which specifies a particular part of something, to introduce the thing that it is a part of. 用于名词后以指明某物的某部分 [n PREP n] ❑ *...the other side of the square.* …广场的另一边。❑ *...the beginning of the year.* …那年年初。

10 PREP You use **of** after some verbs to indicate someone or something else involved in the action. 用于某些动词后以表示动作所涉及的人或事物 ❑ *He'd been dreaming of her.* 他一直在梦想着她。 ❑ *Listen, I shall be thinking of you always.* 听着，我会一直想着你。 **11** PREP You use **of** after some adjectives to indicate the thing that a feeling or quality relates to. 用于某些形容词后以表示与某情感或特质所系之物 [adj PREP n/-ing] ❑ *I have grown very fond of Alec.* 我已变得很喜欢亚力克。 ❑ *His father was quite naturally very proud of him.* 他父亲很自然地为他感到自豪。 **12** PREP You use **of** before a word referring to the person who performed an action when saying what you think about the action. 用于指执行了某动作的人的词前以表达对该动作的评价 ❑ *This has been so nice, so terribly kind of you.* 你这样实在是太好了。 **13** PREP If something is **more of** or **less of** a particular thing, it is that thing to a greater or smaller degree. 用以表示具有某事物的特征 ["more/less" PREP "a" n] ❑ *Your extra fat may be more of a health risk than you realize.* 多余的脂肪可能是一种比你认识到的更严重的健康威胁。 **14** PREP You use **of** to indicate a characteristic or quality that someone or something has. 用以表示某人或某事物具有的某种特性和性质 ❑ *...the worth of their music.* …他们音乐的价值。 ❑ *She is a woman of enviable beauty.* 她这个女人美丽得让人羡慕。 **15** PREP You use **of** to specify an amount, value, or age. 用以说明某数量、价值或年龄 [n PREP amount] ❑ *Last Thursday, Nick announced record revenues of $3.4 billion.* 上周四，尼克宣布了34亿美元的创纪录收入。 ❑ *...young people under the age of 16 years.* …16岁以下的年轻人。 **16** PREP You use **of** after a noun such as "month" or "year" to indicate the length of time that some state or activity continues. 用于**month**、**year**等名词后以表示某状态或活动持续的时长 [n PREP n/-ing] ❑ *...eight bruising years of war.* …坚苦卓绝的8年战争。 **17** PREP You can use **of** to say what time it is by indicating how many minutes there are before the hour mentioned. 用于通过表示所提钟点之前有多少分钟来表达时间 [AM]

in BRIT, use **to**

❑ *At about a quarter of eight in the evening Joe Urber calls.* 在晚上大约八点差一刻时乔・乌尔贝打了电话。

of course ♦♦♦ **1** ADV You say **of course** to suggest that something is normal, obvious, or well-known, and should therefore not surprise the person you are talking to. 当然 [ADV with cl] [SPOKEN] ❑ *Of course there were lots of other interesting things at the exhibition.* 当然该展览会上有很多其他有趣的东西。 ❑ *"I have read about you in the newspapers of course," Charlie said.* "我当然在各报纸读过关于你的报道，"查理说。 **2** CONVENTION You use **of course** as a polite way of giving permission. 当然可以 [SPOKEN, FORMULAE] ❑ *"Can I just say something about the game on Saturday?"—"Yes, of course you can."* "我可以就说说关于星期六的那场比赛吗？"——"可以，当然可以。" **3** ADV You use **of course** in order to emphasize a statement that you are making, especially when you are agreeing or disagreeing with someone. 当然（用于强调）[SPOKEN, EMPHASIS] ❑ *"I guess you're right."—"Of course I'm right!"* "我想你是对的。"——"当然我是对的。" ❑ *Of course I'm not afraid!* 当然我不怕！ **4** CONVENTION **Of course not** is an emphatic way of saying no. 当然（不）[SPOKEN, EMPHASIS] ❑ *"You're not really seriously considering this thing, are you?"—"No, of course not."* "你没有真正认真地考虑这件事，对吧？"——"没有，当然没有。"

off
1 AWAY FROM
2 OTHER USES

1 off ♦♦♦

The preposition is pronounced /ɔf/. The adverb is pronounced /ɔf/.

介词读作 /ɔf/。副词读作 /ɔf/。

1 PREP If something is taken **off** something else or moves **off** it, it is no longer touching that thing. （从某物）下来 ❑ *He took his feet off the desk.* 他把双脚从书桌上移开。 ❑ *I took the key for the room off a rack above her head.* 我从她头顶上方的一个架子上拿下了该房间的钥匙。 ● ADV **Off** is also an adverb. 下 [ADV after v] ❑ *Lee broke off a small piece of orange and held it out to him.* 李掰下一小瓣橘子递给他。 **2** PREP When you get **off** a bus, train, or plane, you come out of it or leave it after you have been traveling on it. 下（公车、火车、飞机等） ❑ *Don't try to get on or off a moving train!* 火车运行中勿要上下！ ● ADV **Off** is also an adverb. 下（公车、火车、飞机等）[ADV after v] ❑ *At the next stop the man got off too and introduced himself.* 在下一站那个男人也下了，并介绍了他自己。 **3** PREP If you keep **off** a street or piece of land, you do not step on it or go there. 不在（某街道、某地等）上 ❑ *Locking up men does nothing more than keep them off the streets.* 把男人锁起来只是不让他们上街而已。 ● ADV **Off** is also an adverb. 不在（某街道、某地等）上地 ❑ *...a sign saying "Keep Off."* …一个写着"勿靠近"的牌子。 **4** PREP If something is situated **off** a place such as a coast, room, or road, it is near to it or next to it, but not exactly in it. 在离（某地）不远处 ❑ *The boat was anchored off the northern coast of the peninsula.* 那只船停泊在了离半岛北海岸不远处。 ❑ *Lily lives in a penthouse just off Park Avenue.* 莉莉住在离公园大街不远的一处顶层公寓里。 **5** ADV If you go **off**, you leave a place. 离开 ❑ *He was just about to drive off when the secretary came running out.* 他正要开车离去，这时秘书跑了出来。 ❑ *She was off again, to Kenya.* 她又走了，去肯尼亚。 **6** ADV When you take **off** clothing or jewelry that you are wearing, you remove it from your body. （从身体上脱、摘）下 [ADV after v] ❑ *He took off his spectacles and rubbed frantically at the lens.* 他摘下眼镜慌乱地擦镜片。 **7** ADV If you have time **off** or a particular day **off**, you do not go to work or school, for example, because you are sick or it is a day when you do not usually work. 不在工作中地；不在学习中地 ❑ *The rest of the men had the day off.* 其余的人放假一天。 ❑ *I'm off tomorrow.* 我明天休息。 ● PREP **Off** is also a preposition. 不在工作中；不在学习中 ❑ *He could not get time off work to go on vacation.* 他难以从工作中抽出时间去休假。 **8** PREP If you keep **off** a subject, you deliberately avoid talking about it. 避开（某话题） ❑ *Keep off the subject of politics.* 避开政治话题。 **9** PREP If there is money **off** something, its price is reduced by the amount specified. 减（价）[amount PREP n] ❑ *20 per cent off all jackets this Saturday.* 这个星期六所有上衣减价20%。 ● ADV **Off** is also an adverb. 减（价） ❑ *Take $5 off the regular price of any membership.* 从会员正价中减$5。 **10** ADV If something is a long way **off**, it is a long distance away from you. 离（某处）远 [n/amount ADV] ❑ *Florida was a long way off.* 佛罗里达离得很远。 **11** ADV If something is a long time **off**, it will not happen for a long time. 离（某时）远 [n/amount ADV] ❑ *An end to the crisis seems a long way off.* 危机的结束似乎还要一长段时间。 **12** PREP If you get something **off** someone, you obtain it from them. 从（某人那里得到）[SPOKEN] ❑ *I don't really get a lot of information, and if I do I get it off Mark.* 我真没得到很多信息，即便有也是从马克那里得到的。

2 off ♦♦♦

The preposition is pronounced /ɔf/. The adverb is pronounced /ɔf/.

介词读作 /ɔf/。副词读作 /ɔf/。

1 ADV If something such as an agreement or a sports event is **off**, it is canceled. （协议、运动事件等）取消 ❑ *Until Pointon is completely happy, however, the deal's off.* 等到波因顿完全高兴起来，那笔交易却取消了。 ❑ *She decided to call off the wedding at the last minute.* 她在最后一刻决定取消婚礼。 **2** PREP If someone is **off** something harmful such as a drug, they have stopped taking or using it. 停服（药物） ❑ *She felt better and the psychiatrist took her off antidepressants.* 她感觉好些了，于是精神科医师给她停用了抗抑郁药。 **3** PREP If you are **off** something, you have stopped liking it. 不再喜欢（某物） ❑ *I'm off coffee at the moment.* 我暂时不再喜欢咖啡。 **4** ADV When something such as a machine or electric light is **off**, it is not functioning or in use. When you switch it **off**, you stop it from functioning. （机器、电灯等）关闭着 ❑ *As he pulled into the driveway, he saw her bedroom light was off.* 当他驶入车道时，他看见她卧室的灯关着。 ❑ *We used sail power and turned the engine off to save our fuel.* 我们关掉了发动机，用帆航行以节省燃料。 **5** ADJ If food has gone **off**, it tastes and smells bad because it is no longer fresh enough to be eaten. （食物）变质了的 [mainly BRIT]

in AM, usually use **spoiled, bad**

6 PREP If you live **off** a particular kind of food, you eat it in order to live. If you live **off** a particular source of money, you use it to live. 靠（某种食物、某种资金等生存）[V PREP n] ❑ *Her husband's memories are of living off roast chicken and drinking whiskey.* 她丈夫所记得的是靠吃烤鸡喝威士忌过日子。 **7** PREP If a machine runs **off** a particular kind of fuel or power, it uses that power in order to function. （机器）靠（某种燃料或动力运行）[V PREP n] ❑ *The electric armor runs off the tank's power supply.* 该电动装甲车靠这坦克的动力供应运转。 **8** PHRASE If something happens **on and off**, or **off and on**, it happens occasionally, or only for part of a period of time, not in a regular or continuous way. 有时 ❑ *I was still working on and off as a waitress to support myself.* 我仍然有时做女招待来维持生活。

In addition to the uses shown here, **off** is used after some verbs and nouns in order to introduce extra information. **Off** is also used in phrasal verbs such as "get off," "pair off," and "sleep off."

of·fal /ɔfəl/ 1 N-UNCOUNT **Offal** is the parts of animals' bodies that are thrown away after the animals have been butchered. (不供食用而扔掉的) 动物杂碎 ❑ *...all the blood and offal the butchers shove down in the gutters.* …屠夫们倒入下水道的所有血和杂碎。 2 N-UNCOUNT **Offal** is the internal organs of animals, for example, their hearts and livers, when they are cooked and eaten. (供食用的) 动物内脏

off-balance also **off balance** 1 ADJ If someone or something is **off-balance**, they can easily fall or be knocked over because they are not standing firmly. 失去平衡的 [v n ADJ, v-link ADJ] ❑ *He tried to use his own weight to push his attacker off but he was off balance.* 他试图利用自己的重量推开袭击者，但他失去了平衡。 2 ADJ If someone is caught **off-balance**, they are extremely surprised or upset by a particular event or piece of news they are not expecting. 大为吃惊的 ❑ *Mullins knocked me off-balance with his abrupt change of subject.* 马林斯突然改变话题让我大为吃惊。

off-duty ADJ When someone such as a soldier or police officer is **off-duty**, they are not working. 不当班的 ❑ *The place is the haunt of off-duty policemen.* 那个地方是不当班的警察们的常去之地。

of·fence /əfɛns/ [BRIT] → see **offense**

Word Link *fend ≈ striking : defend, fender, offend*

of·fend /əfɛnd/ (**offends, offending, offended**) 1 V-T/V-I If you **offend** someone, you say or do something rude which upsets or embarrasses them. 冒犯；使人不安 ❑ *He apologizes for his comments and says he had no intention of offending the community.* 他为自己的评论道歉，并且说他无意冒犯那个团体。 ❑ *In the great effort not to offend, we end up saying nothing.* 为了尽量不冒犯人，我们最终什么也没说。 ● **of·fend·ed** ADJ 被冒犯了的 [v-link ADJ] ❑ *She is terribly offended, angered and hurt by this.* 她被此深深地触犯、触怒并伤害了。 2 V-I If someone **offends**, they commit a crime. 犯罪 [no cont] [FORMAL] ❑ *In Western countries girls are far less likely to offend than boys.* 在西方国家，女孩们远不像男孩们那样容易犯罪。

of·fend·er /əfɛndər/ (**offenders**) 1 N-COUNT An **offender** is a person who has committed a crime. 罪犯 ❑ *The authorities often know that sex offenders will attack again when they are released.* 当局通常知道性犯罪者被释放后还会再犯。 2 N-COUNT You can refer to someone or something which you think is causing a problem as an **offender**. 制造麻烦者；造成麻烦之物 ❑ *The plant's leaves can often turn brown, and I sometimes cut off the worst offenders.* 那种植物的叶子常会变成褐色，我有时会把最有问题的剪掉。

of·fense ♦◇◇ /əfɛns/ (**offenses**)

Pronounced /ɔfɛns/ for meaning 3.

义项3读作 /ɔfɛns/。

in BRIT, use **offence**

1 N-COUNT An **offense** is a crime that breaks a particular law and requires a particular punishment. 犯罪行为 ❑ *A first offense carries a fine of $1,000.* 初犯要罚款$1000。 2 N-VAR **Offense** or an **offense** is behavior that causes people to be upset or embarrassed. 冒犯行为 ❑ *He said he didn't mean to give offense.* 他说他无意冒犯。 3 N-SING In sports such as football or basketball, **the offense** is the team which has possession of the ball and is trying to score. (足球、篮球等运动中的) 进攻方 ["the" N] [AM] ❑ *Between plays the coach was talking to the offense in the huddle.* 赛间休息时，教练对围拢的攻方队员讲话。 4 CONVENTION Some people say "**no offense**" to make it clear that they do not want to upset you, although what they are saying may seem rude. 无意冒犯 [FORMULAE] ❑ *"No offense," she said, "but your sister seems a little gloomy."* "没有冒犯的意思，"她说："不过你妹妹似乎有点悲观。" 5 PHRASE If someone **takes offense at** something you say or do, they feel upset, often unnecessarily, because they think you are being rude to them. 生气 ❑ *Instead of taking offense, the woman smiled.* 那女人不但不生气反而笑了。

Thesaurus *offense* 另参见：
N. crime, infraction, violation, wrongdoing 1
assault, attack, insult, put-down, snub 2

Word Partnership *offense* 的常用搭配：
ADJ. **criminal** offense 1
serious offense 1 2
V. **commit an** offense 1 2
take offense 5

of·fen·sive ♦◇◇ /əfɛnsɪv/ (**offensives**) 1 ADJ Something that is **offensive** upsets or embarrasses people because it is rude or insulting. 冒犯性的 ❑ *Some friends of his found the play horribly offensive.* 他的一些朋友觉得那部戏让人很不舒服。 2 N-COUNT A military **offensive** is a carefully planned attack made by a large group of soldiers. (军事) 进攻 ❑ *Its latest military offensive against rebel forces is aimed at re-opening important trade routes.* 其最近对叛军的军事进攻旨在重新开辟重要的贸易路线。 3 N-COUNT If you conduct an **offensive**, you take strong action to show how angry you are about something or how much you disapprove of something. 强硬行动 ❑ *Republicans acknowledged that they had little choice but to mount an all-out offensive on the Democratic nominee.* 共和党人承认他们别无选择，只有对民主党提名人全力发起一场强硬行动。 4 PHRASE If you **go on the offensive, go over to the offensive**, or **take the offensive**, you begin to take strong action against people who have been attacking you. 采取攻势 ❑ *The West African forces went on the offensive in response to attacks on them.* 西非武装力量发起进攻以回应袭击。

Word Partnership *offensive* 的常用搭配：
N. offensive **language** 1
offensive **capability, ground** offensive, offensive **operations**, offensive **weapons** 2
V. **launch an** offensive, **mount an** offensive 2 3
take the offensive 4

of·fer ♦♦♦ /ɔfər/ (**offers, offering, offered**) 1 V-T If you **offer** something to someone, you ask them if they would like to have it or use it. 提供 (某物给某人) ❑ *He has offered seats at the conference table to the Russian leader and the president of Kazakhstan.* 他已给俄罗斯领导人和哈萨克斯坦总统提供了大会席位。 ❑ *The number of companies offering them work increased.* 给他们提供工作的公司的数量增多了。 2 V-T If you **offer to** do something, you say that you are willing to do it. 表示愿意 (做某事) ❑ *Peter offered to teach them water-skiing.* 彼得表示愿意教他们滑水。 3 N-COUNT An **offer** is something that someone says they will give you or do for you. 提议；提供物 ❑ *The offer of talks with Moscow marks a significant change from the previous Western position.* 与莫斯科会谈的提议标志着先前西方立场的一个重大转变。 ❑ *"I ought to reconsider her offer to move in," he mused.* "我应该重新考虑她搬进来的提议，"他若有所思地说。 4 V-T If you **offer** someone information, advice, or praise, you give it to them, usually because you feel that they need it or deserve it. 提供 (信息、忠告等)；给予 (表扬等) ❑ *They manage a company offering advice on mergers and acquisitions.* 他们经营一家公司，为并购和收购提供咨询。 ❑ *She offered him emotional and practical support in countless ways.* 她以无数种方式给予他情感支持和实际支持。 5 V-T If you **offer** someone something such as love or friendship, you show them that you feel that way toward them. 表示 (爱、友谊等) ❑ *The president has offered his sympathy to the Georgian people.* 总统已对格鲁吉亚人民表示了同情。 ❑ *It must be better to be able to offer them love and security.* 能给他们爱心和安全感肯定会更好。 6 V-T If people **offer** prayers, praise, or a sacrifice to God or a god, they speak to or give something to their god. (向上帝或神) 奉上 (祈祷、赞美、祭品等) ❑ *Church leaders offered prayers and condemned the bloodshed.* 教会领袖们奉上祈祷并谴责了那次流血事件。 ● PHRASAL VERB **Offer up** means the same as **offer**. 同**offer** ❑ *He should consider offering up a prayer to St. Lambert.* 他该考虑向圣·兰伯特奉上祈祷。 7 V-T If an organization **offers** something such as a service or product, it provides it. 提供 (服务、产品等) ❑ *We have been successful because we are offering a quality service.* 我们一直是成功的，因为我们在提供优质服务。 ❑ *The grocery store is offering customers 5 cents for each shopping bag re-used.* 该杂货店为顾客重复使用每个购物袋给5美分。 8 N-COUNT An **offer** in a store is a specially low price for a specific product or something extra that you get if you buy a certain product. (商店提供的) 特价；赠品 [oft supp N, also "on" N] ❑ *This month's offers include a pork loin and avocados.* 这个月的特价品包括猪后臀肉和鳄梨。 ❑ *Today's special offer gives you a choice of three destinations.* 今天的特惠为您提供3个可选目的地。 9 V-T If you **offer** a particular amount of money for something, you say that you will pay that much to buy it. 出价 (某数量的钱) ❑ *He is in a position to offer $825,000 for the bankrupt airline's assets.* 他能为这家破产航空公司的资产出价

O

82.5万美元。 ❑ *They are offering farmers $2.15 a bushel for corn.* 他们给农民们出每蒲式耳$2.15的价购买玉米。 10 N-COUNT An **offer** is the amount of money that someone says they will pay to buy something. 出价 ❑ *The real estate agents say no one else will make me an offer.* 各房产中介说别人都不会给我出价了。 11 PHRASE If you **have** something **to offer**, you have a quality or ability that makes you important, attractive, or useful. 有某种重要的品质或能力 ❑ *In your free time, explore all that this incredible city has to offer.* 闲暇时，探索一下这座美妙城市的所有奇妙之处吧。 12 PHRASE If there is something **on offer**, it is available to be used or bought. (某物) 在供 ❑ *They are making trips to check out the merchandise on offer.* 他们奔波各地，检查供售商品。 13 PHRASE If you are **open to offers**, you are willing to do something if someone will pay you an amount of money that you think is reasonable. 愿考虑买主的出价 ❑ *It seems that while the Dodgers are eager to have him, he is still open to offers.* 似乎道奇队很想要他，而他仍在考虑其他队的出价。

of·fer·ing ♦◇◇ /ɔfərɪŋ/ (**offerings**) 1 N-COUNT An **offering** is something that is being sold. 出售物 ❑ *It was very, very good, far better than vegetarian offerings in many an expensive restaurant.* 那道菜非常非常好，远远好过许多豪华饭店的素菜。 2 N-COUNT An **offering** is a gift that people offer to their God or gods as a form of worship. 祭品 ❑ *...the holiest of the Shinto rituals, where offerings are made at night to the great Sun.* …神道教仪式中最神圣的部分，祭品在夜间献给伟大的太阳神。

of·fer price (**offer prices**) 1 N-COUNT The **offer price** for a particular stock or share is the price that the person selling it says that they want for it. (股票等的) 卖方要价 [BUSINESS] ❑ *The company stunned the technology world by increasing its offer price to $26.* 该公司将卖方要价提高到$26，震惊了技术界。 2 → see also **asking price, bid price**

of·fice ♦♦♦ /ɔfɪs/ (**offices**) 1 N-COUNT An **office** is a room or a part of a building where people work sitting at desks. 办公室 ❑ *By the time Flynn arrived at his office it was 5:30.* 弗林到达办公室时已经5:30了。 ❑ *Telephone their head office for more details.* 给他们总部打电话询问更多的详细情况。 2 N-COUNT An **office** is a department of an organization, especially the government, where people deal with a particular kind of administrative work. (尤指政府的) 行政部门 [N-IN-NAMES] ❑ *Thousands have registered with unemployment offices.* 数千人已在失业服务处登记了。 ❑ *...the Congressional Budget Office.* …国会预算办公室。 3 N-COUNT An **office** is a small building or room where people can go for information, tickets, or a service of some kind. 服务处 ❑ *The tourist office operates a useful room-finding service.* 这个旅游办事处开办了实用的找房业务。 4 N-COUNT A doctor's or dentist's **office** is a place where a doctor or dentist sees their patients. 诊所 [AM]

in BRIT, use **surgery**

❑ *The chance of getting AIDS at the doctor's or dentist's office is extremely low.* 在诊所或牙医诊所感染艾滋病的可能性极小。 5 N-UNCOUNT If someone holds **office** in a government, they have an important job or position of authority. 公职 ❑ *The events to mark the president's four years in office went ahead as planned.* 纪念总统执政4年的活动按计划举行。 ❑ *The treasurer shall hold office for five years.* 财务主管将任职5年。 6 → see also **box office, post office**
→ see Picture Dictionary: **office**

of·fice hours N-PLURAL **Office hours** are the times when an office or similar place is open for business. For example, office hours in the United States and Britain are usually between 9 o'clock and 5 o'clock from Monday to Friday. 办公时间 ❑ *If you have any questions, please call Anne Fisher at 555-6203 during office hours.* 如有疑问，请在办公时间致电555-6203找安妮・费希尔。

of·fic·er ♦♦♦ /ɔfɪsər/ (**officers**) 1 N-COUNT In the armed forces, an **officer** is a person in a position of authority. 军官 ❑ *...a retired army officer.* …一位退役陆军军官。 2 N-COUNT Members of the police force can be referred to as **officers**. 警察；警官 ❑ *The officer saw no obvious signs of a break-in.* 那个警察没看到任何闯的明显痕迹。 ❑ *Officer Montoya was first on the scene.* 蒙托亚警官是第一个到达现场的人。 3 N-COUNT An **officer** is a person who has a responsible position in an organization, especially a government organization. (尤指政府部门的) 官员 ❑ *...a local authority education officer.* …一名地方政府教育官员。 4 → see also **police officer, probation officer**

of·fi·cial ♦♦♦ /əfɪʃəl/ (**officials**) 1 ADJ **Official** means approved by the government or by someone in authority. 官方的；正式的 ❑ *According to the official figures, over one thousand people died during the revolution.* 根据官方数字，有一千多人在革命中丧命。 ❑ *An official announcement is expected in the next few days.* 一份官方声明预计会在接下来的几天内发表。 ● **of·fi·cial·ly** ADV 正式地 ❑ *The election results have still not been officially announced.* 选举结果仍未正式宣布。 2 ADJ **Official** activities are carried out by a person in authority as part of their job. 公务的 [ADJ n] ❑ *The president is in Brazil for an official two-day visit.* 总统正在巴西进行为期两天的正式访问。 3 ADJ **Official** things are used by a person in authority as part of their job. 官员的 [ADJ n] ❑ *...the official residence of the head of state.* …国家元首的官邸。 4 ADJ If you describe someone's explanation or reason for something as the **official** explanation, you are suggesting that it is probably not true, but is used because the real explanation is embarrassing. 对外宣称的 [ADJ n] ❑ *They realized that the official explanation left facts unexplained.* 他们意识到那个对外宣称的解释没有对事实做出解释。 ● **of·fi·cial·ly** ADV 对外宣称地 [ADV with cl/group] ❑ *Officially, the guard was to protect us. In fact, they were there to report on our movements.* 据宣称，警卫是来保护我们的。实际上，他们是来监视我们的行动的。 5 N-COUNT An **official** is a person who holds a position of authority in an organization. 官员 ❑ *A senior UN official hopes to visit Baghdad this month.* 联合国一位高级官员希望本月访问巴格达。 6 N-COUNT An **official** at a sports event is a referee, umpire, or other person who checks that the players follow the rules. 裁判 ❑ *Officials suspended the game because of safety concerns.* 出于安全考虑，裁判暂停了那场比赛。

O

Picture Dictionary office

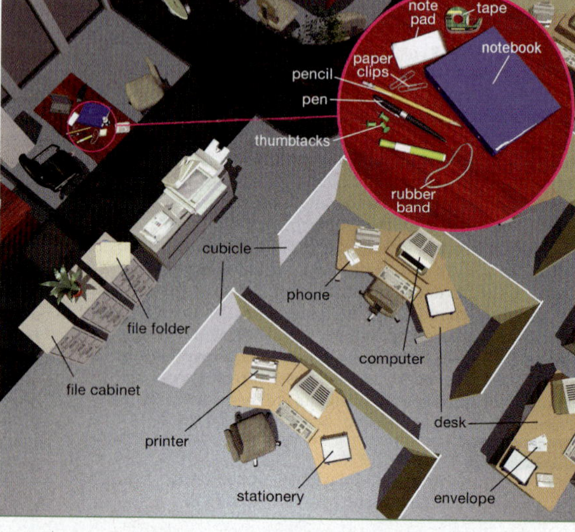

Thesaurus *official* 另参见:

ADJ. authentic, formal, legitimate, valid; (ant.) unauthorized, unofficial 1
N. administrator, director, executive, manager 5

Word Partnership *official* 的常用搭配:

N. official **documents**, official **language**, official **report**, official **sources**, official **statement** 1
official **duties**, official **visit** 2
administration official, **city** official, **government** official, **military** official 5
ADJ. **elected** official, **federal** official, **local** official, **senior** official, **top** official 5

off-licence (off-licences) N-COUNT An **off-licence** is a store that sells beer, wine, and other alcoholic drinks. 持有卖酒执照的商店 [BRIT]

in AM, use **liquor store**

off·line /ɒflaɪn/ 1 ADJ If a computer is **offline**, it is not connected to the Internet. Compare **online**. 脱机的 [COMPUTING] ❑ *Initially the system was offline for a number of days.* 最初系统有几天没有联网。 ● ADV **Offline** is also an adverb. 脱机地 [ADV with v] ❑ *Most software programs allow you to compose e-mails offline.* 大部分软件程序允许在脱机状态下写邮件。 2 **off line** → see **line** ❷ **8**

off-peak ADJ You use **off-peak** to describe something that happens or that is used at times when there is least demand for it. Prices at off-peak times are often lower than at other times. 非高峰时间的 [ADJ n] ❑ *Callers now pay 33 cents during peak hours and 30 cents during off-peak hours.* 现在，主叫方在高峰时段支付33美分话费；而非高峰时段则是30美分。 ❑ *...off-peak electricity.* …非高峰时间的电。 ● ADV **Off-peak** is also an adverb. 非高峰时间地 [ADV after v] ❑ *Each tape lasts three minutes and costs 36 cents per minute off-peak and 48 cents at all other times.* 每盘磁带持续3分钟，非高峰时间每分钟36美分，其他时间48美分。

★ **off·set** /ɔfsɛt/ (**offsets, offsetting**)

The form **offset** is used in the present tense and is the past tense and past participle of the verb.

V-T If one thing **is offset** by another, the effect of the first thing is reduced by the second, so that any advantage or disadvantage is canceled out. 抵消 ❑ *The increase in pay costs was more than offset by higher productivity.* 工资成本的增加远非更高的生产率所能抵消的。

off·shoot /ɔfʃut/ (**offshoots**) N-COUNT If one thing is an **offshoot** of another, it has developed from that other thing. 衍生物；分支 ❑ *Psychology began as a purely academic offshoot of natural philosophy.* 心理学形成之初是作为自然哲学的一个纯学术分支。

off·shore /ɔfʃɔr/ 1 ADJ **Offshore** means situated or happening in the sea, near to the coast. 海上的；近海的 [ADJ n] ❑ *...the offshore oil industry.* …近海石油业。 ❑ *...offshore islands.* …近海岛屿。 ● ADV **Offshore** is also an adverb. 海上地；近海地 ❑ *One day a larger ship anchored offshore.* 一天，一艘更大的船在近海抛锚。 2 ADJ **Offshore** investments or companies are located in a place, usually an island, which has fewer tax regulations than most other countries. (公司) 设在海外的 (尤指设在岛上，有较少税制的) [ADJ n] [BUSINESS] ❑ *The island offers a wide range of offshore banking facilities.* 这座岛提供广泛的海外银行业务。

off·shor·ing /ɒfʃɔrɪŋ, ɔf-/ N-UNCOUNT **Offshoring** is the practice of moving a company's work to a foreign country where labor costs are cheaper. 离岸外包 [BUSINESS] ❑ *Offshoring provides an opportunity to obtain I.T. services at low cost.* 离岸外包为低价获得信息技术服务提供了一个机会。

off·side /ɔfsaɪd/ also **off-side** 1 ADJ In football, a player is **offside** if they cross the line of scrimmage before a play begins. (橄榄球比赛中) 越位的 2 ADJ In games such as soccer or hockey, when an attacking player is **offside**, they have broken the rules by being nearer to the goal than a defending player when the ball is passed to them. (足球、曲棍球比赛中) 越位的 ❑ *The goal was disallowed because Wark was offside.* 那个进球被判无效，因为沃克越位了。 ● ADV **Offside** is also an adverb. 越位地 [ADV after v] ❑ *Yoon was standing at least ten yards offside.* 耀恩当时站的位置至少越位十码。 ● N-UNCOUNT **Offside** is also a noun. 越位 ❑ *Rush had a 45th-minute goal disallowed for offside.* 拉什第45分钟的一个进球由于越位被判无效。

★ **off·spring** /ɔfsprɪŋ/

Offspring is both the singular and the plural form.

N-COUNT You can refer to a person's children or to an animal's young as their **offspring**. 子女；幼崽 [FORMAL] ❑ *Eleanor was now less anxious about her offspring than she had once been.* 这时，埃莉诺已不像以前那样为子女担忧了。

of·ten ♦♦♦ /ɔfᵊn/

Often is usually used before the verb, but it may be used after the verb when it has a word like "less" or "more" before it, or when the clause is negative.

1 ADV If something **often** happens, it happens many times or much of the time. 经常 ❑ *They often spent Christmas together.* 他们经常一起过圣诞节。 ❑ *That doesn't happen very often.* 那不常发生。 2 ADV You use **how often** to ask questions about frequency. You also use **often** in reported clauses and other statements to give information about the frequency of something. 时常的 ❑ *How often do you brush your teeth?* 你多久刷一次牙？

You do not use **often** to talk about something that happens several times within a short period of time. You do not say, for example, "I often phoned her yesterday." You say "**I phoned her several times yesterday**" or "**I kept phoning her yesterday**."

3 PHRASE If something happens **every so often**, it happens regularly, but with fairly long intervals between each occasion. 偶尔 ❑ *She's going to come back every so often.* 她会偶尔回来一下。 4 PHRASE If you say that something happens **as often as not**, or **more often than not**, you mean that it happens fairly frequently, and that this can be considered as typical. 往往 ❑ *Yet, as often as not, they find themselves the target of persecution rather than praise.* 然而，他们往往发现自己是迫害对象，而不是表扬对象。

Thesaurus *often* 另参见:

ADV. regularly, repeatedly, usually; (ant.) never, rarely, seldom 1

oh ♦♦◇ /oʊ/ 1 CONVENTION You use **oh** to introduce a response or a comment on something that has just been said. (引出答话、评语) 哦 [SPOKEN] ❑ *"Had you seen the car before?"—"Oh yes, it was always in the driveway."* "你以前见过这辆车吗？"——"哦，见过。它总在车道上。" 2 EXCLAM You use **oh** to express a feeling such as surprise, pain, annoyance, or happiness. (表达情绪) 哎呀 [SPOKEN, FEELINGS] ❑ *"Oh!" Kenny blinked. "Has everyone gone?"* "哎呀！"肯尼眨了眨眼，"大家都走了吗？" 3 CONVENTION You use **oh** when you are hesitating while speaking, for example, because you are trying to estimate something, or because you are searching for the right word. (表示犹豫) 呃 [SPOKEN] ❑ *I've been here, oh, since the end of June.* 我是，呃，从6月底到这儿来的。

OHP /oʊ eɪtʃ pi/ (**OHPs**) N-COUNT An **OHP** is the same as an **overhead projector**. 高射投影仪

oil ♦♦♦ /ɔɪl/ (**oils, oiling, oiled**) 1 N-MASS **Oil** is a smooth, thick liquid that is used as a fuel and for making the parts of machines move smoothly. Oil is found underground. 石油 ❑ *The company buys and sells about 600,000 barrels of oil a day.* 这家公司一天买卖约六十万桶石油。 ❑ *...the rapid rise in prices for oil and gasoline.* …石油和汽油价格的飙涨。 2 V-T If you **oil** something, you put oil onto or into it, for example, to make it work smoothly or to protect it. 给某物上油 ❑ *A crew of assistants oiled and adjusted the release mechanism until it worked perfectly.* 助手们给排放装置加了润滑油并做了调节，直到其运转良好。 3 N-MASS **Oil** is a smooth, thick liquid made from plants and is often used for cooking. 植物油 ❑ *Combine the beans, chopped mint, and oil in a large bowl.* 将豆子、剁碎的薄荷和植物油混在一个大碗里。 4 N-MASS **Oil** is a smooth, thick liquid, often with a pleasant smell, that you rub into your skin or add to your bath. 润肤油；沐浴液 5 → see also **crude oil, olive oil** 6 **to burn the midnight oil** → see **midnight**
→ see Word Web: **oil**

oil paint (**oil paints**) N-UNCOUNT **Oil paint** is a thick paint used by artists. It is made from colored powder and linseed oil. 油画颜料 [also N in pl]

oil paint·ing (**oil paintings**) N-COUNT An **oil painting** is a picture which has been painted using oil paints. 油画 ❑ *Several magnificent oil paintings adorn the walls.* 几张华丽的油画使墙壁熠熠生辉。

O

Word Web oil

There is a great demand for **petroleum** in the world today. Companies are constantly **drilling oil wells** in oilfields on land and on the ocean floor. Some offshore drilling **rigs** or oil platforms sit on a concrete or metal foundation on a man-made island. Others float on a ship. The **crude oil** obtained from these wells goes to **refineries** through **pipelines** or in huge **tanker** ships. At the refinery, the crude oil is processed into a variety of products including **gasoline, aviation fuel**, and **plastics**.

oil rig (oil rigs) N-COUNT An **oil rig** is a structure on land or in the sea that is used when getting oil from the ground. 石油钻塔

oil slick (oil slicks) N-COUNT An **oil slick** is a layer of oil that is floating on the sea or on a lake because it has accidentally come out of a ship or container. (因事故泄露在水面的) 浮油 ❑ *The oil slick is now 35 miles long.* 这层浮油目前长35英里。

oily /ɔɪli/ (oilier, oiliest) 1 ADJ Something that is **oily** is covered with oil or contains oil. 涂满油的; 含油的 ❑ *He was wiping his hands on an oily rag.* 他在一块油乎乎的抹布上擦着双手。 2 ADJ **Oily** means looking, feeling, tasting, or smelling like oil. 油状的; 似油的 ❑ *...traces of an oily substance.* …一种油状物质的痕迹。

oint·ment /ɔɪntmənt/ (ointments) 1 N-MASS An **ointment** is a smooth thick substance that is put on sore skin or a wound to help it heal. 药膏 ❑ *A range of ointments and creams is available for the treatment of eczema.* 有一系列的药膏和乳剂可用于湿疹的治疗。 2 PHRASE If you describe someone or something as a **fly in the ointment**, you think they spoil a situation and prevent it from being as successful as you had hoped. 扫兴的人或事; 美中不足之处 ❑ *Rachel seems to be the one fly in the ointment of Caroline's smooth life.* 雷切尔似乎是卡罗琳平静生活中惟一的破坏因素。

okay ♦♦◊ /oʊkeɪ/ (okays, okaying, okayed) also **OK, O.K., ok** 1 ADJ If you say that something is **okay**, you find it satisfactory or acceptable. 不错的; 可以的 [INFORMAL] ❑ *...a shooting range where it's OK to use weapons.* …一个可以使用武器的靶场。 ❑ *Is it okay if I come by myself?* 我独自来行吗? ● ADV **Okay** is also an adverb. 不错; 可以 [ADV after v] ❑ *We seemed to manage okay for the first year or so after David was born.* 戴维出生后的第一年左右, 我们好像过得还可以。 2 ADJ If you say that someone is **okay**, you mean that they are safe and well. 安全的; 状况好的 [v-link ADJ] [INFORMAL] ❑ *Check that the baby's okay.* 看一下婴儿是否没事。 3 CONVENTION You can say **"Okay"** to show that you agree to something. (表示同意) 行 [INFORMAL, FORMULAE] ❑ *"Just tell him I would like to talk to him."—"OK."* "你就告诉他我想跟他谈谈。" —— "行。" 4 CONVENTION You can say **"Okay?"** to check whether the person you are talking to understands what you have said and accepts it. 行吗 [INFORMAL] ❑ *We'll get together next week, OK?* 我们下星期聚一聚, 好吗? 5 CONVENTION You can use **okay** to indicate that you want to start talking about something else or doing something else. 好了 [INFORMAL] ❑ *OK. Now, let's talk some business.* 好了。现在, 咱们谈点正事吧。 6 CONVENTION You can use **okay** to stop someone from arguing with you by showing that you accept the point they are making, though you do not necessarily regard it as very important. 好吧 [INFORMAL] ❑ *Okay, there is a slight difference.* 好吧, 是有稍稍的不同。 7 V-T If someone in authority **okays** something, they officially agree to it or allow it to happen. 批准 [INFORMAL] ❑ *His doctor wouldn't OK the trip.* 他的医生不会同意这趟旅行的。 ● N-SING **Okay** is also a noun. 批准 ❑ *He gave the okay to issue a new press release.* 他做出批准发表一篇新的新闻稿。

old ♦♦♦ /oʊld/ (older, oldest) 1 ADJ Someone who is **old** has lived for many years and is no longer young. 年老的 ❑ *...a white-haired old man.* …一位白发老人。 ● N-PLURAL **The old** are people who are old. 老年人 ❑ *...providing a caring response for the needs of the old and the handicapped.* …对老年人和残疾人的需要做出一个充满关怀的回应。 2 ADJ You use **old** to talk about how many days, weeks, months, or years someone or something has lived or existed. …岁的; …久的 ❑ *He was abandoned by his father when he was three months old.* 他3个月大的时候被父亲遗弃了。 ❑ *How old are you now?* 你现在多大了? ❑ *Bill was six years older than David.* 比尔比戴维大6岁。 3 ADJ Something that is **old** has existed for a long time. 古老的 ❑ *She loved the big old house.* 她喜爱那座古老的大房子。 ❑ *These books must be very old.* 这些书一定年头很久了。 4 ADJ Something that is **old** is no longer in good condition because of its age or because it has been used a lot. 破旧的 ❑ *He took a bunch of keys from the pocket of his old corduroy trousers.* 他从他那条破旧的灯心绒裤子口袋里掏出了一串钥匙。 5 ADJ You use **old** to refer to something that is no longer used, that no longer exists, or that has been replaced by something else. 废弃的; 过时的 [ADJ n] ❑ *The old road had disappeared under grass and heather.* 这条废弃的道路已消失在草丛和石南花中。 6 ADJ You use **old** to refer to something that used to belong to you, or to a person or thing that used to have a particular role in your life. 从前 (拥有或珍惜) 的 [poss ADJ n] ❑ *I'll make up the bed in your old room.* 我会把你以前房间的床铺收拾好。 ❑ *I still have affection for my old school.* 我对母校依然很有感情。 7 ADJ An **old** friend, enemy, or rival is someone who has been your friend, enemy, or rival for a long time. 多年的 [ADJ n] ❑ *I called my old friend John Horner.* 我给老朋友约翰·霍纳打了个电话。 ❑ *Mr. Brownson, I assure you, King's an old enemy of mine.* 布朗森先生, 我向你保证, 金是我的夙敌。 8 ADJ You can use **old** to express affection when talking to or about someone you know. (表示亲昵) 老… [BRIT, INFORMAL, FEELINGS] 9 PHRASE You use **any old** to emphasize that the quality or type of something is not important. If you say that a particular thing is **not any old** thing, you are emphasizing how special or famous it is. 随便的/非同一般的 [INFORMAL, EMPHASIS] ❑ *Any old paper will do.* 随便一张纸就行。 10 PHRASE **In the old days** means in the past, before things changed. 以前 ❑ *In the old days, doctors made housecalls.* 以前, 医生们都上门看病。 11 PHRASE When people refer to **the good old days**, they are referring to a time in the past when they think that life was better than it is now. 过去的好时光 ❑ *He remembers the good old days when everyone in his village knew him and you could leave your door open at night.* 他常想起过去的好时光。那时, 村里人都认识他, 而且大家夜不闭户。 12 **good old** → see **good** 13 **to settle an old score** → see **score**

Thesaurus *old* 另参见:

ADJ. elderly, mature, senior; *(ant.)* young 1
ancient, antique, archaic, dated, old-fashioned, outdated, traditional; *(ant.)* new 5

old age N-UNCOUNT Your **old age** is the period of years toward the end of your life. 晚年 ❑ *They worry about how they will support themselves in their old age.* 他们担心自己到了晚年该如何来维持生计。

old-fashioned 1 ADJ Something such as a style, method, or device that is **old-fashioned** is no longer used, done, or admired by most people, because it has been replaced by something that is more modern. 旧式的; 过时的 ❑ *The house was dull, old-fashioned and in bad condition.* 那幢房子阴暗、老式, 并且破烂。 2 ADJ **Old-fashioned** ideas, customs, or values are the ideas, customs, and values of the past. 守旧的 ❑ *She has some old-fashioned values and can be a strict disciplinarian.* 她有一些守旧的观念, 可能还是个严守纪律的人。

★ **ol·ive** /ɒlɪv/ (olives) 1 N-VAR **Olives** are small green or black fruits with a bitter taste. Olives are often pressed to make olive oil. 橄榄 ❑ *...a pile of black olives.* …一堆黑橄榄。 2 N-COUNT An **olive tree** or an **olive** is a tree on which olives grow. 橄榄树 ❑ *Olives look romantic on a hillside in Provence.* 在普罗旺斯的一个山坡上橄榄树看起来很浪漫。 3 COLOR Something that is **olive** is yellowish-green in color. 橄榄色的 ❑ *...glowing colors such as deep red, olive, saffron and ocher.* …鲜艳颜色, 如深红色、橄榄色、橘黄色和赭石色。 ● COMB IN COLOR **Olive** is also a combining form. (用于构成表示颜色的复合词) 橄榄色的 ❑ *She wore an olive-green T-shirt.* 她穿了一件橄榄绿的T恤衫。 4 ADJ If someone has **olive** skin, the color of their skin is yellowish brown. (皮肤) 黄褐色的 ❑ *They are handsome with dark,* shining hair, olive skin and fine brown eyes. 他们很帅，有着乌黑闪亮的头发，黄褐色的皮肤，迷人的棕色眼睛。

ol·ive oil (olive oils) N-MASS **Olive oil** is oil that is obtained by pressing olives. It is used for putting on salads or in cooking. 橄榄油

Olym·pic ♦◇◇ /əlɪmpɪk/ (**Olympics**) 1 ADJ **Olympic** means relating to the Olympic Games. 奥林匹克运动会的 [ADJ n] ❑ *...the reigning Olympic champion.* …本届奥运会冠军。 2 N-PROPER **The Olympics** are the Olympic Games. 奥林匹克运动会 ❑ *Have you been watching the Olympics?* 你一直在看奥运会吗？

Olym·pic Games N-PROPER-COLL **The Olympic Games** are a set of international sports competitions which take place every four years, each time in a different city. 奥林匹克运动会 ❑ *At the 1968 Olympic Games she had won gold medals in races at 200, 400, and 800 meters.* 1968年的奥运会上，她夺得了200米、400米和800米赛跑的金牌。

om·buds·man /ɒmbʊdzmən/ (**ombudsmen**) N-COUNT **The ombudsman** is an independent official who has been appointed to investigate complaints that people make against the government or public organizations. (调查公众对政府或公共机构投诉的) 调查官 ❑ *The leaflet explains how to complain to the banking ombudsman.* 该手册说明了如何向银行调查官投诉。

★ **ome·let** /ɒmlɪt, ɒməlɪt/ (**omelets**) also **omelette** N-COUNT An **omelet** is a type of food made by beating eggs and cooking them in a flat frying pan. 煎蛋饼 ❑ *...a cheese omelet.* …一份奶酪煎蛋饼。 → see **egg**

omen /oʊmən/ (**omens**) N-COUNT If you say that something is an **omen**, you think it indicates what is likely to happen in the future and whether it will be good or bad. 预兆 ❑ *Her appearance at this moment is an omen of disaster.* 她此时的出现是灾难的预兆。

omi·nous /ɒmɪnəs/ ADJ If you describe something as **ominous**, you mean that it worries you because it makes you think that something bad is going to happen. 不祥的 ❑ *There was an ominous silence at the other end of the phone.* 电话那端是一阵不祥的沉默。

● **omi·nous·ly** ADV 不祥地 ❑ *The bar seemed ominously quiet.* 那个酒吧似乎寂静得让人觉得不祥。

★ **omis·sion** /oʊmɪʃən/ (**omissions**) 1 N-COUNT An **omission** is something that has not been included or has not been done, either deliberately or accidentally. 删节；遗漏 ❑ *He was surprised by his wife's omission from the guest list.* 他对于宾客名单上他夫人名字的遗漏感到吃惊。 2 N-VAR **Omission** is the act of not including a particular person or thing or of not doing something. 省略；排除 ❑ *...the prosecution's seemingly malicious omission of recorded evidence.* …控方对在案证据似为恶意的疏略。

omit /oʊmɪt/ (**omits, omitting, omitted**) 1 V-T If you **omit** something, you do not include it in an activity or piece of work, deliberately or accidentally. 删节；省略；遗漏 ❑ *Omit the salt in this recipe.* 去掉这个食谱中的盐。 2 V-T If you **omit to** do something, you do not do it. 未 (做) [FORMAL] ❑ *His new girlfriend had omitted to tell him she was married.* 他的新任女友没有跟他说她已经结婚。

Thesaurus *omit* 另参见：
v. forget, leave out, miss; (*ant.*) add, include 1

on
1. DESCRIBING POSITIONS AND LOCATIONS
2. TALKING ABOUT HOW OR WHEN SOMETHING HAPPENS
3. OTHER USES
4. PHRASES

1 on ♦♦♦

The preposition is pronounced /ɒn/. The adverb and the adjective are pronounced /ɒn/.

介词读作 /ɒn/。副词和形容词读作 /ɒn/。

1 PREP If someone or something is **on** a surface or object, the surface or object is immediately below them and is supporting their weight. (表示接触、支撑) 在…上 ❑ *He is sitting beside her on the sofa.* 他正挨着她坐在沙发上。 ❑ *On top of the cupboards are straw baskets.* 橱柜顶上是几个草篮子。 2 PREP If something is **on** a surface or object, it is stuck to it or attached to it. (表示粘贴、附着) 在…上 ❑ *I stared at the peeling paint on the ceiling.* 我盯着天花板上剥落的油漆。 ❑ *The clock on the wall showed one minute to twelve.* 墙上的钟显示11：59。 ● ADV **On** is also an adverb. 在…上 [ADV after v] ❑ *I know how to sew a button on.* 我知道怎么缝上扣子。 3 PREP If you put, throw, or drop something **on** a surface, you move it or drop it so that it is then supported by the surface. (表示方向) 到…上 ❑ *He got his winter jacket from the closet and dropped it on the sofa.* 他从衣柜里拿出冬天的夹克，把它扔到沙发上。 4 PREP You use **on** to say what part of your body is supporting your weight. 倚在 (身体某部位) 之上 ❑ *He continued to lie on his back and look at clouds.* 他继续仰面朝天躺着，看着云彩。 ❑ *He raised himself on his elbows, squinting into the sun.* 他用双肘撑起身体，眯起眼睛看着太阳。 5 PREP You use **on** to say that someone or something touches a part of a person's body. 与 (身体某部位) 接触 ❑ *He leaned down and kissed her lightly on the mouth.* 他斜下身子，轻轻地吻了她的嘴。 6 PREP If someone has a particular expression **on** their face, their face has that expression. (表情) 在 (脸) 上 [n PREP n] ❑ *The maid looked at him, a nervous smile on her face.* 侍女看着他，脸上带着紧张的微笑。 7 ADV When you put a piece of clothing **on**, you place it over part of your body in order to wear it. If you have it **on**, you are wearing it. (穿) 上；(戴) 上 [ADV after v] ❑ *He put his coat on while she opened the front door.* 她打开前门时，他穿上了他的外套。 8 PREP You can say that you have something **on** you if you are carrying it in your pocket or in a purse. 带在…身上 [PREP pron] ❑ *I didn't have any money on me.* 我身上一点儿钱也没带。 9 PREP If someone's eyes are **on** you, they are looking or staring at you. (视线) 在…上 ❑ *Everyone's eyes were fixed on him.* 大家的目光都锁定在他身上。 10 PREP If you hurt yourself **on** something, you accidentally hit a part of your body against it and that thing causes damage to you. (身体某部位碰撞) 到某物上 ❑ *Mr. Pendle hit his head on a wall as he fell.* 彭德尔先生摔倒时，头撞到了墙上。 11 PREP If you are **on** an area of land, you are there. 在 (区域) 上 ❑ *He was able to spend only a few days on the island.* 他只能在这个岛上待几天。 ❑ *You lived on the farm until you came back to America?* 回美国之前你一直住在农场？ 12 PREP If something is situated **on** a place such as a road or coast, it forms part of it or is by the side of it. (坐落) 在…上；在…旁 ❑ *Bergdorf Goodman has opened a men's store on Fifth Avenue.* 伯格多夫・古德曼在第五大道上开了一家男装店。 ❑ *The hotel is on the coast.* 那家宾馆在海边。 13 PREP If you get **on** a bus, train, or plane, you go into it in order to travel somewhere. If you are **on** it, you are traveling in it. 在 (交通工具) 上 ❑ *We waited till twelve and we finally got on the plane.* 我们一直等到12点，终于登上了飞机。 ● ADV **On** is also an adverb. (登) 上 [ADV after v] ❑ *He showed his ticket to the conductor and got on.* 他向乘务员出示了车票，就上了车。 14 PREP If there is something **on** a piece of paper, it has been written or printed there. (写或印) 在…上 ❑ *The writing on the back of the card was cramped but scrupulously neat.* 卡片背面的字迹密密麻麻，但却工整干净。 15 PREP If something is **on** a list, it is included in it. 在 (名单) 上 ❑ *I've seen your name on the list of deportees.* 我已经在被驱逐出境人员名单上见到你的名字了。

2 on ♦♦♦

The preposition is pronounced /ɒn/. The adverb and the adjective are pronounced /ɒn/.

介词读作 /ɒn/。副词和形容词读作 /ɒn/。

1 PREP You use **on** to introduce the method, principle, or system which is used to do something. 以…方式 ❑ *...a television that we bought on credit two months ago.* …我们两个月前以赊购的方式买的一台电视机。 ❑ *They want all groups to be treated on an equal basis.* 他们希望所有的族群都能以一种平等的原则受到对待。 2 PREP If something is done **on** an instrument or a machine, it is done using that instrument or machine. 借助 (仪器或机械) ❑ *...songs that I could just sit down and play on the piano.* …我一坐下来就可以用钢琴弹奏的歌曲。 3 PREP If information is, for example, **on** tape or **on** computer, that is the way that it is stored. (储存) 在…上 ❑ *We've got her statement on tape.* 我们已经把她的陈述录在磁带上了。 4 PREP If something is being broadcast, you can say that it is **on** the radio or television. 通过 (广播、电视) 播出 ❑ *Every sporting event on television and satellite over the next seven days is listed.* 未来7天通过电视和卫星转播的每个体育赛事均已列出。 ● ADJ **On** is also an adjective. 播出的 [v-link ADJ] ❑ *...teenagers complaining there's nothing good on.* …抱怨没什么好节目播出的青少年。 5 ADJ When an activity is taking place, you can say that it is **on**. 正在发生的 [v-link ADJ] ❑ *There's an exciting match on at Wimbledon right now.* 有一场精彩的比赛

此刻正在温布尔顿正进行着。**6** ADV You use **on** in expressions such as "**have a lot going on**" and "**not have very much on**" to indicate how busy someone is. 用在**have a lot going on**和**not have very much on**中，表示忙碌 [SPOKEN] ❑ *I have a lot on in the next week.* 下星期我会非常地忙。**7** PREP You use **on** to introduce an activity that someone is doing, particularly traveling. 在从事（旅行等活动）中 ❑ *I've always wanted to go on a cruise.* 我一直想去乘船旅游。❑ *We're going on a trip next month.* 我们下个月要去旅行。**8** PREP You can indicate when something happens by saying that it happens **on** a particular day, date, or part of the week. 在（某日）❑ *This year's event will take place on June 19th, a week earlier than usual.* 今年的比赛将在6月19日进行，比往常提前一个星期。❑ *I was born on Christmas Day.* 我出生在圣诞节。❑ *The highway is often lined with cars on the weekend.* 这条公路在周末常排满了汽车。**9** PREP You use **on** when mentioning an event that was followed by another one. 在…之后 [PREP n/-ing] ❑ *She waited in her hotel to welcome her children on their arrival from Vancouver.* 她在旅馆等着迎接将从温哥华回来的孩子们。**10** ADV You use **on** to say that someone is continuing to do something. （继续）下去 [ADV after v] ❑ *They walked on in silence for a while.* 他们默默地继续走了一会儿。❑ *We worked on into the night.* 我们一直工作到夜里。**11** ADV You use **on** in expressions such as **from now on** and **from then on** to indicate that something starts to happen at the time mentioned and continues to happen afterward. （从某时）起 ["from" n ADV] ❑ *Perhaps it would be best not to see much of you from now on.* 或许从现在开始最好少和你见面。❑ *We can expect trouble from this moment on.* 从此时开始，我们可能会有麻烦。**12** ADV You often use **on** after the adverbs "early," "late," "far," and their comparative forms, especially at the beginning or end of a sentence, or before a preposition. 常用在副词**early**，**late**，**far**及其比较级后，尤置于句子开头、结尾或介词后 [adv ADV] ❑ *The market square is a riot of color and animation from early on in the morning.* 这个集市广场从一大早就色彩缤纷，生机勃勃。❑ *Later on I learned how to read music.* 后来我学会了识谱。

❸ on ♦♦♦

> The preposition is pronounced /ɒn/. The adverb and the adjective are pronounced /ɒn/.

> 介词读作 /ɒn/。副词和形容词读作 /ɒn/。

1 PREP Books, discussions, or ideas **on** a particular subject are concerned with that subject. 关于 ❑ *They offer free counseling on legal matters.* 他们提供有关法律事务的免费咨询。❑ *He declined to give any information on the presidential election.* 他拒绝透露有关总统选举的任何信息。**2** ADV When something such as a machine or an electric light is **on**, it is functioning or in use. When you switch it **on**, it starts functioning. （机器、电器等）工作着 ❑ *The light was on and the door was open.* 灯亮着，门开着。❑ *The heating's been turned off. I've turned it on again.* 暖气已经被关掉了，我已经又把它打开了。**3** PREP If you are **on** a committee or council, you are a member of it. 是…的成员 ❑ *Claire and Alita were on the organizing committee.* 克莱尔和阿利塔都曾是组委会成员。**4** PREP Someone who is **on** a drug takes it regularly. 定期服用 ❑ *She was on antibiotics for an eye infection that wouldn't go away.* 她为持续不愈的眼部感染定期服用抗生素。**5** PREP If you live **on** a particular kind of food, you eat it. If a machine runs **on** a particular kind of power or fuel, it uses it in order to function. 靠（某食物为生）；用（某动力运转）[V PREP n] ❑ *The caterpillars feed on a wide range of trees, shrubs and plants.* 毛虫以各种树木、灌木丛和植物为食。❑ *He lived on a diet of water and canned fish.* 他靠水和罐头鱼为生。**6** PREP If you are **on** a particular income, that is the income that you have. 拥有（某程度收入）[BRIT] ❑ *...young people who are unemployed or on low wages.* …失业或低收入的年轻人。❑ *He's on three hundred a week.* 他每周有300元的收入。**7** PREP Taxes or profits that are obtained from something are referred to as taxes or profits **on** it. 从某事物中获得（税收或利润）[n PREP n] ❑ *...a general strike to protest a tax on food and medicine.* …一次抗议对食物和药品征税的大罢工。**8** PREP When you buy something or pay for something, you spend money **on** it. 为某事物（花钱）[PREP n/-ing] ❑ *I resolved not to waste money on a hotel.* 我决定不因住旅馆浪费钱。❑ *He spent more on feeding the dog than he spent on feeding himself.* 他养狗花的钱比养自己花的钱还多。**9** PREP When you spend time or energy **on** a particular activity, you spend time or energy doing it. 在…方面（花时间或精力）[PREP n/-ing] ❑ *People complain about how children spend so much time on computer games.* 人们抱怨孩子怎么花那么多时间玩电脑游戏。❑ *You all know why I am here, so I won't waste time on preliminaries.* 你们都知道我为什么来这儿，因此我就不浪费时间作介绍了。

❹ on ♦♦♦ /ɒn/

➪ **Please look at meanings 4 – 6 to see if the expression you are looking for is shown under another headword.** **1** PHRASE If you say that something happens **on and on**, you mean that it continues to happen for a very long time. 不停地 ❑ *...designers, builders, fitters – the list goes on and on.* …设计师，建筑工，装配工——名单长得没完没了。❑ *Lobell drove on and on through the dense and blowing snow.* 洛贝尔迎着浓密、纷飞的雪花不停地开车。**2** PHRASE If you say that something is **not on** or is **just not on**, you mean that it is unacceptable or impossible. 不被接受的；不可能的 [BRIT, INFORMAL] **3** **on behalf of** → see **behalf** **4** **on and off** → see **off** **5** **and so on** → see **so** **6** **on top of** → see **top**

> In addition to the uses shown here, **on** is used after some verbs, nouns, and adjectives in order to introduce extra information. **On** is also used in phrasal verbs such as "keep on" and "sign on."

once ♦♦♦ /wʌns/ **1** ADV If something happens **once**, it happens one time only. 一次 [ADV with v] ❑ *I met Miquela once, briefly.* 我见过蜜凯拉一次，时间很短。❑ *Since that evening I haven't once slept through the night.* 自那晚之后，我再也没睡过一次囫囵觉。● PRON **Once** is also a pronoun. 一次 ["the/this" PRON] ❑ *"Have they been to visit you yet?"—"Just the once, yeah."* "他们已经去看过你了吗？"——"来过，就那一次。" **2** ADV You use **once** with "a" and words like "day," "week," and "month" to indicate that something happens regularly, one time in each day, week, or month. 每隔…一次 [ADV "a" n] ❑ *Lung cells die and are replaced about once a week.* 肺细胞约每周死亡、更新一次。**3** ADV If something was **once** true, it was true at some time in the past, but is no longer true. 从前 ❑ *Her parents once ran a store.* 她父母从前开过一家商店。❑ *I lived there once myself, before I got married.* 我从前自己住在那儿，没结婚前。**4** ADV If someone **once** did something, they did it at some time in the past. 曾经 [ADV with v] ❑ *I once went camping at Lake Michigan with a friend.* 我曾和一个朋友去密执安湖野营。❑ *We once walked across the frozen pond at two in the morning.* 我们曾在凌晨2点徒步横穿冰冻的池塘。**5** CONJ If something happens **once** another thing has happened, it happens immediately afterward. 一…就 ❑ *The decision had taken about 10 seconds once he'd read a market research study.* 他读完一份市场调研报告后，10秒钟就做出了决定。**6** PHRASE If something happens **all at once**, it happens suddenly, often when you are not expecting it to happen. 突然 ❑ *All at once there was someone knocking on the door.* 突然有人敲门。**7** PHRASE If you do something **at once**, you do it immediately. 立刻 ❑ *I have to go at once.* 我得马上走。❑ *Remove from the heat, add the parsley, toss and serve at once.* 从火上端下来，加入香芹，搅拌后立刻上桌。**8** PHRASE If a number of different things happen **at once** or **all at once**, they all happen at the same time. 同时 ❑ *You can't be doing two things at once.* 你不能同时做两件事。**9** PHRASE **For once** is used to emphasize that something happens on this particular occasion, that it has never happened before, and may never happen again. 就此一次 [EMPHASIS] ❑ *For once, Dad is not complaining.* 就这一次，爸爸没有抱怨。**10** PHRASE If something happens **once again** or **once more**, it happens again. 再一次 ❑ *Amy picked up the hairbrush and brushed her hair once more.* 艾米拿起梳子，又梳了一遍头发。**11** PHRASE If something happens **once and for all**, it happens completely or finally. 最终地 [EMPHASIS] ❑ *We have to resolve this matter once and for all.* 我们必须彻底解决这件事情。**12** PHRASE If something happens **once in a while**, it happens sometimes, but not very often. 偶尔 ❑ *Your body, like any other machine, needs a full service once in a while.* 你的身体就像其他机器一样，偶尔也需要一次全面保养。**13** PHRASE If you have done something **once or twice**, you have done it a few times, but not very often. 一两次；几次 ❑ *I visited once or twice.* 我参观过一两次。❑ *Once or twice she had caught a flash of interest in William's eyes.* 有一两次，她捕捉到威廉眼中一闪的关注。

> **one**
> ❶ NUMBER
> ❷ PRONOUN, DETERMINER AND ADJECTIVE USES
> ❸ PHRASES

❶ one ♦♦♦ /wʌn/ (**ones**) NUM **One** is the number 1. 1 ❑ *They had three sons and one daughter.* 他们有3儿1女。❑ *...one thousand years ago.* …1000年以前。

❷ **one** ♦♦♦ /wʌn/ (ones)

➪ **Please look at meaning 11 to see if the expression you are looking for is shown under another headword.** 1 ADJ If you say that someone or something is the **one** person or thing of a particular kind, you are emphasizing that they are the only person or thing of that kind. 惟一的 [det ADJ] [EMPHASIS] ❑ *They had alienated the one man who knew the business.* 他们已经疏远了那个惟一懂这行的人。 2 DET **One** can be used instead of "a" to emphasize the following noun. 用来代替**a**，强调后接的名词 [EMPHASIS] ❑ *There is one thing I would like to know – What is it about Tim that you find so irresistible?* 有一件事我想知道——蒂姆到底有什么让你觉得那么不可抗拒？ 3 DET You can use **one** instead of "a" to emphasize the following adjective or expression. 用来代替**a**，强调后接的形容词或短语 [INFORMAL, EMPHASIS] ❑ *If we ever get married we'll have one terrific wedding.* 如果我们结婚，我们会举办一场盛大的婚礼。 4 DET You can use **one** to refer to the first of two or more things that you are comparing. (表示与其他事物作比较) 这个 ❑ *Prices vary from one shop to another.* 各家商店价格不同。 ● ADJ **One** is also an adjective. 这个 [det ADJ] ❑ *The one thing that she accomplished was raising money to update our facilities.* 她完成的这项工作就是募集资金来更新我们的设备。 ● PRON **One** is also a pronoun. 这一个 ❑ *The twins were dressed differently and one was thinner than the other.* 这对双胞胎穿着各异，而且其中一个比另一个瘦。 5 PRON You can use **one** or **ones** instead of a noun when it is clear what type of thing or person you are referring to and you are describing them or giving more information about them. 用来替代名词所指的很明确的人、物 ❑ *They are selling their house to move to a smaller one.* 他们要卖掉他们的房子，搬到一个小点的房子去住。 6 PRON You use **ones** to refer to people in general. 人们 ❑ *We are the only ones who know.* 我们是惟一知情的人。 7 PRON You can use **one** instead of a noun group when you have just mentioned something and you want to describe it or give more information about it. 用以替代名词词组表示的刚提到的且要详细描述的事物 [PRON "of" n, PRON that] ❑ *The issue of land reform was one that dominated Hungary's parliamentary elections.* 土地改革是一个左右匈牙利议会选举的问题。 8 DET You can use **one** when you have been talking or writing about a group of people or things and you want to say something about a particular member of the group. (特定的一群人或事物中的) 一个 ❑ *"A college degree isn't enough," said one honors student.* "只有一个大学的学位还不够，"一位优等生说。 ● PRON **One** is also a pronoun. 一个 ❑ *Some of them couldn't eat a thing. One couldn't even drink.* 他们中有些人一点东西都不能吃，有一人甚至连水都不能喝。 9 QUANT You use **one** in expressions such as **"one of the biggest airports"** or **"one of the most experienced players"** to indicate that something or someone is bigger or more experienced than most other things or people of the same kind. (最…) 之一 [QUANT "of" adj-superl] ❑ *Subaru is one of the smallest Japanese car makers.* 斯巴鲁是最小的日本汽车制造商之一。 10 DET You can use **one** when referring to a time in the past or in the future. For example, if you say that you did something **one day**, you mean that you did it on a day in the past. 某一个 (过去或将来的时间) ❑ *How would you like to have dinner one night, just you and me?* 哪天晚上一起吃饭怎么样，就你和我？ 11 **one day** → see **day** 12 PRON You use **one** to make statements about people in general which also apply to themselves. **One** can be used as the subject or object of a sentence. 人们 [FORMAL] ❑ *If one looks at the bigger picture, a lot of positive things are happening.* 如果人们从更宏观的角度看，许多积极的事情正在发生。 ❑ *Where does one go from there?* 人们从那儿能去哪里？

> **One** or **you** is used when making statements that are true of any individual person. **One** is more formal than **you**. ❑ *I suppose one can't blame him… A crisis can make you stop and take a look at your life.* **People** is used to talk about everyone in general, or about a particular group. ❑ *…the amount of bread people buy… Don't go on about it. People may get embarrassed.*

❸ **one** ♦♦♦ /wʌn/

➪ **Please look at meanings 10 – 13 to see if the expression you are looking for is shown under another headword.** 1 PHRASE You can use **for one** to emphasize that a particular person is definitely reacting or behaving in a particular way, even if other people are not. 就某人来说 [EMPHASIS] ❑ *I, for one, hope you don't get the job.* 就我来说，我不希望你得到那份工作。 2 PHRASE You can use expressions such as **a hundred and one**, **a thousand and one**, and **a million and one** to emphasize that you are talking about a large number of things or people. (表示强调) 很多 [EMPHASIS] ❑ *There are a hundred and one ways in which you can raise money.* 有很多你可以筹钱的办法。 3 PHRASE You can use **in one** to indicate that something is a single unit, but is made up of several different parts or has several different functions. 集为一体 ❑ *…a love story and an adventure all in one.* …一个集爱情与冒险于一体的故事。 4 PHRASE You use **one after the other** or **one after another** to say that actions or events happen with very little time between them. 一个接一个地 ❑ *My three guitars broke one after the other.* 我的3把吉它一个接着一个地坏了。 5 PHRASE **The one and only** can be used in front of the name of an actor, singer, or other famous person when they are being introduced on a show. (用在演出前的介绍中) 独一无二的 ❑ *…one of the greatest ever rock performers, the one and only Tina Turner.* …有史以来最伟大的摇滚歌手之一，举世无双的蒂纳・特纳。 6 PHRASE You can use **one by one** to indicate that people do things or that things happen in sequence, not all at the same time. 依次地 ❑ *We went into the room one by one.* 我们依次走进了房间。 7 PHRASE You use **one or other** to refer to one or more things or people in a group, when it does not matter which particular one or ones are thought of or chosen. 或者这个或者那个 ❑ *One or other of the two women was wrong.* 这两个妇女中总有一个错了。 8 PHRASE **One or two** means a few. 几个 ❑ *We may make one or two changes.* 我们可以作几处改变。 ❑ *I've also sold one or two to a publisher.* 我也卖了几个给一位出版商。 9 PHRASE If you try to get **one up on** someone, you try to gain an advantage over them. 略胜某人一筹 ❑ *…the competitive kind who will see this as the opportunity to be one up on you.* …那种会把这视为一次胜过你的机会的好胜者。 10 **one another** → see **another** 11 **one thing after another** → see **another** 12 **of one mind** → see **mind** 13 **in one piece** → see **piece**

one-off (one-offs) 1 N-COUNT You can refer to something as a **one-off** when it is made or happens only once. 一次性事物 ❑ *Our survey revealed that these allergies were mainly one-offs.* 我们的调查显示，这些过敏大多是一次性反应。 2 ADJ A **one-off** thing is made or happens only once. 一次性的 [mainly BRIT]

> in AM, usually use **one-time**

on·er·ous /ɒnərəs, oʊnər-/ ADJ If you describe a task as **onerous**, you dislike having to do it because you find it difficult or unpleasant. 繁重的；费力的 [FORMAL] ❑ *…parents who have had the onerous task of bringing up a very difficult child.* …那些身负重任要养育一个非常难调教的孩子的父母。

one's ♦◇◇ /wʌnz/ 1 DET Speakers and writers use **one's** to indicate that something belongs or relates to people in general, or to themselves in particular. 人们的；自己的 [FORMAL] ❑ *…a feeling of responsibility for the welfare of others in one's community.* …为自己社区里其他人谋福利的责任感。 2 **One's** can be used as a spoken form of "one is" or "one has," especially when "has" is an auxiliary verb. **one is**或**one has**的口语形式，尤当**has**作助动词时 ❑ *No one's going to hurt you.* 没人要伤害你。 → see **one**

one·self /wʌnsɛlf/

> **Oneself** is a third person singular reflexive pronoun.

1 PRON-REFL **Oneself** is used to mean "any person in general" as the object of a verb or preposition, when this refers to the same person as the subject of the verb. (回指前文主语) 自己 [FORMAL] ❑ *One must apply oneself to the present and keep one's eyes firmly fixed on one's future goals.* 人们必须让自己立足于现在，把眼光坚定地锁定未来目标。 2 PRON-REFL **Oneself** is used to mean "any person in general" as the object of a verb or preposition, when "one" is not present but is understood to be the subject of the verb. (前文无指涉主语) 自己 [FORMAL] ❑ *The historic feeling of the town makes it a pleasant place to base oneself for summer vacations.* 这个小镇的历史氛围使其成为在暑假沉浸自己的一个好去处。

one-sided 1 ADJ If you say that an activity or relationship is **one-sided**, you think that one of the people or groups involved does much more than the other or is much stronger than the other. 一边倒的；悬殊的 ❑ *The negotiating was completely one-sided.* 该谈判完全呈一边倒之势。 2 ADJ If you describe someone as **one-sided**, you are critical of what they say or do because you think it shows that they have considered only one side of an issue or event. 偏袒的；片面的 [DISAPPROVAL] ❑ *The organization still believes the government is being one-sided.* 该组织仍然认为政府有偏袒之处。

one-time also **onetime** 1 ADJ **One-time** is used to describe something which happened in the past, or something such as a

O

job, position, or role which someone used to have. 以前的 [ADJ n] [JOURNALISM] ❑ *The legislative body had voted to oust the country's onetime rulers.* 立法机构已投票罢黜了该国以前的统治者们。 **2** ADJ A **one-time** thing is made or happens only once. 一次性的 [ADJ n] [mainly AM] ❑ *...a one-time charge.* …一次性收费。

one-to-one **1** ADJ In a **one-to-one** relationship, one person deals directly with only one other person. 一对一的 [ADJ n] ❑ *...one-to-one training.* …一对一的训练。 ● ADV **One-to-one** is also an adverb. 一对一地 [ADV after v] ❑ *She would like to talk to people one to one.* 她想和人们一对一地谈话。 **2** ADJ If there is a **one-to-one** match between two sets of things, each member of one set matches a member of the other set. 对应的 [ADJ n] ❑ *In English, there is not a consistent one-to-one match between each written symbol and each distinct spoken sound.* 在英语中，每一个书写符号和每一个独特的发音之间不存在固定的一一对应关系。

one-way **1** ADJ In **one-way** streets or traffic systems, vehicles can only travel along in one direction. 单向行驶的 [ADJ n] ❑ *...Gotham's maze of one-way streets.* …纽约市的单行道迷宫。 **2** ADJ **One-way** describes trips which go to just one place, rather than to that place and then back again. (旅行) 单程的 ❑ *The trailers will be rented for one-way trips.* 这些拖车将被租用于单程旅行。 **3** ADJ A **one-way** ticket or fare is for a trip from one place to another, but not back again. (车票、车费) 单程的 [mainly AM] ❑ *...a one-way ticket from New York to Los Angeles.* …从纽约到洛杉矶的一张单程票。 ● ADV **One-way** is also an adverb. 单程地 [ADV after v]

in BRIT, usually use **single**

❑ *Unrestricted fares will be increased as much as $80 one-way.* 弹性票价将增加至高达单程$80。

on·going /ɒ̱ngoʊɪŋ/ ADJ An **ongoing** situation has been happening for quite a long time and seems likely to continue for some time in the future. 进行中的; 继续存在的 ❑ *There is an ongoing debate on the issue.* 关于这个问题争论还在继续。

on·ion /ʌ̱nyən/ (**onions**) N-VAR An **onion** is a round vegetable with a light brown skin. It has many white layers on its inside which have a strong, sharp smell and taste. 洋葱 ❑ *You grind the onion and the raw cranberries together.* 你把洋葱和新鲜越橘一起磨碎。 → see **spice**

on·line ♦♦♦ /ɒ̱nlaɪn/ also **on-line** **1** ADJ If a company goes **online**, its services become available on the Internet. (公司服务) 在网上开通的 [BUSINESS, COMPUTING] ❑ *...the first bank to go online.* …第一家开通网上业务的银行。 ❑ *...an online shopping center.* …一个在线购物中心。 **2** ADJ If you are **online**, your computer is connected to the Internet. Compare **offline**. 在线的 [COMPUTING] ❑ *You can chat to other people who are online.* 你可以与其他在线的人聊天。 ● ADV **Online** is also an adverb. 在线地 [ADV after v] ❑ *...the cool stuff you find online.* …你在网上找到的好东西。 **3** **on line** → see **line** → see **bank**

on·looker /ɒ̱nlʊkər/ (**onlookers**) N-COUNT An **onlooker** is someone who watches an event take place but does not take part in it. 旁观者 ❑ *A handful of onlookers stand in the field watching.* 少数旁观者站在场地里观看。

only

❶ ADVERB AND ADJECTIVE USES
❷ CONJUNCTIONS
❸ PHRASES

❶ only ♦♦♦ /oʊ̱nli/

In written English, **only** is usually placed immediately before the word it qualifies. In spoken English, however, you can use stress to indicate what **only** qualifies, so its position is not so important.

1 ADV You use **only** to indicate the one thing that is true, appropriate, or necessary in a particular situation, in contrast to all the other things that are not true, appropriate, or necessary. 只有 ❑ *Only the president could authorize the use of the atomic bomb.* 只有总统能授权原子弹的使用。 ❑ *A business can only be built and expanded on a sound financial base.* 一家企业只有在稳定的财政基础上才能开办并扩大规模。 **2** ADV You use **only** to introduce the thing which must happen before the thing mentioned in the main part of the sentence can happen. 只有…才 [ADV cl/prep] ❑ *The lawyer is paid only if he wins.* 律师只有打赢官司才会被付费。 ❑ *The Bank of England insists that it will cut interest rates only when it is ready.* 英格兰银行坚持只有在它做好准备时才会降低利率。

When **only** is used as an adverb, its position in the sentence depends on the word or phrase it applies to. If **only** applies to the subject of a clause, you put it in front of the subject. ❑ *Only strong characters can make such decisions.* Otherwise, you normally put it in front of the verb, after the first auxiliary, or after the verb **be**. ❑ *I only want my son back, that is all... He had only agreed to see me because we had met before... I was only able to wash four times in 66 days.* However, some people think it is more correct to put **only** directly in front of the word or phrase it applies to. This is the best position if you want to be quite clear or emphatic. ❑ *It applies only to passengers carrying British passports... She'd done it only because it was necessary.* For extra emphasis, you can put **only** after the word or phrase it applies to. ❑ *The event will be for women only... I'll say this once and once only.*

3 ADJ If you talk about **the only** person or thing involved in a particular situation, you mean there are no others involved in it. 惟一的 [det ADJ] ❑ *She was the only woman in Shell's legal department.* 她曾是壳牌公司法律部惟一的女性。 **4** ADJ An **only** child is a child who has no brothers or sisters. 独生的 [ADJ n] ❑ *The actor, an only child, grew up in the Bronx.* 那位演员是位独生子，在布朗克斯区长大。 **5** ADV You use **only** to indicate that something is no more important, interesting, or difficult, for example, than you say it is, especially when you want to correct a wrong idea that someone has or may get. 仅仅…而已 ❑ *At the moment it is only a theory.* 眼下，它还只是个理论而已。 ❑ *"I'm only a sergeant," said Clements.* "我不过是个中士，" 克莱门茨说。 **6** ADV You use **only** to emphasize how small an amount is or how short a length of time is. (强调数量小或时间短) 仅仅 [ADV n/adv] [EMPHASIS] ❑ *Child car seats only cost about $10 a week to rent.* 儿童汽车座椅租用一周仅花费约$10。 ❑ *...spacecraft guidance systems weighing only a few grams.* …重量只有几克的宇宙飞船导航系统。 **7** ADV You use **only** to emphasize that you are talking about a small part of an amount or group, not the whole of it. (强调只是一小部分而非全部) 仅仅 [ADV n] [EMPHASIS] ❑ *These are only a few of the possibilities.* 这些只是其中的几个可能性。 **8** ADV **Only** is used after "can" or "could" to emphasize that it is impossible to do anything except the rather inadequate or limited action that is mentioned. (用于**can**或**could**之后，强调除此之外别无他法) 只 [modal ADV inf] [EMPHASIS] ❑ *For a moment I could say nothing. I could only stand and look.* 一时间我什么也说不出来，只能站在那儿看着。 **9** ADV You can use **only** in the expressions **I only wish** or **I only hope** in order to emphasize what you are hoping or wishing. (强调愿望或希望) 确实 [ADV before v] [EMPHASIS] ❑ *I only wish he were here now that things are getting better for me.* 既然我的情况正在好转，我真希望他在这儿。 **10** ADV You can use **only** before an infinitive to introduce an event which happens immediately after one you have just mentioned, and which is surprising or unfortunate. (用于不定式前) 不料 [ADV to-inf] ❑ *Ron tried the embassy, only to be told that Hugh was in a meeting.* 罗恩到使馆试了试，不料被告知休正在开会。 **11** ADV You can use **only** to emphasize how appropriate a certain course of action or type of behavior is. (用来强调适宜性) 很 [EMPHASIS] ❑ *It's only fair to let her know that you intend to apply.* 让她知道你有意申请是很公平的。 **12** ADV You can use **only** in front of a verb to indicate that the result of something is unfortunate or undesirable and is likely to make the situation worse rather than better. (用于动词前) 反而 [ADV before v] ❑ *The embargo would only hurt innocent civilians.* 禁运反而会伤及无辜的平民。

Thesaurus *only* 另参见：
ADJ. alone, individual, single, solitary, unique ❶ **3**

❷ only ♦♦♦ /oʊ̱nli/ **1** CONJ **Only** can be used to add a comment which slightly changes or limits what you have just said. (用来补充) 只是 [INFORMAL] ❑ *It's just as dramatic as a movie, only it's real.* 这真和电影一样富有戏剧性，只不过它是现实。 ❑ *It's a bit like my house, only nicer.* 这有点儿像我的房子，不过更漂亮些。 **2** CONJ **Only** can be used after a clause with "would" to indicate why something is not done. 要不是 [SPOKEN] ❑ *I'd invite you to come with me, only it's such a long way.* 要不是路途太远，我就请你和我一起去了。

❸ only ♦♦♦ /oʊ̱nli/ **1** PHRASE If you say you **only have to** do one thing in order to achieve or prove a second thing, you are emphasizing how easily the second thing can be achieved or proved. 只要…即可 [EMPHASIS] ❑ *Any time you want a babysitter, dear,* you only have to ask. 亲爱的，任何时候你想要一个临时照看孩子的人，只要开口说就是了。 **2** PHRASE You can say that something has **only just** happened when you want to emphasize that it happened a very short time ago. 刚刚 [EMPHASIS] ❑ *I've only just arrived.* 我刚刚才到。 **3** PHRASE You use **only just** to emphasize that something is true, but by such a small degree that it is almost not true at all. 勉强 [EMPHASIS] ❑ *For centuries farmers there have only just managed to survive.* 几个世纪以来，那儿的农民勉强能维持生存。 ❑ *I am old enough to remember the War, but only just.* 我这个年龄足以记住那场战争，不过只是勉强记得。 **4** PHRASE You can use **only too** to emphasize that something is true or exists to a much greater extent than you would expect or like. 极其 [EMPHASIS] ❑ *I know only too well that plans can easily go wrong.* 我非常清楚，计划会很容易出问题。 **5** PHRASE You can say that you are **only too** happy to do something to emphasize how willing you are to do it. (强调乐意做某事) 太 [EMPHASIS] ❑ *I'll be only too pleased to help them out with any questions.* 我将十分乐意为他们解决任何问题。 **6 if only** → see **if** **7 not only** → see **not** **8 the one and only** → see **one**

on-screen also **onscreen** **1** ADJ **On-screen** means appearing on the screen of a television, movie theater, or computer. 屏幕上的 [ADJ n] ❑ *Read the on-screen lyrics and sing along.* 看着屏幕上的歌词，跟着唱。 **2** ADJ **On-screen** means relating to the roles played by film or television actors, in contrast with their real lives. 银幕上的 [ADJ n] ❑ *...her first on-screen kiss.* …她的银幕初吻。 ● ADV **On-screen** is also an adverb. 银幕上地 [ADV with cl] ❑ *He was immensely attractive to women, on-screen and off-screen.* 银幕上下，他对女士都极具吸引力。

★ **on·set** /ɒnsɛt/ N-SING **The onset of** something is the beginning of it, used especially to refer to something unpleasant. (尤指不愉快事情的) 开始 ❑ *Most of the passes have been closed with the onset of winter.* 随着冬天的来临，大多数的关卡都已经关闭。

on·shore /ɒnʃɔr/ ADJ **Onshore** means happening on land, rather than at sea. 在陆地上的 ❑ *...Western Europe's biggest onshore oilfield.* …西欧最大的陆上油田。 ● ADV **Onshore** is also an adverb. 在陆地上 [ADV after v] ❑ *They missed the ferry and remained onshore.* 他们没赶上渡船，滞留在了岸上。

on·slaught /ɒnslɔt/ (**onslaughts**) **1** N-COUNT An **onslaught** on someone or something is a very violent, forceful attack against them. 猛攻 ❑ *The press launched another vicious onslaught on the president.* 新闻界对这位总统进行了新一轮的恶毒抨击。 **2** N-COUNT If you refer to an **onslaught of** something, you mean that there is a large amount of it, often so that it is very difficult to deal with. (常指难以应付的) 大量 ❑ *...the constant onslaught of ads on TV.* …电视上连续不断的大量广告。

onto ♦◇◇ /ɒntu/

The spelling **on to** is also used.

In addition to the uses shown below, **onto** is used in phrasal verbs such as "hold onto" and "latch onto."

1 PREP If something moves **onto** or is put **onto** an object or surface, it is then on that object or surface. 到…之上 ❑ *I took my bags inside, lowered myself onto the bed and switched on the TV.* 我把我的包拿进去，坐到了床上，打开了电视。 **2** PREP You can sometimes use **onto** to mention the place or area that someone moves into. 移向 (某处) ❑ *The players jogged onto the field.* 运动员们慢慢跑进赛场。 ❑ *At exactly 6:00 p.m., Marcia drove onto the freeway.* 下午6点整，马西娅开车上了高速公路。 **3** PREP You can use **onto** to introduce the place toward which a light or someone's look is directed. (光线或视线) 朝向 ❑ *...the metal part of the door onto which the sun had been shining.* …阳光一直照耀着的门的金属部分。 ❑ *The colors rotated around on a disc and were reflected onto the wall behind.* 那些色彩在一张圆盘上旋转，并被反射到后面的墙上。 **4** PREP If a door or room opens **onto** a place, that place is directly in front of it. (门或房间) 对着… [V PREP n] ❑ *The door opened onto a well-lit hallway.* 这扇门对着一个照明很好的门厅。 **5** PREP When you change the position of your body, you use **onto** to introduce the part your body which is now supporting you. (身体重心) 移向 ❑ *As he stepped backwards she fell onto her knees, then onto her face.* 他往后退步时，她双膝跪倒在地，接着脸也着地。 ❑ *Puffing a little, Mabel shifted her weight onto her feet.* 梅布尔有些气喘，将她身体的重量移到了双脚上。 **6** PREP When you get **onto** a bus, train, or plane, you enter it in order to travel somewhere. 登上 (交通工具) ❑ *As he got on to the plane, he asked me how I was feeling.* 他上飞机时问我感觉如何。 **7** PREP **Onto** is used after verbs such as "hold," "hang," and "cling" to indicate what someone is holding firmly or where something is being held firmly. 用于**hold**，**hang**，**cling**等动词之后，表示某人紧握或某物被紧握 ❑ *The reflector is held onto the sides of the spacecraft with a frame.* 反光器被一个框紧紧地固定在宇宙飞船的各个侧面。 **8** PREP If people who are talking get **onto** a different subject, they begin talking about it. 转向 (新的话题) ❑ *Let's get on to more important matters.* 咱们谈些更重要的事吧。 **9** PREP You can sometimes use **onto** to indicate that something or someone becomes included as a part of a list or system. 成为…的一部分 ❑ *The Macedonian question had failed to get on to the agenda.* 马其顿问题没能提到议事日程上来。 ❑ *The pill itself has changed a lot since it first came onto the market.* 自从投放市场以来，这种片剂本身已经改变了许多。 **10** PREP If someone **is onto** something, they are about to discover something important. 将要发现 ["be" PREP n] [INFORMAL] ❑ *He leaned across the table and whispered to me, "I'm really onto something."* 他隔着桌子探过身悄悄地跟我说，"我真的要有重大发现了。" **11** PREP If someone **is onto** you, they have discovered that you are doing something illegal or wrong. (对某人做的坏事) 已经明白了 ["be" PREP n] [INFORMAL] ❑ *I had told people what he had been doing, so now the police were onto him.* 我已经告诉人们他一直在从事的勾当，所以现在警察都对他很清楚了。

onus /oʊnəs/ N-SING If you say that **the onus is on** someone **to** do something, you mean it is their duty or responsibility to do it. 责任；义务 [FORMAL] ❑ *The onus is on companies and consumers to keep up with anti-virus updates.* 公司和用户有责任跟上杀毒软件的更新。

★ **on·ward** /ɒnwərd/

The form **onwards** can also be used as an adverb.

1 ADJ **Onward** means moving forward or continuing a journey. 向前的；(旅程) 继续进行的 ❑ *American Airlines have two flights a day to Bangkok, and there are onward flights to Phnom Penh.* 美国航空公司每天有两个航班飞到曼谷，还有接着飞金边的航班。 ● ADV **Onward** is also an adverb. 向前地；(旅程) 继续进行地 [ADV after v] ❑ *The bus continued onward.* 公交车继续前行。 **2** ADJ **Onward** means developing, progressing, or becoming more important over a period of time. 发展的 ❑ *...the onward march of progress in the aircraft industry.* …航空工业的发展进程。 ● ADV **Onward** is also an adverb. 发展地 [ADV after v] ❑ *From here, it has been onward and upward all the way.* 由此开始，它一直在发展、高升。 **3** ADV If something happens from a particular time **onward** or **onwards**, it begins to happen at that time and continues to happen afterward. 从…以后 ["from" n ADV] ❑ *From the turn of the century onward, she shared the life of the aborigines.* 从世纪之交以后，她就过着和土著人一样的生活。

oops /ʊps, ups/ EXCLAM You say "**oops**" to indicate that there has been a slight accident or mistake, or to apologize to someone for it. 哎哟 [INFORMAL, FEELINGS] ❑ *Today they're saying, "Oops, we made a mistake."* 今天他们一直在说："哎哟，我们犯了个错。"

ooze /uz/ (**oozes, oozing, oozed**) **1** V-T/V-I When a thick or sticky liquid **oozes** from something or when something **oozes** it, the liquid flows slowly and in small quantities. 使流出；流出 ❑ *Blood was still oozing from the wound.* 血还在从伤口渗出。 ❑ *The lava will just ooze gently out of the crater.* 熔岩只会缓缓地从火山口流出来。 **2** V-T/V-I If you say that someone or something **oozes** a quality or characteristic, or **oozes** with it, you mean that they show it very strongly. 强烈表现出；强烈表现 ❑ *The Southern plantation house oozes charm.* 南部种植园的那所房子散发出很大魅力。

▲ **opaque** /oʊpeɪk/ **1** ADJ If an object or substance is **opaque**, you cannot see through it. 不透明的 ❑ *You can always use opaque glass if you need to block a street view.* 如果你需要挡住外面的街景，你随时可以使用不透明玻璃。 **2** ADJ If you say that something is **opaque**, you mean that it is difficult to understand. 难理解的 ❑ *...the opaque language of the inspector's reports.* …检查员报告中晦涩难懂的语言。

op. cit. /ɒp sɪt/ In reference books, **op. cit.** is used after an author's name to refer to a book of theirs which has already been mentioned. 见前引书 [FORMAL] ❑ *...quoted in Iyer, op. cit., p. 332.* …引自伊耶，见前引书332页。

OPEC /oʊpɛk/ N-PROPER **OPEC** is an organization of countries that produce oil. It tries to develop a common policy and system of prices. **OPEC** is an abbreviation for "Organization of Petroleum-Exporting Countries." 石油输出国组织 ❑ *Each member of OPEC would seek to maximize its own production.* 石油输出国组织的每个成员国都会设法将本国产量增到最大。

open

❶ DESCRIBING A POSITION OR MOVEMENT
❷ ACCESSIBLE OR AVAILABLE; NOT HIDDEN, BLOCKED, ETC.
❸ BEGIN, START
❹ PHRASES AND PHRASAL VERBS

❶ **open ♦♦♦** /oʊpən/ (**opens, opening, opened**) 1 V-T/V-I If you **open** something such as a door, window, or lid, or if it **opens**, its position is changed so that it no longer covers a hole or gap. 打开 ❑ *He opened the window and looked out.* 他打开窗户往外看。● ADJ **Open** is also an adjective. 开着的 ❑ *...an open window.* …一扇开着的窗户。2 V-T If you **open** something such as a bottle, box, parcel, or envelope, you move, remove, or cut part of it so you can take out what is inside. 开封 ❑ *I opened the letter.* 我拆开了那封信。● ADJ **Open** is also an adjective. 打开的 ❑ *...an open bottle of milk.* …一瓶打开的牛奶。● PHRASAL VERB **Open up** means the same as **open**. 同**open** ❑ *He opened up a cage and lifted out a 6ft python.* 他打开一个笼子，提起了一条6英尺长的蟒蛇。3 V-T/V-I If you **open** something such as a book, an umbrella, or your hand, or if it **opens**, the different parts of it move away from each other so that the inside of it can be seen. 打开；张开 ❑ *He opened the heavy Bible.* 他翻开了那本厚厚的《圣经》。❑ *The flower opens to reveal a bee.* 花开了，露出来一只蜜蜂。● ADJ **Open** is also an adjective. 张开的 ❑ *Without warning, Bardo smacked his fist into his open hand.* 毫无预警地，巴多用拳头啪地猛击了他张开的手。● PHRASAL VERB **Open out** means the same as **open**. 同**open** ❑ *Keith took a map from the dashboard and opened it out on his knees.* 基思从仪表板上拿了张地图，摊开放在了膝盖上。4 V-T If you **open** a computer file, you give the computer an instruction to display it on the screen. 打开(电脑文件) [COMPUTING] ❑ *Double click on the icon to open the file.* 双击图标来打开文件。

> Note that you do not use **open** as a verb or adjective to talk about electrical devices. If someone causes an electrical device to work by pressing a switch, you say that they **put** it **on**, **switch** it **on**, or **turn** it **on**. ❑ *It's too easy just to switch on the television.* If the device is already working, you say that it is **on**. ❑ *The answering machine is on... He cannot sleep with the light on.*

5 V-T/V-I When you **open** your eyes or your eyes **open**, you move your eyelids upward, for example, when you wake up, so that you can see. 睁开 ❑ *When I opened my eyes I saw Melissa standing at the end of my bed.* 我睁开双眼时，看见梅利莎站在我的床脚。● ADJ **Open** is also an adjective. 睁着的 ❑ *As soon as he saw that her eyes were open he sat up.* 一看见她眼睛睁着，他马上坐了起来。6 V-T If you **open** your arms, you stretch them wide apart in front of you, usually in order to put them around someone. 张开(双臂) ❑ *She opened her arms and gave me a big hug.* 她张开双臂，紧紧地拥抱了我。7 V-T If you **open** your shirt or coat, you undo the buttons or pull down the zipper. 解开(衣服) ❑ *I opened my coat and let him see the belt.* 我解开外套，让他看了看腰带。● ADJ **Open** is also an adjective. 解开的 [ADJ n, V-link ADJ] ❑ *The top can be worn buttoned up or open over a T-shirt.* 这件上衣可以系上扣子或不系扣子套在T恤衫的外面穿。

❷ **open ♦♦♦** /oʊpən/ (**opens, opening, opened**) 1 V-T/V-I If people **open** something such as a blocked road or a border, or if it **opens**, people can then pass along it or through it. 开放(被封锁的道路、边界等) ❑ *The rebels have opened the road from Monrovia to the Ivory Coast.* 叛乱分子开放了从蒙罗维亚到科特迪瓦的公路。● ADJ **Open** is also an adjective. 畅通的 ❑ *We were part of an entire regiment that had nothing else to do but to keep that highway open.* 我们是整个团的一部分，这个团无其他任务，只是保证公路畅通。● PHRASAL VERB **Open up** means the same as **open**. 同**open** ❑ *As rescue workers opened up roads today, it became apparent that some small towns were totally devastated.* 今天营救人员清除路障时发现，显然有些小镇已完全沦为废墟。2 V-I If a place **opens into** another, larger place, you can move from one directly into the other. 通向(更大的地方) ❑ *The corridor opened into a low smoky room.* 这条走廊通向一个既低矮又烟雾弥漫的房间。● PHRASAL VERB **Open out** means the same as **open**. 同**open** ❑ *...narrow streets opening out into charming squares.* …通向迷人的广场的狭窄街道。3 ADJ An **open** area is a large area that does not have many buildings or trees in it. 开阔的 ❑ *Officers will also continue their search of nearby open ground.* 警察们也会继续搜寻附近的开阔地。4 ADJ An **open** structure or object is not covered or enclosed. 无遮盖的 [ADJ n] ❑ *Don't leave a child alone in a room with an open fire.* 别把小孩单独放在有明火的房间里。5 V-T/V-I When a store, office, or public building **opens** or **is opened**, its doors are unlocked and the public can go in. 使开门营业；开门营业 ❑ *Banks closed on Friday afternoon and did not open again until Monday morning.* 银行星期五下午关门，直到星期一早上才会再开门营业。❑ *I'd been waiting for him to open the shop.* 我一直在等他开门营业。● ADJ **Open** is also an adjective. 营业中的 ❑ *The gallery is open Monday through Friday, 9 am to 6 pm.* 美术馆的开放时间为周一到周五，上午9点到下午6点。6 V-T/V-I When a public building, factory, or company **opens** or when someone **opens** it, it starts operating for the first time. 使开张；开张 ❑ *The original station opened in 1954.* 原来的车站是1954年启用的。❑ *The complex opens to the public tomorrow.* 该建筑群明天向公众开放。7 ADJ If a factory or company remains **open**, it continues to operate. 运营中的 [V-link ADJ] ❑ *The government says it's no longer willing to spend $170 million a month to keep the pits open.* 政府宣称将不愿再每月花费1.7亿美元维持这些矿井的运转。❑ *...any operating subsidy required to keep the airline open.* …维持航空公司运行所需要的任何运营补贴。● **open·ing** N-COUNT (**openings**) 运营的开始 ❑ *He was there, though, for the official opening.* 然而，他到了那儿是为了参加正式开幕。8 ADJ If you describe a person or their character as **open**, you mean they are honest and do not want or try to hide anything or to deceive anyone. 坦诚的 ❑ *He had always been open with her and she always felt she would know if he lied.* 他对她一向很坦诚。而她也一直觉得如果他撒谎了，她是会知道的。● **open·ness** N-UNCOUNT 坦率 ❑ *...a relationship based on honesty and openness.* …一种在诚实、坦率的基础上建立起来的关系。9 ADJ If you describe a situation, attitude, or way of behaving as **open**, you mean it is not kept hidden or secret. 公然的；公开的 [ADJ n] ❑ *The action is an open violation of the Vienna Convention.* 这次行动是对《维也纳公约》的公然违犯。● **open·ness** N-UNCOUNT 公开性 ❑ *...the new climate of political openness.* …政治透明的新气象。10 ADJ If you are **open to** suggestions or ideas, you are ready and willing to consider or accept them. 愿意接受的 [V-link ADJ "to" n] ❑ *They are open to suggestions on how working conditions might be improved.* 他们愿意接受有关工作条件如何改善的建议。11 ADJ If you say that a system, person, or idea is **open to** something such as abuse or criticism, you mean they might receive abuse or criticism because of their qualities, effects, or actions. 容易受到(辱骂、批评)的 [V-link ADJ "to" n] ❑ *The system, though well-meaning, is open to abuse.* 尽管这个制度立意很好，却容易遭到滥用。12 ADJ If you say that a fact or question is **open to** debate, interpretation, or discussion, you mean that people are uncertain whether it is true, what it means, or what the answer is. 有(讨论、解释)的余地 ❑ *Her interpretation of the facts may be open to doubt.* 她对事实的解释可能有待质疑。13 ADJ You can use **open** to describe something that anyone is allowed to take part in or accept. 对公众开放的 ❑ *It's an open meeting, everybody's invited.* 这是一个开放的会议，谁来都欢迎。❑ *...an open invitation.* …一个公开的邀请。14 ADJ If something such as an offer or job is **open**, it is available for someone to accept or apply for. (报价)可用的；(职位)空缺的 [V-link ADJ] ❑ *The offer will remain open until further notice.* 该报价将一直有效，直到另有通知。15 → see also **opening 6** 16 ADJ If an opportunity or choice **is open to** you, you are able to do a particular thing if you choose to. 可供…利用的 [V-link ADJ "to" n] ❑ *There are a wide range of career opportunities open to young people.* 有广泛的求职机会可供年轻人选择。17 V-T To **open** opportunities or possibilities means the same as to **open** them **up**. 提供(机会) ❑ *The Chief of Naval Operations wants to open opportunities for women in the navy.* 海军作战部部长想给海军中的女性提供机会。

Thesaurus *open* 另参见：

V.	crack, reveal, unblock ❶ 1
	extend, stretch ❶ 3
ADJ.	friendly, outgoing ❷ 8

❸ **open ♦♦♦** /oʊpən/ (**opens, opening, opened**) 1 V-T/V-I If something such as a meeting or series of talks **opens**, or if someone **opens** it, it begins. 召开；开始 ❑ *...an emergency session of the Russian Parliament due to open later this morning.* …将于今天上午晚些时候开始的一次俄罗斯议会紧急会议。● **open·ing** N-SING 开始 ❑ *...a statement issued at the opening of the talks.* …会谈开始时发表的一项声明。2 V-T/V-I If an event such as a meeting or discussion **opens with** a particular activity, that activity is the first thing that happens or is dealt with. You can also say that someone such as a speaker or singer **opens by** doing a particular thing. (活动或活动表演者)以…开始；开始 ❑ *The service opened with a hymn.* 礼拜式以唱赞美诗开始。❑ *I opened by saying, "Honey, you look sensational."* 我以这句

O

话作为开场白："宝贝，你看起来真是棒极了！" 3 V-I On the stock exchange, the price at which currencies, shares, or commodities **open** is their value at the start of that day's trading. 开盘 [BUSINESS] ❑ *Gold declined $2 in Zurich to open at $385.50.* 苏黎世证券交易所的金价跌了$2，以$385.50开盘。 4 V-I When a movie, play, or other public event **opens**, it begins to be shown, be performed, or take place for a limited period of time. 开演 ❑ *A photographic exhibition opens at the Smithsonian on Wednesday.* 一个摄影展周三在史密森尼博物馆开幕。 ● **open·ing** N-SING 开幕 ["the" N "of" n] ❑ *He is due to attend the opening of the Asian Games on Saturday.* 他定于星期六出席亚运会的开幕式。 5 V-T If you **open** an account with a bank or a commercial organization, you begin to use their services. 开立(账户) ❑ *He tried to open an account at the branch of his bank nearest to his workplace.* 他试图在离他工作地点最近的银行分行开立账户。

❹ **open** ♦♦♦ /oʊpən/ (**opens, opening, opened**)
➪ **Please look at meanings 5 – 14 to see if the expression you are looking for is shown under another headword.** 1 PHRASE If you do something **in the open** or **out in the open**, you do it outdoors rather than in a house or other building. 在户外 ❑ *Many are sleeping in the open because they have no shelter.* 许多人因为没有栖身之所而睡在户外。 2 PHRASE If an attitude or situation is **in the open** or **out in the open**, people know about it and it is no longer kept secret. 公开的 ❑ *They had advised us to keep it a secret, but we wanted it out in the open.* 他们曾建议我们对其保密，但我们却想将它公之于众。 3 PHRASE If something is **wide open**, it is open to its full extent. 大开的 ❑ *The child had left the inner door wide open.* 这个孩子让里面的门大开着。 4 PHRASE If you say that a competition, race, or election is **wide open**, you mean that anyone could win it, because there is no competitor who seems to be much better than the others. 胜负不确定的 ❑ *The competition has been thrown wide open by the absence of the world champion.* 世界冠军的缺席使这场比赛变得胜负难定。 5 **with open arms** → see **arm** 6 **to keep your eyes open** → see **eye** 7 **with your eyes open** → see **eye** 8 **to open your eyes** → see **eye** 9 **to open fire** → see **fire** 10 **to open your heart** → see **heart** 11 **the heavens open** → see **heaven** 12 **an open mind** → see **mind** 13 **to open your mind** → see **mind** 14 **to keep your options open** → see **option**
▸ **open out** → see **open** ❶ 3, ❷ 2
▸ **open up** 1 → see **open** ❶ 2, ❷ 1 2 PHRASAL VERB If a place, economy, or area of interest **opens up**, or if someone **opens** it **up**, more people can go there or become involved in it. 开放 ❑ *As the market opens up, I think people are going to be able to spend more money on consumer goods.* 随着市场的开放，我想人们将能够花更多的钱购置消费品。 ❑ *He said he wanted to see how Albania was opening up to the world.* 他说他想看到阿尔巴尼亚如何向世界开放。 3 PHRASAL VERB If something **opens up** opportunities or possibilities, or if they **open up**, they are created. 提供(机会)；(机会、可能性) 出现 ❑ *It was also felt that the collapse of the system opened up new possibilities.* 也感觉到制度的崩溃提供了新的可能。 4 PHRASAL VERB When you **open up** a building, you unlock and open the door so that people can get in. 开(店门等) ❑ *Several customers were waiting when I arrived to open up the shop.* 我到店里开门时，几个顾客已在等侯。 5 PHRASAL VERB If someone **opens up**, they start to say exactly what they think or feel. 自由自在地谈 ❑ *Lorna found that people were willing to open up to her.* 洛娜发现人们愿意向她敞开心扉畅谈。

open-air also **open air** 1 ADJ An **open-air** place or event is outside rather than in a building. 户外的 ❑ *...an open air concert in brilliant sunshine.* …明媚阳光下的一场露天音乐会。 2 N-SING If you are **in the open air**, you are outside rather than in a building. 户外 ❑ *We sleep out under the stars, and eat our meals in the open air.* 我们露宿在星空下，在户外用餐。

open-door also **open door** ADJ If a country or organization has an **open-door** policy toward people or goods, it allows them to come there freely, without any restrictions. 对外开放的 [ADJ n] ❑ *...reformers who have advocated an open door economic policy.* …提倡对外开放的经济政策的改革者们。 ● N-SING **Open door** is also a noun. 对外开放 ❑ *...an open door to further foreign investment.* …推动国外投资的对外开放。

open-ended ADJ When people begin an **open-ended** discussion or activity, they do not start with any intention of achieving a particular decision or result. 无预期结论的 ❑ *...an open-ended commitment to the security of the Gulf.* …对海湾安全的一个可依实际需要修改的承诺。

open·er /oʊpənər/ (**openers**) 1 N-COUNT An **opener** is a tool which is used to open containers such as cans or bottles. 起子 [usu n N] ❑ *...a can opener.* …一个罐头起子。 2 → see also **eye-opener**

open·ing ♦◊◊ /oʊpənɪŋ/ (**openings**) 1 ADJ The **opening** event, item, day, or week in a series is the first one. 第一个的 [ADJ n] ❑ *They returned to play in the season's opening game.* 他们回来参加了本赛季的首场比赛。 2 N-COUNT **The opening of** something such as a book, play, or concert is the first part of it. (书、戏剧、音乐会的) 开始部分 ❑ *The opening of the scene depicts Akhnaten and his family in a moment of intimacy.* 开头一幕描述阿肯那顿及其家人亲密无间的一个时刻。 3 N-COUNT An **opening** is a hole or empty space through which things or people can pass. 缺口 ❑ *He squeezed through a narrow opening in the fence.* 他从围栏的一个狭窄缺口挤了过去。 4 N-COUNT An **opening** in a forest is a small area where there are no trees or bushes. (林中) 空地 [mainly AM]

in BRIT, usually use **clearing**

❑ *I glanced down at the beach as we passed an opening in the trees.* 我们穿过林中空地时，我向下瞥了一眼海滩。 5 N-COUNT An **opening** is a good opportunity to do something, for example, to show people how good you are. 机遇 ❑ *Her capabilities were always there; all she needed was an opening to show them.* 她的能力一直就在那儿；她所需要的只是一个展示它们的机会。 6 N-COUNT An **opening** is a job that is available. 空缺的职位 ❑ *We don't have any openings now, but we'll call you if something comes up.* 眼下我们没有空缺的职位。如果有了，我们会给你打电话的。 7 → see also **open**

Thesaurus *opening* 另参见：
N. cut, door, gap, slot, space, window 3
clearing, glade 4
job, position 6

open·ing hours N-PLURAL **Opening hours** are the times during which a shop, bank, library, or bar is open for business. 营业时间 [mainly BRIT]

in AM, use **business hours**

open·ly /oʊpənli/ ADV If you do something **openly**, you do it without hiding any facts or hiding your feelings. 公开地 ❑ *She openly criticized other athletes.* 她公开批评过其他运动员。

open mar·ket N-SING Goods that are bought and sold on **the open market** are advertised and sold to anyone who wants to buy them. 公开市场 [BUSINESS] ❑ *On the open market, this would be worth much more.* 在公开市场上它的价格会高得多。

open-minded ADJ If you describe someone as **open-minded**, you approve of them because they are willing to listen to and consider other people's ideas and suggestions. 思想开明的 [APPROVAL] ❑ *He was very open-minded about other people's work.* 他对其他人的工作成果不抱任何成见。 ● **open-mindedness** N-UNCOUNT 思想开明 ❑ *He was praised for his enthusiasm and his open-mindedness.* 他由于为人热情、思想开明受到了赞扬。

open-plan ADJ An **open-plan** building, office, or room has no internal walls dividing it into smaller areas. 敞开式的 (室内空间) ❑ *The firm's top managers share the same open-plan office.* 公司的高层管理者们共用同一个没有隔间的办公室。

Word Link *oper ≈ work : cooperate, opera, operation*

op·era ♦◊◊ /ɒpərə, ɒprə/ (**operas**)

Pronounced /ɒpərə/ or /oʊpərə/ for meaning 3.

义项3读作 /ɒpərə/或 /oʊpərə/。

1 N-VAR An **opera** is a play with music in which all the words are sung. 歌剧 ❑ *...a one-act opera about contemporary women in America.* …关于当代美国妇女的一部独幕歌剧。 ❑ *...an opera singer.* …一名歌剧演员。 2 → see also **soap opera** 3 **Opera** is an alternative plural of **opus**. **opus**的两种复数形式之一
→ see **music**

op·er·ate ♦♦♦ /ɒpəreɪt/ (**operates, operating, operated**)
1 V-T/V-I If you **operate** a business or organization, you work to keep it running. If a business or organization **operates**, it carries out its work. 经营；运营 ❑ *Until his death in 1986 Greenwood owned and operated an enormous pear orchard.* 直到1986年去世，格林伍德一直拥有并经营着一个规模巨大的梨园。 ❑ *...allowing commercial banks to operate in the country.* …允许商业银行在本国运营。 ● **op·era·tion** /ɒpəreɪʃ°n/ N-UNCOUNT 经营 ❑ *Company finance is to provide funds for the everyday operation of the business.* 公司财务将为公司业务的日常运转提供资金。

O

2 V-I The way that something **operates** is the way that it works or has a particular effect. 起作用 ❑ *Ceiling and wall lights can operate independently.* 天花板和墙上的灯能够独立操控。 ❑ *How do accounting records operate?* 结算记录是如何运作的？ ● **op·era·tion** N-UNCOUNT 运行 ❑ *No money can be spent on the construction and operation of the streetcar.* 没有钱可以用于有轨电车的建设和运行。 3 V-T/V-I When you **operate** a machine or device, or when it **operates**, you make it work. 操作；运转 ❑ *A massive rock fall trapped the men as they operated a tunneling machine.* 那些男人在驾驶隧道掘进机时，一次大面积的岩崩困住了他们。 ● **op·era·tion** N-UNCOUNT 操作 ❑ *...over 1,000 dials monitoring every aspect of the operation of the airplane.* …监控着飞机每项操作的1000多个调节控制器。 4 V-I When surgeons **operate on** a patient in a hospital, they cut open a patient's body in order to remove, replace, or repair a diseased or damaged part. 动手术 ❑ *In March 2005, surgeons operated on Max for a brain aneurysm.* 2005年3月，外科医生们为马克斯做了脑部动脉瘤手术。

Thesaurus *operate* 另参见：

V. function, perform, run, work; *(ant.)* break down, fail 2 3

Word Partnership *operate* 的常用搭配：

N. operate **a business/company, schools** operate 1
forces operate 1 2
ADV. operate **efficiently** 1 2
operate **independently** 2
V. ***be* allowed to** operate, **continue to** operate 1 2 4

op·er·at·ic /ɒpəræ̱tɪk/ ADJ **Operatic** means relating to opera. 歌剧的 ❑ *...the local amateur operatic society.* …地方业余歌剧爱好者协会。

op·er·at·ing /ɒ̱pəreɪtɪŋ/ ADJ **Operating** profits and costs are the money that a company earns and spends in carrying out its ordinary trading activities, in contrast to such things as interest and investment. 营业收支的 [ADJ n] [BUSINESS] ❑ *The group made operating profits of $80M before interest.* 这个集团赚得了8000万美元的息前营业利润。

op·er·at·ing room (operating rooms) N-COUNT An **operating room** is a special room in a hospital where surgeons carry out medical operations. 手术室

in BRIT, use **operating theatre**

op·er·at·ing sys·tem (operating systems) N-COUNT The **operating system** of a computer is its most basic program, which it needs in order to function and run other programs. 操作系统 [COMPUTING] ❑ *...Microsoft's Windows NT operating system.* …微软公司的视窗NT操作系统。

op·er·at·ing thea·tre (operating theatres) N-COUNT An **operating theatre** is the same as an **operating room.** 手术室 [BRIT]

Word Link *oper ≈ work : cooperate, opera, operation*

op·era·tion ♦♦♦ /ɒpəreɪʃən/ (operations) 1 N-COUNT An **operation** is a highly organized activity that involves many people doing different things. 行动 ❑ *The rescue operation began on Friday afternoon.* 营救行动星期五下午展开。 ❑ *The soldiers were engaged in a military operation close to the Ugandan border.* 士兵们在靠近乌干达边界的地区开展军事行动。 ❑ *...a big operation against the drugs trade.* …一次反对毒品贸易的大行动。 2 N-COUNT A business or company can be referred to as an **operation.** 公司 [BUSINESS] ❑ *Thorn's electronics operation employs around 5,000 people.* 索恩的电子公司雇佣了大约五千名员工。 ❑ *The two parent groups now run their business as a single combined operation.* 那两家母公司现在合并为一家经营。 3 N-COUNT When a patient has an **operation**, a surgeon cuts open their body in order to remove, replace, or repair a diseased or damaged part. 手术 ❑ *Charles was at the clinic recovering from an operation on his arm.* 查尔斯在诊所，进行手臂的术后恢复。 4 N-UNCOUNT If a system is **in operation**, it is being used. 实施中 ❑ *...the free banking system that has been in operation since the early eighties.* …从80年代初就开始实施的自由银行制度。 5 N-UNCOUNT If a machine or device is **in operation**, it is working. 运转中 ❑ *There are three ski lifts in operation.* 有3辆滑雪缆车在运行。 6 → see also **operative** 7 PHRASE When a rule, system, or plan **comes into operation** or you **put** it **into operation**, you begin to use it. 开始实施 ❑ *The Financial Services Act came into operation four years ago.* 《金融服务法》4年前开始生效。

Word Partnership *operation* 的常用搭配：

N. **relief** operation, **rescue** operation 1
ADJ. **covert** operation, **massive** operation, **military** operation, **undercover** operation 1
major operation, **successful** operation 1 – 3
emergency operation 1 3
V. **carry out an** operation, **plan an** operation 1
perform an operation 1 3

op·era·tion·al /ɒpəreɪʃənəl/ 1 ADJ A machine or piece of equipment that is **operational** is in use or is ready for use. （机器、设备）使用中的；可以使用的 ❑ *The whole system will be fully operational by December.* 整个系统将于12月全面投入使用。 2 ADJ **Operational** factors or problems relate to the working of a system, device, or plan. 操作上的 ❑ *The nuclear industry was required to prove that every operational and safety aspect had been fully researched.* 核工业需要证明每一个操作和安全项目都已全面调查过。 ● **op·era·tion·al·ly** ADV 操作上地 ❑ *...goods which are economically or operationally impractical to transport.* …那些从经济角度和可操作角度来说都不适合运输的商品。

★ **op·era·tive** /ɒpərətɪv, -əreɪtɪv/ (operatives) 1 ADJ A system or service that is **operative** is working or having an effect. （系统、服务）起作用的 [FORMAL] ❑ *The commercial telephone service was no longer operative.* 商务电话服务已经不再使用了。 2 N-COUNT An **operative** is a worker, especially one who does work with their hands. 技工 [FORMAL] ❑ *In an automated car plant there is not a human operative to be seen.* 在全自动汽车制造厂，一个工人也看不到。 3 N-COUNT An **operative** is someone who works for a government agency such as the intelligence service. 特工人员 [mainly AM] ❑ *Naturally the CIA wants to protect its operatives.* 中央情报局当然想保护自己的特工人员。 4 PHRASE If you describe a word as **the operative word**, you want to draw attention to it because you think it is important or exactly true in a particular situation. 关键词 ❑ *As long as the operative word is "greed," you can't count on people keeping the costs down.* 只要关键词是"贪婪"，你就不能指望人们降低开销。

op·era·tor ♦◇◇ /ɒpəreɪtər/ (operators) 1 N-COUNT An **operator** is a person who connects telephone calls at a telephone exchange or in a place such as an office or hotel. 电话接线员 ❑ *He dialed the operator and put in a call to Rome.* 他拨通了接线员，往罗马打了一个电话。 2 N-COUNT An **operator** is a person who is employed to operate or control a machine. 操作员 ❑ *...computer operators.* …电脑操作员。 3 N-COUNT An **operator** is a person or a company that runs a business. 经营者 [BUSINESS] ❑ *...the nation's largest cable TV operator.* …全国最大的有线电视运营商。 4 N-COUNT If you call someone a smooth or shrewd **operator**, you mean that they are skillful at achieving what they want, often in a slightly dishonest way. 精明圆滑的人 [INFORMAL] ❑ *He is a smooth operator. Don't underestimate him.* 他是个精明圆滑的人，别低估他。

opin·ion ♦♦◇ /əpɪnyən/ (opinions) 1 N-COUNT Your **opinion** about something is what you think or believe about it. 看法 ❑ *I wasn't asking for your opinion, Mike.* 我不是在问你的看法，迈克。 ❑ *He held the opinion that a government should think before introducing a tax.* 他的看法是政府在推行一项税制前应先作考虑。 2 N-SING Your **opinion of** someone is your judgment of their character or ability. 评价 ❑ *That improved Mrs. Goole's already favorable opinion of him.* 那更提高了古尔太太对他原有的好评。 3 N-UNCOUNT You can refer to the beliefs or views that people have as **opinion.** 舆论 ❑ *Some, I suppose, might even be in positions to influence opinion.* 我认为，有些甚至可以影响舆论。 4 N-COUNT An **opinion** from an expert is the advice or judgment that they give you in the subject that they know a lot about. （专家的）意见 ❑ *Even if you have had a regular physical check-up recently, you should still seek a medical opinion.* 即使你最近已经进行了常规体检，也还是应该听听医学专家的意见。 5 → see also **public opinion, second opinion** 6 PHRASE You add expressions such as **"in my opinion"** or **"in their opinion"** to a statement in order to indicate that it is what you or someone else thinks, and is not necessarily a fact. 据…的意见 ❑ *The book is, in Henry's opinion, the best book on the subject.* 在亨利看来，这本书是关于这个学科最好的一本。 7 PHRASE If someone is **of the opinion that** something is the case, that is what they believe. 持…观点 [FORMAL] ❑ *Frank is of the opinion that Romero should have won.* 弗兰克认为，罗梅罗本来应该获胜的。

Thesaurus *opinion* 另参见:

N. estimation, feeling, judgment, thought, viewpoint 1 – 4

Word Partnership *opinion* 的常用搭配:

ADJ. **favorable** opinion 1
expert opinion, **legal** opinion, **majority** opinion, **medical** opinion 3 4

V. **express an** opinion, **give an** opinion, **share an** opinion 1 2
ask for an opinion 1 2 4

★ **opin·ion·at·ed** /əpɪnyəneɪtɪd/ ADJ If you describe someone as **opinionated**, you mean that they have very strong opinions and refuse to accept that they may be wrong. 固执己见的 ❑ *Sue is the extrovert in the family; opinionated, talkative, and passionate about politics.* 休是那个家庭里性格外向的一位：她固执、健谈、热心政治。

opin·ion poll (**opinion polls**) N-COUNT An **opinion poll** involves asking people's opinions on a particular subject, especially one concerning politics. 民意测验 ❑ *Nearly three-quarters of people questioned in an opinion poll agreed with the government's decision.* 在一项民意测验中，被调查到的近四分之三的人同意政府的决策。

★ **opium** /oʊpiəm/ N-UNCOUNT **Opium** is a powerful drug made from the seeds of a type of poppy. Opium is used in medicines that relieve pain or help someone sleep. 鸦片

op·po·nent ♦◇◇ /əpoʊnənt/ (**opponents**) 1 N-COUNT A politician's **opponents** are other politicians who belong to a different party or who have different aims or policies. (政) 敌 ❑ *...Mr. Kennedy's opponent in the leadership contest.* …肯尼迪先生在领导权竞争中的对手。 2 N-COUNT In a sports contest, your **opponent** is the person who is playing against you. (体育比赛中的) 对手 ❑ *Norris twice knocked down his opponent in the early rounds of the fight.* 诺里斯在拳击赛的头几个回合中，曾两度击倒他的对手。 3 N-COUNT The **opponents of** an idea or policy do not agree with it and do not want it to be carried out. 反对者 ❑ *...opponents of the spread of nuclear weapons.* …核武器扩散的反对者们。
→ see **chess**

op·por·tun·ist /ɒpərtunɪst/ (**opportunists**) ADJ If you describe someone as **opportunist**, you are critical of them because they take advantage of any situation in order to gain money or power, without considering whether their actions are right or wrong. 机会主义的 [DISAPPROVAL] ❑ *...corrupt and opportunist politicians.* …腐败、投机的政客们。● N-COUNT An **opportunist** is someone who is opportunist. 机会主义者 ❑ *Like most successful politicians, Sinclair was an opportunist.* 和大多数成功的政客一样，辛克莱也是个机会主义者。

op·por·tun·is·tic /ɒpərtunɪstɪk/ ADJ If you describe someone's behavior as **opportunistic**, you are critical of them because they take advantage of situations in order to gain money or power, without thinking about whether their actions are right or wrong. 机会主义的 [DISAPPROVAL] ❑ *Many of the party's members joined only for opportunistic reasons.* 这个政党的许多成员入党纯粹是出于投机。

op·por·tu·nity ♦♦◇ /ɒpərtunɪti/ (**opportunities**) N-VAR An **opportunity** is a situation in which it is possible for you to do something that you want to do. 机会 ❑ *I had an opportunity to go to New York and study.* 我曾有过一个去纽约学习的机会。 ❑ *...equal opportunities in employment.* …平等的就业机会。

Word Partnership *opportunity* 的常用搭配:

N. **business** opportunity, **employment** opportunity, **investment** opportunity

ADJ. **economic** opportunity, **educational** opportunity, **equal** opportunity, **golden** opportunity, **great** opportunity, **lost** opportunity, **rare** opportunity, **unique** opportunity

V. **have an** opportunity, **miss an** opportunity, **see an** opportunity, **seize an** opportunity, opportunity **to speak**, **take advantage of an** opportunity

op·pose ♦◇◇ /əpoʊz/ (**opposes, opposing, opposed**) V-T If you **oppose** someone or **oppose** their plans or ideas, you disagree with what they want to do and try to prevent them from doing it. 反对 ❑ *Mr. Taylor was not bitter toward those who had opposed him.* 泰勒先生并不仇恨那些曾经反对过他的人。

op·posed ♦◇◇ /əpoʊzd/ 1 ADJ If you **are opposed to** something, you disagree with it or disapprove of it. 反对的 [v-link ADJ "to" n/-ing] ❑ *I am utterly opposed to any form of terrorism.* 我坚决反对任何形式的恐怖主义。 2 ADJ You say that two ideas or systems are **opposed** when they are opposite to each other or very different from each other. 对立的 ❑ *...people with policies almost diametrically opposed to his own.* …那些持有与他自己几乎截然相反政策的人们。 3 PHRASE You use **as opposed to** when you want to make it clear that you are talking about one particular thing and not something else. 而不是… ❑ *We ate in the restaurant, as opposed to the bistro.* 我们是在饭店吃的饭，而不是在小酒馆。

op·pos·ing /əpoʊzɪŋ/ 1 ADJ **Opposing** ideas or tendencies are totally different from each other. 相反的 [ADJ n] ❑ *I have a friend who has the opposing view and felt that the war was immoral.* 我有一个朋友持完全相反的观点，他认为战争是不道德的。 2 ADJ **Opposing** groups of people disagree about something or are in competition with one another. 对立的 [ADJ n] ❑ *The Georgian leader said in a radio broadcast that he still favored dialogue between the opposing sides.* 这位格鲁吉亚领导人在一次广播中说，他还是赞同对立的双方进行对话。

op·po·site ♦◇◇ /ɒpəzɪt/ (**opposites**) 1 PREP If one thing is **opposite** another, it is on the other side of a space from it. 在…对面 ❑ *Jennie had sat opposite her at breakfast.* 吃早餐时，珍妮已坐在她的对面。● ADV **Opposite** is also an adverb. 在对面地 ❑ *He looked up at the buildings opposite, but could see no open window.* 他抬头看了看对面那些楼，但看不见一扇开着的窗户。 2 ADJ The **opposite** side or part of something is the side or part that is furthest away from you. 对面的 [ADJ n] ❑ *...the opposite corner of the room.* …房间里的另一个对角。 3 ADJ **Opposite** is used to describe things of the same kind which are completely different in a particular way. For example, north and south are opposite directions, and winning and losing are opposite results in a game. 截然相反的 ❑ *All the cars driving in the opposite direction had their headlights on.* 所有迎面开来的车都开着前灯。 4 N-COUNT **The opposite of** someone or something is the person or thing that is most different from them. 正好相反的人或事物 ❑ *Ritter was a very complex man but Marius was the opposite, a simple farmer.* 里特是个非常复杂的人，而马里厄斯则恰恰相反，是个单纯的农民。 ❑ *Well, whatever he says you can bet he's thinking the opposite.* 哦，无论他说什么，你都能肯定他想的是另外一套。

Word Partnership *opposite* 的常用搭配:

ADJ. **directly** opposite 1
exactly (the) opposite, **precisely (the)** opposite, **quite the** opposite 1 3 4
complete opposite, **exact** opposite 3 4

N. opposite **corner**, opposite **end**, opposite **side** 2
opposite **direction**, opposite **effect** 3

PREP. **the** opposite **of** ***someone/something*** 4

op·po·site sex N-SING If you are talking about men and refer to **the opposite sex**, you mean women. If you are talking about women and refer to **the opposite sex**, you mean men. 异性 ❑ *Body language can also be used to attract members of the opposite sex.* 肢体语言也可以被用来吸引异性。

op·po·si·tion ♦♦◇ /ɒpəzɪʃᵊn/ (**oppositions**) 1 N-UNCOUNT **Opposition** is strong, angry, or violent disagreement and disapproval. 强烈的反对 ❑ *There is bitter opposition from local business to the plan.* 有来自当地企业对此计划的强烈反对。 2 N-COUNT-COLL **The opposition** is the political parties or groups that are opposed to a government. 反对党 ❑ *The main opposition parties boycotted the election, saying it would not be conducted fairly.* 主要的反对党抵制了选举，声称选举不会公平进行。 3 N-COUNT-COLL In countries with a parliament, such as Britain, **the opposition** refers to the politicians or political parties that form part of the parliament, but are not the government. 在野党 ❑ *...the Leader of the Opposition.* …在野党领袖。 4 N-SING-COLL **The opposition** is the person or team you are competing against in a sports event. 对手 ❑ *The coach says his team is not underestimating the opposition.* 教练说他的队没在低估对手。

★ **op·press** /əprɛs/ (**oppresses, oppressing, oppressed**) V-T To **oppress** people means to treat them cruelly, or to prevent them from having the same opportunities, freedom, and benefits as others. 压迫 ❑ *These people often are oppressed by the governments of the countries they find themselves in.* 这些人经常受到他们所在国家政府的压迫。

op·pressed /əprɛ̱st/ ADJ People who are **oppressed** are treated cruelly or are prevented from having the same opportunities, freedom, and benefits as others. 被压迫的 ❑ *Before they took power, they felt oppressed by the white English speakers who controlled things.* 在掌握政权之前，他们觉得受到那些控制一切的、讲英语的白人的压迫。 ● N-PLURAL **The oppressed** are people who are oppressed. 被压迫者 ❑ *...a sense of community with the poor and oppressed.* …同属于被压迫的穷人的感觉。

op·pres·sion /əprɛ̱ʃᵊn/ N-UNCOUNT **Oppression** is the cruel or unfair treatment of a group of people. 压迫 ❑ *...an attempt to escape political oppression.* …逃避政治压迫的一次尝试。

op·pres·sive /əprɛ̱sɪv/ **1** ADJ If you describe a society, its laws, or customs as **oppressive**, you think they treat people cruelly and unfairly. 压迫的 ❑ *The new laws will be just as oppressive as those they replace.* 新法律将跟被它所取代的那些法律一样不公正。 **2** ADJ If you describe the weather or the atmosphere in a room as **oppressive**, you mean that it is unpleasantly hot and damp. 湿热的 ❑ *The oppressive afternoon heat had tired him out.* 湿热的午后暑气使他筋疲力尽。 **3** ADJ An **oppressive** situation makes you feel depressed and uncomfortable. 令人感到压抑的 ❑ *...the oppressive sadness that weighed upon him like a physical pain.* …像肉体疼痛一样沉重地压着他、令他抑郁的悲伤。

Word Link *opt ≈ choosing : adopt, opt, optional*

▲ **opt** ♦◇◇ /ɒ̱pt/ (**opts, opting, opted**) V-T/V-I If you **opt for** something, or **opt to** do something, you choose it or decide to do it in preference to anything else. 选择 ❑ *Depending on your circumstances you can opt for one method or the other.* 根据自己的情况，你可以选择这种或那种方法。

▸ **opt out** PHRASAL VERB If you **opt out of** something, you choose to be no longer involved in it. 决定退出 ❑ *The rich can opt out of the public school system.* 有钱人可以选择退出公立学校体系。

Word Link *op ≈ eye : optic, optical, optician*

★ **op·tic** /ɒ̱ptɪk/ ADJ **Optic** means relating to the eyes or to sight. 视觉的; 视力的 [ADJ n] ❑ *The optic nerve is a part of the brain.* 视觉神经是大脑的一部分。
→ see **eye, laser**

op·ti·cal /ɒ̱ptɪkᵊl/ ADJ **Optical** devices, processes, and effects involve or relate to vision, light, or images. 视力的; 光学的 ❑ *...optical telescopes.* …光学望远镜。 ❑ *...an optical scanner.* …一台光学扫描仪。

op·ti·cian /ɒptɪ̱ʃᵊn/ (**opticians**) **1** N-COUNT An **optician** is someone whose job is to make and sell glasses and contact lenses. 眼镜商 **2** N-COUNT An **optician** is someone whose job is to test people's eyesight. 验光师 [BRIT]

in AM, use **optometrist**

3 N-COUNT An **optician** is a store where you can have your eyes tested and buy glasses and contact lenses. 眼镜店

▲ **op·ti·mal** /ɒ̱ptɪmᵊl/ → see **optimum**

op·ti·mise /ɒ̱ptɪmaɪz/ [BRIT] → see **optimize**

Word Link *ism ≈ action or state : communism, optimism, patriotism*

★ **op·ti·mism** /ɒ̱ptɪmɪzəm/ N-UNCOUNT **Optimism** is the feeling of being hopeful about the future or about the success of something in particular. 乐观主义 ❑ *The Indian prime minister has expressed optimism about India's future relations with the U.S.* 印度总理表达了对未来印美关系的乐观态度。

op·ti·mist /ɒ̱ptɪmɪst/ (**optimists**) N-COUNT An **optimist** is someone who is hopeful about the future. 乐观主义者 ❑ *He has the upbeat manner of an eternal optimist.* 他永远都持乐观主义者的那种快乐态度。

op·ti·mis·tic ♦◇◇ /ɒ̱ptɪmɪ̱stɪk/ ADJ Someone who is **optimistic** is hopeful about the future or the success of something in particular. 乐观主义的 ❑ *The president says she is optimistic that an agreement can be worked out soon.* 总统说，她对很快能达成协议持乐观态度。
● **op·ti·mis·ti·cal·ly** ADV 乐观主义地 [ADV with v] ❑ *Both sides have spoken optimistically about the talks.* 双方都对本次会谈表示乐观。

op·ti·mize /ɒ̱ptɪmaɪz/ (**optimizes, optimizing, optimized**)

in BRIT, also use **optimise**

V-T To **optimize** a plan, system, or machine means to arrange or design it so that it operates as smoothly and efficiently as possible. 使优化 [FORMAL] ❑ *The new systems have been optimized for running Microsoft Windows.* 新系统已经被优化，以便运行微软视窗系统。

Word Link *optim ≈ the best : optimism, optimum, optimize*

★ **op·ti·mum** /ɒ̱ptɪməm/ or **optimal** ADJ The **optimum** or **optimal** level or state of something is the best level or state that it could achieve. 最佳的 [FORMAL] ❑ *Try to do some physical activity three times a week for optimum health.* 试着每星期锻炼身体3次，以达到最佳的健康状态。

op·tion ♦♦◇ /ɒ̱pʃᵊn/ (**options**) **1** N-COUNT An **option** is something that you can choose to do in preference to one or more alternatives. 供选择的东西 ❑ *He's argued from the start that the US and its allies are putting too much emphasis on the military option.* 他从一开始就争论说美国及其盟国过于看重军事这个选项。 **2** N-SING If you have the **option** of doing something, you can choose whether to do it or not. 选择权 ❑ *Criminals are given the option of going to jail or facing public humiliation.* 罪犯们被给予进监狱或面对公众羞辱的选择权。 **3** N-COUNT In business, an **option** is an agreement or contract that gives someone the right to buy or sell something such as property or shares at a future date. 购买权; 出售权; 期权 [BUSINESS] ❑ *Each bank has granted the other an option on 19.9% of its shares.* 每家银行都已把自己股份的19.9%的期权给予另一家银行。 **4** N-COUNT An **option** is one of a number of subjects which a student can choose to study as a part of his or her course. 选修课 [mainly BRIT] ❑ *Several options are offered for the student's senior year.* 好几门选修课开给毕业班的学生。 **5** PHRASE If you **keep** your **options open** or **leave** your **options open**, you delay making a decision about something. 暂不做决定 ❑ *I am keeping my options open; I can decide in a few months.* 我保留选择的权利；我可以几个月后再作出决定。

Thesaurus *option* 另参见:
N. alternative, choice, opportunity, preference, selection **1** **2**

Word Partnership *option* 的常用搭配:
ADJ. **available** option, **best** option, **other** option, **viable** option **1** **2**
V. **have an/the** option **1** **2**
choose an option **1** **4**
option **to buy/purchase, exercise an** option **3**

op·tion·al /ɒ̱pʃənᵊl/ ADJ If something is **optional**, you can choose whether or not you do it or have it. 可选择的 ❑ *Sex education is a sensitive area for some parents, and thus it should remain optional.* 性教育对一些家长来说是个敏感的话题，因此应该还是非强制性的。

Word Link *ulent ≈ full of : fraudulent, opulent, virulent*

opu·lent /ɒ̱pyələnt/ ADJ **Opulent** things or places look grand and expensive. 豪华的 [FORMAL] ❑ *Heavy silverplate adds an opulent touch to a formal dinner party.* 沉甸甸的镀银餐具给正式晚宴增加一种奢华感。 ● **opu·lence** N-UNCOUNT 豪华 ❑ *...the elegant opulence of the embassy.* …大使馆的典雅、体面。

or ♦♦♦ /ər, STRONG ɔr/ **1** CONJ You use **or** to link two or more alternatives. 或者 ❑ *"Tea or coffee?" John asked.* "喝茶还是喝咖啡？"约翰问。 ❑ *He said he would try to write or call as soon as he reached the Canary Islands.* 他说他一到加那利群岛就会尽快写信或打电话过来。 **2** CONJ You use **or** to give another alternative, when the first alternative is introduced by "either" or "whether." 还是 (与either或whether连用) ❑ *Items like bread, milk and meat were either unavailable or could be obtained only on the black market.* 像面包、牛奶和肉这样的食品要么没有，要么只有从黑市才能买到。 ❑ *Either you can talk to him, or I will.* 要么你和他谈，要么我来。

You do not use **or** after **neither**. You use **nor** instead. ❑ *He speaks neither English nor German.*

3 CONJ You use **or** between two numbers to indicate that you are giving an approximate amount. 或 (表示大概的数量) ❑ *Everyone benefited from limiting their intake of coffee to just one or two cups a day.* 每个人都从每天限量喝一杯或两杯咖啡的做法中受益了。 ❑ *When I was nine or ten someone explained to me that when you are grown up you have to work.* 在我9岁或10岁的时候，有人跟我解释说，人长大之后必须工作。 **4** CONJ You use **or** to introduce a comment which corrects or modifies what you have just said. 抑或 (用于更正刚说过的话) ❑ *The man was a fool, he thought, or at least incompetent.* 他想，那人是个傻子，或者至少是无能。 **5** CONJ If you say that someone should do something **or** something bad will happen, you are warning them that if they do not do it, the bad thing will happen. 否则(引导一个表示警告的从句) ❑ *She had to have the operation, or she would die.* 她必须进行手术，否则会死的。 **6** CONJ You use **or** to introduce something which is evidence for the truth of a statement you have just made. 否则(引导用作解释、辩护的一件事) ❑ *He must have thought Jane was worth it or he wouldn't have wasted time on her, I suppose.* 我想，他当时肯定认为简值得他费心思，否则他就不会在她身上浪费时间了。 **7** PHRASE You use **or not** to emphasize that a particular thing makes no difference to what is going to happen. …也好(表示某事对要发生的事无关紧要) [EMPHASIS] ❑ *Like it or not, you're in charge.* 喜欢也好，不喜欢也罢，反正是你负责。 **8** PHRASE You use **or no** between two occurrences of the same noun in order to say that whether something is true or not makes no difference to a situation. 不管有没有…(表示某事对形势无关紧要) ❑ *The next day, rain or no rain, it was business as usual.* 不管第二天下不下雨，一切事情照旧。 **9** **or else** → see **else** **10** **or other** → see **other** **11** **or so** → see **so** **12** **or something** → see **something**

★ **ora·cle** /ɔrəkᵊl/ (**oracles**) N-COUNT In ancient Greece, an **oracle** was a priest or priestess who made statements about future events or about the truth. (古希腊传达神谕的) 祭司

oral /ɔrəl/ (**orals**) **1** ADJ **Oral** communication is spoken rather than written. 口头的 ❑ *...the written and oral traditions of ancient cultures.* …古代文化的文字记载和口述传统。 ●**oral·ly** ADV 口头地 [ADV after v] ❑ *...their ability to present ideas orally and in writing.* …他们通过口头和笔头表达观点的能力。 **2** N-COUNT An **oral** is an examination, especially in a foreign language, that is spoken rather than written. 口试 ❑ *I spoke privately to the candidate after the oral.* 口试结束后，我私下和那个考生说了几句话。 **3** ADJ You use **oral** to indicate that something is done with a person's mouth or relates to a person's mouth. 用口的; 与口有关的 ❑ *...good oral hygiene.* …良好的口腔卫生。 ●**oral·ly** ADV 用口地; 与口有关地 ❑ *...antibiotic tablets taken orally.* …口服抗生素片。

or·ange ♦♦◇ /ɔrɪndʒ/ (**oranges**) **1** COLOR Something that is **orange** is of a color between red and yellow. 橙色的 ❑ *...men in bright orange uniforms.* …身穿鲜艳橙色制服的男人们。 **2** N-VAR An **orange** is a round juicy fruit with a thick, orange-colored skin. 柑; 橘; 橙 ❑ *...orange trees.* …橘树。

→ see **color, rainbow**

ora·tory /ɔrətɔri/ (**oratories**) **1** N-UNCOUNT **Oratory** is the art of making formal speeches which strongly affect people's feelings and beliefs. 演讲术 [FORMAL] ❑ *He displayed determination as well as powerful oratory.* 他既展示了雄辩的演讲术又显示了决心。 **2** N-COUNT An **oratory** is a room or building where Christians go to pray. 祈祷室 [mainly BRIT]

or·bit /ɔrbɪt/ (**orbits, orbiting, orbited**) **1** N-COUNT An **orbit** is the curved path in space that is followed by an object going around and around a planet, moon, or star. (天体运行的) 轨道 [also "in/into" N] ❑ *Mars and Earth have orbits which change with time.* 火星和地球的轨道随着时间而发生改变。 **2** V-T If something such as a satellite **orbits** a planet, moon, or sun, it moves around it in a continuous, curving path. 环绕…的轨道运行 ❑ *In 1957 the Soviet Union launched the first satellite to orbit the earth.* 1957年，苏联发射了第一颗环绕地球运行的人造卫星。

→ see **satellite, solar**

▲ **or·chard** /ɔrtʃərd/ (**orchards**) N-COUNT An **orchard** is an area of land on which fruit trees are grown. 果园

→ see **barn**

or·ches·tra /ɔrkɪstrə/ (**orchestras**) **1** N-COUNT An **orchestra** is a large group of musicians who play a variety of different instruments together. Orchestras usually play classical music. 管弦乐队 ❑ *...the Los Angeles Philharmonic Orchestra.* …洛杉矶爱乐乐团。 **2** → see also **symphony orchestra** **3** N-SING **The orchestra** or **the orchestra seats** in a theater or concert hall are the seats on the first floor directly in front of the stage. 舞台前方一楼座位 [mainly AM]

in BRIT, usually use **stalls**

❑ *With the balcony blocked off, patrons filled most of the orchestra seats.* 楼厅包厢被封闭了，赞助人几乎坐满了舞台前方的一楼座位。

→ see Word Web: **orchestra**

or·ches·tral /ɔrkɛstrəl/ ADJ **Orchestral** means relating to an orchestra and the music it plays. 管弦乐的 [ADJ n] ❑ *...an orchestral concert.* …一场管弦音乐会。

or·ches·trate /ɔrkɪstreɪt/ (**orchestrates, orchestrating, orchestrated**) V-T If you say that someone **orchestrates** an event or situation, you mean that they carefully organize it in a way that will produce the result that they want. 精心组织 ❑ *The colonel was able to orchestrate a rebellion from inside an army jail.* 上校得以在陆军监狱里精心组织了一场叛乱。 ●**or·ches·tra·tion** N-UNCOUNT 精心的安排 ❑ *...his skilful orchestration of latent nationalist feeling.* …他对潜在的民族主义情绪的熟练控制。

or·ches·tra·tion /ɔrkɪstreɪʃᵊn/ (**orchestrations**) N-COUNT An **orchestration** is a piece of music that has been rewritten so that it can be played by an orchestra. 改编成的管弦乐曲 ❑ *Mahler's own imaginative orchestration was heard in the same concert.* 在同一场音乐会上，听到了马勒自己改编的充满想像力的管弦乐曲。

or·chid /ɔrkɪd/ (**orchids**) N-COUNT **Orchids** are plants with brightly colored, unusually shaped flowers. 兰科植物

or·dain /ɔrdeɪn/ (**ordains, ordaining, ordained**) **1** V-T When someone **is ordained**, they are made a member of the clergy in a religious ceremony. 任命…为牧师 ❑ *He was ordained a Catholic priest in 1982.* 他在1982年被任命为天主教神父。 ❑ *Women have been ordained for many years in the Presbyterian Church.* 女性在基督教长老会里任神职已有好多年了。 **2** V-T If some authority or power **ordains** something, they decide that it should happen or be in existence. 命令 [FORMAL] ❑ *Nehru ordained that socialism should rule.* 尼赫鲁下命实行社会主义制度。 ❑ *His rule was ordained by heaven.* 他的统治是天命的。

▲ **or·deal** /ɔrdil/ (**ordeals**) N-COUNT If you describe an experience or situation as an **ordeal**, you think it is difficult and stressful. 煎熬 ❑ *...the painful ordeal of the last eight months.* …过去8个月里令人痛苦的煎熬。

order

1. SUBORDINATING CONJUNCTION USES
2. COMMANDS AND REQUESTS
3. ARRANGEMENTS, SITUATIONS, AND GROUPINGS

❶ **or·der** ♦♦◇ /ɔrdər/ **1** PHRASE If you do something **in order to** achieve a particular thing or **in order that** something can happen, you do it because you want to achieve that thing. 为了 ❑ *Most schools are extremely unwilling to cut down on staff in order to cut costs.* 大多数学校都极不愿意为了减少开支而裁员。 **2** PHRASE If someone

Word Web **orchestra**

The modern **symphony orchestra** usually has from 60 to 100 **musicians**. The largest group of musicians are in the **string** section. It gives the orchestra its rich, flowing sound. String **instruments** include **violins, violas, cellos**, and usually **double basses. Flutes**, oboes, **clarinets**, and bassoons make up the woodwind section. The **brass** section is usually quite small. Too much of this sound could overwhelm the more delicate strings. Brass **instruments** include the French horn, **trumpet, trombone**, and tuba. The size of the **percussion** section depends on the **composition** being performed. However, there is almost always a timpani player.

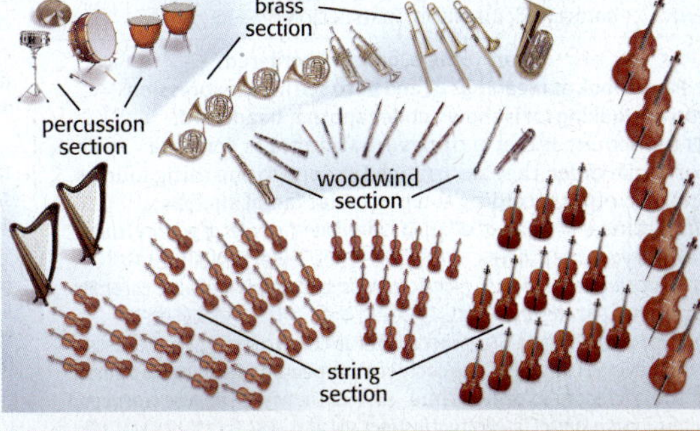

O

must be in a particular situation **in order to** achieve something they want, they cannot achieve that thing if they are not in that situation. (唯有…) 才能 ❑ *We need to get rid of the idea that we must be liked all the time in order to be worthwhile.* 我们需要摆脱那种必须一直受人爱戴才有价值的观念。 3 PHRASE If something must happen **in order for** something else to happen, the second thing cannot happen if the first thing does not happen. 为了使 ❑ *In order for their computers to trace a person's records, they need both the name and address of the individual.* 为了使他们的计算机跟踪某个人的记录，他们需要这个人的名字和地址。

❷ or·der ♦♦♦ /ɔrdər/ (**orders, ordering, ordered**)

➪ **Please look at meaning 12 to see if the expression you are looking for is shown under another headword.** 1 V-T If a person in authority **orders** someone **to** do something, they tell them to do it. 命令 ❑ *Williams ordered him to leave.* 威廉斯命令他离开。 2 V-T If someone in authority **orders** something, they give instructions that it should be done. 下达指示 ❑ *The president has ordered a full investigation.* 总统已下达指示进行彻底调查。 3 N-COUNT If someone in authority gives you an **order**, they tell you to do something. 命令 ❑ *The activists were shot when they refused to obey an order to halt.* 当那些激进分子拒绝听从要他们停下来的命令时，他们遭到了射击。 ❑ *As darkness fell, Clinton gave orders for his men to rest.* 夜幕降临时，克林顿下命令让自己的人休息。 4 N-COUNT A court **order** is a legal instruction stating that something must be done. (法院) 决议 ❑ *She has decided not to appeal against a court order banning her from keeping animals.* 她已决定不对禁止她养动物的判决上诉。 5 V-T/V-I When you **order** something that you are going to pay for, you ask for it to be brought to you, sent to you, or obtained for you. 订购; 点 (餐) ❑ *The couple ordered a new set of sterling silver rings from Tiffany for $200 each.* 这对夫妇从蒂芙尼珠宝店订购了一套新的纯银戒指，每只$200。 ❑ *The waitress appeared. "Are you ready to order?"* 女服务员走了过来，"你们准备好点菜了吗？" 6 N-COUNT An **order** is a request for something to be brought, made, or obtained for you in return for money. 订购 ❑ *The city is going to place an order for a hundred and eighty-eight buses.* 这个城市将下单订购188辆公交车。 7 N-COUNT Someone's **order** is what they have asked to be brought, made, or obtained for them in return for money. 所订的货 ❑ *The waiter returned with their order and Graham signed the bill.* 服务员拿着他们点的东西回来，接着格雷厄姆签了单。 8 → see also **mail order, postal order** 9 PHRASE Something that is **on order** at a store or factory has been asked for but has not yet been supplied. 订购中 ❑ *The airlines still have 2,500 new planes on order.* 航空公司还有已订购的2500架新飞机。 10 PHRASE If you do something **to order**, you do it whenever you are asked to do it. 按要求 ❑ *She now makes wonderful dried flower arrangements to order.* 她现在按订单要求制作精美的干花插花。 11 PHRASE If you are **under orders to** do something, you have been told to do it by someone in authority. 奉命

in BRIT, also use **order about**

❑ *I am under orders not to discuss his mission or his location with anyone.* 我奉命不得跟任何人谈论他的任务或去向。 12 **a tall order** → see **tall**

▸ **order around** PHRASAL VERB If you say that someone **is ordering** you **around**, you mean they are telling you what to do as if they have authority over you, and you dislike this. 支使某人 ❑ *When we're out he gets really bossy and starts ordering me around.* 我们一出来，他就变得很跋扈，开始支使我。

Thesaurus *order* 另参见:

V.	charge, command, direct, tell ❷ 1
	buy, request ❷ 5
N.	command, direction, instruction ❷ 3 4

❸ or·der ♦♦◇ /ɔrdər/ (**orders, ordering, ordered**)

➪ **Please look at meanings 15 and 16 to see if the expression you are looking for is shown under another headword.** 1 N-UNCOUNT If a set of things are arranged or done **in** a particular **order**, they are arranged or done so one thing follows another, often according to a particular factor such as importance. 顺序 [also "a" N] ❑ *Write down (in order of priority) the qualities you'd like to have.* （按先后顺序）写下你所希望拥有的品质。 ❑ *Music shops should arrange their recordings in simple alphabetical order, rather than by category.* 音像店应按照简单的字母顺序摆放其唱片，而不是按类别。 2 N-UNCOUNT **Order** is the situation that exists when everything is in the correct or expected place, or happens at the correct or expected time. 秩序 ❑ *The wish to impose order upon confusion is a kind of intellectual instinct.* 对混乱进行有序管理的希望是一种高智力的本能。 3 N-UNCOUNT **Order** is the situation that exists when people obey the law and do not fight or riot. 治安 ❑ *Troops were sent to the islands to restore order last November.* 部队去年11月份被派到岛上去恢复治安。 4 N-SING When people talk about a particular **order**, they mean the way society is organized at a particular time. 社会秩序 ❑ *The end of the Cold War has produced the prospect of a new world order based on international co-operation.* 冷战的结束使得基于国际合作的世界新秩序成为可能。 5 V-T The way that something **is ordered** is the way that it is organized and structured. 安排 ❑ *...a society which is ordered by hierarchy.* …一个等级森严的社会。 ❑ *We know the French order things differently.* 我们知道法国人处理事情的方式是不同的。 6 N-COUNT A religious **order** is a group of monks or nuns who live according to a particular set of rules. 修道会 ❑ *...the Benedictine order of monks.* …本笃会。 7 → see also **law and order** 8 PHRASE If you put or keep something **in order**, you make sure that it is neat or well organized. 有条理的 ❑ *Now he has a chance to put his life back in order.* 现在，他有机会使自己的生活重新走上正轨。 9 PHRASE If you think something is **in order**, you think it should happen or be provided. 应当发生的 ❑ *Reforms are clearly in order.* 改革显然是顺理成章的。 10 PHRASE You use **in the order of** or **on the order of** when mentioning an approximate figure. 大约 ❑ *They borrowed something in the order of $10 million.* 他们大约借了一千万美元。 11 PHRASE If something is **in good order**, it is in good condition. 处于良好状态 ❑ *The vessel's safety equipment was not in good order.* 这艘船的安全设备出了故障。 12 PHRASE A machine or device that is **in working order** is functioning properly and is not broken. 处于良好的工作状态 ❑ *Only half of the spacecraft's six science instruments are still in working order.* 宇宙飞船的6种科学仪器中，只有一半还能正常运转。 13 PHRASE A machine or device that is **out of order** is broken and does not work. 出现故障 ❑ *Their phone's out of order.* 他们的电话出故障了。 14 PHRASE If you say that someone or their behavior is **out of order**, you mean that their behavior is unacceptable. 不合常规 [INFORMAL] ❑ *Kent, you're out of order.* 肯特，你太过分了。 15 **to put your house in order** → see **house** 16 **order of magnitude** → see **magnitude**

or·der book (**order books**) N-COUNT When you talk about the state of a company's **order book** or **order books**, you are talking about how many orders for their goods the company has. 订货簿 [BRIT, BUSINESS]

or·dered /ɔrdərd/ ADJ An **ordered** society or system is well-organized and has a clear structure. 井然有序的 [usu ADJ n] ❑ *An objective set of rules is necessary for any ordered society.* 一套客观设定的规则是每个有秩序的社会所必需的。

or·der·ly /ɔrdərli/ (**orderlies**) 1 ADJ If something is done in an **orderly** fashion or manner, it is done in a well-organized and controlled way. 有秩序的 ❑ *The organizers guided them in an orderly fashion out of the building.* 组织者们带领他们井然有序地走出了大楼。 2 ADJ Something that is **orderly** is neat or arranged in a neat way. 整齐的 ❑ *It's a beautiful, clean and orderly city.* 这是一座美丽、干净、整齐的城市。 ● **or·der·li·ness** N-UNCOUNT 整齐 ❑ *A balance is achieved in the painting between orderliness and unpredictability.* 这幅画在整齐和变幻间取得了平衡。 3 N-COUNT An **orderly** is a person who works in a hospital and does jobs that do not require special medical training. 护理员 ❑ *For most of his life, he was a hospital orderly.* 他做了大半辈子的医院护理员。

or·di·nance /ɔrdənəns/ (**ordinances**) N-COUNT An **ordinance** is an official rule or order, especially from a local government. (地方性) 法规 [FORMAL] ❑ *...ordinances that restrict building development.* …限制楼房建设的法规。

or·di·nari·ly /ɔrdənɛrɪli/ ADV If you say what is **ordinarily** the case, you are saying what is normally the case. 通常地 ❑ *The streets would ordinarily have been full of people, but now they were empty.* 街上通常都是熙熙攘攘的人群，但那时却空无一人。

or·di·nary ♦◇◇ /ɔrdənɛri/ 1 ADJ **Ordinary** people or things are normal and not special or different in any way. 普通的 ❑ *I strongly suspect that most ordinary people would agree with me.* 我强烈地感到大多数普通老百姓会赞同我。 ❑ *It has 25 calories less than ordinary ice cream.* 它的热量比普通的冰淇淋少25卡路里。 2 PHRASE Something that is **out of the ordinary** is unusual or different. 不寻常的 ❑ *The boy's knowledge was out of the ordinary.* 这个男孩的知识面非同寻常。

Thesaurus *ordinary* 另参见:

ADJ.	common, everyday, normal, regular, standard, typical, usual; *(ant.)* abnormal, unusual 1

O

Word Partnership *ordinary* 的常用搭配:

N. ordinary **Americans**, ordinary **circumstances**, ordinary **citizens**, ordinary **day**, ordinary **expenses**, ordinary **folk**, ordinary **life**, ordinary **people**, ordinary **person** 1

PREP. **out of the** ordinary 2

or·di·nary shares N-PLURAL **Ordinary shares** are shares in a company that are owned by people who have a right to vote at the company's meetings and to receive part of the company's profits after the holders of preference shares have been paid. Compare **preference shares**. 普通股 [BRIT, BUSINESS]

in AM, use **common stock**

or·di·na·tion /ɔrdəneɪʃən/ (**ordinations**) N-VAR When someone's **ordination** takes place, they are made a minister, priest, or rabbi. 圣职授予 ❑ *...supporters of the ordination of women.* …女性担任圣职的支持者们。

ore /ɔr/ (**ores**) N-MASS **Ore** is rock or earth from which metal can be obtained. 矿石 ❑ *...a huge iron ore mine.* …一个储量巨大的铁矿。

→ see **metal**

or·gan /ɔrgən/ (**organs**) 1 N-COUNT An **organ** is a part of your body that has a particular purpose or function, for example, your heart or lungs. 器官 ❑ *...damage to the muscles and internal organs.* …对肌肉和内脏的损伤。 ❑ *...the reproductive organs.* …生殖器官。 2 N-COUNT An **organ** is a large musical instrument with pipes of different lengths through which air is forced. It has keys and pedals like a piano. 风琴; 管风琴 ❑ *...the church organ.* …教堂管风琴。 3 N-COUNT You refer to a newspaper or organization as **the organ of** the government or another group when it is used by them as a means of giving information or getting things done. (政府、集团的)新闻媒体

→ see **donor, keyboard, nervous system**

or·gan·ic /ɔrgænɪk/ 1 ADJ **Organic** methods of farming and gardening do not use pesticides, chemical fertilizers, growth hormones, or antibiotics, so that the food produced does not contain toxic chemicals. 有机种植的 ❑ *Organic farming is expanding everywhere.* 有机农业在各处发展。 ● **or·gani·cal·ly** ADV 有机地 ❑ *...organically grown vegetables.* …有机种植的蔬菜。

Food that is produced without chemicals is called **organic** or **natural** food. Organic food was once sold only in special shops known as **health food stores** at high prices. These days some of these foods and other low-impact products are sold in ordinary supermarkets.

2 ADJ **Organic** substances are produced by or found in living things. 有机的 ❑ *Incorporating organic material into chalky soils will reduce the alkalinity.* 将有机物质掺入白垩质土壤中将会降低碱性。 3 ADJ **Organic** change or development happens gradually and naturally rather than suddenly. 自然演进的 [FORMAL] ❑ *...to manage the company and supervise its organic growth.* …管理公司并指导其逐步发展。

or·gani·sa·tion /ɔrgənɪzeɪʃən/ [BRIT] → see **organization**

or·gani·sa·tion·al /ɔrgənɪzeɪʃənəl/ [BRIT] → see **organizational**

or·gan·ise /ɔrgənaɪz/ [BRIT] → see **organize**

or·ga·nised /ɔ:rgənaɪzd/ [BRIT] → see **organized**

or·gan·is·er /ɔrgənaɪzər/ [BRIT] → see **organizer**

or·gan·ism /ɔrgənɪzəm/ (**organisms**) N-COUNT An **organism** is an animal or plant, especially one that is so small that you cannot see it without using a microscope. 生物; 微生物 ❑ *Not all chemicals normally present in living organisms are harmless.* 并非所有正常存在于活的有机体中的化学物质都是无害的。

or·gan·ist /ɔrgənɪst/ (**organists**) N-COUNT An **organist** is someone who plays the organ. 风琴演奏者

or·gani·za·tion ♦♦◊ /ɔrgənɪzeɪʃən/ (**organizations**)

in BRIT, also use **organisation**

1 N-COUNT An **organization** is an official group of people, for example, a political party, a business, a charity, or a club. 组织(指团体机构等) ❑ *Most of the food for the homeless is provided by voluntary organizations.* 给无家可归者的大部分食物是由志愿组织提供的。 2 N-UNCOUNT The **organization** of an event or activity involves making all the necessary arrangements for it. (活动的)组织 ❑ *...the exceptional attention to detail that goes into the organization of this event.* …对此项活动组织细节的格外关注。 3 N-UNCOUNT The **organization of** something is the way in which its different parts are arranged or relate to each other. 结构 ❑ *I am aware that the organization of the book leaves something to be desired.* 我知道这本书的结构还有待完善。

or·gani·za·tion·al /ɔrgənɪzeɪʃənəl/

in BRIT, also use **organisational**

1 ADJ **Organizational** abilities and methods relate to the way that work, activities, or events are planned and arranged. 组织方面的(能力、方法等) [ADJ n] ❑ *Evelyn's excellent organizational skills were soon spotted by her employers.* 伊夫琳出色的组织才干很快就被她的雇主发现了。 2 ADJ **Organizational** means relating to the structure of an organization. 组织结构方面的 [ADJ n] ❑ *The police now recognize that big organizational changes are needed.* 警方现在认识到需要大的结构方面的改变。 3 ADJ **Organizational** means relating to organizations, rather than individuals. 组织上的(相对个体而言) [ADJ n] ❑ *This problem needs to be dealt with at an organizational level.* 这个问题需要在组织层面上解决。

or·gan·ize ♦♦◊ /ɔrgənaɪz/ (**organizes, organizing, organized**)

in BRIT, also use **organise**

1 V-T If you **organize** an event or activity, you make sure that the necessary arrangements are made. 组织 ❑ *In the end, we all decided to organize a concert for Easter.* 最后，我们一致决定为复活节组织一场音乐会。 ❑ *...a two-day meeting organized by the United Nations.* …一个由联合国组织的，为期两天的会议。 2 V-T If you **organize** something that someone wants or needs, you make sure that it is provided. 安排 ❑ *I will organize transportation.* 我来安排运输。 3 V-T If you **organize** a set of things, you arrange them in an ordered way or give them a structure. 整理 ❑ *He began to organize his materials.* 他开始整理他的材料。 ❑ *She took a hasty cup of coffee and tried to organize her scattered thoughts.* 她急急忙忙喝了杯咖啡，设法整理散乱的思绪。 4 V-T If you **organize** yourself, you plan your work and activities in an ordered, efficient way. 规划(自己的工作和活动) ❑ *...changing the way you organize yourself.* …改变你规划自己的方式。 ❑ *Go right ahead, I'm sure you don't need me to organize you.* 尽管干，我确信你不需要我来帮你规划。

Thesaurus *organize* 另参见:

V. coordinate, plan, set up 1 2
arrange, line up, straighten out 3

or·ga·nized ♦◊◊ /ɔrgənaɪzd/

in BRIT, also use **organised**

1 ADJ An **organized** activity or group involves a number of people doing something together in a structured way, rather than doing it by themselves. 有组织的 [ADJ n] ❑ *...organized groups of art thieves.* …有组织的艺术品盗窃团伙。 ❑ *...organized religion.* …有组织的宗教。 2 ADJ Someone who is **organized** plans their work and activities efficiently. 有条理的 ❑ *These people are very efficient, very organized, and excellent time managers.* 这些人效率很高、很有条理，时间安排得非常好。

or·gan·iz·er ♦◊◊ /ɔrgənaɪzər/ (**organizers**)

in BRIT, also use **organiser**

1 N-COUNT The **organizer** of an event or activity is the person who makes sure that the necessary arrangements are made. 组织者 ❑ *He became an organizer for the Democratic Party.* 他成了民主党的一名组织者。 2 → see also **personal organizer**

→ see **union**

or·gasm /ɔrgæzəm/ (**orgasms**) N-VAR An **orgasm** is the moment of greatest pleasure and excitement in sexual activity. 性高潮 ❑ *...the ability to reach orgasm.* …达到性高潮的能力。

orgy /ɔrdʒi/ (**orgies**) N-COUNT An **orgy** is a party in which people behave in a very uncontrolled way, especially one involving sexual activity. 狂欢会 ❑ *It was reminiscent of a scene from a Roman orgy.* 这让人联想起罗马狂欢会的一个场面。

★ **ori·ent** /ɔriənt, -ɛnt/ (**orients, orienting, oriented**) 1 V-T When you **orient yourself to** a new situation or course of action, you learn about it and prepare to deal with it. 适应 [FORMAL] ❑ *You will need the time to orient yourself to your new way of eating.* 你需要时间适应新的吃法。 2 → see also **oriented**

★ **ori·en·tal** /ɔriɛntəl/ ADJ **Oriental** means coming from or associated with eastern Asia, especially China and Japan. 东方的(尤指中国和日本的) ❑ *There were Oriental carpets on the floors.* 地板上铺着东方的地毯。

ori·en·tat·ed /ɔrienteɪtɪd/ **Orientated** means the same as **oriented**. 朝某方向的

★ **ori·en·ta·tion** /ɔriənteɪʃ^ən/ (**orientations**) **1** N-VAR If you talk about the **orientation** of an organization or country, you are talking about the kinds of aims and interests it has. 方向；目标 ❑ *...a marketing orientation.* …一个营销目标。 ❑ *To a society which has lost its orientation he has much to offer.* 对一个迷失了方向的社会，他有许多要做的。 **2** N-VAR Someone's **orientation** is their basic beliefs or preferences. 基本信仰；取向 ❑ *...legislation that would have made discrimination on the basis of sexual orientation illegal.* …原本可以使基于性取向的歧视不合法的立法。 **3** N-UNCOUNT **Orientation** is basic information or training that is given to people starting a new job, school, or course. (任职、上学等之前的) 情况介绍；训练 ❑ *They give their new employees a day or two of orientation.* 他们对新员工进行一两天的培训。 **4** N-COUNT The **orientation** of a structure or object is the direction it faces. 朝向 ❑ *Farnese had the orientation of the church changed so that the front would face a square.* 法尔内塞把教堂的朝向改了，使其正面对着一个广场。

ori·ent·ed /ɔriɛntɪd/

The form **orientated** is also used.

ADJ If someone **is oriented toward** or **oriented to** a particular thing or person, they are mainly concerned with that thing or person. 以…为方向的；重视…的 [v-link ADJ "toward/to" n] ❑ *It seems almost inevitable that North African economies will still be primarily oriented toward Europe.* 看来可以预见的是，北非经济仍会主要面向欧洲。

ori·gin ♦◇◇ /ɔrɪdʒɪn/ (**origins**) **1** N-COUNT You can refer to the beginning, cause, or source of something as its **origin** or **origins**. 起源；起因 ❑ *...theories about the origin of life.* …有关生命起源的各种理论。 ❑ *Their medical problems are basically physical in origin.* 他们的疾病基本是身体上的问题造成的。 **2** N-COUNT When you talk about a person's **origin** or **origins**, you are referring to the country, race, or living conditions of their parents or ancestors. 出身；血统 [usu poss N, also "of/in" N] ❑ *Thomas has not forgotten his humble origins.* 托马斯没有忘记他卑微的出身。 ❑ *...people of Asian origin.* …亚洲血统的人。

Word Partnership *origin* 的常用搭配：

N.	origin **of life**, **point of** origin, origin **of the universe** 1 **country of** origin, **family of** origin 2
ADJ.	**unknown** origin 1 2 **ethnic** origin, **Hispanic** origin, **national** origin 2

O

origi·nal ♦♦◇ /ərɪdʒɪn^əl/ (**originals**) **1** ADJ You use **original** when referring to something that existed at the beginning of a process or activity, or the characteristics that something had when it began or was made. 起初的 [det ADJ] ❑ *The original plan was to go by bus.* 起初的计划是乘公交车去。 **2** N-COUNT If something such as a document, a work of art, or a piece of writing is an **original**, it is not a copy or a later version. 原件；原作 ❑ *When you have filled in the questionnaire, copy it and send the original to your employer.* 填好问卷调查表之后，复印并将原件交给你的雇主。 **3** ADJ An **original** document or work of art is not a copy. 原件的；原作的 ❑ *...an original movie poster.* …一张原版的电影海报。 **4** ADJ An **original** piece of writing or music was written recently and has not been published or performed before. 新创作的 ❑ *...with catchy original songs by Richard Warner.* …配有几首由理查德·沃纳新创作的朗朗上口的歌曲。 **5** ADJ If you describe someone or their work as **original**, you mean that they are very imaginative and have new ideas. 原创的；创新的 [APPROVAL] ❑ *It is one of the most original works of imagination in the language.* 这是用这种语言创作的最具想像力的原创作品之一。 ● **origi·nal·ity** /ərɪdʒɪnælɪti/ N-UNCOUNT 原创性 ❑ *He was capable of writing things of startling originality.* 他能写出有惊人原创性的作品。

Thesaurus *original* 另参见：

ADJ.	early, first, initial 1 2 authentic, genuine 3 creative, unique 5
N.	master; *(ant.)* copy 2

origi·nal·ly ♦◇◇ /ərɪdʒɪn^əli/ ADV When you say what happened or was the case **originally**, you are saying what happened or was the case when something began or came into existence, often to contrast it with what happened later. 起初 ❑ *The plane has been kept in service far longer than originally intended.* 这架飞机的服役时间已经远远超过了起初的预料。

★ **origi·nate** /ərɪdʒɪneɪt/ (**originates, originating, originated**) V-T/V-I When something **originates** or when someone **originates** it, it begins to happen or exist. 始创；起源 [FORMAL] ❑ *The disease originated in Africa.* 这种疾病起源于非洲。 ❑ *All carbohydrates originate from plants.* 所有的碳水化合物均来源于植物。

or·na·ment /ɔrnəmənt/ (**ornaments**) **1** N-COUNT An **ornament** is an attractive object that you display in your home or in your garden. 装饰品 ❑ *...a shelf containing a few photographs and ornaments.* …一个放有几张照片和几件装饰品的架子。 **2** N-UNCOUNT Decorations and patterns on a building or a piece of furniture can be referred to as **ornament**. (建筑、家具上的) 装饰 [FORMAL] ❑ *...walls of glass overlaid with ornament.* …覆有装饰的玻璃墙。

▲ **or·na·men·tal** /ɔrnəmɛnt^əl/ ADJ Something that is **ornamental** is attractive and decorative. 装饰性的 ❑ *...an ornamental fountain.* …一个装饰性喷泉。

or·nate /ɔrneɪt/ ADJ An **ornate** building, piece of furniture, or object is decorated with complicated patterns or shapes. 装饰华丽的 ❑ *...an ornate iron staircase.* …一个装饰华丽的铁楼梯。

▲ **or·phan** /ɔrfən/ (**orphans, orphaned**) **1** N-COUNT An **orphan** is a child whose parents are dead. 孤儿 ❑ *...a young orphan girl brought up by peasants.* …她是由农民养大的孤儿。 **2** V-T PASSIVE If a child **is orphaned**, their parents die, or their remaining parent dies. 使成为孤儿 [no cont] ❑ *...a fifteen-year-old boy left orphaned by the recent disaster.* …这个15岁的男孩因最近的灾难而成为孤儿。

or·phan·age /ɔrfənɪdʒ/ (**orphanages**) N-COUNT An **orphanage** is a place where orphans live and are cared for. 孤儿院

★ **ortho·dox** /ɔrθədɒks/

The spelling **Orthodox** is also used for meanings **2** and **3**.

1 ADJ **Orthodox** beliefs, methods, or systems are ones which are accepted or used by most people. 正统的 (观念、方法、制度等) ❑ *Many of these ideas are now being incorporated into orthodox medical treatment.* 这些理念有许多正被吸收进正统的医疗中。 **2** ADJ If you describe someone as **orthodox**, you mean that they hold the older and more traditional ideas of their religion or party. 正统的 (人) ❑ *...Orthodox Jews.* …正统的犹太教徒。 **3** ADJ The **Orthodox** churches are Christian churches from Eastern Europe which separated from the western church in the eleventh century. 东正教的 ❑ *...the Greek Orthodox Church.* …希腊东正教会。

Word Link *dox ≈ opinion : orthodoxy, paradox, unorthodox*

ortho·doxy /ɔrθədɒksi/ (**orthodoxies**) **1** N-VAR An **orthodoxy** is an accepted view about something. 正统观念 ❑ *These ideas rapidly became the new orthodoxy in linguistics.* 这些观点很快就成了语言学中新的正统观念。 **2** N-UNCOUNT The old, traditional beliefs of a religion, political party, or philosophy can be referred to as **orthodoxy**. 正统信仰 ❑ *...a conflict between Nat's religious orthodoxy and Rube's belief that his mission is to make money.* …纳特的宗教正统信仰和鲁布以赚钱为己任的信仰之间的冲突。

os·ten·ta·tious /ɒstɛnteɪʃəs/ **1** ADJ If you describe something as **ostentatious**, you disapprove of it because it is expensive and is intended to impress people. 铺张的 [DISAPPROVAL] ❑ *...his house, which, however elaborate, is less ostentatious than the preserves of other Dallas tycoons.* …他的房子无论多精美，还是不如达拉斯其他大亨的独宅铺张奢侈。 **2** ADJ If you describe someone as **ostentatious**, you disapprove of them because they want to impress people with their wealth or importance. 炫耀的 [DISAPPROVAL] ❑ *Obviously he had plenty of money and was generous in its use without being ostentatious.* 显而易见，他有很多钱，花钱虽大方却不摆阔。 ● **os·ten·ta·tious·ly** ADV 炫耀地 ❑ *Her servants were similarly, if less ostentatiously attired.* 她的仆人们穿着相似，只是没那么华丽耀眼。 **3** ADJ You can describe an action or behavior as **ostentatious** when it is done in an exaggerated way to attract people's attention. 招摇的 ❑ *His wife was fairly quiet but she is not an ostentatious person anyway.* 他的妻子过去相当文静，而现在也不是一个爱招摇的人。 ● **os·ten·ta·tious·ly** ADV 招摇地 ❑ *Harry stopped under a street lamp and ostentatiously began inspecting the contents of his bag.* 哈里在一盏路灯下停了下来，开始招摇地翻看他包里的东西。

os·tra·cise /ɒstrəsaɪz/ [BRIT] → see **ostracize**

os·tra·cize /ɒstrəsaɪz/ (**ostracizes, ostracizing, ostracized**)

in BRIT, also use **ostracise**

V-T If someone **is ostracized**, people deliberately behave in an unfriendly way toward them and do not allow them to take part in any of their social activities. 排斥 [usu passive] ❑ *She claims she's being ostracized by some members of her local community.* 她声称遭到自己所在社区的一些成员排斥。

os·trich /ɒstrɪtʃ/ (**ostriches**) N-COUNT An **ostrich** is a very large, long-necked African bird that cannot fly. 鸵鸟

oth·er ♦♦♦ /ʌðər/ (**others**)

> When **other** follows the determiner **an**, it is written as one word: see **another**.

1 ADJ You use **other** to refer to an additional thing or person of the same type as one that has been mentioned or is known about. 其他的（指属于同一类别的）[det ADJ, ADJ n] ❑ *They were just like any other young couple.* 他们那时就和其他任何年轻夫妇一样。● PRON **Other** is also a pronoun. 其他 ❑ *Four crewmen were killed, one other was injured.* 四名船员被杀，另外一个受了伤。2 ADJ You use **other** to indicate that a thing or person is not the one already mentioned, but a different one. 别的（指属于不同类型的）[det ADJ, ADJ n] ❑ *The authorities insist that the discussions must not be linked to any other issue.* 官方坚持这些讨论绝不能和任何别的问题联系起来。❑ *He would have to accept it; there was no other way.* 他不得不接受它，没有别的办法。● PRON **Other** is also a pronoun. 别的 ❑ *This issue, more than any other, has divided her cabinet.* 正是这个问题，而不是任何别的问题，使她的内阁产生了分裂。3 ADJ You use **the other** to refer to the second of two things or people when the identity of the first is already known or understood, or has already been mentioned. （两个中）另一个的 [det ADJ] ❑ *The captain was at the other end of the room.* 队长在房间的另一头。❑ *You deliberately went in the other direction.* 你故意朝另一个方向走了。● PRON-SING **The other** is also a pronoun. 另一个 ["the" PRON] ❑ *Almost everybody had a cigarette in one hand and a martini in the other.* 几乎每个人都是一手一支香烟，一手一杯马提尼酒。4 ADJ You use **other** at the end of a list or a group of examples, to refer generally to people or things like the ones just mentioned. （泛指）其他的 [det ADJ, ADJ n] ❑ *The new Station Center will have shops, restaurants and other amenities.* 新的中央车站将会有商店、饭店及其他设施。● PRON **Other** is also a pronoun. 其他 ❑ *Descartes received his stimulus from the new physics and astronomy of Copernicus, Galileo, and others.* 笛卡儿从哥白尼、伽利略和其他科学家的新物理学和天文学中获得了灵感。5 ADJ You use **the other** to refer to the rest of the people or things in a group, when you are talking about one particular person or thing. 其余的 [det ADJ] ❑ *When the other kids were taken to the zoo, he was left behind.* 其余的孩子被带去动物园时，他被留了下来。● PRON **The others** is also a pronoun. 其余 ["the" PRON] ❑ *Aubrey's on his way here, with the others.* 奥布里和其余的人正在来这儿的路上。6 ADJ **Other** people are people in general, as opposed to yourself or a person you have already mentioned. （总称）他人的 [ADJ n] ❑ *The suffering of other people appalls me.* 他人的苦难使我大为震惊。● PRON-PLURAL **Others** means the same as **other people**. 他人 ❑ *His humor depended on contempt for others.* 他的幽默基于对他人的蔑视。

> Do not confuse **other** and **another**. You use **other** to refer to more than one type of person or thing. ❑ *Other boys were arriving now.* When you are talking about two people or things and have already referred to one of them, you refer to the second one as **the other** or **the other one**. When you are talking about several people or things and have already referred to one or more of them, you usually refer to the remaining ones as **the others**. **Another** person or thing means one more person or thing of the same kind. It is usually followed by a singular count noun, "one," "few," or a number larger than one. ❑ *Rick's got another camera… She had a drink and then another one… I waited another few minutes… They raised another $15,000.*

7 ADJ You use **other** in informal expressions of time such as **the other day**, **the other evening**, or **the other week** to refer to a day, evening, or week in the recent past. （不久）以前的 ["the" ADJ n] ❑ *I called her the other day and she said she'd like to come over.* 我前几天给她打电话，她说她想过来。8 PHRASE You use expressions like **among other things** or **among others** to indicate that there are several more facts, things, or people like the one or ones mentioned, but that you do not intend to mention them all. 除了别的以外（表省略不多言）[VAGUENESS] ❑ *He moved to Ohio in 2005 where, among other things, he worked as a journalist.* 他2005年搬到了俄亥俄州。在那儿除了做其他事情外，他还当了记者。❑ *His travels took him to Peru, among other places.* 他除了去其他地方之外，还旅行到了秘鲁。9 PHRASE If something happens, for example, **every other day** or **every other month**, there is a day or month when it does not happen between each day or month when it happens. 每隔一天（或一周、一月等）❑ *Their food is adequate. It includes meat at least every other day, vegetables and fruit.* 他们的食物足够了，有蔬菜和水果，至少每隔一天还有肉。10 PHRASE You use **every other** to emphasize that you are referring to all the rest of the people or things in a group. 所有其他的 [EMPHASIS] ❑ *The same will apply in every other country.* 这同样将适用于所有其他的国家。11 PHRASE You use **nothing other than** and **no other than** when you are going to mention a course of action, decision, or description and emphasize that it is the only one possible in the situation. 只有 [EMPHASIS] ❑ *Nothing other than an immediate custodial sentence could be justified.* 只有立即判处监禁才合理。❑ *The rebels would not be happy with anything other than the complete removal of the current regime.* 叛乱者们只有彻底推翻现政权才会高兴。12 PHRASE You use **or other** in expressions like **somehow or other** and **someone or other** to indicate that you cannot or do not want to be more precise about the information that you are giving. 什么什么的（指模糊说法）[VAGUENESS] ❑ *I was going to have him called away from the house on some pretext or other.* 我当时正打算用什么借口，让人把他从房子里叫出去。❑ *The foundation is holding a dinner in honor of something or other.* 基金会正设宴庆祝着什么。13 PHRASE You use **other than** after a negative statement to say that the person, item, or thing that follows is the only exception to the statement. 除了…之外 ❑ *She makes no reference to any feminist work other than her own.* 除了自己的作品之外，她根本不提任何其他女权主义作品。14 **each other** → see **each** 15 **one after the other** → see **one** 16 **one or other** → see **one** 17 **this, that and the other** → see **this** 18 **in other words** → see **word**

> **Word Link** ***wise* ≈ *in the direction or manner of* : *clockwise, likewise, otherwise***

other·wise ♦♦◊ /ʌðərwaɪz/ 1 ADV You use **otherwise** after mentioning a situation or telling someone to do something, in order to say what the result or consequence would be if the situation did not exist or the person did not do as you say. 否则 [ADV with cl] ❑ *Make a note of the questions you want to ask; you will invariably forget some of them otherwise.* 把你想问的问题记下来；否则你准会忘记其中几个。❑ *I'm lucky that I'm interested in school work, otherwise I'd go crazy.* 幸好我对学校作业还感兴趣，不然会疯的。2 ADV You use **otherwise** before stating the general condition or quality of something, when you are also mentioning an exception to this general condition or quality. 除此以外 [ADV group] ❑ *The decorations for the games have lent a splash of color to an otherwise drab city.* 运动会的装饰为这个平时乏味的城市增添了几抹色彩。3 ADV You use **otherwise** to refer in a general way to actions or situations that are very different from, or the opposite to, your main statement. 以不同方式 [ADV with v] [WRITTEN] ❑ *Take approximately 60 mg up to four times a day, unless advised otherwise by a doctor.* 每天4次，每次约60毫克，或遵医嘱。❑ *There is no way anything would ever happen between us, and believe me I've tried to convince myself otherwise.* 无论如何，我们之间不会发生什么。而且，相信我，我已经努力说服自己了。4 ADV You use **otherwise** to indicate that other ways of doing something are possible in addition to the way already mentioned. 用别的方法 [ADV before v] ❑ *The studio could punish its players by keeping them out of work, and otherwise controlling their lives.* 电影公司可以通过让演员无角色可演或其他途径控制他们的生活，以惩罚他们。5 PHRASE You use **or otherwise** or **and otherwise** to mention something that is not the thing just referred to or is the opposite of that thing. 或其相反 ❑ *It was for the police to assess the validity or otherwise of the evidence.* 应由警方来评价证据的有效与否。

ouch /aʊtʃ/ EXCLAM **"Ouch!"** is used in writing to represent the noise that people make when they suddenly feel pain. （表示突然感到的疼痛）哎哟 ❑ *She was barefoot and stones dug into her feet. "Ouch, ouch!" she cried.* 当时她光着双脚，石头扎了她的脚。"哎哟！哎哟！"她大喊起来。

ought ♦◊◊ /ɔt/

> **Ought to** is a phrasal modal verb. It is used with the base form of a verb.

1 PHRASE You use **ought to** to mean that it is morally right to do a particular thing or that it is morally right for a particular situation to exist, especially when giving or asking for advice or opinions. （指合乎道义）应该 ❑ *Mark, you've got a good wife. You ought to take care of her.* 马克，你娶了个好太太，应该好好照顾她啊。❑ *The people who already own a bit of money or land ought to have a voice in saying where it goes.* 已经有了点儿钱或土地的人对之有发言权。2 PHRASE

You use **ought to** when saying that you think it is a good idea and important for you or someone else to do a particular thing, especially when giving or asking for advice or opinions. (表示建议、愿望) 应该 ❑ *You don't have to be alone with him and I don't think you ought to be.* 你没必要和他单独相处，而且我认为你不应该和他单独相处。❑ *You ought to ask a lawyer's advice.* 你应该去问问律师的意见。 3 PHRASE You use **ought to** to indicate that you expect something to be true or to happen. (表示可能性、希望) 该 ❑ *"This ought to be fun," he told Alex, eyes gleaming.* "这应该会有趣。"他对亚历克斯说着，两眼闪着光。 4 PHRASE You use **ought to** to indicate that you think that something should be the case, but might not be. (表示推测) 应该 ❑ *They ought to win easily today, but nothing in life is certain.* 他们今天应该能轻而易举地取胜，但世事难料。 5 PHRASE You use **ought to** to indicate that you think that something has happened because of what you know about the situation, but you are not certain. (对已发生的事情做出推测) 应该 [VAGUENESS] ❑ *He ought to have reached the house some time ago.* 他到达那所房子应该有一段时间了。 6 PHRASE You use **ought to have** with a past participle to indicate that something was expected to happen or be the case, but it did not happen or was not the case. (某事) 本应该 (表示虚拟语气) ❑ *Basically the system ought to have worked.* 实际上，这个制度本来应该可行。 7 PHRASE You use **ought to have** with a past participle to indicate that although it was best or correct for someone to do something in the past, they did not actually do it. (某人) 本应该 (表示虚拟语气) ❑ *I realize I ought to have told you about it.* 我意识到我本该告诉你这件事的。 ❑ *I ought not to have asked you a thing like that. I'm sorry.* 我本不应该问你这样一件事。对不起。 8 PHRASE You use **ought to** when politely telling someone that you must do something, for example, that you must leave. 应当 (礼貌用语) [POLITENESS] ❑ *I really ought to be getting back now.* 现在我真应该回去了。

oughtn't /ɔtᵊnt/ **Oughtn't** is a spoken form of "ought not." **Oughtn't**是**ought not**的口语形式

ounce /aʊns/ (**ounces**) 1 N-COUNT An **ounce** is a unit of weight used in the U.S. and Britain. There are sixteen ounces in a pound and one ounce is equal to 28.35 grams. 盎司 ❑ *...four ounces of sugar.* …4盎司的糖。 2 N-SING You can refer to a very small amount of something, such as a quality or characteristic, as an **ounce**. 一点点 ❑ *If only my father had possessed an ounce of business sense.* 要是我父亲有一点点商业头脑就好了。

O

our ♦♦♦ /aʊər/

Our is the first person plural possessive determiner.

1 DET You use **our** to indicate that something belongs or relates both to yourself and to one or more other people. 我们的 ❑ *We're expecting our first baby.* 我们要生第一个孩子了。 2 DET A speaker or writer sometimes uses **our** to indicate that something belongs or relates to people in general. (用于泛指) 我们的 ❑ *We are all entirely responsible for our actions, and for our reactions.* 我们都对自己的行为、自己的反应完全负责。

ours /aʊərz/

Ours is the first person plural possessive pronoun.

PRON-POSS You use **ours** to refer to something that belongs or relates both to yourself and to one or more other people. 属于我们的东西 ❑ *That car is ours.* 那辆车是我们的。 ❑ *There are few strangers in a town like ours.* 像我们这样的镇上，没什么陌生人的。

our·selves ♦◇◇ /aʊərsɛlvz/

Ourselves is the first person plural reflexive pronoun.

1 PRON-REFL You use **ourselves** to refer to yourself and one or more other people as a group. 我们自己 [V PRON, prep PRON] ❑ *We sat around the fire to keep ourselves warm.* 我们围火而坐取暖。 2 PRON-REFL A speaker or writer sometimes uses **ourselves** to refer to people in general. **Ourselves** is used as the object of a verb or preposition when the subject refers to the same people. (泛指) 我们自己 [V PRON, prep PRON] ❑ *We all know that when we exert ourselves our heart rate increases.* 大家都知道，当我们竭尽全力时，心率会加速。 3 PRON-REFL-EMPH You use **ourselves** to emphasize a first person plural subject. In more formal English, **ourselves** is sometimes used instead of "us" as the object of a verb or preposition, for emphasis. (正式英语中，替代**us**作动词或介词宾语，用以强调) 我们自己 [EMPHASIS] ❑ *Others are feeling just the way we ourselves would feel in the same situation.* 他人现在所感受的，我们自己在相同的情况下也会同样感受到。 4 PRON-REFL-EMPH If you say something such as "We did it **ourselves**," you are indicating that the people you are referring to did it, rather than anyone else. 我们亲自 ❑ *We villagers built that ourselves, we had no help from anyone.* 那是我们这些村民自己修建的，没有用任何人帮忙。

★ **oust** /aʊst/ (**ousts, ousting, ousted**) V-T If someone **is ousted** from a position of power, job, or place, they are forced to leave it. 罢黜；把…撤职；驱逐 [JOURNALISM] ❑ *The leaders have been ousted from power by nationalists.* 那些领导人已被民族主义者赶下了台。 ❑ *The Republicans may oust him in November.* 共和党人可能在11月罢免他。 ● **oust·er** N-COUNT (**ousters**) 罢黜；撤职；驱逐 [usu sing with poss] [AM] ❑ *The group has called for the ouster of the trust's board.* 该集团已要求罢免信托董事会。 ● **oust·ing** N-UNCOUNT 罢黜 ❑ *The ousting of his predecessor was one of the most dramatic coups the business world had seen in years.* 对他前任的罢免曾是商界数年来见到的最具戏剧性的妙举之一。

out
1 ADVERB USES
2 ADJECTIVE AND ADVERB USES
3 VERB USE
4 PREPOSITION USES

❶ **out** ♦♦♦ /aʊt/

Out is often used with verbs of movement, such as "walk" and "pull," and also in phrasal verbs such as "give out" and "run out."

1 ADV When something is in a particular place and you take it **out**, you remove it from that place. (拿) 出 [ADV after v] ❑ *I like the pop you get when you pull out a cork.* 我喜欢你拔出瓶塞时弄出的那"砰"的一声。 ❑ *He took out his notebook and flipped the pages.* 他拿出了笔记本，快速地翻着页。 2 ADV You can use **out** to indicate that you are talking about the situation outside, rather than inside buildings. 在室外 [ADV after v] ❑ *It's hot out – very hot, very humid.* 外面热烘烘的——非常热，非常潮湿。 3 ADV If you are **out**, you are not at home or not at your usual place of work. 不在 (家或工作地) ❑ *I tried to get in touch with you yesterday evening, but I think you were out.* 我昨晚联系过你，但你那时可能不在家。 4 ADV If you say that someone is **out** in a particular place, you mean that they are in a different place, usually one far away. 远在 [ADV adv/prep] ❑ *The police tell me they've finished their investigations out there.* 警方告诉我他们已经完成了在那边的调查。 5 ADV When the sea or tide goes **out**, the sea moves away from the shore. (潮水) 退去 ❑ *The tide was out and they walked among the rock pools.* 潮水退了，他们在岩石区的潮水潭间散步。 6 ADV If you are **out** a particular amount of money, you have that amount less than you should or than you did. 缺少 (一笔钱) [ADV n] [mainly AM, INFORMAL] ❑ *I'm out ten thousand dollars, with nothing to show for it!* 我缺1万美元，没啥可说的！

❷ **out** ♦♦♦ /aʊt/ 1 ADJ If a light or fire is **out** or goes **out**, it is no longer shining or burning. (灯、火等) 熄灭的 [v-link ADJ] ❑ *All the lights were out in the house.* 房里所有的灯都熄灭了。 2 ADJ If flowers are **out**, their petals have opened. (花) 盛开的 [v-link ADJ] ❑ *Well, the daffodils are out in the gardens and they're always a beautiful show.* 哇，花园里的水仙开了，它们总是一道亮丽的风景。 ● ADV **Out** is also an adverb. 盛开地 [ADV after v] ❑ *I usually put it in my diary when I see the wild flowers coming out.* 我看到野花盛开时，通常会记在日记本里。 3 ADJ If something such as a book or CD is **out**, it is available for people to buy. 面市的 [v-link ADJ] ❑ *Their new album is out now.* 他们的新专辑现已面市。 ● ADV **Out** is also an adverb. 面市地 [ADV after v] ❑ *The French edition came out in early 2006.* 法文版在2006年初面市。 4 ADJ In a game or sport, if someone is **out**, they can no longer take part either because they are unable to or because they have been defeated. 不能参赛的；出局的 [v-link ADJ] 5 ADJ In baseball, a player is **out** if they do not reach a base safely. When three players on a team are out in an inning, then the team is **out**. (棒球比赛中) 出局的 6 ADJ If you say that a proposal or suggestion is **out**, you mean that it is unacceptable. (提议等) 不能被接受的 [v-link ADJ] ❑ *That idea is out, I'm afraid.* 那个观点恐怕是不能接受的。 7 ADJ If you say that a particular thing is **out**, you mean that it is no longer fashionable at the present time. 过时的 [v-link ADJ] ❑ *Romance is making a comeback. Reality is out.* 浪漫正回归；现实已过时。 8 ADJ If you say that a calculation or measurement is **out**, you mean that it is incorrect. (计算、测量) 不准确的 [v-link ADJ] ❑ *When the two ends of the tunnel met in the middle they were only a few inches out.* 隧道两端在中间相接时，只有几英寸的误差。 9 ADJ If someone is **out** to do something, they intend to do it. 打算做…的 [v-link ADJ to-inf] [INFORMAL] ❑ *Most companies these days are just out to make a quick profit.* 大多数公司如今只图快速获利。 **10** ADJ If news or information about something is **out**, information about it has been made public. 被公开的 [v-link ADJ] ❑ *The word is out that she has fled the country.* 有消息说，她已经逃离了那个国家。

❸ **out** /aʊt/ (**outs, outing, outed**) V-T If a group of people **out** a public figure or famous person, they reveal that person's homosexuality against their wishes. 揭露（名人的同性恋身份） ❑ *The New York gay action group "Queer Nation" recently outed an American Congressman.* 纽约同性恋行动团体"酷儿国度"最近揭露了一位美国国会议员的同性恋身份。 ● **out·ing**▲ N-UNCOUNT 揭露 ❑ *The gay and lesbian rights group, Stonewall, sees outing as completely unhelpful.* 男女同性恋权利团体"石墙"认为揭露同性恋身份是完全无用的。

❹ **out** ♦♦♦ /aʊt/

> **Out of** is used with verbs of movement, such as "walk" and "pull," and also in phrasal verbs such as "get out of" and "grow out of." **Out** is often used instead of **out of**, for example in "He looked out the window."

1 PHRASE If you go **out of** a place, you leave it. 从…离开 ❑ *She let him out of the house.* 她让他离开了那座房子。 **2** PHRASE If you take something **out of** the container or place where it has been, you remove it so that it is no longer there. 从…（拿）出来 ❑ *I always took my key out of my bag and put it in my pocket.* 我总是把钥匙从包里拿出来再放进口袋里。 **3** PHRASE If you look or shout **out of** a window, you look or shout away from the room where you are toward the outside. 向…外面（看或喊） ❑ *He went on staring out of the window.* 他依旧凝视着窗外。 **4** PHRASE If you are **out of** the sun, the rain, or the wind, you are sheltered from it. 躲开（阳光、雨、风等） ❑ *People can keep out of the sun to avoid skin cancer.* 人们可以通过躲开阳光来避免患上皮肤癌。 **5** PHRASE If someone or something gets **out of** a situation, especially an unpleasant one, they are then no longer in it. If they keep **out of** it, they do not start being in it. 摆脱 ❑ *In the past army troops have relied heavily on air support to get them out of trouble.* 过去，陆军部队严重依赖空中支援来摆脱困境。 ❑ *The economy is starting to climb out of recession.* 经济正开始慢慢走出萧条。 **6** PHRASE You can use **out of** to say that someone leaves an institution. 从…离开 ❑ *That is precisely what I came out of college thinking I was supposed to do.* 那正是我大学毕业时认为自己应该做的。 **7** PHRASE If you are **out of** range of something, you are beyond the limits of that range. 在…之外 ❑ *Shaun was in the bedroom, out of earshot, watching television.* 肖恩在卧室里看电视，听不到。 **8** PHRASE You use **out of** to say what feeling or reason causes someone to do something. For example, if you do something **out of** pity, you do it because you pity someone. 出于 ❑ *He took up office out of a sense of duty.* 他任职是出于一种责任感。 **9** PHRASE If you get something such as information or work **out of** someone, you manage to make them give it to you, usually when they are unwilling to give it. 从…那里（获得信息、工作等） ❑ *"Where is she being held prisoner?" I asked. "Did you get it out of him?"* "她现在被囚禁在哪里？"我问道。"你从他那儿打听到了吗？" **10** PHRASE If you get pleasure or an advantage **out of** something, you get it as a result of being involved with that thing or making use of it. 从…中（得到快乐、好处等） ❑ *Jenkins hasn't let the pressure take the fun out of the sport.* 詹金斯没有让压力夺走这项运动的乐趣。 **11** PHRASE If you are **out of** something, you no longer have any of it. 没有 ❑ *I can't find the sugar – and we're out of milk.* 我找不到糖，而且我们也没有牛奶了。 **12** PHRASE If something is made **out of** a particular material, it consists of that material because it has been formed or constructed from it. 用（制成） ❑ *Would you advise people to make a building out of wood or stone?* 你会建议人们用木头还是石头造房子？ **13** PHRASE You use **out of** to indicate what proportion of a group of things something is true of. For example, if something is true of one **out of** five things, it is true of one fifth of all things of that kind. 从…中（挑出一个或一组等） ❑ *Two out of five thought the business would be sold privately on their retirement or death.* 2/5的人认为该企业会在他们退休或去世后被私下卖掉。

out·age /aʊtɪdʒ/ (**outages**) N-COUNT An **outage** is a period of time when the electricity supply to a building or area is interrupted, for example, because of damage to the cables. 电力供应中断期 [AM]

> in BRIT, use **power cut**

❑ *A windstorm in Washington is causing power outages throughout the region.* 一场暴风造成整个华盛顿地区的电力供应中断。

out·back /aʊtbæk/ N-SING The parts of Australia that are far away from towns are referred to as **the outback**. （澳大利亚的）偏远地区 ❑ *Are there many people living in the outback?* 有很多人居住在澳大利亚的偏远地区吗？

out·bid /aʊtbɪd/ (**outbids, outbidding**)

> The form **outbid** is used in the present tense and is the past tense and past participle.

V-T If you **outbid** someone, you offer more money than they do for something that you both want to buy. 出价高于… ❑ *The Museum has antagonized rivals by outbidding them for the world's greatest art treasures.* 这家博物馆由于为世界最珍贵的艺术瑰宝出了更高的价格，从而招致了竞争对手的怨恨。

out·bound /aʊtbaʊnd/ ADJ An **outbound** flight is one that is leaving or about to leave a particular place. 开往某地的 ❑ *Airport officials say at least 20 outbound flights were delayed.* 机场官员说，至少有二十个离港航班被延误。

★ **out·break** /aʊtbreɪk/ (**outbreaks**) N-COUNT If there is an **outbreak of** something unpleasant, such as violence or a disease, it suddenly starts to happen. （暴动、疾病等的）爆发 ❑ *The four-day festival ended a day early after an outbreak of violence involving hundreds of youths.* 由于一起数百名年轻人参与的暴力事件的爆发，为期4天的庆祝活动提前1天结束。 ❑ *...an outbreak of chickenpox.* …水痘的暴发。

out·burst /aʊtbɜrst/ (**outbursts**) **1** N-COUNT An **outburst** of an emotion, especially anger, is a sudden strong expression of that emotion. （情感的）爆发 ❑ *...a spontaneous outburst of cheers and applause.* …由衷爆发出的欢呼声和掌声。 **2** N-COUNT An **outburst of** violent activity is a sudden period of this activity. （暴力活动的）爆发期 ❑ *Five people were reported killed today in a fresh outburst of violence.* 据报道今天有5人死于一起新的暴力事件。

out·cast /aʊtkæst/ (**outcasts**) N-COUNT An **outcast** is someone who is not accepted by a group of people or by society. 被排斥的人 ❑ *He had always been an outcast, unwanted and alone.* 他一直是个被排斥的人，无人理睬，孤孤单单。

out·come ♦◇◇ /aʊtkʌm/ (**outcomes**) N-COUNT The **outcome** of an activity, process, or situation is the situation that exists at the end of it. 结果 ❑ *Mr. Singh said he was pleased with the outcome.* 西恩先生说他对此结果感到满意。 ❑ *It's too early to know the outcome of her illness.* 现在还不知道她的病情结果。

out·cry /aʊtkraɪ/ (**outcries**) N-VAR An **outcry** is a reaction of strong disapproval and anger shown by the public or media about a recent event. 强烈的抗议 ❑ *The killing caused an international outcry.* 该起谋杀引起了国际上强烈的抗议。

★ **out·dat·ed** /aʊtdeɪtɪd/ ADJ If you describe something as **outdated**, you mean that you think it is old-fashioned and no longer useful or relevant to modern life. 过时的 ❑ *...outdated and inefficient factories.* …过时的、效率低下的工厂。 ❑ *...outdated attitudes.* …过时的看法。

out·do /aʊtdu/ (**outdoes, outdoing, outdid, outdone**) **1** V-T If you **outdo** someone, you are a lot more successful than they are at a particular activity. 超过 ❑ *It was important for me to outdo them, to feel better than they were.* 对我来说重要的是超过他们，感觉比他们更好。 **2** PHRASE You use **not to be outdone** to introduce an action which someone takes in response to a previous action. 不甘落后 ❑ *She wore a lovely tiara but the groom, not to be outdone, had on a very smart embroidered waistcoat.* 她戴着一个漂亮的冕状头饰，而新郎也不甘示弱，穿了一件很潇洒的刺绣马甲。

out·door /aʊtdɔr/ ADJ **Outdoor** activities or things happen or are used outside and not in a building. 户外的 [ADJ n] ❑ *If you enjoy outdoor activities, this is the trip for you.* 如果你喜欢户外活动，那么这个旅行适合你。

out·doors /aʊtdɔrz/ **1** ADV If something happens **outdoors**, it happens outside in the fresh air rather than in a building. 在户外 ❑ *It was warm enough to be outdoors all afternoon.* 天气暖洋洋的，整个下午都可以在户外。 **2** N-SING You refer to **the outdoors** when talking about activities that take place outside away from buildings. 户外活动 ❑ *I'm a lover of the outdoors.* 我是个户外活动爱好者。

out·er /aʊtər/ ADJ The **outer** parts of something are the parts which contain or enclose the other parts, and which are furthest from the center. 外面的 [ADJ n] ❑ *He heard a voice in the outer room.* 他听到外屋有人声。
→ see **core**

O

out·er space N-UNCOUNT **Outer space** is the area outside the Earth's atmosphere where the other planets and stars are situated. 外层空间 ❑ *In 1957, the Soviets launched Sputnik 1 into outer space.* 1957年，苏联人将"人造卫星1号"发射到外太空。
→ see **satellite**

★ **out·fit** /aʊtfɪt/ (**outfits**) 1 N-COUNT An **outfit** is a set of clothes. 全套服装 ❑ *She was wearing an outfit she'd bought the previous day.* 她穿着前一天买的一套服装。 2 N-COUNT You can refer to an organization as an **outfit**. 机构 ❑ *He works for a private security outfit.* 他在一家私人保安公司工作。

★ **out·flow** /aʊtfloʊ/ (**outflows**) N-COUNT When there is an **outflow of** money or people, a large amount of money or people move from one place to another. (钱或人的) 外流 ❑ *There was a net outflow of about $650m.* 净外流量大约是6亿5千万美元。

★ **out·going** /aʊtgoʊɪŋ/ 1 ADJ **Outgoing** things such as planes, mail, and passengers are leaving or being sent somewhere. 往外去的 [ADJ n] ❑ *All outgoing flights were grounded.* 所有的离港航班都停飞了。 2 ADJ Someone who is **outgoing** is very friendly and likes meeting and talking to people. 友好的; 喜欢交际的 ❑ *She's very outgoing.* 她非常友好。 3 ADJ You use **outgoing** to describe a person in charge of something who is soon going to leave that position. 行将离职的 [ADJ n] ❑ *...the outgoing director of the International Folk Festival.* …即将卸任的国际民俗节负责人。

out·go·ings /aʊtgoʊɪŋz/ N-PLURAL Your **outgoings** are the regular amounts of money which you have to spend every week or every month, for example, in order to pay your rent or bills. 常规开支 [BRIT]

in AM, use **outlay, expenses**

out·grow /aʊtgroʊ/ (**outgrows, outgrowing, outgrew, outgrown**) 1 V-T If a child **outgrows** a piece of clothing, they grow bigger, so that it no longer fits them. 长大而穿不下 (衣服) ❑ *She outgrew her clothes so rapidly that Patsy was always having to buy new ones.* 她长得太快，衣服很快就穿不下了，帕齐总得给她买新的。 2 V-T If you **outgrow** a particular way of behaving or thinking, you change and become more mature, so that you no longer behave or think in that way. 长大而不再具有 ❑ *The girl may or may not outgrow her interest in fashion.* 那个女孩可能会，也可能不会因长大而失去她对时尚的兴趣。

O

▲ **out·ing** /aʊtɪŋ/ (**outings**) 1 N-COUNT An **outing** is a short trip, usually with a group of people, away from your home, school, or place of work. (常指集体的) 短途旅行; 外出 ❑ *One evening, she made a rare outing to the local night club.* 一天晚上，她难得地去了一趟当地的夜总会。 2 → see also **out** 3

▲ **out·law** /aʊtlɔ/ (**outlaws, outlawing, outlawed**) 1 V-T When something **is outlawed**, it is made illegal. 宣布…为非法 ❑ *In some states gambling was outlawed.* 在一些州赌博被宣布为非法。 ❑ *The German government has outlawed some fascist groups.* 德国政府已宣布一些法西斯团体为非法。 2 N-COUNT An **outlaw** is a criminal who is hiding from the authorities. 逃犯 [OLD-FASHIONED] ❑ *Jesse was an outlaw, a bandit, a criminal.* 杰西曾是个逃犯、土匪、罪犯。

out·lay /aʊtleɪ/ (**outlays**) N-VAR **Outlay** is the amount of money that you have to spend in order to buy something or start a project. (必要的) 费用 ❑ *Apart from the capital outlay of buying the machine, dishwashers can actually save you money.* 抛开购买的费用不讲，洗碗机实际上能给你省钱。

out·let /aʊtlɛt, -lɪt/ (**outlets**) 1 N-COUNT An **outlet** is a store or organization which sells the goods made by a particular manufacturer or at a discount price, often direct from the manufacturer. 专卖店; 直销店 ❑ *...the largest retail outlet in the city.* …该市最大的零售专卖店。 ❑ *At the factory outlet you'll find discounted items at up to 75% off regular prices.* 在工厂的直销店里，你会找到比常规价低75%的打折商品。 2 N-COUNT If someone has an **outlet for** their feelings or ideas, they have a means of expressing and releasing them. (感情的) 发泄途径; (思想的) 表达途径 ❑ *Her father had found an outlet for his ambition in his work.* 她父亲在工作中找到了施展抱负的途径。 3 N-COUNT An **outlet** is a hole or pipe through which liquid or air can flow away. 出水口; 排气口 ❑ *...a warm air outlet.* …一个热气排气口。 4 N-COUNT An **outlet** is a place, usually in a wall, where you can connect electrical devices to the electricity supply. 电源插座 [mainly AM]

in BRIT, usually use **socket**

❑ *Just plug it into any electric outlet.* 就把它插入任何一个电源插座。

out·line ♦◇◇ /aʊtlaɪn/ (**outlines, outlining, outlined**) 1 V-T If you **outline** an idea or a plan, you explain it in a general way. 概述 ❑ *The mayor outlined his plan to clean up the town's image.* 市长概述了他清理整顿该市形象的计划。 2 N-COUNT An **outline** is a general explanation or description of something. 概要 [also "in" N] ❑ *Following is an outline of the survey findings.* 以下是调查结果的概要。 3 V-T PASSIVE You say that an object **is outlined** when you can see its general shape because there is light behind it. 映衬出…的轮廓 ❑ *The Ritz was outlined against the lights up there.* 里兹饭店的轮廓被上方的灯光映衬了出来。 4 N-COUNT The **outline** of something is its general shape, especially when it cannot be clearly seen. 轮廓 ❑ *He could see only the hazy outline of the goalposts.* 他只能看见球门柱模糊的轮廓。

Word Partnership *outline* 的常用搭配:

N.	outline **a paper**, outline **a plan** 1
	chapter outline 2
V.	**write an** outline 2
ADJ.	**broad** outline, **detailed** outline, **general** outline 2 4

out·live /aʊtlɪv/ (**outlives, outliving, outlived**) V-T If one person **outlives** another, they are still alive after the second person has died. If one thing **outlives** another thing, the first thing continues to exist after the second has disappeared or been replaced. 比…活得长; 比…经久 ❑ *I'm sure Rose will outlive many of us.* 我肯定罗斯会比我们中的很多人活得长。

out·look /aʊtlʊk/ (**outlooks**) 1 N-COUNT Your **outlook** is your general attitude toward life. 人生观 [usu sing, with supp, also "in" N] ❑ *I adopted a positive outlook on life.* 我选择了一种积极的人生观。 2 N-SING The **outlook** for something is what people think will happen in relation to it. 前景 ❑ *The economic outlook is one of rising unemployment.* 经济前景恶化，失业率不断增长。

out·ly·ing /aʊtlaɪɪŋ/ ADJ **Outlying** places are far away from the main cities of a country. 边远的 [ADJ n] ❑ *Tourists can visit outlying areas like the Napa Valley Wine Country.* 游客可以去纳帕谷酒乡这样的边远地区。

out·num·ber /aʊtnʌmbər/ (**outnumbers, outnumbering, outnumbered**) V-T If one group of people or things **outnumbers** another, the first group has more people or things in it than the second group. 在数量上超过 ❑ *...a town where men outnumber women four to one.* …一个男女比例为4比1的城镇。

out of → see **out**

out of date also **out-of-date** ADJ Something that is **out of date** is old-fashioned and no longer useful. 过时的 ❑ *The regulations were out of date and confusing.* 那些规定已经过时，而且令人费解。

out of touch 1 ADJ Someone who is **out of touch with** a situation is not aware of recent changes in it. 不了解的 [v-link ADJ] ❑ *Washington politicians are out of touch with the American people.* 华盛顿的政客们不了解美国人民。 2 ADJ If you are **out of touch** with someone, you have not been in contact with them recently and are not familiar with their present situation. 不联系的 [v-link ADJ] ❑ *James and I have been out of touch for years.* 我和詹姆斯已经多年没有联系了。

out of work ADJ Someone who is **out of work** does not have a job. 失业的 ❑ *...a town where half the men are usually out of work.* …一个半数人通常都失业的城镇。

out·pa·tient /aʊtpeɪʃənt/ (**outpatients**) also **out-patient** N-COUNT An **outpatient** is someone who receives treatment at a hospital but does not spend the night there. 门诊病人 ❑ *...the outpatient clinic.* …诊所。
→ see **hospital**

▲ **out·per·form** /aʊtpərfɔrm/ (**outperforms, outperforming, outperformed**) V-T If one thing **outperforms** another, the first is more successful or efficient than the second. 胜过 [JOURNALISM] ❑ *In recent years the Austrian economy has outperformed most other industrial economies.* 近年来奥地利的经济已经超过了其他大多数的工业经济。

out·place·ment /aʊtpleɪsmənt/ N-UNCOUNT An **outplacement** agency gives advice to managers and other professional people who have recently become unemployed, and helps them find new jobs. (为失业者提供就业咨询的) 新职介绍 [BUSINESS] ❑ *...an outplacement firm in Denver.* …丹佛的一家新职介绍所。

★ **out·post** /aʊtpoʊst/ (**outposts**) 1 N-COUNT An **outpost** is a small group of buildings used for trading or military purposes, either in a distant part of your own country or in a foreign country.（设在国内边远地区或国外的）军事基地；贸易基地 ❑ *...a remote mountain outpost, linked to the outside world by the poorest of roads.* …一个偏远山区的军事基地，靠着糟糕透顶的公路与外界相连。 2 N-COUNT An **outpost** is a small settlement or community that is situated in a remote part of a country. 边远居民点 ❑ *This rural outpost, 400 miles northeast of Helena, has one stoplight.* 这个在赫勒拿东北400英里处的农村居民点有一个交通信号灯。

out·put ♦◇◇ /aʊtpʊt/ (**outputs**) 1 N-VAR **Output** is used to refer to the amount of something that a person or thing produces. 产量 ❑ *Government statistics show the largest drop in industrial output for ten years.* 政府的统计数字显示出10年来工业产量最大幅度的下降。 2 N-VAR The **output** of a computer or word processor is the information that it displays on a screen or prints on paper as a result of a particular program.（计算机或文字处理机的）输出信息 ❑ *You run the software, you look at the output, you make modifications.* 运行这个软件，看看输出信息，并做修改。

★ **out·rage** (**outrages, outraging, outraged**)

The verb is pronounced /aʊtreɪdʒ/. The noun is pronounced /aʊtreɪdʒ/.

动词读作 /aʊtreɪdʒ/。名词读作 /aʊtreɪdʒ/。

1 V-T If you **are outraged** by something, it makes you extremely angry and shocked. 使震怒 ❑ *Many people have been outraged by some of the things that have been said.* 许多人曾为其所听说的一些事情所震怒。 ● **out·raged** ADJ 震怒的 ❑ *He is truly outraged about what's happened to him.* 他确实为发生在他身上的事情而震怒。 2 N-UNCOUNT **Outrage** is an intense feeling of anger and shock. 震怒 ❑ *The decision provoked outrage from women and human rights groups.* 该决定激起了妇女和各人权组织的震怒。 3 N-COUNT You can refer to an act or event that angers and shocks you as an **outrage**. 令人震怒之举；令人震怒之事 ❑ *The latest outrage was to have been a coordinated gun and bomb attack on the station.* 最近令人震怒的事件是一次对该车站枪弹并用的袭击。

out·ra·geous /aʊtreɪdʒəs/ ADJ If you describe something as **outrageous**, you are emphasizing that it is unacceptable or very shocking. 不可接受的；令人震惊的 [EMPHASIS] ❑ *By diplomatic standards, this was outrageous behavior.* 按外交标准，这是不可接受的行为。 ● **out·ra·geous·ly** ADV 不可接受地；令人震惊地 ❑ *...outrageously expensive skin care items.* …贵得不可接受的护肤品。

★ **out·reach** /aʊtritʃ/ N-UNCOUNT **Outreach** programs and plans try to find people who need help or advice rather than waiting for those people to come and ask for help. 主动帮助 [usu N n] ❑ *Their brief is to undertake outreach work aimed at young African Americans.* 他们的任务是承担主动帮助年轻美国黑人的工作。

▲ **out·right**

The adjective is pronounced /aʊtraɪt/. The adverb is pronounced /aʊtraɪt/.

形容词读作 /aʊtraɪt/。副词读作 /aʊtraɪt/。

1 ADJ You use **outright** to describe behavior and actions that are open and direct, rather than indirect. 直率的 [ADJ n] ❑ *Kawaguchi finally resorted to an outright lie.* 川口最后干脆公开撒谎。 ● ADV **Outright** is also an adverb. 直率地 [ADV after v] ❑ *Why are you so mysterious? Why don't you tell me outright?* 你为什么这么神神秘秘？为什么不直截了当地告诉我？ 2 ADJ **Outright** means complete and total. 完全彻底的 [ADJ n] ❑ *She had failed to win an outright victory.* 她没能大获全胜。 ● ADV **Outright** is also an adverb. 完全彻底地 [ADV after v] ❑ *The peace plan wasn't rejected outright.* 该和平计划没有被全盘否定。 ● PHRASE If someone **is killed outright**, they die immediately, for example, in an accident. 当即死亡

out·sell /aʊtsɛl/ (**outsells, outselling, outsold**) V-T If one product **outsells** another product, the first product is sold more quickly or in larger quantities than the second. 卖的比…好 [BUSINESS] ❑ *The team's products easily outsell those of other American baseball teams overseas.* 该队的产品在海外轻松卖过美国其他棒球队的产品。

out·set /aʊtsɛt/ PHRASE If something happens **at the outset** of an event, process, or period of time, it happens at the beginning of it. If something happens **from the outset** it happens from the beginning and continues to happen. 在开始时；从一开始 ❑ *Decide at the outset what kind of learning program you want to follow.* 一开始就要定下你的学习计划。

out·side ♦♦♦ /aʊtsaɪd/ (**outsides**)

The form **outside of** can also be used as a preposition.

1 N-COUNT The **outside** of something is the part which surrounds or encloses the rest of it. 外部 ❑ *...the outside of the building.* …该建筑物的外部。 ● ADJ **Outside** is also an adjective. 外部的 [ADJ n] ❑ *...high up on the outside wall.* …在外墙上很高的地方。 2 ADV If you are **outside**, you are not inside a building but are quite close to it. 在外面 ❑ *I stepped outside and pulled up my collar against the cold mist.* 我走到外面，拉起衣领以抵御寒雾。 ❑ *Outside, the light was fading rapidly.* 在外面，光在快速消失。 ● PREP **Outside** is also a preposition. 在…外面 ❑ *The victim was outside a shop when he was attacked.* 受害人被袭击时正在一家商店外面。 ● ADJ **Outside** is also an adjective. 外面的 [ADJ n] ❑ *...the outside temperature.* …外面的温度。 3 PREP If you are **outside** a room, you are not in it but are in the passage or area next to it. 在（房间）外面 ❑ *She'd sent him outside the classroom.* 她叫他到教室外面去。 ● ADV **Outside** is also an adverb. 在外面 ❑ *They heard voices coming from outside in the corridor.* 他们听到来自外面走廊的说话声。 4 ADJ When you talk about the **outside** world, you are referring to things that happen or exist in places other than your own home or community. 外界的 [ADJ n] ❑ *...a side of Morris's character she hid carefully from the outside world.* …莫里斯对外界小心掩藏的其性格的一面。 ● ADV **Outside** is also an adverb. 在外界 [ADV after v] ❑ *The scheme was good for the prisoners because it brought them outside into the community.* 该方案对犯人们有益，因为这能让他们到外界去融入社会。 5 PREP People or things **outside** a country, town, or region are not in it. 在（某国、城市、地区）之外 [n/-ed PREP n] ❑ *...an old castle outside Budapest.* …布达佩斯外的一座古堡。 ● N-SING **Outside** is also a noun. 外部 ["the" N] ❑ *Peace cannot be imposed from the outside by the United States or anyone else.* 和平不能由美国或其他任何国家从外部强加。 6 ADJ **Outside** people or organizations are not part of a particular organization or group. 外来的；外聘的 [ADJ n] ❑ *The company now makes much greater use of outside consultants.* 该公司现在更多地利用外聘顾问。 ● PREP **Outside** is also a preposition. 从外面来；从外面聘 ❑ *He is hoping to recruit a chairman from outside the company.* 他在希望从公司之外招聘一位董事长。 7 PREP **Outside** a particular institution or field of activity means in other fields of activity or in general life. 在（某机构或领域）以外 ❑ *...the largest merger ever to take place outside the oil industry.* …石油行业以外有史以来最大的合并。 8 PREP Something that is **outside** a particular range of things is not included within it. 在（某范围）以外 ❑ *She is a beautiful boat, but way, way outside my price range.* 她是条漂亮的船，但远在我的价格承受范围以外。 9 PREP Something that happens **outside** a particular period of time happens at a different time from the one mentioned. 在（某时期）以外 ❑ *They are open outside normal daily banking hours.* 它们在银行日常营业时间以外开放。

Thesaurus *outside* 另参见：

ADJ. exterior, outdoor; (*ant.*) inside, interior 1
PREP. beyond, near; (*ant.*) inside 2 3 5

Word Partnership *outside* 的常用搭配：

N. **the** outside **of a building** 1
outside **a building,** outside **a car,** outside **a room,** outside **a store** 2 3
outside **interests, the** outside **world** 4
outside **a city/town,** outside **a country** 5
outside **sources** 6
ADJ. **cold** outside, **dark** outside 2
V. **gather** outside, **go** outside, **park** outside, **sit** outside, **stand** outside, **step** outside, **wait** outside 2 3

out·sid·er /aʊtsaɪdər/ (**outsiders**) 1 N-COUNT An **outsider** is someone who does not belong to a particular group or organization.（不属于某组织或团体的）外部人士 ❑ *The most likely outcome may be to subcontract much of the work to an outsider.* 最有可能的结果是把大量工作分包给外部人员。 2 N-COUNT An **outsider** is someone who is not accepted by a particular group, or who feels that they do not belong in it.（未被某组织接受或自感不属其内的）外人 ❑ *Malone, a cop, felt as much an outsider as any of them.* 马隆，一个警察，跟他们中任何人一样感到自己是个外人。 3 N-COUNT In a competition, an **outsider** is a competitor who is unlikely to win.（在比赛中）无望获胜者 ❑ *He was an outsider in the race to be the new UN Secretary-General.* 他在本届新联合国秘书长的角逐中是无望获胜者。

O

▲ **out·skirts** /aʊtskɜrts/ N-PLURAL **The outskirts of** a city or town are the parts of it that are farthest away from its center. (市、镇的) 外围地带 ❑ *Hours later we reached the outskirts of New York.* 数小时后我们到达了纽约市的外围地带。

out·source /aʊtsɔrs/ (**outsources, outsourcing, outsourced**) V-T/V-I If a company **outsources** work or things, it pays workers from outside the company and often outside the country to do the work or supply the things. 外包 [BUSINESS] ❑ *...companies that outsource IT functions.* …将信息技术方面的工作外包的公司。❑ *The company began looking for ways to cut costs, which led to the decision to outsource.* 该公司开始寻找降低成本的途径，这使他们决定外包。
● **out·sourc·ing** N-UNCOUNT 外包 ❑ *The difficulties of outsourcing have been compounded by the increasing resistance of labor unions.* 外包困难加重，因为工会的抵制不断增强。

out·spo·ken /aʊtspoʊkən/ ADJ Someone who is **outspoken** gives their opinions about things openly and honestly, even if they are likely to shock or offend people. 直言不讳的 ❑ *Some church leaders have been outspoken in their support for political reform in Kenya.* 一些宗教领袖在对肯尼亚政治改革的支持上一直直言不讳。
● **out·spo·ken·ness** N-UNCOUNT 直言不讳 ❑ *Their outspokenness on behalf of civil rights sometimes cost them their jobs.* 他们为争取民权直言不讳，这有时会使他们失去工作。

out·stand·ing ♦◇◇ /aʊtstændɪŋ/ **1** ADJ If you describe someone or something as **outstanding**, you think that they are very remarkable and impressive. 杰出的 ❑ *Derartu is an outstanding athlete and deserved to win.* 德拉图是位杰出的运动员，他理应获胜。 **2** ADJ Money that is **outstanding** has not yet been paid and is still owed to someone. 尚未偿还的 ❑ *The total debt outstanding is $70 billion.* 尚未偿还的总债务额是700亿美元。 **3** ADJ **Outstanding** issues or problems have not yet been resolved. 尚未解决的 ❑ *We still have some outstanding issues to resolve before we'll have a treaty that is ready to sign.* 我们在签署这份条约之前还有一些悬而未决的问题要解决。 **4** ADJ **Outstanding** means very important or obvious. 突出的 ❑ *The company is an outstanding example of a small business that grew into a big one.* 该公司是小企业成长为大公司的突出例子。

out·stand·ing·ly /aʊtstændɪŋli/ ADV You use **outstandingly** to emphasize how good, or occasionally how bad, something is. 极其 [ADV adj/adv] [EMPHASIS] ❑ *Guatemala is an outstandingly beautiful place to visit.* 危地马拉是一个极其漂亮的游览胜地。

O

out·stretched /aʊtstrɛtʃt/ ADJ If a part of the body of a person or animal is **outstretched**, it is stretched out as far as possible. 伸展开的 ❑ *She was staring into the fire muttering, and holding her arms outstretched to warm her hands.* 她凝视着那火，喃喃自语着，伸出双臂暖手。

out·strip /aʊtstrɪp/ (**outstrips, outstripping, outstripped**) V-T If one thing **outstrips** another, the first thing becomes larger in amount, or more successful or important, than the second thing. 超过 ❑ *In 1989 and 1990 demand outstripped supply, and prices went up by more than a third.* 1989和1990年，需求大于供给，物价上涨了三分之一多。

out tray (**out trays**) also **out-tray** N-COUNT An **out tray** is a shallow container used in offices to put letters and documents in when they have been dealt with and are ready to be sent somewhere else. Compare **in tray**. 发文篮 [mainly BRIT]

in AM, usually use **out box**

out·ward /aʊtwərd/

The form **outwards** can also be used for meanings **3** and **4**.

1 ADJ The **outward** feelings, qualities, or attitudes of someone or something are the ones they appear to have rather than the ones that they actually have. 表面看起来的 [ADJ n] ❑ *In spite of my outward calm I was very shaken.* 尽管表面看似镇静，我内心却非常慌乱。 **2** ADJ The **outward** features of something are the ones that you can see from the outside. 外在的 [ADJ n] ❑ *Mark was lying unconscious but with no outward sign of injury.* 马克躺着，神志不清，但却没有外在的受伤迹象。 **3** ADV If something moves or faces **outward**, it moves or faces away from the place you are in or the place you are talking about. 向外(移动) 地; (面) 向外地 [ADV after v] ❑ *The top door opened outward.* 最上面的门向外开着。 **4** ADV If you say that a person or a group of people, such as a government, looks **outward**, you mean that they turn their attention to another group that they are interested in or would like greater involvement with. 向外(看) 地 [ADV after v] ❑ *Other poor countries looked outward, strengthening their ties to the economic superpowers.* 其他的穷国向外看，加强它们和经济大国的联系。 **5** ADJ An **outward** flight or journey is one that you make away from a place that you are intending to return to later. 外出的 [ADJ n]

out·ward·ly /aʊtwərdli/ ADV You use **outwardly** to indicate the feelings or qualities that a person or situation may appear to have, rather than the ones that they actually have. 表面上 ❑ *They may feel tired, and though outwardly calm, can be irritable.* 他们可能觉得累，所以尽管表面上平静，却可能容易发怒。

out·weigh /aʊtweɪ/ (**outweighs, outweighing, outweighed**) **1** V-T If one thing **outweighs** another, the first thing is of greater importance, benefit, or significance than the second thing. (在重要性或意义上) 超过 [FORMAL] ❑ *The advantages of this deal largely outweigh the disadvantages.* 这笔交易的利远大于弊。 **2** V-T If you **outweigh** someone, you are heavier than them. 比(某人) 重 ❑ *Young outweighed her opponent by about 60 pounds.* 杨比她的对手重约60磅。

out·wit /aʊtwɪt/ (**outwits, outwitting, outwitted**) V-T If you **outwit** someone, you use your intelligence or a trick to defeat them or to gain an advantage over them. 智胜; 骗过 ❑ *To win the presidency he first had to outwit his rivals within the Socialist Party.* 要想当上总统，他首先要在社会党党内智胜他的竞争对手们。

oval /oʊvᵊl/ (**ovals**) ADJ **Oval** things have a shape that is like a circle but is wider in one direction than the other. 椭圆的 ❑ *...the small oval framed picture of a little boy.* …一个小男孩的镶在椭圆形框架里的小幅照片。 ● N-COUNT **Oval** is also a noun. 椭圆 ❑ *Using 2 spoons, form the cheese into small balls or ovals.* 用两把勺把干酪挤成小圆球状或椭圆球状。
→ see **circle, shape**

ova·ry /oʊvəri/ (**ovaries**) N-COUNT A woman's **ovaries** are the two organs in her body that produce eggs. 卵巢 ❑ *...women who have had their ovaries removed.* …已摘除卵巢的女性。

ova·tion /oʊveɪʃᵊn/ (**ovations**) N-COUNT An **ovation** is a large amount of applause from an audience for a particular performer or speaker. 欢呼 [FORMAL] ❑ *They became civic heroes and received a tumultuous ovation on their appearance in New York City.* 他们成了平民英雄，在纽约市一露面就迎来了一阵激动的欢呼。

oven /ʌvᵊn/ (**ovens**) N-COUNT An **oven** is a device for cooking that is like a box with a door. You heat it and cook food inside it. 烤箱 ❑ *Put the onions and ginger in the oven and let them roast for thirty minutes.* 把洋葱与生姜放入烤箱中烤30分钟。

over

❶ POSITION AND MOVEMENT
❷ AMOUNTS AND OCCURRENCES
❸ OTHER USES

❶ **over** ♦♦♦ /oʊvər/

In addition to the uses shown below, **over** is used after some verbs, nouns, and adjectives in order to introduce extra information. **Over** is also used in phrasal verbs such as "hand over" and "glaze over."

1 PREP If one thing is **over** another thing or is moving **over** it, the first thing is directly above the second, either resting on it, or with a space between them. 在…之上 ❑ *He looked at himself in the mirror over the table.* 他看着桌子上方镜子中的自己。 ● ADV **Over** is also an adverb. 越过 [ADV after v] ❑ *...planes flying over every 10 or 15 minutes.* …每隔10或15分钟飞越上空的飞机。 **2** PREP If one thing is **over** another thing, it is supported by it and its ends are hanging down on each side of it. (搭或挂) 在…上 ❑ *A grey raincoat was folded over her arm.* 一件灰色的雨衣被折叠着搭在她的手臂上。 **3** PREP If one thing is **over** another thing, it covers part or all of it. (部分或全部地覆盖) 在…之上 ❑ *Mix the ingredients and pour over the mushrooms.* 把这些调料混合然后倒在蘑菇上。 ❑ *He was wearing a light-grey suit over a shirt.* 他在衬衣外面套了件浅灰色的西装。 ● ADV **Over** is also an adverb. (部分或全部地覆盖) 在…之上 [ADV after v] ❑ *Heat this syrup and pour it over.* 把糖浆加热然后倒上去。 **4** PREP If you lean **over** an object, you bend your body so that the top part of it is above the object. (身体探) 在…之上 [V PREP n] ❑ *They stopped to lean over a gate.* 他们停下来，将身子从一个栅栏门上面探出去。 ● ADV **Over** is also an adverb. (身体探) 在…之上 [ADV after v] ❑ *Sam leaned over to open the door of the car.* 萨姆探出身子去打开车门。 **5** PREP If you look **over** or talk **over** an object, you look or talk across the top of it. 越过…上方 ❑ *I went and stood beside him, looking over his shoulder.* 我走过去站在他身旁，从他的肩头上方望了过去。 **6** PREP If a window has a view over an area of land or water, you can see the land or water through the window. 从一边到另一边 [n PREP n, v PREP n] ❑ *...a light and airy bar with a wonderful view over the river.* …一个明亮通风而且看得见优美河景的酒吧。 7 PREP If someone or something goes **over** a barrier, obstacle, or boundary, they get to the other side of it by going across it, or across the top of it. 越过 [v PREP n] ❑ *I stepped over a broken piece of wood.* 我迈过一根断裂的木头。 ❑ *Nearly one million people crossed over the river into Moldavia.* 近一百万人渡过了这条河，进入摩尔达维亚。 ● ADV **Over** is also an adverb. 越过 [ADV after v] ❑ *I climbed over into the back seat.* 我爬过去坐在了后座上。 8 PREP If someone or something moves **over** an area or surface, they move across it, from one side to the other. 穿过 ❑ *She ran swiftly over the lawn to the gate.* 她轻快地跑过草坪，来到大门口。 9 PREP If something is on the opposite side of a road or river, you can say that it is **over** the road or river. 在…的另一边 ❑ *...a fashionable neighborhood, just over the river from Manhattan.* …一个时尚街区，正好与曼哈顿隔河相望。 10 ADV If you go **over** to a place, you go to that place. 到… ❑ *I got out the car and drove over to Greg's place.* 我把车开出来，驱车到格雷格那儿去。 ❑ *I thought you might have invited her over.* 我想你大概已经邀请过她到这里来。 11 ADV You can use **over** to indicate a particular position or place a short distance away from someone or something. 在那边 ❑ *He noticed Rolfe standing silently over by the window.* 他注意到罗尔夫默默地站在窗旁。 ❑ *John reached over and took Joanna's hand.* 约翰伸过手去牵起了乔安娜的手。 12 ADV You use **over** to say that someone or something falls toward or onto the ground, often suddenly or violently. (突然或猛然) 倒下 [ADV after v] ❑ *If he drinks more than two glasses of wine he falls over.* 他喝两杯以上的酒就会醉倒。 ❑ *She pushed past me, almost knocking me over.* 她从我身边挤过去，差点把我撞倒。 13 ADV If something rolls **over** or is turned **over**, its position changes so that the part that was facing upward is now facing downward. 翻转倒置 [ADV after v] ❑ *His car rolled over after a tire was punctured.* 在一个车胎被扎破之后，他的车翻了个底朝天。

> **Over** and **above** are both used to talk about position and height. If something is higher than something else and the two things are imagined as being positioned along a vertical line, you can use either **above** or **over**. ❑ *He opened a cupboard above the sink... She leaned forward until her face was over the basin.* However, if something is higher than something else but the two things are regarded as being wide or horizontal rather than tall or vertical, you have to use **above**. ❑ *The trees rose above the row of houses.* **Above** and **over** are both used to talk about measurements, for example, when you are talking about a point that is higher than another point on a scale. ❑ *Any money earned over that level is taxed. ...everybody above five feet eight inches in height.* You use **over** to say that a distance or period of time is longer than the one mentioned. ❑ *...a height of over twelve thousand feet... Our relationship lasted for over a year.* **Above** and **over** are also both used to talk about people's rank or importance. You use **above** to talk about people who are more important and in a higher position than other people. ❑ *...behaving as if she was in a position above the other staff.* If someone is **over** you, they give orders or instructions to you. ❑ *...an officer in authority over him.*

14 PHRASE **All over** a place means in every part of it. 遍及各处 ❑ *...doctors who work all over the country.* …工作在全国各地的医生们。 15 PHRASE **Over here** means near you, or in the country you are in. 这里; 在国内 ❑ *Why don't you come over here tomorrow evening.* 你明晚到这里来吧。 16 PHRASE **Over there** means in a place a short distance away from you, or in another country. 那边; 在别国 ❑ *The cafe is just across the road over there.* 咖啡馆就在马路对面那边。

❷ **over** ♦♦♦ /oʊvər/ 1 PREP If something is **over** a particular amount, measurement, or age, it is more than that amount, measurement, or age. 超过 [PREP amount] ❑ *They say that tobacco will kill over 4 million people worldwide this year.* 他们说烟草今年将在全球范围内夺去超过400万人的生命。 ❑ *His family have accumulated property worth well over $1 million.* 他家已经积累了价值远远超过一百万美元的财产。 ● ADV **Over** is also an adverb. 以上 [amount "and" ADV] ❑ *...people aged 65 and over.* …65岁及以上的人。 2 PHRASE **Over and above** an amount, especially a normal amount, means more than that amount or in addition to it. 多于; 除…之外 ❑ *Expenditure on education has gone up by seven point eight per cent over and above inflation.* 教育支出增长率比通货膨胀率高出7.8%。 3 ADV If you say that you have some food or money **over** or left **over**, you mean that it remains after you have used all that you need. 剩余地 ❑ *The Larsons pay me well enough, but there's not much left over for luxuries.* 拉森家给我的报酬不错，但是剩不下多少钱来买奢侈品。 4 ADV If you do something **over**, you do it again or start doing it again from the beginning. 再一次 [ADV after v] [AM] ❑ *She said if she had the chance to do it over, she would have hired a press secretary.* 她说如果她有机会再做一遍此事，她会雇一个新闻秘书。 5 PHRASE If you say that something happened **twice over, three times over** and so on, you are stating the number of times that it happened and emphasizing that it happened more than once. 两遍 [mainly BRIT, EMPHASIS] ❑ *James had to have everything spelled out twice over for him.* 詹姆斯不得不让人把每个单词都为他拼写两遍。 6 PHRASE If you do something **over again**, you do it again or start doing it again from the beginning. 重新 ❑ *If I could live my life over again, I would do things exactly the same way.* 如果我可以重新活一次，我还会以完全一样的方式来处事。 7 PHRASE If you say that something is happening **all over again**, you are emphasizing that it is happening again, and you are suggesting that it is tiring, boring, or unpleasant. 又一次 [EMPHASIS] ❑ *The whole process started all over again.* 整个过程又重新开始了。 8 PHRASE If you say that something happened **over and over** or **over and over again**, you are emphasizing that it happened many times. 反复地 [EMPHASIS] ❑ *He plays the same songs over and over.* 他反复演奏同样的几首歌曲。

❸ **over** ♦♦♦ /oʊvər/ 1 ADJ If an activity is **over** or **all over**, it is completely finished. 结束的 [v-link ADJ] ❑ *Warplanes that have landed there will be kept until the war is over.* 已经着陆在那里的军用飞机将被留到战争结束。 ❑ *I am glad it's all over.* 我真高兴，一切都结束了。 2 PREP If you are **over** an illness or an experience, it has finished and you have recovered from its effects. 从…中恢复 ❑ *I'm glad that you're over the flu.* 我很高兴你的流感好了。 3 PREP If you have control or influence **over** someone or something, you are able to control them or influence them. 对… [n PREP n] ❑ *He's never had any influence over her.* 他对她从没有过任何影响。 4 PREP You use **over** to indicate what a disagreement or feeling relates to or is caused by. 对于 [n PREP n, v PREP n] ❑ *...concern over recent events in the Dominican Republic.* …对于多米尼加共和国最近若干事件的关注。 ❑ *Staff at some air and sea ports are beginning to protest over pay.* 一些机场和海港的工作人员开始就工资进行抗议。 5 PREP If something happens **over** a particular period of time or **over** something such as a meal, it happens during that time or during the meal. 在…期间 ❑ *The number of attacks on the capital had gone down over the past week.* 在过去一周里对首都的袭击次数下降了。 6 PREP You use **over** to indicate that you give or receive information using a telephone, radio, or other piece of electrical equipment. 通过… ❑ *I'm not prepared to discuss this over the telephone.* 我不准备通过电话来讨论这件事。 ❑ *The head of state addressed the nation over the radio.* 国家元首通过广播向全国人民发表了讲话。 7 PHRASE The presenter of a radio or television program says "**over to** someone" to indicate the person who will speak next. 交由 (某人) 播报 ❑ *With the rest of the sports news, over to Mike Martinez.* 其余的体育新闻，由迈克・马丁内斯播报。 8 CONVENTION When people such as the police or the army are using a radio to communicate, they say "**Over**" to indicate that they have finished speaking and are waiting for a reply. 完毕 (无线电联络的交接用语) [FORMULAE]

> **Thesaurus** *over* 另参见:
> PREP. above, beyond, higher than; (*ant.*) below, under ❶ 1
> ADJ. completed, concluded, done with, ended, finished ❸ 1

over·all ♦♦◇ (**overalls**)

> The adjective and adverb are pronounced /oʊvərɔl/. The noun is pronounced /oʊvərɔl/.

> 形容词和副词读作 /oʊvərɔl/。名词读作 /oʊvərɔl/。

1 ADJ You use **overall** to indicate that you are talking about a situation in general or about the whole of something. 总的 [ADJ n] ❑ *...the overall rise in unemployment.* …失业人数的总体上升。 ● ADV **Overall** is also an adverb. 总体上地 [ADV with cl] ❑ *Overall I was disappointed.* 总的来说，我感到失望。 2 N-PLURAL **Overalls** are pants that are attached to a piece of cloth which covers your chest and which has straps going over your shoulders. 工装裤 [also "a pair of" N] [AM]

> in BRIT, use **dungarees**

O

❑ *An elderly man dressed in faded overalls took the witness stand.* 一位身着褪色工装裤的老人站在了证人席上。 **3** N-PLURAL **Overalls** consist of a single piece of clothing that combines pants and a jacket. You wear overalls over your clothes in order to protect them while you are working. (连体的) 防护服 [also "a pair of" N]

over·awe /oʊvərɔ/ (**overawes, overawing, overawed**) V-T If you **are overawed by** something or someone, you are very impressed by them and a little afraid of them. 敬畏 [usu passive] ❑ *Don't be overawed by people in authority, however important they are.* 无论他们有多么了不起，也不要被有权势的人吓倒。

over·board /oʊvərbɔrd/ **1** ADV If you fall **overboard**, you fall over the side of a boat into the water. 从船上(落) 入水中 [ADV after v] ❑ *His sailing instructor fell overboard and nearly drowned during a lesson.* 他的帆船教练在一次课上落水，差点溺死。 **2** PHRASE If you say that someone **goes overboard**, you mean that they do something to a greater extent than is necessary or reasonable. 过分 [INFORMAL] ❑ *Women sometimes damage their skin by going overboard with abrasive cleansers.* 女性有时因为过度使用研磨型的洁面乳而损害了皮肤。

over·came /oʊvərkeɪm/ **Overcame** is the past tense of **overcome**. **overcome**的过去式

over·ca·pac·ity /oʊvərkəpæsɪti/ N-UNCOUNT If there is **overcapacity** in a particular industry or area, more goods have been produced than are needed, and the industry is therefore less profitable than it could be. 生产能力过剩 [BUSINESS] ❑ *There is huge overcapacity in the world car industry.* 世界汽车工业存在巨大的生产能力过剩。

over·charge /oʊvərtʃɑrdʒ/ (**overcharges, overcharging, overcharged**) V-T If someone **overcharges** you, they charge you too much for their goods or services. 对…要价太高 ❑ *If you feel a taxi driver has overcharged you, say so.* 如果你觉得出租车司机多收了你的钱，要说出来。

over·coat /oʊvərkoʊt/ (**overcoats**) N-COUNT An **overcoat** is a thick warm coat that you wear in winter. 大衣

over·come ♦◇◇ /oʊvərkʌm/ (**overcomes, overcoming, overcame**)

> The form **overcome** is used in the present tense and is also the past participle.

1 V-T If you **overcome** a problem or a feeling, you successfully deal with it and control it. 克服 ❑ *Molly had fought and overcome her fear of flying.* 莫莉经过努力克服了对飞行的恐惧。 **2** V-T If you **are overcome by** a feeling or event, it is so strong or has such a strong effect that you cannot think clearly. 困扰 ❑ *The night before the test I was overcome by fear and despair.* 考试的前一晚我被恐惧与绝望困扰着。 **3** V-T If you **are overcome by** smoke or a poisonous gas, you become very ill or die from breathing it in. 熏倒；熏死 [usu passive] ❑ *The residents were trying to escape from the fire but were overcome by smoke.* 居民们正设法逃出大火，却被烟熏倒了。

> **Word Partnership** *overcome* 的常用搭配：
> ADJ. **difficult to** overcome, **hard to** overcome **1**
> N. overcome **difficulties**, overcome **a fear**, overcome **an obstacle/problem**, overcome **opposition** **1**
> overcome **by emotion**, overcome **by fear** **2**

over·crowd·ed /oʊvərkraʊdɪd/ ADJ An **overcrowded** place has too many things or people in it. 过于拥挤的 ❑ *...a windswept, overcrowded, unattractive beach.* …一个刮着大风，拥挤不堪，缺乏吸引力的海滩。

over·crowd·ing /oʊvərkraʊdɪŋ/ N-UNCOUNT If there is a problem of **overcrowding**, there are more people living in a place than it was designed for. 过度拥挤 ❑ *Students were protesting at overcrowding in the dorms.* 学生们抗议宿舍里过度拥挤。

over·do /oʊvərdu/ (**overdoes, overdoing, overdid, overdone**) **1** V-T If someone **overdoes** something, they behave in an exaggerated or extreme way. 把…做得过头 ❑ *The extent of the rise might indicate that it had been overdone.* 上涨的程度可能显示事情做得过头了。 **2** V-T If you **overdo** an activity, you try to do more than you can physically manage. 过度地做 ❑ *It is important never to overdo new exercises.* 重要的是，千万不要过度进行一项新的锻炼。 ❑ *It's important to study hard, but don't overdo it.* 刻苦学习很重要，但不要超过极限。

over·dose /oʊvərdoʊs/ (**overdoses, overdosing, overdosed**) **1** N-COUNT If someone takes an **overdose** of a drug, they take more of it than is safe. (用药) 过量 ❑ *Each year, one in 100 girls ages 15-19 takes an overdose.* 每年，100个15至19岁的女孩中就有1个用药过量。 **2** V-I If someone **overdoses on** a drug, they take more of it than is safe. 过量服用 ❑ *He'd overdosed on heroin.* 他过量吸食了海洛因。 **3** N-COUNT You can refer to too much of something, especially something harmful, as an **overdose**. 太多的(有害) 物质 ❑ *An overdose of sun, sea, sand and chlorine can give lighter hair a green tinge.* 过多的阳光、海水、沙和氯会给更浅色的头发带来点绿色。 **4** V-I You can say that someone **overdoses on** something if they have or do too much of it. 过度拥有；过度从事 ❑ *The city, he concluded, had overdosed on design.* 他下结论说，这座城市进行了过度的设计。

over·draft /oʊvərdræft/ (**overdrafts**) N-COUNT If you have an **overdraft**, you have spent more money than you have in your bank account, and so you are in debt to the bank. 透支 ❑ *Her bank warned that unless she repaid the overdraft she could face legal action.* 她的银行警告说除非她偿还透支款，否则她可能要面临诉讼。

over·drawn /oʊvərdrɔn/ ADJ If you are **overdrawn** or if your bank account is **overdrawn**, you have spent more money than you have in your account, and so you are in debt to the bank. 透支的 ❑ *Nick's bank sent him a letter saying he was $500 overdrawn.* 尼克的银行给他寄了一封信，说他透支了500元。

▲ **over·due** /oʊvərdu/ **1** ADJ If you say that a change or an event is **overdue**, you mean that you think it should have happened before now. 早该发生的 ❑ *This debate is long overdue.* 这场辩论早就应该进行了。 **2** ADJ **Overdue** sums of money have not been paid, even though it is later than the date on which they should have been paid. 到期未付的 ❑ *There is a 2% interest charge on overdue balances.* 到期未付的余款加收2%的利息。 **3** ADJ An **overdue** library book has not been returned to the library, even though the date on which it should have been returned has passed. 逾期未还的 ❑ *...a library book now weeks overdue.* …一本逾期数周尚未归还的图书馆藏书。

over·eat /oʊvərit/ (**overeats, overeating, overate, overeaten**) V-I If you say that someone **overeats**, you mean they eat more than they need to or more than is healthy. 吃得过多 ❑ *If you tend to overeat because of depression, first take steps to recognize the source of your sadness.* 如果你因为沮丧而打算暴食的话，首先要设法弄清你悲伤的来源。

over·es·ti·mate (**overestimates, overestimating, overestimated**)

> The verb is pronounced /oʊvərɛstɪmeɪt/. The noun is pronounced /oʊvərɛstɪmɪt/.

> 动词读作 /oʊvərɛstɪmeɪt/。名词读作 /oʊvərɛstɪmɪt/。

1 V-T/V-I If you say that someone **overestimates** something, you mean that they think it is greater in amount or importance than it really is. 高估 ❑ *He was overestimating their desire for peace.* 他高估了他们对和平的渴望。 ❑ *If they overestimate, they lose revenue.* 如果他们过高地估算，就会损失收入。 ● N-COUNT **Overestimate** is also a noun. 过高的估计 ❑ *Twenty-five thousand turned out to be an overestimate.* 25000这个数字被证实是过高的估计。 **2** V-T If you say that something **cannot be overestimated**, you are emphasizing that you think it is very important. 无论怎样高估也不为过 [with brd-neg] [EMPHASIS] ❑ *The importance of the media in communicating antidrug messages cannot be overestimated.* 对于媒体在传播反毒品讯息方面的重要性，再高估也不过分。 **3** V-T If you **overestimate** someone, you think that they have more of a skill or quality than they really have. 对…评价过高 ❑ *I think you overestimate me, Fred.* 我想你把我看高了，弗雷德。

★ **over·flow** (**overflows, overflowing, overflowed**)

> The verb is pronounced /oʊvərfloʊ/. The noun is pronounced /oʊvərfloʊ/.

> 动词读作 /oʊvərfloʊ/。名词读作 /oʊvərfloʊ/。

1 V-T/V-I If a liquid or a river **overflows**, it flows over the edges of the container or place it is in. 溢出；漫出 [no passive] ❑ *Pour in some of the broth, but not all of it, because it will probably overflow.* 倒入部分肉汤，不要全部，因为很可能会溢出来。 ❑ *The rivers overflowed their banks.* 那些河里的水漫过了河岸。 **2** V-I If a place or container **is overflowing with** people or things, it is too full of them. 挤满 [usu cont] ❑ *Schreiber addressed an auditorium overflowing with journalists.* 施赖伯向挤满了新闻记者的观众席致辞。 **3** N-COUNT The **overflow** is the extra people or things that something cannot contain or deal with because it is not large enough. (因空间所限) 无法容纳或安顿下

的人或物 ❑ *Tents have been set up next to hospitals to handle the overflow.* 医院旁搭起了帐篷以收治医院里住不下的人。 **4** PHRASE If a place or container is filled **to overflowing**, it is so full of people or things that no more can fit in. 满满地 ❑ *The kitchen garden was full to overflowing with fresh vegetables.* 菜园里长满了新鲜的蔬菜。

over·grown /o͟ʊvərgro͟ʊn/ **1** ADJ If a garden or other place is **overgrown**, it is covered with a lot of unruly plants because it has not been cared for. (无人照料而野草) 漫生的 ❑ *We hurried on until we reached a courtyard overgrown with weeds.* 我们一路急行，直到来到一个杂草丛生的庭院。 **2** ADJ If you describe an adult as an **overgrown** child, you mean that their behavior and attitudes are like those of a child, and that you dislike this. 长得过大的 [ADJ n] [DISAPPROVAL] ❑ *...a bunch of overgrown kids.* …一帮大孩子。

over·hang (**overhangs, overhanging, overhung**)

The verb is pronounced /o͟ʊvərhæ̱ŋ/. The noun is pronounced /o͟ʊvərhæŋ/.

动词读作 /o͟ʊvərhæ̱ŋ/。名词读作 /o͟ʊvərhæŋ/。

1 V-T If one thing **overhangs** another, it sticks out over and above it. 悬于…之上 ❑ *Part of the rock wall overhung the path at one point.* 部分岩壁悬在了小径一处的上方。 **2** N-COUNT An **overhang** is the part of something that sticks out over and above something else. 在上方的伸出部分 ❑ *A sharp overhang of rock gave them cover.* 岩石上方一处尖尖的突起给他们提供了掩护。

▲ **over·haul** (**overhauls, overhauling, overhauled**)

The verb is pronounced /o͟ʊvərhɔ̱l/. The noun is pronounced /o͟ʊvərhɔl/.

动词读作 /o͟ʊvərhɔ̱l/。名词读作 /o͟ʊvərhɔl/。

1 V-T If a piece of equipment **is overhauled**, it is cleaned, checked thoroughly, and repaired if necessary. 全面检修 [usu passive] ❑ *They had ensured the plumbing was overhauled a year ago.* 他们确保管道设备一年前已被彻底检修过。 ● N-COUNT **Overhaul** is also a noun. 全面检修 ❑ *...the overhaul of a cruiser.* …一艘巡洋舰的全面检修。 **2** V-T If you **overhaul** a system or method, you examine it carefully and make many changes in it in order to improve it. 改革；修订 ❑ *...proposals to overhaul bank regulations.* …修订银行规章的提议。 ● N-COUNT **Overhaul** is also a noun. 改革；修订 ❑ *The study says there must be a complete overhaul of air traffic control systems.* 研究称必须对航空交通管理系统进行彻底的改革。

over·head

The adjective and noun are pronounced /o͟ʊvərhɛd/. The adverb is pronounced /o͟ʊvərhɛ̱d/.

形容词和名词读作 /o͟ʊvərhɛd/。副词读作 /o͟ʊvərhɛ̱d/。

1 ADJ You use **overhead** to indicate that something is above you or above the place that you are talking about. 头顶上的 [ADJ n] ❑ *She turned on the overhead light and looked around the little room.* 她打开顶灯，环视这间小屋。 ● ADV **Overhead** is also an adverb. 在头顶 ❑ *...planes passing overhead.* …飞过头顶的飞机。 **2** N-UNCOUNT The **overhead** of a business is its regular and essential expenses, such as salaries, rent, electricity, and telephone bills. (企业的) 日常费用 [BUSINESS]

in BRIT, use **overheads**

❑ *Private insurers spend 27 cents of every dollar on overhead.* 私有保险公司每花掉一美元就有27美分用于日常费用。

over·head pro·jec·tor (**overhead projectors**) N-COUNT An **overhead projector** is a machine that has a light inside it and makes the writing or pictures on a sheet of plastic appear on a screen or wall. The abbreviation **OHP** is also used. 高射投影仪

over·heads /o͟ʊvəʳhedz/ [BRIT] → see **overhead**

★ **over·hear** /o͟ʊvərhɪ͟ər/ (**overhears, overhearing, overheard**) V-T If you **overhear** someone, you hear what they are saying when they are not talking to you and they do not know that you are listening. 无意中听到 ❑ *I overheard two doctors discussing my case.* 我无意中听到两个医生在讨论我的病例。

over·heat /o͟ʊvərhi͟t/ (**overheats, overheating, overheated**) **1** V-T/V-I If something **overheats** or if you **overheat** it, it becomes hotter than is necessary or desirable. 使过热；变得过热 ❑ *The engine was overheating and the car was not handling well.* 引擎过热，汽车运转不正常。 ● **over·heat·ed** ADJ 过热的 ❑ *...that stuffy, overheated apartment.* …那所令人窒息，闷热难耐的公寓。 **2** V-T/V-I If a country's economy **overheats** or if conditions **overheat** it, it grows so rapidly that inflation and interest rates rise very quickly. 使(经济) 过热；(经济) 过热 [BUSINESS] ❑ *The private sector is increasing its spending so sharply that the economy is overheating.* 私营经济支出急剧地攀升导致经济过热。 ● **over·heat·ed** ADJ 过热的 ❑ *...the disastrous consequences of an overheated market.* …一个发展过热市场的灾难性后果。

over·heat·ed /o͟ʊvərhi͟tɪd/ ADJ Someone who is **overheated** is very angry about something. 极其愤怒的 ❑ *I think the reaction has been a little overheated.* 我认为这个反应有点过于愤怒了。

over·hung /o͟ʊvərhʌ͟ŋ/ **Overhung** is the past tense and past participle of **overhang**. **overhang**的过去式和过去分词

over·joyed /o͟ʊvərdʒɔ͟ɪd/ ADJ If you are **overjoyed**, you are extremely happy about something. 狂喜的 [v-link ADJ] ❑ *Shelley was overjoyed to see me.* 谢莉看见我高兴极了。

over·land /o͟ʊvərlænd/ ADJ An **overland** journey is made across land rather than by ship or airplane. 陆路的 [ADJ n] ❑ *...an overland journey through Iraq, Turkey, Iran and Pakistan.* …一趟途经伊拉克、土耳其、伊朗和巴基斯坦的陆路旅程。 ● ADV **Overland** is also an adverb. 通过陆路 [ADV after v] ❑ *They're traveling to Baghdad overland.* 他们通过陆路旅行去巴格达。

★ **over·lap** (**overlaps, overlapping, overlapped**)

The verb is pronounced /o͟ʊvərlæ̱p/. The noun is pronounced /o͟ʊvərlæp/.

动词读作 /o͟ʊvərlæ̱p/。名词读作 /o͟ʊvərlæp/。

1 V-RECIP If one thing **overlaps** another, or if you **overlap** them, a part of the first thing occupies the same area as a part of the other thing. You can also say that two things **overlap**. 重叠 ❑ *When the bag is folded, the bottom overlaps one side.* 把包折叠起来时，其底部与一边就重合了。 ❑ *Overlap the slices carefully so there are no gaps.* 把薄片小心地叠放在一起，那样就没有间隙。 **2** V-RECIP If one idea or activity **overlaps** another, or **overlaps** with another, they involve some of the same subjects, people, or periods of time. 与…重合 ❑ *Christian Holy Week overlaps with the beginning of the Jewish holiday of Passover.* 基督教的圣周与犹太教逾越节的开始时间是重合的。 ❑ *The needs of patients invariably overlap.* 患者们的各种需求总是相互重合的。 ● N-VAR **Overlap** is also a noun. 重合 ❑ *...the overlap between civil and military technology.* …民用技术与军用技术之间的重合。

over·leaf /o͟ʊvərli͟f/ ADV **Overleaf** is used in books and magazines to say that something is on the other side of the page you are reading. 在背面 [FORMAL] ❑ *Answer the questionnaire overleaf.* 回答本页背面的调查问卷。

over·load (**overloads, overloading, overloaded**)

The verb is pronounced /o͟ʊvərlo͟ʊd/. The noun is pronounced /o͟ʊvərloʊd/.

动词读作 /o͟ʊvərlo͟ʊd/。名词读作 /o͟ʊvərloʊd/。

1 V-T If you **overload** something such as a vehicle, you put more things or people into it than it was designed to carry. 使超载 ❑ *Don't overload the boat or it will sink.* 别让船超载了，否则它会沉。 ● **over·load·ed** ADJ 超载的 ❑ *Some trains were so overloaded that their suspension collapsed.* 有些列车超载如此严重，以至于它们的悬架都被压垮了。 **2** V-T To **overload** someone **with** work, problems, or information means to give them more work, problems, or information than they can cope with. 使负担过重 ❑ *...an effective method that will not overload staff with yet more paperwork.* …一个不会使员工背负更多案牍工作的有效方法。 ● N-UNCOUNT **Overload** is also a noun. 过重的负担 ❑ *57 percent complained of work overload.* 57%的人抱怨工作负担过重。 ● **over·load·ed** ADJ 负担过重的 ❑ *The bar waiter was already overloaded with orders.* 这名酒吧侍者已经不堪应付过多的点单了。 **3** V-T If you **overload** an electrical system, you cause too much electricity to flow through it, and so damage it. 使(电气系统) 负荷过重 ❑ *Never overload an electrical outlet.* 绝不要超负荷使用一个电源插座。

over·look /o͟ʊvərlʊ͟k/ (**overlooks, overlooking, overlooked**) **1** V-T If a building or window **overlooks** a place, you can see the place clearly from the building or window. 俯瞰 ❑ *Pretty and comfortable rooms overlook a flower-filled garden.* 那些漂亮、舒适的房间俯瞰着一个花团锦簇的花园。 **2** V-T If you **overlook** a fact or problem, you do not notice it, or do not realize how important it

O

is. 忽视 ❑ *We overlook all sorts of warning signals about our own health.* 我们会忽视关于我们健康的各种警报信号。 **3** V-T If you **overlook** someone's faults or bad behavior, you forgive them and take no action. 不理会 ❑ *...satisfying relationships that enable them to overlook each other's faults.* …能使他们忽略彼此过错的称心如意的关系。

over·ly /oʊvərli/ ADV **Overly** means more than is normal, necessary, or reasonable. 过度地 [ADV adj/adv/-ed] ❑ *Employers may become overly cautious about taking on new staff.* 雇主在雇用新员工的问题上可能会过于谨慎。

over·night ♦◇◇ /oʊvərnaɪt/ **1** ADV If something happens **overnight**, it happens throughout the night or at some point during the night. 通宵地; 在夜间 [ADV after v] ❑ *The decision was reached overnight.* 这个决定是夜间做出的。 ● ADJ **Overnight** is also an adjective. 通宵的; 夜间的 [ADJ n] ❑ *Travel and overnight accommodation are included.* 旅行及夜间住宿是包含在内的。 **2** ADV You can say that something happens **overnight** when it happens very quickly and unexpectedly. 突然地 [ADV after v] ❑ *The rules are not going to change overnight.* 这些规则是不会突然改变的。 ● ADJ **Overnight** is also an adjective. 突然的 [ADJ n] ❑ *In 1970 he became an overnight success in America.* 1970年他在美国一夜之间成了成功人士。 **3** ADJ **Overnight** bags or clothes are ones that you take when you go and stay somewhere for one or two nights. 外出住宿一两晚的 (包或衣服) [ADJ n] ❑ *He realized he'd left his overnight bag at Mary's house.* 他意识到他把自己的短途旅行包落在玛丽家里了。

over·paid /oʊvərpeɪd/ ADJ If you say that someone is **overpaid**, you mean that you think they are paid more than they deserve for the work they do. 报酬过高的 ❑ *...grossly overpaid corporate lawyers.* …报酬高得过头的公司法律顾问们。

★ **over·pass** /oʊvərpæs/ (**overpasses**) N-COUNT An **overpass** is a structure which carries one road over the top of another one. 高架桥 [mainly AM]

in BRIT, usually use **flyover**

❑ *...a $16 million highway overpass over Route 1.* …一座跨越一号线的耗资1600万美元的公路高架桥。

over·pow·er /oʊvərpaʊər/ (**overpowers, overpowering, overpowered**) **1** V-T If you **overpower** someone, you manage to take hold of and keep hold of them, although they struggle a lot. 制服 ❑ *It took ten guardsmen to overpower him.* 动用了10个守卫才将他制服。 **2** V-T If a feeling **overpowers** you, it suddenly affects you very strongly. 突然极为强烈地影响 ❑ *A sudden dizziness overpowered him.* 一阵突然的晕眩令他难以忍受。 **3** V-T In a sports match, when one team or player **overpowers** the other, they play much better than the other and beat them easily. 轻松击败 ❑ *Britain's tennis No 1 yesterday overpowered American Brian Garrow 7-6, 6-3.* 英国网球头号种子选手昨天以7-6和6-3轻松击败美国选手布莱恩·盖罗。 **4** V-T If something such as a color or flavor **overpowers** another color or flavor, it is so strong that it makes the second one less noticeable. (色彩或风味上) 压过 ❑ *A delicate wine will be overpowered by strong food.* 一种精美的葡萄酒会被味道浓烈的食物压过。

over·pow·er·ing /oʊvərpaʊərɪŋ/ **1** ADJ An **overpowering** feeling is so strong that you cannot resist it. 抵挡不住的 ❑ *The desire for revenge can be overpowering.* 复仇的愿望会是抵挡不住的。 **2** ADJ An **overpowering** smell or sound is so strong that you cannot smell or hear anything else. 压倒一切的 (味道或声音) ❑ *There was an overpowering smell of alcohol.* 有一股极为强烈的酒精味。 **3** ADJ An **overpowering** person makes other people feel uncomfortable because they have such a strong personality. 强悍的 ❑ *Mrs. Winter was large and somewhat overpowering.* 温特夫人身材高大，而且有些强悍。

over·priced /oʊvərpraɪst/ ADJ If you say that something is **overpriced**, you mean that you think it costs much more than it should. 价格过高的 ❑ *I went and had an overpriced cup of coffee in the hotel cafeteria.* 我到宾馆的自助餐厅里喝了杯过于昂贵的咖啡。

over·ran /oʊvərræn/ **Overran** is the past tense of **overrun**. **overran**为**overrun**的过去式。

over·rate /oʊvərreɪt/ (**overrates, overrating, overrated**) also **over-rate** V-T If you say that something or someone **is overrated**, you mean that people have a higher opinion of them than they deserve. 高估 ❑ *More men are finding out that the joys of work have been overrated.* 更多的男士正发现工作的种种乐趣被高估了。 ● **over·rat·ed** ADJ 被高估的 ❑ *Life in the wild is vastly overrated.* 野外生活被大大地高估了。

over·react /oʊvərriækt/ (**overreacts, overreacting, overreacted**) V-I If you say that someone **overreacts to** something, you mean that they have and show more of an emotion than is necessary or appropriate. 反应过激 ❑ *I overreact to anything sad.* 我对任何悲伤的事情都反应过激。

▲ **over·ride** (**overrides, overriding, overrode, overridden**)

The verb is pronounced /oʊvəˈraɪd/. The noun is pronounced /oʊvəˈraɪd/.

动词读作 /oʊvəˈraɪd/。名词读作 /oʊvəˈraɪd/。

1 V-T If one thing in a situation **overrides** other things, it is more important than they are. 比…更重要 ❑ *The welfare of a child should always override the wishes of its parents.* 孩子的幸福应该永远比其父母的心愿更重要。 **2** V-T If someone in authority **overrides** a person or their decisions, they cancel their decisions. 推翻 ❑ *The president vetoed the bill, and the Senate failed by a single vote to override his veto.* 总统否决了议案，而参议院因一票之差未能推翻他的否决。 **3** N-COUNT An **override** is an attempt to cancel someone's decisions by using your authority over them or by gaining more votes than they do in an election or contest. 推翻 [AM] ❑ *The bill now goes to the House where an override vote is expected to fail.* 议案现在到了众议院，预计在这里推翻表决会失败。

over·rid·ing /oʊvərraɪdɪŋ/ ADJ In a particular situation, the **overriding** factor is the one that is the most important. 最重要的 ❑ *My overriding concern is to raise the standards of state education.* 我最关心的是提高国民教育水平。

over·rule /oʊvərrul/ (**overrules, overruling, overruled**) V-T If someone in authority **overrules** a person or their decision, they officially decide that the decision is incorrect or not valid. 否决 ❑ *In 1991, the Court of Appeal overruled this decision.* 1991年，上诉法院否决了此项决议。

over·run /oʊvərrʌn/ (**overruns, overrunning, overran**) **1** V-T If an army or an armed force **overruns** a place, area, or country, it succeeds in occupying it very quickly. 迅速占领 ❑ *A group of rebels overran the port area and most of the northern suburbs.* 一群叛乱分子迅速占领了港口地区及绝大部分北部郊区。 **2** ADJ If you say that a place **is overrun with** things that you consider undesirable, you mean that there are a large number of them there. 泛滥成灾的 [v-link ADJ] ❑ *The hotel has been ordered to close because it is overrun by mice and rats.* 这家旅馆因为到处都是老鼠，已经被勒令关闭。 **3** V-T/V-I If costs **overrun**, they are higher than was planned or expected. (费用) 超支 [BUSINESS] ❑ *We should stop the nonsense of taxpayers trying to finance joint weapons whose costs always overrun hugely.* 我们应该制止纳税人设法资助费用总是大大超支的联合武器开发的这种胡闹。 ❑ *Costs overran the budget by about 30%.* 花费超出了预算约30%。 ● N-COUNT **Overrun** is also a noun. 超支 ❑ *He was stunned to discover cost overruns of at least $1 billion.* 他吃惊地发现至少有$10亿的费用超支。 **4** V-I If an event or meeting **overruns** by, for example, ten minutes, it continues for ten minutes longer than it was intended to. 超时 [BRIT]

over·seas ♦◇◇ /oʊvərsiz/ **1** ADJ You use **overseas** to describe things that involve or are in foreign countries, usually across a sea or an ocean. 海外的 [ADJ n] ❑ *He has returned to South Africa from his long overseas trip.* 他结束了漫长的海外旅行回到了南非。 ● ADV **Overseas** is also an adverb. 在海外 ❑ *If you're staying for more than three months or working overseas, a full 10-year passport is required.* 如果你在海外居留超过3个月或工作，须持有效期整10年的护照。 **2** ADJ An **overseas** student or visitor comes from a foreign country, usually across a sea or an ocean. 海外的 [ADJ n] ❑ *Every year nine million overseas visitors come to the city.* 每年有900万的海外游客来到这座城市。

★ **over·see** /oʊvərsi/ (**oversees, overseeing, oversaw, overseen**) V-T If someone in authority **oversees** a job or an activity, they make sure that it is done properly. 监督 ❑ *Use a surveyor or architect to oversee and inspect the different stages of the work.* 用一名监察员或建筑师去监督和检查工程的不同阶段。

over·shad·ow /oʊvərʃædoʊ/ (**overshadows, overshadowing, overshadowed**) **1** V-T If an unpleasant event or feeling **overshadows** something, it makes it less happy or enjoyable. 给…蒙上阴影 ❑ *Fears for the president's safety could overshadow his peace-making mission.* 对总统安全的担心会给他的和平促进任务蒙上阴影。 **2** V-T If you **are overshadowed by** a person or thing, you are less successful, important, or impressive than they are. 使黯然失色 [usu passive] ❑ *Hester is overshadowed by her younger and more attractive* sister. 她那更年轻而且更有魅力的妹妹使赫斯特黯然失色。 3 V-T If one building, tree, or large structure **overshadows** another, it stands near it, is much taller than it, and casts a shadow over it. 遮蔽 ❑ *She said stations should be in the open, near housing, not overshadowed by trees or walls.* 她说车站应该建在开阔、靠近住宅区的地方，不要被树木或墙遮挡。

★ **over·sight** /oʊvərsaɪt/ (**oversights**) 1 N-COUNT If there has been an **oversight**, someone has forgotten to do something which they should have done. 疏忽 ❑ *William was angered and embarrassed by his oversight.* 威廉对自己的疏忽感到恼火和尴尬。 2 ADJ An **oversight** committee or board is responsible for making sure that a process or system works efficiently and correctly. 监督的 [ADJ n] ❑ *The bill creates an oversight board with the authority to investigate and punish accounting firms.* 该法案创建了一个有权调查并处罚会计师事务所的监督委员会。

over·spend (**overspends, overspending, overspent**)

The verb is pronounced /oʊvərspɛnd/. The noun is pronounced /oʊvərspɛnd/.

动词读作 /oʊvərspɛnd/。名词读作 /oʊvərspɛnd/。

1 V-I If you **overspend**, you spend more money than you can afford to. 花钱过多 ❑ *Don't overspend on your home and expect to get the money back when you sell.* 不要在房子上花费太多，别指望你卖掉房子时还能把这笔钱收回来。 2 N-COUNT If an organization or business has an **overspend**, it spends more money than was planned or allowed in its budget. 超支 [BRIT, BUSINESS]

in AM, use **overrun**

★ **over·state** /oʊvərsteɪt/ (**overstates, overstating, overstated**) V-T If you say that someone **is overstating** something, you mean they are describing it in a way that makes it seem more important or serious than it really is. 夸大 ❑ *The authors no doubt overstated their case with a view to catching the public's attention.* 作者们毫无疑问地夸大了他们的情形以吸引公众的注意力。

★ **overt** /oʊvɜrt/ ADJ An **overt** action or attitude is done or shown in an open and obvious way. 公开的；明显的 ❑ *Although there is no overt hostility, black and white students do not mix much.* 虽然没有明显的敌意，但黑人学生和白人学生还是交往不多。 ● **overt·ly** ADV 公开地；明显地 ❑ *He's written a few overtly political lyrics over the years.* 他几年来写了几篇政治性明显的歌词。

over·take /oʊvərteɪk/ (**overtakes, overtaking, overtook, overtaken**) 1 V-T If someone or something **overtakes** a competitor, they become more successful than them. 超过 ❑ *Lung cancer has now overtaken breast cancer as a cause of death for women in the U.S.* 肺癌作为一种美国女性死亡原因现已超过了乳腺癌。 2 V-T If a feeling **overtakes** you, it affects you very strongly. 强烈影响 [LITERARY] ❑ *Something like panic overtook me in a flood.* 一种类似恐慌的感觉在一次洪水中压倒了我。 3 V-T/V-I If you **overtake**, or **overtake** a vehicle or a person that is ahead of you and moving in the same direction, you pass them. 超过 [mainly BRIT]

in AM, usually use **pass**

★ **over·throw** (**overthrows, overthrowing, overthrew, overthrown**)

The verb is pronounced /oʊvərθroʊ/. The noun is pronounced /oʊvərθroʊ/.

动词读作 /oʊvərθroʊ/。名词读作 /oʊvərθroʊ/。

V-T When a government or leader **is overthrown**, they are removed from power by force. 颠覆 ❑ *That government was overthrown in a military coup three years ago.* 该政府在3年前的一次军事政变中被颠覆了。 ● N-SING **Overthrow** is also a noun. 颠覆 ❑ *They were charged with plotting the overthrow of the state.* 他们被控密谋颠覆国家。

★ **over·time** /oʊvərtaɪm/ 1 N-UNCOUNT **Overtime** is time that you spend doing your job in addition to your normal working hours. 加班 ❑ *He would work overtime, without pay, to finish a job.* 他会无偿地加班把一件工作完成。 2 PHRASE If you say that someone **is working overtime** to do something, you mean that they are using a lot of energy, effort, or enthusiasm trying to do it. 全力以赴地做 [INFORMAL] ❑ *We had to battle very hard and our defense worked overtime to keep us in the game.* 我们只得苦战，我们的防守队员全力以赴确保我们不被淘汰。

A salaried worker is paid for a standard number of hours each month. When he or she works **overtime**, instead of additional money the worker is allowed to take time off from the job to compensate for the extra time worked. This is called **comp time** in the US, and **time off in lieu** in the UK.

3 N-UNCOUNT **Overtime** is an additional period of time that is added to the end of a sports game in which the score is tied, so that one team can score and win the game. 加时赛 ❑ *Denver had won the championship in overtime.* 丹佛队对通过加时赛赢得了冠军。

over·tone /oʊvərtoʊn/ (**overtones**) N-COUNT If something has **overtones of** a particular thing or quality, it suggests that thing or quality but does not openly express it. 暗示之意 ❑ *The strike has taken on overtones of a civil rights campaign.* 这次罢工带有民权运动的意味。

over·took /oʊvərtʊk/ **Overtook** is the past tense of **overtake**. **overtake**的过去式

over·ture /oʊvərtʃər, -tʃʊər/ (**overtures**) N-COUNT; N-IN-NAMES An **overture** is a piece of music, often one that is the introduction to an opera or play. (歌剧、戏剧等的) 序曲 ❑ *...Wagner's Mastersingers Overture.* …瓦格纳的《名歌手序曲》。

★ **over·turn** /oʊvərtɜrn/ (**overturns, overturning, overturned**) 1 V-T/V-I If something **overturns** or if you **overturn** it, it turns upside down or on its side. 打翻；翻倒 ❑ *The motorcycle veered out of control, overturned and smashed into a wall.* 摩托车转向失去了控制，翻倒在地，然后猛地撞到一面墙上。 ❑ *Alex jumped up so violently that he overturned his glass of wine.* 亚历克斯跃起得太猛，以至于打翻了他的那杯葡萄酒。 2 V-T If someone in authority **overturns** a legal decision, they officially decide that that decision is incorrect or not valid. 推翻 ❑ *When the courts overturned his decision, he backed down.* 当法院推翻了他的决定时，他让步了。

over·view /oʊvərvyu/ (**overviews**) N-COUNT An **overview of** a situation is a general understanding or description of it as a whole. 概述 ❑ *The central section of the book is a historical overview of drug use.* 本书的中心部分是对药物使用的一个历史概述。

over·weight /oʊvərweɪt/ ADJ Someone who is **overweight** weighs more than is considered healthy or attractive. 超重的 ❑ *Being even moderately overweight increases your risk of developing high blood pressure.* 即便只是稍微超重也会增加你患上高血压的风险。
→ see **diet**

over·whelm /oʊvərwɛlm/ (**overwhelms, overwhelming, overwhelmed**) 1 V-T If you **are overwhelmed by** a feeling or event, it affects you very strongly, and you do not know how to deal with it. (强烈地影响而) 使不知所措 ❑ *He was overwhelmed by a longing for times past.* 他陷入了一种对过去的渴望而不能自拔。 ● **over·whelmed** ADJ (强烈地影响而使) 不知所措的 ❑ *Sightseers may be a little overwhelmed by the crowds and noise.* 观光者可能被人群和噪声搞得有点不知所措。 2 V-T If a group of people **overwhelm** a place or another group, they gain complete control or victory over them. 彻底制服；击败 ❑ *It was clear that one massive Allied offensive would overwhelm the weakened enemy.* 显然同盟国一次大规模的进攻就会彻底击败已被削弱的敌军。

★ **over·whelm·ing** ♦◇◇ /oʊvərwɛlmɪŋ/ 1 ADJ If something is **overwhelming**, it affects you very strongly, and you do not know how to deal with it. 强悍而令人难以应对的 ❑ *The task won't feel so overwhelming if you break it down into small, easy-to-accomplish steps.* 如果你把这个任务分解成一个个容易完成的小步骤，就不会觉得那么难以应对。 ● **over·whelm·ing·ly** ADV 强悍而令人难以应对地 [ADV adj] ❑ *The other women all seemed overwhelmingly confident.* 其他的女士们似乎都令人难以应对地自信。 2 ADJ You can use **overwhelming** to emphasize that an amount or quantity is much greater than other amounts or quantities. (数量上) 压倒性的 [EMPHASIS] ❑ *The overwhelming majority of small businesses go broke within the first twenty-four months.* 绝大多数的小公司在最初的24个月里破产。 ● **over·whelm·ing·ly** ADV (数量上) 压倒性地 ❑ *The people voted overwhelmingly for change.* 人们以绝对多数投票赞成变革。

Word Partnership *overwhelming* 的常用搭配：

N. overwhelming **desire**, overwhelming **response**, overwhelming **responsibility** 1
overwhelming **approval**, overwhelming **force**, overwhelming **majority**, overwhelming **odds**, overwhelming **support**, overwhelming **victory** 2

O

over·work /oʊvərwɜrk/ (**overworks, overworking, overworked**) V-T/V-I If you **overwork** or if someone **overworks** you, you work too hard, and are likely to become very tired or sick. 使工作过度；工作过度 ❑ *He's overworking and has a lot on his mind.* 他在过度工作，有许多事要操心。● N-UNCOUNT **Overwork** is also a noun. 过度工作 ❑ *He died of a heart attack brought on by overwork.* 他死于过度工作导致的一次心脏病发作。● **over·worked** ADJ 过度工作的 ❑ *...an overworked doctor.* …一位过度工作的医生。

over·worked /oʊvərwɜrkt/ ADJ If you describe a word, expression, or idea as **overworked**, you mean it has been used so often that it no longer has much effect or meaning. 滥用的 ❑ *"Ecological" has become one of the most overworked adjectives among manufacturers of garden supplies.* "生态的"已成为园艺用品制造商最为滥用的形容词之一。

ovu·late /ɒvyəleɪt, oʊv-/ (**ovulates, ovulating, ovulated**) V-I When a woman or female animal **ovulates**, an egg is produced from one of her ovaries. 排卵 ❑ *Some girls may first ovulate even before they menstruate.* 有些女孩初次排卵可能甚至早于她们的月经。● **ovu·la·tion** /ɒvyəleɪʃən, oʊv-/ N-UNCOUNT 排卵 ❑ *By noticing these changes, the woman can tell when ovulation is about to occur.* 通过观察这些变化，这名妇女能判断出何时排卵。

ow /aʊ/ EXCLAM **"Ow!"** is used in writing to represent the noise that people make when they suddenly feel pain. 哎哟（书面语中表示突然疼痛时的叫声）❑ *Ow! Don't do that!* 哎哟！别那样做！

owe ♦◇◇ /oʊ/ (**owes, owing, owed**) **1** V-T If you **owe** money **to** someone, they have lent it to you and you have not yet paid it back. 欠 ❑ *The company owes money to more than 60 banks.* 这家公司欠六十多家银行的钱。❑ *Blake already owed him nearly $50.* 布莱克已经欠了他近$50。**2** V-T If someone or something **owes** a particular quality or their success **to** a person or thing, they only have it because of that person or thing. 把…归功于 [no passive] ❑ *I always suspected she owed her first job to her friendship with Roger.* 我总是觉得她得到她的第一份工作是由于她与罗杰的友谊。❑ *He owed his survival to his strength as a swimmer.* 他把自己幸免遇难归功于自己会游泳。**3** V-T If you say that you **owe a** great deal **to** someone or something, you mean that they have helped you or influenced you a lot, and you feel very grateful to them. 感激 ❑ *As a musician I owe much to the radio station in my home town.* 作为一名音乐家，我非常感激我家乡的广播电台。**4** V-T If you say that something **owes** a great deal to a person or thing, you mean that it exists, is successful, or has its particular form mainly because of them. 得益于 ❑ *The island's present economy owes a good deal to tourism.* 该岛现在的经济大大得益于旅游业。**5** V-T If you say that you **owe** someone gratitude, respect, or loyalty, you mean that they deserve it from you. 应给予 ❑ *Perhaps we owe these people more respect.* 也许我们应该给予这些人更多的尊敬。❑ *I owe you an apology; you must have found my attitude very annoying.* 我应向你道歉，你一定觉得我的态度挺让人讨厌的。**6** V-T If you say that you **owe it to** someone to do something, you mean that you should do that thing because they deserve it. 该为（某人做某事）[no passive] ❑ *I can't go; I owe it to him to stay.* 我不能走，为了他我该留下来。❑ *You owe it to yourself to get some professional help.* 你为了自己着想也该去寻求一些专业的帮助了。**7** PHRASE You use **owing to** when you are introducing the reason for something. 由于 ❑ *Owing to staff shortages, there was no food on the plane.* 由于工作人员不足，飞机上没有食物。

Word Partnership *owe* 的常用搭配：

N.	owe **a debt**, owe **money**, owe **taxes** **1**
	owe **a great deal to** ***someone*** **3 4**
	owe ***someone*** **an apology** **5**

★ **owl** /aʊl/ (**owls**) N-COUNT An **owl** is a bird with a flat face, large eyes, and a small sharp beak. Most owls obtain their food by hunting small animals at night. 猫头鹰

own ♦♦♦ /oʊn/ (**owns, owning, owned**) **1** ADJ You use **own** to indicate that something belongs to a particular person or thing. 自己的 [poss ADJ] ❑ *My wife decided I should have my own shop.* 我妻子决定我应该有自己的店铺。❑ *He could no longer trust his own judgement.* 他再也不相信自己的判断了。● PRON **Own** is also a pronoun. 自己的 [poss PRON] ❑ *He saw the major's face a few inches from his own.* 他看到少校的脸离他自己的脸只有几英寸。**2** ADJ You use **own** to indicate that something is used by, or is characteristic of, only one person, thing, or group. 自己独有的 [poss ADJ] ❑ *Jennifer insisted on her own room.* 詹尼弗坚持要自己专用的房间。❑ *Each nation has its own peculiarities when it comes to doing business.* 说到做生意，每个民族都有它自己独有的一些特性。● PRON **Own** is also a pronoun. 自己独有的 [poss PRON] ❑ *This young lady has a sense of style that is very much her own.* 这位年轻女士具有一种她自己独有的时尚观。**3** ADJ You use **own** to indicate that someone does something without any help from other people. 自己的 [poss ADJ] ❑ *They enjoy making their own decisions.* 他们喜欢做他们自己的决定。● PRON **Own** is also a pronoun. 自己的 [poss PRON] ❑ *There's no career structure; you have to create your own.* 没有什么职业架构，你必须创造你自己的。**4** V-T If you **own** something, it is your property. 拥有 ❑ *His father owns a local video store.* 他父亲拥有一家当地的音像店。**5** PHRASE If you have something you can **call** your **own**, it belongs only to you, rather than being controlled by or shared with someone else. 专属于自己的 ❑ *I would like a place I could call my own.* 我想要一个只属于我自己的地方。**6** PHRASE If someone or something **comes into** their **own**, they become very successful or start to perform very well because the circumstances are right. 得心应手 ❑ *Many women have come into their own as teachers, healers, and leaders.* 许多女性成为很成功的教师、医师和领导者。**7** PHRASE If you **get** your **own back** on someone, you have your revenge on them because of something bad that they have done to you. 报复 [BRIT, INFORMAL] **8** PHRASE If you say that someone has a particular thing **of** their **own**, you mean that that thing belongs or relates to them, rather than to other people. 属于自己的 ❑ *He set out in search of ideas for starting a company of his own.* 他开始着手想办法创办属于自己的一家公司。**9** PHRASE If someone or something has a particular quality or characteristic **of** their **own**, that quality or characteristic is especially theirs, rather than being shared by other things or people of that type. 特有的 ❑ *The cries of the seagulls gave this part of the harbor a fascinating character of its own.* 海鸥的鸣叫声赋予海港的这边一种特有的迷人特质。**10** PHRASE When you are **on** your **own**, you are alone. 独自地 ❑ *He lives on his own.* 他独自居住。❑ *I felt pretty lonely last year being on my own.* 我去年独自生活时感到特别孤独。**11** PHRASE If you do something **on** your **own**, you do it without any help from other people. 独立地 ❑ *I work best on my own.* 我独立工作最出色。**12** to **hold** your **own** → see **hold**

▸ **own up** PHRASAL VERB If you **own up** to something wrong that you have done, you admit that you did it. 承认 ❑ *The teacher is waiting for someone to own up to the graffiti.* 老师在等着有人承认乱涂乱画的行为。

Thesaurus *own* 另参见：

ADJ.	individual, personal, private **1 2**
V.	have, possess **4**

own brand (**own brands**) N-COUNT **Own brands** are products which have the trademark or label of the store which sells them, especially a supermarket chain. They are normally cheaper than other popular brands. （商店、超市）自有品牌商品 [BRIT, BUSINESS]

in AM, use **store brand**

own·er ♦♦◇ /oʊnər/ (**owners**) N-COUNT If you are the **owner** of something, it belongs to you. 所有者 ❑ *The owner of the store was sweeping his floor when I walked in.* 我走进去的时候店主正在扫地。

own·er·ship ♦◇◇ /oʊnərʃɪp/ N-UNCOUNT **Ownership** of something is the state of owning it. 所有权 ❑ *On January 23rd, the U.S. decided to relax its rules on the foreign ownership of its airlines.* 1月23日，美国决定放宽对其航空公司外国所有权的规定。❑ *...the growth of home ownership.* …住房拥有率的增长。

own la·bel (**own labels**) N-COUNT **Own label** is the same as **own brand.** 自有品牌商品 [BUSINESS] ❑ *People will trade down to own labels which are cheaper.* 人们会转向购买更便宜的自有品牌商品。

ox /ɒks/ (**oxen** /ɒksən/) N-COUNT An **ox** is a bull that has been castrated. Oxen are used in some countries for pulling vehicles or carrying things. 阉公牛

★ **ox·ide** /ɒksaɪd/ (**oxides**) N-MASS An **oxide** is a compound of oxygen and another chemical element. 氧化物 [usu supp N]

oxy·gen /ɒksɪdʒən/ N-UNCOUNT **Oxygen** is a colorless gas that exists in large quantities in the air. All plants and animals need oxygen in order to live. 氧气 ❑ *The human brain needs to be without oxygen for only four minutes before permanent damage occurs.* 人脑缺氧只需4分钟就会造成永久性损伤。
→ see **air, earth, respiratory**

▲ **oys·ter** /ɔɪstər/ (**oysters**) **1** N-COUNT An **oyster** is a large flat shellfish. Some oysters can be eaten and others produce valuable objects called pearls. 牡蛎 ❑ *He had two dozen oysters and enjoyed every one of them.* 他吃了两打牡蛎，每一个都吃得津津有味。**2** PHRASE

If you say that **the world is** someone's **oyster**, you mean that they can do anything or go anywhere that they want to. 某人可以随心所欲 ❑ *You're young, you've got a lot of opportunity. The world is your oyster.* 你年轻，又得到了很多机会。你可以随心所欲地施展自己。

oz **Oz** is a written abbreviation for **ounce**. 盎司 ❑ *Whisk 1 oz of butter into the sauce.* 将1盎司的黄油搅拌进调味汁里。

★ **ozone** /o͟uzoun/ N-UNCOUNT **Ozone** is a colorless gas which is a form of oxygen. There is a layer of ozone high above the Earth's surface, that protects us from harmful radiation from the sun. 臭氧 ❑ *What they find could provide clues to what might happen worldwide if ozone depletion continues.* 如果臭氧的损耗继续下去，他们的发现能为全世界可能发生的情况提供线索。

ozone-fri͟endly ADJ **Ozone-friendly** chemicals, products, or technology do not cause harm to the ozone layer. 不破坏臭氧层的 ❑ *...ozone-friendly chemicals for fridges and air conditioners.* …冰箱和空调使用的不破坏臭氧层的化学制品。

o͟zone lay·er N-SING **The ozone layer** is the part of the Earth's atmosphere that has the most ozone in it. The ozone layer protects living things from the harmful radiation of the sun. 臭氧层 ❑ *...the hole in the ozone layer.* …臭氧层空洞。

Pp

P also **p** /piː/ (**P's, p's**) N-VAR **P** is the sixteenth letter of the English alphabet. 英语字母表中第16个字母

PA /piː eɪ/ (**PAs**) N-COUNT If you refer to the **PA** or the **PA system** in a place, you are referring to the public address system. 有线广播系统 [usu "the" N in sing] ❑ *A voice came booming over the PA.* 一个声音从有线广播里大声地传了出来。

p.a. **p.a.** is a written abbreviation for **per annum**. 每年

pace ♦◇◇ /peɪs/ (**paces, pacing, paced**) **1** N-SING The **pace** of something is the speed at which it happens or is done. 速度；节奏 [usu with supp] ❑ *Many people were not satisfied with the pace of change.* 许多人都不满意变化的速度。 ❑ *They could not stand the pace or the workload.* 他们受不了工作的节奏和负荷。 **2** N-SING Your **pace** is the speed at which you walk. 步速 [usu with supp] ❑ *He moved at a brisk pace down the rue St. Antoine.* 他沿着圣安托万街轻快地走着。 **3** N-COUNT A **pace** is the distance that you move when you take one step. 步距 [usu with supp] ❑ *He'd only gone a few paces before he stopped again.* 他只走了几步就又停了下来。 **4** V-T/V-I If you **pace** a small area, you keep walking up and down it, because you are anxious or impatient. (因焦虑或不耐烦) 在…走来走去 ❑ *As they waited, Kravis paced the room nervously.* 在他们等着时，克拉维斯在房间里紧张不安地走来走去。 ❑ *He found John pacing around the house, unable to sleep.* 他发现约翰正在房子里四下踱步，无法入眠。 **5** V-T If you **pace yourself** when doing something, you do it at a steady rate. 放稳(自己) 的步调 ❑ *It was a tough race and I had to pace myself.* 那是一场艰难的比赛，我必须放稳自己的步调。 **6** PHRASE If something **keeps pace with** something else that is changing, it changes quickly in response to it. 与…保持同步 ❑ *The earnings of the average American have failed to keep pace with the rate of inflation.* 一般美国人的收入跟不上通货膨胀的速度。 **7** PHRASE If you **keep pace with** someone who is walking or running, you succeed in going as fast as them, so that you remain close to them. 与…并驾齐驱 ❑ *With four laps to go, he kept pace with the leaders.* 还有4圈要跑，他与那些领先者并驾齐驱。 **8** PHRASE If you do something **at** your **own pace**, you do it at a speed that is comfortable for you. 按自己的速度 ❑ *The computer will give students the opportunity to learn at their own pace.* 计算机将给予学生们按照自己的速度学习的机会。 **9** **at a snail's pace** → see **snail**

Word Partnership *pace* 的常用搭配：

N.	pace **of change** 1
ADJ.	**brisk** pace, **fast** pace, **record** pace, **slow** pace 1 2
V.	**pick up the** pace, **set a** pace 1 2
	keep pace **with** *something* 6
	keep pace **with** *someone* 7

paci·fi·er /pæsɪfaɪər/ (**pacifiers**) N-COUNT A **pacifier** is a rubber or plastic object that you give to a baby to suck so that he or she feels comforted. 安抚奶嘴 [AM]

in BRIT, use **dummy**

paci·fism /pæsɪfɪzəm/ N-UNCOUNT **Pacifism** is the belief that war and violence are always wrong. 和平主义 ❑ *...a leading exponent of pacifism.* …一个主要的和平主义倡导者。

paci·fist /pæsɪfɪst/ (**pacifists**) **1** N-COUNT A **pacifist** is someone who believes that violence is wrong and refuses to take part in wars. 和平主义者；反战者 ❑ *Many protesters insist they are pacifists, opposed to war in all forms.* 许多抗议者坚持说他们是和平主义者，反对一切形式的战争。 **2** ADJ If someone has **pacifist** views, they believe that war and violence are always wrong. 和平主义的；反战的 ❑ *...his mother's pacifist ideals.* …他母亲的和平主义理想。

pack ♦♦◇ /pæk/ (**packs, packing, packed**) **1** V-T/V-I When you **pack** a bag, you put clothes and other things into it, because you are leaving a place or going on vacation. 打点 (行装) ❑ *When I was 17, I packed my bags and left home.* 在我17岁的时候，打起行囊离开了家。 ❑ *I began to pack a few things for the trip.* 我开始为旅行收拾些东西。 ● **pack·ing** N-UNCOUNT 打包；包装 ❑ *She left Frances to finish her packing.* 她让弗朗西斯把她的行李收拾完。 **2** V-T When people **pack** things, for example, in a factory, they put them into containers or boxes so that they can be shipped and sold. 包装；把…装箱 ❑ *They offered me a job packing boxes in a warehouse.* 他们为我提供了一份在仓库装箱的工作。 ❑ *Machines now exist to pack olives in jars.* 现在有可以把橄榄装进罐里的机器。 ● **pack·ing** N-UNCOUNT 包装；装箱 ❑ *The shipping and packing costs are passed along in the item price.* 运输和装箱费用已经含在单价中了。 **3** V-T/V-I If people or things **pack into** a place or if they **pack** a place, there are so many of them that the place is full. 挤满 ❑ *Hundreds of people packed into the mosque.* 成百上千的人挤进了清真寺。 **4** N-COUNT A **pack of** things is a collection of them that is sold or given together in a box or bag. 盒；包 ❑ *The club will send a free information pack.* 俱乐部将赠送一个免费的信息包。 ❑ *...a pack of cigarettes.* …一包香烟。 **5** N-COUNT You can refer to a group of people who go around together as a **pack**, especially when it is a large group that you feel threatened by. 一群 (尤指令人感到受到威胁的) ❑ *He thus avoided a pack of journalists eager to question him.* 他就这样避开了一群急于向他提问的记者。 **6** N-COUNT A **pack of** wolves or dogs is a group of them that hunt together. 一群 (狼或狗) ❑ *...a pack of stray dogs.* …一群流浪狗。 **7** N-COUNT A **pack of** playing cards is a complete set of playing cards. 一副 (纸牌) [mainly BRIT]

in AM, usually use **deck**

8 → see also **packed, packing** **9** PHRASE If you say that an account is **a pack of lies**, you mean that it is completely untrue. 一派胡言 ❑ *You told me a pack of lies.* 你跟我说的是一派胡言。 **10** PHRASE If you **send** someone **packing**, you make them go away. 打发 (某人) 离开 [INFORMAL] ❑ *I decided I wanted to live alone and I sent him packing.* 我决定要独自生活，所以我把他打发走了。

pack·age ♦♦◇ /pækɪdʒ/ (**packages, packaging, packaged**) **1** N-COUNT A **package** is something wrapped in paper, in a bag or large envelope, or in a box, usually so that it can be sent to someone by mail. 包裹 ❑ *I tore open the package.* 我撕开了那个包裹。 **2** N-COUNT A **package** is a small container in which a quantity of something is sold. Packages are either small boxes made of thin cardboard, or bags or envelopes made of paper or plastic. 小包 [mainly AM]

in BRIT, usually use **packet**

❑ *...a package of doughnuts.* …一包炸面圈。 **3** N-COUNT A **package** is a set of proposals that are made by a government or organization and that must be accepted or rejected as a group. 一揽子建议 ❑ *...a package of measures to help the movie industry.* …一揽子帮助电影业的措施。 **4** V-T When a product **is packaged**, it is put into containers to be sold. 包装 (产品) [usu passive] ❑ *The beans are then ground and packaged for sale as ground coffee.* 咖啡豆接着被磨碎、包装，以研磨咖啡销售。 **5** V-T If something **is packaged** in a particular way, it is presented or advertised in that way in order to make it seem attractive or interesting. (为使某物吸引人而) 包装 [usu passive] ❑ *A city is like any product, it has to be packaged properly to be attractive to the consumer.* 一座城市就像任何产品一样，需要适当地加以包装来吸引消费者。 **6** N-COUNT A **package** tour is a vacation in which your travel and your accommodations are booked for you. 包价 (旅游) ❑ *...package tours to Egypt.* …去埃及的包价旅游。

Thesaurus *package* 另参见：

N.	batch, bundle, container, pack, parcel 1 2

pack·ag·ing /pækɪdʒɪŋ/ N-UNCOUNT **Packaging** is the container or covering that something is sold in. 包装 ❑ *It is selling very well, in part because the packaging is so attractive.* 它卖得非常好，部分原因在于包装很吸引人。

packed /pækt/ **1** ADJ A place that is **packed** is very crowded. 拥挤的 ❑ *The place is packed at lunchtime.* 这个地方在午餐时间非常拥挤。 ❑ *...a packed meeting in Detroit.* …一个在底特律召开的座无虚席的会议。

2 ADJ Something that is **packed with** things contains a very large number of them. 充满的 [v-link ADJ "with" n] ❑ *The encyclopedia is packed with clear illustrations and over 250 recipes.* 这本百科全书充满了清晰的插图，还有二百五十多个食谱。

packed lunch [BRIT] → see **box lunch**

pack·et /pækɪt/ (**packets**) **1** N-COUNT An information **packet** is a set of information about a particular subject that is given to people who are interested in that subject. (信息) 包 [with supp] [AM]

in BRIT, use **pack**

❑ *Call us for a free information packet that tells you more.* 打电话给我们索要为你提供更多信息的免费信息包。 ❑ *...a 23-page packet of topics to be discussed.* ···一份23页的需要讨论的主题。 **2** N-COUNT A **packet** is a small container in which a quantity of something is sold. Packets are either small boxes made of thin cardboard, or bags or envelopes made of paper or plastic. 小盒子；包装袋 [mainly BRIT] ❑ *...sugar packets.* ···糖盒。 **3** N-COUNT You can use **packet** to refer to a packet and its contents, or to the contents only. 包裹 [mainly BRIT]

in AM, usually use **pack, package**

pack·ing /pækɪŋ/ **1** N-UNCOUNT **Packing** is the paper, plastic, or other material that is put around things that are being sent somewhere to protect them. 包装材料 ❑ *My fingers shook as I pulled the packing from the box.* 当我把盒子上的包装撕下来的时候，我的手指在颤抖。 **2** → see also **pack**

★ **pact** ♦◇◇ /pækt/ (**pacts**) N-COUNT A **pact** is a formal agreement between two or more people, organizations, or governments to do a particular thing or to help each other. 条约；协议 ❑ *Last month he signed a new non-aggression pact with Germany.* 上个月他与德国签署了一份新的互不侵犯条约。

pad /pæd/ (**pads, padding, padded**) **1** N-COUNT A **pad** is a fairly thick, flat piece of a material such as cloth or rubber. Pads are used, for example, to clean things, to protect things, or to change their shape. (清洗、保护或防止变形用的) 垫；护垫 ❑ *He withdrew the needle and placed a pad of cotton over the spot.* 他把针拔出来，将一块药棉盖在针眼上。 ❑ *...a scouring pad.* ···一个擦洗垫。 **2** N-COUNT A **pad of** paper is a number of pieces of paper attached together along the top or the side, so that each piece can be torn off when it has been used. 便笺簿 ❑ *She wrote on a pad of paper.* 她写在了一本便笺簿上。 ❑ *Have a pad and pencil ready and jot down some of your thoughts.* 准备一本便笺簿和一支铅笔，迅速地记下你的一些想法。 **3** V-I When someone **pads** somewhere, they walk there with steps that are fairly quick, light, and quiet. 轻步快走 ❑ *Freddy speaks very quietly and pads around in soft velvet slippers.* 弗雷迪一边非常小声地说着，一边穿着柔软的天鹅绒拖鞋轻快地四处走着。 ❑ *...a dog padding through the streets.* ···一只轻快穿过街道的狗。 **4** N-COUNT A **pad** is a platform or an area of flat, hard ground where helicopters take off and land or rockets are launched. (直升机) 停机坪；(火箭) 发射台 ❑ *...a little round helicopter pad.* ···一个小的圆形直升机停机坪。 ❑ *...a landing pad on the back of the ship.* ···一个位于船尾的停机坪。 **5** N-COUNT The **pads of** a person's fingers and toes or of an animal's feet are the soft, fleshy parts of them. 指头肚；爪垫 ❑ *Tap your cheeks all over with the pads of your fingers.* 用你的指头肚轻拍你的整个面颊。 **6** V-T If you **pad** something, you put something soft in it or over it in order to make it less hard, to protect it, or to give it a different shape. (用软物) 填充；垫衬 ❑ *Pad the back of a car seat with a pillow.* 在汽车座椅靠背上垫一个头枕。 ● **pad·ded** ADJ 填充的；有衬垫的 ❑ *...a padded jacket.* ···一件有衬垫的夹克。 **7** V-T If you **pad** or **pad out** a piece of writing or a speech **with** unnecessary words or pieces of information, you include them to make it longer and hide the fact that you do not have very much to say. (添加不必要的词句或信息以) 拉长 (文章或演讲) ❑ *Quotations should be used to make points, not to pad the essay.* 引语应该是用来陈述观点的，而不是为了拉长文章。 ❑ *The reviewer padded out his review with a lengthy biography of the author.* 那位评论家用冗长的作者生平来拉长他的评论。 **8** V-T If an employee with an expense account **pads** their expenses, they claim that their expenses are greater than they really are in order to get more money from their employer. 虚报 (花费) ❑ *She was fired for padding her expenses.* 她因为虚报她的花费而被解雇。 **9** → see also **padding**

→ see **skateboarding**

▸ **pad out** PHRASAL VERB → see **pad 7**

pad·ding /pædɪŋ/ N-UNCOUNT **Padding** is soft material put on something or inside it in order to make it less hard, to protect it, or to give it a different shape. (柔软的) 填充物；衬垫 ❑ *...the foam rubber padding on the headphones.* ···耳机上的海绵橡胶衬垫。 ❑ *Players must wear padding to protect them from injury.* 运动员们必须戴上护垫以保护自己不受伤害。

▲ **pad·dle** /pædᵊl/ (**paddles, paddling, paddled**) **1** N-COUNT A **paddle** is a short pole with a wide flat part at one end or at both ends. You hold it in your hands and use it as an oar to move a small boat through water. 短桨 ❑ *We might be able to push ourselves across with the paddle.* 我们或许可以自己划桨过去。 **2** V-T/V-I If you **paddle** a boat, you move it through water using a paddle. 用桨划 ❑ *...the skills you will use to paddle the canoe.* ···你将使用到的划独木舟的技巧。 **3** N-COUNT A **paddle** is a specially shaped piece of wood that is used for hitting the ball in table tennis. 乒乓球拍 [AM]

in BRIT, use **bat**

→ see **boat**

pad·dock /pædək/ (**paddocks**) N-COUNT A **paddock** is a small field where horses are kept. (放牧马匹的) 小围场 ❑ *The family kept horses in the paddock in front of the house.* 这家人在房子前面的小围场养马。

pad·dy /pædi/ (**paddies**) N-COUNT A **paddy** or a **paddy field** is a field that is kept flooded with water and is used for growing rice. 稻田 ❑ *...the paddy fields of China.* ···中国的稻田。

pad·lock /pædlɒk/ (**padlocks, padlocking, padlocked**) **1** N-COUNT A **padlock** is a lock that is used for fastening two things together. It consists of a block of metal with a U-shaped bar attached to it. One end of the bar is released by turning a key in the lock. 挂锁 ❑ *They had put a padlock on the door of his house.* 他们已经在他家房门上了一把挂锁。 **2** V-T If you **padlock** something, you lock it or fasten it to something else using a padlock. 用挂锁锁上 ❑ *Eddie parked his bicycle against a lamppost and padlocked it.* 艾迪把他的自行车停靠在一根路灯柱上，然后用挂锁锁上了。

pae·dia·tri·cian /piːdiətrɪʃᵊn/ [BRIT] → see **pediatrician**

pae·do·phile /piːdəfaɪl/ [BRIT] → see **pedophile**

pae·do·philia /piːdəfɪliə/ [BRIT] → see **pedophilia**

pa·gan /peɪgən/ (**pagans**) **1** ADJ **Pagan** beliefs and activities do not belong to any of the main religions of the world. They are older, or are believed to be older, than other religions. 异教徒的 ❑ *The Christian church has adapted many pagan ideas over the centuries.* 几个世纪以来，基督教会已经采用并改编许多异教思想。 **2** N-COUNT In former times, **pagans** were people who did not believe in Christianity and whom many Christians considered to be inferior people. 异教徒 ❑ *The pagans used torchlight parades and bonfires to celebrate important events.* 异教徒们用火把游行和篝火来庆祝重大的事件。

page ♦♦♦ /peɪdʒ/ (**pages, paging, paged**) **1** N-COUNT A **page** is one side of one of the pieces of paper in a book, magazine, or newspaper. Each page usually has a number printed at the top or bottom. (书、报刊等的) 页；版 ❑ *Take out your book and turn to page 4.* 拿出你的书，翻到第4页。 ❑ *...the front page of USA Today.* ···《今日美国》的头版。 **2** N-COUNT The **pages** of a book, magazine, or newspaper are the pieces of paper it consists of. (书、报刊等的) 纸页 ❑ *He turned the pages of his notebook.* 他翻着他笔记本的纸页。 **3** N-COUNT You can refer to an important event or period of time as a **page** of history. (历史的) 一页 [LITERARY] ❑ *...a new page in the country's political history.* ···这个国家政治历史上新的一页。 **4** V-T If someone who is in a public place **is paged**, they receive a message, often over a speaker, telling them that someone is trying to contact them. (在公共场合通过扬声器) 呼叫 ❑ *He was paged repeatedly as the flight was boarding.* 登机时，他被反复地呼叫着。 **5** N-COUNT A **page** is a young person who takes messages or does small jobs for members of the United States Congress or state legislatures. (美国国会或州立法机关的) 青年助理 [AM] **6** N-COUNT A **page** is a small boy who accompanies the bride at a wedding. 男小傧相

→ see **printing**

pag·eant /pædʒənt/ (**pageants**) **1** N-COUNT A **pageant** or a **beauty pageant** is a competition in which young women are judged to decide which one is the most beautiful. 选美大赛 ❑ *...the Miss Universe beauty pageant.* ···环球小姐选美大赛。 **2** N-COUNT A **pageant** is a colorful public procession, show, or ceremony. Pageants are usually held outdoors and often celebrate events or people from history. 盛大庆典 (通常为露天的)

pag·er /peɪdʒər/ (**pagers**) N-COUNT A **pager** is a small electronic device that you can carry around with you and that gives you a number or a message when someone is trying to contact you. 寻呼机 ❑ *Scores of messages on his pager have not been answered.* 他寻呼机上的许多信息都还没有回复。

paid /peɪd/ 1 **Paid** is the past tense and past participle of **pay**. **pay**的过去式和过去分词 2 ADJ **Paid** workers, or people who do **paid** work, receive money for the work that they do. 有薪酬的 [ADJ n] ❑ *Apart from a small team of paid staff, the organization consists of unpaid volunteers.* 除了一小部分有薪酬的工作人员，这个机构还包含没有薪酬的志愿者。 3 ADJ If you are given **paid** vacation, you get your wages or salary even though you are not at work. (假期) 带薪的 [ADJ n] ❑ *He agreed to hire her at slightly over minimum wage with two weeks' paid vacation.* 他同意以略高于最低工资的薪资雇用她，外加两周带薪假。 4 ADJ If you are well **paid**, you receive a lot of money for the work that you do. If you are badly **paid**, you do not receive much money. 薪水(高或低) 的 [adv ADJ] ❑ *...a well-paid accountant.* …一名高薪的会计师。 ❑ *Travel and tourism employees are among the worst paid in the developed world.* 旅行和旅游业的雇员们在发达国家属于薪酬最低的行列。

pain ♦♦◊ /peɪn/ (**pains, pained**) 1 N-VAR **Pain** is the feeling of great discomfort you have, for example, when you have been hurt or when you are ill. 疼痛 ❑ *...back pain.* …背痛。 ❑ *To help ease the pain, heat can be applied to the area with a hot water bottle.* 可以用一个热水瓶在疼痛部位热敷来缓解疼痛。 ❑ *I felt a sharp pain in my lower back.* 我感到背的下部一阵剧痛。 ● PHRASE If you are **in pain**, you feel pain in a part of your body because you are injured or ill. 感到疼痛 ❑ *She was writhing in pain, bathed in perspiration.* 她正痛得扭动着，大汗淋漓。 2 N-UNCOUNT **Pain** is the feeling of unhappiness that you have when something unpleasant or upsetting happens. 痛苦 ❑ *...gray eyes that seemed filled with pain.* …似乎充满了痛苦的灰色眼睛。 3 V-T If a fact or idea **pains** you, it makes you feel upset and disappointed. 使痛苦；使苦恼 [no cont] ❑ *This public acknowledgment of Ted's disability pained my mother.* 特德残疾的公开使我母亲感到痛苦。 4 PHRASE In informal English, if you call someone or something **a pain** or **a pain in the neck**, you mean that they are very annoying or irritating. Expressions such as **a pain in the ass** and **a pain in the butt** are also used, but most people consider them offensive. 讨厌鬼；烦心事 [INFORMAL, DISAPPROVAL] ❑ *Getting rid of unwanted applications from your PC can be a real pain.* 从你的个人电脑上删除不需要的应用程序可以是一件很烦人的事。 5 PHRASE If you **take pains to** do something or **go to great pains to** do something, you try hard to do it, because you think it is important to do it. 下苦功 ❑ *He took great pains to see that he got it right.* 他下了很大的功夫以确保他弄对了。

Thesaurus *pain* 另参见:

N.	ache, agony, discomfort 1
	anguish, distress, heartache, suffering 2
V.	bother, distress, grieve, hurt, upset, wound 3

pained /peɪnd/ ADJ If you have a **pained** expression or look, you look upset, worried, or slightly annoyed. 痛苦的；苦恼的 ❑ *Tanya put on a pained look, as though the subject was too delicate to be spoken about.* 塔尼娅表现出一副痛苦的表情，好像这个话题太微妙了不便讨论。

pain·ful ♦◊◊ /peɪnfəl/ 1 ADJ If a part of your body is **painful**, it hurts because it is injured or because there is something wrong with it. 疼痛的 ❑ *Her glands were swollen and painful.* 她的腺体肿胀且疼痛。 ● **pain·ful·ly** ADV 疼痛地 [ADV with v] ❑ *His tooth had started to throb painfully again.* 他的牙又开始抽痛了。 2 ADJ If something such as an illness, injury, or operation is **painful**, it causes you a lot of physical pain. 令人疼痛的 ❑ *...a painful back injury.* …令人疼痛的背伤。 ● **pain·ful·ly** ADV 令人疼痛地 [ADV with v] ❑ *...cracking his head painfully against the cupboard.* …他的头撞到碗柜上，很痛。 3 ADJ Situations, memories, or experiences that are **painful** are difficult and unpleasant to deal with, and often make you feel sad and upset. (情形、记忆或经历) 痛苦的 ❑ *Remarks like that brought back painful memories.* 像那样的评论勾起了痛苦的记忆。 ❑ *...the painful transition to democracy.* …迈向民主的艰难过渡期。 ● **pain·ful·ly** ADV 痛苦地；令人难过地 [ADV with v] ❑ *...their old relationship, which he had painfully broken off.* …他们之间已经被他痛苦地斩断了的老关系。

Word Partnership *painful* 的常用搭配:

ADV.	**extremely** painful, **less/more** painful, **often** painful,
	sometimes painful, **too** painful, **very** painful 1 – 3
N.	painful **death**, painful **experience**, painful **feelings**,
	painful **lesson**, painful **memory**, painful **process** 3

pain·ful·ly /peɪnfəli/ 1 ADV You use **painfully** to emphasize a quality or situation that is undesirable. (用以强调不好的性质或情形) 非常 [ADV adv/adj] [EMPHASIS] ❑ *Things are moving painfully slowly.* 事情进展得极其缓慢。 ❑ *...a painfully shy young man.* …一个非常害羞的年轻男子。 2 → see also **painful**

pain·killer /peɪnkɪlər/ (**painkillers**) N-COUNT A **painkiller** is a drug that reduces or stops physical pain. 止痛药

pain·less /peɪnlɪs/ 1 ADJ If something such as a treatment is **painless** it causes no physical pain. 无痛的 ❑ *Acupuncture treatment is gentle, painless, and relaxing.* 针灸治疗很温和，无痛，也很放松。 ❑ *The operation itself is a brief, painless procedure.* 手术本身是一个短暂、无痛的过程。 ● **pain·less·ly** ADV 无痛地 [ADV with v] ❑ *...a technique to eliminate unwanted facial hair quickly and painlessly.* …一项迅速且无痛地去除面部多余汗毛的技术。 2 ADJ If a process or activity is **painless**, there are no difficulties involved, and you do not have to make a great effort or suffer in any way. 不费劲的 ❑ *The journey is relatively painless, even with children.* 这趟旅程相对轻松，即使是带着孩子。 ● **pain·less·ly** ADV 不费劲地 [ADV with v] ❑ *...a game for children that painlessly teaches essential pre-reading skills.* …轻松地教给孩子们必要的读前技巧的一个游戏。

pains·taking /peɪnzteɪkɪŋ, peɪnsteɪ-/ ADJ A **painstaking** search, examination, or investigation is done extremely carefully and thoroughly. 十分小心的；极其仔细的 ❑ *Forensic experts carried out a painstaking search of the debris.* 法医专家们对残骸进行了极其仔细的研究。 ● **pains·taking·ly** ADV 十分小心地；极其仔细地 ❑ *Broken bones were painstakingly pieced together and reshaped.* 断裂的骨头被十分小心地拼凑到一起重新成形。

paint ♦♦◊ /peɪnt/ (**paints, painting, painted**) 1 N-MASS **Paint** is a colored liquid that you put onto a surface with a brush in order to protect the surface or to make it look nice, or that you use to produce a picture. 油漆；涂料 ❑ *...a can of red paint.* …一罐红色油漆。 ❑ *They saw some large letters in white paint.* 他们看见了几个用白漆写的大大的字母。 2 N-SING On a wall or object, **the paint** is the covering of dried paint on it. 油漆层；涂层 ❑ *The paint was peeling on the window frames.* 窗框上的油漆正在剥落。 3 V-T/V-I If you **paint** a wall or an object, you cover it with paint. 给…刷油漆；给…刷涂料 ❑ *They started to mend the woodwork and paint the walls.* 他们开始修理木建部分并粉刷墙壁。 ❑ *I had come here to paint.* 我到这儿来是刷漆的。 4 V-T If you **paint** something or **paint** a picture of it, you produce a picture of it using paint. 画 ❑ *He is painting a huge volcano.* 他正在画一座巨型火山。 ❑ *Why do people paint pictures?* 为什么人们要画画？ 5 V-T When you **paint** a design or message on a surface, you put it on the surface using paint. 用颜料画；用颜料写 ❑ *...a machine for painting white lines on roads.* …一台用来在马路上画白线的机器。 ❑ *They went around painting rude slogans on cars.* 他们到处用颜料在轿车上写粗鲁的标语。 6 V-T If you **paint** a grim or vivid picture of something, you give a description of it that is grim or vivid. 把…描绘成 ❑ *The report paints a grim picture of life there.* 该报道把那里的生活描绘成一副阴森的画面。 7 → see also **gloss paint, oil paint, painting**
→ see **painting**

Word Partnership *paint* 的常用搭配:

ADJ.	**blue/green/red/white/yellow** paint 1
	fresh paint, **peeling** paint 2
N.	**can of** paint 1
	coat of paint 2
	paint **a picture**, paint **a portrait** 4

paint·brush /peɪntbrʌʃ/ (**paintbrushes**) N-COUNT A **paintbrush** is a brush that you use for painting. 画笔；油漆刷
→ see **painting**

paint·er /peɪntər/ (**painters**) 1 N-COUNT A **painter** is an artist who paints pictures. 画家 ❑ *...the French painter Claude Monet.* …法国画家克劳德・莫奈。 2 N-COUNT A **painter** is someone who paints walls, doors, and some other parts of buildings as their job. 油漆工 ❑ *...the son of a painter and decorator.* …一个油漆工兼装修工的儿子。
→ see **art**

paint·ing ♦♦◊ /peɪntɪŋ/ (**paintings**) 1 N-COUNT A **painting** is a picture that someone has painted. 画作 ❑ *...a large painting of Dwight Eisenhower.* …一幅巨大的德怀特・艾森豪威尔的画像。 2 N-UNCOUNT **Painting** is the activity of painting pictures. 绘画 ❑ *...two hobbies she really enjoyed, painting and gardening.* …她真正乐此不疲的两个爱好：绘画和园艺。 3 N-UNCOUNT **Painting** is the activity of painting doors, walls, and some other parts of buildings. 刷油漆 ❑ *...painting and decorating.* …刷漆和装修。
→ see Word Web: **painting**
→ see **art, gallery**

Word Web painting

Oil **painting** involves special tools and techniques. Trained artists start by stretching a piece of **canvas** over a wooden **frame**. Then they cover the surface with a **coat** of white **paint**. When it dries, they put it

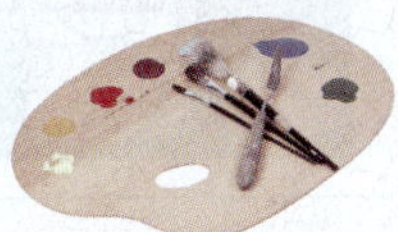

on an **easel**. Most painters use a **palette knife** on a **palette** to mix different **colors** together. They then apply the paint to the canvas using soft bristle **paintbrushes**. When finished, they use turpentine to clean up the brushes and the palette. Three common oil painting styles are the **still life**, the **landscape**, and the **portrait**.

pair ♦♦◇ /pɛər/ (**pairs, pairing, paired**) 1 N-COUNT **A pair of** things are two things of the same size and shape that are used together or are both part of something, for example, shoes, earrings, or parts of the body. 双；对 ❑ *...a pair of socks.* …一双袜子 ❑ *...earrings that cost $142.50 a pair.* …价值$142.50一对的耳环。 2 N-COUNT Some objects that have two main parts of the same size and shape are referred to as a **pair**, for example, **a pair of pants** or **a pair of scissors**. 副；条（裤子）❑ *...a pair of faded jeans.* …一条退色的牛仔裤。 3 N-SING You can refer to two people as a **pair** when they are standing or walking together or when they have some kind of relationship with each other. （站或走在一起的）两人；（有某种关系的）一对 ❑ *A pair of teenage boys were smoking cigarettes.* 两个青少年正在抽烟。 ❑ *The pair admitted that their three-year-old marriage was going through "a difficult time."* 那对夫妇承认他们3年的婚姻正在经历一个困难时期。

The noun **pair** can take either a singular verb or a plural verb, depending on whether it refers to one thing seen as a unit or a collection of two things or people. ❑ *A good, supportive and protective pair of sneakers is essential... The pair are still friends and attend functions together.*

4 V-T If one thing **is paired with** another, it is put with it or considered with it. 把…配对 [usu passive] ❑ *The trainees will then be paired with experienced managers.* 这些实习生之后将被配给有经验的经理们。 5 → see also **au pair**

Thesaurus *pair* 另参见：

N. combination, couple, duo, match, two, twosome 1 3
V. combine, join, match up, put together, team 4

pa·jam·as /pədʒɑməz/ N-PLURAL A pair of **pajamas** consists of loose pants and a top that people wear to bed. 睡衣 [also "a" "pair" "of" N]

in BRIT, use **pyjamas**

❑ *I don't want to get out of my pajamas in the morning.* 我不想在早晨脱下我的睡衣。

pal /pæl/ (**pals**) N-COUNT Your **pals** are your friends. 朋友 [INFORMAL, OLD-FASHIONED] ❑ *They talked like old pals.* 他们像老朋友一样交谈。

pal·ace ♦◇◇ /pælɪs/ (**palaces**) N-COUNT A **palace** is a very large impressive house, especially one that is the official home of a king, queen, or president. 宫殿 ❑ *...Buckingham Palace.* …白金汉宫。

pal·at·able /pælətəbᵊl/ 1 ADJ If you describe food or drink as **palatable**, you mean that it tastes pleasant. 美味的 [FORMAL] ❑ *...flavorings and preservatives, designed to make the food look more palatable.* …用来使食物看起来更美味的调味品和防腐剂。 2 ADJ If you describe something such as an idea or method as **palatable**, you mean that people are willing to accept it. 可接受的 ❑ *...a palatable way of firing employees.* …一种可接受的解雇雇员的方式。

pal·ate /pælɪt/ (**palates**) 1 N-COUNT Your **palate** is the top part of the inside of your mouth. 上颚 2 N-COUNT You can refer to someone's **palate** as a way of talking about their ability to judge good food or drink. 味觉 ❑ *...fresh pasta sauces to tempt more demanding palates.* …诱惑较为挑剔的味觉的新鲜面食调味酱。

pale ♦◇◇ /peɪl/ (**paler, palest, pales, paling, paled**) 1 ADJ If something is **pale**, it is very light in color or almost white. 浅色的；灰白的 ❑ *Migrating birds filled the pale sky.* 迁徙的鸟布满了灰白的天空。 ❑ *As we age, our skin becomes paler.* 随着我们变老，我们的皮肤变得更加苍白。 ● COMB IN COLOR **Pale** is also a combining form. （用于构成合成词）浅…色的 ❑ *...a pale blue sailor dress.* …一件浅蓝色的水手服。 2 ADJ If someone looks **pale**, their face looks a lighter color than usual, usually because they are ill, frightened, or shocked. （脸色）苍白的 ❑ *She looked pale and tired.* 她看起来苍白而疲惫。 3 V-I If one thing **pales** in comparison with another, it is made to seem much less important, serious, or good by it. 显得逊色；相形见绌 ❑ *When someone you love has a life-threatening illness, everything else pales in comparison.* 当你所爱的人得了致命的疾病时，其他的一切就都显得不重要了。

pal·ette /pælɪt/ (**palettes**) 1 N-COUNT A **palette** is a flat piece of wood or plastic on which an artist mixes paints. 调色盘 ❑ *The painter's right hand holds the brush, the left the palette.* 那位画家的右手握着画笔，左手拿着调色盘。 2 N-COUNT You can refer to the range of colors that are used by a particular artist or group of artists as their **palette**. （画家使用的）色彩范围 ❑ *He paints from a palette consisting almost exclusively of gray and mud brown.* 他画画几乎只用包含灰色和土褐色的色调。
→ see **painting**

palm /pɑm/ (**palms**) 1 N-COUNT A **palm** or a **palm tree** is a tree that grows in hot countries. It has long leaves growing at the top, and no branches. 棕榈树 ❑ *...golden sands and swaying palms.* …金色的沙滩和摇曳的棕榈树。 2 N-COUNT **The palm of** your hand is the inside part of your hand, between your fingers and your wrist. 手掌 ❑ *Dornberg slapped the table with the palm of his hand.* 多恩伯格用他的手掌拍了一下桌子。 3 PHRASE If you have someone or something **in the palm of** your **hand**, you have control over them. 在（某人的）掌控之中 ❑ *Johnson thought he had the board of directors in the palm of his hand.* 约翰逊以为他已把董事会控制在他的掌中。
→ see **desert, hand**

palm·top /pɑmtɒp/ (**palmtops**) N-COUNT A **palmtop** is a small computer that you can hold in your hand. 掌上电脑

pal·pable /pælpəbᵊl/ ADJ You describe something as **palpable** when it is obvious or intense and easily noticed. 可感知的；明显的 ❑ *The tension between Amy and Jim is palpable.* 埃米和吉姆之间的紧张关系是显而易见的。 ● **pal·pably** /pælpəbli/ ADV 可感知地；显然地 [ADV with cl/group] ❑ *The scene was palpably intense to watch.* 那场面看起来显然很激烈。

pal·try /pɔltri/ ADJ A **paltry** amount of money or of something else is one that you consider to be very small. 微小的；微不足道的 ❑ *...a paltry fine of $150.* …区区一笔$150的罚款。

pam·per /pæmpər/ (**pampers, pampering, pampered**) V-T If you **pamper** someone, you make them feel comfortable by doing things for them or giving them expensive or luxurious things. 溺爱；细心照顾 ❑ *Why don't you let your mother pamper you for a while?* 为什么你不让你妈妈照顾你一会儿呢？ ❑ *Pamper yourself with our luxury gifts.* 用我们奢华的礼物纵容你自己吧。 ● **pam·pered** ADJ 被溺爱的；被细心照顾的 ❑ *...today's pampered superstars.* …当今被娇惯的超级明星们。

Word Link *let ≈ little : booklet, droplet, pamphlet*

★ **pam·phlet** /pæmflɪt/ (**pamphlets**) N-COUNT A **pamphlet** is a very thin book with a paper cover that gives information about something. 小册子 ❑ *...a pamphlet about smoking.* …一本关于吸烟的小册子。

pan ♦◇◇ /pæn/ (**pans, panning, panned**) 1 N-COUNT A **pan** is a round metal container with a long handle, that is used for cooking things in, usually on top of a stove. 平底锅 ❑ *Heat the butter and oil in a large pan.* 在一个大平底锅里加热黄油和食用油。 2 V-T If something such as a movie or a book **is panned** by journalists, they say it is very bad. 抨击；批评 [usu passive] [INFORMAL] ❑ *His first high-budget movie, called "Brain Donors," was panned by the critics.* 他的第一部巨资电影名为《撞板三舞男》，遭到了批评家们的抨击。 3 V-T/V-I If you **pan** a movie or television camera or if it **pans** somewhere, it moves slowly around so that a wide area is filmed. 使（摄像机）摇摄；摇摄

Word Web pan

No **saucepan** or **frying pan** is perfect. **Copper pans** conduct heat extremely well. This makes them a popular choice for stovetop cooking. However, copper also reacts with the acid in some foods and wines. For this reason, the best copper pans have a thin layer of **tin** covering the copper. **Cast iron** pans are very heavy and **heat up** slowly. But once hot, they stay hot for a long time. Some people like **stainless steel** pans because they heat up quickly and don't react with chemicals in food. However, the bottom of a stainless pan may not heat up evenly.

❑ *The camera panned along the line of players.* 摄像机沿着球员们的队列摇摄。 ❑ *A television camera panned the stadium.* 一台电视摄像机摇摄体育场。

→ see Word Web: pan

pana·cea /pænəsiə/ (**panaceas**) N-COUNT If you say that something is a **panacea for** a set of problems, you mean that it will solve all those problems. 万灵丹 ❑ *Trade is not a panacea for the world's economic or social ills.* 贸易不是世界经济或社会弊端的万灵丹。

pa·nache /pənæʃ/ N-UNCOUNT If you do something **with panache**, you do it in a confident, stylish, and elegant way. 神气十足; 派头 ❑ *The orchestra played with great panache.* 管弦乐队神气十足地演奏着。

pan·cake /pænkeɪk/ (**pancakes**) N-COUNT A **pancake** is a thin, flat, circular piece of cooked batter made from milk, flour, and eggs. Pancakes are usually eaten for breakfast, with butter and syrup. 薄煎饼

▲ **pan·da** /pændə/ (**pandas**) N-COUNT A **panda** or a **giant panda** is a large animal like a bear that has black and white fur and lives in the bamboo forests of China. 大熊猫

→ see **zoo**

pan·der /pændər/ (**panders, pandering, pandered**) V-I If you **pander to** someone or **to** their wishes, you do everything that they want, often to get some advantage for yourself. 迎合 [DISAPPROVAL] ❑ *He has offended the party's traditional base by pandering to the rich and the middle classes.* 他迎合富人和中产阶级，触犯了该党的传统基础。

pane /peɪn/ (**panes**) N-COUNT A **pane** of glass is a flat sheet of glass in a window or door. (门、窗上的) 一块(玻璃) ❑ *I watch my reflection in a pane of glass.* 我在一块玻璃里看着我的映像。

pan·el ♦◊◊ /pænᵊl/ (**panels**) **1** N-COUNT-COLL A **panel** is a small group of people who are chosen to do something, for example, to discuss something in public or to make a decision. 专门小组 ❑ *He assembled a panel of scholars to advise him.* 他集结了一个学者小组为他出谋划策。 ❑ *All the writers on the panel agreed that Quinn's book should be singled out for special praise.* 专门小组中的所有作家都同意奎因的书应该被挑出来予以特别表扬。 **2** N-COUNT A **panel** is a flat rectangular piece of wood or other material that forms part of a larger object such as a door. (门等的) 镶板; 嵌板 ❑ *...the frosted glass panel set in the center of the door.* …嵌在门中心的毛玻璃板。 **3** N-COUNT A control **panel** or instrument **panel** is a board or surface that contains switches and controls to operate a machine or piece of equipment. (控制) 面板; (仪表) 板 [n N] ❑ *The equipment was extremely sophisticated and was monitored from a central control panel.* 这台设备极其复杂，是由中央控制面板监控的。

pan·eled /pænᵊld/ also **panelled** **1** ADJ A **paneled** room has decorative wooden panels covering its walls. (房间) 有墙裙的 ❑ *...their cozy paneled den.* …他们温暖舒适的、有墙裙的小窝。 ● COMB IN ADJ **-paneled** combines with nouns to form adjectives that describe the way a room or wall is decorated or the way a door or window is made. (与名词构成合成形容词) …墙群的; …门窗的 ❑ *...an elegant wood-paneled library.* …一个雅致的、有木头墙群的图书馆。 **2** ADJ A **paneled** wall, door, or window does not have a flat surface but has square or rectangular areas set into its surface. (墙、门窗等) 镶板的 ❑ *...an oil landscape on the paneled wall.* …挂在有镶板的墙上的一幅风景油画。

▲ **pang** /pæŋ/ (**pangs**) N-COUNT A **pang** is a sudden strong feeling or emotion, for example, of sadness or pain. 突然的痛苦; 突然的剧痛 ❑ *For a moment she felt a pang of guilt about the way she was treating him.* 有那么一会儿她为自己对待他的方式感到一阵突然的愧疚。

pan·han·dler /pænhændlər/ (**panhandlers**) N-COUNT A **panhandler** is a person who stops people in the street and asks them for money. 叫花子 [mainly AM, INFORMAL]

in BRIT, usually use **beggar**

pan·ic ♦◊◊ /pænɪk/ (**panics, panicking, panicked**) **1** N-VAR **Panic** is a very strong feeling of anxiety or fear that makes you act without thinking carefully. 惊慌 ❑ *An earthquake has hit the capital, causing damage to buildings and panic among the population.* 一场地震袭击了首都，造成建筑物的损坏和人们的惊慌。 **2** N-UNCOUNT **Panic** or **a panic** is a situation in which people are affected by a strong feeling of anxiety. 恐慌局面 [also a N] ❑ *There was a moment of panic as it became clear just how vulnerable the nation was.* 随着国家如此脆弱变得明显，出现了一阵恐慌局面。 ❑ *I'm in a panic about getting everything done in time.* 我处于一阵要把一切及时安排就绪的恐慌中。 **3** V-T/V-I If you **panic** or if someone **panics** you, you suddenly feel anxious or afraid, and act quickly and without thinking carefully. 使惊慌; 惊慌 ❑ *Guests panicked and screamed when the bomb exploded.* 炸弹爆炸的时候，客人们惊慌失措，惊声尖叫。 ❑ *The unexpected and sudden memory briefly panicked her.* 这突如其来的记忆使她一时惊慌失措。

Thesaurus *panic* 另参见:

N. agitation, alarm, dread, fear, fright; *(ant.)* calm **1**
V. alarm, fear, terrify, unnerve; *(ant.)* relax **3**

▲ **pano·ra·ma** /pænərɑmə, -ræmə/ (**panoramas**) **1** N-COUNT A **panorama** is a view in which you can see a long way over a wide area of land, usually because you are on high ground. 全景; 远景 ❑ *Horton looked out over a panorama of fertile valleys and gentle hills.* 霍顿眺望着那一片肥沃山谷和平缓山脉的景象。 **2** N-COUNT A **panorama** is a broad view of a state of affairs or of a constantly changing series of events. 概述; 全貌 ❑ *The play presents a panorama of the history of communism.* 这出戏展现了共产主义历史的全貌。

pano·ram·ic /pænəræmɪk/ ADJ If you have a **panoramic** view, you can see a long way over a wide area. 全景的; 远景的 ❑ *The terrain's high points provide a panoramic view of Los Angeles.* 这一地带的制高点可以看见洛杉矶的全景。

▲ **pant** /pænt/ (**pants, panting, panted**) **1** V-I If you **pant**, you breathe quickly and loudly with your mouth open, because you have been doing something energetic. 喘息 ❑ *She climbed rapidly until she was panting with the effort.* 她飞快地爬着，直到她气喘吁吁。 **2** → see also **pants**

panties /pæntiz/ N-PLURAL **Panties** are short, close-fitting underpants worn by women or girls. (女式) 内裤 [mainly AM]

in BRIT, usually use **pants, knickers**

❑ *...a pair of white panties.* …一条白色女式内裤。

Word Link *mim ≈ copying : mime, mimic, pantomime*

pan·to·mime /pæntəmaɪm/ N-SING If you say that a situation or a person's behavior is a **pantomime**, you mean that it is silly or exaggerated and that there is something false about it. 闹剧 [mainly BRIT] ❑ *They were made welcome with the usual pantomime of exaggerated smiles and gestures.* 他们以那种具有夸张的微笑和动作的一般闹剧受到欢迎。

pants /pænts/ **1** N-PLURAL **Pants** are a piece of clothing that covers the lower part of your body and each leg. 长裤 [also "a pair of" N] [AM]

in BRIT, use **trousers**

❑ *She described him as wearing brown corduroy pants and a white cotton shirt.* 她描述说他穿着棕色的灯芯绒长裤和一件白色的棉衬衫。

2 N-PLURAL **Pants** are a piece of underwear which have two holes to put your legs through and elastic around the top to hold them up around your waist or hips. 内裤 [also "a pair of" N] [BRIT]

in AM, usually use **underpants**

→ see **clothing**

pan·ty·hose /pæntihoʊz/ also **panty hose** N-PLURAL **Pantyhose** are a piece of clothing worn by women and girls. They are usually made of flesh-colored nylon and cover the hips, legs and feet. 连裤袜 [also "a pair of" N] [mainly AM]

in BRIT, usually use **tights**

❑ *She told him her pantyhose were slipping.* 她告诉他说她的连裤袜正在下滑。

pa·pa /pɑpə/ (**papas**) N-FAMILY Some people refer to or address their father as **papa**. 爸爸 [OLD-FASHIONED] ❑ *He was so much older than me, older even than my papa.* 他比我老那么多，甚至比我爸爸还老。

pa·pal /peɪpəl/ ADJ **Papal** is used to describe things relating to the Pope. 教皇的 [ADJ n] ❑ *...the doctrine of papal infallibility.* …教皇不谬性的学说。

pa·pa·raz·zi /pɑpərɑtsi/ N-PLURAL **The paparazzi** are photographers who follow famous people around, hoping to take interesting or shocking photographs of them that they can sell to a newspaper. 狗仔队 ❑ *The paparazzi pursue Beckham wherever he travels.* 贝克汗姆到哪里，狗仔队就追到哪里。

pa·per ♦♦♦ /peɪpər/ (**papers, papering, papered**) **1** N-UNCOUNT **Paper** is a material that you write on or wrap things with. The pages of this book are made of paper. 纸 ❑ *He wrote his name down on a piece of paper for me.* 他把他的名字写在一张纸上给我。 ❑ *...a paper bag.* …一个纸袋。 **2** N-COUNT A **paper** is a newspaper. 报纸 ❑ *I might get a paper in the town.* 我或许能在城里买到一份报纸。 **3** N-COUNT You can refer to newspapers in general as **the paper** or **the papers**. (总称) 报纸 ❑ *You can't believe everything you read in the paper.* 你不能相信在报纸上读到的所有内容。 **4** N-PLURAL Your **papers** are sheets of paper with information on them that you might keep in a safe place at home. 资料 ❑ *After her death, her papers – including unpublished articles and correspondence – were deposited at the library.* 她死后，她的资料——包括未发表的文章和信函——都被存放在图书馆里。 **5** N-PLURAL Your **papers** are official documents, such as your passport or identity card, that prove who you are or that give you official permission to do something. 身份证件；证明 ❑ *A young Moroccan stopped by police refused to show his papers.* 一个被警察拦住的摩洛哥青年拒绝出示他的身份证件。 **6** N-COUNT A **paper** is a long, formal piece of writing about an academic subject. 论文 ❑ *He just published a paper in the journal Nature analyzing the fires.* 他刚刚在《自然》杂志上发表了一篇分析火灾的论文。 **7** N-COUNT A **paper** is an essay written by a student. (学生) 作文 [mainly AM] ❑ *...the ten common errors that appear most frequently in student papers.* …最常出现在学生作文中的10个错误。 **8** N-COUNT A **paper** prepared by a government or a committee is a report on a question they have been considering or a set of proposals for changes in the law. (政府) 文件 ❑ *...a new government paper on electoral reform.* …一份关于选举改革的新的政府文件。 **9** ADJ **Paper** agreements, qualifications, or profits are ones that are stated by official documents to exist, although they may not really be effective or useful. (协议、资格或利益等) 书面的 [ADJ n] ❑ *They expressed deep mistrust of the paper promises.* 他们对书面的承诺表示出十分的不信任。 **10** V-T If you **paper** a wall, you put wallpaper on it. 给…贴墙纸 ❑ *We papered all four bedrooms.* 我们给4个卧室都贴了墙纸。 ❑ *We have papered this bedroom in softest gray.* 我们给这间卧室贴上了最柔和的灰色墙纸。 **11** PHRASE If you put your thoughts down **on paper**, you write them down. 在纸上 ❑ *It is important to get something down on paper.* 重要的是要把一些事情写在纸上。 **12** PHRASE If something seems to be the case **on paper**, it seems to be the case from what you read or hear about it, but it may not really be the case. 在理论上 ❑ *On paper, their country is a multi-party democracy.* 从理论上讲，他们的国家是一个多党派民主国家。

→ see Word Web: **paper**

→ see **copy**

Word Partnership *paper* 的常用搭配：

ADJ. **blank** paper, **brown** paper, **colored** paper, **recycled** paper **1**
daily paper **2**
V. **fold the** paper **1**
read the paper **2**
present a paper, **publish a** paper **6**
draft a paper, **write a** paper **6** **7**
N. **morning** paper **2**
research paper **6** **7**

★ **paper·back** /peɪpərbæk/ (**paperbacks**) N-COUNT A **paperback** is a book with a thin cardboard or paper cover. Compare **hardback**. 平装书 [also "in" N] ❑ *She said she would buy the book when it comes out in paperback.* 她说等那本书的平装本面市后她会买一本。

pa·per clip (**paper clips**) also **paper-clip, paperclip** N-COUNT A **paper clip** is a small piece of bent wire that is used to hold papers together. 回形针

→ see **office**

paper·work /peɪpərwɜrk/ N-UNCOUNT **Paperwork** is the routine part of a job that involves writing or dealing with letters, reports, and records. 文书工作 ❑ *At every stage in the production there will be paperwork—forms to fill in, permissions to obtain, letters to write.* 在生产的每一阶段都将有文书工作——要填的表格，要获得的许可，要写的信。

Pap smear (**Pap smears**) also **Pap test** N-COUNT A **Pap smear** is a medical test in which cells are taken from a woman's cervix and analyzed to see if any cancer cells are present. (排查宫颈癌的) 刮片检查 [AM]

in BRIT, use **smear**

par /pɑr/ **1** PHRASE If you say that two people or things are **on a par with** each other, you mean that they are equally good or bad, or equally important. 与…同样 ❑ *The water park will be on a par with some of the best public swim facilities around.* 这个水上公园将与周围那些最好的公共游泳场所一样好。 **2** N-UNCOUNT In golf, **par** is the number of strokes that a good player should take to get the ball into a hole or into all the holes on a particular golf course. (高尔夫球的) 标准杆数 [N with num, "under/over" N] ❑ *He was five under par after the first round.* 第一轮过后他低于标准杆5杆。 **3** PHRASE If you say that someone or something is **below par** or **under par**, you are disappointed in them because they are below the standard you expected. 低于预期标准的 ❑ *Duffy's primitive guitar playing is well below par.* 达菲简单的吉他演奏远远低于预期的标准。 ❑ *A teacher's job is relatively safe, even if they perform under par in the classroom.* 教师的工作是相对保险的，即使他们在教室里的表现低于预期的标准。 **4** PHRASE If you say that someone or something is not **up to par**, you are disappointed in them because they are below the standard you expected. 达到标准的 ❑ *It's a constant struggle to try to keep them up to par.* 要使他们达到标准是一场持久战。 **5** PHRASE If you **feel below par** or **under par** or **not up to par**, you feel tired and unable to perform as well as you normally do. (因感到劳累而) 不如平常 ❑ *After the birth of her baby she felt generally under par.* 生过孩子以后她感到大体上不如平常了。

para·ble /pærəbəl/ (**parables**) N-COUNT A **parable** is a short story, that is told in order to make a moral or religious point, like those in the Bible. 寓言 ❑ *...the parable of the Good Samaritan.* …善良的撒玛利亚人的寓言。

★ **para·chute** /pærəʃut/ (**parachutes, parachuting, parachuted**) **1** N-COUNT A **parachute** is a device that enables a person to jump from an aircraft and float safely to the ground. It consists of a large piece of thin cloth attached to your body by

P

Word Web paper

Around 3000 BC, Egyptians began using the papyrus plant to produce **paper**. They cut the stems of the plant into thin slices and pressed them into **sheets**. A very different Chinese technique developed about the same time. It more closely resembles today's manufacturing process. Chinese paper makers cooked **fiber** made of tree bark. Then they pressed it into molds and let it dry. Around 200 BC, a third technique developed in the Middle East. Craftsmen started using animal skins to make parchment. Today, paper manufacturing destroys millions of trees every year. This has led to **recycling** programs and paperless offices.

strings. 降落伞 ❑ *They fell 41,000 ft. before opening their parachutes.* 他们下落了41000英尺才打开他们的降落伞。 **2** V-T/V-I If a person **parachutes** or someone **parachutes** them somewhere, they jump from an aircraft using a parachute. 使空降; 跳伞 ❑ *He was a courier for the Polish underground and parachuted into Warsaw.* 他是波兰地下组织的信使，被空降到了华沙。 **3** V-T To **parachute** something somewhere means to drop it somewhere by parachute. 空投 ❑ *Planes parachuted food, clothing, blankets, medicine, and water into the rugged mountainous border region.* 飞机把食物、衣服、毯子、药和水空投到崎岖的边界山区。 **4** V-T/V-I If a person **parachutes into** an organization or if they **are parachuted into** it, they are brought in suddenly in order to help it. 突然派到(某机构以帮助该机构) ❑ *...a consultant who parachutes into corporations and helps provide strategic thinking.* …一个突然派到公司去帮助提供战略思想的顾问。 ❑ *Executives with political influence are parachuted into the company.* 有政治影响的主管们被突然派进公司。
→ see **fly**

pa·rade /pəreɪd/ (**parades, parading, paraded**) **1** N-COUNT A **parade** is a procession of people or vehicles moving through a public place in order to celebrate an important day or event. 游行 ❑ *A military parade marched slowly and solemnly down Pennsylvania Avenue.* 一个军事阅兵队伍沿着宾夕法尼亚大街缓慢而庄严地行进。 **2** V-I When people **parade** somewhere, they walk together in a formal group or a line, usually with other people watching them. 游行 ❑ *More than four thousand soldiers, sailors, and airmen paraded down the Champs Elysées.* 超过四千名士兵、水手和飞行员沿着香榭丽舍大街游行。 **3** N-VAR **Parade** is a formal occasion when soldiers stand in lines to be seen by an officer or important person, or march in a group. 阅兵式 [oft "on" N] ❑ *He had them on parade at six o'clock in the morning.* 他让他们在早上6点接受检阅。 **4** V-T If prisoners **are paraded** through the streets of a town or on television, they are shown to the public, usually in order to make the people who are holding them seem more powerful or important. 把…游街; 把…示众 [usu passive] ❑ *Five leading fighter pilots have been captured and paraded before the media.* 5名领先的战斗机飞行员被俘，并在媒体前示众。 **5** V-T If you say that someone **parades** a person, you mean that they show that person to others only in order to gain some advantage for themselves. (为使自己获益而) 展示 [usu passive] ❑ *Captured prisoners were paraded before television cameras.* 被捕获的罪犯们被展示在电视摄像机前。 **6** V-T If people **parade** something, they show it in public so that it can be admired. (为炫耀而) 展示 ❑ *Valentino is eager to see celebrities parading his clothes at big occasions.* 瓦伦蒂诺渴望看到名人们在盛大场合展示他的服装。 **7** V-T/V-I If you say that something **parades as** or **is paraded as** a good or important thing, you mean that some people say that it is good or important but you think it probably is not. 吹嘘; 夸耀 ❑ *...all the fashions that parade as modern movements in art.* …所有被吹嘘成现代艺术运动的风尚。

▲ **para·digm** /pærədaɪm/ (**paradigms**) N-VAR A **paradigm** is a model for something that explains it or shows how it can be produced. 范例 [FORMAL] ❑ *...a new paradigm of production.* …一种新的生产范例。

★ **para·dise** /pærədaɪs/ (**paradises**) **1** N-PROPER According to some religions, **paradise** is a wonderful place where people go after they die, if they have led good lives. 天堂 ❑ *The Koran describes paradise as a place containing a garden of delight.* 《古兰经》把天堂描绘成一个拥有快乐花园的地方。 **2** N-VAR You can refer to a place or situation that seems beautiful or perfect as **paradise** or a **paradise**. 乐园; 至福境地 ❑ *Bali is one of the world's great natural paradises.* 巴厘岛是世界最大的自然乐园之一。

Word Link *dox ≈ opinion : orthodoxy, paradox, unorthodox*

Word Link *para ≈ beside : paradox, parallel, paramedic*

★ **para·dox** /pærədɒks/ (**paradoxes**) **1** N-COUNT You describe a situation as a **paradox** when it involves two or more facts or qualities that seem to contradict each other. 自相矛盾 ❑ *The paradox is that the region's most dynamic economies have the most primitive financial systems.* 矛盾的是，该地区最具活力的经济体制有着最原始的金融体系。 ❑ *The paradox of exercise is that while using a lot of energy it seems to generate more.* 锻炼的矛盾之处在于消耗很多能量却似乎又产生更多能量。 **2** N-VAR A **paradox** is a statement in which it seems that if one part of it is true, the other part of it cannot be true. 悖论 ❑ *The story contains many levels of paradox.* 这个故事包含很多层面的悖论。

para·doxi·cal /pærədɒksɪkᵊl/ ADJ If something is **paradoxical**, it involves two facts or qualities that seem to contradict each other. 自相矛盾的 ❑ *Some sedatives produce the paradoxical effect of making the person more anxious.* 一些镇静剂产生出使人更紧张这样自相矛盾的结果。 ● **para·doxi·cal·ly** /pærədɒksɪkli/ ADV 自相矛盾地 ❑ *Paradoxically, the less you have to do the more you may resent the work that does come your way.* 自相矛盾的是，你要做的事情越少，就越是对突然落在你身上的工作不满。

par·af·fin /pærəfɪn/ **1** N-UNCOUNT **Paraffin** is a white wax obtained from petroleum or coal. It is used to make candles, to form seals, and in beauty treatments. 石蜡 **2** N-UNCOUNT **Paraffin** is a strong-smelling liquid which is used as a fuel in heaters, lamps, and engines. 煤油 [mainly BRIT]

in AM, use **kerosene**

para·gon /pærəgɒn/ (**paragons**) N-COUNT If you refer to someone as a **paragon**, you mean that they are perfect or have a lot of a good qualities. 完人; 杰出典范 ❑ *We don't expect candidates to be paragons of virtue.* 我们不指望候选人都是道德完人。 ❑ *Our administrator is a paragon of neatness, efficiency, and reliability.* 我们的管理者是整洁、高效、真实可信的杰出典范。

para·graph /pærəgræf/ (**paragraphs**) N-COUNT A **paragraph** is a section of a piece of writing. A paragraph always begins on a new line and contains at least one sentence. 段落 ❑ *The length of a paragraph depends on the information it conveys.* 段落的长度取决于它传达的信息。

par·al·lel /pærəlɛl/ (**parallels, paralleling, paralleled**) **1** N-COUNT If something has a **parallel**, it is similar to something else, but exists or happens in a different place or at a different time. If it has **no parallel** or is **without parallel**, it is not similar to anything else. (存在或发生在不同地点或不同时间的) 类似的事情 ❑ *Readers familiar with military conflict will find a vague parallel to the Vietnam War.* 熟悉军事冲突的读者们会发现一个和越南战争大致相似的事件。 ❑ *It's an ecological disaster with no parallel anywhere else in the world.* 这是一场世界其他任何地方均无等同的生态灾难。 **2** N-COUNT If there are **parallels** between two things, they are similar in some ways. 相似之处 ❑ *Detailed study of folk music from a variety of countries reveals many close parallels.* 对不同国家的民乐的详细研究表明它们有很多相似之处。 ❑ *There are significant parallels with the 1980s.* 与20世纪80年代有显著的相似之处。 **3** V-T If one thing **parallels** another, they happen at the same time or are similar, and often seem to be connected. 与…同时发生 ❑ *Often there are emotional reasons paralleling the financial ones.* 经济原因的常常伴有情感原因。 ❑ *His remarks paralleled those of the president.* 他的评论与总统的评论相同。 **4** ADJ **Parallel** events or situations happen at the same time as one another, or are similar to one another. 同时发生的; 相似的 ❑ *...parallel talks between the two countries' foreign ministers.* …两国外长之间相似的谈话。 ❑ *Their instincts do not always run parallel with ours.* 他们的直觉并不总是与我们的同步。 **5** ADJ If two lines, two objects, or two lines of movement are **parallel**, they are the same distance apart along their whole length. 平行的 ❑ *...seventy-two ships, drawn up in two parallel lines.* …72艘船，停靠成两条平行线。 ❑ *Remsen Street is parallel with Montague Street.* 雷姆森大街与蒙塔古大街是平行的。 **6** N-COUNT A **parallel** is an imaginary line round the earth that is parallel to the equator. Parallels are shown on maps. 纬线 [usu "the" ord N] ❑ *...the area south of the 38th parallel.* …38度纬线以南的地区。
→ see **globe**

Thesaurus *parallel* 另参见：
N. analogy, correlation, resemblance, similarity **1** **2**

★ **para·lyse** /pærəlaɪz/ [BRIT] → see **paralyze**

pa·raly·sis /pərælәsɪs/ **1** N-UNCOUNT **Paralysis** is the loss of the ability to move and feel in all or part of your body. 瘫痪 ❑ *...paralysis of the leg.* …腿部的瘫痪。 **2** N-UNCOUNT **Paralysis** is the state of being unable to act or function properly. 瘫痪状态 ❑ *The paralysis of the leadership leaves the army without its supreme command.* 领导层的瘫痪使得军队没有了最高统帅。

★ **para·lyze** /pærəlaɪz/ (**paralyzes, paralyzing, paralyzed**)

in BRIT, use **paralyse**

1 V-T If someone **is paralyzed** by an accident or an illness, they have no feeling in their body, or in part of their body, and are unable to move. 使瘫痪 ❑ *She is paralyzed from the waist down.* 她从腰部以下瘫痪。 ● **para·lyzed** ADJ 瘫痪的 ❑ *A guy with paralyzed legs is not*

P

supposed to ride horses. 一个双腿瘫痪的人不该骑马。 2 V-T If a person, place, or organization **is paralyzed by** something, they become unable to act or function properly. 使丧失活动能力 ❑ *The city has been virtually paralyzed by sudden snowstorms.* 这座城市实际上已因突降的暴雪而瘫痪。 ❑ *She was paralyzed by fear and love.* 她因为恐惧和爱而感到瘫痪。 ● **para·lyzed** ADJ 丧失活动能力的 ❑ *He sat in his chair, paralyzed with dread.* 他坐在他的椅子上，吓瘫了。

→ see **disability**

para·med·ic /pærəmɛdɪk/ (**paramedics**) N-COUNT A **paramedic** is a person whose training is similar to that of a nurse and who helps to do medical work. (医疗) 护理人员 ❑ *We intend to have a paramedic on every ambulance within the next three years.* 我们计划在今后的3年内在每辆救护车里配备一名护理人员。

★ **pa·ram·eter** /pəræmɪtər/ (**parameters**) N-COUNT **Parameters** are factors or limits that affect the way something can be done or made. 参数; 界限 [FORMAL] ❑ *...some of the parameters that determine the taste of a wine.* …一些决定葡萄酒味道的参数。

para·mili·tary /pærəmɪlɪtɛri/ (**paramilitaries**) 1 ADJ A **paramilitary** organization is organized like an army and performs either civil or military functions in a country. (组织) 准军事性的 [ADJ n] ❑ *Searches by the army and paramilitary forces have continued today.* 军队和准军事部队的搜索今天仍然继续着。 ● N-COUNT **Paramilitaries** are members of a paramilitary organization. 准军事组织成员 ❑ *Paramilitaries and army recruits patrolled the village.* 准军事组织成员和部队的新兵在村子里巡逻。 2 ADJ A **paramilitary** organization is an illegal group that is organized like an army. 非法军事组织的 [ADJ n] ❑ *...a law which said that all paramilitary groups must be disarmed.* …一个要求所有非法军事组织必须解除武装的法律。 ● N-COUNT **Paramilitaries** are members of an illegal paramilitary organization. 非法军事组织成员 ❑ *Paramilitaries were blamed for the shooting.* 非法军事组织成员因为这次开枪事件而遭谴责。

▲ **para·mount** /pærəmaʊnt/ ADJ Something that is **paramount** or of **paramount** importance is more important than anything else. 首要的 ❑ *The children's welfare must be seen as paramount.* 孩子们的福利必须被视为是最为重要的。

para·noia /pærənɔɪə/ 1 N-UNCOUNT If you say that someone suffers from **paranoia**, you think that they are too suspicious and afraid of other people. 多疑; 恐惧 ❑ *The mood is one of paranoia and expectation of war.* 这种情绪是一种对战争的恐惧和盼望。 2 N-UNCOUNT In psychology, if someone suffers from **paranoia**, they wrongly believe that other people are trying to harm them, or believe themselves to be much more important than they really are. 偏执狂; 妄想狂

para·noid /pærənɔɪd/ (**paranoids**) 1 ADJ If you say that someone is **paranoid**, you mean that they are extremely suspicious and afraid of other people. 多疑的; 恐惧的 ❑ *I'm not going to get paranoid about it.* 我不会对此过分猜疑的。 ❑ *...a paranoid politician who saw enemies all around him.* …一个把自己周围的人都视为敌人的多疑的政治家。 2 ADJ Someone who is **paranoid** suffers from the mental illness of paranoia. 患偏执狂的; 患妄想狂的 ❑ *...paranoid delusions.* …偏执狂的错觉。 ● N-COUNT A **paranoid** is someone who is paranoid. 偏执狂; 妄想狂 ❑ *...these sad, deluded paranoids.* …这些可悲的、被蒙蔽的妄想狂们。

para·pher·na·lia /pærəfərneɪlyə, -fəneɪl-/ N-UNCOUNT You can refer to a large number of objects that someone has with them or that are connected with a particular activity as **paraphernalia**. (与某活动有关的) 大量用品 ❑ *...a large courtyard full of builders' paraphernalia.* …一个充满建筑装备的大院子

para·phrase /pærəfreɪz/ (**paraphrases, paraphrasing, paraphrased**) 1 V-T If you **paraphrase** someone or **paraphrase** something that they have said or written, you express what they have said or written in a different way. 释义; 改述 ❑ *To paraphrase President Bush, we must restore confidence in our economic sector.* 布什总统的意思是，我们必须在我们的经济领域恢复自信。 ❑ *Baxter paraphrased the contents of the press release.* 巴克斯特解释了新闻发布的内容。 2 N-COUNT A **paraphrase** of something written or spoken is the same thing expressed in a different way. 释义; 改述 ❑ *The last two clauses were an exact quote rather than a paraphrase of Mr. Forth's remarks.* 最后两个分句是对福思先生言论的准确引用而不是改述。

para·plegic /pærəplidʒɪk/ (**paraplegics**) N-COUNT A **paraplegic** is someone who cannot move the lower half of their body, for example, because of an injury to their spine. 下身瘫痪者 ❑ *Theoretically, such equipment could help paraplegics regain movement.* 从理论上说，这样的器械可以帮助下身瘫痪者重新获得活动能力。 ● ADJ **Paraplegic** is also an adjective. 下身瘫痪的 ❑ *A passenger was injured so badly he will be paraplegic for the rest of his life.* 一名乘客受伤非常严重，他的后半生都将下身瘫痪。

★ **para·site** /pærəsaɪt/ (**parasites**) 1 N-COUNT A **parasite** is small animal or plant that lives on or inside a larger animal or plant, and gets its food from it. 寄生虫; 寄生植物 ❑ *Kangaroos harbor a vast range of parasites.* 袋鼠身上有各种各样的寄生虫。 2 N-COUNT If you disapprove of someone because you think that they get money or other things from other people but do not do anything in return, you can call them a **parasite**. 靠他人为生的人; 寄生虫 [DISAPPROVAL] ❑ *...a parasite, who produced nothing but lived on the work of others.* …一个什么都不做而靠他人的劳动为生的寄生虫。

para·sit·ic /pærəsɪtɪk/ also **parasitical** 1 ADJ **Parasitic** diseases are caused by parasites. 寄生生物引起的 ❑ *Will global warming mean the spread of tropical parasitic diseases?* 全球变暖将会意味着热带寄生虫病的传播吗？ 2 ADJ **Parasitic** animals and plants live on or inside larger animals or plants and get their food from them. 寄生的 ❑ *...tiny parasitic insects.* …微小的寄生昆虫。 3 ADJ If you describe a person or organization as **parasitic**, you mean that they get money or other things from people without doing anything in return. 寄生性的 [DISAPPROVAL] ❑ *...a parasitic new middle class of consultants and experts.* …由顾问和专家组成的新的寄生性的中产阶级。

para·troop·er /pærətrupər/ (**paratroopers**) N-COUNT **Paratroopers** are soldiers who are trained to be dropped by parachute into battle or into enemy territory. 伞兵

par·cel /pɑrsəl/ (**parcels**) 1 N-COUNT A **parcel** is something wrapped in paper, in a bag or large envelope, or in a box, usually so that it can be sent to someone by mail. 包裹; 邮包 ❑ *They also sent parcels of food and clothing.* 他们还寄送了成包的食物和衣物。 2 PHRASE If you say that something is **part and parcel of** something else, you are emphasizing that it is involved or included in it. 重要部分 [EMPHASIS] ❑ *Learning about life in a new culture is part and parcel of what newcomers to America face.* 学习在一种新的文化中生活是每一个新来美国的人要面对的事情中的重要部分。

parched /pɑrtʃt/ 1 ADJ If something, especially the ground or a plant, is **parched**, it is very dry, because there has been no rain. 干透的 ❑ *The clouds gathered and showers poured down upon the parched earth.* 云聚积起来，大雨倾泄在干透了的大地上。 2 ADJ If your mouth, throat, or lips are **parched**, they are unpleasantly dry. 干的 ❑ *Her throat was parched, and she was exhausted from all the walking.* 她的喉咙发干，走了那么多路后筋疲力尽了。 3 ADJ If you say that you are **parched**, you mean that you are very thirsty. 干渴的 [v-link ADJ] [INFORMAL] ❑ *When I told them I was parched, they went and got me a bottle of mineral water.* 当我跟他们说我口渴时，他们去给我拿了一瓶矿泉水。

Word Link *don ≈ giving : donate, donor, pardon*

par·don /pɑrdən/ (**pardons, pardoning, pardoned**) 1 CONVENTION You say **Pardon?, I beg your pardon?**, or **Pardon me?** when you want someone to repeat what they have just said because you have not heard or understood it. (表示没有听见或不明白，请求重说一遍) 对不起 [SPOKEN, FORMULAE] ❑ *"Will you let me open it?"—"Pardon?"—"Can I open it?"* "让我来打开它，好吗？"——"对不起，你说什么？"——"我能打开它吗？" 2 CONVENTION People say "**I beg your pardon?**" when they are surprised or offended by something that someone has just said. (表示惊讶或者受了冒犯) 什么 [SPOKEN, FEELINGS] ❑ *"Would you get undressed, please?"—"I beg your pardon?"—"Will you get undressed?"* "请你脱下衣服，好吗？"——"什么？"——"你能脱下衣服吗？" 3 CONVENTION You say "**I beg your pardon**" as a way of apologizing for accidentally doing something wrong, such as disturbing someone or making a mistake. 对不起 [SPOKEN, FORMULAE] ❑ *I beg your pardon. I thought you were someone else.* 对不起，我把你当成别人了。 4 CONVENTION Some people say "**Pardon me**" instead of "Excuse me" when they want to politely get someone's attention or interrupt them. 对不起 (以引起注意或者打断一下) [SPOKEN, FORMULAE] ❑ *Pardon me, are you finished, madam?* 对不起，您好了吗，太太？ 5 V-T If someone who has been found guilty of a crime **is pardoned**, they are officially allowed to go free and are not punished. 赦免 [usu passive] ❑ *Hundreds of political prisoners were pardoned and released.* 许多政治犯被赦免和释放了。 ● N-COUNT **Pardon** is also a noun. 赦免 ❑ *They lobbied the government on his behalf and he was granted a presidential pardon.* 他们为他游说政府，他因之得到了总统特赦。

P

pare /pɛər/ (**pares, paring, pared**) **1** V-T When you **pare** something, or **pare** part of it **off** or **away**, you cut off its skin or its outer layer. 削皮；去掉…外层 ❑ *Pare the brown skin from the meat with a very sharp knife.* 用一把非常锋利的刀削掉肉上褐色的皮。 ❑ *He took out a slab of cheese, pared off a slice and ate it hastily.* 他拿出厚厚的一块奶酪，切下一片急匆匆地吃了。 **2** V-T If you **pare** something **down** or **back**, or if you **pare** it, you reduce it. 削减 ❑ *The governor's campaign fund could be pared down to $500.* 州长竞选活动基金可能会被削减到$500。 ❑ *The luxury tax won't really do much to pare down the budget deficit.* 奢侈品税不能真的在削减预算赤字上起到多大作用。

par·ent ♦♦♦ /pɛərənt, pær-/ (**parents**) **1** N-COUNT Your **parents** are your mother and father. 父母亲 ❑ *Children need their parents.* 孩子们需要父母。 ❑ *This is where a lot of parents go wrong.* 正是在这一点上许多父母都错了。 **2** → see also **single parent** **3** ADJ An organization's **parent** organization is the organization that created it and usually still controls it. 创始的（组织）；母（公司）[ADJ n] ❑ *Each unit including the parent company has its own, local management.* 每家单位，包括母公司，都有自己的地方管理层。
→ see **child**

▲ **par·ent·age** /pɛərəntɪdʒ, pær-/ N-UNCOUNT Your **parentage** is the identity and origins of your parents. For example, if you are of Greek **parentage**, your parents are Greek. 出身 [oft "of" adj N] ❑ *...children of mixed parentage.* …混血儿童。

★ **pa·ren·tal** /pərɛntᵊl/ ADJ **Parental** is used to describe something that relates to parents in general, or to one or both of the parents of a particular child. 父母的；父或母的 ❑ *Medical treatment was sometimes given to children without parental consent.* 有时候没有征得父母的同意就对孩子进行了医疗救治。

pa·ren·tal leave N-UNCOUNT **Parental leave** is time away from work, usually without pay, that parents are allowed in order to care for their children. 产假 [BUSINESS] ❑ *Parents are entitled to 13 weeks' parental leave to be taken during the first five years of a child's life.* 孩子出生后的头5年父母有权享受13周的产假。

▲ **pa·ren·thesis** /pərɛnθəsɪs/ (**parentheses** /pərɛnθəsiz/) N-COUNT **Parentheses** are a pair of curved marks that you put around words or numbers to indicate that they are additional, separate, or less important. (This sentence is in parentheses.) 括号

par·ent·hood /pɛərənthʊd, pær-/ N-UNCOUNT **Parenthood** is the state of being a parent. 父母的身份 ❑ *She may feel unready for the responsibilities of parenthood.* 她可能觉得还没有准备好担当人母的责任。

par·ent·ing /pɛərəntɪŋ, pær-/ N-UNCOUNT **Parenting** is the activity of bringing up and taking care of your child. 养育子女 ❑ *Parenting is not fully valued by society.* 养育子女还没有得到社会的充分重视。

P

▲ **par·ish** /pærɪʃ/ (**parishes**) **1** N-COUNT A **parish** is part of a city or town that has its own Catholic church and priest. 教区 ❑ *...Good Shepherd, a parish of about 450 members.* …古德谢泼德，一个有着约四百五十人的教区。 ❑ *...a parish priest.* …一个教区牧师。 **2** N-COUNT In some parts of the United States, a **parish** is a small region within a state which has its own local government. （在美国的某些地区）地方行政区 [AM] ❑ *...the middle-class parishes of northern Louisiana.* …北路易斯安那的中产阶级行政区。

par·ity /pærɪti/ N-UNCOUNT If there is **parity** between two things, they are equal. 平等；相等 [FORMAL] ❑ *Women have yet to achieve wage or occupational parity in many fields.* 妇女们在许多领域尚有待获得薪酬或职业的平等。

park ♦♦◇ /pɑrk/ (**parks, parking, parked**) **1** N-COUNT A **park** is a public area of land with grass and trees, usually in a town, where people go in order to relax and enjoy themselves. 公园 ❑ *...Central Park.* …中央公园。 ❑ *...a brisk walk with the dog around the park.* …带着狗在公园里的一次轻快的散步。 **2** N-COUNT You can refer to a place where a particular activity is carried out as a **park**. （作为专用场地的）…区；…园 [supp N] ❑ *...a science and technology park.* …一个科技园。 **3** V-T/V-I When you **park** a vehicle or **park** somewhere, you drive the vehicle into a position where it can stay for a period of time, and leave it there. 停车 ❑ *Greenfield turned into the next side street and parked.* 格林菲尔德拐进下一个小巷停了车。 ❑ *He found a place to park the car.* 他找到了一个停车的地方。 ❑ *Ben parked across the street.* 本把车停到了街对面。 **4** V-T If you **park yourself** somewhere, you sit there. 坐下 [INFORMAL] ❑ *Every Friday, I would park myself in front of the TV.* 每个周五，我都会坐在电视前。 **5** → see also **ballpark, national park**
→ see Word Web: **park**

> Note that you do not use the word "parking" to refer to a place where cars are parked. Instead, you talk about a **parking lot** in American English and a **car park** in British English. **Parking** is used only to refer to the action of parking your car, or to the state of being parked. ❑ *...a "No Parking" sign.*

park·ing /pɑrkɪŋ/ **1** N-UNCOUNT **Parking** is the action of moving a vehicle into a place in a garage or by the side of the road where it can be left. 停车 ❑ *In many towns parking is allowed only on one side of the street.* 在很多小镇里，只能允许在街道的一侧停车。 **2** N-UNCOUNT **Parking** is space for parking a vehicle in. 停车位 ❑ *Cars allowed, but parking is limited.* 汽车可以得到，但是停车位是有限的。

park·ing gar·age (**parking garages**) N-COUNT A **parking garage** is a building where people can leave their cars. 车库 [AM]
in BRIT, use **car park, multi-storey car park**
❑ *...a multi-level parking garage.* …一个多层车库。

park·ing lot (**parking lots**) N-COUNT A **parking lot** is an area of ground where people can leave their cars. 停车场 [AM]
in BRIT, use **car park**
❑ *A block up the street I found a parking lot.* 在街道北边的一个街区我找到了一个停车场。

park·ing me·ter (**parking meters**) N-COUNT A **parking meter** is a device that you put money into when you park in a parking space. 停车收费器

par·lia·ment ♦♦◇ /pɑrləmənt/ (**parliaments**) also **Parliament** **1** N-COUNT; N-PROPER The **parliament** of some countries is the group of people who make or change its laws, and decide what policies the country should follow. 议会 ❑ *The Bangladesh Parliament today approved the policy, but it has not yet become law.* 孟加拉共和国议会今天批准了这项政策，但它还没有成为法律。 **2** → see also **Member of Parliament** **3** N-COUNT A particular **parliament** is a particular period of time in which a parliament is doing its work, between two elections or between two periods of vacation. 一届议会的任期；（两次大选之间的）一届议会 ❑ *The legislation is expected to be passed in the next parliament.* 这项法规有望在下届议会中通过。

★ **par·lia·men·ta·ry** ♦◇◇ /pɑrləmɛntəri/ ADJ **Parliamentary** is used to describe things that are connected with a parliament or with members of parliament. 议会的；议员的 [ADJ n] ❑ *He used his*

Word Web **park**

In 1858, Central Park* became the first planned urban **park** in the United States. At first only a few wealthy families lived close enough to enjoy it. Today over 20 million visitors of all ages and backgrounds use the park for **recreation** each year. Children love the many **playgrounds**, the **carousel**, and the petting **zoo**. Families spread blankets on the grass for **picnics**. Couples row around the lake in rented rowboats. Seniors **stroll** through the **gardens**. Players fill the **tennis courts** and baseball diamonds all summer. **Cyclists** and **runners** use Central Park Drive* when it's closed to car traffic on weekends.

Central Park: an 843-acre park in New York City.
Central Park Drive: a road in Central Park.

influence to make sure she was not selected as a parliamentary candidate. 他利用自己的影响来确保她不会被选为议员候选人。

▲ **par·lor** /pɑrlər/ (**parlors**)

in BRIT, use **parlour**

N-COUNT **Parlor** is used in the names of some types of stores that provide a service, rather than selling things. (提供服务而不卖货物的) 店堂 [N N] ❑ *...a funeral parlor.* …一家殡仪馆。

▲ **par·lour** /pɑːˈləʳ/ [BRIT] → see **parlor**

pa·ro·chial /pəroʊkiəl/ **1** ADJ If you describe someone as **parochial**, you are critical of them because you think they are too concerned with their own affairs and should be thinking about more important things. 思想偏狭的 [DISAPPROVAL] ❑ *When her brother arrives home on a visit from Hong Kong, he sneers at her parochial existence.* 她哥哥从香港回家探访时，讥笑她偏狭的生活方式。 **2** ADJ **Parochial** is used to describe things that relate to the parish connected with a particular church. 教区的 [ADJ n] ❑ *She was a secretary on the local parochial church council.* 她是当地教区教堂理事会的秘书。 ❑ *Their children attend a Jewish parochial school.* 他们的孩子在一所犹太教区学校上学。

paro·dy /pærədi/ (**parodies, parodying, parodied**) **1** N-VAR A **parody** is a humorous piece of writing, drama, or music that imitates the style of a well-known person or represents a familiar situation in an exaggerated way. 滑稽模仿作品 (指文章、戏剧、音乐作品的滑稽模仿作) ❑ *It was like a parody of the balcony scene from Romeo and Juliet.* 它就像《罗密欧与朱丽叶》阳台上那一幕的模仿作。 **2** V-T When someone **parodies** a particular work, thing, or person, they imitate it in an amusing or exaggerated way. 夸张地演绎；滑稽地模仿 ❑ *...a sketch parodying the views of Donald Rumsfeld.* …一部夸张地演绎唐纳德·拉姆斯菲尔德观点的滑稽短剧。

▲ **pa·role** /pəroʊl/ (**paroles, paroling, paroled**) **1** N-UNCOUNT If a prisoner is given **parole**, he or she is released before the official end of their prison sentence and has to promise to behave well. 假释 ❑ *Although sentenced to life, he will become eligible for parole after serving 10 years.* 尽管被判无期，服刑10年后他将有资格获得假释。 ❑ *...a parole violation.* …一次假释违纪。 ● PHRASE If a prisoner is **on parole**, he or she is released before the official end of their prison sentence and will not be sent back to prison if their behavior is good. 获假释 **2** V-T If a prisoner **is paroled**, he or she is given parole. 获假释 [usu passive] ❑ *He faces at most 12 years in prison and could be paroled after eight years.* 他面临最多12年的监禁，可以在8年后获得假释。

▲ **par·rot** /pærət/ (**parrots, parroting, parroted**) **1** N-COUNT A **parrot** is a tropical bird with a curved beak and brightly-colored or gray feathers. Parrots can be kept as pets. Some parrots are able to copy what people say. 鹦鹉 **2** V-T If you disapprove of the fact that someone is just repeating what someone else has said, often without really understanding it, you can say that they **are parroting** it. 鹦鹉学舌般地重复 [DISAPPROVAL] ❑ *Generations of students have learned to parrot the standard explanations.* 一届又一届的学生学会了鹦鹉学舌般地重复标准的解释。

pars·ley /pɑrsli/ N-UNCOUNT **Parsley** is a small plant with curly leaves that are used for flavoring or decorating food. 欧芹 ❑ *...rice with fresh parsley.* …米饭加新鲜的欧芹。

pars·nip /pɑrsnɪp/ (**parsnips**) N-COUNT A **parsnip** is a long cream-colored root vegetable. 欧洲防风草

Word Link *par ≈ equal : compare, disparate, part*

part
❶ NOUN USES, QUANTIFIER USES, AND PHRASES
❷ VERB USES

❶ **part** ♦♦♦ /pɑrt/ (**parts**)

➪ **Please look at meaning 16 to see if the expression you are looking for is shown under another headword.** **1** N-COUNT A **part of** something is one of the pieces, sections, or elements that it consists of. 部分 ❑ *I like that part of Cape Town.* 我喜欢开普敦的那个地方。 ❑ *Respect is a very important part of any relationship.* 尊重是任何一种人际关系中非常重要的部分。 **2** N-COUNT A **part** for a machine or vehicle is one of the smaller pieces that is used to make it. 零件 ❑ *...spare parts for military equipment.* …军事设备的备用零件。 **3** QUANT **Part of** something is some of it. 一部分 ❑ *It was a very severe accident and he lost part of his foot.* 那是一起严重的事故，他的一只脚残了。 ❑ *Perry spent part of his childhood in Canada.* 佩里在加拿大度过了童年的部分时光。 **4** ADV If you say that something is **part** one thing, **part** another, you mean that it is to some extent the first thing and to some extent the second thing. 一半 ❑ *The television producer today has to be part news person, part educator.* 今天的电视制作人必须一半是新闻人，一半是教育者。 **5** N-COUNT You can use **part** when you are talking about the proportions of substances in a mixture. For example, if you are told to use five **parts** water to one **part** paint, the mixture should contain five times as much water as paint. (等分中的) 一份 ❑ *Use turpentine and linseed oil, three parts to two.* 用松节油和亚麻籽油，三份松节油兑两份亚麻籽油。 **6** N-COUNT A **part** in a play or movie is one of the roles in it which an actor or actress can perform. 角色 ❑ *Alf Sjoberg offered her a large part in the play he was directing.* 阿尔夫·肖博格在他执导的戏里给了她一个重要角色。 ❑ *He was just right for the part.* 他正好适合那个角色。 **7** N-SING Your **part in** something that happens is your involvement in it. 参与 [poss N "in" n] ❑ *If only he could conceal his part in the accident.* 如果他能掩盖他在那次事故中有份参与就好了。 ❑ *He felt a sense of relief that his part in this business was now over.* 他在这项业务的部分现在结束了，他感到如释重负。 **8** N-UNCOUNT If something or someone is **part of a** group or organization, they belong to it or are included in it. 成员 [also "a" N, N "of" n] ❑ *Annie had never been part of the in-crowd.* 安妮从未成为那个小圈子的一员。 **9** N-COUNT The **part** in someone's hair is the line running from the front to the back of their head where their hair lies in different directions. 分发线 [AM]

in BRIT, use **parting**

❑ *The straight white part in her ebony hair seemed to divide the back of her head in half.* 她乌黑头发中笔直的白色分发线似乎把她的后脑勺分成了两半。 **10** PHRASE If something or someone **plays** a large or important **part in** an event or situation, they are very involved in it and have an important effect on what happens. 起作用 ❑ *These days work plays an important part in a single woman's life.* 现今，工作在一个单身妇女的生活中起着重要作用。 **11** PHRASE If you **take part in** an activity, you do it together with other people. 参加 ❑ *Thousands of students have taken part in demonstrations.* 成千上万的学生参加了游行。 **12** PHRASE If you **do** your **part**, you do something that, to a small or limited extent, helps to achieve something. 尽你的本分；做你应该做的 ❑ *Each of you is going to have to do your part in keeping the community crime-free.* 你们每一个人都要尽自己的本分，让社区内没有犯罪。 **13** PHRASE When you are describing people's thoughts or actions, you can say **for** her **part** or **for** my **part**, for example, to introduce what a particular person thinks or does. 就某人而言 [FORMAL] ❑ *For my part, I feel elated and close to tears.* 就我而言，我感觉兴高采烈，都快哭出来了。 **14** PHRASE If you talk about a feeling or action **on** someone's **part**, you are referring to something that they feel or do. 某人所做的 ❑ *...techniques on their part to keep us from knowing exactly what's going on.* …他们那些防止我们确切了解事态进展的技术。 ❑ *There is no need for any further instructions on my part.* 我不需要做任何进一步的指示。 **15** PHRASE You use **in part** to indicate that something exists or happens to some extent but not completely. 在某种程度上 [FORMAL] ❑ *The levels of blood glucose depend in part on what you eat and when you eat.* 血糖水平在一定程度上依赖于你吃什么及什么时候吃。 **16** **part and parcel** → see **parcel**

❷ **part** ♦◇◇ /pɑrt/ (**parts, parting, parted**) **1** V-T/V-I If things that are next to each other **part** or if you **part** them, they move in opposite directions, so that there is a space between them. 分开 ❑ *Her lips parted as if she were about to take a deep breath.* 她张开了嘴，好像要做深呼吸。 **2** V-T If you **part** your hair in the middle or at one side, you make it lie in two different directions so that there is a straight line running from the front of your head to the back. 把 (头发) 分开 ❑ *Picking up a brush, Joanna parted her hair.* 拿起一把刷子，乔安娜把头发分开了。 **3** V-RECIP When two people **part**, or if one person **parts from** another, they leave each other. 分手 [FORMAL] ❑ *He gave me the envelope and we parted.* 他把信封给我，我们就分手了。 **4** V-RECIP If you **are parted from** someone you love, you are prevented from being with them. 被分开 ❑ *I don't believe Laverne and I will ever be parted.* 我相信拉弗内和我永远都不会分开。 **5** → see also **parting**

▸ **part with** PHRASAL VERB If you **part with** something that is valuable or that you would prefer to keep, you give it or sell it to someone else. 送掉；卖掉 ❑ *Buyers might require further assurances before parting with their cash.* 买主在付款前也许需要更多的保证。

Thesaurus *part* 另参见：
N. component, fraction, half, ingredient, piece, portion, section; (*ant.*) entirety, whole ❶ 1
role, share ❶ 7
V. break up, separate, split, tear ❷ 3

par·tial /pɑrʃəl/ 1 ADJ You use **partial** to refer to something that is not complete or whole. 部分的 ❑ *He managed to reach a partial agreement with both republics.* 他设法跟两个共和国达成了部分共识。 ❑ *...a partial ban on the use of cars in the city.* …城市内部分地区禁止使用轿车。 2 ADJ If you are **partial to** something, you like it. 偏爱的 [v-link ADJ "to" n/-ing] ❑ *He's partial to sporty women with blue eyes.* 他对蓝眼睛的、运动型的女人是偏爱的。 ❑ *Mollie confesses she is rather partial to pink.* 莫莉承认她对粉红色是相当偏爱的。 3 ADJ Someone who is **partial** supports a particular person or thing, for example, in a competition or dispute, instead of being completely fair. 偏袒的 [v-link ADJ] ❑ *I might be accused of being partial.* 我可能会被人指责是偏袒的。

par·tial·ly /pɑrʃəli/ ADV If something happens or exists **partially**, it happens or exists to some extent, but not completely. 在一定程度上地 [ADV with cl/group] ❑ *Lisa is deaf in one ear and partially blind.* 莉萨一只耳朵聋了，并且在一定程度上失明了。

★ **par·tici·pant** /pɑrtɪsɪpənt/ (**participants**) N-COUNT The **participants** in an activity are the people who take part in it. 参加者 ❑ *40 of the course participants are offered employment with the company.* 参加课程学习的人中有40名得到了在该公司工作的机会。

par·tici·pate ♦◇◇ /pɑrtɪsɪpeɪt/ (**participates, participating, participated**) V-I If you **participate in** an activity, you take part in it. 参加 ❑ *They expected him to participate in the ceremony.* 他们希望他参加这个典礼。 ❑ *Over half the population of this country participate in sports.* 这个国家一半以上的人参加体育运动。 ● **par·tici·pa·tion** /pɑrtɪsɪpeɪʃən/ N-UNCOUNT 参加 ❑ *...participation in religious activities.* …对宗教活动的参与。

Thesaurus *participate* 另参见：
V. compete, cooperate, join in, partake, perform, share; (*ant.*) observe

par·ti·ci·ple /pɑrtɪsɪpəl/ (**participles**) N-COUNT In grammar, a **participle** is a form of a verb that can be used in compound tenses of the verb. There are two participles in English: the past participle, which usually ends in "-ed," and the present participle, which ends in "-ing." 分词

P

Word Link *cle ≈ small : article, cubicle, particle*

par·ti·cle /pɑrtɪkəl/ (**particles**) 1 N-COUNT A **particle of** something is a very small piece or amount of it. 微粒；极小量 ❑ *...a particle of hot metal.* …热金属微粒。 ❑ *There is a particle of truth in his statement.* 在他的声明中只有极少的事实。 2 N-COUNT In physics, a **particle** is a piece of matter smaller than an atom such as an electron or a proton. 粒子 [TECHNICAL] ❑ *...the sub-atomic particles that make up matter.* …构成物质的次原子微粒。
→ see **lightning**

par·ticu·lar ♦♦◇ /pərtɪkyələr/ 1 ADJ You use **particular** to emphasize that you are talking about one thing or one kind of thing rather than other similar ones. 专指的 [ADJ n] [EMPHASIS] ❑ *I remembered a particular story about a mailman who was a murderer.* 我记得一个故事，关于一个邮递员是杀人犯。 ❑ *I have to know exactly why it is I'm doing a particular job.* 我必须确切地知道我为什么做某项工作。 2 ADJ If a person or thing has a **particular** quality or possession, it is distinct and belongs only to them. 独特的 [ADJ n] ❑ *I have a particular responsibility to ensure I make the right decision.* 我有特别责任要确保做出正确的决定。 3 ADJ You can use **particular** to emphasize that something is greater or more intense than usual. 非同寻常的 [ADJ n] [EMPHASIS] ❑ *Particular emphasis will be placed on oral language training.* 口语训练将给予非同寻常的重视。 4 ADJ If you say that someone is **particular**, you mean that they choose things and do things very carefully, and are not easily satisfied. 挑剔的 ❑ *Ted was very particular about the colors he used.* 特德对于他使用的颜色是非常挑剔的。 5 → see also **particulars** 6 PHRASE You use **in particular** to indicate that what you are saying applies especially to one thing or person. 特别 ❑ *The situation in Ethiopia in particular is worrisome.* 埃塞俄比亚的局势特别令人担忧。 ❑ *Why should he notice her car in particular?* 他为什么要特别注意她的轿车呢？

Thesaurus *particular* 另参见：
ADJ. distinct, precise, specific; (*ant.*) general 1 2
choosy, finicky, demanding, fussy, picky; (*ant.*) easygoing, laid-back 4

par·ticu·lar·ly ♦♦◇ /pərtɪkyələrli/ 1 ADV You use **particularly** to indicate that what you are saying applies especially to one thing or situation. 特别 [ADV with cl/group] ❑ *Keep your office space looking good, particularly your desk.* 保持你办公的地方整洁美观，特别是办公桌。 ❑ *More local employment will be created, particularly in service industries.* 更多的面向当地的就业将被创造出来，尤其是在服务业。 2 ADV **Particularly** means more than usual or more than other things. 格外；异乎寻常地 [ADV with cl/group] [EMPHASIS] ❑ *Progress has been particularly disappointing.* 进展一直格外令人失望。

par·ticu·lars /pərtɪkyələrz/ N-PLURAL The **particulars** of something or someone are facts or details about them that are written down and kept as a record. 细节；详情 ❑ *You will find all the particulars in Chapter 9.* 你将在第9章里读到所有的细节。

part·ing /pɑrtɪŋ/ (**partings**) 1 N-VAR **Parting** is the act of leaving a particular person or place. A **parting** is an occasion when this happens. 离别 ❑ *Parting from any one of you for even a short time is hard.* 与你们当中的任何一个人离别，即使是很短的时间，也很令人难过。 2 ADJ Your **parting** words or actions are the things that you say or do as you are leaving a place or person. 离别的 [ADJ n] ❑ *Her parting words left him feeling empty and alone.* 她离别的话让他感到空虚、孤单。 3 N-COUNT The **parting** in someone's hair is the line running from the front to the back of their head where their hair lies in different directions. (头发的) 分缝 [BRIT]
in AM, use **part**

▲ **par·ti·san** /pɑrtɪzən/ (**partisans**) 1 ADJ Someone who is **partisan** strongly supports a particular person or cause, often without thinking carefully about the matter. 盲目拥护的 ❑ *He is clearly too partisan to be a referee.* 他明显地过于偏袒，不适合担任裁判。 2 N-COUNT **Partisans** are ordinary people, rather than soldiers, who join together to fight enemy soldiers who are occupying their country. 游击队员 ❑ *He was rescued by some Italian partisans.* 他被一些意大利游击队员救了。

★ **par·ti·tion** /pɑrtɪʃən/ (**partitions, partitioning, partitioned**) 1 N-COUNT A **partition** is a wall, screen, or divider that separates one part of a room, vehicle, or other space from another. 隔断 ❑ *...new offices divided only by glass partitions.* …仅仅用玻璃隔板隔开的新办公室。 2 V-T If you **partition** a room, you separate one part of it from another by means of a partition. (用隔断) 隔开 ❑ *Bedrooms have again been created by partitioning a single larger room.* 通过用隔断分隔一间大房，几间卧室又被创造出来。 3 V-T If a country **is partitioned**, it is divided into two or more independent countries. 分割 ❑ *Korea was partitioned in 1945.* 朝鲜是1945年被分割的。 ❑ *...Churchill's plans to partition the German state.* …丘吉尔分割德国的计划。 ● N-UNCOUNT **Partition** is also a noun. 分裂 ❑ *...fighting which followed the partition of India.* …印度分裂后的争斗。

part·ly ♦◇◇ /pɑrtli/ ADV You use **partly** to indicate that something happens or exists to some extent, but not completely. 在一定程度上 [ADV with cl/group] ❑ *It's partly my fault.* 在一定程度上是我的错。 ❑ *I have not worried so much this year, partly because I have had other things to think about.* 今年我不那么担心了，在一定程度上是因为我还有其他的事情要考虑。

part·ner ♦♦◇ /pɑrtnər/ (**partners, partnering, partnered**) 1 N-COUNT Your **partner** is the person you are married to or are having a romantic or sexual relationship with. 配偶；情人；性伴侣 ❑ *Wanting other friends doesn't mean you don't love your partner.* 需要其他朋友并不意味着你不爱你的伴侣。 2 N-COUNT Your **partner** is the person you are doing something with, for example, dancing with or playing with in a game against two other people. 搭档 ❑ *...to dance with a partner.* …与一名搭档跳舞。 ❑ *Her partner for the game was Venus Williams.* 她的比赛搭档是维纳斯•威廉姆斯。 3 N-COUNT The **partners** in a firm or business are the people who share the ownership of it. 合伙人 [BUSINESS] ❑ *He's a partner in a Chicago law firm.* 他是芝加哥一家律师事务所的合伙人。 4 N-COUNT The **partner** of a country or organization is another country or organization with which they work or do business. 盟友 ❑ *Spain has been one of Cuba's major trading partners.* 西班牙一直是古巴的主要贸易伙伴之一。 5 V-T If you **partner** someone, you are their partner in a game or in a dance. 与…搭档 ❑ *He had partnered the famous*

Russian ballerina. 他曾与著名的俄罗斯芭蕾舞女演员搭挡。 ❑ *He will be partnered by Ian Baker, the defending champion.* 他将与卫冕冠军伊恩•贝克搭档。

▲ **part·ner·ship** ♦◇◇ /pɑrtnərʃɪp/ (**partnerships**) N-VAR **Partnership** or a **partnership** is a relationship in which two or more people, organizations, or countries work together as partners. 伙伴关系 ❑ *...the partnership between Germany's banks and its businesses.* …德国的各银行与德国企业之间的伙伴关系。

part-time

> The adverb is also spelled **part time.**

ADJ If someone is a **part-time** worker or has a **part-time** job, they work for only part of each day or week. 部分时间的; 兼职的 ❑ *Many businesses are cutting back by employing lower-paid part-time workers.* 许多商家正通过雇佣低工资的兼职工来削减开支。 ❑ *Part-time work is generally hard to find.* 兼职工作一般很难找。 ● ADV **Part-time** is also an adverb. 部分时间地; 兼职地 [ADV after v] ❑ *I want to work part-time.* 我想做兼职。

par·ty ♦♦♦ /pɑrti/ (**parties, partying, partied**) **1** N-COUNT A **party** is a political organization whose members have similar aims and beliefs. Usually the organization tries to get its members elected to the legislature of a country. 政党 ❑ *...a member of the Republican Party.* …一名共和党党员。 ❑ *...opposition parties.* …反对党们。 **2** N-COUNT A **party** is a social event, often in someone's home, at which people enjoy themselves doing things such as eating, drinking, dancing, talking, or playing games. 派对 ❑ *The couple met at a party.* 这对夫妇相识于一个派对。 ❑ *We threw a huge birthday party.* 我们举办了一次盛大的生日派对。 **3** V-I If you **party**, you enjoy yourself doing things such as going out to parties, drinking, dancing, and talking to people. 尽情欢乐 ❑ *They come to eat and drink, to swim, to party.* 他们来吃饭、喝酒、游泳，尽情欢乐。 **4** N-COUNT A **party of** people is a group of people who are doing something together, for example, traveling together. 群; 队; 组 ❑ *They became separated from their party.* 他们跟他们团队走散了。 ❑ *...a party of sightseers.* …一群游客。 **5** → see also **search party** **6** N-COUNT One of the people involved in a legal agreement or dispute can be referred to as a particular **party.** (契约或争论的)一方 [LEGAL] ❑ *It has to be proved that they are the guilty party.* 尚需证明他们是有过错的一方。 ❑ *...he was the injured party.* …他是受害方。 **7** PHRASE Someone who **is a party to** or **is party to** an action or agreement is involved in it, and therefore partly responsible for it. 参与 ❑ *You were the one that brought up the idea of blackmail. I'd never be a party to such a thing.* 你是那个提出敲诈主意的人。我从来没想过参与这种事。

Word Partnership *party* 的常用搭配:

V. **form** a party, **join** a party, **vote for** a party **1**
attend/go to a party, **have/host/throw** a party, **invite** *someone* **to** a party **2**

N. party **officials, opposition** party, party **platform** **1**
birthday party, **victory** party **2**
wedding party **4**

ADJ. **governing** party, **political** party **1**
responsible party **6**

pass

❶ VERB USES
❷ NOUN USES
❸ PHRASAL VERBS

❶ **pass** ♦♦♦ /pæs/ (**passes, passing, passed**)
➪ **Please look at meanings 21 and 22 to see if the expression you are looking for is shown under another headword.** **1** V-T/V-I To **pass** someone or something means to go past them without stopping. 经过 ❑ *As she passed the library door, the telephone began to ring.* 她经过图书馆门口时，电话开始响铃了。 ❑ *Jane stood aside to let her pass.* 简站到一边让她过去。 ❑ *I sat in the park, and watched the passing cars.* 我座在公园，观察经过的汽车。 **2** V-I When someone or something **passes** in a particular direction, they move in that direction. 穿过 ❑ *He passed through the doorway into the kitchen.* 他穿过门道去厨房。 ❑ *He passed down the tunnel.* 他穿过隧道。 **3** V-I If something such as a road or pipe **passes** along a particular route, it goes along that route. (沿某路线) 穿过 ❑ *A dirt road passes through the town.* 一条土路穿过那座城镇。 ❑ *The road passes a farm.* 该公路经过一个农场。 **4** V-T If you **pass** something through, over, or around something else, you move or push it through, over, or around that thing. 穿; 越; 绕 ❑ *She passed the needle through the rough cloth, back and forth.* 她用针在那块粗布上来来回回地穿进穿出。 ❑ *"I don't understand," the detective mumbled, passing a hand through his hair.* "我不明白，"那个侦探嘟囔着，同时用一只手捋头发。 **5** V-T If you **pass** something **to** someone, you take it in your hand and give it to them. 传递 ❑ *Ken passed the books to Sergeant Wong.* 肯把那些书递给了黄巡佐。 ❑ *Pass me that bottle.* 把那个瓶子递给我。 **6** V-T/V-I If something **passes** or **is passed from** one person **to** another, the second person then has it instead of the first. 转给 ❑ *His mother's small estate had passed to him after her death.* 他母亲死后，微薄的财产转给了他。 ❑ *These powers were eventually passed to municipalities.* 这些权力最终转给了市政当局。 **7** V-T If you **pass** information **to** someone, you give it to them because it concerns them. 传达 ❑ *Officials failed to pass vital information to their superiors.* 官员们没能把重要情报传达给他们的上司。 ● PHRASAL VERB **Pass on** means the same as **pass.** 传达 ❑ *I do not know what to do with the information if I cannot pass it on.* 如果无法传送出去，我不知道该拿这情报怎么办。 ❑ *From time to time he passed on confidential information to him.* 他不时地传送机密情报给他。 **8** V-T/V-I If you **pass,** or **pass** the ball **to** someone on your team in a game such as football or basketball, you throw it to them. 传(球) 给 ❑ *Your partner should then pass the ball back to you.* 你的伙伴该把球回传给你。 **9** V-I When a period of time **passes,** it happens and finishes. (时间) 消逝 ❑ *He couldn't imagine why he had let so much time pass without contacting her.* 他想像不出为什么他这么长时间没跟她联系。 ❑ *As the years passed he felt trapped by certain realities of marriage.* 随着岁月的流逝，他感到受困于某些婚姻的现实情况。 **10** V-T If you **pass** a period of time in a particular way, you spend it in that way. 消磨 (时间) ❑ *The children passed the time playing in the streets.* 孩子们在街上玩耍消磨时间。 **11** V-I If you **pass through** a stage of development or a period of time, you experience it. 经历 ❑ *The country was passing through a grave crisis.* 那个国家正经历着一场严重的危机。 **12** V-T If an amount **passes** a particular total or level, it becomes greater than that total or level. 超过 ❑ *They became the first company in their field to pass the $2 billion turn-over mark.* 他们成为他们那个领域第一家市场营业额超过$20亿的公司。 **13** V-T If someone or something **passes** a test, they are considered to be of an acceptable standard. 通过 (考试) ❑ *Kevin has just passed his driving test.* 凯文刚刚通过驾驶考试。 ❑ *...new drugs which have passed early tests to show that they are safe.* …已经通过了早期试验显示是安全的新药。 **14** V-T If someone in authority **passes** a person or thing, they declare that they are of an acceptable standard or have reached an acceptable standard. 宣布…合格 ❑ *Several popular beaches were found unfit for swimming although the government passed them last year.* 好几个人气很旺的海滩被发现不适合游泳，尽管去年官方宣布他们都合格。 **15** V-T When people in authority **pass** a new law or a proposal, they formally agree to it or approve it. 批准; 认可 ❑ *The Estonian parliament has passed a resolution declaring the republic fully independent.* 爱沙尼亚议会已经批准了一项决议，宣布该共和国完全独立。 **16** V-T When a judge **passes** sentence on someone, he or she says what their punishment will be. 宣布 (判决) ❑ *Passing sentence, the judge said it all had the appearance of a con trick.* 宣判时，法官说这个事情具有一个骗局所有的全部外在形式。 **17** V-I If someone or something **passes for** or **passes as** something that they are not, they are accepted as that thing or mistaken for that thing. 被当作 ❑ *Children's toy guns now look so realistic that they can often pass for the real thing.* 孩子们的玩具枪现在看起来那么真以至于常可被当作真枪。 ❑ *It is doubtful whether Ted, even with his fluent French, passed for one of the locals.* 让人存疑的是特德——即使法语说得很流利——能否被人当作一名当地人。 **18** V-I If someone makes you an offer or asks you a question and you say that you will **pass on** it, you mean that you do not want to accept or answer it now. 对…不接受; 对…不予理会 [INFORMAL] ❑ *I think I'll pass on the swimming.* 我想我不会去游泳。 ❑ *"You can join us if you like." Brad shook his head. "I'll pass, thanks."* "如果喜欢，你可以加入我们。"布拉德摇摇头说。"我不去了，谢谢。" **19** V-I In some card games and other games, if you **pass,** you choose not to play at that stage in the game. 不出牌 **20** V-T If you **pass** comment or **pass** a comment, you say something. 评论 [BRIT] **21** to **pass the buck** → see **buck** **22** to **pass judgment** → see **judgment**

Do not confuse **pass** and **spend**. If you do something while you are waiting for something else, you can say you do it to "**pass** the time." ❑ *He had brought along a book to pass the time.* You can say that time **has passed** in order to show that a period of time has finished. ❑ *The first few days passed... The time seems to have passed so quickly.* If you **spend** a period of time doing something or **spend** time in a place, you do that thing or stay in that place for all of the time you are talking about. ❑ *I spent three days cleaning our flat. ...a hotel where we could spend the night.*

❷ **pass** ♦♦♦ /pæs/ (**passes**) **1** N-COUNT A **pass** in an examination, test, or course is a successful result in it. 考试通过 ❑ *He's been allowed to re-take the exam, and he's going to get a pass.* 他已经被允许再参加一次这个考试，他将得到考试通过的结果。 **2** N-COUNT A **pass** is a document that allows you to do something. 通行证；许可证 ❑ *I got myself a pass into the barracks.* 我搞到一张进兵营的通行证。 **3** N-COUNT A **pass** in a game such as football or basketball is an act of throwing the ball to someone on your team. 传球 ❑ *Hirst rolled a short pass to Merson.* 赫斯特给默森传了个短球。 **4** N-COUNT; N-IN-NAMES A **pass** is a narrow path or route between mountains. 山坳通道 ❑ *The monastery is in a remote mountain pass.* 那僧院在一个偏远的山坳通道处。

→ see **mountain**

❸ **pass** ♦♦♦ /pæs/ (**passes, passing, passed**)

▸ **pass away** PHRASAL VERB You can say that someone **passed away** to mean that they died, if you want to avoid using the word "die" because you think it might upset or offend people. 去世 ❑ *He unfortunately passed away last year.* 他不幸于去年去世了。

▸ **pass off** PHRASAL VERB If an event **passes off** without any trouble, it happens and ends without any trouble. (顺利) 进行；举行 [BRIT]

▸ **pass off as** PHRASAL VERB If you **pass** something **off as** another thing, you convince people that it is that other thing. 把…冒充为 ❑ *He passed himself off as a senior psychologist.* 他自己冒充是一名资深心理学家。 ❑ *I've tried to pass off my accent as a New York one.* 我试图把我的口音冒充为纽约口音。

▸ **pass on** **1** PHRASAL VERB If you **pass** something **on to** someone, you give it to them so that they have it instead of you. 传给 ❑ *The winner is passing the money on to a selection of her favorite charities.* 获胜者将把钱捐给几个她最喜欢的慈善机构。 ❑ *The late governor passed on much of his fortune to his daughter.* 已故州长把财产的大部分传给了他的女儿。 **2** PHRASAL VERB You can say that someone **passed on** to mean that they died, if you want to avoid using the word "die" because you think it might upset or offend people. 去世 ❑ *He passed on at the age of 72.* 他72岁时去世。 **3** → see also **pass** ❶ 7

▸ **pass out** PHRASAL VERB If you **pass out**, you faint or collapse. 昏倒 ❑ *He felt sick and dizzy and then passed out.* 他感觉恶心，眩晕，接着就昏倒了。

▸ **pass over** **1** PHRASAL VERB If someone **is passed over for** a job or position, they do not get the job or position and someone younger or less experienced is chosen instead. (任命或晋升时) 对…未加考虑 ❑ *She claimed she was repeatedly passed over for promotion while less experienced white male colleagues were made partners.* 她声称多次升职都未被考虑，而那些比她资历差的白人男同事却已经晋升成为合伙人了。 **2** PHRASAL VERB If you **pass over** a topic in a conversation or speech, you do not talk about it. 避而不谈 ❑ *He largely passed over the government's record.* 他对政府的相关记录基本上是避而不谈。

▸ **pass up** PHRASAL VERB If you **pass up** a chance or an opportunity, you do not take advantage of it. 放弃 (机会) ❑ *The official urged the government not to pass up the opportunity that has now presented itself.* 那位官员敦促政府不要放弃目前摆在他们面前的机会。

pas·sage ♦◊◊ /pæsɪdʒ/ (**passages**) **1** N-COUNT A **passage** is a long narrow space with walls or fences on both sides, that connects one place or room with another. 过道；走廊 ❑ *Harry stepped into the passage and closed the door behind him.* 哈里走进走廊，关上他身后的门。 **2** N-COUNT A **passage** in a book, speech, or piece of music is a section of it that you are considering separately from the rest. 章节；段落；乐段 ❑ *He read a passage from Emerson.* 他读了一段爱默生的作品。 ❑ *...the passage in which the author speaks of the world of imagination.* …作者谈论幻想世界的那个段落。 **3** N-COUNT A **passage** is a long narrow hole or tube in your body, that air or liquid can pass along. (人体内的) 道 ❑ *...cells that line the air passages.* …沿着通气管排列的细胞。 **4** N-COUNT A **passage through** a crowd of people or things is an empty space that allows you to move through them. 通路 ❑ *He cleared a passage for himself through the crammed streets.* 他在拥挤的大街他为自己清出一条通路。 **5** N-UNCOUNT The **passage** of someone or something is their movement from one place to another. 通过；经过 ❑ *Germany had not requested Franco's consent for the passage of troops through Spain.* 德国未曾请求弗朗哥同意他们的军队通过西班牙。 **6** N-UNCOUNT The **passage** of someone or something is their progress from one situation or one stage in their development to another. 过渡 ❑ *...to ease their passage to a market economy.* …使他们向市场经济平稳过渡。 **7** N-UNCOUNT The **passage** of a bill is its progress through Congress so that it can become a law. (法案等的) 通过 ❑ *...a Medicare bill expected to get final passage in Congress today.* …一个预期今天在国会得到最后通过的医保法案。 **8** N-SING **The passage of** a period of time is its passing. (时间的) 推移 ❑ *...an asset that increases in value with the passage of time.* …一项随着时间的推移而增值的资产。 **9** N-COUNT A **passage** is a journey by ship. 航程 ❑ *We'd arrived the day before after a 10-hour passage from Anchorage.* 从安克雷奇出发经过10小时航程后，我们于前天到达。 **10** N-UNCOUNT If you are granted **passage** through a country or area of land, you are given permission to go through it. 通行许可 ❑ *Mr. Thomas would be given safe passage to and from Jaffna.* 托马斯先生将会得到往返于贾夫纳的安全通行许可。

passage·way /pæsɪdʒweɪ/ (**passageways**) N-COUNT A **passageway** is a long narrow space with walls or fences on both sides, that connects one place or room with another. 过道；走廊 ❑ *Outside, in the passageway, I could hear people moving around.* 外面，在走廊里，我能听见人们走来走去。

pas·sen·ger ♦◊◊ /pæsɪndʒər/ (**passengers**) **1** N-COUNT A **passenger** in a vehicle such as a bus, boat, or plane is a person who is traveling in it, but who is not driving it or working on it. 乘客 ❑ *Mr. Fullemann was a passenger in the car when it crashed.* 汽车撞毁时，富勒曼先生是这辆车里的一名乘客。 **2** ADJ **Passenger** is used to describe something that is designed for passengers, rather than for drivers or freight. 旅客的 [ADJ n] ❑ *I sat in the passenger seat.* 我坐在旅客座位上。

→ see **fly, train**

★ **pass·er·by** /pɑsərbaɪ, pæs-/ (**passersby**) also **passer-by** N-COUNT A **passerby** is a person who is walking past someone or something. 过路人 ❑ *A passerby described what he saw moments after the car bomb had exploded.* 一个过路人描述了汽车炸弹爆炸后瞬间他所看到的情景。

pass·ing /pæsɪŋ/ **1** ADJ A **passing** fashion, activity, or feeling lasts for only a short period of time and is not worth taking very seriously. 一时的 [ADJ n] ❑ *Hamnett does not believe environmental concern is a passing fad.* 哈姆内特相信对环境的关注不是一时的风尚。 **2** N-SING The **passing** of something such as a time or system is the fact of its coming to an end. 结束 ❑ *It was an historic day, yet its passing was not marked by the slightest excitement.* 这是有历史意义的一天，然而这一天的结束却没有被赋予丝毫的兴奋感。 **3** N-SING You can refer to someone's death as their **passing**, if you want to avoid using the word "death" because you think it might upset or offend people. 去世 ❑ *His passing will be mourned by many people.* 他的去世将为许多人所悼念。 **4** N-SING **The passing of** a period of time is the fact or process of its going by. (时光的) 流逝 ❑ *The passing of time brought a sense of emptiness.* 时光的流逝带来了空虚的感觉。 **5** ADJ A **passing** mention or reference is brief and is made while you are talking or writing about something else. 顺便的 [ADJ n] ❑ *It was just a passing comment, he didn't expand.* 那只是顺便提到的评论，他没有展开。 **6** → see also **pass** **7** PHRASE If you mention something **in passing**, you mention it briefly while you are talking or writing about something else. 顺便 ❑ *The army is only mentioned in passing.* 军队只是顺便被谈及。

pas·sion ♦◊◊ /pæʃ°n/ (**passions**) **1** N-UNCOUNT **Passion** is strong sexual feelings toward someone. 强烈的情欲 [also N in pl] ❑ *...my passion for a dark-haired, slender boy named Josh.* …我对一个黑头发、身材修长名叫乔希的男孩的强烈的情欲。 ❑ *...the expression of love and passion.* …爱与情欲的表白。 **2** N-UNCOUNT **Passion** is a very strong feeling about something or a strong belief in something. 强烈的感情；强烈的信任 [also N in pl] ❑ *He spoke with great passion.* 他激情洋溢地讲话。 **3** N-COUNT If you have a **passion for** something, you have a very strong interest in it and like it very much. 酷爱 ❑ *She had a passion for gardening.* 她对于园艺有一份热爱。

P

Thesaurus *passion* 另参见：
N. affection, desire, love, lust 1
enthusiasm, fondness, interest 2 3

▲**pas·sion·ate** /pæʃənɪt/ 1 ADJ A **passionate** person has very strong feelings about something or a strong belief in something. 狂热的；热诚的 ❑ *...his passionate commitment to peace.* …他对和平事业的狂热信奉。 ❑ *He is very passionate about the project.* 他对这个项目非常热诚。 ● **pas·sion·ate·ly** ADV 狂热地；热诚地 ❑ *I am passionately opposed to the death penalty.* 我强烈地反对死刑。 2 ADJ A **passionate** person has strong romantic or sexual feelings and expresses them in their behavior. 非常浪漫的；性欲强的 ❑ *...a beautiful, passionate woman of twenty-six.* …一位美丽的、非常浪漫的26岁的妇女。 ● **pas·sion·ate·ly** ADV 非常浪漫地；性欲强地 ❑ *He was passionately in love with her.* 他热恋着她。

pas·sive /pæsɪv/ 1 ADJ If you describe someone as **passive**, you mean that they do not take action but instead let things happen to them. 被动的 [DISAPPROVAL] ❑ *His passive attitude made things easier for me.* 他的被动态度使我办起事来容易多了。 ● **pas·sive·ly** ADV 被动地 ❑ *He sat there passively, content to wait for his father to make the opening move.* 他被动地坐在那里，心满意足地等着他父亲走第一步棋。 2 ADJ A **passive** activity involves watching, looking at, or listening to things rather than doing things. 消极的 [ADJ n] ❑ *They want less passive ways of filling their time.* 他们需要不那么消极的方式来打发时间。 3 ADJ **Passive** resistance involves showing opposition to the people in power in your country by not cooperating with them and protesting in nonviolent ways. 非暴力的 [ADJ n] ❑ *They made it clear that they would only exercise passive resistance in the event of a military takeover.* 他们声明假若发生军事接管，他们只采取非暴力抵抗行动。 4 N-SING In grammar, **the passive** or **the passive voice** is formed using "be" and the past participle of a verb. The subject of a passive clause does not perform the action expressed by the verb but is affected by it. For example, in "He's been murdered," the verb is in the passive. Compare **active**. 被动语态

pass·port /pæspɔrt/ (**passports**) N-COUNT Your **passport** is an official document containing your name, photograph, and personal details, which you need to show when you enter or leave a country. 护照 ❑ *You should take your passport with you when changing money.* 你换钱的时候应该带着护照。

pass·word /pæswɜrd/ (**passwords**) N-COUNT A **password** is a secret word or phrase that you must know in order to be allowed to enter a place such as a military base, or to be allowed to use a computer system. 口令 ❑ *Advance and give the password.* 向前走，说口令！
→ see **Internet**

past ♦♦♦ /pæst/ (**pasts**)

In addition to the uses shown below, **past** is used in the phrasal verb "run past."

1 N-SING **The past** is the time before the present, and the things that have happened. 过去 ❑ *In the past, about a third of the babies born to women with diabetes died.* 在过去，患有糖尿病的妇女生的婴儿中大约有三分之一都死了。 ● PHRASE If you accuse someone of **living in the past**, you mean that they think too much about the past or believe that things are the same as they were in the past. 活在过去 [DISAPPROVAL] ❑ *What was the point in living in the past, thinking about what had or had not happened?* 活在过去有什么意义，思考已经发生的或者没有发生的事情？ 2 N-COUNT Your **past** consists of all the things that you have done or that have happened to you. 经历 ❑ *...revelations about his past.* …关于他的过往经历的揭露。 3 ADJ **Past** events and things happened or existed before the present time. 以前的 [ADJ n] ❑ *I knew from past experience that alternative therapies could help.* 我知道根据以前的经验其他的治疗方法可能有效。 ❑ *...a return to the turbulence of past centuries.* …回到过去几个中世纪的动荡。 4 ADJ You use **past** to talk about a period of time that has just finished. For example, if you talk about the **past five years**, you mean the period of five years that has just finished. 刚过去的 [det ADJ n] ❑ *Most stores have remained closed for the past three days.* 在刚过去的3天里大多数商店一直关着门。 5 PREP You use **past** when you are stating a time that is thirty minutes or less after a particular hour. For example, if it is **twenty past** six, it is twenty minutes after six o'clock. (指钟点)过 [num PREP num] ❑ *It's ten past eleven.* 11：10了。 ● ADV **Past** is also an adverb. 过了 [num ADV] ❑ *I have my lunch at half past.* 我半点的时候吃午餐。 6 PREP If it is **past** a particular time, it is later than that time. 晚于 ❑ *It was past midnight.* 过了午夜。 7 PREP If you go **past** someone or something, you go near them and keep moving, so that they are then behind you. 经过 ❑ *I dashed past him and out of the door.* 我飞奔着经过他，跑出门外。 ❑ *A steady procession of people filed past the coffin.* 稳步前行的人们排成一行，经过灵柩。 ● ADV **Past** is also an adverb. 经过 ❑ *An ambulance drove past.* 一辆救护车驶了过去。 8 PREP If you look or point **past** a person or thing, you look or point at something behind them. 越过 [V PREP n] ❑ *She stared past Christine at the bed.* 她越过克里斯蒂娜盯着那张床。 9 PREP If something is **past** a place, it is on the other side of it. 在…另一侧 [v-link PREP n] ❑ *Go north on I-15 to the exit just past Barstow.* 顺着I-15公路向北走，出口就在巴斯托的另一侧。 10 PREP If someone or something is **past** a particular point or stage, they are no longer at that point or stage. 超过(某一点或阶段) ❑ *He was well past retirement age.* 他大大超过了退休年龄。
→ see **history**

pas·ta /pɑstə/ (**pastas**) N-MASS **Pasta** is a type of food made from a mixture of flour, eggs, and water that is formed into different shapes and then boiled. Spaghetti, macaroni, and noodles are types of pasta. 面食

Pasta comes in dozens of shapes and sizes but generally the same recipe is used: water, flour, and sometimes eggs or other flavors. Pasta is cooked in boiling water. Some of the most popular types of pasta are **spaghetti** (long, thin pasta noodles); **macaroni** (short tubes of pasta, often eaten with a cheese sauce) and **lasagne** (flat sheets of pasta, eaten in a dish made of layers of lasagne and meat sauce).

paste /peɪst/ (**pastes, pasting, pasted**) 1 N-MASS **Paste** is a soft, wet, sticky mixture of a substance and a liquid, that can be spread easily. Some types of paste are used to stick things together. 面团；糨糊 ❑ *Blend a little milk with the custard powder to form a paste.* 用蛋奶粉和一点牛奶混合成一个面团。 2 N-MASS **Paste** is a soft smooth mixture made of crushed meat, fruit, or vegetables. You can, for example, spread it onto bread or use it in cooking. 酱 ❑ *...tomato paste.* …番茄酱。 3 V-T If you **paste** something on a surface, you put glue or paste on it and stick it on the surface. (用胶水或糨糊)粘贴 ❑ *...pasting labels on bottles.* …在瓶子上贴标签。

pas·tel /pæstɛl/ (**pastels**) ADJ **Pastel** colors are pale rather than dark or bright. (色彩) 淡的 [ADJ n, ADJ color] ❑ *...delicate pastel shades.* …柔和的淡色调。 ❑ *...pastel pink, blue, peach, and green.* …淡粉色、蓝色、桃色和绿色。 ● N-COUNT **Pastel** is also a noun. 淡色彩 ❑ *The lobby is decorated in pastels.* 门厅用柔和的淡色彩装饰。
→ see **drawing**

★ **pas·time** /pæstaɪm/ (**pastimes**) N-COUNT A **pastime** is something that you do in your spare time because you enjoy it or are interested in it. 消遣 ❑ *His favorite pastime is golf.* 他最喜欢的消遣是打高尔夫。

pas·to·ral /pæstərəl, pæstɔr-/ 1 ADJ The **pastoral** duties of a priest or other religious leader involve looking after the people he or she has responsibility for, especially by helping them with their personal problems. 牧师职责的 [ADJ n] ❑ *...the pastoral care of the sick.* …牧师对病人的照料。 2 ADJ A **pastoral** place, atmosphere, or idea is characteristic of peaceful country life and scenery. 田园生活的；田园风光的 [ADJ n] ❑ *...a tranquil pastoral scene.* …宁静的田园风光。

★ **pas·try** /peɪstri/ (**pastries**) 1 N-UNCOUNT **Pastry** is a food made from flour, fat, and water that is mixed together, rolled flat, and baked in the oven. It is used, for example, for making pies. 油酥面团 2 N-COUNT A **pastry** is a small cake made with sweet pastry. 油酥糕点 ❑ *...a wide range of cakes and pastries.* …各种各样的蛋糕和油酥糕点。

★ **pas·ture** /pæstʃər/ (**pastures**) N-VAR **Pasture** is land with grass growing on it for farm animals to eat. 牧场 ❑ *The cows are out now, grazing in the pasture.* 牛群现在出去了，正在牧场上吃草。
→ see **barn**

pat /pæt/ (**pats, patting, patted**) 1 V-T If you **pat** something or someone, you tap them lightly, usually with your hand held flat. 轻拍 ❑ *"Don't you worry about any of this," she said patting me on the knee.* "不要为这事操什么心了，"她说道，轻轻拍了拍我的膝盖。 ❑ *The landlady patted her hair nervously.* 女房东不安地轻拍着她的头发。 ● N-COUNT **Pat** is also a noun. 轻拍 ❑ *He gave her an encouraging pat on the* shoulder. 他轻拍她肩膀以示鼓励。 2 N-COUNT A **pat of** butter or something else that is soft is a small lump of it. (奶油等) 小块 ❑ *Terreano put a pat of butter on his plate.* 特里诺把一小块奶油放在他盘子里。 3 PHRASE If you give someone **a pat on the back** or if you **pat** them **on the back**, you show them that you think they have done well and deserve to be praised. 表扬 [APPROVAL] ❑ *The players deserve a pat on the back.* 运动员们值得表扬。

patch /pætʃ/ (**patches, patching, patched**) 1 N-COUNT A **patch** on a surface is a part of it that is different in appearance from the area around it. (与周围不同的) 块; 片 ❑ *...the bald patch on the top of his head.* …他头顶上那块秃斑。 ❑ *There was a small patch of blue in the gray clouds.* 乌云中透着一小块蓝天。 2 N-COUNT A **patch of** land is a small area of land where a particular plant or crop grows. 小块田地 ❑ *...a patch of land covered in forest.* …一块长着树林的田地。 ❑ *...the little vegetable patch in her backyard.* …在她后院的小块菜地。 3 N-COUNT A **patch** is a piece of material that you use to cover a hole in something. 补丁 ❑ *...jackets with patches on the elbows.* …肘部打着补丁的夹克。 4 N-COUNT A **patch** is a small piece of material that you wear to cover an injured eye. (保护受伤眼睛的) 眼罩 ❑ *She went to the hospital and found him lying down with a patch over his eye.* 她去医院看见他躺着，眼睛上蒙着眼罩。 5 V-T If you **patch** something that has a hole in it, you repair it by fastening a patch over the hole. 打补丁 ❑ *He and Walker patched the barn roof.* 他和沃克修补了那个谷仓的顶。 ❑ *One of the mechanics took off the damaged tire, and took it back to the station to be patched.* 其中一个机械师取下受损轮胎，把它拿到站里修补。 6 N-COUNT A **patch** is a piece of computer program code written as a temporary solution for dealing with a computer virus and distributed by the makers of the original program. (对付计算机病毒的) 补丁 [COMPUTING] ❑ *Older machines will need a software patch to correct the date.* 旧的机器需要软件补丁来修正日期。 7 PHRASE If you have or go through **a rough patch**, you have a lot of problems for a time. 一段艰难时期 ❑ *His marriage was going through a rough patch.* 他的婚姻正处于一段艰难时期。

▸ **patch up** 1 PHRASAL VERB If you **patch up** an argument or relationship, you try to be friendly again and not to argue anymore. 平息 (争吵); 修补 (关系) ❑ *She has gone on vacation with her husband to try to patch up their marriage.* 她跟她丈夫度假去了，以补救他们的婚姻。 ❑ *France patched things up with New Zealand.* 法国与新西兰重修旧好。 2 PHRASAL VERB If you **patch up** something that is damaged, you repair it or patch it. 修理; 修补 ❑ *We can patch up those holes.* 我们能补上那些漏洞。 3 PHRASAL VERB If doctors **patch** someone **up** or **patch** their wounds **up**, they treat their injuries. 处理 (伤口) ❑ *...the medical staff who patched her up after the accident.* …事故发生后为她包扎伤口的医疗人员。

P

patch·work /pætʃwɜrk/ ADJ A **patchwork** quilt, cushion, or piece of clothing is made by sewing together small pieces of material of different colors or patterns. 拼缝的 [ADJ n] ❑ *...beds covered in patchwork quilts.* …一些铺着百衲被子的床。 ● N-UNCOUNT **Patchwork** is also a noun. 拼缝 ❑ *For centuries, quilting and patchwork have been popular needlecrafts.* 几个世纪以来，被褥绗缝和拼缝一直是流行的针线活。

patchy /pætʃi/ 1 ADJ A **patchy** substance or color exists in some places but not in others, or is thick in some places and thin in others. 分布不均衡的 ❑ *Thick patchy fog and irresponsible driving were to blame.* 浓重的分布不均的雾和不负责任的驾驶应受到责难。 ❑ *...the brown, patchy grass.* …分布不均的棕色草地。 2 ADJ If something is **patchy**, it is not completely reliable or satisfactory because it is not always good. 不很可靠的; 不很令人满意的 ❑ *The evidence is patchy.* 这个证据不很可靠。

★ **pa·tent** /pæt³nt/ (**patents, patenting, patented**) 1 N-COUNT A **patent** is an official right to be the only person or company allowed to make or sell a new product for a certain period of time. 专利 ❑ *P&G applied for a patent on its cookies.* 宝洁公司为其饼干申请了专利。 ❑ *He held a number of patents for his many innovations.* 他为他的许多革新申请了几项专利。 2 V-T If you **patent** something, you obtain a patent for it. 得到…专利 ❑ *He patented the idea that the atom could be split.* 他得到了原子可以分裂的这个见解的专利。 ❑ *The invention has been patented by the university.* 那项发明已经由那所大学获取了专利。 3 ADJ You use **patent** to describe something, especially something bad, in order to indicate in an emphatic way that you think its nature or existence is clear and obvious. 显而易见的 [EMPHASIS] ❑ *This was patent nonsense.* 这显然是一派胡言。 ● **pa·tent·ly** ADV 显而易见地 ❑ *He made his displeasure patently obvious.* 他清楚地表明了他的不悦。

Word Link *pater, patr ≈ father : expatriate, paternal, patronize*

pa·ter·nal /pətɜrn³l/ 1 ADJ **Paternal** is used to describe feelings or actions that are typical of those of a kind father toward his child. 父亲的 ❑ *...paternal love for his children.* …对他孩子们的父爱。 2 ADJ A **paternal** relative is one that is related through a person's father rather than their mother. 父系的; 父亲一方的 [ADJ n] ❑ *...my paternal grandparents.* …我的祖父母。

pa·ter·nity leave /pətɜrnɪti liv/ N-UNCOUNT If a man has **paternity leave**, his employer allows him some time off work because his child has just been born. (因家中刚生了孩子) 父亲享有的产假 [BUSINESS] ❑ *Paternity leave is rare and, where it does exist, it's unlikely to be for any longer than two weeks.* 父亲享有的产假很难得，而且即便有，也不可能超过两周。

path ♦◇◇ /pæθ/ (**paths**) 1 N-COUNT A **path** is a long strip of ground that people walk along to get from one place to another. 小径 ❑ *We followed the path along the clifftops.* 我们沿着悬崖顶的小径行进。 ❑ *Feet had worn a path in the rock.* 脚步已在岩石里踏出一条小径。 2 N-COUNT Your **path** is the space ahead of you as you move along. (前面的) 道路 ❑ *A group of reporters blocked his path.* 一群记者堵住了他的路。 3 N-COUNT The **path** of something is the line that it moves along in a particular direction. 路线; 轨道 ❑ *He stepped without looking into the path of a reversing car.* 他一步迈了出去，连看都没看一眼一辆正在倒车的汽车。 ❑ *...people who live near airports or under the flight path of airplanes.* …住在机场附近或者飞机的飞行线路下面的人们。 4 N-COUNT A **path** that you take is a particular course of action or way of achieving something. 行动路线; 途径 ❑ *They appear to have chosen the path of cooperation rather than confrontation.* 他们好像选择了合作而不是对抗的行动路线。

★ **pa·thet·ic** /pəθɛtɪk/ 1 ADJ If you describe a person or animal as **pathetic**, you mean that they are sad and weak or helpless, and they make you feel very sorry for them. 可怜的 ❑ *...a pathetic little dog with a curly tail.* …一只可怜的卷尾小狗。 ❑ *The small group of onlookers presented a pathetic sight.* 那一小群旁观者显出一幅可怜的样子。 ● **pa·theti·cal·ly** /pəθɛtɪkli/ ADV 可怜地 ❑ *She was pathetically thin.* 她那时瘦弱得可怜。 2 ADJ If you describe someone or something as **pathetic**, you mean that they make you feel impatient or angry, often because they are weak or not very good. 差劲的; 无力的 [DISAPPROVAL] ❑ *What pathetic excuses.* 多么无力的借口！ ❑ *Don't be so pathetic.* 别那么差劲。 ● **pa·theti·cal·ly** ADV 差劲地; 无力地 [ADV adj] ❑ *Five women in a group of 18 people is a pathetically small number.* 18个人中5位女性是个小得可怜的数目。

patho·logi·cal /pæθəlɒdʒɪk³l/ 1 ADJ You describe a person or their behavior as **pathological** when they behave in an extreme and unacceptable way, and have very powerful feelings that they cannot control. 病态的 ❑ *He experiences chronic, almost pathological jealousy.* 他经受着长期的、近乎病态的嫉妒。 ❑ *He's a pathological liar.* 他是个说谎成性者。 2 ADJ **Pathological** means relating to pathology or illness. 病理学的; 病理的 [MEDICAL] ❑ *...pathological conditions in animals.* …动物的病理状况。

pa·tholo·gist /pəθɒlədʒɪst/ (**pathologists**) N-COUNT A **pathologist** is someone who studies or investigates diseases and illnesses, or who examines dead bodies in order to find out the cause of death. 病理学家

▲ **pa·thol·ogy** /pəθɒlədʒi/ N-UNCOUNT **Pathology** is the study of the way diseases and illnesses develop. 病理学 [MEDICAL]

pa·thos /peɪθɒs/ N-UNCOUNT **Pathos** is a quality in a situation, movie, or play that makes people feel sadness and pity. (情形、电影或戏剧中) 令人感伤的特质 ❑ *...the pathos of man's isolation.* …人类孤离的令人感伤性。

path·way /pæθweɪ/ (**pathways**) 1 N-COUNT A **pathway** is a path that you can walk along or a route that you can take. 路径 ❑ *Richard was coming up the pathway.* 理查德正沿路走来。 2 N-COUNT A **pathway** is a particular course of action or a way of achieving something. 途径 ❑ *Diplomacy will smooth your pathway to success.* 良好的交际会铺平你的成功之路。

pa·tience /peɪʃ³ns/ 1 N-UNCOUNT If you have **patience**, you are able to stay calm and not get annoyed, for example, when something takes a long time, or when someone is not doing what you want them to do. 耐心 ❑ *He doesn't have the patience to wait.* 他没有耐心等。 2 PHRASE If someone **tries** your **patience** or **tests** your **patience**, they annoy you so much that it is very difficult for you to stay calm. 考验某人的耐心极限 ❑ *He tended to stutter whenever he spoke to her, which tried her patience.* 他一跟她讲话就结巴，这考验了她耐心极限。

pa·tient ♦♦◇ /peɪʃᵊnt/ (**patients**) **1** N-COUNT A **patient** is a person who is receiving medical treatment from a doctor or hospital. A **patient** is also someone who is taken care of by a particular doctor. 病人 ❑ *The earlier the treatment is given, the better the patient's chances.* 治疗给得越早，病人机遇越好。 ❑ *She was tough but wonderful with her patients.* 她很严厉，但对病人很好。 **2** ADJ If you are **patient**, you stay calm and do not get annoyed, for example, when something takes a long time, or when someone is not doing what you want them to do. 耐心的 ❑ *Please be patient – your check will arrive.* 请耐心点儿——你的支票会到的。 ● **pa·tient·ly** ADV 耐心地 [ADV with V] ❑ *She waited patiently for Frances to finish.* 她耐心地等弗朗西丝完成。
→ see **diagnosis, illness**

pa·tio /pætioʊ/ (**patios**) N-COUNT A **patio** is an area of flat blocks of stone or concrete next to a house, where people can sit and relax or eat. 露台

★ **pa·tri·ot** /peɪtriət/ (**patriots**) N-COUNT Someone who is a **patriot** loves their country and feels very loyal toward it. 爱国者 ❑ *It has been suggested the founders were not true patriots but men out to protect their own interests.* 有人指出创建者并非真正的爱国者，而是一些维护自己利益的人。

Word Link *otic ≈ affecting, causing : erotic, neurotic, patriotic*

★ **pat·ri·ot·ic** /peɪtriɒtɪk/ ADJ Someone who is **patriotic** loves their country and feels very loyal toward it. 爱国的 ❑ *Winona is fiercely patriotic.* 威诺娜极度爱国。

Word Link *ism ≈ action or state : communism, optimism, patriotism*

★ **pat·ri·ot·ism** /peɪtriətɪzəm/ N-UNCOUNT **Patriotism** is love for your country and loyalty toward it. 爱国心 ❑ *He was a country boy who had joined the army out of a sense of patriotism and adventure.* 他是个乡下小伙子，出于爱国心和冒险精神参了军。

★ **pa·trol** /pətroʊl/ (**patrols, patrolling, patrolled**) **1** V-T When soldiers, police, or guards **patrol** an area or building, they move around it in order to make sure that there is no trouble there. 在…巡逻 ❑ *Prison officers continued to patrol the grounds within the jail.* 狱警们继续在监狱内的场地里巡逻。 ● N-COUNT **Patrol** is also a noun. 巡逻 ❑ *He failed to return from a patrol.* 他没能从一次巡逻中回来。 **2** PHRASE Soldiers, police, or guards who are **on patrol** are patrolling an area. 在巡逻 ❑ *The army is now on patrol in Srinagar and a curfew has been imposed.* 军队现在在斯利那加巡逻，宵禁也已实行。 **3** N-COUNT A **patrol** is a group of soldiers or vehicles that are patrolling an area. 巡逻队 ❑ *Guerrillas attacked a patrol with hand grenades.* 游击队用手榴弹袭击了一支巡逻队。

★ **pa·tron** /peɪtrən/ (**patrons**) **1** N-COUNT A **patron** is a person who supports and gives money to artists, writers, or musicians. (艺术家、作家、音乐家等的) 资助人 ❑ *Catherine the Great was a patron of the arts and sciences.* 凯瑟琳大帝是艺术和科学的赞助人。 **2** N-COUNT The **patron** of a charity, group, or campaign is an important person who allows his or her name to be used for publicity. (慈善机构、团体、运动等的) 名誉赞助人 ❑ *He has now become one of the patrons of the association.* 他如今已成为该协会的名誉赞助人之一。 **3** N-COUNT The **patrons** of a place such as a bar or hotel are its customers. (酒吧、旅馆等的) 顾客 ❑ *Few patrons of a high-priced hotel can be led to expect anything other than luxury service.* 高价旅馆的顾客几乎没有人会被引导去期待奢侈服务以外的任何东西。

Word Link *age ≈ state of, related to : courage, marriage, patronage*

pat·ron·age /peɪtrənɪdʒ, pæt-/ N-UNCOUNT **Patronage** is the support and money given by someone to a person or a group such as a charity. 赞助 ❑ *...government patronage of the arts in Europe.* …在欧洲政府对艺术的资助。

▲ **pat·ron·ise** /pætrənaɪz/ [BRIT] → see **patronize**

pat·ron·is·ing /pætrənaɪzɪŋ/ [BRIT] → see **patronizing**

▲ **pat·ron·ize** /peɪtrənaɪz/ (**patronizes, patronizing, patronized**)

in BRIT, also use **patronise**

1 V-T If someone **patronizes** you, they speak or behave toward you in a way that seems friendly, but that shows that they think they are superior to you in some way. 屈尊对待 [DISAPPROVAL] ❑ *Don't you patronize me!* 你不要屈尊对待我。 **2** V-T Someone who **patronizes** artists, writers, or musicians supports them and gives them money. 赞助 [FORMAL] ❑ *The Japanese imperial family patronizes the Japanese Art Association.* 日本皇室资助日本艺术协会。 **3** V-T If someone **patronizes** a place such as a bar, store, or hotel, they are one of its customers. 光顾 ❑ *The ladies of Berne liked to patronize the palace for tea and little cakes.* 伯尔尼的女士们喜欢光顾这个地方喝茶吃点心。

pat·ron·iz·ing /peɪtrənaɪzɪŋ/

in BRIT, also use **patronising**

ADJ If someone is **patronizing**, they speak or behave toward you in a way that seems friendly, but that shows that they think they are superior to you. 屈尊的 [DISAPPROVAL] ❑ *The tone of the interview was unnecessarily patronizing.* 这场会面的语气屈尊得很没必要。

pat·ter /pætər/ (**patters, pattering, pattered**) **1** V-I If something **patters** on a surface, it hits it quickly several times, making quiet, tapping sounds. 急速拍打 ❑ *Rain pattered gently outside, dripping onto the roof from the pines.* 雨在外面沙沙地下着，从松树上滴落在房顶上。 **2** N-SING A **patter** is a series of quick, quiet, tapping sounds. 急速击打声 ❑ *...the patter of the driving rain on the roof.* …大雨在屋顶上的急速击打声。 **3** N-SING Someone's **patter** is a series of things that they say quickly and easily, usually in order to entertain people or to persuade them to buy or do something. 顺口溜 ❑ *Women found him charming. It must have been his patter because he's not good-looking.* 女人们觉得他有魅力。这肯定是因为他的顺口溜，因为他并不好看。

pat·tern ♦♦◇ /pætərn/ (**patterns**) **1** N-COUNT A **pattern** is the repeated or regular way in which something happens or is done. 模式 ❑ *All three attacks followed the same pattern.* 3次袭击都依照同一模式。 **2** N-COUNT A **pattern** is an arrangement of lines or shapes, especially a design in which the same shape is repeated at regular intervals over a surface. 图案 ❑ *...a golden robe embroidered with red and purple thread stitched into a pattern of flames.* …一件用红紫相间的线镶了火焰图案的边的金色长袍。 **3** N-COUNT A **pattern** is a diagram or shape that you can use as a guide when you are making something such as a model or a piece of clothing. 参照图形 ❑ *...cutting out a pattern for slacks.* …剪出一个便裤的纸样。 ❑ *Send for our free patterns to knit yourself.* 索取我们免费的参照图形以便自己织。
→ see **quilt**

Word Partnership *pattern* 的常用搭配:
ADJ. **familiar** pattern, **normal** pattern, **typical** pattern **1**
different pattern, **same** pattern, **similar** pattern **1** **2**
V. **change a** pattern, **fit a** pattern, **see a** pattern **1**
follow a pattern **1**–**3**

pat·terned /pætərnd/ **1** ADJ Something that is **patterned** is covered with a pattern or design. 饰有图案的 ❑ *...a plain carpet with a patterned border.* …一块有饰边的素色地毯。 **2** V-T PASSIVE If something new **is patterned on** something else that already exists, it is deliberately made so that it has similar features. 使照…设计 [mainly AM] ❑ *New York City announced a 10-point policy patterned on the federal bill of rights for taxpayers.* 纽约市公布了一项以联邦纳税人权利法案为范本而制定的10点政策。

pause ♦◇◇ /pɔz/ (**pauses, pausing, paused**) **1** V-I If you **pause** while you are doing something, you stop for a short period and then continue. 停顿 ❑ *"It's rather embarrassing," he began, and paused.* "这很让人尴尬，" 他开始说道，又停顿了片刻。 ❑ *He talked for two hours without pausing for breath.* 他谈了两个小时，没有停下来喘口气。 **2** N-COUNT A **pause** is a short period when you stop doing something before continuing. 停顿 ❑ *After a pause Al said sharply: "I'm sorry if I've upset you."* 停了一下之后艾尔突然说："如果我让你不安了，我很抱歉。"

Word Partnership *pause* 的常用搭配:
ADJ. **awkward** pause, **brief** pause, **long** pause, **short** pause, **slight** pause **2**

pave /peɪv/ (**paves, paving, paved**) V-T If a road or an area of ground **has been paved**, it has been covered with asphalt or concrete, so that it is suitable for walking or driving on. 铺(路) [usu passive] ❑ *The avenue had never been paved, and deep mud made it impassable in winter.* 这条大街从来没有铺过，深泥使其在冬天无法通行。

P

pave·ment /peɪvmənt/ (**pavements**) 1 N-COUNT The **pavement** is the hard surface of a road. 路面 [AM] ❑ *The tires of Lenny's bike hissed over the wet pavement.* 伦尼的自行车轮胎嘶嘶地驶过湿漉漉的路面。 2 N-COUNT A **pavement** is a path with a hard surface, usually by the side of a road. 人行道 [BRIT]

in AM, use **sidewalk**

pav·er /peɪvər/ (**pavers**) N-COUNT **Pavers** are flat pieces of stone or concrete, usually square in shape, that are put on the ground, for example, to make a path. (方形的) 铺路的石板或混凝土板

pa·vil·ion /pəvɪlyən/ (**pavilions**) 1 N-COUNT A **pavilion** is a large temporary structure such as a tent that is used at outdoor public events. (为举行户外活动而搭建的诸如帐篷的) 大的临时建筑物 ❑ *...heading across the beautiful green lawn toward the International Pavilion.* …穿过美丽的绿草坪前往国际展篷。 2 N-COUNT A **pavilion** is an ornamental building in a garden or park. 亭子 ❑ *Despite persistent rain showers, the lawn and pavilion were packed with fans.* 尽管有持续阵雨，草坪上和亭子里还是挤满了仰慕者。

pav·ing /peɪvɪŋ/ N-UNCOUNT **Paving** is flat blocks of stone or concrete covering an area. 铺路的石板或混凝土板 [oft supp N] ❑ *...concrete paving.* …铺路的混凝土板。

paw /pɔ/ (**paws, pawing, pawed**) 1 N-COUNT The **paws** of an animal such as a cat, dog, or bear are its feet, which have claws for gripping things and soft pads for walking on. 脚爪 ❑ *The kitten was black with white front paws and a white splotch on her chest.* 那只小猫除了白色前爪和胸部的一块白色区域外是黑色的。 2 V-T/V-I If an animal **paws** something, or **paws** at it, it draws its foot over it or down it. 用脚抓; 用脚刨 ❑ *Madigan's horse pawed the ground.* 马迪根的马刨了地。 3 V-T/V-I If one person **paws** another, or **paws** at them, they touch or stroke them in a way that the other person finds offensive. (冒犯性地) 抚摸 [DISAPPROVAL] ❑ *Stop pawing me, Geraldo!* 杰拉尔多，别摸我！

pawn /pɔn/ (**pawns, pawning, pawned**) 1 V-T If you **pawn** something that you own, you leave it with a pawnbroker, who gives you money for it and who can sell it if you do not pay back the money before a certain time. 典当 ❑ *He is contemplating pawning his watch.* 他在考虑把手表当了。 2 N-COUNT In chess, a **pawn** is the smallest and least valuable playing piece. Each player has eight pawns at the start of the game. (国际象棋中的) 卒; 兵 3 N-COUNT If you say that someone is using you as a **pawn**, you mean that they are using you for their own advantage. 马前卒 ❑ *It looks as though he is being used as a political pawn by the president.* 看来似乎他在被总统用作政治卒子。

→ see **chess**

P

▸ **pawn off** PHRASAL VERB If you **pawn off** something or someone that you do not want **on** another person, you persuade the person to accept them. 使 (自己不想要的人或物) 脱手 [DISAPPROVAL] ❑ *The factories produce hugely subsidized rubbish they can't pawn off on anybody but the Russians.* 这些工厂生产享受了巨额补贴的垃圾产品，除了兜售给俄国人外，找不到其他买主。 ❑ *Are you trying to pawn me off on somebody?* 你在试图把我硬塞给别人吗？

pawn·broker /pɔnbroʊkər/ (**pawnbrokers**) N-COUNT A **pawnbroker** is a person who lends people money. People give the pawnbroker something they own, which can be sold if they do not pay back the money before a certain time. 典当商

pawnshop /pɔnʃɒp/ (**pawnshops**) N-COUNT A **pawnshop** is a pawnbroker's shop. 当铺

paw·paw /pɔpɔ/ (**pawpaws**) also **paw-paw** N-COUNT A **pawpaw** is a tree that grows in the eastern United States or the oval yellow fruit of this tree. 宝爪果树; 宝爪果

pay ♦♦♦ /peɪ/ (**pays, paying, paid**) 1 V-T/V-I When you **pay** an amount of money **to** someone, you give it to them because you are buying something from them or because you owe it to them. When you **pay** something such as a bill or a debt, you pay the amount that you owe. 支付; 偿还 ❑ *Owners who have already paid for repairs will be reimbursed.* 已经付了修缮费的业主将会得到退费。 ❑ *The wealthier may have to pay a little more in taxes.* 更有钱的人可能得多交点税。 2 V-T When you **are paid**, you get your wages or salary from your employer. 给…支付工薪 ❑ *The lawyer was paid a huge salary.* 这个律师拿了很高的薪金。 ❑ *I get paid monthly.* 我拿月薪。 3 N-UNCOUNT Your **pay** is the money that you get from your employer as wages or salary. 薪水 ❑ *...their complaints about their pay and conditions.* …他们对薪水和工作条件的不满。

When used as a noun, **pay** is a general word which you can use to refer to the money you get from your employer for doing your job. Professional people and office workers receive a **salary**, which is paid monthly. However, when talking about someone's salary, you usually give the annual figure. ❑ *I'm paid a salary of $15,000 a year.* Manual workers are paid **wages**, or **a wage**. The plural is more common than the singular, especially when you are talking about the actual cash that someone receives. ❑ *Every week he handed all his wages in cash to his wife.* Wages are usually paid, and quoted, as an hourly or a weekly sum. ❑ *...a starting wage of five dollars an hour.* Your **income** consists of all the money you receive from all sources, including your pay.

4 V-T If you **are paid to** do something, someone gives you some money so that you will help them or perform some service for them. 雇佣 ❑ *There are people who are paid to sit around and play games.* 有人受雇闲坐着玩游戏。 5 V-I If a government or organization makes someone **pay for** something, it makes them responsible for providing the money for it, for example, by increasing prices or taxes. 承担费用 ❑ *...a legally binding international treaty that establishes who must pay for environmental damage.* …一项规定谁必须为环境的破坏承担费用的具有法律约束力的国际公约。 6 V-T/V-I If a job, deal, or investment **pays** a particular amount, it brings you that amount of money. 带来 (某数量的钱); 带来钱 ❑ *We're stuck in jobs that don't pay very well.* 我们被困在钱给得很少的工作中。 ❑ *The banks don't pay interest on those accounts.* 银行对那些账户不支付利息。 7 V-I If a job, deal, or investment **pays**, it brings you a profit or earns you some money. 给报酬 ❑ *There are some agencies now specializing in helping older people to find jobs which pay.* 现在有一些机构专门帮助年纪较大的人找到有酬工作。 8 V-T/V-I If a course of action **pays**, it results in some advantage or benefit for you. (某种做法) 有好处 ❑ *It pays to invest in protective clothing.* 在防护服上投资值。 ❑ *We must demonstrate that aggression will not pay.* 我们必须证明侵犯是没有好处的。 9 V-T/V-I If you **pay for** something that you do or have, you suffer as a result of it. (为…) 付出代价 ❑ *He was to pay dearly for his lack of resolve.* 他将为自己缺乏决心付出高昂的代价。 ❑ *Why should I pay the penalty for somebody else's mistake?* 我为什么要为别人的错误而受罚呢？ 10 V-T If you **pay** money **down** when you are buying something, you pay only a part of the total cost. You then finish paying for it later, usually by paying a certain amount every month. 首付 (商品部份金额) [AM] ❑ *We paid $500 down and $100 a month after that.* 我们首付了$500，以后每月付$100。 11 V-T You use **pay** with some nouns, such as in the expressions **pay a visit** and **pay attention**, to indicate that something is given or done. (与名词连用) 进行; 给予 ❑ *Pay us a visit next time you're in Portland.* 下次来波特兰的时候来看看我们。 ❑ *He felt a heavy bump, but paid no attention to it.* 他感觉重重地撞了一下，但没有在意。 12 → see also **paid, sick pay** 13 PHRASE If something that you buy or invest in **pays for itself** after a period of time, the money you gain from it, or save because you have it, is greater than the amount you originally spent or invested. 赚回本钱 ❑ *...investments in energy efficiency that would pay for themselves within five years.* …5年内能回本的、在能效方面的投资。 14 **to pay dividends** → see **dividend** 15 **to pay through the nose** → see **nose**

Do not confuse **pay** and **buy**. If you **pay** someone, **pay** them money, or **pay for** something, you give someone money for something they are selling to you. ❑ *I paid the taxi driver... I need some money to pay the window cleaner... Some people are forced to pay for their own medicines.* If you **pay** a bill or debt, you pay the amount of money that is owed. ❑ *He paid his bill and left... We were paying $50 for a single room.* If you **buy** something, you obtain it by paying money for it. ❑ *Gary's bought a bicycle.*

▸ **pay back** 1 PHRASAL VERB If you **pay back** some money that you have borrowed or taken from someone, you give them an equal sum of money at a later time. 偿还 ❑ *He burst into tears, begging her to forgive him and swearing to pay back everything he had stolen.* 他突然哭了起来，求她原谅他并发誓要偿还他偷的所有东西。 2 PHRASAL VERB If you **pay** someone **back for** doing something unpleasant to you, you take your revenge on them or make them suffer for what they did. 报复 ❑ *Some day I'll pay you back for this!* 总有一天我会为此报复你的！

▸ **pay down** PHRASAL VERB If you **pay down** a debt, or **pay down** part of a debt, you give someone part of or all of the money that you owe them. 偿还 [AM] ❑ *The Treasury plans to pay down about $1.58 billion on the federal debt.* 财政部计划偿还约十五亿八千万美元的联邦债务。

▸ **pay off** 1 PHRASAL VERB If you **pay off** a debt, you give someone all the money that you owe them. 还清 ❑ *It would take him the rest of his life to pay off that loan.* 还清那笔贷款将花费他的余生。 2 PHRASAL VERB If an action **pays off**, it is successful or profitable after a period of time. (某行动) 取得成功; 带来好结果 ❑ *Sandra was determined to become a doctor and her persistence paid off.* 桑德拉决心成为一名医生，她的坚持不懈终于带来了成功。 3 → see also **payoff**

▸ **pay out** 1 PHRASAL VERB If you **pay out** money, usually a large amount, you spend it on something. 付出 (巨款) ❑ *The insurance industry will pay out billions of dollars for damage caused by Hurricane Katrina.* 保险业将为卡特里娜飓风造成的损失赔付数十亿美元。 2 → see also **payout**

▸ **pay up** PHRASAL VERB If you **pay up**, you give someone the money that you owe them or that they are entitled to, even though you would prefer not to give it. (不情愿地) 偿付 ❑ *We claimed a refund from the association, but they would not pay up.* 我们向该协会要求退款，但他们不肯把钱吐出来。

Thesaurus *pay* 另参见:
V. clear, remit, settle 1
N. compensation, salary, wages 3

pay·able /peɪəbᵊl/ 1 ADJ If an amount of money is **payable**, it has to be paid or it can be paid. 应支付的; 可支付的 [v-link ADJ] ❑ *The money is not payable until January 31.* 这钱要到1月31日才可支付。 2 ADJ If a check or money order is made **payable to** you, it has your name written on it to indicate that you are the person who will receive the money. 应支付 (给某人) 的 [v N ADJ, n ADJ, ADJ "to" n] ❑ *Make your check payable to "Stanford Alumni Association."* 把支票开给"斯坦福校友会"。

pay·back /peɪbæk/ (**paybacks**) 1 N-COUNT You can use **payback** to refer to the profit or benefit that you obtain from something that you have spent money, time, or effort on. 收益; 收效 [mainly AM] ❑ *There is a substantial payback in terms of employee and union relations.* 就雇员和工会的关系而言有可观的收效。 2 ADJ The **payback** period of a loan is the time in which you are required or allowed to pay it back. 偿付的 (时期) [ADJ n] ❑ *The payback period can be as short as seven years.* 偿付期可以短至7年。 3 PHRASE **Payback time** is when someone has to take the consequences of what they have done in the past. You can use this expression to talk about good or bad consequences. 自食 (好或坏) 结果之时 [INFORMAL] ❑ *This was payback time. I've proved once and for all I can become champion.* 这是回报之时。我已经一劳永逸地证明我能成为冠军。

pay·check /peɪtʃɛk/ (**paychecks**)
in BRIT, use **paycheque**
N-COUNT Your **paycheck** is a piece of paper that your employer gives you as your wages or salary, and which you can then cash at a bank. You can also use **paycheck** as a way of referring to your wages or salary. 工资支票; 工薪 ❑ *I just get a small paycheck every month.* 我每个月只得到一份菲薄的工薪。 ❑ *He says his expenses are rising faster than his paycheck.* 他说他的花销比工薪增长快。

pay cheque [BRIT] → see **paycheck**

pay·day /peɪdeɪ/ (**paydays**) N-UNCOUNT **Payday** is the day of the week or month on which you receive your wages or salary. 发薪日 [also N in pl] ❑ *Until next payday, I was literally without any money.* 到下一个发薪日之前，我是名符其实身无分文了。

Word Link *ee ≈ one who receives : employee, payee, refugee*

payee /peɪi/ (**payees**) N-COUNT The **payee** of a check or similar document is the person who should receive the money. 收款人 [FORMAL] ❑ *On the check, write the name of the payee and then sign your name.* 在支票上写上收款人的名字然后签上你的名字。

pay en·velope (**pay envelopes**) N-COUNT Your **pay envelope** is the envelope containing your wages that your employer gives you. 工薪袋 [AM]
in BRIT, use **pay packet**

pay·er /peɪər/ (**payers**) 1 N-COUNT You can refer to someone as a **payer** if they pay a particular kind of bill or fee. For example, a mortgage **payer** is someone who pays a mortgage. 支付人 ❑ *Lower interest rates pleased millions of mortgage payers.* 较低利率使上百万抵押贷款支付人高兴了。 2 → see also **taxpayer** 3 N-COUNT A **good payer** pays you quickly or pays you a lot of money. A **bad payer** takes a long time to pay you, or does not pay you very much. (好的、差的等) 付款人 ❑ *Small businesses, hit hard by the recession, blame the government, banks, and late payers.* 受到经济衰退沉重打击的小企业指责政府、银行和那些迟付款的人。

pay·ment ♦♦◇ /peɪmənt/ (**payments**) 1 N-COUNT A **payment** is an amount of money that is paid to someone, or the act of paying this money. 支付的款项; 支付 ❑ *Thousands of its customers are behind with loans and mortgage payments.* 其数千客户未按时支付贷款和按揭款。 2 N-UNCOUNT **Payment** is the act of paying money to someone or of being paid. 支付 ❑ *He had sought to obtain payment of a sum which he had claimed was owed to him.* 他曾试图获得一笔他声称是欠他的钱。 3 → see also **balance of payments, down payment**

Word Partnership *payment* 的常用搭配:
V. **accept** payment, **make a** payment, **receive** payment 1
ADJ. **late** payment, **minimum** payment, **monthly** payment 1
N. payment **in cash**, payment **by check**, **mortgage** payment 1
payment **date** 1 2
payment **method**, payment **plan** 2

pay·off /peɪɔf/ (**payoffs**) also **pay-off** 1 N-COUNT The **payoff from** an action is the advantage or benefit that you get from it. (某行动的) 收益 ❑ *If such materials became generally available to the optics industry the payoffs from such a breakthrough would be enormous.* 如果此类材料能够普遍用于光学产业，这一突破带来的收益将是巨大的。 2 N-COUNT A **payoff** is a payment made to someone, often secretly or illegally, so that they will not cause trouble. 贿赂钱 ❑ *Soldiers in both countries supplement their incomes with payoffs from drugs exporters.* 两国士兵们都靠来自毒品出口贩的贿赂来增补收入。 3 N-COUNT A **payoff** is a large payment made to someone by their employer when the person has been forced to leave their job. 辞退补偿金 ❑ *The ousted chairman received a $1.5 million payoff from the loss-making oil company.* 被辞退的董事长从亏损中的石油公司获得了一笔150万美元的辞退补偿金。

pay·out /peɪaʊt/ (**payouts**) N-COUNT A **payout** is a sum of money, especially a large one, that is paid to someone, for example, by an insurance company or as a prize. (尤指大笔) 钱款 ❑ *...long delays in receiving insurance payouts.* …收取保险赔偿金的长期拖延。
→ see **lottery**

pay pack·et (**pay packets**) 1 N-COUNT Your **pay packet** is the envelope containing your wages that your employer gives you at the end of every week. 工薪袋 [BRIT]
in AM, use **pay envelope**
2 N-COUNT You can refer to someone's wages or salary as their **pay packet**. 工薪 [BRIT]
in AM, use **paycheck, pay**

pay-per-view N-UNCOUNT **Pay-per-view** is a cable or satellite television service in which you pay a fee to watch a particular program. The abbreviation **PPV** is also used. 收看付费 (电视) ❑ *The match appeared on pay-per-view television.* 这场比赛出现在了收看付费电视上。

pay·phone /peɪfoʊn/ (**payphones**) also **pay phone** N-COUNT A **payphone** is a telephone that you put coins or a card into before you can make a call. Payphones are usually in public places. (投币式或插卡式) 公用电话

▲ **pay·roll** /peɪroʊl/ (**payrolls**) N-COUNT The people **on the payroll** of a company or an organization are the people who work for it and are paid by it. 在职人员工薪名册 [BUSINESS] ❑ *They had 87,000 employees on the payroll.* 他们有87000人在在职人员工薪名册上。

pay·slip /peɪslɪp/ (**payslips**) also **pay slip** N-COUNT A **payslip** is the same as a **paystub**. 工资条 [BRIT]

pay·stub /peɪstʌb/ (**paystubs**) also **pay stub** N-COUNT A **paystub** is a piece of paper given to an employee when he or she is paid stating how much money has been earned and how much has been taken from that sum for things such as tax. 工资条 [AM]
in BRIT, use **payslip**

PC /pi si/ (**PCs**) 1 N-COUNT A **PC** is a computer that is used by one person at a time in a business, a school, or at home. **PC** is an abbreviation for **personal computer**. 个人电脑 ❑ *The price of a PC has fallen by an average of 25% a year since 1982.* 1982年以来个人电脑的价格平均每年下降25%。 2 ADJ If you say that someone is **PC**, you mean that they are extremely careful not to offend or upset any group of people in society who have a disadvantage. **PC** is an abbreviation for **politically correct.** 政治上正确的 ❑ *Certainly, when you're with a group of guys and you're talking about women, you're not PC.* 当然，当你跟一帮哥们在一起，而你却在谈论女人，你就不是政治上正确了。

pd. **pd.** is a written abbreviation for **paid**. It is written on a bill to indicate that it has been paid. 已付

PDA /pi di eɪ/ (**PDAs**) N-COUNT A **PDA** is a handheld computer, used mainly for storing and accessing personal information such as addresses, telephone numbers, and memos. **PDA** is an abbreviation for **personal digital assistant.** 个人数字助理 ❑ *A typical PDA can function as a cellphone and a personal organizer.* 一部典型的个人数字助理可以兼具手机和个人记事簿功能。

PDF /pi di ɛf/ N-UNCOUNT **PDF** files are computer documents which look exactly like the original documents, regardless of which software or operating system was used to create the original documents. **PDF** is an abbreviation for 'Portable Document Format'. 可移植文档格式 [USU N n] [COMPUTING] ❑ *The leaflet is in PDF format.* 这个传单用的是可移植文档格式。

pea /pi/ (**peas**) N-COUNT **Peas** are round green seeds that grow in long thin cases and are eaten as a vegetable. 豌豆

peace ♦♦♦ /pis/ **1** N-UNCOUNT If countries or groups involved in a war or violent conflict are discussing **peace**, they are talking to each other in order to try to end the conflict. 和平问题 ❑ *Peace talks involving other rebel leaders and government representatives broke up without agreement last week, but are due to resume shortly.* 有其他叛军领袖和政府代表参加的和平谈判于上周未能达成协议而破裂，但不久之后将恢复。 ❑ *Leaders of some rival factions signed a peace agreement last week.* 一些对立派别的领导人于上周签署了一项和平协议。 **2** N-UNCOUNT If there is **peace** in a country or in the world, there are no wars or violent conflicts going on. 和平状态 ❑ *The president spoke of a shared commitment to world peace and economic development.* 总统谈到了一项促进世界和平和经济发展的共同承诺。 **3** N-UNCOUNT If you disapprove of weapons, especially nuclear weapons, you can use **peace** to refer to campaigns and other activities intended to reduce their numbers or stop their use. (尤指阻止核武器使用的) 和平运动 ❑ *...two peace campaigners accused of causing damage to an F1-11 nuclear bomber.* …被指控造成一架F1-11核轰炸机受损的两位和平运动家。 **4** N-UNCOUNT If you have **peace**, you are not being disturbed, and you are in calm, quiet surroundings. 安宁 ❑ *All I want is to have some peace and quiet and spend a couple of nice days with my grandchildren.* 我只想有一些安宁与平静并和我的孙子孙女们过几天好日子。 **5** N-UNCOUNT If you have a feeling of **peace**, you feel contented and calm and not at all worried. You can also say that you are **at peace**. 平和 ❑ *I had a wonderful feeling of peace and serenity when I saw my husband.* 我看到我的丈夫就有一种平和安详的美妙感觉。 **6** N-UNCOUNT If there is **peace** among a group of people, they live or work together in a friendly way and do not argue. You can also say that people live or work **in peace with** each other. 相安无事 ❑ *...a period of relative peace in the country's industrial relations.* …该国产业关系中一段相对平静的时期。 **7** PHRASE If someone in authority, such as the army or the police, **keeps the peace**, they make sure that people behave and do not fight or quarrel with each other. 维持和平 ❑ *...the first U.N. contingent assigned to help keep the peace in Cambodia.* …第一支派往柬埔寨帮助维持和平的联合国分队。 **8** PHRASE If something gives you **peace of mind**, it stops you from worrying about a particular problem or difficulty. 心灵的平静 ❑ *The main appeal these bonds hold for individual investors is the safety and peace of mind they offer.* 这些债券对于个人投资者的主要吸引力在于它们提供的安全感和心灵的平静。

peace·ful ♦◇◇ /pisfəl/ **1** ADJ **Peaceful** activities and situations do not involve war. 和平的 (活动、局面) ❑ *He has attempted to find a peaceful solution to the Ossetian conflict.* 他曾试图找到一个解决奥塞梯冲突的和平的办法。 ● **peace·ful·ly** ADV 和平地 [ADV with v] ❑ *The U.S. military expects the matter to be resolved peacefully.* 美国军方期望这一事件能和平解决。 **2** ADJ **Peaceful** occasions happen without violence or serious disorder. 和平的 (场景) ❑ *The farmers staged a noisy but peaceful protest outside the headquarters of the organization.* 农民们在该组织总部外举行了一次喧闹但和平的抗议活动。 ● **peace·ful·ly** ADV 和平地 [ADV with v] ❑ *The governor asked the crowd of protestors to leave peacefully.* 州长要求抗议人群和平离开。 **3** ADJ **Peaceful** people are not violent and try to avoid arguing or fighting with other people. 和平的 (人们) ❑ *...warriors who killed or enslaved the peaceful farmers.* …杀死或奴役和平的农民们的那些武士。 ● **peace·ful·ly** ADV 和平地 [ADV with v] ❑ *They've been living and working peacefully with members of various ethnic groups.* 他们一直与各种族群的成员们和平地生活和工作。 **4** ADJ A **peaceful** place or time is quiet, calm, and free from disturbance. 安宁的 (地方、时期) ❑ *...a peaceful house in the heart of the Ozarks.* …在欧扎克山脉中心地带的一幢安宁的房子。 ● **peace·ful·ly** ADV 安宁地 [ADV after v] ❑ *Except for traffic noise the night passed peacefully.* 除了交通噪音，那夜安宁地过去了。

> **Thesaurus** *peaceful* 另参见：
> ADJ. calm, friendly, gentle, harmonious, nonviolent, placid, quiet, tranquil; *(ant.)* hostile, warring **1**–**4**

peace·ful·ly /pisfəli/ **1** ADV If you say that someone died **peacefully**, you mean that they suffered no pain or violence when they died. 安详地 (死去) [ADV after v] ❑ *He died peacefully on December 10 after a short illness.* 他在一场短病后于12月10日安详地离开了人世。 **2** → see also **peaceful**

peach /pitʃ/ (**peaches**) **1** N-COUNT A **peach** is a soft, round, slightly furry fruit with sweet yellow flesh and pinky-orange skin. Peaches grow in warm countries. 桃 **2** COLOR Something that is **peach** is pale pinky-orange in color. 桃红色的 ❑ *...a peach silk blouse.* …一件桃红色的丝绸衫。

peak ♦◇◇ /pik/ (**peaks, peaking, peaked**) **1** N-COUNT The **peak** of a process or an activity is the point at which it is at its strongest, most successful, or most fully developed. (过程、活动的) 顶峰 ❑ *The firm has slashed its workforce from a peak of 150,000 in 2000.* 2000年那家公司把其员工从15万峰值进行了大幅裁减。 ❑ *...a flourishing career that was at its peak at the time of his death.* …在他去世时处于鼎盛时期的兴旺事业。 **2** V-I When something **peaks**, it reaches its highest value or its highest level. 达到峰值 ❑ *Temperatures have peaked at over 90 degrees.* 温度已达到峰值，超过了90度。 **3** ADJ The **peak** level or value of something is its highest level or value. 峰值的 [ADJ n] ❑ *Today's price is 59% lower than the peak level of $1.5 million.* 今天的价格比150万美元的峰值水平低了59%。 **4** ADJ **Peak** times are the times when there is most demand for something or most use of something. 高峰的 (时期) [ADJ n] ❑ *It's always crowded at peak times.* 在高峰期总是很拥挤。 **5** N-COUNT A **peak** is a mountain or the top of a mountain. 山峰 ❑ *...the snow-covered peaks.* …白雪覆盖的山峰。
→ see **mountain**

peal /pil/ (**peals, pealing, pealed**) **1** V-I When bells **peal**, they ring one after another, making a musical sound. (钟等) 一声接一声地鸣响 ❑ *Church bells pealed at the stroke of midnight.* 午夜时钟一敲响，教堂的钟声便一声接一声地响起来。 ● N-COUNT **Peal** is also a noun. 一声接一声的钟鸣声 ❑ *...the great peal of the abbey bells.* …修道院一声接一声的洪亮的钟鸣声。 **2** N-COUNT A **peal of** laughter or thunder consists of a long, loud series of sounds. 一长串霍响亮的 (笑、雷的) 声音 ❑ *I heard a peal of laughter.* 我听到一长串响亮的笑声。

★ **pea·nut** /pinʌt, -nət/ (**peanuts**) N-COUNT **Peanuts** are small nuts that grow under the ground. Peanuts are often eaten as a

> **Word Web** peanut
>
> The **peanut** is not actually a **nut**. It is a legume and grows under the ground. Peanuts originated in South America about 3,500 years ago. Explorers took them to Africa. Later, African slaves introduced the peanut into North America. At first only poor people ate them. However, by 1900 they had become a popular **snack**. You could buy **roasted** peanuts on city streets and at baseball games and circuses. Some scientists believe that roasted peanuts cause more **allergic** reactions than boiled peanuts. George Washington Carver, an African-American scientist, found 325 different uses for peanuts—including **peanut butter**.

snack, especially roasted and salted, and their oil is used in cooking. 花生 ❑ *...a packet of peanuts.* …一袋花生。
→ see Word Web: **peanut**

In the early 20th century, African-American scientist George Washington Carver ground **peanuts** into a smooth paste. This food, called **peanut butter**, is used to make sandwiches. Peanut butter and jelly sandwiches are a popular food with American children.

pear /pɛər/ (**pears**) N-COUNT A **pear** is a sweet, juicy fruit that is narrow near its stalk, and wider and rounded at the bottom. Pears have white flesh and thin green, yellow, or brown skin. 梨

★ **pearl** /pɜrl/ (**pearls**) **1** N-COUNT A **pearl** is a hard round object that is shiny and creamy white in color. Pearls grow inside the shell of an oyster and are used for making expensive jewelry. 珍珠 ❑ *She wore a string of pearls at her throat.* 她那时脖子上带着一串珍珠。 **2** ADJ **Pearl** is used to describe something that looks like a pearl. 珍珠般的 ❑ *...tiny pearl buttons.* …珍珠般的小扣子

peas·ant /pɛzᵊnt/ (**peasants**) N-COUNT A **peasant** is a poor person of low social status who works on the land; used to refer to people who live in countries where farming is still a common way of life. 农民 ❑ *...the peasants in the Peruvian highlands.* …秘鲁高原地区的农民们。

peat /pit/ N-UNCOUNT **Peat** is decaying plant material that is found under the ground in some cool, wet regions. Peat can be added to soil to help plants grow, or can be burned to produce coal. 泥炭 ❑ *...a peat fire.* …一堆泥炭火。
→ see **wetland**

▲ **peb·ble** /pɛbᵊl/ (**pebbles**) N-COUNT A **pebble** is a small, smooth, round stone which is found on beaches and at the bottom of rivers. 卵石
→ see **beach**

▲ **peck** /pɛk/ (**pecks, pecking, pecked**) **1** V-T/V-I If a bird **pecks at** something or **pecks** something, it moves its beak forward quickly and bites at it. 啄; 啄食 ❑ *It was winter and the sparrows were pecking at whatever they could find.* 已是冬天了，麻雀们能找到什么就啄食什么。 ❑ *Chickens pecked in the dust.* 小鸡们在尘土中啄食。 ❑ *It pecked his leg.* 它啄了他的腿。 **2** V-T If you **peck** someone **on** the cheek, you give them a quick, light kiss. 快速轻吻 ❑ *Elizabeth walked up to him and pecked him on the cheek.* 伊丽莎白走近他，快速轻吻了他的脸颊。 ● N-COUNT **Peck** is also a noun. 快速轻吻 ❑ *He gave me a little peck on the cheek.* 他给了我一个脸上快速轻吻。

pe·cu·liar /pɪkyulyər/ **1** ADJ If you describe someone or something as **peculiar**, you think that they are strange or unusual, sometimes in an unpleasant way. 不寻常的; 古怪的 ❑ *Mr. Kennet has a rather peculiar sense of humor.* 肯尼特先生有一种相当不寻常的幽默感。 ● **pe·cu·liar·ly** ADV 不寻常地; 奇怪地 ❑ *His face had become peculiarly expressionless.* 他的脸变得异乎寻常地毫无表情。 **2** ADJ If something is **peculiar to** a particular thing, person, or situation, it belongs or relates only to that thing, person, or situation. 特有的; 独特的 ❑ *Punks, soldiers, hippies, and Sumo wrestlers all have distinct hair styles, peculiar to their group.* 朋克摇滚歌手、士兵、嬉皮士和相扑手都留着他们那个群体特有的独特发型。 ● **pe·cu·liar·ly** ADV 特有地; 独特地 ❑ *...a peculiarly American conservatism.* …一种美国特有的保守主义。

★ **pe·cu·li·ar·ity** /pɪkyuliærɪti/ (**peculiarities**) **1** N-COUNT A **peculiarity** that someone or something has is a strange or unusual characteristic or habit. 怪癖; 古怪之处 ❑ *Joe's other peculiarity was that he was constantly munching hard candy.* 乔的另一个怪癖是他不停地嚼硬糖。 **2** N-COUNT A **peculiarity** is a characteristic or quality that belongs or relates only to one person or thing. 独特性; 特性 ❑ *...a strange peculiarity of the U.S. system.* …美国制度的一个奇怪的特性。

pe·cu·ni·ary /pɪkyunieri/ ADJ **Pecuniary** means concerning or involving money. 金钱上的; 金钱方面的 [FORMAL] ❑ *She denies obtaining a pecuniary advantage by deception.* 她否认通过欺骗获得了金钱方面的好处。

Word Link *ped ≈ child : pedagogical, pediatrician, pedophile*

peda·gogi·cal /pɛdəgɒdʒɪkᵊl/ ADJ **Pedagogical** means concerning the methods and theory of teaching. 教学法的 [ADJ n] [FORMAL] ❑ *The school district provides training to help teachers improve their pedagogical methods.* 该学区提供培训以帮助教师们改进教学方法。

Word Link *ped ≈ foot : pedal, pedestal, pedestrian*

★ **ped·al** /pɛdᵊl/ (**pedals, pedaling** or **pedalling, pedaled** or **pedalled**) **1** N-COUNT The **pedals** on a bicycle are the two parts that you push with your feet in order to make the bicycle move. (自行车的) 踏板 **2** V-T/V-I When you **pedal** a bicycle, you push the pedals around with your feet to make it move. 踩 (自行车) 踏板 ❑ *She climbed on her bike with a feeling of pride and pedaled the five miles home.* 她怀着自豪感跨上自行车，蹬了5英里回到家。 **3** N-COUNT A **pedal** in a car or on a machine is a lever that you press with your foot in order to control the car or machine. (汽车、机器的) 踏板 ❑ *...the brake or accelerator pedals.* …刹车或加速器踏板。
→ see **bicycle**

pe·dan·tic /pɪdæntɪk/ ADJ If you say someone is **pedantic**, you mean that they are too concerned with unimportant details or traditional rules, especially in connection with academic subjects. 学究气的 [DISAPPROVAL] ❑ *His lecture was so pedantic and uninteresting.* 他的讲座学究气十足且没趣。

▲ **ped·dle** /pɛdᵊl/ (**peddles, peddling, peddled**) **1** V-T Someone who **peddles** things goes from place to place trying to sell them. 兜售 ❑ *His attempts to peddle his paintings around Laramie's tiny gallery scene proved unsuccessful.* 他在拉勒米的小画廊现场周围兜售其画作的企图证明不成功。 **2** V-T Someone who **peddles** drugs sells illegal drugs. 贩卖 (非法药品) ❑ *When a drug pusher offered the Los Angeles youngster $100 to peddle drugs, Jack refused.* 当一名毒贩子给这位洛杉矶小伙子杰克$100让他贩卖毒品时，他拒绝了。 ● **ped·dling** N-UNCOUNT 贩卖 ❑ *The war against drug peddling is all about cash.* 反对毒品贩卖的斗争完全是个钱的问题。 **3** V-T If someone **peddles** an idea or a piece of information, they try to get people to accept it. 散布 (某观点或信息) [DISAPPROVAL] ❑ *They even set up their own news agency to peddle anti-isolationist propaganda.* 他们甚至建立了自己的新闻机构以散布反孤立主义思想。

ped·es·tal /pɛdɪstᵊl/ (**pedestals**) **1** N-COUNT A **pedestal** is the base on which something such as a statue stands. (雕像等的) 基座 ❑ *...a larger than life-sized bronze statue on a granite pedestal.* …在花岗岩基座上的一尊比真人大的铜像。 **2** N-COUNT If you put someone **on a pedestal**, you admire them very much and think that they cannot be criticized. If someone is knocked **off a pedestal** they are no longer admired. 崇高地位 ❑ *Since childhood, I put my own parents on a pedestal. I felt they could do no wrong.* 自童年起我就把我父母当偶像崇拜。我觉得他们不会做错事。

Word Link *an, ian ≈ one of, relating to : Christian, pedestrian, Roman*

★ **pe·des·trian** /pɪdɛstriən/ (**pedestrians**) **1** N-COUNT A **pedestrian** is a person who is walking, especially in a town or city, rather than traveling in a vehicle. 行人 ❑ *Ingrid was a walker, even in Los Angeles, where a pedestrian is a rare sight.* 英格丽德是个步行者，即使在行人少见的洛杉矶也是如此。 **2** ADJ If you describe something as **pedestrian**, you mean that it is ordinary and not at all interesting. 平庸乏味的 [DISAPPROVAL] ❑ *His style is so pedestrian that the book becomes a real bore.* 他的文风很平庸，以致那本书成了一本真正乏味的书。

pe·dia·tri·cian /pidiətrɪʃᵊn/ (**pediatricians**)

in BRIT, use **paediatrician**

N-COUNT A **pediatrician** is a doctor who specializes in treating children. 儿科医生

Word Link *iatr ≈ healing : geriatric, pediatrics, psychiatrist*

▲ **pe·di·at·rics** /pidiætrɪks/

The form **pediatric** is used as a modifier.

N-UNCOUNT **Pediatrics** is the area of medicine that is concerned with the treatment of children. 儿科学 ❑ *...a career in pediatrics.* …一段儿科学职业生涯。
→ see **hospital**

pedi·gree /pɛdɪgri/ (**pedigrees**) **1** N-COUNT If a dog, cat, or other animal has a **pedigree**, its ancestors are known and recorded. An animal is considered to have a good pedigree when all its known ancestors are of the same type. (狗、猫等动物的) 血统记录; 纯种系谱 ❑ *60 percent of dogs and ten percent of cats have pedigrees.* 60%的狗和10%的猫都有血统记录。 **2** N-COUNT Someone's **pedigree** is their background or their ancestors. (人的) 背景; 出身 ❑ *Hammer's business pedigree almost guaranteed him the acquaintance of presidents.* 哈默的商业背景几乎保证了他与几位总统的相识。

P

Word Link *ped ≈ child : pedagogical, pediatrician, pedophile*

pe·do·phile /pidəfaɪl/ (**pedophiles**)
in BRIT, use **paedophile**
N-COUNT A **pedophile** is a person, usually a man, who is sexually attracted to children. 恋童癖患者

pe·do·philia /pidəfɪliə/
in BRIT, use **paedophilia**
N-UNCOUNT **Pedophilia** is sexual activity with children or the condition of being sexually attracted to children. 恋童癖 *...allegations of his pedophilia.* …有关他的恋童癖的各种指称。 ❑ *He addressed the clinical aspects of pedophilia and abuse.* 他谈及了恋童癖和虐待的临床方面。

peek /pik/ (**peeks, peeking, peeked**) V-I If you **peek at** something or someone, you take a quick look at them, often secretly. (常指偷偷地) 瞥一眼 ❑ *On two occasions she had peeked at him through a crack in the wall.* 有两次她曾透过墙上的一个裂缝偷窥了他。 ● N-COUNT **Peek** is also a noun. 一瞥 ❑ *Companies have been paying outrageous fees for a peek at the technical data.* 各公司一直在为该技术资料的一窥支付惊人的费用。

★ **peel** /pil/ (**peels, peeling, peeled**) **1** N-VAR The **peel** of a fruit such as a lemon or an apple is its skin. You can also refer to a **peel**. (果) 皮 ❑ *...grated lemon peel.* …磨碎了的柠檬皮。 ❑ *...a banana peel.* …一块香蕉皮。 **2** V-T When you **peel** fruit or vegetables, you remove their skins. 将 (水果、蔬菜等) 去皮 ❑ *She sat down in the kitchen and began peeling potatoes.* 她在厨房里坐下，开始削土豆。 **3** V-T/V-I If you **peel off** something that has been sticking to a surface or if it **peels off**, it comes away from the surface. 剥掉；剥落 ❑ *One of the kids was peeling plaster off the wall.* 其中一个孩子在剥墙上的灰泥。 ❑ *It took me two days to peel off the labels.* 我花了两天时间才剥掉那些标签。 ❑ *Paint was peeling off the walls.* 漆在从墙上剥落。 **4** V-I If a surface **is peeling**, the paint on it is coming away. (表面) 掉漆 [usu cont] ❑ *Its once-elegant white pillars are peeling.* 其一度典雅的白色立柱在掉漆。 **5** V-I If you **are peeling** or if your skin **is peeling**, small pieces of skin are coming off, usually because you have been burned by the sun. (人) 脱皮；(皮) 脱落 [usu cont] ❑ *His face was peeling from sunburn.* 他的脸因日晒而在脱皮。
→ see **cut**

▲ **peep** /pip/ (**peeps, peeping, peeped**) **1** V-I If you **peep**, or **peep at** something, you take a quick look at it, often secretly and quietly. (常指悄悄地) 瞥一眼 ❑ *Children came to peep at him around the doorway.* 孩子们来到门口偷看他。 ● N-SING **Peep** is also a noun. 一瞥 ["a" N] ❑ *"Fourteen minutes," Chris said, taking a peep at his watch.* "十四分钟，" 克里斯瞥了一眼手表说道。 **2** V-I If something **peeps** out from behind or under something, a small part of it is visible or becomes visible. (从后面或下面) 探出；露出 ❑ *Purple and yellow flowers peeped up between rocks.* 紫色与黄色的花从岩石之间探了出来。 **3** PHRASE If you say that you **don't hear a peep from** someone, you mean that they do not say anything or make any noise. 听到一点声音 [INFORMAL] ❑ *You don't hear a peep from her once she's gone to bed.* 她一上床你就不会听见她吭一声。

peer ♦◇◇ /pɪər/ (**peers, peering, peered**) **1** V-I If you **peer at** something, you look at it very hard, usually because it is difficult to see clearly. 费力地看 ❑ *I had been peering at a computer print-out that made no sense at all.* 我一直在费力地看一份毫无意义的电脑打印稿。 **2** N-COUNT Your **peers** are the people who are the same age as you or who have the same status as you. 同龄人；同等地位的人 ❑ *His engaging personality made him popular with his peers.* 他迷人的个性使他很受同龄人欢迎。

★ **peg** ♦◇◇ /pɛg/ (**pegs, pegging, pegged**) **1** N-COUNT A **peg** is a small piece of wood or metal that is used for fastening something to something else. 销钉 ❑ *He builds furniture using wooden pegs instead of nails.* 他用木钉而不是铁钉制作家具。 **2** N-COUNT A **peg** is a small hook or knob that is attached to a wall or door and is used for hanging things on. 挂钩；挂环 ❑ *His work jacket hung on the peg in the kitchen.* 他的工作服挂在厨房里的挂钩上。 **3** N-COUNT A **peg** is a small device that you use to fasten clothes to a clothes line. 衣夹 [mainly BRIT]
in AM, usually use **clothespin**
4 V-T If you **peg** something somewhere or **peg** it **down**, you fix it there with pegs. 用衣夹夹住；用销钉固定 ❑ *Peg down netting over the top to keep out leaves.* 把网子用销钉固定在顶部以防止树叶掉入。 ❑ *...a tent pegged to the ground nearby for the kids.* …用销钉固定在附近的地上给孩子们用的一个帐篷。 **5** V-T If a price or amount of something **is pegged at** a particular level, it is fixed at that level. 固定 (价格、数量等) ❑ *Its currency is pegged to the dollar.* 其货币与美元的汇率固定了。 ❑ *The Bank wants to peg rates at 9%.* 该银行想要把利率固定在9%。

pel·let /pɛlɪt/ (**pellets**) N-COUNT A **pellet** is a small ball of paper, mud, lead, or other material. 小团；丸 ❑ *He was shot in the head by an air gun pellet.* 他被一粒气枪弹丸射中了头部。

pelt /pɛlt/ (**pelts, pelting, pelted**) **1** N-COUNT The **pelt** of an animal is its skin, which can be used to make clothing or rugs. (动物的) 皮 ❑ *...a bed covered with beaver pelts.* …一张铺着海狸皮的床。 **2** V-T If you **pelt** someone **with** things, you throw things at them. 扔 ❑ *Some of the younger men began to pelt one another with snowballs.* 一些年纪稍轻的人开始用雪球互相扔。 **3** V-I If the rain **is pelting down**, it is raining very hard. (雨) 猛烈地下 [usu cont] [INFORMAL] ❑ *The rain now was pelting down.* 雨这时正哗哗地下。

pel·vic /pɛlvɪk/ ADJ **Pelvic** means near or relating to your pelvis. 靠近骨盆的；有关骨盆的 [ADJ n] ❑ *...an inflammation of the pelvic region.* …一种骨盆区炎症。

pel·vis /pɛlvɪs/ (**pelvises**) N-COUNT Your **pelvis** is the wide, curved group of bones at the level of your hips. 骨盆

pen ♦◇◇ /pɛn/ (**pens, penning, penned**) **1** N-COUNT A **pen** is a long thin object which you use to write in ink. 钢笔 **2** **felt-tip pen** → see **felt-tip** **3** V-T If someone **pens** a letter, article, or book, they write it. 撰写 [FORMAL] ❑ *I really intended to pen this letter to you early this morning.* 我本来真的打算今天一大早就给你撰写这封信的。 **4** N-COUNT A **pen** is a small area with a fence around it in which farm animals are kept for a short time. (临时圈养牲畜的) 圈 ❑ *...a holding pen for sheep.* …一个羊群候宰圈。 **5** V-T If people or animals **are penned** somewhere or **are penned up**, they are forced to remain in a very small area. 关 (人、动物) [usu passive] ❑ *The cattle were penned for the night.* 这头牛晚上被关了起来。 ❑ *The animals were penned up in cages.* 这些动物被关在了笼子里。
→ see **drawing, office**

Thesaurus *pen* 另参见:

N.	cage, coop, corral, enclosure, fence **4**
V.	cage, enclose, shut in **5**

pe·nal /pinəl/ ADJ **Penal** means relating to the punishment of criminals. 有关刑罚的 ❑ *...penal and legal systems.* …刑罚与法律体系。

▲ **pe·nal·ise** /pinəlaɪz/ [BRIT] → see **penalize**

▲ **pe·nal·ize** /pinəlaɪz/ (**penalizes, penalizing, penalized**)
in BRIT, also use **penalise**
V-T If a person or group **is penalized** for something, they are made to suffer in some way because of it. 处罚 [usu passive] ❑ *Some of the players may, on occasion, break the rules and be penalized.* 一些选手可能偶尔会犯规并受到处罚。

pen·al·ty ♦◇◇ /pɛnəlti/ (**penalties**) **1** N-COUNT A **penalty** is a punishment that someone is given for doing something which is against a law or rule. 刑罚 ❑ *One of those arrested could face the death penalty.* 那些被捕之人其中的一个可能会面临死刑。 **2** N-COUNT In sports such as soccer, football, and hockey, a **penalty** is a disadvantage forced on the team that breaks a rule. (体育比赛中的) 罚球 ❑ *Referee Michael Reed had no hesitation in awarding a penalty.* 裁判迈克尔・里德毫不犹豫地判了罚球。 **3** N-COUNT **The penalty** that you pay for something you have done is something unpleasant that you experience as a result. 惩罚 ❑ *Why should I pay the penalty for somebody else's mistake?* 我为什么要为别人的错误而接受惩罚呢？

pence /pɛns/ N-PLURAL **Pence** is the plural form of penny, a British coin worth one hundredth of a pound. 便士 (**penny**的复数形式) ❑ *Matches cost only a few pence.* 火柴只需几便士。

pen·chant /pɛntʃənt/ N-SING If someone has a **penchant for** something, they have a special liking for it or a tendency to do it. 特别的喜好 [FORMAL] ❑ *...a stylish woman with a penchant for dark glasses.* …一位对墨镜有特别喜好的时髦女子。

pen·cil /pɛnsəl/ (**pencils**) N-COUNT A **pencil** is an object that you write or draw with. It consists of a thin piece of wood with a rod of a black or colored substance through the middle. If you write or draw something **in pencil**, you do it using a pencil. 铅笔 [also "in" N] ❑ *I found a pencil and some blank paper in her desk.* 我在她的书桌里找到了一支铅笔和一些白纸。
→ see **drawing, office**

P

Word Link *pend ≈ hanging : appendix, depend, pendant*

pen·dant /pɛndənt/ (**pendants**) N-COUNT A **pendant** is an ornament on a chain that you wear around your neck. 坠饰；挂件 → see **jewelry**

▲ **pend·ing** /pɛndɪŋ/ 1 ADJ If something such as a legal procedure is **pending**, it is waiting to be dealt with or settled. 待处理的 [FORMAL] ❑ *She had a libel action against the magazine pending.* 她有一项针对那家杂志的诽谤诉讼待处理。 ❑ *In 2006, the court had 600 pending cases.* 2006年，该法院有600件未结的案子。 2 PREP If something is done **pending** a future event, it is done until that event happens. 待(某未来事件)发生 [FORMAL] ❑ *A judge has suspended the ban pending a full inquiry.* 一名法官已暂时取消了此项禁令，等待一次全面调查。 3 ADJ Something that is **pending** is going to happen soon. 即将发生的 [FORMAL] ❑ *A growing number of customers have been inquiring about the pending price rises.* 越来越多的顾客在询问即将出现的价格上涨问题。

★ **pen·du·lum** /pɛndʒələm/ (**pendulums**) 1 N-COUNT The **pendulum** of a clock is a rod with a weight at the end which swings from side to side in order to make the clock work. 钟摆 2 N-SING You can use the idea of a **pendulum** and the way it swings regularly as a way of talking about regular changes in a situation or in people's opinions. (事态、舆论等的) 摇摆 ❑ *The political pendulum has swung in favor of the liberals.* 政治的钟摆已经摆向了自由派。

pen·etrate /pɛnɪtreɪt/ (**penetrates, penetrating, penetrated**) 1 V-T If something or someone **penetrates** a physical object or an area, they succeed in getting into it or passing through it. 进入；穿透 ❑ *X-rays can penetrate many objects.* X射线能穿透很多物体。 ● **pen·etra·tion** /pɛnɪtreɪʃən/ N-UNCOUNT (**penetrations**) 进入；穿透 [also N in pl] ❑ *The thick walls prevented penetration by debris from the hurricane.* 一堵堵厚墙阻挡了飓风带来的碎片的穿透。 2 V-T If someone **penetrates** an organization, a group, or a profession, they succeed in entering it although it is difficult to do so. (排除困难) 进入 ❑ *...the continuing failure of women to penetrate the higher levels of engineering.* …女性跻身工程业较高层级的连续失败。 3 V-T If someone **penetrates** an enemy group or a rival organization, they succeed in joining it in order to get information or cause trouble. 打入(敌对组织) ❑ *The CIA had requested our help to penetrate a drug ring operating out of Munich.* 中情局曾要求我们协助打入在慕尼黑外活动的一个贩毒团伙。 ● **pen·etra·tion** N-UNCOUNT 打入 ❑ *...the successful penetration by the KGB of the French intelligence service.* …克格勃向法国情报机构的成功渗入。 4 V-T If a company or country **penetrates** a market or area, they succeed in selling their products there. 打入(某市场或地区) [BUSINESS] ❑ *There have been around 15 attempts from outside Idaho to penetrate the market.* 已有约十五次从爱达荷州以外打入该市场的企图。 ● **pen·etra·tion** N-UNCOUNT 打入 ❑ *...import penetration across a broad range of heavy industries.* …横跨广泛重工业领域的进口渗入。

pen·etrat·ing /pɛnɪtreɪtɪŋ/ 1 ADJ A **penetrating** sound is loud and usually high-pitched. 刺耳的 ❑ *Mary heard the penetrating siren of an ambulance.* 玛丽听到了救护车刺耳的警报声。 2 ADJ If someone gives you a **penetrating** look, it makes you think that they know what you are thinking. 穿透人心的(目光) ❑ *He gazed at me with a sharp, penetrating look that made my heart pound.* 他用一种犀利的、穿透人心的、使得我的心怦怦直跳的目光注视着我。

pen-friend (**pen-friends**) also **penfriend** N-COUNT A **pen-friend** is the same as a **pen pal**. 笔友 [BRIT]

★ **pen·guin** /pɛŋgwɪn/ (**penguins**) N-COUNT A **penguin** is a type of large black and white sea bird found mainly in the Antarctic. Penguins cannot fly but use their short wings for swimming. 企鹅

peni·cil·lin /pɛnɪsɪlɪn/ N-UNCOUNT **Penicillin** is a drug that kills bacteria and is used to treat infections. 青霉素

Word Link *insula ≈ island : insular, insulate, peninsula*

★ **pen·in·su·la** /pənɪnsələ, -nɪnsyə-/ (**peninsulas**) N-COUNT A **peninsula** is a long narrow piece of land that sticks out from a larger piece of land and is almost completely surrounded by water. 半岛 ❑ *...the political situation in the Korean peninsula.* …朝鲜半岛的政治局势。

pe·nis /pinɪs/ (**penises**) N-COUNT A man's **penis** is the part of his body that he uses when he urinates and when he has sex. 阴茎

pen·ni·less /pɛnilɪs/ ADJ Someone who is **penniless** has hardly any money at all. 身无分文的 ❑ *They'd soon be penniless and homeless if she couldn't find suitable work.* 如果她找不到合适的工作，他们很快就会身无分文、无家可归。

pen·ny ♦◇◇ /pɛni/ (**pennies, pence**) 1 N-COUNT A **penny** is one cent, or a coin worth one cent. 便士 [AM, INFORMAL] ❑ *Unleaded gasoline rose more than a penny a gallon.* 无铅汽油每加仑涨了一个多便士。 2 N-SING If you say, for example, that you do not have **a penny**, or that something does not cost **a penny**, you are emphasizing that you do not have any money at all, or that something did not cost you any money at all. 分文 [EMPHASIS] ❑ *From the day you arrive at my house, you need not spend a single penny.* 从你到我家的那一天起，你就分文不需花了。

pen·ny stock N-PLURAL A **penny stock** is a stock whose shares are offered for sale at a very low price. 便士股 [BUSINESS]

pen·sion ♦◇◇ /pɛnʃən/ (**pensions**) N-COUNT Someone who has a **pension** receives a regular sum of money from a former employer because they have retired or because they are widowed or disabled. 养老金；抚恤金 ❑ *...struggling by on a pension.* …靠养老金艰难度日。

★ **pen·sion·er** /pɛnʃənər/ (**pensioners**) N-COUNT A **pensioner** is someone who receives a pension, especially a pension paid by the state to retired people. 养老金领取者；抚恤金领取者 [mainly BRIT]

pen·sion plan (**pension plans**) N-COUNT A **pension plan** is an arrangement to receive a pension from an organization such as an insurance company or a former employer in return for making regular payments to them over a number of years. 养老金计划 [BUSINESS] ❑ *I would have been much wiser to start my own pension plan when I was younger.* 我要是更年轻的时就开始我自己的养老金计划就明智得多了。

Pen·ta·gon N-PROPER **The Pentagon** is the main building of the U.S. Defense Department, in Washington DC. The U.S. Defense Department is often referred to as **the Pentagon**. 五角大楼 (美国国防部的代称) ❑ *...a news conference at the Pentagon.* …在五角大楼的一场记者招待会。

pent·house /pɛnthaʊs/ (**penthouses**) N-COUNT A **penthouse** or a **penthouse** apartment or suite is a luxurious apartment or set of rooms at the top of a tall building. 顶层豪华公寓；顶层豪华套间 ❑ *...her swanky Manhattan penthouse.* …她的曼哈顿豪华顶层公寓。

pent-up /pɛnt ʌp/ ADJ **Pent-up** emotions, energies, or forces have been held back and not expressed, used, or released. 被压抑的 ❑ *He still had a lot of pent-up anger to release.* 他仍有许多被压抑的愤怒要发泄。

Word Link *ultim ≈ end, last : penultimate, ultimate, ultimatum*

pe·nul·ti·mate /pɪnʌltɪmɪt/ ADJ The **penultimate** thing in a series of things is the second to the last. 倒数第二的 [det ADJ] [FORMAL] ❑ *...on the penultimate day of the Asian Games.* …在亚运会的倒数第二天。

peo·ple ♦♦♦ /pipəl/ (**peoples, peopling, peopled**) 1 N-PLURAL **People** are men, women, and children. **People** is normally used as the plural of **person**, instead of "persons." 人们 ❑ *Millions of people have lost their homes.* 数百万人失去了家园。 ❑ *...the people of Angola.* …安哥拉人。 2 N-PLURAL **The people** is sometimes used to refer to ordinary men and women, in contrast to the government or the military. 人民 ❑ *...the will of the people.* …人民的意愿。 3 N-COUNT-COLL A **people** is all the men, women, and children of a particular country or race. 国民；民族 ❑ *...the native peoples of Central and South America.* …中美洲和南美洲的各本土民族。 4 V-T If a place or country **is peopled by** a particular group of people, that group of people live there. 居住 [usu passive] ❑ *It was peopled by a fiercely independent race of peace-loving Buddhists.* 那里由极其独立的一群热爱和平的佛教徒居住着。

peo·ple skills N-PLURAL **People skills** are the ability to deal with, influence, and communicate effectively with other people. 人际交往技巧 [BUSINESS] ❑ *She has very good people skills and is able to manage a team.* 她有很好的人际交往技巧并能管理一个团队。

pep·per ♦◇◇ /pɛpər/ (**peppers, peppering, peppered**) 1 N-UNCOUNT **Pepper** or **black pepper** is a hot-tasting spice used to flavor food. 胡椒 ❑ *Season with salt and pepper.* 用盐和胡椒调味。 2 N-COUNT A **pepper**, or a **bell pepper**, is a hollow green, red, or yellow vegetable with seeds inside it. 椒类 ❑ *...2 red or green peppers,*

P

sliced. …2个切成片了的红椒或青椒。 **3** V-T If something **is peppered with** small objects, a lot of those objects hit it. (以小物体) 大量击中 [usu passive] ❑ *He was wounded in both legs and severely peppered with shrapnel.* 他两条腿都受伤了，受到了弹片重创。
→ see **spice**

pepper·mint /pɛpərmɪnt/ (**peppermints**) **1** N-UNCOUNT **Peppermint** is a strong, sharp flavoring from the peppermint plant. 胡椒薄荷 **2** N-COUNT A **peppermint** is a peppermint-flavored piece of candy. 胡椒薄荷糖

pep talk (**pep talks**) also **pep-talk** N-COUNT A **pep talk** is a speech intended to encourage someone to make more effort or feel more confident. 鼓舞士气的讲话 [INFORMAL] ❑ *Powell and Cheney spent the day giving pep talks to the troops.* 鲍威尔和切尼花了一整天给部队作鼓舞士气的讲话。

per ♦♦◊ /pər, STRONG pɜr/ **1** PREP You use **per** to express rates and ratios. For example, if something costs $50 **per** year, you must pay $50 each year for it. If a vehicle is traveling at 40 miles **per** hour, it travels 40 miles each hour. 每 [amount PREP n] ❑ *...$6 per week for lunch.* …每周$6吃午饭。 **2** **per head** → see **head**

per an·num /pər ænəm/ ADV A particular amount **per annum** means that amount each year. 每年 [amount ADV] ❑ *...a fee of $35 per annum.* …每年$35的费用。

per capi·ta /pər kæpɪtə/ ADJ The **per capita** amount of something is the total amount of it in a country or area divided by the number of people in that country or area. 人均的 [ADJ n] ❑ *They have the world's largest per capita income.* 他们有世界上最高的人均收入。 ● ADV **Per capita** is also an adverb. 人均地 [n ADV] ❑ *Ethiopia has almost the lowest oil consumption per capita in the world.* 埃塞俄比亚有几乎是世界上最低的人均石油消费。

Word Link *per ≈ through, thoroughly : perceive, perfect, permit*

per·ceive /pərsiv/ (**perceives, perceiving, perceived**) **1** V-T If you **perceive** something, you see, notice, or realize it, especially when it is not obvious. 感知到 ❑ *Students must perceive for themselves the relationship between success and effort.* 学生们必须自己去认识到成功与努力之间的关系。 **2** V-T If you **perceive** someone or something **as** doing or being a particular thing, it is your opinion that they do this thing or that they are that thing. 认为 ❑ *Stress is widely perceived as contributing to coronary heart disease.* 压力普遍被认为能造成冠心病。

Word Link *cent ≈ hundred : cent, century, percent*

percent ♦♦♦ /pərsɛnt/ (**percent**) N-COUNT You use **percent** to talk about amounts. For example, if an amount is 10 percent (10%) of a larger amount, it is equal to 10 hundredths of the larger amount. 百分数 (通常用%表示) ❑ *Sixteen percent of children live in poverty in this country.* 这个国家百分之十六的孩子生活在贫困中。 ❑ *Sales of new homes fell by 1.4 percent in August.* 新房的销售量在8月份下降了1.4%。 ● ADJ **Percent** is also an adjective. 百分之…的 [ADJ n] ❑ *...a 15 percent increase in border patrols.* …边境巡逻15%的增加。 ● ADV **Percent** is also an adverb. 百分之…地 [ADV with v]

in BRIT, usually use **per cent**

❑ *He predicted sales will fall 2 percent to 6 percent in the second quarter.* 他预计第二季度的销售量将下降2%至6%。

per·cent·age ♦◊◊ /pərsɛntɪdʒ/ (**percentages**) N-COUNT A **percentage** is a fraction of an amount expressed as a particular number of hundredths of that amount. 百分比 ❑ *Only a few vegetable-origin foods have such a high percentage of protein.* 只有几种来源于植物的食品含有如此高百分比的蛋白质。

per·cep·tion /pərsɛpʃən/ (**perceptions**) **1** N-COUNT Your **perception of** something is the way that you think about it or the impression you have of it. 理解; 看法 ❑ *He is interested in how our perceptions of death affect the way we live.* 他对我们的死亡观如何影响我们的生活方式感兴趣。 **2** N-UNCOUNT Someone who has **perception** realizes or notices things that are not obvious. 洞察力 ❑ *It did not require a lot of perception to realize the interview was over.* 不需要很强的洞察力就可以意识到面试结束了。 **3** N-COUNT **Perception** is the recognition of things using your senses, especially the sense of sight. (尤指通过视觉的) 感知

per·cep·tive /pərsɛptɪv/ ADJ If you describe a person or their remarks or thoughts as **perceptive**, you think that they are good at noticing or realizing things, especially things that are not obvious. 有洞察力的 [APPROVAL] ❑ *He was one of the most perceptive U.S. political commentators.* 他曾是美国最具洞察力的政治评论员之一。

▲ **perch** /pɜrtʃ/ (**perches, perching, perched**)

The form **perch** is used for both the singular and plural in meaning **6**.

1 V-I If you **perch on** something, you sit down lightly on the very edge or tip of it. 轻坐在; 轻落在 (边上或顶上) ❑ *He lit a cigarette and perched on the corner of the desk.* 他点了一支烟，轻轻地坐在书桌角上。 ❑ *He perched himself on the side of the bed.* 他轻轻地坐在了床边上。 **2** V-I To **perch** somewhere means to be on the top or edge of something. 坐落于 (某物顶部或边缘) ❑ *...the vast slums that perch precariously on top of the hills around which the city was built.* …摇摇欲坠地坐落于城市中心群山之顶的大片贫民窟。 **3** V-T If you **perch** something **on** something else, you put or balance it on the top or edge of that thing. 把…稳置于 (某物顶部或边缘) ❑ *The use of steel and concrete has allowed the builders to perch a light concrete dome on eight slender columns.* 钢筋混凝土的使用使建筑者们能将一个轻巧的混凝土穹顶架在8根细柱上。 **4** V-I When a bird **perches on** something such as a branch or a wall, it lands on it and stands there. (鸟) 栖息 ❑ *A blackbird flew down and perched on the parapet outside his window.* 一只乌鸫飞下来，栖息在他家窗外的矮墙上。 **5** N-COUNT A **perch** is a short rod for a bird to stand on. (鸟的) 栖木 ❑ *A small, yellow bird in a cage sat on its perch outside the house.* 屋外，一只小黄鸟站在鸟笼的栖木上。 **6** N-COUNT A **perch** is an edible fish. There are several kinds of perch. 河鲈

per·cus·sion /pərkʌʃən/ N-UNCOUNT **Percussion** instruments are musical instruments that you hit, such as drums. 打击乐器 ❑ *...a large orchestra, with a vast percussion section.* …一支有很大的打击乐器组的大型管弦乐队。
→ see **drum, orchestra**

per diem /pɜr diəm, pər/ N-SING A **per diem** is an amount of money that someone is given to cover their daily expenses while they are working. 日津贴 [mainly AM] ❑ *He received a per diem allowance to cover his travel expenses.* 他收到一笔按日计算的差旅费用补贴。

Word Link *enn ≈ year : centennial, millennium, perennial*

per·en·nial /pərɛniəl/ (**perennials**) **1** ADJ You use **perennial** to describe situations or states that keep occurring or that seem to exist all the time; used especially to describe problems or difficulties. 不断出现的; 长期存在的 (问题、困难) ❑ *...the perennial urban problems of drugs and homelessness.* …城市长期存在的毒品和无家可归的问题。 **2** ADJ A **perennial** plant lives for several years and has flowers each year. (植物) 多年生的 ❑ *...a perennial herb with greenish-yellow flowers.* …一种开黄绿色花的多年生草本植物。 ● N-COUNT **Perennial** is also a noun. 多年生植物 ❑ *...a low-growing perennial.* …一种长不高的多年生植物。
→ see **plant**

per·fect ♦♦◊ (**perfects, perfecting, perfected**)

The adjective is pronounced /pɜrfɪkt/. The verb is pronounced /pərfɛkt/.

形容词读作 /pɜrfɪkt/。动词读作 /pərfɛkt/。

1 ADJ Something that is **perfect** is as good as it could possibly be. 完美的 ❑ *He spoke perfect English.* 他讲一口纯正的英语。 ❑ *Nobody is perfect.* 人无完人。 ❑ *Hiring her has turned out to be the perfect solution.* 雇用她结果证明是最适合的解决方案。 **2** ADJ If you say that something is **perfect for** a particular person, thing, or activity, you are emphasizing that it is very suitable for them or for that activity. 最适合的 [EMPHASIS] ❑ *The pool area is perfect for entertaining.* 游泳池一带最适合娱乐。 **3** ADJ If an object or surface is **perfect**, it does not have any marks on it, or does not have any lumps, hollows, or cracks in it. 无瑕疵的 ❑ *Use only clean, Grade A, perfect eggs.* 只用洁净的、一级的、无瑕疵的鸡蛋。 **4** ADJ You can use **perfect** to give emphasis to the noun following it. (用以强调所修饰名词) 完全的 [ADJ n] [EMPHASIS] ❑ *She was a perfect fool.* 她是个十足的傻瓜。 ❑ *Some people are always coming up to perfect strangers and asking them what they do.* 有些人总是走近完全不认识的人跟前，问人家是干什么的。 **5** V-T If you **perfect** something, you improve it so that it becomes as good as it can possibly be. 使完美 ❑ *We perfected a hand-signal system so that he could keep me informed of hazards.* 我们完善了一套手语体系，以便他能告知我危险。 ❑ *I removed the fibroid tumors, using the techniques that I have perfected.* 我用我完善过的技术切除了这些纤维瘤。

Thesaurus *perfect* 另参见：

ADJ. flawless, ideal; *(ant.)* defective, faulty **1**
complete, undamaged; *(ant.)* damaged **3**

per·fec·tion /pərfɛkʃən/ **1** N-UNCOUNT **Perfection** is the quality of being as good as it is possible for something of a particular kind to be. 完美 ❑ *His quest for perfection is relentless.* 他对完美的追求是不懈的。 **2** N-UNCOUNT **The perfection of** something such as a skill, system, or product involves making it as good as it could possibly be. 完善 ❑ *Madame Clicquot is credited with the perfection of this technique.* 这项工艺的完善要归功于克利科夫人。

per·fec·tion·ist /pərfɛkʃənɪst/ (**perfectionists**) N-COUNT Someone who is a **perfectionist** refuses to do or accept anything that is not as good as it could possibly be. 完美主义者 ❑ *He was such a perfectionist that he published only those results that satisfied him completely.* 他是个完美主义者，只发表那些令他完全满意的成果。

per·fect·ly ♦◇◇ /pɜrfɪktli/ **1** ADV You can use **perfectly** to emphasize an adjective or adverb, especially when you think the person you are talking to might doubt what you are saying. 完全地（尤用在认为对方有疑虑时以示强调）[ADV adj/adv] [EMPHASIS] ❑ *There's no reason why you can't have a perfectly normal child.* 没有理由说明你生不出一个完全正常的孩子。 ❑ *You know perfectly well what happened.* 你完全清楚发生了什么。 **2** ADV If something is done **perfectly**, it is done so well that it could not possibly be done better. 完美地 [ADV with v] ❑ *This ambitious adaptation perfectly captures the spirit of Kurt Vonnegut's acclaimed novel.* 这次大胆的改编完美地把握住了库尔特・冯内古特那部广为称赞的小说的精髓。

per·form ♦♦◇ /pərfɔrm/ (**performs, performing, performed**) **1** V-T When you **perform** a task or action, especially a complicated one, you do it. 做；执行（尤指复杂的任务或行动）❑ *We're looking for people of all ages who have performed outstanding acts of bravery, kindness, or courage.* 我们正在寻找各个年龄的、曾有过无畏、善良或英勇之举的杰出人士。 ❑ *His council had had to perform miracles on a tiny budget.* 他的委员会不得不靠一笔微薄的预算来创造奇迹。 **2** V-T If something **performs** a particular function, it has that function. 行使（某种功能）❑ *An engine has many parts, each performing a different function.* 一部发动机有很多部件，各自行使不同的功能。 **3** V-T If you **perform** a play, a piece of music, or a dance, you do it in front of an audience. 演出；演奏 ❑ *Gardiner has pursued relentlessly high standards in performing classical music.* 加德纳在演奏古典音乐方面始终不懈地追求高标准。 ❑ *This play was first performed in 411 BC.* 该剧于公元前411年首次上演。 **4** V-I If someone or something **performs well**, they work well or achieve a good result. If they **perform badly**, they work badly or achieve a poor result. 表现（好/不好）❑ *He had not performed well in his exams.* 过去考试他都考得不好。 ❑ *State-owned industries will always perform poorly.* 国有工业将始终经营不善。

Word Partnership *perform* 的常用搭配：

N. perform **miracles**, perform **tasks** **1**
ADJ. **able to** perform **1**–**3**
V. **continue to** perform **1**–**3**
ADV. perform **well** **4**

Word Link *ance ≈ quality, state : defiance, performance, resistance*

per·for·mance ♦♦◇ /pərfɔrməns/ (**performances**) **1** N-COUNT A **performance** involves entertaining an audience by doing something such as singing, dancing, or acting. 表演 ❑ *Inside the theater, they were giving a performance of Bizet's Carmen.* 他们正在剧院里演出比才的《卡门》。 ❑ *...her performance as the betrayed Medea.* …她出演被出卖的美狄亚。 **2** N-VAR Someone's or something's **performance** is how successful they are or how well they do something. 业绩；性能 ❑ *That study looked at the performance of 18 surgeons.* 那项研究着眼于18位外科医生的业绩。 ❑ *The poor performance has been blamed on the recession and cheaper sports car imports.* 业绩惨淡归咎于经济衰退和更便宜跑车的进口。 **3** N-SING **The performance of** a task is the fact or action of doing it. 执行；实施 ❑ *He devoted in excess of seventy hours a week to the performance of his duties.* 他每周在自己职责的执行上投入超过70个小时。
→ see **concert, theater**

Word Partnership *performance* 的常用搭配：

ADJ. **live** performance **1**
good performance, **poor** performance, **strong** performance **1**–**3**
academic performance, **economic** performance, **sexual** performance **2**
N. performance **appraisal**, **company** performance, **job** performance **2**

perfo̲rmance-related pa̲y N-UNCOUNT **Performance-related pay** is a rate of pay which is based on how well someone does their job. 绩效工资 [BUSINESS] ❑ *...plans to introduce performance-related pay for teachers.* …推行教师绩效工资的计划。

per·form·er /pərfɔrmər/ (**performers**) **1** N-COUNT A **performer** is a person who acts, sings, or does other entertainment in front of audiences. 表演者 ❑ *A performer plays classical selections on the violin.* 一位表演者用小提琴演奏古典音乐选段。 **2** N-COUNT You can use **performer** when describing someone or something in a way that indicates how well they do a particular thing. 表现…者 ❑ *Until 1987, Canada's industry had been the star performer.* 直到1987年，加拿大的工业一直是明星产业。

★ **per·fume** /pɜrfyum, pərfyum/ (**perfumes, perfuming, perfumed**) **1** N-MASS **Perfume** is a pleasant-smelling liquid that women put on their skin to make themselves smell nice. 香水 ❑ *The hall smelled of her mother's perfume.* 大厅里弥漫着她母亲的香水味。 ❑ *...a bottle of perfume.* …一瓶香水。 **2** N-MASS **Perfume** is the ingredient that is added to some products to make them smell nice. 香料 ❑ *...a delicate white soap without perfume.* …一块不含香料的气味清淡的白色肥皂。 **3** V-T If something is used to **perfume** a product, it is added to the product to make it smell nice. 给…添加香味 ❑ *The oil is used to flavor and perfume soaps, foam baths, and scents.* 这种油用来给肥皂、泡沫浴液和香水添加特殊气味和香味。

per·haps ♦♦♦ /pərhæps, præps/ **1** ADV You use **perhaps** to express uncertainty, for example, when you do not know that something is definitely true, or when you are mentioning something that may possibly happen in the future in the way you describe. 可能 [ADV with cl/group] [VAGUENESS] ❑ *In the end they lose millions, perhaps billions.* 最终他们损失了数百万，也许数亿。 ❑ *Perhaps, in time, the message will get through.* 可能，过一段时间，这消息将会送到。 **2** ADV You use **perhaps** in opinions and remarks to make them appear less definite or more polite. （用于表示不确定性或礼貌）或许 [ADV with cl/group] [VAGUENESS] ❑ *Perhaps the most important lesson to be learned is that you simply cannot please everyone.* 或许应吸取的最重要的教训是你不可能取悦每一个人。 ❑ *His very last paintings are perhaps the most puzzling.* 他最后的那些绘画作品也许是最令人费解的。 **3** ADV You use **perhaps** when you are making suggestions or giving advice. **Perhaps** is also used in formal English to introduce requests. （用于提出建议或请求）也许 [ADV with cl] [POLITENESS] ❑ *Perhaps I may be permitted a few suggestions.* 也许能容许我提几条建议。 ❑ *Well, perhaps you'll come and see us at our place?* 呃，也许你会来我们住的地方看看我们？

▲ **per·il** /pɛrɪl/ (**perils**) N-VAR **Perils** are great dangers. 极大危险 [FORMAL] ❑ *...the perils of the sea.* …海洋的严重危险。 ❑ *In spite of great peril, I have survived.* 尽管危险巨大，我还是活了下来。

peri·lous /pɛrɪləs/ ADJ Something that is **perilous** is very dangerous. 险恶的 [LITERARY] ❑ *...a perilous journey across the war zone.* …一段穿越战区的艰险旅途。 ❑ *The road grew even steeper and more perilous.* 这条路变得更陡更险了。 ● **peri·lous·ly** ADV 险恶地 ❑ *The track snaked perilously upwards.* 这条小道绝险地蜿蜒而上。

Word Link *meter ≈ measuring : kilometer, meter, perimeter*

Word Link *peri ≈ around : perimeter, periodic, periphery*

pe·rim·eter /pərɪmɪtər/ (**perimeters**) N-COUNT The **perimeter** of an area of land is the whole of its outer edge or boundary. 周边；周界 ❑ *...the perimeter of the airport.* …机场周边。
→ see **area**

pe·ri·od ♦♦◇ /pɪəriəd/ (**periods**) **1** N-COUNT A **period** is a length of time. 一段时间 [usu with supp] ❑ *This crisis might last for a long period of time.* 此次危机可能会持续很长一段时间。 ❑ *...a period of a few months.* …几个月的时间。 **2** N-COUNT A **period** in the life of a person, organization, or society is a length of time that is remembered for a particular situation or activity. （个人、组织或社

P

会的）时期 ❑ *...a period of economic good health and expansion.* …一段经济健康发展和扩张时期。❑ *He went through a period of wanting to be accepted.* 他经历了一段渴望得到接受的时期。 3 N-COUNT A particular length of time in history is sometimes called a **period**. For example, you can talk about **the Civil War period** or **the Prohibition period** in the U.S. (历史) 时期 ❑ *The novel is set in the Roman period.* 该小说的背景是罗马时期。❑ *No reference to their existence appears in any literature of the period.* 该时期的任何文献中都没有提及他们的存在。 4 ADJ **Period** costumes, furniture, and instruments were made at an earlier time in history, or look as if they were made then. 具特定历史时期特点的 [ADJ n] ❑ *The characters were dressed in full period costume.* 剧中人物全都身着具有时代特色的服装。 5 N-COUNT Exercise, training, or study **periods** are lengths of time that are set aside for exercise, training, or study. (练习、训练或学习的) 时段 ❑ *They accompanied him during his exercise periods.* 在他的练习时段，他们都陪着他。 6 N-COUNT A **period** is the punctuation mark (.) that you use at the end of a sentence when it is not a question or an exclamation. 句号 [AM]

in BRIT, use **full stop**

7 N-COUNT When a woman has a **period**, she bleeds from her uterus. This usually happens once a month, unless she is pregnant. 经期 ❑ *Can you get pregnant if you have sex during your period?* 经期性交会怀孕吗？

Thesaurus *period* 另参见：
N. age, course, epoch, era, term, time 1–3

Word Link *peri ≈ around : perimeter, periodic, periphery*

★ **pe·ri·od·ic** /pɪəriɒdɪk/ ADJ **Periodic** events or situations happen occasionally, at fairly regular intervals. 周期性的 ❑ *Periodic checks are taken to ensure that high standards are maintained.* 进行周期性检查以确保高标准得以维持。

pe·ri·odi·cal /pɪəriɒdɪkəl/ (**periodicals**) 1 N-COUNT **Periodicals** are magazines, especially serious or academic ones, that are published at regular intervals. (尤指内容严肃或学术性的) 期刊 ❑ *The walls would be lined with books and periodicals.* 沿这几面墙将排放书籍和期刊。 2 ADJ **Periodical** events or situations happen occasionally, at fairly regular intervals. 定期的 ❑ *She made periodical visits to her dentist.* 她定期去看牙医。● **pe·ri·odi·cal·ly** /pɪəriɒdɪkli/ ADV 定期地 [ADV with v] ❑ *Meetings are held periodically to monitor progress on the case.* 定期召开会议监控案件的进展情况。
→ see **library**

P

▲ **pe·riph·er·al** /pərɪfərəl/ (**peripherals**) 1 ADJ A **peripheral** activity or issue is one that is not very important compared with other activities or issues. 次要的 ❑ *Companies are increasingly eager to contract out peripheral activities like training.* 公司越来越渴望把像培训这样的次要活动外包出去。❑ *...peripheral and boring information.* …无关紧要且无聊的信息。 2 ADJ **Peripheral** areas of land are ones that are on the edge of a larger area. 周边的 ❑ *...urban development in the outer peripheral areas of large towns.* …大城市外部周边地区的城市发展。 3 N-COUNT **Peripherals** are devices that can be attached to computers. (计算机的) 外围设备 [COMPUTING] ❑ *...peripherals to expand the use of our computers.* …扩展计算机用途的外围设备。

pe·riph·ery /pərɪfəri/ (**peripheries**) N-COUNT If something is on the **periphery** of an area, place, or thing, it is on the edge of it. 边缘 [FORMAL] ❑ *Taste buds are concentrated at the tip and rear of the tongue and around its periphery.* 味蕾集中在舌尖、舌根及舌边。

★ **per·ish** /pɛrɪʃ/ (**perishes, perishing, perished**) V-I If people or animals **perish**, they die as a result of very harsh conditions or as the result of an accident. (因恶劣条件或事故) 死亡 [WRITTEN] ❑ *Most of the butterflies perish in the first frosts of autumn.* 大多数蝴蝶在秋季初霜来临时死亡。

per·jury /pɜrdʒəri/ N-UNCOUNT If someone who is giving evidence in a court of law commits **perjury**, they lie. 伪证 [LEGAL] ❑ *This witness has committed perjury and no reliance can be placed on her evidence.* 该证人作了伪证，她提供的证据不可信。

perk /pɜrk/ (**perks, perking, perked**) N-COUNT **Perks** are special benefits that are given to people who have a particular job or belong to a particular group. 特殊待遇 ❑ *...a company car, health insurance and other perks.* …一辆公司配车、健康保险以及其他特殊待遇。

▸ **perk up** 1 PHRASAL VERB If something **perks** you **up** or if you **perk up**, you become cheerful and lively, after feeling tired, bored, or depressed. 使振作；振作 ❑ *He perks up and jokes with them.* 他振作起来，和他们开着玩笑。 2 PHRASAL VERB If you **perk** something **up**, you make it more interesting. 使更有趣 ❑ *To make the bland taste more interesting, the locals began perking it up with local produce.* 为了使平淡的口味更有味道，当地人开始加些土特产来调味。 3 PHRASAL VERB If sales, prices, or economies **perk up**, or if something **perks** them **up**, they begin to increase or improve. 增长 [JOURNALISM] ❑ *House prices could perk up during the fall.* 秋季房价可能会上涨。

perm /pɜrm/ (**perms, perming, permed**) 1 N-COUNT If you have a **perm**, your hair is curled and treated with chemicals so that it stays curly for several months. 烫的卷发 ❑ *...a middle-aged lady with a perm.* …一位烫卷发的中年女士。 2 V-T When a hairstylist **perms** someone's hair, they curl it and treat it with chemicals so that it stays curly for several months. 烫 (卷发) ❑ *She had her hair permed.* 她烫了卷发。

per·ma·nent ♦◇◇ /pɜrmənənt/ (**permanents**) 1 ADJ Something that is **permanent** lasts forever. 永久的 ❑ *Heavy drinking can cause permanent damage to the brain.* 饮酒过量可能造成永久性脑损伤。❑ *...a permanent solution to the problem.* …一个解决该问题的永久性办法。● **per·ma·nent·ly** ADV 永久地 ❑ *His confidence had been permanently affected by the ordeal.* 他的信心已永久地被这次磨难影响了。● **per·ma·nence** N-UNCOUNT 永久性 ❑ *Anything which threatens the permanence of the treaty is a threat to stability and to peace.* 任何威胁该条约持久性的东西都是对稳定与和平的威胁。 2 ADJ You use **permanent** to describe situations or states that keep occurring or that seem to exist all the time; used especially to describe problems or difficulties. (问题或困难) 不断发生的；一直存在的 ❑ *...a permanent state of tension.* …长期的紧张状态。❑ *They feel under permanent threat.* 他们感觉处在持续不断的威胁之下。● **per·ma·nent·ly** ADV (问题或困难) 不断发生地；一直存在地 ❑ *...the heavy, permanently locked gate.* …这扇厚重的、长年锁着的大门。 3 ADJ A **permanent** employee is one who is employed for an unlimited length of time. 终身的 [ADJ n] ❑ *At the end of the probationary period you will become a permanent employee.* 试用期结束后，你将成为终身雇员。● **per·ma·nent·ly** ADV 终身地 [ADV with v] ❑ *...permanently employed lifeguards.* …终身雇用的救生员。 4 ADJ Your **permanent** home or your **permanent** address is the one at which you spend most of your time or the one that you return to after having stayed in other places. 固定的 (住所或地址) [ADJ n] ❑ *They had no permanent address.* 他们没有固定的地址。 5 N-COUNT A **permanent** is a treatment in which a hairstylist curls your hair and treats it with a chemical so that it stays curly for several months. 烫发 [AM] ❑ *Her hair had had a permanent, but had grown out.* 她的头发曾经烫卷过，但又长出新的了。

Thesaurus *permanent* 另参见：
ADJ. constant, continual, everlasting; (*ant.*) fleeting, temporary 1

★ **per·me·ate** /pɜrmieɪt/ (**permeates, permeating, permeated**) 1 V-T If an idea, feeling, or attitude **permeates** a system or **permeates** society, it affects every part of it or is present throughout it. (思想、情感或态度) 全面影响 ❑ *Bias against women permeates every level of the judicial system.* 对妇女的偏见全面影响司法体系的各个层面。 2 V-T If something **permeates** a place, it spreads throughout it. 弥漫 ❑ *The smell of roast beef permeated the air.* 烤牛肉的气味弥漫在空气中。

★ **per·mis·sible** /pərmɪsəbəl/ ADJ If something is **permissible**, it is considered to be acceptable because it does not break any laws or rules. 可允许的 ❑ *Religious practices are permissible under the Constitution.* 根据宪法，宗教行为是可允许的。

per·mis·sion ♦◇◇ /pərmɪʃən/ N-UNCOUNT If someone who has authority over you gives you **permission to** do something, they say that they will allow you to do it. 许可 ❑ *He asked permission to leave the room.* 他请求离开房间的许可。❑ *They cannot leave the country without permission.* 没有许可他们不得离开这个国家。

Word Partnership *permission* 的常用搭配：
V. **ask (for)** permission, **get** permission, permission **to leave**, **need** permission, **obtain** permission, **receive** permission, **request** permission, **seek** permission
ADJ. **special** permission, **written** permission

per·mis·sive /pərmɪsɪv/ ADJ A **permissive** person, society, or way of behaving allows or tolerates things that other people disapprove of. 宽容的；放任的 ❑ *The call for law and order replaced the "permissive tolerance" of the 1960s.* 对法治的呼吁取代了20世纪60年

代的“姑息忍让”。● **per·mis·sive·ness** N-UNCOUNT 宽容；放任 ❑ *Permissiveness and democracy go together.* 宽容和民主并存。

Word Link *per ≈ through, thoroughly : perceive, perfect, permit*

per·mit ♦◇◇ (**permits, permitting, permitted**)

The verb is pronounced /pərmɪt/. The noun is pronounced /pɜrmɪt/.

动词读作 /pərmɪt/。名词读作 /pɜrmɪt/。

1 V-T If someone **permits** something, they allow it to happen. If they **permit** you **to** do something, they allow you to do it. 允许 [FORMAL] ❑ *He can let the court's decision stand and permit the execution.* 他能让法院的判决成立，并允许处决。❑ *The guards permitted me to bring my camera and tape recorder.* 守卫允许我带上相机和录音机。 2 N-COUNT A **permit** is an official document which says that you may do something. For example, you usually need a **permit** to work in a foreign country. 许可证 ❑ *He has to apply for a permit, and we have to find him a job.* 他必须申请一个许可证，而我们必须给他找一份工作。 3 V-T/V-I If a situation **permits** something, it makes it possible for that thing to exist, happen, or be done or it provides the opportunity for it. 使成为可能；成为可能 [FORMAL] ❑ *Try to go out for a walk at lunchtime, if the weather permits.* 如果天气条件允许，午饭时尽量出去散散步。❑ *This method of cooking also permits heat to penetrate evenly from both sides.* 这种烹调方法还能使两面均匀受热。

Thesaurus *permit* 另参见：
V. allow, authorize, let; *(ant.)* ban, forbid, prohibit 1 3
N. authorization, consent, permission 2

per·ni·cious /pərnɪʃəs/ ADJ If you describe something as **pernicious**, you mean that it is very harmful. 极为有害的 [FORMAL] ❑ *I did what I could, but her mother's influence was pernicious.* 我已尽我所能，但她母亲造成的影响是很极为不利的。

per·pe·trate /pɜrpɪtreɪt/ (**perpetrates, perpetrating, perpetrated**) V-T If someone **perpetrates** a crime or any other immoral or harmful act, they do it. 犯（罪）；做（不道德、有害之事）[FORMAL] ❑ *A high proportion of crime in any country is perpetrated by young males in their teens and twenties.* 在任何国家，很大比例的罪行都是十几岁和二十几岁的青年男子所为。● **per·pe·tra·tor** N-COUNT (**perpetrators**) 罪犯；作恶的人 ❑ *The perpetrator of the crime does not have to be traced before you can claim compensation.* 不一定非要抓住罪犯之后你才能够索赔。

★ **per·pet·ual** /pərpɛtʃuəl/ 1 ADJ A **perpetual** feeling, state, or quality is one that never ends or changes. 永恒的 ❑ *...the creation of a perpetual union.* …一个永久性工会的创立。● **per·pet·ual·ly** ADV 永恒地 ❑ *They were all perpetually starving.* 他们一直都在挨饿。 2 ADJ A **perpetual** act, situation, or state is one that happens again and again and so seems never to end. 反复不断的；无休止的 ❑ *I thought her perpetual complaints were going to prove too much for me.* 我觉得她那永无休止的抱怨会让我吃不消的。● **per·pet·ual·ly** ADV 反复不断地；无休止地 ❑ *He perpetually interferes in political affairs.* 他不断地干涉政治事务。

per·petu·ate /pərpɛtʃueɪt/ (**perpetuates, perpetuating, perpetuated**) V-T If someone or something **perpetuates** a situation, system, or belief, especially a bad one, they cause it to continue. 使继续（尤指不好的情形、体系或信仰）❑ *We must not perpetuate the religious divisions of the past.* 我们绝不能使过去的宗教分裂继续下去。

★ **per·plex** /pərplɛks/ (**perplexes, perplexing, perplexed**) V-T If something **perplexes** you, it confuses and worries you because you do not understand it or because it causes you difficulty. 使困惑和忧虑 ❑ *It perplexed him because he was tackling it the wrong way.* 这件事令他困惑和忧虑因为他处理得不对。

per·plexed /pərplɛkst/ ADJ If you are **perplexed**, you feel confused and slightly worried by something because you do not understand it. 困惑不解的 ❑ *She is perplexed about what to do for her daughter.* 她很困惑，不知该为女儿做些什么。

per se /pɜr seɪ, pər-/ ADV **Per se** means "by itself" or "in itself," and is used when you are talking about the qualities of one thing considered on its own, rather than in connection with other things. 本身；本质上 ❑ *I don't work out per se, but I'm very active physically.* 我本身不锻炼，但我体能上很有力。

▲ **per·secute** /pɜrsɪkyut/ (**persecutes, persecuting, persecuted**) V-T If someone **is persecuted**, they are treated cruelly and unfairly, often because of their race or beliefs. (因种族或信仰) 迫害 ❑ *Mr. Weaver and his family have been persecuted by the authorities for their beliefs.* 韦弗先生及其家人因为他们的信仰而遭当局迫害。❑ *They began by brutally persecuting the Catholic Church.* 他们以残酷迫害天主教会作为开始。

★ **per·secu·tion** /pɜrsɪkyuʃən/ (**persecutions**) N-COUNT **Persecution** is cruel and unfair treatment of a person or group, especially because of their religious or political beliefs, or their race. (尤指因宗教、政治信仰或种族而遭受的) 迫害 ❑ *...the persecution of minorities.* …对少数派的迫害。❑ *...victims of political persecution.* …政治迫害的受害者。

per·sever·ance /pɜrsɪvɪərəns/ N-UNCOUNT **Perseverance** is the quality of continuing with something even though it is difficult. 坚持不懈 ❑ *He has never stopped trying and showed great perseverance.* 他从未停止努力，表现出了极大的毅力。

▲ **per·severe** /pɜrsɪvɪər/ (**perseveres, persevering, persevered**) V-I If you **persevere with** something, you keep trying to do it and do not give up, even though it is difficult. 坚持不懈 ❑ *This ability to persevere despite obstacles and setbacks is the quality people most admire in others.* 这种不管障碍和挫折的锲而不舍的能力是人们最为钦佩的品质。❑ *...a school with a reputation for persevering with difficult and disruptive children.* …一所因坚持不懈地教诲难管捣蛋的学生而闻名的学校。

per·sist /pərsɪst/ (**persists, persisting, persisted**) 1 V-I If something undesirable **persists**, it continues to exist. (尤指不合意的事物) 继续存在 ❑ *Contact your doctor if the cough persists.* 如果持续咳嗽，就与医生联系。 2 V-I If you **persist in** doing something, you continue to do it, even though it is difficult or other people are against it. 坚持；执意 ❑ *Why do people persist in begging for money in the street?* 为什么人们非要在街上讨钱呢？❑ *He urged the United States to persist with its efforts to bring about peace.* 他敦促美国坚持努力实现和平。

per·sis·tence /pərsɪstəns/ 1 N-UNCOUNT If you have **persistence**, you continue to do something even though it is difficult or other people are against it. 坚持不懈；执著 ❑ *Skill comes only with practice, patience, and persistence.* 只有通过练习、耐心和坚持不懈才能获得技能。 2 N-UNCOUNT **The persistence of** something, especially something bad, is the fact of its continuing to exist for a long time. (尤指坏事物的) 持续存在 ❑ *...an expression of concern at the persistence of inflation and high interest rates.* …对持续通货膨胀和高利率所表示的关注。

★ **per·sis·tent** /pərsɪstənt/ 1 ADJ Something that is **persistent** continues to exist or happen for a long time; used especially about bad or undesirable states or situations. (坏的或令人不悦的状态或情形) 持续存在的 ❑ *Her position as national leader has been weakened by persistent fears of another coup attempt.* 她国家领导人的地位因为人们一直担心再次的政变企图而被削弱了。❑ *His cough grew more persistent until it never stopped.* 他的咳嗽愈来愈频繁，直到咳个不停。 2 ADJ Someone who is **persistent** continues trying to do something, even though it is difficult or other people are against it. 坚持不懈的；执著的 ❑ *...a persistent critic of the president.* …一个执著的批评总统的人。

per·sis·tent·ly /pərsɪstəntli/ 1 ADV If something happens **persistently**, it happens again and again or for a long time. 反复地；一直 ❑ *The allegations have been persistently denied by ministers.* 这些说法一次次地被部长们否认。 2 ADV If someone does something **persistently**, they do it with determination even though it is difficult or other people are against it. 坚定地 [ADV with v] ❑ *Rachel gently but persistently imposed her will on Doug.* 雷切尔温和而坚定地将她的意志强加在道格身上。

per·son ♦♦♦ /pɜrsən/ (**people** or **persons**)

The usual word for "more than one person" is **people**. The form **persons** is used as the plural in formal or legal language.

1 N-COUNT A **person** is a man, woman, or child. 人 ❑ *At least one person died and several others were injured.* 至少一人死亡，另有几人受伤。❑ *They were both lovely, friendly people.* 他们俩都是可爱、友好的人。 2 N-PLURAL **Persons** is used as the plural of **person** in formal, legal, and technical writing. **person**的复数形式，用于正式、法律和技术文体中 ❑ *...removal of the right of accused persons to remain silent.* …对被告人沉默权的剥夺。 3 N-COUNT If you talk about someone **as a person**, you are considering them from the point of view of their real nature. (从其真正本质出发而言的) 人 ❑ *Robin didn't feel good about herself as a person.* 罗宾对她自己的为人感觉不佳。 4 PHRASE If you do something **in person**, you do it yourself rather

P

than letting someone else do it for you. 亲自 ❑ *You must collect the mail in person and take along some form of identification.* 你必须亲自去取邮件，并带上某种身份证明。 **5** PHRASE If you meet, hear, or see someone **in person**, you are in the same place as them, rather than, for example, speaking to them on the telephone, writing to them, or seeing them on television. 当面；本人 ❑ *It was the first time she had seen him in person.* 这是她第一次见到他本人。 **6** N-COUNT Your **person** is your body. 身体 [FORMAL] ❑ *The suspect had refused to give any details of his identity and had carried no documents on his person.* 嫌疑犯拒绝交代任何有关他身份的细节，身上也没带任何证件。 **7** N-COUNT In grammar, we use the term **first person** when referring to "I" and "we," **second person** when referring to "you," and **third person** when referring to "he," "she," "it," "they," and all other noun groups. **Person** is also used like this when referring to the verb forms that go with these pronouns and noun groups. (语法中的) 人称

per·so·na /pərsoʊnə/ (**personas** or **personae** /pərsoʊni/) N-COUNT Someone's **persona** is the aspect of their character or nature that they present to other people, perhaps in contrast to their real character or nature. (同本人真实品性不一致的) 表面形象 [FORMAL] ❑ *The contradictions between her private life and the public persona are not always fully explored.* 她私生活和公众形象的不一致并非总能得到充分的探究。

per·son·al ♦♦◇ /pɜrsənəl/ **1** ADJ A **personal** opinion, quality, or thing belongs or relates to one particular person rather than to other people. 个人的；私人的 [ADJ n] ❑ *He learned this lesson the hard way – from his own personal experience.* 他惨痛地得到了这一教训——从他自己的亲身经历中得来的。 ❑ *That's my personal opinion.* 这是我的个人意见。 **2** ADJ If you give something your **personal** care or attention, you deal with it yourself rather than letting someone else deal with it. 亲自的 ❑ *...a business that requires a lot of personal contact.* …一桩需要很多亲自联络的生意。 ❑ *...a personal letter from the president's secretary.* …一封来自总统秘书的亲笔信。 **3** ADJ **Personal** matters relate to your feelings, relationships, and health. 有关个人的 ❑ *...teaching young people about marriage and personal relationships.* …教导年轻人婚姻和人际关系。 ❑ *You never allow personal problems to affect your performance.* 绝不容许个人问题影响你的表现。 **4** ADJ **Personal** comments refer to someone's appearance or character in an offensive way. 人身的 ❑ *Newspapers resorted to personal abuse.* 报纸搞起了人身攻击。 **5** ADJ **Personal** care involves taking care of your body and appearance. 个人体貌的 [ADJ n] ❑ *...the new breed of men who take as much time and trouble over personal hygiene as the women in their lives.* …生活中，和女人花一样多时间和精力在个人卫生上的新型男士。 **6** ADJ A **personal** relationship is one that is not connected with your job or public life. 与公务无关的；私人的 ❑ *He was a great and valued personal friend whom I've known for many years.* 他是个非常好的、很宝贵的私人朋友，我们已相识多年。 **7** ADJ If someone has a **personal** shopper or a **personal** trainer, they employ another person to shop for them or to help them keep fit. 属于个人的 [ADJ n] ❑ *Another way of escaping the crowds and the changing rooms is to employ a personal shopper.* 另一个逃避人群和更衣室的办法是雇一个私人采购专员。 ❑ *The best clubs also offer personal trainers to help motivate and ensure that exercises are properly performed.* 最好的俱乐部还提供私人教练，来帮助激发动力，并确保训练适当地进行。

per·son·al as·sis·tant (**personal assistants**) N-COUNT A **personal assistant** is a person who does office work and administrative work for someone. The abbreviation **PA** is also used. 私人助理 [BUSINESS] ❑ *She was a hard-pressed personal assistant to a frenetic company chairman.* 她给一位疯狂的公司总裁当私人助理，有很大的压力。

per·son·al com·put·er (**personal computers**) N-COUNT A **personal computer** is a computer that is used by one person at a time in a business, a school, or at home. The abbreviation **PC** is also used. 个人电脑

per·son·al digi·tal as·sis·tant (**personal digital assistants**) N-COUNT A **personal digital assistant** is a handheld computer, used mainly for storing and accessing personal information such as addresses, telephone numbers, and memos. The abbreviation **PDA** is also used. 个人数字助理；掌上电脑 ❑ *...devices such as cellphones and personal digital assistants.* …诸如手机和掌上电脑之类的设备。

per·son·al·ity ♦◇◇ /pɜrsənælɪti/ (**personalities**) **1** N-VAR Your **personality** is your whole character and nature. 性格；品性 ❑ *She has such a kind, friendly personality.* 她有着如此友善的性格。 ❑ *The contest was as much about personalities as it was about politics.* 这次竞赛既比政治策略，又比品质性格。 **2** N-VAR If someone has **personality** or is **a personality**, they have a strong and lively character. (坚强、活泼的) 个性 ❑ *...a woman of great personality.* …一个很有个性的女人。 **3** N-COUNT You can refer to a famous person, especially in entertainment, broadcasting, or sports, as a **personality**. (尤指娱乐、广播、体育界) 名人 ❑ *...the radio and television personality, Johnny Carson.* …广播电视名人约翰尼·卡森。

Word Partnership *personality* 的常用搭配：

N.	personality **trait** **1** **radio** personality, **television/TV** personality **3**
ADJ.	**strong** personality, **unique** personality **1** **2**

per·son·al·ly ♦◇◇ /pɜrsənəli/ **1** ADV You use **personally** to emphasize that you are giving your own opinion. 在个人看来 [ADV with cl] [EMPHASIS] ❑ *Personally I think it's a waste of time.* 在我看来，我认为这是浪费时间。 ❑ *You can disagree about them, and I personally do, but they are great ideas that have made people think.* 你可以… **2** ADV If you do something **personally**, you do it yourself rather than letting someone else do it. 亲自 [ADV with v] ❑ *He is returning to Paris to answer the allegations personally.* 他将回巴黎来亲自回应这些指控。 ❑ *When the great man arrived, the club's manager personally escorted him upstairs.* 当那位大人物到达时，俱乐部的经理亲自护送他上楼。 **3** ADV If you meet or know someone **personally**, you meet or know them in real life, rather than knowing about them or knowing their work. 当面地；本人直接地 [ADV with v] ❑ *He did not know them personally, but he was familiar with their reputation.* 他并不直接认识他们，但久闻他们的大名。 **4** ADV You can use **personally** to say that something refers to an individual person rather than to other people. 关于个人地 ❑ *He was personally responsible for all that people suffered under his rule.* 他个人对在他统治下受苦难的人民有全部的责任。 **5** ADV You can use **personally** to show that you are talking about someone's private life rather than their professional or public life. 涉及私生活地 ❑ *This has taken a great toll on me personally and professionally.* 这让我在私人生活和事业上造成了巨大的损失。 **6** PHRASE If you **take** someone's remarks **personally**, you are upset because you think that they are criticizing you in particular. 视 (言论等) 针对自己而不悦 ❑ *I take everything too personally.* 我过于把什么都看成是冲着自己而来的。

per·son·al or·gan·iz·er (**personal organizers**) N-COUNT A **personal organizer** is a book containing personal or business information, that you can add pages to or remove pages from to keep the information up-to-date. Small computers with a similar function are also called **personal organizers**. 活页记事本；电子记事簿

per·son·al ste·reo (**personal stereos**) N-COUNT A **personal stereo** is a small cassette or CD player with very light headphones, that people carry around so that they can listen to music while doing something else. 随身听

per·soni·fi·ca·tion /pərsɒnɪfɪkeɪʃən/ N-SING If you say that someone is **the personification of** a particular thing or quality, you mean that they are a perfect example of that thing or that they have a lot of that quality. 典型；化身 ❑ *Janis Joplin was the personification of the '60s female rock singer.* 贾尼斯·乔普林是60年代女摇滚歌手的典型。

per·soni·fy /pərsɒnɪfaɪ/ (**personifies, personifying, personified**) V-T If you say that someone **personifies** a particular thing or quality, you mean that they seem to be a perfect example of that thing, or to have that quality to a very large degree. 是…的化身；体现 ❑ *She seemed to personify goodness and nobility.* 她似乎是善良和高贵的化身。

per·son·nel ♦◇◇ /pɜrsənɛl/ **1** N-PLURAL The **personnel** of an organization are the people who work for it. 人员 ❑ *Since 1954 Japan has never dispatched military personnel abroad.* 自1954年以来，日本再也没有向海外派遣过军事人员。 ❑ *There has been very little renewal of personnel in higher education.* 高等教育事业中人员更新很少。 **2** N-UNCOUNT **Personnel** is the department in a large company or organization that deals with employees, keeps their records, and helps with any problems they might have. 人事部门 [OLD-FASHIONED, BUSINESS] ❑ *Her first job was in personnel.* 她的第一份工作是在人事部。

per·spec·tive ♦◇◇ /pərspɛktɪv/ (**perspectives**) **1** N-COUNT A particular **perspective** is a particular way of thinking about something, especially one that is influenced by your beliefs or experiences. 思维方式；看法 ❑ *He says the death of his father 18 months ago has given him a new perspective on life.* 他说 1 8 个月前他父亲的去世

使他对人生产生了新的看法。 ❑ *...two different perspectives on the nature of adolescent development.* …关于青春期发育特点的两种不同观点。
2 PHRASE If you get something **in perspective** or **into perspective**, you judge its real importance by considering it in relation to everything else. If you get something **out of perspective**, you fail to judge its real importance in relation to everything else. (看待事物) 正确/不正确地 ❑ *Remember to keep things in perspective.* 记住要正确地看待事物。 ❑ *I let things get out of perspective.* 我没能正确地看待事物。

Thesaurus *perspective* 另参见:
N. attitude, mindset, outlook, viewpoint 1

per·spi·ra·tion /pɜrspɪreɪʃ°n/ N-UNCOUNT **Perspiration** is the liquid that comes out on the surface of your skin when you are hot or frightened. 汗水 [FORMAL] ❑ *His hands were wet with perspiration.* 他的双手被汗水浸湿了。
→ see **sweat**

Word Link *suad, suas ≈ urging : dissuade, persuade, persuasive*

per·suade ♦◇◇ /pərsweɪd/ (**persuades, persuading, persuaded**)
1 V-T If you **persuade** someone **to** do something, you cause them to do it by giving them good reasons for doing it. 说服 ❑ *My husband persuaded me to come.* 我丈夫说服我来的。 ❑ *We're trying to persuade manufacturers to sell them here.* 我们正试图说服制造商们在这里销售它们。
2 V-T If something **persuades** someone **to** take a particular course of action, it causes them to take that course of action because it is a good reason for doing so. 引发 (某人采取行动) ❑ *It was the lack of privacy that eventually persuaded us to move after Ben was born.* 正是因为缺少隐私感才最终迫使我们在本出生后搬了家。 3 V-T If you **persuade** someone that something is true, you say things that eventually make them believe that it is true. 使相信 ❑ *I've persuaded Mrs. Tennant that it's time she retired.* 我已经使坦南特夫人相信是她该退休的时候了。 ❑ *We had managed to persuade them that it was worth working with us.* 我们已经设法使他们相信和我们一起共事是值得的。

Thesaurus *persuade* 另参见:
V. cajole, convince, influence, sway, talk into, win over; *(ant.)* discourage, dissuade 1 3

Word Partnership *persuade* 的常用搭配:
V. **attempt to** persuade, **be able to** persuade, **fail to** persuade, **try to** persuade 1 3

per·sua·sion /pərsweɪʒ°n/ (**persuasions**) 1 N-UNCOUNT **Persuasion** is the act of persuading someone to do something or to believe that something is true. 说服 ❑ *Only after much persuasion from Ellis had she agreed to hold a show at all.* 直到埃利斯进行了大量的游说之后她才同意举办一次展览。 2 N-COUNT If you are **of** a particular **persuasion**, you have a particular belief or set of beliefs. 信仰; 信念 [FORMAL] ❑ *It is a national movement and has within it people of all political persuasions.* 这是一项全国性的运动，参加的人们政治信仰各不相同。

★ **per·sua·sive** /pərsweɪsɪv/ ADJ Someone or something that is **persuasive** is likely to persuade a person to believe or do a particular thing. 有说服力的 ❑ *What do you think were some of the more persuasive arguments on the other side?* 你觉得对方哪些论点更有说服力? ❑ *I can be very persuasive when I want to be.* 当我想要的时候，我会很有说服力的。 ● **per·sua·sive·ly** ADV 有说服力地 [ADV with V] ❑ *...a trained lawyer who can present arguments persuasively.* …一位训练有素、能令人信服地陈述辩词的律师。

▲ **per·tain** /pərteɪn/ (**pertains, pertaining, pertained**) V-I If one thing **pertains to** another, it relates, belongs, or applies to it. 与…相关; 属于; 适于 [FORMAL] ❑ *...matters pertaining to naval district defense.* …与海军区域防卫有关的问题。

▲ **per·ti·nent** /pɜrt°nənt/ ADJ Something that is **pertinent** is relevant to a particular subject. 相关的 [FORMAL] ❑ *She had asked some pertinent questions.* 她问了一些相关的问题。 ❑ *...name, address, and other pertinent information.* …姓名、地址及其他相关信息。

per·vade /pərveɪd/ (**pervades, pervading, pervaded**) V-T If something **pervades** a place or thing, it is a noticeable feature throughout it. 弥漫; 充满 [FORMAL] ❑ *The smell of sawdust and glue pervaded the factory.* 锯屑和胶水的气味弥漫在工厂里。

★ **per·va·sive** /pərveɪsɪv/ ADJ Something, especially something bad, that is **pervasive** is present or felt throughout a place or thing. (尤指不好的事物) 无处不在的 [FORMAL] ❑ *...the pervasive influence of the army in national life.* …军队在国民生活中无处不在的影响。

per·verse /pərvɜrs/ ADJ Someone who is **perverse** deliberately does things that are unreasonable or that result in harm for themselves. 乖戾的; 有悖常理的 [DISAPPROVAL] ❑ *It would be perverse to stop this healthy trend.* 阻止这一健康的趋势是有悖常理的。 ❑ *He seemed to take a perverse pleasure in being disagreeable.* 他似乎在招人厌恶中得到一种反常的乐趣。 ● **per·verse·ly** ADV 乖戾地; 有悖常理地 ❑ *She was perversely pleased to be causing trouble.* 她反常地乐在制造麻烦中。

per·ver·sion /pərvɜrʒ°n, -ʃ°n/ (**perversions**) 1 N-VAR You can refer to a sexual desire or action that you consider to be abnormal and unacceptable as a **perversion**. 性变态 [DISAPPROVAL] ❑ *The book was the authority on sexual perversions.* 这本书是关于性变态的权威著作。
2 N-VAR A **perversion of** something is a form of it that is bad or wrong, or the changing of it into this form. 歪曲 [DISAPPROVAL] ❑ *Critics say that the system is a dangerous perversion of democracy.* 批评家们说，这种体系是对民主的危险的歪曲。

per·vert (**perverts, perverting, perverted**)

The verb is pronounced /pərvɜrt/. The noun is pronounced /pɜrvərt/.

动词读作 /pərvɜrt/。名词读作 /pɜrvərt/。

1 V-T If you **pervert** something such as a process or society, you interfere with it so that it is not as good as it used to be or as it should be. 使败坏 [FORMAL, DISAPPROVAL] ❑ *Any reform will destroy and pervert our constitution.* 任何改革都将破坏、败坏我们的宪法。
2 N-COUNT If you say that someone is a **pervert**, you mean that you consider their behavior, especially their sexual behavior, to be immoral or unacceptable. (尤在性行为方面) 变态的人 [DISAPPROVAL] ❑ *I hope the police track down these perverts and charge them with rape.* 我希望警方追查这些性变态者，并以强奸罪起诉他们。

per·vert·ed /pərvɜrtɪd/ 1 ADJ If you say that someone is **perverted**, you mean that you consider their behavior, especially their sexual behavior, to be immoral or unacceptable. (尤指性行为) 变态的 [DISAPPROVAL] ❑ *You've been protecting sick and perverted men.* 你们一直在保护恶心的性变态的男人们。 2 ADJ You can use **perverted** to describe actions or ideas which you think are wrong, unnatural, or harmful. 反常的 [DISAPPROVAL] ❑ *...a perverted form of knowledge.* …一种反常的知识形式。

pes·si·mism /pɛsɪmɪzəm/ N-UNCOUNT **Pessimism** is the belief that bad things are going to happen. 悲观主义 ❑ *...universal pessimism about the economy.* …对经济形势普遍的悲观看法。

pes·si·mist /pɛsɪmɪst/ (**pessimists**) N-COUNT A **pessimist** is someone who thinks that bad things are going to happen. 悲观主义者 ❑ *I'm a natural pessimist; I usually expect the worst.* 我是个天生的悲观主义者，我总是往最坏的方面想。

pes·si·mis·tic /pɛsɪmɪstɪk/ ADJ Someone who is **pessimistic** thinks that bad things are going to happen. 悲观的 ❑ *Not everyone is so pessimistic about the future.* 并非每个人都对未来如此悲观。 ❑ *Hardy has often been criticized for an excessively pessimistic view of life.* 哈迪因其过分悲观的人生观而经常受到批评。

★ **pest** /pɛst/ (**pests**) 1 N-COUNT **Pests** are insects or small animals that damage crops or food supplies. 害虫; 有害的小动物 ❑ *...crops which are resistant to some of the major insect pests and diseases.* …能抵抗一些主要病虫害的庄稼。 ❑ *Each year ten percent of the crop is lost to a pest called corn rootworm.* 每年有10%的作物受损于一种叫做玉米根虫的害虫。 2 N-COUNT You can describe someone, especially a child, as a **pest** if they keep bothering you. 讨厌鬼 (尤指小孩) [INFORMAL, DISAPPROVAL] ❑ *He climbed on the table, pulled my hair, and was generally a pest.* 他爬上桌子，揪我的头发，真是个讨厌鬼。
→ see **farm**

▲ **pes·ter** /pɛstər/ (**pesters, pestering, pestered**) V-T If you say that someone **is pestering** you, you mean that they keep asking you to do something, or keep talking to you, and you find this annoying. 纠缠 [DISAPPROVAL] ❑ *I thought she'd stop pestering me, but it only seemed to make her worse.* 我以为她会停止纠缠我，但似乎只是让她变本加厉了。 ❑ *I know he gets fed up with people pestering him for money.* 我知道他烦透了那些缠着他要钱的人。

Word Link *cide ≈ killing : genocide, homicide, pesticide*

▲ **pes·ti·cide** /pɛstɪsaɪd/ (**pesticides**) N-MASS **Pesticides** are chemicals that farmers put on their crops to kill harmful insects. 杀虫剂
→ see **pollution**

pet ♦◇◇ /pɛt/ (**pets, petting, petted**) **1** N-COUNT A **pet** is an animal that you keep in your home to give you company and pleasure. 宠物 ❑ *It is plainly cruel to keep turtles as pets.* 把海龟当宠物养显然是残忍的。 ❑ *...a bachelor living alone in a house with his pet dog.* …一个与宠物狗独住一栋房子的单身汉。 **2** ADJ Someone's **pet** theory, project, or subject is one that they particularly support or like. 钟爱的(理论、项目、学科等) ❑ *He would not stand by and let his pet project be killed off.* 他不会袖手旁观，任由自己钟爱的项目被否决。 **3** V-T If you **pet** a person or animal, you touch them in an affectionate way. 爱抚 ❑ *The policeman reached down and petted the wolfhound.* 警察伸出手，摸了摸那条猎狼犬。
→ see Word Web: **pet**

▲ **pet·al** /pɛtᵊl/ (**petals**) N-COUNT The **petals** of a flower are the thin colored or white parts that together form the flower. 花瓣 ❑ *...bowls of dried rose petals.* …一碗碗干玫瑰花瓣。

pe·ter /pitər/ (**peters, petering, petered**)
▸ **peter out** PHRASAL VERB If something **peters out**, it gradually comes to an end. 逐渐停息 ❑ *The six-month strike seemed to be petering out.* 持续了6个月的罢工似乎在逐渐停息。

pe·tite /pətit/ ADJ If you describe a woman as **petite**, you are politely saying that she is small and is not fat. 娇小的 ❑ *She was of below average height, petite and slender.* 她低于平均身高，娇小且苗条。

★ **pe·ti·tion** /pətɪʃᵊn/ (**petitions, petitioning, petitioned**) **1** N-COUNT A **petition** is a document signed by a lot of people that asks a government or other official group to do a particular thing. 请愿书 ❑ *People feel so strongly that we recently presented the government with a petition signed by 4,500 people.* 人们感受如此强烈，以至我们最近向政府提交了一份由4500人签名的请愿书。 **2** N-COUNT A **petition** is a formal request made to a court of law for some legal action to be taken. 诉状；(向法院提出的) 申请 [LEGAL] ❑ *His lawyers filed a petition for all charges to be dropped.* 他的律师们提出申请要求撤销所有指控。 **3** V-T/V-I If you **petition** someone in authority, you make a formal request to them. 正式请求 [LEGAL] ❑ *...couples petitioning for divorce.* …申请离婚的几对夫妇。 ❑ *All the attempts to petition Congress had failed.* 所有向国会提出请求的努力都已失败了。

★ **pe·ti·tion·er** /pətɪʃənər/ (**petitioners**) **1** N-COUNT A **petitioner** is a person who presents or signs a petition. 请愿者 **2** N-COUNT A **petitioner** is a person who brings a legal case to a court of law. 起诉人 [LEGAL] ❑ *The judge awarded the costs of the case to the petitioners.* 那位法官把案子的费用判给了起诉方。

pet·ri·fied /pɛtrɪfaɪd/ **1** ADJ If you are **petrified**, you are extremely frightened, perhaps so frightened that you cannot think or move. 吓呆了的 ❑ *I've always been petrified of being alone.* 我总是非常害怕独处。 **2** ADJ A **petrified** plant or animal has died and has gradually turned into stone. 石化了的 [ADJ n] ❑ *...a block of petrified wood.* …一块石化了的木头。

★ **pet·ro·chemi·cal** /pɛtroʊkɛmɪkᵊl/ (**petrochemicals**) also **petro-chemical** N-COUNT **Petrochemicals** are chemicals that are obtained from petroleum or natural gas. 石油化工产品 [usu pl]

pet·rol /pɛtrəl/ N-UNCOUNT **Petrol** is the same as **gasoline**. 汽油 [BRIT]

pe·tro·leum /pətroʊliəm/ N-UNCOUNT **Petroleum** is oil that is found under the surface of the earth or under the sea bed. Gasoline and kerosene are obtained from petroleum. 石油
→ see **energy, oil**

pet·rol sta·tion [BRIT] → see **gas station**

★ **pet·ty** /pɛti/ (**pettier, pettiest**) **1** ADJ You can use **petty** to describe things such as problems, rules, or arguments that you think are unimportant or relate to unimportant things. 不重要的 [DISAPPROVAL] ❑ *He was miserable all the time and fights would start over petty things.* 他一直都很闷闷不乐，常为一些鸡毛蒜皮的事吵架。 ❑ *...endless rules and petty regulations.* …没完没了的规则和无足轻重的规定。 **2** ADJ If you describe someone's behavior as **petty**, you mean that they care too much about small, unimportant things and perhaps that they are unnecessarily unkind. 过分在乎琐事的 [DISAPPROVAL] ❑ *He was petty-minded and obsessed with detail.* 他谨小慎微，过于在意细节。 ● **pet·ti·ness** N-UNCOUNT 狭隘 ❑ *Never had she met such spite and pettiness.* 她以前从来没有碰到过这样的恶意和狭隘。 **3** ADJ **Petty** is used of people or actions that are less important, serious, or great than others. (人或行动) 次要的 [ADJ n] ❑ *...petty crime, such as purse-snatching and minor break-ins.* …诸如抢钱包、不严重的入室盗窃之类的轻罪。

pet·ty cash N-UNCOUNT **Petty cash** is money that is kept in the office of a company, for making small payments in cash when necessary. (办公室存放的) 小额备用金 [BUSINESS] ❑ *After having her expense claims overruled, she took the money from petty cash.* 在她的费用申请被驳回后，她从小额备用金中取了钱。

petu·lant /pɛtʃələnt/ ADJ Someone who is **petulant** is unreasonably angry and upset in a childish way. 使小性子的 ❑ *His critics say he's just being silly and petulant.* 批评他的人说，他真是又愚蠢又任性。

pew /pyu/ (**pews**) N-COUNT A **pew** is a long wooden seat with a back that people sit on in church. (教堂里的) 靠背长椅 ❑ *Charlene sat in the front pew.* 查伦坐在前排的靠背长椅上。

pew·ter /pyutər/ N-UNCOUNT **Pewter** is a grey metal that is made by mixing tin and lead. Pewter was often used in former times to make ornaments or containers for eating and drinking. 锡铅合金 ❑ *...pewter plates.* …锡铅合金盘子。

phan·tom /fæntəm/ (**phantoms**) **1** N-COUNT A **phantom** is a ghost. 幽灵 ❑ *They vanished down the stairs like two phantoms.* 他们像两个幽灵似的下楼不见了。 **2** ADJ You use **phantom** to describe something that you think you experience but that is not real. 幻觉的 [ADJ n] ❑ *...phantom pregnancies.* …精神性假妊娠。 **3** ADJ **Phantom** is used to describe business organizations, agreements, or goods that do not really exist, but that someone pretends do exist in order to cheat people. (企业、协议或商品等) 有名无实的 [ADJ n] ❑ *A phantom trading scheme at a Wall Street investment bank went unnoticed for three years.* 一家华尔街投资银行的虚构的交易方案历经3年都未被察觉。

phar·aoh /fɛəroʊ, færoʊ, feɪ-/ (**pharaohs**) N-COUNT; N-PROPER A **pharaoh** was a king of ancient Egypt. 法老 (古埃及国王) ❑ *...Rameses II, Pharaoh of All Egypt.* …古埃及法老拉美西斯二世。

Word Link *pharma ≈ drug : **pharma**ceutical, **pharma**cist, **pharma**cy*

phar·ma·ceu·ti·cal /fɑrməsutɪkᵊl/ (**pharmaceuticals**) **1** ADJ **Pharmaceutical** means connected with the industrial production of medicines. 制药的 [ADJ n] ❑ *...a Swiss pharmaceutical company.* …一家瑞士制药公司。 **2** N-PLURAL **Pharmaceuticals** are medicines. 药品 ❑ *Antibiotics were of no use, neither were other pharmaceuticals.* 抗生素没有用，其他药物也没有用。

Word Link *ist ≈ one who practices : art**ist**, chem**ist**, pharmac**ist***

phar·ma·cist /fɑrməsɪst/ (**pharmacists**) N-COUNT A **pharmacist** is a person who is qualified to prepare and sell medicines. 药剂师 ❑ *Ask your pharmacist for advice.* 向你的药剂师征询意见吧。

Word Web **pet**

Americans love **pets**. They own more than 51 million **dogs**, 56 million **cats**, 45 million **birds**, 75 million small **mammals** and **reptiles**, and millions of **fish**. Recent studies have shown that adult pet owners are healthier overall than those who don't have **companion animals**. One study (Katcher, 1982) suggests that owning a pet lowers blood pressure. The 2001 German Socio-Economic Panel Survey found that pet owners made fewer doctor visits than others in the group. And a study in the *American Journal of Cardiology* found that male dog owners were less likely to die within a year after a heart attack than people who didn't own dogs.

Word Web philosophy

Philosophy helps us **understand** ourselves and the purpose of our lives. **Philosophers** have studied the same **issues** for thousands of years. The Chinese philosopher Confucius* wrote about personal and **political morals**. He taught that people should love others and honor their parents. They should do what is right, not what is best for themselves. He thought that a ruler who had to use force had already failed as a ruler. The Greek philosopher Plato* wrote about politics and science. Later, Aristotle* outlined a system of **logic** and **reasoning**. He wanted to be absolutely sure what is true and what isn't.

Confucius (551-479 BC)
Plato (427-347 BC)
Aristotle (384-322 BC)

Plato

Aristotle

Confucius

▲ **phar·ma·cy** /fɑ̲rməsi/ (**pharmacies**) **1** N-COUNT A **pharmacy** is a store or a department in a store where medicines are sold or given out. 药店；药房 ❑ *Pick up the medicine from the pharmacy.* 从药房取药。 **2** N-UNCOUNT **Pharmacy** is the job or the science of preparing medicines. 制药业；药剂学 ❑ *He spent four years studying pharmacy.* 他花了4年时间学习药剂学。

> In American English, the usual way of referring to a store where medicines are sold is a **drugstore**. ❑ *She went into a drugstore and bought some aspirin.* **Pharmacy** refers specifically to a part of the drugstore where you get prescription medicines. Pharmacies are often located in stores that mainly sell other merchandise, such as supermarkets and discount centers. In Britain, the nearest equivalent of a drugstore is a **chemist's**.

phase ♦◇◇ /fe̲ɪz/ (**phases, phasing, phased**) N-COUNT A **phase** is a particular stage in a process or in the gradual development of something. 阶段 ❑ *This fall, 6000 residents will participate in the first phase of the project.* 今年秋季，6000名居民将参与这项计划的第一阶段。 ❑ *The crisis is entering a crucial, critical phase.* 危机正进入一个至关重要的决定性阶段。

▸ **phase in** PHRASAL VERB If a new way of doing something **is phased in**, it is introduced gradually. 逐步采用 ❑ *The reforms would be phased in over three years.* 改革将在3年内逐步实施。

▸ **phase out** PHRASAL VERB If something **is phased out**, people gradually stop using it. 逐步淘汰 ❑ *They said the present system of military conscription should be phased out.* 他们说现行的征兵体系应该逐步淘汰。

> **Thesaurus** *phase* 另参见：
> N. chapter, juncture, period, point, stage, time

Ph.D. /pi̲ eɪtʃ di̲/ (**Ph.D.s**) also **PhD** **1** N-COUNT A **Ph.D.** is a degree awarded to people who have done advanced research into a particular subject. **Ph.D.** is an abbreviation for **Doctor of Philosophy**. 博士学位 ❑ *He is more highly educated, with a Ph.D. in chemistry.* 他受过更高的教育，拥有化学博士学位。 **2** **Ph.D.** is written after someone's name to indicate that they have a Ph.D. 博士（用于人名之后） ❑ *...R.D. Combes, Ph.D.* …R. D. 库姆斯博士。
→ see **graduation**

pheas·ant /fɛ̲zᵊnt/ (**pheasants**)

> **Pheasant** can also be used as the plural form.

N-COUNT A **pheasant** is a bird with a long tail. Pheasants are often shot as a sport and then eaten. 野鸡 ● N-UNCOUNT **Pheasant** is the flesh of this bird eaten as food. 野鸡肉 ❑ *...roast pheasant.* …烤野鸡肉。

phe·nom·enal /fɪnɒ̲mɪnᵊl/ ADJ Something that is **phenomenal** is unusually great or good. 非凡的；杰出的 [EMPHASIS] ❑ *Exports of Australian wine are growing at a phenomenal rate.* 澳大利亚葡萄酒的出口正以惊人的速度增长。 ● **phe·nom·enal·ly** ADV 非凡地；杰出地 ❑ *Annie, 37, has recently re-launched her phenomenally successful singing career.* 37岁的安妮最近又重新开始了她极其成功的演唱生涯。

phe·nom·enon /fɪnɒ̲mɪnɒn/ (**phenomena**) N-COUNT A **phenomenon** is something that is observed to happen or exist. 现象 [FORMAL] ❑ *...scientific explanations of natural phenomena.* …自然现象的科学解释。
→ see **experiment, science**

phi·loso·pher /fɪlɒ̲səfər/ (**philosophers**) **1** N-COUNT A **philosopher** is a person who studies or writes about philosophy. 哲学家 ❑ *...the Greek philosopher Plato.* …希腊哲学家柏拉图。 **2** N-COUNT If you refer to someone as a **philosopher**, you mean that they think deeply and seriously about life and other basic matters. 哲人 ❑ *Carlos was something of a philosopher.* 卡洛斯有几分哲人气质。
→ see **philosophy**

> **Word Link** *soph ≈ wise : philosophical, philosophy, sophisticated*

philo·sophi·cal /fɪ̲ləsɒ̲fɪkᵊl/ **1** ADJ **Philosophical** means concerned with or relating to philosophy. 哲学的 ❑ *He was more accustomed to cocktail party chatter than to political or philosophical discussions.* 比起政治或者哲学讨论，他更习惯于鸡尾酒会上的闲谈。 ● **philo·sophi·cal·ly** /fɪ̲ləsɒ̲fɪkli/ ADV 哲学地 ❑ *Wilbur says he's not a coward, but that he's philosophically opposed to war.* 威尔伯说他不是个懦夫，但他在哲学观念上反对战争。 **2** ADJ Someone who is **philosophical** does not get upset when disappointing or disturbing things happen. 泰然自若的 [APPROVAL] ❑ *Lewis has grown philosophical about life.* 刘易斯对生活已经变得豁达了。 ● **philo·sophi·cal·ly** ADV 泰然自若地 [ADV after v] ❑ *She says philosophically: "It could have been far worse."* 她泰然自若地说，"情况本来可能会糟得多。"

phi·loso·phy ♦◇◇ /fɪlɒ̲səfi/ (**philosophies**) **1** N-UNCOUNT **Philosophy** is the study or creation of theories about basic things such as the nature of existence, knowledge, and thought, or about how people should live. 哲学 ❑ *He studied philosophy and psychology at Yale.* 他在耶鲁大学学习哲学和心理学。 **2** N-COUNT A **philosophy** is a particular set of ideas that a philosopher has. 哲学思想 ❑ *...the philosophies of Socrates, Plato, and Aristotle.* …苏格拉底、柏拉图和亚里士多德的哲学思想。 **3** N-COUNT A **philosophy** is a particular theory that someone has about how to live or how to deal with a particular situation. 人生哲学；处事原则 ❑ *The best philosophy is to change your food habits to a low-sugar diet.* 最好的生活方式是将你的饮食习惯改成食用低糖食品。
→ see Word Web: **philosophy**

> **Thesaurus** *philosophy* 另参见：
> N. attitude, outlook, reasoning **3**

phish·ing /fɪ̲ʃɪŋ/ N-UNCOUNT **Phishing** is the practice of trying to trick people into giving secret financial information by sending e-mails that look as if they come from a bank, credit-card account, etc. The details are then used to steal people's money, or to steal their identity in order to commit crimes. 网络钓鱼 [COMPUTING]

> **Word Link** *phob ≈ fear : homophobic, phobia, xenophobia*

pho·bia /fo̲ʊbiə/ (**phobias**) N-COUNT A **phobia** is a very strong irrational fear or hatred of something. 恐惧症 ❑ *The man had a phobia about flying.* 这个男人有飞行恐惧症。

★ **phoe·nix** /fi̲nɪks/ (**phoenixes**) **1** N-COUNT A **phoenix** is an imaginary bird that, according to ancient stories, burns itself to ashes every five hundred years and is then born again. 凤凰 [usu sing] **2** N-SING If you describe someone or something as a **phoenix**, you mean that they return again after seeming to disappear or be destroyed. 失而复现或毁而再生者 [LITERARY] ❑ *Out of the ashes of the economic shambles, a phoenix of recovery can arise.* 复苏之风会从经济废墟的灰烬中腾飞而起。

phone ♦♦◊ /foʊn/ (**phones, phoning, phoned**) 1 N-SING The **phone** is an electrical system that you use to talk to someone else in another place, by dialing a number on a piece of equipment and speaking into it. 电话 [usu "the" N, also "by" N] ❑ *"I didn't tell you over the phone," she said. "I didn't know who might be listening."* "我没有在电话里告诉你，"她说。"我不知道谁会在听。" ❑ *She looked forward to talking to her daughter by phone.* 她盼望着和女儿通电话交谈。 2 N-COUNT The **phone** is the piece of equipment that you use when you dial someone's phone number and talk to them. 电话机 ❑ *Two minutes later the phone rang.* 两分钟后，电话铃响了。 3 → see also **cellular phone** 4 N-SING If you say that someone picks up or puts down **the phone**, you mean that they lift or replace the receiver. 电话听筒 ❑ *She picked up the phone, and began to dial Maurice's number.* 她拿起电话听筒，开始拨莫里斯的号码。 5 V-T/V-I When you **phone** someone, you dial their phone number and speak to them by phone. 给…打电话 ❑ *He'd phoned Laura to see if she was better.* 他给劳拉打过电话，看她是不是好些了。 6 PHRASE If you say that someone is **on the phone**, you mean that they are speaking to someone by phone. 在打电话 ❑ *She's always on the phone, wanting to know what I've been up to.* 她总是打电话，想知道我忙了些什么。

→ see **office**

▸ **phone in** 1 PHRASAL VERB If you **phone in** to a radio or television show, you telephone the show in order to give your opinion on a matter that the show has raised. (给电视台或电台)打电话(发表意见) ❑ *Listeners have been invited to phone in to pick the winner.* 听众受邀请打进电话选出获胜者。 2 PHRASAL VERB If you **phone in** to a place, you make a telephone call to that place. (给某处) 打电话 ❑ *He has phoned in to say he is thinking over his options.* 他已经打来电话说他正在考虑他的选择。 3 PHRASAL VERB If you **phone in** an order for something, you place the order by telephone. 电话预订 ❑ *Just phone in your order three or more days prior to departure.* 在出发前3天或更早打电话预订即可。

▸ **phone up** PHRASAL VERB When you **phone** someone **up**, you dial their phone number and speak to them by phone. 给…打电话 ❑ *Phone him up and tell him to come and have dinner with you one night.* 给他打电话，叫他哪天晚上过来和你一起吃晚饭。

phone book (**phone books**) N-COUNT A **phone book** is a book that contains an alphabetical list of the names, addresses, and telephone numbers of the people and businesses in a town or area. 电话簿

P

phone booth (**phone booths**) 1 N-COUNT A **phone booth** is a place in a station, hotel, or other public building where there is a public telephone. 公用电话间 2 N-COUNT A **phone booth** is a small shelter outdoors or in a building in which there is a public telephone. 公用电话亭 [AM]

phone box (**phone boxes**) N-COUNT A **phone box** is the same as a **phone booth** 公用电话亭 [BRIT]

phone call (**phone calls**) N-COUNT If you make a **phone call**, you dial someone's phone number and speak to them by phone. (打)电话 ❑ *Wait there for a minute. I have to make a phone call.* 在那儿等会儿，我得打个电话。

phone·card /foʊnkɑrd/ (**phonecards**) also **phone card** N-COUNT A **phonecard** is a plastic card that you can use instead of money to pay for telephone calls in some public telephones. 电话卡

phone-in (**phone-ins**) N-COUNT A **phone-in** is a program on radio or television in which people telephone with questions or opinions and their calls are broadcast. (电台或电视台的) 听众或观众来电直播节目 ❑ *She took part in a radio phone-in program.* 她参加了电台的听众来电直播节目。

pho·ney /foʊni/ → see **phony**

phos·phate /fɒsfeɪt/ (**phosphates**) N-MASS A **phosphate** is a chemical compound that contains phosphorus. Phosphates are often used in fertilizers. 磷酸盐

pho·to ♦♦♦ /foʊtoʊ/ (**photos**) N-COUNT A **photo** is the same as a **photograph**. 照片 ❑ *Let's take a photo!* 我们拍张照片吧！

→ see **photography**

Word Link *photo ≈ light : photocopier, photograph, photovoltaic*

photo·copi·er /foʊtəkɒpiər/ (**photocopiers**) N-COUNT A **photocopier** is a machine that quickly copies documents onto paper by photographing them. 复印机

→ see **copy**

photo·copy /foʊtəkɒpi/ (**photocopies, photocopying, photocopied**) 1 N-COUNT A **photocopy** is a copy of a document made using a photocopier. 复印件 ❑ *He was shown a photocopy of the certificate.* 给他看了证书的复印件。 2 V-T If you **photocopy** a document, you make a copy of it using a photocopier. 复印 ❑ *Staff photocopied the check before cashing it.* 工作人员在兑现支票前先把它复印了。

photo·graph ♦♦◊ /foʊtəgræf/ (**photographs, photographing, photographed**) 1 N-COUNT A **photograph** is a picture that is made using a camera. 照片 ❑ *He wants to take some photographs of the house.* 他想给这所房子拍一些照片。 2 V-T When you **photograph** someone or something, you use a camera to obtain a picture of them. 给…照相 [FORMAL] ❑ *She photographed the children.* 她给孩子们照了相。 ❑ *I hate being photographed.* 我讨厌被拍照。

pho·tog·ra·pher ♦◊◊ /fətɒgrəfər/ (**photographers**) N-COUNT A **photographer** is someone who takes photographs as a job or hobby. 摄影师; 摄影爱好者 ❑ *...a professional photographer.* …一名专业摄影师。 ❑ *...an amateur photographer.* …一名业余摄影爱好者。

→ see **photography**

photo·graph·ic /foʊtəgræfɪk/ 1 ADJ **Photographic** means connected with photographs or photography. 摄影的; 照片的 ❑ *...photographic equipment.* …摄影器材。 2 ADJ If you have a **photographic memory**, you are able to remember things in great detail after you have seen them. 摄影般精确的记忆力 ❑ *He had a photographic memory for maps.* 他对地图具有摄影般精确的记忆力。

pho·tog·ra·phy /fətɒgrəfi/ N-UNCOUNT **Photography** is the skill, job, or process of producing photographs. 摄影术; 摄影 ❑ *Photography is one of her hobbies.* 摄影是她的爱好之一。

→ see Word Web: **photography**

photovoltaic /foʊtoʊvɒlteɪk/ ADJ A **photovoltaic** cell or panel is a device that uses sunlight to cause a chemical reaction which produces electricity. 光电的 [ADJ n] [TECHNICAL]

→ see **solar system**

phras·al verb /freɪzᵊl vɜrb/ (**phrasal verbs**) N-COUNT A **phrasal verb** is a combination of a verb and an adverb or preposition, for example, "shut up" or "knock back," which together have a particular meaning. 短语动词

phrase ♦◊◊ /freɪz/ (**phrases, phrasing, phrased**) 1 N-COUNT A **phrase** is a short group of words that people often use as a way of saying something. The meaning of a phrase is often not obvious from the meaning of the individual words in it. 惯用语; 警句 ❑ *He used a phrase I hate: "You have to be cruel to be kind."* 他用了一句我讨厌的习语："要想善良，就得残忍。" 2 N-COUNT A **phrase** is a small group of words that forms a unit, either on its own or

Word Web photography

It's easy to **take** a **picture** with a digital **camera**. You just look through the viewfinder and push the **shutter button**. But professional **photographers** need to produce high quality **photos**. So their job is more difficult. First they decide on the correct **film** for the job and **load** the camera. Then they check the **lighting** and carefully **focus** the camera. They usually take several **shots**, one after another. Then it's time to **develop** the film and make **prints**. Sometimes a photographer will **crop** a photo or **enlarge** it to create a more striking **image**.

within a sentence. 短语；词组 ❑ *A writer spends many hours going over and over a scene—changing a phrase here, a word there.* 作家花许多个小时反复润色一个场景——这儿改个短语，那儿改个单词。 **3** V-T If you **phrase** something in a particular way, you express it in words in that way. 用言语表达 ❑ *I would have phrased it quite differently.* 我则会用完全不同的话来表达它。 ❑ *The speech was carefully phrased.* 这篇讲话措辞谨慎。 **4** PHRASE If someone has a particular **turn of phrase**, they have a particular way of expressing themselves in words. 表述方式 ❑ *...Schwarzkopf's distinctive turn of phrase.* …施瓦茨科普夫与众不同的表述方式。 **5** to **coin a phrase** → see **coin**

Word Link *physi ≈ of nature : physical, physician, physiology*

physi·cal ♦♦◇ /fɪzɪkᵊl/ (**physicals**) **1** ADJ **Physical** qualities, actions, or things are connected with a person's body, rather than with their mind. 肉体的；身体的 ❑ *...the physical and mental problems caused by the illness.* …这种疾病引起的生理和心理问题。 ❑ *Physical activity promotes good health.* 身体运动促进健康。 ● **physi·cal·ly** ADV 身体上地 ❑ *You may be physically and mentally exhausted after a long flight.* 长途飞行后你可能身心都很疲惫。 **2** ADJ **Physical** things are real things that can be touched and seen, rather than ideas or spoken words. 实物的；有形的 ❑ *Physical and ideological barriers had come down in Eastern Europe.* 物质和意识形态上的障碍在东欧都已减少。 ❑ *...physical evidence to support the story.* …支持这种说法的实物证据。 ● **physi·cal·ly** ADV 有形地 ❑ *...physically cut off from every other country.* …地理上与所有其他国家分割开来。 **3** ADJ **Physical** means relating to the structure, size, or shape of something that can be touched and seen. 物理的 [ADJ n] ❑ *...the physical characteristics of the terrain.* …这一地形的物理特点。 **4** ADJ **Physical** means connected with physics or the laws of physics. 物理学的 [ADJ n] ❑ *...the physical laws of combustion and thermodynamics.* …燃烧和热力学的物理定律。 **5** ADJ Someone who is **physical** touches people a lot, either in an affectionate way or in a rough way. (以温柔或粗鲁的方式) 有大量身体接触的 ❑ *We decided that in the game we would be physical and aggressive.* 我们决定，在比赛中我们将积极拼抢，大胆进攻。 **6** ADJ **Physical** is used in expressions such as **physical love** and **physical relationships** to refer to sexual relationships between people. 性的 [ADJ n] ❑ *It had been years since they had shared any meaningful form of physical relationship.* 他们已经多年没有真正意义上的性关系了。 **7** N-COUNT A **physical** is a medical examination by your doctor to make sure that there is nothing wrong with your health, or a medical examination to make sure you are fit enough to do a particular job. 体格检查 ❑ *Bob failed his physical.* 鲍勃没有通过体格检查。

→ see **diagnosis**

Thesaurus *physical* 另参见：

ADJ. bodily, earthly, mortal, visceral; *(ant.)* mental **1**
concrete, natural, real, solid, tangible, visible; *(ant.)* intangible, theoretical **2**

Word Link *ician ≈ person who works at : electrician, musician, physician*

phy·si·cian /fɪzɪʃᵊn/ (**physicians**) N-COUNT A **physician** is a medical doctor. 内科医生 [FORMAL] ❑ *...your family physician.* …你的家庭医生。

→ see **diagnosis, hospital, medicine**

physi·cist /fɪzɪsɪst/ (**physicists**) N-COUNT A **physicist** is a person who does research connected with physics or who studies physics. 物理学家 ❑ *...a nuclear physicist.* …一位核物理学家。

phys·ics /fɪzɪks/ N-UNCOUNT **Physics** is the scientific study of forces such as heat, light, sound, pressure, gravity, and electricity, and the way that they affect objects. 物理学 ❑ *...the laws of physics.* …物理学定律。

physi·ol·ogy /fɪziɒlədʒi/ **1** N-UNCOUNT **Physiology** is the scientific study of how people's and animals' bodies function, and of how plants function. 生理学 ❑ *...the Nobel Prize for Medicine and Physiology.* …诺贝尔医学和生理学奖。 **2** N-UNCOUNT The **physiology** of a human or animal's body or of a plant is the way that it functions. 生理机能 ❑ *...the physiology of respiration.* …呼吸的生理机能。

● **physio·logi·cal** ★ /fɪziəlɒdʒɪkᵊl/ ADJ 生理的 ❑ *...the physiological effects of stress.* …压力的生理影响。

physio·thera·py /fɪzioʊθɛrəpi/ N-UNCOUNT **Physiotherapy** is the same as **physical therapy**. 物理疗法 [BRIT]

phy·sique /fɪzik/ (**physiques**) N-COUNT Someone's **physique** is the shape and size of their body. 体格；体形 ❑ *He has the physique and energy of a man half his age.* 他有着小他一半年纪的人的体格和精力。

pia·nist /piænɪst, piənɪst/ (**pianists**) N-COUNT A **pianist** is a person who plays the piano. 钢琴演奏者 ❑ *She was an accomplished pianist, a superb swimmer, and a gifted artist.* 她曾是一位很有造诣的钢琴家、一流的游泳健将和天才艺术家。

pi·ano /piænoʊ, pyænoʊ/ (**pianos**) N-VAR A **piano** is a large musical instrument with a row of black and white keys. When you press these keys with your fingers, little hammers hit wire strings inside the piano which vibrate to produce musical notes. 钢琴 ❑ *I taught myself how to play the piano.* 我自学弹钢琴。 ❑ *He started piano lessons at the age of 7.* 他7岁开始学弹钢琴。

→ see **keyboard, music**

pick ♦♦◇ /pɪk/ (**picks, picking, picked**) **1** V-T If you **pick** a particular person or thing, you choose that one. 挑选 ❑ *Mr. Nowell had picked ten people to interview for six sales jobs in Dallas.* 诺埃尔先生为在达拉斯的6个销售职位挑选了10人进行面试。 **2** N-SING You can refer to the best things or people in a particular group as **the pick of** that group. 精华；精英 ❑ *The boys here are the pick of the high school's soccer players.* 这儿的男孩都是该中学足球队的精英。 **3** V-T When you **pick** flowers, fruit, or leaves, you break them off the plant or tree and collect them. 采摘 ❑ *She used to pick flowers in the Adirondacks.* 她以前常去阿迪朗达克山采花。 **4** V-T If you **pick** something from a place, you remove it from there with your fingers or your hand. 拿走 ❑ *He picked the napkin from his lap and placed it alongside his plate.* 他从腿上拿起餐巾，放在他的盘子旁边。 **5** V-T If you **pick** your **nose** or **teeth**, you remove substances from inside your nose or between your teeth. 抠 (鼻子)；剔 (牙) ❑ *Edgar, don't pick your nose, dear.* 埃德加，不要抠鼻子，亲爱的。 **6** V-T If you **pick** a **fight with** someone, you deliberately cause one. 挑衅 ❑ *He picked a fight with a waiter and landed in jail.* 他找茬儿和服务员打架，结果锒铛入狱。 **7** V-T If someone such as a thief **picks** a lock, they open it without a key, for example, by using a piece of wire. 撬 (锁) ❑ *He picked each lock deftly, and rifled the papers within each drawer.* 他熟练地撬开每一把锁，偷走了每个抽屉里的文件。 **8** N-COUNT A **pick** is the same as a **pickax**. 镐 **9** PHRASE If you are told to **take** your **pick**, you can choose any one that you like from a group of things. 任意挑选 ❑ *Accountants can take their pick of company cars.* 会计们可以任意挑选公司的汽车。 **10** to **pick holes in** something → see **hole** **11** to **pick** someone's **pocket** → see **pocket**

▸ **pick on** PHRASAL VERB If someone **picks on** you, they repeatedly criticize you unfairly or treat you unkindly. 刁难；欺负 [INFORMAL] ❑ *Bullies pick on younger children.* 恃强凌弱的家伙欺负更年幼的孩子。

▸ **pick out** **1** PHRASAL VERB If you **pick out** someone or something, you recognize them when it is difficult to see them, for example, because they are among a large group. 辨认出 ❑ *The detective picked out the words with difficulty.* 侦探费力地辨认出这些字。 **2** PHRASAL VERB If you **pick out** someone or something, you choose them from a group of people or things. 挑选 ❑ *I have been picked out to represent the whole team.* 我被挑选出来代表全队。

▸ **pick up** **1** PHRASAL VERB When you **pick** something **up**, you lift it up. 拾起 ❑ *He picked his cap up from the floor and stuck it back on his head.* 他从地板上捡起帽子，重新戴在头上。 **2** PHRASAL VERB When you **pick yourself up** after you have fallen or been knocked down, you stand up rather slowly. (跌倒或被击倒后) 慢慢站起身 ❑ *Tony picked himself up and set off along the track.* 托尼慢慢站起，沿道跑起来。 **3** PHRASAL VERB When you **pick up** someone or something that is waiting to be collected, you go to the place where they are and take them away, often in a car. (开车) 接；取 ❑ *She was going over to her parents' house to pick up some clean clothes for Oskar.* 她正要去父母家为奥斯卡取几件干净的衣服。 **4** PHRASAL VERB If someone **is picked up** by the police, they are arrested and taken to a police station. 逮捕 ❑ *Rawlings had been picked up by police at his office.* 罗林斯在他的办公室被警察逮捕了。 **5** PHRASAL VERB If you **pick up** something such as a skill or an idea, you acquire it without effort over a period of time. (不费力地) 学会；获得 [INFORMAL] ❑ *Where did you pick up your English?* 你是在哪儿学得英语？ **6** PHRASAL VERB If you **pick up** someone you do not know, you talk to them and try to start a sexual relationship with them. 勾搭 [INFORMAL] ❑ *He had picked her up at a nightclub, where she worked as a singer.* 他是在一家夜总会勾搭上她的，她在那儿当歌女。 **7** PHRASAL VERB If you **pick up** an illness, you get it from somewhere or something. 染上 (疾病) ❑ *They've picked up a really nasty infection from something they've eaten.* 他们因食用某物而染上非常严重的传染病。 **8** PHRASAL VERB If a piece of equipment, for example, a radio or a microphone, **picks up** a signal or sound, it receives it or detects it. 接收(信号或声音) ❑ *We can pick up Mexican television.* 我们可以接收到墨西哥电视。 **9** PHRASAL VERB If you **pick up** something, such as a feature or a pattern, you discover or identify it. 发现；识别 ❑ *Some groups of consumers are slow to pick up trends in the use of information technology.* 有些顾客群对信息技术应用方面的潮流反应迟钝。 **10** PHRASAL VERB If someone **picks up** a point or topic that has already been mentioned, or if they **pick up on** it, they refer to it or develop it. 接起(某观点、话题) ❑ *Can I just pick up that guy's point?* 我能接着谈一下那个人的观点吗？ **11** PHRASAL VERB If trade or the economy of a country **picks up**, it improves. (贸易、经济) 改善 ❑ *Industrial production is beginning to pick up.* 工业生产正在开始好转。 **12** PHRASAL VERB If you **pick up** a room or house, you tidy it. 整理(房间、房子) [AM] ❑ *She decided to start picking up the house from the top down.* 她决定开始彻底收拾那房子。 **13** → see also **pickup** **14** PHRASE When a vehicle **picks up speed**, it begins to move more quickly. 加速 ❑ *Brian started the engine and pulled away slowly, but picked up speed once he entered Oakwood Drive.* 布赖恩发动引擎，慢慢驶离，但上了奥克伍德大道后就开始加速。

Thesaurus *pick* 另参见：
V. choose, decide on, elect, select **1**
collect, gather, harvest, pull **3**

pick·ax /pɪkæks/ (**pickaxes**) also **pickaxe** N-COUNT A **pickax** is a large tool consisting of a curved, pointed piece of metal with a long handle attached to the middle. Pickaxes are used for breaking up rocks or the ground. 镐

▲ **pick·et** /pɪkɪt/ (**pickets, picketing, picketed**) **1** V-T/V-I When a group of people, usually labor union members, **picket**, or **picket** a place of work, they stand outside it in order to protest about something, to prevent people from going in, or to persuade the workers to join a strike. 聚集在…外抗议；在…外设立罢工纠察队 ❑ *A few dozen employees picketed the company's headquarters.* 几十名雇员聚集在公司总部的外面示威抗议。 ● N-COUNT **Picket** is also a noun. 示威抗议行为；罢工纠察队 ❑ *...forty demonstrators who have set up a twenty-four hour picket.* …组建了一支24小时纠察队的40名示威者。 **2** N-COUNT **Pickets** are people who are picketing a place of work. 示威抗议者；罢工纠察队员 ❑ *The strikers agreed to remove their pickets and hold talks with the company.* 罢工者同意撤走纠察队员，和公司进行会谈。

pick·et line (**picket lines**) N-COUNT A **picket line** is a group of pickets outside a place of work. (由罢工纠察队员组成的) 纠察线 ❑ *No one tried to cross the picket lines.* 没有人试图越过纠察线。

pick·le /pɪkᵊl/ (**pickles, pickling, pickled**) **1** N-PLURAL **Pickles** are vegetables or fruit, sometimes cut into pieces, which have been kept in vinegar or salt water for a long time so that they have a strong, sharp taste. 泡菜 ❑ *...a bowl of sliced pickles in lemon juice.* …一碗浸在柠檬汁中的泡菜片。 **2** N-MASS **Pickle** is a cold spicy sauce with pieces of vegetables and fruit in it. 泡菜酱 ❑ *...jars of pickle.* …成罐的泡菜酱。 **3** V-T When you **pickle** food, you keep it in vinegar or salt water so that it does not go bad and it develops a strong, sharp taste. 腌制 ❑ *Select your favorite fruit or veg and pickle them while they are still fresh.* 挑选你最喜欢的水果或蔬菜，趁新鲜腌制起来。

pick·led /pɪkᵊld/ ADJ **Pickled** food, such as vegetables, fruit, and fish, has been kept in vinegar or salt water to preserve it. 腌制的 ❑ *...a jar of pickled fruit.* …一罐腌制的水果。

pick·pocket /pɪkpɒkɪt/ (**pickpockets**) N-COUNT A **pickpocket** is a person who steals things from people's pockets or bags in public places. 扒手 ❑ *Beware of pickpockets, especially when making a purchase.* 当心扒手，尤其是在购物的时候。

pick·up ♦◇◇ /pɪkʌp/ (**pickups**) **1** N-COUNT A **pickup** or a **pickup truck** is a small truck with low sides that can be easily loaded and unloaded. 轻型货车 **2** N-SING A **pickup in** trade or **in** a country's economy is an improvement in it. (贸易或经济的) 改善 ❑ *...a pickup in the housing market.* …房地产市场的好转。 **3** N-COUNT A **pickup** takes place when someone picks up a person or thing that is waiting to be collected. (人或物的) 接取 ❑ *The company had pickup points in most cities.* 公司在大多数城市都有接取点。
→ see **car**

pic·nic /pɪknɪk/ (**picnics, picnicking, picnicked**) **1** N-COUNT When people have a **picnic**, they eat a meal outdoors, usually in a park or a forest, or at the beach. 野餐 ❑ *We're going on a picnic tomorrow.* 我们明天去野餐。 **2** V-I When people **picnic** somewhere, they have a picnic. 野餐 ❑ *Afterwards, we picnicked on the riverbank.* 之后，我们在河岸上野餐。
→ see **park**

pic·to·gram /pɪktəgræm/ (**pictograms**) or **pic+to+graph** /pɪktəgræf, -grɑf/ N-COUNT A **pictogram** is a simple drawing that represents something. Pictograms were used as the earliest form of writing. 象形图画 ❑ *...a pictogram of a pine tree.* …一幅代表一棵松树的象形图画。

pic·to·rial /pɪktɔriəl/ ADJ **Pictorial** means using or relating to pictures. 图示的；与图片有关的 ❑ *...a pictorial history of the Jewish people.* …一部犹太民族的图解历史。

Word Link *pict ≈ painting : depict, picture, picturesque*

pic·ture ♦♦◇ /pɪktʃər/ (**pictures, picturing, pictured**) **1** N-COUNT A **picture** consists of lines and shapes that are drawn, painted, or printed on a surface and show a person, thing, or scene. 图画 ❑ *...drawing a small picture with colored chalk.* …用彩色粉笔画一幅小画。 **2** N-COUNT A **picture** is a photograph. 照片 ❑ *The tourists have nothing to do but take pictures of each other.* 游客们无事可做，只有相互拍照。 **3** N-COUNT Television **pictures** are the scenes that you see on a television screen. (电视) 画面 ❑ *...heartrending television pictures of human suffering.* …令人心碎的人类受难的电视画面。 **4** V-T To **be pictured** somewhere, for example, in a newspaper or magazine, means to appear in a photograph or picture. (在报纸、杂志上) 登载照片 [usu passive] ❑ *The golfer is pictured on many of the front pages, kissing his trophy as he holds it aloft.* 这位高尔夫球手高举奖杯亲吻的照片被刊登在许多报纸的头版上。 ❑ *...a woman who claimed she had been pictured dancing with a celebrity in a nightclub.* …一位声称自己和一位名人在夜总会跳舞的照片被刊登的女人。 ❑ *The chair pictured here costs $125.* 这里刊登的椅子值125美元。 **5** N-COUNT You can refer to a movie as a **picture**. 电影 ❑ *...a director of epic action pictures.* …一位大制作动作片的导演。 **6** N-COUNT If you have a **picture** of something in your mind, you have a clear idea or memory of it in your mind as if you were actually seeing it. (头脑中的) 影像 ❑ *We are just trying to get our picture of the whole afternoon straight.* 我们正努力在脑海中理清整个下午的情景。 **7** V-T If you **picture** something in your mind, you think of it and have such a clear memory or idea of it that you seem to be able to see it. 想像 ❑ *He pictured her with long black braided hair.* 他想像她扎着长长的黑麻花辫。 ❑ *He pictured Carrie sitting out in the car, waiting for him.* 他想像卡丽正坐在外面的车里等他的情景。 **8** N-COUNT A **picture** of something is a description of it or an indication of what it is like. 描述 ❑ *I'll try and give you a better picture of what the boys do.* 我会尽力给你一个关于这些男孩所作事情的更好描述。 **9** N-SING When you refer to the **picture** in a particular place, you are referring to the situation there. 局面；情况 ❑ *It's a similar picture across the border in Ethiopia.* 在边界那边的埃塞俄比亚也是类似的局面。 **10** PHRASE If you say that someone is **in the picture**, you mean that they are involved in the situation that you are talking about. If you say that they are **out of the picture**, you mean that they are not involved in the situation you are talking about. 在/不在其中 [v-link PHR, PHR after v] ❑ *Meyerson is back in the picture after disappearing in July.* 继7月份失踪后，迈耶森又重回其中。 ❑ *His dad had been out of the picture since he was eight.* 自从他8岁时起，他的爸爸就一直不在其中。 **11** PHRASE If you **put** someone **in the picture**, you tell them about a situation which they need to know about. 使…了解内情 ❑ *Has anyone put you in the picture?* 有人把内情告诉你了吗？
→ see **photography**

Thesaurus *picture* 另参见：
N. drawing, illustration, image, painting **1**
photograph **2**
V. envision, imagine, visualize **7**

Word Partnership *picture* 的常用搭配：
ADJ. pretty as a picture **1**
mental picture **6**
clear picture **6** **8**
accurate picture, **complete** picture, **different** picture, **larger** picture, **overall** picture, **vivid** picture, **whole** picture **6** **8** **9**
the big picture **8**

▲ **pic·tur·esque** /pɪktʃərɛsk/ ADJ A **picturesque** place is attractive and interesting, and has no ugly modern buildings. 古雅的 ❑ *...a picturesque mountain village.* …一个古雅的山村。 ● N-SING You can refer to picturesque things as **the picturesque**. 古雅的事物 ❑ *...lovers of the picturesque.* …古雅物品的爱好者。

P

pie /paɪ/ (**pies**) **1** N-VAR A **pie** consists of fruit, meat, or vegetables baked in pastry. 馅饼 ❑ *...a slice of apple pie.* …一片苹果馅饼。 **2** to **eat humble pie** → see **humble**
→ see **dessert**

piece ♦♦◇ /pis/ (**pieces, piecing, pieced**) **1** N-COUNT A **piece of** something is an amount of it that has been broken off, torn off, or cut off. (从某物上拆下、撕下或切下的) 块; 片; 段 ❑ *...a piece of cake.* …一块蛋糕。 ❑ *Cut the ham into pieces.* 把火腿切成片。 **2** N-COUNT A **piece** of an object is one of the individual parts or sections that it is made of, especially a part that can be removed. 部件 ❑ *...assembling objects out of standard pieces.* …用标准部件组装物品。 **3** N-COUNT A **piece of** land is an area of land. (一) 块 (土地) ❑ *People struggle to get the best piece of land.* 人们竞相争夺最好的一块土地。 **4** N-COUNT You can use **piece of** with many uncount nouns to refer to an individual thing of a particular kind. For example, you can refer to some advice as a **piece of advice**. 与不可数名词搭配，表示某种事物的个体 ❑ *When I produced this piece of work, my lecturers were very critical.* 当我创作这件作品的时候，我的老师们批评甚多。 ❑ *...an interesting piece of information.* …一条有趣的信息。 **5** N-COUNT You can refer to an article in a newspaper or magazine, some music written by someone, a broadcast, or a play as a **piece**. (报纸、杂志上的) 文章; 作品 ❑ *She wrote a piece on Gwyneth Paltrow for the New Yorker.* 她为《纽约客》写了一篇关于格温妮丝·帕尔特罗的文章。 ❑ *...a vaguely familiar orchestral piece.* …一首隐约熟悉的管弦乐曲。 **6** N-COUNT You can refer to a work of art as a **piece**. 艺术品 [FORMAL] ❑ *Each piece is unique, an exquisite painting of a real person, done on ivory.* 每件艺术品都很独特，均为绘在象牙上的真人精致画像。 **7** N-COUNT You can refer to specific coins as **pieces**. For example, a 5 cent **piece** is a coin that is worth 5 cents. 硬币 ❑ *...lots of 10 cent, 20 cent, and 50 cent pieces.* …很多10分、20分和50分的硬币。 **8** N-COUNT The **pieces** that you use when you play a board game such as chess are the specially made objects that you move around on the board. 棋子 ❑ *How many pieces does each player have in backgammon?* 西洋双陆棋里每方各有多少枚棋子? **9** PHRASE If you **give** someone **a piece of** your **mind**, you tell them very clearly that you think they have behaved badly. 鲜明地批评 [INFORMAL] ❑ *How very thoughtless. I'll give him a piece of my mind.* 太欠考虑了。我要狠狠地批评他。 **10** PHRASE If someone or something is still **in one piece** after a dangerous journey or experience, they are safe and not damaged or hurt. 完好无损 ❑ *...providing that my brother gets back alive and in one piece from his mission.* …假若我哥哥完成任务后，活着安然无恙地回来的话。 **11** PHRASE You use **to pieces** in expressions such as "smash to pieces," or "take something to pieces," when you are describing how something is broken or comes apart so that it is in separate pieces. 成为片 **12** PHRASE If you **go to pieces**, you are so upset or nervous that you lose control of yourself and cannot do what you should do. (因紧张不安而) 崩溃 [INFORMAL] ❑ *She's a strong woman, but she nearly went to pieces when Arnie died.* 她是个坚强的女人，但阿尼死的时候她几乎崩溃了。 **13** **a piece of the action** → see **action** **14** **bits and pieces** → see **bit**
→ see **chess**

▸ **piece together** **1** PHRASAL VERB If you **piece together** the truth about something, you gradually discover it. 渐渐弄清 (真相) ❑ *They've pieced together his movements for the last few days before his death.* 他们已经渐渐查明了他死前最后几天里的行踪。 ❑ *In the following days, Frankie was able to piece together what had happened.* 在接下来的几天里，弗朗姬能够渐渐弄清所发生的事情了。 **2** PHRASAL VERB If you **piece** something **together**, you gradually make it by joining several things or parts together. 拼凑 ❑ *This process is akin to piecing together a jigsaw puzzle.* 这过程类似于拼七巧板。

> **Thesaurus** *piece* 另参见:
> N. bit, fragment, part, portion, section, segment; (*ant.*) whole **1** **2**
> arrangement, article, creation, production, work **5** **6**

piece·meal /pismil/ ADJ If you describe a change or process as **piecemeal**, you disapprove of it because it happens gradually, usually at irregular intervals, and is probably not satisfactory. (变化或过程) 逐渐而零碎的 [DISAPPROVAL] ❑ *These piecemeal solutions won't work.* 这些零敲碎打的解决办法不会有效。 ● ADV **Piecemeal** is also an adverb. 逐渐而零碎地 [ADV after V] ❑ *It was built piecemeal over some 130 years.* 它是在大约一百三十年间一点一点建造起来的。

pie chart (**pie charts**) N-COUNT A **pie chart** is a circle divided into sections to show the relative proportions of a set of things. (显示各部分比例关系的) 饼分图

▲ **pier** /pɪər/ (**piers**) N-COUNT A **pier** is a platform sticking out into water that people walk along or use when getting onto or off boats. 凸式码头 ❑ *...Chicago's Navy Pier.* …芝加哥的海军码头。

pierce /pɪərs/ (**pierces, piercing, pierced**) **1** V-T If a sharp object **pierces** something, or if you **pierce** something **with** a sharp object, the object goes into it and makes a hole in it. 刺穿 ❑ *One bullet pierced the left side of his chest.* 一颗子弹射入了他的左胸。 **2** V-T If you have your ears or some other part of your body **pierced**, you have a small hole made through them so that you can wear a piece of jewelry in them. 穿孔 ❑ *I'm having my ears pierced on Saturday.* 我星期六要去扎耳洞。 ● **pierc·ing** N-VAR (**piercings**) 穿孔 ❑ *...health risks from needles used in piercing and tattooing.* …穿孔和纹身中使用针而带来的健康风险。

pierc·ing /pɪərsɪŋ/ **1** ADJ A **piercing** sound or voice is high-pitched and very sharp and clear in an unpleasant way. 刺耳的 ❑ *A piercing scream split the air.* 一声刺耳的尖叫划破天空。 **2** ADJ If someone has **piercing** eyes or a **piercing** stare, they seem to look at you very intensely. (目光) 锐利的 [WRITTEN] ❑ *...his sandy blond hair and piercing blue eyes.* …他那淡金色的头发和犀利的蓝眼睛。 **3** ADJ A **piercing** wind makes you feel very cold. 刺骨的 ❑ *Warm clothing is recommended as the wind can be piercing.* 寒风刺骨，建议穿暖和些的衣服。 **4** → see **pierce 2**

▲ **pi·ety** /paɪɪti/ N-UNCOUNT **Piety** is strong religious belief, or behavior that is religious or morally correct. 虔诚 ❑ *Known for her piety, she would walk miles to attend communion services in the neighboring villages.* 她的虔诚是出了名的，她会步行几英里去参加邻村的圣餐仪式。

pig /pɪg/ (**pigs, pigging, pigged**) **1** N-COUNT A **pig** is a pink or black animal with short legs and not much hair on its skin. Pigs are often kept on farms for their meat, which is called pork, ham, or bacon. 猪 ❑ *...the grunting of the pigs.* …猪的哼哼声。 **2** → see also **guinea pig** **3** N-COUNT If you call someone a **pig**, you think that they are unpleasant in some way, especially that they are greedy or unkind. 猪 (用来比喻贪婪、刻薄的人) [INFORMAL, DISAPPROVAL] ❑ *These guys destroyed the company. They're all a bunch of greedy pigs.* 这些家伙毁了公司。他们是一群贪婪的猪。 **4** PHRASE If you say "**when pigs fly**" after someone has said that something might happen, you are emphasizing that you think it is very unlikely. 等到猴年马月 [HUMOROUS, INFORMAL, EMPHASIS] ❑ *When would they be hired again? Perhaps, as the saying goes, when pigs fly.* 他们什么时候会被重新雇用? 也许正像俗话说的，等到猴年马月吧。 **5** PHRASE If you say that someone **is making a pig of themselves**, you are criticizing them for eating a very large amount at one meal. 狼吞虎咽 [INFORMAL, DISAPPROVAL] ❑ *I'm afraid I made a pig of myself at dinner.* 恐怕晚饭我是狼吞虎咽了。
→ see **barn, meat**

▸ **pig out** PHRASAL VERB If you say that people **are pigging out**, you are criticizing them for eating a very large amount at one meal or over a short period of time. 暴饮暴食 [INFORMAL, DISAPPROVAL] ❑ *Some are so accustomed to pigging out, they can't cut back.* 有些人习惯暴饮暴食了，他们不可能缩减食量。

pi·geon /pɪdʒɪn/ (**pigeons**) N-COUNT A **pigeon** is a bird, usually gray in color, that has a fat body. Pigeons often live in cities and towns. 鸽子

pigeon·hole /pɪdʒɪnhoʊl/ (**pigeonholes, pigeonholing, pigeonholed**) also **pigeon-hole** **1** N-COUNT A **pigeonhole** is one of the sections in a frame on a wall where letters and messages can be left for someone, or one of the sections in a writing desk where you can keep documents. (墙上挂的) 信件架; (书桌上摆放的) 文件格 **2** V-T To **pigeonhole** someone or something means to decide that they belong to a particular class or category, often without considering all their qualities or characteristics. (常指不考虑所有特性地) 给…分类 ❑ *He felt they had pigeonholed him.* 他感觉他们已经将他归入某一类了。

pig·ment /pɪgmənt/ (**pigments**) N-MASS A **pigment** is a substance that gives something a particular color. 颜料 [FORMAL] ❑ *The Romans used natural pigments on their fabrics and walls.* 罗马人使用天然颜料染布和刷墙。

pike /paɪk/ (**pike**)

> The plural can also be **pikes**.

N-VAR A **pike** is a large fish that lives in rivers and lakes and eats other fish. 狗鱼 ● N-UNCOUNT **Pike** is this fish eaten as food. 狗鱼肉 ❑ *...a mousse of pike.* …一块狗鱼慕思。

Pilates /pɪlɑtiz/ N-UNCOUNT **Pilates** is a type of exercise similar to yoga. 普拉提 ❑ *She'd never done Pilates before.* 她以前从未做过普拉提。

pile ♦◇◇ /paɪl/ (**piles, piling, piled**) **1** N-COUNT A **pile of** things is a mass of them that is high in the middle and has sloping sides. 堆 ❑ *...a pile of sand.* …一堆沙子。 ❑ *...a little pile of crumbs.* …一小堆面包屑。 **2** N-COUNT A **pile of** things is a quantity of things that have been put neatly somewhere so that each thing is on top of the one below. 摞 ❑ *...a pile of boxes.* …一摞盒子。 ❑ *We sat in Sam's study, among the piles of books.* 我们坐在萨姆的书房里，周围是一摞摞的书。

> A **pile** of things can be tidy or untidy. ❑ *...a neat pile of clothes.* A **heap** is usually untidy, and often has the shape of a hill or mound. ❑ *Now, the house is a heap of rubble.* A **stack** is usually tidy, and often consists of flat objects placed directly on top of each other. ❑ *...a neat stack of dishes.*

3 V-T If you **pile** things somewhere, you put them there so that they form a pile. 堆放 ❑ *He was piling clothes into the suitcase.* 他正把衣服叠放到手提箱中去。 **4** V-T If something **is piled with** things, it is covered or filled with piles of things. 堆满 [usu passive] ❑ *Tables were piled high with local produce.* 桌子上高高地堆满了土特产。 **5** V-I If a group of people **pile into** or **out of** a vehicle, they all get into it or out of it in a disorganized way. 涌入/出 ❑ *They all piled into Jerry's car.* 他们都挤进了杰里的车里。 **6** N-COUNT **Piles** are wooden, concrete, or metal posts that are pushed into the ground and on which buildings or bridges are built. Piles are often used in very wet areas so that the buildings do not flood. (房屋、桥梁的) 地桩 ❑ *...settlements of wooden houses, set on piles along the shore.* …沿岸而建的吊脚木屋居民区。 **7** N-PLURAL **Piles** is an informal word meaning **hemorrhoids**. 痔疮 **8** N-SING The **pile** of a carpet or of a fabric such as velvet is its soft surface. It consists of a lot of little threads standing on end. (地毯或织物的) 绒面 ❑ *...the carpet's thick pile.* …地毯厚厚的绒面。 **9** PHRASE Someone who is **at the bottom of the pile** is low down in society or low down in an organization. Someone who is **at the top of the pile** is high up in society or high up in an organization. 处于(社会或组织的) 下层/上层 [INFORMAL] ❑ *These workers are fed up with being at the bottom of the pile when it comes to pay.* 这些工人受够了收入水平处于底层的苦恼。

▸ **pile up** **1** PHRASAL VERB If you **pile up** a quantity of things or if they **pile up**, they gradually form a pile. 堆积 ❑ *Bulldozers piled up huge mounds of dirt.* 推土机堆起了一个个大土堆。 **2** PHRASAL VERB If you **pile up** work, problems, or losses or if they **pile up**, you get more and more of them. (工作、问题、损失等) 积累 ❑ *Problems were piling up at work.* 工作中的问题越积越多。

P

Thesaurus *pile* 另参见：

N.	accumulation, buildup, collection, heap, quantity, stack **1** **2**
V.	assemble, collect, heap, stack **3**

★ **pil·grim** /pɪlgrɪm/ (**pilgrims**) N-COUNT **Pilgrims** are people who journey to a holy place for a religious reason. 朝圣者 ❑ *This is where pilgrims to the abbey would pay their first devotions.* 这儿就是来此修道院的朝圣者做第一次祈祷的地方。

pil·grim·age /pɪlgrɪmɪdʒ/ (**pilgrimages**) **1** N-COUNT If you make a **pilgrimage** to a holy place, you go there for a religious reason. 朝圣 ❑ *...the pilgrimage to Mecca.* …前往麦加的朝圣。 **2** N-COUNT A **pilgrimage** is a trip that someone makes to a place that is very important to them. (去重要地方的) 出行 ❑ *...a private pilgrimage to family graves.* …一次对祖坟的私下参拜。

pill ♦◇◇ /pɪl/ (**pills**) **1** N-COUNT **Pills** are small solid round masses of medicine or vitamins that you swallow without chewing. 药丸 ❑ *Why do I have to take all these pills?* 我为什么非得吃了所有这些药丸？ **2** N-SING If a woman is **on the pill**, she takes a special pill that prevents her from becoming pregnant. 避孕药 ❑ *She had been on the pill for three years.* 她曾服了3年的避孕药。 **3** PHRASE If a person or group has to accept a failure or an unpleasant piece of news, you can say that it was **a bitter pill** or **a bitter pill to swallow**. 不得不承受的苦事 ❑ *You're too old to be given a job. That's a bitter pill to swallow.* 你年龄太大，不能给你工作了。这是你不得不接受的现实。 **4** PHRASE If someone does something to **sweeten the pill**, they do it to make some unpleasant news or an unpleasant measure more acceptable. 使不愉快的事变得更容易接受 ❑ *A few words of praise help to sweeten the pill of criticism.* 几句赞赏的话有助于使批评更容易被接受。

pil·lar /pɪlər/ (**pillars**) **1** N-COUNT A **pillar** is a tall solid structure that is usually used to support part of a building. 柱子 ❑ *...the pillars supporting the roof.* …支撑屋顶的柱子。 **2** N-COUNT If something is the **pillar of** a system or agreement, it is the most important part of it or what makes it strong and successful. (系统、协议的) 核心 ❑ *The pillar of her economic policy was keeping tight control over money supply.* 她的经济政策的核心就是严格控制货币供应。 **3** N-COUNT If you describe someone as a **pillar of** society or as a **pillar of** the community, you approve of them because they play an important and active part in society or in the community. 栋梁 [APPROVAL] ❑ *My father is a pillar of the community.* 我父亲是社区的顶梁柱。

pil·low /pɪloʊ/ (**pillows**) N-COUNT A **pillow** is a rectangular cushion that you rest your head on when you are in bed. 枕头
→ see **bed, sleep**

pi·lot ♦◇◇ /paɪlət/ (**pilots, piloting, piloted**) **1** N-COUNT A **pilot** is a person who is trained to fly an aircraft. 飞行员 ❑ *He spent seventeen years as an airline pilot.* 他当了17年的航空公司飞行员。 **2** N-COUNT A **pilot** is a person who steers a ship through a difficult stretch of water, for example, the entrance to a harbor. 领航员 ❑ *It seemed that the pilot had another ship to take up the river that evening.* 似乎该领航员那天晚上还要引领另一艘船沿河而上。 **3** V-T If someone **pilots** an aircraft or ship, they act as its pilot. 驾驶(飞机); 为(船只) 领航 ❑ *He piloted his own plane part of the way to Washington.* 他驾驶自己的飞机飞行了去华盛顿的部分路程。 **4** ADJ A **pilot** plan or a **pilot** project is one that is used to test an idea before deciding whether to introduce it on a larger scale. 试验性的 ❑ *The plan is to launch a pilot program next summer.* 计划是在明年夏天实施一个试验性方案。 **5** V-T If a government or organization **pilots** a program or project, they test it, before deciding whether to introduce it on a larger scale. 试行 (计划或方案) ❑ *Teachers are piloting a literature-based reading program.* 老师们正在试开一门以文学为基础的阅读课程。

pimp /pɪmp/ (**pimps, pimping, pimped**) **1** N-COUNT A **pimp** is a man who gets clients for prostitutes and takes some of the money the prostitutes earn. 皮条客 **2** V-I Someone who **pimps** gets clients for prostitutes and takes some of the money the prostitutes earn. 拉皮条 ❑ *He stole, lied, deceived, and pimped his way out of poverty.* 他靠偷窃、行骗、欺诈和拉皮条摆脱了贫穷。

pin ♦◇◇ /pɪn/ (**pins, pinning, pinned**) **1** N-COUNT **Pins** are very small thin pointed pieces of metal. They are used in sewing to fasten pieces of material together until they have been sewn. 别针 ❑ *...a box of needles and pins.* …一盒缝衣针和别针。 **2** V-T If you **pin** something **on** or **to** something, you attach it with a pin, a safety pin or a thumbtack. 用别针别住; 用图钉钉住 ❑ *They pinned a notice to the door.* 他们把通知钉在门上。 ❑ *Everyone was supposed to dance with the bride and pin money on her dress.* 每个人都应该和新娘跳舞并把钱别在她的衣服上。 **3** V-T If someone **pins** you to something, they press you against a surface so that you cannot move. 按住; 使不能动弹 ❑ *I pinned him against the wall.* 我把他按在墙上。 ❑ *I'd try to get away and he'd pin me down, saying he would kill me.* 我会试图逃走，而他会把我按倒，说要杀了我。 **4** N-COUNT A **pin** is any long narrow piece of metal or wood that is not sharp, especially one that is used to fasten two things together. (把两件物品固定在一起的) 销; 钉; 栓 ❑ *...the 18-inch steel pin holding his left leg together.* …将他的左腿固定起来的18英寸长的钢钉。 **5** V-T If someone tries to **pin** something **on** you or to **pin the blame on** you, they say, often unfairly, that you were responsible for something bad or illegal. 把…归罪于 ❑ *They're trying to pin it on us.* 他们正试图把这件事归罪于我们。 **6** V-T If you **pin** your hopes **on** something or **pin** your faith **on** something, you hope very much that it will produce the result you want. 寄(希望、信念) 于 ❑ *The Democrats are pinning their hopes on the next election.* 民主党人正寄希望于下一次选举。 **7** N-COUNT A **pin** is something worn on your clothing, for example, as jewelry, which is fastened with a pointed piece of metal. 胸针 [AM] ❑ *...necklaces, bracelets, and pins.* …项链、手镯和胸针。 **8** → see also **safety pin**
→ see **jewelry**

▸ **pin down** **1** PHRASAL VERB If you try to **pin** something **down**, you try to discover exactly what, where, or when it is. 弄明确 ❑ *It has taken until now to pin down its exact location.* 一直到现在才确定了它的准确位置。 ❑ *I can only pin it down to between 1936 and 1942.* 我只能将其确定在1936年到1942年之间。 **2** PHRASAL VERB If you **pin** someone **down**, you force them to make a decision or to tell you what their decision is, when they have been trying to avoid doing this. 迫使…明确表态 ❑ *She couldn't pin him down to a date.* 她未能迫使他确定下日期。

PIN /pɪn/ N-SING Someone's **PIN** or **PIN number** is a secret number that they can use, for example, with a bank card to withdraw money from a cash machine or ATM. **PIN** is an abbreviation for "personal identification number." 密码 [oft N n] ❑ *To use the service you'll need a PIN number.* 使用该服务需要一个密码。

pina·fore /pɪnəfɔr/ (**pinafores**) N-COUNT A **pinafore** is a sleeveless dress. It is worn over a blouse or sweater. (穿在罩衫或针织衫外的)无袖女装

pin·cer /pɪnsər/ (**pincers**) **1** N-PLURAL **Pincers** consist of two pieces of metal that are hinged in the middle. They are used as a tool for gripping things or for pulling things out. 镊子; 钳子 [also "a pair of" N] ❑ *His surgical instruments were a knife and a pair of pincers.* 他的手术器械是一把刀和一把镊子。 **2** N-COUNT The **pincers** of an animal such as a crab or a lobster are its front claws. (蟹或虾的) 螯

pinch /pɪntʃ/ (**pinches, pinching, pinched**) **1** V-T If you **pinch** a part of someone's body, you take a piece of their skin between your thumb and first finger and give it a short squeeze. 掐; 拧 ❑ *She pinched his arm as hard as she could.* 她使出全力拧他的胳膊。 ● N-COUNT **Pinch** is also a noun. 掐; 拧 ❑ *She gave him a little pinch.* 她轻轻地拧了他一下。 **2** N-COUNT A **pinch of** an ingredient such as salt is the amount of it that you can hold between your thumb and your first finger. 撮 ❑ *Put all the ingredients, including a pinch of salt, into a food processor.* 将所有的配料，连同一撮盐，放进食品加工机里。 **3** to **take** something **with a pinch of salt** → see **salt** **4** V-T To **pinch** something, especially something of little value, means to steal it. 偷拿 (尤为不太值钱的东西) [INFORMAL] ❑ *Do you remember when I pinched your glasses?* 你还记得我偷拿过你的眼镜吗？ **5** PHRASE If a person or company **is feeling the pinch**, they do not have as much money as they used to, and so they cannot buy the things they would like to buy. 感到手头拮据 ❑ *Consumers are spending less and merchants are feeling the pinch.* 消费者花钱少了，商家感到手头拮据。

pine /paɪn/ (**pines, pining, pined**) **1** N-VAR A **pine tree** or a **pine** is a tall tree that has very thin, sharp leaves called needles and a fresh smell. Pine trees have leaves all year round. 松树 ❑ *...high mountains covered in pine trees.* …长满松树的高山。 ● N-UNCOUNT **Pine** is the wood of this tree. 松木 ❑ *...a big pine table.* …一张大松木桌子。 **2** V-I If you **pine for** someone who has died or gone away, you want them to be with you very much and feel sad because they are not there. 苦苦思念 ❑ *She'd be sitting at home pining for her lost husband.* 她会一直坐在家里苦苦思念着她死去的丈夫。 **3** V-I If you **pine for** something, you want it very much, especially when it is unlikely that you will be able to have it. 渴望 (尤指不可能得到的东西) ❑ *I pine for the countryside.* 我渴望乡下的生活。

▲ **pine·apple** /paɪnæpᵊl/ (**pineapples**) N-VAR A **pineapple** is a large oval fruit that grows in hot countries. It is sweet, juicy, and yellow inside. It has a thick brownish skin. 菠萝

pink ♦♦◇ /pɪŋk/ (**pinks, pinker, pinkest**) **1** COLOR **Pink** is the color between red and white. 粉红色 (的) ❑ *...pink lipstick.* …粉红色口红。 ❑ *...white flowers edged in pink.* …带粉边的白花。 **2** ADJ **Pink** is used to refer to things relating to or connected with gay people. 与男同性恋有关的 [BRIT]

pin·na·cle /pɪnɪkəl/ (**pinnacles**) **1** N-COUNT A **pinnacle** is a pointed piece of stone or rock that is high above the ground. 尖锥形石块 ❑ *A walker broke his arms, legs, and pelvis yesterday when he plunged 80 feet from a rocky pinnacle.* 一位步行者昨天从80英尺高的尖锥形岩石上摔下来，摔断了胳膊、腿和骨盆。 **2** N-COUNT If someone reaches **the pinnacle of** their career or **the pinnacle of** a particular area of life, they are at the highest point of it. 顶峰 ❑ *She was still at the pinnacle of her career.* 她依然处在事业的巅峰时期。

▲ **pin·point** /pɪnpɔɪnt/ (**pinpoints, pinpointing, pinpointed**) **1** V-T If you **pinpoint** the cause of something, you discover or explain the cause exactly. 准确指出 (原因) ❑ *It was almost impossible to pinpoint the cause of death.* 几乎不可能确定死因。 ❑ *...if you can pinpoint exactly what the anger is about.* …如果你能确切说明生气的原因。 **2** V-T If you **pinpoint** something or its position, you discover or show exactly where it is. 给…准确定位 ❑ *I could pinpoint his precise location on a map.* 我能在地图上指出他的确切位置。

pin·stripe /pɪnstraɪp/ (**pinstripes**) also **pin-stripe** N-COUNT **Pinstripes** are very narrow vertical stripes found on certain types of clothing. Businessmen's suits often have pinstripes. (织物上的) 垂直细条纹 ❑ *He wore an expensive, dark blue pinstripe suit.* 他穿着一套昂贵的、深蓝色细条纹西装。

pint /paɪnt/ (**pints**) N-COUNT A **pint** is a unit of measurement for liquids. It is equal to 473 cubic centimeters or one eighth of a gallon. 品脱 (液量单位，1品脱等于473立方厘米或1/8加仑) ❑ *...a pint of ice cream.* …一品脱冰淇淋。

pin-up (**pin-ups**) also **pinup** N-COUNT A **pin-up** is an attractive man or woman who appears on posters, often wearing very few clothes. 海报上的性感男女 ❑ *...pin-up boys.* …海报上的性感男孩们。

pio·neer /paɪənɪər/ (**pioneers, pioneering, pioneered**) **1** N-COUNT Someone who is referred to as a **pioneer** in a particular area of activity is one of the first people to be involved in it and develop it. 先驱 ❑ *...one of the leading pioneers of photojournalism.* …摄影新闻界的主要先驱之一。 **2** V-T Someone who **pioneers** a new activity, invention, or process is one of the first people to do it. 倡导 ❑ *...Professor Alec Jeffreys, who invented and pioneered DNA tests.* …发明和倡导DNA测试的亚历克・杰弗里斯教授。 **3** N-COUNT **Pioneers** are people who leave their own country or the place where they were living, and go and live in a place that has not been lived in before. 拓荒者 ❑ *...abandoned settlements of early European pioneers.* …已废弃的早期欧洲拓荒者的居住地。

pio·neer·ing /paɪənɪərɪŋ/ ADJ **Pioneering** work or a **pioneering** individual does something that has not been done before, for example, by developing or using new methods or techniques. 开创性的 ❑ *The school has won awards for its pioneering work with the community.* 该校因与社区开创性合作而获奖。

pi·ous /paɪəs/ ADJ Someone who is **pious** is very religious and moral. 虔诚的 ❑ *He was brought up by pious female relatives.* 他是由虔诚的女性亲属抚养大的。 ● **pi·ous·ly** ADV 虔诚地 [ADV with v] ❑ *Conti kneeled and crossed himself piously.* 康蒂跪下，虔诚地在身上划十字。

pipe ♦◇◇ /paɪp/ (**pipes, piping, piped**) **1** N-COUNT A **pipe** is a long, round, hollow object, usually made of metal or plastic, through which a liquid or gas can flow. 管子 ❑ *The liquid can't escape into the air, because it's inside a pipe.* 液体不会漏到空气中，因为它在管子里。 **2** N-COUNT A **pipe** is an object that is used for smoking tobacco. You put the tobacco into the cup-shaped part at the end of the pipe, light it, and breathe in the smoke through a narrow tube. 烟斗 ❑ *Do you smoke a pipe?* 你抽烟斗吗？ **3** N-COUNT A **pipe** is a simple musical instrument in the shape of a tube with holes in it. You play a pipe by blowing into it while covering and uncovering the holes with your fingers. 管乐器 **4** N-COUNT An **organ pipe** is one of the long hollow tubes in which air vibrates and produces a musical note. 管风琴的音管 **5** V-T If liquid or gas **is piped** somewhere, it is transferred from one place to another through a pipe. 用管道输送 ❑ *The heated gas is piped through a coil surrounded by water.* 受热气体通过水中的一根螺旋管输送。 ❑ *The Communists brought electricity to his village and piped in drinking water from the reservoir.* 共产党员们把电接入了他的村子，还用管道从水库送来饮用水。 **6** → see also **piping**

→ see **plumbing**

★ **pipe·line** /paɪplaɪn/ (**pipelines**) **1** N-COUNT A **pipeline** is a large pipe that is used for carrying oil or gas over a long distance, often underground. (长距离输送石油、天然气等的地下) 管道 ❑ *A consortium plans to build a natural-gas pipeline from Russia to supply eastern Germany.* 一家财团计划修建一条从俄罗斯向德国东部供应天然气的管道。 **2** PHRASE If something is **in the pipeline**, it has already been planned or begun. 已筹划的; 已实施的 ❑ *Already in the pipeline is a 2.9 percent pay increase for teachers.* 已在筹划之中的是教师收入将增长2.9%。

→ see **oil**

pip·ing /paɪpɪŋ/ N-UNCOUNT **Piping** is metal, plastic, or another substance made in the shape of a pipe or tube. (金属、塑料等的) 管子 ❑ *...rolls of bright yellow plastic piping.* …成卷的亮黄色塑料管子。

pi·ra·cy /paɪrəsi/ **1** N-UNCOUNT **Piracy** is robbery at sea carried out by pirates. 海盗行为 ❑ *Seven of the fishermen have been formally charged with piracy.* 其中7名渔民已被正式指控犯有海盗罪。 **2** N-UNCOUNT You can refer to the illegal copying of things such as DVDs and computer programs as **piracy**. 盗版行为 ❑ *...protection against piracy of books, films, and other intellectual property.* …对书籍、影片以及其他知识产权免遭侵权的保护。

★ **pi·rate** /paɪrɪt/ (**pirates, pirating, pirated**) **1** N-COUNT **Pirates** are sailors who attack other ships and steal property from them.

海盗 ❑ *In the nineteenth century, pirates roamed the seas.* 19世纪，海盗很猖獗。 **2** V-T Someone who **pirates** CDs, DVDs, books, or computer programs copies and sells them when they have no right to do so. 盗版(CD、DVD、书籍、计算机程序等) ❑ *Computer crimes include data theft and pirating software.* 计算机犯罪包括数据窃取和盗版软件。 ● **pi·rat·ed** ADJ 非法复制的 ❑ *New technology makes it possible to make pirated copies of music and movies.* 新技术使制作盗版音乐和影片成为可能。 **3** ADJ A **pirate** version of something is an illegal copy of it. 盗版的 [ADJ n] ❑ *Pirate copies of the DVD are already being sold.* 该DVD的盗版已经有售了。

piss /pɪs/ (**pisses, pissing, pissed**) V-I To **piss** means to urinate. 撒尿 [INFORMAL, VULGAR] ❑ *A man pissed against a wall.* 一个男人对着墙撒尿。

▸ **piss off** **1** PHRASAL VERB If someone or something **pisses** you **off**, they annoy you. 使恼火；使厌烦 [INFORMAL, VULGAR] ❑ *It pisses me off when they start moaning about going to war.* 当他们开始抱怨起参战的时候，我很恼火。● **pissed off** ADJ 恼火的；厌烦的 ❑ *I was really pissed off.* 我真地厌烦了。 **2** PHRASAL VERB If someone tells a person to **piss off**, they are telling the person in a rude way to go away. 滚开 [INFORMAL, VULGAR]

pissed /pɪst/ ADJ If you say that someone is **pissed**, you mean that they are annoyed. 恼火的；厌烦的 [V-link ADJ] [AM, INFORMAL, VULGAR] ❑ *You know Molly's pissed at you.* 你知道莫莉对你很厌烦。

piste /pist/ (**pistes**) N-COUNT A **piste** is a track of firm snow for skiing on. 滑雪道 ❑ *...confident skiers who want to move off the piste.* …想脱离滑雪道滑行的自信的滑雪者们。

pis·tol /pɪstᵊl/ (**pistols**) N-COUNT A **pistol** is a small gun. 手枪

▲ **pis·ton** /pɪstᵊn/ (**pistons**) N-COUNT A **piston** is a cylinder or metal disk that is part of an engine. Pistons slide up and down inside tubes and cause various parts of the engine to move. 活塞

pit ♦◇◇ /pɪt/ (**pits, pitting, pitted**) **1** N-COUNT A **pit** is the underground part of a mine, especially a coal mine. (尤指煤矿的)矿井 **2** N-COUNT A **gravel pit** or **clay pit** is a very large hole that is left where gravel or clay has been dug from the ground. (挖出沙砾或黏土后留下的) 大坑 ❑ *This area of former farmland was worked as a gravel pit until 1964.* 这片昔日的农田在1964年前是被用作沙砾坑的。 **3** V-T If two opposing things or people **are pitted against** one another, they are in conflict. 使对立；使竞争 [usu passive] ❑ *You will be pitted against two, three, or four people who are every bit as good as you are.* 你将和2个、3个或者4个和你一样优秀的对手竞争。 **4** N-COUNT A **pit** is a large hole that is dug in the ground. 大坑 ❑ *Eric lost his footing and began to slide into the pit.* 埃里克一失足，开始滑进坑里。 **5** N-PLURAL In auto racing, **the pits** are the areas at the side of the track where drivers stop to get more fuel and to repair their cars during races. (赛车道旁的) 检修加油站 ❑ *He moved quickly into the pits and climbed rapidly out of the car.* 他急速驶入检修加油站，迅速爬出赛车。 **6** N-COUNT A **pit** is the large hard seed of a fruit or vegetable. 核 [AM] ❑ *...cherry pits.* …樱桃核。 **7** → see also **orchestra pit, pitted** **8** PHRASE If you **pit** your **wits against** someone, you compete with them in a test of knowledge or intelligence. 与…斗智 ❑ *I'd like to manage at the very highest level and pit my wits against the best.* 我希望在最高水平上管理，与最优秀的人斗智。 **9** PHRASE If you have a feeling **in the pit of** your **stomach**, you have a tight or sick feeling in your stomach, usually because you are afraid or anxious. 在胸口；在心窝 ❑ *I had a funny feeling in the pit of my stomach.* 我内心深处有种奇怪的感觉。
→ see **fruit**

pitch ♦◇◇ /pɪtʃ/ (**pitches, pitching, pitched**) **1** V-T If you **pitch** something somewhere, you throw it with some force, usually aiming it carefully. 投掷 ❑ *Simon pitched the empty bottle into the lake.* 西蒙把空瓶子投进湖里。 **2** V-T In the game of baseball, when you **pitch** the ball, you throw it to the batter for them to hit it. 投(球)给击球手 ❑ *We passed long, hot afternoons pitching a baseball.* 我们打棒球来消磨一个个漫长、炎热的下午。 **3** V-T/V-I To **pitch** somewhere means to fall forwards suddenly and with a lot of force. (向前)跌倒 ❑ *The movement took him by surprise, and he pitched forward.* 突然的移动让他猝不及防，向前跌倒。 ❑ *Alan staggered sideways, pitched head-first over the low wall and fell into the lake.* 艾伦摇晃着歪向一侧，一头栽过矮墙，掉进湖里。 **4** V-T If someone **is pitched into** a new situation, they are suddenly forced into it. 迫使进入(一种新的处境) ❑ *They were being pitched into a new adventure in which they would have to fight the whole world.* 他们当时在受迫参与到一次将不得不与整个世界为敌的新冒险中。 **5** N-UNCOUNT The **pitch** of a sound is how high or low it is. 音高 ❑ *He raised his voice to an even higher pitch.* 他将嗓门提得更高了。 **6** V-T If a sound **is pitched at** a particular level, it is produced at the level indicated. 使(声音) 提高(到指定高度) [usu passive] ❑ *His cry is pitched at a level that makes it impossible to ignore.* 他哭声之大让人不可能置若罔闻。 ❑ *His voice was pitched high, the words muffled by his crying.* 他的嗓门提得很高，说的话都被他的叫喊声压得听不清了。 **7** → see also **high-pitched** **8** V-T If something **is pitched at** a particular level or degree of difficulty, it is set at that level. 给…设定水平(或难度) ❑ *While this is very important material, I think it's probably pitched at too high a level for our students.* 尽管这是个很重要的材料，但我认为它的难度太大，不适合我们的学生。 **9** N-SING If something such as a feeling or a situation rises to a high **pitch**, it rises to a high level. (感情、形势等的) 程度 ❑ *The public's feelings were at a high pitch of indignation.* 公众的愤怒情绪达到了极点。 **10** V-T If someone **pitches** an idea for something such as a new product, they try to persuade people to accept the idea. 推荐(某主张) ❑ *My agent has pitched the idea to my editor in New York.* 我的代理人已向我在纽约的编辑力荐这个主张。 **11** N-COUNT A **pitch** is an area of ground that is marked out and used for playing a game such as soccer, cricket, or hockey. 比赛场地 [BRIT]

in AM, use **field**

12 PHRASE If someone **makes a pitch for** something, they try to persuade people to do or buy it. 推销 ❑ *The president speaks in New York today, making another pitch for his economic program.* 总统今天在纽约发表讲话，再一次推销他的经济计划。 **13** → see also **sales pitch**

▸ **pitch for** PHRASAL VERB If someone is **pitching for** something, they are trying to persuade other people to give it to them. 争取 ❑ *It was middle-class votes they were pitching for.* 他们试图争取的是中产阶级的选票。

▸ **pitch in** PHRASAL VERB If you **pitch in**, you join in and help with an activity. 参与并帮助 [INFORMAL] ❑ *The agency says international relief agencies also have pitched in.* 该机构说，一些国际救援机构也参与其中并提供了帮助。

pitch·er /pɪtʃər/ (**pitchers**) **1** N-COUNT A **pitcher** is a cylindrical container with a handle and is used for holding and pouring liquids. 壶 [mainly AM] ❑ *My sister fetched a pitcher of iced water.* 我妹妹取来一壶冰水。 **2** N-COUNT In baseball, the **pitcher** is the person who throws the ball to the batter, who tries to hit it. (棒球) 投手
→ see **baseball**

▲ **pit·fall** /pɪtfɔl/ (**pitfalls**) N-COUNT The **pitfalls** involved in a particular activity or situation are the things that may go wrong or may cause problems. 隐患 ❑ *The pitfalls of working abroad are numerous.* 在国外工作有很多隐患。

piti·ful /pɪtɪfəl/ **1** ADJ Someone or something that is **pitiful** is so sad, weak, or small that you feel pity for them. 令人同情的；可怜的 ❑ *He sounded both pitiful and eager to get what he wanted.* 他听上去可怜兮兮地迫切想得到他所想要的。● **piti·ful·ly** ADV 令人同情地；可怜地 ❑ *His legs were pitifully thin compared to the rest of his bulk.* 他的双腿和他魁梧的上身相比细得可怜。 **2** ADJ If you describe something as **pitiful**, you mean that it is completely inadequate. 极度欠缺的 [DISAPPROVAL] ❑ *The choice is pitiful and the quality of some of the products is very low.* 选择余地很小，而且有些产品的质量很差。
● **piti·ful·ly** ADV 极度欠缺地 ❑ *State help for the mentally handicapped is pitifully inadequate.* 国家对智障者的帮助少得可怜。

pit·ted /pɪtɪd/ **1** ADJ **Pitted** fruits have had their pits removed. 去核的 [ADJ n] ❑ *...green and black pitted olives.* …绿色的和黑色的去核橄榄。 **2** ADJ If the surface of something is **pitted**, it is covered with a lot of small, shallow holes. 坑坑洼洼的；有凹陷的 ❑ *Everywhere building facades are pitted with shell and bullet holes.* 各处建筑物的正面都布满了炮弹孔。

pity /pɪti/ (**pities, pitying, pitied**) **1** N-UNCOUNT If you feel **pity for** someone, you feel very sorry for them. 同情心 ❑ *He felt a sudden tender pity for her.* 他突然对她起了温柔的同情心。 **2** → see also **self-pity** **3** V-T If you **pity** someone, you feel very sorry for them. 同情 ❑ *I don't know whether to hate or pity him.* 我不知道是该恨他还是该同情他。 **4** N-SING If you say that it is **a pity** that something is the case, you mean that you feel disappointment or regret about it. 遗憾的事 [FEELINGS] ❑ *It is a great pity that all students in the city cannot have the same chances.* 很遗憾的是，并非该市所有学生都能拥有同样的机会。 ❑ *It's a pity you've arrived so late in the year.* 真遗憾，你这一年来得太迟了。 **5** N-UNCOUNT If someone shows **pity**, they do not harm or punish someone they have power over. 仁慈；怜悯 ❑ *Noncommunist forces have some pity toward people here.* 非共产主义者

的军队有些怜悯这里的人们。 6 PHRASE If you **take pity on** someone, you feel sorry for them and help them. 同情 ❑ *No woman had ever felt the need to take pity on him before.* 之前，没有哪个女人觉得有必要同情他。

piv·ot /pɪvət/ (**pivots, pivoting, pivoted**) 1 N-COUNT **The pivot** in a situation is the most important thing that everything else is based on or arranged around. 中心点 ❑ *Forming the pivot of the exhibition is a large group of watercolors.* 构成这个展览核心的是一大批水彩画。 2 V-I If something or someone **pivots**, they balance or turn on a central point. 绕支点运动 ❑ *The wheels pivot for easy maneuvering.* 这些轮子绕轴转动，以方便操控。 ❑ *He pivoted on his heels and walked on down the hall.* 他以脚跟着地转身，沿着走廊走去。 3 N-COUNT A **pivot** is the pin or the central point on which something balances or turns. 枢轴；支点 ❑ *The pedal had sheared off at the pivot.* 这个踏板已经在轴处断裂。

piv·ot·al /pɪvətəl/ ADJ A **pivotal** role, point, or figure in something is one that is very important and affects the success of that thing. 关键的 ❑ *The elections may prove to be pivotal in Colombia's political history.* 这些选举也许会证明其在哥伦比亚政治史上是至关重要的。

pix·el /pɪksəl/ (**pixels**) N-COUNT A **pixel** is the smallest area on a computer screen that can be given a separate color by the computer. 像素 [COMPUTING] ❑ *...a display screen that measures one million pixels.* …一个达到1百万像素的显示屏。
→ see **television**

▲ **piz·za** /pitsə/ (**pizzas**) N-VAR A **pizza** is a flat, round piece of dough covered with tomatoes, cheese, and other toppings, and then baked in an oven. 比萨饼 ❑ *...the last piece of pizza.* …最后一块比萨饼。

pkg. **Pkg.** is a written abbreviation for **package**. 包裹

plac·ard /plækard, -kərd/ (**placards**) N-COUNT A **placard** is a large notice that is carried in a march or displayed in a public place. 标语牌；布告 ❑ *The protesters sang songs and waved placards.* 抗议者们唱着歌并挥舞标语牌。

Word Link *plac ≈ pleasing : complacent, placate, placid*

pla·cate /pleɪkeɪt/ (**placates, placating, placated**) V-T If you **placate** someone, you do or say something to make them stop feeling angry. 安抚 [FORMAL] ❑ *He smiled, and made a gesture intended to placate me.* 他微笑了一下，做了一个意在安抚我的手势。

place
❶ NOUN USES
❷ VERB USES
❸ PHRASES

❶ **place** ♦♦♦ /pleɪs/ (**places**) 1 N-COUNT A **place** is any point, building, area, town, or country. (任何) 地方 ❑ *...a list of museums and places of interest.* …一份博物馆和名胜地的列表。 ❑ *We're going to a place called Platoro.* 我们要去一个叫普拉托罗的地方。 ❑ *The pain is always in the same place.* 疼痛总是在同一个地方。 2 N-SING You can use **the place** to refer to the point, building, area, town, or country that you have already mentioned. (提到过的点、建筑、地区、城镇、国家等) 地方 ❑ *Except for the remarkably tidy kitchen, the place was a mess.* 除了异常整洁的厨房外，这个地方一团糟。 3 N-COUNT You can refer to somewhere that provides a service, such as a hotel, restaurant, or institution, as a particular kind of **place**. (旅馆、饭店、机构等某种提供服务的) 地方 ❑ *He found a bed-and-breakfast place.* 他找到一个提供住宿带早餐的地方。 ❑ *My wife and I discovered some superb places to eat.* 我妻子和我发现了一些很棒的吃饭的地方。 4 PHRASE When something **takes place**, it happens, especially in a controlled or organized way. (尤指在控制或组织下) 发生；进行 ❑ *The discussion took place in a famous villa on the lake's shore.* 讨论在湖滨一座著名别墅举行。 ❑ *She wanted Randy's wedding to take place quickly.* 她想让兰迪的婚礼马上举行。 5 N-SING **Place** can be used after "any," "no," "some," or "every" to mean "anywhere," "nowhere," "somewhere," or "everywhere." 用在**any**，**no**，**some**或**every**之后，分别表示**anywhere**，**nowhere**，**somewhere**或**everywhere** [mainly AM, INFORMAL] ❑ *The poor guy obviously didn't have any place to go for Easter.* 这个可怜的家伙显然复活节没有任何地方可去。 6 ADV If you go **places**, you visit pleasant or interesting places. (去) 各地 [ADV after v] [mainly AM] ❑ *I don't have money to go places.* 我没有钱到处玩。 7 N-COUNT You can refer to the position where something belongs, or where it is supposed to be, as its **place**. (常处的、应在的) 位置 ❑ *He returned the album to its place on the shelf.* 他将像册放回到架上原来的地方。 8 N-COUNT A **place** is a seat or position that is available for someone to occupy. (空闲的) 座位；位置 ❑ *He walked back to the table and sat at the nearest of two empty places.* 他走回桌旁，在两个空位中就近的一个位子上坐下。

> You can use **place** or, more often, **seat** to refer to somewhere where someone can sit. ❑ *The women looked around for a place to sit... There was only one seat free on the train.* More generally, you can refer to a **space** which someone or something can occupy. ❑ *He was clearing a space for her to lie down.* You do not use **place** as an uncount noun to refer to an open or empty area. You should use **room** or **space** instead. **Room** is more likely to be used when you are talking about space inside an enclosed area. ❑ *There's not enough room in the bathroom for both of us... Leave plenty of space between you and the car in front.*

9 N-COUNT Someone's or something's **place** in a society, system, or situation is their position in relation to other people or things. 地位 ❑ *They want to see more women take their place higher up the corporate or professional ladder.* 他们希望看到更多女性担任公司或职业阶梯上更高的职位。 10 N-COUNT Your **place** in a race or competition is your position in relation to the other competitors. If you are in first place, you are ahead of all the other competitors. 排名 ❑ *He has risen to second place in the opinion polls.* 他在民意调查中排名已升至第二位。 11 N-COUNT If you get a **place** on a team, on a committee, or in an institution, for example, you are accepted as a member of the team or committee or as a resident of the institution. (在团队、委员会或机构等中的) 位置 ❑ *Derek had lost his place on the team.* 德里克已经丢了他在那个队的位置。 ❑ *They should be in residential care but there are no places available.* 他们应该得到住院护理，但是没有空床位。 12 N-SING A good **place to** do something in a situation or activity is a good time or stage at which to do it. (适当的) 时机 ❑ *It seemed an appropriate place to end somehow.* 似乎是到了该结束的时候了。 13 N-COUNT Your **place** is the house or apartment where you live. (居住地) 地方 [INFORMAL] ❑ *Let's all go back to my place!* 咱们都回我的住处吧！ 14 N-COUNT Your **place in** a book or speech is the point you have reached in reading the book or making the speech. (书读到的或话说到的) 地方 ❑ *...her finger marking her place in the book.* …她的手指指着书上她读到的地方。 15 N-COUNT If you say how many decimal **places** there are in a number, you are saying how many numbers there are to the right of the decimal point. (数) 位 ❑ *A pocket calculator only works to eight decimal places.* 袖珍计算器只计算到小数点后8位。
→ see **election, vote, zero**

❷ **place** ♦♦♦ /pleɪs/ (**places, placing, placed**) 1 V-T If you **place** something somewhere, you put it in a particular position, especially in a careful, firm, or deliberate way. (小心地、稳妥地或从容地) 放置 ❑ *Brand folded it in his handkerchief and placed it in the inside pocket of his jacket.* 布兰德把它包在手绢里，放进了他夹克衫的内兜。 2 V-T To **place** a person or thing in a particular state means to cause them to be in it. 使处于 (某种状态) ❑ *Widespread protests have placed the president under serious pressure.* 大范围的抗议已经使总统处于巨大的压力之下。 ❑ *The crisis could well place the relationship at risk.* 这场危机很可能使这个关系岌岌可危。 3 V-T You can use **place** instead of "put" or "lay" in certain expressions where the meaning is carried by the following noun. For example, if you **place emphasis on** something, you emphasize it, and if you **place the blame on** someone, you blame them. 替代**put**或**lay**，用于**place emphasis on**、**place the blame on**等由其后的名词决定意思的短语中 ❑ *He placed great emphasis on the importance of family life and ties.* 他非常重视家庭生活和家庭纽带。 ❑ *She seemed to be placing most of the blame on her mother.* 她好像是在把大部分责任推到她母亲身上。 4 V-T If you **place** someone or something in a particular class or group, you label or judge them in that way. 评定 ❑ *The authorities have placed the drug in Class A, the same category as heroin and cocaine.* 当局已把这种毒品定为A级，与海洛因和可卡因属同一类。 5 V-T If a competitor in a race or competition **is placed** first, second, or third, they finish first, second or third. If a horse **is placed** in a race, it finishes second. 取得名次；(马在赛跑中) 位居第二 [usu passive] ❑ *I had been placed 2nd and 3rd a few times but had never won.* 我得过几次第二名和第三名，但是从来没有得过第一。 6 V-T If you **place an order for** a product or **for** a meal, you ask for it to be sent or brought to you. 订 (产品或餐) ❑ *It is a good idea to place your order well in advance as delivery can often take months rather than weeks.* 早早提前订购是个好主意，因为交货常常

P

要花几个月的时间，而不是几星期。 **7** V-T If you **place an advertisement in** a newspaper, you arrange for the advertisement to appear in the newspaper. 登广告 ❑ *They placed an advertisement in the local paper for a secretary.* 他们把一则秘书招聘广告登在当地报纸上。 **8** V-T If you **place a bet**, you bet money on something. 下赌注 ❑ *For this race, though, he had already placed a bet on one of the horses.* 不过，这次赛马，他已经在其中的一匹马上下了注。 **9** V-T If an agency or organization **places** someone, it finds them a job or somewhere to live. 安置(工作或住所) ❑ *They managed to place fourteen women in paid positions.* 他们设法为14名妇女安排了有报酬的工作。

❸ **place** ♦♦♦ /pleɪs/ **1** PHRASE If something is happening **all over the place**, it is happening in many different places. 到处 ❑ *Businesses are closing down all over the place.* 到处都有企业在倒闭。 **2** PHRASE If things are **all over the place**, they are spread over a very large area, usually in a disorganized way. 遍地 ❑ *Our fingerprints are probably all over the place.* 我们的指纹很可能到处都有。 **3** PHRASE If you **change places with** another person, you start being in their situation or role, and they start being in yours. 互换角色 ❑ *With his door key in his hand, knowing Millie and the kids awaited him, he wouldn't change places with anyone.* 手里拿着门钥匙，知道米莉和孩子们正等着自己，他决不会同任何人互换位置。 **4** PHRASE If you have been trying to understand something puzzling and then everything **falls into place** or **clicks into place**, you suddenly understand how different pieces of information are connected and everything becomes clearer. (情况) 豁然开朗 ❑ *When the reasons behind the decision were explained, of course, it all fell into place.* 当这个决定背后的原因得到了解释后，当然，一切都变得豁然开朗了。 **5** PHRASE If things **fall into place**, events happen naturally to produce a situation you want. (事情) 顺理成章 ❑ *Once the decision was made, things fell into place rapidly.* 一旦决定了，事情很快顺理成章。 **6** PHRASE If you say that someone **is going places**, you mean that they are showing a lot of talent or ability and are likely to become very successful. 出色 ❑ *You always knew Barbara was going places, she was different.* 你一直知道芭芭拉很出色，她与众不同。 **7** PHRASE People **in high places** are people who have powerful and influential positions in a government, society, or organization. (在政府、社会或组织中) 身居高位 ❑ *He had friends in high places.* 他有一些高层的朋友。 **8** PHRASE If something is **in place**, it is in its correct or usual position. If it is **out of place**, it is not in its correct or usual position. 在恰当/不恰当的位置 ❑ *Gary hastily pushed the drawer back into place.* 加里匆忙把抽屉推回去。 **9** PHRASE If something such as a law, a policy, or an administrative structure is **in place**, it is working or able to be used. (法律、政策、行政机构等) 在运行 ❑ *Similar legislation is already in place in Utah.* 类似的法规已在犹他州实施。 **10** PHRASE If one thing or person is used or does something **in place of** another, they replace the other thing or person. 替代 ❑ *Cooked kidney beans can be used in place of French beans.* 做熟的四季豆可以用来代替菜豆。 **11** PHRASE If something has particular characteristics or features **in places**, it has them at several points within an area. 在几处 ❑ *Even now the snow along the roadside was five or six feet deep in places.* 即使现在，路边的雪有的地方有五六英尺深。 **12** PHRASE If you say what you would have done **in** someone else's **place**, you say what you would have done if you had been in their situation and had been experiencing what they were experiencing. 处于(某人的) 位置 ❑ *In her place I wouldn't have been able to resist it.* 若处在她的位置上，我也会无法抵挡它的。 **13** PHRASE You say **in the first place** when you are talking about the beginning of a situation or about the situation as it was before a series of events. 最初 ❑ *What brought you to Washington in the first place?* 最初是什么使你来到华盛顿？ **14** PHRASE You say **in the first place** and **in the second place** to introduce the first and second in a series of points or reasons. **In the first place** can also be used to emphasize a very important point or reason. 首先/其次 (用于列举，首先也可以用于强调) ❑ *In the first place you are not old, Conway. And in the second place, you are a very strong and appealing man.* 首先，你不老，康韦。其次，你是个非常强壮、有魅力的男人。 **15** PHRASE If you say that **it is not** your **place to** do something, you mean that it is not right or appropriate for you to do it, or that it is not your responsibility to do it. 不是(某人) 该做的事 ❑ *He says that it is not his place to comment on government commitment to further funds.* 他说，他不便评论政府对进一步提供资金的承诺。 **16** PHRASE If someone or something seems **out of place** in a particular situation, they do not seem to belong there or to be suitable for that situation. 不属于；不适宜 ❑ *I felt out of place in my suit and tie.* 穿着西装打着领带，我感到不自在。 **17** PHRASE If you **place** one thing **above**, **before**, or **over** another, you think that the first thing is more important than the second and you show this in your behavior. 置…于…之上/前 ❑ *He continued to place security above all other objectives.* 他继续将安全置于其他所有目标之上。 **18** PHRASE If you **put** someone **in** their **place**, you show them that they are less important or clever than they think they are. 使(某人) 有自知之明 ❑ *In a few words she had put him in his place.* 几句话她就让他安分了下来。 **19** PHRASE If you say that someone should **be shown** their **place** or **be kept in** their **place**, you are saying, often in a humorous way, that they should be made aware of their low status. (以幽默的方式) 使(某人) 识相 ❑ *...an uppity bartender who needs to be shown his place.* …一个盛气凌人的需要有点自知之明的酒吧招待。 **20** PHRASE If one thing **takes second place to** another, it is considered to be less important and is given less attention than the other thing. 居次要地位 ❑ *My personal life has had to take second place to my career.* 我的个人生活得让位于我的事业。 **21** PHRASE If one thing or person **takes the place of** another or **takes** another's **place**, they replace the other thing or person. 替代 ❑ *Optimism was gradually taking the place of pessimism.* 乐观正逐渐替代悲观。

place·ment /pleɪsmənt/ (**placements**) **1** N-UNCOUNT **The placement of** something or someone is the act of putting them in a particular place or position. (物的) 安放；(人的) 安排 ❑ *The treatment involves the placement of twenty-two electrodes in the inner ear.* 治疗包括在内耳安放22个电极。 **2** N-UNCOUNT The **placement** of someone in a job, home, or school is the act or process of finding them a job, home, or school. (对某人工作、家庭或学校的) 安置 ❑ *The children were waiting for placement in a foster care home.* 孩子们正在等待被安置到寄养家庭里。 **3** N-COUNT If someone gets a **placement**, they get a job for a short period of time to gain experience. 实习职位 ❑ *He spent a year studying Japanese in Tokyo, followed by a six-month work placement with the Japanese government.* 他花了1年时间在东京学日语，接着是在日本政府6个月的实习工作。

→ see **advertising**

Word Link *plac ≈ pleasing : complacent, placate, placid*

plac·id /plæsɪd/ **1** ADJ A **placid** person or animal is calm and does not easily become excited, angry, or upset. 温和的 ❑ *She was a placid child who rarely cried.* 她是个温和的孩子，很少哭。 **2** ADJ A **placid** place, area of water, or life is calm and peaceful. 平静的 ❑ *...the placid waters of Lake Erie.* …伊利湖平静的湖水。

pla·gia·rise /pleɪdʒəraɪz/ [BRIT] → see **plagiarize**

pla·gia·rism /pleɪdʒərɪzəm/ N-UNCOUNT **Plagiarism** is the practice of using or copying someone else's idea or work and pretending that you thought of it or created it. 剽窃 ❑ *Now he's in real trouble. He's accused of plagiarism.* 现在他陷入真正的麻烦了。他被指控剽窃。

> Writing a paper entirely or partly composed of the words of others without giving them credit for their work is called **plagiarism**. It is a punishable offense at American colleges and universities where students will be asked to leave. Professional writers who are caught cheating in this way may lose their jobs.

pla·gia·rize /pleɪdʒəraɪz/ (**plagiarizes, plagiarizing, plagiarized**) in BRIT, also use **plagiarise**

V-T If someone **plagiarizes** another person's idea or work, they use it or copy it and pretend that they thought of it or created it. 剽窃 ❑ *The students denied plagiarizing papers.* 学生们不承认抄袭试卷。

plague /pleɪg/ (**plagues, plaguing, plagued**) **1** N-UNCOUNT **Plague** or **the plague** is a very infectious disease that usually results in death. The patient has a severe fever and swellings on his or her body. 瘟疫 [also "the" N] ❑ *...a fresh outbreak of plague.* …瘟疫的新一轮爆发。 **2** N-COUNT **A plague of** unpleasant things is a large number of them that arrive or happen at the same time. 泛滥 ❑ *The city is under threat from a plague of rats.* 这座城市面临着鼠患的威胁。 **3** V-T If you **are plagued by** unpleasant things, they continually cause you a lot of trouble or suffering. 使困扰 ❑ *She was plagued by weakness, fatigue, and dizziness.* 她被虚弱、疲劳和眩晕折磨。

plaice /pleɪs/ (**plaice**)

> **Plaice** is both the singular and the plural form.

N-VAR **Plaice** are a type of flat sea fish. 鲽鱼 (一种体形扁平的海鱼) ● N-UNCOUNT **Plaice** is this fish eaten as food. 鲽鱼肉。

P

plain ♦◇◇ /pleɪn/ (**plainer, plainest, plains**) **1** ADJ A **plain** object, surface, or fabric is entirely in one color and has no pattern, design, or writing on it. 纯色的 ❑ *In general, a plain carpet makes a room look bigger.* 一般来讲，纯色的地毯使房间显得更大。 ❑ *He placed the paper in a plain envelope.* 他把论文放在一个空白的信封里。 **2** ADJ Something that is **plain** is very simple in style. 朴素的 ❑ *It was a plain, gray stone house.* 这是一座简朴的灰色石头房子。 ● **plain·ly** ADV 朴素地 [ADV -ed] ❑ *He was very tall and plainly dressed.* 他个子很高，穿着朴素。 **3** ADJ If a fact, situation, or statement is **plain**, it is easy to recognize or understand. 清楚的 ❑ *It was plain to him that I was having a nervous breakdown.* 我那时神经衰弱，他是清楚的。 **4** ADJ If you describe someone as **plain**, you think they look ordinary and not at all beautiful. 相貌平平的 ❑ *...a shy, rather plain girl with a pale complexion.* …一个害羞、相貌平平、脸色苍白的女孩。 **5** N-COUNT A **plain** is a large flat area of land with very few trees on it. 平原 ❑ *Once there were 70 million buffalo on the plains.* 在这片草原上曾经生活着7000万头水牛。 **6** PHRASE If a police officer is **in plain clothes**, he or she is wearing ordinary clothes instead of a police uniform. (警察) 穿便衣的 ❑ *Three officers in plain clothes told me to get out of the car.* 三名便衣警官叫我从车上下来。 **7** **plain sailing** → see **sailing**

Thesaurus *plain* 另参见：

ADJ. bare, common, everyday, modest, ordinary, simple, usual; (*ant.*) elaborate, fancy **2**
clear, distinct, evident, transparent **3**

Word Partnership *plain* 的常用搭配：

N. plain **style** **2**
plain **English**, plain **language**, plain **speech**, plain **truth** **3**

plain·ly /pleɪnli/ **1** ADV You use **plainly** to indicate that you believe something is obviously true, often when you are trying to convince someone else that it is true. 显而易见地 [EMPHASIS] ❑ *The judge's conclusion was plainly wrong.* 法官的结论显然是错误的。 ❑ *Plainly, a more objective method of description must be adopted.* 显然，必须采用一种更客观的描述方法。 **2** ADV You use **plainly** to indicate that something is easily seen, noticed, or recognized. 明显地 ❑ *He was plainly annoyed.* 他明显是生气了。 ❑ *I could plainly see him turning his head to the right and left.* 我可以清楚地看到他将头向右转然后又向左转。 **3** → see also **plain**

plain·tiff /pleɪntɪf/ (**plaintiffs**) N-COUNT A **plaintiff** is a person who brings a legal case against someone in a court of law. 原告 ❑ *The lead plaintiff of the lawsuit is the University of California.* 这次诉讼的第一原告是加利福尼亚大学。
→ see **trial**

plain·tive /pleɪntɪv/ ADJ A **plaintive** sound or voice sounds sad. (声音或嗓音) 哀伤的 [LITERARY] ❑ *They lay on the firm sands, listening to the plaintive cry of the seagulls.* 他们躺在坚实的沙滩上，听着海鸥的哀鸣。

plait /pleɪt/ (**plaits, plaiting, plaited**) **1** V-T If you **plait** three or more lengths of hair, rope, or other material together, you twist them over and under each other to make one thick length. 编 (头发、绳子等) 成辫 [mainly BRIT]

in AM, usually use **braid**

2 N-COUNT A **plait** is a length of hair that has been plaited. 辫子 [mainly BRIT]

in AM, usually use **braid**

plan ♦♦♦ /plæn/ (**plans, planning, planned**) **1** N-COUNT A **plan** is a method of achieving something that you have worked out in detail beforehand. 计划；方案 ❑ *The three leaders had worked out a peace plan.* 这3位领导人已制定出了一份和平计划。 ❑ *He maintains that everything is going according to plan.* 他坚持说一切都在按计划进行。 **2** V-T/V-I If you **plan** what you are going to do, you decide in detail what you are going to do, and you intend to do it. 计划 ❑ *If you plan what you're going to eat, you reduce your chances of overeating.* 如果你对要吃的东西加以计划，饮食过度的几率就会减少。 ❑ *He planned to leave Baghdad on Monday.* 他计划星期一离开巴格达。 ❑ *Moderate Republicans gathered together to plan for the future.* 温和的共和党人集会筹划未来。 **3** N-PLURAL If you have **plans**, you are intending to do a particular thing. (具体) 安排 ❑ *"I'm sorry," she said. "I have plans for tonight."* "抱歉，"她说。"我今晚有安排。" **4** V-T When you **plan** something that you are going to make, build, or create, you decide what the main parts of it will be and do a drawing of how it should be made. 规划 ❑ *It is no use trying to plan an 18-hole golf course on a 120-acre site if you have to ruin the environment to do it.* 要规划一个占地120公顷、拥有18洞的高尔夫球场如果必须破坏环境才能做到，那就毫无益处了。 **5** N-COUNT A **plan of** something that is going to be built or made is a detailed diagram or drawing of it. 设计图 ❑ *...when you have drawn a plan of the garden.* …在你画完这个花园的设计图时。 **6** → see also **planning**

▶ **plan on** PHRASAL VERB If you **plan on** doing something, you intend to do it. 打算 ❑ *They were planning on getting married.* 他们正打算结婚。

Thesaurus *plan* 另参见：

N. aim, deal, idea, intention, procedure, strategy, system **1**
blueprint, diagram, illustration, layout, sketch **5**
V. intend, propose **2**
design, devise, draft, prepare **4**

plane ♦♦◇ /pleɪn/ (**planes, planing, planed**) **1** N-COUNT A **plane** is a vehicle with wings and one or more engines that can fly through the air. 飞机 ❑ *He had plenty of time to catch his plane.* 他有足够的时间赶飞机。 ❑ *Her mother was killed in a plane crash.* 她的母亲死于一次飞机失事。 **2** N-COUNT A **plane** is a flat, level surface that may be sloping at a particular angle. (可能有坡度的) 平面 ❑ *...a building with angled planes.* …一个表面有一定角度的建筑物。 **3** N-SING If a number of points are in the same **plane**, one line or one flat surface could pass through them all. 平面 ❑ *All the planets orbit the Sun in roughly the same plane, around its equator.* 所有行星基本在同一个平面上围绕太阳赤道运转。 **4** N-COUNT A **plane** is a tool that has a flat bottom with a sharp blade in it. You move the plane over a piece of wood in order to remove thin pieces of its surface. 刨子 **5** V-T If you **plane** a piece of wood, you make it smaller or smoother by using a plane. 刨 ❑ *She watches him plane the surface of a walnut board.* 她看着他刨一块胡桃木板。 **6** N-COUNT A **plane** or a **plane tree** is the same as a sycamore. 悬铃木

Thesaurus *plane* 另参见：

N. aircraft, airplane, craft, jet **1**
horizontal, level, surface **2**

plan·et ♦◇◇ /plænɪt/ (**planets**) N-COUNT A **planet** is a large, round object in space that moves around a star. The Earth is a planet. 行星 ❑ *The picture shows six of the nine planets in the solar system.* 这张图片展示太阳系9个行星中的6个行星。
→ see **astronomer, galaxy, satellite, solar**

★ **plan·etary** /plænɪtɛri/ ADJ **Planetary** means relating to or belonging to planets. 行星的 [ADJ n] ❑ *Within our own galaxy there are probably tens of thousands of planetary systems.* 在我们所在的银河系中，很可能存在数以万计的行星系。

▲ **plank** /plæŋk/ (**planks**) **1** N-COUNT A **plank** is a long, flat, rectangular piece of wood. 长方形木板 ❑ *It was very strong, made of three solid planks of wood.* 它非常结实，是用3块长条木板做成的。 **2** N-COUNT The main **plank of** a particular group or political party is the main principle on which it bases its policy, or its main aim. (社团或政党的) 政纲 [JOURNALISM] ❑ *The Saudi authorities have made agricultural development a central plank of policy to make the country less dependent on imports.* 沙特阿拉伯当局已经将农业发展作为其政策的核心纲领，以减少该国对进口的依赖。

plan·ner /plænər/ (**planners**) N-COUNT **Planners** are people whose job is to make decisions about what is going to be done in the future. For example, town planners decide how land should be used and what new buildings should be built. 规划者 ❑ *...a panel that includes city planners, art experts, and historians.* …一个由城市规划者、艺术专家和历史学家组成的专门小组。

plan·ning ♦◇◇ /plænɪŋ/ **1** N-UNCOUNT **Planning** is the process of deciding in detail how to do something before you actually start to do it. 计划 ❑ *The trip needs careful planning.* 这次旅行需要认真计划。 **2** → see also **family planning** **3** N-UNCOUNT **Planning** is control by the local government of the way that land is used in an area and of what new buildings are built there. 市政规划 ❑ *New York City's Planning Commissions rejected the builder's proposals.* 纽约市市政规划委员会拒绝了那个建筑商的提案。

plant ♦♦♦ /plænt/ (**plants, planting, planted**) **1** N-COUNT A **plant** is a living thing that grows in the earth and has a stem, leaves, and roots. 植物 ❑ *Water each plant as often as required.* 按要求经

常给每棵植物浇水。**2** V-T When you **plant** a seed, plant, or young tree, you put it into the ground so that it will grow there. 栽种 ❑ *He says he plans to plant fruit trees and vegetables.* 他说他计划栽种果树和蔬菜。● **plant·ing** N-UNCOUNT 栽种 ❑ *Extensive flooding in the country has delayed planting and many crops are still under water.* 该国大范围的洪水已经延误了栽种，许多庄稼现在还泡在水中。**3** V-T When someone **plants** land **with** a particular type of plant or crop, they put plants, seeds, or young trees into the land to grow them there. 将(土地)种植(植被) ❑ *They plan to plant the area with grass and trees.* 他们计划在这个地区植树种草。❑ *Recently much of their energy has gone into planting a large vegetable garden.* 最近，他们的大部分精力已经花在种植一个大型蔬菜园上。**4** N-COUNT A **plant** is a factory or a place where power is produced. 工厂；电厂 ❑ *...Ford's car assembly plants.* …福特公司的汽车装配厂。**5** N-UNCOUNT **Plant** is large machinery that is used in industrial processes. (工业用) 大型机械设备 ❑ *Companies may start to invest in plant and equipment abroad where costs may be lower.* 各公司可能要开始在国外投资大型机械设备，那里成本可能低一些。**6** V-T If you **plant** something somewhere, you put it there firmly. (稳固地) 放置 ❑ *She planted her feet wide and bent her knees slightly.* 她双脚大步稳稳分开，双膝微微弯曲。**7** V-T To **plant** something such as a bomb means to hide it somewhere so that it explodes or works there. 埋设 (炸弹等) ❑ *So far no one has admitted planting the bomb.* 到目前为止，没有人承认埋设了炸弹。**8** V-T If something such as a weapon or drugs **is planted** on someone, it is put among their possessions or in their house so that they will be wrongly accused of a crime. 放置 (武器、毒品等以栽赃) [oft passive] ❑ *He always protested his innocence and claimed that the drugs had been planted to incriminate him.* 他一直坚称自己是清白的，声称毒品是有人放置要栽赃于他。**9** V-T If an organization **plants** someone somewhere, they send that person there so that they can get information or watch someone secretly. 安插 (卧底) ❑ *Journalists informed police who planted an undercover detective to trap Smith.* 记者们向警方提供了信息，警方安插了一名卧底侦探诱捕史密斯。
→ see **earth, farm, food, tide, tree**

plan·ta·tion /plænteɪʃ°n/ (**plantations**) **1** N-COUNT A **plantation** is a large piece of land, especially in a tropical country, where crops such as rubber, coffee, tea, or sugar are grown. (尤指热带国家的橡胶、咖啡、茶、甘蔗) 种植园 ❑ *...banana plantations in Costa Rica.* …在哥斯达黎加的香蕉种植园。**2** N-COUNT A **plantation** is a large number of trees that have been planted together. 人工林 ❑ *...a plantation of almond trees.* …一片人工杏树林。

plaque /plæk/ (**plaques**) **1** N-COUNT A **plaque** is a flat piece of metal or stone with writing on it which is fixed to a wall or other structure to remind people of an important person or event. (金属或石质的) 匾额 ❑ *The First Lady unveiled a commemorative plaque.* 第一夫人为纪念牌匾揭了幕。**2** N-UNCOUNT **Plaque** is a substance containing bacteria that forms on the surface of your teeth. 牙菌斑 ❑ *Deposits of plaque build up between the tooth and the gum.* 牙菌斑的沉积物在牙齿和牙龈间形成。
→ see **teeth**

plas·ma /plæzmə/ N-UNCOUNT **Plasma** is the clear liquid part of blood that contains the blood cells. 血浆

plas·ma screen (**plasma screens**) or **plasma display** N-COUNT A **plasma screen** is a type of thin television screen or computer screen that produces high-quality images. 等离子屏幕 ❑ *...a 50-inch plasma screen.* …一个50英寸的等离子屏幕。❑ *...flat-panel TVs using thin plasma displays.* …使用很薄的等离子屏幕的平面电视。

★ **plas·ter** /plæstər/ (**plasters, plastering, plastered**) **1** N-UNCOUNT **Plaster** is a smooth paste made of sand, lime, and water that gets hard when it dries. Plaster is used to cover walls and ceilings and is also used to make sculptures. 灰泥 ❑ *There were huge cracks in the plaster, and the green shutters were faded.* 灰泥上有巨大的裂缝，绿色的百叶窗也褪色了。**2** V-T If you **plaster** a wall or ceiling, you cover it with a layer of plaster. 往…上抹灰泥 ❑ *The ceiling he had just plastered fell in and knocked him off his ladder.* 他刚抹过灰泥的那块天花板脱落了，把他从梯子上砸了下来。**3** V-T If you **plaster** a surface or a place **with** posters or pictures, you stick a lot of them all over it. 到处张贴 (海报、图画等) ❑ *He has plastered the city with posters proclaiming his qualifications and experience.* 他已在城中各处张贴了声明自己资质和阅历的海报。**4** V-T If you **plaster yourself** in some kind of sticky substance, you cover yourself in it. (给自己) 涂抹 ❑ *She gets sunburned even when she plasters herself from head to toe in factor 7 sun lotion.* 即使她从头到脚涂抹上防晒系数是7的防晒霜，她也会被晒伤。**5** N-COUNT A **plaster** is a strip of sticky material used for covering small cuts or sores on your body. 膏药 [BRIT]
in AM, usually use **Band-aid**
6 → see also **plastered**

plas·tered /plæstərd/ **1** ADJ If something is **plastered to** a surface, it is sticking to the surface. 粘贴了的 [v-link ADJ prep/adv] ❑ *His hair was plastered down to his scalp by the rain.* 雨水使他的头发紧贴在头皮上。**2** ADJ If something or someone is **plastered with** a sticky substance, they are covered with it. 粘满…的 [v-link ADJ] ❑ *My hands, boots, and pants were plastered with mud.* 我的双手、两只靴子和裤子上都粘满了泥。**3** ADJ If a story or photograph is **plastered all over** the front page of a newspaper, it is given a lot of space on the page and made very noticeable. (报道、照片) 醒目刊载的 [v-link ADJ prep/adv] ❑ *His picture was plastered all over the newspapers.* 他的照片被醒目地刊登在各家报纸上。**4** ADJ If someone gets **plastered**, they get very drunk. 大醉的 [v-link ADJ] [INFORMAL] ❑ *I decided to get some beer. Seems a good night to get plastered.* 我决定弄些啤酒来。似乎是个很好的不醉不休之夜。

plas·tic ♦◇◇ /plæstɪk/ (**plastics**) **1** N-MASS **Plastic** is a material that is produced from oil by a chemical process and that is used to make many objects. It is light in weight and does not break easily. 塑料 ❑ *...a wooden crate, sheltered from rain by sheets of plastic.* …一只板条木箱，用塑料膜盖着遮雨。❑ *A lot of the plastics that carmakers are using cannot be recycled.* 汽车制造商们正在使用的很多塑料制品是无法回收再用的。**2** ADJ If you describe something as **plastic**, you mean that you think it looks or tastes unnatural or not real. (样子或味道) 不自然的 [DISAPPROVAL] ❑ *You wanted proper home-cooked meals, you said you had enough plastic hotel food and airline food.* 你想吃地道的家常饭菜，你说你吃够了宾馆里和航班上味道不纯的食品。**3** N-UNCOUNT If you use **plastic** or **plastic money** to pay for something, you pay for it with a credit card instead of using cash. 信用卡 [INFORMAL] ❑ *Using plastic to pay for an order is simplicity itself.* 使用信用卡支付订单本身就很简单。**4** ADJ Something that is **plastic** is soft and can easily be made into different shapes. 柔软易塑的 ❑ *You can also enjoy mud packs with the natural mud, smooth, gray, soft, and plastic as butter.* 你还可以享受天然泥制面膜，灰色的泥，光滑、柔软，像黄油一样易塑。
→ see **oil**

plas·tic sur·gery N-UNCOUNT **Plastic surgery** is the practice of performing operations to repair or replace skin that has been damaged, or to improve people's appearance. 整形手术 ❑ *She even had plastic surgery to change the shape of her nose.* 她甚至做过整形手术来改变鼻子的形状。

plas·tic wrap N-UNCOUNT **Plastic wrap** is a thin, clear, stretchy plastic that you use to cover food to keep it fresh. 保鲜膜 [AM]
in BRIT, use **clingfilm**

plate ♦◇◇ /pleɪt/ (**plates**) **1** N-COUNT A **plate** is a round or oval flat dish that is used to hold food. (盛食物的) 盘子 ❑ *Anita pushed her plate away; she had eaten virtually nothing.* 安妮塔把盘子推开；她其实什么都没吃。**2** N-COUNT A **plate of** food is the amount of food on a plate. 一盘子的量 ❑ *...a huge plate of bacon and eggs.* …一大盘子咸肉和鸡蛋。**3** N-COUNT A **plate** is a flat piece of metal, especially on machinery or a building. (尤指机械或建筑上的) 金属板 ❑ *...a recess covered by a brass plate.* …一个被一块铜板覆盖着的壁龛。**4** N-COUNT A **plate** is a small, flat piece of metal with someone's name written on it, which you usually find beside the front door of an office or house. (金属制的刻有姓名的) 牌子 ❑ *...a brass plate by the front door bearing his name.* …大门旁一块刻有他名字的铜牌。**5** N-PLURAL On a road vehicle, the **plates** are the panels on the front and back that display the license number. (车辆) 牌照 ❑ *...dusty-looking cars with New Jersey plates.* …挂着新泽西牌照的落满灰尘的汽车。**6** → see also **license plate** **7** N-COUNT A **plate** in a book is a picture or photograph that takes up a whole page and is usually printed on better quality paper than the rest of the book. (书中通常用质地比正文好的纸印刷的) 整页插图 ❑ *The book has 55 color plates.* 这本书有55页彩色整页插图。**8** PHRASE If you **have enough on** your **plate** or **have a lot on** your **plate**, you have a lot of work to do or a lot of things to deal with. 有许多事等着做 ❑ *We have enough on our plate. There is plenty of work to be done on what we have.* 我们有许多事干。我们手头就有大量的工作要做。
→ see **continent, dish, earthquake, rock**

★ **plat·eau** /plætoʊ/ (**plateaus** or **plateaux**) **1** N-COUNT A **plateau** is a large area of high and fairly flat land. 高原 ❑ *A broad valley opened up leading to a high, flat plateau of cultivated land.* 一个宽阔

的山谷展开，通向一片平坦的高原耕地。**2** N-COUNT If you say that an activity or process has reached a **plateau**, you mean that it has reached a stage where there is no further change or development. (不再有变化或进展的) 稳定阶段 ❑ *The U.S. heroin market now appears to have reached a plateau.* 美国的海洛因市场目前似乎已进入了一个稳定阶段。

-plated /-pleɪtɪd/ COMB IN ADJ Something made of metal that is **plated** is covered with a thin layer of another type of metal such as gold and silver. (金属制品) 镀…的 ❑ *...a gold-plated watch.* …一块镀金手表。

plat·form ♦◇◇ /plætfɔrm/ (**platforms**) **1** N-COUNT A **platform** is a flat raised structure, usually made of wood, that people stand on when they make speeches or give a performance. 讲台；舞台 ❑ *Nick finished what he was saying and jumped down from the platform.* 尼克讲完话，从讲台上跳了下来。**2** N-COUNT A **platform** is a flat raised structure or area, usually one that something can stand on or land on. (用于放置物品或着陆的) 平台 ❑ *They found a spot on a rocky platform where they could pitch their tents.* 他们在一个岩石平台上找到了一处可以搭帐篷的地方。**3** N-COUNT A **platform** is a structure built for people to work and live on when drilling for oil or gas at sea, or when extracting it. (在海上为钻探石油或天然气而建的) 平台 ❑ *The platform began to produce oil in 1994.* 1994年，这个钻井平台开始产油。**4** N-COUNT A **platform** in a train or subway station is the area beside the tracks where you wait for or get off a train. (火车或地铁站的) 站台 ❑ *The train was about to leave and I was not even on the platform.* 火车就要开了，而我甚至还没有赶到站台上。**5** N-COUNT The **platform** of a political party is what they say they will do if they are elected. (政党的) 施政纲领 ❑ *The party has announced a platform of political and economic reforms.* 该党已宣布了一份关于政治和经济改革的施政纲领。**6** N-COUNT If someone has a **platform**, they have an opportunity to tell people what they think or want. 发表意见的机会 ❑ *The demonstration provided a platform for a broad cross-section of speakers.* 那次示威为广泛代表各方的发言者们提供了一个发表意见的机会。

→ see **skateboarding**

Thesaurus *platform* 另参见：

N. floor, podium, staging, table **1**
objective, policy, principle, program, promise **5**

plati·num /plætɪnəm, plætnəm/ N-UNCOUNT **Platinum** is a very valuable, silvery-gray metal. It is often used for making jewelry. 铂；白金

plati·tude /plætɪtud/ (**platitudes**) N-COUNT A **platitude** is a statement that is considered meaningless and boring because it has been made many times before in similar situations. 陈词滥调 [DISAPPROVAL] ❑ *Why couldn't he say something vital and original instead of just spouting the same old platitudes?* 他为什么不能说点重要的、有新意的东西，而不只是喋喋不休地讲些陈词滥调呢？

pla·ton·ic /plətɒnɪk/ ADJ **Platonic** relationships or feelings of affection do not involve sex. 柏拉图式的 ❑ *She values the platonic friendship she has had with Chris for ten years.* 她珍视她同克里斯之间已经长达10年的柏拉图式的友谊。

plat·ter /plætər/ (**platters**) **1** N-COUNT A **platter** is a large flat plate used for serving food. (盛食物的) 大浅盘 [mainly AM] ❑ *The food was being served on silver platters.* 食物是用银质大浅盘端上来的。**2** N-COUNT A **platter of** food is the amount of food on a platter. 一大浅盘子的量 ❑ *They were served platters of cheese and fruit.* 给他们上了几大盘奶酪和水果。**3** PHRASE If you say that someone has things **handed to** them **on a platter**, you disapprove of them because they get good things easily. 毫不费力地得到 [DISAPPROVAL] ❑ *Even the presidency was handed to him on a platter.* 甚至连总统的职位也让他轻易到手。

→ see **dish**

plau·sible /plɔzɪbᵊl/ **1** ADJ An explanation or statement that is **plausible** seems likely to be true or valid. (解释或叙述) 看似合理的 ❑ *A more plausible explanation would seem to be that people are fed up with the administration.* 一个更合理的解释似乎是人们对行政机关感到厌倦。

● **plau·sibly** /plɔzɪbli/ ADV 看似合理地 [ADV with v] ❑ *Having bluffed his way in without paying, he could not plausibly demand his money back.* 没付钱混了进去，他不大可能理直气壮地要回自己的钱。

● **plau·sibil·ity** /plɔzɪbɪlɪti/ N-UNCOUNT 看似合理性 ❑ *...the plausibility of the theory.* …这个理论的看似合理性。**2** ADJ If you say that someone is **plausible**, you mean that they seem to be telling the truth and to be sincere and honest. (人) 看似可信的 ❑ *All I can say is that he was so plausible it wasn't just me that he conned.* 我只能说，他看上去好像那么可信，他骗的可不只我一个。

play ♦♦♦ /pleɪ/ (**plays, playing, played**) **1** V-I When children, animals, or adults **play**, they spend time doing enjoyable things, such as using toys and taking part in games. 玩耍 ❑ *...invite the children over to play.* …邀请孩子们过来玩。❑ *They played in the little garden.* 他们在小花园里玩耍。● N-UNCOUNT **Play** is also a noun. 玩 ❑ *...a few hours of play until the babysitter puts them to bed.* …直到保姆让他们上床睡觉之前的几小时的玩耍。**2** V-RECIP When you **play** a sport, game, or match, you take part in it. 参加 (体育运动、游戏、比赛等) ❑ *While the twins played cards, Leona sat reading.* 那对双胞胎玩牌的时候，利昂娜坐着看书。❑ *I used to play basketball.* 我过去常打篮球。

● N-UNCOUNT **Play** is also a noun. (对运动、游戏、比赛等的) 参加 ❑ *They've got more exciting players and a more exciting style of play.* 他们有更精彩的选手和更精彩的比赛风格。**3** V-T/V-I When one person or team **plays** another or **plays against** them, they compete against them in a sport or game. 与…比赛 ❑ *Dallas will play Green Bay.* 达拉斯队将迎战绿湾队。● N-UNCOUNT **Play** is also a noun. 比赛 ❑ *Fischer won after 5 hours and 41 minutes of play.* 费希尔在5小时41分钟的较量后获胜。**4** V-T If you **play** a joke or a trick on someone, you deceive them or give them a surprise in a way that you think is funny, but that often causes problems for them or annoys them. 开 (玩笑)；搞 (恶作剧) ❑ *Someone had played a trick on her, stretched a piece of string at the top of those steps.* 有人对她搞恶作剧，在那些台阶的顶部拉了一根绳子。**5** V-I If you **play with** an object or with your hair, you keep moving it or touching it with your fingers, perhaps because you are bored or nervous. 摆弄 ❑ *She stared at the floor, idly playing with the strap of her handbag.* 她盯着地板，随手摆弄着手提包的提带。**6** N-COUNT A **play** is a piece of writing performed in a theater, on the radio, or on television. 戏剧 ❑ *It's my favorite Shakespeare play.* 这是我最喜欢的莎士比亚剧。**7** V-T If an actor **plays** a role or character in a play or movie, he or she performs the part of that character. (在戏剧或电影中) 扮演 (角色) ❑ *...Dr. Jekyll and Mr. Hyde, in which he played Hyde.* …他在其中扮演海德的《化身博士》。**8** V-LINK You can use **play** to describe how someone behaves, when they are deliberately behaving in a certain way or like a certain type of person. For example, to **play the innocent**, means to pretend to be innocent, and to **play deaf** means to pretend not to hear something. 假装 ❑ *Hill tried to play the peacemaker.* 希尔试图假扮成和事佬。❑ *She was just playing the devoted mother.* 她只是在装成一位负责的母亲。**9** V-T You can describe how someone deals with a situation by saying that they **play it** in a certain way. For example, if someone **plays it cool**, they keep calm and do not show much emotion, and if someone **plays it straight**, they behave in an honest and direct way. 对待 ❑ *Investors are playing it cautious, and they're playing it smart.* 投资者们在谨慎应对，同时他们也在巧妙应对。**10** V-T/V-I If you **play** a musical instrument or **play** a tune on a musical instrument, or if a musical instrument **plays**, music is produced from it. 演奏 (乐器或乐曲)；奏响 ❑ *Nina had been playing the piano.* 尼娜一直在弹钢琴。❑ *He played for me.* 他为我弹奏。**11** V-T/V-I If you **play** a record, a CD, or a DVD, you put it into a machine and sound and sometimes pictures are produced. If a record, CD, or DVD **is playing**, sound and sometimes pictures are being produced from it. 播放 ❑ *She played her records too loudly.* 她放唱片的声音太大。❑ *There is classical music playing in the background.* 背景中正在播放古典音乐。**12** V-T/V-I If a musician or group of musicians **plays** or **plays** a concert, they perform music for people to listen or dance to. (在音乐会上) 演奏 ❑ *A band was playing.* 一支乐队正在演奏。**13** PHRASE When something **comes into play** or **is brought into play**, it begins to be used or to have an effect. 开始起作用 ❑ *The real existence of a military option will come into play.* 现有的军事手段将开始起作用。**14** PHRASE If something or someone **plays a part** or **plays a role in** a situation, they are involved in it and have an effect on it. 起作用 ❑ *They played a part in the life of their community.* 他们在自己的社区生活中发挥了作用。❑ *The U.N. would play a major role in monitoring a ceasefire.* 联合国将在监督停火方面发挥主要作用。**15** to **play ball** → see **ball** **16** to **play the fool** → see **fool** **17** to **play to the gallery** → see **gallery** **18** to **play hard to get** → see **hard** **19** to **play havoc** → see **havoc** **20** to **play hooky** → see **hooky** **21** to **play host** → see **host** **22** to **play possum** → see **possum** **23** to **play safe** → see **safe**

→ see **DVD, lottery, theater**

▸ **play around** **1** PHRASAL VERB If you **play around**, you behave in a silly way to amuse yourself or other people. 胡闹 [INFORMAL] ❑ *Stop playing around and eat!* 别胡闹了，吃饭吧！❑ *There was no doubt*

P

he was serious, it wasn't just playing around. 无疑，他是认真的，而不是在闹着玩。 2 PHRASAL VERB If you **play around with** a problem or an arrangement of objects, you try different ways of organizing it in order to find the best solution or arrangement. 对…尝试不同方法以找到最佳方案 [INFORMAL] ❑ *I can play around with the pictures in all sorts of ways to make them more eye-catching.* 我可以试着用各种不同的方式来摆放这些图片，使它们更引人注目。 3 PHRASAL VERB If someone **plays around**, they have sex with people other than the person they are married to or having a serious relationship with. 鬼混(和配偶以外的人发生性关系) [INFORMAL] ❑ *Up to 75 percent of married men may be playing around.* 75%以上的已婚男人可能有外遇。 ❑ *Robert was playing around with another woman.* 罗伯特正和另一个女人厮混。

▸ **play at** 1 PHRASAL VERB If you say that someone **is playing at** something, you disapprove of the fact that they are doing it casually and not very seriously. 把…当儿戏 [no passive] [DISAPPROVAL] ❑ *We were still playing at war – dropping leaflets instead of bombs.* 我们仍然在把战争当儿戏——在空投传单而不是在投炸弹。 2 PHRASAL VERB If someone, especially a child, **plays at** being someone or doing something, they pretend to be that person or do that thing as a game. 扮…玩 [no passive] ❑ *Ed played at being a pirate.* 埃德假扮海盗。 3 PHRASAL VERB If you do not know what someone **is playing at**, you do not understand what they are doing or what they are trying to achieve. 搞(什么) [INFORMAL] ❑ *She began to wonder what he was playing at.* 她开始纳闷他在搞什么。

▸ **play back** PHRASAL VERB When you **play back** a tape or film, you listen to the sounds or watch the pictures after recording them. 回放(磁带、电影) ❑ *He bought an answering machine that plays back his messages when he calls.* 他买了一台可以在他打过去时回放给他的留言的电话应答机。 ❑ *Ted might benefit from hearing his own voice recorded and played back.* 特德也许能从听到自己声音的录音回放中受益。

▸ **play down** PHRASAL VERB If you **play down** something, you try to make people believe that it is not particularly important. 贬低 ❑ *Western diplomats have played down the significance of the reports.* 西方的外交官们已贬低了这些报告的重要性。

▸ **play on** PHRASAL VERB If you **play on** someone's fears, weaknesses, or faults, you deliberately use them in order to persuade that person to do something, or to achieve what you want. 有意利用(别人的恐惧、弱点或过错) ❑ *...a campaign which plays on the population's fear of change.* …一场有意利用人们对变化的恐惧的运动。

▸ **play up** PHRASAL VERB If you **play up** something, you emphasize it and try to make people believe that it is important. 强调 ❑ *The media played up the prospects for a settlement.* 媒体夸大了和解的前景。

play·er ♦♦♦ /pleɪər/ (**players**) 1 N-COUNT A **player** in a sport or game is a person who takes part, either as a job or for fun. 选手 ❑ *...his greatness as a player.* …他作为运动员的伟大。 ❑ *She was a good golfer and tennis player.* 她曾是一名优秀的高尔夫球手和网球运动员。 2 N-COUNT You can use **player** to refer to a musician. For example, a **piano player** is someone who plays the piano. 演奏者 ❑ *...a professional trumpet player.* …一个职业小号手。 3 N-COUNT If a person, country, or organization is a **player in** something, they are involved in it and important in it. 重要参与者 ❑ *Big business has become a major player in the art market.* 大公司已经成为艺术市场中的重要参与者。 4 N-COUNT You can refer to a person who spends a lot of time enjoying themselves, especially by having a lot of sexual relationships, as a **player**. 寻欢作乐者 [AM, INFORMAL] ❑ *He was a ladies' man. A cheater. A player.* 他曾是个花花公子，一个骗子，一个四处寻欢作乐的浪子。 5 → see also **CD player, record player**

→ see **chess, football, soccer**

play·ful /pleɪfəl/ 1 ADJ A **playful** gesture or person is friendly or humorous. 闹着玩的 ❑ *...a playful kiss on the tip of his nose.* …在他鼻尖上的戏吻。 ❑ *...a playful fight.* …一场闹着玩的打闹。 ● **play·ful·ly** ADV 闹着玩地 ❑ *She pushed him away playfully.* 她开玩笑地将他推开。 ● **play·ful·ness** N-UNCOUNT 顽皮 ❑ *...the child's natural playfulness.* …那个孩子天生的顽皮。 2 ADJ A **playful** animal is lively and cheerful. 顽皮的 ❑ *...a playful puppy.* …一只顽皮的小狗。

play·ground /pleɪgraʊnd/ (**playgrounds**) N-COUNT A **playground** is a piece of land, at school or in a public area, where children can play. 游戏场 ❑ *...a seven-year-old boy playing in a school playground.* …一个在学校操场上玩耍的7岁男孩。

→ see **park**

play·group /pleɪgrup/ (**playgroups**) also **play group** N-COUNT A **playgroup** is an informal school for very young children, where they learn things by playing. (幼儿)游戏组 [also prep N]

play·ing card (**playing cards**) N-COUNT **Playing cards** are thin pieces of cardboard with numbers or pictures printed on them that are used to play various games. 扑克牌 ❑ *...a deck of playing cards.* …一副扑克牌。

play·ing field (**playing fields**) 1 N-COUNT A **playing field** is a large area of grass where people play sports. 运动草场 ❑ *Jefferson County has three grass playing fields for 18 varsity football teams.* 杰斐逊县有3个运动草场，供18支大学足球队使用。 2 PHRASE You talk about **a level playing field** to mean a situation that is fair, because no competitor or opponent in it has an advantage over another. 平等竞争环境 ❑ *American businessmen ask for a level playing field when they compete with foreign companies.* 美国商人与外国公司竞争时要求平等竞争的环境。

play·list /pleɪlɪst/ (**playlists**) N-COUNT A **playlist** is a list of songs, albums, and artists that a radio station broadcasts. (电台的)音乐播放列表 ❑ *The radio station's playlist is dominated by top-selling youth-orientated groups.* 这个广播电台主要播放面向年轻人的乐队所演唱的畅销曲目。

play·off ♦♦◇ /pleɪɔf/ (**playoffs**) 1 N-COUNT A **playoff** is an extra game that is played to decide the winner of a sports competition when two or more people have the same score. 加时赛 ❑ *Nick Faldo was beaten by Peter Baker in a playoff.* 尼克·福尔多在加时赛中被彼得·贝克击败。 2 N-COUNT You use **playoffs** to refer to a series of games that are played to decide the winner of a championship. 夺标决赛 ❑ *It's been a long time since these two teams faced each other in the playoffs.* 这两个队已经有很长时间没在夺标决赛中相遇了。

Play·Sta·tion /pleɪsteɪʃən/ (**PlayStations**) N-VAR A **PlayStation** is a type of games console. 游戏站(一种游戏机) [COMPUTING, TRADEMARK] ❑ *He spends most of his pocket money on PlayStation games.* 他将大部分的零花钱花在买游戏站的游戏上。

play·wright /pleɪraɪt/ (**playwrights**) N-COUNT A **playwright** is a person who writes plays. 剧作家

★ **pla·za** /plɑzə, plæzə/ (**plazas**) 1 N-COUNT A **plaza** is an open square in a city. (城市中的)露天广场 ❑ *Across the busy plaza, vendors sell hot dogs and croissant sandwiches.* 忙碌的露天广场对面，小贩们在卖热狗和新月形面包三明治。 2 N-COUNT A **plaza** is a group of stores or buildings that are joined together or share common areas. (店铺或建筑毗邻的)广场 [AM] ❑ *...a new retail plaza.* …一个新的零售广场。

★ **plea** /pli/ (**pleas**) 1 N-COUNT A **plea** is an appeal or request for something, made in an intense or emotional way. 恳求 [JOURNALISM] ❑ *Mr. Nicholas made his emotional plea for help in solving the killing.* 尼古拉斯先生发出了令人感动的呼吁，恳求帮助破解这桩杀人案。 2 N-COUNT In a court of law, a person's **plea** is the answer that they give when they have been charged with a crime, saying whether or not they are guilty of that crime. (法庭上表明是否认罪的)抗辩 ❑ *The judge questioned him about his guilty plea.* 法官就他的认罪答辩对他提出质疑。 ❑ *We will enter a plea of not guilty.* 我们将进行无罪抗辩。 3 N-COUNT A **plea** is a reason given, to a court of law or to other people, as an excuse for doing something or for not doing something. (向法庭或其他人说明是否做某事的)托辞 ❑ *Phillips murdered his wife, but got off on a plea of insanity.* 菲利普斯谋杀了自己的妻子，但以精神错乱为由逃脱了罪责。

→ see **trial**

★ **plead** /plid/ (**pleads, pleading, pleaded, pled**) 1 V-I If you **plead with** someone to do something, you ask them in an intense, emotional way to do it. 恳求 ❑ *The lady pleaded with her daughter to come back home.* 那位女士恳求她的女儿回家。 ❑ *He was kneeling on the floor pleading for mercy.* 他正跪在地板上请求宽恕。 2 V-I When someone charged with a crime **pleads guilty** or **not guilty** in a court of law, they officially state that they are guilty or not guilty of the crime. 表示服罪/不服罪 ❑ *Morris had pleaded guilty to robbery.* 莫里斯已经承认犯有抢劫罪。 3 V-T If you **plead the case** or **cause** of someone or something, you speak out in their support or defense. 为…辩护 ❑ *He appeared before the committee to plead his case.* 他出现在委员会上为他的案子辩护。 4 V-T If you **plead** a particular thing as the reason for doing or not doing something, you give it as your excuse. 以…为借口 ❑ *Mr. Giles pleads ignorance as his excuse.* 贾尔斯先生以不知情作为他的借口。

plead·ing /plidɪŋ/ (**pleadings**) 1 ADJ A **pleading** expression or gesture shows someone that you want something very much.

恳求的 ❑ ...*his pleading eyes.* …他恳求的目光。 ❑ ...*the pleading expression on her face.* …她脸上恳求的表情。 2 N-UNCOUNT **Pleading** is asking someone for something you want very much, in an intense or emotional way. 恳求 [also N in pl] ❑ *He simply ignored Sid's pleading.* 他完全不理会锡德的恳求。

pleas·ant ♦◇◇ /plɛzᵊnt/ (**pleasanter, pleasantest**) 1 ADJ Something that is **pleasant** is nice, enjoyable, or attractive. 令人愉快的 ❑ *I've got a pleasant little apartment.* 我有一套舒适的小公寓。 ● **pleas·ant·ly** ADV 令人愉快地 ❑ *We talked pleasantly of old times.* 我们愉快地谈论着过去的时光。 2 ADJ Someone who is **pleasant** is friendly and likeable. 友善的 ❑ *The woman had a pleasant face.* 那个女人长着一张和善的脸。

> **Thesaurus** *pleasant* 另参见:
> ADJ. agreeable, cheerful, delightful, likable, friendly, nice; (*ant.*) unpleasant 2

please ♦♦◇ /pliz/ (**pleases, pleasing, pleased**) 1 ADV You say **please** when you are politely asking or inviting someone to do something. 请 (用于礼貌地请求或邀请某人做某事) [ADV with cl] [POLITENESS] ❑ *Can you help us please?* 能请你帮助我们吗? ❑ *Please come in.* 请进。 ❑ *Can we have the bill please?* 请给我们账单好吗? 2 ADV You say **please** when you are accepting something politely. 有请 (用于礼貌地接受某物) [FORMULAE] ❑ *"Tea?"—"Yes, please."* "要茶吗?" —— "好的, 有请。" 3 CONVENTION You can say **please** to indicate that you want someone to stop doing something or stop speaking. You would say this if, for example, what they are doing or saying makes you angry or upset. 求你了 (请求别人停止做某事或停止讲话) [FEELINGS] ❑ *Please, Mary, this is all so unnecessary.* 求你了, 玛丽, 这一切根本没有必要。 4 CONVENTION You can say **please** in order to attract someone's attention politely. 对不起 (用以引起某人注意) [POLITENESS] ❑ *Please, Miss Smith, a moment.* 对不起, 史密斯小姐, 稍等。 5 V-T/V-I If someone or something **pleases** you, they make you feel happy and satisfied. 使高兴; 讨好 ❑ *More than anything, I want to please you.* 最重要的是, 我想让你高兴。 ❑ *It pleased him to talk to her.* 和她谈话让他高兴。 ❑ *He appeared anxious to please.* 他似乎急于讨好。 6 PHRASE You use **please** in expressions such as **as she pleases, whatever you please**, and **anything he pleases** to indicate that someone can do or have whatever they want. 随 (某人) 喜欢 ❑ *Women should be free to dress and act as they please.* 女人应该有自由随自己的意愿着装和行事。 ❑ *He does whatever he pleases.* 他想做什么就做什么。

pleased ♦◇◇ /plizd/ 1 ADJ If you are **pleased**, you are happy about something or satisfied with something. 开心的 ❑ *Felicity seemed pleased at the suggestion.* 费利西蒂似乎对这个建议很满意。 ❑ *I think he's going to be pleased that we identified the real problems.* 我想他会为我们找到真正的问题所在高兴的。 2 ADJ If you say you will be **pleased to** do something, you are saying in a polite way that you are willing to do it. 乐意 (做某事) 的 [v-link ADJ to-inf] [POLITENESS] ❑ *We will be pleased to answer any questions you may have.* 我们将愿意回答你可能有的任何问题。 3 ADJ You can tell someone that you are **pleased with** something they have done in order to express your approval. 满意的 [v-link ADJ] [FEELINGS] ❑ *I'm pleased with the way things have been going.* 我对事情的进展状况感到满意。 ❑ *I am very pleased about the result.* 我对结果很满意。 ❑ *We are pleased that the problems have been resolved.* 我们很高兴问题已经得到了解决。 4 ADJ When you are about to give someone some news that you know will please them, you can say that you are **pleased to** tell them the news or that they will be **pleased to** hear it. 高兴的 (告诉或听到消息) [v-link ADJ to-inf] ❑ *I'm pleased to say that he is now doing well.* 我很高兴地告诉你, 他现在很好。 5 ADJ In official letters, people often say they will be **pleased to** do something, as a polite way of introducing what they are going to do or inviting people to do something. 愿意的 (用于官方信函中礼貌地介绍打算要做的事或邀请人们做某事) [v-link ADJ to-inf] [POLITENESS] ❑ *We will be pleased to delete the charge from the original invoice.* 我们将愿意将这笔收费从原来的发票中删去。 6 PHRASE If someone seems very satisfied with something they have done, you can say that they are **pleased with themselves**, especially if you think they are more satisfied than they should be. 洋洋自得 ❑ *"Sophie was glad to see you," he said, pleased with himself again for having remembered her name.* "索菲很高兴见到你," 他说, 为自己记住了她的名字又暗自得意。 7 CONVENTION You can say "**Pleased to meet you**" as a polite way of greeting someone who you are meeting for the first time. 很高兴见到你 (用于初次见面问候对方) [FORMULAE]

pleas·ing /plizɪŋ/ ADJ Something that is **pleasing** gives you pleasure and satisfaction. 令人愉快的 ❑ *This area of France has a pleasing climate in August.* 法国这个地区在8月气候宜人。 ❑ *Such a view is pleasing.* 这样一种风景令人愉快。 ● **pleas·ing·ly** ADV 令人愉快地 ❑ *The interior design is pleasingly simple.* 这种室内设计简约宜人。

pleas·ur·able /plɛʒərəbᵊl/ ADJ **Pleasurable** experiences or sensations are pleasant and enjoyable. 令人愉悦的 (经历或感受) ❑ *The most pleasurable experience of the evening was the wonderful fireworks display.* 那天晚上最令人愉悦的经历是精彩的焰火表演。

pleas·ure ♦◇◇ /plɛʒər/ (**pleasures**) 1 N-UNCOUNT If something gives you **pleasure**, you get a feeling of happiness, satisfaction, or enjoyment from it. 愉悦 ❑ *Watching sports gave him great pleasure.* 观看体育运动带给他极大的愉悦。 ❑ *Everybody takes pleasure in eating.* 每个人都在吃中获得愉悦。 2 N-UNCOUNT **Pleasure** is the activity of enjoying yourself, especially rather than working or doing what you have a duty to do. 娱乐 ❑ *He mixed business and pleasure in a perfect and dynamic way.* 他把工作和娱乐以一种完美而活跃的方式结合了起来。 3 N-COUNT A **pleasure** is an activity, experience, or aspect of something that you find very enjoyable or satisfying. 乐事 ❑ *Watching TV is our only pleasure.* 看电视是我们惟一的乐趣。 ❑ ...*the pleasure of seeing a smiling face.* …看到一张笑脸的那种愉悦。 4 CONVENTION If you meet someone for the first time, you can say, as a way of being polite, that it is **a pleasure to meet** them. You can also ask for **the pleasure of** someone's **company** as a polite and formal way of inviting them somewhere. 荣幸 (用于初次见面礼貌地打招呼) [POLITENESS] ❑ *"A pleasure to meet you, sir," he said.* "很荣幸见到您, 先生," 他说。 5 CONVENTION You can say "**It's a pleasure**" or "**My pleasure**" as a polite way of replying to someone who has just thanked you for doing something. 乐意效劳 (用作回应别人的感谢时的礼貌用语) [FORMULAE] ❑ *"Thanks very much anyhow."—"It's a pleasure."* "无论如何, 非常感谢你。" —— "不客气。"

> **Word Partnership** *pleasure* 的常用搭配:
> ADJ. **great** pleasure, **intense** pleasure, **simple** pleasure 1 2
> **sexual** pleasure 3

pleat /plit/ (**pleats**) N-COUNT A **pleat** in a piece of clothing is a permanent fold that is made in the cloth by folding one part over the other and sewing across the top end of the fold. 褶 ❑ *Her skirt hangs in perfect wide pleats.* 她的裙子打着漂亮的宽褶自然下垂。

pleat·ed /plitɪd/ ADJ A **pleated** piece of clothing has pleats in it. 有褶的 ❑ ...*a short white pleated skirt.* …一条白色的有褶短裙。

pledge ♦◇◇ /plɛdʒ/ (**pledges, pledging, pledged**) 1 N-COUNT When someone makes a **pledge**, they make a serious promise that they will do something. 誓言 ❑ *The meeting ended with a pledge to step up cooperation between the six states of the region.* 会议以加快该地区6个州之间合作的承诺结束。 2 V-T When someone **pledges to** do something, they promise in a serious way to do it. When they **pledge** something, they promise to give it. 保证 (做某事); 保证给予 (某物) ❑ *The Communists have pledged to support the opposition's motion.* 共产党员们已经承诺支持反对党的动议。 ❑ *Philip pledges support and offers to help in any way that he can.* 菲利普承诺给予支持并提供力所能及的帮助。 3 V-T If you **pledge** a sum of money to an organization or activity, you promise to pay that amount of money to it at a particular time or over a particular period. 承诺支付 (一笔款) ❑ *The French president is pledging $150 million in French aid next year.* 法国总统承诺来年将拨款1.5亿美元用于法国援助。 ● N-COUNT **Pledge** is also a noun. 承诺拨款 ❑ ...*a pledge of forty two million dollars a month.* …一个每月拨款4200万美元的承诺。 4 V-T If you **pledge yourself to** something, you commit yourself to following a particular course of action or to supporting a particular person, group, or idea. 保证 ❑ *The president pledged himself to increase taxes for the rich but not the middle classes.* 总统保证增加富人而不是中产阶级的税收。 5 V-T If you **pledge** something such as a valuable possession or a sum of money, you leave it with someone as a guarantee that you will repay money that you have borrowed. 抵押 ❑ *He asked her to pledge the house as security for a loan.* 他要她抵押房子作为贷款担保。

> **Thesaurus** *pledge* 另参见:
> N. agreement, covenant, guarantee, promise 1
> V. contract, guarantee, promise, swear, vow 2 3

▲ **ple·na·ry** /plinəri, plɛn-/ (**plenaries**) ADJ A **plenary session** or **plenary meeting** is one that is attended by everyone who has the right to attend. 全体出席的 [ADJ n] [TECHNICAL] ❑ ...*a plenary session*

P

of the Central Committee. …一次中央委员会全会。● N-COUNT **Plenary** is also a noun. 全体会议 ❑ *There'll be another plenary at the end of the afternoon after the workshop.* 傍晚专题讨论会后将另有一个全体会议。

Word Link *plen ≈ full : plentiful, plenty, replenish*

plen·ti·ful /plɛ̱ntɪfəl/ ADJ Things that are **plentiful** exist in such large amounts or numbers that there is enough for people's wants or needs. 富足的 ❑ *Fish are plentiful in the lake.* 这个湖里鱼很多。

plen·ty ♦◇◇ /plɛ̱nti/ QUANT If there is **plenty of** something, there is a large amount of it. If there are **plenty of** things, there are many of them. **Plenty** is used especially to indicate that there is enough of something, or more than you need. 大量的; 充裕的 ❑ *There was still plenty of time to take Jill out for pizza.* 还有充裕的时间带吉尔出去吃比萨。❑ *Most businesses face plenty of competition.* 多数企业都面临大量的竞争。● PRON **Plenty** is also a pronoun. 充裕 ❑ *I don't believe in long interviews. Fifteen minutes is plenty.* 我不相信长时间的面试会有什么好处，15分钟就足够了。

Thesaurus *plenty* 另参见：
QUANT. abundance, capacity, quantity; *(ant.)* scarcity

pletho·ra /plɛ̱θərə/ N-SING A **plethora of** something is a large amount of it, especially an amount of it that is greater than you need, want, or can cope with. 过剩 [FORMAL] ❑ *A plethora of new operators will be allowed to enter the market.* 过多的新经营者将获准进入市场。

pli·able /plaɪ̱əbᵊl/ ADJ If something is **pliable**, you can bend it easily without cracking or breaking it. 柔韧的 ❑ *As your baby grows bigger, his bones become less pliable.* 随着你的宝宝慢慢长大，他的骨头柔韧性会变弱。

pli·ers /plaɪ̱ərz/ N-PLURAL **Pliers** are a tool with two handles at one end and two hard, flat, metal parts at the other. Pliers are used for holding or pulling out things such as nails, or for bending or cutting wire. 钳子 [also "a pair of" N]
→ see **tool**

★ **plight** /plaɪ̱t/ (**plights**) N-COUNT If you refer to someone's **plight**, you mean that they are in a difficult or distressing situation that is full of problems. 困境 ❑ *The nation saw the plight of the farmers, whose crops had died.* 全国上下都看到了农民因庄稼死亡而陷入困境。

Thesaurus *plight* 另参见：
N. difficulty, dilemma, problem, situation

P

plod /plɒ̱d/ (**plods, plodding, plodded**) 1 V-I If someone **plods**, they walk slowly and heavily. 缓慢沉重地走 ❑ *Crowds of people plodded around in yellow plastic raincoats.* 一群群身穿黄色塑料雨衣的人在四下里吃力地走着。2 V-I If you say that someone **plods on** or **plods along** with a job, you mean that the job is taking a long time. 苦干 ❑ *He is plodding on with negotiations.* 他正进行艰苦的谈判。

plot ♦◇◇ /plɒ̱t/ (**plots, plotting, plotted**) 1 N-COUNT A **plot** is a secret plan by a group of people to do something that is illegal or wrong, usually against a person or a government. 阴谋 ❑ *Security forces have uncovered a plot to overthrow the government.* 安全部队已经揭穿了一个推翻政府的阴谋。2 V-T If people **plot to** do something or **plot** something that is illegal or wrong, they plan secretly to do it. 密谋 ❑ *Prosecutors in the trial allege the defendants plotted to overthrow the government.* 审判的公诉人指称被告曾密谋推翻政府。❑ *The military were plotting a coup.* 军方当时正在密谋政变。3 V-T When people **plot** a strategy or a course of action, they carefully plan each step of it. 制订 ❑ *Yesterday's meeting was intended to plot a survival strategy for the party.* 昨天的会议旨在制订该党的生存策略。4 N-VAR The **plot** of a movie, novel, or play is the connected series of events which make up the story. (电影、小说、戏剧的) 情节 ❑ *He began to tell me the plot of his new book.* 他开始向我讲述他新书的情节。5 N-COUNT A **plot of** land is a small piece of land, especially one that has been measured or marked out for a special purpose, such as building houses or growing vegetables. (有特定用途的) 小块土地 ❑ *I thought that I'd buy myself a small plot of land and build a house on it.* 我觉得我应该给自己买一小块地，在上面盖一所房子。6 V-T When someone **plots** something on a graph, they mark certain points on it and then join the points up. (在曲线图上) 绘制 ❑ *We plotted about eight points on the graph.* 我们在图表上绘出了大约有八个点的曲线。7 V-T When someone **plots** the position or course of a plane or ship, they mark it on a map using instruments to obtain accurate information. (在地图上) 标绘 (飞机或船只的位置和航线) ❑ *We were trying to plot the course of the submarine.* 我们当时正试图标绘出那艘潜艇的航线。8 V-T If someone **plots** the progress or development of something, they make a diagram or a plan which shows how it has developed in order to give some indication of how it will develop in the future. 用图表展示 (进展) ❑ *They used a computer to plot the movements of everyone in the police station on December 24, 1990.* 他们使用计算机绘制了图表，来显示1990年12月24日警察局中每个人的行动。

plough /plaʊ̱/ [BRIT] → see **plow**

plow /plaʊ̱/ (**plows, plowing, plowed**)
in BRIT, use **plough**

1 N-COUNT A **plow** is a large farming tool with sharp blades that is pulled across the soil to turn it over, usually before seeds are planted. 犁 ❑ *There are new tractors and new plows in the machinery lot.* 机器设备场里有新拖拉机和新耕犁。2 → see also **snowplow** 3 V-T When someone **plows** an area of land, they turn over the soil using a plow. 犁 (地) ❑ *They were no longer using mules and horses to plow their fields.* 他们那时已不再用骡子和马来犁地了。
→ see **barn**

▸ **plow back** PHRASAL VERB If profits **are plowed back into** a business, they are used to increase the size of the business or to improve it. 把…再投资 [usu passive] [BUSINESS] ❑ *...cash profits that are quickly plowed back into the market.* …很快又投资到市场中去的现金收益。

ploy /plɔ̱ɪ/ (**ploys**) N-COUNT A **ploy** is a way of behaving that someone plans carefully and secretly in order to gain an advantage for themselves. 计策; 手段 ❑ *Christmas should be a time of excitement and wonder, not a cynical marketing ploy.* 圣诞节应该是激动人心的奇妙时刻，而不是自私牟利的营销计谋。

pls. **Pls.** is a written abbreviation for **please**. **please**的缩写 ❑ *Have you moved yet? Pls. advise address, phone no., etc.* 你已经搬家了吗？请告知你的地址、电话号码等。

▲ **pluck** /plʌ̱k/ (**plucks, plucking, plucked**) 1 V-T If you **pluck** a fruit, flower, or leaf, you take it between your fingers and pull it in order to remove it from its stalk where it is growing. 采摘 [WRITTEN] ❑ *I plucked a lemon from the tree.* 我从树上摘下一枚柠檬。2 V-T If you **pluck** something from somewhere, you take it between your fingers and pull it sharply from where it is. 拔; 扯 [WRITTEN] ❑ *He plucked the cigarette from his mouth and tossed it out into the street.* 他从嘴上扯下了香烟，扔在外面的街上。❑ *He plucked the baby out of my arms.* 他从我的怀中夺走了孩子。3 V-T If you **pluck** a guitar or other musical instrument, you pull the strings with your fingers and let them go, so that they make a sound. 弹; 拨 (乐器) ❑ *Nell was plucking a harp.* 内尔那时在弹竖琴。4 V-T If you **pluck** a chicken or other dead bird, you pull its feathers out to prepare it for cooking. 拔除 (禽类的羽毛) ❑ *She looked relaxed as she plucked a chicken.* 她拔鸡毛的时候看上去很轻松。5 V-T If a woman **plucks** her **eyebrows**, she pulls out some of the hairs using tweezers. (用镊子) 拔 (眉毛) ❑ *You've plucked your eyebrows at last!* 你终于修了眉！6 PHRASE If you **pluck up the courage to** do something that you feel nervous about, you make an effort to be brave enough to do it. 鼓起勇气 ❑ *It took me about two hours to pluck up the courage to call.* 大约两小时后我才鼓起勇气打了电话。

plug /plʌ̱g/ (**plugs, plugging, plugged**) 1 N-COUNT A **plug** on a piece of electrical equipment is a small plastic object with two or three metal pins that fit into the holes of an electric outlet and connects the equipment to the electricity supply. 插头 ❑ *I used to go around and take every plug out at night.* 过去我常在夜里巡视一番，拔掉所有的插头。2 N-COUNT A **plug** is an electric outlet. 插座 [INFORMAL] ❑ *Then Bob spotted the problem - the plug in the wall hadn't been switched on.* 然后鲍勃发现了问题——墙上的插座没有打开。3 N-COUNT A **plug** is a thick, circular piece of rubber or plastic that you use to block the hole in a bathtub or sink when it is filled with water. (浴缸、洗涤槽的) 塞子 ❑ *She put the plug in the sink and filled it with cold water.* 她用塞子塞住水池，并将其注满冷水。4 N-COUNT A **plug** is a small, round piece of wood, plastic, or wax that is used to block holes. (木头、塑料或腊制的) 塞子 ❑ *A plug had been inserted in the drill hole.* 那个钻孔里已经塞上了塞子。5 V-T If you **plug** a hole, you block it with something. 堵; 塞 ❑ *Crews are working to plug a major oil leak.* 机组人员正在努力堵一个漏油的大洞。6 V-T If someone **plugs** a commercial product, especially a book or a movie, they praise it in order to encourage people to buy it or see it because they have an interest in it doing well. 大力宣传 (商品，

尤为图书或电影) ❑ *We did not want people on the show who are purely interested in plugging a book or movie.* 我们不想让那种纯粹只对宣传某书籍或电影感兴趣的人上节目。 ● N-COUNT **Plug** is also a noun. 大力宣传 ❑ *Let's do this show tonight and it'll be a great plug, a great promotion.* 让我们今晚进行这场演出吧。这将会是一场盛大而绝妙的宣传。 **7** PHRASE If someone in a position of power **pulls the plug on** a project or **on** someone's activities, they use their power to stop them from continuing. (利用权力) 终止(方案或活动) ❑ *The banks have the power to pull the plug on the project.* 银行有权终止该项目。

▶ **plug in** or **plug into** **1** PHRASAL VERB If you **plug** a piece of electrical equipment **into** an electricity supply or if you **plug it in**, you push its plug into an electric outlet so that it can work. (将插头插入插座) 给…接通电源 ❑ *They plugged in their tape-recorders.* 他们给磁带录音机接通了电源。 ❑ *I had a TV set but there was no place to plug it in.* 那时我有一台电视机，但没有接通电源的插座。 **2** PHRASAL VERB If you **plug** one piece of electrical equipment **into** another or if you **plug it in**, you make it work by connecting the two. 将…与…接通 ❑ *They plugged their guitars into amplifiers.* 他们将吉他接到了扩音器上。 **3** PHRASAL VERB If one piece of electrical equipment **plugs in** or **plugs into** another piece of electrical equipment, it works by being connected by an electrical cord or lead to an electricity supply or to the other piece of equipment. (用插头) 与电源接通; (用导线) 和另一电器相接 ❑ *The device looks like a video recorder and plugs into the home television and stereo system.* 该装置看上去像录像机，连接在家用电视机和立体音箱上。 ❑ *They plug into a laptop, desktop, or handheld computer.* 它们可以连接在便携式电脑、台式电脑或掌上电脑上。 **4** PHRASAL VERB If you **plug** something **into** a hole, you push it into the hole. 将…塞入 ❑ *Her instructor plugged live bullets into the gun's chamber.* 她的教官将实弹装入了枪膛。 **5** → see also **plug-in**

plug-and-play ADJ **Plug-and-play** is used to describe computer equipment, for example, a printer, that is ready to use immediately when you connect it to a computer. 即插即用的 [ADJ n] [COMPUTING] ❑ *...a plug-and-play USB camera.* …一台具有即插即用USB端口的照相机。

plug-in (**plug-ins**) **1** ADJ A **plug-in** machine is a piece of electrical equipment that is operated by being connected to an electricity supply or to another piece of electrical equipment by means of a plug. (指接上电源或另一电子设备就可以工作的) 插入式的; 带插头接点的 [ADJ n] ❑ *...a plug-in radio.* …一台可外接电源的收音机。 **2** N-COUNT A **plug-in** is something such as a piece of software that can be added to a computer system to give extra features or functions. (计算机软件的) 插件 [COMPUTING] ❑ *Some websites make it seem like you need to download a plug-in or program to access the site.* 有些网站设计得似乎需要下载一个插件或程序才能进入访问。

▲ **plum** /plʌm/ (**plums**) **1** N-COUNT A **plum** is a small, sweet fruit with a smooth purple, red, or yellow skin and a pit in the middle. 李子 **2** COLOR Something that is **plum** or **plum-colored** is a dark reddish-purple color. 紫红色的 ❑ *...plum-colored silk.* …紫红色的丝绸。

▲ **plumb·er** /plʌmər/ (**plumbers**) N-COUNT A **plumber** is a person whose job is to connect and repair things such as water and drainage pipes, bathtubs, and toilets. 管子工; 水暖工

plumb·ing /plʌmɪŋ/ **1** N-UNCOUNT The **plumbing** in a building consists of the water and drainage pipes, bathtubs, and toilets in it. 管道系统; 水暖设备 ❑ *The wiring and the plumbing were sound but everything else had to be cleaned up.* 电路和管道都还行，但其他的都必须清理。 **2** N-UNCOUNT **Plumbing** is the work of connecting and repairing things such as water and drainage pipes, baths, and toilets. 管道工程 ❑ *She learned the rudiments of bricklaying, wiring, and plumbing.* 她学过一些砌砖、布线和管道工程的基本技术。
→ see Word Web: **plumbing**

▲ **plume** /plum/ (**plumes**) **1** N-COUNT A **plume of** smoke, dust, fire, or water is a large quantity of it that rises into the air in a column. 一缕(烟雾、尘土等); 一股(水柱); 一道(火光) ❑ *The rising plume of black smoke could be seen all over Kabul.* 那股升起的黑烟整个喀布尔都可以看到。 **2** N-COUNT A **plume** is a large, soft bird's feather. 大而柔的羽毛 ❑ *...broad straw hats decorated with ostrich plumes.* …装饰着鸵鸟毛的宽沿草帽。

plum·met /plʌmɪt/ (**plummets, plummeting, plummeted**) V-I If an amount, rate, or price **plummets**, it decreases quickly by a large amount. (数量、比率、价格) 暴跌 [JOURNALISM] ❑ *In Tokyo share prices have plummeted for the sixth successive day.* 在东京，股价已经是连续第6天暴跌了。 ❑ *The president's popularity has plummeted to an all-time low in recent weeks.* 总统的声望最近几周已骤然跌至前所未有的低点。

▲ **plump** /plʌmp/ (**plumper, plumpest, plumps, plumping, plumped**) **1** ADJ You can describe someone or something as **plump** to indicate that they are somewhat fat or rounded. 丰满的 ❑ *Maria was a pretty little thing, small and plump with a mass of curly hair.* 玛丽亚是个漂亮的小家伙，小小的，胖乎乎的，生着一头浓密的卷发。 ❑ *He pushed a plump little hand toward me.* 他向我伸出一只胖乎乎的小手。 **2** V-T If you **plump** a pillow or cushion, you shake it and hit it gently so that it goes back into a rounded shape. 使(枕头、靠垫等)蓬松 ❑ *She patted all the seats and plumped all the cushions.* 她把所有的坐垫和靠垫都拍得松松的。 ● PHRASAL VERB **Plump up** means the same as **plump**. 使(枕头、靠垫等) 蓬松 ❑ *"You need to rest," she told him reassuringly as she moved to plump up his pillows.* "你需要休息，" 她劝他说，一边走过去将他的枕头拍得松松的。

▲ **plun·der** /plʌndər/ (**plunders, plundering, plundered**) V-T If someone **plunders** a place or **plunders** things **from** a place, they steal things from it. 掠夺 [LITERARY] ❑ *He plundered the palaces and ransacked the treasuries.* 他洗劫了各个宫殿，将那些财宝掠夺一空。 ❑ *She faces charges of helping to plunder her country's treasury of billions of dollars.* 她面临协助从窃取国库中数十亿美元的指控。 ● N-UNCOUNT **Plunder** is also a noun. 掠夺 ❑ *...a guerrilla group infamous for torture and plunder.* …一支以酷刑和掠夺而臭名昭著的游击队。

plunge ♦◇◇ /plʌndʒ/ (**plunges, plunging, plunged**) **1** V-I If something or someone **plunges** in a particular direction, especially into water, they fall, rush, or throw themselves in that direction. 纵身跳向; 猛冲向 ❑ *At least 50 people died when a bus plunged into a river.* 一辆公共汽车冲进了河里，至少有50人死亡。 ● N-COUNT **Plunge** is also a noun. 投入(水中); 俯冲 ❑ *...a plunge into cold water.* …向着冰冷的水中的纵身一跳。 **2** V-T If you **plunge** an object **into** something, you push it quickly or violently into it. (猛地) 将…推入 ❑ *A soldier plunged a bayonet into his body.* 一名士兵猛地将刺刀刺入了他的身体。 ❑ *She plunged her face into a bowl of cold water.* 她猛地把脸浸入一盆冷水中。 **3** V-T/V-I If a person or thing **is plunged into** a particular state or situation, or if they **plunge into** it, they are suddenly in that state or situation. 使突然陷入; 突然陷入 ❑ *The government's political and economic reforms threaten to plunge the country into chaos.* 该政府的政治和经济改革有可能使这个国家陷入混乱之中。 ❑ *Eddy found himself plunged into a world of brutal violence.* 埃迪发现自己突然陷入了一个残酷暴力的世界。 ● N-COUNT **Plunge** is also a noun. 突然陷入 ❑ *That peace often looked like a brief truce before the next plunge into war.* 那种和平看起来常常像是投入新一轮战争前的短暂停火期。 **4** V-T/V-I If you **plunge into** an activity or **are plunged into**

P

Word Web **plumbing**

Babylonian* homes of 4,000 years ago had **bathrooms** where people bathed themselves with **water**. The waste water **drained** off through a hole in the floor. At about the same time, the Minoans* in Crete* invented the **flush toilet**. It used rain water held in cisterns. The early Egyptians discovered how to make **pipes** out of clay and **basins** out of **copper**. Some homes in ancient Greece contained latrines that drained into a sewer beneath the street. The Romans were the first to use **lead** for **plumbing** purposes. The word "plumbing" comes from *plumbus*, the Latin word for "lead."

Babylonian: from the ancient city of Babylon.
Minoans (3000 BC – 1100 BC): people who lived on Crete.
Crete: an island in the eastern Mediterranean Sea.

it, you suddenly get very involved in it. 使突然开始；突然开始 ❑ *The two men plunged into discussion.* 这两个男人突然投入了讨论。 ❑ *The prince should be plunged into work.* 应该赶紧让王子投入工作。
● N-COUNT **Plunge** is also a noun. 突然开始 ❑ *His sudden plunge into the field of international diplomacy is a major surprise.* 他突然进入了国际外交领域，让人十分意外。 **5** V-I If an amount or rate **plunges**, it decreases quickly and suddenly. 骤降 ❑ *His weight began to plunge.* 他的体重开始骤然下降。 ❑ *The Peso plunged to a new low on the foreign exchange markets yesterday.* 昨天，比索在外汇市场上暴跌到了历史新低。
● N-COUNT **Plunge** is also a noun. 骤降 ❑ *Japan's banks are in trouble because of bad loans and the stock market plunge.* 日本各家银行处于困境，缘于不良贷款以及股市的暴跌。 **6** PHRASE If you **take the plunge**, you decide to do something that you consider difficult or risky. 决定冒险一试 ❑ *If you have been thinking about buying mutual funds, now could be the time to take the plunge.* 如果你一直在考虑购买共同基金，现在也许是冒险一试的时候了。

plu·ral /plʊərəl/ (**plurals**) **1** ADJ The **plural** form of a word is the form that is used when referring to more than one person or thing. 复数的 ❑ *"Data" is the Latin plural form of "datum."* "**Data**"是"**datum**"的拉丁语复数形式。 **2** N-COUNT The **plural** of a noun is the form of it that is used to refer to more than one person or thing. 复数形式 ❑ *What is the plural of "person"?* "**person**"的复数形式是什么？

plu·ral·ism /plʊərəlɪzəm/ N-UNCOUNT If there is **pluralism** within a society, it has many different groups and political parties. 多元化；多样性 [FORMAL] ❑ *...as the country shifts toward political pluralism.* …随着该国转向政治多元化。

plus ♦♦◊ /plʌs/ (**pluses** or **plusses**) **1** CONJ You say **plus** to show that one number or quantity is being added to another. 加 ❑ *...$5 for a small locker, plus a $3 deposit.* …带锁的小柜子$5，外加$3的押金。 **2** ADJ **Plus** before a number or quantity means that the number or quantity is greater than zero. 正的 [ADJ amount] ❑ *The aircraft was subjected to temperatures of minus 65 degrees and plus 120 degrees.* 这架飞机经受过零下65度和零上120度的考验。 **3** CONJ You can use **plus** when mentioning an additional item or fact. 外加 [INFORMAL] ❑ *There's easily enough room for two adults and three children, plus a dog in the trunk.* 有足够的空间容纳2个大人和3个小孩。另外，行李箱里还能容纳1只狗。 **4** ADJ You use **plus** after a number or quantity to indicate that the actual number or quantity is greater than the one mentioned. 略多一些的 [amount ADJ] ❑ *There are only 35 staff to serve 30,000-plus customers.* 只有35名员工为3万多位顾客服务。 **5** ADJ Teachers use **plus** in grading work in schools and colleges. "B plus" is a better grade than "B," but it is not as good as "A." 略好一些的 **6** N-COUNT A **plus** is an advantage or benefit. 优势；益处 [INFORMAL] ❑ *Well-known figures would be a big plus for the new board.* 名人会成为新董事会的一大优势。

P

plush /plʌʃ/ (**plusher, plushest**) ADJ If you describe something as **plush**, you mean that it is very comfortable and expensive. 豪华舒适的 ❑ *...their plush new training facility.* …他们豪华舒适的新训练设施。

plu·to·nium /plutoʊniəm/ N-UNCOUNT **Plutonium** is a radioactive element used especially in nuclear weapons and as a fuel in nuclear power stations. 钚（一种放射性元素）

ply /plaɪ/ (**plies, plying, plied**) **1** V-T If you **ply** someone **with** food or drink, you keep giving them more of it. 不断供给 ❑ *Elsie, who had been told that Maria wasn't well, plied her with food.* 埃尔茜听说玛丽亚身体不好，就不停地给她食物。 **2** V-T If you **ply** someone **with** questions, you keep asking them questions. 盘问 ❑ *Giovanni plied him with questions and comments with the deliberate intention of prolonging his stay.* 乔瓦尼不停地向他问问题并发表意见，故意拖住他。

ply·wood /plaɪwʊd/ N-UNCOUNT **Plywood** is wood that consists of thin layers of wood stuck together. 胶合板 ❑ *...a sheet of plywood.* …一张胶合板。

p.m. /pi ɛm/ also **pm** ADV **p.m.** is used after a number to show that you are referring to a particular time between 12 noon and 12 midnight. Compare **a.m.** 午后（从正午到午夜之间的钟点）[num ADV] ❑ *The spa is open from 7:00 a.m. to 9:00 p.m. every day of the year.* 温泉区全年从早上7:00到晚上9:00开放。

▲**pneu·mo·nia** /nʊmoʊnyə, -moʊniə/ N-UNCOUNT **Pneumonia** is a serious disease that affects your lungs and makes it difficult for you to breathe. 肺炎 ❑ *She nearly died of pneumonia.* 她差点死于肺炎。

poach /poʊtʃ/ (**poaches, poaching, poached**) **1** V-T/V-I If someone **poaches** fish, animals, or birds, they illegally catch them on someone else's property. 偷猎 ❑ *Many national parks set up to provide a refuge for wildlife are regularly invaded by people poaching game.* 很多旨在为野生动物提供庇护的国家公园经常受到偷猎者的入侵。
● **poach·er** N-COUNT (**poachers**) 偷猎者 ❑ *Security cameras have been installed to guard against poachers.* 已经安装了安防摄像机来防范偷猎者。
● **poach·ing** N-UNCOUNT 偷猎行为 ❑ *The poaching of elephants for their tusks could start to decline soon.* 偷猎大象获取象牙的行为可能很快就会开始减少。 **2** V-T If an organization **poaches** members or customers **from** another organization, they secretly or dishonestly persuade them to join them or become their customers. （通过不正当的手段或秘密）挖走（其他组织的成员或顾客）❑ *Companies sometimes poach employees from one another.* 一些公司有时会相互挖走对方的雇员。
● **poach·ing** N-UNCOUNT 挖人 ❑ *The union was accused of poaching.* 该工会被指控有挖人行径。 **3** V-T If someone **poaches** an idea, they dishonestly or illegally use the idea. 窃取（别人的想法）❑ *They've poached all our best ideas.* 他们已经窃取了我们所有最好的想法。 **4** V-T If you **poach** food such as fish, you cook it gently in boiling water, milk, or other liquid. 小火煮 ❑ *Poach the chicken until just cooked.* 把鸡用小火煮到刚刚熟。 ❑ *...a pear poached in red wine.* …用红酒煮过的梨。
● **poach·ing** N-UNCOUNT 烹煮 ❑ *You will need a pot of broth for poaching.* 你需要用一锅汤来煮食物。

PO Box /pi oʊ bɒks/ also **P.O. Box** **PO Box** is used before a number as a kind of address. The Post Office keeps letters addressed to the PO Box until they are collected by the person who has paid for the service. 邮政信箱（用在数字之前）❑ *Send your order and a check to PO Box 2855, Sunnyvale 94087.* 将你的订单和支票寄至桑尼维尔市第2855号信箱，邮编94087。

pock·et ♦◊◊ /pɒkɪt/ (**pockets, pocketing, pocketed**) **1** N-COUNT A **pocket** is a kind of small bag that forms part of a piece of clothing, and that is used for carrying small things such as money or a handkerchief. 衣兜 ❑ *He took his flashlight from his jacket pocket and switched it on.* 他从上衣口袋里拿出手电筒并将其打开。 **2** N-COUNT You can use **pocket** in a lot of different ways to refer to money that people have, get, or spend. For example, if someone gives or pays a lot of money, you can say that they **dig deep into** their **pocket**. If you approve of something because it is very cheap to buy, you can say that it **suits people's pockets**. 财力 ❑ *When you come to choosing a dining table, it really is worth digging deep into your pocket for the best you can afford.* 说到选择餐桌，的确值得尽你的财力买张最好的。 ❑ *...ladies' fashions to suit all shapes, sizes, and pockets.* …适合所有体形、尺寸和价格选择的女士时装。 **3** ADJ You use **pocket** to describe something that is small enough to fit into a pocket, often something that is a smaller version of a larger item. 袖珍的 [ADJ n] ❑ *...a pocket calculator.* …一个袖珍计算器。 **4** N-COUNT A **pocket of** something is a small area where something is happening, or a small area which has a particular quality, and which is different from the other areas around it. （与周围区域不同或孤立的）小块地区 ❑ *Trapped in a pocket of air, they had only 40 minutes before the tide flooded the chamber.* 他们被困在有一点空气的弹丸之地，再过40分钟洪水就会淹没这间屋子了。 **5** V-T If someone who is in possession of something valuable such as a sum of money **pockets** it, they steal it or take it for themselves, even though it does not belong to them. 将…据为己有 ❑ *Banks have passed some of the savings on to customers and pocketed the rest.* 银行将部分存款转给顾客，其余的则据为己有。 **6** V-T If you say that someone **pockets** something such as a prize or sum of money, you mean that they win or obtain it, often without needing to make much effort or in a way that seems unfair. （轻松或不公正地）获得（奖赏、金钱等）[JOURNALISM] ❑ *He pocketed more money from this tournament than in his entire three years as a professional.* 他从这次锦标赛中捞到的钱比他作为一名职业运动员整整3年赚的还要多。 **7** V-T If someone **pockets** something, they put it in their pocket, for example, because they want to steal it or hide it. 把…放入衣袋 ❑ *Anthony snatched his letters and pocketed them.* 安东尼抓过他的信，放进了衣袋中。 **8** PHRASE If you say that a person or organization has **deep pockets**, you mean that they have a lot of money with which to pay for something. 雄厚的财力 ❑ *The church will do anything to avoid scandal – and everyone knows it has deep pockets.* 教会将不惜一切来避开丑闻——大家都知道它有的是钱。 ❑ *...investors with deep pockets.* …财力雄厚的投资者们。 **9** PHRASE If you are **out of pocket**, you have less money than you should have or than you intended, for example, because you have spent too much or because of a mistake. 缺钱的 ❑ *Make sure you are not out of pocket for your expenses.* 你要确保别把日常开销的钱都花没了。 **10** PHRASE If someone **picks** your **pocket**, they steal something from your pocket, usually without you noticing. 扒窃 ❑ *They were more in danger of having their pockets picked than being shot at.* 他们遭遇扒窃的危险大于遭受枪击。

Word Partnership *pocket* 的常用搭配:
N. **back** pocket, **hip** pocket, **jacket** pocket, **pants** pocket, **shirt** pocket 1

pocket·book /pɒkɪtbʊk/ (**pocketbooks**) 1 N-COUNT You can use **pocketbook** to refer to people's concerns about the money they have or hope to earn. 对钱袋的顾虑 [AM, JOURNALISM] ❑ *People feel pinched in their pocketbooks and insecure about their futures.* 人们感到钱袋紧缩，对未来缺少安全感。❑ *...the voters' concerns over pocketbook issues.* …选民们对钱袋问题的关心。2 N-COUNT A **pocketbook** is a small bag that a woman uses to carry things such as her money and keys in when she goes out. 女式手提包 [AM]

in BRIT, use **handbag, bag**

pock·et mon·ey 1 N-UNCOUNT **Pocket money** is money for buying small things that you find you want or need. 零用钱 ❑ *They earned themselves a little pocket money by selling cigarettes.* 他们靠卖香烟赚点零用钱。2 → see **allowance**

pod /pɒd/ (**pods**) N-COUNT A **pod** is a seed container that grows on plants such as peas or beans. 豆荚 ❑ *...fresh peas in the pod.* …豆荚中的新鲜豌豆。

pod·cast /pɒdkæst/ (**podcasts**) N-COUNT A **podcast** is an audio file similar to a radio broadcast, that can be downloaded and listened to on a computer or iPod. 播客 ❑ *Now there are thousands of podcasts available daily.* 现在每天有数千个播客可供下载。

po·dium /poʊdiəm/ (**podiums**) N-COUNT A **podium** is a small platform on which someone stands in order to give a lecture or conduct an orchestra. 讲台; (乐队) 指挥台 ❑ *Unsteadily he mounted the podium, adjusted the microphone, coughed, and went completely blank.* 他摇摇晃晃地走上讲台，调好麦克风，咳嗽了几声，接着脑子就一片空白。

poem ♦◇◇ /poʊəm/ (**poems**) N-COUNT A **poem** is a piece of writing in which the words are chosen for their beauty and sound and are carefully arranged, often in short lines that rhyme. 诗 ❑ *...a book of love poems.* …一本爱情诗集。

poet ♦◇◇ /poʊɪt/ (**poets**) N-COUNT A **poet** is a person who writes poems. 诗人 ❑ *He was a painter and poet.* 他是一位画家兼诗人。

po·et·ic /poʊɛtɪk/ 1 ADJ Something that is **poetic** is very beautiful and expresses emotions in a sensitive or moving way. 富有诗意的 ❑ *Nikolai Demidenko gave an exciting yet poetic performance.* 尼古拉・德米丹柯献上了一场激动人心而又富有诗意的演出。2 ADJ **Poetic** means relating to poetry. 诗歌的 ❑ *...Keats' famous poetic lines.* …济慈的著名诗句。

po·et·ry ♦◇◇ /poʊɪtri/ 1 N-UNCOUNT Poems, considered as a form of literature, are referred to as **poetry**. 诗歌 ❑ *...Russian poetry.* …俄罗斯诗歌。2 N-UNCOUNT You can describe something very beautiful as **poetry**. 富有诗意的东西 ❑ *His music is purer poetry than a poem in words.* 他的音乐比诗文更具诗意。
→ see **genre**

▲ **poign·ant** /pɔɪnyənt/ ADJ Something that is **poignant** affects you deeply and makes you feel sadness or regret. 辛酸的 ❑ *...a poignant combination of beautiful surroundings and tragic history.* …优美环境与悲怆历史的辛酸结合。❑ *...a poignant love story.* …一个令人感伤的爱情故事。

point
❶ NOUN USES
❷ VERB USES
❸ PHRASES

❶ **point** ♦♦♦ /pɔɪnt/ (**points**) 1 N-COUNT You use **point** to refer to something that someone has said or written. 看法 ❑ *We disagree with every point she makes.* 我们不同意她提出的任何观点。❑ *The following account will clearly illustrate this point.* 以下的陈述将清楚地阐明这一看法。2 N-SING If you say that someone **has a point**, or if you **take** their **point**, you mean that you accept that what they have said is important and should be considered. 重要性 ❑ *"If he'd already killed once, surely he'd have killed Sarah?" She had a point there.* "如果他已经杀过一次人，莎拉就一定是他杀的了吗？" 她这句话有道理。3 N-SING **The point** of what you are saying or discussing is the most important part that provides a reason or explanation for the rest. 要点 ❑ *"Did I ask you to talk to me?"—"That's not the point."* "我要你跟我说了吗？" —— "问题不在这儿。" 4 N-SING If you ask what **the point of** something is, or say that there is **no point in** it, you are indicating that a particular action has no purpose or would not be useful. 意义; 目的 ❑ *What was the point of thinking about him?* 想着他有什么意义呢？5 N-COUNT A **point** is a detail, aspect, or quality of something or someone. 细节 (之处) ❑ *Many of the points in the report are correct.* 报告中的很多细节是正确的。❑ *The most interesting point about the village was its religion.* 这个村庄最有趣的一点是它的宗教。6 N-COUNT A **point** is a particular place or position where something happens. 地点 ❑ *I'm sure there's another point we could meet at, but not there.* 我确信我们还有别的地点可以会面，但不是那儿。7 N-SING You use **point** to refer to a particular time, or to a particular stage in the development of something. 时刻; 阶段 ❑ *We're all going to die at some point.* 我们都会在某一时刻死去的。❑ *It got to the point where he had to leave.* 到了他不得不离开的时候了。8 N-COUNT The **point** of something such as a pin, needle, or knife is the thin, sharp end of it. (别针、针、刀等的) 尖端 ❑ *Put the tomatoes into a bowl and stab each one with the point of a knife.* 把那些西红柿放在一只碗里，然后用刀尖把每个都划开。9 In spoken English, you use **point** to refer to the dot or mark in a decimal number that separates the whole numbers from the fractions. 点; 小数点 ❑ *This is FM stereo one oh three point seven.* 这里是调频立体声广播103.7兆赫。10 N-COUNT In some sports, competitions, and games, a **point** is one of the single marks that are added together to give the total score. (体育比赛中的) 得分 ❑ *Chamberlain scored 50 or more points four times in the season.* 张伯伦在那个赛季中4次得分在50或50以上。11 N-COUNT The **points of the compass** are directions such as North, South, East, and West. (罗盘的) 方位点 ❑ *Sightseers arrived from all points of the compass.* 观光客从四面八方赶了过来。12 N-PLURAL On a railroad track, the **points** are the levers and rails at a place where two tracks join or separate. The points enable a train to move from one track to another. (铁轨的) 接点 [BRIT]

in AM, use **switches**

13 → see also **breaking point, focal point, point of sale, point of view, sticking point, vantage point**

Thesaurus *point* 另参见:
N. argument, gist, topic ❶ 3
location, place, position, spot ❶ 6

❷ **point** ♦♦♦ /pɔɪnt/ (**points, pointing, pointed**) 1 V-I If you **point at** a person or thing, you hold out your finger toward them in order to make someone notice them. (用手指) 指向 ❑ *I pointed at the boy sitting nearest me.* 我指了指坐得离我最近的那个男孩。❑ *He pointed at me with the stem of his pipe.* 他用他的烟斗柄指着我。2 V-T If you **point** something **at** someone, you aim the tip or end of it toward them. 对准 ❑ *David pointed his finger at Mary.* 戴维手指着玛丽。3 V-I If something **points to** a place or **points** in a particular direction, it shows where that place is or it faces in that direction. 指向 ❑ *An arrow pointed to the toilets.* 一个箭头指向了厕所。❑ *He controlled the car until it was pointing forward again.* 他控制住了汽车，直到车头再次朝向前方。4 V-I If something **points to** a particular situation, it suggests that the situation exists or is likely to occur. 表明; 显示 ❑ *Earlier reports pointed to students working harder, more continuously, and with enthusiasm.* 早期的报告显示学生学习更刻苦、持续的时间更长，而且兴致高昂。5 V-I If you **point to** something that has happened or that is happening, you are using it as proof that a particular situation exists. 着重指出 ❑ *George Fodor points to other weaknesses in the campaign.* 乔治・福多尔着重指出了这场活动的其他缺点。
6 → see also **pointed**

❸ **point** ♦♦♦ /pɔɪnt/
➪ **Please look at meanings 8 – 10 to see if the expression you are looking for is shown under another headword.** 1 PHRASE If you say that something is **beside the point**, you mean that it is not relevant to the subject that you are discussing. 不相关的 ❑ *Brian didn't like it, but that was beside the point.* 布赖恩是不喜欢它，但这同讨论的问题不相关。2 PHRASE When someone **comes to the point** or **gets to the point**, they start talking about the thing that is most important to them. 谈正题; 言归正传 ❑ *He came to the point at once. "You did a splendid job on this case."* 他立刻切入正题。"你这件事情干得真棒。" 3 PHRASE If you **make** your **point** or **prove** your **point**, you prove that something is true, either by arguing about it or by your actions or behavior. 证明自己的论点 ❑ *I think you've made your point, dear.* 我想你已经证明了你的论点，亲爱的。❑ *Dr. David McCleland studied one-hundred people, aged eighteen to sixty, to prove the point.*

戴维·麦克莱兰博士对100个年龄在18岁到60岁之间的人进行了研究，以证明自己的论点。 4 PHRASE If you **make a point of** doing something, you do it in a very deliberate or obvious way. 有意 ❑ *She made a point of spending as much time as possible away from Oklahoma.* 她有意尽可能长时间地呆在俄克拉何马以外的地方。 5 PHRASE If you are **on the point of** doing something, you are about to do it. 正要…之际 ❑ *He was on the point of saying something when the phone rang.* 他正要说些什么的时候，电话响了。 6 PHRASE Something that is **to the point** is relevant to the subject that you are discussing, or expressed neatly without wasting words or time. 中肯的 ❑ *The description which he had been given was brief and to the point.* 对他所作的描述简要、中肯。 7 PHRASE If you say that something is true **up to a point**, you mean that it is partly but not completely true. 在一定程度上 ❑ *"Was she good?"—"Mmm. Up to a point."* "她优秀吗？"——"嗯，还过得去。" 8 **in point of fact** → see **fact** 9 **to point the finger at** someone → see **finger** 10 **a sore point** → see **sore**

▸ **point out** 1 PHRASAL VERB If you **point out** an object or place, you make people look at it or show them where it is. 指出；指明 ❑ *They kept standing up to take pictures and point things out to each other.* 他们不停地站起来照相，还相互指些东西给对方看。 2 PHRASAL VERB If you **point out** a fact or mistake, you tell someone about it or draw their attention to it. 指出（事实、错误）❑ *I should point out that these estimates cover just the hospital expenditures.* 我应该指出，这些估价只包括医院的开支。

point-and-click ADJ **Point-and-click** refers to the way a computer mouse can be used to do things quickly and easily on a computer. 即点即击的 [COMPUTING] ❑ *...a simple point-and-click interface.* …一个简单的即点即击界面。

point-blank 1 ADV If you say something **point-blank**, you say it very directly or rudely, without explaining or apologizing. 直截了当地 [ADV after v] ❑ *The army apparently refused point-blank to do what was required of them.* 军方显然直截了当地拒绝了对他们提出的要求。 ● ADJ **Point-blank** is also an adjective. 直截了当的 [ADJ n] ❑ *...a point-blank refusal.* …直截了当的拒绝。 2 ADV If someone or something is shot **point-blank**, they are shot when the gun is touching them or extremely close to them. 近距离地 [ADV after v] ❑ *He put a gun through the open window of the car and fired point-blank at Bernadette.* 他把枪伸出车窗，近距离向贝尔纳黛特开枪。 ● ADJ **Point-blank** is also an adjective. 近距离的 [ADJ n] ❑ *He had been shot at point-blank range in the back of the head.* 他被近距离射中了后脑勺。

point·ed /pɔɪntɪd/ 1 ADJ Something that is **pointed** has a point at one end. 尖的 ❑ *...a pointed roof.* …一个尖屋顶。 2 ADJ **Pointed** comments or behavior express criticism in a clear and direct way. （批评等）尖锐的 ❑ *I couldn't help notice the pointed remarks slung in my direction.* 我不可能注意不到那些针对我的尖锐评论。 ● **point·ed·ly** ADV 尖锐地 ❑ *They were pointedly absent from the news conference.* 他们有意缺席了那场新闻发布会。

P

point·er /pɔɪntər/ (pointers) 1 N-COUNT A **pointer** is a piece of advice or information that helps you to understand a situation or to find a way of making progress. 建议；提示；线索 ❑ *I hope at least my daughter was able to offer you some useful pointers.* 我希望至少我女儿能够给你提供一些有用的线索。 2 N-COUNT A **pointer** is a long stick that is used to point at something such as a large chart or diagram when explaining something to people. 指示棒；教鞭 ❑ *She tapped on the world map with her pointer.* 她用教鞭轻点在那张世界地图上。 3 N-COUNT The **pointer** on a measuring instrument is the long, thin piece of metal that points to the numbers. （钟表、仪表等的）指针 ❑ *A series of levers joined to a pointer shows pressure on a dial.* 一系列控制杆连着一枚指针，在刻度盘上显示出压力数。

point·less /pɔɪntlɪs/ ADJ If you say that something is **pointless**, you are criticizing it because it has no sense or purpose. 无意义的；无益的 [DISAPPROVAL] ❑ *Violence is always pointless.* 暴力总是毫无意义的。 ❑ *Without an audience the performance is pointless.* 没有观众，演出是没有意义的。 ● **point·less·ly** ADV 无意义地 ❑ *Chemicals were pointlessly poisoning the soil.* 化学物品毫无意义地毒化着土壤。

point of sale (points of sale) 1 N-COUNT The **point of sale** is the place in a store where a product is passed from the seller to the customer. The abbreviation **POS** is also used. 销售点；收银处 [BUSINESS] ❑ *...information on consumer behavior at the point of sale.* …关于收银处顾客行为的信息。 2 N-UNCOUNT **Point-of-sale** is used to describe things that occur or are located or used at the place where you buy something. The abbreviation **POS** is also used. 收银处情况；销售点设施 [usu N n] [BUSINESS] ❑ *Introduction of electronic point-of-sale systems is improving efficiency.* 电子售货系统的引进提高了工作效率。

point of view ♦◇◇ (points of view) 1 N-COUNT You can refer to the opinions or attitudes that you have about something as your **point of view**. 观点；看法 ❑ *Thanks for your point of view, John.* 谢谢你的观点，约翰。 2 N-COUNT If you consider something **from** a particular **point of view**, you are using one aspect of a situation in order to judge that situation. （思考的）角度 ❑ *Do you think that, from the point of view of results, this exercise was worth the cost?* 从效果来看，你认为这种锻炼值得花这笔钱吗？
→ see **history**

▲ **poise** /pɔɪz/ N-UNCOUNT If someone has **poise**, they are calm, dignified, and self-controlled. 镇定；镇静 ❑ *What amazed him even more than her appearance was her poise.* 比她的长相更让他惊讶的是她的沉着镇定。

poised /pɔɪzd/ 1 ADJ If a part of your body is **poised**, it is completely still but ready to move at any moment. 摆好姿势准备行动的 ❑ *He studied the keyboard carefully, one finger poised.* 他仔细审视着键盘，一根手指摆好了姿势。 2 ADJ If someone is **poised to** do something, they are ready to take action at any moment. 随时准备行动的 [v-link ADJ] ❑ *U.S. forces are poised for a massive air, land, and sea assault.* 美军做好了随时从空中、陆地和海上发动大规模攻击的准备。 3 ADJ If you are **poised**, you are calm, dignified, and self-controlled. 镇定的 ❑ *She was self-assured, poised, almost self-satisfied.* 她自信、沉着，几乎有些自满了。

poi·son /pɔɪzᵊn/ (poisons, poisoning, poisoned) 1 N-MASS **Poison** is a substance that harms or kills people or animals if they swallow it or absorb it. 毒药 ❑ *Poison from the fish causes paralysis, swelling, and nausea.* 这种鱼的毒素会引起瘫痪、肿胀、恶心。 2 V-T If someone **poisons** another person, they kill the person or make them ill by giving them poison. 毒死 ❑ *The rumors that she had poisoned him could never be proved.* 说她毒死了他的谣言永远不可能得到证实。 ● **poi·son·ing** N-UNCOUNT 投毒 ❑ *She was sentenced to twenty years' imprisonment for poisoning and attempted murder.* 她因投毒和谋杀未遂而被判处了20年监禁。 3 V-T If you **are poisoned by** a substance, it makes you very ill and sometimes kills you. 使中毒 ❑ *Employees were taken to the hospital yesterday after being poisoned by fumes.* 雇员们昨天在烟雾中毒后被送进了医院。 ● **poi·son·ing** N-UNCOUNT 中毒 ❑ *...acute alcohol poisoning.* …急性酒精中毒。 4 V-T If someone **poisons** a food, drink, or weapon, they add poison to it so that it can be used to kill someone. 在…中下毒 ❑ *If I was your wife I would poison your coffee.* 如果我是你的妻子，我会在你的咖啡里下毒。 5 V-T To **poison** water, air, or land means to damage it with harmful substances such as chemicals. 污染 ❑ *...the textile and fiber industries that taint the air, poison the water, and use vast amounts of natural resources.* …污染空气、水源并消耗大量自然资源的纺织业和纤维制造业。 ❑ *The land has been completely poisoned by chemicals.* 这块土地已完全被化学品污染了。 6 V-T Something that **poisons** a good situation or relationship spoils it or destroys it. 玷污；破坏 ❑ *The whole atmosphere has really been poisoned.* 整个气氛已经完全被破坏了。

poi·son·ous /pɔɪzᵊnəs/ 1 ADJ Something that is **poisonous** will kill you or make you ill if you swallow or absorb it. （某物）有毒的 ❑ *All parts of the yew tree are poisonous, including the berries.* 紫杉树全身都有毒，包括其果实。 2 ADJ An animal that is **poisonous** produces a poison that will kill you or make you ill if the animal bites you. （动物）产生毒的 ❑ *There are hundreds of poisonous spiders and snakes.* 有数百种毒蜘蛛和毒蛇。 3 ADJ If you describe something as **poisonous**, you mean that it is extremely unpleasant and likely to spoil or destroy a good relationship or situation. 令人厌恶的；恶毒的 ❑ *...poisonous comments.* …恶毒的评论。 ❑ *...lying awake half the night tormented by poisonous suspicions.* …半个晚上躺着都不能入眠，被恶毒的猜疑所煎熬。

poi·son pill (poison pills) N-COUNT A **poison pill** refers to what some companies do to reduce their value in order to prevent themselves being taken over by another company. （指一些公司为避免被兼并而贬低自身价值的）毒丸策略 [BUSINESS] ❑ *Some believe this level of compensation is essentially a poison pill to put off any rival bidders.* 一些人相信这种程度的补偿本质上是一个毒丸策略，旨在阻止一切竞标对手。

★ **poke** /poʊk/ (pokes, poking, poked) 1 V-T If you **poke** someone or something, you quickly push them with your finger or with a sharp object. 戳；捅 ❑ *Lindy poked him in the ribs.* 林迪戳了戳

他的肋骨。● N-COUNT **Poke** is also a noun. 戳 ❑ *John smiled at them and gave Richard a playful poke.* 约翰冲他们笑了笑，还顽皮地捅了理查德一下。 **2** V-T If you **poke** one thing **into** another, you push the first thing into the second thing. 把…戳进 ❑ *He poked his finger into the hole.* 他把手指戳进洞里。 **3** V-I If something **pokes out of** or **through** another thing, you can see part of it appearing from behind or underneath the other thing. 伸出；露出 ❑ *He saw the dog's twitching nose poke out of the basket.* 他看见那条狗颤搐的鼻子从篮子里露出来。 **4** V-T/V-I If you **poke** your head through an opening or if it **pokes** through an opening, you push it through, often so that you can see something more easily. 探出(头)；(头) 探出 ❑ *Julie tapped on my door and poked her head in.* 朱莉敲了敲我的房门，接着将头探了进来。 **5** to **poke fun at** → see **fun** **6** to **poke** your **nose into** something → see **nose**

pok·er /poʊkər/ (**pokers**) **1** N-UNCOUNT **Poker** is a card game that people usually play in order to win money. 扑克牌游戏 ❑ *Lon and I play in the same weekly poker game.* 朗与我每周玩一次扑克牌。 **2** N-COUNT A **poker** is a metal bar that you use to move coal or wood in a stove or fireplace in order to make it burn better. 拨火棍 ❑ *Niigata stirred the wood with a poker, and put another log on.* 尼加塔用拨火棍搅了一下柴火，接着又加了一根木柴。

★ **po·lar** /poʊlər/ **1** ADJ **Polar** means near the North or South Poles. 极地的 [ADJ n] ❑ *...the rigors of life in the polar regions.* …极地的艰苦生活。 ❑ *There was a period of excessive warmth which melted some of the polar ice.* 有段时期温度过高，融化了极地的部分冰层。 **2** ADJ **Polar** is used to describe things that are completely opposite in character, quality, or type. (性格、质量或类型) 正好相反的 [ADJ n] [FORMAL] ❑ *The nomads' lifestyle was the polar opposite of collectivization.* 游牧民的生活方式同集体化的生活方式刚好相反。
→ see **arctic**

po·lar·ise /poʊləraɪz/ [BRIT] → see **polarize**

po·lar·ize /poʊləraɪz/ (**polarizes, polarizing, polarized**)
in BRIT, also use **polarise**
V-T/V-I If something **polarizes** people or if something **polarizes**, two separate groups are formed with opposite opinions or positions. 使两级分化；两级分化 ❑ *Missile deployment did much to further polarize opinion.* 导弹的部署进一步地加剧了意见的分化。 ❑ *As the car rental industry polarizes, business will go to the bigger companies.* 随着汽车租赁行业的两级分化，业务会流向大一些的公司。
● **po·lari·za·tion** /poʊlərɪzeɪʃən/ N-UNCOUNT 分化 ❑ *...the increasing polarization between rich and poor.* …不断加剧的贫富分化。

pole ♦◇◇ /poʊl/ (**poles**) **1** N-COUNT A **pole** is a long thin piece of wood or metal, used especially for supporting things. 柱；杆 ❑ *The truck crashed into a telegraph pole.* 卡车撞上了电线杆。 **2** N-COUNT The Earth's **poles** are the two opposite ends of its axis, its most northern and southern points. 地极 ❑ *For six months of the year, there is hardly any light at the poles.* 一年中的6个月里，地球的两极几乎没有任何光线。 **3** N-COUNT The two **poles** of a magnet are the two ends of the magnet where the magnetic force is strongest. 磁极 ❑ *The important fact is that the two poles of the magnet work in opposite ways.* 重要的事实是，磁体两极的运行方式完全相反。 **4** N-COUNT The two **poles** of a range of qualities, opinions, or beliefs are the completely opposite qualities, opinions, or beliefs at either end of the range. (品质、观点或信仰) 截然相反的两极 ❑ *The two politicians represent opposite poles of the political spectrum.* 这两位政治家代表了各种政治倾向中的两个极端。 **5** PHRASE If you say that two people or things are **poles apart**, you mean that they have completely different beliefs, opinions, or qualities. (信仰、观点或品质) 截然相反的 [EMPHASIS]
→ see **magnet**

po·lem·ic /pəlɛmɪk/ (**polemics**) N-VAR A **polemic** is a very strong written or spoken attack on, or defense of, a particular belief or opinion. (口头或书面的) 猛烈抨击；辩护 ❑ *...a polemic against the danger of secret societies.* …一次对秘密社团的危害所进行的猛烈抨击。

Word Link *poli ≈ city : metropolis, police, policy*

po·lice ♦♦♦ /pəlis/ (**polices, policing, policed**) **1** N-SING-COLL The **police** are the official organization that is responsible for making sure that people obey the law. 警方 ❑ *The police are also looking for a second car.* 警方也在寻找第二辆车。 ❑ *Police say they have arrested twenty people following the disturbances.* 警方称他们已经在骚乱后逮捕了20个人。 **2** N-PLURAL **Police** are men and women who are members of the official organization that is responsible for making sure that people obey the law. 警察 ❑ *More than one hundred police have ringed the area.* 一百多名警察已经包围了这个地区。 **3** V-T If the police or military forces **police** an area or event, they make sure that law and order is preserved in that area or at that event. 维持…的治安 ❑ *...the tiny U.N. observer force whose job it is to police the border.* …维持边界治安的那一小支联合国观察部队。 **4** V-T If a person or group in authority **polices** a law or an area of public life, they make sure that what is done is fair and legal. 监督 ❑ *...the self-regulatory body that polices the investment management business.* …监督投资管理事务的自律机构。 **5** → see also **secret police**

po·lice force (**police forces**) N-COUNT A **police force** is the police organization in a particular country or area. 警察部队 ❑ *...the Wichita police force.* …威奇托警察部队。

police·man ♦◇◇ /pəlismən/ (**policemen**) N-COUNT A **policeman** is a man who is a member of the police force. 警察

po·lice of·fic·er ♦◇◇ (**police officers**) N-COUNT A **police officer** is a member of the police force. 警察 ❑ *...a meeting of senior police officers.* …一个高级警官会议。

po·lice sta·tion (**police stations**) N-COUNT A **police station** is the local office of a police force in a particular area. 警察局 ❑ *Two police officers arrested him and took him to Gettysburg police station.* 两名警察逮捕了他，并把他带到了葛底斯堡警察局。

police·woman /pəliswʊmən/ (**policewomen**) N-COUNT A **policewoman** is a woman who is a member of the police force. 女警

poli·cy ♦♦♦ /pɒlɪsi/ (**policies**) **1** N-VAR A **policy** is a set of ideas or plans that is used as a basis for making decisions, especially in politics, economics, or business. 政策 ❑ *...plans that include changes in foreign policy and economic reforms.* …包括外交政策调整和经济改革的计划。 **2** N-COUNT An official organization's **policy** on a particular issue or toward a country is their attitude and actions regarding that issue or country. 方针 ❑ *...the organization's future policy toward South Africa.* …该组织未来的南非政策。 ❑ *...the government's policy on repatriation.* …该政府的遣返政策。 **3** N-COUNT An insurance **policy** is a document that shows the agreement that you have made with an insurance company. 保险单 [BUSINESS] ❑ *You are advised to read the small print of homeowner and car insurance policies.* 建议你读一下房主保险单和汽车保险单上的小号印刷字。

Word Partnership *policy* 的常用搭配：
ADJ. **domestic** policy, **economic** policy, **educational** policy, **foreign** policy, **new** policy, **official** policy, **public** policy **1**
N. policy **analyst**, **defense** policy, **energy** policy, **immigration** policy **1**
policy **change** (*or* **change of** policy), policy **objectives**, policy **shift** **1** **2**
administration policy, **government** policy **2**
insurance policy **3**

policy·holder /pɒlɪsihoʊldər/ (**policyholders**) N-COUNT A **policyholder** is a person who has an insurance policy with an insurance company. 投保人 [BUSINESS] ❑ *The first 10 percent of legal fees will be paid by the policyholder.* 第一笔10%的法律费用将由投保人支付。

policy·maker /pɒlɪsimeɪkər/ (**policymakers**) also **policy-maker** N-COUNT In politics, **policymakers** are people who are involved in making policies and policy decisions. 决策者 [usu pl] ❑ *...top economic policymakers.* …最高经济决策者们。

po·lio /poʊlioʊ/ N-UNCOUNT **Polio** is a serious infectious disease that often makes people unable to use their legs. 小儿麻痹症 ❑ *Gladys was crippled by polio at the age of 3.* 格拉迪丝3岁时因小儿麻痹症而瘸了。
→ see **hospital**

pol·ish /pɒlɪʃ/ (**polishes, polishing, polished**) **1** N-MASS **Polish** is a substance that you put on the surface of an object in order to clean it, protect it, and make it shine. 抛光剂；亮漆 ❑ *The still air smelled faintly of furniture polish.* 久未流通的空气中有股淡淡的家具漆的气味。 **2** V-T If you **polish** something, you put polish on it or rub it with a cloth to make it shine. (用抛光剂等) 擦亮 ❑ *Each morning he shaved and polished his shoes.* 每天早晨他都刮胡子、擦皮鞋。 ● N-SING **Polish** is also a noun. 擦亮；磨光 ❑ *He gave his counter a polish with a soft duster.* 他用柔软的抹布将柜台擦得亮亮的。 ● **pol·ished** ADJ 擦亮的；磨光的 ❑ *...a highly polished floor.* …一块擦得很亮的地板。

P

3 N-UNCOUNT If you say that a performance or piece of work has **polish**, you mean that it is of a very high standard. 完美；上乘境界 [APPROVAL] ❑ *The opera lacks the polish of his later work.* 这部歌剧缺少他后期作品中所具有的上乘境界。 **4** V-T If you **polish** your technique, performance, or skill at doing something, you work on improving it. 使完美；改进 ❑ *They just need to polish their technique.* 他们只需要改进一下自己的技艺。 ● PHRASAL VERB **Polish up** means the same as **polish**. 使完美；改进 ❑ *Polish up your writing skills on a one-week professional course.* 上一周的专业课程来增强你的写作技能。 **5** → see also **polished**

pol·ished /pɒlɪʃt/ **1** ADJ Someone who is **polished** shows confidence and knows how to behave socially. 幽雅的；有教养的 [APPROVAL] ❑ *He is polished, charming, articulate, and an excellent negotiator.* 他举止幽雅、富有魅力、善于表达，是个杰出的谈判者。 **2** ADJ If you describe a performance, ability, or skill as **polished**, you mean that it is of a very high standard. (表演、能力或技艺)完美的 [APPROVAL] ❑ *...a very polished performance.* …一场完美的表演。 **3** → see also **polish**

po·lite /pəlaɪt/ (**politer, politest**) ADJ Someone who is **polite** has good manners and behaves in a way that is socially correct and not rude to other people. 有礼貌的 ❑ *Everyone around him was trying to be polite, but you could tell they were all bored.* 他身边的每一个人都尽力表现得彬彬有礼，但你可以看出他们都厌倦了。 ❑ *Gonzales, a quiet and very polite young man, made a favorable impression.* 冈萨雷斯是个文静而又很有礼貌的年轻人，给人留下了很好的印象。 ● **po·lite·ly** ADV 礼貌地 ❑ *"Your home is beautiful," I said politely.* "你的家很漂亮，"我客气地说。 ● **po·lite·ness** N-UNCOUNT 礼貌 ❑ *She listened to him, but only out of politeness.* 她听他讲着，但只是出于礼貌而已。

Thesaurus *polite* 另参见：
ADJ. considerate, courteous, gracious, respectful, well-mannered; *(ant.)* brash, impolite, rude

po·liti·cal ♦♦♦ /pəlɪtɪkᵊl/ **1** ADJ **Political** means relating to the way power is achieved and used in a country or society. 政治的 ❑ *All other political parties there have been completely banned.* 那里的其他所有政党都已经完全被取缔了。 ❑ *The government is facing another political crisis.* 该政府正面临着另一场政治危机。 ● **po·liti·cal·ly** /pəlɪtɪkli/ ADV 政治上地 ❑ *They do not believe the killings were politically motivated.* 他们相信这些谋杀案没有什么政治动机。 **2** ADJ Someone who is **political** is interested or involved in politics and holds strong beliefs about it. 对政治感兴趣的；有坚定政治信仰的 ❑ *Oh I'm not political, I take no interest in politics.* 哦，我不关心政治，对政治不感兴趣。
→ see **empire, philosophy**

P

po·liti·cal asy·lum N-UNCOUNT **Political asylum** is the right to live in a foreign country and is given by the government of that country to people who have to leave their own country for political reasons. 政治避难 ❑ *...a university teacher who is seeking political asylum in California.* …正在加州寻求政治避难的一名大学教师。

po·liti·cal econo·my N-UNCOUNT **Political economy** is the study of the way in which a government influences or organizes a nation's wealth. 政治经济学

po·liti·cal·ly cor·rect ADJ If you say that someone is **politically correct**, you mean that they are extremely careful not to offend or upset any group of people in society who have a disadvantage, or who have been treated differently because of their sex, race, or disability. The abbreviation **PC** is also used. 政治上正确的 (指力求避免冒犯处于不利地位或被歧视的群体) ❑ *...environmentalists and politically correct liberals.* …环保主义者和保持政治上正确的自由主义者们。 ● N-PLURAL **The politically correct** are people who are politically correct. 政治上正确的人 ["the" N] ❑ *...the hypocrisy of the politically correct.* …政治上正确的人的虚伪性。

poli·ti·cian ♦♦◊ /pɒlɪtɪʃᵊn/ (**politicians**) N-COUNT A **politician** is a person whose job is in politics, especially a member of the government. 政客 (尤指政府成员)；政治家 ❑ *They have arrested a number of leading opposition politicians.* 他们已经逮捕了一些主要的反对党政治家。

poli·tics ♦♦◊ /pɒlɪtɪks/ **1** N-PLURAL **Politics** are the actions or activities concerned with achieving and using power in a country or society. The verb that follows **politics** may be either singular or plural. 政治 ❑ *Many people think Nixon transformed American politics.* 许多人认为尼克松改变了美国的政治。 ❑ *He quickly involved himself in local politics.* 他很快就参与到地方政治活动中去了。 **2** N-PLURAL Your **politics** are your beliefs about how a country ought to be governed. 政治观点 ❑ *My politics are well to the left of center.* 我的政治观点很靠左翼。 **3** N-UNCOUNT **Politics** is the study of the ways in which countries are governed. 政治学 ❑ *He began studying politics and medieval history.* 他开始学习政治学和中世纪史。 **4** N-PLURAL **Politics** can be used to talk about the ways that power is shared in an organization and the ways it is affected by personal relationships between people who work together. The verb that follows **politics** may be either singular or plural. 权术 ❑ *You need to understand how office politics influence the working environment.* 你需要明白办公室权术怎样影响工作环境。

poll ♦♦◊ /poʊl/ (**polls, polling, polled**) **1** N-COUNT A **poll** is a survey in which people are asked their opinions about something, usually in order to find out how popular something is or what people intend to do in the future. 民意测验 ❑ *Polls show that the European treaty has gained support in Denmark.* 民意测验显示，欧洲条约已经在丹麦获得支持。 ❑ *We are doing a weekly poll on the president, and clearly his popularity has declined.* 我们正在对总统进行每周一次的民意测验，很显然他的受欢迎度已经下降了。 **2** → see also **opinion poll** **3** V-T If you **are polled on** something, you are asked what you think about it as part of a survey. 对…进行民意测验 [usu passive] ❑ *More than 18,000 people were polled.* 18000多人接受了民意测验。 ❑ *Audiences were going to be polled on which of three pieces of contemporary music they liked best.* 听众将就3首现代乐曲中最喜欢哪一首接受民意调查。 **4** N-PLURAL **The polls** means an election for a country's government, or the place where people go to vote in an election. 政治大选；投票地点 ❑ *Incumbent officeholders are difficult to defeat at the polls.* 现任官员很难在选举中被击败。 ❑ *Voters are due to go to the polls on Sunday to elect a new president.* 选民们按计划将于周日前往投票站选举新总统。 **5** V-T If a political party or a candidate **polls** a particular number or percentage of votes, they get that number or percentage of votes in an election. 获得…选票 ❑ *The result showed he had polled enough votes to force a second ballot.* 结果显示他获得了足够的选票来促使第二轮选举。 **6** → see also **polling**

pol·len /pɒlən/ (**pollens**) N-MASS **Pollen** is a fine powder produced by flowers. It fertilizes other flowers of the same species so that they produce seeds. 花粉

poll·ing /poʊlɪŋ/ N-UNCOUNT **Polling** is the act of voting in an election. 投票 ❑ *There has been a busy start to polling in today's local elections.* 今天地方选举开始时投票就非常踊跃。
→ see **election, vote**

★ **pol·lu·tant** /pəluːtᵊnt/ (**pollutants**) N-VAR **Pollutants** are substances that pollute the environment, especially gases from vehicles and poisonous chemicals produced as waste by industrial processes. 污染物 (尤指车辆尾气和化学工业废料) ❑ *Industrial pollutants are responsible for a sizable proportion of all cancers.* 工业污染物会引发多种癌症。

pol·lute /pəluːt/ (**pollutes, polluting, polluted**) V-T To **pollute** water, air, or land means to make it dirty and dangerous to live in or to use, especially with poisonous chemicals or sewage. 污染 ❑ *Heavy industry pollutes our rivers with noxious chemicals.* 重工业排放的有毒化学物质污染着我们的河流。 ● **pol·lut·ed** ADJ 受污染的 ❑ *The police have warned the city's inhabitants not to bathe in the polluted river.* 警方已经警告本市居民不要在那条被污染的河里游泳。

pol·lu·tion ♦◊◊ /pəluːʃᵊn/ **1** N-UNCOUNT **Pollution** is the process of polluting water, air, or land, especially with poisonous chemicals. 污染 ❑ *The fine was for the company's pollution of the air near its plants.* 公司被罚款是因为它的工厂污染了周围的空气。 **2** N-UNCOUNT **Pollution** is poisonous or dirty substances that are polluting the water, air, or land somewhere. 污染物 ❑ *The level of pollution in the river was falling.* 该河流受污染的程度其时正在降低。
→ see Word Web: **pollution**
→ see **air, factory, solar system**

polo /poʊloʊ/ N-UNCOUNT **Polo** is a game played between two teams of players. The players ride horses and use wooden hammers with long handles to hit a ball. 马球

▲ **poly·es·ter** /pɒliɛstər/ (**polyesters**) N-MASS **Polyester** is a type of synthetic cloth used especially to make clothes. 涤纶 ❑ *...a green polyester shirt.* …一件绿色的涤纶衬衫。

poly·eth·yl·ene /pɒliɛθɪliːn/ N-UNCOUNT **Polyethylene** is a type of plastic made into thin sheets or bags and used especially to keep food fresh or to keep things dry. 聚乙烯 [mainly AM]
in BRIT, usually use **polythene**

Word Web pollution

Pollution affects all aspects of the **environment**. **Airborne emissions** from industrial plants and vehicle **exhaust** cause air pollution. When these smoky **emissions** combine with fog, the result is **smog**. Airborne pollutants can travel long distances. **Acid rain** caused by factories in the Midwest falls on states to the east. There it damages trees and kills fish in lakes. Chemical waste from factories, **sewage**, and **garbage** have polluted the water and land in many areas. The overuse of **pesticides** and **fertilizers** has added to the problem. These chemicals accumulate in the soil and poison the earth.

★ **poly·tech·nic** /pɒlɪtɛknɪk/ (**polytechnics**) N-VAR A **polytechnic** is the name for a school, college, or university that specializes in courses in science and technology. 理工院校 [oft in names]

poly·thene /pɒlɪθin/ N-UNCOUNT **Polythene** is the same as **polyethylene**. 聚乙烯 [mainly BRIT]

pomp /pɒmp/ N-UNCOUNT **Pomp** is the use of a lot of ceremony, fine clothes, and decorations, especially on a special occasion. 排场 ❑ *I hate all this pomp and ceremony.* 我讨厌所有这些排场和仪式。

pom·pos·ity /pɒmpɒsɪti/ N-UNCOUNT **Pomposity** means speaking or behaving in a very serious manner that shows you think you are more important than you really are. 摆架子 [DISAPPROVAL] ❑ *Einstein was a scientist who hated pomposity and disliked being called a genius.* 科学家爱因斯坦不喜欢摆架子，也不喜欢被称为天才。

pomp·ous /pɒmpəs/ **1** ADJ If you describe someone as **pompous**, you mean that they behave or speak in a very serious way because they think they are more important than they really are. 爱摆架子的 [DISAPPROVAL] ❑ *He was somewhat pompous and had a high opinion of his own capabilities.* 他有些爱摆架子，并且高估自己的能力。 ● **pomp·ous·ly** ADV 爱摆架子地 ❑ *Robin told me firmly and pompously that he had an important business appointment.* 罗宾一本正经地对我显摆说他有个重要的商务约会。 **2** ADJ A **pompous** building or ceremony is very grand and elaborate. (建筑物) 气派的; (仪式) 盛大铺张的 ❑ *The service was grand without being pompous.* 该仪式盛大而不铺张。

pond /pɒnd/ (**ponds**) **1** N-COUNT A **pond** is a small area of water that is smaller than a lake. Ponds are often made artificially. 池塘 ❑ *She chose a bench beside the duck pond and sat down.* 她选了鸭池旁的一张长椅坐了下来。 **2** N-SING People sometimes refer to the Atlantic Ocean as **the pond**. 大西洋 [mainly JOURNALISM] ❑ *Tourist numbers from across the pond have dropped dramatically.* 来自大西洋彼岸的游客数量已急剧减少。

★ **pon·der** /pɒndər/ (**ponders, pondering, pondered**) V-T/V-I If you **ponder** something, you think about it carefully. 仔细思考 ❑ *I found myself constantly pondering the question: "How could anyone do these things?"* 我发现自己不停地思索着这个问题："怎么会有人做出这些事情？" ❑ *He pondered over the difficulties involved.* 他仔细思考了有关的种种困难。

pon·der·ous /pɒndərəs/ ADJ **Ponderous** writing or speech is very serious, uses more words than necessary, and is dull. (文章、话语) 冗长沉闷的 [DISAPPROVAL] ❑ *He had a dense, ponderous style.* 他的风格是词藻堆砌、冗长沉闷。

▲ **pony** /poʊni/ (**ponies**) N-COUNT A **pony** is a small or young horse. 小马

pony·tail /poʊniteɪl/ (**ponytails**) N-COUNT A **ponytail** is a hairstyle in which someone's hair is tied up at the back of the head and hangs down like a tail. 马尾发型 ❑ *Her long, fine hair was swept back in a ponytail.* 她那漂亮的长发向后梳成了一个马尾辫。

poo·dle /pudᵊl/ (**poodles**) N-COUNT A **poodle** is a type of dog with thick curly hair. 鬈毛狗

pool ♦◇◇ /pul/ (**pools, pooling, pooled**) **1** N-COUNT A **pool** is the same as a **swimming pool**. 游泳池 ❑ *...a heated indoor pool.* …一个室内温水游泳池。 **2** N-COUNT A **pool** is a fairly small area of still water. 水池 ❑ *The pool had dried up and was full of bracken and reeds.* 该水池已经干涸，长满了欧洲蕨和芦苇。 **3** N-COUNT A **pool of** liquid or light is a small area of it on the ground or on a surface. 一滩 (液体); 一片 (光) ❑ *She was found lying in a pool of blood.* 她被发现躺在一滩血泊中。 ❑ *It was raining quietly and steadily and there were little pools of water on the gravel drive.* 雨一直静静地下着，砂砾车道上积了一滩滩的水。 **4** N-COUNT A **pool of** people, money, or things is a quantity or number of them that is available for an organization or group to use. 一拨人; 一笔钱; 一笔物资; ❑ *The available pool of healthy manpower was not as large as military officials had expected.* 一拨可用的健康劳力人数达不到军方官员们的期望值。 **5** → see also **carpool** **6** V-T If a group of people or organizations **pool** their money, knowledge, or equipment, they share it or put it together so that it can be used for a particular purpose. 凑集 (资金、知识、设备等) ❑ *We pooled ideas and information.* 我们汇集了意见和信息。

poor ♦♦◇ /pʊər/ (**poorer, poorest**) **1** ADJ Someone who is **poor** has very little money and few possessions. (人) 贫穷的 ❑ *The reason our schools cannot afford better teachers is because people here are poor.* 我们学校请不起更好的老师是因为这里的人穷。 ● N-PLURAL **The poor** are people who are poor. 穷人 (与**the**连用) ❑ *Even the poor have their pride.* 即使穷人也有他们的自尊。 **2** ADJ The people in a **poor** country or area have very little money and few possessions. 贫困的 (国家、地区等) ❑ *Many countries in the Third World are as poor as they have ever been.* 许多第三世界国家一如既往地贫困。 **3** ADJ You use **poor** to express your sympathy for someone. 可怜的 [ADJ n] [FEELINGS] ❑ *I feel sorry for that poor child.* 我为那个可怜的孩子感到难过。 ❑ *It was way too much for the poor guy to overcome.* 它对那个可怜的家伙来讲太难克服。 **4** ADJ If you describe something as **poor**, you mean that it is of a low quality or standard or that it is in bad condition. (质量、水准、条件等) 差的 ❑ *...the poor state of the economy.* …经济的不良状况。 ❑ *The gap between the best and poorest childcare provision has widened.* 儿童保育供给的最佳和最低水准之间加大了差距。 ● **poor·ly** ADV 差地 ❑ *Some are living in poorly built dormitories, even in tents.* 一些人住在建得很差的宿舍里，甚至住在帐篷里。 **5** ADJ If you describe an amount, rate, or number as **poor**, you mean that it is less than expected or less than is considered reasonable. 低的 (数量或比率) ❑ *...poor wages and working conditions.* …低的工资和差的工作条件。 ● **poor·ly** ADV 低地 ❑ *During the first week, the evening meetings were poorly attended.* 第一个星期晚间会议出勤率低。 **6** ADJ You use **poor** to describe someone who is not very skillful in a particular activity. (技术) 差劲的 ❑ *He was a poor actor.* 他是个差劲的演员。 ● **poor·ly** ADV 差劲地 [ADV after v] ❑ *Cheetahs breed very poorly in captivity.* 猎豹在圈养的情况下繁殖力很差。 **7** ADJ If something is **poor in** a particular quality or substance, it contains very little of the quality or substance. (某特质或物质) 贫乏的 [v-link ADJ "in" n] ❑ *Fats and sugar are very rich in energy but poor in vitamins and minerals.* 脂肪和糖富含热量，但缺乏维生素和矿物质。

Thesaurus *poor* 另参见：

ADJ. impoverished, penniless; *(ant.)* rich, wealthy **1** **2**
inferior **4**

poor·ly /pʊərli/ ADJ If someone is **poorly**, they are ill. 病的 [mainly BRIT, INFORMAL]

pop ♦◇◇ /pɒp/ (**pops, popping, popped**) **1** N-UNCOUNT **Pop** is modern music that usually has a strong rhythm and uses electronic equipment. 流行乐 ❑ *...the perfect combination of Caribbean rhythms, European pop, and American soul.* …加勒比旋律、欧洲流行乐及美国灵乐的完美结合。 ❑ *...a life-size poster of a pop star.* …一张如真人大小的流行歌星招贴画。 **2** N-UNCOUNT You can refer to carbonated drinks such as cola as **pop**. 汽水 [BRIT, INFORMAL] ❑ *...a can of pop.* …一听汽水。 **3** N-COUNT; SOUND **Pop** is used to represent a short sharp sound such as the sound made by bursting a balloon or by pulling a cork out of a bottle. 爆裂声 ❑ *Each corn kernel will make a loud pop when cooked.* 每颗玉米粒爆炒的时候都会发出很响的爆裂声。 **4** V-I If something **pops**, it makes a short sharp sound. 发爆裂声 ❑ *He untwisted the wire off the champagne bottle, and the cork popped and* *shot to the ceiling.* 他拧开香槟酒瓶，瓶塞砰的一声冲到了天花板上。 **5** V-I If your eyes **pop**, you look very surprised or excited when you see something. (眼睛因惊讶或兴奋而) 鼓出；瞪(眼) [INFORMAL] ❑ *My eyes popped at the sight of the rich variety of food on show.* 我瞪眼看着各色各样的食物展品。 **6** V-T If you **pop** something somewhere, you put it there quickly. 迅速放置 [INFORMAL] ❑ *Marianne got a couple of mugs from the cupboard and popped a teabag into each of them.* 玛丽安娜从碗柜中拿出了几个马克杯，把袋泡茶迅速地放入每个杯子中。 **7** N-FAMILY Some people call their father **pop**. 爸爸 [mainly AM, INFORMAL] ❑ *I looked at Pop and he had big tears in his eyes.* 我看了看爸爸，他眼里噙着大滴的泪珠。 **8** to **pop the question** → see **question**

▸ **pop up** PHRASAL VERB If someone or something **pops up**, they appear in a place or situation unexpectedly. 突然出现 [INFORMAL] ❑ *She was startled when Lisa popped up at the door all smiles.* 莉萨满面笑容地突然出现在门口时她吃了一惊。

POP /pi oʊ pi/ (**POPs**) N-COUNT **POP** is something that proves that you have paid for something. **POP** is an abbreviation for "proof of purchase." 购买凭证

▲ **pop·corn** /pɒpkɔrn/ N-UNCOUNT **Popcorn** is a snack that consists of grains of corn that have been heated until they have burst and become large and light. 爆米花

pope /poʊp/ (**popes**) N-COUNT **The pope** is the head of the Roman Catholic Church. 罗马天主教教皇 [usu "the" N; N-TITLE] ❑ *The highlight of the pope's visit will be his message to the people.* 教皇访问的亮点是，他将给人们传达训诫。

pop·py /pɒpi/ (**poppies**) N-COUNT A **poppy** is a plant with a large, delicate flower, usually red in color. The drug opium is obtained from one type of poppy. 罂粟 ❑ *...a field of poppies.* …一块罂粟地。

Pop·si·cle /pɒpsɪkᵊl/ (**Popsicles**) N-COUNT A **Popsicle** is a piece of flavored ice on a stick. 冰棍 [AM, TRADEMARK]

in BRIT, use **ice lolly**

Word Link *popul ≈ people : populace, popular, population*

popu·lace /pɒpyələs/ N-UNCOUNT **The populace** of a country is its people. 平民 [FORMAL] ❑ *...a large proportion of the populace.* …平民中的很大一部分。

popu·lar ♦♦◇ /pɒpyələr/ **1** ADJ Something that is **popular** is enjoyed or liked by a lot of people. (物) 广受喜爱的 ❑ *Chocolate sauce is always popular with youngsters.* 巧克力酱总是受年轻人喜爱。 ● **popu·lar·ity** /pɒpyəlærɪti/ N-UNCOUNT (物的) 受喜爱度 ❑ *...the growing popularity of Australian wines among consumers.* …澳大利亚葡萄酒越来越受消费者青睐。 **2** ADJ Someone who is **popular** is liked by most people, or by most people in a particular group. (人) 广受喜爱的 ❑ *He remained the most popular politician in Arkansas.* 他仍是阿肯色州最广受喜爱的政治家。 ● **popu·lar·ity** N-UNCOUNT (人的) 受喜爱度 ❑ *It is his popularity with ordinary people that sets him apart.* 他深受普通群众的喜爱，正是这一点使他与众不同。 **3** ADJ **Popular** newspapers, television programs, or forms of art are aimed at ordinary people and not at experts or intellectuals. 面向大众的；通俗的 [ADJ n] ❑ *Once again the popular press in Britain has been rife with stories about their marriage.* 英国大众媒体中又充斥着他们的婚事报导。 ❑ *...one of the classics of modern popular music.* …现代通俗音乐的经典之一。 **4** ADJ **Popular** ideas, feelings, or attitudes are approved of or held by most people. 广受赞同的 ❑ *Contrary to popular belief, the oil companies can't control the price of crude.* 和大众的想法相反，各石油公司控制不了原油的价格。 ❑ *The military government has been unable to win popular support.* 军政府没能赢得公众的支持。 ● **popu·lar·ity** N-UNCOUNT 受赞同度 ❑ *Over time, though, Watson's views gained in popularity.* 然而，随着时间的推移，沃森的观点越来越受到赞同。 **5** ADJ **Popular** is used to describe political activities that involve the ordinary people of a country, and not just members of political parties. 民众的 (政治活动) [ADJ n] ❑ *The late president Ferdinand Marcos was overthrown by a popular uprising in 1986.* 已故总统费迪南德·马科斯于1986年被民众起义所推翻。

→ see **genre**

Word Partnership *popular* 的常用搭配：

ADV. **extremely** popular, **increasingly** popular, **more** popular, **most** popular, **wildly** popular **1** **2** **4**

N. popular **culture**, popular **magazine**, popular **movie**, popular **music**, popular **novel**, popular **restaurant**, popular **show**, popular **song** **1** **3**

popu·lar·ise /pɒpjʊləraɪz/ [BRIT] → see **popularize**

popu·lar·ize /pɒpyələraɪz/ (**popularizes, popularizing, popularized**)

in BRIT, also use **popularise**

V-T To **popularize** something means to make a lot of people interested in it and able to enjoy it. 推广 ❑ *Irving Brokaw, who had studied figure skating in Europe, returned to the U.S. and popularized the new sport.* 欧文·布罗考在欧洲学习了花样滑冰，回到美国后推广了这项新的体育运动。 ● **popu·lari·za·tion** /pɒpyʊlərɪzeɪʃᵊn/ N-UNCOUNT 推广 ❑ *...the popularization of sports through television.* …通过电视对体育运动的推广。

popu·lar·ly /pɒpyələrli/ **1** ADV If something or someone is **popularly** known as something, most people call them that, although it is not their official name or title. 通俗地 [ADV with -ed] ❑ *...the Mesozoic era, more popularly known as the age of dinosaurs.* …中生代，俗称恐龙时代。 ❑ *...an infection popularly called mad cow disease.* …俗称疯牛病的一种传染病。 **2** ADV If something is **popularly** believed or supposed to be the case, most people believe or suppose it to be the case, although it may not be true. 普遍地 (认为) [ADV -ed] ❑ *Schizophrenia is not a "split mind" as is popularly believed.* 精神分裂症并不是普遍认为的"分裂了的精神"。 **3** ADV A **popularly elected** leader or government has been elected by a majority of the people in a country. 由广大人民选举的 [ADV -ed] ❑ *Walesa was Poland's first popularly elected president.* 瓦文萨是波兰的第一位普选总统。

★ **popu·late** /pɒpyəleɪt/ (**populates, populating, populated**) **1** V-T If an area **is populated by** certain people or animals, those people or animals live there, often in large numbers. 聚居；栖息 ❑ *Before all this the island was populated by native American Arawaks.* 在所有这一切之前，该岛聚居着土著美洲阿拉瓦克人。 ● **popu·lat·ed** ADJ 聚居了的；栖息了的 [adv ADJ] ❑ *The southeast is the most densely populated area.* 东南部是最稠密的居住区。 **2** V-T To **populate** an area means to cause people to live there. 使聚居 ❑ *Successive regimes annexed the region and populated it with lowland people.* 后继政权吞并了这个地区并让低地居民聚居于此。

popu·la·tion ♦♦◇ /pɒpyəleɪʃᵊn/ (**populations**) **1** N-COUNT The **population** of a country or area is all the people who live in it. 人口 ❑ *Bangladesh now has a population of about 110 million.* 孟加拉国现有约一亿一千万人口。 ❑ *...the annual rate of population growth.* …人口年增长率。 **2** N-COUNT If you refer to a particular type of **population** in a country or area, you are referring to all the people or animals of that type there. (某种) 人群；种群 [FORMAL] ❑ *...75.6 percent of the male population over sixteen.* …16岁以上男性人群的75.6%。 ❑ *...areas with a large black population.* …有大批黑人群体的的各地区。

→ see Word Web: **population**

→ see **country**

▲ **popu·lous** /pɒpyələs/ ADJ A **populous** country or area has a lot of people living in it. 人口众多的 [usu ADJ n] [FORMAL] ❑ *Indonesia, with 216 million people, is the fourth most populous country in the world.* 印度尼西亚，2.16亿人口，是人口占世界第4位的国家。

Word Web population

In 1987 the world's **population** was 5 billion. By the year 2000, it had climbed to 6 billion. Demographers predict that the total will top 9 billion by the year 2050. Improvements in medicine, sanitation, and nutrition have caused a decline in **death rates**. At the same time, there has been no overall decrease in **birth rates**. In a few countries, like Japan, the birth rate has dropped dramatically. As Japan's population ages, its workforce shrinks. India has the opposite problem. With its population **trend**, it has more young people wanting to join the workforce than there are jobs available.

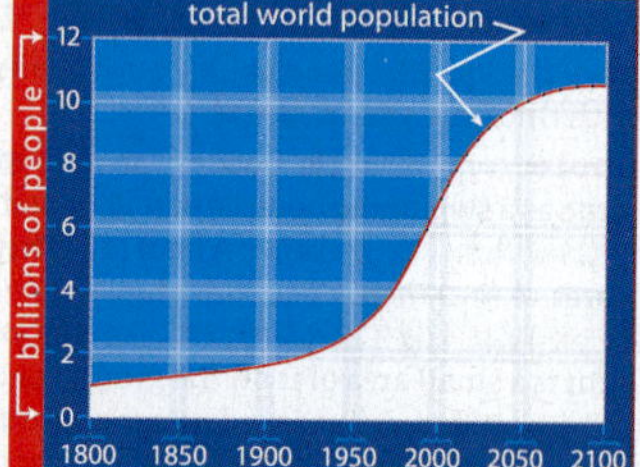

P

pop-up 1 ADJ A **pop-up** book, usually a children's book, has pictures that stand up when you open the pages. 弹起立体图片的(书) [ADJ n] 2 ADJ On a computer screen, a **pop-up** menu or advertisement is a small window containing a menu or advertisement that appears on the screen when you perform particular operations. (计算机屏幕上) 弹出的(菜单、广告) [ADJ n] [COMPUTING] ❑ *...a program for stopping pop-up ads.* …阻挡弹出广告的程序。

▲ **porce·lain** /pɔrsəlɪn, pɔrslɪn/ N-UNCOUNT **Porcelain** is a hard, shiny substance made by heating clay. It is used to make delicate cups, plates, and ornaments. 瓷 ❑ *There were lilies everywhere in tall white porcelain vases.* 到处都是插在白瓷高花瓶里的百合花。

→ see **pottery**

★ **porch** /pɔrtʃ/ (**porches**) 1 N-COUNT A **porch** is a sheltered area at the entrance to a building. It has a roof and sometimes has walls. 门廊 ❑ *She huddled inside the porch as she rang the bell.* 她一边按门铃一边蜷缩进门廊里。 2 N-COUNT A **porch** is a raised platform built along the outside wall of a house and often covered with a roof. 走廊 [AM]

in BRIT, usually use **veranda**

❑ *He was standing on the porch, waving as we drove away.* 我们开车离开的时候，他站在走廊上向我们挥手。

▲ **pore** /pɔr/ (**pores, poring, pored**) 1 N-COUNT Your **pores** are the tiny holes in your skin. 毛孔 ❑ *The size of your pores is determined by the amount of oil they produce.* 毛孔的大小取决于毛孔分泌油脂的多少。 2 V-I If you **pore over** or **through** information, you look at it and study it very carefully. 仔细研究 ❑ *We spent hours poring over travel brochures.* 我们花了几个小时仔细研究旅游宣传册。

pork /pɔrk/ N-UNCOUNT **Pork** is meat from a pig, usually fresh and not smoked or salted. (常为新鲜的未熏过、未腌过的) 猪肉 ❑ *...fried pork chops.* …炸猪排。

→ see **meat**

porn /pɔrn/ N-UNCOUNT **Porn** is the same as **pornography**. 色情作品 [INFORMAL] ❑ *...a porn cinema.* …色情影院。

por·no·graph·ic /pɔrnəgræfɪk/ ADJ **Pornographic** materials such as movies, DVDs, and magazines are designed to cause sexual excitement by showing naked people or referring to sexual acts. 色情的 [DISAPPROVAL] ❑ *I found out he'd been watching pornographic videos.* 我发现他一直在看色情录像。

por·nog·ra·phy /pɔrnɒgrəfi/ N-UNCOUNT **Pornography** refers to books, magazines, and movies that are designed to cause sexual excitement by showing naked people or referring to sexual acts. 色情作品 [DISAPPROVAL] ❑ *The country's leading newspaper has called for a new campaign against child pornography.* 该国最大的报纸已呼吁开展一场新运动反对儿童色情作品。

po·rous /pɔrəs/ ADJ Something that is **porous** has many small holes in it that water and air can pass through. 多孔的 ❑ *The local limestone is so porous that all the rainwater immediately sinks below ground.* 当地的石灰岩如此多孔以致所有的雨水很快渗到地下。

→ see **pottery**

★ **por·ridge** /pɔrɪdʒ/ N-UNCOUNT **Porridge** is a thick sticky food made from oats cooked in water or milk and eaten hot, especially for breakfast. 麦片粥 [mainly BRIT]

in AM, usually use **oatmeal**

port ♦◇◇ /pɔrt/ (**ports**) 1 N-COUNT A **port** is a town by the sea or on a river that has a harbor. 港口城市 ❑ *...the Mediterranean port of Marseilles.* …地中海港口城市马赛。 2 N-COUNT A **port** is a harbor area where ships load and unload goods or passengers. 港口 ❑ *...the bridges that link the port area to the rest of the city.* …连接城市港口和其余地区的各桥梁。 3 N-COUNT A **port** on a computer is a place where you can attach another piece of equipment such as a printer. (计算机的) 端口 [COMPUTING] ❑ *The devices, attached to a PC through standard ports, print bar codes onto envelopes.* 这些设备通过标准端口和个人电脑相连，将条形码打印到信封上。 4 ADJ In sailing, the **port** side of a ship is the left side when you are on it and facing toward the front. (轮船) 左舷的 [TECHNICAL] ❑ *Her official number is carved on the port side of the forecabin.* 她的正式编号刻在前舱的左舷上。

● N-UNCOUNT **Port** is also a noun. 左舷 ❑ *USS Ogden turned to port.* 美国奥格登号舰向左转了。 5 N-UNCOUNT **Port** is a type of strong, sweet red wine. 波尔特 (葡萄酒) ❑ *He asked for a glass of port after dinner.* 他饭后要了一杯波尔特葡萄酒。

→ see **ship**

Word Link *able ≈ able to be : incurable, portable, unavoidable*

Word Link *port ≈ carrying : export, import, portable*

port·able /pɔrtəbᵊl/ (**portables**) 1 ADJ A **portable** machine or device is designed to be easily carried or moved. 便携式的 ❑ *There was a little portable television switched on behind the bar.* 吧台后有一台便携式小电视机开着。 2 N-COUNT A **portable** is something such as a television, radio, or computer that can be easily carried or moved. 便携式设备 ❑ *We bought a portable for the bedroom.* 我们卧室里买了台便携设备。

por·tal /pɔrtᵊl/ (**portals**) N-COUNT On the Internet, a **portal** is a website that consists of links to other sites. (互联网上的) 门户网站 [COMPUTING] ❑ *The site acts as a portal for thousands of online dealers.* 该站点为数千名网络交易者的门户网站。

por·ter /pɔrtər/ (**porters**) 1 N-COUNT A **porter** is a person whose job is to carry things, for example, people's luggage at a train station or in a hotel. 搬运工 ❑ *Our taxi pulled up at Old Delhi station and a porter sprinted to the door.* 我们的出租车停在老德里车站，一个搬运工快步朝车门跑过来。 2 N-COUNT In a hospital, a **porter** is someone whose job is to move patients from place to place. (医院里的) 护工 [BRIT]

in AM, use **orderly**

3 N-COUNT A **porter** is a person whose job is to be in charge of the entrance of a building such as a hotel. 看门人 [BRIT]

in AM, use **doorman**

★ **port·fo·lio** /pɔrtfoʊlioʊ/ (**portfolios**) 1 N-COUNT A **portfolio** is a set of pictures by someone, photographs of their work, or examples of their writing, which they use when entering competitions or applying for work. (用于参赛或求职的) 作品选辑 ❑ *After dinner that evening, Edith showed them a portfolio of her own political cartoons.* 那天晚饭后，伊迪丝给他们看了她自己的政治漫画选辑。 2 N-COUNT In finance, a **portfolio** is the combination of investments that a particular person or company owns. 投资组合 [BUSINESS] ❑ *...Roger Early, a portfolio manager at Federated Investors Corp.* …罗杰・厄尔利，联合投资者公司的投资组合经理。 3 N-COUNT In politics, a **portfolio** is a high-ranking official's responsibility for a particular area of a government's activities. (高官的) 职责 ❑ *He has held the defense portfolio since the first free elections in 1990.* 自从1990年的首次自由选举以来他一直担任国防部长一职。 4 N-COUNT A company's **portfolio** of products or designs is their range of products or designs. (产品或设计的) 系列 [BUSINESS] ❑ *The company has continued to invest heavily in a strong portfolio of products.* 该公司继续大力投资一个强大的产品系列。

por·tion /pɔrʃᵊn/ (**portions**) 1 N-COUNT A **portion of** something is a part of it. 部分 ❑ *Damage was confined to a small portion of the castle.* 城堡仅有一小部分受到了损坏。 ❑ *I have spent a considerable portion of my life here.* 我已在这里度过了一生中的大部分时光。 2 N-COUNT A **portion** is the amount of food that is given to one person at a meal. (食物的) 一份 ❑ *Desserts can be substituted by a portion of fresh fruit.* 甜点可以替换成一份新鲜水果。 ❑ *The portions were generous.* 份量很足。

por·trait ♦◇◇ /pɔrtrɪt, -treɪt/ (**portraits**) 1 N-COUNT A **portrait** is a painting, drawing, or photograph of a particular person. 画像；像片 ❑ *...badly painted family portraits.* …绘制得很差的全家福画像。 2 N-COUNT A **portrait** of a person, place, or thing is a verbal description of them. 文字描述 [usu N of n] ❑ *...this gripping, funny portrait of Jewish life in 1950s Hoboken.* …这段文字引人入胜、妙趣横生地描述了20世纪50年代霍博肯犹太人的生活。

→ see **painting**

★ **por·tray** /pɔrtreɪ/ (**portrays, portraying, portrayed**) 1 V-T When an actor or actress **portrays** someone, he or she plays that person in a play or movie. 扮演 ❑ *In 1975 he portrayed the king in a Los Angeles revival of "Camelot."* 1975年他在洛杉矶重演的戏剧《卡米洛特》中扮演国王。 2 V-T When a writer or artist **portrays** something, he or she writes a description or produces a painting of it. 描绘(事物) ❑ *The film portrays a culture of young people who live in lower Manhattan.* 这部电影描绘了在下曼哈顿地区生活的青年人文化。 3 V-T If a movie, book, or television program **portrays** someone in a certain way, it represents them in that way. (以某种方式) 刻画(某人) ❑ *...complaints about the way women are portrayed in ads.* …不满于广告中对妇女的刻画方式。

P

por·tray·al /pɔrtreɪəl/ (**portrayals**) 1 N-COUNT An actor's **portrayal of** a character in a play or movie is the way that he or she plays the character. 扮演 ❑ *Mr. Ying is well-known for his portrayal of a prison guard in the film "The Last Emperor."* 英先生因在《末代皇帝》中扮演一个监狱看守而出名。 2 N-COUNT An artist's **portrayal of** something is a drawing, painting, or photograph of it. 绘画；照片 ❑ *...a moving portrayal of St. John the Evangelist by Simone Martini.* …西蒙纳・马蒂尼创作的福音传道者圣约翰的感人画像。 3 N-COUNT The **portrayal of** something in a book or movie is the act of describing it or showing it. 描绘；展示 ❑ *...an accurate portrayal of family life.* …对家庭生活的精确描绘。 4 N-COUNT The **portrayal of** something in a book, movie, or program is the way that it is made to appear. 刻画 ❑ *The media persists in its portrayal of us as muggers, dope sellers, and gangsters.* 媒体坚持将我们刻画成抢劫犯、毒品贩和匪徒。

POS /pi oʊ ɛs/ 1 The **POS** is the place in a store where a product is passed from the seller to the customer. **POS** is an abbreviation for **point of sale**. 售货点；收银台 [BUSINESS] ❑ *...a POS system that doubles as an inventory and sales control system.* …一个兼作库存和销售控制的收银系统。

pose ♦◇◇ /poʊz/ (**poses, posing, posed**) 1 V-T If something **poses** a problem or a danger, it is the cause of that problem or danger. 造成（问题、危险）❑ *This could pose a threat to jobs in the coal industry.* 这可能对煤炭行业的就业造成威胁。 2 V-T If you **pose** a question, you ask it. If you **pose** an issue that needs considering, you mention the issue. 提出（问题）[FORMAL] ❑ *When I finally posed the question, "Why?" he merely shrugged.* 当我最终提出"为什么"这个问题时，他只是耸耸肩。 3 V-I If you **pose as** someone, you pretend to be that person in order to deceive people. 假扮 ❑ *The team posed as drug dealers to trap the ringleaders.* 专案组成员们假扮毒品贩子来诱捕犯罪头目。 4 V-I If you **pose for** a photograph or painting, you stay in a particular position so that someone can photograph you or paint you. 摆姿势（以供人摄影或绘画）❑ *Before going into their meeting the six foreign ministers posed for photographs.* 开会前6国外长摆姿势照了相。 5 N-COUNT A **pose** is a particular way that you stand, sit, or lie, for example, when you are being photographed or painted. 姿势 ❑ *We have had several preliminary sittings in various poses.* 我们已经预拍了几种不同的姿势。

posh /pɒʃ/ (**posher, poshest**) 1 ADJ If you describe something as **posh**, you mean that it is elegant, fashionable, and expensive. 时髦的；豪华的 [INFORMAL] ❑ *Celebrating a promotion, I took her to a posh hotel for a cocktail.* 为庆祝晋升，我带她去了一家豪华酒店喝鸡尾酒。 2 ADJ If you describe a person as **posh**, you mean that they belong to or behave as if they belong to the upper classes. 上流社会的；看似上流社会的 [mainly BRIT, INFORMAL] ❑ *I wouldn't have thought she had such posh friends.* 我没有想到她有这样一些上流社会的朋友。

P

po·si·tion ♦♦♦ /pəzɪʃᵊn/ (**positions, positioning, positioned**) 1 N-COUNT The **position** of someone or something is the place where they are in relation to other things. 位置 ❑ *The ship was identified, and its name and position were reported to the Coast Guard.* 该轮船的身份已得到确认，其名称和位置已报告给了海岸警卫队。 2 N-COUNT When someone or something is in a particular **position**, they are sitting, lying, or arranged in that way. 姿势 ❑ *It is crucial that the upper back and neck are held in an erect position to give support for the head.* 重要的是：上背和颈部要挺直以支撑头部，这一点很重要。 ❑ *Mr. Dambar had raised himself to a sitting position.* 丹巴先生已坐了起来。 3 V-T If you **position** something somewhere, you put it there carefully, so that it is in the right place or position. 小心放置 ❑ *Position the cursor where you want the new margins to begin.* 将光标放在你所要的新页边空白开端。 4 N-COUNT Your **position** in society is the role and the importance that you have in it. （社会）地位 ❑ *Adjustment to their changing role and position in society can be painful for some old people.* 对有些老年人适应他们在社会中不断变化的角色和地位可能是痛苦的。 5 N-COUNT A **position** in a company or organization is a job. 职位 [FORMAL] ❑ *He left a career in teaching to take up a position with the NEH.* 他放弃了教职，以便在国家人文基金会任职。 6 N-COUNT Your **position** in a race or competition is how well you did in relation to the other competitors or how well you are doing. （比赛、竞赛中的）名次 ❑ *By the ninth hour the car was running in eighth position.* 比赛进行到第9个小时的时候该赛车跑在第8位。 7 N-COUNT You can describe your situation at a particular time by saying that you are in a particular **position**. 处境；状况 ❑ *He's going to be in a very difficult position if things go badly for him.* 他处境将非常困难，如果情况变糟的话。 ❑ *Companies should be made to reveal more about their financial position.* 应该要求各公司披露更多的财务状况资料。 8 N-COUNT Your **position on** a particular matter is your attitude toward it or your opinion of it. 态度；看法 [FORMAL] ❑ *He could be depended on to take a moderate position on most of the key issues.* 可以相信，他会在大多数关键问题上持温和态度。 9 N-SING If you are **in a position to** do something, you are able to do it. If you are **in no position to** do something, you are unable to do it. （做某事的）适当位置 ❑ *I am not in a position to comment.* 我不便发表评论。 10 PHRASE If someone or something is **in position**, they are in their correct or usual place or arrangement. 在合适的位置上 ❑ *28,000 U.S. troops are moving into position.* 2.8万名美国士兵即将到位。

→ see **navigation**

Word Partnership	*position* 的常用搭配:
ADJ.	**better** position 1 2 4 – 7
	fetal position 2
	(un)comfortable position 2 7
	difficult position, **financial** position 7
	official position 8

posi·tive ♦♦◇ /pɒzɪtɪv/ 1 ADJ If you are **positive about** things, you are hopeful and confident, and think of the good aspects of a situation rather than the bad ones. （心态）积极的 ❑ *Be positive about your future and get on with living a normal life.* 要积极面对未来，习惯过一种平常生活。 ❑ *Her husband became much more positive and was soon back in full-time employment.* 她丈夫变得积极多了，并且很快又干起了全职工作。 ● **posi·tive·ly** ADV 积极地 [ADV after v] ❑ *You really must try to start thinking positively.* 你真得开始努力地积极思考问题。 2 ADJ A **positive** fact, situation, or experience is pleasant and helpful to you in some way. 积极的（事实、情形、经历）❑ *The parting from his sister had a positive effect on John.* 和姐姐的分开对约翰有积极的影响。 ● N-SING **The positive** in a situation is the good and pleasant aspects of it. 积极面 ["the" N] ❑ *He prefers to focus on the positive.* 他更愿意关注积极面。 3 ADJ If you make a **positive** decision or take **positive** action, you do something definite in order to deal with a task or problem. 积极的（决定、行动等）❑ *There are positive changes that should be implemented in the rearing of animals.* 应该积极改变动物的饲养方式。 4 ADJ A **positive** response to something indicates agreement, approval, or encouragement. 积极的（回应）❑ *There's been a positive response to the U.N. Secretary-General's recent peace efforts.* 对联合国秘书长最近的和平努力已有积极回应。 ● **posi·tive·ly** ADV 积极地 [ADV after v] ❑ *He responded positively and accepted the fee of $1,000 I had offered.* 他作出了积极回应，接受了我提供的$1000的费用。 5 ADJ If you are **positive** about something, you are completely sure about it. 肯定的 [v-link ADJ] ❑ *"Judith's never late. You sure she said eight?"—"Positive."* "朱迪丝从来不迟到，你肯定她说的是8点？"——"肯定。" 6 ADJ **Positive** evidence gives definite proof of the truth or identity of something. 确凿的（证据）[ADJ n] ❑ *There was no positive evidence that any birth defects had arisen as a result of Vitamin A intake.* 没有确凿证据表明摄入维生素A会导致先天缺陷。 ● **posi·tive·ly** ADV 确凿地 [ADV with v] ❑ *He has positively identified the body as that of his wife.* 他已确认那具尸体是他妻子的。 7 ADJ If a medical or scientific test is **positive**, it shows that something has happened or is present. （化验结果）阳性的 ❑ *If the test is positive, a course of antibiotics may be prescribed.* 如果化验结果呈阳性，可能要开一个疗程的抗生素。 8 **HIV positive** → see **HIV** 9 ADJ A **positive** number is greater than zero. 正的（数字）[ADJ n] ❑ *It's really a simple numbers game with negative and positive numbers.* 这其实是一种正负数的简单数字游戏。 10 ADJ If something has a **positive** electrical charge, it has the same charge as a proton and the opposite charge to a neutron. 正的（电荷）[TECHNICAL]

→ see **lightning, magnet**

posi·tive dis·crimi·na·tion N-UNCOUNT **Positive discrimination** means making sure that people such as women, members of smaller racial groups, and disabled people get a fair share of the opportunities available. （使妇女、少数民族、残疾人获公平机会的）积极性区别对待 [BRIT]

in AM, use **affirmative action**

posi·tive·ly /pɒzɪtɪvli/ 1 ADV You use **positively** to emphasize that you really mean what you are saying. 绝对地 [ADV adj-superl] [EMPHASIS] ❑ *This is positively the last chance for the industry to establish such a system.* 这绝对是该行业建立此机制的最后一次机会。 2 ADV You use **positively** to emphasize that something really is the case, although it may sound surprising or extreme. 真正地 [EMPHASIS]

❑ *Mike's changed since he came back – he seems positively cheerful.* 迈克自从回来后就变了——他看上去真是喜气洋洋。

pos·sess /pəzɛs/ (**possesses, possessing, possessed**) V-T If you **possess** something, you have it or own it. 拥有 [no passive] ❑ *He was then arrested and charged with possessing an offensive weapon.* 他之后被逮捕了并被指控拥有攻击性武器。

pos·ses·sion /pəzɛʃᵊn/ (**possessions**) 1 N-UNCOUNT If you are **in possession of** something, you have it, because you have obtained it or because it belongs to you. 拥有 [FORMAL] ❑ *Those documents are now in the possession of the Washington Post.* 那些文件现在归《华盛顿邮报》所有。 ❑ *He was also charged with illegal possession of firearms.* 他还被指控非法拥有火器。 2 N-COUNT Your **possessions** are the things that you own or have with you at a particular time. 财产；所有物 ❑ *People had lost their homes and all their possessions.* 人们已失去了家园和所有的财产。

Word Partnership *possession* 的常用搭配：

N. **cocaine** possession, **drug** possession, possession **of a firearm**, possession **of illegal drugs**, **marijuana** possession, possession **of property**, **weapons** possession 1

pos·ses·sive /pəzɛsɪv/ 1 ADJ Someone who is **possessive about** another person wants all that person's love and attention. (对某人) 独占欲强的 ❑ *Danny could be very jealous and possessive about me.* 丹尼会很嫉妒，对我独占欲极强。 ● **pos·ses·sive·ness** N-UNCOUNT 独占欲 ❑ *I've ruined every relationship with my possessiveness.* 我的独占欲每次都毁掉了两人关系。 2 ADJ Someone who is **possessive about** things that they own does not like other people to use them. (对物) 独享欲强的 ❑ *People were very possessive about their coupons.* 人们极爱独享优惠券。 3 ADJ In grammar, a **possessive determiner** or **possessive adjective** is a word such as "my" or "his" that shows who or what something belongs to or is connected with. The **possessive** form of a name or noun has **'s** added to it, as in "Jenny's" or "cat's." (语法中) 物主性的 (限定词、形容词) [ADJ n]

pos·sibil·ity ◆◆◇ /pɒsɪbɪlɪti/ (**possibilities**) 1 N-COUNT If you say there is a **possibility that** something is the case or **that** something will happen, you mean that it might be the case or it might happen. 可能性 ❑ *We were not in the least worried about the possibility that candy could rot the teeth.* 我们一点也不担心糖果可能会腐蚀牙齿。 2 N-COUNT A **possibility** is one of several different things that could be done. 可以做的事 ❑ *There were several possibilities open to each manufacturer.* 每个制造商都有几种可能的选择。

Note that you do not use **possibility** in sentences like "I had the possibility to do it." The words you need are **opportunity** or **chance**. **Opportunity** is more formal. ❑ *Later Donald had the opportunity of driving the car... The people of Northern Ireland would have the chance to shape their own future.*

Word Link *ible ≈ able to be : audible, flexible, possible*

pos·sible ◆◆◆ /pɒsɪbᵊl/ (**possibles**) 1 ADJ If it is **possible** to do something, it can be done. (做某事) 可能的 ❑ *If it is possible to find out where your brother is, we will.* 如果有可能找到你哥哥的下落，我们会找的。 ❑ *Everything is possible if we want it enough.* 如果我们非常想要的话，任何事都是有可能的。 2 ADJ A **possible** event is one that might happen. 可能 (发生) 的 ❑ *He referred the matter to the attorney general for possible action against several newspapers.* 他将此事交给首席检察官处理，以求可能诉讼几家报社。 ❑ *One possible solution, if all else fails, is to take legal action.* 如果其他方案都不行，一个可能的解决办法就是提起诉讼。 3 ADJ If you say that it is **possible that** something is true or correct, you mean that although you do not know whether it is true or correct, you accept that it might be. 可能 (真实) 的 [v-link ADJ] [VAGUENESS] ❑ *It is possible that there's an explanation for all this.* 这一切可能真有个解释。 4 ADJ If you do something **as soon as possible**, you do it as soon as you can. If you get **as much as possible** of something, you get as much of it as you can. 尽可能的 (早、多等) ["as" adv/pron "as" ADJ] ❑ *Please make your decision as soon as possible.* 请尽可能快地出你们的决定。 ❑ *Mrs. Pollard decided to learn as much as possible about the country before going there.* 波拉德夫人决定尽可能多地了解那个国家后再去那儿。 5 ADJ You use **possible** with superlative adjectives to emphasize that something has more or less of a quality than anything else of its kind. 和形容词最高级连用，表示"最…不过" [EMPHASIS] ❑ *They have joined the job market at the worst possible time.* 他们在一个最遭糕不过的时候进入了职场。 ❑ *We expressed in the clearest possible way our disappointment, hurt, and anger.* 我们以最清晰不过的方式表达了我们的失望、伤痛和愤怒。 6 ADJ If you describe someone as, for example, a **possible** governor, you mean that they could be elected as governor. 可能 (当选) 的 [ADJ n] ❑ *Government sources are now openly speculating about a possible successor for Dr. Lawrence.* 各官方消息源现在正公开地推测继劳伦斯博士之任的可能人选。 ● N-COUNT **Possible** is also a noun. 可能的人 ❑ *Kennedy, who divorced wife Joan in 1982, was tipped as a presidential possible.* 1982年和妻子琼离婚的肯尼迪被认为最可能成为总统人选。 7 N-SING **The possible** is everything that can be done in a situation. 可能的事 ❑ *He is a Democrat with the skill, nerve, and ingenuity to push the limits of the possible.* 作为民主党人，他有着技巧、胆量和智谋来利用一切可能性。

Thesaurus *possible* 另参见：

ADJ. achievable, attainable, feasible, likely; (*ant.*) impossible, unlikely 1

pos·sibly ◆◆◇ /pɒsɪbli/ 1 ADV You use **possibly** to indicate that you are not sure whether something is true or might happen. 可能地 (表示没把握) [VAGUENESS] ❑ *Exercise will not only lower blood pressure but possibly protect against heart attacks.* 运动不仅会降低血压，而且能防止心脏病发作。 ❑ *They were casually dressed; possibly students.* 他们穿着随意，可能是学生。 2 ADV You use **possibly** to emphasize that you are surprised, puzzled, or shocked by something that you have seen or heard. 可能地 (强调惊讶、迷惑或震惊) [ADV before v] [EMPHASIS] ❑ *It was the most unexpected piece of news one could possibly imagine.* 可以想像，这是最出人意料的一则消息。 3 ADV You use **possibly** to emphasize that someone has tried their hardest to do something, or has done it as well as they can. (最大) 可能地 [ADV before v] [EMPHASIS] ❑ *They've done everything they can possibly think of.* 凡是可能想得到的，他们都已经做了。 4 ADV You use **possibly** to emphasize that something definitely cannot happen or definitely cannot be done. (完全不) 可能地 [with brd-neg, ADV before v] [EMPHASIS] ❑ *No I really can't possibly answer that!* 不，我真地根本不可能回答那个问题。

post

1 LETTERS, PARCELS, AND INFORMATION
2 JOBS AND PLACES
3 POLES

1 **post** ◆◆◇ /poʊst/ (**posts, posting, posted**) 1 V-T If you **post** notices, signs, or other pieces of information somewhere, you attach them to a wall or board so that everyone can see them. 张贴 ❑ *Officials began posting warning notices.* 官员们开始张贴警示布告。 ● PHRASAL VERB **Post up** means the same as **post**. 张贴 ❑ *He has posted a sign up that says "No Fishing."* 他已经张贴了一个标牌，写着"禁止钓鱼。" 2 V-T If you **post** information on the Internet, you make the information available to other people on the Internet. (在互联网上) 贴 (信息) [COMPUTING] ❑ *A consultation paper has been posted on the Internet inviting input from users.* 一份咨询文件已经贴上了互联网，恳请用户们提供信息。 3 PHRASE If you **keep** someone **posted**, you keep giving them the latest information about a situation that they are interested in. 让 (某人) 及时获悉 ❑ *Keep me posted on your progress.* 及时让我知道你的进展。 4 N-UNCOUNT You can use **post** to refer to letters and packages that are delivered to you. 邮件 [mainly BRIT]

in AM, usually use **mail**

5 V-T If you **post** a letter or package, you send it to someone by putting it in a mailbox or by taking it to a post office. 投寄；邮寄 [mainly BRIT]

in AM, usually use **mail**

2 **post** ◆◆◇ /poʊst/ (**posts, posting, posted**) 1 N-COUNT A **post** in a company or organization is a job or official position in it, usually one that involves responsibility. 职位；职务 [FORMAL] ❑ *She had earlier resigned her post as President Menem's assistant.* 她已于早些时候辞去了梅内姆总统助理的职务。 2 V-T If you **are posted** somewhere, you are sent there by the organization that you work for and usually work there for several years. 派遣 [usu passive] ❑ *After training she was posted to Biloxi.* 培训之后，她被派到了比洛克西。 3 V-T If a soldier, guard, or other person **is posted** somewhere, they are told to stand there, in order to supervise an activity or

guard a place. 安置…站岗 ❑ *Police have now been posted outside all temples.* 已经在所有庙宇外安置了警察站岗。❑ *They had to post a signalman at the entrance to the tunnel.* 他们不得不在隧道入口处安置一名信号员站岗。 **4** → see also **posting**

❸ post /poʊst/ (**posts**) **1** N-COUNT A **post** is a strong upright pole made of wood or metal that is dug into the ground. (金属或木头的) 柱子 ❑ *The device is fixed to a post.* 该设备固定在一根柱子上。 **2** N-COUNT A **post** is the same as a **goalpost**. 球门柱 ❑ *Jenkins missed a penalty, hitting the post in the thirteenth minute.* 詹金斯在第13分钟时罚球不中，打在了球门柱上。 **3** N-SING On a horse-racing track, **the post** is a pole that marks the finishing point. (赛马比赛的) 终点柱

post·age /poʊstɪdʒ/ N-UNCOUNT **Postage** is the money that you pay for sending letters and packages by mail. 邮资 ❑ *All prices include postage and handling.* 所有价格都包含邮资和手续费。

post·al /poʊstᵊl/ **1** ADJ **Postal** is used to describe things or people connected with the public service of carrying letters and packages from one place to another. 邮政的 [ADJ n] ❑ *Compensation for lost or damaged mail will be handled by the postal service.* 丢失或损坏邮件的赔偿事宜将由邮政部门处理。 **2** ADJ **Postal** is used to describe activities that involve sending things by mail. 邮寄的 [ADJ n] ❑ *...free postal delivery.* …免费邮递。

post·al or·der (**postal orders**) N-COUNT A **postal order** is a piece of paper representing a sum of money which you can buy at a post office and send to someone as a way of sending them money by mail. 邮政汇票 [BRIT]

in AM, use **money order**

post·box /poʊstbɒks/ (**postboxes**) also **post box** N-COUNT A **postbox** is a metal box in a public place, where you put letters and small parcels to be collected. They are then sorted and delivered. Compare **letterbox**. 邮箱 [BRIT]

in AM, use **mailbox**

post·card /poʊstkard/ (**postcards**) also **post card** N-COUNT A **postcard** is a thin card, often with a picture on one side, which you can write on and mail to people without using an envelope. 明信片

post·code /poʊstkoʊd/ (**postcodes**) also **post code** N-COUNT A **postcode** is a short sequence of numbers and letters at the end of an address. 邮政编码 [BRIT]

in AM, use **zip code**

post·dated /poʊstdeɪtɪd/ ADJ On a **postdated** check, the date is a later one than the date when the check was actually written. You write a postdated check to allow a period of time before the money is taken from your account. 延期的 (支票)

post·er /poʊstər/ (**posters**) N-COUNT A **poster** is a large notice or picture that you stick on a wall or board, often in order to advertise something. 海报；招贴 ❑ *I had seen the poster for the jazz festival in Monterey.* 我已经见到了蒙特雷爵士音乐节的海报。 → see **advertising**

post·er child (**poster children**) or **poster boy, poster girl** N-COUNT If someone is a **poster child for** a particular cause, characteristic, or activity, they are seen as a very good or typical example of it. 榜样 [mainly AM] ❑ *Zidane has become the poster child for a whole generation of French-born youths of North African extraction.* 齐达内已成为法国出生、北非血统的一整代青年的榜样。

pos·ter·ity /pɒstɛrɪti/ N-UNCOUNT You can refer to everyone who will be alive in the future as **posterity**. 子孙后代 [FORMAL] ❑ *A photographer recorded the scene on video for posterity.* 一位摄影师为子孙后代摄下了这个场面。

Word Link *post ≈ after : postgraduate, postpone, postwar*

post·gradu·ate /poʊstgrædʒuɪt/ (**postgraduates**) also **post-graduate** **1** ADJ **Postgraduate** study or research is done by a student who has a bachelor's degree and is studying or doing research at a more advanced level. 研究生阶段的 [ADJ n] **2** N-COUNT A **postgraduate** or a **postgraduate student** is a student with a first degree from a university who is studying or doing research at a more advanced level. 研究生 [BRIT]

in AM, use **graduate student**

post·ing /poʊstɪŋ/ (**postings**) **1** N-COUNT If a member of an armed force gets a **posting to** a particular place, they are sent to live and work there for a period. (军事成员的) 派驻 ❑ *...awaiting his posting to a field ambulance corps in early 1941.* …1941年初他等着被派驻到野战救护队去。 **2** N-COUNT A **posting** is a message that is placed on the Internet, for example, on a newsgroup or website, for everyone to read. (在互联网上的) 帖子 [COMPUTING] ❑ *Postings on the Internet can be accessed from anywhere in the world.* 互联网上的帖子可以从世界任何地方看到。 **3** N-COUNT If you get a **posting to** a different town or country, your employers send you to work there, usually for several years. (雇员的) 派驻 [mainly BRIT]

in AM, usually use **assignment**

post·man /poʊstmən/ (**postmen**) N-COUNT A **postman** is a man whose job is to collect and deliver letters and packages that are sent by mail. 邮递员 [mainly BRIT]

in AM, usually use **letter carrier, mailman**

post·mor·tem /poʊstmɔrtəm/ (**postmortems**) **1** N-COUNT A **postmortem** is a medical examination of a dead person's body in order to find out how they died. 尸检 ❑ *A postmortem was carried out to establish the cause of death.* 进行了尸检以确定死因。 **2** N-COUNT A **postmortem** is an examination of something that has recently happened, especially something that has failed or gone wrong. 事后调查 ❑ *The postmortem on the presidential campaign is under way.* 对总统竞选的事后调查正在进行。

post of·fice (**post offices**) **1** N-COUNT A **post office** is a building where you can buy stamps, mail letters and packages, and use other services provided by the national postal service. 邮局 ❑ *She rushed to get to the post office before it closed.* 她赶在邮局关门之前到达邮局。 **2** N-SING **The Post Office** is sometimes used to refer to the U.S. Postal Service, which operates post offices. 美国邮政局 ❑ *The Post Office has confirmed that up to fifteen thousand jobs could be lost.* 美国邮政局已证实可能会丧失多达15000个就业岗位。

post of·fice box (**post office boxes**) N-COUNT A **post office box** is a numbered box in a post office where a person's mail is kept for them until they come to collect it. 邮政信箱

post·pone /poʊstpoʊn, poʊspoʊn/ (**postpones, postponing, postponed**) V-T If you **postpone** an event, you delay it or arrange for it to take place at a later time than was originally planned. 推迟 ❑ *He decided to postpone the expedition until the following day.* 他决定将探险活动推迟到第二天。

> If you **cancel** or **call off** an arrangement or an appointment, you stop it from happening. ❑ *His failing health forced him to cancel the meeting... The European Community has threatened to call off peace talks.* If you **postpone** or **put off** an arrangement or an appointment, you make another arrangement for it to happen at a later time. ❑ *Elections have been postponed until next year... The senate put off a vote on the nomination for one week.* If you **delay** something that has been arranged, you make it happen later than planned. ❑ *Space agency managers decided to delay the launch of the space shuttle.* If something **delays** you or **holds** you **up**, you start or finish what you are doing later than you planned. ❑ *He was delayed in traffic... Delivery of equipment had been held up by delays and disputes.*

post·pone·ment /poʊstpoʊnmənt, poʊspoʊn-/ (**postponements**) N-VAR The **postponement** of an event is the act of delaying it or arranging for it to take place at a later time than originally planned. 延期 ❑ *The postponement was due to a dispute over where the talks should be held.* 延期是因为在会议地点上有争议。

▲ post·script /poʊstskrɪpt/ (**postscripts**) **1** N-COUNT A **postscript** is something written at the end of a letter after you have signed your name. You usually write "P.S." in front of it. (信末的) 附言 ❑ *A brief, handwritten postscript lay beneath his signature.* 一段简短的手写体附言位于他的签名下方。 **2** N-COUNT A **postscript** is an addition to a finished story, account, or statement, that gives further information. (故事、陈述等的) 补笔；跋 ❑ *Let me add a postscript to this section on diet.* 让我对饮食这一部分加个补笔。

pos·tu·late /pɒstʃəleɪt/ (**postulates, postulating, postulated**) V-T If you **postulate** something, you suggest it as the basis for a theory, argument, or calculation, or assume that it is the basis. 假定 [FORMAL] ❑ *He dismissed arguments postulating differing standards for human rights in different cultures and regions.* 他无法接受的是假定人权标准在不同文化和地区有所不同。

★ pos·ture /pɒstʃər/ (**postures, posturing, postured**) **1** N-VAR Your **posture** is the position in which you stand or sit. (站或坐的) 姿势 ❑ *You can make your stomach look flatter instantly by improving your*

P

posture. 你可以改善坐姿，腹部就会马上显得平些。❑ *Exercise, fresh air, and good posture are all helpful.* 体育运动、新鲜空气和良好姿势都很有效果。 2 N-COUNT A **posture** is an attitude that you have toward something. 态度 [FORMAL] ❑ *The military machine is ready to change its defensive posture to one prepared for action.* 军事当局已准备从防御态势变为备战态势。 3 V-I You can say that someone **is posturing** when you disapprove of their behavior because you think they are trying to give a particular impression in order to deceive people. 作态 [usu cont] [FORMAL, DISAPPROVAL] ❑ *She says the president may just be posturing.* 她说总统也许只是在作态。
→ see **brain**

post·war /poʊstwɔr/ ADJ **Postwar** is used to describe things that happened, existed, or were made in the period immediately after a war, especially World War II, 1939-45. (尤指二战) 战后的 ❑ *Anesthetics and bottle feeding were popular in the early postwar years.* 麻醉药和奶瓶喂养在战后早些年代非常流行。

pot ♦◇◇ /pɒt/ (**pots, potting, potted**) 1 N-COUNT A **pot** is a deep round container used for cooking stews, soups, and other food. (深而圆的) 锅 ❑ *...metal cooking pots.* …金属烹饪锅。 2 N-COUNT You can use **pot** to refer to the pot and its contents, or to the contents only. (一) 锅; (一) 锅之物 ❑ *He was stirring a pot of soup.* 他当时在搅一锅汤。 3 N-COUNT A **pot of** coffee or tea is an amount of it contained in a pot. (一) 壶 ❑ *He spilt a pot of coffee.* 他洒了一壶咖啡。 ● N-COUNT You can use **pot** to refer to a coffeepot or teapot. (咖啡、茶) 壶 ❑ *There's tea in the pot.* 壶里有茶。 4 N-UNCOUNT **Pot** is sometimes used to refer to the drug marijuana or the cannabis plant. 大麻 [INFORMAL] ❑ *I started smoking pot when I was about eleven.* 我大约十一岁的时候开始吸大麻。 5 N-SING In a card game, **the pot** is the money from all the players which the winner of the game will take as a prize. (纸牌游戏一局的) 赌注总额 ["the" N] 6 V-T If you **pot** a young plant, or part of a plant, you put it into a container filled with soil, so it can grow there. 将…移盆 ❑ *Pot the cuttings individually.* 将这些切条分别移盆。 ● **pot·ted** ADJ 盆栽的 [ADJ n] ❑ *...potted plants.* …盆栽植物。 7 → see also **melting pot**

po·ta·to ♦◇◇ /pəteɪtoʊ/ (**potatoes**) 1 N-VAR **Potatoes** are round vegetables with brown or red skins and white insides. They grow under the ground. 土豆 2 PHRASE You can refer to a difficult subject that people disagree on as a **hot potato**. 烫手山芋 ❑ *...a political hot potato such as abortion.* …像堕胎这样的政治性烫手山芋。

po·ta·to chip (**potato chips**) 1 N-COUNT **Potato chips** are very thin slices of potato that have been fried until they are hard, dry, and crisp. 薯片 [AM]

in BRIT, use **crisps**

2 N-COUNT **Potato chips** are long, thin pieces of potato fried in oil or fat and eaten hot, usually with a meal. 炸薯条 [BRIT]

in AM, use **French fries**

po·ten·cy /poʊtᵊnsi/ 1 N-UNCOUNT **Potency** is the power and influence that a person, action, or idea has to affect or change people's lives, feelings, or beliefs. 影响力 ❑ *All their songs have a lingering potency.* 他们所有的歌曲都有挥之不去的影响力。 2 N-UNCOUNT The **potency** of a drug, poison, or other chemical is its strength. (毒品、药品等的) 效力 ❑ *Sunscreen can lose its potency if left over winter in the bathroom cabinet.* 防晒霜在盥洗室柜子里放置一个冬天后会失去效力。

Word Link *potent ≈ ability, power : impotent, potent, potential*

▲ **po·tent** /poʊtᵊnt/ ADJ Something that is **potent** is very effective and powerful. 效力强的 ❑ *Their most potent weapon was the Exocet missile.* 他们效力最强的武器是飞鱼导弹。

po·ten·tial ♦♦◇ /pətɛnʃᵊl/ 1 ADJ You use **potential** to say that someone or something is capable of developing into the particular kind of person or thing mentioned. 潜在的 [ADJ n] ❑ *The company has identified 60 potential customers.* 该公司已确定了60位潜在的客户。 ❑ *We are aware of the potential problems and have taken every precaution.* 我们意识到了潜在的问题，已经采取了一切防范措施。 ● **po·ten·tial·ly** ADV 潜在地 [ADV with cl/group] ❑ *Clearly this is a potentially dangerous situation.* 显然这是一种具有潜在危险的局势。 2 N-UNCOUNT If you say that someone or something has **potential**, you mean that they have the necessary abilities or qualities to become successful or useful in the future. 潜力; 潜质 ❑ *The boy has great potential.* 这个男孩有很大的潜力。 ❑ *The school strives to treat students as individuals and to help each one to achieve their full potential.* 学校力图因材施教，并帮助每位学生发挥他们的全部潜能。 3 N-UNCOUNT If you say that someone or something has **potential for** doing a particular thing, you mean that it is possible they may do it. If there is **the potential for** something, it may happen. 潜在性 ❑ *John seemed as horrified as I about his potential for violence.* 和我一样，约翰对他的暴力倾向感到恐惧。

po·tion /poʊʃᵊn/ (**potions**) N-COUNT A **potion** is a drink that contains medicine, poison, or something that is supposed to have magic powers. (含药、毒或有魔力的) 饮剂 ❑ *...a magic potion that will make Siegfried forget Brunnhilde and fall in love with Gutrune.* …一种会使齐格弗里德忘掉布伦希尔德而爱上古特鲁内娜的魔剂。

▲ **pot·tery** /pɒtəri/ (**potteries**) 1 N-UNCOUNT You can use **pottery** to refer to pots, dishes, and other objects made from clay and then baked in an oven until they are hard. 陶器 ❑ *...a fine range of pottery.* …一系列的优质陶器。 2 N-UNCOUNT You can use **pottery** to refer to the hard clay that some pots, dishes, and other objects are made of. 陶土 ❑ *Some bowls were made of pottery and wood.* 一些碗是用陶土和木头做的。 3 N-UNCOUNT **Pottery** is the craft or activity of making objects out of clay. 制陶; 陶器制造术 ❑ *He became interested in sculpting and pottery.* 他变得对雕刻和制陶感兴趣了。 4 N-COUNT A **pottery** is a factory or other place where pottery is made. 制陶厂 ❑ *...the many galleries and potteries which sell pieces by local artists.* …出售本地艺术家作品的诸多画廊和制陶厂。
→ see Word Web: **pottery**

pot·ty /pɒti/ (**potties**) N-COUNT A **potty** is a deep bowl that a small child uses instead of a toilet. 幼儿便盆

pouch /paʊtʃ/ (**pouches**) 1 N-COUNT A **pouch** is a flexible container like a small bag. 小袋 ❑ *Joe Bob took out his pipe and dug it into a pouch of tobacco.* 乔・鲍勃拿出他的烟斗伸进一个烟袋中。 2 N-COUNT The **pouch** of an animal such as a kangaroo or a koala bear is the pocket of skin on its stomach in which its baby grows. (袋鼠、树袋熊等的) 育儿袋 ❑ *...a kangaroo, with a baby in its pouch.* …育儿袋里有只幼崽的袋鼠。

▲ **poul·try** /poʊltri/ N-PLURAL You can refer to chickens, ducks, and other birds that are kept for their eggs and meat as **poultry**. 家禽 ❑ *...a poultry farm.* …一个家禽饲养场。 ● N-UNCOUNT Meat from these birds is also referred to as **poultry**. 家禽肉 ❑ *The menu features roast meats and poultry.* 菜单以各种烤肉和家禽肉为特色。
→ see **meat**

pounce /paʊns/ (**pounces, pouncing, pounced**) 1 V-I If someone **pounces on** you, they come up toward you suddenly and take hold of you. (向某人) 猛扑 ❑ *He pounced on the photographer, beat him up, and smashed his camera.* 他猛扑向那个摄影师，揍了他，并砸碎了他的相机。 2 V-I If someone **pounces on** something such as a mistake, they quickly draw attention to it, usually in order to gain an advantage for themselves or to prove that they are right.

P

Word Web pottery

There are three basic types of **pottery**. Earthenware **dishes** are made from **clay** and **fired** at a relatively low temperature. They are **porous** and require a **glaze** in order to hold water. Potters first created earthenware objects about 15,000 years ago. Stoneware pieces are heavier and are fired at a higher temperature. They are impermeable even without a glaze. **Porcelain ceramics** are more fragile. They have thin walls and are **translucent**. Stoneware and porcelain are not as old as earthenware. They appeared about 2,000 years ago when the Chinese started building high-temperature kilns. Another name for porcelain is **china**.

(对某事) 抓住不放 ❑ *The Democrats were ready to pounce on any Republican failings or mistakes.* 民主党人准备要抓住共和党人的瑕疵或错误不放。 3 V-I When an animal or bird **pounces on** something, it jumps on it and holds it, in order to kill it. (动物、鸟等) 猛扑 (以捕杀) ❑ *...like a tiger pouncing on its prey.* …宛如老虎扑猎物。

pound ♦♦♦ /paʊnd/ (**pounds, pounding, pounded**) 1 N-COUNT A **pound** is a unit of weight used mainly in the U.S., Britain and other countries where English is spoken. One pound is equal to 0.454 kilograms. A **pound of** something is a quantity of it that weighs one pound. 磅 (英美等国的重量单位，等于0.454公斤); 一磅的量 ❑ *Her weight was under ninety pounds.* 她的体重不足90磅。 ❑ *...a pound of cheese.* …一磅奶酪。 2 N-COUNT The **pound** is the unit of money which is used in Britain. It is represented by the symbol £. One British pound is divided into a hundred pence. Some other countries, for example, Egypt, also have a unit of money called a **pound**. 英镑 (英国货币单位，等于100便士) ❑ *...multi-million pound profits.* …数百万英镑的利润。 ❑ *...a pound coin.* …一英镑的硬币。 ❑ *Beer costs three pounds a bottle.* 啤酒3镑一瓶。 ❑ *A thousand pounds worth of jewelry and silver has been stolen.* 价值1000英镑的珠宝和白银被盗。 3 N-SING **The pound** is used to refer to the British currency system, and sometimes to the currency systems of other countries which use pounds. 镑制 (英国等国的币制) ❑ *The pound is expected to continue to increase against most other currencies.* 英镑对多数其他货币的汇率有望继续上升。 4 N-COUNT A **pound** is a place where dogs and cats found wandering in the street are taken and kept until they are claimed by their owners. (走失猫狗的) 认领处 ❑ *...cages at the local pound.* …本地走失猫狗认领处的笼子。 5 N-COUNT A **pound** is a place where cars that have been parked illegally are taken by the police and kept until they have been claimed by their owners. (被扣押的违章停放车辆的) 认领处 ❑ *The car remained in the police pound for a month.* 那辆汽车在警察局违章车辆认领处停放了一个月。 6 V-T/V-I If you **pound** something or **pound on** it, you hit it with great force, usually loudly and repeatedly. 连续重击 ❑ *He pounded the table with his fist.* 他用拳头猛扎桌子。 ❑ *Somebody began pounding on the front door.* 有人开始猛敲前门。 7 V-T If you **pound** something, you crush it into a paste or a powder or into very small pieces. 捣碎 ❑ *She pounded the corn kernels.* 她捣碎了玉米粒。 8 V-I If your heart **is pounding**, it is beating with an unusually strong and fast rhythm, usually because you are afraid. (心脏) 怦怦跳 ❑ *I'm sweating, my heart is pounding. I can't breathe.* 我在流汗、心脏也怦怦跳，透不过气来。

pour ♦◇◇ /pɔr/ (**pours, pouring, poured**) 1 V-T If you **pour** a liquid or other substance, you make it flow steadily out of a container by holding the container at an angle. 倒 (液体等) ❑ *Pour a pool of sauce on two plates and arrange the meat neatly.* 倒一些酱到两个盘子里，然后把肉摆放整齐。 ❑ *Don poured a generous measure of scotch into a fresh glass.* 唐往新杯子里倒了很多苏格兰威士忌。 2 V-T If you **pour** someone a drink, you put some of the drink in a cup or glass so that they can drink it. (给某人) 倒 (一杯饮料) ❑ *He got up and poured himself another drink.* 他站起身来，给自己又倒了一杯。 ❑ *She asked Tillie to pour her a cup of coffee.* 她叫蒂莉给她倒一杯咖啡。 3 V-I When a liquid or other substance **pours** somewhere, for example, through a hole, it flows quickly and in large quantities. 喷涌 ❑ *Blood was pouring from his broken nose.* 血正从他破了的鼻子里喷涌而出。 ❑ *Tears poured down both our faces.* 眼泪在我们两人脸上哗哗地流。 4 V-I When it rains very heavily, you can say that **it is pouring**. (雨) 倾盆而下 [usu cont] ❑ *It was still pouring outside.* 外面依旧大雨倾盆。 ❑ *The rain was pouring down.* 雨在倾盆而下。 5 V-I If people **pour** into or out of a place, they go there quickly and in large numbers. (人) 大量涌至 ❑ *Any day now, the Northern forces may pour across the new border.* 如今任何一天，北方军队都可能大量涌过新边界。 ❑ *At six p.m. large groups poured from the numerous offices.* 下午6:00，大批人群从无数的办公室涌出。 6 V-I If something such as information **pours** into a place, a lot of it is obtained or given. (信息等) 大量涌至 ❑ *Martin, 78, died yesterday. Tributes poured in from around the globe.* 78岁的马丁于昨日辞世，各种吊唁从全球各地大量涌来。 7 **to pour cold water on** something → see **water**

→ see **coffee**

▸ **pour out** 1 PHRASAL VERB If you **pour out** a drink, you put some of it in a cup or glass. 倒出 (一杯饮料) ❑ *Larry was pouring out four glasses of champagne.* 拉里在倒4杯香槟。 2 PHRASAL VERB If you **pour out** your thoughts, feelings, or experiences, you tell someone all about them. 倒出 (想法、情感、经历等) ❑ *I poured my thoughts out on paper in an attempt to rationalize my feelings.* 我将自己的想法倒出，写在纸上以求理顺情绪。

Word Partnership *pour* 的常用搭配：

N. pour **a liquid**, pour **a mixture**, pour **water** 1
pour **coffee**, pour **a drink** 2

pout /paʊt/ (**pouts, pouting, pouted**) V-I If someone **pouts**, they stick out their lips, usually in order to show that they are annoyed or to make themselves sexually attractive. 撅嘴 ❑ *Like one of the kids, he whined and pouted when he did not get what he wanted.* 他若没有得到他想要的，就会像孩子一般又是哼唧又是撅嘴。 ● N-COUNT **Pout** is also a noun. 撅嘴 ❑ *She shot me a reproachful pout.* 她作责备状地冲我噘了个嘴。

pov·er·ty ♦◇◇ /pɒvərti/ 1 N-UNCOUNT **Poverty** is the state of being extremely poor. 贫穷 ❑ *According to World Bank figures, 41 percent of Brazilians live in absolute poverty.* 根据世界银行的统计数字，41%的巴西人生活在极度贫困之中。 2 N-SING You can use **poverty** to refer to any situation in which there is not enough of something or its quality is poor. 贫乏 [also no det, N "of" n] [FORMAL] ❑ *...a poverty of ideas.* …思想的贫乏。

pow·der /paʊdər/ (**powders, powdering, powdered**) 1 N-MASS **Powder** consists of many tiny particles of a solid substance. 粉末 ❑ *Put a small amount of the powder into a container and mix with water.* 将少许该粉末放入容器里与水混合。 ❑ *...cocoa powder.* …可可粉。 2 V-T If a woman **powders** her face or some other part of her body, she puts face powder or talcum powder on it. 往…上搽粉 ❑ *She powdered her face and applied her lipstick and rouge.* 她往脸上搽了粉，又涂了她的口红和胭脂。

pow·dered /paʊdərd/ ADJ A **powdered** substance is one that is in the form of a powder although it can come in a different form. 粉状的 ❑ *There are only two boxes of powdered milk left.* 只剩两盒奶粉了。

pow·er ♦♦♦ /paʊər/ (**powers, powering, powered**) 1 N-UNCOUNT If someone has **power**, they have a lot of control over people and activities. 权力 ❑ *In a democracy, power must be divided.* 在民主政体中，权力必须被分散。 2 N-UNCOUNT Your **power to** do something is your ability to do it. 能力 ❑ *Human societies have the power to solve the problems confronting them.* 人类社会有能力解决他们面临的问题。 ❑ *Fathers have the power to dominate children and young people.* 父辈们有控制孩子们和年轻人的能力。 3 N-UNCOUNT If it is **in** or **within** your **power to** do something, you are able to do it or you have the resources to deal with it. 能力范围 ❑ *Your debt situation is only temporary, and it is within your power to resolve it.* 你的债务状况只是暂时的，解决它在你的能力范围里。 4 N-UNCOUNT If someone in authority has the **power** to do something, they have the legal right to do it. (法律赋予的) 权力 [also N in pl] ❑ *The police have the power of arrest.* 警察有逮捕权。 5 N-UNCOUNT If people take **power** or come to **power**, they take charge of a country's affairs. If a group of people are **in power**, they are in charge of a country's affairs. 政权 ❑ *Idi Amin came into power several years later.* 伊迪·阿明几年后执掌了政权。 ❑ *He first assumed power in 1970.* 他于1970年首次执掌了政权。 6 N-COUNT You can use **power** to refer to a country that is very rich or important, or has strong military forces. 强国 ❑ *....the emergence of the new major economic power, Japan.* …新的主要经济强国日本的崛起。 7 N-UNCOUNT The **power** of something is the ability that it has to move or affect things. 动力 ❑ *The vehicle had better power, better tires, and better brakes.* 这种车辆有更好的动力、更好的轮胎和更好的刹车。 8 N-UNCOUNT **Power** is energy, especially electricity, that is obtained in large quantities from a fuel source and used to operate lights, heating, and machinery. (尤指电) 能量 ❑ *Nuclear power is cleaner than coal.* 核能比煤更清洁。 ❑ *Power has been restored to most parts that were hit last night by high winds.* 昨天夜里受到强风袭击的大部分地区已经恢复了供电。 9 V-T The device or fuel that **powers** a machine provides the energy that the machine needs in order to work. 为…提供动力 ❑ *The "flywheel" battery, it is said, could power an electric car for 600 miles on a single charge.* 据说，"飞轮"电池每充电一次可驱动一辆电动汽车行驶600英里。 10 ADJ **Power** tools are operated by electricity. 电动的 [ADJ n] ❑ *...large power tools, such as chainsaws.* …大型电动工具，如链锯。

→ see **electricity, energy, solar system**

▸ **power up** PHRASAL VERB When you **power up** something such as a computer or a machine, you connect it to a power supply and switch it on. 将…接通电源 ❑ *Simply power up your laptop and continue work.* 只要把你的手提电脑接通电源就能继续工作。

Thesaurus *power* 另参见:

N. authority, control 1
energy, force, intensity, potency, strength 7

Word Partnership *power* 的常用搭配:

ADJ. **divine** power, **political** power 1
real power 1 2
tremendous power 1 2 7
absolute power, power **hungry** 1 5
economic power, **military** power 1 6
electric(al) power, **nuclear** power, **solar** power 8
V. **exercise** power, **wield** power 1 4 5
come into power, **hold** power, **maintain** power, **remain in** power, **restore to** power, **rise to** power, **seize** power, **share** power, **take** power, **transfer** power 5

pow·er bro·ker (power brokers) N-COUNT A **power broker** is someone who has a lot of influence, especially in politics, and uses it to help other people gain power. 权力经纪人 ❑ *Jackson had been a major power broker in the presidential elections.* 杰克逊曾是总统竞选中一名主要的权力经纪人。

pow·er cut (power cuts) N-COUNT A **power cut** is a period of time when the electricity supply to a particular building or area is stopped, sometimes deliberately. 停电 [mainly BRIT]
in AM, usually use **outage**

pow·er·ful ♦♦◇ /paʊərfəl/ 1 ADJ A **powerful** person or organization is able to control or influence people and events. 有影响力的 ❑ *You're a powerful man – people will listen to you.* 你是个有影响力的人——人们会听你的。 ❑ *...Russia and India, two large, powerful countries.* …俄罗斯和印度——两个有影响力的大国。 2 ADJ You say that someone's body is **powerful** when it is physically strong. 强壮的 ❑ *Hans flexed his powerful muscles.* 汉斯放松了他强壮的肌肉。 ● **pow·er·ful·ly** ADV 强壮地 [ADV with v] ❑ *He is described as a strong, powerfully-built man of 60.* 他被描述成一个身强力壮的60岁的人。 3 ADJ A **powerful** machine or substance is effective because it is very strong. 效力强大的 ❑ *The more powerful the car the more difficult it is to handle.* 汽车的功效越大，操纵起来越难。 ❑ *...powerful computer systems.* …强大的计算机系统。 ● **pow·er·ful·ly** ADV 效力大地 [ADV adj] ❑ *Crack is a much cheaper, smokable form of cocaine which is powerfully addictive.* 强效可卡因是一种便宜得多的可吸食性可卡因，非常容易上瘾。 4 ADJ A **powerful** smell is very strong. 浓烈的 ❑ *There was a powerful smell of stale beer.* 有一股浓烈的馊啤酒的气味。 ● **pow·er·ful·ly** ADV 强烈地 [ADV after v] ❑ *The air smelled powerfully of dry dust.* 空气中弥漫着浓烈的尘土味。 5 ADJ A **powerful** voice is loud and can be heard from a long way away. 洪亮的 ❑ *At that moment Mrs. Jones's powerful voice interrupted them, announcing a visitor.* 这时，琼斯太太洪亮的嗓音打断了他们，说有位客人来了。 6 ADJ You describe a piece of writing, speech, or work of art as **powerful** when it has a strong effect on people's feelings or beliefs. 有感染力的 ❑ *...a powerful 11-part drama about a corrupt city leader.* …一部有关一位腐败的市领导、有感染力的、由11部分组成的戏剧作品。 ● **pow·er·ful·ly** ADV 有感染力地 ❑ *It's a play – painful, funny, and powerfully acted.* 这是一出戏——令人痛苦而又逗人发笑，演得很有感染力。

pow·er·less /paʊərlɪs/ 1 ADJ Someone who is **powerless** is unable to control or influence events. 无能为力的 ❑ *If you don't have money, you're powerless.* 如果你没有钱，你就无能为力。 ● **pow·er·less·ness** N-UNCOUNT 无能为力 ❑ *If we can't bring our problems under control, feelings of powerlessness and despair often ensue.* 如果我们不能将我们的问题控制住，无能为力和绝望感往往就会随之而来。 2 ADJ If you are **powerless to** do something, you are completely unable to do it. 不能的 [ADJ to-inf] ❑ *People are being murdered every day and I am powerless to stop it.* 每天都有人被杀害，而我却无力制止。

pow·er line (power lines) N-COUNT A **power line** is a cable, especially above ground, along which electricity is passed to an area or building. 输电线

pow·er plant (power plants) N-COUNT A **power plant** is the same as a **power station**. 发电站

power-sharing also **power sharing** N-UNCOUNT **Power-sharing** is a political arrangement in which different or opposing groups all take part in government together. 权力分享 ❑ *They agreed a power-sharing arrangement, but it collapsed after five months.* 他们达成了一项权力分享协议，但5个月后该协议就破产了。

pow·er sta·tion (power stations) N-COUNT A **power station** is a place where electricity is produced. 发电站
→ see **electricity**

pow·er steer·ing N-UNCOUNT In a vehicle, **power steering** is a system for steering that uses power from the engine so that it is easier for the driver to steer the vehicle. 动力转向系统

pp. ♦◇◇ pp. is the plural of "p." and means "pages." 页(复数) [WRITTEN] ❑ *See chapter 6, pp. 137–41.* 见第6章第137–41页。

PR /pi ɑr/ N-UNCOUNT **PR** is an abbreviation for **public relations**. 公关 [BUSINESS] ❑ *It will be good PR.* 这将是很好的公关。

★ **prac·ti·cable** /præktɪkəb^əl/ ADJ If a task, plan, or idea is **practicable**, people are able to carry it out. 可行的 [FORMAL] ❑ *It is not practicable to offer her the original job back.* 让她重回原工作岗位是不可行的。

prac·ti·cal ♦◇◇ /præktɪk^əl/ 1 ADJ The **practical** aspects of something involve real situations and events, rather than just ideas and theories. 实际的 ❑ *...practical suggestions on how to increase the fiber in your daily diet.* …有关如何增加日常饮食中的纤维素的实际建议。 2 ADJ You describe people as **practical** when they make sensible decisions and deal effectively with problems. 务实的 [APPROVAL] ❑ *You were always so practical, Maria.* 你总是那么务实，玛丽亚。 ❑ *How could she be so practical when he'd just told her something so shattering?* 他刚对她讲了那么令人震惊的事情，她怎么还能这么务实？ 3 ADJ **Practical** ideas and methods are likely to be effective or successful in a real situation. (主意、方法) 有实效的 ❑ *Although the causes of cancer are being uncovered, we do not yet have any practical way to prevent it.* 尽管癌症的病因正被揭开，但我们还没有任何预防它的有效的方法。 4 ADJ You can describe clothes and things in your house as **practical** when they are suitable for a particular purpose rather than just being fashionable or attractive. (衣物等) 实用的 ❑ *...lightweight, practical clothes.* …质轻、实用的服装。

Thesaurus *practical* 另参见:

ADJ. businesslike, pragmatic, reasonable, sensible, systematic; *(ant.)* impractical 2 3

prac·ti·cal·ity /præktɪkælɪti/ (**practicalities**) N-VAR The **practicalities of** a situation are the practical aspects of it, as opposed to its theoretical aspects. 现实 ❑ *Decisions about your children should be based on the practicalities of everyday life.* 有关你的孩子们的决定应以日常生活的现实为依据。

prac·ti·cal·ly /præktɪkli/ 1 ADV **Practically** means almost, but not completely or exactly. 几乎 [ADV with group/cl] ❑ *He'd known the old man practically all his life.* 他几乎从小就认识那位老人。 2 ADV You use **practically** to describe something that involves real actions or events rather than ideas or theories. 实际地 [ADV adj/-ed] ❑ *The course is more practically based than the master's degree.* 这一课程比硕士学位更注重实际。

prac·tice ♦♦♦ /præktɪs/ (**practices, practicing, practiced**)
in BRIT, use **practise** for meaning 7, 8, 9, 10, 11.
1 N-COUNT You can refer to something that people do regularly as a **practice**. 做法 ❑ *Some firms have reached agreements to cut workers' pay below the level set in their contract, a practice that is illegal in Germany.* 有些公司已达成一致意见将工人的工资削减到低于合同中规定的水平，这种做法在德国是违法的。 2 N-VAR **Practice** means doing something regularly in order to be able to do it better. A **practice** is one of these periods of doing something. 练习 ❑ *She was taking all three of her daughters to basketball practice every day.* 她那时每天带她的3个女儿去进行篮球训练。 ❑ *...the hard practice necessary to develop from a learner to an accomplished musician.* …从初学者成长为有造诣的音乐家所必需的艰苦练习。 3 N-UNCOUNT The work done by doctors and lawyers is referred to as the **practice** of medicine and law. People's religious activities are referred to as the **practice** of a religion. (医疗或法律的) 业务; (宗教) 活动 ❑ *...maintaining or improving his skills in the practice of internal medicine.* …保持或提高他在内科医疗业务方面的技能。 ❑ *I eventually realized I had to change my attitude toward medical practice.* 我终于认识到我得改变我对医务工作的态度。 4 N-COUNT A doctor's or lawyer's **practice** is his or her business, often shared with other doctors or lawyers. 医生的诊所; 律师的事务所 ❑ *The new doctor's practice was miles away from where I lived.* 那位新医生的诊所离我的住处有数英里远。 5 PHRASE What happens **in practice** is what actually happens, in contrast to what is supposed to happen. 实际上 ❑ *...the difference between foreign policy*

as presented to the public and foreign policy in actual practice. …呈现给公众的外交政策和实际上实行的外交政策之间的区别。 6 PHRASE If you **put** a belief or method **into practice**, you behave or act in accordance with it. 付诸实践 ❑ *Now that he is back, the mayor has another chance to put his new ideas into practice.* 现在市长回来了，他就又有了一次机会将他的新思想付诸实践。 7 V-T/V-I If you **practice**, or **practice** something, you keep doing it regularly in order to be able to do it better. 练习 ❑ *She practiced the piano in the grade school basement.* 她在小学的地下室里练习弹钢琴。 8 → see also **practiced**
9 V-T When people **practice** something such as a custom, craft, or religion, they take part in the activities associated with it. 遵循；信奉；从事 ❑ *Her parents had yearned to be free to practice their religion.* 她父母曾渴望能自由信奉他们的宗教。 ❑ *He was brought up in a family that practiced traditional Judaism.* 他在一个信奉传统犹太教的家庭里长大。 ● **prac·tic·ing** ADJ 信奉的 [ADJ n] ❑ *And he was more or less a practicing Muslim throughout his life.* 而他差不多一生都是个信奉穆斯林的人。 10 V-T If something cruel is regularly done to people, you can say that it **is practiced on** them. 施行 [usu passive] ❑ *Female circumcision is practiced on 2 million girls a year.* 每年有2百万个女孩被施行女性割礼手术。 11 V-T/V-I Someone who **practices** medicine or law works as a doctor or a lawyer. 从事(医药、法律等工作) ❑ *He doesn't practice medicine for the money.* 他不为赚钱而行医。 ❑ *...the obligations of my license to practice as a lawyer.* …我的律师从业执照规定的义务。

Thesaurus *practice* 另参见：
N. custom, habit, method, procedure, system, way 1
exercise, rehearsal, training, workout 2

Word Partnership *practice* 的常用搭配：
PREP. **after** practice, **during** practice 2
ADJ. **clinical** practice, **legal** practice, **medical** practice, **private** practice 3

prac·ticed /præktɪst/
in BRIT, use **practised**
ADJ Someone who is **practiced at** doing something is good at it because they have had experience and have developed their skill at it. 擅长的 ❑ *She worked for years as a bookkeeper, so she's practiced at budgeting.* 她做了多年簿记员，因此她擅长预算。

prac·tise /præktɪs/ [BRIT] → see **practice**

▲ **prac·ti·tion·er** /præktɪʃənər/ (**practitioners**) N-COUNT Doctors are sometimes referred to as **practitioners** or **medical practitioners**. 行医者 [FORMAL]

▲ **prag·mat·ic** /prægmætɪk/ ADJ A **pragmatic** way of dealing with something is based on practical considerations, rather than theoretical ones. A **pragmatic** person deals with things in a practical way. 务实的 ❑ *Robin took a pragmatic look at her situation.* 罗宾从务实的角度看待她的状况。 ● **prag·mati·cal·ly** /prægmætɪkli/ ADV 务实地 ❑ *"I can't ever see us doing anything else," stated Brian pragmatically.* "我看不出我们还能做别的什么事情，"布赖恩务实地说。

prag·ma·tism /prægmətɪzəm/ N-UNCOUNT **Pragmatism** means thinking of or dealing with problems in a practical way, rather than by using theory or abstract principles. 实用主义 [FORMAL] ❑ *She had a reputation for clear thinking and pragmatism.* 她因思维清晰和实用主义而闻名。 ● **prag·ma·tist** N-COUNT (**pragmatists**) 实用主义者 ❑ *He is a political pragmatist, not an idealist.* 他是个政治上的实用主义者，而不是个理想主义者。

▲ **prai·rie** /prɛəri/ (**prairies**) N-VAR A **prairie** is a large area of flat, grassy land in North America. Prairies have very few trees. 北美大草原

praise ♦◇◇ /preɪz/ (**praises, praising, praised**) 1 V-T If you **praise** someone or something, you express approval for their achievements or qualities. 称赞 ❑ *The American president praised Turkey for its courage.* 美国总统称赞了土耳其的勇气。 ❑ *Many others praised Sanford for taking a strong stand.* 还有许多人称赞桑福德立场坚定。
2 N-UNCOUNT **Praise** is what you say or write about someone when you are praising them. 赞美 ❑ *All the ladies are full of praise for the staff and service they received.* 所有女士对工作人员和她们得到的服务赞不绝口。 ❑ *I have nothing but praise for the police.* 我对警察只有赞扬。

Thesaurus *praise* 另参见：
N. applause, compliment, congratulations;
(ant.) criticism, insult 2

pram /præm/ (**prams**) N-COUNT A **pram** is the same as a **baby carriage**. 婴儿车 [BRIT]

prank /præŋk/ (**pranks**) N-COUNT A **prank** is a childish trick. 恶作剧 [OLD-FASHIONED] ❑ *Their pranks are amusing at times.* 他们的恶作剧有时很逗。

▲ **prawn** /prɔn/ (**prawns**) N-COUNT A **prawn** is a small shellfish with a long tail and many legs, which can be eaten. 虾 [BRIT]
in AM, use **shrimp**

prawn cock·tail [BRIT] → see **shrimp cocktail**

pray /preɪ/ (**prays, praying, prayed**) 1 V-I When people **pray**, they speak to God in order to give thanks or to ask for his help. 祈祷 ❑ *He spent his time in prison praying and studying.* 他把在狱中的时间花在了祈祷和学习上。 ❑ *Now all we have to do is help ourselves and pray to God.* 现在我们要做的是自救和向上帝祈祷。 2 V-T When someone is hoping very much that something will happen, you can say that they **are praying** that it will happen. 祈望 [usu cont] ❑ *I'm just praying that somebody in Congress will do something before it's too late.* 我只祈望国会中有人在还来得及的时候做点什么。
→ see **religion**

prayer /prɛər/ (**prayers**) 1 N-UNCOUNT **Prayer** is the activity of speaking to God. 祈祷 ❑ *They had joined a religious order and dedicated their lives to prayer and good works.* 他们参加了一个宗教团体，献身于祈祷和做善事。 2 N-COUNT A **prayer** is the words a person says when they speak to God. 祷词 ❑ *They should take a little time and say a prayer for the people on both sides.* 他们应该花点儿时间为双方人民祈祷。
3 N-COUNT You can refer to a strong hope that you have as your **prayer**. 祈求 ❑ *This drug could be the answer to our prayers.* 这种药也许是对我们的祈求的回答。 4 N-PLURAL A short religious service at which people gather to pray can be referred to as **prayers**. 祈祷仪式 ❑ *He promised that the boy would be back at school in time for evening prayers.* 他承诺孩子会及时回到学校参加晚上的祈祷仪式。

★ **preach** /pritʃ/ (**preaches, preaching, preached**) 1 V-T/V-I When a member of the clergy **preaches** a sermon, he or she gives a talk on a religious or moral subject during a religious service. 布(道)；布道 ❑ *At High Mass the priest preached a sermon on the devil.* 在大弥撒仪式上，牧师布了一次有关魔鬼的道。 ❑ *The bishop preached to a crowd of several hundred local people.* 主教向一群几百名当地人布道。
2 V-T/V-I When people **preach** a belief or a course of action, they try to persuade other people to accept the belief or to take the course of action. 宣扬 ❑ *He said he was trying to preach peace and tolerance to his people.* 他说他正试图向他的人民宣扬和平与宽容。
❑ *Health experts are now preaching that even a little exercise is far better than none at all.* 如今，健康专家宣扬说，即使少量的运动也比一点不运动要好得多。 3 V-I If someone gives you advice in a very serious, boring way, you can say that they **are preaching at** you. 说教 [DISAPPROVAL] ❑ *"Don't preach at me," he shouted.* "不要对我说教，"他喊道。

preach·er /pritʃər/ (**preachers**) N-COUNT A **preacher** is a person, usually a member of the clergy, who preaches sermons as part of a church service. 传道士

▲ **pre·cari·ous** /prɪkɛəriəs/ 1 ADJ If your situation is **precarious**, you are not in complete control of events and might fail in what you are doing at any moment. (情况) 不稳定的 ❑ *Our financial situation had become precarious.* 我们的财政状况已经不稳定了。
● **pre·cari·ous·ly** ADV 不稳定地 ❑ *We lived precariously. I suppose I wanted to squeeze as much pleasure from each day as I possibly could.* 我们过着动荡不安的生活。我想我那时候是想从每一天中获取尽量多的快乐。
2 ADJ Something that is **precarious** is not securely held in place and seems likely to fall or collapse at any moment. 不稳固的
❑ *They looked really comical as they crawled up precarious ladders.* 他们爬上摇摇晃晃的梯子时，看起来真滑稽。 ● **pre·cari·ous·ly** ADV 不稳固地
❑ *One of my grocery bags was still precariously perched on the car bumper.* 我的一只购物袋还很不牢靠地悬挂在汽车保险杠上。

Word Link *caut ≈ taking care : caution, cautious, precaution*

Word Link *pre ≈ before : precaution, precede, prefix*

pre·cau·tion /prɪkɔʃən/ (**precautions**) N-COUNT A **precaution** is an action that is intended to prevent something dangerous or unpleasant from happening. 防范行动 ❑ *Could he not, just as a precaution, move to a place of safety?* 难道他不能就当是一种防范搬到一个安全的地方去吗？

P

Word Partnership *precaution* 的常用搭配：
ADV. **(just) as a** precaution
V. **take every** precaution

★ **pre·cede** /prɪsi̱d/ (precedes, preceding, preceded) 1 V-T If one event or period of time **precedes** another, it happens before it. (某事件) 先于 (另一事件) 而发生; (某时段) 先于 (另一时段) 而存在 [FORMAL] ❑ *Intensive negotiations between the main parties preceded the vote.* 投票之前，主要政党间进行了深入细致的磋商。 ❑ *The earthquake was preceded by a loud roar and lasted 20 seconds.* 地震之前有一声巨响，持续了20秒钟。 2 V-T If you **precede** someone somewhere, you go in front of them. 走在…的前面 [FORMAL] ❑ *He gestured to Alice to precede them from the room.* 他示意艾丽斯从房间里出来走在他们前面。 3 V-T A sentence, paragraph, or chapter that **precedes** another one comes just before it. (句、段、章) 处于 (另一句、段、章) 之前 ❑ *Look at the information that precedes the paragraph in question.* 请看所谈这一段之前的信息。

prec·edence /pre̱sɪdəns/ N-UNCOUNT If one thing takes **precedence over** another, it is regarded as more important than the other thing. 优先性 ❑ *Have as much fun as possible at college, but don't let it take precedence over work.* 在大学里尽情地玩，但别让玩乐优先于学习。

★ **prec·edent** /pre̱sɪdənt/ (precedents) N-VAR If there is a **precedent for** an action or event, it has happened before, and this can be regarded as an argument for doing it again. 先例 [FORMAL] ❑ *The trial could set an important precedent for dealing with similar cases.* 这次审判能为处理类似案件开创一个重要先例。

pre·ced·ing /prɪsi̱dɪŋ/ ADJ You refer to the period of time or the thing immediately before the one that you are talking about as the **preceding** one. 前面的 ❑ *As we saw in the preceding chapter, groups can be powerful agents of socialization.* 如我们在前一章所见，团组可以是社会化的有力动因。 ❑ *She informed us that eighteen members of the staff had left during the preceding year.* 她当时告知我们，18位教职员在此前的一年里离开了。

pre·cept /pri̱sɛpt/ (precepts) N-COUNT A **precept** is a general rule that helps you to decide how you should behave in particular circumstances. 准则 [FORMAL] ❑ *...an electoral process based on the central precept that all people are born equal.* …以所有人生而平等这一核心准则为基础的一种选举程序。

pre·cinct /pri̱sɪŋkt/ (precincts) N-COUNT A **precinct** is a part of a city or town that has its own police force. 警区 [AM] ❑ *The shooting occurred in the 34th Precinct.* 该枪击事件发生在第34警区。

pre·cious /pre̱ʃəs/ 1 ADJ If you say that something such as a resource is **precious**, you mean that it is valuable and should not be wasted or used badly. (资源等) 宝贵的 ❑ *After four months in foreign parts, every hour at home was precious.* 在境外待了4个月之后，在家的每个小时都是宝贵的。 ❑ *A family break allows you to spend precious time together.* 一次家庭休假使你有机会和家人共度宝贵时光。 2 ADJ **Precious** objects and materials are worth a lot of money because they are rare. (物品、材料等) 珍贵的 ❑ *...jewelry and precious objects belonging to her mother.* …属于她母亲的首饰和珍贵物品。 3 ADJ If something is **precious** to you, you regard it as important and do not want to lose it. (对某人来讲) 珍贵的 ❑ *Her family's support is particularly precious to Josie.* 家人的支持对乔茜尤为珍贵。

▲ **pre·cipi·tate** (precipitates, precipitating, precipitated)

> The verb is pronounced /prɪsɪpəteɪt/. The adjective is pronounced /prɪsɪpɪtɪt/.

> 动词读作 /prɪsɪpəteɪt/。形容词读作 /prɪsɪpɪtɪt/。

1 V-T If something **precipitates** an event or situation, usually a bad one, it causes it to happen suddenly or sooner than normal. 造成…仓促发生 [FORMAL] ❑ *The killings in Vilnius have precipitated the worst crisis yet.* 维尔纽斯的杀戮事件快速引发了迄今为止最严重的危机。 ❑ *A slight mistake could precipitate a disaster.* 一个小错误可能导致一场灾难。 2 ADJ A **precipitate** action or decision happens or is made more quickly or suddenly than most people think is sensible. 仓促的 [FORMAL] ❑ *I don't think we should make precipitate decisions.* 我认为我们不应该做出仓促的决定。

pre·cise /prɪsa̱ɪs/ 1 ADJ You use **precise** to emphasize that you are referring to an exact thing, rather than something vague. 确切的 [ADJ n] [EMPHASIS] ❑ *I can remember the precise moment when my daughter came to see me and her new baby brother in the hospital.* 我还记得我女儿来医院看望我和她刚出生的弟弟的那确切的一刻。 ❑ *The precise location of the wreck was discovered in 1988.* 船舶失事的确切地点是在1988年发现的。 2 ADJ Something that is **precise** is exact and accurate in all its details. 精确的 ❑ *They speak very precise English.* 他们说非常标准的英语。

pre·cise·ly ♦◇◇ /prɪsa̱ɪsli/ 1 ADV **Precisely** means accurately and exactly. 准确地 ❑ *Nobody knows precisely how many people are still living in the camp.* 没有人准确地知道有多少人还生活在那个营地。 ❑ *The first bell rang at precisely 10:29 a.m.* 第一遍铃声在上午10：29准时响起。 2 ADV You can use **precisely** to emphasize that a reason or fact is the only important one there is, or that it is obvious. 正是 [ADV with cl/group] [EMPHASIS] ❑ *Children come to zoos precisely to see captive animals.* 孩子们到动物园来正是为了看那些被关起来的动物。 3 ADV You can say "**precisely**" to confirm in an emphatic way that what someone has just said is true. 正是地 [as reply] [EMPHASIS] ❑ *"All I did was write the truth."—"Precisely! Now everyone knows."* "我所做的就是把真相写出来。"——"正是！现在大家都知道了。"

pre·ci·sion /prɪsɪ̱ʒ^{ə}n/ N-UNCOUNT If you do something **with precision**, you do it exactly as it should be done. 准确性 ❑ *The choir sang with precision.* 合唱团的演唱准确无误。

★ **pre·clude** /prɪklu̱d/ (precludes, precluding, precluded) 1 V-T If something **precludes** an event or action, it prevents the event or action from happening. 阻止 (某事件或行动发生) [FORMAL] ❑ *At 84, John feels his age precludes too much travel.* 在84岁时，约翰感觉到他的年龄不允许他作太多的旅行。 2 V-T If something **precludes** you **from** doing something or going somewhere, it prevents you from doing it or going there. 阻止 (某人做某事或去某地) [FORMAL] ❑ *A constitutional amendment precludes any president from serving more than two terms.* 宪法的一项修订条款规定任何总统不得连任两届以上。

pre·co·cious /prɪkoʊ̱ʃəs/ ADJ A **precocious** child is very clever, mature, or good at something, often in a way that you usually only expect to find in an adult. 早熟的 ❑ *Margaret was always a precocious child.* 玛格丽特一直是个早熟的孩子。 ❑ *She burst on to the world tennis scene as a precocious 14-year-old.* 她作为一个14岁的早熟孩子突然出现在了世界网坛上。

pre·con·cep·tion /pri̱kənsɛ̱pʃ^{ə}n/ (preconceptions) N-COUNT Your **preconceptions** about something are beliefs formed about it before you have enough information or experience. 先入之见 ❑ *Did you have any preconceptions about the sort of people who did computing?* 你对那些使用计算机的人有什么先入之见吗？

pre·con·di·tion /pri̱kəndɪ̱ʃ^{ə}n/ (preconditions) N-COUNT If one thing is a **precondition for** another, it must happen or be done before the second thing can happen or exist. 先决条件 [FORMAL] ❑ *They have demanded the release of three prisoners as a precondition for any negotiation.* 他们要求释放3名囚犯作为谈判的先决条件。

pre·cur·sor /prɪkɜ̱rsər/ (precursors) N-COUNT A **precursor** of something is a similar thing that happened or existed before it, often something that led to the existence or development of that thing. 前兆 ❑ *He said that the deal should not be seen as a precursor to a merger.* 他说这次交易不应该被看作是合并的前兆。

preda·tor /pre̱dətər/ (predators) 1 N-COUNT A **predator** is an animal that kills and eats other animals. 食肉动物 ❑ *With no natural predators on the island, the herd increased rapidly.* 由于岛上没有天然食肉动物，牧群的数量迅速增加。 2 N-COUNT People sometimes refer to predatory people or organizations as **predators**. 掠夺者 ❑ *Rumors of a takeover by Hanson are probably far-fetched, but the company is worried about other predators.* 被汉森公司收购的谣言可能是捕风捉影，但公司仍担心其他觊觎者。
→ see **food, shark**

Word Link *ory ≈ relating to : advisory, contradictory, predatory*

▲ **preda·tory** /pre̱dətɔri/ 1 ADJ **Predatory** animals live by killing other animals for food. 食肉的 ❑ *...predatory birds like the eagle.* …像鹰这样的食肉飞禽。 2 ADJ **Predatory** people or organizations are eager to gain something out of someone else's weakness or suffering. 掠夺性的 ❑ *People will not set up new businesses while they are frightened by the predatory behavior of the banks.* 人们在被银行的掠夺行为惊吓的情况下是不会开办新企业的。

★ **pre·de·ces·sor** /pre̱dɪsɛsər/ (predecessors) 1 N-COUNT Your **predecessor** is the person who had your job before you. 前任 ❑ *He maintained that he learned everything he knew from his predecessor.* 他坚称他所知道的一切都是从他的前任那儿学到的。 2 N-COUNT The **predecessor** of an object or machine is the object or machine that came before it in a sequence or process of development. 前一代

❑ *Although the car is some 2 inches shorter than its predecessor, its trunk is 20 percent larger.* 尽管这款汽车比其上一代产品短2英寸，但它的行李箱大了20%。

pre·dica·ment /prɪdɪkəmənt/ (**predicaments**) N-COUNT If you are in a **predicament**, you are in an unpleasant situation that is difficult to get out of. 困境 ❑ *Hank explained our predicament.* 汉克说明了我们的困境。

Word Link *dict ≈ speaking : contradict, dictate, predict*

pre·dict ♦◇◇ /prɪdɪkt/ (**predicts, predicting, predicted**) V-T If you **predict** an event, you say that it will happen. 预言 ❑ *The latest opinion polls are predicting a very close contest.* 最新的民意测验预言将是一场势均力敌的竞赛。 ❑ *He predicted that my hair would grow back "in no time."* 他预言我的头发会"马上"再长出来。

→ see **experiment, forecast**

pre·dict·able /prɪdɪktəbᵊl/ ADJ If you say that an event is **predictable**, you mean that it is obvious in advance that it will happen. 可预见的 ❑ *This was a predictable reaction, given the bitter hostility between the two countries.* 考虑到两国之间的强烈敌意，这种反应是可以预见的。 ● **pre·dict·ably** ADV 可预见地 ❑ *His article is, predictably, a scathing attack on capitalism.* 可以预见，他的文章会是对资本主义的猛烈抨击。 ● **pre·dict·abil·ity** /prɪdɪktəbɪlɪti/ N-UNCOUNT 可预见性 ❑ *Your mother values the predictability of your Sunday calls.* 你母亲很看重你周日电话的可预知性。

★ **pre·dic·tion** /prɪdɪkʃᵊn/ (**predictions**) N-VAR If you make a **prediction** about something, you say what you think will happen. 预言 ❑ *He was unwilling to make a prediction for the coming year.* 他不愿对来年作出预言。 ❑ *Weather prediction has never been a perfect science.* 天气预报从来都不是一门准确无误的科学。

→ see **science**

pre·dis·pose /pri̲dɪspo̲ʊz/ (**predisposes, predisposing, predisposed**) **1** V-T If something **predisposes** you **to** think or behave in a particular way, it makes it likely that you will think or behave in that way. 使…很可能 (以某方式思考或行事) [FORMAL] ❑ *They take pains to hire people whose personalities predispose them to serve customers well.* 他们煞费苦心雇用那些具备把顾客服务好的个性的人。 ● **pre·dis·posed** ADJ 有…倾向的 [v-link ADJ] ❑ *...people who are predisposed to violent crime.* …有暴力犯罪倾向的人们。 **2** V-T If something **predisposes** you **to** a disease or illness, it makes it likely that you will suffer from that disease or illness. 使…很可能患 (某疾病) [FORMAL] ❑ *...a gene that predisposes people to alcoholism.* …使易于嗜酒的基因。 ● **pre·dis·posed** ADJ 易患…的 [v-link ADJ] ❑ *Some people are genetically predisposed to diabetes.* 有些人先天性易患糖尿病。

P

pre·dis·po·si·tion /pri̲dɪspəzɪʃᵊn/ (**predispositions**) **1** N-COUNT If you have a **predisposition to** behave in a particular way, you tend to behave like that because of the kind of person you are or the attitudes you have. (以某方式行事的) 倾向 [FORMAL] ❑ *There is a thin dividing line between educating the public and creating a predisposition to panic.* 教育公众和营造恐慌倾向之间只有细小的区别。 **2** N-COUNT If you have a **predisposition to** a disease or illness, it is likely that you will suffer from that disease or illness. (患某种疾病的) 倾向 [FORMAL] ❑ *...a genetic predisposition to lung cancer.* …一种遗传性患肺癌的倾向。

Word Link *domin ≈ rule, master : dominate, dominion, predominant*

★ **pre·domi·nant** /prɪdɒmɪnənt/ ADJ If something is **predominant**, it is more important or noticeable than anything else in a set of people or things. 主导性的 ❑ *Mandy's predominant emotion was confusion.* 曼迪的主导情绪是困惑。

pre·domi·nant·ly /prɪdɒmɪnəntli/ ADV You use **predominantly** to indicate which feature or quality is most noticeable in a situation. 主导性地 ❑ *The landscape has remained predominantly rural in appearance.* 该风景看上去主要保留了乡村风貌。

pre·domi·nate /prɪdɒmɪneɪt/ (**predominates, predominating, predominated**) **1** V-I If one type of person or thing **predominates** in a group, there is more of that type of person or thing in the group than of any other. (在数量上) 占优势 [FORMAL] ❑ *In older age groups women predominate because men tend to die younger.* 在年龄较大的人群中，女性占多数，因为男性的寿命倾向于短些。 **2** V-I When a feature or quality **predominates**, it is the most important or noticeable one in a situation. 占主导地位 [FORMAL] ❑ *He wants to create a society where Islamic principles predominate.* 他想创建一个伊斯兰教信念占主导地位的社会。

pre·emi·nent /pri̲ɛ̲mɪnənt/ also **pre-eminent** ADJ If someone or something is **preeminent** in a group, they are more important, powerful, or capable than other people or things in the group. 杰出的 [FORMAL] ❑ *...some of the preeminent names in baseball.* …棒球史上一些杰出的名字。 ● **pre·emi·nence** /pri̲ɛ̲mɪnəns/ N-UNCOUNT 杰出 ❑ *Europe was poised to reassert its traditional preeminence in Western art.* 欧洲准备重新确立其在西方艺术上的传统卓越地位。

pre·empt /pri̲ɛ̲mpt/ (**preempts, preempting, preempted**) also **pre-empt** V-T If you **preempt** an action, you prevent it from happening by doing something that makes it unnecessary or impossible. 预先制止 ❑ *The law would preempt stronger local rules.* 该法律将预先制止更强硬的地方性法规。 ❑ *"the survival of the fittest," a slogan that virtually preempted all debate.* "适者生存"，一个几乎无可辩驳的口号。

pre·emp·tive /pri̲ɛ̲mptɪv/ also **pre-emptive** ADJ A **preemptive** attack or strike is intended to weaken or damage an enemy or opponent, for example, by destroying their weapons before they can do any harm. 先发制人的 ❑ *A preemptive strike against a sovereign nation raises moral and legal issues.* 对一个主权国家进行先发制人的攻击会引起道德和法律上的争议。

pref·ace /prɛ̲fɪs/ (**prefaces, prefacing, prefaced**) **1** N-COUNT A **preface** is an introduction at the beginning of a book that explains what the book is about or why it was written. 前言 ❑ *...the preface to Kelman's novel.* …凯尔曼小说的前言。 **2** V-T If you **preface** an action or speech **with** something else, you do or say this other thing first. 说…作为开场白；做…作为开始 ❑ *I will preface what I am going to say with a few lines from Shakespeare.* 我将引用莎士比亚的几行诗作为我讲话的开场白。

pre·fer ♦♦◇ /prɪfɜ̲r/ (**prefers, preferring, preferred**) V-T If you **prefer** someone or something, you like that person or thing better than another, and so you are more likely to choose them if there is a choice. 更喜欢 [no cont] ❑ *Does he prefer a particular sort of music?* 他更喜欢某种特别的音乐吗？ ❑ *I became a teacher because I preferred books and people to politics.* 我成为了一名教师是因为我更喜欢书籍和人而不是政治。 ❑ *I prefer to think of peace not war.* 我更喜欢思考和平而不是战争。 ❑ *I would prefer him to be with us next season.* 我更希望他在下个赛季和我们在一起。

Note that **prefer** can often sound rather formal in ordinary conversation. Verbal expressions such as **like...better** and **would rather** are used more frequently. For example, instead of saying "I prefer football to tennis," you can say "**I like football better than tennis.**" Instead of "I'd prefer an apple," you can say "**I'd rather have an apple**," and instead of "I'd prefer to walk," you can say "**I'd rather walk.**"

pref·er·able /prɛ̲fərəbᵊl, prɛ̲frə-, prɪfɜ̲rə-/ ADJ If you say that one thing is **preferable to** another, you mean that it is more desirable or suitable. 更合心意的；更适合的 ❑ *A big earthquake a long way off is preferable to a smaller one nearby.* 远处的大地震要比近处的小地震好。 ❑ *Prevention of a problem is always preferable to trying to cure it.* 防止出现问题总是比试图解决问题更可取。 ● **pref·er·ably** /prɛ̲fərəbli, prɛ̲frə-, prɪfɜ̲rə-/ ADV 更可取地 ❑ *Do something creative or take exercise, preferably in the fresh air.* 做一些有创意的事或者进行体育锻炼，在新鲜的空气中更好。

pref·er·ence /prɛ̲fərəns/ (**preferences**) **1** N-VAR If you have a **preference for** something, you would like to have or do that thing rather than something else. 偏爱 ❑ *It upset her when men revealed a preference for her sister.* 当男人们显露出偏爱她妹妹的时候，她很不高兴。 **2** N-UNCOUNT If you **give preference to** someone with a particular qualification or feature, you choose them rather than someone else. 优先考虑 ❑ *The Pentagon has said it will give preference to companies with which it can do business electronically.* 五角大楼已经宣布它将优先考虑能与之进行电子交易的公司。

pref·er·ence shares **1** N-PLURAL **Preference shares** are the same as **preferred stock**. 优先股 [BRIT, BUSINESS] **2** → see also **ordinary shares**

pref·er·en·tial /prɛ̲fərɛ̲nʃᵊl/ ADJ If you get **preferential** treatment, you are treated better than other people and therefore have an advantage over them. 优等的 ❑ *Firstborn sons received preferential treatment.* 长子们受到了优等待遇。

pref·erred stock N-UNCOUNT **Preferred stock** is the shares in a company that are owned by people who have the right to receive part of the company's profits before the holders of common stock. They also have the right to have their capital repaid if the company fails and has to close. Compare **common stock**. 优先股 [AM, BUSINESS]

in BRIT, use **preference shares**

Word Link *fix ≈ fastening : affix, prefix, suffix*

Word Link *pre ≈ before : precaution, precede, prefix*

▲ **pre·fix** /prifɪks/ (**prefixes**) **1** N-COUNT A **prefix** is a letter or group of letters, for example, "un-" or "multi-," that is added to the beginning of a word in order to form a different word. For example, the prefix "un-" is added to "happy" to form "unhappy." Compare **affix** and **suffix**. 前缀 **2** N-COUNT A **prefix** is one or more numbers or letters added to the beginning of a code number to indicate, for example, what area something belongs to. 前置代码 ❑ *To telephone from the U.S. use the prefix 011 33 before the numbers given here.* 从美国拨出电话，请在所给号码前加拨前置代码011 33。

▲ **preg·nan·cy** ♦◇◇ /prɛgnənsi/ (**pregnancies**) N-VAR **Pregnancy** is the condition of being pregnant or the period of time during which a female is pregnant. 怀孕；怀孕期 ❑ *It would be wiser to cut out all alcohol during pregnancy.* 怀孕期间最好完全戒酒。

preg·nant ♦◇◇ /prɛgnənt/ **1** ADJ If a woman or female animal is **pregnant**, she has a baby or babies developing in her body. 怀孕的 ❑ *Lena got pregnant and married.* 莉娜怀了孕并结了婚。 **2** ADJ A **pregnant** silence or moment has a special meaning that is not obvious but that people are aware of. 耐人寻味的 [ADJ n, v-link ADJ "with" n] ❑ *There was a long, pregnant silence, which Mrs. Madrigal punctuated by reaching for the check.* 马德里加尔太太伸手去拿那支票，打破了那一阵长时间的、耐人寻味的沉默。

Word Partnership *pregnant* 的常用搭配：

N. pregnant **with a baby/child**, pregnant **mother**, pregnant **wife**, pregnant **woman** **1**

V. **be** pregnant, **become** pregnant, **get** pregnant **1**

pre·heat /prihit/ (**preheats, preheating, preheated**) V-T If you **preheat** an oven, you switch it on and allow it to reach a certain temperature before you put food inside it. 预热 ❑ *Preheat the oven to 400 degrees.* 将烤箱预热到400度。

pre·his·tor·ic /prihɪstɔrɪk/ ADJ **Prehistoric** people and things existed at a time before information was written down. 史前的 ❑ *...the famous prehistoric cave paintings of Lascaux.* …拉斯科著名的史前洞穴绘画。

preju·dice /prɛdʒədɪs/ (**prejudices, prejudicing, prejudiced**) **1** N-VAR **Prejudice** is an unreasonable dislike of a particular group of people or things, or a preference for one group of people or things over another. 偏见 ❑ *There was a deep-rooted racial prejudice long before the two countries went to war.* 早在两国交战之前就有了根深蒂固的种族偏见。 ❑ *There is widespread prejudice against workers over 45.* 对年龄超过45岁的工人有普遍的偏见。 **2** V-T If you **prejudice** someone or something, you influence them so that they are unfair in some way. 使…有偏见 ❑ *I think your upbringing has prejudiced you.* 我认为你的教养使你抱有偏见。 ❑ *The report was held back for fear of prejudicing his trial.* 因为担心会使他的审判带有偏见，该报告没有公开。 **3** V-T If someone **prejudices** another person's situation, they do something that makes it worse than it should be. 损害 [FORMAL] ❑ *Her study was not in any way intended to prejudice the future development of the college.* 她的研究绝对无意损害该学院的未来发展。

Thesaurus *prejudice* 另参见：

N. bias, bigotry, disapproval, intolerance; (*ant.*) tolerance **1**

preju·diced /prɛdʒədɪst/ ADJ A person who is **prejudiced** against someone from a different racial group has an unreasonable dislike of them. 有偏见的 ❑ *Some landlords and landladies are racially prejudiced.* 有些房东有种族偏见。

pre·limi·nary /prɪlɪmɪnɛri/ (**preliminaries**) **1** ADJ **Preliminary** activities or discussions take place at the beginning of an event, often as a form of preparation. 初步的 ❑ *Preliminary results show the Republican Party with 11 percent of the vote.* 初步结果显示共和党得到11%的选票。 **2** N-COUNT A **preliminary** is something that you do at the beginning of an activity, often as a form of preparation. (程序性或礼节性的) 预备事务 ❑ *You all know why I am here. So I won't waste time on preliminaries.* 你们都知道我为什么在这里。所以我就不浪费时间讲客套话了。

prel·ude /prɛlyud, preɪlud/ (**preludes**) N-COUNT You can describe an event as a **prelude to** another event or activity when it happens before it and acts as an introduction to it. 前奏 ❑ *For him, reading was a necessary prelude to sleep.* 对他来说，阅读是入睡的必要前奏。

★ **prema·ture** /primətʃʊər/ **1** ADJ Something that is **premature** happens earlier than usual or earlier than people expect. 提早的 ❑ *Accidents are still the number one cause of premature death for Americans.* 事故仍然是美国人非自然死亡的首要原因。 ❑ *His career was brought to a premature end by a succession of knee injuries.* 他的职业生涯因连续的膝伤过早地结束了。 ● **prema·ture·ly** ADV 提早地 ❑ *The war and the years in the harsh mountains had prematurely aged him.* 战争和深山老林的岁月使他提早衰老了。 **2** ADJ You can say that something is **premature** when it happens too early and is therefore inappropriate. 过早的 ❑ *It now seems their optimism was premature.* 目前，他们的乐观好像还为时过早。 ● **prema·ture·ly** ADV 过早地 ❑ *He was careful not to celebrate prematurely.* 他很谨慎，没有过早地举行庆祝活动。 **3** ADJ A **premature** baby is one that was born before the date when it was expected to be born. 早产的 ❑ *Even very young premature babies respond to their mother's presence.* 即使很小的早产儿也会对母亲的在场有所反应。 ● **prema·ture·ly** ADV 早产地 [ADV after v] ❑ *Danny was born prematurely, weighing only 3lb 3oz.* 丹尼是早产的，体重只有3磅3盎司。

★ **prem·ier** ♦◇◇ /prɪmɪər/ (**premiers**) **1** N-COUNT The leader of the government of a country is sometimes referred to as the country's **premier**. 总理 ❑ *...Australian premier Paul Keating.* …澳大利亚总理保罗・基廷。 **2** ADJ **Premier** is used to describe something that is considered to be the best or most important thing of a particular type. 最好的；首要的 [ADJ n] ❑ *...the country's premier opera company.* …这个国家最好的歌剧团。

premi·ere /prɪmɪər, prɪmyɛər/ (**premieres, premiering, premiered**) **1** N-COUNT The **premiere** of a new play or movie is the first public performance of it. 首次公演 ❑ *Four astronauts visited for last week's premiere of the movie Space Station.* 四位宇航员到场参加了上个星期举行的电影《空间站》的首映式。 **2** V-T/V-I When a movie or show **premieres** or **is premiered**, it is shown to an audience for the first time. 首次上映；首次上演 ❑ *The documentary premiered at the Jerusalem Film Festival.* 那部记录片在耶路撒冷电影节上首映。

prem·ier·ship /prɪmɪərʃɪp/ N-SING The **premiership** of a leader of a government is the period of time during which they are the leader. 总理任期 ❑ *...the final years of Margaret Thatcher's premiership.* …玛格丽特・撒切尔夫人首相任期的最后几年。

★ **prem·ise** /prɛmɪs/ (**premises**) **1** N-PLURAL The **premises** of a business or an institution are all the buildings and land that it occupies in one place. 经营场所；办公场所 ❑ *There is a kitchen on the premises.* 营业场所内有一个厨房。 **2** N-COUNT A **premise** is something that you suppose is true and that you use as a basis for developing an idea. 前提 [FORMAL] ❑ *The premise is that schools will work harder to improve if they must compete.* 前提是各学校如必须竞争就会更加努力改进。

★ **pre·mium** ♦◇◇ /primiəm/ (**premiums**) **1** N-COUNT A **premium** is a sum of money that you pay regularly to an insurance company for an insurance policy. 保险费 ❑ *It is too early to say whether insurance premiums will be affected.* 保险费会不会受到影响现在判定还为时过早。 **2** N-COUNT A **premium** is a sum of money that you have to pay for something in addition to the normal cost. 附加费 ❑ *Even if customers want "solutions," most are not willing to pay a premium for them.* 即使顾客们想要"解决方案"，大部分人不愿意为此支付附加费。 **3** ADJ **Premium** products are of a higher than usual quality and are often expensive. 高端的 [ADJ n] ❑ *At the premium end of the market, business is booming.* 在市场的高端销售区，生意火暴。 **4** PHRASE If something is **at a premium**, it is wanted or needed, but is difficult to get or achieve. 求之难得 ❑ *If space is at a premium, choose adaptable furniture that won't fill the room.* 如果空间很有限，就选购不太占地方的可改装家具。 **5** PHRASE If you buy or sell something **at a premium**, you buy or sell it at a higher price than usual, for example, because it is in short supply. 以高价 (买、卖) ❑ *He eventually sold the shares back to the bank at a premium.* 他最终以高价将股票返售给了银行。

P

premo·ni·tion /prɪmənɪʃᵊn, prɛm-/ (**premonitions**) N-COUNT If you have a **premonition**, you have a feeling that something is going to happen, often something unpleasant. (常为不祥的) 预感 ❑ *He had an unshakable premonition that he would die.* 他有一种强烈的预感：他就要死了。

Word Link *nat ≈ being born : innate, native, prenatal*

pre·na·tal /priːneɪtᵊl/ ADJ **Prenatal** is used to describe things relating to the medical care of women during pregnancy. 产前的 ❑ *I'd met her briefly in a prenatal class.* 我在孕期培训班上匆匆见了她一面。

pre·oc·cu·pa·tion /priɒkyəpeɪʃᵊn/ (**preoccupations**) **1** N-COUNT If you have a **preoccupation with** something or someone, you keep thinking about them because they are important to you. 关注 ❑ *Karouzos's poetry shows a profound preoccupation with the Orthodox Church.* 卡鲁佐斯的诗歌表现出对东正教的深切关注。 **2** N-UNCOUNT **Preoccupation** is a state of mind in which you think about something so much that you do not consider other things to be important. 专注 ❑ *The arrest of Senator Pinochet has created a climate of preoccupation among our citizens.* 对参议员皮诺切特的逮捕引起了我国公民的极大专注。

pre·oc·cu·pied /priɒkyəpaɪd/ ADJ If you are **preoccupied**, you are thinking a lot about something or someone, and so you hardly notice other things. 专注的 ❑ *Tom Banbury was preoccupied with the missing Shepherd child and did not want to devote time to the new murder.* 汤姆·班伯里一心专注着谢泼德家失踪的孩子，不想在新的谋杀案上花时间。

▲ **pre·oc·cu·py** /priɒkyəpaɪ/ (**preoccupies, preoccupying, preoccupied**) V-T If something **is preoccupying** you, you are thinking about it a lot. 占据(某人的思绪) ❑ *Crime and the fear of crime preoccupy the community.* 犯罪和对犯罪的恐惧占据了这个社区的思绪。

pre·pack·aged /pripækɪdʒd/ ADJ **Prepackaged** foods have been prepared in advance and put in plastic or cardboard containers to be sold. (食品) 预先包装好的

pre·paid /pripeɪd/ ADJ **Prepaid** items are paid for in advance, before the time when you would normally pay for them. 预付了的 ❑ *...prepaid funerals.* …预付了费用的葬礼。

prepa·ra·tion ♦◇◇ /prɛpəreɪʃᵊn/ (**preparations**) **1** N-UNCOUNT **Preparation** is the process of getting something ready for use or for a particular purpose, or making arrangements for something. 准备 ❑ *Rub the surface of the wood in preparation for the varnish.* 打磨木头的表面为上油漆做准备。 ❑ *Few things distracted the pastor from the preparation of his weekly sermons.* 几乎没有什么事情使该牧师从他每周布道的准备中分心。 **2** N-PLURAL **Preparations** are all the arrangements that are made for a future event. 准备工作 ❑ *The United States is making preparations for a large-scale airlift of 1,200 American citizens.* 美国在为一次1200名美国公民的大规模空运做准备。 **3** N-COUNT A **preparation** is a mixture that has been prepared for use as food, medicine, or a cosmetic. (用作食品、药品或化妆品的) 配制品 ❑ *...anti-aging creams and sensitive-skin preparations.* …抗衰老面霜和针对敏感皮肤的制剂。

pre·para·tory /prɪpærətɔri, prɛpərə-/ ADJ **Preparatory** actions are done before doing something else as a form of preparation or as an introduction. 准备性的 ❑ *At least a year's preparatory work will be necessary before building can start.* 在建造开始之前至少需要一年的准备工作。

pre·pare ♦♦◇ /prɪpɛər/ (**prepares, preparing, prepared**) **1** V-T If you **prepare** something, you make it ready for something that is going to happen. 准备 ❑ *Two technicians were preparing a videotape recording of last week's program.* 两名技师正在准备上周节目的录像。 ❑ *On average each report requires 1,000 hours to prepare.* 平均每份报告需要1000个小时来准备。 **2** V-T/V-I If you **prepare for** an event or action that will happen soon, you get yourself ready for it or make the necessary arrangements. (为…) 作准备；准备 (做某事) ❑ *The party leadership is using management consultants to help prepare for the next election.* 该政党的领导层正聘用管理顾问来帮助准备下一次选举。 ❑ *He had to go back to his hotel and prepare to catch a train for New York.* 他不得不回宾馆准备赶火车去纽约。 **3** V-T When you **prepare** food, you get it ready to be eaten, for example, by cooking it. 准备 (食物) ❑ *She made her way to the kitchen, hoping to find someone preparing dinner.* 她朝厨房走去，希望看到有人在准备晚餐。

Thesaurus *prepare* 另参见：

V. arrange, fix, plan, ready **1**

Word Partnership *prepare* 的常用搭配：

N. prepare **a list**, prepare **a plan**, prepare **a report** **1**
prepare **for battle/war**, prepare **for the future**, prepare **for the worst** **2**
prepare **dinner**, prepare **food**, prepare **a meal** **3**

pre·pared ♦♦◇ /prɪpɛərd/ **1** ADJ If you are **prepared to** do something, you are willing to do it if necessary. 愿意的 [v-link ADJ to-inf] ❑ *Are you prepared to take industrial action?* 你们愿意采取劳工行动吗？ **2** ADJ If you are **prepared for** something that you think is going to happen, you are ready for it. 作好准备的 [v-link ADJ "for" n] ❑ *Police are prepared for large numbers of demonstrators.* 警察对大批示威者有准备。 **3** ADJ You can describe something as **prepared** when it has been done or made beforehand, so that it is ready when it is needed. 预先准备好的 [ADJ n] ❑ *He ended his prepared statement by thanking the police.* 他以感谢警方结束了他事先准备好的声明。

Word Link *pos ≈ placing : deposit, preposition, repository*

prepo·si·tion /prɛpəzɪʃᵊn/ (**prepositions**) N-COUNT A **preposition** is a word such as "by," "for," "into," or "with" that usually has a noun group as its object. 介词 ❑ *There is nothing in the rules of grammar to suggest that ending a sentence with a preposition is wrong.* 在语法规则中没有哪一条表明以介词结束一个句子是错误的。

pre·pos·ter·ous /prɪpɒstərəs, -trəs/ ADJ If you describe something as **preposterous**, you mean that it is extremely unreasonable and foolish. 荒谬的 [DISAPPROVAL] ❑ *The whole idea was preposterous.* 整个想法都是荒谬的。 ● **pre·pos·ter·ous·ly** ADV 荒谬地 ❑ *Some prices are preposterously high.* 有些价格高得离谱。

prep school /prɛp skul/ (**prep schools**) **1** N-VAR In the United States, a **prep school** is a private school for students who intend to go to college after they leave. (在美国为意欲上大学的学生提供教育的) 私立预科学校 ❑ *...an exclusive prep school in Washington.* …华盛顿一所高级的私立预科学校。 **2** N-VAR In Britain, a **prep school** is a private school where children are educated until the age of 11 or 13. (在英国为11或13岁之前的孩子提供教育的) 私立预备学校

▲ **pre·requi·site** /prirɛkwɪzɪt/ (**prerequisites**) N-COUNT If one thing is a **prerequisite for** another, it must happen or exist before the other thing is possible. 先决条件 ❑ *Good self-esteem is a prerequisite for a happy life.* 良好的自尊心是幸福生活的先决条件。

pre·roga·tive /prɪrɒgətɪv/ (**prerogatives**) N-COUNT If something is the **prerogative** of a particular person or group, it is a privilege or a power that only they have. 特权 [FORMAL] ❑ *It is your prerogative to stop seeing that particular therapist and find another one.* 不再去见那位疗法师而去找另一位是你的特权。

pre·scribe /prɪskraɪb/ (**prescribes, prescribing, prescribed**) **1** V-T If a doctor **prescribes** medicine or treatment for you, he or she tells you what medicine or treatment to have. 开 (药、处方) ❑ *The physician examines the patient then diagnoses the disease and prescribes medication.* 内科医生检查了病人，然后对疾病作出诊断，并开出药方。 ❑ *She took twice the prescribed dose of sleeping tablets.* 她服用了所开剂量两倍的安眠药。 **2** V-T If a person or set of laws or rules **prescribes** an action or duty, they state that it must be carried out. 规定 [FORMAL] ❑ *...article II of the constitution, which prescribes the method of electing a president.* …规定总统选举办法的宪法第二条。

★ **pre·scrip·tion** /prɪskrɪpʃᵊn/ (**prescriptions**) **1** N-COUNT A **prescription** is the piece of paper on which your doctor writes an order for medicine and which you give to a pharmacist to get the medicine. 处方 ❑ *The new drug will not require a physician's prescription.* 这种新药不需要医生的处方。 **2** N-COUNT A **prescription** is a medicine that a doctor has told you to take. 处方药 ❑ *I'm not sleeping even with the prescription Ackerman gave me.* 我服用了阿克曼开给我的处方药还是睡不着。 ● PHRASE If a medicine is available **by** or **on prescription**, you can only get it from a pharmacist if a doctor gives you a prescription for it. 凭处方 **3** N-COUNT A **prescription** is a proposal or a plan that gives ideas about how to solve a problem or improve a situation. 方案 ❑ *There's not much difference in the economic prescriptions of Ireland's two main political parties.* 爱尔兰两大政党的经济方案没有多大差异。

pres·ence ♦♦◇ /prɛzᵊns/ (**presences**) **1** N-SING Someone's **presence** in a place is the fact that they are there. 在场 ❑ *They argued that his presence in the town could only stir up trouble.* 他们争辩说他在城里出现只会搅起麻烦。 **2** N-UNCOUNT If you say that someone has **presence**, you mean that they impress people by their appearance and manner. 风采 [APPROVAL] ❑ *They do not seem to have the vast, authoritative presence of those great men.* 他们似乎没有那些大人物的轩昂威严的风采。 **3** N-COUNT A **presence** is a person or creature that you cannot see, but that you are aware of. 幽灵 [LITERARY] ❑ *She started to be affected by the ghostly presence she could feel in the house.* 她开始受到那个幽灵的困扰，她能感觉到它就在屋子里。 **4** N-SING If a country has a military **presence** in another country, it has some of its armed forces there. 驻扎 ❑ *The Philippine government wants the U.S. to maintain a military presence in Southeast Asia.* 菲律宾政府希望美国保留在东南亚的驻军。 **5** N-UNCOUNT If you refer to the **presence** of a substance in another thing, you mean that it is in that thing. 存在 ❑ *The somewhat acid flavor is caused by the presence of lactic acid.* 略有的酸味是由乳酸的存在造成的。 **6** PHRASE If you are **in** someone's **presence**, you are in the same place as that person, and are close enough to them to be seen or heard. 在某人面前 ❑ *The talks took place in the presence of a diplomatic observer.* 会谈是在一位外交观察家在场的情况下进行的。

present
❶ EXISTING OR HAPPENING NOW
❷ BEING SOMEWHERE
❸ GIFT
❹ VERB USES

❶ **pres·ent** ♦♦◇ /prɛzᵊnt/ **1** ADJ You use **present** to describe things and people that exist now, rather than those that existed in the past or those that may exist in the future. 目前的 [ADJ n] ❑ *He has brought much of the present crisis on himself.* 他目前的危机大多是他自己造成的。 ❑ *...the government's present economic difficulties.* …政府目前的经济困难。 **2** N-SING **The present** is the period of time that we are in now and the things that are happening now. 现在 ❑ *...his struggle to reconcile the past with the present.* …他将过去和现在调和的斗争。 ❑ *...continuing right up to the present.* …一直持续到现在。 **3** PHRASE A situation that exists **at present** exists now, although it may change. 目前 ❑ *There is no way at present of predicting which individuals will develop the disease.* 目前还没有办法预言哪些人会患这种病。 **4** PHRASE **The present day** is the period of history that we are in now. 现代 ❑ *...Western European art from the period of Giotto to the present day.* …从乔托时代到现代的西欧艺术。 **5** PHRASE Something that exists or will be done **for the present** exists now or will continue for a while, although the situation may change later. 暂时 ❑ *The cabinet had expressed the view that sanctions should remain in place for the present.* 内阁曾表示说制裁会暂时保留。

❷ **pres·ent** ♦♦◇ /prɛzᵊnt/ **1** ADJ If someone is **present at** an event, they are there. 在场的 [v-link ADJ] ❑ *The president was not present at the meeting.* 总统没有出席该会议。 ❑ *Nearly 85 percent of men are present at the birth of their children.* 将近85%的男性在他们的孩子出生时在场。 **2** ADJ If something, especially a substance or disease, is **present in** something else, it exists within that thing. 存在的 [v-link ADJ] ❑ *This special form of vitamin D is naturally present in breast milk.* 这种特殊形式的维生素D天然存在于母乳中。

❸ **pres·ent** /prɛzᵊnt/ (**presents**) N-COUNT A **present** is something that you give to someone, for example, at Christmas or when you visit them. 礼物 ❑ *The carpet was a wedding present from Jack's parents.* 地毯是杰克的父母送的结婚礼物。 ❑ *She bought a birthday present for her mother.* 她为她母亲买了一件生日礼物。

❹ **pre·sent** ♦♦◇ /prɪzɛnt/ (**presents, presenting, presented**) **1** V-T If you **present** someone **with** something such as a prize or document, or if you **present** it **to** them, you formally give it to them. 颁发 ❑ *The mayor presented him with a gold medal at an official city reception.* 市长在一次正式的市招待会上给他颁发了一枚金质奖章。 ❑ *Betty will present the prizes to the winners.* 贝蒂将给获胜者颁奖。 ● **pres·en·ta·tion** /prizɛnteɪʃᵊn/ N-UNCOUNT 颁发 ❑ *Then came the presentation of the awards by the First Lady.* 接下来是第一夫人的颁奖。 **2** V-T If something **presents** a difficulty, challenge, or opportunity, it causes it or provides it. 带来 ❑ *This presents a problem for many financial consumers.* 这给许多金融消费者带来了麻烦。 ❑ *The future is going to be one that presents many challenges.* 未来将会带来许多挑战。 **3** V-T If an opportunity or problem **presents itself**, it occurs, often when you do not expect it. (机会、问题) 呈现出来 ❑ *Their colleagues insulted them whenever the opportunity presented itself.* 他们的同事们一有机会就侮辱他们。 **4** V-T When you **present** information, you give it to people in a formal way. 展示 ❑ *We spend the time collating and presenting the information in a variety of chart forms.* 我们把时间花在以各种图表形式比照和展示信息上。 ❑ *We presented three options to the unions for discussion.* 我们向工会提出了3种选择以供讨论。 ● **pres·en·ta·tion** N-VAR (**presentations**) 陈述 ❑ *...in his first presentation of the theory to the Berlin Academy.* …在他第一次向柏林科学院陈述该理论时。 ❑ *...a fair presentation of the facts to a jury.* …向陪审团对事实的公正的陈述。 **5** V-T If you **present** someone or something in a particular way, you describe them in that way. 描述 ❑ *The government has presented these changes as major reforms.* 政府将这些变化描述成重大改革。 **6** V-T The way you **present yourself** is the way you speak and act when meeting new people. 展示 (自己) ❑ *...all those tricks which would help him to present himself in a more confident way in public.* …所有那些可以帮助他在公共场合更自信地展示自己的窍门。 **7** V-T If someone or something **presents** a particular appearance or image, that is how they appear or try to appear. 表现出 ❑ *The small group of onlookers presented a pathetic sight.* 那一小撮旁观者表现出一副可怜的样子。 ❑ *Cohen was making an effort to present a kinder, gentler image.* 科恩在努力表现出一副更和善、更温柔的形象。 **8** V-T If you **present yourself** somewhere, you officially arrive there, for example, for an appointment. 出席 ❑ *Get word to him right away that he's to present himself at City Hall by tomorrow afternoon.* 立即通知他，他得于明天下午之前到市政厅来。 **9** V-T If someone **presents** a program on television or radio, they introduce each item in it. 主持 (电视或广播节目) [mainly BRIT]

in AM, usually use **host, introduce**

10 V-T When someone **presents** something such as a production of a play or an exhibition, they organize it. 上演; 展出 ❑ *They threatened to close any theater presenting a play with gay characters.* 他们威胁要关闭任何上演有同性恋角色戏剧的剧院。 **11** V-T If you **present** someone **to** someone else, often an important person, you formally introduce them. 正式介绍 ❑ *Fox stepped forward, welcomed him in Malay, and presented him to Jack.* 福克斯向前跨了一步，用马来语对他表示了欢迎，接着把他正式介绍给了杰克。

Word Partnership *present* 的常用搭配:

N. present **century**, present **circumstances**, present **location**, present **position**, present **situation**, present **time** ❶ **1**
present **a check** ❹ **1**
present **a challenge**, present **a danger**, present **an opportunity**, present **a problem**, present **a threat** ❹ **2**
present **an argument**, present **evidence**, present **a plan** ❹ **4**

pres·en·ta·tion /prizɛnteɪʃᵊn/ (**presentations**) **1** N-UNCOUNT **Presentation** is the appearance of something, that someone has worked to create. 外观 ❑ *We serve traditional French food cooked in a lighter way, keeping the presentation simple.* 我们提供传统法国美食，风味清淡，外观简洁。 **2** N-COUNT A **presentation** is a formal event at which someone is given a prize or award. 颁奖仪式 ❑ *...after receiving his award at a presentation in Kansas City yesterday.* …昨天在堪萨斯城的一个颁奖仪式上接受了他的奖项之后。 **3** N-COUNT When someone gives a **presentation**, they give a formal talk, often in order to sell something or get support for a proposal. 讲座 ❑ *James Watson, Philip Mayo and I gave a slide and video presentation.* 詹姆斯·沃森、菲利普·梅奥和我一起做了一场有幻灯和录像片的讲座。 **4** → see also **present**

present-day ADJ **Present-day** things, situations, and people exist at the time in history we are now in. 现今的 [ADJ n] ❑ *Even by present-day standards these were large aircraft.* 即使按现今的标准，这些也是大型飞机。 ❑ *...a huge area of northern India, stretching from present-day Afghanistan to Bengal.* …印度北部一片广阔的地域，从现今的阿富汗一直延伸到孟加拉。

pre·sent·er /prɪzɛntər/ (**presenters**) N-COUNT A radio or television **presenter** is a person who introduces the items in a particular program. (广播、电视) 节目主持人 [mainly BRIT]

in AM, usually use **host, anchor**

pres·ent·ly /prɛzᵊntli/ **1** ADV If you say that something is **presently** happening, you mean that it is happening now. 目前 ❑ *She is presently developing a number of projects.* 她目前在开发好几个项目。 ❑ *The island is presently uninhabited.* 那个岛目前还没人居住。 **2** ADV You use **presently** to indicate that something happened a short time after the time or event that you have just mentioned. 之后不久 [ADV with cl] [WRITTEN] ❑ *He was shown to a small office.*

Presently, a young woman in a white coat came in. 他被带到一间小办公室。之后不久，一个穿白色上衣的年轻女子走进来。

pre·serva·tive /prɪzɜrvətɪv/ (**preservatives**) N-MASS A **preservative** is a chemical that prevents things from decaying. Some preservatives are added to food, and others are used to treat wood or metal. 防腐剂 ❑ *Nitrates are used as preservatives in food processing.* 硝酸盐在食品加工中被用作防腐剂。
→ see **salt**

Word Link *serv ≈ keeping : conserve, observe, preserve*

pre·serve ♦◇◇ /prɪzɜrv/ (**preserves, preserving, preserved**) **1** V-T If you **preserve** a situation or condition, you make sure that it remains as it is, and does not change or end. 维护 ❑ *We will do everything to preserve peace.* 我们将竭尽全力维护和平。 ● **pres·er·va·tion** ★ /prɛzərveɪʃən/ N-UNCOUNT 维护 ❑ *...the preservation of the status quo.* …现状的维护。 **2** V-T If you **preserve** something, you take action to save it or protect it from damage or decay. 保护 ❑ *We need to preserve the forest.* 我们需要保护森林。 ● **pres·er·va·tion** ★ N-UNCOUNT 保护 ❑ *...the preservation of buildings of architectural or historic interest.* …对具有建筑学或历史意义的建筑物的保护。 **3** V-T If you **preserve** food, you treat it in order to prevent it from decaying so that you can store it for a long time. 保藏 ❑ *I like to make puree, using only enough sugar to preserve the plums.* 我喜欢做果酱，只用足够的糖来保藏李子。 **4** N-PLURAL **Preserves** are foods made by cooking fruit with a large amount of sugar so that they can be stored for a long time. 果酱 ❑ *She decided to make peach preserves for Christmas gifts.* 她决定做桃子果酱作圣诞礼物。 **5** N-COUNT If you say that a job or activity is the **preserve of** a particular person or group of people, you mean that they are the only ones who take part in it. 独揽之事；独占的活动 ❑ *The making and conduct of foreign policy is largely the preserve of the president.* 外交政策的制定和实施很大程度上是总统的独揽之事。
→ see **can**

Word Link *sid ≈ sitting : preside, president, reside*

★ **pre·side** /prɪzaɪd/ (**presides, presiding, presided**) V-I If you **preside over** a meeting or an event, you are in charge. 做主持 ❑ *The PM returned to Downing Street to preside over a meeting of his inner cabinet.* 首相回到唐宁街去主持一场核心内阁会议。

presi·den·cy ♦◇◇ /prɛzɪdənsi/ (**presidencies**) N-COUNT The **presidency** of a country or organization is the position of being the president or the period of time during which someone is president. (某国、某组织的) 最高职位；最高职位任期 ❑ *He is a candidate for the presidency of the organization.* 他是该组织最高职位候选人。

presi·dent ♦♦♦ /prɛzɪdənt/ (**presidents**) **1** N-TITLE; N-COUNT The **president** of a country that has no king or queen is the person who is the head of state of that country. 总统 [oft "the" N; N-VOC] ❑ *...President Mubarak.* …穆巴拉克总统。 **2** N-COUNT The **president** of an organization is the person who has the highest position in it. (某组织的) 最高权力人 ❑ *...Alexandre de Merode, the president of the medical commission.* …亚历山大・德梅罗德，医学委员会主席。
→ see **election**

★ **presi·den·tial** ♦♦◇ /prɛzɪdɛnʃəl/ ADJ **Presidential** activities or things relate or belong to a president. 最高权力人的 [ADJ n] ❑ *...campaigning for Peru's presidential election.* …秘鲁总统选举竞选活动。
→ see **election**

press ♦♦♦ /prɛs/ (**presses, pressing, pressed**) **1** V-T If you **press** something somewhere, you push it firmly against something else. 推；挤 ❑ *He pressed his back against the door.* 他将背顶在了门上。 **2** V-T If you **press** a button or switch, you push it with your finger in order to make a machine or device work. 按压 ❑ *Drago pressed a button and the door closed.* 德拉戈按了一个按钮，门关上了。 ● N-COUNT **Press** is also a noun. 按压 ❑ *...a TV which rises from a table at the press of a button.* …按一个按钮就会从桌上升起的一台电视机。 **3** V-T/V-I If you **press** something or **press down on** it, you push hard against it with your foot or hand. 用力按；用力踩 ❑ *The engine stalled. He pressed the accelerator hard.* 引擎熄火了。他猛踩油门。 **4** V-I If you **press for** something, you try hard to persuade someone to give it to you or to agree to it. 竭力争取 ❑ *Police might now press for changes in the law.* 警方现在可能会竭力争取法律的修改。 **5** V-T If you **press** someone, you try hard to persuade them to do something. 极力劝说 ❑ *Trade unions are pressing him to stand firm.* 各工会在极力劝说他坚持立场。 ❑ *Mr. Kurtz seems certain to be pressed for further details.* 库尔茨先生似乎肯定会被极力劝说说出更多细节。 **6** V-T If someone **presses** their claim, demand, or point, they state it in a very forceful way. 有力陈述 ❑ *The protest campaign has used mass strikes and demonstrations to press its demands.* 抗议活动采用了大规模罢工和示威游行来有力地表明其要求。 **7** V-T If you **press** something **on** someone, you give it to them and insist that they take it. 硬塞 ❑ *All I had was money, which I pressed on her reluctant mother.* 我只有钱，硬塞给了她那不肯接受我钱的母亲。 **8** V-T If you **press** clothes, you iron them in order to get rid of the creases. 熨 ❑ *Vera pressed his shirt.* 薇拉熨了他的衬衣。 ❑ *There's a couple of dresses to be pressed.* 有几条连衣裙要熨。 **9** N-SING-COLL Newspapers are referred to as **the press**. 报纸 ["the" N] ❑ *...interviews in the local and foreign press.* …当地和国外报纸中的采访。 ❑ *...freedom of the press.* …新闻自由。 **10** N-SING-COLL Journalists and reporters are referred to as **the press**. 新闻工作者 ❑ *Christie looked relaxed and calm as she faced the press afterwards.* 克里斯蒂之后面对新闻工作者时看上去轻松平静。 **11** N-COUNT A **press** or a **printing press** is a machine used for printing things such as books and newspapers. 印刷机 **12** → see also **pressed, pressing** **13** PHRASE If someone or something **gets bad press**, they are criticized, especially in the newspapers, on television, or on radio. If they **get good press**, they are praised. 受到媒体批评/好评 ❑ *...the bad press that career women consistently get in this country.* …在这个国家职业女性一贯受到的媒体批评一家先前不知名。 **14** PHRASE If you **press charges against** someone, you make an official accusation against them that has to be decided in a court of law. 起诉 ❑ *I could have pressed charges against him.* 我原本可以起诉他的。 **15** PHRASE When a newspaper or magazine **goes to press**, it starts being printed. 付印 ❑ *We check prices at the time of going to press.* 我们在付印时核对价格。
→ see **newspaper, printing**

Word Partnership *press* 的常用搭配：
N. press **a button**, **at the** press **of a button** **2**
press **accounts**, press **coverage**, **freedom of the** press, press **reports** **9** **10**
press **charges** **14**

press con·fer·ence (**press conferences**) N-COUNT A **press conference** is a meeting held by a famous or important person in which they answer reporters' questions. 新闻发布会 ❑ *She gave her reaction to his release at a press conference.* 她在一次新闻发布会上就他的释放做出了回应。

pressed /prɛst/ **1** ADJ If you say that you are **pressed for** time or **pressed for** money, you mean that you do not have enough time or money at the moment. 紧缺的 [v-link ADJ] ❑ *Are you pressed for time? If not, I suggest we have lunch.* 你时间紧吗？如果不紧的话，我建议我们一起吃午饭。 **2** → see also **hard-pressed**

press·ing /prɛsɪŋ/ **1** ADJ A **pressing** problem, need, or issue has to be dealt with immediately. 紧迫的 ❑ *It is one of the most pressing problems facing this country.* 它是该国面临的最紧迫的问题之一。 **2** → see also **press**

press of·fic·er (**press officers**) N-COUNT A **press officer** is a person who is employed by an organization to give information about that organization to the press. 新闻发布官 ❑ *...the press officer of the Bavarian Government.* …巴伐利亚州政府的新闻发布官。

press re·lease (**press releases**) **1** N-COUNT A **press release** is a written statement about a matter of public interest that is given to the press by an organization concerned with the matter. (向记者发布的) 新闻稿 ❑ *The next day, Fox issued a press release saying the show had sold out in 24 hours.* 第二天，福克斯公司发布新闻稿称该演出门票已在24小时内卖空。 **2** → see also **news release**

press sec·re·tary (**press secretaries**) N-COUNT A government's or political leader's **press secretary** is someone who is employed by them to give information to the press. 媒体秘书 ❑ *The press secretary told reporters that a majority of one would be a sufficient mandate.* 该媒体秘书告诉记者们，超出一票的多数就足以获得授权。

press-up (**press-ups**) N-COUNT **Press-ups** are the same as **push-ups**. 俯卧撑 [BRIT]

pres·sure ♦♦♦ /prɛʃər/ (**pressures, pressuring, pressured**) **1** N-UNCOUNT **Pressure** is force that you produce when you press hard on something. (用力按压而产生的) 压力 ❑ *She kicked at the door with her foot, and the pressure was enough to open it.* 她用脚踢门，其产生的压力足以把门打开。 ❑ *The pressure of his fingers had relaxed.* 他手指的压力已经减弱了。 **2** N-UNCOUNT The **pressure** in a place or container is the force produced by the quantity of gas or liquid in that place or container. (某地或某容器内的气体或液体产生的) 压力

P

[also N in pl] ❑ *The window in the cockpit had blown in and the pressure dropped dramatically.* 驾驶舱的窗子已向内破裂，气压骤然下降。 3 N-UNCOUNT If there is **pressure on** a person, someone is trying to persuade or force them to do something. (因极力劝说或强迫某人做某事而造成的) 压力 [also N in pl] ❑ *He may have put pressure on her to agree.* 他可能已对她施压让她同意。 ❑ *A lot of dot-coms were under pressure from their investors.* 很多网络公司那时都在承受着来自其投资者的压力。 4 N-UNCOUNT If you are experiencing **pressure**, you feel that you must do a lot of tasks or make a lot of decisions in very little time, or that people expect a lot from you. (因任务紧、决策时间短或别人的期望多而感到的) 压力 [also N in pl] ❑ *Can you work under pressure?* 你能在压力下工作吗？ ❑ *Even if I had the talent to play tennis I couldn't stand the pressure.* 即使我有打网球的天资，我也承受不了那种压力。 5 V-T If you **pressure** someone **to** do something, you try forcefully to persuade them to do it. 对…施加压力 ❑ *He will never pressure you to get married.* 他永远也不会给你施加压力让你结婚。 ❑ *The Senate should not be pressured into making hasty decisions.* 参议院不应受压而做出草率的决定。 ● **pres·sured** ADJ 受压的 ❑ *You're likely to feel anxious and pressured.* 你可能会感到焦虑并且有压力。 6 → see also **blood pressure**

→ see **flight, forecast, weather**

pres·sure group (**pressure groups**) N-COUNT A **pressure group** is an organized group of people who are trying to persuade a government or other authority to do something, for example, to change a law. 施压集团 ❑ *...the environmental pressure group Greenpeace.* …绿色和平组织这个环保施压集团。

pres·sur·ised /prɛ̲ʃəraɪzd/ [BRIT] → see **pressurized**

pres·sur·ized /prɛ̲ʃəraɪzd/

in BRIT, also use **pressurised**

ADJ In a **pressurized** container or area, the pressure inside is different from the pressure outside. 加压了的 ❑ *Certain types of foods are also dispensed in pressurized canisters.* 某些类型的食品也被装在压力罐中分发出去。

★ **pres·tige** /prɛsti̲ʒ, -sti̲dʒ/ 1 N-UNCOUNT If a person, a country, or an organization has **prestige**, they are admired and respected because of the position they hold or the things they have achieved. 威望 ❑ *...efforts to build up the prestige of the United Nations.* …为树立联合国威望而做的努力。 ❑ *It was his responsibility for foreign affairs that gained him international prestige.* 是他在外交事务中的尽职尽责为他赢得了国际声望。 2 ADJ **Prestige** is used to describe products, places, or activities that people admire because they are associated with being rich or having a high social position. 名贵的 [ADJ n] ❑ *...such prestige cars as Cadillac, Mercedes, Porsche, and Jaguar.* …像凯迪拉克、梅赛德斯、保时捷和捷豹这样的名贵轿车。

pres·tig·ious /prɛstɪ̲dʒəs, -sti̲dʒəs/ ADJ A **prestigious** institution, job, or activity is respected and admired by people. 有声望的 ❑ *It's one of the best equipped and most prestigious schools in the country.* 它是该国设备最好、最有声望的学校之一。

pre·sum·ably ♦◇◇ /prɪzu̲məbli/ ADV If you say that something is **presumably** the case, you mean that you think it is very likely to be the case, although you are not certain. 很可能 [VAGUENESS] ❑ *The spear is presumably the murder weapon.* 这矛很可能就是凶器。

Word Link *sume ≈ taking : assume, consume, presume*

★ **pre·sume** /prɪzu̲m/ (**presumes, presuming, presumed**) 1 V-T If you **presume that** something is the case, you think that it is the case, although you are not certain. 推测 ❑ *I presume you're here on business.* 我想你是来这儿出差的吧。 ❑ *"Had he been home all week?"—"I presume so."* "他整个星期都在家吗？"——"我想是。" 2 V-T If you say that someone **presumes to** do something, you mean that they do it even though they have no right to do it. 擅自 (做某事) [FORMAL] ❑ *They're resentful that outsiders presume to meddle in their affairs.* 他们对外人擅自干预他们的事务怨恨不已。 3 V-T If an idea, theory, or plan **presumes** certain facts, it regards them as true so that they can be used as a basis for further ideas and theories. 假定 (某事实) 为真 [FORMAL] ❑ *The legal definition of "know" often presumes mental control.* "知情"的法律界定通常以思维控制力为前提。

Word Link *sumpt ≈ taking : assumption, consumption, presumption*

★ **pre·sump·tion** /prɪzʌ̲mpʃən/ (**presumptions**) N-COUNT A **presumption** is something that is accepted as true but is not certain to be true. 假定 ❑ *...the presumption that a defendant is innocent until proved guilty.* …在被证明有罪之前被告为无罪的假定。

pre·sump·tu·ous /prɪzʌ̲mptʃuəs/ ADJ If you describe someone or their behavior as **presumptuous**, you disapprove of them because they are doing something that they have no right or authority to do. 擅自作主的 [DISAPPROVAL] ❑ *It would be presumptuous to judge what the outcome will be.* 断定结果将会如何未免冒失。

pre·tax /pri̲tæ̲ks/ also **pre-tax** ADJ **Pretax** profits or losses are the total profits or losses made by a company before tax has been taken away. 税前的 [ADJ n] [BUSINESS] ❑ *They announced a fall in pretax profits.* 他们宣布了税前利润的下降。 ● ADV **Pretax** is also an adverb. 税前地 [ADV after v] ❑ *Last year it made $2.5 million pretax.* 去年，他们税前赚了250万美元。

pre·tence /prɪtɛ̲ns, pri̲tɛns/ [BRIT] → see **pretense**

pre·tend /prɪtɛ̲nd/ (**pretends, pretending, pretended**) 1 V-T If you **pretend that** something is the case, you act in a way that is intended to make people believe that it is the case, although in fact it is not. 假装 (某事是事实) ❑ *I pretend that things are really okay when they're not.* 我在情况不好的时候假装一切真地没事。 ❑ *Sometimes the boy pretended to be asleep.* 有时候那个男孩子假装睡着了。 2 V-T If children or adults **pretend that** they are doing something, they imagine that they are doing it, for example, as part of a game. 假装 (在做某事) ❑ *She can sunbathe and pretend she's in Cancun.* 她会进行日光浴并假装她是在坎昆。 3 V-T If you do not **pretend that** something is the case, you do not claim that it is the case. 假称 [with neg] ❑ *We do not pretend that the past six years have been without problems for us.* 我们不假称过去的6年对我们来讲是没有问题的。

pre·tense /prɪtɛ̲ns, pri̲tɛns/ (**pretenses**)

in BRIT, use **pretence**

1 N-VAR A **pretense** is an action or way of behaving that is intended to make people believe something that is not true. 假装 ❑ *He goes to the library and makes a pretense of reading some Thoreau.* 他去图书馆假装读梭罗的书。 ❑ *On the eighth day of questioning, she dropped the pretense that she was Japanese.* 在审问的第8天，她不再假装她是日本人。 2 PHRASE If you do something **under false pretenses**, you do it when people do not know the truth about you and your intentions. 欺骗 ❑ *This interview was conducted under false pretenses.* 这次采访是以欺骗手段进行的。

pre·ten·sion /prɪtɛ̲nʃən/ (**pretensions**) 1 N-VAR If you say that someone has **pretensions**, you disapprove of them because they claim or pretend that they are more important than they really are. 做作 [DISAPPROVAL] ❑ *Her wide-eyed innocence soon exposes the pretensions of the art world.* 她的天真无邪很快就暴露出艺术界的做作。 2 N-PLURAL If someone has **pretensions to** something, they claim to be or do that thing. 声称 ❑ *The city has unrealistic pretensions to world-class status.* 该城市不切实际地声称为世界一流城市。

P

▲ **pre·ten·tious** /prɪtɛ̲nʃəs/ ADJ If you say that someone or something is **pretentious**, you mean that they try to seem important or significant, but you do not think that they are. 做作的 [DISAPPROVAL] ❑ *His response was full of pretentious nonsense.* 他的回答尽是些装腔作势的胡说八道。

★ **pre·text** /pri̲tɛkst/ (**pretexts**) N-COUNT A **pretext** is a reason that you pretend has caused you to do something. 托词 ❑ *They wanted a pretext for subduing the region by force.* 他们需要一个用武力征服那个地区的托词。

pret·ty ♦♦◇ /prɪ̲ti/ (**prettier, prettiest**) 1 ADJ If you describe someone, especially a girl, as **pretty**, you mean that they look nice and are attractive in a delicate way. (尤指女孩) 漂亮的 ❑ *She's a very charming and very pretty girl.* 她是一个非常迷人、非常漂亮的姑娘。 ● **pret·ti·ly** /prɪ̲tɪli/ ADV 漂亮地 ❑ *She smiled again, prettily.* 她又笑了，很美。

When you are describing someone's appearance, you generally use **pretty** and **beautiful** to describe women, girls, and babies. **Beautiful** is a much stronger word than **pretty**. The equivalent word for a man is **handsome**. **Good-looking** and **attractive** can be used to describe people of either sex. **Pretty** can also be used to modify adjectives and adverbs but is less strong than **very**. In this sense, **pretty** is informal.

2 ADJ A place or a thing that is **pretty** is attractive and pleasant, in a charming but not particularly unusual way. (某地、某物) 漂亮的 ❑ *...a very pretty little town.* …一座非常漂亮的小镇。 ● **pret·ti·ly** ADV 漂亮地 ❑ *The living-room was prettily decorated.* 客厅装饰得很漂亮。

3 ADV You can use **pretty** before an adjective or adverb to slightly lessen its force. 颇 [ADV adj/adv] [INFORMAL] ❑ *I had a pretty good idea what she was going to do.* 我颇清楚她打算做什么。

Thesaurus *pretty* 另参见：
ADJ. beautiful, cute, lovely **1**
beautiful, charming, pleasant **2**

pre·vail /prɪveɪl/ (**prevails, prevailing, prevailed**) **1** V-I If a proposal, principle, or opinion **prevails**, it gains influence or is accepted, often after a struggle or argument. 占上风 ❑ *We hoped that common sense would prevail.* 我们希望常识能占上风。 ❑ *Rick still believes that justice will prevail.* 里克仍然相信正义会占上风。 **2** V-I If a situation, attitude, or custom **prevails** in a particular place at a particular time, it is normal or most common in that place at that time. 盛行；普遍存在 ❑ *A similar situation prevails in Canada.* 同样的情况在加拿大也普遍存在。 ❑ *...the confusion which had prevailed at the time of the revolution.* …在革命时期普遍存在的混乱。 **3** V-I If one side in a battle, contest, or dispute **prevails**, it wins. 获胜 ❑ *He appears to have the votes he needs to prevail.* 他看来有他胜出所需要的选票。

★ **preva·lent** /prɛvələnt/ ADJ A condition, practice, or belief that is **prevalent** is common. 盛行的；普遍存在的 ❑ *This condition is more prevalent in women than in men.* 这种情况在女性中比在男性中更为普遍。 ❑ *Smoking is becoming increasingly prevalent among younger women.* 吸烟在年轻女性中正变得越来越盛行。 ● **preva·lence** ▲ N-UNCOUNT 盛行 ❑ *...the prevalence of cocaine abuse in the 1980s.* …20世纪80年代可卡因滥用的盛行。

pre·vent ♦♦◊ /prɪvɛnt/ (**prevents, preventing, prevented**) **1** V-T To **prevent** something means to ensure that it does not happen. 预防 ❑ *These methods prevent pregnancy.* 这些方法预防怀孕。 ❑ *Further treatment will prevent cancer from developing.* 进一步治疗将预防癌症恶化。 ● **pre·ven·tion** N-UNCOUNT 预防 ❑ *...the prevention of heart disease.* …心脏病的预防。 **2** V-T To **prevent** someone **from** doing something means to make it impossible for them to do it. 阻止 ❑ *He said this would prevent companies from creating new jobs.* 他说这将阻止各公司创造新的职位。 ❑ *Its nationals may be prevented from leaving the country.* 其公民可能会被阻止离开该国。

Thesaurus *prevent* 另参见：
V. avoid, hold off, stop **1**

Word Partnership *prevent* 的常用搭配：
N. prevent **attacks**, prevent **cancer**, prevent **damage**, prevent **disease**, prevent **infection**, prevent **injuries**, prevent **loss**, prevent **pregnancy**, prevent **problems**, prevent **violence**, prevent **war** **1**

P

pre·ven·ta·tive /prɪvɛntətɪv/ ADJ **Preventative** means the same as **preventive**. 预防性的

pre·ven·tive /prɪvɛntɪv/ ADJ **Preventive** actions are intended to help prevent things such as disease or crime. 预防性的 ❑ *Too much is spent on curative medicine and too little on preventive medicine.* 在治疗医学上花费太多，而在预防医学上花费太少。

★ **pre·view** /priːvyu/ (**previews**) N-COUNT A **preview** is an opportunity to see something such as a movie, exhibition, or invention before it is open or available to the public. 预先观看 ❑ *He had gone to see the preview of a play.* 他去看过一出戏的预演。

pre·vi·ous ♦♦◊ /priːviəs/ **1** ADJ A **previous** event or thing is one that happened or existed before the one that you are talking about. 前一次的 [ADJ n] ❑ *She has a teenage daughter from a previous marriage.* 她有个出自前一次婚姻的十几岁的女儿。 **2** ADJ You refer to the period of time or the thing immediately before the one that you are talking about as the **previous** one. 前一个的 [det ADJ] ❑ *It was a surprisingly dry day after the rain of the previous week.* 这是继前一周的降雨之后出奇干燥的一天。

pre·vi·ous·ly ♦◊◊ /priːviəsli/ **1** ADV **Previously** means at some time before the period that you are talking about. 先前地 ❑ *Guyana's railways were previously owned by private companies.* 圭亚那的铁路先前为私营公司所拥有。 ❑ *The contract was awarded to a previously unknown company.* 该合同给了一家先前不知名的公司。 **2** ADV You can use **previously** to say how much earlier one event was than another event. (某时长) 之前 [n ADV] ❑ *He had first entered the House 12 years previously.* 他12年前首次进入了众议院。

pre·war /priːwɔr/ also **pre-war** ADJ **Prewar** is used to describe things that happened, existed, or were made in the period immediately before a war, especially World War II, 1939-45. 战 (尤指第二次世界大战) 前的 ❑ *...Poland's prewar leader.* …波兰的战前领导人。

★ **prey** /preɪ/ (**preys, preying, preyed**) **1** N-UNCOUNT-COLL A creature's **prey** are the creatures that it hunts and eats in order to live. 猎物 ❑ *Electric rays stun their prey with huge electrical discharges.* 电鳐释放大量的电荷将他们的猎物击昏。 **2** V-I A creature that **preys on** other creatures lives by catching and eating them. 捕食 ❑ *The effect was to disrupt the food chain, starving many animals and those that preyed on them.* 后果是打断食物链，使许多动物和捕食它们的动物饿死。 **3** N-UNCOUNT You can refer to the people who someone tries to harm or trick as their **prey**. (某人的) 坑害对象 ❑ *Police officers lie in wait for the gangs who stalk their prey at night.* 警官们埋伏起来等待捉拿那些夜间悄悄追踪作案对象的黑帮成员。 **4** V-I If someone **preys on** other people, especially people who are unable to protect themselves, they take advantage of them or harm them in some way. 坑害 [DISAPPROVAL] ❑ *Pam had never learned that there were men who preyed on young runaways.* 帕姆从未了解到有些人专门坑害那些年轻的离家出走者。 **5** V-I If something **preys on** your mind, you cannot stop thinking and worrying about it. 困扰 ❑ *It was a misunderstanding and it preyed on his conscience.* 这是个误会，让他的良心很不安。
→ see **shark**

price ♦♦♦ /praɪs/ (**prices, pricing, priced**) **1** N-COUNT The **price** of something is the amount of money that you have to pay in order to buy it. 价格 ❑ *...a sharp increase in the price of gas.* …燃气价格的一次猛涨。 ❑ *They expected house prices to rise.* 他们预期房价会上涨。 **2** N-SING The **price** that you pay for something that you want is an unpleasant thing that you have to do or suffer in order to get it. 代价 ❑ *There may be a price to pay for such relentless activity, perhaps ill health or even divorce.* 这种没完没了的活动可能是要付出代价的，也许是不良健康状况甚至是离婚。 **3** V-T If something **is priced at** a particular amount, the price is set at that amount. 将…定价 ❑ *The bond is currently priced at $900.* 这种债券当前定价为$900。 ❑ *Analysts predict that Digital will price the new line at less than half the cost of comparable IBM mainframes.* 分析家们预测迪吉多公司会将其新线产品的价格定在低于可比的IBM公司大型主机成本的一半的水平。 ● **pric·ing** N-UNCOUNT 定价 ❑ *It's hard to maintain competitive pricing.* 很难保持有竞争力的定价。 **4** → see also **retail price index, selling price** **5** PHRASE If you want something **at any price**, you are determined to get it, even if unpleasant things happen as a result. 不惜任何代价 ❑ *If they wanted a deal at any price, they would have to face the consequences.* 如果他们不惜任何代价想要一笔生意，他们将得面对其后果。 **6** PHRASE If you can buy something that you want **at a price**, it is for sale, but it is extremely expensive. 以极高的价格 ❑ *Most goods are available, but at a price.* 大部分商品都可以买到，但价格昂贵。 **7** PHRASE If you get something that you want **at a price**, you get it but something unpleasant happens as a result. 以一定代价 ❑ *Fame comes at a price.* 成名是要付出代价的。 **8** to **price** yourself **out of the market** → see **market**

> The **price** of something is the amount of money that the seller is asking people to pay in order to buy it. ❑ *The price marked on the box was $5.* When you are referring to services, or to things that you pay to use, you usually talk about a **charge** or a **fee**, rather than a **price**. ❑ *There is a one dollar handling charge for telephone reservations. ...$400 in unpaid consulting fees.* The **cost** of something is the amount of money that you actually pay, or would pay, for it. ❑ *The total cost of modernizing the room came to just $800.* See also note at **cost**.

price·less /praɪslɪs/ **1** ADJ If you say that something is **priceless**, you are emphasizing that it is worth a very large amount of money, or that it is very important to you although it has little financial value. 无价的 [EMPHASIS] ❑ *They are priceless, unique and irreplaceable.* 它们是无价的、独一无二的，不可替代的。 ❑ *Did Mom throw away your priceless Dungeons and Dragons magazine?.* 妈妈扔掉了你那本宝贝杂志《龙与地下城》吗？ **2** ADJ If you say that something is **priceless**, you approve of it because it is extremely useful. 宝贵的 [APPROVAL] ❑ *They are a priceless record of a brief period in Colorado history.* 它们是科罗拉多历史上一段短暂时期的宝贵记录。

price tag (**price tags**) **1** N-COUNT If something has a **price tag** of a particular amount, that is the amount that you must pay in order to buy it. 标价 [WRITTEN] ❑ *The monorail can be completed at the price tag of $1.7 billion.* 该单轨铁路能以标价17亿美元完成。 **2** N-COUNT

In a store, the **price tag** on an article for sale is a small piece of card or paper attached to the article with the price written on it. 价格标签

price war (**price wars**) N-COUNT If competing companies are involved in a **price war**, they each try to gain an advantage by lowering their prices as much as possible in order to sell more of their products and damage their competitors financially. 价格战 [BUSINESS] ❑ *Their loss was partly due to a vicious price war between manufacturers that has cut margins to the bone.* 他们的亏损部分是因为制造商之间把利润空间削减到了极点的一场恶性价格战。

pricey /praɪsi/ (**pricier, priciest**) also **pricy** ADJ If you say that something is **pricey**, you mean that it is expensive. 价格高的 [INFORMAL] ❑ *Medical insurance is very pricey.* 医疗保险很昂贵。

▲ **prick** /prɪk/ (**pricks, pricking, pricked**) 1 V-T If you **prick** something or **prick** holes in it, you make small holes in it with a sharp object such as a pin. 扎（某物）；戳（洞）❑ *Prick the potatoes and rub the skins with salt.* 在这些土豆扎些洞，然后用盐擦它们的皮。 2 V-T If something sharp **pricks** you or if you **prick yourself with** something sharp, it sticks into you or presses your skin and causes you pain. 扎（人）❑ *She had just pricked her finger with the needle.* 她刚用针扎了她的手指。 3 N-COUNT A **prick** is a small, sharp pain that you get when something pricks you. 刺痛 ❑ *At the same time she felt a prick on her neck.* 同时她感到脖子上一阵刺痛。 4 N-COUNT If you call someone a **prick**, you are insulting them because you think they are mean and spiteful or stupid, or you do not like them. 小气鬼；可恶之人；蠢货 [INFORMAL, VERY RUDE, DISAPPROVAL] 5 N-COUNT A man's **prick** is his penis. 阴茎 [POSS N] [INFORMAL, VULGAR]

prick·ly /prɪkli/ 1 ADJ Something that is **prickly** feels rough and uncomfortable, as if it has a lot of prickles. 扎人的 ❑ *The bunk mattress was hard, the blankets prickly and slightly damp.* 铺位上的床垫很硬，毛毯扎人且有点潮湿。 2 ADJ Someone who is **prickly** loses their temper or gets upset very easily. 易怒的；易生气的 ❑ *You know how prickly she is.* 你知道她多么容易生气。 3 ADJ A **prickly** issue or subject is one that is rather complicated and difficult to discuss or resolve. 棘手的 ❑ *The issue is likely to prove a prickly one.* 这个问题很可能是棘手的。

pricy /praɪsi/ → see **pricey**

pride ♦◇◇ /praɪd/ (**prides, priding, prided**) 1 N-UNCOUNT **Pride** is a feeling of satisfaction that you have because you or people close to you have done something good or possess something good. 自豪 ❑ *...the sense of pride in a job well done.* …因一项工作完成得很好而感到的自豪。 ❑ *We take pride in offering you the highest standards.* 我们以向您提供最高标准的服务而自豪。 2 N-UNCOUNT **Pride** is a sense of the respect that other people have for you, and that you have for yourself. 尊严 ❑ *Davis had to salvage his pride.* 戴维斯不得不挽回自己的尊严。 3 N-UNCOUNT Someone's **pride** is the feeling that they have that they are better or more important than other people. 傲慢 [DISAPPROVAL] ❑ *His pride may still be his downfall.* 他的傲慢仍可能是他垮台的原因。 4 V-T If you **pride** yourself **on** a quality or skill that you have, you are very proud of it. 以…而自豪 ❑ *Suarez prides himself on being able to organize his own life.* 苏亚雷斯为能安排好自己的生活而自豪。

Word Partnership *pride* 的常用搭配：
- V. **take** pride **in** ***something*** 1
- **feel** pride 1 2
- N. **sense of** pride, **source of** pride 1 – 3

priest ♦◇◇ /prist/ (**priests**) 1 N-COUNT A **priest** is a member of the Christian clergy in the Catholic, Anglican, or Orthodox church. （圣公会教的）牧师；（天主教、东正教的）神父 ❑ *He had trained to be a Catholic priest.* 他接受培训成了一名天主教神父。 2 N-COUNT In many non-Christian religions a **priest** is a man who has particular duties and responsibilities in a place where people worship. （非基督教的）祭司 ❑ *...a New Age priest or priestess.* …一个"新世纪"男祭司或女祭司。

priest·ess /pristɪs/ (**priestesses**) N-COUNT A **priestess** is a woman in a non-Christian religion who has particular duties and responsibilities in a place where people worship. （非基督教的）女祭司 ❑ *...the priestess of the temple.* …该寺院里的女祭司。

priest·hood /pristhʊd/ 1 N-UNCOUNT **Priesthood** is the position of being a priest or the period of time during which someone is a priest. 教士身份 ❑ *...the early rites of priesthood.* …早期的教士任职仪式。 2 N-SING **The priesthood** is all the members of the Christian clergy, especially in a particular church. （基督教的）全体教士 ❑ *Should the General Synod vote women into the priesthood?* 英国教会应该选妇女作教士吗？

prim /prɪm/ ADJ If you describe someone as **prim**, you disapprove of them because they behave too correctly and are too easily shocked by anything vulgar. 古板的 [DISAPPROVAL] ❑ *We tend to imagine that the Victorians were very prim and proper.* 我们往往认为维多利亚时代的人非常古板、循规蹈矩。 ● **prim·ly** ADV 古板地 [ADV with V] ❑ *We sat primly at either end of a long bench.* 我们古板地坐在一张长凳的两端。

pri·mal /praɪməl/ ADJ **Primal** is used to describe something that relates to the origins of things or that is very basic. 原始的 [FORMAL] ❑ *Jealousy is a primal emotion.* 嫉妒是一种原始情感。

pri·mari·ly /praɪmɛrɪli/ ADV You use **primarily** to say what is mainly true in a particular situation. 主要地 ❑ *...a book aimed primarily at high-energy physicists.* …一本主要以高能物理学家为目标对象的书。 ❑ *Public order is primarily an urban problem.* 公共秩序主要是一种城市问题。

Word Link *prim ≈ first : primary, primate, prime*

pri·ma·ry ♦◇◇ /praɪmɛri, -məri/ (**primaries**) 1 ADJ You use **primary** to describe something that is very important. 首要的 [ADJ n] [FORMAL] ❑ *That's the primary reason the company's share price has held up so well.* 这就是那家公司的股票价格一直保持得这么好的首要原因。 ❑ *His misunderstanding of language was the primary cause of his other problems.* 他对语言的误解是他其他问题的主要原因。 2 ADJ **Primary** education is the first few years of formal education for children. 初级的 [ADJ n] ❑ *The content of primary education should be the same for everyone.* 初级教育的内容对每个人都应该是相同的。 ❑ *Ninety-nine percent of primary pupils now have hands-on experience of computers.* 99%的小学生如今都有电脑实际操作经验。 3 ADJ **Primary** is used to describe something that occurs first. 最初的 [ADJ n] ❑ *It is not the primary tumor that kills, but secondary growths elsewhere in the body.* 致命的并不是原发肿瘤，而是在身体其他部位的继发。 4 N-COUNT A **primary** or a **primary election** is an election in an American state in which people vote for someone to become a candidate for a political office. Compare **general election**. （美国各州的）初选 ❑ *...the 1968 New Hampshire primary.* …1968年新罕布什尔州的初选。

pri·ma·ry school (**primary schools**) N-VAR A **primary school** is a school for children in the first four or five years of their education. 小学 [mainly BRIT]

in AM, usually use **elementary school**

pri·mate /praɪmeɪt/ (**primates**)

The pronunciation /praɪmɪt/ is also used for meaning 2.

读法 /praɪmɪt/亦被用于义项2。

Word Web primate

The classification **primate** includes **monkeys**, **apes**, and **humans**. Scientists have shown that humans and the other primates share some surprising similarities. We used to believe that only humans favor one hand over the other. However, researchers carefully observed a group of 66 **chimpanzees**. They found that chimps are also right-handed and left-handed. Other researchers have learned that chimpanzee groups have different cultures. In 1972 a female **gorilla** named Koko began to learn sign language from a college student. Today Koko understands about 2,000 words and can sign about 500 of them. She makes up sentences using three to six words.

P

1 N-COUNT A **primate** is a member of the group of mammals that includes humans, monkeys, and apes. 灵长目动物 ❑ *The woolly spider monkey is the largest primate in the Americas.* 绒毛蛛猴是美洲最大的灵长目动物。 **2** N-COUNT **The Primate of** a particular country or region is the most important priest in that country or region. 大主教 ❑ *...the Roman Catholic Primate of All Ireland.* …全爱尔兰罗马天主教大主教。

→ see Word Web: **primate**

prime ♦◇◇ /praɪm/ (**primes, priming, primed**) **1** ADJ You use **prime** to describe something that is most important in a situation. 主要的 [ADJ n] ❑ *Political stability, meanwhile, will be a prime concern.* 与此同时，政治稳定将是头等大事。 ❑ *It could be a prime target for guerrilla attack.* 它会是游击队进攻的一个主要目标。 **2** ADJ You use **prime** to describe something that is of the best possible quality. 最佳的 [ADJ n] ❑ *The location of these beaches makes them prime sites for development.* 这些海滩的位置使它们成为开发的最佳选址。 **3** ADJ You use **prime** to describe an example of a particular kind of thing that is absolutely typical. 最典型的 [ADJ n] ❑ *The prime example is Macy's, once the undisputed king of California retailers.* 最典型的例子是梅西百货，曾是加州零售商们公认的王者。 **4** N-UNCOUNT If someone or something is **in their prime**, they are at the stage in their existence when they are at their strongest, most active, or most successful. 鼎盛时期 ❑ *Maybe I'm just coming into my prime now.* 可能我刚迈入我的最佳时期。 ❑ *We've had a series of athletes trying to come back well past their prime.* 我们有不少早已过了鼎盛时期的运动员在试图复出。 **5** V-T If you **prime** someone **to** do something, you prepare them to do it, for example, by giving them information about it beforehand. 事先交代 (某人做某事) ❑ *Claire wished she'd primed Sarah beforehand.* 克莱尔希望她事先交代过萨拉。 ❑ *Marianne had not known until Arnold primed her for her duties that she was to be the sole female.* 直到阿诺德向她交待她的职责时，玛丽安娜才知道她将是惟一的女性。 **6** V-T If someone **primes a bomb** or **a gun**, they prepare it so that it is ready to explode or fire. 事先准备 (炸弹、枪) ❑ *He was priming the bomb to go off in an hour's time.* 他在事先准备炸弹在一小时后爆炸。 ❑ *He kept a primed shotgun in his office.* 他在办公室放了一杆装好子弹的散弹猎枪。

prime min·is·ter ♦♦♦ (**prime ministers**) N-COUNT; N-TITLE The leader of the government in some countries is called **the prime minister**. 总理；首相 ❑ *...the former prime minister of Pakistan, Miss Benazir Bhutto.* …巴基斯坦前总理贝娜齐尔・布托小姐。

prime rate (**prime rates**) N-COUNT A bank's **prime rate** is the lowest rate of interest that it charges at a particular time and that is offered only to certain customers. 最低贷款利率 [BUSINESS] ❑ *At least one bank cut its prime rate today.* 至少有一家银行今天降低了自己的最低贷款利率。

P

prime time also **primetime** N-UNCOUNT **Prime time** television or radio programs are broadcast when the greatest number of people are watching television or listening to the radio, usually in the evenings. 黄金时段 ❑ *...a prime-time television show.* …一个黄金时段的电视节目。

primi·tive /prɪmɪtɪv/ **1** ADJ **Primitive** means belonging to a society in which people live in a very simple way, usually without industries or a writing system. 原始的 (社会) ❑ *...studies of primitive societies.* …对原始社会的研究。 **2** ADJ **Primitive** means belonging to a very early period in the development of an animal or plant. 原始的 (动物、植物) ❑ *...primitive whales.* …原始鲸。 ❑ *Primitive humans needed to be able to react like this to escape from dangerous animals.* 原始人们需要能够像这样反应以逃脱危险的动物。 **3** ADJ If you describe something as **primitive**, you mean that it is very simple in style or very old-fashioned. 简陋的；旧式的 ❑ *The conditions are primitive by any standards.* 这些条件以任何标准衡量都是简陋的。

prim·rose /prɪmroʊz/ (**primroses**) N-VAR A **primrose** is a wild plant that has pale yellow flowers in the spring. 报春花

prince ♦♦◇ /prɪns/ (**princes**) **1** N-TITLE; N-COUNT A **prince** is a male member of a royal family, especially the son of the king or queen of a country. 王子 ❑ *...Prince Edward and other royal guests.* …爱德华王子和其他王室贵宾。 **2** N-TITLE; N-COUNT A **prince** is the male royal ruler of a small country or state. (小国的) 君王 ❑ *He was speaking without the prince's authority.* 他在未经君王许可而发言。

Word Link *ess ≈ female : actress, heiress, princess*

prin·cess ♦♦◇ /prɪnsɪs, -sɛs/ (**princesses**) N-TITLE; N-COUNT A **princess** is a female member of a royal family, usually the daughter of a king or queen or the wife of a prince. 公主；王妃 ❑ *Princess Anne topped the guest list.* 安妮公主的名字位于来宾名单之首。

prin·ci·pal ♦◇◇ /prɪnsɪpᵊl/ (**principals**) **1** ADJ **Principal** means first in order of importance. 最重要的 [ADJ n] ❑ *The principal reason for my change of mind is this.* 我改变主意的最重要原因就是这个。 ❑ *...the country's principal source of foreign exchange earnings.* …该国最重要的外汇交易收入来源。 **2** N-COUNT The **principal** of a school is the person in charge of the school or college. 校长 ❑ *Donald King is the principal of Dartmouth High School.* 唐纳德・金是达特茅斯中学的校长。 **3** N-COUNT The **principal** of a loan is the original amount of the loan, on which you pay interest. (贷款的) 本金 [usu sing] [FINANCE]

→ see **bank, interest rate**

prin·ci·pal·ly /prɪnsɪpli/ ADV **Principally** means more than anything else. 最主要地 [ADV with cl/group] ❑ *This is principally because the major export markets are slowing.* 这最主要是因为主要出口市场越来越不景气。

prin·ci·ple ♦♦◇ /prɪnsɪpᵊl/ (**principles**) **1** N-VAR A **principle** is a general belief about the way you should behave, which influences your behavior. 原则 ❑ *Buck never allowed himself to be bullied into doing anything that went against his principles.* 巴克从来不让自己被迫做任何违背自己原则的事。 ❑ *It's not just a matter of principle.* 这不仅仅是个原则问题。 **2** N-COUNT The **principles of** a particular theory or philosophy are its basic rules or laws. (理论或哲学) 原理 ❑ *...a violation of the basic principles of Marxism.* …对马克思主义基本原理的一种违背。 **3** N-COUNT Scientific **principles** are general scientific laws which explain how something happens or works. (科学) 原理 ❑ *These people lack all understanding of scientific principles.* 这些人缺乏对科学原理的全面理解。 **4** PHRASE If you agree with something **in principle**, you agree in general terms to the idea of it, although you do not yet know the details or know if it will be possible. 原则上 ❑ *I agree with it in principle but I doubt if it will happen in practice.* 我原则上是同意它的，但我怀疑在实践中它是否会发生。 **5** PHRASE If something is possible **in principle**, there is no known reason why it should not happen, even though it has not happened before. 在理论上 ❑ *Even assuming this to be in principle possible, it will not be achieved soon.* 即使假定这在理论上是可能的，它也不会很快就能实现。 **6** PHRASE If you refuse to do something **on principle**, you refuse to do it because of a particular belief that you have. 依据原则 ❑ *He would vote against it on principle.* 他会依据原则投票反对它。

prin·ci·pled /prɪnsɪpᵊld/ ADJ If you describe someone as **principled**, you approve of them because they have strong moral principles. 有原则的 [APPROVAL] ❑ *She was a strong, principled woman.* 她是个坚强、有原则的女人。

print ♦♦◇ /prɪnt/ (**prints, printing, printed**) **1** V-T If someone **prints** something such as a book or newspaper, they produce it in large quantities using a machine. 印刷 ❑ *He started to print his own posters to distribute abroad.* 他开始印刷他自己的宣传海报以在国外散发。 ❑ *Our brochure is printed on environmentally-friendly paper.* 我们的宣传手册是用环保纸印刷的。 ● PHRASAL VERB In American English, **print up** means the same as **print**. 印刷 ❑ *Community workers here are printing up pamphlets for peace demonstrations.* 这里的社区工作者们正在印制和平示威游行用的小册子。 ● **print·ing** N-UNCOUNT 印刷 [oft N n] ❑ *His brother ran a printing and publishing company.* 他兄弟开办过一家印刷出版公司。 **2** V-T If a newspaper or magazine **prints** a piece of writing, it includes it or publishes it. 发表；刊登 ❑ *We can only print letters which are accompanied by the writer's name and address.* 我们只能发表有作者姓名和地址的信件。 **3** V-T If numbers, letters, or designs **are printed on** a surface, they are put on it in ink or dye using a machine. You can also say that a surface **is printed with** numbers, letters, or designs. 印 (数字、字母或图案) ❑ *...the number printed on the receipt.* …印在发票上的编号。 ❑ *The company has for some time printed its phone number on its products.* 这家公司将其电话号码印在其产品上已有一段时间了。 **4** N-COUNT A **print** is a piece of clothing or material with a pattern printed on it. You can also refer to the pattern itself as a **print**. 印花布料；印花 ❑ *Her mother wore one of her dark summer prints.* 她母亲穿了她的一件深色印花布夏装。 ❑ *In this living room we've mixed glorious floral prints.* 在这客厅里我们将各种漂亮的花卉图案搭配在了一起。 **5** V-T When you **print** a photograph, you produce it from a negative. 冲印 ❑ *Printing a black-and-white negative on to color paper produces a similar monochrome effect.* 将黑白底片冲印在彩色纸上产生一种类似的单色效果。 **6** N-COUNT A **print** is a photograph from a film that has been developed. 冲印出的照片

❑ *...black and white prints of Margaret and Jean as children.* …玛格丽特和琼小时候的黑白照片。 **7** N-COUNT A **print** is one of a number of copies of a particular picture. It can be either a photograph, something such as a painting, or a picture made by an artist who puts ink on a prepared surface and presses it against paper. 版画；印出来的画 ❑ *...12 original copper plates engraved by William Hogarth for his famous series of prints.* …由威廉·霍格思为他著名的系列版画刻制的12块原始铜板。 **8** N-UNCOUNT **Print** is used to refer to letters and numbers as they appear on the pages of a book, newspaper, or printed document. 印刷字 ❑ *...columns of tiny print.* …一栏栏极小的印刷字。 **9** ADJ The **print** media consists of newspapers and magazines, but not television or radio. 印刷的 (媒体) [ADJ n] ❑ *I have been convinced that the print media are more accurate and more reliable than television.* 我一直深信印刷媒体比电视更准确、更可靠。 **10** V-T If you **print** words, you write in letters that are not joined together. 用印刷体书写 ❑ *Print your name and address on a postcard and send it to us.* 用印刷体将你的名字和地址写在一张明信片上寄给我们。 **11** N-COUNT You can refer to a mark left by someone's foot as a **print**. 脚印 ❑ *He crawled from print to print, sniffing at the earth, following the scent left in the tracks.* 他从一个脚印爬到另一个脚印，嗅着泥土，跟着路上留下的气味。 **12** N-COUNT You can refer to oily marks left by someone's fingers as their **prints**. 指印 ❑ *Fresh prints of both girls were found in the house.* 两个女孩刚留下的指印都在屋子里找到了。 **13** → see also **printing** **14** PHRASE If you appear **in print**, or get **into print**, what you say or write is published in a book, newspaper, or magazine. (出现在) 印刷媒体 ❑ *Many of these poets appeared in print only long after their deaths.* 这些诗人中许多只是在去世很久之后才出现在印刷媒体上。 **15** PHRASE The **small print** or the **fine print** of something such as an advertisement or a contract consists of the technical details and legal conditions, which are often printed in much smaller letters than the rest of the text. (广告、合同里的技术细节、法律条款等) 小体印刷的内容 ❑ *I'm looking at the small print; I don't want to sign anything that I shouldn't sign.* 我在读小体印刷的细则，我不想在不该签的文件上签字。

→ see **photography**

▸ **print out** **1** PHRASAL VERB If a computer or a machine attached to a computer **prints** something **out**, it produces a copy of it on paper. 打印出来 ❑ *You measure yourself, enter measurements and the computer will print out the pattern.* 你量一量自己，输入量得的数据，然后电脑就会将样式打印出来。 **2** → see also **printout**

print·er /prɪntər/ (**printers**) **1** N-COUNT A **printer** is a machine that can be connected to a computer in order to make copies on paper of documents or other information held by the computer. 打印机 **2** → see also **laser printer** **3** N-COUNT A **printer** is a person or company whose job is printing things such as books. 印刷工；印刷公司 ❑ *The manuscript had already been sent off to the printer.* 手稿已经送到印刷厂去了。

→ see **office, printing**

print·ing /prɪntɪŋ/ (**printings**) **1** N-COUNT If copies of a book are printed and published on a number of different occasions, you can refer to each of these occasions as a **printing**. (一次) 印刷 ❑ *"Cloud Street" is already in its third printing.* 《云街》已经是第3次印刷了。 **2** → see also **print**

→ see Word Web: **printing**

print·out /prɪntaʊt/ (**printouts**) also **print-out** N-COUNT A **printout** is a piece of paper on which information from a computer or similar device has been printed. 打印件 ❑ *...a computer printout of various financial projections.* …各种财务规划的一份电脑打印件。

pri·or ♦◇◇ /praɪər/ **1** ADJ You use **prior** to indicate that something has already happened, or must happen, before another event takes place. 事先的 [ADJ n] ❑ *He claimed he had no prior knowledge of the protest.* 他声称他事先对那次抗议一无所知。 ❑ *The Constitution requires the president to seek the prior approval of Congress for military action.* 宪法要求总统寻求国会对军事行动的事先批准。 **2** ADJ A **prior** claim or duty is more important than other claims or duties and needs to be dealt with first. 优先的 [ADJ n] ❑ *The firm I wanted to use had prior commitments.* 我选择的那家公司有优先承诺。 **3** PHRASE If something happens **prior to** a particular time or event, it happens before that time or event. 在 (某时间或事件) 之前 [FORMAL] ❑ *A death prior to 65 is considered to be a premature death.* 65岁以前的死亡被认为是过早死亡。

> **Word Partnership** *prior* 的常用搭配：
> N. prior **approval**, prior **experience**, prior **knowledge**, prior **notice**, prior **year** **1**
> prior **commitment** **2**

pri·ori·tise /praɪɒrɪtaɪz/ [BRIT] → see **prioritize**

pri·ori·tize /praɪɒrɪtaɪz/ (**prioritizes, prioritizing, prioritized**) in BRIT, also use **prioritise**

1 V-T If you **prioritize** something, you treat it as more important than other things. 优先考虑 ❑ *Prioritize your own wants rather than constantly thinking about others.* 优先考虑你自己的需要，而不要总想着别人。 **2** V-T If you **prioritize** the tasks that you have to do, you decide which are the most important and do them first. 确定 (任务) 优先顺序 ❑ *Make lists of what to do and prioritize your tasks.* 把你要做的事情列出来，确定任务的轻重缓急。

pri·or·ity ♦◇◇ /praɪɒrɪti/ (**priorities**) **1** N-COUNT If something is a **priority**, it is the most important thing you have to do or deal with, or must be done or dealt with before everything else you have to do. 优先处理的事 ❑ *Being a parent is her first priority.* 做母亲是她的头等大事。 ❑ *The government's priority is to build more power plants.* 政府的当务之急是建造更多的发电厂。 **2** PHRASE If you **give priority to** something or someone, you treat them as more important than anything or anyone else. 优先考虑 ❑ *Women are more likely to give priority to child care and education policies.* 女性更可能给孩子的照料和教育方案以优先考虑。 **3** PHRASE If something **takes priority** or **has priority over** other things, it is regarded as being more important than them and is dealt with first. 有优先性 ❑ *The fight against inflation took priority over measures to combat the deepening recession.* 对抗通货膨胀的斗争比对抗日益加深的经济衰退措施更具优先性。

prise /praɪz/ [mainly BRIT] → see **prize 5**

pris·on ♦♦◇ /prɪzᵊn/ (**prisons**) N-VAR A **prison** is a building where criminals are kept as punishment. 监狱 ❑ *The prison's inmates are being kept in their cells.* 监狱里的囚犯们被关在各自的牢房里。

> **Word Partnership** *prison* 的常用搭配：
> N. **life in** prison, prison **officials**, prison **population**, prison **reform**, prison **sentence**, prison **time**
> V. **die in** prison, **escape from** prison, **face** prison, **go to** prison, **release *someone* from** prison, **send *someone* to** prison, **serve/spend time in** prison

pris·on·er ♦♦◇ /prɪzənər/ (**prisoners**) **1** N-COUNT A **prisoner** is a person who is kept in a prison as a punishment for a crime that they have committed. 囚犯 ❑ *The committee is concerned about the large number of prisoners sharing cells.* 该委员会很关心共用牢房的大量犯人。 **2** N-COUNT A **prisoner** is a person who has been captured by an enemy, for example, in war. 俘虏 [also "hold/take" n N] ❑ *...wartime hostages and concentration-camp prisoners.* …战时的人质们和集中营的战俘们。

→ see **war**

Word Web **printing**

Before the invention of **printing**, scribes wrote **documents** by hand. The earliest **printers** were the Chinese. They used pieces of wood with rows of **characters** carved into them. Later, they started using **movable type** made of baked clay. They created full **pages** by lining up rows of type. A German named Gutenberg expanded on the idea of movable type. He produced the first metal type. He also introduced the **printing press**. The idea came from the centuries-old wine press. In the 1500s, printed advertisements first appeared in the form of handbills. The earliest newspapers were **published** in the 1600s.

pris·tine /prɪstin, prɪstin/ ADJ **Pristine** things are extremely clean or new. 崭新的 [FORMAL] ❑ *Now the house is in pristine condition.* 现在该房子是崭新的。

★ **pri·va·cy** /praɪvəsi/ N-UNCOUNT If you have **privacy**, you are in a place or situation that allows you to do things without other people seeing you or disturbing you. 隐私；私人空间 ❑ *He resented the publication of this book, which he saw as an embarrassing invasion of his privacy.* 他憎恨这本书的出版，它将此看作是对其隐私的令人难堪的侵犯。 ❑ *Thatched pavilions provide shady retreats for relaxing and reading in privacy.* 茅亭为独自放松和看书提供阴凉的幽僻之所。

pri·vate ♦♦◊ /praɪvɪt/ (**privates**) **1** ADJ **Private** companies, industries, and services are owned or controlled by individuals or stockholders, rather than by the government or an official organization. 私有的 [BUSINESS] ❑ *...a joint venture with private industry.* …一个与私有企业合资的企业。 ❑ *They sent their children to private schools.* 他们送孩子们上私立学校。 ● **pri·vate·ly** ADV 私有地 [ADV with v] ❑ *No other European country had so much state ownership and so few privately owned businesses.* 没有任何别的欧洲国家有这么多的国有企业和这么少的私有企业。 **2** ADJ **Private** individuals are acting only for themselves, and are not representing any group, company, or organization. 代表个人行事的 [ADJ n] ❑ *Private individuals with money to lend are more difficult to find than traditional lenders.* 有钱借的个人比传统的放贷者更难找。 ❑ *The king was on a private visit to enable him to pray at the tombs of his ancestors.* 国王在做一次私访以便能祭拜其祖坟。 **3** ADJ Your **private** things belong only to you, or may only be used by you. 私人的（财物） ❑ *They want more state control over private property.* 他们想要对私人财产更多国家控制。 **4** ADJ **Private** places or gatherings may be attended only by a particular group of people, rather than by the general public. 不对外开放的 ❑ *673 private golf clubs took part in a recent study.* 673家不对外开放的高尔夫俱乐部参加了最近的一次调查。 ❑ *The door is marked "Private."* 门上写着"闲人免进"。 **5** ADJ **Private** meetings, discussions, and other activities involve only a small number of people, and very little information about them is given to other people. 私下的（会晤、讨论等） ❑ *Don't bug private conversations, and don't buy papers that reprint them.* 不要窃听私下谈话，也不要买翻印这种谈话的报纸。 ● **pri·vate·ly** ADV 私下地 ❑ *Few senior figures have issued any public statements but privately the resignation's been welcomed.* 几乎没有高级人物发表过任何公开声明，但私底下辞职是受欢迎的。 **6** ADJ Your **private life** is that part of your life that is concerned with your personal relationships and activities, rather than with your work or business. 私人的（生活） ❑ *I've always kept my private and professional life separate.* 我一向将我的私生活和职业生涯分开。 **7** ADJ Your **private** thoughts or feelings are ones that you do not talk about to other people. 私下的（想法、情感） ❑ *We all felt as if we were intruding on his private grief.* 我们都觉得好像我们在触犯他的个人悲痛。 ● **pri·vate·ly** ADV 私下地 ❑ *Privately, she worries about whether she's really good enough.* 私下里，她担心她是不是真的够好。 **8** ADJ If you describe a place as **private**, or as somewhere where you can be **private**, you mean that it is a quiet place and you can be alone there without being disturbed. 无他人打扰的（地方） ❑ *It was the only reasonably private place they could find.* 这是他们能找到的惟一颇不受他人打扰的地方。 **9** ADJ If you describe someone as a **private** person, you mean that they are very quiet by nature and do not reveal their thoughts and feelings to other people. 孤僻的 ❑ *Gould was an intensely private individual.* 古尔德曾是个相当孤僻的人。 **10** N-COUNT; N-TITLE A **private** is a soldier of the lowest rank in an army or the marines. 列兵 ❑ *He was a private in the U.S. Army.* 他是美国陆军中的一名列兵。 **11** → see also **privately** **12** PHRASE If you do something **in private**, you do it without other people being present, often because it is something that you want to keep secret. 私下地 ❑ *Some of what we're talking about might better be discussed in private.* 我们正在谈论的有些事也许私下讨论更好。

pri·vate en·ter·prise N-UNCOUNT **Private enterprise** is industry and business that is owned by individuals or stockholders, and not by the government or an official organization. 私有企业 [BUSINESS] ❑ *...the encouragement of private enterprise.* …对私有企业的鼓励。

pri·vate·ly /praɪvɪtli/ **1** ADV If you buy or sell something **privately**, you buy it from or sell it to another person directly, rather than in a store or through a business. 私下地（买、卖） [ADV after v] ❑ *The whole process makes buying a car privately as painless as buying from a garage.* 这整个过程使得私下买车和从汽车行买一样轻松。 **2** → see also **private**

pri·vate·ly held cor·po·ra·tion (**privately held corporations**) N-COUNT A **privately held corporation** is a company whose shares cannot be bought by the general public. 私人持股公司 [AM] → see **company**

pri·vate school (**private schools**) N-VAR A **private school** is a school that is not supported financially by the government and that parents have to pay for their children to go to. 私立学校 ❑ *...an exclusive private school.* …一家昂贵的私立学校。

pri·vate sec·tor N-SING **The private sector** is the part of a country's economy that consists of industries and commercial companies that are not owned or controlled by the government. （经济的）私营部分 [BUSINESS] ❑ *...small firms in the private sector.* …私营部分的各小公司。

pri·vat·ise /praɪvətaɪz/ [BRIT] → see **privatize**

pri·vat·ize ♦◊◊ /praɪvətaɪz/ (**privatizes, privatizing, privatized**)

in BRIT, also use **privatise**

V-T If a company, industry, or service that is owned by the state **is privatized**, the government sells it and makes it a private company. 使私有化 [BUSINESS] ❑ *Many state-owned companies were privatized.* 许多国有公司被私有化了。 ❑ *...a move to privatize prisons.* …一项使监狱私有化的举措。 ● **pri·vati·za·tion** ▲ /praɪvətɪzeɪʃən/ N-VAR (**privatizations**) 私有化 ❑ *...the privatization of government services.* …政府服务事业的私有化。

privi·lege /prɪvɪlɪdʒ, prɪvlɪdʒ/ (**privileges**) **1** N-COUNT A **privilege** is a special right or advantage that only one person or group has. （某人、某团体拥有的）特权 ❑ *The Russian Federation has issued a decree abolishing special privileges for government officials.* 俄罗斯联邦已颁布了一条取消政府官员特权的法令。 **2** N-UNCOUNT If you talk about **privilege**, you are talking about the power and advantage that only a small group of people have, usually because of their wealth or their connections with powerful people. （一小部分人因其财富或与有权人的关系而拥有的）特权 ❑ *Pironi was the son of privilege and wealth, and it showed.* 皮罗尼是富贵人家的子弟，这一点明摆着。 **3** N-SING You can use **privilege** in expressions such as **be a privilege** or **have the privilege** when you want to show your appreciation of someone or something, or to show your respect. 荣幸 ❑ *It must be a privilege to know such a man.* 认识这样一个人必是一种荣幸。

Word Partnership *privilege* 的常用搭配：

ADJ.	**special** privilege **1**
N.	**attorney-client** privilege, **executive** privilege **1**
	power and privilege **2**

★ **privi·leged** /prɪvɪlɪdʒd, prɪvlɪdʒd/ **1** ADJ Someone who is **privileged** has an advantage or opportunity that most other people do not have, often because of their wealth or connections with powerful people. 有特权的 ❑ *They were, by and large, a very wealthy, privileged elite.* 他们一般都属于一个非常富有的特权阶层。 ● N-PLURAL **The privileged** are people who are privileged. 有特权的人 ❑ *They are only interested in preserving the power of the privileged and the well off.* 他们只对保护特权阶层和富人的权力感兴趣。 **2** ADJ **Privileged** information is known by only a small group of people, who are not legally required to give it to anyone else. 特许保密的 ❑ *The data is privileged information, not to be shared with the general public.* 这些数据是特许保密的信息，不能让公众知道。

prize ♦♦◊ /praɪz/ (**prizes, prizing, prized**) **1** N-COUNT A **prize** is money or something valuable that is given to someone who has the best results in a competition or game, or as a reward for doing good work. 奖品；奖金 ❑ *You must claim your prize by telephoning our claims line.* 你必须通过打我们的领奖热线来领取奖品。 ❑ *He was awarded the Nobel Prize for Physics in 1985.* 他获得了1985年诺贝尔物理学奖。 **2** ADJ You use **prize** to describe things that are of such good quality that they win prizes or deserve to win prizes. 获奖的；应获奖的 [ADJ n] ❑ *...a prize bull.* …一头获奖的公牛。 **3** N-COUNT You can refer to someone or something as a **prize** when people consider them to be of great value or importance. 有价值之人；有价值之物 ❑ *With no lands of his own, he was no great matrimonial prize.* 没有自己的土地，他绝不是个有价值的结婚对象。 **4** V-T Something that **is prized** is wanted and admired because it is considered to be very valuable or very good quality. 青睐 [usu passive] ❑ *Military figures made out of lead are prized by collectors.* 用铅做的军人塑像很受收藏者们青睐。 **5** V-T If you **prize** something **open** or **prize** it away from a surface, you force it to open or force it to come away from the surface. 撬 [mainly BRIT]

in AM, usually use **pry**

Word Partnership *prize* 的常用搭配：

V. **award a** prize, **claim a** prize, **receive a** prize, **share a** prize, **win a** prize 1

ADJ. **grand** prize, **top** prize 1

pro /proʊ/ (**pros**) 1 N-COUNT A **pro** is a professional. 专业人员 [INFORMAL] ❑ *In the professional theater, there is a tremendous need to prove that you're a pro.* 在专业剧院里，证明自己是个专业人士是非常必要的。 2 ADJ A **pro** player is a professional athlete. You can also use **pro** to refer to sports that are played by professional athletes. 职业的 [ADJ n] [AM] ❑ *...a former college and pro basketball player.* …一名前大学及职业篮球队员。 3 PREP If you are **pro** a particular course of action or belief, you agree with it or support it. 支持；赞成 ❑ *Americans have always been very pro business, pro competition, pro free market.* 美国人一向很支持商业、支持竞争、支持自由市场。 4 PHRASE The **pros and cons** of something are its advantages and disadvantages, which you consider carefully so that you can make a sensible decision. 利弊 ❑ *Motherhood has both its pros and cons.* 做母亲有利也有弊。

Word Link *pro ≈ in front, before : proactive, proceed, produce*

pro·ac·tive /proʊæktɪv/ ADJ **Proactive** actions are intended to cause changes, rather than just reacting to change. 积极行动的 ❑ *In order to survive the competition a company should be proactive not reactive.* 为了能在竞争中立于不败之地，一个公司应积极行动而非被动应变。

Word Link *prob ≈ testing : probability, probation, probe*

★ **prob·abil·ity** /prɒbəbɪlɪti/ (**probabilities**) 1 N-VAR The **probability of** something happening is how likely it is to happen, sometimes expressed as a fraction or a percentage. 概率 ❑ *Without a transfusion, the victim's probability of dying was 100%.* 不输血的话，该患者的死亡概率是100%。 ❑ *The probabilities of crime or victimization are higher with some situations than with others.* 犯罪或实施伤害的概率在有些情况下比其他情况下要大一些。 2 N-VAR You say that there is a **probability that** something will happen when it is likely to happen. 可能性 [VAGUENESS] ❑ *If you've owned property for several years, the probability is that values have increased.* 如果你已拥有财产几年了，很可能价值已经增涨了。 ❑ *Formal talks are still said to be a possibility, not a probability.* 正式谈判据说仍有可能，但不是很可能。 3 PHRASE If you say that something will happen **in all probability**, you mean that you think it is very likely to happen. 很可能 [VAGUENESS] ❑ *The Republicans had better get used to the fact that in all probability, they are going to lose.* 共和党人最好习惯他们很可能会失败的事实。

prob·able /prɒbəbᵊl/ 1 ADJ If you say that something is **probable**, you mean that it is likely to be true or likely to happen. 可能(是真实、发生) 的 [VAGUENESS] ❑ *It is probable that the medication will suppress the symptom without treating the condition.* 可能该药物只治标而不治本。 2 ADJ You can use **probable** to describe a role or function that someone or something is likely to have. 可能(拥有) 的 [ADJ n] ❑ *...their probable presidential candidate.* …他们可能的总统候选人。

prob·ably ♦♦♦ /prɒbəbli/ 1 ADV If you say that something is **probably** the case, you think that it is likely to be the case, although you are not sure. 可能 (为事实) 地 [ADV with cl/group] [VAGUENESS] ❑ *The White House probably won't make this plan public until July.* 白宫可能要到7月份才会公布这项计划。 ❑ *Van Gogh is probably the best-known painter in the world.* 梵高可能是世界上最知名的画家。 2 ADV You can use **probably** when you want to make your opinion sound less forceful or definite, so that you do not offend people. 可能 (用以缓和语气) [ADV with cl/group] [VAGUENESS] ❑ *What would he think of their story? He'd probably think she and Lenny were both crazy!* 他会怎么看他们的故事呢。他可能会想她和伦尼都疯了！

▲ **pro·ba·tion** /proʊbeɪʃᵊn/ 1 N-UNCOUNT **Probation** is a period of time during which a person who has committed a crime has to obey the law and be supervised by a probation officer, rather than being sent to prison. 缓刑期 ❑ *A young woman admitted three theft charges and was put on probation for two years.* 一名年轻的妇女承认了3宗盗窃指控，被处以2年缓刑。 2 N-UNCOUNT **Probation** is a period of time during which someone is judging your character and ability while you work, in order to see if you are suitable for that type of work. 试用期 ❑ *Employee appointment to the council will be subject to a term of probation of 6 months.* 到该理事会任职须经过6个月的试用期。

pro·ba·tion of·fic·er (**probation officers**) N-COUNT A **probation officer** is a person whose job is to supervise and help people who have committed crimes and been put on probation. 缓刑监助官

probe /proʊb/ (**probes, probing, probed**) 1 V-I If you **probe into** something, you ask questions or try to discover facts about it. 调查；探寻 ❑ *The more they probed into his background, the more inflamed their suspicions would become.* 他们越深入调查他的背景，对他的怀疑就会越强烈。 ❑ *For three years, I have probed for understanding.* 3年来我一直在寻求理解。 ● N-COUNT **Probe** is also a noun. 调查；探寻 ❑ *...a federal grand-jury probe into corruption within the FDA.* …联邦大陪审团对食品及药品管理局内部腐败的一次调查。 2 V-I If a doctor or dentist **probes**, he or she uses a long instrument to examine part of a patient's body. 用探针探查 ❑ *The surgeon would pick up his instruments, probe, repair, and stitch up again.* 外科医生会拿起器械进行探查、修复，然后再缝合。 ❑ *Dr. Amid probed around the sensitive area.* 阿米德医生在敏感部位周围做了探查。 3 N-COUNT A **probe** is a long thin instrument that doctors and dentists use to examine parts of the body. 探针 ❑ *...a fiber-optic probe.* …一根光纤探针。 4 V-T If you **probe** a place, you search it in order to find someone or something that you are looking for. 搜索 ❑ *A flashlight beam probed the underbrush only yards away from their hiding place.* 一束手电光搜索了离他们藏身之处仅几码远的低矮灌丛。

prob·lem ♦♦♦ /prɒbləm/ (**problems**) 1 N-COUNT A **problem** is a situation that is unsatisfactory and causes difficulties for people. 问题 ❑ *...the economic problems of the inner city.* …内城的经济问题。 ❑ *I do not have a simple solution to the drug problem.* 我并没有一个简单的解决毒品问题的方法。 2 N-COUNT A **problem** is a puzzle that requires logical thought or mathematics to solve it. 题目 ❑ *With mathematical problems, you can save time by approximating.* 对于数学题，你可以用近似法省时间。

Thesaurus *problem* 另参见：

N. complication, difficulty, hitch 1
brain-teaser, puzzle, question, riddle 2

★ **prob·lem·at·ic** /prɒbləmætɪk/ ADJ Something that is **problematic** involves problems and difficulties. 有问题的 ❑ *Some places are more problematic than others for women traveling alone.* 对独自旅行的妇女来说，有些地方比其他地方更容易出问题。

pro·cedur·al /prəsidʒərəl/ ADJ **Procedural** means involving a formal procedure. 程序的 [FORMAL] ❑ *A Spanish judge rejected the suit on procedural grounds.* 一名西班牙法官以程序理由驳回了该起诉。

pro·cedure ♦◇◇ /prəsidʒər/ (**procedures**) N-VAR A **procedure** is a way of doing something, especially the usual or correct way. 程序 ❑ *A biopsy is usually a minor surgical procedure.* 活组织切除通常是一个较小的外科手术。 ❑ *Police insist that Michael did not follow the correct procedure in applying for a visa.* 警方坚持认为迈克尔没有按正确的程序申请签证。

Word Partnership *procedure* 的常用搭配：

V. **follow a** procedure, **perform a** procedure, **use a** procedure

ADJ. **simple** procedure, **standard (operating)** procedure, **surgical** procedure

pro·ceed ♦◇◇ (**proceeds, proceeding, proceeded**)

The verb is pronounced /prəsid/. The plural noun in meaning 4 is pronounced /proʊsidz/.

动词读作 /prəsid/。义项4的复数名词读作 /proʊsidz/。

1 V-T If you **proceed to** do something, you do it, often after doing something else first. (做完某事之后) 接着 (做另一事) ❑ *He proceeded to tell me of my birth.* 他接着给我讲了我的出生。 2 V-I If you **proceed with** a course of action, you continue with it. 继续进行 (某行动) [FORMAL] ❑ *The group proceeded with a march they knew would lead to bloodshed.* 这群人继续进行他们知道会导致流血事件的一次游行。 3 V-I If an activity, process, or event **proceeds**, it goes on and does not stop. (活动、过程、事件等) 继续 ❑ *The ideas were not new. Their development had proceeded steadily since the war.* 这些想法并不新。它们的发展自开战以来一直在稳步地继续。 4 N-PLURAL **The proceeds** of an event or activity are the money that has been obtained from it. (某事件或活动带来的) 收入 ❑ *The proceeds of the concert went to charity.* 音乐会的收入给了慈善机构。

★ **pro·ceed·ing** /prəsiːdɪŋ/ (**proceedings**) 1 N-COUNT Legal **proceedings** are legal action taken against someone. 诉讼 [FORMAL] ❑ *...criminal proceedings against the former prime minister.* …对前首相的刑事诉讼。 2 N-COUNT **The proceedings** are an organized series of events that take place in a particular place. 行动 [FORMAL] ❑ *The proceedings of the inquiry will take place in private.* 调查行动将秘密进行。 3 N-PLURAL You can refer to a written record of the discussions at a meeting or conference as **the proceedings**. 会议记录 ❑ *The DOT is to publish the conference proceedings.* 运输部将公布会议记录。

pro·cess ♦♦♦ /prɒsɛs/ (**processes, processing, processed**) 1 N-COUNT A **process** is a series of actions which are carried out in order to achieve a particular result. (行动) 过程 ❑ *There was total agreement to start the peace process as soon as possible.* 全体同意尽快启动和平进程。 ❑ *They decided to spread the building process over three years.* 他们决定在3年内分期完成该建造过程。 2 N-COUNT A **process** is a series of things that happen naturally and result in a biological or chemical change. (发展) 过程 ❑ *It occurs in elderly men, apparently as part of the aging process.* 它明显作为衰老过程的一部分发生在老年男性身上。 3 V-T When raw materials or foods **are processed**, they are prepared in factories before they are used or sold. 加工 (原材料、食品) ❑ *...fish which are processed by the best methods: from freezing to canning and smoking.* …用从冷冻到装罐和熏制等最好的方法加工的鱼。 ❑ *The material will be processed into plastic pellets.* 该原料将被加工成塑料颗粒。 ● N-COUNT **Process** is also a noun. 过程 ❑ *...the cost of reengineering the production process.* …重新设计生产过程的成本。 ● **pro·cess·ing** N-UNCOUNT 加工 [usu with supp] ❑ *America sent cotton to England for processing.* 美国把棉花运到英格兰加工。 4 V-T When people **process** information, they put it through a system or into a computer in order to deal with it. 处理 (信息) ❑ *...facilities to process the data, and the right to publish the results.* …处理数据的设备和公布结果的权利。 ● **pro·cess·ing** N-UNCOUNT 处理 ❑ *...data processing.* …数据处理。 5 → see also **word processing** 6 V-T When people **are processed** by officials, their case is dealt with in stages and they pass from one stage of the process to the next. 按程序处理 [usu passive] ❑ *Patients took more than two hours to be processed through the department.* 病人们花了两个多小时才走完那个科室程序。 7 PHRASE If you are **in the process of** doing something, you have started to do it and are still doing it. 在…过程中 ❑ *The administration is in the process of drawing up a peace plan.* 政府正在起草一项和平计划。 8 PHRASE If you are doing something and you do something else **in the process**, you do the second thing as part of doing the first thing. 在此过程中 ❑ *You have to let us struggle for ourselves, even if we must die in the process.* 你得让我们自己去奋斗，即使在此过程中我们得死。

Word Partnership *process* 的常用搭配:

ADJ. **difficult** process, **political** process 1
complicated process, **gradual** process, **long** process, **normal** process, **slow** process, **whole** process 1 2
V. **participate in a** process 1
begin a process, **complete a** process, **control a** process, **describe a** process, **start a** process 1 2
N. **application** process, **approval** process, **decision** process, **learning** process, **planning** process 1
process **information** 4

pro·ces·sion /prəsɛʃən/ (**processions**) N-COUNT A **procession** is a group of people who are walking, riding, or driving in a line as part of a public event. (行走、骑行、开车等的) 队伍 ❑ *...a funeral procession.* …一行送葬队伍。

pro·ces·sor /prɒsɛsər/ (**processors**) 1 N-COUNT A **processor** is the part of a computer that interprets commands and performs the processes the user has requested. (电脑) 处理器 [COMPUTING] 2 → see also **food processor, word processor** 3 N-COUNT A **processor** is someone or something which carries out a process. 加工者; 加工物 ❑ *The frozen-food industry could be supplied entirely by growers and processors outside the country.* 冷冻食品行业可以完全由国外的种植者们和加工者们供应。

pro·claim /proʊkleɪm/ (**proclaims, proclaiming, proclaimed**) 1 V-T If people **proclaim** something, they formally make it known to the public. 宣布 ❑ *The new government in Venezuela set up its own army and proclaimed its independence.* 委内瑞拉新政府建立了自己的军队并宣布独立。 ❑ *Britain proudly proclaims that it is a nation of animal lovers.* 英国自豪地宣称它是个热爱动物的国家。 2 V-T If you **proclaim** something, you state it in an emphatic way. 强调 ❑ *"I think we have been heard today," he proclaimed.* "我想我们所说的今天大家都听到了，"他强调说。

proc·la·ma·tion /prɒkləmeɪʃən/ (**proclamations**) N-COUNT A **proclamation** is a public announcement about something important, often about something of national importance. 声明 ❑ *The proclamation of independence was broadcast over the radio.* 独立声明在广播里播出了。

pro·cure /prəkyʊər/ (**procures, procuring, procured**) V-T If you **procure** something, especially something that is difficult to get, you obtain it. 获得 (尤指难以获得的东西) [FORMAL] ❑ *It remained very difficult to procure food, fuel, and other daily necessities.* 当时仍然很难获得食品、燃料和其他日用必需品。

▲ **pro·cure·ment** /prəkyʊərmənt/ N-UNCOUNT **Procurement** is the act of obtaining something such as supplies for an army or other organization. 获得 (军需品等的) 行为 [FORMAL] ❑ *Russia was cutting procurement of new weapons "by about 80 percent," he said.* 他说俄罗斯正"以大约百分之八十的幅度"削减新武器的补给。

prod /prɒd/ (**prods, prodding, prodded**) 1 V-T If you **prod** someone or something, you give them a quick push with your finger or with a pointed object. (用手指或尖物) 捅 ❑ *He prodded Murray with the shotgun.* 他用猎枪捅了默里一下。 ❑ *Prod the windowsills to check for signs of rot.* 捅一捅窗台，看有没有腐烂迹象。 ● N-COUNT **Prod** is also a noun. 捅 ❑ *He gave the donkey a mighty prod in the backside.* 他在驴的屁股上狠狠地捅了一下。 2 V-T If you **prod** someone **into** doing something, you remind or persuade them to do it. 敦促 ❑ *The question is intended to prod students into examining the concept of freedom.* 这个问题旨在敦促学生探究自由这个概念。

pro·di·gious /prədɪdʒəs/ ADJ Something that is **prodigious** is very large or impressive. 巨大的; 给人印象深刻的 [LITERARY] ❑ *This business generates cash in prodigious amounts.* 这生意带来大量现金。 ● **pro·di·gious·ly** ADV 巨大地; 给人印象深刻地 ❑ *She ate prodigiously.* 她真能吃。

▲ **prodi·gy** /prɒdɪdʒi/ (**prodigies**) N-COUNT A **prodigy** is someone young who has a great natural ability for something such as music, mathematics, or sports. (有极大的音乐、数学、运动等天赋的) 奇才 ❑ *The Russian tennis prodigy is well on the way to becoming the youngest world champion of all time.* 这位俄罗斯网球奇才已很有望成为历史上最年轻的世界冠军。

Word Link *pro ≈ in front, before : proactive, proceed, produce*

pro·duce ♦♦♦ (**produces, producing, produced**)

The verb is pronounced /prədus/. The noun is pronounced /prɒdus/ or /proʊdus/.

动词读作 /prədus/。名词读作 /prɒdus/或 /proʊdus/。

1 V-T To **produce** something means to cause it to happen. 使发生 ❑ *The drug is known to produce side-effects in women.* 众所周知，这种药会在女性身上产生各种副作用。 2 V-T If you **produce** something, you make or create it. 生产 ❑ *The company produced circuitry for communications systems.* 这家公司为通讯系统生产电路系统。 3 V-T When things or people **produce** something, it comes from them or slowly forms from them, especially as the result of a biological or chemical process. 生长出; 生育出 ❑ *These plants are then pollinated and allowed to mature and produce seed.* 这些植物之后被授粉，使其成熟、结籽。 4 V-T If you **produce** evidence or an argument, you show it or explain it to people in order to make them agree with you. 给出 (证据、论据等) ❑ *They challenged him to produce evidence to support his allegations.* 他们要求他给出证据来支撑他的断言。 5 V-T If you **produce** an object from somewhere, you show it or bring it out so that it can be seen. 出示 ❑ *To rent a car you must produce a passport and a current driver's license.* 要租一辆车你必须出示护照和现有驾照。 6 V-T If someone **produces** something such as a movie, a magazine, or a CD, they organize it and decide how it should be done. 制作 (电影、杂志、唱片等) ❑ *He has produced his own sports magazine.* 他已经创办了自己的体育杂志。 7 N-UNCOUNT **Produce** is fruit and vegetables that are grown in large quantities to be sold. 农产品 ❑ *We manage to get most of our produce in farmers' markets.* 我们设法在农贸市场弄到大部分我们需要的农产品。

pro·duc·er ♦♦◊ /prədusər/ (**producers**) 1 N-COUNT A **producer** is a person whose job is to produce plays, movies, programs, or

CDs. (戏剧、电影、节目、唱片等的) 制作人 ❑ *...a freelance film producer.* …一名独立电影制片人。 **2** N-COUNT A **producer** of a food or material is a company or country that grows or manufactures a large amount of it. (食品、材料等的) 生产者 ❑ *...Saudi Arabia, the world's leading oil producer.* …沙特阿拉伯，世界上最重要的石油生产国。

prod·uct ♦♦♦ /prɒdʌkt/ (**products**) **1** N-COUNT A **product** is something that is produced and sold in large quantities, often as a result of a manufacturing process. 产品 ❑ *Try to get the best product at the lowest price.* 尽力以最低的价格买到最好的产品。 **2** N-COUNT If you say that someone or something is a **product of** a situation or process, you mean that the situation or process has had a significant effect in making them what they are. 产物 ❑ *We are all products of our time.* 我们都是我们时代的产物。

→ see **advertising, industry, inventor**

pro·duc·tion ♦♦◊ /prədʌkʃ^ən/ (**productions**) **1** N-UNCOUNT **Production** is the process of manufacturing or growing something in large quantities. 生产 ❑ *That model won't go into production before late 2007.* 那种型号要到2007年底才会投入生产。 **2** N-UNCOUNT **Production** is the amount of goods manufactured or grown by a company or country. 产量 ❑ *We needed to increase the volume of production.* 我们必须增加产量。 **3** N-UNCOUNT The **production of** something is its creation as the result of a natural process. 产生；生成 ❑ *These proteins stimulate the production of blood cells.* 这些蛋白质促进血细胞的生成。 **4** N-UNCOUNT **Production** is the process of organizing and preparing a play, movie, program, or CD, in order to present it to the public. (戏剧、电影、节目等的) 制作 ❑ *She is head of the production company.* 她是该制片公司的头儿。 **5** N-COUNT A **production** is a play, opera, or other show that is performed in a theater. 演出 ❑ *...a critically acclaimed production of Othello.* …一场受到评论界好评的《奥赛罗》的演出。 **6** PHRASE When you can do something **on production of** or **on the production of** documents, you need to show someone those documents in order to be able to do that thing. 凭某物的出示 ❑ *Entry to the show is free to members on production of their membership cards.* 该演出会员凭其会员证的出示免费入场。

→ see **theater**

pro·duc·tion line (**production lines**) N-COUNT A **production line** is an arrangement of machines in a factory where the products pass from machine to machine until they are finished. 生产线 ❑ *Honda added a production line this year, hoping to boost domestic sales.* 本田公司今年增加了一条生产线，希望提高国内的销售额。

pro·duc·tive /prədʌktɪv/ **1** ADJ Someone or something that is **productive** produces or does a lot for the amount of resources used. 生产力高的 ❑ *Training makes workers highly productive.* 培训使工人们生产力很高。 ❑ *More productive farmers have been able to provide cheaper food.* 生产力更高的农民们已能提供更便宜的食品。 **2** ADJ If you say that a relationship between people is **productive**, you mean that a lot of good or useful things happen as a result of it. 富有成效的 ❑ *He was hopeful that the next round of talks would also be productive.* 他对下一轮会谈也会富有成效充满了希望。

prod·uc·tiv·ity /prɒdʊktɪvɪti/ N-UNCOUNT **Productivity** is the rate at which goods are produced. 生产率 ❑ *The third-quarter results reflect continued improvements in productivity.* 第三季度的结果反映了生产率的持续提高。

prod·uct line (**product lines**) N-COUNT A **product line** is a group of related products produced by one manufacturer, for example, products that are intended to be used for similar purposes or to be sold in similar types of stores. 产品线 [BUSINESS] ❑ *...the company's most successful product lines.* …该公司最成功的产品线。

prod·uct place·ment (**product placements**) N-VAR **Product placement** is a form of advertising in which a company has its product placed where it can be clearly seen during a movie or television program. (电影或电视节目中的) 植入式广告 [BUSINESS] ❑ *It was the first movie to feature onscreen product placement for its own merchandise.* 这是第一部为自己的商品做银幕植入式广告的电影。

▲ **pro·fess** /prəfɛs/ (**professes, professing, professed**) **1** V-T If you **profess to** do or have something, you claim that you do it or have it, often when you do not. (常不真实地) 声称 [FORMAL] ❑ *She professed to hate her nickname.* 她声称讨厌她的绰号。 ❑ *Why do organizations profess that they care?* 为什么一些组织声称他们关心呢？ **2** V-T If you **profess** a feeling, opinion, or belief, you express it. 表示 (某感情、观点、信仰等) [FORMAL] ❑ *He professed to be content with the arrangement.* 他表示对该安排满意。 ❑ *Miller professed himself dissatisfied with Broadway theater.* 米勒表示他对百老汇剧院不满。

pro·fes·sion ♦◊◊ /prəfɛʃ^ən/ (**professions**) **1** N-COUNT A **profession** is a type of job that requires advanced education or training. 职业 [also "by" N] ❑ *Harper was a teacher by profession.* 哈珀的职业是教师。 **2** N-COUNT-COLL You can use **profession** to refer to all the people who have the same profession. 同业的全体人员 ❑ *The attitude of the medical profession is very much more liberal now.* 医学人士的态度如今开放多了。

pro·fes·sion·al ♦♦◊ /prəfɛʃən^əl/ (**professionals**) **1** ADJ **Professional** means relating to a person's work, especially work that requires special training. 有关职业的 [ADJ n] ❑ *His professional career started at Colgate University.* 他的职业生涯始于科尔盖特大学。 ● **pro·fes·sion·al·ly** ADV 职业上地 ❑ *...a professionally-qualified architect.* …一名职业上合格的建筑师。 **2** ADJ **Professional** people have jobs that require advanced education or training. 专业的 (人士) [ADJ n] ❑ *...highly qualified professional people like doctors and engineers.* …像医生和工程师这样高资历的专业人士。 ● N-COUNT **Professional** is also a noun. 专业人士 ❑ *My father wanted me to become a professional and have more stability.* 我父亲希望我成为一名专业人士，有更多稳定性。 **3** ADJ You use **professional** to describe people who do a particular thing to earn money rather than as a hobby. 职业的 (运动员等) ❑ *This has been my worst time for injuries since I started as a professional player.* 这是我成为职业球员以来受伤最严重的一次。 ● N-COUNT **Professional** is also a noun. 职业人士 ❑ *He had been a professional since March 1985.* 他自1985年3月以来一直是一名职业人士。 ● **pro·fes·sion·al·ly** ADV 作为职业地 [ADV after v] ❑ *By age 16 he was playing professionally with bands in Greenwich Village.* 到16岁时，他已在与格林尼治村的各乐队进行职业演出了。 **4** ADJ **Professional** sports are played for money rather than as a hobby. 职业的 (运动等) [ADJ n] ❑ *...an art student who had played professional football for a short time.* …曾短期踢过职业足球的艺术生。 **5** ADJ If you say something that someone does or produces is **professional**, you approve of it because you think that it is of a very high standard. 专业水准的 [APPROVAL] ❑ *They run it with a truly professional but personal touch.* 他们以真正专业而个性化的方式经营它。 ● N-COUNT **Professional** is also a noun. 有专业水准的人 ❑ *...a dedicated professional who worked harmoniously with the cast and crew.* …一位和全体演职人员合作融洽、敬业、有专业水准的人。 ● **pro·fes·sion·al·ly** ADV 有专业水准地 [ADV with v] ❑ *These tickets have been produced very professionally.* 这些标签制作得很专业。

pro·fes·sion·al·ism /prəfɛʃən^əlɪzəm/ N-UNCOUNT **Professionalism** in a job is a combination of skill and high standards. 专业性 [APPROVAL] ❑ *American companies pride themselves on their professionalism.* 美国的公司为他们的专业性而自豪。

pro·fes·sor ♦♦◊ /prəfɛsər/ (**professors**) **1** N-COUNT; N-TITLE; N-VOC A **professor** in an American or Canadian university or college is a teacher of the highest rank. (美国大学的) 教授 ❑ *Robert Dunn is a professor of economics at George Washington University.* 罗伯特・邓恩是乔治・华盛顿大学的经济学教授。 **2** N-TITLE; N-COUNT; N-VOC A **professor** in a British university is the most senior teacher in a department. (英国大学的) 系主任 ❑ *...Professor Cameron.* …卡梅伦主任。

→ see **graduation**

prof·fer /prɒfər/ (**proffers, proffering, proffered**) **1** V-T If you **proffer** something to someone, you hold it toward them so that they can take it or touch it. 递上 [FORMAL] ❑ *He rose and proffered a silver box full of cigarettes.* 他站起来递上了一个装满香烟的银盒子。 **2** V-T If you **proffer** something such as advice to someone, you offer it to them. 提供 (建议等) [FORMAL] ❑ *The army has not yet proffered an explanation of how and why the accident happened.* 军队还没有提供对该事故如何发生以及为什么发生的解释。

pro·fi·cien·cy /prəfɪʃ^ənsi/ N-UNCOUNT If you show **proficiency** in something, you show ability or skill at it. 水平 ❑ *Evidence of basic proficiency in English is part of the admissions requirement.* 基本英语水平的证明是录取条件的一部分。

pro·fi·cient /prəfɪʃənt/ ADJ If you are **proficient in** something, you can do it well. 精通的 ❑ *A great number of Egyptians are proficient in foreign languages.* 大量埃及人精通外语。

pro·file ♦◊◊ /proʊfaɪl/ (**profiles**) **1** N-COUNT Your **profile** is the outline of your face as it is seen when someone is looking at you from the side. (面部的) 侧面轮廓 ❑ *His handsome profile was turned away from us.* 他英俊的侧面轮廓转离了我们。 **2** N-UNCOUNT If you see someone **in profile**, you see them from the side. 从侧面 ❑ *This*

P

picture shows the girl in profile. 这张照片从侧面显示该女孩。 3 N-COUNT A **profile of** someone is a short article or program in which their life and character are described. (有关某人的) 简介 ❑ *A Washington newspaper published comparative profiles of the candidates' wives.* 一家华盛顿的报纸刊登了候选人妻子们的对比简介。 4 N-COUNT If the police make a **profile of** someone they are looking for, they write a description of the sort of person they are looking for. (书面的) 描述 [oft N "of" n] ❑ *...the FBI profile of the anthrax killer.* …联邦调查局对那名炭疽杀人犯的描述。 ● **pro·fil·ing** /proʊfaɪlɪŋ/ N-UNCOUNT 进行描画 [usu with supp] ❑ *...a former FBI agent who pioneered psychological profiling in the 1970s.* …在20世纪70年代开创了犯罪心理描画的一名前联邦调查局特工。 ❑ *DNA profiling would now be added to the struggle against vandalism.* DNA描画如今也许会被加到对抗故意破坏公共财物的斗争中。 5 PHRASE If someone has a **high profile**, people notice them and what they do. If you **keep a low profile**, you avoid doing things that will make people notice you. 高关注度 ❑ *...a move that would give Egypt a much higher profile in the upcoming peace talks.* …会给埃及在即将到来的和平谈判中高关注度的一个行动。 6 → see also **high-profile**

prof·it ♦♦◇ /prɒfɪt/ (**profits, profiting, profited**) 1 N-VAR A **profit** is an amount of money that you gain when you are paid more for something than it cost you to make, get, or do it. 利润 ❑ *The bank made pre-tax profits of $6.5 million.* 该银行获得了税前650万美元的利润。 ❑ *You can improve your chances of profit by sensible planning.* 你可以通过合理的计划增加盈利的机会。 2 V-I If you **profit from** something, you earn a profit from it. (从…中) 获利 ❑ *No one was profiting inordinately from the war effort.* 没有人在从战争中发大财。 ❑ *He has profited by selling his holdings to other investors.* 他已通过将他所持有的卖给其他投资者们而获利。 3 V-T/V-I If you **profit from** something, or it **profits** you, you gain some advantage or benefit from it. 使 (某人) 获利; 获利 [FORMAL] ❑ *Jennifer wasn't yet totally convinced that she'd profit from a more relaxed lifestyle.* 珍妮弗还没有完全相信她会从更放松的生活方式中获益。 ❑ *So far the French alliance had profited the rebels little.* 到那时为止，法联盟还没让叛军得到多少好处。

→ see **company**

Word Partnership *profit* 的常用搭配:

N. **decline in** profit, profit **and loss**, profit **margin**, **operating** profit, profit **sharing** 1
V. **make a** profit, **maximize** profit, **post a** profit, **report a** profit, **turn a** profit 1

★ **prof·it·able** /prɒfɪtəbᵊl/ 1 ADJ A **profitable** organization or practice makes a profit. 可盈利的 ❑ *Drug manufacturing is the most profitable business in the U.S.* 药品生产是美国最赚钱的行业。 ● **prof·it·ably** /prɒfɪtəbli/ ADV 可盈利地 [ADV with v] ❑ *The 28 French stores are trading profitably.* 那28家法国商店在盈利。 ● **prof·it·abil·ity** /prɒfɪtəbɪlɪti/ N-UNCOUNT 盈利能力 ❑ *Changes were made in operating methods in an effort to increase profitability.* 在经营方式上做了一些改变以增加盈利能力。 2 ADJ Something that is **profitable** results in some benefit for you. 能带来利益的 ❑ *...close collaboration with industry which leads to a profitable exchange of personnel and ideas.* …能带来人员和理念上有益交流的与企业的密切合作。 ● **prof·it·ably** ADV 能带来利益地 [ADV with v] ❑ *In fact he could scarcely have spent his time more profitably.* 事实上他几乎不可能把他的时间花得更有益了。

prof·it·eer·ing /prɒfɪtɪərɪŋ/ N-UNCOUNT **Profiteering** involves making large profits by charging high prices for goods that are hard to get. 投机倒把 [BUSINESS, DISAPPROVAL] ❑ *There's been a wave of profiteering and corruption.* 曾有一股投机倒把和腐败之风。

profit-making 1 ADJ A **profit-making** business or organization makes a profit. 盈利的 [BUSINESS] ❑ *He wants to set up a profit-making company, owned mostly by the university.* 他想开办一家能赚钱的公司，主要由该大学所有。 2 → see also **nonprofit**

prof·it mar·gin (**profit margins**) N-COUNT A **profit margin** is the difference between the selling price of a product and the cost of producing and marketing it. 利润空间 [BUSINESS] ❑ *The group had a net profit margin of 30% last year.* 该集团去年的净利润空间为30%。

profit-sharing N-UNCOUNT **Profit-sharing** is a system by which all the people who work in a company have a share in its profits. 分红制 [BUSINESS] ❑ *...the bank's profit-sharing plan.* …该银行的分红计划。

profit-taking N-UNCOUNT **Profit-taking** is the selling of stocks and shares at a profit after their value has risen or just before their value falls. 套利 [BUSINESS] ❑ *The market was held down by profit-taking in the banking sector yesterday.* 股市昨天因银行方面套利持续走低。

★ **pro·found** /prəfaʊnd/ (**profounder, profoundest**) 1 ADJ You use **profound** to emphasize that something is very great or intense. 深刻的; 极大的 [EMPHASIS] ❑ *...discoveries which had a profound effect on many areas of medicine.* …对医学的许多领域都有深刻影响的一些发现。 ❑ *...profound disagreement.* …极大的分歧。 ● **pro·found·ly** ADV 深刻地; 极大地 ❑ *This has profoundly affected my life.* 这已极大地影响了我的生活。 2 ADJ A **profound** idea, work, or person shows great intellectual depth and understanding. 高深的 ❑ *This is a book full of profound, original, and challenging insights.* 这是一本充满高深、新颖且富有挑战性见解的书。

pro·fuse /prəfyus/ 1 ADJ **Profuse** sweating, bleeding, or vomiting is sweating, bleeding, or vomiting large amounts. 大量的 (出汗、流血、呕吐) ❑ *...a remedy that produces profuse sweating.* …一种让人大量出汗的疗法。 ● **pro·fuse·ly** ADV 大量地 [ADV after v] ❑ *He was bleeding profusely.* 他当时在大量出血。 2 ADJ If you offer **profuse** apologies or thanks, you apologize or thank someone a lot. 多次的 (感谢或道歉) ❑ *Then the policeman recognized me, breaking into profuse apologies.* 然后警察认出了我，开始一再道歉。 ● **pro·fuse·ly** ADV 多次地 [ADV after v] ❑ *They were very grateful and thanked me profusely.* 他们非常感激，不停地谢我。

prog·no·sis /prɒgnoʊsɪs/ (**prognoses** /prɒgnoʊsiz/) N-COUNT A **prognosis** is an estimate of the future of someone or something, especially about whether a patient will recover from an illness. (尤指对病人能否康复的) 预后 [FORMAL] ❑ *The doctor's prognosis was that Laurence might walk within 12 months.* 该医生的预后是劳伦斯可能在12个月之内能走动。

Word Link *gram ≈ writing : diagram, program, telegram*

pro·gram ♦♦◇ /proʊgræm, -grəm/ (**programs, programming, programmed**)

in BRIT, use **programme** for meanings 1, 2, 3

1 N-COUNT A **program** of actions or events is a series of actions or events that are planned to be done. 计划 ❑ *The nation's largest training and education program for adults.* 该国最大的成人培训与教育计划。 2 N-COUNT A television or radio **program** is something that is broadcast on television or radio. (电视、广播) 节目 ❑ *...a network television program.* …一个网络电视节目。 3 N-COUNT A theater or concert **program** is a small book or sheet of paper that gives information about the play or concert you are attending. (戏剧、音乐会的) 节目单 ❑ *When you go to concerts, it's helpful to read the program.* 去音乐会的时候，看看节目单是有帮助的。 4 V-T When you **program** a machine or system, you set its controls so that it will work in a particular way. 设定 (机器、系统等的) 程序 ❑ *Parents can program the machine not to turn on at certain times.* 父母可设定机器在某些时候不启动。 5 N-COUNT A **program** is a set of instructions that a computer follows in order to perform a particular task. (计算机) 程序 [COMPUTING] ❑ *The chances of an error occurring in a computer program increase with the size of the program.* 计算机程序出错的几率随程序的增大而增高。 6 V-T When you **program** a computer, you give it a set of instructions to make it able to perform a particular task. 给 (计算机) 编程 [COMPUTING] ❑ *He programmed his computer to compare the 1,431 possible combinations of pairs in this population.* 他给他的计算机编了程来比较这些人中1431种可能的成对组合。 ❑ *...45 million people, about half of whom can program their own computers.* 4500万人，其中约有一半会给他们自己的计算机编程。 ● **pro·gram·ming** N-UNCOUNT 编程 ❑ *...programming skills.* …编程技巧。

→ see **radio**

Word Partnership *program* 的常用搭配:

V. **create a** program, **expand a** program, **implement a** program, **launch a** program, **run a** program 1 5
N. **computer** program, **software** program 5
program **a computer** 6

pro·gramme /proʊgræm/ [mainly BRIT] → see **program**

pro·gram·mer /proʊgræmər/ (**programmers**) N-COUNT A computer **programmer** is a person whose job involves writing programs for computers. (计算机) 程序员 [COMPUTING]

pro·gress ♦♦◇ (**progresses, progressing, progressed**)

The noun is pronounced /prɒgrɛs/. The verb is pronounced /prəgrɛs/.

名词读作 /prɒgres/，动词读作 /prəgrɛs/。

1 N-UNCOUNT **Progress** is the process of gradually improving or getting nearer to achieving or completing something. 进步 ❑ *The medical community continues to make progress in the fight against cancer.* 医学界继续在抗癌斗争中取得进步。 2 N-SING **The progress of** a situation or action is the way in which it develops. 进展 ❑ *The president is reported to have been delighted with the progress of the first day's talks.* 据报道，总统对第一天会谈的进展很满意。 3 V-I **To progress** means to move over a period of time to a stronger, more advanced, or more desirable state. 进展 ❑ *He will visit once every two weeks to see how his new employees are progressing.* 他将每两周视察一次以看看他的新雇员们进展如何。 4 V-I If events **progress**, they continue to happen gradually over a period of time. 继续进行 ❑ *As the evening progressed, sadness turned to rage.* 随着夜晚的来临，悲伤变成了愤怒。 5 V-T If you **progress** something, you cause it to develop. 使…发展 [BRIT, FORMAL] 6 PHRASE If something **is in progress**, it has started and is still continuing. 在进行中 ❑ *The game was already in progress when we took our seats.* 比赛在我们坐下时已经在进行了。

pro·gres·sion /prəgrɛʃ^{ə}n/ (**progressions**) N-COUNT A **progression** is a gradual development from one state to another. (从一状态到另一状态的) 逐步发展 ❑ *Both drugs slow the progression of HIV, but neither cures the disease.* 两种药都能减缓艾滋病病毒的发展，但都不能治愈艾滋病。

pro·gres·sive /prəgrɛsɪv/ (**progressives**) 1 ADJ Someone who is **progressive** or has **progressive** ideas has modern ideas about how things should be done, rather than traditional ones. 进步的 ❑ *...a progressive businessman who had voted for Roosevelt in 1932 and 1936.* …在1932年和1936年投票支持罗斯福的一位进步商人。 ❑ *Willan was able to point to the progressive changes he had already introduced.* 威兰能够指出他已经带来的有进步意义的变化。 ● N-COUNT A **progressive** is someone who is progressive. 进步人士 ❑ *The Republicans were deeply split between progressives and conservatives.* 共和党进步派和保守派之间分歧很大。 2 ADJ A **progressive** change happens gradually over a period of time. 逐步的 ❑ *One prominent symptom of the disease is progressive loss of memory.* 这种病的一个突出症状是记忆的逐步丧失。 ● **pro·gres·sive·ly** ADV 逐步地 ❑ *Her symptoms became progressively worse.* 她的症状逐步恶化。

pro·hib·it /proʊhɪbɪt/ (**prohibits, prohibiting, prohibited**) V-T If a law or someone in authority **prohibits** something, they forbid it or make it illegal. 禁止 [FORMAL] ❑ *...a law that prohibits tobacco advertising in newspapers and magazines.* …一项禁止在报纸和杂志上刊登烟草广告的法律。 ❑ *Fishing is prohibited.* 捕鱼是受禁止的。 ● **pro·hi·bi·tion** N-UNCOUNT 禁止 ❑ *The air force and the navy retain their prohibition of women on air combat missions.* 空军和海军都保留了对女性空中作战任务的禁止。

pro·hi·bi·tion /proʊɪbɪʃ^{ə}n/ (**prohibitions**) 1 N-COUNT A **prohibition** is a law or rule forbidding something. 禁令 ❑ *...a prohibition on discrimination.* …一项对歧视的禁令。 2 → see also **prohibit**

pro·hibi·tive /proʊhɪbɪtɪv/ ADJ If the cost of something is **prohibitive**, it is so high that many people cannot afford it. (费用) 高得负担不起的 [FORMAL] ❑ *The cost of private treatment can be prohibitive.* 私人治疗的费用会高得负担不起。 ● **pro·hibi·tive·ly** ADV 高得负担不起地 [ADV adj] ❑ *Meat and butter were prohibitively expensive.* 肉和奶油都贵得买不起。

proj·ect ♦♦◊ (**projects, projecting, projected**)

The noun is pronounced /prɒdʒɛkt/. The verb is pronounced /prədʒɛkt/.

名词读作 /prɒdʒɛkt/，动词读作 /prədʒɛkt/。

1 N-COUNT A **project** is a task that requires a lot of time and effort. 项目 ❑ *Money will also go into local development projects in Vietnam.* 资金也会流入越南本地开发项目。 ❑ *...an international science project.* …一个国际科研项目。 2 N-COUNT A **project** is a detailed study of a subject by a student. (学生研究的) 课题 ❑ *Students complete projects for a personal tutor, working at home at their own pace.* 学生们为个人导师完成课题研究，在家里按自己的速度工作。 3 V-T If something **is projected**, it is planned or expected. 计划；预计 ❑ *13% of Americans are over 65; this number is projected to reach 22% by the year 2030.* 13%的美国人在65岁以上；这个数字预计到2030年会达到22%。 ❑ *The government had been projecting a 5% consumer price increase for the entire year.* 政府一直在预计全年5%的消费价格增长。 4 V-T If you **project** someone or something in a particular way, you try to make people see them in that way. If you **project** a particular feeling or quality, you show it in your behavior. (以某方式) 呈现 ❑ *Bradley projects a natural warmth and sincerity.* 布拉德利表现出一种自然的热情和真诚。 ❑ *He just hasn't been able to project himself as the strong leader.* 他只是还没能把自己表现得是个强有力的领导。 5 V-T If you **project** a film or picture **onto** a screen or wall, you make it appear there. 投映 ❑ *The team tried projecting the maps with two different projectors onto the same screen.* 该组尝试用两台不同的放映机将地图投映在同一屏幕上。 6 V-I If something **projects**, it sticks out above or beyond a surface or edge. 突出 [FORMAL] ❑ *...a narrow ledge that projected out from the bank of the river.* …河岸边突出来的一块狭长的岩脊。

Word Partnership *project* 的常用搭配：

V. **approve a** project, **launch a** project 1
complete a project, **involved in a** project, **start a** project 1 2

N. **construction** project, **development** project, project **director/manager** 1
research project, **science** project, **writing** project 1 2

ADJ. **latest** project, **new** project, **special** project 1 2

pro·jec·tion /prədʒɛkʃ^{ə}n/ (**projections**) 1 N-COUNT A **projection** is an estimate of a future amount. 预计 ❑ *...the company's projection of 11 million visitors for the first year.* …公司对第一年1100万游客的预计。 2 N-UNCOUNT The **projection** of a film or picture is the act of projecting it onto a screen or wall. 投映 ❑ *They took me into a projection room to see a picture.* 他们将我带进了一个投映室去看一张图片。

pro·jec·tor /prədʒɛktər/ (**projectors**) 1 N-COUNT A **projector** is a machine that projects films or slides onto a screen or wall. 放映机；投影仪 ❑ *...a slide projector.* …幻灯机。 2 → see also **overhead projector**

▲ **pro·lif·er·ate** /prəlɪfəreɪt/ (**proliferates, proliferating, proliferated**) V-I If things **proliferate**, they increase in number very quickly. 激增 [FORMAL] ❑ *Computerized databases are proliferating fast.* 计算机化的数据库在迅速激增。 ● **pro·lif·era·tion** /prəlɪfəreɪʃ^{ə}n/ N-UNCOUNT 激增 ❑ *...the proliferation of nuclear weapons.* …核武器的激增。

pro·lif·ic /prəlɪfɪk/ 1 ADJ A **prolific** writer, artist, or composer produces a large number of works. (作家、艺术家或作曲家) 多产的 ❑ *She is a prolific writer of novels and short stories.* 她是位多产的长篇和短篇小说家。 2 ADJ An animal, person, or plant that is **prolific** produces a large number of babies, young plants, or fruit. (动物、人、植物) 多产的 ❑ *They are prolific breeders, with many hens laying up to six eggs.* 他们是多产的培育者，有许多能下多达6个蛋的母鸡。

pro·logue /proʊlɔg/ (**prologues**) also **prolog** N-COUNT A **prologue** is a speech or section of text that introduces a play or book. 开场白；前言 ❑ *The prologue to the novel is written in the form of a newspaper account.* 该小说的前言是以新闻报道的形式写的。

★ **pro·long** /prəlɔŋ/ (**prolongs, prolonging, prolonged**) V-T To **prolong** something means to make it last longer. 延长 ❑ *Mr. Chesler said foreign military aid was prolonging the war.* 切斯勒先生说外国的军事援助正在延长这场战争。

pro·longed /prəlɔŋd/ ADJ A **prolonged** event or situation continues for a long time, or for longer than expected. 长期的；延长了的 ❑ *...a prolonged period of low interest rates.* …一段很长的低利率期。

promi·nence /prɒmɪnəns/ N-UNCOUNT If someone or something is in a position of **prominence**, they are well-known and important. 著名；重要性 ❑ *He came to prominence during the World Cup.* 他在该世界杯期间一举成名。 ❑ *Crime prevention had to be given more prominence.* 犯罪预防得给予更多重视。

promi·nent ♦◊◊ /prɒmɪnənt/ 1 ADJ Someone who is **prominent** is important and well-known. 重要的；著名的 ❑ *...the children of very prominent or successful parents.* …非常知名或成功的人士们的孩子们。 2 ADJ Something that is **prominent** is very noticeable or is an important part of something else. 突出的 ❑ *Here the window plays a prominent part in the design.* 这里，窗户在设计中有着突出的作用。 ● **promi·nent·ly** ADV 突出地 [ADV with v] ❑ *Trade will figure prominently in the second day of talks in Washington.* 贸易在华盛顿会谈的第二天将成为突出的议题。

P

pro·mis·cu·ous /prəmɪskyuəs/ ADJ Someone who is **promiscuous** has sex with many different people. 淫乱的 [DISAPPROVAL] ❑ *She is perceived as vain, spoiled, and promiscuous.* 她被认为是个虚荣、娇生惯养、淫乱的女人。● **promis·cu·ity** /prɒmɪskyuɪti/ N-UNCOUNT 淫乱

prom·ise ♦♦◇ /prɒmɪs/ (**promises, promising, promised**) 1 V-T/V-I If you **promise that** you will do something, you say to someone that you will definitely do it. 承诺 ❑ *The post office has promised to resume first class mail delivery to the area on Friday.* 邮局已承诺在星期五恢复该地区第一类邮件的递送。❑ *He had promised that the rich and privileged would no longer get preferential treatment.* 他已承诺富人和特权阶层将不会再得到优待。❑ *Promise me you will not waste your time.* 向我承诺你不会浪费你的时间。❑ *I'll call you back, I promise.* 我会给你回电话的，我保证。2 V-T If you **promise** someone something, you tell them that you will definitely give it to them or make sure that they have it. 向(某人)承诺(给予他们某物); 向(某人)保证(他们获得某物) ❑ *In 1920 the great powers promised them an independent state.* 1920年，列强们曾答应让他们成为一个独立国家。3 N-COUNT A **promise** is a statement that you make to a person in which you say that you will definitely do something or give them something. 诺言 ❑ *If you make a promise, you should keep it.* 如果你许下一个诺言，你就应该遵守它。4 V-T If a situation or event **promises to** have a particular quality or **to** be a particular thing, it shows signs that it will have that quality or be that thing. 预示 ❑ *While it will be fun, the seminar also promises to be most instructive.* 这次专题讨论会将会很有趣，也一定会非常有启发性。5 N-UNCOUNT If someone or something shows **promise**, they seem likely to be very good or successful. (显示出) 成功的迹象 ❑ *The boy first showed promise as an athlete in grade school.* 这个男孩最初是在小学显示出成为一名成功的运动员的迹象。

Word Partnership *promise* 的常用搭配:

N. **campaign** promise 3

V. **break** a promise, **deliver on** a promise, **keep** a promise, **make** a promise 3
hold promise, **show** promise 5

ADJ. **broken** promise, **empty** promise, **false** promise 3
enormous promise, **great** promise, **real** promise 5

prom·is·ing /prɒmɪsɪŋ/ ADJ Someone or something that is **promising** seems likely to be very good or successful. 有望成功的; 前景很好的 ❑ *A school has honored one of its brightest and most promising former students.* 一所学校给其培养过的最聪明、最有前途的学生中的一位颁了奖。

P

prom·is·sory note /prɒmɪsɔri noʊt/ (**promissory notes**) N-COUNT A **promissory note** is a written, dated promise to pay a specific sum of money to a particular person. 期票 [mainly AM, BUSINESS] ❑ *...a $36.4 million, five-year promissory note.* …一张3640万美元的5年期期票。

Word Link *mot ≈ moving : motion, motivate, promote*

pro·mote ♦♦◇ /prəmoʊt/ (**promotes, promoting, promoted**) 1 V-T If people **promote** something, they help or encourage it to happen, increase, or spread. 促进 ❑ *You don't have to sacrifice environmental protection to promote economic growth.* 你们没有必要牺牲环保来促进经济增长。● **pro·mo·tion** N-UNCOUNT 促进 ❑ *The government has pledged to give the promotion of democracy higher priority.* 政府已承诺要给民主的促进以更高的优先级。2 V-T If a firm **promotes** a product, it tries to increase the sales or popularity of that product. 促销 ❑ *...a tour to promote his second solo album.* …一场促销他第二张个人专辑的巡回演出。3 V-T If someone **is promoted**, they are given a more important job or rank in the organization that they work for. 晋升 [usu passive] ❑ *I was promoted to editor and then editorial director.* 我晋升为编辑，之后又晋升为编辑部主任。

Word Partnership *promote* 的常用搭配:

N. promote **competition**, promote **democracy**, promote **development**, promote **education**, promote **growth**, promote **health**, promote **peace**, promote **stability**, promote **trade**, promote **understanding** 1
promote **a product** 2

pro·mot·er /prəmoʊtər/ (**promoters**) 1 N-COUNT A **promoter** is a person who helps organize and finance an event, especially a sports event. (尤指体育赛事的) 承办者 ❑ *...one of the top boxing promoters in Las Vegas.* …拉斯维加斯顶尖的拳击比赛的承办者之一。2 N-COUNT The **promoter of** a cause or idea tries to make it become popular. 倡导者 ❑ *Aaron Copland was always the most energetic promoter of American music.* 阿伦·柯普兰一直是美国音乐最积极的倡导者。
→ see **concert**

pro·mo·tion ♦◇◇ /prəmoʊʃən/ (**promotions**) 1 N-VAR If you are given **promotion** or **a promotion** in your job, you are given a more important job or rank in the organization that you work for. 晋升 ❑ *Consider changing jobs or trying for promotion.* 考虑换工作或者争取晋升。2 N-VAR A **promotion** is an attempt to make a product or event popular or successful, especially by advertising. 促销; 推广 [BUSINESS] ❑ *Advertising and promotion are what American business does best.* 打广告和促销是美国企业做得最好的事情。3 → see also **promote**

pro·mo·tion·al /prəmoʊʃənəl/ ADJ **Promotional** material, events, or ideas are designed to increase the sales of a product or service. 促销的 ❑ *"Jeans," according to one company's promotional material, "are designed and made to be worn hard."* 根据一家公司促销材料上所说的，"牛仔裤为耐穿而设计和制作。"

prompt ♦◇◇ /prɒmpt/ (**prompts, prompting, prompted**) 1 V-T To **prompt** someone **to** do something means to make them decide to do it. 促使 ❑ *Japan's recession has prompted consumers to cut back on buying cars.* 日本的经济衰退已促使消费者们削减购车花销。2 V-T If you **prompt** someone when they stop speaking, you encourage or help them to continue. If you **prompt** an actor, you tell them what their next line is when they have forgotten what comes next. 提示; 给(演员)提示词 ❑ *"You wouldn't have wanted to bring those people to justice anyway, would you?" Brand prompted him.* "你本不想将那些人绳之以法的，是吧？"布兰德提示他说。3 ADJ A **prompt** action is done without any delay. 立即的(行动) ❑ *It is not too late, but prompt action is needed.* 还不太晚，但需要立即行动。4 ADJ If you are **prompt** to do something, you do it without delay or you are not late. (做某事)迅速的 [v-link ADJ] ❑ *You have been so prompt in carrying out all these commissions.* 你执行所有这些任务非常迅速。

prompt·ing /prɒmptɪŋ/ (**promptings**) N-UNCOUNT If you respond to **prompting**, you do what someone encourages or reminds you to do. 鼓励; 提醒 [also N in pl] ❑ *The New York team needed little prompting from their coach Bill Parcells.* 纽约队几乎不需要教练比尔·帕索斯的提醒。

prompt·ly /prɒmptli/ 1 ADV If you do something **promptly**, you do it immediately. 立即 [ADV with v] ❑ *Sister Francesca entered the chapel, took her seat, and promptly fell asleep.* 弗朗西丝卡修女走进小教堂，就了座，很快就睡着了。2 ADV If you do something **promptly at** a particular time, you do it at exactly that time. 准点地 ❑ *Promptly at a quarter past seven, we left the hotel.* 我们在7：15准点离开了旅馆。

★ **prone** /proʊn/ 1 ADJ To be **prone to** something, usually something bad, means to have a tendency to be affected by it or to do it. 易于(受某事物影响或做某事)的 [v-link ADJ] ❑ *For all her experience as a television reporter, she was still prone to camera nerves.* 尽管有丰富的做电视记者的经验，她仍然倾向于在镜头前紧张。● COMB IN ADJ **-prone** combines with nouns to make adjectives that describe people who are frequently affected by something bad. 易受…影响的(与名词结合构成形容词) ❑ *...the most injury-prone rider on the circuit.* …赛车道上最容易受伤的车手。2 ADJ If you are lying **prone**, you are lying on your front. 面朝下的 [ADJ after v, ADJ n] [FORMAL] ❑ *Bob slid from his chair and lay prone on the floor.* 鲍勃从椅子上滑下来，面朝下躺在了地板上。

pro·noun /proʊnaʊn/ (**pronouns**) N-COUNT A **pronoun** is a word that you use to refer to someone or something when you do not need to use a noun, often because the person or thing has been mentioned earlier. Examples are "it," "she," "something," and "myself." 代词

Word Link *nounce ≈ reporting : announce, denounce, pronounce*

pro·nounce /prənaʊns/ (**pronounces, pronouncing, pronounced**) 1 V-T To **pronounce** a word means to say it using particular sounds. 发(某字或词的)音 ❑ *Have I pronounced your name correctly?* 我把你的名字读对了吗？2 V-T If you **pronounce** something to be true, you state that it is the case. 宣布 [FORMAL] ❑ *A specialist has now pronounced him fully fit.* 一位专家已宣布他完全康复了。
→ see **trial**

pro·nounced /prənaʊnst/ ADJ Something that is **pronounced** is very noticeable. 明显的 ❑ *Most of the art exhibitions have a* pronounced Appalachian theme. 大部分艺术展品都有一种明显的阿巴拉契亚主题。

pro·nounce·ment /prənaʊnsmənt/ (**pronouncements**) N-COUNT **Pronouncements** are public or official statements on an important subject. 公告 ❑ *...the president's latest pronouncements about the protection of minorities.* …总统关于少数民族保护的最新公告。

pro·nun·cia·tion /prənʌnsieɪʃ°n/ (**pronunciations**) N-VAR The **pronunciation** of a word or language is the way it is pronounced. 发音 ❑ *She gave the word its French pronunciation.* 她给出了这个单词的法语发音。

proof ♦◇◇ /pruf/ (**proofs**) **1** N-VAR **Proof** is a fact, argument, or piece of evidence showing that something is definitely true or definitely exists. 证明 ❑ *You have to have proof of residence in the state of Texas, such as a Texas ID card.* 你必须有在德克萨斯州的居住证明，例如一张得克萨斯州的身份证。 ❑ *This is not necessarily proof that he is wrong.* 这未必是他错了的证明。 **2** ADJ **Proof** is used after a number of degrees or a percentage, when indicating the strength of a strong alcoholic drink such as whiskey. (用于度数或百分比之后) 标准酒精度的 [amount ADJ] ❑ *...a glass of Wild Turkey bourbon: 101 proof.* …一杯101标准酒精度的野火鸡牌波旁威士忌。

Word Partnership *proof* 的常用搭配：
ADJ. **convincing** proof, **final** proof, **living** proof, proof **positive** **1**
V. **have** proof, **need** proof, **offer** proof, **provide** proof, **require** proof, **show** proof **1**

-proof /-pruf/ (**-proofs, -proofing, -proofed**) **1** COMB IN ADJ **-proof** combines with nouns and verbs to form adjectives indicating that something cannot be damaged or badly affected by the thing or action mentioned. 抗…的 (与名词或动词结合构成形容词) ❑ *...a bomb-proof aircraft.* …防弹飞机。 ❑ *In a large microwave-proof dish, melt butter for 20 seconds.* 在一个耐微波的大盘子里，将奶油融化20秒。 **2** COMB IN VERB **-proof** combines with nouns to form verbs that refer to protecting something against being damaged or badly affected by the thing mentioned. 抗… (与名词结合构成动词) ❑ *They recommended that the viaduct be replaced rather than quake-proofed.* 他们建议更换这座高架桥，而不要对其做抗震处理。 **3** → see also **bulletproof, waterproof**

▲ **prop** /prɒp/ (**props, propping, propped**) **1** V-T If you **prop** an object **on** or **against** something, you support it by putting something underneath it or by resting it somewhere. 架；搁 ❑ *He rocked back in the chair and propped his feet on the desk.* 他往椅背上一靠，将双脚搁在了桌子上。 ● PHRASAL VERB **Prop up** means the same as **prop**. 支撑；维持 ❑ *Sam slouched back and propped his elbows up on the bench behind him.* 萨姆懒懒地往后一靠，将他的两胳膊肘撑在了他背后的长凳上。 **2** N-COUNT A **prop** is a stick or other object that you use to support something. 支撑物 ❑ *Using the table as a prop, he dragged himself to his feet.* 他用桌子作支撑，缓慢费力地站了起来。 **3** N-COUNT To be a **prop** for a system, institution, or person means to be the main thing that keeps them strong or helps them survive. 支柱 ❑ *The army is one of the main props of the government.* 军队是政府的主要支柱之一。 **4** N-COUNT The **props** in a play or movie are all the objects or pieces of furniture that are used in it. (戏剧、电影中的) 道具 ❑ *...the backdrop and props for a stage show.* …一场舞台剧的背景幕和道具。

▸ **prop up** **1** PHRASAL VERB To **prop up** something means to support it or help it to survive. 支撑；维持 ❑ *Investments in the U.S. money market have propped up the American dollar.* 对美国货币市场的投资一直在支撑着美元。 **2** → see **prop 1**

★ **propa·gan·da** /prɒpəgændə/ N-UNCOUNT **Propaganda** is information, often inaccurate information, that a political organization publishes or broadcasts in order to influence people. (政治组织的) 宣传 [DISAPPROVAL] ❑ *The party adopted an aggressive propaganda campaign against its rivals.* 该党采用了一场对抗其对手的咄咄逼人的宣传运动。

★ **propa·gate** /prɒpəgeɪt/ (**propagates, propagating, propagated**) **1** V-T If people **propagate** an idea or piece of information, they spread it and try to make people believe it or support it. 宣传 [FORMAL] ❑ *They propagated political doctrines that promised to tear apart the fabric of society.* 他们宣传有可能摧毁社会结构的政治学说。 ● **propa·ga·tion** /prɒpəgeɪʃ°n/ N-UNCOUNT 宣传 ❑ *These two countries must work together toward the propagation of true Buddhism.* 这两个国家必须携手进行真正的佛教教义的宣传。 **2** V-T If you **propagate** plants, you grow more of them from the original ones. 繁殖 [TECHNICAL] ❑ *The easiest way to propagate a vine is to take hardwood cuttings.* 繁殖葡萄藤最容易的办法就是采取硬木扦插。

Word Link *pel ≈ driving, forcing : compel, expel, propel*

★ **pro·pel** /prəpɛl/ (**propels, propelling, propelled**) V-T To **propel** something in a particular direction means to cause it to move in that direction. 推进 ❑ *The tiny rocket is attached to the spacecraft and is designed to propel it toward Mars.* 微型火箭附在宇宙飞船上，用来推进飞船飞向火星。 ● COMB IN ADJ **-propelled** combines with nouns to form adjectives that indicate how something, especially a weapon, is propelled. (与名词结合构成形容词) …推进的 ❑ *...rocket-propelled grenades.* …火箭推进的榴弹。

pro·pel·ler /prəpɛlər/ (**propellers**) N-COUNT A **propeller** is a device with blades attached to a boat or aircraft. The engine makes the propeller spin around and causes the boat or aircraft to move. 螺旋桨 ❑ *...a fixed three-bladed propeller.* …一个固定的三叶螺旋桨。 → see **flight**

pro·pen·sity /prəpɛnsɪti/ (**propensities**) N-COUNT A **propensity to** do something or a **propensity for** something is a natural tendency to behave in a particular way. (行为) 倾向 [FORMAL] ❑ *Mr. Bint has a propensity to put off decisions to the last minute.* 宾特先生有一种将决定拖到最后一分钟的倾向。

prop·er ♦◇◇ /prɒpər/ **1** ADJ You use **proper** to describe things that you consider to be real and satisfactory rather than inadequate in some way. 像样的 [ADJ n] ❑ *Two out of five people lack a proper job.* 2/5的人缺乏一份像样的工作。 **2** ADJ The **proper** thing is the one that is correct or most suitable. 正规的 [ADJ n] ❑ *The Supreme Court will ensure that the proper procedures have been followed.* 最高法院将保证正规的程序得到遵守。 **3** ADJ If you say that a way of behaving is **proper**, you mean that it is considered socially acceptable and right. 适宜的 ❑ *In those days it was not thought entirely proper for a woman to be on the stage.* 在那时，女人登台演出不被认为是完全适宜的。 **4** ADJ You can add **proper** after a word to indicate that you are referring to the central and most important part of a place, event, or object and want to distinguish it from other things that are not regarded as being important or central to it. 严格意义上的 [n ADJ] ❑ *A distinction must be made between archaeology proper and science-based archaeology.* 必须对严格意义上的考古学和以科学为基础的考古学加以区分。

prop·er·ly ♦◇◇ /prɒpərli/ **1** ADV If something is done **properly**, it is done in a correct and satisfactory way. 合宜地 ❑ *You're too thin. You're not eating properly.* 你太瘦了。你没有好好吃饭。 **2** ADV If someone behaves **properly**, they behave in a way that is considered acceptable and not rude. 得当地 [ADV after v] ❑ *He's a spoiled brat and it's about time he learned to behave properly.* 他是个被宠坏的顽劣孩子，该是他学着行为得当的时候了。

prop·er noun (**proper nouns**) N-COUNT A **proper noun** is the name of a particular person, place, organization, or thing. Proper nouns begin with a capital letter. Examples are "Peggy," "Tucson," and "the United Nations." Compare **common noun**. 专有名词

Word Link *proper, propr ≈ owning : property, proprietary, proprietor*

prop·er·ty ♦♦◇ /prɒpərti/ (**properties**) **1** N-UNCOUNT Someone's **property** is all the things that belong to them or something that belongs to them. 财产 [FORMAL] ❑ *Richard could easily destroy her personal property to punish her for walking out on him.* 理查德可以轻而易举地毁掉她的私有财产作为对她背叛他的惩罚。 **2** N-VAR A **property** is a building and the land belonging to it. 房地产 [FORMAL] ❑ *Cecil inherited a family property near Stamford.* 塞西尔继承了斯坦福附近的一处家族房产。 **3** N-COUNT The **properties** of a substance or object are the ways in which it behaves in particular conditions. (物质、物体的) 特性 ❑ *A radio signal has both electrical and magnetic properties.* 无线电信号既具有电的特性也具有磁的特性。 → see **element**

▲ **proph·ecy** /prɒfɪsi/ (**prophecies**) N-VAR A **prophecy** is a statement in which someone says they strongly believe that a particular thing will happen. 预言 ❑ *Will the teacher's prophecy be fulfilled?* 那位老师的预言会实现吗？

proph·esy /prɒfɪsaɪ/ (**prophesies, prophesying, prophesied**) V-T If you **prophesy** that something will happen, you say that you strongly believe that it will happen. 预言 ❑ *He prophesied that within*

P

five years his opponent would either be dead or in prison. 他预言说在5年之内他的对手不是死就会蹲监狱。

★ **proph·et** /prɒfɪt/ (**prophets**) N-COUNT A **prophet** is a person who is believed to be chosen by God to say the things that God wants to tell people. 先知 ❑ *...the sacred name of the Holy Prophet of Islam.* …伊斯兰教神圣先知之圣名。

pro·phet·ic /prəfɛtɪk/ ADJ If something was **prophetic**, it described or suggested something that did actually happen later. 有预见性的 ❑ *This ominous warning soon proved prophetic.* 这一不详的警示不久就证明有预见性。

▲ **pro·po·nent** /prəpoʊnənt/ (**proponents**) N-COUNT If you are a **proponent of** a particular idea or course of action, you actively support it. (某观念或行为的) 支持者 [FORMAL] ❑ *Halsey was identified as a leading proponent of the values of progressive education.* 哈尔西被认为是进步教育价值观的首要支持者。

pro·por·tion ♦◇◇ /prəpɔrʃ^ən/ (**proportions**) **1** N-COUNT A **proportion of** a group or an amount is a part of it. 部分 [FORMAL] ❑ *A large proportion of the dolphins in that area will eventually die.* 那个地区的很大一部分海豚最终都会死去。 **2** N-COUNT The **proportion of** one kind of person or thing in a group is the number of people or things of that kind compared to the total number of people or things in the group. (某部分在总体中所占的) 比例 ❑ *The proportion of women in the profession had risen to 17.3%.* 从事那个职业的女性比例已经增长到17.3%。 **3** N-COUNT The **proportion of** one amount **to** another is the relationship between the size of the two amounts. (一个量与另一个量的) 比值 ❑ *Women's bodies tend to have a higher proportion of fat to water.* 女性体内往往有更高的脂肪与水的比值。 **4** N-PLURAL If you refer to the **proportions** of something, you are referring to its size, usually when this is extremely large. (某物的) 大小 [WRITTEN] ❑ *In the tropics plants grow to huge proportions.* 在热带，植物长得很高大。 **5** PHRASE If one thing increases or decreases **in proportion to** another thing, it increases or decreases to the same degree as that thing. (与…) 成比例地 ❑ *The pressure in the cylinders would go up in proportion to the boiler pressure.* 汽缸内的压力会与锅炉的压力成比例上升。 **6** PHRASE If something is small or large **in proportion to** something else, it is small or large when compared with that thing. (与…) 比 ❑ *Children tend to have relatively larger heads than adults in proportion to the rest of their body.* 与身体其余部位相比，孩子头部所占比例往往比成人大。 **7** PHRASE If you say that something is **out of all proportion to** something else, you think that it is far greater or more serious than it should be. (与…) 完全不成比例 ❑ *The punishment was out of all proportion to the crime.* 惩罚和罪行完全不成比例。

→ see ratio

P

Word Partnership *proportion* 的常用搭配：

N. proportion **of the population** **1**
proportion **of adults/children/men/women** **1** **2**
ADJ. **large** proportion, **significant** proportion, **small** proportion **1** **2**
greater proportion, **higher** proportion, **larger** proportion **3**
in direct proportion **5** **6**

pro·por·tion·al /prəpɔrʃən^əl/ ADJ If one amount is **proportional to** another, the two amounts increase and decrease at the same rate so there is always the same relationship between them. (与…) 成比例的 [FORMAL] ❑ *Loss of weight is directly proportional to the rate at which the disease is progressing.* 体重减轻和该病的发展速度成比例。

pro·por·tion·al rep·re·sen·ta·tion N-UNCOUNT **Proportional representation** is a system of voting in which each political party is represented in a legislature or parliament in proportion to the number of people who vote for it in an election. 比例代表制 (指每个政党在议会中的席位与其得票数成比例的制度)

pro·por·tion·ate /prəpɔrʃənɪt/ ADJ **Proportionate** means the same as **proportional**. (与…) 成比例的 ❑ *Republics will have voting rights proportionate to the size of their economies.* 各共和国将拥有与其经济规模成比例的选举权。 ● **pro·por·tion·ate·ly** ADV 成比例地 ❑ *We have increased the number of teachers but the size of the classes hasn't changed proportionately.* 我们已增加了教师的数量，但班级的大小并没有成比例地改变。

pro·po·sal ♦♦◇ /prəpoʊz^əl/ (**proposals**) **1** N-COUNT A **proposal** is a plan or an idea, often a formal or written one, which is suggested for people to think about and decide upon. (常为正式书面的) 提议 ❑ *The president is to put forward new proposals for resolving the country's constitutional crisis.* 总统将提出解决国家宪法危机的新议案。 ❑ *...the governor's proposal to restrict cigarette sales.* …州长关于限制香烟销售的提案。 **2** N-COUNT A **proposal** is the act of asking someone to marry you. 求婚 ❑ *After a three-weekend courtship, Pam accepted Randy's proposal of marriage.* 经过一段为期3个周末的恋爱，帕姆接受了兰迪的求婚。

Word Partnership *proposal* 的常用搭配：

ADJ. **new** proposal, **original** proposal **1**
V. **adopt a** proposal, **approve a** proposal, **support a** proposal, **vote on a** proposal **1**
accept a proposal, **make a** proposal, **reject a** proposal **1** **2**
N. **budget** proposal, **peace** proposal **1**
marriage proposal **2**

pro·pose ♦♦◇ /prəpoʊz/ (**proposes, proposing, proposed**) **1** V-T If you **propose** something such as a plan or an idea, you suggest it for people to think about and decide upon. 建议 ❑ *Hamilton proposed a change in the traditional debating format.* 汉密尔顿建议对传统的辩论形式作一个改变。 **2** V-T If you **propose** to do something, you intend to do it. 打算 ❑ *It's still far from clear what action the government proposes to take over the affair.* 尚不清楚政府打算采取什么行动接手这件事。 **3** V-T If you **propose** a motion for debate, or a candidate for election, you begin the debate or the election procedure by formally stating your support for that motion or candidate. 提出；提名 ❑ *He has proposed a resolution limiting the role of U.S. troops.* 他提出了一项限制美军作用的决议。 **4** V-T/V-I If you **propose to** someone, or **propose marriage to** them, you ask them to marry you. 求婚 ❑ *He proposed to his girlfriend over a public-address system.* 他在有线广播系统上向女友求婚。

Word Partnership *propose* 的常用搭配：

N. propose **changes**, propose **legislation**, propose **a plan**, propose **a solution**, propose **a tax**, propose **a theory**, propose **a toast** **1** **2**
propose **marriage** **4**

★ **propo·si·tion** /prɒpəzɪʃ^ən/ (**propositions**) **1** N-COUNT If you describe something such as a task or an activity as, for example, a difficult **proposition** or an attractive **proposition**, you mean that it is difficult or pleasant to do. 事情 ❑ *Making easy money has always been an attractive proposition.* 轻轻松松地赚钱一直是令人向往的事。 **2** N-COUNT A **proposition** is a statement or an idea that people can consider or discuss to decide whether it is true. 主张；观点 [FORMAL] ❑ *The proposition that democracies do not fight each other is based on a tiny historical sample.* 民主国家间互不交战的观点是基于一个微不足道的历史实例。 **3** N-COUNT A **proposition** is a question or statement about an issue of public policy that appears on a voting paper so that people can vote for or against it. 提案 ❑ *Vote Yes on Proposition 136, but No on Propositions 129, 133, and 134.* 对136号提案投赞成票，但对129、133和134号提案投反对票。 **4** N-COUNT A **proposition** is an offer or a suggestion that someone makes to you, usually concerning some work or business that you might be able to do together. 建议 ❑ *You came to see me at my office the other day with a business proposition.* 你几天前到我的办公室来看我，带着一份业务上的建议。

Word Link *proper, propr ≈ owning : property, proprietary, proprietor*

▲ **pro·pri·etary** /prəpraɪətɛri/ ADJ **Proprietary** substances or products are sold under a brand name. 品牌专卖的 [ADJ n] [FORMAL] ❑ *...some proprietary brands of dog food.* …一些专卖狗粮的品牌。

pro·pri·etor /prəpraɪətər/ (**proprietors**) N-COUNT The **proprietor** of a hotel, store, newspaper, or other business is the person who owns it. 业主 [FORMAL] ❑ *...the proprietor of a local restaurant.* …一家当地餐馆的业主。

pro·pri·etress /prəpraɪətrɪs/ (**proprietresses**) N-COUNT The **proprietress** of a hotel, store, or business is the woman who owns it. 女业主 [FORMAL] ❑ *The proprietress was alone in the bar.* 女业主独自一人在酒吧里。

pro ra·ta /proʊ reɪtə/ ADV If something is distributed **pro rata**, it is distributed in proportion to the amount or size of something. 按比例地 [ADV after v] [FORMAL] ❑ *All part-timers should be paid the* same, pro rata, as full-timers doing the same job. 所有兼职人员都应按比例地与全职人员同工同酬。● ADJ **Pro-rata** is also an adjective. 按比例的 [ADJ n] ❑ *They are paid their salaries and are entitled to fringe benefits on a pro-rata basis.* 他们领工资，同时还能按比例享受附加福利。

pro·sa·ic /proʊzeɪɪk/ ADJ Something that is **prosaic** is dull and uninteresting. 枯燥乏味的 [FORMAL] ❑ *His instructor offered a more prosaic explanation for the surge in interest.* 他的老师对利率的急剧上升给出了一个更枯燥乏味的解释。

★ **prose** /proʊz/ N-UNCOUNT **Prose** is ordinary written language, in contrast to poetry. 散文 ❑ *Shute's prose is stark and chillingly unsentimental.* 舒特的散文刻板而冷峻。

★ **pros·ecute** /prɒsɪkyut/ (**prosecutes, prosecuting, prosecuted**) **1** V-T/V-I If the authorities **prosecute** someone, they charge them with a crime and put them on trial. 对…提起公诉；提起公诉 ❑ *The police have decided not to prosecute because the evidence is not strong enough.* 警方已决定不起诉，因为证据不够充分。❑ *Photographs taken by roadside cameras will soon be enough to prosecute drivers for speeding.* 路边摄像机所拍到的照片不久将足以用来起诉超速的司机。**2** V-T When a lawyer **prosecutes** a case, he or she tries to prove that the person who is on trial is guilty. (原告律师) 起诉 ❑ *The attorney who will prosecute the case says he cannot reveal how much money is involved.* 即将起诉这件案子的原告律师说他不能透漏涉案金额。

★ **pros·ecu·tion** ◆◇◇ /prɒsɪkyuʃən/ (**prosecutions**) **1** N-VAR **Prosecution** is the action of charging someone with a crime and putting them on trial. 起诉 ❑ *Yesterday the head of government called for the prosecution of those responsible for the deaths.* 政府首脑昨日要求对那些造成死亡的责任人进行起诉。**2** N-SING The lawyers who try to prove that a person on trial is guilty are called **the prosecution**. 原告律师 ❑ *The star witness for the prosecution took the stand.* 原告律师传讯的主要证人站到了证人席上。

pros·ecu·tor /prɒsɪkyutər/ (**prosecutors**) N-COUNT In some countries, a **prosecutor** is a lawyer or official who brings charges against someone or tries to prove in a trial that they are guilty. 起诉人；检察官

pros·pect ◆◆◇ /prɑspɛkt/ (**prospects, prospecting, prospected**) **1** N-VAR If there is some **prospect of** something happening, there is a possibility that it will happen. 可能性；前景 ❑ *Unfortunately, there is little prospect of seeing these big questions answered.* 遗憾的是，几乎没有可能看到这些重大问题得到解答。❑ *The prospects for peace in the country's eight-year civil war are becoming brighter.* 在该国的8年内战中，和平的前景正变得越来越光明。**2** N-SING A particular **prospect** is something that you expect or know is going to happen. 将要发生的事 ❑ *There was a mixed reaction to the prospect of having new neighbors.* 对于将要有新邻居这件事有多种反应。**3** N-PLURAL Someone's **prospects** are their chances of being successful, especially in their career. 成功的机会；前途 ❑ *I chose to work abroad to improve my career prospects.* 我选择到国外工作，以增进我的事业成功的机会。**4** V-I When people **prospect for** oil, gold, or some other valuable substance, they look for it in the ground or under the sea. 勘探 ❑ *He had prospected for minerals everywhere from the Gobi Desert to the Transvaal.* 他在世界各地探过矿，从戈壁沙漠到德兰士瓦。

Word Partnership *prospect* 的常用搭配：

V.	prospect **of being** ***something***, prospect **of having** ***something*** **1**
N.	prospect **for/of peace**, prospect **for/of war** **1**

★ **pro·spec·tive** /prəspɛktɪv/ **1** ADJ You use **prospective** to describe someone who wants to be the thing mentioned or who is likely to be the thing mentioned. 预期的 [ADJ n] ❑ *The story should act as a warning to other prospective buyers.* 这篇报道应该可以对其他可能的购买者起到警告作用。**2** ADJ You use **prospective** to describe something that is likely to happen soon. 可能很快发生的 [ADJ n] ❑ *The terms of the prospective deal are most clearly spelled out in Business Week.* 这笔即将达成的交易条款在《商业周刊》上清楚地阐述了。

pro·spec·tus /prəspɛktəs/ (**prospectuses**) N-COUNT A **prospectus** is a detailed document produced by a company, college, or school, which gives details about it. (公司或学校的) 介绍说明文件 ❑ *...a prospectus for a new issue of stock.* …新发行股票的招股说明书。

▲ **pros·per** /prɒspər/ (**prospers, prospering, prospered**) V-I If people or businesses **prosper**, they are successful and do well. 兴隆；成功 [FORMAL] ❑ *His business continued to prosper.* 他的生意持续兴隆。

Word Link *sper ≈ hope : desperate, exasperate, prosperity*

pros·per·ity /prɒspɛrɪti/ N-UNCOUNT **Prosperity** is a condition in which a person or community is doing well financially. 繁荣 ❑ *...a new era of peace and prosperity.* …一个和平与繁荣的新时代。

pros·per·ous /prɒspərəs/ ADJ **Prosperous** people, places, and economies are rich and successful. 富裕的；成功的 [FORMAL] ❑ *...the youngest son of a relatively prosperous family.* …一个相对富裕的家庭里的小儿子。

pros·ti·tute /prɒstɪtut/ (**prostitutes**) N-COUNT A **prostitute** is a person, usually a woman, who has sex with men in exchange for money. 娼妓 ❑ *He admitted last week he paid for sex with a prostitute.* 他承认上星期曾和一名妓女有过性交易。

pros·ti·tu·tion /prɒstɪtuʃən/ N-UNCOUNT **Prostitution** means having sex with people in exchange for money. 卖淫 ❑ *She eventually drifted into prostitution.* 她最终沦落风尘。

Word Link *agon ≈ struggling : agonize, antagonist, protagonist*

pro·tago·nist /proʊtægənɪst/ (**protagonists**) **1** N-COUNT Someone who is a **protagonist of** an idea or movement is a supporter of it. 倡导者；拥护者 [FORMAL] ❑ *...the main protagonists of their countries' integration into the world market.* …将他们的国家融入世界市场的主要倡导者。**2** N-COUNT A **protagonist** in a play, novel, or real event is one of the main people in it. (戏剧、小说或真实事件里的) 主人公 [FORMAL] ❑ *...the protagonist of J. D. Salinger's novel "The Catcher in the Rye."* …J・D・塞林格的小说《麦田里的守望者》的主人公。

Word Link *tect ≈ covering : detect, protect, protective*

pro·tect ◆◆◇ /prətɛkt/ (**protects, protecting, protected**) **1** V-T To **protect** someone or something means to prevent them from being harmed or damaged. 保护 ❑ *So, what can women do to protect themselves from heart disease?* 那么，女性能做什么来保护自己不患心脏病呢？ ❑ *A long thin wool coat and a purple headscarf protected her against the wind.* 一件薄薄的羊毛长大衣和一条紫色头巾为她挡风。**2** V-T If an insurance policy **protects** you **against** an event such as death, injury, fire, or theft, the insurance company will give you or your family money if that event happens. 为…保险 ❑ *Many manufacturers have policies to protect themselves against blackmailers.* 许多制造商都有为敲诈勒索保险的保单。

→ see **hero**

Word Partnership *protect* 的常用搭配：

N.	protect **against attacks**, protect **children**, protect **citizens**, **duty to** protect, **efforts to** protect, protect **the environment**, **laws** protect, protect **people**, protect **privacy**, protect **women**, protect **workers** **1** protect **property** **1** **2**
ADJ.	**designed to** protect, **necessary to** protect, **supposed to** protect **1** **2**

pro·tec·tion ◆◆◇ /prətɛkʃən/ (**protections**) **1** N-VAR To give or be **protection** against something unpleasant means to prevent people or things from being harmed or damaged by it. 保护 ❑ *Such a diet is widely believed to offer protection against a number of cancers.* 这样的日常饮食被广泛认为可以预防多种癌症。 ❑ *It is clear that the primary duty of parents is to provide protection for our children.* 很明显，父母的首要职责就是为孩子提供保护。**2** N-UNCOUNT If an insurance policy gives you **protection against** an event such as death, injury, fire, or theft, the insurance company will give you or your family money if that event happens. (保险单提供的) 保险 [oft N "against" n] ❑ *Insurance can be purchased to provide protection against such risks.* 买保险可以应对此类风险。**3** N-UNCOUNT If a government has a policy of **protection**, it helps its own industries by putting a tax on imported goods or by restricting imports in some other way. 贸易保护 [BUSINESS] ❑ *Over the same period trade protection has increased in the rich countries.* 在同一时期，富国的贸易保护增强了。

pro·tec·tion·ism /prətɛkʃənɪzəm/ N-UNCOUNT **Protectionism** is the policy some countries have of helping their own industries by putting a large tax on imported goods or by restricting imports in some other way. 贸易保护主义 [BUSINESS] ❑ *The aim of the current round of talks is to promote free trade and to avert the threat of increasing protectionism.* 本轮会谈的目的是促进自由贸易，消除日益加剧的贸易保护主义的威胁。

P

pro·tec·tion·ist /prətɛkʃənɪst/ (**protectionists**) 1 N-COUNT A **protectionist** is someone who agrees with and supports protectionism. 贸易保护主义者 [BUSINESS] ❑ *Trade frictions between the two countries had been caused by trade protectionists.* 两国间的贸易摩擦是由贸易保护主义者引起的。 2 ADJ **Protectionist** policies, measures, and laws are meant to stop or reduce imports. 贸易保护主义的 [BUSINESS] ❑ *The administration may be moving away from free trade and toward more protectionist policies.* 该政府可能正在放弃自由贸易而走向贸易保护主义的政策。

Word Link *tect ≈ covering : detect, protect, protective*

pro·tec·tive /prətɛktɪv/ 1 ADJ **Protective** means designed or intended to protect something or someone from harm. 起保护作用的 ❑ *Protective gloves reduce the absorption of chemicals through the skin.* 防护手套可以减少皮肤对化学物质的吸收。 2 ADJ If someone is **protective toward** you, they look after you and show a strong desire to keep you safe. 爱护备至的 ❑ *He is very protective toward his mother.* 他对母亲爱护备至。

pro·tec·tor /prətɛktər/ (**protectors**) 1 N-COUNT If you refer to someone as your **protector**, you mean that they protect you from being harmed. 保护人 ❑ *Many mothers see their son as a potential protector and provider.* 许多母亲将她们的儿子看作是潜在的保护人和赡养人。 2 N-COUNT A **protector** is a device that protects someone or something from physical harm. 保护装置 ❑ *He was the only National League umpire to wear an outside chest protector.* 他是惟一穿着外层护胸的全国联盟裁判。

pro·tein ♦◇◇ /proʊtin/ (**proteins**) N-MASS **Protein** is a substance found in food and drink such as meat, eggs, and milk. You need protein in order to grow and be healthy. 蛋白质 ❑ *Fish was a major source of protein for the working man.* 鱼曾是劳动者获取蛋白质的主要来源。

→ see **calorie, diet**

pro·test ♦♦◇ (**protests, protesting, protested**)

The verb is usually pronounced /prətɛst/. The noun, and sometimes the verb, is pronounced /proʊtɛst/.

动词通常读作 /prətɛst/。名词、有时动词读作 /proʊtɛst/。

1 V-T/V-I If you **protest** something or **protest against** something, you say or show publicly that you object to it. 抗议 ❑ *They were protesting soaring prices.* 他们在抗议不断飞涨的物价。 2 N-VAR A **protest** is the act of saying or showing publicly that you object to something. 抗议 ❑ *The opposition now seems too weak to stage any serious protests against the government.* 反对党现在似乎太弱小，无力针对政府组织什么重大的抗议。 ❑ *The Mexican president canceled a trip to Texas in protest at the state's execution of a Mexican national.* 墨西哥总统取消了得克萨斯之行，以抗议该州对一名墨西哥侨民的处决。 3 V-T If you **protest** that something is the case, you insist that it is the case, when other people think that it may not be. 断言 ❑ *When we tried to protest that Mo was beaten up they didn't believe us.* 当我们坚持说莫遭到了毒打时，他们都不相信。 ❑ *"I never said any of that to her," he protested.* "我从来没有对她说过那种话，" 他断然否认。

Word Partnership *protest* 的常用搭配：

N. **workers** protest 1
protest **demonstrations**, protest **groups**, protest **march**, protest **rally** 2

ADJ. **anti-government** protest, **anti-war** protest, **organized** protest, **peaceful** protest, **political** protest 2

▲ **Prot·es·tant** /prɒtɪstənt/ (**Protestants**) 1 N-COUNT A **Protestant** is a Christian who belongs to the branch of the Christian church that separated from the Catholic church in the sixteenth century. 新教徒 2 ADJ **Protestant** means relating to Protestants or their churches. 新教的; 新教徒的 ❑ *Most Protestant churches now have some women ministers.* 如今，大部分新教教堂都有一些女牧师。

pro·test·er /prətɛstər/ (**protesters**) also **protestor** N-COUNT **Protesters** are people who protest publicly about an issue. 抗议者 ❑ *The protesters say the government is corrupt and inefficient.* 抗议者指责政府腐败无能。

▲ **proto·col** /proʊtəkɔl/ (**protocols**) 1 N-VAR **Protocol** is a system of rules about the correct way to act in formal situations. 礼节 ❑ *He has become a stickler for the finer observances of Washington protocol.* 他成了拘泥于华盛顿外交礼节的人。 2 N-COUNT A **protocol** is a set of rules for exchanging information between computers. (计算机间交换信息的) 协议 [COMPUTING] ❑ *...a computer protocol which could communicate across different languages.* …一个可以在不同的语言之间传递信息的计算机协议。 3 N-COUNT A **protocol** is a written record of a treaty or agreement that has been made by two or more countries. 议定书 [FORMAL] ❑ *...the Montreal Protocol to phase out use and production of CFCs.* …逐步停止使用和生产含氯氟烃的《蒙特利尔议定书》。 4 N-COUNT A **protocol** is a plan for a course of medical treatment, or a plan for a scientific experiment. 医疗方案; 科学试验计划 [AM, FORMAL] ❑ *...the detoxification protocol.* …戒毒方案。

★ **proto·type** /proʊtətaɪp/ (**prototypes**) N-COUNT A **prototype** is a new type of machine or device that is not yet ready to be made in large numbers and sold. 样机 ❑ *Chris Retzler has built a prototype of a machine called the wave rotor.* 克里斯·雷兹勒做出了一台叫做波转子的样机。

pro·tract·ed /proʊtræktɪd/ ADJ Something, usually something unpleasant, that is **protracted** lasts a long time, especially longer than usual or longer than you hoped. 拖拉的 [FORMAL] ❑ *However, after protracted negotiations Ogden got the deal he wanted.* 然而，经过拖拉的谈判，奥格登还是得到了他想要的那笔交易。 ❑ *...a protracted civil war.* …一场旷日持久的内战。

pro·trude /proʊtrud, prə-/ (**protrudes, protruding, protruded**) V-I If something **protrudes from** somewhere, it sticks out. 突出 [FORMAL] ❑ *...a huge round mass of smooth rock protruding from the water.* …从水中突出来的一块光滑的圆形巨石。

proud ♦◇◇ /praʊd/ (**prouder, proudest**) 1 ADJ If you feel **proud**, you feel pleased about something good that you possess or have done, or about something good that a person close to you has done. 自豪的 ❑ *I felt proud of his efforts.* 我为他的努力感到自豪。 ❑ *They are proud that she is doing well at school.* 他们为她在学校功课好而自豪。 ● **proud·ly** ADV 自豪地 [ADV with v] ❑ *"That's the first part finished," he said proudly.* "那是完成的第一部分，" 他自豪地说。 2 ADJ Your **proudest** moments or achievements are the ones that you are most proud of. 最自豪的 [ADJ n] ❑ *This must have been one of the proudest moments of his busy and hard-working life.* 在他忙碌、勤奋的一生中，这可能是他最自豪的时刻之一。 3 ADJ Someone who is **proud** has respect for themselves and does not want to lose the respect that other people have for them. 有自尊心的 ❑ *He was too proud to ask his family for help and support.* 他自尊心太高，不肯请求家里人的帮助和支持。 4 ADJ Someone who is **proud** feels that they are better or more important than other people. 骄傲的 [DISAPPROVAL] ❑ *She was said to be proud and arrogant.* 据说，她骄傲且自大。

prove ♦♦◇ /pruv/ (**proves, proving, proved, proven**)

The forms **proved** and **proven** can both be used as a past participle.

1 V-LINK If something **proves to** be true or **to** have a particular quality, it becomes clear after a period of time that it is true or has that quality. 证明是 ❑ *We have been accused of exaggerating before, but unfortunately all our reports proved to be true.* 我们曾被指责夸大其词，但遗憾的是，我们所有的报告都证明是真实的。 ❑ *In the past this process of transition has often proven difficult.* 在过去，这种转变过程常证明是艰难的。 2 V-T If you **prove that** something is true, you show by means of argument or evidence that it is definitely true. 证明 ❑ *You brought this charge. You prove it!* 你提出了这一指控。你来证明它！ ❑ *The results prove that regulation of the salmon farming industry is inadequate.* 结果证明，大马哈鱼养殖业的管理是失当的。 ❑ *That made me hopping mad and determined to prove him wrong.* 这使我暴跳如雷并且使我下决心要证明他错了。 3 V-T If you **prove yourself** to have a certain good quality, you show by your actions that you have it. 显示 (优点) ❑ *Margie proved herself to be a good mother.* 玛吉显示了自己是个好母亲。 ❑ *As a composer he proved himself adept at large dramatic forms.* 作为一名作曲家，他显示出自己擅长创作大型的戏剧体裁。

→ see **science**

Word Partnership *prove* 的常用搭配：

ADJ. prove **(to be) difficult**, prove **helpful**, prove **useful**, prove **worthy** 1
difficult to prove, **hard to** prove 2

V. **have *something* to** prove, **have to** prove, **try to** prove 2
able to prove 2 3

Word Link *verb ≈ word : proverb, verbal, verbatim*

▲ **prov·erb** /prɒvɜrb/ (**proverbs**) N-COUNT A **proverb** is a short sentence that people often quote, because it gives advice or tells you something about life. 谚语 ❑ *An old Arab proverb says, "The enemy of my enemy is my friend."* 有一句古老的阿拉伯谚语说："我敌人的敌人是我的朋友。"

pro·ver·bial /prəvɜrbiəl/ ADJ You use **proverbial** to show that you know the way you are describing something is one that is often used or is part of a popular saying. 谚语的 [ADJ n] ❑ *The limousine sped off down the road in the proverbial cloud of dust.* 那辆豪华轿车沿着公路向前飞驰而去，车后扬起了俗话说的滚滚尘土。

pro·vide ♦♦♦ /prəvaɪd/ (**provides, providing, provided**) 1 V-T If you **provide** something that someone needs or wants, or if you **provide** them **with** it, you give it to them or make it available to them. 提供 ❑ *I'll be glad to provide a copy of this.* 我将很乐意提供这东西的一个副本。 ❑ *They would not provide any details.* 他们不肯提供任何细节。 ❑ *They provided him with a car and driver.* 他们为他提供了一辆汽车和一位司机。 2 V-T If a law or agreement **provides that** something will happen, it states that it will happen. 规定 [FORMAL] ❑ *The treaty provides that, by the end of the century, the United States must have removed its bases.* 这项条约规定，到本世纪末，美国必须撤走其基地。 3 → see also **provided, providing**

▸ **provide for** 1 PHRASAL VERB If you **provide for** someone, you support them financially and make sure that they have the things that they need. 供养 ❑ *Elaine wouldn't let him provide for her.* 伊莱恩不肯让他供养她。 2 PHRASAL VERB If you **provide for** something that might happen or that might need to be done, you make arrangements to deal with it. 为…做准备 ❑ *Jim had provided for just such an emergency.* 吉姆已经为这样的突发事件做好了准备。

pro·vid·ed /prəvaɪdɪd/ CONJ If you say that something will happen **provided** or **provided that** something else happens, you mean that the first thing will happen only if the second thing also happens. 如果…才会… ❑ *The other banks are going to be very eager to help, provided that they see that he has a specific plan.* 如果他有一个具体的计划，其他的银行才会非常渴望提供资助。

provi·dence /prɒvɪdəns/ N-UNCOUNT **Providence** is God, or a force that is believed by some people to arrange the things that happen to us. 上帝; 天意 [LITERARY] ❑ *These women regard his death as an act of providence.* 这些妇女将他的死看成是天意的展现。

pro·vid·ing /prəvaɪdɪŋ/ CONJ If you say that something will happen **providing** or **providing that** something else happens, you mean that the first thing will happen only if the second thing also happens. 如果…才会… ❑ *I do believe in people being able to do what they want to do, providing they're not hurting someone else.* 我确实相信人们可以做他们想做的事，只要他们不伤害他人。

prov·ince ♦◊◊ /prɒvɪns/ (**provinces**) 1 N-COUNT A **province** is a large section of a country that has its own administration. 省 ❑ *...the Algarve, Portugal's southernmost province.* …阿尔加维，葡萄牙最南端的一个省。 2 N-PLURAL **The provinces** are all the parts of a country except the part where the capital is situated. 外省 ❑ *The government plans to transfer some 30,000 government jobs from Paris to the provinces.* 政府计划将30000个政府职位从巴黎下放到外省去。 3 N-SING If you say that a subject or activity is a particular person's **province**, you mean that this person has a special interest in it, a special knowledge of it, or a special responsibility for it. (学识或活动的) 领域; (兴趣或职责的) 范围 ❑ *Tattooing is not just the province of sailors.* 纹身不只是水手们才感兴趣的事。

★ **pro·vin·cial** /prəvɪnʃəl/ 1 ADJ **Provincial** means connected with the parts of a country away from the capital city. 省的 [ADJ n] ❑ *...the Quebec and Ontario provincial police.* …魁北克和安大略省的警察。 2 ADJ If you describe someone or something as **provincial**, you disapprove of them because you think that they are old-fashioned and boring. 守旧的 [DISAPPROVAL] ❑ *He decided to revamp the company's provincial image.* 他决定改变公司守旧的形象。

pro·vi·sion ♦◊◊ /prəvɪʒən/ (**provisions**) 1 N-UNCOUNT The **provision of** something is the act of giving it or making it available to people who need or want it. 提供 [also "a" N] ❑ *The department is responsible for the provision of residential care services.* 该部门负责住宿照顾服务的提供。 2 N-VAR If you make **provision for** something that might happen or that might need to be done, you make arrangements to deal with it. 准备 ❑ *Mr. Kurtz asked if it had ever occurred to her to make provision for her retirement.* 库尔茨先生问她是否想过要为退休做好准备。 3 N-UNCOUNT If you make **provision for** someone, you support them financially and make sure that they have the things that they need. 供给 [also N in pl, N "for" n] ❑ *Special provision should be made for children.* 应该给孩子们特别的供给。 4 N-COUNT A **provision** in a law or an agreement is an arrangement which is included in it. 规定 ❑ *He backed a provision that would allow judges to delay granting a divorce decree in some cases.* 他支持允许法官在有些情况下推迟离婚判决的规定。

▲ **pro·vi·sion·al** /prəvɪʒənəl/ ADJ You use **provisional** to describe something that has been arranged or appointed for the present, but may be changed in the future. 临时的; 暂时的 ❑ *...the possibility of setting up a provisional coalition government.* …建立一个临时的联合政府的可能性。 ❑ *These times are provisional and subject to confirmation.* 这些期限是暂定的，还有待确认。 ● **pro·vi·sion·al·ly** ADV 临时地; 暂时地 [ADV with v] ❑ *The U.S. and Japan provisionally agreed to add new chartered flights to serve their major cities.* 美国和日本临时同意增加包机航班，为各大城市服务。

provo·ca·tion /prɒvəkeɪʃən/ (**provocations**) N-VAR If you describe a person's action as **provocation** or a **provocation**, you mean that it is a reason for someone else to react angrily, violently, or emotionally. 挑衅 ❑ *He denies murder on the grounds of provocation.* 他以受到了挑衅为理由而否认谋杀。

★ **pro·voca·tive** /prəvɒkətɪv/ 1 ADJ If you describe something as **provocative**, you mean that it is intended to make people react angrily or argue against it. 挑衅的 ❑ *He has made a string of outspoken and sometimes provocative speeches in recent years.* 他最近几年做了一系列直言不讳的、有时带有挑衅的演说。 2 ADJ If you describe someone's clothing or behavior as **provocative**, you mean that it is intended to make someone feel sexual desire. 挑逗的 ❑ *Some adolescents might be more sexually mature and provocative than others.* 有些青少年可能比其他人在性方面是更成熟、更挑逗的。

pro·voke ♦◊◊ /prəvoʊk/ (**provokes, provoking, provoked**) 1 V-T If you **provoke** someone, you deliberately annoy them and try to make them behave aggressively. 对…挑衅 ❑ *He started beating me when I was about fifteen but I didn't do anything to provoke him.* 我大约十五岁时，他开始打我，但我并没有做什么招惹他的事情。 2 V-T If something **provokes** a reaction, it causes it. 引起 ❑ *His election success has provoked a shocked reaction.* 他的竞选胜利已经引起了震惊的反应。

prow·ess /praʊɪs/ N-UNCOUNT Someone's **prowess** is their great skill at doing something. 杰出的技能 [FORMAL] ❑ *He's always bragging about his prowess as a hunter.* 他老是吹嘘自己作为猎手的高超技能。

prowl /praʊl/ (**prowls, prowling, prowled**) V-I If an animal or a person **prowls around**, they move around quietly, for example, when they are hunting. 悄悄巡行 ❑ *He prowled around the room, not sure what he was looking for or even why he was there.* 他在房间里悄悄地走来走去，不知道自己在找什么，甚至不知道自己为什么在那里。

Word Link *proxim ≈ near : approximate, approximation, proximity*

★ **prox·im·ity** /prɒksɪmɪti/ N-UNCOUNT **Proximity to** a place or person is nearness to that place or person. 接近 [FORMAL] ❑ *Part of the attraction is Darwin's proximity to Asia.* 达尔文港的部分吸引力在于她与亚洲比邻。 ❑ *He became aware of the proximity of the Afghans.* 他开始意识到那些阿富汗人的接近。

proxy /prɒksi/ N-UNCOUNT If you do something **by proxy**, you arrange for someone else to do it for you. 代理权 ❑ *Those not attending the meeting may vote by proxy.* 没有到会的人可由别人代为投票。

prude /prud/ (**prudes**) N-COUNT If you call someone a **prude**, you mean that they are too easily shocked by things relating to sex. (尤指在性问题上) 一本正经的人 [DISAPPROVAL] ❑ *Caroline was very much a prude. She wouldn't let me see her naked.* 卡罗琳是个过于一本正经的人。她不肯让我看到她的裸体。

pru·dence /prudəns/ N-UNCOUNT **Prudence** is care and good sense that someone shows when making a decision or taking action. 谨慎 [FORMAL] ❑ *Western businessmen are showing remarkable prudence in investing in the region.* 西方商人对投资那个地区正表现出异常的谨慎。

▲ **pru·dent** /prudənt/ ADJ Someone who is **prudent** is sensible and careful. 谨慎的 ❑ *It is clearly prudent to take all precautions.* 采取一切防范措施显然是慎重的。 ● **pru·dent·ly** ADV 谨慎地 ❑ *I believe it is essential that we act prudently.* 我认为我们必须谨慎地行事。

P

★ **prune** /prun/ (prunes, pruning, pruned) 1 N-COUNT A **prune** is a dried plum. 李子干 2 V-T/V-I When you **prune**, or **prune** a tree or bush, you cut off some of the branches so that it will grow better the next year. 修剪(树木) ❑ *You have to prune a bush if you want fruit.* 如果你想要果树结果，你就得给它剪枝。 ● PHRASAL VERB **Prune back** means the same as **prune**. 修剪(树木) ❑ *Apples, pears, and cherries can be pruned back when they've lost their leaves.* 苹果树、梨树和樱桃树在落叶之后就可以被修剪。 3 V-T If you **prune** something, you cut out all the parts that you do not need. 删减 ❑ *Companies are cutting investment and pruning their product ranges.* 公司都在削减投资并减少产品种类。 ● PHRASAL VERB **Prune back** means the same as **prune**. 删减 ❑ *The company has pruned back its workforce by 20,000 since 2003.* 公司自2003年以来已经裁减了2万名员工。

prun·ing shears N-PLURAL **Pruning shears** are a gardening tool that look like a pair of strong, heavy scissors. Pruning shears are used for cutting the stems of plants. 整枝剪 [AM]

in BRIT, use **secateurs**

▲ **pry** /praɪ/ (pries, prying, pried) 1 V-I If someone **pries**, they try to find out about someone else's private affairs, or look at their personal possessions. 刺探；窥探 ❑ *We do not want people prying into our affairs.* 我们不想让人刺探我们的私事。 ❑ *Imelda might think she was prying.* 伊梅尔达可能认为她在窥探。 2 V-T If you **pry** something **open** or **pry** it away from a surface, you force it open or away from a surface. 撬 ❑ *They pried open a sticky can of blue paint.* 他们撬开了一个装着蓝色油漆的黏糊糊的罐子。 ❑ *They pried the bars apart to free the dog.* 他们撬开了栏栅，把狗放出来。

PS /pi ɛs/ also **P.S.** You write **PS** to introduce something that you add at the end of a letter after you have signed it. 又及(信末，签名后的附言标识) ❑ *PS Please show your friends this letter and the enclosed leaflet.* 又及：请将这封信和随附的传单拿给你的朋友们看。

pseudo·nym /sudənɪm/ (pseudonyms) N-COUNT A **pseudonym** is a name that someone, usually a writer, uses instead of his or her real name. 假名；笔名 ❑ *Both plays were published under the pseudonym of Philip Dayre.* 两个剧本都是以菲利普・戴尔的笔名发表的。

Word Link *psych ≈ mind : psyche, psychiatrist, psychic*

psy·che /saɪki/ (psyches) N-COUNT In psychology, your **psyche** is your mind and your deepest feelings and attitudes. 心灵 [TECHNICAL] ❑ *His exploration of the myth brings insight into the American psyche.* 他对那个神话的探索揭示了美国人的心理。

psychedel·ic /saɪkədɛlɪk/ 1 ADJ **Psychedelic** means relating to drugs such as LSD that have a strong effect on your mind, often making you see things that are not there. 幻觉的 ❑ *...his first real, full-blown psychedelic experience.* …他第一次真正的、充分的迷幻体验。 2 ADJ **Psychedelic** art has bright colors and strange patterns. 有迷幻色彩的 ❑ *...psychedelic patterns.* …光怪陆离的图案。

▲ **psy·chi·at·ric** /saɪkiætrɪk/ 1 ADJ **Psychiatric** means relating to psychiatry. 治疗精神病的 [ADJ n] ❑ *We finally insisted that he seek psychiatric help.* 我们最后坚持让他寻求精神病治疗方面的帮助。 2 ADJ **Psychiatric** means involving mental illness. 精神病的 [ADJ n] ❑ *About 4% of the prison population have chronic psychiatric illnesses.* 约有百分之四的监狱犯人患有慢性精神疾病。

Word Link *iatr ≈ healing : geriatric, pediatrics, psychiatrist*

★ **psy·chia·trist** /sɪkaɪətrɪst/ (psychiatrists) N-COUNT A **psychiatrist** is a doctor who treats people suffering from mental illness. 精神病医生

psy·chia·try /sɪkaɪətri/ N-UNCOUNT **Psychiatry** is the branch of medicine concerned with the treatment of mental illness. 精神病学

psy·chic /saɪkɪk/ (psychics) 1 ADJ If you believe that someone is **psychic** or has **psychic** powers, you believe that they have strange mental powers, such as being able to read the minds of other people or to see into the future. 有特异功能的 ❑ *The woman helped police by using her psychic powers.* 那位妇女用她的特异功能帮助警察。 ● N-COUNT A **psychic** is someone who seems to be psychic. 有特异功能的人 ❑ *...her latest role as a psychic who can foretell the future.* …她最新的角色是扮演一个有特异功能可以预言未来的人。 2 ADJ **Psychic** means relating to ghosts and the spirits of the dead. 通灵的 ❑ *He declared his total disbelief in psychic phenomena.* 他宣称他完全不相信通灵现象。

psycho·analy·sis /saɪkoʊənælɪsɪs/ N-UNCOUNT **Psychoanalysis** is the treatment of someone who has mental problems by asking them about their feelings and their past in order to try to discover what may be causing their condition. 精神分析

psycho·ana·lyst /saɪkoʊænəlɪst/ (psychoanalysts) N-COUNT A **psychoanalyst** is someone who treats people who have mental problems using psychoanalysis. 精神分析学家

psycho·logi·cal ♦◇◇ /saɪkəlɒdʒɪkəl/ 1 ADJ **Psychological** means concerned with a person's mind and thoughts. 心理的 ❑ *John received constant physical and psychological abuse from his father.* 约翰受到来自他父亲的不断的身心摧残。 ● **psycho·logi·cal·ly** /saɪkəlɒdʒɪkli/ ADV 心理上地 ❑ *It was very important psychologically for us to succeed.* 取得成功，在心理上对我们非常重要。 2 ADJ **Psychological** means relating to psychology. 心理学的 [ADJ n] ❑ *...psychological testing.* …心理学测试。

→ see **myth**

psy·cholo·gist /saɪkɒlədʒɪst/ (psychologists) N-COUNT A **psychologist** is a person who studies the human mind and tries to explain why people behave in the way that they do. 心理学家

psy·chol·ogy /saɪkɒlədʒi/ 1 N-UNCOUNT **Psychology** is the scientific study of the human mind and the reasons for people's behavior. 心理学 ❑ *...Professor of Psychology at Haverford College.* …海沃福德学院的心理学教授。 2 N-UNCOUNT The **psychology of a** person is the kind of mind that they have, which makes them think or behave in the way that they do. 心理 ❑ *...a fascination with the psychology of murderers.* …对谋杀犯心理的强烈兴趣。

psycho·path /saɪkəpæθ/ (psychopaths) N-COUNT A **psychopath** is someone who has serious mental problems and who may act in a violent way without feeling sorry for what they have done. 精神变态者 ❑ *She was abducted by a dangerous psychopath.* 她被一名危险的精神变态者劫持了。

Word Link *osis ≈ state or condition : hypnosis, metamorphosis, psychosis*

psy·cho·sis /saɪkoʊsɪs/ (psychoses) N-VAR **Psychosis** is mental illness of a severe kind that can make people lose contact with reality. 精神错乱 [MEDICAL] ❑ *He may have some kind of neurosis or psychosis later in life.* 他在以后的生活中可能会有某种神经官能症或精神错乱。

psycho·thera·pist /saɪkoʊθɛrəpɪst/ (psychotherapists) N-COUNT A **psychotherapist** is a person who treats people who are mentally ill using psychotherapy. 心理治疗师

psycho·thera·py /saɪkoʊθɛrəpi/ N-UNCOUNT **Psychotherapy** is the use of psychological methods in treating people who are mentally ill, rather than using physical methods such as drugs or surgery. 心理疗法 ❑ *For milder depressions, certain forms of psychotherapy do work well.* 对于比较轻微的抑郁症，某些形式的心理疗法确实很有效。

psy·chot·ic /saɪkɒtɪk/ ADJ Someone who is **psychotic** has a type of severe mental illness. 精神错乱的 [MEDICAL] ❑ *The man, who police believe is psychotic, is thought to be responsible for eight attacks.* 警方相信有精神错乱的那个男人，被认为要为8起攻击事件负责。

pub ♦◇◇ /pʌb/ (pubs) N-COUNT A **pub** is a building where people can have drinks, especially alcoholic drinks, and talk to their friends. Many pubs also serve food. 酒馆 [mainly BRIT] ❑ *He was in the pub until closing time.* 他在酒馆里待到打烊。

> During **happy hour** customers in pubs, bars and cafés can buy alcoholic drinks more cheaply than usual. This practice was introduced by owners and managers to entice people into their bars. Happy hour is usually during the late afternoon or early evening, the exact time being chosen by the bar; strangely, it quite often lasts more than an hour.

pu·ber·ty /pyubərti/ N-UNCOUNT **Puberty** is the stage in someone's life when their body starts to become physically mature. 青春期 ❑ *Moesha had reached the age of puberty.* 莫莎已到了青春期年龄。

pub·lic ♦♦♦ /pʌblɪk/ 1 N-SING-COLL You can refer to people in general, or to all the people in a particular country or community, as **the public**. 公众 ❑ *The park is now open to the public.* 那公园现在对公众开放了。 ❑ *Pure alcohol is not for sale to the general public.* 纯酒精是不对大众销售的。 2 N-SING-COLL You can refer to a set of people in a country who share a common interest, activity, or characteristic as a particular kind of **public**. 群体 ❑ *Market research showed that 93%*

of the viewing public wanted a hit movie channel. 市场调查显示，93%的收视群体希望有一个热门电影频道。 3 ADJ **Public** means relating to all the people in a country or community. 公众的 [ADJ n] ❑ *The president is attempting to drum up public support for his economic program.* 总统正试图为他的经济计划争取公众的支持。 4 ADJ **Public** means relating to the government or state, or things that are done for the people by the state. 政府的 [ADJ n] ❑ *The social services account for a substantial part of public spending.* 社会服务性事业占政府开支的相当大的一部分。 ● **pub·lic·ly** ADV 政府地 [ADV -ed] ❑ *...publicly funded legal services.* …政府资助的法律服务。 5 ADJ **Public** buildings and services are provided for everyone to use. (建筑、服务) 公共的 [ADJ n] ❑ *...the New York Public Library.* …纽约公共图书馆。 ❑ *The new museum must be accessible by public transportation.* 新博物馆必须能通公共交通。 6 ADJ A **public** place is one where people can go about freely and where you can easily be seen and heard. (地方) 公共的 ❑ *...the heavily congested public areas of international airports.* …国际机场里严重拥挤的公共区域。 7 ADJ If someone is a **public figure** or in **public life**, many people know who they are because they are often mentioned in newspapers and on television. 公众熟悉的 [ADJ n] ❑ *He hit out at public figures who commit adultery.* 他猛烈抨击犯通奸的公众人物。 8 ADJ **Public** is used to describe statements, actions, and events that are made or done in such a way that any member of the public can see them or be aware of them. (陈述、行为、事件) 公开的 [ADJ n] ❑ *...a public inquiry into the most grievous breakdown in security our nation has ever known.* …对我们国家迄今所知最严重的安全体系崩溃的公开的调查。 ❑ *The comments were the governor's first detailed public statement on the subject.* 这些评论是州长在这个问题上的首个详尽的、公开的声明。 ● **pub·lic·ly** ADV 公开地 ❑ *He never spoke publicly about the affair.* 他从未公开地谈论过此事。 9 ADJ If a fact is made **public** or becomes **public**, it becomes known to everyone rather than being kept secret. (事实) 公开的 [v-link ADJ] ❑ *The facts could cause embarrassment if they ever became public.* 如果公开的话，这些事实可能会引起尴尬。 10 PHRASE If a company **goes public**, it starts selling its shares on the stock exchange. 上市 [BUSINESS] ❑ *The company went public at $21 per share.* 这家公司以每股$21的价格上市了。 11 PHRASE If you say or do something **in public**, you say or do it when a group of people are present. 当众 ❑ *I probably won't be performing in public much.* 我很可能不会再经常当众演出。
→ see **library**

pub·lic ad·dress sys·tem (**public address systems**) N-COUNT A **public address system** is a set of electrical equipment which allows someone's voice, or music, to be heard throughout a large building or area. The abbreviation **PA** is also used. 有线广播系统

pub·li·ca·tion ♦◊◊ /pʌblɪkeɪʃ°n/ (**publications**) 1 N-UNCOUNT The **publication** of a book or magazine is the act of printing it and sending it to stores to be sold. 出版 ❑ *The guide is being translated into several languages for publication near Christmas.* 这本指南正被翻译成好几种语言，准备在圣诞节前后出版。 2 N-COUNT A **publication** is a book or magazine that has been published. 出版物 ❑ *They have started legal proceedings against two publications which spoke of an affair.* 他们已开始对提及一件绯闻的两本出版物进行法律诉讼。 3 N-UNCOUNT The **publication of** something such as information is the act of making it known to the public, for example, by informing journalists or by publishing a government document. 公开 ❑ *A spokesman said: "We have no comment regarding the publication of these photographs."* 一位发言人说："关于这些照片的公开，我们无可奉告。"

pub·lic com·pa·ny (**public companies**) N-COUNT A **public company** is a company whose shares can be bought by the general public. 上市公司 [BUSINESS]

★ **pub·li·cise** /pʌblɪsaɪz/ [BRIT] → see **publicize**

pub·li·cist /pʌblɪsɪst/ (**publicists**) N-COUNT A **publicist** is a person whose job involves getting publicity for people, events, or things such as movies or books. 宣传员 ❑ *...Larry Kaplan, a publicist for "Cold Mountain."* …拉里·卡普兰，《冷山》的宣传员。

pub·lic·ity ♦◊◊ /pʌblɪsɪti/ 1 N-UNCOUNT **Publicity** is information or actions that are intended to attract the public's attention to someone or something. 宣传 ❑ *Much advance publicity was given to the talks.* 会谈之前做了大量的宣传。 ❑ *...government publicity campaigns.* …政府的宣传活动。 2 N-UNCOUNT When the news media and the public show a lot of interest in something, you can say that it is receiving **publicity**. 公众的关注 ❑ *The case has generated enormous publicity in Brazil.* 这起犯罪事件已在巴西引起了公众的极大关注。

> **Word Partnership** *publicity* 的常用搭配:
> V. **generate** publicity 1 2
> **get** publicity, **receive** publicity, publicity **surrounding** *someone/something* 2
> ADJ. **bad** publicity, **negative** publicity 2

★ **pub·li·cize** /pʌblɪsaɪz/ (**publicizes, publicizing, publicized**)
in BRIT, also use **publicise**
V-T If you **publicize** a fact or event, you make it widely known to the public. 宣传；公布 ❑ *The author appeared on television to publicize her latest book.* 作者出现在电视上宣传她的新书。 ❑ *He never publicized his plans.* 他从未将他的计划公之于众。

pub·lic lim·it·ed com·pa·ny (**public limited companies**) N-COUNT A **public limited company** is the same as a **public company**. The abbreviation **plc** is used after such companies' names. 上市公司 [BRIT, BUSINESS]

pub·lic opin·ion N-UNCOUNT **Public opinion** is the opinion or attitude of the public regarding a particular matter. 舆论 ❑ *He mobilized public opinion all over the world against hydrogen-bomb tests.* 他动员起世界各地的舆论，反对氢弹试验。

pub·lic re·la·tions 1 N-UNCOUNT **Public relations** is the part of an organization's work that is concerned with obtaining the public's approval for what it does. The abbreviation **PR** is often used. 公关工作 [BUSINESS] ❑ *The move was good public relations.* 这一举措是很好的公关工作。 2 N-PLURAL You can refer to the opinion that the public has of an organization as **public relations**. 公关形象 ❑ *Limiting casualties is important for public relations.* 减少伤亡事故对公关形象很重要。

pub·lic school (**public schools**) 1 N-VAR In the United States, Australia, and many other countries, a **public school** is a school that is supported financially by the government and usually provides free education. (美国、澳大利亚等国的) 公立学校 ❑ *...Milwaukee's public school system.* …密尔沃基市的公立学校制度。 2 N-VAR In Britain, a **public school** is a private school that provides secondary education that parents have to pay for. The students often live at the school during the school term. (英国的私立寄宿中学) 公学 ❑ *He was headmaster of a public school in the West of England.* 他曾是英格兰西部一所公学的校长。

pub·lic sec·tor N-SING **The public sector** is the part of a country's economy which is controlled or supported financially by the government. (国民经济中的) 公营部分 [BUSINESS] ❑ *...Carlos Menem's policy of reducing the public sector and opening up the economy to free-market forces.* …卡洛斯·梅内姆的减少公营部分、将经济开放给自由市场力量的政策。

pub·lic ser·vice (**public services**) 1 N-COUNT A **public service** is something such as health care, transportation, or the removal of waste, which is organized by the government or an official body in order to benefit all the people in a particular society or community. 公用事业 ❑ *The money is used by local authorities to pay for public services.* 这笔资金被地方当局用来支付公用事业。 2 N-UNCOUNT You use **public service** to refer to activities and jobs that are provided or paid for by a government, especially through the civil service. 公职 [oft N n] ❑ *...a distinguished career in public service.* …一段政绩卓越的公职生涯。 3 N-UNCOUNT **Public service** activities and types of work are concerned with helping people and providing them with what they need, rather than making a profit. 公益服务 ❑ *...the notion of public service and obligation which has been under such attack.* …备受抨击的公益服务和公民义务观念。

pub·lic util·ity (**public utilities**) N-COUNT **Public utilities** are services that are regulated by the government or state, such as the supply of electricity, gas, or water. 公用事业 ❑ *Officials said water supplies and other public utilities in the capital were badly affected.* 官员们说首都的供水和其他公用事业都受到了严重影响。

pub·lish ♦♦◊ /pʌblɪʃ/ (**publishes, publishing, published**) 1 V-T When a company **publishes** a book or magazine, it prints copies of it, which are sent to stores to be sold. 出版 ❑ *They publish reference books.* 他们出版参考书。 2 V-T When the people in charge of a newspaper or magazine **publish** a piece of writing or a photograph, they print it in their newspaper or magazine. 刊登 ❑ *Womens' magazines just don't publish articles on the harmful effects of smoking.* 女性杂志就是不刊登关于吸烟有害的文章。 3 V-T If someone **publishes** a book or an article that they have written, they

arrange to have it published. 出版；发表 ❑ *Walker has published four books of her verse.* 沃克已经出版了4本诗集。 **4** V-T If you **publish** information or an opinion, you make it known to the public by having it printed in a newspaper, magazine, or official document. 公开 ❑ *The demonstrators called on the government to publish a list of registered voters.* 示威者要求政府公开已登记的选民名单。
→ see **laboratory, printing**

pub·lish·er ♦◇◇ /pʌblɪʃər/ (**publishers**) N-COUNT A **publisher** is a person or a company that publishes books, newspapers, or magazines. 出版者；出版公司 ❑ *The publishers planned to produce the journal on a weekly basis.* 出版社计划将这份杂志做成周刊。

pub·lish·ing ♦◇◇ /pʌblɪʃɪŋ/ N-UNCOUNT **Publishing** is the profession of publishing books. 出版业 ❑ *I had a very high-powered job in publishing.* 我曾在出版业有一份位高权重的工作。
→ see **newspaper**

pub·lish·ing house (**publishing houses**) N-COUNT A **publishing house** is a company that publishes books. 出版社

★ **pud·ding** /pʊdɪŋ/ (**puddings**) N-VAR A **pudding** is a cooked sweet food made from ingredients such as milk, sugar, flour, and eggs, and is served either hot or cold. 布丁 ❑ *...a banana vanilla pudding.* …一份香蕉香草布丁。

▲ **pud·dle** /pʌdᵊl/ (**puddles**) N-COUNT A **puddle** is a small, shallow pool of liquid that has spread on the ground. 水坑 ❑ *The road was shiny with puddles, but the rain was at an end.* 路上尽是明晃晃的水坑，但雨已经停了。

▲ **puff** /pʌf/ (**puffs, puffing, puffed**) **1** V-I If someone **puffs on** or **at** a cigarette, cigar, or pipe, they smoke it. 抽（香烟、雪茄、烟斗等） ❑ *He lit a cigar and puffed on it twice.* 他点上一支雪茄，抽了两口。 ● N-COUNT **Puff** is also a noun. 一口烟 ❑ *I took a puff on the cigarette and started coughing.* 我抽了一口烟就开始咳嗽起来。 **2** V-T/V-I If you **puff** smoke or moisture from your mouth or if it **puffs** from your mouth, you breathe it out. （从口中）喷出 ❑ *Richard lit another cigarette and puffed smoke toward the ceiling.* 理查德点上另一支烟，将烟雾喷向天花板。 ● PHRASAL VERB **Puff out** means the same as **puff**. （从口中）喷出 ❑ *He drew heavily on his cigarette and puffed out a cloud of smoke.* 他深深地吸了一口烟，喷出了一团烟雾。 **3** V-T If an engine, chimney, or stove **puffs** smoke or steam, clouds of smoke or steam come out of it. （发动机、烟囱或炉子等）喷 ❑ *As I completed my 26th lap the Porsche puffed blue smoke.* 我跑完第26圈时，保时捷车喷起了蓝色的烟雾。 **4** N-COUNT A **puff of** something such as air or smoke is a small amount of it that is blown out from somewhere. 一股 ❑ *Wind caught the sudden puff of dust and blew it inland.* 风夹裹着那股突然扬起的尘土，把它吹向内陆。 **5** V-I If you **are puffing**, you are breathing loudly and quickly with your mouth open because you are out of breath after a lot of physical effort. 喘粗气 [usu cont] ❑ *I know nothing about boxing, but I could see he was unfit, because he was puffing.* 我对拳击一无所知，但我看得出他身体不行，因为他直喘粗气。

pull ♦♦◇ /pʊl/ (**pulls, pulling, pulled**) **1** V-T/V-I When you **pull** something, you hold it firmly and use force in order to move it toward you or away from its previous position. 拉；拔 ❑ *They have pulled out patients' teeth unnecessarily.* 他们毫无必要地拔掉了病人的牙。 ❑ *Erica was solemn, pulling at her blonde curls.* 埃丽卡表情严肃，拉扯着她金黄色的卷发。 ❑ *I helped pull him out of the water.* 我帮着把他从水里拉了出来。 ❑ *Someone pulled her hair.* 有人揪她的头发。 ● N-COUNT **Pull** is also a noun. 拉；拔 ❑ *The feather must be removed with a straight, firm pull.* 羽毛必须笔直地用力一拔才能拔掉。 **2** V-T When you **pull** an object from a bag, pocket, or cabinet, you put your hand in and bring the object out. 掏出 ❑ *Jack pulled the slip of paper from his shirt pocket.* 杰克从衬衣口袋里掏出那张纸条。 **3** V-T When a vehicle, animal, or person **pulls** a cart or piece of machinery, they are attached to it or hold it, so that it moves along behind them when they move forward. 拉 ❑ *He pulls a rickshaw, probably the oldest form of human taxi service.* 他拉一辆黄包车，这可能是最古老形式的人类出租车服务。 **4** V-T If you **pull yourself** or **pull** a part of your body in a particular direction, you move your body or a part of your body with effort or force. （使劲）移动 ❑ *Hughes pulled himself slowly to his feet.* 休斯挪动身体，慢慢地站了起来。 ❑ *He pulled his arms out of the sleeves.* 他把双臂从袖子里抽了出来。 **5** V-I When a driver or vehicle **pulls to** a stop or a halt, the vehicle stops. 停车 ❑ *He pulled to a stop behind a pickup truck.* 他把车停在了一辆小型货车后面。 **6** V-I In a race or contest, if you **pull ahead of** or **pull away from** an opponent, you gradually increase the amount by which you are ahead of them. 逐渐拉开（领先的距离） ❑ *He pulled away, extending his lead to 15 seconds.* 他甩开了对手，领先优势扩大到了15秒。 **7** V-T If you **pull** something **apart**, you break or divide it into small pieces, often in order to put them back together again in a different way. 拆下 ❑ *If I wanted to improve the car significantly I would have to pull it apart and start again.* 如果我想大大提高这辆车的性能，我就得将它拆开来重新组装。 **8** V-T To **pull** crowds, viewers, or voters means to attract them. 吸引 [INFORMAL] ❑ *The organizers have to employ performers to pull a crowd.* 那些组织者不得不雇表演者来吸引群众。 ● PHRASAL VERB **Pull in** means the same as **pull**. 吸引 ❑ *They provided a far better news service and pulled in many more viewers.* 他们提供了好得多的新闻节目，吸引了更多的观众。 **9** N-COUNT A **pull** is a strong physical force that causes things to move in a particular direction. 引力 ❑ *...the pull of gravity.* …地心引力。 **10** to **pull a face** → see **face** **11** to **pull** someone's **leg** → see **leg** **12** to **pull strings** → see **string** **13** to **pull** your **weight** → see **weight**

▸ **pull away** **1** PHRASAL VERB When a vehicle or driver **pulls away**, the vehicle starts moving forward. 开走 ❑ *I stood in the driveway and watched him back out and pull away.* 我站在车道上，看着他把车倒出来，然后开走。 **2** PHRASAL VERB If you **pull away from** someone that you have had close links with, you deliberately become less close to them. 疏远 ❑ *Other daughters, faced with their mother's emotional hunger, pull away.* 其他几个女儿在面对母亲对感情的渴望时躲开了。

▸ **pull back** **1** PHRASAL VERB If someone **pulls back from** an action, they decide not to do it or continue with it, because it could have bad consequences. 打退堂鼓；中止 ❑ *They will plead with him to pull back from confrontation.* 他们会恳求他不要再对抗下去。 **2** PHRASAL VERB If troops **pull back** or if their leader **pulls** them **back**, they go some or all of the way back to their own territory. 撤退 ❑ *They were asked to pull back from their artillery positions around the city.* 他们被要求从城市四周的炮兵阵地上撤退。

▸ **pull down** PHRASAL VERB To **pull down** a building or statue means to deliberately destroy it. 拆毁 ❑ *They'd pulled the registrar's office down which then left an open space.* 他们拆除了教务主任的办公室，于是就留出了一块空地。

▸ **pull in** **1** PHRASAL VERB When a vehicle or driver **pulls in** somewhere, the vehicle stops there. 停下 ❑ *He pulled in at the side of the road.* 他将车停在路旁。 **2** → see **pull 8**

▸ **pull into** PHRASAL VERB When a vehicle or driver **pulls into** a place, the vehicle moves into the place and stops there. 驶入…后停下 ❑ *He pulled into the driveway in front of her garage.* 他把车开进她家车库前的车道上停在那里。

▸ **pull off** **1** PHRASAL VERB If you **pull off** something very difficult, you succeed in achieving it. 做成（某件难事） ❑ *The National League for Democracy pulled off a landslide victory.* 国家民主联盟取得了压倒性优势的胜利。 **2** PHRASAL VERB If a vehicle or driver **pulls off** the road, the vehicle stops by the side of the road. 停靠路边 ❑ *I pulled off the road at a scenic overlook.* 在一个可以眺望优美风景的地方，我将车停在了路旁。

▸ **pull out** **1** PHRASAL VERB When a vehicle or driver **pulls out**, the vehicle moves out into the road or nearer the center of the road. 驶入主路 ❑ *She pulled out into the street.* 她将车开到了街上。 **2** PHRASAL VERB If you **pull out of** an agreement, a contest, or an organization, you withdraw from it. 从…退出 ❑ *The World Bank should pull out of the project.* 世界银行应该退出这个项目。 ❑ *France was going to pull out of NATO.* 法国准备退出北大西洋公约组织。 **3** PHRASAL VERB If troops **pull out of** a place or if their leader **pulls** them **out**, they leave it. 撤离 ❑ *The militia in Lebanon has agreed to pull out of Beirut.* 黎巴嫩的民兵组织已经同意撤出贝鲁特。 ❑ *Economic sanctions will be lifted once two-thirds of their forces have pulled out.* 一旦他们的部队撤出2/3，经济制裁就会解除。 **4** PHRASAL VERB If you **pull out of** a bad situation or if someone **pulls** you **out**, you begin to recover from it. 摆脱（困境）；由…康复 ❑ *I pulled out of the depression very quickly with treatment.* 经过治疗，我很快就摆脱了抑郁症。 ❑ *Sterling has been hit by the economy's failure to pull out of recession.* 由于经济没能摆脱衰退，英镑遭受了重创。

▸ **pull over** **1** PHRASAL VERB When a vehicle or driver **pulls over**, or when a police officer **pulls** them **over**, the vehicle moves closer to the side of the road and stops there. 靠边停车 ❑ *He noticed a man behind him in a blue Ford gesticulating to pull over.* 他注意到后面一辆蓝色福特车里的一个男人示意他靠边停车。 **2** → see also **pullover**

▸ **pull through** PHRASAL VERB If someone with a serious illness or someone in a very difficult situation **pulls through**, they recover. 恢复健康；渡过难关 ❑ *Everyone was very concerned whether he*

P

would pull through or not. 每个人都很关心他是否能恢复健康。 ❑ *It is only our determination to fight that has pulled us through.* 是我们战斗的决心才使我们渡过了难关。

▶ **pull together** 1 PHRASAL VERB If people **pull together**, they help each other or work together in order to deal with a difficult situation. 同心协力 ❑ *The nation was urged to pull together to avoid a slide into complete chaos.* 敦促全体国民同心协力，避免陷入全面的混乱之中。 2 PHRASAL VERB If you are upset or depressed and someone tells you to **pull yourself together**, they are telling you to control your feelings and behave calmly again. 冷静下来；重新振作起来 ❑ *Pull yourself together, you stupid woman!* 振作起来，你这个蠢女人！

▶ **pull up** 1 PHRASAL VERB When a vehicle or driver **pulls up**, the vehicle slows down and stops. 慢慢停下 ❑ *The cab pulled up and the driver jumped out.* 出租车慢慢停了下来，司机跳下了车。 2 PHRASAL VERB If you **pull up** a chair, you move it closer to something or someone and sit on it. (将椅子) 挪近然后坐下 ❑ *He pulled up a chair behind her and put his chin on her shoulder.* 他把椅子挪到她后面坐下，把下巴放在她肩上。

Thesaurus *pull* 另参见：
v. drag, haul, lug, tow; *(ant.)* push 1 3
attract, draw, lure; *(ant.)* repel 8

pull·over /pʊloʊvər/ (**pullovers**) N-COUNT A **pullover** is a piece of clothing that covers the upper part of your body and your arms. You put it on by pulling it over your head. 套衫

▲ **pulp** /pʌlp/ (**pulps, pulping, pulped**) 1 N-SING If an object is pressed into a **pulp**, it is crushed or beaten until it is soft, smooth, and wet. 浆 ❑ *The olives are crushed to a pulp by stone rollers.* 橄榄由石磙碾成浆。 2 N-SING In fruit or vegetables, **the pulp** is the soft part inside the skin. 果肉 ❑ *Make maximum use of the whole fruit, including the pulp which is high in fiber.* 最大限度地利用整个水果，包括富含纤维的果肉部分。 3 N-UNCOUNT **Wood pulp** is material made from crushed wood. It is used to make paper. 木浆 4 ADJ People refer to stories or novels as **pulp** fiction when they consider them to be of poor quality and intentionally shocking or sensational. 低俗的 (小说等) [ADJ n] ❑ *...lurid '50s pulp novels.* …50年代耸人听闻的低俗小说。 5 V-T If vegetables or fruit **are pulped**, they are crushed into a smooth, wet paste. 将…捣成浆 [usu passive] ❑ *Onions can be boiled and pulped to a puree.* 洋葱可以煮熟，捣成泥。 6 V-T If paper, books, or documents **are pulped**, they are destroyed. 把…化为纸浆 [usu passive] ❑ *The first edition had to be pulped because it contained inaccuracies.* 第一版不得不化为纸浆，因为里面有差错。 7 PHRASE If someone **is beaten to a pulp**, they are hit repeatedly until they are very badly injured. 把某人打成重伤 ❑ *I tried to talk myself out of a fight and got beaten to a pulp instead by three other boys.* 我试图说服自己不要打架，结果却被另外3个男孩子打得遍体鳞伤。

pul·pit /pʊlpɪt, pʌl-/ (**pulpits**) N-COUNT A **pulpit** is a small raised platform with a rail or barrier around it in a church, where a member of the clergy stands to speak. 布道坛 ❑ *The time came for the sermon and he ascended the pulpit steps.* 布道的时间到了，他迈上了讲坛的台阶。

pul·sate /pʌlseɪt/ (**pulsates, pulsating, pulsated**) V-I If something **pulsates**, it beats, moves in and out, or shakes with strong, regular movements. 有节奏地跳动 ❑ *The Pole Star appears to be changing from a star that pulsates.* 北极星似乎由一颗脉动的恒星衍变而来。

pulse /pʌls/ (**pulses, pulsing, pulsed**) 1 N-COUNT Your **pulse** is the regular beating of blood through your body, which you can feel when you touch particular parts of your body, especially your wrist. 脉搏 ❑ *Mahoney's pulse was racing, and he felt confused.* 马奥尼的脉搏跳得很快，他感到很慌乱。 2 N-COUNT In music, a **pulse** is a regular beat, often produced by a drum. 节拍 ❑ *...the repetitive pulse of the music.* …乐曲的重复节拍。 3 N-COUNT A **pulse of** electrical current, light, or sound is a temporary increase in its level. 脉冲 ❑ *The switch works by passing a pulse of current between the tip and the surface.* 电源开关的工作原理是让电流脉冲穿过触点和触面之间。 4 N-SING If you refer to **the pulse of** a group in society, you mean the ideas, opinions, or feelings they have at a particular time. 意向 ❑ *The White House insists that the president is in touch with the pulse of the black community.* 白宫坚持说总统了解黑人社区的民意。 5 V-I If something **pulses**, it moves, appears, or makes a sound with a strong regular rhythm. 有节奏地跳动 ❑ *His temples pulsed a little, threatening a headache.* 他的太阳穴跳动得有点厉害，预示着要头痛了。 6 N-PLURAL Some seeds that can be cooked and eaten are called **pulses**, for example, peas, beans, and lentils. 可食用的豆子 [mainly BRIT]

in AM, usually use **legumes**

pump ♦◇◇ /pʌmp/ (**pumps, pumping, pumped**) 1 N-COUNT A **pump** is a machine or device that is used to force a liquid or gas to flow in a particular direction. 泵 ❑ *...pumps that circulate the fuel around in the engine.* …使燃料在发动机内循环的气泵。 ❑ *There was no water in the building, just a pump in the courtyard.* 楼里没水，只在院子里有个水泵。 2 V-T To **pump** a liquid or gas in a particular direction means to force it to flow in that direction using a pump. (用泵) 抽送 ❑ *It's not enough to get rid of raw sewage by pumping it out to sea.* 仅用水泵将未经处理的污水排入海中是不够的。 ❑ *The money raised will be used to dig bore holes to pump water into the dried-up lake.* 筹到的钱款将用来挖井眼，再将水抽入干涸的湖中。 3 N-COUNT A fuel or gas **pump** is a machine with a tube attached to it that you use to fill a car with gasoline. 汽油加油泵 ❑ *The average price for all grades of gas at the pump was $3.49 a gallon.* 加油泵所有等级的汽油平均价格为1加仑$3.49。 4 V-T If someone **has** their stomach **pumped**, doctors remove the contents of their stomach, for example, because they have swallowed poison or drugs. 用泵灌洗 (胃) [usu passive] ❑ *One woman was rushed to the emergency room to have her stomach pumped.* 一名妇女被紧急送进了急诊室去洗胃。 5 N-COUNT **Pumps** are women's shoes that do not cover the top part of the foot and are usually made of plain leather. 女式浅口便鞋 [mainly AM]

in BRIT, usually use **court shoes**

▶ **pump out** PHRASAL VERB To **pump out** something means to produce or supply it continually and in large amounts. 不断地大量推出 ❑ *Japanese companies have been pumping out plenty of innovative products.* 日本的公司一直在不断推出各种新款的产品。

▶ **pump up** PHRASAL VERB If you **pump up** something such as a tire, you fill it with air using a pump. 给 (轮胎等) 打气 ❑ *Pump all the tires up.* 给所有的轮胎打气。

★ **pump·kin** /pʌmpkɪn/ (**pumpkins**) N-VAR A **pumpkin** is a large, round, orange vegetable with a thick skin. 南瓜 ❑ *Quarter the pumpkin and remove the seeds.* 把南瓜一切四块，把南瓜子取出来。

pun /pʌn/ (**puns**) N-COUNT A **pun** is a clever and amusing use of a word or phrase with two meanings, or of words with the same sound but different meanings. For example, if someone says "The peasants are revolting," this is a pun because it can be interpreted as meaning either that the peasants are fighting against authority, or that they are disgusting. 双关语 ❑ *He spoke of a hatchet job, which may be a pun on some senator's name.* 他提到"恶毒诽谤"一词，这可能和某个参议员的名字有一语双关的联系。

punch ♦◇◇ /pʌntʃ/ (**punches, punching, punched**) 1 V-T If you **punch** someone or something, you hit them hard with your fist. 用拳猛击 ❑ *After punching him on the chin she wound up hitting him over the head.* 她对准他的下巴猛击一拳，最后又在他的头上打了一拳。 ● N-COUNT **Punch** is also a noun. 一拳 ❑ *He was hurting Johansson with body punches in the fourth round.* 他在第4个回合猛击约翰逊的身体。 ● PHRASAL VERB **Punch out** means the same as **punch**. 用拳猛击 ❑ *"I almost lost my job today."—"What happened?"—"Oh, I punched out this guy."* "我今天差点丢了工作。"——"怎么回事？"——"噢，我把那个家伙狠揍了一顿。" 2 V-T If you **punch** something such as the buttons on a keyboard, you touch them in order to store information on a machine such as a computer or to give the machine a command to do something. 按 (键或钮) ❑ *Mrs. Baylor strode to the elevator and punched the button.* 贝勒太太大步走到电梯前按了一下按钮。 3 V-T If you **punch** holes **in** something, you make holes in it by pushing or pressing it with something sharp. 在…上打孔 ❑ *I took a ballpoint pen and punched a hole in the carton.* 我拿了一支圆珠笔在纸板箱上戳了个孔。 4 N-COUNT A **punch** is a tool that you use for making holes in something. 打孔器 ❑ *Make two holes with a hole punch.* 用打孔器打两个孔。 5 N-UNCOUNT If you say that something has **punch**, you mean that it has force or effectiveness. 力量；效力 ❑ *My nervousness made me deliver the vital points of my address without sufficient punch.* 我太紧张，讲到演说关键地方时不够有力。 6 N-MASS **Punch** is a drink made from wine, spirits, or fruit juice, mixed with things such as sugar and spices. 潘趣酒 ❑ *...a bowl of punch.* …一碗潘趣酒。

▶ **punch in** 1 PHRASAL VERB If you **punch in** a number on a machine or **punch** numbers **into** it, you push the machine's buttons or keys in order to give it a command to do something. 按键输入 ❑ *You can bank by phone in the U.S., punching in account numbers*

P

on the phone. 在美国，你可以用电话完成银行业务，通过在电话上输入账号的方式。 2 PHRASAL VERB When you **punch in** at work, you arrive there and put a special card into a device to show what time you arrived. 打卡上班 ❑ *He would get up and get ready for work, eat, and punch in at 6 p.m.* 他通常起床、准备上班、吃饭，然后在下午6:00打卡上班。

Word Partnership *punch* 的常用搭配：

V.	**pack** a punch, **throw** a punch 1
N.	punch **a button** 2
	punch **a hole in** *something* 3

punc·tu·al /pʌŋktʃuəl/ ADJ If you are **punctual**, you do something or arrive somewhere at the right time and are not late. 准时的 ❑ *He's always very punctual. I'll see if he's here yet.* 他一向很准时。我要看看他是不是已经来了。 ● **punc·tu·al·ly** ADV 准时地 ❑ *My guest arrived punctually.* 我的客人准时到了。

★ **punc·tu·al·ity** /pʌŋktʃuælɪti/ N-UNCOUNT **Punctuality** is the quality of being punctual. 准时性 ❑ *The airline hopes to improve punctuality next year.* 这家航空公司希望明年在准点上做出改善。

★ **punc·tu·ate** /pʌŋktʃueɪt/ (**punctuates, punctuating, punctuated**) V-T If an activity or situation **is punctuated by** particular things, it is interrupted by them at intervals. 不时打断 [usu passive] [WRITTEN] ❑ *The game was punctuated by a series of injuries.* 那场比赛因不时有人受伤而中断。

punc·tua·tion /pʌŋktʃueɪʃᵊn/ 1 N-UNCOUNT **Punctuation** is the use of symbols such as periods, commas, or question marks to divide written words into sentences and clauses. 标点符号的使用 ❑ *He was known for his poor grammar and punctuation.* 他以很差的语法和标点符号使用而出名。 2 N-UNCOUNT **Punctuation** is the symbols that you use to divide written words into sentences and clauses. 标点符号 ❑ *Jessica had rapidly scanned the lines, none of which boasted a capital letter or any punctuation.* 杰西卡已经迅速浏览了那几行，其中既无大写字母也无任何标点符号。

punc·tua·tion mark (**punctuation marks**) N-COUNT A **punctuation mark** is a symbol such as a period, comma, or question mark that you use to divide written words into sentences and clauses. 标点符号

punc·ture /pʌŋktʃər/ (**punctures, puncturing, punctured**) 1 N-COUNT A **puncture** is a small hole in a car tire or bicycle tire that has been made by a sharp object. (车胎上的) 刺孔 ❑ *Somebody helped me to mend the puncture.* 有人帮我补了车胎上的洞。 2 N-COUNT A **puncture** is a small hole in someone's skin that has been made by or with a sharp object. (皮肤上的) 扎孔 ❑ *An instrument called a trocar makes a puncture in the abdominal wall.* 一种叫作套管针的器械会在腹壁上扎一个小孔。 3 V-T If a sharp object **punctures** something, it makes a hole in it. 刺破 ❑ *The bullet punctured the skull.* 子弹射穿了头骨。 4 V-T/V-I If a car tire or bicycle tire **punctures** or if something **punctures** it, a hole is made in the tire. 扎破 ❑ *His bike's rear tire punctured.* 他的自行车的后胎被扎破了。

P

pun·dit /pʌndɪt/ (**pundits**) N-COUNT A **pundit** is a person who knows a lot about a subject and is often asked to give information or opinions about it to the public. 权威；专家 ❑ *...a well-known political pundit.* …一位著名的政治权威。

pun·gent /pʌndʒᵊnt/ ADJ Something that is **pungent** has a strong, sharp smell or taste which is often so strong that it is unpleasant. 刺鼻的；刺激味觉的 ❑ *The more herbs you use, the more pungent the sauce will be.* 你用的香草越多，沙司的味道就越刺鼻。

pun·ish /pʌnɪʃ/ (**punishes, punishing, punished**) 1 V-T To **punish** someone means to make them suffer in some way because they have done something wrong. 惩罚 ❑ *I don't believe that George ever had to punish the children.* 我不相信乔治曾不得不惩罚这些孩子。 ❑ *According to present law, the authorities can only punish smugglers with small fines.* 根据现行法律，当局只能对走私者处以小额罚款。 2 V-T To **punish** a crime means to punish anyone who commits that crime. 惩处 ❑ *...federal laws to punish crimes such as murder and assault.* …惩处诸如谋杀和强奸等罪的联邦法律。

pun·ish·ing /pʌnɪʃɪŋ/ ADJ A **punishing** schedule, activity, or experience requires a lot of physical effort and makes you very tired or weak. 繁重费力的；令人疲惫的 ❑ *He claimed his punishing work schedule had made him resort to taking the drug.* 他声称，繁重的工作日程使他不得不服用药物。

pun·ish·ment /pʌnɪʃmənt/ (**punishments**) 1 N-UNCOUNT **Punishment** is the act of punishing someone or of being punished. 惩罚 ❑ *...a group that campaigns against the physical punishment of children.* …一个发起运动反对体罚儿童的组织。 2 N-VAR A **punishment** is a particular way of punishing someone. 处罚方式 ❑ *The government is proposing tougher punishments for officials convicted of corruption.* 该政府正在提议对被判贪污罪的官员予以更严厉的处罚。 3 N-UNCOUNT You can use **punishment** to refer to severe physical treatment of any kind. 虐待；糟蹋 ❑ *Don't expect these boots to take the punishment that gardening will give them.* 别指望这样的靴子能经得起园艺活儿的糟蹋。 4 → see also **capital punishment, corporal punishment**

pu·ni·tive /pyunɪtɪv/ ADJ **Punitive** actions are intended to punish people. 惩罚性的 [FORMAL] ❑ *...a punitive bombing raid.* …一场惩罚性的空袭。

punk /pʌŋk/ (**punks**) 1 N-UNCOUNT **Punk** or **punk rock** is rock music that is played in a fast, loud, and aggressive way and is often a protest against conventional attitudes and behavior. Punk rock was particularly popular in the late 1970s. 朋客摇滚乐 (流行于20世纪70年代末的一种反传统摇滚乐，节奏快、喧闹而激进) ❑ *I was never really into punk.* 我从未真正喜欢过朋客摇滚乐。 2 N-COUNT A **punk** or a **punk rocker** is a young person who likes punk music and dresses in a very noticeable and unconventional way, for example, by having brightly colored hair and wearing metal chains. 朋客青年 (指喜欢朋克音乐、衣着打扮另类的年轻人) ❑ *In the 1970s, punks wore safety pins through their cheeks.* 在20世纪70年代，朋客青年把安全别针别在面颊上。

pup /pʌp/ (**pups**) 1 N-COUNT A **pup** is a young dog. 幼犬 ❑ *I'll get you an Alsatian pup for Christmas.* 我将送你一只德国牧羊犬幼仔作为圣诞礼物。 2 N-COUNT The young of some other animals, for example, seals, are called **pups**. 幼兽 ❑ *Two thousand gray seal pups are born there every fall.* 2000只灰色海豹幼仔每年秋天在那里出生。

pu·pil ♦◇◇ /pyupɪl/ (**pupils**) 1 N-COUNT A **pupil** of a painter, musician, or other expert is someone who studies under that expert and learns his or her skills. (画家、音乐家等的) 弟子 ❑ *After his education, Goldschmidt became a pupil of the composer Franz Schreker.* 上完学后，戈尔德施密特成了作曲家弗朗兹·施雷克的弟子。 2 N-COUNT The **pupils** of a school are the children who go to it. 学生 ❑ *...schools with over 1,000 pupils.* …有1000多名学生的学校。 3 N-COUNT The **pupils** of your eyes are the small, round, black holes in the center of them. 瞳孔 ❑ *The sick man's pupils were dilated.* 病人的瞳孔放大了。 → see **eye**

▲ **pup·pet** /pʌpɪt/ (**puppets**) 1 N-COUNT A **puppet** is a doll that you can move, either by pulling strings that are attached to it or by putting your hand inside its body and moving your fingers. 木偶 2 N-COUNT You can refer to a person or country as a **puppet** when you mean that their actions are controlled by a more powerful person or government, even though they may appear to be independent. 傀儡 [DISAPPROVAL] ❑ *When the invasion occurred he seized power and ruled the country as a puppet of the occupiers.* 他趁入侵之时夺取了政权，作为占领者的傀儡统治着这个国家。

▲ **pup·py** /pʌpi/ (**puppies**) N-COUNT A **puppy** is a young dog. 幼犬 ❑ *One Sunday he began trying to teach the two puppies to walk on a leash.* 一个星期天，他开始试着教两只幼犬栓着皮带走路。

pur·chase ♦♦◇ /pɜrtʃɪs/ (**purchases, purchasing, purchased**) 1 V-T When you **purchase** something, you buy it. 购买 [FORMAL] ❑ *He purchased a ticket and went up on the top deck.* 他买了张票，上了顶层。 ● **pur·chas·er** N-COUNT (**purchasers**) 购买者 ❑ *The broker will get 5% if he finds a purchaser.* 这个中间人如果找到一个买主就将提成5%。 2 N-UNCOUNT The **purchase of** something is the act of buying it. 购买 [FORMAL] ❑ *This week he is to visit China to discuss the purchase of military supplies.* 本周他将访问中国，讨论军用物资的采购。 3 N-COUNT A **purchase** is something that you buy. 购买的东西 [FORMAL] ❑ *She opened the tie box and looked at her purchase. It was silk, with maroon stripes.* 她打开领带盒子，看着自己买的东西。那是真丝的，有栗色的条纹。

pur·chas·ing pow·er 1 N-UNCOUNT The **purchasing power** of a currency is the amount of goods or services that you can buy with it. (货币的) 购买力 [BUSINESS] ❑ *The real purchasing power of the rouble has plummeted.* 卢布的实际购买力已直线下降。 2 N-UNCOUNT The **purchasing power** of a person or group of people is the amount of goods or services that they can afford to buy. (人或人群的) 购买力 [BUSINESS] ❑ *Wage rates must be maintained in order to maintain the purchasing power of the consumer.* 必须维持工资率以保持消费者的购买力。

pure ◆◇◇ /pyʊər/ (**purer, purest**) **1** ADJ A **pure** substance is not mixed with anything else. 纯粹的 ❑ *...a carton of pure orange juice.* …一箱纯橙汁。 **2** ADJ Something that is **pure** is clean and does not contain any harmful substances. 洁净的 ❑ *In remote regions, the air is pure and the crops are free of poisonous insecticides.* 在偏远地区，空气是纯净的，庄稼也不用有毒的杀虫剂。 ● **pu·rity** ★ /pyʊərɪti/ N-UNCOUNT 洁净 [with poss] ❑ *They worried about the purity of tap water.* 他们担心自来水是否洁净。 **3** ADJ If you describe something such as a color, a sound, or a type of light as **pure**, you mean that it is very clear and represents a perfect example of its type. 纯的 ❑ *She was dressed in pure white clothes.* 她穿着纯白的衣服。 ● **pu·rity** ★ N-UNCOUNT 清亮 ❑ *The soaring purity of her voice conjured up the frozen bleakness of the Far North.* 她高亢、清亮的声音使人们想到了遥远的北方萧瑟的冰天雪地。 **4** ADJ **Pure** science or **pure** research is concerned only with theory and not with how this theory can be used in practical ways. 纯理论的 [ADJ n] ❑ *Physics isn't just about pure science with no immediate applications.* 物理学并非没有直接应用价值的纯科学。 **5** ADJ **Pure** means complete and total. 完全的 [EMPHASIS] ❑ *The old man turned to give her a look of pure surprise.* 那位老人回过头来非常吃惊地看了她一眼。
→ see **science**

pu·ree /pyʊreɪ, -ri/ (**purees, pureeing, pureed**) also **purée** **1** N-VAR **Puree** is food that has been crushed or beaten so that it forms a thick, smooth liquid. (食物捣烂而成的) 泥; 酱 ❑ *...a can of tomato puree.* …一罐番茄酱。 **2** V-T If you **puree** food, you make it into a puree. 把…捣成泥 ❑ *In a blender, puree the fruit with the orange juice.* 将水果和橙汁放在一个搅拌器里搅成泥。

pure·ly /pyʊərli/ ADV You use **purely** to emphasize that the thing you are mentioning is the most important feature or that it is the only thing which should be considered. 纯粹地; 完全地 [ADV with cl/group] [EMPHASIS] ❑ *It is a racing machine, designed purely for speed.* 那是一部赛车，完全是为速度而设计的。

▲ **purge** /pɜrdʒ/ (**purges, purging, purged**) **1** V-T To **purge** an organization **of** its unacceptable members means to remove them from it. You can also talk about **purging** people **from** an organization. (从组织中) 清除 (异己成员) ❑ *The leadership voted to purge the party of "hostile and antiparty elements."* 领导层投票来清除党内"有敌意的反党分子"。 ❑ *He recently purged the armed forces, sending hundreds of officers into retirement.* 他最近肃清了武装部队，打发数百名军官退了役。 ● N-COUNT **Purge** is also a noun. 清除 ❑ *The army have called for a more thorough purge of people associated with the late president.* 军队已要求对已故总统的关联人物来一次更彻底地清除。 **2** V-T If you **purge** something **of** undesirable things, you get rid of them. 清除 (不合意的事物) ❑ *He closed his eyes and lay still, trying to purge his mind of anxiety.* 他闭上眼睛躺着不动，试图清除心里的焦虑。

★ **pu·ri·fy** /pyʊərɪfaɪ/ (**purifies, purifying, purified**) V-T If you **purify** a substance, you make it pure by removing any harmful, dirty, or inferior substances from it. 净化 ❑ *I take wheat and yeast tablets daily to purify the blood.* 我每天服用小麦酵母片来净化血液。 ● **pu·ri·fi·ca·tion** /pyʊərɪfɪkeɪʃən/ N-UNCOUNT 净化 ❑ *...a water purification plant.* …一家净化水工厂。

pur·ist /pyʊərɪst/ (**purists**) **1** N-COUNT A **purist** is a person who wants something to be totally correct or unchanged, especially something they know a lot about. 纯粹主义者 ❑ *The new edition of the dictionary carries 7,000 additions to the language, which purists say is under threat.* 新版词典为该语种增加了7000个词条，纯粹派说该语种正受到威胁。 **2** ADJ **Purist** attitudes are the kind of attitudes that purists have. 纯粹主义的 ❑ *...a peculiarly purist argument.* …一个纯粹主义的典型论点。

pu·ri·tan /pyʊərɪtən/ (**puritans**) **1** N-COUNT You describe someone as a **puritan** when they live according to strict moral or religious principles, especially when they disapprove of physical pleasures. (生活上严格遵守道德或宗教准则、尤指反对物质享受的) 清教徒式的人 [DISAPPROVAL] ❑ *Bykov had forgotten that Malinin was something of a puritan.* 贝科夫忘记了马利宁是个近乎清教徒式的人。 **2** ADJ **Puritan** attitudes are based on strict moral or religious principles and often involve disapproval of physical pleasures. 清教徒式的 [DISAPPROVAL] ❑ *Paul was someone who certainly had a puritan streak in him.* 保罗这人的确有点清教徒式的性格。

pu·ri·tani·cal /pyʊərɪtænɪkəl/ ADJ If you describe someone as **puritanical**, you mean that they have very strict moral principles, and often try to make other people behave in a more moral way. 有严格道德原则的 [DISAPPROVAL] ❑ *He has a puritanical attitude toward sex.* 他对性持严格刻板的态度。

★ **pu·rity** /pyʊərɪti/ → see **pure**

pur·ple ◆◆◇ /pɜrpəl/ (**purples**) COLOR Something that is **purple** is of a reddish-blue color. 紫色的 ❑ *She wore purple and green silk.* 她穿着紫色和绿色的丝绸。
→ see **color**

pur·port /pərpɔrt/ (**purports, purporting, purported**) V-T If you say that someone or something **purports to** do or be a particular thing, you mean that they claim to do or be that thing, although you may not always believe that claim. 声称 [FORMAL] ❑ *...a book that purports to tell the whole truth.* …一本声称讲出全部真相的书。

pur·pose ◆◆◇ /pɜrpəs/ (**purposes**) **1** N-COUNT The **purpose** of something is the reason for which it is made or done. 目的; 用途 ❑ *The purpose of the occasion was to raise money for medical supplies.* 此次活动的目的是为医疗用品筹款。 ❑ *...the use of nuclear energy for military purposes.* …军事用途的核能的使用。 **2** N-COUNT Your **purpose** is the thing that you want to achieve. 目标 ❑ *They might well be prepared to do you harm in order to achieve their purpose.* 他们很可能有备而来伤害你，以实现其目标。 **3** N-UNCOUNT **Purpose** is the feeling of having a definite aim and of being determined to achieve it. 意志 ❑ *The teachers are enthusiastic and have a sense of purpose.* 教师们热情高涨，感到很有奔头。 **4** PHRASE If you do something **on purpose**, you do it intentionally. 故意地 ❑ *Was it an accident or did David do it on purpose?* 这是个意外呢，还是戴维故意干的？

Word Partnership *purpose* 的常用搭配：

V. **serve a** purpose **1**
accomplish a purpose, **achieve a** purpose **2**
ADJ. **main** purpose, **original** purpose, **primary** purpose, **real** purpose, **sole** purpose **1** **2**

purpose-built ADJ A **purpose-built** building has been specially designed and built for a particular use. 为特定目的建造的 [mainly BRIT]
in AM, usually use **custom-built**

pur·pose·ful /pɜrpəsfəl/ ADJ If someone is **purposeful**, they show that they have a definite aim and a strong desire to achieve it. 有意图的; 志在必得的 ❑ *She had a purposeful air, and it became evident that this was not a casual visit.* 她一副志在必得的样子，显然这不是一次随意造访。 ● **pur·pose·ful·ly** ADV 有意图地; 志在必得地 ❑ *He strode purposefully toward the barn.* 他有意朝谷仓大步走去。

purr /pɜr/ (**purrs, purring, purred**) **1** V-I When a cat **purrs**, it makes a low vibrating sound with its throat because it is contented. (猫满足地) 发呼噜声 ❑ *The kitten had settled comfortably in her arms and was purring enthusiastically.* 小猫舒服地卧在她怀里，起劲地打着呼噜。 **2** V-I When the engine of a machine such as a car **purrs**, it is working and making a quiet, continuous, vibrating sound. (发动机、机器等工作时) 发出翁翁声 ❑ *Both boats purred out of the cave mouth and into open water.* 两条小船翁翁地驶出洞口，到了开阔的水面上。 ● N-SING **Purr** is also a noun. 翁翁声 ❑ *Carmela heard the purr of a motorcycle coming up the drive.* 卡梅拉听到摩托车开上快车道的翁翁声。

purse /pɜrs/ (**purses, pursing, pursed**) **1** N-COUNT A **purse** is a small bag or a handbag that women carry. 女式手袋 [AM]
in BRIT, use **bag, handbag**
❑ *She looked at me and then reached in her purse for cigarettes.* 她看了看我，然后从手袋里掏香烟。 **2** N-COUNT A **purse** is a very small bag that people, especially women, keep their money in. (尤指女式) 钱包 [mainly BRIT]
in AM, usually use **wallet**
3 N-SING **Purse** is used to refer to the total amount of money that a country, family, or group has. (国家、家庭、团体等的) 财力 ❑ *The money could simply go into the public purse, helping to lower taxes.* 这笔钱可以直接划入国库，来帮助降低税收。 **4** V-T If you **purse** your **lips**, you move them into a small, rounded shape, usually because you disapprove of something or when you are thinking. 撅 (嘴) ❑ *She pursed her lips in disapproval.* 她噘起嘴唇反对。

pur·sue ◆◇◇ /pərsu/ (**pursues, pursuing, pursued**) **1** V-T If you **pursue** an activity, interest, or plan, you carry it out or follow it. 执行; 贯彻 [FORMAL] ❑ *He said Japan would continue to pursue the policies laid down at the London summit.* 他说日本将继续贯彻伦敦峰会上确定的方针。 **2** V-T If you **pursue** a particular aim or result, you make efforts to achieve it, often over a long period of time. 追求; 努力实现 [FORMAL] ❑ *He will pursue a trade policy that protects American*

P

workers. 他将努力实行保护美国工人的贸易政策。 3 V-T If you **pursue** a particular topic, you try to find out more about it by asking questions. 追问 [FORMAL] ❑ *If your original request is denied, don't be afraid to pursue the matter.* 如果你最初的要求被拒绝了，不要害怕去追问这件事情。 4 V-T If you **pursue** a person, vehicle, or animal, you follow them, usually in order to catch them. 追赶 [FORMAL] ❑ *She pursued the man who had stolen a woman's bag.* 她追赶那个偷了一女士钱包的男子。

pur·su·er /pərsuər/ (**pursuers**) N-COUNT Your **pursuers** are the people who are chasing or searching for you. 追踪者 [FORMAL] ❑ *They had shaken off their pursuers.* 他们甩掉了追踪者。

★ **pur·suit** /pərsut/ (**pursuits**) 1 N-UNCOUNT Your **pursuit of** something is your attempts at achieving it. If you do something **in pursuit of** a particular result, you do it in order to achieve that result. 追求 ❑ *...a young man whose relentless pursuit of excellence is conducted with single-minded determination.* …一个一心一意不断追求卓越的年轻男子。 2 N-UNCOUNT The **pursuit of** an activity, interest, or plan consists of all the things that you do when you are carrying it out. 执行 ❑ *The vigorous pursuit of policies is no guarantee of success.* 政策的严格执行并非成功的保障。 3 N-UNCOUNT Someone who is **in pursuit of** a person, vehicle, or animal is chasing them. 追赶 ❑ *...a police officer who drove a patrol car at more than 120 mph in pursuit of a motorcycle.* …一位开着巡逻车以120英里以上的时速追赶一辆摩托车的警官。 4 N-COUNT Your **pursuits** are your activities, usually activities that you enjoy when you are not working. 消遣活动 ❑ *They both love outdoor pursuits.* 他们俩都喜欢户外活动。

pur·vey·or /pərveɪər/ (**purveyors**) N-COUNT A **purveyor of** goods or services is a person or company that provides them. 供应者 [FORMAL] ❑ *...purveyors of gourmet foods.* …美食供应者们。

push ♦♦◊ /pʊʃ/ (**pushes, pushing, pushed**) 1 V-T/V-I When you **push** something, you use force to make it move away from you or away from its previous position. 推 ❑ *The woman pushed back her chair and stood up.* 那女人把椅子向后一推，站了起来。 ❑ *They pushed him into the car.* 他们把他推进了汽车。 ❑ *...a pregnant woman pushing a stroller.* …一位推着婴儿车的孕妇。 ● N-COUNT **Push** is also a noun. 推 ❑ *He gave me a sharp push.* 他猛地推了我一下。 2 V-T/V-I If you **push through** things that are blocking your way or **push** your **way through** them, you use force in order to move past them. 挤过 ❑ *I pushed through the crowds and on to the escalator.* 我挤过人群，上了自动扶梯。 ❑ *Dix pushed forward carrying a glass.* 迪克斯拿着一个玻璃杯往前挤。 3 V-I If an army **pushes into** a country or area that it is attacking or invading, it moves further into it. 挺进 ❑ *One detachment pushed into the eastern suburbs toward the airfield.* 一支小分队挺进了东郊往机场去。 ● N-COUNT **Push** is also a noun. 挺进 ❑ *All that was needed was one final push, and the enemy would be vanquished once and for all.* 只需要最后一次挺进，敌军就将被彻底击败。 4 V-T To **push** a value or amount **up** or **down** means to cause it to increase or decrease. 推动(价值、数量上升或下降) ❑ *Any shortage could push up grain prices.* 任何短缺都会推动粮价上涨。 ❑ *The government had done everything it could to push down inflation.* 政府已经竭尽全力遏制通货膨胀。 5 V-T If someone or something **pushes** an idea or project in a particular direction, they cause it to develop or progress in a particular way. 使发展；推进 ❑ *China would use its influence to help push forward the peace process.* 中国将会利用其影响力帮助推进和平进程。 6 V-T If you **push** someone **to** do something or **push** them **into** doing it, you encourage or force them to do it. 鼓励；逼迫 ❑ *She thanks her parents for keeping her in school and pushing her to study.* 她感谢她的父母一直让她上学，并鼓励她学习。 ❑ *Jason did not push her into stealing the money.* 贾森并没有逼迫她去偷那钱。 ● N-COUNT **Push** is also a noun. 鼓励；逼迫 ❑ *We need a push to take the first step.* 我们需要鼓励来迈出第一步。 7 V-I If you **push for** something, you try very hard to achieve it or to persuade someone to do it. 努力争取；力劝…做 ❑ *Doctors are pushing for a ban on all cigarette advertising.* 医生们正力求禁止所有香烟广告。 ● N-COUNT **Push** is also a noun. 努力；劝服 ❑ *In its push for economic growth it has ignored projects that would improve living standards.* 在努力追求经济增长的同时却忽视了改善生活水平的项目。 8 V-T If someone **pushes** an idea, a point, or a product, they try in a forceful way to convince people to accept it or buy it. 力劝…接受(思想、论点)；推销(产品) ❑ *The commissioners will push the case for opening the plant.* 委员们将力陈开办此厂的理由。 9 V-T When someone **pushes** drugs, they sell them illegally. 贩卖(毒品) [INFORMAL] ❑ *You would be on welfare with your kids pushing drugs to pay the rent.* 你将靠福利救济过活，靠你的孩子们贩毒来支付租金。 10 → see also **pushed** 11 if **push comes to shove** → see **shove**

▸ **push ahead** or **push forward** PHRASAL VERB If you **push ahead** or **push forward with** something, you make progress with it. 推进 ❑ *The government intends to push ahead with its reform program.* 该政府打算推进其改革计划。

▸ **push on** PHRASAL VERB When you **push on**, you continue with a trip or task. 继续前进；继续进行 ❑ *Although the journey was a long and lonely one, Tumalo pushed on.* 尽管路途漫长而孤单，图马洛仍继续行进。

▸ **push over** PHRASAL VERB If you **push** someone or something **over**, you push them so that they fall onto the ground. 推倒 ❑ *We have had trouble with people damaging hedges, uprooting trees and pushing over walls.* 我们与毁篱、拔树、推墙之徒发生了纠纷。

▸ **push through** PHRASAL VERB If someone **pushes through** a law, they succeed in getting it accepted although some people oppose it. 使…被通过 ❑ *The Democratic majority pushed through a law permitting the sale of arms.* 民主党以多数票通过了允许武器销售的法案。

Thesaurus *push* 另参见：

V. drive, force, move, pressure, propel, shove, thrust; (*ant.*) pull 1 2
encourage, urge 6 – 8

Word Partnership *push* 的常用搭配：

N. push **a button, at the** push **of a button,** push **a door** 1
push **prices,** push **rates** 4
push **an agenda,** push **legislation** 8
push **drugs** 9

push·chair /pʊʃtʃɛər/ (**pushchairs**) N-COUNT A **pushchair** is a small chair on wheels, in which a baby or small child can sit and be wheeled around. 婴儿车 [BRIT]

in AM, use **stroller**

pushed /pʊʃt/ ADJ If you are **pushed for** something such as time or money, you do not have enough of it. (时间、金钱) 不够的 [v-link ADJ] [BRIT, INFORMAL]

in AM, use **pressed for**

❑ *He's going to be a bit pushed for money.* 他手头将会有点拮据。

push·er /pʊʃər/ (**pushers**) N-COUNT A **pusher** is a person who sells illegal drugs. 毒贩子 [INFORMAL] ❑ *His father accused him of acting as a carrier for some drug pushers.* 他父亲指责他为某些毒贩子充当毒品送递人。

push-up (**push-ups**) N-COUNT **Push-ups** are exercises to strengthen your arms and chest muscles. They are done by lying with your face toward the floor and pushing with your hands to raise your body until your arms are straight. 俯卧撑 ❑ *He did push-ups after games.* 他在赛后做了俯卧撑。

put ♦♦♦ /pʊt/ (**puts, putting**)

The form **put** is used in the present tense and is the past tense and past participle.

Put is used in a large number of expressions that are explained under other words in this dictionary. For example, the expression **to put someone in the picture** is explained at **picture**.

1 V-T When you **put** something in a particular place or position, you move it into that place or position. 放置 ❑ *Leaphorn put the photograph on the desk.* 利普霍恩把那张照片放在桌子上。 ❑ *She hesitated, then put her hand on Grace's arm.* 她犹豫了一下，然后把手搭在格雷斯的臂膀上。 2 V-T If you **put** someone somewhere, you cause them to go there and to stay there for a period of time. 安置 ❑ *Rather than put him in the hospital, she had been caring for him at home.* 她没有把他送进医院，而是一直在家里照料他。 3 V-T To **put** someone or something in a particular state or situation means to cause them to be in that state or situation. 致使(…处于某种状态) ❑ *This is going to put them out of business.* 这将使他们歇业。 ❑ *He was putting himself at risk.* 他在把自己置于危险境地。 4 V-T To **put** something **on** people or things means to cause them to have it, or to cause them to be affected by it. 把…施加给；使受…的影响 ❑ *He didn't put any pressure on her.* 他并没有给她施加任何压力。 ❑ *Be aware of the terrible strain it can put on a child when you expect the best grades.* 当你期盼最佳成绩时，要意识到这可能给孩子带来的可怕压力。 5 V-T If you **put** your trust, faith, or confidence **in** someone or something, you trust them or have faith or confidence in them. 把(信任、信仰、信心等)寄托在

P

❑ *He had decided long ago that he would put his trust in socialism when the time came.* 他很久以前就已决定，他到时候将信仰社会主义。 6 V-T If you **put** time, strength, or energy **into** an activity, you use it in doing that activity. 把（时间、体力或精力）用于 ❑ *We're not saying that activists should put all their effort and time into party politics.* 我们并不是说，积极分子们应把他们所有的精力和时间都投入到党政工作。 7 V-T If you **put** money **into** a business or project, you invest money in it. 投入（资金）❑ *Investors should consider putting some money into an annuity.* 投资者们应考虑在年金上投入一些资金。 8 V-T When you **put** an idea or remark in a particular way, you express it in that way. You can use expressions like **to put it simply** and **to put it bluntly** before saying something when you want to explain how you are going to express it. 表达 ❑ *I had already met Pete a couple of times through – how should I put it – friends in low places.* 我已经见过皮特好几次了，通过——怎么说呢——底层社会的朋友们。 ❑ *He admitted the security forces might have made some mistakes, as he put it.* 如他所说的，他承认治安部队可能犯了一些错误。 9 V-T When you **put a question to** someone, you ask them the question. 提出（问题）❑ *Is this fair? Well, I put that question today to the mayor.* 这公平吗？好吧，我今天就向市长提出那个问题。 10 V-T If you **put** a case, opinion, or proposal, you explain it and list the reasons why you support or believe it. 解释 ❑ *He always put his point of view with clarity and with courage.* 他一贯勇于清晰地阐释自己的观点。 ❑ *He put the case to the Saudi foreign minister.* 他向沙特外交部长解释了此事。 11 V-T If you **put** something **at** a particular value or **in** a particular category, you consider that it has that value or that it belongs in that category. 给…估（值）；把…归（类）❑ *I would put her age at about 50 or so.* 我估计她的年纪大约是五十岁左右。 ❑ *All the more technically advanced countries put a high value on science.* 所有技术更发达的国家都高度重视科学。 12 V-T If you **put** written information somewhere, you write, type, or print it there. 写下；用打字机打下；印下 ❑ *Mary's family was so pleased that they put an announcement in the local paper to thank them.* 玛丽的家人如此高兴，以至于在当地报纸上登了一则启事感谢他们。 ❑ *I think what I put in that book is now pretty much the agenda for this country.* 我认为我在那本书里写的正是该国目前亟待解决的问题。 13 PHRASE If you **put it to** someone **that** something is true, you suggest that it is true, especially when you think that they will be unwilling to admit this. 向…指出 ❑ *But I put it to you that they're useless.* 但我要告诉你，他们没用。 14 PHRASE If you say that something is bigger or better than several other things **put together**, you mean that it is bigger or has more good qualities than all of those other things if they are added together. 加在一起 ❑ *Mary ate more than the rest of us put together.* 玛丽吃得比我们其他人加在一起还要多。

▸ **put across** or **put over** PHRASAL VERB When you **put** something **across** or **put** it **over**, you succeed in describing or explaining it to someone. 描述清楚；解释明白 ❑ *He has taken out a half-page advertisement in his local paper to put his point across.* 他拿出了当地报纸上的半版广告来阐释他的观点。

▸ **put aside** PHRASAL VERB If you **put** something **aside**, you keep it to be dealt with or used at a later time. 把…暂放一边；把…留作后用 ❑ *Encourage children to put aside some of their allowance to buy Christmas presents.* 鼓励孩子们留下部分零用钱来买圣诞礼物。

▸ **put away** PHRASAL VERB If you **put** something **away**, you put it into the place where it is normally kept when it is not being used, for example, in a drawer. 把…收拾起来 ❑ *She finished putting the milk away and turned around.* 她把牛奶收拾完后转过身来。 ❑ *"Yes, Mom," replied Cheryl as she slowly put away her doll.* "是的，妈妈，"谢里尔一边回答，一边慢慢地把她的玩具娃娃收起来。

▸ **put back** PHRASAL VERB To **put** something **back** means to delay it or arrange for it to happen later than you previously planned. 推迟 ❑ *There are always new projects which seem to put the reunion back further.* 总是有一些新项目，似乎还要把这次团聚再往后推迟。

▸ **put down** 1 PHRASAL VERB If you **put** something **down** somewhere, you write or type it there. 写下；用打字机打下 ❑ *Never put anything down on paper which might be used in evidence against you at a later date.* 不要在纸上写下任何东西，免得日后成为对你不利的证据。 ❑ *The journalists simply put down what they thought they heard.* 记者们只是记下他们认为自己听到的东西。 2 PHRASAL VERB If you **put down** some money, you pay part of the price of something, and will pay the rest later. 付订金 ❑ *He bought an investment property for $100,000 and put down $20,000.* 他买了一处价值$10万的投资性房产，并支付了$2万的订金。 3 PHRASAL VERB When soldiers, police, or the government **put down** a riot or rebellion, they stop it by using force. 镇压（暴动、叛乱）❑ *Soldiers went in to put down a rebellion.* 士兵们攻进去镇压了一场叛乱。 4 PHRASAL VERB If someone **puts** you **down**, they treat you in an unpleasant way by criticizing you in front of other people or making you appear foolish. 当众批评；捉弄 ❑ *I know that I do put people down occasionally.* 我知道我有时候确实会伤人面子。 ❑ *Racist jokes come from wanting to put down other kinds of people we feel threatened by.* 种族笑话源于我们想捉弄那些我们感到有威胁的异族人。 5 → see also **put-down** 6 PHRASAL VERB When an animal **is put down**, it is killed because it is dangerous or very ill. 杀死（危险或病重的动物）❑ *The judge ordered their dog Samson to be put down immediately.* 该法官下令立即杀掉他们的狗萨姆森。

▸ **put down to** PHRASAL VERB If you **put** something **down to** a particular thing, you believe that it is caused by that thing. 把…归因于 ❑ *You may be a skeptic and put it down to life's inequalities.* 你可能是个怀疑论者，并将其归因于生活的种种不平等。

▸ **put forward** PHRASAL VERB If you **put forward** a plan, proposal, or name, you suggest that it should be considered for a particular purpose or job. 提出（计划、建议、名称）❑ *He has put forward new peace proposals.* 他已提出了新的和平建议。

▸ **put in** 1 PHRASAL VERB If you **put in** an amount of time or effort doing something, you spend that time or effort doing it. 投入（时间、精力）❑ *Wade was going to be paid a salary, instead of by the hour, whether he put in forty hours or not.* 韦德将领月薪，而不是小时工资，无论他是否干够40个小时。 ❑ *They've put in time and effort to keep the strike going.* 他们已投入了时间和精力使这次罢工继续进行。 2 PHRASAL VERB If you **put in** a request or **put in for** something, you formally request or apply for that thing. 提出（请求）❑ *I also put in a request for some overtime.* 我也提出了支付加班费的请求。 3 PHRASAL VERB If you **put in** a remark, you interrupt someone or add to what they have said with the remark. 插嘴；补充 ❑ *"He was a lawyer before that," Mary Ann put in.* "在那之前他是个律师，"玛丽・安补充道。

▸ **put off** 1 PHRASAL VERB If you **put** something **off**, you delay doing it. 推迟 ❑ *Women who put off having a baby often make the best mothers.* 晚育的妇女常常会成为最佳母亲。 2 PHRASAL VERB If you **put** someone **off**, you make them wait for something that they want. 使…等待；把…搪塞过去 ❑ *The old priest tried to put them off, saying that the hour was late.* 那位老牧师试图把他们搪塞过去，说时间太晚了。 3 PHRASAL VERB If something **puts** you **off** something, it makes you dislike it, or decide not to do or have it. 使反感；使对…失去兴趣 ❑ *The high divorce figures don't seem to be putting people off marriage.* 高离婚率好像并没有使人们对婚姻望而却步。 ❑ *His personal habits put them off.* 他的个人习惯让他们反感。 4 PHRASAL VERB If someone or something **puts** you **off**, they take your attention from what you are trying to do and make it more difficult for you to do it. 使分心 ❑ *She asked me to be serious – said it put her off if I laughed.* 她要我严肃一点——说如果我大笑会让她分心。

▸ **put on** 1 PHRASAL VERB When you **put on** clothing or makeup, you place it on your body in order to wear it. 穿戴；涂抹（化妆品）❑ *She put on her coat and went out.* 她穿上外套，出去了。 ❑ *Maximo put on a pair of glasses.* 马克西莫戴上了一副眼镜。 2 PHRASAL VERB When people **put on** a show, exhibition, or service, they perform it or organize it. 举办（演出、展览）；提供（服务）❑ *The band is hoping to put on a show before the end of the year.* 该乐队正希望在年底之前举行一场演出。 3 PHRASAL VERB If someone **puts on** weight, they become heavier. 增加（体重）❑ *I can eat what I want but I never put on weight.* 我想吃什么就能吃什么，而体重从不增加。 4 PHRASAL VERB If you **put on** a piece of equipment or a device, you make it start working, for example, by pressing a switch or turning a knob. 打开（开关）❑ *I put the radio on.* 我打开了收音机。 5 PHRASAL VERB If you **put** a record, tape, or CD **on**, you place it in a record, tape, or CD player and listen to it. 播放 ❑ *She poured them drinks, and put a record on loud.* 她给他们倒了饮料，把唱片的声音放得很大。

▸ **put out** 1 PHRASAL VERB If you **put out** an announcement or story, you make it known to a lot of people. 发布 ❑ *No one put out a press release aimed at the public.* 没有人发布针对公众的新闻稿。 2 PHRASAL VERB If you **put out** a fire, candle, or cigarette, you make it stop burning. 熄灭 ❑ *Firemen tried to free the injured and put out the blaze.* 消防员们竭力救出伤者，扑灭大火。 3 PHRASAL VERB If you **put out** an electric light, you make it stop shining by pressing a switch. 关闭（电灯等）❑ *He crossed to the nightstand and put out the light.* 他走到床头柜边，把灯关掉。 4 PHRASAL VERB If you **put out** things that will be needed, you place them somewhere ready to be used. 把…放好备用 ❑ *Paula had put out her luggage for the bus.* 葆拉放好了行李准备乘公车。 5 PHRASAL VERB If you **put out** your **hand**, you move it forward, away from your body. 伸（手）❑ *He put out his*

P

hand to Alfred. 他把手伸向艾尔弗雷德。 **6** PHRASAL VERB If you **put** someone **out**, you cause them trouble because they have to do something for you. 给…带来麻烦 ❑ *It is a very sociable diet to follow because you don't have to put anyone out.* 这是一种非常大众化的食谱，因为你不会给任何人带来麻烦。

▸ **put over** → see **put across**

▸ **put through** **1** PHRASAL VERB When someone **puts through** someone who is making a telephone call, they make the connection that allows the telephone call to take place. 给…接通电话 ❑ *The operator will put you through.* 接线员将为你接通电话。 **2** PHRASAL VERB If someone **puts** you **through** an unpleasant experience, they make you experience it. 使…遭受 ❑ *She wouldn't want to put them through the ordeal of a huge ceremony.* 她不想让他们遭受一次盛大典礼的煎熬。

▸ **put together** **1** PHRASAL VERB If you **put** something **together**, you join its different parts to each other so that it can be used. 装配 ❑ *He took it apart brick by brick, and put it back together again.* 他一块砖一块砖地把它拆开，又重新把它砌好。 **2** PHRASAL VERB If you **put together** a group of people or things, you form them into a team or collection. 组建 ❑ *It will be able to put together a governing coalition.* 它将能够组建一个执政联盟。 **3** PHRASAL VERB If you **put together** an agreement, plan, or product, you design and create it. 拟定；设计制造 ❑ *We wouldn't have time to put together an agreement.* 我们不会有时间拟定一份协议。 ❑ *Reports speak of Berlin putting together an aid package for Moscow.* 报告提到柏林正在拟定一份援助莫斯科的一揽子计划。 **4** → see also **put 14**

▸ **put up** **1** PHRASAL VERB If people **put up** a wall, building, tent, or other structure, they construct it so that it is upright. 建造 ❑ *Protesters have been putting up barricades across a number of major intersections.* 抗议者们已在许多主要十字路口搭建了路障。 **2** PHRASAL VERB If you **put up** a poster or notice, you attach it to a wall or board. 张贴 ❑ *They're putting new street signs up.* 他们正在张贴新的路标。 **3** PHRASAL VERB To **put up** resistance to something means to resist it. 进行（抵抗） ❑ *In the end the Kurds surrendered without putting up any resistance.* 最终，库尔德人未做任何抵抗就投降了。 ❑ *He'd put up a real fight to keep you there.* 他为了让你留在那儿，进行了一场实实在在的斗争。 **4** PHRASAL VERB If you **put up** money for something, you provide the money that is needed to pay for it. 提供 ❑ *The state agreed to put up $69,000 to start his company.* 国家同意出资$69000创办他的公司。 **5** PHRASAL VERB To **put up** the price of something means to cause it to increase. 提高（价格） ❑ *Their friends suggested they should put up their prices.* 他们的朋友们建议他们提高价格。 **6** PHRASAL VERB If a person or hotel **puts** you **up** or if you **put up** somewhere, you stay there for one or more nights. 留宿 ❑ *I wanted to know if she could put me up for a few days.* 我想知道她能否让我留宿几天。 ❑ *Hundreds of commuters had to be put up in hotel rooms.* 数百名往返者只得留宿在旅馆的房间里。 **7** PHRASAL VERB If a political party **puts up** a candidate in an election or if the candidate **puts up**, the candidate takes part in the election. 提名（为选举侯选人）；参加选举 ❑ *Barnes put up a candidate of his own for this post.* 巴恩斯为这个职位提出了自己的一名候选人。

▸ **put up with** PHRASAL VERB If you **put up with** something, you tolerate or accept it, even though you find it unpleasant or unsatisfactory. 容忍 ❑ *They had put up with behavior from their son which they would not have tolerated from anyone else.* 他们容忍了自己儿子的行为，而换作别的任何人，他们才不会容忍。

put out ADJ If you feel **put out**, you feel annoyed or upset. 生气的；心烦的 [v-link ADJ] ❑ *I did not blame him for feeling put out.* 我不是因为生气而责怪他。

putt /pʌt/ (**putts, putting, putted**) **1** N-COUNT A **putt** is a stroke in golf that you make when the ball has reached the green in an attempt to get the ball in the hole. （高尔夫球的）轻击 ❑ *...a 5-foot putt.* …一次5英尺远的轻击。 **2** V-T/V-I In golf, when you **putt**, or **putt** the ball, you hit a putt. 轻击（高尔夫球） ❑ *Turner, however, putted superbly, twice holing from 40 feet.* 然而，特纳两次在40英尺之外漂亮地把球轻击入洞。

puz·zle /pʌz°l/ (**puzzles**) **1** V-T If something **puzzles** you, you do not understand it and feel confused. 使…迷惑不解 ❑ *My sister puzzles me and causes me anxiety.* 我的妹妹常会让我不解，使我焦虑。 ● **puz·zling** ADJ 令人迷惑不解的 ❑ *His letter poses a number of puzzling questions.* 他的信中提出了几个令人迷惑不解的问题。 **2** V-I If you **puzzle over** something, you try hard to think of the answer to it or the explanation for it. 对…苦苦思索 ❑ *In rehearsing Shakespeare, I puzzle over the complexities of his verse and prose.* 排演莎士比亚戏剧时，我苦苦地思索着他诗歌和散文中的复杂难懂之处。 **3** N-COUNT A **puzzle** is a question, game, or toy that you have to think about carefully in order to answer it correctly or put it together properly. 智力问题（或游戏、玩具） [oft supp N] ❑ *...a word puzzle.* …一条字谜。 **4** → see also **crossword, jigsaw** **5** N-SING You can describe a person or thing that is hard to understand as **a puzzle**. 谜一样的人或事物 ["a" N] ❑ *The rise in accidents remains a puzzle.* 事故的增多仍是个谜。

puz·zled /pʌz°ld/ ADJ Someone who is **puzzled** is confused because they do not understand something. 感到困惑的 ❑ *Critics remain puzzled by the election results.* 评论家们对选举结果仍感到困惑。

PVC /pi vi si/ N-UNCOUNT **PVC** is a plastic material that is used for many purposes, for example, to make clothing or shoes or to cover chairs. **PVC** is an abbreviation for "polyvinyl chloride." 聚氯乙烯

py·ja·mas /pɪdʒɑməz/ [mainly BRIT] → see **pajamas**

▲ **pyra·mid** /pɪrəmɪd/ (**pyramids**) **1** N-COUNT **Pyramids** are ancient stone buildings with four triangular sloping sides. The most famous pyramids are those built in ancient Egypt to contain the bodies of their kings and queens. 金字塔 ❑ *We set off to see the Pyramids and Sphinx.* 我们出发去看金字塔和狮身人面像。 **2** N-COUNT A **pyramid** is a shape, object, or pile of things with a flat base and sloping triangular sides that meet at a point. 角锥形；角锥体 ❑ *On a plate in front of him was piled a pyramid of flat white crackers.* 他面前盘子里的白色薄饼干堆成了金字塔形。 **3** N-COUNT You can describe something as a **pyramid** when it is organized so that there are fewer people at each level as you go toward the top. 金字塔形结构 ❑ *Traditionally, the Brahmins, or the priestly class, are set at the top of the social pyramid.* 传统上，婆罗门或僧侣阶层位于社会金字塔的顶层。

→ see **solid, volume**

pyra·mid scheme N-UNCOUNT A **Pyramid scheme** is a method of selling in which one person buys a supply of a particular product directly from the manufacturer and then sells it to a number of other people at an increased price. These people sell it on to others in a similar way, but eventually the final buyers are only able to sell the product for less than they paid for it. 金字塔式销售（指价格逐级提升地转售产品，最高一级只能低于进价销售） [BUSINESS] ❑ *The pyramid scheme was marketed through a home page on the World Wide Web.* 这个金字塔式销售是通过万维网的一个主页进行交易的。

py·thon /paɪθɒn, -θən/ (**pythons**) N-COUNT A **python** is a large snake that kills animals by squeezing them with its body. 蟒蛇

P

Qq

Q also **q** /kyu/ (**Q's, q's**) N-VAR **Q** is the seventeenth letter of the English alphabet. 英文字母表第17个字母

Q & A /kyu ən eɪ/ also **Q and A** N-UNCOUNT **Q & A** is a situation in which a person or group of people asks questions and another person or group of people answers them. **Q & A** is short for "question and answer." 问与答

quad·ru·ple /kwɒdrʌpəl, -drupᵊl, kwɒdrupᵊl/ (**quadruples, quadrupling, quadrupled**) **1** V-T/V-I If someone **quadruples** an amount or if it **quadruples**, it becomes four times bigger. 使成4倍；成为4倍 ❑ *China seeks to quadruple its income in twenty years.* 中国力求在20年内将其收入翻两番。 **2** PREDET If one amount is **quadruple** another amount, it is four times bigger. 4倍的 [PREDET det n] ❑ *Fifty-nine percent of its residents have attended graduate school – quadruple the national average.* 该地区59%的居民读过研究生——是全国平均水平的4倍。 **3** ADJ You use **quadruple** to indicate that something has four parts or happens four times. 由4部分组成的；发生4次的 [ADJ n] ❑ *The quadruple murder has replaced property prices as the sole topic of interest.* 这4起连环谋杀案已经取代房价成为了人们惟一感兴趣的话题。

▲ **quaint** /kweɪnt/ (**quainter, quaintest**) ADJ Something that is **quaint** is attractive because it is old-fashioned. 古雅的 ❑ *...a small, quaint town with narrow streets and traditional half-timbered houses.* …一座古朴的小镇，有着狭窄的街道和传统的半木制房屋。

quake /kweɪk/ (**quakes, quaking, quaked**) **1** N-COUNT A **quake** is the same as an **earthquake**. 地震 [INFORMAL] ❑ *The quake destroyed mud buildings in many remote villages.* 地震摧毁了许多偏远村庄的泥土房屋。 **2** V-I If you **quake**, you shake, usually because you are very afraid. (常指因害怕而) 发抖 ❑ *I just stood there quaking with fear.* 我站在那儿，吓得发抖。 **3** PHRASE If you **are quaking in** your **boots** or **quaking in** your **shoes**, you feel very nervous or afraid, and may be feeling slightly weak as a result. (因紧张、害怕而) 发抖 ❑ *If you stand up straight, you'll give an impression of self-confidence, even if you're quaking in your boots.* 只要你站直了，就会给人一种自信的印象，哪怕你正紧张得发抖。

quali·fi·ca·tion /kwɒlɪfɪkeɪʃᵊn/ (**qualifications**) **1** N-COUNT Your **qualifications** are the official documents or titles you have that show your level of education and training. 资格；学历 ❑ *"Do you have any qualifications?"—"Yes, I'm certified to teach high school."* "你有资格吗？"——"有，我有资格教高中。" **2** N-UNCOUNT **Qualification** is the act of passing the examinations you need to work in a particular profession. 资格取得 ❑ *She has met the minimum educational requirements for qualification.* 她已达到了资格取得所需的最低教育水准。 **3** N-COUNT The **qualifications** you need for an activity or task are the qualities and skills that you need to be able to do it. 素质；技能 ❑ *Responsibility and reliability are necessary qualifications, as well as a friendly and outgoing personality.* 责任感和可靠性是必需的素质，友善和外向的性格也必不可少。 **4** N-VAR A **qualification** is a detail or explanation that you add to a statement to make it less strong or less general. 限制条件 ❑ *The empirical evidence considered here is subject to many qualifications.* 这里所考虑的经验证据有许多限制条件。 **5** N-COUNT Your **qualifications** are the examinations that you have passed. (已通过的) 资格考试 [BRIT] ❑ *Lucy Thomson, 16, wants to study theater but needs more qualifications.* 露西·汤姆森16岁，想学戏剧，但还需要通过更多的资格考试。

Thesaurus *qualification* 另参见：

N.	capability, proficiency, skill **3** condition, provision, stipulation **4**

Word Partnership *qualification* 的常用搭配：

N.	qualification **for a job, standards for** qualification **3**
ADJ.	**necessary** qualification **3**
PREP.	**without** qualification **3 4**

quali·fied ♦◇◇ /kwɒlɪfaɪd/ **1** ADJ Someone who is **qualified** has a certificate, license, diploma or degree in order to work in a particular profession. 有资格的；有文凭的 ❑ *Demand has far outstripped supply of qualified teachers.* 对有资格教师的需求远远超过了供应。 ❑ *Are you qualified for this job?* 你有资格担任这项工作吗？ **2** ADJ If you give someone or something **qualified** support or approval, your support or approval is not total because you have some doubts. 有限度的；有保留的 [ADJ n] ❑ *The government has in the past given qualified support to the idea of tightening the legislation.* 政府过去对加强立法的观点给予了有保留的支持。 **3** PHRASE If you describe something as a **qualified success**, you mean that it is only partly successful. 局部成功 ❑ *Even as a humanitarian mission it has been only a qualified success.* 即使是一项人道主义任务，也只是局部成功。

quali·fi·er /kwɒlɪfaɪər/ (**qualifiers**) **1** N-COUNT A **qualifier** is an early round or match in some competitions. The players or teams who are successful are able to continue to the next round or to the main competition. 预选赛 ❑ *Crew Stadium hosted the U.S.-Mexico qualifier.* 在船员体育场举行了美国对墨西哥的预选赛。 **2** → see also **qualify**

quali·fy ♦◇◇ /kwɒlɪfaɪ/ (**qualifies, qualifying, qualified**) **1** V-I If you **qualify** in a competition, you are successful in one part of it and go on to the next stage. 通过预赛；取得下一轮比赛资格 ❑ *We qualified for the final by beating Stanford on Tuesday.* 我们在星期二击败了斯坦福队，取得了决赛资格。 ● **quali·fi·er** N-COUNT (**qualifiers**) 通过预赛者 ❑ *Kenya's Robert Kibe was the fastest qualifier for the 800 meters final.* 肯尼亚的罗伯特·凯布是800米决赛入围者中速度最快的选手。 **2** V-T/V-I To **qualify as** something or to **be qualified as** something means to have all the features that are needed to be that thing. 使…符合(某物的全部特征)；符合 ❑ *13 percent of American households qualify as poor, says Mr. Mishel.* 13%的美国家庭称得上是贫民，米歇尔先生说。 **3** V-T If you **qualify** a statement, you make it less strong or less general by adding a detail or explanation to it. (通过增加细节、解释) 使语气缓和；使…不太笼统 ❑ *I would qualify that by putting it into context.* 我会把它放入上下文中加以解释。 ❑ *Boyd qualified his opinion, noting that the evidence could be interpreted in other ways.* 博伊德补充说明了他的观点，指出证据可以用其他方式加以解释。 **4** V-T/V-I If you **qualify** for something or if something **qualifies** you for it, you have the right to do it or have it. (使) 有权做；(使) 有资格拥有 ❑ *To qualify for maternity leave you must have worked for the same employer for two years.* 你必须为同一雇主工作两年才有资格休产假。 ❑ *The basic course does not qualify you to practice as a therapist.* 这门基础课程并不能使你有资格当一名治疗师。 **5** V-I When someone **qualifies**, they receive the certificate, license, diploma, or degree that they need to be able to work in a particular profession. 取得资格；获得文凭 ❑ *But when I'd qualified and started teaching it was a different story.* 但是当我取得资格并开始从教时，情况就完全不同了。 **6** → see also **qualified**

Word Partnership *qualify* 的常用搭配：

V.	**chance to** qualify, **fail to** qualify **1 2 4 5**
PREP.	qualify **as *something*** **2** qualify **for *something*** **4**

★ **quali·ta·tive** /kwɒlɪteɪtɪv/ ADJ **Qualitative** means relating to the nature or standard of something, rather than to its quantity. 质的；品质上的 [FORMAL] ❑ *There are qualitative differences in the way children of different ages and adults think.* 不同年龄的儿童和成人在思维方式上有着质的差异。

qual·ity ♦♦◇ /kwɒlɪti/ (**qualities**) **1** N-UNCOUNT The **quality** of something is how good or bad it is. 质量 ❑ *Everyone can greatly improve the quality of life.* 人人都能大幅提高生活质量。 ❑ *Other services vary dramatically in quality.* 其它服务在质量上差异很大。 **2** N-UNCOUNT Something of **quality** is of a high standard. 优质 ❑ *...a college of quality.* …一所优质学院 **3** N-COUNT Someone's **qualities** are the good characteristics that they have which are part of their nature. 优良品质 ❑ *Sometimes you wonder where your kids get their good qualities.* 有时候你会奇怪，自己的孩子是在哪里养成那些优良品德的。 4 N-COUNT You can describe a particular characteristic of a person or thing as a **quality**. 个性；特性 ❑ *...a childlike quality.* …孩子般的个性

Thesaurus *quality* 另参见：
N. class, kind, position, rank, virtue, worth 1
aspect, attribute, characteristic, feature, trait 4

Word Partnership *quality* 的常用搭配：
N. **air** quality, quality **of life**, quality **of service**, **water** quality, quality **of work** 1
ADJ. **best/better/good** quality, **high/higher/highest** quality, **low** quality, **poor** quality, **top** quality 1

qual·ity con·trol N-UNCOUNT **Quality control** is the activity of checking that goods or services are of an acceptable standard. 质量控制；质量管理 [BUSINESS] ❑ *The message is you need better quality control.* 这条信息是说你们需要加强质量管理。

qual·ity time N-UNCOUNT If people spend **quality time** together, they spend a period of time relaxing or doing things that they both enjoy, and not worrying about work or other responsibilities. 开心时光（指放松娱乐的时间）[APPROVAL] ❑ *Today I can spend quality time with my family for a change.* 今天我可以调剂一下，与我的家人一起享受天伦之乐了。

qualm /kwɑm/ (**qualms**) N-COUNT If you have no **qualms** about doing something, you are not worried that it may be wrong in some way. 疑虑 ❑ *I have no qualms about recommending the same approach to other doctors.* 我对把同一方法推荐给其他医生没有任何疑虑。

Word Link *quant ≈ how much : quantify, quantitative, quantity*

★ **quan·ti·fy** /kwɒntɪfaɪ/ (**quantifies, quantifying, quantified**) V-T If you try to **quantify** something, you try to calculate how much of it there is. 确定…的数量 [usu with brd-neg] ❑ *It is difficult to quantify an exact figure as firms are reluctant to declare their losses.* 很难确定一个准确的数字，因为各家公司不愿公布它们的亏损情况。

★ **quan·ti·ta·tive** /kwɒntɪteɪtɪv/ ADJ **Quantitative** means relating to different sizes or amounts of things. 数量的；与数有关的 [FORMAL] ❑ *...the advantages of quantitative and qualitative research.* …定量和定性研究的优点。

quan·tity ♦◊◊ /kwɒntɪti/ (**quantities**) 1 N-VAR A **quantity** is an amount. 数量 ❑ *...a small quantity of water.* …少量的水。 2 N-UNCOUNT Things that are produced or available in **quantity** are produced or available in large amounts. 大量 ❑ *After some initial problems, acetone was successfully produced in quantity.* 解决了最初的一些问题后，成功地生产出了大量丙酮。 3 N-UNCOUNT You can use **quantity** to refer to the amount of something that there is, especially when you want to contrast it with its quality. (尤指相对于质量而言的) 数量 ❑ *...the less discerning drinker who prefers quantity to quality.* …重量不重质、识别力较差的饮酒者。 4 PHRASE If you say that someone or something is an **unknown quantity**, you mean that not much is known about what they are like or how they will behave. 未知量；未知数 ❑ *She had known Max for some years now, but he was still pretty much an unknown quantity.* 她现在认识马克斯也好几年了，但是他仍然是个大大的未知数。
→ see **mathematics**

quan·tum /kwɒntəm/ 1 ADJ In physics, **quantum** theory and **quantum** mechanics are concerned with the behavior of atomic particles. 量子的 [ADJ n] ❑ *Both quantum mechanics and chaos theory suggest a world constantly in flux.* 量子力学和混沌理论都指出世界处在不断变化中。 2 ADJ A **quantum leap** or **quantum jump** in something is a very great and sudden increase in its size, amount, or quality. (大小、数量的) 猛然剧增；(质量的) 突飞猛进 [ADJ n] ❑ *A vaccine which can halt this suffering represents a quantum leap in healthcare in this country.* 一种能终结这种苦楚的疫苗代表了该国在医疗保健方面的一次巨大进步。

▲ **quar·an·tine** /kwɔrəntin/ (**quarantines, quarantining, quarantined**) 1 N-UNCOUNT If a person or animal is **in quarantine**, they are being kept separate from other people or animals for a set period of time, usually because they have or may have a disease that could spread. 隔离 ❑ *She was sent home and put in quarantine.* 她被送回家实施隔离。 2 V-T If people or animals **are quarantined**, they are stopped from having contact with other people or animals. If a place **is quarantined**, people and animals are prevented from entering or leaving it. 对…进行隔离 [usu passive] ❑ *Dogs have to be quarantined for six months before they'll let them in.* 狗必须被隔离6个月后他们才会放它们进来。
→ see **illness**

quar·rel /kwɔrəl/ (**quarrels, quarreling** or **quarrelling, quarreled** or **quarrelled**) 1 N-COUNT A **quarrel** is an angry argument between two or more friends or family members. 争吵 ❑ *I had a terrible quarrel with my other brothers.* 我和其他几个兄弟大吵了一架。 2 V-RECIP When two or more people **quarrel**, they have an angry argument. 争论 ❑ *At one point we quarreled, over something silly.* 有一次，我们为了一件愚蠢的事争论起来。 3 N-SING If you say that you have no **quarrel** with someone or something, you mean that you do not disagree with them. 分歧 ❑ *We have no quarrel with the people of Spain or of any other country.* 我们和西班牙人民或其它任何国家的人民都没有分歧。 4 N-COUNT **Quarrels** between countries or groups of people are disagreements, which may be diplomatic or include fighting. 争端 [JOURNALISM] ❑ *New Zealand's quarrel with France over the Rainbow Warrior incident was formally ended.* 新西兰和法国之间关于"彩虹勇士号"事件的争端得已正式了结。

▲ **quar·ry** /kwɔri/ (**quarries, quarrying, quarried**) 1 N-COUNT A **quarry** is an area that is dug out from a piece of land or the side of a mountain in order to get stone or minerals. 采石场；矿场 ❑ *...an old limestone quarry.* …一处老的石灰岩开采场。 2 V-T When stone or minerals **are quarried** or when an area **is quarried** for them, they are removed from the area by digging, drilling, or using explosives. 开采；在…处开采 ❑ *The large limestone caves are also quarried for cement.* 这些大石灰岩洞也用来开采水泥原料。

Word Link *quart ≈ four : quart, quarter, quarterfinal*

★ **quart** /kwɔrt/ (**quarts**) N-COUNT A **quart** is a unit of volume that is equal to two pints. There are four quarts in a gallon. The abbreviation **qt.** is also used. 夸脱（容量单位，等于2品脱或1/4加仑）❑ *Pick up a quart of milk and a loaf of bread.* 买一夸脱牛奶和一条面包。

quar·ter ♦♦◊ /kwɔrtər/ (**quarters, quartering, quartered**) 1 FRACTION A **quarter** is one of four equal parts of something. 1/4 ❑ *A quarter of the residents are over 55 years old.* 1/4的居民在55岁以上。 ❑ *Prices have fallen by a quarter since January.* 自1月份以来，物价下降了1/4。 ● PREDET **Quarter** is also a predeterminer. 四分之一 ❑ *The largest asteroid is Ceres, which is about a quarter the size of the moon.* 最大的小行星是谷神星，其体积大约是月球的四分之一。 ● ADJ **Quarter** is also an adjective. 四分之一的 [ADJ n] ❑ *...the past quarter century.* …过去的四分之一世纪。 2 N-COUNT A **quarter** is an American or Canadian coin that is worth 25 cents. (美国或加拿大) 25分的硬币 ❑ *I dropped a quarter into the slot of the pay phone.* 我往付费电话的投币口里投了一枚25分的硬币。 3 N-COUNT A **quarter** is a fixed period of three months. Companies often divide their financial year into four quarters. 季度 ❑ *The group said results for the third quarter are due on October 29.* 该集团说第3季度的结果将于10月29日公布。 4 N-UNCOUNT When you are telling the time, you use **quarter** to talk about the fifteen minutes before or after an hour. For example, 8:15 is **quarter after** eight and 8:45 is a **quarter of** or a **quarter to** nine. You can also say that 8:15 is **quarter past** eight, and 8:45 is **quarter to** nine. 一刻钟 [also "a" N] ❑ *It was a quarter to six.* 当时是5:45。 5 V-T If you **quarter** something such as a fruit or a vegetable, you cut it into four roughly equal parts. 把…切成4等份 ❑ *Chop the mushrooms and quarter the tomatoes.* 把蘑菇剁碎，把番茄切成四块。 6 V-T If the number or size of something **is quartered**, it is reduced to about a quarter of its previous number or size. 把…减至四分之一 [usu passive] ❑ *The doses I suggested for adults could be halved or quartered.* 我建议的成人剂量可以减半或减至四分之一。 7 N-COUNT A particular **quarter** of a town is a part of the town where a particular group of people traditionally live or work. (某一人群生活或工作的) 地区 ❑ *We wandered through the Chinese quarter.* 我们在华人区逛了一圈。 8 PHRASE If you do something **at close quarters**, you do it very near to a particular person or thing. 接近地 ❑ *You can watch aircraft take off or land at close quarters.* 你可以近距离地观看飞机起飞或降落。

Word Partnership *quarter* 的常用搭配：
N. quarter **(of a) century**, quarter **(of a) pound** 1
ADJ. **first/fourth/second/third** quarter 3
PREP. **for the** quarter, **in the** quarter 3
quarter **after**, quarter **of**, quarter **past**, quarter **to** 4

quarter·final /kwɔrtərfaɪnᵊl/ (**quarterfinals**)
in BRIT, use **quarter-final**
N-COUNT A **quarterfinal** is one of the four matches in a competition which decides which four players or teams will compete in the semifinal. 1/4决赛 ❑ *The very least I'm looking for at the Open is to reach the quarterfinals.* 我期望在这次公开赛上最少进入1/4决赛。

★ **quar·ter·ly** /kwɔrtərli/ (**quarterlies**) 1 ADJ A **quarterly** event happens four times a year, at intervals of three months. 一年四次的；每季的 ❑ *...the latest Bank of Japan quarterly survey of 5,000 companies.* …日本银行对5000家公司最新的季度调查。● ADV **Quarterly** is also an adverb. 一年四次地；每季地 [ADV after v] ❑ *It makes no difference whether dividends are paid quarterly or annually.* 红利是按季度还是按年度支付没有区别。 2 N-COUNT A **quarterly** is a magazine that is published four times a year, at intervals of three months. 季刊 ❑ *The quarterly had been a forum for sound academic debate.* 这份季刊曾经是正统学术辩论的论坛。

quar·tet /kwɔrtɛt/ (**quartets**) 1 N-COUNT-COLL A **quartet** is a group of four people who play musical instruments or sing together. 四重奏乐团；四重唱小组 ❑ *...a string quartet.* …一个四重奏弦乐队。 2 N-COUNT A **quartet** is a piece of music for four instruments or four singers. 四重奏曲；四重唱曲 ❑ *The String Quartet No. 1 is an early work, composed in California in 1941.* 弦乐四重奏曲1号是一个早期作品，1941年创作于加利福尼亚。

★ **quartz** /kwɔrts/ N-UNCOUNT **Quartz** is a mineral in the form of a hard, shiny crystal. It is used in making electronic equipment and very accurate watches and clocks. 石英 ❑ *...a quartz crystal.* …一块石英晶体。

quash /kwɒʃ/ (**quashes, quashing, quashed**) 1 V-T If a court or someone in authority **quashes** a decision or judgment, they officially reject it. 撤销；废止 ❑ *The Appeal Court has quashed the convictions of all eleven people.* 上诉法院已经撤销了对所有11人的判决。 2 V-T If someone **quashes** rumors, they say or do something to demonstrate that the rumors are not true. 澄清（谣言）❑ *Graham attempted to quash rumors of growing discontent in the dressing room.* 格雷厄姆试图澄清化妆室里日益增长的不满情绪的谣言。 3 V-T To **quash** a rebellion or protest means to stop it, often in a violent way. 镇压；平息 ❑ *Troops were displaying an obvious reluctance to get involved in quashing demonstrations.* 部队明确表示不愿卷入镇压示威活动。

▲ **quay** /ki/ (**quays**) N-COUNT A **quay** is a long platform beside the sea or a river where boats can be tied up and loaded or unloaded. 码头 ❑ *Jack and Stephen were waiting for them on the quay.* 杰克和斯蒂芬正在码头等他们。

queen ♦♦◊ /kwin/ (**queens**) 1 N-TITLE; N-COUNT A **queen** is a woman who rules a country as its monarch. 女王 ❑ *...Queen Victoria.* …维多利亚女王。 2 N-TITLE; N-COUNT A **queen** is a woman who is married to a king. 王后 ❑ *The king and queen had fled.* 国王和王后已经逃跑。 3 N-COUNT If you refer to a woman as **the queen of** a particular activity, you mean that she is well-known for being very good at it. 出众的女子 ❑ *...the queen of crime writing.* …犯罪小说之王。 4 N-COUNT A **queen** is a male homosexual who dresses and speaks rather like a woman. 男同性恋中的女性角色 [INFORMAL] 5 N-COUNT In chess, the **queen** is the most powerful piece. It can be moved in any direction. （国际象棋中的）后 ❑ *Chris will either have to take his queen's knight and lose his own knight, or he'll lose a rook.* 克里斯要么吃掉他的后翼马而失去自己的马，要么失去一个车。 6 N-COUNT A **queen** is a playing card with a picture of a queen on it. （纸牌中的）王后 ❑ *...the queen of spades.* …黑桃王后。 7 N-COUNT A **queen** or a **queen bee** is a large female bee which can lay eggs. 蜂王 ❑ *Glass hives offer a close-up view of the bees at work, with the queen bee in each hive marked by a white dot.* 玻璃蜂房可以近距离观察工作中的蜜蜂，每个蜂房的蜂王都被打上白点标记。
→ see **chess**

★ **queer** /kwɪər/ (**queerer, queerest, queers**) 1 ADJ Something that is **queer** is strange. 奇怪的 [OLD-FASHIONED] ❑ *If you ask me, there's something kind of queer going on.* 如果问起来的话，是有点奇怪。 2 N-COUNT People sometimes call homosexual men **queers**. 男同性恋 ● ADJ **Queer** is also an adjective. 男同性恋的 [INFORMAL, OFFENSIVE] ❑ *...America's first queer country music star.* …美国头号男同性恋、乡村乐手。

▲ **quell** /kwɛl/ (**quells, quelling, quelled**) 1 V-T To **quell** opposition or violent behavior means to stop it. 镇压 ❑ *Troops eventually quelled the unrest.* 部队最终镇压了动乱。 2 V-T If you **quell** an unpleasant feeling such as fear or anger, you stop yourself or other people from having that feeling. 消除（恐惧、愤怒等）❑ *The government is trying to quell fears of a looming oil crisis.* 该政府正努力消除日益临近的石油危机而带来的恐惧。

★ **quench** /kwɛntʃ/ (**quenches, quenching, quenched**) V-T If someone who is thirsty **quenches** their **thirst**, they lose their thirst by having a drink. （通过喝水）解（渴）❑ *He stopped to quench his thirst at a stream.* 他停在一条小溪边喝水解渴。

▲ **que·ry** /kwɪəri/ (**queries, querying, queried**) 1 N-COUNT A **query** is a question, especially one that you ask an organization, publication, or expert. 疑问 ❑ *If you have any queries about this insurance, please contact our call center.* 如果你对此项保险有任何疑问，请联系我们的呼叫中心。 2 V-T If you **query** something, you check it by asking about it because you are not sure if it is correct. 对…提出疑问 ❑ *It's got a number you can call to query your bill.* 你可以拨打一个号码，对账单提出质疑。 3 V-T To **query** means to ask a question. 询问 ❑ *"Is there something else?" Ray queried as Helen stopped speaking.* 海伦话音刚落，雷便问道："还有别的什么吗？"

quest /kwɛst/ (**quests**) 1 N-COUNT A **quest** is a long and difficult search for something. （长久而艰难的）搜寻；探求 [LITERARY or HUMOROUS] ❑ *My quest for a better bank continues.* 我继续在搜寻一家更好的银行。 ❑ *...the quest for the Holy Grail.* …对圣杯的探求 ● PHRASE If you go **in quest of** something, you try to find or obtain it. 寻找；寻求 2 V-I If you **are questing for** something, you are searching for it. 搜寻；探求 [usu cont] [LITERARY] ❑ *He had been questing for religious belief from an early age.* 他从早年开始就一直在寻求宗教信仰。 ❑ *...his questing mind and boundless enthusiasm.* …他的探索型头脑和无限的热情

ques·tion ♦♦♦ /kwɛstʃᵊn/ (**questions, questioning, questioned**)
1 N-COUNT A **question** is something that you say or write in order to ask a person about something. 问题 ❑ *They asked a lot of questions about China.* 他们问了许多有关中国的问题。 2 V-T If you **question** someone, you ask them a lot of questions about something. 询问 ❑ *This led the therapist to question Jim about his parents and their marriage.* 这让治疗师询问起吉姆关于其父母以及他们的婚姻情况。 ● **ques·tion·ing** N-UNCOUNT 询问 ❑ *The police have detained thirty-two people for questioning.* 警方拘留了32个人进行审问。 3 V-T If you **question** something, you have or express doubts about whether it is true, reasonable, or worthwhile. 怀疑 ❑ *It never occurs to them to question the doctor's decisions.* 他们从来没有想到去怀疑那个医生的决定。 4 N-SING If you say that there is some **question** about something, you mean that there is doubt or uncertainty about it. If something is **in question** or has been **called into question**, doubt or uncertainty has been expressed about it. 疑问；不确定 ❑ *There's no question about their success.* 他们毫无疑问会成功。 ❑ *Her political future is in question.* 她的政治前途还是个疑问。 ❑ *My integrity has been called into question by people who have never spoken to me.* 我的正直品行竟遭到素昧平生之人的质疑。 5 N-COUNT A **question** is a problem, matter, or point which needs to be considered. （需考虑的）问题 ❑ *But the whole question of aid is a tricky political one.* 但是整个援助问题是个棘手的政治问题。 6 N-COUNT The **questions** on an examination are the problems that test your knowledge or ability. 试题 ❑ *That question did come up on the test.* 那道题真的在试卷上出现了。 7 → see also **questioning** 8 PHRASE The person, thing, or time **in question** is one which you have just been talking about or which is relevant. 正被提及的；有关的 ❑ *Add up all the income you've received over the period in question.* 把相关时期内你获得的所有收入加起来。 9 PHRASE If you say that something is **out of the question**, you are emphasizing that it is completely impossible or unacceptable. 完全不可能的；不能接受的 [EMPHASIS] ❑ *For the homeless, private medical care is simply out of the question.* 对于无家可归的人来说，私人医疗保健简直就是天方夜谭。 10 PHRASE If you **pop the question**, you ask someone to marry you. 求婚 [INFORMAL] ❑ *Stuart got serious quickly and popped the question six months later.* 斯图尔特很快认真起来，6个月后就求婚了。 11 PHRASE If you say **there is no question of** something happening, you are emphasizing that it is not going to happen. …是不可能的 [EMPHASIS] ❑ *There was no question of my blaming Janet.* 我不可能责备珍妮特。

Thesaurus *question* 另参见：
N. query 1
V. ask, inquire; *(ant.)* answer 2
doubt 3

Word Partnership *question* 的常用搭配：

V. **answer** a question, **ask** a question, **beg the** question, **pose** a question, **raise** a question 1
N. **answer/response to** a question 1
ADJ. **difficult** question, **good** question, **important** question 1

ques·tion·able /kwɛstʃənəbᵊl/ ADJ If you say that something is **questionable**, you mean that it is not completely honest, reasonable, or acceptable. 可疑的；不合理的；不能接受的 [FORMAL] ❑ *He has been dogged by allegations of questionable business practices.* 他一直被有可疑商业行为的传言困扰着。

Thesaurus *questionable* 另参见：
ADJ. doubtful, dubious, problematic, uncertain

ques·tion·ing /kwɛstʃənɪŋ/ 1 ADJ If someone has a **questioning** expression on their face, they look as if they want to know the answer to a question. 询问的（表情）[ADJ n] [WRITTEN] ❑ *He raised a questioning eyebrow.* 他探询地扬起眉毛。 2 → see also **question**

ques·tion mark (**question marks**) 1 N-COUNT A **question mark** is the punctuation mark ? which is used in writing at the end of a question. 问号 ❑ *Who invented the question mark?* 谁发明了问号？ 2 N-COUNT If there is doubt or uncertainty about something, you can say that there is a **question mark over** it. 疑问；不确定性 ❑ *There are bound to be question marks over his future.* 他的未来肯定会有很多问号。

★ **ques·tion·naire** /kwɛstʃənɛər/ (**questionnaires**) N-COUNT A **questionnaire** is a written list of questions which are answered by a lot of people in order to provide information for a report or a survey. 调查问卷 ❑ *Teachers will be asked to fill in a questionnaire.* 教师们将被要求填写一份调查问卷。
→ see **census**

queue /kyu/ (**queues, queuing, queued**)

Queueing can also be used as the continuous form.

1 N-COUNT A **queue** is a list of computer tasks which will be done in order. 队列（指等待计算机逐个处理的任务列表）[COMPUTING] ❑ *Your print job has already been sent from your PC to the network print queue.* 你的打印任务已经从你的个人电脑输送到网络打印队列了。 2 V-T To **queue** a number of computer tasks means to arrange them to be done in order. 将（计算机任务）排序 [COMPUTING] 3 N-COUNT A **queue** is a line of people or vehicles that are waiting for something. （等候的）一队人；一列车辆 [mainly BRIT]

in AM, usually use **line**

4 N-COUNT If you say there is a **queue of** people who want to do or have something, you mean that a lot of people are waiting for an opportunity to do it or have it. 众多 [mainly BRIT]

in AM, usually use **line**

5 V-I When people **queue**, they stand in a line waiting for something. 排队等候 ● PHRASAL VERB **Queue up** means the same as **queue**. 排队等候 [mainly BRIT]

in AM, usually use **stand in line, line up**

quib·ble /kwɪbᵊl/ (**quibbles, quibbling, quibbled**) 1 V-RECIP When people **quibble over** a small matter, they argue about it even though it is not important. （为琐事）争辩 ❑ *Lawmakers spent the day quibbling over the final wording of the resolution.* 立法者们花了一天争辩决议的最后措词。 2 N-COUNT A **quibble** is a small and unimportant complaint about something. 微不足道的抱怨 ❑ *These are minor quibbles.* 这都是些微不足道的抱怨。

quick ♦♦♦ /kwɪk/ (**quicker, quickest**) 1 ADJ Someone or something that is **quick** moves or does things with great speed. 快的；迅速的 ❑ *You'll have to be quick. The flight leaves in about three hours.* 你得快点了，那个航班大约3小时后就起飞了。 ● **quick·ly** ADV 快地；迅速地 [ADV with v] ❑ *Cussane worked quickly and methodically.* 丘萨恩干得快而且有条不紊。 ● **quick·ness** N-UNCOUNT 快；迅速 ❑ *...the natural quickness of his mind.* …他天生敏捷的思维。 2 ADV **Quicker** is sometimes used to mean "at a greater speed," and **quickest** to mean "at the greatest speed." **Quick** is sometimes used to mean "with great speed." Some people consider this to be non-standard. 有时分别用**quick**、**quicker**和**quickest**表示"以很快的速度"，"以更快的速度"和"以最快的速度"，但有人认为此用法并不规范 [ADV after v] [INFORMAL] ❑ *Warm the sugar slightly first to make it dissolve quicker.* 首先把糖微微加热让它更快地溶化。 3 ADJ Something that is **quick** takes or lasts only a short time. 短暂的 ❑ *He took one last quick look around the room.* 他朝房间匆匆扫了最后一眼。 ● **quick·ly** ADV 短暂地 [ADV with v] ❑ *You can get in shape quite quickly and easily.* 你能又快又容易地恢复好身段。 4 ADJ **Quick** means happening without delay or with very little delay. 立刻发生的；很快发生的 ❑ *Officials played down any hope for a quick end to the bloodshed.* 官员们对快速了结这场流血冲突不抱太大希望。 ● **quick·ly** ADV 立刻 [ADV with v] ❑ *We need to get it back as quickly as possible.* 我们需要尽快把它拿回来。 5 ADV **Quick** is sometimes used to mean "with very little delay." 马上 [ADV after v] [INFORMAL] ❑ *I got away as quick as I could.* 我尽快地离开了。 6 ADJ If you are **quick to** do something, you do not hesitate to do it. 毫不迟疑的 [v-link ADJ] ❑ *Mark says the ideas are Katie's own, and is quick to praise her talent.* 马克说这些主意都是凯蒂自己的，接着便毫不迟疑地称赞她的才干。 7 ADJ If someone has a **quick** temper, they are easily made angry. （性情）暴躁的；易怒的 [ADJ n] ❑ *He readily admitted to the interviewer that he had a quick temper, with a tendency toward violence.* 他欣然向采访者承认他性情暴躁，有暴力倾向。 8 **quick as a flash** → see **flash**

Thesaurus *quick* 另参见：
ADJ. brisk, fast, rapid, speedy, swift; (*ant.*) slow 1

Word Partnership *quick* 的常用搭配：

N. quick **learner** 1
quick **glance**, quick **kiss**, quick **look**, quick **question**, quick **smile** 3
quick **action**, quick **profit**, quick **response**, quick **start**, quick **thinking** 4
V. **think** quick 5

quick·en /kwɪkən/ (**quickens, quickening, quickened**) V-T/V-I If something **quickens** or if you **quicken** it, it becomes faster or moves at a greater speed. 加快 ❑ *Ann's pulse quickened in alarm.* 安的脉搏因惊恐而加快了。

quick fix (**quick fixes**) N-COUNT If you refer to a **quick fix** to a problem, you mean a way of solving a problem that is easy but temporary or inadequate. （不完善的）应急解决办法；权宜之计 [DISAPPROVAL] ❑ *Any tax measures enacted now as a quick fix would only be reversed in a few years when the economy picks up.* 现在作为权宜之计颁布的任何税收措施等几年后经济好转时就会被撤消。

▲ **quid** /kwɪd/ (**quid**) N-COUNT A **quid** is a pound in money. 英镑 [BRIT, INFORMAL] ❑ *It cost him five hundred quid.* 它花费了他500英镑。

qui·et ♦♦◊ /kwaɪɪt/ (**quieter, quietest, quiets, quieting, quieted**) 1 ADJ Someone or something that is **quiet** makes only a small amount of noise. 轻声的；安静的 ❑ *Tania kept the children reasonably quiet and contented.* 塔妮娅把孩子们料理得安心而满足。 ● **qui·et·ly** ADV 轻声地；安静地 [ADV with v] ❑ *"This is goodbye, isn't it?" she said quietly.* "这就算告别了，不是吗？"她轻声地说道。 ● **qui·et·ness** N-UNCOUNT 轻声；安静 ❑ *...the smoothness and quietness of the flight.* …飞行的平稳和安静。 2 ADJ If a place is **quiet**, there is very little noise there. 寂静的 ❑ *She was received in a small, quiet office.* 她在一间寂静的小办公室里受到接见。 ● **qui·et·ness** N-UNCOUNT 寂静 ❑ *I miss the quietness of the countryside.* 我怀念农村的寂静。 3 ADJ If a place, situation, or time is **quiet**, there is no excitement, activity, or trouble. 平静的；清静的 ❑ *...a quiet rural backwater.* …一个清静的乡间隐蔽处。 ● **qui·et·ly** ADV 平静地；清静地 [ADV with v] ❑ *His most prized time, though, will be spent quietly on his farm.* 不过，他最珍贵的时光将在自己的农场上平静地度过。 ● **qui·et·ness** N-UNCOUNT 平静；清静 ❑ *He stretched, taking pleasure in the quietness of the morning hour.* 他伸了伸懒腰，享受着清晨时分的宁静。 4 N-UNCOUNT **Quiet** is silence. 安静 ❑ *He called for quiet and announced that the next song was in our honor.* 他要求静下来，并宣布下一首歌是献给我们的。 5 ADJ If you are **quiet**, you are not saying anything. 不出声的 [v-link ADJ] ❑ *I told them to be quiet and go to sleep.* 我叫他们不要说话，去睡觉。 ● **qui·et·ly** ADV 不出声地 [ADV with v] ❑ *Amy stood quietly in the doorway watching him.* 艾米一声不响地站在门口看着他。 6 ADJ A **quiet** person behaves in a calm way and is not easily made angry or upset. 冷静的；不易动怒的 ❑ *He's a nice quiet man.* 他是个冷静的好男人。 7 V-T/V-I If someone or something **quiets** or if you **quiet** them, they become less noisy, less active, or silent. 使安静；安静 [mainly AM]

in BRIT, usually use **quieten**

❑ *The wind dropped and the sea quieted.* 风势减弱了，大海平静下来。

8 V-T To **quiet** fears or complaints means to persuade people that there is no good reason for them. 消除(恐惧); 平息(抱怨) [mainly AM]

in BRIT, usually use **quieten**

❑ *Supporters of the constitution had to quiet fears that aristocrats plotted to steal the fruits of the revolution.* 宪法的支持者们不得不消除人们对贵族阴谋窃取革命成果的恐惧。 **9** PHRASE If you **keep quiet about** something or **keep** something **quiet**, you do not say anything about it. 保守秘密 ❑ *I told her to keep quiet about it.* 我叫她对此保守秘密。 **10** PHRASE If something is done **on the quiet**, it is done secretly or in such a way that people do not notice it. 秘密地 ❑ *She'd promised to give him driving lessons, on the quiet, when no one could see.* 她答应在无人看见时秘密地给他上驾驶课。

Thesaurus *quiet* 另参见:
ADJ. low, silent, soft; (ant.) loud **1**
calm, serene, tranquil; (ant.) busy **3** **6**
N. calm, hush, lull **4**
V. calm, hush, soothe; (ant.) agitate, excite, stir up **7** **8**

Word Partnership *quiet* 的常用搭配:
ADV. **real** quiet, **relatively** quiet, **too** quiet, **very** quiet **1** – **3** **5**
V. **be** quiet, **keep** quiet **1** **5**
N. quiet **neighborhood/street**, quiet **place/spot** **2** – **4**
quiet **day/evening/night**, quiet **life** **3**
peace and quiet **4**

qui·et·en /kwaɪəᵗn/ [BRIT] → see **quiet 7, 8**

▲ **quilt** /kwɪlt/ (**quilts, quilting, quilted**) **1** N-COUNT A **quilt** is a bed cover made by sewing layers of cloth together, usually with different colors sewn together to make a design. 被子 ❑ *...an old patchwork quilt.* …一条旧的拼布被子。 **2** N-COUNT A **quilt** is the same as a **comforter**. (羽绒或其他类似材料填充的) 夹被 [mainly BRIT] **3** V-T/V-I If you **quilt**, or if you **quilt** a piece of fabric, you make a quilt. 缝制(织物、被子); 缝制被子 ❑ *Maggie knows how to quilt.* 玛吉知道怎样缝制被子。 ❑ *Quilting a bed cover can be laborious.* 缝制一个床罩会很费力的。
→ see Word Web: **quilt**

quip /kwɪp/ (**quips**) N-COUNT A **quip** is a remark that is intended be amusing or clever. 俏皮话; 妙语 [WRITTEN] ❑ *The commentators make endless quips about the players' appearance.* 解说员们对球员们的外貌没完没了地说着俏皮话。

quirk /kwɜrk/ (**quirks**) **1** N-COUNT A **quirk** is something unusual or interesting that happens by chance. (偶然发生的) 怪事; 趣事 ❑ *By a tantalizing quirk of fate, the pair have been drawn to meet in the first round of the championship.* 由于命运的捉弄，这对选手被抽中在锦标赛的第一轮相遇。 **2** N-COUNT A **quirk** is a habit or aspect of a person's character which is odd or unusual. 怪癖; 古怪的性格 ❑ *Brown was always fascinated by the quirks and foibles of people in everyday situations.* 布朗总是着迷于日常环境中人们的古怪性格和怪癖。

quirky /kwɜrki/ (**quirkier, quirkiest**) ADJ Something or someone that is **quirky** is odd or unpredictable in their appearance, character, or behavior. (外貌、性格或行为) 古怪的; 难料的 ❑ *We've developed a reputation for being quirky and original.* 我们因古怪、新颖而获得了声誉。 ● **quirki·ness** N-UNCOUNT (外貌、性格或行为的) 古怪; 难料 ❑ *You will probably notice an element of quirkiness in his behavior.* 你很可能会注意到他行为的古怪之处。

quit /kwɪt/ (**quits, quitting**)

The form **quit** is used in the present tense and is the past tense and past participle.

1 V-T/V-I If you **quit**, or **quit** your job, you choose to leave it. 辞去(工作); 辞职 [INFORMAL] ❑ *He quit his job as an office boy.* 他辞去了办公室勤杂员的工作。 **2** V-T If you **quit** an activity or **quit** doing something, you stop doing it. 停止 [mainly AM] ❑ *A nicotine spray can help smokers quit the habit.* 一种尼古丁喷剂可以帮助吸烟者戒烟。 ❑ *Quit acting like you didn't know.* 别装得像你不知道似的。 ❑ *Quit it! That hurts!* 戒掉它吧！这东西害人！ **3** V-T If you **quit** a place, you leave it completely and do not go back to it. 彻底离开 ❑ *Science fiction writers have long dreamed that humans might one day quit the earth to colonize other planets.* 科幻小说作家们长期以来一直梦想着人类有一天可以离开地球移居到其它星球上。 **4** PHRASE If you say that you are going to **call it quits**, you mean that you have decided to stop doing something or being involved in something. 叫停 ❑ *They raised $630,000 through listener donations, and then called it quits.* 他们通过听众募捐筹集到了63万美元，之后就叫停了。

Thesaurus *quit* 另参见:
V. resign, vacate **1**
break off, cease, discontinue **2**
abandon, leave **3**

quite ♦♦♦ /kwaɪt/ **1** ADV You use **quite** to indicate that something is the case to a fairly great extent. **Quite** is less emphatic than "very" and "extremely." 相当; 颇 [VAGUENESS] ❑ *I felt quite bitter about it at the time.* 当时我对此感到相当痛苦。 ❑ *Well, actually it requires quite a bit of work and research.* 呃，实际上这需要相当多的工作和研究。 **2** ADV You use **quite** to emphasize what you are saying. 用于强调 [EMPHASIS] ❑ *It is quite clear that we were firing in self defense.* 非常清楚，我们当时是自卫还击。 ❑ *My position is quite different.* 我的立场完全不同。 **3** ADV You use **quite** after a negative to make what you are saying weaker or less definite. 用于否定词之后表示语气较弱或不确定 [VAGUENESS] ❑ *Something here is not quite right.* 这儿有什么不太对劲儿。 **4** PREDET You use **quite** in front of a noun group to emphasize that a person or thing is very impressive or unusual. 出众的; 不同寻常的 [PREDET "a" n] [APPROVAL] ❑ *"Oh, he's quite a character," Sean replied.* "哦，他真是一个不同寻常的人。"肖恩答道。 **5** ADV You can say **quite** to express your agreement with someone. 正是这样; 可不是嘛 [ADV as reply] [mainly BRIT, SPOKEN, FORMULAE] ❑ *"It's your choice isn't it."—"Quite."* "这是你的选择，不是吗？"——"可不是嘛。"

Thesaurus *quite* 另参见:
ADV. entirely, extremely, wholly **2**

quiv·er /kwɪvər/ (**quivers, quivering, quivered**) **1** V-I If something **quivers**, it shakes with very small movements. 颤抖 ❑ *Her bottom lip quivered and big tears rolled down her cheeks.* 她的下嘴唇颤动着，大滴大滴的泪珠顺着脸颊流了下来。 **2** V-I If you say that someone or their voice **is quivering with** an emotion such as rage or excitement, you mean that they are strongly affected by this emotion and show it in their appearance or voice. (人或声音因愤怒、激动而) 颤抖 ❑ *Cooper arrived, quivering with rage.* 库珀来了，气得浑身发抖。 ● N-COUNT **Quiver** is also a noun. 颤抖 ❑ *I recognized it instantly and felt a quiver of panic.* 我立刻认出它了，感到一阵惊恐的颤抖。

quiz /kwɪz/ (**quizzes, quizzing, quizzed**) **1** N-COUNT A **quiz** is a test, game, or competition in which someone tests your

Word Web quilt

The Hmong* tribes are famous for their colorful **quilts**. Many people think of a quilt as a bed covering. However, these **textiles** feature pictures that tell stories about the people who made them. A favorite story shows how the Hmong fled from China to southeast Asia in the early 1800s. The story sometimes shows the quiltmaker's arrival in a new country. The seamstress **sews** small pieces of colorful **fabric** together to make the **design**. The needlework is very elaborate. It includes cross-stitching, **embroidery**, and appliqué. A common border **pattern** is a design that represents mountains—the Hmong's original home.

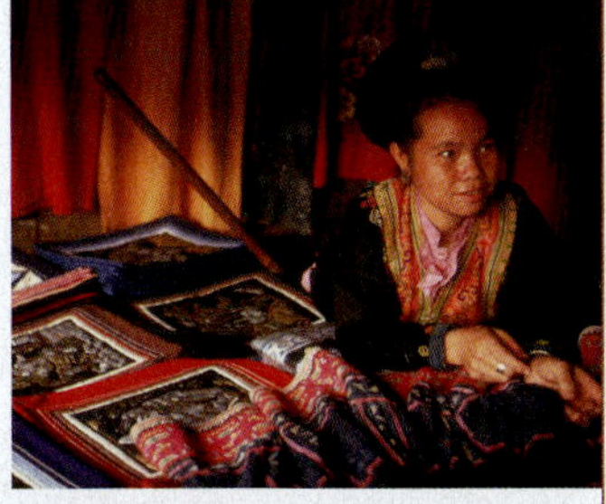

Hmong: a group of people who live in the mountains of China, Vietnam, Laos, and Thailand.

q

knowledge by asking you questions. 测试；知识竞赛 ❑ *We'll have a quiz at the end of class.* 下课前我们将进行一次测试。 2 V-T If you **are quizzed** by someone about something, they ask you questions about it. 询问 ❑ *He was quizzed about his income, debts and eligibility for financial aid.* 他被询问了收入、债务以及经济补助资格等。

★ **quo·ta** /kwoʊtə/ (**quotas**) 1 N-COUNT A **quota** is the limited number or quantity of something which is officially allowed. 限额 ❑ *The quota of four tickets per person had been reduced to two.* 每人4张票的限额已减少到了2张。 2 N-COUNT A **quota** is a fixed maximum or minimum proportion of people from a particular group who are allowed to do something, such as come and live in a country or work for the government. 配额 ❑ *The bill would force employers to adopt a quota system when recruiting workers.* 该法案将迫使雇主们在录用工人时采取配额制。 3 N-COUNT Someone's **quota of** something is their expected or deserved share of it. (预期或应得的)份额 ❑ *They have the usual quota of human weaknesses, no doubt.* 他们毫无疑问也有人类通常的弱点。

quo·ta·tion /kwoʊteɪʃn/ (**quotations**) 1 N-COUNT A **quotation** is a sentence or phrase taken from a book, poem, speech, or play, which is repeated by someone else. 引文；引语 ❑ *He illustrated his argument with quotations from Martin Luther King Jr.* 他引用小马丁·路德·金的话阐述了自己的观点。 2 N-COUNT When someone gives you a **quotation**, they tell you how much they will charge to do a particular piece of work. 报价 ❑ *Get several written quotations and check exactly what's included in the cost.* 弄几份书面报价来，并查清楚成本中包含哪些内容。

quo·ta·tion mark (**quotation marks**) N-COUNT **Quotation marks** are punctuation marks that are used in writing to show where speech or a quotation begins and ends. They are usually written or printed as "...". 引号 ❑ *Make sure you have quotation marks at both the beginning and the end of quotes.* 务必在引文的开始和结尾处加上引号。

quote ♦♦◇ /kwoʊt/ (**quotes, quoting, quoted**) 1 V-T/V-I If you **quote** someone as saying something, you repeat what they have written or said. 引用；引述 ❑ *He quoted Mr. Polay as saying that peace negotiations were already underway.* 他引用波利先生的话说，和平谈判已在进行。 ❑ *I gave the letter to the local press and they quoted from it.* 我把信交给了当地的报社，他们从中引用了内容。 2 N-COUNT A **quote from** a book, poem, play, or speech is a passage or phrase from it. 引文；引语 ❑ *The paper starts its editorial comment with a quote from an unnamed member of the House.* 该报社论以一位匿名议员的引语展开。 3 V-T If you **quote** something such as a law or a fact, you state it because it supports what you are saying. 引用(法律条款、事实等) ❑ *The Congresswoman quoted statistics saying that the standard of living of the poorest people had fallen.* 这位女国会议员援引统计数据说，赤贫人口的生活水平已经下降。 4 V-T If someone **quotes** a price **for** doing something, they say how much money they would charge you for a service they are offering or a for a job that you want them to do. 报(价) ❑ *A travel agent quoted her $260 for a flight from Boston to New Jersey.* 一家旅行社给她从波士顿到新泽西的航班报价$260。 5 N-COUNT A **quote for** a piece of work is the price that someone says they will charge you to do the work. 报价 ❑ *Always get a written quote for any repairs needed.* 对任何所需的修理都索取一份书面报价。 6 V-T PASSIVE If a company's shares, a substance, or a currency **is quoted** at a particular price, that is its current market price. 报(公司股票、物质、货币)的牌价 [BUSINESS] ❑ *In early trading in Hong Kong yesterday, gold was quoted at $368.20 an ounce.* 昨天在香港早市的交易中，黄金被报出每盎司$368.20的牌价。 7 N-PLURAL **Quotes** are the same as **quotation marks.** 引号 [INFORMAL] ❑ *The word "remembered" is in quotes.* "**remembered**"一词是打了引号的。

Thesaurus *quote* 另参见：
V. cite, recite, repeat, retell 1 3
N. estimate, price 5

Quran /kɔrɑn, -ræn, kʊ-/ also **Koran, Qur'an** N-PROPER **The Quran** is the holy book on which the religion of Islam is based. (伊斯兰教的)《古兰经》 ❑ *Still a devout Muslim, Lindh reads the Quran and prays every day.* 林德仍是一名虔诚的穆斯林，每天诵读《古兰经》并且做祷告。

QWER·TY /kwɜrti/ also **Qwerty, qwerty** ADJ A **QWERTY** keyboard on a typewriter or computer is the standard English language keyboard, on which the top line of keys begins with the letters q, w, e, r, t, and y. (首行以**q**，**w**，**e**，**r**，**t**和**y**开头的) 标准键盘 [ADJ n] ❑ *You can enter text on the QWERTY keyboard or simply write on the screen.* 你可以用标准键盘输入文本或者直接写在屏幕上。

Q

Rr

R also **r** /ɑr/ (**R's, r's**) N-VAR **R** is the eighteenth letter of the English alphabet. 英语字母表的第18个字母

rab·bi /ræbaɪ/ (**rabbis**) N-COUNT; N-TITLE A **rabbi** is a Jewish religious leader, usually one who is in charge of a synagogue, one who is qualified to teach Judaism, or one who is an expert on Jewish law. 拉比(犹太宗教领袖，尤指有资格传授犹太教义，或精于犹太法典之犹太教堂主管)

rab·bit /ræbɪt/ (**rabbits**) N-COUNT A **rabbit** is a small, furry animal with long ears. Rabbits are sometimes kept as pets, or live wild in holes in the ground. 兔子

rab·ble /ræbᵊl/ N-SING A **rabble** is a crowd of noisy people who seem likely to cause trouble. 乌合之众 ❑ *He seems to attract a rabble of supporters more loyal to the man than to the cause.* 他似乎吸引了一群忠于他个人超过忠于事业的乱糟糟的拥护者。

ra·bies /reɪbiz/ N-UNCOUNT **Rabies** is a serious disease that causes people and animals to go mad and die. 狂犬病

race ♦♦♦ /reɪs/ (**races, racing, raced**) **1** N-COUNT A **race** is a competition to see who is the fastest, for example in running, swimming, or driving. (速度的) 比赛 ❑ *The women's race was won by the only American in the field, Patti Sue Plumer.* 女子赛跑被田赛场上惟一的一名美国人帕蒂·休·普卢默赢得了。 **2** V-T/V-I If you **race**, you take part in a race. 参赛; 与…比赛 ❑ *In the 10 years I raced in Europe, 30 drivers were killed.* 我在欧洲参赛的10年间，有30名车手身亡。 ❑ *We raced them to the summit.* 我们和他们一路赛跑到最高点。 **3** N-PLURAL **The races** are a series of horse races that are held in a particular place on a particular day. People go to watch and to bet on which horse will win. 赛马会 ❑ *The high point of this trip was a day at the races.* 这次旅行的高潮是在赛马会上度过的一天。 **4** N-COUNT A **race** is a situation in which people or organizations compete with each other for power or control. 竞争 ❑ *The race for the White House begins in earnest today.* 为入主白宫而展开的竞选今天正式开始。 **5** → see also **rat race** **6** N-VAR A **race** is one of the major groups which human beings can be divided into according to their physical features, such as the color of their skin. 种族 ❑ *The college welcomes students of all races, faiths, and nationalities.* 该学院欢迎来自各种族、有各种宗教信仰和国籍的学生。 **7** → see also **human race, race relations** **8** V-I If you **race** somewhere, you go there as quickly as possible. 疾走 ❑ *He raced across town to the State House building.* 他急速穿过市区去州议会大厦。 **9** V-I If something **races** toward a particular state or position, it moves very fast toward that state or position. (向某种状态或位置) 快速发展; 快速运动 ❑ *Do they realize we are racing toward complete economic collapse?* 他们是否意识到我们正迅速走向彻底的经济崩溃? **10** V-T If you **race** a vehicle or animal, you prepare it for races and make it take part in races. 使参赛 (多指车辆或动物) ❑ *He still raced sports cars as often as he could.* 他仍然尽可能频繁地开着跑车参加比赛。 **11** V-I If your mind **races**, or if thoughts **race** through your mind, you think very fast about something, especially when you are in a difficult or dangerous situation. (尤指在面临困难或危险时大脑) 急速运转 ❑ *I made sure I sounded calm but my mind was racing.* 我确保自己听起来很平静，但大脑却在急速运转。 **12** V-I If your heart **races**, it beats very quickly because you are excited or afraid. (心脏因激动或恐惧而) 急速跳动 ❑ *Her heart raced uncontrollably.* 她的心脏难以控制地急速跳动起来。 **13** → see also **racing** **14** PHRASE You describe a situation as a **race against time** when you have to work very fast in order to do something before a particular time, or before another thing happens. 与时间赛跑 ❑ *A spokesman said the rescue operation was a race against time.* 一位发言人说该营救工作是在与时间赛跑。

★ **race·course** /reɪskɔrs/ (**racecourses**) N-COUNT A **racecourse** is a track on which horses race. 赛马场; 赛马跑道 [mainly BRIT]

in AM, usually use **racetrack**

race·horse /reɪshɔrs/ (**racehorses**) N-COUNT A **racehorse** is a horse that is trained to run in races. 赛马

rac·er /reɪsər/ (**racers**) **1** N-COUNT A **racer** is a person or animal that takes part in races. 参赛者; 参赛动物 ❑ *Tim Powell is a former champion powerboat racer.* 蒂姆·鲍威尔曾是汽艇比赛的冠军。 **2** N-COUNT A **racer** is a vehicle such as a car or bicycle that is designed to be used in races and therefore travels fast. (比赛用的) 车辆; 赛艇 ❑ *...everything from small boats to ocean racers.* …从小船到海洋赛艇等所有的一切。

race re·la·tions N-PLURAL **Race relations** are the ways in which people of different races living together in the same community behave toward one another. 种族关系 ❑ *...a breakdown in race relations.* …一次种族关系的破裂。

race·track /reɪstræk/ (**racetracks**) also **race track** **1** N-COUNT A **racetrack** is a track on which horses race. 赛马跑道; 赛马场 [AM]

in BRIT, use **racecourse**

❑ *...the Breeders' Cup, run Oct. 26 at Arlington racetrack near Chicago.* …育马者杯比赛，于10月26日在芝加哥附近的阿灵顿赛马场举行。 **2** N-COUNT A **racetrack** is a track for races, for example car or bicycle races. 赛车道; 赛车场 ❑ *...the sound of cars roaring around a racetrack.* …汽车围绕赛车跑道奔驰的轰鸣声。

race·way /reɪsweɪ/ (**raceways**) N-IN-NAMES A **raceway** is a racetrack. 赛场; 赛道 ❑ *...the garage area of Pocono Raceway.* …波科诺赛车场的车库区域。

ra·cial ♦◇◇ /reɪʃᵊl/ ADJ **Racial** describes things relating to people's race. 种族的 ❑ *...the protection of national and racial minorities.* …对少数民族和少数种族的保护。 ● **ra·cial·ly** ADV 种族地 ❑ *We are both children of racially mixed marriages.* 我们俩都是不同种族通婚所生的孩子。

Word Partnership	*racial* 的常用搭配:
N.	racial **differences**, racial **discrimination**, racial **diversity**, racial **equality**, racial **groups**, racial **minorities**, racial **prejudice**, racial **tensions**

rac·ing ♦◇◇ /reɪsɪŋ/ N-UNCOUNT **Racing** refers to races between animals, especially horses, or between vehicles. 动物赛跑比赛 (尤指赛马); 赛车 ❑ *Four horse racing tracks operate in Pennsylvania.* 4个赛马跑道运营在宾西法尼亚。
→ see **bicycle**

▲ **rac·ism** /reɪsɪzəm/ N-UNCOUNT **Racism** is the belief that people of some races are inferior to others, and the behavior which is the result of this belief. 种族主义; 种族歧视 ❑ *There is a feeling among some black people that the level of racism is declining.* 有些黑人感觉到种族歧视的程度正在减轻。

rac·ist /reɪsɪst/ (**racists**) ADJ If you describe people, things, or behavior as **racist**, you mean that they are influenced by the belief that some people are inferior because they belong to a particular race. 种族主义的 [DISAPPROVAL] ❑ *You have to acknowledge that we live in a racist society.* 你不得不承认我们生活在一个有种族歧视的社会。 ● N-COUNT A **racist** is someone who is racist. 种族主义者 ❑ *He has a hard core of support among white racists.* 他得到了白人种族主义分子强有力的支持。

rack /ræk/ (**racks, racking, racked**)

The spelling **wrack** is also used for meanings **2** and **3**.

1 N-COUNT A **rack** is a frame or shelf, usually with bars or hooks, that is used for holding things or for hanging things on. 搁物架; 挂物架 ❑ *A luggage rack is a sensible option.* 行李架是个明智的选择。 **2** V-T If someone **is racked by** something such as illness or anxiety, it causes them great suffering or pain. 使痛苦 [usu passive] ❑ *His already infirm body was racked by high fever.* 他已经很孱弱的身体受到高烧的折磨。 **3** PHRASE If you **rack** your **brains**, you try very hard to think of something. 绞尽脑汁 ❑ *She began to rack her brains to remember what had happened at the nursing home.* 她开始绞尽脑汁地回忆在疗养院发生的事。

▶ **rack up** PHRASAL VERB If a business **racks up** profits, losses, or sales, it makes a lot of them. If a sportsman, sportswoman, or team **racks up** wins, they win a lot of games or races. 大量获得(利润); 严重遭受(损失); (体育中) 多次赢得(比赛) [no passive] ❑ *Lower rates mean that firms are more likely to rack up profits in the coming months.* 更低的费率意味着各公司更有可能在未来的几个月里获得大量利润。

★ **rack·et** /rækɪt/ (**rackets**)

> The spelling **racquet** is also used for meaning **3**.

1 N-SING A **racket** is a loud, unpleasant noise. 喧闹 ❑ *He makes such a racket I'm afraid he disturbs the neighbors.* 他如此大声喧哗，我担心他骚扰到邻居。 **2** N-COUNT You can refer to an illegal activity used to make money as a **racket**. 非法的赚钱勾当 [INFORMAL] ❑ *I'm sure he'll admit he was in the drug racket in the end.* 我敢肯定最终他会承认他在从事非法毒品买卖。 **3** N-COUNT A **racket** is an oval-shaped bat with strings across it. Rackets are used in tennis, squash, and badminton. (网球、壁球、羽毛球等的) 球拍 ❑ *Tennis rackets and balls are provided.* 提供网球拍和网球。

rack·et·eer·ing /rækɪtɪərɪŋ/ N-UNCOUNT **Racketeering** is making money from illegal activities such as threatening people or selling worthless, immoral, or illegal goods or services. 敲诈勒索; 诈骗 ❑ *Edwards was indicted on racketeering charges but never convicted.* 爱德华兹被指控犯敲诈罪但从未被判有罪。

racy /reɪsi/ (**racier, raciest**) ADJ **Racy** writing or behavior is lively, amusing, and slightly shocking. 生动活泼的; (写作风格或举止) 有趣动人的 ❑ *He listened to David Bright's racy stories about life in the navy.* 他听戴维・布赖特讲有关海军生活的有趣的故事。

> **Word Link** *rad ≈ ray : radar, radiant, radius*

ra·dar /reɪdɑr/ (**radars**) N-VAR **Radar** is a way of discovering the position or speed of objects such as aircraft or ships when they cannot be seen, by using radio signals. 雷达 ❑ *...a ship's radar screen.* …一艘船的雷达显示屏。

→ see **bat, forecast**

ra·di·ance /reɪdiəns/ **1** N-UNCOUNT **Radiance** is great happiness which shows in someone's face and makes them look very attractive. 容光焕发 [also "a" N] ❑ *She has the vigor and radiance of someone young enough to be her granddaughter.* 她精力充沛、容光焕发，就像小到可以做她孙女的年轻人那样。 **2** N-UNCOUNT **Radiance** is a glowing light shining from something. 光辉 [also "a" N] ❑ *The dim bulb of the bedside lamp cast a soft radiance over his face.* 床头灯微弱的灯光给他的脸上涂上了一层柔和的光辉。

★ **ra·di·ant** /reɪdiənt/ **1** ADJ Someone who is **radiant** is so happy that their happiness shows in their face. 容光焕发的 ❑ *On her wedding day the bride looked truly radiant.* 在她婚礼那天，新娘看起来真的是容光焕发。 **2** ADJ Something that is **radiant** glows brightly. 光芒四射的 ❑ *The evening sun warms the old red brick wall to a radiant glow.* 傍晚的阳光照暖了那道旧红砖墙，使它熠熠生辉。

★ **ra·di·ate** /reɪdieɪt/ (**radiates, radiating, radiated**) **1** V-I If things **radiate** out **from** a place, they form a pattern that is like lines drawn from the center of a circle to various points on its edge. 辐射 ❑ *Many kinds of woodland can be seen on the various walks which radiate from the Heritage Center.* 从遗产中心向外伸展的各条走道上可以看到多种林地。 **2** V-T/V-I If you **radiate** an emotion or quality or if it **radiates from** you, people can see it very clearly in your face and in your behavior. 显现(特质); 流露(情感) ❑ *She radiates happiness and health.* 她浑身洋溢着快乐与健康。 **3** V-T If something **radiates** heat or light, heat or light comes from it. 散发出 (光或热)

ra·dia·tion /reɪdieɪʃᵊn/ **1** N-UNCOUNT **Radiation** consists of very small particles of a radioactive substance. Large amounts of radiation can cause illness and death. 辐射物 ❑ *They suffer from health problems and fear the long term effects of radiation.* 他们受健康问题的困扰，还担心遭受辐射造成的长期影响。 **2** N-UNCOUNT **Radiation** is energy, especially heat, that comes from a particular source. 辐射能 (尤指热能) ❑ *The $617 million satellite will study energy radiation from the most violent stars in the universe.* 这个价值6.17亿美元的人造卫星将研究宇宙中活动最剧烈的恒星所发出的辐射能。

→ see **cancer, greenhouse effect, wave**

> **Word Partnership** *radiation* 的常用搭配:
>
> ADJ. **nuclear** radiation **1**
>
> N. radiation **levels**, radiation **therapy/treatment** **1**
> radiation **damage, effects of** radiation, **exposure to** radiation **1** **2**

ra·dia·tor /reɪdieɪtər/ (**radiators**) **1** N-COUNT A **radiator** is a hollow metal device, usually connected by pipes to a central heating system, that is used to heat a room. 暖气片 **2** N-COUNT The **radiator** in a car is the part of the engine that is filled with water in order to cool the engine. (汽车引擎的) 水箱

radi·cal ◆◆◇ /rædɪkᵊl/ (**radicals**) **1** ADJ **Radical** changes and differences are very important and great in degree. 重大的; 彻底的 ❑ *The country needs a period of calm without more surges of radical change.* 这个国家需要一段平静的时期，不再有重大变化所引发的动荡。 ● **radi·cal·ly** /rædɪkli/ ADV 重大地; 彻底地 ❑ *...two large groups of people with radically different beliefs and cultures.* …信仰与文化彻底不同的两大群体。 **2** ADJ **Radical** people believe that there should be great changes in society and try to bring about these changes. 激进的 ❑ *...threats by left-wing radical groups to disrupt the proceedings.* …左翼激进团体要扰乱这些活动的威胁。 ● N-COUNT A **radical** is someone who has radical views. 激进分子 ❑ *Vanessa and I had been student radicals together at Berkeley from 1965 to 1967.* 瓦妮莎和我在1965年至1967年期间都是伯克利大学的学生激进分子。

ra·dii /reɪdiaɪ/ **Radii** is the plural of **radius**. **radius**的复数形式

ra·dio ◆◆◆ /reɪdioʊ/ (**radios, radioing, radioed**) **1** N-UNCOUNT **Radio** is the broadcasting of programs for the public to listen to, by sending out signals from a transmitter. 无线电广播 ❑ *The last 12 months have been difficult ones for local radio.* 最近的12个月对地方广播电台来说是艰难的。 **2** N-SING You can refer to the programs broadcast by radio stations as **the radio**. 无线电广播节目 ❑ *A lot of people listen to the radio in the mornings.* 很多人早上收听广播节目。 **3** N-COUNT A **radio** is the piece of equipment that you use in order to listen to radio programs. 收音机 ❑ *He sat down in the armchair and turned on the radio.* 他在扶手椅上坐下来，打开了收音机。 **4** N-UNCOUNT **Radio** is a system of sending sound over a distance by transmitting electrical signals. 无线电通信系统 ❑ *They are in twice daily radio contact with the rebel leader.* 他们一天两次通过无线电通信系统与反叛者领导人保持联系。 **5** N-COUNT A **radio** is a piece of equipment that is used for sending and receiving messages. 无线电收发装置 ❑ *Judge Bruce Laughland praised the courage of the young policeman, who managed to raise the alarm on his radio.* 布鲁斯・劳赫兰法官赞扬了那名年轻警察的勇气，该警察设法通过自己的无线电收发装置发出了警报。 **6** V-T/V-I If you **radio** someone, you send a message to them by radio. 用无线电发送 ❑ *The officer radioed for advice.* 那名军官发电请求指示。

→ see Word Web: **radio**

→ see **telescope, wave**

> **Word Web** radio
>
> **Radio** originally provided **communication** between ships at sea. Ships could also contact **stations** on the land. In 1912, the *Titanic* sank in the North Atlantic with over 2,000 people on board. However, a radio call to a nearby ship helped save a third of the passengers. What we call a radio is actually a **receiver**. The **waves** it receives come from a **transmitter**. Radio is an important source of **entertainment**. AM radio carries all kinds of radio **programs**. However, **listeners** often prefer musical programs on the FM waveband or from **satellites** because the sound quality is better.

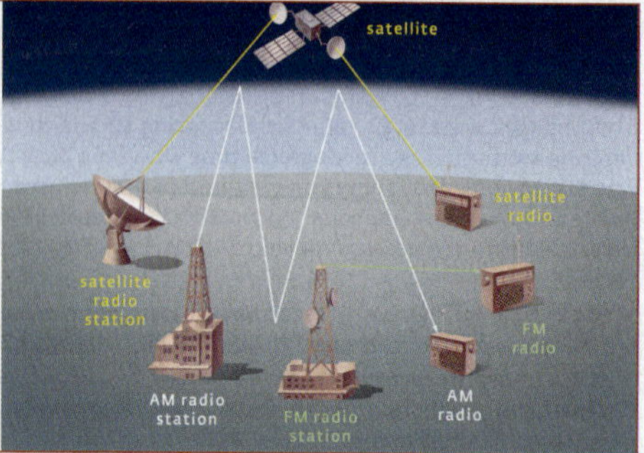

★ **radio·ac·tive** /reɪdioʊæktɪv/ ADJ Something that is **radioactive** contains a substance that produces energy in the form of powerful and harmful rays. 放射性的 ❑ *The government has been storing radioactive waste at Fernald for 50 years.* 该政府50年来一直在弗纳德储存放射性废物。● **radio·ac·tiv·ity** /reɪdioʊæktɪvɪti/ N-UNCOUNT 放射性 ❑ *...the storage and disposal of solid waste that is contaminated with low levels of radioactivity.* …对受到低水平放射污染的固体废弃物的储存和处置。

ra·di·og·ra·pher /reɪdiɒgrəfər/ (**radiographers**) N-COUNT A **radiographer** is a person who is trained to take X-rays. X射线照相技师

ra·di·og·ra·phy /reɪdiɒgrəfi/ N-UNCOUNT **Radiography** is the process of taking X-rays. X射线照相

★ **ra·dium** /reɪdiəm/ N-UNCOUNT **Radium** is a radioactive element which is used in the treatment of cancer. 镭

★ **ra·dius** /reɪdiəs/ (**radii** /reɪdiaɪ/) 1 N-SING The **radius** around a particular point is the distance from it in any direction. 范围 ❑ *Nick has searched for work in a ten-mile radius around his home.* 尼克已经在以家为中心10英里的范围内寻找工作。 2 N-COUNT The **radius** of a circle is the distance from its center to its outside edge. 半径 ❑ *He indicated a semicircle with a radius of about thirty miles.* 他标示出一个半径大约三十英里的半圆。
→ see **area**

▲ **raf·fle** /ræfᵊl/ (**raffles, raffling, raffled**) 1 N-COUNT A **raffle** is a competition in which you buy tickets with numbers on them. Afterward some numbers are chosen, and if your ticket has one of these numbers on it, you win a prize. 买彩票抽奖 ❑ *Any more raffle tickets? Twenty-five cents each or five for a dollar.* 还要抽奖彩票吗？每张25美分或1美元5张。 2 V-T If someone **raffles** something, they give it as a prize in a raffle. 通过抽彩奖给 ❑ *During each show we will be raffling a fabulous prize.* 每次展览我们都会通过抽彩送出惊人的奖品。

▲ **raft** /ræft/ (**rafts**) 1 N-COUNT A **raft** is a floating platform made from large pieces of wood or other materials tied together. 木排；筏 ❑ *...a river trip on bamboo rafts through dense rainforest.* …一次乘着竹筏穿过茂密雨林的河上旅行。 2 N-COUNT A **raft** is a small rubber or plastic boat that you blow air into to make it float. (橡皮或塑料的) 小型充气船 ❑ *The crew spent two days and nights in their raft.* 船员们在他们的小充气船上度过了两天两夜。
→ see **boat**

raft·er /ræftər/ (**rafters**) N-COUNT **Rafters** are the sloping pieces of wood that support a roof. 椽子 ❑ *From the rafters of the thatched roofs hung strings of dried onions and garlic.* 从茅草屋顶的椽子上垂挂下一串一串的干洋葱和大蒜。

rag /ræg/ (**rags, ragging, ragged**) 1 N-VAR A **rag** is a piece of old cloth which you can use to clean or wipe things. 抹布 ❑ *He was wiping his hands on an oily rag.* 他正用一块油腻腻的抹布擦手。 2 N-PLURAL **Rags** are old torn clothes. 破烂衣服 ❑ *There were men, women, and small children, some dressed in rags.* 有男人、女人和孩子，其中一些人穿着破烂的衣服。 3 N-COUNT People refer to a newspaper as a **rag** when they have a poor opinion of it. 质量低劣的报纸 [INFORMAL, DISAPPROVAL] ❑ *"This man Tom works for a local rag," he said.* "那个叫汤姆的人为当地一家小报干活，"他说。 4 V-T If someone **rags** you, they tease you in a friendly way. (善意的) 揶揄 [INFORMAL] ❑ *"They always rag me about my car," he says.* "他们总拿我的汽车取笑我，"他说。
▸ **rag on** PHRASAL VERB If you **rag on** someone, you speak angrily to them because they have done something wrong. 责备 [AM, INFORMAL] ❑ *Ma, quit ragging on Ruthie.* 妈，不要再责备鲁西了。

rage ♦◇◇ /reɪdʒ/ (**rages, raging, raged**) 1 N-VAR **Rage** is strong anger that is difficult to control. 盛怒 ❑ *He was red-cheeked with rage.* 他因盛怒而满脸通红。 2 V-I You say that something powerful or unpleasant **rages** when it continues with great force or violence. 肆虐 ❑ *Train service was halted as the fire raged for more than four hours.* 火车停运了，因为大火肆虐了四个多小时。 3 V-I If you **rage** about something, you speak or think very angrily about it. 发怒；怒斥 ❑ *Monroe was on the phone, raging about her mistreatment by the brothers.* 门罗正在打电话，愤怒地诉说兄弟们对她的虐待。 ❑ *Inside, Frannie was raging.* 内心里，弗兰尼怒不可遏。 4 N-UNCOUNT You can refer to the strong anger that someone feels in a particular situation as a particular **rage**, especially when this results in violent or aggressive behavior. (尤指导致暴力或侵略性行为的) 狂怒 ❑ *Cabin crews are reporting up to nine cases of air rage a week.* 乘务人员们报告每周有多达9起的乘客情绪失控事件。 5 → see also **road rage** 6 → see also **raging**
→ see **anger**

Thesaurus	*rage* 另参见:
N.	anger, frenzy, madness, tantrum 1 4
V.	fume, scream, yell 3

▲ **rag·ged** /rægɪd/ 1 ADJ Someone who is **ragged** looks messy and is wearing clothes that are old and torn. 衣衫褴褛的 ❑ *The five survivors eventually reached safety, ragged, half-starved, and exhausted.* 这5名幸存者最终到达了安全地带，衣衫褴褛、饿得半死、筋疲力尽。 2 ADJ **Ragged** clothes are old and torn. 破旧的 ❑ *...an elderly, bearded man in ragged clothes.* …一个上了年纪、留着胡须、穿着破旧衣服的男人。 3 ADJ You can say that something is **ragged** when it is rough or uneven. 粗糙的；参差不齐的 ❑ *O'Brien formed the men into a ragged line.* 奥布赖恩把这些男人排成了歪歪扭扭的一排。

rag·ing /reɪdʒɪŋ/ 1 ADJ **Raging** water moves very forcefully and violently. 汹涌的 [ADJ n] ❑ *The field trip involved crossing a raging torrent.* 越野旅行包括跨越一条汹涌的急流。 2 ADJ **Raging** fire is very hot and fierce. 熊熊燃烧的 [ADJ n] ❑ *As he came closer he saw a gigantic wall of raging flame before him.* 当他走近时，他看到面前是一堵巨大的、熊熊燃烧的火墙。 3 ADJ **Raging** is used to describe things, especially bad things, that are very intense. 严重的 (尤指坏事) [ADJ n] ❑ *If raging inflation returns, then interest rates will shoot up.* 如果严重的通货膨胀再发生，利率就会暴涨。 4 → see also **rage**

raid ♦◇◇ /reɪd/ (**raids, raiding, raided**) 1 V-T When soldiers **raid** a place, they make a sudden armed attack against it, with the aim of causing damage rather than occupying any of the enemy's land. 突袭 ❑ *The guerrillas raided banks and destroyed a police barracks and an electricity substation.* 游击队员们突袭了多家银行，摧毁了一个警察营房和一座变电站。● N-COUNT **Raid** is also a noun. 突袭 ❑ *The rebels attempted a surprise raid on a military camp.* 反叛者们曾经试图对兵营发动一场突然袭击。 2 → see also **air raid** 3 V-T If the police **raid** a building, they enter it suddenly and by force in order to look for dangerous criminals or for evidence of something illegal, such as drugs or weapons. 突击搜查 ❑ *Police raided their headquarters and other offices.* 警察突击搜查了他们的总部和其他办公场所。● N-COUNT **Raid** is also a noun. 突击搜查 ❑ *They were arrested early this morning after a raid on a house by thirty armed police.* 他们于今天凌晨，在30名武装警察突击搜查了一所住宅后被捕。

raid·er /reɪdər/ → see **corporate raider**

rail ♦◇◇ /reɪl/ (**rails**) 1 N-COUNT A **rail** is a horizontal bar attached to posts or around the edge of something as a fence or support. 栏杆 ❑ *They had to walk across an emergency footbridge, holding onto a rope that served as a rail.* 他们不得不抓着当作栏杆用的绳子，走过一架应急人行桥。 2 N-COUNT A **rail** is a horizontal bar that you hang things on. (挂物用的) 横杆 ❑ *This pair of curtains will fit a rail up to 7 ft 6 in wide.* 这副窗帘适合安装在宽度为7英尺6英寸的横杆上。 3 N-COUNT **Rails** are the steel bars which trains run on. 铁轨 ❑ *The train left the rails but somehow forced its way back onto the line.* 火车偏离了铁轨，但又设法回到了原来的轨道上。 4 N-UNCOUNT If you travel or send something **by rail**, you travel or send it on a train. 乘火车；用火车 (运送) ❑ *The president traveled by rail to his home town.* 总统乘火车回到了家乡。 5 PHRASE If something is **back on the rails**, it is beginning to be successful again after a period when it almost failed. 东山再起 [mainly BRIT, JOURNALISM]
in AM, use **back on track**
6 PHRASE If someone **goes off the rails**, they start to behave in a way that other people think is unacceptable or very strange, for example, they start taking drugs or breaking the law. 行为出轨 [mainly BRIT] ❑ *They've got to do something about these children because clearly they've gone off the rails.* 他们必须对这些孩子采取点行动，因为很明显他们的行为已经出轨了。
→ see **skateboarding, train, transportation**

rail·ing /reɪlɪŋ/ (**railings**) N-COUNT A fence made from metal bars is called a **railing** or **railings**. (金属的) 栏杆 ❑ *He walked out on to the balcony where he rested his arms on the railing.* 他走出屋外到阳台上，把胳膊搭在栏杆上。

rail·road /reɪlroʊd/ (**railroads, railroading, railroaded**) 1 N-COUNT A **railroad** is a route between two places along which trains travel on steel rails. 铁路 [AM]
in BRIT, use **railway**
2 N-COUNT A **railroad** is a company or organization that operates railroad routes. 铁路公司 [AM]
in BRIT, use **railway**

r

❑ *The Chicago and Northwestern Railroad wouldn't go along with that arrangement and said it would shut down completely.* 芝加哥西北铁路公司不同意那项安排并说要彻底停止。 **3** V-T If you **railroad** someone **into** doing something, you make them do it although they do not really want to, by hurrying them and putting pressure on them. (通过催促和施压) 迫使某人做某事 ❑ *He more or less railroaded the rest of Europe into recognizing the new "independent" states.* 他或多或少地强迫了欧洲其他国家承认这些新"独立"的国家。 ❑ *He railroaded the reforms through.* 他强行实施了改革。

rail·way ♦◇◇ /reɪlweɪ/ (**railways**) **1** N-COUNT A **railway** is the system and network of tracks that trains travel on. 铁路网 [mainly AM] **2** N-COUNT A **railway** is a route between two places along which trains travel on steel rails. 铁路 [mainly BRIT]

in AM, usually use **railroad**

3 N-COUNT A **railway** is a company or organization that operates railroad routes. 铁路公司 [BRIT]

in AM, use **railroad**

→ see **train**

rain ♦♦◇ /reɪn/ (**rains, raining, rained**) **1** N-UNCOUNT **Rain** is water that falls from the clouds in small drops. 雨 [also "the" N] ❑ *I hope you didn't get soaked standing out in the rain.* 我希望你站在外面雨里没淋得浑身透湿。 **2** N-PLURAL In countries where rain only falls in certain seasons, this rain is referred to as **the rains**. 雨季 ❑ *...the spring, when the rains came.* …春天，雨季来临时。 **3** V-I When rain falls, you can say that **it is raining**. 下雨 ❑ *It was raining hard, and she didn't have an umbrella.* 雨下得很大，而她没有带伞。 **4** V-T/V-I If someone **rains** blows, kicks, or bombs **on** a person or place, the person or place is attacked by many blows, kicks, or bombs. You can also say that blows, kicks, or bombs **rain on** a person or place. 使像雨点般落下; 像雨点般落下 ❑ *The police, raining blows on rioters and spectators alike, cleared the park.* 警察对暴乱者和旁观者都一阵猛打，清空了公园。 ● PHRASAL VERB **Rain down** means the same as **rain**. 同**rain** ❑ *Fighter aircraft rained down high explosives.* 战斗机如雨点般投下烈性炸弹。

→ see **disaster, storm, water**

Thesaurus *rain* 另参见:

N. drizzle, precipitation, shower, sleet **1**

rain·bow /reɪnboʊ/ (**rainbows**) N-COUNT A **rainbow** is an arch of different colors that you can sometimes see in the sky when it is raining. 彩虹 ❑ *...silk and satin in every shade of the rainbow.* …如彩虹般五颜六色的丝绸与锦缎。

→ see Word Web: **rainbow**

rain check PHRASE If you say you will take a **rain check** on an offer or suggestion, you mean that you do not want to accept it now, but you might accept it at another time. 目前无法接受，但可日后接受的邀请或建议 ❑ *I was planning to ask you in for a brandy, but if you want to take a rain check, that's fine.* 我本想请你来喝杯白兰地，但如果你想改日再来，也行。

R

rain·coat /reɪnkoʊt/ (**raincoats**) N-COUNT A **raincoat** is a waterproof coat. 雨衣

→ see **clothing**

rain·drop /reɪndrɒp/ (**raindrops**) N-COUNT A **raindrop** is a single drop of rain. 雨滴

rain·fall /reɪnfɔl/ N-UNCOUNT **Rainfall** is the amount of rain that falls in a place during a particular period. 降雨量 ❑ *There have been four years of below average rainfall.* 已经有4年降雨量低于平均水平了。

→ see **erosion, storm**

rain for·est (**rain forests**) also **rainforest** N-VAR A **rain forest** is a thick forest of tall trees which is found mainly in tropical areas where there is a lot of rain. 热带雨林 ❑ *...the destruction of the Amazon rain forest.* …对亚马逊河流域热带雨林的破坏。

rainy /reɪni/ (**rainier, rainiest**) ADJ During a **rainy** day, season, or period it rains a lot. 多雨的 ❑ *The rainy season in the Andes normally starts in December.* 安第斯山脉的雨季一般从12月开始。

raise ♦♦♦ /reɪz/ (**raises, raising, raised**) **1** V-T If you **raise** something, you move it so that it is in a higher position. 举起 ❑ *He raised his hand to wave.* 他举起手来挥动。 ❑ *Milton raised the glass to his lips.* 米尔顿举起杯子放到嘴唇边。 **2** V-T If you **raise** a flag, you display it by moving it up a pole or into a high place where it can be seen. 升起 ❑ *They had raised the white flag in surrender.* 他们已经升起白旗投降。 **3** V-T If you **raise yourself**, you lift your body so that you are standing up straight, or so that you are no longer lying flat. 站立; 起身 ❑ *He raised himself into a sitting position.* 他起身坐了起来。 **4** V-T If you **raise** the rate or level of something, you increase it. 增加 ❑ *The Federal Reserve Board is expected to raise interest rates.* 联邦储备委员会预计将增加利率。 **5** V-T To **raise** the standard of something means to improve it. 提高 (水平) ❑ *...a new drive to raise standards of literacy in New York's schools.* …一场提高纽约各学校文化程度的新运动。 **6** V-T If you **raise** your **voice**, you speak more loudly, usually because you are angry. (常指因生气) 提高 (嗓门) ❑ *Don't you raise your voice to me!* 别对我高声大气！ **7** N-COUNT A **raise** is an increase in your wages or salary. 加薪 [AM]

in BRIT, use **rise**

❑ *Within two months Kelly got a raise.* 两个月内凯利就获得了加薪。 **8** V-T If you **raise** money **for** a charity or an institution, you ask people for money which you collect on its behalf. 筹募 (资金) ❑ *...events held to raise money for flood victims.* …为水患灾民募捐而举行的活动。 **9** V-T If a person or company **raises** money that they need, they manage to get it, for example by selling their property or by borrowing. 筹措 (资金) ❑ *They raised the money to buy the house and two hundred acres of land.* 他们筹措了资金来购买房子和200英亩土地。 **10** V-T If an event **raises** a particular emotion or question, it makes people feel the emotion or consider the question. 唤起; 引发 ❑ *The agreement has raised hopes that the war may end soon.* 合约唤起了战争也许很快会结束的希望。 **11** V-T If you **raise** a subject, an objection, or a question, you mention it or bring it to someone's attention. 提出 ❑ *He had been consulted and had raised no objections.* 他已经被征询意见，并没有提出异议。 **12** V-T Someone who **raises** a child takes care of it until it is grown up. 抚养 ❑ *My mother was an amazing woman. She raised four of us kids virtually singlehandedly.* 我母亲是个了不起的女人。她几乎是独自抚养大了我们4个孩子。 **13** V-T If someone **raises** a particular type of animal or crop, they breed that type of animal or grow that type of crop. 饲养; 种植 ❑ *He raises 2,000 acres of wheat and hay.* 他种植了2000英亩的小麦和饲料用草。 **14** **to raise the alarm** → see **alarm** **15** **to raise** your **eyebrows** → see **eyebrow** **16** **to raise a finger** → see **finger** → see **union**

You should be careful not to confuse the verbs **raise** and **rise**. **Raise** is a transitive verb and usually followed by an object, whereas **rise** is an intransitive verb and not followed by an object. **Rise** also can not be used in the passive. ❑ *...the government's decision to raise prices... The number of dead is likely to rise.* Both **raise** and **rise** can be used as nouns meaning "pay increase". **Raise** is used in American English, and **rise** is used in British English. ❑ *Millions of Americans get a pay raise today. ...a rise of at least 12 percent.*

Thesaurus *raise* 另参见:

V. elevate, hold up, lift **1**
N. addition, hike, increase **7**

Word Web rainbow

Sunlight contains all of the colors. When a **ray** of sunlight passes through a prism, it splits into separate colors. This is also what happens when light passes through the drops of water in the air. The light is refracted, and we see a **rainbow**. The colors of the rainbow are **red**, **orange**, **yellow**, **green**, **blue**, indigo, and **violet**. One tradition says that there is a pot of gold at the end of the rainbow. Other myths say that the rainbow is a bridge between Earth and the land of the gods.

Word Partnership *raise* 的常用搭配：

N. raise *your* **hand** 1
raise **fares**, raise **interest rates**, raise **the level of** *something*, raise **prices**, raise **taxes** 4
raise **your voice** 6
pay raise 7
raise **money** 8 9
raise **capital/revenue** 9
raise **awareness**, raise **doubts**, raise **eyebrows**, raise **hopes** 10
raise **concerns**, raise **an issue**, raise **questions** 10 11
raise **objections** 11
raise **a children/family/kids** 12
raise **crops** 13

rai·sin /reɪzᵊn/ (**raisins**) N-COUNT **Raisins** are dried grapes. 葡萄干 ❑ *...homemade oatmeal with brown sugar and raisins.* …自家煮的放有红糖和葡萄干的麦片粥。

▲ **rake** /reɪk/ (**rakes, raking, raked**) 1 N-COUNT A **rake** is a garden tool consisting of a row of metal or wooden teeth attached to a long handle. You can use a rake to make the earth smooth and level before you put plants in, or to gather leaves together. (长柄) 耙子 2 V-T If you **rake** a surface, you move a rake across it in order to make it smooth and level. 耙平 ❑ *Rake the soil, press the seed into it, then cover it lightly.* 耙平土，把种子按进土里，然后再把它轻轻地盖上。 3 V-T If you **rake** leaves or ashes, you move them somewhere using a rake or a similar tool. 耙 ❑ *I watched the men rake leaves into heaps.* 我看见男人们把树叶耙成堆。

▸ **rake in** PHRASAL VERB If you say that someone **is raking in** money, you mean that they are making a lot of money very easily, more easily than you think they should. 轻易地大捞 (钱财) [INFORMAL] ❑ *The privatization allowed companies to rake in huge profits.* 私有化使各公司轻易地捞到了巨额利润。

rake-off (**rake-offs**) N-COUNT If someone who has helped to arrange a business deal takes or gets a **rake-off**, they illegally or unfairly take a share of the profits. (非法或不正当获得的) 回扣 [INFORMAL] ❑ *Hall takes a rake-off, often amounting to tens of thousands of dollars on most project deals.* 霍尔收取回扣，在大多数的项目交易中经常达到数万美元。

ral·ly ♦◇◇ /ræli/ (**rallies, rallying, rallied**) 1 N-COUNT A **rally** is a large public meeting that is held in order to show support for something such as a political party. 集会 ❑ *About three thousand people held a rally to mark international human rights day.* 大约三千人举行集会以纪念国际人权日。 2 V-T/V-I When people **rally to** something or when something **rallies** them, they unite to support it. 一致支持；团结起来 ❑ *Her cabinet colleagues have continued to rally to her support.* 她的内阁同僚们继续团结一致地支持她。 3 V-I When someone or something **rallies**, they begin to recover or improve after having been weak. 恢复健康；好转 ❑ *He rallied enough to thank his doctors.* 他身体恢复得能向医生们道谢了。 ● N-COUNT **Rally** is also a noun. 恢复健康；好转 ❑ *After a brief rally the shares returned to $2.15.* 短暂的反弹之后，股票回到了$2.15。 4 N-COUNT A **rally** in tennis, badminton, or squash is a continuous series of shots that the players exchange without stopping. (网球、羽毛球、壁球中的) 连续对打 ❑ *...a long rally.* …一阵长时间的连续对打。 5 N-COUNT A **rally** is a competition in which vehicles are driven over public roads. 公路车赛 ❑ *Carlos Sainz of Spain has won the New Zealand Motor Rally.* 西班牙的卡洛斯·赛恩斯在新西兰摩托车公路赛中获胜。

▸ **rally around** PHRASAL VERB When people **rally around**, they work as a group in order to support someone or something at a difficult time. 集体声援 ❑ *So many people have rallied around to help the family.* 如此多的人团结在一起帮助这家人。

Word Partnership *rally* 的常用搭配：

ADJ. **political** rally 1
N. **campaign** rally, **protest** rally, rally **in support of** *someone/something* 1
prices/stocks rally 3
PREP. rally **behind** *someone/something* 2

ram /ræm/ (**rams, ramming, rammed**) 1 V-T If a vehicle **rams** something such as another vehicle, it crashes into it with a lot of force, usually deliberately. (通常指故意地) 猛烈撞击 ❑ *The thieves fled, ramming the policeman's car.* 小偷们撞了警车，逃跑了。 2 V-T If you **ram** something somewhere, you push it there with great force. 猛推 ❑ *He rammed the key into the lock and kicked the front door open.* 他猛地把钥匙插进锁里，踢开了前门。 3 N-COUNT A **ram** is an adult male sheep. 公羊 4 PHRASE If something **rams home** a message or a point, it makes it clear in a way that is very forceful and that people are likely to listen to. 充分讲明 ❑ *The report by the chairman will ram this point home.* 主席的报告将充分地讲明这一点。 5 to **ram** something **down** someone's **throat** → see **throat**

RAM /ræm/ N-UNCOUNT **RAM** is the part of a computer in which information is stored while you are using it. **RAM** is an abbreviation for "Random Access Memory." 随机存取存贮器 [COMPUTING] ❑ *...a PC with 512 MB RAM.* …一台内存为512MB的个人电脑。

ram·ble /ræmbᵊl/ (**rambles, rambling, rambled**) 1 N-COUNT A **ramble** is a long walk in the countryside. (乡间的) 漫步 ❑ *...an hour's ramble through the woods.* …1小时穿过树林的漫步。 2 V-I If you **ramble**, you go on a long walk in the countryside. (在乡间) 漫步 ❑ *...freedom to ramble across the rolling hills.* …跨越起伏的丘陵漫步的自由。 3 V-I If you say that a person **rambles** in their speech or writing, you mean they do not make much sense because they keep going off the subject in a confused way. 漫谈 ❑ *Sometimes she spoke sensibly; sometimes she rambled.* 有时她说话很有道理；有时却漫无边际。

rami·fi·ca·tion /ræmɪfɪkeɪʃᵊn/ (**ramifications**) N-COUNT The **ramifications** of a decision, plan, or event are all its consequences and effects, especially ones that are not obvious at first. (尤指最初并不明显的) 后果 ❑ *The book analyzes the social and political ramifications of AIDS for the gay community.* 这本书分析了同性恋团体中艾滋病引发的社会和政治后果。

▲ **ramp** /ræmp/ (**ramps**) N-COUNT A **ramp** is a sloping surface between two places that are at different levels. 斜坡 ❑ *Lillian was coming down the ramp from the museum.* 莉莲正从博物馆沿着斜坡走下来。 → see **disability, skateboarding, traffic**

ram·page (**rampages, rampaging, rampaged**)

Pronounced /ræmpeɪdʒ/ for meaning 1, and /ræmpeɪdʒ/ for meaning 2.

义项1读作 /ræmpeɪdʒ/，义项2读作 /ræmpeɪdʒ/。

1 V-I When people or animals **rampage** through a place, they rush around there in a wild or violent way, causing damage or destruction. 横冲直撞 ❑ *Hundreds of youths rampaged through the town, smashing store windows and overturning cars.* 数百名年轻人在镇上横冲直撞，捣毁商店的橱窗，掀翻汽车。 2 PHRASE If people go **on a rampage**, they rush around in a wild or violent way, causing damage or destruction. 横冲直撞 ❑ *The prisoners went on a rampage destroying everything in their way.* 犯人们横冲直撞，捣毁一切妨碍他们的东西。

▲ **ram·pant** /ræmpənt/ ADJ If you describe something bad, such as a crime or disease, as **rampant**, you mean that it is very common and is increasing in an uncontrolled way. 猖獗的；泛滥的 ❑ *Inflation is rampant and industry in decline.* 通货膨胀肆虐，工业生产下降。

ram·shack·le /ræmʃækᵊl/ 1 ADJ A **ramshackle** building is badly made or in bad condition, and looks as if it is likely to fall down. 摇摇欲坠的 ❑ *They entered the shop, which was a curious ramshackle building.* 他们走进商店，那是一所奇怪、摇摇欲坠的房子。 2 ADJ A **ramshackle** system, union, or collection of things has been put together without much thought and is not likely to work very well. 拼凑的 ❑ *They joined with a ramshackle alliance of other rebels.* 他们加入了一个其他反叛分子拼凑起来的联盟。

ran /ræn/ **Ran** is the past tense of **run**. **run**的过去式

▲ **ranch** /ræntʃ/ (**ranches**) N-COUNT A **ranch** is a large farm used for raising animals, especially cattle, horses, or sheep. (尤指饲养牛、马或羊的) 大牧场 ❑ *He lives on a cattle ranch in Texas.* 他住在德克萨斯州的一个养牛的大牧场里。

R & D /ɑr ən di/ also **R and D** N-UNCOUNT **R & D** refers to the research and development work or department within a large company or organization. **R & D** is an abbreviation for "Research and Development." 研究与开发；研究与开发部门 ❑ *Businesses need to train their workers better, and spend more on R & D.* 各企业需要更好地培训其员工，并且在研发上有更多的投入。

★ **ran·dom** /rændəm/ 1 ADJ A **random** sample or method is one in which all the people or things involved have an equal chance of being chosen. 随机的 ❑ *The survey used a random sample* *of two thousand people across the Midwest.* 这项调查使用的是对中西部地区2000人的随机取样。 ● **ran·dom·ly** ADV 随机地 [ADV with v] ❑ *...interviews with a randomly selected sample of 30 girls aged between 13 and 18.* …对随机抽取的30名年龄在13至18岁之间的女孩的访谈。 **2** ADJ If you describe events as **random**, you mean that they do not seem to follow a definite plan or pattern. 随意的 ❑ *...random violence against innocent victims.* …对无辜受害者的随意攻击。 ● **ran·dom·ly** ADV 随意地 [ADV with v] ❑ *...drinks and magazines left scattered randomly around.* …随意四处散落的饮料和杂志。 **3** PHRASE If you choose people or things **at random**, you do not use any particular method, so they all have an equal chance of being chosen. 随机地 ❑ *We received several answers, and we picked one at random.* 我们收到了好几个答案，就随机地拣选了一个。 **4** PHRASE If something happens **at random**, it happens without a definite plan or pattern. 随意地 ❑ *Three African-Americans were killed by shots fired at random from a minibus.* 3名非洲裔美国人被从一辆小型公共汽车中胡乱射出的子弹打死了。

rang /ræŋ/ **Rang** is the past tense of **ring**. ring的过去式

range ♦♦◊ /reɪndʒ/ (**ranges, ranging, ranged**) **1** N-COUNT A **range of** things is a number of different things of the same general kind. (同类事物的) 一系列 ❑ *A wide range of colors and patterns are available.* 一系列各种各样的颜色和图案都有。 **2** N-COUNT A **range** is the complete group that is included between two points on a scale of measurement or quality. 范围 ❑ *The average age range is between 35 and 55.* 平均年龄范围是35至55岁。 **3** N-COUNT The **range of** something is the maximum area in which it can reach things or detect things. (能够到达或探知的) 最大范围 ❑ *The 120mm mortar has a range of 18,000 yards.* 口径120毫米的迫击炮的射程是1.8万码。 **4** V-I If things **range between** two points or **range from** one point **to** another, they vary within these points on a scale of measurement or quality. (在一定幅度内) 变化 ❑ *They range in price from \$3 to \$15.* 它们的价格在\$3到\$15之间变化。 ❑ *...offering merchandise ranging from the everyday to the esoteric.* …出售的商品包括日常用品到少数人使用的特别物品。 **5** N-COUNT A **range** of mountains or hills is a line of them. 山脉 ❑ *...the massive mountain ranges to the north.* …连绵向北的巨大山脉。 **6** N-COUNT A rifle **range** or a shooting **range** is a place where people can practice shooting at targets. 射击场 ❑ *It reminds me of my days on the rifle range preparing for duty in Vietnam.* 这使我回想起在射击场上训练准备去越南服役的那些日子。 **7** N-COUNT A **range** is a large area of open land, especially land in the United States, where cattle are kept. (尤指美国的) 大牧场 ❑ *He grazed his cattle on the open range.* 他在开阔的大牧场上放牧他的牛群。 **8** N-COUNT A **range** or **kitchen range** is a large metal device for cooking food using gas or electricity. A range consists of a broiler, an oven, and some gas or electric burners. 炉灶 [AM]

in BRIT, usually use **cooker**

9 → see also **free-range** **10** PHRASE If something is **in range** or **within range**, it is near enough to be reached or detected. If it is **out of range**, it is too far away to be reached or detected. 在可触及的范围内/外 ❑ *Cars are driven through the mess, splashing everyone within range.* 车子从泥泞中开过，把泥点溅到附近能溅得到的每个人身上。 **11** PHRASE If you see or hit something **at close range** or **from close range**, you are very close to it when you see it or hit it. If you do something **at a range of** half a mile, for example, you are half a mile away from it when you do it. 近距离内 ❑ *He was shot in the head at close range.* 他被近距离射中头部。

→ see **graph**

Word Partnership *range* 的常用搭配：

ADJ.	**broad** range, **limited** range, **narrow** range, **wide** range **1**
	full range, **normal** range, **whole** range **2**
N.	range **of emotions**, range **of possibilities** **1**
	age range, **price** range, **temperature** range **2**

▲**rang·er** /reɪndʒər/ (**rangers**) N-COUNT A **ranger** is a person whose job is to take care of a forest or large park. 护林员；公园管理员 ❑ *Bill Justice is a park ranger at the Carlsbad Caverns National Park.* 比尔·贾斯蒂斯是卡尔斯巴德洞穴国家公园的管理员。

rank ♦◊◊ /ræŋk/ (**ranks, ranking, ranked**) **1** N-VAR Someone's **rank** is the position or grade that they have in an organization. 职位；级别 ❑ *He eventually rose to the rank of captain.* 他最终升到了船长的职位。 **2** N-VAR Someone's **rank** is the social class, especially the high social class, that they belong to. (尤指较高的) 社会地位 [FORMAL] ❑ *He must be treated as a hostage of high rank, not as a common prisoner.* 他一定要作为一个高级人质而不是一般囚徒来对待。 **3** V-T/V-I If an official organization **ranks** someone or something 1st, 5th, or 50th, for example, they calculate that the person or thing has that position on a scale. You can also say that someone or something **ranks** 1st, 5th, or 50th, for example. 给…排名；名列 ❑ *The report ranks the U.S. 20th out of 22 advanced nations.* 这份报告把美国排在22个发达国家的第20位。 ❑ *...the only Canadian woman to be ranked in the top 50 of the women's world rankings.* …进入世界妇女排行榜前50名的惟一的加拿大妇女。 **4** V-T/V-I If you say that someone or something **ranks** high or low on a scale, you are saying how good or important you think they are. 给…排等级；位列 ❑ *His prices rank high among those of other contemporary photographers.* 他的要价与其他同时代的摄影师相比居高。 ❑ *Investors ranked South Korea high among Asian nations.* 投资者在亚洲国家中更看重韩国。 ❑ *St. Petersburg's night life ranks as more exciting than the capital's.* 圣彼得堡的夜生活比首都的更令人激动。 **5** N-PLURAL The **ranks** of a group or organization are the people who belong to it. 成员 ❑ *There were some misgivings within the ranks of the media too.* 媒体内部成员也有一些担忧。 **6** N-PLURAL **The ranks** are the ordinary members of an organization, especially of the armed forces. 普通成员 (尤指军队的普通士兵) ❑ *Most store managers have worked their way up through the ranks.* 大部分的商店经理都是从普通员工干上来的。 **7** N-COUNT A **rank of** people or things is a row of them. 排 ❑ *Ranks of police in riot gear stood nervously by.* 一排排配有防暴设备的警察紧张地站在一边。 **8** N-COUNT A **taxi rank** is a place on a city street where taxis park when they are available. 计程车停车处 [mainly BRIT]

in AM, use **stand**

9 PHRASE If you say that a member of a group or organization **breaks ranks**, you mean that they disobey the instructions of their group or organization. 违背指令 ❑ *Britain appears unlikely to break ranks with other members of the European Union.* 英国似乎不会背弃欧盟其他成员国。 **10** PHRASE If you say that the members of a group **close ranks**, you mean that they are supporting each other only because their group is being criticized. (受批评时) 紧密团结 ❑ *Institutions tend to close ranks when a member has been accused of misconduct.* 各个机构在其某一成员被指控行为不当时都会同心合力。

Thesaurus *rank* 另参见：

N.	class, grade, position, status **1** **2**
V.	assign, place **3**

Word Partnership *rank* 的常用搭配：

ADJ.	**high** rank, **top** rank **1** **2**
ADV.	rank **above**, rank **below** **3**
	rank **high** **4**

rank and file N-SING **The rank and file** are the ordinary members of an organization or the ordinary workers in a company, as opposed to its leaders or managers. 普通成员 [JOURNALISM] ❑ *There was widespread support for him among the rank and file.* 在普通员工中他得到广泛的支持。

ran·sack /rænsæk/ (**ransacks, ransacking, ransacked**) V-T If people **ransack** a building, they damage things in it or make it very messy, often because they are looking for something in a quick and careless way. 洗劫 ❑ *Demonstrators ransacked and burned the house where he was staying.* 示威者们洗劫并焚烧了他住的那所房子。

▲**ran·som** /rænsəm/ (**ransoms, ransoming, ransomed**) **1** N-VAR A **ransom** is the money that has to be paid to someone so that they will set free a person they have kidnapped. 赎金 ❑ *Her kidnapper successfully extorted a \$250,000 ransom for her release.* 绑架者们成功地勒索了25万美元的赎金才释放她。 **2** V-T If you **ransom** someone who has been kidnapped, you pay the money to set them free. 赎出 ❑ *The same system was used for ransoming or exchanging captives.* 同一系统也被用来赎回或交换俘虏。 **3** PHRASE If a kidnapper **is holding** a person **for ransom**, they keep that person prisoner until they are given what they want. 劫持某人以勒取赎金 ❑ *He is charged with kidnapping a businessman last year and holding him for ransom.* 他被指控去年绑架了一名商人并挟持他以勒索赎金。

rant /rænt/ (**rants, ranting, ranted**) V-T/V-I If you say that someone **rants**, you mean that they talk loudly or angrily, and exaggerate or say foolish things. 咆哮；夸夸其谈 ❑ *As the boss began to rant, I stood up and went out.* 老板开始咆哮时，我站起来走了出去。 ❑ *Even their three dogs got bored and fell asleep as he ranted on.* 甚至他们的

3条狗在他不停地夸夸其谈时，都觉得厌烦并睡着了。❑ *"Let's get it over and done with," he ranted.* "让我们就此了结这件事情，"他咆哮道。● N-COUNT **Rant** is also a noun. 咆哮；夸夸其谈 ❑ *Part I is a rant against organized religion.* 第一部分是对有组织的宗教的怒斥。● **rant·ing** N-VAR (**rantings**) 咆哮；夸夸其谈 ❑ *He had been listening to Goldstone's rantings all night.* 他整晚都在听戈德斯通的夸夸其谈。

★ **rap** /ræp/ (**raps, rapping, rapped**) **1** N-UNCOUNT **Rap** is a type of music in which the words are not sung but are spoken in a rapid, rhythmic way. 说唱音乐 ❑ *Her favorite music was by Run DMC, a rap group.* 她最喜欢的音乐是一个说唱音乐组合**Run DMC**的音乐。**2** V-I Someone who **raps** performs rap music. 表演说唱音乐 ❑ *They rap about life in the inner city.* 他们演唱了有关市区生活的说唱乐。**3** N-COUNT A **rap** is a piece of music performed in rap style, or the words that are used in it. 以说唱方式表演的乐曲；(说唱音乐中的) 歌词 ❑ *Every member contributes to the rap, singing either solo or as part of a rap chorus.* 每个成员都在为这首说唱乐出力，或者独唱，或者参与说唱合唱。**4** V-T/V-I If you **rap on** something or **rap** it, you hit it with a series of quick blows. 急速敲打 ❑ *Mary Ann turned and rapped on Charlie's door.* 玛丽・安转过身急敲查理的门。❑ *...rapping the glass with the knuckles of his right hand.* …用他右手的指关节敲击玻璃。● N-COUNT **Rap** is also a noun. 急敲 ❑ *There was a sharp rap on the door.* 有一阵猛烈的敲门声。**5** N-UNCOUNT A rap is a statement in a court of law that someone has committed a particular crime, or the punishment for committing it. 指控；刑罚 [AM, INFORMAL] ❑ *With that old man dead, you're up against a murder rap.* 那个老头死了，你现在面临谋杀的指控。**6** N-COUNT A **rap** is an act of criticizing or blaming someone or something. 批评 [JOURNALISM] ❑ *Bad corks get the rap for as much as 15 percent of tainted wine.* 坏木塞被指造成多达15%的葡萄酒受污染。**7** V-T If you **rap** someone **for** something, you criticize or blame them for it. 批评 [JOURNALISM] ❑ *Water industry chiefs were rapped yesterday for failing their customers.* 供水业的头头们由于未能满足顾客的需要昨天受到了批评。**8** PHRASE If someone in authority **raps** your **knuckles** or **raps** you **on the knuckles**, they criticize you or blame you for doing something they think is wrong. 训斥 [JOURNALISM] ❑ *I joined the workers on strike and was rapped on the knuckles.* 我加入了工人们的罢工，结果遭到了训斥。**9** PHRASE If you say that someone has gotten **a bum rap**, you mean that they have been treated unfairly or punished unfairly. 受冤枉 [mainly AM, INFORMAL] ❑ *She's gotten kind of a bum rap, you know. She's not at all the person she's perceived to be.* 她受到了些冤枉，你知道的。她完全不像人们所想的那样。**10** PHRASE If you **take the rap**, you are blamed or punished for something, especially something that is not your fault or for which other people are equally guilty. 背黑锅 [INFORMAL] ❑ *When the client was murdered, his wife took the rap, but did she really do it?* 那名客户被谋杀后，他的妻子背了黑锅，但她真的做了吗？**11** PHRASE If you **beat the rap**, you avoid being blamed for something wrong that you have done. 逃脱责罚 [INFORMAL] ❑ *...an attorney who boasts he can beat any rap, for a $5,000 fee.* …一个吹嘘只要5000美元就可以让人逃脱任何责罚的律师。
→ see **genre**

★ **rape** ♦◇◇ /reɪp/ (**rapes, raping, raped**) **1** V-T If someone **is raped**, they are forced to have sex, usually by violence or threats of violence. 强奸 ❑ *A young woman was brutally raped in her own home.* 一个年轻妇女在自己家中被粗暴地强奸了。**2** N-VAR **Rape** is the crime of forcing someone to have sex. 强奸罪 ❑ *Almost 90 percent of all rapes and violent assaults went unreported.* 几乎百分之九十的强奸和暴力攻击都没有报警。**3** N-COUNT **Rape** is a plant with yellow flowers which is grown as a crop. Its seeds are crushed to make cooking oil. 油菜

rap·id ♦♦◇ /ræpɪd/ **1** ADJ A **rapid** change is one that happens very quickly. (变化) 快速的 ❑ *...the country's rapid economic growth in the 1980s.* …这个国家在20世纪80年代快速的经济增长。● **rap·id·ly** ADV 快速地 ❑ *...countries with rapidly growing populations.* …人口快速增长的国家。❑ *Try to rip it apart as rapidly as possible.* 试着尽快把它撕开。● **ra·pid·ity** /rəpɪdɪti/ N-UNCOUNT 快速 ❑ *...the rapidity with which the weather can change.* …天气以极快的速度发生变化。**2** ADJ A **rapid** movement is one that is very fast. (动作) 迅速的 ❑ *He walked at a rapid pace along Charles Street.* 他沿着查尔斯大街快步行走。● **rap·id·ly** ADV 迅速地 [ADV with v] ❑ *He was moving rapidly around the room.* 他正在房间里快速地来回走着。● **ra·pid·ity** N-UNCOUNT 迅速 ❑ *The water rushed through the holes with great rapidity.* 水流急速地冲过这些洞口。

Thesaurus *rapid* 另参见：

ADJ. fast, speedy, swift; (*ant.*) slow **1** **2**

Word Partnership *rapid* 的常用搭配：

N. rapid **change**, rapid **decline**, rapid **development**, rapid **expansion**, rapid **growth**, rapid **increase**, rapid **progress** **1**
rapid **pace**, rapid **pulse** **2**

rap·ids /ræpɪdz/ N-PLURAL **Rapids** are a section of a river where the water moves very fast, often over rocks. 急流 ❑ *His canoe was there, on the river below the rapids.* 他的独木舟就在那儿，在河中急流下面的地方。

rap·ist /reɪpɪst/ (**rapists**) N-COUNT A **rapist** is a man who has raped someone. 强奸犯 ❑ *The convicted murderer and rapist is scheduled to be executed next Friday.* 那名被判有罪的强奸杀人犯定于下周五执行死刑。

rap·per /ræpər/ (**rappers**) N-COUNT A **rapper** is a person who performs rap music. 说唱乐手 ❑ *The charts have been dominated by rappers in recent months.* 唱片排行榜最近几个月都被说唱乐歌手占据了。

rap·port /ræpɔr/ N-SING If two people or groups have a **rapport**, they have a good relationship in which they are able to understand each other's ideas or feelings very well. 融洽 [also no det, oft N "with/between" n] ❑ *The success depends on good rapport between interviewer and interviewee.* 成功取决于采访者和被采访者之间的融洽。

rap·ture /ræptʃər/ N-UNCOUNT **Rapture** is a feeling of extreme happiness or pleasure. 狂喜 [LITERARY] ❑ *The film was shown to gasps of rapture at the Democratic Convention.* 这部电影在民主党大会上的放映使与会者欢天喜地。❑ *His speech was received with rapture by his supporters.* 他的演说受到了其支持者的热烈欢呼。

rap·tur·ous /ræptʃərəs/ ADJ A **rapturous** feeling or reaction is one of extreme happiness or enthusiasm. 狂喜的；狂热的 [JOURNALISM] ❑ *The students gave him a rapturous welcome.* 学生们给了他热烈的欢迎。

rare ♦◇◇ /rɛər/ (**rarer, rarest**) **1** ADJ Something that is **rare** is not common and is therefore interesting or valuable. 稀有的 ❑ *...the black-necked crane, one of the rarest species in the world.* …黑颈鹤，世界上最珍稀的物种之一。**2** ADJ An event or situation that is **rare** does not occur very often. 罕见的 ❑ *...on those rare occasions when he did eat alone.* …在他独自吃饭的那些不常有的时候。**3** ADJ You use **rare** to emphasize an extremely good or remarkable quality. 极好的 (素质) [ADJ n] [EMPHASIS] ❑ *Ferris has a rare ability to record her observations on paper.* 费里斯有将自己的观察结果以书面形式记录下来的杰出能力。**4** ADJ Meat that is **rare** is cooked very lightly so that the inside is still red. (肉类) 半熟的 ❑ *Thick tuna steaks are eaten rare, like beef.* 厚厚的金枪鱼片要半熟吃，就像牛肉一样。

Thesaurus *rare* 另参见：

ADJ. incomparable, unique; (*ant.*) commonplace, ordinary **1**
few, infrequent, uncommon, unusual; (*ant.*) common, frequent **2**
raw, undercooked; (*ant.*) well-done **4**

rare·ly ♦◇◇ /rɛərli/ ADV If something **rarely** happens, it does not happen very often. 少见地 ❑ *They battled against other Indian tribes, but rarely fought with the whites.* 他们与其他印第安部落交战，但很少与白人作战。

rar·ity /rɛərɪti/ (**rarities**) **1** N-COUNT If someone or something is a **rarity**, they are interesting or valuable because they are so unusual. 稀有物；罕见之人 [JOURNALISM] ❑ *Sontag has always been that rarity, a glamorous intellectual.* 桑塔格一直都是那种与众不同、极有魅力的知识分子。**2** N-UNCOUNT The **rarity** of something is the fact that it is very uncommon. 稀有 ❑ *It was a real prize due to its rarity and good condition.* 它是一件真正的稀世珍品，因为它不但稀有而且保存完好。

★ **rash** /ræʃ/ (**rashes**) **1** ADJ If someone is **rash** or does **rash** things, they act without thinking carefully first, and therefore make mistakes or behave foolishly. 轻率的 ❑ *It would be rash to rely on such evidence.* 依靠这样的证据太轻率了。● **rash·ly** ADV 轻率地 ❑ *I made a lot of money, but I rashly gave most of it away.* 我赚了很多钱，但我轻率地挥霍了其中的大部分。**2** N-COUNT A **rash** is an area of red spots that appears on your skin when you are ill or have a bad reaction to something that you have eaten or touched. 疹子 ❑ *He may break out in a rash when he eats these nuts.* 他吃了这些坚果以后可能会长出疹子。**3** N-SING If you talk about a **rash of** events or things,

r

you mean a large number of unpleasant events or undesirable things, which have happened or appeared within a short period of time. (短期内出现的) 一连串 (不悦之事) ❑ *...one of the few major airlines left untouched by the industry's rash of takeovers.* …在这一连串的行业兼并中剩下的少数几个未被波及的大航空公司之一。

rasp /ræsp/ **(rasps, rasping, rasped)** 1 V-T/V-I If someone **rasps**, their voice or breathing is harsh and unpleasant to listen to. 刺耳地说; 发出刺耳声 ❑ *"Where did you put it?" he rasped.* "你把它放在哪儿了?" 他尖声地问。● N-SING **Rasp** is also a noun. 刺耳的声音 ❑ *He was still laughing when he heard the rasp of Rennie's voice.* 他听到伦尼刺耳的声音时还在大笑。 2 V-T/V-I If something **rasps** or if you **rasp** it, it makes a harsh, unpleasant sound as it rubs against something hard or rough. 使发出刺耳的刮擦声; 发出刺耳的刮擦声 ❑ *The key rasped in the lock and the door swung open.* 钥匙在锁孔里发出刺耳的刮擦声，门猛地一下开了。❑ *Frank rasped a hand across his chin.* 弗兰克用一只手蹭着下巴发出擦擦的声音。● N-SING **Rasp** is also a noun. 刺耳的刮擦声 ❑ *...the rasp of something being drawn across the sand.* …东西被拖过沙地时刺耳的刮擦声。

rasp·berry /ræzbɛri/ **(raspberries)** 1 N-COUNT **Raspberries** are small, soft, red fruit that grow on bushes. 树莓 2 → see also **Bronx cheer**

rat /ræt/ **(rats, ratting, ratted)** 1 N-COUNT A **rat** is an animal which has a long tail and looks like a large mouse. 老鼠 ❑ *This was demonstrated in a laboratory experiment with rats.* 这点通过在实验室中用老鼠做试验得到证明。 2 N-COUNT If you call someone a **rat**, you mean that you are angry with them or dislike them, often because they have cheated you or betrayed you. 卑鄙小人 [INFORMAL, DISAPPROVAL] ❑ *What did you do with the gun you took from that little rat Turner?* 你要用从卑鄙小人特纳那里弄来的那支枪干什么呢? 3 V-I If someone **rats on** you, they tell someone in authority about things that you have done, especially bad things. 告发 [INFORMAL] ❑ *They were accused of encouraging children to rat on their parents.* 他们被指控怂恿孩子们告发他们的父母。 4 V-I If someone **rats on** an agreement, they do not do what they said they would do. 违约 [INFORMAL] ❑ *She claims he ratted on their divorce settlement.* 她声称他违背了他们的离婚协议。 5 PHRASE If you **smell a rat**, you begin to suspect or realize that something is wrong in a particular situation, for example that someone is trying to deceive you or harm you. 感觉事情不妙 ❑ *If I don't send a picture, he will smell a rat.* 如果我不寄张照片，他会起疑心。

rate ♦♦♦ /reɪt/ **(rates, rating, rated)** 1 N-COUNT The **rate** at which something happens is the speed with which it happens. 速度 ❑ *The rate at which hair grows can be agonizingly slow.* 头发生长的速度可以慢得令人苦恼。 2 N-COUNT The **rate** at which something happens is the number of times it happens over a period of time. 频率 ❑ *New diet books appear at a rate of nearly one a week.* 饮食方面的新书以几乎每周一本的频率出版。 3 N-COUNT A **rate** is the amount of money that is charged for goods or services. 价格 ❑ *A special weekend rate is available from mid-November.* 周末特价从11月中旬就有了。 4 → see also **exchange rate** 5 N-COUNT The **rate** of taxation or interest is the amount of tax or interest that needs to be paid. It is expressed as a percentage of the amount that is earned, gained as profit, or borrowed. 税率; 利率 [BUSINESS] ❑ *The government insisted that it would not be panicked into interest rate cuts.* 政府坚持说它不会因恐慌而降低利率。 6 V-T/V-I If you **rate** someone or something as good or bad, you consider them to be good or bad. You can also say that someone or something **rates** as good or bad. 评价; 被评价 [no cont] ❑ *Of all the men in the survey, they rate themselves the least fun-loving and the most responsible.* 在所有参与调查的人中，他们认为自己是最不喜欢玩乐而最负责任的人。❑ *Most rated it a hit.* 大部分人认为那是一次辉煌的成功。❑ *We rate him as one of the best.* 我们认为他是最优秀者之一。 7 V-T PASSIVE If someone or something **is rated** at a particular position or rank, they are calculated or considered to be in that position on a list. 被评定为; 被看作 [no cont] ❑ *He is generally rated the country's No. 3 industrialist.* 他被大家普遍看成该国的第3大实业家。 8 V-T If you say that someone or something **rates** a particular reaction, you mean that this is the reaction you consider to be appropriate. 值得 [no cont] ❑ *This is so extraordinary, it rates a medal and a phone call from the president.* 这太了不起了，应该颁发一枚奖章并接受总统的电话祝贺。 9 → see also **rating** 10 PHRASE You use **at any rate** to indicate that what you have just said might be incorrect or unclear in some way, and that you are now being more precise. 无论如何 ❑ *His friends liked her – well, most of them at any rate.* 他的朋友们很喜欢她——嗯，无论如何大部分是这样的。 11 PHRASE If you say that **at this rate** something bad or extreme will happen, you mean that it will happen if things continue to develop as they have been doing. 照这样下去 ❑ *At this rate they'd be lucky to get home before eight-thirty or nine.* 照这样下去，他们能在8：30或9：00前到家就很走运了。 → see **interest rate, motion**

Word Partnership *rate* 的常用搭配:

N.	rate **of change** 1
	birth rate, **crime** rate, **dropout** rate, **heart** rate, **pulse** rate, **survival** rate, **unemployment** rate 2
	interest rate 5
ADJ.	**average** rate, **faster** rate, **slow** rate, **steady** rate 1 2
	high rate, **low** rate 1 – 3 5

rate of re·turn **(rates of return)** N-COUNT The **rate of return** on an investment is the amount of profit it makes, often shown as a percentage of the original investment. 回报率 [BUSINESS] ❑ *High rates of return can be earned on these investments.* 这些投资能够带来很高的回报率。

ra·ther ♦♦♦ /ræðər/ 1 PHRASE You use **rather than** when you are contrasting two things or situations. **Rather than** introduces the thing or situation that is not true or that you do not want. 而不是 ❑ *The problem was psychological rather than physiological.* 这是个心理而不是生理问题。● CONJ **Rather** is also a conjunction. 而不是 ❑ *She made students think for themselves, rather than telling them what to think.* 她让学生们自己思考，而不是告诉他们思考什么。 2 ADV You use **rather** when you are correcting something that you have just said, especially when you are describing a particular situation after saying what it is not. (尤指修正上文时) 更确切地说 [ADV with cl/group] ❑ *Twenty million years ago, Idaho was not the arid place it is now. Rather, it was warm and damp, populated by dense primordial forest.* 2000万年前，爱达荷州不像现在这样干旱。确切地说，它那时温暖潮湿，生长着茂密的原始森林。 3 PHRASE If you say that you **would rather** do something or you**'d rather** do it, you mean that you would prefer to do it. If you say that you **would rather not** do something, you mean that you do not want to do it. 宁愿/宁愿不 ❑ *If it's all the same to you, I'd rather work at home.* 如果对你来说都一样，我宁愿在家工作。❑ *Kids would rather play than study.* 孩子们宁愿玩而不愿学习。 4 ADV You use **rather** to indicate that something is true to a fairly great extent, especially when you are talking about something unpleasant or undesirable. (尤指谈论令人不快的事时) 相当地 ❑ *I grew up in rather unusual circumstances.* 我在相当不寻常的环境中长大。❑ *I'm afraid it's a rather long story.* 我恐怕这是个相当长的故事。 5 ADV You use **rather** before verbs that introduce your thoughts and feelings, in order to express your opinion politely, especially when a different opinion has been expressed. (尤指有礼貌地表达相反意见) 或多或少地 [ADV before v] [mainly BRIT, POLITENESS] ❑ *I rather think he was telling the truth.* 我或多或少地相信他在说真话。

▲ rati·fi·ca·tion /rætɪfɪkeɪʃən/ **(ratifications)** N-VAR The **ratification** of a treaty or written agreement is the process of ratifying it. 批准 ❑ *We welcome this development and we look forward to early ratification of the treaty by China.* 我们欢迎这一进展并期望中国早日批准本条约。

▲ rati·fy /rætɪfaɪ/ **(ratifies, ratifying, ratified)** V-T When national leaders or organizations **ratify** a treaty or written agreement, they make it official by giving their formal approval to it, usually by signing it or voting for it. 批准 (条约或书面协议) ❑ *The parliaments of Australia and Indonesia have yet to ratify the treaty.* 澳大利亚和印度尼西亚议会还未批准该条约。

★ rat·ing ♦◇◇ /reɪtɪŋ/ **(ratings)** 1 N-COUNT A **rating** of something is a score or measurement of how good or popular it is. (针对受欢迎度和优劣性的) 评分 ❑ *New public opinion polls show the president's approval rating at its lowest point since he took office.* 新的民意测验表明总统的支持率处在他就职以来的最低点。 2 → see also **credit rating** 3 N-PLURAL The **ratings** are the statistics published each week which show how popular each television program is. (电视节目的) 收视率 ❑ *CBS's ratings again showed huge improvement over the previous year.* 哥伦比亚广播公司的收视率比过去的一年又有了大幅提高。

Word Partnership *rating* 的常用搭配:

N.	**approval** rating 1
ADJ.	**high** rating, **low** rating, **poor** rating, **top** rating 1

R

Word Web ratio

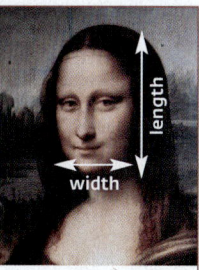

The golden **ratio** is a phrase invented by the ancient Greeks. It refers to a specific mathematical **proportion**— 1:1.618. **Mathematicians** named this number "Phi" in honor of the sculptor Phidias*. He frequently used this ratio in his sculptures. Architects and artists find this proportion attractive. The floor plan of the Parthenon is 1.618 times as **long** as it is **wide**. Drawing a **rectangle** around the face of da Vinci's* "Mona Lisa"* results in the same ratio. The golden ratio is even found in the comparison of the **width** and the **length** of an egg.

Phidias (490-430 BC): a Greek sculptor.
Leonardo da Vinci (1452-1519): an Italian artist and inventor.
"Mona Lisa": a famous painting of a woman.

ra·tio /reɪʃoʊ, -ʃioʊ/ (**ratios**) N-COUNT A **ratio** is a relationship between two things when it is expressed in numbers or amounts. For example, if there are ten boys and thirty girls in a room, the ratio of boys to girls is 1:3, or one to three. 比率 ❑ *The adult to child ratio is one to six.* 成人与儿童之比是1比6。
→ see Word Web: **ratio**

▲ **ra·tion** /ræʃ^ə^n, reɪ-/ (**rations, rationing, rationed**) **1** N-COUNT When there is not enough of something, your **ration** of it is the amount that you are allowed to have. (物资紧缺时的) 配给量 ❑ *The meat ration was down to one pound per person per week.* 肉类的配给量降到了每人每周一磅。 **2** V-T When something **is rationed** by a person or government, you are only allowed to have a limited amount of it, usually because there is not enough of it. (常指因紧缺) 定量配给 ❑ *Staples such as bread, rice, and tea are already being rationed.* 面包、米、茶等主要食品已经是定量配给。 ❑ *The City Council of Moscow has decided that it will begin rationing bread, butter, and meat.* 莫斯科市议会已经决定开始定量配给面包、黄油和肉。 **3** N-PLURAL **Rations** are the food that is given to people who do not have enough food or to soldiers. (给食物不足者的) 配给品; (给士兵的) 给养 ❑ *Aid officials said that the first emergency food rations of wheat and oil were handed out here last month.* 援助官员们说第一批面粉和食用油等紧急救援食品配给已于上月在此发放。 **4** N-COUNT Your **ration of** something is the amount of it that you normally have. 应得份额 ❑ *...after consuming his ration of junk food and two cigarettes.* …吃完他那份垃圾食品、抽完两支烟后。 **5** → see also **rationing**

Word Link *ratio ≈ reasoning : irrational, rational, rationale*

ra·tion·al /ræʃən^ə^l/ **1** ADJ **Rational** decisions and thoughts are based on reason rather than on emotion. 理性的 ❑ *He's asking you to look at both sides of the case and come to a rational decision.* 他是在要求你看到问题的两面，然后做出理性的决定。 ● **ra·tion·al·ly** ADV 理性地 ❑ *It can be very hard to think rationally when you're feeling so vulnerable and alone.* 在你感到如此脆弱和孤单的时候很难理性地思考问题。 ● **ra·tion·al·ity** /ræʃənælɪti/ N-UNCOUNT 理性 ❑ *We live in an era of rationality.* 我们生活在一个理性的时代。 **2** ADJ A **rational** person is someone who is sensible and is able to make decisions based on intelligent thinking rather than on emotion. 理智的 ❑ *Did he come across as a sane, rational person?* 他看上去是不是一个头脑清醒而理智的人?

Word Partnership *rational* 的常用搭配:
N. rational **approach**, rational **choice**, rational **decision**, rational **explanation** **1**
rational **human being**, rational **person** **2**

ra·tion·ale /ræʃənæl, -næl/ (**rationales**) N-COUNT The **rationale** for a course of action, practice, or belief is the set of reasons on which it is based. 全部理由; 根本原因 [FORMAL] ❑ *However, the rationale for such initiatives is not, of course, solely economic.* 但是，这些积极行动的根本原因当然不全是出于经济目的。

ra·tion·al·ise /ræʃənəlaɪz/ [BRIT] → see **rationalize**

ra·tion·al·ist /ræʃən^ə^lɪst/ (**rationalists**) **1** ADJ If you describe someone as **rationalist**, you mean that their beliefs are based on reason and logic rather than emotion or religion. (人) 理性主义的; 唯理论的 ❑ *White was both visionary and rationalist.* 怀特既有远见又有理性。 **2** N-COUNT If you describe someone as a **rationalist**, you mean that they base their life on rationalist beliefs. 理性主义者; 唯理论者 ❑ *...the rationalists and scientists of the nineteenth century.* …19世纪的理性主义者和科学家们。

ra·tion·al·ize /ræʃən^ə^laɪz/ (**rationalizes, rationalizing, rationalized**)
in BRIT, also use **rationalise**
V-T If you try to **rationalize** attitudes or actions that are difficult to accept, you think of reasons to justify or explain them. 使合理化; 为…做合理解释 ❑ *He further rationalized his activity by convincing himself that he was actually promoting peace.* 他通过说服自己确实是在促进和平来进一步使自己的行为合理化。

ra·tion·ing /ræʃənɪŋ/ N-UNCOUNT **Rationing** is the system of limiting the amount of food, water, gasoline, or other necessary substances that each person is allowed to have or buy when there is not enough of them. 配给制 ❑ *The municipal authorities here are preparing for food rationing.* 此地的市政当局正为食物配给制做准备。

rat race N-SING If you talk about getting out of **the rat race**, you mean leaving a job or way of life in which people compete aggressively with each other to be successful. 激烈的竞争; 你争我夺的生活 ❑ *I had to get out of the rat race and take a look at the real world again.* 我必须退出这种你争我夺的生活，重新看看真实的世界。

▲ **rat·tle** /ræt^ə^l/ (**rattles, rattling, rattled**) **1** V-T/V-I When something **rattles** or when you **rattle** it, it makes short, sharp, knocking sounds because it is being shaken or it keeps hitting against something hard. 使发出嘎嘎声; 发出嘎嘎声 ❑ *She slams the kitchen door so hard I hear dishes rattle.* 她砰地一下使劲关上厨房门，我听到盘子都震得嘎嘎响。 ● N-COUNT **Rattle** is also a noun. 嘎嘎声 ❑ *There was a rattle of rifle fire.* 有步枪射击发出的嘎嘎声。 **2** N-COUNT A **rattle** is a baby's toy with small, loose objects inside which make a noise when the baby shakes it. 拨浪鼓 **3** V-T If something or someone **rattles** you, they make you nervous. 使紧张 ❑ *Officials are not normally rattled by any reporter's question.* 官员们一般不会因为任何记者的提问而紧张不安。 ● **rat·tled** ADJ 紧张的 ❑ *He swore in Spanish, an indication that he was rattled.* 他用西班牙语宣誓，这表明他很紧张。

rau·cous /rɔkəs/ ADJ A **raucous** sound is loud, harsh, and rather unpleasant. 刺耳的 ❑ *They heard a bottle being smashed, then more raucous laughter.* 他们听到瓶子被打碎的声音，然后是更多刺耳的笑声。 ● **rau·cous·ly** ADV 刺耳地 ❑ *They laughed together raucously.* 他们一起大声笑起来，声音很刺耳。

▲ **rav·age** /rævɪdʒ/ (**ravages, ravaging, ravaged**) V-T A town, country, or economy that **has been ravaged** is one that has been damaged so much that it is almost completely destroyed. 摧毁 [usu passive] ❑ *The country has been ravaged by civil war.* 这个国家被内战摧毁了。

rav·ages /rævɪdʒɪz/ N-PLURAL **The ravages of** time, war, or the weather are the damaging effects that they have. (时间、战争或天气造成的) 破坏 ❑ *...the ravages of two world wars.* …两次世界大战造成的破坏。

▲ **rave** /reɪv/ (**raves, raving, raved**) **1** V-T/V-I If someone **raves**, they talk in an excited and uncontrolled way. 狂乱地说 ❑ *She cried and raved for weeks, and people did not know what to do.* 她又哭又叫了好几个星期，大家不知道怎么办。 ❑ *"What is wrong with you, acting like that," she raved.* "你是怎么了，会那样做事?" 她狂吼道。 **2** V-T/V-I If you **rave about** something, you speak or write about it with great enthusiasm. 热烈谈论 ❑ *Rachel raved about the new foods she ate while she was there.* 雷切尔大谈特谈她在那里吃到的新食物。 ❑ *"I'd no idea Milan was so wonderful," he raved.* "我之前不知道米兰是那么棒，" 他感叹道。 **3** N-COUNT A **rave** is a big event at which young people dance to electronic music in a large building or in the open air.

Raves are often associated with illegal drugs. (常涉及吸毒的) 狂欢聚会 ❑ *...an all-night rave.* …一场通宵狂欢晚会。 **4** → see also **raving**

ra·ven /reɪvᵊn/ (**ravens**) N-COUNT A **raven** is a large bird with shiny black feathers and a deep harsh call. 渡鸦

ra·vine /rəvin/ (**ravines**) N-COUNT A **ravine** is a very deep, narrow valley with steep sides. 沟壑；深谷 ❑ *The bus overturned and fell into a ravine.* 这辆公共汽车翻了车，掉进了一处深谷。

rav·ing /reɪvɪŋ/ **1** ADJ You use **raving** to describe someone who you think is completely mad. 胡言乱语的；精神错乱的 [INFORMAL] ❑ *Malcolm looked at her as if she were a raving lunatic.* 马尔科姆看着她，好像她是一个胡言乱语的疯子。 ● ADV **Raving** is also an adverb. 完全地 [ADV adj] ❑ *I'm afraid Paul has gone raving mad.* 我恐怕保罗已经彻底疯了。 **2** → see also **rave**

raw ♦◇◇ /rɔ/ (**rawer, rawest**) **1** ADJ **Raw** materials or substances are in their natural state before being processed or used in manufacturing. 未加工的 ❑ *We import raw materials and energy and export mainly industrial products.* 我们进口原材料和能源，主要出口工业产品。 **2** ADJ **Raw** food is food that is eaten uncooked, that has not yet been cooked, or that has not been cooked enough. (食物) 生的 ❑ *...a popular dish made of raw fish.* …由生鱼做的一道很受欢迎的菜肴。 **3** ADJ If a part of your body is **raw**, it is red and painful, perhaps because the skin has come off or has been burned. (身体某部因破皮或烫着等) 红且疼的 ❑ *...the drag of the rope against the raw flesh of my shoulders.* …绳子勒磨在我肩上又红又疼的肉上。 **4** ADJ **Raw** emotions are strong basic feelings or responses which are not weakened by other influences. 强烈直露的 (情感) ❑ *Her grief was still raw and he did not know how to help her.* 她的悲伤仍然强烈直露，他不知道如何帮助她好。 **5** ADJ If you describe something as **raw**, you mean that it is simple, powerful, and real. (用以描述事物) 质朴的；强大的；真实的 ❑ *...the raw power of instinct.* …本能的强大力量。 **6** ADJ **Raw** data is facts or information that has not yet been sorted, analyzed, or prepared for use. (数据等) 未整理的；原始的 ❑ *Analyses were conducted on the raw data.* 对原始数据进行了分析。 **7** ADJ If you describe someone in a new job as **raw**, or as a **raw** recruit, you mean that they lack experience in that job. 无经验的 ❑ *...replacing experienced men with raw recruits.* …用没有经验的新成员代替有经验的人。 **8** ADJ **Raw** weather feels unpleasantly cold. 阴冷的 ❑ *...a raw December morning.* …12月份一个阴冷的早晨。 **9** ADJ **Raw** sewage is sewage that has not been treated to make it cleaner. 未处理的 (污水) [ADJ n] ❑ *...contamination of drinking water by raw sewage.* …饮用水被未处理的污水所污染。 **10** PHRASE If you say that you are getting **a raw deal**, you mean that you are being treated unfairly. 不公平的待遇 [INFORMAL] ❑ *I think women have a raw deal.* 我认为妇女受到了不公平的待遇。

Thesaurus *raw* 另参见：

ADJ. natural **1**
fresh, uncooked; (*ant.*) cooked **2**
scraped, skinned **3**

R

ray ♦◇◇ /reɪ/ (**rays**) **1** N-COUNT **Rays** of light are narrow beams of light. 光线 ❑ *The sun's rays can penetrate water up to 10 feet.* 阳光的光线一直能透射到水下10英尺处。 **2** → see also **X-ray** **3** N-COUNT **A ray of** hope, comfort, or other positive quality is a small amount of it that you welcome because it makes a bad situation seem less bad. 一丝 (希望、安慰等其他积极因素) ❑ *They could provide a ray of hope amid the general economic gloom.* 他们能在普遍的经济低迷中带来一丝希望。
→ see **rainbow, telescope**

▲ **ra·zor** /reɪzər/ (**razors**) N-COUNT A **razor** is a tool that people use for shaving. 剃刀 ❑ *...a plastic disposable razor.* …一把一次性的塑料剃刀。

Rd. also **Rd** **Rd.** is a written abbreviation for **road**. It is used especially in addresses and on maps or signs. 公路 (常用于地址、地图或路标) ❑ *Chicago Botanic Garden, Lake Cook Rd., Glencoe.* 格伦科，雷克库克路，芝加哥植物园。

re /ri/ PREP You use **re** in documents such as business letters, e-mails, faxes and memos to introduce a subject or item which you are going to discuss or refer to in detail. 关于 (用在商务信函、电子邮件、传真、备忘录中，引出所要谈论的话题) ❑ *Dear Mrs. Cox, Re: Homeowners Insurance. We note from our files that we have not yet received your renewal instructions.* 亲爱的考克斯夫人，关于房主保险一事。我们从自己的资料中注意到我们还没有收到你续保的通知。

-'re /ər/ **-'re** is the usual spoken form of "are." It is added to the end of the pronoun or noun which is the subject of the verb. For example, "they are" can be shortened to "they're." **are**的缩写

reach ♦♦♦ /ritʃ/ (**reaches, reaching, reached**) **1** V-T When someone or something **reaches** a place, they arrive there. 到达 (某地) ❑ *He did not stop until he reached the door.* 他到门口才停住。 **2** V-T If someone or something has **reached** a certain stage, level, or amount, they are at that stage, level, or amount. 达到 (某一阶段、水平或数量) ❑ *The process of political change in South Africa has reached the stage where it is irreversible.* 南非的政治变革进程已经到了不可逆转的阶段。 **3** V-I If you **reach** somewhere, you move your arm and hand to take or touch something. 伸手去 (拿或够东西) ❑ *Judy reached into her handbag and handed me a small, printed leaflet.* 朱迪把手伸进手提袋中，递给我一张小小的印刷传单。 **4** V-T If you can **reach** something, you are able to touch it by stretching out your arm or leg. (伸展手臂或腿) 够到 ❑ *Can you reach your toes with your fingertips?* 你能用手指尖触到脚趾头吗？

> You use both **reach** and **arrive** to talk about coming to a particular place. **Reach** is always followed by a noun or pronoun referring to a place, and you can use it to emphasize the effort required to get there. ❑ *To reach the capital might not be easy.* You can use **arrive** to emphasize being in a place rather than traveling to it. ❑ *When I arrived in England I was exhausted.* **Arrive at** and **reach** can also be used to say that someone eventually makes a decision or finds the answer to something. ❑ *It took hours to arrive at a decision... They were unable to reach a decision.*

5 V-T If you try to **reach** someone, you try to contact them, usually by telephone. (常指通过电话) 联系上 (某人) ❑ *Has the doctor told you how to reach him or her in emergencies?* 医生有没有告诉你在紧急状况下如何联系上他或她？ **6** V-T/V-I If something **reaches** a place, point, or level, it extends as far as that place, point, or level. 延伸到；延伸 ❑ *...a nightshirt that reached to his knees.* …一件长及他膝盖的男用睡衣。 **7** V-T When people **reach** an agreement or a decision, they succeed in achieving it. 达成 ❑ *A meeting of agriculture ministers has so far failed to reach agreement over farm subsidies.* 农业部长们的会议到目前为止还没有达成有关农业补贴的协议。 **8** N-UNCOUNT Someone's or something's **reach** is the distance or limit to which they can stretch, extend, or travel. (人或物所能及的) 距离；限度 ❑ *Isabelle placed a wine cup on the table within his reach.* 伊莎贝尔把一只酒杯放在桌上他伸手可及的地方。 **9** N-UNCOUNT If a place or thing is within **reach**, it is possible to have it or get to it. If it is out of **reach**, it is not possible to have it or get to it. 可及的范围 ❑ *It is located within reach of many important Norman towns, including Bayeux.* 它位于诺曼许多重要城镇的附近，包括巴约。

Thesaurus *reach* 另参见：

V. arrive, enter, get in **1**
arrive, succeed **2**
extend to, hold out, stretch **3**
call, contact **5**

Word Partnership *reach* 的常用搭配：

N. reach **a destination** **1**
reach **a goal**, reach ***one's* potential** **2**
reach **(an) agreement**, reach **a compromise**, reach **a conclusion**, reach **a consensus**, reach **a decision** **7**

re·act ♦◇◇ /riækt/ (**reacts, reacting, reacted**) **1** V-I When you **react to** something that has happened to you, you behave in a particular way because of it. 作出反应 ❑ *They reacted violently to the news.* 他们对这条新闻反应强烈。 **2** V-I If you **react against** someone's way of behaving, you deliberately behave in a different way because you do not like the way they behave. 反抗 ❑ *My father never saved money and perhaps I reacted against that.* 我父亲从不攒钱，也许我反对这种做法。 **3** V-I If you **react to** a substance such as a drug, or **to** something you have touched, you are affected unpleasantly or made ill by it. (对药物或其他所碰触的东西等) 起不良反应 ❑ *Someone allergic to milk is likely to react to cheese.* 对牛奶过敏的人可能会对奶酪也有不良反应。 **4** V-RECIP When one chemical substance **reacts with** another, or when two chemical substances **react**, they combine chemically to form another substance. 起化学反应 ❑ *Calcium reacts with water but less violently than sodium and potassium do.* 钙能与水产生化学反应但不如钠以及钾那么剧烈。

Word Partnership *react* 的常用搭配：

ADJ. **slow** to react 1
N. react **to news**, react **to a situation** 1
ADV. react **differently**, react **emotionally**, **how** to react, react **negatively**, react **positively**, react **quickly** 1 react **strongly**, react **violently** 1 3 4

re·ac·tion ♦♦◇ /riækʃᵊn/ (**reactions**) 1 N-VAR Your **reaction to** something that has happened or something that you have experienced is what you feel, say, or do because of it. 反应 ❑ *Reaction to the visit is mixed.* 对这次访问的反应不一。 2 N-COUNT A **reaction against** something is a way of behaving or doing something that is deliberately different from what has been done before. 反抗 ❑ *All new fashion starts out as a reaction against existing convention.* 所有新时尚都是从反抗现存习俗开始的。 3 N-SING If there is a **reaction against** something, it becomes unpopular. 抵触 [also no det, N "against" n] ❑ *Premature moves in this respect might well provoke a reaction against the reform.* 在这方面过早的行动可能会激起对改革的抵触。 4 N-PLURAL Your **reactions** are your ability to move quickly in response to something, for example when you are in danger. 反应能力；应变能力 ❑ *The sport requires very fast reactions.* 这项运动要求很快的反应能力。 5 N-UNCOUNT **Reaction** is the belief that the political or social system of your country should not change. 保守思想 [DISAPPROVAL] ❑ *Thus, he aided reaction and thwarted progress.* 所以他支持保守思想，反对进步。 6 N-COUNT A chemical **reaction** is a process in which two substances combine together chemically to form another substance. (化学)反应 ❑ *Ozone is produced by the reaction between oxygen and ultraviolet light.* 臭氧是氧气与紫外线发生化学反应而产生的。 7 N-COUNT If you have a **reaction to** a substance such as a drug, or **to** something you have touched, you are affected unpleasantly or made ill by it. (对药物或所碰触的东西等的) 不良反应 ❑ *Every year, 5,000 people have life-threatening reactions to anesthetics.* 每年，有5000人会对麻醉剂产生致命的不良反应。

→ see **motion**

Word Partnership *reaction* 的常用搭配：

ADJ. **emotional** reaction, **initial** reaction, **mixed** reaction, **negative** reaction, **positive** reaction 1 **chemical** reaction 6 **allergic** reaction 7

★ **re·ac·tion·ary** /riækʃənɛri/ (**reactionaries**) ADJ A **reactionary** person or group tries to prevent changes in the political or social system of their country. 反动的；保守的 [DISAPPROVAL] ❑ *It became clear to everyone that the chairman was too reactionary, too blinkered.* 现在每人都看清了主席太保守、太狭隘。 ● N-COUNT A **reactionary** is someone with reactionary views. 反动分子；保守分子 ❑ *Critics viewed him as a reactionary, even a monarchist.* 批评者们把他看成是反动分子，甚至是君主主义者。

re·ac·tor /riæktər/ (**reactors**) N-COUNT A **reactor** is the same as a **nuclear reactor**. 核反应堆

read ♦♦♦ (**reads, reading**)

The form **read** is pronounced /rid/ when it is the present tense, and /rɛd/ when it is the past tense and past participle.

read此词形为现在时时读作 /rid/，为过去时和过去完成时时读作 /rɛd/。

1 V-T/V-I When you **read** something such as a book or article, you look at and understand the words that are written there. 阅读 ❑ *Have you read this book?* 你读过这本书吗？ ❑ *I read about it in the paper.* 我在报上读到有关它的消息。 ❑ *She spends her days reading and watching television.* 她每天就是看书和看电视。 ● N-SING **Read** is also a noun. 阅读 ❑ *I settled down to have a good read.* 我舒舒服服地坐下来，想好好读书。 2 V-T/V-I When you **read** a piece of writing to someone, you say the words aloud. 朗读 ❑ *Jay reads poetry so beautifully.* 杰伊朗读诗歌非常动听。 ❑ *I like it when she reads to us.* 我很喜欢她读书给我们听。 3 V-T/V-I People who can **read** have the ability to look at and understand written words. 识字 ❑ *He couldn't read or write.* 他不识字，也不会写字。 ❑ *The kid can read words, but did miserably on the test.* 这孩子能认字，但考试时却一塌糊涂。 4 V-T If you can **read** music, you have the ability to look at and understand the symbols that are used in written music to represent musical sounds. 识(乐谱) ❑ *Later on I learned how to read music.* 后来我学会了如何识乐谱。 5 V-T When a computer **reads** a file or a document, it takes information from a disk or tape. (电脑) 读取 (文件或文档) [COMPUTING] ❑ *How can I read an Excel file on a computer that only has Word installed?* 我怎么在只装了**Word**文字处理软件的电脑上读取**Excel**表格文件呢？ 6 V-T You can use **read** when saying what is written on something or in something. For example, if a notice **reads** "Entrance," the word "Entrance" is written on it. 写着 [no cont] ❑ *The sign on the bus read "Private: Not In Service."* 公共汽车上的标志写着"私人所有：不运营。" 7 V-I If you refer to how a piece of writing **reads**, you are referring to its style. (作品) 读起来 (有…风格) ❑ *The book reads like a ballad.* 这本书读起来像民谣的风格。 8 N-COUNT If you say that a book or magazine is a good **read**, you mean that it is very enjoyable to read. 读物 [adj N] ❑ *Ben Okri's latest novel is a good read.* 本・奥克里的最新小说是本好读物。 9 V-T If something **is read** in a particular way, it is understood or interpreted in that way. 理解；诠释 ❑ *The play is being widely read as an allegory of imperialist conquest.* 这出戏正被广泛地诠释为帝国主义征服的寓言。 10 V-T If you **read** someone's mind or thoughts, you know exactly what they are thinking without them telling you. 看透 (心思或想法) ❑ *From behind her, as if he could read her thoughts, Benny said, "You're free to go any time you like, Madame."* 从她身后，好像他可以看透她的想法，本尼说道，"你什么时候想走都可以，夫人。" 11 V-T If you can **read** someone or you can **read** their gestures, you can understand what they are thinking or feeling by the way they behave or the things they say. 领会 (某人或其言谈举止的意图) ❑ *If you have to work as part of a team, you must learn to read people.* 如果你不得不在一个团队中工作，你必须学会领会别人的意图。 12 V-T When you **read** a measuring device, you look at it to see what the figure or measurement on it is. 查看；读出 (测量仪器的数字) ❑ *It is essential that you are able to read a thermometer.* 能读出温度计上的温度是基本要求。 13 V-T If a measuring device **reads** a particular amount, it shows that amount. (测量仪表) 显示为；标明 ❑ *The thermometer read 105 degrees Fahrenheit.* 温度计显示为华氏105度。 14 → see also **reading**

▸ **read into** PHRASAL VERB If you **read** a meaning **into** something, you think it is there although it may not actually be there. 认为包含；对…加入 (某种实际并不存在的含义) ❑ *It is dangerous to read too much into one year's figures.* 对一年的数据加入太多并不存在的含义是危险的。

▸ **read out** PHRASAL VERB If you **read out** a piece of writing, you say it aloud. 大声读出 ❑ *He's obliged to take his turn at reading out the announcements.* 他不得不依次等着轮到自己大声读出通知。

▸ **read up on** PHRASAL VERB If you **read up on** a subject, you read a lot about it so that you become informed about it. 钻研；熟读 ❑ *I've read up on the dangers of all these drugs.* 我已熟知所有这些药物的危险之处。

Thesaurus *read* 另参见：

V. scan, skim, study 1 comprehend 1 3 4

Word Partnership *read* 的常用搭配：

ADV. read **carefully**, read **silently** 1
N. read **a book/magazine/(news)paper**, read **a sentence**, read **a sign**, read **a statement** 1 2 read **a verdict** 2 **ability** to read 3 4
V. **like** to read, **want** to read 1 2 **listen to** *someone* read 2 **learn (how)** to read 3 4

read·able /ridəbᵊl/ 1 ADJ If you say that a book or article is **readable**, you mean that it is enjoyable and easy to read. 易读的；有可读性的 ❑ *This is a well researched and very readable book.* 这是一本研究深刻、可读性强的书。 2 ADJ A piece of writing that is **readable** is written or printed clearly and can be read easily. 字迹清晰的；容易辨认的 ❑ *My secretary worked long hours translating my almost illegible writing into a typewritten and readable script.* 我的秘书花了很长时间将我那几乎辨别不清的书写稿转换成打印的、字迹清晰的文稿。

read·er ♦♦◇ /ridər/ (**readers**) 1 N-COUNT The **readers** of a newspaper, magazine, or book are the people who read it. 读者 ❑ *These texts give the reader an insight into the Chinese mind.* 这些文章让读者对中国式的思维有了深入了解。 ❑ *The paper's success is simple: we give our readers what they want.* 本报的成功很简单：我们给读者他们想要的东西。 2 N-COUNT A **reader** is a person who reads, especially one

r

who reads for pleasure. 读书的人(尤指为获得乐趣) ❑ *Thanks to that job I became an avid reader.* 多亏那项工作我成了一个爱读书的人。

read·er·ship /riːdərʃɪp/ (**readerships**) N-COUNT The **readership** of a book, newspaper, or magazine is the number or type of people who read it. 读者数; 读者群 ❑ *Its readership has grown to over 15,000 subscribers.* 它的读者数已超过一万五千订户。

read·ily /rɛdɪli/ **1** ADV If you do something **readily**, you do it in a way which shows that you are very willing to do it. 乐意地 [ADV with v] ❑ *I asked her if she would allow me to interview her, and she readily agreed.* 我问她是否允许我采访她，她欣然同意了。 **2** ADV You also use **readily** to say that something can be done or obtained quickly and easily. For example, if you say that something can be readily understood, you mean that people can understand it quickly and easily. 容易地; 迅速地 ❑ *The components are readily available in hardware stores.* 这些零件在五金商店容易买到。

Word Partnership *readily* 的常用搭配:

V.	readily **accept**, readily **admit**, readily **agree** **1**
ADV.	readily **apparent** **2**
ADJ.	***be*** readily **available**, **make** readily **available** **2**

readi·ness /rɛdinɪs/ **1** N-UNCOUNT If someone is very willing to do something, you can talk about their **readiness to** do it. 乐意 ❑ *...their readiness to co-operate with the new U.S. envoy.* …他们乐意与美国的新特使合作。 **2** N-UNCOUNT If you do something **in readiness for** a future event, you do it so that you are prepared for that event. 准备就绪 ❑ *Security tightened in the capital in readiness for the president's arrival.* 首都的安全加强了，为总统的到来做好了准备。

read·ing ♦◇◇ /riːdɪŋ/ (**readings**) **1** N-UNCOUNT **Reading** is the activity of reading books. 读书 ❑ *I have always loved reading.* 我一直很喜欢读书。 **2** N-COUNT A **reading** is an event at which poetry or extracts from books are read to an audience. 朗诵会 ❑ *...a poetry reading.* …一场诗歌朗诵会。 **3** N-COUNT Your **reading of** a word, text, or situation is the way in which you understand or interpret it. 诠释; 理解 ❑ *My reading of her character makes me feel that she was too responsible a person to do those things.* 我对她性格的了解使我觉得她是个非常负责、绝不会干那些事的人。 **4** N-COUNT The **reading** on a measuring device is the figure or measurement that it shows. (测量仪器上的) 读数 ❑ *The gauge must be giving a faulty reading.* 标尺一定是给出了一个错误的读数。

re·adjust /riːədʒʌst/ (**readjusts, readjusting, readjusted**) **1** V-I When you **readjust to** a new situation, usually one you have been in before, you adapt to it. 重新适应 ❑ *I can understand why astronauts find it difficult to readjust to life on earth.* 我能明白为什么宇航员们发现难以重新适应地球上的生活。 **2** V-T If you **readjust** the level of something, your attitude to something, or the way you do something, you change it to make it more effective or appropriate. 调整 ❑ *In the end you have to readjust your expectations.* 最后你得调整你的期望值。 **3** V-T If you **readjust** something such as a piece of clothing or a mechanical device, you correct or alter its position or setting. 校准; 重置 ❑ *Readjust your watch. You are now on Moscow time.* 校准你的手表。你现在正处于莫斯科时间。

re·adjust·ment /riːədʒʌstmənt/ (**readjustments**) N-VAR **Readjustment** is the process of adapting to a new situation, usually one that you have been in before. 重新适应 ❑ *The next few weeks will be a period of readjustment, and will probably not be easy.* 接下来的几周是重新适应的时期，很可能不会容易。

ready ♦♦◇ /rɛdi/ (**readier, readiest, readies, readying, readied**) **1** ADJ If someone is **ready**, they are properly prepared for something. If something is **ready**, it has been properly prepared and is now able to be used. 准备好的 [v-link ADJ] ❑ *It took her a long time to get ready for church.* 她花了很长时间才准备好去教堂。 ❑ *Are you ready to board, Mr. Daly?* 准备好上飞机了吗，戴利先生？ **2** ADJ If you are **ready for** something or **ready to** do something, you have enough experience to do it or you are old enough and sensible enough to do it. 胜任的; 准备好的 [v-link ADJ] ❑ *She says she's not ready for marriage.* 她说她还没有准备好结婚。 **3** ADJ If you are **ready to** do something, you are willing to do it. 乐意的 [v-link ADJ to-inf] ❑ *They were ready to die for their beliefs.* 他们愿意为信仰而献身。 **4** ADJ If you are **ready for** something, you need it or want it. 需要的 [v-link ADJ "for" n] ❑ *I don't know about you, but I'm ready for bed.* 我不知道你怎样，但我想去睡了。 **5** ADJ To be **ready to** do something means to be about to do it or likely to do it. 即将…的; 可能…的 [v-link ADJ to-inf] ❑ *She looked ready to cry.* 她看起来将要哭了。 **6** ADJ You use **ready** to describe things that are able to be used very quickly and easily. 现成的 [ADJ n] ❑ *I didn't have a ready answer for this dilemma.* 我没有现成的答案来解决这个进退两难的问题。 **7** V-T When you **ready** something, you prepare it for a particular purpose. 使准备好 [FORMAL] ❑ *John's soldiers were readying themselves for the final assault.* 约翰的士兵们正在为最后的进攻做好准备。

Word Partnership *ready* 的常用搭配:

V.	**get** ready **1**
	ready **to begin**, ready **to fight**, ready **to go/leave**, ready **to play**, ready **to start** **1**–**5**
	ready **to burst** **5**
ADV.	**always** ready, **not quite** ready, **not** ready **yet** **1**–**5**
N.	ready **for bed**, ready **for dinner** **1** **4**

ready-made **1** ADJ If something that you buy is **ready-made**, you can use it immediately, because the work you would normally have to do has already been done. 现成的; 预先做好的 ❑ *We rely quite a bit on ready-made meals – they are so convenient.* 我们相当依赖现成的熟食——它们如此方便。 **2** ADJ **Ready-made** means extremely convenient or useful for a particular purpose. 极其方便的; 极其有用的 ❑ *Those wishing to study urban development have a ready-made example on their doorstep.* 那些想研究城市开发的人眼前有一个极其方便的例子。

re·affirm /riːəfɜːrm/ (**reaffirms, reaffirming, reaffirmed**) V-T If you **reaffirm** something, you state it again clearly and firmly. 重申 [FORMAL] ❑ *He reaffirmed his commitment to the country's economic reform program.* 他重申了对这个国家经济改革计划的承诺。

real ♦♦♦ /riːl/ **1** ADJ Something that is **real** actually exists and is not imagined, invented, or theoretical. 真实的 ❑ *No, it wasn't a dream. It was real.* 不，那不是梦。它是真实的。 **2** ADJ If something is **real to** someone, they experience it as though it really exists or happens, even though it does not. 逼真的 ❑ *Whitechild's life becomes increasingly real to the reader.* 怀特莱尔德的生活在读者看来越来越像是真的。 **3** ADJ A material or object that is **real** is natural or functioning, and not artificial or an imitation. 天然的; 非仿制的 ❑ *...the smell of real leather.* …真皮的气味。 **4** ADJ You can use **real** to describe someone or something that has all the characteristics or qualities that such a person or thing typically has. 名副其实的; 真正的 [ADJ n] ❑ *...his first real girlfriend.* …他的第一个名副其实的女朋友。 **5** ADJ You can use **real** to describe something that is the true or original thing of its kind, in contrast to one that someone wants you to believe is true. 真实的; 最初的 [ADJ n] ❑ *This was the real reason for her call.* 这是她打电话的真实原因。 **6** ADJ You can use **real** to describe something that is the most important or typical part of a thing. 最重要的; 最典型的 [ADJ n] ❑ *When he talks, he only gives glimpses of his real self.* 他讲话时只是偶尔流露出真实的自我。 **7** ADJ You can use **real** when you are talking about a situation or feeling to emphasize that it exists and is important or serious. 确实存在的; 真切而严重的 [EMPHASIS] ❑ *Global warming is a real problem.* 全球变暖是个确实存在的问题。 ❑ *The prospect of civil war is very real.* 内战爆发的可能性确实存在。 **8** ADJ You can use **real** to emphasize a quality that is genuine and sincere. 真实的; 真诚的 [ADJ n] [EMPHASIS] ❑ *You've been drifting from job to job without any real commitment.* 你从一个工作换到另一个工作，从没有真正地投入过。 **9** ADJ You can use **real** before nouns to emphasize your description of something or someone. (用在名词前) 十足的 [ADJ n] [mainly SPOKEN, EMPHASIS] ❑ *"You must think I'm a real idiot."* "你一定认为我是个十足的傻瓜。" **10** ADJ The **real** cost or value of something is its cost or value after other amounts have been added or subtracted and when factors such as the level of inflation have been considered. (成本或价值) 实际的; 净的 [ADJ n] ❑ *...the real cost of borrowing.* …借款的实际成本。 ● PHRASE You can also talk about the cost or value of something **in real terms**. 实(价) ❑ *In real terms the cost of driving is cheaper than a decade ago.* 驾车的实际花费比10年前要少。 **11** ADV You can use **real** to emphasize an adjective or adverb. 非常 (用以强调形容词或副词) [ADV adj/adv] [AM, INFORMAL, EMPHASIS] ❑ *He is finding prison life "real tough."* 他现在发现监狱生活"非常艰苦。" **12** PHRASE If you say that someone does something **for real**, you mean that they actually do it and do not just pretend to do it. 确实地; 真正地 [INFORMAL] ❑ *I have gone to premieres in my dreams but I never thought I'd do it for real.* 我在梦中多次参加过首演，但我从没想到我会真的参加。

Do not confuse **real** and **actual**. You use **real** to describe things that exist rather than being imagined or theoretical. ❑ *Robert squealed in mock terror, then in real pain.* You use **actual** to emphasize that what you are referring to is real or genuine, for example, the **actual** cost of something is what it costs rather than what you expect it to cost. You can also use **actual** to contrast different aspects of something, for example, the time taken to prepare for something and to do something. ❑ *The actual boat trip takes around forty-five minutes.*

real es·tate ♦♦◊ **1** N-UNCOUNT **Real estate** is property in the form of land and buildings, rather than personal possessions. 不动产；房地产 [mainly AM] ❑ *By investing in real estate, he was one of the richest men in the United States.* 通过投资房地产，他成了美国最富的人之一。 **2** N-UNCOUNT **Real estate** businesses or **real estate** agents sell houses, buildings, and land. 房地产 [AM]

in BRIT, use **estate agency, estate agents**

❑ *...the real estate agent who sold you your house.* …卖给你房子的那个房地产经纪人。

→ see **skyscraper**

re·al·is·able /riːəlaɪzəbᵊl/ [BRIT] → see **realizable**

re·al·ise /riəlaɪz/ [mainly BRIT] → see **realize**

★ **re·al·ism** /riəlɪzəm/ **1** N-UNCOUNT When people show **realism** in their behavior, they recognize and accept the true nature of a situation and try to deal with it in a practical way. 现实态度；务实精神 [APPROVAL] ❑ *It was time now to show more political realism.* 是表现出更多的政治务实精神的时候了。 **2** N-UNCOUNT If things and people are presented with **realism** in paintings, stories, or movies, they are presented in a way that is like real life. (绘画、小说或电影中的) 现实主义 [APPROVAL] ❑ *Greene's stories had an edge of realism that made it easy to forget they were fiction.* 格林的故事带有现实主义的色彩，使人容易忘记它们是虚构的。

→ see **genre**

re·al·ist /riəlɪst/ (**realists**) **1** N-COUNT A **realist** is someone who recognizes and accepts the true nature of a situation and tries to deal with it in a practical way. 现实主义者；务实的人 [APPROVAL] ❑ *I see myself not as a cynic but as a realist.* 我把自己看成是现实主义者而不是愤世嫉俗的人。 **2** ADJ A **realist** painter or writer is one who represents things and people in a way that is like real life. 现实主义的 (画家或作家) [ADJ n] ❑ *...perhaps the foremost realist painter of our time.* …也许我们这个时代最重要的现实主义画家。

re·al·is·tic /riəlɪstɪk/ **1** ADJ If you are **realistic** about a situation, you recognize and accept its true nature and try to deal with it in a practical way. 现实的；务实的 ❑ *Police have to be realistic about violent crime.* 警察对暴力犯罪不得不采取务实的态度 ❑ *It's only realistic to acknowledge that something, some time, will go wrong.* 承认有些事情，有些时候会出错是现实的。 ● **re·al·is·ti·cal·ly** ADV 现实地；务实地 ❑ *As an adult, you can assess the situation realistically.* 作为成年人，你可以现实地估量这个局势。 **2** ADJ Something such as a goal or target that is **realistic** is one that you can sensibly expect to achieve. 现实可行的 ❑ *A more realistic figure is 11 million.* 一个更现实可行的数字是1100万。 **3** ADJ You say that a painting, story, or movie is **realistic** when the people and things in it are like people and things in real life. 逼真的 ❑ *...extraordinarily realistic paintings of Indians.* …关于印第安人的极其逼真的绘画。 ● **re·al·is·ti·cal·ly** ADV 逼真地 ❑ *The film starts off realistically and then develops into a ridiculous fantasy.* 电影开始的时候比较逼真，然后却发展成为荒谬的幻想。

→ see **art, fantasy**

Word Partnership *realistic* 的常用搭配：

V.	**be** realistic **1**
ADV.	**more** realistic, **very** realistic **1**–**3**
N.	realistic **assessment**, realistic **expectations**, realistic **goals**, realistic **view** **2**

re·al·is·ti·cal·ly /riəlɪstɪkli/ **1** ADV You use **realistically** when you want to emphasize that what you are saying is true, even though you would prefer it not to be true. 实际上 (用以强调尽管不希望，但所说内容却是真实的) [ADV with cl] [EMPHASIS] ❑ *Realistically, there is never one right answer.* 实际上，从来没有一个正确的答案。 **2** → see also **realistic**

Word Link *real ≈ actual : reality, realize, really*

re·al·ity ♦♦◊ /riælɪti/ (**realities**) **1** N-UNCOUNT You use **reality** to refer to real things or the real nature of things rather than imagined, invented, or theoretical ideas. 现实 ❑ *Fiction and reality were increasingly blurred.* 小说与现实越来越混淆难分。 **2** → see also **virtual reality** **3** N-COUNT **The reality of** a situation is the truth about it, especially when it is unpleasant or difficult to deal with. (尤指令人不快或难对付的) 真实情形 ❑ *...the harsh reality of top international competition.* …顶级的国际竞争的残酷现实。 **4** N-SING You say that something has become a **reality** when it actually exists or is actually happening. 事实存在；真实发生的事 ❑ *...the whole procedure that made this book become a reality.* …使这本书的出版成为现实的整个过程。 **5** PHRASE You can use **in reality** to introduce a statement about the real nature of something, when it contrasts with something incorrect that has just been described. 事实上；实际上 ❑ *He came across as streetwise, but in reality he was not.* 他看似适应都市的生活，但事实上他不是。

→ see **fantasy**

Word Partnership *reality* 的常用搭配：

ADJ.	**virtual** reality **1**
V.	**distort** reality **1**
	become a reality **4**
N.	reality **of life**, reality **of war** **3**
PREP.	**in** reality **5**

re·al·ity TV N-UNCOUNT **Reality TV** is a type of television programming that aims to show how ordinary people behave in everyday life, or in situations, often created by the program makers, which are intended to represent everyday life. (电视) 真人秀 (节目)

re·al·iz·able /riəlaɪzəbᵊl/

in BRIT, also use **realisable**

1 ADJ If your hopes or aims are **realizable**, there is a possibility that the things that you want to happen will happen. (希望、目标等) 可实现的 [FORMAL] ❑ *...the reasonless assumption that one's dreams and desires were realizable.* …一个人的梦想与欲望都是可以实现的这种不合理的假设。 **2** ADJ **Realizable** wealth is money that can be easily obtained by selling something. 可变现的 (财富) [FORMAL] ❑ *In many cases this realizable wealth is not realized during the lifetime of the home owner.* 在很多情况下，这种可变现的财富在房主一生中都没有成为现实。

re·al·ize ♦♦◊ /riəlaɪz/ (**realizes, realizing, realized**)

in BRIT, also use **realise**

1 V-T/V-I If you **realize** that something is true, you become aware of that fact or understand it. 意识到 ❑ *As soon as we realized something was wrong, we moved the children away.* 我们一意识到出了问题，就立即把孩子们转移开了。 ❑ *People don't realize how serious this recession has actually been.* 人们没有意识到这次经济衰退有多么严重。 ● **re·ali·za·tion** /riəlɪzeɪʃᵊn/ N-VAR (**realizations**) 认识 ❑ *There is now a growing realization that things cannot go on like this for much longer.* 人们越来越认识到事情不可能再这样发展下去了。 **2** V-T If your hopes, desires, or fears **are realized**, the things that you hope for, desire, or fear actually happen. (希望、渴望或恐惧) 变成现实 [usu passive] ❑ *All his worst fears were realized.* 他最担心的事情都变成了现实。 ● **re·ali·za·tion** N-UNCOUNT 成为现实 ❑ *In Kravis's venomous tone he recognized the realization of his worst fears.* 从克拉维斯恶毒的语调中他意识到他最害怕的事情发生了。 **3** V-T When someone **realizes** a design or an idea, they make or organize something based on that design or idea. 使成为现实 [FORMAL] ❑ *I knew the technique that I would have to create in order to realize that structure.* 我了解为了使这种结构成为现实，我必须开发的技术。 **4** V-T If someone or something **realizes** their potential, they do everything they are capable of doing, because they have been given the opportunity to do so. 发挥 (潜能) ❑ *The support systems to enable women to realize their potential at work are seriously inadequate.* 使妇女发挥其工作潜能的支持系统严重不足。 **5** V-T If something **realizes** a particular amount of money when it is sold, that amount of money is paid for it. 赚取 (指通过出售某物赚钱) [FORMAL] ❑ *A selection of correspondence from P.G. Wodehouse realized 2,000 dollars.* 佩·格·沃德豪斯的书信选集卖了2000美元。 ● **re·ali·za·tion** N-VAR 赚取 ❑ *...a total cash realization of about $23 million.* …一共赚了大约两千三百万美元的现金。

in BRIT, also use **realisation**

Thesaurus *realize* 另参见：

V. pick up, see, understand 1

Word Partnership *realize* 的常用搭配：

V. **come** to realize, **make** *someone* realize 1
begin to realize, **fail** to realize 1 4
ADV. **suddenly** realize 1
finally realize, **fully** realize 1 4
N. realize **a dream** 2
realize **your potential** 4

real life N-UNCOUNT If something happens **in real life**, it actually happens and is not just in a story or in someone's imagination. 现实生活 ❑ *In real life men like Richard Gere don't marry hookers.* 在现实生活中，像理查德·盖尔这种人不会和妓女结婚。● ADJ **Real life** is also an adjective. 现实生活的 [ADJ n] ❑ *...a real-life horror story.* …一个现实生活中的恐怖故事。

re·allo·cate /riæləkeɪt/ (**reallocates, reallocating, reallocated**) V-T When organizations **reallocate** money or resources, they decide to change the way they spend the money or use the resources. 再分配(金钱或资源) ❑ *...a cost-cutting program to reallocate people and resources within the company.* …在公司内部重新分配人员和资源的节省开支计划。

Word Link *real ≈ actual : reality, realize, really*

re·al·ly ♦♦♦ /riəli/ 1 ADV You can use **really** to emphasize a statement. 的确(用于强调) [SPOKEN, EMPHASIS] ❑ *I'm very sorry. I really am.* 我很抱歉。真的。 2 ADV You can use **really** to emphasize an adjective or adverb. (用于强调形容词或副词) 非常 [ADV adj/adv] [EMPHASIS] ❑ *It was really good.* 这非常好。 3 ADV You use **really** when you are discussing the real facts about something, in contrast to the ones someone wants you to believe. 实际上 ❑ *My father didn't really love her.* 我父亲实际上并不爱她。 4 ADV People use **really** in questions and negative statements when they want you to answer "no." 果真(用在疑问句和否定句中，引出否定回答) [ADV before v] [EMPHASIS] ❑ *Do you really think he would be that stupid?* 你果真认为他那么蠢吗？ 5 ADV If you refer to a time when something **really** begins to happen, you are emphasizing that it starts to happen at that time to a much greater extent and much more seriously than before. 真正地(用于强调事情的发生较以前有所扩大且变得更严重) [ADV before v] [EMPHASIS] ❑ *That's when the pressure really started.* 那是压力真正开始的时候。 6 ADV People sometimes use **really** to slightly reduce the force of a negative statement. 真地(用在否定句中，减轻语气) [SPOKEN, VAGUENESS] ❑ *I'm not really surprised.* 我并不真地惊讶。 7 CONVENTION You can say **really** to express surprise or disbelief at what someone has said. 真的(表示惊讶或对别人的话不相信) [SPOKEN, FEELINGS] ❑ *"We discovered it was totally the wrong decision."—"Really?"* "我们发现那完全是个错误的决定。"——"真的吗？"

R

Note that **really** and **actually** are both used to emphasize statements. You use **really** in conversation to emphasize something that you are saying. ❑ *I really think he's sick.* Note that when **really** is used in a negative sentence, its position in relation to the verb affects the meaning. For instance, if you say "**I really don't like Richard**," with **really** in front of the verb, you are emphasizing how much you dislike Richard. However, if you say "**I don't really like Richard**," with **really** coming after the negative, you are still saying that you dislike Richard, but the feeling is not particularly strong. When you use **really** in front of an adjective or adverb, it has a similar meaning to **very**. ❑ *This is really serious.* **Actually** is used to emphasize what is true or genuine in a situation, often when this is surprising, or a contrast with what has just been said. ❑ *All the characters in the novel actually existed... He actually began to cry.* It can also be used to be precise or to correct someone. ❑ *No one was actually drunk... We couldn't actually see the garden.*

realm /rɛlm/ (**realms**) 1 N-COUNT You can use **realm** to refer to any area of activity, interest, or thought. (活动、兴趣、思想的) 领域 [FORMAL] ❑ *...the realm of politics.* …政治领域。 2 N-COUNT A **realm** is a country that has a king or queen. 王国 [FORMAL] ❑ *Defense of the realm is crucial.* 王国的防御是至关重要的。

real prop·er·ty N-UNCOUNT **Real property** is property in the form of land and buildings, rather than personal possessions. 不动产 [AM] ❑ *...the owner or tenant of a piece of real property.* …一处不动产的主人或承租人。

real-time ADJ **Real-time** processing is a type of computer programming or data processing in which the information received is processed by the computer almost immediately. (计算机数据处理) 实时的 [ADJ n] [COMPUTING] ❑ *...real-time language translations.* …实时语言转换。

Real·tor /riəltər, -tɔr/ (**Realtors**) also **realtor** N-COUNT A **Realtor** is a person whose job is to sell houses, buildings, and land, and who is a member of the National Association of Realtors. 房地产经纪人(尤指美国房地产行业工会成员) [AM, TRADEMARK]

in BRIT, use **estate agent**

❑ *When the Realtor showed us this house, we knew we wanted it right away.* 当房地产经纪人带我们看这所房子时，我们就知道要立刻买下它。

real world N-SING If you talk about **the real world**, you are referring to the world and life in general, in contrast to a particular person's own life, experience, and ideas, which may seem untypical and unrealistic. 现实世界；现实生活 ❑ *When they eventually leave the school they will be totally ill-equipped to deal with the real world.* 当他们最终离开学校的时候，他们将完全没有准备好应付现实世界。

reap /rip/ (**reaps, reaping, reaped**) V-T If you **reap** the benefits or the rewards of something, you enjoy the good things that happen as a result of it. 获得 ❑ *You'll soon begin to reap the benefits of being fitter.* 你很快就会获得身体更健康带来的好处。

re·appear /riəpɪər/ (**reappears, reappearing, reappeared**) V-I When people or things **reappear**, they return again after they have been away or out of sight for some time. 再次露面 ❑ *Thirty seconds later she reappeared and beckoned them forward.* 30秒钟后她再次露面，招呼他们向前走。

re·appear·ance /riəpɪərəns/ (**reappearances**) N-COUNT The **reappearance** of someone or something is their return after they have been away or out of sight for some time. 再次露面 ❑ *His sudden reappearance must have been a shock.* 他的突然再次露面一定引起了震动。

rear ♦◇◇ /rɪər/ (**rears, rearing, reared**) 1 N-SING The **rear** of something such as a building or vehicle is the back part of it. (建筑物或机动车等的) 后部 ❑ *He settled back in the rear of the taxi.* 他在出租车后座，往后靠着坐好了。● ADJ **Rear** is also an adjective. 后部的 [ADJ n] ❑ *Manufacturers have been obliged to fit rear seat belts in all new cars.* 生产商不得不在所有的新车上安装后部座椅安全带。 2 N-SING If you are at the **rear** of a moving line of people, you are the last person in it. (队列的) 尾部 [FORMAL] ❑ *Musicians played at the front and rear of the procession.* 乐师们在游行队伍的前面和后面演奏。 3 N-COUNT Your **rear** is the part of your body that you sit on. 臀部 [INFORMAL] ❑ *I saw him pat a waitress on her rear.* 我看见他拍一个女服务生的屁股。 4 V-T If you **rear** children, you take care of them until they are old enough to take care of themselves. 抚养 ❑ *She reared sixteen children, six her own and ten her husband's.* 她抚养大了16个孩子，6个她自己的，10个她丈夫的。 5 V-T If you **rear** a young animal, you keep and take care of it until it is old enough to be used for work or food, or until it can look after itself. 饲养 ❑ *She spends a lot of time rearing animals.* 她花很多时间饲养动物。 6 V-I When a horse **rears**, it moves the front part of its body upward, so that its front legs are high in the air and it is standing on its back legs. (指马) 后腿直立 ❑ *The horse reared and threw off its rider.* 那匹马后腿直立，把骑手摔了下去。 7 PHRASE If a person or vehicle **is bringing up the rear**, they are the last person or vehicle in a moving line of them. 殿后 ❑ *...police motorcyclists bringing up the rear of the procession.* …警用摩托车为游行队伍殿后。

re·arrange /riəreɪndʒ/ (**rearranges, rearranging, rearranged**) 1 V-T If you **rearrange** things, you change the way in which they are organized or ordered. 重新整理 ❑ *When she returned, she found Malcolm had rearranged all her furniture.* 她回来时发现马尔科姆重新摆放了她所有的家具。 2 V-T If you **rearrange** a meeting or an appointment, you arrange for it to take place at a different time from that originally intended. 重新安排 ❑ *You may cancel or rearrange the appointment.* 你可以取消或重新安排这次预约。

re·arrange·ment /riəreɪndʒmənt/ (**rearrangements**) N-VAR A **rearrangement** is a change in the way that something is arranged or organized. 重新安排；重新整理 ❑ *...a rearrangement of the job structure.* …对工作结构的重新安排。

rear·view mir·ror /rɪərvyu/ (**rearview mirrors**) N-COUNT Inside a car, the **rearview mirror** is the mirror that enables you to see the traffic behind when you are driving. (汽车的) 后视镜

rea·son ♦♦♦ /riːzᵊn/ (**reasons, reasoning, reasoned**) 1 N-COUNT The **reason for** something is a fact or situation which explains why it happens or what causes it to happen. 原因 ❑ *There is a reason for every important thing that happens.* 发生的每一件重要事情都是有原因的。 2 N-UNCOUNT If you say that you have **reason to** believe something or **to** have a particular emotion, you mean that you have evidence for your belief or there is a definite cause of your feeling. 道理；理由 ❑ *They had reason to believe there could be trouble.* 他们有理由相信会有麻烦。 3 N-UNCOUNT The ability that people have to think and to make sensible judgments can be referred to as **reason**. 理智 ❑ *...a conflict between emotion and reason.* …情感与理智的冲突。 4 V-T If you **reason that** something is true, you decide that it is true after thinking carefully about all the facts. 推断 ❑ *I reasoned that changing my diet would lower my cholesterol level.* 我推断改变我的饮食会降低我的胆固醇水平。 5 → see also **reasoned, reasoning** 6 PHRASE If one thing happens **by reason of** another, it happens because of it. 因为 [FORMAL] ❑ *The boss retains enormous influence by reason of his position.* 老板因为职位的关系保持着巨大的影响力。 7 PHRASE If you try to make someone **listen to reason**, you try to persuade them to listen to sensible arguments and be influenced by them. 听从道理 ❑ *The company's top executives had refused to listen to reason.* 公司的高级主管们拒绝听从道理。 8 PHRASE If you say that something happened or was done **for no reason, for no good reason**, or **for no reason at all**, you mean that there was no obvious reason why it happened or was done. 无缘无故 ❑ *The guards, he said, would punch them for no reason.* 他说看守人员们会无缘无故地用拳头打他们。 9 PHRASE If you say that you will do anything **within reason**, you mean that you will do anything that is fair or reasonable and not too extreme. 合情合理的；正当的 ❑ *I will take any job that comes along, within reason.* 我有什么工作就干什么，只要是正当的。 10 **to see reason** → see **see** 11 **it stands to reason** → see **stand**

▸ **reason with** PHRASAL VERB If you try to **reason with** someone, you try to persuade them to do or accept something by using sensible arguments. 说服；与…讲道理 ❑ *He's impossible. I can't reason with him.* 他这人难以理喻。我没法跟他讲道理。

Thesaurus *reason* 另参见：

N. apology, argument, defense, excuse, explanation 1
analysis, comprehension, intellect, logic 3

Word Partnership *reason* 的常用搭配：

ADJ. **main** reason, **major** reason, **obvious** reason, **only** reason, **primary** reason, **real** reason, **same** reason, **simple** reason 1
compelling reason, **good** reason, **sufficient** reason 1 2

rea·son·able ♦◇◇ /riːzənəbᵊl/ 1 ADJ If you think that someone is fair and sensible you can say that they are **reasonable**. 通情达理的 ❑ *He's a reasonable sort of person.* 他是那种通情达理的人。
● **rea·son·ably** /riːzənəbli/ ADV 通情达理地 ❑ *"I'm sorry, Andrew," she said reasonably.* "对不起，安德鲁，"她通情达理地说。
● **rea·son·able·ness** N-UNCOUNT 通情达理 ❑ *"I can understand how you feel," Dan said with great reasonableness.* "我能明白你的感受，"丹非常通情达理地说。 2 ADJ If you say that a decision or action is **reasonable**, you mean that it is fair and sensible. (决定或行动) 合理的 ❑ *...a perfectly reasonable decision.* …一个完全合理的决定。
3 ADJ If you say that an expectation or explanation is **reasonable**, you mean that there are good reasons why it may be correct. (期望或解释) 有道理的 ❑ *It seems reasonable to expect rapid urban growth.* 看起来期待城市会飞速发展是有道理的。 ● **rea·son·ably** ADV 有道理地 [ADV with v] ❑ *You can reasonably expect your goods to arrive within six to eight weeks.* 你有理由预期你的货品会在6至8周内运到。 4 ADJ If you say that the price of something is **reasonable**, you mean that it is fair and not too high. (价钱) 公道的 ❑ *You get a good meal for a reasonable price.* 你能以公道的价格好好地吃一顿。 ● **rea·son·ably** ADV 公道地 [ADV with v] ❑ *...reasonably priced accommodations.* …定价公道的住宿。 5 ADJ You can use **reasonable** to describe something that is fairly good, but not very good. 还算好的 ❑ *The boy answered him in reasonable French.* 那男孩用过得去的法语回答了他的问题。
● **rea·son·ably** ADV 还算好地 [ADV adj/adv] ❑ *I can dance reasonably well.* 我舞跳得还算不错。 6 ADJ A **reasonable** amount of something is a fairly large amount of it. 相当大的 ❑ *They will need a reasonable amount of desk area and good light.* 他们将需要相当大的桌区和充足的光线。
● **rea·son·ably** ADV 相当地 [ADV adj/adv] ❑ *From now on events moved reasonably quickly.* 从此，事情发展得相当快。

Thesaurus *reasonable* 另参见：

ADJ. level-headed, rational 1
acceptable, fair, sensible; (*ant.*) unreasonable 2
likely, probable, right 3
fair, inexpensive 4

Word Partnership *reasonable* 的常用搭配：

N. reasonable **person** 1
beyond a reasonable **doubt**, reasonable **expectation**, reasonable **explanation** 3
reasonable **cost**, reasonable **price**, reasonable **rates** 4
reasonable **amount** 4 6
reasonable **chance**, reasonable **time** 5

rea·soned /riːzᵊnd/ ADJ A **reasoned** discussion or argument is based on sensible reasons, rather than on an appeal to people's emotions. (讨论或观点) 缜密的；理由充分的 [APPROVAL] ❑ *Their opinions are not based on reasoned argument.* 他们的意见不是以缜密的推断为基础的。

rea·son·ing /riːzənɪŋ/ (**reasonings**) N-VAR **Reasoning** is the process by which you reach a conclusion after thinking about all the facts. 推理；论证 ❑ *...the reasoning behind the decision.* …该决定背后的论证。
→ see **philosophy**

re·as·sert /riːəsɜrt/ (**reasserts, reasserting, reasserted**) 1 V-T If you **reassert** your control or authority, you make it clear that you are still in a position of power, or you strengthen the power that you had. 重申 (地位、权力) ❑ *...the government's continuing effort to reassert its control in the region.* …政府不断努力重申对该地区的控制权。 2 V-T If something such as an idea or habit **reasserts itself**, it becomes noticeable again. (想法或习惯等) 再次显现 ❑ *His sense of humor was beginning to reassert itself.* 他的幽默感又开始显现了。

re·as·sess /riːəsɛs/ (**reassesses, reassessing, reassessed**) V-T If you **reassess** something, you think about it and decide whether you need to change your opinion about it. 重新评价 ❑ *I will reassess the situation when I get home.* 我回家之后将对情况重新评估一番。

re·as·sess·ment /riːəsɛsmənt/ (**reassessments**) N-VAR If you make a **reassessment** of something, you think about it and decide whether you need to change your opinion about it. 重新评价 ❑ *There's a total reassessment of what people want out of life.* 对于人们对生活有什么样的期待有了重新评价。

re·assur·ance /riːəʃʊərəns/ (**reassurances**) 1 N-UNCOUNT If someone needs **reassurance**, they are very worried and need someone to help them stop worrying by saying kind or helpful things. 安慰 ❑ *She needed reassurance that she belonged somewhere.* 她需要让她有归属感的安慰。 2 N-COUNT **Reassurances** are things that you say to help people stop worrying about something. 安慰的话 ❑ *...reassurances that pesticides are not harmful.* …杀虫剂没有危害的宽慰的话。

★ **re·assure** /riːəʃʊər/ (**reassures, reassuring, reassured**) V-T If you **reassure** someone, you say or do things to make them stop worrying about something. 使安心；使消除疑虑 ❑ *I tried to reassure her, "Don't worry about it. We won't let it happen again."* 我尽力使她安心，"别担心，我们不会允许它再发生的。"

Word Partnership *reassure* 的常用搭配：

N. reassure **citizens**, reassure **customers**, reassure **investors**, reassure **the public**
V. **seek to** reassure, **try to** reassure

re·assured /riːəʃʊərd/ ADJ If you feel **reassured**, you feel less worried about something, usually because you have received help or advice. (常因获得了帮助或建议而感到) 放心的 ❑ *I feel much more reassured when I've had a physical exam.* 我做完身体检查后觉得放心多了。

re·assur·ing /riːəʃʊərɪŋ/ ADJ If you find someone's words or actions **reassuring**, they make you feel less worried about something. 安慰的 ❑ *It was reassuring to hear John's familiar voice.* 听到约翰熟悉的声音令人感到安慰。 ● **re·assur·ing·ly** ADV 安慰地 ❑ *"It's okay now," he said reassuringly.* "现在没事了，"他安慰地说。

re·bate /ribeɪt/ (**rebates**) N-COUNT A **rebate** is an amount of money which is returned to you after you have paid for goods or services or after you have paid tax or rent. (支付后的) 退款; (税金或租金的) 返还部分 ❑ *Citicorp will guarantee its credit card customers a rebate on a number of products.* 花旗银行将保证其信用卡用户在一些商品上得到退款。

re·bel ♦♦◊ (**rebels, rebelling, rebelled**)

The noun is pronounced /rɛbəl/. The verb is pronounced /rɪbɛl/.

名词读作 /rɛbəl/。动词读作 /rɪbɛl/。

1 N-COUNT **Rebels** are people who are fighting against their own country's army in order to change the political system there. 反叛者 ❑ *...fighting between rebels and government forces.* …叛军与政府军之间的战斗。 **2** N-COUNT Politicians who oppose some of their own party's policies can be referred to as **rebels**. (政党内部的) 反对者 ❑ *The rebels want another 1% cut in interest rates.* 反对派希望能再降低1%的利率。 **3** V-I If politicians **rebel** against one of their own party's policies, they show that they oppose it. (因不同政见) 反对 ❑ *Voters rebelled against high property taxes.* 投票者们反对高额财产税。 **4** N-COUNT You can say that someone is a **rebel** if you think that they behave differently from other people and have rejected the values of society or of their parents. 叛逆者 ❑ *She had been a rebel at school.* 她在学校时就是个叛逆者。 **5** V-I When someone **rebels**, they start to behave differently from other people and reject the values of society or of their parents. 叛逆 ❑ *The child who rebels is unlikely to be overlooked.* 叛逆的孩子不太可能被忽视。

★ **re·bel·lion** /rɪbɛlyən/ (**rebellions**) **1** N-VAR A **rebellion** is a violent organized action by a large group of people who are trying to change their country's political system. 叛乱 ❑ *The government soon put down the rebellion.* 政府很快镇压了这次叛乱。 **2** N-VAR A situation in which people show their opposition to the way things have been done in the past can be referred to as a **rebellion**. 反抗 ❑ *Women are waging a quiet rebellion against the traditional roles their mothers have played.* 妇女们正悄悄地发动一场反抗她们的母亲们所扮演的传统角色的运动。

re·bel·lious /rɪbɛlyəs/ **1** ADJ If you think someone behaves in an unacceptable way and does not do what they are told, you can say they are **rebellious**. 叛逆的 ❑ *...a rebellious teenager.* …一个叛逆的青少年。 ● **re·bel·lious·ness** N-UNCOUNT 叛逆性 ❑ *...the normal rebelliousness of youth.* …年轻人正常的叛逆性。 **2** ADJ A **rebellious** group of people is a group involved in taking violent action against the rulers of their own country, usually in order to change the system of government there. (通常指为改变现行政治体制而) 反叛的 [ADJ n] ❑ *The rebellious officers, having seized the radio station, broadcast the news of the overthrow of the monarchy.* 反叛的军官们占领广播电台后播发了推翻君主制的消息。

R

re·birth /ribɜrθ/ N-UNCOUNT You can refer to a change that leads to a new period of growth and improvement in something as its **rebirth**. 复兴; 再生 ❑ *...the rebirth of democracy in Latin America.* …民主在拉丁美洲的复兴。

★ **re·bound** /rɪbaʊnd/ (**rebounds, rebounding, rebounded**) **1** V-I If something **rebounds** from a solid surface, it bounces or springs back from it. 弹回 ❑ *His shot in the 21st minute of the game rebounded from a post.* 他在比赛21分钟时的射门从球门柱上弹了回来。 **2** V-I If an action or situation **rebounds on** you, it has an unpleasant effect on you, especially when this effect was intended for someone else. 反作用于 (尤指对自己产生本想施与别人的不良影响) ❑ *Mia realized her trick had rebounded on her.* 米娅意识到她的伎俩反而害了自己。

re·brand /ribrænd/ (**rebrands, rebranding, rebranded**) V-T To **rebrand** a product or organization means to present it to the public in a new way, for example by changing its name or appearance. 重塑 (某产品或机构) [BUSINESS] ❑ *There are plans to rebrand many Texas stores.* 有计划要重塑得克萨斯州的许多商店。

re·brand·ing /ribrændɪŋ/ N-UNCOUNT **Rebranding** is the process of giving a product or an organization a new image, in order to make it more attractive or successful. 重塑 [BUSINESS] ❑ *A complete rebranding of the school is expected within two years.* 有望在两年内完全重塑该校的形象。

▲ **re·buff** /rɪbʌf/ (**rebuffs, rebuffing, rebuffed**) V-T If you **rebuff** someone or **rebuff** a suggestion that they make, you refuse to do what they suggest. 拒绝 ❑ *His proposals have already been rebuffed by the governor.* 他的建议已被州长拒绝了。 ● N-VAR **Rebuff** is also a noun. 拒绝 ❑ *The results of the poll dealt a humiliating rebuff to Mr. Jones.* 民意测验的结果对琼斯先生来说是一个羞辱性的拒绝。

re·build /ribɪld/ (**rebuilds, rebuilding, rebuilt**) **1** V-T When people **rebuild** something such as a building or a city, they build it again after it has been damaged or destroyed. 重建 (房屋或城市等) ❑ *They say they will stay to rebuild their homes rather than retreat to refugee camps.* 他们说要留下来重建家园而不是撤到难民营中。 ❑ *The old south grandstand must be rebuilt.* 破旧的南看台一定要重建。 **2** V-T When people **rebuild** something such as an institution, a system, or an aspect of their lives, they take action to bring it back to its previous condition. 重建 (组织、制度和生活等) ❑ *The president's message was that everyone would have to work hard together to rebuild the economy.* 总统所传达的信息是每个人都应一起努力工作重建经济。

▲ **re·buke** /rɪbyuk/ (**rebukes, rebuking, rebuked**) V-T If you **rebuke** someone, you speak severely to them because they have said or done something that you do not approve of. 谴责 [FORMAL] ❑ *The president rebuked the House and Senate for not passing those bills within 100 days.* 总统谴责参众两院未在100天内通过那些法案。 ● N-VAR **Rebuke** is also a noun. 谴责 ❑ *His statements drew a stinging rebuke from the chairman.* 他的申明受到了主席严厉的谴责。

re·call ♦♦◊ (**recalls, recalling, recalled**)

The verb is pronounced /rɪkɔl/. The noun is pronounced /rikɔl/.

动词读作 /rɪkɔl/。名词读作 /rikɔl/。

1 V-T/V-I When you **recall** something, you remember it and tell others about it. 记起; 回忆道 ❑ *Henderson recalled that he first met Pollard during a business trip to Washington.* 亨德森记起他是在一次去华盛顿出差的途中第一次与波拉德结识的。 ❑ *His mother later recalled: "He used to stay up until two o'clock in the morning playing these war games."* 他的母亲后来回忆道: "他过去常常熬夜到凌晨2点玩这些打仗的游戏。" ❑ *"What was his name?"—"I don't recall."* "他叫什么名字?" — "我想不起来了。" **2** N-UNCOUNT **Recall** is the ability to remember something that has happened in the past or the act of remembering it. 记忆力; 回忆 ❑ *He had a good memory, and total recall of her spoken words.* 他有好记性, 能完全回忆出她说过的话。 **3** V-T If you **are recalled** to your home, country, or the place where you work, you are ordered to return there. 召回 (某人) ❑ *The U. S. envoy was recalled to Washington.* 该美国特使被召回了华盛顿。 ● N-SING **Recall** is also a noun. 召回 ❑ *The recall of Ambassador Alan Green is a public signal of America's concern.* 艾伦・格林大使的召回是美国关注此事的公开信号。 **4** V-T If a company **recalls** a product, it asks the stores or the people who have bought that product to return it because there is something wrong with it. 召回 (产品) ❑ *The company said it was recalling one of its drugs and had stopped selling two others.* 该公司说它正在召回它的一种药品, 而且已经停售了另外两种药品。 ● N-COUNT **Recall** is also a noun. 召回 ❑ *...a recall of the laptops due to defective supply parts.* …因为有缺陷的配件而对笔记本电脑的召回。

re·cap /rikæp/ (**recaps, recapping, recapped**) V-T/V-I You can say that you are going to **recap** when you want to draw people's attention to the fact that you are going to repeat the main points of an explanation, argument, or description, as a summary of it. 概括 ❑ *To recap briefly, the agreement was rejected 10 days ago.* 简短概括就是, 这项协议10天前被否决了。 ❑ *Can you recap the points included in the proposal?* 你能概括一下这个提议中包括的要点吗? ● N-SING **Recap** is also a noun. 概要 ❑ *Each report starts with a recap of how we did versus our projections.* 每一份报道都以一个概要开头, 讲述和预期相比我们的表现如何。

re·capi·tal·ize /rikæpɪtᵊlaɪz/ (**recapitalizes, recapitalizing, recapitalized**) V-T/V-I If a company **recapitalizes**, it changes the way it manages its financial affairs, for example by borrowing money or reissuing shares. 调整…的资本结构; 调整资本结构 [AM, BUSINESS] ❑ *Mr. Warnock resigned as the company abandoned a plan to recapitalize.* 沃诺克先生辞职了, 因为公司放弃了资本重组的计划。 ❑ *He plans to recapitalize the insurance fund.* 他计划调整保险基金的资本结构。 ● **re·capi·tali·za·tion** /rikæpɪtᵊlɪzeɪʃᵊn/ N-COUNT (**recapitalizations**) 资本重组 ❑ *A substantial thrust of the effort of management is to explore a recapitalization of the company.* 管理层努力的一个重点是探索公司的资本重组。

re·ca·pitu·late /rikəpɪtʃəleɪt/ (**recapitulates, recapitulating, recapitulated**) V-T/V-I You can say that you are going to

recapitulate the main points of an explanation, argument, or description when you want to draw attention to the fact that you are going to repeat the most important points as a summary. 概括 ❑ *Let's just recapitulate the essential points.* 让我们只概述一下基本要点吧。 ❑ *It will be put up for sale under the terms already communicated to you, which, to recapitulate, call for a very minimum of publicity.* 其销售将按照已讲的条件进行，概括地说，就是要求尽量少宣传。
● **re·ca·pitu·la·tion** /ri̲kəpɪtʃəle̲ɪʃən/ N-SING 概括 ❑ *Chapter nine provides a valuable recapitulation of the material already presented.* 第9章对已经陈述过的材料进行了有价值的概括。

re·cap·ture /ri̲kæ̲ptʃər/ (**recaptures, recapturing, recaptured**) **1** V-T When soldiers **recapture** an area of land or a place, they gain control of it again from an opposing army who had taken it from them. 重新占领 ❑ *They said the bodies were found when rebels recaptured the area.* 他们说这些尸体是在反叛者们重新占领这个地区时被发现的。● N-SING **Recapture** is also a noun. 重新占领 ❑ *...an offensive to be launched for the recapture of the city.* …为重新占领这座城市而即将发起的进攻。 **2** V-T When people **recapture** something that they have lost to a competitor, they get it back again. (从竞争对手处)夺回 ❑ *I believe that he would be the best possibility to recapture the center vote in the upcoming election.* 我相信他将是在即将来临的选举中最有可能夺回中间选票的人。 **3** V-T To **recapture** a person or animal which has escaped from somewhere means to catch them again. 抓回 ❑ *Police have recaptured Alan Lewis, who escaped from a jail cell in Boston.* 警察们已经抓回了从波士顿一个监狱牢房中逃跑的艾伦·刘易斯。● N-SING **Recapture** is also a noun. 重新抓获 ❑ *...the recapture of a renegade police chief in Panama.* …在巴拿马叛变警局的重新抓获。

★ **re·cede** /rɪsi̲d/ (**recedes, receding, receded**) **1** V-I If something **recedes** from you, it moves away. 远离 ❑ *Luke's footsteps receded into the night.* 卢克的脚步声渐渐消失在夜色中。 ❑ *As she receded he waved goodbye.* 当她离去时，他挥手告别。 **2** V-I When something such as a quality, problem, or illness **recedes**, it becomes weaker, smaller, or less intense. (品质) 减弱；(问题或疾病等) 好转 ❑ *Just as I started to think that I was never going to get well, the illness began to recede.* 就在我开始认为我将永远不会好起来的时候，我的病开始好转。 **3** V-I If a man's hair starts to **recede**, it no longer grows on the front of his head. 谢顶 ❑ *...a youngish man with dark hair just beginning to recede.* …一个前额黑发刚开始脱落的相当年轻的男人。

re·ceipt /rɪsi̲t/ (**receipts**) **1** N-COUNT A **receipt** is a piece of paper that you get from someone as proof that they have received money or goods from you. 收据 ❑ *I wrote her a receipt for the money.* 我为那笔钱给她开了张收据。 **2** N-PLURAL **Receipts** are the amount of money received during a particular period, for example by a store or theater. 收入 ❑ *He was tallying the day's receipts.* 他正在结算当天的收入。 **3** N-UNCOUNT The **receipt** of something is the act of receiving it. 收到 [FORMAL] ❑ *Goods should be supplied within 28 days after the receipt of your order.* 收到你的订单28天内供货。 **4** PHRASE If you are **in receipt of** something, you have received it or you receive it regularly. 已收到；定期收到 [FORMAL] ❑ *We are taking action, having been in receipt of a letter from him.* 收到他的信之后，我们正采取行动。

re·ceive ♦♦♦ /rɪsi̲v/ (**receives, receiving, received**) **1** V-T When you **receive** something, you get it after someone gives it to you or sends it to you. 接到；收到 ❑ *They will receive their awards at a ceremony in Stockholm.* 他们将在斯德哥尔摩的典礼上接受给他们的奖励。 **2** V-T You can use **receive** to say that certain kinds of things happen to someone. For example if they are injured, you can say that they **received** an injury. 受到；遭受 ❑ *He received more of the blame than anyone when the plan failed to work.* 当计划失败之后他受到的指责比任何人都多。 **3** V-T When you **receive** a visitor or a guest, you greet them. 接待；迎接 ❑ *The following evening the hotel was again receiving guests.* 第二天晚上饭店又接待起客人来。 **4** V-T If you say that something **is received** in a particular way, you mean that people react to it in that way. (用某种特定方式) 回应 [usu passive] ❑ *The resolution had been received with great disappointment within the PLO.* 巴勒斯坦解放组织内部对此决议感到极其失望。 **5** V-T When a radio or television **receives** signals that are being transmitted, it picks them up and converts them into sound or pictures. 接收 (信号) ❑ *The reception was a little faint but clear enough for him to receive the signal.* 接收有些弱，但是足够清晰到使他能够接收信号。 **6** PHRASE If you **are on the receiving end** or **at the receiving end** of something unpleasant, you are the person that it happens to. 成为 (不愉快事件的) 承受方 ❑ *You saw hate in their eyes and you were on the receiving end of that hate.* 你在他们的眼中看到仇恨，而你就是那仇恨的对象。

Thesaurus *receive* 另参见：	
V.	accept, collect, get, take; *(ant.)* give, present **1** entertain, take in, welcome **3**

re·ceiv·er /rɪsi̲vər/ (**receivers**) **1** N-COUNT A telephone's **receiver** is the part that you hold near to your ear and speak into. 电话听筒 ❑ *She picked up the receiver and started to dial.* 她拿起听筒开始拨号。 **2** N-COUNT A **receiver** is the part of a radio or television that picks up signals and converts them into sound or pictures. (收音机或电视机的) 信号接收器 ❑ *Auto-tuning VHF receivers are now common in cars.* 自动调谐的超高频信号接收器现普遍使用在小汽车上。 **3** N-COUNT **The receiver** is someone who is appointed by a court of law to manage the affairs of a business, usually when it is facing financial failure. (法庭指定的) 破产接管人 [usu "the" N] [BUSINESS] ❑ *...the receivers handling his bankruptcy case.* …处理他破产案子的接管人员们。
→ see **radio, television, tennis**

re·ceiv·er·ship /rɪsi̲vərʃɪp/ (**receiverships**) N-VAR If a company goes **into receivership**, it faces financial failure and the administration of its business is handled by the receiver. 破产管理 [BUSINESS] ❑ *The company has now gone into receivership with debts of several million.* 这家公司负债几百万，已接受了破产管理。

re·cent ♦♦♦ /ri̲sənt/ ADJ A **recent** event or period of time happened only a short while ago. 最近的 ❑ *In the most recent attack, one man was shot dead and two others were wounded.* 在最近的这次袭击中有1人被打死，另2人受伤。

re·cent·ly ♦♦◊ /ri̲səntli/ ADV If you have done something **recently** or if something happened **recently**, it happened only a short time ago. 最近 ❑ *The bank recently opened a branch in Miami.* 这家银行最近在迈阿密开了一家分行。

re·cep·tion /rɪse̲pʃən/ (**receptions**) **1** N-COUNT A **reception** is a formal party which is given to welcome someone or to celebrate a special event. 招待会 ❑ *At the reception they served smoked salmon.* 在招待会上，他们端上了熏三文鱼。 **2** N-SING **Reception** in a hotel is the desk or office that books rooms for people and answers their questions. (酒店) 接待处；服务台 ["the" N, oft N n, also "at" N] ❑ *Have him bring a car around to reception.* 让他开辆车到接待处附近来。 **3** N-SING **Reception** in an office or hospital is the place where people's appointments and questions are dealt with. (办公室或医院的) 服务台 ["the" N, oft N n, also "at" N] ❑ *Wait at reception for me.* 在服务台等我。 **4** N-COUNT If someone or something has a particular kind of **reception**, that is the way that people react to them. 接待 ❑ *Mr. Mandela was given a warm reception in Washington.* 曼德拉先生在华盛顿受到了热情接待。 **5** N-UNCOUNT If you get good **reception** from your radio or television, the sound or picture is clear because the signal is strong. If the **reception** is poor, the sound or picture is unclear because the signal is weak. (收音机或电视机的) 接收效果 ❑ *...poor radio reception.* …糟糕的广播接收效果。
→ see **wedding**

re·cep·tion·ist /rɪse̲pʃənɪst/ (**receptionists**) **1** N-COUNT In an office or hospital, the **receptionist** is the person whose job is to answer the telephone, arrange appointments, and deal with people when they first arrive. (办公室或医院) 接待员 **2** N-COUNT In a hotel, the **receptionist** is the person whose job is to reserve rooms for people and answer their questions. (宾馆前台) 接待员

▲ **re·cep·tive** /rɪse̲ptɪv/ **1** ADJ Someone who is **receptive to** new ideas or suggestions is prepared to consider them or accept them. (对新思想或建议) 乐于接受的 ❑ *The voters had seemed receptive to his ideas.* 选民似乎愿意接受他的想法。 **2** ADJ If someone who is ill is **receptive to** treatment, they start to get better when they are given treatment. (对治疗) 有反映的 [v-link ADJ "to" n] ❑ *For those patients who are not receptive to treatment, the chance for improvement is small.* 那些对治疗没反应的病人，好转的机会很小。

★ **re·cep·tor** /rɪse̲ptər/ (**receptors**) N-COUNT **Receptors** are nerve endings in your body which react to changes and stimuli and make your body respond in a particular way. 感受器 [TECHNICAL] ❑ *...the information receptors in our brain.* …我们大脑中的信息感受器。

▲ **re·cess** /ri̲sɛs, rɪsɛ̲s/ (**recesses, recessing, recessed**) **1** N-COUNT A **recess** is a break between the periods of work of an official body such as a committee, a court of law, or a government. (会议、法庭或政府等官方机构的) 休息 [also "in/from" N] ❑ *The conference broke for a recess, but the 10-minute break*

r

stretched to two hours. 会议暂时休会，但10分钟的休息延长到了两小时。 2 N-VAR In a school, **recess** is the period of time between classes when the children are allowed to play. 课间休息 [AM] ❑ *She decides to visit the school library during recess.* 她准备课间休息的时候去参观学校图书馆。 ❑ *...the children's first morning recess.* …那些孩子们上午的第一次课间休息。 3 V-I When formal meetings or court cases **recess**, they stop temporarily. 暂时休会；休庭 [FORMAL] ❑ *The hearings have now recessed for dinner.* 听证会现已暂时休会以便大家吃饭。 4 N-COUNT In a room, a **recess** is part of a wall which is built further back than the rest of the wall. Recesses are often used as a place to put furniture such as shelves. 壁龛 ❑ *...a discreet recess next to a fireplace.* …一座壁炉旁的一个隐秘的壁龛。 5 N-COUNT **The recesses of** something or somewhere are the parts of it that are hard to see because light does not reach them or they are hidden from view. 暗处；隐蔽处 ❑ *He emerged from the dark recesses of the garage.* 他从那间车库漆黑的隐蔽处走了出来。 6 N-COUNT If you refer to **the recesses of** someone's mind or soul, you are referring to thoughts or feelings they have which are hidden or difficult to describe. (思想、灵魂的) 深处 ❑ *There was something in the darker recesses of his unconscious that was troubling him.* 在他潜意识的隐秘的深处有一些东西让他觉得不安。

re·ces·sion ♦♦◇ /rɪsɛʃᵊn/ (**recessions**) N-VAR A **recession** is a period when the economy of a country is doing badly, for example because industry is producing less and more people are becoming unemployed. 经济衰退；萧条 ❑ *The oil price increases sent Europe into deep recession.* 石油价格的上涨使欧洲陷入严重的经济衰退。

★ **reci·pe** /rɛsɪpi/ (**recipes**) 1 N-COUNT A **recipe** is a list of ingredients and a set of instructions that tell you how to cook something. 食谱 ❑ *...a traditional recipe for buttermilk biscuits.* …一个酪乳饼干的传统烹饪法。 2 N-SING If you say that something is **a recipe for** a particular situation, you mean that it is likely to result in that situation. 方法 ❑ *Large-scale inflation is a recipe for disaster.* 大规模的通货膨胀有可能导致灾难。

★ **re·cipi·ent** /rɪsɪpiənt/ (**recipients**) N-COUNT The **recipient** of something is the person who receives it. 接受者 [FORMAL] ❑ *...the largest recipient of U.S. foreign aid.* …最大的美国对外援助接受方。
→ see **donor**

★ **re·cip·ro·cal** /rɪsɪprəkᵊl/ ADJ A **reciprocal** action or agreement involves two people or groups who do the same thing to each other or agree to help each another in a similar way. 相互的；互惠的 [FORMAL] ❑ *They expected a reciprocal gesture before more hostages could be freed.* 他们期望在更多的人质被释放之前有互惠的表示。

re·cip·ro·cate /rɪsɪprəkeɪt/ (**reciprocates, reciprocating, reciprocated**) V-T/V-I If your feelings or actions toward someone **are reciprocated**, the other person feels or behaves in the same way toward you as you have felt or behaved toward them. 同等回应；回报 ❑ *I would like to think the way I treat people is reciprocated.* 我愿意认为我对待别人的方式得到了同等的回应。 ❑ *He needs these people to fulfill his ambitions and reciprocates by bringing out the best in each of them.* 他需要这些人来实现他的雄心，作为回报他让他们每个人得到最佳的发挥。

re·cit·al /rɪsaɪtᵊl/ (**recitals**) N-COUNT A **recital** is a performance of music or poetry, usually given by one person. (通常是一个人的) 朗诵会；演奏会 ❑ *...a solo recital by the harpsichordist Maggie Cole.* …一场大键琴手玛吉・科尔的独奏会。

★ **re·cite** /rɪsaɪt/ (**recites, reciting, recited**) 1 V-T When someone **recites** a poem or other piece of writing, they say it aloud after they have learned it. 出声背诵 ❑ *They recited poetry to one another.* 他们互相为对方背诵诗歌。 2 V-T If you **recite** something such as a list, you say it aloud. 说出；口头列举 ❑ *All he could do was recite a list of government failings.* 他所有能做的就是逐一说出政府的过失。

★ **reck·less** /rɛklɪs/ ADJ If you say that someone is **reckless**, you mean that they act in a way which shows that they do not care about danger or the effect their behavior will have on other people. 鲁莽的；不顾后果的 ❑ *He is charged with reckless driving.* 他被控莽撞驾驶。 ● **reck·less·ly** ADV 鲁莽地；不计后果地 ❑ *He was leaning recklessly out of the open window.* 他鲁莽地从开着的窗户探出身子。 ● **reck·less·ness** N-UNCOUNT 鲁莽 ❑ *He felt a surge of recklessness.* 他感觉到一阵不顾一切的冲动。

reck·on ♦◇◇ /rɛkən/ (**reckons, reckoning, reckoned**) 1 V-T If you **reckon** that something is true, you think that it is true. 想 [INFORMAL] ❑ *Toni reckoned that it must be about three o'clock.* 托尼想一定是3点钟左右了。 2 V-T If something **is reckoned** to be a particular figure, it is calculated to be roughly that amount. 估算 [usu passive] ❑ *The market is reckoned to be worth $1.4 bn in the U.S. alone.* 这个市场仅在美国的价值估计就有14亿美元。
▸ **reckon with** 1 PHRASAL VERB If you say that you had not **reckoned with** something, you mean that you had not expected it and so were not prepared for it. 料想到 [with brd-neg] ❑ *Gary had not reckoned with the strength of Sally's feelings for him.* 加里没有料想到萨莉对他的感情如此强烈。 2 PHRASE If you say that there is someone or something **to be reckoned with**, you mean that they must be dealt with and it will be difficult. 认真处理；小心对付 ❑ *This act was a signal to his victim's friends that he was someone to be reckoned with.* 这一举动是给为他所害者的朋友们的一个信号，告诉他们他是个必须被小心对付的人。

reck·on·ing /rɛkənɪŋ/ (**reckonings**) N-VAR Someone's **reckoning** is a calculation they make about something, especially a calculation that is not very exact. 估算 ❑ *By my reckoning we were seven or eight miles from the campground.* 据我估算我们离露营地大约七八英里远。

★ **re·claim** /rɪkleɪm/ (**reclaims, reclaiming, reclaimed**) 1 V-T If you **reclaim** something that you have lost or that has been taken away from you, you succeed in getting it back. 拿回；收回 ❑ *In 1986, they got the right to reclaim South African citizenship.* 1986年，他们得到了恢复南非公民身份的权利。 2 V-T If you **reclaim** an amount of money, for example tax that you have paid, you claim it back. 要求归还 ❑ *The good news for the industry was that investors don't seem to be in any hurry to reclaim their money.* 对该行业来说，好消息是投资者们似乎不急于要求收回他们的钱。 3 V-T When people **reclaim** land, they make it suitable for a purpose such as farming or building, for example by draining it or by building a barrier against the sea. 开垦；改造 ❑ *The Netherlands has been reclaiming farmland from water.* 荷兰一直在围海造田。 4 V-T If a piece of land that was used for farming or building **is reclaimed by** a desert, forest, or the sea, it turns back into desert, forest, or sea. 重新变成 (沙漠、森林、海洋) [usu passive] ❑ *The diamond towns are gradually being reclaimed by the desert.* 那些开采钻石的小镇逐渐被沙漠重新吞噬了。

Word Link *clin ≈ leaning : decline, incline, recline*

re·cline /rɪklaɪn/ (**reclines, reclining, reclined**) 1 V-I If you **recline on** something, you sit or lie on it with the upper part of your body supported at an angle. 斜靠 ❑ *She proceeded to recline on a chaise longue.* 她开始斜靠在一个躺椅上。 2 V-T/V-I When a seat **reclines** or when you **recline** it, you lower the back so that it is more comfortable to sit in. 使向后倾斜；向后倾斜 ❑ *Air France first-class seats recline almost like beds.* 法国航空公司头等舱座位的靠背可以向后倾斜得几乎像床一样。 ❑ *Ramesh had reclined his seat and was lying back smoking.* 拉米许已经把椅背向后调了，正仰靠着吸着烟。

re·cluse /rɪklus, rɛklus/ (**recluses**) N-COUNT A **recluse** is a person who lives alone and deliberately avoids other people. 隐居者 ❑ *His widow became a virtual recluse for the remainder of her life.* 他的遗孀在其余生成了一名实际上的隐居者。

re·clu·sive /rɪklusɪv/ ADJ A **reclusive** person or animal lives alone and deliberately avoids the company of others. 独处的；隐居的 ❑ *All that neighbors knew about the reclusive man was that he had lived in the building for about 20 years.* 关于那名隐居者邻居们所知道的就是他已经在那栋楼里住了大约二十年了。

rec·og·nis·able /rɛkəgnaɪzəbᵊl/ [BRIT] → see **recognizable**

rec·og·nise /rɛkəgnaɪz/ [mainly BRIT] → see **recognize**

rec·og·ni·tion ♦◇◇ /rɛkəgnɪʃᵊn/ 1 N-UNCOUNT **Recognition** is the act of recognizing someone or identifying something when you see it. 认出；识别 ❑ *He searched for a sign of recognition on her face, but there was none.* 他在她的脸上搜寻她认出来的迹象，但没有。 2 N-UNCOUNT **Recognition of** something is an understanding and acceptance of it. 认可；接受 ❑ *Recognition of the importance of career development is increasing.* 对职业发展重要性的认可在不断增加。 3 N-UNCOUNT When a government gives diplomatic **recognition** to another country, they officially accept that its status is valid. (国际上的) 正式承认 ❑ *His government did not receive full recognition by the United States until July.* 他的政府直到7月才得到美国的完全承认。 4 N-UNCOUNT When a person receives **recognition** for the things that they have done, people acknowledge the value or skill of their work. 赞赏；赏识 ❑ *At last, her father's work has received popular recognition.* 最终，她父亲的工作得到了大家的普遍赞赏。 5 PHRASE If something is done **in recognition of** someone's achievements, it is done as a way of showing official appreciation of them. 用以肯定 ❑ *...a small plaque in recognition of her contribution to the university.* …一枚用以肯定她对该大学所做贡献的奖章。

Word Partnership *recognition* 的常用搭配：
V. **deserve** recognition, **receive** recognition 2 – 4
ADJ. **formal** recognition, **full** recognition 3
growing recognition, **special** recognition 4

rec·og·niz·able /rɛkəgnaɪzəbᵊl/
in BRIT, also use **recognisable**
ADJ If something can be easily recognized or identified, you can say that it is easily **recognizable**. 可辨认的；可认出的 ❑ *The vault was opened and the body found to be well preserved, his features easily recognizable.* 地窖被打开了，尸体被发现保存完好，他的面容很容易辨认。

Word Link *cogn ≈ knowing : cognitive, recognize, unrecognizable*

rec·og·nize ♦♦◇ /rɛkəgnaɪz/ (**recognizes, recognizing, recognized**)
in BRIT, also use **recognise**
1 V-T If you **recognize** someone or something, you know who that person is or what that thing is. 认出 [no cont] ❑ *The receptionist recognized him at once.* 那名接待员马上认出了他。 2 V-T If someone says that they **recognize** something, they acknowledge that it exists or that it is true. 承认 [no cont] ❑ *I recognize my own shortcomings.* 我承认我自己的那些缺点。 3 V-T If people or organizations **recognize** something as valid, they officially accept it or approve of it. 承认；赞成 ❑ *Many doctors recognize homeopathy as a legitimate form of medicine.* 许多医生承认顺势疗法是一种合理的医疗形式。 ❑ *France is on the point of recognizing the independence of the Baltic States.* 法国即将承认波罗的海各国的独立。 4 V-T When people **recognize** the work that someone has done, they show their appreciation of it, often by giving that person an award of some kind. 赏识；表彰 ❑ *The army recognized him as an outstandingly able engineer.* 军队称赞他为杰出能干的工程师。

Thesaurus *recognize* 另参见：
V. acknowledge, identify, know, notice; *(ant.)* ignore 1
accept, believe, understand 2 3

re·coil (**recoils, recoiling, recoiled**)
The verb is pronounced /rɪkɔɪl/. The noun is pronounced /ri̲kɔɪl/.
动词读作 /rɪkɔ̲ɪl/。名词读作 /ri̲kɔɪl/。
1 V-I If something makes you **recoil**, you move your body quickly away from it because it frightens, offends, or hurts you. 躲闪；畏缩 ❑ *For a moment I thought he was going to kiss me. I recoiled in horror.* 一时间我认为他要吻我。我惊恐地躲开了。 ● N-UNCOUNT **Recoil** is also a noun. 躲闪；畏缩 ❑ *...his small body jerking in recoil from the volume of his shouting.* …他小小身体在他大声的叫喊中畏缩地抽搐着。 2 V-I If you **recoil from** doing something or **recoil at** the idea of something, you refuse to do it or accept it because you dislike it so much. (因厌恶而) 拒绝 ❑ *People used to recoil from the idea of getting into debt.* 人们过去一想到要负债就会因厌恶而拒绝。

rec·ol·lect /rɛkəlɛkt/ (**recollects, recollecting, recollected**) V-T If you **recollect** something, you remember it. 回忆起 ❑ *Ramona spoke with warmth when she recollected the doctor who used to be at the community hospital.* 当回忆起曾在社区医院工作的那位医生时，拉蒙纳话语中流露出温情。

rec·ol·lec·tion /rɛkəlɛkʃᵊn/ (**recollections**) N-VAR If you have a **recollection of** something, you remember it. 记忆 ❑ *Pat has vivid recollections of the trip, and remembers some of the frightening aspects I had forgotten.* 帕特对这次旅行的记忆生动清晰，他还记得一些我已经忘却的可怕的事情。

rec·om·mend ♦♦◇ /rɛkəmɛnd/ (**recommends, recommending, recommended**) 1 V-T If someone **recommends** a person or thing to you, they suggest that you would find that person or thing good or useful. 推荐 ❑ *I just spent a vacation there and would recommend it to anyone.* 我刚在那儿度过一个假期，愿意向任何人推荐那里。 ❑ *"You're a good worker," he told him. "I'll recommend you for a promotion."* "你是名好员工，"他说。"我要推荐你升职。" ● **rec·om·mend·ed** ADJ 被推崇的 ❑ *Though ten years old, this book is highly recommended.* 尽管已出版10年了，这本书仍备受推崇。 2 V-T If you **recommend** that something is done, you suggest that it should be done. 建议 ❑ *The judge recommended that he serve 20 years in prison.* 法官建议判他入狱服刑20年。 ❑ *We strongly recommend reporting the incident to the police.* 我们强烈建议将此事报警。 3 V-T If something or someone has a particular quality to **recommend** them, that quality makes them attractive or gives them an advantage over similar things or people. 使受欢迎；使有优势 ❑ *La Cucina restaurant has much to recommend it.* 拉库奇那餐馆有许多值得称道的地方。

Thesaurus *recommend* 另参见：
V. endorse, put forward, suggest 1
advise, urge 2

Word Partnership *recommend* 的常用搭配：
N. **doctors** recommend, **experts** recommend 1 2
recommend **changes** 2
ADV. **highly** recommend, **strongly** recommend 1 – 3

rec·om·men·da·tion ♦◇◇ /rɛkəmɛndeɪʃᵊn/ (**recommendations**) 1 N-VAR The **recommendations** of a person or a committee are their suggestions or advice on what is the best thing to do. 建议；劝告 ❑ *The committee's recommendations are unlikely to be made public.* 委员会的建议很可能不会公之于众。 2 N-VAR A **recommendation** of something is the suggestion that someone should have or use it because it is good. 推荐 ❑ *The best way of finding a lawyer is through personal recommendation.* 找律师的最好方法是通过个人推荐。

rec·om·pense /rɛkəmpɛns/ (**recompenses, recompensing, recompensed**) 1 N-UNCOUNT If you are given something, usually money, **in recompense**, you are given it as a reward or because you have suffered. 奖赏；补偿 [FORMAL] ❑ *He demands no financial recompense for his troubles.* 他对遭受到的麻烦没有要求经济补偿。 2 V-T If you **recompense** someone **for** their efforts or their loss, you give them something, usually money, as a payment or reward. 报酬；赔偿 [FORMAL] ❑ *If they succeed in court, they will be fully recompensed for their loss.* 如果他们在法庭上胜诉，他们的损失就会得到全额赔偿。

rec·on·cile /rɛkənsaɪl/ (**reconciles, reconciling, reconciled**) 1 V-T If you **reconcile** two beliefs, facts, or demands that seem to be opposed or completely different, you find a way in which they can both be true or both be successful. 使和谐一致；调和 ❑ *It's difficult to reconcile the demands of my job and the desire to be a good father.* 协调我工作的要求与我当个好父亲的愿望很难。 2 V-RECIP-PASSIVE If you **are reconciled with** someone, you become friendly with them again after a quarrel or disagreement. 与…和好 ❑ *He never believed he and Susan would be reconciled.* 他不认为他和苏珊会和好。 3 V-T If you **reconcile** two people, you make them become friends again after a quarrel or disagreement. 使和解 ❑ *...my attempt to reconcile him with Toby.* …我使他与托比和解的努力。 4 V-T If you **reconcile yourself to** an unpleasant situation, you accept it, although it does not make you happy to do so. 妥协；将就 ❑ *She had reconciled herself to never seeing him again.* 她不情愿地接受了再也不和他见面的事实。 ● **rec·on·ciled** ADJ 妥协的；将就的 [v-link ADJ "to" n/-ing] ❑ *She felt, if not grateful for her own situation, at least a little more reconciled to it.* 她觉得，即便对自己的处境不心存感激，至少能将就一些了。

★ **rec·on·cilia·tion** /rɛkənsɪlieɪʃᵊn/ (**reconciliations**) 1 N-VAR **Reconciliation** between two people or countries who have quarreled is the process of their becoming friends again. A **reconciliation** is an instance of this. 和解 ❑ *...an appeal for reconciliation between Catholics and Protestants.* …一个对天主教徒和新教徒之间和解的呼吁。 2 N-SING The **reconciliation** of two beliefs, facts, or demands that seem to be opposed is the process of finding a way in which they can both be true or both be successful. 调和；一致 ❑ *...the ideal of democracy based upon a reconciliation of the values of equality and liberty.* …平等和自由两种价值观和谐统一基础上的民主观念。

re·con·nais·sance /rɪkɒnɪsəns/ N-UNCOUNT **Reconnaissance** is the activity of obtaining military information about a place by sending soldiers or planes there, or by the use of satellites. 侦察 ❑ *The helicopter was returning from a reconnaissance mission.* 那架直升机执行完一项侦察任务正在返回。

re·con·sid·er /ri̲kənsɪdər/ (**reconsiders, reconsidering, reconsidered**) V-T/V-I If you **reconsider** a decision or opinion, you think about it and try to decide whether it should be changed.

重新考虑 ❑ *We want you to reconsider your decision to resign from the board.* 我们希望你能重新考虑从董事会辞职的决定。❑ *If at the end of two years you still feel the same, we will reconsider.* 如果两年后你仍然有同样的感觉，我们将重新考虑。

re·con·struct /ri̱kənstrʌ̱kt/ (**reconstructs, reconstructing, reconstructed**) **1** V-T If you **reconstruct** something that has been destroyed or badly damaged, you build it and make it work again. 重建；修复 ❑ *The government must reconstruct the shattered economy.* 政府必须重建垮掉的经济。**2** V-T To **reconstruct** a system or policy means to change it so that it works in a different way. 改造 ❑ *She actually wanted to reconstruct the state and transform society.* 她其实想改造这个国家并完全改变社会。**3** V-T If you **reconstruct** an event that happened in the past, you try to get a complete understanding of it by combining a lot of small pieces of information. 使再现 ❑ *He began to reconstruct the events of December 21, 1988, when flight 103 disappeared.* 他开始重现1988年12月21日103航班失踪时所发生的事情。

re·con·struc·tion /ri̱kənstrʌ̱kʃᵊn/ (**reconstructions**) **1** N-UNCOUNT **Reconstruction** is the process of making a country normal again after a war, for example by making the economy stronger and by replacing buildings that have been damaged. （战后国家的）重建 ❑ *...America's part in the postwar reconstruction of Germany.* …美国在战后德国重建中扮演的角色。❑ *...the Reconstruction period immediately following the Civil War.* …美国内战后紧随而来的重建期。**2** N-UNCOUNT The **reconstruction** of a building, structure, or road is the activity of building it again, because it has been damaged. 修复；重修（建筑、道路等）❑ *Work began on the reconstruction of the road.* 重修这条路的工作已经开始了。**3** N-COUNT The **reconstruction** of a crime or event is when people try to understand or show exactly what happened, often by acting it out. （犯罪过程的）再现 ❑ *Mrs. Kerr was too upset to take part in a reconstruction of her ordeal.* 克尔夫人过于悲痛以至不能参加对她受折磨场面的再现。

re·con·vene /ri̱kənvi̱n/ (**reconvenes, reconvening, reconvened**) V-T/V-I If a legislature, court, or conference **reconvenes** or if someone **reconvenes** it, it meets again after a break. 重新集合；重新召集 ❑ *The conference might reconvene after its opening session.* 会议可能会在开幕式之后重新召集。

rec·ord ♦♦♦ (**records, recording, recorded**)

The noun is pronounced /re̱kərd/. The verb is pronounced /rɪkɔ̱rd/.

名词读作 /re̱kərd/。动词读作 /rɪkɔ̱rd/。

1 N-COUNT If you keep a **record of** something, you keep a written account or photographs of it so that it can be referred to later. 记录；记载 ❑ *Keep a record of all the payments.* 对所有付款做一个记录。❑ *There's no record of any marriage or children.* 没有任何有关结婚或子女的记录。**2** V-T If you **record** a piece of information or an event, you write it down, photograph it, or put it into a computer so that in the future people can refer to it. 记录；记载 ❑ *Her letters record the domestic and social details of diplomatic life in China.* 她的信件记录了在中国的外交生活中家庭和社会活动的细节。**3** V-T If you **record** something such as a speech or performance, you put it on tape or film so that it can be heard or seen again later. 录音；录像 ❑ *There is nothing to stop viewers from recording the films on videotape.* 没有办法阻止观众用录像带录下电影。**4** V-T If a musician or performer **records** a piece of music or a television or radio show, they perform it so that it can be put onto CD, tape, or film. 录制 ❑ *It took the musicians two and a half days to record their soundtrack for the film.* 音乐家们花了两天半的时间录制电影的配乐。**5** N-COUNT A **record** is a round, flat piece of black plastic on which sound, especially music, is stored, and which can be played on a record player. You can also refer to the music stored on this piece of plastic as a **record**. 唱片 ❑ *This is one of my favorite records.* 这是我最喜欢的唱片之一。**6** V-T If a dial or other measuring device **records** a certain measurement or value, it shows that measurement or value. 标明；显示 ❑ *The test records the electrical activity of the brain.* 这个测试显示出大脑的电流活动。**7** N-COUNT A **record** is the best result that has ever been achieved in a particular sport or activity, for example the fastest time, the farthest distance, or the greatest number of victories. 纪录 ❑ *Roger Kingdom set the world record of 12.92 seconds.* 罗杰·金顿创下了12.92秒的世界纪录。**8** ADJ You use **record** to say that something is higher, lower, better, or worse than has ever been achieved before. 创纪录的 [ADJ n] ❑ *Profits were at record levels.* 利润水平是创纪录的。**9** N-COUNT Someone's **record** is the facts that are known about their achievements or character. 经历；履历 ❑ *His record reveals a tough streak.* 他的经历说明他个性坚强。**10** N-COUNT If someone has a criminal **record**, it is officially known that they have committed crimes in the past. （犯罪）记录 ❑ *...a heroin addict with a criminal record going back 15 years.* …一名15年前留有案底的海洛因吸食成瘾者。**11** → see also **recording, track record** **12** PHRASE If you say that what you are going to say next is **for the record**, you mean that you are saying it publicly and officially and you want it to be written down and remembered. 供记录在案 ❑ *We're willing to state for the record that it has enormous value.* 我们愿意申明它有巨大的价值并望其能被记录在案。**13** PHRASE If you give some information **for the record**, you give it in case people might find it useful at a later time, although it is not a very important part of what you are talking about. 顺便说一下；仅供参考 ❑ *For the record, most Moscow girls leave school at about 18.* 随便说一下，多数莫斯科女孩大约十八岁离开学校。**14** PHRASE If something that you say is **off the record**, you do not intend it to be considered as official, or published with your name attached to it. 非正式的；不得公开引用的 ❑ *May I speak off the record?* 我可以私下里说吗？**15** PHRASE If you are **on record as** saying something, you have said it publicly and officially and it has been written down. 公开宣布并记录在案的 ❑ *The president is on record as saying that the increase in unemployment is "a price worth paying" to keep inflation down.* 总统公开说失业率的上升是遏制通货膨胀"值得付出的代价"。**16** PHRASE If you keep information **on record**, you write it down or store it in a computer so that it can be used later. 记录在案的 ❑ *The practice is to keep on record any analysis of samples.* 这项工作是为了记录下对样品的所有分析。

→ see **diary, history**

Word Partnership *record* 的常用搭配：

N. record **a song** **4**
record **album**, record **company**, **hit** record, record **industry**, record **label**, record **producer**, record **store** **5**
world record **7**
record **earnings**, record **high**, record **low**, record **numbers**, record **temperatures**, record **time** **8**
criminal record **10**

V. **break a** record, **set a** record **7**

re·cord·er /rɪkɔ̱rdər/ (**recorders**) **1** N-COUNT You can refer to a cassette recorder, a tape recorder, or a video recorder as a **recorder**. 录音机；录像机 ❑ *Rodney put the recorder on the desk top and pushed the play button.* 罗德尼把录音机放在桌面上，按下了播放键。**2** → see also **tape recorder, video recorder** **3** N-VAR A **recorder** is a wooden or plastic musical instrument in the shape of a pipe. You play the recorder by blowing into the top of it and covering and uncovering the holes with your fingers. 竖笛 **4** N-COUNT A **recorder** is a machine or instrument that keeps a record of something, for example in an experiment or on a vehicle. 记录仪器 ❑ *Data recorders also pinpoint mechanical faults rapidly, reducing repair times.* 数据记录仪器也能很快查明机械故障，减少维修时间。

re·cord·ing ♦◇◇ /rɪkɔ̱rdɪŋ/ (**recordings**) **1** N-COUNT A **recording of** something is a record, CD, tape, or video of it. 唱片；录音带；录像带 ❑ *...a video recording of a police interview.* …一盘警察询问的录像带。**2** N-UNCOUNT **Recording** is the process of making records, CDs, tapes, or videos. 录音；录像 ❑ *...the recording industry.* …音像业。

rec̱ord play·er (**record players**) N-COUNT A **record player** is a machine on which you can play a record in order to listen to the music or other sounds on it. 唱机 ❑ *His parents had no record player or television.* 他的父母没有唱机，也没有电视。

★ **re·count** (**recounts, recounting, recounted**)

The verb is pronounced /rɪka̱ʊnt/. The noun is pronounced /ri̱kaʊnt/.

动词读作 /rɪka̱ʊnt/。名词读作 /ri̱kaʊnt/。

1 V-T If you **recount** a story or event, you tell or describe it to people. 叙述；描述 [FORMAL] ❑ *He then recounted the story of the interview for his first job.* 他然后叙述了有关他第一份工作面试的故事。**2** N-COUNT A **recount** is a second count of votes in an election when the result is very close. 重新计票 ❑ *She wanted a recount. She couldn't believe that I got more votes than she did.* 她要求重新计票。她不相信我比她得票多。

re·coup /rɪkuːp/ (**recoups, recouping, recouped**) V-T If you **recoup** a sum of money that you have spent or lost, you get it back. 弥补；收回 ❑ *Insurance companies are trying to recoup their losses by increasing premiums.* 保险公司正试图通过增加保费来弥补损失。

re·course /rɪkɔrs/ N-UNCOUNT If you achieve something without **recourse to** a particular course of action, you succeed without carrying out that action. To have **recourse to** a particular course of action means to have to do that action in order to achieve something. 依靠 [FORMAL] ❑ *It enabled its members to settle their differences without recourse to war.* 它使其成员不必诉诸战争来解决他们的分歧。

re·cov·er ♦◇◇ /rɪkʌvər/ (**recovers, recovering, recovered**) **1** V-I When you **recover from** an illness or an injury, you become well again. 痊愈；恢复健康 ❑ *He is recovering from a knee injury.* 他的膝伤正在痊愈。

> **Recover** is a fairly formal word. In conversation, you usually say that someone **gets better**. ❑ *Qualified nurses help patients get better more quickly.*

2 V-I If you **recover from** an unhappy or unpleasant experience, you stop being upset by it. (从不愉快的经历中) 恢复 ❑ *...a tragedy from which he never fully recovered.* …一场他再也没有完全从中恢复过来的悲剧。 **3** V-I If something **recovers from** a period of weakness or difficulty, it improves or gets stronger again. (从弱势或困境中) 好转 ❑ *He recovered from a 4-2 deficit to reach the quarter-finals.* 他从4—2的失利中恢复过来，进入1/4决赛。 **4** V-T If you **recover** something that has been lost or stolen, you find it or get it back. 重新找回 ❑ *Police raided five houses in Brooklyn and recovered stolen goods.* 警察突击搜查了位于布鲁克林的5栋住宅，找回了被盗物品。 **5** V-T If you **recover** a mental or physical state, it comes back again. For example, if you **recover** consciousness, you become conscious again. 恢复 (身心状态或意识) ❑ *She had a severe attack of asthma and it took an hour to recover her breath.* 她犯了一次严重的哮喘，一个小时之后才恢复正常呼吸。 **6** V-T If you **recover** money that you have spent, invested, or lent to someone, you get the same amount back. 收回 (花掉、投资或借出的钱) ❑ *Legal action is being taken to recover the money.* 正采取法律措施来收回那笔钱。

> **Thesaurus** *recover* 另参见：
> v. recuperate **1**
> get over **2**
> get, back, reclaim **4**–**6**

re·cov·ery ♦◇◇ /rɪkʌvəri/ (**recoveries**) **1** N-VAR If a sick person makes a **recovery**, he or she becomes well again. 痊愈 ❑ *He made a remarkable recovery from a shin injury.* 他胫骨伤恢复得相当好。 **2** N-VAR When there is a **recovery** in a country's economy, it improves. 好转；复苏 ❑ *Interest-rate cuts have failed to bring about economic recovery.* 利率的降低未能带来经济的复苏。 **3** N-UNCOUNT You talk about the **recovery of** something when you get it back after it has been lost or stolen. 失而复得 ❑ *A substantial reward is being offered for the recovery of a painting by Turner.* 一笔巨额悬赏正被用来找回特纳的一幅油画。 **4** N-UNCOUNT You talk about the **recovery of** someone's physical or mental state when they return to this state. 复原；恢复 ❑ *...the abrupt loss and recovery of consciousness.* …意识的突然失去和恢复。 **5** PHRASE If someone is **in recovery**, they are being given a course of treatment to help them recover from something such as a drug habit or mental illness. 在恢复中 ❑ *...Carole, a compulsive pot smoker and alcoholic in recovery.* …卡萝尔，一名正在恢复的吸食大麻成瘾者和酗酒者。

> **Word Link** *creat ≈ making : creation, creature, recreate*

re·cre·ate /rikrieɪt/ (**recreates, recreating, recreated**) V-T If you **recreate** something, you succeed in making it exist or seem to exist in a different time or place from its original time or place. 再现；重建 ❑ *I am trying to recreate family life far from home.* 我正试图在远离家的地方重建家庭生活。

rec·rea·tion (**recreations**)

> Pronounced /rɛkrieɪʃən/ for meaning **1**. Pronounced /rikrieɪʃən/ and hyphenated re·crea·tion for meaning **2**.

> 义项**1**读作 /rɛkrieɪʃən/。义项**2**读作 /rikrieɪʃən/且连字符添加方式为 re·crea·tion。

1 N-VAR **Recreation** consists of things that you do in your spare time to relax. 娱乐 ❑ *Saturday afternoon is for recreation and outings.* 周六下午是娱乐和外出的时间。 **2** N-COUNT A **recreation of** something is the process of making it exist or seem to exist again in a different time or place. 重现；重建 ❑ *They are planning to build a faithful recreation of the original frontier town.* 他们正计划建造一座和原来边境城镇一模一样的复制品。
→ see **park**

rec·rea·tion·al /rɛkrieɪʃənəl/ ADJ **Recreational** means relating to things people do in their spare time to relax. 娱乐的 ❑ *...parks and other recreational facilities.* …公园及其它娱乐设施。 ❑ *...recreational use of alcohol.* …娱乐性饮酒。

rec·rea·tion·al drug (**recreational drugs**) N-COUNT **Recreational drugs** are illegal drugs such as cannabis or cocaine that people take occasionally for enjoyment, especially when they are spending time socially with other people. (在社交中偶尔使用的) 消遣性毒品 ❑ *Society largely turns a blind eye to recreational drug use.* 社会大体上对消遣性毒品的使用视而不见。

re·crimi·na·tion /rɪkrɪmɪneɪʃən/ (**recriminations**) N-UNCOUNT **Recriminations** are accusations that two people or groups make about each other. 互相指责 [also N in pl] ❑ *The bitter arguments and recriminations have finally ended the relationship.* 充满仇恨的争吵和互相指责最终结束了这段关系。

re·cruit ♦◇◇ /rɪkrut/ (**recruits, recruiting, recruited**) **1** V-T If you **recruit** people for an organization, you select them and persuade them to join it or work for it. 招收；招募 ❑ *The police are trying to recruit more black and Hispanic officers.* 警方正试图招收更多的黑人和西班牙裔的警官。 ❑ *She set up her stand to recruit students to the Anarchist Association.* 她搭了一个摊位招募学生加入无政府主义者协会。 ● **re·cruit·ing** N-UNCOUNT 招收；招募 ❑ *A bomb exploded at an army recruiting office.* 一枚炸弹在一个征兵办公室爆炸了。 **2** N-COUNT A **recruit** is a person who has recently joined an organization or an army. 新成员；新兵 ❑ *...a new recruit to the LA Police Department.* …洛杉矶警察局的一名新警员。

★ **re·cruit·ment** /rɪkrutmənt/ N-UNCOUNT The **recruitment** of workers, soldiers, or members is the act or process of selecting them for an organization or army and persuading them to join. 招聘 ❑ *...the examination system for the recruitment of civil servants.* …公务员招聘的考试体系。

> **Word Link** *rect ≈ right, straight : correct, rectangle, rectify*

▲ **rec·tan·gle** /rɛktæŋgəl/ (**rectangles**) N-COUNT A **rectangle** is a four-sided shape whose corners are all ninety-degree angles. Each side of a rectangle is the same length as the one opposite to it. 长方形
→ see **ratio, shape, volume**

★ **rec·tan·gu·lar** /rɛktæŋgyələr/ ADJ Something that is **rectangular** is shaped like a rectangle. 长方形的 ❑ *...a rectangular table.* …一张长方形的桌子。

★ **rec·ti·fy** /rɛktɪfaɪ/ (**rectifies, rectifying, rectified**) V-T If you **rectify** something that is wrong, you change it so that it becomes correct or satisfactory. 矫正；改正 ❑ *Only an act of Congress could rectify the situation.* 只有国会的法案才能扭转这种局面。

re·cu·per·ate /rɪkupəreɪt/ (**recuperates, recuperating, recuperated**) V-I When you **recuperate**, you recover your health or strength after you have been ill or injured. 康复；复原 ❑ *I went away to the country to recuperate.* 我离开到乡下去养病。 ● **re·cu·pera·tion** /rɪkupəreɪʃən/ N-UNCOUNT 康复；复原 ❑ *Leonard was very pleased with his powers of recuperation.* 伦纳德对他的康复能力很满意。

★ **re·cur** /rɪkɜr/ (**recurs, recurring, recurred**) V-I If something **recurs**, it happens more than once. 再现；屡次发生 ❑ *...a theme that was to recur frequently in his work.* …一个将在他的作品中多次出现的主题。

re·cur·rence /rɪkɜrəns/ (**recurrences**) N-VAR If there is a **recurrence of** something, it happens again. 再次发生 ❑ *Police are out in force to prevent a recurrence of the violence.* 警察大规模地行动防止暴力的再次发生。

re·cur·rent /rɪkɜrənt/ ADJ A **recurrent** event or feeling happens or is experienced more than once. (情感) 反复出现的；(事情) 一再发生的 ❑ *Race is a recurrent theme in the work.* 种族是该作品中反复出现的一个主题。

★ **re·cy·clable** /risaɪkləbəl/ ADJ **Recyclable** waste or materials can be processed and used again. 可再生的 ❑ *...a separate bin for recyclable waste products.* …一个专门装可再生废物的垃圾桶。

r

re·cy·cle /risaɪkᵊl/ (**recycles, recycling, recycled**) V-T If you **recycle** things that have already been used, such as bottles or sheets of paper, you process them so that they can be used again. 回收利用；循环使用 ❑ *The objective would be to recycle 98 percent of domestic waste.* 该目标是循环使用98%的生活垃圾。● **re·cy·cling** N-UNCOUNT 回收利用；循环使用 ❑ *...a recycling plan.* …一项回收利用计划。

→ see **dump, paper**

> **Recycling** has become so common in North America that many communities have special procedures for sorting and collecting the trash. Glass, metal, paper and plastic can be separated and used again. In some places, residents must pay a fine if they do not recycle.

red ♦♦♦ /rɛd/ (**reds, redder, reddest**) **1** COLOR Something that is **red** is the color of blood or fire. 红色（的）❑ *...a bunch of red roses.* …一束红色的玫瑰花。**2** ADJ If you say that someone's face is **red**, you mean that it is redder than its normal color, because they are embarrassed, angry, or out of breath. 脸红的 ❑ *With a bright red face I was forced to admit that I had no real idea.* 我满脸通红，被迫承认我其实没有什么想法。**3** ADJ You describe someone's hair as **red** when it is between red and brown in color. （头发）红褐色的 ❑ *...a girl with red hair.* …一位红褐色头发的女孩。**4** N-MASS You can refer to red wine as **red**. 红葡萄酒 ❑ *The spicy flavors in these dishes call for reds rather than whites.* 这些菜肴味道辛辣，宜配红葡萄酒而不是白葡萄酒。**5** ADJ If a U.S. state is described as **red**, it means that the majority of its residents vote for the Republican Party in elections, especially in the presidential elections. 支持共和党的 ❑ *...policies that could guarantee her enough support in red states to win the White House in 2008.* …保证她能在支持共和党的各个州获得足够支持以在2008年白宫的竞选中获胜的政策。**6** PHRASE If a person or company is **in the red** or if their bank account is **in the red**, they have spent more money than they have in their account and therefore they owe money to the bank. 负债的 ❑ *The theater is $500,000 in the red.* 剧院负债50万美元。**7** PHRASE If you **see red**, you suddenly become very angry. 勃然大怒 ❑ *I didn't mean to break his nose. I just saw red.* 我不是有意打破他的鼻子的。我只是一时愤怒。

→ see **color, rainbow**

red card (**red cards**) N-COUNT In soccer, if a player is shown the **red card**, the referee holds up a red card to indicate that the player must leave the field for breaking the rules. （足球比赛的）红牌 ❑ *He was shown a red card for a rough tackle.* 他因为粗暴抢球而被红牌罚下。

red·dish /rɛdɪʃ/ ADJ **Reddish** means slightly red in color. 微红的 ❑ *He had reddish brown hair.* 他有一头略带红色的褐发。

▲ **re·deem** /rɪdim/ (**redeems, redeeming, redeemed**) **1** V-T If you **redeem yourself** or your reputation, you do something that makes people have a good opinion of you again after you have behaved or performed badly. 挽回声誉；改善形象 ❑ *He realized the mistake he had made and wanted to redeem himself.* 他认识到自己所犯的错误并想挽回声誉。**2** V-T When something **redeems** an unpleasant thing or situation, it prevents it from being completely bad. 弥补；补救 ❑ *Work is the way that people seek to redeem their lives from futility.* 工作是人们寻求用以弥补生活使之不至于毫无意义的途径。**3** V-T If you **redeem** a debt or money that you have promised to someone, you pay money that you owe or that you promised to pay. 偿还（债务或钱）[FORMAL] ❑ *The amount required to redeem the mortgage was $358,587.* 偿还抵押贷款所需的金额是$358587。**4** V-T In religions such as Christianity, to **redeem** someone means to save them by freeing them from sin and evil. 救赎 ❑ *...a new female spiritual force to redeem the world.* …一股挽救世界的新的女性精神力量。

R

re·deem·able /rɪdiməbᵊl/ ADJ If something is **redeemable**, it can be exchanged for a particular sum of money or for goods worth a particular sum. 可兑换现金的；可兑换其他物品的 ❑ *Their full catalog costs $5, redeemable against a first order.* 他们的完整目录要5美元，首次订购金额可充兑。

re·demp·tion /rɪdɛmpʃᵊn/ (**redemptions**) **1** N-VAR **Redemption** is the act of redeeming something or of being redeemed by something. 救赎；偿还 [FORMAL] ❑ *He craves redemption for his sins.* 他渴望对其罪孽的救赎。❑ *...redemption of the loan.* …该贷款的偿还。**2** PHRASE If you say that someone or something is **beyond redemption**, you mean that they are so bad it is unlikely that anything can be done to improve them. 无可挽回的；不可救药的 ❑ *No man is beyond redemption.* 没有人是不可救药的。

re·devel·op·ment /ridɪvɛləpmənt/ N-UNCOUNT When **redevelopment** takes place, the buildings in one area of a town are knocked down and new ones are built in their place. 重新开发；重建 ❑ *The group's intention is to clear the site for redevelopment.* 这个集团的意图是清空这片地以重新开发。

red-hot **1** ADJ **Red-hot** metal or rock has been heated to such a high temperature that it has turned red. 烧红的；炽热的 ❑ *...red-hot iron.* …烧红的铁。**2** ADJ A **red-hot** object is too hot to be touched safely. 炽热的；烫的 ❑ *In the main rooms red-hot radiators were left exposed.* 在那些主房间里炽热的散热器被暴露放在那儿。**3** ADJ **Red-hot** is used to describe a person or thing that is very popular, especially someone who is very good at what they do or something that is new and exciting. 炙手可热的；热门的 [JOURNALISM] ❑ *Some traders are already stacking the red-hot book on their shelves.* 一些书商已经在往他们的架上放这本热门畅销书了。

re·di·rect /ridɪrɛkt, -daɪ-/ (**redirects, redirecting, redirected**) **1** V-T If you **redirect** your energy, resources, or ability, you begin doing something different or trying to achieve something different. 使转向 ❑ *Controls were used to redistribute or redirect resources.* 采取了管制措施来重新分配资源或转变资源投放方向。**2** V-T If you **redirect** someone or something, you change their course or destination. 使改变方向；使改变线路 ❑ *She redirected them to the men's department.* 她让他们转向到了男装部。

re·dis·trib·ute /ridɪstrɪbyut/ (**redistributes, redistributing, redistributed**) V-T If something such as money or property **is redistributed**, it is shared among people or organizations in a different way from the way that it was previously shared. 重新分配 ❑ *Wealth was redistributed more equitably among society.* 财富在社会上被更公平地重新分配。● **re·dis·tri·bu·tion** /ridɪstrɪbyuʃᵊn/ N-UNCOUNT 重新分配 ❑ *One of government's primary duties is the redistribution of income, so that the better off can help the worse off out of poverty.* 政府的主要职责之一就是收入的重新分配，这样富裕的人能帮助贫穷的人摆脱贫困。

re·dress /rɪdrɛs/ (**redresses, redressing, redressed**)

> The noun is also pronounced /ridrɛs/ in American English.

> 名词在美国英语中亦读作 /ridrɛs/。

1 V-T If you **redress** something such as a wrong or a complaint, you do something to correct it or to improve things for the person who has been badly treated. 纠正；补救 [FORMAL] ❑ *More and more victims turn to litigation to redress wrongs done to them.* 越来越多的受害者诉诸法律以获得平反。**2** V-T If you **redress** the balance or the imbalance between two things that have become unfair or unequal, you make them fair and equal again. 使恢复（平衡）[FORMAL] ❑ *So we're trying to redress the balance and to give teachers a sense that both spoken and written language are equally important.* 所以我们正力求平衡，让老师们感觉到口语和书面语同样重要。**3** N-UNCOUNT **Redress** is money that someone pays you because they have caused you harm or loss. 赔款；赔偿 [FORMAL] ❑ *They are continuing their legal battle to seek some redress from the government.* 他们正继续打官司以向政府寻求一些赔偿。

red tape N-UNCOUNT You refer to official rules and procedures as **red tape** when they seem unnecessary and cause delay. （官方的）繁文缛节 [DISAPPROVAL] ❑ *The little money that was available was tied up in bureaucratic red tape.* 可支配的那点点钱都花在官僚主义的繁文缛节上了。

re·duce ♦♦◊ /rɪdus/ (**reduces, reducing, reduced**) **1** V-T If you **reduce** something, you make it smaller in size or amount, or less in degree. 使变小 ❑ *It reduces the risks of heart disease.* 它减小了犯心脏病的危险。**2** V-T If someone **is reduced to** a weaker or inferior state, they become weaker or inferior as a result of something that happens to them. 使陷入 [usu passive] ❑ *They were reduced to extreme poverty.* 他们沦落到极度贫困的地步。**3** V-T If you say that someone **is reduced to** doing something, you mean that they have to do it, although it is unpleasant or embarrassing. 迫使 [usu passive] ❑ *He was reduced to begging for a living.* 他不得不以乞讨为生。**4** V-T If something is changed to a different or less complicated form, you can say that it **is reduced to** that form. 使变成；使简化为 [usu passive] ❑ *All the buildings in the town have been reduced to rubble.* 镇上所有的建筑都变成了瓦砾。**5** V-T/V-I If you **reduce** liquid when you are cooking, or if it **reduces**, it is boiled in order to make it less in quantity and thicker. 使变稠；收汁

❑ *Boil the liquid in a small saucepan to reduce it by half.* 在小炖锅中煮沸汤汁使其收到一半的量。 **6** PHRASE If someone or something **reduces** you **to tears**, they make you feel so unhappy that you cry. 使…流泪 ❑ *The attentions of the media reduced her to tears.* 媒体的关注使她流下了眼泪。

→ see **mineral**

Thesaurus *reduce* 另参见：

V. cut back, decrease, lessen, lower **1**

Word Partnership *reduce* 的常用搭配：

N. reduce **anxiety**, reduce **costs**, reduce **crime**, reduce **debt**, reduce **pain**, reduce **spending**, reduce **stress**, reduce **taxes**, reduce **violence**, reduce **waste** **1**

ADV. **dramatically** reduce, **greatly** reduce, **significantly** reduce, **substantially** reduce **1**

V. **help** reduce, **plan to** reduce, **try to** reduce **1**

re·duc·tion ♦◇◇ /rɪdʌkʃᵊn/ (**reductions**) **1** N-COUNT When there is a **reduction in** something, it is made smaller. 缩减 ❑ *...a future reduction in interest rates.* …一次未来利率的降低。 **2** N-UNCOUNT **Reduction** is the act of making something smaller in size or amount, or less in degree. (尺寸、数量或程度上的)削减 ❑ *...a new strategic arms reduction agreement.* …一项新的战略武器削减协议。

→ see **dump**

Word Partnership *reduction* 的常用搭配：

N. **arms** reduction, **budget** reduction, **cost** reduction, **debt** reduction, **deficit** reduction, **noise** reduction, **rate** reduction, **risk** reduction, **tax** reduction **2**

▲ **re·dun·dan·cy** /rɪdʌndənsi/ (**redundancies**) **1** N-UNCOUNT **Redundancy** means being made redundant. 裁员 [BUSINESS] ❑ *Thousands of bank employees are facing redundancy as their employers cut costs.* 数千名银行职员面临裁员，因为他们的雇主要削减成本。 **2** N-COUNT When there are **redundancies**, an organization tells some of its employees to leave because their jobs are no longer necessary or because the organization can no longer afford to pay them. 多余的员工 [BRIT, BUSINESS]

in AM, use **dismissals**, **layoffs**

★ **re·dun·dant** /rɪdʌndənt/ **1** ADJ Something that is **redundant** is unnecessary, for example, because it is no longer needed or because its job is being done by something else. 多余的 ❑ *Changes in technology may mean that once-valued skills are now redundant.* 技术的变化可能意味着从前受重视的技巧现在变得多余了。 **2** ADJ If you are made **redundant**, your employer tells you to leave because your job is no longer necessary or because your employer cannot afford to keep paying you. 被裁减的 [BRIT, BUSINESS]

in AM, use **be dismissed**, **be laid off**

▲ **reed** /rid/ (**reeds**) **1** N-COUNT **Reeds** are tall plants that grow in large groups in shallow water or on ground that is always wet and soft. They have strong, hollow stems that can be used for making things such as mats or baskets. 芦苇 **2** N-COUNT A **reed** is a small piece of cane or metal inserted into the mouthpiece of a woodwind instrument. The reed vibrates when you blow through it and makes a sound. (木管乐器的) 簧片

▲ **reef** /rif/ (**reefs**) N-COUNT A **reef** is a long line of rocks or sand, the top of which is just above or just below the surface of the sea. 礁 ❑ *An unspoiled coral reef encloses the bay.* 一道完好的珊瑚礁围绕着海湾。

reek /rik/ (**reeks, reeking, reeked**) **1** V-I To **reek of** something, usually something unpleasant, means to smell very strongly of it. 散发出 (强烈难闻的气味) ❑ *Your breath reeks of stale cigar smoke.* 你的呼吸中散发出雪茄烟的臭味。 ● N-SING **Reek** is also a noun. 臭气 ❑ *He smelled the reek of whiskey.* 他散发出威士忌酒味。 **2** V-I If you say that something **reeks of** unpleasant ideas, feelings, or practices, you disapprove of it because it gives a strong impression that it involves those ideas, feelings, or practices. 明显带有 (令人不快的特性) [DISAPPROVAL] ❑ *The whole thing reeks of hypocrisy.* 整件事充满了虚伪。

★ **reel** ♦◇◇ /ril/ (**reels, reeling, reeled**) **1** N-COUNT A **reel** is a cylindrical object around which you wrap something such as movie film, magnetic tape, or fishing line. 卷轴 ❑ *...a 30-meter reel of cable.* …一卷30米长的电缆。 **2** V-I If someone **reels**, they move about in an unsteady way as if they are going to fall. 踉跄 ❑ *He was reeling a little. He must be very drunk.* 他有点踉跄。一定醉得很厉害。 **3** V-I If you **are reeling** from a shock, you are feeling extremely surprised or upset because of it. 感到震惊；心烦意乱 [usu cont] ❑ *I'm still reeling from the shock of hearing about it.* 我现在仍然因为听到这个消息而震惊不已。 **4** V-I If you say that your brain or your mind **is reeling**, you mean that you are very confused because you have too many things to think about. 混乱 ❑ *His mind reeled at the question.* 他的脑子被这个问题搅混了。

▸ **reel off** PHRASAL VERB If you **reel off** information, you repeat it from memory quickly and easily. 不费力地讲出；流利地背出 ❑ *She reeled off the titles of a dozen or so of the novels.* 她脱口说出了十来本小说的书名。

re·elect /riɪlɛkt/ (**reelects, reelecting, reelected**) also **re-elect** V-T When someone such as a politician or an official who has been elected **is reelected**, they win another election and are therefore able to continue in their position as, for example, president, or an official in an organization. 再次当选 ❑ *He needs 51 percent to be reelected.* 他需要51%的选票以再度当选。 ❑ *James Rhodes was reelected governor of Ohio.* 詹姆斯·罗兹再度当选俄亥俄州的州长。 ● **re·elec·tion** /riɪlɛkʃᵊn/ N-UNCOUNT 再次当选 ❑ *He is heavily favored to win reelection.* 他再次当选的条件极其有利。

re·ex·am·ine /riɪgzæmɪn/ (**reexamines, reexamining, reexamined**) also **re-examine** V-T If a person or group of people **reexamines** their ideas, beliefs, or attitudes, they think about them carefully because they are no longer sure if they are correct. 重新审视 ❑ *The marriage will cause Drew to reexamine his life.* 这场婚姻将让德鲁重新审视他的生活。 ● **re·ex·ami·na·tion** /riɪgzæmɪneɪʃᵊn/ N-VAR (**reexaminations**) 重新审视 ❑ *The issue has led to a reexamination of censorship rules.* 这件事导致了对审查制度的重新审视。

ref /rɛf/ (**refs**) **1** **Ref.** is an abbreviation for **reference**. It is written in front of a code at the top of business letters and documents. The code refers to a file where all the letters and documents about the same matter are kept. 文件编号 [BUSINESS] ❑ *Our Ref: JAH/JW.* 我们的编号是：JAH/JW。 **2** N-COUNT The **ref** in a sports game, such as football, soccer, or boxing, is the same as the **referee**. 裁判员 [INFORMAL] ❑ *The ref said it was a fumble.* 裁判员判定为失球。

re·fer ♦♦◇ /rɪfɜr/ (**refers, referring, referred**) **1** V-I If you **refer to** a particular subject or person, you talk about them or mention them. 谈及 ❑ *In his speech, he referred to a recent trip to Canada.* 在他的讲话中，他提到了最近的加拿大之行。 **2** V-I If you **refer to** someone or something **as** a particular thing, you use a particular word, expression, or name to mention or describe them. 称 ❑ *Marcia had referred to him as a dear friend.* 玛西娅把他称为好朋友。 **3** V-I If a word **refers to** a particular thing, situation, or idea, it describes it in some way. 描述 ❑ *The term electronics refers to electrically induced action.* 电子学描述的是电力产生的作用。 **4** V-T If a person who is ill **is referred to** a hospital or a specialist, they are sent there by a doctor in order to be treated. 把…送往 [usu passive] ❑ *She was referred to the hospital by a neighborhood clinic.* 她被一家社区诊所送往医院救诊了。 **5** V-T If you **refer** a task or a problem **to** a person or an organization, you formally tell them about it, so that they can deal with it. 提交 ❑ *He could refer the matter to the high court.* 他可以把这件事提交高等法院。 **6** V-T If you **refer** someone **to** a person or organization, you send them there for the help they need. 介绍 ❑ *Now and then I referred a client to him.* 我不时地介绍客户给他。 **7** V-I If you **refer to** a book or other source of information, you look at it in order to find something out. 参考；查看 ❑ *He referred briefly to his notebook.* 他迅速查看了一下他的笔记。 **8** V-T If you **refer** someone **to** a source of information, you tell them the place where they will find the information they need or that you think will interest them. 指点…查阅 ❑ *Mr. Bryan also referred me to a book by the American journalist Anthony Scaduto.* 布赖恩先生还要我去查阅美国记者安东尼·斯卡杜托写的一本书。

★ **ref·eree** /rɛfəri/ (**referees, refereeing, refereed**) **1** N-COUNT The **referee** is the official who controls a sports event such as a football game or a boxing match. 裁判员 **2** V-T/V-I When someone **referees** a sports event or contest, they act as referee. 担任裁判 ❑ *Vautrot has refereed in two World Cups.* 沃特罗特已经在两届世界杯比赛中担任过裁判。 **3** N-COUNT A **referee** is a person who gives you a reference, for example when you are applying for a job. 介绍人；推荐人 [BRIT]

in AM, use **reference**

→ see **football**, **tennis**

ref·er·ence ♦◇◇ /rɛfərəns, rɛfrəns/ (**references**) 1 N-VAR **Reference to** someone or something is the act of talking about them or mentioning them. A **reference** is a particular example of this. 提及 ❑ *He made no reference to any agreement.* 他没有提到任何协议。 2 N-UNCOUNT **Reference** is the act of consulting someone or something in order to get information or advice. 咨询；查阅 ❑ *Please keep this sheet in a safe place for reference.* 请把这张纸放在稳妥的地方以备查阅。 3 ADJ **Reference** books are ones that you look at when you need specific information or facts about a subject. 供参考的 [ADJ n] ❑ *...a useful reference work for teachers.* …一本对老师们有用处的参考资料。 4 N-COUNT A **reference** is a word, phrase, or idea which comes from something such as a book, poem, or play and which you use when making a point about something. 引文；引文出处 ❑ *...a reference from the Koran.* …一段《可兰经》的引文。 5 N-COUNT A **reference** is something such as a number or a name that tells you where you can obtain the information you want. 编号；标记 ❑ *Make a note of the reference number shown on the form.* 记下表格上的编码。 6 N-COUNT A **reference** is a letter that is written by someone who knows you and which describes your character and abilities. When you apply for a job, an employer might ask for **references**. 推荐信 ❑ *The firm offered to give her a reference.* 公司提出给她开一封推荐信。 7 N-COUNT A **reference** is a person who gives you a reference, for example when you are applying for a job. 证明人 [mainly AM]

in BRIT, usually use **referee**

❑ *The official at the American embassy asked me for two references.* 美国大使馆的官员要我提供两名证明人。 8 PHRASE You use **with reference to** or **in reference to** in order to indicate what something relates to. 关于… ❑ *I am writing with reference to your article on salaries for scientists.* 我给你写信是要谈谈你写的有关科学家工资的那篇文章。 9 → see also **cross-reference**

Word Partnership *reference* 的常用搭配：

ADJ.	**clear** reference, **specific** reference 1 4
	quick reference 2
N.	reference **books**, reference **materials** 3
	reference **number** 5

▲ **ref·er·en·dum** ♦◇◇ /rɛfərɛndəm/ (**referendums** or **referenda** /rɛfərɛndə/) N-COUNT If a country holds a **referendum** on a particular policy, they ask the people to vote on the policy and show whether or not they agree with it. 公民投票；全民公决 ❑ *Estonia said today it too plans to hold a referendum on independence.* 爱沙尼亚今天称它也计划要就独立进行全民公决。

re·fer·ral /rɪfɜrəl/ (**referrals**) N-VAR **Referral** is the act of officially sending someone to a person or authority that is qualified to deal with them. A **referral** is an instance of this. 移交；送交 ❑ *Legal Aid can often provide referral to other types of agencies.* 法律援助机构能经常提供向其他类型机构的移交。

R

re·fill (**refills, refilling, refilled**)

The verb is pronounced /rifɪl/. The noun is pronounced /rifɪl/.

动词读作 /rifɪl/。名词读作 /rifɪl/。

1 V-T If you **refill** something, you fill it again after it has been emptied. 重新装满 ❑ *I refilled our wine glasses.* 我重新斟满了我们的酒杯。 ● N-COUNT **Refill** is also a noun. 重新装满 [INFORMAL] ❑ *Max held out his cup for a refill.* 马克斯伸出他的杯子要求再满上。 2 N-COUNT A **refill** of a particular product is a quantity of that product sold in a cheaper container than the one it is usually sold in. You use a refill to fill the more permanent container when it is empty. 补充剂 ❑ *Refill packs are cheaper and lighter.* 补充剂包装更便宜，更轻。

re·fi·nance /rifənæns, rifaɪnæns/ (**refinances, refinancing, refinanced**) V-T/V-I If a person or a company **refinances** a debt or if they **refinance**, they borrow money in order to pay the debt. 再筹资金 [BUSINESS] ❑ *A loan was arranged to refinance existing debt.* 一笔贷款被安排来偿还已有的债务。

re·fine /rɪfaɪn/ (**refines, refining, refined**) 1 V-T When a substance **is refined**, it is made pure by having all other substances removed from it. 提炼 [usu passive] ❑ *Oil is refined to remove naturally occurring impurities.* 油经过提炼去除天然生成的杂质。 ● **re·fin·ing** N-UNCOUNT 提炼 ❑ *...oil refining.* …炼油。 2 V-T If something such as a process, theory, or machine **is refined**, it is improved by having small changes made to it. 完善 [usu passive] ❑ *Surgical techniques are constantly being refined.* 外科手术技术正在不断得到完善。
→ see **sugar**

re·fined /rɪfaɪnd/ 1 ADJ A **refined** substance has been made pure by having other substances removed from it. 去掉杂质的；精炼的 ❑ *...refined sugar.* …精制糖。 2 ADJ If you say that someone is **refined**, you mean that they are very polite and have good manners and good taste. 彬彬有礼的；举止文雅的 ❑ *...refined and well-dressed ladies.* …举止文雅、衣着考究的女士们。 3 ADJ If you describe a machine or a process as **refined**, you mean that it has been carefully developed and is therefore very efficient or elegant. 精密的 ❑ *This technique is becoming more refined and more acceptable all the time.* 这项技术变得越来越精密和受人欢迎。

re·fine·ment /rɪfaɪnmənt/ (**refinements**) 1 N-VAR **Refinements** are small changes or additions that you make to something in order to improve it. **Refinement** is the process of making refinements. 改进；完善 ❑ *Older cars inevitably lack the latest safety refinements.* 较老式的汽车难免缺乏最新的安全改进。 2 N-UNCOUNT **Refinement** is politeness and good manners. 彬彬有礼；举止文雅

Word Link *ery ≈ place where something happens : bakery, fishery, refinery*

★ **re·fin·ery** /rɪfaɪnəri/ (**refineries**) N-COUNT A **refinery** is a factory where a substance such as oil or sugar is refined. 精炼厂 ❑ *...an oil refinery.* …一家炼油厂。
→ see **industry, mineral, oil**

re·fit (**refits, refitting, refitted**)

The verb is pronounced /rifɪt/. The noun is pronounced /rifɪt/.

动词读作 /rifɪt/。名词读作 /rifɪt/。

V-T When a ship **is refitted**, it is repaired or is given new parts, equipment, or furniture. 整修；改装 [usu passive] ❑ *During the war, navy ships were refitted here.* 战争期间海军战舰曾在这里整修。 ● N-COUNT **Refit** is also a noun. 整修；改装 ❑ *The ship finished an extensive refit last year.* 去年这艘船完成了一次全面整修。

Word Link *re ≈ back, again : reflect, repay, restate*

re·flect ♦♦◇ /rɪflɛkt/ (**reflects, reflecting, reflected**) 1 V-T If something **reflects** an attitude or situation, it shows that the attitude or situation exists or it shows what it is like. 反映；表现；显示 ❑ *A newspaper report seems to reflect the view of most members of Congress.* 报纸的一篇报导似乎反映了国会多数议员的观点。 2 V-T/V-I When light, heat, or other rays **reflect** off a surface or when a surface **reflects** them, they are sent back from the surface and do not pass through it. 反射 ❑ *The sun reflected off the snow-covered mountains.* 阳光从被雪覆盖的山峦反射回来。 3 V-T When something **is reflected** in a mirror or in water, you can see its image in the mirror or in the water. 映出 [usu passive] ❑ *His image was reflected many times in the mirror.* 他的影像在那面镜子里映出了很多个。 4 V-I When you **reflect on** something, you think deeply about it. 深思 ❑ *We should all give ourselves time to reflect.* 我们都应该给自己时间来深思。 5 V-T You can use **reflect** to indicate that a particular thought occurs to someone. 想到（某事） ❑ *Things were very much changed since before the war, he reflected.* 从战争开始前情况就已经发生了很大的变化，他想到。 6 V-I If an action or situation **reflects** in a particular way **on** someone or something, it gives people a good or bad impression of them. 使对…产生某种印象 ❑ *The affair hardly reflected well on the president.* 这个事件很难让人对那位总统有好印象。
→ see **echo, telescope**

re·flec·tion /rɪflɛkʃən/ (**reflections**) 1 N-COUNT A **reflection** is an image that you can see in a mirror or in glass or water. 影像；映像 ❑ *Meg stared at her reflection in the bedroom mirror.* 梅格端详着自己映在卧室镜子中的影像。 2 N-UNCOUNT **Reflection** is the process by which light and heat are sent back from a surface and do not pass through it. 反射 ❑ *...the reflection of a beam of light off a mirror.* …一束光线在镜面上的反射。 3 N-COUNT If you say that something is a **reflection of** a particular person's attitude or **of** a situation, you mean that it is caused by that attitude or situation and therefore reveals something about it. 反映 ❑ *Inhibition in adulthood seems to be a reflection of a person's experiences as a child.* 成年期的压抑似乎是一个人童年经历的一种反映。 4 N-SING If something is a **reflection** or a

sad reflection on a person or thing, it gives a bad impression of them. 坏的影响 ❑ *Infection with head lice is no reflection on personal hygiene.* 染上头虱并不会给个人卫生带来不好的影响。 5 N-UNCOUNT **Reflection** is careful thought about a particular subject. Your **reflections** are your thoughts about a particular subject. 认真思考 [also N in pl] ❑ *After days of reflection she decided to write back.* 经过几天的认真思考，她决定回信。 ● PHRASE If someone admits or accepts something **on reflection**, they admit or accept it after having thought carefully about it. 经过认真思考 ❑ *While the news at first shocked me, on reflection it made perfect sense.* 虽然一开始这个消息令我震惊，但经过认真思考，觉得它也很有道理。
→ see **echo**

re·flec·tive /rɪflɛktɪv/ 1 ADJ If you are **reflective**, you are thinking deeply about something. 沉思的 [WRITTEN] ❑ *I walked on in a reflective mood to the car, thinking about the poor honeymooners.* 我若有所思地朝那辆汽车走去，心里想着那些可怜的度蜜月的人们。 2 ADJ If something is **reflective of** a particular situation or attitude, it is typical of that situation or attitude, or is a consequence of it. 反映的 [v-link ADJ "of" n] ❑ *The German government's support of the U.S. is not entirely reflective of German public opinion.* 德国政府对美国的支持并没有完全反映出德国的民意。 3 ADJ A **reflective** surface or material sends back light or heat. 反射的 [FORMAL] ❑ *Avoid using pans with a shiny, reflective base as the heat will be reflected back.* 避免使用底部闪亮、能反射的锅，因为热量会被反射回去。

Word Link *flex ≈ bending : flex, flexible, reflex*

re·flex /rifleks/ (reflexes) 1 N-COUNT A **reflex** or a **reflex action** is something that you do automatically and without thinking, as a habit or as a reaction to something. 下意识反应；习惯性动作 ❑ *Walt fumbled in his pocket, a reflex from his smoking days.* 沃尔特在口袋里摸索，一个他以前抽烟时形成的习惯性动作。 2 N-COUNT A **reflex** or a **reflex action** is a normal, uncontrollable reaction of your body to something that you feel, see, or experience. 反射动作 ❑ *...tests for reflexes, like tapping the knee or the heel with a rubber hammer.* …反射动作的测试，比如用橡胶锤敲击膝盖或脚踵。 3 N-PLURAL Your **reflexes** are your ability to react quickly with your body when something unexpected happens, for example when you are involved in sports or when you are driving a car. 迅速反应能力 ❑ *It takes great skill, cool nerves, and the reflexes of an athlete.* 这需要运动员娴熟的技巧、冷静的头脑以及迅速反应的能力。

re·form ♦♦◊ /rɪfɔrm/ (reforms, reforming, reformed) 1 N-VAR **Reform** consists of changes and improvements to a law, social system, or institution. A **reform** is an instance of such a change or improvement. 改革；改良 ❑ *The party embarked on a program of economic reform.* 这个政党开始了一个经济改革的计划。 2 V-T If someone **reforms** something such as a law, social system, or institution, they change or improve it. 改革；改良 ❑ *...his plans to reform the country's economy.* …他改革国家经济的计划。 3 V-T/V-I When someone **reforms** or when something **reforms** them, they stop doing things that society does not approve of, such as breaking the law or drinking too much alcohol. 改造；改过自新 ❑ *When his court case was coming up, James promised to reform.* 当他的案件即将被审理时，詹姆斯承诺要改过自新。 ● **re·formed** ADJ 改过自新的 ❑ *...a reformed alcoholic.* …一个改过自新的酗酒者。

Word Partnership *reform* 的常用搭配：

ADJ. **economic** reform, **political** reform 1
N. **education** reform, **election** reform, **health care** reform, reform **movement**, **party** reform, **prison** reform, **tax** reform 1

re·form·er /rɪfɔrmər/ (reformers) N-COUNT A **reformer** is someone who tries to change and improve something such as a law or a social system. 改革者；改良者 ❑ *How could he be a reformer and a defender of established interests at the same time?* 他怎么可能既是改革者，又是既得利益的维护者呢？

★ **re·frain** /rɪfreɪn/ (refrains, refraining, refrained) 1 V-I If you **refrain from** doing something, you deliberately do not do it. 忍住；克制 ❑ *Mrs. Hardie refrained from making any comment.* 哈迪太太忍住了没做任何评论。 2 N-COUNT A **refrain** is a short, simple part of a song, which is repeated many times. 副歌 ❑ *...a refrain from an old song.* …一首老歌的副歌。 3 N-COUNT A **refrain** is a comment or saying that people often repeat. 一再重复的话 ❑ *Rosa's constant refrain is that she doesn't have a life.* 罗莎总是不断重复的一句话就是她生活得很无聊。

re·fresh /rɪfrɛʃ/ (refreshes, refreshing, refreshed) 1 V-T If something **refreshes** you when you are hot, tired, or thirsty, it makes you feel cooler or more energetic. 使清爽；使精神振作 ❑ *The lotion cools and refreshes the skin.* 润肤液使皮肤凉爽清新。 ● **re·freshed** ADJ 清爽的；精神振作的 ❑ *He awoke feeling completely refreshed.* 他醒来感觉精神完全恢复了。 2 V-T If you **refresh** something old or dull, you make it as good as it was when it was new. 使更新 ❑ *Many view these meetings as an occasion to share ideas and refresh friendship.* 很多人把这些聚会看作是交流思想、重叙友情的机会。 3 V-T If someone **refreshes** your memory, they tell you something that you had forgotten. 使重新想起 ❑ *He walked on the opposite side of the street to refresh his memory of the building.* 他走在街对面，以唤起对这栋大楼的记忆。 4 V-T If you **refresh** a web page, you click a button in order to get the most recent version of the page. 刷新 [COMPUTING] ❑ *I've refreshed the page a few times and still see no comments.* 这一页我已经反复刷新了几次，但是仍未见到任何评论。

re·fresh·er course (refresher courses) N-COUNT A **refresher course** is a training course in which people improve their knowledge or skills and learn about new developments that are related to the job that they do. 进修课程

re·fresh·ing /rɪfrɛʃɪŋ/ 1 ADJ You say that something is **refreshing** when it is pleasantly different from what you are used to. 使人耳目一新的 ❑ *It's refreshing to hear somebody speaking common sense.* 听到有人说出大家本应知道的道理，让人耳目一新。 ● **re·fresh·ing·ly** ADV 使人耳目一新地 ❑ *He was refreshingly honest.* 他诚实得让人耳目一新。 2 ADJ A **refreshing** bath or drink makes you feel energetic or cool again after you have been tired or hot. 使人感到清爽的；使人精神恢复的 ❑ *Herbs have been used for centuries to make refreshing drinks.* 草药用于调制清凉饮料已有几百年的历史了。

★ **re·fresh·ment** /rɪfrɛʃmənt/ (refreshments) 1 N-PLURAL **Refreshments** are drinks and small amounts of food that are provided, for example, during a meeting or a trip. 茶点 ❑ *Lunch and refreshments will be provided.* 将提供午餐和茶点。 2 N-UNCOUNT You can refer to food and drink as **refreshment**. 食物和饮料 [FORMAL] ❑ *May I offer you some refreshment?* 可以请您吃点喝点什么吗？

re·frig·er·ate /rɪfrɪdʒəreɪt/ (refrigerates, refrigerating, refrigerated) V-T If you **refrigerate** food, you make it cold by putting it in a refrigerator, usually in order to preserve it. 冷藏 ❑ *Refrigerate the dough overnight.* 把生面团冷藏一整夜。
→ see **dairy**

re·frig·era·tor /rɪfrɪdʒəreɪtər/ (refrigerators) N-COUNT A **refrigerator** is a large container which is kept cool inside, usually by electricity, so that the food and drink in it stays fresh. 冰箱
→ see Word Web: **refrigerator**

Word Web refrigerator

Refrigerators and **freezers cool** and **freeze** food, but how do they work? A gas passes through coils inside the walls of the refrigerator or freezer. As it does so, it absorbs heat and **chills** the interior. Then a pump compresses the gas, which raises its **temperature**. It pushes the gas through coils on the outside of the refrigerator. There it expands and becomes a liquid. At the same time, it gives off heat into the surrounding air. The liquid then flows through a valve into a low pressure area. There it becomes a gas again. Then the cycle repeats itself.

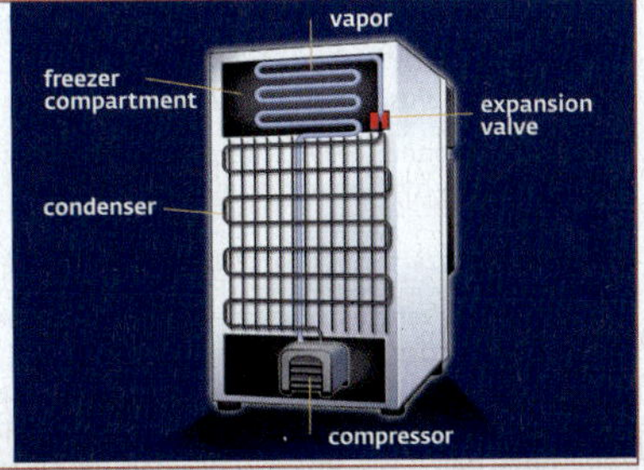

re·fu·el /rɪfyuəl/ (**refuels, refueling** or **refuelling, refueled** or **refuelled**) V-T/V-I When an aircraft or other vehicle **refuels** or when someone **refuels** it, it is filled with more fuel so that it can continue its journey. 使加燃料；加燃料 ❑ *His plane stopped in Hawaii to refuel.* 他的飞机在夏威夷停下来加燃料。● **re·fu·el·ing** N-UNCOUNT 加燃料 ❑ *...nighttime refueling of vehicles.* …为机动车提供的夜间加油服务。

★ **ref·uge** /rɛfyudʒ/ (**refuges**) 1 N-UNCOUNT If you take **refuge** somewhere, you try to protect yourself from physical harm by going there. 避难 ❑ *They took refuge in a bomb shelter.* 他们在一个防空洞里避难。 2 N-COUNT A **refuge** is a place where you go for safety and protection, for example from violence or from bad weather. 避难所；收容所 ❑ *Eventually Suzanne fled to a refuge for battered women.* 最后苏珊娜逃到了一家受虐妇女收容所。 3 N-UNCOUNT If you take **refuge in** a particular way of behaving or thinking, you try to protect yourself from unhappiness or unpleasantness by behaving or thinking in that way. 庇护 ❑ *All too often, they get bored and seek refuge in drink and drugs.* 多数时间，他们感觉厌倦便借酒和毒品得以逃避。

Word Link *ee ≈ one who receives : employee, payee, refugee*

refu·gee ♦♦◇ /rɛfyudʒi/ (**refugees**) N-COUNT **Refugees** are people who have been forced to leave their homes or their country, either because there is a war there, because of their political or religious beliefs, or because of natural disaster. 难民 ❑ *A political refugee from Cameroon has moved into our neighborhood.* 一个喀麦隆的政治难民已经搬进了我们小区。

★ **re·fund** (**refunds, refunding, refunded**)

The noun is pronounced /rifʌnd/. The verb is pronounced /rɪfʌnd/.

名词读作 /rifʌnd/。动词读作 /rɪfʌnd/。

1 N-COUNT A **refund** is a sum of money that is returned to you, for example because you have paid too much or because you have returned goods to a store. 退款 ❑ *Face it – you'll just have to take those cowboy boots back and ask for a refund.* 面对现实吧——你不过是要把那些牛仔靴拿回去，要求退款。 2 V-T If someone **refunds** your money, they return it to you, for example because you have paid too much or because you have returned goods to a store. 退还 ❑ *We guarantee to refund your money if you're not delighted with your purchase.* 如果你对购买的商品不满意，我们保证退款。

Thesaurus *refund* 另参见：
N. payment, reimbursement 1
V. give back, pay back, reimburse 2

re·fund·able /rɪfʌndəbᵊl/ ADJ A **refundable** payment will be paid back to you in certain circumstances. 可退还的 ❑ *A refundable deposit is payable on arrival.* 货一到就把可退还的押金退给你。

re·fur·bish /rifɜrbɪʃ/ (**refurbishes, refurbishing, refurbished**) V-T To **refurbish** a building or room means to clean it and decorate it and make it more attractive or better equipped. 翻新（建筑物或房间）❑ *We have spent money on refurbishing the offices.* 我们已在这些办公室的翻新上花了钱。

re·fus·al /rɪfyuzᵊl/ (**refusals**) 1 N-VAR Someone's **refusal to** do something is the fact of them showing or saying that they will not do it, allow it, or accept it. 拒绝 ❑ *Her country suffered through her refusal to accept change.* 她的国家因为她拒绝接受变革而受了害。 2 PHRASE If someone has **first refusal** on something that is being sold or offered, they have the right to decide whether or not to buy it or take it before it is offered to anyone else. 优先购买权 ❑ *A tenant may have a right of first refusal if a property is offered for sale.* 如果房产要出售，房客可以有优先购买权。

re·fuse ♦♦◇ (**refuses, refusing, refused**)

The verb is pronounced /rɪfyuz/. The noun is pronounced /rɛfyus/ and is hyphenated ref·use.

动词读作 /rɪfyuz/。名词读作 /rɛfyus/且连字符添加方式为**ref·use**。

1 V-T/V-I If you **refuse to** do something, you deliberately do not do it, or you say firmly that you will not do it. 拒绝 ❑ *He refused to comment after the trial.* 该审判之后他拒绝发表评论。 ❑ *I could hardly refuse, could I?* 我很难拒绝，是不是？ 2 V-T If someone **refuses** you something, they do not give it to you or do not allow you to have it. 拒绝给予 ❑ *The United States has refused him a visa.* 美国当局已拒绝给予他签证。 3 V-T If you **refuse** something that is offered to you, you do not accept it. 拒绝 ❑ *The patient has the right to refuse treatment.* 病人有权拒绝治疗。 4 N-UNCOUNT **Refuse** consists of the trash and all the things that are not wanted in a house, store, or factory, and that are regularly thrown away; used mainly in official language. 垃圾；废料 ❑ *The town made a weekly collection of refuse.* 该镇每周收一次垃圾。
→ see **dump**

Do not confuse **refuse** and **deny**. If you **refuse** to do something, you deliberately do not do it, or you say firmly that you will not do it. ❑ *...people who refuse to change their opinions... He refused to condemn them.* You can **refuse** something that someone offers you. ❑ *The patient has the right to refuse treatment.* If someone does not allow you to have something you ask for, or to do something you have asked to do, you can say that they **refuse** you. ❑ *He can run to Dad for money if I refuse him.* If you **deny** something, you say that it is not true. ❑ *The allegation was denied by government spokesmen.* If someone **denies** you something, they do not allow you to have it. ❑ *I never denied her anything.*

Thesaurus *refuse* 另参见：
V. decline, reject, turn down; (*ant.*) accept 1 3
N. garbage, rubbish, trash 4

Word Partnership *refuse* 的常用搭配：
V. refuse **to answer**, refuse **to cooperate**, refuse **to go**, refuse **to participate**, refuse **to pay** 1
refuse **to allow**, refuse **to give** 1 2
refuse **to accept** 1 3

★ **re·fute** /rɪfyut/ (**refutes, refuting, refuted**) 1 V-T If you **refute** an argument, accusation, or theory, you prove that it is wrong or untrue. 驳倒 [FORMAL] ❑ *It was the kind of rumor that it is impossible to refute.* 这是那种不可能推翻的谣言。 2 V-T If you **refute** an argument or accusation, you say that it is not true. 否认 [FORMAL] ❑ *Isabelle is quick to refute any suggestion of intellectual snobbery.* 对于任何暗示她恃才傲物的话，伊莎贝尔都立即予以否认。

re·gain /rɪgeɪn/ (**regains, regaining, regained**) V-T If you **regain** something that you have lost, you get it back again. 重新获得 ❑ *Troops have regained control of the city.* 军队已重新获得对那座城市的控制。

Word Link *reg ≈ rule : regal, regime, regulation*

re·gal /rigᵊl/ ADJ If you describe something as **regal**, you mean that it is suitable for a king or queen, because it is very impressive or beautiful. 王者的 ❑ *He sat with such regal dignity.* 他以王者之尊严就座。

re·gard ♦♦◇ /rɪgard/ (**regards, regarding, regarded**) 1 V-T If you **regard** someone or something **as** being a particular thing or **as** having a particular quality, you believe that they are that thing or have that quality. 看待 ❑ *He was regarded as the most successful president of modern times.* 他被看成是近代最成功的总统。 ❑ *I regard creativity both as a gift and as a skill.* 我把创造力当作一件礼物，也当作一种技巧。 2 V-T If you **regard** something or someone **with** a feeling such as dislike or respect, you have that feeling about them. （以某种感情）看待 ❑ *He regarded drug dealers with loathing.* 他带着憎恶去看待毒贩子。 3 N-UNCOUNT If you have **regard for** someone or something, you respect them and care about them. If you hold someone **in high regard**, you have a lot of respect for them. 尊重 ❑ *I have a very high regard for him and what he has achieved.* 我非常尊重他和他所取得的成就。 4 N-PLURAL **Regards** are greetings. You use **regards** in expressions such as **best regards** and **with kind regards** as a way of expressing friendly feelings toward someone, especially in a letter. 用在**best regards**和**with kind regards**等表达方式中，表示对某人的良好祝愿，多用于书信中 [FORMULAE] ❑ *Give my regards to your family.* 请代我向您的家人问好。 5 PHRASE You can use **as regards** to indicate the subject that is being talked or written about. 关于；至于 ❑ *As regards the war, Haig believed in victory at any price.* 关于这场战争，黑格认为应不惜任何代价获胜。 6 PHRASE You can use **with regard to** or **in regard to** to indicate the subject that is being talked or written about. 关于；至于 ❑ *The department is reviewing its policy with regard to immunization.* 该部门正在重新审查其有关免疫注射的政策。

Word Partnership *regard* 的常用搭配：

PREP. regard **as** 1
regard **with** 2
regard **for** 3
in/with regard **to**, **with/without** regard 6

re·gard·ing /rɪgɑrdɪŋ/ PREP You can use **regarding** to indicate the subject that is being talked or written about. 关于；至于 ❑ *He refused to divulge any information regarding the man's whereabouts.* 他拒绝透露任何关于那个男人下落的消息。

re·gard·less /rɪgɑrdlɪs/ 1 PHRASE If something happens **regardless of** something else, it is not affected or influenced at all by that other thing. 不管；无论 ❑ *It takes in anybody regardless of religion, color, or creed.* 这个组织接纳任何人，不管其宗教、肤色或信仰。 2 ADV If you say that someone did something **regardless**, you mean that they did it even though there were problems or factors that could have stopped them, or perhaps should have stopped them. 不顾一切地 [ADV after v] ❑ *Despite her recent surgery she has been carrying on regardless.* 尽管她最近动了手术，她却一直在不顾一切地继续工作。

re·gen·er·ate /rɪdʒɛnəreɪt/ (**regenerates, regenerating, regenerated**) 1 V-T To **regenerate** something means to develop and improve it to make it more active, successful, or important, especially after a period when it has been getting worse. 重建；复兴 ❑ *The government will continue to try to regenerate inner-city areas.* 政府将继续努力重建市区内部。 ●**re·gen·era·tion** /rɪdʒɛnəreɪʃən/ N-UNCOUNT 重建；复兴 ❑ *...the physical and economic regeneration of the area.* …该地区的物理重建和经济复兴。 2 V-T/V-I If organs or tissues **regenerate** or if something **regenerates** them, they heal and grow again after they have been damaged. 使再生；再生 ❑ *Nerve cells have limited ability to regenerate if destroyed.* 神经细胞如果被破坏其再生能力有限。 ●**re·gen·era·tion** N-UNCOUNT 再生 ❑ *Vitamin B assists in red-blood-cell regeneration.* 维生素B有助于红细胞的再生。

reg·gae /rɛgeɪ/ N-UNCOUNT **Reggae** is a kind of West Indian popular music with a very strong beat. 雷盖音乐 ❑ *Many people will remember Bob Marley for giving them their first taste of reggae music.* 许多人将会记住鲍勃·马利，因为正是他让他们第一次体验雷盖音乐。

★ **re·gime** ♦◊◊ /rəʒim, reɪ-/ (**regimes**) 1 N-COUNT If you refer to a government or system of running a country as a **regime**, you are critical of it because you think it is not democratic and uses unacceptable methods. 统治 [DISAPPROVAL] ❑ *...the collapse of the Fascist regime at the end of the war.* …战争结束时法西斯统治的崩溃。 2 N-COUNT A **regime** is the way that something such as an institution, company, or economy is run, especially when it involves tough or severe action. (机构、公司或经济等的) 管理方式 ❑ *The authorities moved him to the less rigid regime of an open prison.* 当局把他移送到管理相对宽松的不设防监狱。 3 N-COUNT A **regime** is a set of rules about food, exercise, or beauty that some people follow in order to stay healthy or attractive. 养生法 ❑ *He has a new fitness regime to strengthen his back.* 他有一套新的健康养生法来加强他的背部力量。

★ **regi·ment** /rɛdʒɪmənt/ (**regiments**) 1 N-COUNT A **regiment** is a large group of soldiers that is commanded by a colonel. 团 2 N-COUNT A **regiment of** people is a large number of them. 一大批 ❑ *...robust food, good enough to satisfy a regiment of hungry customers.* …足够让一大批饥饿的顾客吃饱的丰盛食物。

regi·men·tal /rɛdʒɪmɛntəl/ ADJ **Regimental** means belonging to a particular regiment. 团的 [ADJ n] ❑ *Mills was regimental colonel.* 米尔斯曾是上校团长。

re·gion ♦♦◊ /ridʒən/ (**regions**) 1 N-COUNT A **region** is a large area of land that is different from other areas of land, for example because it is one of the different parts of a country with its own customs and characteristics, or because it has a particular geographical feature. 地区 ❑ *...Barcelona, capital of the autonomous region of Catalonia.* …巴塞罗那，加泰罗尼亚自治区的首府。 2 N-COUNT You can refer to a part of your body as a **region**. (身体)部位 ❑ *...the pelvic region.* …骨盆部位。 3 PHRASE You say **in the region of** to indicate that an amount that you are stating is approximate. (数量) 在…左右 [VAGUENESS] ❑ *The plan will cost in the region of six million dollars.* 这项计划将花费大约六百万美元。

re·gion·al ♦♦◊ /ridʒənəl/ ADJ **Regional** is used to describe things which relate to a particular area of a country or of the world. 地区的 ❑ *The Garden's menu is based on Hawaiian regional cuisine.* 花园饭店的菜肴以夏威夷地区的烹饪风格为基础。

reg·is·ter ♦◊◊ /rɛdʒɪstər/ (**registers, registering, registered**) 1 N-COUNT A **register** is an official list or record of people or things. 登记簿 ❑ *...registers of births, deaths, and marriages.* …出生、死亡及结婚登记簿。 2 V-T/V-I If you **register** to do something, you put your name on an official list, in order to be able to do that thing or to receive a service. 登记；注册 ❑ *Have you come to register at the school?* 你到学校来注册过了吗？ ❑ *Thousands lined up to register to vote.* 数千人排队登记投票。 3 V-T If you **register** something, such as the name of a person who has just died or information about something you own, you have these facts recorded on an official list. 登记 ❑ *In order to register a car in Japan, the owner must have somewhere to park it.* 在日本要想登记一辆汽车，车主必须要有停车的地方。 4 V-T/V-I When something **registers on** a scale or measuring instrument, it shows on the scale or instrument. (在仪表上) 显示 ❑ *It will only register on sophisticated X-ray equipment.* 只有在先进的X光设备上它才会显示出来。 ❑ *The earthquake registered 5.7 on the Richter scale.* 这次地震显示为里氏5.7级。 5 V-T If you **register** your feelings or opinions about something, you do something that makes them clear to other people. 表示 (感情或看法) ❑ *Voters wish to register their dissatisfaction with the ruling party.* 选民们希望表达他们对执政党的不满。 6 V-I If a feeling **registers on** someone's face, their expression shows clearly that they have that feeling. (面部表情)流露 ❑ *Surprise again registered on Rodney's face.* 罗德尼的脸上再次流露出惊讶的表情。 7 V-T/V-I If a piece of information does not **register** or if you do not **register** it, you do not really pay attention to it, and so you do not remember it or react to it. 留意；留下印象 ❑ *It wasn't that she couldn't hear me, it was just that what I said sometimes didn't register in her brain.* 并不是她听不到我说话，而是我的话有时候没有在她脑子里留下印象。 8 → see also **cash register** → see **bank**

Word Partnership *register* 的常用搭配：

V. register **to vote** 2
N. **voters** register 2

reg·is·trar /rɛdʒɪstrɑr/ (**registrars**) N-COUNT A **registrar** is an administrative official in a college or university who is responsible for student records. 注册主任

reg·is·tra·tion /rɛdʒɪstreɪʃən/ N-UNCOUNT The **registration** of something such as a person's name or the details of an event is the recording of it in an official list. 登记；注册 ❑ *They have campaigned strongly for compulsory registration of dogs.* 他们大力开展了狗的强制性登记活动。 ❑ *With the high voter registration, many will be voting for the first time.* 由于高的投票者登记率，很多人将是第一次投票。

reg·is·tra·tion num·ber [BRIT] → see **license number**

reg·is·try /rɛdʒɪstri/ (**registries**) N-COUNT A **registry** is a collection of all the official records relating to something, or the place where they are kept. 记录收藏；记录保管处 ❑ *There is no international registry of stolen art.* 没有一个国际性的被盗艺术品记录保管处。

re·gress /rɪgrɛs/ (**regresses, regressing, regressed**) V-I When people or things **regress**, they return to an earlier and less advanced stage of development. 退步 [FORMAL] ❑ *If your child regresses to babyish behavior, all you know for certain is that the child is under stress.* 如果你的孩子退步到幼稚的行为，你可以肯定的是孩子正处在压力之下。 ●**re·gres·sion** /rɪgrɛʃən/ N-VAR (**regressions**) 退步 ❑ *Calderdale accepts that this can cause regression in a student's learning process.* 考尔德戴尔承认这会在学生的学习过程中引起退步。

re·gret ♦◊◊ /rɪgrɛt/ (**regrets, regretting, regretted**) 1 V-T If you **regret** something that you have done, you wish that you had not done it. 后悔 ❑ *I simply gave in to him, and I've regretted it ever since.* 当时我轻易向他屈服了，到现在我一直后悔。 ❑ *Ellis seemed to be regretting that he had asked the question.* 埃利斯当时似乎正后悔不该问那个问题。 2 N-VAR **Regret** is a feeling of sadness or disappointment, which is caused by something that has happened or something that you have done or not done. 遗憾；惋惜；后悔 ❑ *Larry said he had no regrets about retiring.* 拉里曾说他对于退休没有任何遗憾。 3 V-T You can say that you **regret** something as a polite way of saying that you are sorry about it. You use expressions such as **I regret to say** or **I regret to inform you** to show that you are sorry about something. 对…感到遗憾 [POLITENESS] ❑ *"I very much regret the injuries he sustained," he said.* 他说："我对他所遭受的伤害感到非常遗憾。" ❑ *I regret that the United States has added its voice to such protests.* 我很遗憾美国也附和了这样的抗议。

r

Word Partnership *regret* 的常用搭配：

N. regret **a decision**, regret **a loss** 1
V. **come to** regret 1
express regret 2

re·gret·ful /rɪgrɛtfəl/ ADJ If you are **regretful**, you show that you regret something. 遗憾的 [oft ADJ "about" n, ADJ that] ❑ *Mr. Griffin gave a regretful smile.* 格里芬先生露出遗憾的笑容。 ● **re·gret·ful·ly** ADV 遗憾地 ❑ *He shook his head regretfully.* 他遗憾地摇了摇头。

re·gret·table /rɪgrɛtəbᵊl/ ADJ You describe something as **regrettable** when you think that it is bad and that it should not happen or have happened. 不幸的 [FORMAL, FEELINGS] ❑ *The army said it had started an investigation into what it described as a regrettable incident.* 军方说已经开始调查这起据称的不幸事件。 ● **re·gret·tably** ADV 不幸地 ❑ *Regrettably we could find no sign of the man and the search was terminated.* 不幸，我们无法找到这个人的任何踪迹因此搜寻停止了。

re·group /rigrup/ (**regroups, regrouping, regrouped**) V-T/V-I When people, especially soldiers, **regroup**, or when someone **regroups** them, they form an organized group again, in order to continue fighting. 重新部署 ❑ *Now the rebel army has regrouped and reorganized.* 现在叛军已经重新部署和改编。

regu·lar ♦♦◇ /rɛgyələr/ (**regulars**) 1 ADJ **Regular** events have equal amounts of time between them, so that they happen, for example, at the same time each day or each week. 定期的 ❑ *Get regular exercise.* 定期进行锻炼。 ❑ *We're going to be meeting there on a regular basis.* 我们将定期在那里见面。 ● **regu·lar·ly** ADV 定期地 [ADV with v] ❑ *He also writes regularly for "International Management" magazine.* 他也定期为《国际管理》杂志写稿。 ● **regu·lar·ity** N-UNCOUNT 规律性 ❑ *The overdraft arrangements had been generous because of the regularity of the half-yearly payments.* 由于半年内规律性的付款，透支额度给得一直很高。 2 ADJ **Regular** events happen often. 经常的 ❑ *Although it may look unpleasant, this condition is harmless and usually clears up with regular shampooing.* 这可能不好看，但这种情况是无害的并且经常的洗头通常可以消除它。 ● **regu·lar·ly** ADV 经常地 [ADV with v] ❑ *Fox, badger, and weasel are regularly seen here.* 这里经常看得到狐狸、獾和黄鼠狼。 ● **regu·lar·ity** N-UNCOUNT 经常性 ❑ *Closures and job losses are again being announced with monotonous regularity.* 停业和失业再次被一成不变地经常性地通告着。 3 ADJ If you are, for example, a **regular** customer at a store or a **regular** visitor to a place, you go there often. 经常的（顾客或来访者）[ADJ n] ❑ *She has become a regular visitor to Houghton Hall.* 她已成为霍顿府邸的一名常客。 4 N-COUNT The **regulars** at a place or on a team are the people who often go to the place or are often on the team. 常客；正式队员 ❑ *Regulars at his local bar have set up a fund to help out.* 他的当地酒吧的常客们已经设立了一项基金来帮忙解决困难。 5 ADJ You use **regular** when referring to the thing, person, time, or place that is usually used by someone. For example, someone's **regular** place is the place where they usually sit. 固定的 [det ADJ n] ❑ *The man shook his hand and then sat at his regular table near the windows.* 这个人握了握他的手，然后坐在他固定的靠窗的桌子旁。 6 ADJ A **regular** rhythm consists of a series of sounds or movements with equal periods of time between them. 均匀的 ❑ *...a very regular beat.* …非常均匀的节拍。 ● **regu·lar·ly** ADV 均匀地 [ADV with v] ❑ *Remember to breathe regularly.* 记住要均匀地呼吸。 ● **regu·lar·ity** N-UNCOUNT 规律性 ❑ *Experimenters have succeeded in controlling the rate and regularity of the heartbeat.* 实验者们已经成功地控制了心跳的速度和规律性。 7 ADJ **Regular** is used to mean "normal." 普通的 [ADJ n] [mainly AM] ❑ *The product looks and burns like a regular cigarette.* 这种产品看上去和点起来都像一支普通的香烟。 8 ADJ In some restaurants, a **regular** drink or quantity of food is of medium size. 中份的 [ADJ n] [mainly AM] ❑ *...a cheeseburger and regular fries.* …一个干酪汉堡包和中份的炸薯条。 9 ADJ A **regular** pattern or arrangement consists of a series of things with equal spaces between them. 间隔一致的 ❑ *The village was laid out in regular patterns.* 这个村庄街道和房屋被以相等的间隔整齐地加以布局。 10 ADJ If something has a **regular** shape, both halves are the same and it has straight edges or a smooth outline. 规则的 ❑ *...some regular geometrical shape.* …一些规则的几何图形。 ● **regu·lar·ity** N-UNCOUNT 规则性 ❑ *...the chessboard regularity of their fields.* …国际象棋棋盘的规则性。 11 ADJ In grammar, a **regular** verb, noun, or adjective inflects in the same way as most verbs, nouns, or adjectives in the language. （动词、名词或形容词）按规则变化的

Word Partnership *regular* 的常用搭配：

N. regular **basis**, regular **checkups**, regular **exercise**, regular **meetings**, regular **schedule**, regular **visits** 1 2
regular **customer**, regular **visitor** 3
regular **coffee**, regular **guy**, regular **hours**, regular **mail**, regular **season** 7
regular **verbs** 11

regu·late /rɛgyəleɪt/ (**regulates, regulating, regulated**) V-T To **regulate** an activity or process means to control it, especially by means of rules. 控制（尤指通过规则）❑ *Under such a plan, the government would regulate competition among insurance companies so that everyone gets care at lower cost.* 根据这样一个计划，政府会控制保险公司之间的竞争，这样每个人都能以较低价格获得保险。

Word Link *reg ≈ rule : regal, regime, regulation*

regu·la·tion ♦◇◇ /rɛgyəleɪʃᵊn/ (**regulations**) 1 N-COUNT **Regulations** are rules made by a government or other authority in order to control the way something is done or the way people behave. 法规；条例 ❑ *The European Union has proposed new regulations to control the hours worked by its employees.* 欧盟已经提出了新的法规来控制其雇员的工作时间。 2 N-UNCOUNT **Regulation** is the controlling of an activity or process, usually by means of rules. 管理 ❑ *Some in the market now want government regulation in order to reduce costs.* 市场上现在有人想要政府来管理以降低成本。
→ see **factory**

Word Partnership *regulation* 的常用搭配：

ADJ. **new** regulation 1
federal regulation, **financial** regulation, **strict** regulation 1 2
N. **banking** regulation, **government** regulation, **industry** regulation 1 2

regu·la·tor ♦◇◇ /rɛgyəleɪtər/ (**regulators**) N-COUNT A **regulator** is a person or organization appointed by a government to regulate an area of activity such as banking or industry. 监管人；监管机构 ❑ *An independent regulator will be appointed to ensure fair competition.* 一个独立的监管机构将受委派来确保公平竞争。 ● **regu·la·tory** ★ /rɛgyələtɔri/ ADJ 监管的 [ADJ n] ❑ *...the U.S.'s financial regulatory system.* …美国的金融监管系统。

re·hab /rihæb/ (**rehabs, rehabbing, rehabbed**) 1 N-UNCOUNT **Rehab** is the process of helping someone to lead a normal life again after they have been ill, or when they have had a drug or alcohol problem. **Rehab** is short for **rehabilitation**. 复原 [INFORMAL] ❑ *...a hospital rehab program.* …一项医院康复计划。 2 V-T If you **rehab** an old building, you repair and improve it and get it back into good condition. 修缮 [AM, INFORMAL] ❑ *People are improving and rehabbing homes throughout the city.* 那座城市到处都在改进和修缮房子。

▲ **re·ha·bili·tate** /rihəbɪlɪteɪt/ (**rehabilitates, rehabilitating, rehabilitated**) V-T To **rehabilitate** someone who has been ill or in prison means to help them to live a normal life again. To **rehabilitate** someone who has a drug or alcohol problem means to help them stop using drugs or alcohol. 使康复；使戒毒；使戒酒 ❑ *Considerable efforts have been made to rehabilitate patients who have suffered in this way.* 为使受这种苦的病人康复已经付出了相当大的努力。 ● **re·ha·bili·ta·tion** ▲ /rihəbɪlɪteɪʃᵊn/ N-UNCOUNT 复原 ❑ *A number of other techniques are now being used by psychologists in the rehabilitation of young offenders.* 一些别的技术现正被心理学家们用于年轻罪犯的复原。

★ **re·hears·al** /rɪhɜrsᵊl/ (**rehearsals**) 1 N-VAR A **rehearsal** of a play, dance, or piece of music is a practice of it in preparation for a performance. 排练 ❑ *The band was scheduled to begin rehearsals for a concert tour.* 乐队按计划开始了为巡回音乐会进行的排练。 2 → see also **dress rehearsal** 3 N-COUNT You can describe an event or object that is a preparation for a more important event or object as a **rehearsal for** it. （重大事件的）预演 ❑ *Daydreams may seem to be rehearsals for real-life situations, but we know they are not.* 白日梦可能看上去像是真实生活境遇的预演，但我们知道它们不是。

★ **re·hearse** /rɪhɜrs/ (**rehearses, rehearsing, rehearsed**) 1 V-T/V-I When people **rehearse** a play, dance, or piece of music, they practice it in order to prepare for a performance. 排练 ❑ *In his version, a group of actors are rehearsing a play about Joan of Arc.* 按他说，

一群演员正在排练一出关于圣女贞德的戏。❑ *Tens of thousands of people have been rehearsing for the opening ceremony in the new stadium.* 数万人一直在新体育场里为开幕式进行排练。**2** V-T If you **rehearse** something that you are going to say or do, you silently practice it by imagining that you are saying or doing it. 在心里预演 ❑ *Anticipate any tough questions and rehearse your answers.* 事先预想会有任何难的问题，然后在心里预演你的答复。

→ see **memory**

★ **reign** /reɪn/ (**reigns, reigning, reigned**) **1** V-I If you say, for example, that silence **reigns** in a place or confusion **reigns** in a situation, you mean that the place is silent or the situation is confused. 主宰 [WRITTEN] ❑ *Last night confusion reigned about how the debate, which continues today, would end.* 昨晚，这场在今天继续进行的辩论将如何结束的问题令人困惑。**2** V-I When a king or queen **reigns**, he or she rules a country. 在位统治 ❑ *...Henry II, who reigned from 1154 to 1189.* …1154年至1189年在位统治的亨利二世。● N-COUNT **Reign** is also a noun. 统治时期 ❑ *...Queen Victoria's reign.* …维多利亚女王的统治时期。

re·im·burse /riɪmbɜrs/ (**reimburses, reimbursing, reimbursed**) V-T If you **reimburse** someone **for** something, you pay them back the money that they have spent or lost because of it. 报销；偿还 [FORMAL] ❑ *I'll be happy to reimburse you for any expenses you've had.* 我很乐意报销你的所有花费。

re·im·burse·ment /riɪmbɜrsmənt/ (**reimbursements**) N-VAR If you receive **reimbursement for** money that you have spent, you get your money back, for example because the money should have been paid by someone else. 报销；偿还 [FORMAL] ❑ *She is demanding reimbursement for medical and other expenses.* 她在要求医疗和其他费用的报销。

★ **rein** /reɪn/ (**reins, reining, reined**) **1** N-PLURAL **Reins** are the thin leather straps attached around a horse's neck which are used to control the horse. 缰绳 ❑ *Cord held the reins while the stallion tugged and snorted.* 当那匹牡马使劲挣扎，打着响鼻的时候，科德勒紧了缰绳。**2** N-PLURAL Journalists sometimes use the expression **the reins** or **the reins of power** to refer to the control of a country or organization. 执政；掌权 ❑ *He was determined to see the party keep a hold on the reins of power.* 他决心要确保该党继续执掌政权。**3** PHRASE If you **give free rein to** someone, you give them a lot of freedom to do what they want. 给（某人）充分的自由 ❑ *The government continued to believe it should give free rein to the private sector in transportation.* 政府继续认为应该给私营运输部门充分的自由。**4** PHRASE If you **keep a tight rein on** someone, you control them firmly. 严格控制 ❑ *Her parents kept her on a tight rein with their narrow and inflexible views.* 她的父母目光短浅而又固执地严格控制着她。

▸ **rein back** PHRASAL VERB To **rein back** something such as spending means to control it strictly. 严格控制（开支等）❑ *He promised that between now and the end of the year the government would try to rein back inflation.* 他承诺从现在起到年底政府将努力严格控制通货膨胀。

▸ **rein in** PHRASAL VERB To **rein in** something means to control it. 控制 ❑ *Many people have begun looking for long-term ways to rein in spending.* 很多人已经开始寻找控制开支的长远方式。

Word Link	*carn ≈ flesh : carnage, incarnation, reincarnation*

re·incar·na·tion /riɪnkɑrneɪʃən/ (**reincarnations**) **1** N-UNCOUNT If you believe in **reincarnation**, you believe that you will be reincarnated after you die. 转世再生 ❑ *Many African tribes believe in reincarnation.* 很多非洲部落相信转世再生。**2** N-COUNT A **reincarnation** is a person or animal whose body is believed to contain the spirit of a dead person. （灵魂转世的）化身 ❑ *Another little girl, believed to be the reincarnation of her grandmother, was obsessed with sewing.* 另外一个据说是她祖母转世化身的小女孩痴迷于缝纫。

rein·deer /reɪndɪər/ (**reindeer**)

Reindeer is both the singular and the plural form.

N-COUNT A **reindeer** is a deer with large horns called antlers that lives in northern areas of Europe, Asia, and America. 驯鹿 ❑ *...a herd of reindeer.* …一群驯鹿。

re·inforce /riɪnfɔrs/ (**reinforces, reinforcing, reinforced**) **1** V-T If something **reinforces** a feeling, situation, or process, it makes it stronger or more intense. 加强 ❑ *I hope this will reinforce Indonesian determination to deal with this kind of threat.* 我希望这会加强印度尼西亚对付这类威胁的决心。**2** V-T If something **reinforces** an idea or point of view, it provides more evidence or support for it. 巩固 ❑ *The delegation hopes to reinforce the idea that human rights are not purely internal matters.* 代表团希望巩固人权不完全是国家内政的观念。**3** V-T To **reinforce** an object means to make it stronger or harder. 加固 ❑ *Eventually, they had to reinforce the walls with exterior beams.* 最后，他们不得不用外梁来加固那些墙壁。**4** V-T To **reinforce** an army or a police force means to make it stronger by increasing its size or providing it with more weapons. To **reinforce** a position or place means to make it stronger by sending more soldiers or weapons. 增援 ❑ *Both sides have been reinforcing their positions after yesterday's fierce fighting.* 在昨天的激战后，双方一直在增援各自的阵地。

Word Partnership	*reinforce* 的常用搭配：
N.	reinforce **behaviors** **1**
	reinforce **a belief**, reinforce **a message**, reinforce **a stereotype** **2**

re·inforce·ment /riɪnfɔrsmənt/ (**reinforcements**) **1** N-PLURAL **Reinforcements** are soldiers or police officers who are sent to join an army or group of police in order to make it stronger. 增援部队 ❑ *Mr. Vlok promised new measures to protect residents, including the dispatch of police and troop reinforcements.* 乌洛克先生答应了新的保护居民的措施，包括派遣增援的警察和军队。**2** N-VAR The **reinforcement** of something is the process of making it stronger. 巩固 ❑ *I am sure that this meeting will contribute to the reinforcement of peace and security all over the world.* 我确信这次会晤将为全世界和平与安全的巩固做出贡献。

▲ **re·instate** /riɪnsteɪt/ (**reinstates, reinstating, reinstated**) **1** V-T If you **reinstate** someone, you give them back a job or position that had been taken away from them. 使复职 ❑ *The governor is said to have agreed to reinstate five senior workers who were dismissed.* 据说州长已经同意让被解雇的5位高级工人复职。**2** V-T To **reinstate** a law, facility, or practice means to start having it again. 恢复（法律、机构或条例等）❑ *She says the public response was a factor in the decision to reinstate the grant.* 她说公众的反应是决定恢复补助金的一个因素。

re·instate·ment /riɪnsteɪtmənt/ **1** N-UNCOUNT **Reinstatement** is the act of giving someone back a job or position that has been taken away from them. 复职 ❑ *Parents campaigned in vain for her reinstatement.* 家长们为她的复职而奔波，但是毫无结果。**2** N-UNCOUNT The **reinstatement** of a law, facility, or practice is the act of causing it to exist again. （法律、机构或条例等的）恢复 ❑ *He welcomed the reinstatement of the 10 percent bank base rate.* 他对于10%的银行基本利率的恢复表示欢迎。

▲ **re·it·er·ate** /riɪtəreɪt/ (**reiterates, reiterating, reiterated**) V-T If you **reiterate** something, you say it again, usually in order to emphasize it. 重申 [FORMAL, JOURNALISM] ❑ *He reiterated his opposition to the creation of a central bank.* 他重申了他对创办中央银行的反对。

re·ject ◆◆◇ (**rejects, rejecting, rejected**)

The verb is pronounced /rɪdʒɛkt/. The noun is pronounced /ridʒɛkt/.

动词读作 /rɪdʒɛkt/。名词读作 /ridʒɛkt/。

1 V-T If you **reject** something such as a proposal, a request, or an offer, you do not accept it or you do not agree to it. 拒绝；不同意 ❑ *The government is expected to reject the idea of state subsidy for a new high-speed railroad.* 预期该政府不会同意向一条新建高速铁路提供国家补助的意见。● **re·jec·tion** /rɪdʒɛkʃən/ N-VAR (**rejections**) 拒绝；不同意 ❑ *The rejection of such initiatives by no means indicates that voters are unconcerned about the environment.* 对这些提案的不同意决不意味着选民们不关心环境。**2** V-T If you **reject** a belief or a political system, you refuse to believe in it or to live by its rules. 摈弃 ❑ *...the children of Eastern European immigrants who had rejected their parents' political and religious beliefs.* …已经摈弃了其父母的政治和宗教信仰的东欧移民的子女们。● **re·jec·tion** N-VAR 摈弃 ❑ *His rejection of our values is far more complete than that of D. H. Lawrence.* 他对于我们价值观的摈弃远比D. H. 劳伦斯更彻底。**3** V-T If someone **is rejected** for a job or course of study, it is not offered to them. 拒绝（录用或录取）❑ *One of my most able students was rejected by another university.* 我的一个最有能力的学生被另外一所大学拒绝了。● **re·jec·tion** N-COUNT 拒绝 ❑ *Be prepared for lots of rejections before you land a job.* 在你找到一份工作之前要做好多次被拒绝的准备。**4** V-T If someone **rejects** another person who expects affection from them, they are cold and unfriendly toward them. 拒绝(某人的爱情) ❑ *...people who had been rejected by their lovers.* …遭到他们的恋人拒绝的人们。 ● **re·jec·tion** N-VAR 拒绝 ❑ *These feelings of rejection and hurt remain.* 这些遭到拒绝和伤害的感觉仍然存在。 **5** V-T If a person's body **rejects** something such as a new heart that has been transplanted into it, it tries to attack and destroy it. 排斥(移植的器官等) ❑ *It was feared his body was rejecting a kidney he received in a transplant four years ago.* 人们担心他的身体在排斥他4年前在一项移植中接受的一个肾脏。 ● **re·jec·tion** N-VAR 排斥 ❑ *...a special drug which stops rejection of transplanted organs.* …一种阻止对移植器官的排斥的专用药物。 **6** N-COUNT A **reject** is a product that has not been accepted for use or sale, because there is something wrong with it. 不合格品 ❑ *The check shirt is a reject - too small.* 这件格子衬衣是个不合格品，太小。

Thesaurus *reject* 另参见：

V. decline, refuse, turn down; (*ant.*) accept **1**

Word Partnership *reject* 的常用搭配：

V. **vote to** reject **1**

N. reject **an offer**, reject **a plan**, reject **a proposal**, **voters** reject **1**
reject **an idea** **1** **2**
reject **an application** **3**

★ **re·joice** /rɪdʒɔɪs/ (**rejoices, rejoicing, rejoiced**) V-T/V-I If you **rejoice**, you are very pleased about something and you show it in your behavior. 欣喜 ❑ *Garbo plays the queen, rejoicing in the love she has found with Antonio.* 嘉宝饰演沉浸在与安东尼奥爱情的欣喜中的王后。 ❑ *Party activists in New Hampshire rejoiced that the presidential campaign had finally started.* 新罕布什尔州的党派积极分子们为总统竞选活动终于开始而欣喜。 ● **re·joic·ing** N-UNCOUNT 欣喜 ❑ *There was general rejoicing at the news.* 这个消息带来一片欣喜。

re·ju·venate /rɪdʒuvəneɪt/ (**rejuvenates, rejuvenating, rejuvenated**) **1** V-T If something **rejuvenates** you, it makes you feel or look young again. 使年轻 ❑ *Shelley was advised that the Italian climate would rejuvenate him.* 有人建议雪莱说意大利的气候会使他年轻。 **2** V-T If you **rejuvenate** an organization or system, you make it more lively and more efficient, for example by introducing new ideas. 使恢复活力 ❑ *The government pushed through plans to rejuvenate the inner cities.* 该政府努力完成了使市中心恢复活力的一些计划。

re·kin·dle /rikɪndᵊl/ (**rekindles, rekindling, rekindled**) **1** V-T If something **rekindles** an interest, feeling, or thought that you used to have, it makes you think about it or feel it again. 使恢复 ❑ *Ben Brantley's article on Sir Ian McKellen rekindled many memories.* 本•布兰特利关于伊恩•麦凯伦爵士的文章唤回许多记忆。 **2** V-T If something **rekindles** an unpleasant situation, it makes the unpleasant situation happen again. 重新引发 ❑ *There are fears that the series could rekindle animosity between the two countries.* 有人担心这一系列的事情可能会重新引发两国之间的敌意。

re·lapse /rɪlæps/ (**relapses, relapsing, relapsed**)

The noun can be pronounced /rɪlæps/ or /rilæps/.

名词可读作 /rɪlæps/或 /rilæps/。

1 V-I If you say that someone **relapses into** a way of behaving that is undesirable, you mean that they start to behave in that way again. 复发 ❑ *"I wish I did," said Phil Jordan, relapsing into his usual gloom.* "我要是做了就好了，"菲尔•乔丹说着，回到平时的忧郁中。 ● N-COUNT **Relapse** is also a noun. 复发 ❑ *...a relapse into the nationalism of the nineteenth century.* …一个回到19世纪民族主义的倒退。 **2** V-I If a sick person **relapses**, their health suddenly gets worse after it had been improving. (旧病) 复发 ❑ *In 90 percent of cases the patient will relapse within six months.* 90%的病人会在6个月内旧病复发。 ● N-VAR **Relapse** is also a noun. (旧病的) 复发 ❑ *The treatment is usually given to women with a high risk of relapse after surgery.* 该治疗通常用于术后复发可能性高的女性。

re·late ♦◇◇ /rɪleɪt/ (**relates, relating, related**) **1** V-I If something **relates to** a particular subject, it concerns that subject. 与…有关 ❑ *Other recommendations relate to the details of how such data is stored.* 其他建议与如何存储这种数据的一些细节有关。 **2** V-RECIP The way that two things **relate**, or the way that one thing **relates to** another, is the sort of connection that exists between them. 发生联系；与…相联系 ❑ *I don't think he understood the dynamics of how the police and the city administration relate.* 我认为他不理解警方与市政部门如何发生联系的动态原理。 ❑ *Trainees should be invited to relate new ideas to their past experiences.* 应该要求实习生把新想法与他们的以往经历相联系。 **3** V-RECIP If you can **relate to** someone, you can understand how they feel or behave so that you are able to communicate with them or deal with them easily. 与…息息相通 ❑ *He is unable to relate to other people.* 他不能够与别人沟通。

re·lat·ed ♦◇◇ /rɪleɪtɪd/ **1** ADJ If two or more things are **related**, there is a connection between them. 有联系的 ❑ *The philosophical problems of chance and of free will are closely related.* 关于偶然性和自由意志的哲学问题是紧密相联的。 **2** ADJ People who are **related** belong to the same family. 有亲属关系的 [v-link ADJ] ❑ *The children, although not related to us by blood, had become as dear to us as our own.* 这些孩子，虽然和我们没有血缘上的亲属关系，也变得像我们亲生的一样亲了。 **3** ADJ If you say that different types of things, such as languages, are **related**, you mean that they developed from the same language. (语言) 同源的 ❑ *He recognized that Sanskrit, the language of India, was related very closely to Latin, Greek, and the Germanic and Celtic languages.* 他认识到梵语，即印度的语言，与拉丁语、希腊语、日尔曼语和凯尔特语密切同源。

-related /-rɪleɪtɪd/ COMB IN ADJ **-related** combines with nouns to form adjectives with the meaning "connected with the thing referred to by the noun." 与…相关的 ❑ *More than 50 arrests were made, mostly for drug-related offenses.* 超过五十人被捕，大部分是因为与毒品相关的犯罪。

re·la·tion ♦♦◇ /rɪleɪʃᵊn/ (**relations**) **1** N-COUNT **Relations** between people, groups, or countries are contacts between them and the way in which they behave toward each other. 关系 ❑ *Greece has established full diplomatic relations with Israel.* 希腊已经和以色列建立了全面的外交关系。 **2** → see also **industrial relations, public relations, race relations** **3** N-COUNT If you talk about the **relation of** one thing **to** another, you are talking about the ways in which they are connected. 关系 ❑ *It is a question of the relation of ethics to economics.* 这是个道德和经济之间关系的问题。 **4** N-COUNT Your **relations** are the members of your family. 亲属 ❑ *...visits to friends and relations.* …对亲友的拜访。 **5** PHRASE You can talk about something **in relation to** something else when you want to compare the size, condition, or position of the two things. 与…相比 ❑ *The money he'd been ordered to pay was minimal in relation to his salary.* 他被要求支付的钱与他的薪水相比是少的。 **6** PHRASE If something is said or done **in relation to** a subject, it is said or done in connection with that subject. 关于 ❑ *...a question that has been asked many times in relation to Irish affairs.* …一个多次被问到的关于爱尔兰事务的问题。

Word Partnership *relation* 的常用搭配：

PREP. relation **between** *someone/something* **and** *someone/something* **1**
relation **of** *something* **to** *something* **3**
in relation **to** *something* **5** **6**

V. **bear a** relation **3**

re·la·tion·ship ♦♦◇ /rɪleɪʃᵊnʃɪp/ (**relationships**) **1** N-COUNT The **relationship** between two people or groups is the way in which they feel and behave toward each other. 关系 ❑ *...the friendly relationship between France and Britain.* …英法间的友好关系。 **2** N-COUNT A **relationship** is a close friendship between two people, especially one involving romantic or sexual feelings. (尤指爱情或性的) 关系 ❑ *We had been together for two years, but both of us felt the relationship wasn't really going anywhere.* 我们在一起已经两年了，但是我们俩都觉得这种关系实在不会有什么结果。 **3** N-COUNT The **relationship** between two things is the way in which they are connected. 联系 ❑ *A number of small-scale studies have already indicated that there is a relationship between diet and cancer.* 一些小规模的研究已经表明，饮食和癌症之间有一种联系。

Word Partnership *relationship* 的常用搭配：

ADJ. **professional** relationship, **working** relationship **1**
abusive relationship, **good** relationship, **healthy** relationship, **loving** relationship **1** **2**
close relationship, **intimate** relationship **1** – **3**
romantic relationship, **sexual** relationship **2**

V. **develop a** relationship, **end a** relationship, **have a** relationship, **maintain a** relationship **1** **2**
establish a relationship **1** – **3**

rela·tive ♦◇◇ /rɛlətɪv/ (**relatives**) 1 N-COUNT Your **relatives** are the members of your family. 亲属 ❏ *Get a relative to look after the children.* 找个亲戚来照看这些孩子。 2 ADJ You use **relative** to say that something is true to a certain degree, especially when compared with other things of the same kind. 相对的 [ADJ n] ❏ *The fighting resumed after a period of relative calm.* 战斗在一段相对的平静之后重新开始。 3 ADJ You use **relative** when you are comparing the quality or size of two things. 比较而言的 [ADJ n] ❏ *They chatted about the relative merits of London and Paris as places to live.* 他们闲聊伦敦与巴黎作为居住地各自相对的优点。 4 PHRASE **Relative to** something means with reference to it or in comparison with it. 与…相比 ❏ *Japanese interest rates rose relative to America's.* 日本的利率与美国相比有所上升。 5 ADJ If you say that something is **relative**, you mean that it needs to be considered and judged in relation to other things. 相对的 ❏ *Fitness is relative; one must always ask "Fit for what?"* 适宜是相对的；始终必须问问："适宜什么？" 6 N-COUNT If one animal, plant, language, or invention is a **relative of** another, they have both developed from the same type of animal, plant, language, or invention. 亲缘物种；同源事物 ❏ *The pheasant is a close relative of the guinea hen.* 这种雉鸡和这种珍珠鸡是亲缘物种。

Word Partnership *relative* 的常用搭配：

ADJ.	**close** relative, **distant** relative 1
N.	**friend and** relative 1
	relative **calm**, relative **ease**, relative **safety**, relative **stability** 2

rela·tive clause (**relative clauses**) N-COUNT In grammar, a **relative clause** is a subordinate clause which specifies or gives information about a person or thing. Relative clauses come after a noun or pronoun and, in English, often begin with a relative pronoun such as "who," "which," or "that." 关系从句

rela·tive·ly ♦◇◇ /rɛlətɪvli/ ADV **Relatively** means to a certain degree, especially when compared with other things of the same kind. 相对地 [ADV adj/adv] ❏ *The sums needed are relatively small.* 所需金额相对较小。

rela·tiv·ity /rɛlətɪvɪti/ N-UNCOUNT The theory of **relativity** is Einstein's theory concerning space, time, and motion. 相对论 [TECHNICAL]

re·launch /rilɔntʃ/ (**relaunches, relaunching, relaunched**) V-T To **relaunch** something such as a company, a product, or a program means to start it again or to produce it in a different way. 重新开始；重新开发 ❏ *He is hoping to relaunch his film career with a remake of the 1971 British thriller.* 他正希望通过重拍那部1971年的英国恐怖片来重新开始他的电影事业。 ● N-COUNT **Relaunch** is also a noun. 重新开始；重新开发 ❏ *Relaunches are often simply a way of boosting sales.* 产品的重新开发常常只是一种刺激销售的方法。

Word Link *lax ≈ allowing, loosening : lax, laxative, relax*

re·lax ♦◇◇ /rɪlæks/ (**relaxes, relaxing, relaxed**) 1 V-T/V-I If you **relax** or if something **relaxes** you, you feel more calm and less worried or tense. 使放心；放心 ❏ *I ought to relax and stop worrying about it.* 我应该放心，不再为它担忧。 2 V-T/V-I When a part of your body **relaxes**, or when you **relax** it, it becomes less stiff or firm. 使放松；放松 ❏ *Massage is used to relax muscles, relieve stress and improve the circulation.* 按摩可用于放松肌肉、减轻压力和促进血液循环。 3 V-T If you **relax** your grip or hold on something, you hold it less tightly than before. 松开 ❏ *He gradually relaxed his grip on the arms of the chair.* 他渐渐松开了那把椅子的一对扶手。 4 V-T/V-I If you **relax** a rule or your control over something, or if it **relaxes**, it becomes less firm or strong. 放松（规定或控制）；变宽松 ❏ *Rules governing student conduct have relaxed somewhat in recent years.* 管理学生操行的规定最近几年已经稍微变得宽松了。 5 → see also **relaxed, relaxing** → see **muscle**

Thesaurus *relax* 另参见：

V.	calm down, rest, unwind 1
	ease off, loosen 3 4

Word Partnership *relax* 的常用搭配：

V.	**sit back and** relax 1
	begin to relax, **try to** relax 1 2
N.	**time to** relax 1
	relax ***your* body, muscles** relax 2

Word Link *ation ≈ state of : celebration, elevation, relaxation*

re·laxa·tion /rilækseɪʃᵊn/ 1 N-UNCOUNT **Relaxation** is a way of spending time in which you rest and feel comfortable. 休息 ❏ *You should be able to find the odd moment for relaxation.* 你应该能找到零碎的休息时间。 2 N-UNCOUNT If there is **relaxation** of a rule or control, it is made less firm or strong. （规定或控制的）放松 ❏ *The relaxation of travel restrictions means they are free to travel and work.* 旅游限制的放松意味着他们可以自由地旅游和工作。

re·laxed /rɪlækst/ 1 ADJ If you are **relaxed**, you are calm and not worried or tense. 放松的 ❏ *As soon as I had made the final decision, I felt a lot more relaxed.* 我一做出最后的决定，就觉得轻松了许多。 2 ADJ If a place or situation is **relaxed**, it is calm and peaceful. 平静的；轻松的 ❏ *The atmosphere at lunch was relaxed.* 午餐时的气氛是轻松的。

re·lax·ing /rɪlæksɪŋ/ ADJ Something that is **relaxing** is pleasant and helps you to relax. 令人放松的 ❏ *I find cooking very relaxing.* 我发现烹饪非常令人放松。

★ **re·lay** (**relays, relaying, relayed**)

The noun is pronounced /rileɪ/. The verb is pronounced /rɪleɪ/.

名词读作 /rileɪ/。动词读作 /rɪleɪ/。

1 N-COUNT A **relay** or a **relay race** is a race between two or more teams, for example teams of runners or swimmers. Each member of the team runs or swims one section of the race. 接力赛 ❏ *Britain's prospects of beating the United States in the relay looked poor.* 英国队在接力赛中战胜美国队的希望看上去不大。 2 V-T To **relay** television or radio signals means to send them or broadcast them. 转播 ❏ *The satellite will be used mainly to relay television programs.* 这颗卫星将主要用来转播电视节目。 3 V-T If you **relay** something that has been said to you, you repeat it to another person. 转告 [FORMAL] ❏ *She relayed the message, then frowned.* 她转告了那个消息，然后皱了皱眉。

re·lease ♦♦♦ /rɪlis/ (**releases, releasing, released**) 1 V-T If a person or animal **is released** from somewhere where they have been locked up or cared for, they are set free or allowed to go. 放走 [usu passive] ❏ *He was released from custody the next day.* 他第二天被从拘留中释放。 2 N-COUNT When someone is released, you refer to their **release**. 释放 [with supp] ❏ *He called for the immediate release of all political prisoners.* 他要求立即释放所有的政治犯。 3 V-T If someone or something **releases** you **from** a duty, task, or feeling, they free you from it. 解除 [FORMAL] ❏ *Divorce releases both the husband and wife from all marital obligations to each other.* 离婚解除了夫妻相互之间的所有婚姻义务。 ● N-UNCOUNT **Release** is also a noun. 解除 [also "a" N, oft N "from" N] ❏ *Our therapeutic style offers release from stored tensions, traumas, and grief.* 我们的治疗方式意在解除蓄积的压力、创伤和悲痛。 4 V-T To **release** feelings or abilities means to allow them to be expressed. 释放 ❏ *Becoming your own person releases your creativity.* 保持你自己的本色可以释放出你的创造力。 ● N-UNCOUNT **Release** is also a noun. 释放 ❏ *She felt the sudden sweet release of her own tears.* 她感到自己的眼泪突然而甜蜜地流出来。 5 V-T If someone in authority **releases** something such as a document or information, they make it available. 发放 ❏ *They're not releasing any more details yet.* 他们还不准备发放更多详情。 ● N-COUNT **Release** is also a noun. 发放 ❏ *Action had been taken to speed up the release of checks.* 已采取行动来加速支票的发放。 6 V-T If you **release** someone or something, you stop holding them. 放开 [FORMAL] ❏ *He stopped and faced her, releasing her wrist.* 他停下来面对着她，放开了她的手腕。 7 V-T If something **releases** gas, heat, or a substance, it causes it to leave its container or the substance that it was part of and enter the surrounding atmosphere or area. 释放 ❏ *...a weapon that releases toxic nerve gas.* …一种释放神经毒气的武器。 ● N-COUNT **Release** is also a noun. 释放 ❏ *Under the agreement, releases of cancer-causing chemicals will be cut by about 80 percent.* 根据这个协议，致癌化学物的释放将被削减80%左右。 8 V-T When an entertainer or company **releases** a new CD, DVD, or movie, it becomes available so that people can buy it or see it. 发行 ❏ *He is releasing an album of love songs.* 他将发行一张情歌专辑。 9 N-COUNT A new **release** is a new CD, DVD, or movie that has just become available for people to buy or see. 发行物 ❏ *Of the new releases that are out there now, which do you think are really good?* 现在外面新的发行物中，你觉得哪些真正好呢？ 10 → see also **press release**

r

Thesaurus *release* 另参见:
V. clear, excuse, free; *(ant.)* detain, imprison 1
N. acquittal, liberation; *(ant.)* detention, imprisonment 2

▲ **rel·egate** /rɛlɪgeɪt/ (**relegates, relegating, relegated**) V-T If you **relegate** someone or something **to** a less important position, you give them this position. 使降级 ❑ *Might it not be better to relegate the king to a purely ceremonial function?* 使该国王降级到一种纯粹礼仪性的职能难道不更好吗?

re·lent /rɪlɛnt/ (**relents, relenting, relented**) V-I If you **relent**, you allow someone to do something that you had previously refused to allow them to do. 发慈悲 ❑ *Finally his mother relented and gave permission for her youngest son to marry.* 他的母亲终于发慈悲，允许她最小的儿子结婚。

▲ **re·lent·less** /rɪlɛntlɪs/ 1 ADJ Something bad that is **relentless** never stops or never becomes less intense. 毫不留情的 ❑ *The pressure now was relentless.* 压力现在毫无减弱之意。 ● **re·lent·less·ly** ADV 毫不留情地 ❑ *The sun is beating down relentlessly.* 太阳正无情地照射下来。 2 ADJ Someone who is **relentless** is determined to do something and refuses to give up, even if what they are doing is unpleasant or cruel. 坚持不懈的 ❑ *Relentless in his pursuit of quality, his technical ability was remarkable.* 由于对质量的坚持不懈的追求，他的技术能力非同凡响。 ● **re·lent·less·ly** ADV 坚持不懈地 ❑ *She always questioned me relentlessly.* 她总是无休止地问我。

rel·evance /rɛləvᵊns/ N-UNCOUNT Something's **relevance to** a situation or person is its importance or significance in that situation or to that person. 相关性 ❑ *Politicians' private lives have no relevance to their public roles.* 政治家的私生活与他们的公众角色没有相关性。

rel·evant /rɛləvᵊnt/ ADJ Something that is **relevant to** a situation or person is important or significant in that situation or to that person. 相关的

re·li·able ♦◇◇ /rɪlaɪəbᵊl/ 1 ADJ People or things that are **reliable** can be trusted to work well or to behave in the way that you want them to. 可靠的 ❑ *She was efficient and reliable.* 她既能干又可靠。 ● **re·li·ably** /rɪlaɪəbli/ ADV 可靠地 ❑ *It's been working reliably for years.* 它多年来一直可靠地运转着。 ● **re·li·abil·ity** /rɪlaɪəbɪlɪti/ N-UNCOUNT 可靠性 ❑ *He's not at all worried about his car's reliability.* 他根本就不担心他的汽车的可靠性。 2 ADJ Information that is **reliable** or that is from a **reliable** source is very likely to be correct. (信息)可靠的 ❑ *There is no reliable information about civilian casualties.* 还没有关于平民伤亡的可靠信息。 ● **re·li·ably** ADV 可靠地 ❑ *Sonia, we are reliably informed, loves her family very much.* 我们得到可靠消息，索尼亚非常爱她的家人。 ● **re·li·abil·ity** N-UNCOUNT 可靠性 ❑ *Both questioned the reliability of recent opinion polls.* 双方都怀疑最近民意测验的可靠性。

Word Partnership *reliable* 的常用搭配:
N. reliable **service** 1
reliable **data**, reliable **information**, reliable **source** 2
ADV. **highly** reliable, **less/more/most** reliable, **usually** reliable, **very** reliable 1 2

★ **re·li·ance** /rɪlaɪəns/ N-UNCOUNT A person's or thing's **reliance on** something is the fact that they need it and often cannot live or work without it. 依赖; 依靠 ❑ *...the country's increasing reliance on foreign aid.* …这个国家日益依赖外来援助。

re·li·ant /rɪlaɪənt/ ADJ A person or thing that is **reliant on** something needs it and often cannot live or work without it. 依赖的; 依靠的 [v-link ADJ "on/upon" n] ❑ *These people are not wholly reliant on Western charity.* 这些人并非完全依赖西方的施舍。

▲ **rel·ic** /rɛlɪk/ (**relics**) 1 N-COUNT If you refer to something or someone as a **relic of** an earlier period, you mean that they belonged to that period but have survived into the present. 遗物; 遗迹 ❑ *Germany's asylum law is a relic of an era in European history that has passed.* 德国的避难法是欧洲历史上一个逝去时代的遗留物。 2 N-COUNT A **relic** is something which was made or used a long time ago and which is kept for its historical significance. 纪念物 ❑ *...a museum of war relics.* …一个战争纪念物博物馆。

re·lief ♦♦◇ /rɪlif/ (**reliefs**) 1 N-UNCOUNT If you feel a sense of **relief**, you feel happy because something unpleasant has not happened or is no longer happening. 宽慰; 安心 [also "a" N] ❑ *I breathed a sigh of relief.* 我安心地松了一口气。 2 N-UNCOUNT If something provides **relief from** pain or distress, it stops the pain or distress. (痛苦、悲痛的) 解除 ❑ *...a self-help program which can give lasting relief from the torment of hay fever.* …一个可以永久解除花粉热折磨的自助疗方。 3 N-UNCOUNT **Relief** is money, food, or clothing that is provided for people who are very poor, or who have been affected by war or a natural disaster. 救济金; 救济物资 ❑ *Relief agencies are stepping up efforts to provide food, shelter, and agricultural equipment.* 救济机构正在加紧努力提供食物、住处和农业设备。 4 N-COUNT A **relief** worker is someone who does your work when you go home, or who is employed to do it instead of you when you are sick. 换班人; 接替人 ❑ *No relief drivers were available.* 没有换班的司机。

Word Partnership *relief* 的常用搭配:
V. **express** relief 1
feel relief, **seek** relief 1 2
bring relief, **get** relief, **provide** relief 1 – 3
supply relief 2 3
N. **sense of** relief, **sigh of** relief 1
pain relief, relief **from symptoms**, relief **from tension** 2
disaster relief, **emergency** relief 3

re·lieve /rɪliv/ (**relieves, relieving, relieved**) 1 V-T If something **relieves** an unpleasant feeling or situation, it makes it less unpleasant or causes it to disappear completely. 缓解; 减轻; 解除 ❑ *Drugs can relieve much of the pain.* 药物可以大大缓解疼痛。 2 V-T If someone or something **relieves** you **of** an unpleasant feeling or difficult task, they take it from you. 使解脱; 使摆脱 ❑ *A part-time bookkeeper will relieve you of the burden of chasing unpaid invoices.* 一名兼职簿记员将使你摆脱追讨欠款的负担。 3 V-T If you **relieve** someone, you take their place and continue to do the job or duty that they have been doing. 接(某人)的班; 接替 ❑ *At seven o'clock the night nurse came in to relieve her.* 7点钟时值夜班的护士进来接了她的班。 4 V-T If someone **is relieved of** their duties or **is relieved of** their post, they are told that they are no longer required to continue in their job. 使解除(职务); 使免除(职位) [usu passive] [FORMAL] ❑ *The officer involved was relieved of his duties because he had violated strict guidelines.* 该名军官因违反了严格的准则而被解除了职务。

re·lieved /rɪlivd/ ADJ If you are **relieved**, you feel happy because something unpleasant has not happened or is no longer happening. 感到宽慰的; 感到安心的 ❑ *We are all relieved to be back home.* 回到家我们都松了一口气。

re·li·gion ♦◇◇ /rɪlɪdʒᵊn/ (**religions**) 1 N-UNCOUNT **Religion** is belief in a god or gods and the activities that are connected with this belief, such as praying or worshiping in a building such as a

Word Web religion

Today the world's population is about 33% **Christian**, 21% **Islamic**, 16% **agnostic**, and 14% **Hindu**. Christians believe in one **god**, but they also **pray** to his son, Jesus Christ. Followers of **Islam** believe in a single god, Allah, and follow the teachings of the prophet Muhammad. Their **divine scripture** is the Koran. They also honor parts of the **Jewish** and Christian **Bible**. Hinduism recognizes a single **deity** along with other gods and **goddesses**. **Buddhism** developed after Hinduism in India and does not include a god figure. All religions seem to share one traditional **belief**—the idea of treating others the way we wish to be treated.

Buddhism

Christianity

Judaism

Hinduism

R

church or temple. 宗教 ❑ ...*his understanding of Indian philosophy and religion.* …他对于印度哲学和宗教的理解。 2 N-COUNT A **religion** is a particular system of belief in a god or gods and the activities that are connected with this system. (一种) 宗教 ❑ ...*the Christian religion.* …基督教。

→ see Word Web: **religion**

re·li·gious ♦♦◊ /rɪlɪdʒəs/ 1 ADJ You use **religious** to describe things that are connected with religion or with one particular religion. 宗教的 [ADJ n] ❑ *Religious groups are now able to meet quite openly.* 宗教团体现在可以公开集会了。 2 ADJ Someone who is **religious** has a strong belief in a god or gods. 虔诚的; 笃信宗教的 ❑ *They are both very religious and felt it was a gift from God.* 他们俩都很虔诚，觉得这是上帝赐予的礼物。

re·lin·quish /rɪlɪŋkwɪʃ/ (**relinquishes, relinquishing, relinquished**) V-T If you **relinquish** something such as power or control, you give it up. 放弃 (权力或控制) [FORMAL] ❑ *He does not intend to relinquish power.* 他不打算放弃权力。

★ **rel·ish** /rɛlɪʃ/ (**relishes, relishing, relished**) V-T If you **relish** something, you get a lot of enjoyment from it. 喜爱; 乐于; 玩赏 ❑ *I relish the challenge of doing jobs that others turn down.* 我喜欢接受挑战做别人拒绝做的工作。 ● N-UNCOUNT **Relish** is also a noun. 喜爱; 爱好 ❑ *The three men ate with relish.* 那3个人吃得津津有味。

re·live /riliv/ (**relives, reliving, relived**) V-T If you **relive** something that has happened to you in the past, you remember it and imagine that you are experiencing it again. 重温; 回味 ❑ *There is no point in reliving the past.* 回味过去毫无意义。

re·lo·cate /riloʊkeɪt/ (**relocates, relocating, relocated**) V-T/V-I If people or businesses **relocate** or if someone **relocates** them, they move to a different place. 迁移; 重新安置 ❑ *If the company was to relocate, most employees would move.* 如果公司要迁移，大多数员工得搬家。 ● **re·lo·ca·tion** /riloʊkeɪʃᵊn/ N-UNCOUNT (**relocations**) 迁移; 重新安置 ❑ *The company says the cost of relocation will be negligible.* 公司说迁移的费用微不足道。

re·lo·ca·tion ex·penses N-PLURAL **Relocation expenses** are a sum of money that a company pays to someone who moves to a new area in order to work for the company. The money is to help them pay for moving their belongings. (公司付给员工为工作而搬家所需的) 搬迁费 [BUSINESS] ❑ *Relocation expenses were paid to encourage senior staff to move to the region.* 支付搬迁费是为了鼓励资深职员搬到那个地区去。

re·luc·tant ♦◊◊ /rɪlʌktənt/ ADJ If you are **reluctant to** do something, you are unwilling to do it and hesitate before doing it, or do it slowly and without enthusiasm. 不愿意的; 勉强的 ❑ *Mr. Spero was reluctant to ask for help.* 斯珀洛先生不愿意请求帮助。 ● **re·luc·tant·ly** ADV 不愿意地; 勉强地 [ADV with v] ❑ *We have reluctantly agreed to let him go.* 我们已勉强同意让他走了。 ● **re·luc·tance** N-UNCOUNT 不愿意; 勉强 ❑ *Committee members have shown extreme reluctance to explain their position to the media.* 委员会成员表现地极不情愿向媒体解释他们的立场。

Thesaurus *reluctant* 另参见:
ADJ. hesitant, unwilling; *(ant.)* eager, willing

rely ♦◊◊ /rɪlaɪ/ (**relies, relying, relied**) 1 V-I If you **rely on** someone or something, you need them and depend on them in order to live or work properly. 依赖; 依靠 ❑ *They relied heavily on the advice of their professional advisers.* 他们非常依赖专业顾问的建议。 2 V-I If you can **rely on** someone to work well or to behave as you want them to, you can trust them to do this. 信任; 信赖 ❑ *I know I can rely on you to sort it out.* 我知道我可以信赖你来处理此事。

re·main ♦♦♦ /rɪmeɪn/ (**remains, remaining, remained**) 1 V-LINK If someone or something **remains** in a particular state or condition, they stay in that state or condition and do not change. 继续; 保持 ❑ *The three men remained silent.* 这3个人保持沉默。 ❑ *The government remained in control.* 政府继续控制着局势。 2 V-I If you **remain** in a place, you stay there and do not move away. 留在; 停留 ❑ *They have asked the residents to remain in their homes.* 他们已经要求居民待在自己家里。 3 V-I You can say that something **remains** when it still exists. 继续存在; 仍然存在 ❑ *The wider problem remains.* 更广泛的问题依然存在。 4 V-LINK If something **remains to be** done, it has not yet been done and still needs to be done. 剩下; 余留; 待做 ❑ *Major questions remain to be answered about his work.* 关于他工作的主要问题仍有待回答。 5 N-PLURAL **The remains of** something are the parts of it that are left after most of it has been taken away or destroyed. 残余; 残迹 ❑ *They were cleaning up the remains of their picnic.* 他们正在打扫野餐的残余物。 6 N-PLURAL The **remains** of a person or animal are the parts of their body that are left after they have died, sometimes after they have been dead for a long time. (人的) 遗体; (动物的) 残骸 ❑ *The unrecognizable remains of a man had been found.* 发现了一具无法辨认的男子的遗体。 7 → see also **remaining**

Thesaurus *remain* 另参见:
V. last, linger, stay; *(ant.)* depart, leave 2

★ **re·main·der** /rɪmeɪndər/ QUANT **The remainder of** a group are the things or people that still remain after the other things or people have gone or have been dealt with. 剩余部分 [QUANT "of" def-n] ❑ *He gulped down the remainder of his coffee.* 他一口喝完了剩下的咖啡。 ● PRON **Remainder** is also a pronoun. 剩余部分 ❑ *Only 5.9 percent of the area is now covered in trees. Most of the remainder is farmland.* 该地区现在的树木覆盖率仅为5.9%。剩余部分大多是农田。

re·main·ing ♦◊◊ /rɪmeɪnɪŋ/ 1 ADJ The **remaining** things or people out of a group are the things or people that still exist, are still present, or have not yet been dealt with. 剩余的; 剩下的 [ADJ n] ❑ *The three parties will meet next month to work out remaining differences.* 这3个党派将在下月会晤来解决剩下的分歧。 2 → see also **remain**

re·mand /rɪmænd/ (**remands, remanding, remanded**) 1 V-T If a person who is accused of a crime **is remanded** in custody, they are kept in prison until their trial begins. If a person **is remanded on bail**, they are told to return to the court at a later date, when their trial will take place. 使取保候审; 羁押 [usu passive] ❑ *Carter was remanded in custody for seven days.* 卡特被取保候审了7天。 2 N-UNCOUNT **Remand** is used to refer to the process of remanding someone in custody or on bail, or to the period of time until their trial begins. 取保候审; 取保候审期 ❑ *The remand hearing is often over in three minutes.* 取保候审听证会通常在3分钟内结束。

re·mark ♦◊◊ /rɪmɑrk/ (**remarks, remarking, remarked**) 1 V-T/V-I If you **remark** that something is the case, you say that it is the case. 说; 评论 ❑ *I remarked that I would go shopping that afternoon.* 我说过那天下午我要去买东西。 ❑ *On several occasions she had remarked on the boy's improvement.* 有几次她说起过那个男孩的进步。 2 N-COUNT If you make a **remark** about something, you say something about it. 议论; 评论 ❑ *She has made outspoken remarks about the legalization of marijuana.* 她直言不讳地评论过大麻合法化问题。

If you **remark** on something, or make a **remark** about it, you say what you think or what you have noticed, often in a casual way. ❑ *Visitors remark on how well the children look... General Sutton's remarks about the conflict.* If you **comment** on a situation, or make a **comment** about it, you give your opinion on it. ❑ *Mr. Cook has not commented on these reports... I was wondering whether you had any comments.* If you **mention** something, you say it, but only briefly, especially when you have not talked about it before. ❑ *He mentioned that he might go to New York.*

Word Partnership *remark* 的常用搭配:
ADJ. **casual** remark, **offhand** remark 2
V. **hear a** remark, **make a** remark 2

re·mark·able ♦◊◊ /rɪmɑrkəbᵊl/ ADJ Someone or something that is **remarkable** is unusual or special in a way that makes people notice them and be surprised or impressed. 不同寻常的; 非凡卓越的; 引人注目的 ❑ *He was a remarkable man.* 他是个非凡卓越的人。 ● **re·mark·ably** /rɪmɑrkəbli/ ADV 不同寻常地; 非凡卓越地; 引人注目地 ❑ *Herbal remedies are remarkably successful in treating eczema.* 草药疗法医治湿疹非常成功。

re·match /rimætʃ/ (**rematches**) 1 N-COUNT A **rematch** is a second game that is played between two people or teams, for example because their first match was a draw or because there was a dispute about some aspect of it. 重赛 ❑ *Duff said he would be demanding a rematch.* 达夫说他会要求重赛。 2 N-COUNT A **rematch** is a second game or contest between two people or teams who have already faced each other. 复赛 [mainly AM]

in BRIT, usually use **return match**

❑ *Stanford will face UCLA in a rematch.* 斯坦福大学代表队将在复赛中对阵加利福尼亚大学洛杉矶分校代表队。

re·medial /rɪmidiəl/ 1 ADJ **Remedial** action is intended to correct something that has been done wrong or that has not been successful. 补救的; 纠正的 [FORMAL] ❑ *Some authorities are now having* *to take remedial action.* 一些当局现在不得不采取补救行动。 2 ADJ **Remedial** education is intended to improve a person's ability to read, write, or do mathematics, especially when they find these things difficult. 补习的；辅导的 ❑ *...children who required remedial education.* …需要补习辅导的孩子们。

rem·edy /rɛmədi/ (**remedies, remedying, remedied**) 1 N-COUNT A **remedy** is a successful way of dealing with a problem. 解决办法 ❑ *The remedy lies in the hands of the government.* 解决办法就在政府手中。 2 N-COUNT A **remedy** is something that is intended to cure you when you are ill or in pain. 治疗；疗法；药品 ❑ *There are many different kinds of natural remedies to help overcome winter infections.* 很多不同种类的天然药物有助于克服冬季传染病。 3 V-T If you **remedy** something that is wrong or harmful, you correct it or improve it. 补救；纠正；改善 ❑ *A great deal has been done internally to remedy the situation.* 内部已经采取了很多措施来挽救局面。

re·mem·ber ♦♦♦ /rɪmɛmbər/ (**remembers, remembering, remembered**) 1 V-T/V-I If you **remember** people or events from the past, you still have an idea of them in your mind and you are able to think about them. 记得 ❑ *You wouldn't remember me. I was in another group.* 你不会记得我的，我当时在另一个组。 ❑ *I remembered that we had made the last of the coffee the day before.* 我记得我们前一天刚煮完了最后一点咖啡。 ❑ *What a day that was, do you remember?* 那是怎样的一天，你还记得吗？ 2 V-T If you **remember** that something is the case, you become aware of it again after a time when you did not think about it. 忆起；回想起 ❑ *She remembered that she was going to the club that evening.* 她回想起那天晚上她要去俱乐部。 3 V-T/V-I If you cannot **remember** something, you are not able to bring it back into your mind when you make an effort to do so. 记住 [usu with brd-neg] ❑ *If you can't remember your number, write it in code in an appointment book.* 如果你记不住你的号码，就用密码把它写在预约本里。 ❑ *I can't remember what I said.* 我记不起我说过什么了。 ❑ *Don't tell me you can't remember.* 别告诉我你不记得了。 4 V-T If you **remember to** do something, you do it when you intend to. 记住（做某事） ❑ *Please remember to enclose a stamped self-addressed envelope when writing.* 请记住写信的时候附上一个贴好邮票、写好自己姓名地址的信封。 5 V-T You tell someone to **remember that** something is the case when you want to emphasize its importance. It may be something that they already know about or a new piece of information. 要记住（表示强调重要性） [EMPHASIS] ❑ *It is important to remember that each person reacts differently.* 重要的是要记住每个人的反应不同。

→ see **memory**

> Do not confuse **remember** and **remind**. If you **remember** something, you are able to bring it back into your mind. ❑ *He remembers everything that happened... I could not remember her name.* If you **remember** to do something, you do what you are meant to do without forgetting or needing to be told to do it. ❑ *He remembered to turn the gas off... Remember to put all your tools away.* If someone **reminds** you of someone or something, they make you think about that person or thing. ❑ *He reminds me of Maurice Fitzgerald... The pink dress reminds me of when I was a chauffeur in New York.* You cannot use 'remember' in this way. You can use **remember** with the 'to' infinitive or the '-ing' form of the verb, but note that they have different meanings. If you **remember** to do something, you do it when you intend to. ❑ *He remembered to buy his wife chocolates.* If you **remember** doing something, you are thinking back to the past. ❑ *I remember reading the newspaper aloud to my father at five.*

Thesaurus *remember* 另参见：

V. look back, recall, think back; *(ant.)* forget 1 3

Word Partnership *remember* 的常用搭配：

CONJ. remember **what**, remember **when**, remember **where**, remember **why** 1 – 3

ADJ. **easy to** remember, **important to** remember 1 2 4 5

ADV. remember **clearly**, remember **correctly**, remember **exactly**, **still** remember, remember **vividly** 1 3
always remember 1 4 5

re·mem·brance /rɪmɛmbrəns/ N-UNCOUNT If you do something **in remembrance of** a dead person, you do it as a way of showing that you want to remember them and that you respect them. 纪念；怀念 [FORMAL] ❑ *They wore black in remembrance of those who had died.* 他们穿一身黑服以纪念死者。

re·mind ♦◇◇ /rɪmaɪnd/ (**reminds, reminding, reminded**) 1 V-T If someone **reminds** you **of** a fact or event that you already know about, they say something which makes you think about it. 使记起；使想起 ❑ *So she simply welcomed Tim and reminded him of the last time they had met.* 因此她只是欢迎了蒂姆，让他想起他们上次的相遇。 2 V-T You use **remind** in expressions such as **Let me remind you that** and **May I remind you that** to introduce a piece of information that you want to emphasize. It may be something that the hearer already knows about or a new piece of information. Sometimes these expressions can sound unfriendly. 提醒（表强调，语气较强硬） [SPOKEN, EMPHASIS] ❑ *"Let me remind you," said Marianne, "that Milwaukee is also my home town."* "让我提醒你，"玛丽安娜说，"密尔沃基也是我的家乡。" 3 V-T If someone **reminds** you **to** do a particular thing, they say something which makes you remember to do it. 提醒 ❑ *Can you remind me to buy a bottle of wine?* 你能提醒我买一瓶葡萄酒吗？ 4 V-T If you say that someone or something **reminds** you **of** another person or thing, you mean that they are similar to the other person or thing and that they make you think about them. 使想起 ❑ *She reminds me of the wife of the pilot who used to work for you.* 她使我想起曾为你工作过的飞行员之妻。

> Do not confuse **remind** and **remember**. If someone **reminds** you **of** someone or something, they make you think about that person or thing. ❑ *He reminds me of Maurice Fitzgerald... The pink dress reminds me of when I was a chauffeur in New York.* If you **remember** something, you are able to bring it back into your mind. ❑ *He remembers everything that happened... I could not remember her name.* If you **remember** to do something, you do what you are meant to do without forgetting or needing to be told to do it. ❑ *He remembered to turn the gas off... Remember to put all your tools away.*

Word Partnership *remind* 的常用搭配：

PREP. remind ***someone*** **of** ***something*** 1
remind ***you of someone/something*** 4

V. **let me** remind **you, may I** remind **you** 2

re·mind·er /rɪmaɪndər/ (**reminders**) 1 N-COUNT Something that serves as a **reminder of** another thing makes you think about the other thing. 提醒人记忆之物 [WRITTEN] ❑ *The last thing you'd want is a constant reminder of a bad experience.* 你最不想要的就是不断让你想起一段糟糕经历的东西。 2 N-COUNT A **reminder** is a letter or note that is sent to tell you that you have not done something such as pay a bill or return library books. 催缴单；催费单 ❑ *...the final reminder for the gas bill.* …煤气费的最后催缴单。

remi·nisce /rɛmɪnɪs/ (**reminisces, reminiscing, reminisced**) V-I If you **reminisce** about something from your past, you write or talk about it, often with pleasure. 缅怀往事；叙旧 [FORMAL] ❑ *I don't like reminiscing because it makes me feel old.* 我不喜欢回忆旧事，因为这让我觉得我老了。

★ **remi·nis·cence** /rɛmɪnɪsəns/ (**reminiscences**) N-VAR Someone's **reminiscences** are things that they remember from the past, and which they talk or write about. **Reminiscence** is the process of remembering these things and talking or writing about them. 回忆录；缅怀往事的谈话 [FORMAL] ❑ *Here I am boring you with my reminiscences.* 我的这些陈年老事让你烦了吧。

▲ **remi·nis·cent** /rɛmɪnɪsənt/ ADJ If you say that one thing is **reminiscent of** another, you mean that it reminds you of it. 令人想起的 [v-link ADJ "of" n] [FORMAL] ❑ *We drank from wax-coated paper cups reminiscent of a visit to the dentist.* 我们喝水用的蜡纸杯让我想起了那次去看牙医的事。

re·mis·sion /rɪmɪʃən/ (**remissions**) N-VAR If someone who has had a serious disease such as cancer is **in remission** or if the disease is **in remission**, the disease has been controlled so that they are not as ill as they were. 缓解 ❑ *Brain scans have confirmed that the disease is in remission.* 脑部扫描已经证实疾病有所缓解。

▲ **re·mit** /rɪmɪt/ (**remits, remitting, remitted**) V-T If you **remit** money to someone, you send it to them. 汇（款） [FORMAL] ❑ *Many immigrants regularly remit money to their families.* 很多移民定期给他们的家人寄钱。

re·mit·tance /rɪmɪtəns/ (**remittances**) N-VAR A **remittance** is a sum of money that you send to someone. 汇款 [FORMAL] ❑ *Please enclose your remittance, making checks payable to Valley Technology Services.* 请随信附上您的汇款，支票收款方为瓦利科技服务公司。

R

★ **rem·nant** /rɛmnənt/ (**remnants**) N-COUNT The **remnants of** something are small parts of it that are left over when the main part has disappeared or has been used or destroyed. 残余部分；残迹 ❑ *Beneath the present church were remnants of Roman flooring.* 在目前的这座教堂下面还有残余的古罗马地板。

▲ **re·morse** /rɪmɔrs/ N-UNCOUNT **Remorse** is a strong feeling of sadness and regret about something wrong that you have done. 懊悔；悔恨；自责 ❑ *He was full of remorse and asked Beatrice what he could do to make amends.* 他悔恨不已，问比阿特丽斯他可以做点什么来弥补。

re·mote ♦◇◇ /rɪmoʊt/ (**remoter, remotest, remotes**) 1 ADJ **Remote** areas are far away from cities and places where most people live, and are therefore difficult to get to. 边远的；偏僻的 ❑ *Landslides have cut off many villages in remote areas.* 塌方已切断了边远地区许多村庄与外界的联系。 2 ADJ The **remote** past or **remote** future is a time that is many years distant from the present. 遥远的；久远的 ❑ *Slabs of rock had slipped sideways in the remote past and formed this hole.* 在遥远的过去，大块的岩石向旁边滑落，形成了这个洞。 3 ADJ If something is **remote from** a particular subject or area of experience, it is not relevant to it because it is very different. (关系) 疏远的 ❑ *This government depends on the wishes of a few who are remote from the people.* 这个政府按照那几个疏远群众之人的愿望行事。 4 ADJ If you say that there is a **remote** possibility or chance that something will happen, you are emphasizing that there is only a very small chance that it will happen. 极小的；(可能性或机会) 微乎其微的 [EMPHASIS] ❑ *I use sunscreen whenever there is even a remote possibility that I will be in the sun.* 我无论什么时候都用防晒霜，哪怕是有一点点晒到太阳的可能。 5 ADJ If you describe someone as **remote**, you mean that they behave as if they do not want to be friendly or closely involved with other people. 与人疏远的；孤傲的 ❑ *She looked so beautiful, and at the same time so remote.* 她看上去如此漂亮，但同时又那么孤傲。 6 N-COUNT A **remote** is the same as a **remote control**. 遥控器 ❑ *He flipped through the channels with the remote.* 他用遥控器快速浏览了各个频道。

re·mote ac·cess N-UNCOUNT **Remote access** is a system that allows you to gain access to a particular computer or network using a separate computer. 远程访问 [COMPUTING] ❑ *The diploma course would offer remote access to course materials via the Internet's world wide web.* 该学位课程将通过互联网来提供可远程访问的课程资料。

re·mote con·trol (**remote controls**) 1 N-UNCOUNT **Remote control** is a system of controlling a machine or a vehicle from a distance by using radio or electronic signals. 遥控 ❑ *The bomb was detonated by remote control.* 炸弹通过遥控引爆。 2 N-COUNT The **remote control** for a television or other equipment is the device that you use to control the machine from a distance, by pressing the buttons on it. 遥控器 ❑ *Richard picked up the remote control and turned on the television.* 理查德拿起遥控器，打开了电视机。

re·mote·ly /rɪmoʊtli/ 1 ADV You use **remotely** with a negative statement to emphasize the statement. 丝毫；根本 (用于强调否定) [EMPHASIS] ❑ *We had never seen anything remotely like it before.* 我们以前从未见过同它有丝毫相似的东西。 2 ADV If someone or something is **remotely** placed or situated, they are a long way from other people or places. 偏远的 [ADV -ed] ❑ *...the remotely situated, five bedroom house.* …那幢位置偏远的5居室的房子。

re·mov·al /rɪmuvᵊl/ (**removals**) 1 N-UNCOUNT The **removal** of something is the act of removing it. 移动；搬动；去除 ❑ *What they expected to be the removal of a small lump turned out to be major surgery.* 他们本以为只是切除一个小肿块，结果却成了个大手术。 2 N-VAR **Removal** is the process of transporting furniture or equipment from one building to another. (家具、设备的) 搬运 [BRIT]

in AM, use **moving**

re·move ♦♦◇ /rɪmuv/ (**removes, removing, removed**) 1 V-T If you **remove** something from a place, you take it away. 移开 [WRITTEN] ❑ *As soon as the cake is done, remove it from the oven.* 蛋糕一烤好，就把它从烤箱里移出来。 2 V-T If you **remove** clothing, you take it off. 脱下；摘下 [WRITTEN] ❑ *He removed his jacket.* 他脱掉了夹克。 3 V-T If you **remove** a stain from something, you make the stain disappear by treating it with a chemical or by washing it. 去除 (痕迹)；洗掉 (污渍) ❑ *This treatment removes the most stubborn stains.* 这个处理方法能洗掉最顽固的污渍。 4 V-T If people **remove** someone **from** power or **from** something such as a committee, they stop them from being in power or being a member of the committee. 把…免职 ❑ *The student senate voted to remove Fuller from office.* 大学评议会投票将富勒免职了。 5 V-T If you **remove** an obstacle, a restriction, or a problem, you get rid of it. 去除 (障碍或限制)；解决 (问题) ❑ *The agreement removes the last serious obstacle to the signing of the arms treaty.* 该协议为武器条约的签署去除了最后一个重大障碍。

Thesaurus	*remove* 另参见：
V.	take away, take out 1 take off, undress 2

re·moved /rɪmuvd/ ADJ If you say that an idea or situation is far **removed from** something, you mean that it is very different from it. 非常不同的 [v-link adv ADJ "from" n] ❑ *Central office was too far removed from operating decisions at the department level.* 总部办公室与部门级别对运行的决策大相径庭。

re·mu·ner·ate /rɪmyunəreɪt/ (**remunerates, remunerating, remunerated**) V-T If you **are remunerated** for work that you do, you are paid for it. 给…报酬 [usu passive] [FORMAL] ❑ *You will be remunerated and so will your staff.* 你将会得到报酬，你的员工也会。

re·mu·nera·tion /rɪmyunəreɪʃᵊn/ (**remunerations**) N-VAR Someone's **remuneration** is the amount of money that they are paid for the work that they do. 报酬；酬金 [FORMAL] ❑ *...the continuing marked increases in the remuneration of the company's directors.* …公司主管们薪酬的持续显著增加。

★ **re·nais·sance** /rɛnɪsɑns/ 1 N-PROPER **The Renaissance** was the period in Europe, especially Italy, in the 14th, 15th, and 16th centuries, when there was a new interest in art, literature, science, and learning. 文艺复兴时期 ❑ *...the Renaissance masterpieces in London's galleries.* …伦敦美术馆里文艺复兴时期的杰作。 2 N-SING If something experiences a **renaissance**, it becomes popular or successful again after a time when people were not interested in it. 复兴 ❑ *Popular art is experiencing a renaissance.* 通俗艺术正在复兴。

ren·der /rɛndər/ (**renders, rendering, rendered**) V-T You can use **render** with an adjective that describes a particular state to say that someone or something is changed into that state. For example, if someone or something makes a thing harmless, you can say that they **render** it harmless. 使成为；使变得 ❑ *It contained so many errors as to render it worthless.* 太多的错误使之变得毫无价值。

ren·dez·vous /rɒndeɪvu/ (**rendezvousing, rendezvoused**)

The form **rendezvous** is pronounced /rɒndeɪvuz/ when it is the plural of the noun or the third person singular of the verb.

名词复数或动词第三人称单数时，**rendezvous**此词形读作/rɒndeɪvuz/。

1 N-COUNT A **rendezvous** is a meeting, often a secret one, that you have arranged with someone for a particular time and place. (常指秘密的) 会面 ❑ *I had almost decided to keep my rendezvous with Tony.* 我几乎已经决定要保持和托尼的秘密会面。 2 N-COUNT A **rendezvous** is the place where you have arranged to meet someone, often secretly. 会面地点 ❑ *Their rendezvous would be the Plaza Hotel.* 他们的会面地点将是广场大酒店。 3 V-RECIP If you **rendezvous with** someone or if the two of you **rendezvous**, you meet them at a time and place that you have arranged. (与…) 会面 ❑ *The plan was to rendezvous with him on Sunday afternoon.* 计划是在星期天下午和他会面。 ❑ *She wondered where they were going to rendezvous afterward.* 她不清楚他们以后会在哪里会面。

ren·egade /rɛnɪgeɪd/ (**renegades**) N-COUNT A **renegade** is a person who abandons the religious, political, or philosophical beliefs that he or she used to have, and accepts opposing or different beliefs. 叛徒；叛逆者；改变信仰者 ❑ *He has shown himself to be a renegade without respect for the rule of law.* 他已经表现出自己是个毫不尊重法规的叛逆者。

re·nege /rɪnɪg/ (**reneges, reneging, reneged**) V-I If someone **reneges on** a promise or an agreement, they do not do what they have promised or agreed to do. 违约；背信；食言 ❑ *He reneged on a promise to leave his wife.* 他背弃了诺言，离开了他的妻子。 ❑ *If someone reneged on a deal, they could never trade here again.* 如果谁违背了一笔交易，他就不能再在这里做生意了。

re·new ♦◇◇ /rɪnu/ (**renews, renewing, renewed**) 1 V-T If you **renew** an activity, you begin it again. 重新开始 ❑ *He renewed his attack on government policy toward Europe.* 他重新开始抨击政府的欧洲政策。 2 V-RECIP If you **renew** a relationship **with** someone, you start it again after you have not seen them or have not been friendly with them for some time. 恢复 (关系) ❑ *When the two men met again after the war they renewed their friendship.* 当这两个男人战后重

逢时，他们恢复了友谊。 3 V-T When you **renew** something such as a license or a contract, you extend the period of time for which it is valid. 延长（执照、合同的）有效期 ❑ *Larry's landlord threatened not to renew his lease.* 拉里的房东威胁说不再让他续租。 4 V-T You can say that something **is renewed** when it grows again or is replaced after it has been destroyed or lost. 获得新生；（遭毁坏或损失后）再生 [usu passive] ❑ *Nature's repair process is slow and steady, with cells being constantly renewed.* 自然的修复过程缓慢而稳定，在此过程中细胞不断再生。

Thesaurus *renew* 另参见：
V. continue, resume, revive 1 – 4

★ **re·new·able** /rɪnuəbᵊl/ 1 ADJ **Renewable** resources are natural ones such as wind, water, and sunlight which are always available. （资源）可再生的 ❑ *...renewable energy sources.* …可再生能源。 2 ADJ If a contract or agreement is **renewable**, it can be extended when it reaches the end of a fixed period of time. （合同、协议）可延长有效期的 ❑ *A formal contract is signed which is renewable annually.* 签署的一份正式合同每年可续签一次。

re·new·al /rɪnuəl/ (**renewals**) 1 N-SING If there is a **renewal of** an activity or a situation, it starts again. 重新开始；恢复 ❑ *They will discuss the possible renewal of diplomatic relations.* 他们将讨论恢复外交关系的可能性。 2 N-VAR The **renewal** of a document such as a license or a contract is an official increase in the period of time for which it remains valid. （有效期的）延长 ❑ *His contract came up for renewal.* 他的合同交上来要求延期。 3 N-UNCOUNT **Renewal** of something lost, dead, or destroyed is the process of it growing again or being replaced. 新生；复兴 ❑ *...a political lobbyist concentrating on urban renewal and regeneration.* …一个专门就城市复兴与重建而游说的政客。

▲ **re·nounce** /rɪnaʊns/ (**renounces, renouncing, renounced**) 1 V-T If you **renounce** a belief or a way of behaving, you decide and declare publicly that you no longer have that belief or will no longer behave in that way. 宣布放弃（信仰、行为方式） ❑ *After a period of imprisonment she renounced terrorism.* 被监禁了一段时间后她宣布放弃恐怖主义。 2 V-T If you **renounce** a claim, rank, or title, you officially give it up. （正式的）放弃 ❑ *He renounced his claim to the French throne.* 他宣布放弃法国王位。

Word Link *nov ≈ new : innovate, novel, renovate*

▲ **reno·vate** /rɛnəveɪt/ (**renovates, renovating, renovated**) V-T If someone **renovates** an old building, they repair and improve it and get it back into good condition. 修复；整修 ❑ *The couple spent thousands renovating the house.* 这对夫妻花了几千元来整修房子。 ● **reno·va·tion** /rɛnəveɪʃᵊn/ N-VAR (**renovations**) 修复；整修 ❑ *...a property which will need extensive renovation.* …一处需要大范围整修的房产。

R

▲ **re·nown** /rɪnaʊn/ N-UNCOUNT A person **of renown** is well known, usually because they do or have done something good. 名望；声誉 ❑ *She used to be a singer of some renown.* 她过去是个小有名气的歌手。

★ **re·nowned** /rɪnaʊnd/ ADJ A person or place that is **renowned for** something, usually something good, is well known because of it. 有名望的；有声誉的 ❑ *The area is renowned for its Romanesque churches.* 这个地区以其罗马式教堂闻名。

rent ♦◇◇ /rɛnt/ (**rents, renting, rented**) 1 V-T If you **rent** something, you regularly pay its owner a sum of money in order to be able to have it and use it yourself. 租；租借 ❑ *She rents a house with three other girls.* 她和另外3个女孩合租了一套房子。 2 V-T If you **rent** something **to** someone, you let them have it and use it in exchange for a sum of money which they pay you regularly. 租给；出租 ❑ *She rented rooms to university students.* 她曾把房间租给大学生。 ● PHRASAL VERB **Rent out** means the same as **rent**. 租给；出租 ❑ *Last summer Brian Williams rented out his house and went camping.* 去年夏天，布赖恩·威廉斯把自己的房子租出去，然后去露营。 3 N-VAR **Rent** is the amount of money that you pay regularly to use a house, apartment, or piece of land. 租金；房租 ❑ *She worked to pay the rent while I went to college.* 当我读大学时，她工作挣钱来付租金。 4 PHRASE If something is **for rent**, it is available for you to use in exchange for a sum of money. 待租的；供出租的 [mainly AM]

in BRIT, usually use **for hire**

❑ *Helmets will be available for rent at all Vail Resort ski areas.* 在韦尔度假村的所有滑雪场里都有头盔供出租。

Do not confuse **rent**, **hire**, and **let**. If you make a series of payments to use something for a long time, you say that you **rent** it. ❑ *...the apartment he had rented... He rented a TV.* You can say that you **rent** or **rent out** a house or room to someone when they pay you money to live there. ❑ *We rented our house to a college professor.* In British English, it is more common to say that you **let** it. ❑ *They were letting a room to a school teacher.* Americans also use **rent** when you pay a sum of money to use something for a short time. ❑ *He rented a car for the weekend.* In British English, if you pay a sum of money to use something for a short time, you usually say that you **hire** it. ❑ *He was unable to hire another car.*

rent·al /rɛntᵊl/ (**rentals**) 1 N-UNCOUNT The **rental** of something such as a car or piece of equipment is the activity or process of renting it. 出租；租借 [also N in pl] ❑ *We can arrange car rental from Chicago's O'Hare Airport.* 我们可以安排从芝加哥奥黑尔机场租车。 2 N-COUNT The **rental** is the amount of money that you pay when you rent something such as a car, property, or piece of equipment. 租金 ❑ *It has been let at an annual rental of $393,000.* 它已经以每年$393000的租金租出去了。 3 ADJ You use **rental** to describe things that are connected with the renting out of goods, properties, and services. 出租的；租赁业的 [ADJ n] ❑ *A friend drove her to Atlanta, where she picked up a rental car.* 一个朋友开车送她去了亚特兰大，在那里她租到了一辆车。

re·or·gan·ise /riɔːʳgənaɪz/ [BRIT] → see **reorganize**

re·or·gan·ize /riɔrgənaɪz/ (**reorganizes, reorganizing, reorganized**)

in BRIT, also use **reorganise**

V-T/V-I To **reorganize** something means to change the way in which it is organized, arranged, or done. 重组；改编；重新安排 ❑ *It is the mother who is expected to reorganize her busy schedule.* 应该让妈妈来重新安排她繁忙的日程。 ❑ *Four thousand troops have been reorganized into a fighting force.* 4000人的军队已经被改编成了一支战斗力强的精锐部队。 ● **re·or·gani·za·tion** /riɔrgənɪzeɪʃᵊn/ N-VAR (**reorganizations**) 重组；改编；整顿 ❑ *...the reorganization of the legal system.* …法律体系的整顿。

rep /rɛp/ (**reps**) 1 N-COUNT A **rep** is a person whose job is to sell a company's products or services, especially by traveling around and visiting other companies. **Rep** is short for **representative**. 销售代表 ❑ *I'd been working as a sales rep for a photographic company.* 我一直在担任一家摄影公司的销售代表。 2 N-COUNT A **rep** is a person who acts as a representative for a group of people, usually a group of people who work together. 代表 ❑ *Contact the health and safety rep at your union.* 请联系你们工会的健康安全代表。

re·paid /rɪpeɪd/ **Repaid** is the past tense and past participle of **repay**. **repay**的过去式和过去分词

re·pair ♦◇◇ /rɪpɛər/ (**repairs, repairing, repaired**) 1 V-T If you **repair** something that has been damaged or is not working properly, you fix it. 修理；修补；整修 ❑ *Goldsmith has repaired the roof to ensure the house is windproof.* 戈德史密斯已经修理了房顶以确保房子可以抵御狂风。 ● **re·pair·er** N-COUNT (**repairers**) 修理工 ❑ *...services provided by builders, plumbers, and TV repairers.* …建筑工、水暖工和电视修理工提供的服务。 2 V-T If you **repair** a relationship or someone's reputation after it has been damaged, you do something to improve it. 弥补；补救 ❑ *The administration continued to try to repair the damage caused by the secretary's interview.* 该政府继续努力去弥补因秘书访谈而造成的损失。 3 N-VAR A **repair** is something that you do to mend a machine, building, piece of clothing, or other thing that has been damaged or is not working properly. 修理；修补；整修 ❑ *Many women know how to make repairs on their cars.* 很多女性知道如何修理汽车。

Word Partnership *repair* 的常用搭配：
N. repair **a chimney**, repair **equipment**, repair **parts**, repair **a roof** 1
repair **damage** 1 2
repair **a relationship** 2
auto repair, **car** repair, **home** repair, **road** repair, repair **service**, repair **shop** 3

re·pat·ri·ate /ripeɪtrieɪt/ (**repatriates, repatriating, repatriated**) 1 V-T If a country **repatriates** someone, it sends them back to their home country. 遣返 ❑ *It was not the policy of the government to repatriate genuine refugees.* 遣返真正的难民并不是政府的

政策。● **re·pat·ria·tion** /riːpeɪtrieɪʃᵊn/ N-VAR (**repatriations**) 遣返 ❑ *Today they begin the forced repatriation of Vietnamese boat people.* 今天他们开始强制遣返越南船民。 2 V-T If someone **repatriates** money that is invested in another country, they change their investments so that the money is invested in their own country. 调资回国

Word Link *re* ≈ *back, again* : ***re**flect, **re**pay, **re**state*

★ **re·pay** /rɪpeɪ/ (**repays, repaying, repaid**) 1 V-T If you **repay** a loan or a debt, you pay back the money that you owe to the person who you borrowed or took it from. 付还；偿还（贷款、债务） ❑ *He advanced funds of his own to his company, which was unable to repay him.* 他把自己的资金预付给公司，公司却未能偿还给他。 2 V-T If you **repay** a favor that someone did for you, you do something for them in return. 报答；回报 ❑ *It was very kind. I don't know how I can ever repay you.* 太好了。我不知道怎样才能报答你。

re·pay·able /rɪpeɪəbᵊl/ ADJ A loan that is **repayable** within a certain period of time must be paid back within that time. 可偿还的 [mainly BRIT] ❑ *The loan is repayable over twenty years.* 该贷款20年内偿清。

in AM, usually use **payable**

re·pay·ment /rɪpeɪmənt/ (**repayments**) 1 N-COUNT **Repayments** are amounts of money which you pay at regular intervals to a person or organization in order to repay a debt. （债务的）分期还款 [mainly BRIT] ❑ *They were unable to meet their mortgage repayments.* 他们没能支付抵押贷款的偿还。

in AM, usually use **payment**

2 N-UNCOUNT The **repayment of** money is the act or process of paying it back to the person you owe it to. 偿还 ❑ *He failed to meet last Friday's deadline for repayment of a $114 million loan.* 他在上周五的最后期限内未能偿还$1.14亿的贷款。

▲ **re·peal** /rɪpiːl/ (**repeals, repealing, repealed**) V-T If the government **repeals** a law, it officially ends it, so that it is no longer valid. 撤销；废止（法令） ❑ *The government has just repealed the law segregating public facilities.* 政府刚刚废除了隔离公共设施的法令。 ● N-UNCOUNT **Repeal** is also a noun. 撤销；（法令的）废止 ❑ *Next year will be the 60th anniversary of the repeal of Prohibition.* 明年将是禁酒令废止的60周年。

re·peat ◆◆◇ /rɪpiːt/ (**repeats, repeating, repeated**) 1 V-T If you **repeat** something, you say or write it again. You can say **I repeat** to show that you feel strongly about what you are repeating. 重复；重说；重写 ❑ *He repeated that he had been misquoted.* 他反复地说他的话被错误地引用了。 ❑ *She repeated her call yesterday for an investigation into the incident.* 她昨天反复要求对那起事件进行调查。 2 V-T If you **repeat** something that someone else has said or written, you say or write the same thing, or tell it to another person. 照着说；照着写；把…告诉别人 ❑ *She had an irritating habit of repeating everything I said to her.* 她有个令人恼火的毛病，就是把我对她说的每一件事都告诉别人。 ❑ *I trust you not to repeat that to anyone else.* 我相信你不会把这事告诉别人。 3 V-T If you **repeat yourself**, you say something which you have said before, usually by mistake. （常指失误造成的）反复地讲 ❑ *He spoke well to begin with, but then started rambling and repeating himself.* 开始他说得很好，但是后来开始闲扯，一句话翻来覆去地讲。 4 V-T/V-I If you **repeat** an action, you do it again. 再做；重做 ❑ *The next day I repeated the procedure.* 第二天我重复了这个程序。 ❑ *Move the leg up and down several times and rotate the foot. Repeat on the right leg.* 把腿上下移动几次并转动脚。然后换右腿重做一遍。 5 V-T If an event or series of events **repeats itself**, it happens again. 再次发生；重演 ❑ *The UN will have to work hard to stop history from repeating itself.* 联合国必须努力工作以阻止历史重演。 6 N-COUNT If there is a **repeat of** an event, usually an undesirable event, it happens again. （尤指不受欢迎的事情）重演 ❑ *There were fears that there might be a repeat of last year's campaign of strikes.* 有人担心去年的罢工或许会重演。 7 ADJ If a company gets **repeat** business or **repeat** customers, people who have bought their goods or services before buy them again. （顾客）回头的；（生意）回头客的 [ADJ n] [BUSINESS] ❑ *Nearly 60% of our bookings come from repeat business and personal recommendation.* 我们近60%的预订来自于回头客生意或个人推荐。 8 N-COUNT A **repeat** is a television or radio program that has been broadcast before. （电视或电台节目的）重播

Thesaurus *repeat* 另参见：
V. reiterate, restate, retell 1 2
N. encore, rerun 8

re·peat·ed /rɪpiːtɪd/ ADJ **Repeated** actions or events are ones that happen many times. 反复的；屡次的 [ADJ n] ❑ *Mr. Lawssi apparently did not return the money, despite repeated reminders.* 劳斯先生显然还没有还钱，尽管已经反复提醒过。

re·peat·ed·ly /rɪpiːtɪdli/ ADV If you do something **repeatedly**, you do it many times. 反复地；再三地 [ADV with v] ❑ *Both men have repeatedly denied the allegations.* 两个人都再三地否认这些指控。

re·peat of·fend·er (**repeat offenders**) N-COUNT A **repeat offender** is someone who commits the same sort of crime more than once. 惯犯 ❑ *We need to ensure that repeat offenders spend longer behind bars, even for relatively minor crimes.* 我们需要确保惯犯坐更多年牢，即使针对相对轻的罪行。

★ **re·pel** /rɪpel/ (**repels, repelling, repelled**) 1 V-T When an army **repels** an attack, they successfully fight and drive back soldiers from another army who have attacked them. 击退；打退 [FORMAL] ❑ *They have fifty thousand troops along the border ready to repel any attack.* 他们沿边界有5万军队，随时准备击退任何进攻。 2 V-T If something **repels** you, you find it horrible and disgusting. 使厌恶；使反感 [no cont] ❑ *...a violent excitement that frightened and repelled her.* …使她害怕和厌恶的一次暴力骚动。 ● **re·pelled** ADJ 厌恶的；反感的 ❑ *She was very striking but in some way I felt repelled.* 她非常吸引人，但是我觉得有些反感。 3 V-RECIP When a magnetic pole **repels** another magnetic pole, it gives out a force that pushes the other pole away. You can also say that two magnetic poles **repel** each other or that they **repel**. 排斥；（磁极间）相斥 [TECHNICAL]
→ see **magnet**

re·pel·lent /rɪpelənt/ (**repellents**) also **repellant** 1 ADJ If you think that something is horrible and disgusting you can say that it is **repellent**. 令人厌恶的 [FORMAL] ❑ *...a very large, very repellent toad.* …一只又大又令人厌恶的蟾蜍。 2 N-MASS Insect **repellent** is a product containing chemicals that you spray into the air or on your body in order to keep insects away. 驱虫剂 ❑ *...mosquito repellent.* …驱蚊剂。

re·pent /rɪpent/ (**repents, repenting, repented**) V-I If you **repent**, you show or say that you are sorry for something wrong you have done. 悔悟；悔恨；忏悔 ❑ *Those who refuse to repent, he said, will be punished.* 他说，那些不肯悔悟的人将受到惩罚。

re·pent·ance /rɪpentəns/ N-UNCOUNT If you show **repentance** for something wrong that you have done, you make it clear that you are sorry for doing it. 悔悟；悔恨；忏悔 ❑ *They showed no repentance during their trial.* 他们在受审期间没有表现出任何悔悟。

re·pent·ant /rɪpentənt/ ADJ Someone who is **repentant** shows or says that they are sorry for something wrong that they have done. 悔悟的；悔恨的；忏悔的 ❑ *He was feeling guilty and depressed, repentant and scared.* 他现在觉得既内疚又沮丧，既悔恨又害怕。

▲ **re·per·cus·sion** /riːpərkʌʃᵊn/ (**repercussions**) N-COUNT If an action or event has **repercussions**, it causes unpleasant things to happen some time after the original action or event. 后果 [usu pl] [FORMAL] ❑ *It was an effort which was to have painful repercussions.* 那是一个将产生沉痛后果的尝试。

★ **rep·er·toire** /repərtwɑr/ (**repertoires**) N-COUNT A performer's **repertoire** is all the plays or pieces of music that he or she has learned and can perform. （表演者的）全部曲目；保留剧目 ❑ *Meredith D'Ambrosio has thousands of songs in her repertoire.* 梅雷迪思•丹布罗西奥的全部曲目达到几千首。

rep·er·tory /repərtɔri/ N-UNCOUNT A **repertory** company is a group of actors and actresses who perform a small number of plays for just a few weeks at a time. They work in a **repertory** theater. 保留剧目轮演 [usu N n] ❑ *...a well-known repertory company in Boston.* …波士顿一个著名的保留剧目轮演剧团。

rep·eti·tion /repɪtɪʃᵊn/ (**repetitions**) 1 N-VAR If there is a **repetition of** an event, usually an undesirable event, it happens again. （尤指令人不快的事情）重演 ❑ *Today the city government has taken measures to prevent a repetition of last year's confrontation.* 今天市政府已经采取了措施来防止去年的冲突重演。 2 N-VAR **Repetition** means using the same words again. 重复的语句 ❑ *He could also have cut out much of the repetition and thus saved many pages.* 他本来也可以删掉很多重复的语句，省去很多页数。

re·peti·tive /rɪpetɪtɪv/ 1 ADJ Something that is **repetitive** involves actions or elements that are repeated many times and is therefore boring. 重复（因而乏味）的 [DISAPPROVAL] ❑ *...factory workers who do repetitive jobs.* …做重复工作的工人们。 2 ADJ **Repetitive** movements or sounds are repeated many times.

重复的 ❑ *This technique is particularly successful where problems occur as the result of repetitive movements.* 这项技术的成功之处在于能解决重复运动引起的问题。

re·place ♦♦◇ /rɪpleɪs/ **(replaces, replacing, replaced)** 1 V-T If one thing or person **replaces** another, the first is used or acts instead of the second. 代替；取代 ❑ *One species of tree replaces another as a forest ages.* 随着森林老化，一种树会取代另一种树。 ❑ *...the lawyer who replaced Robert as chairman of the company.* …取代罗伯特成为公司主席的那位律师。 2 V-T If you **replace** one thing or person **with** another, you put something or someone else in their place to do their job. 用…代替；用…替换 ❑ *I clean out all the grease and replace it with oil so it works better in very low temperatures.* 我清除掉了所有的油脂，以油替换，因此它在很低的温度下运转得更好。 3 V-T If you **replace** something that is broken, damaged, or lost, you get a new one to use instead. 换下（坏的）；换上（新的） ❑ *The shower that we put in a few years back has broken and we cannot afford to replace it.* 我们几年前安装的淋浴器坏了，但没钱换新的。 4 V-T If you **replace** something, you put it back where it was before. 把…放回原处 ❑ *Replace the caps on the bottles.* 把瓶盖盖回到瓶子上。

re·place·ment ♦◇◇ /rɪpleɪsmənt/ **(replacements)** 1 N-UNCOUNT If you refer to the **replacement** of one thing by another, you mean that the second thing takes the place of the first. 代替；取代；更换 [with supp] ❑ *...the replacement of damaged or lost books.* …受损或遗失书籍的更换。 2 N-COUNT Someone who takes someone else's place in an organization, government, or team can be referred to as their **replacement**. 接替者 ❑ *Taylor has nominated Adams as his replacement.* 泰勒已经提名亚当斯为接替者。

re·play **(replays, replaying, replayed)**

The verb is pronounced /ripleɪ/. The noun is pronounced /ripleɪ/.

动词读作 /ripleɪ/。名词读作 /ripleɪ/。

1 V-T If a game or match between two sports teams **is replayed**, the two teams play it again, because neither team won the first time, or because the game was stopped because of bad weather. 重新举行（比赛） [usu passive] ❑ *The game had to be replayed at the end of the season.* 这场比赛不得不在赛季末重新举行。 ● N-COUNT You can refer to a game that is replayed as a **replay**. 重赛 ❑ *If there has to be a replay we are confident of victory.* 如果不得不重赛，我们有信心赢。 2 V-T If you **replay** something that you have recorded on film or tape, you play it again in order to watch it or listen to it. 重新播放（电影或磁带） ❑ *He stopped the machine and replayed the message.* 他停下机器，重新播放了那条消息。 ● N-COUNT **Replay** is also a noun. （电影或磁带的）重新播放；回放 ❑ *I watched a slow-motion videotape replay of his fall.* 我看了他跌倒时的慢动作录像回放。 3 V-T If you **replay** an event in your mind, you think about it again and again. 反复回想 ❑ *She spends her nights lying in bed, replaying the fire in her mind.* 她很多个晚上躺在床上，反复回想着那场火灾。

R

Word Link *plen ≈ full : plentiful, plenty, replenish*

re·plen·ish /rɪplenɪʃ/ **(replenishes, replenishing, replenished)** V-T If you **replenish** something, you make it full or complete again. 重新充满；再度装满 [FORMAL] ❑ *Three hundred thousand tons of cereals are needed to replenish stocks.* 需要30万吨谷物才能重新装满仓库。

rep·li·ca /replɪkə/ **(replicas)** N-COUNT A **replica of** something such as a statue, building, or weapon is an accurate copy of it. （雕像、建筑物或武器等的）复制品 ❑ *...a human-sized replica of the Statue of Liberty.* …一件真人大小的自由女神像的复制品。

re·ply ♦♦◇ /rɪplaɪ/ **(replies, replying, replied)** 1 V-T/V-I When you **reply to** something that someone has said or written to you, you say or write an answer to them. 回答；答复 ❑ *"That's a nice dress," said Michael. "Thanks," she replied solemnly.* "那连衣裙很漂亮，"迈克尔说。"谢谢，"她郑重地回答。 ❑ *He replied that this was absolutely impossible.* 他回答说这绝对不可能。 ❑ *He never replied to the letters.* 他从来都不回信。 2 N-COUNT A **reply** is something that you say or write when you answer someone or answer a letter or advertisement. 回答；答复 [oft N "to/from" n, also "in" N] ❑ *I called out a challenge, but there was no reply.* 我发起了一个挑战，但是没人回应。 ❑ *He said in reply that the question was unfair.* 他回答说这个问题不公平。 3 V-I If you **reply to** something such as an attack **with** violence or **with** another action, you do something in response. 做出回应；（以行动）回击 ❑ *During a number of violent incidents farmers threw eggs and empty bottles at police, who replied with tear gas.* 在多次暴力事件中，农场主们朝警察扔鸡蛋和空瓶子，而警察则以催泪瓦斯回击。

Thesaurus *reply* 另参见：

V. acknowledge, answer, respond, return 1
N. acknowledgement, answer, response 2

Word Partnership *reply* 的常用搭配：

N. reply **card**, reply **envelope**, reply **form** 2
V. **make a** reply, **receive a** reply 2

re·port ♦♦♦ /rɪpɔrt/ **(reports, reporting, reported)** 1 V-T If you **report** something that has happened, you tell people about it. 报告；告知 ❑ *I reported the theft to the police.* 我向警察报告了这起盗窃案。 ❑ *The officials also reported that two more ships were apparently heading for Malta.* 官员们也报告说另有两艘船显然正朝马耳他驶去。 ❑ *"He seems to be all right now," reported a relieved Taylor.* "他现在似乎完全好了，"泰勒放心地报告说。 ❑ *She reported him missing the next day.* 她第二天报告说他失踪了。 2 V-I If you **report on** an event or subject, you tell people about it, because it is your job or duty to do so. 报道；（工作或职责上）汇报 ❑ *Many journalists based outside of Sudan have been refused visas to enter the country to report on political affairs.* 很多驻在苏丹境外的记者遭到拒签，无法进入该国报道政治事件。 3 N-COUNT A **report** is a news article or broadcast which gives information about something that has just happened. （报刊或广播电视上的）报道 ❑ *According to a report in the newspaper, he still has control over the remaining shares.* 根据报纸上的报道，他依然控制着剩余的股份。 4 N-COUNT A **report** is an official document which a group of people issue after investigating a situation or event. （调查）报告 ❑ *The education committee will today publish its report on the supply of teachers for the next decade.* 教育委员会今天将公布关于今后十年师资储备的报告。 5 N-COUNT If you give someone a **report** on something, you tell them what has been happening. 报告；告知 ❑ *She came back to give us a progress report on how the project is going.* 她回来给我们做了项目进展情况的报告。 6 N-COUNT If you say that there are **reports** that something has happened, you mean that some people say it has happened but you have no direct evidence of it. 传闻 [VAGUENESS] ❑ *There are unconfirmed reports that two people have been shot in the neighboring town of Springfield.* 根据未经证实的传闻，有两个人在邻近斯普林菲尔德的城镇遭到枪击。 7 V-T If someone **reports** you **to** a person in authority, they tell that person about something wrong that you have done. 告发；控告 ❑ *His ex-wife reported him to police a few days later.* 他前妻几天后向警察告发了他。 8 V-I If you **report to** a person or place, you go to that person or place and say that you are ready to start work or say that you are present. 报到 ❑ *Mr. Ashwell has to surrender his passport and report to the police every five days.* 阿什维尔先生不得不交出他的护照，而且每5天去警察局报到一次。 9 V-I If you say that one employee **reports to** another, you mean that the first employee is told what to do by the second one and is responsible to them. 隶属；被…领导 [no cont] [FORMAL] ❑ *He reported to a section chief, who reported to a division chief, and so on up the line.* 他受科长领导，科长受处长领导，如此逐级向上。 10 → see also **report card, reporting**

Thesaurus *report* 另参见：

V. broadcast, cover, narrate, publish 1 2
appear, arrive, show up 8
N. announcement, communication, release, story 3 – 5

re·port card **(report cards)** 1 N-COUNT A **report card** is an official written account of how well or how badly a student has done during the term or year that has just finished. 成绩单 [AM]

in BRIT, use **report**

❑ *The only time I got their attention was when I brought home straight A's on my report card.* 我仅有一次引起他们注意的是在我把全A的成绩单拿回家的时候。 2 N-COUNT A **report card** is a report on how well a person, organization, or country has been doing recently. 工作报告 [AM, JOURNALISM] ❑ *The president today issued his final report card on the state of the economy.* 总统今天发表了他的最后一份关于经济状况的工作报告。

re·port·ed·ly /rɪpɔrtɪdli/ ADV If you say that something is **reportedly** true, you mean that someone has said that it is true, but you have no direct evidence of it. 据报道；据说 [FORMAL, VAGUENESS] ❑ *More than two hundred people have reportedly been killed in the past week's fighting.* 据报道有两百多人在上周的战斗中丧生。

re·port·er ♦♦◊ /rɪpɔrtər/ (**reporters**) N-COUNT A **reporter** is someone who writes news articles or who broadcasts news reports. 记者 ❑ *...a TV reporter.* ···一名电视台记者。

re·port·ing ♦♦◊ /rɪpɔrtɪŋ/ N-UNCOUNT **Reporting** is the presenting of news in newspapers, on radio, and on television. 新闻报道 ❑ *This newspaper has achieved a reputation for honest and impartial political reporting.* 这家报纸凭诚实公正的政治报道赢得了声誉。

Word Link *pos ≈ placing : deposit, preposition, repository*

re·posi·tory /rɪpɒzɪtɔri/ (**repositories**) N-COUNT A **repository** is a place where something is kept safely. 贮存处; 存放处 [FORMAL] ❑ *A church in Moscow became a repository for police files.* 莫斯科的一座教堂成为警察局档案的存放处。

re·pos·sess /ripəzɛs/ (**repossesses, repossessing, repossessed**) V-T If your car or house **is repossessed**, the people who supplied it take it back because they are still owed money for it. 收回 (汽车或房子) [usu passive] ❑ *His car was repossessed by the company.* 他的汽车被公司收回去了。

re·pos·ses·sion /ripəzɛʃᵊn/ (**repossessions**) N-VAR The **repossession** of someone's house or car is the act of repossessing it. 收回 ❑ *...the problem of home repossessions.* ···收回住宅的问题。

rep·re·sent ♦♦◊ /rɛprɪzɛnt/ (**represents, representing, represented**) **1** V-T If someone such as a lawyer or a politician **represents** a person, a group of people, or a place, they act on behalf of that person, group, or place. 代表; 代理 ❑ *...the politicians we elect to represent us.* ···我们所选的代表我们的政治家。 ❑ *...Richard Bolling, a Democrat who represented Missouri in Congress.* ···理查德·博林，一个在国会中代表密苏里州的民主党人。 **2** V-T If you **represent** a person or group at an official event, you go there on their behalf. 代表 (出席) ❑ *The general secretary may represent the president at official ceremonies.* 秘书长可以在官方仪式上代表主席。 **3** V-T If you **represent** your country or city in a competition or sports event, you take part in it on behalf of the country or city where you live. 代表 (参赛) ❑ *My only aim is to represent the United States at the Olympics.* 我惟一的目标就是代表美国参加奥运会。 **4** V-T PASSIVE If a group of people or things **is** well **represented** in a particular activity or in a particular place, a lot of them can be found there. 使有代表性 ❑ *Women are already well represented in the area of TV drama.* 女性在电视戏剧领域已经占有很大比例。 **5** V-T If a sign or symbol **represents** something, it is accepted as meaning that thing. 代表; 表示; 象征 [no cont] ❑ *...a black dot in the middle of the circle is supposed to represent the source of the radiation.* ···圆圈中央的黑点应该表示射线的来源。 **6** V-T To **represent** an idea or quality means to be a symbol or an expression of that idea or quality. 代表; 象征; 反映 [no cont, no passive] ❑ *New York represents everything that's great about America.* 纽约象征着美国伟大的一切。 **7** V-T If you **represent** a person or thing **as** a particular thing, you describe them as being that thing. 描写; 描绘 ❑ *The popular press tends to represent him as an environmental guru.* 大众媒体倾向于把他描绘成环保领袖。

rep·re·sen·ta·tion /rɛprɪzɛnteɪʃᵊn/ (**representations**) **1** N-UNCOUNT If a group or person has **representation** in a legislature or on a committee, someone in the legislature or on the committee supports them and makes decisions on their behalf. 代表 ❑ *Puerto Ricans are U.S. citizens but they have no representation in Congress.* 波多黎各人是美国公民，但是他们在国会中没有代表。 **2** → see also **proportional representation** **3** N-COUNT You can describe a picture, model, or statue of a person or thing as a **representation of** them. 描写; 描绘 [FORMAL] ❑ *...a lifelike representation of Christ.* ···对基督的生动描绘。

rep·re·senta·tive ♦♦◊ /rɛprɪzɛntətɪv/ (**representatives**) **1** N-COUNT A **representative** is a person who has been chosen to act or make decisions on behalf of another person or a group of people. 代表; 代理人 ❑ *...labor union representatives.* ···工会代表们。 **2** N-COUNT A **representative** is a person whose job is to sell a company's products or services, especially by traveling around and visiting other companies. 销售代理 [FORMAL] ❑ *She had a stressful job as a sales representative.* 作为一名销售代理，她的工作压力很大。 **3** N-COUNT In the United States, a **representative** is a member of the House of Representatives, the less powerful of the two parts of Congress. 众议院议员 ❑ *...a Republican representative from Wyoming.* ···一位来自怀俄明州的共和党众议员。 **4** ADJ A **representative** group consists of a small number of people who have been chosen to make decisions on behalf of a larger group. 代表制的; 代议制的 [ADJ n] ❑ *The new head of state should be chosen by an 87-member representative council.* 新的国家元首应该由87人组成的代表委员会选出。 **5** ADJ Someone who is typical of the group to which they belong can be described as **representative**. 有代表性的 ❑ *He was in no way representative of dog trainers in general.* 他绝不能代表大多数的驯狗师。 **6** → see also **House of Representatives**

re·press /rɪprɛs/ (**represses, repressing, repressed**) **1** V-T If you **repress** a feeling, you make a deliberate effort not to show or have this feeling. 抑制 (感情) ❑ *It is anger that is repressed that leads to violence and loss of control.* 正是被抑制的愤怒导致暴力和失控。 **2** V-T If you **repress** a smile, sigh, or moan, you try hard not to smile, sigh, or moan. 忍住 (笑、叹气或呻吟) ❑ *He repressed a smile.* 他忍住没有笑。 **3** V-T If a section of society **is repressed**, their freedom is restricted by the people who have authority over them. 镇压; 压制 [DISAPPROVAL] ❑ *...a UN resolution banning him from repressing his people.* ···联合国的一项禁止他镇压人民的决议。

re·pressed /rɪprɛst/ ADJ A **repressed** person is someone who does not allow themselves to have natural feelings and desires, especially sexual ones. (感情、欲望等) 受到压抑的 ❑ *Some have charged that the Puritans were sexually repressed.* 有些人指责说清教徒性欲受到压抑。

★ **re·pres·sion** /rɪprɛʃᵊn/ (**repressions**) **1** N-UNCOUNT **Repression** is the use of force to restrict and control a society or other group of people. 镇压; 压制 [DISAPPROVAL] ❑ *...a society conditioned by violence and repression.* ···处于暴力和压迫中的一个社会。 **2** N-UNCOUNT **Repression** of feelings, especially sexual ones, is a person's unwillingness to allow themselves to have natural feelings and desires. (对感情、欲望等的) 压抑 ❑ *Much of the anger he's felt during his life has stemmed from the repression of his feelings about men.* 他一生中的大多愤怒源于对男人的情感压抑。

★ **re·pres·sive** /rɪprɛsɪv/ ADJ A **repressive** government is one that restricts people's freedom and controls them by using force. (政府) 镇压的; 压迫的 [DISAPPROVAL] ❑ *The military regime in power was unpopular and repressive.* 执政的军事政权不得民心，镇压人民。

re·prieve /rɪpriv/ (**reprieves, reprieving, reprieved**) **1** V-T If someone who has been sentenced in a court **is reprieved**, their punishment is officially delayed or canceled. (被判) 缓刑; 撤销 (刑罚) [no cont] ❑ *Fourteen people, waiting to be hanged for the murder of a former prime minister, have been reprieved.* 因谋杀前总理而等受绞刑的十四个人获得缓刑。 ● N-VAR **Reprieve** is also a noun. 缓刑; (刑罚) 撤销 ❑ *A man awaiting death by lethal injection has been saved by a last-minute reprieve.* 一名等待被注射处死的男子因为最后一刻的缓刑而获救。 **2** N-COUNT A **reprieve** is a delay before a very unpleasant or difficult situation which may or may not take place. 暂缓; 暂缓令 ❑ *It looked as though the college would have to shut, but this week it was given a reprieve.* 看上去这所学院将不得不关闭，但本周却收到了暂缓令。

rep·ri·mand /rɛprɪmænd/ (**reprimands, reprimanding, reprimanded**) V-T If someone **is reprimanded**, they are spoken to angrily or seriously for doing something wrong, usually by a person in authority. 训斥; 谴责 [FORMAL] ❑ *He was reprimanded by a teacher for talking in the corridor.* 他因在走廊里说话而被一位老师训斥。 ● N-VAR **Reprimand** is also a noun. 训斥; 谴责 ❑ *He has been fined five thousand dollars and given a severe reprimand.* 他被罚款5000美元，并且受到严厉的训斥。

re·print (**reprints, reprinting, reprinted**)

The verb is pronounced /riprɪnt/. The noun is pronounced /riprɪnt/.

动词读作 /riprɪnt/。名词读作 /riprɪnt/。

1 V-T If a book **is reprinted**, further copies of it are printed when all the other ones have been sold. 重印; 再版 [usu passive] ❑ *It remained an exceptionally rare book until it was reprinted in 1918.* 在1918年再版之前，这本书一直非常罕见。 **2** N-COUNT A **reprint** is a process in which new copies of a book or article are printed because all the other ones have been sold. 重印; 再版 ❑ *Demand picked up and a reprint was required last November.* 因需求量上升，去年11月要求重印。 **3** N-COUNT A **reprint** is a new copy of a book or article, printed because all the other ones have been sold or because minor changes have been made to the original. 重印本; 再版本 ❑ *...a reprint of a 1962 novel.* ···一部1962年小说的重印本。

▲ **re·pris·al** /rɪpraɪzᵊl/ (**reprisals**) N-VAR If you do something to a person **in reprisal**, you hurt or punish them because they have done something violent or unpleasant to you. 报复 ❑ *There were fears that some of the Western hostages might be killed in reprisal.* 有人担心，一些西方人质可能会被报复杀害。

★ **re·proach** /rɪproʊtʃ/ (**reproaches, reproaching, reproached**) **1** V-T If you **reproach** someone, you say or show that you are disappointed, upset, or angry because they have done something wrong. 责备；指责 ❑ *She is quick to reproach anyone who doesn't live up to her own high standards.* 她动不动就指责达不到她高标准的人。 **2** N-VAR If you look at or speak to someone with **reproach**, you show or say that you are disappointed, upset, or angry because they have done something wrong. 责备；指责 ❑ *He looked at her with reproach.* 他用责备的目光看着她。 **3** V-T If you **reproach yourself**, you think with regret about something you have done wrong. 责备(自己) ❑ *You've no reason to reproach yourself, no reason to feel shame.* 你没有理由责备自己，也没有理由感到羞愧。

re·pro·duce /riprədus/ (**reproduces, reproducing, reproduced**) **1** V-T If you try to **reproduce** something, you try to copy it. 复制；再造 ❑ *The effect has proved hard to reproduce.* 这种效果经证实很难再造。 **2** V-T If you **reproduce** a picture, speech, or piece of writing, you make a photograph or printed copy of it. 复制；复印 ❑ *We are grateful to you for permission to reproduce this article.* 我们很感激您允许我们复印这篇文章。 **3** V-T If you **reproduce** an action or an achievement, you repeat it. 重演 ❑ *If we can reproduce the form we have shown in the last couple of months we will be successful.* 如果我们能够重演上两个月表现出来的状态，我们就会成功。 **4** V-T/V-I When people, animals, or plants **reproduce**, they produce young. 生育；繁殖 ❑ *...a society where women are defined by their ability to reproduce.* …一个以生育能力来定位妇女角色的社会。 ❑ *We are reproducing ourselves at such a rate that our numbers threaten the ecology of the planet.* 我们繁衍得如此之快，以至于人口数量威胁到地球的生态系统。 ● **re·pro·duc·tion** /riprədʌkʃən/ N-UNCOUNT 生育；繁殖 ❑ *Treatments using assisted reproduction techniques jumped 30 percent.* 使用辅助技术的生育疗法猛增了30%。

re·pro·duc·tion /riprədʌkʃən/ (**reproductions**) **1** N-COUNT A **reproduction** is a copy of something such as a piece of furniture or a work of art. (家具或艺术品的) 复制品 ❑ *...a reproduction of a popular religious painting.* …一幅通俗宗教画的复制品。 **2** → see also **reproduce**

→ see **flower**

re·pro·duc·tive /riprədʌktɪv/ ADJ **Reproductive** processes and organs are concerned with the reproduction of living things. 生殖的；繁殖的 ❑ *...the female reproductive system.* …雌性生殖系统。

▲ **rep·tile** /rɛptaɪl, -tɪl/ (**reptiles**) N-COUNT **Reptiles** are a group of cold-blooded animals which lay eggs and have skins covered with small, hard plates called scales. Snakes, lizards, and crocodiles are reptiles. 爬行动物

→ see **pet**

re·pub·lic ♦♦◇ /rɪpʌblɪk/ (**republics**) N-COUNT A **republic** is a country where power is held by the people or the representatives that they elect. Republics have presidents who are elected, rather than kings or queens. 共和国 ❑ *In 1918, Austria became a republic.* 1918年奥地利成为共和国。 ❑ *...the Baltic republics.* …波罗的海各共和国。

re·pub·li·can ♦♦◇ /rɪpʌblɪkən/ (**republicans**) **1** ADJ **Republican** means relating to a republic. In **republican** systems of government, power is held by the people or the representatives that they elect. 共和的 ❑ *...the nations that had adopted the republican form of government.* …采用了共和制政体的国家。 **2** ADJ If someone is **Republican**, they belong to or support the Republican Party. 共和党的 ❑ *Lower taxes made Republican voters happier with their party.* 更低的税率使共和党选民对该党更加满意。 ● N-COUNT A **Republican** is someone who supports or belongs to the Republican Party. 共和党人 ❑ *What made you decide to become a Republican, as opposed to a Democrat?* 是什么使你决定成为共和党人，而不是民主党人呢？

re·pu·di·ate /rɪpyudieɪt/ (**repudiates, repudiating, repudiated**) V-T If you **repudiate** something or someone, you show that you strongly disagree with them and do not want to be connected with them in any way. 批判 [FORMAL OR WRITTEN] ❑ *Leaders urged people to turn out in large numbers to repudiate the violence.* 领导们力劝人们集体出面来声讨该暴力。 ● **re·pu·dia·tion** /rɪpyudieɪʃən/ N-VAR (**repudiations**) 批判 ❑ *He believes his public repudiation of the conference decision will enhance his standing as a leader.* 他认为他对大会决议的公开批判将提高他作为一名领导的声望。

re·pul·sive /rɪpʌlsɪv/ ADJ If you describe something or someone as **repulsive**, you mean that they are horrible and disgusting and you want to avoid them. 令人厌恶的 ❑ *...repulsive, fat, white slugs.* …令人讨厌的、肥胖的白色蛞蝓。

repu·table /rɛpyətəbəl/ ADJ A **reputable** company or person is reliable and can be trusted. 声誉好的 ❑ *You are well advised to buy your car through a reputable dealer.* 你通过一个声誉好的经销商来买车是明智的。

repu·ta·tion ♦◇◇ /rɛpyəteɪʃən/ (**reputations**) **1** N-COUNT To have a **reputation for** something means to be known or remembered for it. 名声 ❑ *Alice Munro has a reputation for being a very depressing writer.* 艾丽斯·门罗有文风抑郁的名声。 **2** N-COUNT Something's or someone's **reputation** is the opinion that people have about how good they are. If they have a good reputation, people think they are good. 声誉 ❑ *This college has a good academic reputation.* 这所大学拥有良好的学术声誉。 **3** PHRASE If you know someone **by reputation**, you have never met them but you have heard of their reputation. 久闻 ❑ *She was by reputation a good organizer.* 久闻她是个出色的组织者。

Word Partnership *reputation* 的常用搭配：

V. **acquire a** reputation, **build a** reputation, **damage** ***someone's*** reputation, **earn a** reputation, **establish a** reputation, **gain a** reputation, **have a** reputation, **ruin** ***someone's*** reputation, **tarnish** ***someone's*** reputation **1** **2**

ADJ. **bad** reputation, **good** reputation **2**

re·put·ed /rɪpyutɪd/ V-T PASSIVE If you say that something **is reputed to** be true, you mean that people say it is true, but you do not know if it is definitely true. 据说 [FORMAL, VAGUENESS] ❑ *He was reputed to be a fine cook.* 他据说是个好厨师。 ● **re·put·ed·ly** /rɪpyutɪdli/ ADV 据说地 ❑ *He reputedly earns two million dollars a year.* 他据说一年赚200万美元。

re·quest ♦♦◇ /rɪkwɛst/ (**requests, requesting, requested**) **1** V-T If you **request** something, you ask for it politely or formally. 请求；正式要求 [FORMAL] ❑ *Mr. Dennis said he had requested access to a telephone.* 丹尼斯先生说他已正式要求要能够使用一部电话。 **2** V-T If you **request** someone **to** do something, you politely or formally ask them to do it. 要求 [FORMAL] ❑ *Students are requested to park at the rear of the building.* 学生们被要求在那座楼后面停车。 **3** N-COUNT If you make a **request**, you politely or formally ask someone to do something. 请求 ❑ *France had agreed to his request for political asylum.* 法国已经同意了他政治避难的请求。 **4** PHRASE If you do something **at** someone's **request**, you do it because they have asked you to. 应某人的要求 ❑ *The evacuation is being organized at the request of the United Nations Secretary General.* 应联合国秘书长的要求，该撤离正在进行中。 **5** PHRASE If something is given or done **on request**, it is given or done whenever you ask for it. 应要求 ❑ *Details are available on request.* 详情备索。

Word Partnership *request* 的常用搭配：

N. request **aid**, request **a hearing**, request **information**, request **permission**, request **a response** **1**

V. **agree to a** request, **consider a** request, **deny a** request, **grant a** request, **make a** request, **refuse a** request, **reject a** request, **respond to a** request, **send a** request, **submit a** request **3**

re·quire ♦♦◇ /rɪkwaɪər/ (**requires, requiring, required**) **1** V-T If you **require** something or if something **is required**, you need it or it is necessary. 需要 [FORMAL] ❑ *If you require further information, you should consult the registrar.* 如果你需要进一步的信息，你应该向注册主任咨询。 ❑ *This isn't the kind of crisis that requires us to drop everything else.* 这不是需要我们抛下其他一切的那种危机。 **2** V-T If a law or rule **requires** you **to** do something, you have to do it. 要求 [FORMAL] ❑ *The rules also require employers to provide safety training.* 这些规定也要求雇主们提供安全训练。 ❑ *At least 35 manufacturers have flouted a law requiring prompt reporting of such malfunctions.* 至少有三十五位制造商已经对要求即刻汇报这类故障的规定嗤之以鼻了。

re·quire·ment ♦◇◇ /rɪkwaɪərmənt/ (**requirements**) **1** N-COUNT A **requirement** is a quality or qualification that you must have in order to be allowed to do something or to be suitable for something. 必备条件 ❑ *Its products met all legal requirements.* 它的产品满足了所有法定的必备条件。 **2** N-COUNT Your **requirements** are the things that you need. 需要；必需品 [FORMAL] ❑ *Variations of this program can be arranged to suit your requirements.* 这个软件可以被设置成各种各样的形式以适应你们的需要。

Word Partnership *requirement* 的常用搭配:

ADJ. **legal** requirement, **minimum** requirement 1
V. **meet a** requirement 1

requi·site /rɛkwɪzɪt/ (**requisites**) 1 ADJ You can use **requisite** to indicate that something is necessary for a particular purpose. 必要的 [FORMAL] ❑ *She filled in the requisite paperwork.* 她填写了必要的文件。 2 N-COUNT A **requisite** is something that is necessary for a particular purpose. 必需品 [FORMAL] ❑ *An understanding of accounting techniques is a requisite for the work of the analysts.* 对核算技术的理解对于分析师的工作是必需的。

re·sale /riseɪl/ N-UNCOUNT The **resale** price of something that you own is the amount of money that you would get if you sold it. 转卖 ❑ *...a well-maintained used car with a good resale value.* …一部维护良好的、可以转卖个好价钱的旧车。

re·sched·ule /riʃɛdʒul, -dʒuəl/ (**reschedules, rescheduling, rescheduled**) 1 V-T If someone **reschedules** an event, they change the time at which it is supposed to happen. 重订…的时间表 ❑ *Since I'll be away, I'd like to reschedule the meeting.* 既然我将要离开，我想重新安排一下这次会议的时间。 2 V-T To **reschedule** a debt means to arrange for the person, organization, or country that owes money to pay it back over a longer period because they are in financial difficulty. 安排缓期偿还 ❑ *...companies that have gone bust or had to reschedule their debts.* …已经破产的或者不得不安排缓期还债的公司。

res·cue ♦◇◇ /rɛskyu/ (**rescues, rescuing, rescued**) 1 V-T If you **rescue** someone, you get them out of a dangerous or unpleasant situation. 营救 ❑ *Helicopters rescued nearly 20 people from the roof of the burning building.* 直升机从着火的楼顶救出来了将近二十个人。 ●**res·cu·er** ★ N-COUNT (**rescuers**) 救援者 ❑ *It took rescuers 90 minutes to reach the trapped men.* 救援者们花了90分钟才来到那些被困的男子身边。 2 N-UNCOUNT **Rescue** is help which gets someone out of a dangerous or unpleasant situation. 营救 ❑ *A big rescue operation has been launched for a trawler missing in the North Atlantic.* 为了一艘在北大西洋失踪的拖网渔船，已经开始了一项大的营救行动。 3 N-COUNT A **rescue** is an attempt to save someone from a dangerous or unpleasant situation. 营救行动 ❑ *A major air-sea rescue is under way.* 一项重要的海空营救行动正在进行中。 4 PHRASE If you **go to** someone's **rescue** or **come to** their **rescue**, you help them when they are in danger or difficulty. 营救某人 ❑ *The 23-year-old's screams alerted a passerby who went to her rescue.* 那名23岁女孩的尖叫声引起了一个过路人的警觉，他救了她。

Word Partnership *rescue* 的常用搭配:

N. **firefighters** rescue, rescue **a hostage**, rescue **miners**, rescue **people**, **police** rescue, **volunteers** rescue, rescue **wildlife** 1
rescue **attempt**, rescue **crews**, rescue **effort**, rescue **mission**, rescue **operation**, rescue **teams**, rescue **workers** 2

re·search ♦♦♦ /rɪsɜrtʃ, risɜrtʃ/ (**researches, researching, researched**) 1 N-UNCOUNT **Research** is work that involves studying something and trying to discover facts about it. 研究 [also N in pl] ❑ *Sixty-five percent of the 1987 budget went for nuclear weapons research and production.* 1987年预算的65%用在了核武器的研制上。 2 V-T If you **research** something, you try to discover facts about it. 研究 ❑ *She spent two years in South Florida researching and filming her documentary.* 她在南佛罗里达花了两年的时间研究和拍摄纪录片。 ●**re·search·er** N-COUNT (**researchers**) 研究员 ❑ *He chose to join the company as a market researcher.* 他选择加入这家公司当一名市场研究员。 → see **hospital, inventor, laboratory, medicine, science, zoo**

Word Partnership *research* 的常用搭配:

N. **animal** research, **cancer** research, research **and development**, research **facility**, research **findings**, **laboratory** research, research **methods**, research **paper**, research **project**, research **report**, research **results**, research **scientist** 1
ADJ. **biological** research, **clinical** research, **current** research, **experimental** research, **medical** research, **recent** research, **scientific** research 1

re·sell /risɛl/ (**resells, reselling, resold**) V-T/V-I If you **resell** something that you have bought, you sell it again. 转卖 ❑ *Storekeepers buy them in bulk and resell them for $150 each.* 店主大批买进这些，又以每件$150的价格转卖出去。 ❑ *It makes sense to buy at dealer prices so you can maximize your profits if you resell.* 以批发价格买进是有道理的，如果你再转卖就可以最大化你的利润。

★ **re·sem·blance** /rɪzɛmbləns/ (**resemblances**) N-VAR If there is a **resemblance** between two people or things, they are similar to each other. 相似之处 ❑ *There was a remarkable resemblance between him and Pete.* 他和皮特有一个惊人的相似之处。

re·sem·ble /rɪzɛmbᵊl/ (**resembles, resembling, resembled**) V-T If one thing or person **resembles** another, they are similar to each other. 像 [no cont] ❑ *Some of the commercially produced venison resembles beef in flavor.* 一些商业化生产的鹿肉味道像牛肉。

re·sent /rɪzɛnt/ (**resents, resenting, resented**) V-T If you **resent** someone or something, you feel bitter and angry about them. 憎恨 ❑ *She resents her mother for being so tough on her.* 她恨她的妈妈对她如此苛刻。

re·sent·ful /rɪzɛntfəl/ ADJ If you are **resentful**, you feel resentment. 怨恨的 ❑ *At first I felt very resentful and angry about losing my job.* 起初，我对丢掉工作感到非常怨恨和恼怒。

★ **re·sent·ment** /rɪzɛntmənt/ (**resentments**) N-UNCOUNT **Resentment** is bitterness and anger that someone feels about something. 怨恨 [also N in pl] ❑ *She expressed resentment at being interviewed by a social worker.* 她对于被一个社会工作者面试表示了怨恨。

res·er·va·tion /rɛzərveɪʃᵊn/ (**reservations**) 1 N-VAR If you have **reservations about** something, you are not sure that it is entirely good or right. 保留意见 ❑ *I told him my main reservation about his film was the ending.* 我告诉了他我主要对他电影的结局有所保留。 2 N-COUNT If you make a **reservation**, you arrange for something such as a table in a restaurant or a room in a hotel to be kept for you. 预订 ❑ *He went to the desk to inquire and make a reservation.* 他到前台去咨询并做了预订。 3 N-COUNT A **reservation** is an area of land that is kept separate for a particular group of people to live in. 保留地 ❑ *Seventeen thousand Indians live in Arizona on a reservation.* 17000名印第安人居住在亚利桑那州的保留地内。 → see **hotel**

re·serve ♦♦◇ /rɪzɜrv/ (**reserves, reserving, reserved**) 1 V-T If something **is reserved for** a particular person or purpose, it is kept specially for that person or purpose. 预留 [usu passive] ❑ *A double room with a balcony overlooking the sea had been reserved for him.* 一个带一座阳台的海景双人间已被预留给他了。 2 V-T If you **reserve** something such as a table, ticket, or magazine, you arrange for it to be kept specially for you, rather than sold or given to someone else. 预订 ❑ *I'll reserve a table for five.* 我要预订一个5人的餐位。 3 N-COUNT A **reserve** is a supply of something that is available for use when it is needed. 储备 ❑ *The Persian Gulf has 65 percent of the world's oil reserves.* 波斯湾拥有全世界石油储备的65%。 4 N-COUNT A nature **reserve** is an area of land where the animals, birds, and plants are officially protected. 保护区 [mainly BRIT]
in AM, use **preserve**
5 N-UNCOUNT If someone shows **reserve**, they keep their feelings hidden. 矜持 ❑ *I hope that you'll overcome your reserve and let me know.* 我希望你能克服矜持，让我知道。 6 PHRASE If you have something **in reserve**, you have it available for use when it is needed. 保留备用 ❑ *He poked around the top of his cabinet for the bottle of whiskey that he kept in reserve.* 他在壁橱的上面翻找他留的那瓶威士忌。 7 **to reserve judgment** → see **judgment** 8 **to reserve the right** → see **right**

Thesaurus *reserve* 另参见:

V. hold, save, set aside 1 2
N. stock, store, supply 3

re·served /rɪzɜrvd/ 1 ADJ Someone who is **reserved** keeps their feelings hidden. 矜持的 ❑ *He was unemotional, quiet, and reserved.* 他不动感情、安静而矜持。 2 ADJ A table in a restaurant or a seat in a theater that is **reserved** is being kept for someone rather than given or sold to anyone else. 预订的 ❑ *Seats, or sometimes entire tables, were reserved.* 座位，有时候全部的桌子，都被预订了。

res·er·voir /rɛzərvwɑr/ (**reservoirs**) 1 N-COUNT A **reservoir** is a lake that is used for storing water before it is supplied to people. 水库 2 N-COUNT A **reservoir of** something is a large quantity of it that is available for use when needed. 大量储备 ❑ *...the huge oil reservoir beneath the Kuwaiti desert.* …科威特沙漠下面大量的石油储备。 → see **dam**

★ **re·shuf·fle** /riʃʌfᵊl/ (**reshuffles, reshuffling, reshuffled**) V-T When a political leader **reshuffles** the ministers in a government, he or she changes their jobs so that some of the ministers change their responsibilities. 改组 [mainly BRIT] ❑ *The prime minister told reporters this morning that he plans to reshuffle his entire cabinet.* 首相今晨告诉记者们他计划改组全体内阁。● N-COUNT **Reshuffle** is also a noun. 改组 [usu sing, with supp] ❑ *He has carried out a partial cabinet reshuffle.* 他对内阁进行了一次部分改组。

Word Link *sid ≈ sitting : preside, president, reside*

★ **re·side** /rɪzaɪd/ (**resides, residing, resided**) **1** V-I If someone **resides** somewhere, they live there or are staying there. 居住 [FORMAL] ❑ *Margaret resides with her invalid mother in a Seattle suburb.* 玛格丽特和她有病的妈妈住在西雅图郊区。 **2** V-I If a quality **resides in** something, the thing has that quality. 存在 [no cont] [FORMAL] ❑ *Happiness does not reside in strength or money.* 幸福不存在于力量或金钱之中。

resi·dence /rɛzɪdəns/ (**residences**) **1** N-COUNT A **residence** is a house where people live. 住宅 [FORMAL] ❑ *The house is currently run as a country inn, but could easily convert back into a private residence.* 这栋房子目前被当作一家乡村客栈用，但可以容易地改回成一所私用住宅。 **2** N-UNCOUNT Your place of **residence** is the place where you live. 住所 [FORMAL] ❑ *There were significant differences among women based on age, place of residence, and educational levels.* 基于年龄、住处和教育水平，妇女们之间存在显著的差异。 **3** N-UNCOUNT Someone's **residence** in a particular place is the fact that they live there or that they are officially allowed to live there. 居住 ❑ *They had entered the country and had applied for permanent residence.* 他们已进入了那个国家，并已经申请了永久居住权。 **4** → see also **residence hall** **5** PHRASE If someone is **in residence** in a particular place, they are living there. 住在(某处) ❑ *The king and queen of Jordan are in residence.* 约旦的国王和王后住在宫邸。

resi·dence hall (**residence halls**) N-COUNT **Residence halls** are buildings with rooms or apartments, usually built by universities or colleges, in which students live during the school year. 学生宿舍楼 [AM]

in BRIT, use **hall of residence**

❑ *A freshman adviser lives in each residence hall.* 每栋学生宿舍楼里住着一位新生指导老师。

Word Link *ent ≈ one who does, has : dependent, resident, superintendent*

resi·dent ♦♦◇ /rɛzɪdənt/ (**residents**) **1** N-COUNT The **residents** of a house or area are the people who live there. 居民 ❑ *The archbishop called on the government to build more low cost homes for local residents.* 这位大主教呼吁该政府为当地居民建更多的廉价住宅。 **2** ADJ Someone who is **resident in** a country or a town lives there. 居住的 [v-link ADJ] ❑ *He moved to the United States in 1990 to live with his son, who had been resident in Baltimore since 1967.* 他1990年移居美国去和从1967年就住在巴尔的摩的儿子一起住。 **3** N-COUNT A **resident** or a **resident** doctor is a doctor who is receiving a period of specialized training in a hospital after completing his or her internship. 住院医师 [AM] ❑ *Many resident doctors complain that they are assigned too many duties that are usually not performed by physicians.* 很多住院医师抱怨他们被指派了太多通常不由内科医生完成的职责。
→ see **country, hospital**

★ **resi·den·tial** /rɛzɪdɛnʃᵊl/ **1** ADJ A **residential** area contains houses rather than offices or factories. 住宅的 ❑ *...a posh residential area 20 minutes from the White House.* …距离白宫20分钟路程的一个豪华住宅区。 **2** ADJ A **residential** institution is one where people live while they are studying there or being cared for there. 寄宿制的 ❑ *Training involves a two-year residential course.* 培训包括两年的住校课程。

re·sid·ual /rɪzɪdʒuəl/ ADJ **Residual** is used to describe what remains of something when most of it has gone. 残留的 ❑ *...residual radiation from nuclear weapons testing.* …来自核武器试验的残留放射物。

▲ **resi·due** /rɛzɪdu, -dyu/ (**residues**) N-COUNT A **residue** of something is a small amount that remains after most of it has gone. 残留物 ❑ *Always using the same shampoo means that a residue can build up on the hair.* 总是用同一种洗发水意味着残留物会在头发上越积越多。

re·sign ♦◇◇ /rɪzaɪn/ (**resigns, resigning, resigned**) **1** V-T/V-I If you **resign** from a job or position, you formally announce that you are leaving it. 辞职 ❑ *A hospital administrator has resigned over claims he lied to get the job.* 一位医院主管因为有人声称他的职位是骗来的而辞职了。 ❑ *Mr Robb resigned his position last month.* 罗布先生上个月辞去了他的职位。 **2** V-T If you **resign yourself to** an unpleasant situation or fact, you accept it because you realize that you cannot change it. 使屈从 ❑ *Pat and I resigned ourselves to yet another summer without a boat.* 帕特和我将就着又过了一个没有船的夏天。 **3** → see also **resigned**

Do not confuse **resign** and **retire**. If someone **resigns** from their job, they leave it after saying that they do not want to do it any more. ❑ *He hasn't decided whether he will resign.* You can **resign** from your job at any age, and perhaps start another job soon afterward. When someone **retires**, they leave their job and stop working, often because they have reached the age when they can get a pension. ❑ *He had been planning for some time to retire at around age 60.* When professional athletes stop playing sport as their job, you can also say that they **retire**, even if they are fairly young ❑ *A heart attack at the age of 36 forced him to retire from tennis.*

Thesaurus *resign* 另参见：
V. leave, quit, step down **1**

★ **res·ig·na·tion** ♦◇◇ /rɛzɪgneɪʃᵊn/ (**resignations**) **1** N-VAR Your **resignation** is a formal statement of your intention to leave a job or position. 辞呈 ❑ *Bob Morgan has offered his resignation and it has been accepted.* 鲍勃·摩根已递交了辞呈，并且已被批准了。 **2** N-UNCOUNT **Resignation** is the acceptance of an unpleasant situation or fact because you realize that you cannot change it. 无奈的顺从 ❑ *He sighed with profound resignation.* 他极度无奈地叹气。

re·signed /rɪzaɪnd/ ADJ If you are **resigned to** an unpleasant situation or fact, you accept it without complaining because you realize that you cannot change it. 逆来顺受的 ❑ *He is resigned to the noise, the mess, the constant upheaval.* 他对噪音、杂乱和持续动荡逆来顺受。

re·sili·ent /rɪzɪlyənt/ **1** ADJ Something that is **resilient** is strong and not easily damaged by being hit, stretched, or squeezed. 有弹性的 ❑ *...an armchair of some resilient plastic material.* …一把由某种弹性塑料制成的扶手椅。● **re·sili·ence** N-UNCOUNT 弹性 [also "a" N] ❑ *Do you feel that your muscles do not have the strength and resilience that they should have?* 你觉得你的肌肉不具备它应有的力量和弹性了吗？ **2** ADJ People and things that are **resilient** are able to recover easily and quickly from unpleasant or damaging events. 立即复原的 ❑ *When the U.S. stock market collapsed in October 1987, the Japanese stock market was the most resilient.* 当美国股市在1987年10月崩盘时，日本股市是最快复苏的。● **re·sili·ence** N-UNCOUNT 复原能力 [also "a" N] ❑ *...the resilience of human beings to fight after they've been attacked.* …人类遭受袭击后进行抵抗的复原能力。

res·in /rɛzɪn/ (**resins**) **1** N-MASS **Resin** is a sticky substance that is produced by some trees. 树脂 ❑ *...a tropical tree that is bled regularly for its resin.* …定期被采割树脂的一棵热带树。 **2** N-MASS **Resin** is a substance that is produced chemically and used to make plastics. 合成树脂 ❑ *The plastic resin is used in a wide range of products, including electrical wire insulation.* 塑料合成树脂被广泛应用到各种产品中，包括电线的绝缘层。

re·sist ♦◇◇ /rɪzɪst/ (**resists, resisting, resisted**) **1** V-T If you **resist** something such as a change, you refuse to accept it and try to prevent it. 抵制 ❑ *They resisted our attempts to modernize the distribution of books.* 他们抵制我们将书籍发行现代化的努力。 **2** V-T/V-I If you **resist** someone or **resist** an attack by them, you fight back against them. 反抗 ❑ *The man was shot outside his house as he tried to resist arrest.* 那个男人因为试图拒捕在他住宅外被击中。 ❑ *When she attempted to cut his nails he resisted.* 当她试图给他剪指甲时，他反抗了。 **3** V-T If you **resist** doing something, or **resist** the temptation to do it, you stop yourself from doing it although you would like to do it. 抗拒 [oft with neg] ❑ *Congress should resist the temptation to try quick economic fixes.* 国会应该抗拒尝试快速经济调整的诱惑。 **4** V-T If someone or something **resists** damage of some kind, they are not damaged. 抵抗住 ❑ *...bodies trained and toughened to resist the cold.* …经过锻炼和强化能抵抗寒冷的身体。

Word Link *ance ≈ quality, state : defiance, performance, resistance*

re·sist·ance ♦◇◇ /rɪzɪstəns/ (**resistances**) **1** N-UNCOUNT **Resistance** to something such as a change or a new idea is a refusal to accept it. 抵制 ❑ *The U.S. wants big cuts in European* *agricultural export subsidies, but this is meeting resistance.* 美国想要在欧洲农业出口补贴上的大幅度削减，但这正遭遇抵制。 2 N-UNCOUNT **Resistance** to an attack consists of fighting back against the people who have attacked you. 抵抗 ❑ *A CBS correspondent in Colombo says the troops are encountering stiff resistance.* 哥伦比亚广播公司驻科伦坡的一名记者报道说，军队正遭遇顽强的抵抗。 3 N-UNCOUNT The **resistance** of your body **to** germs or diseases is its power to remain unharmed or unaffected by them. 抵抗力；免疫力 ❑ *This disease is surprisingly difficult to catch, as most people have a natural resistance to it.* 这种病令人惊讶的难以患上，因为大多数人对它有一种先天的免疫力。 4 N-UNCOUNT Wind or air **resistance** is a force which slows down a moving object or vehicle. 阻力 ❑ *The design of the bicycle reduces the effects of wind resistance and drag.* 这种自行车的设计减少了风阻及曳力的影响。 5 N-VAR In electrical engineering or physics, **resistance** is the ability of a substance or an electrical circuit to stop the flow of an electrical current through it. 电阻 ❑ *The salt reduces the electrical resistance of the water.* 盐使水的电阻减小。

→ see **bicycle, flight**

re·sist·ant /rɪzɪstənt/ 1 ADJ Someone who is **resistant to** something is opposed to it and wants to prevent it. 抵制的 ❑ *Some people are very resistant to the idea of exercise.* 一些人对锻炼的主意非常抵制。 2 ADJ If something is **resistant to** a particular thing, it is not harmed by it. 有抵抗力的 ❑ *...how to improve plants to make them more resistant to disease.* …如何改良植物来使它们对疾病更有抵抗力。

re·skill /riskɪl/ (**reskills, reskilling, reskilled**) V-T/V-I If you **reskill**, or if someone **reskills** you, you learn new skills, so that you can do a different job or do your old job in a different way. 再培训 [BRIT, BUSINESS]

in AM, use **retrain**

reso·lute /rɛzəlut/ ADJ If you describe someone as **resolute**, you approve of them because they are very determined not to change their mind or not to give up a course of action. 坚定的 [FORMAL] ❑ *Voters perceive him as a decisive and resolute international leader.* 选民认识到他是一位果断、坚定的国际领袖。 ● **reso·lute·ly** ADV 坚定地 ❑ *He resolutely refused to speak English unless forced to.* 除非被逼迫，他坚决拒绝说英语。

reso·lu·tion ♦♦◊ /rɛzəluʃᵊn/ (**resolutions**) 1 N-COUNT A **resolution** is a formal decision made at a meeting by means of a vote. 决议 ❑ *He replied that the UN had passed two major resolutions calling for a complete withdrawal.* 他回复说联合国已经通过要求完全撤军的两项重大决议。 2 N-COUNT If you make a **resolution**, you decide to try very hard to do something. 决心 ❑ *They made a resolution to lose all the weight gained during the Christmas holidays.* 他们下了一个决心要减掉圣诞节期间增加的全部体重。 3 N-UNCOUNT **Resolution** is determination to do something or not do something. 决心 ❑ *"I think I'll try a hypnotist," I said with sudden resolution.* "我想我要找个催眠师试试，"我突然坚决地说。 4 N-SING The **resolution** of a problem or difficulty is the final solving of it. 最终解决 [FORMAL] ❑ *...the successful resolution of a dispute involving UN inspectors in Baghdad.* …对涉及联合国驻巴格达调查员的一项争议的成功解决。

re·solve ♦◊◊ /rɪzɒlv/ (**resolves, resolving, resolved**) 1 V-T To **resolve** a problem, argument, or difficulty means to find a solution to it. 解决 [FORMAL] ❑ *We must find a way to resolve these problems before it's too late.* 我们必须找到一个办法去解决这些问题，不然就太晚了。 2 V-T If you **resolve to** do something, you make a firm decision to do it. 下决心 [FORMAL] ❑ *She resolved to report the matter to the hospital's nursing supervisor.* 她决心把这件事向该医院的护士长汇报。 3 N-VAR **Resolve** is determination to do what you have decided to do. 决心 [FORMAL] ❑ *So you're saying this will strengthen the American public's resolve to go to war if necessary?* 那么你是说，这将会坚定美国公众在必要时参战的决心？

re·solved /rɪzɒlvd/ ADJ If you are **resolved to** do something, you are determined to do it. 坚决的 [v-link ADJ to-inf] [FORMAL] ❑ *Most people with property to lose were resolved to defend it.* 大多数有财产的人都坚决地捍卫它。

▲ **reso·nance** /rɛzənəns/ (**resonances**) 1 N-VAR If something has a **resonance for** someone, it has a special meaning or is particularly important to them. 共鸣 ❑ *The ideas of order, security, family, religion and country had the same resonance for them as for Michael.* 秩序、安全、家庭、宗教和国家这些概念在他们心里产生了和迈克尔一样的共鸣。 2 N-UNCOUNT If a sound has **resonance**, it is deep, clear, and strong. 洪亮 ❑ *His voice had lost its resonance; it was tense and strained.* 他的声音失去了原有的洪亮，紧张而做作。

reso·nant /rɛzənənt/ ADJ A sound that is **resonant** is deep and strong. 洪亮的 ❑ *His voice sounded oddly resonant in the empty room.* 他的声音在空房间里听起来奇特地洪亮。

Word Link son ≈ sound : resonate, sonata, supersonic

reso·nate /rɛzəneɪt/ (**resonates, resonating, resonated**) 1 V-I If something **resonates**, it vibrates and produces a deep, strong sound. 共振 ❑ *The bass guitar began to thump so loudly that it resonated in my head.* 低音吉他开始砰然作响，震得我的脑袋嗡嗡的。 2 V-I You say that something **resonates** when it has a special meaning or when it is particularly important to someone. (对某人)有重要性 ❑ *What are the issues resonating with voters?* 什么是投票者特别关心的问题？

re·sort ♦◊◊ /rɪzɔrt/ (**resorts, resorting, resorted**) 1 V-I If you **resort to** a course of action that you do not really approve of, you adopt it because you cannot see any other way of achieving what you want. 不得不求助 ❑ *His punishing work schedule had made him resort to drugs.* 他那累人的工作日程已经使他不得不求助于毒品了。 2 N-UNCOUNT If you achieve something without **resort to** a particular course of action, you succeed without carrying out that action. To have **resort to** a particular course of action means to have to do that action in order to achieve something. 诉诸 ❑ *Congress has a responsibility to ensure that all peaceful options are exhausted before resort to war.* 国会有责任确保在所有和平的手段用尽之后再诉诸武力。 3 PHRASE If you do something **as a last resort**, you do it because you can find no other way of getting out of a difficult situation or of solving a problem. 作为最后手段 ❑ *Nuclear weapons should be used only as a last resort.* 核武器应该只被用作最后手段。 4 N-COUNT A **resort** is a place where a lot of people spend their vacation. (度假) 胜地 ❑ *The ski resorts are expanding to meet the growing number of skiers that come here.* 该滑雪胜地正在扩建以应付来这里滑雪的不断增长的人数。

re·sound·ing /rɪzaʊndɪŋ/ 1 ADJ A **resounding** sound is loud and clear. 响亮清晰的 ❑ *There was a resounding slap as Andrew struck him violently across the face.* 安德鲁狠狠地打了他一记耳光，声音清晰响亮。 2 ADJ You can refer to a very great success as a **resounding** success. 彻底的 [EMPHASIS] ❑ *The good weather helped to make the occasion a resounding success.* 好天气帮助这次活动获得了彻底的成功。

re·source ♦♦◊ /rɪsɔrs/ (**resources**) 1 N-COUNT The **resources** of an organization or person are the materials, money, and other things that they have and can use in order to function properly. 财力 ❑ *Some families don't have the resources to feed themselves adequately.* 一些家庭没有钱填饱肚子。 2 N-COUNT A country's **resources** are the things that it has and can use to increase its wealth, such as coal, oil, or land. 资源 ❑ *...resources like coal, tungsten, oil, and copper.* …像煤、钨、石油和铜等资源。

★ **re·source·ful** /rɪsɔrsfəl/ ADJ Someone who is **resourceful** is good at finding ways of dealing with problems. 足智多谋的 ❑ *He was amazingly inventive and resourceful, and played a major role in my career.* 他极具创造力又足智多谋，在我的职业生涯中起了重要的作用。 ● **re·source·ful·ness** N-UNCOUNT 足智多谋 ❑ *Because of his adventures, he is a person of far greater experience and resourcefulness.* 由于他的各种冒险经历，他是个在经验和足智多谋上都远胜一筹的人。

re·spect ♦♦◊ /rɪspɛkt/ (**respects, respecting, respected**) 1 V-T If you **respect** someone, you have a good opinion of their character or ideas. 尊重 ❑ *I want him to respect me as a career woman.* 我要他把我作为一个职业女性来尊重。 2 N-UNCOUNT If you have **respect for** someone, you have a good opinion of them. 敬重 ❑ *I have tremendous respect for Dean.* 我非常敬重迪安。 3 → see also **self-respect** 4 V-T If you **respect** someone's wishes, rights, or customs, you avoid doing things that they would dislike or regard as wrong. 尊重 ❑ *Finally, trying to respect her wishes, I said I'd leave.* 最后，设法尊重她的意愿，我说我会离开。 5 N-UNCOUNT If you show **respect for** someone's wishes, rights, or customs, you avoid doing anything they would dislike or regard as wrong. 尊重 ❑ *They will campaign for respect for aboriginal rights and customs.* 他们将开展尊重土著居民权利和风俗的活动。 6 V-T If you **respect** a law or moral principle, you agree not to break it. 遵守 ❑ *It is about time tour operators respected the law and their own code of conduct.* 现在该是旅行社经营者们遵守法律和他们自己的行业规范的时候了。 ● N-UNCOUNT **Respect** is also a noun. 遵守 ❑ *...respect for the law and the rejection of the use of violence.* …对法律的遵守和对使用暴力的摒弃。 7 PHRASE You can say **with all due respect** when you are politely disagreeing with someone or criticizing them. 请恕我冒犯 [POLITENESS]

❑ *With all due respect, I hardly think that's the point.* 请恕我冒犯，我不认为那是要点。 **8** PHRASE If you **pay** your **respects to** someone, you go to see them or speak to them. You usually do this to be polite, and not necessarily because you want to do it. 表示某人的敬意 [FORMAL] ❑ *Carl had asked him to visit the hospital and to pay his respects to Francis.* 卡尔已要求他去那所医院向弗朗西斯表示他的敬意。 **9** PHRASE You use expressions like **in this respect** and **in many respects** to indicate that what you are saying applies to the feature you have just mentioned or to many features of something. 在这方面；在许多方面 ❑ *Within the Department of Justice are several drug-fighting agencies. The lead agency in this respect is the DEA.* 司法部内部有几个禁毒机构，在这方面的领导机构是禁毒执行中心。 **10** PHRASE You use **with respect to** to say what something relates to. 关于；至于 [FORMAL] ❑ *Parents often have little choice with respect to the way their child is medically treated.* 至于他们孩子被医治的方式，父母通常少有选择的余地。 **11** → see also **respected**

Thesaurus *respect* 另参见：

V. admire, esteem **1**

N. consideration, courtesy, esteem **4**

Word Partnership *respect* 的常用搭配：

V. **deserve** respect, **earn** respect, **gain** respect **2**
lack respect **for** ***someone/something***, **show** respect **for** ***someone/something***, **treat** ***someone/something*** **with** respect **2** **5**

N. **lack** of respect **2** **5**
respect ***someone's*** **privacy**, respect ***someone's*** **rights**, respect ***someone's*** **wishes** **4**
respect **the law** **6**

★ **re·spect·able** /rɪspɛktəbəl/ **1** ADJ Someone or something that is **respectable** is approved of by society and considered to be morally correct. 体面的 ❑ *He came from a perfectly respectable middle-class family.* 他来自一个非常体面的中产阶级家庭。 ● **re·spect·abil·ity** /rɪspɛktəbɪlɪti/ N-UNCOUNT 体面 ❑ *If she divorced Tony, she would lose the respectability she had as Mrs. Tony Tatterton.* 如果她和托尼离婚，她将会失去作为托尼·塔特顿太太的体面。 **2** ADJ You can say that something is **respectable** when you mean that it is good enough or acceptable. 可接受的 ❑ *...investments that offer respectable and highly attractive rates of return.* …提供不错的、极具吸引力的回报率的投资。

re·spect·ed /rɪspɛktɪd/ ADJ Someone or something that is **respected** is admired and considered important by many people. 受到广泛尊重的 ❑ *He is highly respected for his novels and plays as well as his translations of American novels.* 他因他的小说、戏剧和美国小说译作而极受敬重。

★ **re·spect·ful** /rɪspɛktfəl/ ADJ If you are **respectful**, you show respect for someone. 恭敬的 ❑ *The children in our family are always respectful to their elders.* 我们家的孩子们总是很尊敬他们的长辈。 ● **re·spect·ful·ly** ADV 恭敬地 ❑ *"You are an artist," she said respectfully.* "您是一位艺术家，"她毕恭毕敬地说。

re·spec·tive /rɪspɛktɪv/ ADJ **Respective** means relating or belonging separately to the individual people you have just mentioned. 各自的 [ADJ n] ❑ *Steve and I were at very different stages in our respective careers.* 史蒂夫和我处在各自事业的迥然不同的阶段。

re·spec·tive·ly /rɪspɛktɪvli/ ADV **Respectively** means in the same order as the items that you have just mentioned. 分别地 [ADV with cl/group] ❑ *Their sons were three and six respectively.* 他们的儿子们分别是3岁和6岁。

Word Link *spir ≈ breath : aspire, inspire, respiratory*

▲ **res·pira·tory** /rɛspərətɔri/ ADJ **Respiratory** means relating to breathing. 呼吸的 [ADJ n] [MEDICAL] ❑ *...people with severe respiratory problems.* …有严重呼吸问题的人们。
→ see Word Web: **respiratory system**

res·pite /rɛspɪt/ **1** N-SING A **respite** is a short period of rest from something unpleasant. (某种不快中的) 小间歇 [also no det, oft N "from" n] [FORMAL] ❑ *It was some weeks now since they'd had any respite from shellfire.* 他们数周在炮火中，中间没任何小的间歇。 **2** N-SING A **respite** is a short delay before a very unpleasant or difficult situation which may or may not take place. 暂缓 [also no det] [FORMAL] ❑ *Devaluation would only give the economy a brief respite.* 货币贬值只会给经济一个短时间的暂缓。

re·spond ♦♦◇ /rɪspɒnd/ (**responds, responding, responded**) **1** V-T/V-I When you **respond** to something that is done or said, you react to it by doing or saying something yourself. 回应 ❑ *They are likely to respond positively to the president's request for aid.* 他们有可能积极地回应该总统的援助请求。 ❑ *The army responded with gunfire and tear gas.* 军方以炮火和催泪弹回应。 ❑ *"I have no idea," she responded.* "我不知道，"她回应道。 **2** V-I When you **respond to** a need, crisis, or challenge, you take the necessary or appropriate action. 应对 ❑ *This modest group size allows our teachers to respond to the needs of each student.* 这个适中的小组规模使得我们的老师们可以应对每个学生的需要。 **3** V-I If a patient or their injury or illness **is responding to** treatment, the treatment is working and they are getting better. 作出反映 ❑ *I'm pleased to say that he is now doing well and responding to treatment.* 我很高兴地说他现在正在顺利恢复，治疗是有效果的。

★ **re·spond·ent** /rɪspɒndənt/ (**respondents**) N-COUNT A **respondent** is a person who replies to something such as a survey or set of questions. 被调查人 [usu pl] ❑ *Sixty percent of the respondents said they disapproved of the president's performance.* 60%的被调查人说他们不赞成总统的表现。

re·sponse ♦♦◇ /rɪspɒns/ (**responses**) N-COUNT Your **response** to an event or to something that is said is your reply or reaction to it. 反应 [oft N "to/from" n, also "in" N] ❑ *There has been no response to his remarks from the government.* 政府方面对他的评论一直没有反应。

Word Partnership *response* 的常用搭配：

ADJ. **correct** response, **enthusiastic** response, **immediate** response, **military** response, **negative/positive** response, **overwhelming** response, **quick** response, **written** response

re·sponse time (**response times**) **1** N-COUNT The **response time** of an emergency service such as the police or the fire department is the length of time it takes them to arrive at an incident such as a crime or a fire after it has been reported to them. 响应时间 ❑ *Kyle says the average 911 response time is about 9.2 minutes.* 凯尔说911的平均响应时间为9.2分钟。 **2** N-COUNT **Response time** is the time taken for a computer to do something after you have given an instruction. 反应时间 [COMPUTING] ❑ *The only flaw is the slightly slow response times when you press the buttons.* 惟一的缺陷就是当你按按钮时稍慢的反应时间。

re·spon·sibil·ity ♦♦◇ /rɪspɒnsɪbɪlɪti/ (**responsibilities**) **1** N-UNCOUNT If you have **responsibility** for something or someone, or if they are your **responsibility**, it is your job or duty to deal with them and to make decisions relating to them. 责任 ❑ *Each manager had responsibility for just under 600 properties.* 每位经理对差一点不到六百处房产负责。 **2** N-UNCOUNT If you accept

Word Web respiratory system

Respiration moves **air** in and out of the **lungs**. Air comes in through the **nose** or **mouth**. Then it travels down the windpipe and into the lungs. In the lungs **oxygen** absorbs into the bloodstream. Blood carries oxygen to the heart and other organs. The lungs also remove **carbon dioxide** from the blood. This gas is then **exhaled** through the mouth. During inhalation the **diaphragm** moves downward and the lungs fill with air. During exhalation the diaphragm relaxes and air flows out. Adult humans **breathe** about six liters of air each minute.

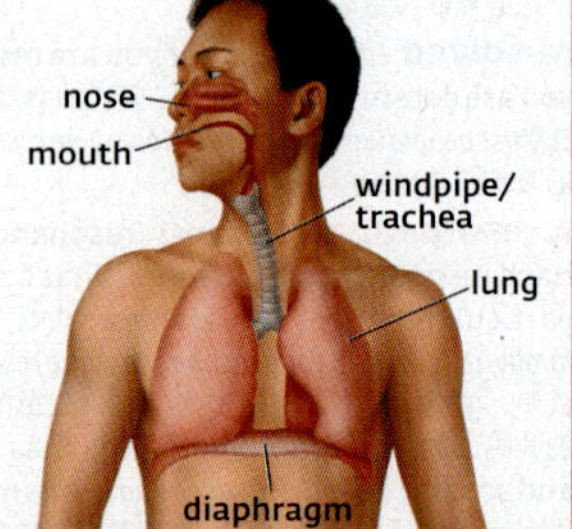

R

responsibility for something that has happened, you agree that you were to blame for it or you caused it. 责任 ❑ *No one admitted responsibility for the attacks.* 没有人对这些袭击负责。 **3** N-PLURAL Your **responsibilities** are the duties that you have because of your job or position. 职责 ❑ *I am told that he handled his responsibilities as a counselor in a highly intelligent and caring fashion.* 我被告知，他以一种高度的智慧和富有同情心的方式对待他作为一名顾问的职责。 **4** N-UNCOUNT If someone is given **responsibility**, they are given the right or opportunity to make important decisions or to take action without having to get permission from anyone else. 职权 ❑ *She would have loved to have a better-paying job with more responsibility.* 她本想有一份薪水更高职权更多的工作。 **5** N-SING If you think that you have a **responsibility to** do something, you feel that you ought to do it because it is morally right to do it. 责任 ❑ *The court feels it has a responsibility to ensure that customers are not misled.* 该法院觉得其有责任确保消费者们不被误导。 **6** N-SING If you think that you have a **responsibility to** someone, you feel that it is your duty to take action that will protect their interests. 义务 ❑ *She had decided that as a doctor she had a responsibility to her fellow creatures.* 她决定作为一名医生她对同胞们负有义务。

Word Partnership *responsibility* 的常用搭配：

V. **assume** responsibility, **bear** responsibility, **share** responsibility, **take** responsibility **1** – **4**
have (a) responsibility **1** **4** – **6**
accept responsibility, **claim** responsibility **2**
be given responsibility **4**
ADJ. **financial** responsibility, **personal** responsibility **1** **4**
moral responsibility **5**

re·spon·sible ♦♦◇ /rɪspɒnsɪbᵊl/ **1** ADJ If someone or something is **responsible for** a particular event or situation, they are the cause of it or they can be blamed for it. 负有责任的 [v-link ADJ] ❑ *He still felt responsible for her death.* 他依然觉得对她的死负有责任。 **2** ADJ If you are **responsible for** something, it is your job or duty to deal with it and make decisions relating to it. 负责的 [v-link ADJ] ❑ *...the cabinet member responsible for the environment.* …负责环境的内阁成员。 **3** ADJ If you are **responsible to** a person or group, they have authority over you and you have to report to them about what you do. 向…汇报的 [v-link ADJ "to" n] ❑ *I'm responsible to my board of directors.* 我向我的董事会汇报。 **4** ADJ **Responsible** people behave properly and sensibly, without needing to be supervised. 有责任心的 ❑ *He feels that the media should be more responsible in what they report.* 他觉得媒体应该对他们的报道更负责些。 ● **re·spon·sibly** ADV 有责任心地 [ADV with v] ❑ *He urged everyone to act responsibly.* 他力劝每一个人做事要负责。 **5** ADJ **Responsible** jobs involve making important decisions or carrying out important tasks. 责任重大的 [ADJ n] ❑ *You are too young for such a responsible position.* 对于这样一个责任重大的职位，你太年轻了。

★ **re·spon·sive** /rɪspɒnsɪv/ **1** ADJ A **responsive** person is quick to react to people or events and to show emotions such as pleasure and affection. 敏感的 ❑ *Harriet was an easy, responsive little girl.* 哈丽特是个随和、敏感的小姑娘。 ● **re·spon·sive·ness** N-UNCOUNT 敏感 ❑ *This condition decreases sexual desire and responsiveness.* 这种情况会降低性的欲望和敏感。 **2** ADJ If someone or something is **responsive**, they react quickly and favorably. 迅速积极反应的 ❑ *With an election coming soon, your representative should be very responsive to your request.* 大选在即，你们的代表应该对你们的要求作出迅速积极的反应。 ● **re·spon·sive·ness** N-UNCOUNT 迅速积极的反应 ❑ *Such responsiveness to public pressure is extraordinary.* 对公众压力如此快速积极的反应是非凡的。

rest
❶ QUANTIFIER USES
❷ VERB AND NOUN USES

❶ **rest** ♦♦◇ /rɛst/ **1** QUANT **The rest** is used to refer to all the parts of something or all the things in a group that remain or that you have not already mentioned. 其余部分 [QUANT "of" def-n] ❑ *It was an experience I will treasure for the rest of my life.* 这是一次我将终生珍视的经历。 ● PRON **Rest** is also a pronoun. 其余部分 ❑ *The first payment was made yesterday, and the rest will be paid next month.* 第一笔款在昨天支付了，其余部分将在下个月支付。 **2** PHRASE You can add **and the rest** or **all the rest of it** to the end of a statement or list when you want to refer in a vague way to other things that are associated with the ones you have already mentioned. 诸如此类；如此等等 [SPOKEN, VAGUENESS] ❑ *...a man with nice clothes, an SUV, and the rest.* …一个衣着考究、开一辆四轮驱动，诸如此类的男人。

If you are talking about an uncountable noun, for example "food," the verb following **rest** is singular. ❑ *The rest of the food was delicious.* If you are talking about a countable noun, such as "boys," the verb is plural. ❑ *The rest of the boys were delighted.*

❷ **rest** ♦♦◇ /rɛst/ (**rests, resting, rested**)
➪ **Please look at meanings 14 and 15 to see if the expression you are looking for is shown under another headword.** **1** V-T/V-I If you **rest** or if you **rest** your body, you do not do anything active for a time. 休息 ❑ *He's tired and exhausted, and has been advised to rest for two weeks.* 他劳累而疲惫，被建议休息两个星期。 **2** N-VAR If you get some **rest** or have a **rest**, you do not do anything active for a time. 休息 ❑ *"You're worn out, Laura," he said. "Go home and get some rest."* "你太累了，劳拉，"他说。"回家休息一下吧。" **3** V-I If something such as a theory or someone's success **rests on** a particular thing, it depends on that thing. 依赖 [FORMAL] ❑ *Such a view rests on a number of incorrect assumptions.* 这一观点基于一些错误的假定。 **4** V-I If authority, a responsibility, or a decision **rests with** you, you have that authority or responsibility, or you are the one who will make that decision. 取决 [FORMAL] ❑ *The final decision rested with the president.* 最终决定取决于该总统。 **5** V-T If you **rest** something somewhere, you put it there so that its weight is supported. 使倚靠 ❑ *He rested his arms on the back of the chair.* 他把他的两条胳膊倚在那把椅子的靠背上。 **6** V-T/V-I If something **is resting** somewhere, or if you **are resting** it there, it is in a position where its weight is supported. 靠放 ❑ *His head was resting on her shoulder.* 他的头正靠在她的肩上。 **7** V-I If you **rest** on or against someone or something, you lean on them so that they support the weight of your body. 倚靠 ❑ *He rested on his pickax for a while.* 他在他的镐上倚靠了一会儿。 **8** N-COUNT A **rest** is an object that is used to support something, especially your head, arms, or feet. 支架 ❑ *When you are sitting, keep your elbow on the arm rest.* 当你坐着的时候，把胳膊肘靠在扶手上。 **9** V-I If your eyes **rest on** a particular person or object, you look directly at them, rather than somewhere else. (目光) 停留 [WRITTEN] ❑ *As she spoke, her eyes rested on her husband's face.* 当她说话的时候，目光停留在她丈夫的脸上。 **10** → see also **rested** **11** PHRASE When an object that has been moving **comes to rest**, it finally stops. 停止 [FORMAL] ❑ *The plane had plowed a path through a patch of forest before coming to rest in a field.* 该飞机从一小块森林中间犁出一条小径，而后停在一片旷野上。 **12** PHRASE If someone refuses to **let** a subject **rest**, they refuse to stop talking about it, especially after they have been talking about it for a long time. 停止谈论 ❑ *I am not prepared to let this matter rest.* 我不准备停止谈论这件事。 **13** PHRASE To **put** someone's **mind at rest** or **set** their **mind at rest** means to tell them something that stops them from worrying. 使某人安心 ❑ *A brain scan last Friday finally set his mind at rest.* 上周五进行的一次脑部扫描终于让他安心了。 **14** **rest assured** → see **assured** **15** to **rest on** your **laurels** → see **laurel**
→ see **motion, sleep**

Thesaurus *rest* 另参见：
V. lie down, relax ❷ **1**

rest area (**rest areas**) N-COUNT A **rest area** is a place beside a highway where you can buy gas and other things, use a toilet or have a meal. (高速公路旁的) 服务区 [mainly AM]
in BRIT, use **services**
❑ *...a freeway rest area in Texas Canyon.* …德克萨斯峡谷内的一个高速公路服务区。

Word Link *re ≈ back, again : reflect, repay, restate*

re·state /ristelt/ (**restates, restating, restated**) V-T If you **restate** something, you say it again in words or writing, usually in a slightly different way. 重申 [FORMAL] ❑ *He continued throughout to restate his opposition to violence.* 他一直不断重申他对暴力的反对。

res·tau·rant ♦♦◇ /rɛstərənt, -tərɑnt, -trɑnt/ (**restaurants**) N-COUNT A **restaurant** is a place where you can eat a meal and pay for it. In restaurants, your food is usually served to you at your table by a waiter or waitress. 餐馆 ❑ *They ate in an Italian restaurant in Forth Street.* 他们在福斯大街的一家意大利餐馆吃了饭。
→ see Word Web: **restaurant**
→ see **city**

r

Word Web restaurant

There are over 900,000 **restaurants** in the United States. These include traditional sit-down eateries as well as **coffee shops**, **cafeterias**, and **takeout** places. Here are some more key statistics. Forty percent of American adults have worked in a restaurant at some point in their lives. Only the government employs more people than the food service business. The restaurant industry has more minority **managers** than any other industry. In 2005, the average **tip** received by a **waiter** or **waitress** was 18%. The average **meal** cost $31.51. The most popular **cuisine** was Italian (31% preferred it), followed by Asian (25%).

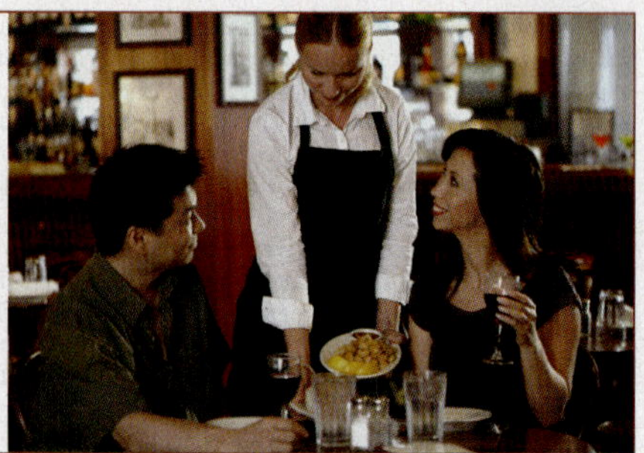

The **salad bar** is a popular feature of American restaurants, and allows the customer to choose what kind of and how much salad to eat for a set price. Salad bars may offer bread, soup, or dessert as well.

rest·ed /rɛstɪd/ ADJ If you feel **rested**, you feel more energetic because you have just had a rest. 精力恢复的 [v-link ADJ] ❑ *He looked tanned and well rested after his vacation.* 假期过后他看上去晒黑了，精力恢复得不错。

rest·less /rɛstlɪs/ **1** ADJ If you are **restless**, you are bored, impatient, or dissatisfied, and you want to do something else. 焦躁不安的 ❑ *By 1982, she was restless and needed a new impetus for her talent.* 到1982年，她焦躁不安，需要一个新的对其才华的推动力。 ● **rest·less·ness** N-UNCOUNT 焦躁不安 ❑ *From the audience came increasing sounds of restlessness.* 从观众中传来了越来越大的焦躁不安的声音。 **2** ADJ If someone is **restless**, they keep moving around because they find it difficult to keep still. 坐立不安的 ❑ *My father seemed very restless and excited.* 我父亲似乎非常坐立不安和兴奋。 ● **rest·less·ness** N-UNCOUNT 坐立不安 ❑ *Karen complained of hyperactivity and restlessness.* 卡伦抱怨说自己过分好动和不安宁。 ● **rest·less·ly** ADV 坐立不安地 ❑ *He paced up and down restlessly, trying to put his thoughts in order.* 他坐立不安地走来走去，试图理清思路。

re·stock /ristɒk/ (**restocks, restocking, restocked**) V-T/V-I If you **restock** something such as a shelf, refrigerator, or store, you fill it with food or other goods to replace what you have used or sold. 补充；重新进货 ❑ *I have to restock the freezer.* 我得补充冷冻柜里的东西了。 ❑ *Manufacturers are testing a system that tracks products leaving the shelves and alerts employees to restock.* 制造商们正在测试一个系统，它可以追踪离架的货品并提醒雇员补充上货。

re·store ♦◇◇ /rɪstɔr/ (**restores, restoring, restored**) **1** V-T To **restore** a situation or practice means to cause it to exist again. 恢复 ❑ *The army has recently been brought in to restore order.* 该军队最近被调来恢复秩序。 ● **res·to·ra·tion** ★ /rɛstəreɪʃ°n/ N-UNCOUNT 恢复 ❑ *His visit is expected to lead to the restoration of diplomatic relations.* 他的访问预计会导致外交关系的恢复。 **2** V-T To **restore** someone or something **to** a previous condition or place means to cause them to be in that condition or place once again. 使复原 ❑ *We will restore her to health but it may take time.* 我们会让她恢复健康，但这或许需要时间。 ● **res·to·ra·tion** ★ N-UNCOUNT 复原 ❑ *I owe the restoration of my hearing to this remarkable new technique.* 我把我听力的复原归功于这项非凡的新技术。 **3** V-T When someone **restores** something such as an old building, painting, or piece of furniture, they repair and clean it, so that it looks like it did when it was new. 修复 ❑ *...experts who specialize in examining and restoring ancient parchments.* …专门研究和修复古羊皮纸手稿的专家们。 ● **res·to·ra·tion** ★ N-VAR (**restorations**) 修复 ❑ *I specialized in the restoration of old houses.* 我擅长旧房的修复。 ● **re·stored** /rɪstɔrd/ ADJ 修复的 ❑ *The restored building helps people understand the historic significance of our neighborhood.* 那座修复的建筑帮助人们了解我们这个社区的历史重要性。 **4** V-T If something that was lost or stolen **is restored to** its owner, it is returned to them. 归还 [usu passive] [FORMAL] ❑ *The following day their horses and goods were restored to them.* 第二天他们的马匹和货物被归还给了他们。

re·strain /rɪstreɪn/ (**restrains, restraining, restrained**) **1** V-T If you **restrain** someone, you stop them from doing what they intended or wanted to do, usually by using your physical strength. 制止 ❑ *Wally gripped my arm, partly to restrain me and partly to reassure me.* 沃利抓住了我的胳膊，部分是想制止我，部分是想安慰我。 **2** V-T If you **restrain** an emotion or you **restrain yourself from** doing something, you prevent yourself from showing that emotion or doing what you wanted or intended to do. 抑制 ❑ *She was unable to restrain her desperate anger.* 她无法抑制她那不顾一切的愤怒。 **3** V-T To **restrain** something that is growing or increasing means to prevent it from getting too large. 限制 ❑ *The radical 500-day plan was very clear on how it intended to try to restrain inflation.* 这项激进的500天计划在其想要如何试图限制通货膨胀上是非常清晰的。

re·strained /rɪstreɪnd/ **1** ADJ Someone who is **restrained** is very calm and unemotional. 克制的 ❑ *Under the circumstances, he felt he'd been very restrained.* 在这种环境下，他觉得他一直很克制。 **2** ADJ If you describe someone's clothes or the decorations in a house as **restrained**, you mean that you like them because they are simple and not too brightly colored. 素净的 [APPROVAL] ❑ *Her black suit was restrained and expensive.* 她的黑色套装素净且昂贵。

re·straint /rɪstreɪnt/ (**restraints**) **1** N-VAR **Restraints** are rules or conditions that limit or restrict someone or something. 限制 ❑ *The president is calling for spending restraints in some areas.* 该总统要求在一些领域限制开支。 **2** N-UNCOUNT **Restraint** is calm, controlled, and unemotional behavior. 克制 ❑ *They behaved with more restraint than I'd expected.* 他们表现了比我预想还多的克制。

re·strict /rɪstrɪkt/ (**restricts, restricting, restricted**) **1** V-T If you **restrict** something, you put a limit on it in order to reduce it or prevent it from becoming too great. 限制 ❑ *There is talk of raising the admission requirements to restrict the number of students on campus.* 有提高录取条件来限制校园里学生数量的说法。 ● **re·stric·tion** /rɪstrɪkʃ°n/ N-UNCOUNT 限制 ❑ *Since the costs of science were rising faster than inflation, some restriction on funding was necessary.* 既然科学成本上涨快于通货膨胀，资助上的一些限制是必要的。 **2** V-T To **restrict** the movement or actions of someone or something means to prevent them from moving or acting freely. 限制 ❑ *The government imprisoned dissidents, forbade travel, and restricted the press.* 政府关押了持不同政见者，禁止了出游，限制了新闻自由。 ● **re·stric·tion** N-UNCOUNT 限制 ❑ *...the justification for this restriction of individual liberty.* …对限制个人自由的辩护。 **3** V-T If you **restrict** someone or their activities **to** one thing, they can only do, have, or deal with that thing. If you **restrict** them **to** one place, they cannot go anywhere else. 限制（在某范围）❑ *For the first two weeks, patients are restricted to the grounds.* 最初两周病人们被限制在院内活动。 **4** V-T If you **restrict** something **to** a particular group, only that group can do it or have it. If you **restrict** something **to** a particular place, it is allowed only in that place. 限定 ❑ *Trustees had decided to restrict university entry to about 30 percent of applicants.* 董事们已经决定把大学入学率限定在申请人数的30%左右。

re·strict·ed /rɪstrɪktɪd/ **1** ADJ Something that is **restricted** is quite small or limited. 受限制的 ❑ *...the monotony of a heavily restricted diet.* …严重受限制的饮食的单调乏味。 **2** ADJ If something is **restricted to** a particular group, only members of that group have it. If it is **restricted to** a particular place, it exists only in that place. 仅限的 [v-link ADJ "to" n] ❑ *Discipline problems are by no means restricted to children in families dependent on benefits.* 纪律问题绝不仅限于依赖救济家庭的孩子。 **3** ADJ A **restricted** area is one that only people with special permission can enter. 不对外开放的 ❑ *...a highly restricted area close to the old naval airfield.* …靠近旧海军机场的一个高度戒备地区。

re·stric·tion ♦◇◇ /rɪstrɪkʃ°n/ (**restrictions**) **1** N-COUNT A **restriction** is an official rule that limits what you can do or that limits the amount or size of something. 限制条例 ❑ *...the lifting of restrictions on political parties and the news media.* …政党和新闻媒体限制条例的取消。 **2** N-COUNT You can refer to anything that limits

R

what you can do as a **restriction**. 限制 ❑ *His parents are trying to make up to him for the restrictions of urban living.* 他的父母正试图为城市生活的诸多限制而补偿他。 **3** → see also **restrict**

re·stric·tive /rɪstrɪktɪv/ ADJ Something that is **restrictive** prevents people from doing what they want to do, or from moving freely. 约束性的 ❑ *The state will adopt a more restrictive policy on arms sales.* 这个州将对武器销售采取一项更具约束性的政策。

rest·room /rɛstrum, -rʊm/ (**restrooms**) also **rest room** N-COUNT In a restaurant, theater, or other public place, a **restroom** is a room with a toilet for customers to use. 公共厕所 [AM]

in BRIT, usually use **toilet**

★ **re·struc·ture** /ristrʌktʃər/ (**restructures, restructuring, restructured**) V-T To **restructure** an organization or system means to change the way it is organized, usually in order to make it work more effectively. 重新建构 ❑ *The president called on educators and politicians to help him restructure American education.* 该总统号召教育家和政治家们帮助他重新建构美国的教育。 ●**re·struc·tur·ing** N-VAR (**restructurings**) 重新建构 ❑ *The company is to lay off 1,520 workers as part of a restructuring.* 作为改组的一部分，这家公司将解雇1520名工人。

re·sult ♦♦♦ /rɪzʌlt/ (**results, resulting, resulted**) **1** N-COUNT A **result** is something that happens or exists because of something else that has happened. 结果 ❑ *Compensation is available for people who have developed asthma as a direct result of their work.* 那些由于工作而导致患上哮喘的人可以得到补偿。 **2** V-I If something **results in** a particular situation or event, it causes that situation or event to happen. 致使 ❑ *Fifty percent of road accidents result in head injuries.* 50%的公路交通事故致使头部受伤。 **3** V-I If something **results from** a particular event or action, it is caused by that event or action. 起因 ❑ *Many hair problems result from what you eat.* 很多头发问题是由你吃的东西引起的。 **4** N-COUNT A **result** is the situation that exists at the end of a contest. 结果 ❑ *The final election results will be announced on Friday.* 最终选举结果将在周五被公布。 **5** N-COUNT A **result** is the number that you get when you do a calculation. 答案 ❑ *They found their computers producing different results from exactly the same calculation.* 他们发现他们的电脑从完全相同的计算得出了不同的答案。 **6** N-COUNT Your **results** are the marks or grades that you get for examinations you have taken. 成绩 [mainly BRIT]

in AM, usually use **scores**

Thesaurus *result* 另参见：

N. by-product, consequence **1**
V. come about, produce, turn out, wind up **3**

★ **re·sult·ant** /rɪzʌltənt/ ADJ **Resultant** means caused by the event just mentioned. 由此导致的 [ADJ n] [FORMAL] ❑ *At least a quarter of a million people have died in the fighting and the resultant famines.* 至少25万人死于这场战斗，由此导致的是饥荒。

re·sume ♦◇◇ /rɪzum/ (**resumes, resuming, resumed**) **1** V-T/V-I If you **resume** an activity or if it **resumes**, it begins again. 重新开始 [FORMAL] ❑ *After the war he resumed his duties at Wellesley College.* 那场战争之后，他恢复了在韦尔斯利学院的任职。 ●**re·sump·tion** ▲ /rɪzʌmpʃən/ N-UNCOUNT 重新开始 ❑ *It is premature to speculate about the resumption of negotiations.* 考虑谈判的恢复还太早。 **2** V-T If you **resume** your seat or position, you return to the seat or position you were in before you moved. 重返 [FORMAL] ❑ *"I changed my mind," Blanche said, resuming her seat.* "我改主意了，"布兰奇说，返回到她的座位上。

★ **ré·su·mé** /rɛzumeɪ/ (**résumés**) also **resumé, resume** **1** N-COUNT A **résumé** is a short account, either spoken or written, of something that has happened or that someone has said or written. 摘要 [oft N of n/wh] ❑ *I will leave with you a résumé of his most recent speech.* 我将留给你一份他最近一次讲演的摘要。 **2** N-COUNT Your **résumé** is a brief account of your personal details, your education, and the jobs you have had. You are often asked to send a résumé when you are applying for a job. 简历 [mainly AM]

in BRIT, usually use **curriculum vitae**

re·sur·gence /rɪsɜrdʒəns/ N-SING If there is a **resurgence of** an attitude or activity, it reappears and grows. 复苏 [also no det, oft N "of" n] [FORMAL] ❑ *Police say drugs traffickers are behind the resurgence of violence.* 警方说毒贩是暴力事件增加的原因。

res·ur·rect /rɛzərɛkt/ (**resurrects, resurrecting, resurrected**) V-T If you **resurrect** something, you cause it to exist again after it had disappeared or ended. 复兴 ❑ *Attempts to resurrect the ceasefire have already failed once.* 为恢复停战所作的努力已经失败过一次了。 ●**res·ur·rec·tion** /rɛzərɛkʃən/ N-UNCOUNT 复兴 ❑ *This is a resurrection of an old story from the mid-70s.* 这是70年代中期的一个老故事的再现。

re·sus·ci·tate /rɪsʌsɪteɪt/ (**resuscitates, resuscitating, resuscitated**) **1** V-T If you **resuscitate** someone who has stopped breathing, you cause them to start breathing again. 救醒 ❑ *A policeman and then a paramedic tried to resuscitate her.* 一名警察，接着是一名医护人员试图把她救醒。 ●**re·sus·ci·ta·tion** /rɪsʌsɪteɪʃən/ N-UNCOUNT 救醒 ❑ *They must even now be rushing her to the hospital for resuscitation and treatment.* 他们肯定在我说话这会儿正火速把她送往那家医院抢救治疗。 **2** V-T If you **resuscitate** something, you cause it to become active or successful again. 使复兴 ❑ *He has submitted a bid to resuscitate the weekly magazine, which closed in April with losses of $1 million a year.* 他已经竞标以使由于100万美元1年的损失于4月份停刊了的那个周刊起死回生。 ●**re·sus·ci·ta·tion** N-UNCOUNT 复兴 ❑ *The economy needs vigorous resuscitation.* 该经济需要强劲的复兴。

re·tail ♦◇◇ /riteɪl/ (**retails, retailing, retailed**) **1** N-UNCOUNT **Retail** is the activity of selling products direct to the public, usually in small quantities. Compare **wholesale**. 零售 [BUSINESS] ❑ *Retail stores usually count on the Christmas season to make up to half of their annual profits.* 零售商店通常指望圣诞节期间来赚取一半的年利润。 **2** ADV If something is sold **retail**, it is sold in ordinary stores direct to the public. 以零售方式地 [ADV after v] [BUSINESS] ❑ *We sell wholesale to several chains that sell retail to the public.* 我们批发给几家向公众零售的连锁店。 **3** V-I If an item in a store **retails at** or **for** a particular price, it is for sale at that price. (按某种价格) 零售 [BUSINESS] ❑ *It originally retailed at $23.50.* 它起初按$23.50的价格零售。 **4** → see also **retailing**

★ **re·tail·er** /riteɪlər/ (**retailers**) N-COUNT A **retailer** is a person or business that sells goods to the public. 零售商 [BUSINESS] ❑ *Furniture and carpet retailers are among those reporting the sharpest annual decline in sales.* 家具和地毯零售商们是在那些报告最大年销售下滑的商家之中。

re·tail·ing /riteɪlɪŋ/ N-UNCOUNT **Retailing** is the activity of selling products direct to the public, usually in small quantities. Compare **wholesaling**. 零售 [BUSINESS] ❑ *She spent fourteen years in retailing.* 她做了14年的零售。

re·tail park (**retail parks**) N-COUNT A **retail park** is a large, specially built area, usually at the edge of a town or city, where there are a lot of large stores and sometimes other facilities such as movie theaters and restaurants. 购物广场 [BRIT]

in AM, use **shopping mall**

re·tail price in·dex N-PROPER **The retail price index** is a list of the prices of typical goods which shows how much the cost of living changes from one month to the next. 零售价格指数 [BRIT, BUSINESS]

re·tain ♦◇◇ /rɪteɪn/ (**retains, retaining, retained**) V-T To **retain** something means to continue to have that thing. 保留 [FORMAL] ❑ *The interior of the shop still retains a nineteenth-century atmosphere.* 那家商店内部依然保持着19世纪的格调。

Thesaurus *retain* 另参见：

V. hold, keep, maintain, remember, save; (*ant.*) give up, lose

re·tain·er /rɪteɪnər/ (**retainers**) N-COUNT A **retainer** is a fee that you pay to someone in order to make sure that they will be available to do work for you if you need them to. 预付聘金 ❑ *I'll need a five-hundred-dollar retainer.* 我将需要一笔500美元的预付聘金。

▲ **re·tali·ate** /rɪtælieɪt/ (**retaliates, retaliating, retaliated**) V-I If you **retaliate** when someone harms or annoys you, you do something which harms or annoys them in return. 报复 ❑ *I was sorely tempted to retaliate.* 我非常想报复。 ❑ *The company would retaliate against employees who joined a union.* 该公司将对加入工会的员工们进行报复。 ●**re·talia·tion** ▲ /rɪtælieɪʃən/ N-UNCOUNT 报复 ❑ *Police said they believed the attack was in retaliation for the death of the drug trafficker.* 警方说他们认为这起袭击是为那个毒贩的死而实施的报复。

▲ **re·tard·ed** /rɪtɑrdɪd/ ADJ Someone who is **retarded** is much less advanced mentally than most people of their age. 弱智的 [OLD-FASHIONED] ❑ *...a special school for mentally retarded children.* …一家弱智儿童的特殊学校

re·tell /ritɛl/ (**retells, retelling, retold**) V-T If you **retell** a story, you write it, tell it, or present it again, often in a different way

r

from its original form. 重述 ❑ *Lucilla often asks her sisters to retell the story.* 陆希拉经常叫她的姐姐们重讲那个故事。

★ **re·ten·tion** /rɪtɛnʃᵊn/ N-UNCOUNT The **retention of** something is the keeping of it. 保留 [FORMAL] ❑ *The Citizens' Forum supported special powers for Quebec but also argued for the retention of a strong central government.* 《市民论坛》支持魁北克的特殊权力，但是也主张保留一个强有力的中央政府。

re·think /riθɪŋk/ (**rethinks, rethinking, rethought**) **1** V-T If you **rethink** something such as a problem, a plan, or a policy, you think about it again and change it. 重新考虑 ❑ *Both major political parties are having to rethink their policies.* 两个主要政党都必须重新考虑他们的政策。 **2** N-SING If you have a **rethink** of a problem, a plan, or a policy, you think about it again and change it. 重新考虑 [JOURNALISM] ❑ *There must be a rethink of government policy toward this vulnerable group.* 对这一弱势群体的政府政策一定要进行重新思考。

reti·cent /rɛtɪsənt/ ADJ Someone who is **reticent** does not tell people about things. 缄默的 ❑ *She is so reticent about her achievements.* 她对于自己的成就如此缄默。 ● **reti·cence** N-UNCOUNT 缄默 ❑ *Pearl didn't mind his reticence; in fact she liked it.* 珀尔不介意他的沉默，事实上她喜欢这一点。

reti·na /rɛtɪnə/ (**retinas**) N-COUNT Your **retina** is the area at the back of your eye. It receives the image that you see and then sends the image to your brain. 视网膜 ❑ *Bruno had to have eye surgery on a torn retina two years ago.* 布鲁诺两年前因为视网膜破裂不得不进行了一次眼部手术。

→ see **eye**

re·tire ♦◇◇ /rɪtaɪər/ (**retires, retiring, retired**) **1** V-I When older people **retire**, they leave their job and usually stop working completely. 退休 ❑ *At the age when most people retire, he is ready to face a new career.* 在大多数人退休的年纪，他准备要面对一项新事业。 **2** V-I When an athlete **retires from** their sport, they stop playing in competitions. When they **retire from** a race or a game, they stop competing in it. 退役 ❑ *I have decided to retire from Formula One racing at the end of the season.* 我已经决定这个赛季末退出一级方程式赛车。 **3** V-I When a jury in a court of law **retires**, the members of it leave the court in order to decide whether someone is guilty or innocent. (陪审团) 退庭 ❑ *The jury will retire to consider its verdict today.* 该陪审团今天将退庭来考虑其裁决。 **4** → see also **retired**

> Do not confuse **retire** and **resign**. When someone **retires**, they leave their job and stop working, often because they have reached the age when they can get a pension. ❑ *He had been planning for some time to retire at around age 60.* When professional sportsmen and women stop playing sport as their job, you can also say that they **retire**, even if they are fairly young. ❑ *A heart attack at the age of 36 forced him to retire from tennis.* If someone **resigns** from their job, they leave it after saying that they do not want to do it any more. ❑ *He hasn't decided whether he will resign.* You can **resign** from your job at any age, and perhaps start another job soon afterward.

R

Thesaurus *retire* 另参见：

v. finish, leave, stop, quit **1** **2**

re·tired /rɪtaɪərd/ **1** ADJ A **retired** person is an older person who has left his or her job and has usually stopped working completely. 退休的 ❑ *...a seventy-three-year-old retired teacher from Florida.* …一位来自佛罗里达的73岁的退休教师。 **2** → see also **retire**

re·tire·ment ♦◇◇ /rɪtaɪərmənt/ (**retirements**) **1** N-VAR **Retirement** is the time when a worker retires. 退休 ❑ *The proportion of the population who are over retirement age has grown tremendously in the past few years.* 超过退休年龄的人口的比例在过去几年中已急剧增长。 **2** N-UNCOUNT A person's **retirement** is the period in their life after they have retired. 退休生活 ❑ *"Growing Older" considered the needs of the elderly for financial support during retirement.* 《进入老年》考虑到了老年人在退休期间对经济资助的需要。

★ **re·tort** /rɪtɔrt/ (**retorts, retorting, retorted**) V-T To **retort** means to reply angrily to someone. 反驳 [WRITTEN] ❑ *"You can't smoke in here," Shaw said.—"Don't worry, it's not tobacco," he retorted.* "你不能在这儿吸烟，" 肖说道。——"别担心，这不是烟叶，" 他反驳道。 ● N-COUNT **Retort** is also a noun. 反驳 ❑ *His sharp retort clearly made an impact.* 他的尖锐反驳显然起了作用。

re·trace /rɪtreɪs/ (**retraces, retracing, retraced**) V-T If you **retrace** your steps or **retrace** your way, you return to the place you started from by going back along the same route. 折返 ❑ *He retraced his steps to the spot where he'd left the case.* 他折回到他留下箱子的地方。

re·tract /rɪtrækt/ (**retracts, retracting, retracted**) **1** V-T/V-I If you **retract** something that you have said or written, you say that you did not mean it. 收回；撤回说出的话 [FORMAL] ❑ *Mr. Smith hurriedly sought to retract the statement, but it had just been broadcast on national radio.* 史密斯先生急忙试图收回声明，但它刚刚已经在国家电台播出了。 ❑ *He's hoping that if he makes me feel guilty, I'll retract.* 他希望如果他使我感到愧疚，我就会收回自己的话。 ● **re·trac·tion** /rɪtrækʃᵊn/ N-COUNT (**retractions**) 收回 ❑ *Miss Pearce said she expected an unqualified retraction of his comments within twenty-four hours.* 皮尔斯小姐称她希望他在24小时内无条件收回他的言论。 **2** V-T/V-I When a part of a machine or a part of a person's body **retracts** or **is retracted**, it moves inward or becomes shorter. 使缩回；缩回 [FORMAL] ❑ *Torn muscles retract and lose strength, structure, and tightness.* 撕裂了的肌肉会收缩，进而丧失力量、结构和紧实度。

re·train /ritreɪn/ (**retrains, retraining, retrained**) V-T/V-I If you **retrain**, or if someone **retrains** you, you learn new skills, especially in order to get a new job. 再培训；接受再培训 ❑ *Look at what you can do to retrain for a job that will make you happier.* 看看你能做些什么来接受再培训，以便找到让你更快乐的工作。 ● **re·train·ing** N-UNCOUNT 再培训 ❑ *...measures such as the retraining of the workforce at their place of work.* …对劳动力进行在岗再培训等措施。

re·treat ♦◇◇ /rɪtrit/ (**retreats, retreating, retreated**) **1** V-I If you **retreat**, you move away from something or someone. 退出；离开 ❑ *"I've already got a job," I said quickly, and retreated from the room.* "我已经有了工作，" 我迅速说道，然后就从房间里退了出来。 **2** V-I When an army **retreats**, it moves away from enemy forces in order to avoid fighting them. 撤退 ❑ *The French, suddenly outnumbered, were forced to retreat.* 法军在人数上突然处于劣势，被迫撤退了。 ● N-VAR **Retreat** is also a noun. 撤退 ❑ *In June 1942, the British 8th Army was in full retreat.* 1942年6月，英军第8军全线撤退。 **3** V-I If you **retreat from** something such as a plan or a way of life, you give it up, usually in order to do something safer or less extreme. 放弃 ❑ *She retreated from public life.* 她放弃了社会生活。 ● N-VAR **Retreat** is also a noun. 放弃 ❑ *The president's remarks appear to signal that there will be no retreat from his position.* 总统的话似乎暗示他不会放弃自己的职位。 **4** N-COUNT A **retreat** is a quiet, isolated place that you go to in order to rest or to do things in private. 隐居处；休养处 ❑ *He spent yesterday hidden away in his country retreat.* 他躲在乡间的休养地度过了昨天。

re·trench /rɪtrɛntʃ/ (**retrenches, retrenching, retrenched**) V-I If a person or organization **retrenches**, they spend less money. 紧缩开支 [FORMAL] ❑ *Shortly afterwards, cuts in defense spending forced the aerospace industry to retrench.* 此后不久，国防开支的削减迫使航空航天业紧缩开支。

ret·ri·bu·tion /rɛtrɪbyuʃᵊn/ N-UNCOUNT **Retribution** is punishment for a crime, especially punishment that is carried out by someone other than the official authorities. 惩罚；报应 [FORMAL] ❑ *He didn't want any further involvement for fear of retribution.* 由于害怕遭到惩罚，他不想进一步卷进去。

★ **re·triev·al** /rɪtrivᵊl/ **1** N-UNCOUNT The **retrieval** of information from a computer is the process of getting it back. (电脑中信息的) 读取 ❑ *...electronic storage and retrieval systems.* …电子存储和读取系统。 **2** N-UNCOUNT The **retrieval** of something is the process of getting it back from a particular place, especially from a place where it should not be. 找回；取回 ❑ *Its real purpose is the launching and retrieval of small airplanes in flight.* 它的真正目的是发射和找回飞行中的小型飞机。

★ **re·trieve** /rɪtriv/ (**retrieves, retrieving, retrieved**) **1** V-T If you **retrieve** something, you get it back from the place where you left it. 找回；取回 ❑ *The men were trying to retrieve weapons left when the army abandoned the island.* 那些人正试图找回该军队撤离这个岛时留下的武器。 **2** V-T If you manage to **retrieve** a situation, you succeed in bringing it back into a more acceptable state. 挽回 ❑ *He, the one man who could retrieve that situation, might receive the call.* 他这个惟一能挽回那个局面的人可能会接到这个电话。 **3** V-T To **retrieve** information from a computer or from your memory means to get it back. (从电脑中) 读取 (信息) ❑ *Computers can instantly retrieve millions of information bits.* 计算机能立刻读取数百万条信息。

ret·ro /rɛtroʊ/ ADJ **Retro** clothes, music, and objects are based on the styles of the past. 复古风格的 [JOURNALISM] ❑ *...clothing* *stores where original versions of many of today's retro looks can be found for a fraction of the price.* …能以低价买到许多复古式样的原创版的服装店。

★ **retro·spect** /rɛtrəspɛkt/ PHRASE When you consider something **in retrospect**, you think about it afterward, and often have a different opinion about it from the one that you had at the time. 回想 ❑ *In retrospect, I wish that I had thought about alternative courses of action.* 回想起来，我真希望自己当初考虑过其他的行动方案。

★ **retro·spec·tive** /rɛtrəspɛktɪv/ (**retrospectives**) **1** N-COUNT A **retrospective** is an exhibition or showing of work done by an artist over many years, rather than his or her most recent work. (艺术家作品的) 回顾展 ❑ *...a retrospective of the films of Judy Garland.* …朱迪·嘉兰影片回顾展。 **2** ADJ **Retrospective** feelings or opinions concern things that happened in the past. 回顾的 ❑ *Afterwards, retrospective fear of the responsibility would make her feel almost faint.* 后来，对要负的责任的后怕常使她几乎晕倒。 ● **retro·spec·tive·ly** ADV 回顾地 ❑ *Retrospectively, it seems as if they probably were negligent.* 回想起来，似乎他们可能是疏忽了。 **3** ADJ **Retrospective** laws or legal actions take effect from a date before the date when they are officially approved. 有追溯力的 (法律) [mainly BRIT]

in AM, use **retroactive**

re·turn ♦♦♦ /rɪtɜrn/ (**returns, returning, returned**) **1** V-I When you **return to** a place, you go back there after you have been away. 返回 ❑ *There are unconfirmed reports that Aziz will return to Moscow within hours.* 有未经证实的报道称阿齐兹将在数小时内返回莫斯科。 **2** N-SING Your **return** is your arrival back at a place where you had been before. 返回 ❑ *Kenny explained the reason for his sudden return to Dallas.* 肯尼解释了他突然返回达拉斯的理由。 **3** V-T If you **return** something that you have borrowed or taken, you give it back or put it back. 归还 ❑ *I enjoyed the book and said so when I returned it.* 我很喜欢这本书，归还它的时候就这么说了。 ● N-SING **Return** is also a noun. 归还 ❑ *The main demand of the Indians is for the return of one-and-a-half-million acres of forest to their communities.* 印第安人的主要要求是把150万英亩的森林归还给他们的族群。 **4** V-T If you **return** something somewhere, you put it back where it was. 放回 ❑ *He returned the notebook to his jacket.* 他把笔记本放回自己的夹克里。 **5** V-T If you **return** someone's action, you do the same thing to them as they have just done to you. If you **return** someone's feelings, you feel the same way toward them as they feel toward you. 回应; 回报 ❑ *Back at the station the chief inspector returned the call.* 回到警察局后，督察长回了电话。 **6** V-I If a feeling or situation **returns**, it comes back or happens again after a period when it was not present. 再现; 恢复 ❑ *Official reports in Algeria suggest that calm is returning to the country.* 阿尔及利亚官方的报道暗示该国正在恢复平静。 ● N-SING **Return** is also a noun. 再现; 恢复 ❑ *It was like the return of his youth.* 这好像是他青年重现。 **7** V-I If you **return to** a state that you were in before, you start being in that state again. 恢复 ❑ *Life has improved and returned to normal.* 生活改善了且恢复了正常。 ● N-SING **Return** is also a noun. 恢复 ❑ *He made an uneventful return to normal health.* 他顺利地恢复到了正常健康状态。 **8** V-I If you **return to** a subject that you have mentioned before, you begin talking about it again. 回到 (前面的话题) ❑ *The power of the church is one theme all these writers return to.* 教会的权力是所有这些作家回归的一个主题。 **9** V-I If you **return to** an activity that you were doing before, you start doing it again. 重新开始; 继续 (做) ❑ *At that stage he will be 52, young enough to return to politics if he wishes to do so.* 到那时候他将是52岁，足够年轻，只要他愿意还可以继续从政。 ● N-SING **Return** is also a noun. 重新开始; 继续 ❑ *He has not ruled out the shock possibility of a return to football.* 他没有排除重返足坛的这个惊人的可能性。 **10** V-T When a judge or jury **returns** a verdict, they announce whether they think the person on trial is guilty or not. 宣布 (裁决) ❑ *They returned a verdict of not guilty.* 他们宣布了无罪判决。 **11** ADJ A **return** ticket is a ticket for a trip from one place to another and then back again. 往返的 [mainly BRIT]

in AM, usually use **round trip**

12 ADJ The **return** trip is the part of a trip that takes you back to where you started from. 返程的 [ADJ n] ❑ *Buy an extra ticket for the return trip.* 额外再买一张返程票。 **13** N-COUNT The **return on** an investment is the profit that you get from it. 返利; 收益 [BUSINESS] ❑ *Profits have picked up this year but the return on capital remains tiny.* 利润本年度上升了，但资本收益仍然很少。 **14** PHRASE If you do something **in return for** what someone else has done for you, you do it because they did that thing for you. 作为回报 ❑ *You pay regular premiums and in return the insurance company will pay out a lump sum.* 你定期交纳保险费，作为回报，保险公司会一次性付给你一笔钱。 **15** **to return fire** → see **fire**

→ see **library**

Thesaurus *return* 另参见：

V. come again, come back, go back, reappear **1**
give back, hand back, pay back; (*ant.*) keep **3**
N. arrival, homecoming; (*ant.*) departure **2**

Word Partnership *return* 的常用搭配：

V. **decide to** return, **plan to** return, **want to** return **1** **3**–**5** **9**
N. return **a (phone) call** **5**
return **to work** **9**
return **trip** **12**
return **on an investment, rate of** return **13**

re·turn match [BRIT] → see **rematch**

re·uni·fi·ca·tion /riyunɪfɪkeɪʃən/ N-UNCOUNT The **reunification** of a country or city that has been divided into two or more parts for some time is the joining of it together again. 重新统一 [with supp] ❑ *...the reunification of East and West Beirut in 1991.* …1991年东、西贝鲁特的重新统一。

re·union /riyunyən/ (**reunions**) **1** N-COUNT A **reunion** is a party attended by members of the same family, school, or other group who have not seen each other for a long time. (家庭、学校及其他团体成员的) 重聚会 ❑ *The association holds an annual reunion.* 这个协会每年举行一次重聚会。 **2** N-VAR A **reunion** is a meeting between people who have been separated for some time. 重逢 ❑ *The children weren't allowed to see her for nearly a week. It was a very emotional reunion.* 孩子们将近一周都没被允许见她。这是一次非常令人激动的重逢。

re·unite /riyunaɪt/ (**reunites, reuniting, reunited**) **1** V-T If people **are reunited**, or if they **reunite**, they meet each other again after they have been separated for some time. 重聚 ❑ *She and her youngest son were finally allowed to be reunited with their family.* 她和她的小儿子最终被允许和他们的家庭团聚。 **2** V-T/V-I If a divided organization or country **is reunited**, or if it **reunites**, it becomes one united organization or country again. 使重新统一; 重新联合 ❑ *As of this evening, Germany is reunited. In Berlin they're celebrating.* 从今晚起，德国统一了。他们正在柏林庆祝。 ❑ *His first job will be to reunite the army.* 他的第一项任务将是重新统一军队。

re·value /rivælyu/ (**revalues, revaluing, revalued**) **1** V-T When a country **revalues** its currency, it increases the currency's value so that it can buy more foreign currency than before. 调高 (货币的) 价值 ❑ *Countries enjoying surpluses will be under no pressure to revalue their currencies.* 享有贸易顺差的国家将不会受到调高本国货币币值的压力。 **2** V-T To **revalue** something means to increase the amount that you calculate it is worth so that its value stays roughly the same in comparison with other things, even if there is inflation. 调高 (某物的) 价值 ❑ *It is now usual to revalue property assets on a more regular basis.* 目前更经常地调高固定资产的价值是很平常的。

re·vamp /rivæmp/ (**revamps, revamping, revamped**) V-T If someone **revamps** something, they make changes to it in order to try and improve it. 修改; 改进 ❑ *All the country's political parties have accepted that it is time to revamp the system.* 这个国家的所有政党都认可现在是改革这一体制的时候了。 ● N-SING **Revamp** is also a noun. 修改; 改进 ❑ *The revamp includes replacing the old navy uniform with a crisp blue and white cotton outfit.* 改进的内容包括将旧海军制服换成清新的蓝白相间的棉套装。

re·veal ♦♦◊ /rɪvil/ (**reveals, revealing, revealed**) **1** V-T To **reveal** something means to make people aware of it. 透露; 显示 ❑ *She has refused to reveal the whereabouts of her daughter.* 她已拒绝透露她女儿的行踪。 ❑ *A survey of the American diet has revealed that a growing number of people are overweight.* 一项有关美国人日常饮食的调查表明越来越多的人超重。 **2** V-T If you **reveal** something that has been out of sight, you uncover it so that people can see it. 使显露; 揭露 ❑ *In the principal room, a gray carpet was removed to reveal the original pine floor.* 在主房间里，一块灰色的地毯被挪开了，使原有的松木地板露了出来。

re·veal·ing /rɪvilɪŋ/ ADJ A **revealing** statement, account, or action tells you something that you did not know, especially about the person doing it or making it. 透露内情的 ❑ *...a revealing interview.* …一次透露内幕的采访。

rev·el /rɛvᵊl/ (**revels, reveling** or **revelling, reveled** or **revelled**) V-I If you **revel in** a situation or experience, you enjoy it very much. 陶醉；沉湎 ❑ *Annie was smiling and laughing, clearly reveling in the attention.* 安妮时而微笑，时而大笑，显然为受到瞩目而陶醉。

★ **rev·ela·tion** /rɛvəleɪʃᵊn/ (**revelations**) **1** N-COUNT A **revelation** is a surprising or interesting fact that is made known to people. 被透露的事实；被泄露的秘密 ❑ *...the seemingly everlasting revelations about his private life.* …有关他私生活的似乎永无休止的披露。 **2** N-VAR The **revelation of** something is the act of making it known. 揭露；透露 ❑ *...following the revelation of his affair with a former secretary.* …在他和前任秘书的风流韵事被揭露之后。 **3** N-SING If you say that something you experienced was **a revelation**, you are saying that it was very surprising or very good. (惊人的、极好的) 发现 ❑ *Degas's work had been a revelation to her.* 德各斯的工作曾是她的一大发现。

★ **re·venge** /rɪvɛndʒ/ (**revenges, revenging, revenged**) **1** N-UNCOUNT **Revenge** involves hurting or punishing someone who has hurt or harmed you. 报复 ❑ *The attackers were said to be taking revenge on the 14-year-old, claiming he was a school bully.* 攻击者被称是在报复一名14岁男孩，称他是学校一霸。 **2** V-T If you **revenge** yourself on someone who has hurt you, you hurt them in return. 报复 [WRITTEN] ❑ *The paper accused her of trying to revenge herself on her former lover.* 这家报纸指责她企图报复她以前的情人。

rev·enue ♦◇◇ /rɛvənyu/ (**revenues**) **1** N-UNCOUNT **Revenue** is money that a company, organization, or government receives from people. (公司、组织或政府的) 收入 [also N in pl] [BUSINESS] ❑ *...a boom year at the movies, with record advertising revenue and the highest ticket sales since 1980.* …电影业欣欣向荣的一年，广告及票房收入都创下1980年以来的最高纪录。 **2** → see also **Internal Revenue Service**

re·ver·ber·ate /rɪvɜrbəreɪt/ (**reverberates, reverberating, reverberated**) **1** V-I When a loud sound **reverberates** through a place, it echoes through it. 回响 ❑ *Day in and day out, the flat crack of the tank guns reverberates through the little Bavarian town.* 日复一日地，单调的坦克炮的轰隆声在巴伐利亚的这个小镇上空回响着。 **2** V-I You can say that an event or idea **reverberates** when it has a powerful effect which lasts a long time. 产生反响 ❑ *The controversy surrounding the takeover yesterday continued to reverberate around the television industry.* 围绕昨天的接管问题的争议继续在电视业产生反响。

Word Link *vere ≈ fear, awe : irreverent, revere, reverence*

▲ **re·vere** /rɪvɪər/ (**reveres, revering, revered**) V-T If you **revere** someone or something, you respect and admire them greatly. 崇敬 [FORMAL] ❑ *The Chinese revered corn as a gift from heaven.* 中国人将谷物奉为天赐礼物。 ● **re·vered** ADJ 受尊崇的 ❑ *...some of the country's most revered institutions.* …该国一些最受尊崇的机构。

rev·er·ence /rɛvərəns/ N-UNCOUNT **Reverence for** someone or something is a feeling of great respect for them. 尊崇 [FORMAL] ❑ *We stand together now in mutual support and in reverence for the dead.* 出于相互支持和对逝者的敬意，我们现在站到了一起。

Rev·er·end /rɛvərənd/ N-TITLE **Reverend** is a title used before the name or rank of an officially appointed Christian religious leader. The abbreviation **Rev.** is also used. …大人 (用于正式任命的基督教领袖的名字或头衔前，其缩略为**Rev.**) ❑ *The service was led by the Reverend Jim Simons.* 这次礼拜仪式由吉姆•西蒙斯牧师大人主持。

re·ver·sal /rɪvɜrsᵊl/ (**reversals**) **1** N-COUNT A **reversal of** a process, policy, or trend is a complete change in it. 彻底改变；逆转 ❑ *The paper says the move represents a complete reversal of previous U.S. policy.* 报上说这一举动反映了之前美国政策的彻底逆转。 **2** N-COUNT When there is a role **reversal** or a **reversal of** roles, two people or groups exchange their positions or functions. (位置或功能的) 转变 ❑ *When children end up taking care of their parents, it is a strange role reversal indeed.* 当孩子们最终照看起父母来的时候，这确实是一个奇怪的角色转变。

re·verse ♦◇◇ /rɪvɜrs/ (**reverses, reversing, reversed**) **1** V-T When someone or something **reverses** a decision, policy, or trend, they change it to the opposite decision, policy, or trend. 使 (决定、政策、趋势) 转向；逆转 ❑ *They have made it clear they will not reverse the decision to increase prices.* 他们已经明确表示不会为了提高价格而转变这一决定。 **2** V-T If you **reverse** the order of a set of things, you arrange them in the opposite order, so that the first thing comes last. 颠倒 (顺序) ❑ *Because the normal word order is reversed in passive sentences, they are sometimes hard to follow.* 由于正常语序在被动句中被颠倒过来了，所以有时很难理解。 **3** V-T If you **reverse** the positions or functions of two things, you change them so that each thing has the position or function that the other one had. 调换 (位置、功能) ❑ *He reversed the position of the two stamps.* 他调换了两张邮票的位置。 **4** V-T/V-I When a car **reverses** or when you **reverse** it, the car is driven backward. 倒 (车)；(车) 倒过来 [mainly BRIT]

in AM, usually use **back up**

5 N-UNCOUNT If your car is **in reverse**, you have changed gears so that you can drive it backward. (汽车的) 倒档 ❑ *He lurched the car in reverse along the ruts to the access road.* 他沿着车辙颠簸着倒行到通行道。 **6** ADJ **Reverse** means opposite from what you expect or to what has just been described. 相反的 ❑ *The wrong attitude will have exactly the reverse effect.* 这种错误的态度会得到恰好相反的结果。 **7** N-SING If you say that one thing is **the reverse** of another, you are emphasizing that the first thing is the complete opposite of the second thing. 相反物；相反面 ❑ *He was not at all jolly. Quite the reverse.* 他一点儿也不高兴。恰恰相反。 **8** N-SING **The reverse** or **the reverse side** of a flat object which has two sides is the less important or the other side. 背面；反面 ❑ *A chart on the reverse of this letter highlights your savings.* 这封信背面的图表着重写明了你的存款情况。 **9** PHRASE If something happens **in reverse** or goes **into reverse**, things happen in the opposite way from what usually happens or from what has been happening. 朝相反方向；反向地 (发展) ❑ *Amis tells the story in reverse, from the moment the man dies.* 埃米斯以倒叙方式讲这个故事，从那个男人死去的那一刻开始。 **10** PHRASE If you **reverse the charges** when you make a telephone call, the person who you are phoning pays the cost of the call and not you. 对方付费电话；受话人付费 [mainly BRIT]

in AM, usually use **call collect**

★ **re·vers·ible** /rɪvɜrsɪbᵊl/ **1** ADJ If a process or an action is **reversible**, its effects can be reversed so that the original situation returns. 可逆的 ❑ *Heart disease is reversible in some cases, according to a study published last summer.* 根据去年夏天发表的一项研究，心脏病有时是可逆的。 **2** ADJ **Reversible** clothes or materials have been made so that either side can be worn or shown as the outside. 可两面穿用的 ❑ *...a reversible vest.* …一件两面穿马甲。

★ **re·vert** /rɪvɜrt/ (**reverts, reverting, reverted**) **1** V-I When people or things **revert to** a previous state, system, or type of behavior, they go back to it. 恢复 (先前的状态、制度或行为) ❑ *Jackson said her boss became increasingly depressed and reverted to smoking heavily.* 杰克逊说她的老板变得越来越抑郁，又重新大量吸烟了。 **2** V-I When someone **reverts to** a previous topic, they start talking or thinking about it again. 重回 (先前的话题) [WRITTEN] ❑ *In the car she reverted to the subject uppermost in her mind. "You know, I really believe what Grandma told you."* 在车里她又提起了她头脑里最重要的话题："你知道，我确实相信奶奶告诉你的那些事。" **3** V-I If property, rights, or money **revert to** someone, they become that person's again after someone else has had them for a period of time. 归还 [LEGAL] ❑ *When the lease ends, the property reverts to the owner.* 租约到期后，房屋归还业主。

re·view ♦♦◇ /rɪvyu/ (**reviews, reviewing, reviewed**) **1** N-COUNT A **review of** a situation or system is its formal examination by people in authority. This is usually done in order to see whether it can be improved or corrected. (上级的) 审查 [oft N "of" n, also prep N] ❑ *The president ordered a review of U.S. economic aid to Jordan.* 总统下令对美国向约旦提供的经济援助进行一次审查。 **2** V-T If you **review** a situation or system, you consider it carefully to see what is wrong with it or how it could be improved. 审裁；审度 ❑ *The president reviewed the situation with his cabinet yesterday.* 总统昨天与他的内阁成员审度了局势。 **3** N-COUNT A **review** is a report in the media in which someone gives their opinion of something such as a new book or movie. 评论 ❑ *We've never had a good review in the music press.* 我们在音乐媒体内未曾得到过好评。 **4** V-T If someone **reviews** something such as a new book or movie, they write a report or give a talk on television or radio in which they express their opinion of it. 对 (新作品) 作评论 ❑ *Richard Coles reviews all the latest video releases.* 理查德•科尔斯对最近发行的所有录像做了评论。 **5** V-T/V-I When you **review for** an examination, you read things again and make notes in order to be prepared for the examination. 复习 [AM] ❑ *Reviewing for exams gives you a chance to bring together all the individual parts of the course.* 考前复习给你一个把课程各独立部分融会贯通的机会。 ❑ *Review all the notes you need to cover for each course.* 复习所有你需要涵盖的每门课的笔记。 ● N-COUNT **Review** is also a noun. 复习

in BRIT, use **revise**

R

❑ *If you have to cover 12 chapters in American history, begin by planning on three two-hour reviews with four chapters per session.* 如果你必须涵盖美国史的12个章节，首先计划3次2小时的复习，每次4章。

Thesaurus *review* 另参见:
N. analysis, evaluation, inspection, study 1
V. prepare, read, study 5

Word Partnership *review* 的常用搭配:
N. **performance** review 1
review **a case**, review **evidence** 2
book review, **film/movie** review, **restaurant** review 3
review **questions** 5

re·view·er /rɪvyuər/ (**reviewers**) N-COUNT A **reviewer** is a person who reviews new books, movies, television programs, CDs, plays, or concerts. 评论员 ❑ *...the reviewer for Atlantic Monthly.* …《大西洋月刊》的评论员。

re·vise /rɪvaɪz/ (**revises, revising, revised**) 1 V-T If you **revise** the way you think about something, you adjust your thoughts, usually in order to make them better or more suited to how things are. 修正（对某事的想法）❑ *With time he came to revise his opinion of the profession.* 随着时间的推移，他开始修正自己对这一职业的看法。 2 V-T If you **revise** a price, amount, or estimate, you change it to make it more fair, realistic, or accurate. 调整（使更合理、实际、准确）❑ *They realized that some of their prices were higher than their competitors' and revised prices accordingly.* 他们意识到他们的部分价格比竞争对手的高，就相应地调整了价格。 3 V-T When you **revise** an article, a book, a law, or a piece of music, you change it in order to improve it, make it more modern, or make it more suitable for a particular purpose. 修改；修订（使改进、更时尚、更适于某目的）❑ *Three editors handled the work of revising the articles for publication.* 3名编辑负责对要出版的文章进行修订的工作。 4 V-I When you **revise for** an examination, you read things again and make notes in order to be prepared for the examination. （为考试）复习 [BRIT]
in AM, use **review**

▲ **re·vi·sion** /rɪvɪʒən/ (**revisions**) 1 N-VAR To make a **revision of** something that is written or something that has been decided means to make changes to it in order to improve it, make it more modern, or make it more suitable for a particular purpose. 修改；修正 ❑ *The phase of writing that is actually most important is revision.* 写作中真正最重要的阶段是修改。 2 N-UNCOUNT When people who are studying do **revision**, they read things again and make notes in order to prepare for an examination. 复习 [BRIT]
in AM, use **review**

re·vis·it /rivɪzɪt/ (**revisits, revisiting, revisited**) 1 V-T If you **revisit** a place, you return there for a visit after you have been away for a long time, often after the place has changed a lot. 重游 ❑ *In the summer, when we returned to Canada, we revisited this lake at dawn.* 夏天，我们回到加拿大后，在黎明时分重游了这个湖。 2 V-T If you **revisit** a subject or topic, you discuss it again or consider it again. 重新讨论；重新考虑 ❑ *The committee agreed to revisit the issue at their next meeting.* 该委员会同意在他们下次会议上重新讨论这个问题。

▲ **re·vi·tal·ise** /rivaɪtəlaɪz/ [BRIT] → see **revitalize**

Word Link *vita ≈ life : revitalize, vital, vitality*

▲ **re·vi·tal·ize** /rivaɪtəlaɪz/ (**revitalizes, revitalizing, revitalized**)
in BRIT, also use **revitalise**
V-T To **revitalize** something that has lost its activity or its health means to make it active or healthy again. 使恢复元气；使复苏 ❑ *This hair conditioner is excellent for revitalizing dry, lifeless hair.* 这种护发素对使干枯、无生气的头发重新焕发光彩非常有效。

Word Link *viv ≈ living : revival, survive, vivacious*

re·viv·al /rɪvaɪvəl/ (**revivals**) 1 N-COUNT When there is a **revival of** something, it becomes active or popular again. 再流行；复兴 ❑ *This return to realism has produced a revival of interest in a number of artists.* 这次向现实主义的回归引起了对许多艺术家兴趣的复苏。 2 N-COUNT A **revival** is a new production of a play, an opera, or a ballet. 新版演出 ❑ *...John Clement's revival of Chekhov's "The Seagull."* …约翰·克莱门的新版特契诃夫的《海鸥》。 3 N-UNCOUNT A **revival** meeting is a public religious event that is intended to make people more interested in Christianity. 奋兴（布道会）❑ *He toured the country organizing revival meetings.* 他巡游全国，组织奋兴布道会。

★ **re·vive** /rɪvaɪv/ (**revives, reviving, revived**) 1 V-T/V-I When something such as the economy, a business, a trend, or a feeling **is revived** or when it **revives**, it becomes active, popular, or successful again. 恢复；复兴 ❑ *...an attempt to revive the economy.* …一次重振经济的尝试。 2 V-T When someone **revives** a play, opera, or ballet, they present a new production of it. 重新上演（作品的新版）❑ *His plays continue to be revived both here and abroad.* 他的剧作在国内外继续重新上演。 3 V-T/V-I If you **revive** someone who has fainted or if they **revive**, they become conscious again. 使苏醒；苏醒 ❑ *She and a neighbor tried in vain to revive him.* 她和一个邻居试图使他苏醒过来，却没有成功。

▲ **re·voke** /rɪvoʊk/ (**revokes, revoking, revoked**) V-T When people in authority **revoke** something such as a license, a law, or an agreement, they cancel it. 撤销；废除 [FORMAL] ❑ *The government revoked her husband's license to operate migrant labor crews.* 政府撤销了她丈夫经营流动劳工团队的许可证。

re·volt /rɪvoʊlt/ (**revolts, revolting, revolted**) 1 N-VAR A **revolt** is an illegal and often violent attempt by a group of people to change their country's political system. 造反；叛乱 ❑ *It was undeniably a revolt by ordinary people against their leaders.* 不可否认，这是一场普通百姓反抗领导人的起义。 2 V-I When people **revolt**, they make an illegal and often violent attempt to change their country's political system. 造反；叛乱 ❑ *In 1375 the townspeople revolted.* 1375年，市民造反了。 3 N-VAR A **revolt** by a person or group against someone or something is a refusal to accept the authority of that person or thing. 反抗；抵制 ❑ *Conservative Republicans had led the revolt against the budget package.* 保守共和党带领了对这一预算计划的抵制。 4 V-I When people **revolt against** someone or something, they reject the authority of that person or reject that thing. 反抗；抵制 ❑ *In 1978 California taxpayers revolted against higher taxes.* 1978年加利福尼亚的纳税人抵制了高税费。

re·volt·ing /rɪvoʊltɪŋ/ ADJ If you say that something or someone is **revolting**, you mean you think they are horrible and disgusting. 令人厌恶的 ❑ *The smell in the cell was revolting.* 这间牢房里的味道令人作呕。

revo·lu·tion ♦◇◇ /rɛvəluʃən/ (**revolutions**) 1 N-COUNT A **revolution** is a successful attempt by a large group of people to change the political system of their country by force. 革命 ❑ *The period since the revolution has been one of political turmoil.* 自革命以来的这一段时期是一个政治动荡的时期。 2 N-COUNT A **revolution** in a particular area of human activity is an important change in that area. 重大变革 ❑ *The nineteenth century witnessed a revolution in ship design and propulsion.* 19世纪经历了船舶设计和推进上的一次重大变革。

revo·lu·tion·ary ♦◇◇ /rɛvəluʃəneri/ (**revolutionaries**) 1 ADJ **Revolutionary** activities, organizations, or people have the aim of causing a political revolution. 革命的 ❑ *Do you know anything about the revolutionary movement?* 你对这次革命运动有什么了解吗？ 2 N-COUNT A **revolutionary** is a person who tries to cause a revolution or who takes an active part in one. 革命者 ❑ *The revolutionaries laid down their arms and their leaders went into voluntary exile.* 这些革命者们放下了武器，他们的领袖们自愿流亡。 3 ADJ **Revolutionary** ideas and developments involve great changes in the way that something is done or made. 革命性的 ❑ *Invented in 1951, the rotary engine is a revolutionary concept in internal combustion.* 1951年发明的旋转引擎是内燃领域的一个革命性观念。

revo·lu·tion·ise /rɛvəluʃənaɪz/ [BRIT] → see **revolutionize**

revo·lu·tion·ize /rɛvəluʃənaɪz/ (**revolutionizes, revolutionizing, revolutionized**)
in BRIT, also use **revolutionise**
V-T When something **revolutionizes** an activity, it causes great changes in the way that it is done. 彻底改变 ❑ *Over the past forty years plastics have revolutionised the way we live.* 在过去40年里，塑料完全改变了我们的生活方式。

re·volve /rɪvɒlv/ (**revolves, revolving, revolved**) 1 V-I If you say that one thing **revolves around** another thing, you mean that the second thing is the main feature or focus of the first thing. 以…为中心 ❑ *Since childhood, her life has revolved around tennis.* 从孩提时代起，她的生活就一直以网球为中心。 2 V-I If a discussion or conversation **revolves around** a particular topic, it is mainly about that topic. 围绕（某个主题）❑ *The debate revolves around specific accounting techniques.* 这场讨论围绕具体的会计技巧。 3 V-I If one object **revolves around** another object, the first object turns in a circle

r

around the second object. 围绕…转 ❑ *The satellite revolves around the earth once every hundred minutes.* 该人造卫星每100分钟绕地球旋转一圈。 **4** V-T/V-I When something **revolves** or when you **revolve** it, it moves or turns in a circle around a central point or line. 使旋转; 旋转 ❑ *Overhead, the fan revolved slowly.* 头顶上，电扇缓慢地旋转着。

re·volv·er /rɪvɒlvər/ (**revolvers**) N-COUNT A **revolver** is a kind of hand gun. Its bullets are kept in a revolving cylinder in the gun. 左轮手枪

re·vue /rɪvyu/ (**revues**) N-COUNT A **revue** is a theatrical performance consisting of songs, dances, and jokes about recent events. 时事讽刺歌舞剧

re·vul·sion /rɪvʌlʃən/ N-UNCOUNT Someone's **revulsion** at something is the strong feeling of disgust or disapproval they have toward it. 极端厌恶 ❑ *...their revulsion at the act of desecration.* …他们对亵渎行为的极端厌恶。

re·ward ♦◇◇ /rɪwɔrd/ (**rewards, rewarding, rewarded**) **1** N-COUNT A **reward** is something that you are given, for example because you have behaved well, worked hard, or provided a service to the community. 奖励 ❑ *A bonus of up to five percent can be added to a student's final exam score as a reward for good spelling, punctuation, and grammar.* 作为对正确的拼写、标点和语法的奖励，多达5分的加分可以加到学生期末考试成绩中。 **2** N-COUNT A **reward** is a sum of money offered to anyone who can give information about lost or stolen property, a missing person, or someone who is wanted by the police. 赏金 ❑ *The firm last night offered a $10,000 reward for information leading to the conviction of the killer.* 这家公司昨晚对能将凶手定罪的信息悬赏1万美元。 **3** V-T If you do something and **are rewarded** with a particular benefit, you receive that benefit as a result of doing that thing. 回报 ❑ *Make the extra effort to impress the buyer and you will be rewarded with a quicker sale at a better price.* 格外卖力地给买主一个好印象，你就会被报以用更佳的价格更快地卖掉商品。 **4** N-COUNT The **rewards** of something are the benefits that you receive as a result of doing or having that thing. 回报 ❑ *The company is just starting to reap the rewards of long-term investments.* 这家公司正开始收获长期投资的回报。

Thesaurus *reward* 另参见:

N. bonus, prize; (*ant.*) punishment **1**

Word Partnership *reward* 的常用搭配:

N. reward **for good behavior, risk and** reward **1**
reward **for information** **2**
V. **give** *someone* **a** reward, **offer a** reward **1** **2**

re·ward·ing /rɪwɔrdɪŋ/ ADJ An experience or action that is **rewarding** gives you satisfaction or brings you benefits. 令人满意的; 令人有所收获的 ❑ *...a career that she found stimulating and rewarding.* …一项她感到激发人的、令人有所收获的职业。

R

re·wind /riwaɪnd/ (**rewinds, rewinding, rewound**) V-T/V-I When the tape in a video or tape recorder **rewinds** or when you **rewind** it, the tape goes backwards so that you can play it again. Compare **fast forward**. 把(录像带、录音带)倒回去; 倒带 ❑ *Wendy rewound the tape and played the message again.* 温迪把录音带倒了回去，把那条留言又放了一遍。

re·work /riwɜrk/ (**reworks, reworking, reworked**) V-T If you **rework** something such as an idea or a piece of writing, you reorganize it and make changes to it in order to improve it or bring it up to date. 修改; 重写 ❑ *See if you can rework your schedule and come up with practical ways to reduce the number of hours you're on call.* 看看你能否修改你的时间表，想出切实可行的方法来减少你待命的时间。

re·write /riraɪt/ (**rewrites, rewriting, rewrote, rewritten**) **1** V-T If someone **rewrites** a piece of writing such as a book, an article, or a law, they write it in a different way in order to improve it. 重写 ❑ *Following this critique, students rewrite their papers and submit them for final evaluation.* 遵照这一评语，学生们重写他们的论文并交上去以接受终审。 **2** V-T If you accuse someone such as a government of **rewriting** history, you are criticizing them for selecting and presenting particular historical events in a way that suits their own purposes. 篡改(历史) [DISAPPROVAL] ❑ *We have always been an independent people, no matter how they rewrite history.* 无论他们如何篡改历史，我们一直都是一个独立的民族。

▲ **rheto·ric** /rɛtərɪk/ **1** N-UNCOUNT If you refer to speech or writing as **rhetoric**, you disapprove of it because it is intended to convince and impress people but may not be sincere or honest. 虚华词藻 [DISAPPROVAL] ❑ *The change is largely cosmetic, a matter of acceptable political rhetoric rather than social reality.* 这一变化主要是表面文章，不过是受欢迎的政治性虚华词藻而非社会现实。 **2** N-UNCOUNT **Rhetoric** is the skill or art of using language effectively. 修辞艺术 [FORMAL] ❑ *...the noble institutions of political life, such as political rhetoric, public office, and public service.* …政治生活中令人尊崇的机制，诸如政治修辞艺术、政府机构以及公益服务。

rhe·tori·cal /rɪtɔrɪkəl/ **1** ADJ A **rhetorical** question is one that is asked in order to make a statement rather than to get an answer. 修辞上的(设问); 反问的 ❑ *He grimaced slightly, obviously expecting no answer to his rhetorical question.* 他稍稍做了个苦相，显然并不指望对他的修辞性设问有所回答。 ● **rhe·tori·cal·ly** /rɪtɔrɪkli/ ADV 修辞上地(设问); 反问地 [ADV **with** v] ❑ *"Do these kids know how lucky they are?" Jackson asked rhetorically.* "这些孩子知道他们有多幸运吗？"杰克逊反问道。 **2** ADJ **Rhetorical** language is intended to be grand and impressive. 词藻华丽的; 修辞性的(语言) [FORMAL] ❑ *These arguments may have been used as a rhetorical device to argue for a perpetuation of a United Nations role.* 这些争论可能已被用作支持联合国角色永存的一种修辞手段。 ● **rhe·tori·cal·ly** ADV 词藻华丽地; (语言)修辞性地 ❑ *Suddenly, the narrator speaks in his most rhetorically elevated mode.* 突然，讲述者以其最华丽的措辞方式讲起来。

rhi·no /raɪnoʊ/ (**rhinos**) N-COUNT A **rhino** is the same as a **rhinoceros**. 犀牛 [INFORMAL]

rhi·noc·er·os /raɪnɒsərəs/ (**rhinoceroses**) N-COUNT A **rhinoceros** is a large Asian or African animal with thick, gray skin and a horn, or two horns, on its nose. 犀牛

▲ **rhyme** /raɪm/ (**rhymes, rhyming, rhymed**) **1** V-RECIP If one word **rhymes with** another or if two words **rhyme**, they have a very similar sound. Words that rhyme with each other are often used in poems. (字、词) 押韵 ❑ *June always rhymes with moon in old love songs.* **June** (六月) 在古老的情歌中总是和**moon** (月亮) 押韵。 ❑ *...the sort of people who give their children names that rhyme: Donnie, Ronnie, Connie.* …给孩子们起押韵名字 (如多尼、罗尼、康尼) 的那种人。 **2** V-I If a poem or song **rhymes**, the lines end with words that have very similar sounds. (诗、歌曲) 押韵 ❑ *In his efforts to make it rhyme, he seems to have chosen the first word that came into his head.* 为了努力使其押韵，他似乎选择了进到他脑袋里的第一个词。 **3** N-COUNT A **rhyme** is a word which rhymes with another word, or a set of lines which rhyme. 押韵词 ❑ *The one rhyme for passion is fashion.* 与passion押韵的词是fashion。 **4** N-COUNT A **rhyme** is a short poem which has rhyming words at the ends of its lines. 押韵短诗 ❑ *He was teaching Helen a little rhyme.* 他在教海伦一首短小的押韵诗。 **5** N-UNCOUNT **Rhyme** is the use of rhyming words as a technique in poetry. If something is written **in rhyme**, it is written as a poem in which the lines rhyme. (诗歌中的) 用韵; 押韵 ❑ *The plays are in rhyme.* 这些剧作是用韵文写成的。

rhythm ♦◇◇ /rɪðəm/ (**rhythms**) **1** N-VAR A **rhythm** is a regular series of sounds or movements. 节奏 ❑ *His music of that period fused the rhythms of Jazz with classical forms.* 他那段时期的音乐融合了爵士乐的节奏和古典音乐的形式。 **2** N-COUNT A **rhythm** is a regular pattern of changes, for example changes in your body, in the seasons, or in the tides. (身体、季节等的) 规律性变化 ❑ *Begin to listen to your own body rhythms.* 开始聆听你自己身体的规律性变化。
→ see **drum**

rhyth·mic /rɪðmɪk/ or **rhythmical** /rɪðmɪkəl/ ADJ A **rhythmic** movement or sound is repeated at regular intervals, forming a regular pattern or beat. 有节奏的 ❑ *Good breathing is slow, rhythmic and deep.* 良好的呼吸缓慢、有节奏并且深沉。 ● **rhyth·mi·cal·ly** /rɪðmɪkli/ ADV 有节奏地 [ADV **after** v] ❑ *She stood, swaying her hips, moving rhythmically.* 她站着，摇摆着臀部，有节奏地动着。

rib /rɪb/ (**ribs**) **1** N-COUNT Your **ribs** are the 12 pairs of curved bones that surround your chest. 肋骨 ❑ *Her heart was thumping against her ribs.* 当时她的心挨着她的肋骨砰砰直跳。 **2** N-COUNT A **rib of** meat such as beef or pork is a piece that has been cut to include one of the animal's ribs. 排骨 ❑ *...a rib of beef.* …一块牛小排。 ❑ *...pork ribs.* …猪排骨。

rib·bon /rɪbən/ (**ribbons**) **1** N-VAR A **ribbon** is a long, narrow piece of cloth that you use for tying things together or as a decoration. 装饰带 ❑ *She had tied back her hair with a peach satin ribbon.* 她用一条桃红色的缎带把头发扎在了脑后。 **2** N-COUNT A typewriter or printer **ribbon** is a long, narrow piece of cloth containing ink and is used in a typewriter or printer. 色带

Word Web rice

An ancient Chinese myth says that an animal gave humans the gift of **rice**. Once a large flood destroyed all the crops. When the people returned from the hills, they saw a dog. It had bunches of rice **seeds** in its tail. They planted this new **grain** and were never hungry again. In many Asian countries the words for rice and **food** are identical. Rice has many non-food uses. It is the main ingredient in some kinds of laundry **starch**. The Japanese make a liquor called saké from it. And in Thailand, rice **straw** is made into hats and shoes.

rice ♦◇◇ /raɪs/ (**rices**) N-MASS **Rice** consists of white or brown grains taken from a cereal plant. You cook rice and usually eat it with meat or vegetables. 米 ❑ *...a meal consisting of chicken, rice, and vegetables.* …有鸡肉、米饭和蔬菜的一餐。
→ see Word Web: **rice**
→ see **grain**

rich ♦♦◇ /rɪtʃ/ (**richer, richest, riches**) 1 ADJ A **rich** person has a lot of money or valuable possessions. 富的 ❑ *You're going to be a very rich man.* 你将成为一个非常富的人。 ● N-PLURAL **The rich** are rich people. 富人 ❑ *This is a system in which the rich are taken care of and the poor are left to suffer.* 这是个富人受关照，而穷人遭罪的制度。 2 N-PLURAL **Riches** are valuable possessions or large amounts of money. 财富 ❑ *An Olympic gold medal can lead to untold riches for an athlete.* 一枚奥运金牌能为一名运动员带来数不尽的财富。 3 ADJ A **rich** country has a strong economy and produces a lot of wealth, so many people who live there have a high standard of living. 富强的 ❑ *There is hunger in many parts of the world, even in rich countries.* 饥饿在世界许多地方都存在，甚至在一些富国。 4 N-PLURAL If you talk about the Earth's **riches**, you are referring to things that exist naturally in large quantities and that are useful and valuable, for example minerals, wood, and oil. (自然) 资源 ❑ *...Russia's vast natural riches.* …俄罗斯巨大的自然资源。 5 ADJ If something is **rich in** a useful or valuable substance or is a **rich source of** it, it contains a lot of it. 富含的 [v-link ADJ "in" n, ADJ n] ❑ *Liver and kidneys are particularly rich in vitamin A.* 肝脏和肾脏尤其富含维生素A。 6 ADJ **Rich** food contains a lot of fat or oil. (食物) 油腻的 ❑ *Additional cream would make it too rich.* 额外的奶油会使它过于油腻。 ● **rich·ness** N-UNCOUNT 油腻 ❑ *A squeeze of fresh lime juice cuts the richness of the avocado.* 挤一点鲜青柠汁能减少鳄梨的油腻。 ❑ *...the richness of the pudding.* …布丁的油腻。 7 ADJ **Rich** soil contains large amounts of substances that make it good for growing crops or flowers. (土壤) 肥沃的 ❑ *Farmers grow rice in the rich soil.* 农民们在肥沃的土地上种水稻。 8 ADJ A **rich** deposit of a mineral or other substance is a large amount of it. 富饶的 (矿藏等) ❑ *...the country's rich deposits of the metal lithium.* …该国富饶的锂金属矿藏。 ● **rich·ness** N-UNCOUNT 富饶 ❑ *...the richness of Tibet's mineral deposits.* …西藏矿藏之富饶。 9 ADJ If you say that something is a **rich** vein or source of something such as humor, ideas, or information, you mean that it can provide a lot of that thing. 丰富的 (来源) [ADJ n] ❑ *The director discovered a rich vein of sentimentality.* 导演发现了多愁善感的丰富源泉。 10 ADJ **Rich** smells are strong and very pleasant. **Rich** colors and sounds are deep and very pleasant. 浓郁的 (气味); 浓厚的 (色彩) ❑ *...a rich and luxuriously perfumed bath essence.* …一种浓郁的、富含香气的沐浴精华乳。 ● **rich·ness** N-UNCOUNT (气味的) 浓郁; (色彩的) 浓厚 ❑ *His musicals were infused with richness of color and visual detail.* 他的音乐剧充满了浓厚色彩与视觉细节。 11 ADJ A **rich** life or history is one that is interesting because it is full of different events and activities. 丰富多彩的 (生活、历史) ❑ *A rich and varied cultural life is essential for this couple.* 丰富多彩的、多样化的文化生活对于这对夫妇而言是必不可少的。 ● **rich·ness** N-UNCOUNT 丰富多彩性 ❑ *It all adds to the richness of human life.* 这都增添了人类生活的丰富多彩性。 12 ADJ A **rich** collection or mixture contains a wide and interesting variety of different things. 各种各样的; 丰富的 (种类) ❑ *Visitors can view a rich and colorful array of aquatic plants and animals.* 参观者可以观赏到一系列各种各样、色彩斑斓的水生动植物。 ● **rich·ness** N-UNCOUNT 丰富性; 多样性 ❑ *...a huge country, containing a richness of culture and diversity of landscape.* …一个具有文化丰富性和地貌多样性的大国。

Thesaurus *rich* 另参见:

ADJ. affluent, wealthy; (*ant.*) poor 1 3

Word Partnership *rich* 的常用搭配:

ADJ. rich **and beautiful**, rich **and famous**, rich **and powerful** 1
V. **become** rich, **get** rich **(quick)** 1
N. rich **kids**, rich **man/people**, rich **and poor** 1
rich **country/nation** 3
rich **in natural resources** 5
rich **diet**, rich **food** 6
rich **color** 10
rich **culture**, rich **heritage**, rich **history**, rich **tradition** 11

rich·ly /rɪtʃli/ 1 ADV If something is **richly** colored, flavored, or perfumed, it has a pleasantly strong color, flavor, or perfume. 浓厚地; 浓郁地 ❑ *...Renaissance masterpieces, so richly colored and lustrous.* …文艺复兴时期的杰作，如此地色彩鲜艳而且光泽柔和。 2 ADV If something is **richly** decorated, patterned, or furnished, it has a lot of elaborate and beautiful decoration, patterns, or furniture. 繁丽地; 华丽地 ❑ *Coffee steamed in the richly decorated silver pot.* 咖啡在装饰华丽的银壶里冒着热气。 3 ADV If you say that someone **richly** deserves an award, success, or victory, you approve of what they have done and feel very strongly that they deserve it. 完全地 [FEELINGS] ❑ *He achieved the success he so richly deserved.* 他获得了他完全应得的成功。 4 ADV If you are **richly** rewarded for doing something, you get something very valuable or pleasant in return for doing it. 丰厚地 ❑ *It is a difficult book to read, but it richly rewards the effort.* 这是本难读的书，不过它会丰厚回报为之所付出的努力。

rick·ety /rɪkɪti/ ADJ A **rickety** structure or piece of furniture is not very strong or well made, and seems likely to collapse or break. 摇晃的; 不稳固的 ❑ *Mona climbed the rickety wooden stairs.* 莫娜爬上了摇摇晃晃的木楼梯。

rid ♦◇◇ /rɪd/ (**rids, ridding**)

The form **rid** is used in the present tense and is the past tense and past participle of the verb.

1 PHRASE When you **get rid of** something that you do not want or do not like, you take action so that you no longer have it or suffer from it. 处理掉某物; 摆脱掉某物 ❑ *The owner needs to get rid of the car for financial reasons.* 出于经济原因，车主需要处理掉这辆车。 2 PHRASE If you **get rid of** someone who is causing problems for you or who you do not like, you do something to prevent them from affecting you anymore, for example by making them leave. 摆脱掉某人; 撵走某人 ❑ *He believed that his manager wanted to get rid of him for personal reasons.* 他认为他的经理出于个人原因想要撵走他。 3 V-T If you **rid** a place or person **of** something undesirable or unwanted, you succeed in removing it completely from that place or person. 使 (某地、某人) 摆脱 ❑ *The proposals are an attempt to rid the country of political corruption.* 这些提议是使该国摆脱政治腐败的一种尝试。 4 V-T If you **rid yourself of** something you do not want, you take action so that you no longer have it or are no longer affected by it. 使 (自己) 摆脱 ❑ *Why couldn't he ever rid himself of those thoughts, those worries?* 为什么他始终摆脱不了那些想法、那些担忧呢? 5 ADJ If you **are rid of** someone or something that you did not want or that caused problems for you, they are no longer with you or causing problems for you. 摆脱了的 [v-link ADJ "of" n] ❑ *The family had sought a way to be rid of her and the problems she had caused them.* 这家人寻求了一个摆脱她以及她给他们制造的麻烦的办法。

rid·den /rɪdᵊn/ **Ridden** is the past participle of **ride**. **ride**的过去分词

-ridden /-rɪdᵊn/ COMB IN ADJ **-ridden** combines with nouns to form adjectives that describe something as having a lot of a

r

particular undesirable thing or quality, or suffering very much because of it. 为…所困扰的（与名词连用构成形容词）❑ *...the debt-ridden economies of Latin America.* …为债务所困扰的拉美经济。

▲**rid·dle** /rɪdᵊl/ (**riddles, riddling, riddled**) 1 N-COUNT A **riddle** is a puzzle or joke in which you ask a question that seems to be nonsense but which has a clever or amusing answer. 谜语 ❑ *All comers to the Sphinx were asked a riddle, and failure to solve it meant death.* 所有来到斯芬克斯面前的人都被问了一个谜语，解答不了就意味着死亡。 2 N-COUNT You can describe something as a **riddle** if people have been trying to understand or explain it but have not been able to. 谜 ❑ *Scientists claimed yesterday to have solved the riddle of the birth of the universe.* 科学家们昨天宣布已经解开了宇宙诞生之谜。 3 V-T If someone **riddles** something **with** bullets or bullet holes, they fire a lot of bullets into it. （用子弹）把…打得千疮百孔 ❑ *Unknown attackers riddled two homes with gunfire.* 不明来路的袭击者用枪把两座房屋打得千疮百孔。

rid·dled /rɪdᵊld/ 1 ADJ If something is **riddled with** bullets or bullet holes, it is full of bullet holes. 布满（枪眼）的 ❑ *The bodies of four people were found riddled with bullets.* 4个人的尸体被发现时布满了枪眼。 2 ADJ If something is **riddled with** undesirable qualities or features, it is full of them. 充满（不好的特质或特征）的 [v-link ADJ "with" n] ❑ *They were the principal shareholders in a bank riddled with corruption.* 他们是一家腐败成风的银行的主要股东。

ride ♦♦◇ /raɪd/ (**rides, riding, rode, ridden**) 1 V-T/V-I When you **ride** a horse, you sit on it and control its movements. 骑（马）；骑马 ❑ *I saw a girl riding a horse.* 我看见一个骑着马的女孩。 ❑ *Can you ride?* 你会骑马吗？ 2 V-T/V-I When you **ride** a bicycle or a motorcycle, you sit on it, control it, and travel along on it. 骑（自行车或摩托车）；骑车 ❑ *Riding a bike is great exercise.* 骑自行车是很好的锻炼。 ❑ *Two men riding on motorcycles opened fire on him.* 两个骑在摩托车上的人向他开了枪。 3 V-I When you **ride in** a vehicle such as a car, you travel in it. 乘坐 ❑ *He prefers traveling on the subway to riding in a limousine.* 他宁愿乘坐地铁出行而不愿乘坐豪华加长轿车。

> When you want to say that someone is controlling a horse, bicycle, or motorbike, you can use **ride** as a transitive verb, with the object coming immediately after it. ❑ *Whether you ride a motorbike, scooter, or moped, get yourself properly trained.* However, if you want to say that someone is a passenger in a vehicle, **ride** must be followed by a preposition. ❑ *I was riding on the back of a friend's bicycle... We are still letting our children ride in the front seat of our cars.* If **ride** is used without an object, a preposition, or any other phrase that specifies the context, it usually refers to the activity of riding a horse. ❑ *"Do you ride?"—"No, I've never been on a horse."*

4 N-COUNT A **ride** is a trip on a horse or bicycle, or in a vehicle. （骑马、骑车、乘车的）旅程 ❑ *She took some friends for a ride in the family car.* 她用私家车载了朋友们一程。 5 N-COUNT In an amusement park, a **ride** is a large machine that people ride on for fun. （游乐园中的）飞车 ❑ *...roller coasters or other thrill rides at amusement parks.* …游乐园里的过山车或其他的飞车娱乐。 6 V-I If you say that one thing **is riding on** another, you mean that the first thing depends on the second thing. 依赖于；取决于 [oft cont] ❑ *Billions of dollars are riding on the outcome of the election.* 数十亿美元取决于选举的结果。 7 → see also **riding** 8 PHRASE If you say that someone faces **a rough ride**, you mean that things are going to be difficult for them because people will criticize them a lot or treat them badly. 难关 [INFORMAL] ❑ *The president could face a rough ride unless the plan works.* 除非计划奏效，否则该总统会面临一个难关。 9 PHRASE If you describe something as **a free ride**, you mean that things are going to be very easy and that people will take advantage of this. 顺利无阻的事 [INFORMAL] ❑ *I've had an opponent every time. I've never had a free ride. I've had to fight.* 每次我都有一个对手。我从未遇到一件一帆风顺的事。我一直都得奋斗。 10 PHRASE If you say that someone **has been taken for a ride**, you mean that they have been deceived or cheated. 受骗 [INFORMAL] ❑ *You got taken for a ride. Why did you give him five thousand dollars?* 你受骗了。你为什么要给他5000美元？ 11 PHRASE If someone **rides herd on** other people or their actions, they supervise them or watch them closely. 监督；严管 [PHR n] [AM] ❑ *...state efforts to ride herd on the oil companies.* …国家严管石油公司的努力。 ❑ *...Hank, who often stayed late riding herd on the day-to-day business of the magazine.* …经常为监督杂志社的日常事务而工作到很晚的汉克。 12 PHRASE Someone who **rides the rails** travels by train, especially over a long period of time and without buying a ticket. （长期乘火车）逃票 [AM] ❑ *It is 1933, the height of the Great Depression, and the hobos are busy riding the rails.* 那是1933年，经济大萧条的高峰期，流动工人们加紧在火车上逃票。

▸ **ride out** PHRASAL VERB If someone **rides out** a storm or a crisis, they manage to survive a difficult period without suffering serious harm. 安然度过 ❑ *The Republicans think they can ride out the political storm.* 共和党人认为他们能安然度过这场政治风暴。

Word Partnership *ride* 的常用搭配：

N.	**bus/car/subway/train** ride, ride **home** 4
V.	**give** *someone* a ride, **go for** a ride, **offer** *someone* a ride 4
ADJ.	**long** ride, **scenic** ride, **short** ride, **smooth** ride 4

rid·er ♦◇◇ /raɪdər/ (**riders**) N-COUNT A **rider** is someone who rides a horse, a bicycle, or a motorcycle as a hobby or job. You can also refer to someone who is riding a horse, a bicycle, or a motorcycle as a rider. 骑手；骑（马、自行车、摩托车）的人 ❑ *She is a very good and experienced rider.* 她是一个有经验的优秀骑手。

ridge /rɪdʒ/ (**ridges**) 1 N-COUNT A **ridge** is a long, narrow piece of raised land. 脊；山脉 ❑ *...a high road along a mountain ridge.* …一条沿山脊而建的公路。 2 N-COUNT A **ridge** is a raised line on a flat surface. （平面上的）隆起线 ❑ *...the bony ridge of the eye socket.* …眼窝的骨质隆起线。

→ see **mountain**

Word Link *cule ≈ small : minuscule, molecule, ridicule*

Word Link *rid, ris ≈ laughing : deride, derision, ridicule*

ridi·cule /rɪdɪkyul/ (**ridicules, ridiculing, ridiculed**) 1 V-T If you **ridicule** someone or **ridicule** their ideas or beliefs, you make fun of them in an unkind way. 嘲笑 ❑ *I admired her all the more for allowing them to ridicule her and never striking back.* 我更加钦佩她了，因为她能够容许让他们嘲笑她而从不回击。 2 N-UNCOUNT If someone or something is an object of **ridicule** or is held up to **ridicule**, someone makes fun of them in an unkind way. 嘲笑 ❑ *As a heavy child, she became the object of ridicule from classmates.* 作为一个胖孩子，她成了同学们的笑柄。

Thesaurus *ridicule* 另参见：

V.	humiliate, mimic, mock; *(ant.)* praise 1

ri·dicu·lous /rɪdɪkyələs/ ADJ If you say that something or someone is **ridiculous**, you mean that they are very foolish. 荒唐可笑的 ❑ *It is ridiculous to suggest we are having a romance.* 说我们之间有风流韵事真是荒唐可笑。

ri·dicu·lous·ly /rɪdɪkyələsli/ ADV You use **ridiculously** to emphasize the fact that you think something is unreasonable or very surprising. 荒唐可笑地 [EMPHASIS] ❑ *Dana bought rolls of silk that seemed ridiculously cheap.* 德娜买了看起来便宜得简直可笑的成卷的丝绸。

rid·ing /raɪdɪŋ/ N-UNCOUNT **Riding** is the activity or sport of riding horses. 骑马 ❑ *The next morning we went riding again.* 第二天早上我们又去骑马了。

rife /raɪf/ ADJ If you say that something, usually something bad, is **rife** in a place or that the place is **rife with** it, you mean that it is very common. （常指坏事）普遍的；猖獗的 [v-link ADJ] ❑ *Speculation is rife that he will be fired.* 他将被解雇的猜测盛行。

ri·fle /raɪfᵊl/ (**rifles, rifling, rifled**) 1 N-COUNT A **rifle** is a gun with a long barrel. 来复枪；步枪 ❑ *They shot him at point blank range with an automatic rifle.* 他们用一支自动步枪在近距离射程内射中了他。 2 V-T/V-I If you **rifle through** things or **rifle** them, you make a quick search among them in order to find something or steal something. 匆忙搜寻 ❑ *I discovered my husband rifling through the filing cabinet.* 我发现我丈夫在档案柜里匆忙地翻找。

rift /rɪft/ (**rifts**) 1 N-COUNT A **rift** between people or countries is a serious quarrel or disagreement that stops them from having a good relationship. 不和 ❑ *The interview reflected a growing rift between the president and Congress.* 这次会见反映出总统与国会间日益加深的不和。 2 N-COUNT A **rift** is a split that appears in something solid, especially in the ground. （尤指地面上的）裂缝 ❑ *The earth convulsed uncontrollably, a rift opened suddenly and, with a horrid sucking sound, swallowed the entire pool.* 大地失控地剧烈震动，一条裂缝突然出现，随着一声可怕的吞吸声，吞噬了整个池塘。

▲**rig** /rɪg/ (**rigs, rigging, rigged**) 1 V-T If someone **rigs** an election, a job appointment, or a game, they dishonestly arrange

it to get the result they want or to give someone an unfair advantage. (欺骗性地) 幕后操纵 ❑ *She accused her opponents of rigging the vote.* 她指责对手幕后操纵了这次选举。 **2** N-COUNT A **rig** is a large structure that is used for looking for oil or gas and for taking it out of the ground or the sea bed. 钻塔 ❑ *...a supply vessel for oil rigs in the Gulf of Mexico.* …一艘墨西哥湾石油钻塔的供给船。 **3** N-COUNT A **rig** is a truck that is made in two or more sections which are jointed together by metal bars, so that the vehicle can turn more easily. 重型铰接式卡车 [AM] ❑ *An inspection of his rig showed that three of the brakes were faulty.* 对他的重型卡车的检查显示有3处刹车存在问题。
→ see **oil**

rig·ging /rɪgɪŋ/ **1** N-UNCOUNT Vote or ballot **rigging** is the act of dishonestly organizing an election to get a particular result. (对投票的) 幕后操纵 [usu supp N] ❑ *She was accused of corruption, of vote rigging on a massive scale.* 她被控腐败以及对投票的大规模幕后操纵。 **2** N-UNCOUNT On a ship, the **rigging** is the ropes which support the ship's masts and sails. (船的) 索具 ❑ *...the howling of the wind in the rigging.* …风吹打船上索具发出的呼啸声。

right
❶ CORRECT, APPROPRIATE, OR ACCEPTABLE
❷ DIRECTION AND POLITICAL GROUPINGS
❸ ENTITLEMENT
❹ DISCOURSE USES
❺ USED FOR EMPHASIS

❶ right ♦♦♦ /raɪt/ (**rights, righting, righted**)
➪ **Please look at meanings 15 and 16 to see if the expression you are looking for is shown under another headword.** **1** ADJ If something is **right**, it is correct and agrees with the facts. 正确的 ❑ *That's absolutely right.* 那是完全正确的。 ❑ *Clocks never told the right time.* 时钟从来都不报正确的时间。 ● ADV **Right** is also an adverb. 正确地 [ADV after v] ❑ *He guessed right about some things.* 他对有些事情猜对了。 **2** ADJ If you do something in the **right** way or in the **right** place, you do it as or where it should be done or was planned to be done. 适当的; 恰当的 ❑ *Walking, done in the right way, is a form of aerobic exercise.* 走路方法得当的话是一种有氧锻炼。 ❑ *They have computerized systems to ensure delivery of the right pizza to the right place.* 他们有计算机化的系统来确保把相应的比萨饼送到相应的地方。 ● ADV **Right** is also an adverb. 适当地; 恰当地 [ADV after v] ❑ *To make sure I did everything right, I bought a fat instruction book.* 为了确保每件事情都做对，我买了一本厚厚的说明书。 **3** ADJ If you say that someone is seen in **all the right** places or knows **all the right** people, you mean that they go to places that are socially acceptable or know people who are socially acceptable. 入流的 ❑ *He was always to be seen in the right places.* 他总是在入流的场所露面。 **4** ADJ If someone is **right about** something, they are correct in what they say or think about it. (说法或想法) 正确的 ❑ *Ron has been right about the result of every general election but one.* 除了一次以外，罗恩对每次大选的结果都判断正确。 **5** ADJ If something such as a choice, action, or decision is the **right** one, it is the best or most suitable one. 最好的; 最恰当的 ❑ *She'd made the right choice in leaving New York.* 她在离开纽约这件事上做出了正确的选择。 **6** ADJ If something is **not right**, there is something unsatisfactory about the situation or thing that you are talking about. 对劲的 [v-link ADJ, with brd-neg] ❑ *Ratatouille doesn't taste right with any other oil.* 普罗旺斯杂烩用其他任何油做出的味道都不正。 **7** ADJ If you think that someone was **right to** do something, you think that there were good moral reasons why they did it. (道德上) 对的; 正当的 [v-link ADJ] ❑ *You were right to do what you did, under the circumstances.* 在那种情况下，你所做的是对的。 **8** ADJ **Right** is used to refer to activities or actions that are considered to be morally good and acceptable. (道德上) 正确的 [v-link ADJ, oft with brd-neg] ❑ *It's not right, leaving her like this.* 这样抛弃她是不对的。 ● N-UNCOUNT **Right** is also a noun. 正确 ❑ *At least he knew right from wrong.* 至少他明白是非。 ● **right·ness** N-UNCOUNT 正确性 ❑ *Many people have very strong opinions about the rightness or wrongness of abortion.* 许多人对于堕胎的对与错有着十分鲜明的意见。 **9** V-T If you **right** something or if it **rights itself**, it returns to its normal or correct state, after being in an undesirable state. 纠正; 矫正 ❑ *They recognize the urgency of righting the economy.* 他们认识到整顿经济的迫切性。 **10** V-T If you **right** a wrong, you do something to make up for a mistake or something bad that you did in the past. 改正 ❑ *We've made progress in righting the wrongs of the past.* 我们已经在改正过去的错误方面取得了进展。 **11** V-T If you **right** something that has fallen or rolled over, or if it **rights itself**, it returns to its normal upright position. 扶正 ❑ *He righted the yacht and continued the race.* 他扶正了帆船，继续比赛。 **12** ADJ The **right** side of a material is the side that is intended to be seen and that faces outward when it is made into something. 正面的 [ADJ n] ❑ *Trim off excess fabric and turn the right side out.* 修剪掉多余的料子，把正面翻出来。 **13** PHRASE If you say that things **are going right**, you mean that your life or a situation is developing as you intended or expected and you are pleased with it. 进展顺利 ❑ *I can't think of anything in my life that's going right.* 我想不出我的生活中有任何进展顺利的事。 **14** PHRASE If you **put** something **right**, you correct something that was wrong or that was causing problems. 纠正某事 ❑ *We've discovered what went wrong and are going to put it right.* 我们已经发现错误所在并会将其纠正。 **15** **heart in the right place** → see **heart** **16** **it serves you right** → see **serve**

❷ right ♦♦♦ /raɪt/

The spelling **Right** is also used for meaning **3**.

1 N-SING The **right** is one of two opposite directions, sides, or positions. If you are facing north and you turn to the right, you will be facing east. In the word "to," the "o" is to the right of the "t." 右边; 右侧 ❑ *Ahead of you on the right will be a lovely garden.* 你的右前方将是一个可爱的花园。 ● ADV **Right** is also an adverb. 向右 [ADV after v] ❑ *Turn right into the street.* 向右拐进那条街。 **2** ADJ Your **right** arm, leg, or ear, for example, is the one which is on the right side of your body. Your **right** shoe or glove is the one which is intended to be worn on your right foot or hand. 右边的 [ADJ n] ❑ *She shattered her right leg in a fall.* 她摔断了右腿。 **3** N-SING-COLL You can refer to people who support the political ideals of capitalism and conservatism as **the right**. They are often contrasted with **the left**, who support the political ideals of socialism. 右翼分子 ❑ *The Republican Right despise him.* 共和党右翼分子看不起他。

Thesaurus *right* 另参见:
ADJ. appropriate, correct, just, true; *(ant.)* unjust, wrong ❶ **1** **2** **5**
conservative, right-wing; *(ant.)* left, liberal ❷ **3**

❸ right ♦♦♦ /raɪt/ (**rights**) **1** N-PLURAL Your **rights** are what you are morally or legally entitled to do or to have. (道德或法律赋予的) 权利 ❑ *They don't know their rights.* 他们不知道自己的权利。 **2** N-SING If you have a **right to** do or to have something, you are morally or legally entitled to do it or to have it. (做某事、拥有某物的) 权利 ❑ *...a woman's right to choose.* …妇女的选择权。 **3** N-PLURAL If someone has **the rights to** a story or book, they are legally allowed to publish it or reproduce it in another form, and nobody else can do so without their permission. 版权 ❑ *An agent bought the rights to his life.* 一个代理商购买了他生平传记的出版权。 **4** PHRASE If something is not the case but you think that it should be, you can say that **by rights** it should be the case. 按理说 ❑ *She did work which by rights should be done by someone else.* 她做了按理本应由其他人做的工作。 **5** PHRASE If someone is a successful or respected person **in** their **own right**, they are successful or respected because of their own efforts and talents rather than those of the people they are closely connected with. 全凭自己地 ❑ *Although now a celebrity in her own right, actress Lynn Redgrave knows the difficulties of living in the shadow of her famous older sister.* 尽管现在女演员林恩·雷德格雷夫依靠自己的努力成了名人，但她明白生活在她那著名的姐姐的阴影之下的艰难。 **6** PHRASE If you say that you **reserve the right to** do something, you mean that you will do it if you feel that it is necessary. 保留 (做某事) 的权利 ❑ *He reserved the right to change his mind.* 他保留了改变主意的权利。 **7** PHRASE If you say that someone is **within** their **rights to** do something, you mean that they are morally or legally entitled to do it. 在某人的权限之内; 某人有权 (做某事) ❑ *You were quite within your rights to refuse to cooperate with him.* 你完全有权拒绝与他合作。

❹ right ♦♦♦ /raɪt/ **1** ADV You use **right** in order to attract someone's attention or to indicate that you have dealt with one thing so you can go on to another. 好; 好了 [ADV cl] [SPOKEN] ❑ *Right, I'll be back in a minute.* 好，我马上回来。 **2** CONVENTION You can use **right** to check whether what you have just said is correct. 对吧; 是吧 [SPOKEN] ❑ *They have a small plane, right?* 他们有一架小型飞机，

对吧？ 3 ADV You can say "**right**" to show that you are listening to what someone is saying and that you accept it or understand it. 对；嗯 [ADV as reply] [SPOKEN] ❏ *"It was probably much harder for older people. Don't you think?"—"Right."* "这对老年人来说可能要困难得多。你不这么认为吗？"——"对。" 4 → see also **all right**

❻ **right** ♦♦♦ /raɪt/ 1 ADV You can use **right** to emphasize the precise place, position, or time of something. (地点、位置、时间) 正好 [ADV adv/prep] [EMPHASIS] ❏ *The back of a car appeared right in front of him.* 一辆车的尾部正好出现在他面前。 2 ADV You can use **right** to emphasize how far something moves or extends or how long it continues. (强调长度) 一直；径直 [ADV prep/adv] [EMPHASIS] ❏ *...the highway that runs through the neutral zone right to the army positions.* …穿越中立区一直通到军队阵营的公路。 3 ADV You can use **right** to emphasize that an action or state is complete. 完全地 (强调动作或状态已结束) [ADV adv/prep] [EMPHASIS] ❏ *The candle had burned right down.* 这支蜡烛已全烧完了。 4 ADV If you say that something happened **right after** a particular time or event or **right before** it, you mean that it happened immediately after or before it. (指发生时间) 恰好；就在 [ADV prep/adv] [EMPHASIS] ❏ *All of a sudden, right after the summer, Mother gets married.* 突然之间，夏天刚过完母亲就结婚了。 5 ADV If you say **I'll be right there** or **I'll be right back**, you mean that you will get to a place or get back to it in a very short time. 马上就；立即就 [ADV adv] [EMPHASIS] ❏ *I'm going to get some water. I'll be right back.* 我去拿些水，马上就回来。 6 PHRASE If you do something **right away**, you do it immediately. 马上；立刻 [INFORMAL, EMPHASIS] ❏ *He wants to see you right away.* 他想立刻见你。 7 PHRASE You can use **right now** to emphasize that you are referring to the present moment. 此刻 [INFORMAL, EMPHASIS] ❏ *Right now I'm feeling very excited.* 此刻我感到非常激动。

right an·gle (**right angles**) 1 N-COUNT A **right angle** is an angle of ninety degrees. A square has four right angles. 直角 2 PHRASE If two things are **at right angles**, they are situated so that they form an angle of 90° where they touch each other. You can also say that one thing is **at right angles to** another. 成直角地 ❏ *...two lasers at right angles.* …两束成直角的激光。

right-angled tri·an·gle [BRIT] → see **right triangle**

right-click (**right-clicks, right-clicking, right-clicked**) V-I To **right-click** or to **right-click on** something means to press the right-hand button on a computer mouse. 右击 (电脑鼠标) [COMPUTING] ❏ *All you have to do is right-click on the desktop and select New Folder.* 你惟一需要做的是在桌面上右击鼠标，然后选择"新建文件夹"。

▲ **right·eous** /raɪtʃəs/ ADJ If you think that someone behaves or lives in a way that is morally good, you can say that they are **righteous**. People sometimes use **righteous** to express their disapproval when they think someone is only behaving in this way so that others will admire or support them. 正直的；(有时指) 假正经的 [FORMAL] ❏ *Aren't you afraid of being seen as a righteous crusader?* 难道你不怕被人看成是一个装腔作势的改革者吗？

R

right·ful /raɪtfəl/ ADJ If you say that someone or something has returned to its **rightful** place or position, they have returned to the place or position that you think they should have. 理应的；本来应有的 [ADJ n] ❏ *We have restored Hamill to his rightful place as editor.* 我们已经把哈米尔恢复到他本应有的编辑职位。 ● **right·ful·ly** ADV 理应地；本来应有地 [ADV group] ❏ *Jealousy is the feeling that someone else has something that rightfully belongs to you.* 嫉妒是一种认为别人占有了本应属于自己的东西的情感。

right-hand ADJ If something is on the **right-hand** side of something, it is positioned on the right of it. 右侧的 [ADJ n] ❏ *...a church on the right-hand side of the road.* …道路右侧的一座教堂。

right-handed ADJ Someone who is **right-handed** uses their right hand rather than their left hand for activities such as writing and sports, and for picking things up. 用右手的 ● ADV **Right-handed** is also an adverb. 用右手地 [ADV after v] ❏ *I batted left-handed and bowled right-handed.* 我左手击球，右手投球。

right-hand man (**right-hand men**) N-COUNT Someone's **right-hand man** is the person who acts as their chief assistant and helps and supports them a lot in their work. 得力助手 ❏ *He is Rupert Murdoch's right-hand man at News International.* 他是鲁珀特•默多克在新闻国际公司的得力助手。

right·ist /raɪtɪst/ (**rightists**) 1 N-COUNT If someone is described as a **rightist**, they are politically conservative and traditional. Rightists support the ideals of capitalism. 右派 2 ADJ If someone has **rightist** views or takes part in **rightist** activities, they are politically conservative and traditional and support the ideas of capitalism. 右派的 [usu ADJ n]

right tri·an·gle (**right triangles**) N-COUNT A **right triangle** has one angle that is a right angle. 直三角形 [AM]

in BRIT, use **right-angled triangle**

→ see **shape**

right-wing ♦◇◇

The spelling **right wing** is also used for meaning 2.

1 ADJ A **right-wing** person or group has conservative or capitalist views. 右翼的；右派的 ❏ *...a right-wing government.* …一个右翼政府。 2 N-SING **The right wing** of a political party consists of the members who have the most conservative or the most capitalist views. 右翼；右派 ❏ *...the right wing of the Republican Party.* …共和党右翼。

right-winger (**right-wingers**) N-COUNT If you think someone has views which are more right-wing than most other members of their party, you can say they are a **right-winger**. 右翼分子；右派分子 ❏ *Across Europe, hard-line right-wingers are gaining power.* 在整个欧洲，主张强硬路线的右翼分子正在赢得政权。

rig·id /rɪdʒɪd/ 1 ADJ Laws, rules, or systems that are **rigid** cannot be changed or varied, and are therefore considered to be rather severe. (法律、规章或制度) 僵死的；过于严格的 [DISAPPROVAL] ❏ *Several colleges in our study have rigid rules about student conduct.* 我们调查中的几所学院对学生行为举止都有过于严格的规定。 ● **ri·gid·ity** /rɪdʒɪdɪti/ N-UNCOUNT (法律、规章或制度的) 僵死；过于严格 ❏ *...the rigidity of government policy.* …政府政策的僵化。 ● **rig·id·ly** ADV 僵死地；过于严格地 [ADV with v] ❏ *The caste system was so rigidly enforced that non-Hindus were not even allowed inside a Hindu house.* 种姓制度执行得太过严格，非印度教徒甚至不得进入印度教徒的家中。 2 ADJ If you disapprove of someone because you think they are not willing to change their way of thinking or behaving, you can describe them as **rigid**. (人) 刻板的；头脑僵化的 [DISAPPROVAL] ❏ *She was a fairly rigid person who had strong religious views.* 她是个相当刻板、有着很强宗教观念的人。 3 ADJ A **rigid** substance or object is stiff and does not bend, stretch, or twist easily. 僵硬的 ❏ *...rigid plastic containers.* …坚硬的塑料容器。 ● **ri·gid·ity** N-UNCOUNT 硬度 ❏ *...the strength and rigidity of glass.* …玻璃的强度与硬度。

rig·or /rɪgər/ (**rigors**)

in BRIT, use **rigour**

1 N-PLURAL If you refer to **the rigors of** an activity or job, you mean the difficult, demanding, or unpleasant things that are associated with it. 艰辛；严酷 ❏ *They're accustomed to the rigors of army life.* 他们已习惯了军旅生活的艰辛。 2 N-UNCOUNT If something is done with **rigor**, it is done in a strict, thorough way. 严谨 ❏ *The prince had performed his social duties with professional rigor.* 王子以职业性的严谨履行了他的社会职责。

★ **rig·or·ous** /rɪgərəs/ 1 ADJ A test, system, or procedure that is **rigorous** is very thorough and strict. (测试、制度、程序) 严格缜密的 ❏ *The selection process is based on rigorous tests of competence and experience.* 挑选过程是建立在对能力和经验严格缜密的考核的基础之上的。 ● **rig·or·ous·ly** ADV 严格缜密地 ❏ *...rigorously conducted research.* …严格进行的研究。 2 ADJ If someone is **rigorous** in the way that they do something, they are very careful and thorough. 一丝不苟的；缜密的 ❏ *He is rigorous in his control of expenditure.* 他在控制开支方面一丝不苟。

ri·gour /rɪgər/ [mainly BRIT] → see **rigor**

★ **rim** /rɪm/ (**rims**) 1 N-COUNT The **rim** of a container such as a cup or glass is the edge that goes all the way around the top. (容器的) 上缘 ❏ *She looked at him over the rim of her glass.* 她沿玻璃杯口看着他。 2 N-COUNT The **rim** of a circular object is its outside edge. (圆形物体的) 外缘；外框 ❏ *...a round mirror with white metal rim.* …一面有白色金属边框的圆镜子。

rind /raɪnd/ (**rinds**) 1 N-VAR The **rind** of a fruit such as a lemon or orange is its thick outer skin. (柠檬、橘子等的) 厚皮 ❏ *...grated lemon rind.* …擦碎的柠檬皮。 2 N-VAR The **rind** of cheese or bacon is the hard outer edge which you do not usually eat. (奶酪、熏肉的) 外皮 ❏ *...a cream cheese with a soft rind.* …一种有松软外皮的奶油奶酪。

ring
❶ TELEPHONING OR MAKING A SOUND
❷ SHAPES AND GROUPS

❶ **ring** ♦♦◇ /rɪŋ/ (**rings, ringing, rang, rung**)
➪ **Please look at meaning 9 to see if the expression you are looking for is shown under another headword.** 1 V-I When a telephone **rings**, it makes a sound to let you know that someone is phoning you. (电话) 响铃 ❑ *As soon as he got home, the phone rang.* 他刚一到家，电话就响了。 ● N-COUNT **Ring** is also a noun. (电话) 响铃声 ❑ *After at least eight rings, an ancient-sounding maid answered the phone.* 在至少八声响铃后，一名听上去很老的女仆接了电话。 ● **ring·ing** N-UNCOUNT (电话) 响铃 ❑ *She was jolted out of her sleep by the ringing of the telephone.* 她被电话响铃惊醒了。 2 V-T/V-I When you **ring** someone, you telephone them. 给…打电话; 打电话 [mainly BRIT]

in AM, usually use **call**

● PHRASAL VERB **Ring up** means the same as **ring**. 给…打电话; 打电话 3 V-T/V-I When you **ring** a bell or when a bell **rings**, it makes a sound. 使 (铃) 响; (铃) 响 ❑ *He heard the school bell ring.* 他听见学校的铃响了。 ● N-COUNT **Ring** is also a noun. (铃的) 响声 ❑ *There was a ring of the bell.* 有铃声。 ● **ring·ing** N-UNCOUNT (铃) 响 ❑ *...the ringing of church bells.* …教堂的钟响。 4 V-I If you say that a place **is ringing with** sound, usually pleasant sound, you mean that the place is completely filled with that sound. (优美的声音) 回荡 [LITERARY] ❑ *The whole place was ringing with music.* 整个地方回荡着音乐声。 5 N-SING You can use **ring** to describe a quality that something such as a statement, discussion, or argument seems to have. For example, if an argument **has a familiar ring**, it seems familiar. 感觉 ❑ *His proud boast of leading "the party of low taxation" has a hollow ring.* 他有关领导"主张低税收的政党"的豪言有空洞的感觉。 6 PHRASE If you **give** someone **a ring**, you phone them. 给某人电话 [mainly BRIT, INFORMAL]

in AM, usually use **call**

❑ *We'll give him a ring as soon as we get back.* 我们一回来就会给他电话。 7 PHRASE If a statement **rings true**, it seems to be true or genuine. If it **rings hollow**, it does not seem to be true or genuine. 听起来真实/不真实 ❑ *Joanna's denial rang true.* 乔安娜的否认听上去像是真的。 8 → see also **ringing** 9 **to ring a bell** → see **bell**

▸ **ring back** PHRASAL VERB If you **ring** someone **back**, you phone them either because they phoned you earlier and you were not there or because you did not finish an earlier telephone conversation. 回电话 [no passive] [BRIT]

in AM, use **call back**

▸ **ring in** PHRASAL VERB If you **ring in**, you phone a place, such as the place where you work. 给某个地方打电话 (如工作单位等) [BRIT]

in AM, use **call in**

▸ **ring off** PHRASAL VERB When you **ring off**, you put down the receiver at the end of a telephone call. 挂断电话 [BRIT]

in AM, use **hang up**

▸ **ring round** or **ring around** PHRASAL VERB If you **ring round** or **ring around**, you phone several people, usually when you are trying to organize something or to find some information. (为组织某事或询问信息) 打很多人电话 [BRIT]

in AM, use **call around**

▸ **ring up** 1 → see **ring** ❶ 2 2 PHRASAL VERB If a store clerk **rings up** a sale on a cash register, he or she presses the keys in order to record the amount that is being spent. 把 (销售额) 记入 (收款机) ❑ *She was ringing up her sale on an ancient cash register.* 她在把销售额记入那台老旧的收款机。 3 PHRASAL VERB If a company **rings up** an amount of money, usually a large amount of money, it makes that amount of money in sales or profits. 挣得 (大笔钱) ❑ *The advertising agency rang up 1.4 billion dollars in yearly sales.* 这家广告代理商的年销售额达14亿美元。

❷ **ring** ♦◇◇ /rɪŋ/ (**rings, ringing, ringed**) 1 N-COUNT A **ring** is a small circle of metal or other substance that you wear on your finger as jewelry. 戒指 ❑ *...a gold wedding ring.* …一枚黄金婚戒。 2 N-COUNT An object or substance that is in the shape of a circle can be described as a **ring**. 环状物; 圈 ❑ *Frank took a large ring of keys from his pocket.* 弗兰克从口袋里拿出了一个大串钥匙。 3 N-COUNT A group of people or things arranged in a circle can be described as a **ring**. (人或物围成的) 圈 ❑ *They then formed a ring around the square.* 他们随后沿广场围成了一圈。 4 N-COUNT At a boxing or wrestling match or a circus, the **ring** is the place where the contest or performance takes place. It consists of an enclosed space with seats around it. 圆形 (表演、竞技) 场地 ❑ *He will never again be allowed inside a boxing ring.* 他将再也不会被允许进入拳击场了。 5 N-COUNT You can refer to an organized group of people who are involved in an illegal activity as a **ring**. 团伙 ❑ *Police are investigating the suspected drug ring at the school.* 警方正在调查这所学校受到贩毒嫌疑的团伙。 6 N-COUNT [BRIT] → see **burner** 7 V-T If a building or place **is ringed with** or **by** something, it is surrounded by it. 围住 [usu passive] ❑ *The areas are sealed off and ringed by troops.* 这一地区被封锁了，被军队包围了。
→ see **circle, jewelry**

ring bind·er (**ring binders**) N-COUNT A **ring binder** is a file with hard covers, which you can insert pages into. The pages are held in by metal rings on a bar attached to the inside of the file. 活页夹

ring·ing /rɪŋɪŋ/ 1 ADJ A **ringing** sound is loud and can be heard very clearly. 响亮的 [ADJ n] ❑ *He hit the metal steps with a ringing crash.* 他很响的一声撞在了金属台阶上。 2 ADJ A **ringing** statement or declaration is one that is made forcefully and is intended to make a powerful impression. (声明、宣言等) 强有力的 [ADJ n] ❑ *...the party's 14th congress, which gave a ringing endorsement to capitalist-style economic reforms.* …对资本主义式经济改革给予了强有力支持的该党的第14次代表大会。

ring road (**ring roads**) also **ringroad** N-COUNT A **ring road** is a road that goes around the edge of a city or town so that traffic does not have to go through the center. 环路 [mainly BRIT]

in AM, usually use **beltway**

ring tone (**ring tones**) N-COUNT The **ring tone** is the sound made by a telephone, especially a cell phone, when it rings. (电话，尤指手机) 铃音 ❑ *They offer 70 hours' standby time, 2hr. 50min. talk time, and 15 ring tones.* 它们给70小时的待机时间、2小时50分钟通话时间以及15种铃音。

rink /rɪŋk/ (**rinks**) N-COUNT A **rink** is a large area covered with ice where people go to ice-skate, or a large area of concrete where people go to roller-skate. 溜冰场; 旱冰场 ❑ *The other skaters were ordered off the rink.* 其他溜冰者被勒令离开溜冰场。

▲ **rinse** /rɪns/ (**rinses, rinsing, rinsed**) 1 V-T When you **rinse** something, you wash it in clean water in order to remove dirt or soap from it. 冲洗 ❑ *It's important to rinse the rice to remove the starch.* 淘洗大米去掉淀粉很重要。 ● N-COUNT **Rinse** is also a noun. 冲洗 ❑ *Clean skin means plenty of lather followed by a rinse with water.* 清洁的皮肤意味着用大量的皂沫清洗，然后用水冲洗。 2 V-T If you **rinse** your mouth, you wash it by filling your mouth with water or with a liquid that kills germs, then spitting it out. 漱 (口) ❑ *Use a toothbrush on your tongue as well, and rinse your mouth frequently.* 用牙刷在舌头上也刷刷，然后频频漱口。 ● PHRASAL VERB **Rinse out** means the same as **rinse**. 漱 (口) ❑ *After her meal she invariably rinsed out her mouth.* 饭后她总漱口。 ● N-MASS **Rinse** is also a noun. 漱口液 ❑ *...mouth rinses with fluoride.* …有氟化物的漱口液。

riot ♦◇◇ /raɪət/ (**riots, rioting, rioted**) 1 N-COUNT When there is a **riot**, a crowd of people behave violently in a public place, for example they fight, throw stones, or damage buildings and vehicles. 暴乱 ❑ *Twelve inmates have been killed during a riot at the prison.* 十二名囚犯在该监狱里的一次暴乱中丧生。 2 V-I If people **riot**, they behave violently in a public place. 闹事 ❑ *Last year 600 inmates rioted, starting fires and building barricades.* 去年600名囚犯闹事，放火并制造路障。 ● **ri·ot·er** N-COUNT (**rioters**) 闹事者 ❑ *The militia dispersed the rioters.* 民兵驱散了闹事者。 ● **ri·ot·ing** N-UNCOUNT 闹事 ❑ *At least fifteen people are now known to have died in three days of rioting.* 目前已知至少有15人在3天的骚乱中丧生。 3 N-SING If you say that there is a **riot of** something pleasant such as color, you mean that there is a large amount of various types of it. (颜色等) 丰富多样 [APPROVAL] ❑ *It would be a riot of color, of poppies and irises and flowers of every kind.* 那将会是五彩斑斓的颜色，由罂粟花、鸢尾花以及各种花卉组成。 4 PHRASE If someone in authority **reads** you **the riot act**, they tell you that you will be punished unless you start behaving properly. 向某人提出不良行为警告 ❑ *I'm glad you read the riot act to Billy. He's still a kid and still needs to be told what to do.* 我很高兴你向比利提出了不良行为警告。他还是个孩子，还是需要有人指导。 5 PHRASE If people **run riot**, they behave in a wild and uncontrolled manner. 肆意撒野 ❑ *Rampaging prisoners ran riot through the jail.* 闹事的囚犯在监狱里肆意

撒野。 **6** PHRASE If something such as your imagination **runs riot**, it is not limited or controlled, and produces ideas that are new or exciting, rather than sensible. (想像力等) 肆意驰骋 ❑ *She dressed strictly for comfort and economy, but let her imagination run riot with costume jewelry.* 她穿衣服严格地追求舒适和经济，但是在佩戴时装首饰方面则让其想像力肆意发挥。

rip /rɪp/ (**rips, ripping, ripped**) **1** V-T/V-I When something **rips** or when you **rip** it, you tear it forcefully with your hands or with a tool such as a knife. 撕；撕裂 ❑ *I felt the banner rip as we were pushed in opposite directions.* 当我们被挤向相反的方向的时候，我感到横幅撕裂了。 **2** N-COUNT A **rip** is a long cut or split in something made of cloth or paper. (布或纸上的) 裂口 ❑ *Looking at the rip in her new dress, she flew into a rage.* 看着新连衣裙上的裂口，她勃然大怒。 **3** V-T If you **rip** something away, you remove it quickly and forcefully. 拚；扯 (掉) ❑ *He ripped away a wire that led to the alarm button.* 他扯掉了连接报警按钮的电线。 **4** V-I If something **rips** into someone or something or **rips** through them, it enters that person or thing so quickly and forcefully that it often goes completely through them. 穿 (过)；穿 (透) ❑ *A volley of bullets ripped into the facing wall.* 一排子弹穿透了对面的墙。 **5** PHRASE If you **let it rip**, you do something forcefully and without trying to control yourself. 尽情地干；敞开地干 [INFORMAL] ❑ *Turn the guitars up full and let it rip.* 把吉他的音量调到最大，尽情地来。

▸ **rip off** **1** PHRASAL VERB If someone **rips** you **off**, they cheat you by charging you too much money for something or by selling you something that is broken or damaged. 宰人；坑人 [INFORMAL] ❑ *The bigger, more reputable online casinos are not going to rip you off.* 规模更大、声誉更好的网上赌场不会宰你。 **2** → see also **rip-off**

▸ **rip up** PHRASAL VERB If you **rip** something **up**, you tear it into small pieces. 撕碎 ❑ *If we wrote, I think he would rip up the letter.* 如果我们写信，我想他会把信撕得粉碎。

→ see **cut**

ripe /raɪp/ (**riper, ripest**) **1** ADJ **Ripe** fruit or grain is fully grown and ready to eat. (水果、谷物) 成熟的 ❑ *Always choose firm, but ripe fruit.* 总该挑选坚挺但成熟的水果。 **2** ADJ If a situation is **ripe for** a particular development or event, you mean that development or event is likely to happen soon. (事态) 成熟的 [v-link ADJ "for" n/-ing] ❑ *A hospital consultant said conditions were ripe for an outbreak of cholera and typhoid.* 一位医院的专家医师说霍乱和伤寒爆发的条件已经成熟。 **3** PHRASE If someone lives to a **ripe old age**, they live until they are very old. 高龄 ❑ *He lived to the ripe old age of 95.* 他活到了95岁的高龄。

rip·en /raɪpən/ (**ripens, ripening, ripened**) V-T/V-I When crops **ripen** or when the sun **ripens** them, they become ripe. (指庄稼) 成熟 ❑ *I'm waiting for the apples to ripen.* 我在等这些苹果成熟。

rip-off (**rip-offs**) N-COUNT If you say that something that you bought was a **rip-off**, you mean that you were charged too much money or that it was of very poor quality. 宰人货 [INFORMAL] ❑ *The service charge is a rip-off, but I'm willing to pay if I'm guaranteed a seat.* 这项服务费是宰人的，但要是能保证我有座位我就愿意付钱。

R

▲ **rip·ple** /rɪpᵊl/ (**ripples, rippling, rippled**) **1** N-COUNT **Ripples** are little waves on the surface of water caused by the wind or by something moving in or on the water. 涟漪 ❑ *Gleaming ripples cut the lake's surface.* 闪着微光的涟漪打破了湖面的平静。 **2** V-T/V-I When the surface of an area of water **ripples** or when something **ripples** it, a number of little waves appear on it. 使泛起涟漪；泛起涟漪 ❑ *You throw a pebble in a pool and it ripples.* 你把卵石扔进水池里，水面就泛起涟漪。 **3** V-I If something such as a feeling **ripples** over someone's body, it moves across it or through it. (感觉等) 扩散全身 [LITERARY] ❑ *A chill shiver rippled over his skin.* 一阵寒颤传遍了他的肌肤。 **4** N-COUNT If an event causes **ripples**, its effects gradually spread, causing several other events to happen one after the other. 涟漪反应 ❑ *If Brazil defaults on its foreign debt, it will cause ripples throughout the world.* 如果巴西不还外债的话，这将在全世界引起涟漪反应。

rise ♦♦♦ /raɪz/ (**rises, rising, rose, risen**) **1** V-I If something **rises**, it moves upward. 上升；升起 ❑ *Wilson's ice-cold eyes watched the smoke rise from his cigarette.* 威尔逊那双冰冷的眼睛注视着烟雾从他的香烟中冒出。 ● PHRASAL VERB **Rise up** means the same as **rise**. 上升；升起 ❑ *Spray rose up from the surface of the water.* 水花从水面上溅起来。 **2** V-I When you **rise**, you stand up. 起身 [FORMAL] ❑ *Luther rose slowly from the chair.* 卢瑟慢慢从椅子上站起身来。 ● PHRASAL VERB **Rise up** means the same as **rise**. 起身 ❑ *The only thing I wanted was to rise up from the table and leave this house.* 我惟一想做的是从餐桌旁站起身来，离开这所房子。 **3** V-I When you **rise**, you get out of bed. 起床 [FORMAL] ❑ *Tony had risen early and gone to the cottage to work.* 托尼很早就起床去那间小屋干活了。 **4** V-I When the sun or moon **rises**, it appears in the sky. (太阳或月亮) 升起 ❑ *He wanted to be over the line of the ridge before the sun had risen.* 他想赶在太阳升起前翻过那山脊。 **5** V-I You can say that something **rises** when it appears as a large, tall shape. 耸立 [LITERARY] ❑ *The building rose before him, tall and stately.* 那栋大楼耸立在他面前，高大而又雄伟。 ● PHRASAL VERB **Rise up** means the same as **rise**. 耸立 ❑ *The White Mountains rose up before me.* 怀特山耸立在我面前。 **6** V-I If the level of something such as the water in a river **rises**, it becomes higher. (河水等) 上涨 ❑ *The waters continue to rise as more than 1,000 people are evacuated.* 在1000多人被疏散的同时，河水持续上涨。 **7** V-I If land **rises**, it slopes upward. (地面) 隆起 ❑ *He looked up the slope of land that rose from the house.* 他抬头看了看从那所房子向上隆起的斜坡。 **8** V-I If an amount **rises**, it increases. (数量) 增加；上涨 ❑ *Interest rates rise from 4% to 5%.* 利率从4%上升到5%。 ❑ *Tourist trips of all kinds rose by 10.5% between 1977 and 1987.* 各类旅游在1977至1987年间增长了10.5%。 ❑ *Exports rose 23%.* 出口货品增长了23%。 **9** N-COUNT A **rise in** the amount of something is an increase in it. 增长；上涨 ❑ *...the prospect of another rise in interest rates.* …又一次利率上升的可能性。 **10** N-SING **The rise of** a movement or activity is an increase in its popularity or influence. (运动或行为的) 兴起；抬头 ❑ *The rise of racism in America is a serious concern.* 美洲种族主义的抬头是一个严重忧患。 **11** N-COUNT A **rise** is an increase in your wages or your salary. (薪水、工资的) 增加 [BRIT] in AM, use **raise**

12 V-I If the wind **rises**, it becomes stronger. (风力) 增强 ❑ *The wind was still rising, approaching a force nine gale.* 风力仍在增强，接近九级。 **13** V-I If a sound **rises** or if someone's voice **rises**, it becomes louder or higher. (声音或噪音) 升高 ❑ *"Bernard?" Her voice rose hysterically.* "伯纳德？" 她的嗓门歇斯底里地升高了。 **14** V-I When the people in a country **rise**, they try to defeat the government or army that is controlling them. 起义 ❑ *President Bush had encouraged the Panamanian military to rise against General Noriega.* 布什总统曾鼓动巴拿马军方起来反抗诺列加将军。 ● PHRASAL VERB **Rise up** means the same as **rise**. 起义 ❑ *He warned that if the government moved against him the people would rise up.* 他警告说如果政府对他采取行动，人民将起来反抗。 **15** V-I If someone **rises to** a higher position or status, they become more important, successful, or powerful. (职位、地位) 升高 ❑ *She is a strong woman who has risen to the top of a deeply sexist organization.* 她是一位坚强的女性，在一个性别歧视严重的组织中升到了顶层。 ● PHRASAL VERB **Rise up** means the same as **rise**. (职位、地位) 升高 ❑ *I started with Hoover 26 years ago in sales and rose up through the ranks.* 我26年前加入胡佛公司作销售，而后一步步晋升。 **16** N-SING The **rise** of someone is the process by which they become more important, successful, or powerful. 崛起 ❑ *Haig's rise was fueled by an all-consuming sense of patriotic duty.* 黑格的崛起被一种压倒一切的爱国责任感推动着。 **17** PHRASE If something **gives rise to** an event or situation, it causes that event or situation to happen. 引发 ❑ *Low levels of choline in the body can give rise to high blood pressure.* 体内胆碱含量低可引发高血压。 **18** **to rise to the challenge** → see **challenge** **19** **to rise to the occasion** → see **occasion**

> You should be careful not to confuse the verbs **rise** and **raise**. **Rise** is an intransitive verb and cannot be followed by an object, whereas **raise** is a transitive verb and is usually followed by an object. **Rise** can also not be used in the passive. ❑ *The number of dead is likely to rise.* *...the government's decision to raise prices.* Both **raise** and **rise** can be used as nouns with meaning pay increase. **Raise** is used in American English, and **rise** is used in British English. ❑ *Millions of Americans get a pay raise today.* *...a rise of at least 12 per cent.*

▸ **rise above** PHRASAL VERB If you **rise above** a difficulty or problem, you manage not to let it affect you. 克服 ❑ *It tells the story of an aspiring young man's attempt to rise above the squalor of the street.* 它讲述了一个有志青年试图超越其街头穷困生活的故事。

▸ **rise up** → see **rise** 1, 2, 5, 14, 15

risk ♦♦◊ /rɪsk/ (**risks, risking, risked**) **1** N-VAR If there is a **risk of** something unpleasant, there is a possibility that it will happen. 风险 ❑ *There is a small risk of brain damage from the procedure.* 存在该手术导致脑损伤的小风险。 **2** N-COUNT If something that you do is a **risk**, it might have unpleasant or undesirable results. 危险 ❑ *You're taking a big risk showing this to Kravis.* 你在冒很大的危险把这给克拉维斯看。 **3** N-COUNT If you say that something or someone is a **risk**, you mean they are likely to cause harm. 风险因素 ❑ *It's being obese* *that constitutes a health risk.* 是痴肥构成的健康风险。 4 N-COUNT If you are considered a good **risk**, a bank or store thinks that it is safe to lend you money or let you have goods without paying for them at the time. (风险大或小的) 信贷对象 ❑ *Before providing the cash, they will have to decide whether you are a good or bad risk.* 提供资金之前，他们得确定你是风险小还是大的信贷对象。 5 V-T If you **risk** something unpleasant, you do something which might result in that thing happening or affecting you. 冒遭受…的风险 ❑ *Those who fail to register risk severe penalties.* 那些没登记的人冒着受重罚的风险。 6 V-T If you **risk** doing something, you do it, even though you know that it might have undesirable consequences. 冒险 (做某事) ❑ *The skipper was not willing to risk taking his ship through the straits until he could see where he was going.* 这位船长不愿意冒险在看不见方向之前将船开过海峡。 7 V-T If you **risk** your life or something else important, you behave in a way that might result in it being lost or harmed. 冒失去…的危险 ❑ *She risked her own life to help a disabled woman.* 她冒着失去自己生命的危险帮助了一位残疾妇女。 8 PHRASE To be **at risk** means to be in a situation where something unpleasant might happen. 受到威胁 ❑ *Up to 25,000 jobs are still at risk.* 多达25000职位仍受到威胁。 9 PHRASE If you do something **at the risk of** something unpleasant happening, you do it even though you know that the unpleasant thing might happen as a result. 冒着 (发生不快事件的) 风险地 ❑ *At the risk of being repetitive, I will say again that statistics are only a guide.* 尽管会被认为罗嗦，我还得再说一遍：统计数字只是指向。 10 PHRASE If you tell someone that they are doing something **at** their **own risk**, you are warning them that, if they are harmed, it will be their own responsibility. 自担风险地 ❑ *Those who wish to come here will do so at their own risk.* 那些想来这里的人来的话将要自担风险。 11 PHRASE If you **run** the **risk of** doing or experiencing something undesirable, you do something knowing that the undesirable thing might happen as a result. 冒着风险 ❑ *The officers had run the risk of being dismissed.* 官员们曾冒着被解职的风险。

Thesaurus *risk* 另参见：
N. danger, gamble, hazard; *(ant.)* safety 2 3
V. chance, endanger, gamble, jeopardize 5 – 7

risk man·age·ment N-UNCOUNT **Risk management** is the skill or job of deciding what the risks are in a particular situation and taking action to prevent or reduce them. 风险管理 ❑ *Good risk management and higher sales can both boost profits.* 良好的风险管理和更高的销售额都能增加赢利。

risky /rɪski/ (**riskier, riskiest**) ADJ If an activity or action is **risky**, it is dangerous or likely to fail. 冒险的；有危险的 ❑ *Investing in airlines is a very risky business.* 投资航空公司是非常冒险的生意。

rite /raɪt/ (**rites**) N-COUNT A **rite** is a traditional ceremony that is carried out by a particular group or within a particular society. 传统仪式 ❑ *Most traditional societies have transition rites at puberty.* 大多数传统社会在青春期举行过渡仪式。

ritu·al /rɪtʃuəl/ (**rituals**) 1 N-VAR A **ritual** is a religious service or other ceremony which involves a series of actions performed in a fixed order. 宗教仪式；典礼 ❑ *This is the most ancient, and holiest of the Shinto rituals.* 这是最古老、最神圣的神道教仪式。 2 ADJ **Ritual** activities happen as part of a ritual or tradition. 仪式性的；传统的 [ADJ n] ❑ *...fasting and ritual dancing.* …斋戒和仪式性舞蹈。 3 N-VAR A **ritual** is a way of behaving or a series of actions that people regularly carry out in a particular situation, because it is their custom to do so. 习俗 ❑ *The whole Italian culture revolves around the ritual of eating.* 整个意大利文化是围绕着饮食习俗的。 4 ADJ You can describe something as a **ritual** action when it is done in exactly the same way whenever a particular situation occurs. 例行公事般的；习惯性的 [ADJ n] ❑ *I realized that here the conventions required me to make the ritual noises.* 我意识到这里的习俗要求我得说套话。
→ see **myth**

ri·val ♦♦◊ /raɪvᵊl/ (**rivals, rivaling, rivaled**)
in BRIT, use **rivalling, rivalled**
1 N-COUNT Your **rival** is a person, business, or organization who you are competing or fighting against in the same area or for the same things. 对手 ❑ *The world champion finished more than two seconds ahead of his nearest rival.* 这位世界冠军领先离他最近的对手两秒多钟冲过终点。 2 N-COUNT If you say that someone or something has **no rivals** or is **without rival**, you mean that it is best of its type. 可匹敌者 ❑ *The area is famous for its wonderfully fragrant wine which has no rivals in the Rhone.* 这一地区以其极为醇香的葡萄酒而闻名，这种酒在罗纳河流域没有可匹敌者。 3 V-T If you say that one thing **rivals** another, you mean that they are both of the same standard or quality. 与…相匹敌 ❑ *Cassette recorders cannot rival the sound quality of CDs.* 盒式磁带录音机在音质上无法与CD相媲美。

★ **ri·val·ry** /raɪvᵊlri/ (**rivalries**) N-VAR **Rivalry** is competition or fighting between people, businesses, or organizations who are in the same area or want the same things. 竞争；斗争 ❑ *The rivalry between the Inkatha and the ANC has resulted in violence in the black townships.* 英卡塔自由党与非洲国民大会之间的斗争导致了黑人城镇之间的暴力冲突。

riv·er ♦♦◊ /rɪvər/ (**rivers**) N-COUNT A **river** is a large amount of fresh water flowing continuously in a long line across the land. 河；江 ❑ *...a chemical plant on the banks of the river.* …这条河岸上的一家化工厂。
→ see Picture Dictionary: **river**

river·side /rɪvərsaɪd/ N-SING The **riverside** is the area of land by the banks of a river. 河边 ❑ *They walked back along the riverside.* 他们沿着河边往回走。

riv·et /rɪvɪt/ (**rivets, riveting, riveted**) V-T If you **are riveted** by something, it fascinates you and holds your interest completely. 迷住 ❑ *As a child I remember being riveted by my grandfather's appearance.* 我记得孩提时我曾被我祖父的模样所迷住。 ❑ *He was riveted to the John Wayne movie.* 他痴迷于约翰•韦恩的电影。

Picture Dictionary river

riv·et·ing /rɪvɪtɪŋ/ ADJ If you describe something as **riveting**, you mean that it is extremely interesting and exciting, and that it holds your attention completely. 引人入胜的 ❑ *...Jeffrey Wolf's riveting new novel.* …杰弗里•沃尔夫引人入胜的新小说。

roach /roʊtʃ/ (**roaches**) N-COUNT A **roach** is the same as a **cockroach**. 蟑螂 [mainly AM] ❑ *He found his brother in a seedy, roach-infested apartment.* 他发现他的兄弟住在一套蟑螂横行的破旧公寓里。

road ♦♦♦ /roʊd/ (**roads**) **1** N-COUNT A **road** is a long piece of hard ground that is built between two places so that people can drive or ride easily from one place to the other. 公路 ❑ *There was very little traffic on the roads.* 那时这些公路上车辆很少。 ❑ *We just go straight up the Boston Post Road.* 我们就径直沿着波士顿邮政大道走。 **2** N-COUNT The **road to** a particular result is the means of achieving it or the process of achieving it. 途径; 过程 ❑ *We are bound to see some ups and downs along the road to recovery.* 在复苏的道路上我们一定会经历一些波折起伏。 **3** PHRASE If you say that someone is **on the road to** something, you mean that they are likely to achieve it. 在 (取得成功的) 的道路上 ❑ *The government took another step on the road to political reform.* 政府又在政治改革的道路上迈进了一步。 **4** **the end of the road** → see **end**
→ see **traffic**

road rage N-UNCOUNT **Road rage** is anger or violent behavior caused by someone else's bad driving or the stress of being in heavy traffic. 道路暴行; 道路愤慨 ❑ *Two women were being hunted by police after a road rage attack on a male motorist.* 两名妇女因在一次道路暴行中袭击一名男司机而正被警方追捕。

road·side /roʊdsaɪd/ (**roadsides**) N-COUNT **The roadside** is the area at the edge of a road. 路边 ❑ *Bob was forced to leave the car at the roadside and run for help.* 鲍勃被迫把车停在路边，跑去求助。

road·work /roʊdwɜrk/ N-UNCOUNT **Roadwork** is repairs or other work being done on a road. 道路施工 ❑ *The traffic was stationary due to three sets of roadwork in less than a mile.* 车辆静止不动，由于不到一英里内有3处道路施工。

▲ **roam** /roʊm/ (**roams, roaming, roamed**) V-T/V-I If you **roam** an area or **roam around** it, you wander or travel around it without having a particular purpose. 闲逛; 漫游 ❑ *Barefoot children roamed the streets.* 光着脚的孩子们在街上闲逛。 ❑ *I spent a couple of years roaming around the countryside.* 我花了几年时间在乡村漫游。

roam·ing /roʊmɪŋ/ N-UNCOUNT **Roaming** refers to the service provided by a cellphone company which makes it possible for you to use your cellphone when you travel. (移动电话) 漫游 ❑ *Ignorance of roaming call charges is common.* 不知道漫游电话收费情况很普遍。

roar /rɔr/ (**roars, roaring, roared**) **1** V-I If something, usually a vehicle, **roars** somewhere, it goes there very fast, making a loud noise. (常指车辆) 呼啸疾驰 [WRITTEN] ❑ *A police car roared past.* 一辆警车呼啸而过。 **2** V-I If something **roars**, it makes a very loud noise. 咆哮; 轰鸣 [WRITTEN] ❑ *The engine roared, and the vehicle leapt forward.* 引擎轰鸣，车子猛地向前驶去。 ● N-COUNT **Roar** is also a noun. 咆哮声; 轰鸣声 ❑ *...the roar of traffic.* …车辆的轰鸣声。 **3** V-I If someone **roars with** laughter, they laugh in a very noisy way. 哄然 (大笑) ❑ *Max threw back his head and roared with laughter.* 马克斯把头向后一甩，哄然大笑。 ● N-COUNT **Roar** is also a noun. (笑声) 哄然 ❑ *There were roars of laughter as he stood up.* 他站起来时出现阵阵哄堂大笑。 **4** V-T/V-I If someone **roars**, they shout something in a very loud voice. (人) 吼道; 吼 [WRITTEN] ❑ *"I'll kill you for that," he roared.* "我要为此杀了你，" 他吼道。 ❑ *During the playing of the national anthem the crowd roared and whistled.* 奏国歌时，人群又吼又吹口哨。 ● N-COUNT **Roar** is also a noun. 吼叫声 ❑ *There was a roar of approval.* 响起了一片表示赞成的喊叫声。 **5** V-I When a lion **roars**, it makes the loud sound that lions typically make. (狮子) 吼叫 ❑ *The lion roared once, and sprang.* 狮子吼了一声，跳了起来。 ● N-COUNT **Roar** is also a noun. (狮子的) 吼叫声 ❑ *...the roar of lions in the distance.* …远处的狮吼声。

R

roar·ing /rɔrɪŋ/ **1** ADJ A **roaring** fire has large flames and sends out a lot of heat. 熊熊燃烧的 (火) [ADJ n] ❑ *...nighttime beach parties, with a roaring fire.* …有熊熊篝火的沙滩晚会。 **2** ADJ If something is a **roaring** success, it is extremely successful. 极其巨大的 (成功) [ADJ n] ❑ *The government's first effort to privatize a company has been a roaring success.* 政府首次使公司私有化的尝试已大获成功。 **3** → see also **roar**

roast /roʊst/ (**roasts, roasting, roasted**) **1** V-T When you **roast** meat or other food, you cook it by dry heat in an oven or over a fire. 烤 ❑ *I personally would rather roast a chicken whole.* 我个人更愿意烤整鸡。 **2** ADJ **Roast** meat has been cooked by roasting. 烤熟了的 [ADJ n] ❑ *They serve the most delicious roast beef.* 他们做最美味的烤牛肉。 **3** N-COUNT A **roast** is a piece of meat that is cooked by roasting. 烤肉 ❑ *Come into the kitchen. I've got to put the roast in.* 到厨房里来。我得把烤肉放进去。
→ see **cook, peanut**

rob /rɒb/ (**robs, robbing, robbed**) **1** V-T If someone **is robbed**, they have money or property stolen from them. 盗窃; 抢劫 ❑ *Mrs. Yacoub was robbed of her designer watch at her Westchester home.* 雅各布夫人的名牌手表在她威斯特切斯特的家中被人盗走了。 **2** V-T If someone **is robbed of** something that they deserve, have, or need, it is taken away from them. 抢走 ❑ *When Miles Davis died jazz was robbed of its most distinctive voice.* 当迈尔斯•戴维斯去世时，爵士乐里最具特色的声音也被夺走了。

> Do not confuse **rob** and **steal**. If someone **robs** someone or somewhere, they take something, often violently, from that person or place without asking and without intending to give it back. ❑ *They planned to rob an old widow... They joined forces to rob a factory.* You can also say that someone **robs** you of something when referring to what has been taken. ❑ *The two men were robbed of more than $700.* If someone **steals** something, for example, money or a car, they take it without asking and without intending to give it back. ❑ *My car was stolen on Friday evening.* Note that you cannot say that someone **steals** someone.

rob·ber /rɒbər/ (**robbers**) N-COUNT A **robber** is someone who steals money or property from a bank, store, or vehicle, often by using force or threats. 抢劫者 ❑ *Armed robbers broke into a jeweler's through a hole in the wall.* 武装劫匪从墙上的一个洞闯入了一家珠宝行。

> Anyone who steals can be called a **thief**. A **robber** often uses violence or the threat of violence to steal things from places such as banks or businesses. A **burglar** breaks into houses or other buildings and steals things.

★ **rob·bery** /rɒbəri/ (**robberies**) N-VAR **Robbery** is the crime of stealing money or property from a bank, store, or vehicle, often by using force or threats. 抢劫; 抢劫罪 ❑ *The gang members committed dozens of armed robberies over the past year.* 该团伙成员在过去一年中犯下了数十起持械抢劫罪。

▲ **robe** /roʊb/ (**robes**) **1** N-COUNT A **robe** is a loose piece of clothing that covers all of your body and reaches the ground. You can describe someone as wearing a **robe** or as wearing **robes**. 长袍 [FORMAL] ❑ *Pope John Paul II knelt in his white robes before the simple altar.* 约翰•保罗二世教皇身着白色长袍跪在简朴的祭坛前。 **2** N-COUNT A **robe** is a piece of clothing, usually made of toweling, which people wear in the house, especially when they have just gotten up or taken a bath. 睡袍; 浴衣 ❑ *Kyle put on a robe and went down to the kitchen.* 凯尔穿上睡袍，下楼去了厨房。

ro·bot /roʊbət, -bɒt/ (**robots**) N-COUNT A **robot** is a machine that is programmed to move and perform certain tasks automatically. 机器人 ❑ *...very lightweight robots that we could send to the moon for planetary exploration.* …我们能够送上月球用于行星探索的重量很轻的机器人。
→ see **mass production**

★ **ro·bust** /roʊbʌst, roʊbʌst/ **1** ADJ Someone or something that is **robust** is very strong or healthy. 健壮的 ❑ *He was always the robust one, physically strong and mentally sharp.* 他一向是个健壮的人，身体强壮、头脑敏锐。 **2** ADJ **Robust** views or opinions are strongly held and forcefully expressed. 强有力的 (观点、见解) ❑ *The Secretary of State has made a robust defense of the agreement.* 国务卿对这项协议进行了强有力的辩护。

rock ♦♦◊ /rɒk/ (**rocks, rocking, rocked**) **1** N-UNCOUNT **Rock** is the hard substance which the earth is made of. 岩石 ❑ *The hills above the valley are bare rock.* 河谷上面的山是光秃秃的岩石。 **2** N-COUNT A **rock** is a large piece of rock that sticks up out of the ground or the sea, or that has broken away from a mountain or a cliff. 巨石 ❑ *She sat cross-legged on the rock.* 她盘着腿坐在那块巨石上。 **3** N-COUNT A **rock** is a piece of rock that is small enough for you to pick up. 小石块 ❑ *She bent down, picked up a rock, and threw it into the trees.* 她弯下腰，拣起一块小石头，把它扔进了树林里。 **4** V-T/V-I When something **rocks** or when you **rock** it, it moves slowly and regularly backward and forward or from side to side. 使摇晃; 摇晃 ❑ *His body rocked from side to side with the train.* 他的身体随着火车

Word Web rock

igneous

sedimentary

metamorphic

Rocks are made of **minerals**. They may consist of a single **element**. However, they usually contain **compounds** of several elements. Each type of rock also has a unique **crystal** structure. Rock is constantly in the process of changing. When **lava erupts** from a **volcano**, it forms igneous rock. Wind, water, and ice **erode** this type of rock. The resulting **sediment** collects in rivers. As these layers of particles build up, they form sedimentary rock. When tectonic plates move around, they create heat and pressure. This melting and crushing changes sedimentary rock into metamorphic rock.

左右晃动。 5 V-T/V-I If an explosion or an earthquake **rocks** a building or an area, it causes the building or area to shake. 使震动; 震动 [JOURNALISM] ❑ *Three people were injured yesterday when an explosion rocked the factory.* 3名工人昨天在爆炸震动了这座工厂时受伤。 ❑ *In Taipei buildings rocked back and forth.* 在台北，各建筑物前后摇晃。 6 V-T If an event or a piece of news **rocks** a group or society, it shocks them or makes them feel less secure. 震惊 [JOURNALISM] ❑ *His death rocked the fashion business.* 他的死震惊了时装界。 7 N-UNCOUNT **Rock** is loud music with a strong beat that is usually played and sung by a small group of people using instruments such as electric guitars and drums. 摇滚乐 ❑ *...a rock concert.* …一场摇滚音乐会。
→ see Word Web: **rock**
→ see **crystal, earth, fossil, genre**

rock and roll also **rock'n'roll** N-UNCOUNT **Rock and roll** is a kind of popular music developed in the 1950s which has a strong beat and is played on electrical instruments. 摇滚流行乐 ❑ *...Elvis Presley – the King of Rock and Roll.* …埃尔维斯•普雷斯利——摇滚流行乐之王。

rock bot·tom also **rock-bottom** 1 N-UNCOUNT If something has reached **rock bottom**, it is at such a low level that it cannot go any lower. 最低谷 ❑ *Morale in the armed forces was at rock bottom.* 那时军队的士气处在最低谷。 2 ADJ A **rock-bottom** price or level is a very low one, mainly in advertisements. 底线的 (价格、水平) [APPROVAL] ❑ *What they do offer is a good product at a rock-bottom price.* 他们真正提供的是一种以价格在底线的优质产品。

rock·et ♦◇◇ /rɒkɪt/ (**rockets, rocketing, rocketed**) 1 N-COUNT A **rocket** is a space vehicle that is shaped like a long tube. 火箭 ❑ *...the Apollo 12 rocket that took astronauts to the moon.* …将宇航员送上了月球的阿波罗12号火箭。 2 N-COUNT A **rocket** is a missile containing explosives that is powered by gas. 火箭弹 ❑ *There has been a renewed rocket attack on the capital.* 发生了对首都的新一轮火箭弹攻击。 3 N-COUNT A **rocket** is a firework that quickly goes high into the air and then explodes. 火箭弹烟花 4 V-I If things such as prices or social problems **rocket**, they increase very quickly and suddenly. 飞速增加; 飞速上涨 [JOURNALISM] ❑ *Fresh food is so scarce that prices have rocketed.* 新鲜食物如此稀缺以致价格飞涨。 5 V-I If something such as a vehicle **rockets** somewhere, it moves there very quickly. (车辆等) 疾驰; 飞奔 ❑ *A train rocketed by, shaking the walls of the row houses.* 一辆火车疾驰而过，震动着排房的墙壁。 6 N-UNCOUNT **Rocket** is the same as **arugula**. 芝麻菜 [BRIT]

rocky /rɒki/ (**rockier, rockiest**) 1 ADJ A **rocky** place is covered with rocks or consists of large areas of rock and has nothing growing on it. 多岩石的 ❑ *The paths are often very rocky so strong boots are advisable.* 这些道路通常多岩石，所以建议穿结实的靴子。 2 ADJ A **rocky** situation or relationship is unstable and full of difficulties. 不稳定的; 艰难的 ❑ *They had gone through some rocky times together when Ann was first married.* 当安刚结婚的时候，他们已经一起度过了一些感情不稳定的日子。

rod /rɒd/ (**rods**) N-COUNT A **rod** is a long, thin, metal or wooden bar. 长杆; 长棒 ❑ *...a 15-foot thick roof that was reinforced with steel rods.* …用钢条加固了的15英尺厚的屋顶。

rode /roʊd/ **Rode** is the past tense of **ride**. **ride**的过去式

ro·dent /roʊdᵊnt/ (**rodents**) N-COUNT **Rodents** are small mammals which have sharp front teeth. Rats, mice, and squirrels are rodents. 啮齿动物

ro·deo /roʊdioʊ, roʊdeɪoʊ/ (**rodeos**) N-COUNT A **rodeo** is a public entertainment event in which cowboys show different skills, including riding wild horses and catching cattle with ropes. 牛仔竞技表演

▲ **rogue** /roʊg/ (**rogues**) 1 N-COUNT A **rogue** is a man who behaves in a dishonest or criminal way. 流氓; 无赖 ❑ *Mr. Ward wasn't a rogue at all.* 沃德先生根本不是个无赖。 2 N-COUNT If a man behaves in a way that you do not approve of but you still like him, you can refer to him as a **rogue**. 捣蛋鬼; 小坏蛋 [FEELINGS] ❑ *...Falstaff, the lovable rogue.* …福斯塔夫，这个可爱的捣蛋鬼。 3 ADJ A **rogue** element is someone or something that behaves differently from others of its kind, often causing damage. 行为异常的 [ADJ n] ❑ *Computer systems throughout the country are being affected by a series of mysterious rogue programs, known as viruses.* 全国的计算机系统正受到一系列称做病毒的神秘的异常程序的影响。

role ♦♦♦ /roʊl/ (**roles**) 1 N-COUNT If you have a **role** in a situation or in society, you have a particular position and function in it. 功能; 作用 ❑ *Until now scientists had very little clear evidence about the drug's role in preventing more serious effects of infection.* 到目前为止，科学家们几乎没有该药物在防止更严重的感染后果的功能的明确证据。 2 N-COUNT A **role** is one of the characters that an actor or singer can play in a movie, play, or opera. 角色 ❑ *She has just landed the lead role in their latest production.* 她刚在他们最新的作品中取得了主角。
→ see **theater**

Word Partnership *role* 的常用搭配:

N. **leadership** role, role **reversal** 1
lead role 2
ADJ. **active** role, **key** role, **parental** role, **positive** role, **significant** role, **traditional** role, **vital** role 1
bigger/larger role, **leading** role, **major** role 1 2
starring role 2
V. **play a** role, **take on a** role 1 2

role mod·el (**role models**) N-COUNT A **role model** is someone you admire and try to imitate. 楷模 ❑ *Five out of the ten top role models for teenagers are black.* 十大青少年楷模中有5位是黑人。

roll ♦♦◇ /roʊl/ (**rolls, rolling, rolled**) 1 V-T/V-I When something **rolls** or when you **roll** it, it moves along a surface, turning over many times. 滚动 ❑ *The ball rolled into the net.* 球滚进了网。 2 V-I If you **roll** somewhere, you move on a surface while lying down, turning your body over and over, so that you are sometimes on your back, sometimes on your side, and sometimes on your front. 打滚 ❑ *When I was a little kid I rolled down a hill and broke my leg.* 我小的时候曾滚下山摔断了腿。 3 V-I When vehicles **roll** along, they move along slowly. (车辆) 缓行 ❑ *The truck quietly rolled forward and demolished all the old wooden fencing.* 卡车静静地缓慢前行，毁了所有旧木栅栏。 4 V-I If a machine **rolls**, it is operating. (机器) 运转 ❑ *He slipped and fell on the step as the cameras rolled.* 在相机拍摄时，他滑倒在了台阶上。 5 V-I If drops of liquid **roll** down a surface, they move quickly down it. (液体) 滚落 ❑ *She looked at Ginny and tears rolled down her cheeks.* 她看着金尼，泪珠顺着脸颊淌下。 6 V-T If you **roll** something flexible **into** a cylinder or a ball, you form it into a cylinder or a ball by wrapping it several times around itself or by shaping it between your hands. 卷; 绕 (成柱形或团) ❑ *He took off his sweater, rolled it into a pillow, and lay down on the grass.* 他脱下毛衣，卷成一个枕头，然后在草地上躺了下来。 ● PHRASAL VERB **Roll up** means the same as **roll**. 卷; 绕 (成柱形或团) ❑ *Stein rolled up the paper bag with the money inside.* 斯坦把装着钱的纸袋卷了起来。 7 N-COUNT A **roll of** paper, plastic, cloth, or wire is a long piece of it that has been wrapped many times around itself or around a tube. (一) 卷 ❑ *The photographers had already shot a dozen rolls of film.* 摄影师们已经拍完了一打胶卷。 8 V-T If you **roll up** something such as a car window or a blind, you cause it to move upward by turning a handle. If you **roll** it **down**, you cause it to move downward by turning a handle.

摇(车窗、卷帘等) ❑ *In mid-afternoon, shopkeepers began to roll down their shutters.* 下午三点钟左右，店主们开始摇下百叶窗。 **9** V-T/V-I If you **roll** your eyes or if your eyes **roll**, they move around and upward. People sometimes roll their eyes when they are frightened, bored, or annoyed. (指眼睛) 翻转 [WRITTEN] ❑ *People may roll their eyes and talk about overprotective, interfering grandmothers.* 人们可能会翻着白眼讨论过分呵护、事事插手的祖母们。 **10** N-COUNT A **roll** is a small piece of bread that is round or long and is made to be eaten by one person. Rolls can be eaten plain, with butter, or with a filling. 面包卷 ❑ *He sipped at his coffee and spread butter and marmalade on a roll.* 他抿了一口咖啡，将黄油和果酱涂在了面包卷上。 **11** N-COUNT A **roll of** drums is a long, low, fairly loud sound made by drums. 低缓的轰隆鼓声 ❑ *As the town clock struck two, they heard the roll of drums.* 当镇上的钟敲响了两点时，他们听到了隆隆的鼓声。 **12** N-COUNT A **roll** is an official list of people's names. 名册 ❑ *Pro-democracy activists say a new electoral roll should be drawn up.* 亲民主派活动分子们说应当起草一份新的候选人名单。 **13** → see also **rolling, rock and roll** **14** PHRASE If something is several things **rolled into one**, it combines the main features or qualities of those things. 集于一体 ❑ *This is our kitchen, living room, and dining room all rolled into one.* 这是我们的厨房、客厅和餐厅都融为一体的房间。 **15** **heads will roll** → see **head**

▸ **roll back** PHRASAL VERB To **roll back** prices, taxes, or benefits means to reduce them. 削减 [mainly AM] ❑ *One provision of the law was to roll back taxes to the 1975 level.* 该法律的一项条款是把税收削减至1975年的水平。

▸ **roll in** PHRASAL VERB If something such as money **is rolling in**, it is appearing or being received in large quantities. (金钱等) 大量涌进 [INFORMAL] ❑ *Don't forget, I have always kept the money rolling in.* 别忘了，我总是在让钱财滚滚而来。

▸ **roll out** PHRASAL VERB If a company **rolls out** a new product or service, or if the product or service **rolls out**, it is made available to the public. 推出(新产品或服务) ❑ *On Thursday Microsoft rolls out its new operating system.* 在星期四微软推出了它的新操作系统。 ❑ *Northern Telecom says its products will roll out over 18 months beginning early next year.* 北方电讯公司表示其产品将从明年初起用18个多月的时间推出。

▸ **roll over** **1** PHRASAL VERB If you are lying down and you **roll over**, you turn your body so that a different part of you is facing upward. (身体) 翻过来 ❑ *I rolled over and went back to sleep.* 我翻了个身接着又睡着了。 **2** PHRASAL VERB If a moving vehicle such as a car **rolls over**, it turns over many times, usually because it has crashed. (车出事故而) 翻筋斗 ❑ *Those kinds of vehicles are more likely to roll over than passenger cars.* 那些种类的车辆比客车更容易翻筋斗。 **3** PHRASAL VERB If you say that someone **rolls over**, you mean that they stop resisting someone and do what the other person wants them to do. 转而听命 ❑ *That's why most people and organizations just roll over and give up when they're challenged or attacked by the I.R.S.* 那就是为什么大部分人和组织遇到国内收入署的质疑和责问时转而听命并且放弃的原因。 **4** PHRASAL VERB If you **roll over** a loan or other financial arrangement, you extend it, for example by adding it to another loan. (贷款等) 续期; 展期 [BUSINESS] ❑ *There seems to be no way to spread out the tax or roll over the cash into another pension plan.* 看来无法更长期地收这项税收，并把取得的现金续到另一项退休金计划里。 **5** PHRASAL VERB In lotteries and similar games, if a jackpot **rolls over**, it is not won by anyone and the money is added to the prize money for the next lottery. (彩票等) 滚计 ❑ *If the jackpot isn't won this week it will roll over again to next week.* 如果本周没有人获得彩票头奖，头奖将再次滚计到下周。 **6** → see also **rollover**

▸ **roll up** **1** PHRASAL VERB If you **roll up** your sleeves or pant legs, you fold the ends back several times, making them shorter. 卷起(袖子或裤腿) ❑ *The jacket was too big for him so he rolled up the cuffs.* 这件夹克对他来说太大了，所以他卷起了袖口。 **2** PHRASAL VERB If people **roll up** somewhere, they arrive there, especially in a car and often late. (尤指开车晚点) 到达 [INFORMAL] ❑ *They eventually rolled up two hours late.* 他们最终晚来了两小时。 **3** → see also **roll 6**

roll·er /roʊlər/ (**rollers**) **1** N-COUNT A **roller** is a cylinder that turns around in a machine or device. 滚筒 **2** N-COUNT **Rollers** are hollow tubes that women roll their hair round in order to make it curly. 发卷 ❑ *She gets up every morning and puts her hair in rollers.* 她每天早晨起床后把头发缠进发卷里。

Roll·er·blade /roʊlərbleɪd/ (**Rollerblades**) N-COUNT **Rollerblades** are a type of roller skates with a single line of wheels along the bottom. 单排滚轴旱冰鞋 ● **roll·er·blad·ing** N-UNCOUNT 滚轴溜冰 [TRADEMARK] ❑ *Rollerblading is great for all ages.* 滚轴溜冰老少皆宜。

roll·er coast·er (**roller coasters**) **1** N-COUNT A **roller coaster** is a small railroad at an amusement park that goes up and down steep slopes fast and that people ride on for pleasure or excitement. 过山车 ❑ *It's great to go on the roller coaster five times and not be sick.* 能坐5次过山车而不吐真够棒的。 **2** N-COUNT If you say that someone or something is on a **roller coaster**, you mean that they go through many sudden or extreme changes in a short time. (指人或事急转突变) 过山车 [JOURNALISM] ❑ *I've been on an emotional roller coaster since I've been here.* 自从我到这里以来，情绪像坐上了过山车。

roller skate (**roller skates, roller-skates, roller-skating, roller-skated**) **1** N-COUNT **Roller skates** are shoes with four small wheels on the bottom. 双排四轮旱冰鞋 ❑ *A boy of about ten came up on roller skates.* 一个大约十岁的男孩穿着双排四轮旱冰鞋滑了过来。 **2** V-I If you **roller-skate**, you move over a flat surface wearing roller skates. 滑旱冰 ❑ *On the day of the accident, my son Gary was roller-skating outside our house.* 在出事的那天，我的儿子格雷正在我们家外面滑旱冰。

roll·ing /roʊlɪŋ/ ADJ **Rolling** hills are small hills with gentle slopes that extend a long way into the distance. (山丘) 绵延起伏的 [ADJ n] ❑ *...the rolling countryside of southwestern France.* …法国西南部绵延起伏的乡村。

ROM /rɒm/ **1** N-UNCOUNT **ROM** is the permanent part of a computer's memory. The information stored there can be read but not changed. **ROM** is an abbreviation for "read-only memory." (机算机的) 只读存储器 [COMPUTING] ❑ *It's got 256 megabytes of ROM and 512 megabytes of RAM.* 它装有256兆字节的只读存储器和512兆字节的随机存取存储器。 **2** → see also **CD-ROM**

Word Link	*an, ian ≈ one of, relating to : Christian, pedestrian, Roman*

Ro·man ♦◇◇ /roʊmən/ (**Romans**) **1** ADJ **Roman** means related to or connected with ancient Rome and its empire. 古罗马的 ❑ *...the fall of the Roman Empire.* …罗马帝国的灭亡。 ● N-COUNT A **Roman** was a citizen of ancient Rome or its empire. 古罗马人 ❑ *When they conquered Britain, the Romans brought this custom with them.* 当古罗马人征服不列颠时，他们把这一习俗也带了过去。 **2** ADJ **Roman** means related to or connected with modern Rome. 罗马的 ❑ *...a Roman hotel room.* …一家罗马酒店的客房。 ● N-COUNT A **Roman** is someone who lives in or comes from Rome. 罗马人 ❑ *...soccer-mad Romans.* …对迷恋足球的罗马人。

Ro·man Cath·o·lic (**Roman Catholics**) **1** ADJ The **Roman Catholic** Church is the same as the **Catholic** Church. 天主教的 ❑ *...a Roman Catholic priest.* …一名天主教神父。 **2** N-COUNT A **Roman Catholic** is the same as a **Catholic**. 天主教徒 ❑ *Like her, Maria was a Roman Catholic.* 和她一样，玛丽亚也是一名天主教徒。

★ **ro·mance** /roʊmæns, roʊmæns/ (**romances**) **1** N-COUNT A **romance** is a relationship between two people who are in love with each other but who are not married to each other. 恋爱 ❑ *After a whirlwind romance the couple announced their engagement in July.* 在旋风式的恋爱之后，这对情侣在7月宣布定婚。 **2** N-UNCOUNT **Romance** refers to the actions and feelings of people who are in love, especially behavior that is very caring or affectionate. (爱情中) 浪漫的感觉 ❑ *He still finds time for romance by cooking candlelit dinners for his girlfriend.* 他仍有时间为女友做烛光晚餐来制造浪漫。 **3** N-UNCOUNT You can refer to the pleasure and excitement of doing something new or exciting as **romance**. 浪漫新奇的感受 ❑ *We want to recreate the romance and excitement that used to be part of rail journeys.* 我们想重新营造过去乘火车旅行的那份浪漫新奇和刺激。 **4** N-COUNT A **romance** is a novel or movie about a love affair. 爱情小说; 爱情电影 ❑ *Her taste in fiction was for chunky historical romances.* 她喜爱的小说类型是厚重的历史爱情小说。 → see **love**

Ro·man nu·mer·al /roʊmən numərəl/ (**Roman numerals**) N-COUNT **Roman numerals** are the letters used by the ancient Romans to represent numbers, for example I, IV, VIII, and XL, which represent 1, 4, 8, and 40. Roman numerals are still sometimes used today. 罗马数字 [usu pl] → see Picture Dictionary: **Roman numerals**

ro·man·tic ♦◇◇ /roʊmæntɪk/ (**romantics**) **1** ADJ Someone who is **romantic** or does **romantic** things says and does things that make their wife, husband, girlfriend, or boyfriend feel special and loved. 浪漫的 ❑ *When we're together, all he talks about is*

R

Picture Dictionary Roman numerals

I	1	XI	11	XXI	21	XL	40
II	2	XII	12	XXII	22	L	50
III	3	XIII	13	XXIII	23	LX	60
IV	4	XIV	14	XXIV	24	LXX	70
V	5	XV	15	XXV	25	LXXX	80
VI	6	XVI	16	XXVI	26	XC	90
VII	7	XVII	17	XXVII	27	C	100
VIII	8	XVIII	18	XXVIII	28	D	500
IX	9	XIX	19	XXIX	29	M	1000
X	10	XX	20	XXX	30	MMIX	2009

business. I wish he were more romantic. 我们在一起时，他只谈生意上的事。我希望他能更浪漫一点。 2 ADJ **Romantic** means connected with sexual love. 有关性爱的 [ADJ n] ❑ *He was not interested in a romantic relationship with Ingrid.* 他不想和英格丽德有性爱关系。
● **ro·man·ti·cal·ly** ADV 性爱上地 ❑ *We are not romantically involved.* 我们没有性爱关系。 3 ADJ A **romantic** play, movie, or story describes or represents a love affair. 关于爱情的（戏剧、影片或故事）[ADJ n] ❑ *It is a lovely romantic comedy, well worth seeing.* 这是一部好看的爱情喜剧，很值得一看。 4 ADJ If you say that someone has a **romantic** view or idea of something, you are critical of them because their view of it is unrealistic and they think that thing is better or more exciting than it really is. 浪漫主义的；不切实际的 [DISAPPROVAL] ❑ *He has a romantic view of rural society.* 他对于乡村地区有种不切实际的看法。 ● N-COUNT A **romantic** is a person who has romantic views. 浪漫主义者；不切实际的人 ❑ *You're a hopeless romantic.* 你是个无可救药的浪漫主义者。 5 ADJ Something that is **romantic** is beautiful in a way that strongly affects your feelings. 有浪漫情调的 ❑ *It is considered one of the most romantic restaurants in the city.* 它被认为是这座城市里最有浪漫情调的餐厅之一。
● **ro·man·ti·cal·ly** ADV 有浪漫情调地 ❑ *...the romantically named, but very muddy, Cave of the Wild Horses.* …这个取名浪漫但泥泞不堪的“野马洞”。
→ see **love**

romp /rɒmp/ (**romps, romping, romped**) 1 V-I Journalists use **romp** in expressions like **romp home**, **romp in**, or **romp to victory**, to say that a person or horse has won a race or competition very easily. 轻松取胜 ❑ *Mr. Foster romped home with 141 votes.* 福斯特先生以141票轻松获胜。 2 V-I When children or animals **romp**, they play noisily and happily. 嬉戏喧闹 ❑ *Dogs and little children romped happily in the garden.* 小孩子们和狗们在那座花园里嬉戏喧闹。

roof ♦◇◇ /ruf/ (**roofs**)

> The plural can be pronounced /rufs/ or /ruvz/.

> 复数可读作 /rufs/或 /ruvz/。

1 N-COUNT The **roof** of a building is the covering on top of it that protects the people and things inside from the weather. 屋顶 ❑ *...a small stone cottage with a red slate roof.* …一座有一个红石板屋顶的小石屋。 2 N-COUNT The **roof** of a car or other vehicle is the top part of it, which protects passengers or goods from the weather. （车的）顶篷 ❑ *The car rolled onto its roof, trapping him.* 那辆小汽车翻了个底朝天，把他困在里面。 3 N-COUNT **The roof of** your mouth is the highest part of the inside of your mouth. 上腭 ❑ *She clicked her tongue against the roof of her mouth.* 她用舌头抵着上腭发出咔哒声。 4 PHRASE If the level of something such as the price of a product or the rate of inflation **goes through the roof**, it suddenly increases very rapidly indeed. 突然猛涨 [INFORMAL] ❑ *Prices for Korean art have gone through the roof.* 韩国艺术品价格突然猛涨了。 5 PHRASE If you **hit the roof** or **go through the roof**, you become very angry, and usually show your anger by shouting at someone. 怒气冲天 [INFORMAL] ❑ *Sergeant Long will hit the roof when I tell him you've gone off.* 如果我告诉朗警官你已经走了，他一定会怒火冲天的。 6 PHRASE If a number of things or people are **under one roof** or **under the same roof**, they are in the same building. 在同一建筑物里 ❑ *The firms intend to open either together under one roof or alongside each other in shopping malls.* 这些公司打算要么开在同一栋楼里，要么在商业街上比邻而开。

Word Partnership *roof* 的常用搭配：

N.	roof **of a building/house**, **metal** roof, **rain on a** roof, **slate** roof, **tin** roof 1
V.	roof **collapses**, roof **leaks**, **repair a** roof 1
ADJ.	**retractable** roof 1 2

roof·er /rufər/ (**roofers**) N-COUNT A **roofer** is a person whose job is to put roofs on buildings and to repair damaged roofs. 盖屋顶的人；修屋顶的人

roof gar·den (**roof gardens**) N-COUNT A **roof garden** is a garden on the flat roof of a building. 屋顶花园

roof rack (**roof racks**) also **roof-rack** N-COUNT A **roof rack** is a metal frame that is fixed on top of a car and used for carrying large objects. 车顶支架 [mainly BRIT]

> in AM, usually use **luggage rack**

rookie /ruki/ (**rookies**) 1 N-COUNT A **rookie** is someone who has just started doing a job and does not have much experience, especially someone who has just joined the army or police force. 新手 [mainly AM, INFORMAL] ❑ *I don't want to have another rookie to train.* 我不想再训练一个新手。 2 N-COUNT A **rookie** is a person who has been competing in a professional sport for less than a year. 新人 [AM] ❑ *...the oldest rookie on the European Tour.* …欧洲巡回赛中年纪最大的新人。

room ♦♦♦ /rum/ (**rooms, rooming, roomed**) 1 N-COUNT A **room** is one of the separate sections or parts of the inside of a building. Rooms have their own walls, ceilings, floors, and doors, and are usually used for particular activities. You can refer to all the people who are in a room as **the room**. 房间 ❑ *A minute later he excused himself and left the room.* 一分钟后他告辞了，离开了房间。 ❑ *The largest conference room could seat 5,000 people.* 最大的会议室可坐5千人。 2 N-COUNT If you talk about your **room**, you are referring to the room that you alone use, especially your bedroom at home or your office at work. （我的）房间 ❑ *If you're running upstairs, go to my room and bring down my sweater, please.* 如果你要上楼的话，请到我的房间把我的毛衣拿下来。 3 N-COUNT A **room** is a bedroom in a hotel. （酒店的）客房 ❑ *Toni reserved a room in a hotel not far from Arzfeld.* 托妮在离阿茨费尔德不远的酒店预定了一个房间。 4 V-I If you **room with** someone, you share a rented room, apartment, or house with them, for example when you are a student. 合住 [AM] ❑ *I had roomed with him in New Haven when we were both at Yale Law School.* 我们俩在耶鲁法学院上学的时候，我和他在纽黑文合住。 5 N-UNCOUNT If there is **room** somewhere, there is enough empty space there for people or things to be fitted in, or for people to move freely or do what they want to. 空间 ❑ *There is usually room to accommodate up to 80 visitors.* 通常可以多能容纳80名来宾。 6 N-UNCOUNT If there is **room for** a particular kind of behavior or action, people are able to behave in that way or to take that action. 机会 ❑ *The intensity of the work left little room for personal grief or anxiety.* 该工作的强度很少给个人留下悲伤或忧虑的机会。 7 → see also **chat room, dining room, drawing room, emergency room, living room, restroom**

r

You should use **room** or **space** to refer to an open or empty area. You do not use **place** as an uncount noun in this sense. **Room** is more likely to be used when you are talking about space inside an enclosed area. ❑ *There's not enough room in the bathroom for both of us... Leave plenty of space between you and the car in front.*

room·mate /rummeɪt/ (**roommates**) N-COUNT Your **roommate** is the person you share a room, apartment, or house with, for example when you are in college. 室友 [AM] ❑ *Derek and I are close; we were roommates for two years.* 德里克和我关系密切，我们曾是两年的室友。

room ser·vice N-UNCOUNT **Room service** is a service in a hotel by which meals or drinks are provided for guests in their rooms. (宾馆的）客房服务 ❑ *The hotel did not normally provide room service.* 那家宾馆通常不提供客房服务。

→ see **hotel**

roomy /rumi/ (**roomier, roomiest**) ADJ If you describe a place as **roomy**, you mean that you like it because it is large inside and you can move around freely and comfortably. 宽敞的 [APPROVAL] ❑ *The car is roomy and a good choice for anyone who needs to carry equipment.* 这车内部宽敞，对于任何需要携带设备的人来说是个不错的选择。

roost /rust/ (**roosts, roosting, roosted**) **1** N-COUNT A **roost** is a place where birds or bats rest or sleep. 栖息处 ❑ *Something disturbed the bird on its roost.* 什么东西惊扰了那只栖息的鸟。 **2** V-I When birds or bats **roost** somewhere, they rest or sleep there. 栖息 ❑ *The peacocks roost in nearby shrubs.* 那只孔雀在附近的灌木丛里栖息。 **3** PHRASE If bad or wrong things that someone has done in the past **have come home to roost**, or if their **chickens have come home to roost**, they are now experiencing the unpleasant effects of these actions. 自食其果 ❑ *Appeasement has come home to roost.* 绥靖已自食其果。 **4** PHRASE If you say that someone **rules the roost** in a particular place, you mean that they have control and authority over the people there. 大权在握 [INFORMAL] ❑ *Today the country's nationalists rule the roost and hand out the jobs.* 如今这个国家的民族主义者掌握大权，分派那些工作。

→ see **bat**

★ **roost·er** /rustər/ (**roosters**) N-COUNT A **rooster** is an adult male chicken. 公鸡 [AM]

in BRIT, use **cock**

root ♦◇◇ /rut/ (**roots, rooting, rooted**) **1** N-COUNT The **roots** of a plant are the parts of it that grow under the ground. (植物的）根 ❑ *...the twisted roots of an apple tree.* …一棵苹果树的那些弯曲的树根。 **2** V-T/V-I If you **root** a plant or cutting or if it **roots**, roots form on the bottom of its stem and it starts to grow. 使生根；生根 ❑ *Most plants will root in about six to eight weeks.* 大多数植物会在6到8周内生根。 **3** ADJ **Root** vegetables or **root** crops are grown for their roots, which are large and can be eaten. 块根的 [ADJ n] ❑ *...root crops such as carrots and potatoes.* …胡萝卜、土豆等块根作物。 **4** N-COUNT The **root** of a hair or tooth is the part of it that is underneath the skin. (发、牙）根 ❑ *...decay around the roots of teeth.* …那些牙根周围的蛀蚀。 **5** N-PLURAL You can refer to the place or culture that a person or their family comes from as their **roots**. (指某人或家族的）根 ❑ *I am proud of my Brazilian roots.* 我为自己的巴西血统而自豪。 **6** N-COUNT You can refer to the cause of a problem or of an unpleasant situation as **the root of** it or **the roots of** it. (问题的）根源 ❑ *We got to the root of the problem.* 我们触及了这个问题的根源。 **7** V-I If you **root through** or **in** something, you search for something by moving other things around. 搜；翻 ❑ *She rooted through the bag, found what she wanted, and headed toward the door.* 她在那个包里搜寻了一番，找到了她想要的东西，然后朝门口走去。 **8** → see also **grassroots, rooted, square root** **9** PHRASE If someone **puts down roots**, they make a place their home, for example by taking part in activities there or by making a lot of friends there. 扎根 ❑ *When they got to Montana, they put down roots and built a life.* 到达蒙大拿后，他们便在那里扎根，过上了日子。 **10** PHRASE If an idea, belief, or custom **takes root**, it becomes established among a group of people. 深入人心 ❑ *Time would be needed for democracy to take root.* 民主深入人心需要时间。

▸ **root out** **1** PHRASAL VERB If you **root out** a person, you find them and force them from the place they are in, usually in order to punish them. 纠出 ❑ *The generals have to root out traitors.* 那些将军们必须纠出叛徒们。 **2** PHRASAL VERB If you **root out** a problem or an unpleasant situation, you find out who or what is the cause of it and put an end to it. 根除 ❑ *There would be a major drive to root out corruption.* 将会有一场根除腐败的大规模的运动。

Word Partnership *root* 的常用搭配：

N. **tree** root **1**
root **canal** **4**
root **cause of** ***something***, root **of a problem** **6**

V. **take** root **10**

root·ed /rutɪd/ **1** ADJ If you say that one thing is **rooted in** another, you mean that it is strongly influenced by it or has developed from it. 源于…的 [v-link ADJ "in" n] ❑ *The crisis is rooted in deep rivalries between the two groups.* 这次危机的根源在于两个集团间的严重对立。 **2** ADJ If someone has deeply **rooted** opinions or feelings, they believe or feel something extremely strongly and are unlikely to change. 根深蒂固的 ❑ *Racism is a deeply rooted prejudice which has existed for thousands of years.* 种族主义是一种已存在了数千年的根深蒂固的偏见。 **3** PHRASE If you are **rooted to the spot**, you are unable to move because you are very frightened or shocked. 呆着不动的 ❑ *We just stopped there, rooted to the spot.* 我们只是停在那里，呆着不动。

rope /roʊp/ (**ropes, roping, roped**) **1** N-VAR A **rope** is a thick cord or wire that is made by twisting together several thinner cords or wires. Ropes are used for jobs such as pulling cars, tying up boats, or tying things together. 缆绳 ❑ *He tied the rope around his waist.* 他把那条缆绳系在他的腰上。 **2** V-T If you **rope** one thing **to** another, you tie the two things together with a rope. (用绳）系 ❑ *I roped myself to the chimney.* 我用绳子将自己系在了那个烟囱上。 **3** PHRASE If you **give** someone **enough rope to hang themselves**, you give them the freedom to do a job in their own way because you hope that their attempts will fail and that they will look foolish. 任某人自作自受 ❑ *The king has merely given the politicians enough rope to hang themselves.* 那位国王不过是任那些政客自作自受。 **4** PHRASE If you **are learning the ropes**, you are learning how a particular task or job is done. 熟悉门道 [INFORMAL] ❑ *He tried hiring more salesmen to push his radio products, but they took too much time to learn the ropes.* 他试图雇佣更多的销售员来推销无线电产品，但那些人用了太多时间熟悉门道。 **5** PHRASE If you **know the ropes**, you know how a particular job or task should be done. 懂行 [INFORMAL] ❑ *The moment she got to know the ropes, there was no stopping her.* 一旦她懂了行，她就一往无前了。 **6** PHRASE If you **show** someone **the ropes**, you show them how to do a particular job or task. 给某人指点门道 [INFORMAL]

Word Web rope

Rope consists of a number of **threads, strands,** or **fiber.** A machine twists the strands around one another in such a way that they won't **unravel.** Natural materials like hemp and synthetic ones like **nylon** are used. Rope has played a central role in the history of humanity. The Egyptians used it to help build the pyramids. The ships Columbus* discovered America with required rope to raise the sails. Early mountain climbers used thick **cords** to reach high peaks. Using rope always involves making **knots.** The square knot and clove hitch are two of the most common knots.

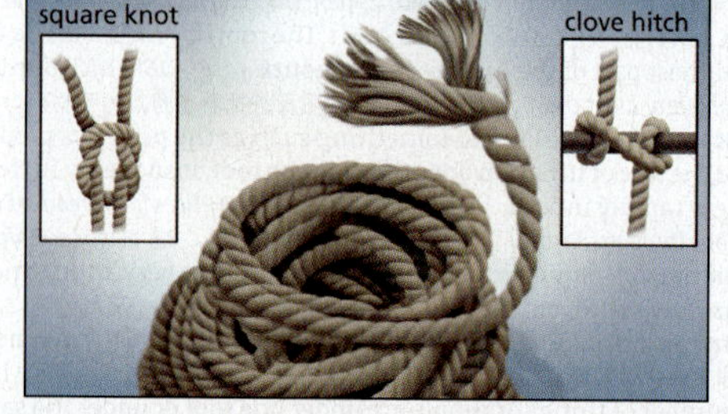

Christopher Columbus (1451-1506): an Italian explorer.

❑ *We had a patrol out on the border, breaking in some young soldiers, showing them the ropes.* 我们在边境上进行了一次巡逻，训练一些年轻士兵，对他们做了指点。

→ see Word Web: **rope**

▸ **rope in** PHRASAL VERB If you say that you **were roped in to** do a particular task, you mean that someone persuaded you to help them do that task. 拉…来帮忙 [INFORMAL] ❑ *Visitors were roped in for potato picking and harvesting.* 参观者们被拉来帮助挖土豆和收获。

rose ♦◇◇ /roʊz/ (**roses**) **1** **Rose** is the past tense of **rise**. **rise**的过去式 **2** N-COUNT A **rose** is a flower, often with a pleasant smell, which grows on a bush with stems that have sharp points called thorns on them. 玫瑰花 ❑ *She bent to pick a red rose.* 她弯下腰摘了一朵红玫瑰。 **3** N-COUNT A **rose** is a bush that roses grow on. 玫瑰丛 ❑ *Prune rambling roses when the flowers have faded.* 花儿已经凋谢了的时候，修剪那些散漫的玫瑰枝。 **4** COLOR Something that is **rose** is reddish pink in color. 玫瑰色(的) [LITERARY] ❑ *...the rose and violet hues of a twilight sky.* …微明的天空上的玫瑰色和紫色。 **5** PHRASE If you say that a situation is not **a bed of roses**, you mean that it is not as pleasant as it seems, and that there are some unpleasant aspects to it. 尽如人意 ❑ *We all knew that life was unlikely to be a bed of roses back in Nebraska.* 我们都知道回到内布拉斯加生活不太可能尽如人意。

→ see **plant**

Word Link *ette ≈ small : cigarette, diskette, rosette*

ro·sette /roʊzɛt/ (**rosettes**) N-COUNT A **rosette** is a large, circular decoration made from colored ribbons which is given as a prize in a competition, or is worn to show support for a political party or sports team. 玫瑰花形饰物 ❑ *Marjorie stood on the porch with a big yellow rosette tied around the post.* 马乔里站在柱子上系着一个巨大的黄色玫瑰花形饰物的门廊里。

ros·ter /rɒstər/ (**rosters**) **1** N-COUNT A **roster** is a list which gives details of the order in which different people have to do a particular job. 值勤表 ❑ *The next day he put himself first on the new roster for domestic chores.* 次日，他在新的内务值勤表上把自己排在第一个。 **2** N-COUNT A **roster** is a list, especially of the people who work for a particular organization or are available to do a particular job. It can also be a list of the athletes who are available for a particular team. 花名册；(运动员) 名单 [mainly AM] ❑ *The Amateur Softball Association's roster of umpires has declined to 57,000.* 业余垒球协会的裁判员名单上的人数减少到了5.7万人。

rosy /roʊzi/ (**rosier, rosiest**) **1** ADJ If you say that someone has a **rosy** face, you mean that they have pink cheeks and look very healthy. (面色) 红润的 [h2] ❑ *Bethan's round, rosy face seemed hardly to have aged at all.* 贝森那张红润的圆脸看上去几乎一点儿也没有变老。 **2** ADJ If you say that a situation looks **rosy** or that the picture looks **rosy**, you mean that the situation seems likely to be good or successful. 乐观的 ❑ *The job prospects for those graduating in engineering are far less rosy now than they used to be.* 那些工科毕业生的就业前景远不如以往那么乐观。

★ **rot** /rɒt/ (**rots, rotting, rotted**) **1** V-T/V-I When food, wood, or another substance **rots**, or when something **rots** it, it becomes softer and is gradually destroyed. 使腐烂；腐烂 ❑ *If we don't unload it soon, the grain will start rotting in the silos.* 如果我们不马上卸货，这些粮食在仓中将开始腐烂。 **2** N-UNCOUNT If there is **rot** in something, especially something that is made of wood, parts of it have decayed and fallen apart. 腐朽 ❑ *Investigations had revealed extensive rot in the beams under the ground floor.* 调查显示了一楼下面的横梁已经有大面积的腐烂。 **3** N-SING You can use **the rot** to refer to the way something gradually gets worse. For example, if you are talking about the time when **the rot set in**, you are talking about the time when a situation began to get steadily worse and worse. 逐步恶化 ❑ *In many schools, the rot is beginning to set in. Standards are falling all the time.* 在许多学校，情况正在逐步恶化，水准在不断降低。 **4** V-I If you say that someone is being left to **rot** in a particular place, especially in a prison, you mean that they are being left there and their physical and mental condition is being allowed to get worse and worse. 身心退化 ❑ *Most governments simply leave the long-term jobless to rot.* 大多数政府只能任由长期失业者腐烂下去。

Word Link *rot ≈ turning : rotary, rotate, rotation*

★ **ro·ta·ry** /roʊtəri/ **1** ADJ **Rotary** means turning or able to turn around a fixed point. 旋转的 [ADJ n] ❑ *...turning linear into rotary motion.* …变直线运动为旋转运动。 **2** ADJ **Rotary** is used in the names of some machines that have parts that turn around a fixed point. 转… (用于机器名) [ADJ n] ❑ *...a rotary engine.* …一台转缸式发动机。

ro·tate /roʊteɪt/ (**rotates, rotating, rotated**) **1** V-T/V-I When something **rotates** or when you **rotate** it, it turns with a circular movement. 旋转 ❑ *The earth rotates around the sun.* 地球围绕太阳旋转。 **2** V-T/V-I If people or things **rotate**, or if someone **rotates** them, they take turns to do a particular job or serve a particular purpose. 使轮流；轮流 ❑ *The members of the club can rotate and one person can do all the preparation for the evening.* 该俱乐部的成员可轮流工作，一个人可做晚会所有的准备工作。

→ see **moon**

ro·ta·tion /roʊteɪʃ°n/ (**rotations**) **1** N-VAR **Rotation** is circular movement. A **rotation** is the movement of something through one complete circle. 旋转；转动 ❑ *...the daily rotation of the earth upon its axis.* …地球围绕地轴的每日自转。 **2** N-UNCOUNT The **rotation** of a group of things or people is the fact of them taking turns to do a particular job or serve a particular purpose. If people do something **in rotation**, they take turns to do it. 轮流 ❑ *He grew a different crop on the same field five years in a row, what researchers call crop rotation.* 他连续5年在同一块地上轮流种植不同作物，研究人员称之为轮作。

rot·ten /rɒt°n/ **1** ADJ If food, wood, or another substance is **rotten**, it has decayed and can no longer be used. 腐烂了的 ❑ *The smell outside this building is overwhelming – like rotten eggs.* 这栋大楼外的气味势不可挡——像臭鸡蛋。 **2** ADJ If you describe something as **rotten**, you think it is very unpleasant or of very poor quality. 极差的 [INFORMAL] ❑ *I personally think it's a rotten idea.* 我个人认为这是个馊主意。 **3** ADJ If you feel **rotten**, you feel bad, either because you are ill or because you are sorry about something. 糟糕的 [INFORMAL] ❑ *I had rheumatic fever and spent that year feeling rotten.* 我得了风湿热，那一年感觉很糟。

Thesaurus *rotten* 另参见：
ADJ. decomposed, spoiled; (*ant.*) fresh **1**

▲ **rouge** /ruʒ/ (**rouges, rouging, rouged**) **1** N-UNCOUNT **Rouge** is a red powder or cream which women and actors can put on their cheeks in order to give them more color. 胭脂 [OLD-FASHIONED] **2** V-T If a woman or an actor **rouges** their cheeks or lips, they put red powder or cream on them to give them more color. 给…搽胭脂 ❑ *Florentine women rouged their earlobes.* 佛罗伦萨的妇女往她们的耳垂上搽胭脂。 ❑ *She had curly black hair and rouged cheeks.* 她有卷曲的黑发和涂脂的双颊。

→ see **makeup**

rough ♦◇◇ /rʌf/ (**rougher, roughest**) **1** ADJ If a surface is **rough**, it is uneven and not smooth. 粗糙的 ❑ *His hands were rough and callused, from years of karate practice.* 他的双手由于多年的空手道练习，粗糙而布满老茧。 ● **rough·ness** N-UNCOUNT 粗糙 ❑ *She rested her cheek against the roughness of his jacket.* 她把脸靠在了他粗糙的夹克上。 **2** ADJ You say that people or their actions are **rough** when they use too much force and not enough care or gentleness. 粗暴的；粗野的 ❑ *Football's a rough game at the best of times.* 在最好的情况下足球也是一项粗野的运动。 ● **rough·ly** ★ ADV 粗暴地；粗野地 ❑ *They roughly pushed her forward.* 他们粗暴地向前推她。 ● **rough·ness** N-UNCOUNT 粗暴；粗野 ❑ *He regretted his roughness.* 他为自己的粗暴而感到懊悔。 **3** ADJ A **rough** area, city, school, or other place is unpleasant and dangerous because there is a lot of violence or crime there. (治安) 乱的 ❑ *It was quite a rough part of our town.* 那是我们镇上相当乱的一个地方。 **4** ADJ If you say that someone has had a **rough** time, you mean that they have had some difficult or unpleasant experiences. 艰难的 ❑ *All women have a rough time in our society.* 我们社会所有妇女都过着艰难的日子。 **5** ADJ A **rough** calculation or guess is approximately correct, but not exact. 粗略的 ❑ *We were only able to make a rough estimate of how much fuel would be required.* 我们只能对所需燃料的量作一个粗略估计。 ● **rough·ly** ★ ADV 粗略地 [ADV with cl/group] ❑ *Gambling and tourism pay roughly half the entire state budget.* 博彩业和旅游业为整个国家预算提供大致一半的资金来源。 **6** ADJ If you give someone a **rough** idea, description, or drawing of something, you indicate only the most important features, without much detail. 大致的 ❑ *I've got a rough idea of what he looks like.* 我对他的样子有了个大致的概念。 ● **rough·ly** ★ ADV 大致地 ❑ *He knew roughly what was about to be said.* 他大致知道该说些什么。 **7** ADJ You can say that something is **rough** when it is not neat and well made. 粗糙的 ❑ *The bench had a rough wooden table in front of it.* 那长椅前有张粗糙的木桌。 ● **rough·ly** ★ ADV 粗糙地 [ADV with v] ❑ *Roughly*

r

chop the tomatoes and add them to the casserole. 把这些西红柿粗切一下，添到那个砂锅里。 **8** ADJ If the sea or the weather at sea is **rough**, the weather is windy or stormy and there are very big waves. 风浪大的 ❑ *A fishing vessel and a cargo ship collided in rough seas.* 一艘渔船与一艘货轮在风大浪急的海上相撞了。 **9** PHRASE If you have to **rough it**, you have to live without the possessions and comforts that you normally have. 将就 [INFORMAL] ❑ *There is a campsite but, if you prefer not to rough it, the Lake Hotel is nearby.* 有一个营地，不过如果你不想将就，湖滨酒店就在附近。 **10** **rough justice** → see **justice**

▸ **rough up** PHRASAL VERB If someone **roughs** you **up**, they attack you and hit or beat you. 殴打 [INFORMAL] ❑ *They threw him in a cell and roughed him up a bit.* 他们将他投入牢房，打了他一顿。 ❑ *He was fired from his job after roughing up a colleague.* 殴打一名同事后，他被辞退了。

Thesaurus	*rough* 另参见：
ADJ.	coarse, harsh; *(ant.)* smooth **1**
	approximate, estimated, vague; *(ant.)* exact **5** **6**

rou·lette /ruˈlet/ N-UNCOUNT **Roulette** is a gambling game in which a ball is dropped onto a wheel with numbered holes in it while the wheel is spinning around. The players bet on which hole the ball will be in when the wheel stops spinning. 轮盘赌 ❑ *I had been playing roulette at the casino.* 我过去一直在那家赌场玩轮盘赌。

round
❶ PHRASE
❷ NOUN USE
❸ ADJECTIVE USES
❹ VERB USES

❶ round ◆◆◇ /raʊnd/

Round is used mainly in British English. See **around**.

PHRASE If something happens **all year round**, it happens throughout the year. 全年 ❑ *Many of these plants are evergreen, so you can enjoy them all year round.* 这些植物中有许多都是四季常青的，所以可以全年观赏。

❷ round ◆◆◇ /raʊnd/ (**rounds**) **1** N-COUNT A **round of** events is a series of related events, especially one which comes after or before a similar series of events. (一) 轮 ❑ *It was agreed that another round of preliminary talks would be held in Beijing.* 商定了又一轮预备会谈将在北京举行。 **2** N-COUNT In sports, a **round** is a series of games in a competition. The winners of these games go on to play in the next round, and so on, until only one player or team is left. (运动比赛的) 一轮；一场 ❑ *...in the third round of the Ryder Cup.* …莱德杯高尔夫球赛的第三轮。 **3** N-COUNT In a boxing or wrestling match, a **round** is one of the periods during which the boxers or wrestlers fight. (拳击或摔跤比赛的) 回合 ❑ *He was declared the victor in the 11th round.* 他在第11个回合被宣布为获胜者。 **4** N-COUNT A **round of** golf is one game, usually including 18 holes. (高尔夫球赛的) 一场 ❑ *...two rounds of golf.* …两场高尔夫球赛。 **5** N-COUNT If you do your **rounds** or your **round**, you make a series of visits to different places or people, for example as part of your job. 巡访 ❑ *The doctors still did their morning rounds.* 医生们依旧做晨访。 **6** N-COUNT If you buy a **round of** drinks, you buy a drink for each member of the group of people that you are with. (一) 巡 (饮料) ❑ *They sat on thesnd clubhouse terrace, downing a round of drinks.* 他们都坐在那个俱乐部会所的露台上，豪饮着一巡饮料。 **7** N-COUNT A **round of** ammunition is the bullet or bullets released when a gun is fired. 射击一次的量 ❑ *...firing 1,650 rounds of ammunition during a period of ten minutes.* …10分钟发射1650堂弹药。 **8** N-COUNT If there is a **round of applause**, everyone claps their hands to welcome someone or to show that they have enjoyed something. (一) 阵 (掌声) ❑ *Sue got a sympathetic round of applause.* 苏获得了一阵同情的掌声。 **9** PHRASE If you **make the rounds** or **do the rounds**, you visit a series of different places. 巡访 ❑ *After school, I had picked up Nick and Ted and made the rounds of the dry cleaner and the food stores.* 放学后，我接了尼克和特德，然后去了那干洗店和食品店。

❸ round /raʊnd/ (**rounder, roundest**) **1** ADJ Something that is **round** is shaped like a circle or ball. 圆形的 ❑ *She had small feet and hands and a flat, round face.* 她有一对小手小脚和一张扁平的圆脸。 **2** ADJ A **round** number is a multiple of 10, 100, 1,000, and so on. Round numbers are used instead of precise ones to give the general idea of a quantity or proportion. 整十，整百，整千…的数 [ADJ n] ❑ *I asked how much silver could be bought for a million dollars, which seemed a suitably round number.* 我问了100万美元，这似乎是个合适的整数，能买多少白银。

❹ round /raʊnd/ (**rounds, rounding, rounded**) **1** V-T If you **round** a place or obstacle, you move in a curve past the edge or corner of it. 绕过 ❑ *The house disappeared from sight as we rounded a corner.* 那栋房屋在我们绕过街角时从视线中消失了。 **2** V-T If you **round** an amount **up** or **down**, or if you **round** it **off**, you change it to the nearest whole number or nearest multiple of 10, 100, 1000, and so on. 四舍五入 ❑ *We needed to do decimals to round up and round down numbers.* 我们需要把小数四舍五入成整数。 ❑ *The fraction was then multiplied by 100 and rounded to the nearest half or whole number.* 该分数然后被乘以100，再四舍五入成半数或者整数。 **3** → see also **rounded**

▸ **round up** **1** PHRASAL VERB If the police or army **round up** a number of people, they arrest or capture them. 逮捕 ❑ *The police rounded up a number of suspects.* 警察逮捕了几个嫌疑犯。 **2** PHRASAL VERB If you **round up** animals or things, you gather them together. 使聚拢 ❑ *He had sought work as a cowboy, rounding up cattle.* 他曾经找过一份当牛仔的工作，负责看牛不让其失散。 **3** → see also **round ❹ 2** → see also **roundup**

▲ **round·about** /raʊndəbaʊt/ (**roundabouts**) **1** ADJ If you go somewhere by a **roundabout** route, you do not go there by the shortest and quickest route. 迂回的 ❑ *He left today on a roundabout route for Jordan and is also due soon in Egypt.* 他今天绕道前往约旦，也将很快到达埃及。 **2** ADJ If you do or say something in a **roundabout** way, you do not do or say it in a simple, clear, and direct way. 拐弯抹角的 ❑ *We made a little fuss in a roundabout way.* 我们拐弯抹角地发了点牢骚。 **3** N-COUNT A **roundabout** is a circular structure in the road at a place where several roads meet. You drive around it until you come to the road that you want. (交通) 环岛 [BRIT]

in AM, use **traffic circle, rotary**

4 N-COUNT A **roundabout** at an amusement park is a large, circular mechanical device with seats, often in the shape of animals or cars, on which children sit and go around and around. (游乐园的) 旋转木马 [BRIT]

in AM, use **merry-go-round, carousel**

5 N-COUNT A **roundabout** in a park or school play area is a circular platform that children sit or stand on. People push the platform to make it spin around. (公园、学校的) 转椅 [BRIT]

in AM, use **merry-go-round**

6 **round about** → see **round**

round·ed /raʊndɪd/ **1** ADJ Something that is **rounded** is curved in shape, without any points or sharp edges. 圆形的 ❑ *...a low, rounded hill.* …一座矮的圆形山丘。 **2** ADJ You describe something or someone as **rounded** when you are expressing approval of them because they have a personality which is fully developed in all aspects. (个性) 全面发展的 [APPROVAL] ❑ *...his carefully organized narrative, full of rounded, believable, and interesting characters.* …他那精心编排的故事，充满了完美、可信而有趣的人物。

round trip (**round trips**) **1** N-COUNT If you make a **round trip**, you travel to a place and then back again. 往返旅行 ❑ *The train operates the 2,400-mile round trip once a week.* 这列火车每周进行一次2400英里的往返旅行。 **2** ADJ A **round-trip** ticket is a ticket for a train, bus, or plane that allows you to travel to a particular place and then back again. 往返的 [ADJ n] [AM]

in BRIT, use **return**

❑ *Mexicana Airlines has announced cheaper round-trip tickets between Los Angeles and cities it serves in Mexico.* 墨西哥航空公司已宣布降价出售从洛杉矶到该公司设有航班的墨西哥各城市的往返机票。

round·up /raʊndʌp/ (**roundups**) N-COUNT In journalism, especially television or radio, a **roundup** of news is a summary of the main events that have happened. (新闻) 综述 ❑ *First, we have this roundup of the day's news.* 首先是今日新闻综述。

rouse /raʊz/ (**rouses, rousing, roused**) **1** V-T/V-I If someone **rouses** you when you are sleeping or if you **rouse**, you wake up. 使醒来；醒来 [LITERARY] ❑ *Hilton roused him at eight-thirty by rapping on the door.* 希尔顿8:30急敲门把他弄醒了。 **2** V-T If you **rouse yourself**, you stop being inactive and start doing something. 使振作起来 ❑ *She seemed to be unable to rouse herself to do anything.* 她似乎打不起精神做任何事情。 **3** V-T If something or someone **rouses** you, they make you very emotional or excited. 使激动 ❑ *He did more to rouse the crowd there than anybody else.* 他比其他任何人都更卖力地鼓动那里的群众。 • **rous·ing** ADJ 激动人心的 ❑ *...a rousing speech to the convention in support of the president.* …在那次大会上作的支持这位总统的一次振奋人心的演讲。 **4** V-T If something **rouses** a feeling in you, it causes

R

you to have that feeling. 激起；唤起 ❑ *It roused a feeling of rebellion in him.* 这激起了他的叛逆感。

→ see **dream**

rout /raʊt/ (**routs, routing, routed**) V-T If an army, sports team, or other group **routs** its opponents, it defeats them completely and easily. 一举击败 ❑ *...the Battle of Hastings at which the Norman army routed the English opposition.* …诺曼军队一举击败英格兰军队的黑斯廷斯战役。 ● N-COUNT **Rout** is also a noun. 一举击败 ❑ *One after another the Italian bases in the desert fell as the retreat turned into a rout.* 当撤退转变为溃败时，意大利在那个沙漠中的基地接连失守。

route ♦♦◇ /rut, raʊt/ (**routes, routing, routed**) 1 N-COUNT A **route** is a way from one place to another. 路线 ❑ *...the most direct route to the center of town.* …去镇中心最直接的路线。 2 N-COUNT A bus, air, or shipping **route** is the way between two places along which buses, planes, or ships travel regularly. (公共汽车的) 行车路线；(飞机、轮船的) 航线 ❑ *...the main shipping routes to Japan.* …去往日本的主要轮船航线。 3 N-IN-NAMES In the United States, **Route** is used in front of a number in the names of main roads between major cities. (…号) 公路 ❑ *From San Francisco take the freeway to the Broadway-Webster exit on Route 580.* 从旧金山走高速公路到580号公路百老汇–韦伯斯特出口。 4 N-COUNT Your **route** is the series of visits you make to different people or places, as part of your job. 巡访 [mainly AM]

in BRIT, usually use **round, rounds**

❑ *He began cracking open big blue tins of butter cookies and feeding the dogs on his route.* 他开始打开装着奶油曲奇的蓝色大罐子，巡访途中喂起那些狗来。 5 N-COUNT You can refer to a way of achieving something as a **route**. 途径 ❑ *Researchers are trying to get at the same information through an indirect route.* 研究者们正试图通过一条间接途径获取同样的信息。 6 V-T If vehicles, goods, or passengers **are routed** in a particular direction, they are made to travel in that direction. 为…规定路线 [usu passive] ❑ *Trains are taking a lot of freight that used to be routed via trucks.* 火车正在运送过去由卡车运送的大批货物。 7 PHRASE **En route to** a place means on the way to that place. **En route** is sometimes spelled **on route** in nonstandard English. 在途中 ❑ *They have arrived in London en route to the United States.* 他们在前往美国的途中已中途到达伦敦。 8 PHRASE Journalists sometimes use **en route** when they are mentioning an event that happened as part of a longer process or before another event. 在…的过程中；在…之前 ❑ *The German set three tournament records and equaled two others en route to grabbing golf's richest prize.* 这个德国人在赢取高尔夫球赛最高奖的过程中刷新了3项、平了2项锦标赛记录。

Thesaurus *route* 另参见：

N. path, road, trail 1 2

Word Partnership *route* 的常用搭配：

N. **escape** route, **parade** route 1

ADJ. **scenic** route 1

main route 1 2

alternative route, **different** route, **direct** route, **shortest** route 1 2 5

rou·tine ♦◇◇ /rutin/ (**routines**) 1 N-VAR A **routine** is the usual series of things that you do at a particular time. A **routine** is also the practice of regularly doing things in a fixed order. 惯例；常规 ❑ *The players had to change their daily routine and lifestyle.* 这些运动员不得不改变他们的每日常规和生活方式。 2 ADJ You use **routine** to describe activities that are done as a normal part of a job or process. 常规的 ❑ *...a series of routine medical tests including X-rays and blood tests.* …一系列包括X光和验血在内的常规医学检查。 3 ADJ A **routine** situation, action, or event is one which seems completely ordinary, rather than interesting, exciting, or different. 平淡的 [DISAPPROVAL] ❑ *So many days are routine and uninteresting, especially in winter.* 太多的日子都是平淡和无趣，尤其是在冬季。 4 N-VAR You use **routine** to refer to a way of life that is uninteresting and ordinary, or hardly ever changes. 平淡乏味 [DISAPPROVAL] ❑ *...the mundane routine of her life.* …她生活的平常乏味。 5 N-COUNT A **routine** is a computer program, or part of a program, that performs a specific function. 程序 [COMPUTING] ❑ *...an installation routine.* …一个安装程序。 6 N-COUNT A **routine** is a short sequence of jokes, remarks, actions, or movements that forms part of a longer performance. (一) 套 ❑ *...an athletic dance routine.* …一套体育舞蹈动作。

Word Partnership *routine* 的常用搭配：

ADJ. **daily** routine, **normal** routine, **regular** routine, **usual** routine 1

N. **exercise** routine, **morning** routine, **work** routine 1

routine **maintenance**, routine **tests** 2

routine **day** 3

comedy routine, **dance** routine 6

★ **rou·tine·ly** /rutinli/ 1 ADV If something is **routinely** done, it is done as a normal part of a job or process. 例行地；常规性地 ❑ *Vitamin K is routinely given in the first week of life to prevent bleeding.* 维生素K是在婴儿出生的第一周内常规性地补充以防出血。 2 ADV If something happens **routinely**, it happens repeatedly and is not surprising, unnatural, or new. 照例地 [ADV with v] ❑ *Any outside criticism is routinely dismissed as interference.* 任何外来批评照例都被当作干涉而不予理睬。

rov·ing /roʊvɪŋ/ ADJ You use **roving** to describe a person who travels around, rather than staying in a fixed place. (人) 流动的 [ADJ n] ❑ *He is to join NBC to cover the Olympic Games in Barcelona next month as a roving reporter.* 他将于下月作为一名流动记者加入国家广播公司报道巴塞罗纳奥运会。

row

❶ ARRANGEMENT OR SEQUENCE

❷ MAKING A BOAT MOVE

❶ **row** ♦◇◇ /roʊ/ (**rows**) 1 N-COUNT A **row of** things or people is a number of them arranged in a line. 排 ❑ *...a row of pretty little cottages.* …一排漂亮的小村舍。 2 N-IN-NAMES **Row** is sometimes used in the names of streets. …街 (用于街道名) ❑ *...the house at 236 Larch Row.* …位于拉齐街236号的那栋房子。 3 → see also **death row** 4 PHRASE If something happens several times **in a row**, it happens that number of times without a break. If something happens several days **in a row**, it happens on each of those days. 连续地 ❑ *They have won five championships in a row.* 他们已经赢得了五连冠。

❷ **row** /roʊ/ (**rows, rowing, rowed**) 1 V-T/V-I When you **row**, you sit in a boat and make it move through the water by using oars. If you **row** someone somewhere, you take them there in a boat, using oars. 划船运送；划船 ❑ *He rowed as quickly as he could to the shore.* 他尽可能快速地将船划向了岸边。 ❑ *The boatman refused to row him back.* 那船夫拒绝划船送他回去。 ● N-COUNT **Row** is also a noun. 划船 ❑ *I took Daniel for a row.* 我带丹尼尔去划船了。 2 → see also **rowing**

row·dy /raʊdi/ (**rowdier, rowdiest**) ADJ When people are **rowdy**, they are noisy, rough, and likely to cause trouble. 吵闹的 ❑ *He has complained to the police about rowdy neighbors.* 他已向警察投诉了吵闹的邻居。

row house (**row houses**) N-COUNT A **row house** is one of a row of similar houses that are joined together by both of their side walls. 排屋 [AM]

in BRIT, use **terraced house**

❑ *...a city block of row houses.* …一个排屋组成的城市街区。

row·ing /roʊɪŋ/ N-UNCOUNT **Rowing** is a sport in which people or teams race against each other in boats with oars. 划船 (运动) ❑ *...competitions in rowing, swimming, and water skiing.* …划船、游泳和滑水比赛。

Word Link *roy ≈ king : royal, royalist, royalty*

roy·al ♦♦◇ /rɔɪəl/ (**royals**) 1 ADJ **Royal** is used to indicate that something is connected with a king, queen, or emperor, or their family. A **royal** person is a king, queen, or emperor, or a member of their family. 王室的 ❑ *...an invitation to a royal garden party.* …一张参加皇家花园聚会的请帖。 2 ADJ **Royal** is used in the names of institutions or organizations that are officially appointed or supported by a member of a royal family. 皇家的 [ADJ n] ❑ *...the Royal Academy of Music.* …皇家音乐学院。 3 N-COUNT Members of the royal family are sometimes referred to as **royals**. 王室成员 [INFORMAL] ❑ *The royals have always been patrons of charities pulling in large donations.* 王室成员一直都是慈善机构的资助人，注入大量捐赠。

roy·al·ist /rɔɪəlɪst/ (**royalists**) N-COUNT A **royalist** is someone who supports their country's royal family or who believes that their country should have a king or queen. 保皇主义者；保皇党人 ❑ *He was hated by the royalists and mistrusted by the communists.* 他遭保皇党人痛恨，也不被共产党人信任。

r

Word Link *roy ≈ king : royal, royalist, royalty*

★ **roy·al·ty** /rɔɪəlti/ (**royalties**) **1** N-UNCOUNT The members of royal families are sometimes referred to as **royalty**. 王室 ❑ *Royalty and government leaders from all around the world are gathering in Japan.* 来自世界各国的王室和政府首脑们正聚集日本。 **2** N-PLURAL **Royalties** are payments made to authors and musicians when their work is sold or performed. They usually receive a fixed percentage of the profits from these sales or performances. 版税 ❑ *I lived on about $5,000 a year from the royalties on my book.* 我靠的大约五千美元的出书版税生活。 **3** N-COUNT Payments made to someone whose invention, idea, or property is used by a commercial company can be referred to as **royalties**. (发明、创意、财产等的) 使用费 ❑ *The royalties enabled the inventor to re-establish himself in business.* 这些使用费使这名发明者能再次立足商界。

RSI /ɑr ɛs aɪ/ N-UNCOUNT People who suffer from **RSI** have pain in their hands and arms as a result of repeating similar movements over a long period of time, usually as part of their job. **RSI** is an abbreviation for **repetitive strain injury**. 重复性劳损 ❑ *The women developed painful RSI because of poor working conditions.* 这些妇女因恶劣的工作条件而患上了折磨人的重复性劳损。

RSVP /ɑr ɛs vi pi/ also **R.S.V.P.** **1** **RSVP** is an abbreviation for "répondez s'il vous plaît," which means "please reply." It is written on the bottom of a card inviting you to a party or special occasion. 敬请赐复 [FORMAL]

> When **RSVP** appears on an invitation, the sender needs to know whether or not the guest will come to the event. The guest should answer in plenty of time so the host can make plans. If the note **BYOB** also appears, it means the host wants the guest to "Bring Your Own Bottle" if they wish to drink alcoholic drinks.

rub /rʌb/ (**rubs, rubbing, rubbed**) **1** V-T/V-I If you **rub** a part of your body or if you **rub at** it, you move your hand or fingers backward and forward over it while pressing firmly. 揉 ❑ *He rubbed his arms and stiff legs.* 他揉了揉他的两条胳膊和两条僵硬的腿。 **2** V-T/V-I If you **rub against** a surface or **rub** a part of your body **against** a surface, you move it backward and forward while pressing it against the surface. 蹭 ❑ *A cat was rubbing against my leg.* 一只猫当时在我腿上蹭来蹭去。 **3** V-T/V-I If you **rub** an object or a surface or you **rub at** it, you move a cloth backward and forward over it in order to clean or dry it. 擦 ❑ *She took off her glasses and rubbed them hard.* 她摘下了她的眼镜，用力擦着。 **4** V-T If you **rub** a substance **into** a surface or **rub** something such as dirt **from** a surface, you spread it over the surface or remove it from the surface using your hand or something such as a cloth. 抹 ❑ *He rubbed oil into my back.* 他在我的背上抹上了油。 **5** V-T/V-I If you **rub** two things **together** or if they **rub together**, they move backward and forward, pressing against each other. 揉搓 ❑ *He rubbed his hands together a few times.* 他把双手搓了好几遍。 **6** V-I If something you are wearing or holding **rubs**, it makes you sore because it keeps moving backward and forward against your skin. 蹭得疼 ❑ *It should be comfortable against the skin without rubbing, chafing, or cutting into anything.* 它贴身穿应是舒服的，不会蹭伤、磨伤或划伤皮肤。 **7** N-COUNT A massage can be referred to as a **rub**. 按摩 ❑ *She sometimes asks if I want a back rub.* 她有时问我是否想要一次背部按摩。 **8** PHRASE If you **rub shoulders with** famous people, you meet them and talk to them. You can also say that you **rub elbows with** someone. 与某人接触 ❑ *He regularly rubbed shoulders with the likes of Elizabeth Taylor and Kylie Minogue.* 他常与伊丽莎白•泰勒和凯莉•米洛之类的人接触。 **9** PHRASE If you **rub** someone **the wrong way**, you offend or annoy them without intending to. 无意中冒犯某人 [INFORMAL] ❑ *What are you going to get out of him if you rub him the wrong way?* 如果你无意中惹恼了他，你能从他那里得到什么呢？ **10** to **rub** someone's **nose in** it → see **nose**

▸ **rub out** PHRASAL VERB If you **rub out** something that you have written on paper or a board, you remove it using an eraser. 擦掉 [BRIT]

in AM, use **erase**

Word Partnership *rub* 的常用搭配：

PREP.	rub against **2**
	rub off, rub with **4**
ADV.	rub together **5**

rub·ber /rʌbər/ (**rubbers**) **1** N-UNCOUNT **Rubber** is a strong, waterproof, elastic substance made from the juice of a tropical tree or produced chemically. It is used for making tires, boots, and other products. 橡胶 ❑ *...the smell of burning rubber.* …橡胶烧着的气味 **2** N-COUNT A **rubber** is a condom. 避孕套 [AM, INFORMAL] **3** N-COUNT A **rubber** is a small piece of rubber or other material that is used to remove mistakes that you have made while writing, drawing, or typing. 橡皮 [BRIT]

in AM, use **eraser**

rub·ber band (**rubber bands**) N-COUNT A **rubber band** is a thin circle of very elastic rubber. You put it around things such as papers in order to keep them together. 橡皮筋

→ see **office**

rub·ber stamp (**rubber stamps, rubber stamping, rubber stamped**) also **rubber-stamp** **1** N-COUNT A **rubber stamp** is a small device with a name, date, or symbol on it. You press it onto an ink pad and then on to a document in order to show that the document has been officially dealt with. 橡皮图章 ❑ *In post offices, virtually every document that's passed across the counter is stamped with a rubber stamp.* 在邮局，基本上每个交到柜面的文件都会用一个橡皮图章盖上印。 **2** V-T When someone in authority **rubber-stamps** a decision, plan, or law, they agree to it without thinking about it much. (不多加思考而) 盖章批准 ❑ *The board's job is to rubber-stamp his decisions.* 该委员会的工作就是例行公事式地盖章批准他的决定。

rub·bish /rʌbɪʃ/ (**rubbishes, rubbishing, rubbished**) **1** N-UNCOUNT **Rubbish** consists of unwanted things or waste material such as used paper, empty cans and bottles, and waste food. 垃圾 [mainly BRIT]

in AM, usually use **garbage, trash**

2 N-UNCOUNT If you think that something is of very poor quality, you can say that it is **rubbish**. 垃圾 (强调质量极差) [mainly BRIT, INFORMAL] **3** V-T If you **rubbish** a person, their ideas or their work, you say they are of little value. 把…说得一文不值 [BRIT, INFORMAL]

in AM, use **trash**

> In British English, **rubbish** is the word most commonly used to refer to waste material that is thrown away. In American English, the words **garbage** and **trash** are more usual. ❑ *...the smell of rotting garbage... She threw the bottle into the trash.* **Garbage** and **trash** are sometimes used in British English, but only informally and metaphorically. ❑ *I don't have to listen to this garbage... The book was trash.*

rub·bish tip [BRIT] → see **garbage dump**

rub·ble /rʌbəl/ **1** N-UNCOUNT When a building is destroyed, the pieces of brick, stone, or other materials that remain are referred to as **rubble**. 瓦砾 ❑ *Thousands of bodies are still buried under the rubble.* 数千具尸体还埋在瓦砾下。 **2** N-UNCOUNT **Rubble** is used to refer to the small pieces of bricks and stones that are used as a bottom layer on which to build roads, paths, or houses. (铺路、建房用的) 碎石；碎砖 ❑ *Brick rubble is useful as the base for paths and patios.* 碎砖可用作道路和天井的基石。

▲ **ruby** /rubi/ (**rubies**) **1** N-COUNT A **ruby** is a dark red jewel. 红宝石 ❑ *...a ruby and diamond ring.* …一枚红宝石钻戒。 **2** COLOR Something that is **ruby** is dark red in color. 深红色 (的) ❑ *...a glass of ruby-red Cabernet Sauvignon.* …一杯深红色的赤霞珠红葡萄酒。

ruck·sack /rʌksæk/ (**rucksacks**) N-COUNT A **rucksack** is a bag with straps that go over your shoulders, so that you can carry things on your back, for example when you are walking or climbing. 双肩背 [BRIT]

in AM, usually use **backpack, knapsack, pack**

rud·der /rʌdər/ (**rudders**) **1** N-COUNT A **rudder** is a device for steering a boat. It consists of a vertical piece of wood or metal at the back of the boat. 舵 **2** N-COUNT An airplane's **rudder** is a vertical piece of metal at the back which is used to make the plane turn to the right or to the left. (飞机的) 方向舵

rud·dy /rʌdi/ (**ruddier, ruddiest**) ADJ If you describe someone's face as **ruddy**, you mean that their face is a reddish color, usually because they are healthy or have been working hard, or because they are angry or embarrassed. (面色) 红的 ❑ *He had a naturally ruddy complexion, even more flushed now from dancing.* 他的面色天生红润，现在跳了舞就更红了。

rude /rud/ (**ruder, rudest**) **1** ADJ When people are **rude**, they act in an impolite way toward other people or say impolite things about them. 无礼的；粗鲁的 ❑ *He's rude to her friends and obsessively jealous.* 他对她的朋友粗鲁无礼而且过分嫉妒。 ● **rude·ly** ADV 无礼地；粗鲁地 ❑ *I could not understand why she felt compelled to behave so rudely to a friend.* 我不能理解为什么她非要如此粗鲁地对待一位朋友。 ● **rude·ness** N-UNCOUNT 无礼；粗鲁 ❑ *Mother is annoyed at Caleb's rudeness, but I can forgive it.* 母亲为卡勒布的无礼生气，我倒是能原谅。 **2** ADJ **Rude** is used to describe words and behavior that are likely to embarrass or offend people, because they relate to sex or to body functions. 下流的 ❑ *Fred keeps cracking rude jokes with the guests.* 弗雷德不停地和那些客人开下流的玩笑。 **3** ADJ If someone receives a **rude** shock, something unpleasant happens unexpectedly. 令人不快的 [ADJ n] ❑ *It will come as a rude shock when their salary or income-tax refund cannot be cashed.* 如果他们的薪水或所得税返还不能兑现，那对他们将是一个晴天霹雳。 ● **rude·ly** ADV 令人不快地 [ADV with v] ❑ *People were rudely awakened by a siren just outside their window.* 人们被窗外的一声警报惊醒了。 **4** **rude awakening** → see **awakening**

Thesaurus *rude* 另参见：
ADJ. disrespectful, impolite, vulgar; (*ant.*) polite **1** **2**

ru·di·men·ta·ry /rudɪmɛntəri, -tri/ **1** ADJ **Rudimentary** things are very basic or simple and are therefore unsatisfactory. 简陋的 [FORMAL] ❑ *The earth surface of the courtyard extended into a kind of rudimentary kitchen.* 院子的泥土地面延伸进一间类似简易厨房的地方。 **2** ADJ **Rudimentary** knowledge includes only the simplest and most basic facts. 最基本的 [FORMAL] ❑ *He had only a rudimentary knowledge of French.* 他只有最基本的法语知识。

▲ **ruf·fle** /rʌfᵊl/ (**ruffles, ruffling, ruffled**) **1** V-T If you **ruffle** someone's hair, you move your hand backward and forward through it as a way of showing your affection toward them. 抚弄（头发） ❑ *"Don't let that get you down," he said, ruffling Ben's dark curls.* "别因那事而沮丧，"他抚弄着本的黑色卷发说道。 **2** V-T When the wind **ruffles** something such as the surface of the sea, it causes it to move gently in a wavelike motion. 使起皱 [LITERARY] ❑ *The evening breeze ruffled the pond.* 那傍晚的微风吹皱了水塘的表面。 **3** V-T If something **ruffles** someone, it causes them to panic and lose their confidence or to become angry or upset. 使惊慌失措；使沮丧；激怒 ❑ *I could tell that my refusal to allow him to ruffle me infuriated him.* 我可以断定，我拒绝让他激怒我使他很恼火。 **4** V-T/V-I If a bird **ruffles** its feathers or if its feathers **ruffle**, they stand out on its body, for example when it is cleaning itself or when it is frightened. 竖起 ❑ *Tame birds, when approached, will stretch out their necks and ruffle their neck feathering.* 驯化的鸟在人靠近时会伸长脖子，竖起脖子上的羽毛。 **5** N-COUNT **Ruffles** are folds of cloth at the neck or the ends of the arms of a piece of clothing, or are sometimes sewn on things as a decoration. （衣服领口、袖口的）褶边；装饰 ❑ *...a white blouse with ruffles at the neck and cuffs.* …一件领口和袖口上有褶边的白色女式衬衣。 **6** PHRASE To **ruffle** someone's **feathers** means to cause them to become very angry, nervous, or upset. 使某人愤怒；紧张；沮丧 ❑ *His direct, often abrasive approach will doubtless ruffle a few feathers.* 他那直截了当、常常很粗鲁的方式无疑会激怒一些人。

ruf·fled /rʌfᵊld/ ADJ Something that is **ruffled** is no longer smooth or neat. 弄皱了的；弄乱了的 ❑ *Her short hair was oddly ruffled and then flattened around her head.* 她的短发被怪怪地弄乱然后压平在头上。

rug /rʌg/ (**rugs**) **1** N-COUNT A **rug** is a piece of thick material that you put on a floor. It is like a carpet but covers a smaller area. 小地毯 ❑ *A Persian rug covered the hardwood floors.* 一张波斯小地毯铺在了那硬木地板上。 **2** N-COUNT A **rug** is a small blanket which you use to cover your shoulders or your knees to keep them warm. （盖在肩上或膝上的）小毛毯 [mainly BRIT] ❑ *The old lady was seated in her chair at the window, a rug over her knees.* 这位老妇人坐在靠窗的椅子上，膝上盖着一块小毛毯。 **3** PHRASE If someone **pulls the rug from under** a person or thing or **pulls the rug from under** someone's **feet**, they stop giving their help or support. 不再帮助或支持某人 ❑ *If the banks opt to pull the rug from under the ill-fated project, it will go into liquidation.* 如果这些银行选择不再支持那项倒霉的工程，它就将破产。 **4** to **sweep** something **under the rug** → see **sweep**

▲ **rug·by** ♦◇◇ /rʌgbi/ N-UNCOUNT **Rugby** or **rugby football** is a game played by two teams using an oval ball. Players try to score points by carrying the ball to their opponents' end of the field, or by kicking it over a bar fixed between two posts. 英式橄榄球（运动）

rug·ged /rʌgɪd/ **1** ADJ A **rugged** area of land is uneven and covered with rocks, with few trees or plants. 崎岖多岩的 [LITERARY] ❑ *We left the rough track and bumped our way over a rugged mountainous terrain.* 我们驶离坎坷的小道，又颠簸过了崎岖多岩的山地。 **2** ADJ If you describe a man as **rugged**, you mean that he has strong, masculine features. （男子）粗犷的 [LITERARY, APPROVAL] ❑ *A look of pure disbelief crossed Shankly's rugged face.* 尚克利粗犷的脸上掠过一副完全不信任的表情。 **3** ADJ If you describe someone's character as **rugged**, you mean that they are strong and determined, and have the ability to cope with difficult situations. 坚毅的 [APPROVAL] ❑ *Rugged individualism forged America's frontier society.* 坚定的个人主义铸就了美国这个前沿社会。 **4** ADJ A **rugged** piece of equipment is strong and is designed to last a long time, even if it is treated roughly. 结实耐用的 ❑ *The camera combines rugged reliability with unequaled optical performance and speed.* 这款照相机集经久可靠性、无与伦比的光学性能和速度于一身。

ruin ♦◇◇ /ruɪn/ (**ruins, ruining, ruined**) **1** V-T To **ruin** something means to severely harm, damage, or spoil it. 毁坏 ❑ *My wife was ruining her health through worry.* 我妻子的忧虑正在损害着她的健康。 **2** V-T To **ruin** someone means to cause them to no longer have any money. 使倾家荡产 ❑ *She accused him of ruining her financially with his taste for the high life.* 她指责他因其对高档生活的追求使得她倾家荡产。 **3** N-UNCOUNT **Ruin** is the state of no longer having any money. 破产 ❑ *The farmers say recent inflation has driven them to the brink of ruin.* 那些农民们说最近的通货膨胀已经把他们逼到了破产的边缘。 **4** N-UNCOUNT **Ruin** is the state of being severely damaged or spoiled, or the process of reaching this state. 毁坏；破落 ❑ *The vineyards were falling into ruin.* 那些葡萄园当时正日渐没落。 **5** N-PLURAL **The ruins of** something are the parts of it that remain after it has been severely damaged or weakened. 残存部分 ❑ *The new Turkish republic he helped to build emerged from the ruins of a great empire.* 他帮助创建的新土耳其共和国是在大帝国残存的领土上建立起来的。 **6** N-COUNT **The ruins** of a building are the parts of it that remain after the rest has fallen down or been destroyed. 废墟 ❑ *One dead child was found in the ruins almost two hours after the explosion.* 一名遇难儿童在爆炸发生近两小时后在废墟中被找到。 **7** → see also **ruined** **8** PHRASE If something is **in ruins**, it is completely spoiled. 毁灭了的 ❑ *Its heavily subsidized economy is in ruins.* 它的严重依赖于资助的经济已崩溃了。 **9** PHRASE If a building or place is **in ruins**, most of it has been destroyed and only parts of it remain. 成为废墟了的 ❑ *The abbey was in ruins.* 这座修道院成了一片废墟。

Thesaurus *ruin* 另参见：
V. destroy, smash, wreck **1**

ruined /ruɪnd/ ADJ A **ruined** building or place has been very badly damaged or has gradually fallen down because no one has taken care of it. 坍塌的；荒废的 [ADJ n] ❑ *...a ruined church.* …一座荒废的教堂。

rule ♦♦♦ /rul/ (**rules, ruling, ruled**) **1** N-COUNT **Rules** are instructions that tell you what you are allowed to do and what you are not allowed to do. 规则 ❑ *...a thirty-two-page pamphlet explaining the rules of basketball.* …一本说明篮球规则的32页的小册子。 **2** N-COUNT A **rule** is a statement telling people what they should do in order to achieve success or a benefit of some kind. 原则；准则 ❑ *An important rule is to drink plenty of water during any flight.* 一条重要的原则是在任何一次飞行中都要喝大量的水。 **3** N-COUNT The **rules of** something such as a language or a science are statements that describe the way that things usually happen in a particular situation. 规律；法则 ❑ *...according to the rules of quantum theory.* …根据量子论的法则。 **4** N-SING If something is **the rule**, it is the normal state of affairs. 常规；惯例 ❑ *However, for many Americans today, weekend work has unfortunately become the rule rather than the exception.* 然而，如今对许多美国人而言，周末工作已不幸成为惯例而不是特例。 **5** V-T/V-I The person or group that **rules** a country controls its affairs. 统治 ❑ *For four centuries, he says, foreigners have ruled Angola.* 他说4个世纪以来外国人一直统治着安哥拉。 ❑ *He ruled for eight months.* 他在位了8个月。 ● N-UNCOUNT **Rule** is also a noun. 统治 ❑ *...demands for an end to one-party rule.* …结束一党统治的要求。 **6** V-T If something **rules** your life, it influences or restricts your actions in a way that is not good for you. 严重影响；制约 ❑ *Scientists have always been aware of how fear can rule our lives and make us ill.* 科学家们从来都知道恐惧是如何严重影响我们的生活并使我们患病的。 **7** V-T/V-I When someone in authority **rules** that something is true or should happen, they state that they have officially decided that it is true or should happen. 裁定 [FORMAL] ❑ *The court* *ruled that laws passed by the assembly remained valid.* 该法庭裁定由议会通过的法律仍然有效。 ❑ *The Israeli court has not yet ruled on the case.* 以色列法院尚未对此案做出裁决。 **8** V-T If you **rule** a straight line, you draw it using something that has a straight edge. 画 ❑ *...a ruled grid of horizontal and vertical lines.* …一个画好的由水平线及垂直线构成的网格。 **9** → see also **golden rule, ground rule, ruling** **10** PHRASE If you say that something happens **as a rule**, you mean that it usually happens. 通常 ❑ *As a rule, however, such attacks have been aimed at causing damage rather than taking life.* 然而，通常此类攻击意在造成破坏而非要人性命。 **11** PHRASE If someone in authority **bends the rules** or **stretches the rules**, they do something even though it is against the rules. 变通规则；通融 ❑ *There happens to be a particular urgency in this case, and it would help if you could bend the rules.* 这次碰巧有紧急情况，如果你能通融一下将会很有帮助。 **12** PHRASE A **rule of thumb** is a rule or principle that you follow which is not based on exact calculations, but rather on experience. 经验法则 ❑ *A good rule of thumb is that a broker must generate sales of ten times his salary if his employer is to make a profit.* 一个很好的经验法则是，雇主要获取利润的话，其中间人必须创造10倍于自己薪水的销售额。

▸ **rule out** **1** PHRASAL VERB If you **rule out** a course of action, an idea, or a solution, you decide that it is impossible or unsuitable. 不考虑；排除 ❑ *The Treasury Department has ruled out using a weak dollar as the main solution for the country's trade problems.* 财政部已经不考虑使用疲软美元作为解决该国贸易问题的主要办法。 **2** PHRASAL VERB If something **rules out** a situation, it prevents it from happening or from being possible. 阻止…发生；使…不可能 ❑ *A serious car accident in 1986 ruled out a permanent future for him in farming.* 1986年的一起严重车祸使他永远无法务农了。

Thesaurus *rule* 另参见：

N.	guideline, law, standard **1** **2**
	authority, leadership **5**
V.	command, dictate, govern **5** **6**

Word Partnership *rule* 的常用搭配：

V.	**break** a rule, **change** a rule, **follow** a rule **1**
N.	**gag** rule **1**
	exception to a rule **1**–**4**
	majority rule, **minority** rule **5**
	courts rule, **judges** rule **7**
	rule **of thumb** **12**
PREP.	**against** a rule, **under** a rule **1**
	rule **over** ***something*** **5**

rul·er /ru̲lər/ (**rulers**) **1** N-COUNT The **ruler** of a country is the person who rules the country. 统治者 ❑ *The former military ruler of Lesotho has been placed under house arrest.* 莱索托前军事统治者已被软禁了。 **2** N-COUNT A **ruler** is a long, flat piece of wood, metal, or plastic with straight edges marked in or inches or centimeters. Rulers are used to measure things and to draw straight lines. 尺 ❑ *...a twelve-inch ruler.* …一把12英寸长的尺子。

rul·ing ♦◇◇ /ru̲lɪŋ/ (**rulings**) **1** ADJ The **ruling** group of people in a country or organization is the group that controls its affairs. 统治的 [ADJ n] ❑ *...the Mexican voters' growing dissatisfaction with the ruling party.* …墨西哥选民们对执政党的日益增长的不满。 **2** N-COUNT A **ruling** is an official decision made by a judge or court. 裁决 ❑ *Goodwin tried to have the court ruling overturned.* 古德温试图推翻法院的裁决。 **3** ADJ Someone's **ruling** passion or emotion is the feeling they have most strongly, which influences their actions. 最强烈的；主导的 [ADJ n] ❑ *Even my love of literary fame, my ruling passion, never soured my temper.* 甚至我对文学声誉的热衷，即我的主导激情，从未使我的脾气变坏。

rum /rʌm/ (**rums**) N-MASS **Rum** is an alcoholic drink made from sugar. 朗姆酒 ❑ *...a bottle of rum.* …一瓶朗姆酒。

▲ **rum·ble** /rʌmbᵊl/ (**rumbles, rumbling, rumbled**) **1** N-COUNT A **rumble** is a low, continuous noise. 隆隆声 ❑ *The silence of the night was punctuated by the distant rumble of traffic.* 夜晚的宁静被远处车辆的隆隆声所打破。 **2** V-I If a vehicle **rumbles** somewhere, it moves slowly forward while making a low, continuous noise. 轰隆着缓慢行进 ❑ *A bus rumbled along the road.* 一辆公共汽车轰隆着缓慢行驶在路上。 **3** V-I If something **rumbles**, it makes a low, continuous noise. 隆隆作响 ❑ *The sky, swollen like a black bladder, rumbled and crackled.* 天空胀得像个黑色的气囊，发出隆隆声和劈啪声。 **4** V-I If your stomach **rumbles**, it makes a vibrating noise, usually because you are hungry. (肚子因饥饿) 发咕咕声 ❑ *Her stomach rumbled. She hadn't eaten any breakfast.* 她的肚子咕咕直叫。她早上什么也没吃。

rum·bling /rʌmblɪŋ/ (**rumblings**) **1** N-COUNT A **rumbling** is a low, continuous noise. 咕噜声 ❑ *...the rumbling of an empty stomach.* …空腹发出的咕噜声。 **2** N-COUNT **Rumblings** are signs that a bad situation is developing or that people are becoming annoyed or unhappy. 风声；迹象 ❑ *Even Baldwin had become aware that there were rumblings of discontent within the ranks.* 就连鲍德温也开始意识到内部成员有不满的迹象。

▲ **rum·mage** /rʌmɪdʒ/ (**rummages, rummaging, rummaged**) V-I If you **rummage through** something, you search for something you want by moving things around in a careless or hurried way. 翻找 ❑ *They rummage through piles of secondhand clothes for something that fits.* 他们在成堆的二手衣服中翻找合身的衣服。 ● N-SING **Rummage** is also a noun. 翻找 ❑ *A brief rummage will provide several pairs of gloves.* 稍许翻一下就会找到几副手套。 ● PHRASAL VERB **Rummage around** means the same as **rummage**. 翻找 ❑ *I opened the fridge and rummaged around.* 我打开了冰箱到处翻。

People trying to raise funds for charity, for a school (for example, to buy a computer), or for a church (to repair the roof, perhaps) may come up with the idea of holding a **rummage sale** (or **jumble sale** in the UK) in the school or church hall. Items such as clothing, toys, books, and household goods are donated by people who no longer need them, and shoppers come along in the hope of finding a second-hand bargain.

ru·mor ♦◇◇ /ru̲mər/ (**rumors**)

in BRIT, use **rumour**

N-VAR A **rumor** is a story or piece of information that may or may not be true, but that people are talking about. 传闻 ❑ *U.S. officials are discounting rumors of a coup.* 美国政府官员对一场政变的传闻将信将疑。

Word Partnership *rumor* 的常用搭配：

ADJ.	**false** rumor
V.	**hear** a rumor, **spread** a rumor, **start** a rumor

ru·mored /ru̲mərd/

in BRIT, use **rumoured**

V-T PASSIVE If something **is rumored to** be the case, people are suggesting that it is the case, but they do not know for certain. 据传 ❑ *The company is rumored to be a takeover target.* 这家公司据传是并购的对象。

ru·mour /ru̲ːməʳ/ [BRIT] → see **rumor**

ru·moured /ru̲ːməʳd/ [BRIT] → see **rumored**

rump /rʌmp/ (**rumps**) **1** N-COUNT An animal's **rump** is its rear end. (动物的) 臀部 ❑ *The cows' rumps were marked with their owner's initials and a number.* 这些奶牛的臀部上标有它们主人姓名的首字母和一个数字。 **2** N-UNCOUNT **Rump** or **rump steak** is meat cut from the rear end of a cow. 牛后臀尖 ❑ *...a pound of rump.* …一磅牛后臀尖。 **3** N-SING The **rump of** a group, organization, or country consists of the members who remain in it after the rest have left. (集团、组织或国家的) 残余部分 [mainly BRIT] ❑ *The rump of the party does in fact still have considerable assets.* 该党的残余分子事实上仍拥有大量财产。

run

❶ VERB USES
❷ NOUN USES
❸ PHRASES
❹ PHRASAL VERBS

❶ **run** ♦♦♦ /rʌn/ (**runs, running, ran**)

The form **run** is used in the present tense and is also the past participle of the verb.

1 V-T/V-I When you **run**, you move more quickly than when you walk, for example because you are in a hurry to get somewhere, or for exercise. 跑 ❑ *I excused myself and ran back to the telephone.* 我道了歉，跑回去接电话。 ❑ *He ran the last block to the White House with two cases of gear.* 他带着两箱工具跑过最后一个街区到了白宫。 **2** V-T/V-I When someone **runs** in a race, they run in competition with other people. 参加…赛跑；赛跑 ❑ *...when I was running in the New York Marathon.* …当我正参加纽约马拉松赛跑时。 ❑ *He ran a tremendous race.* 他参加了一场大规模赛跑。 **3** V-T/V-I When a horse **runs** in a race or when its owner **runs** it, it competes in a race. 使(马) 参加比赛；

R

(马) 参加比赛 ❑ *He was overruled by the owner, Peter Bolton, who insisted on Cool Ground running in the Gold Cup.* 他的意见被坚持让酷地参加金杯赛的主人彼得•博尔顿否决了。 4 V-I If you say that something long, such as a road, **runs** in a particular direction, you are describing its course or position. You can also say that something **runs** the length or width of something else. (道路等) 延伸 ❑ *...the sun-dappled trail which ran through the beech woods.* …一条穿过山毛榉树林的阳光斑驳的小路。 5 V-T If you **run** a wire or tube somewhere, you attach it or pull it from, to, or across a particular place. 铺设(电线、管道等) ❑ *Our host ran a long extension cord out from the house and set up a screen and a projector.* 我们的主人从那所房子里牵出了一条长的延长导线，安置了一块屏幕和一个投影仪。 6 V-T If you **run** your hand or an object **through** something, you move your hand or the object through it. 移动 ❑ *He laughed and ran his fingers through his hair.* 他大笑了并用手指梳理他的头发。 7 V-T If you **run** something through a machine, process, or series of tests, you make it go through the machine, process, or tests. 运行 ❑ *They have gathered the best statistics they can find and run them through their own computers.* 他们已经搜集了他们所能找到的最佳数据并将其在他们自己的电脑里运行。 8 V-I If someone **runs for** office in an election, they take part as a candidate. 竞选 ❑ *It was only last February that he announced he would run for president.* 直到去年2月他才宣布自己将竞选总统。 ❑ *It is no easy job to run against John Glenn, Ohio's Democratic senator.* 与俄亥俄州民主党参议员约翰•格伦竞选绝非易事。 9 V-T If you **run** something such as a business or an activity, you are in charge of it or you organize it. 经营; 管理 ❑ *His stepfather ran a prosperous paint business.* 他的继父曾经营一家生意兴旺的涂料公司。 ❑ *...a well-run, profitable organization.* …一家经营很好的赢利机构。 10 V-I If you talk about how a system, an organization, or someone's life **is running**, you are saying how well it is operating or progressing. 运作; 运转 [usu cont] ❑ *Officials in charge of the camps say the system is now running extremely smoothly.* 负责营房的官员说这一体制目前运作得相当顺利。 11 V-T/V-I If you **run** an experiment, computer program, or other process, or start it **running**, you start it and let it continue. 进行; 运行 ❑ *He ran a lot of tests and it turned out I had an infection called mycoplasma.* 他进行了许多化验，结果证明我感染了支原体病毒。 12 V-T/V-I When a machine **is running** or when you **are running** it, it is switched on and is working. 使(机器) 运转; (机器) 运转 [usu cont] ❑ *We told him to wait out front with the engine running.* 我们告诉他在入口外等候，不要熄火。 13 V-I A machine or equipment that **runs on** or **off** a particular source of energy functions using that source of energy. 运转 ❑ *The buses run on diesel.* 这些公共汽车使用的是柴油。 14 V-I When you say that vehicles such as trains and buses **run** from one place to another, you mean they regularly travel along that route. 行驶 ❑ *A shuttle bus runs frequently between the inn and the country club.* 一辆区间往返公共汽车频繁地往来于小客栈与乡村俱乐部之间。 15 V-T If you **run** someone somewhere in a car, you drive them there. (开车) 送 [INFORMAL] ❑ *Could you run me up to Baltimore?* 你能开车送我去巴尔的摩吗？ 16 V-I If you **run** over or down to a place that is quite near, you drive there. 驾车去 [INFORMAL] ❑ *I'll run over to Short Mountain and check on Mrs. Adams.* 我将开车去肖特山看看亚当斯夫人。 17 V-I If a liquid **runs** in a particular direction, it flows in that direction. (液体) 流 ❑ *Tears were running down her cheeks.* 泪水当时正沿着她的脸颊流下。 18 V-T If you **run** water, or if you **run** a faucet or a bath, you cause water to flow from a faucet. 从水管放 (水) ❑ *She went to the sink and ran water into her empty glass.* 她走到了洗涤槽边，往空玻璃杯里灌水。 19 V-I If a faucet or a bath **is running**, water is coming out of a faucet. 流水 [only cont] ❑ *The kitchen sink had been stopped up and the faucet left running, so water spilled over onto the floor.* 那厨房的洗涤槽堵塞了，而水龙头在那里流水，所以水溢满流到了地板上。 20 V-I If your nose **is running**, liquid is flowing out of it, usually because you have a cold. 流鼻涕 [usu cont] ❑ *Timothy was crying, mostly from exhaustion, and his nose was running.* 蒂莫西在哭，主要是因为太累了，而且在流鼻涕。 21 V-I If a surface **is running with** a liquid, that liquid is flowing down it. 流下 [usu cont] ❑ *After an hour he realized he was completely running with sweat.* 一个小时后，他发现自己已是大汗淋漓。 22 V-T/V-I When you **run** a cassette or videotape or when it **runs**, it moves through the machine as the machine operates. 播放 ❑ *Leaphorn pushed the play button again, ran the tape, pushed stop, pushed rewind.* 利福恩又按下播放按钮，播放了磁带，接着按了停止键，然后又按下倒带键。 23 V-I If the dye in some cloth or the ink on some paper **runs**, it comes off or spreads when the cloth or paper gets wet. 渗开 ❑ *The ink had run on the wet paper.* 墨迹在那张湿纸上渗开了。 24 V-I If a feeling **runs through** your body or a thought **runs through** your mind, you experience it or think it quickly. (感觉) 传遍; (念头) 掠过 ❑ *She felt a surge of excitement run through her.* 她感到一阵激动传遍全身。 25 V-I If a feeling or noise **runs through** a group of people, it spreads among them. (感受、噪音等) 传开 ❑ *A buzz of excitement ran through the crowd.* 一阵兴奋的嗡嗡声在人群中蔓延开来。 26 V-I If a theme or feature **runs through** something such as someone's actions or writing, it is present in all of it. 贯穿 ❑ *Another thread running through this series is the role of doctors in the treatment of the mentally ill.* 贯穿这部连续剧的另一主线是医生们在心理疾病患者的治疗过程中的作用。 27 V-T/V-I When newspapers or magazines **run** a particular item or story or if it **runs**, it is published or printed. 刊登; 发表 ❑ *The New Orleans Times-Picayune ran a series of four scathing editorials entitled "The Choice of Our Lives."* 《新奥尔良时代花絮报》连续刊登了题为"我们生活的选择"的4篇尖刻的社论。 28 V-I If an amount **is running** at a particular level, it is at that level. 处于 (某一水平) ❑ *Today's figures show inflation running at 10.9 percent.* 今天的数据显示通货膨胀率为10.9%。 29 V-I If a play, event, or legal contract **runs** for a particular period of time, it lasts for that period of time. (戏剧、事件、法律合同等) 延续 ❑ *It pleased critics but ran for only three months on Broadway.* 它得到了评论家的好评，但在百老汇只上演了3个月。 ❑ *The contract was to run from 1992 to 2020.* 该合同从1992年至2020年有效。 30 V-I If someone or something **is running** late, they have taken more time than had been planned. If they **are running** on time or ahead of time, they have taken the time planned or less than the time planned. 进展 [usu cont] ❑ *Tell her I'll call her back later, I'm running late again.* 告诉她我待会儿再给她回电话，我又要晚了。 31 V-T If you **are running** a temperature or a fever, you have a high temperature because you are ill. 患 ❑ *The little girl is running a fever and she needs help.* 这个小女孩正在发烧，她需要帮助。 32 → see also **running**

Thesaurus *run* 另参见:

v. dash, jog, sprint ❶ 1
follow, go ❶ 4
administer, conduct, manage ❶ 9

❷ **run** ♦♦♦ /rʌn/ (**runs**) 1 N-COUNT A **run** is a time when you move somewhere on foot more quickly than when you walk, usually for exercise. 跑步 ❑ *After a six-mile run, Jackie returns home for a substantial breakfast.* 6英里跑之后，杰基回家吃一顿丰盛的早餐。 2 N-SING A **run for** office is an attempt to be elected to office. 竞选 [N "for" n] [mainly AM]

in BRIT, usually use **bid**

❑ *He was already preparing his run for the presidency.* 他已经在为总统竞选做准备。 3 N-COUNT A **run** is a trip somewhere. 出行 ❑ *...doing the morning school run.* …早上去学校。 4 N-COUNT A **run** of a play or television program is the period of time during which performances are given or programmes are shown. (戏剧或电视节目的) 演出期; 播放期 ❑ *The show will transfer to Broadway on October 9, after a month's run in Philadelphia.* 这出戏在费城为期一个月的演出之后，将于10月9日转到百老汇上演。 5 N-SING A **run of** successes or failures is a series of successes or failures. 一连串 (成功或失败) ❑ *The team is haunted by a run of low scores.* 这个队被一连串的低分所折磨。 6 N-COUNT A **run** of a product is the amount that a company or factory decides to produce at one time. (产品的) 批量 ❑ *Wayne plans to increase the print run to 1,000.* 韦恩计划将印量增加到1千册。 7 N-COUNT In baseball or cricket, a **run** is a score of one, which is made by players running between marked places on the field after hitting the ball. (棒球或板球比赛中跑动得到的) 一分 ❑ *The Padres scored four runs off Terry Adams in the last 2 innings.* 在最后2个回合中，教士队力挫特里•亚当斯，跑垒得4分。 8 N-SING If someone gives you **the run of** a place, they give you permission to go where you like in it and use it as you wish. (对某地的) 使用权 ❑ *He had the run of the house and the pool.* 他曾有这座房子和游泳池的使用权。 9 N-SING If there is a **run on** something, a lot of people want to buy it or get it at the same time. 抢购; 争先获取 ❑ *A run on the dollar has killed off hopes of a rate cut.* 对美元的挤兑使降息彻底无望了。 10 N-COUNT A **run** is a hole or torn part in a woman's stocking or pantyhose, where some the vertical threads have broken, leaving only the horizontal threads. (长筒袜或连裤袜的) 抽丝 ❑ *I had a run in my stocking.* 我的长筒袜有抽丝了。 11 N-COUNT A ski **run** or bobsled **run** is a course or route that has been designed for skiing or for riding in a bobsled. (滑雪或乘雪橇的) 滑道 ❑ *...an avalanche on Colorado's highest ski run.* …一次在科罗拉多州最高的滑雪道上发生的雪崩。

❸ **run** ♦♦♦ /rʌn/ (**runs, running, ran**)

The form **run** is used in the present tense and is also the past participle of the verb.

➪ **Please look at meanings 12 – 17 to see if the expression you are looking for is shown under another headword.** 1 PHRASE If you **run** someone **a close second**, or **run a close second**, you almost beat them in a race or competition. (比赛中) 以极小劣势位居第二 ❑ *While "Nightly" has led in the ratings all season, "World News Tonight" is running a close second.* 《晚间新闻》全年收视率名列前茅，而《今夜世界新闻》紧随其后。 2 PHRASE If a river or well **runs dry**, it no longer has any water in it. If an oil well **runs dry**, it no longer produces any oil. (河流、井) 干涸; (油井) 枯竭 ❑ *Streams had run dry for the first time in memory.* 溪流在记忆中第一次干涸了。 3 PHRASE If a source of information or money **runs dry**, no more information or money can be obtained from it. (信息或资金) 枯竭 ❑ *Three days into production, the kitty had run dry.* 投产3天，资金已经用完了。 4 PHRASE If a characteristic **runs in** someone's **family**, it often occurs in members of that family, in different generations. 在某人的家族中遗传 ❑ *The insanity which ran in his family haunted him.* 家族世代相袭的精神病令他惴惴不安。 5 PHRASE If you **make a run for it** or if you **run for it**, you run away in order to escape from someone or something. 逃离 ❑ *A helicopter hovered overhead as one of the gang made a run for it.* 那伙人中的一个逃跑的时候，一架直升飞机在头顶上空盘旋。 6 PHRASE If people's feelings **are running high**, they are very angry, concerned, or excited. (情绪) 高涨 ❑ *Feelings there have been running high in the wake of last week's killing.* 紧随上周杀人事件之后，那里已是群情激愤。 7 PHRASE If you talk about what will happen **in the long run**, you are saying what you think will happen over a long period of time in the future. If you talk about what will happen **in the short run**, you are saying what you think will happen in the near future. 从长期/短期来看 ❑ *Sometimes expensive drugs or other treatments can be economical in the long run.* 有时昂贵的药物或其他疗法从长远来看是省钱的。 8 PHRASE If you say that someone could **give** someone else **a run for** their **money**, you mean you think they are almost as good as the other person. 几乎比得上某人 ❑ *...a youngster who even now could give Meryl Streep a run for her money.* …一位现在就几乎能与梅里尔•斯特里普相媲美的年轻人。 9 PHRASE If someone is **on the run**, they are trying to escape or hide from someone such as the police or an enemy. 在逃 ❑ *Fifteen-year-old Danny is on the run from a juvenile detention center.* 15岁的丹尼从少年犯拘留所逃了出来。 10 PHRASE If someone is **on the run**, they are being severely defeated in a contest or competition. 惨败 ❑ *I knew I had him on the run.* 我知道我已打得他落花流水。 11 PHRASE If you **are running short of** something or **running low on** something, you do not have much of it left. If a supply of something **is running short** or **running low**, there is not much of it left. 所剩无几 ❑ *Government forces are running short of ammunition and fuel.* 政府军所剩弹药和燃料已不多。 12 **to run deep** → **see deep** 13 **to run an errand** → **see errand** 14 **to run the gauntlet** → **see gauntlet** 15 **to run riot** → **see riot** 16 **to run a risk** → **see risk** 17 **to run wild** → **see wild**

R

❹ **run** ♦♦♦ /rʌn/ (**runs, running, ran**)

The form **run** is used in the present tense and is also the past participle of the verb.

▸ **run across** PHRASAL VERB If you **run across** someone or something, you meet them or find them unexpectedly. 偶然遇见 ❑ *We ran across some old friends in the village.* 我们在村子里撞见了一些老朋友。

▸ **run around** PHRASAL VERB If you **run around**, you go to a lot of places and do a lot of things, often in a rushed or disorganized way. 东奔西走 ❑ *We had been running around cleaning up.* 我们一直忙来忙去做清洁。 ❑ *Jessica was running around with the camera snapping pictures.* 杰茜卡拿着照相机四处抓拍。 ❑ *I will not have you running around the countryside without my authority.* 我不允许你未经我批准在乡下到处乱跑。

▸ **run away** 1 PHRASAL VERB If you **run away** from a place, you leave it because you are unhappy there. 出走 ❑ *I ran away from home when I was sixteen.* 我16岁时离家出走。 ❑ *After his beating, Colin ran away and hasn't been heard of since.* 挨打后科林出走了，从此杳无音信。 2 PHRASAL VERB If you **run away** with someone, you secretly go away with them in order to live with them or marry them. 私奔 ❑ *She ran away with a man called McTavish last year.* 她去年和一个叫麦克塔维什的男人私奔了。 3 PHRASAL VERB If you **run away from** something unpleasant or new, you try to avoid dealing with it or thinking about it. 避开 ❑ *They run away from the problem, hoping it will disappear of its own accord.* 他们回避了这个问题，希望它会自行消失。 4 → **see also runaway**

▸ **run away with** PHRASAL VERB If you let your imagination or your emotions **run away with** you, you fail to control them and cannot think sensibly. (想像、情感等) 不受(某人) 控制 ❑ *You're letting your imagination run away with you.* 你在让自己胡思乱想。

▸ **run by** PHRASAL VERB If you **run** something **by** someone, you tell them about it or mention it, to see if they think it is a good idea, or can understand it. 把(某事) 告诉(某人) 以征求意见 ❑ *I'm definitely interested, but I'll have to run it by Larry Estes.* 我肯定有兴趣，但我得告诉拉里•埃斯蒂斯，听听他的意见。

▸ **run down** 1 PHRASAL VERB If you **run** people or things **down**, you criticize them strongly. 强烈指责 ❑ *I'm always running myself down.* 我总是深深自责。 2 PHRASAL VERB If a vehicle or its driver **runs** someone **down**, the vehicle hits them and injures them. (车) 撞(某人) ❑ *Lozano claimed that motorcycle driver Clement Lloyd was trying to run him down.* 洛扎诺声称摩托车手克莱门特•劳埃德当时正试图撞他。 3 PHRASAL VERB If a machine or device **runs down**, it gradually loses power or works more slowly. (机器或装置) 逐渐耗尽能量; 运转渐慢 ❑ *The batteries are running down.* 电池快耗完了。 4 PHRASAL VERB If people **run down** an industry or an organization, they deliberately reduce its size or the amount of work that it does. 缩减 ❑ *The government is cynically running down Sweden's welfare system.* 该政府正在自私地缩减瑞典福利体系。 5 PHRASAL VERB If someone **runs down** an amount of something, they reduce it or allow it to decrease. 减少; 任(某物的数量) 降低 ❑ *But the survey also revealed firms were running down stocks instead of making new products.* 但该调查也显示各企业正在任其库存减少而不生产新的产品。 6 → **see also run-down**

▸ **run into** 1 PHRASAL VERB If you **run into** problems or difficulties, you unexpectedly begin to experience them. 遇上 ❑ *Wang agreed to sell IBM Systems last year after it ran into financial problems.* IBM公司遭遇财政问题后，王去年同意出售该公司的操作系统。 2 PHRASAL VERB If you **run into** someone, you meet them unexpectedly. 撞见 ❑ *He ran into Krettner in the corridor a few minutes later.* 几分钟后他在走廊里撞见了克雷特勒。 3 PHRASAL VERB If a vehicle **runs into** something, it accidentally hits it. 撞上 ❑ *The driver failed to negotiate a bend and ran into a tree.* 该司机没能顺利转过一个弯，撞上了一棵树。 4 PHRASAL VERB You use **run into** when indicating that the cost or amount of something is very great. (金额) 高达 ❑ *He said companies should face punitive civil penalties running into millions of dollars.* 他说各公司应当面临高达上百万美元的惩罚性民事处罚。

▸ **run off** 1 PHRASAL VERB If you **run off** with someone, you secretly go away with them in order to live with them or marry them. (与某人) 私奔 ❑ *The last thing I'm going to do is run off with somebody's husband.* 我绝不会和某人的丈夫私奔。 2 PHRASAL VERB If you **run off** copies of a piece of writing, you produce them using a machine. 复印 ❑ *If you want to run off a copy sometime today, you're welcome to.* 如果你想今天某个时候复印文件，欢迎你来印。 3 PHRASE If you say that someone **is running off at the mouth**, you are criticizing them for talking too much. 喋喋不休 [V inflects] [DISAPPROVAL] ❑ *That was when she really started running off at the mouth. I'll bet she hasn't shut up yet.* 那就是她真正开始唠叨的时候。我敢说她还没闭嘴。

▸ **run out** 1 PHRASAL VERB If you **run out of** something, you have no more of it left. 用完 ❑ *They have run out of ideas.* 他们已经想不出办法了。 ❑ *We're running out of time.* 我们没时间了。 2 **to run out of steam** → **see steam** 3 PHRASAL VERB If something **runs out**, it becomes used up so that there is no more left. 耗尽 ❑ *Conditions are getting worse and supplies are running out.* 情况越来越糟，给养也快耗尽了。 4 PHRASAL VERB When a legal document **runs out**, it stops being valid. (法律文件) 到期 ❑ *When the lease ran out the family moved to Cleveland.* 租赁合同到期后，这家人搬到了克利夫兰。

▸ **run over** PHRASAL VERB If a vehicle or its driver **runs** a person or animal **over**, it knocks them down or drives over them. 撞倒; 轧过 ❑ *You can always run him over and make it look like an accident.* 你总是可以把他轧死并使之看起来像一起事故。

▸ **run through** 1 PHRASAL VERB If you **run through** a list of items, you read or mention all the items quickly. 过一遍 ❑ *I ran through the options with him.* 我和他过了一遍那些选项。 2 PHRASAL VERB If you **run through** a performance or a series of actions, you practice it. 排练 ❑ *Doug stood still while I ran through the handover procedure.* 我排练交接程序的时候，道格站在那儿一动不动。

▸ **run up** **1** PHRASAL VERB If someone **runs up** bills or debts, they acquire them by buying a lot of things or borrowing money. 积欠(债务) ❑ *She managed to run up a credit card debt of $60,000.* 她竟然用信用卡透支了6万美元。 **2** → see also **run-up**

▸ **run up against** PHRASAL VERB If you **run up against** problems, you suddenly begin to experience them. 遇到 ❑ *I ran up against the problem of getting taken seriously long before I became a writer.* 还远没有成为作家我就碰到了得到重视的问题。

run·away /rʌnəweɪ/ (**runaways**) **1** ADJ You use **runaway** to describe a situation in which something increases or develops very quickly and cannot be controlled. 迅猛发展而难以控制的 [ADJ n] ❑ *Our June sale was a runaway success.* 我们6月份的促销大获成功。 **2** N-COUNT A **runaway** is someone, especially a child, who leaves home without telling anyone or without permission. 离家出走者 ❑ *...a teenage runaway.* …一名十来岁的离家出走者。 **3** ADJ A **runaway** vehicle or animal is moving forward quickly, and its driver or rider has lost control of it. (车辆或动物) 失控的 [ADJ n] ❑ *The runaway car careered into a bench, hitting an elderly couple.* 那辆失控的轿车疾速撞上了一条长凳，撞了一对老夫妇。

run-down

The spelling **rundown** is also used. The adjective is pronounced /rʌn daʊn/. The noun is pronounced /rʌn daʊn/.

1 ADJ If someone is **run-down**, they are tired or slightly ill. 疲惫的；略感不适的 [INFORMAL] ❑ *When 23-year-old Marilyn Brown started to feel run-down last December, it never occurred to her that she could have tuberculosis.* 当23岁的玛丽莲•布朗去年12月开始感到疲惫的时候，她未曾想到她会得肺结核。 **2** ADJ A **run-down** building or area is in very poor condition. (房屋等) 破败的 ❑ *They have put substantial funds into rebuilding one of the most run-down areas.* 他们已投入大量的资金用于重建最破败的地区之一。 **3** ADJ A **run-down** place of business is not as active as it used to be or does not have many customers. 萧条的 ❑ *...a run-down slate quarry.* …一座萧条的板岩采石场。 **4** N-SING If you give someone a **rundown of** a group of things or a **rundown on** something, you give them details about it. 详细情况 [INFORMAL] ❑ *Here's a rundown of the options.* 这是可选项目的一个详细情况。

rung /rʌŋ/ (**rungs**) **1** **Rung** is the past participle of **ring**. ring的过去分词 **2** N-COUNT The **rungs** on a ladder are the wooden or metal bars that form the steps. 梯级 ❑ *I swung myself onto the ladder and felt for the next rung.* 我荡到那个梯子上，然后摸索下一级阶梯。 **3** N-COUNT If you reach a particular **rung** in your career, in an organization, or in a process, you reach that level in it. (职业、组织、过程的) 阶段 ❑ *I first worked with him in 1971 when we were both on the lowest rung of our careers.* 我第一次和他共事是在1971年，当时我们都处在职业生涯的起步阶段。

run-in (**run-ins**) N-COUNT A **run-in** is an argument or quarrel with someone. 口角 [INFORMAL] ❑ *I had a monumental run-in with him a couple of years ago.* 我几年前和他大吵过一场。

run·ner ♦◇◇ /rʌnər/ (**runners**) **1** N-COUNT A **runner** is a person who runs, especially for sport or pleasure. 跑步者 ❑ *...a marathon runner.* …一个马拉松赛跑选手。 **2** N-COUNT The **runners** in a horse race are the horses taking part. 赛马 ❑ *There are 18 runners in the top race of the day.* 在那天的最高级别的比赛中有18匹赛马参加。 **3** N-COUNT A drug **runner** or gun **runner** is someone who illegally takes drugs or guns into a country. 走私者 ❑ *...a gang of evil gun runners.* …一伙邪恶的走私枪支的人。 **4** N-COUNT Someone who is a **runner** for a particular person or company is employed to take messages, collect money, or do other small tasks for them. 听差 ❑ *...a bookie's runner.* …一名赌注登记人的听差。 **5** N-COUNT **Runners** are thin strips of wood or metal underneath something which help it to move smoothly. 滑板 ❑ *...the runners of his sled.* …他雪橇下面的滑板。
→ see **park**

runner-up (**runners-up**) N-COUNT A **runner-up** is someone who has finished in second place in a race or competition. 亚军 ❑ *The ten runners-up will receive a case of wine.* 那10名亚军将得到一箱葡萄酒。

run·ning ♦♦◇ /rʌnɪŋ/ **1** N-UNCOUNT **Running** is the activity of moving fast on foot, especially as a sport. 跑 ❑ *We chose to do cross-country running.* 我们选择进行越野赛跑。 **2** N-SING **The running of** something such as a business is the managing or organizing of it. 经营 ❑ *...the committee in charge of the day-to-day running of the party.* …负责该党日常运作的委员会。 **3** ADJ You use **running** to describe things that continue or keep occurring over a period of time. 连续的；不断的 [ADJ n] ❑ *He also began a running feud with Dean Acheson.* 他也开始和艾奇逊院长发生接连不断的争执。 **4** ADJ A **running** total is a total which changes because numbers keep being added to it as something progresses. 流水式的 [ADJ n] ❑ *He kept a running tally of who had called him, who had visited, who had sent flowers.* 他记录着关于谁给他打过电话、谁看望过、谁送过花的一本流水账。 **5** ADV You can use **running** when indicating that something keeps happening. For example, if something has happened every day for three days, you can say that it has happened for the third day **running** or for three days **running**. 连续地 [n ADV] ❑ *He said drought had led to severe crop failure for the second year running.* 他说干旱已连续两年造成严重农作物歉收。 **6** ADJ **Running** water is water that is flowing rather than standing still. 流动的(水) [ADJ n] ❑ *The forest was filled with the sound of running water.* 该森林里充满了流水声。 **7** ADJ If a house has **running** water, water is supplied to the house through pipes and faucets. 自来(水) [ADJ n] ❑ *...a house without electricity or running water in a tiny African village.* …一座在非洲一个小村庄里、没有电和自来水的房子。 **8** PHRASE If someone is **in the running for** something, they have a good chance of winning or obtaining it. If they are **out of the running for** something, they have no chance of winning or obtaining it. 有望获胜/无望获胜 ❑ *Until this week he appeared to have ruled himself out of the running because of his age.* 直到本周他似乎才因为自己年龄关系排除了自己获胜的可能性。 **9** PHRASE If something such as a system or place is **up and running**, it is operating normally. 正常运转 ❑ *We're trying to get the medical facilities up and running again.* 我们正在尽力让这些医疗设施恢复正常运转。

run·ning costs N-PLURAL The **running costs** of a business are the amount of money that is regularly spent on things such as salaries, heating, lighting, and rent. 运营成本 [BRIT, BUSINESS]
in AM, use **overhead**

run·ning mate (**running mates**) N-COUNT In an election campaign, a candidate's **running mate** is the person that they have chosen to help them in the election. If the candidate wins, the running mate will become the second most important person after the winner. 竞选伙伴 [mainly AM] ❑ *...Clinton's selection of Al Gore as his running mate.* …克林顿选择阿尔•戈尔作为他的竞选伙伴。

run·ny /rʌni/ (**runnier, runniest**) **1** ADJ Something that is **runny** is more liquid than usual or than was intended. 过稀的 ❑ *Warm the honey until it becomes runny.* 把蜂蜜加热到它变稀为止。 **2** ADJ If someone has a **runny** nose or **runny** eyes, liquid is flowing from their nose or eyes. (鼻、眼) 流出液体的 ❑ *Symptoms are streaming eyes, a runny nose, headache, and a cough.* 症状是流泪、流鼻涕、头疼和咳嗽。

run time (**run times**) N-COUNT **Run time** is the time during which a computer program is running. (计算机) 运行时间 [COMPUTING] ❑ *With run time for most applications lasting days or weeks, the queue fills up quickly.* 由于大多数应用程序的运行时间要持续数天或数周，队列很快就满了。

run-up (**run-ups**) N-SING **The run-up to** an event is the period of time just before it. 前夕 [mainly BRIT] ❑ *The company believes the products will sell well in the run-up to Christmas.* 该公司相信这些产品在圣诞节前夕将会销得很好。

▲ **run·way** /rʌnweɪ/ (**runways**) N-COUNT At an airport, the **runway** is the long strip of ground with a hard surface which an airplane takes off from or lands on. (机场的) 跑道 ❑ *The plane started taxiing down the runway.* 该飞机开始沿跑道滑行。

★ **rup·ture** /rʌptʃər/ (**ruptures, rupturing, ruptured**) **1** N-COUNT A **rupture** is a severe injury in which an internal part of your body tears or bursts open, especially the part between the bowels and the abdomen. (体内组织) 破裂 ❑ *He died of an abdominal infection caused by a rupture of his stomach.* 他死于由一次胃穿孔引发的腹部感染。 **2** V-T/V-I If a person or animal **ruptures** a part of their body or if it **ruptures**, it tears or bursts open. 使(体内组织) 破裂；(体内组织) 破裂 ❑ *His stomach might rupture from all the acid.* 他的胃可能会因为所有这些酸而穿孔。 ❑ *While playing badminton, I ruptured my Achilles tendon.* 打羽毛球的时候，我把跟腱撕裂了。 **3** V-T If you **rupture yourself**, you rupture a part of your body, usually because you have lifted something heavy. 使患疝气 ❑ *He ruptured himself playing football.* 他因踢足球而发了疝气。 **4** V-T/V-I If an object **ruptures** or if something **ruptures** it, it bursts open. 使爆裂；爆裂 ❑ *Certain gasoline tanks in trucks can rupture and burn in a collision.* 卡车内的某些油箱会在一次碰撞中爆裂起火。 **5** N-COUNT If there is a **rupture** between people, relations between them get much worse or end completely. (关系) 破裂；决裂 ❑ *The incidents have not yet*

caused a major rupture in the political ties between countries. 这些事件尚未造成各国间政治联系的严重破裂。 6 V-T If someone or something **ruptures** relations between people, they damage them, causing them to become worse or to end. 使(关系)破裂；使决裂 ❑ *Brutal clashes between squatters and police yesterday ruptured the city's governing coalition.* 昨天私自占地者与警察的野蛮冲突使这座城市的执政联盟破裂。
→ see **crash**

ru·ral ♦◇◇ /rʊərəl/ 1 ADJ **Rural** places are far away from large towns or cities. 乡村的 ❑ *These plants have a tendency to grow in the more rural areas.* 这些植物倾向于生长在更偏远的乡村地区。 2 ADJ **Rural** means having features which are typical of areas that are far away from large towns or cities. 有乡村特色的 [ADJ n] ❑ *...the old rural way of life.* …古老的乡村生活方式。

ruse /ruz, rus/ (**ruses**) N-COUNT A **ruse** is an action or plan which is intended to deceive someone. 诡计 [FORMAL] ❑ *It is now clear that this was a ruse to divide them.* 现在清楚了，这是分裂他们的诡计。

rush ♦◇◇ /rʌʃ/ (**rushes, rushing, rushed**) 1 V-T/V-I If you **rush** somewhere, you go there quickly. 迅速地走 ❑ *A schoolgirl rushed into a burning apartment to save a man's life.* 一名女学童冲进一栋着火的公寓去救一个男子的命。 ❑ *I've got to rush. Got a meeting in a few minutes.* 我得赶快走。几分钟后有一个会。 ❑ *I rushed to get the 7:00 a.m. train.* 我急急忙忙去赶早上7点的火车。 2 V-T If people **rush to** do something, they do it as soon as they can, because they are very eager to do it. 急着(做) ❑ *Russian banks rushed to buy as many dollars as they could.* 俄罗斯各银行急着尽可能多地买入美元。 3 N-SING A **rush** is a situation in which you need to go somewhere or do something very quickly. 匆忙 ❑ *The men left in a rush.* 这些男人在匆忙中离开了。 4 N-SING If there is a **rush for** something, many people suddenly try to get it or do it. 争抢 ❑ *Record stores are expecting a huge rush for the single.* 各唱片店正期待着这张单曲唱片的一个大抢购。 5 N-SING **The rush** is a period of time when many people go somewhere or do something. 高峰期 ❑ *The store's opening coincided with the Christmas rush.* 这家商店的开张正赶上圣诞节购物高峰。 6 V-T/V-I If you **rush** something, you do it in a hurry, often too quickly and without much care. 忙碌 ❑ *You can't rush a search.* 你不能匆忙做搜寻工作。 ❑ *Instead of rushing at life, I wanted something more meaningful.* 我不想在生活中忙忙碌碌，而想做更有意义的事。 ● **rushed** ADJ 忙碌的 ❑ *The report had all the hallmarks of a rushed job.* 这份报告有着急就章的一切特点。 7 V-T If you **rush** someone or something to a place, you take them there quickly. 迅速送 ❑ *They had rushed him to a hospital for a lifesaving operation.* 他们迅速送他到了医院进行急救手术。 8 V-T/V-I If you **rush into** something or **are rushed into** it, you do it without thinking about it for long enough. 使仓促行事；仓促行事 ❑ *He will not rush into any decisions.* 他不会仓促做出任何决定。 ❑ *They had rushed in without adequate appreciation of the task.* 他们没有充分了解这项任务就仓促行动了。 ● **rushed** ADJ 仓促的 ❑ *At no time did I feel rushed or under pressure.* 我从未感到仓促或有压力。 9 V-T/V-I If you **rush** something or someone, or **rush at** them, you move quickly and forcefully at them, often in order to attack them. 冲向；冲 ❑ *They rushed the entrance and forced their way in.* 他们冲向了入口并强行闯了进去。 ❑ *Reporters rushed at him and he ran back inside.* 记者向他冲，他就跑回里面去了。 10 V-I If air or liquid **rushes** somewhere, it flows there suddenly and quickly. 奔涌 ❑ *Water rushes out of huge tunnels.* 水从巨大的隧道奔涌而出。 ● N-COUNT **Rush** is also a noun. 急流 ❑ *A rush of air on my face woke me.* 脸上的一股急促的气流惊醒了我。 11 N-COUNT If you experience a **rush of** a feeling, you suddenly experience it very strongly. (感情) 迸发 ❑ *A rush of pure affection swept over him.* 一股强烈的真爱掠过了他的心田。

Word Partnership *rush* 的常用搭配：

ADJ.	**mad** rush 3 4
	sudden rush 3 4 10 11
N.	**evening** rush, **morning** rush 5
	rush **to judgment** 6
	rush **of air**, rush **of water** 10
	rush **of adrenaline** 11

rush hour (**rush hours**) N-COUNT The **rush hour** is one of the periods of the day when most people are traveling to or from work. (上下班交通) 高峰期 [also "at/during" N] ❑ *During the evening rush hour it was often solid with vehicles.* 在傍晚高峰期，车辆经常堵得水泄不通。

rust /rʌst/ (**rusts, rusting, rusted**) 1 N-UNCOUNT **Rust** is a brown substance that forms on iron or steel, for example when it comes into contact with water. 锈 ❑ *...a decaying tractor, red with rust.* …一辆腐朽的拖拉机，因生锈而呈红色。 2 V-I When a metal object **rusts**, it becomes covered in rust and often loses its strength. 生锈 ❑ *Copper nails are better than iron nails because the iron rusts.* 铜钉比铁钉好，因为铁钉会生锈。 3 COLOR **Rust** is sometimes used to describe things that are reddish brown in color. 铁锈色(的) ❑ *...rust and gold leaves from the maples.* …铁锈色和金黄色相间的枫叶。

▲ **rus·tic** /rʌstɪk/ ADJ You can use **rustic** to describe things or people that you approve of because they are simple or unsophisticated in a way that is typical of the countryside. 质朴的 [APPROVAL] ❑ *...the rustic charm of a country lifestyle.* …乡村生活方式的质朴魅力。

▲ **rus·tle** /rʌsᵊl/ (**rustles, rustling, rustled**) V-T/V-I When something thin and dry **rustles** or when you **rustle** it, it makes soft sounds as it moves. 使沙沙作响；沙沙作响 ❑ *The leaves rustled in the wind.* 那些树叶在风中沙沙作响。 ❑ *She rustled her papers impatiently.* 她不耐烦地把文件翻得沙沙响。 ● N-COUNT **Rustle** is also a noun. 沙沙声 ❑ *She sat perfectly still, without even a rustle of her frilled petticoats.* 她一动不动地坐着，就连她那褶边长裙也无一丝窸窣。 ● **rus·tling** N-VAR (**rustlings**) 沙沙声 ❑ *We were all terrified by a rustling sound coming from beneath one of the seats.* 我们都被从一个座位下发出的沙沙声吓坏了。

▸ **rustle up** PHRASAL VERB If you **rustle up** something to eat or drink, you make or prepare it quickly, with very little planning. 未经准备很快做成(吃的或喝的) ❑ *Let's see if somebody can rustle up a cup of coffee.* 看看是否有人能临时很快弄一杯咖啡。

rusty /rʌsti/ (**rustier, rustiest**) 1 ADJ A **rusty** metal object such as a car or a machine is covered with rust, which is a brown substance that forms on iron or steel when it comes into contact with water. 生锈的 ❑ *...a rusty iron gate.* …一扇生锈的铁门。 2 ADJ If a skill that you have or your knowledge of something is **rusty**, it is not as good as it used to be, because you have not used it for a long time. 生疏的 ❑ *You may be a little rusty, but past experience and teaching skills won't have been lost.* 你可能会有点生疏，但过去的经验和教学技巧不会丢了的。

▲ **rut** /rʌt/ (**ruts**) 1 N-COUNT If you say that someone is **in a rut**, you disapprove of the fact that they have become fixed in their way of thinking and doing things, and find it difficult to change. You can also say that someone's life or career is **in a rut**. (思维、做事方式的) 刻板状态；(生活、事业) 一成不变状态 [DISAPPROVAL] ❑ *I don't like being in a rut – I like to keep moving on.* 我不喜欢一成不变——我喜欢不断前进。 2 N-COUNT A **rut** is a deep, narrow mark made in the ground by the wheels of a vehicle. 车辙 ❑ *Our driver slowed up as we approached the ruts in the road.* 我们的司机在我们靠近路上的车辙时放慢了车速。

▲ **ruth·less** /ruθlɪs/ 1 ADJ If you say that someone is **ruthless**, you mean that you disapprove of them because they are very harsh or cruel, and will do anything that is necessary to achieve what they want. 残酷的 [DISAPPROVAL] ❑ *The president was ruthless in dealing with any hint of internal political dissent.* 这位总统对任何内部政治分歧的苗头都毫不留情。 ● **ruth·less·ly** ADV 残酷地 [ADV with v] ❑ *The party has ruthlessly crushed any sign of organized opposition.* 该党残酷地将任何有组织反抗都消灭在了萌芽状态。 ● **ruth·less·ness** N-UNCOUNT 残酷 ❑ *...a powerful political figure with a reputation for ruthlessness.* …一个以残酷无情闻名的强权政治人物。 2 ADJ A **ruthless** action or activity is done forcefully and thoroughly, without much concern for its effects on other people. 坚决无情的 ❑ *Her lawyers have been ruthless in thrashing out a divorce settlement.* 她的律师们在协商离婚协议上毫不留情。 ● **ruth·less·ly** ADV 坚决无情地 ❑ *Gloria showed signs of turning into the ruthlessly efficient woman her father wanted her to be.* 格洛丽亚有迹象变成为她父亲所期望的那种坚决无情、办事利落的女人。 ● **ruth·less·ness** N-UNCOUNT 坚决无情 ❑ *...a woman with a brain and business acumen and a certain healthy ruthlessness.* …一个有头脑、生意眼光和一定魄力的女人。

RV /ɑr vi/ (**RVs**) N-COUNT An **RV** is a van that is equipped with such things as beds and cooking equipment, so that people can live in it, usually while they are on vacation. **RV** is an abbreviation for **recreational vehicle**. 旅行房车 [mainly AM]

in BRIT, usually use **camper, camper van**

❑ *...a group of RVs pulled over on the side of the highway.* …一队停在公路边的旅行房车。

rye /raɪ/ 1 N-UNCOUNT **Rye** is a cereal grown in cold countries. Its grains can be used to make flour, bread, or other foods. 黑麦 ❑ *One of the first crops that I grew when we came here was rye.* 我们来到这里时，我种的第一批作物中就有黑麦。 2 N-UNCOUNT **Rye** is bread made from rye. 黑麦面包 [AM] ❑ *I was eating ham and Swiss cheese on rye.* 我当时正在吃夹火腿和瑞士乳酪的黑麦面包。

Ss

S also **s** /ɛs/ (**S's, s's**) N-VAR **S** is the nineteenth letter of the English alphabet. 英文字母表第19个字母

Sab·bath /sæbəθ/ N-PROPER **The Sabbath** is the day of the week when members of some religious groups do not work. The Jewish Sabbath is on Saturday and the Christian Sabbath is on Sunday. 安息日 ❑ *...a deeply religious man who will not discuss politics on the Sabbath.* …一个笃信宗教、不会在安息日讨论政治的男人。

sab·bati·cal /səbætɪkᵊl/ (**sabbaticals**) N-COUNT A **sabbatical** is a period of time during which someone such as a university teacher can leave their ordinary work and travel or study. (大学教师等的) 休假 [also "on" N] ❑ *He took a year's sabbatical from teaching to write a book.* 他停教休假了一年去写一本书。

★ **sabo·tage** /sæbətɑʒ/ (**sabotages, sabotaging, sabotaged**) **1** V-T If a machine, railroad line, or bridge **is sabotaged**, it is deliberately damaged or destroyed, for example, in a war or as a protest. 蓄意破坏 [usu passive] ❑ *The main pipeline supplying water was sabotaged by rebels.* 主供水管道被叛乱分子故意破坏了。 ● N-UNCOUNT **Sabotage** is also a noun. 蓄意的破坏 ❑ *The bombing was a spectacular act of sabotage.* 这次爆炸是一次惊人的蓄意破坏行为。 **2** V-T If someone **sabotages** a plan or a meeting, they deliberately prevent it from being successful. 阻挠 ❑ *He accused the opposition of doing everything they could to sabotage the election.* 他指责反对派正在竭尽全力阻挠选举的进行。

sa·chet /sæʃeɪ/ (**sachets**) N-COUNT A **sachet** is a small soft bag containing a perfumed powder or other substance placed in drawers to give clothing a pleasant smell. (熏衣服用的) 小香袋 [AM] ❑ *...a lilac sachet.* …一个丁香香袋。

sack ♦◇◇ /sæk/ (**sacks, sacking, sacked**) **1** N-COUNT A **sack** is a large bag made of thick paper or rough material. Sacks are used to carry or store things such as food or groceries. 大麻袋; 大厚纸袋 ❑ *...a sack of potatoes.* …一大袋土豆。 **2** V-T If your employers **sack** you, they tell you that you can no longer work for them because you have done something that they did not like or because your work was not good enough. 开除 [mainly BRIT, INFORMAL]

in AM, usually use **fire**

● N-SING **Sack** is also a noun. 开除

sack·ing /sækɪŋ/ (**sackings**) **1** N-UNCOUNT **Sacking** is rough woven material that is used to make sacks. 粗麻布 ❑ *...a piece of sacking.* …一块粗麻布。 **2** N-COUNT A **sacking** is when an employer tells a worker to leave their job. 开除 [mainly BRIT, INFORMAL]

in AM, usually use **firing**

★ **sa·cred** /seɪkrɪd/ **1** ADJ Something that is **sacred** is believed to be holy and to have a special connection with God. 神圣的 ❑ *The owl is sacred for many Californian Indian people.* 猫头鹰对于很多加利福利亚的印第安人来说是神圣的。 **2** ADJ Something connected with religion or used in religious ceremonies is described as **sacred**. 宗教的 [ADJ n] ❑ *...sacred art.* …宗教艺术。 **3** ADJ You can describe something as **sacred** when it is regarded as too important to be changed or interfered with. 不容更改的; 不容干涉的 ❑ *My memories are sacred.* 我的记忆不能泯灭。

sac·ri·fice ♦◇◇ /sækrɪfaɪs/ (**sacrifices, sacrificing, sacrificed**) **1** V-T To **sacrifice** an animal or person means to kill them in a special religious ceremony as an offering to a god. 献祭 ❑ *The priest sacrificed a chicken.* 牧师献祭了一只鸡。 ● N-COUNT **Sacrifice** is also a noun. 祭品 ❑ *...animal sacrifices to the gods.* …献给众神的动物祭品。 **2** V-T If you **sacrifice** something that is valuable or important, you give it up, usually to obtain something else for yourself or for other people. 舍弃; 牺牲 ❑ *She sacrificed family life to her career.* 她为了她的事业牺牲了家庭生活。 ❑ *Kitty Aldridge has sacrificed all for her first film.* 姬蒂•奥尔德里奇为了她的第一部电影牺牲了一切。 ● N-VAR **Sacrifice** is also a noun. 舍弃; 牺牲 ❑ *She made many sacrifices to get Anita a good education.* 为了让安尼塔受到良好教育，她做出了很多牺牲。

sac·ri·fi·cial /sækrɪfɪʃᵊl/ ADJ **Sacrificial** means connected with or used in a sacrifice. 献祭的 [ADJ n] ❑ *...the sacrificial altar.* …祭坛。

sad ♦♦◇ /sæd/ (**sadder, saddest**) **1** ADJ If you are **sad**, you feel unhappy, usually because something has happened that you do not like. 悲伤的; 难过的 ❑ *The relationship had been important to me and its loss left me feeling sad and empty.* 这种关系对我一直都很重要，失去它让我感到难过而空虚。 ❑ *I'm sad that Julie's marriage is on the verge of splitting up.* 我为朱莉的婚姻处于破裂的边缘感到难过。 ● **sad·ly** ADV 悲伤地; 难过地 ❑ *...a gallant man who will be sadly missed by all his comrades.* …一位将被他所有的同志沉痛怀念的勇士。 ● **sad·ness** N-UNCOUNT 悲哀 ❑ *It is with a mixture of sadness and joy that I say farewell.* 我是怀着悲喜交加的心情告别的。 **2** ADJ **Sad** stories and **sad** news make you feel sad. 令人难过的 ❑ *...a desperately humorous, impossibly sad novel.* …一部极其幽默又催人泪下的小说。 **3** ADJ A **sad** event or situation is unfortunate or undesirable. 不幸的; 令人遗憾的 ❑ *It's a sad truth that children are the biggest victims of passive smoking.* 可悲的事实是，孩子们是被动吸烟的最大受害者。 ● **sad·ly** ADV 不幸地; 令人遗憾地 ❑ *Sadly, bamboo plants die after flowering.* 令人遗憾的是，竹子开花后就会死亡。 **4** ADJ If you describe someone as **sad**, you do not have any respect for them and think their behavior or ideas are ridiculous. 荒唐的 [INFORMAL, DISAPPROVAL] ❑ *...sad old bikers and youngsters who think that Jim Morrison is God.* …视吉姆•莫里森为上帝的那些荒唐的老车手和年轻人。

→ see **cry, emotion**

Thesaurus *sad* 另参见:

ADJ.	depressed, down, gloomy, unhappy; (*ant.*) cheerful, happy **1**
	miserable, tragic, unhappy **3**

Word Partnership *sad* 的常用搭配:

V.	**feel** sad, **seem** sad **1**
	look sad **1** **4**
ADV.	**kind of** sad, **a little** sad, **really** sad, **so** sad, **too** sad, **very** sad **1**–**4**
N.	sad **news**, sad **story** **2**
	sad **day**, sad **eyes**, sad **face**, sad **fact**, sad **truth** **3**

sad·den /sædᵊn/ (**saddens, saddened**) V-T If something **saddens** you, it makes you feel sad. 使悲伤; 使难过 [no cont] ❑ *The cruelty in the world saddens me incredibly.* 世间的残酷令我悲伤不已。 ● **sad·dened** ADJ 悲伤的; 难过的 [v-link ADJ] ❑ *He was disappointed and saddened that legal argument had stopped the trial.* 让他失望又难过的是，法庭辩论中止了审判。

sad·dle /sædᵊl/ (**saddles, saddling, saddled**) **1** N-COUNT A **saddle** is a leather seat that you put on the back of an animal so that you can ride the animal. 鞍 **2** V-T If you **saddle** a horse, you put a saddle on it so that you can ride it. 给 (马) 配鞍 ❑ *Why don't we saddle a couple of horses and go for a ride?* 为什么我们不给几匹马配上鞍骑着转转? ● PHRASAL VERB **Saddle up** means the same as **saddle**. 同**saddle** ❑ *I want to be gone from here as soon as we can saddle up.* 我想一配好鞍就离开这儿。 **3** N-COUNT A **saddle** is a seat on a bicycle or motorcycle. (自行车或摩托车的) 车座

→ see **horse**

sad·ism /seɪdɪzəm, sæd-/ N-UNCOUNT **Sadism** is a type of behavior in which a person obtains pleasure from hurting other people and making them suffer physically or mentally. 施虐狂 ❑ *Psychoanalysts tend to regard both sadism and masochism as arising from childhood deprivation.* 精神分析专家们倾向于认为施虐狂和受虐狂均由童年时期缺乏关爱所致。 ● **sad·ist** /seɪdɪst, sæd-/ N-COUNT (**sadists**) 施虐狂 ❑ *The man was a sadist who tortured animals and people.* 这个男人是个施虐狂，折磨动物也折磨人。

sa·dis·tic /sədɪstɪk/ ADJ A **sadistic** person obtains pleasure from hurting other people and making them suffer physically or mentally. 有施虐狂的 ❑ *The prisoners rioted against mistreatment by sadistic guards.* 囚犯们发动了暴乱反抗施虐狂狱警的虐待。

s.a.e. /ɛs eɪ iː/ (**s.a.e.s**) N-COUNT An **s.a.e.** is the same as an **SASE.** (贴好邮票写明自己姓名和地址的) 回信信封 [BRIT]

sa·fa·ri /səfɑːri/ (**safaris**) N-COUNT A **safari** is a trip to observe or hunt wild animals, especially in East Africa. (尤指在东非的) 游猎 [also "on" N] ❑ *He'd like to go on safari to photograph snakes and tigers.* 他想去游猎以拍摄蛇和老虎。

safe ♦♦◇ /seɪf/ (**safer, safest, safes**) **1** ADJ Something that is **safe** does not cause physical harm or danger. 安全的 ❑ *Officials arrived to assess whether it is safe to bring emergency food supplies into the city.* 官员们过来评估调拨紧急救济食品进入该市是否安全。 ❑ *Most foods that we eat are safe for birds.* 我们吃的绝大部分食物对鸟类是安全的。 **2** ADJ If a person or thing is **safe from** something, they cannot be harmed or damaged by it. 不会受损伤的 [v-link ADJ] ❑ *They are safe from the violence that threatened them.* 他们不会受到威胁性暴力的伤害。 **3** ADJ If you are **safe**, you have not been harmed, or you are not in danger of being harmed. 未受伤害的; 安全的 [v-link ADJ] ❑ *Where is Sophy? Is she safe?* 索菲在哪儿? 她没受到伤害吧? ● **safe·ly** ADV 未受伤害地; 安全地 [ADV with v] ❑ *All 140 guests were brought out of the building safely by firemen.* 140位客人全部被消防人员安然无恙地救出了大楼。 **4** ADJ A **safe** place is one where it is unlikely that any harm, damage, or unpleasant things will happen to the people or things that are there. (地方) 安全的 ❑ *The continuing tension has prompted more than half the inhabitants of the refugee camp to flee to safer areas.* 持续的紧张局势已经促使难民营中一半以上的人逃往了更安全的地区。 ● **safe·ly** ADV 安全地 [ADV after v] ❑ *The banker keeps the money tucked safely under his bed.* 那位银行家把钱安置在他的床下。 **5** ADJ If people or things have a **safe** trip, they reach their destination without harm, damage, or unpleasant things happening to them. (旅途) 平安的 [ADJ n] ❑ *I told him good night, come back any time, and have a safe trip home.* 我祝他晚安、回家一路平安，并告诉他可以随时回来。 ● **safe·ly** ADV 平安地 ❑ *The space shuttle returned safely today from a 10-day mission.* 航天飞机在为期10天的任务之后于今日平安返回。 **6** ADJ If you are at a **safe** distance from something or someone, you are far enough away from them to avoid any danger, harm, or unpleasant effects. (距离) 安全的 [ADJ n] ❑ *I shall conceal myself at a safe distance from the battlefield.* 我将把自己藏在一个远离战场的安全地带。 **7** ADJ If something you have or expect to obtain is **safe**, you cannot lose it or be prevented from having it. 保险的; 不会失去的 ❑ *We as consumers need to feel confident that our jobs are safe before we will spend spare cash.* 我们作为消费者需要确信我们的工作是不会丢的，这样才会去花闲钱。 **8** ADJ A **safe** course of action is one in which there is very little risk of loss or failure. 稳妥的; 风险小的 ❑ *Electricity shares are still a safe investment.* 电力股仍然是小风险投资。 ● **safe·ly** ADV 稳妥地; 风险小地 ❑ *We reveal only as much information as we can safely risk at a given time.* 我们只透露那些在特定时期我们可以稳妥地承担风险的信息。 **9** ADJ If **it is safe to** say or assume something, you can say it with very little risk of being wrong. 有把握的 ❑ *I think it is safe to say that very few students expend the effort to do quality work in school.* 我认为有把握这么说，几乎没有学生能在学校用心读书。 ● **safe·ly** ADV 有把握地 [ADV before v] ❑ *I think you can safely say she will not be appearing in another of my films.* 我想你可以有把握地说她不会在我的另一部电影中现身了。 **10** N-COUNT A **safe** is a strong metal cabinet with special locks, in which you keep money, jewelry, or other valuable things. 保险柜 ❑ *The files are now in a safe to which only he has the key.* 那些文件如今在一个保险柜里，只有他有钥匙。 **11** → see also **safely** **12** PHRASE If you say that a person or thing is **in safe hands**, or is **safe in** someone's **hands**, you mean that they are being taken care of by a reliable person and will not be harmed. 得到(某可靠之人的) 妥善照顾 ❑ *I had a huge responsibility to ensure these packets remained in safe hands.* 我有重大责任保证这些包裹在可靠的人手里。 **13** PHRASE If you **play safe** or **play it safe**, you do not take any risks. 万无一失 ❑ *If you want to play safe, cut down on the amount of salt you eat.* 如果你想万无一失，就少吃盐。 **14** PHRASE If you say you are doing something **to be on the safe side**, you mean that you are doing it in case something undesirable happens, even though this may be unnecessary. 为保险起见 ❑ *You might still want to go for an X-ray, however, just to be on the safe side.* 但你也许还想去拍张X光片，为保险起见。 **15** PHRASE If you say **"it's better to be safe than sorry,"** you are advising someone to take action in order to avoid possible unpleasant consequences later, even if this seems unnecessary. 免吃后悔药 ❑ *Don't be afraid to have this checked by a doctor – better safe than sorry!* 别怕把这个让医生检查一下——以免吃后悔药！ **16** PHRASE You say that someone is **safe and sound** when they are still alive or unharmed after being in danger. 安然无恙地 ❑ *All I'm hoping for is that wherever Trevor is he will come home safe and sound.* 我所希望的是不论特雷弗在哪儿他都能安然无恙地回家。

Word Partnership *safe* 的常用搭配:

N. safe **drinking water**, safe **operation** **1**
children/kids are safe, safe **at home** **3**
safe **environment**, safe **neighborhood**, safe **place**, safe **streets** **4**
safe **bet**, safe **investment** **8**

ADV. **completely** safe, **perfectly** safe, **reasonably** safe, **relatively** safe **1** **3** **4**

safe de·pos·it box (**safe deposit boxes**) N-COUNT A **safe deposit box** is a small box, usually kept in a special room in a bank, in which you can store valuable objects. (银行) 保管箱

★ **safe·guard** /seɪfgɑrd/ (**safeguards, safeguarding, safeguarded**) **1** V-T To **safeguard** something or someone means to protect them from being harmed, lost, or badly treated. 保护; 保卫 [FORMAL] ❑ *They will press for international action to safeguard the ozone layer.* 他们将竭力要求国际行动来保护臭氧层。 **2** N-COUNT A **safeguard** is a law, rule, or measure intended to prevent someone or something from being harmed. 安全条例; 防护措施 ❑ *As an additional safeguard against weeds you can always use an underlay of heavy duty polyethylene.* 作为另外一种预防杂草的防护措施，你可以一直使用一层厚重耐磨的聚乙烯底垫。

safe ha·ven (**safe havens**) **1** N-COUNT If part of a country is declared a **safe haven**, people who need to escape from a dangerous situation such as a war can go there and be protected. (躲避战争等危险活动的) 安全区 ❑ *Countries overwhelmed by the human tide of refugees want safe havens set up at once.* 那些被难民潮席卷的国家想要立即建立安全区。 **2** N-UNCOUNT If a country provides **safe haven** for people from another country who have been in danger, it allows them to stay there under its official protection. 避难所 [AM] ❑ *Some Democrats support granting the Haitians temporary safe haven in the U.S.* 一些民主党人支持为海地人提供在美国的临时避难所。 **3** N-COUNT A **safe haven** is a place, a situation, or an activity which provides people with an opportunity to escape from things that they find unpleasant or worrying. 避风港 ❑ *...the idea of the family as a safe haven from the brutal outside world.* …把家庭当作避风港、摆脱残酷尘世的观念。

safe·ly /seɪfli/ **1** ADV If something is done **safely**, it is done in a way that makes it unlikely that anyone will be harmed. 安全地 ❑ *The waste is safely locked away until it is no longer radioactive.* 废料被安全地封存，直到其不再有辐射。 ❑ *"Drive safely," he said and waved goodbye.* "开车小心，"他说着挥手告别。 **2** ADV You also use **safely** to say that there is no risk of a situation being changed. 稳定地 ❑ *Once events are safely in the past, this idea seems to become less alarming.* 一旦事件稳稳地尘封为历史，这种想法似乎就变得不那么令人惊慌了。 **3** → see also **safe**

safe sex also **safer sex** N-UNCOUNT **Safe sex** is sexual activity in which people protect themselves against the risk of AIDS and other diseases, usually by using condoms. (常指使用安全套的) 安全性交 ❑ *You must practice safe sex and know your partner well.* 你必须进行安全性交并充分了解你的性伴侣。

safe·ty ♦♦◇ /seɪfti/ **1** N-UNCOUNT **Safety** is the state of being safe from harm or danger. 安全; 平安 ❑ *The report goes on to make a number of recommendations to improve safety on aircraft.* 该报告接着提出了几点建议来加强飞行安全。 **2** N-UNCOUNT If you reach **safety**, you reach a place where you are safe from danger. 安全场所 ❑ *He stumbled through smoke and fumes to pull her to safety.* 他跌跌撞撞地穿过重重烟雾把她拖到了安全的地方。 ❑ *People scurried for safety as the firing started.* 人们在交火发生时急忙跑向安全地带。 **3** N-SING If you are concerned about the **safety** of something, you are concerned that it might be harmful or dangerous. 安全性 ❑ *...consumers are showing growing concern about the safety of the food they buy.* …消费者越来越关注所购食品的安全性。 **4** N-SING If you are concerned for someone's **safety**, you are concerned that they might be in danger. 安危 ❑ *There is grave concern for the safety of witnesses.* 证人们的安危受到严重关注。 **5** ADJ **Safety** features or measures are intended to make something less dangerous. 安全的 (特性或措施) [ADJ n] ❑ *The built-in safety device compensates for a fall in water pressure.* 这个内置的安全装置可以补偿水压的下降。

S

Word Partnership *safety* 的常用搭配：

V. **improve** safety, **provide** safety 1
ensure safety 1 3 4
fear for ***someone's*** safety 4

N. **child** safety, **fire** safety, **health and** safety, **highway/traffic** safety, safety **measures**, **public** safety, safety **regulations**, safety **standards**, **workplace** safety 1
safety **concerns**, **food** safety 3
safety **device**, safety **equipment** 5

safe·ty belt (safety belts) also **safety-belt** N-COUNT A **safety belt** is a strap attached to a seat in a car or airplane. You fasten it around your body and it stops you from being thrown forward if there is an accident. 安全带 ❑ *Please return to your seats and fasten your safety belts.* 请回到你们的座位上并系好安全带。

safe·ty net (safety nets) 1 N-COUNT A **safety net** is something that you can rely on to help you if you get into a difficult situation. 安全保障 ❑ *Welfare is the only real safety net for low-income workers.* 福利是低收入工人们惟一真正的安全保障。 2 N-COUNT In a circus, a **safety net** is a large net that is placed below performers on a high wire or trapeze in order to catch them and prevent them being injured if they fall off. (马戏团杂技表演使用的）安全网

safe·ty of·fic·er (safety officers) N-COUNT The **safety officer** in a company or an organization is the person who is responsible for the safety of the people who work or visit there. 安全员 ❑ *Organizers had consulted widely with police and safety officers to ensure tight security.* 组织者们已广泛咨询了警方和安全员们以确保绝对的安全。

safe·ty pin (safety pins) N-COUNT A **safety pin** is a bent metal pin used for fastening things together. The point of the pin has a cover so that when the pin is closed it cannot hurt anyone. 安全别针 ❑ *...trousers which were held together with safety pins.* …用几个安全别针别起来的裤子。

▲ **sag** /sæg/ (sags, sagging, sagged) V-I When something **sags**, it hangs down loosely or sinks downward in the middle. (中间部分）下垂；下陷 ❑ *The shirt's cuffs won't sag and lose their shape after washing.* 这件衬衫的袖口洗后不会松垂变形。

saga /sɑgə/ (sagas) 1 N-COUNT A **saga** is a long story, account, or sequence of events. 长篇故事；长篇记叙；一长串事件 ❑ *...a 600 page saga about 18th century slavery.* …一个关于18世纪奴隶制的600页的长篇故事。 2 N-COUNT A **saga** is a long story composed in medieval times in Norway or Iceland. 萨迦（中世纪挪威、冰岛的长篇传说） ❑ *...a Nordic saga of giants and trolls.* …一个关于巨人和巨怪的北欧萨迦。

sage /seɪdʒ/ N-UNCOUNT **Sage** is a herb used in cooking. (用于烹调的）鼠尾草

said /sɛd/ **Said** is the past tense and past participle of **say**. **say**的过去式和过去分词

sail ♦◇◇ /seɪl/ (sails, sailing, sailed) 1 N-COUNT **Sails** are large pieces of material attached to the mast of a ship. The wind blows against the sails and pushes the ship along. 帆 ❑ *The white sails billow with the breezes they catch.* 片片白帆随风扬起。 2 V-I You say a ship **sails** when it moves over the sea. 航行 ❑ *The trawler had sailed from the port of Zeebrugge.* 那只拖网渔船已经从泽布吕赫港启航。 3 V-T/V-I If you **sail** a boat or if a boat **sails**, it moves across water using its sails. 驾驶（船）；（船）扬帆航行 ❑ *His crew's job is to sail the boat.* 他的船员的职责是驾船。 ❑ *I'd buy a big boat and sail around the world.* 我要买条大船航游世界。 4 → see also **sailing** 5 PHRASE When a ship **sets sail**, it leaves a port. 启航 ❑ *He loaded his vessel with another cargo and set sail.* 他又往他的船上装了一件货就启航了。

▸ **sail through** PHRASAL VERB If someone or something **sails through** a difficult situation or experience, they deal with it easily and successfully. 轻易完成；顺利通过 ❑ *While she sailed through her exams, he struggled.* 她顺利通过了考试，而他却奋力挣扎。

sail·ing /seɪlɪŋ/ (sailings) 1 N-UNCOUNT **Sailing** is the activity or sport of sailing boats. 驾船；帆船运动 ❑ *There was swimming and sailing down on the lake.* 湖上有游泳的和驾船的。 2 N-COUNT **Sailings** are trips made by a ship carrying passengers. 水运航班 ❑ *Ferry companies are providing extra sailings from Calais.* 轮渡公司正在投放从加来出发的加运航班。 3 PHRASE If you say that a task was not all **plain sailing**, you mean that it was not very easy. 轻而易举；一帆风顺 ❑ *Pregnancy wasn't all plain sailing and once again there were problems.* 怀孕并非一帆风顺，又一次出现了若干问题。

→ see **boat**

sail·or /seɪlər/ (sailors) N-COUNT A **sailor** is someone who works on a ship or sails a boat. 船员；船只驾驶员 ❑ *...sailors, marines and Coast Guard personnel.* …船员们、海军陆战队士兵们和海岸警卫队人员。

saint ♦◇◇ /seɪnt/ (saints) 1 N-COUNT; N-TITLE A **saint** is someone who has died and been officially recognized and honored by the Christian church because his or her life was a perfect example of the way Christians should live. (基督教教会正式追封的）圣人 ❑ *Every parish was named after a saint.* 每个教区都以一个圣徒的名字命名。 2 N-COUNT If you refer to a living person as a **saint**, you mean that they are extremely kind, patient, and unselfish. 圣人 [APPROVAL] ❑ *My girlfriend Geraldine is a saint to put up with me.* 我的女友杰拉尔丁是个能包容我的圣人。

saint·ly /seɪntli/ ADJ A **saintly** person behaves in a very good or very holy way. 神圣的；高尚的 [APPROVAL] ❑ *She has been saintly in her self-restraint.* 她一直似圣徒般能自我克制。

sake ♦◇◇ /seɪk/ (sakes) 1 PHRASE If you do something **for the sake of** something, you do it for that purpose or in order to achieve that result. You can also say that you do it **for** something's **sake**. 为了…的目的 ❑ *Let's assume for the sake of argument that we manage to build a satisfactory database.* 让我们为了讨论假定我们设法构建了一个令人满意的数据库。 ❑ *For the sake of historical accuracy, please permit us to state the true facts.* 为了历史的准确性，请允许我们说出事实真相。 2 PHRASE If you do something **for** its **own sake**, you do it because you want to, or because you enjoy it, and not for any other reason. You can also talk about, for example, **art for art's sake** or **sport for sport's sake**. 由于自身原因 ❑ *Economic change for its own sake did not appeal to him.* 经济变化本身并没有吸引他。 3 PHRASE When you do something **for** someone's **sake**, you do it in order to help them or make them happy. 为帮助某人；为使某人开心 ❑ *I trust you to do a good job for Stan's sake.* 我相信你会为了斯坦把工作做好。 4 PHRASE Some people use expressions such as **for God's sake**, **for heaven's sake**, **for goodness' sake**, or **for Pete's sake** in order to express annoyance or impatience, or to add force to a question or request. The expressions "for God's sake" and "for Christ's sake" could cause offense. (用以加强质问或请求的语气，表示厌恶或烦躁）看在上帝的份上 [INFORMAL, FEELINGS] ❑ *For goodness' sake, why didn't you call me?* 天哪，你为什么没给我打电话？

sal·ad /sæləd/ (salads) N-VAR A **salad** is a mixture of cold foods such as lettuce, tomatoes, or cold cooked potatoes, cut up and mixed with a dressing. It is often served with other food as part of a meal. 色拉 ❑ *...a salad of tomato, onion and cucumber.* …一份番茄、洋葱和黄瓜色拉。

→ see **dish**

sala·ried /sælərid/ ADJ **Salaried** people receive a salary from their job. 拿薪金的 [BUSINESS] ❑ *...salaried employees.* …拿薪金的雇员们。

sala·ry ♦◇◇ /sæləri/ (salaries) N-VAR A **salary** is the money that someone earns each month or year from their employer. (按月或按年支付的）薪水 [BUSINESS] ❑ *The lawyer was paid a huge salary.* 这位律师被付了一大笔薪水。

→ see **salt**

Professional people and office workers receive a **salary**, which is paid monthly. However, when talking about someone's salary, you usually give the annual figure. ❑ *I'm paid a salary of $29,000 a year.* **Pay** is a general noun which you can use to refer to the money you get from your employer for doing your job. Manual workers are paid **wages**, or **a wage**. The plural is more common than the singular, especially when you are talking about the actual cash that someone receives. ❑ *Every week he handed all his wages in cash to his wife.* Wages are usually paid, and quoted, as an hourly or a weekly sum. ❑ *...a starting wage of five dollars an hour.* Your **income** consists of all the money you receive from all sources, including your pay.

sale ♦♦♦ /seɪl/ (sales) 1 N-SING The **sale** of goods is the act of selling them for money. 销售 ❑ *Efforts were made to limit the sale of alcohol.* 做出努力来限制酒的销售。 ❑ *...a proposed arms sale to Saudi Arabia.* …拟议中对沙特阿拉伯的武器销售。 2 N-PLURAL The **sales** of a product are the quantity of it that is sold. 销售量 ❑ *The newspaper has sales of 1.72 million.* 该报有172万份的销售量。 ❑ *...the huge Christmas sales of computer games.* …电脑游戏在圣诞节的巨额销售量。 3 N-PLURAL The part of a company that deals with **sales** deals with selling the company's products. 销售部门 ❑ *Until 1983 he worked in sales and marketing.* 到1983年为止他一直供职于市场营销部。

4 N-COUNT A **sale** is an occasion when a store sells things at less than their normal price. 减价出售 ❑ *...a pair of jeans bought half-price in a sale.* …一条减价时半价买的牛仔裤。 **5** N-COUNT A **sale** is an event when goods are sold to the person who offers the highest price. 拍卖 ❑ *The Old Master was bought by dealers at the Christie's sale.* 这幅早期名画被商人们在克里斯蒂的拍卖会上买走。 **6** PHRASE If something is **for sale**, it is being offered to people to buy. 供出售 ❑ *The yacht is for sale at a price of 1.7 million dollars.* 这艘游艇以170万美元的价格待售。 **7** PHRASE If products in a store are **on sale**, they can be bought for less than their normal price. 减价出售 ❑ *A good shopper doesn't just buy things because they're on sale.* 善于购物的人不会仅仅因为商品减价出售就买。 **8** PHRASE Products that are **on sale** can be bought. 出售 ❑ *English textbooks and dictionaries are on sale everywhere.* 英语教材和词典到处都有出售。 ❑ *Tickets go on sale this week.* 票本周开始出售。 **9** PHRASE If a property or company is **up for sale**, its owner is trying to sell it. 待售 ❑ *The mansion has been put up for sale.* 该豪宅已待售。

sales·clerk /seɪlzklɜrk/ (**salesclerks**) also **sales clerk** N-COUNT A **salesclerk** is a person who works in a store selling things to customers and helping them to find what they want. 售货员 [AM]

in BRIT, use **shop assistant**

sales force (**sales forces**) also **salesforce** N-COUNT A company's **sales force** is all the people that work for that company selling its products. (全体) 销售人员 [BUSINESS] ❑ *His sales force is signing up schools at the rate of 25 a day.* 他的销售人员正以每天25个的速度和多所学校签约。

sales·man /seɪlzmən/ (**salesmen**) N-COUNT A **salesman** is a man whose job is to sell things, especially directly to stores or other businesses on behalf of a company. 男推销员 ❑ *...an insurance salesman.* …一位男保险推销员。

sales·person /seɪlzpɜrsən/ (**salespeople** or **salespersons**) N-COUNT A **salesperson** is a person who sells things, either in a store or directly to customers on behalf of a company. 售货员; 推销员 [BUSINESS] ❑ *They will usually send a salesperson out to measure your bathroom.* 他们通常会派一名推销员去测量你的浴室。

sales pitch (**sales pitches**) N-COUNT A salesperson's **sales pitch** is what they say in order to persuade someone to buy something from them. 推销辞令 ❑ *His sales pitch was smooth and convincing.* 他的推销辞令流畅且令人信服。

sales slip (**sales slips**) N-COUNT A **sales slip** is a piece of paper that you are given when you buy something in a store, which shows when you bought it and how much you paid. 销售凭证 [AM]

sales tax (**sales taxes**) N-VAR The **sales tax** on things that you buy is the percentage of money that you pay to the local or state government. 销售税 [BUSINESS] ❑ *The state's unpopular sales tax on snacks has ended.* 该州不得人心的快餐销售税已经取消。

sales·wom·an /seɪlzwʊmən/ (**saleswomen**) N-COUNT A **saleswoman** is a woman who sells things, either in a store or directly to customers on behalf of a company. 女售货员; 女推销员 [BUSINESS] ❑ *...an insurance saleswoman.* …一位女保险推销员。

S

▲**sa·li·ent** /seɪliənt, seɪlyənt/ ADJ The **salient** points or facts of a situation are the most important ones. 最重要的; 突出的 [FORMAL] ❑ *He read the salient facts quickly.* 他迅速地阅读了那些最重要的事实。

sa·li·va /səlaɪvə/ N-UNCOUNT **Saliva** is the watery liquid that forms in your mouth and helps you to chew and digest food. 唾液 ❑ *He noticed a lot of saliva settling in his mouth.* 他注意到有很多唾液滞留在他的嘴里。

▲**salm·on** /sæmən/ (**salmon**)

Salmon is both the singular and the plural form.

N-COUNT A **salmon** is a large silver-colored fish. 三文鱼 ● N-UNCOUNT **Salmon** is the orangey-pink flesh of this fish which is eaten as food. It is often smoked and eaten raw. 鲑鱼肉 ❑ *He gave them a splendid lunch of smoked salmon.* 他款待了他们一顿极好的熏三文鱼午餐。

▲**sa·lon** /səlɒn/ (**salons**) N-COUNT A **salon** is a place where people have their hair cut or colored, or have beauty treatments. 美发厅; 美容院 ❑ *...a new hair salon.* …一家新美发厅。

▲**sa·loon** /səlun/ (**saloons**) N-COUNT A **saloon** is a place where alcoholic drinks are sold and drunk. 酒馆 [AM, OLD-FASHIONED] ❑ *In the saloon, he drank whiskey and let his eyes become accustomed to the dimness.* 在酒馆里，他喝了威士忌，双眼也变得适应昏暗。

salt ♦◇◇ /sɔlt/ (**salts, salting, salted**) **1** N-UNCOUNT **Salt** is a strong-tasting substance, in the form of white powder or crystals, which is used to improve the flavor of food or to preserve it. Salt occurs naturally in sea water. 食盐 ❑ *Season lightly with salt and pepper.* 用盐和胡椒稍微调一下味。 **2** V-T When you **salt** food, you add salt to it. (给食物) 加盐 ❑ *Salt the stock to your taste and leave it simmering very gently.* 按照你的口味在原汤里加盐，然后用文火慢炖。 ● **salt·ed** ADJ 加了盐的 ❑ *Put a pan of salted water on to boil.* 把一锅加了盐的水放上去煮沸。 **3** N-COUNT **Salts** are substances that are formed when an acid reacts with an alkali. 盐 ❑ *The rock is rich in mineral salts.* 这种岩石富含矿物盐。 **4** PHRASE If you **take** something **with a grain of salt**, you do not believe that it is completely accurate or true. 对…半信半疑 ❑ *You have to take these findings with a grain of salt because respondents tend to give the answers they feel they should.* 你必须对这些结果有所保留，因为调查对象们倾向于给出他们认为应该给的答案。 **5** PHRASE If you say, for example, that any doctor **worth** his or her **salt** would do something, you mean that any doctor who was good at his or her job or who deserved respect would do it. 称职的; 值得尊敬的 ❑ *No golf teacher worth his salt would ever recommend that you grip the club tightly.* 没有哪位称职的高尔夫教练会建议你紧紧地握住球杆。

→ see Word Web: salt
→ see **crystal, ocean, sweat, wetland**

Word Partnership *salt* 的常用搭配:

V.	**add** salt, **season with** salt, **sprinkle** salt, **taste** salt **1**
N.	salt **air**, salt **and pepper**, **pinch of** salt, **teaspoon of** salt **1**

salty /sɔlti/ (**saltier, saltiest**) ADJ Something that is **salty** contains salt or tastes of salt. 含盐的; 咸的 ❑ *...salty foods such as ham and bacon.* …例如火腿和熏肉这样的咸味食品。

→ see **taste**

★**sa·lute** /səlut/ (**salutes, saluting, saluted**) **1** V-T/V-I If you **salute** someone, you greet them or show your respect with a formal sign. Soldiers usually salute officers by raising their right hand so that their fingers touch their forehead. 向…打招呼; 向…行军礼 ❑ *One of the company stepped out and saluted the General.* 队中的一人站出来，向那位将军行军礼。 ● N-COUNT **Salute** is also a noun. 招呼; 军礼 [also "in" N] ❑ *He gave his salute and left.* 他打了招呼然后离开了。 **2** V-T To **salute** a person or their achievements means to publicly show or state your admiration for them. 对…表示敬意 ❑ *I salute the governor for the leadership role that he is taking.* 我对州长的领导风范表示敬意。

▲**sal·vage** /sælvɪdʒ/ (**salvages, salvaging, salvaged**) **1** V-T If something **is salvaged**, someone manages to save it, for example, from a ship that has sunk, or from a building that has been damaged. 抢救 (沉船或被毁楼房中的财物) [usu passive] ❑ *The team's first task was to decide what equipment could be salvaged.* 该队的首要任务是决定要抢救出什么设备。 **2** N-UNCOUNT **Salvage** is the act of salvaging things from somewhere such as a damaged ship or

Word Web salt

Since prehistoric times, **salt** has been used for a **seasoning**, a **preservative**, and even **money**. A book about salt published in China around 2700 BC describes methods of producing salt that are strikingly similar to current methods. The ancient Greeks exchanged salt for slaves, giving rise to the expression, "not worth his salt." Roman soldiers received *salarium argentum* (salt money), which is the source of the English word **salary**. And salt has altered the course of history. For example, the salt tax was one major cause of the French Revolution.

building. (对沉船或被毁楼房中财物的) 抢救 ❑ *The salvage operation went on.* 抢救作业继续进行。 **3** N-UNCOUNT The **salvage** from somewhere such as a damaged ship or building is the things that are saved from it. (从沉船或被毁楼房中) 抢救出的财物 ❑ *They climbed up on the rock with their salvage.* 他们带着抢救出来的财物爬到了礁石上。 **4** V-T If you manage to **salvage** a difficult situation, you manage to get something useful from it so that it is not a complete failure. 挽救 (败局) ❑ *Officials tried to salvage the situation.* 官员们努力挽救这个局面。 **5** V-T If you **salvage** something such as your pride or your reputation, you manage to keep it even though it seems likely you will lose it, or you get it back after losing it. 挽回 (自尊、声誉等) ❑ *We definitely wanted to salvage some pride for American tennis.* 我们当然想为美国网球挽回些尊严。

★ **sal·va·tion** /sælveɪʃən/ **1** N-UNCOUNT In Christianity, **salvation** is the fact that Christ has saved a person from evil. (基督教中) 灵魂的拯救 ❑ *The church's message of salvation has changed the lives of many.* 这个教会的灵魂得救的训诫已经改变了很多人的一生。 **2** N-UNCOUNT The **salvation** of someone or something is the act of saving them from harm, destruction, or an unpleasant situation. 解救; 拯救 ❑ *...those whose marriages are beyond salvation.* …那些婚姻无法拯救的人。 **3** N-SING If someone or something is your **salvation**, they are responsible for saving you from harm, destruction, or an unpleasant situation. 救星; 解救物 ❑ *The country's salvation lies in forcing through democratic reforms.* 拯救该国在于强制推行民主改革。

same ♦♦♦ /seɪm/ **1** ADJ If two or more things, actions, or qualities are **the same**, or if one is **the same as** another, they are very like each other in some way. 一样的; 极相似的 ❑ *The houses were all the same – square, close to the street, needing paint.* 这些房子都是一样的——四方形、邻街、需要粉刷。 ❑ *People with the same experience in the job should be paid the same.* 同等工作经验的人应该报酬相等。 **2** PHRASE If something is happening **the same as** something else, the two things are happening in a way that is similar or exactly the same. 和…相似; 跟…一样 ❑ *I mean, it's a relationship, the same as a marriage is a relationship.* 我是说，这是一种关系，跟婚姻是一种关系一样。 **3** ADJ You use **same** to indicate that you are referring to only one place, time, or thing, and not to different ones. 同一的 ❑ *Bernard works at the same institution as Arlette.* 伯纳德与阿莱特在同一个机构工作。 ❑ *It's impossible to get everybody together at the same time.* 不可能把每个人同时召集在一起。 **4** ADJ Something that is still **the same** has not changed in any way. 毫无变化的 ["the" ADJ] ❑ *Taking ingredients from the same source means the beers stay the same.* 从同一来源选取原料意味着啤酒保持不变。 **5** PRON You use **the same** to refer to something that has previously been mentioned or suggested. 一样 ["the" PRON] ❑ *We made the decision which was right for us. Other parents must do the same.* 我们做了适合我们的决定。其他家长一定也会如此。 ❑ *In the United States small bookstores survive quite well. The same applies to small publishers.* 在美国小书店生存得很好。小出版商也是一样。 ● ADJ **Same** is also an adjective. 同前的; 前面提到的 ["the" ADJ] ❑ *He's so effective. I admire Ginny for pretty much the same reason.* 他真有效。我佩服金尼也出于此因。 **6** CONVENTION You say "**same here**" in order to suggest that you feel the same way about something as the person who has just spoken to you, or that you have done the same thing. 我也一样 [INFORMAL, SPOKEN, FORMULAE] ❑ *"Nice to meet you," said Michael. "Same here," said Mary Ann.* "很高兴见到你，" 迈克尔说。"我也一样，" 玛丽·安说。 **7** CONVENTION You say "**same to you**" in response to someone who wishes you well with something. (用于致以对方同样的祝愿) 你也一样 [INFORMAL, SPOKEN, FORMULAE] ❑ *"Have a nice Easter."—"And the same to you Bridie."* "复活节快乐。" —— "你也一样，布赖迪。" **8** PHRASE You say "**same again**" when you want to order another drink of the same kind as the one you have just had. 再来一份 (同样的酒水) [INFORMAL, SPOKEN] ❑ *Give Roger another pint, Imogen, and I'll have the same again.* 给罗杰再来一品脱，伊摩根，我也再来一个。 **9** PHRASE You can say **all the same** or **just the same** to introduce a statement which indicates that a situation or your opinion has not changed, in spite of what has happened or what has just been said. (尽管如此…) 同样; 依然 ❑ *I arranged to pay him the dollars when he got there, a purely private arrangement. All the same, it was illegal.* 我安排好了，他到那儿就付给他钱，纯粹的个人安排。同样，这是违法的。 **10** PHRASE If you say "**It's all the same to me**," you mean that you do not care which of several things happens or is chosen. 我无所谓; 对我来说都一样 [mainly SPOKEN] ❑ *Whether I've got a mustache or not it's all the same to me.* 我留不留胡子对自己来说都一样。 **11** **at the same time**
→ see **time**

Thesaurus *same* 另参见:

ADJ. alike, equal, identical; *(ant.)* different **1**
constant, unchanged; *(ant.)* different **4**

sam·ple ♦◇◇ /sæmpəl/ (**samples, sampling, sampled**) **1** N-COUNT A **sample** of a substance or product is a small quantity of it that shows you what it is like. 样品; 样本 ❑ *You'll receive samples of paint, curtains and upholstery.* 你将收到涂料、窗帘和座套的样品。 ❑ *We're giving away 2,000 free samples.* 我们正在赠送2000件免费样品。 **2** N-COUNT A **sample** of a substance is a small amount of it that is examined and analyzed scientifically. (用于检验、分析的) 试样 ❑ *They took samples of my blood.* 他们采了我的血样。 **3** N-COUNT A **sample** of people or things is a number of them chosen out of a larger group and then used in tests or used to provide information about the whole group. 抽样 ❑ *We based our analysis on a random sample of more than 200 males.* 我们把我们的分析基于二百多名男性的一组随机抽样。 **4** V-T If you **sample** food or drink, you taste a small amount of it in order to find out if you like it. 品尝 ❑ *We sampled a selection of different bottled waters.* 我们品尝了挑选出来的各种瓶装水。 **5** V-T If you **sample** a place or situation, you experience it for a short time in order to find out about it. 体验 ❑ *...the chance to sample a different way of life.* …体验一种不同生活方式的机会。
→ see **DVD, laboratory**

Thesaurus *sample* 另参见:

N. bit, piece, portion, specimen **1** **2**
V. experience, taste, try **4** **5**

sanc·tion ♦♦◇ /sæŋkʃən/ (**sanctions, sanctioning, sanctioned**) **1** V-T If someone in authority **sanctions** an action or practice, they officially approve of it and allow it to be done. 批准; 认可 ❑ *He may now be ready to sanction the use of force.* 他或许现在正准备批准使用武力。 ● N-UNCOUNT **Sanction** is also a noun. 批准; 认可 ❑ *...a newspaper run by citizens without the sanction of the government.* …未经政府许可的一家民办报纸。 **2** N-PLURAL **Sanctions** are measures taken by countries to restrict trade and official contact with a country that has broken international law. 国际制裁 ❑ *The continued abuse of human rights has now led the United States to impose sanctions against the regime.* 对人权的不断践踏现已导致美国对该政权实施国际制裁。

Word Partnership *sanction* 的常用搭配:

ADJ. **legal** sanction, **official** sanction, **proposed** sanction **1**
PREP. **without** sanction **1**
sanctions **against** **2**
V. **impose** sanctions, **lift** sanctions **2**

sanc·tity /sæŋktɪti/ N-UNCOUNT If you talk about **the sanctity of** something, you mean that it is very important and must be treated with respect. 神圣 ❑ *...the sanctity of human life.* …人类生命的神圣。

▲ **sanc·tu·ary** /sæŋktʃueri/ (**sanctuaries**) **1** N-COUNT A **sanctuary** is a place where people who are in danger from other people can go to be safe. 避难所 ❑ *His church became a sanctuary for thousands of people who fled the civil war.* 他的教堂成了数千逃避内战的人们的一个避难所。 **2** N-UNCOUNT **Sanctuary** is the safety provided in a sanctuary. 庇护 ❑ *Some of them have sought sanctuary in the church.* 他们中的一些人已在教堂里寻求庇护。 **3** N-COUNT A **sanctuary** is a place where birds or animals are protected and allowed to live freely. 鸟兽禁猎区 ❑ *...a bird sanctuary.* …一个鸟类禁猎区。

sand ♦◇◇ /sænd/ (**sands, sanding, sanded**) **1** N-UNCOUNT **Sand** is a substance that looks like powder, and consists of extremely small pieces of stone. Some deserts and many beaches are made up of sand. 沙 ❑ *They all walked barefoot across the damp sand to the water's edge.* 他们都光着脚走过潮湿的沙地来到了水边。 **2** N-PLURAL **Sands** are a large area of sand, for example, a beach. 沙滩 ❑ *...miles of golden sands.* …数英里的金色沙滩。 **3** V-T If you **sand** a wood or metal surface, you rub sandpaper over it in order to make it smooth or clean. 用砂纸打磨 ❑ *Sand the surface softly and carefully.* 轻轻地、小心地用砂纸打磨表面。 ● PHRASAL VERB **Sand down** means the same as **sand**. 同**sand** ❑ *I was going to sand down the chairs and repaint them.* 我打算用砂纸打磨这些椅子然后重新刷漆。
→ see **beach, desert, erosion, glass**

▲ **san·dal** /sændəl/ (**sandals**) N-COUNT **Sandals** are light shoes that you wear in warm weather, which have straps instead of a solid part over the top of your foot. 凉鞋 ❑ *...a pair of old sandals.* …一双旧凉鞋。

S & L /ɛs ən ɛl/ (**S & Ls**) N-COUNT **S & L** is an abbreviation for **savings and loan.** 储蓄贷款社 [BUSINESS]

sand·paper /sændpeɪpər/ N-UNCOUNT **Sandpaper** is strong paper that has a coating of sand on it. It is used for rubbing wood or metal surfaces to make them smoother. 砂纸 ❏ *...a piece of sandpaper.* …一张砂纸。

sand·stone /sændstoʊn/ (**sandstones**) N-MASS **Sandstone** is a type of rock which contains a lot of sand. It is often used for building houses and walls. 砂岩 ❏ *...the reddish sandstone walls.* …微红的砂岩墙。

sand·storm /sændstɔrm/ (**sandstorms**) N-COUNT A **sandstorm** is a strong wind in a desert area, which carries sand through the air. 沙暴

sand·wich /sænwɪtʃ, sænd-/ (**sandwiches, sandwiching, sandwiched**) **1** N-COUNT A **sandwich** usually consists of two slices of bread with a layer of food such as cheese or meat between them. 三明治 ❏ *...a ham sandwich.* …一个火腿三明治。 **2** V-T If you **sandwich** two things **together** with something else, you put that other thing between them. If you **sandwich** one thing between two other things, you put it between them. 夹住; 把…插入 (两者之间) ❏ *Carefully split the sponge ring, then sandwich the two halves together with whipped cream.* 小心地切开海绵蛋糕圈，然后在两半中间夹上生奶油。
→ see **meal**

sandy /sændi/ (**sandier, sandiest**) ADJ A **sandy** area is covered with sand. 覆盖着沙的 ❏ *...long, sandy beaches.* …长长的沙地海滩。

Word Link *san ≈ health : insane, sane, sanitation*

▲ **sane** /seɪn/ (**saner, sanest**) **1** ADJ Someone who is **sane** is able to think and behave normally and reasonably, and is not mentally ill. 心智健全的; 神志正常的 ❏ *He seemed perfectly sane.* 他看来心智非常健全。 **2** ADJ If you refer to a **sane** person, action, or system, you mean one that you think is reasonable and sensible. 理智的; 合乎情理的 ❏ *No sane person wishes to see conflict or casualties.* 理智的人都不希望看到冲突或伤亡。

sang /sæŋ/ **Sang** is the past tense of **sing**. **sing**的过去式

sani·tary /sænɪteri/ **1** ADJ **Sanitary** means concerned with keeping things clean and healthy, especially by providing a sewage system and a clean water supply. 公共卫生的; 有益于健康的 [ADJ n] ❏ *Sanitary conditions are appalling.* 卫生条件非常恶劣。 **2** ADJ If you say that a place is not **sanitary**, you mean that it is not very clean. 干净的 ❏ *It's not the most sanitary place one could swim.* 这不是最干净的游泳之地。

sani·tary nap·kin (**sanitary napkins**) N-COUNT A **sanitary napkin** is a pad of thick soft material which women wear to absorb the blood during their periods. 卫生巾 [AM]
in BRIT, use **sanitary towel**

sani·tary tow·el (**sanitary towels**) N-COUNT A **sanitary towel** is the same as a **sanitary napkin**. 卫生巾 [BRIT]

▲ **sani·ta·tion** /sænɪteɪʃən/ N-UNCOUNT **Sanitation** is the process of keeping places clean and healthy, especially by providing a sewage system and a clean water supply. (尤指通过提供排污系统和洁净水源的) 公共卫生 ❏ *...the hazards of contaminated water and poor sanitation.* …污水和不良公共卫生的危害。

S

san·ity /sænɪti/ N-UNCOUNT A person's **sanity** is their ability to think and behave normally and reasonably. 心智健全; 神志正常 ❏ *He and his wife finally had to move from their apartment just to preserve their sanity.* 他和妻子最后不得不搬离其公寓，只是为了保持精神正常。

sank /sæŋk/ **Sank** is the past tense of **sink**. **sink**的过去式

sap /sæp/ (**saps, sapping, sapped**) **1** V-T If something **saps** your strength or confidence, it gradually weakens or destroys it. 消耗; 削弱 ❏ *I was afraid the sickness had sapped my strength.* 恐怕这场病已经消耗了我的力气。 **2** N-UNCOUNT **Sap** is the watery liquid in plants and trees. (植物的) 汁液 ❏ *The leaves, bark and sap are also common ingredients of local herbal remedies.* 树叶、树皮和树液也是当地草药疗法的常用药材。

sap·phire /sæfaɪər/ (**sapphires**) **1** N-VAR A **sapphire** is a precious stone which is blue in color. 蓝宝石 ❏ *...a sapphire engagement ring.* …一枚蓝宝石订婚戒指。 **2** COLOR Something that is **sapphire** is bright blue in color. 天蓝色的 [LITERARY] ❏ *...white snow and sapphire skies.* …白雪和蓝天。

★ **sar·casm** /sɑrkæzəm/ N-UNCOUNT **Sarcasm** is speech or writing which actually means the opposite of what it seems to say. Sarcasm is usually intended to mock or insult someone. 挖苦; 讽刺 ❏ *Sarcasm and demeaning remarks have no place in parenting.* 挖苦和贬损的言语不应用来教育子女。

▲ **sar·cas·tic** /sɑrkæstɪk/ ADJ Someone who is **sarcastic** says or does the opposite of what they really mean in order to mock or insult someone. 挖苦的; 讽刺的 ❏ *She poked fun at people's shortcomings with sarcastic remarks.* 她用挖苦的话来取笑别人的缺点。
● **sar·cas·ti·cal·ly** /sɑrkæstɪkli/ ADV 挖苦地; 讽刺地 ❏ *"What a surprise!" Caroline murmured sarcastically.* "多么惊喜呀！" 卡罗琳讽刺地嘟囔。

sar·dine /sɑrdin/ (**sardines**) N-COUNT **Sardines** are a kind of small sea fish, often eaten as food. 沙丁鱼 ❏ *They opened a can of sardines.* 他们打开了一罐沙丁鱼。

sar·don·ic /sɑrdɒnɪk/ ADJ If you describe someone as **sardonic**, you mean their attitude to people or things is humorous but rather critical. 讥讽的 ❏ *He was a big, sardonic man, who intimidated even the most self-confident students.* 他身材高大、爱讽刺人，甚至震慑住了最自信的学生们。

★ **SARS** /sɑrz/ N-UNCOUNT **SARS** is a serious disease which affects your ability to breathe. **SARS** is an abbreviation for "severe acute respiratory syndrome." 非典型性肺炎; 严重急性呼吸系统综合症

SASE /ɛs eɪ ɛs i/ (**SASEs**) N-SING An **SASE** is an envelope on which you have stuck a stamp and written your own name and address. You send it to a person or organization so that they can reply to you in it. **SASE** is an abbreviation for "self-addressed stamped envelope." (贴好邮票写明自己姓名和地址的) 回信信封 [AM]
in BRIT, use **s.a.e.**

sash /sæʃ/ (**sashes**) N-COUNT A **sash** is a long piece of cloth which people wear around their waist or over one shoulder, especially with formal or official clothes. 腰带; 背带 ❏ *She wore a white dress with a thin blue sash.* 她穿着一条白连衣裙，系着一根蓝色的细腰带。

sas·sy /sæsi/ ADJ If an older person describes a younger person as **sassy**, they mean that they are disrespectful in a lively, confident way. 不敬的; 无礼的 [AM, INFORMAL] ❏ *Are you that sassy with your parents, young lady?* 你对你的父母也这样无礼吗，小姑娘？

sat /sæt/ **Sat** is the past tense and past participle of **sit**. **sit**的过去式和过去分词

SAT /ɛs eɪ ti/ (**SATs**) N-PROPER The **SAT** is a set of examinations which are usually taken by students who wish to enter a college or university. (大学的) 入学考试 [AM] ❏ *The average SAT score among 2004's freshman class was 1,200.* 2004级新生入学考试平均分为1200。

Sat. **Sat.** is a written abbreviation for **Saturday**. 星期六

Satan /seɪtᵊn/ N-PROPER In the Christian religion, **Satan** is the Devil, a powerful evil being who is the chief opponent of God. 撒旦 (基督教中与上帝为敌的魔王)

sa·tan·ic /sətænɪk, seɪ-/ ADJ Something that is **satanic** is considered to be caused by or influenced by Satan. 撒旦引起的; 撒旦般的 ❏ *...satanic cults.* …邪教。

sat·el·lite ♦◇◇ /sætᵊlaɪt/ (**satellites**) **1** N-COUNT A **satellite** is an object which has been sent into space in order to collect information or to be part of a communications system. Satellites move continually around the earth or around another planet. 人造卫星 [also "by" N] ❏ *The rocket launched two communications satellites.* 火箭发射了两颗通信卫星。 **2** ADJ **Satellite** television is broadcast using a satellite. 卫星的 [ADJ n] ❏ *They have four satellite channels.* 他们有4个卫星频道。 **3** N-COUNT A **satellite** is a natural object in space that moves around a planet or star. 卫星 ❏ *...the satellites of Jupiter.* …木星的卫星。 **4** N-COUNT You can refer to a country, area, or organization as a **satellite** when it is controlled by or depends on a larger and more powerful one. 卫星国; 附属区; 卫星组织 ❏ *Some companies are outfitting their satellite offices with wireless LANs.* 一些公司正在为其办事处装备无线局域网。
→ see Word Web: **satellite**
→ see **astronomer, forecast, navigation, radio, television**

sat·el·lite dish (**satellite dishes**) N-COUNT A **satellite dish** is a piece of equipment which people have on their house in order to receive satellite television. 圆盘式卫星电视接收天线

sat·in /sætᵊn/ (**satins**) **1** N-MASS **Satin** is a smooth, shiny kind of cloth, usually made from silk. 缎子 ❏ *...a peach satin ribbon.* …一根桃色缎带。 **2** ADJ If something such as a paint, wax, or cosmetic

Word Web satellite

The **moon** is the earth's best-known **satellite**. However, humans began **launching** other objects into **space** starting in 1957. That's when the first artificial satellite, Sputnik, began to **orbit** the earth. Today, hundreds of satellites circle the **planet**. The largest of these is the International **Space Station**. It completes an orbit about every 90 minutes and sometimes can be seen from the earth. Others, such as the Hubbel Telescope, help us learn more about **outer space**. The NOAA 12 monitors the earth's climate. Most TV weather forecasts feature images taken from satellites. Today, many TV programs are also broadcast by satellite.

gives something a **satin** finish, it reflects light to some extent but is not very shiny. 缎子般光泽的 [ADJ n] ❑ *The final stage of waxing left it with a satin sheen.* 最后一道打蜡使之有了缎子般的光泽。

▲ **sat·ire** /sætaɪər/ (**satires**) 1 N-UNCOUNT **Satire** is the use of humor or exaggeration in order to show how foolish or wicked some people's behavior or ideas are. 讽刺 ❑ *The commercial side of the Christmas season is an easy target for satire.* 圣诞节期间商业化的一面很容易成为讽刺的对象。 2 N-COUNT A **satire** is a play, movie, or novel in which humor or exaggeration is used to criticize something. 讽刺作品 ❑ *...a sharp satire on the American political process.* …一部关于美国政治进程的尖锐的讽刺作品。

sa·tir·ic /sətɪrɪk/ ADJ **Satiric** means the same as **satirical**. 讽刺的 ❑ *...Ibsen's satiric attack on bourgeois convention.* …易卜生对资产阶级习俗的讽刺性攻击。

sa·tiri·cal /sətɪrɪkᵊl/ ADJ A **satirical** drawing, piece of writing, or comedy show is one in which humor or exaggeration is used to criticize something. 讽刺的 ❑ *...a satirical novel about New York life in the late 80s.* …一部关于80年代末纽约生活的讽刺小说。

sat·is·fac·tion /sætɪsfækʃᵊn/ 1 N-UNCOUNT **Satisfaction** is the pleasure that you feel when you do something or get something that you wanted or needed to do or get. 满意 ❑ *She felt a small glow of satisfaction.* 她感到了一丝满足的喜悦。 ❑ *Both sides expressed satisfaction with the progress so far.* 双方都对目前的进展表示满意。 2 N-UNCOUNT If you get **satisfaction** from someone, you get money or an apology from them because you have been treated badly. 赔偿；补偿 ❑ *If you can't get any satisfaction, complain to the park owner.* 如果你得不到任何赔偿，就向公园的所有者投诉。 3 PHRASE If you do something **to** someone's **satisfaction**, they are happy with the way that you have done it. 令某人满意 ❑ *She never could seem to do anything right or to his satisfaction.* 她似乎从来不会做任何正确或令他满意的事情。

sat·is·fac·tory /sætɪsfæktəri/ ADJ Something that is **satisfactory** is acceptable to you or fulfills a particular need or purpose. 令人满意的；合适的 ❑ *I never got a satisfactory answer.* 我从未得到过一个满意的回答。

sat·is·fied ♦◇◇ /sætɪsfaɪd/ 1 ADJ If you are **satisfied with** something, you are happy because you have gotten what you wanted or needed. 满意的 ❑ *We are not satisfied with these results.* 我们对这些结果不满意。 2 ADJ If you are **satisfied that** something is true or has been done properly, you are convinced about this after checking it. 确信的 [v-link ADJ] ❑ *People must be satisfied that the treatment is safe.* 人们一定要确信这种疗法是安全的。

Word Link *sat, satis ≈ enough : dissatisfaction, insatiable, satisfy*

sat·is·fy /sætɪsfaɪ/ (**satisfies, satisfying, satisfied**) 1 V-T If someone or something **satisfies** you, they give you enough of what you want or need to make you pleased or contented. 使满意 ❑ *The pace of change has not been quick enough to satisfy everyone.* 变化的速度还没有快到让所有人都满意。 2 V-T To **satisfy** someone **that** something is true or has been done properly means to convince them by giving them more information or by showing them what has been done. 使确信 ❑ *He has to satisfy the environmental lobby that real progress will be made to cut emissions.* 他必须使环境游说团确信，将采取实质性行动来降低排放量。 3 V-T If you **satisfy** the requirements for something, you are good enough or have the right qualities to fulfill these requirements. 满足（要求） ❑ *The executive committee recommends that the procedures should satisfy certain basic requirements.* 执行委员会建议，这些程序应该满足某些基本要求。

Word Partnership *satisfy* 的常用搭配：

N. satisfy **an appetite**, satisfy **demands**, satisfy a **desire** 1
satisfy **a need** 1 3
satisfy **critics**, satisfy *someone's* **curiosity** 2

sat·is·fy·ing /sætɪsfaɪɪŋ/ ADJ Something that is **satisfying** makes you feel happy, especially because you feel you have achieved something. 令人满意的 ❑ *I found wood carving satisfying.* 我发觉木雕让我很开心。

sat·nav /sætnæv/ N-UNCOUNT **Satnav** is a system that uses information from satellites to find the best way of getting to a place. It is often found in cars. **Satnav** is an abbreviation for "satellite navigation". 卫星导航系统 ❑ *We didn't have satnav, so the traditional map and compass took over.* 我们没有卫星导航系统，所以就用传统的地图和指南针了。

★ **satu·rate** /sætʃəreɪt/ (**saturates, saturating, saturated**) 1 V-T If people or things **saturate** a place or object, they fill it completely so that no more can be added. 使饱和；使充满 ❑ *In the last days before the vote, both sides are saturating the airwaves.* 在投票前的最后几天，双方的宣传充斥着各个广播频道。 2 V-T If someone or something **is saturated**, they become extremely wet. 使湿透 ❑ *If the filter has been saturated with motor oil, it should be discarded and replaced.* 如果过滤器已被机油浸透，就应该丢掉并更换一个。

satu·ra·tion /sætʃəreɪʃᵊn/ 1 N-UNCOUNT **Saturation** is the process or state that occurs when a place or thing is filled completely with people or things, so that no more can be added. 饱和 ❑ *Japanese car makers have been equally blind to the saturation of their markets at home and abroad.* 日本的汽车制造商对国内外市场的饱和同样视而不见。 2 ADJ **Saturation** is used to describe a campaign or other activity that is carried out very thoroughly, so that nothing is missed. （运动、活动）彻底的 [ADJ n] ❑ *The concept of saturation marketing makes perfect sense.* 饱和营销的概念很有道理。

Sat·ur·day ♦♦♦ /sætərdeɪ, -di/ (**Saturdays**) N-VAR **Saturday** is the day after Friday and before Sunday. 星期六 ❑ *He called her on Saturday morning at the studio.* 他星期六早上在工作室给她打电话。 ❑ *Every Saturday dad made a beautiful pea and ham soup.* 每个星期六爸爸都做一道鲜美的豌豆火腿汤。

sauce ♦◇◇ /sɔs/ (**sauces**) N-MASS A **sauce** is a thick liquid which is served with other food. 酱；调味汁 ❑ *...pasta cooked in a sauce of garlic, tomatoes, and cheese.* …用大蒜、番茄和奶酪调味汁煮的意大利面。

▲ **sauce·pan** /sɔspæn/ (**saucepans**) N-COUNT A **saucepan** is a deep metal cooking pot, usually with a long handle and a lid. （常指有长柄和盖且较深的）炖锅 ❑ *Place the potatoes and turnips in a large saucepan, cover with cold water and bring to the boil.* 把这些土豆和萝卜放在一只大炖锅里，用冷水盖没，然后煮沸。
→ see **pan**

sau·cer /sɔsər/ (**saucers**) N-COUNT A **saucer** is a small curved plate on which you stand a cup. 茶碟 ❑ *Rae's coffee cup clattered against the saucer as she picked it up.* 蕾把咖啡杯拿起来的时候杯子碰响了茶碟。
→ see **dish**

saucy /sɔsi/ (**saucier, sauciest**) ADJ Someone or something that is **saucy** refers to sex in a light-hearted, amusing way. 开色情玩笑的；色情的 ❑ *...a saucy joke.* …一个黄色笑话。

sau·na /sɔnə/ (**saunas**) 1 N-COUNT If you have a **sauna**, you sit or lie in a room that is so hot that it makes you sweat. People have saunas in order to relax and to clean their skin thoroughly. 桑拿 ❑ *Every month I have a sauna.* 我每个月洗一次桑拿。 **2** N-COUNT A **sauna** is a room or building where you can have a sauna. 桑拿浴室 ❑ *The hotel has a sauna, solarium and heated indoor swimming pool.* 这家旅馆有一个桑拿浴室、日光浴室和室内温水游泳池。

saun·ter /sɔntər/ (**saunters, sauntering, sauntered**) V-I If you **saunter** somewhere, you walk there in a slow, casual way. 漫步 ❑ *We watched our fellow students saunter into the building.* 我们看着同学们漫步走进了那栋楼。

sau·sage /sɔsɪdʒ/ (**sausages**) N-VAR A **sausage** consists of minced meat, usually pork, mixed with other ingredients and is contained in a tube made of skin or a similar material. 香肠；腊肠 ❑ *...sausages and fries.* …香肠和炸薯条。

sau·té /sɔteɪ/ (**sautés, sautéing, sautéed**) V-T When you **sauté** food, you fry it quickly in hot oil or butter. 炒；嫩煎 ❑ *Sauté the chicken until golden brown.* 把鸡肉煎至金黄色。

★ **sav·age** /sævɪdʒ/ (**savages, savaging, savaged**) **1** ADJ Someone or something that is **savage** is extremely cruel, violent, and uncontrolled. 野蛮的；残暴的 ❑ *This was a savage attack on a defenseless young girl.* 这是对一个无力自卫的小姑娘的野蛮袭击。 ❑ *...the savage wave of violence that swept the country in November 1987.* …1987年11月席卷了该国的野蛮暴力浪潮。 ● **sav·age·ly** ADV 野蛮地；残暴地 ❑ *He was savagely beaten.* 他被毒打了。 **2** N-COUNT If you refer to people as **savages**, you dislike them because you think that they do not have an advanced society and are violent. 野蛮人；残暴的人 [DISAPPROVAL] ❑ *...their conviction that the area was a frozen desert peopled with uncouth savages.* …他们深信该地区是一片冰冷的沙漠，住着一些没有教养的野蛮人。 **3** V-T If someone **is savaged** by a dog or other animal, the animal attacks them violently. (动物)凶猛地攻击 [usu passive] ❑ *The animal then turned on him and he was savaged to death.* 那只兽接而扑向他，把他攻击至死。

sav·age·ry /sævɪdʒri/ N-UNCOUNT **Savagery** is extremely cruel and violent behavior. 暴行 ❑ *...the sheer savagery of war.* …战争极度的残暴。

save ◆◆◇ /seɪv/ (**saves, saving, saved**) **1** V-T If you **save** someone or something, you help them to avoid harm or to escape from a dangerous or unpleasant situation. 救助；拯救 ❑ *...an austerity program designed to save the country's failing economy.* …一个旨在拯救该国衰退的经济的紧缩计划。 ❑ *The meeting is an attempt to mobilize nations to save children from death by disease and malnutrition.* 该会议试图动员各国救助儿童，以免死于疾病和营养不良。 **2** V-T/V-I If you **save**, you gradually collect money by spending less than you get, usually in order to buy something that you want. 储蓄 ❑ *The majority of people intend to save, but find that by the end of the month there is nothing left.* 大多数人都想要储蓄，但到月底的时候却发现已经一分不剩了。 ❑ *Tim and Barbara are now saving for a house in the suburbs.* 蒂姆和芭芭拉眼下正为郊区的一所房子攒钱。 ❑ *I was trying to save money to go to college.* 我当时正努力攒钱去上大学。 ● PHRASAL VERB **Save up** means the same as **save**. 同**save** ❑ *Julie wanted to put some of her money aside for holidays or save up for something special.* 朱莉想留出一些钱去度假或是存些钱以备专门之需。 **3** V-T/V-I If you **save** something such as time or money, you prevent the loss or waste of it. 节约 ❑ *It saves time in the kitchen to have things you use a lot within reach.* 在厨房里把常用的东西放在手边可以节省时间。 ❑ *I'll try to save him the expense of a flight from Perth.* 我会想办法给他省下从珀斯过来的机票费用。 ❑ *A new filter can save on energy bills.* 一个新的过滤器能节省能源开支。 **4** V-T If you **save** something, you keep it because it will be needed later. 保留(备用) ❑ *Drain the beans thoroughly and save the stock for soup.* 把豆子彻底滤干，留下豆汁做汤。 **5** V-T If someone or something **saves** you **from** an unpleasant action or experience, they change the situation so that you do not have to do it or experience it. 免去 ❑ *The scanner will reduce the need for exploratory operations which will save risk and pain for patients.* 扫描仪将减少所需的探查手术，从而为病患者免除风险和疼痛。 ❑ *She was hoping that something might save her from having to make a decision.* 她真希望有什么可以使自己免于作决定。 **6** V-T/V-I If you **save** data in a computer, you give the computer an instruction to store the data on a tape or disk. 保存；存盘 [COMPUTING] ❑ *Try to get into the habit of saving your work regularly.* 要努力养成经常保存工作内容的习惯。 ❑ *Save frequently when you are creating graphics.* 当你在制图的时候要经常存盘。 **7** V-T/V-I If a goalkeeper **saves**, or **saves** a shot, they succeed in preventing the ball from going into the goal. 救球；扑救 ❑ *He saved one shot when the ball hit him on the head.* 他扑住了一次射门，球打在了他的头上。 ● N-COUNT **Save** is also a noun. 救球；扑救 ❑ *The goalie made some great saves.* 这名守门员扑住了几个好球。 **8** to **save the day** → see **day** **9** to **save face** → see **face**

▸ **save up** → see **save 2**

Thesaurus *save* 另参见：

v. defend, protect, rescue **1**
conserve, economize, hoard; (*ant.*) waste **2**–**4**

sav·er /seɪvər/ (**savers**) N-COUNT A **saver** is a person who regularly saves money, especially by paying it into a bank account. 储户 ❑ *Low interest rates are bad news for savers, who have seen their income halved over the last year.* 低利率对储户来说是个坏消息，他们在过去一年就看到了收入减半。

sav·ing ◆◇◇ /seɪvɪŋ/ (**savings**) **1** N-COUNT A **saving** is a reduction in the amount of time or money that is used or needed. 节省 ❑ *You can enjoy a year's membership for just $28 – a saving of $7 off the regular rate.* 你只需花$28就可以享受一年的会员资格——比正常会费节省了$7。 **2** N-PLURAL Your **savings** are the money that you have saved, especially in a bank or a building society. 积蓄；存款 ❑ *Her savings were in the First National Bank.* 她的存款以前在第一国民银行。 → see **bank**

sav·ings and loan (**savings and loans**) N-COUNT A **savings and loan** association is a business where people save money to earn interest, and which lends money to savers to buy houses. Compare **building society**. 储蓄贷款社(向存款者支付利息，同时可向存款者提供购房贷款的合作社) [mainly AM, BUSINESS]

sav·ior /seɪvyər/ (**saviors**)

in BRIT, use **saviour**

N-COUNT A **savior** is a person who saves someone or something from danger, ruin, or defeat. 拯救者；救星 ❑ *...the savior of his country.* …他的国家的救星。

sav·iour /seɪvjəʳ/ [BRIT] → see **savior**

▲ **sa·vor** /seɪvər/ (**savors, savoring, savored**)

in BRIT, use **savour**

1 V-T If you **savor** an experience, you enjoy it as much as you can. 尽情享受 ❑ *She savored her newfound freedom.* 她体味到了她新获得的自由。 **2** V-T If you **savor** food or drink, you eat or drink it slowly in order to taste its full flavor and to enjoy it properly. 品尝 ❑ *Just relax, eat slowly and savor the full flavor of your food.* 只要放松，慢慢地吃，充分品尝食物的滋味。

Word Link *vor ≈ eating : herbivorous, savory, voracious*

sa·vory /seɪvəri/

in BRIT, use **savoury**

ADJ **Savory** food has a salty or spicy flavor rather than a sweet one. 咸味的；辛辣的 ❑ *...all sorts of sweet and savory breads.* …各种甜味和咸味的面包。

▲ **sa·vour** /seɪvəʳ/ [BRIT] → see **savor**

sa·voury /seɪvəri/ [BRIT] → see **savory**

saw /sɔ/ (**saws, sawing, sawed, sawed** or **sawn**) **1** **Saw** is the past tense of **see**. **see**的过去式 **2** N-COUNT A **saw** is a tool for cutting wood, which has a blade with sharp teeth along one edge. Some saws are pushed backward and forward by hand, and others are powered by electricity. 锯 **3** V-T/V-I If you **saw** something, you cut it with a saw. 锯 ❑ *He escaped by sawing through the bars of his cell.* 他锯断牢房的铁栅逃跑了。 → see **cut, tool**

saw·dust /sɔdʌst/ N-UNCOUNT **Sawdust** is dust and very small pieces of wood which are produced when you saw wood. 锯末 ❑ *...a layer of sawdust.* …一层锯末。

sawn /sɔn/ **Sawn** is the past participle of **saw**. **saw**的过去分词 [mainly BRIT]

sax /sæks/ (**saxes**) N-COUNT A **sax** is the same as a **saxophone**. 萨克斯管 [INFORMAL]

★ **saxo·phone** /sæksəfoʊn/ (**saxophones**) N-VAR A **saxophone** is a musical instrument in the shape of a curved metal tube with a narrower part that you blow into and keys that you press. 萨克斯管

sax·opho·nist /sæksəfoʊnɪst/ (**saxophonists**) N-COUNT A **saxophonist** is someone who plays the saxophone. 萨克斯管吹奏者

say
❶ VERB AND NOUN USES
❷ PHRASES AND CONVENTIONS

❶ **say** ♦♦♦ /seɪ/ (**says** /sɛz/, **saying**, **said** /sɛd/) 1 V-T When you **say** something, you speak words. 说 ❑ *"I'm sorry," he said.* "我很抱歉，"他说。 ❑ *She said they were very impressed.* 她说他们被深深打动了。 ❑ *Forty-one people are said to have been seriously hurt.* 据说有41人严重受伤。 ❑ *I packed and said goodbye to Charlie.* 我收拾好行装，跟查理说了再见。 2 V-T You use **say** in expressions such as **I would just like to say** to introduce what you are actually saying, or to indicate that you are expressing an opinion or admitting a fact. If you state that you **can't say** something or you **wouldn't say** something, you are indicating in a polite or indirect way that it is not the case. (表达观点或陈述事实，否定用法表示婉转陈述某事并非事实) 说 ❑ *I would just like to say that this is the most hypocritical thing I have ever heard in my life.* 我只想说这是我一生中听到过的最虚伪的事。 ❑ *I must say that rather shocked me, too.* 我得说那件事也让我颇为震惊。 3 V-T You can mention the contents of a piece of writing by mentioning what it **says** or what someone **says** in it. 宣称 ❑ *The report says there is widespread and routine torture of political prisoners in the country.* 报告称在那个国家存在着普遍的、惯常的虐待政治犯的现象。 ❑ *You can't have one without the other, as the song says.* 正如那首歌所唱的，二者你不能只取其一。 4 V-T If you **say** something **to yourself**, you think it. 心中暗想 ❑ *Perhaps I'm still dreaming, I said to myself.* 我心中暗想，可能我仍在做梦吧。 5 N-SING If you have **a say in** something, you have the right to give your opinion and influence decisions relating to it. 发言权 [usu "a" N, also "more/some" N] ❑ *You can get married at sixteen, and yet you haven't got a say in the running of the country.* 你可以在16岁结婚，然而对国家的管理你还没有发言权。 6 V-T You indicate the information given by something such as a clock, dial, or map by mentioning what it **says**. (钟，地图等) 表明 ❑ *The clock said four minutes past eleven when we set off.* 我们出发时，时钟显示11点4分。 7 V-T If something **says** something **about** a person, situation, or thing, it gives important information about them. 说明 ❑ *I think that says a lot about how well Safin is playing.* 我认为那足以说明萨芬表现得有多出色。 8 V-T If something **says** a lot **for** a person or thing, it shows that this person or thing is very good or has a lot of good qualities. 说明 (某人或某物有很多优点) ❑ *That the Escort is still the nation's bestselling car in 1992 says a lot for the power of Ford's marketing people.* 雅仕车仍是1992年全国销售得最好的汽车，这足以说明福特公司营销人员的非凡的能力。 9 V-T You use **say** in expressions such as **I'll say that for them** and **you can say this for them** after or before you mention a good quality that someone has, usually when you think they do not have many good qualities. 有一点该肯定 (用于表扬没有多少优点的人) ❑ *He's usually well-dressed, I'll say that for him.* 有一点该肯定的是，他通常穿着很考究。 10 V-T You can use **say** when you want to discuss something that might possibly happen or be true. 假定 [only imper] ❑ *Say you were buying a new car, would your discussion begin and end with the monthly payment?* 假定你要买辆新车，你开始和结束讨论时的问题会是按月付款的数额吗？ 11 PHRASE You can use **say** or **let's say** when you mention something as an example. 比如说 ❑ *To see the problem here more clearly, let's look at a different biological system, say, an acorn.* 为了把这里的问题看得更清楚，让我们看一种不同的生物系统，比如说，橡实。

Note that, with the verb **say**, if you want to mention the person who is being addressed, you should use the preposition **to**. "What did she say you?" is wrong. "**What did she say to you?**" is correct. The verb **tell**, however, is usually followed by a direct object indicating the person who is being addressed. ❑ *He told Alison he was suffering from leukemia... What did she tell you?* "What did she tell to you?" is wrong. **Say** is the most general verb for reporting the words that someone speaks. **Tell** is used to report information that is given to someone. ❑ *The manufacturer told me that the product did not contain corn.* **Tell** can also be used with a "to" infinitive to report an order or instruction. ❑ *My mother told me to shut up and eat my dinner.*

Thesaurus *say* 另参见：
v. announce, communicate, declare, speak ❶ 1

❷ **say** ♦♦♦ /seɪ/ (**says** /sɛz/, **saying**, **said** /sɛd/) 1 PHRASE If you say that something **says it all**, you mean that it shows you very clearly the truth about a situation or someone's feelings. 清楚说明事实 ❑ *This is my third visit in a week, which says it all.* 这是我一周内的第三次来访，这本身就说明了一切。 2 CONVENTION You can use "**You don't say**" to express surprise at what someone has told you. People often use this expression to indicate that in fact they are not surprised. 真的吗 (用于并不太惊讶时) [FEELINGS] ❑ *"I'm a writer."—"You don't say. What kind of book are you writing?"* "我是个作家。"——"真的吗，你在写什么样的书呢？" 3 PHRASE If you say there is a lot **to be said for** something, you mean you think it has a lot of good qualities or aspects. 有很多优点 ❑ *There's a lot to be said for being based in the country.* 以农村为依托有很多优势。 4 PHRASE If someone asks **what** you **have to say for yourself**, they are asking what excuse you have for what you have done. 某人有何要为自己辩解的 ❑ *"Well," she said eventually, "what have you to say for yourself?"* "好了，"她最后说，"你有什么要为自己说的？" 5 PHRASE If something **goes without saying**, it is obvious. 不言而喻 ❑ *It goes without saying that if someone has lung problems they should not smoke.* 肺部有了问题就不该抽烟，这是不言而喻的。 6 PHRASE When one of the people or groups involved in a discussion **has** their **say**, they give their opinion. 发表意见 ❑ *Voters were finally having their say today.* 选民们今天终于发表他们的意见了。 7 CONVENTION You use "**I wouldn't say no**" to indicate that you would like something, especially something that has just been offered to you. 我不反对 [INFORMAL, FORMULAE] ❑ *I wouldn't say no to a drink.* 我不反对喝一杯。 8 PHRASE You use **that is to say** or **that's to say** to indicate that you are about to express the same idea more clearly or precisely. 也就是说 [FORMAL] ❑ *That would mean voting no, that is to say, using the veto.* 那就意味着投反对票，也就是说，行使否决权。 9 CONVENTION You can use "**You can say that again**" to express strong agreement with what someone has just said. 说得太对了 [INFORMAL, EMPHASIS] ❑ *"You are in enough trouble already."—"You can say that again," sighed Richard.* "你现在麻烦已经够多的。"——"说得太对了，"理查德叹息着说。

say·ing /seɪɪŋ/ (**sayings**) N-COUNT A **saying** is a sentence that people often say and that gives advice or information about human life and experience. 谚语；格言 ❑ *We also realize the truth of that old saying: Charity begins at home.* 我们也明白那句老话很有道理：仁爱始于家庭。

scab /skæb/ (**scabs**) N-COUNT A **scab** is a hard, dry covering that forms over the surface of a wound. 痂 ❑ *The area can be very painful until scabs form after about ten days.* 这个部位会非常疼痛，直到大约十天后结了痂为止。

scaf·fold /skæfəld, -oʊld/ (**scaffolds**) 1 N-COUNT A **scaffold** was a raised platform on which criminals were hanged or had their heads cut off. 绞刑台 ❑ *Ascending the shaky ladder to the scaffold, More addressed the executioner.* 摩尔沿着摇摇晃晃的梯子登上绞刑台，跟行刑人说了话。 2 N-COUNT A **scaffold** is a temporary raised platform on which workers stand to paint, repair, or build high parts of a building. 脚手架 ❑ *They were standing on top of a giant scaffold.* 他们站在一个巨大的脚手架顶上。

scaf·fold·ing /skæfəldɪŋ/ N-UNCOUNT **Scaffolding** consists of poles and boards made into a temporary framework that is used by workers when they are painting, repairing, or building high parts of a building, usually outside. 脚手架 ❑ *Workers have erected scaffolding around the base of the tower below the roadway.* 工人们已经在车行道下的塔基四周竖起了脚手架。

Word Link *cal, caul ≈ hot, heat : calorie, cauldron, scald*

scald /skɔld/ (**scalds, scalding, scalded**) 1 V-T If you **scald yourself**, you burn yourself with very hot liquid or steam. 烫伤 ❑ *A patient jumped into a bath being prepared by a member of staff and scalded herself.* 一位病人跳进了工作人员正在给她准备的洗澡水中把自己烫伤了。 2 N-COUNT A **scald** is a burn caused by very hot liquid or steam. 烫伤 ❑ *Scalds, burns and poisoning can all be life-threatening.* 烫伤、烧伤和中毒都有可能危及生命。

Word Link *scal, scala ≈ ladder, stairs : escalate, escalator, scale*

scale ♦♦◊ /skeɪl/ (**scales, scaling, scaled**) 1 N-SING If you refer to the **scale** of something, you are referring to its size or extent, especially when it is very big. 规模；范围 ❑ *However, he underestimates the scale of the problem.* 然而，他却低估了问题的严重性。 ❑ *The breakdown of law and order could result in killing on a massive scale.* 法律和秩序的崩溃可能会导致大规模的杀戮。 2 → see also **full-scale, large-scale, small-scale** 3 N-COUNT A **scale** is a set of levels or numbers which are used in a particular system of measuring things or are used when comparing things. 等级 ❑ *...an earthquake measuring 5.5 on the Richter scale.* …一次里氏5.5级地震。 ❑ *The patient rates the therapies on a scale of zero to ten.* 这位患者按0到10分给这些疗法分级。 **4** → see also **timescale** **5** N-COUNT A pay **scale** or **scale of** fees is a list that shows how much someone should be paid, depending, for example, on their age or what work they do. 工资级别 ❑ *...those on the high end of the pay scale.* …那些在高工资级别端的人。 **6** N-COUNT The **scale** of a map, plan, or model is the relationship between the size of something in the map, plan, or model and its size in the real world. 比例尺 ❑ *The map, on a scale of 1:10,000, shows over 5,000 individual paths.* 这张比例尺为1:10000的地图显示了5000条以上的独立小径。 **7** → see also **full-scale, large-scale** **8** ADJ A **scale** model or **scale** replica of a building or object is a model of it which is smaller than the real thing but has all the same parts and features. 按比例缩小的 [ADJ n] ❑ *Franklin made his mother an intricately detailed scale model of the house.* 富兰克林为他的母亲制作了一个按这座房子比例缩小的精巧逼真的模型。 **9** N-COUNT In music, a **scale** is a fixed sequence of musical notes, each one higher than the next, which begins at a particular note. 音阶 ❑ *...the scale of C major.* …C大调音阶。 **10** N-COUNT The **scales** of a fish or reptile are the small, flat pieces of hard skin that cover its body. 鳞 ❑ *Remove any excess scales from the fish skin.* 刮掉鱼皮上任何多余的鳞。 **11** N-COUNT A **scale** is a piece of equipment used for weighing things, for example, for weighing amounts of food that you need in order to make a particular meal. 秤 [usu pl] ❑ *...a pair of kitchen scales.* …一台厨用天平秤。 ❑ *...a bathroom scale.* …一台浴室磅秤。 **12** V-T If you **scale** something such as a mountain or a wall, you climb up it or over it. 攀登 [WRITTEN] ❑ *...Rebecca Stephens, the first British woman to scale Everest.* …丽贝卡·斯蒂芬斯，第一位登上珠穆朗玛峰的英国女性。 **13** PHRASE If something is **out of scale with** the things near it, it is too big or too small in relation to them. 与…不成比例；与…不相称 ❑ *The tiny church was out of scale with the new banks and offices around it.* 这座小教堂与周围那些新的银行和办公楼很不相称。 **14** PHRASE If the different parts of a map, drawing, or model are **to scale**, they are the right size in relation to each other. 按比例 ❑ *...a miniature garden, with little pagodas and bridges all to scale.* …一个盆景，里面的小宝塔和小桥也都是按比例制作的。

→ see **graph**

▸ **scale down** PHRASAL VERB If you **scale down** something, you make it smaller in size, amount, or extent than it used to be. 缩小；缩减 ❑ *One factory has had to scale down its workforce from six hundred to only six.* 一家工厂已不得不把工人总数从600裁减到仅剩6人。

▸ **scale up** PHRASAL VERB If you **scale up** something, you make it greater in size, amount, or extent than it used to be. 增加；放大 ❑ *...a major push to scale up treatment programs for people in poor countries.* …一项为贫困国家人民增加医疗项目的重大努力。

scalp /skælp/ (**scalps, scalping, scalped**) **1** N-COUNT Your **scalp** is the skin under the hair on your head. 头皮 ❑ *He smoothed his hair back over his scalp.* 他把头发顺着头皮往后捋平。 **2** V-T If someone **scalps** tickets, they sell them outside a sports stadium or theater, usually for more than their original value. 倒卖（票） [AM]

in BRIT, use **tout**

❑ *He was trying to pick up some cash scalping tickets.* 他那时在筹集现金倒卖票。

→ see **hair**

scal·pel /skælpᵊl/ (**scalpels**) N-COUNT A **scalpel** is a knife with a short, thin, sharp blade. Scalpels are used by surgeons during operations. 手术刀

scalp·er /skælpər/ (**scalpers**) N-COUNT A **scalper** is someone who sells tickets outside a sports stadium or theater, usually for more than their original value. 倒票者 [AM]

in BRIT, use **tout**

❑ *Another scalper said he'd charge $1,000 for a $125 ticket.* 另一个票贩子说一张$125的票他要价$1000。

scam /skæm/ (**scams, scamming, scammed**) **1** V-T If someone **scams** a person or organization, they deceive them in order to get something valuable from them, especially money. 欺诈；骗 [INFORMAL] ❑ *When I told them they were being scammed, they couldn't believe it.* 当我告诉他们被人骗了时，他们简直无法相信。 ❑ *Ryan's campaign fund allegedly scammed the state out of a million dollars.* 据称，瑞安的竞选基金管理机构骗了国家100万美元。 ❑ *...a prisoner who scammed his way out of court.* …一名靠欺骗获得法庭释放的刑犯。 **2** N-COUNT A **scam** is an illegal trick, usually with the purpose of getting money from people or avoiding paying tax. （通常以诈财或逃税为目的的）骗局 [INFORMAL] ❑ *They believed they were participating in an insurance scam, not a murder.* 他们认为他们只是在参与保险骗局，而不是谋杀。

scamp·er /skæmpər/ (**scampers, scampering, scampered**) V-I When people or small animals **scamper** somewhere, they move there quickly with small, light steps. （轻快地）奔跑；疾走 ❑ *Children scampered off the yellow school bus and into the playground.* 孩子们跑下黄颜色的校车，奔跑进了操场。

scan /skæn/ (**scans, scanning, scanned**) **1** V-T/V-I When you **scan** written material, you look through it quickly in order to find important or interesting information. 浏览 ❑ *She scanned the advertisement pages of the newspapers.* 她浏览了报纸的广告页。 ● N-SING **Scan** is also a noun. 浏览 ❑ *I just had a quick scan through your book again.* 我刚刚把你的书又作了一次浏览。 **2** V-T/V-I When you **scan** a place or group of people, you look at it carefully, usually because you are looking for something or someone. 仔细察看 [no passive] ❑ *The officer scanned the room.* 警察仔细察看了那个房间。 ❑ *She was nervous and kept scanning the crowd for Paul.* 她很紧张，一直在人群中寻找保罗。 **3** V-T If people **scan** something such as luggage, they examine it using a machine that can show or find things inside it that cannot be seen from the outside. （用机器）扫描（行李等） ❑ *Their approach is to scan every checked-in bag with a bomb detector.* 他们的做法是用炸弹探测器扫描每一个办理了登机手续的箱包。 **4** V-T If a computer disk **is scanned**, a program on the computer checks the disk to make sure that it does not contain a virus. 扫描（计算机磁盘以查病毒） [COMPUTING] ❑ *Not all ISPs are equipped to scan for viruses.* 并非所有的因特网服务供应商都有装备来扫描病毒。 **5** V-T If a picture or document **is scanned** into a computer, a machine passes a beam of light over it to make a copy of it in the computer. 扫描（图片或文件） [usu passive] [COMPUTING] ❑ *The entire paper contents of all libraries will eventually be scanned into computers.* 所有图书馆的全部纸质内容最终都会被扫描进电脑。 **6** V-T If a radar or sonar machine **scans** an area, it examines or searches it by sending radar or sonar beams over it. （用雷达或声纳波束）扫描 ❑ *The ship's radar scanned the sea ahead.* 船上的雷达扫描了前方海域。 **7** N-COUNT A **scan** is a medical test in which a machine sends a beam of X-rays over a part of your body in order to check that it is healthy. （身体）扫描检查 ❑ *A brain scan revealed the blood clot.* 脑部扫描检查发现了那个血块。

scan·dal ♦◇◇ /skændᵊl/ (**scandals**) **1** N-COUNT A **scandal** is a situation or event that is thought to be shocking and immoral and that everyone knows about. 丑闻 ❑ *...a financial scandal.* …一桩金融丑闻。 **2** N-UNCOUNT **Scandal** is talk about the shocking and immoral aspects of someone's behavior or something that has happened. 流言蜚语 ❑ *He loved gossip and scandal.* 他喜欢闲话和流言蜚语。

scan·dal·ous /skændᵊləs/ **1** ADJ **Scandalous** behavior or activity is considered immoral and shocking. 不道德的；令人震惊的 ❑ *They would be sacked for criminal or scandalous behavior.* 他们会因犯罪行为或不道德的行为而遭解雇。 ● **scan·dal·ous·ly** ADV 不道德地；令人震惊地 [ADV with v] ❑ *He asked only that Ingrid stop behaving so scandalously.* 他只要求英格里德停止表现得如此不道德。 **2** ADJ **Scandalous** stories or remarks are concerned with the immoral and shocking aspects of someone's behavior or something that has happened. 涉及丑闻的 ❑ *Newspaper columns were full of scandalous tales.* 报纸专栏上尽是与丑闻有关的故事。

scan·dal sheet (**scandal sheets**) N-COUNT You can refer to newspapers and magazines which print mainly stories about sex and crime as **scandal sheets**. 花边报刊 [AM]

in BRIT, use **gutter press**

❑ *What if someone sells the story to the scandal sheets?* 如果有人把这个故事卖给花边报刊怎么办？

scan·ner /skænər/ (**scanners**) **1** N-COUNT A **scanner** is a machine which is used to examine, identify, or record things, for example by using a beam of light, sound, or X-rays. 扫描设备 ❑ *...brain scanners.* …大脑扫描仪。 **2** N-COUNT A **scanner** is a piece of computer equipment that you use for copying a picture or document into a computer. 扫描仪 [COMPUTING] ❑ *...a color printer and scanner.* …一台彩色打印机和扫描仪。

→ see **laser**

▲ **scant** /skænt/ ADJ You use **scant** to indicate that there is very little of something or not as much of something as there should be. 少量的；不足的 ❑ *She began to berate the police for paying scant attention to the theft from her car.* 她开始严厉斥责警方对她车内东西失窃一案关注不足。

scape·goat /skeɪpgoʊt/ (**scapegoats, scapegoating, scapegoated**) **1** N-COUNT If you say that someone is made a **scapegoat for** something bad that has happened, you mean that people blame them and may punish them for it although it may not be their fault. 替罪羊 ❑ *I don't think I deserve to be made the scapegoat for a couple of bad results.* 我认为我不该为出现的一些不良后果充当替罪羊。 **2** V-T To **scapegoat** someone means to blame them publicly for something bad that has happened, even though it was not their fault. 使成为替罪羊 ❑ *...a climate where ethnic minorities are continually scapegoated for the lack of jobs and housing problems.* …一种屡屡把缺少工作职位和住房问题归罪于少数族裔的风气。

★ **scar** /skɑr/ (**scars, scarring, scarred**) **1** N-COUNT A **scar** is a mark on the skin which is left after a wound has healed. 伤疤 ❑ *He had a scar on his forehead.* 他前额上有个伤疤。 **2** V-T If your skin **is scarred**, it is badly marked as a result of a wound. 在…留下伤疤 [usu passive] ❑ *He was scarred for life during a fight.* 他在一次打架中留下了一辈子的疤痕。 **3** V-T If a surface **is scarred**, it is damaged and there are ugly marks on it. 留下损伤痕迹 [usu passive] ❑ *The arena was scarred by deep muddy ruts.* 竞技场上留下了深深的车辙泥痕。 **4** N-COUNT If an unpleasant physical or emotional experience leaves a **scar** on someone, it has a permanent effect on their mind. (肉体或情感上的) 创伤 ❑ *The early years of fear and the hostility left a deep scar on the young boy.* 早年的恐惧和这种敌意在这个小男孩的心灵上留下了深深的创伤。 **5** V-T If an unpleasant physical or emotional experience **scars** you, it has a permanent effect on your mind. 给…留下精神创伤 ❑ *This is something that's going to scar him forever.* 这将会是永远给他留下心灵创伤的事情。

scarce /skɛərs/ (**scarcer, scarcest**) **1** ADJ If something is **scarce**, there is not enough of it. 短缺的 ❑ *Food was scarce and expensive.* 食物匮乏而且昂贵。 ❑ *Jobs are becoming increasingly scarce.* 工作职位变得越来越少。 **2** PHRASE If you **make yourself scarce**, you quickly leave the place you are in, usually in order to avoid a difficult or embarrassing situation. 溜走 [INFORMAL] ❑ *It probably would be a good idea if you made yourself scarce.* 如果你溜走倒可能是个好主意。

scarce·ly /skɛərsli/ **1** ADV You use **scarcely** to emphasize that something is only just true or only just the case. 几乎不；简直不 [EMPHASIS] ❑ *He could scarcely breathe.* 他几乎喘不过气来。 ❑ *I scarcely knew him.* 我几乎不认识他。 **2** ADV You can use **scarcely** to say that something is not true or is not the case, in a humorous or critical way. 决不 ❑ *It can scarcely be coincidence.* 这决不可能是巧合。 **3** ADV If you say **scarcely had** one thing happened when something else happened, you mean that the first event was followed immediately by the second. 刚…就… [ADV before v] ❑ *Scarcely had the votes been counted, when the telephone rang.* 选票刚一统计好，电话就响了。

★ **scar·city** /skɛərsɪti/ (**scarcities**) N-VAR If there is a **scarcity of** something, there is not enough of it for the people who need it or want it. 缺乏；稀少 [FORMAL] ❑ *...an ever increasing scarcity of water.* …越来越匮乏的水资源。

scare /skɛər/ (**scares, scaring, scared**) **1** V-T If something **scares** you, it frightens or worries you. 惊吓 ❑ *You're scaring me.* 你吓着我了。 ❑ *The prospect of failure scares me rigid.* 失败的可能吓得我都僵了。 ● PHRASE If you want to emphasize that something scares you a lot, you can say that it **scares the hell out of** you or **scares the life out of** you. 吓死了 [INFORMAL, EMPHASIS] **2** N-SING If a sudden unpleasant experience gives you a **scare**, it frightens you. 惊吓 ❑ *Don't you realize what a scare you've given us all?* 你难道没意识到你给了我们大家一个什么样的惊吓吗？ **3** N-COUNT A **scare** is a situation in which many people are afraid or worried because they think something dangerous is happening which will affect them all. 恐慌；恐惧 ❑ *The news set off a continent-wide health scare.* 这一消息引起了整个大陆的健康恐慌。 **4** N-COUNT A bomb **scare** or a security **scare** is a situation in which there is believed to be a bomb in a place. (炸弹或安全) 恐慌 ❑ *Despite many recent bomb scares, no one has yet been hurt.* 尽管最近发生多次炸弹恐慌，但至今为止还没有人员受伤。 **5** → see also **scared**

▸ **scare away** → see **scare off 1**

▸ **scare off** **1** PHRASAL VERB If you **scare off** or **scare away** a person or animal, you frighten them so that they go away. 吓跑 ❑ *...an alarm to scare off an attacker.* …把一个袭击者吓跑的警报。 **2** PHRASAL VERB If you **scare** someone **off**, you accidentally make them unwilling to become involved with you. 吓跑 ❑ *I don't think that revealing your past to your boyfriend scared him off.* 我并不认为是因为你把自己的过去告诉了你的男朋友才把他吓跑的。

scare·crow /skɛərkroʊ/ (**scarecrows**) N-COUNT A **scarecrow** is an object in the shape of a person, which is put in a field where crops are growing in order to frighten birds away. 稻草人

scared /skɛərd/ **1** ADJ If you are **scared of** someone or something, you are frightened of them. 害怕的 ❑ *I'm certainly not scared of him.* 我当然不怕他。 ❑ *I was too scared to move.* 我吓得动弹不得。 **2** ADJ If you are **scared that** something unpleasant might happen, you are nervous and worried because you think that it might happen. 担心的；害怕的 ❑ *I was scared that I might be sick.* 我担心我可能病了。

scare·monger·ing /skɛərmʌŋgərɪŋ, -mɒŋ-/ N-UNCOUNT If one person or group accuses another person or group of **scaremongering**, they accuse them of deliberately spreading worrying stories to try and frighten people. 散布骇人听闻的消息 ❑ *The government yesterday accused Greenpeace of scaremongering.* 政府昨天指责"绿色和平"组织危言耸听。

▲ **scarf** /skɑrf/ (**scarfs** or **scarves**) N-COUNT A **scarf** is a piece of cloth that you wear around your neck or head, usually to keep yourself warm. 围巾 ❑ *He reached up to loosen the scarf around his neck.* 他伸出手松开围在脖子上的围巾。

scar·let /skɑrlɪt/ (**scarlets**) COLOR Something that is **scarlet** is bright red. 猩红 (的)；鲜红 (的) ❑ *...her scarlet lipstick.* …她的鲜红的唇膏。

scarves /skɑrvz/ **Scarves** is a plural of **scarf**. **scarf**的复数形式

scary /skɛəri/ (**scarier, scariest**) ADJ Something that is **scary** is rather frightening. 可怕的 [INFORMAL] ❑ *I think prison is going to be a scary thing for Harry.* 我认为蹲监狱对哈利来说会是件很可怕的事。 ❑ *There's something very scary about him.* 他身上有种非常吓人的东西。

scath·ing /skeɪðɪŋ/ ADJ If you say that someone is being **scathing** about something, you mean that they are being very critical of it. 尖锐的；刻薄的 ❑ *Republican senators were scathing in their criticism of today's hearing.* 共和党参议员们对今天听证会的批评很尖锐。

scat·ter /skætər/ (**scatters, scattering, scattered**) **1** V-T If you **scatter** things over an area, you throw or drop them so that they spread all over the area. 撒 ❑ *She tore the rose apart and scattered the petals over the grave.* 她掰开玫瑰花，把花瓣撒在坟墓上。 ❑ *They've been scattering toys everywhere.* 他们总是把玩具分散得到处都是。 **2** V-T/V-I If a group of people **scatter** or if you **scatter** them, they suddenly separate and move in different directions. 使散开；散开 ❑ *After dinner, everyone scattered.* 吃完饭，每个人都散开了。 **3** → see also **scattered, scattering**

scat·tered /skætərd/ **1** ADJ **Scattered** things are spread over an area in an untidy or irregular way. 分散的 [ADJ n] ❑ *He picked up the scattered toys.* 他把散落的玩具捡了起来。 ❑ *Tomorrow there will be a few scattered showers.* 明天局部地区将会有阵雨。 **2** ADJ If something is **scattered with** a lot of small things, they are spread all over it. 布满…的 [v-link ADJ "with" n] ❑ *Every surface is scattered with photographs.* 每面都贴满了照片。

scat·ter·ing /skætərɪŋ/ (**scatterings**) N-COUNT A **scattering of** things or people is a small number of them spread over an area. 分散零落的少数 ❑ *...the scattering of houses east of the village.* …村东零零散散的几间房舍。

scav·enge /skævɪndʒ/ (**scavenges, scavenging, scavenged**) V-T/V-I If people or animals **scavenge for** things, they collect them by searching among waste or unwanted objects. (在垃圾或废物中) 捡拾 ❑ *Many are orphans, their parents killed as they scavenged for food.* 很多人是孤儿，他们的父母在垃圾中捡食物时丢了性命。 ❑ *Children scavenge through garbage.* 孩子们在垃圾中捡破烂。 ● **scav·en·ger** N-COUNT (**scavengers**) 捡破烂的人；食腐动物 ❑ *...scavengers such as rats.* …老鼠之类的食腐动物。

★ **sce·nario** /sɪnɛərioʊ/ (**scenarios**) N-COUNT If you talk about a likely or possible **scenario**, you are talking about the way in which a situation may develop. 设想；可能的情况 ❑ *The conflict degenerating into civil war is everybody's nightmare scenario.* 这场冲突恶化成内战成为每个人的恶梦。

scene ◆◆◇ /sin/ (**scenes**) **1** N-COUNT A **scene** in a play, movie, or book is part of it in which a series of events happen in the same place. 场面；片断 ❑ *...the opening scene of "A Christmas Carol."* …《圣诞颂歌》的开场。 ❑ *...Act I, scene 1.* …第1幕，第1场。 **2** N-COUNT You refer to a place as a **scene** when you are describing its appearance and indicating what impression it makes on you. 景象 ❑ *It's a*

S

scene of complete devastation. 那是一幅满目疮痍的景象。❑ *Thick black smoke billowed over the scene.* 黑色的浓烟从现场滚滚升起。 3 N-COUNT You can describe an event that you see, or that is broadcast or shown in a picture, as a **scene** of a particular kind. 场面；事件 ❑ *There were emotional scenes as the refugees enjoyed their first breath of freedom.* 难民们享受第一口自由的呼吸时，有一些感人至深的场面。 ❑ *Television broadcasters were warned to exercise caution over depicting scenes of violence.* 电视台受到警告，在描述暴力场面时要采取谨慎态度。 4 N-COUNT The **scene of** an event is the place where it happened. 现场 ❑ *The area has been the scene of fierce fighting for three months.* 这个地区是3个月来激烈战斗的现场。 ❑ *...traces left at the scene of a crime.* …在犯罪现场留下的痕迹。 5 N-SING You can refer to an area of activity as a particular type of **scene**. 活动领域 ❑ *Sandman's experimentation has made him something of a cult figure on the local music scene.* 桑德曼的实验已经使他成为当地音乐领域颇受人崇拜的人物。 6 N-COUNT If you make a **scene**, you embarrass people by publicly showing your anger about something. 发脾气；当众吵闹 ❑ *I'm sorry I made such a scene.* 很抱歉我刚才发了这么一通火。 7 PHRASE If something is done **behind the scenes**, it is done secretly rather than publicly. 秘密地；在幕后 ❑ *But behind the scenes Mr. Cain will be working quietly to try to get a deal done.* 但在幕后，凯恩先生将会不声不响地工作，努力把交易做成。 8 PHRASE If you refer to what happens **behind the scenes**, you are referring to what happens during the making of a movie, play, or radio or television program. 在幕后；在后台 ❑ *It's an exciting opportunity to learn what goes on behind the scenes.* 这是个令人激动的机会，可以了解幕后发生的事情。 9 PHRASE If you have **a change of scene**, you go somewhere different after being in a particular place for a long time. 换个环境 ❑ *What you need is a change of scene. Why not go on a cruise?* 你需要的是换个环境。为何不乘游轮去旅行呢？ 10 PHRASE Something that **sets the scene for** a particular event creates the conditions in which the event is likely to happen. 为…做好准备 ❑ *An improving economy helped set the scene for his re-election.* 好转的经济为他的再选铺平了道路。 11 PHRASE When a person or thing appears **on the scene**, they come into being or become involved in something. When they disappear **from the scene**, they are no longer there or are no longer involved. 登场/离场；到场/消失 ❑ *He could react jealously when and if another child comes on the scene.* 如果有别的孩子加入其中，他可能会表现得相当嫉妒。
→ see **animation**, **drawing**

Word Partnership *scene* 的常用搭配：

N. **movie** scene, **sex** scene 1
scene **of an accident**, **crime** scene, scene **of a murder**, scene **of a shooting** 4
music scene 5
ADJ. **final** scene, **first/opening** scene, **nude** scene 1
political scene 5
V. **describe** a scene 2 3
arrive at a scene, **leave** a scene, **rush to** a scene 4

scen·ery /siːnəri/ 1 N-UNCOUNT The **scenery** in a country area is the land, water, or plants that you can see around you. 风景；景色 ❑ *...the island's spectacular scenery.* …岛上壮美的景色。 2 N-UNCOUNT In a theater, the **scenery** consists of the structures and painted backgrounds that show where the action in the play takes place. 舞台布景 ❑ *Instead of stagehands, the actors will move the scenery right in front of the audience.* 演员们将替代舞台工作人员，当着观众的面置换布景。

> Do not confuse **scenery**, **landscape**, **countryside**, and **nature**. With **landscape**, the emphasis is on the physical features of the land, while **scenery** includes everything you can see when you look out over an area of land. ❑ *...the landscape of steep woods and distant mountains. ...unattractive urban scenery.* **Countryside** is land which is away from towns and cities. ❑ *...3,500 acres of mostly flat countryside.* **Nature** includes the landscape, the weather, animals, and plants, which are not created by man. ❑ *These creatures roamed the Earth as the finest and rarest wonders of nature.*

3 PHRASE If you have **a change of scenery**, you go somewhere different after being in a particular place for a long time. 换个环境 ❑ *A change of scenery might do you good.* 换个环境可能会对你有好处。

sce·nic /siːnɪk/ 1 ADJ A **scenic** place has attractive scenery. 风景优美的 ❑ *This is an extremely scenic part of America.* 这是美国风景极其优美的一个地区。 2 ADJ A **scenic** route goes through attractive scenery and has nice views. 观光的（路线）❑ *It was even marked on the map as a scenic route.* 它在地图上甚至被标明为一条观光路线。

★ **scent** /sɛnt/ (**scents, scenting, scented**) 1 N-COUNT The **scent** of something is the pleasant smell that it has. 香味 ❑ *Flowers are chosen for their scent as well as their look.* 花儿不仅凭外观也凭香味而被选中。 2 V-T If something **scents** a place or thing, it makes it smell pleasant. 使充满香味 ❑ *Jasmine flowers scent the air.* 茉莉花使空气充满芳香。 3 N-MASS **Scent** is a liquid which women put on their necks and wrists to make themselves smell nice. 香水 ❑ *She dabbed herself with scent.* 她在自己身上擦了点香水。 4 N-VAR The **scent** of a person or animal is the smell that they leave and that other people sometimes follow when looking for them. （人的）气味；（动物留下的）臭迹 ❑ *A police dog picked up the murderer's scent.* 一条警犬嗅出了凶手的气味。 5 V-T When an animal **scents** something, it becomes aware of it by smelling it. 嗅到 [no cont] ❑ *...dogs which scent the hidden birds.* …嗅到隐藏的鸟的狗。
→ see **flower**

scent·ed /sɛntɪd/ ADJ **Scented** things have a pleasant smell, either naturally or because perfume has been added to them. 芳香的 ❑ *The white flowers are pleasantly scented.* 那些白色的花芳香怡人。

scep·tic /skɛptɪk/ [mainly BRIT] → see **skeptic**

★ **scep·ti·cal** /skɛptɪkəl/ [mainly BRIT] → see **skeptical**

scep·ti·cism /skɛptɪsɪzəm/ [mainly BRIT] → see **skepticism**

sched·ule ♦♦◇ /skɛdʒul, -uəl/ (**schedules, scheduling, scheduled**) 1 N-COUNT A **schedule** is a plan that gives a list of events or tasks and the times at which each one should happen or be done. 日程安排 ❑ *He has been forced to adjust his schedule.* 他已被迫调整了日程安排。 2 N-UNCOUNT You can use **schedule** to refer to the time or way something is planned to be done. For example, if something is completed **on schedule**, it is completed at the time planned. 计划的时间 ❑ *The jet arrived in Johannesburg two minutes ahead of schedule.* 那架喷气式飞机比预定时间提前两分钟到达了约翰内斯堡。 ❑ *Everything went according to schedule.* 一切都是按计划进行的。 3 V-T If something **is scheduled** to happen at a particular time, arrangements are made for it to happen at that time. 计划；安排 [usu passive] ❑ *The space shuttle had been scheduled to blast off at 04:38.* 这架航天飞机计划于04:38发射升空。 ❑ *A presidential election was scheduled for last December.* 一场总统大选计划在去年12月举行。 4 N-COUNT A **schedule** is a written list of things, for example, a list of prices, details, or conditions. （价格、细节或条件的）明细表 ❑ *Ticket plans and a pricing schedule will not be released until later this year.* 售票计划和价目表要到今年晚些时候才会公布。 5 N-COUNT A **schedule** is a list of all the times when trains, boats, buses, or aircraft are supposed to arrive at or leave a particular place. 时刻表 [mainly AM]

in BRIT, usually use **timetable**

❑ *...a bus schedule.* …一份公共汽车时刻表。 6 N-COUNT In a school or college, a **schedule** is a diagram that shows the times in the week at which particular subjects are taught. 课程表 [AM]

in BRIT, usually use **timetable**

❑ *He began college with a schedule that included biology, calculus and political science.* 他开始了大学生活，课程表上包括生物、微积分和政治学。

Word Partnership *schedule* 的常用搭配：

ADJ. **busy** schedule, **hectic** schedule 1
regular schedule 1 5
N. **change of** schedule, schedule **of events**, **payment** schedule, **playoff** schedule, **work** schedule 1 4
bus schedule, **train** schedule 5
PREP. **according to** schedule, **ahead of** schedule, **behind** schedule, **on** schedule 2

scheme ♦♦◇ /skim/ (**schemes, scheming, schemed**) 1 N-COUNT A **scheme** is someone's plan for achieving something, especially something that will bring them some benefit. 计划 ❑ *...a quick money-making scheme to get us through the summer.* …一个能让我们迅速赚到钱以顺利度过这个夏季的计划。 ❑ *They would first have to work out some scheme for getting the treasure out.* 他们首先得想出某种计划把珍宝取出来。 2 V-T/V-I If you say that people **are scheming**, you mean that they are making secret plans in order to gain something for themselves. 密谋 [oft cont] [DISAPPROVAL] ❑ *Everyone's always scheming and plotting.* 每个人时刻都在算计和谋划。 ❑ *The bride's family were scheming to prevent a wedding.* 新娘的家人在密谋阻止婚礼。 3 N-COUNT A **scheme** is a plan or arrangement involving many people which is made by a government or other organization. （政府或其他机构的）大规模计划 [BRIT]

in AM, use **plan**, **program**

❑ ...*a private pension scheme.* …一个私人养老金计划。 **4** PHRASE When people talk about **the scheme of things** or **the grand scheme of things**, they are referring to the way that everything in the world seems to be organized. 天地万物的格局 ❑ *We realize that we are infinitely small within the scheme of things.* 我们认识到在大千世界中我们是极其渺小的。

Thesaurus *scheme* 另参见：
N. design, plan, strategy **1**

schizo·phre·nia /skɪtsəfriniə/ N-UNCOUNT **Schizophrenia** is a serious mental illness. People who suffer from it are unable to relate their thoughts and feelings to what is happening around them and often withdraw from society. 精神分裂症

schizo·phren·ic /skɪtsəfrɛnɪk/ (**schizophrenics**) N-COUNT A **schizophrenic** is a person who is suffering from schizophrenia. 精神分裂症患者 ❑ *He was diagnosed as a paranoid schizophrenic.* 他被诊断为偏执性精神分裂症患者。● ADJ **Schizophrenic** is also an adjective. 患精神分裂症的 ❑ ...*a schizophrenic patient.* …一位精神分裂症患者。

Word Link *schol ≈ school : scholar, scholarship, scholastic*

schol·ar /skɒlər/ (**scholars**) N-COUNT A **scholar** is a person who studies an academic subject and knows a lot about it. 学者 [FORMAL] ❑ *The library attracts thousands of scholars and researchers.* 这家图书馆吸引了数千名学者和研究人员。
→ see **history**

★ **schol·ar·ly** /skɒlərli/ **1** ADJ A **scholarly** person spends a lot of time studying and knows a lot about academic subjects. 好学的；博学的 ❑ *He was an intellectual, scholarly man.* 他是一个聪明博学的人。 **2** ADJ A **scholarly** book or article contains a lot of academic information and is intended for academic readers. (书籍或文章) 学术的 ❑ ...*the more scholarly academic journals.* …学术性较强的学术期刊。 **3** ADJ **Scholarly** matters and activities involve people who do academic research. (问题或活动) 学术性的 ❑ *This has been the subject of intense scholarly debate.* 这一直是学术讨论的热门话题。

schol·ar·ship /skɒlərʃɪp/ (**scholarships**) **1** N-COUNT If you get a **scholarship** to a school or university, your studies are paid for by the school or university or by some other organization. 奖学金 ❑ *He got a scholarship to the Pratt Institute of Art.* 他得到了一笔普拉特艺术学院的奖学金。 **2** N-UNCOUNT **Scholarship** is serious academic study and the knowledge that is obtained from it. 学术研究；学问成就 ❑ *I want to take advantage of your lifetime of scholarship.* 我想从您一生的学术成就中获益。

scho·las·tic /skəlæstɪk/ ADJ Your **scholastic** achievement or ability is your academic achievement or ability while you are at school. 学业的；学术的 [ADJ n] [FORMAL] ❑ ...*the values which encouraged her scholastic achievement.* …激励了她的学术成就的价值观。

school ♦♦♦ /skul/ (**schools, schooling, schooled**) **1** N-VAR A **school** is a place where children are educated. You usually refer to this place as **school** when you are talking about the time that children spend there and the activities that they do there. 学校 ❑ ...*a boy who was in my class at school.* …上学时我班上的一个男孩。 ❑ *Even the good students say homework is what they most dislike about school.* 就连好学生也说家庭作业是他们最讨厌学校的一点。 ❑ ...*a school built in the Sixties.* …一所建于六十年代的学校。

In public education in the United States, most schools are **co-educational** or **coed**, that is they allow both male and female students to enroll. Schools that are not coed are usually private schools.

2 N-COUNT-COLL A **school** is the students or staff at a school. 全校师生 ❑ *Deirdre, the whole school's going to hate you.* 迪尔德丽，全校师生都要恨你了。 **3** N-COUNT; N-IN-NAMES A privately-run place where a particular skill or subject is taught can be referred to as a **school**. 私立专科学校 ❑ ...*a riding school.* …一所私立骑术学校。 **4** N-VAR; N-IN-NAMES A university, college, or university department specializing in a particular type of subject can be referred to as a **school**. 学院；系 ❑ ...*a lecturer in the school of veterinary medicine at the University of Pennsylvania.* …宾夕法尼亚大学兽医学系的一名讲师。 **5** N-UNCOUNT **School** is used to refer to college. 大学 [AM] ❑ *Jack eventually graduated from school, got married, and got his first real job.* 杰克终于大学毕了业，结了婚，找到了第一份真正的工作。 **6** N-COUNT-COLL A particular **school of** writers, artists, or thinkers is a group of them whose work, opinions, or theories are similar. 学派；流派 [usu with supp] ❑ ...*the Chicago school of economists.* …芝加哥经济学派。 **7** V-T If you **school** someone **in** something, you train or educate them to have a certain skill, type of behavior, or way of thinking. 训练；教育 [WRITTEN] ❑ *Many mothers schooled their daughters in the myth of female inferiority.* 许多母亲用男尊女卑的错误观念教育女儿。 **8** → see also **schooling, boarding school, grade school, graduate school, grammar school, high school, nursery school, prep school, primary school, private school, public school, state school**

school board (**school boards**) N-COUNT-COLL A **school board** is a committee in charge of education in a particular city or area, or in a particular school, especially in the United States. 地方教育董事会 [AM] ❑ *Colonel Richard Nelson served on the school board until this year.* 理查德・纳尔逊上校在地方教育董事会任职至今年为止。

school·boy /skulbɔɪ/ (**schoolboys**) N-COUNT A **schoolboy** is a boy who goes to school. 男学生

school·child /skultʃaɪld/ (**schoolchildren**) N-COUNT **Schoolchildren** are children who go to school. 小学生 ❑ *Last year I had an audience of schoolchildren and they laughed at everything.* 去年我有一群小学生听众，他们听到什么都哈哈大笑。

school·days /skuldeɪz/ also **school days** N-PLURAL Your **schooldays** are the period of your life when you were at school. 学生时代 ❑ *He was happily married to a girl he had known since his schooldays.* 他和一个从学生时代就认识的女孩幸福地结了婚。

school friend (**school friends**) also **schoolfriend** N-COUNT A **school friend** is a friend of yours who is at the same school as you, or who used to be at the same school when you were children. 同窗好友 ❑ *I spent the evening with an old school friend.* 我和一位老同学一起度过了那个夜晚。

school·girl /skulgɜrl/ (**schoolgirls**) N-COUNT A **schoolgirl** is a girl who goes to school. 女学生 ❑ ...*half a dozen giggling schoolgirls.* …6个咯咯笑的女学生。

school·ing /skulɪŋ/ N-UNCOUNT **Schooling** is education that children receive at school. 学校教育 ❑ *His formal schooling continued erratically until he reached the age of eleven.* 他的正式学校教育断断续续地持续到了他11岁时。

school·teacher /skultitʃər/ (**schoolteachers**) N-COUNT A **schoolteacher** is a teacher in a school. 教师

Word Link *sci ≈ knowing : conscience, science, unconscious*

sci·ence ♦♦◊ /saɪəns/ (**sciences**) **1** N-UNCOUNT **Science** is the study of the nature and behavior of natural things and the knowledge that we obtain about them. 科学 ❑ *The best discoveries in science are very simple.* 科学上最好的发现都是非常简单的。 **2** N-COUNT A **science** is a particular branch of science such as physics, chemistry, or biology. (科学的) 学科 ❑ *Physics is the best example of*

S

Word Web science

Science is the study of the laws that govern the natural world. It uses **research** and **experiments** to try to explain various **phenomena**. Scientists follow the **scientific method** which begins with **observation** and measurement. Then they state a **hypothesis**, which is a possible explanation for the observations and measurements. Next, scientists make a **prediction**, which is a logical **deduction** based on the hypothesis. The last step is to conduct experiments which **prove** or **disprove** the hypothesis. Scientists construct and modify **theories** based on **empirical findings**. **Pure** science deals only with theories, while **applied** science has practical applications.

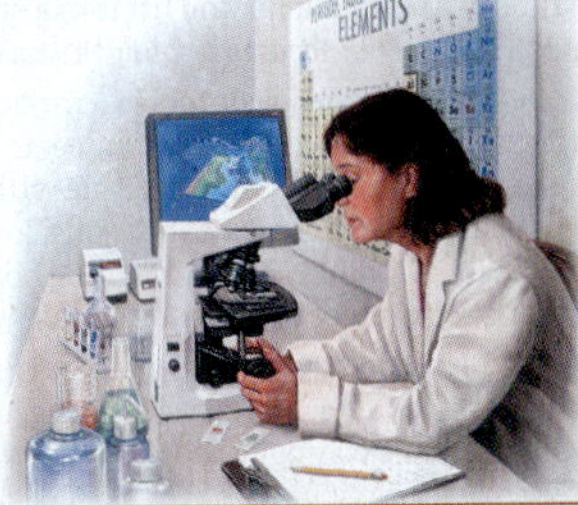

a science which has developed strong, abstract theories. 物理学是一个发展出了强有力的抽象理论的学科的最好例证。 **3** N-COUNT A **science** is the study of some aspect of human behavior, for example, sociology or anthropology. (人类行为的) 科学研究 ❏ *...the modern science of psychology.* …现代心理学。 **4** → see also **social science**
→ see Word Web: **science**

sci·ence fic·tion N-UNCOUNT **Science fiction** consists of stories in books, magazines, and movies about events that take place in the future or in other parts of the universe. 科幻作品

sci·en·tif·ic ♦◊◊ /saɪəntɪfɪk/ **1** ADJ **Scientific** is used to describe things that relate to science or to a particular science. 科学的 ❏ *Scientific research is widely claimed to be the source of the high standard of living in the U.S.* 在美国，科学研究被广泛宣称为高生活水平的来源。 ❏ *...the use of animals in scientific experiments.* …科学实验中对动物的使用。 ● **sci·en·tifi·cal·ly** /saɪəntɪfɪkli/ ADV 科学地 ❏ *...scientifically advanced countries.* …科学发达的国家。 **2** ADJ If you do something in a **scientific** way, you do it carefully and thoroughly, using experiments or tests. 仔细严谨的；使用科学方法的 ❏ *It's not a scientific way to test their opinions.* 这样检验他们的观点不是一个科学的方式。 ● **sci·en·tifi·cal·ly** ADV 细致严谨地；使用科学方法上 ❏ *Efforts are being made to research it scientifically.* 正在努力对它进行科学研究。

sci·en·tist ♦♦◊ /saɪəntɪst/ (**scientists**) N-COUNT A **scientist** is someone who has studied science and whose job is to teach or do research in science. 科学家 ❏ *Scientists say they've already collected more data than had been expected.* 科学家们说他们已经搜集到比预期更多的数据。

sci-fi /saɪ faɪ/ N-UNCOUNT **Sci-fi** is short for **science fiction.** 科幻作品 [INFORMAL] ❏ *...a two-and-a-half hour sci-fi film.* …一部两个半小时长的科幻影片。

scis·sors /sɪzərz/ N-PLURAL **Scissors** are a small cutting tool with two sharp blades that are screwed together. You use scissors for cutting things such as paper and cloth. 剪刀 [also "a pair of" N] ❏ *He told me to get some scissors.* 他叫我去拿几把剪刀。
→ see **office**

▲ **scoff** /skɒf/ (**scoffs, scoffing, scoffed**) V-I If you **scoff at** something, you speak about it in a way that shows you think it is ridiculous or inadequate. 嘲笑 ❏ *At first I scoffed at the notion.* 刚开始时我对那种想法嗤之以鼻。

scold /skoʊld/ (**scolds, scolding, scolded**) V-T If you **scold** someone, you speak angrily to them because they have done something wrong. 责骂 [FORMAL] ❏ *If he finds out, he'll scold me.* 如果他发现了，他会责骂我。 ❏ *Later she scolded her daughter for having talked to her father like that.* 后来她因女儿对她父亲那样讲话而训斥了她。

▲ **scoop** /skuːp/ (**scoops, scooping, scooped**) **1** V-T If you **scoop** something from a container, you remove it with something such as a spoon. (用勺子) 舀 ❏ *...the sound of a spoon scooping dog food out of a can.* …用勺子从罐子里舀狗粮的声音。 **2** N-COUNT A **scoop** is an object like a spoon which is used for picking up a quantity of a food such as ice cream or an ingredient such as flour. 勺 ❏ *...a small ice-cream scoop.* …一把小冰淇淋勺。 **3** N-COUNT You can use **scoop** to refer to an exciting news story which is reported in one newspaper or on one television program before it appears anywhere else. 独家新闻 ❏ *...one of the biggest scoops in the history of newspapers.* …报业史上最大的独家新闻之一。 **4** V-T If you **scoop** a person or thing somewhere, you put your hands or arms under or around them and quickly move them there. (敏捷地) 抱住 ❏ *Michael knelt next to her and scooped her into his arms.* 迈克尔跪在她旁边，一下子把她抱在怀里。

▸ **scoop up** PHRASAL VERB If you **scoop** something **up**, you put your hands or arms under it and lift it in a quick movement. (敏捷地) 抱起来 ❏ *Use both hands to scoop up the leaves.* 用双手捧起叶子来。

scoot·er /skuːtər/ (**scooters**) **1** N-COUNT A **scooter** is a small light motorcycle which has a low seat. 小型摩托车 **2** N-COUNT A **scooter** is a type of child's bicycle which has two wheels joined by a wooden board and a handle on a long pole attached to the front wheel. The child stands on the board with one foot, and uses the other foot to move forward. 踏板车

scope /skoʊp/ **1** N-UNCOUNT If there is **scope for** a particular kind of behavior or activity, people have the opportunity to behave in this way or do that activity. 机会 ❏ *He believed in giving his staff scope for initiative.* 他赞成给他的员工主动的机会。 **2** N-SING The **scope of** an activity, topic, or piece of work is the whole area which it deals with or includes. 范围 ❏ *Mr. Dobson promised to widen the organization's scope of activity.* 多布森先生答应扩大该组织的活动范围。

S

scorch /skɔrtʃ/ (**scorches, scorching, scorched**) **1** V-T To **scorch** something means to burn it slightly. 烧焦 ❏ *The bomb scorched the side of the building.* 炸弹烧焦了建筑物的侧面。 ● **scorched** ADJ 烧焦的 ❏ *...scorched black earth.* …烧焦的黑土。 **2** V-T/V-I If something **scorches** or **is scorched**, it becomes marked or changes color because it is affected by too much heat or by a chemical. 使枯萎；变枯萎 ❏ *The leaves are inclined to scorch in hot sunshine.* 树叶在炙热的阳光下易变枯黄。

scorch·ing /skɔrtʃɪŋ/ ADJ **Scorching** or **scorching hot** weather or temperatures are very hot indeed. 酷热的 [INFORMAL, EMPHASIS] ❏ *That race was run in scorching weather.* 那次赛跑是在酷热的天气里进行的。

> In informal English, if you want to emphasize how hot the weather is, you can say that it is **boiling** or **scorching**. In winter, if the temperature is above average, you can say that it is **mild**. In general, **hot** suggests a higher temperature than **warm**, and **warm** things are usually pleasant. ❏ *...a warm evening.*

score ♦♦◊ /skɔr/ (**scores, scoring, scored**)

> In meaning **9**, the plural form is **score**.

1 V-T/V-I In a sport or game, if a player **scores** a goal or a point, they gain a goal or point. (比赛中) 得分；进球 ❏ *Patten scored his second touchdown of the game.* 帕顿在比赛中第2次持球触地得分。 ❏ *He scored late in the third quarter to cut the gap to 10 points.* 他在第3节快结束时进了一球，把分差缩小到10分。 **2** V-T/V-I If you **score** a particular number or amount, for example, as a mark in a test, you achieve that number or amount. (测试) 得分 ❏ *Kelly had scored an average of 147 on three separate IQ tests.* 凯利在3次单独进行的智商测试中平均得到147分。 ❏ *Congress scores low in public opinion polls.* 国会在民意测验中得分很低。 **3** N-COUNT Someone's **score** in a game or test is a number, for example, a number of points or runs, which shows what they have achieved or what level they have reached. 得分；分数 ❏ *The U.S. Open golf tournament was won by Ben Hogan, with a score of 287.* 美国高尔夫球公开赛由本·霍根以287分夺冠。 ❏ *He won this year's title with a score of 9.687.* 他以9.687分赢得本年度的冠军。 **4** N-COUNT The **score** in a game is the result of it or the current situation, as indicated by the number of goals, runs, or points obtained by the two teams or players. 比分 ❏ *4-1 was the final score.* 最终比分是4:1。 ❏ *They beat the Giants by a score of 7 to 3.* 他们以7比3战胜了巨人队。 **5** V-T If you **score** a success, a victory, or a hit, you are successful in what you are doing. 赢得 [WRITTEN] ❏ *His abiding passion was ocean racing, at which he scored many successes.* 他长期的爱好是海上赛艇，并曾赢得多次胜利。 **6** N-COUNT The **score** of a movie, play, or similar production is the music which is written or used for it. (电影、戏剧等演出的) 配乐 ❏ *The dance is accompanied by an original score by Henry Torgue.* 舞蹈由亨利·托尔格的一支原创配乐作搭配。 **7** N-COUNT The **score** of a piece of music is the written version of it. 乐谱 ❏ *He recognizes enough notation to be able to follow a score.* 他认识足够多的音乐符号，能看懂乐谱。 **8** QUANT If you refer to **scores of** things or people, you are emphasizing that there are very many of them. 大量 [QUANT "of" pl-n] [WRITTEN, EMPHASIS] ❏ *Campaigners lit scores of bonfires in ceremonies to mark the anniversary.* 参加活动的人们在仪式上点起了许多堆篝火，以庆祝这一周年纪念日。 **9** NUM A **score** is twenty or approximately twenty. 二十；二十左右 [WRITTEN] ❏ *A score of countries may be either producing or planning to obtain chemical weapons.* 约有二十个国家可能在生产或计划获取化学武器。 **10** V-T If you **score** a surface with something sharp, you cut a line or number of lines in it. 划线于；刻痕于 ❏ *Lightly score the surface of the steaks with a sharp cook's knife.* 用一把锋利的菜刀在牛排表面上轻轻打花刀。 **11** PHRASE If you **keep score** of the number of things that are happening in a certain situation, you count them and record them. 记数 ❏ *You can keep score of your baby's movements before birth by recording them on a kick chart.* 你可以在胎动图表上记下分娩前胎儿的活动次数。 **12** PHRASE If you **know the score**, you know what the real facts of a situation are and how they affect you, even though you may not like them. 了解实情 [SPOKEN] ❏ *I don't feel sorry for Carl. He knew the score, he knew what he had to do and couldn't do it.* 我并不为卡尔感到难过。他了解实情，他知道他必须做什么，但又没能做成。 **13** PHRASE You can use **on that score** or **on this score** to refer to something that has just been mentioned, especially an

area of difficulty or concern. 在那/这一点上 ❑ *I became pregnant easily. At least I've had no problems on that score.* 我很容易就怀孕了。至少在那一点上我是没问题的。 14 PHRASE If you **settle a score** or **settle an old score with** someone, you take revenge on them for something they have done in the past. 报复 ❑ *The groups had historic scores to settle with each other.* 这两伙人之间有一些陈年老账要算。
→ see **music**

score·board /skɔrbɔrd/ (**scoreboards**) N-COUNT A **scoreboard** is a large board, for example, at a sports arena or stadium, which shows the score in a game or competition. 记分牌 ❑ *The figures flash up on the scoreboard.* 数字在记分牌上闪亮。

scor·er /skɔrər/ (**scorers**) 1 N-COUNT In football, hockey, and many other sports and games, a **scorer** is a player who scores a goal, runs, or points. 得分者; 进球者 ❑ *...David Hirst, the scorer of 11 goals this season.* …戴维・赫斯特，本赛季进了11个球的得分手。 2 N-COUNT A **scorer** is an official who writes down the score of a game or competition as it is being played. 记分员

★ **scorn** /skɔrn/ (**scorns, scorning, scorned**) 1 N-UNCOUNT If you treat someone or something **with scorn**, you show contempt for them. 轻蔑; 鄙视 ❑ *Researchers greeted the proposal with scorn.* 研究者们对这个提议报以轻蔑的态度。 2 V-T If you **scorn** someone or something, you feel or show contempt for them. 鄙视; 看不起 ❑ *Several leading officers have quite openly scorned the peace talks.* 几名高级官员曾相当公开地鄙视和平谈判。 3 V-T If you **scorn** something, you refuse to have it or accept it because you think it is not good enough or suitable for you. 摈弃 ❑ *...people who scorned traditional methods.* …摈弃传统做法的人们。

scorn·ful /skɔrnfəl/ ADJ If you are **scornful** of someone or something, you show contempt for them. 轻蔑的; 嘲笑的 ❑ *He is deeply scornful of politicians.* 他对政客是很不屑的。

scotch /skɒtʃ/ (**scotches, scotching, scotched**) V-T If you **scotch** a rumor, plan, or idea, you put an end to it before it can develop any further. 结束; 制止 ❑ *They have scotched rumors that they are planning a special show.* 他们辟谣说他们并没有在筹划一场特别的演出。

Scotch /skɒtʃ/ (**Scotches**) N-MASS **Scotch** or **Scotch whisky** is whiskey made in Scotland. 苏格兰威士忌 ❑ *...a bottle of Scotch.* …一瓶苏格兰威士忌。 ● N-COUNT A **Scotch** is a glass of Scotch. 一杯苏格兰威士忌。 ❑ *He poured himself a Scotch.* 他给自己倒了一杯苏格兰威士忌。

scot-free /skɒt fri/ ADV If you say that someone got away **scot-free**, you are emphasizing that they escaped punishment for something that you believe they should have been punished for. 免于受罚地; 安然无恙地 [ADV after V] [EMPHASIS] ❑ *Others who were guilty were being allowed to get off scot-free.* 其他有罪的人获准免于受罚。

▲ **scour** /skaʊər/ (**scours, scouring, scoured**) 1 V-T If you **scour** something such as a place or a book, you make a thorough search of it to try to find what you are looking for. 四处搜索 ❑ *Rescue crews had scoured an area of 30 square miles.* 救援人员已经搜遍了30平方英里的范围。 2 V-T If you **scour** something such as a sink, floor, or pan, you clean its surface by rubbing it hard with something rough. (费力地) 擦洗 ❑ *He decided to scour the sink.* 他决定把水池擦洗干净。

▲ **scourge** /skɜrdʒ/ (**scourges, scourging, scourged**) 1 N-COUNT A **scourge** is something that causes a lot of trouble or suffering to a group of people. 灾难 [oft N "of" n] ❑ *...the best chance in 20 years to end the scourge of terrorism.* …20年来结束恐怖主义灾难的最佳机会。 2 V-T If something **scourges** a place or group of people, it causes great pain and suffering to people. 折磨 ❑ *Economic anarchy scourged the post-war world.* 经济混乱蹂躏战后世界。

scout /skaʊt/ (**scouts, scouting, scouted**) 1 N-COUNT A **scout** is someone who is sent to an area of countryside to find out the position of an enemy army. 侦察员 ❑ *They set off, two men out in front as scouts, two behind in case of any attack from the rear.* 他们出发了，两人在前作为侦察员，两人殿后以防后方攻击。 2 V-T/V-I If you **scout** somewhere **for** something, you go through that area searching for it. 搜寻 ❑ *I wouldn't have time to scout the area for junk.* 我不会有时间在那个地区找废物。 ❑ *A team of four was sent to scout for a nuclear test site.* 一个四人小组被派去寻找核试验基地。

▲ **scowl** /skaʊl/ (**scowls, scowling, scowled**) V-I When someone **scowls**, an angry or hostile expression appears on their face. 作怒容; 绷着脸 ❑ *He scowled, and slammed the door behind him.* 他怒气冲冲，摔门而去。 ● N-COUNT **Scowl** is also a noun. 怒容 ❑ *Chris met the remark with a scowl.* 克里斯听到这句话面带怒容。

★ **scram·ble** /skræmbəl/ (**scrambles, scrambling, scrambled**) 1 V-I If you **scramble** over rocks or up a hill, you move quickly over them or up it using your hands to help you. 攀爬 ❑ *Tourists were scrambling over the rocks looking for the perfect camera angle.* 旅行者们爬上岩石，寻找最完美的拍摄角度。 2 V-I If you **scramble** to a different place or position, you move there in a hurried, awkward way. 仓促行动 ❑ *Ann threw back the covers and scrambled out of bed.* 安掀开被子，急忙下了床。 3 V-T/V-I If a number of people **scramble for** something, they compete energetically with each other for it. 争夺 ❑ *More than three million fans are expected to scramble for tickets.* 预计会有三百万以上的歌迷抢购门票。 ● N-COUNT **Scramble** is also a noun. 争夺 ❑ *...the scramble for jobs.* …工作的竞争。 4 V-T If you **scramble** eggs, you break them, mix them together and then cook them in butter. 炒 (蛋) ❑ *Make the toast and scramble the eggs.* 烤面包，炒鸡蛋。 ● **scram·bled** ADJ 炒的 ❑ *...scrambled eggs and bacon.* …炒蛋和熏咸肉。 5 V-T If a device **scrambles** a radio or telephone message, it interferes with the sound so that the message can only be understood by someone with special equipment. 对 (无线电或电话信号) 作扰频处理 ❑ *The system lets you encrypt or scramble the data that's sent between machines.* 这个系统可以让你对机器间互发的数据作加密或扰频处理。
→ see **egg**

★ **scrap** /skræp/ (**scraps, scrapping, scrapped**) 1 N-COUNT A **scrap of** something is a very small piece or amount of it. 小块; 碎片 ❑ *A crumpled scrap of paper was found in her handbag.* 在她的手提包里找到了一张弄皱的小纸片。 2 N-PLURAL **Scraps** are pieces of unwanted food which are thrown away or given to animals. 残羹剩饭 ❑ *...the scraps from the Sunday dinner table.* …周日餐桌上的残羹剩饭。 3 V-T If you **scrap** something, you get rid of it or cancel it. 取消; 放弃 [JOURNALISM] ❑ *President Hussein called on all countries in the Middle East to scrap nuclear or chemical weapons.* 侯赛因总统呼吁中东各国放弃核武器或化学武器。 4 ADJ **Scrap** metal or paper is no longer wanted for its original purpose, but may have some other use. 废弃的; 剩余的 [ADJ n] ❑ *There's always tons of scrap paper in Dad's office.* 爸爸的办公室里总有大量的废纸。 5 N-UNCOUNT **Scrap** is metal from old or damaged machinery or cars. 废金属 ❑ *Thousands of tanks, artillery pieces and armored vehicles will be cut up for scrap.* 成千上万的坦克、大炮和装甲车将被切割成废金属。 6 N-UNCOUNT You can refer to a fight or a quarrel as a **scrap**, especially if it is not very serious. 打架; 斗嘴 [INFORMAL] ❑ *He had suffered a mild concussion in a scrap for a loose ball.* 在一次争球引起的打架中他被打成轻度脑震荡。 ● V-I **Scrap** is also a verb. 打架; 斗嘴 ❑ *Our guys scrapped and competed and went right to the wire.* 我们的小伙子们一边吵着，一边比赛，一直到比赛结束。

scrap·book /skræpbʊk/ (**scrapbooks**) N-COUNT A **scrapbook** is a book with empty pages on which you can stick things such as pictures or newspaper articles in order to keep them. 剪贴簿 ❑ *...a large scrapbook of press clippings and photographs.* …一大本贴着剪报和照片的剪贴簿。

scrape /skreɪp/ (**scrapes, scraping, scraped**) 1 V-T If you **scrape** something from a surface, you remove it, especially by pulling a sharp object over the surface. 刮掉 ❑ *She went around the car scraping the frost off the windows.* 她绕着车刮掉车窗上的霜。 2 V-T/V-I If something **scrapes** against something else, it rubs against it, making a noise or causing slight damage. 刮擦 ❑ *The only sound is that of knives and forks scraping against china.* 惟一的声音是刀叉刮擦瓷器的声音。 ❑ *The car hurtled past us, scraping the wall and screeching to a halt.* 那辆汽车从我们身旁疾驰而过，刮擦着墙嘎然停下。 3 V-T If you **scrape** a part of your body, you accidentally rub it against something hard and rough, and damage it slightly. 擦伤 ❑ *She stumbled and fell, scraping her palms and knees.* 她绊了一跤摔倒了，擦伤了双掌和双膝。

▸ **scrape through** PHRASAL VERB If you **scrape through** an examination, you just succeed in passing it. If you **scrape through** a competition or a vote, you just succeed in winning it. 勉强通过 (考试); 勉强赢得 (竞赛或选举) ❑ *He was a poor student, barely scraping through his final year.* 他是个差生，仅勉强修完最后一年。

▸ **scrape together** PHRASAL VERB If you **scrape together** an amount of money or a number of things, you succeed in obtaining it with difficulty. 艰难地凑齐 (一笔钱等) ❑ *They only just managed to scrape the money together.* 他们只刚好设法勉强凑够了那笔钱。

scrap·heap /skræphip/ also **scrap heap** 1 N-SING If you say that someone has been thrown on **the scrapheap**, you mean that they have been forced to leave their job by an uncaring employer

S

and are unlikely to get other work. 被解雇人群 ❑ *Thousands of miners have been thrown on the scrapheap with no jobs and no prospects.* 数千矿工被解雇，没有工作，也没有前途。 2 N-SING If things such as machines or weapons are thrown on **the scrapheap**, they are thrown away because they are no longer needed. 废物堆 ❑ *Thousands of Europe's tanks and guns are going to the scrap heap.* 成千上万的欧洲坦克和枪炮将被废弃。

scratch /skrætʃ/ (**scratches, scratching, scratched**) 1 V-T If you **scratch yourself**, you rub your fingernails against your skin because it is itching. 挠 ❑ *He scratched himself under his arm.* 他在自己腋下挠了挠。 ❑ *The old man lifted his cardigan to scratch his side.* 那位老人撩起他的开襟毛衣挠了挠身子侧面。 2 V-T If a sharp object **scratches** someone or something, it makes small shallow cuts on their skin or surface. 划破 ❑ *The branches tore at my jacket and scratched my hands and face.* 那些树枝挂了我的夹克，划破了我的双手和脸。 3 N-COUNT **Scratches** on someone or something are small shallow cuts. 划伤 ❑ *The seven-year-old was found crying with scratches on his face and neck.* 那个7岁的孩子被找到时正在哭，脸上和颈上都有划伤。 4 PHRASE If you do something **from scratch**, you do it without making use of anything that has been done before. 从零开始 ❑ *Building a home from scratch can be both exciting and challenging.* 白手起家既激动人心又具有挑战性。 5 PHRASE If you say that someone is **scratching** their **head**, you mean that they are thinking hard and trying to solve a problem or puzzle. 绞尽脑汁思考 ❑ *The Institute spends a lot of time scratching its head about how to boost American productivity.* 这家研究所花大量时间绞尽脑汁思考怎样推进美国的生产力。

scratch card (**scratch cards**) also **scratchcard** N-COUNT A **scratch card** is a card with hidden words or symbols on it. You scratch the surface off to reveal the words or symbols and find out if you have won a prize. (刮开表层查看是否中奖的) 刮刮卡

scrawl /skrɔl/ (**scrawls, scrawling, scrawled**) 1 V-T If you **scrawl** something, you write it in a careless and messy way. 潦草地写 ❑ *He scrawled a hasty note to his wife.* 他草草写了张便条给他妻子。 ❑ *Someone had scrawled "Scum" on his car.* 有人已在他的车上涂写了"人渣"字样。 2 N-VAR You can refer to writing that looks careless and messy as a **scrawl**. 潦草的字迹 ❑ *The letter was handwritten, in a hasty, barely decipherable scrawl.* 这封信是手写的，字迹潦草，几乎无法辨认。

scrawny /skrɔni/ (**scrawnier, scrawniest**) ADJ If you describe a person or animal as **scrawny**, you mean that they look unattractive because they are so thin. 瘦骨嶙峋的 [DISAPPROVAL] ❑ *...a scrawny woman with dyed black hair.* …一个留着染成黑色的头发、瘦骨嶙峋的女人。

scream ♦◇◇ /skrim/ (**screams, screaming, screamed**) 1 V-I When someone **screams**, they make a very loud, high-pitched cry, for example, because they are in pain or are very frightened. (人因痛苦或恐惧而) 尖叫 ❑ *Women were screaming; some of the houses nearest the bridge were on fire.* 女人们在尖叫；最靠近桥的一些房屋在燃烧。 ● N-COUNT **Scream** is also a noun. 尖叫 ❑ *Hilda let out a scream.* 希尔达发出了一声尖叫。 2 V-T If you **scream** something, you shout it in a loud, high-pitched voice. 尖声说 ❑ *"Brigid!" she screamed. "Get up!"* "布里吉德！"她尖声叫道。"起床！"

S

▲ **screech** /skritʃ/ (**screeches, screeching, screeched**) 1 V-I If a vehicle **screeches** somewhere or if its tires **screech**, its tires make an unpleasant high-pitched noise on the road. (车辆轮胎摩擦路面而) 发嘎吱声 ❑ *A black Mercedes screeched to a halt beside the helicopter.* 一辆黑色梅赛德斯轿车在那辆直升机旁嘎然停下。 2 V-T When you **screech** something, you shout it in a loud, unpleasant, high-pitched voice. (人) 尖声喊 ❑ *"Get me some water, Jeremy!" I screeched.* "给我弄些水，杰里米！"我尖声喊道。 ● N-COUNT **Screech** is also a noun. 尖声喊 ❑ *The figure gave a screech.* 那个人影发出了一声尖叫。 3 V-I When a bird, animal, or thing **screeches**, it makes a loud, unpleasant, high-pitched noise. (鸟、动物、物体等) 发出尖而刺耳的叫声 ❑ *A macaw screeched at him from its perch.* 一只金刚鹦鹉从栖枝上冲他尖叫。 ● N-COUNT **Screech** is also a noun. (鸟、动物、物体等发出的) 尖而刺耳的叫声 ❑ *He heard the screech of brakes.* 他听到了刹车的尖而刺耳声。

screen ♦♦◇ /skrin/ (**screens, screening, screened**) 1 N-COUNT A **screen** is a flat vertical surface on which pictures or words are shown. Television sets and computers have screens, and movies are shown on a screen in movie theaters. (电视、电脑、影院等的) 屏幕 2 → see also **widescreen** 3 N-SING You can refer to movies or television as **the screen**. 影视 ["the" N, also "on/off" N] ❑ *Many viewers have strong opinions about violence on the screen.* 许多观众对影视暴力有强烈意见。 4 V-T When a movie or a television program **is screened**, it is shown in the movie theater or broadcast on television. 上映 (影片)；播放 (电视节目) ❑ *The series is likely to be screened in January.* 这部系列剧可能在1月份播放。 ● **screen·ing** N-COUNT (**screenings**) 放映；播放 ❑ *The film-makers will be present at the screenings to introduce their works.* 电影制作人将在放映时到场介绍他们的作品。 5 N-COUNT A **screen** is a vertical panel which can be moved around. It is used to keep cold air away from part of a room, or to create a smaller area within a room. 屏风 ❑ *They put a screen in front of me so I couldn't see what was going on.* 他们在我面前放置了一扇屏风，因此我看不见在发生什么。 6 V-T If something **is screened by** another thing, it is behind it and hidden by it. 屏蔽；遮挡 [usu passive] ❑ *Most of the road behind the hotel was screened by an apartment block.* 旅馆后面那条路的大部分都被一排公寓楼挡住了。 7 V-I To **screen for** a disease means to examine people to make sure that they do not have it. (为确定是否患有某病而) 做检查 ❑ *...a quick saliva test that would screen for people at risk of tooth decay.* …一项能查出有患牙蚀风险的人群的快速唾液化验。 ● **screen·ing** N-VAR 检查 ❑ *Our country has an enviable record on breast screening for cancer.* 我们国家在乳腺癌检查方面有着令人羡慕的纪录。 8 V-T When an organization **screens** people who apply to join it, it investigates them to make sure that they are not likely to cause problems. 审查 (申请加入者) ❑ *They will screen all their candidates.* 他们将审查他们所有的求职者。 9 V-T To **screen** people or luggage means to check them using special equipment to make sure they are not carrying a weapon or a bomb. (为确保没有携带武器等而) 检查 (人、行李) ❑ *The airline had not been searching unaccompanied baggage by hand, but only screening it on X-ray machines.* 这家航空公司一直没有手工检查非随身行李，只是在X光机上检查。
→ see **computer, television**

screen·play /skrinpleɪ/ (**screenplays**) N-COUNT A **screenplay** is the words to be spoken in a movie, and instructions about what will be seen in it. 电影剧本

screen·saver /skrinseɪvər/ (**screensavers**) also **screen saver** N-COUNT A **screensaver** is a moving picture which appears or is put on a computer screen when the computer is not used for a while. (计算机上的) 屏幕保护程序 [COMPUTING]

screen·writer /skrinraɪtər/ (**screenwriters**) N-COUNT A **screenwriter** is a person who writes screenplays. 电影剧本作家

screw /skru/ (**screws, screwing, screwed**) 1 N-COUNT A **screw** is a metal object similar to a nail, with a raised spiral line around it. You turn a screw using a screwdriver so that it goes through two things, for example, two pieces of wood, and fastens them together. 螺钉 ❑ *Each bracket is fixed to the wall with just three screws.* 每个托架只用3颗螺钉固定在墙上。 2 V-T/V-I If you **screw** something somewhere or if it **screws** somewhere, you fix it in place by means of a screw or screws. 用螺钉固定 ❑ *I had screwed the shelf on the wall myself.* 我自己用螺钉把架子固定在了墙上。 ❑ *Screw down any loose floorboards.* 用螺钉钉紧任何松动的地板。 3 ADJ A **screw** lid or fitting is one that has a raised spiral line on the inside or outside of it, so that it can be fixed in place by twisting. 带螺旋的 (盖子、配件等) [ADJ n] ❑ *...an ordinary jam jar with a screw lid.* …一个带螺旋盖的普通果酱罐。 4 V-T/V-I If you **screw** something somewhere or if it **screws** somewhere, you fix it in place by twisting it around and around. 拧紧 ❑ *"Yes, I know that," Kelly said, screwing the silencer onto the pistol.* "是的，我知道那事。"凯利一边把消音器拧到手枪上一边说道。 ❑ *Screw down the lid fairly tightly.* 把盖子拧到很紧。 5 V-T If you **screw** something such as a piece of paper **into** a ball, you squeeze it or twist it tightly so that it is in the shape of a ball. 把 (纸片等) 揉成 (一团) ❑ *He screwed the paper into a ball and tossed it into the fire.* 他把那片纸揉成一团扔进了火里。 6 V-T If you **screw** your face or your eyes **into** a particular expression, you tighten the muscles of your face to form that expression, for example, because you are in pain or because the light is too bright. 把 (脸、眼睛等) 扭曲成 (某表情) ❑ *He screwed his face into an expression of mock pain.* 他把他的脸扭曲成假痛苦状。 7 V-RECIP If someone **screws** someone else or if two people **screw**, they have sex together. 与…性交；性交 [INFORMAL, VULGAR] ❑ *"Are you screwing her?" she said.* "你是不是和她上床了？"她说。 8 V-T Some people use **screw** in expressions such as **screw you** or **screw that** to show that they are not concerned about someone or something or that they feel contempt for them. 去 (你、它等) 的 (表示不关心或蔑视) [only imper] [INFORMAL, VULGAR, FEELINGS] ❑ *Something inside me snapped. "Well, screw you then!"* 我忍不住爆发

了。"好，那么去你的吧！" **9** V-T If someone **screws** something, especially money, **out of** you, they get it from you by putting pressure on you. 敲诈 [INFORMAL] ❑ *After decades of rich nations screwing money out of poor nations, it's about time some went the other way.* 富国从穷国敲诈钱财已数十年，该是有些国家反其道而行之的时候了。

▸ **screw up** **1** PHRASAL VERB If you **screw up** your eyes or your face, you tighten your eye or face muscles, for example, because you are in pain or because the light is too bright. (因痛苦、光太强等) 锁起 (眼睛、脸) ❑ *She had screwed up her eyes, as if she found the sunshine too bright.* 她已眯起眼睛，似乎她发现阳光太强。 ❑ *Close your eyes and screw them up tight.* 合上你的双眼，把它们紧紧闭上。 **2** PHRASAL VERB If you **screw up** a piece of paper, you squeeze it tightly so that it becomes very creased and no longer flat, usually when you are throwing it away. 把 (纸片) 揉成团 ❑ *He would start writing to his family and would screw the letter up in frustration.* 他一次次开始给家里写信，又一次次懊恼地把信揉成团。 **3** PHRASAL VERB To **screw** something **up**, or to **screw up**, means to cause something to fail or be spoiled. 弄糟；破坏 [INFORMAL] ❑ *You can't open the window because it screws up the air conditioning.* 你不能开窗，因为那样会破坏空调。 ❑ *Get out. Haven't you screwed things up enough already, you idiot!* 出去。难道你把事情弄得还不够糟吗？你这个白痴！

screw·driver /skrudraɪvər/ (**screwdrivers**) N-COUNT A **screwdriver** is a tool that is used for turning screws. It consists of a metal rod with a flat or cross-shaped end that fits into the top of the screw. 螺丝刀

→ see **tool**

screwed up ADJ If you say that someone is **screwed up**, you mean that they are very confused or worried, or that they have psychological problems. 心烦意乱的 [INFORMAL] ❑ *He was really screwed up with his emotional problems.* 他真的被感情问题弄得心烦意乱。

Word Link *scrib ≈ writing : inscribe, scribble, transcribe*

scrib·ble /skrɪbəl/ (**scribbles, scribbling, scribbled**) **1** V-T/V-I If you **scribble** something, you write it quickly and roughly. 草草地写 ❑ *She scribbled a note to tell Mom she'd gone out.* 她草草地写了个便条告诉妈妈，她出去了。 **2** V-I To **scribble** means to make meaningless marks or rough drawings using a pencil or pen. 乱涂乱画 ❑ *When Caroline was five she scribbled on a wall.* 卡罗琳5岁时在墙上乱涂乱画。 **3** N-VAR **Scribble** is something that has been written or drawn quickly and roughly. 潦草的字迹；胡乱的涂画 ❑ *I'm sorry what I wrote was such a scribble.* 很抱歉我写的东西太潦草了。

scrip /skrɪp/ (**scrips**) N-COUNT A **scrip** is a certificate which shows that an investor owns part of a share or stock. 股票临时凭证 [BUSINESS] ❑ *The cash or scrip would be offered as part of a pro rata return of capital to shareholders.* 现金或临时凭证会提供给股东作为资本按比例收益的一部分。

script ♦◇◇ /skrɪpt/ (**scripts, scripting, scripted**) **1** N-COUNT The **script** of a play, movie, or television program is the written version of it. 脚本 ❑ *Jenny's writing a film script.* 珍妮在写一个电影脚本。 **2** V-T The person who **scripts** a movie or a radio or television play writes it. 为(电影、广播、电视等) 写脚本 ❑ *...James Cameron, who scripted and directed both films.* …为这两部电影写脚本并执导的詹姆斯・卡梅伦。 **3** N-VAR You can refer to a particular system of writing as a particular **script**. 文字系统 [usu adj N] ❑ *...a text in the Malay language but written in Arabic script.* …一段用阿拉伯文书写的马来语文本。 **4** N-VAR **Script** is handwriting in which the letters are joined together. 连写体 ❑ *When you're writing in script, there are four letters of the alphabet that you can't complete in one stroke.* 当你用连写体书写时，字母表里有4个字母你不能一笔写完。

→ see **animation**

Word Link *script ≈ writing : manuscript, scripture, transcript*

scrip·ture /skrɪptʃər/ (**scriptures**) N-VAR **Scripture** or **the scriptures** refers to writings that are regarded as holy in a particular religion, for example, the Bible in Christianity. (宗教) 圣典 ❑ *...a quote from scripture.* …出自圣典的引文。

→ see **religion**

scroll /skroʊl/ (**scrolls, scrolling, scrolled**) **1** N-COUNT A **scroll** is a long roll of paper or a similar material with writing on it. (写有文字的) 卷轴 ❑ *Ancient scrolls were found in caves by the Dead Sea.* 在死海边的洞穴里发现了古代的卷轴。 **2** N-COUNT A **scroll** is a painted or carved decoration made to look like a scroll. 卷轴形装饰 ❑ *...a handsome suite of chairs incised with Grecian scrolls.* …一套漂亮的刻有古希腊式卷轴形装饰的椅子。 **3** V-I If you **scroll** through text on a computer screen, you move the text up or down to find the information that you need. (在计算机屏幕上的文本中) 滚动 [COMPUTING] ❑ *I scrolled down to find "United States of America."* 我向下滚动以寻找**United States of America**。

→ see **book**

scroll bar (**scroll bars**) N-COUNT On a computer screen, a **scroll bar** is a long thin box along one edge of a window, which you click on with the mouse to move the text up, down, or across the window. (计算机上的) 滚动条 [COMPUTING]

scrounge /skraʊndʒ/ (**scrounges, scrounging, scrounged**) V-T/V-I If you say that someone **scrounges** something such as food or money, you disapprove of them because they get it by asking for it, rather than by buying it or earning it. 讨要 (食物、钱等) [INFORMAL, DISAPPROVAL] ❑ *We managed to scrounge every piece of gear you requested.* 我们设法要来了你要求的每一件用具。

★ **scrub** /skrʌb/ (**scrubs, scrubbing, scrubbed**) **1** V-T If you **scrub** something, you rub it hard in order to clean it, using a stiff brush and water. 用力刷洗 ❑ *Surgeons began to scrub their hands and arms with soap and water before operating.* 外科医生们在手术前开始用肥皂和水清洗他们的手和手臂。 ● N-SING **Scrub** is also a noun. 用力刷洗 ❑ *The walls needed a good scrub.* 这些墙需要一次好好的刷洗。 **2** V-T If you **scrub** dirt or stains **off** something, you remove them by rubbing hard. (将污渍等从某物上) 用力擦 (除) ❑ *I started to scrub off the dirt.* 我开始用力擦除污物。 **3** N-UNCOUNT **Scrub** consists of low trees and bushes, especially in an area that has very little rain. (尤指少雨地区的) 矮灌木丛 ❑ *There is an area of scrub and woodland beside the railroad.* 那条铁路旁边有一片矮灌木丛和林地。 **4** N-PLURAL **Scrubs** are the protective clothes that surgeons and other hospital staff wear in operating rooms. 手术服 [mainly AM, INFORMAL] ❑ *...a man wearing blue hospital scrubs.* …一个穿着蓝色的医院手术服的男子。

scruffy /skrʌfi/ (**scruffier, scruffiest**) ADJ Someone or something that is **scruffy** is dirty and messy. 脏乱的 ❑ *...a young man, pale, scruffy and unshaven.* …一个面色苍白、邋里邋遢、胡子拉碴的年轻男子。

scrunch /skrʌntʃ/ (**scrunches, scrunching, scrunched**)

▸ **scrunch up** PHRASAL VERB If you **scrunch** something **up**, you squeeze it or bend it so that it is no longer in its natural shape and is often crushed. 压碎；弄弯 ❑ *She scrunched up three pages of notes and threw them in the bin.* 她把3页笔记揉成团并把它们扔进了垃圾箱。

scru·ple /skrupəl/ (**scruples**) N-VAR **Scruples** are moral principles or beliefs that make you unwilling to do something that seems wrong. 道德良知 ❑ *...a man with no moral scruples.* …一个毫无道德良知的男人。

scru·pu·lous /skrupyələs/ **1** ADJ Someone who is **scrupulous** takes great care to do what is fair, honest, or morally right. 讲良心的 [APPROVAL] ❑ *You're being very scrupulous, but to what end?* 你表现得很讲良心，但目的是什么呢？ ❑ *I have been scrupulous about telling them the dangers.* 我告诉他们这些危险是很讲良心的。 **2** ADJ **Scrupulous** means thorough, exact, and careful about details. 谨小慎微的 ❑ *Both readers commend Knutson for his scrupulous attention to detail.* 两位读者都称赞克努森对细节谨小慎微的关注。

S

▲ **scru·ti·nise** /skru:tɪnaɪz/ [BRIT] → see **scrutinize**

▲ **scru·ti·nize** /skrutənaɪz/ (**scrutinizes, scrutinizing, scrutinized**)

in BRIT, also use **scrutinise**

V-T If you **scrutinize** something, you examine it very carefully, often to find out some information from it or about it. 仔细察看 ❑ *Her purpose was to scrutinize his features to see if he was an honest man.* 她的目的是仔细察看他的特征看他是不是个诚实的人。

★ **scru·ti·ny** /skrutəni/ N-UNCOUNT If a person or thing is under **scrutiny**, they are being studied or observed very carefully. 仔细研究；仔细观察 ❑ *His private life came under media scrutiny.* 他的私生活开始受到媒体的密切关注。

scu·ba div·ing /skubə daɪvɪŋ/ N-UNCOUNT **Scuba diving** is the activity of swimming underwater using special breathing equipment. The equipment consists of cylinders of air which you carry on your back and which are connected to your mouth by rubber tubes. 戴水肺潜水

→ see Picture Dictionary: **scuba diving**

scuf·fle /skʌfəl/ (**scuffles, scuffling, scuffled**) **1** N-COUNT A **scuffle** is a short, disorganized fight or struggle. 打斗；混战 ❑ *Violent scuffles broke out between rival groups demonstrating for and*

Picture Dictionary scuba diving

scuba mask

air tank

pressure gauge

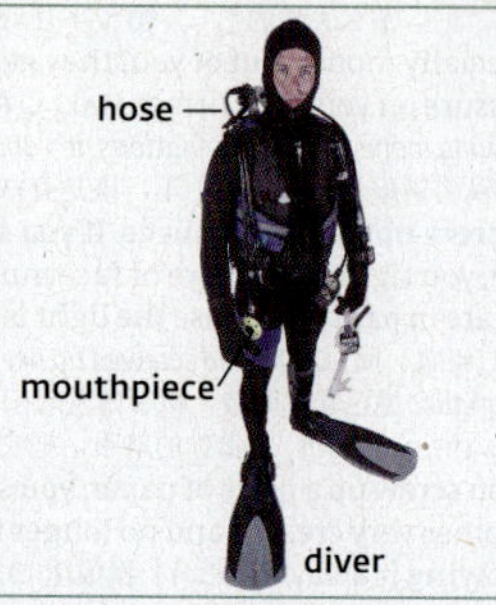

diver

against independence. 在支持和反对独立的两派示威者之间爆发了激烈混战。 2 V-RECIP If people **scuffle**, they fight for a short time in a disorganized way. 打斗；混战 ❑ *Police scuffled with some of the protesters.* 警察和一些抗议者打了起来。

sculpt /skʌlpt/ (**sculpts, sculpting, sculpted**) 1 V-T/V-I When an artist **sculpts**, or **sculpts** something, they carve or shape it out of a material such as stone or clay. 雕塑 ❑ *An artist sculpted a full-size replica of her head.* 一位艺术家雕塑了一尊她头部的全幅头像。 2 V-T If something **is sculpted**, it is made into a particular shape. 使成形 ❑ *More familiar landscapes have been sculpted by surface erosion.* 更多熟悉的地形是由地表侵蚀形成的。

sculp·tor /skʌlptər/ (**sculptors**) N-COUNT A **sculptor** is someone who creates sculptures. 雕塑家

★ **sculp·ture** /skʌlptʃər/ (**sculptures**) 1 N-VAR A **sculpture** is a work of art that is produced by carving or shaping stone, wood, clay, or other materials. 雕塑 ❑ *...stone sculptures of figures and animals.* …人物及动物石雕。 2 N-UNCOUNT **Sculpture** is the art of creating sculptures. 雕塑（艺术） ❑ *Both studied sculpture.* 两人都学过雕塑。

→ see **gallery**

scum /skʌm/ 1 N-PLURAL If you refer to people as **scum**, you are expressing your feelings of dislike and disgust for them. 令人厌恶的人 [INFORMAL, DISAPPROVAL] ❑ *She never would have even spoken to scum like him when Mom was alive.* 妈妈活着的时候她是绝不会和像他这样令人厌恶的人说话的。 2 N-UNCOUNT **Scum** is a layer of a dirty or unpleasant-looking substance on the surface of a liquid. （液体表面的）浮垢 ❑ *...scum marks around the bath.* …浴缸周围的垢迹。

scum·bag /skʌmbæg/ (**scumbags**) N-COUNT If you refer to someone as a **scumbag**, you are expressing your feelings of dislike and disgust for them. 令人讨厌的家伙 [INFORMAL, DISAPPROVAL]

scur·ry /skɜri/ (**scurries, scurrying, scurried**) V-I When people or small animals **scurry** somewhere, they move there quickly and hurriedly, especially because they are frightened. （尤指因受惊而）急促跑 [WRITTEN] ❑ *The attack began, sending residents scurrying for cover.* 袭击开始了，使得居民们急促奔跑寻找藏身之处。

scut·tle /skʌtᵊl/ (**scuttles, scuttling, scuttled**) 1 V-I When people or small animals **scuttle** somewhere, they run there with short quick steps. 碎步疾跑 ❑ *Two very small children scuttled away in front of them.* 两个很小的孩子在他们面前迈着又碎又快的步子跑开了。 2 V-T To **scuttle** a plan or a proposal means to make it fail or cause it to stop. 破坏（计划、提议） ❑ *Such threats could scuttle the peace conference.* 这样的威胁可能会破坏和平会议。

sea ♦♦◊ /si/ (**seas**) 1 N-SING **The sea** is the salty water that covers about three-quarters of the Earth's surface. 海洋 ["the" N, also "by" N] ❑ *Most of the kids have never seen the sea.* 这些孩子中的大多数从没见过大海。 2 N-PLURAL You use **seas** when you are describing the sea at a particular time or in a particular area. （某时、某区域的）海 [LITERARY] ❑ *He drowned after 30 minutes in the rough seas.* 他在波涛汹涌的海里挣扎了30分钟后溺死了。 3 N-COUNT; N-IN-NAMES A **sea** is a large area of salty water that is part of an ocean or is surrounded by land. （作为海洋的一部分的或陆地围起来的）海 ❑ *...the North Sea.* …北海。 4 PHRASE **At sea** means on or under the sea, far away from land. 在海上；在海里 ❑ *The boats remain at sea for an average of ten days at a time.* 这些船平均每次在海上呆10天。 5 PHRASE If you go or look out **to sea**, you go or look across the sea. 到海上/向海上 ❑ *...fishermen who go to sea for two weeks at a time.* …每次出海两周的渔民们。

Word Partnership *sea* 的常用搭配：

PREP. **above the sea, across the sea, below the sea, beneath the sea, by sea, from the sea, into the sea, near the sea, over the sea** 1
N. **sea air, sea coast, land and sea, sea voyage** 1
ADJ. **calm sea, deep sea** 1

sea·bed /sibɛd/ also **sea bed** N-SING **The seabed** is the ground under the sea. 海床 ❑ *The wreck was raised from the seabed in June 2000.* 沉船于2000年6月从海底打捞上来。

sea change (**sea changes**) N-COUNT A **sea change** in someone's attitudes or behavior is a complete change. （在态度、行为上的）彻底改变 ❑ *A sea change has taken place in young people's attitudes to their parents.* 年轻人对父母的态度已发生了彻底的改变。

sea·food /sifud/ (**seafoods**) N-UNCOUNT **Seafood** is shellfish such as lobsters, mussels, and crabs, and sometimes other sea creatures that you can eat. 海产食品 ❑ *...a seafood restaurant.* …一家海鲜餐馆。

sea·front /sifrʌnt/ (**seafronts**) N-COUNT **The seafront** is the part of a seaside town that is nearest to the sea. It usually consists of a road with buildings that face the sea. （城镇的）滨海区 ❑ *They decided to meet on the seafront.* 他们决定在滨海区见面。

sea·gull /sigʌl/ (**seagulls**) N-COUNT A **seagull** is a common kind of bird with white or gray feathers. 海鸥

1 **seal** ♦◊◊ /sil/ (**seals, sealing, sealed**) 1 V-T When you **seal** an envelope, you close it by folding part of it over and sticking it down, so that it cannot be opened without being torn. 封（信封） ❑ *He sealed the envelope and put on a stamp.* 他封好信封，贴了张邮票。 ❑ *Write your letter and seal it in a blank envelope.* 写好你的信，然后将其封入一个空信封。 2 V-T If you **seal** a container or an opening, you cover it with something in order to prevent air, liquid, or other material from getting in or out. If you **seal** something **in** a container, you put it inside and then close the container tightly. 封（容器、开口）；将（某物）封入（某容器中） ❑ *She filled the containers, sealed them with a cork, and stuck on labels.* 她装满那些容器，用塞子封了口，然后贴上了标签。 ❑ *A woman picks them up and seals them in plastic bags.* 一位女士拣起它们，然后把它们封入各塑料袋中。 3 N-COUNT The **seal** on a container or opening is the part where it has been sealed. （容器、开口等）封了的部分 ❑ *When assembling the pie, wet the edges where the two crusts join, to form a seal.* 捏合馅饼时，弄湿两块面皮封合的边缘，以形成一个封口。 4 N-COUNT A **seal** is a device or a piece of material, for example, in a machine, which closes an opening tightly so that air, liquid, or other substances cannot get in or out. （机器上防止气体或液体渗入或露出的）密封装置 [oft N "on" n] ❑ *Check seals on fridges and freezers regularly.* 定期检查冰箱和冰柜的密封装置。 5 N-COUNT A **seal** is something such as a piece of sticky paper or wax that is fixed to a container or door and must be broken before the container or door can be opened. （封条、封蜡等）封口物 [oft N "on" n] ❑ *The seal on the box broke when it fell from its hiding-place.* 盒子从隐藏处掉下时上面的封口破了。 6 N-COUNT A **seal** is a special mark or design, for example, on a document, representing someone or something. It may be used to show that something is genuine or officially approved. 印章

S

❑ *...a supply of note paper bearing the presidential seal.* …一批盖有总统印章的便条纸。 **7** V-T If someone in authority **seals** an area, they stop people entering or passing through it, for example, by placing barriers in the way. 封锁(某地区) ❑ *The soldiers were deployed to help paramilitary police seal the border.* 这些士兵们被调去协助准军事警察封锁边境。 ● PHRASAL VERB **Seal off** means the same as **seal**. 封锁(某地区) ❑ *Police and troops sealed off the area after the attack.* 警察和军队在袭击发生后封锁了该地区。 **8** V-T To **seal** something means to make it definite or confirm how it is going to be. 确定 [WRITTEN] ❑ *McLaren are close to sealing a deal with Renault.* 麦克拉伦即将和雷诺尔特达成一笔交易。 ❑ *A general election will be held which will seal his destiny one way or the other.* 一场将左右他命运的大选即将举行。

→ see **arctic, can**

▸ **seal off** **1** PHRASAL VERB If one object or area **is sealed off** from another, there is a physical barrier between them, so that nothing can pass between them. 封闭 ❑ *Windows are usually sealed off.* 窗户通常是封闭的。 **2** → see **seal ❶ 7**

❷ seal /siːl/ (**seals**) N-COUNT A **seal** is a large animal with a rounded body and flat legs called flippers. Seals eat fish and live in and near the sea, usually in cold parts of the world. 海豹

sea lev·el also **sea-level** N-UNCOUNT **Sea level** is the average level of the sea with respect to the land. The height of mountains or other areas is calculated in relation to **sea level**. 海平面 ❑ *The stadium was 5,000 feet above sea level.* 该体育场海拔5000英尺。 ❑ *The whole place is at sea level.* 整个地区与海平面持平。

→ see **glacier**

★ **seam** /siːm/ (**seams**) **1** N-COUNT A **seam** is a line of stitches which joins two pieces of cloth together. 缝合线 ❑ *The skirt ripped along a seam.* 那条裙子沿一条缝合线裂开了。 **2** N-COUNT A **seam** of coal is a long, narrow layer of it underneath the ground. (煤) 层 ❑ *The average coal seam here is three feet thick.* 这里的煤层平均为3英尺厚。 **3** PHRASE If something **is coming apart at the seams** or **is falling apart at the seams**, it is no longer working properly and may soon stop working completely. 散架；崩溃 ❑ *Our university system is in danger of falling apart at the seams.* 我们的大学体系处在崩溃的危险之中。 **4** PHRASE If a place is very full, you can say that it **is bursting at the seams**. 爆满 ❑ *The hotels of Warsaw, Prague and Budapest were bursting at the seams.* 华沙、布拉格和布达佩斯的旅馆已经爆满。

sea·man /siːmən/ (**seamen**) N-COUNT A **seaman** is a sailor, especially one who is not an officer. 海员 ❑ *The men emigrate to work as seamen.* 这些男人移居国外当海员。

seam·less /siːmlɪs/ ADJ You use **seamless** to describe something that has no breaks or gaps in it or which continues without stopping. 无缝的；不停顿的 ❑ *It was a seamless procession of wonderful electronic music.* 那是一曲流畅美妙的电子音乐。 ● **seam·less·ly** ADV 无缝地；不停顿地 [ADV with v] ❑ *It's a class move, allowing new and old to blend seamlessly.* 这是一次班级活动，让新老同学亲密无间地融合在一起。

search ♦♦◇ /sɜːrtʃ/ (**searches, searching, searched**) **1** V-I If you **search for** something or someone, you look carefully for them. 搜寻 ❑ *The Turkish security forces have started searching for the missing men.* 土耳其安全部队已经开始搜寻失踪人员。 ❑ *They searched for a spot where they could sit on the floor.* 他们在地板上寻找一个能够坐下的地方。 **2** V-T/V-I If you **search** a place, you look carefully for something or someone there. 在(某地) 搜寻；搜查(某地) ❑ *Armed troops searched the hospital yesterday.* 武装部队昨天搜查了这家医院。 ❑ *She searched her desk for the necessary information.* 她在她的书桌里搜寻必要的资料。 ❑ *Relief workers are still searching through collapsed buildings.* 救援人员仍在塌了的建筑物里搜寻。 **3** N-COUNT A **search** is an attempt to find something or someone by looking for them carefully. 搜寻 ❑ *There was no chance of him being found alive and the search was abandoned.* 没有他活着被找到的可能了，于是放弃了搜寻。 **4** V-T If a police officer or someone else in authority **searches** you, they look carefully to see whether you have something hidden on you. 搜(某人) 身 ❑ *The man took her suitcase from her and then searched her.* 那个人从她手上拿走了她的手提箱然后搜了她的身。 **5** V-I If you **search for** information on a computer, you give the computer an instruction to find that information. (在计算机上) 搜索 [COMPUTING] ❑ *You can use a directory service to search for people on the Internet.* 你可以使用目录服务在因特网上搜索人。 ● N-COUNT **Search** is also a noun. 搜索 ❑ *He came across this story while he was doing a computer search of local news articles.* 他在电脑上搜索地方新闻文章时碰到了这篇报道。 **6** → see also **searching** **7** PHRASE If you go **in search of** something or someone, you try to find them. 寻找 ❑ *Miserable, and unexpectedly lonely, she went in search of Jean-Paul.* 由于痛苦和突如其来的孤独，她去找让-保罗了。 **8** CONVENTION You say "**search me**" when someone asks you a question and you want to emphasize that you do not know the answer. 我哪知道 [INFORMAL, EMPHASIS] ❑ *"So why did he get interested all of a sudden?"—"Search me."* "那么他为什么突然感兴趣了呢？"——"我哪知道。"

Thesaurus *search* 另参见：

V. hunt, inspect, look for, seek **1 2**
N. exploration, hunt, inspection, quest **3**

Word Partnership *search* 的常用搭配：

N. search **for a job, talent** search, search **for the truth** **1**
search **an area**, search **for clues** **1 2**
search **for information** **1 2 5**
investigators search, **police** search, search **suspects** **4**
computer search, search **criteria**, search **the Internet, online** search **5**
V. **conduct a** search **3**

search en·gine (**search engines**) N-COUNT A **search engine** is a computer program that searches for documents containing a particular word or words on the Internet. (计算机) 搜索引擎 [COMPUTING]

search·ing /sɜːrtʃɪŋ/ ADJ A **searching** question or look is intended to discover the truth about something. 探寻的 (问题、目光) ❑ *They asked her some searching questions on moral philosophy and logic.* 他们就道德哲学和逻辑学问了她一些探寻性的问题。

search·light /sɜːrtʃlaɪt/ (**searchlights**) N-COUNT A **searchlight** is a large powerful light that can be turned to shine a long way in any direction. 探照灯 ❑ *Helicopters threw searchlights over the meadows and the lake.* 直升飞机将探照灯光投射在草地和湖上。

search par·ty (**search parties**) N-COUNT A **search party** is an organized group of people who are searching for someone who is missing. 搜寻队

search war·rant (**search warrants**) N-COUNT A **search warrant** is a special document that gives the police permission to search a house or other building. 搜查证 ❑ *Officers armed with a search warrant entered the apartment.* 持有搜查证的警官们进入了那间公寓。

sear·ing /sɪərɪŋ/ **1** ADJ **Searing** is used to indicate that something such as pain or heat is very intense. (疼痛、热量等) 强烈的 [ADJ n] ❑ *She woke to feel a searing pain in her feet.* 她醒来后感到脚上一阵剧烈疼痛。 **2** ADJ A **searing** speech or piece of writing is very critical. (话语、文字) 尖刻的 [ADJ n] ❑ *There's a searing column in today's paper about the president's decision.* 今天的报纸上有一篇关于总统的决定的尖刻的专栏文章。

sea·shell /siːʃɛl/ (**seashells**) N-COUNT **Seashells** are the empty shells of small sea creatures. 海贝壳 [usu pl]

sea·shore /siːʃɔr/ (**seashores**) N-COUNT **The seashore** is the part of a coast where the land slopes down into the sea. 海岸边 ❑ *She takes her inspiration from shells and stones she finds on the seashore.* 她从她在海岸边发现的贝壳和石头里获取灵感。

sea·sick /siːsɪk/ ADJ If someone is **seasick** when they are traveling in a boat, they vomit or feel sick because of the way the boat is moving. 晕船的 ❑ *It was quite rough at times, and she was seasick.* 海上有时波涛汹涌，她就晕船。 ● **sea·sick·ness** N-UNCOUNT 晕船 ❑ *He was very prone to seasickness and already felt queasy.* 他很容易晕船，此时已经感到恶心了。

sea·side /siːsaɪd/ N-SING You can refer to an area that is close to the sea, especially one where people go for their vacation, as **the seaside**. (尤指作为度假地的) 海边 ❑ *I went to spend a few days at the seaside.* 我去海边呆了几天。

sea·son ♦♦♦ /siːzᵊn/ (**seasons, seasoning, seasoned**) **1** N-COUNT The **seasons** are the main periods into which a year can be divided and which each have their own typical weather conditions. (一年中有某典型天气状况的) 季 ❑ *Fall is my favorite season.* 秋季是我最喜欢的季节。 ❑ *...the only region of Brazil where all four seasons are clearly defined.* …巴西惟一四季分明的地区。 **2** N-COUNT You can use **season** to refer to the period during each year when a particular activity or event takes place. For example, the planting **season** is the period when a particular plant or crop is planted. (一年中某活动或事件发生的) 季节 ❑ *...birds arriving for the breeding*

S

season. …为繁殖季节而到来的鸟类。 **3** N-COUNT You can use **season** to refer to the period when a particular fruit, vegetable, or other food is ready for eating and is widely available. (水果、蔬菜或其他食物的) 当季期 [n N, also "in/out of" N] ❑ *The plum season is about to begin.* 李子的当季期就要开始了。 **4** N-COUNT You can use **season** to refer to a fixed period during each year when a particular sport is played or when a particular activity is allowed. (一年中某体育比赛或某活动被允许的) 季节 ❑ *...the baseball season.* …棒球赛季。 ❑ *Deer hunting season is only a couple of weeks long.* 猎鹿季节只有几个星期长。 **5** N-COUNT A **season** is a period in which a play or show, or a series of plays or shows, is performed in one place. (戏剧、演出的) 上演期 ❑ *...a season of three new plays.* …3出新戏剧的上演期。 **6** N-COUNT A **season of** movies is several of them shown as a series because they are connected in some way. (影片的) 连续上映期 ❑ *...a brief season of films in which Artaud appeared.* …阿尔托出演的影片的一个短暂的连续上映期。 **7** N-COUNT The vacation **season** is the time when most people take their vacation. (多数人休假的) 时期 [usu sing, usu supp N, also "in/out of" N] ❑ *...the peak vacation season.* …休假高峰期。 **8** V-T If you **season** food with salt, pepper, or spices, you add them to it in order to improve its flavor. 给 (食物) 调味 ❑ *Season the meat with salt and pepper.* 用盐和胡椒粉给肉调味。 **9** → see also **seasoned, seasoning** **10** PHRASE If a female animal is **in season**, she is in a state where she is ready to have sex. (雌性动物) 在发情期 ❑ *There are a few ideas around on how to treat fillies and mares in season.* 关于如何对待发情期的小母马和母马有几种观点。

→ see **plant**

sea·son·al /siːzənᵊl/ ADJ A **seasonal** factor, event, or change occurs during one particular time of the year. 季节性的 [ADJ n] ❑ *The figures aren't adjusted for seasonal variations.* 这些数字未作季节性变化调整。 ● **sea·son·al·ly** ADV 季节性地 ❑ *The seasonally adjusted unemployment figures show a rise of twelve-hundred.* 作了季节性调整的失业数字显示出1200人的增长。

sea·soned /siːzᵊnd/ ADJ You can use **seasoned** to describe a person who has a lot of experience of something. For example, a **seasoned** traveler is a person who has traveled a lot. 经验丰富的 ❑ *The author is a seasoned academic.* 作者是位经验丰富的大学教师。

sea·son·ing /siːzənɪŋ/ (**seasonings**) N-MASS **Seasoning** is salt, pepper, or other spices that are added to food to improve its flavor. 佐料 ❑ *Mix the meat with the onion, carrot, and some seasoning.* 将肉、洋葱、胡萝卜及一些佐料拌在一起。

→ see **salt**

sea·son tick·et (**season tickets**) N-COUNT A **season ticket** is a ticket that you can use repeatedly during a certain period, without having to pay each time. You can buy **season tickets** for things such as buses, trains, regular sports events, or theater performances. (在规定时期内可重复使用的) 定期票 ❑ *We went to renew our monthly season ticket.* 我们去续了月票。

seat ♦♦◊ /siːt/ (**seats, seating, seated**) **1** N-COUNT A **seat** is an object that you can sit on, for example, a chair. 座位 ❑ *Stephen returned to his seat.* 斯蒂芬回到了他的座位上。 **2** N-COUNT The **seat** of a chair is the part that you sit on. (椅子的) 坐部 ❑ *The stool had a torn, red plastic seat.* 这条无靠背凳子有一个破了的、红色的塑料坐部。 **3** V-T If you **seat yourself** somewhere, you sit down. 使 (自己) 坐下 [WRITTEN] ❑ *He waved toward a chair, and seated himself at the desk.* 他朝一把椅子一挥手，在桌旁坐了下来。 **4** V-T A building or vehicle that **seats** a particular number of people has enough seats for that number. (建筑物、车等) 提供 (一定数量的) 坐席 ❑ *The theater seats 570.* 这家剧院可容纳570名观众。 **5** N-SING **The seat of** a piece of clothing is the part that covers your bottom. (衣物的) 臀部 [usu "the" N "of" n] ❑ *Then he got up, brushed off the seat of his jeans, and headed slowly down the slope.* 接着他站了起来，拍了拍他牛仔裤的臀部，然后沿山坡缓缓而下。 **6** N-COUNT When someone is elected to a legislature you can say that they, or their party, have won a **seat**. (立法机构的) 席位 ❑ *Independent candidates won the majority of seats on the local council.* 独立派候选人赢得了地方议会的多数席位。 **7** N-COUNT If someone has a **seat** on the board of a company or on a committee, they are a member of it. (董事会、委员会) 席位 ❑ *He has been unsuccessful in his attempt to win a seat on the board of the company.* 他在该公司董事会谋得一席之地的企图未能成功。 **8** N-COUNT The **seat** of an organization, a wealthy family, or an activity is its base. (组织、富裕家庭、活动的) 基地 ❑ *Gunfire broke out early this morning around the seat of government in Lagos.* 今天清晨在拉各斯政府基地周围爆发了枪战。 **9** → see also **deep-seated** **10** PHRASE If you **take a back seat**, you allow other people to have all the power and to make all the decisions. 退居次位 ❑ *You need to take a back seat and think about both past and future.* 你需要退居次位思考过去和将来。 **11** PHRASE If you **take a seat**, you sit down. 坐下 [FORMAL] ❑ *"Take a seat," he said in a bored tone.* "坐下，" 他以一种厌倦的口气说道。

Word Partnership *seat* 的常用搭配：

ADJ. **back** seat, **empty** seat, **front** seat **1**
vacant seat, **vacated** seat **1 6 7**
congressional seat **6**

N. **car** seat, **child** seat, **driver's** seat, **passenger** seat, seat **at a table, theater** seat, **toilet** seat **1**
seat **in the House/Senate** **6**
seat **on the board** **7**

seat belt (**seat belts**) also **seatbelt** N-COUNT A **seat belt** is a strap attached to a seat in a car or an aircraft. You fasten it across your body in order to prevent yourself being thrown out of the seat if there is a sudden movement or stop. (汽车、飞机座椅上的) 安全带 ❑ *The fact I was wearing a seat belt saved my life.* 我系着安全带，幸免于难。

→ see **car**

> Laws have been passed in most of the US requiring motorists and their passengers to wear **seat belts** while in a moving vehicle. For small children's safety, **car seats** especially designed with belts to fit them must be used. Those caught not using seat belts are liable for a heavy fine.

seat·ing /siːtɪŋ/ **1** N-UNCOUNT You can refer to the seats in a place as the **seating**. (某地的) 座席 ❑ *The stadium has been fitted with seating for over eighty thousand spectators.* 这个体育场装了八万多观众座席。 **2** N-UNCOUNT The **seating** at a public place or a formal occasion is the arrangement of where people will sit. (公共场所、正式场合的) 座席安排 ❑ *She made a mental note to check the seating arrangements before the guests filed into the dining-room.* 她在脑子里记下了要在客人们鱼贯进入餐厅前查看一下座席的安排。

sea·weed /siːwiːd/ (**seaweeds**) N-MASS **Seaweed** is a plant that grows in the sea. There are many kinds of seaweed. 海草 ❑ *...seaweed washed up on a beach.* …被冲上海滩的海草。

sec /sɛk/ (**secs**) N-COUNT If you ask someone to wait a **sec**, you are asking them to wait for a very short time. 片刻 [INFORMAL] ❑ *Can you just hang on a sec?* 您能稍等一下吗？

sec. /sɛk/ (**secs**) **Sec.** is a written abbreviation for **second** or **seconds**. 秒 ❑ *The first woman to finish was Grete Waitz of Norway, with a time of 2 hrs, 29 min., 30 sec.* 第1个完成的女性是挪威的格雷特・瓦伊茨，用时2小时29分30秒。

seca·teurs /sɛkətɜrz/ N-PLURAL **Secateurs** are the same as **pruning shears**. 整枝剪刀 [BRIT]

se·clud·ed /sɪkluːdɪd/ ADJ A **secluded** place is quiet and private. 僻静的 ❑ *We were tucked away in a secluded corner of the room.* 我们被塞进了那个房间一个僻静的角落里。

se·clu·sion /sɪkluːʒᵊn/ N-UNCOUNT If you are living **in seclusion**, you are in a quiet place away from other people. 与世隔绝 ❑ *She lived in seclusion with her husband on their farm in Panama.* 她和她丈夫隐居在他们在巴拿马的农场里。

second
❶ PART OF A MINUTE
❷ COMING AFTER SOMETHING ELSE

❶ **sec·ond** ♦♦♦ /sɛkənd/ (**seconds**) N-COUNT A **second** is one of the sixty parts that a minute is divided into. People often say "**a second**" or "**seconds**" when they simply mean a very short time. 秒；片刻 ❑ *For a few seconds nobody said anything.* 有几秒钟没一个人说话。 ❑ *It only takes forty seconds.* 这只需40秒。

❷ **sec·ond** ♦♦♦ /sɛkənd/ (**seconds, seconding, seconded**)
➪ **Please look at meanings 12 and 13 to see if the expression you are looking for is shown under another headword.** **1** ORD The **second** item in a series is the one that you count as number two. 第二 ❑ *...the second day of his visit to Delhi.* …他访问德里的第二天。 ❑ *...their second child.* …他们的第二个孩子。 ❑ *...the Second World War.* …第二次世界大战。 **2** ORD **Second** is used before superlative

S

adjectives to indicate that there is only one thing better or larger than the thing you are referring to. 第二…的 (用于形容词最高级前) [ORD adj-superl] ❑ *The party is still the second strongest in Italy.* 该党仍是意大利第二大党。 **3** ADV You say **second** when you want to make a second point or give a second reason for something. 第二; 其次 [ADV cl] ❑ *First, the weapons should be intended for use only in retaliation after a nuclear attack. Second, the possession of the weapons must be a temporary expedient.* 首先，这些武器应当只在遭受核袭击后反击时才使用。其次，这些武器的拥有必须是一种临时的应急手段。 **4** N-PLURAL If you have **seconds**, you have a second helping of food. (食物) 第二份 [INFORMAL] ❑ *There's seconds if you want them.* 你想要的话还有。 **5** N-COUNT **Seconds** are goods that are sold cheaply in stores because they have slight faults. 次品 ❑ *These are not seconds, or unbranded goods, but first-quality products.* 这些既不是次品也不是无牌货，而是质量一流的产品。 **6** V-T If you **second** a proposal in a meeting or debate, you formally express your agreement with it so that it can then be discussed or voted on. 附议 ❑ *...Bryan Sutton, who seconded the motion against fox hunting.* …附议反对猎狐动议的布赖恩・萨顿。 **7** V-T If you **second** what someone has said, you say that you agree with them or say the same thing yourself. 赞同 ❑ *The UN secretary-general seconded the appeal for peace.* 联合国秘书长支持这项和平呼吁。 **8** PHRASE If you experience something **at second hand**, you are told about it by other people rather than experiencing it yourself. 间接地 ❑ *Most of them, after all, had not been at the battle and had only heard of the massacre at second hand.* 他们中的大多数毕竟没有亲历那场战争而只是间接听说过那场大屠杀。 **9** → see also **secondhand** **10** PHRASE If you say that something is **second to none**, you are emphasizing that it is very good indeed or the best that there is. 不亚于任何一个的 [EMPHASIS] ❑ *Our scientific research is second to none.* 我们的科学研究不亚于任何人。 **11** PHRASE If you say that something is **second only to** something else, you mean that only that thing is better or greater than it. 仅次于某物 ❑ *As a major health risk hepatitis is second only to tobacco.* 肝炎仅次于烟草是主要的健康隐患之一。 **12** **second nature** → see **nature** **13** **in the second place** → see **place**

sec·ond·ary /sɛkənderi/ **1** ADJ If you describe something as **secondary**, you mean that it is less important than something else. 次要的 ❑ *The street erupted in a huge explosion, with secondary explosions in the adjoining buildings.* 街上突然发生了一次巨大爆炸，相邻的建筑物里伴随有一些次级爆炸。 ❑ *They argue that human rights considerations are now of only secondary importance.* 他们争辩说人权考虑现在只是次要的。 **2** ADJ **Secondary** diseases or infections happen as a result of another disease or infection that has already happened. (疾病、感染等) 续发性的 ❑ *These patients had been operated on for the primary cancer but there was evidence of secondary tumors.* 这些病人曾因原发性癌症做过手术，但是又有了继发性肿瘤迹象。 **3** ADJ **Secondary** education is given to students between the ages of 11 or 12 and 17 or 18. (教育) 中等的 ❑ *Examinations are taken after about five years of secondary education.* 经过约五年的中等教育后参加考试。

sec·ond·ary school (**secondary schools**) N-VAR A **secondary school** is a school for students between the ages of 11 or 12 and 17 or 18. 中学 ❑ *She taught history at a secondary school.* 她在一所中学教过历史。

sec·ond best also **second-best** **1** ADJ **Second best** is used to describe something that is not as good as the best thing of its kind but is better than all the other things of that kind. 第二好的 ❑ *He put on his second best suit.* 他穿上了他第二好的西服。 **2** ADJ You can use **second best** to describe something that you have to accept even though you would have preferred something else. 退而求其次的 ❑ *...a messy, second-best solution.* …一个麻烦的、退而求其次的解决办法。 ● N-SING **Second best** is also a noun. 第二好者 ❑ *Oatmeal is a good second best.* 燕麦片是不错的第二选择。

second-class also **second class** **1** ADJ If someone treats you as a **second-class** citizen, they treat you as if you are less valuable and less important than other people. 二等的 (公民) [ADJ n] ❑ *Too many airlines treat our children as second-class citizens.* 太多航空公司把我们的孩子当作二等公民对待。 **2** ADJ If you describe something as **second-class**, you mean that it is of poor quality. 次等的 ❑ *I am not prepared to see children in some parts of this country having to settle for a second-class education.* 我不愿看到在这个国家部分地区的儿童们只能勉强接受次等的教育。 **3** ADJ The **second-class** accommodations on a train or ship are the ordinary accommodations, which are cheaper and less comfortable than the first-class accommodations. 二等的 (车厢、舱位等) [ADJ n] ❑ *He sat in the corner of a second-class compartment.* 他坐在一个二等车厢的角落里。 ❑ *Seven second-class passengers prepared to disembark.* 7名二等舱的旅客准备下船了。 ● ADV **Second class** is also an adverb. 乘二等舱地; 乘二等车厢地 [ADV after v] ❑ *I recently travelled second class from Pisa to Ventimiglia.* 我最近乘二等舱旅行从比萨到了文蒂米利亚。 ● N-UNCOUNT **Second-class** is second-class accommodations on a train or ship. 二等车厢; 二等舱 ❑ *"Is there any chance of a compartment to myself?"—"Not in second class."* "有没有可能买个我个人的包厢?" —— "二等车厢里不行。" **4** ADJ **Second-class** postage is a slower and cheaper type of postage. 二类的 (邮资) [ADJ n] [BRIT]

second·hand /sɛkəndhænd/ also **second-hand** **1** ADJ **Secondhand** things are not new and have been owned by someone else. 二手的 ❑ *They could afford a secondhand car, she thought.* 他们能买得起一辆二手车，她想。 ● ADV **Secondhand** is also an adverb. 二手地 [ADV after v] ❑ *Household appliances were bought secondhand and are outdated.* 家用电器曾是二手买的，现在已经过时了。 **2** ADJ A **secondhand** store sells secondhand goods. 经营二手货的 [ADJ n] ❑ *...lovingly restored old pieces bought from a secondhand store.* …从二手货店买来的一些精心修复了的旧东西。 **3** ADJ **Secondhand** stories, information, or opinions are those you learn about from other people rather than directly or from your own experience. 间接的; 二手的 (故事、信息、观点等) ❑ *He urged the committee to discount any secondhand knowledge or hearsay.* 他敦促该委员会不要相信任何二手的消息或传闻。 ● ADV **Secondhand** is also an adverb. 间接地; 二手地 [ADV after v] ❑ *I only heard about it secondhand.* 我只间接听说了这件事。 **4** **at second hand** → see **second**

sec·ond lan·guage (**second languages**) N-COUNT Someone's **second language** is a language which is not their native language but which they use at work or at school. 第二语言 ❑ *Lucy teaches English as a second language.* 露西教作为第二语言的英语。

sec·ond·ly /sɛkəndli/ ADV You say **secondly** when you want to make a second point or give a second reason for something. 其次; 第二 ❑ *It makes you look firstly at how you're treated and secondly how you treat everybody else.* 它让你首先看到别人怎样对待你，其次看你怎样对待别人。

sec·ond opin·ion (**second opinions**) N-COUNT If you get a **second opinion**, you ask another qualified person for their opinion about something such as your health. (来自另一个有资格者的) 第二意见 ❑ *I would like to see a specialist for a second opinion on my doctor's diagnosis.* 我想就我的医生诊断去见一位专家寻求第二意见。

second-rate ADJ If you describe something as **second-rate**, you mean that it is of poor quality. 二流的 ❑ *...second-rate restaurants.* …二流餐馆。

sec·ond thought (**second thoughts**) **1** N-SING If you do something without **a second thought**, you do it without thinking about it carefully, usually because you do not have enough time or you do not care very much. 再次考虑 ❑ *This murderous lunatic could kill them both without a second thought.* 这个杀人狂会毫不犹豫地把他们两人都杀掉。 **2** N-PLURAL If you have **second thoughts about** a decision that you have made, you begin to doubt whether it was the best thing to do. 转念 ❑ *I had never had second thoughts about my decision to leave the company.* 我从未对离开那家公司的决定有过别的想法。 **3** PHRASE You can say **on second thoughts** or **on second thought** when you suddenly change your mind about something that you are saying or something that you have decided to do. 转念一想 ❑ *"Wait there!" Kathryn rose. "No, on second thought, follow me."* "等等！" 凯瑟琳站了起来。"不，转念一想，跟我来吧。"

★ **se·cre·cy** /sikrəsi/ N-UNCOUNT **Secrecy** is the act of keeping something secret, or the state of being kept secret. 保密; 秘密 ❑ *The government has thrown a blanket of secrecy over the details.* 政府已对这些细节严加保密。

se·cret ♦♦◇ /sikrɪt/ (**secrets**) **1** ADJ If something is **secret**, it is known about by only a small number of people, and is not told or shown to anyone else. 秘密的; 保密的 ❑ *Soldiers have been training at a secret location.* 士兵们一直在一个秘密的地方训练。 **2** → see also **top secret** ● **se·cret·ly** ADV 秘密地 ❑ *He wore a hidden microphone to secretly tape-record conversations.* 他戴了一个窃听器秘密录下了谈话。 **3** N-COUNT A **secret** is a fact that is known by only a small number of people, and is not told to anyone else. 秘密 ❑ *I think he enjoyed keeping our love a secret.* 我想他喜欢对我们的恋情保密。 **4** N-SING If you say that a particular way of doing things is **the secret of** achieving something, you mean that it is the best or only way to achieve it. 秘诀 ❑ *The secret of success is honesty and fair* *dealing.* 成功的秘诀是诚实和公平交易。 **5** N-COUNT Something's **secrets** are the things about it which have never been fully explained. 奥秘 ❑ *We have an opportunity now to really unlock the secrets of the universe.* 我们现在有机会真正揭开宇宙的奥秘。 **6** PHRASE If you do something **in secret**, you do it without anyone else knowing. 秘密地 ❑ *Dan found out that I had been meeting my ex-boyfriend in secret.* 丹发现了我一直和前男友秘密见面。 **7** PHRASE If you say that someone can **keep a secret**, you mean that they can be trusted not to tell other people a secret that you have told them. 保守秘密 ❑ *Tom was utterly indiscreet, and could never keep a secret.* 汤姆言行完全不慎重，从来守不住秘密。 **8** PHRASE If you **make no secret** of something, you tell others about it openly and clearly. 不保密 ❑ *His wife made no secret of her hatred for the formal occasions.* 他的妻子不隐瞒她对正式场合的厌恶。

Thesaurus *secret* 另参见:
ADJ. hidden, private, unknown; *(ant.)* known **1**

sec·re·tar·ial /sɛkrɪtɛəriəl/ ADJ **Secretarial** work is the work done by a secretary in an office. 秘书的 [ADJ n] ❑ *I was doing temporary secretarial work.* 我在做临时的秘书工作。

sec·re·tari·at /sɛkrɪtɛəriət/ (**secretariats**) N-COUNT A **secretariat** is a department that is responsible for the administration of an international political organization. 秘书处 ❑ *...the UN secretariat.* …联合国秘书处。

sec·re·tary ♦♦♦ /sɛkrɪtɛri/ (**secretaries**) **1** N-COUNT A **secretary** is a person who is employed to do office work, such as typing letters, answering phone calls, and arranging meetings. 秘书 **2** N-COUNT The **secretary** of a company is the person who has the legal duty of keeping the company's records. (公司负责保管各种记录的) 干事 **3** N-COUNT; N-TITLE **Secretary** is used in the titles of high officials who are in charge of main government departments. 大臣; 部长 ❑ *...a former Venezuelan foreign secretary.* …一位前任委内瑞拉外交部长。

secretary-general ♦◇◇ (**secretaries-general**) also **Secretary General** N-COUNT **The secretary-general** of an international political organization is the person in charge of its administration. 秘书长 ❑ *...the United Nations Secretary-General.* …联合国秘书长。

Sec·re·tary of State ♦◇◇ (**Secretaries of State**) N-COUNT In the United States, **the Secretary of State** is the head of the government department which deals with foreign affairs. (美国) 国务卿

se·crete /sɪkrit/ (**secretes, secreting, secreted**) **1** V-T If part of a plant, animal, or human **secretes** a liquid, it produces it. 分泌 ❑ *The sweat glands secrete water.* 汗腺分泌汗液。 **2** V-T If you **secrete** something somewhere, you hide it there so that nobody will find it. 隐藏 [LITERARY] ❑ *She secreted the gun in the kitchen cabinet.* 她把枪藏在了厨房的橱柜里。

se·cre·tion /sɪkriʃ ͦn/ (**secretions**) **1** N-UNCOUNT **Secretion** is the process by which certain liquid substances are produced by parts of plants or from the bodies of people or animals. 分泌 ❑ *...the secretion of adrenaline.* …肾上腺素的分泌。 **2** N-PLURAL **Secretions** are liquid substances produced by parts of plants or bodies. 分泌物 ❑ *...gastric secretions.* …胃的分泌物。

S

se·cre·tive /sikrətɪv, sɪkrit-/ ADJ If you are **secretive**, you like to have secrets and to keep your knowledge, feelings, or intentions hidden. 藏而不露的; 讳莫如深的 ❑ *Billionaires are usually fairly secretive about the exact amount that they're worth.* 亿万富翁们通常对有关他们身价的确切数字讳莫如深。

se·cret po·lice N-UNCOUNT **The secret police** is a police force in some countries that works secretly and deals with political crimes committed against the government. 秘密警察 [also "the" N] ❑ *...former members of the secret police.* …前秘密警察成员。

se·cret ser·vice (**secret services**) **1** N-COUNT A country's **secret service** is a secret government department whose job is to find out enemy secrets and to prevent its own government's secrets from being discovered. 情报处 ❑ *...French secret service agents.* …法国情报特工。 **2** N-COUNT **The Secret Service** is the government department in the United States which protects the president, the vice president, and their families. 特工处 (指美国负责保护总统及其家人的政府部门) [AM] ❑ *He finished his career as head of the Secret Service team assigned to President Reagan.* 他结束了特工处里根总统特派队队长生涯。

▲ **sect** /sɛkt/ (**sects**) N-COUNT A **sect** is a group of people that has separated from a larger group and has a particular set of religious or political beliefs. (有某种宗教或政治信仰的) 派系

sec·tar·ian /sɛktɛəriən/ ADJ **Sectarian** means resulting from the differences between different religions. 派系的 ❑ *He was the fifth person to be killed in sectarian violence last week.* 他是上周派系暴力的第5个遇害者。 ❑ *The police said the murder was sectarian.* 警方说这是一起派系谋杀。

Word Link *sect ≈ cutting : dissect, intersect, section*

sec·tion ♦♦◇ /sɛkʃ ͦn/ (**sections, sectioning, sectioned**) **1** N-COUNT A **section** of something is one of the parts into which it is divided or from which it is formed. 部分 ❑ *He said it was wrong to single out any section of society for AIDS testing.* 他说挑出社会任何一部份人做艾滋病检查都是错误的。 ❑ *...the Georgetown section of Washington, D.C.* …华盛顿特区的乔治敦区。 **2** → see also **cross-section** **3** V-T If something **is sectioned**, it is divided into sections. 分 (成若干部分) [usu passive] ❑ *It holds vegetables in place while they are being peeled or sectioned.* 它在蔬菜被去皮或切分时将他们固定。 **4** N-COUNT A **section** is a diagram of something such as a building or a part of the body. It shows how the object would appear to you if it were cut from top to bottom and looked at from the side. 剖面图 ❑ *For some buildings a vertical section is more informative than a plan.* 对一些建筑物来说，垂直剖面图比平面图提供的信息更多。

Word Partnership *section* 的常用搭配:
N. section **of a city**, section **of a coast**, **rhythm** section, **sports** section **1**
ADJ. **main** section, **new** section, **special** section, **thin** section **1**

sec·tor ♦♦◇ /sɛktər/ (**sectors**) **1** N-COUNT A particular **sector** of a country's economy is the part connected with that specified type of industry. (经济的) 部门 ❑ *...the nation's manufacturing sector.* …该国的制造部门。 **2** → see also **public sector, private sector** **3** N-COUNT A **sector** of a large group is a smaller group which is part of it. 部分 ❑ *Workers who went to the Gulf came from the poorest sectors of Pakistani society.* 去海湾的工人们来自巴基斯坦社会最贫穷的阶层。 **4** N-COUNT A **sector** is an area of a city or country which is controlled by a military force. 军事管制区 ❑ *Officers were going to retake sectors of the city.* 军官们打算收回该市的一些军事管制区。

Word Partnership *sector* 的常用搭配:
N. **banking** sector, **business** sector, **government** sector, **growth in a** sector, **job in a** sector, **manufacturing** sector, **technology** sector, **telecommunications** sector **1**

★ **secu·lar** /sɛkyələr/ ADJ You use **secular** to describe things that have no connection with religion. 非宗教的 ❑ *He spoke about preserving the country as a secular state.* 他谈到保持该国的非宗教国性质。

se·cure ♦♦◇ /sɪkyʊər/ (**secures, securing, secured**) **1** V-T If you **secure** something that you want or need, you obtain it, often after a lot of effort. 争取到 [FORMAL] ❑ *Federal leaders continued their efforts to secure a ceasefire.* 联邦政府的领导人们继续他们争取停火的努力。 **2** V-T If you **secure** a place, you make it safe from harm or attack. 使 (某地) 免遭伤害或攻击 [FORMAL] ❑ *Staff withdrew from the main part of the prison but secured the perimeter.* 工作人员从监狱的主体区域撤了出来，但封锁了监狱四周。 **3** ADJ A **secure** place is tightly locked or well protected, so that people cannot enter it or leave it. 锁牢了的; 严密保护的 ❑ *We'll make sure our home is as secure as possible from now on.* 我们将从现在起确保我们的家尽可能安全。 ● **se·cure·ly** ADV 锁牢了地; 严密保护地 ❑ *He locked the heavy door securely and kept the key in his pocket.* 他锁牢了那扇重门把钥匙放在了他的口袋里。 **4** V-T If you **secure** an object, you fasten it firmly to another object. 缚牢 ❑ *He helped her close the cases up, and then he secured the canvas straps as tight as they would go.* 他帮她关上箱子，然后他又把帆布带尽可能缚紧。 **5** ADJ If an object is **secure**, it is fixed firmly in position. 牢固的 ❑ *Check that joints are secure and the wood is sound.* 检查接头是否牢固，木头是否完好。 ● **se·cure·ly** ADV 牢固地 [ADV with v] ❑ *Ensure that the frame is securely fixed to the ground with bolts.* 确保框架用螺栓牢牢地固定在地面上。 **6** ADJ If you describe something such as a job as **secure**, it is certain not to change or end. (工作等) 稳定的 ❑ *...demands for secure wages and employment.* …对稳定的工资和就业的要求。 ❑ *Senior citizens long for a more predictable and secure future.* 老年人渴望一

个更可预知、更稳定的未来。**7** ADJ A **secure** base or foundation is strong and reliable. 坚实的（基础）❏ *He was determined to give his family a secure and solid base.* 他决心为他的家庭打下一个坚实牢固的基础。**8** ADJ If you feel **secure**, you feel safe and happy and are not worried about life. (感觉) 安全的 ❏ *She felt secure and protected when she was with him.* 她和他在一起的时候感到很安全。**9** V-T If a loan **is secured**, the person who lends the money may take property such as a house from the person who borrows the money if they fail to repay it. 以…作抵押 [usu passive] [BUSINESS] ❏ *The loan is secured against your home.* 这笔贷款以你的房屋作抵押。

Thesaurus *secure* 另参见：

V. catch, get, obtain; (*ant.*) lose **1**
attach, fasten **4**
ADJ. safe, sheltered **3**
locked, tight **5**

Word Partnership *secure* 的常用搭配：

N. secure **a job/place/position**, secure **peace**, secure ***your* rights** **1**
secure **a loan** **1** **9**
secure **borders** **3**
secure **future**, secure **jobs** **6**
ADV. **less** secure, **more** secure **3** **5** **7** **8**
financially secure **6** **8**

se·cu·rity ♦♦♦ /sɪkyʊ̲ərɪti/ (**securities**) **1** N-UNCOUNT **Security** refers to all the measures that are taken to protect a place, or to ensure that only people with permission enter it or leave it. 保安措施；安全措施 ❏ *They are now under a great deal of pressure to tighten their airport security.* 他们目前承受着加强机场保安措施的巨大压力。❏ *Strict security measures are in force in the capital.* 严格的安全措施在首都实施。**2** N-UNCOUNT A feeling of **security** is a feeling of being safe and free from worry. 安全感 ❏ *He loves the security of a happy home life.* 他非常喜欢幸福的家庭生活所来的那种安全感。❏ *If an alarm gives you that feeling of security, then it's worth carrying.* 如果一个报警器能给你那种安全感，那就值得携带。● PHRASE If something gives you **a false sense of security**, it makes you believe that you are safe when you are not. 虚假的安全感 **3** N-UNCOUNT If something is **security** for a loan, you promise to give that thing to the person who lends you money, if you fail to pay the money back. 抵押品 [BUSINESS] ❏ *The central bank will provide special loans, and the banks will pledge the land as security.* 中央银行将提供特别贷款，而各家银行将以土地作为抵押品。**4** N-PLURAL **Securities** are stocks, shares, bonds, or other certificates that you buy in order to earn regular interest from them or to sell them later for a profit. 有价证券 [BUSINESS] ❏ *National banks can package their own mortgages and underwrite them as securities.* 国家银行可以组合包装自己的的抵押贷款，以证券形式承销。**5** → see also **Social Security**

se·cu·rity cam·era (**security cameras**) N-COUNT A **security camera** is a video camera that records people's activities in order to detect and prevent crime. 监控录像机

Se·cu·rity Coun·cil ♦◇◇ N-PROPER **The Security Council** is the committee which governs the United Nations. It has permanent representatives from the United States, Russia, China, France, and the United Kingdom, and temporary representatives from some other countries. 联合国安全理事会

se·cu·rity guard (**security guards**) N-COUNT A **security guard** is someone whose job is to protect a building or to collect and deliver large amounts of money. 保安人员

se·cu·rity risk (**security risks**) N-COUNT If you describe someone as a **security risk**, you mean that they may be a threat to the safety of a country or organization. (危及国家、机构安全的) 危险分子 ❏ *Individuals considered a security risk will have to report to immigration authorities within 30 days.* 被视为危险分子的个人将必须在30天之内向移民当局报到。

se·dan /sɪdæ̲n/ (**sedans**) N-COUNT A **sedan** is a car with seats for four or more people, a fixed roof, and a trunk that is separate from the part of the car that you sit in. 箱式小货车 [AM]

in BRIT, use **saloon**

→ see **car**

se·date /sɪde̲ɪt/ (**sedates, sedating, sedated**) **1** ADJ If you describe someone or something as **sedate**, you mean that they are quiet and rather dignified, though perhaps a bit dull. 沉静的；庄重的；不苟言笑的 ❏ *She took them to visit her sedate, elderly cousins.* 她带他们去探望她那些不苟言笑的表哥表姐们。❏ *Her life was sedate, almost mundane.* 她的生活很平静，几乎有些枯燥。**2** ADJ If you move along at a **sedate** pace, you move slowly, in a controlled way. 不慌不忙的 ❏ *We set off again at a more sedate pace.* 我们又一次出发了，步调更加缓慢。**3** V-T If someone **is sedated**, they are given a drug to calm them or to make them sleep. (用镇静剂) 使镇静 ❏ *The patient is sedated with intravenous use of sedative drugs.* 这名患者在静脉注射了镇静剂后镇静了下来。

se·da·tion /sɪde̲ɪʃᵊn/ N-UNCOUNT If someone is **under sedation**, they have been given medicine or drugs in order to calm them or make them sleep. (靠药物保持) 镇静状态 ❏ *His mother was under sedation after the boy's body was brought back from Germany.* 男孩的尸体从德国被运回后，他的母亲一直靠服药保持镇静。

seda·tive /sɛ̲dətɪv/ (**sedatives**) N-COUNT A **sedative** is a medicine or drug that calms you or makes you sleep. 镇静剂 ❏ *They use opium as a sedative, rather than as a narcotic.* 他们把鸦片作为镇静剂，而不是作为麻醉剂。

sed·en·tary /sɛ̲dᵊntɛri/ ADJ Someone who has a **sedentary** lifestyle or job sits down a lot of the time and does not do much exercise. 需要久坐的 ❏ *Obesity and a sedentary lifestyle has been linked with an increased risk of heart disease.* 肥胖和久坐的生活方式被认为会增加患心脏病的几率。

▲ **sedi·ment** /sɛ̲dɪmənt/ (**sediments**) N-VAR **Sediment** is solid material that settles at the bottom of a liquid, especially earth and pieces of rock that have been carried along and then left somewhere by water, ice, or wind. 沉淀物；沉渣 ❏ *Many organisms that die in the sea are soon buried by sediment.* 许多在海里死亡的生物很快便被沉淀物掩埋。
→ see **rock**

▲ **se·duce** /sɪdu̲s/ (**seduces, seducing, seduced**) **1** V-T If something **seduces** you, it is so attractive that it makes you do something that you would not otherwise do. 诱惑 ❏ *The view of lake and plunging cliffs seduces visitors.* 湖水和陡峭的悬崖景观吸引着游客。● **se·duc·tion** /sɪdʌ̲kʃᵊn/ N-VAR (**seductions**) 诱惑 ❏ *...the seduction of words.* …言语的诱惑。**2** V-T If someone **seduces** another person, they use their charm to persuade that person to have sex with them. 勾引；诱奸 ❏ *She has set out to seduce Stephen.* 她已开始勾引斯蒂芬。● **se·duc·tion** N-VAR 勾引 ❏ *Her methods of seduction are subtle.* 她勾引人的手法很巧妙。

se·duc·tive /sɪdʌ̲ktɪv/ **1** ADJ Something that is **seductive** is very attractive or makes you want to do something that you would not otherwise do. 诱人的 ❏ *It's a seductive argument.* 这是一个很有诱惑力的论点。● **se·duc·tive·ly** ADV 有诱惑力地 ❏ *...his seductively simple assertion.* …他的简单而又有诱惑力的主张。**2** ADJ A person who is **seductive** is very attractive sexually. 性感的 ❏ *...a seductive woman.* …一位性感的女子。● **se·duc·tive·ly** ADV 性感地 ❏ *...looking seductively over her shoulder.* …她性感地回首一望。

see

❶ VERB USES
❷ EXPRESSIONS, PHRASES AND CONVENTIONS
❸ PHRASAL VERBS

❶ **see** ♦♦♦ /si/ (**sees, seeing, saw, seen**) **1** V-T/V-I When you **see** something, you notice it using your eyes. 看见 [no cont] ❏ *You can't see colors at night.* 你在夜间看不见颜色。❏ *She can see, hear, touch, smell, and taste.* 她看得见、听得到、有触觉、嗅觉和味觉。**2** V-T If you **see** someone, you visit them or meet them. 看望；会见 ❏ *I saw him yesterday.* 我昨天见了他了。❏ *Mick wants to see you in his office right away.* 米克要你马上去他的办公室见他。**3** V-T If you **see** an entertainment such as a play, movie, concert, or sports game, you watch it. 观看 [no cont] ❏ *I haven't been to see a movie in 10 years.* 我已有10年没去看电影了。**4** V-T/V-I If you **see** that something is true or exists, you realize by observing it that it is true or exists. 看出 [no cont] ❏ *I could see she was lonely.* 我能看出她很寂寞。❏ *...a lot of people saw what was happening but did nothing about it.* …很多人都看到发生了什么事，但却袖手旁观。❏ *My taste has changed a bit over the years as you can see.* 就像你看到的，这些年来我的品味有些改变。**5** V-T If you **see** what someone means or **see** why something happened, you understand what they mean or understand why it happened. 明白 [no cont, no passive] ❏ *Oh, I see what you're saying.* 哦，我明白你

S

说的了。❑ *I really don't see any reason for changing it.* 我实在想不出有任何理由要改变它。 **6** V-T If you **see** someone or something **as** a certain thing, you have the opinion that they are that thing. 认为；视为 ❑ *She saw him as a visionary, but her father saw him as a man who couldn't make a living.* 她认为他是个梦想家，但她的父亲却认为他没有谋生的能力。❑ *Others saw it as a betrayal.* 其他人都视它为一种背叛。❑ *As I see it, Steve has three choices open to him.* 我认为，史蒂夫有3种选择。 **7** V-T If you **see** a particular quality **in** someone, you believe they have that quality. If you ask what someone **sees in** a particular person or thing, you want to know what they find attractive about that person or thing. 看中；欣赏 [no cont, no passive] ❑ *Frankly, I don't know what Paul sees in her.* 坦白地说，我不知道保罗看中她什么了。 **8** V-T If you **see** something happening in the future, you imagine it, or predict that it will happen. 想像；预测 [no cont] ❑ *A good idea, but can you see Taylor trying it?* 主意很好，但是你能想像泰勒试着做吗？ **9** V-T If a period of time or a person **sees** a particular change or event, it takes place during that period of time or while that person is alive. 历经；目睹 [no passive] ❑ *Yesterday saw the resignation of the chief financial officer.* 昨天，首席财政长官辞职了。❑ *He had worked with the general for three years and was sorry to see him go.* 他与将军一起共事3年，看他离去很难过。 **10** V-T If you **see that** something is done or if you **see to it that** it is done, you make sure that it is done. 确保 ❑ *See that you take care of him.* 你一定要好好照顾他。 **11** V-T If you **see** someone to a particular place, you accompany them to make sure that they get there safely, or to show politeness. 陪同；护送 ❑ *He didn't offer to see her to her car.* 他没有表示要送她上她的汽车。 **12** V-T If you **see** a lot **of** someone, you often meet each other or visit each other. 遇到；拜访 ❑ *We used to see quite a lot of his wife, Carolyn.* 我们过去经常见到他的妻子卡罗琳。 **13** V-T If you **are seeing** someone, you spend time with them socially, and are having a romantic or sexual relationship. 与…交往；与…有恋情 ❑ *My husband was still seeing her and he was having an affair with her.* 当时我丈夫仍与她交往，并跟她有暧昧关系。 **14** V-T **See** is used in books to indicate to readers that they should look at another part of the book, or at another book, because more information is given there. 参见 [only imper] ❑ *Surveys consistently find that men report feeling safe on the street after dark. See, for example, Hindelang and Garofalo (1978, p.127).* 调查一致显示，男性天黑后在街上感到安全。可参见如欣德朗和加罗法洛的著作(1978年，127页)。

Thesaurus *see* 另参见：
V. glimpse, look, observe, watch ❶ **1**
grasp, observe, understand ❶ **5**

❷ **see** ♦♦♦ /si/ (sees, seeing, saw, seen)
➪ **Please look at meanings 12 – 19 to see if the expression you are looking for is shown under another headword.** **1** V-T You can use **see** in expressions to do with finding out information. For example, if you say "**I'll see what's happening**," you mean that you intend to find out what is happening. 察看 ❑ *Let me just see what the next song is.* 让我看看下一首歌是什么。❑ *Every time we asked our mother, she said, "Well, see what your father says."* 每次我们问母亲，她总是说："喔，看看你父亲怎么说。" **2** V-T You can use **see** in expressions in which you promise to try and help someone. For example, if you say "**I'll see if I can do it**," you mean that you will try to do the thing concerned. 试试看 ❑ *I'll see if I can call her for you.* 我试试看能不能帮你叫她来。 **3** V-T Some writers use **see** in expressions such as **we saw** and **as we have seen** to refer to something that has already been explained or described. (如上所) 述 ❑ *We saw in Chapter 16 how annual cash budgets are produced.* 在第16章我们已经了解了年度现金预算是如何制定的。❑ *Laws are often not clear, as we saw in Chapter 1.* 正如第1章中所述，法律往往是含糊不清的。 **4** PHRASE You can use **seeing that** or **seeing as** to introduce a reason for what you are saying. 既然 [INFORMAL, SPOKEN] ❑ *Seeing as Mr. Moreton is a doctor, I assume he is reasonably intelligent.* 既然莫尔顿先生是个医生，我猜想他应该相当聪明。 **5** CONVENTION You can say "**I see**" to indicate that you understand what someone is telling you. 我明白 [SPOKEN, FORMULAE] ❑ *"He came home in my car."—"I see."* "他坐我的车回的家。"——"哦，是这样。" **6** CONVENTION People say "**I'll see**" or "**We'll see**" to indicate that they do not intend to make a decision immediately, and will decide later. 看看再说 ❑ *We'll see. It's a possibility.* 看看再说吧，这有可能。 **7** CONVENTION People say "**let me see**" or "**let's see**" when they are trying to remember something, or are trying to find something. 让我想一想；让我看看 ❑ *Let's see, they're six – no, make that five hours ahead of us.* 让我想想，他们比我们早了6个小时——不，就算是6个小时吧。 **8** PHRASE If you try to make someone **see sense** or **see reason**, you try to make them realize that they are wrong or are being stupid. 认识到错误；明白事理 ❑ *He was hopeful that by sitting together they could both see sense and live as good neighbors.* 他希望通过坐在一起沟通，他们双方都能认识到自己的错误，成为和睦相处的好邻居。 **9** CONVENTION You can say "**you see**" when you are explaining something to someone, to encourage them to listen and understand. (用于解释时) 你瞧 [SPOKEN] ❑ *Well, you see, you shouldn't really feel that way about it.* 好了，你瞧，你真的不该有那种感觉。 **10** CONVENTION "**See you**," "**be seeing you**," and "**see you later**" are ways of saying goodbye to someone when you expect to meet them again soon. 再见；回头见 [INFORMAL, SPOKEN, FORMULAE] ❑ *"Talk to you later."—"All right. See you love."* "以后再聊"。——"好的。回头见，亲爱的。" **11** CONVENTION You can say "**You'll see**" to someone if they do not agree with you about what you think will happen in the future, and you believe that you will be proved right. 你等着瞧吧 ❑ *The thrill wears off after a few years of marriage. You'll see.* 那股兴奋劲儿结婚几年后就会慢慢消失，你等着瞧吧。 **12** **to have seen better days** → see **day** **13** **to be seen dead** → see **dead** **14** **as far as the eye can see** → see **eye** **15** **to see eye to eye** → see **eye** **16** **as far as I can see** → see **far** **17** **to see fit** → see **fit** **18** **to see red** → see **red** **19** **wait and see** → see **wait**

You use **see** to talk about things that you are aware of because a visual impression reaches your eyes. You often use **can** in this case. ❑ *I can see the fax here on the desk.* If you want to say that someone is paying attention to something they can see, you say that they **are looking at** it or **are watching** it. In general, you **look at** something that is not moving, while you **watch** something that is moving or changing. ❑ *I asked him to look at the picture above his bed... He watched Blake run down the stairs.*

❸ **see** ♦♦♦ /si/ (sees, seeing, saw, seen)
▸ **see about** PHRASAL VERB When you **see about** something, you arrange for it to be done or provided. 安排；办理 ❑ *Tony announced it was time to see about lunch.* 托尼宣布该吃午饭了。
▸ **see off** PHRASAL VERB When you **see** someone **off**, you go with them to the station, airport, or port that they are leaving from, and say goodbye to them there. 为…送行 ❑ *Ben had planned a steak dinner for himself after seeing Jackie off on her plane.* 本已计划好在把杰基送上飞机后自己吃顿牛排晚餐。
▸ **see out** PHRASAL VERB If you **see out** a period of time, you continue to do what you are doing until that period of time is over. 持续到…结束 ❑ *The lease runs for 21 years, and they are committed to seeing out that time.* 租约为期21年，他们将信守合同直到期满。
▸ **see through** **1** PHRASAL VERB If you **see through** someone or their behavior, you realize what their intentions are, even though they are trying to hide them. 看穿；识破 ❑ *I saw through your little ruse from the start.* 从一开始我就识破了你的小诡计。 **2** → see also **see-through**
▸ **see to** PHRASAL VERB If you **see to** something that needs attention, you deal with it. 照料；办理 ❑ *While Franklin saw to the luggage, Sara took Eleanor home.* 弗兰克林处理行李，萨拉则带埃莉诺回家了。

seed ♦♦◇ /sid/ (seeds, seeding, seeded) **1** N-VAR A **seed** is the small, hard part of a plant from which a new plant grows. 种子 ❑ *I sow the seed in pots of soil-based compost.* 我把种子种在一盆盆施有堆肥的土里。 **2** V-T If you **seed** a piece of land, you plant seeds in it. 在(地里)播种 ❑ *Men mowed the wide lawns and seeded them.* 男人们修剪了大片的草坪，然后在上面播了种。❑ *The primroses should begin to seed themselves down the steep hillside.* 报春花应该开始沿那个陡峭的山坡一路撒播种子了。 **3** N-PLURAL You can refer to the **seeds of** something when you want to talk about the beginning of a feeling or process that gradually develops and becomes stronger or more important. (事物的) 起源 [LITERARY] ❑ *He raised questions meant to plant seeds of doubts in the minds of jurors.* 他提出了一些问题，意欲引起陪审员的疑心。 **4** N-COUNT In sports such as tennis or badminton, a **seed** is a player who has been ranked according to his or her ability. 种子选手 ❑ *...Roger Federer, Wimbledon's top seed and the world No.1.* …罗杰・费德勒，温布尔登网球赛的头号种子选手，世界排名第一。 **5** V-T When a player or a team **is seeded** in a sports competition, they are ranked according to their ability. 将(选手或球队)排列名次 [usu passive] ❑ *The Longhorns have won a national title and are seeded first overall.* 朗霍恩队曾得过一次全国冠军，整体排名第一。❑ *He is seeded second, behind Brad Beven.* 他排名第二，位于布拉德・贝文之后。

S

6 PHRASE If vegetable plants **go to seed**, they produce flowers and seeds as well as leaves. 开花结籽 ❑ *...plants that had long since flowered, gone to seed, and died.* …已经开花好久、结过籽并死去的植物。 **7** PHRASE If you say that someone or something **has gone to seed**, you mean that they have become much less attractive, healthy, or efficient. 衰退；退化 ❑ *He says the economy has gone to seed.* 他说经济已经走向衰退。 ❑ *...a retired cop who has gone to seed.* …一名衰老的退休警察。
→ see **flower, fruit, plant, rice**

seed capi·tal N-UNCOUNT **Seed capital** is an amount of money that a new company needs to pay for the costs of producing a business plan so that they can raise further capital to develop the company. 种子资本 [BUSINESS] ❑ *I am negotiating with financiers to raise seed capital for my latest venture.* 我正同一些金融家协商，为我最新的风险企业筹集种子资金。

seed·ling /si̱dlɪŋ/ (**seedlings**) N-COUNT A **seedling** is a young plant that has been grown from a seed. 幼苗

seed mon·ey N-UNCOUNT **Seed money** is money that is given to someone to help them start a new business or project. 本钱 [BUSINESS] ❑ *The government will give seed money to the project.* 政府将为这个项目提供本钱。

seedy /si̱di/ (**seedier, seediest**) ADJ If you describe a person or place as **seedy**, you disapprove of them because they look dirty and messy, or they have a bad reputation. 肮脏的；声名狼藉的 [DISAPPROVAL] ❑ *Frank ran errands for a seedy local villain.* 弗兰克为当地一个声名狼藉的恶棍跑腿。 ❑ *We were staying in a seedy hotel close to the red light district.* 我们住在靠近红灯区的一家脏乱的旅馆里。

See·ing Eye dog (**Seeing Eye dogs**) also **Seeing-Eye dog** N-COUNT A **Seeing Eye dog** is a dog that has been trained to lead a blind person. 导盲犬 [AM, TRADEMARK]
in BRIT, use **guide dog**
→ see **disability**

seek ♦◇◇ /si̱k/ (**seeks, seeking, sought**) **1** V-T If you **seek** something such as a job or a place to live, you try to find one. 寻找 [FORMAL] ❑ *They have had to seek work as laborers.* 他们只好找体力活来做。 ❑ *Four people who sought refuge in the Italian embassy have left voluntarily.* 到意大利大使馆寻求避难的四个人已经自愿离开了。 **2** V-T When someone **seeks** something, they try to obtain it. 谋求 [FORMAL] ❑ *The prosecutors have warned they will seek the death penalty.* 原告已警告说他们会努力争取死刑。 **3** V-T If you **seek** someone's help or advice, you contact them in order to ask for it. 请求；征求 [FORMAL] ❑ *Always seek professional legal advice before entering into any agreement.* 在签订任何协议之前，一定要征求法律专家的意见。 ❑ *On important issues, they seek a second opinion.* 在重要问题上，他们都征求别人的意见。 **4** V-T If you **seek to** do something, you try to do it. 力图；设法 [FORMAL] ❑ *He also denied that he would seek to annex the country.* 他还否认了他企图并吞该国。
▸ **seek out** PHRASAL VERB If you **seek out** someone or something or **seek** them **out**, you keep looking for them until you find them. 追寻到；找到 ❑ *Now is the time for local companies to seek out business opportunities in Europe.* 现在是当地公司在欧洲寻求商机的时候了。

Word Partnership *seek* 的常用搭配：
N. seek **asylum**, seek **election**, seek **employment**, seek **shelter** **1** **2**
seek **justice**, seek **revenge** **2**
seek **advice**, seek **approval**, seek **assistance/help**, seek **counseling**, seek **permission**, seek **protection**, seek **support** **3**

seek·er /si̱kər/ (**seekers**) **1** N-COUNT A **seeker** is someone who is looking for or trying to get something. 追求者 ❑ *I am a seeker after truth.* 我是一名真理的追求者。 **2** → see also **asylum seeker**

seem ♦♦♦ /si̱m/ (**seems, seeming, seemed**) **1** V-LINK You use **seem** to say that someone or something gives the impression of having a particular quality, or of happening in the way you describe. 似乎；看起来 [no cont] ❑ *The explosions seemed quite close by.* 爆炸似乎就在近旁。 ❑ *To everyone who knew them, they seemed an ideal couple.* 在每个认识他们的人看来，他们似乎是一对佳偶。 ❑ *The calming effect seemed to last for about ten minutes.* 镇静效果好像持续了大约10分钟。 ❑ *It seems that the attack was carefully planned.* 看起来，这次袭击是精心策划的。 ❑ *It seemed as if she'd been gone forever.* 好像她已经永远地离开了一样。 **2** V-LINK You use **seem** when you are describing your own feelings or thoughts, or describing something that has happened to you, in order to make your statement less forceful. 感觉好像 [no cont] [VAGUENESS] ❑ *I seem to have lost all my self-confidence.* 我好像已经丧失了所有的自信。 ❑ *I seem to remember giving you very precise instructions.* 我好像记得曾给过你非常明确的指示。 **3** PHRASE If you say that you **cannot seem** or **could not seem to** do something, you mean that you have tried to do it and were unable to. 好像总是不能 ❑ *No matter how hard I try I cannot seem to catch up on all the bills.* 不管我怎么努力，我好像总也无法付清所有的账单。

seem·ing /si̱mɪŋ/ ADJ **Seeming** means appearing to be the case, but not necessarily the case. For example, if you talk about someone's **seeming** ability to do something, you mean that they appear to be able to do it, but you are not certain. 表面上的；貌似的 [ADJ n] [FORMAL, VAGUENESS] ❑ *Wall Street analysts have been highly critical of the company's seeming inability to control costs.* 华尔街的分析家们对该公司似乎无力控制成本一事一直批评甚多。

seem·ing·ly /si̱mɪŋli/ **1** ADV If something is **seemingly** the case, you mean that it appears to be the case, even though it may not really be so. 好似；看上去 [ADV adj/adv] ❑ *A seemingly endless line of trucks waits in vain to load up.* 看上去没有尽头的一排卡车徒劳地等着装货。 **2** ADV You use **seemingly** when you want to say that something seems to be true. 似乎 [VAGUENESS] ❑ *He has moved to Spain, seemingly to enjoy a slower style of life.* 他已移居西班牙，似乎是想过一种节奏较慢的生活。

seen /si̱n/ **Seen** is the past participle of **see**. see的过去分词

seep /si̱p/ (**seeps, seeping, seeped**) **1** V-I If something such as liquid or gas **seeps** somewhere, it flows slowly and in small amounts into a place where it should not go. 渗透 ❑ *Radioactive water had seeped into underground reservoirs.* 放射性水已渗入了地下蓄水池。 ❑ *The gas is seeping out of the rocks.* 气体正从岩石里渗出。
● N-COUNT **Seep** is also a noun. 渗透 ❑ *...an oil seep.* …一次石油渗漏。 **2** V-I If something such as information or an emotion **seeps** into or out of a place, it enters or leaves it gradually. 逐渐外泄；逐渐进入 ❑ *Many of us thrive on competition, but it can seep into areas of our lives where we do not want it.* 我们许多人靠竞争而发展，但竞争也会逐渐侵入到我们生活中不需要它的一些方面。

see·saw /si̱sɔ/ (**seesaws**) also **see-saw** N-COUNT A **seesaw** is a long board which is balanced in the middle. To play on it, a child sits on each end, and when one end goes up, the other goes down. 跷跷板 ❑ *There was a sandpit, a seesaw and a swing in the playground.* 操场上有一个沙坑，一副跷跷板和一架秋千。

▲ **seethe** /si̱ð/ (**seethes, seething, seethed**) V-I When you **are seething**, you are very angry about something but do not express your feelings about it. 怒火中烧 ❑ *She took it calmly at first but under the surface was seething.* 她起初处之泰然，但内心却是气呼呼的。 ❑ *She put a hand on her hip, grinning derisively, while I seethed with rage.* 她把一只手叉着腰，嘲弄地咧嘴而笑，而此时我已怒火中烧。

see-through ADJ **See-through** clothes are made of thin cloth, so that you can see a person's body or underwear through them. (衣服) 薄得透明的 ❑ *She was wearing a white, see-through blouse, a red bra showing beneath.* 她穿着一件白色透明的衬衫，里面的红色胸罩透了出来。

seg·ment ♦◇◇ /sɛ̱gmənt/ (**segments**) **1** N-COUNT A **segment of** something is one part of it, considered separately from the rest. 部分 ❑ *...the poorer segments of society.* …社会中的较贫困阶层。 **2** N-COUNT A **segment** of fruit such as an orange or grapefruit is one of the sections into which it is easily divided. (水果的) 瓣 ❑ *Peel all the fruit except the lime and separate into segments.* 除了酸橙之外，把所有的水果剥皮并分成瓣。 **3** N-COUNT A **segment** of a circle is one of the two parts into which it is divided when you draw a straight line through it. 圆缺 ❑ *The other children stood around the circle, one in each segment.* 其他孩子围着圆圈而站，每一半圈里站着一个孩子。

★ **seg·re·gate** /sɛ̱grɪgeɪt/ (**segregates, segregating, segregated**) V-T To **segregate** two groups of people or things means to keep them physically apart from each other. 隔离；分开 ❑ *A large detachment of police was used to segregate the two rival camps of protesters.* 一大队分遣警察被派来隔离两群敌对的抗议者。

seg·re·gat·ed /sɛ̱grɪgeɪtɪd/ ADJ **Segregated** buildings or areas are kept for the use of one group of people who are the same race, sex, or religion, and no other group is allowed to use them. (因种族、性别或宗教不同而) 隔离的 ❑ *...racially segregated schools.* …实行种族隔离的学校。

S

★ **seg·re·ga·tion** /sɛgrɪgeɪʃən/ N-UNCOUNT **Segregation** is the official practice of keeping people apart, usually people of different sexes, races, or religions. (因种族、性别或宗教不同而采取的) 隔离 ❑ *The Supreme Court unanimously ruled that racial segregation in schools was unconstitutional.* 最高法院一致裁定学校实施的种族隔离措施违反宪法。

seis·mic /saɪzmɪk/ 1 ADJ **Seismic** means caused by or relating to an earthquake. 地震的; 地震引起的 [ADJ n] ❑ *Earthquakes produce two types of seismic waves.* 地震产生两种类型的地震波。 2 ADJ A **seismic** shift or change is a very sudden or dramatic change. 突然的 [usu ADJ n] ❑ *I have never seen such a seismic shift in public opinion in such a short period of time.* 我从来没有见过公众舆论在这么短的时间内发生如此突然的转变。
→ see **earthquake**

seize ♦◇◇ /siz/ (**seizes, seizing, seized**) 1 V-T If you **seize** something, you take hold of it quickly, firmly, and forcefully. 抓住 ❑ *"Leigh," he said seizing my arm to hold me back.* "莉，"他说着便抓住我的胳膊把我拉了回来。 2 V-T When a group of people **seize** a place or **seize** control of it, they take control of it quickly and suddenly, using force. 攻占; 夺取 ❑ *Troops have seized the airport and railroad terminals.* 军队已经占领了机场和铁路终点站。 3 V-T If a government or other authority **seize** someone's property, they take it from them, often by force. 没收; 查封 ❑ *Police were reported to have seized all copies of this morning's edition of the newspaper.* 据报道警方已没收了该报纸今早所有的出刊。 4 V-T When someone **is seized**, they are arrested or captured. 逮捕; 俘获 ❑ *UN officials say two military observers were seized by the Khmer Rouge yesterday.* 联合国官员称，昨天有两名军事观察员被红色高棉组织俘获。 5 V-T When you **seize** an opportunity, you take advantage of it and do something that you want to do. 抓住 (机会) ❑ *During the riots hundreds of people seized the opportunity to steal property.* 暴乱期间数以百计的人乘机窃取财物。

▶ **seize on** PHRASAL VERB If you **seize on** something or **seize upon** it, you show great interest in it, often because it is useful to you. 利用 ❑ *Newspapers seized on the results as proof that global warming wasn't really happening.* 报纸用这些结果作为全球变暖并未真正发生的证据。

▶ **seize up** 1 PHRASAL VERB If a part of your body **seizes up**, it suddenly stops working, because you have strained it or because you are getting old. (人体某部位) 发僵 ❑ *After two days' exertions, it's the arms and hands that seize up, not the legs.* 两天的劳累之后，突然发僵的是胳膊和手，并不是双腿。 2 PHRASAL VERB If something such as an engine **seizes up**, it stops working, because it has not been properly cared for. (机器) 失灵 ❑ *She put diesel fuel, instead of gasoline, into the tank causing the motor to seize up.* 她把柴油代替汽油灌入油箱，造成发动机失灵。

▲ **sei·zure** /siʒər/ (**seizures**) 1 N-COUNT If someone has a **seizure**, they have a sudden violent attack of an illness, especially one that affects their heart or brain. (心脏病、脑部疾病等的) 突然发作 ❑ *...a mild cardiac seizure.* …一次轻度心脏病发作。 2 N-COUNT If there is a **seizure of** power or a **seizure of** an area of land, a group of people suddenly take control of the place, using force. 占领 ❑ *...the seizure of territory through force.* …对领土的武装占领。 3 N-COUNT When an organization such as the police or customs makes a **seizure of** illegal goods, they find them and take them away. 缴获; 没收 ❑ *Police have made one of the biggest seizures of heroin there's ever been.* 警方这次缴获的海洛因是迄今为止数目最大的几宗之一。

sel·dom /sɛldəm/ ADV If something **seldom** happens, it happens only occasionally. 很少; 不常 ❑ *They seldom speak.* 他们很少说话。 ❑ *I've seldom felt so happy.* 我很少感到过这么快乐了。

se·lect ♦◇◇ /sɪlɛkt/ (**selects, selecting, selected**) 1 V-T If you **select** something, you choose it from a number of things of the same kind. 挑选; 选择 ❑ *Voters are selecting candidates for both U.S. Senate seats and for 52 congressional seats.* 选民们正在选举美国参议院议席的候选人和52个众议院席位的候选人。 ❑ *With a difficult tee shot, select a club which will keep you short of the trouble.* 开球难度较大时，选择一根用起来能不给你添乱的高尔夫球杆。 2 V-T If you **select** a file or a piece of text on a computer screen, you click on it so that it is marked in a different color, usually in order for you to give the computer an instruction relating to that file or piece of text. (在计算机屏幕上) 选定 (某文件或某段文章以作特别处理) [COMPUTING] ❑ *I selected a file and pressed the delete key.* 我选定了一份文件，然后按下了删除键。 3 ADJ A **select** group is a small group of some of the best people or things of their kind. 精选的 [ADJ n] ❑ *...a select group of French cheeses.* …一组精选的法国奶酪。 4 ADJ If you describe something as **select**, you mean it has many desirable features, but is available only to people who have a lot of money or who belong to a high social class. 第一流的; 只为富人、上层人士而设的 ❑ *Christian Lacroix is throwing a very lavish and very select party.* 克里斯琴·拉克鲁瓦正在举行一个上层人士参加的非常豪华的聚会。

Thesaurus *select* 另参见:

V.	choose, pick out, take 1
ADJ.	best, exclusive 3 4

se·lec·tion ♦◇◇ /sɪlɛkʃən/ (**selections**) 1 N-UNCOUNT **Selection** is the act of selecting one or more people or things from a group. 挑选; 选择 ❑ *...Darwin's principles of natural selection.* …达尔文的物竞天择理论。 ❑ *Dr. Sullivan's selection to head the Department of Health was greeted with satisfaction.* 由沙利文博士担任卫生部部长的这项选择很令人满意。 2 N-COUNT A **selection of** people or things is a set of them that have been selected from a larger group. 挑选出的一群 ❑ *...this selection of popular songs.* …这组精选的通俗歌曲。 3 N-COUNT The **selection of** goods in a store is the particular range of goods that it has available and from which you can choose what you want. (商店内) 可供选择的商品范围 ❑ *It offers the widest selection of antiques of every description in a one day market.* 在为时一天的集市上，它提供了选择范围广泛的各式古董。 4 N-COUNT In computing, a **selection** is an area of the screen that you have highlighted, for example because you want to copy it to another file. (计算机屏幕上) 选定的板块 [COMPUTING]

se·lec·tive /sɪlɛktɪv/ 1 ADJ A **selective** process applies only to a few things or people. 选择性的 [ADJ n] ❑ *Selective breeding may result in a greyhound running faster and seeing better than a wolf.* 选择育种可能会培育出一种比狼跑得更快、视力更好的灵缇。 ● **se·lec·tive·ly** ADV 有选择地 ❑ *Within the project, trees are selectively cut on a 25-year rotation.* 在这一计划中，会以25年为周期有选择地砍伐树木。 2 ADJ When someone is **selective**, they choose things carefully, for example, the things that they buy or do. 仔细挑选的; 讲究的 ❑ *Sales still happen, but buyers are more selective.* 销售仍在进行，但买家更挑剔了。 ● **se·lec·tive·ly** ADV 仔细挑选地 [ADV with v] ❑ *...people on small incomes who wanted to shop selectively.* …购物时需要仔细挑选的低收入人群。 3 ADJ If you say that someone has a **selective** memory, you disapprove of the fact that they remember certain facts about something and deliberately forget others, often because it is convenient for them to do so. 选择性的 (记忆) [DISAPPROVAL] ❑ *We seem to have a selective memory for the best bits of the past.* 我们似乎对过去最美好的时光有选择性的记忆。 ● **se·lec·tive·ly** ADV 有选择性地 [ADV with v] ❑ *...a tendency to remember only the pleasurable effects of the drug and selectively forget all the adverse effects.* …一种只记住毒品带来的快感而有选择性地忘掉其所有负面作用的倾向。

self ♦◇◇ /sɛlf/ (**selves**) 1 N-COUNT Your **self** is your basic personality or nature, especially considered in terms of what you are really like as a person. 自身; 本性 ❑ *You're looking more like your usual self.* 你现在看上去更像你平常的样子了。 2 N-COUNT A person's **self** is the essential part of their nature which makes them different from everyone and everything else. 个性 ❑ *I want to explore and get in touch with my inner self.* 我想认真探索，了解我内在的个性。 ❑ *The face is the true self visible to others.* 面孔是外人能看到的真实自我。

self-adhesive ADJ Something that is **self-adhesive** is covered on one side with a sticky substance like glue, so that it will stick to surfaces. 自粘的 ❑ *...self-adhesive labels.* …自粘标签。

self-assured ADJ Someone who is **self-assured** shows confidence in what they say and do because they are sure of their own abilities. 自信的 ❑ *He's a self-assured, confident negotiator.* 他是个胸有成竹、很有信心的谈判者。

self-centered
in BRIT, use **self-centred**
ADJ Someone who is **self-centered** is only concerned with their own wants and needs and never thinks about other people. 自我中心的; 自私自利的 [DISAPPROVAL] ❑ *It's very self-centered to think that people are talking about you.* 你认为人们都在谈论你，那是过于以自我为中心了。

self-confessed ADJ If you describe someone as a **self-confessed** murderer or a **self-confessed** romantic, for example, you mean that they admit openly that they are a murderer or a romantic. 不打自招的; 公开承认的 [ADJ n] ❑ *The self-confessed drug addict was arrested 13 months ago.* 那个招认自己是瘾君子的人13个月前被抓起来了。

self-confidence N-UNCOUNT If you have **self-confidence**, you behave confidently because you feel sure of your abilities or value. 自信 ❑ *With the end of my love affair, I lost all the self-confidence I once had.* 随着恋情的结束，我失去了所有曾经拥有的自信。

self-confident ADJ Someone who is **self-confident** behaves confidently because they feel sure of their abilities or value. 自信的 ❑ *She'd blossomed into a self-confident young woman.* 她已出落成一个自信的年轻女性。

self-conscious ADJ Someone who is **self-conscious** is easily embarrassed and nervous because they feel that everyone is looking at them and judging them. 难为情的; 不自在的 ❑ *I felt a bit self-conscious in my bikini.* 穿着比基尼，我感到有点难为情。

self-contained **1** ADJ You can describe someone or something as **self-contained** when they are complete and separate and do not need help or resources from outside. 独立自足的 ❑ *He seems completely self-contained and he doesn't miss you when you're not there.* 他似乎完全独立，你不在的时候他并不想念你。 **2** ADJ **Self-contained** accommodations such as an apartment have all their own facilities, so that a person living there does not have to share rooms such as a kitchen or bathroom with other people. 独门独户的 (指毋须与他人共享厨房、厕所等) ❑ *Her family lives in a self-contained three-bedroom suite in the back of the main house.* 她一家人住在主宅后面一个独立的三居室套房里。

self-control N-UNCOUNT **Self-control** is the ability to not show your feelings or not do the things that your feelings make you want to do. 自制力 ❑ *His self-control, reserve and aloofness were almost inhuman.* 他的自制力、矜持和孤傲几乎有些不近人情。

self-defence [BRIT] → see **self-defense**

self-defense

in BRIT, use **self-defence**

1 N-UNCOUNT **Self-defense** is the use of force to protect yourself against someone who is attacking you. 自卫 ❑ *The women acted in self-defense after years of abuse.* 这些妇女遭受了多年的虐待后终于起来自卫了。 **2** N-UNCOUNT **Self-defense** is the action of protecting yourself against something bad. 自卫行动 ❑ *Tai Chi is an ancient form of self-defense.* 太极拳是一种古老的自卫手段。

self-determination N-UNCOUNT **Self-determination** is the right of a country to be independent, instead of being controlled by a foreign country, and to choose its own form of government. (民族独立的) 自决权 ❑ *...Lithuania's right to self-determination.* …立陶宛的民族自决权。

self-employed ADJ If you are **self-employed**, you organize your own work and taxes and are paid by people for a service you provide, rather than being paid a regular salary by a person or a firm. 个体经营的; 自雇的 [BUSINESS] ❑ *There are no paid holidays or sick leave if you are self-employed.* 如果你是个体经营的，那就没有带薪休假或病假了。 ● N-PLURAL **The self-employed** are people who are self-employed. 个体经营者 ❑ *We want more support for the self-employed.* 我们需要更多给个体经营者的支持

self-esteem N-UNCOUNT Your **self-esteem** is how you feel about yourself. For example, if you have low **self-esteem**, you do not like yourself, you do not think that you are a valuable person, and therefore you do not behave confidently. 自尊 ❑ *Poor self-esteem is at the center of many of the difficulties we experience in our relationships.* 缺乏自尊心是我们在社交中所经历的许多困难的核心所在。

self-evident ADJ A fact or situation that is **self-evident** is so obvious that there is no need for proof or explanation. 不证自明的; 不言而喻的 ❑ *It is self-evident that we will never have enough resources to meet the demand.* 不言而喻，我们将永远不会有足够的资源来满足需求。

self-explanatory ADJ Something that is **self-explanatory** is clear and easy to understand without needing any extra information or explanation. 无需解释的; 不释自明的 ❑ *I hope the graphs on the following pages are self-explanatory.* 我希望以下几页图表能一目了然。

self-help N-UNCOUNT **Self-help** consists of people providing support and help for each other in an informal way, rather than relying on the government, authorities, or other official organizations. 互助 ❑ *She set up a self-help group for parents with overweight children.* 她成立了一个由超重儿童家长组成的互助会。

self-image (**self-images**) N-COUNT Your **self-image** is the set of ideas you have about your own qualities and abilities. 自我形象 ❑ *Children who have a positive self-image are less likely to present behavior and discipline problems.* 有着正面自我形象的儿童较不可能出现行为和纪律的问题。

self-important ADJ If you say that someone is **self-important**, you disapprove of them because they behave as if they are more important than they really are. 妄自尊大的 [DISAPPROVAL] ❑ *He was self-important, vain and ignorant.* 他自大、虚荣、而且无知。 ● **self-importance** N-UNCOUNT 妄自尊大 ❑ *Many visitors complained of his bad manners and self-importance.* 许多访客抱怨他的不礼貌和妄自尊大。

self-imposed ADJ A **self-imposed** restriction, task, or situation is one that you have deliberately created or accepted for yourself. 自愿承担的; 自己强加的 ❑ *He returned home after eleven years of self-imposed exile.* 经历了11年的自我流放后他回家了。

self-indulgence (**self-indulgences**) N-VAR **Self-indulgence** is the act of allowing yourself to have or do the things that you enjoy very much. 自我放纵 ❑ *He prayed to be saved from self-indulgence.* 他祈祷能从自我放纵中解脱出来。

self-indulgent ADJ If you say that someone is **self-indulgent**, you mean that they allow themselves to have or do the things that they enjoy very much. 自我放纵的 ❑ *Why give publicity to this self-indulgent, adolescent oaf?* 为什么要宣传这个自我放纵的傻小子？

self-inflicted ADJ A **self-inflicted** wound or injury is one that you do to yourself deliberately. 自己造成的 ❑ *He is being treated for a self-inflicted gunshot wound.* 他因开枪自残正在接受治疗。

self-interest N-UNCOUNT If you accuse someone of **self-interest**, you disapprove of them because they always want to do what is best for themselves rather than for anyone else. 自私自利 [DISAPPROVAL] ❑ *Their current protests are motivated purely by self-interest.* 他们目前的抗议纯粹是受私利驱使的。

self·ish /sɛlfɪʃ/ ADJ If you say that someone is **selfish**, you mean that he or she cares only about himself or herself, and not about other people. 自私的 [DISAPPROVAL] ❑ *I think I've been very selfish. I've been mainly concerned with myself.* 我觉得我一直很自私。我总是只关心自己。 ● **self·ish·ly** ADV 自私地 ❑ *Someone has selfishly emptied the cookie jar.* 有人自私地吃光了饼干罐里的饼干。 ● **self·ish·ness** N-UNCOUNT 自私 ❑ *The arrogance and selfishness of different interest groups never ceases to amaze me.* 不同利益集团的傲慢与自私总是令我惊讶不已。

self·less /sɛlflɪs/ ADJ If you say that someone is **selfless**, you approve of them because they care about other people more than themselves. 无私的 [APPROVAL] ❑ *She was a wonderful companion and her generosity to me was entirely selfless.* 她是一位极好的伴侣，她对我的宽容完全是无私的。

self-pity N-UNCOUNT **Self-pity** is a feeling of unhappiness that you have about yourself and your problems, especially when this is unnecessary or greatly exaggerated. (常指过度的) 自哀; 自怜 [DISAPPROVAL] ❑ *I was unable to shake off my self-pity.* 我无法从自怜中摆脱出来。

self-portrait (**self-portraits**) N-COUNT A **self-portrait** is a drawing, painting, or written description that you do of yourself. 自画像; 自我描述

self-regulation N-UNCOUNT **Self-regulation** is the controlling of a process or activity by the people or organizations that are involved in it rather than by an outside organization such as the government. 自我调节 ❑ *Competition between companies is too fierce for self-regulation to work.* 公司之间的竞争过于激烈，难以进行自我调节。

self-respect N-UNCOUNT **Self-respect** is a feeling of confidence and pride in your own ability and worth. 自尊 (心) ❑ *They have lost not only their jobs, but their homes, their self-respect and even their reason for living.* 他们不仅失去了工作，还失去了家园、自尊心，甚至活下去的理由。

self-righteous ADJ If you describe someone as **self-righteous**, you disapprove of them because they are convinced that they are right in their beliefs, attitudes, and behavior and that other people are wrong. 自以为是的; 自命正直的 [DISAPPROVAL] ❑ *He is critical of the monks, whom he considers narrow-minded and self-righteous.* 他对僧侣们颇有微词，认为他们心胸狭隘，自以为是。 ● **self-righteousness** N-UNCOUNT 自以为是; 自命正直 ❑ *Her aggressiveness and self-righteousness caused prickles of anger at the back of his neck.* 她的咄咄逼人和自以为是让他很生气。

self-service ADJ A **self-service** store, restaurant, or garage is one where you get things for yourself rather than being served by another person. 自我服务的; 自助的 ❑ *...a self-service cafeteria with a wide choice.* …一家菜品繁多的自助餐厅。

S

> Gasoline stations in the North America offer **full-service** and **self-service**. In **self-service** gas stations, the customer pumps his own gasoline and pays the attendant. Self-serve gasoline is cheaper than gas pumped by the attendant.

self-study N-UNCOUNT **Self-study** is study that you do on your own, without a teacher. 自学 ❑ *Individuals can enrol on self-study courses in the university's language institute.* 人们可以报名参加这所大学的语言学院的自学课程。

self-styled ADJ If you describe someone as a **self-styled** leader or expert, you disapprove of them because they claim to be a leader or expert but they do not actually have the right to call themselves this. 自封的; 自诩的 [ADJ n] [DISAPPROVAL] ❑ *Two of those arrested are said to be self-styled area commanders.* 据说被捕者中有两人自称是地区指挥官。

self-sufficiency /sɛlf səfɪʃᵊnsi/ N-UNCOUNT **Self-sufficiency** is the state of being self-sufficient. 自给自足

self-sufficient 1 ADJ If a country or group is **self-sufficient**, it is able to produce or make everything that it needs. 自给自足的 ❑ *This enabled the country to become self-sufficient in sugar.* 这使得该国在食糖方面变得自给自足了。 2 ADJ Someone who is **self-sufficient** is able to live happily without anyone else. 自给自足的; 自立的 ❑ *Although she had various boyfriends, Madeleine was, and remains, fiercely self-sufficient.* 尽管有过各种各样男朋友，马德琳过去和现在一直都非常自立。

sell ♦♦♦ /sɛl/ (**sells, selling, sold**) 1 V-T/V-I If you **sell** something that you own, you let someone have it in return for money. 卖 ❑ *Catlin sold the paintings to Philadelphia industrialist Joseph Harrison.* 卡特林把这些画卖给了费城实业家约瑟夫·哈里森。 ❑ *The directors sold the business for $14.8 million.* 董事们把这个公司以1480万美元卖掉了。 ❑ *When is the best time to sell?* 什么时候才是出售的最佳时机呢？ 2 V-T If a store **sells** a particular thing, it is available for people to buy there. 出售; 经销 ❑ *It sells everything from hair ribbons to oriental rugs.* 这里出售各种商品，从扎头发的发带到东方小地毯都有。 3 V-I If something **sells for** a particular price, that price is paid for it. 售价为… ❑ *Unmodernized property can sell for up to 40 percent of its modernized market value.* 未经现代化改造的房地产售价至多是其现代化改造后市价的40%。 4 V-I If something **sells**, it is bought by the public, usually in fairly large quantities. 有销路; 行销 ❑ *Even if this album doesn't sell and the critics don't like it, we wouldn't ever change.* 即使这张专辑没有销路，并且也不讨评论家们喜欢，我们也决不会改变。 5 V-T/V-I Something that **sells** a product makes people want to buy the product. 促进…的销路 ❑ *It is only the sensational that sells news magazines.* 只有轰动性的消息才能促进新闻杂志的销售。 ❑ *...the maxim that safety doesn't sell.* …安全并不意味着畅销的格言。 6 V-T If you **sell** someone an idea or proposal, or **sell** someone **on** an idea, you convince them that it is a good one. 推荐; 使接受 ❑ *She tried to sell me the idea of buying my own paper shredder.* 她努力向我灌输买一台自己的碎纸机的想法。 ❑ *She is hoping she can sell the idea to clients.* 她希望她能使客户接受这一想法。 7 PHRASE If someone **sells** their **body**, they have sex for money. 出卖肉体 ❑ *85 percent said they would rather not sell their bodies for a living.* 85%的人说她们不会出卖肉体以谋生。 8 PHRASE If you talk about someone **selling** their **soul** in order to get something, you are criticizing them for abandoning their principles. 出卖灵魂 [DISAPPROVAL] ❑ *...a man who would sell his soul for political viability.* …一个为了政治前途甘愿出卖灵魂的人。

▸ **sell off** 1 PHRASAL VERB If you **sell** something **off**, you sell it because you need the money. 甩卖; 变卖 ❑ *The company is selling off some sites and concentrating on cutting debts.* 该公司正在变卖一些地皮，全力削减债务。 2 → see also **sell-off**

▸ **sell on** PHRASAL VERB If you buy something and then **sell it on**, you sell it to someone else soon after buying it, usually in order to make a profit. 转卖 ❑ *Mr. Farrier bought cars at auctions and sold them on.* 法里尔先生在拍卖会上买了一些汽车，然后再把他们转卖出去。

▸ **sell out** 1 PHRASAL VERB If a store **sells out** of something, it sells all its stocks of it, so that there is no longer any left for people to buy. 销售一空 ❑ *Hardware stores have sold out of water pumps and tarpaulins.* 五金商店的水泵和防水油布已经销售一空。 2 PHRASAL VERB If a performance, sports event, or other entertainment **sells out**, all the tickets for it are sold. (票等) 售完 ❑ *Football games often sell out well in advance.* 足球比赛的门票常常提前销售一空。 3 PHRASAL VERB When things **sell out**, all of them that are available are sold. 售完; 不再有存货 ❑ *Sleeping bags sold out almost immediately.* 睡袋几乎马上就卖完了。 4 PHRASAL VERB If you accuse someone of **selling out**, you disapprove of the fact that they do something which used to be against their principles, or give in to an opposing group. 出卖; 背叛 [DISAPPROVAL] ❑ *You don't have to sell out and work for some corporation.* 你没有必要出卖自己为某公司工作。 5 PHRASAL VERB If you **sell out**, you sell everything you have, such as your house or your business, because you need the money. 变卖全部财产 ❑ *I'll have a going out of business sale. I'll sell out and move out of here.* 我要举行一场歇业大甩卖。我要变卖全部财产，然后从这里搬走。 6 → see also **sell-out, sold out**

> **Thesaurus** *sell* 另参见：
> V. barter, exchange, retail; *(ant.)* buy 1 2

sell-by date (**sell-by dates**) N-COUNT The **sell-by date** on a food container is the date by which the food should be sold or eaten before it starts to decay. 最迟销售日期 ❑ *...a piece of cheese four weeks past its sell-by date.* …一块超过最迟销售日期4个星期的奶酪。

> **Word Link** *ar, er ≈ one who acts as : buyer, liar, seller*

sell·er /sɛlər/ (**sellers**) 1 N-COUNT A **seller** of a type of thing is a person or company that sells that type of thing. 卖者 ❑ *...a flower seller.* …一个卖花的人。 2 N-COUNT In a business deal, the **seller** is the person who is selling something to someone else. 卖方 ❑ *In theory, the buyer could ask the seller to have a test carried out.* 在理论上，买方可以要求卖方进行一次产品检测。 3 N-COUNT If you describe a product as, for example, a big **seller**, you mean that large numbers of it are being sold. 畅销品 ❑ *The gift store's biggest seller is a photo of Nixon meeting Presley.* 这家礼品店最畅销的商品是一幅尼克松会见普雷斯利的照片。 4 → see also **bestseller**

sel·ler's mar·ket N-SING When there is a **seller's market** for a particular product, there are fewer of the products for sale than people who want to buy them, so buyers have little choice and prices go up. 卖方市场 [BUSINESS] ❑ *It's a seller's market, and no one is forced to discount to remain competitive.* 这是一个卖方市场，没有人被迫打折来保持其竞争力。

sell·ing point (**selling points**) N-COUNT A **selling point** is a desirable quality or feature that something has which makes it likely that people will want to buy it. (指吸引顾客的) 卖点 [BUSINESS] ❑ *A garden is one of the biggest selling points with house-hunters.* 花园是吸引购房者的最大卖点之一。

sell·ing price (**selling prices**) N-COUNT The **selling price** of something is the price for which it is sold. 销售价 [BUSINESS] ❑ *Palm said the average selling price of its devices was $183.* 奔迈公司说其仪器的平均售价为$183。

sell-off (**sell-offs**) also **selloff** N-COUNT The **sell-off** of something, for example, an industry owned by the state or a company's shares, is the selling of it. (国有企业、公司股份等的) 出售 [BUSINESS] ❑ *The privatization of the electricity industry was the biggest sell-off of them all.* 电力行业的私有化是这类出售中最大的一宗。

sell-out (**sell-outs**) also **sellout** 1 N-COUNT If a play, sports event, or other entertainment is a **sell-out**, all the tickets for it are sold. (演出或比赛等的) 满座 ❑ *Their concert there was a sell-out.* 他们在那儿的音乐会座无虚席。 2 N-COUNT If you describe someone's behavior as a **sell-out**, you disapprove of the fact that they have done something which used to be against their principles, or given in to an opposing group. 出卖; 背叛 [DISAPPROVAL] ❑ *For some, his decision to become a Socialist candidate at Sunday's election was simply a sell-out.* 对某些人来说，他决定以社会党候选人的身份参加星期天的选举完全是一种背叛。

selves /sɛlvz/ **Selves** is the plural of **self**. **self**的复数

se·man·tics /sɪmæntɪks/

> The form **semantic** is used as a modifier.

N-UNCOUNT **Semantics** is the branch of linguistics that deals with the meanings of words and sentences. 语义学

sem·blance /sɛmbləns/ N-UNCOUNT If there is a **semblance of** a particular condition or quality, it appears to exist, even though this may be a false impression. 表象; 外观 [FORMAL] ❑ *At least a semblance of normality has been restored to parts of the country.* 这个国家的部分地区至少在表面上已恢复正常。

se·men /simən/ N-UNCOUNT **Semen** is the liquid containing sperm that is produced by the sex organs of men and male animals. 精液

se·mes·ter /sɪmɛstər/ (**semesters**) N-COUNT In colleges and universities in some countries, a **semester** is one of the two main periods into which the year is divided. 学期 ❑ *...February 22nd when most of their students begin their spring semester.* …2月22日，大多数学生开始春季学期时。

semi /sɛmi, sɛmaɪ/ (**semis**) **1** N-COUNT In a sports competition, **the semis** are the semifinals. 半决赛 [INFORMAL] ❑ *He reached the semis after beating Nadal in the quarterfinal.* 他在四分之一决赛中击败纳达尔后进入了半决赛。 **2** N-COUNT A **semi** is the same as a **tractor-trailer.** 牵引式挂车 [AM]

Word Link *semi ≈ half : semicircle, semiconductor, semifinal*

semi·cir·cle /sɛmisɜrkᵊl, sɛmaɪ-/ (**semicircles**) also **semi-circle** N-COUNT A **semicircle** is one half of a circle, or something having the shape of half a circle. 半圆（形） ❑ *They sit cross-legged in a semicircle and share stories.* 他们盘着腿围成半圆坐在一起讲故事。

semi·co·lon /sɛmikoʊlən/ (**semicolons**) N-COUNT A **semicolon** is the punctuation mark ; which is used in writing to separate different parts of a sentence or list or to indicate a pause. 分号（；）

semi·con·duc·tor /sɛmikəndʌktər, sɛmaɪ-/ (**semiconductors**) N-COUNT A **semiconductor** is a substance used in electronics whose ability to conduct electricity increases with greater heat. 半导体

→ see **solar system**

semi-detached /sɛmidɪtætʃt, sɛmaɪ-/ also **semidetached** ADJ A **semi-detached** house is a house that is joined to another house on one side by a shared wall. （与另一房屋共用一堵墙的）半独立式的 [mainly BRIT]

in AM, usually use **duplex**

● N-SING **Semi-detached** is also a noun. 半独立式房屋

semi·fi·nal /sɛmifaɪnᵊl, sɛmaɪ-/ (**semifinals**) N-COUNT A **semifinal** is one of the two games or races in a competition that are held to decide who will compete in the final. 半决赛 ❑ *We want to go into the semifinal, no matter who the rival is.* 我们想要进入半决赛，无论对手是谁。 ● N-PLURAL **The semifinals** is the round of a competition in which these two games or races are held. 半决赛阶段 ❑ *Team USA reached the semifinals by defeating New Zealand in the second round.* 美国队在第二轮击败新西兰后进入了半决赛阶段。

semi·nal /sɛmɪnᵊl/ ADJ **Seminal** is used to describe things such as books, works, events, and experiences that have a great influence in a particular field. （在某一领域内）有重大影响的 [FORMAL] ❑ *...author of the seminal book "Animal Liberation."* …有着巨大影响的《动物解放》一书的作者。

semi·nar /sɛmɪnɑr/ (**seminars**) **1** N-COUNT A **seminar** is a meeting where a group of people discuss a problem or topic. 研讨会；专题讨论会 ❑ *...a series of half-day seminars to help businessmen get the best value from investing in information technology.* …一系列帮助商界人士从投资信息技术中获得最大价值的每次为期半天的专题讨论会。 **2** N-COUNT A **seminar** is a class at a college or university in which the teacher and a small group of students discuss a topic. （大学里由教师指导小组学生参加的）研讨班 ❑ *Students are asked to prepare material in advance of each weekly seminar.* 要求学生为每星期一次的研讨班预先准备好材料。

semi·skilled /sɛmiskɪld, sɛmaɪ-/ ADJ A **semiskilled** worker has some training and skills, but not enough to do specialized work. 半熟练的 [BUSINESS]

Sen·ate ♦♦◊ /sɛnɪt/ (**Senates**) **1** N-PROPER-COLL **The Senate** is the smaller and more important of the two parts of the legislature in some US states and in some countries, for example, the United States and Australia. （美国、澳大利亚等国的）参议院 ❑ *The Senate is expected to pass the bill shortly.* 预计参议院将很快通过这项议案。 **2** N-PROPER-COLL **The Senate** is the governing council at some universities. （某些大学的）评议会 ❑ *By the time I was vice chancellor, the Senate had become a much larger and a much more democratic body.* 到我做副校长的那个时候，大学评议会已经成为一个更大、更民主的机构了。

Word Link *sen ≈ old : senator, senile, senior*

sena·tor ♦◊◊ /sɛnɪtər/ (**senators**) N-COUNT; N-TITLE A **senator** is a member of a political Senate, for example, in the United States or Australia. 参议员 ❑ *...Texas' first black senator.* …得克萨斯州的第一位黑人参议员。

send ♦♦♦ /sɛnd/ (**sends, sending, sent**) **1** V-T When you **send** someone something, you arrange for it to be taken and delivered to them, for example, by mail. 邮寄；发送 ❑ *Myra Cunningham sent me a note thanking me for dinner.* 迈拉・坎宁安寄给了我一封短信，感谢我请她吃饭。 ❑ *I sent a copy to the school principal.* 我寄了一份复印件给校长。 **2** V-T If you **send** someone somewhere, you tell them to go there. 派遣；打发 ❑ *Inspector Banbury came up to see her, but she sent him away.* 班伯里警官过来看她，但她却把他打发走了。 ❑ *...the government's decision to send troops to the region.* …政府向该地区派遣军队的决定。 ❑ *I suggested that he rest, and sent him for an X-ray.* 我建议他休息，并叫他去作一次X光检查。 **3** V-T If you **send** someone **to** an institution such as a school or a prison, you arrange for them to stay there for a period of time. 把…送进（学校、监狱等） ❑ *It's his parents' choice to send him to a boarding school, rather than a convenient day school.* 把他送到寄宿学校而不是去附近的走读学校，是他父母的决定。 **4** V-T To **send** a signal means to cause it to go to a place by means of radio waves or electricity. （通过电波或电）发送（信号） ❑ *The transmitters will send a signal automatically to a local base station.* 发射台会自动将信号发送到地方基站。 **5** V-T If something **sends** things or people in a particular direction, it causes them to move in that direction. 使（向某方向）移动 ❑ *The explosion sent shrapnel flying through the sides of cars on the crowded highway.* 这场爆炸使得炸弹碎片从拥挤公路上的车辆两侧飞过。 ❑ *A left hook sent him reeling.* 一记左钩拳打得他踉踉跄跄。 **6** V-T To **send** someone or something **into** a particular state means to cause them to go into or be in that state. 使进入（某种状态） ❑ *My attempt to fix it sent Lawrence into fits of laughter.* 我尝试着修理它，逗得劳伦斯笑得前仰后合。 ❑ *...before civil war and famine sent the country plunging into anarchy.* …在内战和饥荒让这个国家陷入一片混乱之前。 **7** to **send** someone **packing** → see **pack**

▸ **send away for** → see **send for 2**

▸ **send for** **1** PHRASAL VERB If you **send for** someone, you send them a message asking them to come and see you. 派人去叫；请（某人）来 ❑ *I've sent for the doctor.* 我已经让人去请医生了。 **2** PHRASAL VERB If you **send for** something, or **send away for** it, or **send off for** it, you write and ask for it to be sent to you. 去信索要；让人寄来 ❑ *Send for your free catalog today.* 今天就写信去索要免费目录。

▸ **send in** **1** PHRASAL VERB If you **send in** something such as a competition entry or a letter applying for a job, you mail it to the organization concerned. 呈递；提交 ❑ *Applicants are asked to send in a résumé and a cover letter.* 申请人被要求提交一份简历并附申请信。 **2** PHRASAL VERB When a government **sends in** troops or police officers, it orders them to deal with a crisis or problem somewhere. 派遣（军队或警察） ❑ *He has asked the government to send in troops to end the fighting.* 他已要求政府派部队来平息那场战斗。

▸ **send off** **1** PHRASAL VERB When you **send off** a letter or package, you send it somewhere by mail. 寄出；发出 ❑ *He sent off copies to various people for them to read and make comments.* 他把复印件寄给不同的人，请他们阅读并发表意见。 **2** PHRASAL VERB If a soccer player **is sent off**, the referee makes them leave the field during a game, as a punishment for seriously breaking the rules. 将（足球队员）罚下场 [mainly BRIT]

in AM, use **eject**

▸ **send off for** → see **send for 2**

▸ **send out** **1** PHRASAL VERB If you **send out** things such as letters or bills, you send them to a large number of people at the same time. 分发；散发 ❑ *She had sent out well over four hundred invitations that afternoon.* 那天下午她发出了远不止400份请柬。 **2** PHRASAL VERB To **send out** a signal, sound, light, or heat means to produce it. 发出（信号、声音、光、热等） ❑ *The crew did not send out any distress signals.* 机组人员没有发出任何求救信号。

▸ **send out for** PHRASAL VERB If you **send out for** food, for example, pizza or sandwiches, you phone and ask for it to be delivered to you. 叫外卖 ❑ *Let's send out for a pizza.* 咱们叫外卖送一个比萨饼来吧。

Thesaurus *send* 另参见：

V. issue, mail, ship, transmit; *(ant.)* receive **1** **4**

send·er /sɛndər/ (**senders**) N-COUNT **The sender of** a letter, package, or radio message is the person who sent it. 寄件人 ❑ *The sender of the best letter every week will win a check for $50.* 每周的最佳寄信人将赢得一张$50的支票。

se·nile /sinaɪl/ ADJ If old people become **senile**, they become confused, can no longer remember things, and are unable to take care of themselves. 衰老的；年老糊涂的 ● **se·nil·ity** /sɪnɪlɪti/ N-UNCOUNT 衰老；年老糊涂 ❑ *The old man was forced to resign after*

S

showing unmistakable signs of senility. 那个老头明显有了年老糊涂的迹象后就被迫辞职了。

sen·ior ♦♦◊ /siːnyər/ (**seniors**) 1 ADJ The **senior** people in an organization or profession have the highest and most important jobs. 级别高的; 资深的 [ADJ n] ❑ *...senior officials in the Israeli government.* …以色列政府中的高级官员。 ❑ *...the company's senior management.* …该公司的高级管理人员。 2 ADJ If someone is **senior to** you in an organization or profession, they have a higher and more important job than you or they are considered to be superior to you because they have worked there for longer and have more experience. 职务高于…的; 资格比…老的 ❑ *The position had to be filled by an officer senior to Haig.* 这个位置必须由一名职位比黑格高的军官来填补。 ● N-PLURAL Your **seniors** are the people who are senior to you. 上级; 地位较高者 ❑ *He was described by his seniors as a model officer.* 他被上级称为模范军官。 3 N-SING **Senior** is used when indicating how much older one person is than another. For example, if someone is ten years your **senior**, they are ten years older than you. 年长(岁数) 的人 ❑ *She became involved with a married man many years her senior.* 她与一名比她年长很多的已婚男子坠入情网。 4 N-COUNT **Seniors** are students in a high school, university, or college who are in their fourth year of study. (高中、大学的) 毕业班学生 [AM] ❑ *...the number of high school seniors who go on to college.* …高中毕业班上大学的学生人数。 5 N-COUNT A **senior** is the same as a **senior citizen**. 老年人 ❑ *Tickets at the gate are $10, $7 for seniors (age 55 and up).* 门票价格为$10，老年人(55岁及以上)为$7。 6 ADJ If you take part in a sport at **senior** level, you take part in competitions with adults and people who have reached a high degree of achievement in that sport. (体育比赛) 成人组的 [ADJ n] ❑ *This will be his fifth international championship and his third at senior level.* 这将是他的第五次国际锦标赛，也是他的第三次成人级别比赛。

sen·ior cit·i·zen (**senior citizens**) N-COUNT A **senior citizen** is an older person who has retired or receives social security benefits. 老年人(指已退休或领取养老金的) ❑ *...services for senior citizens.* …为老年人提供的服务。
→ see **age**

★ **sen·ior·ity** /siːnjɔrɪti/ N-UNCOUNT A person's **seniority** in an organization is the importance and power that they have compared with others, or the fact that they have worked there for a long time. 资历; 年资 ❑ *He has said he will fire editorial employees without regard to seniority.* 他说过在解雇编辑人员时他不会考虑其资历如何。

Word Link *sens ≈ feeling : sensation, senseless, sensitive*

★ **sen·sa·tion** /sɛnseɪʃən/ (**sensations**) 1 N-COUNT A **sensation** is a physical feeling. 感觉 ❑ *Floating can be a very pleasant sensation.* 漂浮会给人一种非常愉快的感觉。 2 N-UNCOUNT **Sensation** is your ability to feel things physically, especially through your sense of touch. 感觉能力 ❑ *The pain was so bad that she lost all sensation.* 疼得太厉害了，她完全失去了感觉能力。 3 N-COUNT You can use **sensation** to refer to the general feeling or impression caused by a particular experience. (某种经历所产生的) 整体感觉 ❑ *It's a funny sensation to know someone's talking about you in a language you don't understand.* 知道有人正用一种你不懂的语言谈论你，这种感觉真奇怪。 4 N-COUNT If a person, event, or situation is a **sensation**, it causes great excitement or interest. 引起轰动的人或事物 ❑ *...the film that turned her into an overnight sensation.* …让她一夜成名的影片。 5 N-SING If a person, event, or situation causes **a sensation**, they cause great interest or excitement. 轰动 ❑ *She was just 14 when she caused a sensation at the Montreal Olympics.* 她在蒙特利尔奥运会上引起轰动时，年仅14岁。
→ see **taste**

★ **sen·sa·tion·al** /sɛnseɪʃənəl/ 1 ADJ A **sensational** result, event, or situation is so remarkable that it causes great excitement and interest. 戏剧性的; 轰动性的 ❑ *The world champions suffered a sensational defeat.* 世界冠军们遭到一次戏剧性的失败 ● **sen·sa·tion·al·ly** ADV 戏剧性地; 轰动性地 ❑ *The rape trial was sensationally halted yesterday.* 强奸案审判昨天戏剧性地被中断了。 2 ADJ You can describe stories or reports as **sensational** if you disapprove of them because they present facts in a way that is intended to cause feelings of shock, anger, or excitement. 耸人听闻的; 哗众取宠的 [DISAPPROVAL] ❑ *...sensational tabloid newspaper reports.* …耸人听闻的小报报道。 3 ADJ You can describe something as **sensational** when you think that it is extremely good. 极好的 ❑ *Her voice is sensational.* 她的嗓音极为动听。 ● **sen·sa·tion·al·ly** ADV 极好地 ❑ *...sensationally good food.* …绝佳美食。

sense ♦♦♦ /sɛns/ (**senses, sensing, sensed**) 1 N-COUNT Your **senses** are the physical abilities of sight, smell, hearing, touch, and taste. 感觉功能 ❑ *She stared at him again, unable to believe the evidence of her senses.* 她再次盯着他，不敢相信自己的感觉。 2 V-T If you **sense** something, you become aware of it or you realize it, although it is not very obvious. 觉察到; 意识到 ❑ *She probably sensed that I wasn't telling her the whole story.* 她很可能觉察到我没有告诉她全部真相。 ❑ *He looks about him, sensing danger.* 他环顾四周，觉察到了危险。 3 N-SING If you have a **sense that** something is the case, you think that it is the case, although you may not have firm, clear evidence for this belief. 感觉 ❑ *Suddenly you got this sense that people were drawing themselves away from each other.* 突然你有了这样的感觉即人们正在彼此疏远。 4 N-SING If you have a **sense of** guilt or relief, for example, you feel guilty or relieved. 感觉 ❑ *When your child is struggling for life, you feel this overwhelming sense of guilt.* 当你的孩子为生活而奔波时，你就会有这种强烈的内疚感。 5 N-SING If you have a **sense of** something such as duty or justice, you are aware of it and believe it is important. 意识; 观念 ❑ *My sense of justice was offended.* 我的正义感受到了冒犯。 ❑ *We must keep a sense of proportion about all this.* 我们必须把握好所有这些事情的轻重缓急。 6 N-SING Someone who has a **sense of** timing or style has a natural ability with regard to timing or style. You can also say that someone has a bad **sense of** timing or style. 理解力; 天赋 [N "of" n, also n N] ❑ *He has an impeccable sense of timing.* 他时间感很强。 ❑ *Her dress sense is appalling.* 她的着装品位让人汗颜。 7 → see also **sense of humor** 8 N-UNCOUNT **Sense** is the ability to make good judgments and to behave sensibly. 理智; 判断力 ❑ *...when he was younger and had a bit more sense.* …当他较为年轻、较为理智的时候。 ❑ *When that doesn't work they sometimes have the sense to seek help.* 当那样做行不通时，他们会想到时不时地去寻求帮助。 9 → see also **common sense** 10 N-SING If you say that there is no **sense** or little **sense in** doing something, you mean that it is not a sensible thing to do because nothing useful would be gained by doing it. 意义 ❑ *There's no sense in pretending this doesn't happen.* 假装此事没有发生是没用的。 11 N-COUNT A **sense** of a word or expression is one of its possible meanings. 意义; 含义 ❑ *...a noun which has two senses.* …一个有两种含义的名词。 12 PHRASE **Sense** is used in several expressions to indicate how true your statement is. For example, if you say that something is true **in a sense**, you mean that it is partly true, or true in one way. If you say that something is true **in a general sense**, you mean that it is true in a general way. 在某种意义上; 在一般意义上 ❑ *In a sense, both were right.* 在某种意义上，两者都对。 ❑ *Though his background was modest, it was in no sense deprived.* 他的出身背景一般般，但绝算不上贫穷。 13 PHRASE If something **makes sense**, you can understand it. 有意义; 言之有理 ❑ *He was sitting there saying, "Yes, the figures make sense."* 他坐在那里说："是的，这些数字有其道理。" 14 PHRASE When you **make sense of** something, you succeed in understanding it. 理解 ❑ *Provided you didn't try to make sense of it, it sounded beautiful.* 只要你不试图理解，它听起来是美的。 15 PHRASE If a course of action **makes sense**, it seems sensible. 看来明智 ❑ *It makes sense to look after yourself.* 照顾好你自己是明智的。 ❑ *The project should be re-appraised to see whether it made sound economic sense.* 该项目应重新评估，看看在经济上是否合情合理。 16 PHRASE If you say that someone **has come to** their **senses** or **has been brought to** their **senses**, you mean that they have stopped being foolish and are being sensible again. 恢复理智 ❑ *Eventually the world will come to its senses and get rid of them.* 最终这个世界会恢复理智，除掉它们。 17 PHRASE If you say that someone **talks sense**, you mean that what they say is sensible. 说得有理 ❑ *When he speaks, he talks sense.* 他言之必有理。 18 PHRASE If you **have a sense that** something is true or **get a sense that** something is true, you think that it is true. 意识到 [mainly SPOKEN] ❑ *Do you have the sense that you are loved by the public?* 你意识到自己受公众喜爱了吗? 19 **to see sense** → see **see**
→ see **smell**

Thesaurus *sense* 另参见:
V. notice, perceive, realize 2
N. feeling, sensation 2 3
awareness, feeling, perception 3 – 5

sense·less /sɛnslɪs/ 1 ADJ If you describe an action as **senseless**, you think it is wrong because it has no purpose and produces no benefit. 无意义的 ❑ *...people whose lives have been destroyed by acts of senseless violence.* …被无意义的暴力毁了生活的人们。 2 ADJ If someone is **senseless**, they are unconscious. 失去知觉的;

S

不省人事的 ❑ *They were knocked to the ground, beaten senseless and robbed of their wallets.* 他们被打倒在地、不省人事，还被抢走了钱包。

sense of di·rec·tion N-SING Your **sense of direction** is your ability to know roughly where you are, or which way to go, even when you are in an unfamiliar place. 方向感 ❑ *He had a poor sense of direction and soon got lost.* 他方向感不好，一会儿就迷路了。

sense of hu·mor

in BRIT, use **sense of humour**

N-SING Someone who has a **sense of humor** often finds things amusing, rather than being serious all the time. 幽默感 ❑ *She seems to have a good sense of humor.* 她似乎有很强的幽默感。

sense of hu·mour [BRIT] → see **sense of humor**

sen·sibil·ity /sɛnsɪbɪlɪti/ (**sensibilities**) **1** N-UNCOUNT **Sensibility** is the ability to experience deep feelings. 感受力 ❑ *Everything he writes demonstrates the depth of his sensibility.* 他写的一切都显示出其感受力之深切。 **2** N-VAR Someone's **sensibility** is their tendency to be influenced or offended by things. 敏感性 ❑ *He was unable to control his sensibility.* 他无法控制自己敏锐的情感。

sen·sible ♦◇◇ /sɛnsɪbəl/ **1** ADJ **Sensible** actions or decisions are good because they are based on reasons rather than emotions. 明智的 ❑ *It might be sensible to get a lawyer.* 找个律师可能会是明智的。 ❑ *The sensible thing is to leave them alone.* 明智的做法是不理他们。 ● **sen·sibly** /sɛnsɪbli/ ADV 明智地 ❑ *He sensibly decided to lie low for a while.* 他明智地决定先躲避一段时间。 **2** ADJ **Sensible** people behave in a sensible way. 理智的 ❑ *She was a sensible girl and did not panic.* 她是个理智的女孩子，并没有惊慌失措。 ❑ *Oh come on, let's be sensible about this.* 哦，得了吧，关于这事我们还是理智一点吧。 **3** ADJ **Sensible** shoes or clothes are practical and strong rather than fashionable and attractive. 实用耐穿的 ❑ *Wear loose clothing and sensible footwear.* 穿宽松的衣服和实用耐穿的鞋子。 ● **sen·sibly** ADV 实用耐穿地 ❑ *They were not sensibly dressed.* 他们穿得不实用。

> Take care not to confuse **sensible** and **sensitive**. You do not use **sensible** to describe someone whose feelings or emotions are strongly affected by their experiences. The word you need is **sensitive**. ❑ *...a highly sensitive artist.*

sen·si·tive ♦◇◇ /sɛnsɪtɪv/ **1** ADJ If you are **sensitive to** other people's needs, problems, or feelings, you show understanding and awareness of them. 有感知力的；能理解的 [APPROVAL] ❑ *The classroom teacher must be sensitive to a child's needs.* 课堂教师必须理解孩子的需求。 ● **sen·si·tive·ly** ADV 有感知力地；能理解地 ❑ *The abuse of women needs to be treated seriously and sensitively.* 虐待妇女的问题需要严肃、小心地对待。 ● **sen·si·tiv·ity** ★ /sɛnsɪtɪvɪti/ N-UNCOUNT 感受力；理解 [oft N "for" n] ❑ *A good relationship involves concern and sensitivity for each other's feelings.* 良好的关系包含关心并理解彼此的情感。 **2** ADJ If you are **sensitive about** something, you are easily worried and offended when people talk about it. 敏感的 ❑ *Young people are very sensitive about their appearance.* 年轻人对自己的外貌很敏感。 ● **sen·si·tiv·ity** N-VAR (**sensitivities**) 敏感 ❑ *...people who suffer extreme sensitivity about what others think.* …对别人的看法极为敏感的人。 **3** ADJ A **sensitive** subject or issue needs to be dealt with carefully because it is likely to cause disagreement or make people angry or upset. 敏感的；棘手的 ❑ *Employment is a very sensitive issue.* 就业是一个非常敏感的问题。 ● **sen·si·tiv·ity** N-UNCOUNT 敏感性 [oft N "of" n] ❑ *Due to the obvious sensitivity of the issue he would not divulge any details.* 由于问题带有明显的敏感性，他不肯透露任何细节。 **4** ADJ **Sensitive** documents or reports contain information that needs to be kept secret and dealt with carefully. 机密的 ❑ *He instructed staff to shred sensitive documents.* 他指示员工用碎纸机粉碎机密文件。 **5** ADJ Something that is **sensitive to** a physical force, substance, or treatment is easily affected by it and often harmed by it. 敏感的 ❑ *...a chemical which is sensitive to light.* …一种对光敏感的化学品。 ● **sen·si·tiv·ity** N-UNCOUNT 敏感性 ❑ *...the sensitivity of cells damaged by chemotherapy.* …被化疗损害了的细胞敏感性。 **6** ADJ A **sensitive** piece of scientific equipment is capable of measuring or recording very small changes. 灵敏的 ❑ *...an extremely sensitive microscope.* …一台极为灵敏的显微镜。 ● **sen·si·tiv·ity** N-UNCOUNT 灵敏度 ❑ *...the sensitivity of the detector.* …该探测器的灵敏度。

Thesaurus *sensitive* 另参见：

ADJ. conscious, perceptive, understanding; (*ant.*) insensitive **1**
emotional, irritable, touchy **2**

Word Partnership *sensitive* 的常用搭配：

ADV. **highly** sensitive, **very** sensitive **1**–**6**
politically sensitive **3**
overly sensitive, **so** sensitive, **too** sensitive **2**
environmentally sensitive **5**
N. sensitive **areas**, sensitive **issue** **3**
sensitive **information**, sensitive **material** **4**
heat sensitive, **light** sensitive, sensitive **skin** **5**
sensitive **equipment** **6**

sen·sor /sɛnsər/ (**sensors**) N-COUNT A **sensor** is an instrument which reacts to certain physical conditions or impressions such as heat or light, and which is used to provide information. 传感器 ❑ *The latest Japanese vacuum cleaners contain sensors that detect the amount of dust and type of floor.* 日本最新款吸尘器装有传感器，能测出灰尘量和地板类型。

sen·so·ry /sɛnsəri/ ADJ **Sensory** means relating to the physical senses. 感官的；感觉的 [ADJ n] [FORMAL] ❑ *Almost all sensory information from the trunk and limbs passes through the spinal cord.* 几乎所有来自躯干及四肢的感官信息都经由脊髓传递。
→ see **nervous system, smell**

★ **sen·sual** /sɛnʃuəl/ **1** ADJ Someone or something that is **sensual** shows or suggests a great liking for physical pleasures, especially sexual pleasures. 喜爱感官享受(尤指肉欲)的 ❑ *He was a very sensual person.* 他是个非常喜爱感官享受的人。 ❑ *...the sensual curve of her lips.* …她嘴唇的性感曲线。 ● **sen·su·al·ity** /sɛnʃuælɪti/ N-UNCOUNT 性感 ❑ *The wave and curl of her blonde hair gave her sensuality and youth.* 波浪式的卷曲金发使她显得性感并富有青春活力。 **2** ADJ Something that is **sensual** gives pleasure to your physical senses rather than to your mind. 愉悦感官的 ❑ *It was an opera, very glamorous and very sensual.* 那是一部极富魅力，让人感官非常愉悦的歌剧。 ● **sen·su·al·ity** N-UNCOUNT 感官的愉悦 ❑ *These perfumes have warmth and sensuality.* 这些香水温暖且令人愉悦。

sen·su·ous /sɛnʃuəs/ **1** ADJ Something that is **sensuous** gives pleasure to the mind or body through the senses. 给人快感的 ❑ *The film is ravishing to look at and boasts a sensuous musical score.* 这部电影令人陶醉，配乐也悦耳动听。 ● **sen·su·ous·ly** ADV 给人快感地 ❑ *She lay in the deep bath for a long time, enjoying its sensuously perfumed water.* 她在装满水的浴缸里躺了很长时间，享受着水的宜人芳香。 **2** ADJ Someone or something that is **sensuous** shows or suggests a great liking for sexual pleasure. 性感的 ❑ *...his sensuous young mistress, Marie-Therese.* …他年轻性感的情妇玛丽・泰蕾兹。 ❑ *...wide sensuous lips.* …宽而性感的嘴唇。 ● **sen·su·ous·ly** ADV 性感地 ❑ *The nose was straight, the mouth sensuously wide and full.* 鼻子挺直，嘴唇宽厚性感。

sent /sɛnt/ **Sent** is the past tense and past participle of **send**. **send**的过去式和过去分词

sen·tence ♦♦◇ /sɛntəns/ (**sentences, sentencing, sentenced**) **1** N-COUNT A **sentence** is a group of words which, when they are written down, begin with a capital letter and end with a period, question mark, or exclamation mark. Most sentences contain a subject and a verb. 句子 ❑ *Here we have several sentences incorrectly joined by commas.* 这里有几个误用逗号连接的句子。 **2** N-VAR In a law court, a **sentence** is the punishment that a person receives after they have been found guilty of a crime. 刑罚 ❑ *They are already serving prison sentences for their part in the assassination.* 他们已经因为参与暗杀而在监狱服刑。 ❑ *He was given a four-year sentence.* 他被判处了4年徒刑。 ❑ *The court is expected to pass sentence later today.* 预计法庭将于今天晚些时候宣布判决。 **3** → see also **death sentence** **4** V-T When a judge **sentences** someone, he or she states in court what their punishment will be. 宣判；判决 ❑ *A military court sentenced him to death in his absence.* 一家军事法院在他未到庭的情况下判处他死刑。 ❑ *She was sentenced to nine years in prison.* 她被判处9年监禁。
→ see **trial**

★ **sen·ti·ment** /sɛntɪmənt/ (**sentiments**) **1** N-VAR A **sentiment** that people have is an attitude which is based on their thoughts and feelings. 情绪 ❑ *Public sentiment rapidly turned anti-American.* 公众的情绪迅速转向反美。 ❑ *He's found growing sentiment for military action.* 他已经发现支持军事行动的情绪在日益增长。 **2** N-COUNT A **sentiment** is an idea or feeling that someone expresses in words. 观点；感想 ❑ *I must agree with the sentiments expressed by John Prescott.* 我必须同意约翰・普雷斯科特表达的观点。 **3** N-UNCOUNT **Sentiment** is feelings such as pity or love, especially for things in the past, and may be

S

considered exaggerated and foolish. 伤感; 感情 ❑ *Laura kept that letter out of sentiment.* 劳拉出于伤感保留了那封信。

sen·ti·ment·al /sɛntɪmɛntᵊl/ **1** ADJ Someone or something that is **sentimental** feels or shows pity or love, sometimes to an extent that is considered exaggerated and foolish. 伤感的; 多愁善感的 ❑ *I'm trying not to be sentimental about the past.* 我尽力不为过去的事情而多愁善感。● **sen·ti·men·tal·ly** ADV 伤感地; 多愁善感地 ❑ *Childhood had less freedom and joy than we sentimentally attribute to it.* 童年的自由和欢乐没有我们多愁善感地赋予它的那么多。● **sen·ti·men·tal·ity** /sɛntɪmɛntælɪti/ N-UNCOUNT 伤感; 多愁善感 ❑ *In this book there is no sentimentality.* 在这本书里没有伤感。**2** ADJ **Sentimental** means relating to or involving feelings such as pity or love, especially for things in the past. 情感的 ❑ *Our paintings and photographs are of sentimental value only.* 我们的画和照片只有情感价值。

▲ **sen·try** /sɛntri/ (**sentries**) N-COUNT A **sentry** is a soldier who guards a camp or a building. 哨兵; 警卫 ❑ *The sentry would not let her enter.* 警卫不会让她进来。

sepa·rate ♦♦◊ (**separates, separating, separated**)

> The adjective and noun are pronounced /sɛpərɪt/. The verb is pronounced /sɛpəreɪt/.

> 形容词和名词读作 /sɛpərɪt/。动词读作 /sɛpəreɪt/。

1 ADJ If one thing is **separate from** another, there is a barrier, space, or division between them, so that they are clearly two things. 分开的; 单独的 ❑ *They are now making plans to form their own separate party.* 他们现在正制订计划单独组建自己的政党。❑ *Business bank accounts were kept separate from personal ones.* 银行的商业账户同个人账户是分开存放的。**2** ADJ If you refer to **separate** things, you mean several different things, rather than just one thing. 分开的; 不同的 ❑ *Use separate chopping boards for raw meats, cooked meats, vegetables and salads.* 用不同的砧板切生肉、熟肉、蔬菜和沙拉。❑ *Men and women have separate exercise rooms.* 男士和女士有分开的健身房。**3** V-RECIP If you **separate** people or things that are together, or if they **separate**, they move apart. 分开 ❑ *Police moved in to separate the two groups.* 警察插进来分开了那两群人。❑ *The pans were held in both hands and swirled around to separate gold particles from the dirt.* 淘洗盘被端在两手中旋转，以便将金粒从泥沙中分离出来。❑ *The front end of the car separated from the rest of the vehicle.* 车的前端同车子的其他部分分开了。**4** V-RECIP If you **separate** people or things that have been connected, or if one **separates from** another, the connection between them is ended. 使分离; 脱离 ❑ *They want to separate teaching from research.* 他们要把教学与研究分离开来。❑ *It's very possible that we may see a movement to separate the two parts of the country.* 我们很有可能会看到一场运动将该国一分为二。**5** V-RECIP If a couple who are married or living together **separate**, they decide to live apart. 分居 ❑ *Her parents separated when she was very young.* 在她很小的时候，父母就分居了。**6** V-T An object, obstacle, distance, or period of time which **separates** two people, groups, or things exists between them. 分隔 ❑ *...the white-railed fence that separated the yard from the paddock.* …把院子和围场分隔开来的白色围栏。❑ *They had undoubtedly made progress in the six years that separated the two periods.* 他们无疑在那两个时期之间的6年里取得了进步。**7** V-T If you **separate** one idea or fact **from** another, you clearly see or show the difference between them. 分辨; 区分 ❑ *It is difficult to separate legend from truth.* 传说与事实很难分辨。❑ *...learning how to separate real problems from imaginary illnesses.* …学习如何分辨真实的与想像的疾病。● PHRASAL VERB **Separate out** means the same as **separate**. 分辨; 区分 ❑ *How can one ever separate out the act from the attitudes that surround it?* 如何才能将行动同围绕着它的种种看法区分开来呢？**8** V-T A quality or factor that **separates** one thing **from** another is the reason why the two things are different from each other. 使不同 ❑ *The single most important factor that separates ordinary photographs from good photographs is the lighting.* 区分一般照片和好照片的惟一重要因素是光线效果。**9** V-T If a particular number of points **separate** two teams or competitors, one of them is winning or has won by that number of points. 使分出高下; 使分出输赢 ❑ *In the end only three points separated the two teams.* 最后，两队只以3分之差分出了输赢。**10** V-T/V-I If you **separate** a group of people or things **into** smaller elements, or if a group **separates**, it is divided into smaller elements. 使分散; 分散 ❑ *The police wanted to separate them into smaller groups.* 警察想把他们分成更小的组。❑ *Let's separate into smaller groups.* 让我们分成更小的组吧。● PHRASAL VERB **Separate out** means the same as **separate**. 分开; 分散 ❑ *If prepared many hours ahead, the mixture may separate out.* 如果提前很多小时配制，这种混合物就可能会分离。**11** N-PLURAL **Separates** are clothes such as skirts, pants, and shirts which cover just the top half or the bottom half of your body. 单件衣服 ❑ *She wears coordinated separates instead of a suit.* 她不穿套装，而穿着搭配协调的单件衣服。**12** → see also **separated** **13** PHRASE When two or more people who have been together for some time **go** their **separate ways**, they go to different places or end their relationship. 分道扬镳 ❑ *Sue was 27 when she and her husband decided to go their separate ways.* 27岁时苏与丈夫决定分道扬镳。

▸ **separate out** **1** PHRASAL VERB If you **separate out** something from the other things it is with, you take it out. 使…分开 ❑ *The ability to separate out reusable elements from other waste is crucial.* 将可再次利用的成分从其他废料中分离出来的能力至关重要。**2** → see also **separate 7, 10**

> **Thesaurus** *separate* 另参见：
> ADJ. disconnected, divided **1**
> V. divide, remove, split **3** **4**
> split **5**

sepa·rat·ed /sɛpəreɪtɪd/ **1** ADJ Someone who is **separated** from their wife or husband lives apart from them, but is not divorced. 分居的 [v-link ADJ] ❑ *Most single parents are either divorced or separated.* 大多数单身父母不是离婚的，就是分居的。**2** ADJ If you are **separated** from someone, for example, your family, you are not able to be with them. 分开的 ❑ *The idea of being separated from him, even for a few hours, was torture.* 想到与他分开，哪怕只是几个小时，也是一种折磨。

sepa·rate·ly /sɛpərɪtli/ ADV If people or things are dealt with **separately** or do something **separately**, they are dealt with or do something at different times or places, rather than together. 分别地 ❑ *Cook each vegetable separately until just tender.* 把每样蔬菜单独烹煮，直到煮软就行了。

sepa·ra·tion /sɛpəreɪʃᵊn/ (**separations**) **1** N-VAR The **separation of** two or more things or groups is the fact that they are separate or become separate, and are not linked. 分离; 分开; 隔离 [oft N "of/from/between" n] ❑ *He believes in the separation of the races.* 他信奉种族隔离政策。**2** N-VAR During a **separation**, people who usually live together are not together. 分离期间 ❑ *She wondered if Harry had been unfaithful to her during this long separation.* 她想知道，在分开的漫长岁月里哈里是否已经对她不忠了。**3** N-VAR If a couple who are married or living together have a **separation**, they decide to live apart. 分居 ❑ *They agreed to a trial separation.* 他们同意尝试一次分居。

sepa·ra·tism /sɛpərətɪzəm/ N-UNCOUNT **Separatism** is the beliefs and activities of separatists. 分裂主义; 独立主义 ❑ *...a doctrine of racial separatism.* …一个种族分裂的学说。

▲ **sepa·ra·tist** /sɛpərətɪst/ (**separatists**) **1** ADJ **Separatist** organizations and activities within a country involve members of a group of people who want to establish their own separate government or are trying to do so. 分裂主义的; 独立主义的 [ADJ n] ❑ *Spanish police say they have arrested ten people suspected of being members of the Basque separatist movement.* 西班牙警方说，他们已经逮捕了10名巴斯克独立运动的嫌疑分子。**2** N-COUNT **Separatists** are people who want their own separate government or are involved in separatist activities. 独立主义者 ❑ *The army has come under attack by separatists.* 军队遭到独立分子的袭击。

Sept. **Sept.** is a written abbreviation for **September**. 9月 ❑ *I've booked it for Thurs. Sept. 8th.* 我已经预定了9月8日星期四那天的。

Sep·tem·ber ♦♦♦ /sɛptɛmbər/ (**Septembers**) N-VAR **September** is the ninth month of the year in the Western calendar. 9月 ❑ *Her son, Jerome, was born in September.* 她的儿子杰罗姆出生于9月。❑ *We didn't make the original September 30 release date.* 我们没有赶上原定9月30日的发行日。

sep·tic /sɛptɪk/ ADJ If a wound or a part of your body becomes **septic**, it becomes infected. 受感染的 ❑ *A flake of plaster from the ceiling fell into his eye, which became septic.* 天花板上的一片灰掉进他眼睛里，引起了感染。

> **Word Link** *sequ ≈ following : consequence, sequel, sequence*

se·quel /sikwᵊl/ (**sequels**) N-COUNT A book or movie which is a **sequel to** an earlier one continues the story of the earlier one. (书或电影的) 续篇; 续集 ❑ *She is currently writing a sequel to Daphne du Maurier's "Rebecca."* 她目前正在写达夫妮·杜穆里埃的《蝴蝶梦》续集。

se·quence /sikwəns/ (**sequences**) **1** N-COUNT A **sequence of** events or things is a number of events or things that come one after another in a particular order. 一系列；一连串 ❑ *...the sequence of events which led to the murder.* …导致这起谋杀的一连串事件。 **2** N-COUNT A particular **sequence** is a particular order in which things happen or are arranged. 次序；顺序 ❑ *...the color sequence yellow, orange, purple, blue, green and white.* …黄、橙、紫、蓝、绿和白的颜色顺序。

se·quin /siːkwɪn/ (**sequins**) N-COUNT **Sequins** are small, shiny disks that are sewn on clothes to decorate them. 闪光装饰片。 ❑ *The frocks were covered in sequins, thousands of them.* 连衣裙上缀满了数以千计的闪光装饰片。

▲ **se·rene** /sɪriːn/ ADJ Someone or something that is **serene** is calm and quiet. 安详的；宁静的 ❑ *She looked as calm and serene as she always did.* 她看上去如往常一样安详宁静。 ❑ *He didn't speak much, he just smiled with that serene smile of his.* 他没有多说，仅是面含他特有的安详微笑。 ● **se·rene·ly** ADV 安详地；宁静地 ❑ *We sailed serenely down the river.* 我们乘船平静地沿江而下。 ❑ *She carried on serenely sipping her gin and tonic.* 她继续平静地呷着加奎宁水的杜松子酒。 ● **se·ren·ity** /sɪrɛnɪti/ N-UNCOUNT 安详；平静 ❑ *I had a wonderful feeling of peace and serenity when I saw my husband.* 当我看到丈夫时，有种奇妙的安详与平静的感觉。

★ **ser·geant** /sɑrdʒᵊnt/ (**sergeants**) **1** N-COUNT; N-TITLE; N-VOC A **sergeant** is a non-commissioned officer of middle rank in the army, marines, or air force. 中士 ❑ *A sergeant with a detail of four men came into view.* 1名中士率领由4名士兵组成的小分队进入了视野。 **2** N-COUNT; N-TITLE; N-VOC A **sergeant** is an officer with the rank immediately below a captain. 警官 ❑ *A police sergeant patrolling the area spotted flames at the store.* 在该地区巡逻的一名警官发现那家商店失火了。

ser·geant ma·jor (**sergeant majors**) also **sergeant-major** N-COUNT; N-TITLE; N-VOC A **sergeant major** is a noncommissioned army or marine officer of the highest rank. 上士

★ **se·rial** /sɪəriəl/ (**serials**) **1** N-COUNT A **serial** is a story which is broadcast on television or radio or is published in a magazine or newspaper in a number of parts over a period of time. 连续剧；连载 ❑ *...one of television's most popular serials.* …最受欢迎的电视连续剧之一。 **2** ADJ **Serial** killings or attacks are a series of killings or attacks committed by the same person. This person is known as a **serial** killer or attacker. 连续的；一系列的 [ADJ n] ❑ *...serial murders.* …系列谋杀案。

se·riali·sa·tion /sɪəriəlaɪzeɪʃᵊn/ [BRIT] → see **serialization**

se·rial·ise /sɪəriəlaɪz/ [BRIT] → see **serialize**

se·riali·za·tion /sɪəriəlɪzeɪʃᵊn/ (**serializations**)

in BRIT, also use **serialisation**

1 N-UNCOUNT **Serialization** is the act of serializing a book. 连载 ❑ *It was first written for serialization in a magazine.* 那是原来为在杂志上连载而写的。 **2** N-COUNT A **serialization** is a story, originally written as a book, which is being published or broadcast in a number of parts. 连载；连播 ❑ *...the serialization of Jane Austen's Pride and Prejudice.* …简·奥斯丁《傲慢与偏见》的连播。

se·rial·ize /sɪəriəlaɪz/ (**serializes, serializing, serialized**)

in BRIT, also use **serialise**

V-T If a book **is serialized**, it is broadcast on the radio or television or is published in a magazine or newspaper in a number of parts over a period of time. 连载；连播；连映 [usu passive] ❑ *Attention was first drawn to the book when a condensed version was serialized in The New Yorker.* 这本书的缩写本在《纽约人》上连载时首次引起了人们的注意。

se·rial num·ber (**serial numbers**) **1** N-COUNT The **serial number** of an object is a number on that object which identifies it. 序列号；编号 ❑ *...the gun's serial number.* …这支枪的序列号。 ❑ *...your bike's serial number.* …你的自行车的编号。 **2** N-COUNT The **serial number** of a member of the United States military forces is a number which identifies them. (美国军人的) 入伍编号 ❑ *He could never ever give any responses to his captor other than name, rank, serial number and date of birth.* 除了自己的姓名、军衔、编号和出生日期外，他绝不可能向捕获他的人透露其他任何信息。

se·rial port (**serial ports**) N-COUNT A **serial port** on a computer is a place where you can connect the computer to a device such as a modem or a mouse. 串行端口 [COMPUTING]

se·ries ◆◆◇ /sɪəriz/ (**series**)

Series is both the singular and the plural form.

1 N-COUNT A **series of** things or events is a number of them that come one after the other. 一连串；一系列 ❑ *...a series of meetings with students and political leaders.* …与学生和政治领袖们的一连串会晤。 **2** N-COUNT A radio or television **series** is a set of programs of a particular kind which have the same title. (广播或电视的) 系列节目 ❑ *...Captain Kirk's chair from the TV series "Star Trek."* …电视系列片《星际迷航》中柯克船长的椅子。

se·ri·ous ◆◆◆ /sɪəriəs/ **1** ADJ **Serious** problems or situations are very bad and cause people to be worried or afraid. 严重的；危急的 ❑ *Crime is an increasingly serious problem in Russian society.* 犯罪是俄罗斯社会一个日益严重的问题。 ❑ *The government still face very serious difficulties.* 政府仍面临着非常严重的困难。 ● **se·ri·ous·ly** ADV 严重地；危急地 ❑ *If this ban was to come in it would seriously damage my business.* 这项禁令如果实施，将会严重地损害我的生意。 ● **se·ri·ous·ness** N-UNCOUNT 严重性 [oft N "of" n] ❑ *...the seriousness of the crisis.* …危机的严重性。 **2** ADJ **Serious** matters are important and deserve careful and thoughtful consideration. 重要的 ❑ *I regard this as a serious matter.* 我认为这是一件重要的事情。 ❑ *Don't laugh boy. This is serious.* 不要笑，伙计。这事很重要。 **3** ADJ When important matters are dealt with in a **serious** way, they are given careful and thoughtful consideration. 认真的；严肃的 ❑ *My parents never really faced up to my drug use in any serious way.* 我的父母从未真正认真面对我吸毒的问题。 ❑ *It was a question which deserved serious consideration.* 这是一个值得认真考虑的问题。 ● **se·ri·ous·ly** ADV 认真地；严肃地 [ADV with v] ❑ *The management will have to think seriously about their positions.* 管理层将不得不认真考虑他们的立场。 **4** ADJ **Serious** music or literature requires concentration to understand or appreciate it. 严肃的 [ADJ n] ❑ *...serious classical music.* …严肃的古典音乐。 **5** ADJ If someone is **serious about** something, they are sincere about what they are saying, doing, or intending to do. 真心的；郑重的 ❑ *You really are serious about this, aren't you?* 你对这事确实是认真的，是吧？ ● **se·ri·ous·ly** ADV 真心地；郑重地 ❑ *Are you seriously jealous of Erica?* 你真的妒忌埃里卡吗？ ● **se·ri·ous·ness** N-UNCOUNT 真心；郑重 [oft N "of" n] ❑ *In all seriousness, there is nothing else I can do.* 说真的，能做的我都做了。 **6** ADJ **Serious** people are thoughtful and quiet, and do not laugh very often. 严肃的 ❑ *He's quite a serious person.* 他是一个相当严肃的人。 ● **se·ri·ous·ly** ADV 严肃地 [ADV with v] ❑ *They spoke to me very seriously but politely.* 他们非常严肃但又很有礼貌地与我谈话。

Thesaurus *serious* 另参见：

ADJ. crucial, important, significant; *(ant.)* unimportant **1**
businesslike, humorless, solemn; *(ant.)* cheerful **6**

Word Partnership *serious* 的常用搭配：

N. serious **accident**, serious **condition**, serious **crime**, serious **danger**, serious **harm**, serious **illness**, serious **injury**, serious **mistake**, serious **problem**, serious **threat**, serious **trouble** **1**
serious **matter**, serious **situation** **1** **2**
serious **business**, serious **question** **2**
serious **consideration**, serious **doubts** **3**
serious **expression**, serious **face** **6**

ADV. **potentially** serious **1** **2**
extremely serious, **more** serious, **quite** serious, **really** serious, **very** serious **1**–**3** **5** **6**
deadly serious **2** **5** **6**

se·ri·ous·ly ◆◇◇ /sɪəriəsli/ **1** ADV You use **seriously** to indicate that you are not joking and that you really mean what you say. 说真的 [ADV with cl] ❑ *Seriously, I only smoke in the evenings.* 说真的，我只在晚上抽烟。 **2** CONVENTION You say **"seriously"** when you are surprised by what someone has said, as a way of asking them if they really mean it. 当真 [SPOKEN, FEELINGS] ❑ *"I tried to chat him up at the general store." He laughed. "Seriously?"* "我试图在杂货店同他搭讪。"他笑着说。"当真？" **3** → see also **serious** **4** PHRASE If you **take** someone or something **seriously**, you believe that they are important and deserve attention. 把某人/某事物当回事 ❑ *It's hard to take them seriously in their pretty gray uniforms.* 他们穿着灰灰的制服，很难让人把他们当回事。

▲ **ser·mon** /sɜrmən/ (**sermons**) N-COUNT A **sermon** is a talk on a religious or moral subject that is given by a member of the clergy as part of a church service. 布道；讲道 ❑ *Cardinal Murphy will deliver the sermon on Sunday.* 墨菲红衣主教将在周日布道。

ser·pent /sɜrpənt/ (**serpents**) N-COUNT A **serpent** is a snake. 蛇 [LITERARY] ❑ *...the serpent in the Garden of Eden.* …伊甸园里的那条蛇。

S

se·rum /sɪərəm/ (**serums**) 1 N-VAR A **serum** is a liquid that is injected into someone's blood to protect them against a poison or disease. 免疫血清 ❑ *...painful injections of anti-cancer serum.* …令人痛苦的抗癌血清注射。 2 N-UNCOUNT **Serum** is the watery, pale yellow part of blood. 血清 ❑ *The strip, which accepts blood, serum or plasma, is inserted into the analyzer.* 涂上了血液、血清或血浆的测试带被插入分析器。

serv·ant ♦◇◇ /sɜrvᵊnt/ (**servants**) 1 N-COUNT A **servant** is someone who is employed to work at another person's home, for example, as a cleaner or a gardener. 仆人；佣人 ❑ *...a large Victorian family with several servants.* …一个拥有几名佣人的维多利亚时代的大家庭。 2 N-COUNT You can use **servant** to refer to someone or something that provides a service for people or can be used by them. 雇员 ❑ *Like any other public servants, police must respond to public demand.* 像任何其他公务员一样，警察必须对公众要求作出反应。 3 → see also **civil servant**

serve ♦♦◇ /sɜrv/ (**serves, serving, served**) 1 V-T If you **serve** your country, an organization, or a person, you do useful work for them. 为…服务；为…效力 ❑ *It is unfair to soldiers who have served their country well for many years.* 对忠心效力国家多年的士兵们来说，这是不公平的。 2 V-I If you **serve** in a particular place or as a particular official, you perform official duties, especially in the armed forces, as a civil servant, or as a politician. 服役；任职 ❑ *During the second world war he served with 92nd Airborne.* 第二次世界大战期间，他在第92空降师服役。 ❑ *They have both served on the school board.* 他们俩都曾在学校董事会任职。 3 V-T/V-I If something **serves as** a particular thing or **serves** a particular purpose, it performs a particular function, which is often not its intended function. 对…有用；能起…作用 ❑ *She ushered me into the front room, which served as her office.* 她领我进入前厅，那儿用做她的办公室了。 ❑ *I really do not think that an inquiry would serve any useful purpose.* 我真的认为一场咨询不会起什么作用。 4 V-T If something **serves** people or an area, it provides them with something that they need. 供应；提供 ❑ *This could mean the closure of thousands of small businesses which serve the community.* 这意味着数以千计的为社区提供服务的小企业可能会关闭。 ❑ *...improvements in the public water-supply system serving the Nairobi area.* …内罗毕地区公共供水系统的改善。 5 V-T Something that **serves** someone's interests benefits them. 满足；对…有益 ❑ *The economy should be organized to serve the interests of all the people.* 经济规划应该符合全体民众的利益。 6 V-T/V-I When you **serve** food and drinks, you give people food and drinks. 上(菜、饮料) ❑ *Serve it with French bread.* 这个与法式面包一起上。 ❑ *Serve the cakes warm.* 烤饼要趁热端上来。 ❑ *Refrigerate until ready to serve.* 一直冷藏到准备上桌。 ● PHRASAL VERB **Serve up** means the same as **serve.** 上(菜、饮料) ❑ *After all, it is no use serving up TV dinners if the kids won't eat them.* 归根到底，如果孩子们不肯吃，就是端上即食快餐也没有什么用。 7 V-T **Serve** is used to indicate how much food a recipe produces. For example, a recipe that **serves** six provides enough food for six people. 足以供…人食用 [no cont] ❑ *Garnish with fresh herbs. Serves 4.* 缀上新鲜的香草，供4人食用。 8 V-T/V-I Someone who **serves** customers in a store or a bar helps them and provides them with what they want to buy. 接待(顾客) ❑ *They wouldn't serve me in any bars because I looked too young.* 任何酒吧都不肯接待我，因为我看上去太年轻了。 9 V-T When the police or other officials **serve** someone **with** a legal order or **serve** an order **on** them, they give or send the legal order to them. 送交(令状/传票) [LEGAL] ❑ *Immigration officers tried to serve her with a deportation order.* 移民局官员试图向她交送驱逐出境令。 10 V-T If you **serve** something such as a prison sentence or an apprenticeship, you spend a period of time doing it. 服(刑)；做(学徒) ❑ *...Leo, who is currently serving a life sentence for murder.* …目前正因谋杀罪在服无期徒刑的利奥。 11 V-T/V-I When you **serve** in games such as tennis and badminton, you throw up the ball or shuttlecock and hit it to start play. (网球、羽毛球等) 发球 ❑ *He served 17 double faults.* 他有17次双发失误。 ● N-COUNT **Serve** is also a noun. 发球 ❑ *His second serve clipped the net.* 他的第2次发球擦到了球网。 12 N-COUNT When you describe someone's **serve**, you are indicating how well or how fast they serve a ball or shuttlecock. 发球 ❑ *His powerful serve was too much for the defending champion.* 他有力的发球使卫冕冠军难以招架。 13 → see also **serving** 14 PHRASE If you say **it serves** someone **right** when something unpleasant happens to them, you mean that it is their own fault and you have no sympathy for them. 某人活该受惩罚 [FEELINGS] ❑ *Serves her right for being so stubborn.* 她这么顽固，受到惩罚是活该。

▸ **serve up** → see **serve 6**

Word Partnership *serve* 的常用搭配：

N. serve **a community**, serve **the public** 1 4
serve **a purpose** 3
serve ***someone's* needs** 5
serve **cake**, serve **food** 6

serv·er /sɜrvər/ (**servers**) 1 N-COUNT In computing, a **server** is part of a computer network which does a particular task, such as storing or processing information, for all or part of the network. 服务器 [COMPUTING] 2 N-COUNT A **server** is a person who works in a restaurant, serving people with food and drink. 侍者 [AM] ❑ *A server came by balancing a tray of wineglasses.* 一名侍者平稳地托着一托盘葡萄酒杯走了过来。 3 N-COUNT In tennis and badminton, the **server** is the player whose turn it is to hit the ball or shuttlecock to start play. (网球、羽毛球等的) 发球员 ❑ *...the fastest server in tennis.* …最快的网球发球手。

→ see **Internet, tennis**

service

❶ NOUN AND ADJECTIVE USES
❷ VERB USES
❸ PHRASES

❶ **ser·vice** ♦♦♦ /sɜrvɪs/ (**services**) 1 N-COUNT A **service** is something that the public needs, such as transportation, communications facilities, hospitals, or energy supplies, which is provided in a planned and organized way by the government or an official body. 公共服务机构；公共服务系统 ❑ *The postal service has been trying to cut costs.* 邮政系统一直在试图削减成本。 ❑ *We have started a campaign for better nursery and school services.* 我们已开展了一场运动，以改善幼儿园和学校的服务。 2 N-COUNT You can sometimes refer to an organization or private company as a particular **service** when it provides something for the public or acts on behalf of the government. 官方机构；政府的行政部门 ❑ *The Agriculture Department has ultimate control over the Forest Service.* 农业部对林务局有最终控制权。 3 N-COUNT If an organization or company provides a particular **service**, they can do a particular job or a type of work for you. 服务；服务项目 ❑ *The kitchen maintains a twenty-four hour service and can be contacted via reception.* 厨房提供24小时服务，可通过接待处联系。 4 N-PLURAL **Services** are activities such as tourism, banking, and selling things which are part of a country's economy, but are not concerned with producing or manufacturing goods. 服务性工作；服务性行业 ❑ *Mining rose by 9.1%, manufacturing by 9.4% and services by 4.3%.* 采矿业增长了9.1%，制造业增长了9.4%，服务业增长了4.3%。 5 N-UNCOUNT The level or standard of **service** provided by an organization or company is the amount or quality of the work it can do for you. 服务质量；服务水平 ❑ *Taking risks is the only way employees can provide effective and efficient customer service.* 只有承担风险，雇员们才能提供高效的客户服务。 6 N-COUNT A bus or train **service** is a route or regular trip that is part of a transportation system. 交通线路 ❑ *The local bus service is well run and extensive.* 当地的公交线路运营良好，四通八达。 7 N-PLURAL Your **services** are the things that you do or the skills that you use in your job, which other people find useful and are usually willing to pay you for. 专业性服务 ❑ *I have obtained the services of a top photographer to take our pictures.* 我得到了一位顶级摄影师的服务。 8 N-UNCOUNT If you refer to someone's **service** or **services to** a particular organization or activity, you mean that they have done a lot of work for it or spent a lot of their time on it. 效力；供职 [also N in pl, oft N "to" n] ❑ *You've given a lifetime of service to athletics.* 你一生致力于体育事业。 ❑ *Most employees had long service with the company and were familiar with our products.* 绝大部分雇员在公司供职多年，熟悉我们的产品。 9 N-COUNT **The Services** are the army, the navy, the air force and the marines. (包括陆、海、空军和海军陆战队在内的)军队 ❑ *Some of the money could be spent on persuading key specialists to stay in the Services.* 可以花费一部分资金挽留重要专家在军队工作。 10 N-UNCOUNT **Service** is the work done by people or equipment in the army, navy, or air force, for example, during a war. 兵役；作战 ❑ *Units are being called up today for service in the Gulf.* 今天正在征调一些部队去海湾服役。 11 N-UNCOUNT When you receive **service** in a restaurant, hotel, or store, an employee asks you what you want or gives you what you have ordered. (饭店、酒店、商店等的) 服务 ❑ *Service was attentive and the meal proceeded at a leisurely pace.* 服务很周到，饭吃得悠闲从容。 12 N-COUNT A **service** is a religious

S

ceremony that takes place in a church or synagogue. 宗教仪式；礼拜 [also no det] ❑ *After the hour-long service, his body was taken to a cemetery in the south of the city.* 长达1小时的宗教仪式之后，他的遗体被送往城南的一座公墓里。 13 N-COUNT If a vehicle or machine has a **service**, it is examined, adjusted, and cleaned so that it will keep working efficiently and safely. 保养 [also no det] ❑ *The car needs a service.* 这辆车需要一次保养。 14 N-COUNT A **dinner service** or a **tea service** is a complete set of plates, cups, saucers, and other pieces of china. 整套餐具 ❑ *...a 60-piece dinner service.* …一套60件的餐具。 15 N-COUNT In tennis, badminton, and some other sports, when it is your **service**, it is your turn to serve. (网球、羽毛球等的) 发球 ❑ *She conceded just three points on her service during the first set.* 她在第1局中发球只丢了3分。 16 ADJ **Service** is used to describe the parts of a building or structure that are used by the staff who clean, repair, or take care of it, and are not usually used by the public. 员工专用的 [ADJ n] ❑ *I went out through the kitchen and down the service elevator.* 我穿过厨房，乘员工专用电梯下楼。 17 → see also **civil service, community service, emergency services, in-service, public service, rest area, room service**
→ see **dry-cleaning, economics, industry, library**

❷ **ser·vice** /sɜrvɪs/ (**services, servicing, serviced**) 1 V-T If you have a vehicle or machine **serviced**, you arrange for someone to examine, adjust, and clean it so that it will keep working efficiently and safely. 做保养 ❑ *I had my car serviced at the local garage.* 我在当地的汽车修理厂给我的车做了保修。 2 V-T If someone or something **services** an organization, a project, or a group of people, they provide it with the things that it needs in order to function properly or effectively. 为…效力 ❑ *There are now 400 staff at headquarters, servicing our regional and overseas work.* 目前总部有400名员工致力于我们本地以及海外的工作。

❸ **ser·vice** /sɜrvɪs/ 1 PHRASE If you **do** someone **a service**, you do something that helps or benefits them. 帮某人一个忙 ❑ *You are doing me a great service, and I'm very grateful to you.* 你正在帮我一个大忙，我非常感谢你。 2 PHRASE If a piece of equipment or type of vehicle is **in service**, it is being used or is able to be used. If it is **out of service**, it is not being used, usually because it is not working properly. (不) 在使用中 ❑ *Cuts in funding have meant that equipment has been kept in service long after it should have been replaced.* 拨款减少意味着设备达到该替换的期限后还要使用很长时间。 ❑ *In 1882, the city's first electric tram cars went into service.* 1882年，该市第1批电车投入使用。

ser·vice charge (**service charges**) N-COUNT A **service charge** is an amount that is added to your bill in a restaurant to pay for the work of the person who comes and serves you. 服务费；小费 ❑ *Most restaurants add a 10 percent service charge to the bill.* 大多数餐馆在账单上加收10%的服务费。

ser·vice in·dus·try (**service industries**) N-COUNT A **service industry** is an industry such as banking or insurance that provides a service but does not produce anything. 服务业 ❑ *Seventy-two percent of people now work in service industries.* 72%的人现今从事服务业。

ser·vice·man /sɜrvɪsmən/ (**servicemen**) N-COUNT A **serviceman** is a man who is in the army, navy, air force, or marines. 军人 ❑ *He was an American serviceman based in Vietnam during the war.* 他是一名战争期间在越南基地服役的美国军人。

ser·vice pro·vid·er (**service providers**) N-COUNT A **service provider** is a company that provides a service, especially an Internet service. 服务提供商 [COMPUTING]

ser·vice sta·tion (**service stations**) N-COUNT A **service station** is a place that sells things for vehicles such as gas, oil, and spare parts. Service stations often sell food, drinks, and other products. 加油站；车辆服务站

serv·ing /sɜrvɪŋ/ (**servings**) 1 N-COUNT A **serving** is an amount of food that is given to one person at a meal. (食物的) 一份 ❑ *Quantities will vary according to how many servings of soup you want to prepare.* 数量取决于你要准备多少份汤。 2 ADJ A **serving** spoon or dish is used for giving out food at a meal. 上菜用的 [ADJ n] ❑ *Pile the potatoes into a warm serving dish.* 把土豆堆在一只上菜的热盘子里。

ses·sion ♦♦◊ /sɛʃən/ (**sessions**) 1 N-COUNT A **session** is a meeting of a court, legislature, or other official group. 开庭；会议 [also "in" N] ❑ *After two late night sessions, the Security Council has failed to reach agreement.* 开过两次深夜会议之后，安理会仍未能达成协议。 ❑ *The Arab League is meeting in emergency session today.* 阿拉伯国家联盟今天正在举行紧急会议。 2 N-COUNT A **session** is a period during which the meetings of a court, legislature, or other official group are regularly held. 开庭期；会期 [also "in" N] ❑ *From September until December, Congress remained in session.* 9月到12月国会一直处在开会期。 3 N-COUNT A **session** of a particular activity is a period of that activity. 一场 (活动) ❑ *The two leaders emerged for a photo session.* 两位领导人出场参加了合影。

set
❶ NOUN USES
❷ VERB AND ADJECTIVE USES

❶ **set** ♦♦♦ /sɛt/ (**sets**) 1 N-COUNT A **set of** things is a number of things that belong together or that are thought of as a group. 套；系列 ❑ *There must be one set of laws for the whole of the country.* 必须有一套适用于全国的法律。 ❑ *The mattress and base are normally bought as a set.* 床垫和床基通常成套购买。 ❑ *...a chess set.* …一副国际象棋。 2 N-COUNT In tennis, a **set** is one of the groups of six or more games that form part of a match. (网球赛的) 一盘 ❑ *Graf was leading 5-1 in the first set.* 格拉夫在首盘比赛中以5-1领先。 3 N-COUNT In mathematics, a **set** is a group of mathematical quantities that have some characteristic in common. 集合 ❑ *...the field of set theory.* …集合论领域。 4 N-COUNT The **set** for a play, movie, or television show is the furniture and scenery that is on the stage when the play is being performed or in the studio where filming takes place. (话剧的) 布景；(电影的) 摄影棚；拍片现场 [also "on/off" N] ❑ *From the first moment he got on the set, he wanted to be a director too.* 从踏进摄影棚的第一刻起，他就也想成为一名导演。 ❑ *He achieved fame for his stage sets for the Folies Bergeres.* 他因为为《疯狂的藤椅》设计舞台布景而一举成名。 5 N-COUNT A **set** is an appliance that receives television or radio signals. For example, a television set is a television. 电器装置 (如电视机、收音机) ❑ *Children spend so much time in front of the television set.* 孩子们在电视机前花的时间太多了。

❷ **set** ♦♦♦ /sɛt/ (**sets, setting**)

The form **set** is used in the present tense and is the past tense and past participle of the verb.

➪ **Please look at meanings 22 – 26 to see if the expression you are looking for is shown under another headword.** 1 V-T If you **set** something somewhere, you put it there, especially in a careful or deliberate way. (小心地) 放置 ❑ *He took the case out of her hand and set it on the floor.* 他从她手中接过箱子并置于地板上。 2 ADJ If something is **set** in a particular place or position, it is in that place or position. 处于…的；位于…的 [v-link ADJ prep/adv] ❑ *The castle is set in 25 acres of beautiful grounds.* 城堡坐落于方圆25英亩的宜人场地。 3 ADJ If something is **set into** a surface, it is fixed there and does not stick out. 嵌入的 [v-link ADJ prep/adv] ❑ *The man unlocked a gate set in a high wall and let me through.* 那人打开砌在高墙中的门，放我过去了。 4 V-T You can use **set** to say that a person or thing causes another person or thing to be in a particular condition or situation. For example, to **set** someone free means to cause them to be free, and to **set** something going means to cause it to start working. 使…处于某种状况；使开始 ❑ *Set the kitchen timer going.* 启动厨房定时器。 ❑ *Dozens of people have been injured and many vehicles set on fire.* 已经有几十人受伤，很多车辆被放火焚烧。 5 V-T When you **set** a clock or control, you adjust it to a particular point or level. 拨；调 ❑ *Set the volume as high as possible.* 把音量尽量调大。 6 V-T If you **set** a date, price, goal, or level, you decide what it will be. 决定；确定 ❑ *The conference chairman has set a deadline of noon tomorrow.* 会议主席设定明天中午为最后期限。 ❑ *A date will be set for a future meeting.* 将为未来的会议确定一个日期。 7 V-T If you **set** a certain value **on** something, you think it has that value. 确定 ❑ *She sets a high value on autonomy.* 她高度重视自主权。 8 V-T If you **set** something such as a record, an example, or a precedent, you do something that people will want to copy or try to achieve. 树立 (样板) ❑ *Legal experts said her case would not set a precedent because it was an out-of-court settlement.* 法律专家说她的案子不会开创先例，因为是庭外和解。 9 V-T If someone **sets** you a task or aim or if you **set yourself** a task or aim, you need to succeed in doing it. 分派；制订 ❑ *I have to plan my academic work very rigidly and set myself clear objectives.* 我必须给我的学术工作制订非常严格的计划，并给自己规定明确的目标。 10 ADJ You use **set** to describe something which is fixed and cannot be changed. 固定不变的 ❑ *A set period of fasting is supposed to bring us closer to godliness.* 通常认为一段固定的斋戒期可以使我们更虔诚。

11 ADJ A **set** book must be studied by students taking a particular course. 指定的 [ADJ n] [BRIT]

in AM, use **required**

12 ADJ If a play, movie, or story is **set** in a particular place or period of time, the events in it take place in that place or period. 以…为背景的 [v-link ADJ prep/adv] ❑ *The play is set in a small Midwestern town.* 这出戏是以中西部的一个小城镇为背景的。 13 ADJ If you are **set to** do something, you are ready to do it or are likely to do it. If something is **set to** happen, it is about to happen or likely to happen. 作好准备的; 有可能的 [v-link ADJ to-inf] ❑ *Roberto Baggio was set to become one of the greatest players of all time.* 罗伯特·巴乔有可能成为有史以来最伟大的球星之一。 14 ADJ If you are **set on** something, you are strongly determined to do or have it. If you are **set against** something, you are strongly determined not to do or have it. 执意的 [v-link ADJ "on/against" n/-ing] ❑ *She was set on going to an all-girls school.* 她执意要去一所女子学校读书。 15 V-I When something such as jelly, melted plastic, or cement **sets**, it becomes firm or hard. 凝固; 凝结 ❑ *You can add ingredients to these desserts as they begin to set.* 你可以在那些甜点快凝固时添加一些成分。 16 V-I When the sun **sets**, it goes below the horizon. (太阳) 落下 ❑ *They watched the sun set behind the distant dales.* 他们远观夕阳落下山谷。 17 V-T To **set** a trap means to prepare it to catch someone or something. 设置 ❑ *He seemed to think I was setting some sort of trap for him.* 他似乎认为我正给他设置某种陷阱。 18 V-T When someone **sets** the table, they prepare it for a meal by putting plates and flatware on it. 摆放 ❑ *One would shop and cook, another would set the table and another would wash up.* 一人会购物和烹饪，一人摆桌子，另外一人洗餐具。 19 V-T If someone **sets** a poem or a piece of writing to music, they write music for the words to be sung to. 为…谱曲; 为…配乐 ❑ *He has attracted much interest by setting ancient religious texts to music.* 他为古代宗教经文谱曲，引起了很多人的兴趣。 20 → see also **setting** 21 PHRASE If someone **sets the scene** or **sets the stage for** an event to take place, they make preparations so that it can take place. 为…作好准备; 为…创造条件 ❑ *The Democratic convention has set the scene for a ferocious election campaign this fall.* 民主党全国代表大会已为今秋激烈的竞选活动作好了准备。 22 to **set fire to** something → see **fire** 23 to **set foot** somewhere → see **foot** 24 to **set** your **heart on** something → see **heart** 25 to **set sail** → see **sail** 26 to **set to work** → see **work**

▸ **set aside** 1 PHRASAL VERB If you **set** something **aside for** a special use or purpose, you keep it available for that use or purpose. 省出; 抽出 ❑ *Some doctors advise setting aside a certain hour each day for worry.* 一些医生建议每天抽出一定时间思忧。 2 PHRASAL VERB If you **set aside** a belief, principle, or feeling, you decide that you will not be influenced by it. 把…抛在脑后 ❑ *He urged the participants to set aside minor differences for the sake of achieving peace.* 他敦促与会者把小分歧抛于脑后，以求实现和平。

▸ **set back** 1 PHRASAL VERB If something **sets** you **back** or **sets back** a project or plan, it causes a delay. 延误; 推迟 ❑ *It has set us back in so many respects that I'm not sure how long it will take for us to catch up.* 我们在很多方面都被延误了，不知道需要多久才能赶上。 2 PHRASAL VERB If something **sets** you **back** a certain amount of money, it costs you that much money. 使花费 [INFORMAL] ❑ *A bottle of imported beer will set you back $7.* 一瓶进口啤酒将花费你$7。 3 → see also **setback**

▸ **set down** 1 PHRASAL VERB If a committee or organization **sets down** rules for doing something, it decides what they should be and officially records them. 制定 ❑ *I like to make suggestions rather than setting down laws and forcing people to follow them.* 我喜欢提建议而不是制定法律并强迫人们去遵守。 2 PHRASAL VERB If you **set down** your thoughts or experiences, you write them all down. 把…写下来 ❑ *Old Walter is setting down his memories of village life.* 老瓦尔特正在写他的乡村生活回忆录。

▸ **set in** PHRASAL VERB If something unpleasant **sets in**, it begins and seems likely to continue or develop. (不好的事物) 来了 ❑ *Winter is setting in and the population is facing food and fuel shortages.* 冬天来了，人们正面临着食物和燃料的短缺。

▸ **set off** 1 PHRASAL VERB When you **set off**, you start a journey. 启程; 出发 ❑ *Nichols set off for his remote farmhouse in Connecticut.* 尼科尔斯启程前往他位于康涅狄格州的偏远农舍。 ❑ *The president's envoy set off on another diplomatic trip.* 总统特使再次踏上外交之旅。 2 PHRASAL VERB If something **sets off** something such as an alarm or a bomb, it makes it start working so that, for example, the alarm rings or the bomb explodes. 引爆 (炸弹); 触发 (警报) ❑ *Any escape, once it's detected, sets off the alarm.* 逃跑一旦被侦察到，就会触发警报。 ❑ *Someone set off a fire extinguisher.* 有人打开了灭火器。 3 PHRASAL VERB If something **sets off** an event or a series of events, it causes it to start happening. 引发; 激起 ❑ *The arrival of the charity van set off a minor riot as villagers scrambled for a share of the aid.* 赈济货车一到达，便引发了村民争抢救援物资的小规模骚乱。

▸ **set out** 1 PHRASAL VERB When you **set out**, you start a journey. 启程; 出发 ❑ *When setting out on a long walk, always wear suitable boots.* 出发进行长距离徒步时，一定要穿上合适的靴子。 2 PHRASAL VERB If you **set out to** do something, you start trying to do it. 开始努力 ❑ *He has achieved what he set out to do three years ago.* 他已经完成了3年前开始努力做的事情。 3 PHRASAL VERB If you **set** things **out**, you arrange or display them somewhere. 摆出; 陈列 ❑ *Set out the cakes attractively, using lacy doilies.* 用花边垫子摆蛋糕，好看诱人。 4 PHRASAL VERB If you **set out** a number of facts, beliefs, or arguments, you explain them in writing or speech in a clear, organized way. 阐述; 提出 ❑ *He has written a letter to The Times setting out his views.* 他已经给《泰晤士报》写信，阐述了自己的观点。

▸ **set up** 1 PHRASAL VERB If you **set** something **up**, you create or arrange it. 安排; 创建 ❑ *The two sides agreed to set up a commission to investigate claims.* 双方同意成立一个委员会，调查索赔问题。 ❑ *...an organization which sets up meetings about issues of interest to women.* …一个安排有关妇女利益问题的会议组织。 ● **set·ting up** N-UNCOUNT 设置; 成立 ❑ *The government announced the setting up of a special fund.* 政府宣布设置了一项特别基金。 2 PHRASAL VERB If you **set up** a temporary structure, you place it or build it somewhere. 设立; 设置 ❑ *They took to the streets, setting up roadblocks of burning tires.* 他们走上街头，用燃烧的轮胎设置路障。 3 PHRASAL VERB If you **set up** a device or piece of machinery, you do the things that are necessary for it to be able to start working. 调试 (设备、机器等) ❑ *Setting up the camera can be tricky.* 调试相机可能会很费事。 4 PHRASAL VERB If you **set up** somewhere or **set yourself up** somewhere, you establish yourself in a new business or new area. 开办; 开创事业 ❑ *The mayor's plan offers incentives to firms setting up in lower Manhattan.* 市长的计划是鼓励在下曼哈顿区开公司。 ❑ *He worked as a dance instructor in London before setting himself up in Bucharest.* 在布加勒斯特开创事业之前，他在伦敦当过舞蹈教练。 ❑ *Grandfather set them up in a printing business.* 祖父资助他们开办了一家印刷公司。 5 PHRASAL VERB If you **set up** house or home or **set up** shop, you buy a house or business of your own and start living or working there. (购置房子) 自立门户; 自行开业 ❑ *They married, and set up home in Atlanta.* 他们结了婚，在亚特兰大安了家。 6 PHRASAL VERB If you **are set up** by someone, they make it seem that you have done something wrong when you have not. 陷害; 诬陷 [INFORMAL] ❑ *He claimed yesterday that he had been set up after drugs were discovered at his home.* 家中被查出毒品后，他昨天声称是遭人陷害。 7 → see also **setup**

Thesaurus *set* 另参见:

N.	bunch, group ❶ 1 scene ❶ 4
V.	arrange, place ❷ 1 decide, fix ❷ 6 7
ADJ.	established ❷ 10

★ **set·back** /sɛtbæk/ (**setbacks**) N-COUNT A **setback** is an event that delays your progress or reverses some of the progress that you have made. 挫折; 倒退 [oft N "for/in/to" n] ❑ *The move represents a setback for the Middle East peace process.* 此举意味着中东和平进程的倒退。

set·tee /sɛti/ (**settees**) N-COUNT A **settee** is a long comfortable seat with a back and arms, which two or more people can sit on. 长沙发

set·ting /sɛtɪŋ/ (**settings**) 1 N-COUNT A particular **setting** is a particular place or type of surroundings where something is or takes place. (事件发生的) 背景; 地点 ❑ *Rome is the perfect setting for romance.* 罗马是寻求浪漫的最佳地点。 2 N-COUNT A **setting** is one of the positions to which the controls of a device such as a stove or heater can be adjusted. 挡位 ❑ *You can boil the fish fillets on a high setting.* 你可以设置在高挡位上煮鱼片。

set·tle ♦♦◇ /sɛtᵊl/ (**settles, settling, settled**) 1 V-T If people **settle** an argument or problem, or if something **settles** it, they solve it, for example, by making a decision about who is right or about what to do. 解决 (纠纷、问题等) ❑ *They agreed to try to settle their dispute by negotiation.* 他们同意尽量通过谈判解决他们之间的纠纷。 2 V-T/V-I If people **settle** a legal dispute or if they **settle**, they agree to end the dispute without going to a court of law, for

S

example, by paying some money or by apologizing. (庭外) 和解 ❑ *In an attempt to settle the case, Molken has agreed to pay restitution.* 为了结此案，莫尔肯已同意赔偿。❑ *She got much less than she would have done if she had settled out of court.* 她得到的远不如她若庭外和解得到的多。 **3** V-T/V-I If you **settle** a bill or debt, you pay the amount that you owe. 结算；算清 ❑ *I settled the bill for my coffee and his two glasses of wine.* 我为我的咖啡和他的两杯葡萄酒付了钱。❑ *She has now settled with her landlord.* 她现在已经和她的房东算清了。 **4** V-T If something **is settled**, it has all been decided and arranged. 确定 [usu passive] ❑ *As far as we're concerned, the matter is settled.* 在我们看来，此事已定。 **5** V-T/V-I When people **settle** a place or in a place, or when a government **settles** them there, they start living there permanently. 定居于；使定居；定居 ❑ *Refugees settling in a new country suffer from a number of problems.* 在一个新国家定居的难民们面临许多问题。❑ *He visited Paris and eventually settled there.* 他访问了巴黎并最终在那儿定居了。 **6** V-T/V-I If you **settle yourself** somewhere or **settle** somewhere, you sit down or make yourself comfortable. 安顿；安坐 ❑ *Albert settled himself on the sofa.* 阿尔伯特在沙发安坐下来。 **7** V-T/V-I If something **settles** or if you **settle** it, it sinks slowly down and becomes still. 使沉降；沉降 ❑ *A black dust settled on the walls.* 一团黑色粉尘落到了这些墙上。❑ *Once its impurities had settled, the oil could be graded.* 一旦杂质沉淀下去，油就可以定级了。 **8** V-I If your eyes **settle on** or **upon** something, you stop looking around and look at that thing for some time. (目光) 停留 ❑ *The man let his eyes settle upon Blume's face.* 那个人让自己的目光落在了布卢姆的脸上。 **9** V-I When birds or insects **settle on** something, they land on it from above. (鸟类或昆虫) 飞落；栖息 ❑ *Moths flew in front of it, eventually settling on the rough painted metal.* 飞蛾在它前面飞舞，最后落在了那块粗糙的喷漆金属上。 **10** → see also **settled** **11** **when the dust settles** → see **dust** **12** **to settle a score** → see **score**

▸ **settle down** **1** PHRASAL VERB When someone **settles down**, they start living a quiet life in one place, especially when they get married or buy a house. (尤指因结了婚或买了房而) 安顿下来 ❑ *One day I'll want to settle down and have a family.* 总有一天我会想安顿下来，成个家。 **2** PHRASAL VERB If a situation or a person that has been going through a lot of problems or changes **settles down**, they become calm. 安定下来；平静下来 ❑ *It'd be fun, after the situation in Europe settles down, to take a trip to France.* 欧洲局势平定下来之后，去法国旅行将会很好玩。 **3** PHRASAL VERB If you **settle down to** do something or **to** something, you prepare to do it and concentrate on it. 安下心来 (做某事) ❑ *He got his coffee, came back and settled down to listen.* 他取了咖啡回来安心听了起来。 **4** PHRASAL VERB If you **settle down** for the night, you get ready to lie down and sleep. 安歇 ❑ *They put up their tents and settled down for the night.* 他们搭起帐篷，安歇下来。

▸ **settle for** PHRASAL VERB If you **settle for** something, you choose or accept it, especially when it is not what you really want but there is nothing else available. 勉强接受 ❑ *Virginia was a perfectionist. She was just not prepared to settle for anything mediocre.* 弗吉尼娅是个完美主义者。她就是无法勉强接受任何平庸的东西。

▸ **settle in** PHRASAL VERB If you **settle in**, you become used to living in a new place, doing a new job, or going to a new school. 适应下来 ❑ *I enjoyed school enormously once I'd settled in.* 一旦适应了，我就非常喜欢上学了。

▸ **settle on** PHRASAL VERB If you **settle on** a particular thing, you choose it after considering other possible choices. 选定 ❑ *I finally settled on a Mercedes. It's the ideal car for me.* 我最后选中了一辆奔驰。它是我最理想的轿车。

▸ **settle up** PHRASAL VERB When you **settle up**, you pay a bill or a debt. 付清 ❑ *I'll have to settle up what I owe for the phone.* 我得付清所欠的电话费。

Word Partnership *settle* 的常用搭配:

N. settle **differences**, settle **things** **1**
settle **a dispute**, settle **a matter** **1** **2**
settle **a case**, settle **a claim**, settle **a lawsuit/suit** **2**
V. **agree to** settle, **decide to** settle **1** – **3**

set·tled /sɛtᵊld/ **1** ADJ If you have a **settled** way of life, you stay in one place, in one job, or with one person, rather than moving around or changing. 稳定的；安定的 ❑ *He decided to lead a more settled life with his partner.* 他决定与他的伴侣过一种更为安定的生活。 **2** ADJ A **settled** situation or system stays the same all the time. 稳定不变的 (形势或系统) ❑ *There has been a period of settled weather.* 曾有一段时期天气很稳定。

set·tle·ment ♦♦◇ /sɛtᵊlmənt/ (**settlements**) **1** N-COUNT A **settlement** is an official agreement between two sides who were involved in a conflict or argument. 协议 ❑ *Our objective must be to secure a peace settlement.* 我们的目标必须是确保达成一个和平协议。 **2** N-COUNT A **settlement** is an agreement to end a disagreement or dispute without going to a court of law, for example, by offering someone money. (庭外) 和解 ❑ *She accepted an out-of-court settlement of $40,000.* 她接受了4万美元庭外和解。 **3** N-UNCOUNT The **settlement of** a debt is the act of paying back money that you owe. 清偿 ❑ *...ways to delay the settlement of debts.* …拖延债务清偿的办法。 **4** N-COUNT A **settlement** is a place where people have come to live and have built homes. 定居地 ❑ *The village is a settlement of just fifty houses.* 这个村子是个仅有50家住户的定居地。

set·tler /sɛtlər, sɛtᵊl-/ (**settlers**) N-COUNT **Settlers** are people who go to live in a new country. 移民者 ❑ *The first German village in southwestern Siberia was founded a century ago by settlers from the Volga region.* 西伯利亚西南部的第一个日尔曼村庄是一个世纪前由来自伏尔加地区的移民们建立的。

set-top box (**set-top boxes**) N-COUNT A **set-top box** is a piece of equipment that rests on top of your television and receives digital television signals. 电视机顶盒用来接受数码信号

set·up ♦♦◇ /sɛtʌp/ (**setups**) also **set-up** **1** N-COUNT A particular **setup** is a particular system or way of organizing something. 体制；组织方式 [INFORMAL] ❑ *It appears to be an idyllic domestic setup.* 它看起来是一种田园式的家庭组织方式。 **2** N-COUNT If you describe a situation as a **setup**, you mean that people have planned it in order to deceive you or to make it look as if you have done something wrong. 圈套；陷阱 [INFORMAL] ❑ *He was asked to pick somebody up and bring them to a party, not realizing it was a setup.* 他被叫去开车接人并送他们到一个聚会，没意识到那是个圈套。 **3** N-SING The **setup** of computer hardware or software is the process of installing it and making it ready to use. (电脑硬件或软件的) 安装 [COMPUTING] ❑ *The worst part of the setup is the poor instruction manual.* 安装过程中最糟糕的部分就是差劲的操作手册。

sev·en ♦♦♦ /sɛvᵊn/ (**sevens**) NUM **Seven** is the number 7. 7；七 ❑ *Sarah and Ella have been friends for seven years.* 萨拉和埃拉已经是7年的朋友了。

Word Link ***teen ≈ plus ten, from 13–19 : eighteen, seventeen, teenager***

sev·en·teen ♦♦♦ /sɛvᵊntin/ (**seventeens**) NUM **Seventeen** is the number 17. 17；十七 ❑ *Jenny is seventeen years old.* 珍妮17岁。❑ *I have seventeen pairs of shoes.* 我有17双鞋子。

sev·en·teenth ♦♦◇ /sɛvᵊntinθ/ (**seventeenths**) **1** ORD The **seventeenth** item in a series is the one that you count as number seventeen. 第17；第十七 ❑ *She gave birth to Annabel just after her seventeenth birthday.* 她刚过完17岁生日就生下了安娜贝尔。 **2** FRACTION A **seventeenth** is one of seventeen equal parts of something. 1/17；十七分之一

sev·enth ♦♦◇ /sɛvᵊnθ/ (**sevenths**) **1** ORD The **seventh** item in a series is the one that you count as number seven. 第7；第七 ❑ *I was the seventh child in the family.* 我是家里的第7个孩子。 **2** FRACTION A **seventh** is one of seven equal parts of something. 1/7 ❑ *A million people died, a seventh of the population.* 100万人，即人口的1/7，死了。

sev·en·ti·eth ♦♦◇ /sɛvᵊntiəθ/ (**seventieths**) **1** ORD The **seventieth** item in a series is the one that you count as number seventy. 第70；第七十 ❑ *...the seventieth anniversary of the discovery of Tutankhamun's tomb.* …图坦卡蒙墓发现70周年纪念日。 **2** FRACTION A **seventieth** is one of seventy equal parts of something. 1/70；七十分之一

sev·en·ty ♦♦♦ /sɛvᵊnti/ (**seventies**) **1** NUM **Seventy** is the number 70. 70；七十 ❑ *Seventy people were killed.* 70人丧生。 **2** N-PLURAL When you talk about the **seventies**, you are referring to numbers between 70 and 79. For example, if you are **in** your **seventies**, you are aged between 70 and 79. If the temperature is **in the seventies**, it is between 70 and 79. 70多；七十几 (指70到79之间的数字) ❑ *I thought it was a long way to go for two people in their seventies, but Sylvia loved the idea.* 我认为对于两个七十多岁的人来说这是一段很长的路，但是西尔维娅却喜欢这个主意。 **3** N-PLURAL **The seventies** is the decade between 1970 and 1979. 70年代；七十年代 (指1970 到1979之间的年代) ❑ *In the late Seventies, things had to be new, modern, revolutionary.* 在20世纪70年代末，一切都得新奇、现代、有创意。

Word Link *sever ≈ separating : sever, several, severance*

sev·er /sɛvər/ (**severs, severing, severed**) **1** V-T To **sever** something means to cut completely through it or to cut it completely off. 切断；切掉 [FORMAL] ❑ *Richardson severed his right foot in a motorcycle accident.* 理查森在一次摩托车事故中轧断了右脚。 **2** V-T If you **sever** a relationship or connection that you have with someone, you end it suddenly and completely. 断绝（关系、联系）[FORMAL] ❑ *She severed her ties with her homeland.* 她断绝了与自己祖国的联系。

sev·er·al ♦♦♦ /sɛvrəl/ DET **Several** is used to refer to a number of people or things that is not large but is greater than two. 几；一些 ❑ *I had lived two doors away from this family for several years.* 我与相隔两户的这家人做了几年的邻居。 ❑ *Several blue plastic boxes under the window were filled with CDs.* 窗子下面的几个蓝色塑料盒子里装满了激光唱片。 ● QUANT **Several** is also a quantifier. 几个；若干 [QUANT "of" pl-n] ❑ *The building was picketed by demonstrators, several of whom were well-known actors.* 这座建筑被示威者们包围了起来，其中几位是著名的演员。 ● PRON **Several** is also a pronoun. 几个；几种 ❑ *No one drug will suit or work for everyone and sometimes several may have to be tried.* 没有任何一种药会对每个人都适用或有效，有时得试好几种。

sev·er·ance /sɛvrəns, -ərəns/ ADJ **Severance** pay is a sum of money that a company gives to its employees when it has to stop employing them. 离职的（补偿金）[ADJ n] [BUSINESS] ❑ *We were offered 13 weeks' severance pay.* 我们得了13个星期的离职补偿金。

se·vere ♦♦◇ /sɪvɪər/ (**severer, severest**) **1** ADJ You use **severe** to indicate that something bad or undesirable is great or intense. 严重的 ❑ *...a business with severe cash flow problems.* …一个有严重现金流转问题的企业。 ❑ *Shortages of professional staff are very severe in some places.* 专业人员的短缺在一些地方十分严重。 ● **se·vere·ly** ADV 严重地 ❑ *The UN wants to send food aid to 10 countries in Africa severely affected by the drought.* 联合国想给予10个受旱灾严重影响的非洲国家食品援助。 ❑ *An aircraft overshot the runway and was severely damaged.* 一架飞机冲出了跑道后严重受损。 ● **se·ver·ity** /sɪvɛrɪti/ N-UNCOUNT 严重性 [usu with supp] ❑ *Several drugs are used to lessen the severity of the symptoms.* 几种药被用于缓解这些严重症状。 **2** ADJ **Severe** punishments or criticisms are very strong or harsh. （惩罚、批评）严厉的 ❑ *This was a dreadful crime and a severe sentence is necessary.* 这是一种骇人听闻的罪行，重判是必要的。 ● **se·vere·ly** ADV 严厉地 [ADV with v] ❑ *...a campaign to try to change the law to punish dangerous drivers more severely.* …一场试图修改法律以更加严厉地惩罚危险驾车者的运动。 ● **se·ver·ity** N-UNCOUNT 严厉性 [usu with supp] ❑ *He was sickened by the severity of the sentence.* 他对判刑之重感到恶心。

Thesaurus *severe* 另参见：

ADJ. critical, extreme, intense, tough **1** **2**

Word Partnership *severe* 的常用搭配：

N. severe **consequences**, severe **depression**, severe **disease/illness**, severe **drought**, severe **flooding**, severe **injuries**, severe **pain**, severe **problem**, severe **symptoms**, severe **weather** **1**
severe **penalty**, severe **punishment** **2**

ADV. **less/more/most** severe, **very** severe **1** **2**

sew /soʊ/ (**sews, sewing, sewed, sewn**) V-T/V-I When you **sew** something such as clothes, you make them or repair them by joining pieces of cloth together by passing thread through them with a needle. 缝制；缝补 ❑ *She sewed the dresses on the sewing machine.* 她在缝纫机上缝制了这些衣服。 ❑ *Anyone can sew on a button, including you.* 任何人都能缝钮扣，包括你。
→ see **quilt**

sew·age /suɪdʒ/ N-UNCOUNT **Sewage** is waste matter such as feces or dirty water from homes and factories, which flows away through sewers. （下水道排出的）废物 ❑ *...treatment of raw sewage.* …原始污物的处理。
→ see **pollution**

sew·er /suər/ (**sewers**) N-COUNT A **sewer** is a large underground channel that carries waste matter and rain water away, usually to a place where it is treated and made harmless. 下水道 ❑ *...the city's sewer system.* …该城市的下水道系统。

sew·ing /soʊɪŋ/ **1** N-UNCOUNT **Sewing** is the activity of making or mending clothes or other things using a needle and thread. 缝纫 ❑ *Her mother had always done all the sewing.* 她的母亲一直做所有的针线活。 **2** N-UNCOUNT **Sewing** is clothes or other things that are being sewn. 缝制中的衣物；针线活 ❑ *We all got out our own sewing and sat in front of the log fire.* 我们都拿出自己的针线活，坐在了篝火前。

sewn /soʊn/ **Sewn** is the past participle of **sew**. **sew**的过去分词

sex ♦♦◇ /sɛks/ (**sexes, sexing, sexed**) **1** N-COUNT The two **sexes** are the two groups, male and female, into which people and animals are divided according to the function they have in producing young. （雌、雄、男、女）性 ❑ *...a movie star who appeals to all ages and both sexes.* …一个吸引男女老少的电影明星。 **2** → see also **opposite sex** **3** N-COUNT The **sex** of a person or animal is their characteristic of being either male or female. 性别 ❑ *She continually failed to gain promotion because of her sex.* 由于性别的原因，她频频得不到升职。 ❑ *The new technique has been used to identify the sex of fetuses.* 这项新技术已被用来鉴定胎儿的性别。 **4** N-UNCOUNT **Sex** is the physical activity by which people can produce young. 性行为 ❑ *He was very open in his attitudes about sex.* 他对性的态度很开放。 ❑ *The entire film revolves around drugs, sex and violence.* 整部电影都围绕着毒品、色情和暴力展开。 **5** PHRASE If two people **have sex**, they perform the act of sex. 进行性交 ❑ *Have you ever thought about having sex with someone other than your husband?* 你想过与丈夫之外的人发生性关系吗？

▸ **sex up** PHRASAL VERB To **sex** something **up** means to make it seem more attractive or interesting than it actually is. 包装 [INFORMAL] ❑ *Nintendo is sexing up its U.S. advertising to launch the new handheld device.* 任天堂公司正包装它在美国的广告以推出新的掌上设备。

sex·ism /sɛksɪzəm/ N-UNCOUNT **Sexism** is the belief that the members of one sex, usually women, are less intelligent or less capable than those of the other sex and need not be treated equally. It is also the behavior which is the result of this belief. （尤其对女性的）性别歧视 ❑ *Groups like ours are committed to eradicating homophobia, racism and sexism.* 像我们这样的组织致力于消除同性恋憎恶、种族歧视和性别歧视。

sex·ist /sɛksɪst/ (**sexists**) ADJ If you describe people or their behavior as **sexist**, you mean that they are influenced by the belief that the members of one sex, usually women, are less intelligent or less capable than those of the other sex and need not be treated equally. （尤指对女性）性别歧视的 [DISAPPROVAL] ❑ *Old-fashioned sexist attitudes are still common.* 老套的性别歧视态度仍然很普遍。 ● N-COUNT A **sexist** is someone with sexist views or behavior. 性别歧视者 ❑ *It's got nothing to do with sexism. You know I'm not a sexist.* 这与性别歧视毫无关系。你知道我不是个性别歧视者。

sex sym·bol (**sex symbols**) N-COUNT A **sex symbol** is a famous person, especially an actor or a singer, who is considered by many people to be sexually attractive. 性感偶像 ❑ *...Hollywood sex symbols of the Forties.* …好莱坞40年代的性感偶像们。

sex·ual ♦♦◇ /sɛkʃuəl/ **1** ADJ **Sexual** feelings or activities are connected with the act of sex or with people's desire for sex. 有关性行为的；有关性欲的 ❑ *This was the first sexual relationship I'd had.* 这是我第一次与人发生性关系。 ● **sex·ual·ly** ADV 与性行为有关地；与性欲有关地 ❑ *...sexually transmitted diseases.* …性传播疾病。 **2** ADJ **Sexual** means relating to the differences between male and female people. 与性别有关的 ❑ *Women's groups denounced sexual discrimination.* 妇女组织谴责性别歧视。 ● **sex·ual·ly** ADV 性别上地 [ADV with v] ❑ *If you're sexually harassed, you ought to do something about it.* 如果遭到性骚扰，你应该对其采取行动。 **3** ADJ **Sexual** means relating to the differences between heterosexuals and homosexuals. 有关性取向的 ❑ *...couples of all sexual persuasions.* …有各种性取向的情侣们。 **4** ADJ **Sexual** means relating to the biological process by which people and animals produce young. 有关性繁殖的 ❑ *Girls generally reach sexual maturity two years earlier than boys.* 女孩子通常比男孩子早两年达到性成熟。 ● **sex·ual·ly** ADV 有关性繁殖地 ❑ *The first organisms that reproduced sexually were free-floating plankton.* 最早的有性繁殖生物是自由漂浮的浮游生物。

sex·ual abuse N-UNCOUNT If a child or other person suffers **sexual abuse**, someone forces them to take part in sexual activity with them, often regularly over a period of time. 性虐待 ❑ *...victims of sexual abuse.* …性虐待的受害者们。

sex·ual har·ass·ment N-UNCOUNT **Sexual harassment** is repeated and unwelcome sexual comments, looks, or physical contact at work, usually a man's actions that offend a woman. （常指男性对女性的）性骚扰 ❑ *Sexual harassment of women workers by their bosses is believed to be widespread.* 女员工受其上司性骚扰的情况被认为是广泛存在的。

S

sex·ual inter·course N-UNCOUNT **Sexual intercourse** is the physical act of sex between two people. 性交 [FORMAL] ❑ *I have never had sexual intercourse with her and that is the truth.* 我从未与她发生过性关系，而这是事实。

sexu·al·ity /sɛkʃuælɪti/ **1** N-UNCOUNT A person's **sexuality** is their sexual feelings. 性欲 ❑ *...the growing discussion of women's sexuality.* …日益增多的对女性性欲的讨论。 **2** N-UNCOUNT You can refer to a person's **sexuality** when you are talking about whether they are sexually attracted to people of the same sex or a different sex. 性倾向 ❑ *He believes he has been discriminated against because of his sexuality.* 他认为他因自己的性倾向而受到了歧视。

★ **sexy** /sɛksi/ (**sexier, sexiest**) ADJ You can describe people and things as **sexy** if you think they are sexually exciting or sexually attractive. 性感的 ❑ *She was one of the sexiest women I had seen.* 她是我所见过的最性感的女人之一。

sh /ʃ/ → see **shh**

★ **shab·by** /ʃæbi/ (**shabbier, shabbiest**) ADJ **Shabby** things or places look old and in bad condition. 破旧的；破烂的 ❑ *His clothes were old and shabby.* 他的衣服又旧又破。

▲ **shack** /ʃæk/ (**shacks, shacking, shacked**) N-COUNT A **shack** is a simple hut built from tin, wood, or other materials. 简易的棚屋

▸ **shack up** PHRASAL VERB If someone **has shacked up with** someone else or two people **have shacked up** together, they have started living together as lovers. 同居 [INFORMAL] ❑ *...the deserters who had shacked up with local women.* …那些与当地女人同居的逃兵们。 ❑ *Young people are afraid to get married, so they shack up.* 年轻人害怕结婚，所以他们同居。

▲ **shack·le** /ʃækᵊl/ (**shackles, shackling, shackled**) **1** V-T If you **are shackled by** something, it prevents you from doing what you want to do. 阻碍 [usu passive] [FORMAL] ❑ *The labor unions are shackled by the law.* 该工会被法律所羁绊。 ❑ *...people who find themselves shackled to a high-stress job.* …发现自己为高负荷工作所束缚的人们。 **2** N-PLURAL If you throw off the **shackles of** something, you reject it or free yourself from it because it was preventing you from doing what you wanted to do. 桎梏 [with supp] [LITERARY] ❑ *...a country ready to throw off the shackles of its colonial past.* …一个愿意甩掉其殖民历史的桎梏的国家。 **3** N-PLURAL **Shackles** are two metal rings joined by a chain which are fastened around someone's wrists or ankles in order to prevent them from moving or escaping. 镣铐 ❑ *He unbolted the shackles on Billy's hands.* 他打开比利的手铐。 **4** V-T To **shackle** someone means to put shackles on them. 用镣铐铐 ❑ *...the chains that were shackling his legs.* …铐着他双腿的锁链。

shade ♦◇◇ /ʃeɪd/ (**shades, shading, shaded**) **1** N-COUNT A **shade of** a particular color is one of its different forms. For example, emerald green and olive green are shades of green. 色调 ❑ *In the mornings the sky appeared a heavy shade of mottled gray.* 清晨，天空看上去是斑驳的深灰色调。 ❑ *The walls were painted in two shades of green.* 这些墙壁被涂成了两种色调不同的绿色。 **2** N-UNCOUNT **Shade** is an area of darkness under or next to an object such as a tree, where sunlight does not reach. 阴凉处 ❑ *Temperatures in the shade can reach forty-eight degrees Celsius at this time of year.* 一年中的这个时候，阴凉处的温度能达到48摄氏度。 ❑ *Alexis walked up the coast, and resumed his reading in the shade of an overhanging cliff.* 亚历克西斯沿着海岸向前走，然后在一块凸出的悬崖下的阴凉处重新看起书来。 **3** V-T If you say that a place or person **is shaded** by objects such as trees, you mean that the place or person cannot be reached, harmed, or bothered by strong sunlight because those objects are in the way. 形成阴蔽 ❑ *...a health resort whose beaches are shaded by palm trees.* …一个海滩上棕榈成阴荫的疗养胜地。 **4** V-T If you **shade** your eyes, you put your hand or an object partly in front of your face in order to prevent a bright light from shining into your eyes. 遮蔽(使不受阳光伤害) ❑ *You can't look directly into it; you've got to shade your eyes or close them altogether.* 你不能直视它；你得遮住双眼或者完全闭上眼睛。 **5** N-UNCOUNT **Shade** is darkness or shadows as they are shown in a picture. (图画中的)暗部；投影 ❑ *...Rembrandt's skillful use of light and shade to create the atmosphere of movement.* …伦勃朗巧妙的运用了明与暗来营造动感。 **6** N-COUNT The **shades of** something abstract are its many, slightly different forms. (抽象事物的)略有差异的形式 ❑ *...the capacity to convey subtle shades of meaning.* …表达略有微妙差异的意义的能力。 **7** N-COUNT A **shade** is a piece of stiff cloth or heavy paper that you can pull down over a window as a covering. 遮帘 [AM]

in BRIT, use **blind**

❑ *Nancy left the shades down and the lights off.* 南希放下帘子，关了灯。

shad·ow ♦◇◇ /ʃædoʊ/ (**shadows, shadowing, shadowed**) **1** N-COUNT A **shadow** is a dark shape on a surface that is made when something stands between a light and the surface. 影子；阴影 ❑ *An oak tree cast its shadow over a tiny round pool.* 一棵橡树在一个小圆池塘上投下了它的影子。 ❑ *Nothing would grow in the shadow of the gray wall.* 没有任何东西会在那堵灰墙的阴影里生长。 **2** N-UNCOUNT **Shadow** is darkness in a place caused by something preventing light from reaching it. 背阴 ❑ *Most of the lake was in shadow.* 那个湖的大部分都在背阴中。 **3** V-T If something **shadows** a thing or place, it covers it with a shadow. 遮住 ❑ *The hood shadowed her face.* 风帽遮住了她的脸。 **4** V-T If someone **shadows** you, they follow you very closely wherever you go. 尾随 ❑ *The president is constantly shadowed by bodyguards.* 该总统总是有保镖紧随其后。 **5** ADJ A British Member of Parliament who is a member of the **shadow** cabinet or who is a **shadow** cabinet minister belongs to the main opposition party and takes a special interest in matters which are the responsibility of a particular government minister. 在野党派的(内阁) [ADJ n] ❑ *...the shadow chancellor.* …在野党派的财政大臣。 ● N-COUNT **Shadow** is also a noun. 在野内阁成员 ❑ *Clarke swung at his shadow the accusation that he was "a tabloid politician."* 克拉克指责其在野对手为"煽情政客"。 **6** PHRASE If you say that something is true **without a shadow of a doubt** or **without a shadow of doubt,** you are emphasizing that there is no doubt at all that it is true. 一丝怀疑 [EMPHASIS] ❑ *It was without a shadow of a doubt the best we've played.* 那毫无疑问是我们表现最出色的一次。 **7** PHRASE If you live **in the shadow of** someone or **in** their **shadow**, their achievements and abilities are so great that you are not noticed or valued. 在某人的阴影下 ❑ *He has always lived in the shadow of his brother.* 他一直生活在他哥哥的阴影之下。

Word Partnership *shadow* 的常用搭配：

N.	*someone's* shadow **1**
	shadow of *something* **1** **6**
V.	cast a shadow **1**
	live in the shadow **7**

shad·owy /ʃædoʊi/ **1** ADJ A **shadowy** place is dark or full of shadows. 阴暗的 ❑ *I watched him from a shadowy corner.* 我从一个阴暗的角落观察他。 **2** ADJ A **shadowy** figure or shape is someone or something that you can hardly see because they are in a dark place. 昏暗中的；模糊的 [ADJ n] ❑ *...a tall, shadowy figure silhouetted against the pale wall.* …映在灰白色墙上的一个高大模糊的人影。 **3** ADJ You describe activities and people as **shadowy** when very little is known about them. 神秘的 ❑ *...the shadowy world of spies.* …神秘的间谍世界。

shady /ʃeɪdi/ (**shadier, shadiest**) **1** ADJ You can describe a place as **shady** when you like the fact that it is sheltered from bright sunlight, for example, by trees or buildings. 阴凉的；背阴的 ❑ *After flowering, place the pot in a shady spot in the garden.* 花开过之后，把花盆放到花园的阴凉处。 **2** ADJ You can describe activities as **shady** when you think that they might be dishonest or illegal. You can also use **shady** to describe people who are involved in such activities. 可疑的；不法的 [DISAPPROVAL] ❑ *In the 1980s, the company was notorious for shady deals.* 在20世纪80年代，这个公司因不法交易而臭名昭著。

★ **shaft** /ʃæft/ (**shafts**) **1** N-COUNT A **shaft** is a long vertical passage, for example, for an elevator. (电梯等的) 垂直通道 ❑ *The fire began in an elevator shaft and spread to the roof.* 大火从电梯通道里开始，然后蔓延到了屋顶。 **2** N-COUNT In a machine, a **shaft** is a rod that turns around continually in order to transfer movement in the machine. 轴 ❑ *...a drive shaft.* …一根传动轴。 **3** N-COUNT A **shaft** is a long thin piece of wood or metal that forms part of a spear, ax, golf club, or other object. 杆；柄 ❑ *...golf clubs with steel shafts.* …带钢柄的高尔夫球棒。 **4** N-COUNT A **shaft of** light is a beam of light, for example, sunlight shining through an opening. 一道(光) ❑ *A brilliant shaft of sunlight burst through the doorway.* 一道耀眼的阳光从门口照射进来。

shag·gy /ʃægi/ (**shaggier, shaggiest**) ADJ **Shaggy** hair or fur is long and messy. (毛发等) 又长又乱的 ❑ *Tim, who still has longish, shaggy hair, used to turn up at official dinners in jeans and T-shirt.* 仍然留着蓬乱长发的蒂姆过去常常穿着牛仔服和T恤衫出现在正式宴会上。

shake ♦♦◇ /ʃeɪk/ (**shakes, shaking, shook, shaken**) **1** V-T If you **shake** something, you hold it and move it quickly backward and forward or up and down. You can also **shake** a person, for example, because you are angry with them or because you want them to wake up. 摇晃；抖动；甩动 ❑ *The nurse took the thermometer, shook it, and put it under my armpit.* 护士拿出体温计，甩了甩，然后放在我的腋窝下。 ● N-COUNT **Shake** is also a noun. 摇晃；抖动；甩动 ❑ *She picked up the bag of salad and gave it a shake.* 她拿起了那袋沙拉摇了摇。 **2** V-T If you **shake yourself** or your body, you make a lot of quick, small, repeated movements without moving from the place where you are. 摇晃 (身体) ❑ *As soon as he got inside, the dog shook himself.* 他一进去，那条狗就摇头摆尾。 ● N-COUNT **Shake** is also a noun. 摇晃 ❑ *Take some slow, deep breaths and give your body a bit of a shake.* 做几次慢慢的深呼吸，轻轻晃动身体。 **3** V-T If you **shake** your **head**, you turn it from side to side in order to say "no" or to show disbelief or sadness. 摇 (头) ❑ *"Anything else?" Chris asked. Kathryn shook her head wearily.* "还有别的事吗？" 克里斯问道。凯瑟琳疲惫地摇了摇头。 ● N-COUNT **Shake** is also a noun. 摇动 ❑ *"The elm trees are all dying," said Palmer, with a sad shake of his head.* "这些榆树全都要死了，" 帕尔默说道，难过地摇了摇头。 **4** V-I If you **are shaking**, or a part of your body **is shaking**, you are making quick, small movements that you cannot control, for example, because you are cold or afraid. (因寒冷、害怕等而) 颤抖 ❑ *He roared with laughter, shaking in his chair.* 他放声大笑，身子在椅子里直摇晃。 ❑ *My hand shook so much that I could hardly hold the microphone.* 我的手抖得厉害以至于几乎握不住麦克风。 **5** V-T If you **shake** your fist or an object such as a stick **at** someone, you wave it in the air in front of them because you are angry with them. 挥舞 (拳头、棍棒等) ❑ *The colonel rushed up to Earle and shook his gun at him.* 上校冲到厄尔面前，冲他挥舞着枪。 **6** V-T/V-I If a force **shakes** something, or if something **shakes**, it moves from side to side or up and down with quick, small, but sometimes violent movements. 震动；摇动 ❑ *...an explosion that shook buildings several kilometers away.* …震动了数公里之外的建筑的一次爆炸。 **7** V-T To **shake** something into a certain place or state means to bring it into that place or state by moving it quickly up and down or from side to side. 抖撒 ❑ *She shook some pepper onto her sandwich.* 她在她的三明治上撒了些胡椒。 **8** V-I If your voice **is shaking**, you cannot control it properly and it sounds very unsteady, for example, because you are nervous or angry. (声音) 颤抖 ❑ *His voice shaking with rage, he asked how the committee could keep such a report from the public.* 他气得声音发抖，责问该委员会怎么能向公众隐瞒这样一份报告。 **9** V-T If an event or a piece of news **shakes** you, or **shakes** your confidence, it makes you feel upset and unable to think calmly. 震惊；动摇 (信心) ❑ *There was no doubt that the news of Tandy's escape had shaken them all.* 毫无疑问，坦迪逃跑的消息震惊了他们所有人。 **10** V-T If an event **shakes** a group of people or their beliefs, it causes great uncertainty and makes them question their beliefs. 动摇 (人心、信仰) ❑ *The five years she spent as a news correspondent in Moscow were five years that shook the world.* 她在莫斯科当新闻记者的5年是动摇了世界的5年。 **11** PHRASE If you **shake** someone's **hand** or **shake** someone **by the hand**, you shake hands with them. 握某人的手 ❑ *I said congratulations and walked over to him and shook his hand.* 我向他表示祝贺并走过去和他握手。 **12** PHRASE If you **shake hands with** someone, you take their right hand in your own for a few moments, often moving it up and down slightly, when you are saying hello or goodbye to them, congratulating them, or agreeing on something. You can also say that two people **shake hands.** (与某人) 握手 ❑ *He nodded greetings to Mary Ann and Michael and shook hands with Burke.* 他对玛丽·安和迈克尔点头致意，然后和伯克握了手。

▸ **shake down** **1** PHRASAL VERB If someone **shakes** you **down**, they use threats or search you physically in order to obtain something from you. 勒索；敲诈 [AM] ❑ *He accused the lawyer of shaking him down.* 他指控律师勒索他。 ❑ *...crooks who had tried to shake down other hotels.* …曾试图敲诈其他旅馆的骗子们。 **2** → see also **shakedown**

▸ **shake off** **1** PHRASAL VERB If you **shake off** something that you do not want such as an illness or a bad habit, you manage to recover from it or get rid of it. 摆脱 (疾病、坏习惯等) ❑ *Businessmen are frantically trying to shake off the bad habits learned under six decades of a protected economy.* 商人们拼命想摆脱60年来在保护经济下所养成的这些坏习惯。 **2** PHRASAL VERB If you **shake off** someone who is following you, you manage to get away from them, for example, by running faster than them. 甩掉 (跟踪者、跟随者) ❑ *Although I could pass him I could not shake him off.* 尽管我能超过他，却不能甩掉他。

▸ **shake out** PHRASAL VERB If you wonder how something will **shake out**, you wonder how it will develop and what the outcome will be. 收尾 [AM] ❑ *We don't know how this situation will shake out.* 我们不知道这个局面会如何收尾。

▸ **shake up** **1** PHRASAL VERB If someone **shakes up** something such as an organization, an institution, or a profession, they make major changes to it. 整顿 ❑ *The government wanted to accelerate the reform of the institutions, to find new ways of shaking up the country.* 政府想加快机构改革，以找到整顿国家的新方法。 **2** → see also **shakeup**

Thesaurus *shake* 另参见：
V. jerk, move, ruffle, swing **1** **2**

Word Partnership *shake* 的常用搭配：
V. begin to shake **1** – **3** **5** – **7**
N. shake *your* head **3**
shake *someone's* confidence **9**
shake *someone's* hand **11**
shake hands (with *someone*) **12**

shake·up /ʃeɪkʌp/ (**shakeups**)
in BRIT, use **shake-up**
N-COUNT A **shakeup** is a major set of changes in an organization or a system. (组织) 大改组；(体系) 剧变 [JOURNALISM] ❑ *Community leaders say a complete departmental shakeup is needed.* 社区领导人说需要进行一次彻底的部门大改组。

★ **shaky** /ʃeɪki/ (**shakier, shakiest**) **1** ADJ If you describe a situation as **shaky**, you mean that it is weak or unstable, and seems unlikely to last long or be successful. 不牢靠的 ❑ *A shaky ceasefire is holding after three days of fighting between rival groups.* 敌对组织之间进行了3天的战斗之后，达成了勉强的停火协议。 **2** ADJ If your body or your voice is **shaky**, you cannot control it properly and it shakes, for example, because you are ill or nervous. (身体、声音) 颤抖的 ❑ *We have all had a shaky hand and a dry mouth before speaking in public.* 当众发言之前，我们都曾双手发抖，嘴巴发干。

shall ♦♦◇ /ʃəl, STRONG ʃæl/

Shall is a modal verb. It is used with the base form of a verb.

1 MODAL You use **shall** with "I" and "we" in questions in order to make offers or suggestions, or to ask for advice. 可以 (用于疑问句中 "I" 和 "we" 前，用以提供建议或征求意见) ❑ *Shall I get the keys?* 我拿钥匙可以吗？ ❑ *Well, shall we go?* 那，我们走好吗？ ❑ *Let's have a nice little stroll, shall we?* 咱们去好好散散步，好吗？ **2** MODAL You use **shall**, usually with "I" and "we," when you are referring to something that you intend to do, or when you are referring to something that you are sure will happen to you in the future. 将 (与 "I" 和 "we" 连用，表示意欲做某事或将要发生的事) [FORMAL] ❑ *We shall be landing in Paris in sixteen minutes, exactly on time.* 我们将在16分钟后准时在巴黎降落。 ❑ *I shall know more next month, I hope.* 我希望下个月我将知道更多。 **3** MODAL You use **shall** with "I" or "we" during a speech or piece of writing to say what you are going to discuss or explain later. 将 (与 "I" 和 "we" 连用，表示将要论及或解释的内容) [FORMAL] ❑ *In Chapter 3, I shall describe some of the documentation that I gathered.* 在第3章，我将讲述我所搜集到的一些文献资料。 **4** MODAL You use **shall** to indicate that something must happen, usually because of a rule or law. You use **shall not** to indicate that something must not happen. 将 (指按规定或规律一定会发生) ❑ *The president shall hold office for five years.* 总统将任职5年。 **5** MODAL You use **shall**, usually with "you," when you are telling someone that they will be able to do or have something they want. 可以 (与 "you" 连用，用以告知某人能做某事或拥有想要的东西) ❑ *Very well, if you want to go, go you shall.* 很好，如果你想走的话，你可以走了。

shal·low /ʃæloʊ/ (**shallower, shallowest**) **1** ADJ A **shallow** container, hole, or area of water measures only a short distance from the top to the bottom. 浅的 ❑ *Put the milk in a shallow dish.* 把牛奶倒进一个浅盘里。 **2** ADJ If you describe a person, piece of work, or idea as **shallow**, you disapprove of them because they do not show or involve any serious or careful thought. (人、作品、主意等) 浅薄的 [DISAPPROVAL] ❑ *I think he is shallow, vain and untrustworthy.* 我认为他浅薄、虚荣、不可信。 **3** ADJ If your breathing is **shallow**, you take only a very small amount of air into your lungs at each breath. (呼吸) 浅的 ❑ *She began to hear her own taut, shallow breathing.* 她开始听到自己紧张、短促的呼吸。

sham /ʃæm/ (**shams**) N-COUNT Something that is a **sham** is not real or is not really what it seems to be. 假的东西 [DISAPPROVAL]

❑ *The government's promises were exposed as a hollow sham.* 政府的承诺被揭露为一个空洞的谎言。

sham·bles /ʃæmbᵊlz/ N-SING If a place, event, or situation is **a shambles** or is **in a shambles**, everything is in disorder. 混乱 ❑ *The ship's interior was an utter shambles.* 那艘船的内部一片狼藉。

shame ♦◇◇ /ʃeɪm/ (**shames, shaming, shamed**) **1** N-UNCOUNT **Shame** is an uncomfortable feeling that you get when you have done something wrong or embarrassing, or when someone close to you has. 羞耻；羞愧 ❑ *She felt a deep sense of shame.* 她深感羞耻。 ❑ *Her father and her brothers would die of shame.* 她的父亲和兄弟们会羞愧死的。 **2** N-UNCOUNT If someone brings **shame on** you, they make other people lose their respect for you. 耻辱 ❑ *I don't want to bring shame on the family name.* 我不想给家庭的声誉带来耻辱。 **3** V-T If something **shames** you, it causes you to feel shame. 使羞愧 ❑ *Her son's affair had humiliated and shamed her.* 她儿子的事丢了她的脸、令她羞愧。 **4** V-T If you **shame** someone **into** doing something, you force them to do it by making them feel ashamed not to. 使…感到羞愧（而做某事） ❑ *He would not let neighbors shame him into silence.* 他不会因为邻居的羞辱而默不作声。 **5** N-SING If you say that something is **a shame**, you are expressing your regret about it and indicating that you wish it had happened differently. 令人遗憾的事 [FEELINGS] ❑ *It's a crying shame that police have to put up with these mindless attacks.* 警察不得不容忍这些无谓的攻击，真是件太令人遗憾的事。 **6** CONVENTION You can use **shame** in expressions such as **shame on you** and **shame on him** to indicate that someone ought to feel shame for something they have said or done. 耻辱 [FEELINGS] ❑ *He tried to deny it. Shame on him!* 他想否认此事。真丢人！ **7** PHRASE If someone **puts** you **to shame**, they make you feel ashamed because they do something much better than you do. 使自愧不如 ❑ *His playing really put me to shame.* 他的表现真让我自愧不如。
→ see **emotion**

Word Partnership *shame* 的常用搭配：

V.	**experience** shame, **feel** shame **1**
N.	**feelings of** shame, **sense of** shame **1**

shame·ful /ʃeɪmfəl/ ADJ If you describe a person's action or attitude as **shameful**, you think that it is so bad that the person ought to be ashamed. 可耻的 [DISAPPROVAL] ❑ *...the most shameful episode in U.S. naval history.* …美国海军史上最耻辱的一段历史。
● **shame·ful·ly** ADV 可耻地 ❑ *At times they have been shamefully neglected.* 有时他们被可耻地忽略了。

shame·less /ʃeɪmlɪs/ ADJ If you describe someone as **shameless**, you mean that they should be ashamed of their behavior, which is unacceptable to other people. 无耻的 [DISAPPROVAL] ❑ *...a shameless attempt to stifle democratic debate.* …一个压制民主辩论的无耻企图。
● **shame·less·ly** ADV 无耻地 ❑ *...a shamelessly lazy week-long trip.* …一次长达一周的懒得可耻的旅行。

▲ **sham·poo** /ʃæmpuː/ (**shampoos, shampooing, shampooed**) **1** N-MASS **Shampoo** is a soapy liquid that you use for washing your hair. 洗发液 ❑ *...a bottle of shampoo.* …一瓶洗发水。 **2** V-T When you **shampoo** your hair, you wash it using shampoo. 用洗发水洗 ❑ *Shampoo your hair and dry it.* 用洗发水洗洗你的头发，然后把头发弄干。
→ see **hair**

shan't /ʃænt/ **Shan't** is the usual spoken form of "shall not." **shall not**的常用口语形式

shape ♦♦◇ /ʃeɪp/ (**shapes, shaping, shaped**) **1** N-COUNT The **shape of** an object, a person, or an area is the appearance of their outside edges or surfaces, for example, whether they are round, square, curved, or fat. 外形；形状 [oft N "of" n, also "in" N] ❑ *Each mirror is made to order and can be designed to almost any shape or size.* 每面镜子都是定制做的，而且能设计成几乎任何形状或规格。 ❑ *...little pens in the shape of baseball bats.* …棒球球棒形状的小钢笔。 ❑ *...sofas and chairs of contrasting shapes and colors.* …形状和颜色反差很大的沙发和椅子。 **2** N-COUNT You can refer to something that you can see as a **shape** if you cannot see it clearly, or if its outline is the clearest or most striking aspect of it. （模糊的）影像 ❑ *The great gray shape of a tank rolled out of the village.* 一个坦克状的巨大灰影从村子里开了出来。 **3** N-COUNT A **shape** is a space enclosed by an outline, for example, a circle, a square, or a triangle. 形状 ❑ *Imagine a sort of a kidney shape.* 想像一种类似肾脏的形状。 **4** N-SING The **shape of** something that is planned or organized is its structure and character. （计划或组织的）框架 ❑ *The last two weeks have seen a lot of talk about the future shape of Europe.* 在过去的两周里有许多关于欧洲的未来格局的讨论。 **5** V-T Someone or something that **shapes** a situation or an activity has a very great influence on the way it develops. 塑造 ❑ *Like it or not, our families shape our lives and make us what we are.* 不管喜欢与否，我们的家庭塑造我们的生活并铸就我们的个性。 **6** V-T If you **shape** an object, you give it a particular shape, using your hands or a tool. 使成…形 ❑ *Cut the dough in half and shape each half into a loaf.* 把生面团切成两半，分别捏成长条状。 **7** → see also **shaped** **8** PHRASE If you say, for example, that you will not accept something **in any shape or form**, or **in any way, shape or form**, you are emphasizing that you will not accept it in any circumstances. 以任何形式 [EMPHASIS] ❑ *I don't condone violence in any shape or form.* 我决不容忍任何形式的暴力。 **9** PHRASE If someone or something is **in shape**, or **in good shape**, they are in a good state of health or in a good condition. If they are **in bad shape**, they are in a bad state of health or in a bad condition. （身体、物体）处于（良好/不良）状况 ❑ *...the Fatburner Diet Book, a comprehensive guide to getting in shape.* …《减肥饮食指南》，一本保持健康的综合指南。 ❑ *He was still in better shape than many young men.* 他依然比许多年轻人都健康。 **10** PHRASE If you **lick**, **knock**, or **whip** someone or something **into shape**, you use whatever methods are necessary to change or improve them so that they are in the condition that you want them to be in. 用尽办法塑造 ❑ *You'll have four months in which to lick the*

Picture Dictionary shapes

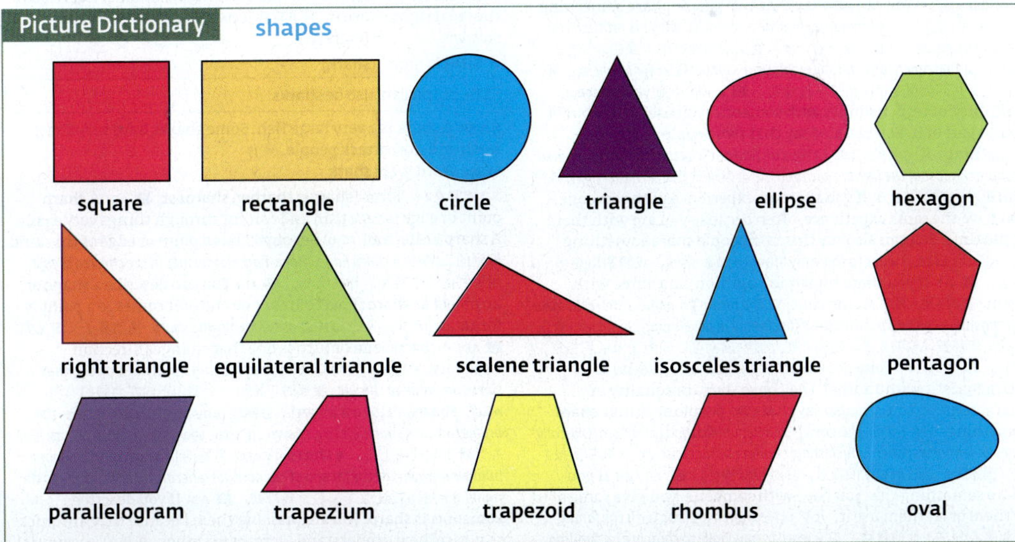

S

recruits into shape. 你将有4个月的时间训练就这些新兵。 11 PHRASE If something is **out of shape**, it is no longer in its proper or original shape, for example, because it has been damaged or wrongly handled. 变形了的 ❑ *Once most wires are bent out of shape, they don't return to the original position.* 大多数电线一旦弯曲变形就恢复不了原状。 12 PHRASE If you are **out of shape**, you are unhealthy and unable to do a lot of physical activity without getting tired. 不健康的 ❑ *I weighed 245 pounds and was out of shape.* 我那时体重245磅，健康状况不佳。 13 PHRASE When something **takes shape**, it develops or starts to appear in such a way that it becomes fairly clear what its final form will be. 成形 ❑ *In 1912 women's events were added, and the modern Olympic program began to take shape.* 1912年增加了女子项目，现代奥林匹克运动会开始初具雏形。
→ see Picture Dictionary: **shapes**
→ see **circle, mathematics**

▸ **shape up** 1 PHRASAL VERB If something **is shaping up**, it is starting to develop or seems likely to happen. 开始形成；酝酿 ❑ *There are also indications that a major tank battle may be shaping up for tonight.* 也有迹象表明今晚很可能有一场坦克大战。 ❑ *The accident is already shaping up as a significant environmental disaster.* 这个事故已经酝酿成为一场重大的环境灾难。 2 PHRASAL VERB If you ask how someone or something **is shaping up**, you want to know how well they are doing in a particular situation or activity. 进展 ❑ *I did have a few worries about how Hugh and I would shape up as parents.* 我对休和我将如何为人父母的确有些担心。 3 PHRASAL VERB If you tell someone to **shape up**, you are telling them to start behaving in a sensible and responsible way. 合理行事；好好表现 ❑ *They were given a year to shape up or risk losing their scholarships.* 他们被给了一年的时间好好表现，否则就有失去奖学金的危险。

Word Partnership *shape* 的常用搭配：
V. **change** shape 1
change the shape **of** ***something*** 4
get in shape 9
ADJ. **dark** shape 2
(pretty) bad/good/great shape, **better/worse** shape, **physical** shape, **terrible** shape 9

shaped ◆◇◇ /ʃeɪpt/ ADJ Something that is **shaped** like a particular object or in a particular way has the shape of that object or a shape of that type. 有…形状的 [v-link ADJ] ❑ *A new perfume from Russia came in a bottle shaped like a tank.* 来自俄罗斯的一种新型香水装在坦克形状的瓶子里。

share ◆◆◆ /ʃɛər/ (**shares, sharing, shared**) 1 N-COUNT A company's **shares** are the many equal parts into which its ownership is divided. Shares can be bought by people as an investment. 股份；股票 [BUSINESS] ❑ *People in China are eager to buy shares in new businesses.* 中国民众热衷于购买新企业的股票。 2 V-RECIP If you **share** something **with** another person, you both have it, use it, or occupy it. You can also say that two people **share** something. 共有；共用；共享 ❑ *...the small income he had shared with his brother from his father's estate.* …他和他兄弟分享从他父亲的地产中得来的一小笔收入。 ❑ *Two Americans will share this year's Nobel Prize for Medicine.* 两位美国人将共同摘得今年的诺贝尔医学奖。 3 V-RECIP If you **share** a task, duty, or responsibility **with** someone, you each carry out or accept part of it. You can also say that two people **share** something. 共同承担；分摊 ❑ *You can find out whether they are prepared to share the cost of the flowers with you.* 你会发现他们是否准备与你分摊鲜花的费用。 4 V-RECIP If you **share** an experience **with** someone, you have the same experience, often because you are with them at the time. You can also say that two people **share** something. 共享（经历） ❑ *Yes, I want to share my life with you.* 是的，我想和你共享生活。 5 V-T If you **share** someone's opinion, you agree with them. 赞同（某人的观点） [no cont] ❑ *The forum's members share his view that business can be a positive force for change in developing countries.* 论坛的成员们都赞同他的观点，即商业在发展中国家可以成为变革的积极推动力。 6 V-RECIP If one person or thing **shares** a quality or characteristic **with** another, they have the same quality or characteristic. You can also say that two people or things **share** something. 共有（特点） [no cont] ❑ *La Repubblica and El Pais are politically independent newspapers which share similar characteristics.* 《共和国报》和《国家报》是政治独立的报纸，具有相似特征。 7 V-T/V-I If you **share** something that you have **with** someone, you give some of it to them or let them use it. 分享 ❑ *He shared his food with the family.* 他和家人分享了他的食物。 ❑ *Scientists now have to compete for funding, and do not share information among themselves.* 科学家们现在不得不为了资金而相互竞争，彼此间不共享信息。 ❑ *I wanted everybody to share.* 我希望大家一起分享。 8 V-T If you **share** something personal such as a thought or a piece of news **with** someone, you tell them about it. 分享（个人感情、消息等） ❑ *It can be beneficial to share your feelings with someone you trust.* 与你信任的人分享你的情感会是有益的。 9 N-COUNT If something is divided or distributed among a number of different people or things, each of them has, or is responsible for, a **share of** it. （若干中的）一份 ❑ *Sara also pays a share of the gas, electricity and phone bills.* 萨拉也交一份煤气、电和电话的费用。 10 N-COUNT If you have or do your **share of** something, you have or do an amount that seems reasonable to you, or to other people. （应拥有或承担的）一份 ❑ *Women must receive their fair share of training for good-paying jobs.* 妇女必须获得找到高收入工作需要的应有的培训。 11 → see also **lion's share, market share, power-sharing**
→ see **company**

▸ **share out** PHRASAL VERB If you **share out** an amount of something, you give each person in a group an equal or fair part of it. 分配；均分

share capi·tal N-UNCOUNT A company's **share capital** is the money that shareholders invest in order to start or expand the business. 股本 [BUSINESS] ❑ *The bank has a share capital of almost 100 million dollars.* 这家银行有差不多一亿美元的股本。

★ **share·holder** ◆◇◇ /ʃɛərhoʊldər/ (**shareholders**) 1 N-COUNT A **shareholder** is a person who owns shares in a company. 股东 [BUSINESS] ❑ *...a shareholders' meeting.* …一次股东会议。 2 → see also **stockholder**

share·holding /ʃɛərhoʊldɪŋ/ (**shareholdings**) N-COUNT If you have a **shareholding** in a company, you own some of its shares. 股权 [BUSINESS] ❑ *She will retain her very significant shareholding in the company.* 她将保留她在该公司的重要股权。

share in·dex (**share indices** or **share indexes**) N-COUNT A **share index** is a number that indicates the state of a stock market. It is based on the combined share prices of a set of companies. 股票指数 [BUSINESS] ❑ *The share index was up 16.4 points to 1,599.6.* 股指上升了16.4点，达到1599.6。

share is·sue (**share issues**) N-COUNT When there is a **share issue**, shares in a company are made available for people to buy. 股票发行 [BUSINESS] ❑ *The deal will be financed by a share issue that will raise $128.9 million.* 这笔交易将由要筹集到1.289亿美元的股票发行来资助。

share op·tion (**share options**) N-COUNT A **share option** is the same as a **stock option**. 优先认股权 [BRIT, BUSINESS]

share shop (**share shops**) N-COUNT A **share shop** is a store or Internet website where members of the public can buy shares in companies. （地面或网上的）股票认购店 [BUSINESS]

share·ware /ʃɛərwɛər/ N-UNCOUNT **Shareware** is computer software that you can try before deciding whether or not to buy the legal right to use it. 共享软件 [COMPUTING] ❑ *...a shareware program.* …一个共享软件程序。

★ **shark** /ʃɑrk/ (**shark**)

The plural can also be **sharks**.

N-VAR A **shark** is a very large fish. Some sharks have very sharp teeth and may attack people. 鲨鱼
→ see Word Web: **shark**

sharp ◆◆◇ /ʃɑrp/ (**sharps, sharper, sharpest**) 1 ADJ A **sharp** point or edge is very thin and can cut through things very easily. A **sharp** knife, tool, or other object has a point or edge of this kind. 锋利的 ❑ *With a sharp knife, make diagonal slashes in the chicken breast.* 用锋利的刀子斜着切开鸡胸脯。 2 ADJ You can describe a shape or an object as **sharp** if part of it or one end of it comes to a point or forms an angle. 尖的 ❑ *His nose was thin and sharp.* 他的鼻子又细又尖。 3 ADJ A **sharp** bend or turn is one that changes direction suddenly. 急剧的（转弯） ❑ *I was approaching a fairly sharp bend that swept downhill to the left.* 我那时正接近一个朝山下向左急转的弯道。 ● ADV **Sharp** is also an adverb. 急剧地 [ADV adv] ❑ *Do not cross the bridge but turn sharp left to go down on to the towpath.* 不要过桥，而是向左急转下到纤道上去。 ● **sharp·ly** ADV 急剧地 [ADV after v] ❑ *Room number nine was at the far end of the corridor where it turned sharply to the right.* 9号房间在过道尽头右急转弯处。 4 ADJ If you describe someone as **sharp**, you are praising them because they are quick to notice, hear, understand, or react to things. 机敏的 [APPROVAL]

S

Word Web shark

Sharks are different from other **fish**. The **skeleton** of a shark is made of **cartilage**, not bone. The flexibility of cartilage allows this **predator** to maneuver around its **prey** easily. Sharks also have several gill **slits** with no flap covering them. Its scales are also much smaller and harder than fish scales. And its teeth are special too. Sharks grow new teeth when they lose old ones. It's almost impossible to escape from a shark. Some of them can swim up to 44 miles per hour. But sharks only kill 50 to 75 people each year worldwide.

❑ *He is very sharp, a quick thinker and swift with repartee.* 他很机敏、思维敏捷并且能机智应答。 5 ADJ If someone says something in a **sharp** way, they say it suddenly and rather firmly or angrily, for example, because they are warning or criticizing you. (说话、措辞等) 严厉的 ❑ *"Don't contradict your mother," was Charles's sharp reprimand.* "不要顶撞你的母亲，"查尔斯严厉的斥责。 ● **sharp·ly** ADV 严厉地 ❑ *"You've known," she said sharply, "and you didn't tell me?"* "你已经知道了，"她严厉地说道，"而你却没有告诉我？" 6 ADJ A **sharp** change, movement, or feeling occurs suddenly, and is great in amount, force, or degree. (变化、动作等) 急剧的; (情感等) 剧烈的 ❑ *There's been a sharp rise in the rate of inflation.* 通货膨胀率急剧上升了。 ❑ *Tennis requires a lot of short sharp movements.* 网球运动需要大量快速而剧烈的动作。 ● **sharp·ly** ADV 急剧地 ❑ *Unemployment has risen sharply in recent years.* 近年来失业率已急剧上升。 7 ADJ A **sharp** difference, image, or sound is very easy to see, hear, or distinguish. (差异、图像、声音等) 清晰可辨的 ❑ *Many people make a sharp distinction between humans and other animals.* 许多人将人类和其他动物截然分开。 ❑ *All the footmarks are quite sharp and clear.* 所有的足迹都很清楚明晰。 ● **sharp·ly** ADV 清晰可辨地 ❑ *Opinions on this are sharply divided.* 对这事的看法迥然各异。 8 ADJ A **sharp** taste or smell is rather strong or bitter, but is often also clear and fresh. (味道、气味等) 浓烈的 ❑ *The apple tasted just as I remembered – sharp, sour, yet sweet.* 这苹果尝起来跟我记忆中的完全一样——味道十足，酸中带甜。 9 ADV **Sharp** is used after stating a particular time to show that something happens at exactly the time stated. (…点) 整 [n ADV] ❑ *She planned to unlock the store at 8:00 sharp this morning.* 她计划今早8点整打开店门。 10 N-COUNT **Sharp** is used after a letter representing a musical note to show that the note should be played or sung half a tone higher. **Sharp** is often represented by the symbol #. 升半音 ❑ *A solitary viola plucks a lonely, soft F sharp.* 一把中提琴独奏出孤寂婉约的升F调。

Word Partnership *sharp* 的常用搭配：

ADV. very sharp 1 – 8
N. sharp **edge**, sharp **point**, sharp **teeth** 1 2
sharp **eyes**, sharp **mind** 4
sharp **criticism** 5
sharp **decline**, sharp **increase**, sharp **pain** 6
sharp **contrast** 7

sharp·en /ʃɑrpən/ (**sharpens, sharpening, sharpened**) 1 V-T/V-I If your senses, understanding, or skills **sharpen** or **are sharpened**, you become better at noticing things, thinking, or doing something. 使敏锐; 增强 ❑ *Her gaze sharpened, as if she had seen something unusual.* 她眼睛一亮，好像看到了不寻常的东西。 ❑ *He will need to sharpen his diplomatic skills in order to work with Congress.* 他将需要增强外交技巧以与国会打交道。 2 V-T If you **sharpen** an object, you make its edge very thin or you make its end pointed. 使变锋利; 弄尖 ❑ *He started to sharpen his knife.* 他开始磨刀。

sharp·en·er /ʃɑrpənər/ (**sharpeners**) N-COUNT A **sharpener** is a tool or machine used for sharpening pencils or knives. 磨具; 卷笔刀 ❑ *...a pencil sharpener.* …一个卷笔刀。

shat /ʃæt/ **Shat** is the past tense and past participle of **shit**. **shit** 的过去式和过去分词

★ **shat·ter** /ʃætər/ (**shatters, shattering, shattered**) 1 V-T/V-I If something **shatters** or **is shattered**, it breaks into a lot of small pieces. 粉碎 ❑ *...safety glass that won't shatter if it's broken.* …安全玻璃即使破了也不会粉碎。 ❑ *The car shattered into a thousand burning pieces in a 200 mph crash.* 这辆轿车在时速200英里的碰撞中裂成了数以千计燃烧着的碎片。 ● **shat·ter·ing** N-UNCOUNT 粉碎 ❑ *...the shattering of glass.* …玻璃的粉碎。 2 V-T If something **shatters** your dreams, hopes, or beliefs, it completely destroys them. 粉碎 (梦想、希望、信仰等) ❑ *A failure would shatter the hopes of many people.* 一次失败会粉碎很多人的希望。 3 V-T If someone **is shattered** by an event, it shocks and upsets them very much. 严重打击 ❑ *He had been shattered by his son's death.* 儿子的死使他很受打击。 4 → see also **shattered, shattering** → see **crash, glass**

shat·tered /ʃætərd/ ADJ If you are **shattered** by something, you are extremely shocked and upset about it. 严重受打击的 ❑ *It is desperately sad news and I am absolutely shattered to hear it.* 这是极为令人悲伤的消息，我听后完全被击垮了。

shave /ʃeɪv/ (**shaves, shaving, shaved**) 1 V-T/V-I When a man **shaves**, he removes the hair from his face using a razor or shaver so that his face is smooth. 刮 (脸); 剃须 ❑ *He took a bath and shaved before dinner.* 他在晚餐前洗了澡并刮了脸。 ❑ *He had shaved his face until it was smooth.* 他把脸刮到光滑为止。 ● N-COUNT **Shave** is also a noun. 剃须; 刮脸 ❑ *He never seemed to need a shave.* 他似乎从不需要刮脸。 ● **shav·ing** N-UNCOUNT 剃须; 刮脸 ❑ *...a range of shaving products.* …一系列剃须产品。 2 V-T If you **shave off** part of a piece of wood or other material, you cut very thin pieces from it. 削掉; 刨掉 ❑ *I set the log on the ground and shaved off the bark.* 我把原木放在地上，然后刨掉树皮。 3 V-T If you **shave** a small amount **off** something such as a record, cost, or price, you reduce it by that amount. 少量削减; 略微降低 ❑ *She's already shaved four seconds off the national record for the mile.* 她已经把1英里赛跑的全国纪录减少了4秒。 4 → see also **shaving** 5 PHRASE If you describe a situation as **a close shave**, you mean that there was nearly an accident or a disaster but it was avoided. 侥幸脱险 ❑ *I can't quite believe the close shaves I've had just recently.* 我几乎不能相信我最近刚经历的几次侥幸脱险。

shav·er /ʃeɪvər/ (**shavers**) N-COUNT A **shaver** is an electric device, used for shaving hair from the face and body. 电动剃须刀 ❑ *...men's electric shavers.* …男用电动剃须刀。

shav·ing /ʃeɪvɪŋ/ (**shavings**) 1 N-COUNT **Shavings** are small very thin pieces of wood or other material which have been cut from a larger piece. 刨花; 削屑 ❑ *The floor was covered with shavings from his wood carvings.* 地板上满是他从木雕上刻下来的碎屑。 2 → see also **shave**

▲ **shawl** /ʃɔl/ (**shawls**) N-COUNT A **shawl** is a large piece of woolen cloth which a woman wears over her shoulders or head, or which is wrapped around a baby to keep it warm. 披肩; 围巾; 襁褓 → see **clothing**

she ◆◆◆ /ʃɪ, STRONG ʃi/

She is a third person singular pronoun. **She** is used as the subject of a verb.

1 PRON-SING You use **she** to refer to a woman, girl, or female animal who has already been mentioned or whose identity is clear. 她 (代指女性或雌性动物) ❑ *When Ann arrived home that night, she found Brian in the house watching TV.* 当安那天晚上回到家时，她发现布赖恩正在屋里看电视。 ❑ *She was seventeen and she had no education or employment.* 她17岁了，既没有受过教育也没有工作。 2 PRON-SING Some writers may use **she** to refer to a person who is not identified as either male or female. They do this because they wish to avoid using the pronoun "he" all the time. Some people dislike this use and prefer to use "he or she" or "they." 她 (代指不分性别的所有人) ❑ *The student may show signs of feeling the strain of responsibility and she may give up.* 学生可能表现出责任带来的压力感的种种迹象，她也许会放弃。 3 PRON-SING **She** is sometimes used to refer to a country or nation. 她 (代指国家或民族) ❑ *The country needs new leadership if she is to play a role in future development.* 该国要在未来的发展中发挥作用的话，她就需要新的领导班子。 4 PRON-SING Some people use **she** to refer to a car or machine. People who sail often use **she** to refer to a ship or boat. 她 (代指汽车、机器或船只) ❑ *The Seaflower was being repaired, but soon she was fit to sail again.* "海花号"当时正在修理，但很快她就又可以航行了。

S

▲ **shear** /ʃɪər/ (**shears, shearing, sheared, sheared** or **shorn**) **1** V-T To **shear** a sheep means to cut its wool off. (给羊) 剪毛 ❑ *Competitors have six minutes to shear four sheep.* 参赛者们有6分钟的时间来给4只羊剪毛。● **shear·ing** N-UNCOUNT 剪羊毛 ❑ *...a display of sheep shearing.* …一场剪羊毛表演。 **2** N-PLURAL A pair of **shears** is a garden tool like a very large pair of scissors. Shears are used especially for cutting hedges. 大剪刀 ❑ *Trim the shrubs with shears.* 用大剪刀修剪这些灌木。

sheath /ʃiθ/ (**sheaths**) N-COUNT A **sheath** is a covering for the blade of a knife. (刀) 鞘

shed ♦◇◇ /ʃɛd/ (**sheds, shedding**)

The form **shed** is used in the present tense and in the past tense and past participle of the verb.

1 N-COUNT A **shed** is a small building that is used for storing things such as garden tools. (用于存放园艺工具等的) 棚屋 ❑ *...a garden shed.* …一个园艺工具棚。 **2** N-COUNT A **shed** is a large shelter or building, for example, at a train station, port, or factory. (车站、港口、工厂等的) 棚式建筑 ❑ *...a vast factory shed.* …一座巨大的厂房。 **3** V-T When a tree **sheds** its leaves, its leaves fall off in the autumn. When an animal **sheds** hair or skin, some of its hair or skin drops off. 落 (叶); 脱 (发); 蜕 (皮) ❑ *Some of the trees were already beginning to shed their leaves.* 有些树已经开始落叶了。 **4** V-T To **shed** something means to get rid of it. 去除; 摆脱 [FORMAL] ❑ *The firm is to shed 700 jobs.* 这个公司将裁掉700个工作岗位。 **5** V-T If you **shed** tears, you cry. 落 (泪) ❑ *They will shed a few tears at their daughter's wedding.* 他们在女儿的婚礼上会落些泪。 **6** V-T To **shed** blood means to kill people in a violent way. If someone **sheds** their blood, they are killed in a violent way, usually when they are fighting in a war. 洒 (热血) [FORMAL] ❑ *...young warriors, eager to shed blood.* …渴望洒热血的年轻武士们。 **7** to **shed light on** something → see **light** → see **cry**

Word Partnership *shed* 的常用搭配:

N. storage shed **1**
shed *your* **clothes**, shed *your* **image**, shed **pounds** **4**
shed **a tear**, shed **tears** **5**
shed **blood** **6**

she'd /ʃid, ʃɪd/ **1** **She'd** is the usual spoken form of "she had," especially when "had" is an auxiliary verb. **she had**的常用口语形式 ❑ *She'd been to clubs all over the world.* 她去过世界各地的俱乐部。 **2** **She'd** is a spoken form of "she would." **she would**的口语形式 ❑ *She'd do anything for a bit of money.* 她为一点点钱什么都肯做。

sheen /ʃin/ N-SING If something has a **sheen**, it has a smooth and gentle brightness on its surface. 光泽 ❑ *The carpet had a silvery sheen to it.* 地毯有种银色的光泽。

sheep /ʃip/ (**sheep**)

Sheep is both the singular and the plural form.

N-COUNT A **sheep** is a farm animal which is covered with thick curly hair called wool. Sheep are kept for their wool or for their meat. 羊 ❑ *...grassland on which a flock of sheep were grazing.* …有一群羊正在吃草的草地。
→ see **barn, meat**

sheep·ish /ʃipɪʃ/ ADJ If you look **sheepish**, you look slightly embarrassed because you feel foolish or you have done something silly. 困窘的 ❑ *I asked him why. He looked a little sheepish when he answered.* 我问他为什么。他回答时看起来有点困窘。

sheer /ʃɪər/ (**sheerer, sheerest**) **1** ADJ You can use **sheer** to emphasize that a state or situation is complete and does not involve or is not mixed with anything else. 纯粹的 [ADJ n] [EMPHASIS] ❑ *His music is sheer delight.* 他的音乐是纯粹的快乐。 ❑ *Sheer chance quite often plays an important part in sparking off an idea.* 纯粹的运气常常在激发思想方面起着重要的作用。 **2** ADJ A **sheer** cliff or drop is extremely steep or completely vertical. 陡峭的; 完全垂直的 ❑ *There was a sheer drop just outside my window.* 就在我的窗外有一个陡坡。 **3** ADJ **Sheer** material is very thin, light, and delicate. 极轻薄的 ❑ *...sheer black tights.* …极薄的黑色紧身衣。

Word Partnership *sheer* 的常用搭配:

N. sheer **delight**, sheer **force**, sheer **luck**, sheer **number**, sheer **pleasure**, sheer **power**, sheer **size**, sheer **strength**, sheer **terror**, sheer **volume** **1**

sheet ♦◇◇ /ʃit/ (**sheets**) **1** N-COUNT A **sheet** is a large rectangular piece of cotton or other cloth that you sleep on or cover yourself with in a bed. 床单; 被单 ❑ *Once a week, a maid changes the sheets.* 女仆每个星期换一次床单。 **2** N-COUNT A **sheet of** paper is a rectangular piece of paper. (一) 张 (纸) ❑ *...a sheet of newspaper.* …一张报纸。 **3** N-COUNT You can use **sheet** to refer to a piece of paper which gives information about something. (一份) 资料 ❑ *...information sheets on each country in the world.* …有关世界各国的情报资料。 **4** N-COUNT A **sheet of** glass, metal, or wood is a large, flat, thin piece of it. (一) 块 (玻璃、金属或木头等) ❑ *...a cracked sheet of glass.* …一块裂开的玻璃。 ❑ *Overhead cranes were lifting giant sheets of steel.* 高架起重机正吊起一块块巨大的钢材。 **5** N-COUNT A **sheet of** something is a thin wide layer of it over the surface of something else. (一) 大层 (覆盖物) ❑ *...a sheet of ice.* …一大层冰。 **6** → see also **balance sheet, broadsheet, fact sheet, spreadsheet, worksheet** → see **bed, glass, paper**

sheikh /ʃik, ʃeɪk/ (**sheikhs**) N-TITLE; N-COUNT A **sheikh** is a male Arab chief or ruler. (阿拉伯的男性) 酋长; 统治者 ❑ *...Sheikh Khalifa.* …酋长哈里发。

shelf /ʃɛlf/ (**shelves**) **1** N-COUNT A **shelf** is a flat piece of wood, metal, or glass which is attached to a wall or to the sides of a cabinet. Shelves are used for keeping things on. 架子 ❑ *He took a book from the shelf.* 他从那个架上拿了一本书。 **2** PHRASE If you buy something **off the shelf**, you buy something that is not specially made for you. 现货出售的 ❑ *Lower-priced jewelry will be sold off the shelf by this fall.* 低价的珠宝到今年秋天就将现货出售。

shell ♦◇◇ /ʃɛl/ (**shells, shelling, shelled**) **1** N-COUNT The **shell** of a nut or egg is the hard covering which surrounds it. (坚果或蛋的) 壳 ❑ *They cracked the nuts and removed their shells.* 他们打破坚果并剥掉果壳。 ● N-UNCOUNT **Shell** is the substance that a shell is made of. 壳料 ❑ *...beads made from ostrich egg shell.* …鸵鸟蛋壳做成的珠子。 **2** N-COUNT The **shell** of an animal such as a tortoise, snail, or crab is the hard protective covering that it has around its body or on its back. (动物的) 甲壳 ❑ *...the spiral form of a snail shell.* …蜗牛壳的螺旋形状。 **3** N-COUNT **Shells** are hard objects found on beaches. They are usually pink, white, or brown and are the coverings which used to surround small sea creatures. 贝壳 ❑ *I collect shells and interesting seaside items.* 我收集贝壳以及海边有趣的东西。 **4** V-T If you **shell** nuts, peas, shrimp, or other food, you remove their natural outer covering. 剥…的壳 ❑ *She shelled and ate a few nuts.* 她剥了一些坚果吃。 **5** N-COUNT If someone comes out of their **shell**, they become more friendly and interested in other people and less quiet, shy, and reserved. 矜持 ❑ *Her normally shy son had come out of his shell.* 她那平时害羞的儿子已经开始活跃起来了。 **6** N-COUNT The **shell** of a building, boat, car, or other structure is the outside frame of it. 框架 ❑ *...the shells of burned buildings.* …被烧毁的建筑物的框架。 **7** N-COUNT A **shell** is a weapon consisting of a metal container filled with explosives that can be fired from a large gun over long distances. 炮弹 ❑ *Tanks fired shells at the house.* 坦克向那座房子发射炮弹。 **8** V-T To **shell** a place means to fire explosive shells at it. 炮击 ❑ *The rebels shelled the densely-populated suburbs near the port.* 那些叛乱者炮击了港口附近人口稠密的郊区。 ● **shell·ing** N-VAR (**shellings**) 炮击 ❑ *Out on the streets, the shelling continued.* 在外面街道上，炮击在继续。

▸ **shell out** PHRASAL VERB If you **shell out for** something, you spend a lot of money on it. 付 (一大笔钱) [INFORMAL] ❑ *You won't have to shell out a fortune for it.* 你将不必为它花一大笔钱。 ❑ *...an insurance policy which saves you from having to shell out for repairs.* …一份可以使你不必为修理花一大笔钱的保险单。

she'll /ʃil, ʃɪl/ **She'll** is the usual spoken form of "she will." **she will**的常用口语形式 ❑ *Sharon was a wonderful lady and I know she'll be greatly missed.* 莎伦是一位出色的女士，我知道她会被深深想念。

shell com·pa·ny (**shell companies**) **1** N-COUNT A **shell company** is a company that another company takes over in order to use its name to gain an advantage. 壳公司 [BUSINESS] ❑ *The U.S. shell company was set up to mount a bid for Kingston Communications.* 那家美国的壳公司为竞购金斯顿通信公司而成立。 **2** N-COUNT A **shell company** is a company which does not conduct legitimate business but which has been officially registered, so that it can be used for fraud. 空壳公司 [BUSINESS]

shell·fish /ʃɛlfɪʃ/ (**shellfish**)

Shellfish is both the singular and the plural form.

S

N-VAR **Shellfish** are small creatures that live in the sea and have a shell. 甲壳类水生动物 ❑ *Fish and shellfish are the specialties.* 鱼和甲壳类水生动物是特产。

shell pro·gram (**shell programs**) N-COUNT A **shell program** is a basic computer program that provides a framework within which the user can develop the program to suit their own needs. 壳程序 [COMPUTING]

shel·ter ♦◇◇ /ʃɛltər/ (**shelters, sheltering, sheltered**) 1 N-COUNT A **shelter** is a small building or covered place which is made to protect people from bad weather or danger. 躲避处 ❑ *The city's bomb shelters were being prepared for possible air raids.* 这座城市的防空掩体正在准备中，以防可能发生的空袭。 2 N-UNCOUNT If a place provides **shelter**, it provides you with a place to stay or live, especially when you need protection from bad weather or danger. 遮蔽；庇护 ❑ *The number of families seeking shelter rose by 17 percent.* 寻求避难的家庭数目上升了17%。 ❑ *Although horses do not generally mind the cold, shelter from rain and wind is important.* 尽管马通常不怕冷，但对风雨的遮挡还是很重要的。 3 N-COUNT A **shelter** is a building where homeless people can sleep and get food. 收容所 ❑ *...a shelter for homeless women.* …一个收留无家可归妇女的收容所。 4 V-I If you **shelter** in a place, you stay there and are protected from bad weather or danger. 躲避 ❑ *...a man sheltering in a doorway.* …躲避在门廊里的一名男子。 5 V-T If a place or thing **is sheltered** by something, it is protected by that thing from wind and rain. 遮蔽 [usu passive] ❑ *...a wooden house, sheltered by a low pointed roof.* …一座由低矮的尖屋顶遮蔽的木房子。 6 V-T If you **shelter** someone, usually someone who is being hunted by police or other people, you provide them with a place to stay or live. 窝藏；庇护 ❑ *A neighbor sheltered the boy for seven days.* 一个邻居将这个男孩藏了7天。

Word Partnership *shelter* 的常用搭配：

N.	**bomb** shelter, **emergency** shelter 1
	shelter **and clothing**, **food and** shelter 2
	homeless shelter 3
ADJ.	**temporary** shelter 1 – 3
V.	**find** shelter, **provide** shelter, **seek** shelter 2

shel·tered /ʃɛltərd/ 1 ADJ A **sheltered** place is protected from wind and rain. 不受风雨侵袭的 ❑ *...a shallow-sloping beach next to a sheltered bay.* …一片不受风雨侵袭的海湾旁边的一个缓坡海滩。 2 ADJ If you say that someone has led a **sheltered** life, you mean that they have been protected from difficult or unpleasant experiences. 受呵护的 ❑ *Perhaps I've just led a really sheltered life.* 也许我只是过上了一种真正受人呵护的生活。 3 ADJ **Sheltered** accommodations or work is designed for old or disabled people. It allows them to be independent but also allows them to get help when they need it. 福利性的（住所或工作）[ADJ n] ❑ *Call the family service agencies to find out if they sponsor this kind of sheltered housing.* 打电话给家庭服务机构，看看他们是否资助这种福利性住房。 4 → see also **shelter**

shelve /ʃɛlv/ (**shelves, shelving, shelved**) 1 V-T If someone **shelves** a plan or project, they decide not to continue with it, either for a while or permanently. 搁置 ❑ *King County has shelved plans to build a driving range.* 金郡已搁置了建造一个高尔夫练习场的计划。 2 **Shelves** is the plural of **shelf**. **shelf**的复数形式

★ **shep·herd** /ʃɛpərd/ (**shepherds, shepherding, shepherded**) 1 N-COUNT A **shepherd** is a person, especially a man, whose job is to take care of sheep. 牧羊人 2 V-T If you **are shepherded** somewhere, someone takes you there to make sure that you arrive at the right place safely. 护送 [usu passive] ❑ *She was shepherded by her guards up the rear ramp of the aircraft.* 她由她的警卫们护送登上飞机后部的活动舷梯。

sher·iff /ʃɛrɪf/ (**sheriffs**) N-COUNT; N-TITLE In the United States, a **sheriff** is a person who is elected to make sure that the law is obeyed in a particular county. （美国的）县治安官 ❑ *...the local sheriff.* …当地的县治安官。

sher·ry /ʃɛri/ (**sherries**) N-MASS **Sherry** is a type of strong wine that is made in southwestern Spain. It is usually drunk before a meal. 雪利酒 ❑ *I poured us a glass of sherry.* 我给我们倒了一杯雪利酒。

she's /ʃiz, ʃɪz/ 1 **She's** is the usual spoken form of "she is." **she is**的常用口语形式 ❑ *She's an exceptionally good cook.* 她是一个特别好的厨师。 2 **She's** is a spoken form of "she has," especially when "has" is an auxiliary verb. **she has**的口语形式（尤其当**has**是助动词时）❑ *She's been married for seven years and has two daughters.* 她已结婚7年并有两个女儿。

shh /ʃ/ also **sh** CONVENTION You can say "**Shh!**" to tell someone to be quiet. 嘘；别作声 [INFORMAL, SPOKEN] ❑ *Shh, don't wake Danny.* 嘘，别吵醒丹尼。

shield /ʃild/ (**shields, shielding, shielded**) 1 N-COUNT Something or someone which is a **shield** against a particular danger or risk provides protection from it. 防护物；保护人 ❑ *He used his left hand as a shield against the reflecting sunlight.* 他用左手遮挡反射过来的阳光。 2 V-T If something or someone **shields** you **from** a danger or risk, they protect you from it. 保护 ❑ *He shielded his head from the sun with an old sack.* 他用一个旧袋子遮住头来防晒。 3 V-T If you **shield** your eyes, you put your hand above your eyes to protect them from direct sunlight. 遮挡 ❑ *He squinted and shielded his eyes.* 他眯着眼并遮住眼睛。 4 N-COUNT A **shield** is a large piece of metal or leather which soldiers used to carry to protect their bodies while they were fighting. 盾 ❑ *He clanged his sword three times on his shield.* 他用他的剑当当当地敲了3下盾。 5 N-COUNT A **shield** is a sports prize or badge that is shaped like a shield. 盾形奖章；盾形徽章 → see **army**

shift ♦◇◇ /ʃɪft/ (**shifts, shifting, shifted**) 1 V-T/V-I If you **shift** something or if it **shifts**, it moves slightly. 稍微移动 ❑ *He stopped, shifting his cane to his left hand.* 他停下来，把手杖移到左手。 ❑ *He shifted from foot to foot.* 他从一只脚换到另一只脚。 2 V-T/V-I If someone's opinion, a situation, or a policy **shifts** or **is shifted**, it changes slightly. 稍微改变 ❑ *Attitudes to mental illness have shifted in recent years.* 对精神病的态度近年来已稍微有所改变。 ● N-COUNT **Shift** is also a noun. 稍微改变 [usu N prep] ❑ *...a shift in government policy.* …政府政策的些许改变。 3 V-T If someone **shifts** the responsibility or blame for something onto you, they unfairly make you responsible or make people blame you for it, instead of them. 推卸；转嫁 [DISAPPROVAL] ❑ *It was a vain attempt to shift the responsibility for the murder to somebody else.* 把这项谋杀的罪责转嫁于他人是徒劳之举。 4 V-T If you **shift** gears in a car, you put the car into a different gear. 换（挡）[AM]

in BRIT, use **change**

❑ *He shifts gears and pulls away slowly.* 他换了挡，慢慢把车开走了。 5 N-COUNT If a group of factory workers, nurses, or other people work **shifts**, they work for a set period before being replaced by another group, so that there is always a group working. Each of these set periods is called a **shift**. You can also use **shift** to refer to a group of workers who work together on a particular shift. 轮班 ❑ *His father worked shifts in a steel mill.* 他的父亲在一家钢铁厂轮班工作。

Word Partnership *shift* 的常用搭配：

N.	shift *your* **weight** 1
	shift *your* **position** 1 2
	shift *your* **attention**, shift **in focus**, **policy** shift, shift **in/of power**, shift **in priorities** 2
	shift **blame** 3
	shift **gears** 4
	shift **change**, **night** shift 5
ADJ.	**dramatic** shift, **major** shift, **significant** shift 2

shim·mer /ʃɪmər/ (**shimmers, shimmering, shimmered**) V-I If something **shimmers**, it shines with a faint, unsteady light or has an unclear, unsteady appearance. 发出微光 ❑ *The lights shimmered on the water.* 那些灯在水面上闪着微光。 ● N-SING **Shimmer** is also a noun. 微光 ❑ *...a shimmer of starlight.* …星光的闪烁。

shin /ʃɪn/ (**shins**) N-COUNT Your **shins** are the front parts of your legs between your knees and your ankles. 胫 ❑ *She punched him on the nose and kicked him in the shins.* 她猛击了他的鼻子又踢了他的胫部。

shine /ʃaɪn/ (**shines, shining, shined** or **shone**) 1 V-I When the sun or a light **shines**, it gives out bright light. 发光 ❑ *It is a mild morning and the sun is shining.* 这是一个和煦的早晨，太阳在照耀着。 2 V-T If you **shine** a flashlight or other light somewhere, you point it there, so that you can see something when it is dark. 用…照射 ❑ *One of the men shone a torch in his face.* 其中一个男子用火把照着他的脸。 ❑ *The man walked slowly toward her, shining the flashlight.* 那个男子照着手电筒慢慢地向她走去。 3 V-I Something that **shines** is very bright and clear because it is reflecting light. （因反光而）发亮 ❑ *Her blue eyes shone and caught the light.* 她的蓝眼睛在光照下闪闪发亮。 ❑ *...a pair of patent leather shoes that shone like mirrors.* …一双像镜子那样闪光的黑漆皮鞋。 4 N-SING Something that has a **shine** is bright and clear because it is reflecting light. 光泽 ❑ *This gel gives a beautiful shine to the hair.* 这种发胶带给头发一种美丽的光泽。 5 V-I

Someone who **shines** at a skill or activity does it extremely well. 干得出色 ❑ *Did you shine at school?* 你在学校出类拔萃吗？ 6 → see also **shining**
→ see **light**

Thesaurus *shine* 另参见：
V. glare, gleam, illuminate, shimmer 1 3
N. light, radiance, sheen 4

shin·gle /ʃɪŋᵍl/ (**shingles**) 1 N-UNCOUNT **Shingle** is a mass of small rough pieces of stone on the shore of a sea or a river. (海边或河边的) 碎石滩 ❑ *...a beach of sand and shingle.* ···一个有沙子和碎石的海滩。 2 N-UNCOUNT **Shingles** is a disease in which painful red spots spread in bands over a person's body, especially around their waist. 带状疱疹 3 N-COUNT **Shingles** are thin pieces of wood or another material which are fixed in rows to cover a roof or wall. 瓦板 [usu pl] ❑ *The roofs had shingles missing.* 屋顶的一些瓦板不见了。 4 N-COUNT A **shingle** is a small sign that is hung outside a building, such as the place where a doctor or lawyer works. (医生或律师等的) 小招牌 [AM] 5 PHRASE If you **hang out** your **shingle** or **hang out** a **shingle**, you start your own business. 开业 [v and n inflect] [AM] ❑ *She hung out her shingle under the name Designs by Pamela.* 她以"帕梅拉设计"的名字开业。 ❑ *The industry isn't regulated, so anybody can hang out a shingle.* 这个行业无制度规范，所以任何人都可以开业。

shin·ing /ʃaɪnɪŋ/ 1 ADJ A **shining** achievement or quality is a very good one which should be greatly admired. 杰出的 ❑ *She is a shining example to us all.* 她是我们所有人的光辉榜样。 2 → see also **shine**

★ **shiny** /ʃaɪni/ (**shinier, shiniest**) ADJ **Shiny** things are bright and reflect light. 闪亮的 ❑ *Her blonde hair was shiny and clean.* 她的金发闪亮而整齐。
→ see **metal**

ship ◆◆◇ /ʃɪp/ (**ships, shipping, shipped**) 1 N-COUNT A **ship** is a large boat which carries passengers or cargo. 轮船 [also "by" N] ❑ *Within ninety minutes the ship was ready for departure.* 90分钟内轮船就准备好了出发。 ❑ *We went by ship over to America.* 我们乘轮船去美国。 2 V-T If people, supplies, or goods **are shipped** somewhere, they are sent there on a ship or by some other means of transportation. 运送 [usu passive] ❑ *We'll ship your order to the address we print on your checks.* 我们将把你预订的货物送到我们印在你单据上的地址。 ❑ *Food is being shipped to drought-stricken Southern Africa.* 食物正被运送到遭受旱灾的南非。 3 → see also **shipping**
→ see Word Web: **ship**

Word Partnership *ship* 的常用搭配：
V. **board** a ship, **build** a ship, ship **docks**, **jump** ship, **sink** a ship 1
N. **bow of** a ship, **captain of** a ship, **cargo** ship, ship's **crew** 1

★ **ship·ment** /ʃɪpmənt/ (**shipments**) 1 N-COUNT A **shipment** is an amount of a particular kind of cargo that is sent to another country on a ship, train, airplane, or other vehicle. 运送的货物 (量) ❑ *After that, food shipments to the port could begin in a matter of weeks.* 之后，到该港口的食物运送可能在几周之内开始。 2 N-UNCOUNT The **shipment** of a cargo or goods somewhere is the sending of it there by ship, train, airplane, or some other vehicle. 运送 ❑ *Bananas are packed before being transported to the docks for shipment overseas.* 香蕉先要装箱，然后送到码头运往海外。

ship·ping /ʃɪpɪŋ/ 1 N-UNCOUNT **Shipping** is the transportation of cargo or goods as a business, especially on ships. 航运业 [usu with supp] ❑ *...the international shipping industry.* ···国际航运业。 ❑ *...a coupon for free shipping of your catalog order.* ···一张可免费运送你在目录中定购的商品的优待券。 2 N-UNCOUNT You can refer to the amount of money that you pay to a company to transport cargo or goods as **shipping**. 运费 ❑ *It is $39.95 plus $3 shipping.* 总共是$39.95加$3的运费。

ship·wreck /ʃɪprɛk/ (**shipwrecks, shipwrecked**) 1 N-VAR If there is a **shipwreck**, a ship is destroyed in an accident at sea. 船只失事 ❑ *He was drowned in a shipwreck off the coast of Spain.* 他在西班牙海岸的一次船只失事中淹死。 2 N-COUNT A **shipwreck** is a ship which has been destroyed in an accident at sea. 遇难船只 ❑ *More than 1,000 shipwrecks litter the coral reef ringing the islands.* 一千多艘遇难船只散布在环绕岛屿的珊瑚礁之中。 3 V-T PASSIVE If someone **is shipwrecked**, their ship is destroyed in an accident at sea but they survive and manage to reach land. 使遭遇海难后幸存 ❑ *He was shipwrecked after visiting the island.* 他参观那座岛屿后遭遇海难并幸存下来。

▲ **ship·yard** /ʃɪpyɑrd/ (**shipyards**) N-COUNT A **shipyard** is a place where ships are built and repaired. 造船厂；修船厂 ❑ *The Queen Mary 2 is currently docked at the shipyard.* "玛丽女王 2 号"现在停泊在修船厂。

shirt ◆◇◇ /ʃɜrt/ (**shirts**) 1 N-COUNT A **shirt** is a piece of clothing that you wear on the upper part of your body. Shirts have a collar, sleeves, and buttons down the front. 衬衫 2 → see also **sweatshirt, T-shirt**
→ see **clothing**

▲ **shit** /ʃɪt/ (**shits, shitting, shat**) 1 N-UNCOUNT Some people use **shit** to refer to solid waste matter from the body of a human being or animal. 粪便 [INFORMAL, VULGAR] ❑ *...a pile of dog shit.* ···一堆狗屎。 2 V-I To **shit** means to get rid of solid waste matter from the body. 拉屎 [INFORMAL, VULGAR] ❑ *...his memories of the yellow dog shitting on the stairs.* ···他的那些关于那只黄狗在楼梯上拉屎的记忆。 3 N-SING To have **a shit** means to get rid of solid waste matter from the body. 拉屎 [INFORMAL, VULGAR] ❑ *Before dying he confesses that he hasn't taken a shit in weeks.* 临终前，他承认自己已经好几周没大便了。 4 N-UNCOUNT People sometimes refer to things that they do not like as **shit**. 令人讨厌的东西 [INFORMAL, VULGAR, DISAPPROVAL] ❑ *This is a load of shit.* 这是一堆废物。

shiv·er /ʃɪvər/ (**shivers, shivering, shivered**) V-I When you **shiver**, your body shakes slightly because you are cold or frightened. (因寒冷或害怕而) 颤抖 ❑ *He shivered in the cold.* 他在寒冷中发抖。 ● N-COUNT **Shiver** is also a noun. 颤抖 ❑ *The emptiness here sent shivers down my spine.* 这里的空寂让我感到脊背一阵颤栗。

Word Partnership *shiver* 的常用搭配：
V. **feel a** shiver, shiver **goes/runs down** ***your*** spine, ***something*** **makes** ***you*** shiver, ***something*** **sends a** shiver **down** ***your*** **spine**

shoal /ʃoʊl/ (**shoals**) N-COUNT A **shoal of** fish is a large group of them swimming together. 鱼群 ❑ *Among them swam shoals of fish.* 在他们之中游动着一群群鱼儿。

shock ◆◆◇ /ʃɒk/ (**shocks, shocking, shocked**) 1 N-COUNT If you have a **shock**, something suddenly happens which is unpleasant, upsetting, or very surprising. 震惊 ❑ *The extent of the violence came as a shock.* 暴力的程度令人震惊。 ❑ *He has never recovered from the shock of your brother's death.* 他从来没有从你兄弟的死所带来的震惊中恢复过来。 2 N-UNCOUNT **Shock** is a person's emotional and physical condition when something very frightening or upsetting has happened to them. (身心受到的) 惊吓 ❑ *The little boy was speechless with shock.* 这个小男孩被吓得说不出话来。 3 N-UNCOUNT If someone is **in shock**, they are suffering from a serious physical

Word Web ship

Large **ocean-going vessels** remain an important way of transporting people and **cargo**. **Oil tankers** and **container ships** are a common sight in many **ports**. **Ocean liners** serve as both transportation and hotel for tourists. Some of these **ships** are several stories tall. The **captain** steers a **cruise ship** from the **bridge**, while passengers enjoy themselves on the promenade deck. Huge **warships** carry thousands of soldiers to battlefields around the world. **Aircraft carriers** include a flight deck where planes can take off and land. **Ferries**, **barges**, fishing **craft**, and research **boats** are also an important part of the **marine** industry.

condition in which their blood is not flowing around their body properly, for example, because they have had a bad injury. 休克 ❑ *He was found beaten and in shock.* 他被发现遭到殴打，处于休克中。
4 V-T If something **shocks** you, it makes you feel very upset, because it involves death or suffering and because you had not expected it. 使震惊 ❑ *After forty years in the police force nothing much shocks me.* 在警察部门干了40年后，没有什么能令我非常震惊了。
● **shocked** ADJ 震惊的 ❑ *This was a nasty attack and the woman is still very shocked.* 这是一次严重的袭击，这个女人仍然感到非常震惊。
5 V-T/V-I If someone or something **shocks** you, it upsets or offends you because you think it is vulgar or morally wrong. 使不快；不快 ❑ *You can't shock me.* 你不会让我生气。 ❑ *They were easily shocked in those days.* 他们那时候容易被激怒。 ❑ *...the desire to shock* …发怒的欲望。 ● **shocked** ADJ 生气的 ❑ *Don't look so shocked.* 别这么生气。 **6** N-VAR A **shock** is the force of something suddenly hitting or pulling something else. 冲击力 ❑ *Steel barriers can bend and absorb the shock.* 铁栅栏会弯曲并吸收冲击力。 **7** N-COUNT A **shock** is the same as an **electric shock**. 电击 **8** → see also **electric shock**

Word Partnership	*shock* 的常用搭配:
V.	**come as a** shock **1** **send a** shock **1** **7** **express** shock, **feel** shock **2**
N.	**in a state of** shock, shock **value** **2**

shock·ing /ʃɒkɪŋ/ **1** ADJ You can say that something is **shocking** if you think that it is very bad. 极坏的 [INFORMAL] ❑ *The media coverage was shocking.* 媒体的报道糟透了。 ● **shock·ing·ly** ADV 极坏地 [ADV adj/adv] ❑ *His memory was becoming shockingly bad.* 他的记忆力正变得很糟。 **2** ADJ You can say that something is **shocking** if you think that it is morally wrong. 令人震惊的；令人愤慨的 ❑ *It is shocking that nothing was said.* 令人震惊的是，什么都没说。 ● **shock·ing·ly** ADV 令人震惊地；令人愤慨地 ❑ *Shockingly, this useless and dangerous surgery did not end until the 1930s.* 令人震惊地，这种毫无作用又危险的外科手术直到20世纪30年代才结束。 **3** → see also **shock**

shock wave (**shock waves**) also **shockwave** **1** N-COUNT A **shock wave** is an area of very high pressure moving through the air, earth, or water. It is caused by an explosion or an earthquake, or by an object traveling faster than sound. 冲击波 ❑ *The shock waves yesterday were felt from Las Vegas to San Diego.* 昨天从拉斯韦加斯到圣地亚哥都能感觉到冲击波。 **2** N-COUNT A **shock wave** is the effect of something surprising, such as a piece of unpleasant news, that causes strong reactions when it spreads through a place. 强烈反应 ❑ *The crime sent shock waves throughout the country.* 这起犯罪在全国引起强烈反应。
→ see **sound**

▲ **shod·dy** /ʃɒdi/ (**shoddier, shoddiest**) ADJ **Shoddy** work or a **shoddy** product has been done or made carelessly or badly. 粗制滥造的 ❑ *I'm normally quick to complain about shoddy service.* 我通常会迅速地投诉劣质的服务。 ● **shod·di·ly** ADV 粗制滥造地 ❑ *These products are shoddily produced.* 这些产品是粗制滥造地生产的。

shoe ♦◇◇ /ʃuː/ (**shoes, shoeing, shoed** or **shod**) **1** N-COUNT **Shoes** are objects which you wear on your feet. They cover most of your foot and you wear them over socks or stockings. 鞋 ❑ *...a pair of shoes.* …一双鞋。 ❑ *Low-heeled comfortable shoes are best.* 舒适的低跟鞋是最好的。 **2** N-COUNT A **shoe** is the same as a **horseshoe**. 马蹄铁 **3** V-T When a blacksmith **shoes** a horse, they attach horseshoes onto their feet. 给…钉蹄铁 ❑ *Blacksmiths spent most of their time repairing tools and shoeing horses.* 铁匠们把他们大部分时间用来修理工具和给马钉蹄铁。 **4** PHRASE If you **fill** someone's **shoes** or **step into** their **shoes**, you take their place by doing the job they were doing. 接替某人的位置 ❑ *No one has been able to fill his shoes.* 没有人能接替他的工作。 **5** PHRASE If you talk about being **in** someone's **shoes**, you talk about what you would do or how you would feel if you were in their situation. 处在某人的境地 ❑ *I wouldn't want to be in his shoes.* 我不愿意处于他的境地。
→ see **clothing**

shoe·string /ʃuːstrɪŋ/ **1** ADJ A **shoestring** budget is one where you have very little money to spend. (预算) 小额的 [ADJ n] ❑ *The movie was made on a shoestring budget.* 这部电影是靠小额预算拍出来的。 **2** PHRASE If you do something or make something **on a shoestring**, you do it using very little money. 用很少的钱 ❑ *The theater will be run on a shoestring.* 这个戏院将小本经营。

shone /ʃoʊn/ **Shone** is the past tense and past participle of **shine**. **shine**的过去式和过去分词

shook /ʃʊk/ **Shook** is the past tense of **shake**. **shake**的过去式

shoot ♦♦◇ /ʃuːt/ (**shoots, shooting, shot**) **1** V-T If someone **shoots** a person or an animal, they kill them or injure them by firing a bullet or arrow at them. 射死；射伤 ❑ *The police had orders to shoot anyone who attacked them.* 警察得到命令可以向任何袭击他们的人开枪。 ❑ *The man was shot dead by the police during a raid on his house.* 这个人在一次对他家的突击搜查时被警察击毙了。 **2** V-I To **shoot** means to fire a bullet from a weapon such as a gun. 射击 ❑ *He taunted armed officers by pointing to his head, as if inviting them to shoot.* 他指着自己的头来奚落武装警察，仿佛是在招惹他们开枪一样。 ❑ *The police came around the corner and they started shooting at us.* 警察来到拐角，他们开始朝我们开枪。 **3** V-I If someone or something **shoots** in a particular direction, they move in that direction quickly and suddenly. 猛冲 ❑ *They had almost reached the boat when a figure shot past them.* 他们几乎快要到达船上时，一个人影冲过他们身旁。 **4** V-T/V-I If you **shoot** something somewhere or if it **shoots** somewhere, it moves there quickly and suddenly. 猛然移动 ❑ *Masters shot a hand across the table and gripped his wrist.* 师傅突然把一只手伸过桌子，抓住他的手腕。 ❑ *As soon as she got close, the old woman's hand shot out.* 她一靠近，那个老妇人的手就猛地伸了出来。 **5** V-T If you **shoot** a look at someone, you look at them quickly and briefly, often in a way that expresses your feelings. 瞥 ❑ *Mary Ann shot him a rueful look.* 玛丽・安悔恨地瞥了他一眼。 **6** V-I If someone **shoots to** fame, they become famous or successful very quickly. 迅速(成名) ❑ *Alina Reyes shot to fame a few years ago with her extraordinary first novel.* 阿丽娜・雷耶斯几年前凭借她那非凡的小说处女作迅速成名。 **7** V-T When people **shoot** a movie or **shoot** photographs, they make a movie or take photographs using a camera. 拍摄 ❑ *He'd love to shoot his film in Cuba.* 他很乐意在古巴拍摄他的电影。 ● N-COUNT **Shoot** is also a noun. 拍摄 ❑ *...a barn presently being used for a video shoot.* …一个目前被用于电视拍摄的谷仓。 **8** N-COUNT **Shoots** are plants that are beginning to grow, or new parts growing from a plant or tree. 新芽 ❑ *Prune established plants annually as new shoots appear.* 每年嫩芽长出来时，要给长成的植物剪枝。 **9** V-I In sports such as soccer or basketball, when someone **shoots**, they try to score by kicking or throwing the ball toward the goal or hoop. 射门；投篮 ❑ *Spencer scuttled away from Singh to shoot wide when he should have scored.* 斯宾塞快速晃开辛格却射门偏出，而他本应该得分的。 **10** → see also **shooting, shot** **11** to **shoot from the hip** → see **hip**

▸ **shoot down** **1** PHRASAL VERB If someone **shoots down** an airplane, a helicopter, or a missile, they make it fall to the ground by hitting it with a bullet or missile. 击落 ❑ *They claimed to have shot down one incoming missile.* 他们声称已经击落了一枚来袭的导弹。 **2** PHRASAL VERB If one person **shoots down** another, they shoot them with a gun. 枪杀 ❑ *He was prepared to suppress rebellion by shooting down protesters.* 他准备枪杀抗议者来镇压叛乱。

▸ **shoot up** PHRASAL VERB If something **shoots up**, it grows or increases very quickly. 快速成长；激增 ❑ *Sales shot up by 9% last month.* 上个月的销售猛增了9%。

Word Partnership	*shoot* 的常用搭配:
V.	**going to** shoot **1** **2** **try to** shoot **1** **2** **7** shoot **to kill** **2**
N.	**orders to** shoot, **soldiers** shoot **1** **2** shoot **a gun**, shoot **missiles** **2** shoot **a film**, **photo** shoot **7**

shoot·ing /ʃuːtɪŋ/ (**shootings**) **1** N-COUNT A **shooting** is an occasion when someone is killed or injured by being shot with a gun. 枪击 ❑ *Two more bodies were found nearby after the shooting.* 附近又有两具尸体在枪击后被找到。 **2** N-UNCOUNT **Shooting** is hunting animals with a gun as a leisure activity. 狩猎 ❑ *Grouse shooting begins in August.* 松鸡狩猎8月份开始。 **3** N-UNCOUNT The **shooting** of a movie is the act of filming it. 拍摄 ❑ *Ingrid was busy learning her lines for the next day's shooting.* 英格里德正忙着背第二天拍摄的台词。 **4** N-UNCOUNT In sports such as basketball and soccer, a player's **shooting** is their ability to score points or goals. 得分 ❑ *When asked whether the injury affected his shooting, Iverson said: "Not at all."* 当被问及受伤是否会影响到他得分时，艾弗森说："根本不会。"

S

shop ♦♦◇ /ʃɒp/ (**shops, shopping, shopped**) **1** N-COUNT A **shop** is a small store that sells one type of merchandise. (卖一种商品的)店 ❑ *...a gift shop.* …一个礼品店。 ❑ *He and his wife run their own antiques shop.* 他和他的妻子经营他们自己的古董店。 **2** N-COUNT A **shop** is a building or part of a building where things are sold. 商店 [mainly BRIT]

in AM, usually use **store**

Americans use **shop** to mean a small business that sells only one product or service, like a record shop or a shoe repair shop. **Store** is used when the business sells a variety of products. A **shopping center** or **mall** will have a department store or two, as well as several kinds of shops and stores at one location.

3 V-I When you **shop**, you go to stores or shops and buy things. 购物 ❑ *He always shopped at the co-op.* 他总在合作社购物。 ❑ *...some advice that's worth bearing in mind when shopping for a new carpet.* …一些在买新地毯时值得记住的建议。 ● **shop·per** N-COUNT (**shoppers**) 购物者 ❑ *...crowds of Christmas shoppers.* …圣诞节的购物人潮。 **4** N-COUNT You can refer to a place where a particular service is offered as a particular type of **shop**. (提供某种服务的)店 ❑ *...the barber shop where Rodney sometimes had his hair cut.* …罗德尼有时去理发的那间理发店。 ❑ *...betting shops.* …彩票销售店。 **5** → see also **shopping, coffee shop** **6** PHRASE If you say that people **are talking shop**, you mean that they are talking about their work, and this is boring for other people who do not do the same work. 谈论本行工作 ❑ *Although I get on well with my colleagues, if you hang around together all the time you just end up talking shop.* 尽管我和同事们相处得很融洽，但如果老呆在一起最后往往就谈论工作了。

▸ **shop around** PHRASAL VERB If you **shop around**, you go to different stores or companies in order to compare the prices and quality of goods or services before you decide to buy them. 货比三家 ❑ *Prices may vary so it's well worth shopping around before you buy.* 价格可能会不一样，所以在购买之前多跑几家商店是很值得的。

Word Partnership *shop* 的常用搭配：

N. **antique** shop, **pet** shop, **souvenir** shop **1**
shop **owner** **1** **2**
auto shop, **barber** shop, **beauty** shop, **repair** shop **4**

shop as·sis·tant (**shop assistants**) N-COUNT A **shop assistant** is a person who works in a store selling things to customers. 售货员 [mainly BRIT]

in AM, usually use **sales clerk**

shop floor also **shop-floor, shopfloor** N-SING The **shop floor** is used to refer to all the ordinary workers in a factory or the area where they work, especially in contrast to the people who are in charge. 全体工人；工作场所 ❑ *Cost must be controlled, not just on the shop floor but in the boardroom too.* 成本必须得到控制，不仅仅是全体工人，还有董事会。

shop·keeper /ʃɒpkipər/ (**shopkeepers**) N-COUNT A **shopkeeper** is a person who owns or manages a shop. 店主；商店经理

shop·lift /ʃɒplɪft/ (**shoplifts, shoplifting, shoplifted**) V-T/V-I If someone **shoplifts**, they steal goods from a store by hiding them in a bag or in their clothes. 在商店偷窃 ❑ *He openly shoplifted from a supermarket.* 他在一家超市公然行窃。 ● **shop·lifter** N-COUNT (**shoplifters**) 在商店行窃的人 ❑ *A persistent shoplifter has been banned from every store in town.* 一个商店行窃惯犯已被禁止进入镇上任何一家商店。

shop·lifting /ʃɒplɪftɪŋ/ N-UNCOUNT **Shoplifting** is stealing from a store by hiding things in a bag or in your clothes. 商店行窃 ❑ *The grocer accused her of shoplifting and demanded to look in her bag.* 这家食品杂货店指控她行窃并要求搜查她的包。

shop·ping ♦◇◇ /ʃɒpɪŋ/ **1** N-UNCOUNT When you do **the shopping**, you go to the stores or shops and buy things. 购物 ❑ *I'll do the shopping this afternoon.* 我今天下午要去购物。 **2** N-UNCOUNT Your **shopping** is the things that you have bought from stores, especially food. 从商店买回来的东西(尤指食品) [mainly BRIT]

in AM, usually use **groceries**

Word Partnership *shopping* 的常用搭配：

N. shopping **bag**, **Christmas** shopping, shopping **district**, **food** shopping, **grocery** shopping, **holiday** shopping, **online** shopping, shopping **spree** **1**

shop·ping cen·ter (**shopping centers**) N-COUNT A **shopping center** is a specially built area containing a lot of different stores. 购物中心 ❑ *They met in the parking lot at the new shopping center.* 他们在新购物中心的停车场见面。

shop·ping chan·nel (**shopping channels**) N-COUNT A **shopping channel** is a television channel that broadcasts programs showing products that you can buy over the phone or online. 电视购物频道

shop·ping mall (**shopping malls**) N-COUNT A **shopping mall** is a specially built covered area containing stores and restaurants which people can walk between, and where cars are not allowed. 大型购物中心

shore ♦◇◇ /ʃɔr/ (**shores, shoring, shored**) N-COUNT The **shores** or the **shore** of a sea, lake, or wide river is the land along the edge of it. Someone who is **on shore** is on the land rather than on a ship. 岸 [also prep N] ❑ *They walked down to the shore.* 他们往下走到了岸边。 ❑ *...elephants living on the shores of Lake Kariba.* …生活在卡里巴湖滨的大象。

You can use **beach, coast**, and **shore** to talk about the piece of land beside a stretch of water. The **shore** is the area of land along the edge of the ocean, a lake, or a wide river. The **coast** is the area of land that lies alongside the ocean. You may be referring just to the land close to the ocean, or to a wider area that extends further inland. A **beach** is a flat area of sand or pebbles next to the ocean.

▸ **shore up** PHRASAL VERB If you **shore up** something that is weak or about to fail, you do something in order to strengthen it or support it. 支持 ❑ *The democracies of the West may find it hard to shore up their defenses.* 西方的民主国家可能发现很难加固自己的防御。

shore·line /ʃɔrlaɪn/ (**shorelines**) N-COUNT A **shoreline** is the edge of a sea, lake, or wide river. 岸线 ❑ *...the rocks along the shoreline.* …海岸线沿线的岩石。

shorn /ʃɔrn/ **Shorn** is the past participle of **shear**. **shear**的过去分词

short

❶ ADJECTIVE AND ADVERB USES
❷ NOUN USES

❶ **short** ♦♦♦ /ʃɔrt/ (**shorter, shortest**)
➪ **Please look at meanings 16 – 20 to see if the expression you are looking for is shown under another headword.** **1** ADJ If something is **short** or lasts for a **short** time, it does not last very long. 短暂的 ❑ *The announcement was made a short time ago.* 这个通告是在不久前刚发布的。 ❑ *Kemp gave a short laugh.* 肯普笑了一下。 **2** ADJ A **short** speech, letter, or book does not have many words or pages in it. 简短的 ❑ *They were performing a short extract from Shakespeare's Two Gentlemen of Verona.* 他们正在表演莎士比亚戏剧《两位维罗纳绅士》中一个简短的片段。 **3** ADJ Someone who is **short** is not as tall as most people are. 矮的 ❑ *I'm tall and thin and he's short and fat.* 我又高又瘦，他又矮又胖。 ❑ *...a short, elderly woman with gray hair.* …一个头发灰白的矮小老妇人。 **4** ADJ Something that is **short** measures only a small amount from one end to the other. 短的 ❑ *The restaurant is only a short distance away.* 那个饭店就在不远处。 ❑ *A short flight of steps led to a grand doorway.* 一段短短的楼梯通向一个宽敞的门道。 **5** ADJ If you are **short of** something or if it is **short**, you do not have enough of it. If you are running **short of** something or if it is running **short**, you do not have much of it left. 短缺的 [v-link ADJ] ❑ *Her father's illness left the family short of money.* 他父亲的病使得全家缺钱。 ❑ *Government forces are running short of ammunition and fuel.* 政府军正缺少弹药和燃料。 **6** ADJ If someone or something is or stops **short of** a place, they have not quite reached it. If they are or fall **short of** an amount, they have not quite achieved it. 未达到的 [v-link ADJ "of" n] ❑ *He stopped a hundred yards short of the building.* 他停在离那座建筑还有100码远的地方。 **7** PHRASE **Short of** a particular thing means except for that thing or without actually doing that thing. 除…外 ❑ *Short of gagging the children, there was not much she could do about the noise.* 除了不让孩子们说话之外，她对那噪音无能为力。 **8** ADV If something is **cut short** or **stops short**, it is stopped before people expect it to or before it has finished. 提早结束地 [ADV after v] ❑ *His glittering career was cut short by a heart attack.* 他辉煌的事业被一次心脏病发作给提早完结了。 **9** ADJ If a name or abbreviation is **short for** another name, it is the short version of that name. 简称的 [v-link ADJ "for" n] ❑ *Her friend Kes (short for Kesewa) was in*

S

tears. 她的朋友凯斯（凯斯瓦的简称）在流泪。 11 ADJ If you have a **short** temper, you get angry very easily. 易怒的 ❑ *...an awkward, self-conscious woman with a short temper.* ⋯一个笨拙忸怩而且脾气暴躁的女人，。 12 ADJ If you are **short with** someone, you speak briefly and rather rudely to them, because you are impatient or angry. 简慢无礼的 [v-link ADJ] ❑ *She seemed nervous or tense, and she was definitely short with me.* 她似乎是紧张或焦急，显然对我简慢无礼。 12 PHRASE If a person or thing is called something **for short**, that is the short version of their name. 作为简称 ❑ *Opposite me was a woman called Jasminder (Jazzy for short).* 我对面是个叫杰丝明德（简称杰丝）的女人。 13 PHRASE You use **in short** when you have been giving a lot of details and you want to give a conclusion or summary. 简而言之 ❑ *Try tennis, badminton or windsurfing. In short, anything challenging.* 试试网球、羽毛球或帆板运动。简而言之，任何有挑战性的东西。 14 PHRASE If someone or something **is short on** a particular good quality, they do not have as much of it as you think they should have. 缺少某物 [DISAPPROVAL] ❑ *The proposals were short on detail.* 这些提议缺少细节。 15 PHRASE If someone **stops short of** doing something, they come close to doing it but do not actually do it. 险些 ❑ *He stopped short of explicitly criticizing the government.* 他险些就直言不讳地批评政府了。 16 **short of breath** → see **breath** 17 **on short notice** → see **notice** 18 **to draw the short straw** → see **straw** 19 **in short supply** → see **supply** 20 **in the short term** → see **term**

Thesaurus *short* 另参见：
ADJ. brief, quick; (*ant.*) long ❶ 1 2
petite, slight, small; (*ant.*) tall ❶ 3

❷ **short** /ʃɔrt/ (**shorts**) 1 N-PLURAL **Shorts** are pants with very short legs that people wear in hot weather or for taking part in sports. 短裤 [also "a pair of" N] ❑ *...two women in bright cotton shorts and tee shirts.* ⋯两个穿着鲜丽棉短裤和T恤的女人。 2 N-PLURAL **Shorts** are men's underpants with short legs. (男子的) 内裤 [also "a pair of" N] [mainly AM] 3 N-COUNT A **short** is a short film, especially one that is shown before the main film at the cinema. (电影院正片前放映的) 短片

short·age ♦◇◇ /ʃɔrtɪdʒ/ (**shortages**) N-VAR If there is a **shortage of** something, there is not enough of it. 短缺 ❑ *A shortage of funds is preventing the UN from monitoring relief.* 资金短缺使得联合国无法监督救济工作。 ❑ *Vietnam is suffering from food shortage.* 越南正遭受食品短缺之苦。

short-change (**short-changes, short-changing, short-changed**) 1 V-T If someone **short-changes** you, they do not give you enough change after you have bought something from them. 少找零钱给⋯ ❑ *The cashier made a mistake and short-changed him.* 那位收银员搞错了，少找给了他钱。 2 V-T If you **are short-changed**, you are treated unfairly or dishonestly, often because you are given less of something than you deserve. 亏待 [usu passive] ❑ *Women are in fact still being short-changed in the press.* 事实上妇女在新闻界仍然受到不公平地对待。

short·coming /ʃɔrtkʌmɪŋ/ (**shortcomings**) N-COUNT Someone's or something's **shortcomings** are the faults or weaknesses which they have. 缺点 ❑ *Marriages usually break down as a result of the shortcomings of both partners.* 婚姻常常因双方的缺点而破裂。

short·cut /ʃɔrtkʌt/ (**shortcuts**) 1 N-COUNT A **shortcut** is a quicker way of getting somewhere than the usual route. 近路 ❑ *I tried to take a shortcut and got lost.* 我试着走近路，结果迷路了。 2 N-COUNT A **shortcut** is a method of achieving something more quickly or more easily than if you use the usual methods. 捷径 ❑ *Fame can be a shortcut to love and money.* 名望可以是得到爱情和金钱的捷径。 3 N-COUNT On a computer, a **shortcut** is an icon on the desktop that allows you to go immediately to a program or document. 快捷方式 [COMPUTING] ❑ *There are any number of ways to move or copy icons or create shortcuts in Windows.* 视窗操作系统中有很多方法来移动或复制图标或创建快捷方式。 4 N-COUNT On a computer, a **shortcut** is a keystroke or a combination of keystrokes that allows you to give commands without using the mouse. 快捷键 [COMPUTING] ❑ *There is a handy keyboard shortcut to save you having to scroll up to the top of the screen.* 有一个方便的键盘快捷键可用，不必滚动到屏幕的顶端。

short·en /ʃɔrtᵊn/ (**shortens, shortening, shortened**) 1 V-T/V-I If you **shorten** an event or the length of time that something lasts, or if it **shortens**, it does not last as long as it would otherwise do or as it used to do. 缩短 ❑ *Smoking can shorten your life.* 吸烟会缩短你的寿命。 ❑ *The trading day is shortened in observance of the Labor Day holiday.* 交易日为了庆祝劳动节而缩短。 2 V-T/V-I If you **shorten** an object or if it **shortens**, it becomes smaller in length. 使变短；变短 ❑ *Her father paid $5,000 for an operation to shorten her nose.* 她父亲为一个缩短她的鼻子的手术花了$5000。 3 V-T If you **shorten** a name or other word, you change it by removing some of the letters. 缩写 ❑ *Originally called Lili, she eventually shortened her name to Lee.* 她原本叫莉莉，最后她把名字缩写成了莉。

short·fall /ʃɔrtfɔl/ (**shortfalls**) N-COUNT If there is a **shortfall in** something, there is less of it than you need. 不足 ❑ *The government has refused to make up a $30,000 shortfall in funding.* 政府已经拒绝补足3万美元的资金短缺。

▲ **short·hand** /ʃɔrthænd/ 1 N-UNCOUNT **Shorthand** is a quick way of writing and uses signs to represent words or syllables. Shorthand is sometimes used by secretaries and journalists to write down what someone is saying. 速记法 ❑ *Ben took notes in shorthand.* 本用速记法记笔记。 2 N-UNCOUNT You can use **shorthand** to mean a quick or simple way of referring to something. 简约表达法 [also "a" N] ❑ *Laslett uses the shorthand of "second age" for the group of younger people who are creating families.* 拉斯莱特用"第二代"来简单指称那些更年轻、正在组建家庭的人。

short-haul ADJ **Short-haul** is used to describe things that involve transporting passengers or goods over short distances. Compare **long-haul**. 短途运输的 [ADJ n] ❑ *...short-haul flights, for example Chicago to Philadelphia.* ⋯短途航班，例如从芝加哥到费城。

short·list /ʃɔrtlɪst/ (**shortlists, shortlisting, shortlisted**) also **short list** 1 N-COUNT If someone is on a **shortlist**, for example, for a job or a prize, they are one of a small group of people who have been chosen from a larger group. The successful person is then chosen from the small group. (工作或获奖的) 候选人名单 ❑ *If you've been asked for an interview you are probably on a shortlist of no more than six.* 如果你已经被要求参加面试，你很可能在不超过6人的候选名单上。 2 V-T If someone or something **is shortlisted for** a job or a prize, they are put on a shortlist. 将⋯列入候选名单 [usu passive] ❑ *He was shortlisted for the Nobel Prize for literature several times.* 他曾数次获得诺贝尔文学奖提名。

short-lived ADJ Something that is **short-lived** does not last very long. 短暂的 ❑ *Any hope that the speech would end the war was short-lived.* 任何关于这次演讲将结束这次战争的希望很快就破灭了。

short·ly ♦◇◇ /ʃɔrtli/ ADV If something happens **shortly** after or before something else, it happens not long after or before it. If something is going to happen **shortly**, it is going to happen soon. 不久 ❑ *Their trial will shortly begin.* 他们的审讯很快就要开始。 ❑ *Shortly after moving into her apartment, she found a job.* 搬进公寓后不久她就找到了一份工作。

short·sighted /ʃɔrtsaɪtɪd/ also **short-sighted** 1 ADJ If someone is **shortsighted** about something, or if their ideas are **shortsighted**, they do not make proper or careful judgments about the future. 目光短浅的 ❑ *Environmentalists fear that this is a shortsighted approach to the problem of global warming.* 环境保护主义者们担心这会是解决全球变暖问题的一个目光短浅的方法。 2 ADJ If you are **short-sighted**, you cannot see things properly when they are far away, because there is something wrong with your eyes. 近视的 [mainly BRIT]

in AM, usually use **nearsighted**

short-term ♦◇◇ ADJ **Short-term** is used to describe things that will last for a short time, or things that will have an effect soon rather than in the distant future. 短期的 ❑ *Investors weren't concerned about short-term profits over the next few years.* 投资者不关心今后几年里的短期收益。 ❑ *The company has 90 staff, almost all on short-term contracts.* 这家公司有90名员工，几乎全部签的是短期合同。
→ see **memory**

short·wave /ʃɔrtweɪv/ also **short-wave** N-UNCOUNT **Shortwave** is a range of short radio wavelengths used for broadcasting. 短波 [oft N n] ❑ *I use the shortwave radio to get the latest war news.* 我用短波收音机收听最新战事新闻。

shot ♦♦◇ /ʃɒt/ (**shots**) 1 **Shot** is the past tense and past participle of **shoot**. **shoot**的过去式和过去分词 2 N-COUNT A **shot** is an act of firing a gun. 开枪 ❑ *He had murdered Perceval at point blank range with a single shot.* 他在近距离只用一枪就射杀了珀西瓦尔。 3 N-COUNT Someone who is a good **shot** can shoot well. Someone

S

who is a bad **shot** cannot shoot well. 射击手 ❏ *He was not a particularly good shot because of his eyesight.* 他由于视力缘故并不是一个特别好的射手。 4 N-COUNT In sports such as soccer, golf, or tennis, a **shot** is an act of kicking, hitting, or throwing the ball, especially in an attempt to score a point. 射门; 击球; 投篮 ❏ *He had only one shot at goal.* 他只有一次射门在门框内。 5 N-COUNT A **shot** is a photograph or a particular sequence of pictures in a movie. 照片; (电影的) 连续镜头 ❏ *I decided to try for a more natural shot of a fox peering from the bushes.* 我决定尝试拍摄一只狐狸从灌木丛中偷窥的一个更自然的镜头。 6 N-COUNT If you have a **shot at** something, you attempt to do it. 尝试 [INFORMAL] ❏ *The heavyweight champion will be given a shot at Holyfield's world title.* 这个重量级拳击冠军将要挑战霍利菲尔德的世界冠军头衔。 7 N-COUNT A **shot of** a drug is an injection of it. 注射 ❏ *He administered a shot of Nembutal.* 他进行了一针"宁必妥"的注射。 8 N-COUNT A **shot of** a strong alcoholic drink is a small glass of it. 一小杯 ❏ *...a shot of vodka.* …一小杯伏特加酒。 9 PHRASE If you **give** something your **best shot**, you do it as well as you possibly can. 尽力做某事 [INFORMAL] ❏ *I don't expect to win. But I am going to give it my best shot.* 我并不期望能赢。但是我要尽力而为。 10 PHRASE The person who **calls the shots** is in a position to tell others what to do. 发号施令 ❏ *The directors call the shots and nothing happens without their say-so.* 董事们发号施令，没有他们的指示什么都不能做。 11 PHRASE If you do something **like a shot**, you do it without any delay or hesitation. 立刻; 毫不迟疑地 [INFORMAL] ❏ *I heard the key turn in the front door and I was out of bed like a shot.* 我听见钥匙开前门的声音，立刻从床上起来了。 12 PHRASE If you describe something as **a long shot**, you mean that it is unlikely to succeed, but is worth trying. 胜算不大的尝试 ❏ *The deal was a long shot, but Bagley had little to lose.* 这宗交易不太可能成功，但巴格莱没什么可损失的。 13 PHRASE People sometimes use the expression **by a long shot** to emphasize the opinion they are giving. 根本 (表示强调) [EMPHASIS] ❏ *The missile-reduction treaty makes sweeping cuts, but the arms race isn't over by a long shot.* 削减导弹条约引起大范围的裁减，但是军备竞赛根本没有结束。
→ see **photography**

Word Partnership *shot* 的常用搭配:

ADJ.	**single** shot, **warning** shot 2 **good** shot 2 3 **winning** shot 4
V.	**fire** a shot, **hear** a shot 2 **miss** a shot 2 4 **take** a shot 2 4 – 8 **block** a shot, **hit** a shot 4 **get** a shot, **give** ***someone*** a shot 6 7

shot·gun /ʃɒtgʌn/ (**shotguns**) N-COUNT A **shotgun** is a gun used for shooting birds and animals which fires a lot of small metal balls at one time. 散弹猎枪

should ♦♦♦ /ʃəd, STRONG ʃʊd/

Should is a modal verb. It is used with the base form of a verb.

1 MODAL You use **should** when you are saying what would be the right thing to do or the right state for something to be in. 应该 ❏ *I should exercise more.* 我应该多锻炼。 ❏ *He's never going to be able to forget it. And I don't think he should.* 他将永远都不会忘记它。而且我认为他也不应该忘记。 ❏ *Should our children be taught to swim at school?* 我们的孩子应该在学校学游泳吗? 2 MODAL You use **should** to give someone an order to do something, or to report an official order. 必须; 应该 ❏ *18-year-olds are sent reminders that they should register to vote.* 给18岁的人派送了通知单，提醒他们应该登记投票。 3 MODAL If you say that something **should have** happened, you mean that it did not happen, but that you wish it had. If you say that something **should not have** happened, you mean that it did happen, but that you wish it had not. (本来) 应该 ❏ *I should have gone this morning but I was feeling a bit ill.* 今早我本应该去的，可是我感到有点不舒服。 ❏ *You should have written to the area manager again.* 你本应该再写信给区域经理。 4 MODAL You use **should** when you are saying that something is probably the case or will probably happen in the way you are describing. If you say that something **should have** happened by a particular time, you mean that it will probably have happened by that time. 应该会 ❏ *You should have no problem with reading this language.* 你读这种语言应该不会有问题。 ❏ *The doctor said it will take six weeks and I should be fine by then.* 医生说这将需要6周时间而我到时应该会康复。 5 MODAL You use **should** in questions when you are asking someone for advice, permission, or information. (用于征求意见、同意、信息等) 该; 可以 ❏ *Should I take out a loan?* 我该去贷款吗? ❏ *What should I do?* 我该怎么办? 6 MODAL You say "**I should**," usually with the expression "if I were you," when you are giving someone advice by telling them what you would do if you were in their position. (通过假设来提建议) 会 [mainly BRIT, FORMAL] ❏ *I should look out if I were you!* 如果我是你，我就会小心的。 7 MODAL You use **should** in conditional clauses when you are talking about things that might happen. 用于条件句，表示事情发生的可能性 [FORMAL] ❏ *If you should be fired, your health and pension benefits will not be automatically cut off.* 如果你失业了，你的健康津贴和养老金将不会自动中断。 8 MODAL You use **should** in "that" clauses after certain verbs, nouns, and adjectives when you are talking about a future event or situation. (用于某些动词、名词和形容词后的that从句中，表示将来的事件或情形) 应该 ❏ *He raised his glass and indicated that I should do the same.* 他举起了他的玻璃杯，暗示我应该照着做。 ❏ *I insisted that we should have a look at every car.* 我坚持我们应该把每辆车都看一看。 9 MODAL You use **should** in expressions such as **I should think** and **I should imagine** to indicate that you think something is true but you are not sure. 用于**I should think**和**I should imagine**中表示不确定的想法 [VAGUENESS] ❏ *I should think it's going to rain soon.* 我觉得很快就会下雨了。 10 MODAL You use **should** in expressions such as **You should have seen us** and **You should have heard him** to emphasize how funny, shocking, or impressive something that you experienced was. (表示强调有趣、惊讶或印象深刻) 真该 [SPOKEN, EMPHASIS] ❏ *You should have heard him last night!* 你真该听到他昨晚说的话!

shoul·der ♦♦◊ /ʃoʊldər/ (**shoulders, shouldering, shouldered**)
1 N-COUNT Your **shoulders** are between your neck and the tops of your arms. 肩 ❏ *She led him to an armchair, with her arm round his shoulder.* 她把他领到扶手椅上，手臂搂住了他的肩膀。 2 N-PLURAL When you talk about someone's problems or responsibilities, you can say that they carry them **on** their **shoulders**. 承担 ❏ *No one suspected the anguish he carried on his shoulders.* 没有人怀疑他所承受的痛苦。 3 V-T If you **shoulder** the responsibility or the blame for something, you accept it. 肩负 ❏ *He has had to shoulder the responsibility of his father's mistakes.* 他不得不肩负起他父亲所犯错误的责任。 4 V-T/V-I If you **shoulder** someone **aside** or if you **shoulder** your **way** somewhere, you push past people roughly using your shoulder. 用肩推; 用肩挤着走 ❏ *The policemen rushed past him, shouldering him aside.* 警察们从他身边匆匆走过，用肩膀把他推到了一边。 ❏ *She could do nothing to stop him as he shouldered his way into the house.* 当他用肩推挤着进那房子时，她根本就阻止不了他。 5 N-VAR A **shoulder** is a cut of meat from the upper part of the front leg of an animal. 前腿肉 ❏ *...shoulder of lamb.* …羊的前腿肉。 6 N-COUNT On a busy road such as a freeway, the **shoulder** is the area at the side of the road where vehicles are allowed to stop in an emergency. (道路两旁的) 紧急停车带 [AM]

in BRIT, use **hard shoulder**

7 PHRASE If someone offers you **a shoulder to cry on** or is **a shoulder to cry on**, they listen sympathetically as you talk about your troubles. 聆听倾诉者 ❏ *Mrs. Barrantes longs to be at her daughter's side to offer her a shoulder to cry on.* 巴兰茨夫人希望能在女儿身边听她的倾诉。 8 PHRASE If you say that someone or something stands **head and shoulders above** other people or things, you mean that they are a lot better than them. 远远 (胜过) ❏ *The two candidates stood head and shoulders above the rest.* 这两名候选人远远胜过其他人。 9 PHRASE If two or more people stand **shoulder to shoulder**, they are next to each other, with their shoulders touching. 肩并肩地 ❏ *They fell into step, walking shoulder to shoulder with their heads bent against the rain.* 他们步伐一致，肩并肩低着头冒雨走着。 10 PHRASE If people work or stand **shoulder to shoulder**, they work together in order to achieve something, or support each other. 同心协力地 ❏ *They could fight shoulder-to-shoulder against a common enemy.* 他们能同心协力地抗击一个共同的敌人。 11 **to rub shoulders with** → see **rub**
→ see **body**

Word Partnership *shoulder* 的常用搭配:

ADJ.	**bare** shoulder, **broken** shoulder, **dislocated** shoulder, **left/right** shoulder 1
N.	**head on** ***someone's*** shoulder 1 shoulder **a burden** 3
V.	**look over** ***your*** shoulder, **tap** ***someone*** **on the** shoulder 1 **cry on** ***someone's*** shoulder 7

shouldn't /ʃʊdᵊnt/ **Shouldn't** is the usual spoken form of "should not." **should not**的常用口语形式

should've /ʃʊdəv/ **Should've** is the usual spoken form of "should have," especially when "have" is an auxiliary verb. **should have**的常用口语形式

shout ♦◇◇ /ʃaʊt/ (**shouts, shouting, shouted**) V-T/V-I If you **shout**, you say something very loudly, usually because you want people a long distance away to hear you or because you are angry. 大声说出；大喊 ❑ *He had to shout to make himself heard above the wind.* 他不得不大喊，好让别人能在风中听见。 ❑ *"She's alive!" he shouted triumphantly.* "她活着！"他狂喜地大喊。 ❑ *Andrew rushed out of the house, shouting for help.* 安德鲁冲出房子大喊救命。 ● N-COUNT **Shout** is also a noun. 大喊 ❑ *The decision was greeted with shouts of protest from the crowd.* 这项决定遭到了人群抗议的呼喊。

▸ **shout out** PHRASAL VERB If you **shout** something **out**, you say it very loudly so that people can hear you clearly. 大喊 ❑ *They shouted out the names of those detained.* 他们大声喊着那些被拘留者的名字。 ❑ *I shouted out "I'm OK!"* 我大声喊道，"我没事！"

Word Partnership *shout* 的常用搭配：

PREP.	shout **at** *someone*
V.	**hear a/***someone* shout, **want to** shout

shove /ʃʌv/ (**shoves, shoving, shoved**) 1 V-T/V-I If you **shove** someone or something, you push them with a quick, violent movement. 猛推 ❑ *He shoved her out of the way.* 他把她推开。 ❑ *He's the one who shoved me.* 他是推我的那个人。 ● N-COUNT **Shove** is also a noun. 猛推 ❑ *She gave Gracie a shove toward the house.* 她把格雷西向那所房子猛地一推。 2 V-T If you **shove** something somewhere, you push it there quickly and carelessly. 乱塞 ❑ *We shoved a copy of the newsletter beneath their door.* 我们在他们的门下塞了一份时事通讯。 3 PHRASE If you talk about what you think will happen **if push comes to shove**, you are talking about what you think will happen if a situation becomes very bad or difficult. 情况不妙时 [INFORMAL] ❑ *If push comes to shove, if you should lose your case in the court, what will you do?* 如果情况不妙，你在法庭上输了官司，你会怎么办？

Word Partnership *shove* 的常用搭配：

ADV.	shove *someone* **down** 1
V.	**give** *someone/something* **a** shove 1
PREP.	shove *someone/something* **into** *someone/something* 1

▲ **shov·el** /ʃʌvᵊl/ (**shovels, shoveling** or **shovelling, shoveled** or **shovelled**) 1 N-COUNT A **shovel** is a tool with a long handle that is used for lifting and moving earth, coal, or snow. 铲 ❑ *...a coal shovel.* …一把煤铲。 2 V-T If you **shovel** earth, coal, or snow, you lift and move it with a shovel. 用铲挖；铲起 ❑ *He has to get out and shovel snow.* 他不得不出去铲雪。 3 V-T If you **shovel** something somewhere, you push a lot of it quickly into that place. 把…大量送入 ❑ *There was silence, except for Randall, who was obliviously shoveling food into his mouth.* 到处一片寂静，除了正在忘乎所以地把食物大口大口地塞进嘴里的兰德尔。

show
1 VERB USES
2 NOUN AND ADJECTIVE USES
3 PHRASAL VERBS

1 **show** ♦♦♦ /ʃoʊ/ (**shows, showing, showed, shown**)
➪ **Please look at meanings 15 and 16 to see if the expression you are looking for is shown under another headword.** 1 V-T If something **shows that** a state of affairs exists, it gives information that proves it or makes it clear to people. 显示；表明 ❑ *Research shows that young people still look to parents as their main source for health information.* 研究表明年轻人仍然指望父母作为他们主要的健康信息来源。 ❑ *These figures show an increase of over one million in unemployment.* 这些数据表明失业人数增长超过100万。 2 V-T If a picture, chart, movie, or piece of writing **shows** something, it represents it or gives information about it. (图画、图表、文章等) 表示 ❑ *Figure 4.1 shows the respiratory system.* 图4.1所示的是呼吸系统。 ❑ *The cushions, shown left, measure 20 x 12 inches and cost $39.95.* 左边展示的垫子尺寸是20 x 12英寸，价格为$39.95。 ❑ *Much of the film shows the painter simply going about his task.* 这部电影主要演的是这位画家只是忙着自己的工作。 3 V-T If you **show** someone something, you give it to them, take them to it, or point to it, so that they can see it or know what you are referring to. 拿给…看；指给…看 ❑ *Cut out this article and show it to your boss.* 把这篇文章剪下来拿给你的老板看。 ❑ *He showed me the apartment he shares with Esther.* 他指给我看他和埃斯特合住的公寓。 4 V-T If you **show** someone to a room or seat, you lead them there. 引领 ❑ *It was very good of you to come. Let me show you to my study.* 你能来真是太好了。让我带你看我的书房。 ❑ *Milton was shown into the office.* 米尔顿被领进了办公室。 5 V-T If you **show** someone how to do something, you do it yourself so that they can watch you and learn how to do it. 向…演示 ❑ *Claire showed us how to make a chocolate cake.* 克莱尔向我们演示如何做巧克力蛋糕。 ❑ *There are seasoned professionals who can teach you and show you what to do.* 有经验丰富的专业人员可以教你，并向你示范做什么。 6 V-T/V-I If something **shows** or if you **show** it, it is visible or noticeable. 显露 ❑ *When he smiled he showed a row of strong white teeth.* 他笑的时候露出了一排结实而洁白的牙齿。 ❑ *Faint glimmers of daylight were showing through the trees.* 微弱的日光从树丛中透出。 7 V-T/V-I If you **show** a particular attitude, quality, or feeling, or if it **shows**, you behave in a way that makes this attitude, quality, or feeling clear to other people. 流露出；表现 ❑ *She showed no interest in her children.* 她流露出对自己的孩子没有兴趣。 ❑ *Ferguson was unhappy and it showed.* 弗格森不高兴，而且表现了出来。 ❑ *You show me respect.* 请你对我尊重点。 8 V-T If something **shows** a quality or characteristic or if that quality or characteristic **shows itself**, it can be noticed or observed. 表露出；显示出 (品质、特征) ❑ *The story shows a strong narrative gift and a vivid eye for detail.* 这个故事显示出很强的叙事才能和对细节的生动观察力。 ❑ *Her popularity clearly shows no sign of waning.* 她的受欢迎程度显然没有显示出下降的迹象。 9 V-T If a company **shows** a profit or a loss, its accounts indicate that it has made a profit or a loss. 出现 (赢利或亏损) ❑ *It is the only one of the three companies expected to show a profit for the quarter.* 这是3家公司中惟一1家有望在本季度出现赢利的公司。 10 V-I If a person you are expecting to meet does not **show**, they do not arrive at the place where you expect to meet them. 露面 [mainly AM] ❑ *There was always a chance he wouldn't show.* 他总有可能不会露面。 ● PHRASAL VERB **Show up** means the same as **show**. 露面 ❑ *We waited until five o'clock, but he did not show up.* 我们一直等到5点，但他却没有露面。 11 V-T/V-I If someone **shows** a film or television program, it is broadcast or appears on television or in the movie theater. 放映；播放 ❑ *The TV news showed the same film clip.* 电视新闻播放了同一个电影短片。 ❑ *The movie is now showing at theaters around the country.* 该部影片目前正在全国各地的影院上映。 12 V-T To **show** things such as works of art means to put them in an exhibition where they can be seen by the public. 展出 ❑ *50 dealers will show oils, watercolors, drawings and prints from 1900 to 1992.* 50位经销商将要展出1900年到1992年的油画、水彩画、素描画和版画。 13 PHRASE If you **have** something **to show for** your efforts, you have achieved something as a result of what you have done. (努力) 收到成效 ❑ *I'm nearly 31 and it's about time I had something to show for my time in my job.* 我快三十一岁了，该是我在工作中的付出收获成果的时候了。 14 PHRASE If you say **it just goes to show** or **it just shows that** something is the case, you mean that what you have just said or experienced demonstrates that it is the case. 这就证明了… ❑ *I forgot all about the ring. Which just goes to show that getting good grades in school doesn't mean you're clever.* 我完全忘了戒指的事情。这证明在校取得好成绩并不意味着你就聪明。 15 **to show** someone **the door** → see **door** 16 **to show** your **face** → see **face**

2 **show** ♦♦♦ /ʃoʊ/ (**shows**) 1 N-COUNT **A show of** a feeling or quality is an attempt by someone to make it clear that they have that feeling or quality. 表示 [usu "a" N "of" n] ❑ *Miners gathered in the center of Bucharest in a show of support for the government.* 矿工聚集在了布加勒斯特市中心表示对政府的支持。 2 N-UNCOUNT If you say that something is **for show**, you mean that it has no real purpose and is done just to give a good impression. 虚饰 ❑ *The change in government is more for show than for real.* 政府的这个变化更多是在装样子而不是真的。 3 N-COUNT A television or radio **show** is a program on television or radio. (电视或广播) 节目 ❑ *I had my own TV show.* 我有过自己的电视节目。 ❑ *...a popular talk show on a Cuban radio station.* …古巴广播电台的一个受欢迎的访谈节目。 4 N-COUNT **A show** in a theater is an entertainment or concert, especially one that includes different items such as music, dancing, and comedy. 演出 ❑ *How about going shopping and seeing a show?* 去购物然后看场演出如何？ 5 N-COUNT **A show** is a public exhibition of things, such as works of art, fashionable clothes, or things that have been entered in a competition. 展览会 [also "on" N] ❑ *Currently, the show is in Boston.* 目前，这场展览会正在波士顿举行。 ❑ *It plans about 30 such*

fashion shows this fall in department stores. 计划今年秋天在百货公司举行大约三十场这样的时装展览会。
→ see **concert, laser, theater**

Thesaurus *show* 另参见:
V. demonstrate, display, exhibit, present ❶ 1 5
N. act, entertainment, production, program ❷ 3 4
demonstration, display, presentation ❷ 5

❸ **show** ◆◆◆ /ʃoʊ/ (**shows, showing, showed, shown**)
▸ **show off** 1 PHRASAL VERB If you say that someone **is showing off**, you are criticizing them for trying to impress people by showing in a very obvious way what they can do or what they own. 卖弄; 炫耀 [DISAPPROVAL] ❑ *All right, there's no need to show off.* 好啦，没有必要炫耀了。 2 PHRASAL VERB If you **show off** something that you have, you show it to a lot of people or make it obvious that you have it, because you are proud of it. 炫耀 ❑ *Naomi was showing off her engagement ring.* 内奥米那时正在炫耀她的订婚戒指。
3 → see also **show-off**
▸ **show up** 1 PHRASAL VERB If something **shows up** or if something **shows it up**, it can be clearly seen or noticed. 使显露; 显露 ❑ *You may have some strange disease that may not show up for 10 or 15 years.* 你可能患上某种10年或15年内都显露不出什么症状来的怪病。 ❑ *The orange color shows up well against most backgrounds.* 橙色在多数背景下都很能突显出来。 2 PHRASAL VERB If someone or something **shows** you **up**, they make you feel embarrassed or ashamed of them. 使难堪 ❑ *He wanted to teach her a lesson for showing him up in front of Leonov.* 他因她在列昂诺夫面前使他难堪而想教训她一顿。
3 → see **show** ❶ 10

show busi·ness N-UNCOUNT **Show business** is the entertainment industry of movies, theater, and television. 娱乐业; 演艺业 ❑ *He started his career in show business by playing the saxophone and singing.* 他以吹萨克斯管和唱歌开始了他的演艺生涯。

show·down /ʃoʊdaʊn/ (**showdowns**) N-COUNT A **showdown** is a big argument or conflict which is intended to settle a dispute that has lasted for a long time. 决战 ❑ *They may be pushing the president toward a final showdown with his party.* 他们可能会逼迫总统与其政党做最后的较量。

show·er /ʃaʊər/ (**showers, showering, showered**) 1 N-COUNT A **shower** is a device for washing yourself. It consists of a pipe which ends in a flat cover with a lot of holes in it so that water comes out in a spray. 淋浴器 ❑ *She heard him turn on the shower.* 她听见他拧开了淋浴器。 2 N-COUNT A **shower** is a small enclosed area containing a shower. 淋浴间 ❑ *Do you sing in the shower?* 你在淋浴间里唱歌吗? 3 N-COUNT **The showers** or **the shower** in a place such as a gym is the area containing showers. (体育馆等的) 浴室 ❑ *The showers are a mess.* 那些浴室一片狼藉。 4 N-COUNT If you take a **shower**, you wash yourself by standing under a spray of water from a shower. 淋浴 ❑ *I think I'll take a shower before dinner.* 我想晚饭前我要来次淋浴。 5 V-I If you **shower**, you wash yourself by standing under a spray of water from a shower. 洗澡 ❑ *There wasn't time to shower or change clothes.* 没时间洗澡或换衣服了。 6 N-COUNT A **shower** is a short period of rain, especially light rain. 阵雨 ❑ *There'll be bright or sunny spells and scattered showers this afternoon.* 今天下午将放晴，间有零星阵雨。 7 N-COUNT You can refer to a lot of things that are falling as a **shower of** them. 大量下落 ❑ *Showers of sparks flew in all directions.* 无数火星儿向四处飞溅。 8 V-T If you are **showered with** a lot of small objects or pieces, they are scattered over you. 抛撒 [usu passive] ❑ *They were showered with rice in the traditional manner.* 人们按照传统习俗朝他们抛撒大米。 9 N-COUNT A **shower** is a party or celebration at which the guests bring gifts. 送礼会 [mainly AM] ❑ *...a baby shower.* …为婴儿举行的送礼会。
→ see **meteor, soap, wedding**

shown /ʃoʊn/ **Shown** is the past participle of **show**. **show**的过去分词

show-off (**show-offs**) also **showoff** N-COUNT If you say that someone is a **show-off**, you are criticizing them for trying to impress people by showing in a very obvious way what they can do or what they own. 爱卖弄的人 [INFORMAL, DISAPPROVAL] ❑ *Many jet ski riders are big show-offs who stick around populated areas so everyone can see their turns and maneuvers.* 许多驾喷气式滑艇者都是极爱卖弄的人，他们总是出现在人多的地方，好让大家都能看到他们的翻转和各种熟练动作。

show·piece /ʃoʊpis/ (**showpieces**) also **show-piece** N-COUNT A **showpiece** is something that is admired because it is the best thing of its type, especially something that is intended to be impressive. 展示的样品 ❑ *The factory was to be a showpiece of Western investment in the East.* 这家工厂将成为西方在东方投资的样板。

show·room /ʃoʊrum/ (**showrooms**) N-COUNT A **showroom** is a store in which goods are displayed for sale, especially goods such as cars or electrical or gas appliances. (汽车、电器或煤气用具的) 展销店 ❑ *...a car showroom.* …汽车展销店。

shrank /ʃræŋk/ **Shrank** is the past tense of **shrink**. **shrink**的过去式

shrap·nel /ʃræpnᵊl/ N-UNCOUNT **Shrapnel** consists of small pieces of metal which are scattered from exploding bombs and shells. (炸弹或炮弹的) 碎片 ❑ *He was hit by shrapnel from a grenade.* 他被一枚手榴弹的弹片击中了。

▲ **shred** /ʃrɛd/ (**shreds, shredding, shredded**) 1 V-T If you **shred** something such as food or paper, you cut it or tear it into very small, narrow pieces. 切碎; 撕碎 ❑ *They may be shredding documents.* 他们也许正在粉碎那些文件。 2 N-COUNT If you cut or tear food or paper **into shreds**, you cut or tear it into small, narrow pieces. 碎片; 细条 ❑ *Cut the cabbage into fine long shreds.* 把这棵卷心菜切成细长条。
3 N-COUNT If there is not a **shred of** something, there is not even a small amount of it. 一丁点儿 ❑ *He said there was not a shred of evidence to support such remarks.* 他说没有一丁点儿支持这些说法的证据。 ❑ *There is not a shred of truth in the story.* 这个故事没有一点真实性。

★ **shrewd** /ʃrud/ (**shrewder, shrewdest**) ADJ A **shrewd** person is able to understand and judge a situation quickly and to use this understanding to their own advantage. 精明的 ❑ *She's a shrewd businesswoman.* 她是一个精明的商人。

shriek /ʃrik/ (**shrieks, shrieking, shrieked**) V-I When someone **shrieks**, they make a short, very loud cry, for example, because they are suddenly surprised, are in pain, or are laughing. 尖叫 ❑ *She shrieked and leapt from the bed.* 她尖叫着从那张床上跳了起来。 ● N-COUNT **Shriek** is also a noun. 尖叫 ❑ *Sue let out a terrific shriek and leapt out of the way.* 苏发出一声恐怖的尖叫，跳了出来。

shrill /ʃrɪl/ (**shriller, shrillest**) ADJ A **shrill** sound is high-pitched and unpleasant. (声音) 刺耳的 ❑ *Shrill cries and startled oaths flew up around us as pandemonium broke out.* 骚动爆发后，我们的周围响起了刺耳的喊叫声和令人惊愕的咒骂声。 ❑ *...the shrill whistle of the engine.* …那发动机的尖啸声。

▲ **shrimp** /ʃrɪmp/ (**shrimp**)

The plural can also be **shrimps**.

N-COUNT **Shrimps** are small shellfish with long tails and many legs. 小虾 ❑ *Add the shrimp and cook for 30 seconds.* 放入小虾，烹饪30秒。

shrimp cock·tail (**shrimp cocktails**) N-VAR A **shrimp cocktail** is a dish that consists of shrimp and a sauce. It is usually eaten at the beginning of a meal. (通常在饭前食用的) 鲜虾盅 [mainly AM]
in BRIT, use **prawn cocktail**

▲ **shrine** /ʃraɪn/ (**shrines**) 1 N-COUNT A **shrine** is a place of worship which is associated with a particular holy person or object. 圣殿 ❑ *...the holy shrine of Mecca.* …麦加的圣殿。 2 N-COUNT A **shrine** is a place that people visit and treat with respect because it is connected with a dead person or with dead people that they want to remember. 圣地 ❑ *The monument has been turned into a shrine to the dead and the missing.* 这座纪念碑已经变成了纪念那些过世或失踪的人的圣地。

shrink /ʃrɪŋk/ (**shrinks, shrinking, shrank, shrunk**) 1 V-I If cloth or clothing **shrinks**, it becomes smaller in size, usually as a result of being washed. 缩水 ❑ *People were short in those days – or else those military uniforms all shrank in the wash!* 那个年代人们很矮——要么就是那些军装在洗涤时全都缩水了！ 2 V-T/V-I If something **shrinks** or something else **shrinks** it, it becomes smaller. 使缩小; 缩小 ❑ *The vast forests of West Africa have shrunk.* 西非那片广袤的森林已经缩小了。
3 V-I If you **shrink away from** someone or something, you move away from them because you are frightened, shocked, or disgusted by them. (因害怕、震惊或厌恶) 避开 ❑ *One child shrinks away from me when I try to talk to him.* 我试着和这个孩子说话时，他避开了我。 4 V-I If you do not **shrink from** a task or duty, you do it even though it is unpleasant or dangerous. 逃避 (不愉快或危险的事) [usu with neg] ❑ *He is decisive and won't shrink from a fight.* 他很果断，而且不会逃避战斗。 5 N-COUNT A **shrink** is a psychiatrist. 精神病医生 [INFORMAL] ❑ *I've seen a shrink already.* 我已经看过了精神病医生。
6 **no shrinking violet** → see **violet**

shriv·el /ʃrɪvᵊl/ (**shrivels, shriveling** or **shrivelling, shriveled** or **shrivelled**) V-T/V-I When something **shrivels** or when something

S

shrivels it, it becomes dryer and smaller, often with lines in its surface, as a result of losing the water it contains. 使皱缩; 使枯萎 皱缩; 枯萎 ❑ *The plant shrivels and dies.* 那棵植物枯死了。 ● PHRASAL VERB **Shrivel up** means the same as **shrivel**. 枯萎 ❑ *The leaves started to shrivel up.* 那些树叶开始枯萎了。 ● **shriv·eled** ADJ 皱缩的; 枯萎的 ❑ *...a shriveled chestnut.* …一颗枯萎的栗子树。

▲ **shroud** /ʃraʊd/ (**shrouds, shrouding, shrouded**) 1 N-COUNT A **shroud** is a cloth which is used for wrapping a dead body. 裹尸布 ❑ *...the burial shroud.* …下葬裹尸布。 2 V-T If something **has been shrouded in** mystery or secrecy, very little information about it has been made available. 掩盖 ❑ *For years the teaching of acting has been shrouded in mystery.* 数年来，表演教学一直被蒙上神秘的色彩。 3 V-T If darkness, fog, or smoke **shrouds** an area, it covers it so that it is difficult to see. 笼罩 ❑ *Mist shrouded the hilltops.* 薄雾笼罩了那些山顶。

★ **shrub** /ʃrʌb/ (**shrubs**) N-COUNT **Shrubs** are plants that have several woody stems. 灌木 ❑ *...flowering shrubs.* …开花的灌木。

shrug /ʃrʌg/ (**shrugs, shrugging, shrugged**) V-T/V-I If you **shrug**, you raise your shoulders to show that you are not interested in something or that you do not know or care about something. 耸肩 ❑ *I shrugged, as if to say, "Why not?"* 我耸了耸肩，好像在说，"为什么不？" ● N-COUNT **Shrug** is also a noun. 耸肩 ❑ *"I suppose so," said Anna with a shrug.* "我想是这样，" 安娜耸耸肩说道。

▸ **shrug off** PHRASAL VERB If you **shrug** something **off**, you ignore it or treat it as if it is not really important or serious. 对…不予理睬 ❑ *He shrugged off the criticism.* 他对批评不予理睬。

shrunk /ʃrʌŋk/ **Shrunk** is the past participle of **shrink**. shrink的过去分词

▲ **shud·der** /ʃʌdər/ (**shudders, shuddering, shuddered**) 1 V-I If you **shudder**, you shake with fear, horror, or disgust, or because you are cold. (因害怕、恐惧、厌恶或寒冷) 发抖 ❑ *Lloyd had urged her to eat caviar. She had shuddered at the thought.* 劳埃德已鼓动她吃鱼子酱。可她一想到这个就打哆嗦了。 ● N-COUNT **Shudder** is also a noun. (因害怕、恐惧、厌恶或寒冷而产生的) 发抖 [usu sing] ❑ *She gave a violent shudder.* 她猛地抖了一下。 2 V-I If something such as a machine or vehicle **shudders**, it shakes suddenly and violently. (机器或车辆) 剧烈震动 ❑ *The train began to pull out of the station – then suddenly shuddered to a halt.* 火车开始驶出车站——然后就突然剧烈震动停了下来。 3 N-COUNT If something sends **a shudder** or **shudders** through a group of people, it makes them worried or afraid. 担忧; 害怕 ❑ *The next crisis sent a shudder of fear through the UN community.* 下一次危机引起了联合国组织的担忧。

shuf·fle /ʃʌfᵊl/ (**shuffles, shuffling, shuffled**) 1 V-I If you **shuffle** somewhere, you walk there without lifting your feet properly off the ground. 拖着脚走 ❑ *Moira shuffled across the kitchen.* 莫伊拉拖着脚走过了厨房。 ● N-SING **Shuffle** is also a noun. 拖着脚走 ❑ *She noticed her own proud walk had become a shuffle.* 她注意到了自己得意的步伐已变成了拖着脚走。 2 V-T/V-I If you **shuffle around**, you move your feet about while standing or you move your bottom about while sitting, often because you feel uncomfortable or embarrassed. (因不舒服或尴尬) 站着的脚来回挪动; 坐立不安 ❑ *He shuffles around in his chair.* 他在椅子上坐立不安。 3 V-T If you **shuffle** playing cards, you mix them up before you begin a game. 洗 (牌) ❑ *There are various ways of shuffling and dealing the cards.* 有各种不同的洗牌和发牌方法。

▲ **shun** /ʃʌn/ (**shuns, shunning, shunned**) V-T If you **shun** someone or something, you deliberately avoid them or keep away from them. 有意回避 ❑ *From that time forward everybody shunned him.* 从那时起，人人都有意回避他。

shunt /ʃʌnt/ (**shunts, shunting, shunted**) V-T If a person or thing **is shunted** somewhere, they are moved or sent there, usually because someone finds them inconvenient. (因嫌碍事) 把…移走或打发走 [usu passive] [DISAPPROVAL] ❑ *He has spent most of his life being shunted between his mother, father and various foster families.* 他生命中大部分时间都在母亲、父亲和各个收养家庭之间被推来推去。

shut ♦◇◇ /ʃʌt/ (**shuts, shutting**)

> The form **shut** is used in the present tense and is the past tense and past participle.

1 V-T/V-I If you **shut** something such as a door or if it **shuts**, it moves so that it fills a hole or a space. 关上; 关闭 ❑ *Just make sure you shut the gate.* 你务必关上那幢大门。 ● ADJ **Shut** is also an adjective. 关闭的 [v-link ADJ] ❑ *They have warned residents to stay inside and keep their doors and windows shut.* 他们已警告居民待在屋内并关好门窗。 2 V-T If you **shut** your eyes, you lower your eyelids so that you cannot see anything. 闭上 (眼睛) ❑ *Lucy shut her eyes so she wouldn't see it happen.* 露西闭上了眼睛，以便不会看到它发生。 ● ADJ **Shut** is also an adjective. 闭合的 [v-link ADJ] ❑ *His eyes were shut and he seemed to have fallen asleep.* 他的双眼闭着，看上去像是已经睡着了。 3 V-T/V-I If your mouth **shuts** or if you **shut** your mouth, you place your lips firmly together. 闭上 (嘴); (嘴) 闭上 ❑ *Daniel's mouth opened, and then shut again.* 丹尼尔的嘴张开后又闭上了。 ● ADJ **Shut** is also an adjective. 合上的 [v-link ADJ] ❑ *She was silent for a moment, lips tight shut, eyes distant.* 她沉默了片刻，双唇紧闭，两眼茫然。 4 V-T/V-I When a store, bar, or other public building **shuts** or when someone **shuts** it, it is closed and you cannot use it until it is open again. 使停止营业; 使关门; 停止营业; 关门 ❑ *There is a tendency to shut museums or shops at a moment's notice.* 有一接到通知就关闭博物馆或商店的趋势。 ❑ *Stores usually shut from noon-3pm, and stay open late.* 商店通常都中午到下午3点关门，然后开到很晚。 ● ADJ **Shut** is also an adjective. 关门的 [v-link ADJ] ❑ *Make sure you have food to tide you over when the local shop may be shut.* 在那家当地商店可能关门时，你一定要确保自己有度过难关的食物。 5 PHRASE If someone tells you to **keep** your **mouth shut** about something, they are telling you not to let anyone else know about it. 保密 ❑ *I don't have to tell you how important it is for you to keep your mouth shut about all this.* 我不必告诉你对这件事保密有多么重要。 6 PHRASE If you **keep** your **mouth shut**, you do not express your opinions about something, even though you would like to. 保持沉默 ❑ *If she had kept her mouth shut she would still have her job now.* 如果她当时能保持沉默，她现在还能有工作。

▸ **shut down** PHRASAL VERB If a factory or business **shuts down** or if someone **shuts** it **down**, work there stops or it is no longer in business. (使) 歇业 ❑ *Smaller contractors had been forced to shut down.* 一些小的承包商已被迫歇业。 ❑ *It is required by law to shut down banks which it regards as chronically short of capital.* 法律规定要关闭资金长期短缺的银行。

▸ **shut in** PHRASAL VERB If you **shut** someone or something **in** a room, you close the door so that they cannot leave it. 把…关在房间里 ❑ *The door enables us to shut the birds in the shelter in bad weather.* 这扇门能让我们在天气不好时把这些鸟关在庇护处。

▸ **shut off** 1 PHRASAL VERB If you **shut off** something such as an engine or an electrical item, you turn it off to stop it from working. 关掉 ❑ *They pulled over and shut off the engine.* 他们把车停到路边并关掉了发动机。 2 PHRASAL VERB If you **shut yourself off**, you avoid seeing other people, usually because you are feeling depressed. 避免见人 ❑ *Billy tends to keep things to himself more and shut himself off.* 比利更加倾向于把事情藏在心里，不与他人来往。 3 PHRASAL VERB If an official organization **shuts off** the supply of something, they no longer send it to the people they supplied in the past. 停止 (供应) ❑ *The State Water Project has shut off all supplies to farmers.* 州水利工程已经停止了对农场主的所有供应。

▸ **shut out** 1 PHRASAL VERB If you **shut** something or someone **out**, you prevent them from getting into a place, for example, by closing the doors. 把…关在门外 ❑ *"I shut him out of the bedroom," says Maureen.* "我把他关在卧室门外，" 莫琳说道。 2 PHRASAL VERB If you **shut out** a thought or a feeling, you prevent yourself from thinking or feeling it. 不让自己 (去想或感受) ❑ *I shut out the memory which was too painful to dwell on.* 我不让自己去回忆那段会引起我太多痛苦的往事。 3 PHRASAL VERB If you **shut** someone **out** of something, you prevent them from having anything to do with it. 把…排除在外 ❑ *She is very reclusive, to the point of shutting me out of her life.* 她很喜欢独处，到了要把我排斥在她的生活之外的程度。 4 PHRASAL VERB In sports such as football and hockey, if one team **shuts out** the team they are playing against, they win and prevent the opposing team from scoring. (足球、曲棍球等) 使不能得分 ❑ *Harvard shut out Yale, 14-0.* 哈佛队让耶鲁队一分未得，以14比0获胜。 5 → see also **shutout**

▸ **shut up** PHRASAL VERB If someone **shuts up** or if someone **shuts** them **up**, they stop talking. You can say **'shut up'** as an impolite way to tell a person to stop talking. 使闭嘴; 闭嘴 ❑ *Just shut up, will you?* 闭嘴，行吗？

Thesaurus *shut* 另参见：

V. close, fasten, secure; (*ant.*) open 1

Word Partnership *shut* 的常用搭配：

N. shut **a door**, shut **a gate**, shut **a window** 1

V. **force** *something* shut, **pull** *something* shut, **push** *something* shut, **slam** *something* shut 1

ADV. shut **tight/tightly** 1–3

shut **temporarily** 4

S

shut·down /ʃʌtdaʊn/ (**shutdowns**) N-COUNT A **shutdown** is the closing of a factory, store, or other business, either for a short time or forever. 歇业 ❑ *The shutdown is the latest in a series of painful budget measures.* 歇业是一连串痛苦的预算措施中刚刚实施的一项。

★ **shut·ter** /ʃʌtər/ (**shutters**) 1 N-COUNT **Shutters** are wooden or metal covers fitted on the outside of a window. They can be opened to let in the light, or closed to keep out the sun or the cold. 百叶窗 ❑ *She opened the shutters and gazed out over village roofs.* 她打开了百叶窗，朝村里的房顶望去。 2 N-COUNT The **shutter** in a camera is the part which opens to allow light through the lens when a photograph is taken. (照相机的) 快门 ❑ *There are a few things you should check before pressing the shutter release.* 在按快门之前，有几件事情你应该检查。
→ see **photography**

★ **shut·tle** /ʃʌtᵊl/ (**shuttles, shuttling, shuttled**) 1 N-COUNT A **shuttle** is the same as a **space shuttle**. 航天飞机 2 N-COUNT A **shuttle** is a plane, bus, or train which makes frequent trips between two places. 穿梭班机；穿梭班车；穿梭火车 ❑ *There is a free 24-hour shuttle between the airport terminals.* 在机场的各航空站之间有24小时的免费穿梭巴士。 3 V-T/V-I If someone or something **shuttles** or **is shuttled** from one place to another place, they frequently go from one place to the other. 使频频往返于两地之间；频频往返于两地之间 ❑ *He and colleagues have shuttled back and forth between the three capitals.* 他和同事们一直来回往返于3个首都之间。

shy /ʃaɪ/ (**shyer, shyest, shies, shying, shied**) 1 ADJ A **shy** person is nervous and uncomfortable in the company of other people. 害羞的；腼腆的 ❑ *She was a shy, quiet girl.* 她是个腼腆安静的女孩。 ❑ *She was a shy and retiring person off-stage.* 台下她是个害羞、沉默寡言的人。 ● **shy·ly** ADV 害羞地；腼腆地 ❑ *The children smiled shyly.* 孩子们腼腆地笑了。 ● **shy·ness** N-UNCOUNT 羞涩；腼腆 ❑ *Eventually he overcame his shyness.* 他终于克服了腼腆。 2 ADJ If you are **shy about** or **shy of** doing something, you are unwilling to do it because you are afraid of what might happen. (因担心后果) 不情愿的 ❑ *They feel shy about showing their feelings.* 他们不愿表达自己的感情。
▶ **shy away from** PHRASAL VERB If you **shy away from** doing something, you avoid doing it, often because you are afraid or not confident enough. (因害怕或信心不足而) 避免 ❑ *We frequently shy away from making decisions.* 我们常常因为害怕而避免做决定。

Thesaurus *shy* 另参见：
ADJ. nervous, quiet, sheepish, uncomfortable; (*ant.*) confident 1

sib·ling /sɪblɪŋ/ (**siblings**) N-COUNT Your **siblings** are your brothers and sisters. 兄弟姐妹 [FORMAL] ❑ *His siblings are in their twenties.* 他的兄弟姐妹都是20来岁。

Note that there is no common English word that can refer to both a brother and a sister. You simply have to use both words. ❑ *She has 13 brothers and sisters.* The word **sibling** exists, but it is very formal. Some Americans use **sib** as an informal substitute for **sibling**. ❑ *All my sibs were home for Thanksgiving.*

S

sick ♦◇◇ /sɪk/ (**sicker, sickest**) 1 ADJ If you are **sick**, you are ill. **Sick** usually means physically ill, but it can sometimes be used to mean mentally ill. (生理上) 有病的；精神不健全的 ❑ *He's very sick. He needs medication.* 他病得很重，需要药物治疗。 ❑ *She found herself with two small children, a sick husband, and no money.* 她发现自己带着2个年幼的孩子和1个有病的丈夫，而且身无分文。 ● N-PLURAL **The sick** are people who are sick. 病人 ❑ *There were no doctors to treat the sick.* 那时没有医生医治病人们。 2 ADJ If you are **sick**, the food that you have eaten comes up from your stomach and out of your mouth. If you **feel sick**, you feel as if you are going to be sick. 恶心的；呕吐的 [v-link ADJ] ❑ *She got up and was sick in the sink.* 她起身往水池里呕吐起来。 ❑ *The very thought of food made him feel sick.* 一想到食物他就想吐。 3 ADJ If you say that you are **sick of** something or **sick and tired of** it, you are emphasizing that you are very annoyed by it and want it to stop. 厌倦的 [v-link ADJ "of" n/-ing] [INFORMAL, EMPHASIS] ❑ *I am sick and tired of hearing all these people moaning.* 我厌倦了听所有这些人抱怨个没完。 4 ADJ If you describe something such as a joke or story as **sick**, you mean that it deals with death or suffering in an unpleasantly humorous way. 令人毛骨悚然的 [DISAPPROVAL] ❑ *...a sick joke about a cat.* …有关猫的一个令人毛骨悚然的笑话。 5 PHRASE If you say that something or someone **makes** you **sick**, you mean that they make you feel angry or disgusted. 使某人生气；使某人厌恶 [INFORMAL] ❑ *It makes me sick that this wasn't disclosed.* 这事被隐瞒了让我很生气。 6 PHRASE If you are **out sick**, you are not at work because you are sick. 因病没上班 [usu v-link PHR] ❑ *That afternoon she was fired from her job as a nurse, because she'd been out sick so much.* 那天下午她因经常生病没去上班被开除，丢掉了护士工作。 7 PHRASE If you say that you are **worried sick**, you are emphasizing that you are extremely worried. 担心得要命 [INFORMAL, EMPHASIS] ❑ *He was worried sick about what our mothers would say.* 他对我们的妈妈们可能要说的话担心得要命。

The words **ill** and **sick** are very similar in meaning, but are used in slightly different ways. **Ill** is generally not used before a noun, and can be used in verbal expressions such as **fall ill** and **be taken ill**. ❑ *He fell ill shortly before Christmas... One of the jury members was taken ill.* **Sick** is often used before a noun. ❑ *...sick children.* In British English, **ill** is a slightly more polite, less direct word than **sick**. **Sick** often suggests the actual physical feeling of being ill, for example nausea or vomiting. ❑ *I spent the next 24 hours in bed, groaning and being sick.* In American English, **sick** is often used where British people would say **ill**. ❑ *Some people get hurt in accidents or get sick.*

Word Partnership *sick* 的常用搭配：
N. sick **children**, sick **mother**, sick **patients**, sick **people**, sick **person** 1
ADV. **really** sick, **very** sick 1
V. **care for the** sick 1
become sick, **feel** sick, **get** sick 1 2
ADJ. **worried** sick 7

sick·en /sɪkən/ (**sickens, sickening, sickened**) V-T If something **sickens** you, it makes you feel disgusted. 使厌恶 ❑ *The notion that art should be controlled by intellectuals sickened him.* 艺术应该由知识分子掌控的观念使他很厌恶。

sick·en·ing /sɪkənɪŋ/ ADJ You describe something as **sickening** when it gives you feelings of horror or disgust, or makes you feel sick. 令人恐惧的；令人恶心的 ❑ *...the sickening rise in the number of suicide bombings.* …自杀式爆炸的数量令人恐惧的增加。

sick leave N-UNCOUNT **Sick leave** is the time that a person spends away from work because of illness or injury. 病假 [BUSINESS] ❑ *I have been on sick leave for seven months with depression.* 我因患抑郁症已休了7个月的病假。

sick·ly /sɪkli/ (**sicklier, sickliest**) 1 ADJ A **sickly** person or animal is weak, unhealthy, and often ill. 体弱多病的 ❑ *He had been a sickly child.* 他过去一直是个体弱多病的孩子。 2 ADJ A **sickly** smell or taste is unpleasant and makes you feel slightly sick, often because it is extremely sweet. (常指因太甜而) 令人有点作呕的 ❑ *...the sickly smell of rum.* …朗姆酒甜得发腻的气味。

sick·ness /sɪknɪs/ (**sicknesses**) 1 N-UNCOUNT **Sickness** is the state of being ill or unhealthy. 生病 ❑ *In fifty-two years of working he had one week of sickness.* 他在52年的工作时间里曾生过1星期的病。 2 N-UNCOUNT **Sickness** is the uncomfortable feeling that you are going to vomit. 恶心 ❑ *After a while, the sickness gradually passed and she struggled to the mirror.* 过了不久，恶心的感觉逐渐消退，她挣扎着来到镜子前。 3 N-VAR A **sickness** is a particular illness. 疾病 ❑ *More than 930 local people are registered as suffering from radiation sickness.* 九百三十多位当地人被注册患有辐射病。

sick pay N-UNCOUNT When you are ill and unable to work, **sick pay** is the money that you get from your employer instead of your normal wages. 病假工资 [BUSINESS] ❑ *They are not eligible for sick pay.* 他们没有资格领病假工资。

side
❶ A SURFACE, POSITION, OR PLACE
❷ ONE ASPECT OR ONE POINT OF VIEW
❸ PHRASES

❶ **side** ♦♦♦ /saɪd/ (**sides**) 1 N-COUNT The **side of** something is a position to the left or right of it, rather than in front of it, behind it, or on it. 一侧 ❑ *On one side of the main entrance there's a red plaque.* 大门口的一侧有块红色匾牌。 ❑ *...a photograph with Joe and Ken on each side of me.* …一张乔和肯在我两侧的照片。 ❑ *...the nations on either side of the Pacific.* …太平洋两岸的国家。 2 N-COUNT The **side** of an object, building, or vehicle is any of its flat surfaces which is not considered to be its front, its back, its top, or its bottom. 侧面 ❑ *We put a notice on the side of the box.* 我们在这箱子的一侧贴了一张通知。 ❑ *A carton of milk lay on its side.* 一盒牛奶侧躺着放在那里。 **3** N-COUNT The **sides** of a hollow or a container are its inside vertical surfaces. 内侧面 ❑ *The rough rock walls were like the sides of a deep canal.* 粗糙的岩壁就像一条很深的运河的两岸。 ❑ *Line the base of the dish with greaseproof paper and lightly grease the sides.* 在盘子的底部垫一层防油纸，并在内侧涂上少许油。 **4** N-COUNT The **sides of** an area or surface are its edges. 边缘 ❑ *Park on the side of the road.* 在那条路边停车。 ❑ *...a small beach on the north side of the peninsula.* …那个半岛北边上的一个小海滩。 **5** N-COUNT The two **sides of** an area, surface, or object are its two halves. (地区、表面或物体的一分为二的) 一半 ❑ *She turned over on her stomach on the other side of the bed.* 她翻身趴到了床的另一半边。 ❑ *The major center for language is in the left side of the brain.* 语言的主要中心在左半脑。 **6** N-COUNT The two **sides** of a road are its two halves on which traffic travels in opposite directions. (往返车道的) 一半 ❑ *It had gone on to the wrong side of the road and hit a car coming in the other direction.* 它驶入了逆行车道，撞上了一辆迎面开来的车。 **7** N-COUNT If you talk about the other **side** of a town, a country, or the world, you mean a part of the town, the country, or the world that is very far from where you are. (城镇、国家或世界的) 一端 ❑ *He lives the other side of town.* 他住在城镇的另一端。 ❑ *He saw the ship that was to transport them to the other side of the world.* 他看到了那艘要把他们载往世界另一端的船。 **8** N-COUNT Your **sides** are the parts of your body between your front and your back, from under your arms to your hips. 肋部 ❑ *His arms were limp at his sides.* 他的手臂无力地垂在两侧。 **9** N-COUNT If someone is **by** your **side** or **at** your **side**, they stay near you and give you comfort or support. 身边 ❑ *He was constantly at his wife's side.* 他那时一直陪伴在他妻子身边。 ❑ *He calls me 20 times a day and needs me by his side in the evening.* 他一天给我打20次电话，晚上还需要我陪在他身边。 **10** N-COUNT The two **sides** of something flat, for example, a piece of paper, are its two flat surfaces. You can also refer to one side of a piece of paper filled with writing as one **side** of writing. (纸张等的) 一面 ❑ *The new copiers only copy onto one side of the paper.* 这批新复印机只能复印到单面纸上。 ❑ *Fry the chops until brown on both sides.* 把排骨的两面煎成棕色。 **11** N-COUNT One **side** of a tape or record is what you can hear or record if you play the tape or record from beginning to end without turning it over. (磁带或唱片的) 一面 ❑ *We want to hear side A.* 我们想听A面。 **12** ADJ **Side** is used to describe things that are not the main or most important ones of their kind. 次要的 [ADJ n] ❑ *She slipped in and out of the theater by a side door.* 她从侧门溜进去又溜出了那家剧院。

❷ side ♦♦♦ /saɪd/ (**sides, siding, sided**) **1** N-COUNT The different **sides** in a war, argument, or negotiation are the groups of people who are opposing each other. (战争、争论或谈判中的) 一方 ❑ *Both sides appealed for a new ceasefire.* 双方都呼吁新一轮的停火。 ❑ *Any solution must be acceptable to all sides.* 任何解决方案都必须使各方能接受。 **2** N-COUNT The different **sides of** an argument or deal are the different points of view or positions involved in it. (争论或交易中的) 一方的观点 ❑ *His words drew sharp reactions from people on both sides of the issue.* 他的言辞激起了问题双方的强烈反应。 **3** V-I If one person or country **sides with** another, they support them in an argument or a war. If people or countries **side against** another person or country, they support each other against them. 支持；站在一起反对 ❑ *There has been much speculation that they might be siding with the rebels.* 有很多猜测说他们可能会支持叛乱者们。 **4** N-COUNT In sports, a **side** is a team. 运动队 [BRIT] **5** N-COUNT A particular **side of** something such as a situation or someone's character is one aspect of it. 方面 ❑ *He is in charge of the civilian side of the UN mission.* 他在联合国使团中负责平民方面的事务。 **6** N-COUNT The **mother's side** and the **father's side** of your family are your mother's relatives and your father's relatives. 家系；血统 ❑ *So was your father's side more well off?* 那么你父亲那边的亲戚以前更富裕？

❸ side ♦♦♦ /saɪd/ (**sides**)
➪ **Please look at meanings 11 – 14 to see if the expression you are looking for is shown under another headword.** **1** PHRASE If two people or things are **side by side**, they are next to each other. 并排 ❑ *We sat side by side on two wicker seats.* 我们并排坐在两张柳条椅上。 **2** PHRASE If people work or live **side by side**, they work or live closely together in a friendly way. 和睦相处 ❑ *...areas where different nationalities have lived side by side for centuries.* …不同民族的人和睦相处了几个世纪的地区。 **3** PHRASE If something moves **from side to side**, it moves repeatedly to the left and to the right. 左右来回 ❑ *She was shaking her head from side to side.* 她那时正左右来回摇着头。 **4** PHRASE If you are **on** someone's **side**, you are supporting them in an argument or a war. (在争论或战争中) 支持 ❑ *He has the Democrats on his side.* 他有民主党人的支持。 **5** PHRASE If something is **on** your **side** or if you have it **on** your **side**, it helps you when you are trying to achieve something. 对你有利 ❑ *The weather is rather on our side.* 这天气对我们很有利。 **6** PHRASE If you say that something is **on the** small **side**, you are saying politely that you think it is slightly too small. If you say that someone is **on the** young **side**, you are saying politely that you think they are slightly too young. 稍有点大或稍有点小等 [POLITENESS] ❑ *He's quiet and a bit on the shy side.* 他很安静，稍微有点害羞。 **7** PHRASE If someone does something **on the side**, they do it in addition to their main work. 兼职 ❑ *...ways of making a little bit of money on the side.* …靠兼职赚点钱的方法。 **8** PHRASE If you **put** something **to one side** or **put** it **on one side**, you temporarily ignore it in order to concentrate on something else. 将某事暂时搁置一边 ❑ *He can now concentrate on a project he'd originally put to one side.* 他现在能集中做他以前暂时搁置一边的一个项目了。 **9** PHRASE If you **take** someone **to one side** or **draw** them **to one side**, you speak to them privately, usually in order to give them advice or a warning. 私下劝告某人 ❑ *He took Sabrina to one side and told her about the safe.* 他把萨博莉娜叫到了一边，私下告诉了她有关安全的事项。 **10** PHRASE If you **take sides** or **take** someone's **side** in an argument or war, you support one of the sides against the other. (在争论或战争中) 支持一方 ❑ *We cannot take sides in a civil war.* 内战中，我们不能支持任何一方。 **11** **the other side of the coin** → see **coin** **12** **to err on the side of** something → see **err** **13** **to be on the safe side** → see **safe** **14** someone's **side of the story** → see **story**

side-effect (**side-effects**) also **side effect** **1** N-COUNT The **side-effects** of a drug are the effects, usually bad ones, that the drug has on you in addition to its function of curing illness or pain. (药物的) 副作用 ❑ *Side-effects include nausea, tiredness, and dizziness.* 副作用包括呕吐、疲倦和头晕。 **2** N-COUNT A **side-effect of** a situation is something unplanned and usually unpleasant that happens in addition to the main effects of that situation. 附带后果 ❑ *One side effect of modern life is stress.* 现代生活的一个附带后果就是压力。

★ **side·line** /saɪdlaɪn/ (**sidelines, sidelining, sidelined**) **1** N-COUNT A **sideline** is something that you do in addition to your main job in order to earn extra money. 兼职 ❑ *It was quite a lucrative sideline.* 那是一份很赚钱的兼职工作。 **2** N-PLURAL The **sidelines** are the lines marking the long sides of the playing area, for example, on a football field or tennis court. (运动场地的) 边线 **3** N-PLURAL If you are **on the sidelines** in a situation, you do not influence events at all, either because you have chosen not to be involved, or because other people have not involved you. 置身事外 ❑ *France no longer wants to be left on the sidelines when critical decisions are made.* 法国再也不想在做出重大决定时被搁置一旁。 **4** V-T If someone or something **is sidelined**, they are made to seem unimportant and not included in what people are doing. 把…排除在外；使靠边 [usu passive] ❑ *For months he had been under pressure to resign and was about to be sidelined anyway.* 几个月以来他一直处在辞职的压力下，他无论如何都是要靠边站了。
→ see **football, soccer, tennis**

side road (**side roads**) N-COUNT A **side road** is a road which leads off a busier, more important road. 旁路

side·step /saɪdstɛp/ (**sidesteps, sidestepping, sidestepped**) also **side-step** V-T If you **sidestep** a problem, you avoid discussing it or dealing with it. 回避 (问题) ❑ *Rarely, if ever, does he sidestep a question.* 他很少回避问题。

side street (**side streets**) N-COUNT A **side street** is a quiet, often narrow street which leads off a busier street. (安静而狭窄的) 小街

side·walk /saɪdwɔk/ (**sidewalks**) N-COUNT A **sidewalk** is a path with a hard surface by the side of a road. 人行道 [AM]

in BRIT, use **pavement**

❑ *Two men and a woman were walking briskly down the sidewalk toward him.* 两个男子和一个女子正轻快地沿着人行道朝他走去。

side·ways /saɪdweɪz/ **1** ADV **Sideways** means from or toward the side of something or someone. 从一旁地；向一旁地 [ADV after v] ❑ *Piercey glanced sideways at her.* 皮尔西斜着眼看了她一下。 ❑ *The ladder blew sideways.* 那梯子从一旁倒下了。 ● ADJ **Sideways** is also an adjective. 从一旁的；向一旁的 [ADJ n] ❑ *Alfred shot him a sideways glance.* 艾尔弗雷德斜着眼看了他一下。 **2** ADV If you are moved **sideways** at work, you move to another job at the same level as your old job. 平级地 [ADV after v] ❑ *He would be moved sideways, rather than demoted.* 他会被平级调动，而非被降职。 ● ADJ **Sideways** is also an adjective. 平级的 [ADJ n] ❑ *...her recent sideways move.* …她最近的平级调动。

siege /siːdʒ/ (**sieges**) **1** N-COUNT A **siege** is a military or police operation in which soldiers or police surround a place in order to force the people there to come out or give up control of the place. 包围 [also "under" N] ❑ *We must do everything possible to lift the siege.* 我们必须尽一切可能解除包围。 **2** PHRASE If police, soldiers, or journalists **lay siege to** a place, they surround it in order to force the people there to come out or give up control of the place. 包围 ❑ *The rebels laid siege to the governor's residence.* 叛乱者们包围了那座总督官邸。

Word Partnership *siege* 的常用搭配：
PREP. **after** a siege, **during** a siege, **under** siege **1**
V. **end** a siege, **lift** a siege **1**

★ **sieve** /sɪv/ (**sieves, sieving, sieved**) **1** N-COUNT A **sieve** is a tool used for separating solids from liquids or larger pieces of something from smaller pieces. It consists of a metal or plastic ring with a wire or plastic net underneath, which the liquid or smaller pieces pass through. 筛子；过滤器 ❑ *Press the raspberries through a fine sieve to form a puree.* 用一把细筛子把黑莓压榨成浓汁。 **2** V-T When you **sieve** a substance, you put it through a sieve. 筛；过滤 ❑ *Cream the margarine in a small bowl, then sieve the powdered sugar into it.* 把人造黄油在小碗里搅成糊状，然后把糖粉筛入其中。

▲ **sift** /sɪft/ (**sifts, sifting, sifted**) **1** V-T If you **sift** a powder such as flour or sand, you put it through a sieve in order to remove large pieces or lumps. 筛（面粉、沙子等）❑ *Sift the flour and baking powder into a medium-sized mixing bowl.* 把面粉和发酵粉筛到一个中号搅拌碗中。 **2** V-T/V-I If you **sift through** something such as evidence, you examine it thoroughly. 细查 ❑ *Police officers have continued to sift through the wreckage following yesterday's bomb attack.* 警官们继续细查了昨天炸弹袭击后留下的残骸。

sigh ♦◇◇ /saɪ/ (**sighs, sighing, sighed**) **1** V-I When you **sigh**, you let out a deep breath, as a way of expressing feelings such as disappointment, tiredness, or pleasure. 叹气 ❑ *Michael sighed wearily.* 迈克尔疲惫地叹了口气。 ❑ *Roberta sighed with relief.* 罗伯塔松了口气。 ● N-COUNT **Sigh** is also a noun. 叹气 ❑ *She kicked off her shoes with a sigh.* 她叹着气踢掉了鞋子。 **2** PHRASE If people breathe or heave a **sigh of relief**, they feel happy that something unpleasant has not happened or is no longer happening. 松了口气 ❑ *With monetary mayhem now retreating into memory, European countries can breathe a collective sigh of relief.* 随着金融混乱已成往事，欧洲国家全都可以松口气了。

Word Partnership *sigh* 的常用搭配：
ADJ. **collective** sigh, **deep** sigh, **long** sigh **1**
V. **breathe** a sigh, **give** a sigh, **hear** a sigh, **heave** a sigh, **let out** a sigh **1** **2**

S

sight ♦♦◇ /saɪt/ (**sights, sighting, sighted**) **1** N-UNCOUNT Someone's **sight** is their ability to see. 视力 ❑ *My sight is failing, and I can't see to read any more.* 我的视力正在下降，不能再看书了。 **2** N-SING **The sight of** something is the act of seeing it or an occasion on which you see it. 看见 ❑ *I faint at the sight of blood.* 我一看见血就晕。 **3** N-COUNT A **sight** is something that you see. 景象 ❑ *The practice of hanging clothes across the street is a common sight in many parts of the city.* 在大街上晾晒衣服在该市的许多地区是很常见的景象。 **4** V-T If you **sight** someone or something, you suddenly see them, often briefly. (在一瞬间) 突然看见 ❑ *The security forces sighted a group of young men that had crossed the border.* 安全部队在一瞬间突然看见了一群越过了边境的年轻人。 **5** N-PLURAL **The sights** are the places that are interesting to see and that are often visited by tourists. 名胜；风景 ❑ *We'd toured the sights of Paris.* 我们已游览了巴黎的名胜。 **6** → see also **sighting** **7** PHRASE If you **catch sight of** someone, you suddenly see them, often briefly. 瞬间内突然看见某人 ❑ *Then he caught sight of her small black velvet hat in the crowd.* 随后他突然看见她的黑色丝绒小帽在人群中闪过。 **8** PHRASE If you say that something seems to have certain characteristics **at first sight**, you mean that it appears to have the features you describe when you first see it but later it is found to be different. 乍一看 ❑ *The theory is not as simple as you might think at first sight.* 这个理论并不像你乍看时想到的那么简单。 **9** PHRASE If something is **in sight** or **within sight**, you can see it. If it is **out of sight**, you cannot see it. 看得见/看不见 ❑ *The sandy beach was in sight.* 那片沙滩映入眼帘。 ❑ *The Atlantic coast is within sight of the hotel.* 从那个酒店可以看见大西洋的海岸线。 **10** PHRASE If a result or a decision is **in sight** or **within sight**, it is likely to happen within a short time. 即将发生 ❑ *An agreement on many aspects of trade policy was in sight.* 有关贸易政策诸多方面的一项协议即将签订了。 **11** PHRASE If you **lose sight of** an important aspect of something, you no longer pay attention to it because you are worrying about less important things. 忽略 ❑ *In some cases, U.S. industry has lost sight of customer needs in designing products.* 在一些情况下，美国工业在设计产品时忽略了顾客的需求。 **12** PHRASE If someone is ordered to do something **on sight**, they have to do it without delay, as soon as a person or thing is seen. 一看见…就 ❑ *Troops shot anyone suspicious on sight.* 军队一见可疑的人就开枪。 **13** PHRASE If you **set your sights on** something, you decide that you want it and try hard to get it. 以某事为奋斗目标 ❑ *They have set their sights on the world record.* 他们把目标瞄向了世界纪录。 **14** PHRASE If you **have** something **in your sights**, you are trying hard to achieve it, and you have a good chance of success. If you **have** someone **in your sights**, you are determined to catch, defeat, or overcome them. 志在取得某事；决意抓获、打败或征服某人 ❑ *The Giants' slugger also has fourth place in his sights, needing 13 homers to move past Frank Robinson's 586.* 巨人队的强击手也对第4名志在必得，需要击出13个本垒打才能超过弗兰克・罗宾逊的586分。 ❑ *Is this knowledge of yours the reason the murderer now has you in his sights?* 就是因为你知道的这些事凶犯才在追杀你吗？

Word Partnership *sight* 的常用搭配：
ADJ. **common** sight, **familiar** sight, **welcome** sight **3**
in plain sight **9**
V. **catch** sight **of** *someone/something* **7**
come into sight, **keep** *someone/something* **in** sight **9** **10**
drop out of sight, **lose** sight **of** *something* **9** **11**
N. **the end is in** sight **10**

sight·ing /saɪtɪŋ/ (**sightings**) N-COUNT A **sighting of** something, especially something unusual or unexpected is an occasion on which it is seen. 见到 ❑ *...the sighting of a rare sea bird at Lundy island.* …在隆地岛见到一种珍稀海鸟。

sight·see·ing /saɪtsiːɪŋ/ N-UNCOUNT If you go **sightseeing** or do some **sightseeing**, you travel around visiting the interesting places that tourists usually visit. 观光 ❑ *...a day's sight-seeing in Venice.* …在威尼斯的一日游。
→ see **city**

sign ♦♦♦ /saɪn/ (**signs, signing, signed**) **1** N-COUNT A **sign** is a mark or shape that always has a particular meaning, for example, in mathematics or music. 符号 ❑ *Equations are generally written with an equal sign.* 等式通常用等号来写。 **2** N-COUNT A **sign** is a movement of your arms, hands, or head which is intended to have a particular meaning. 姿势；手势 ❑ *They gave Lavalle the thumbs-up sign.* 他们给拉瓦列做了一个竖起大拇指的手势。 **3** V-T If you **sign**, you communicate with someone using sign language. If a program or performance **is signed**, someone uses sign language so that deaf people can understand it. 打手势；(节目或表演) 配手势语 ❑ *All programs will be either "signed" or subtitled.* 所有的节目都配有手势语或者字幕。 **4** N-COUNT A **sign** is a piece of wood, metal, or plastic with words or pictures on it. Signs give you information about something, or give you a warning or an instruction. 指示牌 ❑ *...a sign saying that the highway was closed because of snow.* …一个写着公路因大雪封闭的指示牌。 **5** N-VAR If there is a **sign of** something, there is something which shows that it exists or is happening. 迹象；征兆 ❑ *They are prepared to hand back a hundred prisoners of war a day as a sign of good will.* 作为一种友好的表示，他们准备一天遣返100名战犯。 ❑ *His face and movements rarely betrayed a sign of nerves.* 他的表情和行为很少流露出紧张的迹象。 **6** V-T When you **sign** a document, you write your name on it, usually at the end or in a special space. You do this to indicate that you have written the document, that you agree with what is written, or that you were present as a witness. 在…上签名；签署 ❑ *World leaders are expected to sign a treaty pledging to increase environmental protection.* 人们期望世界领导人们能签署一份承诺加强环境保护的条约。 **7** V-T/V-I If an organization **signs** someone or if someone **signs** for an organization, they sign a contract agreeing to work for that organization for a specified period of time. 签约雇用；签约受雇 ❑ *The Minnesota Vikings signed Herschel Walker from the Dallas Cowboys.* 明尼苏达维京人队签约雇用了达拉斯牛仔队的

赫舍尔·沃克。**8** N-COUNT In astrology, a **sign** or a **sign of the zodiac** is one of the twelve areas into which the heavens are divided. 星座 ❏ *The new moon takes place in your opposite sign of Libra on the 15th.* 15日新月会出现在天秤座的对面。 **9** → see also **signing**
10 PHRASE If you say that there is **no sign of** someone, you mean that they have not yet arrived, although you are expecting them to come. 不见某人的踪影 ❏ *The train was on time, but there was no sign of my Finnish friend.* 火车准时到达了，但还没有见到我芬兰朋友的踪影。

▸ **sign for** PHRASAL VERB If you **sign for** something, you officially state that you have received it, by signing a form or book. 签收 ❏ *When the letter carrier delivers your order, check the carton before signing for it.* 当那个邮递员将你订购的货物送到时，签收之前检查那个包装盒。

▸ **sign in** PHRASAL VERB If you **sign in**, you officially indicate that you have arrived at a hotel or club by signing a book or form. (在旅馆或俱乐部) 签到 ❏ *I signed in and crunched across the gravel to my room.* 我签到后便嘎吱嘎吱地穿过砾石路走到我的房间。

▸ **sign over** PHRASAL VERB If you **sign** something **over**, you sign documents that give someone else property, possessions, or rights that were previously yours. 签字转让 (财产或权利) ❏ *Two years ago, he signed over his art collection to the New York Metropolitan Museum of Art.* 两年前，他签字把他的艺术收藏品转让给了纽约大都会艺术博物馆。

▸ **sign up** PHRASAL VERB If you **sign up** for an organization or if an organization **signs** you **up**, you sign a contract officially agreeing to do a job or course of study. 和…签约；报名参加 (课程) ❏ *He signed up as a flight attendant with Korean Air.* 他与大韩航空公司签了约，当机乘员。

Thesaurus *sign* 另参见：

N.	nod, signal, wave **2**
V.	authorize, autograph, endorse **6**

Word Partnership *sign* 的常用搭配：

V.	**give a** sign **2** **hang a** sign, **read a** sign **4** **see a** sign **4 5** **show no** sign **of** *something* **5** **refuse to** sign **6** **see no** sign **of** *someone/something* **10**
N.	sign **on a door**, sign **over an entrance**, **neon** sign, **stop** sign, sign **in a window** **4** sign **an agreement**, sign **an autograph**, sign **a contract**, sign **legislation**, sign *your* **name**, sign **a petition**, sign **a treaty** **6**
ADJ.	**bad/good** sign, **encouraging** sign, **positive** sign, **a sure** sign, **warning** sign **5**
PREP.	sign **of progress**, sign **of the times**, sign **of trouble**, sign **of weakness** **5**

sig·nal ♦◇◇ /sɪgnəl/ (**signals, signaling** or **signalling, signaled** or **signalled**) **1** N-COUNT A **signal** is a gesture, sound, or action which is intended to give a particular message to the person who sees or hears it. 信号 ❏ *They fired three distress signals.* 他们发射了3次遇难求救信号。 ❏ *As soon as it was dark, Mrs. Evans gave the signal.* 天一黑，埃文斯夫人就发出了那个信号。 **2** V-T/V-I If you **signal to** someone, you make a gesture or sound in order to send them a particular message. (打手势或发声音) 向…示意；发信号 ❏ *Mandy started after him, signaling to Jesse to follow.* 曼迪开始追赶他，示意杰西跟上。 ❏ *She signaled to Ted that she was moving forward.* 她向特德示意她要向前走。 **3** N-COUNT If an event or action is a **signal of** something, it suggests that this thing exists or is going to happen. 信号 ❏ *Kurdish leaders saw the visit as an important signal of support.* 库尔德领导人把这次访问看作是表示支持的重要信号。 **4** V-T If someone or something **signals** an event, they suggest that the event is happening or likely to happen. 表示 ❏ *He seemed to be signaling important shifts in U.S. government policy.* 他似乎在表示美国政府的政策将会有些重大变化。 **5** N-COUNT A **signal** is a piece of equipment beside a railroad, which indicates to train drivers whether they should stop the train or not. 铁路的信号灯 ❏ *A signal failure contributed to the crash.* 信号灯故障导致了这次撞车事故。 **6** N-COUNT A **signal** is a series of radio waves, light waves, or changes in electrical current which may carry information. (传输信息的无线电、光波或电流) 信号 ❏ *...high-frequency radio signals.* …高频无线电信号。
→ see **cellphone, television**

Word Partnership *signal* 的常用搭配：

V.	**give a** signal **1 3** **send a** signal **1 3 6**
ADJ.	**wrong** signal **1 3** **clear** signal, **strong** signal **1 3 6** **important** signal **3**

sig·na·tory /sɪgnətɔri/ (**signatories**) N-COUNT The **signatories** of an official document are the people, organizations, or countries that have signed it. 签约人；签约组织；签约国 [FORMAL] ❏ *Both countries are signatories to the Nuclear Non-Proliferation Treaty.* 两个国家都是《防止核扩散条约》的签约国。

sig·na·ture /sɪgnətʃər, -tʃʊər/ (**signatures**) N-COUNT Your **signature** is your name, written in your own characteristic way, often at the end of a document to indicate that you wrote the document or that you agree with what it says. 签名 ❏ *I was writing my signature at the bottom of the page.* 我当时正把我的签名写在本页的底部。

sig·nifi·cance /sɪgnɪfɪkəns/ N-UNCOUNT The **significance** of something is the importance that it has, usually because it will have an effect on a situation or shows something about a situation. 重要性；意义 ❏ *Ideas about the social significance of religion have changed over time.* 有关宗教的社会意义的观念已随时间的流逝发生了改变。

Word Partnership *significance* 的常用搭配：

ADJ.	**cultural** significance, **great** significance, **historic/historical** significance, **political** significance, **religious** significance
V.	**downplay the** significance **of** *something*, **explain the** significance **of** *something*, **understand the** significance **of** *something*

sig·nifi·cant ♦♦◇ /sɪgnɪfɪkənt/ **1** ADJ A **significant** amount or effect is large enough to be important or affect a situation to a noticeable degree. 重大的；显著的 ❏ *Most 11-year-olds are not encouraged to develop reading skills; a small but significant number are illiterate.* 大多数11岁的儿童没有被鼓励去培养阅读技能。有为数不多、但足以引起人们注意的数目的儿童是文盲。● **sig·nifi·cant·ly** ADV 重大地；显著地 ❏ *The number of Senators now supporting him had increased significantly.* 现在支持他的参议员人数已经显著增加了。 **2** ADJ A **significant** fact, event, or thing is one that is important or shows something. 重要的；说明问题的 ❏ *I think it was significant that he never knew his own father.* 我想他从不了解自己的父亲这一点就很说明问题。● **sig·nifi·cant·ly** ADV 重要地；说明问题地 ❏ *Significantly, the company recently opened a huge store in Atlanta.* 重要的是，这家公司最近在亚特兰大开了一家大商店。

Thesaurus *significant* 另参见：

ADJ.	big, important, large; (*ant.*) insignificant, minor, small **1**

★ **sig·ni·fy** /sɪgnɪfaɪ/ (**signifies, signifying, signified**) **1** V-T If an event, a sign, or a symbol **signifies** something, it is a sign of that thing or represents that thing. 表示；意味着 ❏ *These were not the only changes that signified the end of boyhood.* 这些不是表示男孩时代已结束的惟一变化。 **2** V-T If you **signify** something, you make a sign or gesture in order to communicate a particular meaning. (用符号或手势) 表达 ❏ *Two jurors signified their dissent.* 两个陪审员表达了他们的异议。

sign·ing /saɪnɪŋ/ (**signings**) **1** N-UNCOUNT The **signing of** a document is the act of writing your name to indicate that you agree with what it says or to say that you have been present to witness other people writing their signature. 签署 ❏ *Spain's top priority is the signing of the treaty.* 西班牙的当务之急就是这项条约的签署。 **2** N-COUNT A **signing** is someone who has recently signed a contract agreeing to play for a sports team or work for a record company. (运动队或唱片公司的) 签约者 [usu with supp] ❏ *...the salary paid to the club's latest signing.* …付给俱乐部新近签约者的薪水。 **3** N-UNCOUNT The **signing of** a player by a sports team or a group by a record company is the act of drawing up a legal document setting out the length and terms of the association between them. (与运动队或唱片公司) 签约 ❏ *The ranks of professional tennis swelled with the signing of Bobby Riggs.* 博比·里格斯的签约加盟使参加职业网球运动的人数增加了。 **4** N-UNCOUNT **Signing** is the use of sign language to communicate with someone who is deaf. 手势语的使用 ❏ *The two deaf actors converse solely in signing.* 两位聋哑演员只靠打手势语交谈。

S

Picture Dictionary sign language

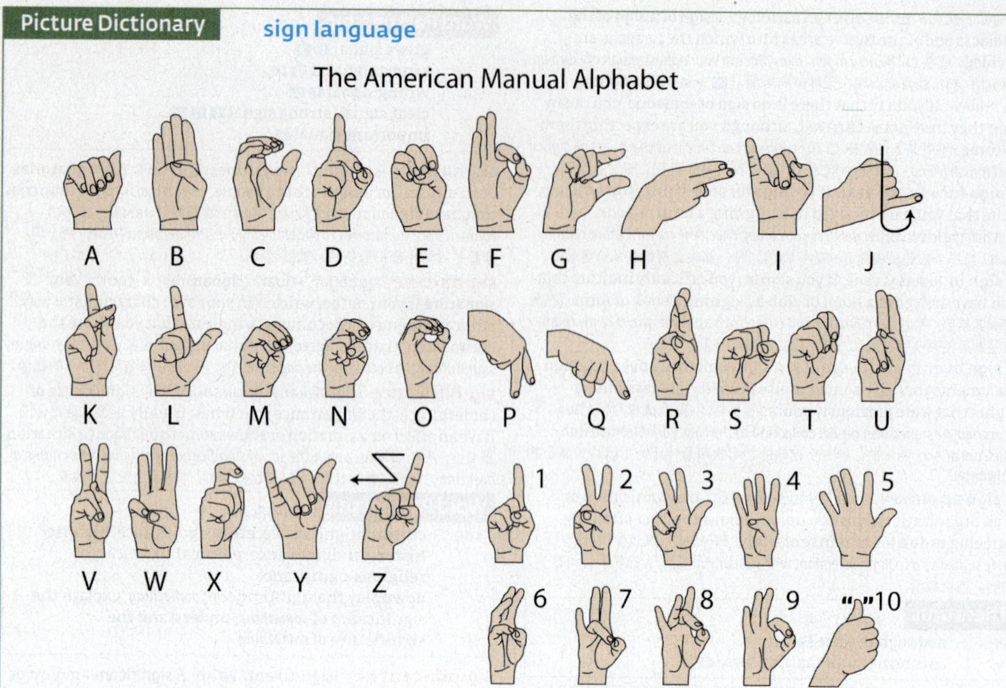

sign lan·guage (**sign languages**) N-VAR **Sign language** is movements of your hands and arms used to communicate. There are several official systems of sign language, used, for example, by deaf people. Movements are also sometimes invented by people when they want to communicate with someone who does not speak the same language. 手势语 ❑ *Her son used sign language to tell her what happened.* 她的儿子用手势语告诉她发生的事情。

→ see Picture Dictionary: **sign language**

★ **sign·post** /saɪnpoʊst/ (**signposts**) N-COUNT A **signpost** is a sign where roads meet that tells you which direction to go in to reach a particular place or different places. 路标 ❑ *Turn off at the signpost for the East 71st Street exit.* 在指向东第71街出口的路标处转弯。

sign·post·ed /saɪnpoʊstɪd/ ADJ A place or route that is **signposted** has signposts beside the road to show the way. (地方或路线) 有路标的 ❑ *The entrance is well signposted and is in Marbury Road.* 入口有清楚的路标，位于马伯里路。

Sikh /sik/ (**Sikhs**) N-COUNT A **Sikh** is a person who follows the Indian religion of Sikhism. 锡克教徒 ❑ *The rise of racism concerns Sikhs because they are such a visible minority.* 种族主义的抬头使锡克教徒很担心，因为他们是如此明显的一个少数民族。 ❑ *...a Sikh temple.* …一座锡克教寺庙。

Sikh·ism /sikɪzəm/ N-UNCOUNT **Sikhism** is an Indian religion which separated from Hinduism in the sixteenth century and which teaches that there is only one God. 锡克教(印度的一种宗教，于16世纪从印度教分离出来，信奉一神论)

si·lence ♦◇◇ /saɪləns/ (**silences, silencing, silenced**) **1** N-VAR If there is **silence**, nobody is speaking. 沉默 ❑ *They stood in silence.* 他们默默地站着。 ❑ *He never lets those long silences develop during dinner.* 他在晚餐时从不会让长时间的沉默出现。 **2** N-UNCOUNT Someone's **silence** about something is their failure or refusal to speak to other people about it. 缄默 ❑ *The district court ruled that Popper's silence in court today should be entered as a plea of not guilty.* 该区法院裁决波珀今天在法庭中的缄默应被看作是进行无罪抗辩。 ● PHRASE If someone **breaks** their **silence** about something, they talk about something that they have not talked about before or for a long time. 打破沉默；开口讲话 **3** V-T If someone **silences** you, they stop you from expressing opinions that they do not agree with. 制止 (发表不同意见) ❑ *Like other tyrants, he tried to silence anyone who spoke out against him.* 像其他暴君一样，他试图压制任何公开反对他的人。

S

Word Partnership *silence* 的常用搭配：

ADJ.	**awkward** silence, **complete** silence, **long** silence, **sudden** silence, **total** silence **1**
V.	silence **falls**, **listen in** silence, **observe a** silence, **sit in** silence, **watch** *something* **in** silence **1** **break a/*your*** silence **2**

si·lent ♦◇◇ /saɪlənt/ **1** ADJ Someone who is **silent** is not speaking. 沉默的 [v-link ADJ] ❑ *Trish was silent because she was reluctant to put her thoughts into words.* 特里希一言不发，因为她不愿意把她的想法说出来。 ❑ *He spoke no English and was completely silent during the visit.* 他不会说英语，在整个参观中一言不发。 ● **si·lent·ly** ADV 沉默地 [ADV with v] ❑ *She and Ned sat silently for a moment, absorbing the peace of the lake.* 她和内德默默地坐了片刻，享受着那湖泊的宁静。 **2** ADJ A place that is **silent** is completely quiet, with no sound at all. Something that is **silent** makes no sound at all. 寂静的 ❑ *The room was silent except for the TV.* 除了电视的声音，那房间里寂静无声。 ● **si·lent·ly** ADV 寂静地 [ADV with v] ❑ *Strange shadows moved silently in the almost permanent darkness.* 奇怪的影子在几乎永远的黑暗中静静地移动。 **3** ADJ A **silent** movie has pictures usually accompanied by music but does not have the actors' voices or any other sounds. (电影) 无声的 [ADJ n] ❑ *...one of the famous silent films of Charlie Chaplin.* …查理・卓别林著名的无声电影之一。 **4** PHRASE If you **give** someone **the silent treatment**, you do not speak to them for a period of time because you are annoyed at something they have done. 长期不跟某人说话 ❑ *He fully expected his mother to give him the silent treatment.* 他完全预料得到他母亲会长时间不跟他讲话。

Thesaurus *silent* 另参见：

ADJ.	hushed, mute, speechless **1** noiseless, quiet **2**

Word Partnership *silent* 的常用搭配：

V.	**go** silent, **keep** silent, **remain** silent, **sit** silent **1**
N.	silent **prayer**, silent **reading** **1**

si·lent part·ner (**silent partners**) N-COUNT A **silent partner** is a person who provides some of the capital for a business but who does not take an active part in managing the business. 隐名合伙人 [AM, BUSINESS]

in BRIT, use **sleeping partner**

❑ *...firms run by his friends in which he was a silent partner.* …由他朋友经营的公司，他是这些公司的隐名合伙人。

sil·hou·ette /sɪlut/ (**silhouettes**) **1** N-COUNT A **silhouette** is the solid dark shape that you see when someone or something has a bright light or pale background behind them. (强光或浅色背景衬托下的) 黑色轮廓 ❑ *The dark silhouette of the castle ruins stood out boldly against the fading light.* 城堡遗迹的黑暗轮廓在暗淡光线下显得格外突出。 **2** N-COUNT The **silhouette** of something is the outline that it has, which often helps you to recognize it. 轮廓 ❑ *...the distinctive silhouette of the Manhattan skyline.* …曼哈顿天际线的清晰轮廓。

sili·con /sɪlɪkən/ N-UNCOUNT **Silicon** is an element that is found in sand and in minerals such as quartz and granite. Silicon is used to make parts of computers and other electronic equipment. 硅 ❑ *The new chip will be made from a piece of silicon about the size of a postage stamp.* 这种新的芯片将由大约邮票大小的一块硅片制成。

> **Silicon Valley** is an area in the US, near San Francisco, where the computer industry dominates the local economy. These days the name may also be given to other locations where computer companies are gathered.

sili·con chip (**silicon chips**) N-COUNT A **silicon chip** is a very small piece of silicon inside a computer. It has electronic circuits on it and can hold large quantities of information or perform mathematical or logical operations. 芯片 ❑ *Today's silicon chip-based computers can't come close.* 现今的基于芯片的计算机根本比不上。

sili·cone /sɪlɪkoʊn/ N-UNCOUNT **Silicone** is a tough artificial substance made from silicon, which is used to make polishes, and also used in cosmetic surgery and plastic surgery. 硅酮 ❑ *...women who suffered health problems from silicone breast implants that leak.* …由于硅酮乳房植入物泄漏而遭受健康问题折磨的妇女们。

silk /sɪlk/ (**silks**) N-MASS **Silk** is a substance which is made into smooth fine cloth and sewing thread. You can also refer to this cloth or thread as **silk**. 丝绸；丝线 ❑ *They continued to get their silks from China.* 他们继续从中国获取丝绸。 ❑ *Pauline wore a silk dress with a strand of pearls.* 保利娜穿了一条带有一串珍珠的丝绸连衣裙。

silky /sɪlki/ (**silkier, silkiest**) ADJ If something has a **silky** texture, it is smooth, soft, and shiny, like silk. 丝质的；柔软光洁的 ❑ *...dresses in seductively silky fabrics.* …诱人的丝绸般的连衣裙。

sill /sɪl/ (**sills**) N-COUNT A **sill** is a shelf along the bottom edge of a window, either inside or outside a building. 窗台 ❑ *Whitlock was perched on the sill of the room's only window.* 惠特洛克栖息在房里惟一窗子的窗台上。

sil·ly /sɪli/ (**sillier, silliest**) ADJ If you say that someone or something is **silly**, you mean that they are foolish, childish, or ridiculous. 愚蠢的；幼稚的；荒唐的 ❑ *My best friend tells me that I am silly to be upset about this.* 我最好的朋友说我为此事心烦太傻了。 ❑ *I thought it would be silly to be too rude at that stage.* 我觉得处在那个阶段上太过粗鲁是很幼稚的。

silt /sɪlt/ N-UNCOUNT **Silt** is fine sand, soil, or mud which is carried along by a river. 泥沙 ❑ *The lake was almost solid with silt and vegetation.* 这个湖几乎填满了泥沙和植被。
→ see **erosion**

sil·ver ♦◇◇ /sɪlvər/ (**silvers**) **1** N-UNCOUNT **Silver** is a valuable pale gray metal that is used for making jewelry and ornaments. 银 ❑ *...a hand-crafted brooch made from silver.* …一枚银制的手工胸针。 ❑ *...amber earrings set in silver.* …镶于银中的琥珀耳环。 **2** N-UNCOUNT **Silver** consists of coins that are made from silver or that look like silver. 银币 ❑ *...the basement where $150,000 in silver was buried.* …埋着15万美元银币的地下室。 **3** N-UNCOUNT You can use **silver** to refer to all the things in a house that are made of silver, especially the flatware and dishes. 银器 [also "the" N] ❑ *He beat the rugs and polished the silver.* 他拍打了地毯，擦亮了银器。 **4** COLOR **Silver** is used to describe things that are shiny and pale gray in color. 银色的 ❑ *He had thick silver hair which needed cutting.* 他有一头需要修剪的浓密银发。
→ see **mineral, money, silverware**

sil·ver med·al (**silver medals**) N-COUNT If you win a **silver medal**, you come second in a competition, especially a sports contest, and are given a medal made of silver as a prize. (尤指在体育比赛中获得的) 银牌 ❑ *Gillingham won the silver medal in the 200 meters at Seoul.* 吉林厄姆在汉城获得了200米的银牌。

> **Word Link** *ware ≈ merchandise : hardware, silverware, software*

silver·ware /sɪlvərwɛər/ N-UNCOUNT You can use **silverware** to refer to all the things in a house that are made of silver, especially the flatware and dishes. 银器；银餐具 ❑ *There was a serving spoon missing when Nina put the silverware back in its box.* 当妮娜将银餐具装回盒子中时，少了一把分菜用的匙子。
→ see Word Web: **silverware**

sil·very /sɪlvəri/ ADJ **Silvery** things look like silver or are the color of silver. 似银的；银色的 ❑ *My father is a small, intense man with silvery hair.* 我父亲是个热情的人，小个子，满头银发。

sim /sɪm/ (**sims**) N-COUNT A **sim** is a computer game that simulates an activity such as playing a sport or flying an aircraft. 电脑模拟游戏 [COMPUTING]

SIM card /sɪm kɑrd/ (**SIM cards**) N-COUNT A **SIM card** is a microchip in a cell phone that connects it to a particular phone network. **SIM** is an abbreviation for "Subscriber Identity Module." SIM卡

simi·lar ♦♦◇ /sɪmɪlər/ ADJ If one thing is **similar to** another, or if two things are **similar**, they have features that are the same. 相似的 ❑ *...a savory cake with a texture similar to that of carrot cake.* …一块口感跟胡萝卜饼差不多的咸味饼。 ❑ *The accident was similar to one that happened in 1973.* 这起事故跟1973年发生的那起相似。

> **Word Link** *simil ≈ similar : assimilate, dissimilar, similarity*

simi·lar·ity /sɪmɪlærɪti/ (**similarities**) **1** N-UNCOUNT If there is a **similarity between** two or more things, they are similar to each other. 相似；类似 ❑ *...the astonishing similarity between my brother and my first-born son.* …我弟弟和我大儿子的惊人相似。 ❑ *There was a very basic similarity in our philosophy.* 我们的人生哲学在根本上很相似。 **2** N-COUNT **Similarities** are features that things have which make them similar to each other. 相似之处 ❑ *There were significant similarities between mother and son.* 母子间有着极其相似的地方。

simi·lar·ly /sɪmɪlərli/ **1** ADV You use **similarly** to say that something is similar to something else. 类似地 ❑ *Most of the men who now gathered around him again were similarly dressed.* 现在重新聚在他周围的大多数人穿着差不多的衣服。 **2** ADV You use **similarly** when mentioning a fact or situation that is similar to the one you have just mentioned. 相同地；同样地 [ADV with cl] ❑ *Same-sex marriages are not recognized. Similarly, marriages of close relatives are not legal.* 同性婚姻得不到承认。同样，近亲结婚也不合法。

S

Word Web silverware

Anthropologists tell us that the first knives were simple cutting instruments made from flint that were first used about two million years ago. The first modern **knife** with a metal **blade** and wooden **handle** appeared about 1000 years BC. During the Middle Ages, people carried their own eating knives with them because no one provided knives for guests. The earliest **spoons** were made from scooped-out bones or shells tied to the end of sticks. Later the Romans introduced bronze and **silver** spoons. The earliest **forks** had only two tines and were used only for carving and serving meat.

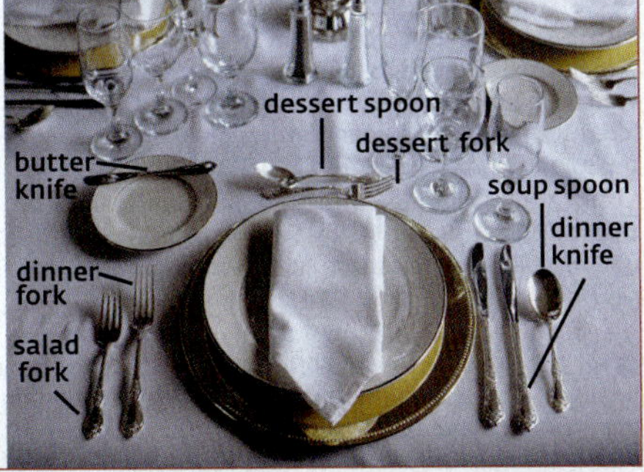

▲**sim·mer** /sɪmər/ (**simmers, simmering, simmered**) **1** V-T/V-I When you **simmer** food or when it **simmers**, you cook it by keeping it at boiling point or just below boiling point. 用文火炖；煨 ❑ *Make an infusion by boiling and simmering the rhubarb and camomile together.* 煮炖大黄和黄春菊来熬成浓汁。● N-SING **Simmer** is also a noun. 炖；煨 ❑ *Combine the stock, whole onion and peppercorns in a pan and bring to a simmer.* 把高汤料、整个洋葱和胡椒粒拌入平底锅内，然后用文火炖。 **2** V-I If a conflict or a quarrel **simmers**, it does not actually happen for a period of time, but eventually builds up to the point where it does. (冲突或争吵) 酝酿；趋于激化 ❑ *...bitter divisions that have simmered for more than half a century.* …酝酿了半个多世纪的严重分歧。

sim·ple ♦♦◊ /sɪmpᵊl/ (**simpler, simplest**) **1** ADJ If you describe something as **simple**, you mean that it is not complicated, and is therefore easy to understand. 简单的；简明的 ❑ *...simple pictures and diagrams.* …简明的图片和图表。❑ *...pages of simple advice on filling in your tax form.* …几页有关填写纳税表格的简单建议。● **simp·ly** ADV 简单地 [ADV with v] ❑ *When applying for a visa extension state simply and clearly the reasons why you need an extension.* 申请签证续签时，简单明了地陈述你需要延期的理由。 **2** ADJ If you describe people or things as **simple**, you mean that they have all the basic or necessary things they require, but nothing extra. 简朴的；朴素的 ❑ *He ate a simple dinner of rice and beans.* 他吃了一顿米饭加豆子的简单晚餐。❑ *...the simple pleasures of childhood.* …童年纯朴的快乐。● **simp·ly** ADV 简朴地；朴素地 [ADV after v] ❑ *The living room is furnished simply with white wicker furniture and blue-and-white fabrics.* 起居室朴素地摆放着白柳条家具和蓝白相间的织物。 **3** ADJ If a problem is **simple** or if its solution is **simple**, the problem can be solved easily. 好办的；易解决的 ❑ *Some puzzles look difficult but are actually quite simple.* 有些谜看似很难，但实际上相当容易解开。 **4** ADJ A **simple** task is easy to do. 容易的；简易的 ❑ *The job itself had been simple enough.* 这工作本身一直就相当容易。● **simp·ly** ADV 简易地；容易地 [ADV after v] ❑ *We can do things that were not possible before, and they can be done simply.* 我们现在可以做以前不可能的事情，而且可以轻而易举地做成。 **5** ADJ You use **simple** to emphasize that the thing you are referring to is the only important or relevant reason for something. 纯粹的；完全的 [ADJ n] [EMPHASIS] ❑ *His refusal to talk was simple stubbornness.* 他拒绝交谈只是出于固执。 **6** ADJ In grammar, **simple** tenses are ones which are formed without an auxiliary verb "be," for example, "I dressed and went for a walk" and "This tastes nice." **Simple** verb groups are used especially to refer to completed actions, regular actions, and situations. Compare **continuous**. 简单的 (时态或动词词组) **7** → see also **simply**

Thesaurus *simple* 另参见：

ADJ.	clear, easy, understandable; *(ant.)* complicated **1** **3** **4** plain **2**

Word Partnership *simple* 的常用搭配：

N.	simple **concept**, simple **explanation**, simple **instructions**, simple **language**, simple **message**, simple **procedure**, simple **steps** **1** simple **life**, simple **pleasure** **2** simple **answer**, simple **question** **3** simple **matter**, simple **task**, simple **test** **3** **4** simple **fact** **5**
ADV.	**rather** simple **1**–**3** **fairly** simple, **pretty** simple, **quite** simple, **really** simple, **relatively** simple, **very** simple **1**–**4** simple **enough**, **so** simple **1** **3** **4**

sim·ple in·ter·est N-UNCOUNT **Simple interest** is interest that is calculated on an original sum of money and not also on interest which has previously been added to the sum. Compare **compound interest**. 单利 (参较**compound interest**) [BUSINESS] ❑ *...an investment that pays only simple interest.* …一项只付单利的投资。

sim·plic·ity /sɪmplɪsɪti/ N-UNCOUNT The **simplicity** of something is the fact that it is not complicated and can be understood or done easily. 简单；简明 ❑ *The apparent simplicity of his plot is deceptive.* 他的阴谋貌似简单，却具有欺骗性。

★**sim·pli·fi·ca·tion** /sɪmplɪfɪkeɪʃᵊn/ (**simplifications**) **1** N-COUNT You can use **simplification** to refer to the thing that is produced when you make something simpler or when you reduce it to its basic elements. 简化了的事物 ❑ *Like any such diagram, it is a simplification.* 正如任何此类图表，这是个简图。 **2** N-UNCOUNT **Simplification** is the act or process of making something simpler. 简化 ❑ *Everyone favors the simplification of court procedures.* 人人都赞成法庭程序的简化。

sim·pli·fy /sɪmplɪfaɪ/ (**simplifies, simplifying, simplified**) V-T If you **simplify** something, you make it easier to understand or you remove the things which make it complex. 简化 ❑ *Our aim is to simplify the complex social security system.* 我们的目的是要简化复杂的社会保险体系。

★**sim·plis·tic** /sɪmplɪstɪk/ ADJ A **simplistic** view or interpretation of something makes it seem much simpler than it really is. 过分简单化的 ❑ *He has a simplistic view of the treatment of eczema.* 他对湿疹治疗所持观点过于简单化。

simp·ly ♦♦◊ /sɪmpli/ **1** ADV You use **simply** to emphasize that something consists of only one thing, happens for only one reason, or is done in only one way. 只不过；仅仅 [EMPHASIS] ❑ *The table is simply a chipboard circle on a base.* 这张桌子只不过是基座加圆形刨花板。❑ *Most of the damage that's occurred was simply because of fallen trees.* 大部分损失仅仅是因横倒在地面的树木造成的。 **2** ADV You use **simply** to emphasize what you are saying. 简直；完全地 [EMPHASIS] ❑ *This sort of increase simply cannot be justified.* 这种增长完全没有道理。 **3** → see also **simple**

★**simu·late** /sɪmyəleɪt/ (**simulates, simulating, simulated**) **1** V-T If you **simulate** an action or a feeling, you pretend that you are doing it or feeling it. 假装 ❑ *They rolled about on the Gilligan Road, simulating a bloodthirsty fight.* 他们在吉利根路上打滚，模拟一场血腥的战斗。 **2** V-T If you **simulate** a set of conditions, you create them artificially, for example, in order to conduct an experiment. 模拟 ❑ *The scientist developed one model to simulate a full year of the globe's climate.* 这位科学家研制出一个模型，能模拟全年地球的气候。

simu·la·tion /sɪmyəleɪʃᵊn/ (**simulations**) N-VAR **Simulation** is the process of simulating something or the result of simulating it. 模拟；模拟结果 ❑ *Training includes realistic simulation of casualty procedures.* 训练包括伤亡处理程序的实际模拟。

★**si·mul·ta·neous** /saɪməlteɪniəs/ ADJ Things which are **simultaneous** happen or exist at the same time. 同时的 ❑ *...the simultaneous release of the book and the CD.* …书与激光唱片的同时发行。● **si·mul·ta·neous·ly** ADV 同时地 ❑ *The two guns fired almost simultaneously.* 两支枪几乎同时开火。

sin /sɪn/ (**sins, sinning, sinned**) **1** N-VAR **Sin** or a **sin** is an action or type of behavior which is believed to break the laws of God. 罪过；罪孽 ❑ *The Vatican's teaching on abortion is clear: it is a sin.* 梵蒂冈有关堕胎的教义是清楚的：这是个罪过。 **2** V-I If you **sin**, you do something that is believed to break the laws of God. 犯戒律 ❑ *The Spanish Inquisition charged him with sinning against God and man.* 西班牙宗教法庭指控他违背了上帝和人类的律法。● **sin·ner** /sɪnər/ N-COUNT (**sinners**) 罪人 ❑ *I was shown that I am a sinner, that I needed to repent of my sins.* 我被证明是个罪人，需要为我的罪孽忏悔。 **3** N-COUNT A **sin** is any action or behavior that people disapprove of or consider morally wrong. 违背道德原则的行为 ❑ *...the sin of arrogant hard-heartedness.* …狂妄冷酷的恶行。

Word Partnership *sin* 的常用搭配：

PREP.	**without** sin **1**
V.	**commit a** sin **1** **live in** sin **3**
ADJ.	**unpardonable** sin **1** **3**

since ♦♦♦ /sɪns/ **1** PREP You use **since** when you are mentioning a time or event in the past and indicating that a situation has continued from then until now. 自…以来；从…以后 ❑ *He's been in exile in India since 1959.* 他自1959年以来一直流亡印度。❑ *She had a sort of breakdown some years ago, and since then she has been very shy.* 她几年前曾遭遇精神崩溃，从那以后她一直怯生生的。● ADV **Since** is also an adverb. 自那时起 [ADV with v] ❑ *They worked together in the 1960s, and have kept in contact ever since.* 他们在20世纪60年代曾一起工作，自那时起就一直保持着联系。● CONJ **Since** is also a conjunction. 自…以来 ❑ *I've earned my own living since I was seven, doing all kinds of jobs.* 我自从7岁就自己谋生，做各种各样的工作。 **2** PREP You use **since** to mention a time or event in the past when you are describing an event or situation that has happened after that time. 自…以来 ❑ *The percentage increase in reported crime this year is the highest since the war.* 今年报道的犯罪增长率是该战争以来最高的。● CONJ **Since** is also a conjunction. 自…以来 ❑ *So much has changed in the sport since I was a teenager.* 自我十几岁以来，该项运动发

生了很大变化。❑ *Since I have become a mother, the sound of children's voices has lost its charm.* 我当了母亲之后，孩子的声音就失去了魅力。 **3** ADV When you are talking about an event or situation in the past, you use **since** to indicate that another event happened at some point later in time. 此后；后来 [ADV with v] ❑ *About six thousand people were arrested, several hundred of whom have since been released.* 约六千人被逮捕，不过他们中有几百人后来被释放了。 **4** CONJ You use **since** to introduce reasons or explanations. 由于；既然 ❑ *I'm forever on a diet, since I put on weight easily.* 我一直在节食，因为我的体重很容易增加。

sin·cere /sɪnsɪər/ ADJ If you say that someone is **sincere**, you approve of them because they really mean the things they say. You can also describe someone's behavior and beliefs as **sincere**. (指人) 真诚的；(指行为、信仰) 诚挚的 [APPROVAL] ❑ *He's sincere in his views.* 他的意见是诚恳的。● **sin·cer·ity** /sɪnsɛrɪti/ N-UNCOUNT 真诚；诚挚 ❑ *I was impressed with his deep sincerity.* 让我铭记在心的是他深切的诚意。

sin·cere·ly /sɪnsɪərli/ **1** ADV If you say or feel something **sincerely**, you really mean or feel it, and are not pretending. 诚恳地；真诚地 ❑ *"Congratulations," he said sincerely.* "祝贺，"他真诚地说道。 ❑ *...sincerely held religious beliefs.* …虔诚遵奉的宗教信仰。 **2** CONVENTION People write "**Sincerely yours**" or "**Sincerely**" before their signature at the end of a formal letter when they have addressed it to someone by name. People sometimes write "**Yours sincerely**" instead. 谨上(在正式信件中，结束语可在签名前用**Sincerely yours**或**Sincerely**，有时也可用**Yours sincerely**) ❑ *Sincerely yours, RobbieWeinz.* 罗比・温兹谨上。

sin·ful /sɪnfəl/ ADJ If you describe someone or something as **sinful**, you mean that they are wicked or immoral. 罪恶的 ❑ *"I am a sinful man, Magda," he said quietly.* "我是个罪人，马格达，"他轻声地说。 ❑ *This is a sinful world.* 这是一个罪恶的世界。● **sin·ful·ness** N-UNCOUNT 罪恶 ❑ *...the sinfulness of apartheid.* …种族隔离的罪恶。

sing ♦♦◊ /sɪŋ/ (**sings, singing, sang, sung**) **1** V-T/V-I When you **sing**, you make musical sounds with your voice, usually producing words that fit a tune. 唱 ❑ *I can't sing.* 我不会唱歌。 ❑ *I sing about love most of the time.* 我大部分时间都在歌唱爱情。 ❑ *They were all singing the same song.* 他们在唱同一首歌。 **2** → see also **singing**

▸ **sing along** PHRASAL VERB If you **sing along with** a piece of music, you sing it while you are listening to someone else perform it. 跟唱 ❑ *We listen to children's shows on the radio, and Janey can sing along with all the tunes.* 我们听着收音机上的儿童演出节目，珍妮能跟着所有的曲子一起哼唱。 ❑ *Would-be Elvis Presleys can sing along to "Jailhouse Rock," "Love me Tender," and "Blue Suede Shoes."* 想要成为猫王的人可以跟着《监狱摇滚》、《温柔地爱我》和《蓝色羊皮鞋》一起唱。

Thesaurus *sing* 另参见：
v. chant, hum **1**

Word Partnership *sing* 的常用搭配：
v. **begin to** sing, **can/can't** sing, **dance and** sing, **hear** *someone* sing, **like to** sing **1**
N. **birds** sing, sing *someone's* **praises**, sing **a song** **1**

sing·er ♦◊◊ /sɪŋər/ (**singers**) N-COUNT A **singer** is a person who sings, especially as a job. 歌手；歌唱家 ❑ *My mother was a singer in a dance band.* 我妈妈是一个舞蹈团的歌手。
→ see **concert**

sing·ing /sɪŋɪŋ/ N-UNCOUNT **Singing** is the activity of making musical sounds with your voice. 歌唱 ❑ *...a people's carnival, with singing and dancing in the streets.* …一次载歌载舞的街头狂欢。 ❑ *...the singing of a traditional hymn.* …一首传统赞美诗的演唱。

sin·gle ♦♦♦ /sɪŋgəl/ (**singles, singling, singled**) **1** ADJ You use **single** to emphasize that you are referring to one thing, and no more than one thing. 单个的；一个的 [ADJ n] [EMPHASIS] ❑ *A single shot rang out.* 一声枪响。 ❑ *Over six hundred people were wounded in a single day.* 一天内六百多人受伤。 **2** ADJ You use **single** to indicate that you are considering something on its own and separately from other things like it. 个别的；一个个的；每一个的 [det ADJ] [EMPHASIS] ❑ *Every single house in town had been damaged.* 镇上的每一座房子都被毁坏了。 **3** ADJ Someone who is **single** is not married. You can also use **single** to describe someone who does not have a girlfriend or boyfriend. 未婚的；单身的 ❑ *Is it difficult being a single mother?* 当单身母亲难吗？ **4** ADJ A **single** room is a room intended for one person to stay or live in. 单人的(房间) ❑ *Each guest has her own single room, or shares, on request, a double room.* 每位客人都有自己的单人房间，经要求也可共用双人间。● N-COUNT **Single** is also a noun. 单人间 ❑ *It's $65 for a single, $98 for a double and $120 for an entire suite.* 单人间$65，双人间$98，套房$120。 **5** ADJ A **single** bed is wide enough for one person to sleep in. 单人的(床) [ADJ n] ❑ *...his bedroom with its single bed.* …他那间有一张单人床的卧室。 **6** ADJ A **single** ticket is a ticket for a trip from one place to another but not back again. 单程的 ● N-COUNT **Single** is also a noun. 单程票 [BRIT]
in AM, use **one-way**
7 N-COUNT A **single** is a small record which has one song on each side. A **single** is also a CD which has a few short songs on it. You can also refer to the main song on a record or CD as a **single**. 单曲唱片；激光唱片；唱片主歌 ❑ *The winners will pocket a cash sum and get a chance to release their debut CD single.* 获胜者将获得一笔现金，并有机会发行他们的首张激光唱片。 **8** N-UNCOUNT **Singles** is a game of tennis or badminton in which one player plays another. The plural **singles** can be used to refer to one or more of these matches. (网球、羽毛球等的) 单打比赛 ❑ *Lleyton Hewitt won the men's singles.* 雷顿・休伊特赢得了男子单打比赛。 **9** → see also **single-** **10** **in single file** → see **file**
→ see **hotel, tennis**

▸ **single out** PHRASAL VERB If you **single** someone **out** from a group, you choose them and give them special attention or treatment. 选出；挑出 ❑ *The gunman had singled Debilly out and waited for him.* 枪手单单挑出德比利，并等着他出现。 ❑ *His immediate superior has singled him out for a special mention.* 他的顶头上司专门提到他。

single- /sɪŋgəl-/ COMB IN ADJ **single-** is used to form words which describe something that has one part or feature, rather than having two or more of them. 单一的；由一个单元或者一种特色构成的 ❑ *The single-engine plane landed in western Arizona.* 单引擎飞机在亚利桑那州西部降落。

single-handed or **single-handedly** ADV If you do something **single-handed**, you do it on your own, without help from anyone else. 单独地 [ADV after v] ❑ *I brought up my seven children single-handed.* 我独自带大了7个孩子。

single-minded ADJ Someone who is **single-minded** has only one aim or purpose and is determined to achieve it. 一心一意的 ❑ *They were effective politicians, ruthless and single-minded in their pursuit of political power.* 他们是注重实效的政治家，无情而专注地追逐着政治权力。

sin·gle par·ent (**single parents**) N-COUNT A **single parent** is someone who is bringing up a child on their own, because the other parent is not living with them. 单亲 ❑ *I was bringing up my three children as a single parent.* 我当时作为一个单亲家长抚养着我的3个孩子。 ❑ *...single-parent families.* …单亲家庭。

sin·gle sup·plement (**single supplements**) also **single person supplement** N-COUNT A **single supplement** is an additional sum of money that a hotel charges for one person to stay in a room meant for two people. 单间附加费(客人独住双人房时旅馆增收的额外费用) ❑ *You can avoid the single supplement by agreeing to share a twin room.* 你如果同意与人共住双人房就可免交单间附加费。

sin·gu·lar /sɪŋgyələr/ **1** ADJ The **singular** form of a word is the form that is used when referring to one person or thing. (名词) 单数的 ❑ *...the fifteen case endings of the singular form of the Finnish noun.* …芬兰语名词单数形式的15种格结尾。 **2** N-SING **The singular** of a noun is the form of it that is used to refer to one person or thing. (名词的) 单数形式 ❑ *The inhabitants of the Arctic are known as the Inuit. The singular is Inuk.* 北极居民被称作**Inuit**，其单数形式是**Inuk**。

▲ **sin·is·ter** /sɪnɪstər/ ADJ Something that is **sinister** seems evil or harmful. 不祥的；险恶的 ❑ *There was something sinister about him that she found disturbing.* 他身上带有某种令她心神不宁的阴险。

sink ♦◊◊ /sɪŋk/ (**sinks, sinking, sank, sunk**) **1** N-COUNT A **sink** is a large fixed container in a kitchen or bathroom, with faucets to supply water. In the kitchen, it is used for washing dishes, and in the bathroom, it is used to wash your hands and face. (固定在厨房里的) 洗涤槽；(固定在浴室里的) 洗脸盆 ❑ *The sink was full of dirty dishes.* 水池里满是脏碟子。 ❑ *The bathroom is furnished with 2 toilets, 2 showers, and 2 sinks.* 卫生间里装有2个便池，2个淋浴器和2个洗脸盆。 **2** V-T/V-I If a boat **sinks** or if someone or something **sinks** it, it disappears below the surface of a mass of water. 使沉没；下沉 ❑ *In a naval battle your aim is to sink the enemy's ship.* 在海战中，你的目标是要击沉敌舰。 ❑ *The boat was beginning to sink fast.* 那艘船开始迅速下沉。 **3** V-I If something **sinks**, it disappears below the surface of a mass of water. 沉没 ❑ *A fresh egg will sink and an old egg will float.* 新鲜鸡蛋会下沉，旧鸡

蛋会浮起来。 4 V-I If something **sinks**, it moves slowly downward. 下沉 ❑ *Far off to the west the sun was sinking.* 远远的，太阳在西边落下。 5 V-I If something **sinks to** a lower level or standard, it falls to that level or standard. 下降 ❑ *Share prices would have sunk – hurting small and big investors.* 股票价格本来会下跌——伤及大大小小的投资者。 ❑ *Pay increases have sunk to around seven percent.* 工资增长已下降到7%左右。 6 V-I If your heart or your spirits **sink**, you become depressed or lose hope. (心情) 沮丧; (情绪) 低落 ❑ *My heart sank because I thought he was going to dump me for another girl.* 我的心情沮丧，因为我认为他要把我甩了，去追求另一个姑娘。 7 V-T/V-I If something sharp **sinks** or **is sunk into** something solid, it goes deeply into it. 深深切入 ❑ *I sank my teeth into a peppermint cream.* 我的牙齿咬住了一块薄荷奶油糖。 8 V-T If someone **sinks** a well, mine, or other large hole, they make a deep hole in the ground, usually by digging or drilling. 打 (水井); 挖 (矿井) ❑ *...the site where Stephenson sank his first mineshaft.* …斯蒂芬森挖第一口矿井时的旧址。 9 V-T If you **sink** money **into** a business or project, you spend money on it in the hope of making more money. 投入 (资金) ❑ *He has already sunk $25 million into the project.* 他已经在这个项目投入了2500万美元。 10 → see also **sinking**, **sunk** 11 PHRASE If you say that someone will have to **sink or swim**, you mean that they will have to succeed through their own efforts, or fail. 自主沉浮 ❑ *I think athletes sink or swim depending on how they motivate themselves.* 我认为运动员的成败取决于他们如何激励自己。 12 **to sink without trace** → see **trace**

▸ **sink in** PHRASAL VERB When a statement or fact **sinks in**, you finally understand or realize it fully. 被充分理解; 被领会 ❑ *The implication took a while to sink in.* 这个含意过了一会儿才被领会。

Word Partnership *sink* 的常用搭配:
N. **bathroom** sink, **dishes in a** sink, **kitchen** sink 1
sink **a ship** 2

sip /sɪp/ (**sips, sipping, sipped**) 1 V-T/V-I If you **sip** a drink or **sip at** it, you drink by taking just a small amount at a time. 小口地喝 ❑ *Jessica sipped her drink thoughtfully.* 杰西卡若有所思地喝了一小口饮料。 ❑ *He sipped at the glass and then put it down.* 他抿了一口，然后放下杯子。 2 N-COUNT A **sip** is a small amount of drink that you take into your mouth. 一小口的量 ❑ *Harry took a sip of bourbon.* 哈里喝了一小口波旁威士忌酒。

si·phon /saɪfᵊn/ (**siphons, siphoning, siphoned**) also **syphon** 1 V-T If you **siphon** liquid from a container, you make it come out through a tube and down into a lower container by enabling the pressure of the air on it to push it out. 用虹吸管抽吸 ❑ *He told police someone had tried to siphon gas from his car.* 他告诉警察有人试图用吸管吸出他汽车里的汽油。 ● PHRASAL VERB **Siphon off** means the same as **siphon**. 用虹吸管抽吸 ❑ *Surgeons siphoned off fluid from his left lung.* 外科医生用虹吸管从他的左肺吸出液体。 2 N-COUNT A **siphon** is a tube that you use for siphoning liquid. 虹吸管 3 V-T If you **siphon** money or resources from something, you cause them to be used for a purpose for which they were not intended. 抽走 (金钱或资源) ❑ *He siphoned $1.2 billion from his companies to prop up his crumbling media empire.* 他从他所有的公司抽调12亿美元用来支持他摇摇欲坠的媒体王国。 ● PHRASAL VERB **Siphon off** means the same as **siphon**. 抽走 (金钱或资源) ❑ *He had siphoned off a small fortune in aid money from the United Nations.* 他从联合国援助基金中抽走了一小笔钱。

sir ♦♦◊ /sɜr/ (**sirs**) 1 N-VOC People sometimes say **sir** as a polite way of addressing a man whose name they do not know, or an older man. For example, a store clerk might address a male customer as **sir**. 先生 (对男性的客气称呼) [POLITENESS] ❑ *Excuse me sir, but would you mind telling me what sort of car that is?* 对不起，先生，您能告诉我那是什么样的汽车吗? 2 N-TITLE **Sir** is the title used in front of the name of a knight or baronet. (爵士或从男爵名字前的头衔) 爵士 ❑ *She introduced me to Sir Tobias and Lady Clarke.* 她把我介绍给托拜厄斯爵士和克拉克夫人。 3 CONVENTION You use the expression **Dear Sir** at the beginning of a formal letter or a business letter when you are writing to a man. 敬启者 (常用于正式函件或商务函件) ❑ *Dear Sir, Enclosed is a copy of my résumé for your consideration.* 敬启者，兹附上我的简历一份，请予以考虑。

▲ **si·ren** /saɪrən/ (**sirens**) N-COUNT A **siren** is a warning device which makes a long, loud noise. Most fire engines, ambulances, and police cars have sirens. (救火车、救护车、警车等上的) 警报器 ❑ *It sounds like an air raid siren.* 这听起来像是空袭警报。

sis·ter ♦♦♦ /sɪstər/ (**sisters**) 1 N-COUNT Your **sister** is a girl or woman who has the same parents as you. 姐; 妹 [oft poss N] ❑ *His sister Sarah helped him.* 他姐姐萨拉帮助了他。 ❑ *...Vanessa Bell, the sister of Virginia Woolf.* …弗吉尼亚・伍尔夫的姐姐瓦内莎・贝尔。 2 → see also **half sister**, **stepsister**

> Note that there is no common English word that can refer to both a brother and a sister. You simply have to use both words. ❑ *She has 13 brothers and sisters.* The word **sibling** exists, but it is very formal. Some Americans use **sib** as an informal substitute for **sibling**. ❑ *All my sibs were home for Thanksgiving.*

3 N-COUNT; N-TITLE; N-VOC **Sister** is a title given to a woman who belongs to a religious community. 修女 ❑ *Sister Francesca entered the chapel.* 弗朗西丝卡修女走进小教堂。 4 N-COUNT You can describe a woman as your **sister** if you feel a connection with her, for example, because she belongs to the same race, religion, country, or profession. 姐妹 (对同种族、宗教、国家，或职业女性的亲切说法); 女同胞 ❑ *Modern woman has been freed from many of the duties that befell her sisters in times past.* 现代女性已从旧时代姐妹们肩负的许多责任中解放出来了。 5 ADJ You can use **sister** to describe something that is of the same type or is connected in some way to another thing you have mentioned. For example, if a company has a **sister** company, they are connected. 同类型的; 姐妹般的 [ADJ n] ❑ *...the International Monetary Fund and its sister organization, the World Bank.* …国际货币基金组织和它的姐妹机构，世界银行。
→ see **family**

sister-in-law (**sisters-in-law**) N-COUNT Someone's **sister-in-law** is the sister of their husband or wife, or the woman who is married to their brother. 丈夫的姐妹; 妻子的姐妹; 兄或弟的妻子
→ see **family**

sit ♦♦♦ /sɪt/ (**sits, sitting, sat**) 1 V-I If you **are sitting** somewhere, for example, in a chair, your bottom is resting on the chair and the upper part of your body is upright. 坐 ❑ *Mother was sitting in her chair in the kitchen.* 妈妈正坐在厨房的椅子上。 ❑ *They had been sitting watching television.* 他们一直坐着看电视。 2 V-I When you **sit** somewhere, you lower your body until you are sitting on something. (在某处) 坐下 ❑ *He set the cases against a wall and sat on them.* 他把箱子靠在墙上，然后坐在上面。 ❑ *Eva pulled over a chair and sat beside her husband.* 伊娃拽过一张椅子，在她丈夫身边坐下。 ● PHRASAL VERB **Sit down** means the same as **sit**. 坐下 (同 **sit**) ❑ *I sat down, stunned.* 我坐了下来，大吃一惊。 3 V-T If you **sit** someone somewhere, you tell them to sit there or put them in a sitting position. 使坐下; 使就位 ❑ *He used to sit me on his lap.* 他过去常常让我坐在他的腿上。 ● PHRASAL VERB To **sit** someone **down** somewhere means to **sit** them there. 使坐下 ❑ *She helped him out of the water and sat him down on the rock.* 她把他从水里拉出来，让他坐在岩石上。 4 V-I If you **sit on** a committee or other official group, you are a member of it. 担任…的成员 [no cont] ❑ *He was asked to sit on numerous committees.* 他应邀担任许多委员会的委员。 5 V-I When a legislature, court, or other official body **sits**, it officially carries out its work. (立法院) 开会; (法院) 开庭 [FORMAL] ❑ *The court sits under tight security in a former museum.* 法院在一所旧时的博物馆开庭，保安措施很严密。 6 PHRASE If you **sit tight**, you remain in the same place or situation and do not take any action, usually because you are waiting for something to happen. 留在原地不动; 不采取任何行动 ❑ *Sit tight. I'll be right back.* 别慌张，我马上回来。 7 **to sit on the fence** → see **fence**

▸ **sit back** PHRASAL VERB If you **sit back** while something is happening, you relax and do not become involved in it. 袖手旁观; 在一旁闲着 [INFORMAL] ❑ *They didn't have to do anything except sit back and enjoy life.* 他们不必做任何事情，只是在一旁闲着，享受生活。

▸ **sit in on** PHRASAL VERB If you **sit in on** a lesson, meeting, or discussion, you are present while it is taking place but do not take part in it. 列席; 旁听 ❑ *Will they permit you to sit in on a few classes as an observer?* 他们会允许你旁听几节课吗?

▸ **sit on** PHRASAL VERB If you say that someone **is sitting on** something, you mean that they are delaying dealing with it. 拖延; 压着不办 [INFORMAL] ❑ *He had been sitting on the document for at least two months.* 他已经把这个文件压了至少两个月。

▸ **sit out** PHRASAL VERB If you **sit** something **out**, you wait for it to finish, without taking any action. 坐等…结束 ❑ *The only thing I can do is keep quiet and sit this one out.* 我能做的只有保持沉默，坐等这件事结束。

▸ **sit through** PHRASAL VERB If you **sit through** something such as a movie, lecture, or meeting, you stay until it is finished although you are not enjoying it. 坐到…结束 ❑ *...movies so bad you* *can hardly bear to sit through them.* …电影非常差劲，你很难能够忍着一直坐到看完。

▸ **sit up** 1 PHRASAL VERB If you **sit up**, you move into a sitting position when you have been leaning back or lying down. 坐起来; 坐直身子 ❑ *Her head spins dizzily as soon as she sits up.* 她一坐起来，就感到天旋地转。 2 PHRASAL VERB If you **sit** someone **up**, you move them into a sitting position when they have been leaning back or lying down. 使坐起来 ❑ *She sat him up and made him comfortable.* 她帮他坐起来，让他舒服些。 3 PHRASAL VERB If you **sit up**, you do not go to bed although it is very late. 熬夜 ❑ *We sat up drinking and talking.* 我们很晚还没睡，一直喝酒聊天。 4 → see also **sit-up**

Thesaurus *sit* 另参见:
V. perch, rest, settle 1 – 3

Word Partnership *sit* 的常用搭配:
ADV. sit **alone**, sit **back**, sit **comfortably**, sit **quietly**, sit **still** 1
PREP. sit **in a circle**, sit **on the porch**, sit **on the sidelines** 1 sit **on a bench**, sit **in a chair**, sit **on the floor**, sit **on** *someone's* **lap**, sit **around/at a table** 1 2
V. sit **and eat**, sit **and enjoy**, sit **and listen**, sit **and talk**, sit **and wait**, sit **and watch** (or sit **watching**) 1 sit **down to dinner/eat**, sit **down and relax** 1 2

site ♦♦◊ /saɪt/ (**sites, siting, sited**) 1 N-COUNT A **site** is a piece of ground that is used for a particular purpose or where a particular thing happens. 场地; 场所 ❑ *I was working as a foreman on a building site.* 我在一个建筑工地当工头。 2 N-COUNT **The site of** an important event is the place where it happened. (事件发生的) 现场; 场所 ❑ *Scientists have described the Aral sea as the site of the worst ecological disaster on earth.* 科学家们把咸海描绘成地球上生态环境最差的地方。 3 N-COUNT A **site** is a piece of ground where something such as a statue or building stands or used to stand. 地点; 遗址; 原址 ❑ *…the site of Moses' tomb.* …摩西墓遗址。 4 N-COUNT A **site** is the same as a **website**. 网站 5 V-T If something **is sited** in a particular place or position, it is put there or built there. 使坐落于; 把…置于 [usu passive] ❑ *He said chemical weapons had never been sited in Germany.* 他说从未在德国部署过化学武器。 ● **sit·ing** N-SING 选址 ❑ *…controls on the siting of gas storage vessels.* …对煤气储存罐选址的种种限制。 6 PHRASE If someone or something is **on site**, they are in a particular area or group of buildings where people work, study, or stay. 在工地上; 在现场 ❑ *It is cheaper to have extra building work done when the builder is on site, rather than bringing him back for a small job.* 趁建筑工人在工地上时叫他们完成额外的建筑工作要比叫他回来做一点小工便宜。 7 PHRASE If someone or something is **off site**, they are away from a particular area or group of buildings where people work, study, or stay. 不在工地上; 不在现场 ❑ *There is ample car parking off site.* 外面有个很大的停车场。

site map (**site maps**) N-COUNT A **site map** is a plan of a website showing what is on it and providing links to the different sections. 网站地图 [COMPUTING]

sit-in (**sit-ins**) N-COUNT A **sit-in** is a protest in which people go to a public place and stay there for a long time. 静坐示威 ❑ *The campaigners held a sit-in outside the Supreme Court.* 运动发起者在最高法院外进行静坐示威。

▲ **sit·ting** /sɪtɪŋ/ (**sittings**) 1 N-COUNT A **sitting** is one of the periods when a meal is served when there is not enough space for everyone to eat at the same time. 就餐时段 ❑ *Dinner was in two sittings.* 晚餐有两个就餐时段。 2 N-COUNT **A sitting** of a legislature, court, or other official body is one of the occasions when it meets in order to carry out its work. 开会; 开庭 [usu N "of" n] ❑ *…the recent emergency sittings of the UN Security Council.* …那些近期的联合国安理会紧急会议。 3 ADJ A **sitting** president or congressman is a present one, not a future or past one. 现任的 [ADJ n] ❑ *…the greatest clash in our history between a sitting president and an ex-president.* …我们历史上在现任总统和前总统之间的最严重的冲突。 4 → see also **sit**

sit·ting room (**sitting rooms**) also **sitting-room** N-COUNT A **sitting room** is a room in a house where people sit and relax. 起居室 [OLD-FASHIONED]

★ **situ·ate** /sɪtʃueɪt/ (**situates, situating, situated**) V-T If you **situate** something such as an idea or fact in a particular context, you relate it to that context, especially in order to understand it better. 使处于 [FORMAL] ❑ *How do we situate Christianity in the context of modern physics and psychology?* 我们如何将基督教置于现代物理学和心理学的背景中呢？

★ **situ·at·ed** /sɪtʃueɪtɪd/ ADJ If something is **situated** in a particular place or position, it is in that place or position. 坐落于…的; 位于…的 ❑ *His hotel is situated in one of the loveliest places on the Loire.* 他的旅馆坐落在卢瓦尔的一个最优美的地方。

Word Link ***site, situ ≈ position, location : campsite, situation, website***

situa·tion ♦♦♦ /sɪtʃueɪʃᵊn/ (**situations**) N-COUNT You use **situation** to refer generally to what is happening in a particular place at a particular time, or to refer to what is happening to you. 情况; 形势 ❑ *Army officers said the situation was under control.* 军方官员说局势已得到控制。 ❑ *And now for a look at the travel situation in the rest of the country.* 现在来看一看该国其他地区的旅行条件。

Thesaurus *situation* 另参见:
N. circumstances, condition, plight, position, state

Word Partnership *situation* 的常用搭配:
ADJ. **bad** situation, **complicated** situation, **current** situation, **dangerous** situation, **difficult** situation, **economic** situation, **financial** situation, **political** situation, **present** situation, **same** situation, **tense** situation, **terrible** situation, **unique** situation, **unusual** situation, **whole** situation
V. **describe a** situation, **discuss a** situation, **handle a** situation, **improve a** situation, **understand a** situation

sit-up (**sit-ups**) also **situp** N-COUNT **Sit-ups** are exercises that you do to strengthen your stomach muscles. They involve sitting up from a lying position while keeping your legs straight on the floor. 仰卧起坐 ❑ *He does 100 sit-ups each day.* 他每天做100个仰卧起坐。

six ♦♦♦ /sɪks/ (**sixes**) NUM **Six** is the number 6. 六; 六个 ❑ *…a glorious career spanning more than six decades.* …六十多年辉煌的职业生涯。

six·teen ♦♦♦ /sɪkstiːn/ (**sixteens**) NUM **Sixteen** is the number 16. 16; 16个 ❑ *…exams taken at the age of sixteen.* …16岁时参加的考试。 ❑ *He worked sixteen hours a day.* 他每天工作16个小时。

six·teenth ♦♦◊ /sɪkstiːnθ/ (**sixteenths**) 1 ORD The **sixteenth** item in a series is the one that you count as number sixteen. 第十六 ❑ *…the sixteenth century AD.* …公元16世纪。 2 FRACTION A **sixteenth** is one of sixteen equal parts of something. 1/16 ❑ *…a sixteenth of a second.* …1/16秒。

sixth ♦♦◊ /sɪksθ/ (**sixths**) 1 ORD The **sixth** item in a series is the one that you count as number six. 第六 ❑ *…the sixth round of the World Cup.* …世界杯足球赛的第6轮比赛。 2 FRACTION A **sixth** is one of six equal parts of something. 1/6 ❑ *The company yesterday shed a sixth of its workforce.* 该公司昨天削减了1/6的劳动力。

sixth form (**sixth forms**) also **sixth-form** N-COUNT The **sixth form** in a British school consists of students aged 16 to 18, usually studying for A levels. (英国中学的) 6年级

six·ti·eth ♦♦◊ /sɪkstiəθ/ (**sixtieths**) 1 ORD The **sixtieth** item in a series is the one that you count as number sixty. 第60 ❑ *He is to retire on his sixtieth birthday.* 他将在60岁生日时退休。 2 FRACTION A **sixtieth** is one of sixty equal parts of something. 1/60

six·ty ♦♦♦ /sɪksti/ (**sixties**) 1 NUM **Sixty** is the number 60. 60; 60个 ❑ *…the sunniest April for more than sixty years.* …六十多年来晴天最多的一个4月。 2 N-PLURAL When you talk about the **sixties**, you are referring to numbers between 60 and 69. For example, if you are **in your sixties**, you are aged between 60 and 69. If the temperature is **in the sixties**, it is between 60 and 69 degrees. (年龄或温度) 60到69的数字 ❑ *…a lively widow in her sixties.* …一位年过花甲精神抖擞的寡妇。 3 N-PLURAL **The sixties** is the decade between 1960 and 1969. (20世纪的) 60年代 ❑ *In the sixties there were the deaths of the two Kennedy brothers and Martin Luther King.* 20世纪60年代发生了肯尼迪两兄弟和马丁·路德·金的死亡事件。

★ **siz·able** /saɪzəbᵊl/ also **sizeable** ADJ **Sizable** means fairly large. 相当大的 ❑ *Harry inherited the house and a sizable piece of land that surrounds it.* 哈里继承了那座房子和房子周围一块相当大的土地。

size ♦♦◊ /saɪz/ (**sizes, sizing, sized**) 1 N-VAR **The size of** something is how big or small it is. Something's size is determined by comparing it to other things, counting it, or

S

measuring it. 大小；规模 ❑ *In 1970 the average size of a French farm was 19 hectares.* 1970年法国农场的平均面积是19公顷。 ❑ *...shelves containing books of various sizes.* …摆放着大大小小书籍的书架。 2 N-UNCOUNT **The size of** something is the fact that it is very large. 巨大；庞大 ❑ *He knows the size of the task.* 他知道任务很重。 3 N-COUNT A **size** is one of a series of graded measurements, especially for things such as clothes or shoes. 尺寸；尺码 ❑ *My sister is the same height but only a size 12.* 我妹妹的身高一样，但只穿12码的。

▸ **size up** PHRASAL VERB If you **size up** a person or situation, you carefully look at the person or think about the situation, so that you can decide how to act. 估计；品评 [INFORMAL] ❑ *Some U.S. manufacturers have been sizing up the UK as a possible market for their clothes.* 一些美国制造商一直把英国视为其服装的潜在市场。

Word Partnership *size* 的常用搭配：

ADJ.	**average** size, **full** size, **mid-size** 1
	sheer size 2
	right size, size **large/medium/small** 3
N.	**bite** size, **class** size, **family** size, **life** size, **pocket** size 1
	size **chart**, **king/queen** size 3
V.	**double in** size, **increase in** size, **vary in** size 1
	a size **fits** 3

size·able /saɪzəbᵊl/ [mainly BRIT] → see **sizable**

siz·zle /sɪzᵊl/ (**sizzles, sizzling, sizzled**) V-I If something such as hot oil or fat **sizzles**, it makes hissing sounds. 发出咝咝声

skate /skeɪt/ (**skates, skating, skated**) 1 N-COUNT **Skates** are ice-skates. 冰鞋；冰刀 2 N-COUNT **Skates** are roller-skates. 旱冰鞋 3 V-I If you **skate**, you move around wearing ice-skates or roller-skates. 滑冰 ❑ *I actually skated, and despite some teetering I did not fall on the ice.* 我的确滑冰了。尽管有些摇摇晃晃，我还是没有摔倒在冰上。 ● **skat·ing** N-UNCOUNT 滑冰 ❑ *They all went skating together in the winter.* 他们冬天都一起去滑冰。 ● **skat·er** N-COUNT (**skaters**) 滑冰者；溜冰者 ❑ *West Lake, an outdoor ice-skating rink, attracts skaters during the day and night.* 西湖，一个室外溜冰场，昼夜都吸引溜冰者。

skate·board /skeɪtbɔrd/ (**skateboards**) N-COUNT A **skateboard** is a narrow board with wheels at each end, which people stand on and ride for pleasure. 滑板

→ see **skateboarding**

skate·board·ing /skeɪtbɔrdɪŋ/ N-UNCOUNT **Skateboarding** is the activity of riding on a skateboard. 滑板运动 ❑ *...a skateboarding competition.* …滑板比赛。

→ see Picture Dictionary: **skateboarding**

skel·etal /skɛlɪtᵊl/ 1 ADJ **Skeletal** means relating to the bones in your body. 骨骼的；骸骨的 [ADJ n] ❑ *...the skeletal remains of seven adults.* …7个成年人的遗骸。 ❑ *...the skeletal system.* …骨骼系统。 2 ADJ A **skeletal** person is so thin that you can see their bones through their skin. 骨瘦如柴的 ❑ *...a hospital filled with skeletal children.* …一所挤满骨瘦如柴的孩子的医院。

→ see **muscle**

skel·eton /skɛlɪtᵊn/ (**skeletons**) 1 N-COUNT Your **skeleton** is the framework of bones in your body. 骨骼 ❑ *...a human skeleton.* …人体骨骼。 2 ADJ A **skeleton** staff is the smallest number of staff necessary in order to run an organization or service. 最起码的(员工) [ADJ n] ❑ *Only a skeleton staff remains to show anyone interested around the site.* 只有极少数的员工留下来带领感兴趣的人参观场地。 3 N-COUNT The **skeleton** of something such as a building or a plan is its basic framework. (楼房或计划的) 构架；框架 ❑ *The town of Rudbar had ceased to exist, with only skeletons of buildings remaining.* 鲁德巴尔城已不存在，只剩一些建筑骨架。

→ see **shark**

skep·tic /skɛptɪk/ (**skeptics**)

in BRIT, use **sceptic**

N-COUNT A **skeptic** is a person who has doubts about things that other people believe. 怀疑论者 ❑ *He is a skeptic who tries to keep an open mind.* 他是一个试图保持开明观点的怀疑论者。

★ **skep·ti·cal** /skɛptɪkᵊl/

in BRIT, use **sceptical**

ADJ If you are **skeptical about** something, you have doubts about it. 表示怀疑的 ❑ *Others here are more skeptical about the chances for justice being done.* 这里的其他人更为怀疑正义能否得到伸张。

skep·ti·cism /skɛptɪsɪzəm/

in BRIT, use **scepticism**

N-UNCOUNT **Skepticism** is great doubt about whether something is true or useful. 怀疑 ❑ *A survey reflects business skepticism about the strength of the economic recovery.* 一份调查反映出商业界对经济恢复能力的怀疑。

sketch /skɛtʃ/ (**sketches, sketching, sketched**) 1 N-COUNT A **sketch** is a drawing that is done quickly without a lot of details. Artists often use sketches as a preparation for a more detailed painting or drawing. 草图；略图；素描 ❑ *...a sketch of a soldier by Orpen.* …一幅奥彭画的一位士兵的素描。 2 V-T/V-I If you **sketch** something, you make a quick, rough drawing of it. 画…的素描；画…的速写 ❑ *Clare and David Astor are sketching a view of far Spanish hills.*

Picture Dictionary skateboarding

S

克莱尔和大卫·阿斯特正在素描远处西班牙山峦景色。 3 N-COUNT A **sketch of** a situation, person, or incident is a brief description of it without many details. 概述 ❑ *...thumbnail sketches of heads of state and political figures.* …国家首脑和政治要员们的简要陈述。 4 V-T If you **sketch** a situation or incident, you give a short description of it, including only the most important facts. 概述；简述 ❑ *Cross sketched the story briefly, telling the facts just as they had happened.* 克罗斯简要地概述了这个事件，如实地讲述了所发生的事情。 ● PHRASAL VERB **Sketch out** means the same as **sketch**. 概述；简述 ❑ *He sketched out plans to give consumers more affordable choices.* 他简述了几个计划，以给顾客提供更多符合其购买力的选择。 5 N-COUNT A **sketch** is a short humorous piece of acting, usually forming part of a comedy show. 幽默短剧；滑稽小品 ❑ *...a five-minute sketch about a folk singer.* …一出有关一位民间歌手的5分钟幽默短剧。

→ see **animation, drawing**

sketchy /skɛtʃi/ (**sketchier, sketchiest**) ADJ **Sketchy** information about something does not include many details and is therefore incomplete or inadequate. 粗略的；不完全的 ❑ *Details of what actually happened are still sketchy.* 究竟发生了什么，细节仍旧不详。

skew /skyu/ (**skews, skewing, skewed**) V-T If something **is skewed**, it is changed or affected to some extent by a new or unusual factor, and so is not correct or normal. 曲解；歪曲 ❑ *The arithmetic of nuclear running costs has been skewed by the fall in the cost of other fuels.* 对核运行费用的计算因其他燃料费用的下降而出现了偏差。

skew·er /skyuər/ (**skewers**) N-COUNT A **skewer** is a long pin made of wood or metal that is used to hold pieces of food together during cooking. 串肉扦；烤肉叉

ski ♦◇◇ /ski/ (**skis, skiing, skied**) 1 N-COUNT **Skis** are long, flat, narrow pieces of wood, metal, or plastic that are fastened to boots so that you can move easily on snow or water. 滑雪板；滑水板 ❑ *...a pair of skis.* …一副滑雪板。 2 V-I When people **ski**, they move over snow or water on skis. 滑雪；滑水 ❑ *They surf, ski and ride.* 他们冲浪、滑水和骑马。 ● **ski·er** /skiər/ N-COUNT (**skiers**) 滑雪者；滑水者 ❑ *He is an enthusiastic skier.* 他是个热情的滑雪爱好者。 ● **ski·ing** N-UNCOUNT 滑雪；滑水 ❑ *My hobbies were skiing and scuba diving.* 我的爱好是滑雪和潜水。 3 ADJ You use **ski** to refer to things that are concerned with skiing. 滑雪用的；滑水用的 [ADJ n] ❑ *...the Swiss ski resort of Klosters.* …瑞士的克洛斯特斯滑雪胜地。 ❑ *...a private ski instructor.* …一位私人滑雪教练。

skid /skɪd/ (**skids, skidding, skidded**) V-I If a vehicle **skids**, it slides sideways or forward while moving, for example, when you are trying to stop it suddenly on a wet road. 侧滑；打滑；(刹车时)滑行 ❑ *The car pulled up too fast and skidded on the dusty shoulder of the road.* 那辆汽车刹车太快，车轮在尘土飞扬的路肩上打滑。 ● N-COUNT **Skid** is also a noun. 打滑；滑行 ❑ *I slammed the brakes on and went into a skid.* 我猛踩刹车，汽车滑向一侧。

skil·ful /skɪlfəl/ [mainly BRIT] → see **skillful**

skill ♦♦◇ /skɪl/ (**skills**) 1 N-COUNT A **skill** is a type of work or activity which requires special training and knowledge. (专门)技术 ❑ *Most of us will know someone who is always learning new skills, or studying new fields.* 我们大多数人都会认识一些总在学习新技术或研究新领域的人。 2 N-UNCOUNT **Skill** is the knowledge and ability that enables you to do something well. 技能；技艺 ❑ *The cut of a diamond depends on the skill of its craftsman.* 切割钻石的好坏取决于工匠的技艺。

Thesaurus *skill* 另参见：

N. ability, proficiency, talent 1 2

skilled /skɪld/ 1 ADJ Someone who is **skilled** has the knowledge and ability to do something well. 有技术的；熟练的 ❑ *Few doctors are actually trained, and not all are skilled, in helping their patients make choices.* 在帮助病人做选择方面，没有几个医生实际受过训练，也并非所有的医生都很熟练。 2 ADJ **Skilled** work can only be done by people who have had some training. 需要熟练能力的；需要专门技术的 ❑ *New industries demanded skilled labor not available locally.* 新兴产业需要熟练技术工人，而当地没有。

skill·ful /skɪlfəl/

in BRIT, use **skilful**

ADJ Someone who is **skillful** at something does it very well. 熟练的 ❑ *He actually is quite a skillful campaigner.* 他实际上是个老练的活动家。 ● **skill·ful·ly** ADV 熟练地 [ADV with v] ❑ *The city's rulers skillfully played both powers off against each other.* 这座城市的统治者巧妙地挑起两派势力之间的争斗。

skim /skɪm/ (**skims, skimming, skimmed**) 1 V-T If you **skim** something **from** the surface of a liquid, you remove it. 撇去(液体表面的浮物) ❑ *Rough seas today prevented specially equipped ships from skimming oil off the water's surface.* 今天汹涌的海浪使特别装备的船只无法撇去浮在水面上的石油。 2 V-T/V-I If something **skims** a surface, it moves quickly along just above it. 掠过 ❑ *...seagulls skimming the waves.* …掠过海浪的海鸥。 ❑ *The little boat was skimming across the sunlit surface of the bay.* 那艘小船略过阳光照耀下的海湾表面。 3 V-T/V-I If you **skim** a piece of writing, you read through it quickly. 略读；浏览 ❑ *He skimmed the pages quickly, then read them again more carefully.* 他很快浏览了几页，然后又仔细地读了一遍。 ❑ *I only had time to skim through the script before I flew over here.* 我只在飞过来之前才有时间略读了讲稿。

▸ **skim off** PHRASAL VERB If someone **skims off** the best part of something, or money which belongs to other people, they take it for themselves. 捞取；偷走(钱) ❑ *The regime was able to skim off about $10 billion in illegal revenue.* 该政权能够捞取一百亿美元左右的非法收入。 ❑ *She admitted she skimmed cash off the top of the fees she collected.* 她承认从所收的款项中捞了钱。

skimmed milk [BRIT] → see **skim milk**

skim milk

in BRIT, and sometimes in AM, use **skimmed milk**

N-UNCOUNT **Skim milk** is milk from which the cream has been removed. 脱脂牛奶

skimpy /skɪmpi/ (**skimpier, skimpiest**) ADJ Something that is **skimpy** is too small in size or quantity. 不足的(尺寸或数量) ❑ *...skimpy underwear.* …太紧的内衣。

skin ♦♦◇ /skɪn/ (**skins, skinning, skinned**) 1 N-VAR Your **skin** is the natural covering of your body. 皮肤 ❑ *His skin is clear and smooth.* 他的皮肤光洁滑润。 ❑ *There are three major types of skin cancer.* 皮肤癌有3大类。 2 N-VAR An animal **skin** is skin which has been removed from a dead animal. Skins are used to make things such as coats and rugs. 兽皮；毛皮 ❑ *That was real crocodile skin.* 那是真正的鳄鱼皮。 3 N-VAR The **skin** of a fruit or vegetable is its outer layer or covering. 果皮；(蔬菜的) 外皮 ❑ *The outer skin of the orange is called the "zest."* 橙子外层皮叫"橙皮"。 4 N-SING If a **skin** forms on the surface of a liquid, a thin, fairly solid layer forms on it. (液体表面凝结的) 薄层；薄皮 ❑ *Stir the custard occasionally to prevent a skin forming.* 不时搅动蛋奶沙司，以免凝结奶皮。 5 V-T If you **skin** a dead animal, you remove its skin. 剥去…的皮 ❑ *...with the expertise of a chef skinning a rabbit.* …具有大厨剥兔皮的专长。

→ see Word Web: **skin**

Word Partnership *skin* 的常用搭配：

ADJ. **dark** skin, **dry** skin, **fair** skin, **oily** skin, **pale** skin, **sensitive** skin, **smooth** skin, **soft** skin 1

N. skin **and bones**, skin **cancer**, skin **cells**, skin **color** (or **color of** *someone's* skin), skin **cream**, skin **problems**, skin **type** 1, **leopard** skin 2

S

Word Web skin

What is the best thing you can do for your **skin**? Stay out of the sun. When skin **cells** grow normally, the skin remains smooth and firm. However, the sun's **ultraviolet** rays sometimes cause damage. This can lead to **sunburn**, **wrinkles**, and skin cancer. The damage may not be apparent for several years. However, doctors have discovered that even a light **suntan** can be dangerous. **Sunlight** makes the melanin in skin turn dark. This is the body's attempt to protect itself from the ultraviolet radiation. Dermatologists recommend limiting exposure to the sun and always using a **sunscreen**.

skin·ny /skɪni/ (**skinnier, skinniest**) ADJ A **skinny** person is extremely thin, often in a way that you find unattractive. 瘦得皮包骨的 [INFORMAL] ❑ *He was quite a skinny little boy.* 他是个骨瘦如柴的小男孩。

skin-tight also **skintight** ADJ **Skin-tight** clothes fit very tightly so that they show the shape of your body. 紧身的（衣服）[usu ADJ n] ❑ *...the guy with the slicked down hair and skin-tight jeans.* …那个头发油光，穿紧身牛仔裤的男子。

★ **skip** /skɪp/ (**skips, skipping, skipped**) **1** V-I If you **skip** along, you move almost as if you are dancing, with a series of little jumps from one foot to the other. 蹦跳；蹦跳着走 ❑ *They saw the man with a little girl skipping along behind him.* 他们看到那个男人身后跟着一个蹦蹦跳跳的小女孩。 ❑ *We went skipping down the street arm in arm.* 我们挽着臂蹦蹦跳跳地沿大街走着。 ● N-COUNT **Skip** is also a noun. 蹦跳 ❑ *The boxer gave a little skip as he came out of his corner.* 那位拳击手轻快地跳出了场角。 **2** V-T When someone **skips rope**, they jump up and down over a rope which they or two other people are holding at each end and turning around and around. 跳（绳）❑ *They skip rope and play catch, waiting for the bell.* 他们又是跳绳又是玩捉迷藏，等着铃声响。 ● **skip·ping** N-UNCOUNT 跳绳 ❑ *We did rope skipping and things like that.* 我们跳绳或做类似的活动。 **3** V-T If you **skip** something that you usually do or something that most people do, you decide not to do it. 不做；逃避 ❑ *It is important not to skip meals.* 重要的是，不能不吃饭。 **4** V-T/V-I If you **skip** or **skip over** a part of something you are reading or a story you are telling, you miss it out or pass over it quickly and move on to something else. 匆匆翻阅；略过 ❑ *You might want to skip the exercises in this chapter.* 你可能想把这一章的练习跳过去。 **5** V-I If you **skip from** one subject or activity to another, you move quickly from one to the other, although there is no obvious connection between them. （无条理地）快速转换 ❑ *She kept up a continuous chatter, skipping from one subject to the next.* 她叽叽咕咕地说个不停，从一个话题跳到另一个话题。 **6** N-COUNT A **skip** is a large, open, metal container which is used to hold and take away large unwanted items and trash. （装大的废弃物的）废料桶；大铁桶 [BRIT] in AM, use **Dumpster**

skip·per /skɪpər/ (**skippers**) N-COUNT; N-VOC You can use **skipper** to refer to the captain of a ship or boat. （小型商船或渔船的）船长 ❑ *...the skipper of an English fishing boat.* …一艘英国渔船的船长。

skir·mish /skɜrmɪʃ/ (**skirmishes, skirmishing, skirmished**) **1** N-COUNT A **skirmish** is a minor battle. 小规模战斗；小冲突 ❑ *Border skirmishes between India and Pakistan were common.* 印巴边境的小冲突曾经是常有的事。 **2** V-RECIP If people **skirmish**, they fight. 进行小规模战斗；发生小冲突 ❑ *They were skirmishing close to the minefield now.* 他们当时正在雷区附近小规模交火。

skirt /skɜrt/ (**skirts, skirting, skirted**) **1** N-COUNT A **skirt** is a piece of clothing worn by women and girls. It fastens at the waist and hangs down around the legs. 裙子 **2** V-T Something that **skirts** an area is situated around the edge of it. 位于…的边缘；围绕 ❑ *We raced across a large field that skirted the slope of a hill.* 我们快速穿越山坡边的一大片旷野。 **3** V-T/V-I If you **skirt** a problem or question, you avoid dealing with it. 回避（问题等）❑ *He skirted the hardest issues, concentrating on areas of possible agreement.* 他避开最难的问题，而专注于可能达成一致意见的领域。
→ see **clothing**

S

★ **skull** /skʌl/ (**skulls**) N-COUNT Your **skull** is the bony part of your head which encloses your brain. 颅骨；头颅 ❑ *Her husband was later treated for a fractured skull.* 她丈夫后来因颅骨碎裂而接受治疗。

sky ♦◇◇ /skaɪ/ (**skies**) N-VAR **The sky** is the space around the earth which you can see when you stand outside and look upward. 天空 ❑ *The sun is already high in the sky.* 太阳早已高挂在天上了。 ❑ *...warm sunshine and clear blue skies.* …温暖的阳光和清澈的蓝天。
→ see **star**

Word Partnership **sky** 的常用搭配：

ADV. sky **above**, the sky **overhead**, **up in the** sky
ADJ. **black** sky, **blue** sky, **bright** sky, **clear** sky, **cloudless** sky, **dark** sky, **empty** sky, **high in the** sky

★ **sky·line** /skaɪlaɪn/ (**skylines**) N-COUNT **The skyline** is the line or shape that is formed where the sky meets buildings or the land. （建筑物等在天空映衬下的）空中轮廓线 ❑ *The village church dominates the skyline.* 那座乡村教堂独绝天际。

▲ **sky·scraper** /skaɪskreɪpər/ (**skyscrapers**) N-COUNT A **skyscraper** is a very tall building in a city. 摩天楼
→ see Word Web: **skyscraper**
→ see **city**

▲ **slab** /slæb/ (**slabs**) N-COUNT A **slab of** something is a thick, flat piece of it. 厚板 [with supp] ❑ *...slabs of stone.* …一块块石板。 ❑ *...huge paving slabs.* …大块大块的铺板。

★ **slack** /slæk/ (**slacker, slackest, slacks, slacking, slacked**) **1** ADJ Something that is **slack** is loose and not firmly stretched or tightly in position. 松散的；松弛的；不紧的 ❑ *The boy's jaw went slack.* 那个男孩的下巴松掉了。 **2** ADJ A **slack** period is one in which there is not much work or activity. 萧条的；（生意、市场等）不景气的 ❑ *The workload can be evened out, instead of the shop having busy times and slack periods.* 工作量可以均衡分配，商店就不会有旺季和淡季。 **3** ADJ Someone who is **slack** in their work does not do it properly. 松懈的；懈怠的 [DISAPPROVAL] ❑ *Many publishers have simply become far too slack.* 许多出版商简直变得过于松松垮垮。 **4** V-I If someone **is slacking**, they are not working as hard as they should. 偷懒 [only cont] [DISAPPROVAL] ❑ *He had never let a foreman see him slacking.* 他从未让工头见到他偷懒过。 ● PHRASAL VERB **Slack off** means the same as **slack**. 偷懒 ❑ *If someone slacks off, Bill comes down hard.* 如果有人偷懒，比尔就会严厉训斥。

slack·en /slækən/ (**slackens, slackening, slackened**) **1** V-T/V-I If something **slackens** or if you **slacken** it, it becomes slower, less active, or less intense. （使）变缓慢；（使）变弱；（使）减轻 ❑ *Inflationary pressures continued to slacken last month.* 通货膨胀的压力上个月持续减轻。 **2** V-T/V-I If your grip or a part of your body **slackens** or if you **slacken** your grip, it becomes looser or more relaxed. 松开；放松 ❑ *Her grip slackened on Arnold's arm.* 她松开了紧拽着阿诺德臂膀的手。

slam /slæm/ (**slams, slamming, slammed**) **1** V-T/V-I If you **slam** a door or window or if it **slams**, it shuts noisily and with great force. 砰地关上；使劲关上 ❑ *She slammed the door and locked it behind her.* 她砰地一声关上门，上了锁。 ❑ *I was relieved to hear the front door slam.* 听到前门砰地一声关上，我才放下了心。 **2** V-T If you **slam** something **down**, you put it there quickly and with great force. 摔；使劲扔 ❑ *She listened in a mixture of shock and anger before slamming the phone down.* 她震惊又气愤地听着，随后啪地挂上电话。 **3** V-T To **slam** someone or something means to criticize them very severely. 严厉批评；猛烈抨击 [JOURNALISM] ❑ *The famed filmmaker slammed the claims as "an outrageous lie."* 那位享有盛名的电影制片人猛烈抨击这些说法，称其为"无耻谰言。" **4** V-T/V-I If one thing **slams** into or against another, it crashes into it with great force. 猛烈撞击 ❑ *The plane slammed into the building after losing an engine shortly after take-off.* 飞机起飞后不久便失去一个引擎，猛地撞到那栋建筑物上。

Word Partnership **slam** 的常用搭配：

N. slam **a door** **1**
V. **hear** *something* slam **1**
ADV. slam *(something)* **shut** **1**

Word Web **skyscraper**

Large American **cities** were expanding rapidly in the early 1900s. As this happened, **land** became scarce and expensive. **Real estate developers** soon felt the need for taller **buildings** and the **skyscraper** was born. Two things made these buildings possible—mass-produced steel and the invention of the **elevator**. The **construction** of the Empire State Building set two important records. At 102 **stories**, it was the tallest building in the world for 41 years. And 3,000 workers completed it in only 14 months. To accomplish this, they worked day and night, seven days a week, including holidays.

slan·der /slændər/ (**slanders, slandering, slandered**) **1** N-VAR **Slander** is an untrue spoken statement about someone which is intended to damage their reputation. Compare **libel**. 诽谤（参较 **libel**）❑ *Dr. Bach is now suing the company for slander.* 巴赫博士现在正在控告该公司犯诽谤罪。 **2** V-T To **slander** someone means to say untrue things about them in order to damage their reputation. 诋毁；诽谤 ❑ *He accused me of slandering him and trying to undermine his position.* 他指控我诽谤他并想削弱他的地位。

▲ **slang** /slæŋ/ N-UNCOUNT **Slang** consists of words, expressions, and meanings that are informal and are used by people who know each other very well or who have the same interests. 俚语；行话 ❑ *Archie liked to think he kept up with current slang.* 阿奇乐于自认为能跟得上时新俚语。

▲ **slant** /slænt/ (**slants, slanting, slanted**) **1** V-I Something that **slants** is sloping, rather than horizontal or vertical. 倾斜 ❑ *The morning sun slanted through the glass roof.* 朝阳透过玻璃屋顶斜射进来。 **2** N-SING If something is **on a slant**, it is in a slanting position. 倾斜 ❑ *...long pockets cut on the slant.* …斜裁的长口袋。 **3** V-T If information or a system **is slanted**, it is made to show favor toward a particular group or opinion. 使有倾向性；使有偏向性 [usu passive] ❑ *The program was deliberately slanted to make the home team look good.* 该节目有意带着倾向性，使主队看上去很不错。 **4** N-SING A particular **slant** on a subject is a particular way of thinking about it, especially one that is unfair. 偏见；偏向 ❑ *The political slant at Focus can be described as center-right.* 对福克斯的政治倾向可以描述成中间偏右。

slap /slæp/ (**slaps, slapping, slapped**) **1** V-T If you **slap** someone, you hit them with the palm of your hand. 掴；（用手掌）拍打 ❑ *He would push or slap her once in a while.* 他时不时地推搡她，或是打她耳光。 ❑ *I slapped him hard across the face.* 我重重地打了他一记耳光。 ● N-COUNT **Slap** is also a noun. 掴；拍打 ❑ *He reached forward and gave her a slap.* 他走上前去，给了她一个耳光。 **2** V-T If you **slap** something **onto** a surface, you put it there quickly, roughly, or carelessly. 重重放下；摔；掼 ❑ *He emptied his drink and slapped the money on the bar.* 他喝光了饮料，然后把钱摔在吧台上。 **3** V-T If journalists say that the authorities **slap** something such as a tax or a ban **on** something, they think it is unreasonable or put on without careful thought. （无理地或者盲目地）强加 [INFORMAL, DISAPPROVAL] ❑ *The government slapped a ban on the export of unprocessed logs.* 政府强制禁止出口未加工过的木料。

Word Partnership *slap* 的常用搭配：

N. a slap **on the back**, a slap **in the face**, a slap **on the wrist** **1**

★ **slash** /slæʃ/ (**slashes, slashing, slashed**) **1** V-T If you **slash** something, you make a long, deep cut in it. 砍；劈 ❑ *He came within two minutes of bleeding to death after slashing his wrists.* 他割腕后不到两分钟就失血而死。 ● N-COUNT **Slash** is also a noun. 劈砍；砍击 ❑ *Make deep slashes in the meat and push in the spice paste.* 把肉剁透，然后挤入调料酱。 **2** V-I If you **slash at** a person or thing, you quickly hit at them with something such as a knife. 挥舞（刀等）击打 ❑ *He slashed at her, aiming carefully.* 他瞄得准准的，朝她挥砍过去。 **3** V-T To **slash** something such as costs or jobs means to reduce them by a large amount. 大幅度削减 [JOURNALISM] ❑ *Car makers could be forced to slash prices.* 汽车制造商可能会被迫大幅度降价。 **4** N-COUNT You say **slash** to refer to a sloping line that separates letters, words, or numbers. For example, if you are giving the number 340/2/K you say "Three four zero, slash two, slash K." 斜线号 [SPOKEN]

▲ **slate** /sleɪt/ (**slates, slating, slated**) **1** N-UNCOUNT **Slate** is a dark gray rock that can be easily split into thin layers. Slate is often used for covering roofs. （常用来作屋顶建材的）石板 ❑ *...a stone-built cottage, with a traditional slate roof.* …一间有传统石板屋顶的石砌村舍。 **2** N-COUNT A **slate** is one of the small flat pieces of slate that are used for covering roofs. 石板瓦 ❑ *Thieves had stolen the slates from the roof.* 窃贼偷走了屋顶的石板瓦。 **3** V-T PASSIVE If something **is slated to** happen, it is planned to happen at a particular time or on a particular occasion. （在特定时间或者条件下）选定 [mainly AM] ❑ *Bromfield was slated to become U.S. Secretary of Agriculture.* 布罗姆菲尔德被内定为美国的农业部长。 **4** PHRASE If you start **with a clean slate**, you do not take account of previous mistakes or failures and make a fresh start. 不计前嫌重新开始；既往不咎 ❑ *The proposal is to pay everything you owe, so that you can start with a clean slate.* 奉劝你还清所有债务，这样你就可以重新开始。

★ **slaugh·ter** /slɔtər/ (**slaughters, slaughtering, slaughtered**) **1** V-T If large numbers of people or animals **are slaughtered**, they are killed in a way that is cruel or unnecessary. 屠杀 [usu passive] ❑ *Thirty four people were slaughtered while lining up to cast their votes.* 有34人在排队投票时遭屠杀。 ● N-UNCOUNT **Slaughter** is also a noun. 屠杀 ❑ *This was only a small part of a war where the slaughter of civilians was commonplace.* 这只是战争的一小部分，在战争中对平民的屠杀已司空见惯。 **2** V-T To **slaughter** animals such as cows and sheep means to kill them for their meat. 屠宰 ❑ *Lack of chicken feed means that chicken farms are having to slaughter their stock.* 饲料不足意味着养鸡场将不得不宰杀鸡。 ● N-UNCOUNT **Slaughter** is also a noun. 屠宰 ❑ *More than 491,000 sheep were exported for slaughter last year.* 去年，超过四十九万一千只羊被出口供屠宰。

slave /sleɪv/ (**slaves, slaving, slaved**) **1** N-COUNT A **slave** is someone who is the property of another person and has to work for that person. 奴隶 ❑ *The state of Liberia was formed a century and a half ago by freed slaves from the United States.* 利比里亚国家是一个半世纪前由来自美国的获得自由的奴隶建立的。 **2** N-COUNT You can describe someone as a **slave** when they are completely under the control of another person or of a powerful influence. 奴隶般受控制的人 ❑ *She may no longer be a slave to the studio system, but she still has a duty to her fans.* 她也许不再受制片公司制度的控制了，但她对其粉丝还负有责任。 **3** V-I If you say that a person **is slaving over** something or **is slaving for** someone, you mean that they are working very hard. 苦干 ❑ *When you're busy all day the last thing you want to do is spend hours slaving over a hot stove.* 当你忙碌了一整天后，你最不愿意做的事就是花好几个钟头在灼热的火炉边辛苦地劳作。 ● PHRASAL VERB **Slave away** means the same as **slave**. 苦干 ❑ *He stares at the hundreds of workers slaving away in the intense sun.* 他凝视着几百个正在烈日下苦干的工人们。

slav·ery /sleɪvəri, sleɪvri/ N-UNCOUNT **Slavery** is the system by which people are owned by other people as slaves. 奴隶制 ❑ *My people have survived 400 years of slavery.* 我的民族历经400年的奴隶制度后幸存了下来。

▲ **slay** /sleɪ/ (**slays, slaying, slew, slayed, slain**) **1** V-T If someone **slays** an animal, they kill it in a violent way. 屠杀 [FORMAL] ❑ *...the hill where St. George slew the dragon.* …圣乔治屠龙之丘。 **2** V-T PASSIVE If someone **has been slain**, they have been murdered. 谋杀 [mainly AM] ❑ *Two Australian tourists were slain.* 两位澳大利亚游客被谋杀了。

sleaze /sliz/ N-UNCOUNT You use **sleaze** to describe activities that you consider immoral, dishonest, or not respectable, especially in politics, business, journalism, or entertainment. （政治、商业、新闻或娱乐业中的）不名誉 [INFORMAL, DISAPPROVAL] ❑ *She claimed that an atmosphere of sleaze and corruption now surrounded the government.* 她声称目前声名狼藉和腐败的氛围笼罩着这个政府。

slea·zy /slizi/ (**sleazier, sleaziest**) **1** ADJ If you describe a place as **sleazy**, you dislike it because it looks dirty and badly cared for, and not respectable. 破烂的 [INFORMAL, DISAPPROVAL] ❑ *...sleazy bars.* … 破烂不堪的酒吧。 **2** ADJ If you describe something or someone as **sleazy**, you disapprove of them because you think they are not respectable and are rather disgusting. 不名誉的；令人厌恶的 [INFORMAL, DISAPPROVAL] ❑ *The accusations are making the government's conduct appear increasingly sleazy.* 种种指责使这个政府的行为看起来越发令人厌恶。

sled /slɛd/ (**sleds, sledding, sledded**)

in BRIT, use **sledge**

1 N-COUNT A **sled** is an object used for traveling over snow. It consists of a framework which slides on two strips of wood or metal. 雪橇 [AM] ❑ *I saw her pulling three children through the snow on a sled.* 我看到她用雪橇拉着3个孩子穿过风雪。 **2** V-I If you **sled** or go **sledding**, you ride on a sled. 乘雪橇 [AM] ❑ *We got home and went sledding on the small hill in our back yard.* 我们回到家，去后院的小山丘上滑雪橇。

sledge /slɛdʒ/ (**sledges, sledging, sledged**) **1** N-COUNT A **sledge** is the same as a **sled**. 雪橇 [BRIT] **2** V-I If you **sledge** or go **sledging**, you ride on a sledge. 滑雪橇 [BRIT]

sleek /slik/ (**sleeker, sleekest**) **1** ADJ **Sleek** hair or fur is smooth and shiny and looks healthy. 光滑的 ❑ *...sleek black hair.* …乌黑光滑的头发。 **2** ADJ If you describe someone as **sleek**, you mean that they look rich and stylish. 时髦的 ❑ *Lord White is as sleek and elegant as any other millionaire businessman.* 怀特勋爵像其他百万富商一样时尚高雅。 **3** ADJ **Sleek** vehicles, furniture, or other objects look smooth, shiny, and expensive. （车辆、家具等）豪华的 ❑ *...a sleek white BMW.* …一辆豪华的白色宝马轿车。

Word Web sleep

Do you ever go to **bed** and then discover you can't **fall asleep**? You start **yawning** and you feel **tired**. But somehow your body isn't ready for a good night's **rest**. You **toss and turn** and pound the **pillow** for hours. After a while you may start to **doze**, but then five minutes later you're **wide awake**. The scientific name for this condition is **insomnia**. There are many causes for sleeplessness like this. If you **nap** too late in the day it may interrupt your normal sleep cycle. Health and job-related worries can also affect sleep patterns.

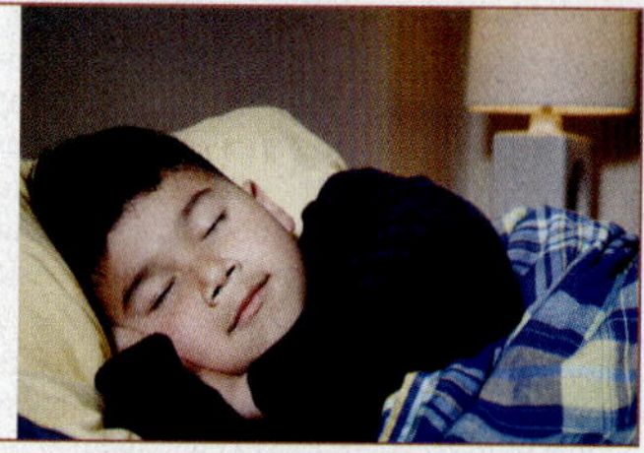

sleep ♦♦◇ /slip/ (**sleeps, sleeping, slept**) **1** N-UNCOUNT **Sleep** is the natural state of rest in which your eyes are closed, your body is inactive, and your mind does not think. 睡眠；睡觉 ❑ *They were exhausted from lack of sleep.* 他们因睡眠不足而疲惫不堪了。❑ *Be quiet and go to sleep.* 安静，睡觉吧。 **2** V-I When you **sleep**, you rest with your eyes closed and your mind and body inactive. 睡着；睡觉 ❑ *During the drive, the baby slept.* 在行驶中那个婴儿睡了。❑ *I've not been able to sleep for the last few nights.* 最近几个晚上我一直无法入睡。 **3** N-COUNT A **sleep** is a period of sleeping. (一段) 睡眠时间 ❑ *I think he may be ready for a sleep soon.* 我想他可能准备好了马上睡一觉。 **4** V-T If a building or room **sleeps** a particular number of people, it has beds for that number of people. 供…住宿 [no cont, no passive] ❑ *The villa sleeps 10.* 这幢别墅可供10人住宿。 **5** → see also **sleeping** **6** PHRASE If you cannot **get to sleep**, you are unable to sleep. 入睡 ❑ *I can't get to sleep with all that singing.* 那样的歌声让我无法入睡。 **7** PHRASE If you say that you didn't **lose** any **sleep over** something, you mean that you did not worry about it at all. 担心 ❑ *I didn't lose too much sleep over that investigation.* 我不太担心那起调查。 **8** PHRASE If you are trying to make a decision and you say that you will **sleep on it**, you mean that you will delay making a decision on it until the following day, so you have time to think about it. 把…留待以后解决 ❑ *I need more time to sleep on it. It's a big decision and I want to make the right one.* 我需要更多的时间再考虑一下。这是个重大的决定，我想做出正确的决定。 **9** PHRASE If a sick or injured animal **is put to sleep**, it is killed by a vet in a way that does not cause it pain. 使 (有病或受伤的动物) 无痛苦地死去 ❑ *I'm going take the dog down to the vet's and have her put to sleep.* 我打算把这只狗带到兽医那儿，让她无痛苦地死去。 **10** to **sleep rough** → see **rough**
→ see Word Web: **sleep**
→ see **dream**

There are several verbal expressions in English using the noun **sleep** which refer to the moment when you start to sleep. When you go to bed at night, you normally **go to sleep** or **fall asleep**. When you **go to sleep**, it is usually a deliberate action. ❑ *He didn't want to go to sleep.* You can **fall asleep** by accident, or at a time when you should be awake. ❑ *I've seen doctors fall asleep in the operating room.* If you have difficulty sleeping, you can say that you cannot **get to sleep**. ❑ *Sometimes the fever prevents the child from getting to sleep.*

S

▸ **sleep around** PHRASAL VERB If you say that someone **sleeps around**, you disapprove of them because they have sex with a lot of different people. 到处乱搞男女关系 [INFORMAL, DISAPPROVAL] ❑ *I don't sleep around.* 我可不到处乱搞男女关系。

▸ **sleep in** PHRASAL VERB If you **sleep in**, you stay asleep in the morning for longer than you usually do. 睡懒觉 ❑ *Yesterday, few players turned up because most slept in.* 昨天，没有几个球员露面，因为大多数都睡了懒觉。

▸ **sleep off** PHRASAL VERB If you **sleep off** the effects of too much traveling, drink, or food, you recover from it by sleeping. 以睡眠消除 (不适) ❑ *It's a good idea to spend the first night of your vacation sleeping off the jet lag.* 你假期的第一天晚上睡觉来消除飞行时差反应是个好主意。

▸ **sleep over** PHRASAL VERB If someone, especially a child, **sleeps over** in a place such as a friend's home, they stay there for one night. (尤指孩子) 不在家过夜 ❑ *She said his friends could sleep over.* 她说他的朋友们可能不回家过夜。

▸ **sleep together** PHRASAL VERB If two people **are sleeping together**, they are having a sexual relationship, but are not usually married to each other. (通常指非婚姻关系的两个人) 一起睡 ❑ *I'm pretty sure they slept together before they were married.* 我很确定他们结婚前就睡在一起。

▸ **sleep with** PHRASAL VERB If you **sleep with** someone, you have sex with them. 与…发生性关系 ❑ *He was old enough to sleep with a girl and make her pregnant.* 他年龄已经够大了，能够跟女孩发生性关系并使她怀孕。

Thesaurus *sleep* 另参见：

N.	nap, rest, slumber **1** **3**
V.	doze, rest, snooze; *(ant.)* awaken, wake **2**

Word Partnership *sleep* 的常用搭配：

V.	**can't/couldn't** sleep **2** **drift off to** sleep, **get enough** sleep, **get some** sleep, **go to** sleep, **need** sleep **1**
N.	sleep **deprivation**, sleep **disorder**, **hours of** sleep, **lack of** sleep **1** sleep **on the floor**, sleep **nights** **2**
ADJ.	**deep** sleep **1** **good** sleep **3**

sleep·er /slipər/ (**sleepers**) N-COUNT You can use **sleeper** to indicate how well someone sleeps. For example, if someone is a light **sleeper**, they are easily woken up. (睡眠质量不同的) 睡眠者 ❑ *I'm a very light sleeper and I can hardly get any sleep at all.* 我是个睡觉非常轻的人，几乎一点儿也睡不着。

sleep·ing bag (**sleeping bags**) N-COUNT A **sleeping bag** is a large deep bag with a warm lining, used for sleeping in, especially when you are camping. 睡袋

sleep·ing part·ner (**sleeping partners**) N-COUNT A **sleeping partner** is the same as a **silent partner**. 不参与具体经营的合伙人 [BRIT, BUSINESS]

sleep·less /sliplɪs/ **1** ADJ A **sleepless** night is one during which you do not sleep. 失眠的 ❑ *I have sleepless nights worrying about her.* 我有好几个不眠之夜都在为她担心。 **2** ADJ Someone who is **sleepless** is unable to sleep. 无法入睡的 ❑ *A sleepless baby can seem to bring little reward.* 睡不着觉的婴儿似乎会令人难以满意。

sleep·over /slipoʊvər/ (**sleepovers**) also **sleep-over** N-COUNT A **sleepover** is an occasion when someone, especially a child, sleeps for one night in a place such as a friend's home. (尤指孩子的) 不在家过夜 ❑ *Emily couldn't ask a friend for a sleepover until she cleaned her room.* 埃米莉直到把房间清理干净了才会叫朋友来过夜。

sleep·walk /slipwɔk/ (**sleepwalks, sleepwalking, sleepwalked**) V-I If someone **is sleepwalking**, they are walking around while they are asleep. 梦游 ❑ *He once sleepwalked to the middle of the road outside his home at 1 a.m.* 他有一次凌晨1点钟梦游到了家外面的那条马路中央。

sleepy /slipi/ (**sleepier, sleepiest**) **1** ADJ If you are **sleepy**, you are very tired and are almost asleep. 困倦的；昏昏欲睡的 ❑ *I was beginning to feel amazingly sleepy.* 我开始感觉到特别困。 ● **sleepi·ly** ADV 困倦地；昏昏欲睡地 [ADV with v] ❑ *Joanna sat up, blinking sleepily.* 乔安娜坐了起来，睡意未消地眨着眼睛。 **2** ADJ A **sleepy** place is quiet and does not have much activity or excitement. 寂静的；不活跃的 ❑ *Valence is a sleepy little town just south of Lyon.* 瓦朗斯是里昂正南方一个寂静的小镇。

sleet /slit/ N-UNCOUNT **Sleet** is rain that is partly frozen. 冻雨 ❑ *...blinding snow, driving sleet and wind.* …迷眼的大雪、猛烈的冻雨和狂风。
→ see **water**

sleeve /sliv/ (**sleeves**) **1** N-COUNT The **sleeves** of a coat, shirt, or other item of clothing are the parts that cover your arms. 袖子 ❑ *His sleeves were rolled up to his elbows.* 他的两只袖子被挽到了肘部。 **2** N-COUNT A record **sleeve** is the stiff cover in which a record is kept. (唱片的) 套子 [mainly BRIT] ❑ *...an album sleeve.* …一个唱片套。 **3** PHRASE If you have something **up** your **sleeve**, you have an idea or plan which you have not told anyone about. You can also say that someone has **an ace, card,** or **trick up** their **sleeve**. 有锦囊妙计；对…胸有成竹 ❑ *He wondered what tricks Shearson had up his sleeve.* 他想知道希尔森有何锦囊妙计。

sleeve·less /sliːvlɪs/ ADJ A **sleeveless** dress, top, or other item of clothing has no sleeves. 无袖的 [usu ADJ n] ❑ *She wore a sleeveless silk dress.* 她穿了一件无袖的丝绸礼服。

sleigh /sleɪ/ (**sleighs**) N-COUNT A **sleigh** is a vehicle which can slide over snow. Sleighs are usually pulled by horses. (通常由马拉的)雪橇

slen·der /slɛndər/ **1** ADJ A **slender** person is attractively thin and graceful. 苗条的；优美的 [WRITTEN, APPROVAL] ❑ *She was slender, with delicate wrists and ankles.* 她身材苗条，有着纤细的手腕和脚踝。❑ *...a tall, slender figure in a straw hat.* …一个戴草帽的高挑的形象。**2** ADJ You can use **slender** to describe a situation which exists but only to a very small degree. 微弱的 [WRITTEN] ❑ *The United States held a slender lead.* 美国稍微领先。

slept /slɛpt/ **Slept** is the past tense and past participle of **sleep**. **sleep**的过去式和过去分词

slice ♦◇◇ /slaɪs/ (**slices, slicing, sliced**) **1** N-COUNT A **slice of** bread, meat, fruit, or other food is a thin piece that has been cut from a larger piece. (切下的食物) 薄片 ❑ *Try to eat at least four slices of bread a day.* 每天尽量吃至少4片面包。**2** V-T If you **slice** bread, meat, fruit, or other food, you cut it into thin pieces. 把(食物) 切成薄片 ❑ *Helen sliced the cake.* 海伦把蛋糕切成了薄片。● PHRASAL VERB **Slice up** means the same as **slice**. 把(食物) 切成薄片 ❑ *I sliced up an onion.* 我把洋葱切成了片。**3** N-COUNT You can use **slice** to refer to a part of a situation or activity. (情况或活动的) 部分 ❑ *Fiction takes up a large slice of the publishing market.* 小说占出版市场的一大部分。**4** **slice of the action** → see **action**
→ see **cut**

Word Partnership *slice* 的常用搭配：

ADJ.	**small** slice, **thin** slice **1**
N.	slice **of bread**, slice **of pie**, slice **of pizza** **1**
	slice **a cake** **2**
	slice **of life** **3**
PREP.	slice **into**, slice **off**, slice **through** **2**

▲ **slick** /slɪk/ (**slicker, slickest**) **1** ADJ A **slick** performance, production, or advertisement is skillful and impressive. 娴熟的 ❑ *There's a big difference between an amateur video and a slick Hollywood production.* 业余录像与娴熟的好莱坞作品之间有天壤之别。**2** ADJ A **slick** action is done quickly and smoothly, and without any obvious effort. 灵巧的 ❑ *They were outplayed by the Colombians' slick passing and decisive finishing.* 他们败给了哥伦比亚人灵巧的传球和决定性的最后一击。**3** ADJ A **slick** person speaks easily in a way that is likely to convince people, but is not sincere. 圆滑的；巧舌如簧的 [DISAPPROVAL] ❑ *Don't be fooled by slick politicians.* 别被巧舌如簧的政客们愚弄了。**4** N-COUNT A **slick** is the same as an **oil slick**. 浮油 ❑ *Experts are trying to devise ways to clean up the huge slick.* 专家们在努力想出清除大面积浮油的办法。

slide ♦◇◇ /slaɪd/ (**slides, sliding, slid**) **1** V-T/V-I When something **slides** somewhere or when you **slide** it there, it moves there smoothly over or against something. 使滑动；滑动 ❑ *She slid the door open.* 她把门滑开了。❑ *I slid the wallet into his pocket.* 我把那钱包滑进了他的口袋。**2** V-I If you **slide** somewhere, you move there smoothly and quietly. 悄悄地溜到 ❑ *He slid into the driver's seat.* 他悄悄地坐到了司机的座位上。**3** V-I To **slide into** a particular mood, attitude, or situation means to gradually start to have that mood, attitude, or situation often without intending to. 不知不觉地陷入(某种情绪、态度或情形) ❑ *She had slid into a depression.* 她不知不觉地抑郁寡欢起来。**4** V-T/V-I If currencies or prices **slide**, they gradually become worse or lower in value. 使减少；下跌 [JOURNALISM] ❑ *The dollar continued to slide.* 美元继续下跌。● N-COUNT **Slide** is also a noun. 下跌 ❑ *...the dangerous slide in oil prices.* …石油价格危险的下跌。**5** N-COUNT A **slide** is a small piece of photographic film which you project onto a screen so that you can see the picture. 幻灯片 ❑ *...a slide show.* …幻灯片放映。**6** N-COUNT A **slide** is a piece of glass on which you put something that you want to examine through a microscope. (显微镜的) 载物玻璃片 ❑ *...a drop of blood on a slide.* …载物玻璃片上的一滴血。**7** N-COUNT A **slide** is a piece of playground equipment that has a steep slope for children to go down for fun. 滑梯 ❑ *...two young children playing on a slide.* …在玩滑梯的两个年幼的孩子。

Word Partnership *slide* 的常用搭配：

V.	**begin to** slide, **continue to** slide **1**–**4**
ADJ.	**downward** slide, **recent** slide, **steep** slide **4**

slight ♦◇◇ /slaɪt/ (**slighter, slightest, slights, slighting, slighted**) **1** ADJ Something that is **slight** is very small in degree or quantity. 轻微的；细微的 ❑ *Doctors say he has made a slight improvement.* 医生说他已经有些轻微的好转。❑ *He's not the slightest bit worried.* 他一点儿也不着急。**2** ADJ A **slight** person has a fairly thin and delicate looking body. 瘦小的；纤细的 ❑ *She is smaller and slighter than Christie.* 她比克里斯蒂更瘦小更纤弱。● **slight·ly** ADV 瘦小地；纤细地 [ADV -ed] ❑ *...a slightly built man.* …一个身材瘦小的男人。**3** V-T If you **are slighted**, someone does or says something that insults you by treating you as if your views or feelings are not important. 轻蔑；怠慢 [usu passive] ❑ *They felt slighted by not being adequately consulted.* 因为没有充分地征求他们的意见，他们感到被怠慢了。● N-COUNT **Slight** is also a noun. 轻视；冷落 ❑ *It's difficult to persuade my husband that it isn't a slight on him that I enjoy my evening class.* 很难劝说我丈夫相信我喜欢去上夜校课程并不是对他的冷落。**4** PHRASE You use **in the slightest** to emphasize a negative statement. (用于加强否定的陈述语气) 一点也 [EMPHASIS] ❑ *That doesn't interest me in the slightest.* 那事儿一点也勾不起我的兴趣。

slight·ly ♦♦◇ /slaɪtli/ ADV **Slightly** means to some degree but not to a very large degree. 轻微地；稍微 ❑ *His family then moved to a slightly larger house.* 他的家后来搬到了一间稍微大一点儿的房子。❑ *Each person learns in a slightly different way.* 每个人学习的方式都略有不同。

slim ♦◇◇ /slɪm/ (**slimmer, slimmest, slims, slimming, slimmed**) **1** ADJ A **slim** person has an attractively thin and well-shaped body. 苗条的；纤细的 [APPROVAL] ❑ *The young woman was tall and slim.* 那个年轻女子个子高挑，身材苗条。**2** ADJ A **slim** book, wallet, or other object is thinner than usual. 薄的 ❑ *The slim booklets describe a range of services and facilities.* 那些薄薄的小册子描述了一系列服务和设施。**3** ADJ A **slim** chance or possibility is a very small one. (机会或可能性) 微小的 ❑ *There's still a slim chance that he may become president.* 仍然有微小的可能他会当上总统。**4** V-T If an organization **slims** its products or workers, it reduces the number of them that it has. 缩减 [BUSINESS] ❑ *The company recently slimmed its product line.* 该公司最近缩减了生产线。

▸ **slim down** **1** PHRASAL VERB If you **slim down**, you lose weight and become thinner. 减轻体重；变苗条 ❑ *People will lose weight when they slim down with a friend.* 人们若和朋友一起减肥，就会减轻体重。**2** PHRASAL VERB If a company or other organization **slims down** or **is slimmed down**, it employs fewer people, in order to save money or become more efficient. (为节省开支或提高效率而) 裁员 [BUSINESS] ❑ *Many firms have had little choice but to slim down.* 许多公司除了裁员已经没有多少选择了。

Word Partnership *slim* 的常用搭配：

ADJ.	**tall and** slim **1**
ADV.	**pretty** slim, **very** slim **1** **3**
N.	slim **chance**, slim **lead**, slim **margin** **3**

slime /slaɪm/ N-UNCOUNT **Slime** is a thick, wet substance which covers a surface or comes from the bodies of animals such as snails. (动物体表分泌的) 黏液；污泥 ❑ *He swam down and retrieved his glasses from the muck and slime at the bottom of the pond.* 他潜下水去，从池塘底部的烂泥污物中找回了眼镜。

slimy /slaɪmi/ (**slimier, slimiest**) ADJ **Slimy** substances are thick, wet, and unpleasant. **Slimy** objects are covered in a slimy substance. 黏糊糊的；覆有黏液的 ❑ *His feet slipped in the slimy mud.* 他因脚下黏糊糊的泥而滑倒了。

▲ **sling** /slɪŋ/ (**slings, slinging, slung**) **1** V-T If you **sling** something somewhere, you throw it there carelessly. (随意) 扔 ❑ *Marla was recently seen slinging her shoes at Trump.* 最近玛拉被看到向特拉普扔她的鞋子。**2** V-T If you **sling** something over your shoulder or over something such as a chair, you hang it there loosely. (松散地)悬起 ❑ *She slung her coat over her desk chair.* 她把外衣搭在了桌椅背上。❑ *He had a small green backpack slung over one shoulder.* 他把一只绿色小背包挂在一边肩上。**3** V-T If a rope, blanket, or other object **is slung** between two points, someone has hung it loosely between them. (在两头之间) 悬挂 [usu passive] ❑ *...two long poles with a blanket slung between them.* …之间挂着一条毯子的两根长杆。**4** N-COUNT A **sling** is an object made of ropes, straps, or cloth that is used for carrying things. 吊索 ❑ *They used slings of rope to lower us from one set of arms to*

S

another. 他们用几条绳索把我们从一组吊臂降到另外一组吊臂。 **5** N-COUNT A **sling** is a piece of cloth which supports someone's broken or injured arm and is tied around their neck. (挂在脖子上支撑伤臂或断臂的) 悬带 ❑ *She was back at work with her arm in a sling.* 她回来上班了，手臂用绷带吊着。

sling·shot /slɪŋʃɒt/ (**slingshots**) N-COUNT A **slingshot** is a device for shooting small stones. It is made of a Y-shaped stick with a piece of elastic tied between the two top posts. 弹弓 [AM]

in BRIT, use **catapult**

slip ♦♦◇ /slɪp/ (**slips, slipping, slipped**) **1** V-I If you **slip**, you accidentally slide and lose your balance. 滑；滑倒 ❑ *He had slipped on an icy pavement.* 他在结冰的人行道上滑倒了。 **2** V-I If something **slips**, it slides out of place or out of your hand. 滑走；滑落 ❑ *His glasses had slipped.* 他的眼镜滑落了。 **3** V-I If you **slip** somewhere, you go there quickly and quietly. 溜走 ❑ *Amy slipped downstairs and out of the house.* 埃米悄悄地下楼，溜出了屋子。 **4** V-T If you **slip** something somewhere, you put it there quickly in a way that does not attract attention. 把…悄悄地放在 ❑ *I slipped a note under Louise's door.* 我悄悄地把一张字条塞到了路易丝的门下。 ❑ *He found a coin in his pocket and slipped it into her hand.* 他在口袋里找到一枚硬币，把它悄悄塞进她的手里。 **5** V-T If you **slip** something **to** someone, you give it to them secretly. 偷偷地给 ❑ *Robert had slipped her a note in school.* 罗伯特上学时偷偷地塞给了她一张字条。 **6** V-I To **slip into** a particular state or situation means to pass gradually into it, in a way that is hardly noticed. (不知不觉地) 陷入 ❑ *It amazed him how easily one could slip into a routine.* 人们竟如此容易就陷入俗套，这使他感到吃惊。 **7** V-T/V-I If something **slips to** a lower level or standard, it falls to that level or standard. 使下降；下降 ❑ *Shares slipped to $1.17.* 股票下跌至$1.17。 ❑ *In June, producer prices slipped 0.1% from May.* 6月份，生产商的价格从5月份下降了0.1%。 ● N-SING **Slip** is also a noun. 下降 ❑ *...a slip in consumer confidence.* …消费者信心的下降。 **8** V-T/V-I If you **slip into** or **out of** clothes or shoes, you put them on or take them off quickly and easily. 迅速轻松地穿上；迅速轻松地脱下 ❑ *She slipped out of the jacket and tossed it on the couch.* 她快速脱下了那件上衣，把它丢在沙发上。 **9** N-COUNT A **slip** is a small or unimportant mistake. 差错；疏漏 ❑ *We must be well prepared, there must be no slips.* 我们必须好好准备，一定不要有差错。 **10** N-COUNT A **slip of** paper is a small piece of paper. 纸条 ❑ *...little slips of paper he had torn from a notebook.* …他从笔记本上撕下的几张小纸片。 ❑ *I put her name on the slip.* 我把她的名字写在那张纸条上。 **11** N-COUNT A **slip** is a thin piece of clothing that a woman wears under her dress or skirt. 衬裙 **12** PHRASE If you **let slip** information, you accidentally tell it to someone, when you wanted to keep it secret. 无意中说出 (秘密) ❑ *I bet he let slip that I'd gone to America.* 我确信他无意中说出了我已去了美国。 **13** PHRASE If something **slips** your **mind**, you forget about it. 被遗忘 ❑ *The reason for my visit had obviously slipped his mind.* 我到访的原因显然被他忘了。

▸ **slip up** PHRASAL VERB If you **slip up**, you make a small or unimportant mistake. 疏忽；出差错 ❑ *There were occasions when we slipped up.* 我们有疏忽的一些时候。

S

Thesaurus *slip* 另参见：

V.	fall, slide, trip **1**
N.	blunder, failure, flub, foul-up, mistake **9**
	leaf, page, paper, sheet **10**

Word Partnership *slip* 的常用搭配：

ADJ.	slip **resistant** **1**
N.	slip **of paper**, **sales** slip **10**
V.	**let** *(something)* slip **12**

slip·page /slɪpɪdʒ/ (**slippages**) N-VAR **Slippage** is a failure to maintain a steady position or rate of progress, so that a particular target or standard is not achieved. (位置、水准等方面) 下降 ❑ *...a substantial slippage in the value of sterling.* … 英国货币的大幅度贬值。

▲ **slip·per** /slɪpər/ (**slippers**) N-COUNT **Slippers** are loose, soft shoes that you wear at home. 拖鞋 ❑ *...a pair of old slippers.* …一双旧拖鞋。

slip·pery /slɪpəri/ **1** ADJ Something that is **slippery** is smooth, wet, or oily and is therefore difficult to walk on or to hold. 滑的；湿滑的 ❑ *The tiled floor was wet and slippery.* 那磁砖地板又湿又滑。 **2** ADJ You can describe someone as **slippery** if you think that they are dishonest in a clever way and cannot be trusted. 狡猾的；不可靠的 [DISAPPROVAL] ❑ *He is a slippery customer, and should be carefully watched.* 他可是个狡猾的主顾，得小心看着他。 **3** PHRASE If someone is on a **slippery slope**, they are involved in a course of action that is difficult to stop and that will eventually lead to failure or trouble. 不断恶化的局势 ❑ *The company started down the slippery slope of believing that they knew better than the customer.* 该公司开始走下坡路了，他们相信自己比顾客更明白。

▲ **slit** /slɪt/ (**slits, slitting**)

The form **slit** is used in the present tense and is the past tense and past participle.

1 V-T If you **slit** something, you make a long narrow cut in it. 切开；撕开 ❑ *They say somebody slit her throat.* 他们说有人割断了她的喉咙。 ❑ *He began to slit open each envelope.* 他开始撕开每个信封。 **2** N-COUNT A **slit** is a long narrow cut. 狭长的切口 ❑ *Make a slit in the stem about half an inch long.* 在树干上割一个约半英寸长的口儿。 **3** N-COUNT A **slit** is a long narrow opening in something. 裂缝；缝隙 ❑ *She watched them through a slit in the curtains.* 她透过窗帘的缝隙注视着他们。

→ see **shark**

slith·er /slɪðər/ (**slithers, slithering, slithered**) **1** V-I If you **slither** somewhere, you slide along in an uneven way. 滑动 ❑ *Robert lost his footing and slithered down the bank.* 罗伯特失足滑下了河岸。 **2** V-I If an animal such as a snake **slithers**, it moves along in a curving way. (蛇等) 蜿蜒地滑行 ❑ *The snake slithered into the water.* 那条蛇蜿蜒滑入了水中。

sliv·er /slɪvər/ (**slivers**) N-COUNT A **sliver of** something is a small thin piece or amount of it. 细片；少量 ❑ *Not a sliver of glass remains where the windows were.* 当时窗户所在的地方现在连一小片玻璃都没留下。

slog /slɒg/ (**slogs, slogging, slogged**) **1** V-T/V-I If you **slog through** something, you work hard and steadily through it. 苦干 [INFORMAL] ❑ *They secure their degrees by slogging through an intensive 11-month course.* 他们通过苦读11个月的强化课程而获得了学位。 ● PHRASAL VERB **Slog away** means the same as **slog**. 苦干 ❑ *Edward slogged away, always learning.* 爱德华埋头苦干，总是在学习。 **2** N-SING If you describe a task as a **slog**, you mean that it is tiring and requires a lot of effort. 苦干 [also no det] [INFORMAL] ❑ *There is little to show for the two years of hard slog.* 这两年的埋头苦干没有什么可展示的。

slo·gan /sloʊgən/ (**slogans**) N-COUNT A **slogan** is a short phrase that is easy to remember. Slogans are used in advertisements and by political parties and other organizations who want people to remember what they are saying or selling. 口号；广告语 ❑ *They could campaign on the slogan "We'll take less of your money."* 他们可以打着"我们将少赚你的钱"的广告语开展宣传攻势。

slop /slɒp/ (**slops, slopping, slopped**) V-T/V-I If liquid **slops** from a container or if you **slop** liquid somewhere, it comes out over the edge of the container, usually accidentally. 使溢出；溢出 ❑ *A little cognac slopped over the edge of the glass.* 少量法国白兰地溢出了那只酒杯。

slope /sloʊp/ (**slopes, sloping, sloped**) **1** N-COUNT A **slope** is the side of a mountain, hill, or valley. (山丘或山谷的) 斜坡 ❑ *Saint-Christo is perched on a mountain slope.* 圣克里斯托坐落在山坡上。 **2** N-COUNT A **slope** is a surface that is at an angle, so that one end is higher than the other. 斜面 ❑ *The street must have been on a slope.* 那条街一定是一直在一个斜坡上。 **3** V-I If a surface **slopes**, it is at an angle, so that one end is higher than the other. 倾斜 ❑ *The bank sloped down sharply to the river.* 那座堤岸陡峭地朝着那条河倾斜下去。 ● **slop·ing** ADJ 倾斜的 ❑ *...a brick building, with a sloping roof.* …一幢斜顶的砖建筑。 **4** V-I If something **slopes**, it leans to the right or to the left rather than being upright. 歪斜 ❑ *The writing sloped backwards.* 那字迹向后斜了。 **5** N-COUNT The **slope** of something is the angle at which it slopes. 斜度；坡度 ❑ *The slope increases as you go up the curve.* 你顺着那条弯路往上走，坡度越来越大。 **6** **slippery slope** → see **slippery**

slop·py /slɒpi/ (**sloppier, sloppiest**) ADJ If you describe someone's work or activities as **sloppy**, you mean they have been done in a careless and lazy way. 慵懒的；马虎的 [DISAPPROVAL] ❑ *He has little patience for sloppy work from colleagues.* 他无法忍耐同事们马虎的工作。

★ **slot** /slɒt/ (**slots, slotting, slotted**) **1** N-COUNT A **slot** is a narrow opening in a machine or container, for example, a hole that you put coins in to make a machine work. (机器或容器上的) 狭槽；投币口 ❑ *He dropped a coin into the slot and dialed.* 他把一枚硬币投进了那个投币口，然后拨了号。 **2** V-T/V-I If you **slot** something into something else, or if it **slots** into it, you put it into a space where it fits. 把…放入狭缝；放入狭缝 ❑ *He was slotting a CD into a CD player.*

他正把一张光盘放入光盘播放器中。❑ *The car seat belt slotted into place easily.* 那个汽车安全带很容易就扣好了。 3 N-COUNT A **slot** in a schedule or program is a place in it where an activity can take place. 时段；(时间表或节目的) 位置 ❑ *Visitors can book a time slot a week or more in advance.* 来访者们可以提前一周或一周以上预约一个时段。

slouch /slaʊtʃ/ (**slouches, slouching, slouched**) V-I If someone **slouches**, they sit or stand with their shoulders and head bent so they look lazy and unattractive. 无精打采地坐；无精打采地站 ❑ *Try not to slouch when you are sitting down.* 你坐下时尽量不要无精打采。

slow ♦♦◇ /sloʊ/ (**slower, slowest, slows, slowing, slowed**) 1 ADJ Something that is **slow** moves, happens, or is done without much speed. 缓慢的 ❑ *The traffic is heavy and slow.* 车很多，走得慢。 ❑ *Electric whisks should be used on a slow speed.* 电子打蛋器应该慢速运转。 ● **slow·ly** ADV 缓慢地 [ADV with v] ❑ *He spoke slowly and deliberately.* 他说得缓慢而慎重。 ● **slow·ness** N-UNCOUNT 缓慢 ❑ *She lowered the glass with calculated slowness.* 她有意慢慢地放下杯子。 2 ADV In informal English, **slower** is used to mean "at a slower speed" and **slowest** is used to mean "at the slowest speed." In nonstandard English, **slow** is used to mean "with little speed." 缓慢地 [ADV after v] ❑ *I began to walk slower and slower.* 我开始走得越来越慢。 3 ADJ Something that is **slow** takes a long time. 漫长的 ❑ *The distribution of passports has been a slow process.* 颁发护照一直是个漫长的过程。 ● **slow·ly** ADV 漫长地 [ADV with v] ❑ *My resentment of her slowly began to fade.* 我对她的怨恨慢慢地开始消退了。 ● **slow·ness** N-UNCOUNT 缓慢 ❑ *...the slowness of political and economic progress.* …政治和经济进展的缓慢。 4 ADJ If someone is **slow** to do something, they do it after a delay. 迟缓的 [v-link ADJ] ❑ *The world community has been slow to respond to the crisis.* 国际社会对该危机的反应向来迟缓。 5 V-T/V-I If something **slows** or if you **slow** it, it starts to move or happen more slowly. 使慢下来；慢下来 ❑ *The rate of bombing has slowed considerably.* 轰炸频率已经放慢了许多。 ❑ *She slowed the car and began driving up a narrow road.* 她放慢了车速，开始驶上一条狭窄的道路。 6 ADJ Someone who is **slow** is not very clever and takes a long time to understand things. 迟钝的 ❑ *He got hit on the head and he's been a bit slow since.* 他的头被打了一下，从那以后，就有点迟钝。 7 ADJ If you describe a situation, place, or activity as **slow**, you mean that it is not very exciting. 乏味的 ❑ *Don't be faint-hearted when things seem a bit slow or boring.* 当事情似乎有点乏味或无聊时，不要胆怯。 8 ADJ If a clock or watch is **slow**, it shows a time that is earlier than the correct time. (钟表) 慢的 ❑ *The clock is about two and a half minutes slow.* 那钟慢两分半左右。 9 **slowly but surely** → see **surely**

▸ **slow down** 1 PHRASAL VERB If something **slows down** or if something **slows** it **down**, it starts to move or happen more slowly. 放慢；使放慢 ❑ *The bus slowed down for the next stop.* 那辆公共汽车慢下来准备停靠下一站。 ❑ *There is no cure for the disease, although drugs can slow down its rate of development.* 这种病没法治，尽管药物可以延缓病情的发展。 2 PHRASAL VERB If someone **slows down** or if something **slows** them **down**, they become less active. 使放松下来；放松下来 ❑ *You will need to slow down for a while.* 你将会需要放松一会儿。 3 → see also **slowdown**

▸ **slow up** PHRASAL VERB **Slow up** means the same as **slow down** 1. 使放慢；使放松下来；放慢；放松下来 ❑ *Sales are slowing up.* 销售正在减慢。

Word Partnership *slow* 的常用搭配：

ADJ. slow **acting**, slow **moving** 1
slow **but steady** 1 3
N. slow **movements**, slow **speed**, slow **traffic** 1
slow **death**, slow **growth**, slow **pace**, slow **process**, slow **progress**, slow **recovery**, slow **response**, slow **sales**, slow **start**, slow **stop** 3

slow·down /sloʊdaʊn/ (**slowdowns**) 1 N-COUNT A **slowdown** is a reduction in speed or activity. 减速；减退 ❑ *There has been a sharp slowdown in economic growth.* 在经济增长方面一直存在急剧的减速。 2 N-COUNT A **slowdown** is a protest in which workers deliberately work slowly and cause problems for their employers. 怠工抗议 [AM, BUSINESS]

in BRIT, use **go-slow**

❑ *It's impossible to assess how many officers are participating in the slowdown.* 不可能估计出有多少官员参加了怠工抗议。

slow mo·tion also **slow-motion** N-UNCOUNT When film or television pictures are shown **in slow motion**, they are shown much more slowly than normal. (电影或电视节目的) 慢动作 ❑ *It seemed almost as if he were falling in slow motion.* 看起来他那时几乎像是在以慢动作倒下。

sludge /slʌdʒ/ (**sludges**) N-VAR **Sludge** is thick mud, sewage, or industrial waste. 淤泥；污水；工业废料 ❑ *More than a million gallons of sludge has seeped into the water.* 超过一百万加仑的工业废料已渗进水中。

slug /slʌg/ (**slugs**) 1 N-COUNT A **slug** is a small slow-moving creature with a long soft body and no legs, like a snail without a shell. 蛞蝓 2 N-COUNT If you take a **slug of** an alcoholic drink, you take a large mouthful of it. 一大口 (饮料) [INFORMAL] ❑ *Edgar took a slug of his drink.* 埃德加喝了一大口饮料。

▲ **slug·gish** /slʌgɪʃ/ ADJ You can describe something as **sluggish** if it moves, works, or reacts much slower than you would like or is normal. 缓慢的；迟钝的 ❑ *The economy remains sluggish.* 经济保持缓慢发展。 ❑ *Circulation is much more sluggish in the feet than in the hands.* 血液循环在脚部要比在手部慢得多。

★ **slum** /slʌm/ (**slums**) N-COUNT A **slum** is an area of a city where living conditions are very bad and where the houses are in bad condition. 贫民区 ❑ *...a slum area of St. Louis.* …圣路易斯的一个贫民区。

slum·ber /slʌmbər/ (**slumbers, slumbering, slumbered**) N-VAR **Slumber** is sleep. 睡眠 [LITERARY] ❑ *He had fallen into exhausted slumber.* 他已经进入了沉睡。 ● V-I **Slumber** is also a verb. 睡觉 ❑ *The older three girls are still slumbering peacefully.* 稍大些的3个女孩仍在平静地睡着。

slum·ber par·ty (**slumber parties**) N-COUNT A **slumber party** is an occasion when a group of young friends spend the night together at the home of one of the group. (一群年轻人在其中一位家里过夜的) 睡衣晚会 [mainly AM] ❑ *I'm having a slumber party for my birthday.* 我正在为我的生日举办睡衣晚会。

★ **slump** /slʌmp/ (**slumps, slumping, slumped**) 1 V-I If something such as the value of something **slumps**, it falls suddenly and by a large amount. (价值等) 暴跌 ❑ *Net profits slumped by 41%.* 净利润暴跌了41%。 ● N-COUNT **Slump** is also a noun. (价值等的) 暴跌 ❑ *The council's land is now worth much less than originally hoped because of a slump in property prices.* 由于地产价格的暴跌，委员会的土地目前大不如原来所希望的那么值钱了。 2 N-COUNT A **slump** is a time when many people in a country are unemployed and poor. 经济萧条时期 ❑ *...the slump of the early 1980s.* …20世纪80年代初期的经济萧条时期。 3 V-T/V-I If you **slump** somewhere, you fall or sit down there heavily, for example, because you are very tired or you feel ill. 瘫倒；(因劳累或生病等) 跌坐 ❑ *She slumped into a chair.* 她瘫倒在一张椅子上。

slung /slʌŋ/ **Slung** is the past tense and past participle of **sling**. **sling**的过去式和过去分词

▲ **slur** /slɜr/ (**slurs, slurring, slurred**) 1 N-COUNT A **slur** is an insulting remark which could damage someone's reputation. 诽谤 ❑ *This is yet another slur on the integrity of the police.* 这将是对警察廉正的又一次毁谤。 2 V-T/V-I If someone **slurs** their speech or if their speech **slurs**, they do not pronounce each word clearly, because they are drunk, ill, or sleepy. (因醉酒、生病或困乏) 含糊地说；(因醉酒、生病或困乏) 发音不清 ❑ *He repeated himself and slurred his words more than usual.* 他重复着自己的话，比平常更加含糊不清地说着。

slurp /slɜrp/ (**slurps, slurping, slurped**) 1 V-T/V-I If you **slurp** a liquid, you drink it noisily. 出声地喝；出声地喝着 ❑ *He blew on his soup before slurping it off the spoon.* 他先吹了吹汤，然后出声地从匙子里喝汤。 2 N-COUNT A **slurp** is a noise that you make with your mouth when you drink noisily, or a mouthful of liquid that you drink noisily. (喝东西时发出的) 声响；(出声喝的) 一口液体 ❑ *He takes a slurp from a cup of black coffee.* 他出声地喝了一口黑咖啡。

slush /slʌʃ/ N-UNCOUNT **Slush** is snow that has begun to melt and is therefore very wet and dirty. 雪泥 ❑ *Front-drive cars work better in the snow and slush.* 前轮驱动的汽车在雪中和雪泥中开得更好。

slush fund (**slush funds**) N-COUNT A **slush fund** is a sum of money collected to pay for an illegal activity, especially in politics or business. (政界或商界的) 贿赂基金 ❑ *He's accused of misusing $17.5 million from a secret government slush fund.* 他被指控从一个秘密政府贿赂基金中滥用1750万美元。

▲ **sly** /slaɪ/ 1 ADJ A **sly** look, expression, or remark shows that you know something that other people do not know or that was meant to be a secret. (眼神、表情或话语) 会意的 ❑ *His lips were spread in a sly smile.* 他的双唇在会心的微笑中张开。 ● **sly·ly** ADV 会意地 ❑ *Anna grinned slyly.* 安娜会意地咧嘴笑了。 2 ADJ If you describe someone as **sly**, you disapprove of them because they keep their

S

feelings or intentions hidden and are clever at deceiving people. 虚伪的；狡诈的 [DISAPPROVAL] ❑ *She is devious and sly and manipulative.* 她阴险、狡诈，而且爱操纵他人。

▲ **smack** /smæk/ (**smacks, smacking, smacked**) **1** V-T If you **smack** someone, you hit them with your hand. (用手) 击打 ❑ *She smacked me on the side of the head.* 她打到了我一边脑袋上。 ● N-COUNT **Smack** is also a noun. (用手) 击打 ❑ *Sometimes he just doesn't listen and I end up shouting at him or giving him a smack.* 有时他就是不听，最后我朝他大喊大叫，或者给他一巴掌。 **2** V-T If you **smack** something somewhere, you put it or throw it there so that it makes a loud, sharp noise. 啪地扔下；啪地放下 ❑ *He smacked his hands down on his knees.* 他把双手啪地放到了双膝上。 **3** V-I If one thing **smacks of** another thing that you consider bad, it reminds you of it or is like it. 带有…迹象；含有…意味 ❑ *The engineers' union was unhappy with the motion, saying it smacked of racism.* 工程师联合会不满意这个提议，说它有种族主义的味道。 **4** ADV Something that is **smack** in a particular place is exactly in that place. 恰好 [ADV prep] [INFORMAL] ❑ *In part that's because industry is smack in the middle of the city.* 部分是因为工业恰恰就在该市的中心地带。 **5** N-UNCOUNT **Smack** is heroin. 海洛因 [INFORMAL] ❑ *...a smack addict.* …一个吸海洛因成瘾的人。 **6** PHRASE If you **smack** your **lips**, you open and close your mouth noisily, especially before or after eating, to show that you are eager to eat or enjoyed eating. (尤指嘴馋或回味而) 咂嘴 ❑ *"I really want some dessert," Keaton says, smacking his lips.* "我真的想要些餐后甜点，"基顿咂着嘴唇说。

small ♦♦♦ /smɔl/ (**smaller, smallest**) **1** ADJ A **small** person, thing, or amount of something is not large in physical size. (体积或规模等) 小的 ❑ *She is small for her age.* 相对她的年龄而言，她个子小了。 ❑ *Stick them on using a small amount of glue.* 用少量胶水把它们粘上。 **2** ADJ A **small** group or quantity consists of only a few people or things. (规模) 小的 ❑ *A small group of students meets regularly to learn Japanese.* 一个小组的学生定期聚在一起学日语。 **3** ADJ A **small** child is a very young child. 幼小的 ❑ *I have a wife and two small children.* 我有妻子和两个年幼的孩子。 **4** ADJ You use **small** to describe something that is not significant or great in degree. (程度上) 不重要的 ❑ *It's quite easy to make quite small changes to the way that you work.* 对你的工作方式做些相当细微的调整是很容易的。 ❑ *No detail was too small to escape her attention.* 最微小的细节也逃不过她的注意。 **5** ADJ **Small** businesses or companies employ a small number of people and do business with a small number of clients. (生意或公司) 小规模的 ❑ *...shops, restaurants and other small businesses.* …商店、餐馆和其他小规模生意。 **6** ADJ If someone makes you look or feel **small**, they make you look or feel stupid or ashamed. 卑微的；感到惭愧的 [v-link ADJ] ❑ *This may just be another of her schemes to make me look small.* 这也许就是她要让我羞愧的又一个诡计。 **7** N-SING **The small of** your **back** is the bottom part of your back that curves in slightly. (人体的) 后腰 ❑ *Place your hands on the small of your back and breathe in.* 把你的双手放在后腰，然后吸气。 **8** **the small hours** → see **hour** **9** **small wonder** → see **wonder**

> You can use the adjective **small** rather than **little** to draw attention to the fact that something is small. For instance, you cannot say "The town is little" or "I have a very little car," but you can say "**The town is small**" or "**I have a very small car.**" **Little** is a less precise word than **small**, and may be used to suggest the speaker's feelings or attitude toward the person or thing being described. For that reason, **little** is often used after another adjective. ❑ *What a nice little house you've got here!... Shut up, you horrible little boy!*

> **Thesaurus** *small* 另参见：
> ADJ. little, minute, petite, slight; *(ant.)* big, large **1**
> young **3**
> insignificant, minor; *(ant.)* important, major, significant **4**

small print N-UNCOUNT **The small print** of a contract or agreement is the part of it that is written in very small print. You refer to it as **the small print** especially when you think that it might include unfavorable conditions which someone might not notice or understand. (合同或协议的) 附属细则 ❑ *Read the small print in your contract to find out exactly what you are insured for.* 读一下你合同中的附属细则，准确找出你投险的内容。

small-scale ADJ A **small-scale** activity or organization is small in size and limited in extent. (活动或组织) 小规模的 ❑ *...the small-scale production of farmhouse cheeses in Vermont.* …佛蒙特州小规模的农家奶酪生产。

smart ♦◇◇ /smɑrt/ (**smarter, smartest, smarts, smarting, smarted**) **1** ADJ You can describe someone who is clever or intelligent as **smart**. 聪明的；机智的 ❑ *He thinks he's smarter than Sarah is.* 他认为他比萨拉更聪明。 **2** ADJ **Smart** people and things are pleasantly neat and clean in appearance. 整洁的 [mainly BRIT] ❑ *He was smart and well groomed but not good looking.* 他时髦而且打扮整齐，但是长得不帅。 ❑ *I was dressed in a smart navy blue suit.* 我穿一身整洁的海军蓝制服。 ● **smart·ly** ADV 整洁地 [ADV with v] ❑ *He dressed very smartly, which was important in those days.* 他穿得非常整洁，这在当时很重要。 **3** ADJ A **smart** place or event is connected with wealthy and fashionable people. 时髦的 [mainly BRIT] ❑ *...smart dinner parties.* …时髦的宴会。 **4** V-I If a part of your body or a wound **smarts**, you feel a sharp stinging pain in it. (身体某部位或伤口) 刺痛 ❑ *My eyes smarted from the smoke.* 我的双眼被烟熏得刺痛。 **5** V-I If you **are smarting from** something such as criticism or failure, you feel upset about it. (因批评或失败) 感到难受 [usu cont] [JOURNALISM] ❑ *The Americans were still smarting from their defeat in the Vietnam War.* 美国人仍在为越战中失利而难受。 **6** **the smart money** → see **smart**

smart card (**smart cards**) N-COUNT A **smart card** is a plastic card which looks like a credit card and can store and process computer data. 智能卡 ❑ *We encourage the use of smart cards for online payments.* 我们鼓励智能卡在网上支付中的使用。

smart·en /smɑrtᵊn/ (**smartens, smartening, smartened**)
▸ **smarten up** PHRASAL VERB If you **smarten yourself** or a place **up**, you make yourself or the place look neater and tidier. 使更整洁；打扮更漂亮潇洒 ❑ *...a 10-year program to smarten up the city.* …一个使这座城市变得更整洁的十年计划。 ❑ *She had wisely smartened herself up.* 她已经聪明地把自己打扮得更漂亮了。

smash ♦◇◇ /smæʃ/ (**smashes, smashing, smashed**) **1** V-T/V-I If you **smash** something or if it **smashes**, it breaks into many pieces, for example, when it is hit or dropped. 打碎；破碎 ❑ *Someone smashed a bottle.* 有人打碎了一个瓶子。 ❑ *A crowd of youths started smashing windows.* 一群年轻人开始打碎窗户。 **2** V-T/V-I If you **smash** through a wall, gate, or door, you get through it by hitting and breaking it. 撞破 (墙或门) 而入 ❑ *The demonstrators used trucks to smash through embassy gates.* 示威者们用卡车撞破大门闯进大使馆。 **3** V-T/V-I If something **smashes** or **is smashed** against something solid, it moves very fast and with great force against it. 使猛撞；撞击 ❑ *The bottle smashed against a wall.* 那瓶子撞到了一面墙上。 **4** V-T To **smash** a political group or system means to deliberately destroy it. 搞垮 (政治集团或体制) [INFORMAL] ❑ *Their attempts to clean up politics and smash the power of party machines failed.* 他们整治政治和搞垮党派组织权力的企图失败了。
▸ **smash up** **1** PHRASAL VERB If you **smash** something **up**, you completely destroy it by hitting it and breaking it into many pieces. 砸碎；弄碎 ❑ *She took revenge on her ex-boyfriend by smashing up his home.* 她通过砸烂前男友的家来报复他。 **2** PHRASAL VERB If you **smash up** your car, you damage it by crashing it into something. 捣毁 ❑ *All you told me was that he'd smashed up yet another car.* 所有你要告诉我的就是他已经又捣毁了另一辆汽车。

▲ **smear** /smɪər/ (**smears, smearing, smeared**) **1** V-T If you **smear** a surface **with** an oily or sticky substance or **smear** the substance onto the surface, you spread a layer of the substance over the surface. 涂抹 ❑ *My sister smeared herself with suntan oil and slept by the swimming pool.* 我妹妹用防晒油涂抹了全身，然后睡在那游泳池边。 **2** N-COUNT A **smear** is a dirty or oily mark. 污迹；油迹 ❑ *There was a smear of gravy on his chin.* 他的下巴上有肉汤渍。 **3** V-T To **smear** someone means to spread unpleasant and untrue rumors or accusations about them in order to damage their reputation. 诽谤；诋毁 [JOURNALISM] ❑ *They planned to smear him by publishing information about his private life.* 他们计划通过公开有关他私生活方面的信息来诋毁他。 **4** N-COUNT A **smear** is an unpleasant and untrue rumor or accusation that is intended to damage someone's reputation. 诽谤；诋毁 [JOURNALISM] ❑ *He puts all the accusations down to a smear campaign by his political opponents.* 他把所有的指控归因于由其政敌发起的诽谤活动。 **5** N-COUNT A **smear** or a **smear test** is a medical test in which a few cells are taken from a woman's cervix and examined to see if any cancer cells are present. (一种从妇女子宫颈膜取样检验有无癌细胞的) 涂片试验 [BRIT]

in AM, use **Pap smear, Pap test**

Word Web smell

Scientists believe that the average person can recognize about 10,000 separate **odors**. Until recently, however, the **sense** of **smell** was a mystery. We now know that most substances release odor molecules into the air. They enter the body through the **nose**. When they reach the **nasal cavity**, they attach to **sensory** cells. The olfactory **nerve** carries the information to the brain and we identify the smell. The eyes, mouth, and throat also contain receptors that add to the olfactory experience. Interestingly, our sense of smell is more accurate later in the day than it is in the morning.

smell ♦◇◇ /smɛl/ (**smells, smelling, smelled**) 1 N-COUNT The **smell** of something is a quality it has which you become aware of when you breathe in through your nose. 气味 ❑ *...the smell of freshly baked bread.* …新烤面包的气味。 ❑ *...horrible smells.* …令人恶心的气味。 2 N-UNCOUNT Your sense of **smell** is the ability that your nose has to detect things. 嗅觉 ❑ *...people who lose their sense of smell.* …失去嗅觉的人们。 3 V-LINK If something **smells** a particular way, it has a quality which you become aware of through your nose. 有…的气味; 闻起来 ❑ *The room smelled of lemons.* 房间有股柠檬的气味。 ❑ *It smells delicious.* 它闻起来真香。 4 V-I If you say that something **smells**, you mean that it smells unpleasant. 有臭味 ❑ *Ma threw that out. She said it smelled.* 妈把那个扔出去了。她说它已经有臭味了。 5 V-T If you **smell** something, you become aware of it when you breathe in through your nose. 闻到 ❑ *As soon as we opened the front door we could smell the gas.* 我们一打开前门就能闻到那煤气味。 6 V-T If you **smell** something, you put your nose near it and breathe in, so that you can discover its smell. (鼻子凑近) 嗅 ❑ *I took a fresh rose out of the vase on our table, and smelled it.* 我从我们桌上的花瓶里取出一支新鲜的玫瑰，闻了闻。 7 **to smell a rat** → see **rat**
→ see Word Web: **smell**
→ see **taste**

Thesaurus *smell* 另参见：

N.	aroma, fragrance, odor, scent 1
V.	reek, stink 4
	breathe, inhale, sniff 5

smelly /smɛli/ (**smellier, smelliest**) ADJ Something that is **smelly** has an unpleasant smell. 有臭味的 ❑ *He had extremely smelly feet.* 他的脚臭气熏天。

smile ♦♦◇ /smaɪl/ (**smiles, smiling, smiled**) 1 V-I When you **smile**, the corners of your mouth curve up and you sometimes show your teeth. People smile when they are pleased or amused, or when they are being friendly. 微笑 ❑ *When he saw me, he smiled and waved.* 他见到我时，他笑了笑，挥了挥手。 ❑ *He rubbed the back of his neck and smiled ruefully at me.* 他揉搓着后脖颈，冲我懊悔地笑了一下。 2 N-COUNT A **smile** is the expression that you have on your face when you smile. 微笑 ❑ *She gave a wry smile.* 她露出苦笑。 ❑ *"There are some sandwiches if you're hungry," she said with a smile.* "如果你饿了，那儿有些三明治，" 她微笑着说。

Word Partnership *smile* 的常用搭配：

V.	smile **and laugh**, **make** *someone* smile, smile **and nod**, **see** *someone* smile, **try to** smile 1
	smile **fades**, **flash a** smile, **give** *someone* **a** smile 2
ADJ.	**big/little/small** smile, **broad** smile, **friendly** smile, **half** smile, **sad** smile, **shy** smile, **warm** smile, **wide** smile, **wry** smile 2

smi·ley /smaɪli/ (**smileys**) 1 ADJ A **smiley** person smiles a lot or is smiling. 总带着笑脸的; 笑着的 [usu ADJ n] [INFORMAL] ❑ *Two smiley babies are waiting for their lunch.* 两个笑着的婴儿在等着午餐。 2 N-COUNT A **smiley** or a **smiley face** is a symbol used in e-mail to show how someone is feeling. :-) is a smiley showing happiness. (电子邮件中表示开心的) 笑脸符号: :-) [COMPUTING]

smirk /smɜrk/ (**smirks, smirking, smirked**) V-I If you **smirk**, you smile in an unpleasant way, often because you believe that you have gained an advantage over someone else or know something that they do not know. 幸灾乐祸地笑; 自鸣得意地笑 ❑ *Two men standing nearby looked at me, nudged each other and smirked.* 站在旁边的两个男人看着我，互相用胳膊肘轻碰对方，幸灾乐祸地笑着。

▲ **smog** /smɒg/ (**smogs**) N-VAR **Smog** is a mixture of fog and smoke which occurs in some busy industrial cities. 烟雾 ❑ *Cars cause pollution, both smog and acid rain.* 汽车引起污染，既有烟雾又有酸雨。
→ see **pollution**

smoke ♦♦◇ /smoʊk/ (**smokes, smoking, smoked**) 1 N-UNCOUNT **Smoke** consists of gas and small bits of solid material that are sent into the air when something burns. 烟 ❑ *A cloud of black smoke blew over the city.* 一团黑烟拂过了这座城市。 2 V-I If something **is smoking**, smoke is coming from it. 冒烟 ❑ *The chimney was smoking fiercely.* 烟囱猛烈地冒着烟。 3 V-T/V-I When someone **smokes** a cigarette, cigar, or pipe, they suck the smoke from it into their mouth and blow it out again. If you **smoke**, you regularly smoke cigarettes, cigars, or a pipe. 吸 (烟); 吸烟 ❑ *He was sitting alone, smoking a big cigar.* 他那时正独自坐着，抽着一根大雪茄。 ❑ *It's not easy to quit smoking.* 戒烟不容易。 ● N-SING **Smoke** is also a noun. 吸烟 ❑ *Someone came out for a smoke.* 有人为了吸烟而出来了。 4 V-T If fish or meat **is smoked**, it is hung over burning wood so that the smoke preserves it and gives it a special flavor. 熏制 (鱼或肉) [usu passive] ❑ *...the grid where the fish were being smoked.* …当时熏鱼所用的烤架。 5 → see also **smoking** 6 PHRASE If someone says **where there's smoke there's fire**, they mean that there are rumors or signs that something is true so it must be at least partly true. 有火就冒烟; 无风不起浪 ❑ *A lot of the stuff in the story is not true, but I have to say that where there's smoke there's fire.* 故事中有许多事情都不是真的，但我不得不说，无风不起浪。 7 PHRASE If something **goes up in smoke**, it is destroyed by fire. 被烧毁 ❑ *The crew were able to put out the fire after only 25 acres had gone up in smoke.* 在仅仅25公顷被烧毁之后，队员们能够将火扑灭了。 8 PHRASE If something that is very important to you **goes up in smoke**, it fails or ends without anything being achieved. 化为乌有 ❑ *I was afraid you'd say no, and my dream would go up in smoke.* 我担心你会说不，那我的梦想就化为乌有了。
→ see **fire**

Word Partnership *smoke* 的常用搭配：

ADJ.	**black** smoke, **dense** smoke, **heavy** smoke, **secondhand** smoke, **thick** smoke 1
N.	**cigarette** smoke, **cloud of** smoke, smoke **damage**, smoke **from a fire**, smoke **inhalation**, **smell of** smoke, **tobacco** smoke 1
	smoke **a cigar/cigarette**, smoke **tobacco** 3
V.	**see** smoke, **smell** smoke 1
	smoke **and drink** 3

smok·ing ♦◇◇ /smoʊkɪŋ/ 1 N-UNCOUNT **Smoking** is the act or habit of smoking cigarettes, cigars, or a pipe. 吸烟 ❑ *Smoking is now banned in many places of work.* 吸烟目前在许多工作场所都被禁止。 2 ADJ A **smoking** area is intended for people who want to smoke. 吸烟的 (区域) [ADJ n] ❑ *California no longer allows smoking areas in restaurants.* 加利福尼亚州不再允许在饭店里设吸烟区。 3 → see also **smoke**

Word Partnership *smoking* 的常用搭配：

V.	**ban** smoking, **quit** smoking, **stop** smoking 1
N.	**ban on** smoking, **dangers of** smoking, smoking **and drinking**, **effects of** smoking, smoking **habits**, **risk of** smoking 1
	(no) smoking **section** 2

smoky /smoʊki/ (**smokier, smokiest**) also **smokey** 1 ADJ A place that is **smoky** has a lot of smoke in the air. 烟雾弥漫的 ❑ *His main problem was the extremely smoky atmosphere at work.* 他的主要问题曾是完全烟雾弥漫的工作环境。 2 ADJ You can use **smoky** to describe something that looks like smoke, for example, because it is slightly blue or gray or because it is not clear. 烟雾状的 [ADJ n, ADJ color] ❑ *At the center of the dial is a piece of smoky glass.* 在拨盘中央是

一块烟雾状的玻璃。 3 ADJ Something that has a **smoky** flavor tastes as if it has been smoked. 烟熏味的 ❑ *The fish had just the right amount of smoky flavor for my taste.* 那条鱼刚好有适量的烟熏味，正对我的口味。

▲**smol·der** /smoʊldər/ (**smolders, smoldering, smoldered**)
in BRIT, use **smoulder**
1 V-I If something **smolders**, it burns slowly, producing smoke but not flames. 闷烧 ❑ *The wreckage was still smoldering several hours after the crash.* 残骸在坠机数小时后还在闷烧着。 2 V-I If a feeling such as anger or hatred **smolders** inside you, you continue to feel it but do not show it. (愤怒或仇恨等情感) 郁积 ❑ *...the guilt that had so long smoldered in her heart.* …她心里郁积已久的愧疚。 3 V-I If you say that someone **smolders**, you mean that they are sexually attractive, usually in a mysterious or very intense way. (神秘或强烈的性吸引而产生的) 放电 ❑ *He was good-looking, with dark eyes which could smolder with just the right intimation of passion.* 他长得很帅，黑色的眼睛只要遇到恰当的激情暗示就会放电。
→ see **fire**

smooth ♦◇◇ /smuð/ (**smoother, smoothest, smooths, smoothing, smoothed**) 1 ADJ A **smooth** surface has no roughness, lumps, or holes. 光滑的 ❑ *...a rich cream that keeps skin soft and smooth.* …一种可以保持皮肤柔软光滑的富含营养的护肤霜。 ❑ *...a smooth surface such as glass.* …玻璃般光滑的表面。 2 ADJ A **smooth** liquid or mixture has been mixed well so that it has no lumps. 均匀的; (液体或混合物) 细腻的 ❑ *Continue whisking until the mixture looks smooth and creamy.* 继续搅拌直至混合物看上去均匀且呈奶油状。 3 ADJ If you describe a drink such as wine, whiskey, or coffee as **smooth**, you mean that it is not bitter and is pleasant to drink. (酒或咖啡等饮料) 醇和的 ❑ *This makes the whiskeys much smoother.* 这使威士忌酒醇和得多。 4 ADJ A **smooth** line or movement has no sudden breaks or changes in direction or speed. (线条或动作) 流畅的 ❑ *This exercise is done in one smooth motion.* 这套体操是由一个流畅的动作完成的。 ●**smooth·ly** ADV 流畅地 [ADV with v] ❑ *Make sure that you execute all movements smoothly and without jerking.* 确保你流畅、无颤动地完成所有动作。 5 ADJ A **smooth** ride, flight, or sea crossing is very comfortable because there are no unpleasant movements. (乘车、飞行或航海) 舒适平稳的 ❑ *The active suspension system gives the car a very smooth ride.* 活动的悬挂系统使汽车行驶起来非常平稳。 6 ADJ You use **smooth** to describe something that is going well and is free of problems or trouble. 顺利的 ❑ *Political hopes for a swift and smooth transition to democracy have been dashed.* 向民主快速顺利的过渡的政治愿望已经破灭了。 ●**smooth·ly** ADV 顺利地 [ADV with v] ❑ *So far, talks at GM have gone smoothly.* 迄今，在通用汽车公司的会谈进展顺利。 7 ADJ If you describe a man as **smooth**, you mean that he is extremely smart, confident, and polite, often in a way that you find rather unpleasant. 精明的; 圆滑的 ❑ *Twelve extremely good-looking, smooth young men have been picked as finalists.* 12个非常英俊精明的男青年已被选为参加决赛的选手。 8 V-T If you **smooth** something, you move your hands over its surface to make it smooth and flat. (用手) 弄平 ❑ *She stood up and smoothed down her frock.* 她站了起来，抚平了自己的连衣裙。
→ see **muscle**

▸ **smooth out** PHRASAL VERB If you **smooth out** a problem or difficulty, you solve it, especially by talking to the people concerned. (尤指通过谈话) 解决 ❑ *Baker was smoothing out differences with European allies.* 贝克尔正在解决与欧洲盟友的分歧。

▸ **smooth over** PHRASAL VERB If you **smooth over** a problem or difficulty, you make it less serious and easier to deal with, especially by talking to the people concerned. 缓和; 减轻 ❑ *...an attempt to smooth over the violent splits that have occurred.* …缓和已经发生的暴力冲突的一次努力。 ❑ *The president is trying to smooth things over.* 这位总统正试图把大事化小。

▲**smoth·er** /smʌðər/ (**smothers, smothering, smothered**) 1 V-T If you **smother** a fire, you cover it with something in order to put it out. 把(火) 闷熄 ❑ *The girl's parents were also burned as they tried to smother the flames.* 女孩的父母在试图闷熄火苗时也被烧伤了。 2 V-T To **smother** someone means to kill them by covering their face with something so that they cannot breathe. 使窒息 ❑ *He tried to smother me with a pillow.* 他企图用枕头闷死我。 3 V-T Things that **smother** something cover it completely. 完全覆盖 ❑ *Once the shrubs begin to smother the little plants, we have to move them.* 一旦灌木开始把小植物完全覆盖，我们不得不将它们移走。 4 V-T If you **smother** someone, you show your love for them too much and protect them too much. 溺爱 ❑ *She loved her own children, almost smothering them with love.* 她爱自己的孩子，几乎爱得让他们透不过气。 5 V-T If you **smother** an emotion or a reaction, you control it so that people do not notice it. 压抑; 抑制 ❑ *She tried to smother her anger and help them resolve their conflicts.* 她试图抑制住怒气，帮助他们解决纠纷。

smoul·der /smoʊldər/ [mainly BRIT] → see **smolder**

SMS /ɛs ɛm ɛs/ N-UNCOUNT **SMS** is a way of sending short written messages from one cellphone to another. **SMS** is an abbreviation for **short message system** or **short message service**. (手机) 短信服务; 短信系统

smudge /smʌdʒ/ (**smudges, smudging, smudged**) 1 N-COUNT A **smudge** is a dirty mark. 污迹 ❑ *There was a dark smudge on his forehead.* 他前额上有一个黑色污点。 2 V-T If you **smudge** a substance such as ink, paint, or make-up that has been put on a surface, you make it less neat by touching or rubbing it. 把(墨水、涂料或化妆品) 弄模糊 ❑ *She rubbed her eyes, smudging her make-up.* 她揉了揉眼睛，把妆弄模糊了。 3 V-T If you **smudge** a surface, you make it dirty by touching it and leaving a substance on it. 弄脏 ❑ *She kissed me, careful not to smudge me with her fresh lipstick.* 她亲吻了我，小心翼翼地不让她新抹的唇膏弄脏我。
→ see **drawing**

smug /smʌg/ ADJ If you say that someone is **smug**, you are criticizing the fact they seem very pleased with how good, clever, or lucky they are. 自鸣得意的 [DISAPPROVAL] ❑ *Thomas and his wife looked at each other in smug satisfaction.* 托马斯和他妻子互相看着对方，面带着自鸣得意的满足。

★**smug·gle** /smʌgᵊl/ (**smuggles, smuggling, smuggled**) V-T If someone **smuggles** things or people into a place or out of it, they take them there illegally or secretly. 走私; 偷运 ❑ *My message is "If you try to smuggle drugs you are stupid."* 我的讯息是，"你若企图走私毒品，那是犯傻。" ❑ *Police have foiled an attempt to smuggle a bomb into Belfast airport.* 警方挫败了一个将炸弹偷带进贝尔法斯特机场的企图。 ●**smug·gling** N-UNCOUNT 走私 ❑ *An air hostess was arrested and charged with drug smuggling.* 一位空姐被抓了起来，并被指控走私毒品。

smug·gler /smʌglər/ (**smugglers**) N-COUNT **Smugglers** are people who take goods into or out of a country illegally. 走私者 ❑ *...drug smugglers.* …毒品走私者。

★**snack** /snæk/ (**snacks, snacking, snacked**) 1 N-COUNT A **snack** is a simple meal that is quick to cook and to eat. 快餐 ❑ *Lunch was a snack in the fields.* 午饭是在野外吃的快餐。 2 N-COUNT A **snack** is something such as a chocolate bar that you eat between meals. (正餐之间的) 小吃 ❑ *Do you eat sweets, cakes or sugary snacks?* 你吃糖果、糕点或甜点心吗？ 3 V-I If you **snack**, you eat snacks between meals. 吃小吃 ❑ *Instead of snacking on crisps and chocolate, nibble on celery or carrot.* 不要吃炸薯片和巧克力这些零食，要啃点芹菜或胡萝卜。
→ see **peanut**

snack bar (**snack bars**) N-COUNT A **snack bar** is a place where you can buy drinks and simple meals such as sandwiches. 小吃店; 快餐店

snag /snæg/ (**snags, snagging, snagged**) 1 N-COUNT A **snag** is a small problem or disadvantage. 小问题; 小挫折 ❑ *A police clampdown on car thieves hit a snag when villains stole one of their cars.* 匪徒偷走了警方一辆汽车后，警方打击盗车贼的行动遇到了一点儿小挫折。 2 V-T/V-I If you **snag** part of your clothing **on** a sharp or rough object or if it **snags**, it gets caught on the object and tears. 钩破 ❑ *She snagged a heel on a root and tumbled to the ground.* 她的鞋后跟绊在树根上，跌倒在地。 ❑ *Brambles snagged his suit.* 刺藤钩破了他的西服。

▲**snail** /sneɪl/ (**snails**) 1 N-COUNT A **snail** is a small animal with a long, soft body, no legs, and a spiral-shaped shell. Snails move very slowly. 蜗牛 2 PHRASE If you say that someone does something **at a snail's pace**, you are emphasizing that they are doing it very slowly, usually when you think it would be better if they did it much more quickly. 慢吞吞地 [EMPHASIS] ❑ *The train was moving now at a snail's pace.* 火车现在正缓慢行驶。

snail mail N-UNCOUNT Some computer users refer to the postal system as **snail mail**, because it is very slow in comparison with e-mail. (与快速电子邮件相对比的) 传统纸本邮件

snake /sneɪk/ (**snakes, snaking, snaked**) 1 N-COUNT A **snake** is a long, thin reptile without legs. 蛇 2 V-I Something that **snakes** in a particular direction goes in that direction in a line with a lot of bends. 蜿蜒行进 [LITERARY] ❑ *The road snaked through forested mountains.* 这条路蜿蜒穿过树林覆盖的群山。
→ see **desert**

S

snap ♦◇◇ /snæp/ (**snaps, snapping, snapped**) **1** V-T/V-I If something **snaps** or if you **snap** it, it breaks suddenly, usually with a sharp cracking noise. 使咯嚓折断；喀嚓折断 ❑ *He shifted his weight and a twig snapped.* 他挪了挪身子，一根树枝随即咯嚓一声折断了。❑ *The brake pedal had just snapped off.* 制动踏板刚才突然断裂了。● N-SING **Snap** is also a noun. 喀嚓的断裂声 ❑ *Every minute or so I could hear a snap, a crack and a crash as another tree went down.* 几乎每隔一分钟，我就会听见又有一棵树倒下时发出的折断声、噼啪声和塌倒声。**2** V-T/V-I If you **snap** something into a particular position, or if it **snaps** into that position, it moves quickly into that position, with a sharp sound. 使发出啪的一声；发出啪的一声 ❑ *He snapped the notebook shut.* 他啪的一声合上笔记本。❑ *He snapped the cap on his ballpoint.* 他吧嗒一声扣上圆珠笔的笔帽。● N-SING **Snap** is also a noun. 吧嗒声 ❑ *He shut the book with a snap and stood up.* 他啪的一声合上书，站了起来。**3** V-T If you **snap** your **fingers**, you make a sharp sound by moving your middle finger quickly across your thumb, for example, in order to accompany music or to order someone to do something. 打响指 ❑ *She had millions of listeners snapping their fingers to her first single.* 数百万的听众和着她的首张单曲打响指。❑ *He snapped his fingers, and Wilson produced a sheet of paper.* 他打了一个响指，威尔逊便拿出一张纸来。● N-SING **Snap** is also a noun. 打响指 [N "of" n] ❑ *I could obtain with the snap of my fingers anything I chose.* 只要打一下响指，我就可以得到我选中的任何东西。**4** V-T/V-I If someone **snaps at** you, they speak to you in a sharp, unfriendly way. 声色俱厉地说 ❑ *"Of course I don't know her," Roger snapped.* "我当然不认识她，"罗杰恶声恶气地说。**5** V-I If someone **snaps**, or if something **snaps** inside them, they suddenly stop being calm and become very angry because the situation has become too tense or too difficult for them. (人) 突然发怒；(物) 突然爆发 ❑ *He finally snapped when she prevented their children from visiting him one weekend.* 当她阻止孩子们在一周末来探望他时，他终于失控发怒了。**6** V-I If an animal such as a dog **snaps at** you, it opens and shuts its jaws quickly near you, as if it were going to bite you. 作势猛咬 ❑ *His teeth clicked as he snapped at my ankle.* 他作势猛咬我的脚踝时，牙齿咔嚓作响。**7** ADJ A **snap** decision or action is one that is taken suddenly, often without careful thought. 仓促的 [ADJ n] ❑ *I think this is too important for a snap decision.* 我认为此事非常重要，不宜仓促地做决定。**8** N-COUNT A **snap** is the same as a **snap fastener**. 按扣 [AM] **9** N-COUNT A **snap** is a photograph. 相片 [INFORMAL] ❑ *...a snap my mother took last year.* …我母亲去年拍的一张相片。

▶ **snap up** PHRASAL VERB If you **snap** something **up**, you buy it quickly because it is cheap or is just what you want. 争购 ❑ *...a millionaire ready to snap them up at the premium price of $200 a gallon.* …一个百万富翁准备以每加仑$200的高价抢购它们。

★ **snap·shot** /snæpʃɒt/ (**snapshots**) **1** N-COUNT A **snapshot** is a photograph that is taken quickly and casually. 快照 ❑ *Let me take a snapshot of you guys, so friends back home can see you.* 让我给你们大家拍张快照，这样家里的朋友们可以看到你们。**2** N-COUNT If something provides you with a **snapshot of** a place or situation, it gives you a brief idea of what that place or situation is like. 简况；大致印象 [usu sing, usu N "of" n] ❑ *The interviews present a remarkable snapshot of Britain in these dark days of recession.* 这些访谈深刻地展现了英国在黑暗的经济大萧条时期的点滴情况。

▲ **snare** /snɛər/ (**snares, snaring, snared**) **1** N-COUNT A **snare** is a trap for catching birds or small animals. It consists of a loop of wire or rope which pulls tight around the animal. (捕捉鸟或小动物的) 罗网 ❑ *I felt like an animal caught in a snare.* 我感到自己像是一头陷入网罗的野兽。**2** N-COUNT If you describe a situation as a **snare**, you mean that it is a trap from which it is difficult to escape. 陷阱 [FORMAL] ❑ *Given data which are free from bias there are further snares to avoid in statistical work.* 就算这些数据不带任何偏见，但是统计工作中还有许多需要避免的陷阱。**3** V-T If someone **snares** an animal, they catch it using a snare. 用罗网捕捉 ❑ *He'd snared a rabbit earlier in the day.* 那天早些时候，他用罗网捕了一只野兔。

▲ **snarl** /snɑrl/ (**snarls, snarling, snarled**) V-I When an animal **snarls**, it makes a fierce, rough sound in its throat while showing its teeth. (动物) 露齿嗥叫 ❑ *He raced ahead up into the bush, barking and snarling.* 它向前冲进了树丛，又吠又嗥叫的。● N-COUNT **Snarl** is also a noun. 露齿嗥叫 ❑ *With a snarl, the second dog made a dive for his heel.* 伴着一声嗥叫，第二条狗扑向了他的脚后跟。

★ **snatch** /snætʃ/ (**snatches, snatching, snatched**) **1** V-T/V-I If you **snatch** something or **snatch at** something, you take it or pull it away quickly. 迅速拿走；夺取 ❑ *Mick snatched the cards from Archie's hand.* 米克一把夺过阿彻手里的牌。❑ *He snatched up the telephone.* 他一把抓起了电话。**2** V-T If something **is snatched** from you, it is stolen, usually using force. If a person **is snatched**, they are taken away by force. 强抢 [usu passive] ❑ *If your bag is snatched, let it go.* 如果你的包被抢走，就随它去吧。**3** V-T If you **snatch** an opportunity, you take it quickly. If you **snatch** something to eat or a rest, you have it quickly in between doing other things. 抓紧 (时机或时间) ❑ *I snatched a glance at the mirror.* 我乘机瞥了一眼镜子。**4** V-T If you **snatch** victory in a competition, you defeat your opponent by a small amount or just before the end of the contest. 侥幸获得 ❑ *The American came from behind to snatch victory by a mere eight seconds.* 美国队后来居上，仅以8秒钟的优势赢得了胜利。**5** N-COUNT A **snatch of** a conversation or a song is a very small piece of it. (谈话或歌曲的) 片断 ❑ *I heard snatches of the conversation.* 我听到几段零星的谈话。

★ **sneak** /snik/ (**sneaks, sneaking, sneaked** or **snuck**)

> The form **snuck** is informal.

1 V-I If you **sneak** somewhere, you go there very quietly on foot, trying to avoid being seen or heard. 偷偷地走 ❑ *Sometimes he would sneak out of his house late at night to be with me.* 有时候他会在深夜偷偷溜出他的家来陪伴我。**2** V-T If you **sneak** something somewhere, you take it there secretly. 偷偷地拿 ❑ *He smuggled papers out each day, photocopied them, and snuck them back.* 他每天都把文件偷带出来，复印后又偷偷送回去。**3** V-T If you **sneak** a look at someone or something, you secretly have a quick look at them. 偷偷地看 ❑ *You sneak a look at your watch to see how long you've got to wait.* 你偷偷看一眼手表，看还要等多久。

★ **sneak·er** /snikər/ (**sneakers**) N-COUNT **Sneakers** are casual shoes with rubber soles that people wear often for running or other sports. 运动鞋 [usu pl] [mainly AM]

> in BRIT, usually use **trainers**

❑ *...a new pair of sneakers.* …一双新的运动鞋。

→ see **clothing**

> Athletic shoes have many names. The simplest name is **sneakers**. Other names may specify where the shoe was designed to be worn: **tennis shoe, gym shoe, basketball shoe, running shoe** and so on. In the UK, the term **trainers** is usually used.

▲ **sneer** /snɪər/ (**sneers, sneering, sneered**) V-T/V-I If you **sneer at** someone or something, you express your contempt for them by the expression on your face or by what you say. 嘲笑 ❑ *Most critics have sneered at the movie, calling it dull and cheaply made.* 大多数批评家都嘲笑这部电影，称其无聊、制作低劣。❑ *"I don't need any help from you," he sneered.* "我不需要你的任何帮助，"他嘲笑道。● N-COUNT **Sneer** is also a noun. 嘲笑；讥讽 ❑ *Canete's mouth twisted in a contemptuous sneer.* 卡内特撇了下嘴，一副蔑视嘲讽的样子。

▲ **sneeze** /sniz/ (**sneezes, sneezing, sneezed**) **1** V-I When you **sneeze**, you suddenly take in your breath and then blow it down your nose noisily without being able to stop yourself, for example, because you have a cold. 打喷嚏 ❑ *What exactly happens when we sneeze?* 我们打喷嚏究竟是怎么回事？● N-COUNT **Sneeze** is also a noun. 打喷嚏 ❑ *Coughs and sneezes spread infections.* 咳嗽和打喷嚏会传播传染病。**2** PHRASE If you say that something is **not to be sneezed at**, you mean that it is worth having. 不容小视 [INFORMAL] ❑ *The money's not to be sneezed at.* 这笔钱可不容小视。

★ **sniff** /snɪf/ (**sniffs, sniffing, sniffed**) **1** V-I When you **sniff**, you breathe in air through your nose hard enough to make a sound, for example, when you are trying not to cry, or in order to show disapproval. 抽鼻子 (用来忍住哭声或表示不赞同) ❑ *She wiped her face and sniffed loudly.* 她擦擦脸，大声地抽着鼻子。❑ *Then he sniffed. There was a smell of burning.* 然后他抽了抽鼻子。空气里有一股烧焦的味道。● N-COUNT **Sniff** is also a noun. 抽鼻子声 ❑ *At last the sobs ceased, to be replaced by sniffs.* 最后呜咽声终于停止了，取而代之的是抽鼻子的声音。**2** V-T/V-I If you **sniff** something or **sniff at** it, you smell it by sniffing. (吸着气) 闻 ❑ *Suddenly, he stopped and sniffed the air.* 突然他停下来，嗅了嗅空气中的味道。**3** V-T You can use **sniff** to indicate that someone says something in a way that shows their disapproval or contempt. 嗤之以鼻地说 ❑ *"Tourists!" she sniffed.* "观光客！"她鄙夷地说。**4** V-T/V-I If you say that something is **not to be sniffed at**, you think it is very good or worth having. If someone **sniffs at** something, they do not think it is good enough, or they express their contempt for it. 轻视 [usu passive, usu with brd-neg]

❑ *The salary was not to be sniffed at either.* 当时的工资也是不容轻视的。 **5** V-T If someone **sniffs** a substance such as glue, they deliberately breathe in the substance or the gases from it as a drug. 用鼻子吸 ❑ *He felt light-headed, as if he'd sniffed glue.* 他觉得头晕，好像吸了胶毒一样。

▸ **sniff out** **1** PHRASAL VERB If you **sniff out** something, you discover it after some searching. 找出 [INFORMAL] ❑ *...journalists who are trained to sniff out scandal.* …专门训练来找出丑闻的记者。 **2** PHRASAL VERB When a dog used by a group such as the police **sniffs out** hidden explosives or drugs, it finds them using its sense of smell. 嗅出 (爆炸物或毒品) ❑ *...a police dog trained to sniff out explosives.* …一条受过训练能嗅出爆炸物的警犬。

snig·ger /snɪgər/ (**sniggers, sniggering, sniggered**) V-I If someone **sniggers**, they laugh quietly in a disrespectful way, for example at something rude or unkind. 窃笑 ❑ *Suddenly, three schoolkids sitting near me started sniggering.* 突然，坐在我身边的3个学童偷偷地笑了起来。 ● N-COUNT **Snigger** is also a noun. 窃笑 ❑ *...trying to suppress a snigger.* …极力按捺一阵窃笑。

snip /snɪp/ (**snips, snipping, snipped**) V-T/V-I If you **snip** something, or if you **snip at** or **through** something, you cut it quickly using sharp scissors. 快速剪 ❑ *He has now begun to snip away at the piece of paper.* 他现在已开始快速剪那张纸。

snipe /snaɪp/ (**snipes, sniping, sniped**) **1** V-I If someone **snipes at** you, they criticize you. 抨击 ❑ *The media were still sniping at the president's adviser yesterday.* 昨天媒体依旧在抨击总统的顾问。 **2** V-I To **snipe at** someone means to shoot at them from a hidden position. 狙击 ❑ *Gunmen have repeatedly sniped at U.S. Army positions.* 枪手不停地向美军阵地放冷枪。

snip·er /snaɪpər/ (**snipers**) N-COUNT A **sniper** is someone who shoots at people from a hidden position. 狙击手 ❑ *...a sniper attack.* …一次狙击手的攻击。

snip·pet /snɪpɪt/ (**snippets**) N-COUNT A **snippet of** something is a small piece of it. 片段 ❑ *...snippets of popular classical music.* …流行古典音乐的片段。

▲ **snob** /snɒb/ (**snobs**) N-COUNT If you call someone a **snob**, you disapprove of them because they behave as if they are superior to other people because of their intelligence, taste, or social status. 自命不凡的人 [DISAPPROVAL] ❑ *She was an intellectual snob.* 她自诩才智高人一等。

snob·bery /snɒbəri/ N-UNCOUNT **Snobbery** is the attitude of a snob. 自命不凡 ❑ *There has often been an element of snobbery in golf.* 高尔夫运动中常常含有自命不凡的意味。

snook·er /snʊkər/ N-UNCOUNT **Snooker** is a game involving balls on a large table. The players use a long stick to hit a white ball, and score points by knocking colored balls into the pockets at the sides of the table. 斯诺克 ❑ *...a game of snooker.* …一场斯诺克台球比赛。

snoop /snup/ (**snoops, snooping, snooped**) **1** V-I If someone **snoops** around a place, they secretly look around it in order to find out things. 窥探 ❑ *Ricardo was the one she'd seen snooping around Kim's hotel room.* 里卡多就是她曾见过的在金的旅馆房间里到处窥探的那个人。 ● N-COUNT **Snoop** is also a noun. 窥探 ❑ *The second house that Grossman had a snoop around contained "strong simple furniture."* 格罗斯曼窥探过的第二所房子有"结实简朴的家具。" ● **snoop·er** N-COUNT (**snoopers**) 窥探者 ❑ *Even if the information is intercepted by a snooper, it is impossible for them to decipher it.* 即使信息被窥探者截获，他们也不可能将其破译。 **2** V-I If someone **snoops on** a person, they watch them secretly in order to find out things about their life. 监视 ❑ *Governments have been known to snoop on and harass innocent citizens in the past.* 众所周知，政府过去一直监视和侵扰无辜市民。

snooze /snuz/ (**snoozes, snoozing, snoozed**) **1** N-COUNT A **snooze** is a short, light sleep, especially during the day. (尤指在白天的) 小睡 [INFORMAL] ❑ *I lay down on the bed with my shoes off to have a snooze.* 我脱了鞋，躺在床上打个盹儿。 **2** V-I If you **snooze**, you sleep lightly for a short period of time. 打盹 [INFORMAL] ❑ *Mark snoozed in front of the television.* 马克在电视机前打起盹儿来。

▲ **snore** /snɔr/ (**snores, snoring, snored**) V-I When someone who is asleep **snores**, they make a loud noise each time they breathe. 打鼾 ❑ *His mouth was open, and he was snoring.* 他张着嘴巴，打着鼾。 ● N-COUNT **Snore** is also a noun. 打鼾 ❑ *Uncle Arthur, after a loud snore, woke suddenly.* 阿瑟大叔响亮地打了个鼾后，突然醒了过来。

snor·kel /snɔrkᵊl/ (**snorkels, snorkeling, snorkeled**) **1** N-COUNT A **snorkel** is a tube through which a person swimming just under the surface of the sea can breathe. (潜水者用的) 呼吸管 **2** V-I When someone **snorkels**, they swim under water using a snorkel. 使用呼吸管潜泳 ❑ *Swim off the side of the ship and snorkel in some of the clearest waters imaginable.* 游离小船边，用呼吸管潜游到可以想像得到的一些最清澈的水域。

▲ **snort** /snɔrt/ (**snorts, snorting, snorted**) **1** V-I When people or animals **snort**, they breathe air noisily out through their noses. People sometimes snort in order to express disapproval or amusement. 喷鼻息 (有时表示不赞同或可笑) ❑ *Harrell snorted with laughter.* 哈雷尔扑哧一声笑了。 ● N-COUNT **Snort** is also a noun. 喷鼻息 ❑ *...snorts of laughter.* …阵阵嗤笑声。 **2** V-T To **snort** a drug such as cocaine means to breathe it in quickly through your nose. 用鼻子吸食 (毒品) ❑ *He died of cardiac arrest after snorting cocaine at a party.* 在一次聚会上鼻吸了可卡因之后，他死于心脏停搏。

snow ◆◇◇ /snoʊ/ (**snows, snowing, snowed**) **1** N-UNCOUNT **Snow** consists of a lot of soft white pieces of frozen water that fall from the sky in cold weather. 雪 ❑ *Six inches of snow blocked roads.* 六英寸的大雪阻塞了道路。 **2** V-I When **it snows**, snow falls from the sky. 下雪 ❑ *It had been snowing all night.* 整个晚上一直在下雪。

→ see **arctic, storm, water**

snow·ball /snoʊbɔl/ (**snowballs, snowballing, snowballed**) **1** N-COUNT A **snowball** is a ball of snow. Children often throw snowballs at each other. 雪球 **2** V-I If something such as a project or campaign **snowballs**, it rapidly increases and grows. 迅速增长 ❑ *From those early days the business has snowballed.* 从早期开始以来，这家企业就一直在像滚雪球似地扩张。

snow·board /snoʊbɔrd/ (**snowboards**) N-COUNT A **snowboard** is a narrow board that you stand on in order to slide quickly down snowy slopes as a sport or for fun. 滑雪板

snow·board·ing /snoʊbɔrdɪŋ/ N-UNCOUNT **Snowboarding** is the sport or activity of traveling down snowy slopes using a snowboard. 滑雪板运动 ❑ *New snowboarding facilities should attract more people.* 新型滑雪板运动设施应该会吸引更多的人。

snow·man /snoʊmæn/ (**snowmen**) N-COUNT A **snowman** is a large shape which is made out of snow, especially by children, and is supposed to look like a person. 雪人

snow·plough /snoʊplaʊ/ [BRIT] → see **snowplow**

snow·plow /snoʊplaʊ/ (**snowplows**)

in BRIT, use **snowplough**

N-COUNT A **snowplow** is a vehicle which is used to push snow off roads or railroad tracks. 扫雪机

snowy /snoʊi/ (**snowier, snowiest**) ADJ A **snowy** place is covered in snow. A **snowy** day is a day when a lot of snow has fallen. 积雪覆盖的；下雪多的 ❑ *...the snowy peaks of the Bighorn Mountains.* …比格霍恩山白雪皑皑的群峰。

snub /snʌb/ (**snubs, snubbing, snubbed**) **1** V-T If you **snub** someone, you deliberately insult them by ignoring them or by behaving or speaking rudely toward them. 冷落；怠慢 ❑ *He snubbed her in public and made her feel an idiot.* 他在公共场合故意冷落她，让她觉得自己像是一个白痴。 **2** N-COUNT If you snub someone, your behavior or your remarks can be referred to as a **snub**. 冷落；怠慢 ❑ *Ryan took it as a snub.* 瑞安视其为对他的怠慢。

snuck /snʌk/ **Snuck** is a past tense and past participle of **sneak**. **sneak**的过去式和过去分词 [INFORMAL]

snuff /snʌf/ (**snuffs, snuffing, snuffed**) N-UNCOUNT **Snuff** is powdered tobacco which people take by breathing it in quickly through their nose. 鼻烟 ❑ *...the old man's habit of taking snuff.* …那位老人吸鼻烟的习惯。

▸ **snuff out** PHRASAL VERB To **snuff out** something such as a disagreement means to stop it, usually in a forceful or sudden way. 消除；扼杀 ❑ *Every time a new flicker of resistance appeared, the government snuffed it out.* 每当新的反抗苗头出现时，政府就迅速将其扑灭。

snug /snʌg/ (**snugger, snuggest**) **1** ADJ If you feel **snug** or are in a **snug** place, you are very warm and comfortable, especially because you are protected from cold weather. 温暖舒适的 ❑ *They lay snug and warm amid the blankets and watched their sister hard at work.* 他们躺在温暖舒服的毯子中，看着姐姐辛苦地干活。 **2** ADJ Something such as a piece of clothing that is **snug** fits very closely or tightly. 贴身的 ❑ *...a snug black T-shirt and skin-tight black jeans.* …一件贴身黑色T恤衫和紧身黑色牛仔裤。

S

snug·gle /snʌgᵊl/ (**snuggles, snuggling, snuggled**) V-I If you **snuggle** somewhere, you settle yourself into a warm, comfortable position, especially by moving closer to another person. 依偎 ❑ *Jane snuggled up against his shoulder.* 简依偎在他的肩膀上。

so ♦♦♦ /soʊ/

Usually pronounced /soʊ/ for meanings **1**, **6**, **7**, **8**, **15** and **16**.

义项**1**、**6**、**7**、**8**、**15**和**16**通常读作 /soʊ/。

1 ADV You use **so** to refer back to something that has just been mentioned. 如此 (用以指代刚刚提及的事) [ADV after v] ❑ *"Do you think that made much of a difference to the family?"—"I think so."* "你认为那样给全家带来了很大变化吗？"——"我觉得是。" ❑ *If you can't play straight, then say so.* 如果你不能做到诚实坦率，那就直说。 **2** ADV You use **so** when you are saying that something which has just been said about one person or thing is also true of another one. 也一样 (用以表示说过的事也适用于另一人或物) [ADV cl] ❑ *I enjoy Ann's company and so does Martin.* 我喜欢有安相伴，马丁也一样。 ❑ *They had a wonderful time and so did I.* 他们玩得很开心，我也是。 **3** CONJ You use the structures **as...so** and **just as...so** when you want to indicate that two events or situations are similar in some way. 也亦然 (用以表示两个事件或情况在某方面相似) ❑ *As computer systems become even more sophisticated, so too do the methods of those who exploit the technology.* 正如计算机系统变得越来越复杂，开发计算机技术的人所采用的方法也日趋复杂。 ❑ *Just as John has changed, so has his wife.* 正如约翰已经变了，他妻子也变了。 **4** ADV If you say that a state of affairs **is so**, you mean that it is the way it has been described. (某一情况) 就是这样 [v-link ADV] ❑ *In those days English dances as well as songs were taught at school, but that seems no longer to be so.* 那时，英语歌曲还有舞蹈都要在学校教授，但现在情况似乎不再是这样了。 ❑ *It is strange to think that he held strong views on many things, but it must have been so.* 想到当时他对许多事情的观点都很强硬，真是很奇怪，但那时应该就是这样。 **5** ADV You can use **so** with actions and gestures to show a person how to do something, or to indicate the size, height, or length of something. 这样 (用以演示如何做某事或展示某物) [ADV after v] ❑ *Clasp the chain like so.* 就像这样抓住链子。 **6** CONJ You use **so** and **so that** to introduce the result of the situation you have just mentioned. 因此 ❑ *I am not an emotional type and so cannot bring myself to tell him I love him.* 我不是情感外露的人，因此难以开口对他说我爱他。 ❑ *People are living longer than ever before, so even people who are 65 or 70 have a surprising amount of time left.* 人们的寿命比以前都要长，所以即便是65或70岁的人，余下光阴也还长得惊人。 **7** CONJ You use **so**, **so that**, and **so as** to introduce the reason for doing the thing that you have just mentioned. 为了 (用以说明理由) ❑ *Come to my suite so I can tell you all about this wonderful play I saw in Boston.* 到我的套房来吧，这样我就可以把我在波士顿看的这部好戏好好跟你说说。 ❑ *He took her arm and hurried her upstairs so that they wouldn't be overheard.* 他抓着她的手臂，急忙将她拉上楼，这样他们就不会被偷听了。 **8** ADV You can use **so** in conversations to introduce a new topic, or to introduce a question or comment about something that has been said. 那么 (用以提出新话题、疑问、评论等) [ADV cl] ❑ *So how was your day?* 那么，你今天怎么样？ ❑ *So you're a runner, huh?* 这么说，你是个跑步爱好者喽？ ❑ *So as for your question, Miles, the answer still has to be no.* 那么至于你的问题，迈尔斯，回答依然是否定的。 **9** ADV You can use **so** in conversations to show that you are accepting what someone has just said. 确实 (用以表示接受某人的说法) [ADV cl] ❑ *"It makes me feel, well, important."—"And so you are."* "这使我觉得，嗯，自己很重要。"——"你确实重要。" ❑ *"You can't possibly use this word."—"So I won't."* "你不可能会用这个词。"——"我确实不会用。" **10** CONVENTION You say **"So?"** and **"So what?"** to indicate that you think that something that someone has said is unimportant. 那又怎样呢？ [INFORMAL] ❑ *"My name's Bruno."—"So?"* "我的名字是布鲁诺。"——"那又怎样？" **11** ADV You can use **so** in front of adjectives and adverbs to emphasize the quality that they are describing. 如此 (用于形容词或副词前，表示强调) [ADV adj/adv] [EMPHASIS] ❑ *He was surprised they had married – they had seemed so different.* 他很吃惊他们居然已经结婚了——他们看上去他们如此不同。 **12** ADV You can use **so...that** and **so...as** to emphasize the degree of something by mentioning the result or consequence of it. 如此…以致… [EMPHASIS] ❑ *The tears were streaming so fast she could not see.* 泪水涌出如此迅速，让她都看不见了。 ❑ *He's not so stupid as to listen to rumors.* 他还没有笨到听信谣言份儿上。 **13** → see also **insofar as** **14** PHRASE You use **and so on** or **and so forth** at the end of a list to indicate that there are other items that you could also mention. 如此等等 ❑ *...the government's policies on such important issues as health, education, tax, and so on.* …政府有关医疗、教育、税收等重大问题的政策。 **15** PHRASE You use **so much** and **so many** when you are saying that there is a definite limit to something but you are not saying what this limit is. 这么多 (用以强调某事的限度) ❑ *There is only so much time in the day for answering letters.* 白天只有这么多时间用来回信。 ❑ *There is only so much fuel in the tank and if you burn it up too quickly you are in trouble.* 油罐里只有这么多燃料了，如果你用得太快，就有麻烦了。 **16** PHRASE You use the structures **not...so much** and **not so much...as** to say that something is one kind of thing rather than another kind. 与其说…不如说是… ❑ *I did not really object to Will's behavior so much as his personality.* 我与其说是反感威尔的行为，还不如说是讨厌他的个性。 **17** PHRASE You use **or so** when you are giving an approximate amount. 大约 [VAGUENESS] ❑ *Though rates are heading down, they still offer real returns of 8% or so.* 尽管利率在下降，但他们仍然给出了8%左右的实际收益率。 **18** **so much the better** → see **better** **19** **so far so good** → see **far** **20** **so long** → see **long** **21** **so much so** → see **much** **22** **every so often** → see **often** **23** **so there** → see **there**

So, **very**, and **too** can all be used to intensify the meaning of an adjective, an adverb, or a word like **much** or **many**. However, they are not used in the same way. **Very** is the simplest intensifier. It has no other meaning beyond that. **So** can suggest an emotional reaction on the part of the speaker, such as pleasure, surprise, or disappointment. ❑ *John makes me so angry!... Oh thank you so much!* **So** can also refer forward to a result clause introduced by **that**. ❑ *The procession was forced to move so slowly that he arrived three hours late.* **Too** suggests an excessive or undesirable amount, often so much that a particular result does not or cannot happen. ❑ *She does wear too much make-up at times... He was too late to save her.*

soak /soʊk/ (**soaks, soaking, soaked**) **1** V-T/V-I If you **soak** something or leave it **to soak**, you put it into a liquid and leave it there. 浸泡 ❑ *Soak the beans for 2 hours.* 把豆子泡上两个小时。 **2** V-T If a liquid **soaks** something or if you **soak** something **with** a liquid, the liquid makes the thing very wet. 使浸湿 ❑ *The water had soaked his jacket and shirt.* 水浸湿了他的夹克和衬衣。 **3** V-I If a liquid **soaks through** something, it passes through it. 渗透 ❑ *There was so much blood it had soaked through my boxer shorts.* 血出得太多，都渗透了我的平脚短裤。 **4** V-I If someone **soaks**, they spend a long time in a hot bath, because they enjoy it. 长时间泡浴 ❑ *What I need is to soak in a hot tub.* 我需要的是在浴盆里泡个热水澡。 ● N-COUNT **Soak** is also a noun. 泡浴 ❑ *I was having a long soak in the bath.* 我当时正在浴室里长时间地泡浴。 **5** → see also **soaked, soaking**

▸ **soak up** **1** PHRASAL VERB If a soft or dry material **soaks up** a liquid, the liquid goes into the substance. 吸收 (液体) ❑ *The cells will promptly start to soak up moisture.* 细胞会很快开始吸收水份。 **2** PHRASAL VERB If you **soak up** the atmosphere in a place that you are visiting, you observe or get involved in the way of life there, because you enjoy it or are interested in it. 感受 (气氛) [INFORMAL] ❑ *Keaton comes here once or twice a year to soak up the atmosphere.* 基顿每年来这里一两次，感受这里的氛围。 **3** PHRASAL VERB If something **soaks up** something such as money or other resources, it uses a great deal of money or other resources. 耗费 (钱或其他资源) ❑ *Defence soaks up 40 percent of the budget.* 国防开支要耗费40%的预算。

soaked /soʊkt/ ADJ If someone or something gets **soaked** or **soaked through**, water or some other liquid makes them extremely wet. 湿透的 ❑ *I have to check my tent – it got soaked last night in the storm.* 我得检查一下我的帐篷——昨晚的暴风雨把它给淋透了。 ❑ *We got soaked to the skin.* 我们浑身湿透了。

soak·ing /soʊkɪŋ/ ADJ If something is **soaking** or **soaking wet**, it is very wet. 湿透的 ❑ *My face and raincoat were soaking wet.* 我的脸上和雨衣上都湿淋淋的。

so-and-so PRON-SING You use **so-and-so** instead of a word, expression, or name when you are talking generally rather than giving a specific example of a particular thing. 某某 (泛指一件事) [INFORMAL] ❑ *It would be a case of "just do so-and-so and here's your cash."* 情况会是"只管做这做那，然后拿钱"。

soap /soʊp/ (**soaps**) **1** N-MASS **Soap** is a substance that you use with water for washing yourself or sometimes for washing clothes. 肥皂 ❑ *...a bar of lavender soap.* …一块熏衣草肥皂。 ❑ *...a large box of soap powder.* …一大盒肥皂粉。 **2** N-COUNT A **soap** is the same as a **soap opera**. 肥皂剧 [INFORMAL]
→ see Word Web: **soap**

Word Web soap

Soap is an important part of everyday life. We **wash** our hands before we eat. We lather up with a **bar** of soap in the **shower** or **tub**. We use liquid **detergent** to **clean** our dishes. We use **laundry** detergent to get our clothes clean. But why do we use soap? How does it work? It works almost like a magnet. Only instead of attracting and repelling metal, soap attracts dirt and grease. It makes a **bubble** around the dirt, and water washes it all away.

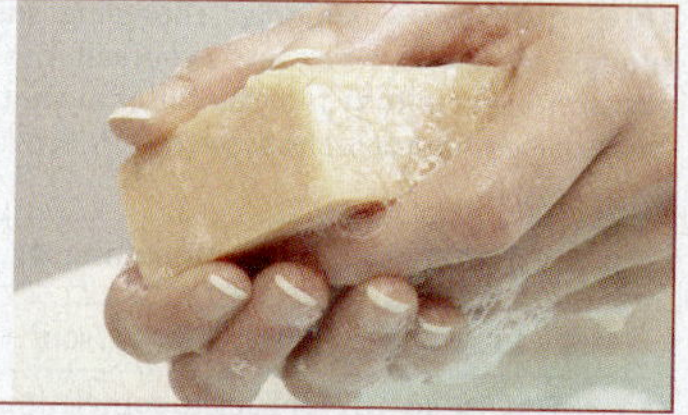

soap op·era (soap operas) N-COUNT A **soap opera** is a popular television drama series about the daily lives and problems of a group of people who live in a particular place. 肥皂剧

soar /sɔr/ (soars, soaring, soared) **1** V-I If the amount, value, level, or volume of something **soars**, it quickly increases by a great deal. 急剧增加 [JOURNALISM] ❑ *Insurance claims are expected to soar.* 预计保险索赔会急剧增加。 ❑ *Shares soared on the New York stock exchange.* 纽约证券交易所股票暴涨。 **2** V-I If something such as a bird **soars** into the air, it goes quickly up into the air. 高飞 [LITERARY] ❑ *If you're lucky, a splendid golden eagle may soar into view.* 幸运的话，一只金色雄鹰会跃入视线。

▲ **sob** /sɒb/ (sobs, sobbing, sobbed) **1** V-I When someone **sobs**, they cry in a noisy way, breathing in short breaths. 抽噎 ❑ *She began to sob again, burying her face in the pillow.* 她又开始抽噎，把脸埋在枕头里。 ● **sob·bing** N-UNCOUNT 抽噎 ❑ *The room was silent except for her sobbing.* 房间里除了她的啜泣声一片寂静。 **2** N-COUNT A **sob** is one of the noises that you make when you are crying. 呜咽声 ❑ *Her sobs grew louder.* 她的呜咽声变得更大了。

★ **so·ber** /soʊbər/ (sobers, sobering, sobered) **1** ADJ When you are **sober**, you are not drunk. 清醒的 ❑ *He'd been drunk when I arrived. Now he was sober.* 我到的时候他已经喝醉了。现在他清醒了。 **2** ADJ A **sober** person is serious and thoughtful. 严肃的 ❑ *We are now far more sober and realistic.* 我们现在严肃多了，也现实多了。 ❑ *It was a room filled with sad, sober faces.* 这是一个满是忧伤和严肃面孔的房间。 ● **so·ber·ly** ADV 严肃地 ❑ *"There's a new development," he said soberly.* "有新的进展，"他严肃地说。 **3** ADJ **Sober** colors and clothes are plain and rather dull. (颜色或衣服) 素淡的 ❑ *He dresses in sober gray suits.* 他穿着一套素净的灰色衣服。 ● **so·ber·ly** ADV 素淡地 [ADV with v] ❑ *She saw Ellis, soberly dressed in a well-cut dark suit.* 她看见了埃利斯，素淡地穿着一套裁剪合体的黑西服。 **4** → see also **sobering**

▸ **sober up** PHRASAL VERB If someone **sobers up**, or if something **sobers** them **up**, they become sober after being drunk. 醒酒 ❑ *He was left to sober up in a police cell.* 他被留在警察局的一间拘留室里醒酒。

so·ber·ing /soʊbərɪŋ/ ADJ You say that something is a **sobering** thought or has a **sobering** effect when a situation seems serious and makes you become serious and thoughtful. 令人深思的 ❑ *It is a sobering thought that in the 17th century she could have been burned as a witch.* 如果是在17世纪，她有可能被当作女巫烧死，这一点是令人深思的。

so-called ♦◇◇ also **so called** **1** ADJ You use **so-called** to indicate that you think a word or expression used to describe someone or something is in fact wrong. 所谓的 [ADJ n] ❑ *These are the facts that explode their so-called economic miracle.* 这些就是戳穿他们所谓的经济奇迹的事实。 **2** ADJ You use **so-called** to indicate that something is generally referred to by the name that you are about to use. 被称为…的 [ADJ n] ❑ *...a summit of the world's seven leading market economies, the so-called G-7.* …世界7个主要市场经济体的峰会，一般称为G-7。

S

soc·cer ♦◇◇ /sɒkər/ N-UNCOUNT **Soccer** is a game played by two teams of eleven players using a round ball. Players kick the ball to each other and try to score goals by kicking the ball into a large net. Outside the United States, this game is also referred to as **football**. 英式足球 ❑ *...a soccer match.* …一场英式足球比赛。

→ see Picture Dictionary: **soccer**

soc·cer play·er /sɒkər pleɪər/ (soccer players) N-COUNT A **soccer player** is a person who plays soccer, especially as a profession. 英式足球运动员 (尤指职业的) [AM]

in BRIT, use **footballer**

▲ **so·cia·ble** /soʊʃəbəl/ ADJ **Sociable** people are friendly and enjoy talking to other people. 友善的；好交际的 ❑ *She was, and remained, extremely sociable, enjoying dancing, golf, tennis, skating, and bicycling.* 她以前是，现在依然是极其好交际，喜欢跳舞、打高尔夫、打网球、滑冰和骑自行车。

Word Link *soci ≈ companion : associate, social, sociology*

so·cial ♦♦♦ /soʊʃəl/ **1** ADJ **Social** means relating to society or to the way society is organized. 社会的 [ADJ n] ❑ *...the worst effects of unemployment, low pay, and other social problems.* …失业、低工资和其他社会问题造成的最坏影响。 ❑ *...long-term social change.* …长期的社会变革。 ❑ *...changing social attitudes.* …变化中的社会观念。 ● **so·cial·ly** ADV 在社会上 [ADV adj/-ed] ❑ *Let's face it – drinking is a socially acceptable habit.* 咱们来面对这个事实吧——饮酒是一种为社会所接受的习俗。 **2** ADJ **Social** means relating to the status or rank that someone has in society. 与社会地位有关的 [ADJ n] ❑ *Higher education is unequally distributed across social classes.* 高等教育是不平等分配给各社会各阶层的。 ● **so·cial·ly** ADV 在社会地位上 ❑ *For socially ambitious couples this is a problem.* 对在社会地位方面有野心的夫妇来说，这是个问题。 **3** ADJ **Social** means relating to leisure activities that involve meeting other people. 社交的 [ADJ n] ❑ *We ought to organize more social events.* 我们应该组织更多的社交活动。 ● **so·cial·ly** ADV 在社交方面 ❑ *We have known each other socially for a long time.* 我们在社交场合相识有很长时间了。 ❑ *...research into housing and social policy.* …研究住房和社会政策。

→ see **kiss, myth, society**

so·cial·ise /soʊʃəlaɪz/ [BRIT] → see **socialize**

so·cial·ism /soʊʃəlɪzəm/ N-UNCOUNT **Socialism** is a set of political principles whose general aim is to create a system in which everyone has an equal opportunity to benefit from a country's wealth. Under socialism, the country's main industries are usually owned by the state. 社会主义

so·cial·ist ♦◇◇ /soʊʃəlɪst/ (socialists) **1** ADJ **Socialist** means based on socialism or relating to socialism. 社会主义的 ❑ *...members of the ruling Socialist Party.* …执政的社会主义党成员。 **2** N-COUNT A **socialist** is a person who believes in socialism or who is a member of a socialist party. 社会主义者；社会主义党成员 ❑ *Esperanto has always been popular among socialists.* 世界语在社会主义者中一直很受欢迎。

Picture Dictionary soccer

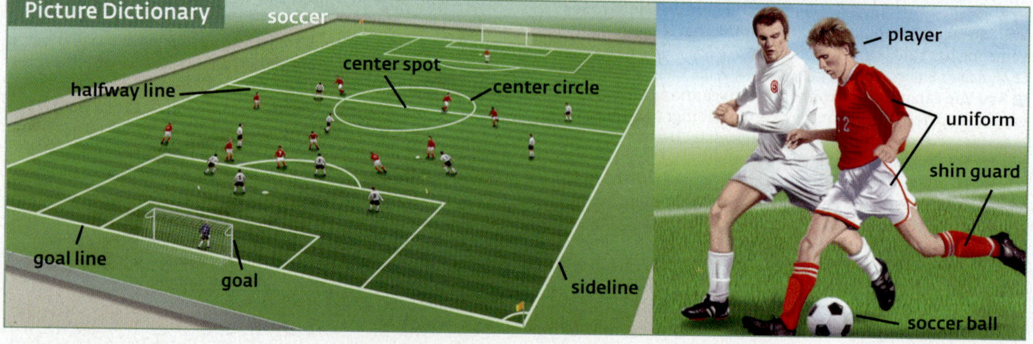

★ **so·cial·ize** /soʊʃəlaɪz/ (**socializes, socializing, socialized**) in BRIT, also use **socialise** V-I If you **socialize**, you meet other people socially, for example at parties. 社交 ❑ *...an open meeting, where members socialized and welcomed any new members.* …让会员们相互交流、欢迎所有新成员的一次公开集会。❑ *It upset her that she no longer socialized with old friends.* 她不再和老朋友们交往，这让她难受。

so·cial sci·ence (**social sciences**) **1** N-UNCOUNT **Social science** is the scientific study of society. 社会科学 ❑ *The research methods of social science generate two kinds of data.* 社会科学的研究方法生成两类数据。**2** N-COUNT The **social sciences** are the various types of social science, for example sociology and politics. 社会科学学科 ❑ *...a degree in a social science.* …一个社会科学学科的学位。

So·cial Se·cu·rity N-UNCOUNT **Social Security** is a system by which workers and employers in the U.S. have to pay money to the government, which gives money to people who are retired, who are disabled, or who cannot work. 社会保障制度 ❑ *My mother never worked, so she's not eligible for Social Security.* 我母亲从未工作过，因此她不符合社会保险资格。❑ *Future retirees are expected to get smaller Social Security benefits than promised.* 预计未来的退休者领取到的社会保险金要比许诺的少。

So·cial Se·cu·rity num·ber (**Social Security numbers**) N-COUNT A **Social Security** number is a nine digit number that is given to U.S. citizens and to people living in the U.S. You need it to get a job, collect Social Security benefits and receive some government services. (美国公民或美国居民的) 社会保险号码 ❑ *Questions such as date of birth and Social Security number are straightforward.* 诸如出生日期和社会保险号码这类问题简单明了。

so·cial ser·vices N-PLURAL **Social services** in a district are the services provided by the local authority or government to help people who have serious family problems or financial problems. 社会福利部门 ❑ *Schools and social services are also struggling to absorb the influx.* 学校和社会福利部门也在努力接纳突然大批涌入的人群。

so·cial work N-UNCOUNT **Social work** is work which involves giving help and advice to people with serious family problems or financial problems. 社会福利工作

so·cial work·er (**social workers**) N-COUNT A **social worker** is a person whose job is to do social work. 社会福利工作者

so·ci·ety ♦♦♦ /səsaɪɪti/ (**societies**) **1** N-UNCOUNT **Society** is people in general, thought of as a large organized group. 社会 (指社会中所有的人) ❑ *This reflects attitudes and values prevailing in society.* 这反映出社会上普遍流行的态度和价值观。**2** N-VAR A **society** is the people who live in a country or region, their organizations, and their way of life. 社会; (生活于某个地区、有自己生活方式的) 群体 ❑ *We live in a capitalist society.* 我们生活在资本主义社会。**3** N-COUNT A **society** is an organization for people who have the same interest or aim. 社团; 协会 ❑ *...the Atlanta Horticultural Society.* …亚特兰大园艺协会。**4** N-UNCOUNT **Society** is the rich, fashionable people in a particular place who meet on social occasions. 上流社会 ❑ *The couple quickly became a fixture in society.* 这对夫妇很快就成为上流社会的常客。
→ see Word Web: **society**

so·cio·eco·nom·ic /soʊsioʊɛkənɒmɪk, -ikə-/ ADJ **Socioeconomic** circumstances or developments involve a combination of social and economic factors. 社会经济的 [ADJ n] ❑ *The age, education, and socioeconomic status of these young mothers led to less satisfactory child care.* 这些年轻妈妈的年龄、教育状况和社会经济地位导致其子女得不到妥帖的照料。

so·ci·ol·ogy /soʊsiɒlədʒi/ N-UNCOUNT **Sociology** is the study of society or of the way society is organized. 社会学 ● **so·cio·logi·cal** /soʊsiəlɒdʒɪkəl/ ADJ 社会学的 ❑ *Psychological and sociological studies were emphasizing the importance of the family.* 心理学和社会学研究都在强调家庭的重要性。● **so·ci·olo·gist** ★ N-COUNT (**sociologists**) 社会学家 ❑ *By the 1950s some sociologists were confident that they had identified the key characteristics of capitalist society.* 到20世纪50年代，一些社会学家深信他们已经确认了资本主义社会的主要特征。

so·cio·po·liti·cal /soʊsioʊpəlɪtɪkəl/ ADJ **Sociopolitical** systems and problems involve a combination of social and political factors. 社会政治的 [ADJ n] ❑ *...contemporary sociopolitical issues such as ecology, human rights, and nuclear arms.* …诸如生态环境、人权和核武器等当代社会政治问题。

sock /sɒk/ (**socks, socking, socked**) **1** N-COUNT **Socks** are pieces of clothing which cover your foot and ankle and are worn inside shoes. 短袜 ❑ *...a pair of knee-high socks.* …一双齐膝的短袜。**2** V-T If you **sock** someone or something, you hit them hard. 重击 [INFORMAL] ❑ *Once, after a boy made a comment, she socked him.* 有一次，一个男孩子发表了一点意见，她就挥拳猛击他。**3** V-T If someone **is socked with** something bad, it happens to them. (遭不利的事) 打击 ❑ *Phil got socked with a bill for nearly $1,000.* 菲尔因一张近$1000的账单蒙受损失。
→ see **clothing**

▲ **sock·et** /sɒkɪt/ (**sockets**) **1** N-COUNT A **socket** is a device on a piece of electrical equipment into which you can put a bulb or plug. 插口; 灯座 ❑ *On the stairway to the basement, he took the light bulb out of the socket.* 在通向地下室的楼梯上，他把灯泡从灯座上拧了下来。**2** N-COUNT A **socket** is a device or point in a wall where you can connect electrical equipment to the power supply. (电源) 插座 [mainly BRIT]
in AM, usually use **outlet**
3 N-COUNT You can refer to any hollow part or opening in a structure which another part fits into as a **socket**. 承槽; 窝 ❑ *Rotate the shoulders in their sockets five times.* 将轴肩在承槽中转动5次。

soda /soʊdə/ (**sodas**) **1** N-MASS **Soda** is a sweet carbonated drink. 汽水 [AM] ❑ *...a glass of diet soda.* …一杯低热量汽水。● N-COUNT A **soda** is a bottle of soda. 一瓶汽水 ❑ *They had liquor for the adults and sodas for the children.* 他们为成年人准备了酒，为孩子们准备了汽水。

> Carbonated drinks containing no alcohol are called **soda** or **soda pop**. They are usually very sweet. Another name is **soft drinks**, and this is the term usually used in the UK.

2 N-UNCOUNT **Soda** is the same as **soda water**. 苏打水 **3** → see also **baking soda, club soda**

soda pop (**soda pops**) N-UNCOUNT **Soda pop** is a sweet carbonated drink. 汽水 [AM] ❑ *Beer and soda pop are served before the bus departs.* 公共汽车出发前有啤酒和汽水供应。● N-COUNT A **soda pop** is a bottle or a glass of soda pop. 一瓶汽水; 一杯汽水 ❑ *He bought me a soda pop.* 他给我买了一瓶汽水。

soda wa·ter also **soda-water** N-UNCOUNT **Soda water** is carbonated water and is often used for mixing with alcoholic drinks and fruit juice. 苏打水

sod·den /sɒdən/ ADJ Something that is **sodden** is extremely wet. 湿透的 ❑ *We stripped off our sodden clothes.* 我们脱掉了湿透的衣服。

so·dium /soʊdiəm/ N-UNCOUNT **Sodium** is a silvery white chemical element which combines with other chemicals. Salt is a sodium compound. 钠 ❑ *The fish or seafood is heavily salted with pure sodium chloride.* 鱼或海产品以厚厚的纯氯化钠盐腌制。

sofa /soʊfə/ (**sofas**) N-COUNT A **sofa** is a long, comfortable seat with a back and usually with arms, which two or three people can sit on. 长沙发

S

Word Web society

Human **social** organizations and **customs** change over time. Early humans established **hunter-gatherer** groups to provide mutual support and improve survival. Later, people in some areas formed family systems like **clans**. In other places people created multi-family groups, or **tribes**. Here leadership came through inheritance, election, or appointment. Some groups were led by women, but these matriarchies are rare today. According to some anthropologists, many societies today are patriarchies where power is held by men. **Feminism** is a societal response seeking to balance power in society. Societies continue to evolve to meet the needs of the people who live within them.

soft ♦♦◇ /sɔft/ (**softer, softest**) 1 ADJ Something that is **soft** is pleasant to touch, and not rough or hard. 柔软的 ❑ *Regular use of a body lotion will keep the skin soft and supple.* 定期使用润肤乳液可以使皮肤保持柔软光滑。 ❑ *When it's dry, brush the hair using a soft, nylon baby brush.* 天气干燥时，用婴儿用的软尼龙刷子梳头发。 ● **soft·ness** N-UNCOUNT 柔软 ❑ *The sea air robbed her hair of its softness.* 海边的空气有损她头发的柔滑。 2 ADJ Something that is **soft** changes shape or bends easily when you press it. 软的 ❑ *She lay down on the soft, comfortable bed.* 她躺到柔软舒适的床上。 ❑ *Add enough milk to form a soft dough.* 加足牛奶，以便揉成一个软面团。 3 ADJ Something that has a **soft** appearance has smooth curves rather than sharp or distinct edges. (外观) 柔和的 ❑ *This is a smart, yet soft and feminine look.* 这是一张透着精明的面孔，但是线条柔和、女性味十足。 ● **soft·ly** ADV 柔和地 [ADV with v] ❑ *She wore a softly tailored suit.* 她穿了件剪裁柔和得体的套装。 4 ADJ Something that is **soft** is very gentle and has no force. For example, a **soft** sound or voice is quiet and not harsh. A **soft** light or color is pleasant to look at because it is not bright. (声音、光线或色彩) 柔和的 ❑ *There was a soft tapping on my door.* 有人在轻轻地敲我的房门。 ● **soft·ly** ADV 柔和地 [ADV with v] ❑ *She crossed the softly lit room.* 她穿过灯光柔和的房间。 5 ADJ If you are **soft on** someone, you do not treat them as strictly or severely as you should. 心慈手软的 [DISAPPROVAL] ❑ *The president says the measure is soft and weak on criminals.* 总统说这项措施对罪犯来说太宽容、软弱了。 6 ADJ If you say that someone has a **soft heart**, you mean that they are sensitive and sympathetic toward other people. 心肠软的; 有同情心的 [APPROVAL] ❑ *Her rather tough and worldly exterior hides a very soft and sensitive heart.* 她那相当坚强而世故的外表下掩藏着一颗非常柔软敏感的心。 7 ADJ You use **soft** to describe a way of life that is easy and involves very little work. 轻松的 ❑ *...a soft life and easy living.* …轻松安逸的生活。 8 ADJ **Soft** water does not contain much of the mineral calcium and so makes bubbles easily when you use soap. (水) 软性的 ❑ *...an area where the water is very soft.* …一个水质很软的地区。 9 ADJ **Soft** drugs are drugs, such as cannabis, which are illegal but which many people do not consider to be strong or harmful. (毒品) 毒性不强的 [ADJ n] [mainly BRIT]

in AM, use **recreational**

Thesaurus *soft* 另参见:
ADJ. fluffy, silky; *(ant.)* firm, hard, rough 1
malleable 2
faint, gentle, light, low; *(ant.)* clear, strong 4

soft·ball /sɔftbɔl/ (**softballs**) 1 N-UNCOUNT **Softball** is a game similar to baseball, but played with a larger, softer ball. 垒球运动 2 N-COUNT A **softball** is the ball used in the game of softball. 垒球

soft drink (**soft drinks**) N-COUNT A **soft drink** is a cold, nonalcoholic drink such as lemonade or fruit juice, or a carbonated drink. (不含酒精的) 软饮料

sof·ten /sɔfᵊn/ (**softens, softening, softened**) 1 V-T/V-I If you **soften** something or if it **softens**, it becomes less hard, stiff, or firm. 使变软; 变软 ❑ *Soften the butter mixture in a small saucepan.* 在小平底锅里将黄油混合物弄软。 2 V-T If one thing **softens** the damaging effect of another thing, it makes the effect less severe. 使减弱 ❑ *There were also pledges to soften the impact of the subsidy cuts on the poorer regions.* 也有保证要减轻消减给较贫困地区补贴所造成的冲击。 3 V-T/V-I If you **soften** your position, if your position **softens**, or if you **soften**, you become more sympathetic and less hostile or critical. 使变温和; 变温和 ❑ *The letter shows no sign that the Germans have softened their position.* 这封信没有任何迹象表明德国人的态度已有所缓和。 ❑ *His party's policy has softened a lot in recent years.* 近年来他所在政党的政策变得温和了许多。 4 V-T/V-I If your voice or expression **softens** or if you **soften** it, it becomes much more gentle and friendly. 使温和; 变温和 ❑ *All at once, Mick's serious expression softened into a grin.* 顷刻间，米克严肃的表情和蔼起来，咧嘴笑了。 5 V-T If you **soften** something such as light, a color, or a sound, you make it less bright or harsh. 使 (光、颜色或声音) 变柔和 ❑ *We wanted to soften the light without destroying the overall effect of space.* 我们希望在不破坏整体空间效果的同时使光线柔和些。 6 V-T Something that **softens** your skin makes it very smooth and pleasant to touch. 使 (皮肤) 变得光滑柔软 ❑ *...products designed to moisturize and soften the skin.* …为滋润柔滑肌肤而设计的产品。

soft land·ing (**soft landings**) N-COUNT In economics, a **soft landing** is a situation in which the economy stops growing but this does not produce a recession. (经济的) 软着陆 ❑ *...the belief that the economy is on course for a so-called soft landing.* …认为经济正在实现所谓的软着陆的观点。

soft loan (**soft loans**) N-COUNT A **soft loan** is a loan with a very low interest rate. Soft loans are usually made to developing countries or to businesses in developing countries. (给发展中国家或其企业的) 软贷款 [BUSINESS]

soft sell also **soft-sell** N-SING A **soft sell** is a method of selling or advertising that involves persuading people in a gentle way rather than putting a lot of pressure on people to buy things. (靠说服而非强迫的) 软性推销 [BUSINESS] ❑ *I think more customers probably prefer a soft sell.* 我想更多的顾客大概更喜欢软推销。

Word Link *ware ≈ merchandise : hardware, silverware, software*

soft·ware ♦◇◇ /sɔftwɛər/ N-UNCOUNT Computer programs are referred to as **software**. Compare **hardware**. 软件 [COMPUTING] ❑ *...the people who write the software for big computer projects.* …大型计算机项目的软件开发人员。
→ see **computer**

sog·gy /sɒgi/ (**soggier, soggiest**) ADJ Something that is **soggy** is unpleasantly wet. 湿乎乎的 ❑ *...soggy cheese sandwiches.* …湿乎乎的乳酪三明治。

soil ♦◇◇ /sɔɪl/ (**soils**) N-MASS **Soil** is the substance on the surface of the earth in which plants grow. 土壤 ❑ *We have the most fertile soil in the Midwest.* 我们在中西部有最肥沃的土壤。
→ see **erosion, farm**

sol·ace /sɒlɪs/ N-UNCOUNT **Solace** is a feeling of comfort that makes you feel less sad. 慰藉 [FORMAL] ❑ *I found solace in writing when my father died three years ago.* 我父亲3年前去世时，我从写作中找到了慰藉。

so·lar /soʊlər/ 1 ADJ **Solar** is used to describe things relating to the sun. 太阳的 ❑ *A total solar eclipse is due to take place some time tomorrow.* 预计日全食会出现在明天的某个时候。 2 ADJ **Solar** power is obtained from the sun's light and heat. 太阳产生的 ❑ *...the financial savings from solar energy.* …使用太阳能带来的资金节约。
→ see Word Web: **solar**
→ see **energy, greenhouse effect, solar system**

so·lar sys·tem (**solar systems**) N-COUNT **The solar system** is the sun and all the planets that go around it. 太阳系 ❑ *Saturn is the second biggest planet in the solar system.* 土星是太阳系的第二大的行星。
→ see Word Web: **solar system**
→ see **galaxy**

sold /soʊld/ **Sold** is the past tense and past participle of **sell**. sell的过去式和过去分词

Word Web **solar**

photovoltaic cells

Traditional **fossil fuel energy** sources are becoming scarce and expensive. They also cause environmental **pollution**. Recently scientists have turned to alternative sources of energy such as **solar power**. There are two ways of using the **sun's energy**. **Thermal** systems produce heat. **Photovoltaic** systems generate electricity. Thermal systems use a **solar collector**. This is an insulated box with a transparent cover. It stores the sun's energy for use in household air or water heating systems. Photovoltaic systems use thin layers of **semiconductor** materials to change the sun's heat into electricity. They are commonly used to power calculators and solar-powered watches.

Word Web solar system

The **sun** formed when a **nebula** turned into a star almost 5 billion years ago. All the **planets, comets,** and asteroids in our **solar system** started out in this nebula. Today they all **orbit** around the sun. The four planets closest to the sun are small and rocky. The next four consist mostly of **gases**. The outermost planet, Pluto, is a dwarf planet. It is composed of rock and ice. Many of the planets have **moons** orbiting them. Most asteroids are irregularly shaped and covered with **craters**. Only about 200 asteroids have diameters of over 100 kilometers.

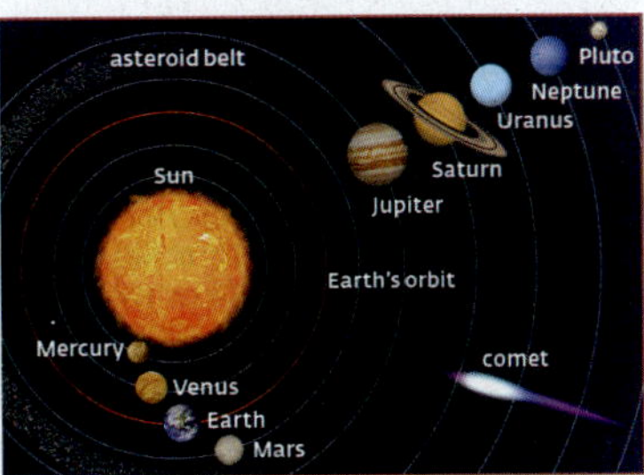

sol·dier ♦♦◇ /soʊldʒər/ (**soldiers**) N-COUNT A **soldier** is a member of an army, especially a person who is not an officer. 士兵
→ see **war**

sold out 1 ADJ If a performance, sports event, or other entertainment is **sold out**, all the tickets for it have been sold. 售完的 [v-link ADJ] ❑ *The premiere on Monday is sold out.* 周一的首映票已经售完。 2 ADJ If a store is **sold out of** something, it has sold all of it that it had. 脱销的 [v-link ADJ] ❑ *The stores are sometimes sold out of certain groceries.* 这些店铺的某些杂货有时会脱销。 3 → see also **sell out**

sole /soʊl/ (**soles**) 1 ADJ The **sole** thing or person of a particular type is the only one of that type. 惟一的 [ADJ n] ❑ *Their sole aim is to destabilize the Indian government.* 他们的惟一目的是要动摇印度政府的统治。 2 ADJ If you have **sole** charge or ownership of something, you are the only person in charge of it or who owns it. 惟一的；独占的 [ADJ n] ❑ *Many women are left as the sole providers in families after their husband has died.* 许多妇女在其丈夫死后成为家庭的惟一扶养人。 3 N-COUNT The **sole** of your foot or of a shoe or sock is the underneath surface of it. 脚掌；鞋底；袜底 ❑ *...shoes with rubber soles.* …橡胶底的鞋子。
→ see **fish, foot**

sole·ly /soʊlli/ ADV If something involves **solely** one thing, it involves only this thing and no others. 惟一地 ❑ *Too often we make decisions based solely upon what we see in the magazines.* 大多数时候，我们仅仅依据在杂志上看到的东西作决定。

sol·emn /sɒləm/ 1 ADJ Someone or something that is **solemn** is very serious rather than cheerful or humorous. (人) 严肃的；(物) 庄严的 ❑ *His solemn little face broke into smiles.* 他那严肃的小脸绽开了笑容。 ●**so·lem·nity** ★ /səlɛmnɪti/ N-UNCOUNT 严肃；庄严 ❑ *The setting for this morning's signing ceremony matched the solemnity of the occasion.* 今天早上签字仪式的布置符合这种场合的庄严气氛。 2 ADJ A **solemn** promise or agreement is one that you make in a very formal, sincere way. 正式的；郑重的 ❑ *She made a solemn promise to him when they became engaged that she would give up cigarettes for good.* 他们订婚时，她向他许下郑重的承诺，说她会永远戒烟。

▲ **so·lic·it** /səlɪsɪt/ (**solicits, soliciting, solicited**) 1 V-T If you **solicit** money, help, support, or an opinion **from** someone, you ask them for it. 请求给予 [FORMAL] ❑ *He's already solicited their support on health care reform.* 他已经请求他们给予医疗保健改革方面的支持。 2 V-I When prostitutes **solicit**, they offer to have sex with people in return for money. (妓女) 拉客 ❑ *Prostitutes were forbidden to solicit on public roads and in public places.* 娼妓被禁止在公路上和公共场所拉客。 ●**so·lic·it·ing** N-UNCOUNT 拉客 ❑ *Girls could get very heavy sentences for soliciting – nine months or more.* 年轻女孩拉客可能会被处以重罚——9个月或更长。

so·lici·ta·tion /səlɪsɪteɪʃən/ (**solicitations**) N-VAR **Solicitation** is the act of asking someone for money, help, support, or an opinion. 请求给予 [mainly AM] ❑ *Republican leaders are making open solicitation of the Italian-American vote.* 共和党领袖正公开地向意大利裔美国人拉票。

★ **so·lici·tor** ♦◇◇ /səlɪsɪtər/ (**solicitors**) N-COUNT In the United States, a **solicitor** is the chief lawyer in a government or city department. (美国政府或市政部门的) 首席法律官员

sol·id ♦◇◇ /sɒlɪd/ (**solids**) 1 ADJ A **solid** substance or object stays the same shape whether it is in a container or not. 固体的 ❑ *...the potential of greatly reducing our solid waste problem.* …大幅度减少我们的固体垃圾问题的可能性。 2 N-COUNT A **solid** is a substance that stays the same shape whether it is in a container or not. 固体 ❑ *Solids turn to liquids at certain temperatures.* 固体在一定温度下转变成液体。 3 ADJ A substance that is **solid** is very hard or firm. 坚固的 ❑ *The snow had melted, but the lake was still frozen solid.* 雪已经融化了，但是湖面上冻得结结实实。 4 ADJ A **solid** object or mass does not have a space inside it, or holes or gaps in it. 实心的 ❑ *...a tunnel carved through 50 ft of solid rock.* …一条凿通了50英尺厚的实心岩石的隧道。 ❑ *The train station was packed solid with people.* 火车站上人挤得水泄不通。 5 ADJ If an object is made of **solid** gold or **solid** wood, for example, it is made of gold or wood all the way through, rather than just on the outside. 纯质的 [ADJ n] ❑ *The faucets appeared to be made of solid gold.* 这些水龙头看上去是纯金做成的。 ❑ *...solid wood doors.* …纯木门。 6 ADJ A structure that is **solid** is strong and is not likely to collapse or fall over. 坚固的 ❑ *Banks are built to look solid to reassure their customers.* 银行修建得看上去很坚固，以使顾客放心。 ●**sol·id·ly** ADV 坚固地 [ADV with v] ❑ *Their house, which was solidly built, resisted the main shock.* 他们的房子修建得很坚固，经受住了主震。 ●**so·lid·ity** /səlɪdɪti/ N-UNCOUNT 坚固性 ❑ *...the solidity of walls and floors.* …墙壁和地板的坚固性。 7 ADJ If you describe someone as **solid**, you mean that they are very reliable and respectable. 可靠的；可敬的 [APPROVAL] ❑ *You want a husband who is solid and stable, someone who will devote himself to you.* 你需要一个可靠而稳重的丈夫，一个全心全意为你的人。 ●**sol·id·ly** ADV 可靠地；可敬地 ❑ *Graham is so solidly consistent.* 格雷厄姆非常可靠稳定。 ●**so·lid·ity** N-UNCOUNT 可靠；可敬 ❑ *He had the proverbial solidity of the English.* 他有着典型英国人的可敬。 8 ADJ **Solid** evidence or information is reliable because it is based on facts. (证据或信息) 真实可靠的 ❑ *We don't have good solid information*

S

Picture Dictionary solids

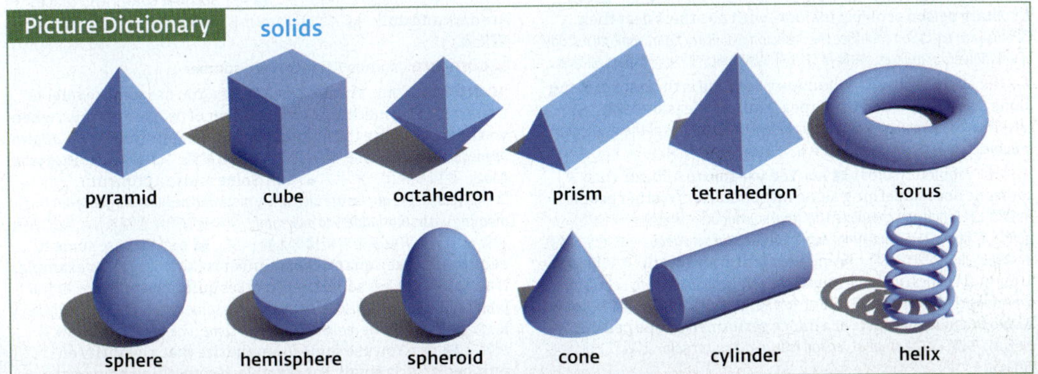

on where the people are. 我们并不掌握有关这些人在哪儿的确切消息。 **9** ADJ You use **solid** to describe something such as advice or a piece of work which is useful and reliable. (建议或工作) 有用可靠的 ❑ *The organization provides churches with solid advice on a wide range of subjects.* 该组织在一系列问题上为教堂提供切实有用的建议。 ● **sol·id·ly** ADV 可靠地 [ADV with v] ❑ *She's played solidly throughout the spring.* 她整个春季都表现得很稳健。 **10** ADJ You use **solid** to describe something such as the basis for a policy or support for an organization when it is strong, because it has been developed carefully and slowly. 坚定的 ❑ *...a Democratic nominee with solid support within the party and broad appeal beyond.* …一位在党内有坚定支持、在党外有广泛吸引力的民主党被提名人。 ● **sol·id·ly** ADV 坚定地 ❑ *The Los Alamos district is solidly Republican.* 洛斯阿拉莫斯地区是坚定的共和党地盘。 ● **so·lid·ity** N-UNCOUNT 坚定 ❑ *...doubts over the solidity of European backing for the American approach.* …对欧洲支持美国方式的坚定性的疑虑。 **11** ADJ If you do something for a **solid** period of time, you do it without any pause or interruption throughout that time. 连续的 [ADJ n, -ed ADJ] ❑ *We had worked together for two solid years.* 我们在一起连续工作了两年。 ● **sol·id·ly** ADV 连续地 [ADV with v] ❑ *People who had worked solidly since Christmas enjoyed the chance of a Friday off.* 自圣诞节连续工作到现在的人们星期五可以有机会放假一天。

→ see Picture Dictionary: solid
→ see **dump, matter**

Word Partnership *solid* 的常用搭配:

N. solid **food**, solid **waste** **1**
solid **ground**, **rock** solid **3**
solid **rock** **4**
solid **base**, solid **foundation** **6** **10**
solid **evidence** **8**
solid **performance** **9**
solid **growth**, solid **majority**, solid **support** **10**
ADJ. **frozen** solid **3**
good and solid **6**–**10**

★ **soli·dar·ity** /sɒlɪdærɪti/ N-UNCOUNT If a group of people show **solidarity**, they show support for each other or for another group, especially in political or international affairs. 团结一致; 相互支持 ❑ *Supporters want to march tomorrow to show solidarity with their leaders.* 支持者有意在明天游行以表现对他们领导的支持。

so·lidi·fy /səlɪdɪfaɪ/ (**solidifies, solidifying, solidified**) **1** V-T/V-I When a liquid **solidifies** or **is solidified**, it changes into a solid. 使凝固; 凝固 ❑ *The thicker lava would have taken two weeks to solidify.* 更厚的熔岩需要两周才会凝固。 ❑ *The Energy Department plans to solidify the deadly waste in a high-tech billion-dollar factory.* 能源部计划在一家斥资10亿美元的高科技工厂里凝固这些致命的废物。 **2** V-T/V-I If something such as a position or opinion **solidifies**, or if something **solidifies** it, it becomes firmer and more definite and unlikely to change. 使稳固; 变稳固 ❑ *Her attitudes solidified through privilege and habit.* 由于特权和习惯, 她的态度愈来愈顽固。 ❑ *...his attempt to solidify his position as chairman.* …他稳固他作为主席的地位的企图。

S

soli·tary /sɒlɪtɛri/ **1** ADJ A person or animal that is **solitary** spends a lot of time alone. 独处的 ❑ *Paul was a shy, pleasant, solitary man.* 保罗是个腼腆的、讨人喜欢的、惯于独处的人。 **2** ADJ A **solitary** activity is one that you do alone. 独自的 [ADJ n] ❑ *His evenings were spent in solitary drinking.* 他的每个夜晚都在独自饮酒中度过。 **3** ADJ A **solitary** person or object is alone, with no others near them. 孤独的 [ADJ n] ❑ *You could see the occasional solitary figure making a study of wildflowers or grasses.* 你偶尔可以看见那个研究野生花草的孤独身影。

▲ **soli·tude** /sɒlɪtud/ N-UNCOUNT **Solitude** is the state of being alone, especially when this is peaceful and pleasant. 独处 ❑ *He enjoyed his moments of solitude before the pressures of the day began in earnest.* 他很喜欢一天的压力真正开始前的独处时刻。

★ **solo** /soʊloʊ/ (**solos**) **1** ADJ You use **solo** to indicate that someone does something alone rather than with other people. 单独的 ❑ *He had just completed his final solo album.* 他刚刚完成他最后一张个人专辑。 ❑ *...Daniel Amokachi's spectacular solo goal.* …丹尼尔·阿莫卡奇精彩的个人进球得分。 ● ADV **Solo** is also an adverb. 单独地 [ADV after v] ❑ *Charles Lindbergh became the very first person to fly solo across the Atlantic.* 查尔斯·林白成为第一个单独飞越大西洋的人。 **2** N-COUNT A **solo** is a piece of music or a dance performed by one person. 独奏曲; 独舞 ❑ *The original version featured a guitar solo.* 原版以吉他独奏为特色。

so·lo·ist /soʊloʊɪst/ (**soloists**) N-COUNT A **soloist** is a musician or dancer who performs a solo. 独奏者; 独舞者 ❑ *...the relationship between soloist and orchestra.* …独奏者与管弦乐队之间的关系。

★ **sol·uble** /sɒlyəbᵊl/ **1** ADJ A substance that is **soluble** will dissolve in a liquid. 可溶解的 ❑ *Uranium is soluble in sea water.* 铀可在海水中溶解。 **2** COMB IN ADJ If something is **water-soluble** or **fat-soluble**, it will dissolve in water or in fat. 水 (脂) 溶性的 ❑ *The red dye on the leather is water-soluble.* 皮革上的红色染料是水溶性的。

so·lu·tion ♦♦◊ /səluʃᵊn/ (**solutions**) **1** N-COUNT A **solution to** a problem or difficult situation is a way of dealing with it so that the difficulty is removed. 解决办法 ❑ *Although he has sought to find a peaceful solution, he is facing pressure to use greater military force.* 虽然他已设法寻找一个和平的解决办法, 但他正面临着使用更大军事力量的压力。 **2** N-COUNT The **solution to** a puzzle is the answer to it. 谜底 ❑ *We invited readers who completed the puzzle to send in their solutions.* 我们邀请解完谜的读者交出谜底。 **3** N-COUNT A **solution** is a liquid in which a solid substance has been dissolved. 溶液 [also "in" N] ❑ *...a warm solution of liquid detergent.* …液体洗洁精的温热稀释溶液。

Word Partnership *solution* 的常用搭配:

ADJ. **best** solution, **peaceful** solution, **perfect** solution, **possible** solution, **practical** solution, **temporary** solution **1**
easy solution, **obvious** solution, **simple** solution **1** **2**
N. solution **to a conflict**, solution **to a crisis** **1**
solution **to a problem** **1** **2**
V. **propose a** solution, **reach a** solution, **seek a** solution **1**
find a solution **1** **2**

solve ♦◊◊ /sɒlv/ (**solves, solving, solved**) V-T If you **solve** a problem or a question, you find a solution or an answer to it. 解决 ❑ *Their domestic reforms did nothing to solve the problem of unemployment.* 他们的国内改革没有采取任何措施以解决失业问题。

Word Partnership *solve* 的常用搭配:

N. **ability to** solve *something*, solve **a crisis**, solve **a mystery**, solve **a problem**, solve **a puzzle**, **way to** solve *something*
V. **attempt/try to** solve *something*, **help** solve *something*

sol·ven·cy /sɒlvᵊnsi/ N-UNCOUNT A person's or organization's **solvency** is their ability to pay their debts. 偿债能力 [BUSINESS] ❑ *...unsound investments that could threaten the company's solvency.* …可能威胁到公司偿债能力的不良投资。

▲ **sol·vent** /sɒlvᵊnt/ (**solvents**) **1** ADJ If a person or a company is **solvent**, they have enough money to pay all their debts. 有偿债能力的 [BUSINESS] ❑ *They're going to have to show that the company is now solvent.* 他们将不得不证明公司现在是具备偿债能力的。 **2** N-MASS A **solvent** is a liquid that can dissolve other substances. 溶剂 ❑ *...a small amount of cleaning solvent.* …少量的清洗剂。

→ see **dry-cleaning**

▲ **som·ber** /sɒmbər/
in BRIT, use **sombre**

1 ADJ If someone is **somber**, they are serious or sad. 沉痛的 ❑ *Spencer cried as she described the somber mood of her co-workers.* 斯宾塞在描述同事们沉痛的情绪时哭了。 **2** ADJ **Somber** colors and places are dark and dull. 灰暗的 ❑ *His room is somber and dark.* 他的房间阴森黑暗。

▲ **som·bre** /sɒmbəʳ/ [BRIT] → see **somber**

some ♦♦♦ /səm, STRONG sʌm/ **1** DET You use **some** to refer to a quantity of something or to a number of people or things, when you are not stating the quantity or number precisely. 一些 ❑ *Robin opened some champagne.* 罗宾打开了一些香槟酒。 ❑ *He went to fetch some books.* 他去取来了一些书。 ● PRON **Some** is also a pronoun. 一些 ❑ *This year all the apples are all red. My niece and nephew are going out this morning with step-ladders to pick some.* 今年所有的苹果都红了。我的侄女和侄子今天上午就要带着折梯出去摘一些。 **2** DET You use **some** to emphasize that a quantity or number is fairly large. For example, if an activity takes **some** time, it takes quite a lot of time. 相当多 [EMPHASIS] ❑ *I have discussed this topic in some detail.* 我已相当详细地讨论过这个话题。 ❑ *He remained silent for some time.* 他好长时间都保持沉默。 **3** DET You use **some** to emphasize that a quantity or number is fairly small. For example, if something happens to

some extent, it happens a little. 一点 [EMPHASIS] ❑ *"Isn't there some chance that William might lead a normal life?" asked Jill.* "威廉难道就没有一点机会可以过一种正常的生活?"吉尔问道。❑ *All mothers share to some extent in the tension of a wedding.* 所有的母亲都有些许程度上的婚礼紧张。 4 QUANT If you refer to **some of** the people or things in a group, you mean a few of them but not all of them. If you refer to **some of** a particular thing, you mean a part of it but not all of it. 一部份 ❑ *Some of the people already in work will lose their jobs.* 一部份已经工作的人将会失去他们的工作。❑ *Remove the cover and spoon some of the sauce into a bowl.* 打开盖子，用勺子舀一部份调味汁放到碗里。● PRON **Some** is also a pronoun. 一部份 ❑ *When the chicken is cooked I'll freeze some.* 鸡肉做熟后我会冷冻一部份。

> You use **not any** instead of **some** in negative sentences. ❑ *There isn't any money.*

5 DET If you refer to **some** person or thing, you are referring to that person or thing but in a vague way, without stating precisely which person or thing you mean. 某些 [VAGUENESS] ❑ *If you are worried about some aspect of your child's health, call us.* 如果你担心孩子的某些健康问题，就给我们打电话。 6 ADV You can use **some** in front of a number to indicate that it is approximate. 大约 [ADV num] [VAGUENESS] ❑ *I have kept birds for some 30 years.* 我养鸟大约有三十年了。 7 ADV **Some** is used to mean to a small extent or degree. 稍微 [ADV after v] [AM] ❑ *If Susanne is off somewhere, I'll kill time by looking around some.* 如果苏珊娜去了别的什么地方，我就稍微逛逛来消磨时间。 8 DET You can use **some** in front of a noun in order to express your approval or disapproval of the person or thing you are mentioning. 在名词前表对该人或事物的褒贬 [INFORMAL, FEELINGS] ❑ *"Some party!"—"Yep. One hell of a party."* "那还算晚会!"——"是啊，晚会简直是一塌糊涂。"

some·body ♦♦◊ /sʌmbɒdi, -bʌdi/ PRON-INDEF **Somebody** means the same as **someone**. 某人

> You use **not anybody** instead of **somebody** in negative sentences. ❑ *There isn't anybody here.*

some·how ♦◊◊ /sʌmhaʊ/ 1 ADV You use **somehow** to say that you do not know or cannot say how something was done or will be done. 不知怎地; 不知以什么方式 ❑ *We'll manage somehow, you and me. I know we will.* 我们总会应付过去的，你和我。我知道我们会的。❑ *Somehow Karin managed to cope with the demands of her career.* 不知怎么地，卡林设法应付了那些来自工作的要求。 2 **somehow or other** → see **other**

some·one ♦♦◊ /sʌmwʌn/

> The form **somebody** is also used.

1 PRON-INDEF You use **someone** or **somebody** to refer to a person without saying exactly who you mean. 某人 ❑ *Her father was shot by someone trying to rob his small retail store.* 她父亲被某个试图抢劫他的小零售店的人开枪打中了。❑ *I need someone to help me.* 我需要有人帮我。 2 PRON-INDEF If you say that a person is **someone** or **somebody in** a particular kind of work or **in** a particular place, you mean that they are considered to be important in that kind of work or in that place. 重要人物 ❑ *"Before she came around," she says, "I was somebody in this town."* "她来这之前，"她说，"我在这个镇上是个人物。"

> You use **not anyone** instead of **someone** in negative sentences. ❑ *There isn't anyone here.*

some·place /sʌmpleɪs/ ADV **Someplace** means the same as **somewhere**. 某地 [ADV after v] [AM] ❑ *Maybe if we could go someplace together, just you and I.* 也许我们可以一起去某个地方，只有你和我。

som·er·sault /sʌmərsɔlt/ (**somersaults, somersaulting, somersaulted**) 1 N-COUNT If someone or something does a **somersault**, they turn over completely in the air. 筋斗 ❑ *Trained dogs did somersaults on a man's shoulders.* 一些受过训练的狗在一个男子的肩膀上翻筋斗。 2 V-I If someone or something **somersaults**, they perform one or more somersaults. 翻筋斗 ❑ *His boat hit a wave and somersaulted.* 他的船撞上了一个波浪，翻了。

some·thing ♦♦♦ /sʌmθɪŋ/ 1 PRON-INDEF You use **something** to refer to a thing, situation, event, or idea, without saying exactly what it is. 某物; 某事 ❑ *He realized right away that there was something wrong.* 他马上意识到有地方不对了。❑ *There was something vaguely familiar about him.* 他身上有某些东西似曾相识。❑ *"You said there was something you wanted to ask me," he said politely.* "你说过有什么事情要问我，"他彬彬有礼地说。 2 PRON-INDEF You can use **something** to say that the description or amount that you are giving is not exact. 有点像; 差不多 [PRON prep] ❑ *Clive made a noise, something like a grunt.* 克莱夫发出了一阵噪声，有点像呼噜声。❑ *Their membership seems to have risen to something over 10,000.* 他们的会员似乎已经增加到差不多超过一万人了。 3 PRON-INDEF If you say that a person or thing is **something** or is really **something**, you mean that you are very impressed by them. 真不错 [INFORMAL] ❑ *You're really something.* 你的确真不错。 4 PRON-INDEF You can use **something** in expressions like "**that's something**" when you think that a situation is not very good but is better than it might have been. 差强人意 ❑ *Well, at least he was in town. That was something.* 哦，至少他还在城里。那也算不错啦。 5 PRON-INDEF If you say that a thing is **something of** a disappointment, you mean that it is quite disappointing. If you say that a person is **something of** an artist, you mean that they are quite good at art. 有点儿 [PRON "of" n] ❑ *The city proved to be something of a disappointment.* 结果这座城市证明有点儿令人失望。 6 PRON-INDEF If you say that there is **something in** an idea or suggestion, you mean that it is quite good and should be considered seriously. (想法或建议) 有道理 [PRON "in" n] ❑ *Could there be something in what he said?* 他说的话是否有道理? 7 PRON-INDEF You use **something** in expressions such as "**or something**" and "**or something like that**" to indicate that you are referring to something similar to what you have just mentioned but you are not being exact. 诸如此类的东西 [VAGUENESS] ❑ *This guy, his name was Briarly or Beardly or something.* 这个家伙，他的名字叫布赖尔利，或比亚特利，或跟这差不多的。 8 **something like** → see **like**

> You use **not anything** instead of **something** in negative sentences. ❑ *There isn't anything here.*

some·time /sʌmtaɪm/ ADV You use **sometime** to refer to a time in the future or the past that is unknown or that has not yet been decided. 某个时候 ❑ *The sales figures won't be released until sometime next month.* 销售数据要到下个月的某个时候才会公布。❑ *Why don't you come and see me sometime.* 你何不在某个时间来看看我?

some·times ♦♦◊ /sʌmtaɪmz/ ADV You use **sometimes** to say that something happens on some occasions rather than all the time. 有时 ❑ *During the summer, my skin sometimes gets greasy.* 在夏季我的皮肤有时会变得多油。❑ *Sometimes I think he dislikes me.* 有时我觉得他不喜欢我。

some·what ♦◊◊ /sʌmwʌt, -wɒt/ ADV You use **somewhat** to indicate that something is the case to a limited extent or degree. 稍微 [ADV with cl/group] [FORMAL] ❑ *He concluded that Oswald was somewhat abnormal.* 他断定奥斯瓦德有点不正常。❑ *He explained somewhat unconvincingly that the company was paying for everything.* 他有点不令人相信地解释说公司正在支付一切费用。

some·where ♦◊◊ /sʌmwɛər/ 1 ADV You use **somewhere** to refer to a place without saying exactly where you mean. 某处 ❑ *I've got a feeling I've seen him before somewhere.* 我有一种感觉，我以前在某个地方见过他。❑ *I'm not going home yet. I have to go somewhere else first.* 我还不会回家。我得先去别的地方。❑ *I needed somewhere to live.* 我需要某个住的地方。 2 ADV You use **somewhere** when giving an approximate amount, number, or time. 大约 [ADV prep] ❑ *He is believed to be worth somewhere between seven million and ten million dollars.* 据说他身价约在700万到1000万美元之间。❑ *Caray is somewhere between 73 and 80 years of age.* 凯瑞大约在73岁到80岁之间。 3 PHRASE If you say that you **are getting somewhere**, you mean that you are making progress toward achieving something. 有些进展 ❑ *At last they were agreeing, at last they were getting somewhere.* 最终他们取得了一致，最终他们取得了一些进展。

> You use **not anywhere** instead of **somewhere** in negative sentences. ❑ *He isn't going anywhere.* Informally, Americans also use the forms **someplace** and **anyplace**.

son ♦♦♦ /sʌn/ (**sons**) 1 N-COUNT Someone's **son** is their male child. 儿子 ❑ *He shared a pizza with his son Laurence.* 他与他的儿子劳伦斯共吃一个比萨饼。❑ *Sam is the seven-year-old son of Eric Davies.* 萨姆是埃里克·戴维斯的7岁儿子。 2 N-COUNT A man, especially a famous man, can be described as a **son** of the place he comes from. 来自某地的人 (尤指名人) [JOURNALISM] ❑ *...New Orleans's most famous son, Louis Armstrong.* …新奥尔良最有名气的人，路易斯·阿姆斯特朗。 3 N-VOC Some people use **son** as a form of address when they are showing kindness or affection to a boy or a man who is younger

than them. 孩子(用于称呼年龄小于自己的男子) [INFORMAL, FEELINGS] ❑ *Don't be frightened by failure, son.* 不要被失败吓倒了，孩子。
→ see **child**

▲ **so·nar** /soʊnɑr/ (**sonars**) N-VAR **Sonar** is equipment on a ship which can calculate the depth of the sea or the position of an underwater object using sound waves. 声纳

Word Link *son ≈ sound : resonate, sonata, supersonic*

so·na·ta /sənɑtə/ (**sonatas**) N-COUNT A **sonata** is a piece of classical music written either for a single instrument, or for one instrument and a piano. 奏鸣曲

song ♦♦◊ /sɔŋ/ (**songs**) **1** N-COUNT A **song** is words and music sung together. 歌曲 ❑ *...a voice singing a Spanish song.* …一个唱着西班牙歌曲的嗓音。 **2** N-UNCOUNT **Song** is the art of singing. 歌唱 ❑ *...dance, music, mime, and song.* …舞蹈、音乐、哑剧和歌唱。 **3** N-COUNT A bird's **song** is the pleasant, musical sounds that it makes. 鸟鸣声 ❑ *It's been a long time since I heard a blackbird's song in the evening.* 我已经好长时间没在晚上听到黑鹂的鸣叫声了。 **4** PHRASE If someone **bursts into song** or **breaks into song**, they start singing. 开始唱歌 ❑ *I feel as if I should break into song.* 我感觉我似乎应该开始歌唱。
→ see **concert**, **music**

Word Partnership *song* 的常用搭配:

ADJ. **beautiful** song, **favorite** song, **old** song, **popular** song **1**
V. **hear** a song, **play** a song, **record** a song, **sing** a song, **write** a song **1**
N. **hit** song, **love** song, song **lyrics**, song **music**, **pop** song, **rap** song, **theme** song, song **title**, **words of a** song **1** **bird's** song **3**

son·ic /sɒnɪk/ ADJ **Sonic** is used to describe things related to sound. 声音的 [ADJ n] [TECHNICAL] ❑ *...the sonic boom of enemy fighter-bombers.* …敌人战斗轰炸机隆隆的轰鸣声。
→ see **sound**

son-in-law (**sons-in-law**) N-COUNT Someone's **son-in-law** is the husband of their daughter. 女婿

son·net /sɒnɪt/ (**sonnets**) N-COUNT A **sonnet** is a poem that has 14 lines. Each line has 10 syllables, and the poem has a fixed pattern of rhymes. 十四行诗

son of a bitch (**sons of bitches**) also **son-of-a-bitch** N-COUNT If someone is very angry with another person, or if they want to insult them, they sometimes call them a **son of a bitch**. 狗娘养的 [INFORMAL, OFFENSIVE, VULGAR, DISAPPROVAL]

soon ♦♦♦ /sun/ (**sooner**, **soonest**) **1** ADV If something is going to happen **soon**, it will happen after a short time. If something happened **soon** after a particular time or event, it happened a short time after it. 不久 ❑ *You'll be hearing from us very soon.* 你很快就会收到我们来信的。 ❑ *This chance has come sooner than I expected.* 这个机会比我预想的来得快。 **2** PHRASE If you say that something happens **as soon as** something else happens, you mean that it happens immediately after the other thing. 一…就 ❑ *As soon as relations improve they will be allowed to go.* 关系一改善他们就会获准离开。 **3** PHRASE If you say that you **would just as soon** do something or you**'d just as soon** do it, you mean that you would prefer to do it. 宁愿 ❑ *These people could afford to retire to Florida but they'd just as soon stay put.* 这些人能负担得起退隐到佛罗里达，但他们宁愿留在原地。 ❑ *I'd just as soon not have to make this public.* 我宁愿不公开此事。

S

soot /sʊt, sut/ N-UNCOUNT **Soot** is black powder which rises in the smoke from a fire and collects usually on the inside of chimneys. 煤烟灰 ❑ *...a wall blackened by soot.* …一堵被煤烟灰熏黑了的墙。

▲ **soothe** /suð/ (**soothes**, **soothing**, **soothed**) **1** V-T If you **soothe** someone who is angry or upset, you make them feel calmer. 使镇定 ❑ *He would take her in his arms and soothe her.* 他就会把她搂在怀里，使她镇定下来。 ● **sooth·ing** ADJ 抚慰的 ❑ *Put on some nice soothing music.* 放些柔和舒缓的音乐。 **2** V-T Something that **soothes** a part of your body where there is pain or discomfort makes the pain or discomfort less severe. 缓和(疼痛或不适) ❑ *...body lotion to soothe dry skin.* …减轻皮肤干燥的润肤露。 ● **sooth·ing** ADJ 缓和的 ❑ *Cold tea is very soothing for burns.* 冷茶对灼伤有镇痛作用。

Word Link *soph ≈ wise : philosophical, philosophy, sophisticated*

so·phis·ti·cat·ed ♦◊◊ /səfɪstɪkeɪtɪd/ **1** ADJ A **sophisticated** machine, device, or method is more advanced or complex than others. 高级的；复杂的 ❑ *Honeybees use one of the most sophisticated communication systems of any insect.* 蜜蜂所使用的交流系统是昆虫中最复杂的之一。 **2** ADJ Someone who is **sophisticated** is comfortable in social situations and knows about culture, fashion, and other matters that are considered socially important. 老练的；久经世故的 ❑ *Claude was a charming, sophisticated companion.* 克劳德是个有魅力、见多识广的伙伴。 **3** ADJ A **sophisticated** person is intelligent and knows a lot, so that they are able to understand complicated situations. 干练的

Thesaurus *sophisticated* 另参见:

ADJ. advanced, complex, elaborate, intricate **1** cultured, experienced, refined, worldly; (*ant.*) backward, crude **2**

so·phis·ti·ca·tion /səfɪstɪkeɪʃᵊn/ N-UNCOUNT The **sophistication** of people, places, machines, or methods is their quality of being sophisticated. 老练；复杂性；先进 ❑ *It would take many decades to build up the level of education and sophistication required.* 要花好几十年的时间来逐步达到所需要的教育和发展水平。

so·pra·no /səprænoʊ, -prɑn-/ (**sopranos**) N-COUNT A **soprano** is a woman, girl, or boy with a high singing voice. 女高音；男童声高音 ❑ *She was the main soprano at the Bolshoi theatre.* 她是波修瓦剧院的主要女高音歌手。

sor·did /sɔrdɪd/ **1** ADJ If you describe someone's behavior as **sordid**, you mean that it is immoral or dishonest. 卑鄙的；不诚实的 [DISAPPROVAL] ❑ *He sat with his head buried in his hands as his sordid double life was revealed.* 当他卑鄙的两面生活被揭发时，他双手掩面地坐着。 **2** ADJ If you describe a place as **sordid**, you mean that it is dirty, unpleasant, or depressing. 肮脏的 [DISAPPROVAL] ❑ *...the attic windows of their sordid little rooms.* …他们那些肮脏小屋的阁楼窗户。

sore /sɔr/ (**sorer**, **sorest**, **sores**) **1** ADJ If part of your body is **sore**, it causes you pain and discomfort. 疼痛的 ❑ *It's years since I've had a sore throat like I did last night.* 我已经好多年没有像昨晚那样嗓子痛了。 **2** ADJ If you are **sore** about something, you are angry and upset about it. 恼怒的 [v-link ADJ] [mainly AM, INFORMAL] ❑ *The result is that they are now all feeling very sore at you.* 结果是他们现在都很生你的气。 **3** N-COUNT A **sore** is a painful place on the body where the skin is infected. 痛处 ❑ *Our backs and hands were covered with sores and burns from the ropes.* 我们的背和手到处是绳索导致的伤口和灼伤。 **4** PHRASE If something is **a sore point with** someone, it is likely to make them angry or embarrassed if you try to discuss it. 令人恼怒的事；令人尴尬的事 ❑ *The continuing presence of American troops on Korean soil remains a very sore point with these students.* 美国军队继续驻留在韩国领土依然是令这些学生极其恼怒的事情。

sore·ly /sɔrli/ ADV **Sorely** is used to emphasize that a feeling such as disappointment or need is very strong. 非常 [EMPHASIS] ❑ *I for one was sorely disappointed.* 拿我来说，我非常失望。 ❑ *He will be sorely missed.* 他会被深深地思念着。

sor·row /sɒroʊ/ N-UNCOUNT **Sorrow** is a feeling of deep sadness or regret. 悲伤；歉疚 ❑ *Words cannot express my sorrow.* 语言不能表达我的悲伤。

sor·rows /sɒroʊz/ **1** N-PLURAL **Sorrows** are events or situations that cause deep sadness. 伤心事 ❑ *...the joys and sorrows of everyday living.* …日常生活的喜与悲。 **2** to **drown** one's **sorrows** → see **drown**

sor·ry ♦♦◊ /sɒri/ (**sorrier**, **sorriest**) **1** CONVENTION You say "**Sorry**" or "**I'm sorry**" as a way of apologizing to someone for something that you have done which has upset them or caused them difficulties, or when you bump into them accidentally. 对不起 [FORMULAE] ❑ *"We're all talking at the same time."—"Yeah. Sorry."* "我们都在同时说话。"——"呃，对不起。" ❑ *Sorry I took so long.* 对不起，我用了这么长时间。 ❑ *I'm really sorry if I said anything wrong.* 真抱歉，如果我有说错的地方。 **2** ADJ If you are **sorry** about a situation, you feel regret, sadness, or disappointment about it. 遗憾的；悲伤的 [v-link ADJ] ❑ *She was very sorry about all the trouble she'd caused.* 她对自己造成的麻烦感到很内疚。 ❑ *I'm sorry he's gone.* 他走了我感到遗憾。 **3** CONVENTION You use **I'm sorry** or **sorry** as an introduction when you are telling a person something that you do not think they will want to hear, for example when you are disagreeing with them or giving them bad news. 抱歉(用于表示不同意或不好的消息) ❑ *No, I'm sorry, I can't* agree with you. 不，抱歉，我不同意你。 ❑ *"I'm sorry," he told the real estate agent, "but we really must go now."* "对不起，"他告诉房地产经纪人，"但我们的确要走了。" **4** PHRASE You use the expression **I'm sorry to say** to express regret together with disappointment or disapproval. 很遗憾 [FEELINGS] ❑ *I've only done half of it, I'm sorry to say.* 我只做了一半，很遗憾。 **5** CONVENTION You say "**I'm sorry**" to express your regret and sadness when you hear sad or unpleasant news. 很难过 [FEELINGS] ❑ *"I'm afraid he's ill."—"I'm sorry to hear that."* "恐怕他病了。"——"听到这个消息我很难过。" **6** ADJ If you feel **sorry for** someone who is unhappy or in an unpleasant situation, you feel sympathy and sadness for them. 同情的 [v-link ADJ "for" n] ❑ *I felt sorry for him and his colleagues – it must have been so frustrating for them.* 我很同情他和他的同事们——这对他们来说肯定是非常令人沮丧。 **7** ADJ You say that someone is feeling **sorry for themselves** when you disapprove of the fact that they keep thinking unhappily about their problems, rather than trying to be cheerful and positive. (自我) 怜悯的 [v-link ADJ] [DISAPPROVAL] ❑ *What he must not do is to sit around at home feeling sorry for himself.* 他绝不该做的事情就是坐在家里自我怜悯。 **8** CONVENTION You say "**Sorry?**" when you have not heard something that someone has said and you want them to repeat it. 抱歉 (请求再讲一遍) [FORMULAE] ❑ *Once or twice I heard her muttering, but when I said, "Sorry? What did you say?" she didn't respond.* 有一两次我听见她在嘀嘀咕咕，但当我说"抱歉？你说什么？"时，她没有回答。 **9** CONVENTION You use **sorry** when you correct yourself and use different words to say what you have just said, especially when what you say the second time does not use the words you would normally choose to use. 抱歉 (用于说话时自我纠正) ❑ *Barcelona will be hoping to bring the trophy back to Spain (sorry, Catalonia) for the first time.* 巴塞罗那将会希望第一次把奖杯带回西班牙（抱歉，是卡塔洛尼亚）。 **10** ADJ If someone or something is in a **sorry** state, they are in a bad state, mentally or physically. 糟糕的 [ADJ n] ❑ *The fire left Kuwait's oil industry in a sorry state.* 大火使科威特的石油工业陷入糟糕的境地。 **11** **better safe than sorry** → see **safe**

sort ♦♦♦ /sɔrt/ (**sorts, sorting, sorted**) **1** N-COUNT If you talk about a particular **sort of** something, you are talking about a class of things that have particular features in common and that belong to a larger group of related things. 种类 ❑ *What sort of school did you go to?* 你上的是哪一类学校？ ❑ *There are so many different sorts of mushrooms available these days.* 这些日子可买到各种各样的蘑菇。 ❑ *A dozen trees of various sorts were planted.* 各类型共12棵树被种下了。 **2** N-SING You describe someone as a particular **sort** when you are describing their character. 类型 [with supp] ❑ *He seemed to be just the right sort for the job.* 他似乎就是该工作的合适人选。 ❑ *She was a very vigorous sort of person.* 她是那种精力非常旺盛的人。 **3** V-T/V-I If you **sort** things, you separate them into different classes, groups, or places, for example so that you can do different things with them. 分类 ❑ *He sorted the materials into their folders.* 他将材料分类放入他们的文件夹里。 ❑ *He unlatched the box and sorted through the papers.* 他打开盒子的锁，在文件里分类拣选。 **4** PHRASE **All sorts of** things or people means a large number of different things or people. 各种各样 ❑ *There are all sorts of animals, including bears, pigs, kangaroos, and penguins.* 有各种各样的动物，包括熊、猪、袋鼠和企鹅。 ❑ *It was used by all sorts of people.* 它被各种人使用。 **5** PHRASE If you describe something as a thing **of sorts** or as a thing **of a sort**, you are suggesting that the thing is of a rather poor quality or standard. (质量) 不怎么样 ❑ *He made a living of sorts selling encyclopedias door-to-door.* 他靠挨家挨户推销百科全书勉强谋生。 **6** PHRASE You use **sort of** when you want to say that your description of something is not very accurate. 有点儿像 [INFORMAL, VAGUENESS] ❑ *You could even order windows from a catalogue – a sort of mail order stained glass service.* 你甚至可以从目录上预订窗户——有点儿像邮购彩色玻璃服务。 **7** **nothing of the sort** → see **nothing**

▸ **sort out** **1** PHRASAL VERB If you **sort out** a group of things, you separate them into different classes, groups, or places, for example so that you can do different things with them. 整理 ❑ *Sort out all your bills, receipts, invoices, and expenses as quickly as possible and keep detailed accounts.* 将你的帐单、收据、发票和花销尽快整理好，并做好详细的账目。 ❑ *Davina was sorting out scraps of material.* 戴维娜正在整理零碎的材料。 **2** PHRASAL VERB If you **sort out** a problem or the details of something, you do what is necessary to solve the problem or organize the details. 解决 ❑ *India and Nepal have sorted out their trade and security dispute.* 印度和尼泊尔已经解决了他们的贸易和安全争端。 **3** PHRASAL VERB If you **sort yourself out**, you organize yourself or calm yourself so that you can act effectively and reasonably. 使平静 ❑ *We're in a state of complete chaos here and I need a little time to sort myself out.* 我们这儿处于一片混乱之中，我需要一些时间让自己平静下来。

sor·tie /sɔrti/ (**sorties**) N-COUNT If a military force makes a **sortie**, it leaves its own position and goes briefly into enemy territory to make an attack. 突袭 [FORMAL] ❑ *His men made a sortie to Guazatan and took a prisoner.* 他的部下对瓜赞坦发动了突袭，并抓获了一名俘虏。

SOS /ɛs oʊ ɛs/ N-SING An **SOS** is a signal which indicates to other people that you are in danger and need help quickly. 紧急呼救信号 ❑ *The ferry did not even have time to send out an SOS.* 这艘渡船甚至没有时间发出紧急呼救信号。

sought /sɔt/ **Sought** is the past tense and past participle of **seek**. **seek**的过去式和过去分词

sought-after ADJ Something that is **sought-after** is in great demand, usually because it is rare or of very good quality. 受青睐的 ❑ *An Olympic gold medal is the most sought-after prize in world sport.* 奥运会金牌是世界体育活动中最受青睐的奖牌。

soul ♦◊◊ /soʊl/ (**souls**) **1** N-COUNT Your **soul** is the part of you that consists of your mind, character, thoughts, and feelings. Many people believe that your soul continues existing after your body is dead. 灵魂 ❑ *She went to pray for the soul of her late husband.* 她去为已故丈夫的灵魂祈祷。 **2** N-COUNT You can refer to someone as a particular kind of **soul** when you are describing their character or condition. 个性 ❑ *He's a jolly soul.* 他是个快活的人。 **3** N-SING You use **soul** in negative statements like **not a soul** to mean nobody at all. 人 (用于否定句中) ❑ *I've never harmed a soul in my life.* 我一生中从未伤害过任何人。 **4** N-UNCOUNT **Soul** is the same as **soul music**. 灵魂音乐 ❑ *...American soul singer Anita Baker.* …美国灵乐歌手安妮塔•贝克。 **5** **to bare one's soul** → see **bare** **6** **body and soul** → see **body**

sound

1 NOUN AND VERB USES
2 ADJECTIVE USES

1 **sound** ♦♦♦ /saʊnd/ (**sounds, sounding, sounded**)
➪ **Please look at meanings 11 and 12 to see if the expression you are looking for is shown under another headword.** **1** N-COUNT A **sound** is something that you hear. 声音 ❑ *Peter heard the sound of gunfire.* 彼得听见了枪炮声。 ❑ *Liza was so frightened she couldn't make a sound.* 莉莎惊吓得发不出任何声音。 **2** N-UNCOUNT **Sound** is energy that travels in waves through air, water, or other substances, and can be heard. 声能 ❑ *The airplane will travel at twice the speed of sound.* 飞机将以两倍于音速的速度飞行。 **3** N-SING **The sound** on a television, radio, or CD player is what you hear coming from the machine. Its loudness can be controlled. (可调大小声的) 播音 ❑ *She went and turned the sound down.* 她过去把声音调小。 **4** N-COUNT A singer's or band's **sound** is the distinctive quality of their music. 音乐风格 ❑ *They have started showing a strong soul element in their sound.* 他们已经开始在音乐风格中展示出一种强烈的灵歌因素。 **5** V-T/V-I If something such as a horn or a bell **sounds** or if you **sound** it, it makes a noise. 使发出声音；发出声音 ❑ *The buzzer sounded in Daniel's office.* 丹尼尔办公室的蜂鸣器响了起来。 **6** V-T If you **sound** a warning, you publicly give it. If you **sound** a note of caution or optimism, you say publicly that you are cautious or optimistic. 宣告 ❑ *The archbishop has sounded a warning to world leaders on third world debt.* 大主教已经发出警告提醒世界领导人注意第三世界的债务。 **7** V-LINK When you are describing a noise, you can talk about the way it **sounds**. 听起来 ❑ *They heard what sounded like a huge explosion.* 他们听见了一种像是巨大爆炸的声音。 ❑ *The creaking of the hinges sounded very loud in that silence.* 铰链的嘎吱声在那寂静中听起来很响。 **8** V-LINK When you talk about the way someone **sounds**, you are describing the impression you have of them when they speak. 听起来 ❑ *She sounded a bit worried.* 她听起来有点焦虑不安。 ❑ *Murphy sounds like a child.* 墨菲听起来像个孩子。 **9** V-LINK When you are describing your impression or opinion of something you have heard about or read about, you can talk about the way it **sounds**. 令人觉得 ❑ *It sounds like a wonderful idea to me, does it really work?* 在我听来那像个好主意，但真管用吗？ ❑ *It sounds as if they might have made a dreadful mistake.* 感觉似乎他们已经犯下了一个大错。 **10** N-SING You can describe your impression of something you have heard about or read about by talking about **the sound of it**. (听到或看到的) 感觉 ❑ *Here's a new idea we liked the sound of.* 这是个新想法，听起来我们就喜欢。 ❑ *I don't like the sound of*

S

Word Web **sound**

Sound is the only form of energy we can hear. It consists of **vibrating** molecules of air. Rapid vibrations called high **frequencies** produce high-pitched sounds. Slower vibrations produce lower frequencies. Sound vibrations travel in waves, just like **waves** in water. Each wave has a **crest** and a **trough**. Amplitude is a measure of how high above the medium line a sound wave moves. When a **sound wave** bounces off an object, it produces an **echo**. When an airplane reaches **supersonic** speed, it generates **shock waves**. As these waves move toward the ground, a sonic boom occurs.

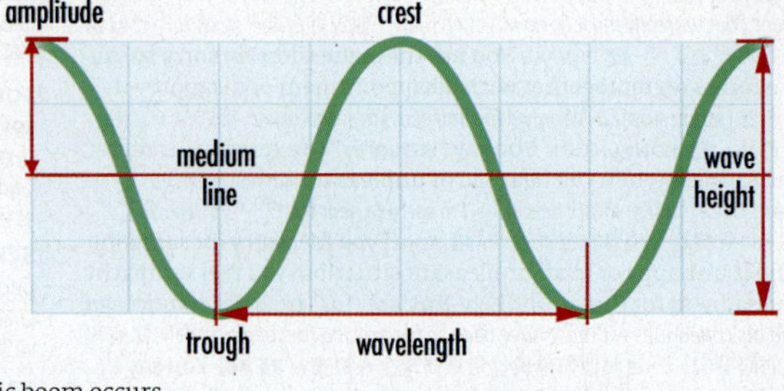

Toby Osborne. 我不喜欢托比•奥斯伯恩的感觉。 11 **to sound the alarm** → see **alarm** 12 **safe and sound** → see **safe**
→ see **concert, ear, echo**
→ see Word Web: **sound**

▸ **sound out** PHRASAL VERB If you **sound** someone **out**, you question them in order to find out what their opinion is about something. 探询 ❑ *He is sounding out Middle Eastern governments on ways to resolve the conflict.* 他正在探询中东各国政府解决这一冲突的方法。

❷ **sound** /saʊnd/ (**sounder, soundest**) 1 ADJ If a structure, part of someone's body, or someone's mind is **sound**, it is in good condition or healthy. 健康的; 状况良好的 ❑ *When we bought the house, it was structurally sound.* 当我们买下这房子时，其结构完好无损。 ❑ *Although the car is basically sound, I was worried about certain areas.* 虽然这辆汽车基本状况完好，但我担心某几个部分。 2 ADJ **Sound** advice, reasoning, or evidence is reliable and sensible. 可靠的 ❑ *They are trained nutritionists who can give sound advice on diets.* 他们是训练有素的营养师，能提供有关饮食的可靠建议。 ❑ *Buy a policy only from an insurance company that is financially sound.* 只买财政状况良好的保险公司的保险。 3 ADJ If you describe someone's ideas as **sound**, you mean that you approve of them and think they are correct. 正确的 [APPROVAL] ❑ *I am not sure that this is sound democratic practice.* 我不能肯定这就是正确的民主做法。 4 ADJ If someone is in a **sound** sleep, they are sleeping very deeply. 酣（睡）的 [ADJ n] ❑ *She had woken me out of a sound sleep.* 她把我从酣睡中叫醒了。 ● ADV **Sound** is also an adverb. 酣（睡）地 [ADV adj] ❑ *He was lying in bed, sound asleep.* 他正躺在床上，睡得很香。 5 → see also **soundly**

Thesaurus *sound* 另参见：
ADJ. safe, sturdy, undamaged, whole ❷ 1
logical, valid, wise; *(ant.)* illogical, unreliable ❷ 2 3

sound·card /saʊndkɑrd/ (**soundcards**) also **sound card** N-COUNT A **soundcard** is a piece of equipment which can be put into a computer so that the computer can produce music or other sounds. （计算机的）声卡 [COMPUTING]

sound·ly /saʊndli/ 1 ADV If someone is **soundly** defeated or beaten, they are defeated or beaten thoroughly. 彻底地 [ADV -ed] ❑ *Needing just a point from their match at St. Helens, they were soundly beaten, going down by 35 points to 10.* 在圣海伦斯比赛时只需要一分就能赢，然而他们却以10比35被彻底击败了。 2 ADV If a decision, opinion, or statement is **soundly** based, there are sensible or reliable reasons behind it. 可靠地 [ADV -ed] [APPROVAL] ❑ *Changes must be soundly based in economic reality.* 变革必须牢靠地建立在经济现实基础之上。 3 ADV If you sleep **soundly**, you sleep deeply and do not wake during your sleep. 酣（睡）地 ❑ *How can he sleep soundly at night? He's the one responsible for all those crimes.* 他晚上怎么能睡得香？他可是所有那些犯罪活动的罪魁祸首啊。

sound sys·tem (**sound systems**) N-COUNT A **sound system** is a set of equipment for playing recorded music, or for making a band's music able to be heard by everyone at a concert. 音响系统

sound·track /saʊndtræk/ (**soundtracks**) also **sound track** N-COUNT The **soundtrack** of a movie is its sound, speech, and music. It is used especially to refer to the music. （电影的）配音 ❑ *...the soundtrack to a movie called "Judgement Night."* …一部名为《夜惊魂》的电影的配音。

soup /sup/ (**soups**) N-MASS **Soup** is liquid food made by boiling meat, fish, or vegetables in water. 汤 ❑ *...home-made chicken soup.* …自家做的鸡汤。

sour /saʊər/ (**sours, souring, soured**) 1 ADJ Something that is **sour** has a sharp, unpleasant taste like the taste of a lemon. 酸的 ❑ *The stewed apple was sour even with honey.* 炖过的苹果即使加了蜂蜜也还是酸的。 2 ADJ **Sour** milk is milk that has an unpleasant taste because it is no longer fresh. 馊的 ❑ *The milk had gone sour.* 牛奶已经馊了。 3 ADJ Someone who is **sour** is bad-tempered and unfriendly. 脾气坏的; 不友好的 ❑ *She made a sour face in his direction.* 她给了他一副不友善的脸色。 ● **sour·ly** ADV 脾气坏地; 不友好地 [ADV with v] ❑ *"Leave my mother out of it," he said sourly.* "不要把我母亲扯进去。" 他生气地说。 4 ADJ If a situation or relationship **turns sour** or **goes sour**, it stops being enjoyable or satisfactory. 令人失望的 ❑ *Everything turned sour for me there.* 对我来说那儿的一切都变得令人失望了。 ❑ *The American dream is beginning to turn sour.* 美国梦正开始破灭。 5 V-T/V-I If a friendship, situation, or attitude **sours** or if something **sours** it, it becomes less friendly, enjoyable, or hopeful. 使变糟; 变糟 ❑ *If anything sours the relationship, it is likely to be real differences in their world-views.* 假如有什么事情使关系恶化的话，那可能就是他们在世界观方面所存在的实质性差异。
→ see **fruit, taste**

source ♦♦◊ /sɔrs/ (**sources, sourcing, sourced**) 1 N-COUNT The **source of** something is the person, place, or thing which you get it from. 来源 ❑ *...over 40 percent of adults use television as their major source of information about the arts.* …超过40%的成年人利用电视作为他们了解艺术信息的主要来源。 ❑ *Renewable sources of energy must be used.* 可再生的能源必须利用。 2 V-T In business, if a person or firm **sources** a product or a raw material, they find someone who will supply it. 寻找…的来源 [BUSINESS] ❑ *Together they travel the world, sourcing clothes for the small, privately owned company.* 他们一起环游世界，为那家小私营公司寻找服装货源。 3 N-COUNT A **source** is a person or book that provides information for a news story or for a piece of research. 消息来源 ❑ *Military sources say the boat was heading south at high speed.* 军方的消息来源说船正向南方快速驶去。 4 N-COUNT The **source of** a difficulty is its cause. 根源 ❑ *This gave me a clue as to the source of the problem.* 这给了我一个关于问题根源的线索。 5 N-COUNT The **source** of a river or stream is the place where it begins. 源头 ❑ *...the source of the Tiber.* …台伯河的源头。
→ see **diary, history**

Thesaurus *source* 另参见：
N. beginning, origin, root, start 1 4

source code (**source codes**) N-VAR **Source code** is the original form of a computer program as it is written by a programmer. It is then converted into code that the computer can understand. 源码 [COMPUTING]

south ♦♦♦ /saʊθ/ also **South** 1 N-UNCOUNT **The south** is the direction which is on your right when you are looking toward the direction where the sun rises. 南方 [also "the" N] ❑ *The town lies ten miles to the south of here.* 该镇位于这里以南10英里。 2 N-SING **The south of** a place, country, or region is the part which is in the south. 南部 [usu "the" N, oft N "of" n] ❑ *...vacations in the south of Mexico.* …在墨西哥南部的假期。 3 ADV If you go **south**, you travel toward the south. 向南 [ADV after v] ❑ *I drove south on Highway 9.* 我在9号高速公路上向南行驶。 4 ADV Something that is **south of** a place is positioned to the south of it. 在…的南方 [ADV "of" n] ❑ *They now own and operate a farm 50 miles south of Rochester.* 他们现在在罗彻斯特南部50英里处拥有并经营一个农场。 5 ADJ The **south** edge, corner, or part of a place or country is the part which is toward the south. 朝南的 [ADJ n] ❑ *...the south coast of Long Island.* …长岛的南海岸。

S

6 ADJ **"South"** is used in the names of some countries, states, and regions in the south of a larger area. 南部的 ❑ *Next week the president will visit five South American countries in six days.* 下周总统将在6天内访问5个南美国家。 7 ADJ A **south** wind is a wind that blows from the south. (风) 来自南方的 ❑ *...a mild south wind.* …一股温暖的南风。 8 N-SING **The South** is used to refer to the poorer, less developed countries of the world. 南方国家 (指较贫穷的不发达国家) ["the" N] ❑ *The debate will pit the industrial North against developing countries in the South.* 这场辩论会使北方的工业国家和南方的发展中国家针锋相对。
→ see **globe**

south·east ◆◆◇ /saʊθiːst/ 1 N-UNCOUNT **The southeast** is the direction which is halfway between south and east. 东南 [also "the" N] ❑ *It shook buildings as far away as Galveston, 90 miles to the southeast.* 它震动了东南方向90英里远的加尔维斯顿的建筑物。 2 N-SING **The southeast of** a place, country, or region is the part which is in the southeast. 东南部 ❑ *Record levels of rainfall fell over the southeast of the country.* 该国东南部降下了最高纪录的雨量。 3 ADV If you go **southeast**, you travel toward the southeast. 朝东南方向 [ADV after v] ❑ *I know we have to go southeast, more or less.* 我知道我们大概得往东南方向走。 4 ADV Something that is **southeast of** a place is positioned to the south-east of it. 在东南方 [ADV "of" n] ❑ *...a vessel that is believed to have sunk 500 miles southeast of Nova Scotia.* …据说在诺瓦斯科西亚东南方500英里处沉没的一艘船。 5 ADJ The **southeast** part of a place, country, or region is the part which is toward the southeast. 东南部的 [ADJ n] ❑ *...rural southeast Kansas.* …堪萨斯东南部的农村。 ❑ *...Southeast Asia.* …东南亚。 6 ADJ A **southeast** wind is a wind that blows from the southeast. (风) 来自东南方的 [ADJ n] ❑ *Thick clothes keeping the chill southeast wind from freezing his bones.* 厚衣服让他不被寒冷的东南风给冻着了。

south·eastern /saʊθiːstərn/ ADJ **Southeastern** means in or from the southeast of a region or country. 东南部的 ❑ *...this city on the southeastern edge of the United States.* …这座位于美国东南边境的城市。

south·er·ly /sʌðərli/ 1 ADJ A **southerly** point, area, or direction is to the south or toward the south. 向南的 ❑ *We set off in a southerly direction.* 我们向南方出发了。 2 ADJ A **southerly** wind is a wind that blows from the south. (风) 来自南方的 ❑ *...a strong southerly wind.* …一股强大的南风。

south·ern ◆◆◇ /sʌðərn/ also **Southern** ADJ **Southern** means in or from the south of a region, state, or country. 南部的 [ADJ n] ❑ *The Everglades National Park stretches across the southern tip of Florida.* 埃弗格莱兹国家公园一直延伸到佛罗里达州南端。

south·ern·er /sʌðərnər/ (**southerners**) N-COUNT A **southerner** is a person who was born in or lives in the south of a country. 南方人 ❑ *Bob Wilson is a southerner, from Texas.* 鲍勃•威尔逊是个南方人，来自得克萨斯州。

south·ward /saʊθwərd/ or **southwards** ADV **Southward** or **southwards** means toward the south. 向南 [ADV after v] ❑ *They drove southward.* 他们向南驶去。 ● ADJ **Southward** is also an adjective. 向南的 ❑ *Instead of her normal southward course towards Alexandria and home, she headed west.* 她不走平常向南去亚历山大和家乡的路，而是向西走。

south·west ◆◆◇ /saʊθwest/ 1 N-UNCOUNT **The southwest** is the direction which is halfway between south and west. 西南 [also "the" N] ❑ *...some 500 kilometers to the southwest of Johannesburg.* …约翰内斯堡西南约五百公里。 2 N-SING **The southwest of** a place, country, or region is the part which is toward the southwest. 西南部 ❑ *...the southwest of France.* …法国的西南部。 3 ADV If you go **southwest**, you travel toward the southwest. 朝西南方 [ADV after v] ❑ *We took a plane southwest across the Anatolian plateau to Cappadocia.* 我们乘飞机朝西南方，越过安纳托利亚高原，飞往卡帕多细亚。 4 ADV Something that is **southwest of** a place is positioned to the southwest of it. 在西南方 [ADV "of" n] ❑ *It's some 65 miles southwest of Houston.* 它位于休斯敦西南方约六十五英里。 5 ADJ The **southwest** part of a place, country, or region is the part which is toward the southwest. 西南部的 [ADJ n] ❑ *...a Labor Day festival in southwest Louisiana.* …路易斯安那州西南部的一个劳动节庆祝活动。 6 ADJ A **southwest** wind is a wind that blows from the southwest. (风) 来自西南方的 [ADJ n] ❑ *Then the southwest wind began to blow.* 接着西南风开始刮起来了。

south·western /saʊθwestərn/ ADJ **Southwestern** means in or from the southwest of a region or country. 西南部的 ❑ *...remote areas in the southwestern part of the country.* …该国西南部的边远地区。

▲ **sou·venir** /suːvənɪər/ (**souvenirs**) N-COUNT A **souvenir** is something which you buy or keep to remind you of a vacation, place, or event. 纪念品 ❑ *...a souvenir of the summer of 1992.* …一个1992年夏天的纪念品。

★ **sov·er·eign** /sɒvrɪn/ (**sovereigns**) 1 ADJ A **sovereign** state or country is independent and not under the authority of any other country. 具有独立主权的 ❑ *Lithuania and Armenia signed a treaty in Vilnius recognizing each other as independent sovereign states.* 立陶宛和亚美尼亚在维尔纽斯签订了一份互相承认各自为独立主权国家的协定。 2 ADJ **Sovereign** is used to describe the person or institution that has the highest power in a country. (人或机构的权力) 至高无上的 ❑ *Sovereign power will continue to lie with the Supreme People's Assembly.* 至高无上的权力将继续掌控在最高人民议会。 3 N-COUNT A **sovereign** is a king, queen, or other royal ruler of a country. 君主 ❑ *In March 1889, she became the first British sovereign to set foot on Spanish soil.* 1889年3月，她成为首位踏上西班牙国土的英国君主。

★ **sov·er·eign·ty** /sɒvrɪnti/ N-UNCOUNT **Sovereignty** is the power that a country has to govern itself or another country or state. 统治权 ❑ *Concern to protect national sovereignty is far from new.* 对捍卫国家主权的关注绝不是新话题。

sow
❶ VERB USES
❷ NOUN USE

❶ **sow** /soʊ/ (**sows, sowing, sowed, sown**) 1 V-T If you **sow** seeds or **sow** an area of land **with** seeds, you plant the seeds in the ground. 播 (种) ❑ *Sow the seed in a warm place in February/March.* 2/3月里把种子播在温暖的地方。 2 V-T If someone **sows** an undesirable feeling or situation, they cause it to begin and develop. 散布 ❑ *He cleverly sowed doubts into the minds of his rivals.* 他巧妙地在他对手们的心里布下了疑云。 3 PHRASE If one thing **sows the seeds of** another, it starts the process which leads eventually to the other thing. 播下某事的种子 ❑ *Rich industrialized countries have sown the seeds of global warming.* 富裕的工业化国家已经播下了使全球变暖的种子。

❷ **sow** /saʊ/ (**sows**) N-COUNT A **sow** is an adult female pig. 成年母猪

spa /spɑ/ (**spas**) 1 N-COUNT A **spa** is a place where water with minerals in it comes out of the ground. People drink the water or go in it in order to improve their health. 矿泉疗养地 ❑ *...Fiuggi, a spa town famous for its water.* …菲乌吉，一个以其水而闻名的矿泉疗养小镇。 2 N-COUNT A health **spa** is a kind of hotel where people go to exercise and have special treatments in order to improve their health. 温泉疗养中心 ❑ *There's also an excellent spa with a large pool, steam room, and sauna.* 那儿还有一家不错的温泉疗养中心，配有一个大的游泳池、蒸汽房和桑拿室。 3 N-COUNT A **spa** is a type of bathtub that can send out jets of water to massage your body. 水流喷射按摩浴缸 ❑ *...a large bathroom with a shower and a spa.* …一间有淋浴和水流喷射按摩浴缸的大型浴室。
→ see **hotel**

space ◆◆◇ /speɪs/ (**spaces, spacing, spaced**) 1 N-VAR You use **space** to refer to an area that is empty or available. The area can be any size. For example, you can refer to a large area outside as a large open **space** or to a small area between two objects as a small **space**. 空间；间隔 ❑ *...cutting down yet more trees to make space for houses.* …砍掉更多的树以腾出空间来盖房屋。 ❑ *I had plenty of space to write and sew.* 我有足够的空间来写作和缝纫。 ❑ *The space underneath could be used as a storage area.* 下面的空间可被用作一个储藏区。

> You should use **space** or **room** to refer to an open or empty area. You do not use **place** as an uncount noun in this sense. **Room** is more likely to be used when you are talking about space inside an enclosed area. ❑ *There's not enough room in the bathroom for both of us... Leave plenty of space between you and the car in front.*

2 N-VAR A particular kind of **space** is the area that is available for a particular activity or for putting a particular kind of thing in. 场所 ❑ *...the high cost of office space.* …办公场所的高额费用。 ❑ *You don't want your living space to look like a bedroom.* 你不会希望你的起居室看上去像一间卧室。 3 N-UNCOUNT If a place gives a feeling of **space**, it gives an impression of being large and open. 宽敞的空间 ❑ *Large paintings can enhance the feeling of space in small rooms.* 大幅画作能增加小房间的宽敞感。 4 N-UNCOUNT If you give someone **space** to think about something or to develop as a person, you allow them

S

the time and freedom to do this. 余地 ❑ *You need space to think everything over.* 你需要留有余地来仔细考虑一切。 **5** N-UNCOUNT The amount of **space** for a topic to be discussed in a document is the number of pages available to discuss the topic. 篇幅 ❑ *We can't promise to publish a reply as space is limited.* 因为篇幅有限，我们无法允诺刊登答复。 **6** N-SING A **space of** time is a period of time. 一段 (时间) ❑ *They've come a long way in a short space of time.* 他们在很短时间内从很远的地方过来了。 **7** N-UNCOUNT **Space** is the area beyond the Earth's atmosphere, where the stars and planets are. 太空 ❑ *The six astronauts on board will spend ten days in space.* 宇宙飞船上的六位宇航员将在太空度过10天的时间。 ❑ *...launching satellites into space.* …发射人造卫星到外层空间。 **8** N-UNCOUNT **Space** is the whole area within which everything exists. 宇宙空间 ❑ *She felt herself transcending time and space.* 她感觉自己正在超越时空。 **9** V-T If you **space** a series of things, you arrange them so that they are not all together but have gaps or intervals of time between them. 使分隔开 ❑ *Women once again are having fewer children and spacing them further apart.* 妇女们又一次开始生育较少的孩子，而且生孩子的时间间隔越来越大。 ● PHRASAL VERB **Space out** means the same as **space**. 使分隔开 ❑ *He talks quite slowly and spaces his words out.* 他说得很慢，词与词之间都有停顿。 **10** → see also **airspace, breathing space, outer space, spacing** **11** PHRASE If you are staring **into space**, you are looking straight in front of you, without actually looking at anything in particular, for example because you are thinking or because you are feeling shocked. 茫然直视 ❑ *He just sat in the dressing room staring into space.* 他就坐在化妆室里，茫然地望着前方。

→ see **meteor, moon, satellite**

space·craft /speɪskræft/ (**spacecraft**)

> **Spacecraft** is both the singular and the plural form.

N-COUNT A **spacecraft** is a rocket or other vehicle that can travel in space. 航天器 ❑ *...the world's largest and most expensive unmanned spacecraft.* …世界上最大、最贵的无人航天器。

space·ship /speɪsʃɪp/ (**spaceships**) N-COUNT A **spaceship** is a spacecraft that carries people through space. 载人宇宙飞船 ❑ *...an alien spaceship.* …一艘外星人的宇宙飞船。

space shut·tle (**space shuttles**) N-COUNT A **space shuttle** or a **shuttle** is a spacecraft that is designed to travel into space and back to earth several times. 航天飞机

space sta·tion (**space stations**) N-COUNT A **space station** is a place built for astronauts to live and work in, which is sent into space and then keeps going around the earth. 太空站

spac·ing /speɪsɪŋ/ **1** N-UNCOUNT **Spacing** refers to the way that typing or printing is arranged on a page, especially in relation to the amount of space that is left between words or lines. (字、行的) 间距 ❑ *Single spacing is used within paragraphs, double spacing between paragraphs.* 单倍行距用于段内，双倍行距用于段与段之间。 **2** → see also **space**

★ **spa·cious** /speɪʃəs/ ADJ A **spacious** room or other place is large in size or area, so that you can move around freely in it. 宽敞的 ❑ *The house has a spacious kitchen and dining area.* 这座住宅有一个宽敞的厨房和用餐区。

spade /speɪd/ (**spades**) **1** N-COUNT A **spade** is a tool used for digging, with a flat metal blade and a long handle. 锹 ❑ *...a garden spade.* …一把花园里使用的锹。 **2** N-UNCOUNT-COLL **Spades** is one of the four suits in a deck of playing cards. Each card in the suit is marked with one or more black symbols: ♠. (扑克牌中的) 黑桃 ❑ *...the ace of spades.* …黑桃A。 ● N-COUNT A **spade** is a playing card of this suit. 黑桃牌 ❑ *He would have done better to play a spade now.* 他要是现在出一张黑桃牌就更好了。

▲ **spa·ghet·ti** /spəgɛti/ N-UNCOUNT **Spaghetti** is a type of pasta. It looks like long pieces of string and is usually served with a sauce. 意大利式细面条

spam /spæm/ (**spams, spamming, spammed**) V-T In computing, to **spam** people or organizations means to send unwanted e-mail to a large number of them, usually as advertising. 群发垃圾邮件 [COMPUTING] ❑ *...programs that let you spam the newspapers.* …使你能够向各家报纸群发垃圾邮件的程序。 ● N-VAR **Spam** is also a noun. 群发的垃圾邮件 ❑ *...a small group of people fighting the spam plague.* …一小群与群发垃圾邮件祸害做斗争的人。 ● **spam·mer** /spæmər/ N-COUNT (**spammers**) 群发垃圾邮件的人 ❑ *The real culprits are the spammers.* 真正的罪魁祸首是群发垃圾邮件的人。

→ see **advertising**

span /spæn/ (**spans, spanning, spanned**) **1** N-COUNT A **span** is the period of time between two dates or events during which something exists, functions, or happens. (两时间点之间的) 时间段 ❑ *The batteries had a life span of six hours.* 电池的使用寿命是6小时。 **2** N-COUNT Your concentration **span** or your attention **span** is the length of time you are able to concentrate on something or be interested in it. (注意力的) 持续时间 ❑ *His ability to absorb information was astonishing, but his concentration span was short.* 他吸收信息的能力让人惊讶，但他的注意力持续时间很短。 **3** V-T If something **spans** a long period of time, it lasts throughout that period of time or relates to that whole period of time. 持续 [no passive] ❑ *His professional career spanned 16 years.* 他的职业生涯持续了16年。 **4** V-T If something **spans** a range of things, all those things are included in it. 包括 [no passive] ❑ *Bernstein's compositions spanned all aspects of music, from symphonies to musicals.* 伯恩斯坦创作的乐曲包括了音乐的所有方面，从交响乐到音乐剧。 **5** N-COUNT The **span** of something that extends or is spread out sideways is the total width of it from one end to the other. 宽距 [usu with supp] ❑ *It is a very pretty butterfly, with a 2 inch wing span.* 它是一只非常漂亮的蝴蝶，翅膀张开有2英寸宽。 **6** V-T A bridge or other structure that **spans** something such as a river or a valley stretches right across it. 横跨 ❑ *Travelers get from one side to the other by walking across a footbridge that spans a little stream.* 旅游者通过一座横跨小溪的人行桥从一边走到另一边。

→ see **bridge**

> **Word Partnership** *span* 的常用搭配:
>
> ADJ. **brief** span **1**
> **short** span **1** **5**
>
> N. **life** span, **time** span **1**
> **attention** span **2**
> span **years** **3**

spank /spæŋk/ (**spanks, spanking, spanked**) V-T If someone **spanks** a child, they punish them by hitting them on the bottom several times with their hand. 用手打 (小孩的) 屁股 ❑ *When I used to do that when I was a kid, my mom would spank me.* 我小时候做那种事时，我妈妈总是打我的屁股。

span·ner /spænər/ (**spanners**) N-COUNT A **spanner** is the same as a **wrench**. 扳手 [mainly BRIT]

spar /spɑr/ (**spars, sparring, sparred**) V-RECIP If you **spar with** someone, you box using fairly gentle blows instead of hitting your opponent hard, either when you are training or when you want to test how quickly your opponent reacts. (练习时或试探对手反应时的) 轻拳出击 ❑ *He entered the ring to spar a few one-minute rounds with an old friend.* 他进了拳击场与一个老朋友练了几个一分钟回合的轻拳出击。

spare ♦◇◇ /spɛər/ (**spares, sparing, spared**) **1** ADJ You use **spare** to describe something that is the same as things that you are already using, but that you do not need yet and are keeping ready in case another one is needed. 备用的 ❑ *If possible keep a spare pair of glasses accessible in case your main pair is broken or lost.* 如有可能留一副备用眼镜以防你常用的那副打碎或丢失。 ❑ *He could have taken a spare key.* 他原本可以带上一把备用钥匙的。 ● N-COUNT **Spare** is also a noun. 备用品 ❑ *Give me the trunk key and I'll get the spare.* 给我行李箱钥匙，我去配一把备用。 **2** ADJ You use **spare** to describe something that is not being used by anyone, and is therefore available for someone to use. 多余的 ❑ *They don't have a lot of spare cash.* 他们并没有很多多余的现金。 ❑ *The spare bedroom is on the second floor.* 闲置的卧室在2楼。 **3** V-I If you have something such as time, money, or space **to spare**, you have some extra time, money, or space that you have not used or which you do not need. 剩下 [only to-inf] ❑ *You got here with ninety seconds to spare.* 你们到达这里时还剩有90秒钟。 **4** V-T If you **spare** time or another resource **for** a particular purpose, you make it available for that purpose. 抽出 ❑ *She said that she could only spare 35 minutes for our meeting.* 她说她只能抽出35分钟给我们的会议。 **5** V-T If a person or a place **is spared**, they are not harmed, even though other people or places have been. 使幸免 [usu passive] [LITERARY] ❑ *We have lost everything, but thank God, our lives have been spared.* 我们失去了一切，但谢天谢地，我们保住了性命。 **6** V-T If you **spare** someone an unpleasant experience, you prevent them from suffering it. 使免遭 ❑ *I wanted to spare Frances the embarrassment of discussing this subject.* 我想使弗朗西丝免遭讨论这个话题的尴尬。 ❑ *Prisoners are spared the indignity of wearing uniforms.* 囚犯们被免于遭受身穿统一服装的侮辱。 **7** → see also **sparing**

S

8 PHRASE If you **spare a thought for** an unfortunate person, you make an effort to think sympathetically about them and their bad luck. 为…着想 ❑ *Spare a thought for the nation's shopkeepers – consumer sales slid again in May.* 为这个国家的店主们着想一下——消费品销售5月份又下滑了。

Thesaurus *spare* 另参见:
ADJ. additional, backup, emergency, extra, reserve **1** **2**

Word Partnership *spare* 的常用搭配:
N. spare **change**, spare **equipment** **1**
spare **bedroom** **2**
a moment to spare, **time to** spare **3**
spare *someone's* **life** **5**

spare part (**spare parts**) N-COUNT **Spare parts** are parts that you can buy separately to replace old or broken parts in a piece of equipment. They are usually parts that are designed to be easily removed or fitted. 备用零件 ❑ *In the future the machines will need spare parts and maintenance.* 这些机器将来会需要备件和维修保养。

spare time N-UNCOUNT Your **spare time** is the time during which you do not have to work and you can do whatever you like. 业余时间 ❑ *In her spare time she read books on cooking.* 她在业余时间读些烹饪方面的书。

spar·ing /spɛərɪŋ/ ADJ Someone who is **sparing with** something uses it or gives it only in very small quantities. 节约的 ❑ *I'm never sparing with the garlic.* 我从不吝啬使用大蒜。 ●**spar·ing·ly** ADV 节约地 [ADV after v] ❑ *Medication is used sparingly.* 药物治疗使用得很少。

spark ♦◇◇ /spɑrk/ (**sparks, sparking, sparked**) **1** N-COUNT **A spark** is a tiny bright piece of burning material that flies up from something that is burning. 火花 ❑ *The fire gradually got bigger and bigger. Sparks flew off in all directions.* 火势逐渐变得越来越大。火花四处飞溅。 **2** N-COUNT **A spark** is a flash of light caused by electricity. It often makes a loud sound. 电火花 ❑ *He passed an electric spark through a mixture of gases.* 他使一束电火花穿过一团气体混合物。 **3** V-I If something **sparks**, sparks of fire or light come from it. 发出火花 ❑ *The wires were sparking above me.* 电线正在我头顶上方冒火花。 **4** V-T If a burning object or electricity **sparks** a fire, it causes a fire. 引发(一场火) ❑ *A dropped cigarette may have sparked the fire.* 一支丢弃的香烟可能引发了这场火灾。 **5** N-COUNT **A spark of** a quality or feeling, especially a desirable one, is a small but noticeable amount of it. 一点(品质或情感) ❑ *His music lacked that vital spark of imagination.* 他的音乐缺乏那关键的一点想像力。 **6** V-T If one thing **sparks** another, the first thing cause the second thing to start happening. 引发 ❑ *My teacher organized a unit on space exploration that really sparked my interest.* 我的老师编排了一个关于太空探测的单元，它真正激发了我的兴趣。 ● PHRASAL VERB **Spark off** means the same as **spark**. 引发(同**spark**) ❑ *That incident sparked it off.* 那一事件引发了它。 **7** PHRASE If **sparks fly** between people, they discuss something in an excited or angry way. 唇枪舌剑地争论 ❑ *They are not afraid to tackle the issues or let the sparks fly when necessary.* 他们不怕应付这些问题，必要时也不惜进行唇枪舌剑的激烈争论。
→ see **engine, fire**

Word Partnership *spark* 的常用搭配:
N. spark **from a fire** **1**
spark **conflict**, spark **debate**, spark **interest**, spark a **reaction** **6**
V. **ignite** a spark, **provide** a spark **5**

★ **spar·kle** /spɑrkᵊl/ (**sparkles, sparkling, sparkled**) **1** V-I If something **sparkles**, it is clear and bright and shines with a lot of very small points of light. 闪闪发光 ❑ *The jewels on her fingers sparkled.* 她手指上的珠宝闪闪发光。 ❑ *His bright eyes sparkled.* 他明亮的双眼炯炯有神。 ● N-UNCOUNT **Sparkle** is also a noun. 闪光 ❑ *...the sparkle of colored glass.* …彩色玻璃的闪光。 **2** N-COUNT **Sparkles** are small points of light caused by light reflecting off a clear bright surface. 闪光; 亮点 ❑ *...sparkles of light.* …光的闪烁 **3** V-I Someone who **sparkles** is lively, intelligent, and witty. 聪慧而有朝气 [APPROVAL] ❑ *She sparkles, and has as much zest as a person half her age.* 她聪慧而有朝气，且有着与比她年龄小一半的人一样多的热情。 ● N-UNCOUNT **Sparkle** is also a noun. 才智与朝气 ❑ *There was little sparkle in their performance.* 他们的表演平庸而了无生气。 ●**spar·kling** ADJ 聪慧而有朝气的 ❑ *He is sparkling and versatile in front of the camera.* 他在摄影机前聪颖机智、多才多艺。

spar·kling /spɑrklɪŋ/ **1** ADJ **Sparkling** drinks are slightly carbonated. (饮料) 起泡的 ❑ *...a glass of sparkling wine.* …一杯起泡的葡萄酒。 **2** → see also **sparkle**

spar·row /spæroʊ/ (**sparrows**) N-COUNT A **sparrow** is a small brown bird that is very common in the United States. 麻雀

sparse /spɑrs/ (**sparser, sparsest**) ADJ Something that is **sparse** is small in number or amount and spread out over an area. 稀疏的 ❑ *Many slopes are rock fields with sparse vegetation.* 许多山坡都是植被稀疏的岩石地。 ❑ *He was a tubby little man in his fifties, with sparse hair.* 他是个50来岁的矮胖男人，头发稀疏。 ●**sparse·ly** ADV 稀疏地 ❑ *...the sparsely populated interior region, where there are few roads.* …人口稀少、几乎没有公路的内陆地区。

spar·tan /spɑrtᵊn/ ADJ A **spartan** lifestyle or existence is very simple or strict, with no luxuries. 简朴的 ❑ *Their spartan lifestyle prohibits a fridge or a phone.* 他们简朴的生活方式使他们不会有冰箱和电话。

spasm /spæzəm/ (**spasms**) N-VAR **A spasm** is a sudden tightening of your muscles, which you cannot control. 痉挛 ❑ *A muscular spasm in the coronary artery can cause a heart attack.* 冠状动脉内肌肉痉挛会导致心脏病发作。

spat /spæt/ **Spat** is a past tense and past participle of **spit**. **spit**的过去式和过去分词

spate /speɪt/ (**spates**) N-COUNT **A spate of** things, especially unpleasant things, is a large number of them that happen or appear within a short period of time. 一连串 ❑ *...the recent spate of attacks on horses.* …最近对马的一连串袭击。

▲ **spa·tial** /speɪʃᵊl/ **1** ADJ **Spatial** is used to describe things relating to areas. 空间的 [ADJ n] ❑ *...the spatial distribution of black employment and population in South Africa.* …南非黑人就业和人口的空间分布。 **2** ADJ Your **spatial** ability is your ability to see and understand the relationships between shapes, spaces, and areas. 感悟空间的(能力) [ADJ n] ❑ *His manual dexterity and fine spatial skills were wasted on routine tasks.* 他的手巧和很好的感悟空间的技能被浪费在日常事务中了。

spat·ter /spætər/ (**spatters, spattering, spattered**) V-T/V-I If a liquid **spatters** a surface or you **spatter** a liquid over a surface, drops of the liquid fall on an area of the surface. 使溅落; 溅落 ❑ *He stared at the rain spattering on the glass.* 他注视着在玻璃上溅落的雨。 ❑ *Gently turn the fish, being careful not to spatter any hot butter on yourself.* 轻轻地把鱼翻过来，小心别让滚烫的黄油溅到你自己身上。

speak ♦♦♦ /spik/ (**speaks, speaking, spoke, spoken**) **1** V-I When you **speak**, you use your voice in order to say something. 说话 ❑ *He tried to speak, but for once, his voice had left him.* 他试图说话，但这一次，他已说不出声。 ❑ *I rang the hotel and spoke to Louie.* 我打电话给宾馆，跟路易通了话。 ❑ *She cried when she spoke of Oliver.* 她提起奥利弗时哭了。 ●**spo·ken** ADJ 口头的 [ADJ n] ❑ *...a marked decline in the standards of written and spoken English.* …书面和口头英语标准的明显下降。 **2** V-I When someone **speaks to** a group of people, they make a speech. 演讲; 发言 ❑ *When speaking to the seminar Mr. Franklin spoke of his experience, gained on a recent visit to Trinidad.* 在研讨会上发言时，富兰克林先生谈到了他最近一次在特立尼达访问时所获得的经验。 ❑ *He's determined to speak at the Democratic Convention.* 他决心在民主党大会上发言。 **3** V-I If you **speak for** a group of people, you make their views and demands known, or represent them. 为…说话; 代表…发言 ❑ *He said it was the job of the Church to speak for the underprivileged.* 他说为弱势群体说话是教会的职责。 ❑ *I speak for all 7,000 members of our organization.* 我代表我们组织的全体7000名成员发言。 **4** V-T If you **speak** a foreign language, you know the language and are able to have a conversation in it. 说(某种语言) ❑ *He doesn't speak English.* 他不说英语。 **5** V-I People sometimes mention something that has been written by saying what the author **speaks of.** 谈及 ❑ *Throughout the book Liu speaks of the abuse of Party power.* 刘在全书中都谈到党权的滥用。 **6** V-RECIP If two people **are not speaking**, they no longer talk to each other because they have argued. (吵架之后) 相互说话 [with neg] ❑ *He is not speaking to his mother because of her friendship with his ex-wife.* 他因母亲跟其前妻的友谊而不跟母亲说话了。 **7** V-I If you say that something **speaks for itself**, you mean that its meaning or quality is so obvious that it does not need explaining or pointing out. (自己) 会说话; (本身) 能说明问题 [no cont] ❑ *...the figures speak for themselves – bleak prospects at home and a worsening outlook for exports.* …这些数字本身就能说明问题——国内暗淡的前景和日益糟糕的出口展望。 **8** PHRASE If a person or thing **is spoken for** or **has been spoken for**, someone has claimed them or asked for them, so no one else can have them. 已有人认领的；已有人请求过的 ❑ *She'd probably drop some comment about her "fiancé" into the conversation so that he'd think she was already spoken for.* 她很可能会在交谈中故意提到她的"未婚夫"，这样他就会知道她已名花有主了。 **9** PHRASE If you **speak well of** someone or **speak highly of** someone, you say good things about them. If you **speak ill of** someone, you criticize them. 说某人好话/坏话 ❑ *Both spoke highly of the Russian president.* 双方都高度评价了那位俄罗斯总统。 **10** PHRASE You use **so to speak** to draw attention to the fact that you are describing or referring to something in a way that may be amusing or unusual rather than completely accurate. 可以说 ❑ *I ought not to tell you but I will, since you're in the family, so to speak.* 我不该告诉你，但我会告诉你，因为说来你也是这个家庭的一员。 **11** to **speak** your **mind** → see **mind** **12** to **speak volumes** → see **volume**

There are some differences in the way the verbs **speak** and **talk** are used. When you **speak**, you could, for example, be addressing someone or making a speech. **Talk** is more likely to be used when you are referring to a conversation or discussion. ❑ *I talked about it with my family at dinner... Sometimes we'd talk all night.* **Talk** can also be used to emphasize the activity of saying things, rather than the words that are spoken. ❑ *She thought I talked too much.*

▸ **speak out** PHRASAL VERB If you **speak out** against something or in favor of something, you say publicly that you think it is bad or good. 公开说出 ❑ *As tempers rose, he spoke out strongly against some of the radical ideas for selling off state-owned property.* 随着火气上升，他公开表达了对某些卖掉国有资产的过激想法的强烈反对。

▸ **speak up** **1** PHRASAL VERB If you **speak up**, you say something, especially to defend a person or protest about something, rather than just saying nothing. (尤指为保护某人或抗议某事而) 说话 ❑ *Uncle Herbert never argued, never spoke up for himself.* 赫伯特叔叔从不争论，从不为自己辩护。 **2** PHRASAL VERB If you ask someone to **speak up**, you are asking them to speak more loudly. 大声点说 [no cont] ❑ *I'm quite deaf – you'll have to speak up.* 我很聋——你得大声点说。

Thesaurus *speak* 另参见:

V. articulate, communicate, declare, talk **1**

Word Partnership *speak* 的常用搭配:

ADV. speak **clearly**, speak **directly**, speak **louder**, speak **slowly** **1**
speak **freely**, speak **publicly** **1** **2**

N. **chance to** speak, **opportunity to** speak, speak **the truth** **1** **2**
speak **English/French/Spanish**, speak **a (foreign) language** **4**

-speak /-spik/ COMB IN N-UNCOUNT **-speak** is used to form nouns which refer to the kind of language used by a particular person or by people involved in a particular activity. You use **-speak** when you disapprove of this kind of language because it is difficult for other people to understand. …腔调 (某个人或某类人说的让其他人很难听懂的) [DISAPPROVAL] ❑ *Team building, motivation, and performance feature widely in modern business-speak.* 团队建设、激励和绩效充斥在现代商业语言中。

speak·er ♦◇◇ /spikər/ (**speakers**) **1** N-COUNT A **speaker** at a meeting, conference, or other gathering is a person who is making a speech or giving a talk. 演讲者；发言者 ❑ *Among the speakers at the gathering was Treasury Secretary Nicholas Brady.* 在那次聚会上发言的人当中有财政部长尼古拉斯•布雷迪。 ❑ *Bruce Wyatt will be the guest speaker at next month's meeting.* 布鲁斯•怀亚特将是下月会议上的特邀发言人。 **2** N-COUNT A **speaker of** a particular language is a person who speaks it, especially one who speaks it as their first language. 说某种语言者 ❑ *...in the Ukraine, where a fifth of the population are Russian speakers.* …在有五分之一的人口说俄语的乌克兰。 **3** N-PROPER; N-VOC In the legislature or parliament of many countries, the **Speaker** is the person who is in charge of meetings. (立法机构或议会的) 议长 ❑ *...the Speaker of the House.* …议院议长。 **4** N-COUNT A **speaker** is a person who is speaking. 说话者 ❑ *From a simple gesture or the speaker's tone of voice, the Japanese listener gleans the whole meaning.* 从一个简单的手势或说话者的声调这位日本听者捕捉到全部含义。 **5** N-COUNT A **speaker** is a piece of electrical equipment, for example part of a radio or set of equipment for playing CDs or tapes, through which sound comes out. 扬声器 ❑ *For a good stereo effect, the speakers should not be too wide apart.* 为了取得好的立体声效果，扬声器之间不应该间隔太宽。

speak·er·phone /spikərfoʊn/ (**speakerphones**) N-VAR A **speakerphone** is a telephone that has a microphone and a loudspeaker, allowing you to talk to someone without putting the phone to your ear, as well as allowing other people to hear the person you are talking to. 免提电话 ❑ *...a 10-channel cordless speakerphone with 13-number memory.* …一台可存储13位电话号码的10频道无绳免提电话。 ❑ *She put me on speakerphone and he heard me talking.* 她让我来到免提电话前，因此他听到了我的讲话。

speak·ing ♦♦◇ /spikɪŋ/ **1** N-UNCOUNT **Speaking** is the activity of giving speeches and talks. 讲话；演讲 ❑ *It would also train women union members in public speaking and decision-making.* 它也将在公开演说和做决策方面培训女工会成员。 ❑ *His work schedule still includes speaking engagements and other public appearances.* 他的工作行程还是包括演讲安排和其他公开场合的露面。 **2** PHRASE You can say "**speaking as a** parent" or "**speaking as** a teacher," for example, to indicate that the opinion you are giving is based on your experience as a parent or as a teacher. 作为…来说 ❑ *Well, speaking as a journalist I'm dismayed by the amount of pressure there is for pictures of combat.* 嗯，作为一名新闻工作者，我为人们对于战斗图片有如此大的需求量而深感不安。 **3** PHRASE You use **speaking** in expressions such as **generally speaking** and **technically speaking** to indicate which things or which particular aspect of something you are talking about. 一般说来/大致说来/等 ❑ *Generally speaking there was no resistance to the idea.* 总的说来没有对这个主意的抵制。 ❑ *Politically speaking, do you think that these moves have been effective?* 从政治上讲，你认为这些行动有效吗？

▲ **spear** /spɪər/ (**spears, spearing, speared**) **1** N-COUNT A **spear** is a weapon consisting of a long pole with a sharp metal point attached to the end. 矛 **2** V-T If you **spear** something, you push or throw a pointed object into it. 刺；叉 (某物) ❑ *Spear a piece of fish with a carving fork and dip it in the batter.* 用切肉叉叉起一片鱼并在面糊里蘸一下。
→ see **army**

spear·head /spɪərhɛd/ (**spearheads, spearheading, spearheaded**) V-T If someone **spearheads** a campaign or an attack, they lead it. 领导 (一场运动或袭击) [JOURNALISM] ❑ *She is spearheading a nationwide campaign against domestic violence.* 她正在领导一场反对家庭暴力的全国性运动。

spec /spɛk/ (**specs**) **1** N-COUNT The **spec** for something, especially a machine or vehicle, is its design and the features included in it. (尤指机器、车辆的) 设计 [INFORMAL] ❑ *The standard spec includes stainless steel holding tanks.* 标准设计包括不锈钢存储器。 **2** N-PLURAL Someone's **specs** are their glasses. 眼镜 [also "a pair of" N] [INFORMAL] ❑ *...a young businessman in his specs and suit.* …一个戴眼镜、穿套装的年轻商人。 **3** PHRASE If you do something **on spec**, you do it hoping to get something that you want, but without being asked or without being certain to get it. 碰运气地 [INFORMAL] ❑ *When searching for a job Adrian favors networking and writing letters on spec.* 寻职时阿德里安更喜欢上网和写信来碰运气。

spe·cial ♦♦♦ /spɛʃəl/ (**specials**) **1** ADJ Someone or something that is **special** is better or more important than other people or things. 特别的 ❑ *You're very special to me, darling.* 你对我来说很特别，亲爱的。 ❑ *My special guest will be Jerry Seinfeld.* 我的特邀嘉宾将是杰瑞•塞菲尔德。 **2** ADJ **Special** means different from normal. 特殊的 [ADJ n] ❑ *In special cases, a husband can deduct the travel expenses of his wife who accompanies him on a business trip.* 在特殊情况下，丈夫可以扣除差旅中随行妻子的旅费。 ❑ *So you didn't notice anything special about him?* 这么说你没有注意到他的特别之处？ **3** ADJ You use **special** to describe someone who is officially appointed or who has a particular position specially created for them. 特派的 [ADJ n] ❑ *Due to his wife's illness, he returned to the State Department as special adviser to the president.* 由于妻子的病，他返回国务院做了总统的特派顾问。 **4** ADJ You use **special** to describe something that relates to one particular person, group, or place. 特有的 [ADJ n] ❑ *Every anxious person will have his or her own special problems or fears.* 每个焦虑的人都将有他/她自己特有的问题或担心。 **5** N-COUNT A **special** is a product, program, or meal which is not normally available, or which is made for a particular purpose. 特产；特别节目；特色菜 ❑ *...complaints about the Halloween special, "Ghostwatch."* …对万圣节特别节目《幽灵观察》的抱怨。 ❑ *Grocery stores have to offer enough specials to bring people into the store.* 杂货店得提供足够多的特色产品以招揽顾客。

Thesaurus *special* 另参见:
ADJ. distinctive, exceptional, unique; (*ant.*) ordinary 1 2 4

spe·cial ef·fect (**special effects**) N-COUNT In a movie, **special effects** are unusual pictures or sounds that are created by using special techniques. (电影中的) 特技效果 ❑ *...a Hollywood horror film with special effects that are not for the nervous.* …具有不适合易紧张者观看的特技效果的一部好莱坞恐怖片。

spe·cial·ise /spɛʃəlaɪz/ [BRIT] → see **specialize**

spe·cial·ised /spɛʃəlaɪzd/ [BRIT] → see **specialized**

spe·cial·ist ♦◇◇ /spɛʃəlɪst/ (**specialists**) N-COUNT A **specialist** is a person who has a particular skill or knows a lot about a particular subject. 专家 ❑ *Peckham, himself a cancer specialist, is well aware of the wide variations in medical practice.* 佩卡姆本人就是个癌症专家，非常清楚医疗实践中的广泛差异。

★ **spe·ci·al·ity** /spɛʃiælɪti/ (**specialities**) N-COUNT A **speciality** is the same as a **specialty**. 专业; 专长 [mainly BRIT]

spe·cial·ize ♦◇◇ /spɛʃəlaɪz/ (**specializes, specializing, specialized**)

in BRIT, also use **specialise**

V-I If you **specialize in** a thing, you know a lot about it and concentrate a great deal of your time and energy on it, especially in your work or when you are studying or training. You also use **specialize** to talk about a restaurant which concentrates on a particular type of food. (在某事物上) 有专长 ❑ *...a University professor who specializes in the history of the Russian empire.* …一位专门研究沙俄历史的大学教授。 ● **spe·ciali·za·tion** ★ /spɛʃəlɪzeɪʃᵊn/ N-VAR (**specializations**) 专门研究 ❑ *This degree offers a major specialization in social policy alongside a course in sociology.* 该学位提供一门社会政策主专业课和一门社会学课程。

spe·cial·ized /spɛʃəlaɪzd/

in BRIT, also use **specialised**

ADJ Someone or something that is **specialized** is trained or developed for a particular purpose or area of knowledge. 专业化的; 专门的 ❑ *Cocaine addicts get specialized support from knowledgeable staff.* 可卡因上瘾者从知识丰富的人员那里得到专业化的帮助。

spe·cial·ly /spɛʃəli/ 1 ADV If something has been done **specially for** a particular person or purpose, it has been done only for that person or purpose. 专门地 ❑ *...a soap specially designed for those with sensitive skin.* …一种专门为敏感肤质者设计的肥皂。 ❑ *Patrick needs to use specially adapted computer equipment.* 帕特里克需要使用专门改装过的电脑设备。 2 ADV **Specially** is used to mean more than usually or more than other things. 特别地 [INFORMAL] ❑ *Stay in bed extra late or get up specially early.* 睡到特别晚或者起得特别早。

spe·cial of·fer (**special offers**) N-COUNT A **special offer** is a product, service, or program that is offered at reduced prices or rates. 特供品; 特供项目 ❑ *Ask about special offers on our new 2-week vacations.* 询问有关我们新的两周假期的特价项目。

★ **spe·cial·ty** /spɛʃᵊlti/ (**specialties**) 1 N-COUNT Someone's **specialty** is a particular type of work that they do most or do best, or a subject that they know a lot about. 专业; 专长 [AM]

in BRIT, use **speciality**

❑ *His specialty is international law.* 他的专业是国际法。 2 N-COUNT A **specialty** of a particular place is a special food or product that is always very good there. 特色食品; 特产 [AM]

in BRIT, use **speciality**

❑ *...seafood, paella, and other specialties.* …海鲜、西班牙肉菜饭及其他特色食品。

spe·cies ♦◇◇ /spiʃiz/ (**species**)

Species is both the singular and the plural form.

N-COUNT A **species** is a class of plants or animals whose members have the same main characteristics and are able to breed with each other. 物种 ❑ *Pandas are an endangered species.* 大熊猫是一种濒危物种。

→ see **plant**, **zoo**

spe·cif·ic ♦♦◇ /spɪsɪfɪk/ 1 ADJ You use **specific** to refer to a particular exact area, problem, or subject. 特定的 (部位、问题、主题等) [ADJ n] ❑ *Massage may help to increase blood flow to specific areas of the body.* 按摩也许会帮助加快血液流向身体各个特定部位。 ❑ *There are several specific problems to be dealt with.* 有好几个特定问题要解决。 2 ADJ If someone is **specific**, they give a description that is precise and exact. You can also use **specific** to describe their description. 确切的 ❑ *She declined to be more specific about the reasons for the separation.* 她拒绝给出导致分手的更确切的原因。 3 ADJ Something that is **specific to** a particular thing is connected with that thing only. 针对…的 ❑ *Send your resume with a cover letter that is specific to that particular job.* 将你的简历和专门为那份工作而写的附信一并寄送。 ● COMB IN ADJ **Specific** is also used after nouns. 针对…的 (用于名词后) ❑ *Most studies of trade have been country-specific.* 大多数贸易研究一直都是针对某个国家的。

spe·cifi·cal·ly ♦◇◇ /spɪsɪfɪkli/ 1 ADV You use **specifically** to emphasize that something is given special attention and considered separately from other things of the same kind. 专门地 [ADV with v] [EMPHASIS] ❑ *...the first nursing home designed specifically for people with AIDS.* …专门为艾滋病患者设计的第一家疗养院。 ❑ *We haven't specifically targeted school children.* 我们没有专门针对学校的孩子。 2 ADV You use **specifically** to add something more precise or exact to what you have already said. 更确切地说 [ADV with group] ❑ *Death frightens me, specifically my own death.* 死亡，更确切地说是我自己的死亡，让我害怕。 ❑ *...the Christian, and specifically Protestant, religion.* …基督教，更确切地说，新教。 3 ADV You use **specifically** to indicate that something has a restricted nature, as opposed to being more general in nature. 仅限地 [ADV adj] ❑ *...a specifically female audience.* …一群仅限女性组成的观众。 4 ADV If you state or describe something **specifically**, you state or describe it precisely and clearly. 明确地 [ADV with v] ❑ *I specifically asked for this steak rare.* 我明确要求了要把这份牛排做成半熟的。

★ **speci·fi·ca·tion** /spɛsɪfɪkeɪʃᵊn/ (**specifications**) N-COUNT A **specification** is a requirement which is clearly stated, for example about the necessary features in the design of something. 具体要求 ❑ *I'd like to buy some land and have a house built to my specification.* 我想买块地并按照我的要求建一座房子。

spe·cif·ics /spɪsɪfɪks/ N-PLURAL The **specifics** of a subject are the details of it that need to be considered. 细节 ❑ *Things improved when we got down to the specifics.* 情况在我们开始认真讨论细节时有了改善。

speci·fy /spɛsɪfaɪ/ (**specifies, specifying, specified**) 1 V-T If you **specify** something, you give information about what is required or should happen in a certain situation. 明确要求 ❑ *They specified a spacious entrance hall.* 他们明确要求门厅要宽敞。 2 V-T If you **specify** what should happen or be done, you explain it in an exact and detailed way. 具体说明 ❑ *Each recipe specifies the size of egg to be used.* 每种食谱都具体说明了所用鸡蛋的大小。 ❑ *A new law specified that houses must be a certain distance back from the water.* 一项新法律详细规定了房子必须与水域相隔一定的距离。

speci·men /spɛsɪmɪn/ (**specimens**) 1 N-COUNT A **specimen** is a single plant or animal which is an example of a particular species or type and is examined by scientists. (动植物的) 标本 [usu with supp] ❑ *200,000 specimens of fungus are kept at the Komarov Botanical Institute.* 20万个真菌标本被保存在科马罗夫植物研究所。 2 N-COUNT A **specimen of** something is an example of it which gives an idea of what the whole of it is like. 样本 [usu with supp] ❑ *Job applicants have to submit a specimen of handwriting.* 求职者必须提交一份笔迹样本。 3 N-COUNT A **specimen** is a small quantity of someone's urine, blood, or other body fluid which is examined in a medical laboratory, in order to find out if they are ill or if they have been drinking alcohol or taking drugs. (供检验用的尿液、血液等的) 抽样 ❑ *He refused to provide a specimen.* 他拒绝提供抽样。

speck /spɛk/ (**specks**) 1 N-COUNT A **speck** is a very small stain, mark, or shape. 污点; 斑迹 [oft N "of" n] ❑ *He has even cut himself shaving. There is a speck of blood by his ear.* 他甚至在刮脸时划伤了自己。他耳边有一点血迹。 2 N-COUNT A **speck** is a very small piece of a powdery substance. (粉状物的) 微粒 [oft N "of" n] ❑ *Billy leaned forward and brushed a speck of dust off his shoes.* 比利俯身刷掉鞋上的一点灰尘。

specs /spɛks/ → see **spec**

Word Link *spect ≈ looking : spectacle, spectacular, spectator*

★ **spec·ta·cle** /spɛktəkᵊl/ (**spectacles**) 1 N-COUNT A **spectacle** is a strange or interesting sight. 奇观 ❑ *It was a spectacle not to be missed.* 它是不可错过的奇观。 2 N-VAR A **spectacle** is a grand and impressive event or performance. 盛大的活动; 盛大的演出 ❑ *Ninety-four thousand people turned up for the spectacle.* 9.4万人参加了这个盛大的活动。 3 N-PLURAL Classes are sometimes referred to as

spectacles. 眼镜 [also "a pair of" N] [OLD-FASHIONED] ❑ *He looked at me over the tops of his spectacles.* 他从眼镜的上方看了看我。

Word Link *spect ≈ looking : spectacle, spectacular, spectator*

spec·tacu·lar ♦◇◇ /spɛktækyələr/ (**spectaculars**) **1** ADJ Something that is **spectacular** is very impressive or dramatic. 壮观的 ❑ *...spectacular views of the Sugar Loaf Mountain.* …甜面包山壮观的景色。 ● **spec·tacu·lar·ly** ADV 可观地 ❑ *My turnover increased spectacularly.* 我的营业额大幅上升。 **2** N-COUNT A **spectacular** is a show or performance which is very grand and impressive. 盛大的演出 [usu n N] ❑ *...a television spectacular.* …一场盛大的电视演出。

Word Link *ator ≈ one who does : creator, innovator, spectator*

★ **spec·ta·tor** /spɛkteɪtər/ (**spectators**) N-COUNT A **spectator** is someone who watches something, especially a sports event. (尤指体育赛事的) 观众 ❑ *Thirty thousand spectators watched the final game.* 3万观众观看了那场决赛。

spec·ter /spɛktər/ (**specters**)

in BRIT, use **spectre**

N-COUNT If you refer to the **specter of** something unpleasant, you are referring to something that you are frightened might occur. (对某事可能会发生而产生的) 萦绕心头的恐惧 [usu "the" N "of" n] ❑ *The arrests raised the specter of revenge attacks.* 拘捕增加了对报复性攻击的恐惧。

spec·tre /spɛktəʳ/ [BRIT] → see **specter**

★ **spec·trum** /spɛktrəm/ (**spectra** or **spectrums**) **1** N-SING **The spectrum** is the range of different colors which is produced when light passes through a glass prism or through a drop of water. A rainbow shows the colors in the spectrum. 光谱 **2** N-COUNT A **spectrum** is a range of a particular type of thing. 范围 ❑ *She'd seen his moods range across the emotional spectrum.* 她见过他在各种情感间的情绪变化。 ❑ *Politicians across the political spectrum have denounced the act.* 政界圈各派政客都谴责了这种行为。

specu·late ♦◇◇ /spɛkyəleɪt/ (**speculates, speculating, speculated**) **1** V-T/V-I If you **speculate** about something, you make guesses about its nature or identity, or about what might happen. 猜测 ❑ *Critics of the project speculate about how many hospitals could be built instead.* 该项目的批评者们则猜想这相当于可以建多少家医院。 ❑ *The doctors speculate that he died of a cerebral hemorrhage caused by a blow on the head.* 医生们猜测他死于头部撞击引起的脑溢血。 ● **specu·la·tion** ★ /spɛkyəleɪʃᵊn/ N-VAR (**speculations**) 猜测 ❑ *The president has gone out of his way to dismiss speculation over the future of the economy.* 总统努力消除对未来经济的悲观估测。 **2** V-I If someone **speculates** financially, they buy property, stocks, or shares, in the hope of being able to sell them again at a higher price and make a profit. 做投机买卖 ❑ *The banks made too many risky loans which now can't be repaid, and they speculated in property whose value has now dropped.* 银行贷出了太多现在无法偿还的风险贷款，而且他们在房地产业做了投机买卖，其价值目前也已经下跌。

Word Partnership *speculate* 的常用搭配：

N. **analysts** speculate, speculate **about a game**, speculate **about an outcome** **1**

★ **specu·la·tive** /spɛkyələtɪv, -lətɪv/ **1** ADJ A piece of information that is **speculative** is based on guesses rather than knowledge. 猜测性的 ❑ *The papers ran speculative stories about the mysterious disappearance of Eddie Donagan.* 各报刊登了有关埃迪•多纳根神秘失踪的猜测性报道。 **2** ADJ **Speculative** is used to describe activities which involve buying goods or shares, or buildings and properties, in the hope of being able to sell them again at a higher price and make a profit. 投机性的 ❑ *Thousands of retirees were persuaded to mortgage their homes to invest in speculative bonds.* 上千的退休人员被劝说抵押他们的房子去投资投机性的债券。

specu·la·tor /spɛkyəleɪtər/ (**speculators**) N-COUNT A **speculator** is a person who speculates financially. 投机者 ❑ *He sold the contracts to another speculator for a profit.* 为了牟利他把合约卖给了另一个投机商。

sped /spɛd/ **Sped** is a past tense and past participle of **speed**. **speed**的过去式和过去分词

speech ♦♦◇ /spitʃ/ (**speeches**) **1** N-UNCOUNT **Speech** is the ability to speak or the act of speaking. 言语能力；说话 ❑ *...the development of speech in children.* …孩子言语能力的发展。 ❑ *Intoxication interferes with speech and coordination.* 醉酒影响言语能力和协调性。 **2** N-SING Your **speech** is the way in which you speak. 说话方式 ❑ *His speech became increasingly thick and nasal.* 他说话变得越来越带口音且鼻音越来越重。 **3** N-UNCOUNT **Speech** is spoken language. 口语 ❑ *He could imitate in speech or writing most of those he admired.* 他能在口语或书写中模仿大多数他崇拜的人。 **4** N-COUNT A **speech** is a formal talk which someone gives to an audience. 演说 ❑ *She is due to make a speech on the economy next week.* 她将在下周作有关经济的演说。 ❑ *He delivered his speech in French.* 他用法语作的演讲。 **5** → see also **direct speech, indirect speech**

→ see **election**

Word Partnership *speech* 的常用搭配：

ADJ. **slurred** speech **1**
free speech **3**
famous speech, **major** speech, **political** speech, **recent** speech **4**

N. **acceptance** speech, **campaign** speech, **keynote** speech, speech **writing** **4**

V. **deliver** a speech, **give** a speech, **make** a speech, **prepare** a speech **4**

speech·less /spitʃlɪs/ ADJ If you are **speechless**, you are temporarily unable to speak, usually because something has shocked you. (常因震惊而) 一时说不出话的 ❑ *Alex was almost speechless with rage and despair.* 亚历克斯一时因愤怒和绝望几乎说不出话来。

speed ♦♦◇ /spid/ (**speeds, speeding, sped** or **speeded**)

The form of the past tense and past participle is **sped** in meaning **5** but **speeded** for the phrasal verb.

1 N-VAR The **speed** of something is the rate at which it moves or travels. (移动、运行的) 速度 ❑ *He drove off at high speed.* 他高速驾车离去了。 ❑ *Wind speeds reached force five.* 风速达到了5级。 **2** N-COUNT The **speed** of something is the rate at which it happens or is done. (发生、完成的) 速度 ❑ *In the late 1850s the speed of technological change quickened.* 在19世纪50年代末，技术变革的速度加快了。 **3** N-UNCOUNT **Speed** is very fast movement or travel. 快速 ❑ *Speed is the essential ingredient of all athletics.* 速度是所有体育运动的基本要素。 ❑ *He put on a burst of speed.* 他暴发出一阵猛冲。 **4** N-UNCOUNT **Speed** is a very fast rate at which something happens or is done. (发生、完成的) 高速 ❑ *I was amazed at his speed of working.* 我对他工作的高速感到惊讶。 **5** V-I If you **speed** somewhere, you move or travel there quickly, usually in a vehicle. (通常指乘车) 迅速疾驰 ❑ *Trains will speed through the tunnel at 186 mph.* 火车将以每小时186英里的速度快速穿过隧道。 **6** V-I Someone who **is speeding** is driving a vehicle faster than the legal speed limit. 超速驾驶 [usu cont] ❑ *This man was not qualified to drive and was speeding.* 这个男子没有资格开车， 而且还在超速驾驶。 ● **speed·ing** N-UNCOUNT 超速驾驶 ❑ *He was fined for speeding last year.* 他去年因超速驾驶被罚了款。 **7** N-UNCOUNT **Speed** is an illegal drug such as amphetamine which some people take to increase their energy and excitement. 快速丸 [INFORMAL] **8** to **pick up speed** → see **pick**

▸ **speed up** **1** PHRASAL VERB When something **speeds up** or when you **speed** it **up**, it moves or travels faster. (某物) 加速；使(某物) 加速 ❑ *You notice that your breathing has speeded up a bit.* 你注意到你的呼吸已加快了一点。 **2** PHRASAL VERB When a process or activity **speeds up** or when something **speeds** it **up**, it happens at a faster rate. (过程、活动) 加速；使 (过程、活动) 加速 ❑ *Job losses are speeding up.* 失业正在加速。 ❑ *I had already taken steps to speed up a solution to the problem.* 我已经采取措施加快解决这个问题。

speed dial (**speed dials**) N-VAR **Speed dial** is a facility on a telephone that allows you to call a number by pressing a single button rather than by dialing the full number. (电话机上的) 快速拨号 ❑ *Who's at the top of your speed-dial list?* 谁在你的电话快速拨号单上位居第一？

speed lim·it (**speed limits**) N-COUNT The **speed limit** on a road is the maximum speed at which you are legally allowed to drive. (道路上的) 限速 ❑ *I was fined $158 for exceeding the speed limit by 15 mph.* 我因超限速15英里每小时被罚了$158。

speed·om·eter /spidɒmɪtər/ (**speedometers**) N-COUNT A **speedometer** is the instrument in a vehicle which shows how fast the vehicle is moving. (车辆的) 速度计

speedy /spidi/ (**speedier, speediest**) ADJ A **speedy** process, event, or action happens or is done very quickly. 迅速的 ❑ *We wish Bill a speedy recovery.* 我们祝比尔早日康复。

spell ♦◇◇ /spɛl/ (**spells, spelling, spelled** or **spelt**) **1** V-T When you **spell** a word, you write or speak each letter in the word in the correct order. 拼写；拼读 ❑ *He gave his name and then helpfully spelled it.* 他说出了他的名字，然后又热心地把它拼读了出来。 ❑ *How do you spell "potato?"* "potato" 怎么拼写？ ● PHRASAL VERB **Spell out** means the same as **spell**. 拼写；拼读 ❑ *If I don't know a word, I ask them to spell it out for me.* 假如我不知道某个词，我请他们替我拼写出来。 **2** V-T/V-I Someone who can **spell** knows the correct order of letters in words. 写；写字 [no cont] ❑ *It's shocking how students can't spell these days.* 如今学生居然不会写字真让人震惊。 ❑ *He can't even spell his own name.* 他甚至不会写自己的名字。 **3** V-T If something **spells** a particular outcome, often an unpleasant one, it suggests that this will be the result. 预示 (通常不好的结果) [no cont] ❑ *If the irrigation plan goes ahead, it could spell disaster for the birds.* 如果该灌溉计划继续的话，这对鸟类可能预示着灾难。 **4** N-COUNT A **spell of** a particular type of weather or a particular activity is a short period of time during which this type of weather or activity occurs. (某种天气或活动的) 短暂发生期 ❑ *There has been a long spell of dry weather.* 干旱天气已持续很长一段时间了。 **5** N-COUNT A **spell** is a situation in which events are controlled by a magical power. 魔 ❑ *They say she died after a witch cast a spell on her.* 人们说一个女巫对她施了魔后她就死了。 **6** → see also **spelling**

▸ **spell out** **1** PHRASAL VERB If you **spell** something **out**, you explain it in detail or in a very clear way. 清楚地解释；详细说明 ❑ *Be assertive and spell out exactly how you feel.* 自信点，把你的真实感受详细说出来。 **2** → see **spell 1**

Thesaurus *spell* 另参见：

N. period, phase **4**

Word Partnership *spell* 的常用搭配：

N. spell **a name/word** **1**
spell **the end of *something***, spell **trouble** **3**
V. **can/can't** spell ***something*** **2**
break a spell, **cast** a spell **5**

spell-check (**spell-checks, spell-checking, spell-checked**) also **spell check** **1** V-T If you **spell-check** something you have written on a computer, you use a special program to check whether you have made any spelling mistakes. (用拼写检查程序) 检查拼写 [COMPUTING] ❑ *This model allows you to spell-check over 100,000 different words.* 这种型号允许你检查十万多个不同单词的拼写。 **2** N-COUNT If you run a **spell-check** over something you have written on a computer, you use a special program to check whether you have made any spelling mistakes. (电脑上的) 拼写检查 [COMPUTING]

spell-checker (**spell-checkers**) also **spell checker** N-COUNT A **spell-checker** is a special program on a computer which you can use to check whether something you have written contains any spelling mistakes. (电脑上的) 拼写检查程序 [COMPUTING]

spell·ing /spɛlɪŋ/ (**spellings**) **1** N-COUNT A **spelling** is the correct order of the letters in a word. 拼写 ❑ *In most languages adjectives have slightly different spellings for masculine and feminine.* 在大多数语言中形容词对于阳性和阴性有略微不同的拼写。 **2** N-UNCOUNT **Spelling** is the ability to spell words in the correct way. It is also an attempt to spell a word in the correct way. 拼写能力；拼写 ❑ *His spelling is very bad.* 他的拼写能力很差。 **3** → see also **spell**

spell·ing bee (**spelling bees**) N-COUNT A **spelling bee** is a competition in which children try to spell words correctly. Anyone who makes a mistake is out and the competition continues until only one person is left. 拼字比赛

spelt /spɛlt/ **Spelt** is a past tense and past participle form of **spell**. **spell**的过去式和过去分词 [mainly BRIT]

spend ♦♦♦ /spɛnd/ (**spends, spending, spent**) **1** V-T When you **spend** money, you pay money for things that you want or need. 花 (钱) ❑ *By the end of the vacation I had spent all my money.* 到那个假期结束时我已经花光了我所有的钱。 ❑ *Businessmen spend enormous amounts advertising their products.* 商人们花巨额资金为他们的产品做广告。 **2** V-T If you **spend** time or energy doing something, you use your time or effort doing it. 花 (时间、精力) ❑ *Engineers spend much time and energy developing brilliant solutions.* 工程师们花大量时间和精力开发出色的解决方案。 **3** V-T If you **spend** a period of time in a place, you stay there for a period of time. 度过 (一段时间) ❑ *We spent the night in a hotel.* 我们在一家宾馆过了夜。

Do not confuse **spend** and **pass**. If you **spend** a period of time doing something or **spend** time in a place, you do that thing or stay in that place for all of the time you are talking about. ❑ *I spent three days cleaning our apartment. ...a hotel where we could spend the night.* If you do something while you are waiting for something else, you can say you do it to "**pass** the time." ❑ *He had brought along a book to pass the time.* You can say that time **has passed** in order to show that a period of time has finished. ❑ *The first few days passed... The time seems to have passed so quickly.*

Word Partnership *spend* 的常用搭配：

N. spend **billions/millions**, **companies** spend, **consumers** spend, spend **money** **1**
spend **an amount** **1** **2**
spend **energy**, spend **time** **2**
spend **a day**, spend **hours/minutes**, spend **months/weeks/years**, spend **a night**, spend **a weekend** **3**
V. **afford to** spend, **expect to** spend, **going to** spend, **plan to** spend **1**–**3**

spend·er /spɛndər/ (**spenders**) N-COUNT If a person or organization is a big **spender** or a compulsive **spender**, for example, they spend a lot of money or are unable to stop themselves from spending money. 花费者 ❑ *The Swiss are Europe's biggest spenders on food.* 瑞士人是欧洲在食品上的最大花费者。

spent /spɛnt/ **Spent** is the past tense and past participle of **spend**. **spend**的过去式和过去分词

sperm /spɜrm/ (**sperms**)

Sperm can also be used as the plural form.

1 N-COUNT A **sperm** is a cell which is produced in the sex organs of a male animal and can enter a female animal's egg and fertilize it. 精子 ❑ *Conception occurs when a single sperm fuses with an egg.* 当一个精子和一个卵子结合时受孕就发生了。 **2** N-UNCOUNT **Sperm** is used to refer to the liquid that contains sperm when it is produced. 精液 ❑ *...a sperm donor.* …精液提供者。

spew /spyu/ (**spews, spewing, spewed**) V-T/V-I When something **spews** out a substance or when a substance **spews** from something, the substance flows out quickly in large quantities. 喷出 ❑ *The volcano spewed out more scorching volcanic ashes, gases, and rocks.* 该火山喷出了更多灼热的火山灰、各种气体和岩石。

Word Link *sphere ≈ ball : atmosphere, hemisphere, sphere*

sphere /sfɪər/ (**spheres**) **1** N-COUNT A **sphere** is an object that is completely round in shape like a ball. 球体 ❑ *Because the earth spins, it is not a perfect sphere.* 因为地球旋转，所以它不是个完完全全的球体。 **2** N-COUNT A **sphere of** activity or interest is a particular area of activity or interest. (活动、兴趣的) 领域 ❑ *...the sphere of international politics.* …国际政治领域。
→ see **solid, volume**

★ **spice** /spaɪs/ (**spices, spicing, spiced**) **1** N-MASS A **spice** is a part of a plant, or a powder made from that part, which you put in food to give it flavor. Cinnamon, ginger, and paprika are spices. 香料 ❑ *...herbs and spices.* …各种香草和香料。 **2** V-T If you **spice** something that you say or do, you add excitement or interest to it. 给…增加趣味 ❑ *They spiced their conversations and discussions with intrigue.* 他们通过设谜为他们的谈话和讨论增加乐趣。 ● PHRASAL VERB **Spice up** means the same as **spice**. 给…增加趣味 (同**spice**) ❑ *Her publisher wants her to spice up her stories with sex.* 她的出版商想要她用色情给她的故事增添趣味。
→ see Word Web: **spice**

spiced /spaɪst/ ADJ Food that is **spiced** has had spices or other strong-tasting foods added to it. 添加了香料的 ❑ *Every dish was served heavily spiced.* 每道菜端上来都是加过很多香料的。

spicy /spaɪsi/ (**spicier, spiciest**) ADJ **Spicy** food is strongly flavored with spices. 香料味重的 ❑ *Thai food is hot and spicy.* 泰国食品很辛辣。
→ see **spice**

spi·der /spaɪdər/ (**spiders**) N-COUNT A **spider** is a small creature with eight legs. Most types of spiders make structures called webs in which they catch insects for food. 蜘蛛

spike /spaɪk/ (**spikes**) N-COUNT A **spike** is a long piece of metal with a sharp point. 长金属锥 ❑ *...a 15-foot wall topped with iron spikes.* …顶上装有长铁锥的15英尺高的墙。

Word Web spice

While researching the use of **spices** in cooking, scientists discovered that many of them have strong disease-prevention properties. Bacteria can grow quickly on food and cause a variety of serious illnesses in humans. The researchers found that many spices are extremely antibacterial. For example, **garlic**, **onion**, allspice, and oregano kill almost all common germs. **Cinnamon**, tarragon, cumin, and **chili peppers** also eliminate about 75% of bacteria. And even common, everyday **black pepper** destroys about 25% of all microbes. The research also found a connection between hot climates and **spicy** food and cold climates and **bland** food.

spike heels N-PLURAL **Spike heels** are the same as **stilettos**. 细高跟女鞋 [also "a pair of" n] [AM]

spiky /spaɪki/ ADJ Something that is **spiky** has one or more sharp points. 有尖端的 ❑ *Her short spiky hair is damp with sweat.* 她又硬又直的短发被汗浸湿了。

spill /spɪl/ (**spills, spilling, spilled** or **spilt**) **1** V-T/V-I If a liquid **spills** or if you **spill** it, it accidentally flows over the edge of a container. 无意洒落；意外溢出 ❑ *Seventy thousand tons of oil spilled from the tanker.* 7万吨油从油轮漏出。 ❑ *He always spilled the drinks.* 他总是不小心把饮料给洒了。 **2** N-COUNT A **spill** is an amount of liquid that has spilled from a container. 洒落的液体 ❑ *She wiped a spill of milkshake off the counter.* 她擦掉柜台上洒落的奶昔。 **3** V-T/V-I If the contents of a bag, box, or other container **spill** or **are spilled**, they come out of the container onto a surface. 使散落；散落 ❑ *A number of bags had split and were spilling their contents.* 许多包裂开了，里面的东西正在散落出来。 **4** V-I If people or things **spill** out of a place, they come out of it in large numbers. 涌出 ❑ *Tears began to spill out of the boy's eyes.* 泪水开始从男孩的眼里涌出。

spill·age /spɪlɪdʒ/ (**spillages**) N-VAR If there is a **spillage**, a substance such as oil escapes from its container. **Spillage** is also used to refer to the substance that escapes. 外溢；溢出物 ❑ *...an oil spillage off the coast of Texas.* …得克萨斯海岸的石油外溢。

spin ♦◇◇ /spɪn/ (**spins, spinning, spun**) **1** V-T/V-I If something **spins** or if you **spin** it, it turns quickly around a central point. 转动 ❑ *The latest disks, used for small portable computers, spin 3,600 times a minute.* 用于小型手提电脑的最新磁盘每分钟转动3600次。 ❑ *He spun the wheel sharply and made a U turn in the middle of the road.* 他猛打方向盘，在路中间掉了个头。 ● N-VAR **Spin** is also a noun. 旋转 ❑ *This driving mode allows you to move off in third gear to reduce wheel-spin in icy conditions.* 这种驾驶方法可以让你用三档发动汽车以减少结冰情况下的车轮打滑。 **2** V-I If your head **is spinning**, you feel unsteady or confused, for example because you are drunk, ill, or excited. 眩晕 ❑ *My head was spinning from the wine.* 当时我因喝了酒而感到眩晕。 **3** N-SING If someone puts a certain **spin** on an event or situation, they interpret it and try to present it in a particular way. (特意做的) 诠释与宣传 [INFORMAL] ❑ *He interpreted the vote as support for the constitution and that is the spin his supporters are putting on the results today.* 他把这次投票结果解释为对宪法的支持，这也是他的支持者们对今天的结果所做的诠释与宣传。 **4** N-UNCOUNT In politics, **spin** is the way in which political parties try to present everything they do in a positive way to the public and the media. (政治) 粉饰 ❑ *The public is sick of spin and tired of promises.* 公众厌倦了粉饰和许诺。 **5** N-SING If you go for **a spin** or take a car for **a spin**, you make a short trip in a car just to enjoy yourself. 兜风 ❑ *Tom Wright celebrated his 99th birthday by going for a spin in his sporty Mazda.* 汤姆·赖特开着他的运动型马自达车出去兜风以庆祝其99岁生日。 **6** V-T When people **spin**, they make thread by twisting together pieces of a fiber such as wool or cotton using a device or machine. 纺；纺线 ❑ *Michelle will also spin a customer's wool fleece to specification at a cost of $2.25 an ounce.* 米歇尔也将以每盎司$2.25的价格按照顾客的要求为其纺羊毛呢。 **7** N-UNCOUNT In a game such as tennis or baseball, if you put **spin** on a ball, you deliberately make it spin rapidly when you hit it or throw it. (击球或投球时故意使球做出的) 快速旋转 ❑ *He threw it back again, putting a slight spin on the ball.* 他把球略带旋转地又投掷了回去。

▸ **spin off** PHRASAL VERB To **spin off** something such as a company means to create a new company that is separate from the original organization. 使脱离 (原组织) 而独立 [BUSINESS] ❑ *He rescued the company and later spun off its textile division into a separate entity.* 他挽救了该公司，后来又把它的纺织部脱离出来组建成一个独立实体。

▸ **spin out** PHRASAL VERB If you **spin** something **out**, you make it last longer than it normally would. 拖延 ❑ *My wife's lawyer was anxious to spin things out for as long as possible.* 我妻子的律师极希望尽可能拖延时间。

Word Partnership spin 的常用搭配：

N.	spin a wheel **1**
ADJ.	positive spin **3** **4**

▲ **spin·ach** /spɪnɪtʃ/ N-UNCOUNT **Spinach** is a vegetable with large dark green leaves. 菠菜

★ **spi·nal** /spaɪnᵊl/ ADJ **Spinal** means relating to your spine. 脊柱的 [ADJ n] ❑ *...spinal fluid.* …脊髓液。

→ see **brain, nervous system**

spin doc·tor (**spin doctors**) N-COUNT In politics, a **spin doctor** is someone who is skilled in public relations and who advises political parties on how to present their policies and actions. 媒体顾问；政治顾问 [INFORMAL] ❑ *...two spin doctors in the majority leader's office.* …在多数党领导人办公室里的两位媒体顾问。

spine /spaɪn/ (**spines**) **1** N-COUNT Your **spine** is the row of bones down your back. 脊柱 ❑ *...injuries to his spine.* …对他的脊柱的创伤。 **2** N-COUNT The **spine** of a book is the narrow stiff part which the pages and covers are attached to. (书) 脊 ❑ *...a book with "Lifestyle" on the spine.* …一本脊上印有"生活方式"的书。 **3** N-COUNT **Spines** are also long, sharp points on an animal's body or on a plant. (动物的) 刺毛；(植物的) 刺 ❑ *An adult hedgehog can boast 7,500 spines.* 一只成年刺猬能有多达7500根刺。

spin·off /spɪnɔf/ (**spinoffs**) **1** N-COUNT A **spinoff** is an unexpected but useful or valuable result of an activity that was designed to achieve something else. 意外收获；意外效应 ❑ *The company put out a report on commercial spinoffs from its research.* 该公司发布了一份关于来自其研究的商业效应的报告。 **2** N-COUNT A **spinoff** is a book, film, or television series that comes after and is related to a successful book, film, or television series. (书、电影或电视连续剧的) 衍生物 ❑ *The film is a spinoff from the TV series "Sabrina The Teenage Witch."* 这部电影是电视连续剧《少年女巫萨布丽娜》的衍生作品。

★ **spi·ral** /spaɪrəl/ (**spirals, spiraling** or **spiralling, spiraled** or **spiralled**) **1** N-COUNT A **spiral** is a shape which winds around and around, with each curve above or outside the previous one. 螺旋形 ❑ *The maze is actually two interlocking spirals.* 这个迷宫实际上是两个连锁的螺旋体。 ● ADJ **Spiral** is also an adjective. 螺旋形的 [ADJ n] ❑ *...a spiral staircase.* …一段旋梯。 **2** V-T/V-I If something **spirals** or **is spiraled** somewhere, it grows or moves in a spiral curve. 使…螺旋式生长或移动；螺旋式生长或移动 ❑ *Vines spiraled upward toward the roof.* 藤蔓螺旋式向上朝屋顶生长。 ❑ *The aircraft began spiraling out of control.* 那架飞机开始做螺旋式飞行，失去了控制。 ● N-COUNT **Spiral** is also a noun. 螺旋式运动 ❑ *Larks were rising in spirals from the ridge.* 云雀在从山脊上盘旋上升。 **3** V-I If an amount or level **spirals**, it rises quickly and at an increasing rate. 加速上升 ❑ *Production costs began* to spiral. 生产成本开始加速上涨。 ❑ *...spiraling health care costs.* …加速上涨的各种保健费用。● N-SING **Spiral** is also a noun. 加速上升 ❑ *...an inflationary spiral.* …一次通胀性的激增。 4 V-I If an amount or level **spirals** downward, it falls quickly and at an increasing rate. 加速下降 ❑ *House prices will continue to spiral downwards.* 房价将继续加速下跌。● N-SING **Spiral** is also a noun. 加速下降 ❑ *...a spiral of debt.* …债务的加剧减少。

→ see **circle**

spire /spaɪər/ (**spires**) N-COUNT The **spire** of a building such as a church is the tall pointed structure on the top. (教堂等建筑物的)尖顶 ❑ *...a church spire poking above the trees.* …伸出树梢的教堂尖顶。

spir·it ♦♦◊ /spɪrɪt/ (**spirits**) 1 N-SING Your **spirit** is the part of you that is not physical and that consists of your character and feelings. 精神(包括性格、情感等) ❑ *The human spirit is virtually indestructible.* 人的精神实际上是不可摧毁的。 2 N-COUNT A person's **spirit** is the nonphysical part of them that is believed to remain alive after their death. 灵魂 ❑ *His spirit has left him and all that remains is the shell of his body.* 他的灵魂已经离开了他，所剩的是他的躯壳。 3 N-COUNT A **spirit** is a ghost or supernatural being. 幽灵 ❑ *In the Middle Ages branches were hung outside country houses as a protection against evil spirits.* 在中世纪树枝被挂在村舍外面作为对邪恶幽灵的防范。 4 N-UNCOUNT **Spirit** is the courage and determination that helps people to survive in difficult times and to keep their way of life and their beliefs. 毅力 ❑ *She was a very brave girl and everyone who knew her admired her spirit.* 她是个很勇敢的女孩，每个认识她的人都钦佩她的毅力。 5 N-UNCOUNT **Spirit** is the liveliness and energy that someone shows in what they do. 活力 ❑ *They played with spirit.* 他们充满活力地进行了比赛。 6 N-SING The **spirit** in which you do something is the attitude you have when you are doing it. 态度 ❑ *Their problem can only be solved in a spirit of compromise.* 他们的问题只能以折衷的态度解决。 7 N-UNCOUNT A particular kind of **spirit** is the feeling of loyalty to a group that is shared by the people who belong to the group. 忠诚 ❑ *There is a great sense of team spirit in the squad.* 这个班有很高的团队忠诚度。 8 N-SING A particular kind of **spirit** is the set of ideas, beliefs, and aims that are held by a group of people. 群体的观念、信仰和目的 ❑ *...the real spirit of the anti-war movement.* …反战运动的真正精神。 9 N-SING **The spirit of** something such as a law or an agreement is the way that it was intended to be interpreted or applied. 宗旨 ❑ *The requirement for work permits violates the spirit of the 1950 treaty.* 对工作许可证的要求违反了1950年条约的宗旨。 10 N-COUNT You can refer to a person as a particular kind of **spirit** if they show a certain characteristic or if they show a lot of enthusiasm in what they are doing. (具有某种特质或热情的)人 ❑ *I like to think of myself as a free spirit.* 我喜欢把自己看成一个无拘无束的人。 11 N-PLURAL Your **spirits** are your feelings at a particular time, especially feelings of happiness or unhappiness. 情绪 ❑ *At supper, everyone was in high spirits.* 晚饭时每个人都情绪高昂。 12 N-PLURAL **Spirits** are strong alcoholic drinks such as whiskey and gin. 烈酒 ❑ *The only problem here is that they don't serve beer - only wine and spirits.* 这儿惟一的问题是他们不供应啤酒——只供应葡萄酒和烈酒。

Word Partnership *spirit* 的常用搭配：

N.	**human** spirit 1 2
	evil spirit 3
	team spirit 7
ADJ.	**free** spirit, **independent** spirit 5 10
	competitive spirit, **generous** spirit 6

spir·it·ed /spɪrɪtɪd/ 1 ADJ A **spirited** action shows great energy and courage. 激烈的 ❑ *This television program provoked a spirited debate.* 这个电视节目引起了激烈的争论。 2 ADJ A **spirited** person is very active, lively, and confident. 生气勃勃的 ❑ *He was by nature a spirited little boy.* 他天生就是个充满活力的小男孩。

spir·itu·al ♦◊◊ /spɪrɪtʃuəl/ 1 ADJ **Spiritual** means relating to people's thoughts and beliefs, rather than to their bodies and physical surroundings. 精神的 ❑ *She lived entirely by spiritual values, in a world of poetry and imagination.* 她完全靠着精神价值生活在一个诗歌和想像的世界里。● **spir·itu·al·ly** ADV 精神地 ❑ *Our whole program is spiritually oriented but not religious.* 我们的整个节目以精神而不是宗教为导向。● **spir·itu·al·ity** /spɪrɪtʃuælɪti/ N-UNCOUNT 精神性 ❑ *...the peaceful spirituality of Japanese culture.* …日本文化的平和的精神性。 2 ADJ **Spiritual** means relating to people's religious beliefs. 宗教的 ❑ *He is the spiritual leader of the world's Catholics.* 他是世界天主教的宗教领袖。

→ see **myth**

spit /spɪt/ (**spits, spitting, spit** or **spat**) 1 N-UNCOUNT **Spit** is the watery liquid produced in your mouth. You usually use **spit** to refer to an amount of it that has been forced out of someone's mouth. 口水 ❑ *A trickle of spit collected at the corner of her mouth.* 一小股口水积聚在了她的嘴角。 2 V-I If someone **spits**, they force an amount of liquid out of their mouth, often to show hatred or contempt. 吐唾沫 ❑ *The gang thought of hitting him too, but decided just to spit.* 那个团伙也想到揍他，但决定只朝他吐唾沫。 ❑ *They spat at me and taunted me.* 他们又朝我吐唾沫又嘲弄我。 3 V-T If you **spit** liquid or food somewhere, you force a small amount of it out of your mouth. 吐出 ❑ *Spit out that gum and pay attention.* 吐掉那口香糖，专心点。 4 N-COUNT A **spit** is a long rod which is pushed through a piece of meat and hung over an open fire to cook the meat. 烤肉扦子 ❑ *She roasted the meat on a spit.* 她在烤肉扦子上烤了那块肉。 5 PHRASE If you say that one person is **the spitting image of** another, you mean that they look very similar. 与某人简直一模一样 [INFORMAL] ❑ *Nina looks the spitting image of Sissy Spacek.* 尼娜看上去简直和茜茜•斯派塞克一模一样。

spite ♦◊◊ /spaɪt/ 1 PHRASE You use **in spite of** to introduce a fact which makes the rest of the statement you are making seem surprising. 尽管 ❑ *Josef Krips at the State Opera hired her in spite of the fact that she had never sung on stage.* 国家歌剧院的约瑟夫•克里普斯雇佣了她，尽管她从未在台上演唱过。 2 PHRASE If you do something **in spite of yourself**, you do it although you did not really intend to or expect to. 不由自主地 ❑ *The blunt comment made Richard laugh in spite of himself.* 那率直的评论使得理查德不由自主地笑了起来。 3 N-UNCOUNT If you do something cruel out of **spite**, you do it because you want to hurt or upset someone. 恶意 ❑ *I refused her a divorce, out of spite I suppose.* 我拒绝了她离婚的要求，我想是出于怨恨。 4 V-T If you do something cruel **to spite** someone, you do it in order to hurt or upset them. 存心伤害 [only to-inf] ❑ *Pantelaras was giving his art collection away for nothing, to spite Marie and her husband.* 潘特拉拉斯将他的艺术收藏品无偿赠送了，存心惹怒玛丽和她的丈夫。

splash /splæʃ/ (**splashes, splashing, splashed**) 1 V-I If you **splash** around or **splash** about in water, you hit or disturb the water in a noisy way, causing some of it to fly up into the air. 泼打戏水 ❑ *A lot of people were in the water, swimming or simply splashing about.* 很多人在水里游泳或者只是戏水。 ❑ *She could hear the voices of her friends as they splashed in a nearby rock pool.* 她能听到她的朋友们在附近的岩石泳池里戏水的声音。 2 V-T/V-I If you **splash** a liquid somewhere or if it **splashes**, it hits someone or something and scatters in a lot of small drops. 使泼溅；溅落 ❑ *He closed his eyes tight, and splashed the water on his face.* 他紧紧地闭上眼睛，把水泼到脸上。 ❑ *A little wave, the first of many, splashed in my face.* 层层波浪中的第一层小浪溅在了我的脸上。 3 N-SING A **splash** is the sound made when something hits water or falls into it. 拍打水的声音；落入水的声音 ❑ *There was a splash and something fell clumsily into the water.* 扑通一声，什么东西重重地掉进了水里。 4 N-COUNT A **splash** of a liquid is a small quantity of it that falls on something or is added to something. (少量液体的)溅落；(少量液体的)添加 ❑ *Wallcoverings and floors should be able to withstand steam and splashes.* 墙纸和地板应该能承受得住蒸汽和液体的泼溅。 5 N-COUNT A **splash of** color is an area of a bright color which contrasts strongly with the colors around it. (与周围颜色形成鲜明对比的)亮色块 ❑ *...shady walks punctuated by splashes of color.* …由鲜艳色彩点缀的条条林荫小径。 6 V-T If a magazine or newspaper **splashes** a story, it prints it in such a way that it is very noticeable. (报刊)以显眼方式刊登 ❑ *The newspapers splashed the story all over their front pages.* 各报都在头版全版以显眼的方式刊登了这个故事。 7 PHRASE If you **make a splash**, you become noticed or become popular because of something that you have done. 引起关注 ❑ *Now she's made a splash in the television show "Civil Wars."* 如今她因在电视节目《内战》中的出现而引起了人们的关注。

splat·ter /splætər/ (**splatters, splattering, splattered**) V-T/V-I If a thick wet substance **splatters** on something or is **splattered** on it, it drops or is thrown over it. 溅洒 ❑ *The rain splattered against the windows.* 雨溅在了窗户上。 ❑ *"Sorry Edward," I said, splattering the cloth with jam.* "对不起，爱德华，"我说道，把果酱溅到了桌布上。

splen·did /splɛndɪd/ ADJ If you say that something is **splendid**, you mean that it is very good. 极好的 ❑ *The book includes a wealth of* *splendid photographs.* 这本书有大量非常好的照片。● **splen·did·ly** ADV 极好地 [ADV with V] ❑ *I have heard him tell people that we get along splendidly.* 我听见他跟人说我们相处得非常好。

splen·dor /splɛndər/ (**splendors**)

in BRIT, use **splendour**

1 N-UNCOUNT The **splendor** of something is its beautiful and impressive appearance. 壮美的外观 ❑ *She gazed down upon the nighttime splendor of the city.* 她往下凝视着这个城市夜晚的壮美。 **2** N-PLURAL The **splendors** of a place or way of life are its beautiful and impressive features. 壮美的特征 ❑ *...such splendors as the Acropolis and the Parthenon.* …像雅典卫城和巴特农神殿那样的壮观。 ❑ *Montagu was extremely impressed by the splendors of the French court.* 法国宫廷的华美给蒙太古留下了极深的印象。

splen·dour /splɛndəʳ/ [BRIT] → see **splendor**

splin·ter /splɪntər/ (**splinters, splintering, splintered**) **1** N-COUNT A **splinter** is a very thin, sharp piece of wood, glass, or other hard substance, which has broken off from a larger piece. 薄而尖的碎片 ❑ *...splinters of glass.* …玻璃碎片。 **2** V-T/V-I If something **splinters** or **is splintered**, it breaks into thin, sharp pieces. 使碎成片；碎成片 ❑ *The ruler cracked and splintered into pieces.* 尺子裂了，碎成了片。

split ♦♦◊ /splɪt/ (**splits, splitting**)

The form **split** is used in the present tense and is the past tense and past participle of the verb.

1 V-T/V-I If something **splits** or if you **split** it, it is divided into two or more parts. 分开 ❑ *In a severe gale the ship split in two.* 在一次强劲的大风中那艘船断成了两半。 ❑ *If the chicken is fairly small, you may simply split it in half.* 要是鸡不太大，你把它分成两半就行。 **2** V-T/V-I If an organization **splits** or **is split**, one group of members disagree strongly with the other members, and may form a group of their own. 分裂 ❑ *Yet it is feared the Republican leadership could split over the agreement.* 然而人们担心共和党领导层可能会因该协议而出现分裂。 ● ADJ **Split** is also an adjective. 分裂的 ❑ *The Kremlin is deeply split in its approach to foreign policy.* 克里姆林宫在对外政策的看法上严重分歧。 **3** N-COUNT A **split in** an organization is a disagreement between its members. 分歧 ❑ *They accused both radicals and conservatives of trying to provoke a split in the party.* 他们指责激进人士和保守人士都企图挑起党内分歧。 **4** N-SING A **split between** two things is a division or difference between them. 区分；区别 ❑ *...a split between what is thought and what is felt.* …所想和所感之间的区别。 **5** V-T/V-I If something such as wood or a piece of clothing **splits** or **is split**, a long crack or tear appears in it. 使裂开；裂开 ❑ *The seat of his gray pants split.* 他的那条灰色裤子的臀部裂开了。 **6** N-COUNT A **split** is a long crack or tear. 裂缝 ❑ *The plastic-covered seat has a few small splits around the corners.* 那个有塑料套的座位的角边周围有几处小裂缝。 **7** V-T If two or more people **split** something, they share it between them. 分摊；分享 ❑ *I would rather pay for a meal than watch nine friends pick over and split a bill.* 我宁愿付整顿饭钱而不愿看着9个朋友仔细算计、分摊账单。

▸ **split up** **1** PHRASAL VERB If two people **split up**, or if someone or something **splits** them **up**, they end their relationship or marriage. 使(两人)分手；(两人)分手 ❑ *Research suggests that children whose parents split up are more likely to drop out of high school.* 研究显示父母离异的孩子更有可能在中学辍学。 ❑ *I was beginning to think that nothing could ever split us up.* 我渐渐开始以为没有什么事情能把我们分开。 **2** PHRASAL VERB If a group of people **split up** or **are split up**, they go away in different directions. 使朝不同方向去；朝不同方向去 ❑ *Did the two of you split up in the woods?* 你们俩在树林里分的道吗？ ❑ *This situation has split up the family.* 此事使这个家庭的成员分道扬镳了。 **3** PHRASAL VERB If you **split** something **up**, or if it **splits up**, you divide it so that it is in a number of smaller separate sections. 使(物)分开；(物)分开 ❑ *Any thought of splitting up the company was unthinkable, they said.* 他们说，任何分裂该公司的想法都是不可思议的。 ❑ *Even though museums have begged to borrow her collection, she could never split it up.* 尽管各博物馆已恳求过借用她的收藏品，她永远都不能把藏品分开。

Thesaurus *split* 另参见：

V.	break, divide, part, separate; (*ant.*) combine **1** **2**
N.	separation **4**
	crack, tear **6**

Word Partnership *split* 的常用搭配：

PREP.	split into **1**
	split over *something* **2**
	split between **4** **7**
	split among **7**
N.	split shares, split wood **1**
	split in a party **3**
ADV.	split apart **1** **2**

split se·cond also **split-second** N-SING A **split second** is an extremely short period of time. 刹那；瞬间 ❑ *Her gaze met Michael's for a split second.* 她与迈克尔目光对视了一刹那。 ❑ *In law enforcement, we have to make split-second decisions.* 在执法中我们不得不做瞬间决定。

splut·ter /splʌtər/ (**splutters, spluttering, spluttered**) **1** V-T/V-I If someone **splutters**, they make short sounds and have difficulty speaking clearly, for example because they are embarrassed or angry. (因尴尬或愤怒而) 结结巴巴地说；结结巴巴地说话 ❑ *"But it cannot be," he spluttered.* "但那不可能，"他结结巴巴地说。 **2** V-I If something **splutters**, it makes a series of short, sharp sounds. 发劈啪声 ❑ *Suddenly the engine coughed, spluttered, and died.* 突然发动机扑哧扑哧、劈啪作响，然后熄火了。

spoil /spɔɪl/ (**spoils, spoiling, spoiled** or **spoilt**) **1** V-T If you **spoil** something, you prevent it from being successful or satisfactory. 毁坏；破坏 ❑ *It's important not to let mistakes spoil your life.* 重要的是不要让错误毁了你的生活。 **2** V-T If you **spoil** children, you give them everything they want or ask for. This is considered to have a bad effect on a child's character. 娇惯 ❑ *Grandparents are often tempted to spoil their grandchildren whenever they come to visit.* 每次祖父母来访，常常禁不住要娇惯孙辈。 **3** V-T If you **spoil yourself** or **spoil** another person, you give yourself or them something nice as a treat or do something special for them. 犒劳；优待 ❑ *Spoil yourself with a new perfume this summer.* 今年夏天买瓶新香水犒劳一下自己吧。 **4** V-T/V-I If food **spoils** or if it **is spoiled**, it is no longer fit to be eaten. 使(食物) 变坏；(食物) 变坏 ❑ *We all know that fats spoil by becoming rancid.* 我们都知道油脂发臭就变坏了。 **5** PHRASE If you say that someone is **spoiled for choice** or **spoilt for choice**, you mean that they have a great many things of the same type to choose from. (因可选的太多而) 不知作何选择是好 [mainly BRIT]

spoilt /spɔɪlt/ **Spoilt** is a past participle and past tense of **spoil**. **spoil**的过去分词和过去式 [BRIT]

spoke /spoʊk/ **1** **Spoke** is the past tense of **speak**. **speak**的过去式 **2** N-COUNT The **spokes** of a wheel are the bars that connect the outer ring to the center. (轮) 辐 [usu pl]

→ see **bicycle, wheel**

spo·ken /spoʊkən/

Spoken is the past participle of **speak**. **speak**的过去分词

spokes·man ♦♦◊ /spoʊksmən/ (**spokesmen**) N-COUNT A **spokesman** is a male spokesperson. 男发言人 ❑ *A UN spokesman said that the mission will carry 20 tons of relief supplies.* 一位联合国男发言人说该行动将运送20吨救济物资。

spokes·person /spoʊkspɜrsᵊn/ (**spokespersons** or **spokespeople**) N-COUNT A **spokesperson** is a person who speaks as the representative of a group or organization. (团体、组织的) 发言人 ❑ *A spokesperson for Amnesty, Norma Johnston, describes some cases.* 大赦国际组织的一位发言人诺尔玛•约翰斯顿描述了一些案例。

spokes·woman ♦♦◊ /spoʊkswʊmən/ (**spokeswomen**) N-COUNT A **spokeswoman** is a female spokesperson. 女发言人 ❑ *A United Nations spokeswoman in New York said the request would be considered.* 一位在纽约的联合国女发言人称该请求会被予以考虑。

sponge /spʌndʒ/ (**sponges, sponging, sponged**) **1** N-COUNT **Sponge** is a very light soft substance with lots of little holes in it, which can be either artificial or natural. It is used to clean things or as a soft layer. 海绵 ❑ *...a sponge mattress.* …一张海绵床垫。 **2** N-COUNT A **sponge** is a piece of sponge that you use for washing yourself or for cleaning things. (洗澡或清洁用的) 海绵块 ❑ *He wiped off the table with a sponge.* 他用一块海绵擦了桌子。 **3** V-T If you **sponge** something, you clean it by wiping it with a wet sponge. 用湿海绵擦拭 ❑ *Fill a bowl with water and gently sponge your face and body.* 装满一碗水，然后用湿海绵轻轻擦洗你的脸和身子。 ● PHRASAL VERB **Sponge down** means the same as **sponge**. 用湿海绵擦洗 ❑ *If your child's temperature rises, sponge her down gently with tepid water.* 如果你孩子的体温升高，用湿海绵沾温水轻轻地擦洗她。

4 V-I If you say that someone **sponges off** other people or **sponges on** them, you mean that they regularly get money from other people when they should be trying to support themselves. 揩油 [INFORMAL, DISAPPROVAL] ❑ *He should just get an honest job and stop sponging off the rest of us!* 他就应该找一份踏实的工作，不要再揩我们其他人的油了！ 5 N-VAR A **sponge** is a light cake or pudding made from flour, eggs, sugar, and sometimes shortening. 松软蛋糕；松软布丁 [BRIT]

in AM, use **sponge cake**

spon·sor ♦◇◇ /spɒnsər/ (**sponsors, sponsoring, sponsored**) 1 V-T If an organization or an individual **sponsors** something such as an event or someone's training, they pay some or all of the expenses connected with it, often in order to get publicity for themselves. 赞助(某事、某人的培训等) ❑ *Dozens of companies, including Hewlett-Packard, are sponsoring the event.* 包括惠普在内的许多公司都在赞助这项赛事。 2 V-T If you **sponsor** someone who is doing something to raise money for charity, for example trying to walk a certain distance, you agree to give them a sum of money for the charity if they succeed in doing it. 赞助(为慈善事业募集资金者) ❑ *Please could you sponsor me for my school's campaign for Help the Aged?* 请问你们能赞助我开展我校的"帮助老年人"活动吗？ 3 V-T If you **sponsor** a proposal or suggestion, you officially put it forward and support it. 倡议 ❑ *Eight senators sponsored legislation to stop the military funding.* 八位参议员倡议立法停拨军费。 4 V-T When a country or an organization such as the United Nations **sponsors** negotiations between countries, it suggests holding the negotiations and organizes them. 提议并组织(商谈) ❑ *Given the strength of pressure on both sides, the superpowers may well have difficulties sponsoring negotiations.* 鉴于双方的强大压力，超级大国可能很难组织谈判。 5 V-T If one country accuses another of **sponsoring** attacks on it, they mean that the other country does not do anything to prevent the attacks, and may even encourage them. 纵容 ❑ *We have to make the states that sponsor terrorism pay a price.* 我们得让那些纵容恐怖主义的国家付出代价。 6 V-T If a company or organization **sponsors** a television program, they pay to have a special advertisement shown at the beginning and end of the program, and at each commercial break. 赞助(电视节目) ❑ *The company plans to sponsor television programs as part of its marketing strategy.* 公司计划赞助电视节目，以此作为营销策略之一。 7 N-COUNT A **sponsor** is a person or organization that sponsors something or someone. 赞助人；赞助机构；倡议人 ❑ *Race officials announced a handful of new sponsors on Tuesday.* 比赛官员们星期二公布了几位新赞助人。

spon·sor·ship /spɒnsərʃɪp/ N-UNCOUNT **Sponsorship** is financial support given by a sponsor. 赞助；资助 [also N in pl] ❑ *Campbell is one of an ever-growing number of skiers in need of sponsorship.* 坎贝尔是日益增多的需要资助的滑雪者之一。

spon·ta·neity /spɒntənɪ̱iti, -neɪ̱-/ N-UNCOUNT **Spontaneity** is spontaneous, natural behavior. 自发行为；自然举动 ❑ *He had the spontaneity of a child.* 他有孩子般的自然举动。

spon·ta·neous /spɒnteɪ̱niəs/ 1 ADJ **Spontaneous** acts are not planned or arranged, but are done because someone suddenly wants to do them. 自然的；自发的(行为) ❑ *Diana's house was crowded with happy people whose spontaneous outbursts of song were accompanied by lively music.* 戴安娜的房子挤满了幸福的人们，他们在欢快音乐的伴奏下不由自主地唱起歌来。 ●**spon·ta·neous·ly** ADV 自然地；自发地 ❑ *Many people spontaneously stood up and cheered.* 许多人自发地站起来欢呼。 2 ADJ A **spontaneous** event happens because of processes within something rather than being caused by things outside it. 自然的(事件) ❑ *I had another spontaneous miscarriage at around the 16th to 18th week.* 在大约第16至18周时我又一次自然流产了。 ●**spon·ta·neous·ly** ADV 自然地 [ADV after v] ❑ *Usually a woman's breasts produce milk spontaneously after the birth.* 通常女性在生孩子后乳房会自然泌乳。

spooky /spuki/ (**spookier, spookiest**) ADJ A place that is **spooky** has a frightening atmosphere, and makes you feel that there are ghosts around. 令人毛骨悚然的 [INFORMAL] ❑ *The whole place has a slightly spooky atmosphere.* 整个地方有点令人毛骨悚然的气氛。

spool /spul/ (**spools**) N-COUNT A **spool** is a round object onto which thread, tape, or film can be wound, especially before it is put into a machine. (线、磁带或胶卷的) 卷轴 ❑ *...the hissing of a tape rewinding on its spool.* …磁带在卷轴上倒转时的嘶嘶声。

spoon /spun/ (**spoons, spooning, spooned**) 1 N-COUNT A **spoon** is an object used for eating, stirring, and serving food. One end of it is shaped like a shallow bowl and it has a long handle. 勺；匙 ❑ *He stirred his coffee with a spoon.* 他用匙搅了搅咖啡。 2 V-T If you **spoon** food into something, you put it there with a spoon. 用勺舀；用匙舀 ❑ *He spooned instant coffee into two of the mugs.* 他用勺把速溶咖啡舀进了两个杯子里。

→ see **silverware**

spo·rad·ic /spəræ̱dɪk/ ADJ **Sporadic** occurrences of something happen at irregular intervals. 零星的 ❑ *...a year of sporadic fighting in the north of the country.* …该国北部有零星战火的一年。 ●**spo·radi·cal·ly** ADV 零星地 [ADV with v] ❑ *The distant thunder from the coast continued sporadically.* 远处海岸仍然零星地传来雷声。

sport ♦♦◇ /spɔ̱rt/ (**sports**) N-VAR **Sports** are games such as football and basketball and other competitive leisure activities which need physical effort and skill. 体育运动 ❑ *I chose boxing because it is my favorite sport.* 我选择了拳击，因为那是我最喜爱的运动。 ❑ *She excels at sports.* 她在体育运动方面很优秀。

sport·ing /spɔ̱rtɪŋ/ ADJ **Sporting** means relating to sports or used for sports. 与体育运动有关的；体育运动用的 [ADJ n] ❑ *...major sporting events, such as the U.S. Open and the World Series.* …主要的体育赛事，例如美国公开赛和世界系列赛。

sports car (**sports cars**) N-COUNT A **sports car** is a low, fast car, usually with room for only two people. 跑车

→ see **car**

sports·man /spɔ̱rtsmən/ (**sportsmen**) N-COUNT A **sportsman** is a man who takes part in sports. 男运动员

sports·woman /spɔ̱rtswʊmən/ (**sportswomen**) N-COUNT A **sportswoman** is a woman who takes part in sports. 女运动员

sporty /spɔ̱rti/ (**sportier, sportiest**) 1 ADJ You can describe a car as **sporty** when it performs like a racing car but can be driven on normal roads. 赛车型的(汽车) ❑ *The steering and braking are exactly what you want from a sporty car.* 转向和刹车装置都完全符合你想要的赛车型汽车的要求。 2 ADJ Someone who is **sporty** likes playing sports. 爱好体育运动的 ❑ *I'm an outdoor, sporty type and don't want to sit behind a desk all day.* 我是个喜爱户外活动、爱好体育运动的人，不想整天坐在桌子后面。

spot ♦♦◇ /spɒ̱t/ (**spots, spotting, spotted**) 1 N-COUNT **Spots** are small, round, colored areas on a surface. 斑点 ❑ *The leaves have yellow areas on the top and underneath are powdery orange spots.* 叶子上端有黄色斑块，下方有粉状橙色斑点。 2 N-COUNT **Spots** on a person's skin are small lumps or marks. (皮肤上的) 小疙瘩；斑

in AM, usually use **pimples**

3 N-COUNT You can refer to a particular place as a **spot**. 地点 ❑ *They stayed at several of the island's top tourist spots.* 他们在岛上几个最好的旅游景点呆过。 4 N-COUNT A **spot** in a television or radio show is a part of it that is regularly reserved for a particular performer or type of entertainment. (电视或广播的) 固定节目档 ❑ *Unsuccessful at screen writing, he got a spot on a CNN show.* 电影剧本创作方面未能成功，之后他在美国有线新闻网得到了一个固定节目档。 5 V-T If you **spot** something or someone, you notice them. 发现 ❑ *Vicenzo failed to spot the error.* 维森佐没能发现这个错误。 6 N-COUNT A **spot of** a liquid is a small amount of it. (液体的) 滴；点 [mainly BRIT] ❑ *Spots of rain had begun to fall.* 雨点已经开始落下来了。 7 PHRASE If you do something **on the spot**, you do it immediately. 当即；当场 ❑ *James was called to see the producer and got the job on the spot.* 詹姆斯被叫去见那个制片人，当即得到了那份工作。 8 **rooted to the spot** → see **rooted**

Word Partnership *spot* 的常用搭配：

ADJ. **good** spot, **perfect** spot, **popular** spot, **quiet** spot, **the right** spot 3
N. **parking** spot, **vacation** spot 3

spot·less /spɒ̱tlɪs/ ADJ Something that is **spotless** is completely clean. 没有污点的；一尘不染的 ❑ *Each morning cleaners make sure everything is spotless.* 每天早上清洁工们确保一切都干干净净。 ●**spot·less·ly** ADV 一尘不染地 [ADV adj] ❑ *The house had huge, spotlessly clean rooms.* 那房子里有着宽敞而且一尘不染的房间。

▲ **spot·light** /spɒ̱tlaɪt/ (**spotlights, spotlighting, spotlighted**) 1 N-COUNT A **spotlight** is a powerful light, for example in a theater, which can be directed so that it lights up a small area. (剧院等的) 聚光灯 2 V-T If something **spotlights** a particular problem or situation, it makes people notice it and think about it. 使备受关注 ❑ *The budget crisis also spotlighted a weakening economy.* 预算

S

危机也使日益衰弱的经济备受关注。 3 PHRASE Someone or something that is **in the spotlight** is getting a great deal of public attention. 瞩目中 ❑ *Webb is back in the spotlight.* 韦布又重新受到瞩目。
→ see **concert**

spouse /spaʊs/ (**spouses**) N-COUNT Someone's **spouse** is the person they are married to. 配偶 ❑ *You, or your spouse, must be at least 60 to participate.* 你或你的配偶至少要有60岁才能加入。

▲ **spout** /spaʊt/ (**spouts, spouting, spouted**) 1 V-T/V-I If something **spouts** liquid or fire, or if liquid or fire **spout** out of something, it comes out very quickly with a lot of force. 喷射(液体、火); (液体、火) 喷射出 ❑ *He replaced the boiler when the last one began to spout flames.* 原来的锅炉开始喷射火焰之后他便更换了一个。 ❑ *The main square has a fountain that spouts water 40 feet into the air.* 主广场有个喷泉，喷水高达40英尺。 2 V-T If you say that a person **spouts** something, you disapprove of them because they say something which you do not agree with or which you think they do not honestly feel. 跌跌不休地说 [DISAPPROVAL] ❑ *My mother would go red in the face and spout bitter recriminations.* 我妈妈会气得脸通红，然后跌跌不休地说些刻薄话。 3 N-COUNT A **spout** is a long, hollow part of a container through which liquids can be poured out easily. (容器的) 嘴; 口 ❑ *She lifted the kettle a little and tilted its spout over the tea-pot.* 她稍稍提起烧水壶，将壶嘴向茶壶倾斜。

sprain /spreɪn/ (**sprains, spraining, sprained**) 1 V-T If you **sprain** a joint such as your ankle or wrist, you accidentally damage it by twisting it or bending it violently. 扭伤 (关节) ❑ *He fell and sprained his ankle.* 他跌了一跤，扭伤了脚踝。 2 N-COUNT A **sprain** is the injury caused by spraining a joint. 扭伤 ❑ *Rubin suffered a right ankle sprain when she rolled over on her ankle.* 鲁宾摔倒时身体压到了脚踝上导致右脚踝扭伤。

sprang /spræŋ/ **Sprang** is the past tense of **spring**. **spring**的过去式

▲ **sprawl** /sprɔːl/ (**sprawls, sprawling, sprawled**) 1 V-I If you **sprawl** somewhere, you sit or lie down with your legs and arms spread out in a careless way. 伸开四肢坐着; 摊开四肢躺着 ❑ *She sprawled on the bed as he had left her, not even moving to cover herself up.* 他离开她后，她摊开四肢躺在床上，甚至懒得动动把自己盖上。 ● PHRASAL VERB **Sprawl out** means the same as **sprawl**. 伸开四肢坐着; 摊开四肢躺着 ❑ *He would take two aspirin and sprawl out on his bed.* 他会吃两片阿斯匹林，然后摊开四肢躺在床上。 2 V-I If you say that a place **sprawls**, you mean that it covers a large area of land. 延伸 ❑ *The State Recreation Area sprawls over 900 acres on the southern tip of Key Biscayne.* 州立休闲区占地九百多英亩，地处基・比斯坎南端。 3 N-UNCOUNT You can use **sprawl** to refer to an area where a city has grown outward in an uncontrolled way. (城市的) 无计划扩张区域 ❑ *The whole urban sprawl of Ankara contains over 2.6 million people.* 整个安卡拉城区总共容纳了260万以上的人口。

spray ♦◇◇ /spreɪ/ (**sprays, spraying, sprayed**) 1 N-VAR **Spray** is a lot of small drops of water which are being thrown into the air. 水雾 ❑ *The moon was casting a rainbow through the spray from the waterfall.* 月光在瀑布溅起的水雾中映出了一道彩虹。 2 N-MASS A **spray** is a liquid kept under pressure in a can or other container, which you can force out in very small drops. 喷剂 ❑ *...hair spray.* …头发喷剂 3 V-T/V-I If you **spray** a liquid somewhere or if it **sprays** somewhere, drops of the liquid cover a place or shower someone. 喷 (液体); (液体) 喷出 ❑ *A sprayer hooked to a tractor can spray five gallons onto ten acres.* 挂在拖拉机上的喷雾器用5加仑液量能喷洒10英亩地。 ❑ *Inmates threw bricks at prison officers who were spraying them with a hose.* 囚犯们朝那些用水管向他们喷水的狱警们抛掷砖头。 4 V-T/V-I If a lot of small things **spray** somewhere or if something **sprays** them, they are scattered somewhere with a lot of force. 使溅出; 溅出 ❑ *A shower of mustard seeds sprayed into the air and fell into the grass.* 许多芥子溅到空中，然后掉进草地里。 ❑ *The intensity of the blaze shattered windows, spraying glass on the streets below.* 熊熊烈焰烧碎了窗户，玻璃碎片飞溅到了下面的街道上。 5 V-T If someone **sprays** bullets somewhere, they fire a lot of bullets at a group of people or things. 大量射出 (子弹) ❑ *He ran to the top of the building, spraying bullets into shoppers below.* 他冲向楼顶，向下面的购物者扫射。 6 V-T If something **is sprayed**, it is painted using paint kept under pressure in a container. 喷漆 [usu passive] ❑ *The bare metal was sprayed with several coats of primer.* 裸露的金属被喷了几层底漆。 7 V-T/V-I When someone **sprays** against insects, they cover plants or crops with a chemical which prevents insects from feeding on them. 给 (作物等) 喷药; 喷药 ❑ *He doesn't spray against pests or diseases.* 他没有喷农药来防治害虫或疾病。 ❑ *Confine the use of insecticides to the evening and do not spray plants that are in flower.* 只限晚间使用杀虫剂，并且不要对花期植物喷药。 8 N-COUNT A **spray** is a piece of equipment for spraying water or another liquid, especially over growing plants. 喷雾器 ❑ *Farmers can use the spray to kill weeds without harming the soy crop.* 农民们能用喷雾器来除草而不伤大豆作物。

Word Partnership *spray* 的常用搭配:
N. spray **bottle**, **bug** spray, spray **can**, **hair** spray, **pepper** spray 2
spray **with water** 3

spread ♦♦◇ /spred/ (**spreads, spreading, spread**) 1 V-T If you **spread** something somewhere, you open it out or arrange it over a place or surface, so that all of it can be seen or used easily. 铺开 ❑ *She spread a towel on the sand and lay on it.* 她把一块浴巾铺在沙地上，然后躺在上面。 ● PHRASAL VERB **Spread out** means the same as **spread**. 铺开 (同**spread**) ❑ *He extracted several glossy prints and spread them out on a low coffee table.* 他抽出几张光面照片铺在一张矮咖啡桌上。 2 V-T If you **spread** your arms, hands, fingers, or legs, you stretch them out until they are far apart. 伸展开 (手臂、手、手指、腿等) ❑ *Sitting on the floor, spread your legs as far as they will go without overstretching.* 坐在地板上，尽可能分开双腿，但不要过度拉伸。 ● PHRASAL VERB **Spread out** means the same as **spread**. 伸展开 ❑ *David made a gesture, spreading out his hands as if he were showing that he had no explanation to make.* 大卫做了个手势，双手一摊，似乎表示他没有什么可解释的。 3 V-T If you **spread** a substance on a surface or **spread** the surface **with** the substance, you put a thin layer of the substance over the surface. 摊; 抹; 敷 ❑ *Spread the mixture in the cake pan and bake for 30 minutes.* 将该混合物摊在蛋糕烤盘里，烤30分钟。 4 V-T/V-I If something **spreads** or **is spread** by people, it gradually reaches or affects a larger and larger area or more and more people. 使扩散; 扩散; 传播 ❑ *The industrial revolution, which started a couple of hundred years ago in Europe, is now spreading across the world.* 几百年前始于欧洲的工业革命现在正向全世界扩散。 ❑ *...the sense of fear spreading in residential neighborhoods.* …在住宅区蔓延的恐惧感。 ● N-SING **Spread** is also a noun. 扩散; 传播 ❑ *The greatest hope for reform is the gradual spread of information.* 改革的最大希望就是信息的逐渐传播。 5 V-T/V-I If something such as a liquid, gas, or smoke **spreads** or **is spread**, it moves outward in all directions so that it covers a larger area. 使蔓延; 蔓延 ❑ *Fire spread rapidly after a chemical truck exploded.* 一辆装有化学品的卡车爆炸后火势迅速蔓延开来。 ❑ *A dark red stain was spreading across his shirt.* 一个暗红色的污渍正在他的衬衫上渗开。 ● N-SING **Spread** is also a noun. 蔓延 ❑ *The situation was complicated by the spread of a serious forest fire.* 形势因一场严重的森林火灾的蔓延而复杂化了。 6 V-T If you **spread** something **over** a period of time, it takes place regularly or continuously over that period, rather than happening at one time. 分散 (于某一时段内) ❑ *There seems to be little difference whether you eat all your calorie allowance at once, or spread it over the day.* 无论你是一次性吃完全天的卡路里限量还是分散在一天里吃，似乎没多大区别。 7 V-T If you **spread** something such as wealth or work, you distribute it evenly or equally. 均分 ❑ *...policies that spread the state's wealth more evenly.* …更加平均地分配国家财富的政策。 ● N-SING **Spread** is also a noun. 均分 ❑ *There are easier ways to encourage the even spread of wealth.* 有更简单的方法来促进财富的平均分配。 8 N-SING **A spread of** ideas, interests, or other things is a wide variety of them. 多样 ❑ *A topic-based approach can be hard to assess in schools with a typical spread of ability.* 在以典型的能力多元化为特征的学校里很难评估一种基于话题的教学方法。 9 N-COUNT A **spread** is two pages of a book, magazine, or newspaper that are opposite each other when you open it at a particular place. (书籍、杂志、报纸等的) 相对的两页 ❑ *There was a double-page spread of a dinner for 46 people.* 有一篇关于46人共进晚餐的横贯两版的文章。 10 N-SING **Spread** is used to refer to the difference between the price that a seller wants someone to pay for a particular stock or share and the price that the buyer is willing to pay. (股票买卖的) 价差 [BUSINESS] ❑ *Market makers earn their livings from the spread between buying and selling prices.* 炒股者赚取股票买卖的价格差。 11 **to spread** your **wings** → see **wing**

▸ **spread out** 1 PHRASAL VERB If people, animals, or vehicles **spread out**, they move apart from each other. 散开 ❑ *Felix watched his men move like soldiers, spreading out into two teams.* 费利克斯看着他的下属像士兵一样移动，散开成两队。 2 PHRASAL VERB If something such as a city or forest **spreads out**, it gets larger and gradually begins to covers a larger area. (城市、森林等) 延伸; 扩展 ❑ *Cities such as Tokyo are spreading out.* 像东京这样的城市正在扩展。 3 → see **spread 1, 2**

Thesaurus *spread* 另参见:
V. arrange, disperse, prepare 1
N. range, variety 8

Word Partnership *spread* 的常用搭配:
ADV. spread **evenly** 1 3 5 7
spread **quickly**, spread **rapidly**, spread **widely** 1 4 5
N. spread **an epidemic**, spread **fear**, **fires** spread, spread **an infection**, spread **a message**, spread **news**, spread **rumors**, spread **technology**, spread **a virus** 4
V. **continue to** spread, **prevent/stop the** spread **of** *something* 4 5

spread out ADJ If people or things are **spread out**, they are a long way apart. 相距很远的; 分散的 ❑ *The Kurds are spread out across five nations.* 库尔德人分散在5个国家。

▲ **spread·sheet** /sprɛdʃit/ (**spreadsheets**) N-COUNT A **spreadsheet** is a computer program that is used for displaying and dealing with numbers. Spreadsheets are used mainly for financial planning. 电子制表 [COMPUTING]

spree /spri/ (**sprees**) N-COUNT If you spend a period of time doing something in an excessive way, you can say that you are going **on** a particular kind of **spree**. 放纵 ❑ *Some people went on a spending spree in December to beat the new tax.* 一些人在12月份抢在新税收政策实施前疯狂消费。

spring ♦♦◊ /sprɪŋ/ (**springs, springing, sprang, sprung**) 1 N-VAR **Spring** is the season between winter and summer when the weather becomes warmer and plants start to grow again. 春季 ❑ *They are planning to move house next spring.* 他们在计划明年春天搬家。 2 N-COUNT A **spring** is a spiral of wire which returns to its original shape after it is pressed or pulled. 弹簧 ❑ *Unfortunately, as a standard mattress wears, the springs soften and so do not support your spine.* 不幸的是，当一张标准床垫用旧后，其弹簧变软，因而不能支撑你的背脊。 3 N-COUNT A **spring** is a place where water comes up through the ground. It is also the water that comes from that place. 泉; 泉水 ❑ *To the north are the hot springs.* 北面是温泉。 4 V-I When a person or animal **springs**, they jump upward or forward suddenly or quickly. (人、动物) 跳 ❑ *He sprang to his feet, grabbing his keys off the coffee table.* 他跳了起来，从咖啡桌上抓起他的钥匙。 ❑ *The lion roared once and sprang.* 狮子吼了一声，跳了起来。 5 V-I If something **springs** in a particular direction, it moves suddenly and quickly. 弹 (向某方向) ❑ *Sadly when the lid of the trunk sprang open, it was empty.* 可惜，当后备箱盖弹开时，里面是空的。 6 V-I If one thing **springs from** another thing, it is the result of it. 起源 ❑ *Ethiopia's art springs from its early Christian as well as its Muslim heritage.* 埃塞俄比亚的艺术起源于其早期的基督教和穆斯林教遗产。 7 V-T If you **spring** some news or a surprise **on** someone, you tell them something that they did not expect to hear, without warning them. 出其不意地告知; 冷不防给 ❑ *McLaren sprang a new idea on him.* 麦克拉伦突然告诉他一个新想法。 8 to **spring to mind** → see **mind**
→ see **river**

▸ **spring up** PHRASAL VERB If something **springs up**, it suddenly appears or begins to exist. 冒出; 涌出 ❑ *New theaters and arts centers sprang up all over the country.* 新的剧院和艺术中心在全国雨后春笋般涌现出来。

Word Partnership *spring* 的常用搭配:
ADJ. **early** spring, **last** spring, **late** spring, **next** spring 1
cold spring, **hot** spring, **warm** spring 1 3
N. spring **day**, spring **flowers**, spring **rains**, spring **semester**, spring **training**, spring **weather** 1
spring **water** 3

spring·board /sprɪŋbɔrd/ (**springboards**) 1 N-COUNT If something is a **springboard for** something else, it makes it possible for that thing to happen or start. (使某事得以开始的) 跳板; 助推因素 ❑ *The 1981 budget was the springboard for an economic miracle.* 1981年的预算造就了一场经济奇迹。 2 N-COUNT A **springboard** is a flexible board from which you jump into a swimming pool or onto a piece of gymnastic equipment. (游泳或体操运动中的) 跳板

★ **sprin·kle** /sprɪŋkᵊl/ (**sprinkles, sprinkling, sprinkled**) 1 V-T If you **sprinkle** a thing **with** something such as a liquid or powder, you scatter the liquid or powder over it. (给…) 洒 (液体); (给…) 撒 (粉末状物) ❑ *Sprinkle the meat with salt and place in the pan.* 给肉撒点盐，然后放进平锅里。 ❑ *At the festival, candles are blessed and sprinkled with holy water.* 在节日里，蜡烛被圣化并被洒上圣水。 2 V-T If something **is sprinkled with** particular things, it has a few of them throughout it and they are far apart from each other. 零星分布 ❑ *Unfortunately, the text is sprinkled with errors.* 遗憾的是，文本有零星的错误。

sprint /sprɪnt/ (**sprints, sprinting, sprinted**) 1 N-SING **The sprint** is a short, fast running race. 短跑赛 ❑ *Rob Harmeling won the sprint in Bordeaux.* 罗布•哈梅林赢得了波尔多短跑赛。 2 N-COUNT A **sprint** is a short race in which the competitors run, drive, ride, or swim very fast. (跑、驾车、骑马、游泳等) 短程赛 ❑ *Lewis will compete in both sprints in Stuttgart.* 刘易斯将参加在斯图加特举行的两项短程赛。 3 N-SING A **sprint** is a fast run that someone does, either at the end of a race or because they are in a hurry. 冲刺; 快跑 ❑ *Gilles Delion, of France, won the Tour of Lombardy in a sprint finish at Monza yesterday.* 法国选手吉勒斯•德利翁昨天在蒙扎最后冲刺时赢得了伦巴第巡回赛冠军。 4 V-I If you **sprint**, you run or ride as fast as you can over a short distance. 快速奔跑; 冲刺 ❑ *Sergeant Horne sprinted to the car.* 霍恩中士冲向那辆汽车。

sprint·er /sprɪntər/ (**sprinters**) N-COUNT A **sprinter** is a person who takes part in short, fast races. 短程赛选手

▲ **sprout** /spraʊt/ (**sprouts, sprouting, sprouted**) 1 V-I When plants, vegetables, or seeds **sprout**, they produce new shoots or leaves. (植物、蔬菜、种子) 发芽 ❑ *It only takes a few days for beans to sprout.* 豆子只需几天就会发芽。 2 V-I When leaves, shoots, or plants **sprout** somewhere, they grow there. (叶子、芽、植株) 长出 ❑ *Leaf-shoots were beginning to sprout on the hawthorn.* 叶芽开始在山楂树上长出来。 3 V-T/V-I If something such as hair **sprouts** from a person or animal, or if they **sprout** it, it grows on them. (人、动物) 长出 (毛发等); (毛发等) 长出来 [no passive] ❑ *She is very old now, with little, round, wire-rimmed glasses and whiskers sprouting from her chin.* 她现在很老了，戴着小而圆的金属丝框眼镜，下巴长出了胡须。 4 N-COUNT **Sprouts** are vegetables that look like tiny cabbages. They are also called **brussels sprouts**. 抱子甘蓝 (也称作**brussels sprouts**) [usu pl]
→ see **tree**

spruce /sprus/ (**spruces, sprucing, spruced**)

Spruce is both the singular and the plural form.

1 N-VAR A **spruce** is a kind of evergreen tree. 云杉 ❑ *Trees such as spruce, pine, and oak have been planted.* 像云杉、松树和橡树之类的树已经种了。 ❑ *...a young blue spruce.* …一株蓝云杉幼苗。 2 ADJ Someone who is **spruce** is very neat and clean in appearance. (人) 整洁的 ❑ *Chris was looking spruce in his stiff-collared black shirt and new short hair cut.* 克里斯穿着那件衣领挺括的黑衬衫加上新剪的短发，看上去很整洁。

▸ **spruce up** PHRASAL VERB If something **is spruced up**, its appearance is improved. If someone **is spruced up**, they have made themselves look very smart. 收拾整洁 ❑ *Many buildings have been spruced up.* 许多建筑物已经焕然一新。

sprung /sprʌŋ/ **Sprung** is the past participle of **spring**. **spring**的过去分词

spun /spʌn/ **Spun** is the past tense and past participle of **spin**. **spin**的过去式和过去分词
→ see **wheel**

spur ♦◊◊ /spɜr/ (**spurs, spurring, spurred**) 1 V-T If one thing **spurs** you **to** do another, it encourages you to do it. 鼓动; 激励 ❑ *It's the money that spurs these fishermen to risk a long ocean journey in their flimsy boats.* 是金钱驱使这些渔民驾驶单薄的小船冒险出海远航。 ● PHRASAL VERB **Spur on** means the same as **spur**. 鼓动; 激励 (同**spur**) ❑ *Their attitude, rather than reining him back, only seemed to spur Philip on.* 他们的态度非但没令菲利普回头，似乎只是激励他继续下去。 2 V-T If something **spurs** a change or event, it makes it happen faster or sooner. 使更快发生; 加速 [JOURNALISM] ❑ *The administration may put more emphasis on spurring economic growth.* 政府可能会更加重视经济的加快增长。 3 N-COUNT Something that acts as a **spur to** something else encourages a person or organization to do that thing or makes it happen more quickly. 促进因素; 推动 ❑ *...a belief in competition as a spur to efficiency.* …一种认为竞争能促进效率提高的观点。 4 PHRASE If you do something **on the spur of the moment**,

S

you do it suddenly, without planning it beforehand. 一时冲动之下 ❑ *They admitted they had taken a vehicle on the spur of the moment.* 他们承认一时冲动之下偷了一辆车。

Word Partnership *spur* 的常用搭配：

N. spur **demand**, spur **development**, spur **economic growth**, spur **the economy**, spur **interest**, spur **investment**, spur **sales** **2**

spu·ri·ous /spyʊəriəs/ **1** ADJ Something that is **spurious** seems to be genuine, but is false. 似是而非的 [DISAPPROVAL] ❑ *He was arrested in 1979 on spurious corruption charges.* 他于1979年因似是而非的腐败指控被拘捕。 **2** ADJ A **spurious** argument or way of reasoning is incorrect, and so the conclusion is probably incorrect. (论据、推理) 不正确的 [DISAPPROVAL] ❑ *...a spurious framework for analysis.* …一个不正确的分析框架。

spurn /spɜrn/ (**spurns, spurning, spurned**) V-T If you **spurn** someone or something, you reject them. 拒绝 ❑ *He spurned the advice of management consultants.* 他拒绝了管理顾问的劝告。

▲ **spurt** /spɜrt/ (**spurts, spurting, spurted**) **1** V-T/V-I When liquid or fire **spurts** from somewhere, it comes out quickly in a thin, powerful stream. 喷出 ❑ *He hit her on the head, causing her to spurt blood.* 他击中了她的头部，使她血流如注。 ❑ *I saw flames spurt from the roof.* 我看见火焰从房顶冒出来。 ● PHRASAL VERB **Spurt out** means the same as **spurt**. 喷出 ❑ *When the washing machine spurts out water at least we can mop it up.* 洗衣机溅出水时，我们至少可以把水擦掉。 **2** N-COUNT A **spurt of** liquid is a stream of it which comes out of something very forcefully. (喷射出的一) 股 ❑ *A spurt of diesel came from one valve and none from the other.* 一股股柴油从一个阀门喷涌而出，但另一个没有。 **3** N-COUNT A **spurt of** activity, effort, or emotion is a sudden, brief period of intense activity, effort, or emotion. (活动、努力、情感的) 迸发 ❑ *The average boy of 14 years old is only beginning his adolescent growth spurt.* 一般14岁的男孩才刚刚开始他青春期的迅猛发育。 **4** V-I If someone or something **spurts** somewhere, they suddenly increase their speed for a short while in order to get there. 冲刺 ❑ *The back wheels spun and the van spurted up the last few feet.* 后轮旋转起来，小货车冲过了最后几英尺。 **5** PHRASE If something happens **in spurts**, there are periods of activity followed by periods in which it does not happen. 时有时无地；一阵阵地 ❑ *The deals came in spurts: three in 1977, none in 1978, three more in 1979.* 交易时有时无：1977年3笔，1978年没有，1979年又有3笔。

spy /spaɪ/ (**spies, spying, spied**) **1** N-COUNT A **spy** is a person whose job is to find out secret information about another country or organization. 间谍 ❑ *He was jailed for five years as an alleged spy.* 他被指控为间谍而被监禁了5年。 **2** ADJ A **spy** satellite or **spy** plane obtains secret information about another country by taking photographs from the sky. 承担间谍任务的 (卫星、飞机) [ADJ n] ❑ *...pictures from unmanned spy planes operated by the U.S. military.* …美国军方操控的无人间谍飞机拍摄到的图片。 **3** V-I Someone who **spies for** a country or organization tries to find out secret information about another country or organization. (为某国、某组织) 从事间谍活动 ❑ *The agent spied for East Germany for more than twenty years.* 该特工为东德从事了二十多年的间谍活动。 ❑ *East and West are still spying on one another.* 东方和西方仍在相互暗中监视着。 ● **spy·ing** N-UNCOUNT 从事间谍活动 ❑ *...a ten-year sentence for spying.* …因从事间谍活动被判的10年监禁。 **4** V-I If you **spy on** someone, you watch them secretly. 秘密监视 ❑ *That day he spied on her while pretending to work on the shrubs.* 那天他假装修剪灌木，却秘密地监视着她。

sq. **sq.** is used as a written abbreviation for **square** when you are giving the measurement of an area. 平方的 ❑ *The building provides about 25,500 sq. ft. of air-conditioned offices.* 这座建筑提供大约2.55万平方英尺的空调办公室。

squab·ble /skwɒbᵊl/ (**squabbles, squabbling, squabbled**) V-RECIP When people **squabble**, they quarrel about something that is not really important. (为琐事) 争吵 ❑ *Mother is devoted to Dad although they squabble all the time.* 妈妈深爱着爸爸，虽然他们总是为琐事争吵。 ❑ *The children were squabbling over the remote-control for the television.* 孩子们正在为争夺电视机的遥控器发生口角。 ● **squab·bling** N-UNCOUNT 争吵 ❑ *In recent months its government has been paralyzed by political squabbling.* 最近几个月其政府因为政治争吵已经瘫痪了。 ● N-COUNT **Squabble** is also a noun. 争吵 ❑ *There have been minor squabbles about phone bills.* 为电话账单已闹过口角。

★ **squad** ♦◇◇ /skwɒd/ (**squads**) **1** N-COUNT A **squad** is a section of a police force that is responsible for dealing with a particular type of crime. (专门处理某类犯罪的) 警察分队 ❑ *The building was evacuated and the bomb squad called.* 那座大楼进行了人员疏散，并通知了拆弹小组。 **2** N-COUNT A **squad** is a group of players from which a sports team will be chosen. (将从中挑选运动员组队参赛的) 运动代表队 ❑ *The American squad has pulled out of the four-day basketball tournament.* 美国运动代表队已经退出了为期4天的篮球锦标赛。

▲ **squad·ron** /skwɒdrən/ (**squadrons**) N-COUNT-COLL A **squadron** is a section of one of the armed forces, especially the air force. (尤指空军的) 中队 ❑ *A squadron of F-15 fighters is on its way home.* 一个F-15战斗机中队正在返程途中。

squal·id /skwɒlɪd/ ADJ A **squalid** place is dirty, untidy, and in bad condition. 脏乱的 ❑ *The early industrial cities were squalid and unhealthy places.* 早期的工业城市曾是些又脏又乱、不利健康的地方。

squal·or /skwɒlər/ N-UNCOUNT You can refer to very dirty, unpleasant conditions as **squalor**. 脏乱环境 ❑ *He was out of work and living in squalor.* 他失业了，生活在脏乱不堪的环境中。

squan·der /skwɒndər/ (**squanders, squandering, squandered**) V-T If you **squander** money, resources, or opportunities, you waste them. 浪费 (金钱、资源或机会) ❑ *Hobbs didn't squander his money on flashy cars or other vices.* 霍布斯没有把钱挥霍在奢华汽车或其他恶习上。

square ♦♦◇ /skwɛər/ (**squares, squaring, squared**) **1** N-COUNT A **square** is a shape with four sides that are all the same length and four corners that are all right angles. 正方形 ❑ *Serve the cake warm or at room temperature, cut in squares.* 端上温的或房间温度的蛋糕，把它切成正方形。 ❑ *There was a calendar on the wall, with large squares around the dates.* 墙上有一副日历，日期周围是大的方框。 **2** N-COUNT; N-IN-NAMES In a town or city, a **square** is a flat open place, often in the shape of a square. 广场 ❑ *The house is located in one of the city's prettiest squares.* 该房子位于市区最漂亮的广场之一。 **3** ADJ Something that is **square** has a shape the same as a square or similar to a square. 正方形的；方形的 ❑ *Round tables seat more people in the same space as a square table.* 在同一空间里，圆桌比方桌可以坐更多的人。 **4** ADJ **Square** is used before units of length when referring to the area of something. For example, if something is three feet long and two feet wide, its area is six square feet. 平方的 (用于长度单位前表示面积) [ADJ n] ❑ *The new complex will provide 10 million square feet of office space.* 这座新的综合建筑群将提供1千万平方英尺的办公空间。 **5** ADJ **Square** is used after units of length when you are giving the length of each side of something that is square in shape. 平方的 (用于长度单位前表示某面面积) [amount ADJ] ❑ *...a linen cushion cover, 45 cm. square.* …一个亚麻坐垫套子，45平方厘米。 **6** V-T To **square** a number means to multiply it by itself. For example, **3 squared** is 3 x 3, or 9. **3 squared** is usually written as 3^2. 乘二次方 ❑ *Take the time in seconds, square it, and multiply by 5.12.* 以秒计时，乘二次方，然后乘以5.12。 **7** N-COUNT The **square of** a number is the number produced when you multiply that number by itself. For example, the square of 3 is 9. 二次方；平方 ❑ *...the square of the speed of light, an exceedingly large number.* …光速的平方，一个极大的数字。 **8** V-T/V-I If you **square** two different ideas or actions **with** each other or if they **square with** each other, they fit or match each other. 使相适配；适配 ❑ *That explanation squares with the facts, doesn't it.* 那种解释与事实相符，是吧。 **9** V-T If you **square** something **with** someone, you ask their permission or check with them that what you are doing is acceptable to them. (就某事) 征求 (某人) 许可 ❑ *I squared it with Dan, who said it was all right so long as I was back next Monday morning.* 我就此事征求过丹的许可，他说只要我能在下周一上午回来就行。 **10** → see also **squarely** **11** PHRASE If you are **back to square one**, you have to start dealing with something from the beginning again because the way you were dealing with it has failed. (因处理失败而) 重新开始 ❑ *If your complaint is not upheld, you may feel you are back to square one.* 如果你的投诉没有得到支持，你可能觉得你又得从新开始。 **12** **fair and square** → see **fair** → see **shape**

square·ly /skwɛərli/ **1** ADV **Squarely** means directly or in the middle, rather than indirectly or at an angle. 垂直正对地；正中地 [ADV with v] ❑ *I kept the gun aimed squarely at his eyes.* 我一直把枪直直瞄准他的眼睛。 **2** ADV If something such as blame or responsibility lies **squarely** with someone, they are definitely the person responsible. 明确地 [ADV with v] ❑ *The president put the blame squarely on his opponent.* 总统明确地指责他的对手。

square root (**square roots**) N-COUNT The **square root of** a number is another number which produces the first number when it is multiplied by itself. For example, the square root of 16 is 4. 平方根

▲**squash** /skwɒʃ/ (**squashes, squashing, squashed**) 1 V-T If someone or something **is squashed**, they are pressed or crushed with such force that they become injured or lose their shape. 压扁；压碎 ❑ *Robert was lucky to escape with just a broken foot after being squashed against a fence by a car.* 罗伯特很幸运，被一辆轿车挤压到一排栅栏上只折了一只脚而脱了险。 ❑ *Whole neighborhoods have been squashed flat by shelling.* 整个的居住区已经被炮火夷为平地。 2 ADJ If people or things are **squashed into** a place, they are put or pushed into a place where there is not enough room for them to be. 挤进去了的 [v-link ADJ "into" n] ❑ *There were 2,000 people squashed into her recent show.* 有2千人挤进了她最近的演出现场。 3 V-T If you **squash** something that is causing you trouble, you put a stop to it, often by force. 镇压 ❑ *The troops would stay in position to squash the first murmur of trouble.* 部队将严阵以待，一有骚乱声音即进行镇压。 4 N-VAR A **squash** is one of a family of vegetables that have thick skin and soft or firm flesh inside. 瓜类蔬菜 5 N-UNCOUNT **Squash** is a game in which two players hit a small rubber ball against the walls of a court using rackets. 壁球 ❑ *I also play squash.* 我也玩壁球。 6 N-SING If you say that getting a number of people into a small space is **a squash**, you mean that it is only just possible for them all to get into it. 塞满 [BRIT, INFORMAL]

in AM, use **squeeze**

▲**squat** /skwɒt/ (**squats, squatting, squatted**) 1 V-I If you **squat**, you lower yourself toward the ground, balancing on your feet with your legs bent. 蹲下 ❑ *We squatted beside the pool and watched the diver sink slowly down.* 我们蹲在池边，看潜水员慢慢沉下水。 ● PHRASAL VERB **Squat down** means the same as **squat**. 蹲下 ❑ *Albert squatted down and examined it.* 阿尔伯特蹲下仔细查看它。 ● N-SING **Squat** is also a noun. 蹲下 ❑ *He bent to a squat and gathered the puppies on his lap.* 他弯腰蹲下，把小狗们聚揽到他的大腿上。 2 ADJ If you describe someone or something as **squat**, you mean they are short and thick, usually in an unattractive way. 矮胖的 ❑ *Eddie was a short squat fellow in his forties with thinning hair.* 埃迪是个矮胖的人，四十来岁，头发稀疏。 3 V-I People who **squat** occupy an unused building or unused land without having a legal right to do so. (对某空建筑、空地) 非法占据 ❑ *You can't simply wander around squatting on other people's property.* 你不能只是四处游荡，非法占据他人房产。

squat·ter /skwɒtər/ (**squatters**) N-COUNT A **squatter** is someone who lives in an unused building without having a legal right to do so and without paying any rent or any property tax. 非法占据者 ❑ *...another violent clash as police evicted squatters from empty buildings.* …警察驱逐空楼里的非法占据者时引发的又一次暴力冲突。

▲**squeak** /skwik/ (**squeaks, squeaking, squeaked**) V-I If something or someone **squeaks**, they make a short, high-pitched sound. 发出短而尖的声音 ❑ *My boots squeaked a little as I walked.* 我走路时靴子有点嘎吱响。 ❑ *The door squeaked open.* 门嘎吱一声开了。 ● N-COUNT **Squeak** is also a noun. 短而尖的声音 ❑ *He gave an outraged squeak.* 他愤怒地发出一声急促的尖叫。

squeal /skwil/ (**squeals, squealing, squealed**) V-I If someone or something **squeals**, they make a long, high-pitched sound. 发出长而尖的声音 ❑ *Jennifer squealed with delight and hugged me.* 珍尼弗高兴地尖叫着，拥抱了我。 ● N-COUNT **Squeal** is also a noun. 长而尖的声音 ❑ *At that moment there was a squeal of brakes and the angry blowing of a car horn.* 那一刻响起了一阵刺耳的刹车声和汽车喇叭愤怒的鸣笛声。

squeam·ish /skwimɪʃ/ ADJ If you are **squeamish**, you are easily upset by unpleasant sights or situations. 神经质的 ❑ *I'm terribly squeamish. I can't bear gory films.* 我很神经质。我不能忍受血腥恐怖片。

squeeze ♦◇◇ /skwiz/ (**squeezes, squeezing, squeezed**) 1 V-T If you **squeeze** something, you press it firmly, usually with your hands. (常指用手) 挤压；紧捏 ❑ *He squeezed her arm reassuringly.* 他安慰地捏了捏她的手臂。 ● N-COUNT **Squeeze** is also a noun. 紧捏；挤压 ❑ *I liked her way of reassuring you with a squeeze of the hand.* 我喜欢她捏捏手来安慰人的方式。 2 V-T If you **squeeze** a liquid or a soft substance out of an object, you get the liquid or substance out by pressing the object. 挤；压榨 (液体等) ❑ *Joe put the plug in the sink and squeezed some detergent over the dishes.* 乔把塞子插进水槽，往盘子上挤了些洗洁精。 3 V-T/V-I If you **squeeze** a person or thing somewhere or if they **squeeze** there, they manage to get through or into a small space. 塞进；挤进 ❑ *They lowered him gradually into the cockpit. Somehow they squeezed him in the tight space, and strapped him in.* 他们缓缓地把他向下放入驾驶舱，设法把他塞进那狭小的空间，并给系上了安全带。 4 N-SING If you say that getting a number of people into a small space is **a squeeze**, you mean that it is only just possible for them all to get into it. 满塞 [INFORMAL] ❑ *It was a squeeze in the car with five of them.* 他们5个人把这小车全部塞满。

▲**squid** /skwɪd/ (**squids**)

Squid can also be used as the plural form.

N-COUNT A **squid** is a sea creature with a long soft body and many soft arms called tentacles. 鱿鱼 ● N-UNCOUNT **Squid** is pieces of this creature eaten as food. (食用的) 鱿鱼 ❑ *Add the prawns and squid and cook for 2 minutes.* 加入虾和鱿鱼，煮2分钟。

squint /skwɪnt/ (**squints, squinting, squinted**) 1 V-I If you **squint at** something, you look at it with your eyes partly closed. 眯着眼看 ❑ *The girl squinted at the photograph.* 女孩眯着眼看了看照片。 ❑ *The bright sunlight made me squint.* 强烈的阳光使我眯起了眼。 2 N-COUNT If someone has **a squint**, their eyes look in different directions from each other. 斜视 ❑ *...a pimple-faced man with a squint.* …一个脸上有粉刺、眼睛斜视的男人。

squirm /skwɜrm/ (**squirms, squirming, squirmed**) 1 V-I If you **squirm**, you move your body from side to side, usually because you are nervous or uncomfortable. (因紧张或不适) 扭来扭去 ❑ *He had squirmed and wriggled and screeched when his father had washed his face.* 父亲给他洗脸时，他扭着身子尖叫着。 ❑ *He gave a feeble shrug and tried to squirm free.* 他微微地耸了耸肩，扭动着试图挣脱。 2 V-I If you **squirm**, you are very embarrassed or ashamed. 感到窘迫；感到羞愧 ❑ *Mentioning religion is a sure way to make him squirm.* 提及宗教肯定会使他感到窘迫。

▲**squir·rel** /skwɜrəl/ (**squirrels**) N-COUNT A **squirrel** is a small animal with a long furry tail. Squirrels live mainly in trees. 松鼠

squirt /skwɜrt/ (**squirts, squirting, squirted**) 1 V-T/V-I If you **squirt** a liquid somewhere or if it **squirts** somewhere, the liquid comes out of a narrow opening in a thin fast stream. 挤；喷出 ❑ *Norman cut open his pie and squirted tomato sauce into it.* 诺曼切开他的馅饼，往里面挤了番茄酱。 ● N-COUNT **Squirt** is also a noun. 挤；喷 ❑ *It just needs a little squirt of oil.* 它只需喷点油。 2 V-T If you **squirt** something **with** a liquid, you squirt the liquid at it. (用某液体) 喷 (某物) ❑ *They squirted each other with soapy water.* 他们相互喷洒肥皂水。

St.

The form **SS** is used as the plural for meaning 2.

1 **St.** is a written abbreviation for **Street**. 街 ❑ *...116 Princess St.* …公主街116号。 2 **St.** is a written abbreviation for **Saint**. 圣… ❑ *...St. Thomas.* …圣托马斯。

★**stab** /stæb/ (**stabs, stabbing, stabbed**) 1 V-T If someone **stabs** you, they push a knife or sharp object into your body. (用刀等利器) 刺；捅 ❑ *Somebody stabbed him in the stomach.* 有人刺了他的腹部。 ❑ *Dean tried to stab him with a screwdriver.* 迪安试图用一把螺丝刀捅他。 2 V-T/V-I If you **stab** something or **stab at** it, you push at it with your finger or with something pointed that you are holding. (用手指或手中尖物) 戳；捅；按 ❑ *Bess stabbed a slice of cucumber.* 贝斯戳起一片黄瓜。 ❑ *Goldstone flipped through the pages and stabbed his thumb at the paragraph he was looking for.* 戈德斯通快速翻动书页，用拇指按住他正在寻找的段落。 3 N-SING If you have **a stab at** something, you try to do it. 尝试 [INFORMAL] ❑ *Several tennis stars have had a stab at acting.* 几位网球明星曾尝试过演戏。 4 N-SING You can refer to a sudden, usually unpleasant feeling as **a stab of** that feeling. 刺痛 [LITERARY] ❑ *...a stab of pain just above his eye.* …他眼睛上方的一阵刺痛。 5 PHRASE If you say that someone **has stabbed** you **in the back**, you mean that they have done something very harmful to you when you thought that you could trust them. You can refer to an action of this kind as **a stab in the back**. 在背后捅某人一刀 ❑ *She felt betrayed, as though her daughter had stabbed her in the back.* 她感到被出卖了，仿佛是她的女儿在背后捅了她一刀。 6 **a stab in the dark** → see **dark**

stab·bing /stæbɪŋ/ (**stabbings**) 1 N-COUNT A **stabbing** is an incident in which someone stabs someone else with a knife. 持刀伤人事件 ❑ *...the victim of a stabbing.* …持刀伤人事件的受害者。 2 ADJ A **stabbing** pain is a sudden sharp pain. (疼痛) 突然而剧烈的 [ADJ n] ❑ *He was struck by a stabbing pain in his midriff.* 他突然感到腹部一阵剧痛。

★**sta·bi·lise** /steɪbɪlaɪz/ [BRIT] → see **stabilize**

sta·bil·ity /stəbɪlɪti/ → see **stable**

S

★ **sta·bi·lize** /steɪbɪlaɪz/ (**stabilizes, stabilizing, stabilized**)
in BRIT, also use **stabilise**
V-T/V-I If something **stabilizes**, or **is stabilized**, it becomes stable. 稳定 ❏ *Although her illness is serious, her condition is beginning to stabilize.* 虽然她的病情很严重，但她的情况正开始稳定下来。
● **sta·bi·li·za·tion** /steɪbɪlɪzeɪʃən/ N-UNCOUNT 稳定 ❏ *...the stabilization of property prices.* …房地产价格的稳定。

sta·ble ♦♦◇ /steɪbəl/ (**stabler, stablest, stables**) 1 ADJ If something is **stable**, it is not likely to change or come to an end suddenly. 稳定的 ❏ *The price of oil should remain stable for the rest of 1992.* 石油价格在1992年余下时间里应该保持稳定。 ● **sta·bil·ity** /stəbɪlɪti/ N-UNCOUNT 稳定 ❏ *It was a time of political stability and progress.* 那是一个政治稳定和进步的时期。 2 ADJ If someone has a **stable** personality, they are calm and reasonable and their mood does not change suddenly. 稳重的 ❏ *Their characters are fully formed and they are both very stable children.* 他们的性格已完全定型，俩人都是很稳重的孩子。 3 ADJ You can describe someone who is seriously ill as **stable** when their condition has stopped getting worse. (病情) 稳定的 ❏ *The injured man was in a stable condition.* 那位受伤男子已处于稳定状态。 4 ADJ Chemical substances are described as **stable** when they tend to remain in the same chemical or atomic state. (化学物质) 稳定的 [TECHNICAL] ❏ *The less stable compounds were converted into a compound called Delta-A THC.* 不太稳定的化合物被转变成了一种称为Delta-A THC的化合物。 5 ADJ If an object is **stable**, it is firmly fixed in position and is not likely to move or fall. 稳固的 ❏ *This structure must be stable.* 这种结构一定很稳固。 6 N-COUNT A **stable** or **stables** is a building in which horses are kept. 马厩 7 N-COUNT A **stable** or **stables** is an organization that breeds and trains horses for racing. (养殖并训练赛马的) 养马场 ❏ *Miss Curling won on two horses from Mick Trickey's stable.* 柯林小姐凭借两匹米克·特里克养马场的马获胜了。

stack /stæk/ (**stacks, stacking, stacked**) 1 N-COUNT A **stack of** things is a pile of them. 摞；堆 ❏ *There were stacks of books on the bedside table and floor.* 床头桌上和地板上有一摞摞的书。 2 V-T If you **stack** a number of things, you arrange them in neat piles. 堆放；摞起 ❏ *Mrs. Cathiard was stacking the clean bottles in crates.* 卡提亚夫人当时正在把干净的瓶子堆放到板条箱里。 ● PHRASAL VERB **Stack up** means the same as **stack**. 堆放；摞起 ❏ *He ordered them to stack up pillows behind his back.* 他命令他们在他背后堆放一些枕头。 3 N-PLURAL If you say that someone has **stacks of** something, you mean that they have a lot of it. 堆 [INFORMAL] ❏ *If the job's that good, you'll have stacks of money.* 如果那份工作真那么好，你就会有成堆的钱。 4 PHRASE If you say that **the odds are stacked against** someone, or that particular factors **are stacked against** them, you mean that they are unlikely to succeed in what they want to do because the conditions are not favorable. 形势对某人不利 ❏ *The odds are stacked against civilians getting a fair trial.* 形势对想得到公正判决的平民不利。

> A **stack** of things is usually tidy, and often consists of flat objects placed directly on top of each other. ❏ *...a neat stack of dishes.* A **heap** of things is usually untidy, and often has the shape of a hill or mound. ❏ *Now, the house is a heap of rubble.* A **pile** can be tidy or untidy. ❏ *...a neat pile of clothes.*

sta·dium ♦◇◇ /steɪdiəm/ (**stadiums** or **stadia**) /steɪdiə/ N-COUNT; N-IN-NAMES A **stadium** is a large sports field with rows of seats all around it. (周围有看台的) 体育场 ❏ *...a baseball stadium.* …一个棒球体育场。

staff ♦♦♦ /stæf/ (**staffs, staffing, staffed**) 1 N-COUNT-COLL The **staff** of an organization are the people who work for it. 全体职员 ❏ *The staff were very good.* 员工们都很棒。 ❏ *The outpatient program has a staff of six people.* 这个门诊部有6名员工。 ❏ *...staff members.* …职工。 2 → see also **chief of staff** 3 N-PLURAL People who are part of a particular staff are often referred to as **staff**. 员工 ❏ *10 staff were allocated to the task.* 10名员工被分派做这项任务。 4 V-T If an organization **is staffed by** particular people, they are the people who work for it. 担当(某机构的) 职员 [usu passive] ❏ *They are staffed by volunteers.* 他们的员工都是志愿者。 ● **staffed** ADJ 配备了职员的 [adv ADJ] ❏ *The house allocated to them was pleasant and spacious, and well staffed.* 分给他们的房子既舒适又宽敞，员工也配备良好。

staff·ing /stæfɪŋ/ N-UNCOUNT **Staffing** refers to the number of workers employed to work in a particular organization or building. 配备的职员人数 [BUSINESS] ❏ *Staffing levels in prisons are too low.* 监狱里的人员配备数量太少。

S

stag /stæg/ (**stags**) N-COUNT A **stag** is an adult male deer belonging to one of the larger species of deer. Stags usually have large branch-like horns called antlers. 成年雄鹿

stage ♦♦♦ /steɪdʒ/ (**stages, staging, staged**) 1 N-COUNT A **stage of** an activity, process, or period is one part of it. (活动、过程、时期的) 阶段 ❏ *The way children talk about or express their feelings depends on their age and stage of development.* 孩子们谈论或表达情感的方式取决于他们的年龄和成长阶段。 2 N-COUNT In a theater, the **stage** is an area where actors or other entertainers perform. 舞台 [also "on" N] ❏ *The road crew needed more than 24 hours to move and rebuild the stage after a concert.* 勤务组在每一场音乐会结束后需要24个小时以上的时间搬运和重搭舞台。 3 V-T If someone **stages** a play or other show, they organize and present a performance of it. 将 (戏剧等) 搬上舞台；上演 ❏ *Maya Angelou first staged the play "And I Still Rise" in the late 1970s.* 玛雅·安吉罗在20世纪70年代末首次将戏剧《我仍将奋起》搬上舞台。 4 V-T If you **stage** an event or ceremony, you organize it and usually take part in it. 主办；举行 ❏ *Russian workers have staged a number of strikes in protest at the republic's declaration of independence.* 俄罗斯工人已经举行了多次罢工，抗议该共和国宣布独立。 5 N-SING You can refer to a particular area of activity as a particular **stage**, especially when you are talking about politics. (尤指政治上的) 活动领域；舞台 ❏ *He was finally forced off the political stage last year by the deterioration of his physical condition.* 他最终因身体状况恶化于去年被迫离开了政治舞台。 6 to **set the stage** → see **set**
→ see **concert**

Word Partnership *stage* 的常用搭配：

ADJ.	**advanced** stage, **critical** stage, **crucial** stage, **early** stage, **final** stage, **late/later** stage 1
V.	**reach** a stage 1 **leave the** stage, **take the** stage 2
N.	stage **of development**, stage **of a disease**, stage **of a process** 1 **actors on** stage, **center** stage, **concert** stage, stage **fright**, stage **manager** 2

stag·fla·tion /stægfleɪʃən/ N-UNCOUNT If an economy is suffering from **stagflation**, inflation is high but there is no increase in the demand for goods or in the number of people who have jobs. 滞胀 [BUSINESS] ❏ *Many of the industrialized economies would be pushed into a cycle of stagflation.* 许多工业化经济将被推入到一个滞胀的循环中。

stag·ger /stægər/ (**staggers, staggering, staggered**) 1 V-I If you **stagger**, you walk very unsteadily, for example because you are ill or drunk. (因生病、醉酒等) 摇晃地走；蹒跚 ❏ *He lost his balance, staggered back against the rail and toppled over.* 他失去了平衡，向后趔趄撞在了栏杆上摔倒了。 2 V-T If something **staggers** you, it surprises you very much. 使震惊 ❏ *The whole thing staggers me.* 整件事让我震惊。 ● **stag·gered** ADJ 震惊的 [v-link ADJ] ❏ *I was simply staggered by the heat of the Argentinian high-summer.* 我只是震惊于阿根廷盛夏的高温。 3 V-T To **stagger** things such as people's vacations or hours of work means to arrange them so that they do not all happen at the same time. 错开 (假期或工作时间) ❏ *During the past few years the university has staggered the summer vacation periods for students.* 在过去几年里该大学已经把学生的暑假时间错开了。

stag·ger·ing /stægərɪŋ/ ADJ Something that is **staggering** is very surprising. 令人震惊的 ❏ *...a staggering $900 million in short- and long-term debt.* …令人震惊的9亿美元的短长期债务。

▲ **stag·nant** /stægnənt/ 1 ADJ If something such as a business or society is **stagnant**, there is little activity or change. (经济、社会等) 停滞不前的 [DISAPPROVAL] ❏ *He is seeking advice on how to revive the stagnant economy.* 他正在征求复苏萧条经济的建议。 2 ADJ **Stagnant** water is not flowing, and therefore often smells unpleasant and is dirty. (水) 不流动而腐浊的 ❏ *...a stagnant pond.* …一个死水塘。

▲ **stag·nate** /stægneɪt/ (**stagnates, stagnating, stagnated**) V-I If something such as a business or society **stagnates**, it stops changing or progressing. (商业、社会等) 停滞不前 [DISAPPROVAL] ❏ *Industrial production is stagnating.* 工业生产停滞不前。
● **stag·na·tion** /stægneɪʃən/ N-UNCOUNT 停滞不前 ❏ *...the stagnation of the steel industry.* …钢铁工业的停滞不前。

staid /steɪd/ ADJ If you say that someone or something is **staid**, you mean that they are serious, dull, and rather old-fashioned. 严肃呆板的；过时的 ❏ *...a staid seaside resort.* …一个了无生气的海滨度假地。

stain /steɪn/ (**stains, staining, stained**) 1 N-COUNT A **stain** is a mark on something that is difficult to remove. 污渍 ❑ *Remove stains by soaking in a mild solution of bleach.* 用温和的漂白溶液浸泡以去除污渍。 2 V-T If a liquid **stains** something, the thing becomes colored or marked by the liquid. (在某物上) 留下污渍 ❑ *Some foods can stain the teeth, as of course can smoking.* 某些食物会使牙齿着色，吸烟当然也会。 ●**stained** ADJ 沾了污渍的 ❑ *His clothing was stained with mud.* 他的衣服沾了泥。 ●**-stained** COMB IN ADJ 被…沾染了的 ❑ *...ink-stained fingers.* …沾染了墨水的手指。
→ see **dry-cleaning**

stained glass also **stained-glass** N-UNCOUNT **Stained glass** consists of pieces of glass of different colors which are fitted together to make decorative windows or other objects. 彩色玻璃 ❑ *...the stained glass window in St. John's Cathedral.* …圣约翰大教堂的彩色玻璃窗。

stain·less steel /steɪnlɪs stil/ N-UNCOUNT **Stainless steel** is a metal made from steel and chromium which does not rust. 不锈钢 ❑ *...a stainless steel sink.* …一个不锈钢水槽。
→ see **pan**

stair /stɛər/ (**stairs**) N-PLURAL **Stairs** are a set of steps inside a building which go from one floor to another. (建筑物内楼层之间的) 楼梯 ❑ *Nancy began to climb the stairs.* 南希开始爬楼梯。 ❑ *We walked up a flight of stairs.* 我们往上走了一段楼梯。

★ **stair·case** /stɛərkeɪs/ (**staircases**) N-COUNT A **staircase** is a set of stairs inside a building. (建筑物内的) 楼梯通道 ❑ *They walked down the staircase together.* 他们一起沿楼梯通道往下走。
→ see **house**

stair·way /stɛərweɪ/ (**stairways**) N-COUNT A **stairway** is a staircase or a flight of steps, inside or outside a building. (建筑物内部或外部的) 楼梯; 一段台阶 ❑ *...the stairway leading to the top floor.* …通往顶层的楼梯。

stake ♦♦◇ /steɪk/ (**stakes, staking, staked**) 1 PHRASE If something is **at stake**, it is being risked and might be lost or damaged if you are not successful. 得失难料 ❑ *The tension was naturally high for a game with so much at stake.* 一场成败如此难料的比赛紧张度自然很高。 2 N-PLURAL The **stakes** involved in a contest or a risky action are the things that can be gained or lost. (竞赛、冒险行为中的) 赌注 ❑ *The game was usually played for high stakes between two large groups.* 这种游戏通常是两大组人为赢得大的赌注而进行的。 3 V-T If you **stake** something such as your money or your reputation **on** the result of something, you risk your money or reputation on it. 以 (金钱、名誉等) 下赌注 ❑ *He has staked his political future on an election victory.* 他已把他的政治前途赌在了一次选举获胜上。 4 N-COUNT If you have a **stake in** something such as a business, it matters to you, for example because you own part of it or because its success or failure will affect you. (商业等中的) 利害关系 ❑ *He was eager to return to a more entrepreneurial role in which he had a big financial stake in his own efforts.* 他渴望回到更具企业家性质的角色，这样他的努力就跟自己有大的金融利害关系。 5 N-PLURAL You can use **stakes** to refer to something that is like a contest. For example, you can refer to the choosing of a leader as **the** leadership **stakes**. 争夺赛 ❑ *We are lagging behind in the childcare stakes.* 我们在儿童保育竞赛中正落在后面。 6 N-COUNT A **stake** is a pointed wooden post which is pushed into the ground, for example in order to support a young tree. 桩 ❑ *His arms were tied to wooden stakes to hold him flat.* 他的双臂被绑在木桩上以便使他平躺着。 7 PHRASE If you **stake a claim**, you say that something is yours or that you have a right to it. 提出所有权要求 ❑ *Jane is determined to stake her claim as an actress.* 简决心提出她作为一名女演员的应有权利。

Word Partnership *stake* 的常用搭配：

N.	**interests at** stake, **issues at** stake 1
	stake **lives on** *something* 3
	stake **in a company/firm, majority/minority** stake 4
ADJ.	**controlling** stake, **personal** stake 4

stake·hold·er /steɪkhoʊldər/ (**stakeholders**) N-COUNT **Stakeholders** are people who have an interest in a company's or organization's affairs. 股东; 利益相关者 [BUSINESS] ❑ *...the Delaware River Port Authority, a major stakeholder in Penn's Landing.* …特拉华河港务局，佩恩码头的一个大股东。

stale /steɪl/ (**staler, stalest**) 1 ADJ **Stale** food is no longer fresh or good to eat. (食物) 不新鲜的; 变味的 ❑ *Their daily diet consisted of a lump of stale bread, a bowl of rice, and stale water.* 他们的日常饮食包括一块不新鲜的面包、一碗米饭，还有不新鲜的水。 2 ADJ **Stale** air or smells are unpleasant because they are no longer fresh. (空气或气味) 不新鲜的 ❑ *...the smell of stale sweat.* …汗臭味。 3 ADJ If you say that a place, an activity, or an idea is **stale**, you mean that it has become boring because it is always the same. (地方、活动、主意) 缺乏新鲜感的 [DISAPPROVAL] ❑ *Her relationship with Mark has become stale.* 她和马克的关系已变得乏味了。

▲ **stale·mate** /steɪlmeɪt/ (**stalemates**) N-VAR **Stalemate** is a situation in which neither side in an argument or contest can win or in which no progress is possible. 僵局 ❑ *The proportional representation system was widely blamed for two inconclusive election results and a year of political stalemate.* 两次无结果的选举和一年的政治僵局使得比例代表制受到广泛地指责。

★ **stalk** /stɔk/ (**stalks, stalking, stalked**) 1 N-COUNT The **stalk** of a flower, leaf, or fruit is the thin part that joins it to the plant or tree. (花、叶、果实与植株相连的) 柄; 梗 ❑ *A single pale blue flower grows up from each joint on a long stalk.* 一根长梗的每个节上都长出了一朵淡蓝色的花。 2 V-T If you **stalk** a person or a wild animal, you follow them quietly in order to kill them, catch them, or observe them carefully. 悄悄跟踪 ❑ *He stalks his victims like a hunter after a deer.* 他像猎人跟踪鹿一样悄悄跟踪他的受害者们。 3 V-T If someone **stalks** someone else, especially a famous person or a person they used to have a relationship with, they keep following them or contacting them in an annoying and frightening way. 骚扰; 纠缠 ❑ *Even after their divorce he continued to stalk and threaten her.* 甚至在他们离婚后，他继续纠缠并恐吓她。

stalk·er /stɔkər/ (**stalkers**) N-COUNT A **stalker** is someone who keeps following or contacting someone else, especially a famous person or a person they used to have a relationship with, in an annoying and frightening way. 骚扰者; 纠缠者 ❑ *She had been followed and then trapped by a stalker.* 她曾被一骚扰者跟踪，然后中了他的圈套。

★ **stall** /stɔl/ (**stalls, stalling, stalled**) 1 V-T/V-I If a process **stalls**, or if someone or something **stalls** it, the process stops but may continue at a later time. 使暂停; 暂停 ❑ *The Social Democratic Party has vowed to try to stall the bill until the current session ends.* 社会民主党已立誓设法暂停该议案直至当前会议结束。 ❑ *...but the peace process stalled.* …但是和平进程暂停了。 2 V-I If you **stall**, you try to avoid doing something until later. 拖延 ❑ *Thomas had spent all week stalling over his decision.* 托马斯花了整周的时间迟迟不做决定。 3 V-T If you **stall** someone, you prevent them from doing something until a later time. 拖住 (某人) ❑ *The store manager stalled the man until the police arrived.* 那个商场经理把那人拖住直到警察赶到为止。 4 V-T/V-I If a vehicle **stalls** or if you accidentally **stall** it, the engine stops suddenly. 使 (发动机) 突然熄火; (发动机) 突然熄火 ❑ *The engine stalled.* 发动机突然熄火了。 5 N-COUNT A **stall** is a large table on which you put goods that you want to sell, or information that you want to give people. 货摊; 咨询台 ❑ *...market stalls selling local fruits.* …出售当地水果的市场摊位。 6 N-PLURAL **The stalls** in a theater or concert hall are the seats on the ground floor directly in front of the stage. (剧院或音乐厅的) 正厅前排座位 [mainly BRIT]

in AM, use **orchestra**

7 N-COUNT A **stall** is a small enclosed area in a room which is used for a particular purpose, for example a shower. (房间内的) 小隔间 [AM]

in BRIT, usually use **cubicle**

❑ *She went into the shower stall, turned on the water, and grabbed the soap.* 她走进淋浴间，打开水，抓起香皂。
→ see **traffic**

stal·lion /stælyən/ (**stallions**) N-COUNT A **stallion** is a male horse, especially one kept for breeding. 牡马 (尤指种马)

stal·wart /stɔlwərt/ (**stalwarts**) N-COUNT A **stalwart** is a loyal worker or supporter of an organization, especially a political party. (尤指某政党的) 忠实拥护者 ❑ *His free-trade policies aroused suspicion among party stalwarts.* 他的自由贸易政策引起了该党忠实拥护者们的怀疑。

stami·na /stæmɪnə/ N-UNCOUNT **Stamina** is the physical or mental energy needed to do a tiring activity for a long time. 毅力 ❑ *You have to have a lot of stamina to be a top-class dancer.* 你得很有毅力才能成为一名顶级舞蹈家。

▲ **stam·mer** /stæmər/ (**stammers, stammering, stammered**) **1** V-T/V-I If you **stammer**, you speak with difficulty, hesitating and repeating words or sounds. 结结巴巴地说；口吃 ❑ *Five percent of children stammer at some point.* 5%的儿童在某个时候都会口吃。 ❑ *"Forgive me," I stammered.* "原谅我吧，"我结结巴巴地说。 ● **stam·mer·ing** N-UNCOUNT 口吃 ❑ *Of all speech impediments stammering is probably the most embarrassing.* 在所有语言障碍中，口吃可能是最让人尴尬的。 **2** N-SING Someone who has a **stammer** tends to stammer when they speak. 口吃 ❑ *A speech therapist cured his stammer.* 一位语言矫治专家治好了他的口吃。

stamp ♦◇◇ /stæmp/ (**stamps, stamping, stamped**) **1** N-COUNT A **stamp** or a **postage stamp** is a small piece of paper which you lick and stick on an envelope or package before you mail it to pay for the cost of the postage. 邮票 ❑ *...a book of stamps.* …一本邮票册。 ❑ *As of February 3rd, the price of a first class stamp will go up to 29 cents.* 自2月3日起，每张一等邮票的价格将上涨到29分。 **2** N-COUNT A **stamp** is a small block of wood or metal which has a pattern or a group of letters on one side. You press it onto a pad of ink and then onto a piece of paper in order to produce a mark on the paper. The mark that you produce is also called a **stamp**. 印章；印记 ❑ *...a date stamp and an ink pad.* …一个日期印章和一个印泥。 **3** V-T If you **stamp** a mark or word on an object, you press the mark or word onto the object using a stamp or other device. 盖（章）；印（某标记）；打上（某字） ❑ *Car manufacturers stamp a vehicle identification number at several places on new cars to help track down stolen vehicles.* 汽车生产商们在新车车身的几个地方打上车辆识别码以帮助追查被盗车辆。 **4** V-T/V-I If you **stamp** or **stamp** your **foot**, you lift your foot and put it down very hard on the ground, for example because you are angry or because your feet are cold. 跺（脚）；跺脚；重重地踩 ❑ *Often he teased me till my temper went and I stamped and screamed, feeling furiously helpless.* 他过去经常取笑我直到我生气，又跺脚又尖叫，感觉非常无助。 ❑ *His foot stamped down on the accelerator.* 他一脚猛地踩下油门。 ● N-COUNT **Stamp** is also a noun. 跺脚 ❑ *...hearing the creak of a door and the stamp of cold feet.* …听到门的吱嘎声和因脚冷而跺脚的声音。 **5** V-I If you **stamp** somewhere, you walk there putting your feet down very hard on the ground because you are angry. （因生气而）顿足 ❑ *"I'm going before things get any worse!" he shouted as he stamped out of the bedroom.* "我要在情况变得更糟前离开！"他叫嚷着顿足走出了卧室。 **6** V-I If you **stamp on** something, you put your foot down on it very hard. （在…上）用力踩 ❑ *He received the original ban last week after stamping on the referee's foot during the final.* 在决赛中狠狠地踩了裁判的脚之后，他上周受到首次禁赛处罚。 **7** N-SING If something bears **the stamp of** a particular quality or person, it clearly has that quality or was done by that person. 印记 ❑ *Most of us want to make our home a familiar place and put the stamp of our personality on its walls.* 我们大多数人都想把我们的家布置成温馨的地方并在墙壁上留下我们个性的印记。 **8** → see also **rubber stamp**

▶ **stamp out** PHRASAL VERB If you **stamp** something **out**, you put an end to it. 杜绝 ❑ *Dr. Muffett stressed that he was opposed to bullying in schools and that action would be taken to stamp it out.* 马费特博士强调他反对学校里恃强凌弱的行为，并说将采取行动杜绝该现象。

S

Word Partnership *stamp* 的常用搭配：

N. stamp **collection**, **postage** stamp **1**
stamp **of approval** **7**

stamped ad·dressed en·velope (**stamped addressed envelopes**) N-COUNT A **stamped addressed envelope** is the same as an **SASE**. （贴好邮票写明自己姓名和地址的）回信信封 [BRIT]

stam·pede /stæmpid/ (**stampedes, stampeding, stampeded**) **1** N-COUNT If there is a **stampede**, a group of people or animals run in a wild, uncontrolled way. （人群或兽群的）狂奔 ❑ *There was a stampede for the exit.* 出现了人群向出口的狂奔。 **2** V-T/V-I If a group of animals or people **stampede** or if something **stampedes** them, they run in a wild, uncontrolled way. 使狂奔；狂奔 ❑ *The crowd stampeded and many were crushed or trampled underfoot.* 人群狂奔起来，很多人被撞倒或踩踏。 ❑ *...a herd of stampeding cattle.* …一群狂奔着的牛。 **3** N-COUNT If a lot of people all do the same thing at the same time, you can describe it as a **stampede**. 热潮 ❑ *...a stampede of consumers rushing to buy merchandise at bargain prices.* …消费者争先恐后购买便宜货的热潮。

▲ **stance** /stæns/ (**stances**) **1** N-COUNT Your **stance** on a particular matter is your attitude to it. （对某事的）态度；立场 ❑ *Congress had agreed to reconsider its stance on the armed struggle.* 国会已经同意重新考虑其对本次武装斗争的态度。 **2** N-COUNT Your **stance** is the way that you are standing. 站姿 [FORMAL] ❑ *Take a comfortably wide stance and flex your knees a little.* 取两腿自然分开的站姿，双膝微屈。

Word Partnership *stance* 的常用搭配：

PREP. stance **against/on/toward** *something* **1**
ADJ. **aggressive** stance, **critical** stance, **hard-line** stance, **tough** stance **1**
V. **adopt** a stance, **take** a stance **1** **2**

stand

❶ VERB USES AND PHRASES
❷ NOUN USES
❸ PHRASAL VERBS

❶ **stand** ♦♦♦ /stænd/ (**stands, standing, stood**)

➪ **Please look at meanings 21 – 25 to see if the expression you are looking for is shown under another headword.** **1** V-I When you **are standing**, your body is upright, your legs are straight, and your weight is supported by your feet. 站立 ❑ *She was standing beside my bed staring down at me.* 她当时站在我床边低头凝视着我。 ❑ *They told me to stand still and not to turn round.* 他们叫我站着不动并且不要转身。 ● PHRASAL VERB **Stand up** means the same as **stand**. 站立 ❑ *We waited, standing up, for an hour.* 我们站着等了一个小时。 **2** V-I When someone who is sitting **stands**, they change their position so that they are upright and on their feet. 站起来 ❑ *Becker stood and shook hands with Ben.* 贝克尔站起来和本握了手。 ● PHRASAL VERB **Stand up** means the same as **stand**. 站起来 ❑ *When I walked in, they all stood up and started clapping.* 我走进去的时候，他们全体起立开始鼓掌。 **3** V-I If you **stand aside** or **stand back**, you move a short distance sideways or backward, so that you are standing in a different place. 往旁边站；往后站 ❑ *I stood aside to let her pass me.* 我往边上站以让她从我身边过去。 **4** V-I If something such as a building or a piece of furniture **stands** somewhere, it is in that position, and is upright. （建筑物、家具等）竖立着 [WRITTEN] ❑ *The house stands alone on top of a small hill.* 那所房子孤零零地立在一座小山顶上。 **5** V-I You can say that a building **is standing** when it remains after other buildings around it have fallen down or been destroyed. （在周围建筑物都已倒下或被摧毁的情况下依然）矗立着 ❑ *The palace, which was damaged by bombs in World War II, still stood.* 这座在二战中被炮火破坏的宫殿依然矗立着。 **6** V-T If you **stand** something somewhere, you put it there in an upright position. 使竖立 ❑ *Stand the plant in the open in a sunny, sheltered place.* 把这株植物立在户外阳光充足、有遮护的地方。 **7** V-I If you leave food or a mixture of something **to stand**, you leave it without disturbing it for some time. 搁置一段时间 ❑ *The salad improves if made in advance and left to stand.* 该色拉如果提前做好并搁上些时候味道会更好。 **8** V-I If you ask someone **where** or **how** they **stand on** a particular issue, you are asking them what their attitude or view is. 持（何种）态度；采取（何种）立场 ❑ *The amendment will force senators to show where they stand on the issue of sexual harassment.* 该修正案将迫使参议员们表明他们在性骚扰问题上采取什么立场。 **9** V-I If you do not know **where** you **stand with** someone, you do not know exactly what their attitude to you is. （在某人心中）处于（何种）位置；被（如何）看待 ❑ *No one knows where they stand with him; he is utterly unpredictable.* 谁也不知道他们在他心中被如何看待，他这个人绝对难以琢磨。 **10** V-LINK You can use **stand** instead of "be" when you are describing the present state or condition of something or someone. 处于（某种状态或状况） ❑ *The alliance stands ready to do what is necessary.* 该联盟已准备好采取必要行动。 **11** V-I If a decision, law, or offer **stands**, it still exists and has not been changed or canceled. （决定、法律或提议）继续有效 ❑ *Although exceptions could be made, the rule still stands.* 尽管有可能有特例，但这条规则继续有效。 **12** V-I If something that can be measured **stands at** a particular level, it is at that level. 处于（某水平） ❑ *The inflation rate now stands at 3.6 percent.* 通货膨胀率现在是3.6%。 **13** V-T If something can **stand** a situation or a test, it is good enough or strong enough to experience it without being damaged, harmed, or shown to be inadequate. 经受住 ❑ *These are the first machines that can stand the wear and tear of continuously crushing glass.* 这些是第一批能经得住连续碾碎玻璃造成的磨损的机器。 **14** V-T If you cannot **stand** something, you cannot bear it or tolerate it. 忍受；容忍（某事物） ❑ *I can't stand any more. I'm going to run away.* 我再也忍受不了了，我打算逃跑。 ❑ *Stoddart can stand any amount of personal criticism.* 斯托达特能容忍针对其个人的无论多少的批评。 **15** V-T If you cannot **stand** someone or something, you dislike them very strongly. 忍受（某人或某事物）[INFORMAL] ❑ *I can't stand that man and his arrogance.* 我受不了那人和他的傲慢态度。 16 V-T If you **stand to gain** something, you are likely to gain it. If you **stand to lose** something, you are likely to lose it. 有可能（获得、失去） ❑ *The management group would stand to gain millions of dollars if the company were sold.* 如果公司被出售的话，管理层有可能获得数百万美元。 17 V-I If you **stand in** an election, you are a candidate in it. 参加（竞选）[BRIT]

in AM, use **run**

18 → see also **standing** 19 PHRASE If you say **it stands to reason that** something is true or likely to happen, you mean that it is obvious. 显然 ❑ *It stands to reason that if you are considerate and friendly to people you will get a lot more back.* 显然，如果你通情达理、对人友善，你会得到比你付出的多得多的回报。 20 PHRASE If you **stand in the way of** something or **stand in** a person's **way**, you prevent that thing from happening or prevent that person from doing something. 阻止某事物/某人 ❑ *The administration would not stand in the way of such a proposal.* 该行政部门不会阻止这样一个提议。
21 to **stand a chance** → see **chance** 22 to **stand firm** → see **firm**
23 to **stand on** your **own two feet** → see **foot** 24 to **stand** your **ground** → see **ground** 25 to **stand** someone **in good stead** → see **stead** 26 to **stand trial** → see **trial**

❷ **stand** ◆◆◆ /stænd/ (**stands**) 1 N-COUNT If you take or make a **stand**, you do something or say something in order to make it clear what your attitude to a particular thing is. 立场 ❑ *He felt the need to make a stand against racism in South Africa.* 他觉得有必要表明反对南非种族主义的立场。 2 N-COUNT A **stand** is a small store or stall, outdoors or in a large public building. 摊位 ❑ *He ran a newspaper stand outside the American Express office.* 他曾在美国运通办公楼外经营一个报摊。 3 N-PLURAL The **stands** at a sports stadium or arena are a large structure where people sit or stand to watch what is happening. （运动场或竞技场的）看台 ❑ *The people in the stands at Candlestick Park are standing and cheering with all their might.* 烛台公园看台上的人们正站着尽情欢呼。 ● N-COUNT In British English, **stand** is used with the same meaning. 看台 ❑ *I was sitting in the stand for the first game.* 我当时正坐在看台上观看首场比赛。 4 N-COUNT A **stand** is an object or piece of furniture that is designed for supporting or holding a particular kind of thing. 托架 ❑ *The teapot came with a stand to catch the drips.* 那把茶壶配有一个接滴水的壶托。 5 N-COUNT A **stand** is an area where taxis or buses can wait to pick up passengers. （出租车或公共汽车）候客处 ❑ *Luckily there was a taxi stand nearby.* 幸好附近有个出租车候客处。 6 N-SING In a law court, **the stand** is the place where a witness sits to answer questions. （法庭上的）证人席 ❑ *When the father took the stand today, he contradicted his son's testimony.* 今天那位父亲出席作证时，他驳斥了他儿子的证词。

❸ **stand** ◆◆◆ /stænd/ (**stands, standing, stood**)

▸ **stand aside** PHRASAL VERB [BRIT]

in AM, use **stand down**

▸ **stand back** PHRASAL VERB If you **stand back** and think about a situation, you think about it as if you were not involved in it. 置身事外（考虑某事） ❑ *Stand back and look objectively at the problem.* 置身事外客观地看待这个问题。

▸ **stand by** 1 PHRASAL VERB If you **are standing by**, you are ready and waiting to provide help or to take action. 做好准备 ❑ *British and American warships are standing by to evacuate their citizens if necessary.* 英美战舰已做好准备一有必要就撤出本国公民。 2 → see also **standby** 3 PHRASAL VERB If you **stand by** and let something bad happen, you do not do anything to stop it. 袖手旁观 [DISAPPROVAL] ❑ *The Secretary of Defense has said that he would not stand by and let democracy be undermined.* 国防部长已经表明他不会袖手旁观，任由民主遭到破坏。 4 PHRASAL VERB If you **stand by** someone, you continue to give them support, especially when they are in trouble. 继续支持（尤指处于困境者）[APPROVAL] ❑ *I wouldn't break the law for a friend, but I would stand by her if she did.* 我不会为朋友而违法，但如果她犯了法我会继续支持她。 5 PHRASAL VERB If you **stand by** an earlier decision, promise, or statement, you continue to support it or keep it. 坚持（原有的决定、承诺或声明） ❑ *The decision has been made and I have got to stand by it.* 这个决定已经作出，我得坚持它。

▸ **stand down** PHRASAL VERB If someone **stands down**, they resign from an important job or position, often in order to let someone else take their place. （从要职上）退下 ❑ *Four days later, the despised leader finally stood down, just 17 days after taking office.* 4天后，这位受鄙视的领导人终于辞职了，就职才只有17天。

▸ **stand for** 1 PHRASAL VERB If you say that a letter **stands for** a particular word, you mean that it is an abbreviation for that word. （某字母）是（某词的）首字母缩写 ❑ *AIDS stands for Acquired Immune Deficiency Syndrome.* AIDS是**Acquired Immune Deficiency Syndrome**的首字母缩写。 ❑ *What does E.U. stand for?* E. U. 是什么意思？ 2 PHRASAL VERB The ideas or attitudes that someone or something **stands for** are the ones that they support or represent. 代表（某观点或态度） ❑ *The party is trying to give the impression that it alone stands for democracy.* 该党正企图让人觉得只有它才代表民主。 3 PHRASAL VERB If you will **not stand for** something, you will not allow it to happen or continue. 不能容忍 [with neg] ❑ *It's outrageous, and we won't stand for it any more.* 这太让人气愤了，我们再也不能容忍下去了。

▸ **stand in** 1 PHRASAL VERB If you **stand in for** someone, you take their place or do their job, because they are sick or away. （因某人生病或离开而）暂时代替 ❑ *I had to stand in for her on Tuesday when she didn't show up.* 星期二那天她没露面，我只好代替她。 ❑ *...the acting president, who's standing in while she's out of the country.* …代理总裁，是她在不在国内时的代理。 2 → see also **stand-in**

▸ **stand out** 1 PHRASAL VERB If something **stands out**, it is very noticeable. 显眼 ❑ *Every tree, wall and fence stood out against dazzling white fields.* 每棵树、每堵墙、每道篱笆在白得耀眼的田野的映衬下都很显眼。 2 PHRASAL VERB If something **stands out** from a surface, it rises up from it. 突出 ❑ *His tendons stood out like rope beneath his skin.* 他的筋像绳子般在皮肤下突出来。

▸ **stand up** 1 → see **stand** ❶ **1, 2** 2 PHRASAL VERB If something such as a claim or a piece of evidence **stands up**, it is accepted as true or satisfactory after being carefully examined. （主张、证据等）经得起检验 ❑ *He made wild accusations that did not stand up.* 他作出了经不起检验的无端的指控。 ❑ *How well does this thesis stand up to close examination?* 这篇论文能在多大程度上经得起仔细检查？ 3 PHRASAL VERB If a boyfriend or girlfriend **stands** you **up**, they fail to keep an arrangement to meet you. （男、女朋友）失约 [INFORMAL] ❑ *We were to have had dinner together yesterday evening, but he stood me up.* 昨晚我们本应该一起用餐，但他失约了。

▸ **stand up for** PHRASAL VERB If you **stand up for** someone or something, you defend them and make your feelings or opinions very clear. 捍卫；为…辩护 [APPROVAL] ❑ *They stood up for what they believed to be right.* 他们捍卫了他们认为正确的东西。

▸ **stand up to** 1 PHRASAL VERB If something **stands up to** bad conditions, it is not damaged or harmed by them. 经受住 ❑ *Is this building going to stand up to the strongest gales?* 这座建筑能经得住最强劲的大风吗？ 2 PHRASAL VERB If you **stand up to** someone, especially someone more powerful than you are, you defend yourself against their attacks or demands. 抵抗 ❑ *He hit me, so I hit him back–the first time in my life I'd stood up to him.* 他打了我，我就还手打了他——这是我生平第一次反抗他。

stand-alone 1 ADJ A **stand-alone** business or organization is independent and does not receive financial support from another organization. （公司、组织）独立的 [ADJ n] [BUSINESS] ❑ *They plan to relaunch it as a stand-alone company.* 他们计划把它重新创办成一家独立的公司。 2 ADJ A **stand-alone** computer is one that can operate on its own and does not have to be part of a network. （电脑）独立的 [ADJ n] [COMPUTING] ❑ *...an operating system that can work on networks and stand-alone machines.* …一套可在网络上和独立机器上运行的操作系统。

stand·ard ◆◆◇ /stændərd/ (**standards**) 1 N-COUNT A **standard** is a level of quality or achievement, especially a level that is thought to be acceptable. （尤指可被接受的）水平 ❑ *The standard of professional cricket has never been lower.* 职业板球的水平从来没这么低过。 2 N-COUNT A **standard** is something that you use in order to judge the quality of something else. 标准 ❑ *...systems that were by later standards absurdly primitive.* …按照后来的标准衡量显得极其原始的系统。 3 N-PLURAL **Standards** are moral principles which affect people's attitudes and behavior. 道德水准 ❑ *My father has always had high moral standards.* 我父亲一直有着很高的道德水准。 4 ADJ You use **standard** to describe things which are usual and normal. 常规的 ❑ *It was standard practice for untrained clerks to advise in serious cases such as murder.* 让未经训练的职员们在诸如谋杀等重案中提出建议是常规的做法。 5 ADJ A **standard** work or text on a particular subject is one that is widely read and often recommended. 权威的；广泛认可的 [ADJ n] ❑ *At twenty he translated Euler's standard work on algebra into English.* 20岁时，他把尤勒的权威代数著作译成了英语。

Word Partnership *standard* 的常用搭配：

V. **become a** standard, **maintain a** standard, **meet a** standard, **raise a** standard, **set a** standard, **use a** standard 1 2

N. standard **of excellence**, **industry** standard 1 2
standard **English**, standard **equipment**, standard **practice**, standard **procedure** 4

stand·ard·ise /stændəʳdaɪz/ [BRIT] → see **standardize**

stand·ard·ize /stændərdaɪz/ (**standardizes, standardizing, standardized**)

in BRIT, also use **standardise**

V-T To **standardize** things means to change them so that they all have the same features. 使标准化 ❑ *There is a drive both to standardize components and to reduce the number of models.* 有一种使零部件标准化并减少型号数量的需求。● **stand·ardi·za·tion** /stændərdɪzeɪʃᵊn/ N-UNCOUNT 标准化 ❑ *...the standardization of working hours.* …工作时间的标准化。

→ see **mass production**

stand·ard of liv·ing (**standards of living**) N-COUNT Your **standard of living** is the level of comfort and wealth which you have. 生活水平 ❑ *We'll continue to fight for a decent standard of living for our members.* 我们将继续为使我们的成员取得较高的生活水平而努力。

stand·ard time N-UNCOUNT **Standard time** is the official local time of a region or country. 标准时间 ❑ *Tonight the nation switches from daylight-saving time to standard time.* 今晚该国从夏令时间改为标准时间。

★ **stand·by** /stændbaɪ/ (**standbys**) also **stand-by** 1 N-COUNT A **standby** is something or someone that is always ready to be used if they are needed. 备用物；后备人员 ❑ *Canned varieties of beans and peas are a good standby.* 各种豆类罐装食品是很好的备用食品。 2 PHRASE If someone or something is **on standby**, they are ready to be used if they are needed. 处于待命状态 ❑ *Five ambulances are on standby at the port.* 五辆救护车在那个港口待命。 3 ADJ A **standby** ticket for something such as the theater or a plane trip is a cheap ticket that you buy just before the performance starts or the plane takes off, if there are still some seats left. （飞机起飞前、剧院演出开始前出售的）剩余廉价的（票） [ADJ n] ❑ *He bought a standby ticket to New York at 5:30 a.m. the following morning and flew to JFK airport six hours later.* 他买了张第2天凌晨5:30飞往纽约的剩余廉价机票，6个小时后飞往肯尼迪机场。● ADV **Standby** is also an adverb. 凭剩余廉价票地 [ADV after v] ❑ *Magda was going to fly standby.* 玛格达将凭剩余廉价机票乘飞机旅行。

stand-in (**stand-ins**) N-COUNT A **stand-in** is a person who takes someone else's place or does someone else's job for a while, for example because the other person is sick or away. 临时替代者 ❑ *He was a stand-in for my regular doctor.* 他是我的固定医生的临时替代者。

stand·ing /stændɪŋ/ (**standings**) 1 N-UNCOUNT Someone's **standing** is their reputation or status. 名声；地位 ❑ *...an artist of international standing.* …一位享有国际声誉的艺术家。 ❑ *He has improved his country's standing abroad.* 他使他的国家在国外的名声得到了提高。 2 N-COUNT A party's or person's **standing** is their popularity. 声望 ❑ *But, as the opinion poll shows, the party's standing with the people at large has never been so low.* 但是，正如民意调查所显示的那样，该党在普通民众中的声望从来没这么低过。 3 ADJ You use **standing** to describe something which is permanently in existence. 常备的；常设的 [ADJ n] ❑ *Israel has a relatively small standing army and its strength is based on its reserves.* 以色列拥有一支规模相对较小的常备军，它的兵力基于其预备役部队。 4 → see also **long-standing**

S

★ **stand·off** /stændɔf/ (**standoffs**) N-COUNT A **standoff** is a situation in which neither of two opposing groups or forces will make a move until the other one does something, so nothing can happen until one of them gives way. 僵局 ❑ *There is no sign of an end to the standoff between Mohawk Indians and the Quebec provincial police.* 莫霍克印第安人和魁北克省警方之间的僵局没有结束的迹象。

stand·point /stændpɔɪnt/ (**standpoints**) N-COUNT **From a particular standpoint** means looking at an event, situation, or idea in a particular way. 观点；角度 ❑ *He believes that from a military standpoint, the situation is under control.* 他认为从军事角度来看，局势已得到控制。

stand·still /stændstɪl/ N-SING If movement or activity comes **to** or is brought to **a standstill**, it stops completely. 停止 ❑ *Abruptly the group ahead of us came to a standstill.* 忽然我们前面的队伍停了下来。

stand-up also **standup** (**stand-ups**) 1 ADJ A **stand-up** comic or comedian stands alone in front of an audience and tells jokes. 单人喜剧表演的 [ADJ n] ❑ *He does all kinds of accents, he can do jokes – he could be a stand-up comic.* 他会模仿各种不同的口音，他会讲笑话——他可以做个单口喜剧演员。 2 N-UNCOUNT **Stand-up** is stand-up comedy. 单人表演的喜剧 ❑ *...likability, professionalism and the kind of nerve you need to do stand-up.* …表演单人喜剧所需要的可爱、专业素养及那种勇气。 3 N-COUNT A **stand-up** is a stand-up comedian. 单人喜剧演员 ❑ *...one of the worst stand-ups alive.* …现有的最蹩脚的单人喜剧演员之一。

stank /stæŋk/ **Stank** is the past tense of **stink**. stink的过去式

★ **sta·ple** /steɪpᵊl/ (**staples, stapling, stapled**) 1 ADJ A **staple** food, product, or activity is one that is basic and important in people's everyday lives. 基本的；主要的（食物、产品、活动）[ADJ n] ❑ *Rice is the staple food of more than half the world's population.* 大米是世界上半数以上人口的主食。 ❑ *The Chinese also eat a type of pasta as part of their staple diet.* 中国人也以一种面食作为他们的部分主食。● N-COUNT **Staple** is also a noun. 主食；主要产品；主要活动 ❑ *Fish is a staple in the diet of many Africans.* 鱼是许多非洲人饮食中的主食。 2 N-COUNT A **staple** is something that forms an important part of something else. 重要部分 ❑ *Political reporting has become a staple of American journalism.* 政治报道已经成为美国新闻业的一个重要内容。 3 N-COUNT **Staples** are small pieces of bent wire that are used mainly for holding sheets of paper together firmly. You put the staples into the paper using a device called a stapler. 订书钉 4 V-T If you **staple** something, you fasten it to something else or fix it in place using staples. 用订书钉订住 ❑ *Staple some sheets of paper together into a book.* 用订书钉把一些纸张订成一本。

sta·pler /steɪplər/ (**staplers**) N-COUNT A **stapler** is a device used for putting staples into sheets of paper. 订书机

→ see **office**

star ♦♦♦ /stɑr/ (**stars, starring, starred**) 1 N-COUNT A **star** is a large ball of burning gas in space. Stars appear to us as small points of light in the sky on clear nights. 星 ❑ *The nights were pure with cold air and lit with stars.* 那些夜晚十分清静，空气清凉、繁星点点。 2 N-COUNT You can refer to a shape or an object as a **star** when it has four, five, or more points sticking out of it in a regular pattern. 星形；星形物 ❑ *Children at school receive colored stars for work well done.* 上学的孩子们表现好会得到彩星。 3 N-COUNT You can say how many **stars** something such as a hotel or restaurant has as a way of talking about its quality, which is often indicated by a number of star-shaped symbols. The more stars something has, the better it is. （宾馆或饭店等的）星级 ❑ *...five star hotels.* …五星级酒店。 4 N-COUNT Famous actors, musicians, and sports players are often referred to as **stars**. 明星 ❑ *...star of the TV series Scrubs.*

Word Web star

Astronomy is the oldest science. It is the study of **stars** and other objects in the **night sky**. People sometimes confuse astronomy and **astrology**. Astrology is the belief that the stars influence people's lives. Long ago people named groups of stars after gods, heroes, and imaginary animals. One of the most famous of these **constellations** is the Big Dipper. Its original name meant "the big bear." It is easy to find and it points toward the North Star*. For centuries sailors have used the North Star to **navigate**. The best-known star in our **galaxy** is the **sun**.

North Star: the star that the earth's northern axis points toward.

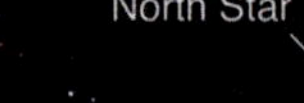

…电视连续剧《实习医生风云》里的明星。❑ *By now Murphy is Hollywood's top male comedy star.* 现在墨菲已是好莱坞顶级男喜剧明星。 **5** V-I If an actor or actress **stars in** a play or movie, he or she has one of the most important parts in it. (在某戏剧、电影中) 扮演主要角色 ❑ *The previous year Adolphson had starred in a play in which Ingrid had been an extra.* 上个年度阿道夫森曾主演了一部戏，在该戏中英格丽德是临时演员。 **6** V-T If a play or movie **stars** a famous actor or actress, he or she has one of the most important parts in it. 由…主演 ❑ *…a Hollywood movie, "The Secret of Santa Vittoria," directed by Stanley Kramer and starring Anthony Quinn.* …一部由斯坦利・克莱默执导、安东尼・奎因主演的名为《圣维多利亚的秘密》的好莱坞影片。 **7** N-PLURAL Predictions about people's lives which are based on astrology and appear regularly in a newspaper or magazine are sometimes referred to as **the stars**. 星相 ❑ *There was nothing in my stars to say I'd have travel problems!* 我的星相上没说我会有旅行问题！

→ see Word Web: **star**

→ see **galaxy, navigation**

Word Partnership *star* 的常用搭配：

ADJ.	**bright** star **1 4** **big** star, **former** star, **rising** star **4**
N.	**bronze** star, **gold** star **2** **all-star cast/game, basketball/football/tennis** star, **film/movie** star, **guest** star, **pop/rap** star, **porn** star, **TV** star **4** star **in a film/movie/show 5**

star·board /stɑrbərd, -bɔrd/ ADJ The **starboard** side of a ship or an aircraft is the right side when you are on it and facing toward the front. (船、飞机) 右舷的 [TECHNICAL] ❑ *He detected a ship moving down the starboard side of the submarine.* 他发现了一艘正沿潜水艇右侧航行的船。 ● N-UNCOUNT **Starboard** is also a noun. 右舷 ❑ *I could see the fishing boat to starboard.* 我能看见右侧的那艘渔船。

▲ **starch** /stɑrtʃ/ (**starches**) **1** N-MASS **Starch** is a substance that is found in foods such as bread, potatoes, pasta, and rice and gives you energy. 淀粉 ❑ *She reorganized her eating so that she was taking more fruit and vegetables and less starch, salt, and fat.* 她重新调整了自己的饮食，在多吃水果蔬菜，少食用淀粉、盐和脂肪。 **2** N-UNCOUNT **Starch** is a substance that is used for making cloth stiffer, especially cotton and linen. (用于使布料挺直的) 浆粉 ❑ *He never puts enough starch in my shirts.* 他从不给我的衬衫上足够的浆粉。

→ see **rice**

star·dom /stɑrdəm/ N-UNCOUNT **Stardom** is the state of being very famous, usually as an actor, musician, or athlete. 明星身份 ❑ *In 1929 she shot to stardom on Broadway in a Noel Coward play.* 1929年，她以一部诺埃尔・科沃德的戏在百老汇一跃成为明星。

stare ◆◇◇ /stɛər/ (**stares, staring, stared**) **1** V-I If you **stare at** someone or something, you look at them for a long time. 盯着看；凝视 ❑ *Tamara stared at him in disbelief, shaking her head.* 塔玛拉摇着头不相信地盯着他看。 ❑ *Ben continued to stare out the window.* 本继续凝视着窗外。 ● N-COUNT **Stare** is also a noun. 盯着看；凝视 ❑ *Hlasek gave him a long, cold stare.* 赫拉塞克冷冷地盯着他看了很久。 **2** PHRASE If a situation or the answer to a problem **is staring** you **in the face**, it is very obvious, although you may not be immediately aware of it. (形势、答案) 明摆在某人面前 [INFORMAL] ❑ *Then the answer hit me. It had been staring me in the face ever since Lullington.* 之后我突然想到了这个答案。自路林顿起这答案就一直明摆在我面前。

The verbs **stare** and **gaze** are both used to talk about looking at something for a long time. If you **stare at** something or someone, it is often because you think they are strange or shocking. ❑ *Various families came out and stared at us.* If you **gaze at** something, it is often because you think it is marvelous or impressive. ❑ *A fresh-faced little girl gazes in wonder at the bright fairground lights.*

Word Partnership *stare* 的常用搭配：

ADJ.	**blank** stare **1**
V.	**continue to** stare, **turn to** stare **1**

▲ **stark** /stɑrk/ (**starker, starkest**) **1** ADJ **Stark** choices or statements are harsh and unpleasant. 严酷的 ❑ *Companies face a stark choice if they want to stay competitive.* 各公司要想保持竞争力就要面临一个严酷的选择。 ❑ *In his celebration speech, he issued a stark warning to Washington and other Western capitals.* 在他的庆典演讲中，他赤裸裸的警告了华盛顿和其他一些西方首府。 ● **stark·ly** ADV 严酷地 ❑ *That issue is presented starkly and brutally by Bob Graham and David Cairns.* 那个问题被鲍勃・格雷厄姆和戴维・凯恩斯冷酷无情地提了出来。 **2** ADJ If two things are in **stark** contrast to one another, they are very different from each other in a way that is very obvious. (对比) 鲜明的 ❑ *…secret cooperation between London and Washington that was in stark contrast to official policy.* …伦敦和华盛顿之间的与官方政策明显相悖的秘密合作。 ● **stark·ly** 鲜明地 ❑ *Angus's child-like paintings contrast starkly with his adult subject matter in these portraits.* 安格斯孩子般的绘画和他这些肖像画里的成人主题对比鲜明。 **3** ADJ Something that is **stark** is very plain in appearance. 普通的 ❑ *…the stark white, characterless fireplace in the drawing room.* …起居室里平淡无奇的白色壁炉。 ● **stark·ly** ADV 普通地 ❑ *The room was starkly furnished.* 那房间布置得很普通。

start ◆◆◆ /stɑrt/ (**starts, starting, started**) **1** V-T If you **start to** do something, you do something that you were not doing before and you continue doing it. 开始 (做某事) ❑ *John then unlocked the front door and I started to follow him up the stairs.* 接着约翰打开前门，我开始随他上楼。 ❑ *It was 1956 when Susanna started the work on the garden.* 苏珊娜是在1956年开始修建那个花园的。 ● N-COUNT **Start** is also a noun. 开始 ❑ *After several starts, she read the report properly.* 几次起头之后，她正确地读了那份报告。 **2** V-T/V-I When something **starts**, or if someone **starts** it, it takes place from a particular time. 使开始发生；开始发生 ❑ *The fire is thought to have started in an upstairs room.* 这火被认为是从楼上的一间房开始的。 ❑ *All of the passengers started the day with a swim.* 所有乘客都以游泳开始了这一天。 ● N-SING **Start** is also a noun. 开始 ❑ *…1918, four years after the start of the Great War.* …第一次世界大战开始4年后的1918年。 **3** V-I If you **start by** doing something, or if you **start with** something, you do that thing first in a series of actions. (以做某事) 开始 ❑ *I started by asking how many day-care centers were located in the United States.* 我以询问在美国有多少日托中心开始。 **4** V-I You use **start** to say what someone's first job was. For example, if their first job was that of a factory worker, you can say that they **started as** a factory worker. (以做…) 开始 (职业生涯) ❑ *Betty started as a shipping clerk at the clothes factory.* 贝蒂以做这家服装厂的运务员开始职业生涯。 ● PHRASAL VERB **Start off** means the same as **start**. 开始 ❑ *Mr. Dambar had started off as an assistant to Mrs. Spear's husband.* 丹巴先生以做斯皮尔夫人的先生的助手开始职业生涯。 **5** V-T When someone **starts** something such as a new business, they create it or cause it to begin. 开办 ❑ *George Granger has started a health center and I know he's looking for qualified staff.* 乔治・格兰杰开了个保健中心，我知道他正在物色合格的员工。 ● PHRASAL VERB **Start up** means the same as **start**. 开办 ❑ *The cost of starting up a day-care center for children ranges from $150,000 to $300,000.* 开办一家儿童日托中心的费用在15到30万美元之间不等。 **6** → see also **startup** **7** V-T/V-I If you **start** an engine, car, or machine, or if it **starts**, it begins to work. 发动 (引擎、汽车、机器等)；(引擎、汽车或机器等) 发动 ❑ *He started the car, which hummed smoothly.* 他发动了汽车，汽车平稳地发出嗡嗡声。 ● PHRASAL VERB **Start up** means the same as **start**. 发动 ❑ *He waited until they went inside the building before starting up the car and driving off.* 他等他们走进那座楼之后才发动汽车开走了。 ❑ *Put the key in the ignition and turn it to start the car up.* 把钥匙插入点火装置，然后转动钥匙发动汽车。 **8** V-I If you **start**, your body suddenly moves slightly as a result of surprise or fear. 惊动 ❑ *She put the bottle on the coffee table beside him, banging it down hard. He started at the sound, his concentration broken.* 她把那个瓶子砰地一声放在他身边的咖啡桌上，他被这声音吓了一跳，注意力被打断了。 ● N-COUNT **Start** is also a noun. 惊动 ❑ *Sylvia woke with a start.* 希尔维娅惊醒了。 **9** → see also **false start, head start** **10** PHRASE You use **for a start** or **to start with** to introduce the first of a number of things or reasons that you want to mention or could mention. 首先；第一 ❑ *You must get her name and address, and that can be a problem for a start.* 你得弄到她的姓名和住址，而这可能就是第一个难题。 **11** PHRASE **To start with** means at the very first stage of an event or process. (事情、过程) 刚开始时 ❑ *To start with, the pressure on her was very heavy, but it's eased off a bit now.* 刚开始时她的压力非常大，但现在轻松些了。 **12** **to get off to a flying start** → see **flying**

Start, begin, and **commence** all have a similar meaning, although **commence** is more formal and is not normally used in conversation. ❑ *The meeting is ready to begin… He tore the list up and started a fresh one… The space probe commenced taking a series of photographs.* Note that **begin, start,** and **commence** can all be followed by an -ing form or a noun, but only **begin** and **start** can be followed by a "to" infinitive.

▶ **start off** 1 PHRASAL VERB If you **start off by** doing something, you do it as the first part of an activity. 以…开始 ❑ *She started off by accusing him of blackmail but he more or less ignored her.* 她以指控他敲诈勒索开始，但他基本上没理会她。 2 PHRASAL VERB To **start** someone **off** means to cause them to begin doing something. 使(某人)开始(做某事) ❑ *Her mother started her off acting in children's theater.* 她母亲让她开始在儿童剧院表演。 3 PHRASAL VERB To **start** something **off** means to cause it to begin. 使(某事)开始 ❑ *He became more aware of the things that started that tension off.* 他对造成那些紧张气氛的因素更加清楚了。 4 → see **start 4**

▶ **start on** PHRASAL VERB If you **start on** something that needs to be done, you start dealing with it. 开始处理 ❑ *Before you start on these chapters, clear your head.* 在你开始这些章之前，先理清思路。

▶ **start out** 1 PHRASAL VERB If someone or something **starts out as** a particular thing, they are that thing at the beginning although they change later. 起初是 ❑ *Daly was a fast-talking Irish-American who had started out as a salesman.* 戴利是个巧舌如簧的爱尔兰裔美国人，他起初是个推销员。 2 PHRASAL VERB If you **start out by** doing something, you do it at the beginning of an activity. 以(做某事)开始 ❑ *I'm careful to start out by saying clearly what I want.* 我小心地以清楚地说出自己想要的东西开始。

▶ **start over** PHRASAL VERB If you **start over** or **start** something **over**, you begin something again from the beginning. 重新开始 [mainly AM]

in BRIT, use **start again**

❑ *...moving the kids to some other schools, closing them down and starting over with a new staff.* …把孩子们转到其他一些学校，关掉它们，然后招一个新员工重新开始。

▶ **start up** → see **start 5, 6**

Thesaurus *start* 另参见：

V.	begin, commence, originate 1 2 establish, found, launch 5
N.	beginning, onset 1 2 jump, scare, shock 8

start·er /stɑrtər/ (**starters**) N-COUNT A **starter** is a small quantity of food that is served as the first course of a meal. 头盘 [mainly BRIT]

in AM, usually use **appetizer**

start·ing point (**starting points**) also **starting-point** 1 N-COUNT Something that is a **starting point for** a discussion or process can be used to begin it or act as a basis for it. (讨论、过程的)起点 ❑ *These proposals represent a realistic starting point for negotiation.* 这些提议代表着谈判的一个现实起点。 2 N-COUNT When you make a journey, your **starting point** is the place from which you start. (旅行的)出发点 ❑ *They had already walked a couple of miles or more from their starting point.* 他们从出发点已走了至少几英里。

star·tle /stɑrtᵊl/ (**startles, startling, startled**) V-T If something sudden and unexpected **startles** you, it surprises and frightens you slightly. 使受惊 ❑ *The telephone startled him.* 电话声吓了他一跳。 ● **star·tled** ADJ 受惊吓了的 ❑ *Martha gave her a startled look.* 玛莎受惊地看了她一眼。

star·tling /stɑrtᵊlɪŋ/ ADJ Something that is **startling** is so different, unexpected, or remarkable that people react to it with surprise. 惊人的 ❑ *Sometimes the results may be rather startling.* 有时结果可能相当惊人。

start·up /stɑrtʌp/ (**startups**) 1 ADJ The **startup** costs of something such as a new business or new product are the costs of starting to run or produce it. 启动所需的(资金) [ADJ n] [BUSINESS] ❑ *That is enough to pay the startup costs for fourteen research projects.* 那足以支付14个研究项目的启动资金。 2 ADJ A **startup** company is a small business that has recently been started by someone. 新创办的(小公司) [ADJ n] [BUSINESS] ❑ *Thousands and thousands of startup firms have poured into the computer market.* 成千上万家新成立的小公司涌入了电脑市场。 ● N-COUNT **Startup** is also a noun. 新创办的小公司 ❑ *For now the only bright spots in the labor market are small businesses and high-tech startups.* 目前劳务市场上仅有的一些亮点是小企业和新创办的高科技公司。

star·va·tion /stɑrveɪʃᵊn/ N-UNCOUNT **Starvation** is extreme suffering or death, caused by lack of food. 饥饿；饿死 ❑ *Over three hundred people have died of starvation since the beginning of the year.* 自那年年初开始，已有三百多人饿死了。

starve /stɑrv/ (**starves, starving, starved**) 1 V-I If people **starve**, they suffer greatly from lack of food which sometimes leads to their death. 挨饿；饿死 ❑ *A number of the prisoners we saw are starving.* 我们看到的许多囚犯都快饿死了。 ❑ *In the 1930s, millions of Ukrainians starved to death or were deported.* 在20世纪30年代，数百万乌克兰人或因饥饿而死，或被驱逐出境。 2 V-T To **starve** someone means not to give them any food. 使挨饿 ❑ *He said the only alternative was to starve the people, and he said this could not be allowed to happen.* 他说惟一的其他办法是饿那些人，但他说这种做法是不允许的。 3 V-T If a person or thing **is starved of** something that they need, they are suffering because they are not getting enough of it. 使极其缺乏 ❑ *The electricity industry is not the only one to have been starved of investment.* 电力行业并不是惟一极其缺乏投资的行业。

starv·ing /stɑrvɪŋ/ ADJ If you say that you are **starving**, you mean that you are very hungry. 极饿的 [v-link ADJ] [INFORMAL] ❑ *Apart from anything else I was starving.* 别的不说，我快饿死了。

stash /stæʃ/ (**stashes, stashing, stashed**) 1 V-T If you **stash** something valuable in a secret place, you store it there to keep it safe. 藏(某物) [INFORMAL] ❑ *We went for the bottle of whiskey that we had stashed behind the bookcase.* 我们去取那瓶我们藏在书柜后面的威士忌。 2 N-COUNT A **stash of** something valuable is a secret store of it. 藏 [INFORMAL] ❑ *A large stash of drugs had been found aboard the yacht.* 在游艇上发现了大量藏匿的毒品。

state ♦♦♦ /steɪt/ (**states, stating, stated**) 1 N-COUNT You can refer to countries as **states**, particularly when you are discussing politics. (政治上所指的)国家 ❑ *Mexico is a secular state and does not have diplomatic relations with the Vatican.* 墨西哥是个非宗教国家，和梵蒂冈没有外交关系。

> **Country** is the most usual word to use when you are talking about the major political units that the world is divided into. **State** is used when you are talking about politics or government institutions. ❑ *...the new German state created by the unification process. ...Italy's state-controlled telecommunications company.* **State** can also refer to a political unit within a particular country. ❑ *...the state of California.* **Nation** is often used when you are talking about a country's inhabitants, and their cultural or ethnic background. ❑ *Wales is a proud nation with its own traditions... A senior government spokesman will address the nation.* **Land** is a less precise and more literary word, which you can use, for example, to talk about the feelings you have for a particular country. ❑ *She was fascinated to learn about this strange land at the edge of Europe.*

2 N-COUNT Some large countries such as the U.S. are divided into smaller areas called **states**. (美国等大国的)州 ❑ *Leaders of the Southern states are meeting in Louisville.* 南部各州的领导人们正在路易斯维尔会晤。 3 N-PROPER The U.S. is sometimes referred to as **the States**. 美国 [INFORMAL] ❑ *She bought it last year in the States.* 她去年在美国买了它。 4 N-SING You can refer to the government of a country as **the state**. 政府 ❑ *The state does not collect enough revenue to cover its expenditure.* 政府没有征到足够的税来支付它的费用。 5 ADJ **State** industries or organizations are financed and organized by the government rather than private companies. 政府的；国家的 [ADJ n] ❑ *...reform of the state social-security system.* …国家社会保障体制的改革。 → see **state school** 6 ADJ A **state** occasion is a formal one involving the head of a country. 国事的 [ADJ n] ❑ *The president of the Czech Republic is in Washington on a state visit.* 捷克共和国总统正在华盛顿进行国事访问。 7 N-COUNT When you talk about the **state of** someone or something, you are referring to the condition they are in or what they are like at a particular time. 状况；状态 ❑ *For the first few months after Daniel died, I was in a state of clinical depression.* 丹尼尔去世后的头几个月，我一直处在临床抑郁状态。 8 V-T If you **state** something, you say or write it in a formal or definite way. 说明；写明 ❑ *Clearly state your address and telephone number.* 清楚地写明你的地址和电话号码。 ❑ *The police report stated that he was arrested for allegedly assaulting his wife.* 警方报告称，他因涉嫌殴打妻子而被捕。 9 → see also **head of state, welfare state** 10 PHRASE If you say that someone **is not in a fit state to** do something, you mean that they are too upset or ill to do it. 不在(做某事的)适宜状态 ❑ *When you left our place, you weren't in a fit state to drive.* 你离开我们家时，你的状态不适合开车。 11 PHRASE If you are **in a state** or if you get **into a state**, you are very upset or nervous about something. 处于苦恼状态；处于焦虑状态 ❑ *I was in a terrible state because nobody could understand why I had this illness.* 我极度不安，因为没人能明白我为什么得了这种病。 12 PHRASE If the dead body of an important person **lies in state**, it is publicly displayed for a few days before it is buried. (要人的遗体)

供瞻仰 ❑ ...the 30,000 people who filed past the cardinal's body while it lay in state last week. …上周红衣主教的遗体供瞻仰时排队瞻仰了的3万民众。

→ see **matter**

Thesaurus *state* 另参见:

N. government, land, nation, republic, sovereignty 1
attitude, condition, mood, situation 7
V. articulate, express, narrate, relate, say, tell 8

State De·part·ment ♦◇◇ N-PROPER In the United States, **the State Department** is the government department that is concerned with foreign affairs. (美国) 国务院 ❑ *Officials at the State Department say the issue is urgent.* 美国国务院的官员们说这个问题紧急。

state·ment ♦♦◇ /steɪtmənt/ (**statements**) 1 N-COUNT A **statement** is something that you say or write which gives information in a formal or definite way. (正式或明确的口头或书面)陈述; 声明 ❑ *Andrew now disowns that statement, saying he was depressed when he made it.* 安德鲁现在否认了那个声明，说那是自己心情沮丧时作的。 2 N-COUNT A **statement** is an official or formal announcement that is issued on a particular occasion. (在特定场合的官方或正式的) 声明 ❑ *The statement by the military denied any involvement in last night's attack.* 军方的声明否认其与昨晚的袭击有任何关系。 3 N-COUNT You can refer to the official account of events which a suspect or a witness gives to the police as a **statement**. (嫌犯或证人向警方提供的) 陈述; 证词 ❑ *The 350-page report was based on statements from witnesses to the events.* 这份350页的报告基于该事件目击者的证词。 4 N-COUNT If you describe an action or thing as a **statement**, you mean that it clearly expresses a particular opinion or idea that you have. (某观点的) 表达 ❑ *The following recipe is a statement of another kind – food is fun!* 下面的食谱是另一种表述——食物就是乐趣！ 5 N-COUNT A printed document showing how much money has been paid into and taken out of a bank or investment account is called a **statement**. 结算清单 ❑ *...the address at the top of your monthly statement.* …你的月结算清单顶端的地址。

→ see **bank**

Word Partnership *statement* 的常用搭配:

N. **mission** statement 1
response to a statement 1 – 4
statement **of support** 1 2
policy statement 2
ADJ. **brief** statement, **formal** statement, **written** statement 1 – 3
political statement, **public** statement, **strong** statement 1 2 4
false/true statement 1 3
official statement 2
financial statement, **monthly** statement 5

state of af·fairs N-SING If you refer to a particular **state of affairs**, you mean the general situation and circumstances connected with someone or something. 事态 ❑ *Some say this state of affairs just can't last.* 有些人说这种事态不会持续多久。

state of mind (**states of mind**) N-COUNT Your **state of mind** is your mood or mental state at a particular time. 心态 ❑ *I want you to get into a whole new state of mind.* 我想让你进入一种全新的心态。

state-of-the-art ADJ If you describe something as **state-of-the-art**, you mean that it is the best available because it has been made using the most modern techniques and technology. (技术上) 最先进的 ❑ *...the production of state-of-the-art military equipment.* …最先进的军事装备的生产。

→ see **technology**

state school (**state schools**) 1 N-COUNT In the United States, a **state school** is a college or university that is part of the public education system provided by the state government. (美国) 州立大学 ❑ *At all 14 state schools, tuition and fees are going up this fall by an average of about 10 percent.* 所有14所州立大学今年秋季的学杂费都将上涨平均约10%。 2 N-COUNT A **state school** is the same as a **public school**. 公立学校 [BRIT]

★ **states·man** /steɪtsmən/ (**statesmen**) N-COUNT A **statesman** is an important and experienced politician, especially one who is widely known and respected. 政治家 ❑ *Hamilton is a great statesman and political thinker.* 汉密尔顿是个伟大的政治家和政治思想家。

state trooper (**state troopers**) N-COUNT In the U.S., a **state trooper** is a member of the police force in one of the states. (美国) 州警察 [AM] ❑ *State troopers said the truck driver was going too fast when he lost control.* 州警察们说那个卡车司机失去控制时开得太快。

state uni·ver·sity (**state universities**) N-COUNT A **state university** is the same as a **state school**. 州立大学 [AM] ❑ *He was a professor at the local state university.* 他曾是当地州立大学的教授。

Word Link *stat ≈ standing : static, station, stationary*

stat·ic /stætɪk/ 1 ADJ Something that is **static** does not move or change. 静止的; 不变的 ❑ *The number of young people obtaining qualifications has remained static or decreased.* 获得各种资格证书的年轻人的数量一直保持不变或者已经减少。 2 N-UNCOUNT **Static** or **static electricity** is electricity which can be caused by things rubbing against each other and which collects on things such as your body or metal objects. 静电 ❑ *When the weather turns cold and dry, my clothes develop a static problem.* 天气变冷变干时，我的衣服就会产生静电问题。 3 N-UNCOUNT If there is **static** on the radio or television, you hear a series of loud noises which spoils the sound. (广播或电视的) 静电噪音 ❑ *After only a minute an authoritative voice came through the static on the radio.* 过了仅一分钟后，透过广播的静电噪音传出了一个威严的声音。

sta·tion ♦♦◇ /steɪʃᵊn/ (**stations, stationing, stationed**) 1 N-COUNT A **station** or a train **station** is a building by a railroad track where trains stop so that people can get on or off. 火车站 ❑ *Ingrid went with him to the train station to see him off.* 英格丽德和他一起去火车站送他。 2 N-COUNT A bus **station** is a building, usually in a town or city, where buses stop, usually for a while, so that people can get on or off. (汽车) 站 ❑ *I walked the two miles back to the bus station and bought a ticket home.* 我走了两英里回到汽车站买了一张回家的票。 3 N-COUNT If you talk about a particular radio or television **station**, you are referring to the company that broadcasts programs. (电、电视) 台 ❑ *...an independent local radio station.* …一家独立的地方广播电台。 4 V-T PASSIVE If soldiers or officials **are stationed** in a place, they are sent there to do a job or to work for a period of time. 派驻 ❑ *Reports from the capital, Lome, say troops are stationed on the streets.* 来自首都洛美的报道说部队驻扎在街道上。 5 → see also **gas station, police station, power station, service station, space station**

→ see **cellphone, radio, satellite, television**

Word Partnership *station* 的常用搭配:

N. **railroad** station, **subway** station 1
radio station, **television/TV** station 3
ADJ. **local** station 3

★ **sta·tion·ary** /steɪʃənɛri/ ADJ Something that is **stationary** is not moving. 静止不动的 ❑ *Stationary cars in traffic jams cause a great deal of pollution.* 交通堵塞中停止不前的车辆造成大量污染。

▲ **sta·tion·ery** /steɪʃənɛri/ N-UNCOUNT **Stationery** is paper, envelopes, and other materials or equipment used for writing. 文具 ❑ *...envelopes and other office stationery.* …信封及其他办公文具。

→ see **office**

sta·tion wag·on (**station wagons**) N-COUNT A **station wagon** is a car with a long body, a door at the rear, and space behind the back seats. 旅行轿车 [AM]

in BRIT, use **estate car**

→ see **car**

sta·tis·tic ♦◇◇ /stətɪstɪk/ (**statistics**) 1 N-COUNT **Statistics** are facts which are obtained from analyzing information expressed in numbers, for example information about the number of times that something happens. 统计数据 ❑ *Official statistics show real wages declining by 24%.* 官方统计数据表明实际工资水平下降了24%。 2 N-UNCOUNT **Statistics** is a branch of mathematics concerned with the study of information that is expressed in numbers. 统计学 ❑ *...a professor of mathematical statistics.* …一位数理统计学教授。

sta·tis·ti·cal /stətɪstɪkᵊl/ ADJ **Statistical** means relating to the use of statistics. 统计的; 统计学的 ❑ *The report contains a great deal of statistical information.* 该报告包含大量统计资料。 ● **sta·tis·ti·cal·ly** /stətɪstɪkli/ ADV 统计上地; 统计学上地 ❑ *The results are not statistically significant.* 这些结果在统计上没有显著意义。

statue /stætʃu/ (**statues**) N-COUNT A **statue** is a large sculpture of a person or an animal, made of stone or metal. (石或金属做的动物或人的) 雕像 ❑ *...a bronze statue of an Arabian horse.* …一座阿拉伯马青铜雕像。

S

▲**stat·ure** /stætʃər/ **1** N-UNCOUNT Someone's **stature** is their height. 身高 ❑ *It's more than his physical stature that makes him remarkable.* 不单单是他的身高使他气宇非凡。 ❑ *Mother was of very small stature, barely five feet tall.* 母亲身材娇小，仅有5英尺高。 **2** N-UNCOUNT The **stature** of a person is the importance and reputation that they have. 名望 ❑ *Who can deny his stature as the world's greatest cellist?* 谁能否认他是世界上最伟大的大提琴演奏家？

sta·tus ♦♦◇ /steɪtəs, stæt-/ **1** N-UNCOUNT Your **status** is your social or professional position. 社会地位；职业地位 ❑ *People of higher status tend more to use certain drugs.* 社会地位较高的人更倾向于使用某些药物。 ❑ *...women and men of wealth and status.* …有钱有势的男男女女。 **2** N-UNCOUNT **Status** is the importance and respect that someone has among the public or a particular group. (在公众中或某一团体中的) 威望；地位 ❑ *Nurses are undervalued, and they never enjoy the same status as doctors.* 护士们没有得到足够重视，她们从未享受和医生一样的地位。 **3** N-UNCOUNT The **status** of something is the importance that people give it. 重要性 ❑ *Those things that can be assessed by external tests are being given unduly high status.* 那些能通过外部测试进行评估的东西受到过高重视。 **4** N-UNCOUNT A particular **status** is an official description that says what category a person, organization, or place belongs to, and gives them particular rights or advantages. 身份 ❑ *The Snoqualmie tribe regained its status as a federally recognized tribe.* 斯诺夸尔米部落重新获得了联邦政府所承认的部落的身份。 **5** N-UNCOUNT The **status** of something is its state of affairs at a particular time. 状况 ❑ *The council unanimously directed city staff to prepare a status report on the project.* 该委员会成员一致要求市政人员准备一份关于这项工程的进展状况报告。

Word Partnership *status* 的常用搭配：

V. **achieve** status, **maintain/preserve** *one's* status **1**
N. **celebrity** status, **wealth and** status **1** **2**
change of status **1** – **5**
tax status **5**
ADJ. **current** status **1** – **5**
economic status, **financial** status, **marital** status **5**

sta·tus quo /steɪtəs kwoʊ, stæt-/ N-SING **The status quo** is the state of affairs that exists at a particular time, especially in contrast to a different possible state of affairs. 现状 ❑ *By 492 votes to 391, the federation voted to maintain the status quo.* 联盟以492票对391票投票决定维持现状。

▲**stat·ute** /stætʃut/ (**statutes**) N-VAR A **statute** is a rule or law which has been made by a government or other organization and formally written down. 法令；规章 ❑ *The new statute covers the care for, raising, and protection of children.* 这项新法令涵盖了儿童的照料、养育和保护。

▲**statu·tory** /stætʃʊtɔri/ ADJ **Statutory** means relating to rules or laws which have been formally written down. 规定的；法定的 [FORMAL] ❑ *The FCC has no statutory authority to regulate the Internet.* 美国联邦通信委员会没有规范因特网的法定权力。

staunch /stɔntʃ/ (**stauncher, staunchest**) ADJ A **staunch** supporter or believer is very loyal to a person, organization, or set of beliefs, and supports them strongly. 坚定的 ❑ *He's a staunch supporter of controls on government spending.* 他是政府开支控制的坚定支持者。 ● **staunch·ly** ADV 坚定地 ❑ *He was staunchly opposed to a public confession.* 他坚决反对公开认错。

stay ♦♦♦ /steɪ/ (**stays, staying, stayed**) **1** V-I If you **stay** where you are, you continue to be there and do not leave. 停留 ❑ *"Stay here," Trish said. "I'll bring the car down the drive to take you back."* "呆在这儿，"特里希说道，"我会把车开下来送你回去。" **2** V-I If you **stay** in a town, or hotel, or at someone's house, you live there for a short time. (在某城市、酒店、某人家里) 暂住；逗留 ❑ *Gordon stayed at The Park Hotel, Milan.* 戈登住在了米兰的帕克酒店。 ❑ *Can't you stay a few more days?* 你不能多住几天吗？ ● N-COUNT **Stay** is also a noun. 暂住；逗留 ❑ *An experienced Indian guide is provided during your stay.* 在你逗留期间给你配备一位经验丰富的印第安向导。 **3** V-LINK If someone or something **stays** in a particular state or situation, they continue to be in it. 保持 (某种状态) ❑ *The Republican candidate said he would "work like crazy to stay ahead."* 该共和党候选人说他将"拼命工作以保持领先地位。" ❑ *...community care networks that offer classes on how to stay healthy.* …提供如何保持健康的课程的社区护理网络。 **4** V-I If you **stay away from** a place, you do not go there. 不去 (某地) ❑ *Management also stayed away from work during the strike.* 管理人员在那次罢工期间也不去上班了。 **5** V-I If you **stay out** of something, you do not get involved in it. 不参与 ❑ *In the past, the UN has stayed out of the internal affairs of countries unless invited in.* 在过去，除非受邀请介入，否则联合国不参与各国的内部事务。 **6** PHRASE If you **stay put**, you remain somewhere. 留在原地 ❑ *He was forced by his condition to stay put and remain out of politics.* 他受自身状况所迫呆在原处，置身政治之外。 **7** PHRASE If you **stay the night** in a place, you sleep there for one night. 住一宿 ❑ *They had invited me to come to supper and stay the night.* 他们已经邀请我共进晚餐并住一宿。

▸ **stay in** PHRASAL VERB If you **stay in** during the evening, you remain at home and do not go out. (夜晚) 呆在家里 ❑ *If I stay in, my boyfriend cooks a wonderful lasagne or chicken or steak.* 我呆在家里的话，我男朋友会做一顿美味的意大利宽面条或鸡肉或牛排。

▸ **stay on** PHRASAL VERB If you **stay on** somewhere, you remain there after other people have left or after the time when you were going to leave. 继续逗留 ❑ *He had managed to arrange to stay on in Adelaide.* 他已设法安排继续在阿德莱德市逗留。

▸ **stay out** PHRASAL VERB If you **stay out** at night, you remain away from home, especially when you are expected to be there. (夜晚) 呆在外面 ❑ *That was the first time Elliot stayed out all night.* 那是埃利奥特第一次彻夜未归。

▸ **stay up** PHRASAL VERB If you **stay up**, you remain out of bed at a time when most people have gone to bed or at a time when you are normally in bed yourself. 熬夜 ❑ *I used to stay up late with my mom and watch movies.* 我过去常和妈妈熬夜看电影。

stead /stɛd/ PHRASE If you say that something will **stand** someone **in good stead**, you mean that it will be very useful to them in the future. 对某人的将来很有用 ❑ *These two games here will stand them in good stead for the future.* 这里的两场比赛对他们的将来很有用。

stead·fast /stɛdfæst/ ADJ If someone is **steadfast in** something that they are doing, they are convinced that what they are doing is right and they refuse to change it or to give up. 坚定的 ❑ *He remained steadfast in his belief that he had done the right thing.* 他仍然坚信自己做了正确的事情。

Word Link *stead ≈ place, stand : homestead, instead, steady*

steady ♦◇◇ /stɛdi/ (**steadier, steadiest, steadies, steadying, steadied**) **1** ADJ A **steady** situation continues or develops gradually without any interruptions and is not likely to change quickly. 稳定的 ❑ *Despite the steady progress of building work, the campaign against it is still going strong.* 尽管建筑工程稳步进行，反工运动却仍然高涨。 ❑ *The improvement in standards has been steady and persistent, but has attracted little comment from educationalists.* 虽然标准在持续稳步提高，但教育者并未对此有何评论。 ● **steadi·ly** /stɛdɪli/ ADV 稳定地 [ADV with v] ❑ *Relax as much as possible and keep breathing steadily.* 尽量放松，保持呼吸平稳。 **2** ADJ If an object is **steady**, it is firm and does not shake or move around. 平稳的 ❑ *Get as close to the subject as you can and hold the camera steady.* 尽可能靠近对象，拿稳相机。 **3** ADJ If you look at someone or speak to them in a **steady** way, you look or speak in a calm, controlled way. 镇定的 ❑ *"Well, go on," said Camilla, her voice fairly steady.* "嗯，继续吧。"卡米拉说道，声音相当镇定。 ● **steadi·ly** ADV 镇定地 [ADV after v] ❑ *He moved back a little and stared steadily at Elaine.* 他往后退了点，镇定地盯着依莱恩。 **4** ADJ If you describe a person as **steady**, you mean that they are sensible and reliable. 可靠的 ❑ *He was firm and steady unlike other men she knew.* 他坚定、可靠，和她所认识的其他男人不同。 **5** V-T/V-I If you **steady** something or if it **steadies**, it stops shaking or moving around. 使平稳；平稳 ❑ *Two men were on the bridge-deck, steadying a ladder.* 两人站在船桥甲板上，扶稳一个梯子。 **6** V-T If you **steady yourself**, you control your voice or expression, so that people will think that you are calm and not nervous. 使镇定 ❑ *Somehow she steadied herself and murmured, "Have you got a cigarette?"* 她设法使自己镇定下来，并低声问道，"你有香烟吗？"

Thesaurus *steady* 另参见：

ADJ. consistent, continuous, uninterrupted **1**
constant, fixed, stable **2**
calm, cool, reserved, sedate **3** **4**

Word Partnership *steady* 的常用搭配：

N. steady **decline/increase**, steady **diet**, steady **growth**, steady **improvement**, steady **income**, steady **progress**, steady **rain**, steady **rate**, steady **supply** **1** **4**
V. **remain** steady **1** **4**
hold/keep *something* steady **2**
hold steady **5**

S

steak /steɪk/ (**steaks**) **1** N-VAR A **steak** is a large flat piece of beef without much fat on it. You cook it by grilling or frying it. 牛排 ❑ *...a steak sizzling on the grill.* …一块儿在烤架上滋滋作响的牛排。 **2** N-COUNT A fish **steak** is a large piece of fish that contains few bones. (鱼) 排 ❑ *...fresh salmon steaks.* …新鲜的三文鱼排。

steal ♦◇◇ /stil/ (**steals, stealing, stole, stolen**) **1** V-T/V-I If you **steal** something **from** someone, you take it away from them without their permission and without intending to return it. 偷 ❑ *He was accused of stealing a small boy's bicycle.* 他被指控偷了一个小男孩的自行车。 ❑ *People who are drug addicts come in and steal.* 吸毒成瘾的人们进来偷东西。 ● **sto·len** ADJ 被盗的 ❑ *We have now found the stolen car.* 我们现已找到被盗的汽车。 **2** V-T If you **steal** someone else's ideas, you pretend that they are your own. 剽窃 ❑ *A writer is suing director Steven Spielberg for allegedly stealing his film idea.* 一个作家正在控告史蒂文・斯皮尔伯格导演剽窃了他的电影创意。

> Do not confuse **steal** and **rob**. If someone **steals** something, for example, money or a car, they take it without asking and without intending to give it back. ❑ *My car was stolen on Friday evening.* Note that you cannot say that someone **steals** someone. If someone **robs** someone or somewhere, they take something, often violently, from that person or place without asking and without intending to give it back. ❑ *They planned to rob an old widow... They joined forces to rob a factory.* You can also say that someone **robs** you of something when referring to what has been taken. ❑ *The two men were robbed of more than $700.*

Thesaurus *steal* 另参见：
V. burglarize, embezzle, swipe, take **1**

steam ♦◇◇ /stim/ (**steams, steaming, steamed**) **1** N-UNCOUNT **Steam** is the hot mist that forms when water boils. **Steam** vehicles and machines are operated using steam as a means of power. 蒸汽 ❑ *In an electric power plant the heat converts water into high-pressure steam.* 在发电厂里，热把水转换成高压水蒸汽。 **2** V-I If something **steams**, it gives off steam. 冒蒸汽 ❑ *...restaurants where coffee pots steamed on their burners.* …饭店里咖啡壶在炉子上冒着热气。 **3** V-T/V-I If you **steam** food or if it **steams**, you cook it in steam rather than in water. 蒸 ❑ *Steam the carrots until they are just beginning to be tender.* 把胡萝卜蒸到刚好变软。 ❑ *Leave the vegetables to steam over the rice for the 20 minutes cooking time.* 把蔬菜放在米饭上蒸20分钟。 **4** PHRASE If something such as a plan or a project goes **full steam ahead**, it progresses quickly. 全速推进 ❑ *The administration was determined to go full steam ahead with its reform program.* 当局决心全速推进其改革方案。 **5** PHRASE If you **run out of steam**, you stop doing something because you have no more energy or enthusiasm left. 筋疲力尽 [INFORMAL] ❑ *I decided to paint the bathroom ceiling but ran out of steam halfway through.* 我决定要粉刷浴室天花板，但干了一半就筋疲力尽了。
→ see **cook, train**
▸ **steam up** PHRASAL VERB When a window, mirror, or pair of glasses **steams up**, it becomes covered with steam or mist. 蒙上水汽 ❑ *...the irritation of living with lenses that steam up when you come in from the cold.* …忍受从冷处进来蒙上水汽的镜片的烦恼。

Word Partnership *steam* 的常用搭配：
N. steam **bath**, **clouds of** steam, steam **engine**, steam **locomotive**, steam **pipes**, steam **turbine** **1**
ADJ. steam **powered**, **rising** steam **1**

steam·er /stimər/ (**steamers**) **1** N-COUNT A **steamer** is a ship that has an engine powered by steam. 汽轮 **2** N-COUNT A **steamer** is a special container used for steaming food such as vegetables and fish. 蒸锅

steamy /stimi/ **1** ADJ **Steamy** means involving exciting sex. 色情的 [INFORMAL] ❑ *He'd had a steamy affair with an office colleague.* 他和办公室的一位同事曾经闹过桃色新闻。 **2** ADJ A **steamy** place has hot, wet air. 湿热的 ❑ *...a steamy cafe.* …一家湿热的咖啡屋。

steel ♦◇◇ /stil/ (**steels, steeling, steeled**) **1** N-MASS **Steel** is a very strong metal which is made mainly from iron. Steel is used for making many things, for example bridges, buildings, vehicles, and flatware. 钢 ❑ *...steel pipes.* …钢管。 ❑ *...the iron and steel industry.* …钢铁工业。 **2** → see also **stainless steel** **3** V-T If you **steel yourself**, you prepare to deal with something unpleasant. 使准备应对 (不愉快之事) ❑ *Those involved are steeling themselves for the coming battle.* 那些参与者正准备应对即将到来的战斗。
→ see **bridge, train**

steely /stili/ ADJ **Steely** is used to emphasize that a person is strong and determined. 坚定的 [EMPHASIS] ❑ *Clad in their black sweatsuits, the Maryland players had a steely determination.* 身着黑色运动服，马里兰队员们有着坚定的决心。

steep /stip/ (**steeper, steepest**) **1** ADJ A **steep** slope rises at a very sharp angle and is difficult to go up. 陡峭的 ❑ *San Francisco is built on 40 hills and some are very steep.* 旧金山建在40座山丘上，其中有些非常陡峭。 ● **steep·ly** ADV 陡峭地 [ADV with v] ❑ *The road climbs steeply, with good views of Orvieto through the trees.* 这条路陡直地向上延伸，透过树丛可以一览奥维多的景色。 ❑ *...steeply terraced valleys.* …陡峭的梯形山谷。 **2** ADJ A **steep** increase or decrease in something is a very big increase or decrease. 急剧的 ❑ *Consumers are rebelling at steep price increases.* 消费者们正在抗议急剧的物价上涨。 ● **steep·ly** ADV 急剧地 [ADV with v] ❑ *Unemployment is rising steeply.* 失业率正在急剧上升。 **3** ADJ If you say that the price of something is **steep**, you mean that it is expensive. (价格) 高昂的 [INFORMAL] ❑ *The annual premium can be a little steep, but will be well worth it if your dog is injured.* 每年的保险费可能有点贵，但是如果您的狗受了伤就很值了。

steeped /stipt/ ADJ If a place or person is **steeped in** a quality or characteristic, they are surrounded by it or deeply influenced by it. 充满…的色彩；深受…浸淫的 [v-link ADJ "in" n] ❑ *The castle is steeped in history and legend.* 这座城堡充满着历史和传奇色彩。

steer /stɪər/ (**steers, steering, steered**) **1** V-T When you **steer** a car, boat, or plane, you control it so that it goes in the direction that you want. 驾驶 ❑ *What is it like to steer a ship this size?* 驾驶这样大小的船会怎么样呢？ **2** V-T If you **steer** people toward a particular course of action or attitude, you try to lead them gently in that direction. 引导 ❑ *The new government is seen as one that will steer the country in the right direction.* 新政府被认为是能将这个国家引向正确的方向。 **3** V-T If you **steer** someone in a particular direction, you guide them there. 引领 ❑ *Nick steered them into the nearest seats.* 尼克领着他们到最近的座位。 **4** PHRASE If you **steer clear of** someone or something, you deliberately avoid them. 有意避开某人/某物 ❑ *I think a lot of people, women in particular, steer clear of these sensitive issues.* 我认为很多人，尤其是女性，有意避开这些敏感问题。

steer·ing wheel (**steering wheels**) N-COUNT In a car or other vehicle, the **steering wheel** is the wheel which the driver holds when he or she is driving. 方向盘

stem ♦◇◇ /stɛm/ (**stems, stemming, stemmed**) **1** V-I If a condition or problem **stems from** something, it was caused originally by that thing. 起源于 ❑ *All my problems stem from drink.* 我所有的问题都是酗酒引起的。 **2** V-T If you **stem** something, you stop it spreading, increasing, or continuing. 阻止 [FORMAL] ❑ *Austria has sent three army battalions to its border with Hungary to stem the flow of illegal immigrants.* 奥地利已派遣3个营到达与匈牙利接壤的边境处，以阻止非法移民的流入。 **3** N-COUNT The **stem** of a plant is the thin, upright part on which the flowers and leaves grow. 茎 ❑ *He stooped down, cut the stem for her with his knife and handed her the flower.* 他弯下腰，用刀替她割下花茎，然后把花递给她。

Word Partnership *stem* 的常用搭配：
N. **charges** stem **from** *something*, **problems** stem **from** *something* **1**
stem **the flow of** *something*, stem **losses**, stem **the tide of** *something* **2**

stem cell (**stem cells**) N-COUNT A **stem cell** is a type of cell that can produce other cells which are able to develop into any kind of cell in the body. 干细胞 ❑ *Stem cell research is supported by many doctors.* 干细胞研究得到很多医生的支持。

stench /stɛntʃ/ (**stenches**) N-COUNT A **stench** is a strong and very unpleasant smell. 臭味 ❑ *The stench of burning rubber was overpowering.* 燃烧橡胶散发出的臭味极其强烈。

sten·cil /stɛnsᵊl/ (**stencils, stenciling** or **stencilling, stenciled** or **stencilled**) **1** N-COUNT A **stencil** is a piece of paper, plastic, or metal which has a design cut out of it. You place the stencil on a surface and paint it so that paint goes through the holes and leaves a design on the surface. 模版 **2** V-T If you **stencil** a design or if you **stencil** a surface **with** a design, you put a design on a surface using a stencil. 用模版印制 ❑ *He then stenciled the ceiling with a moon and stars motif.* 他接着用模版在天花板印上月亮和星星图案。

S

step ♦♦♦ /stɛp/ (**steps, stepping, stepped**) 1 N-COUNT If you take a **step**, you lift your foot and put it down in a different place, for example when you are walking. 脚步 ❑ *I took a step toward him.* 我朝他迈出了一步。 ❑ *She walked on a few steps.* 她继续走了几步。 2 V-I If you **step on** something or **step** in a particular direction, you put your foot on the thing or move your foot in that direction. 踩 ❑ *This was the moment when Neil Armstrong became the first man to step on the Moon.* 正是在这一刻，内尔·阿姆斯特朗成为了登月第一人。 ❑ *She accidentally stepped on his foot on a crowded commuter train.* 她在一辆拥挤的通勤火车上不小心踩到他的脚。 3 N-COUNT **Steps** are a series of surfaces at increasing or decreasing heights, on which you put your feet in order to walk up or down to a different level. 台阶 ❑ *This little room was along a passage and down some steps.* 这小房间在沿着一个过道再走下几级台阶的地方。 4 N-COUNT A **step** is a raised flat surface in front of a door. 门槛 ❑ *A little girl was sitting on the step of the end house.* 有个小女孩坐在最后面那栋房子的门槛上。 5 → see also **doorstep** 6 N-COUNT A **step** is one of a series of actions that you take in order to achieve something. 步骤 ❑ *He greeted the agreement as the first step toward peace.* 他赞称这项协议是迈向和平的第一步。 7 N-COUNT A **step** in a process is one of a series of stages. 阶段 ❑ *The next step is to put the theory into practice.* 下一阶段要把理论付诸实践。 8 N-COUNT The **steps** of a dance are the sequences of foot movements which make it up. 舞步 ❑ *She was a better dancer than Gordon. At least she knew the steps.* 她舞跳得比戈登好，至少她会那些舞步。 9 N-SING Someone's **step** is the way they walk. 步伐 ❑ *He quickened his step.* 他加快了步伐。 10 PHRASE If you stay **one step ahead of** someone or something, you manage to achieve more than they do or avoid competition or danger from them. 领先一步；避开 ❑ *Successful travel is partly a matter of keeping one step ahead of the crowd.* 成功的旅游在某种程度上就是避开众人。 11 PHRASE If people who are walking or dancing are **in step**, they are moving their feet forward at exactly the same time as each other. If they are **out of step**, their feet are moving forward at different times. 步伐（不）一致 ❑ *They were almost the same height and they moved perfectly in step.* 他们身高相仿，而且走路的步伐也完全一致。 12 PHRASE If people are **in step with** each other, their ideas or opinions are the same. If they are **out of step with** each other, their ideas or opinions are different. 意见（不）一致 ❑ *Moscow is anxious to stay in step with Washington.* 莫斯科迫切希望与华盛顿保持一致。 13 PHRASE If you do something **step by step**, you do it by progressing gradually from one stage to the next. 一步一步地 ❑ *I am not rushing things and I'm taking it step by step.* 我没急于求成，我正在一步一步地来。 14 PHRASE If someone tells you to **watch** your **step**, they are warning you to be careful about how you behave or what you say so that you do not get into trouble. 谨慎行事 ❑ *He said I'd come to a bad end, if I didn't watch my step.* 他说如果我不谨慎行事，我的结局会很惨的。

▸ **step aside** → see **stand down**

▸ **step back** PHRASAL VERB If you **step back** and think about a situation, you think about it as if you were not involved in it. 退一步（思考） ❑ *I stepped back and analysed the situation.* 我退一步分析了局势。

▸ **step down** or **step aside** PHRASAL VERB If someone **steps down** or **steps aside**, they resign from an important job or position, often in order to let someone else take their place. 退位 ❑ *Judge Ito said that if his wife was called as a witness, he would step down as trial judge.* 伊托法官说如果自己妻子被传为证人的话，他将辞去审判法官的职位。

▸ **step in** PHRASAL VERB If you **step in**, you get involved in a difficult situation because you think you can or should help with it. 干预 ❑ *If no agreement was reached, the army would step in.* 如果达不成协议，军队将会干预。

▸ **step up** PHRASAL VERB If you **step up** something, you increase it or increase its intensity. 增加 ❑ *He urged donors to step up their efforts to send aid to Somalia.* 他敦促捐赠者再接再厉，将救援物资送往索马里。

Word Partnership *step* 的常用搭配：

ADV.	step **outside** 2
	step **ahead**, step **backward**, step **closer**, step **forward** 2 5 - 7
ADJ.	**big** step, **bold** step, **giant** step, **the right** step 6
	critical step, **important** step, **positive** step 6 7
N.	step **in a process** 7

step·brother /stɛpbrʌðər/ (**stepbrothers**) also **step-brother** N-COUNT Someone's **stepbrother** is the son of their stepfather or stepmother. 继兄；继弟

step·daughter /stɛpdɔtər/ (**stepdaughters**) also **step-daughter** N-COUNT Someone's **stepdaughter** is a daughter that was born to their husband or wife during a previous relationship. 继女

step·family /stɛpfæmɪli, -fæmli/ (**stepfamilies**) N-COUNT A **stepfamily** is a family that consists of a husband and wife and one or more children from a previous marriage or relationship. 重组家庭 ❑ *Stepfamilies are rapidly becoming the norm, not the exception.* 重组家庭正迅速变得司空见惯，不再是个例外。

Word Link *step ≈ related by remarriage : stepfather, stepmother, stepsister*

▲ **step·father** /stɛpfɑðər/ (**stepfathers**) also **step-father** N-COUNT Someone's **stepfather** is the man who has married their mother after the death or divorce of their father. 继父

▲ **step·mother** /stɛpmʌðər/ (**stepmothers**) also **step-mother** N-COUNT Someone's **stepmother** is the woman who has married their father after the death or divorce of their mother. 继母

step·ping stone (**stepping stones**) also **stepping-stone, steppingstone** 1 N-COUNT You can describe a job or event as a **stepping stone** when it helps you to make progress, especially in your career. 垫脚石；进身之阶 ❑ *It is just another stepping stone to bigger and better things.* 这只不过是通往那些更大更好事情的又一块垫脚石。 2 N-COUNT **Stepping stones** are a line of large stones which you can walk on in order to cross a shallow stream or river. （小溪或河流中的）踏脚石

step·sister /stɛpsɪstər/ (**stepsisters**) also **step-sister** N-COUNT Someone's **stepsister** is the daughter of their stepfather or stepmother. 继姐；继妹

step·son /stɛpsʌn/ (**stepsons**) also **step-son** N-COUNT Someone's **stepson** is a son born to their husband or wife during a previous relationship. 继子

★ **ste·reo** /stɛrioʊ, stɪər-/ (**stereos**) 1 ADJ **Stereo** is used to describe a sound system in which the sound is played through two speakers. Compare **mono**. 立体声的 ❑ *...loudspeakers that give all-around stereo sound.* …发出环绕立体声的喇叭。 2 N-COUNT A **stereo** is a CD player with two speakers. 立体音响

ste·reo·type /stɛriətaɪp, stɪər-/ (**stereotypes, stereotyping, stereotyped**) 1 N-COUNT A **stereotype** is a fixed general image or set of characteristics that a lot of people believe represent a particular type of person or thing. 模式化形象；成见 ❑ *There's always been a stereotype about successful businessmen.* 对成功的商人们总有一种成见。 2 V-T If someone **is stereotyped** as something, people form a fixed general idea or image of them, so that it is assumed that they will behave in a particular way. 把…模式化；对…产生成见 [usu passive] ❑ *He was stereotyped by some as a renegade.* 他被一些人带着成见视为一名叛逆者。

ste·reo·typi·cal /stɛriətɪpɪkəl, stɪər-/ ADJ A **stereotypical** idea of a type of person or thing is a fixed general idea that a lot of people have about it, that may be false in many cases. 模式化的；成见的 ❑ *These are men whose masculinity does not conform to stereotypical images of the unfeeling male.* 这些阳刚的男人不符合那种冷血男人的成见形象。

ster·ile /stɛrəl/ 1 ADJ Something that is **sterile** is completely clean and free from germs. 无菌的 ❑ *He always made sure that any cuts were protected by sterile dressings.* 他总是确保所有伤口都用无菌的敷料包好。 ● **ste·ril·ity** /stərɪlɪti/ N-UNCOUNT 无菌 ❑ *...the antiseptic sterility of the hospital.* …医院的无菌消毒。 2 ADJ A person or animal that is **sterile** is unable to have or produce babies. 不育的 ❑ *George was sterile.* 乔治不能生育。 ● **ste·ril·ity** N-UNCOUNT 不育 ❑ *This disease causes sterility in both males and females.* 这种疾病会导致男女不育。

steri·lise /stɛrɪlaɪz/ [BRIT] → see **sterilize**

steri·lize /stɛrɪlaɪz/ (**sterilizes, sterilizing, sterilized**)

in BRIT, also use **sterilise**

1 V-T If you **sterilize** a thing or a place, you make it completely clean and free from germs. 给…消毒 ❑ *Sulfur is also used to sterilize equipment.* 硫磺也用来给设备消毒。 ● **steri·li·za·tion** /stɛrɪlɪzeɪʃən/ N-UNCOUNT 消毒 ❑ *...the pasteurization and sterilization of milk.* …牛奶的巴氏消毒和灭菌处理。 2 V-T If a person or an animal **is sterilized**, they have a medical operation that makes it impossible for them to have or produce babies. 给…做绝育手术 [usu passive] ❑ *My wife was sterilized after the birth of her fourth child.* 我妻子在生了第4个孩子后，

做了绝育手术。 ● **steri·li·za·tion** N-VAR (**sterilizations**) 绝育手术 ❑ *In some cases, a sterilization is performed through the vaginal wall.* 在有些情况下，绝育手术是穿过阴道壁进行的。

▲ **ster·ling** ♦♦◇ /stɜrlɪŋ/ **1** ADJ **Sterling** means very good in quality; used to describe someone's work or character. (工作或品格) 优秀的 [FORMAL, APPROVAL] ❑ *Those are sterling qualities to be admired in anyone.* 那些优秀品质在任何人身上都值得称道。 **2** N-UNCOUNT **Sterling** is the money system of Great Britain. 英镑 ❑ *The stamps had to be paid for in sterling.* 邮票必须用英镑支付。

★ **stern** /stɜrn/ (**sterner, sternest**) **1** ADJ **Stern** words or actions are very severe. (话语或行为) 严厉的 ❑ *Mr. Monroe issued a stern warning to those who persist in violence.* 门罗先生向那些顽守暴力之徒发出严厉警告。 ● **stern·ly** ADV 严厉地 ❑ *"We will take the necessary steps," she said sternly.* "我们将采取必要措施，" 她严厉地说道。 **2** ADJ Someone who is **stern** is very serious and strict. 苛刻的 ❑ *Her father was stern and hard to please.* 她父亲苛刻，不易讨好。

ster·oid /stɪrɔɪd, stɛr-/ (**steroids**) N-COUNT A **steroid** is a type of chemical substance found in your body. Steroids can be artificially introduced into the bodies of athletes to improve their strength. 类固醇

▲ **stew** /stu/ (**stews, stewing, stewed**) **1** N-VAR A **stew** is a meal which you make by cooking meat and vegetables in liquid at a low temperature. 炖煮的菜肴 ❑ *She served him a bowl of beef stew.* 她给他端了一碗炖牛肉。 **2** V-T When you **stew** meat, vegetables, or fruit, you cook them slowly in liquid in a covered pot. 炖 ❑ *Stew the apple and blackberries to make a thick pulp.* 把苹果和黑莓炖成浓稠的果浆。

▲ **stew·ard** /stuərd/ (**stewards**) **1** N-COUNT A **steward** is a man who works on a ship, plane, or train, taking care of passengers and serving meals to them. 男乘务员 **2** N-COUNT A **steward** is a man or woman who helps to organize a race, march, or other public event. (比赛、游行等公共活动的) 组织者 ❑ *The steward at the march stood his ground while the rest of the marchers decided to run.* 当其余的游行者决定跑掉时，游行的组织者坚守了他的位置。

▲ **stew·ard·ess** /stuərdɪs/ (**stewardesses**) N-COUNT A **stewardess** is a woman who works on a ship, plane, or train, taking care of passengers and serving meals to them. 女乘务员

stick

❶ NOUN USES
❷ VERB USES

❶ **stick** ♦◇◇ /stɪk/ (**sticks**) **1** N-COUNT A **stick** is a thin branch which has fallen off a tree. 枝条 ❑ *...people carrying bundles of dried sticks to sell for firewood.* …背着成捆枯枝当柴火卖的人。 **2** N-COUNT A **stick** is a long thin piece of wood which is used for a particular purpose. 棍 ❑ *...lollipop sticks.* …棒棒糖棍。 ❑ *...drum sticks.* …鼓槌。 **3** N-COUNT Some long thin objects that are used in sports are called **sticks**. 球棒 ❑ *...lacrosse sticks.* …长曲棍球球棒。 ❑ *...hockey sticks.* …曲棍球棒。 **4** N-COUNT A **stick of** something is a long thin piece of it. 条状物 ❑ *...a stick of celery.* …一根芹菜。 **5** N-COUNT A **stick** is a long thin piece of wood which is used for supporting someone's weight or for hitting people or animals. 拐杖; (袭击用的) 棍子 [BRIT] in AM, use **cane** **6** PHRASE If someone **gets the wrong end of the stick** or **gets hold of the wrong end of the stick**, they do not understand something correctly and get the wrong idea about it. 误解 [INFORMAL] ❑ *I think someone has got the wrong end of the stick. They should have established the facts before speaking out.* 我想有人误解了。他们本应该在查证事实之后再发表意见。
→ see **drawing**

❷ **stick** ♦♦◇ /stɪk/ (**sticks, sticking, stuck**) **1** V-T If you **stick** something somewhere, you put it there in a rather casual way. 随意放置 [INFORMAL] ❑ *He folded the papers and stuck them in his desk drawer.* 他把文件折起扔进书桌抽屉里。 **2** V-T/V-I If you **stick** a pointed object **in** something, or if it **sticks in** something, it goes into it or through it by making a cut or hole. 使扎入; 扎入 ❑ *They sent in loads of male nurses and stuck a needle in my back.* 他们派来很多男护士，在我的背部扎了根针。 **3** V-I If something **is sticking out** from a surface or object, it extends up or away from it. If something **is sticking into** a surface or object, it is partly in it. 伸出 ❑ *They lay where they had fallen from the crane, sticking out of the water.* 他们位于从那台起重机上摔下的地方，部分露在水面。 **4** V-T If you **stick** one thing to another, you attach it using glue, Scotch tape, or another sticky substance. 粘贴 ❑ *Don't forget to clip the token and stick it on your card.* 别忘了剪下代金券，并贴在你的卡上。 **5** V-I If one thing **sticks to** another, it becomes attached to it and is difficult to remove. 粘住 ❑ *The soil sticks to the blade and blocks the plough.* 土粘在刃上，卡住了犁。 ❑ *Peel away the waxed paper if it has stuck to the bottom of the cake.* 如果蜡纸粘住蛋糕底部，就把它撕掉。 **6** V-I If something **sticks in your** mind, you remember it for a long time. 经久留驻 ❑ *The incident stuck in my mind because it was the first example I had seen of racism in that country.* 那个事件令我难以忘怀，因为那是我看到的那个国家的第一例种族歧视事件。 **7** V-I If something which can usually be moved **sticks**, it becomes fixed in one position. 卡住 ❑ *The needle on the dial went right around to fifty feet, which was as far as it could go, and there it stuck.* 刻度盘上的指针一下转到了50英尺处，即其所能达到的最大刻度，然后卡在了那里。 **8** → see also **stuck**

▸ **stick around** PHRASAL VERB If you **stick around**, you stay where you are, often because you are waiting for something. (为等候) 呆在原地不动 [INFORMAL] ❑ *Stick around a while and see what develops.* 稍呆一会儿，看看会发生什么。

▸ **stick by** **1** PHRASAL VERB If you **stick by** someone, you continue to give them help or support. 继续帮助; 继续支持 ❑ *...friends who stuck by me during the difficult times.* …在困难时继续支持我的朋友们。 **2** PHRASAL VERB If you **stick by** a promise, agreement, decision, or principle, you do what you said you would do, or do not change your mind. 坚持 (诺言、协议、决定或原则) ❑ *But I made my decision then and stuck by it.* 但是我当时做了决定，而且坚持这个决定。

▸ **stick out** **1** PHRASAL VERB If you **stick out** part of your body, you extend it away from your body. 伸出 ❑ *She made a face and stuck out her tongue at him.* 她做了鬼脸，冲他吐了吐舌头。 **2** to **stick** your **neck out** → see **neck** **3** PHRASAL VERB If something **sticks out**, it is very noticeable because it is unusual. 突出显眼 ❑ *What had Cutter done to make him stick out from the crowd?* 卡特做了什么让他在人群中如此显眼？ **4** PHRASE If someone in an unpleasant or difficult situation **sticks it out**, they do not leave or give up. 坚持到底 ❑ *I really didn't like New York, but I wanted to stick it out a little bit longer.* 我真的不喜欢纽约，但我想再稍稍坚持一段时间。

▸ **stick to** **1** PHRASAL VERB If you **stick to** something or someone when you are traveling, you stay close to them. 紧跟 ❑ *Let's stick to the road we know.* 我们沿着熟悉的路走吧。 **2** PHRASAL VERB If you **stick to** something, you continue doing, using, saying, or talking about it, rather than changing to something else. 坚持 ❑ *Perhaps he should have stuck to writing.* 或许他本该坚持写作。 **3** PHRASAL VERB If you **stick to** a promise, agreement, decision, or principle, you do what you said you would do, or do not change your mind. 坚持 (诺言、协议、决定或原则) ❑ *Immigrant support groups are waiting to see if he sticks to his word.* 支持移民的团体正观望他是否遵守诺言。 **4** to **stick to** your **guns** → see **gun**

▸ **stick together** PHRASAL VERB If people **stick together**, they stay with each other and support each other. 团结一致 ❑ *If we all stick together, we ought to be okay.* 如果我们团结一致，应该会没事的。

▸ **stick up for** PHRASAL VERB If you **stick up for** a person or a principle, you support or defend them forcefully. 支持; 捍卫 ❑ *You would think my own father would stick up for me once in a while.* 你会认为我的亲生父亲偶尔也会支持我一下。

▸ **stick with** **1** PHRASAL VERB If you **stick with** something, you do not change to something else. 坚持 ❑ *If you're in a job that keeps you busy, stick with it.* 如果有份让你忙忙碌碌的工作，就要坚持做下去。 **2** PHRASAL VERB If you **stick with** someone, you stay close to them. 紧跟 ❑ *Tugging the woman's arm, she pulled her to her side saying: "You just stick with me, dear."* 她拽着那女人的手臂，把她拉到身边说："亲爱的，你就跟着我吧。"

Word Partnership *stick* 的常用搭配:

PREP.	stick out ❷ 3
	stick to *something* ❷ 5
ADV.	stick together ❷ 5

stick·er /stɪkər/ (**stickers**) N-COUNT A **sticker** is a small piece of paper or plastic, with writing or a picture on one side, that you can stick onto a surface. 小贴纸 ❑ *...a bumper sticker that said, Flowers Make Life Lovelier.* …一张写着"花儿使生活更美好"的保险杠贴纸。

stick·er price (**sticker prices**) N-COUNT The **sticker price** of an item, especially a car, is the price at which is it advertised. (尤指汽车的) 标价 [AM] ❑ *This model carries a sticker price of nearly $27,000.* 这种型号的车标价差不多是$27000。

S

stick·er shock N-UNCOUNT **Sticker shock** is the shock you feel when you find out how expensive something is. 价位震撼 [AM] ❑ *Get over the sticker shock and invest in good kitchen knives.* 别被价格吓坏了，买些好菜刀吧。

stick·ing point (**sticking points**) N-COUNT A **sticking point** in a discussion or series of negotiations is a point on which the people involved cannot agree and which may delay or stop the talks. A **sticking point** is also one aspect of a problem which you have trouble dealing with. 症结；难点 ❑ *The main sticking point was the question of taxes.* 主要的症结是税收问题。

stick-in-the-mud (**stick-in-the-muds**) N-COUNT If you describe someone as a **stick-in-the-mud**, you disapprove of them because they do not like doing anything that is new or fun. 守旧者 [INFORMAL, DISAPPROVAL]

stick shift (**stick shifts**) N-COUNT A **stick shift** is the lever that you use to change gear in a car or other vehicle. 变速杆 [mainly AM]
in BRIT, usually use **gear lever**
❑ *I'm having trouble with this stick shift because I'm left-handed.* 我难于操纵这个变速杆，因为我是左撇子。

sticky /stɪki/ (**stickier, stickiest**) **1** ADJ A **sticky** substance is soft, or thick and liquid, and can stick to other things. **Sticky** things are covered with a sticky substance. 粘的 ❑ *...sticky toffee.* …粘乎乎的太妃糖。 ❑ *If the dough is sticky, add more flour.* 如果面团很粘，就再加些面粉。 **2** ADJ **Sticky** weather is unpleasantly hot and damp. (天气) 湿热的 ❑ *...four desperately hot, sticky days in the middle of August.* …8月中旬极其湿热的4天。 **3** ADJ A **sticky** situation involves problems or is embarrassing. 棘手的；令人尴尬的 [INFORMAL] ❑ *Inevitably the transition will yield some sticky moments.* 转型过程中难免会有棘手的时候。

stiff /stɪf/ (**stiffer, stiffest**) **1** ADJ Something that is **stiff** is firm or does not bend easily. 硬的；不易弯曲的 ❑ *The furniture was stiff, uncomfortable, too delicate, and too neat.* 这家具又硬又不舒服，过分易碎且过于光洁。 ❑ *His gaberdine trousers were brand new and stiff.* 他的华达呢裤子崭新笔直。 ● **stiff·ly** ADV 硬地；不易弯曲地 ❑ *Moira sat stiffly upright in her straight-backed chair.* 莫伊拉直挺挺地坐在直背椅上。 **2** ADJ Something such as a door or drawer that is **stiff** does not move as easily as it should. (门或抽屉) 难移动的 ❑ *Train doors have handles on the inside. They are stiff so that they cannot be opened accidentally.* 火车车门内侧有把手。把手很紧，这样就不会被意外打开了。 **3** ADJ If you are **stiff**, your muscles or joints hurt when you move, because of illness or because of too much exercise. 酸痛的 ❑ *The mud bath is particularly recommended for relieving tension and stiff muscles.* 泥浴被特别推荐用于缓解紧张和肌肉酸痛。 ● **stiff·ly** ADV 酸痛地 ❑ *He climbed stiffly from the Volkswagen.* 他浑身酸痛地从大众汽车里爬出来。 **4** ADJ **Stiff** behavior is rather formal and not very friendly or relaxed. 拘谨的；生硬的 ❑ *They always seemed a little awkward with each other, a bit stiff and formal.* 他们总是彼此显得有点儿别扭，有几分拘谨，不太随意。 ● **stiff·ly** ADV 拘谨地；生硬地 ❑ *"Why don't you borrow your sister's car?" said Cassandra stiffly.* "为什么不借你姐姐的车？"卡珊德拉生硬地说道。 **5** ADJ **Stiff** can be used to mean difficult or severe. 艰难的；激烈的 ❑ *She faces stiff competition in the Best Actress category.* 她在最佳女演员这个奖项上面临着激烈的竞争。 **6** ADV If you are bored **stiff**, worried **stiff**, or scared **stiff**, you are extremely bored, worried, or scared. 极度地 [adj ADV] [INFORMAL, EMPHASIS] ❑ *Anna tried to look interested. Actually, she was bored stiff.* 安娜试图装出感兴趣的样子。实际上她都厌烦透了。 ● ADJ **Stiff** is also an adjective. 极度的 [v n ADJ] ❑ *Even if he bores you stiff, it is good manners not to let him know it.* 即使他把你烦透了，出于礼貌你也不能让他看出来。

stiff·en /stɪfᵊn/ (**stiffens, stiffening, stiffened**) **1** V-I If you **stiffen**, you stop moving and stand or sit with muscles that are suddenly tense, for example because you feel afraid or angry. 僵住 ❑ *Ada stiffened at the sound of his voice.* 听到他的声音，艾达僵住了。 **2** V-I If your muscles or joints **stiffen**, or if something **stiffens** them, they become difficult to bend or move. 难于弯曲或活动 ❑ *The blood supply to the skin is reduced when muscles stiffen.* 肌肉发僵时，皮肤的供血量就会减少。 ● PHRASAL VERB **Stiffen up** means the same as **stiffen**. 难于弯曲或活动 ❑ *These clothes restrict your freedom of movement and stiffen up the whole body.* 这些衣服使你的手脚难于自由活动，使整个身体也僵硬起来。 **3** V-T If something such as cloth **is stiffened**, it is made firm so that it does not bend easily. 使变硬 [usu passive] ❑ *This special paper was actually thin, soft Sugiwara paper that had been stiffened with a kind of paste.* 这种特殊的纸实际上是一种面浆浆过的轻薄柔软的衫原纸。

▲ **sti·fle** /staɪfᵊl/ (**stifles, stifling, stifled**) **1** V-T If someone **stifles** something you consider to be a good thing, they prevent it from continuing. 压制 [DISAPPROVAL] ❑ *Regulations on children stifled creativity.* 对孩子们制定的各种规定压制了创造力。 **2** V-T If you **stifle** a yawn or laugh, you prevent yourself from yawning or laughing. 忍住 (呵欠或笑声) ❑ *She makes no attempt to stifle a yawn.* 她并未试图忍住一个哈欠。 **3** V-T If you **stifle** your natural feelings or behavior, you prevent yourself from having those feelings or behaving in that way. 控制 (感情或行为) ❑ *It is best to stifle curiosity and leave birds' nests alone.* 最好忍住好奇心，别碰鸟巢。

sti·fling /staɪflɪŋ/ **1** ADJ **Stifling** heat is so intense that it makes you feel uncomfortable. You can also use **stifling** to describe a place that is extremely hot. 热得难受的 ❑ *The stifling heat of the little room was beginning to make me nauseous.* 小房间里难以忍受的高温开始令我恶心。 **2** ADJ If a situation is **stifling**, it makes you feel uncomfortable because you cannot do what you want. 令人感到压抑的 ❑ *Life at home with her parents and two sisters was stifling.* 在家里和她父母及两个姊妹生活令人感到压抑。 **3** → see also **stifle**

▲ **stig·ma** /stɪgmə/ (**stigmas**) N-VAR If something has a **stigma** attached to it, people think it is something to be ashamed of. 耻辱的事 ❑ *There is still a stigma attached to cancer.* 癌症仍被人看作是一种见不得人的事。

stig·ma·tise /stɪgmətaɪz/ [BRIT] → see **stigmatize**

stig·ma·tize /stɪgmətaɪz/ (**stigmatizes, stigmatizing, stigmatized**)
in BRIT, also use **stigmatise**
V-T If someone or something **is stigmatized**, they are unfairly regarded by many people as being bad or having something to be ashamed of. 侮辱 ❑ *Children in single-parent families must not be stigmatized.* 单亲家庭的孩子不应该受到侮辱。

stile /staɪl/ (**stiles**) N-COUNT A **stile** is an entrance to a field or path consisting of a step on either side of a fence or wall to help people climb over it. (篱笆或墙) 两侧的阶梯

sti·let·to /stɪletoʊ/ (**stilettos**) N-COUNT **Stilettos** are women's shoes that have high, very narrow heels. 细高跟女鞋 ❑ *Off came her sneakers and on went a pair of stilettos.* 她脱下运动鞋，穿上一双细高跟鞋。

still
❶ ADVERB USES
❷ NOT MOVING OR MAKING A NOISE
❸ EQUIPMENT

❶ **still** ◆◆◆ /stɪl/ **1** ADV If a situation that used to exist **still** exists, it has continued and exists now. 仍然 ❑ *I still dream of home.* 我仍然梦见家。 ❑ *Brian's toe is still badly swollen and he cannot put on his shoe.* 布赖恩的脚趾头仍肿得厉害，不能穿鞋。 **2** ADV If something that has not yet happened could **still** happen, it is possible that it will happen. If something that has not yet happened is **still to** happen, it will happen at a later time. 仍然 [ADV before v] ❑ *Big money could still be made if the crisis keeps oil prices high.* 如果这场危机使得油价居高不下，仍然还是可以挣大钱的。 ❑ *We could still make it, but we won't get there till three.* 我们仍然能去，但3点以前无法到达。 **3** ADV If you say that there **is still** an amount of something left, you are emphasizing that there is that amount left. 还 ["be" ADV n] ❑ *There are still some outstanding problems.* 还有一些突出的问题。 **4** ADV You use **still** to emphasize that something remains the case or is true in spite of what you have just said. 然而 [ADV before v] ❑ *I'm average for my height. But I still feel I'm fatter than I should be.* 我身材中等，但还是觉得胖了些。 **5** ADV You use **still** to indicate that a problem or difficulty is not really worth worrying about. 不过 [ADV with cl] ❑ *Their luck had simply run out. Still, never fear.* 他们的好运已经结束。不过，别害怕。 **6** ADV You use **still** in expressions such as **still further, still another,** and **still more** to show that you find the number or quantity of things you are referring to surprising or excessive. 更加 [ADV n/adv] [EMPHASIS] ❑ *We look forward to strengthening still further our already close co-operation with the police.* 我们期待进一步加强和警方现有的密切合作。 **7** ADV You use **still** with comparatives to indicate that something has even more of a quality than something else. 更加 (与比较级连用) [ADV with compar] [EMPHASIS] ❑ *Formula One motor car racing is supposed to be dangerous. "Indycar" racing is supposed to be more dangerous still.* 一级方程式赛车被认为是危险的。印第赛车则被认为更加危险。

> If you say that something is **still** happening or is **still** the case, you are usually emphasizing your surprise that it has been happening or has been the case for so long. ❑ *She was still looking at me... There are still plenty of horses around here.* **Already** is often used to add emphasis or to suggest that it is surprising that something has happened so soon. ❑ *They were already eating their lunch.* You use **yet** in negative sentences and in questions. It is often used to add emphasis, to suggest surprise that something has not happened, or to say that it will happen later. ❑ *Have you seen it yet?... The troops could not yet see the shore... It isn't dark yet.*

❷ **still** ♦♦♦ /stɪl/ (**stiller, stillest, stills**) **1** ADJ If you stay **still**, you stay in the same position and do not move. 静止不动的 [ADJ after v] ❑ *David had been dancing about like a child, but suddenly he stood still and looked at Brad.* 戴维一直像孩子那样蹦蹦跳跳，但突然伫住，瞧着布拉德。 **2** ADJ If air or water is **still**, it is not moving. 静止的 ❑ *The night air was very still.* 夜晚的空气静止不动。 **3** ADJ If a place is **still**, it is quiet and shows no sign of activity. 安静的 ❑ *In the room it was very still.* 这房间里很安静。 ● **still·ness** N-UNCOUNT 安静 ❑ *Four deafening explosions shattered the stillness of the night air.* 4声震耳欲聋的爆炸打破了夜空的宁静。 **4** ADJ Drinks that are **still** do not contain any bubbles of carbon dioxide. 无碳酸气的 ❑ *...a glass of still water.* …一杯无汽的水。 **5** N-COUNT A **still** is a photograph taken from a movie which is used for publicity purposes. 电影剧照 ❑ *...stills from the James Bond movie series.* …詹姆斯・邦德电影系列片的剧照。

❸ **still** /stɪl/ (**stills**) N-COUNT A **still** is a piece of equipment used to make strong alcoholic drinks by a process called distilling. (制酒的) 蒸馏器

still·born /stɪlbɔrn/ ADJ A **stillborn** baby is dead when it is born. 死产的 ❑ *It was a miracle that she survived the birth of her stillborn baby.* 她生下死产儿后活下来，真是个奇迹。

still life (**still lifes**) N-VAR A **still life** is a painting or drawing of an arrangement of objects such as flowers or fruit. **Still life** refers to this type of painting or drawing. 静物画 ❑ *...a still life by one of France's finest artists.* …一幅法国顶级艺术家之一所创作的静物画。 → see **painting**

▲ **stimu·lant** /stɪmyələnt/ (**stimulants**) N-COUNT A **stimulant** is a drug that makes your body work faster, often increasing your heart rate and making you less likely to sleep. 兴奋剂 ❑ *It is not a good idea to fight fatigue by taking stimulants.* 服兴奋剂来抗疲劳不是个好主意。

stimu·late ♦◇◇ /stɪmyəleɪt/ (**stimulates, stimulating, stimulated**) **1** V-T To **stimulate** something means to encourage it to begin or develop further. 鼓励；刺激 ❑ *America's priority is rightly to stimulate its economy.* 美国的首要任务自然是刺激经济。 ● **stimu·la·tion** /stɪmyəleɪʃən/ N-UNCOUNT 鼓励；刺激 ❑ *...an economy in need of stimulation.* …一个需要刺激的经济。 **2** V-T If you **are stimulated by** something, it makes you feel full of ideas and enthusiasm. 激励 [usu passive] ❑ *Bill was stimulated by the challenge.* 比尔受到该挑战的激励。 ● **stimu·lat·ing** ADJ 激励的 ❑ *It is a complex yet stimulating book.* 这是一本复杂却能引发兴趣的书。 ● **stimu·la·tion** N-UNCOUNT 激励 ❑ *Many enjoy the mental stimulation of a challenging job.* 许多人喜欢挑战性工作带来的心理激励。 **3** V-T If something **stimulates** a part of a person's body, it causes it to move or start working. 刺激 (身体器官) ❑ *Exercise stimulates the digestive and excretory systems.* 运动刺激消化和排泄系统。 ● **stimu·lat·ing** ADJ 刺激的 ❑ *...the stimulating effect of adrenaline.* …肾上腺素的刺激作用。 ● **stimu·la·tion** N-UNCOUNT 刺激 [usu with supp] ❑ *...physical stimulation.* …生理刺激。

stimu·la·tive /stɪmyələtɪv/ ADJ If a government policy has a **stimulative** effect on the economy, it encourages the economy to grow. 刺激性的 ❑ *It is possible that a tax cut might have some stimulative effect.* 减税可能会起到一些刺激作用。

★ **stimu·lus** /stɪmyələs/ (**stimuli** /stɪmyəlaɪ/) N-VAR A **stimulus** is something that encourages activity in people or things. 刺激物 ❑ *Interest rates could fall soon and be a stimulus to the U.S. economy.* 利率很快会下降，并成为美国经济的一个刺激因素。

sting /stɪŋ/ (**stings, stinging, stung**) **1** V-T/V-I If a plant, animal, or insect **stings** you, a sharp part of it, usually covered with poison, is pushed into your skin so that you feel a sharp pain. 刺；叮 ❑ *The nettles stung their legs.* 荨麻刺了他们的腿。 **2** N-COUNT The **sting** of an insect or animal is the part that stings you. 螫刺 ❑ *Remove the bee sting with tweezers.* 用镊子拔掉蜜蜂的螫刺。 **3** N-COUNT If you feel a **sting**, you feel a sharp pain in your skin or other part of your body. 刺；叮 ❑ *This won't hurt – you will just feel a little sting.* 不会痛的——你只会觉得被轻轻刺了一下。 **4** V-T/V-I If a part of your body **stings**, or if a substance **stings** it, you feel a sharp pain there. 使刺痛 ❑ *His cheeks were stinging from the icy wind.* 他的双颊被冰冷的寒风刺痛了。 **5** V-T If someone's remarks **sting** you, they make you feel hurt and annoyed. (话语) 刺伤 [no cont] ❑ *Some of the criticism has stung him.* 有些批评刺伤了他。

stin·gy /stɪndʒi/ (**stingier, stingiest**) ADJ If you describe someone as **stingy**, you are criticizing them for being unwilling to spend money. 吝啬的 [INFORMAL, DISAPPROVAL] ❑ *The West is stingy with aid.* 西方在援助上很吝啬。

▲ **stink** /stɪŋk/ (**stinks, stinking, stank, stunk**) **1** V-I To **stink** means to smell very bad. 发臭 ❑ *We all stank and nobody minded.* 我们大家都很臭，所以也就没人在乎。 ❑ *The place stinks of fried onions.* 这地方有股难闻的炒洋葱味。 ● N-SING **Stink** is also a noun. 臭味 ❑ *He was aware of the stink of stale beer on his breath.* 他注意到自己有变味啤酒般的口臭。 **2** V-I If you say that something **stinks**, you mean that you disapprove of it because it involves ideas, feelings, or practices that you do not like. 令人讨厌 [INFORMAL, DISAPPROVAL] ❑ *I think their methods stink.* 我觉得他们的方法令人讨厌。 **3** N-SING If someone makes **a stink** about something they are angry about, they show their anger in order to make people take notice. 公然表示的愤怒 [INFORMAL] ❑ *The family's making a hell of a stink.* 这家人正在大吵大闹。

stint /stɪnt/ (**stints**) N-COUNT A **stint** is a period of time which you spend doing a particular job or activity or working in a particular place. 一段时间 ❑ *He is returning to this country after a five-year stint in Hong Kong.* 他在香港呆了5年后就要返回这个国家了。

★ **stipu·late** /stɪpyəleɪt/ (**stipulates, stipulating, stipulated**) V-T If you **stipulate** a condition or **stipulate that** something must be done, you say clearly that it must be done. 规定；明确要求 ❑ *She could have stipulated that she would pay when she collected the computer.* 她本可以明确要求取电脑时付款的。 ● **stipu·la·tion** /stɪpyəleɪʃən/ N-COUNT (**stipulations**) 规定；明确要求 ❑ *Clifford's only stipulation is that his clients obey his advice.* 克里弗德惟一的规定是他的客户必须听从自己的建议。

stir ♦◇◇ /stɜr/ (**stirs, stirring, stirred**) **1** V-T If you **stir** a liquid or other substance, you move it around or mix it in a container using something such as a spoon. 搅动；搅拌 ❑ *Stir the soup for a few seconds.* 把汤搅动几秒钟。 ❑ *There was Mrs. Bellingham, stirring sugar into her tea.* 贝林汉姆太太在那儿把糖加入茶中搅拌。 **2** V-I If you **stir**, you move slightly, for example because you are uncomfortable or beginning to wake up. 微动 [WRITTEN] ❑ *Eileen shook him, and he started to stir.* 艾琳摇了摇他，他开始动了动。 **3** V-I If you do not **stir from** a place, you do not move from it. 离开 [usu with brd-neg] [WRITTEN] ❑ *She had not stirred from the house that evening.* 她那天晚上没有离开过那座房子。 **4** V-T/V-I If something **stirs** or if the wind **stirs** it, it moves gently in the wind. 使轻轻拂动；轻轻拂动 [WRITTEN] ❑ *Palm trees stir in the soft Pacific breeze.* 棕榈树在太平洋和煦的微风里轻轻摇动。 **5** V-T/V-I If a particular memory, feeling, or mood **stirs** or **is stirred in** you, you begin to think about it or feel it. 唤起；萌生 [WRITTEN] ❑ *Then a memory stirs in you and you start feeling anxious.* 接着你脑海中涌现出一段回忆，并开始感到不安。 ❑ *Amy remembered the anger he had stirred in her.* 艾米记得他曾惹自己生气。 **6** N-SING If an event causes a **stir**, it causes great excitement, shock, or anger among people. 轰动；愤怒 ❑ *His movie has caused a stir.* 他的电影引起了轰动。 **7** → see also **stirring**

▸ **stir up** **1** PHRASAL VERB If something **stirs up** dust or **stirs up** mud in water, it causes it to rise up and move around. 扬起 ❑ *They saw first a cloud of dust and then the car that was stirring it up.* 他们先是看到一团尘土，接着就看到扬起尘土的那辆车。 **2** PHRASAL VERB If you **stir up** a particular mood or situation, usually a bad one, you cause it. 挑起 [DISAPPROVAL] ❑ *As usual, Harriet is trying to stir up trouble.* 与往常一样，哈里特正在试图挑起事端。

Word Partnership *stir* 的常用搭配：

N.	**stir a mixture, stir in sugar** 1
V.	**cause a stir, create a stir** 6

stir·ring /stɜrɪŋ/ (**stirrings**) **1** ADJ A **stirring** event, performance, or account of something makes people very excited or enthusiastic. (活动、演出或讲述) 激动人心的 ❑ *The president made a stirring speech.* 总统作了一次激动人心的演讲。 **2** N-COUNT A **stirring**

S

of a feeling or thought is the beginning of one. (感情或想法的)开始 [usu N "of" n] ❑ *I feel a stirring of curiosity.* 我开始产生好奇心。

★ **stitch** /stɪtʃ/ (**stitches, stitching, stitched**) 1 V-T/V-I If you **stitch** cloth, you use a needle and thread to join two pieces together or to make a decoration. 缝 ❑ *Fold the fabric and stitch the two layers together.* 把布料对折，将两层缝在一起。❑ *We stitched incessantly.* 我们缝个不停。 2 N-COUNT **Stitches** are the short pieces of thread that have been sewn in a piece of cloth. 针脚 ❑ *...a row of straight stitches.* …一排直直的针脚。 3 N-COUNT In knitting and crochet, a **stitch** is a loop made by one turn of wool around a knitting needle or crochet hook. 一针 ❑ *Her mother counted the stitches on her knitting needles.* 她的母亲数了数编织针上的针数。 4 N-UNCOUNT If you sew or knit something in a particular **stitch**, you sew or knit in a way that produces a particular pattern. 编织法 ❑ *The design can be worked in cross stitch.* 该图案可以用十字针法编织出来。 5 V-T When doctors **stitch** a wound, they use a special needle and thread to sew the skin together. 缝合（伤口）❑ *Jill washed and stitched the wound.* 吉尔清洗并缝合了伤口。 6 N-COUNT A **stitch** is a piece of thread that has been used to sew the skin of a wound together. (缝合伤口的) 一针 ❑ *He had six stitches in a head wound.* 他头部的伤口缝了6针。 7 N-SING A **stitch** is a sharp pain in your side, usually caused by running or laughing a lot. (跑步或大笑引起的) 肋部剧痛 ❑ *One of them was laughing so much he got a stitch.* 他们当中有一个人笑得肋部都疼了。

stock ◆◆◇ /stɒk/ (**stocks, stocking, stocked**) 1 N-COUNT **Stocks** are shares in the ownership of a company, or investments on which a fixed amount of interest will be paid. 股票；证券 [BUSINESS] ❑ *...the buying and selling of stocks and shares.* …证券和股票的买卖。 2 N-UNCOUNT A company's **stock** is the amount of money which the company has through selling shares. (公司的) 股票价值 [BUSINESS] ❑ *Two years later, when Compaq went public, their stock was valued at $38 million.* 两年后康柏公司上市时，他们的股票价值为3800万美元。 3 V-T If a store **stocks** particular products, it keeps a supply of them to sell. 有…存货 [no cont] ❑ *The store stocks everything from cigarettes to recycled paper.* 该商店的存货包括香烟和再生纸等各种商品。 4 N-UNCOUNT A store's **stock** is the total amount of goods which it has available to sell. 存货 ❑ *When a nearby store burned down, our stock was ruined by smoke.* 附近一家商店被烧成灰烬，我们的存货也被浓烟熏坏了。 5 V-T If you **stock** something such as a cupboard, shelf, or room, you fill it with food or other things. 给…装满 ❑ *I worked stocking shelves in a grocery store.* 我在一家杂货店工作，给货架上货。❑ *Some families stocked their cellars with food and water.* 有些家庭在地窖里装满食物和水。 ● PHRASAL VERB **Stock up** means the same as **stock**. 给…装满 ❑ *I had to stock the boat up with food.* 我不得不给小船装满食品。 6 N-COUNT If you have a **stock of** things, you have a supply of them stored in a place ready to be used. 储备 ❑ *I keep a stock of cassette tapes describing various relaxation techniques.* 我储藏着一些讲述各种放松技巧的盒式磁带。 7 ADJ A **stock** answer, expression, or way of doing something is one that is very commonly used, especially because people cannot be bothered to think of something new. (回答、表达或做事方式) 老一套的 [ADJ n] ❑ *My boss had a stock response – "If it ain't broke, don't fix it!"* 我的老板是老一套的回答——"没坏的话就别修了！" 8 N-MASS **Stock** is a liquid, usually made by boiling meat, bones, or vegetables in water, that is used to give flavor to soups and sauces. (以肉、骨头或蔬菜煮成的) 高汤 ❑ *Finally, add the beef stock.* 最后，加入牛肉高汤。 9 → see also **stocking** 10 PHRASE If goods are **in stock**, a store has them available to sell. If they are **out of stock**, it does not. 有货/缺货 ❑ *Check that your size is in stock.* 查查你的尺码是不是有货。 11 PHRASE If you **take stock**, you pause to think about all the aspects of a situation or event before deciding what to do next. 估量 ❑ *It was time to take stock of the situation.* 是估量形势的时候了。 12 **lock, stock, and barrel** → see **barrel**
→ see **company, stock market**

S

▸ **stock up** 1 → see **stock** 5 2 PHRASAL VERB If you **stock up on** something, you buy a lot of it, in case you cannot get it later. 大量储备 ❑ *The authorities have urged people to stock up on fuel.* 当局已敦促人们大量储备燃料。

stock·broker /stɒkbroʊkər/ (**stockbrokers**) N-COUNT A **stockbroker** is a person whose job is to buy and sell stocks and shares for people who want to invest money. 股票经纪人 [BUSINESS]

stock·broking /stɒkbroʊkɪŋ/ N-UNCOUNT **Stockbroking** is the professional activity of buying and selling stocks and shares for clients. 证券经纪业务；股票经纪业务 [BUSINESS] ❑ *His stockbroking firm was hit by the 1987 crash.* 他的证券经纪公司受到了1987年暴跌的打击。

stock con·trol N-UNCOUNT **Stock control** is the activity of making sure that a company always has exactly the right amount of goods available to sell. 库存管理 [BUSINESS] ❑ *Better stock control helped Wal-Mart to reduce its expenses by $2 billion in 1997.* 库存管理的改善使沃尔玛公司在1997年减少了20亿美元的开支。

stock ex·change ◆◇◇ (**stock exchanges**) N-COUNT A **stock exchange** is a place where people buy and sell stocks and shares. **The stock exchange** is also the trading activity that goes on there and the trading organization itself. 股票交易所；股票交易 [BUSINESS] ❑ *The shortage of good stock has kept some investors away from the stock exchange.* 优质股票的缺乏使得一些投资者远离股票交易。❑ *...the New York Stock Exchange.* …纽约证券交易所。
→ see **stock market**

★ **stock·holder** /stɒkhoʊldər/ (**stockholders**) N-COUNT A **stockholder** is a person who owns shares in a company. 股东 [AM, BUSINESS]

in BRIT, use **shareholder**

❑ *He was a stockholder in a hotel corporation.* 他是一家酒店公司的股东。

stock·ing /stɒkɪŋ/ (**stockings**) N-COUNT **Stockings** are items of women's clothing which fit closely over their feet and legs. Stockings are usually made of nylon and are held in place by garters. 长袜 ❑ *...a pair of nylon stockings.* …一双尼龙长袜。

stock mar·ket ◆◇◇ (**stock markets**) N-COUNT **The stock market** consists of the general activity of buying stocks and shares, and the people and institutions that organize it. 股票市场 [BUSINESS] ❑ *He's been studying and playing the stock market since he was 14.* 他自14岁起就一直研究和投资股票市场。
→ see Word Web: **stock market**
→ see **company**

stock op·tion (**stock options**) N-COUNT A **stock option** is an opportunity for the employees of a company to buy shares at a special price. (仅对本公司员工的) 股份认购 [AM, BUSINESS]

in BRIT, use **share option**

❑ *He made a huge profit from the sale of shares purchased in January under the company's stock option program.* 他卖掉于1月份在公司认购的股票，赚了一大笔。

▲ **stock·pile** /stɒkpaɪl/ (**stockpiles, stockpiling, stockpiled**) 1 V-T If people **stockpile** things such as food or weapons, they store large quantities of them for future use. 大量储备 ❑ *People are stockpiling food for the coming winter.* 人们正在为即将到来的冬天大量储备食物。 2 N-COUNT A **stockpile of** things is a large quantity of them that have been stored for future use. 储备物资 ❑ *The two leaders also approved treaties to cut stockpiles of chemical weapons.* 两位领导人也都赞同削减化学武器储备的条约。

stock·taking /stɒkteɪkɪŋ/ N-UNCOUNT **Stocktaking** is the same as doing an **inventory**. 库存 [mainly BRIT, BUSINESS]

stocky /stɒki/ (**stockier, stockiest**) ADJ A **stocky** person has a body that is broad, solid, and often short. 粗壮的 ❑ *...a short stocky man in his forties.* …一位四十来岁的矮壮男子。

Word Web stock market

The Dutch established the first **stock exchange** in Amsterdam in 1611. Its purpose was to raise **capital** to **invest** in the spice trade with the Far East. It also **traded** in metals and grains such as wheat and rye. The Dutch also experienced the world's first **stock market crash**. Tulips were an important **commodity** in seventeenth century Holland. By 1636 a single tulip bulb sold for the equivalent of $76,000. However, **confidence** in the tulip market suddenly dropped. Soon a tulip bulb was worth only $1. **Commerce** in Holland did not recover for many years.

stoke /stoʊk/ (**stokes, stoking, stoked**) **1** V-T If you **stoke** a fire, you add coal or wood to it to keep it burning. 给…添煤；给…添柴火 ❑ *She was stoking the stove with sticks of maple.* 她正在给炉子添枫树枝。 ● PHRASAL VERB **Stoke up** means the same as **stoke**. 给…添煤；给…添柴火 ❑ *He stoked up the fire in the hearth.* 他给壁炉里的火添柴。 **2** V-T If you **stoke** something such as a feeling, you cause it to be felt more strongly. 激起（某种感觉）❑ *These demands are helping to stoke fears of civil war.* 这些要求激起了对内战的恐惧。 ● PHRASAL VERB **Stoke up** means the same as **stoke**. 激起（某种感觉）❑ *He has sent his proposals in the hope of stoking up interest for the idea.* 他已上呈自己的建议，希望能激起人们对这种想法的兴趣。

stole /stoʊl/ **Stole** is the past tense of **steal**. **steal**的过去式

sto·len /stoʊlᵊn/ **Stolen** is the past participle of **steal**. **steal**的过去分词

stom·ach ♦◇◇ /stʌmək/ (**stomachs, stomaching, stomached**) **1** N-COUNT Your **stomach** is the organ inside your body where food is digested before it moves into the intestines. 胃 ❑ *He had an upset stomach.* 他胃部不适。 **2** N-COUNT You can refer to the front part of your body below your waist as your **stomach**. 肚子 ❑ *The children lay down on their stomachs.* 孩子们俯身趴着。 **3** N-COUNT If the front part of your body below your waist feels uncomfortable because you are feeling worried or frightened, you can refer to it as your **stomach**. 心窝 ❑ *His stomach was in knots.* 他的心揪得紧紧的。 **4** N-COUNT If you say that someone has a strong **stomach**, you mean that they are not disgusted by things that disgust most other people. 忍耐力 ❑ *Surgery often demands actual physical strength, as well as the possession of a strong stomach.* 外科手术常常要求有实际体力，也要有很强的忍耐力。 **5** V-T If you cannot **stomach** something, you cannot accept it because you dislike it or disapprove of it. 忍受 [with brd-neg] ❑ *I could never stomach the cruelty involved in the wounding of animals.* 我永远无法忍受伤害动物的残暴行为。 **6** PHRASE If you do something **on an empty stomach**, you do it without having eaten. 空腹 ❑ *Avoid drinking on an empty stomach.* 避免空腹喝酒。

stom·ach ache (**stomach aches**) also **stomachache** N-VAR If you have a **stomach ache**, you have a pain in your stomach. 胃痛

stomp /stɒmp/ (**stomps, stomping, stomped**) V-I If you **stomp** somewhere, you walk there with very heavy steps, often because you are angry. （常指因生气而）迈着重重的脚步走 ❑ *He turned his back on them and stomped off up the hill.* 他转身不理睬他们，迈着重重的脚步走上山去。

stone ♦♦◇ /stoʊn/ (**stones, stoning, stoned**) **1** N-MASS **Stone** is a hard solid substance found in the ground and often used for building houses. 石头 ❑ *He could not tell whether the floor was wood or stone.* 他分不清这地板是木头的还是石头的。 ❑ *People often don't appreciate that marble is a natural stone.* 人们往往不了解大理石是一种天然石头。 **2** N-COUNT A **stone** is a small piece of rock that is found on the ground. 石子 ❑ *He removed a stone from his shoe.* 他清除了鞋中的一粒石子。 **3** N-COUNT A **stone** is a large piece of stone put somewhere in memory of a person or event, or as a religious symbol. 石碑 ❑ *The monument consists of a circle of gigantic stones.* 该纪念碑由一圈巨大的石碑组成。 **4** N-UNCOUNT **Stone** is used in expressions such as **set in stone** and **tablets of stone** to suggest that an idea or rule is firm and fixed, and cannot be changed. （思想或规则）固定不变 ❑ *He is merely throwing the idea forward for discussion, it is not cast in stone.* 他只是抛出个想法供讨论，不是固定不变的。 **5** N-COUNT You can refer to a jewel as a **stone**. 宝石 ❑ *...a diamond ring with three stones.* …一枚有3颗宝石的钻戒。 **6** N-COUNT A **stone** is a small hard ball of minerals and other substances which sometimes forms in a person's kidneys or gallbladder. 结石 ❑ *He had kidney stones.* 他有肾结石。 **7** N-COUNT The **stone** in a plum, cherry, or other fruit is the large hard seed in the middle of it. 果核 [mainly BRIT]

in AM, usually use **pit**

8 V-T If people **stone** someone or something, they throw stones at them. 向…扔石头 ❑ *Youths burned cars and stoned police.* 年轻人烧车辆并向警察扔石头。 **9** → see also **stepping stone, stoned**
→ see **fruit**

stoned /stoʊnd/ ADJ If someone is **stoned**, their mind is greatly affected by a drug such as marijuana. （吸毒而）神智恍惚的 [INFORMAL] ❑ *Half of them were so stoned they couldn't even see.* 他们中一半的人神智恍惚，甚至看不见了。

stony /stoʊni/ (**stonier, stoniest**) **1** ADJ **Stony** ground is rough and contains a lot of stones. 多石的 ❑ *The steep, stony ground is well drained.* 多石陡峭的地面很容易排水。 **2** ADJ A **stony** expression or attitude does not show any sympathy or friendliness. 冷漠的 ❑ *She gave me the stoniest look I ever got.* 她向我投以我所见过的最冷漠的眼神。

stood /stʊd/ **Stood** is the past tense and past participle of **stand**. **stand**的过去式和过去分词

▲ **stool** /stuːl/ (**stools**) N-COUNT A **stool** is a seat with legs but no support for your arms or back. 凳子 ❑ *O'Brien sat on a bar stool and leaned his elbows on the counter.* 奥布赖恩坐在酒吧凳上，肘部依在柜台上。

stoop /stuːp/ (**stoops, stooping, stooped**) **1** V-I If you **stoop**, you stand or walk with your shoulders bent forward. 驼背 ❑ *She was taller than he was and stooped slightly.* 她比他高，但有点儿驼背。 ● N-SING **Stoop** is also a noun. 驼背 ❑ *He was a tall, thin fellow with a slight stoop.* 他是一个有点儿驼背的瘦高个男子。 **2** V-I If you **stoop**, you bend your body forward and downward. 弯腰 ❑ *He stooped to pick up the carrier bag of groceries.* 他弯腰提起装满食品杂货的购物袋。 ❑ *Two men in shirt sleeves stooped over the car.* 两个穿衬衫的男人趴在那辆汽车上。 **3** V-I If you say that a person **stoops to** doing something, you are criticizing them because they do something wrong or immoral that they would not normally do. 卑鄙到… [DISAPPROVAL] ❑ *He had not, until recently, stooped to personal abuse.* 他最近才卑鄙到进行人身攻击。

stop ♦♦♦ /stɒp/ (**stops, stopping, stopped**) **1** V-T/V-I If you have been doing something and then you **stop** doing it, you no longer do it. 停止 ❑ *Stop throwing those stones!* 别再扔那些石头了！ ❑ *Does either of the parties want to stop the fighting?* 双方中有谁想停止战斗呢？ ❑ *She stopped in mid-sentence.* 她说了半句就停下了。 **2** V-T If you **stop** something from happening, or you **stop** something happening, you prevent it from happening or prevent it from continuing. 阻止 ❑ *He proposed a new diplomatic initiative to try to stop the war.* 他提出了一个新的试图阻止战争的外交倡议。 ❑ *He would do what he must to stop her from destroying him.* 他将做该做的事来阻止她把他毁了。 **3** V-I If an activity or process **stops**, it is no longer happening. 停下 ❑ *The rain had stopped and a star or two was visible over the mountains.* 雨停了，山上的天空可见一两颗星星。 ❑ *The system overheated and filming had to stop.* 系统过热，拍摄工作不得不停下。 **4** V-T/V-I If something such as machine **stops** or **is stopped**, it is no longer moving or working. 停止（转动或工作）❑ *The clock stopped at 11:59 Saturday night.* 钟在星期六晚11点59分停了。 ❑ *Arnold stopped the engine and got out of the car.* 阿诺德关闭发动机然后下了车。 **5** V-T/V-I When a moving person or vehicle **stops** or **is stopped**, they no longer move and they remain in the same place. 停下 ❑ *The car failed to stop at an army checkpoint.* 那辆车未能在一个军队检查站停下。 ❑ *He stopped and let her catch up with him.* 他停下了，让她赶上自己。 **6** N-SING If something that is moving comes **to a stop** or is brought **to a stop**, it slows down and no longer moves. 停下 ❑ *People often wrongly open doors before the train has come to a stop.* 人们常常在火车停下之前错误地打开车门。 **7** V-T/V-I If someone does not **stop to** think or **to** explain, they continue with what they are doing without taking any time to think about or explain it. 停下来（思考或解释）❑ *She doesn't stop to think about what she's saying.* 她没有停下来想想自己在说些什么。 ❑ *There is something rather strange about all this if one stops to consider it.* 如果停下来考虑一下，就会发觉这一切相当蹊跷。 **8** V-I If you say that a quality or state **stops** somewhere, you mean that it exists or is true up to that point, but no further. 结束 ❑ *The cafe owner has put up the required "no smoking" signs, but thinks his responsibility stops there.* 咖啡店老板已贴上所要求的"禁止吸烟"的标志，但他认为自己的责任到此为止。 **9** N-COUNT A **stop** is a place where buses or trains regularly stop so that people can get on and off. 车站 ❑ *The closest subway stop is Houston Street.* 最近的地铁站是休斯敦街。 **10** V-I If you **stop** somewhere on a journey, you stay there for a short while. 停留一下 ❑ *He insisted we stop at a small restaurant just outside of Atlanta.* 他坚持要我们在亚特兰大外的一家小餐馆停留一下。 **11** N-COUNT A **stop** is a time or place at which you stop during a journey. 停留时间；停留地 ❑ *The last stop in Mr. Robinson's lengthy tour was Paris.* 鲁滨逊先生漫长旅程的最后一站是巴黎。 **12** PHRASE If you say that someone will **stop at nothing to** get something, you are emphasizing that they are willing to do things that are extreme, wrong, or dangerous in order to get it. 不顾一切 [EMPHASIS] ❑ *Their motive is money, and they will stop at nothing to get it.* 他们的动机是钱，因此他们将不顾一切地捞钱。 **13** PHRASE If you **put a stop to** something that you do not like or approve of, you prevent it from happening or continuing. 制止某事 ❑ *His daughter should have stood up and put a stop to all these rumours.* 他的女儿本应站出来制止所有这些

谣言。**14** PHRASE If you say that someone does not **know when to stop**, you mean that they do not control their own behavior very well and so they often annoy or upset other people. 知道如何把握分寸 ❑ *Like many politicians before him, Mr. Bentley did not know when to stop.* 如他之前的许多政客一样，本特利先生不知道如何把握分寸。 **15** to **stop dead** → see **dead** **16** to **stop short of** → see **short** **17** to **stop** someone **in** their **tracks** → see **track**

When an action comes to an end or **stops**, you can say that someone **stops doing** it. ❑ *She stopped reading and closed the book.* However, if you say that someone **stops to do** something, you mean that they interrupt their movement or another activity in order to do that thing. The "to" infinitive indicates purpose. ❑ *I stopped to read the notices on the bulletin board.*

▸ **stop by** or **stop in** PHRASAL VERB If you **stop by** somewhere, you make a short visit to a person or place. 顺便探访 [INFORMAL] ❑ *Perhaps I'll stop by the hospital.* 也许我会顺便去趟那家医院。

▸ **stop off** PHRASAL VERB If you **stop off** somewhere, you stop for a short time in the middle of a trip. 中途逗留 ❑ *The president stopped off in Poland on his way to Munich for the economic summit.* 总统在前往慕尼黑参加经济峰会的途中在波兰作了短暂停留。

stop·light /stɒplaɪt/ (**stoplights**) also **stop light** N-COUNT A **stoplight** is a set of colored lights which controls the flow of traffic on a road. 交通信号灯 [AM]

in BRIT, use **traffic light**

❑ *Holly waited at a stoplight, impatient for the signal to change.* 霍利在交通信号灯处不耐烦地等着信号改变。

stop·over /stɒpoʊvər/ (**stopovers**) N-COUNT A **stopover** is a short stay in a place in between parts of a trip. 中途停留 ❑ *The Sunday flights will make a stopover in Paris.* 周日航班将在巴黎作一次中途停留。

stop·page /stɒpɪdʒ/ (**stoppages**) **1** N-COUNT When there is a **stoppage**, people stop working because of a disagreement with their employers. 罢工 [BUSINESS] ❑ *Mineworkers in the Ukraine have voted for a one-day stoppage next month.* 乌克兰的矿工们已投票决定下个月罢工一天。 **2** N-COUNT A **stoppage** is the same as **time out**. 暂停 [mainly BRIT]

★ **stop·watch** /stɒpwɒtʃ/ (**stopwatches**) also **stop-watch** N-COUNT A **stopwatch** is a watch with buttons which you press at the beginning and end of an event, so that you can measure exactly how long it takes. 秒表

stor·age /stɔrɪdʒ/ N-UNCOUNT If you refer to the **storage** of something, you mean that it is kept in a special place until it is needed. 贮藏 ❑ *...the storage of toxic waste.* …有毒废弃物的贮藏。 ❑ *Some of the space will at first be used for storage.* 一些空间将首先用于贮藏。

store ♦♦◇ /stɔr/ (**stores, storing, stored**) **1** N-COUNT A **store** is a building or part of a building where things are sold. 商店 ❑ *They are selling them for $10 apiece at a few stores in Texas and Oklahoma.* 得克萨斯和俄克拉何马的一些商店正以每个$10的价钱出售它们。 ❑ *...grocery stores.* …杂货店。 **2** V-T When you **store** things, you put them in a container or other place and leave them there until they are needed. 存放 ❑ *Store the cookies in an airtight tin.* 把曲奇饼干存放在一个密封罐中。 ● PHRASAL VERB **Store away** means the same as **store**. 存放 ❑ *He simply stored the tapes away.* 他只是把那些磁带存放起来。 **3** V-T When you **store** information, you keep it in your memory, in a file, or in a computer. 存储 (信息) ❑ *Where in the brain do we store information about colors?* 我们在大脑的哪个地方存储有关颜色的信息？ **4** N-COUNT A **store of** things is a supply of them that you keep somewhere until you need them. 储存 ❑ *I handed over my secret store of chocolate.* 我交出了我偷偷藏起来的巧克力。 **5** N-COUNT A **store** is a place where things are kept while they are not being used. 储存处 ❑ *...a store for spent fuel from submarines.* …一个潜艇废燃料的储存处。 **6** → see also **department store** **7** PHRASE If something is **in store** for you, it is going to happen at some time in the future. 即将发生 ❑ *Surprises were also in store for me.* 令人吃惊的事也将发生在我身上。 → see **city**

▸ **store away** → see **store 2**

▸ **store up** PHRASAL VERB If you **store** something **up**, you keep it until you think that the time is right to use it. 储备 ❑ *Investors were storing up a lot of cash in anticipation of disaster.* 投资者们预计会发生灾难，正储备大量现金。

Thesaurus *store* 另参见：

N.	business, market, shop **1**
	collection, reserve, stock **4**
V.	accumulate, keep, save **2** **3**

store·card /stɔrkard/ (**storecards**) also **store card** N-COUNT A **storecard** is a plastic card that you use to buy goods on credit from a particular store or group of stores. 购物卡 [mainly BRIT]

in AM, usually use **charge card**

store·keeper /stɔrkipər/ (**storekeepers**) N-COUNT A **storekeeper** is a shopkeeper. 店主 [mainly AM]

sto·rey /stɔri/ [mainly BRIT] → see **story**

storm ♦◇◇ /stɔrm/ (**storms, storming, stormed**) **1** N-COUNT A **storm** is very bad weather, with heavy rain, strong winds, and often thunder and lightning. 暴风雨 ❑ *...the violent storms which whipped the East Coast.* …席卷东海岸的猛烈暴风雨。 **2** N-COUNT If something causes a **storm**, it causes an angry or excited reaction from a large number of people. 强烈的反响 ❑ *The photos caused a storm when they were first published.* 那些照片最初出版时引起强烈的反响。 **3** N-COUNT A **storm of** applause or other noise is a sudden loud amount of it made by an audience or other group of people in reaction to something. 暴风雨般的声音 ❑ *His speech was greeted with a storm of applause.* 他的演讲博得暴风雨般的掌声。 **4** V-I If you **storm into** or **out of** a place, you enter or leave it quickly and noisily, because you are angry. 气冲冲地走 ❑ *After a bit of an argument, he stormed out.* 一次小小的争吵之后，他就气冲冲地走出去。 **5** V-T If a place that is being defended **is stormed**, a group of people attack it, usually in order to get inside it. 猛攻 ❑ *Government buildings have been stormed and looted.* 政府大楼已遭到猛攻和抢掠。 ● **storm·ing** N-UNCOUNT 猛攻 ❑ *...the storming of the Bastille.* …对巴士底狱的猛攻。 **6** PHRASE If someone or something **takes** a place **by storm**, they are extremely successful. 在某处大获成功 ❑ *Kenya's long distance runners have taken the athletics world by storm.* 肯尼亚的长跑运动员在田径界大获成功。

→ see Word Web: **storm**

→ see **disaster, forecast, hurricane, weather**

Word Partnership *storm* 的常用搭配：

ADJ.	**tropical** storm **1**
	gathering storm, **heavy** storm, **severe** storm **1** **2**
N.	storm **clouds**, storm **damage**, **ice/rain/snow** storm, storm **warning**, storm **winds** **1**
	center of a storm, **eye of a** storm **1** **2**
	storm **a building** **5**
V.	**hit by a** storm, **weather the** storm **1** **2**
	cause a storm **2**

stormy /stɔrmi/ (**stormier, stormiest**) **1** ADJ If there is **stormy** weather, there are strong winds and heavy rain. 有暴风雨的 ❑ *It had been a night of stormy weather, with torrential rain and high winds.* 这是一个暴风雨之夜，下着倾盆大雨，刮着强风。 **2** ADJ **Stormy** seas have very large strong waves because there are strong winds. 巨浪

Word Web storm

Here's how to protect yourself and your property when a severe **storm** hits. Listen for warnings from the **weather** service. Strong **wind** may blow trash cans around and **hail** may damage your car. Both should go into the garage. If you are outdoors when a storm strikes, get under cover. If you are in the open, **lightning** could hit you. Heavy **rainfall** can cause **flooding**. After the **rain** has passed, do not drive on flooded roads. The water may be deeper than you think. Be sure to buy food and batteries before a **blizzard** since **snow** may clog the roads.

S

滔天的 ❑ *They make the treacherous journey across stormy seas.* 他们穿越巨浪滔天的大海进行这次危险的旅行。 3 ADJ If you describe a situation as **stormy**, you mean it involves a lot of angry argument or criticism. 群情激愤的 ❑ *The letter was read at a stormy meeting.* 这封信是在一次群情激愤的会上读的。

sto·ry ♦♦♦ /stɔri/ (**stories**) 1 N-COUNT A **story** is a description of imaginary people and events, which is written or told in order to entertain. (虚构的) 故事 ❑ *The second story in the book is titled "The Scholar."* 这本书中的第2个故事标题为《学者》。 ❑ *I shall tell you a story about four little rabbits.* 我将给你讲个关于4只小兔子的故事。 2 N-COUNT A **story** is a description of an event or something that happened to someone, especially a spoken description of it. (尤指口头的) 叙述 ❑ *The parents all shared interesting stories about their children.* 那些家长们都会互相讲起有关自己孩子的趣事。 3 N-COUNT The **story of** something is a description of all the important things that have happened to it since it began. 史话 ❑ *...the story of the women's movement.* …妇女运动的史话。 4 N-COUNT If someone invents a **story**, they give a false explanation or account of something. 谎话 ❑ *He invented some story about a cousin.* 他们编造了一些关于一位表亲的谎话。 5 N-COUNT A news **story** is a piece of news in a newspaper or in a news broadcast. 新闻报道 ❑ *Those are some of the top stories in the news.* 那些都是一些头条新闻报道。 ❑ *They'll do anything for a story.* 他们会为了新闻报道不择手段。 6 N-COUNT A **story** of a building is one of its different levels, which is situated above or below other levels. 楼层

in BRIT, use **storey**

❑ *...long brick buildings, two stories high.* …很长的两层砖楼。 7 PHRASE You use **a different story** to refer to a situation, usually a bad one, which exists in one set of circumstances when you have mentioned that it does not exist in another set of circumstances. 情况不同 ❑ *Where Marcella lives, the rents are fairly cheap, but a little further north it's a different story.* 在马斯拉住的地方房租相当便宜，但再往北一点儿情况就不同了。 8 PHRASE If you say **it's the same old story** or **it's the old story**, you mean that something unpleasant or undesirable seems to happen again and again. 老一套 ❑ *It's the same old story. They want one person to do three people's jobs.* 又是老一套。他们想让一个人干3个人的活儿。 9 PHRASE If you say that something is **only part of the story** or is **not the whole story**, you mean that the explanation or information given is not enough for a situation to be fully understood. 只是部分情况；并非全部情况 ❑ *This may be true but it is only part of the story.* 这也许是真的，但它只是部分情况。 10 PHRASE If someone tells you their **side of the story**, they tell you why they behaved in a particular way and why they think they were right, when other people think that person behaved wrongly. 某人一方的说法 ❑ *He had already made up his mind before even hearing her side of the story.* 他甚至在听到她那一方的说法之前就已下定决心了。

→ see **myth**, **skyscraper**

Thesaurus *story* 另参见：

N. epic, fable, fairy tale, romance, saga, tale 1
account, report 2
fabrication, lie, untruth 4
article, feature 5

Word Partnership *story* 的常用搭配：

N. **character in a** story, story **hour**, story **line**, **narrator of a** story, **title of a** story, story **writer** 1
beginning of a story, **end of a** story, **horror** story, **version of a** story 1–5
life story 2
front page story, **news** story 5
V. **hear a** story, **tell a** story 1–4
publish a story, **read a** story, **write a** story 1 5
ADJ. **classic** story, **compelling** story, **funny** story, **good** story, **interesting** story 1–5
familiar story 2–5
the full story, **untold** story 2 3 5
the whole story 2 3 5 9
big story, **related** story, **top** story 5

▲ **stout** /staʊt/ (**stouter**, **stoutest**) 1 ADJ A **stout** person is rather fat. 肥胖的 ❑ *He was a tall, stout man with gray hair.* 他是一个又高又胖、满头银发的男子。 2 ADJ **Stout** shoes, branches, or other objects are thick and strong. (鞋、枝条等物体) 结实的 ❑ *I hope you've both got stout shoes.* 我希望你们两个都穿结实的鞋。 ❑ *...a stout oak door.* …一扇结实的橡木门。

stove /stoʊv/ (**stoves**) N-COUNT A **stove** is a piece of equipment which provides heat, either for cooking or for heating a room. 炉 ❑ *She put the kettle on the gas stove.* 她把水壶放在煤气炉上。

stow /stoʊ/ (**stows, stowing, stowed**) V-T If you **stow** something somewhere, you carefully put it there until it is needed. 收藏 ❑ *Luke stowed his camera bags into the trunk.* 卢克把他的相机袋收到旅行箱里。

stow·age /stoʊɪdʒ/ N-UNCOUNT **Stowage** is the space that is available for stowing things on a ship or airplane. (船或飞机的) 装载室

stow·away /stoʊəweɪ/ (**stowaways**) N-COUNT A **stowaway** is a person who hides in a ship, airplane, or other vehicle in order to make a journey secretly or without paying. 偷乘者 ❑ *The crew discovered the stowaway about two days into their voyage.* 船员们在航行大约两天后发现了那名偷乘者。

strad·dle /strædᵊl/ (**straddles, straddling, straddled**) 1 V-T If you **straddle** something, you put or have one leg on either side of it. 跨坐 ❑ *He looked at her with a grin and sat down, straddling the chair.* 他咧嘴笑着看她，然后跨坐在那把椅子上。 2 V-T If something **straddles** a river, road, border, or other place, it stretches across it or exists on both sides of it. 横跨 ❑ *A small wooden bridge straddled the dike.* 一座小木桥横跨那个排水渠。 3 V-T Someone or something that **straddles** different periods, groups, or fields of activity exists in, belongs to, or takes elements from them all. 跨越 (不同时期、群体或领域) ❑ *He straddles two cultures, having been brought up in the United States and later converted to Islam.* 他跨越两种文化，从小在美国受教育，后来又改信伊斯兰教。

straight ♦♦◊ /streɪt/ (**straighter, straightest, straights**) 1 ADJ A **straight** line or edge continues in the same direction and does not bend or curve. 笔直的 ❑ *Keep the boat in a straight line.* 让小船直线行驶。 ❑ *His teeth were perfectly straight.* 他的牙齿非常整齐。 ● ADV **Straight** is also an adverb. 直地 [ADV after v] ❑ *Stand straight and stretch the left hand to the right foot.* 站直，伸左手够右脚。 2 ADJ **Straight** hair has no curls or waves in it. (发) 直 ❑ *Grace had long straight dark hair which she wore in a bun.* 格雷斯有一头又长又直的黑发，她把它盘成了一个发髻。 3 ADV You use **straight** to indicate that the way from one place to another is very direct, with no changes of direction. 径直地 [ADV prep/adv] ❑ *...squirting the medicine straight to the back of the child's throat.* …把药直接喷到小孩喉咙后部。 ❑ *He finished his conversation and stood up, looking straight at me.* 他结束了谈话站起来，直视着我。 4 ADV If you go **straight** to a place, you go there immediately. 立即 [ADV prep/adv] ❑ *As always, we went straight to the experts for advice.* 像平时一样，我们立即向那些专家们做了咨询。 5 ADJ If you give someone a **straight** answer, you answer them clearly and honestly. (回答) 直截了当的 [ADJ n] ❑ *What a shifty arguer he is, refusing ever to give a straight answer to a straight question.* 他真是一个狡猾的辩手，一直拒绝对一个直接的问题给予直截了当的回答。 ● ADV **Straight** is also an adverb. 直截了当地 [ADV after v] ❑ *I lost my temper and told him straight that I hadn't been looking for any job.* 我生气了，直截了当地告诉他我一直没找过任何工作。 6 ADJ **Straight** means following one after the other, with no gaps or intervals. 连续的 [ADJ n] ❑ *They'd won 12 straight games before they lost.* 他们在输掉之前已赢了连续12场比赛。 ● ADV **Straight** is also an adverb. 连续地 [n ADV] ❑ *He called from Washington, having been there for 31 hours straight.* 他从华盛顿打来了电话，他已在那里连续呆了31个小时了。 7 ADJ A **straight** choice or a **straight** fight involves only two people or things. 有关两者的 [ADJ n] ❑ *It's a straight choice between low-paid jobs and no jobs.* 这是一个有关低收入工作和没有工作两者之间的选择。 8 ADJ If you describe someone as **straight**, you mean that they are normal and conventional, for example in their opinions and in the way they live. 正统的 ❑ *Dorothy was described as a very straight woman, a very strict Christian who was married to her job.* 多萝西被描述成一位非常正统的女人，一位非常诚笃全心扑在工作上的基督徒。 9 ADJ If you describe someone as **straight**, you mean that they are heterosexual rather than homosexual. 异性恋的 [INFORMAL] ❑ *His sexual orientation was a lot more gay than straight.* 他的性取向更像是同性恋的而非异性恋的。 ● N-COUNT **Straight** is also a noun. 异性恋者 ❑ *...a standard of sexual conduct that applies equally to gays and straights.* …一个同等适用于同性恋者和异性恋者的性行为标准。 10 PHRASE If you **get** something **straight**, you make sure that you understand it properly or that someone else does. 把某事弄清楚 [SPOKEN] ❑ *You need to get your facts straight.* 你需要把你的事实弄清楚。 11 **a straight face** → see **face**

S

Word Partnership *straight* 的常用搭配：

N. straight **line**, straight **nose** 1
second/third straight **loss/victory/win**, **second/third** straight **season/year** 6

V. **drive** straight, **keep going** straight, **look** straight, **point** straight 3

straight ar·row (straight arrows) N-COUNT A **straight arrow** is someone who is very traditional, honest, and moral. 循规蹈矩者 [oft N n] [mainly AM] ❑ *...a well-scrubbed, straight-arrow group of young people.* …一群十分整洁、循规蹈矩的年轻人。

straight away also **straightaway** ADV If you do something **straight away**, you do it immediately and without delay. 立即 [ADV with v] ❑ *I should go and see a doctor straight away.* 我应该立即去看医生。

straight·en /streɪtᵊn/ (**straightens, straightening, straightened**) 1 V-T If you **straighten** something, you make it neat or put it in its proper position. 整理；摆好 ❑ *She sipped her coffee and straightened a picture on the wall.* 她抿了口咖啡，然后把墙上的一幅画扶正。 ● PHRASAL VERB **Straighten up** means the same as **straighten**. 整理；摆好 ❑ *This is my job, to straighten up, to file things.* 这就是我的工作，整理东西，把东西归档。 2 V-I If you are standing in a relaxed or slightly bent position and then you **straighten**, you make your back or body straight and upright. 挺直腰 ❑ *The three men straightened and stood waiting.* 那3个人挺直了腰站着等。 ● PHRASAL VERB **Straighten up** means the same as **straighten**. 挺直腰 ❑ *He straightened up and slipped his hands in his pockets.* 他挺直腰，把双手插进衣兜里。 3 V-T/V-I If you **straighten** something, or it **straightens**, it becomes straight. 使变直；变直 ❑ *Straighten both legs until they are fully extended.* 使双腿挺直，直到他们完全伸展开。 ● PHRASAL VERB **Straighten out** means the same as **straighten**. 使变直；变直 ❑ *No one would dream of straightening out the church's knobbly spire.* 没人会梦想使教堂的圆形尖顶变直。

▸ **straighten out** 1 PHRASAL VERB If you **straighten out** a confused situation, you succeed in getting it organized and cleaned up. 理清 ❑ *He would make an appointment with him to straighten out a couple of things.* 他想同他安排一次约会以理清几件事情。 2 → see **straighten 3**

▸ **straighten up** → see **straighten 2**

★ **straight·forward** /streɪtfɔrwərd/ 1 ADJ If you describe something as **straightforward**, you approve of it because it is easy to do or understand. 容易的；易懂的 [APPROVAL] ❑ *Disposable diapers are fairly straightforward to put on.* 一次性尿布非常容易穿。 ❑ *The question seemed straightforward enough.* 这个问题看起来够容易的了。 2 ADJ If you describe a person or their behavior as **straightforward**, you approve of them because they are honest and direct, and do not try to hide their feelings. 坦率的 [APPROVAL] ❑ *She is very blunt, very straightforward, and very honest.* 她直言不讳，非常坦率，也非常诚实。

strain ♦◇◇ /streɪn/ (**strains, straining, strained**) 1 N-VAR If **strain** is put **on** an organization or system, it has to do more than it is able to do. 压力 ❑ *The prison service is already under considerable strain.* 监狱系统已受到很大的压力。 2 V-T To **strain** something means to make it do more than it is able to do. 使受到压力 ❑ *The volume of scheduled flights is straining the air traffic control system.* 定期航班的数量使空中交通控制系统受到压力。 3 N-UNCOUNT **Strain** is a state of worry and tension caused by a difficult situation. 压力 [also N in pl] ❑ *She was tired and under great strain.* 她疲倦且处于巨大的压力之下。 4 N-SING If you say that a situation is **a strain**, you mean that it makes you worried and tense. 负担 ❑ *I sometimes find it a strain to be responsible for the mortgage.* 我有时发现偿还抵押借款是个负担。 5 N-UNCOUNT **Strain** is a force that pushes, pulls, or stretches something in a way that may damage it. 压力 ❑ *Place your hands under your buttocks to take some of the strain off your back.* 把双手放在臀部下面，以减轻一些背部压力。 6 N-VAR **Strain** is an injury to a muscle in your body, caused by using the muscle too much or twisting it. 损伤；扭伤 ❑ *Avoid muscle strain by warming up with slow jogging.* 通过慢跑热身避免肌肉损伤。 7 V-T If you **strain** a muscle, you injure it by using it too much or twisting it. 损伤；扭伤 ❑ *He strained his back during a practice session.* 他在一次练习课上扭伤了背部。 8 V-T If you **strain to** do something, you make a great effort to do it when it is difficult to do. 努力做 ❑ *I had to strain to hear.* 我不得不努力地听。 9 V-T When you **strain** food, you separate the liquid part of it from the solid parts. 过滤 ❑ *Strain the stock and put it back into the pan.* 滤出原汤，然后把它放回平底锅。 10 N-COUNT A **strain of** a germ, plant, or other organism is a particular type of it. 类型；品种 ❑ *Every year new strains of influenza develop.* 每年都有新的流感类型出现。

Word Partnership *strain* 的常用搭配：

ADJ. **great** strain 1 3 4
virulent strain 10

N. **stress and** strain 3
muscle strain 6
strain **a muscle** 7
strain **of bacteria/virus** 10

strained /streɪnd/ 1 ADJ If someone's appearance, voice, or behavior is **strained**, they seem worried and nervous. 紧张的 ❑ *She looked a little pale and strained.* 她看上去面色有点儿苍白，神情紧张。 ❑ *Gill sensed that something was wrong from her father's strained voice.* 从她父亲紧张的声音中，吉尔感觉到有些不对头。 2 ADJ If relations between people are **strained**, those people do not like or trust each other. （关系）紧张的 ❑ *...a period of strained relations between the mayor and his deputy.* …这位市长和他的副手关系紧张的一段时期。

▲ **strait** /streɪt/ (**straits**) 1 N-COUNT; N-IN-NAMES You can refer to a narrow strip of sea which joins two large areas of sea as a **strait** or **the straits**. 海峡 ❑ *An estimated 1,600 vessels pass through the strait annually.* 估计每年有1600艘船经过这个海峡。 2 N-PLURAL If someone is **in** dire or desperate **straits**, they are in a very difficult situation, usually because they do not have much money. （常指缺钱造成的）困境 [adj N] ❑ *The company's closure has left many small businessmen in desperate financial straits.* 该公司的关闭使得许多小商人陷入经济困境。

strait·jacket /streɪtdʒækɪt/ (**straitjackets**) 1 N-COUNT A **straitjacket** is a special jacket used to tie the arms of a violent person tightly around their body. 约束衣 ❑ *Occasionally his behavior became so uncontrollable that he had to be placed in a straitjacket.* 有时他的行为会如此失控，以至他不得不被穿上一件约束衣。 2 N-COUNT If you describe an idea or a situation as a **straitjacket**, you mean that it is very limited and restricting. 束缚 ❑ *...the ideological straitjacket of religious fundamentalism.* …宗教的原教旨主义意识形态上的束缚。

★ **strand** /strænd/ (**strands, stranding, stranded**) 1 N-COUNT A **strand of** something such as hair, wire, or thread is a single thin piece of it. （头发、电线或纱线的）缕 ❑ *She tried to blow a gray strand of hair from her eyes.* 她试图吹开眼前的一缕白发。 2 V-T If you **are stranded**, you are prevented from leaving a place, for example because of bad weather. 使滞留 ❑ *The climbers had been stranded by a storm.* 这些登山者被暴风雨困住了。
→ see **rope**

strange ♦♦◇ /streɪndʒ/ (**stranger, strangest**) 1 ADJ Something that is **strange** is unusual or unexpected, and makes you feel slightly nervous or afraid. 奇怪的 ❑ *Then a strange thing happened.* 接着一件怪事发生了。 ❑ *There was something strange about the flickering blue light.* 那闪烁的蓝光有点儿奇怪。 ● **strange·ly** ADV 奇怪地 ❑ *She noticed he was acting strangely.* 她注意到他行为怪异。 ● **strange·ness** N-UNCOUNT 奇怪 ❑ *...the breathy strangeness of the music.* …音乐里的奇怪呼吸声。 2 ADJ A **strange** place is one that you have never been to before. A **strange** person is someone that you have never met before. 陌生的 [ADJ n] ❑ *I ended up alone in a strange city.* 我最终是独自呆在了一个陌生的城市。 3 → see also **stranger**

Thesaurus *strange* 另参见：

ADJ. bizarre, different, eccentric, idiosyncratic, odd, peculiar, unusual, weird; *(ant.)* ordinary, usual 1
exotic, foreign, unfamiliar 2

strange·ly /streɪndʒli/ 1 ADV You use **strangely** to emphasize that what you are saying is surprising. 令人奇怪的是 [ADV with cl] [EMPHASIS] ❑ *Strangely, they hadn't invited her to join them.* 令人奇怪的是，他们没邀请她参加。 2 → see also **strange**

stran·ger /streɪndʒər/ (**strangers**) 1 N-COUNT A **stranger** is someone you have never met before. 陌生人 ❑ *Telling a complete stranger about your life is difficult.* 向一位完全陌生的人讲述自己的生活是困难的。 2 N-PLURAL If two people are **strangers**, they do not know each other. 互不相识者 ❑ *The women knew nothing of the dead girl. They were strangers.* 这些妇女对那个死去的女孩一无所知。她们互不相识。 3 N-COUNT If you are a **stranger to** something, you have had no experience of it or do not understand it. 生手 ❑ *He is no stranger to controversy.* 他对争议一点都不陌生。 4 → see also **strange**

You do not use **stranger** to talk about someone who comes from a country which is not your own. You can refer to him or her as a **foreigner**, but this word can sound rather rude. It is better to say specifically where someone comes from. ❑ *He's Egyptian... She's from Finland.*

▲ **stran·gle** /strǽŋgᵊl/ (**strangles, strangling, strangled**) 1 V-T To **strangle** someone means to kill them by squeezing their throat tightly so that they cannot breathe. 扼死 ❑ *He tried to strangle a border policeman and steal his gun.* 他试图扼死一位边防警察并偷走他的枪。 2 V-T To **strangle** something means to prevent it from succeeding or developing. 抑制 ❑ *The country's economic plight is strangling its scientific institutions.* 这个国家的经济困境正在抑制其科研机构的发展。

strangle·hold /strǽŋgᵊlhoʊld/ N-SING To have a **stranglehold on** something means to have control over it and prevent it from being free or from developing. 压制 ❑ *These companies are determined to keep a stranglehold on the banana industry.* 这些公司决定对香蕉业进行压制。

strap /strǽp/ (**straps, strapping, strapped**) 1 N-COUNT A **strap** is a narrow piece of leather, cloth, or other material. Straps are used to carry things, fasten things together, or to hold a piece of clothing in place. 带子 ❑ *Nancy gripped the strap of her beach bag.* 南希抓住自己海滩休闲包的带子。 ❑ *She pulled the strap of her nightgown onto her shoulder.* 她把睡衣的带子拉到她的肩上。 2 V-T If you **strap** something somewhere, you fasten it there with a strap. 用带子绑 ❑ *She strapped the baby seat into the car.* 她把婴儿座椅用带子绑在那辆汽车上。

strap·less /strǽplɪs/ ADJ A **strapless** dress or bra does not have the usual narrow bands of material over the shoulders. 无吊带的 [usu ADJ n]

stra·tegic ♦◇◇ /strətiːdʒɪk/ 1 ADJ **Strategic** means relating to the most important, general aspects of something such as a military operation or political policy, especially when these are decided in advance. 战略上的 ❑ *...the new strategic thinking which NATO leaders produced at the recent London summit.* …北大西洋公约组织领导人在最近伦敦峰会上提出的新的战略思维。 ● **stra·tegi·cal·ly** /strətiːdʒɪkli/ ADV 战略上地 ❑ *...strategically important roads, bridges and buildings.* …战略上具有重要意义的公路、桥梁和建筑物。 2 ADJ **Strategic** weapons are very powerful missiles that can be fired only after a decision to use them has been made by a political leader. 战略性的 ❑ *...strategic nuclear weapons.* …战略性核武器。 3 ADJ If you put something in a **strategic** position, you place it cleverly in a position where it will be most useful or have the most effect. 巧妙的 ❑ *...the marble benches Eve had placed at strategic points throughout the gardens, where the views were spectacular.* …伊夫在花园各个景色优美的巧妙位置安放的大理石长凳。 ● **stra·tegi·cal·ly** ADV 巧妙地 ❑ *We had kept its presence hidden with a strategically placed chair.* 我们用一把巧妙放置的椅子把它隐藏起来。

Word Partnership *strategic* 的常用搭配：

N. strategic **decisions**, strategic **forces**, strategic **interests**, strategic **planning**, strategic **targets**, strategic **thinking** 1
strategic **missiles**, strategic **nuclear weapons** 2
strategic **location**, strategic **position** 3

strat·egist /strǽtədʒɪst/ (**strategists**) N-COUNT A **strategist** is someone who is skilled in planning the best way to gain an advantage or to achieve success, especially in war. 战略家 ❑ *Military strategists had devised a plan that guaranteed a series of stunning victories.* 军事战略家们设计了一个保证了一系列惊人胜利的计划。

strat·egy ♦♦◇ /strǽtədʒi/ (**strategies**) 1 N-VAR A **strategy** is a general plan or set of plans intended to achieve something, especially over a long period. 策略 ❑ *The energy secretary will present the strategy tomorrow afternoon.* 能源部长将于明天下午提出该策略。 2 N-UNCOUNT **Strategy** is the art of planning the best way to gain an advantage or achieve success, especially in war. 战略 ❑ *I've just been explaining the basic principles of strategy to my generals.* 我刚才一直在向我的将军们解释战略的基本原则。

Thesaurus *strategy* 另参见：

N. plan, policy, tactics 1

Word Partnership *strategy* 的常用搭配：

ADJ. **aggressive** strategy, **new** strategy, **political** strategy, **successful** strategy, **winning** strategy 1
V. **adopt a** strategy, **change a** strategy, **develop a** strategy, **plan a** strategy 1
use (a) strategy 1 2
N. **campaign** strategy, **investment** strategy, **marketing** strategy, **part of a** strategy, **pricing** strategy, strategy **shift** 1
military strategy 1 2

straw /strɔ/ (**straws**) 1 N-UNCOUNT **Straw** consists of the dried, yellowish stalks from crops such as wheat or barley. 麦杆；稻草 ❑ *The barn was full of bales of straw.* 这个谷仓堆满了成捆的麦杆。 ❑ *I stumbled through mud to a yard strewn with straw.* 我跌跌撞撞地走过泥泞来到一个散满稻草的院子。 2 N-COUNT A **straw** is a thin tube of paper or plastic, which you use to suck a drink into your mouth. 吸管 ❑ *...a bottle of lemonade with a straw in it.* …一瓶插着吸管的柠檬汽水。 3 PHRASE If you **are clutching at straws** or **grasping at straws**, you are trying unusual or extreme ideas or methods because other ideas or methods have failed. 抓救命稻草 ❑ *...a badly thought-out plan from an administration clutching at straws.* …一个管理部门抓救命稻草而制定的一个考虑不周的计划。 4 PHRASE If an event is **the last straw** or **the straw that broke the camel's back**, it is the latest in a series of unpleasant or undesirable events, and makes you feel that you cannot tolerate a situation any longer. 使人一忍再忍的一系列事件的最后一件 ❑ *For him the Church's decision to allow the ordination of women had been the last straw.* 对他来说，教堂允许妇女被授予圣职的决定使他再也不能容忍下去了。 5 PHRASE If you **draw the short straw**, you are chosen from a number of people to perform a job or duty that you will not enjoy. 下下签 ❑ *...if a few of your guests have drawn the short straw and agreed to drive others home after your summer barbecue.* …如果你的几位客人抽到了下下签，并同意在你的夏日烧烤聚会后开车送其他人回家。
→ see **rice**

▲ **straw·berry** /strɔberi/ (**strawberries**) N-COUNT A **strawberry** is a small red fruit which is soft and juicy and has tiny yellow seeds on its skin. 草莓 ❑ *...strawberries and cream.* …奶油草莓。

★ **stray** /streɪ/ (**strays, straying, strayed**) 1 V-I If someone **strays** somewhere, they wander away from where they are supposed to be. 走失 ❑ *Tourists often get lost and stray into dangerous areas.* 旅游者们经常迷路走进一些危险区域。 2 ADJ A **stray** dog or cat has wandered away from its owner's home. 走失的（狗或猫） [ADJ n] ❑ *A stray dog came up to him.* 一只走失的狗来到他跟前。 ● N-COUNT **Stray** is also a noun. 走失的宠物 ❑ *The dog was a stray which had been adopted.* 这只狗是被收养的流浪狗。 3 V-I If your mind or your eyes **stray**, you do not concentrate on or look at one particular subject, but start thinking about or looking at other things. （思想或视线）不集中 ❑ *Even with the simplest cases I find my mind straying.* 即使对最简单的案例我发现自己的思想也无法集中。 4 ADJ You use **stray** to describe something that exists separated from other similar things. 离群的 [ADJ n] ❑ *An 8-year-old boy was killed by a stray bullet.* 一个8岁的男孩被一颗流弹打死。

streak /striːk/ (**streaks, streaking, streaked**) 1 N-COUNT A **streak** is a long stripe or mark on a surface which contrasts with the surface because it is a different color. 条纹 ❑ *There are these dark streaks on the surface of the moon.* 月亮表面有这些黑色的条纹。 2 V-T If something **streaks** a surface, it makes long stripes or marks on the surface. 在…上留下条痕 ❑ *Rain had begun to streak the windowpanes.* 雨已开始在窗玻璃上留下条痕。 3 N-COUNT If someone has a **streak** of a particular type of behavior, they sometimes behave in that way. 性格特征 [usu sing, with supp] ❑ *We're both alike – there is a streak of madness in us both.* 我们两个很像——我们两人都有一种疯狂的性格特征。 4 V-I If something or someone **streaks** somewhere, they move there very quickly. 疾驰 ❑ *A meteorite streaked across the sky.* 一颗流星划过天空。 5 N-COUNT A winning **streak** or a lucky **streak** is a continuous series of successes, for example in gambling or sports. A losing **streak** or an unlucky **streak** is a series of failures or losses. （赌博或体育比赛中的）运气 ❑ *The casinos had better watch out since I'm obviously on a lucky streak!* 我的手气显然很好，那些赌场最好当心！

stream ♦◇◇ /striːm/ (**streams, streaming, streamed**) 1 N-COUNT A **stream** is a small narrow river. 溪流 ❑ *There was a*

S

small stream at the end of the garden. 这个花园的尽头有一条小溪。 2 N-COUNT A **stream** of smoke, air, or liquid is a narrow moving mass of it. 一股（烟、气或液体）❑ *He breathed out a stream of cigarette smoke.* 他吐出一缕香烟的烟雾。 3 N-COUNT A **stream** of vehicles or people is a long moving line of them. （车或人）流 ❑ *There was a stream of traffic behind him.* 他身后有一股车流。 4 N-COUNT A **stream of** things is a large number of them occurring one after another. 一连串 ❑ *The discovery triggered a stream of readers' letters.* 这个发现引来一连串的读者来信。 ❑ *...a never-ending stream of jokes.* …接连不断的笑话。 5 V-I If a liquid **streams** somewhere, it flows or comes out in large amounts. 流 ❑ *Tears streamed down their faces.* 泪水顺着他们的脸颊流下来。 6 V-I If your eyes **are streaming**, liquid is coming from them, for example because you have a cold. You can also say that your nose **is streaming**. 流眼泪；流鼻涕 [usu cont] ❑ *Her eyes were streaming now from the wind.* 她的眼睛现在被风吹得直流泪。 7 V-I If people or vehicles **stream** somewhere, they move there quickly and in large numbers. （人或车辆）大批流动 ❑ *Refugees have been streaming into Travnik for months.* 难民几个月来一直大量流入特拉弗尼克。 8 V-I When light **streams** into or out of a place, it shines strongly into or out of it. 照射 ❑ *Sunlight was streaming into the courtyard.* 阳光正照进那院子。 9 PHRASE If something such as a new factory or a new system comes **on stream** or is brought **on stream**, it begins to operate or becomes available. 投入生产 ❑ *As new mines come on stream, Chile's share of world copper output will increase sharply.* 随着新矿投产，智利在世界铜产量中所占的份额将大幅度增长。
→ see **river**

★ **stream·line** /striːmlaɪn/ (**streamlines, streamlining, streamlined**) V-T To **streamline** an organization or process means to make it more efficient by removing unnecessary parts of it. 提高…效率 ❑ *They're making efforts to streamline their normally cumbersome bureaucracy.* 他们正努力提高其通常臃肿的官僚机构的效率。
→ see **mass production**

stream·lined /striːmlaɪnd/ ADJ A **streamlined** vehicle, animal, or object has a shape that allows it to move quickly or efficiently through air or water. 流线型的 ❑ *...these beautifully streamlined and efficient cars.* …这些优美的流线型高效能汽车。

street ♦♦♦ /striːt/ (**streets**) 1 N-COUNT; N-IN-NAMES A **street** is a road in a city, town, or village, usually with houses along it. 街道 ❑ *He lived at 66 Bingfield Street.* 他住在宾菲尔德街66号。 2 N-COUNT You can use **street** or **streets** when talking about activities that happen out of doors in a city or town rather than inside a building. 街头 ❑ *Changing money on the street is illegal – always use a bank.* 在街头兑换货币是非法的——始终要去银行。 ❑ *Their aim is to raise a million dollars to get the homeless off the streets.* 他们的目的是募集100万美元以使无家可归者不再流浪街头。 3 → see also **Downing Street, Main Street, Wall Street**

Thesaurus	·street 另参见：
N.	avenue, drive, road 1

street·car /striːtkɑr/ (**streetcars**) N-COUNT A **streetcar** is an electric vehicle for carrying people which travels on rails in the streets of a city or town. 市内有轨电车 [AM]

in BRIT, use **tram**

→ see **transportation**

strength ♦♦◊ /strɛŋkθ, strɛŋθ/ (**strengths**) 1 N-UNCOUNT Your **strength** is the physical energy that you have, which gives you the ability to perform various actions, such as lifting or moving things. 力量 ❑ *She has always been encouraged to swim to build up the strength of her muscles.* 她总是被鼓励去游泳以增强肌肉力量。 ❑ *He threw it forward with all his strength.* 他使尽全部的力气把它向前扔出。 2 N-UNCOUNT Someone's **strength** in a difficult situation is their confidence or courage. （困境中的）勇气 [also "a" N] ❑ *Something gave me the strength to overcome the difficulty.* 有件事给了我克服困难的勇气。 ❑ *He copes incredibly well. His strength is an inspiration to me in my life.* 他处理得非常好。他的勇气对我的人生是一种鼓舞。 3 N-UNCOUNT The **strength** of an object or material is its ability to be treated roughly, or to carry heavy weights, without being damaged or destroyed. 强度 [also N in pl] ❑ *He checked the strength of the cables.* 他检查了缆绳的强度。 4 N-UNCOUNT The **strength** of a person, organization, or country is the power or influence that they have. 实力 [also N in pl] ❑ *America values its economic leadership, and the political and military strength that goes with it.* 美国重视它的经济领导地位以及与其相配的政治和军事实力。 ❑ *The alliance, in its first show of strength, drew a hundred thousand-strong crowd to a rally.* 该联盟在首次实力展示时吸引了多达10万的人群来参加集会。 5 N-UNCOUNT If you refer to the **strength of** a feeling, opinion, or belief, you are talking about how deeply it is felt or believed by people, or how much they are influenced by it. （感情、观点或信念的）强烈程度 ❑ *He was surprised at the strength of his own feeling.* 他对自己感情的强烈程度感到吃惊。 6 N-VAR Someone's **strengths** are the qualities and abilities that they have which are an advantage to them, or which make them successful. 长处 ❑ *Take into account your own strengths and weaknesses.* 考虑一下你自己的长处和弱点。 ❑ *Tact was never Mr. Moore's strength.* 老练从来不是穆尔先生的长处。 7 N-UNCOUNT If you refer to the **strength** of a currency, economy, or industry, you mean that its value or success is steady or increasing. （货币、经济或行业的）走强 ❑ *...the long-term competitive strength of the economy.* …该经济的有竞争力的长期走强。 8 N-UNCOUNT The **strength** of a group of people is the total number of people in it. 人数 [also N in pl] ❑ *...elite forces, comprising about one-tenth of the strength of the army.* …约占军队总人数1/10的精锐部队。 9 N-UNCOUNT The **strength** of a wind, current, or other force is its power or speed. 力 [also N in pl] ❑ *Its oscillation depends on the strength of the gravitational field.* 它的摆动取决于重力场的力。 10 N-UNCOUNT The **strength** of a drink, chemical, or drug is the amount of the particular substance in it that gives it its particular effect. 浓度 [also N in pl] ❑ *It is very alcoholic, sometimes near the strength of port.* 它的酒精度很高，有时接近于波尔图葡萄酒的浓度。 11 PHRASE If a person or organization **goes from strength to strength**, they become more and more successful or confident. 越来越兴旺 ❑ *A decade later, the company has gone from strength to strength.* 10年后，该公司越来越兴旺了。 12 PHRASE If a team or army is at **full strength**, all the members that it needs or usually has are present. 满员 ❑ *He needed more time to bring U.S. forces there up to full strength.* 他需要更多的时间使驻扎在那里的美国部队达到满员。 13 PHRASE If one thing is done **on the strength of** another, it is done because of the influence of that other thing. 凭借 ❑ *He was elected to power on the strength of his charisma.* 他凭借个人魅力当选。
→ see **muscle**

strength·en ♦◊◊ /strɛŋθᵊn/ (**strengthens, strengthening, strengthened**) 1 V-T If something **strengthens** a person or group or if they **strengthen** their position, they become more powerful and secure, or more likely to succeed. 加强 ❑ *Giving the president the authority to go to war would strengthen his hand for peace.* 给予总统发动战争的权利会加强他对于和平的掌控权。 2 V-T If something **strengthens** a case or argument, it supports it by providing more reasons or evidence for it. （提供更多的理由或证据）支持 ❑ *He does not seem to be familiar with research which might have strengthened his own arguments.* 他对本来可使他的论证更有说服力的研究似乎不太熟悉。 3 V-T/V-I If a currency, economy, or industry **strengthens**, or if something **strengthens** it, it increases in value or becomes more successful. 走强 ❑ *The dollar strengthened against most other currencies.* 美元与大多数其它货币相比升值了。 4 V-T If something **strengthens** you or **strengthens** your resolve or character, it makes you more confident and determined. 使变得坚定 ❑ *Any experience can teach and strengthen you, but particularly the more difficult ones.* 任何经历都可以让你学到东西，使你变得坚定，那些更困难的经历尤其如此。 ❑ *This merely strengthens our resolve to win the pennant.* 这只不过坚定了我们赢得锦旗的决心。 5 V-T/V-I If something **strengthens** a relationship or link, or if it **strengthens**, it makes it closer and more likely to last for a long time. 巩固 ❑ *It will draw you closer together, and it will strengthen the bond of your relationship.* 它会拉近你们的距离，而且它会巩固你们联系的纽带。 6 V-T/V-I If something **strengthens** an impression, feeling, or belief, or if it **strengthens**, it becomes greater or affects more people. 加深；增强 ❑ *His speech strengthens the impression he is the main power in the organization.* 他的讲话加深了他是这个组织主要掌权人物的印象。 ❑ *Every day of sunshine strengthens the feelings of optimism.* 每一阳光灿烂的日子都增强着乐观的情绪。 7 V-T If something **strengthens** your body or a part of your body, it makes it healthier, often in such a way that you can move or carry heavier things. 使强健 ❑ *Cycling is good exercise. It strengthens all the muscles of the body.* 骑车是好的锻炼。它使全身肌肉变得强健。 8 V-T If something **strengthens** an object or structure, it makes it able to be treated roughly or able to support heavy weights, without being damaged or destroyed. 加固 ❑ *The builders will have to strengthen the existing joists with additional timber.* 建筑工人们将不得不用额外的木料加固现有的接合处。

S

▲ **strenu·ous** /strɛnyuəs/ ADJ A **strenuous** activity or action involves a lot of energy or effort. 艰苦的; 剧烈的 ❑ *Avoid strenuous exercise in the evening.* 应避免在傍晚进行剧烈的运动。 ❑ *Strenuous efforts had been made to improve conditions in the jail.* 为改善那家监狱里的条件已做了艰苦的努力。

stress ♦♦◇ /strɛs/ (**stresses, stressing, stressed**) **1** V-T If you **stress** a point in a discussion, you put extra emphasis on it because you think it is important. 强调 ❑ *The spokesman stressed that the measures did not amount to an overall ban.* 发言人强调说，这些措施并不等于全面禁止。 ❑ *China's leaders have stressed the need for increased co-operation between Third World countries.* 中国领导人已经强调了增进第三世界国家之间合作的需要。 ● N-VAR **Stress** is also a noun. 重点 ❑ *Japanese car makers are laying ever more stress on overseas sales.* 日本的汽车制造商们把更多的重点放在海外销售上。 **2** N-VAR If you feel under **stress**, you feel worried and tense because of difficulties in your life. 精神压力 ❑ *Katy could think clearly when not under stress.* 凯泰在没有精神压力时能够清晰地思考。 **3** V-T If you **stress** a word or part of a word when you say it, you put emphasis on it so that it sounds slightly louder. 重读 ❑ *She stresses the syllables as though teaching a child.* 她重读这些音节，像教小孩似的。 ● N-VAR **Stress** is also a noun. 重读 ❑ *...the misplaced stress on the first syllable of this last word.* …这个最末单词的第1个音节上的重读错误。 → see **emotion**

Word Partnership *stress* 的常用搭配:

N. stress **the importance of** *something* **1**
anxiety and stress, **effects of** stress, **job/work-related** stress, stress **management**, stress **reduction**, **response to** stress, **symptoms of** stress, stress **test** **2**

V. **cause** stress, **cope with** stress, **deal with** stress, **experience** stress, **induce** stress, **reduce** stress, **relieve** stress **2**

ADJ. **emotional** stress, **excessive** stress, **high** stress, **physical** stress, stress **related, severe** stress **2**

stressed /strɛst/ ADJ If you are **stressed**, you feel tense and anxious because of difficulties in your life. 焦虑不安的 ❑ *Work out what situations or people make you feel stressed and avoid them.* 弄清是什么样的情况或什么样的人使你焦虑不安，并避开他们。

stressed out ADJ If someone is **stressed out**, they are very tense and anxious because of difficulties in their lives. 非常焦虑不安的 [INFORMAL] ❑ *I can't imagine sitting in traffic, getting stressed out.* 我不能想像坐车被堵在路上，变得越来越焦虑不安。

stress·ful /strɛsfəl/ ADJ If a situation or experience is **stressful**, it causes the person involved to feel stress. 压力大的 ❑ *I think I've got one of the most stressful jobs there is.* 我想我找到了一个压力最大的工作。

stretch ♦◇◇ /strɛtʃ/ (**stretches, stretching, stretched**) **1** V-I Something that **stretches** over an area or distance covers or exists in the whole of that area or distance. 延伸 [no cont] ❑ *The procession stretched for several miles.* 游行队伍延伸了数英里。 **2** N-COUNT A **stretch of** road, water, or land is a length or area of it. 一段 ❑ *It's a very dangerous stretch of road.* 这是一段非常危险的路。 **3** V-T/V-I When you **stretch**, you put your arms or legs out straight and tighten your muscles. 伸直 ❑ *He yawned and stretched.* 他打了个哈欠，伸了伸腰。 ❑ *Try stretching your legs and pulling your toes upwards.* 试着伸直双腿并向上拉拉脚趾。 ● N-COUNT **Stretch** is also a noun. 伸展 ❑ *At the end of a workout spend time cooling down with some slow stretches.* 在健身的末尾花时间用一些缓慢的伸展来做缓和。 **4** N-COUNT A **stretch of** time is a period of time. 一段 (时间) ❑ *...after an 18-month stretch in the army.* …在部队呆了18个月后。 **5** V-I If something **stretches from** one time **to** another, it begins at the first time and ends at the second, which is longer than expected. 持续 ❑ *...a working day that stretches from seven in the morning to eight at night.* …从早上7点持续到晚上8点的一个工作日。 **6** V-I If a group of things **stretch from** one type of thing **to** another, the group includes a wide range of things. 涉及 ❑ *...a trading empire, with interests that stretched from chemicals to sugar.* …一个兴趣范围从化学品到食糖的贸易帝国。 **7** V-T/V-I When something soft or elastic **stretches** or **is stretched**, it becomes longer or bigger as well as thinner, usually because it is pulled. 有弹性 ❑ *The cables are designed not to stretch.* 这些缆绳被设计成没有弹性。 **8** V-T/V-I If you **stretch** an amount of something or if it **stretches**, you make it last longer than it usually would by being careful and not wasting any of it. 俭省 ❑ *They're used to stretching their budgets.* 他们习惯于精打细算。 **9** V-T If something **stretches** your money or resources, it uses them up so you have hardly enough for your needs. 耗尽 (钱或资源) ❑ *The drought there is stretching resources.* 那里的干旱正在耗尽财力物力。 **10** V-T If you say that a job or task **stretches** you, you mean that you like it because it makes you work hard and use all your energy and skills so that you do not become bored or achieve less than you should. 使充分发挥 [APPROVAL] ❑ *I'm trying to move on and stretch myself with something different.* 我正试图换个工作，使自己在不同的事情上得到充分发挥。 **11** PHRASE If you say that something is not true or possible **by any stretch of the imagination**, you are emphasizing that it is completely untrue or absolutely impossible. 无论如何想像 [EMPHASIS] ❑ *Her husband was not a womanizer by any stretch of the imagination.* 她的丈夫无论如何想像也不会是个玩弄女性的人。

▸ **stretch out** **1** PHRASAL VERB If you **stretch out** or **stretch yourself out**, you lie with your legs and body in a straight line. (使) 平躺 ❑ *The bathtub was too small to stretch out in.* 这个浴缸太小了躺不下。 **2** PHRASAL VERB If you **stretch out** a part of your body, you hold it out straight. 伸出 ❑ *He was about to stretch out his hand to grab me.* 他正要伸手抓我。

Word Partnership *stretch* 的常用搭配:

PREP. stretch **across** **1** **3**
during a stretch **3** **4**
at a stretch **4**

N. stretch **of highway/road**, stretch **of a river, along a** stretch **of road, down the road a** stretch **2**
stretch ***your* legs** **3**

stretch·er /strɛtʃər/ (**stretchers, stretchered**) **1** N-COUNT A **stretcher** is a long piece of canvas with a pole along each side, which is used to carry an injured or sick person. 担架 ❑ *The two ambulance attendants quickly put Plover on a stretcher and got him into the ambulance.* 这两名救护车的救护员迅速把普洛弗放在担架上并抬进了那辆救护车。 **2** V-T PASSIVE If someone **is stretchered** somewhere, they are carried there on a stretcher. 用担架抬 ❑ *I was close by as Lester was stretchered into the ambulance.* 莱斯特被用担架送进那辆救护车时我在旁边。

strewn /strun/ ADJ If a place is **strewn with** things, they are lying scattered there. 散落的 [v-link ADJ "with" n] ❑ *The front room was strewn with books and clothes.* 前室到处是书和衣服。 ● COMB IN ADJ **Strewn** is also a combining form. 散落着…的 ❑ *...a litter-strewn street.* …一条布满垃圾的街道。

★ **strick·en** /strɪkən/ **1** **Stricken** is the past participle of some meanings of **strike**. 某些义项下，**strike**的过去分词 **2** ADJ If a person or place is **stricken by** something such as an unpleasant feeling, an illness, or a natural disaster, they are severely affected by it. 受侵害的 ❑ *...a family stricken by genetically inherited cancer.* …一个受遗传性癌症侵害的家庭。 ● COMB IN ADJ **Stricken** is also a combining form. 受…侵害的 ❑ *...a leukemia-stricken child.* …一个患白血病的孩子。

strict ♦◇◇ /strɪkt/ (**stricter, strictest**) **1** ADJ A **strict** rule or order is very clear and precise or severe and must always be obeyed completely. 严格的 ❑ *The officials had issued strict instructions that we were not to get out of the jeep.* 这些官员们发出了我们不能从那辆吉普车里出来的严令。 ❑ *French privacy laws are very strict.* 法国的隐私法非常严格。 ● **strict·ly** ADV 严格地 [ADV with v] ❑ *The acceptance of new members is strictly controlled.* 接纳新成员的工作受到严格控制。 **2** ADJ If a parent or other person in authority is **strict**, they regard many actions as unacceptable and do not allow them. 严厉的 ❑ *My parents were very strict.* 我的父母曾非常严厉。 ● **strict·ly** ADV 严厉地 ❑ *My own mother was brought up very strictly and correctly.* 我自己的母亲是被非常严厉且正确地养大的。 **3** ADJ If you talk about the **strict** meaning of something, you mean the precise meaning of it. 确切的 [ADJ n] ❑ *It's not quite peace in the strictest sense of the word, rather the absence of war.* 这个词就其最确切的意义而言不完全是和平，更像是没有战争。 ● **strict·ly** ADV 确切地 [ADV adj] ❑ *Actually, that is not strictly true.* 实际上，那并不完全是真的。 **4** ADJ You use **strict** to describe someone who never does things that are against their beliefs. 恪守信条的 [ADJ n] ❑ *Millions of Americans are now strict vegetarians.* 数百万美国人现在都是严格的素食者。

strict·ly /strɪktli/ ADV You use **strictly** to emphasize that something is of one particular type, or intended for one particular thing or person, rather than any other. 仅限于 [ADV group]

[EMPHASIS] ❑ *He seemed fond of her in a strictly professional way.* 他似乎仅限于以职业的方式喜欢她。

stride /straɪd/ (**strides, striding, strode**) **1** V-I If you **stride** somewhere, you walk there with quick, long steps. 大步走 ❑ *They were joined by a newcomer who came striding across a field.* 他们中又来了个新人，那人穿过一块田地大步走过来。 **2** N-COUNT A **stride** is a long step which you take when you are walking or running. 大步 ❑ *With every stride, runners hit the ground with up to five times their body-weight.* 赛跑者的每一步都以5倍于他们体重的力量撞击地面。 **3** N-COUNT If you **make strides** in something that you are doing, you make rapid progress in it. 进步 ❑ *The country has made enormous strides politically but not economically.* 这个国家在政治上取得了巨大进步，但在经济上却没有。 **4** PHRASE If you **get into** your **stride** or **hit** your **stride**, you start to do something easily and confidently, after being slow and uncertain. 进入状态 ❑ *The campaign is just getting into its stride.* 这场运动刚刚进入状态。 **5** PHRASE If you **take** a problem or difficulty **in stride**, you deal with it calmly and easily. 从容处理某事 ❑ *He took the ridiculous accusation in stride.* 他从容应对那荒谬的指控。

Word Partnership *stride* 的常用搭配：
V. **break** *(your)* stride, **lengthen** *your* stride **2**
ADJ. **long** stride **2**
in full stride **4**

stri·dent /straɪdᵊnt/ ADJ If you use **strident** to describe someone or the way they express themselves, you mean that they make their feelings or opinions known in a very strong way that perhaps makes people uncomfortable. 强硬的 [DISAPPROVAL] ❑ *She was increasingly seen as a strident feminist.* 她越来越被人视为一个强硬的女权主义者。

▲ **strife** /straɪf/ N-UNCOUNT **Strife** is strong disagreement or fighting. 冲突 [FORMAL] ❑ *Money is a major cause of strife in many marriages.* 钱在许多婚姻中是导致冲突的一个主要原因。

strike
❶ NOUN USES
❷ VERB USES AND PHRASES
❸ PHRASAL VERBS

❶ **strike** ♦♦◇ /straɪk/ (**strikes**) **1** N-COUNT When there is a **strike**, workers stop doing their work for a period of time, usually in order to try to get better pay or conditions for themselves. 罢工 [also "on" N] [BUSINESS] ❑ *Air traffic controllers have begun a three-day strike in a dispute over pay.* 空中交通管制员在一场薪酬纠纷中开始了为时3天的罢工。 ❑ *Staff at the hospital went on strike in protest at the incidents.* 这个医院的员工举行罢工，抗议这些事件。 **2** N-COUNT A military **strike** is a military attack, especially an air attack. 袭击 ❑ *...a punitive air strike.* …一次惩罚性空袭。 **3** → see also **hunger strike** → see **union**

❷ **strike** ♦♦◇ /straɪk/ (**strikes, striking, struck, stricken**)

The form **struck** is the past tense and past participle. The form **stricken** can also be used as the past participle for meanings **5** and **13**.

➪ **Please look at meanings 19 and 20 to see if the expression you are looking for is shown under another headword.** **1** V-I When workers **strike**, they go on strike. 罢工 [BUSINESS] ❑ *...their recognition of the workers' right to strike.* …他们对工人罢工权利的承认。 ❑ *They shouldn't be striking for more money.* 他们不该为更多的钱而罢工。

● **strik·er** N-COUNT (**strikers**) 罢工者 ❑ *The strikers want higher wages, which state governments say they can't afford.* 这些罢工者要求得到更高的工资，州政府说他们无力支付。 **2** V-T If you **strike** someone or something, you deliberately hit them. 打；击 [FORMAL] ❑ *She took two quick steps forward and struck him across the mouth.* 她向前快走两步，打了他一记耳光。 ❑ *It is impossible to say who struck the fatal blow.* 不可能确定是谁给了那致命的一击。 **3** V-T If something that is falling or moving **strikes** something, it hits it. 碰撞；击中 [FORMAL] ❑ *His head struck the bottom when he dived into the 6 ft end of the pool.* 当他跳入水池6英尺深的那端时，头撞到池底。 ❑ *One 16-inch shell struck the control tower.* 一发16英寸的炮弹击中了那座指挥塔。 **4** V-T/V-I If you **strike** one thing against another, or if one thing **strikes** against another, the first thing hits the second thing. 碰撞 [FORMAL] ❑ *Wilde fell and struck his head on the stone floor.* 怀尔德跌倒了，头撞在石头地板上。 **5** V-T/V-I If something such as an illness or disaster **strikes**, it suddenly happens. (疾病或灾难) 爆发 ❑ *Fed officials continued to insist that the dollar would soon return to stability but disaster struck.* 联邦政府的官员们仍坚持说美元会很快恢复平稳，但灾难却爆发了。 ❑ *A moderate earthquake struck the northeastern United States early on Saturday.* 美国东北部周六早晨遭遇了一次中等强度的地震。 **6** V-I To **strike** means to attack someone or something quickly and violently. 攻击 ❑ *He was the only cabinet member out of the country when the terrorists struck.* 他在恐怖分子袭击时是惟一人在国外的内阁成员。 **7** V-T If an idea or thought **strikes** you, it suddenly comes into your mind. 使突然想到 [no cont] ❑ *A thought struck her. Was she jealous of her mother, then?* 她突然冒出一个念头。那她是在嫉妒自己的母亲吗？ **8** V-T If something **strikes** you **as** being a particular thing, it gives you the impression of being that thing. 给…印象 ❑ *He struck me as a very serious but friendly person.* 他在我眼里是个非常严肃但友好的人。 **9** V-T If you **are struck** by something, you think it is very impressive, noticeable, or interesting. 把…迷住 ❑ *She was struck by his simple, spellbinding eloquence.* 她被他简洁、富有鼓动性的口才迷住了。 **10** V-RECIP If you **strike** a deal or a bargain with someone, you come to an agreement with them. 达成 (交易或协议) ❑ *They struck a deal with their paper supplier, getting two years of newsprint on credit.* 他们与其纸张供应商达成一个协议，可以赊购两年的新闻纸。 ❑ *The two struck a deal in which Rendell took half of what a manager would.* 这两个人达成一项协议，伦德尔拿一名经理将能得到的一半。 **11** V-T If you **strike** a balance, you do something that is halfway between two extremes. 找到 (某种平衡) ❑ *At times like that you have to strike a balance between sleep and homework.* 在那样的时候，你得在睡眠和家庭作业之间找到一种平衡。 **12** V-T If you **strike** a pose or attitude, you put yourself in a particular position, for example when someone is taking your photograph. 摆出 (姿态) ❑ *She struck a pose, one hand on her hip and the other waving an imaginary cigarette.* 她摆出一个姿势，一只手叉腰，另一只手挥动着一支假想的香烟。 **13** V-T If something **strikes** fear **into** people, it makes them very frightened or anxious. 引起 (恐惧) [LITERARY] ❑ *If there is a single subject guaranteed to strike fear in the hearts of parents, it is drugs.* 如果只有一个话题能保证在家长们的心中引起恐惧的话，那就是毒品。 **14** V-T/V-I When a clock **strikes**, its bells make a sound to indicate what the time is. (钟) 敲响 ❑ *The clock struck nine.* 钟敲了9下。 **15** V-T If you **strike** words **from** a document or an official record, you remove them. 删除 [FORMAL] ❑ *Strike that from the minutes.* 从会议记录中把那个删除。

● PHRASAL VERB **Strike out** means the same as **strike**. 删除 ❑ *The censor struck out the next two lines.* 审查员删除了下面那两行。 **16** V-T When you **strike** a match, you make it produce a flame by moving it quickly against something rough. 擦 (火柴) ❑ *Robina struck a match and held it to the crumpled newspaper in the grate.* 罗比纳擦了一根火柴，将它伸向壁炉中的那些皱报纸。 **17** V-T If someone **strikes** oil or gold, they discover it in the ground as a result of mining or drilling. 发现 (石油或黄金) ❑ *Oil industry sources say that Marathon Oil Company has struck oil in Syria.* 石油业消息人士称马拉松石油公司在叙利亚发现了石油。 **18** → see also **stricken, striking** **19** to **strike a chord** → see **chord** **20** to **strike home** → see **home**

❸ **strike** ♦♦◇ /straɪk/ (**strikes, striking, struck, stricken**)

▸ **strike down** PHRASAL VERB If someone **is struck down**, especially by an illness, they are killed or severely harmed. (尤指因疾病) 使丧命；摧垮 [WRITTEN] ❑ *Frank had been struck down by a massive heart attack.* 弗兰克被严重的心脏病夺去了生命。

▸ **strike out** **1** PHRASAL VERB In baseball, if a batter **strikes out**, they fail three times to hit the ball and end their turn. If a pitcher **strikes out**, they throw three balls that the batter fails to hit, and end the batter's turn. (棒球击球员) 三击不中而出局；(投手) 使 (击球员) 三击不中而出局 ❑ *Trachsel has struck Bonds out on seven occasions.* 特拉赫塞尔已经7次使邦兹三击不中出局了。 ❑ *The third baseman struck out four times.* 三垒手三击不中出局了4次。 ❑ *The Marlin pitcher struck out the first batter he faced.* 那位马林投手使他面对的第一个击球员三击不中而出局。 **2** PHRASAL VERB If you **strike out**, you begin to do something different, often because you want to become more independent. 开辟新路 ❑ *She wanted me to strike out on my own, buy a business.* 她想让我独立开辟新路，购买一家公司。 **3** PHRASAL VERB If you **strike out at** someone, you hit, attack, or speak angrily to them. 愤怒地打；生气地说 ❑ *He seemed always ready to strike out at anyone and for any cause.* 他似乎总是准备好为任何理由打任何人。 **4** → see also **strike** ❷ **15**

▸ **strike up** PHRASAL VERB When you **strike up** a conversation or friendship with someone, you begin one. 开始 (谈话)；建立 (友谊)

[WRITTEN] ❑ *I trailed her into Penney's and struck up a conversation.* 我跟随她进了彭尼家并开始交谈起来。

strik·er /straɪkər/ (**strikers**) 1 N-COUNT In soccer and some other team sports, a **striker** is a player who mainly attacks and scores goals, rather than defends. (足球等运动中的) 前锋 ❑ *...and the striker scored his sixth goal of the season.* …这位前锋进了他本赛季的第6个球。 2 → see also **strike** 2 1

strik·ing ♦◇◇ /straɪkɪŋ/ 1 ADJ Something that is **striking** is very noticeable or unusual. 显著的; 不同寻常的 ❑ *The most striking feature of those statistics is the high proportion of suicides.* 那些统计数据最显著的特征是高自杀率。 ❑ *He bears a striking resemblance to Lenin.* 他与列宁有着不同寻常的相似之处。 ● **strik·ing·ly** ADV 显著地; 不同寻常地 ❑ *In one respect, however, the men really were strikingly similar.* 然而，在一方面，这些男人的确惊人地相似。 ❑ *...a strikingly handsome man.* …一个异乎寻常地英俊的男人。 2 ADJ Someone who is **striking** is very attractive, in a noticeable way. 俊秀的 ❑ *She was a striking woman with long blonde hair.* 她曾是一个留着金色长发的俊秀女子。

string ♦◇◇ /strɪŋ/ (**strings, stringing, strung**) 1 N-VAR **String** is thin rope made of twisted threads, used for tying things together or tying up packages. 细绳 ❑ *He held out a small bag tied with string.* 他递出一个用细绳系着的小包。 2 N-COUNT A **string of** things is a number of them on a piece of string, thread, or wire. 串 ❑ *She wore a string of pearls around her neck.* 她戴了一串珍珠在她的脖子上。 3 N-COUNT A **string of** places or objects is a number of them that form a line. 排 ❑ *The landscape is broken only by a string of villages.* 这风景仅仅是被一排村庄所破坏。 4 N-COUNT A **string of** similar events is a series of them that happen one after the other. 一连串 ❑ *The incident was the latest in a string of attacks.* 该事件是一连串攻击中最近的一起。 5 N-COUNT The **strings** on a musical instrument such as a violin or guitar are the thin pieces of wire or nylon stretched across it that make sounds when the instrument is played. (乐器的) 弦 ❑ *He went off to change a guitar string.* 他离开了去换一根吉他弦。 6 N-PLURAL **The strings** are the section of an orchestra which consists of stringed instruments played with a bow. 弦乐器 ❑ *The strings provided a melodic background to the passages played by the soloist.* 这些弦乐器为那个独奏演员演奏的几个乐段提供了的背景乐。 7 PHRASE If something is offered to you with **no strings attached** or with **no strings**, it is offered without any special conditions. 不带附加条件 ❑ *Aid should be given to developing countries with no strings attached.* 援助应该不带附加条件地被提供给发展中国家。 8 PHRASE If you **pull strings**, you use your influence with other people in order to get something done, often unfairly. 动用关系 ❑ *Tony is sure he can pull a few strings and get you in.* 托尼确信他能动用一些关系把你弄进来。

→ see Picture Dictionary: **strings**

→ see **orchestra**

▸ **string together** PHRASAL VERB If you **string** things **together**, you form something from them by adding them to each other, one at a time. 把…连串起来 ❑ *As speech develops, the child starts to string more words together.* 随着言语的发展，这个孩子开始把更多的词语连串起来。

Thesaurus *string* 另参见:

N. cord, fiber, rope, twine 1
chain, file, line, row, sequence, series 3 4

Word Partnership *string* 的常用搭配:

N. **piece of** string 1
string **of pearls** 2
string **of attacks**, string **of bombings**, string **of losses**, string **of scandals** 4
banjo string, **guitar** string 5

ADJ. **long** string 1 – 4
latest string **of** ***something***, **recent** string **of** ***something*** 4

strin·gent /strɪndʒᵊnt/ ADJ **Stringent** laws, rules, or conditions are very severe or are strictly controlled. (法律、规定或条件) 严格的 [FORMAL] ❑ *He announced that there would be more stringent controls on the possession of weapons.* 他宣布在武器的持有方面将会有更严格的控制。

strip ♦◇◇ /strɪp/ (**strips, stripping, stripped**) 1 N-COUNT A **strip** of something such as paper, cloth, or food is a long, narrow piece of it. (纸、布或食物的) 条 ❑ *...a new kind of manufactured wood made by pressing strips of wood together and baking them.* …一种通过把木条挤压并烘干而制成的新型人造木材。 ❑ *The simplest rag-rugs are made with strips of fabric braided together.* 这些最简单的碎布地毯是由织物条编织而成的。 2 N-COUNT A **strip of** land or water is a long narrow area of it. 狭长 (地带或水域) ❑ *The coastal cities of Liguria sit on narrow strips of land lying under steep mountains.* 利古里亚的那些海滨城市坐落在陡峭山脉下的狭长地带。 3 N-COUNT A **strip** is a long street in a city or town, where there are a lot of stores, restaurants, and hotels. 商业街 [AM] ❑ *...Goff's Charcoal Hamburgers on Lover's Lane, a busy commercial strip in North Dallas.* …在北达拉斯的一条繁忙的商业街——"情人巷"上的戈夫炭烤汉堡店。 4 V-I If you **strip**, you take off your clothes. 脱衣服 ❑ *They stripped completely, and lay and turned in the damp grass.* 他们脱光了衣服，躺在潮湿的草地上翻滚。 ● PHRASAL VERB **Strip off** means the same as **strip**. 脱衣服 ❑ *The children were brazenly stripping off and leaping into the sea.* 这些孩子们那时正无所顾忌地脱掉衣服，跳进海里。 5 V-T If someone **is stripped**, their clothes are taken off by another person, for example in order to search for hidden or illegal things. 脱掉…的衣服 [usu passive] ❑ *One prisoner claimed he'd been dragged to a cell, stripped, and beaten.* 一个犯人声称他曾被拖进一间牢房，被脱掉衣服殴打。 6 V-T To **strip** something means to remove everything that covers it. 剥离 ❑ *After Mike left for work I stripped the beds and vacuumed the carpets.* 迈克去上班后，我揭下了床罩并吸了地毯。 7 V-T If you **strip** an engine or a piece of equipment, you take it to pieces so that it can be cleaned or repaired. 拆卸 ❑ *Volvo's three-man team stripped the car and treated it to a restoration.* 沃尔沃的3人小组拆了那辆汽车并对它进行了修复。 ● PHRASAL VERB **Strip down** means the same as **strip**. 拆卸 ❑ *In five years I had to strip the water pump down four times.* 在5年里我不得不拆卸了那个水泵4次。 8 V-T To **strip** someone **of** their property, rights, or titles means to take those things away from them. 剥夺 (财产、权利); 撤销 (头衔) ❑ *The soldiers have stripped the civilians of their passports, and every other type of document.* 那些士兵们已经夺走了市民的护照以及所有其他证件。

S

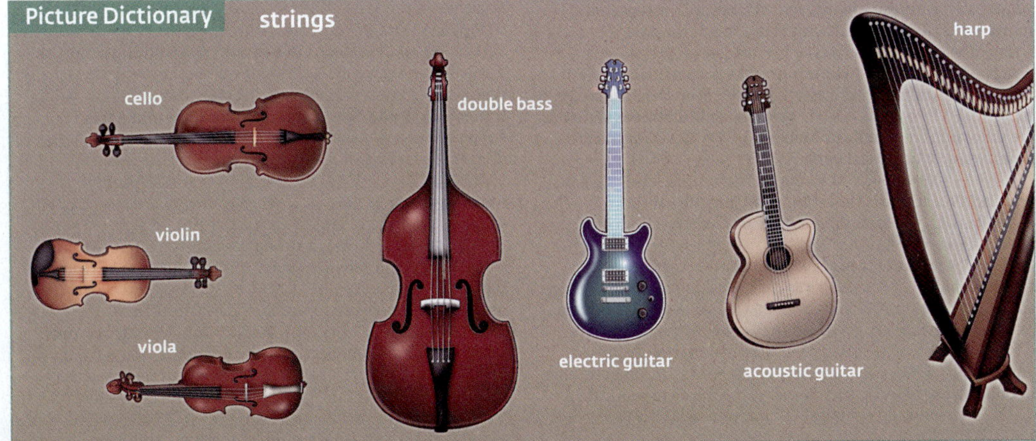

9 N-COUNT In a newspaper or magazine, a **strip** is a series of drawings which tell a story. The words spoken by the characters are often written on the drawings. 连环画 ❑ *...the Doonesbury strip.* …杜恩斯伯利的连环画。

▸ **strip away** PHRASAL VERB To **strip away** something, especially something that hides the true nature of a thing, means to remove it completely. 揭穿 ❑ *Altman strips away the pretense and mythology to expose the film industry as a business like any other.* 奥尔特曼揭穿伪装和神话，把电影业暴露成像其他任何行业一样。

▸ **strip off** **1** PHRASAL VERB If you **strip off** your clothes, you take them off. 脱掉（衣服）❑ *He stripped off his wet clothes and stepped into the shower.* 他脱掉他的湿衣服走进了淋浴间。 **2** → see also **strip 4**

Word Partnership *strip* 的常用搭配：

ADJ. **long** strip, **narrow** strip **1 2**
commercial strip **3**
strip *(someone)* **naked** **4 5**

stripe /straɪp/ (**stripes**) N-COUNT A **stripe** is a long line which is a different color from the areas next to it. 条纹 ❑ *She wore a bright green jogging suit with a white stripe down the sides.* 她穿了一套侧边有一条白色条纹的艳绿色慢跑服。

striped /straɪpt/ ADJ Something that is **striped** has stripes on it. 有条纹的 ❑ *...a bottle green and maroon striped tie.* …一条有深绿色和绛紫色条纹的领带。

strip mall (**strip malls**) N-COUNT A **strip mall** is a shopping area consisting of one or more long buildings. 购物区 [AM] ❑ *...a parking lot outside a strip mall.* …一个购物区外的停车场。

strip·per /strɪpər/ (**strippers**) N-COUNT A **stripper** is a person who earns money by stripping their clothes off. 脱衣舞演员 ❑ *She worked as a stripper and did some acting.* 她当过脱衣舞演员，做过一些表演。

★ **strive** /straɪv/ (**strives, striving**)

The past tense is either **strove** or **strived**, and the past participle is either **striven** or **strived**.

V-T/V-I If you **strive to** do something or **strive for** something, you make a great effort to do it or get it. 努力 ❑ *He strives hard to keep himself very fit.* 他努力使自己保持非常的健康。

strode /stroʊd/ **Strode** is the past tense and past participle of **stride**. **stride**的过去式和过去分词

stroke ♦◇◇ /stroʊk/ (**strokes, stroking, stroked**) **1** V-T If you **stroke** someone or something, you move your hand slowly and gently over them. 轻抚 ❑ *Carla, curled up on the sofa, was smoking a cigarette and stroking her cat.* 卡拉蜷曲在沙发上，抽着一支烟，轻抚着她的猫。 **2** N-COUNT If someone has a **stroke**, a blood vessel in their brain bursts or becomes blocked, which may kill them or make them unable to move one side of their body. 中风 ❑ *He had a minor stroke in 1987, which left him partly paralyzed.* 他在1987年患了轻度中风，这使他半身不遂了。 **3** N-COUNT The **strokes** of a pen or brush are the movements or marks that you make with it when you are writing or painting. 笔画 ❑ *Fill in gaps by using short, upward strokes of the pencil.* 用铅笔画出短的、向上的笔画来填空。 **4** N-COUNT When you are swimming or rowing, your **strokes** are the repeated movements that you make with your arms or the oars. 划水；划桨 ❑ *I turned and swam a few strokes further out to sea.* 我转过身又向海里游了几下。 **5** N-COUNT A swimming **stroke** is a particular style or method of swimming. 游泳姿势 ❑ *She spent hours practicing the breast stroke.* 她花了几个小时练习蛙泳。 **6** N-COUNT The **strokes** of a clock are the sounds that indicate each hour. 钟声 ❑ *On the stroke of 12, fireworks suddenly exploded into the night.* 12点的钟声敲响时，焰火突然冲破了夜空。 **7** N-COUNT In sports such as tennis, baseball, golf, and cricket, a **stroke** is the action of hitting the ball. 击球 ❑ *Compton was sending the ball here, there, and everywhere with each stroke.* 康普顿把球发到这儿，发到那儿，每一次击球都打到不同地方。 **8** N-SING **A stroke of** luck or good fortune is something lucky that happens. 一次（好运）❑ *It didn't rain, which turned out to be a stroke of luck.* 天没下雨，结果成为一次好运。 **9** N-SING **A stroke of** genius or inspiration is a very good idea that someone suddenly has. （天才或灵感的）一举 ❑ *At the time, his appointment seemed a stroke of genius.* 当时，他的任命似乎是天才之举。 **10** PHRASE If someone does not **do a stroke of** work, they are very lazy and do no work at all. 干一点儿 [INFORMAL, EMPHASIS] ❑ *I never did a stroke of work in college.* 我在大学里从来不干一点儿活。

S

Word Partnership *stroke* 的常用搭配：

V. **die from a** stroke, **have a** stroke, **suffer a** stroke **2**
N. **risk of a** stroke **2**
stroke **of a pen** **3**

★ **stroll** /stroʊl/ (**strolls, strolling, strolled**) V-I If you **stroll** somewhere, you walk there in a slow, relaxed way. 溜达 ❑ *He collected some orange juice from the refrigerator and, glass in hand, strolled to the kitchen window.* 他从冰箱里取了些橙汁，然后手拿玻璃杯，溜达到厨房的窗边。 ● N-COUNT **Stroll** is also a noun. 溜达 ❑ *After dinner, I took a stroll round the city.* 晚饭后，我绕着城溜达了一圈。
→ see **park**

stroll·er /stroʊlər/ (**strollers**) N-COUNT A **stroller** is a small chair on wheels, in which a baby or small child can sit and be wheeled around. 婴儿手推车 [AM]

in BRIT, use **pushchair**

strong ♦♦♦ /strɔŋ/ (**stronger** /strɔŋgər/, **strongest** /strɔŋgɪst/) **1** ADJ Someone who is **strong** is healthy with good muscles and can move or carry heavy things, or do hard physical work. 强壮的 ❑ *I'm not strong enough to carry him.* 我不够强壮，抱不动他。 **2** ADJ Someone who is **strong** is confident and determined, and is not easily influenced or worried by other people. 坚定的 ❑ *He is sharp and manipulative with a strong personality.* 他机灵且善于摆布别人，有着很强的个性。 ❑ *It's up to managers to be strong and do what they believe is right.* 立场坚定并做他们认为正确的事情是经理们的责任。 **3** ADJ **Strong** objects or materials are not easily broken and can support a lot of weight or resist a lot of strain. 坚固的 ❑ *The vacuum flask has a strong casing, which won't crack or chip.* 这个真空瓶有一个坚固的外壳，不会破裂。 ❑ *Glue the mirror in with a strong adhesive.* 用牢固的粘合剂把这面镜子粘上。 ● **strong·ly** ADV 坚固地 [ADV -ed] ❑ *The fence was very strongly built, with very large posts.* 这个栅栏用粗大的木桩建得非常坚固。 **4** ADJ A **strong** wind, current, or other force has a lot of power or speed, and can cause heavy things to move. （风、水流等）强劲的 ❑ *Strong winds and torrential rain combined to make conditions terrible for golfers in the Scottish Open.* 强风和暴雨交加使得苏格兰公开赛的环境对高尔夫球员很糟糕。 ❑ *A fairly strong current seemed to be moving the whole boat.* 一股非常强劲的水流似乎要把整只小船冲走。 ● **strong·ly** ADV 强劲地 [ADV with v] ❑ *The metal is strongly attracted to the surface.* 这块金属牢牢地附在表面上。 **5** ADJ A **strong** impression or influence has a great effect on someone. （印象或影响）深刻的；强烈的 ❑ *We're glad if our music makes a strong impression, even if it's a negative one.* 如果我们的音乐能产生一个深刻的印象，即使它是负面的，我们也很高兴。 ❑ *There will be a strong incentive to enter into a process of negotiation.* 将会有一个强烈的刺激来进入谈判的过程。 ● **strong·ly** ADV 深刻地；强烈地 [ADV with v] ❑ *He is strongly influenced by Spanish painters such as Goya and El Greco.* 他被戈雅、艾尔·格列柯等西班牙画家们强烈地影响了。 **6** ADJ If you have **strong** opinions on something or express them using **strong** words, you have extreme or very definite opinions which you are willing to express or defend. （观点、言辞）坚定的 ❑ *She is known to hold strong views on Cuba.* 她因对古巴持有坚定的观点而闻名。 ❑ *I am a strong supporter of the president.* 我是总统的一位坚定的支持者。 ● **strong·ly** ADV 坚定地 ❑ *Obviously you feel very strongly about this.* 显然你对此感觉很坚定。 ❑ *Republicans in the House were strongly opposed to lifting the ban.* 众议院的共和党人们曾坚定地反对解除该禁令。 **7** ADJ If someone in authority takes **strong** action, they act firmly and severely. 坚决的 ❑ *The American public deserves strong action from Congress.* 美国公众应受到来自国会的坚决的行动。 **8** ADJ If there is a **strong** case or argument for something, it is supported by a lot of evidence. 有说服力的 ❑ *The testimony presented offered a strong case for acquitting her on grounds of self-defense.* 所出示的证据为以正当防卫之由宣判她无罪提供了一个有说服力的理由。 ● **strong·ly** ADV 有说服力地 ❑ *He argues strongly for retention of NATO as a guarantee of peace.* 他据理力争北大西洋公约组织作为一个和平保障的保留。 **9** ADJ If there is a **strong** possibility or chance that something is true or will happen, it is very likely to be true or to happen. （可能性、机率）极大的 ❑ *There is a strong possibility that the cat contracted the condition by eating contaminated pet food.* 有一种极大的可能性就是那只猫吃了受污染的宠物食品而染上了病。 **10** ADJ Your **strong** points are your best qualities or talents, or the things you are good at. 优秀的；擅长的 [ADJ n] ❑ *Discretion is not Jeremy's strong point.* 谨慎不是杰里米的长处。 ❑ *Exports may be the only strong point in the economy over the next six to 12 months.* 出口也许是随后的6至12个月经济中的惟一强项。 **11** ADJ A **strong** competitor, candidate, or team is good or likely to succeed. (竞争对手等) 强大的 ❑ *She was a strong contender for the Olympic team.* 她曾是奥林匹克队的一个强大的竞争者。 **12** ADJ If a relationship or link is **strong**, it is close and likely to last for a long time. (关系) 牢固的 ❑ *He felt he had a relationship strong enough to talk frankly to Sarah.* 他觉得他有着一种足够牢固的关系以使他与莎拉坦诚地交谈。 ❑ *This has tested our marriage, and we have come through it stronger than ever.* 这已经考验了我们的婚姻，我们经历它之后比以往更加牢固。 **13** ADJ A **strong** currency, economy, or industry has a high value or is very successful. (货币) 坚挺的; (经济、行业) 有实力的 ❑ *The U.S. dollar continued its strong performance in Tokyo today.* 美元今天在东京继续了其坚挺的表现。 **14** ADJ If something is a **strong** element or part of something else, it is an important or large part of it. (成分) 重要的; 强大的 ❑ *We are especially encouraged by the strong representation, this year, of women in information technology disciplines.* 我们尤其被今年女性在信息技术学科中的重要表现所鼓舞。 **15** ADJ You can use **strong** when you are saying how many people there are in a group. For example, if a group is twenty strong, there are twenty people in it. 多达…的 [num ADJ] ❑ *Ukraine indicated that it would establish its own army, 400,000 strong.* 乌克兰表示它将建立自己的军队，多达40万人。 **16** ADJ A **strong** drink, chemical, or drug contains a lot of the particular substance which makes it effective. (饮品) 浓的; (化学品、药物) 含量高的 ❑ *Strong coffee or tea late at night may cause sleeplessness.* 晚上喝浓咖啡或浓茶可能引起失眠。 **17** ADJ A **strong** color, flavor, smell, sound, or light is intense and easily noticed. (颜色、味道) 浓烈的; 响亮的; (光线) 强烈的 ❑ *As she went past there was a gust of strong perfume.* 当她经过时有一股浓烈的香水味。 ● **strong·ly** ADV 浓烈地; 响亮地; 强烈地 [ADV with v] ❑ *He leaned over her, smelling strongly of sweat.* 他朝她俯下身来，散发着浓烈的汗味。 **18** ADJ If someone has a **strong** accent, they speak in a distinctive way that shows very clearly what country or region they come from. (口音) 浓重的 ❑ *"Good, Mr. Ryle," he said in English with a strong French accent.* "好，赖尔先生，"他用带着浓重的法国口音的英语说道。 **19** PHRASE If someone or something is still **going strong**, they are still alive, in good condition, or popular after a long time. 状况良好; 兴盛不衰 [INFORMAL] ❑ *The old machinery was still going strong.* 这台旧机器依然状况良好。

Thesaurus *strong* 另参见:

ADJ. mighty, powerful, tough; (*ant.*) weak **1**
confident, determined; (*ant.*) cowardly **2**
solid, sturdy **3**

▲ **strong·hold** /strɔŋhoʊld/ (**strongholds**) N-COUNT If you say that a place or region is a **stronghold of** a particular attitude or belief, you mean that most people there share this attitude or belief. (大多数人有共同态度或信仰的) 大本营 ❑ *Florida is a stronghold for pro-choice activists.* 佛罗里达是一个主张堕胎合法的活跃分子们的大本营。

strove /stroʊv/ **Strove** is a past tense of **strive**. **strive**的一种过去式

struck /strʌk/ **Struck** is the past tense and past participle of **strike**. **strike**的过去式和过去分词

struc·tur·al /strʌktʃərəl/ ADJ **Structural** means relating to or affecting the structure of something. 结构上的 ❑ *The explosion caused little structural damage to the office towers themselves.* 这次爆炸对办公大楼本身几乎没有造成结构上的破坏。 ● **struc·tur·al·ly** ADV 在结构上 ❑ *When we bought the house, it was structurally sound, but I decided to redecorate throughout.* 我们买下这个房子时，它在结构上很完好，但我决定全部重新装修。

struc·tur·al en·gi·neer (**structural engineers**) N-COUNT A **structural engineer** is an engineer who works on large structures such as roads, bridges, and large buildings. 结构工程师

struc·ture ♦♦◊ /strʌktʃər/ (**structures, structuring, structured**) **1** N-VAR **The structure of** something is the way in which it is made, built, or organized. 结构 ❑ *The typical family structure of Freud's patients involved two parents and two children.* 弗洛伊德的病人们的典型家庭结构包括一对父母和两个孩子。 **2** N-COUNT A **structure** is something that consists of parts connected together in an ordered way. 结构体 ❑ *The feet are highly specialized structures made up of 26 small delicate bones.* 脚是非常特殊的、由26块细小骨头组成的结构体。 **3** N-COUNT A **structure** is something that has been built. 建筑物 ❑ *About half of those funds has gone to repair public roads, structures, and bridges.* 那些资金中大约一半用于维修公路、建筑物和桥梁。 **4** V-T If you **structure** something, you arrange it in a careful, organized pattern or system. 精心安排; 系统组织 ❑ *By structuring the course this way, we're forced to produce something the companies think is valuable.* 通过这样精心安排进程，我们不得不生产出公司认为有价值的东西。

strug·gle ♦♦◊ /strʌgᵊl/ (**struggles, struggling, struggled**) **1** V-T/V-I If you **struggle to** do something, you try hard to do it, even though other people or things may be making it difficult for you to succeed. 努力; 斗争 ❑ *They had to struggle against all kinds of adversity.* 他们不得不同各种困境斗争。 **2** N-VAR A **struggle** is a long and difficult attempt to achieve something such as freedom or political rights. 努力; 斗争 ❑ *Life became a struggle for survival.* 生活变成了一场争取生存的斗争。 ❑ *...a young boy's struggle to support his poverty-stricken family.* …一个年轻男孩为支撑自己贫穷的家庭所做的努力。 **3** V-I If you **struggle** when you are being held, you twist, kick, and move violently in order to get free. 挣扎 ❑ *I struggled, but he was a tall man, well built.* 我挣扎了，但他是一个高个子男人，很强壮。 **4** V-RECIP If two people **struggle with** each other, they fight. 扭打 ❑ *She screamed at him to "stop it" as they struggled on the ground.* 他们在地上扭打时，她冲他尖叫着"住手"。 ● N-COUNT **Struggle** is also a noun. 扭打 ❑ *He died in a struggle with prison officers less than two months after coming to Britain.* 他来英国不到两个月就死于一次与狱警们的扭打。 **5** V-T/V-I If you **struggle to** move yourself or **to** move a heavy object, you try to do it, but it is difficult. 艰难地移动 ❑ *I could see the young boy struggling to free himself.* 我能看见这个小男孩正使劲挣脱他自己。 **6** V-T/V-I If a person or organization is **struggling**, they are likely to fail in what they are doing, even though they might be trying very hard. 在困境中挣扎; 竭力维持 [only cont] ❑ *The company is struggling to find buyers for its new product.* 这个公司正竭力为它的新产品寻找买主。 ❑ *One in five young adults was struggling with everyday mathematics.* 每5个年轻人中就有1个做日常的数学计算很费劲。 **7** N-SING An action or activity that is **a struggle** is very difficult to do. 很费劲的事 ❑ *Losing weight was a terrible struggle.* 减肥是件很费劲的事。

Word Partnership *struggle* 的常用搭配:

ADJ. **bitter** struggle, **internal** struggle, **long** struggle, **ongoing** struggle, **uphill** struggle **1** **2**
locked in a struggle **1** **2** **4**
political struggle **2**

N. struggle **for democracy**, struggle **for equality**, struggle **for freedom/independence**, **power** struggle, struggle **for survival** **2**

strum /strʌm/ (**strums, strumming, strummed**) V-T If you **strum** a stringed instrument such as a guitar, you play it by moving your fingers backward and forward across the strings. 弹奏 (吉他等弦乐器) ❑ *In the corner, one youth sat alone, softly strumming a guitar.* 在角落里，一个年轻人独自坐着，轻轻地弹着一把吉他。 ❑ *Vaska strummed away on his guitar.* 瓦斯卡过去常常胡乱拨弄他的吉他。

strung /strʌŋ/ **Strung** is the past tense and past participle of **string**. **string**的过去式和过去分词

strut /strʌt/ (**struts, strutting, strutted**) **1** V-I Someone who **struts** walks in a proud way, with their head held high and their chest out, as if they are very important. 趾高气扬地走 [DISAPPROVAL] ❑ *He struts around town like he owns the place.* 他在城里趾高气扬地走着，好像他拥有着这地方似的。 **2** N-COUNT A **strut** is a piece of wood or metal which holds the weight of other pieces in a building or other structure. (建筑物的) 支柱 ❑ *...the struts of a suspension bridge.* …一座悬索桥的支柱。

stub /stʌb/ (**stubs, stubbing, stubbed**) **1** N-COUNT The **stub** of a cigarette or a pencil is the last short piece of it which remains when the rest has been used. (香烟或铅笔的) 残端 ❑ *He pulled the stub of a pencil from behind his ear.* 他从他的耳朵后面抽出了一个铅笔头。 **2** N-COUNT A ticket **stub** is the part that you keep when you go in to watch a performance. 票根 ❑ *Fans who still have their ticket stubs should contact the box office by July 3.* 仍保留着票根的歌迷们应在7月3号前联系售票处。 **3** N-COUNT A check **stub** is the small part that you keep as a record of what you have paid. (支票的) 存根 ❑ *I have every check stub we've written since 1959.* 我有自1959年以来我们填写过的每一张支票存根。 **4** V-T If you **stub** your **toe**, you hurt it by accidentally kicking something. 不小心踢到 ❑ *I stubbed my toes against a table leg.* 我不小心把我的脚趾踢到一条桌腿上。

▸ **stub out** PHRASAL VERB When someone **stubs out** a cigarette, they put it out by pressing it against something hard. 掐灭 (香烟) ❑ *Signs across the entrances warn all visitors to stub out their cigarettes.* 入口处的标牌告诫所有参观者要掐灭他们的香烟。

S

stub·ble /stʌbᵊl/ **1** N-UNCOUNT **Stubble** is the short stalks which are left standing in fields after corn or wheat has been cut. (玉米或小麦收割后的) 残株 ❑ *The stubble was burning in the fields.* 残株在田地里燃烧着。 **2** N-UNCOUNT The very short hairs on a man's face when he has not shaved recently are referred to as **stubble**. 胡子茬 ❑ *His face was covered with the stubble of several nights.* 他脸上布满了几夜的胡子茬。

★ **stub·born** /stʌbərn/ **1** ADJ Someone who is **stubborn** or who behaves in a **stubborn** way is determined to do what they want and is very unwilling to change their mind. 固执的 ❑ *He is a stubborn character used to getting his own way.* 他是一个固执的人，过去常常随心所欲。 ●**stub·born·ly** ADV 固执地 ❑ *He stubbornly refused to tell her how he had come to be in such a state.* 他固执地拒绝告诉她自己是如何落到这种地步的。 ●**stub·born·ness** N-UNCOUNT 固执 ❑ *I couldn't tell if his refusal to talk was simple stubbornness.* 我说不清他对谈话的拒绝是否只是固执。 **2** ADJ A **stubborn** stain or problem is difficult to remove or to deal with. 难去除的；难对付的 ❑ *This treatment removes the most stubborn stains.* 这种处理去掉了最难以去除的污渍。 ●**stub·born·ly** ADV 难去除地；难对付地 ❑ *Some interest rates have remained stubbornly high.* 一些利率仍然一直居高不下。

stuck /stʌk/ **1** **Stuck** is the past tense and past participle of **stick**. **stick**的过去式和过去分词 **2** ADJ If something is **stuck** in a particular position, it is fixed tightly in this position and is unable to move. 动不了的 [v-link ADJ] ❑ *He said his car had gotten stuck in the snow.* 他说他的车已经陷在雪里动不了了。 **3** ADJ If you are **stuck** in a place, you want to get away from it, but are unable to. 被困住的 [v-link ADJ prep/adv] ❑ *I was stuck at home with flu.* 我因流感被困在了家里。 **4** ADJ If you are **stuck** in a boring or unpleasant situation, you are unable to change it or get away from it. 陷入的 [v-link ADJ prep/adv] ❑ *I don't want to get stuck in another job like that.* 我不想陷入另一份那样的工作中。 **5** ADJ If something is **stuck** at a particular level or stage, it is not progressing or changing. 停滞不前的 [v-link ADJ prep/adv] ❑ *I think the economy is stuck on a plateau of slow growth.* 我认为经济在缓慢增长的水平上停滞不前。 ❑ *U.S. unemployment figures for March showed the jobless rate stuck at 7 percent.* 美国3月份的失业数字表明了失业率停滞在7%。 **6** ADJ If you are **stuck with** something that you do not want, you cannot get rid of it. 无法摆脱的 [v-link ADJ "with" n] ❑ *Many people are now stuck with expensive fixed-rate mortgages.* 许多人现在无法摆脱高额的定息按揭。 **7** ADJ If you get **stuck** when you are trying to do something, you are unable to continue doing it because it is too difficult. (因困难) 无法继续的 [v-link ADJ] ❑ *They will be there to help if you get stuck.* 如果你无法继续下去，他们会去帮忙。

stud /stʌd/ (**studs**) **1** N-COUNT **Studs** are small pieces of metal which are attached to a surface for decoration. 金属饰钉 ❑ *You see studs on lots of front doors.* 你能在许多前门上看到金属饰钉。 **2** N-COUNT **Studs** are small round objects attached to the bottom of boots, especially sports boots, so that the person wearing them does not slip. (鞋底的) 防滑钉 [BRIT]

in AM, use **cleats**

3 N-UNCOUNT Horses or other animals that are kept for **stud** are kept to be used for breeding. 种畜 ❑ *He was voted horse of the year and then was retired to stud.* 他被选为年度马，然后就退役作了种马。

S

stud·ded /stʌdɪd/ ADJ Something that is **studded** is decorated with studs or things that look like studs. 用饰钉的；像饰钉的 ❑ *...studded leather jackets.* …有饰钉的皮夹克。

stu·dent ♦♦♦ /studᵊnt/ (**students**) **1** N-COUNT A **student** is a person who is studying at an elementary school, secondary school, college, or university. 学生 ❑ *Warren's eldest son is an art student.* 沃伦的长子是一名学艺术的学生。 **2** → see also **graduate student** **3** N-COUNT Someone who is a **student of** a particular subject is interested in the subject and spends time learning about it. 学者 ❑ *...a passionate student of history and an expert on nineteenth century prime ministers.* …一位热衷历史的学者和一个研究19世纪首相们的专家。
→ see **graduation**

stu·dio ♦♦◇ /studioʊ/ (**studios**) **1** N-COUNT A **studio** is a room where a painter, photographer, or designer works. 工作室 ❑ *She was in her studio again, painting onto a large canvas.* 她又在她的工作室里了，在一块大帆布上画画。 **2** N-COUNT A **studio** is a room where radio or television programs are recorded, CDs are produced, or movies are made. 演播室；制作室 ❑ *She's much happier performing live than in a recording studio.* 她现场表演比在录音棚里更开心。 **3** N-COUNT You can also refer to film-making or recording companies as **studios**. 电影公司；录音公司 ❑ *She wrote to Paramount Studios and asked if they would audition her.* 她写了信给派拉蒙电影公司，问他们是否能让她试镜。 **4** N-COUNT A **studio** or a **studio** apartment is a small apartment with one room for living and sleeping in, a kitchen, and a bathroom. You can also talk about a **studio apartment**. 单间公寓 ❑ *Home for a couple of years was a studio apartment.* 几年来的家就是一个单间公寓。
→ see **art**

Word Partnership *studio* 的常用搭配：

N. studio **album**, studio **audience**, **music** studio, **recording** studio, **television/TV** studio **2**
studio **executives**, **film/movie** studio **3**

study ♦♦♦ /stʌdi/ (**studies, studying, studied**) **1** V-T/V-I If you **study**, you spend time learning about a particular subject or subjects. 学习 ❑ *...a relaxed and happy atmosphere that will allow you to study to your full potential.* …一个将使你学习到充分发挥潜能的轻松又愉快的氛围。 ❑ *He studied History and Economics.* 他学过历史和经济学。 **2** N-UNCOUNT **Study** is the activity of studying. 学习 [also N in pl] ❑ *...the use of maps and visual evidence in the study of local history.* …在当地历史的学习中地图和图像证据的使用。 **3** N-COUNT A **study** of a subject is a piece of research on it. 研究 ❑ *Recent studies suggest that as many as 5 in 1,000 new mothers are likely to have this problem.* 最近的研究表明，1000个新妈妈中有多达5个可能有这个问题。 **4** N-PLURAL You can refer to educational subjects or courses that contain several elements as **studies** of a particular kind. 学科 ❑ *...a center for Islamic studies.* …一个伊斯兰教学科中心。 **5** V-T If you **study** something, you look at it or watch it very carefully, in order to find something out. 端详 ❑ *Debbie studied her friend's face for a moment.* 黛比端详了一会儿她朋友的脸。 **6** V-T If you **study** something, you consider it or observe it carefully in order to be able to understand it fully. 研究；仔细观察 ❑ *I know that you've been studying chimpanzees for thirty years now.* 我知道你研究黑猩猩至今已有30年了。 **7** N-COUNT A **study** is a room in a house which is used for reading, writing, and studying. 书房 ❑ *That evening we sat together in his study.* 那天晚上我们一起坐在他的书房里。 **8** → see also **case study**
→ see **laboratory**

stuff ♦♦◇ /stʌf/ (**stuffs, stuffing, stuffed**) **1** N-UNCOUNT You can use **stuff** to refer to things such as a substance, a collection of things, events, or ideas, or the contents of something in a general way without mentioning the thing itself by name. 东西 [usu with supp] [INFORMAL] ❑ *I'd like some coffee, and I don't object to the powdered stuff if it's all you've got.* 我想要点咖啡，如果你们只有粉状的东西，我也不反对。 ❑ *He pointed to a duffle bag. "That's my stuff."* 他指着一个旅行袋。"那是我的东西。" **2** V-T If you **stuff** something somewhere, you push it there quickly and roughly. 把…塞进 ❑ *I stuffed my hands in my pockets.* 我把双手塞进了我的口袋里。 **3** V-T If you **stuff** a container or space **with** something, you fill it with something or with a quantity of things until it is full. 把…装满 ❑ *He grabbed my purse, opened it and stuffed it full, then gave it back to me.* 他抢走我的钱包，打开并把它装得满满的，然后还给了我。 **4** V-T If you **stuff yourself**, you eat a lot of food. 使吃饱 [INFORMAL] ❑ *I could stuff myself with ten chocolate bars and half an hour later eat a big meal.* 我可以给自己塞下10块巧克力，并在半小时后再大吃一顿。 **5** V-T If you **stuff** a bird such as a chicken or a vegetable such as a pepper, you put a mixture of food inside it before cooking it. 把填料塞入 (鸡或辣椒等) ❑ *Will you stuff the turkey and shove it in the oven for me?* 你能帮我把填料塞进火鸡里，然后把它放进烤箱吗？ **6** V-T If a dead animal **is stuffed**, it is filled with a substance so that it can be preserved and displayed. 把…制成标本 [usu passive] ❑ *...his collections of stamps and books and stuffed birds.* …他的邮票、书和标本鸟的收藏品。 **7** PHRASE If you say that someone **knows** their **stuff**, you mean that they are good at doing something because they know a lot about it. 懂行 [INFORMAL, APPROVAL] ❑ *These guys know their stuff after seven years of war.* 这些家伙在7年的战争之后便懂行了。

Thesaurus *stuff* 另参见：

N. belongings, goods, material, substance **1**
V. crowd, fill, jam, squeeze **2** **3**

stuff·ing /stʌfɪŋ/ (**stuffings**) **1** N-MASS **Stuffing** is a mixture of food that is put inside a bird such as a chicken, or a vegetable such as a pepper, before it is cooked. (放入鸡或辣椒等用于烹饪的) 填料 ❑ *Chestnuts can be used at Christmastime, as a stuffing for turkey, guinea fowl, or chicken.* 栗子可在圣诞节时用作火鸡、珍珠鸡或松鸡的填料。

2 N-UNCOUNT **Stuffing** is material that is used to fill things such as cushions or toys in order to make them firm or solid. 填充物 ❑ *...a rag doll with all the stuffing coming out.* …一个所有的填充物都露出来的破布娃娃。

stuffy /stʌfi/ (**stuffier, stuffiest**) ADJ If it is **stuffy** in a place, it is unpleasantly warm and there is not enough fresh air. 闷热的 ❑ *It was hot and stuffy in the classroom even though two of the windows at the back had been opened.* 尽管后面的两个窗户都已被打开，教室里还是很闷热。

★ **stum·ble** /stʌmbᵊl/ (**stumbles, stumbling, stumbled**) V-I If you **stumble**, you put your foot down awkwardly while you are walking or running and nearly fall over. 踉跄；绊脚 ❑ *He stumbled and almost fell.* 他绊了一下，差点儿摔倒。● N-COUNT **Stumble** is also a noun. 踉跄；绊脚 ❑ *I make it into the darkness with only one stumble.* 我只踉跄了一下就把它弄进了黑暗中。

▸ **stumble across** or **stumble on** PHRASAL VERB If you **stumble across** something or **stumble on** it, you find it or discover it unexpectedly. 意外发现 ❑ *I stumbled across an extremely simple but very exact method for understanding where my money went.* 我意外发现了一种极其简单但又非常准确地知道我的钱去向何处的方法。

stum·bling block (**stumbling blocks**) N-COUNT A **stumbling block** is a problem which stops you from achieving something. 绊脚石 ❑ *The major stumbling block in the talks has been money.* 谈判的主要绊脚石一直是钱。

★ **stump** /stʌmp/ (**stumps, stumping, stumped**) 1 N-COUNT A **stump** is a small part of something that remains when the rest of it has been removed or broken off. 残余部分 ❑ *If you have a tree stump, check it for fungus.* 如果你有一个树桩，就在上面找找菌类。 2 V-T If you **are stumped** by a question or problem, you cannot think of any solution or answer to it. 把…难住 ❑ *John Diamond is stumped by an unexpected question.* 约翰・戴蒙德被一个意想不到的问题难住了。 3 V-I If politicians **stump for** a candidate, they travel around making campaign speeches before an election. (选举前为候选人) 作巡回政治演说 [AM] ❑ *Since September, the president has stumped for Republicans in 23 states.* 自9月以来，这位总统已在23个州为共和党人作了巡回政治演说。

★ **stun** /stʌn/ (**stuns, stunning, stunned**) 1 V-T If you **are stunned** by something, you are extremely shocked or surprised by it and are therefore unable to speak or do anything. 使震惊 [usu passive] ❑ *He's stunned by today's resignation of his longtime ally.* 他被自己的长期助手今天的辞职所震惊。● **stunned** ADJ 惊呆的 ❑ *When they told me she was missing I was totally stunned.* 当他们告诉我她不见了时，我完全惊呆了。 2 V-T If something such as a blow on the head **stuns** you, it makes you unconscious or confused and unsteady. 把…打昏 ❑ *Sam stood his ground and got a blow that stunned him.* 萨姆不让步，遭到一击，把他打昏了。 3 → see also **stunning**

stung /stʌŋ/ **Stung** is the past tense and past participle of **sting**. **sting**的过去式和过去分词

stunk /stʌŋk/ **Stunk** is the past participle of **stink**. **stink**的过去分词

stun·ning /stʌnɪŋ/ 1 ADJ A **stunning** person or thing is extremely beautiful or impressive. 极美的 ❑ *She was 55 and still a stunning woman.* 她55岁，仍是个极美的女人。 2 ADJ A **stunning** event is extremely unusual or unexpected. 令人震惊的 ❑ *He resigned last night after a stunning defeat in Sunday's vote.* 在周日的选举惨败之后，他于昨晚辞职了。

> **Word Partnership** *stunning* 的常用搭配:
> N. stunning **images**, stunning **views** 1
> stunning **blow**, stunning **defeat/loss**, stunning **success**, stunning **upset**, stunning **victory** 2

▲ **stunt** /stʌnt/ (**stunts, stunting, stunted**) 1 N-COUNT A **stunt** is something interesting that is done in order to attract attention and get publicity for the person or company responsible for it. 引人注目的噱头 ❑ *In a bold promotional stunt for the movie, he smashed his car into a passing truck.* 在那部影片大胆的宣传噱头中，他把自己的汽车撞向一辆过路的卡车。 2 N-COUNT A **stunt** is a dangerous and exciting piece of action in a movie. (电影中的) 特技动作 ❑ *Sean Connery insisted on living dangerously for his new film by performing his own stunts.* 肖恩・康纳利坚持通过为他的新影片表演他自己的特技动作而冒险。 3 V-T If something **stunts** the growth or development of a person or thing, it prevents it from growing or developing as much as it should. 阻碍 ❑ *The heart condition had stunted his growth a bit.* 心脏病已经有点儿阻碍他的发育。● **stunt·ed** ADJ 受阻碍的 ❑ *Damage may result in stunted growth and sometimes death of the plant.* 损害会导致植物生长受阻，有时还会导致死亡。

stu·pid ♦◇◇ /stupɪd/ (**stupider, stupidest**) 1 ADJ If you say that someone or something is **stupid**, you mean that they show a lack of good judgment or intelligence and they are not at all sensible. 愚蠢的 ❑ *I'll never do anything so stupid again.* 我再也不会做这么愚蠢的事了。 ❑ *I made a stupid mistake.* 我犯了个愚蠢的错误。● **stu·pid·ly** ADV 愚蠢地 ❑ *We had stupidly been looking at the wrong column of figures.* 我们愚蠢地一直在看那个错的数字栏。● **stu·pid·ity** /stupɪdɪti/ N-VAR (**stupidities**) 愚蠢 ❑ *I stared at him, astonished by his stupidity.* 我盯着他，对他的愚蠢很吃惊。 2 ADJ You say that something is **stupid** to indicate that you do not like it or that it annoys you. 讨厌的 [DISAPPROVAL] ❑ *I wouldn't call it art. It's just stupid and tasteless.* 我不会称它为艺术。它令人讨厌且毫无品味。

> **Word Partnership** *stupid* 的常用搭配:
> V. **(don't) do anything/something** stupid, **feel** stupid, **look** stupid 1
> **think *something* is** stupid 1 2
> N. stupid **idea**, stupid **man**, stupid **mistake**, stupid **people**, stupid **question** 1
> stupid **things** 1 2

★ **stur·dy** /stɜrdi/ (**sturdier, sturdiest**) ADJ Someone or something that is **sturdy** looks strong and is unlikely to be easily injured or damaged. 结实的；坚固的 ❑ *She was a short, sturdy woman in her early sixties.* 她是一位六十出头、矮小结实的女人。● **stur·di·ly** ADV 结实地；坚固地 ❑ *It was a good table too, sturdily constructed of elm.* 它也是一张很好的桌子，榆木做的，很结实。

stut·ter /stʌtər/ (**stutters, stuttering, stuttered**) 1 N-COUNT If someone has a **stutter**, they find it difficult to say the first sound of a word, and so they often hesitate or repeat it two or three times. 口吃 [usu sing] ❑ *He spoke with a pronounced stutter.* 他说话带有明显的口吃。 2 V-I If someone **stutters**, they have difficulty speaking because they find it hard to say the first sound of a word. 结结巴巴地说话 ❑ *I was trembling so hard, I thought I would stutter when I spoke.* 我那时抖得很厉害，我觉得说话时都会结结巴巴。● **stut·ter·ing** N-UNCOUNT 口吃 ❑ *He had to stop talking because if he'd kept on, the stuttering would have started.* 他不得不停止讲话，因为如果他继续下去，口吃就会发作。

style ♦♦◇ /staɪl/ (**styles, styling, styled**) 1 N-COUNT The **style** of something is the general way in which it is done or presented, which often shows the attitudes of the people involved. 方式 ❑ *Our children's different needs and learning styles created many problems.* 我们孩子们不同的需要和学习方式引起了许多问题。 ❑ *Belmont Park is a broad sweeping track which will suit the European style of running.* 贝尔蒙特公园是一条宽阔的弧形跑道，它将会适合欧式的跑步。 2 N-UNCOUNT If people or places have **style**, they are fashionable and elegant. 风度；格调 ❑ *Boston, you have to admit, has style.* 你得承认波士顿很有格调。 ❑ *Both love doing things in style.* 两人都喜爱有风度地做事。 3 N-VAR The **style** of a product is its design. 款式 ❑ *His 50 years of experience have given him strong convictions about style.* 他50年的经验已使他对款式有着坚定的主张。 4 N-COUNT In the arts, a particular **style** is characteristic of a particular period or group of people. (某个时期或群体的艺术) 风格 ❑ *...six scenes in the style of a classical Greek tragedy.* …古典希腊悲剧风格的6个场景。 ❑ *...a mixture of musical styles.* …多种音乐风格的混合。 5 V-T If something such as a piece of clothing, a vehicle, or someone's hair **is styled** in a particular way, it is designed or shaped in that way. 设计式样 [usu passive] ❑ *His thick blond hair had just been styled before his trip.* 他浓密的金发在他旅行前刚被设计了式样。 6 → see also **self-styled**

> **Word Partnership** *style* 的常用搭配:
> N. **leadership** style, **learning** style, style **of life**, **management** style 1
> **differences in** style 1 – 4
> **music** style, **prose** style, **writing** style 4
> ADJ. **distinctive** style, **particular** style, **personal** style 1 – 4

styl·ised /staɪlaɪzd/ [BRIT] → see **stylized**

▲ **styl·ish** /staɪlɪʃ/ ADJ Someone or something that is **stylish** is elegant and fashionable. 有格调的；时髦的 ❑ *...a very attractive and very stylish woman of 27.* …一个非常迷人又非常时髦的27岁女子。

S

• **styl·ish·ly** ADV 有格调地；时髦地 ❑ *...stylishly dressed middle-aged women.* …衣着时髦的中年女人们。

sty·lis·tic /staɪlɪstɪk/ ADJ **Stylistic** describes things relating to the methods and techniques used in creating a piece of writing, music, or art. (文学、音乐或艺术作品) 风格上的 ❑ *There are some stylistic elements in the statue that just don't make sense.* 这座雕像中有一些风格上的成分毫无意义。

styl·ized /st<u>aɪ</u>laɪzd/

in BRIT, also use **stylised**

ADJ Something that is **stylized** is shown or done in a way that is not natural in order to create an artistic effect. 非写实的 ❑ *Some of it has to do with recent stage musicals, which have been very, very stylized.* 其中的一些与最近的舞台音乐剧有关，是极度非写实的。

suave /sw<u>ɑ</u>v/ (**suaver, suavest**) ADJ Someone who is **suave** is charming, polite, and elegant, but may be insincere. 圆滑的 ❑ *He is a suave, cool, and cultured man.* 他是一个圆滑、冷酷、有教养的人。

▲ **sub** /sʌb/ (**subs**) **1** N-COUNT A **sub** is the same as a **substitute teacher**. 代课教师 [AM] **2** N-COUNT In team games such as football, a **sub** is a player who is brought into a game to replace another player. 替补队员 [INFORMAL] ❑ *We had a few injuries and had to use youth team kids as subs.* 我们有几个受伤队员，不得不用青年队的孩子们作替补。 **3** N-COUNT A **sub** is the same as a **submarine**. 潜艇 [INFORMAL]

sub·com·mit·tee /sʌbkəmɪti/ (**subcommittees**) also **sub-committee** N-COUNT-COLL A **subcommittee** is a small committee made up of members of a larger committee. (大委员会内的) 小组委员会

sub·con·scious /sʌbk<u>ɒ</u>nʃəs/ **1** N-SING Your **subconscious** is the part of your mind that can influence you or affect your behavior even though you are not aware of it. 潜意识 ❑ *...the hidden power of the subconscious.* …潜意识的隐藏能量。 **2** ADJ A **subconscious** feeling or action exists in or is influenced by your subconscious. 下意识的 ❑ *He caught her arm in a subconscious attempt to detain her.* 他下意识地抓住了她的胳膊，试图留住她。

• **sub·con·scious·ly** ADV 下意识地 ❑ *Subconsciously I had known that I would not be in personal danger.* 下意识地，我已经知道了我将不会有人身危险。

→ see **hypnosis**

sub·con·tract /sʌbkəntrækt/ (**subcontracts, subcontracting, subcontracted**) V-T If one company **subcontracts** part of its work **to** another company, it pays the other company to do part of the work that it has been employed to do. 把…外包 [BUSINESS] ❑ *The company is subcontracting production of most of the parts.* 这家公司正把大部分零部件的生产外包出去。

sub·con·trac·tor /sʌbk<u>ɑ</u>ntræktər/ (**subcontractors**) N-COUNT A **subcontractor** is a person or company that has a contract to do part of a job which another company is responsible for. 分包人；分包公司 [BUSINESS] ❑ *The company was considered as a possible subcontractor to build the airplane.* 这家公司被认为是可能制造这架飞机的分包公司。

S

sub·cul·ture /sʌbkʌltʃər/ (**subcultures**) N-COUNT A **subculture** is the ideas, art, and way of life of a group of people within a society, which are different from the ideas, art, and way of life of the rest of the society. 亚文化 ❑ *...the latest American subculture.* …最近的美国亚文化。

→ see **culture**

sub·di·vide /sʌbdɪvaɪd/ (**subdivides, subdividing, subdivided**) V-T If something **is subdivided**, it is divided into several smaller areas, parts, or groups. 使细分 [usu passive] ❑ *The verbs were subdivided into transitive and intransitive categories.* 动词被细分为及物和不及物两类。

Word Link	*sub* ≈ *below* : *subdivision*, *submarine*, *subtitle*

sub·di·vi·sion /sʌbdɪvɪʒᵊn/ (**subdivisions**) **1** N-COUNT A **subdivision** is an area, part, or section of something which is itself a part of something larger. 分支；分部 ❑ *Months are a conventional subdivision of the year.* 月份是年的常规分支。 **2** N-COUNT A **subdivision** is an area of land for building houses on. (为建房而划分的) 区域 [AM] ❑ *Rammick lives high on a ridge in a 400-home subdivision.* 拉米克住在高高的山脊上一块有400户的住宅区。

▲ **sub·due** /səbd<u>u</u>/ (**subdues, subduing, subdued**) **1** V-T If soldiers or the police **subdue** a group of people, they defeat them or bring them under control by using force. 制服 ❑ *Senior government officials admit they have not been able to subdue the rebels.* 高级政府官员们承认他们还没能制服反叛者们。 **2** V-T To **subdue** feelings means to make them less strong. 克制 (感情) ❑ *He forced himself to subdue and overcome his fears.* 他强迫自己克制并战胜他的恐惧。

sub·dued /səbd<u>u</u>d/ **1** ADJ Someone who is **subdued** is very quiet, often because they are sad or worried about something. (因难过、担心而) 沉默寡言的 ❑ *He faced the press, initially, in a somewhat subdued mood.* 他起初以一种有点沉默寡言的情绪面对新闻界。 **2** ADJ **Subdued** lights or colors are not very bright. (灯光或颜色) 柔和的 ❑ *The lighting was subdued.* 这灯光很柔和。

sub·group /sʌbgrup/ (**subgroups**) N-COUNT A **subgroup** is a group that is part of a larger group. 子群 ❑ *The Action Group worked by dividing its tasks among a large number of subgroups.* 该行动小组通过把工作分给很多下属组来运作。

sub·hu·man /sʌbhyumən/ ADJ If you describe someone or their situation as **subhuman**, you mean that they behave or live in a much worse way than human beings normally do. 次于人类的 ❑ *The Greeks treated women as subhuman.* 希腊人过去视女人为低等的人类。

sub·ject ♦♦◊ (**subjects, subjecting, subjected**)

The noun and adjective are pronounced /sʌbdʒɪkt/. The verb is pronounced /səbdʒ<u>ɛ</u>kt/.

名词和形容词读作 /sʌbdʒɪkt/。动词读作 /səbdʒ<u>ɛ</u>kt/。

1 N-COUNT The **subject** of something such as a conversation, letter, or book is the thing that is being discussed or written about. 话题；主题 ❑ *It was I who first raised the subject of plastic surgery.* 是我首先提起了整形手术这个话题。 ❑ *...the president's own views on the subject.* …该总统对此问题的个人观点。 **2** N-COUNT Someone or something that is the **subject of** criticism, study, or an investigation is being criticized, studied, or investigated. (批评、研究或调查的) 对象 ❑ *Over the past few years, some of the positions Mr. Meredith has adopted have made him the subject of criticism.* 在过去的几年里，梅雷迪思先生所采取的一些立场已使他成为了被批评的对象。 **3** N-COUNT A **subject** is an area of knowledge or study, especially one that you study in school, or college. (尤指在学校学习的) 科目 ❑ *Surprisingly, math was voted their favorite subject.* 令人吃惊的是，数学被评为他们喜爱的科目。 **4** N-COUNT In an experiment or piece of research, the **subject** is the person or animal that is being tested or studied. 实验对象；研究对象 [FORMAL] ❑ *"White noise" was played into the subject's ears through headphones.* "白色噪音"通过耳机被送进实验对象的耳朵里。 **5** N-COUNT An artist's **subjects** are the people, animals, or objects that he or she paints, models, or photographs. (绘画、摄影等的) 题材 ❑ *Sailboats and fish are popular subjects for local artists.* 帆船和鱼是当地艺术家们喜爱的题材。 **6** N-COUNT In grammar, the **subject** of a clause is the noun group that refers to the person or thing that is doing the action expressed by the verb. For example, in "My cat keeps catching birds," "my cat" is the subject. 主语 **7** ADJ To be **subject to** something means to be affected by it or to be likely to be affected by it. (可能) 受…影响的 [v-link ADJ "to" n] ❑ *Prices may be subject to alteration.* 价格可能会受变更影响。 **8** ADJ If someone is **subject to** a particular set of rules or laws, they have to obey those rules or laws. 受…支配的 [v-link ADJ "to" n] ❑ *The tribunal is unique because Mr. Jones is not subject to the normal police discipline code.* 这个审判很特别，因为琼斯先生不受一般的警务纪律约束。 **9** V-T If you **subject** someone **to** something unpleasant, you make them experience it. 使遭受 ❑ *...the man who had subjected her to four years of beatings and abuse.* …那个使她遭受了4年殴打和辱骂的男人。 **10** N-COUNT The people who live in or belong to a particular country, usually one ruled by a monarch, are the **subjects** of that monarch or country. (常指君主制国家的) 臣民 ❑ *...his subjects regarded him as a great and wise monarch.* …他的臣民把他看成了一位伟大而英明的君主。 **11** PHRASE When someone involved in a conversation **changes the subject**, they start talking about something else, often because the previous subject was embarrassing. 转变话题 ❑ *He tried to change the subject, but she wasn't to be put off.* 他试图转变话题，但她不愿被打断。 **12** PHRASE If an event will take place **subject to** a condition, it will take place only if that thing happens. 取决于 ❑ *They denied a report that Egypt had agreed to a summit, subject to certain conditions.* 他们否认了埃及已同意在特定条件下参加峰会的报道。

→ see **hypnosis**

Word Partnership subject 的常用搭配：

ADJ. **controversial** subject, **favorite** subject, **touchy** subject 1
N. **knowledge of a** subject 1 3
subject **of a debate**, subject **of an investigation** 2
research subject 4
subject **of a sentence**, subject **of a verb** 6
subject **to approval**, subject **to availability**, subject **to laws**, subject **to scrutiny**, subject **to a tax** 7
V. **broach a** subject, **study a** subject 1 3
change the subject 11

★ **sub·jec·tive** /səbdʒɛktɪv/ ADJ Something that is **subjective** is based on personal opinions and feelings rather than on facts. 主观的 ❑ *We know that taste in art is a subjective matter.* 我们知道艺术品味是个主观问题。 ● **sub·jec·tive·ly** ADV 主观地 ❑ *Our preliminary results suggest that people do subjectively find the speech clearer.* 我们的初步结果表明人们的确主观地觉得这个演讲更清楚。 ● **sub·jec·tiv·ity** /sʌbdʒəktɪvɪti/ N-UNCOUNT 主观 ❑ *They accused her of flippancy and subjectivity in her reporting of events in their country.* 他们指责了她在报道他们国家事件时的轻率和主观。

sub·ject mat·ter N-UNCOUNT The **subject matter** of something such as a book, lecture, movie, or painting is the thing that is being written about, discussed, or shown. (著作、讲话、电影或绘画的) 主题 ❑ *Then, attitudes changed and artists were given greater freedom in their choice of subject matter.* 然后，态度转变了，艺术家们在主题的选择上被给予了更大的自由。

▲ **sub·lime** /səblaɪm/ ADJ If you describe something as **sublime**, you mean that it has a wonderful quality that affects you deeply. 绝妙的；令人崇敬的 [LITERARY, APPROVAL] ❑ *Sublime music floats on a scented summer breeze to the spot where you lie.* 美妙的音乐随着夏日芳香的微风飘到你躺着的地方。 ● N-SING You can refer to sublime things as **the sublime**. 绝妙的东西；令人崇敬的事物 ❑ *She elevated every rare small success to the sublime.* 她把每一次少有的微小成功都提升成了非凡的成就。 ● PHRASE If you describe something as going **from the sublime to the ridiculous**, you mean that it involves a change from something very good or serious to something silly or unimportant. 从绝妙到低俗

sub·limi·nal /sʌblɪmɪnəl/ ADJ **Subliminal** influences or messages affect your mind without you being aware of it. 潜意识的 ❑ *Color has a profound, though often subliminal, influence on our senses and moods.* 颜色对我们的感觉和情绪有一种很深远的影响，尽管常常是潜意识的。

→ see **advertising**

Word Link *mar ≈ sea : marine, maritime, submarine*

★ **sub·ma·rine** /sʌbmərin/ (**submarines**) N-COUNT A **submarine** is a type of ship that can travel both above and below the surface of the sea. The abbreviation **sub** is also used. 潜水艇 ❑ *...a nuclear submarine.* …一艘核潜艇。

Word Link *merg ≈ sinking : emerge, merge, submerge*

sub·merge /səbmɜrdʒ/ (**submerges, submerging, submerged**) V-T/V-I If something **submerges** or if you **submerge** it, it goes below the surface of some water or another liquid. 使浸没；淹没 ❑ *Hippos are unable to submerge in the few remaining water holes.* 河马无法淹没在仅存的几个水坑里。

★ **sub·mis·sion** /səbmɪʃən/ (**submissions**) N-UNCOUNT **Submission** is a state in which people can no longer do what they want to do because they have been brought under the control of someone else. 屈服 ❑ *The army intends to take the city or simply starve it into submission.* 这个军队打算占领这座城市或干脆使其挨饿到投降。

sub·mis·sive /səbmɪsɪv/ ADJ If you are **submissive**, you obey someone without arguing. 顺从的 ❑ *Most doctors want their patients to be submissive.* 大多数医生都想让自己的病人们听话。 ● **sub·mis·sive·ly** ADV 顺从地 ❑ *The troops submissively laid down their weapons.* 士兵们顺从地放下了他们的武器。

sub·mit /səbmɪt/ (**submits, submitting, submitted**) 1 V-I If you **submit to** something, you unwillingly allow something to be done to you, or you do what someone wants, for example because you are not powerful enough to resist. 屈从 ❑ *In desperation, Mrs. Jones submitted to an operation on her right knee to relieve the pain.* 绝望中，琼斯夫人不得已接受了一次她右膝的手术以减轻疼痛。 2 V-T If you **submit** a proposal, report, or request **to** someone, you formally send it to them so that they can consider it or decide about it. 提交 (建议、报告或请求) ❑ *They submitted their reports to the chancellor yesterday.* 他们昨天向财政大臣提交了他们的报告。

★ **sub·or·di·nate** (**subordinates, subordinating, subordinated**)

The noun and adjective are pronounced /səbɔrdənɪt/. The verb is pronounced /səbɔrdəneɪt/.

名词和形容词读作 /səbɔrdənɪt/。动词读作 /səbɔrdəneɪt/。

1 N-COUNT If someone is your **subordinate**, they have a less important position than you in the organization that you both work for. 下级 ❑ *Haig tended not to seek guidance from subordinates.* 黑格不想向下属们寻求指导。 2 ADJ Someone who is **subordinate to** you has a less important position than you and has to obey you. 下级的 ❑ *Sixty of his subordinate officers followed his example.* 他的60个下级官员都以他为榜样。 3 ADJ Something that is **subordinate to** something else is less important than the other thing. 次要的；从属的 ❑ *It was an art in which words were subordinate to images.* 它是一种语言比图像次要的艺术。 4 V-T If you **subordinate** something **to** another thing, you regard it or treat it as less important than the other thing. 使从属于；把…列于次要地位 ❑ *He was both willing and able to subordinate all else to this aim.* 他既愿意也能够让别的一切从属于这个目标。 ● **sub·or·di·na·tion** /səbɔrdəneɪʃən/ N-UNCOUNT 从属；次要 ❑ *...the social subordination of women.* …妇女们的社会从属地位。

sub·poe·na /səpinə/ (**subpoenas, subpoenaing, subpoenaed**) 1 N-COUNT A **subpoena** is a legal document telling someone that they must attend a court of law and give evidence as a witness. (传唤出庭作证的) 传票 ❑ *He has been served with a subpoena to answer the charges in court.* 他被送达了一张出庭应诉的传票。 2 V-T If someone **subpoenas** a person, they give them a legal document telling them to attend a court of law and give evidence. If someone **subpoenas** a piece of evidence, the evidence must be produced in a court of law. 传唤 (证人) 出庭；要求 (证据) 到庭 ❑ *Select committees have the power to subpoena witnesses.* 特别委员会有权传唤证人。

★ **sub·scribe** /səbskraɪb/ (**subscribes, subscribing, subscribed**) 1 V-I If you **subscribe to** an opinion or belief, you are one of a number of people who have this opinion or belief. 持有 (意见或信仰) ❑ *I've personally never subscribed to the view that either sex is superior to the other.* 我个人从未持有过一种性别比另一种性别优越的观点。 2 V-I If you **subscribe to** a magazine or a newspaper, you pay to receive copies of it regularly. 订阅 ❑ *My main reason for subscribing to New Scientist is to keep abreast of advances in science.* 我订阅《新科学家》的主要原因是要跟上科学的进步。 3 V-I If you **subscribe to** an online newsgroup or service, you send a message saying that you wish to receive it or belong to it. 申请加入 (在线新闻组)；申请 (在线服务) [COMPUTING] ❑ *Usenet is a collection of discussion groups, known as newsgroups, to which anybody can subscribe.* 新闻组网络是由称为新闻组的讨论组组成，任何人都能申请加入。 4 V-I If you **subscribe for** shares in a company, you apply to buy shares in that company. 申购 (股份) [BUSINESS] ❑ *Employees subscribed for far more shares than were available.* 雇员们申购了远比实际数额还多的股份。

★ **sub·scrib·er** /səbskraɪbər/ (**subscribers**) 1 N-COUNT A magazine's or a newspaper's **subscribers** are the people who pay to receive copies of it regularly. (杂志或报纸的) 订户 ❑ *I have been a subscriber to Newsweek for many years.* 我已是《新闻周刊》一名多年的订户。 2 N-COUNT **Subscribers to** a service are the people who pay to receive the service. 用户 ❑ *China has almost 15 million subscribers to satellite and cable television.* 中国有近一千五百万个卫星和有线电视用户。

★ **sub·scrip·tion** /səbskrɪpʃən/ (**subscriptions**) 1 N-COUNT A **subscription** is an amount of money that you pay regularly in order to belong to an organization, to help a charity or campaign, or to receive copies of a magazine or newspaper. 会员费；捐赠款；征订费 ❑ *You can become a member by paying the yearly subscription.* 你通过支付年度会员费可以成为一名会员。 2 ADJ **Subscription** television is television that you can watch only if you pay a subscription. A **subscription** channel is a channel that you can watch only if you pay a subscription. (电视或频道) 付费的 [ADJ n] ❑ *Premiere, a subscription channel which began in 1991, shows live football covering the top two divisions.* 始于1991年的一个付费频道**Premiere**实况转播两大顶级足球赛。

sub·se·quent ♦◇◇ /sʌbsɪkwənt/ ADJ You use **subsequent** to describe something that happened or existed after the time or event that has just been referred to. 随后的 [ADJ n] [FORMAL] ❑ *...the increase of population in subsequent years.* …随后几年中的人口增长。 ● **sub·se·quent·ly** ADV 后来 ❑ *He subsequently worked on Boeing's 747, 767 and 737 jetliner programs.* 他后来从事了波音747、767 和737喷气式飞机的项目。

sub·ser·vi·ent /səbsɜrviənt/ 1 ADJ If you are **subservient**, you do whatever someone wants you to do. 顺从的 ❑ *Her willingness to be subservient to her children isolated her.* 她对她的孩子们顺从的意愿使她陷于孤立。 ● **sub·ser·vi·ence** /səbsɜrviəns/ N-UNCOUNT 顺从 ❑ *...an austere regime stressing obedience and subservience to authority.* …一个强调对当局的服从和恭顺的严厉政权。 2 ADJ If you treat one thing as **subservient to** another, you treat it as less important than the other thing. 从属的; 次要的 [v-link ADJ "to" n] ❑ *The woman's needs are seen as subservient to the group interest.* 这名妇女的需要被视为从属于集体利益。

sub·set /sʌbsɛt/ (**subsets**) N-COUNT A **subset of** a group of things is a smaller number of things that belong together within that group. 子集 [oft N "of" n] ❑ *...subsets of the population such as men, women, ethnic groups, etc.* …人类的子集，例如男人、女人，种族等。

▲ **sub·side** /səbsaɪd/ (**subsides, subsiding, subsided**) 1 V-I If a feeling or noise **subsides**, it becomes less strong or loud. 减弱 ❑ *The pain had subsided during the night.* 那疼痛在晚间已减轻了。 2 V-I If fighting **subsides**, it becomes less intense or general. 平息 ❑ *Violence has subsided following two days of riots.* 暴力在两天的暴乱之后已经平息了。 3 V-I If the ground or a building **is subsiding**, it is very slowly sinking to a lower level. 下陷 ❑ *Does that mean the whole house is subsiding?* 那意味着整栋房子正在下陷吗？ 4 V-I If a level of water, especially flood water, **subsides**, it goes down. (尤指洪水的水位) 回落 ❑ *Local officials say the flood waters have subsided.* 当地官员们说洪水已经退了。

★ **sub·sidi·ary** /səbsɪdiɛri/ (**subsidiaries**) 1 N-COUNT A **subsidiary** or a **subsidiary** company is a company which is part of a larger and more important company. 子公司 [BUSINESS] ❑ *WM Financial Services is a subsidiary of Washington Mutual.* 华盛顿互惠银行金融服务公司是华盛顿互惠银行的子公司。 2 ADJ If something is **subsidiary**, it is less important than something else with which it is connected. 辅助的 ❑ *The marketing department has always played a subsidiary role to the sales department.* 营销部一直都扮演着销售部的辅助角色。

▲ **sub·si·dise** /sʌbsɪdaɪz/ [BRIT] → see **subsidize**

▲ **sub·si·dize** /sʌbsɪdaɪz/ (**subsidizes, subsidizing, subsidized**)
in BRIT, also use **subsidise**
V-T If a government or other authority **subsidizes** something, they pay part of the cost of it. 补贴 ❑ *Around the world, governments have subsidized the housing of middle- and upper-income groups.* 全世界各政府都补贴过中高收入人群的住房。 ● **sub·si·dized** ADJ 被补贴了的 ❑ *...heavily subsidized prices for housing, bread, and meat.* …受到高额补贴的住房、面包和肉类价格。

S

★ **sub·si·dy** ♦◇◇ /sʌbsɪdi/ (**subsidies**) N-COUNT A **subsidy** is money that is paid by a government or other authority in order to help an industry or business, or to pay for a public service. 补贴金 ❑ *European farmers are planning a massive demonstration against farm subsidy cuts.* 欧洲的农场主们正在策划一场反对削减农场补贴的大游行。

★ **sub·sist·ence** /səbsɪstəns/ 1 N-UNCOUNT **Subsistence** is the condition of just having enough food or money to stay alive. 生存 ❑ *...below the subsistence level.* …在生存线之下。 2 ADJ In **subsistence** farming or **subsistence** agriculture, farmers produce food to eat themselves rather than to sell. 自给自足的 [ADJ n] ❑ *Many Namibians are subsistence farmers who live in the arid borderlands.* 许多纳米比亚人都是自给自足的农民，居住在干旱的边境地区。

sub·stance ♦◇◇ /sʌbstəns/ (**substances**) 1 N-COUNT A **substance** is a solid, powder, liquid, or gas with particular properties. 物质 ❑ *There's absolutely no regulation of cigarettes to make sure that they don't include poisonous substances.* 绝对没有确保香烟不含有毒物质的规定。 2 N-UNCOUNT **Substance** is the quality of being important or significant. 实质 [FORMAL] ❑ *It's questionable whether anything of substance has been achieved.* 是否已取得任何实质性的进展值得质疑。 3 N-SING **The substance of** what someone says or writes is the main thing that they are trying to say. 要旨 ❑ *The substance of his discussions doesn't really matter.* 他讨论的要旨实际并不重要。 4 N-UNCOUNT If you say that something has no **substance**, you mean that it is not true. 正确性 [FORMAL] ❑ *There is no substance in any of these allegations.* 这些指控没有一个是正确的。

Word Partnership *substance* 的常用搭配:
ADJ. **banned** substance, **chemical** substance, **natural** substance 1
N. **lack of** substance 2

sub·stan·tial ♦◇◇ /səbstænʃᵊl/ ADJ **Substantial** means large in amount or degree. 大量的; 很大程度的 [FORMAL] ❑ *A substantial number of mothers with young children are deterred from undertaking paid work because they lack access to childcare.* 很多有小孩的母亲找不到人照顾小孩，从而无法从事有薪工作。

Word Partnership *substantial* 的常用搭配:
N. substantial **amount**, substantial **changes**, substantial **difference**, substantial **evidence**, substantial **improvement**, substantial **increase**, substantial **loss**, substantial **number**, substantial **part**, substantial **progress**, substantial **savings**, substantial **support**
ADV. **fairly** substantial, **very** substantial

sub·stan·tial·ly /səbstænʃəli/ ADV If something changes **substantially** or is **substantially** different, it changes a lot or is very different. 很大程度地 [FORMAL] ❑ *The percentage of girls in engineering has increased substantially.* 工科女生的比例已经大大增长了。

sub·stan·ti·ate /səbstænʃieɪt/ (**substantiates, substantiating, substantiated**) V-T To **substantiate** a statement or a story means to supply evidence which proves that it is true. 证实 [FORMAL] ❑ *There is little scientific evidence to substantiate the claims.* 几乎没有能证实这些断言的科学证据。

★ **sub·stan·tive** /sʌbstəntɪv/ ADJ **Substantive** negotiations or issues deal with the most important and central aspects of a subject. 实质性的 [FORMAL] ❑ *They plan to meet again in Rome very soon to begin substantive negotiations.* 他们计划很快在罗马再次会面以开始实质性的谈判。

sub·sti·tute ♦◇◇ /sʌbstɪtut/ (**substitutes, substituting, substituted**) 1 V-T/V-I If you **substitute** one thing **for** another, or if one thing **substitutes for** another, it takes the place or performs the function of the other thing. 以…代替; 代替 ❑ *They were substituting violence for dialogue.* 他们那时在以暴力代替对话。 ❑ *He was substituting for the injured William Wales.* 他那时在代替受伤的威廉·威尔士。 ● **sub·sti·tu·tion** /sʌbstɪtuʃᵊn/ N-VAR (**substitutions**) 代替 ❑ *In my experience a straight substitution of carob for chocolate doesn't work.* 以我的经验，角豆直接代替巧克力不会奏效。 2 N-COUNT A **substitute** is something that you have or use instead of something else. 替代者 ❑ *She is seeking a substitute for the very man whose departure made her cry.* 他在寻找一个男人的替代者，这个男人的离去曾使她伤心落泪。 3 N-COUNT If you say that one thing is no **substitute for** another, you mean that it does not have certain desirable features that the other thing has, and is therefore unsatisfactory. If you say that there is no **substitute for** something, you mean that it is the only thing which is really satisfactory. 可替代者 ❑ *The printed word is no substitute for personal discussion with a great thinker.* 印刷字无法替代与伟大思想家的当面交流。 4 N-COUNT In team games such as football, a **substitute** is a player who is brought into a game to replace another player. 替补队员 ❑ *Jefferson entered as a substitute in the 60th minute.* 杰斐逊在第60分钟时作为替补队员上了场。

Word Partnership *substitute* 的常用搭配:
ADJ. **good** substitute 2
temporary substitute 2 4
V. **use** *someone/something* **as a** substitute 2 4

sub·sti·tute teach·er (**substitute teachers**) N-COUNT A **substitute teacher** is a teacher whose job is to take the place of other teachers at different schools when they are unable to be there. 代课教师 [AM]
in BRIT, use **supply teacher**

Word Link *terr ≈ earth : subterranean, terrain, terrestrial*

sub·ter·ra·nean /sʌbtəreɪniən/ ADJ A **subterranean** river or tunnel is under the ground. 地下的 [FORMAL] ❑ *The city has 9 miles of such subterranean passages.* 这座城市有9英里这样的地下通道。

Word Link *sub ≈ below : subdivision, submarine, subtitle*

sub·ti·tle /sʌbtaɪtᵊl/ (**subtitles, subtitling, subtitled**) 1 N-COUNT The **subtitle** of a piece of writing is a second title which is often longer and explains more than the main title. 副标题 ❑ *"Kathleen" was, as its 1892 subtitle asserted, "An Irish Drama."* 如其1892年版的副标题所说的，《凯瑟琳》是"一部爱尔兰戏剧"。 2 N-PLURAL **Subtitles** are a printed translation of the words of a foreign film that are shown at the bottom of the picture. (电影的) 字幕 ❑ *The dialogue is in Spanish, with English subtitles.* 这段对话是西班牙语的，配有英语字幕。 3 V-T If you say how a book or play **is subtitled**, you say what its subtitle is. 给…加副标题 ❑ *"Lorna Doone" is subtitled "a Romance of Exmoor."* 《洛娜·杜恩》的副标题是《埃克斯穆尔的一个浪漫故事》。

sub·ti·tled /sʌbtaɪtᵊld/ ADJ If a foreign film is **subtitled**, a printed translation of the words is shown at the bottom of the picture. 配有字幕的 ❑ *Much of the film is subtitled.* 这部电影大部分是配有字幕的。

sub·tle /sʌtᵊl/ (**subtler, subtlest**) 1 ADJ Something that is **subtle** is not immediately obvious or noticeable. 不易察觉的 ❑ *...the slow and subtle changes that take place in all living things.* …所有生物中发生的缓慢而不易察觉的变化。 ● **sub·tly** ADV 不易察觉地 ❑ *The truth is subtly different.* 事实略有不同。 2 ADJ A **subtle** person cleverly uses indirect methods to achieve something. 不露声色的 ❑ *I even began to exploit him in subtle ways.* 我甚至开始不露声色地利用他。 ● **sub·tly** ADV 不露声色地 [ADV with v] ❑ *Nathan is subtly trying to turn her against Barry.* 内森在尽力不露声色地使她转而反对巴里。 3 ADJ **Subtle** smells, tastes, sounds, or colors are pleasantly complex and delicate. 淡的；精妙的 ❑ *...subtle shades of brown.* …各种淡棕色。 ● **sub·tly** ADV 淡地；精妙地 ❑ *...a white sofa teamed with subtly colored rugs.* …一张铺着色彩淡雅的小垫的白色沙发。

sub·tle·ty /sʌtᵊlti/ (**subtleties**) 1 N-COUNT **Subtleties** are very small details or differences which are not obvious. 精妙之处；微妙差异 ❑ *His fascination with the subtleties of human behavior makes him a good storyteller.* 他对人类行为微妙之处的极大兴趣使他成为一个好的作家。 2 N-UNCOUNT **Subtlety** is the quality of being not immediately obvious or noticeable, and therefore difficult to describe. 微妙性 ❑ *African dance is vigorous, but full of subtlety, requiring great strength and control.* 非洲舞蹈很有活力，但充满微妙性，需要很大的力量和很强的控制力。 3 N-UNCOUNT **Subtlety** is the ability to notice and recognize things which are not obvious, especially small differences between things. 敏锐 ❑ *She analyzes herself with great subtlety.* 她非常敏锐地分析了自己。 4 N-UNCOUNT **Subtlety** is the ability to use indirect methods to achieve something, rather than doing something that is obvious. 巧妙 ❑ *They had obviously been hoping to approach the topic with more subtlety.* 他们显然一直在希望更巧妙地切入这个话题。

sub·to·tal /sʌbtoʊtᵊl/ (**subtotals**) N-COUNT A **subtotal** is a figure that is the result of adding some numbers together but is not the final total. 小计 ❑ *...the subtotals for each category of investments.* …每类投资的小计。

Word Link *tract ≈ dragging, drawing : contract, subtract, tractor*

sub·tract /səbtrækt/ (**subtracts, subtracting, subtracted**) V-T If you **subtract** one number **from** another, you do a calculation in which you take it away from the other number. For example, if you subtract 3 from 5, you get 2. (从一数中) 减去 (另一数) ❑ *Mandy subtracted the date of birth from the date of death.* 曼迪从死亡的日期减去了出生的日期。 ● **sub·trac·tion** /səbtrækʃᵊn/ N-VAR (**subtractions**) 减法 ❑ *She's ready to learn simple addition and subtraction.* 她准备学习简单的加法和减法。
→ see **mathematics**

sub·urb /sʌbɜrb/ (**suburbs**) 1 N-COUNT A **suburb of** a city or large town is a smaller area which is part of the city or large town but is outside its center. 市郊 ❑ *Anna was born in 1923 in a suburb of Philadelphia.* 安娜1923年出生在费城市郊。 2 N-PLURAL If you live **in the suburbs**, you live in an area of houses outside the center of a city or large town. 郊区 ❑ *His family lived in the suburbs.* 他家住在郊区。
→ see **city, transportation**

sub·ur·ban /səbɜrbən/ ADJ **Suburban** means relating to a suburb. 郊区的 [ADJ n] ❑ *...a comfortable suburban home.* …一个舒适的位于郊区的家。

sub·ur·bia /səbɜrbiə/ N-UNCOUNT Journalists often use **suburbia** to refer to the suburbs of cities and large towns considered as a whole. 郊区 (总称) ❑ *...summer mornings in leafy suburbia.* …树木繁茂的郊区的夏日早晨。

Word Link *vers ≈ turning : subversion, versatile, version*

▲ **sub·ver·sion** /səbvɜrʒᵊn/ N-UNCOUNT **Subversion** is the attempt to weaken or destroy a political system or a government. 颠覆企图 ❑ *He was arrested on charges of subversion for organizing the demonstration.* 他因组织示威游行被指有颠覆企图而被捕了。

sub·ver·sive /səbvɜrsɪv/ (**subversives**) 1 ADJ Something that is **subversive** is intended to weaken or destroy a political system or government. 颠覆性的 ❑ *The play was promptly banned as subversive and possibly treasonous.* 该剧被认为是颠覆性的且可能是叛国性的而立即被禁演了。 2 N-COUNT **Subversives** are people who attempt to weaken or destroy a political system or government. 颠覆分子 ❑ *Agents regularly rounded up suspected subversives.* 特工们曾定期围捕颠覆嫌疑分子们。

Word Link *verg, vert ≈ turning : converge, diverge, subvert*

▲ **sub·vert** /səbvɜrt/ (**subverts, subverting, subverted**) V-T To **subvert** something means to destroy its power and influence. 颠覆 [FORMAL] ❑ *...an alleged plot to subvert the state.* …一个被指控颠覆国家的阴谋。

sub·way /sʌbweɪ/ (**subways**) 1 N-COUNT A **subway** is an underground railroad. 地铁 [oft N n, also "by" N] [mainly AM]
in BRIT, use **underground, tube**
❑ *I don't ride the subway late at night.* 我深夜不坐地铁。 2 N-COUNT A **subway** is the same as an **underpass**. 地下通道 [BRIT]
→ see **transportation**

suc·ceed ♦♦◊ /səksid/ (**succeeds, succeeding, succeeded**) 1 V-I If you **succeed in** doing something, you manage to do it. (某人在做某事上) 成功 ❑ *We have already succeeded in working out ground rules with the Department of Defense.* 我们已和国防部成功地制定出了基本原则。 2 V-I If something **succeeds**, it works in a satisfactory way or has the result that is intended. (某事物) 成功 ❑ *The talks can succeed if both sides are flexible and serious.* 如果双方都灵活并且认真，这些会谈就能成功。 3 V-I Someone who **succeeds** gains a high position in what they do, for example in business or politics. (某人在商业、政治等方面) 成功 ❑ *...the skills and qualities needed to succeed in small and medium-sized businesses.* …在中小企业中要成功所需的技术和素质。 4 V-T If you **succeed** another person, you are the next person to have their job or position. 接替 ❑ *David Rowland is almost certain to succeed him as chairman on January 1.* 戴维·罗兰几乎肯定会在1月1日接替他当主席。 5 V-T If one thing **is succeeded by** another thing, the other thing happens or comes after it. 继…之后 [usu passive] ❑ *The presentation was succeeded by a roundtable discussion.* 这个讲演之后是一次圆桌讨论。

Thesaurus *succeed* 另参见：
V. accomplish, conquer, master; *(ant.)* fail 1
displace, replace; *(ant.)* precede 4

suc·cess ♦♦◊ /səksɛs/ (**successes**) 1 N-UNCOUNT **Success** is the achievement of something that you have been trying to do. 成效 ❑ *It's important for the success of any diet that you vary your meals.* 膳食多样化对任何饮食的成效都是重要的。 2 N-UNCOUNT **Success** is the achievement of a high position in a particular field, for example in business or politics. (在商业、政治等领域的) 成功 ❑ *We all believed that work was the key to success.* 我们都曾经相信工作是成功的关键。 3 N-UNCOUNT The **success** of something is the fact that it works in a satisfactory way or has the result that is intended. (某事物的) 成功 ❑ *We were amazed by the play's success.* 我们惊叹该剧的成功。 4 N-COUNT Someone or something that is a **success** achieves a high position, makes a lot of money, or is admired a great deal. 成功的人；成功的事物 ❑ *We hope it will be a commercial success.* 我们希望它会是一次商业成功。

Word Partnership *success* 的常用搭配：
N. success **of a business** 1
key to success, success **or failure** 1 2
chance for/of success, **lack of** success, **measure of** success 1 – 4
V. **achieve** success, success **depends on** *something*, **enjoy** success 1 – 4
ADJ. **great** success, **huge** success, **recent** success, **tremendous** success 1 – 4
academic success, **commercial** success 4

S

suc·cess·ful ◆◆◇ /səksɛsfəl/ **1** ADJ Something that is **successful** achieves what it was intended to achieve. Someone who is **successful** achieves what they intended to achieve. 有成效的 ❑ *How successful will this new treatment be?* 这种新疗法将会有多大成效？ ❑ *I am looking forward to a long and successful partnership with him.* 我期待着与他的长期而有成效的合作关系。 ● **suc·cess·ful·ly** ADV 有成效地 [ADV with v] ❑ *The doctors have successfully concluded preliminary tests.* 医生们已成功完成了初步化验。 **2** ADJ Something that is **successful** is popular or makes a lot of money. (事物) 成功的 ❑ *...the hugely successful movie that brought Robert Redford an Oscar for his directing.* …这部使罗伯特·雷德福获得奥斯卡导演奖的极其成功的影片。 **3** ADJ Someone who is **successful** achieves a high position in what they do, for example in business or politics. (人在商业、政治等方面) 成功的 ❑ *Women do not necessarily have to imitate men to be successful in business.* 女人无须非得效仿男人才能在商界成功。

suc·ces·sion /səksɛʃən/ (**successions**) **1** N-SING **A succession of** things of the same kind is a number of them that exist or happen one after the other. 一连串 [oft N "of" n, also "in" N] ❑ *Adams took a succession of jobs which have stood him in good stead.* 亚当斯做了一连串对他很有利的工作。 **2** N-UNCOUNT **Succession** is the act or right of being the next person to have an important job or position. 继任；继任权 ❑ *She is now seventh in line of succession to the throne.* 她目前排在王位继任顺序的第7位。

suc·ces·sive /səksɛsɪv/ ADJ **Successive** means happening or existing one after another without a break. 连续的 ❑ *Jackson was the winner for a second successive year.* 杰克逊是连续第二年的获胜者。

★ **suc·ces·sor** /səksɛsər/ (**successors**) N-COUNT Someone's **successor** is the person who takes their job after they have left. 继任者 ❑ *He set out several principles that he hopes will guide his successors.* 他制定出了几条原则，希望能指导其继任者。

suc·cinct /səksɪŋkt/ ADJ Something that is **succinct** expresses facts or ideas clearly and in few words. 简明的 [APPROVAL] ❑ *The book gives an admirably succinct account of the technology and its history.* 这本书对该项技术及其历史作了极其简明的叙述。 ● **suc·cinct·ly** ADV 简明地 ❑ *He succinctly summed up his manifesto as "Work hard, train hard and play hard."* 他把自己的宣言简明地概括成了"努力工作，努力训练，努力玩耍。"

suc·cu·lent /sʌkyələnt/ ADJ **Succulent** food, especially meat or vegetables, is juicy and good to eat. 多汁味美的 [APPROVAL] ❑ *Cook pieces of succulent chicken with ample garlic and a little sherry.* 用大量的蒜和少量的雪利酒来烹饪多汁味美的鸡块。

▲ **suc·cumb** /səkʌm/ (**succumbs, succumbing, succumbed**) V-I If you **succumb to** temptation or pressure, you do something that you want to do, or that other people want you to do, although you feel it might be wrong. (向诱惑、压力) 屈服 [FORMAL] ❑ *Don't succumb to the temptation to have just one cigarette.* 不要屈服于只抽一支烟的诱惑。

such ◆◆◆ /sʌtʃ/

> When **such** is used as a predeterminer, it is followed by "a" and a count noun in the singular. When it is used as a determiner, it is followed by a count noun in the plural or by an uncountable noun.

S

1 DET You use **such** to refer back to the thing or person that you have just mentioned, or a thing or person like the one that you have just mentioned. You use **such as** and **such...as** to introduce a reference to the person or thing that has just been mentioned. 这样的；如此的 ❑ *There have been previous attempts at coups. We regard such methods as entirely unacceptable.* 先前有过政变企图。我们认为这样的方法完全不可接受。 ● PREDET **Such** is also a predeterminer. 这样的 (作前位限定词) [PREDET "a" n] ❑ *If your request is for information about a child, please contact the registrar to find out how to make such a request.* 如果你寻求的是有关孩子的信息，请与登记员联系以获知如何作这样的请求。 ❑ *She has told us that when she goes back to stay with her family, they make her pay rent. We could not believe such a thing.* 她告诉过我们，当她回去和家人一起住时，他们让她付租金。我们不能相信这样的事。 ● PRON **Such** is also a pronoun used before **be**. 这 (用于**be**前) ❑ *We are scared because we are being watched – such is the atmosphere in Pristina and other cities in Kosovo.* 我们因被监视而害怕——这就是普里什蒂纳和科索沃其他城市的气氛。 **2** DET You use **such...as** or **such as** to link something or someone with a clause in which you give a description of the kind of thing or person that you mean. (像…) 那样的 ❑ *...incentive payments for such activities as planting hardwood trees.* …给予像种植硬木树那样的活动的奖金。 ❑ *Children do not use inflections such as are used in mature adult speech.* 儿童不使用像成年人言语中使用的那些词形变化。 **3** DET You use **such...as** or **such as** to introduce one or more examples of the kind of thing or person that you have just mentioned. (诸如…) 之类的 ❑ *...such careers as teaching, nursing, hairdressing and catering.* …诸如教学、护理、美发和餐饮等事业。 ❑ *...serious offenses, such as assault on a police officer.* …诸如袭击警官等严重违法行为。 **4** DET You use **such** before noun groups to emphasize the extent of something or to emphasize that something is remarkable. 如此的 [EMPHASIS] ❑ *I think most of us don't want to read what's in the newspaper anyway in such detail.* 我想我们中的多数人无论如何都不愿如此详细地去读报纸上的东西。 ❑ *One will never be able to understand why these political issues can acquire such force.* 人们将永远不会明白为什么这些政治问题能获得如此的影响力。 ● PREDET **Such** is also a predeterminer. 如此的 (作前位限定词) [PREDET "a" n] ❑ *It was such a pleasant surprise.* 它是如此一个惊喜。 **5** PREDET You use **such...that** or **such that** in order to emphasize the degree of something by mentioning the result or consequence of it. 如此 (…以至) [PREDET "a" n that] [EMPHASIS] ❑ *This is something where you can earn such a lot of money that there is not any risk that you will lose it.* 这是能赚到很多钱而没有任何亏钱风险的事。 ❑ *Though Vivaldi had earned a great deal in his lifetime, his extravagance was such that he died in poverty.* 尽管维瓦尔蒂一生中挣了许多钱，但其挥霍如此之巨，以至在贫困中死去。 ● DET **Such** is also a determiner. 如此的 (作限定词) ❑ *She looked at him in such distress that he had to look away.* 她如此忧伤地看着他，以至他不得不把目光转向别处。 **6** DET You use **such...that** or **such that** in order to say what the result or consequence of something that you have just mentioned is. 如此这般的 ❑ *The operation has uncovered such backstreet dealing in stolen property that police might now press for changes in the law.* 这次行动发现了如此这般的地下赃物交易以致警方现在可能迫切要求修改法律。 ❑ *Their cost structure is such that they just can't compete with the low-cost carriers.* 他们的成本结构是这样的以致于他们就是没法与那些低成本的运输公司竞争。 ● PREDET **Such** is also a predeterminer. 如此的 (作前位限定词) [PREDET "a" n that/"as to"] ❑ *He could put an idea in such a way that Alan would believe it was his own.* 他能够以这样的方式表达观点，以致于艾伦会相信那是他自己的观点。 **7** PHRASE You use **such and such** to refer to a thing or person when you do not want to be exact or precise. 某某 [SPOKEN, VAGUENESS] ❑ *I said, "Well, what time'll I get to Baltimore?" and he said such and such a time but I missed my connection.* 我说，"那么，我几点会到巴尔的摩呢？"他说了某某时间，可我错过了联运列车。 **8** PHRASE You use **as such** with a negative to indicate that a word or expression is not a very accurate description of the actual situation. 准确意义上的 (与否定词连用) ❑ *I am not a learner as such – I used to ride a bike years ago.* 我不是个准确意义上的初学者——我多年前常常骑自行车。 **9** PHRASE You use **as such** after a noun to indicate that you are considering that thing on its own, separately from other things or factors. 作为…本身 (用于名词后) ❑ *Mr. Simon said he was not against taxes as such, "but I do object when taxation is justified on spurious or dishonest grounds," he says.* 西蒙先生说过他并不反对税收本身，"但我确实反对以无根据或不诚实的理由征税，"他说道。 **10** **no such thing** → see **thing**

> **Such** is followed by **a** when the noun is something that can be counted. ❑ *...such a pleasant surprise.* It is not followed by **a** when the noun is plural or something that cannot be counted. ❑ *...such beautiful girls. ...such power.* You do not use **such** when you are talking about something that is present, or about the place where you are. You need to use the phrases **like that** or **like this**. For example, if you are admiring someone's watch, you do not say "I'd like such a watch." You say "**I'd like a watch like that.**" Similarly, you do not say about the town where you are living "There's not much to do in such a town." You say "**There's not much to do in a town like this.**" **Such** in other contexts is quite formal.

suck /sʌk/ (**sucks, sucking, sucked**) **1** V-T/V-I If you **suck** something, you hold it in your mouth and pull at it with the muscles in your cheeks and tongue, for example in order to get liquid out of it. 吮吸 ❑ *They waited in silence and sucked their sweets.* 他们静静地等着，吮着糖果。 ❑ *He sucked on his cigarette.* 他吸了吸他的香烟。 **2** V-T If something **sucks** a liquid, gas, or object in a particular direction, it draws it there with a powerful force. 吸 (物体)；抽 (液体、气体) ❑ *The pollution-control team is at the scene and is due to start sucking up oil any time now.* 这个污染控制小组已在现场，

随时可以开始抽油。 **3** V-T PASSIVE If you **are sucked into** a bad situation, you are unable to prevent yourself from becoming involved in it. 使卷入 ❑ *...the extent to which they have been sucked into the cycle of violence.* …他们被卷入暴力循环的程度。

sud·den ♦◇◇ /sʌdᵊn/ **1** ADJ **Sudden** means happening quickly and unexpectedly. 突然的 ❑ *He had been deeply affected by the sudden death of his father-in-law.* 他深受其岳父突然辞世的影响。 ❑ *It was all very sudden.* 一切都非常突然。 ● **sud·den·ness** N-UNCOUNT 突然性 ❑ *The enemy seemed stunned by the suddenness of the attack.* 敌人似乎被这次袭击的突如其来惊呆了。 **2** PHRASE If something happens **all of a sudden**, it happens quickly and unexpectedly. 突然地 ❑ *All of a sudden she didn't look sleepy any more.* 突然她看上去不再困倦了。

sud·den·ly ♦♦◇ /sʌdᵊnli/ ADV If something happens **suddenly**, it happens quickly and unexpectedly. 突然地 ❑ *Suddenly, she looked ten years older.* 突然间，她看上去老了10岁。 ❑ *Her expression suddenly altered.* 她的表情突然变了。

★ **sue** /su̲/ (**sues, suing, sued**) V-T/V-I If you **sue** someone, you start a legal case against them, usually in order to claim money from them because they have harmed you in some way. 诉讼 ❑ *Mr. Warren sued for libel over the remarks.* 沃伦先生对那些评论提起诽谤诉讼。 ❑ *The company could be sued for damages.* 该公司会因所造成的损失被起诉。

suede /swe̲ɪd/ N-UNCOUNT **Suede** is leather with a soft, slightly rough surface. 绒面革 ❑ *Albert wore a brown suede jacket and jeans.* 阿尔伯特穿了一件棕色绒面革夹克衫和牛仔裤。

suf·fer ♦♦◇ /sʌfər/ (**suffers, suffering, suffered**) **1** V-T/V-I If you **suffer** pain, you feel it in your body or in your mind. 经受(痛苦); 受苦 ❑ *Within a few days she had become seriously ill, suffering great pain and discomfort.* 在几天时间里她已病得很重，经受了极大的痛苦和不适。 ❑ *He suffered terribly the last few days.* 他过去的几天痛苦不堪。 **2** V-I If you **suffer from** an illness or from some other bad condition, you are badly affected by it. (因疾病等糟糕的处境而) 受苦 ❑ *He was eventually diagnosed as suffering from terminal cancer.* 他最后被诊断为癌症晚期。 **3** V-T If you **suffer** something bad, you are in a situation in which something painful, harmful, or very unpleasant happens to you. 遭受 ❑ *The peace process has suffered a serious blow now.* 该和平进程现已受到一次沉重的打击。 **4** V-I If you **suffer**, you are badly affected by an event or situation. 受难 ❑ *There are few who have not suffered.* 几乎无人免于受难。 **5** V-I If something **suffers**, it becomes worse because it has not been given enough attention or is in a bad situation. 变差 ❑ *I'm not surprised that your studies are suffering.* 你功课变差，我并不感到惊讶。

suf·fer·ing /sʌfərɪŋ/ (**sufferings**) **1** N-UNCOUNT **Suffering** is serious pain which someone feels in their body or their mind. 痛苦 [also N in pl] ❑ *They began to recover slowly from their nightmare of pain and suffering.* 他们开始从痛苦的噩梦中慢慢恢复过来。 ❑ *It has caused terrible suffering to animals.* 它已给动物们造成了可怕的痛苦。 **2** → see also **long-suffering**

★ **suf·fice** /səfa̲ɪs/ (**suffices, sufficing, sufficed**) **1** V-I If you say that something will **suffice**, you mean it will be enough to achieve a purpose or to fulfill a need. 足够 [no cont] [FORMAL] ❑ *A cover letter should never exceed one page; often a far shorter letter will suffice.* 附信绝不应超过一页；通常一封更短的信就足够了。 **2** PHRASE **Suffice it to say** or **suffice to say** is used at the beginning of a statement to indicate that what you are saying is obvious, or that you will only give a short explanation. 不必多言 ❑ *Suffice it to say that afterwards we never met again.* 不必多言，后来我们再也没见过面。

suf·fi·cient ♦◇◇ /səfɪʃᵊnt/ ADJ If something is **sufficient for** a particular purpose, there is enough of it for the purpose. 足够的 ❑ *One yard of fabric is sufficient to cover the exterior of an 18-in.-diameter hatbox.* 一码的布料足够罩住18英寸直径帽盒的外部。 ❑ *Lighting levels should be sufficient for photography without flash.* 照明程度对无闪光灯摄影应该是够了。 ● **suf·fi·cient·ly** ADV 足够地 ❑ *She recovered sufficiently to accompany Chou on his tour of Africa in 1964.* 她康复到足以在周的1964年非洲之旅中伴随他。

Word Link *fix ≈ fastening : affix, prefix, suffix*

suf·fix /sʌfɪks/ (**suffixes**) N-COUNT A **suffix** is a letter or group of letters, for example "-ly" or "-ness," which is added to the end of a word in order to form a different word, often of a different word class. For example, the suffix "-ly" is added to "quick" to form "quickly." Compare **affix** and **prefix**. 后缀

suf·fo·cate /sʌfəkeɪt/ (**suffocates, suffocating, suffocated**) **1** V-T/V-I If someone **suffocates** or **is suffocated**, they die because there is no air for them to breathe. 使窒息而死; 窒息而死 ❑ *He either suffocated, or froze to death.* 他要么窒息而死，要么冻死了。 ● **suf·fo·ca·tion** /sʌfəkeɪʃᵊn/ N-UNCOUNT 窒息 ❑ *Many of the victims died of suffocation.* 受害者中许多死于窒息。 **2** V-T/V-I If you say that you **are suffocating** or that something **is suffocating** you, you mean that you feel very uncomfortable because there is not enough fresh air and it is difficult to breathe. 使感到窒息; 感到窒息 ❑ *That's better. I was suffocating in that cell of a room.* 那样好多了。我刚才在那个小房间里感到窒息。

suf·frage /sʌfrɪdʒ/ N-UNCOUNT **Suffrage** is the right of people to vote for a government or national leader. 选举权 [FORMAL] ❑ *...the women's suffrage movement.* …妇女的选举运动。

sug·ar ♦◇◇ /ʃʊgər/ (**sugars**) **1** N-UNCOUNT **Sugar** is a sweet substance that is used to make food and drinks sweet. It is usually in the form of small white or brown crystals. 食用糖 ❑ *...bags of sugar.* …袋袋食用糖。 **2** N-COUNT If someone has one **sugar** in their tea or coffee, they have one small spoon of sugar or one sugar lump in it. 一匙糖; 一块糖 ❑ *How many sugars do you take?* 你用多少块糖？ **3** N-COUNT **Sugars** are substances that occur naturally in food. When you eat them, the body converts them into energy. 糖 ❑ *Plants produce sugars and starch to provide themselves with energy.* 植物制造糖和淀粉来为自身提供能量。 **4** **to sugar the pill** → see **pill**
→ see Word Web: **sugar**
→ see **coffee, fruit**

sug·gest ♦♦♦ /səgdʒɛst/ (**suggests, suggesting, suggested**) **1** V-T If you **suggest** something, you put forward a plan or idea for someone to think about. 建议 ❑ *He suggested a link between class size and test results of seven-year-olds.* 他建议把7岁儿童的班级大小和考试结果相关联。 ❑ *I suggest you ask him some specific questions about his past.* 我建议你问问他有关他的过去的一些具体问题。 ❑ *No one has suggested how this might occur.* 没有人提议过这事如何开始。 **2** V-T If you **suggest** the name of a person or place, you recommend them to someone. 推荐 ❑ *Could you suggest someone to advise me how to do this?* 你能推荐一个人来建议我怎么做这件事吗？ **3** V-T If you **suggest that** something is the case, you say something which you believe is the case. 认为是 ❑ *I'm not suggesting that is what is happening.* 我并不是说那就是所发生的情况。 ❑ *It is wrong to suggest that there are easy alternatives.* 认为有容易的选择是错误的。 **4** V-T If one thing **suggests** another, it implies it or makes you think that it might be the case. 暗示 ❑ *Earlier reports suggested that a meeting would take place on Sunday.* 早期的报道暗示了一次会议将在周日举行。

Word Web sugar

Sugar cane was discovered in prehistoric New Guinea*. As people migrated across the Pacific Islands and into India and China, they brought sugar cane with them. At first, people just chewed on the cane. They liked the **sweet taste**. When sugar cane reached the Middle East, people discovered how to **refine** it into **crystals**. Brown sugar is created by stopping the refining process earlier. This leaves some of the molasses syrup in the sugar. Today two-fifths of sugar comes from **beets**. Refined sugar is used in many **foods** and **beverages**. The overuse of sugar can cause many problems, such as **obesity** and **diabetes**.

New Guinea: a large island in the southern Pacific Ocean.

S

Note that **suggest** cannot usually be followed directly by a noun or pronoun referring to a person; you generally have to put the preposition **to** in front of it. You do not "suggest someone something," you "**suggest** something **to** someone." ❑ *John Caskey first suggested this idea to me.* Nor do you "suggest someone to do something." You "**suggest that** someone **do** something." ❑ *Beatrice suggested that he spend the summer at their place.* Do not confuse **suggest** and **advise**. If you **suggest** something, you mention it as an idea or plan for someone to think about. If you **advise** someone to do something, you tell them what you think they should do. ❑ *I advised him to leave as soon as possible.*

Word Partnership *suggest* 的常用搭配:
N. **analysts** suggest, **experts** suggest, **researchers** suggest 1-3
data suggest, **findings** suggest, **results** suggest, **studies** suggest, **surveys** suggest 4

sug·ges·tion ♦◇◇ /səgdʒɛstʃᵊn/ (**suggestions**) 1 N-COUNT If you make a **suggestion**, you put forward an idea or plan for someone to think about. 建议 ❑ *The dietitian was helpful, making suggestions as to how I could improve my diet.* 这位饮食学家很有帮助，就我如何能改善膳食提出了建议。 ❑ *Perhaps he'd followed her suggestion of a stroll to the river.* 也许他已听从了她的到河边散步的建议。 2 N-COUNT A **suggestion** is something that a person says which implies that something is the case. 暗示 ❑ *We reject any suggestion that the law needs amending.* 我们拒绝任何该法律需要修订的暗示。 3 N-SING If there is no **suggestion that** something is the case, there is no reason to think that it is the case. 迹象 ❑ *There is no suggestion whatsoever that the two sides are any closer to agreeing.* 没有该双方更接近于达成一致的任何迹象。

Word Partnership *suggestion* 的常用搭配:
V. **follow a** suggestion, **make a** suggestion 1
reject a suggestion 1 2

sug·ges·tive /səgdʒɛstɪv/ 1 ADJ Something that is **suggestive of** something else is quite like it or may be a sign of it. 使人想起…的 [v-link ADJ "of" n] ❑ *The fingers were gnarled, lumpy, with long, curving nails suggestive of animal claws.* 那些手指粗糙、不平，有着又长又弯的使人想起动物爪子的指甲。 2 ADJ **Suggestive** remarks or looks cause people to think about sex, often in a way that makes them feel uncomfortable. 挑逗的 ❑ *...another former employee who claims Thomas made suggestive remarks to her.* …另一位声称托马斯向她讲了挑逗话的前雇员。

sui·cid·al /suɪsaɪdᵊl/ ADJ People who are **suicidal** want to kill themselves. 想自杀的 ❑ *I was suicidal and just couldn't stop crying.* 我想自杀，并忍不住地哭泣。

sui·cide ♦◇◇ /suɪsaɪd/ (**suicides**) N-VAR People who commit **suicide** deliberately kill themselves because they do not want to continue living. 自杀 ❑ *She tried to commit suicide on several occasions.* 她曾几次试图进行自杀。 ❑ *...a case of attempted suicide.* …一个自杀未遂的案子。

S

Word Partnership *suicide* 的常用搭配:
V. **attempt** suicide, **commit** suicide
N. suicide **bomber**, suicide **prevention**, suicide **rate**, **risk** of suicide

suit ♦♦◇ /sut/ (**suits, suiting, suited**) 1 N-COUNT A man's **suit** consists of a jacket, pants, and sometimes a vest, all made from the same fabric. (男) 套装 ❑ *...a dark pin-striped business suit.* …一套黑色细条纹男职业装。 2 N-COUNT A woman's **suit** consists of a jacket and skirt, or sometimes pants, made from the same fabric. (女) 套装 ❑ *I was wearing my tweed suit.* 我那时穿着我的花呢套装。 3 N-COUNT A particular type of **suit** is a piece of clothing that you wear for a particular activity. (特定活动时穿的) 服装 ❑ *The six survivors only lived through their ordeal because of the special rubber suits they were wearing.* 6位幸存者因穿着特殊橡胶服度过了大难。 4 V-T If something **suits** you, it is convenient for you or is the best thing for you in the circumstances. (某事物) 适合 (某人) [no cont] ❑ *They will only release information if it suits them.* 他们只会发布合他们意的消息。 5 V-T If something **suits** you, you like it. (某事物) 合 (某人) 心意 [no cont] ❑ *I don't think a sedentary life would altogether suit me.* 我认为久坐不动的生活方式完全不适合我。 6 V-T If a piece of clothing or a particular style or color **suits** you, it makes you look attractive. (衣服、款式、颜色等) 适合 (某人) [no cont] ❑ *Green suits you.* 绿色适合你。 7 V-T If you **suit yourself**, you do something just because you want to do it, without bothering to consider other people. 按照自己的意愿 ❑ *People have tended to suit themselves, not paying much heed to the reformers.* 人们已趋向于按自己的意愿行事，不太在意改革者们。 8 N-COUNT In a court of law, a **suit** is a case in which someone tries to get a legal decision against a person or company, often so that the person or company will have to pay them money for having done something wrong to them. 诉讼案 ❑ *Up to 2,000 former employees have filed personal injury suits against the company.* 多达2千名前雇员已对该公司提起了个人伤害诉讼。 ● N-UNCOUNT You can also say that someone **files** or **brings suit against** another person. 诉讼 ❑ *One insurance company has already filed suit against the city of Chicago.* 一家保险公司已对芝加哥市提起诉讼。 9 → see also **pantsuit** 10 PHRASE If people **follow suit**, they do the same thing that someone else has just done. 跟着做 ❑ *Efforts to persuade the remainder to follow suit have continued.* 说服其余的人也跟着做的努力在继续。
→ see **clothing**

You do not use the verb **suit** if clothes are simply not the right size for you. The verb you need is **fit**. ❑ *The size 12 gown is gorgeous and fits perfectly... The gloves didn't fit.* You can say that something **suits** a person or place if it looks attractive on that person or in that place. ❑ *It is really feminine and pretty and it certainly suits you.* However, you cannot usually say that one color, pattern, or object **suits** another. The verb you need is **match**. ❑ *She wears a straw hat with a yellow ribbon to match her yellow cotton dress... His clothes don't quite match.*

suit·able ♦◇◇ /sutəbᵊl/ ADJ Someone or something that is **suitable for** a particular purpose or occasion is right or acceptable for it. 适合的 ❑ *Employers usually decide within five minutes whether someone is suitable for the job.* 雇主们通常在5分钟内判断出某人是否适合那份工作。 ● **suit·abil·ity** /sutəbɪlɪti/ N-UNCOUNT 适合 ❑ *...information on the suitability of a product for use in the home.* …有关一项产品家庭适用性的信息。

Word Partnership *suitable* 的常用搭配:
V. **find (a)** suitable *something*, **use (a)** suitable *something*

suit·ably /sutəbli/ ADV You use **suitably** to indicate that someone or something has the right qualities or things for a particular activity, purpose, or situation. 适合地 [ADV adj/-ed] ❑ *There are problems in recruiting suitably qualified scientific officers for our laboratories.* 在为我们实验室招聘恰当合格的科研人员时存在些问题。

Word Link *cas ≈ box, hold* : *case, encase, suitcase*

suit·case /sutkeɪs/ (**suitcases**) N-COUNT A **suitcase** is a box or bag with a handle and a hard frame in which you carry your clothes when you are traveling. 手提箱 ❑ *It did not take Andrew long to pack a suitcase.* 安德鲁没有用多长时间就整理好了手提箱。

★ **suite** /swit/ (**suites**) 1 N-COUNT A **suite** is a set of rooms in a hotel or other building. 套房 ❑ *They had a fabulous time during their week in a suite at the Paris Hilton.* 他们在巴黎希尔顿酒店的套房里度过了非常愉快的一周。 2 N-COUNT A **suite** is a set of matching furniture. 一套家具 ❑ *...a three-piece suite.* …一组三件套家具。 3 N-COUNT A bathroom **suite** is a matching bathtub, sink, and toilet. (浴室) 套件 ❑ *...the horrible pink suite in the bathroom.* …浴室里那组难看的粉红色套件。
→ see **hotel**

suit·ed /sutɪd/ ADJ If something is well **suited to** a particular purpose, it is right or appropriate for that purpose. If someone is well **suited to** a particular job, they are right or appropriate for that job. 适合的 [v-link ADJ] ❑ *The area is well suited to road cycling as well as off-road riding.* 这个地区很适合公路自行车竞赛和越野骑马。

Word Partnership *suited* 的常用搭配:
ADV. **ill** suited, **perfectly** suited, **uniquely** suited, **well** suited
PREP. suited **to** *something*

suit·or /sutər/ (**suitors**) 1 N-COUNT A woman's **suitor** is a man who wants to marry her. (女性的) 求婚者 [OLD-FASHIONED] ❑ *My mother had a suitor who adored her.* 我的母亲曾有一位爱慕她的求婚者。

2 N-COUNT A **suitor** is a company or organization that wants to buy another company. 求购公司 [BUSINESS] ❑ *The company was making little progress in trying to find a suitor.* 该公司在寻找一家求购公司方面进展甚微。

★ **sul·fur** /sʌlfər/

in BRIT, use **sulphur**

N-UNCOUNT **sulfur** is a yellow chemical which has a strong smell. 硫磺 ❑ *Burning sulfur creates poisonous fumes.* 燃烧的硫磺会产生有毒烟雾。

→ see **firework**

sulk /sʌlk/ (**sulks, sulking, sulked**) V-I If you **sulk**, you are silent and bad-tempered for a while because you are annoyed about something. 生闷气 ❑ *He turned his back and sulked.* 他转身生起了闷气。 ● N-COUNT **Sulk** is also a noun. 愠怒 ❑ *He went off in a sulk.* 他带着愠怒走开了。

▲ **sul·len** /sʌlᵊn/ ADJ Someone who is **sullen** is bad-tempered and does not speak much. 愤懑的 ❑ *The offenders lapsed into a sullen silence.* 这些罪犯陷入了愤懑的沉默。

★ **sul·phur** /sʌlfər/ [mainly BRIT] → see **sulfur**

sul·tan /sʌltən/ (**sultans**) N-TITLE; N-COUNT A **sultan** is a ruler in some Muslim countries. 苏丹 (某些穆斯林国家的统治者的称法) ❑ *...during the reign of Sultan Abdul Hamid.* …在苏丹阿布杜勒·哈米德统治时期。

sul·try /sʌltri/ **1** ADJ **Sultry** weather is hot and damp. 闷热潮湿的 [WRITTEN] ❑ *The climax came one sultry August evening.* 高潮在8月一个闷热潮湿的夜晚到来了。 **2** ADJ Someone who is **sultry** is attractive in a way that suggests hidden passion. 撩人的 [WRITTEN] ❑ *...a dark-haired sultry woman.* …一个黑发撩人的女子。

sum ♦◊◊ /sʌm/ (**sums, summing, summed**) **1** N-COUNT A **sum of** money is an amount of money. (一) 笔 (钱) ❑ *Large sums of money were lost.* 大笔大笔的钱损失了。 **2** N-SING In mathematics, **the sum of** two or more numbers is the number that is obtained when they are added together. (数字的) 和 ❑ *The sum of all the angles of a triangle is 180 degrees.* 一个三角形的所有角度之和是180度。 **3** N-SING **The sum of** something is all of it. You often use **sum** in this way to indicate that you are disappointed because the extent of something is rather small, or because it is not very good. 全部 ❑ *To date, the sum of my gardening experience had been futile efforts to rid the flower beds of grass.* 迄今为止，我全部的园艺经验就是给花圃徒劳地除草。 **4** N-COUNT A **sum** is a simple calculation in arithmetic. 简单运算 [BRIT] **5** → see also **lump sum**

▸ **sum up** **1** PHRASAL VERB If you **sum** something **up**, you describe it as briefly as possible. 简述 ❑ *One voter in Brasilia summed up the mood – "Politicians have lost credibility," he complained.* 一位巴西利亚选民简述了人们的心情——"政治家们已丧失信誉，"他抱怨道。 **2** PHRASAL VERB If something **sums** a person or situation **up**, it represents their most typical characteristics. 概括…的最典型特征 ❑ *"I love my wife, my horse and my dog," he said, and that summed him up.* "我爱我的妻子、我的马和我的狗，"他说道。那话概括了他的最典型特征。 **3** PHRASAL VERB If you **sum up** after a speech or at the end of a piece of writing, you briefly state the main points again. When a judge **sums up** after a trial, he reminds the jury of the evidence and the main arguments of the case they have heard. 作总结 ❑ *When the judge summed up, it was clear he wanted a guilty verdict.* 当法官作总结时，显然他想要一个有罪判决。

Word Partnership *sum* 的常用搭配：

ADJ. **equal** sum, **large** sum, **substantial** sum, **undisclosed** sum **1**

N. sum **of money** **1**

sum·ma·rise /sʌməraɪz/ [BRIT] → see **summarize**

sum·ma·rize /sʌməraɪz/ (**summarizes, summarizing, summarized**)

in BRIT, also use **summarise**

V-T/V-I If you **summarize** something, you give a summary of it. 总结 ❑ *Table 3.1 summarizes the information given above.* 表3.1总结了以上所给信息。 ❑ *Basically, the article can be summarized in three sentences.* 基本上，这篇文章可用3句话概括。

Word Link *summ ≈ highest point : consummate, summary, summit*

sum·mary /sʌməri/ (**summaries**) **1** N-COUNT A **summary of** something is a short account of it, which gives the main points but not the details. 总结 ❑ *What follows is a brief summary of the process.* 接下来是对该过程的一个简短总结。 ● PHRASE You use **in summary** to indicate that what you are about to say is a summary of what has just been said. 总之 ❑ *In summary, it is my opinion that this complete treatment process was very successful.* 总之，我认为这整个治疗过程非常成功。 **2** ADJ **Summary** actions are done without delay, often when something else should have been done first or done instead. 从简的 [ADJ n] [FORMAL] ❑ *It says torture and summary execution are common.* 据说酷刑和草草处决很常见。

sum·mer ♦♦◊ /sʌmər/ (**summers**) N-VAR **Summer** is the season between spring and fall. In the summer the weather is usually warm or hot. 夏季 ❑ *I escaped the heatwave in Washington earlier this summer and flew to Maine.* 我今年初夏躲避了华盛顿的热浪，飞到了缅因州。 ❑ *It was a perfect summer's day.* 那是个完美的夏日。

sum·mer camp (**summer camps**) N-COUNT A **summer camp** is a place in the country where parents can pay to send their children during the school summer vacation. The children staying there can take part in many outdoor and social activities. 夏令营 ❑ *We went to summer camp the same two weeks in July every year.* 我们过去都在每年7月相同的两个周去夏令营。

sum·mit ♦♦◊ /sʌmɪt/ (**summits**) **1** N-COUNT A **summit** is a meeting at which the leaders of two or more countries discuss important matters. 峰会 ❑ *...next week's Washington summit.* …下周的华盛顿峰会。 **2** N-COUNT The **summit** of a mountain is the top of it. (山) 峰

→ see **mountain**

★ **sum·mon** /sʌmən/ (**summons, summoning, summoned**) **1** V-T If you **summon** someone, you order them to come to you. 召唤 [FORMAL] ❑ *Howe summoned a doctor and hurried over.* 豪叫了一位医生，匆忙赶过去了。 ❑ *Suddenly we were summoned to the interview room.* 突然我们被召唤进了面试室。 **2** V-T If you **summon** a quality, you make a great effort to have it. For example, if you **summon** the courage or strength to do something, you make a great effort to be brave or strong, so that you will be able to do it. 努力拥有 (某特质); 鼓起 (勇气、力气) ❑ *It took her a full month to summon the courage to tell her mother.* 她用了整整一个月的时间才鼓起勇气告诉了母亲。 ● PHRASAL VERB **Summon up** means the same as **summon.** 努力拥有; 鼓起 (同**summon**) ❑ *Painfully shy, he finally summoned up courage to ask her to a game.* 尽管他非常腼腆，最终还是鼓起了勇气邀她去看一场比赛。

sum·mons /sʌmənz/ (**summonses**) **1** N-COUNT A **summons** is an order to come and see someone. 召见令 ❑ *I received a summons to the Warden's office.* 我接收到了去沃登办公室的召见令。 **2** N-COUNT A **summons** is an official order to appear in court. 传票 ❑ *She had received a summons to appear in court.* 她已接到一张出庭的传票。

sump·tu·ous /sʌmptʃuəs/ ADJ Something that is **sumptuous** is grand and obviously very expensive. 奢华的 ❑ *...a sumptuous feast.* …一场奢华的盛会。

sun ♦♦◊ /sʌn/ **1** N-SING **The sun** is the ball of fire in the sky that the Earth goes around, and that gives us heat and light. 太阳 ❑ *The sun was now high in the southern sky.* 太阳当时正高挂在南面天空上。 ❑ *The sun came out, briefly.* 太阳出来了，时间很短。 **2** N-UNCOUNT You refer to the light and heat that reach us from the sun as **the sun.** 阳光 ❑ *Dena took them into the courtyard to sit in the sun.* 德娜把他们带到院子里坐在阳光下。

→ see Word Web: **sun**

→ see **astronomer, earth, eclipse, navigation, solar, solar system, star**

Sun. **Sun.** is a written abbreviation for **Sunday.** 星期日 ❑ *The museum is open Mon.-Sun.* 这个博物馆周一至周日开放。

sun·bathe /sʌnbeɪð/ (**sunbathes, sunbathing, sunbathed**) V-I When people **sunbathe**, they sit or lie in a place where the sun shines on them, so that their skin becomes browner. 沐日光浴 ❑ *Franklin swam and sunbathed at the pool every morning.* 富兰克林以前每天上午都在游泳池游泳并进行日光浴。 ● **sun·bath·ing** N-UNCOUNT 沐日光浴 ❑ *Nearby there is a stretch of white sand beach perfect for sunbathing.* 附近有一片非常适合沐日光浴的白色沙滩。

sun·burn /sʌnbɜrn/ (**sunburns**) N-VAR If someone has **sunburn**, their skin is bright pink and sore because they have spent too much time in hot sunshine. 晒伤 ❑ *The risk and severity of sunburn depend on the body's natural skin color.* 晒伤的风险和严重程度取决于身体的自然肤色。

→ see **skin**

S

Word Web sun

The **sun**'s core contains **hydrogen** atoms. These atoms combine to form helium. This process is called **fusion**. It produces a core temperature of 15 million degrees Celsius. The corona is a layer of hot, glowing gases surrounding the sun. Large flames called solar flares also burn on the surface. Infrared and **ultraviolet** light are **invisible** parts of **sunlight**. Sometimes dark patches called sunspots appear on the sun. They occur in eleven-year cycles. Scientists believe that sunspots affect the growth of plant life on Earth. They also affect radio transmissions.

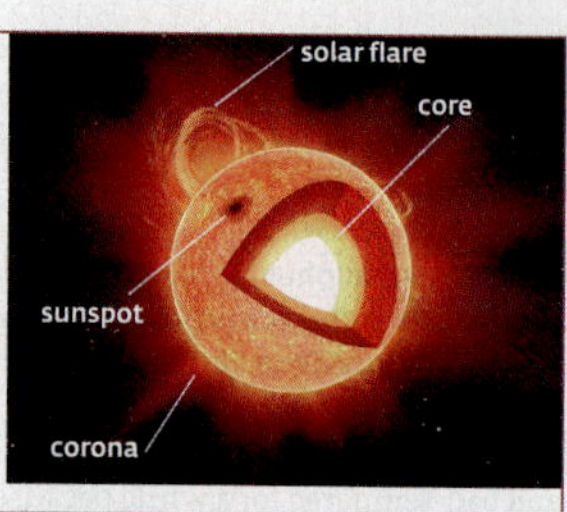

▲ **sun·burned** /sʌnbɜrnd/ also **sunburnt** ADJ Someone who is **sunburned** has sore bright pink skin because they have spent too much time in hot sunshine. 晒伤了的 ❑ *A badly sunburned face or back is extremely painful.* 严重晒伤了的脸或背部是非常疼痛的。

Sun·day ♦♦♦ /sʌndeɪ, -di/ (**Sundays**) N-VAR **Sunday** is the day after Saturday and before Monday. 星期日 ❑ *I thought we might go for a drive on Sunday.* 我原以为我们可能星期日去开车兜风。

sun·dries /sʌndriz/ N-PLURAL When someone is making a list of things, items that are not important enough to be listed separately are sometimes referred to together as **sundries**. 杂项物品 [FORMAL] ❑ *The inn gift shop stocks quality Indian crafts and sundries.* 这个小旅馆的礼品店备有优质的印度工艺品和其他杂品。

sun·dry /sʌndri/ **1** ADJ If someone refers to **sundry** people or things, they are referring to several people or things that are all different from each other. 各异的 [ADJ n] [FORMAL] ❑ *Scientists, business people, and sundry others gathered on Monday for the official opening.* 科学家、商人和其他各类人士星期一聚集一起参加官方的开幕式。 **2** PHRASE **All and sundry** means everyone. 每个人 ❑ *I made tea for all and sundry at the office.* 我为该办公室里的每个人沏了茶。

▲ **sun·flower** /sʌnflaʊər/ (**sunflowers**) N-COUNT A **sunflower** is a very tall plant with large yellow flowers. Oil from sunflower seeds is used in cooking and to make margarine. 向日葵

sung /sʌŋ/ **Sung** is the past participle of **sing**. sing的过去分词

sun·glasses /sʌnglæsɪz/ N-PLURAL **Sunglasses** are glasses with dark lenses which you wear to protect your eyes from bright sunlight. 太阳镜 [also "a pair of" N] ❑ *She slipped on a pair of sunglasses.* 她轻快地戴上了一副太阳镜。

sunk /sʌŋk/ **Sunk** is the past participle of **sink**. sink的过去分词

sunk·en /sʌŋkən/ **1** ADJ **Sunken** ships have sunk to the bottom of a sea, ocean, or lake. 沉没的 [ADJ n] ❑ *The sunken sail boat was a glimmer of white on the bottom.* 这条沉没的帆船在海底呈一道白色微光。 **2** ADJ **Sunken** gardens, roads, or other features are below the level of their surrounding area. 低洼的 [ADJ n] ❑ *Steps lead down to the sunken garden.* 台阶向下通往那个低洼的花园。 **3** ADJ **Sunken** eyes, cheeks, or other parts of the body curve inward and make you look thin and unwell. 凹陷的 ❑ *Her eyes were sunken and black-ringed.* 她的双眼凹陷且有黑眼圈。

sun·light /sʌnlaɪt/ N-UNCOUNT **Sunlight** is the light that comes from the sun during the day. 阳光 ❑ *I saw her sitting at a window table, bathed in sunlight.* 我看见她坐在临窗的桌旁，沐浴在阳光中。
→ see **rainbow, skin, sun**

sun·ny /sʌni/ (**sunnier, sunniest**) **1** ADJ When it is **sunny**, the sun is shining brightly. (天) 晴朗的 ❑ *The weather was surprisingly warm and sunny.* 天气出奇地暖和晴朗。 **2** ADJ **Sunny** places are brightly lit by the sun. (地方) 阳光充足的 ❑ *Most roses like a sunny position in a fairly fertile soil.* 多数玫瑰喜欢土壤肥沃、阳光充足之地。

sun·rise /sʌnraɪz/ (**sunrises**) **1** N-UNCOUNT **Sunrise** is the time in the morning when the sun first appears in the sky. 日出 ❑ *The rain began before sunrise.* 雨是在日出前开始下的。 **2** N-COUNT A **sunrise** is the colors and light that you see in the eastern part of the sky when the sun first appears. 朝霞 ❑ *There was a spectacular sunrise yesterday.* 昨天出现了一片蔚为壮观的朝霞。

sun·roof /sʌnruf/ (**sunroofs**) N-COUNT A **sunroof** is a panel in the roof of a car that opens to let sunshine and air enter the car. (汽车的) 天窗 ❑ *...extras like a sunroof, a CD player, or chrome wheels.* …像天窗、CD唱机或镀铬车轮等附加物。

sun·screen /sʌnskrin/ (**sunscreens**) N-MASS A **sunscreen** is a cream that protects your skin from the sun's rays, especially in hot weather. 防晒霜 ❑ *Use a sunscreen suitable for your skin type.* 使用一款适合你的皮肤类型的防晒霜。
→ see **skin**

sun·set /sʌnsɛt/ (**sunsets**) **1** N-UNCOUNT **Sunset** is the time in the evening when the sun disappears out of sight from the sky. 日落 ❑ *The dance ends at sunset.* 舞会在日落时结束。 **2** N-COUNT A **sunset** is the colors and light that you see in the western part of the sky when the sun disappears in the evening. 晚霞 ❑ *There was a red sunset over Paris.* 巴黎上空有一片红色晚霞。

sun·shine /sʌnʃaɪn/ N-UNCOUNT **Sunshine** is the light and heat that comes from the sun. 阳光 ❑ *In the marina yachts sparkle in the sunshine.* 停靠区里游艇在阳光下闪闪发光。 ❑ *She was sitting outside a cafe in bright sunshine.* 她那时正坐在一个咖啡馆外明媚的阳光里。

sun·stroke /sʌnstroʊk/ N-UNCOUNT **Sunstroke** is an illness caused by spending too much time in hot sunshine. 中暑 ❑ *I was suffering from acute sunstroke, starvation and exhaustion.* 我当时正受着急性中暑、饥饿和疲惫之苦。

sun·tan /sʌntæn/ (**suntans**) **1** N-COUNT If you have a **suntan**, the sun has turned your skin an attractive brown color. 晒黑 ❑ *They want to go to the Bahamas and get a suntan.* 他们想去巴哈马群岛把皮肤晒黑。 **2** ADJ **Suntan** lotion, oil, or cream protects your skin from the sun. 防晒的 (露、油、霜) [ADJ n] ❑ *She playfully rubs suntan lotion on his neck.* 她开玩笑地把防晒露涂在他脖子上。
→ see **skin**

Word Link *super ≈ above : super, superficial, supervise*

su·per ♦◇◇ /supər/ **1** ADV **Super** is used before adjectives to indicate that something has a lot of a quality. 超级地 [ADV adj] ❑ *I'm going to Greece in the summer so I've got to be super slim.* 我这个夏天要去希腊，所以我得变得超级苗条才行。 **2** ADJ **Super** is used before nouns to indicate that something is larger, better, or more advanced than similar things. 超级的 [ADJ n] ❑ *Winners of each regional will advance to the super regionals.* 每个地区分支机构的获胜者们将会晋级为超级地区性人物。 **3** ADJ Some people use **super** to mean very nice or very good. 超好的 [INFORMAL, OLD-FASHIONED] ❑ *We had a super time.* 我们度过了一段超好的时光。 ❑ *That's a super idea.* 那是个超好的想法。

super·an·nua·tion /supərænyueɪʃən/ N-UNCOUNT **Superannuation** is the same as a **retirement fund**. 退休金 [mainly BRIT, BUSINESS]

su·perb ♦◇◇ /supɜrb/ **1** ADJ If something is **superb**, its quality is very good indeed. 极好的 ❑ *There is a superb 18-hole golf course 6 miles away.* 6英里外有个极好的18洞高尔夫球场。 ● **su·perb·ly** ADV 极好地 ❑ *The orchestra played superbly.* 这支管弦乐队演奏得好极了。 **2** ADJ If you say that someone has **superb** confidence, control, or skill, you mean that they have very great confidence, control, or skill. (信心、控制力或技巧) 超凡的 ❑ *With superb skill he managed to make a perfect landing.* 他以超凡的技巧设法完成了一次完美的着陆。 ● **su·perb·ly** ADV 超凡地 ❑ *...his superbly disciplined opponent.* …他的那个受过超凡训练的对手。

super·fi·cial /supərfɪʃəl/ **1** ADJ If you describe someone as **superficial**, you disapprove of them because they do not think deeply, and have little understanding of anything serious or important. (人) 肤浅的 [DISAPPROVAL] ❑ *This guy is a superficial yuppie with no intellect whatsoever.* 这个家伙是个肤浅的雅皮士，没有任何智慧。 **2** ADJ If you describe something such as an action, feeling, or relationship as **superficial**, you mean that it includes only the simplest and most obvious aspects of that thing, and not those aspects which require more effort to deal with or understand. (行动、感情、关系等) 浅表的 ❑ *Their arguments do not withstand the most superficial scrutiny.* 他们的论点经不起最为浅表的细察。 **3** ADJ **Superficial** is used to describe the appearance of something or the impression that it gives, especially if its real nature is very different. 表面上的 ❑ *Despite these superficial resemblances, this is a* darker work than her earlier novels. 尽管有这些表面的相似，这相比她早期的小说是一部更悲观的作品。 **4** ADJ **Superficial** injuries are not very serious, and affect only the surface of the body. You can also describe damage to an object as **superficial**. 表皮的（伤、损坏） ❑ *The 69-year-old clergyman escaped with superficial wounds.* 这位69岁的牧师带着些皮肉伤逃脱了。

▲ **super·flu·ous** /supɜrfluəs/ ADJ Something that is **superfluous** is unnecessary or is no longer needed. 多余的 ❑ *My presence at the afternoon's proceedings was superfluous.* 我在下午的活动中的出席是多余的。

super·high·way /supərhaɪweɪ/ (**superhighways**) **1** N-COUNT A **superhighway** is a large, fast highway or freeway with several lanes. 高速公路 [AM] ❑ *He took off for the city on the eight-lane superhighway.* 他沿着8车道的高速公路朝那座城市驶去了。 **2** N-COUNT The information **superhighway** is the network of computer links that enables computer users all over the world to communicate with each other. （信息）高速公路 [COMPUTING] ❑ *...a superhighway using digital and fiber optic technology to provide new telecommunications links.* …用数字和光纤技术提供新的通讯手段的一条信息高速公路。

super·im·pose /supərɪmpoʊz/ (**superimposes, superimposing, superimposed**) **1** V-T If one image **is superimposed on** another, it is put on top of it so that you can see the second image through it. 叠加 [usu passive] ❑ *The image of a seemingly tiny dancer was superimposed on the image of the table.* 一个看似很小的舞蹈者的影像被叠加在了那张桌子的影像上。 **2** V-T If features or characteristics from one situation **are superimposed onto** or **on** another, they are transferred onto or used in the second situation, though they may not fit. 生搬硬套 [usu passive] ❑ *Patterns of public administration and government are superimposed on traditional societies.* 公共行政与管治模式被生搬硬套于传统社会之上。

Word Link *ent ≈ one who does, has : dependent, resident, superintendent*

★ **super·in·ten·dent** /supərɪntɛndənt, suprɪn-/ (**superintendents**) **1** N-COUNT A **superintendent** is a person who is responsible for a particular thing or the work done in a particular department. 主管 ❑ *He became superintendent of the bank's East African branches.* 他成了这家银行东非分行的主管。 **2** N-COUNT A **superintendent** is a person whose job is to take care of a large building such as a school or an apartment building and deal with small repairs to it. （大楼的）管理员 [AM]

in BRIT, use **caretaker**

❑ *The superintendent, a bundle of keys hanging from his belt, was standing at the door.* 这位管理员正站在门口，腰带上挂着一串钥匙。 **3** N-COUNT; N-TITLE A **superintendent** is the head of a police department. 警长 [BRIT]

su·peri·or ♦◇◇ /supɪəriər/ (**superiors**) **1** ADJ If one thing or person is **superior to** another, the first is better than the second. 比…好的 ❑ *We have a relationship infinitely superior to those of many of our friends.* 我们之间的关系远比我们许多朋友之间的关系好得多。 ● **su·peri·or·ity** ★ N-UNCOUNT 优越性 ❑ *The technical superiority of laser discs over tape is well established.* 光盘相对磁带在技术上的优越性是确定无疑的。 **2** ADJ If you describe something as **superior**, you mean that it is good, and better than other things of the same kind. 上好的 ❑ *A few years ago it was virtually impossible to find superior quality coffee in local shops.* 几年前在当地的商店里几乎不可能买到上好的咖啡。 **3** ADJ A **superior** person or thing is more important than another person or thing in the same organization or system. 上级的 ❑ *...negotiations between the mutineers and their superior officers.* …那些反叛者和他们的上级军官们之间的谈判。 **4** N-COUNT Your **superior** in an organization that you work for is a person who has a higher rank than you. 上级 ❑ *Other army units are completely surrounded and cut-off from communication with their superiors.* 其他部队完全被包围，与上级的联系也被切断了。 **5** ADJ If you describe someone as **superior**, you disapprove of them because they behave as if they are better, more important, or more intelligent than other people. 有优越感的 [DISAPPROVAL] ❑ *Finch gave a superior smile.* 芬奇富有优越感地一笑。 ● **su·peri·or·ity** ★ N-UNCOUNT 优越 ❑ *...a false sense of his superiority over mere journalists.* …他在记者面前才有的虚假的优越感。 **6** ADJ If one group of people has **superior** numbers to another group, the first has more people than the second, and therefore has an advantage over it. （人数）占优势的 [FORMAL] ❑ *The demonstrators fled when they saw the authorities' superior numbers.* 示威者们看到官方占优势的人数时就逃跑了。

Word Partnership *superior* 的常用搭配：

ADV.	**far** superior, **morally** superior, **vastly** superior **1**
N.	superior **performance**, superior **quality**, superior **service** **2**

★ **su·peri·or·ity** /supɪəriɔrɪti/ **1** N-UNCOUNT If one side in a war or conflict has **superiority**, it has an advantage over its enemy, for example because it has more soldiers or better equipment. 优势 [FORMAL] ❑ *We have air superiority.* 我们有空中优势。 **2** → see also **superior**

super·la·tive /supɜrlətɪv/ (**superlatives**) **1** ADJ If you describe something as **superlative**, you mean that it is extremely good. 极好的 ❑ *Some superlative wines are made in this region.* 一些极好的葡萄酒产自这个地区。 **2** N-COUNT If someone uses **superlatives** to describe something, they use adjectives and expressions which indicate that it is extremely good. 盛赞之辞 ❑ *...a spectacle which has critics world-wide reaching for superlatives.* …一种使全世界评论家都极尽盛赞之辞的景象。 **3** ADJ In grammar, the **superlative** form of an adjective or adverb is the form that indicates that something has more of a quality than anything else in a group. For example, "biggest" is the superlative form of "big." Compare **comparative**. （形容词或副词的）最高级的 ● N-COUNT **Superlative** is also a noun. （形容词或副词的）最高级 [ADJ n] ❑ *...his tendency toward superlatives and exaggeration.* …他的使用最高级和夸张言词的倾向。

super·man /supərmæn/ (**supermen**) N-COUNT A **superman** is a man who has very great physical or mental abilities. 超人 ❑ *Collor nurtured the idea that he was a superman, who single-handedly could resolve Brazil's crisis.* 考乐抱有一个想法，即他是可以一手解决巴西危机的超人。

super·mar·ket /supərmɑrkɪt/ (**supermarkets**) N-COUNT A **supermarket** is a large store which sells all kinds of food and some household goods. 超市 ❑ *Most of us do our food shopping in the supermarket.* 我们大多数人在这家超市采购食品。

super·model /supərmɒdᵊl/ (**supermodels**) N-COUNT A **supermodel** is a very famous fashion model. 超级名模

super·natu·ral /supərnætʃərəl, -nætʃrəl/ ADJ **Supernatural** creatures, forces, and events are believed by some people to exist or happen, although they are impossible according to scientific laws. （生物、力量、事件等）超自然的 ❑ *The Nakani were evil spirits who looked like humans and possessed supernatural powers.* 纳卡尼是恶魔，看起来像人类，却具有超自然力量。 ● N-SING **The supernatural** is things that are supernatural. 超自然物 ❑ *He writes short stories with a touch of the supernatural.* 他写带点儿超自然物的短篇故事。

super·pow·er /supərpaʊər/ (**superpowers**) N-COUNT A **superpower** is a very powerful and influential country, usually one that is rich and has nuclear weapons. 超级大国 ❑ *The United States could claim to be both a military and an economic superpower.* 美国可以声称既是军事上也是经济上的一个超级大国。

super·sede /supərsid/ (**supersedes, superseding, superseded**) V-T If something **is superseded by** something newer, it is replaced because it has become old-fashioned or unacceptable. 取代 [usu passive] ❑ *Hand tools are relics of the past that have now been superseded by the machine.* 手工工具是过去的遗物，现在已被机器取代。

Word Link *son ≈ sound : resonate, sonata, supersonic*

★ **super·son·ic** /supərsɒnɪk/ ADJ **Supersonic** aircraft travel faster than the speed of sound. 超音速的 [ADJ n] ❑ *There was a huge bang; it sounded like a supersonic jet.* 发出一声巨响；听起来像一架超音速喷气式飞机。

→ see **sound**

super·star /supərstɑr/ (**superstars**) N-COUNT A **superstar** is a very famous entertainer or athlete. 超级明星 [INFORMAL] ❑ *He was more than a basketball superstar, he was a celebrity.* 他不仅仅是一个篮球超级明星，还是一位名人。

▲ **super·sti·tion** /supərstɪʃᵊn/ (**superstitions**) N-VAR **Superstition** is belief in things that are not real or possible, for example magic. 迷信 ❑ *Fortune-telling is a very much debased art surrounded by superstition.* 算命是一种透着迷信色彩的十分低级的把戏。

super·sti·tious /supərstɪʃəs/ **1** ADJ People who are **superstitious** believe in things that are not real or possible, for example magic. （人）迷信的 ❑ *Jean was extremely superstitious and* believed the color green brought bad luck. 琼极端迷信，认为绿色会带来厄运。 **2** ADJ **Superstitious** fears or beliefs are irrational and not based on fact. (恐惧或信念) 迷信的 [ADJ n] ❑ *A wave of superstitious fear spread among the townspeople.* 一股迷信的恐惧浪潮在城里人中蔓延。

super·store /suːpərstɔr/ (**superstores**) N-COUNT **Superstores** are very large supermarkets or stores selling household goods and equipment. Superstores are usually built outside cities and away from other stores. 大型超市 ❑ *...a Do-It-Yourself superstore.* …一家“自己动手”大型超市。

Word Link *super ≈ above : super, superficial, supervise*

super·vise /suːpərvaɪz/ (**supervises, supervising, supervised**) V-T If you **supervise** an activity or a person, you make sure that the activity is done correctly or that the person is doing a task or behaving correctly. 监督 ❑ *A team was sent to supervise the elections in Nicaragua.* 一队人马被派去监督尼加拉瓜的选举。

super·vi·sion /suːpərvɪʒᵊn/ N-UNCOUNT **Supervision** is the supervising of people, activities, or places. 监督 ❑ *A toddler requires close supervision and firm control at all times.* 刚学走路的孩子需要时刻认真照看，牢牢管住。

★ **super·vi·sor** /suːpərvaɪzər/ (**supervisors**) N-COUNT A **supervisor** is a person who supervises activities or people, especially workers or students. 监督员; 指导者 ❑ *...a full-time job as a supervisor at a factory.* …在一家工厂担任监督员的一项全职工作。

sup·per /sʌpər/ (**suppers**) **1** N-VAR Some people refer to the main meal eaten in the early part of the evening as **supper**. 晚餐 ❑ *Some guests like to dress for supper.* 有些客人喜欢穿礼服出席晚餐。 **2** N-VAR **Supper** is a simple meal eaten just before you go to bed at night. 夜宵 ❑ *She gives the children their supper, then puts them to bed.* 她给孩子们吃了夜宵，然后让他们上床睡觉。

sup·ple /sʌpᵊl/ (**suppler, supplest**) **1** ADJ A **supple** object or material bends or changes shape easily without cracking or breaking. 柔软的 ❑ *The leather is supple and sturdy enough to last for years.* 这种皮革质地柔软结实，足以用上好多年。 **2** ADJ A **supple** person can move and bend their body very easily. 灵活的 ❑ *Paul was incredibly supple and strong.* 保罗非常灵活、强壮。

sup·plement /sʌplɪmənt/ (**supplements, supplementing, supplemented**) **1** V-T If you **supplement** something, you add something to it in order to improve it. 补充 ❑ *...people doing extra jobs outside their regular jobs to supplement their incomes.* …在固定工作之余做兼职以增加收入的人们。 ● N-COUNT **Supplement** is also a noun. 补充 ❑ *Business sponsorship must be a supplement to, not a substitute for, public funding.* 商业赞助必须是公共资助的补充而非替代物。 **2** N-COUNT A **supplement** is a pill that you take or a special kind of food that you eat in order to improve your health. 养生片剂 ❑ *...a multiple vitamin and mineral supplement.* …一种复合维生素和矿物质养生片剂。 **3** N-COUNT A **supplement** is a separate part of a magazine or newspaper, often dealing with a particular topic. (报纸或杂志的) 增刊 ❑ *...a special supplement to a monthly financial magazine.* …一份金融月刊的特别增刊。 **4** N-COUNT A **supplement to** a book is an additional section, written some time after the main text and published either at the end of the book or separately. (书籍的) 附录; 补编 ❑ *...the supplement to the Encyclopedia Britannica.* …《大不列颠百科全书》补编。 **5** N-COUNT A **supplement** is an extra amount of money that you pay in order to obtain special facilities or services, for example when you are traveling or staying at a hotel. (旅行或住宾馆等所付的) 额外费用 ❑ *If you are traveling alone, the single room supplement is $25 a night.* 如果你独自一人旅行，单人间的额外费用是每晚$25。

★ **sup·plemen·ta·ry** /sʌplɪmɛntəri, -tri/ ADJ **Supplementary** things are added to something in order to improve it. 补充的 ❑ *...the question of whether or not we need to take supplementary vitamins.* …我们是否有必要补充维生素的问题。

sup·pli·er /səplaɪər/ (**suppliers**) N-COUNT A **supplier** is a person, company, or organization that sells or supplies something such as goods or equipment to customers. 供应商 [BUSINESS] ❑ *...one of the country's biggest food suppliers.* …该国最大的食品供应商之一。

sup·ply ♦♦◇ /səplaɪ/ (**supplies, supplying, supplied**) **1** V-T If you **supply** someone with something that they want or need, you give them a quantity of it. 供应 ❑ *...an agreement not to produce or supply chemical weapons.* …一份不生产或不供应化学武器的协议。 ❑ *...a pipeline which will supply the major Greek cities with Russian natural gas.* …一条将为希腊各主要城市供应俄罗斯天然气的管道。 **2** N-PLURAL You can use **supplies** to refer to food, equipment, and other essential things that people need, especially when these are provided in large quantities. 补给品 ❑ *What happens when food and gasoline supplies run low?* 食物和汽油这些补给品减少时会发生什么情况呢？ **3** N-VAR A **supply of** something is an amount of it which someone has or which is available for them to use. 供应 ❑ *The brain requires a constant supply of oxygen.* 大脑需要持续的供氧。 **4** N-UNCOUNT **Supply** is the quantity of goods and services that can be made available for people to buy. 供应量 [BUSINESS] ❑ *Prices change according to supply and demand.* 价格根据供应量和需求量而变化。 **5** PHRASE If something is **in short supply**, there is very little of it available and it is difficult to find or obtain. 供应不足 ❑ *Food is in short supply all over the country.* 食品在全国各地都供应不足。

→ see **economics**

Word Partnership *supply* 的常用搭配:

N.	supply **electricity**, supply **equipment**, supply **information** **1**
ADJ.	**abundant** supply, **large** supply, **limited** supply **3**

sup·ply line (**supply lines**) N-COUNT A **supply line** is a route along which goods and equipment are transported to an army during a war. 补给线 ❑ *Soldiers get training setting up supply lines and building roads.* 士兵们接受培训建立补给线和建造公路。

sup·ply teach·er (**supply teachers**) N-COUNT A **supply teacher** is the same as a **substitute teacher**. 代课教师 [BRIT]

sup·port ♦♦♦ /səpɔrt/ (**supports, supporting, supported**) **1** V-T If you **support** someone or their ideas or aims, you agree with them, and perhaps help them because you want them to succeed. 支持 ❑ *The vice president insisted that he supported the hard-working people of New York.* 副总统坚持认为他支持勤劳的纽约人民。 ● N-UNCOUNT **Support** is also a noun. 支持 ❑ *The president gave his full support to the reforms.* 该总统对改革予以了全力的支持。 **2** N-UNCOUNT If you give **support** to someone during a difficult or unhappy time, you are kind to them and help them. (给处境困难或不幸者的) 帮助 ❑ *It was hard to come to terms with her death after all the support she gave to me and the family.* 她曾给我和这个家庭很大的帮助，她的去世让人难以接受。 **3** N-UNCOUNT Financial **support** is money provided to enable an organization to continue. (给组织的) 资助 ❑ *State agencies continue to cut budgets and support to a number of organizations.* 国家机关继续削减对一些组织的预算和资助。 **4** V-T If you **support** someone, you provide them with money or the things that they need. 资助; 供养 ❑ *I have children to support, money to be earned, and a home to be maintained.* 我有一群孩子要供，要赚钱，还要养一所房子。 **5** V-T If a fact **supports** a statement or a theory, it helps to show that it is true or correct. 证实 ❑ *The Freudian theory about daughters falling in love with their father has little evidence to support it.* 弗洛伊德关于女儿恋父的理论没有什么证据来证实。 ● N-UNCOUNT **Support** is also a noun. 证明 ❑ *The two largest powers in any system must always be major rivals. History offers some support for this view.* 任何体制下的两个最高权力者必然永远是主要竞争对手。历史提供了这种观点的一些佐证。 **6** V-T If something **supports** an object, it is underneath the object and holding it up. 支撑 ❑ *...the thick wooden posts that supported the ceiling.* …支撑天花板的那些粗木柱子。 **7** N-COUNT A **support** is a bar or other object that supports something. 支撑物 ❑ *Each slab was nailed to two straight wooden supports.* 每块板都钉在两根垂直的木制支撑物上。 **8** V-T If you **support yourself**, you prevent yourself from falling by holding onto something or by leaning on something. 倚着 ❑ *He supported himself by means of a nearby post.* 他倚在旁边的一根柱子上。 ● N-UNCOUNT **Support** is also a noun. 倚靠 ❑ *Alice, very pale, was leaning against him as if for support.* 爱丽丝脸色非常苍白，正靠在他身上，好像是在寻求倚靠。 **9** V-T If you **support** a sports team, you always want them to win and perhaps go regularly to their games. 支持 (运动队等) ❑ *Tim, 17, supports the Knicks.* 17岁的蒂姆支持尼克斯队。

> If you dislike something very much or get annoyed by it, you do not say "I can't support it." You say "**I can't bear it.**" or "**I can't stand it.**" ❑ *She can't bear the new Republican governor... I cannot stand going shopping.*

sup·port·er ♦♦◇ /səpɔrtər/ (**supporters**) N-COUNT **Supporters** are people who support someone or something, for example a political leader or a sports team. 支持者 ❑ *Attacks against opposition supporters are continuing at levels higher than before the election.* 对反对派支持者的攻击依然持续，程度比竞选前更猛烈。

S

Word Partnership *supporter* 的常用搭配：

ADJ. **active** supporter, **big** supporter, **enthusiastic** supporter, **former** supporter, **longtime** supporter, **staunch** supporter, **strong** supporter

★ **sup·port·ive** /səpɔ̲rtɪv/ ADJ If you are **supportive**, you are kind and helpful to someone at a difficult or unhappy time in their life. (对处境困难或不幸者) 给予帮助的 ❑ *They were always supportive of each other.* 他们总是互相帮助。

sup·pose ♦♦◊ /səpo̲uz/ (**supposes, supposing, supposed**) 1 V-T You can use **suppose** or **supposing** before mentioning a possible situation or action. You usually then go on to consider the effects that this situation or action might have. 假设 ❑ *Suppose someone gave you an egg and asked you to describe exactly what was inside.* 假设某人给你一个蛋并要你准确描述里面的东西。 2 V-T If you **suppose that** something is true, you believe that it is probably true, because of other things that you know. (根据所知) 料想 ❑ *The policy is perfectly clear and I see no reason to suppose that it isn't working.* 这项政策非常明了，我看不出有何理由认为它行不通。 ❑ *I knew very well that the problem was more complex than he supposed.* 我很清楚这个问题比他料想的更复杂。 3 PHRASE You can say "**I suppose**" when you want to express slight uncertainty. 我想 (表示不太确定) [SPOKEN, VAGUENESS] ❑ *I suppose I'd better do some homework.* 我想我最好做点家庭作业。 ❑ *"Is that the right way up?"—"Yeah. I suppose so."* "那是上去的路吗？"——"是的。我想是。" 4 PHRASE You can say "**I suppose**" or "**I don't suppose**" before describing someone's probable thoughts or attitude, when you are impatient or slightly angry with them. 我想 (表示不耐烦或有点生气) [SPOKEN, FEELINGS] ❑ *I suppose you think you're funny.* 我想你认为自己很有趣。 5 PHRASE You can say "**I don't suppose**" as a way of introducing a polite request. 不知 (表示一种礼貌的请求) [SPOKEN, POLITENESS] ❑ *I don't suppose you could tell me where James Street is, could you?* 不知你能不能告诉我詹姆士街在哪儿？ 6 PHRASE You can use "**do you suppose**" to introduce a question when you want someone to give their opinion about something, although you know that they are unlikely to have any more knowledge or information about it than you. 你认为 (用于引出他人观点) [SPOKEN] ❑ *Do you suppose he was telling the truth?* 你认为他在说真话吗？

> Note that when you are using the verb **suppose** with a "that"-clause in order to state a negative opinion or belief, you normally make **suppose** negative, rather than the verb in the "that"-clause. For instance, it is more usual to say ❑ *"I don't suppose he ever saw it."* than "I suppose he didn't ever see it." The same pattern applies to other verbs with a similar meaning, such as **believe**, **consider**, and **think**.

Word Partnership *suppose* 的常用搭配：

V. **let's** suppose 1
ADV. **now** suppose 1

sup·posed ♦♦◊

> Pronounced /səpo̲uzd/ or /səpo̲ust/ for meanings 1 to 4, and /səpo̲uzɪd/ for meaning 5.

> 义项1至4读作 /səpo̲uzd/或 /səpo̲ust/，义项5读作 /səpo̲uzɪd/。

1 PHRASE If you say that something **is supposed to** happen, you mean that it is planned or expected. Sometimes this use suggests that the thing does not really happen in this way. 应该 (表示按计划或期望) ❑ *He produced a hand-written list of nine men he was supposed to kill.* 他手写列出一份他应该杀的9个男子的名单。 2 PHRASE If something **was supposed to** happen, it was planned or intended to happen, but did not in fact happen. 本应该 ❑ *He was supposed to go back to Bergen on the last bus, but of course the accident prevented him.* 他本应坐最后一班公共汽车回卑尔根，但当然，这场意外拦住了他。 3 PHRASE If you say that something **is supposed to** be true, you mean that people say it is true but you do not know for certain that it is true. 据说 ❑ *"The Whipping Block" has never been published, but it's supposed to be a really good poem.* 《鞭笞刑具》从未发表，但据说它是一首相当好的诗。 4 PHRASE You can use "**be supposed to**" to express annoyance at someone's ideas, or because something is not happening in the right way. 还 (表示恼火或失望) [FEELINGS] ❑ *You're supposed to be my friend!* 你还是我的朋友呢！ 5 ADJ You can use **supposed** to suggest that something that people talk about or believe in may not in fact exist, happen, or be as it is described. 所谓的 [ADJ n] ❑ *Not all developing countries are willing to accept the supposed benefits of free trade.* 并非所有发展中国家都愿意接受那些所谓的自由贸易的好处。 ●**sup·pos·ed·ly** /səpo̲uzɪdli/ ADV 所谓地 ❑ *He was more of a victim than any of the women he supposedly offended.* 他和他所谓地冒犯过的女人们中任何一位相比，更是个受害者。

★ **sup·press** /səprɛ̲s/ (**suppresses, suppressing, suppressed**) 1 V-T If someone in authority **suppresses** an activity, they prevent it from continuing, by using force or making it illegal. 镇压；压制 ❑ *...drug traffickers, who continue to flourish despite international attempts to suppress them.* …尽管全世界努力镇压却继续猖獗的毒贩子们。 ●**sup·pres·sion** /səprɛ̲ʃᵊn/ N-UNCOUNT 镇压；压制 ❑ *...people who were imprisoned after the violent suppression of the pro-democracy movement protests.* …赞成民主的抗议活动受暴力镇压后被囚禁的人们。 2 V-T If a natural function or reaction of your body **is suppressed**, it is stopped, for example by drugs or illness. 抑制 (身体功能或反应) ❑ *The reproduction and growth of the cancerous cells can be suppressed by bombarding them with radiation.* 癌细胞的繁殖和生长可通过放射线辐射加以抑制。 ●**sup·pres·sion** N-UNCOUNT 抑制 ❑ *Eye problems can indicate an unhealthy lifestyle with subsequent suppression of the immune system.* 眼睛问题表明一种不健康的生活方式以及随后免疫系统所受的抑制。 3 V-T If you **suppress** your feelings or reactions, you do not express them, even though you might want to. 抑制 (情感或反应) ❑ *Liz thought of Barry and suppressed a smile.* 利兹想到了巴里，强忍住一个微笑。 ●**sup·pres·sion** N-UNCOUNT 抑制 ❑ *A mother's suppression of her own feelings can cause problems.* 一位母亲对她自己情感的压抑可能会导致问题。 4 V-T If someone **suppresses** a piece of information, they prevent other people from learning it. 封锁 ❑ *At no time did they try to persuade me to suppress the information.* 他们从未试图劝我封锁这个消息。 ●**sup·pres·sion** N-UNCOUNT 封锁 ❑ *The inspectors found no evidence which supported any allegation of suppression of official documents.* 这些检察官们找不到证据证明对封锁官方文件的任何指控。 5 V-T If someone or something **suppresses** a process or activity, they stop it continuing or developing. 阻止 (活动)；抑制 (过程) ❑ *The government is suppressing inflation by increasing interest rates.* 政府正通过提高利率来抑制通货膨胀。

su·prema·cy /suprɛ̲məsi/ 1 N-UNCOUNT If one group of people has **supremacy** over another group, they have more political or military power than the other group. 支配地位 ❑ *The conservative old guard had re-established its political supremacy.* 这位保守派的老卫士已重新建立起其政治上的支配地位。 2 N-UNCOUNT If someone or something has **supremacy** over another person or thing, they are better. 优势 ❑ *In the United States Open final, Graf retained overall supremacy.* 在美国网球公开赛的决赛中，格拉芙保持着全面的优势。

su·preme ♦♦◊ /supri̲m/ 1 ADJ **Supreme** is used in the title of a person or an official group to indicate that they are at the highest level in a particular organization or system. 最高的 [ADJ n] ❑ *MacArthur was Supreme Commander for the allied powers in the Pacific.* 麦克阿瑟是太平洋盟军的最高司令官。 ❑ *...the Supreme Court.* …最高法院。 2 ADJ You use **supreme** to emphasize that a quality or thing is very great. 极其的 [EMPHASIS] ❑ *Her approval was of supreme importance.* 她的认可是极其重要的。 ●**su·preme·ly** ADV 极其地 [ADV adj/adv] ❑ *She does her job supremely well.* 她工作得极其出色。

Word Link *sur ≈ above : surcharge, surface, surveillance*

sur·charge /sɜ̲rtʃɑrdʒ/ (**surcharges**) N-COUNT A **surcharge** is an extra payment of money in addition to the usual payment for something. It is added for a specific reason, for example by a company because costs have risen or by a government as a tax. 附加费 ❑ *The government introduced a 15% surcharge on imports.* 政府推出了15%的进口附加费。

sure ♦♦♦ /ʃʊ̲ər/ (**surer, surest**) 1 ADJ If you are **sure** that something is true, you are certain that it is true. If you are not **sure** about something, you do not know for certain what the true situation is. 确定的 [v-link ADJ] ❑ *He'd never been in a class before and he was not even sure that he should have been teaching.* 他以前从未讲过课，他甚至不能确定自己是否应当从事教学。 ❑ *The president has never been sure which direction he wanted to go in on this issue.* 这位总统从未确定在这个问题上自己想要朝哪个方向走。 2 ADJ If someone is **sure of** getting something, they will definitely get it or they think they will definitely get it. 肯定的 [v-link ADJ "of" -ing/n] ❑ *A lot of people think that it's better to pay for their education so that they can be sure of getting quality.* 很多人认为最好是自己掏钱受教育，为的是能肯定得到高

S

品质的教育。 **3** PHRASE If you say that something **is sure to** happen, you are emphasizing your belief that it will happen. 一定 [EMPHASIS] ❏ *With over 80 beaches to choose from, you are sure to find a place to lay your towel.* 有八十多个海滩可供挑选，你一定能找到一个晒日光浴的地方。 **4** ADJ **Sure** is used to emphasize that something such as a sign or ability is reliable or accurate. 可靠的; 准确的 [ADJ n] [EMPHASIS] ❏ *Sharpe's leg and shoulder began to ache, a sure sign of rain.* 夏普的腿和肩开始痛了，这是要下雨的准确迹象。 **5** ADJ If you tell someone to **be sure to** do something, you mean that they must not forget to do it.. 务必的 [v-link ADJ] [EMPHASIS] ❏ *Be sure to read about how mozzarella is made, on page 65.* 务必要阅读第65页上如何制作莫泽雷勒干酪的内容。 **6** CONVENTION **Sure** is an informal way of saying "yes" or "all right." 当然 [FORMULAE] ❏ *"Do you know where she lives?"—"Sure."* "你知道她住在哪儿吗？"——"当然啦！" **7** ADV You can use **sure** in order to emphasize what you are saying. 确实 [ADV before v] [INFORMAL, EMPHASIS] ❏ *"Has the whole world just gone crazy?"—"Sure looks that way, doesn't it."* "整个世界都疯了吗？"——"看起来确实如此，不是吗？" **8** PHRASE You say **sure enough**, especially when telling a story, to confirm that something was really true or was actually happening. (尤用于讲故事时) 果然 ❏ *We found the apple pie pudding too good to resist. Sure enough, it was delicious.* 我们觉得这块苹果馅饼布丁令人无法抗拒。果然，它很美味。 **9** PHRASE If you say that something is **for sure** or that you know it **for sure**, you mean that it is definitely true. 千真万确 ❏ *One thing's for sure, Manilow's vocal style hasn't changed much over the years.* 有一点是千真万确的，马尼洛的演唱风格这些年来没有太大的变化。 **10** PHRASE If you **make sure that** something is done, you take action so that it is done. 确保 ❏ *Make sure that you follow the instructions carefully.* 一定保证你认真遵循这些用法说明。 **11** PHRASE If you **make sure that** something is the way that you want or expect it to be, you check that it is that way. 核实 ❏ *He looked in the bathroom to make sure that he was alone.* 他往那间浴室里看了看，以核实那就他一个人。 **12** PHRASE If you are **sure of yourself**, you are very confident about your own abilities or opinions. 自信 ❏ *I'd never seen him like this, so sure of himself, so in command.* 我从未见过他像这样，如此自信，如此得心应手。

sure·fire /ʃʊərfaɪər/ also **sure-fire** ADJ A **surefire** thing is something that is certain to succeed or win. 一定成功的 [ADJ n] [INFORMAL] ❏ *These products are promoted as surefire cures for various diseases.* 这些产品被当作包治百病的良药来促销。

sure·ly ♦◇◇ /ʃʊərli/ **1** ADV You use **surely** to emphasize that you think something should be true, and you would be surprised if it was not true. 肯定地 [ADV with cl/group] [EMPHASIS] ❏ *You're an intelligent woman, surely you realize by now that I'm helping you.* 你是个聪明的女人，你现在肯定意识到我在帮你。 ❏ *You surely haven't forgotten Dr. Walters?* 你肯定还没忘记沃尔特斯博士吧？ **2** ADV If something will **surely** happen or is **surely** the case, it will definitely happen or is definitely the case. 必定地 [FORMAL] ❏ *He knew that under the surgeon's knife he would surely die.* 他知道在这位外科医生的刀下他会必死无疑。 **3** PHRASE If you say that something is happening **slowly but surely**, you mean that it is happening gradually but it is definitely happening. 缓慢但确实地 ❏ *Slowly but surely she started to fall in love with him.* 虽然缓慢，但她确实开始爱上他了。

> You use **surely** to express disagreement or surprise. ❏ *Surely you care about what happens to her.* You use **certainly** to emphasize that what you say is definitely true. ❏ *His death was certainly not an accident.* Both British and American speakers use **certainly** to agree with requests and statements. ❏ *"It is still a difficult world for women."—"Oh, certainly."* Note that American speakers also use **surely** in this way.

Word Partnership *surely* 的常用搭配:

V. surely **know** *something*, surely **think** *something* **1**
surely **die** **2**

sure·ty /ʃʊərɪti/ (**sureties**) N-VAR A **surety** is money or something valuable which you give to someone to show that you will do what you have promised. 保证金; 担保物 ❏ *The insurance company will take warehouse stocks or treasury bonds as surety.* 保险公司将接受仓库存货或国库券作为担保物。

surf /sɜrf/ (**surfs, surfing, surfed**) **1** N-UNCOUNT **Surf** is the mass of white bubbles that is formed by waves as they fall upon the shore. 拍岸浪花 ❏ *...surf rolling onto white sand beaches.* …翻滚到白色沙滩上的浪花。 **2** V-I If you **surf**, you ride on big waves in the sea on a special board. 冲浪 ❏ *I'm going to buy a surfboard and learn to surf.* 我要去买个冲浪板来学冲浪。 ● **surf·er** N-COUNT (**surfers**) 冲浪者 ❏ *...this small fishing village, which continues to attract painters and surfers.* …这个一直吸引着画家和冲浪者的小渔村。 **3** V-T If you **surf** the Internet, you spend time finding and looking at things on the Internet. (网上) 冲浪 [COMPUTING] ❏ *No one knows how many people currently surf the Net.* 没人知道现在有多少人在网上冲浪。 ● **surf·er** N-COUNT (**surfers**) (网上) 冲浪者 ❏ *Net surfers can use their credit cards to pay for anything from toys to train tickets.* 网上冲浪者可用他们的信用卡购买从玩具到火车票的任何东西。

→ see **beach**

Word Link *sur ≈ above : surcharge, surface, surveillance*

sur·face ♦♦◇ /sɜrfɪs/ (**surfaces, surfacing, surfaced**) **1** N-COUNT The **surface** of something is the flat top part of it or the outside of it. 表面 ❏ *Ozone forms a protective layer between 12 and 30 miles above the Earth's surface.* 臭氧在距地球表面12至30英里的地方形成一个保护层。 ❏ *...tiny little waves on the surface of the water.* …水面的细小波浪。 **2** N-COUNT A work **surface** is a flat area, for example the top of a table, desk, or kitchen counter, on which you can work. 台面 ❏ *It can simply be left on the work surface.* 把它放在操作台面上就行了。 **3** N-SING When you refer to **the surface** of a situation, you are talking about what can be seen easily rather than what is hidden or not immediately obvious. 表面 ❏ *Back home, things appear, on the surface, simpler.* 回到家后，事情表面上看起来简单一些。 **4** V-I If someone or something under water **surfaces**, they come up to the surface of the water. 浮出水面 ❏ *He surfaced, gasping for air.* 他浮出了水面，大口喘着气。 **5** V-I When something such as a piece of news, a feeling, or a problem **surfaces**, it becomes known or becomes obvious. 显现 ❏ *The paper says the evidence, when it surfaces, is certain to cause uproar.* 该报纸说，该证据一旦出现肯定会引起骚动。

Word Partnership *surface* 的常用搭配:

ADJ. **flat** surface, **rough** surface, **smooth** surface **1**
N. surface **area**, **Earth's** surface, surface **of the water** **1**
surface **level** **1** **3**
V. **break** the surface **1**
scratch the surface **1** **3**

sur·face mail N-UNCOUNT **Surface mail** is the system of sending letters and packages by road, rail, or sea, not by air. 平邮 ❏ *Goods may be sent by surface mail or airmail.* 货物可通过平邮或空运发送。

surf·ing /sɜrfɪŋ/ **1** N-UNCOUNT **Surfing** is the sport of riding on the top of a wave while standing or lying on a special board. 冲浪运动 ❏ *...every type of watersport from jetskiing and surfing to sailing and fishing.* …从喷气式快艇、冲浪到帆船运动、钓鱼等各种形式的水上运动。 **2** N-UNCOUNT **Surfing** is the activity of looking at different sites on the Internet, especially when you are not looking for anything in particular. 网上冲浪 [COMPUTING] ❏ *The simple fact is that, for most people, surfing is too expensive to do on a regular basis.* 这个简单的事实是：对大多数人来说，网上冲浪费用太高，无法经常进行。

surge /sɜrdʒ/ (**surges, surging, surged**) **1** N-COUNT A **surge** is a sudden large increase in something that has previously been steady, or has only increased or developed slowly. 剧增 ❏ *Specialists see various reasons for the recent surge in inflation.* 专家认为最近通货膨胀加剧有各种原因。 **2** V-I If something **surges**, it increases suddenly and greatly, after being steady or developing only slowly. 剧增 ❏ *The Freedom Party's electoral support surged from just under 10 percent to nearly 17 percent.* 自由党的选举支持率从只有不到10%剧增到近17%。 **3** V-I If a crowd of people **surge** forward, they suddenly move forward together. 涌动 ❏ *The photographers and cameramen surged forward.* 那些摄影和摄像师们涌向前去。 **4** N-COUNT A **surge** is a sudden powerful movement of a physical force such as wind or water. (风、水等) 突然的涌动 ❏ *The whole car shuddered with an almost frightening surge of power.* 整辆车因受到一股几乎令人惊骇的冲力而颤动。 **5** V-I If a physical force such as water or electricity **surges** through something, it moves through it suddenly and powerfully. (水、电流等) 涌 ❏ *Thousands of volts surged through his car after he careered into a lamp post, ripping out live wires.* 当他急速撞向一个灯柱、扯断了通电的电线之后，几千伏的电流涌过他的汽车。

sur·geon /sɜrdʒᵊn/ (**surgeons**) N-COUNT A **surgeon** is a doctor who is specially trained to perform surgery. 外科医生 ❏ *...a heart surgeon.* …一位心脏外科医生。

S

sur·gery ♦◇◇ /sɜrdʒəri/ (**surgeries**) 1 N-UNCOUNT **Surgery** is medical treatment in which someone's body is cut open so that a doctor can repair, remove, or replace a diseased or damaged part. 外科手术 ❏ *His father has just recovered from heart surgery.* 他父亲刚从心脏手术中恢复过来。 2 → see also **cosmetic surgery, plastic surgery** 3 N-COUNT A **surgery** is the area in a hospital with operating rooms where surgeons operate on their patients. 手术室 [AM]

in BRIT, use **theatre, operating theatre**

4 N-COUNT A **surgery** is the room or house where a doctor or dentist works. 诊室 [BRIT]

in AM, use **doctor's office, dentist's office**

5 N-COUNT A doctor's **surgery** is the period of time each day when a doctor sees patients at his or her surgery. 诊疗时间 [BRIT]

in AM, use **office hours**

→ see **cancer, laser**

★ **sur·gi·cal** /sɜrdʒɪkᵊl/ 1 ADJ **Surgical** equipment and clothing is used in surgery. 外科手术用的 [ADJ n] ❏ *...an array of surgical instruments.* …一批外科手术用的器械。 2 ADJ **Surgical** treatment involves surgery. 外科手术的 [ADJ n] ❏ *A biopsy is usually a minor surgical procedure.* 活组织检查通常是一个小小的外科手术。 ● **sur·gi·cal·ly** ADV 外科手术地 [ADV with v] ❏ *In very severe cases, bunions may be surgically removed.* 在非常严重的情况下，拇趾囊肿可能要手术切除。

sur·mise /sərmaɪz/ (**surmises, surmising, surmised**) 1 V-T If you **surmise** that something is true, you guess it from the available evidence, although you do not know for certain. 猜测 [FORMAL] ❏ *There's so little to go on, we can only surmise what happened.* 几乎没有什么可继续进行的，我们只能猜测发生过的事。 2 N-VAR If you say that a particular conclusion is **surmise**, you mean that it is a guess based on the available evidence and you do not know for certain that it is true. 猜测 [FORMAL] ❏ *It is mere surmise that Bosch had Brant's poem in mind when doing this painting.* 博斯画这幅画时头脑里想着勃朗特的诗，这只是猜测而已。

▲ **sur·name** /sɜrneɪm/ (**surnames**) N-COUNT Your **surname** is the name that you share with other members of your family. In English speaking countries and many other countries it is your last name. 姓 ❏ *She'd never known his surname, only his first name.* 她从来就不知道他姓什么，只知道他的名字。

★ **sur·pass** /sərpæs/ (**surpasses, surpassing, surpassed**) 1 V-T If one person or thing **surpasses** another, the first is better than, or has more of a particular quality than, the second. 优于；超过 ❏ *He was determined to surpass the achievements of his older brothers.* 他决心超过他的几位哥哥的成就。 2 V-T If something **surpasses** expectations, it is much better than it was expected to be. 远远超出（预期） ❏ *Conrad Black gave an excellent party that surpassed expectations.* 康拉德·布莱克办了一次远远超出预期的精彩聚会。

sur·plus ♦◇◇ /sɜrplʌs, -pləs/ (**surpluses**) 1 N-VAR If there is a **surplus of** something, there is more than is needed. 过剩 ❏ *...countries where there is a surplus of labor.* …劳动力过剩的国家。 2 ADJ **Surplus** is used to describe something that is extra or that is more than is needed. 过剩的；多余的 ❏ *Few people have large sums of surplus cash.* 几乎没人有大笔的闲钱。 ❏ *I sell my surplus birds to a local pet shop.* 我把我多余的鸟卖给一家当地的宠物店。 3 N-COUNT If a country has a trade **surplus**, it exports more than it imports. 顺差 ❏ *Japan's annual trade surplus is in the region of 100 billion dollars.* 日本每年的贸易顺差约有一千亿美元。 4 N-COUNT If a government has a budget **surplus**, it has spent less than it received in taxes. 盈余 ❏ *Norway's budget surplus has fallen from 5.9% in 1986 to an expected 0.1% this year.* 挪威的预算盈余已从1986年的5.9%下降到今年预计的0.1%。

sur·prise ♦♦◇ /sərpraɪz/ (**surprises, surprising, surprised**) 1 N-COUNT A **surprise** is an unexpected event, fact, or piece of news. 意外（信息或事件等） ❏ *I have a surprise for you: We are moving to Switzerland!* 我要告诉你一件意想不到的事：我们要搬到瑞士去！ ❏ *It may come as a surprise to some that a normal, healthy child is born with many skills.* 一个正常健康的孩子天生具有很多技艺，这对某些人来说可能是个意外信息。 ● ADJ **Surprise** is also an adjective. 意外的 [ADJ n] ❏ *Baxter arrived here this afternoon, on a surprise visit.* 巴克斯特今天下午突然到了这里，做意外造访。 2 N-UNCOUNT **Surprise** is the feeling that you have when something unexpected happens. 惊讶 ❏ *The Pentagon has expressed surprise at these allegations.* 五角大楼对这些指控表示了惊讶。 ❏ *"You mean he's going to vote against her?" Scobie asked in surprise.* "你的意思是他将投票反对她？"斯考比惊讶地问道。 3 V-T If something **surprises** you, it gives you a feeling of surprise. 使吃惊 ❏ *We'll solve the case ourselves and surprise everyone.* 我们将自己解决这件事，并让所有人吃惊。 ❏ *It surprised me that a driver of Alain's experience should make those mistakes.* 令我吃惊的是，像阿莱恩这样有经验的一位司机竟然会犯那些错误。 4 V-T If you **surprise** someone, you give them, tell them, or do something pleasant that they are not expecting. 使惊喜 ❏ *Surprise a new neighbor with one of your favorite home-made dishes.* 做一道你自己拿手的家常菜，给你的新邻居一个惊喜。 5 N-COUNT If you describe someone or something as a **surprise**, you mean that they are very good or pleasant although you were not expecting this. 惊喜 ❏ *...Senga MacFie, one of the surprises of the World Championships three months ago.* …森加·麦克菲，3个月前世界锦标赛中的惊喜之一。 6 V-T If you **surprise** someone, you attack, capture, or find them when they are not expecting it. 出其不意地抓获（袭击、找到） ❏ *U.S. troops surprised eight enemy fighters in a cave complex.* 美国军队在一个洞穴群里出其不意地抓获了8名敌军士兵。 7 → see also **surprised, surprising** 8 PHRASE If something **takes** you **by surprise**, it happens when you are not expecting it or when you are not prepared for it. 使某人吃惊 ❏ *His question took his two companions by surprise.* 他的提问让他的两位同伴吃了一惊。

Word Partnership *surprise* 的常用搭配:

N. surprise **announcement**, surprise **attack**, surprise **move**, surprise **visit** 1
a bit of a surprise 1 5
element of surprise 2

ADJ. **big** surprise, **complete** surprise, **great** surprise, **pleasant** surprise 1 5

sur·prised ♦◇◇ /sərpraɪzd/ 1 ADJ If you are **surprised** at something, you have a feeling of surprise, because it is unexpected or unusual. 吃惊的 ❏ *This lady was genuinely surprised at what happened to her pet.* 这位女士确实对发生在她宠物身上的事感到吃惊。 2 → see also **surprise**

sur·pris·ing ♦◇◇ /sərpraɪzɪŋ/ 1 ADJ Something that is **surprising** is unexpected or unusual and makes you feel surprised. 令人吃惊的 ❏ *It is not surprising that children learn to read at different rates.* 孩子们以不同速度识字，这并不令人惊讶。 ● **sur·pris·ing·ly** ADV 令人吃惊地 ❏ *The party did surprisingly well in the South.* 该政党在南方做得异常出色。 2 → see also **surprise**

sur·re·al /sərial/ ADJ If you describe something as **surreal**, you mean that the elements in it are combined in a strange way that you would not normally expect, like in a dream. 离奇的 ❏ *"Performance" is one of the most surreal movies ever made.* 《迷幻演出》是有史以来拍摄得最离奇的电影之一。

sur·ren·der ♦◇◇ /sərɛndər/ (**surrenders, surrendering, surrendered**) 1 V-I If you **surrender**, you stop fighting or resisting someone and agree that you have been beaten. 投降；屈服 ❏ *General Martin Bonnet called on the rebels to surrender.* 马丁·邦尼特将军要求反叛分子们投降。 ● N-VAR **Surrender** is also a noun. 投降；屈服 ❏ *...the government's apparent surrender to demands made by the religious militants.* …政府对宗教好战分子所提要求的明显屈从。 2 V-T If you **surrender** something you would rather keep, you give it up or let someone else have it, for example after a struggle. 放弃；交出 ❏ *Nadja had to fill out forms surrendering all rights to her property.* 纳贾不得不填写表格，放弃对她财产的所有权利。 ● N-UNCOUNT **Surrender** is also a noun. 放弃；交出 ❏ *...the sixteen-day deadline for the surrender of weapons and ammunition.* …交出武器弹药的16天期限。 3 V-T If you **surrender** something such as a ticket or your passport, you give it to someone in authority when they ask you to. 交出 [FORMAL] ❏ *They have been ordered to surrender their passports.* 他们已被命令交出他们的护照。

→ see **flag, war**

Thesaurus *surrender* 另参见:

V. abandon, give in, give up 1 2

sur·ren·der value (**surrender values**) N-COUNT The **surrender value** of a life insurance policy is the amount of money you receive if you decide that you no longer wish to continue with the policy. 退保金额 [BUSINESS] ❏ *An ordinary life policy may have a cash surrender value of $50,000.* 一份普通的人寿保险单的退保金额可能有$50000。

sur·ro·gate /sɜrəgeɪt, -gɪt/ (**surrogates**) ADJ You use **surrogate** to describe a person or thing that is given a particular role because the person or thing that should have the role is not available. 替代的 [ADJ n] ❏ *Martin had become Howard Cosell's surrogate*

S

son. 马丁已成为霍华德马考塞尔的代子了。● N-COUNT **Surrogate** is also a noun. 替代者；替代物 ❑ *Arms control should not be made into a surrogate for peace.* 军备控制不应变成和平的替代物。

sur·ro·gate moth·er (surrogate mothers) N-COUNT A **surrogate mother** is a woman who has agreed to give birth to a baby on behalf of another woman. 代孕母亲

sur·round ♦♦◇ /sərau̲nd/ (surrounds, surrounding, surrounded) **1** V-T/V-I If a person or thing **is surrounded** by something, that thing is situated all around them. 围绕 ❑ *The small churchyard was surrounded by a rusted wrought-iron fence.* 这个小墓地被一道生锈的锻铁栅栏围着。 ❑ *The shell surrounding the egg has many important functions.* 包着蛋的外壳有很多重要功能。 ❑ *...Chicago and the surrounding area.* …芝加哥及其周边地区。 **2** V-T If you are **surrounded** by soldiers or police, they spread out so that they are in positions all the way around you. 包围 ❑ *When the car stopped in the town square it was surrounded by soldiers and militiamen.* 当这辆车在城镇广场停下时，它被战士和民兵们包围了。 **3** V-T The circumstances, feelings, or ideas which **surround** something are those that are closely associated with it. 与…紧密联系 ❑ *The decision had been agreed in principle before today's meeting, but some controversy surrounded it.* 在今天的会议之前该决定原则上已获同意，但围绕这项决定还存在一些争议。 **4** V-T If you **surround yourself with** certain people or things, you make sure that you have a lot of them near you all the time. 确保身边总有 ❑ *He had made it his business to surround himself with a hand-picked group of bright young officers.* 他把确保身边有自己亲手挑选的一群聪明的年轻军官当作自己的职责。

sur·round·ings /sərau̲ndɪŋz/ N-PLURAL When you are describing the place where you are at the moment, or the place where you live, you can refer to it as your **surroundings**. 环境 ❑ *Schumacher adapted effortlessly to his new surroundings.* 舒马赫毫不费力地适应了他的新环境。

sur·tax /sɜ̲rtæks/ N-UNCOUNT **Surtax** is an additional tax on incomes higher than the level at which ordinary tax is paid. 附加税 [BUSINESS] ❑ *...a 10% surtax for Americans earning more than $250,000 a year.* …对年收入超过$250000的美国人征收的10%附加税。

Word Link	*sur ≈ above : surcharge, surface, surveillance*

▲ **sur·veil·lance** /sərve̲ɪləns/ N-UNCOUNT **Surveillance** is the careful watching of someone, especially by an organization such as the police or the army. 监视 ❑ *He was arrested after being kept under constant surveillance.* 他在被连续监视之后给逮捕了。 ❑ *Police swooped on the home after a two-week surveillance operation.* 警方经过两周的监视行动后突击搜查了该住宅。

sur·vey ♦♦◇ (surveys, surveying, surveyed)

> The noun is pronounced /sɜ̲rveɪ/. The verb is pronounced /sərve̲ɪ/, and can also be pronounced /sɜ̲rveɪ/ in meanings **2** and **5**.

> 名词读作 /sɜ̲rveɪ/。动词读作 /sərve̲ɪ/，在义项**2**和**5**中亦可读作 /sɜ̲rveɪ/。

1 N-COUNT If you carry out a **survey**, you try to find out detailed information about a lot of different people or things, usually by asking people a series of questions. 调查 ❑ *The council conducted a survey of the uses to which farm buildings are put.* 该委员会对农场建筑的用途进行了一个调查。 **2** V-T If you **survey** a number of people, companies, or organizations, you try to find out information about their opinions or behavior, usually by asking them a series of questions. 调查 ❑ *Business Development Advisers surveyed 211 companies for the report.* 企业发展顾问为这份报告调查了211家公司。 **3** V-T If you **survey** something, you look at or consider the whole of it carefully. 审视 ❑ *He pushed himself to his feet and surveyed the room.* 他站起来审视这个房间。 **4** N-COUNT If someone carries out a **survey** of an area of land, they examine it and measure it, usually in order to make a map of it. 勘测 ❑ *...the organizer of the geological survey of India.* …印度地质勘测的组织者。 **5** V-T If someone **surveys** an area of land, they examine it and measure it, usually in order to make a map of it. 勘测 ❑ *The city council commissioned geological experts earlier this year to survey the cliffs.* 该市议会今年早些时候委托地质专家们对这些悬崖进行勘测。 **6** N-COUNT A **survey** is a careful examination of the condition and structure of a house, usually carried out in order to give information to a person who wants to buy it. (对房屋的) 鉴定 [mainly BRIT] **7** V-T If someone **surveys** a house, they examine it carefully and report on its structure, usually in order to give advice to a person who is thinking of buying it. 鉴定 (房屋) [mainly BRIT]
→ see **census**

sur·vey·or /sərve̲ɪər/ (surveyors) **1** N-COUNT A **surveyor** is a person whose job is to survey land. (土地的) 测量员 ❑ *...the surveyor's maps of the Queen Alexandra Range.* …亚历山德拉皇后山脉勘测图。 **2** N-COUNT A **surveyor** is a person whose job is to survey buildings. (建筑物的) 鉴定人 [BRIT]

> in AM, use **structural engineer**

sur·viv·al ♦◇◇ /sərva̲ɪvəl/ **1** N-UNCOUNT If you refer to the **survival** of something or someone, you mean that they manage to continue or exist in spite of difficult circumstances. (在困境中的) 生存 ❑ *...companies which have been struggling for survival in the advancing recession.* …在不断恶化的萧条期中一直挣扎求生的各家公司。 **2** N-UNCOUNT If you refer to the **survival** of a person or living thing, you mean that they live through a dangerous situation in which it was possible that they might die. 存活 ❑ *If cancers are spotted early there's a high chance of survival.* 如果癌症早被发现，存活的机率就高。

Word Link	*viv ≈ living : revival, survive, vivacious*

sur·vive ♦♦◇ /sərva̲ɪv/ (survives, surviving, survived) **1** V-T/V-I If a person or living thing **survives** in a dangerous situation such as an accident or an illness, they do not die. 存活 ❑ *...the sequence of events that left the eight pupils battling to survive in icy seas for over four hours.* …使4名小学生在冰冷的海洋中挣扎求生超过4个小时的一连串事件。 ❑ *Those organisms that are most suited to the environment will be those that will survive.* 那些最适应环境的生物将是那些存活下来的。 ❑ *He had survived heart bypass surgery.* 他在心脏搭桥手术中活了下来。 **2** V-T/V-I If you **survive** in difficult circumstances, you manage to live or continue in spite of them and do not let them affect you very much. 挺过 ❑ *On my first day here I thought, "Ooh, how will I survive?"* 在这儿的第一天我想："噢，我该怎么挺过去呀？" ❑ *...people who are struggling to survive without jobs.* …挣扎着以挺过失业的人们。 **3** V-T/V-I If something **survives**, it continues to exist even after being in a dangerous situation or existing for a long time. 幸存 ❑ *When the market economy is introduced, many factories will not survive.* 一旦推行市场经济，很多工厂将无法存活下去。 ❑ *No one survived the crash.* 无人在这次撞击中幸免于难。 **4** V-T If you **survive** someone, you continue to live after they have died. 比…活得长 ❑ *Most women will survive their spouses.* 大多数女性比她们的配偶活得长。

sur·vi·vor /sərva̲ɪvər/ (survivors) **1** N-COUNT A **survivor of** a disaster, accident, or illness is someone who continues to live afterward in spite of coming close to death. 幸存者 ❑ *Officials said there were no survivors of the plane crash.* 官员们说这次飞机失事中没有幸存者。 **2** N-COUNT A **survivor of** a very unpleasant experience is a person who has had such an experience, and who is still affected by it. 经受过不幸的人 ❑ *This book is written with survivors of child sexual abuse in mind.* 这本书写的是关于童年时经受过性虐待的人。 **3** N-COUNT A person's **survivors** are the members of their family who continue to live after they have died. (家中) 尚活着的人 [AM] ❑ *The compensation bill offers the miners or their survivors as much as $100,000 apiece.* 这笔赔偿款提供给这些矿工或其尚活着的家人每人$100000。

★ **sus·cep·tible** /səse̲ptɪbəl/ **1** ADJ If you are **susceptible to** something or someone, you are very likely to be influenced by them. 易受…影响的 [v-link ADJ "to" n] ❑ *Young people are the most susceptible to advertisements.* 年轻人最容易受广告影响。 ❑ *James was extremely susceptible to flattery.* 詹姆斯非常容易受奉承话的影响。 **2** ADJ If you are **susceptible to** a disease or injury, you are very likely to be affected by it. 易受 (伤) 的；易患 (病) 的 ❑ *Walking with weights makes the shoulders very susceptible to injury.* 负重行走使肩膀很容易受伤。

sus·pect ♦♦◇ (suspects, suspecting, suspected)

> The verb is pronounced /səspe̲kt/. The noun and adjective are pronounced /sʌ̲spekt/.

> 动词读作 /səspe̲kt/。名词和形容词读作 /sʌ̲spekt/。

1 V-T You use **suspect** when you are stating something that you believe is probably true, in order to make it sound less strong or direct. 觉得 [VAGUENESS] ❑ *I suspect they were right.* 我觉得他们是正确的。 ❑ *The above complaints are, I suspect, just the tip of the iceberg.*

S

上述的这些抱怨，我觉得，不过是冰山的一角。 2 V-T If you **suspect** that something dishonest or unpleasant has been done, you believe that it has probably been done. If you **suspect** someone **of** doing an action of this kind, you believe that they probably did it. 怀疑 ❑ *He suspected that the woman staying in the flat above was using heroin.* 他怀疑住在楼上公寓里的那位女子在吸食海洛因。 ❑ *It was perfectly all right, he said, because the police had not suspected him of anything.* 一点儿没事，他说，因为警察对他没有任何怀疑。 3 N-COUNT A **suspect** is a person who the police or authorities think may be guilty of a crime. 嫌疑犯 ❑ *Police have arrested a suspect in a series of killings and sexual assaults in the city.* 警方逮捕了该城市一系列杀人强奸案件中的一名嫌疑犯。 4 ADJ **Suspect** things or people are ones that you think may be dangerous or may be less good or genuine than they appear. 可疑的 ❑ *Delegates evacuated the building when a suspect package was found.* 一个可疑包裹被发现后，代表们撤离了这栋大楼。

sus·pend ♦◇◇ /səspɛnd/ (**suspends, suspending, suspended**) 1 V-T If you **suspend** something, you delay it or stop it from happening for a while or until a decision is made about it. 暂停 ❑ *The union suspended strike action this week.* 工会本周暂停了罢工行动。 2 V-T If someone **is suspended**, they are prevented from holding a particular job or position for a fixed length of time or until a decision is made about them. 使停职 ❑ *Julie was suspended from her job shortly after the incident.* 该事件发生后不久，朱莉被停职了。 3 V-T If something **is suspended** from a high place, it is hanging from that place. 悬挂 [usu passive] ❑ *...instruments that are suspended on cables.* …悬挂在电缆上的仪器。

sus·pend·er /səspɛndər/ (**suspenders**) 1 N-PLURAL **Suspenders** are a pair of straps that go over someone's shoulders and are fastened to their pants at the front and back to prevent the pants from falling down. 吊裤带 [also "a" "pair" "of" N] [AM]

in BRIT, use **braces**

❑ *He also wore a pair of suspenders.* 他也穿着吊带裤。 2 [BRIT] → see **garter 1**

▲ **sus·pense** /səspɛns/ 1 N-UNCOUNT **Suspense** is a state of excitement or anxiety about something that is going to happen very soon, for example about some news that you are waiting to hear. 悬念 ❑ *The suspense over the two remaining hostages ended last night when the police discovered the bullet ridden bodies.* 有关剩下两名人质的悬念在昨晚警方发现布满弹孔的尸体后结束了。 2 PHRASE If you **keep** or **leave** someone **in suspense**, you deliberately delay telling them something that they are very eager to know about. 让某人心悬着 ❑ *Keppler kept all his men in suspense until that morning before announcing which two would be going.* 科普勒直到那天早上宣布哪两个人要走之前让他所有的手下心悬在空中。

★ **sus·pen·sion** /səspɛnʃ^ən/ (**suspensions**) 1 N-UNCOUNT The **suspension** of something is the act of delaying or stopping it for a while or until a decision is made about it. 延缓; 暂停 ❑ *There's been a temporary suspension of flights out of LA.* 从洛杉矶起飞的飞机已经暂停。 2 N-VAR Someone's **suspension** is their removal from a job or position for a period of time or until a decision is made about them. 停职 ❑ *The minister warned that any civil servant not at his desk faced immediate suspension.* 那位部长警告说任何擅自离岗的公务员面临着立即停职。 3 N-VAR A vehicle's **suspension** consists of the springs and other devices attached to the wheels, which give a smooth ride over uneven ground. (车辆减震的) 悬架 ❑ *...the only small car with independent front suspension.* …惟一的一辆带有独立前悬架的小汽车。

→ see **bridge**

sus·pi·cion ♦◇◇ /səspɪʃ^ən/ (**suspicions**) 1 N-VAR **Suspicion** or a **suspicion** is a belief or feeling that someone has committed a crime or done something wrong. 怀疑 ❑ *There was a suspicion that this runner attempted to avoid the procedures for drug testing.* 存在这名赛跑运动员试图逃避药检的怀疑。 ❑ *The police said their suspicions were aroused because Mr. Owens had other marks on his body.* 警方说他们的怀疑产生于欧文斯先生身上留有其他印迹。 2 N-VAR If there is **suspicion of** someone or something, people do not trust them or consider them to be reliable. 猜疑 ❑ *This tendency in his thought is deepened by his suspicion of all Utopian political programs.* 他思想中这种倾向因他对所有乌托邦政治计划的猜疑而加深。 3 N-COUNT A **suspicion** is a feeling that something is probably true or is likely to happen. 不确定的感觉 ❑ *I have a sneaking suspicion that they are going to succeed.* 我有种隐约的感觉他们会成功。

Word Partnership *suspicion* 的常用搭配：

V.	**arouse** suspicion 1
	view *someone/something* **with** suspicion 2
ADJ.	**sneaking** suspicion 3

★ **sus·pi·cious** /səspɪʃəs/ 1 ADJ If you are **suspicious of** someone or something, you do not trust them, and are careful when dealing with them. 怀疑的 ❑ *He was rightly suspicious of meeting me until I reassured him I was not writing about him.* 他对于见我充满疑虑，直到我向他再次保证我不是在写有关他的东西。 ❑ *He has his father's suspicious nature.* 他有他父亲爱怀疑的脾气。 ● **sus·pi·cious·ly** ADJ 怀疑地 [ADV after v] ❑ *"What is it you want me to do?" Adams asked suspiciously.* "你要我去干的是什么？"亚当斯怀疑地问道。 2 ADJ If you are **suspicious of** someone or something, you believe that they are probably involved in a crime or some dishonest activity. 起疑心的 ❑ *Two officers on patrol became suspicious of two men in a car.* 两位巡警对一辆小汽车内的两名男子起了疑心。 3 ADJ If you describe someone or something as **suspicious**, you mean that there is some aspect of them which makes you think that they are involved in a crime or a dishonest activity. 可疑的 ❑ *He reported that two suspicious-looking characters had approached Callendar.* 他报告说两名看似可疑的人曾靠近过卡兰德。 ● **sus·pi·cious·ly** ADV 可疑地 ❑ *They'll question them as to whether anyone was seen acting suspiciously in the area over the last few days.* 他们将询问这些人过去几天是否在该地区发现行迹可疑的人。

Do not confuse **suspicious, doubtful,** and **dubious.** If you are **suspicious** of a person, you do not trust them and think they might be involved in something dishonest or illegal. ❑ *I am suspicious of his intentions. ...Miss Lenaut had grown suspicious.* If you describe something as **suspicious**, it suggests behavior that is dishonest, illegal, or dangerous. ❑ *He listened for any suspicious sounds. ...in suspicious circumstances.* If you feel **doubtful** about something, you are unsure about it or about whether it will happen or be successful. ❑ *Do you feel insecure and doubtful about your ability?... It was doubtful he would ever see her again.* If you are **dubious** about something, you are not sure whether it is the right thing to do. ❑ *Alison sounded very dubious. ...The men in charge were a bit dubious about taking him on.* If you describe something as **dubious**, you think it is not completely honest, safe, or reliable. ❑ *...his dubious abilities as a teacher.*

sus·pi·cious·ly /səspɪʃəsli/ 1 ADV If you say that one thing looks or sounds **suspiciously** like another thing, you mean that it probably is that thing, or something very similar to it, although it may be intended to seem different. 非常(像) [ADV prep] ❑ *The tan-colored dog looks suspiciously like a pit bull terrier.* 这条棕褐色的狗看起来很像比特犬。 2 ADV You can use **suspiciously** when you are describing something that you think is slightly strange or not as it should be. 出奇地 [ADV adj/adv] ❑ *He lives alone in a suspiciously tidy apartment.* 他独自一人住在一套整洁得出奇的公寓里。 3 → see also **suspicious**

sus·tain ♦◇◇ /səsteɪn/ (**sustains, sustaining, sustained**) 1 V-T If you **sustain** something, you continue it or maintain it for a period of time. 保持 ❑ *He has sustained his fierce social conscience from young adulthood through old age.* 他从青年时代到晚年一直保持着强烈的社会良知。 ❑ *Recovery can't be sustained unless more jobs are created.* 除非有更多的工作机会被创造出来，否则复苏无法保持下去。 2 V-T If you **sustain** something such as a defeat, loss, or injury, it happens to you. 遭受 [FORMAL] ❑ *Every aircraft in there has sustained some damage.* 那里的每架飞机都遭到了一些损坏。 3 V-T If something **sustains** you, it supports you by giving you help, strength, or encouragement. 支撑 [FORMAL] ❑ *The cash dividends they get from the cash crop would sustain them during the lean season.* 他们从经济作物中得到的那些现金红利能支撑他们度过歉收季节。

sus·tain·able /səsteɪnəb^əl/ 1 ADJ You use **sustainable** to describe the use of natural resources when this use is kept at a steady level that is not likely to damage the environment. 可持续的 ❑ *...the management, conservation and sustainable development of forests.* …森林的管理、保护和可持续发展。 ● **sus·tain·abil·ity** /səsteɪnəbɪlɪti/ N-UNCOUNT 可持续性 ❑ *...the issue of long-term environmental sustainability.* …长期的环境可持续性问题。 2 ADJ A **sustainable** plan, method, or system is designed to continue at the same rate or level of activity without any problems. 可持续的 ❑ *The creation of an efficient and sustainable transport system*

S

is critical. 一个高效而可持续发展的交通系统的创建是非常重要的。
● **sus·tain·abil·ity** N-UNCOUNT 可持续性 ❑ *...unease about the sustainability of the American economic recovery.* …对于美国经济复苏的可持续性的担心。

SUV /ɛs yu vi/ (**SUVs**) N-COUNT An **SUV** is a powerful vehicle with four-wheel drive that can be driven over rough ground. **SUV** is an abbreviation for **sport utility vehicle**. 运动型多功能汽车
→ see **car**

swab /swɒb/ (**swabs**) N-COUNT A **swab** is a small piece of cotton used by a doctor or nurse for cleaning a wound or putting a substance on it. 棉签 ❑ *"Okay," he replied and winced as she dabbed the cotton swab over the gash.* 当她用棉签轻擦他的伤口时，他应了一声"行了"，还躲了一下。

swag·ger /swæɡər/ (**swaggers, swaggering, swaggered**) V-I If you **swagger**, you walk in a very proud, confident way, holding your body upright and swinging your hips. 大摇大摆地走 ❑ *A broad shouldered man wearing a dinner jacket swaggered confidently up to the bar.* 一个穿晚礼服上装的宽肩男子大摇大摆自信地走向那个酒吧。● N-SING **Swagger** is also a noun. 大摇大摆 ❑ *He walked with something of a swagger.* 他有点大摇大摆地走着。

swal·low /swɒloʊ/ (**swallows, swallowing, swallowed**)
1 V-T/V-I If you **swallow** something, you cause it to go from your mouth down into your stomach. 吞咽 ❑ *You are asked to swallow a capsule containing vitamin B.* 你被要求吞下一颗含维生素B的胶囊。❑ *Polly took a bite of the apple, chewed, and swallowed.* 波莉咬了一口那个苹果，嚼了嚼吞了下去。● N-COUNT **Swallow** is also a noun. 吞咽 ❑ *Jan lifted her glass and took a quick swallow.* 简举起杯子，迅速咽了一口。**2** V-I If you **swallow**, you make a movement in your throat as if you are swallowing something, often because you are nervous or frightened. (常因紧张或害怕而) 做吞咽动作 ❑ *Nancy swallowed hard and shook her head.* 南希艰难地咽了一下口水，摇了摇她的头。**3** V-T If someone **swallows** a story or a statement, they believe it completely. 完全相信 ❑ *They cast doubt on his words when it suited their case, but swallowed them whole when it did not.* 他的话与他们的情况吻合时他们就怀疑，但不吻合时他们却完全相信。**4** N-COUNT A **swallow** is a kind of small bird with pointed wings and a forked tail. 燕子 **5** **a bitter pill to swallow** → see **pill**
▸ **swallow up** **1** PHRASAL VERB If one thing **is swallowed up** by another, it becomes part of the first thing and no longer has a separate identity of its own. 吞并 ❑ *During the 1980s monster publishing houses started to swallow up smaller companies.* 20世纪80年代期间，巨型的出版公司开始吞并较小的公司。**2** PHRASAL VERB If something **swallows up** money or resources, it uses them entirely while giving very little in return. 用光 (金钱或资源) ❑ *A seven-day TV ad campaign could swallow up the best part of $100,000.* 7天的电视广告宣传能把$100000基本用光。

swam /swæm/ **Swam** is the past tense of **swim**. **swim**的过去式

★ **swamp** /swɒmp/ (**swamps, swamping, swamped**) **1** N-VAR A **swamp** is an area of very wet land with wild plants growing in it. 沼泽地 ❑ *I spent one whole night by a swamp behind the road listening to frogs.* 我整个晚上都在这条路后面的一个沼泽地旁听蛙鸣。**2** V-T If something **swamps** a place or object, it fills it with water. 淹没 ❑ *Their electronic navigation failed and a rogue wave swamped the boat.* 他们的电子导航装置失灵了，一个巨浪吞没了那只船。**3** V-T If you **are swamped** by things or people, you have more of them than you can deal with. 使应接不暇 [usu passive] ❑ *He is swamped with work.* 他工作正忙得不可开交。
→ see **wetland**

swan /swɒn/ (**swans**) N-COUNT A **swan** is a large bird with a very long neck. Swans live on rivers and lakes and are usually white. 天鹅

★ **swap** /swɒp/ (**swaps, swapping, swapped**)
in BRIT, also use **swop**
1 V-RECIP If you **swap** something with someone, you give it to them and receive a different thing in exchange. 交换 ❑ *Next week they will swap places and will repeat the switch weekly.* 下周他们将互换位置，以后将每周换一次。❑ *I know a sculptor who swaps her pieces for drawings by a well-known artist.* 我知道有个雕塑家用她自己的作品去换一位著名画家的画作。● N-COUNT **Swap** is also a noun. 交换 ❑ *Over the long term, a swap of some kind is clearly in the public interest.* 从长远看，有点交换显然是为了公共利益。**2** V-T If you **swap** one thing **for** another, you remove the first thing and replace it with the second, or you stop doing the first thing and start doing the second. 调换 ❑ *Despite the heat, he'd swapped his overalls for a suit and tie.* 尽管天气炎热，他还是把他的工装裤换成了西装和领带。❑ *He has swapped his hectic rock star's lifestyle for that of a country gentleman.* 他已放弃紧张忙碌的摇滚明星的生活，改做乡村绅士。

Word Partnership	*swap* 的常用搭配:
N.	**debt** swap, **interest rate** swap, **stock** swap **1**

▲ **swarm** /swɔrm/ (**swarms, swarming, swarmed**)
1 N-COUNT-COLL A **swarm of** bees or other insects is a large group of them flying together. 大群 (蜜蜂等昆虫) ❑ *...a swarm of locusts.* …一大群蝗虫。**2** V-I When bees or other insects **swarm**, they move or fly in a large group. (蜜蜂或其他昆虫) 大群移动 ❑ *A dark cloud of bees comes swarming out of the hive.* 黑压压的一大群蜜蜂从那座蜂巢涌过来。**3** V-I When people **swarm** somewhere, they move there quickly in a large group. (人群) 涌往 ❑ *People swarmed to the stores, buying up everything in sight.* 人们成群地涌到商场，看到什么就买什么。**4** N-COUNT-COLL A **swarm of** people is a large group of them moving about quickly. (快速移动的) 一大群 ❑ *A swarm of people encircled the hotel.* 一大群人包围了这家酒店。**5** V-I If a place **is swarming with** people, it is full of people moving about in a busy way. 挤满 [usu cont] ❑ *Within minutes the area was swarming with officers who began searching a nearby wood.* 几分钟之内这个地方挤满了警官，他们开始搜查附近的一片树林。

swat /swɒt/ (**swats, swatting, swatted**) V-T If you **swat** something such as an insect, you hit it with a quick, swinging movement, using your hand or a flat object. 拍打 ❑ *Hundreds of flies buzz around us, and the workman keeps swatting them.* 数百只苍蝇围着我们嗡嗡转，这位工人则在不停地拍打它们。

sway /sweɪ/ (**sways, swaying, swayed**) **1** V-I When people or things **sway**, they lean or swing slowly from one side to the other. 摇摆 ❑ *The people swayed back and forth with arms linked.* 人们手拉手前后摇摆着。❑ *The whole boat swayed and tipped.* 整条船摇晃着，然后翻了。**2** V-T If you **are swayed by** someone or something, you are influenced by them. 影响 ❑ *Don't ever be swayed by fashion.* 不要受时尚的影响。**3** PHRASE If someone or something **holds sway**, they have great power or influence over a particular place or activity. 统治 ❑ *Powerful traditional chiefs hold sway over more than 15 million people in rural areas.* 有权势的传统首领们统治着乡村地区的1500万人。

swear /swɛər/ (**swears, swearing, swore, sworn**) **1** V-I If someone **swears**, they use language that is considered to be vulgar or offensive, usually because they are angry. 咒骂 ❑ *It's wrong to swear and shout.* 骂人和喊叫是不对的。**2** V-T If you **swear to** do something, you promise in a serious way that you will do it. 郑重许诺 ❑ *Alan swore that he would do everything in his power to help us.* 艾伦郑重许诺他会尽其所能帮助我们。❑ *We have sworn to fight cruelty wherever we find it.* 我们已郑重许诺，无论在哪儿发现暴行我们都要与其斗争。**3** V-T/V-I If you say that you **swear** that something is true or that you can **swear** to it, you are saying very firmly that it is true. 发誓 [EMPHASIS] ❑ *I swear I've told you all I know.* 我发誓我已经把我所知道的都告诉你了。❑ *I swear on all I hold dear that I had nothing to do with this.* 我拿我所在乎的一切发誓我与这件事情无关。**4** V-T If someone **is sworn to** secrecy or **is sworn to** silence, they promise another person that they will not reveal a secret. 使承诺 (保密) [usu passive] ❑ *She was bursting to announce the news but was sworn to secrecy.* 她忍不住想要发布这条消息，但发过誓要保密。**5** → see also **sworn**
▸ **swear by** PHRASAL VERB If you **swear by** something, you believe that it can be relied on to have a particular effect. 信赖 (某物的效用) [INFORMAL] ❑ *Many people swear by vitamin C's ability to ward off colds.* 很多人深信维生素C能预防感冒。
▸ **swear in** PHRASAL VERB When someone **is sworn in**, they formally promise to fulfill the duties of a new job or appointment. 使宣誓就职 ❑ *Mary Robinson was formally sworn in as Ireland's first woman president.* 玛丽·鲁宾逊正式宣誓就职爱尔兰的首任女总统。

Word Partnership	*swear* 的常用搭配:
N.	swear **words** **1**
	swear **allegiance**, swear **an oath** **2**
ADV.	**solemnly** swear **3**

sweat /swɛt/ (**sweats, sweating, sweated**) **1** N-UNCOUNT **Sweat** is the salty colorless liquid which comes through your skin when you are hot, sick, or afraid. 汗 ❑ *Both horse and rider were dripping with sweat within five minutes.* 马和骑手不到5分钟都大汗淋漓。

Word Web sweat

Vigorous physical activity and unpleasant emotions cause **sweat**. Scientists call it **perspiration**. Tiny **glands** under the skin produce sweat which exits through pores in the epidermis. This liquid then **evaporates** from the surface of the skin and cools the body off. A person living in a cool climate can produce only about a liter of sweat per hour. However, that total can rise to three liters if the person moves to a hot climate. Excess sweating causes **dehydration**. The body must maintain a balance of certain **salts** and water. Perspiration removes large quantities of both from the body.

2 V-I When you **sweat**, sweat comes through your skin. 出汗 ❑ *Already they were sweating as the sun beat down upon them.* 太阳照在他们身上时，他们已经在冒汗了。 ● **sweat·ing** N-UNCOUNT 出汗 ❑ *...symptoms such as sweating, irritability, anxiety, and depression.* …如出汗、易怒、焦虑和抑郁等症状。 3 N-COUNT If someone is **in a sweat**, they are sweating a lot. 满身汗 ❑ *Every morning I would break out in a sweat.* 每天早上我都会突然满身大汗。 ❑ *Cool down very gradually after working up a sweat.* 大量出汗后要慢慢地凉下来。 4 PHRASE If someone is **in a cold sweat** or **in a sweat**, they feel frightened or embarrassed. (害怕或尴尬时) 出冷汗 ❑ *The very thought brought me out in a cold sweat.* 这个念头让我出了一身冷汗。 → see Word Web: sweat

sweat·er /swɛ̲tər/ (**sweaters**) N-COUNT A **sweater** is a warm knitted piece of clothing which covers the upper part of your body and your arms. 毛线衫 → see **clothing**

sweat·shirt /swɛ̲tʃɜrt/ (**sweatshirts**) also **sweat shirt** N-COUNT A **sweatshirt** is a loose warm piece of casual clothing, usually made of thick stretchy cotton, which covers the upper part of your body and your arms. 运动衫 → see **clothing**

sweat·suit /swɛ̲tsut/ (**sweatsuits**) also **sweat suit** N-COUNT A **sweatsuit** is a loose, warm, stretchy suit consisting of long pants and a top which people wear to relax and do exercise. 运动服 [AM] → see **clothing**

sweaty /swɛ̲ti/ (**sweatier, sweatiest**) 1 ADJ If parts of your body or your clothes are **sweaty**, they are soaked or covered with sweat. 出汗的 ❑ *...sweaty hands.* …汗津津的手。 2 ADJ A **sweaty** place or activity makes you sweat because it is hot or tiring. 使出汗的 ❑ *...a sweaty nightclub.* …一个热得让人出汗的夜总会。

sweep ♦◇◇ /swi̲p/ (**sweeps, sweeping, swept**) 1 V-T/V-I If you **sweep** an area of floor or ground, you push dirt or garbage off it using a brush with a long handle. 打扫 ❑ *The owner of the store was sweeping his floor when I walked in.* 当我走进来时，那个店的店主正在扫地板。 ❑ *She was in the kitchen sweeping crumbs into a dust pan.* 她在厨房里正把面包屑扫到一个簸箕里。 2 V-T If you **sweep** things off something, you push them off with a quick smooth movement of your arm. 拂去 ❑ *I swept rainwater off the flat top of a gravestone.* 我拂去一块墓碑平顶上的雨水。 ❑ *With a gesture of frustration, she swept the cards from the table.* 她沮丧地把桌上的那张卡片拂开。 3 V-T If someone with long hair **sweeps** their hair into a particular style, they put it into that style. 梳(头发) ❑ *...stylish ways of sweeping your hair off your face.* …把头发梳开不挡住脸的时髦发式。 4 V-T/V-I If your arm or hand **sweeps** in a particular direction, or if you **sweep** it there, it moves quickly and smoothly in that direction. 挥动 ❑ *His arm swept around the room.* 他的手臂向房间来回挥动。 ❑ *Daniels swept his arm over his friend's shoulder.* 丹尼尔斯一把将手臂搭在他朋友的肩上。 ● N-COUNT **Sweep** is also a noun. 挥动 ❑ *With one sweep of her hand she threw back the sheets.* 她手一挥把那些床单扔了回来。 5 V-T If wind, a stormy sea, or another strong force **sweeps** someone or something along, it moves them quickly along. (风、海浪等) 卷走 ❑ *...landslides that buried homes and swept cars into the sea.* …掩埋了住宅并把汽车卷入海里的山体滑坡。 6 V-T If you **are swept** somewhere, you are taken there very quickly. 快速地带到 ❑ *The visitors were swept past various monuments.* 那些游客们被快速地带着游览了各种纪念碑。 7 V-I If something **sweeps** from one place to another, it moves there extremely quickly. 极快速地移动 [WRITTEN] ❑ *An icy wind swept through the streets.* 一阵寒风扫过那些街道。 8 V-T/V-I If events, ideas, or beliefs **sweep** through a place or **sweep** a place, they spread quickly through it. 使迅速传播；迅速传播 ❑ *A flu epidemic is sweeping through Moscow.* 一场流感正在莫斯科迅速传播。 9 V-T/V-I If a person or group **sweeps** an election or **sweeps to** victory, they win the election easily. 轻松赢得 ❑ *...a man who's promised to make radical changes to benefit the poor has swept the election.* …一个承诺过要进行彻底的变革以造福穷人的男子已轻松赢得该选举。 10 N-COUNT If someone makes a **sweep of** a place, they search it, usually because they are looking for people who are hiding or for an illegal activity. 搜查 ❑ *Two of the soldiers swiftly began making a sweep of the premises.* 其中的两名士兵立即开始对该场所进行搜查。 11 → see also **sweeping** 12 PHRASE If someone **sweeps** something bad or wrong **under the carpet**, or if they **sweep** it **under the rug**, they try to prevent people from hearing about it. 试图掩盖某事 ❑ *For a long time this problem has been swept under the carpet.* 很长一段时间这个问题一直被掩盖着。 13 PHRASE If you **make a clean sweep of** something such as a series of games or tournaments, you win them all. 彻底的胜利 ❑ *...the first club to make a clean sweep of all three trophies.* …第1个赢得全部3个奖杯的俱乐部。 14 **to sweep the board** → see **board**

▸ **sweep up** PHRASAL VERB If you **sweep up** rubbish or dirt, you push it together with a brush and then remove it. 扫除干净 ❑ *Get a broom and sweep up that glass will you?* 拿一把扫帚把那些玻璃扫干净，行吗？

Word Partnership *sweep* 的常用搭配:

ADV.	sweep ***someone/something*** **away** 5 6
PREP.	sweep **into *someplace*** 7
	sweep **through *someplace*** 7 8

sweep·ing /swi̲pɪŋ/ 1 ADJ A **sweeping** curve is a long wide curve. 连绵曲折的 [ADJ n] ❑ *...the long sweeping curve of Rio's Guanabara Bay.* …连绵曲折的里约热内卢瓜纳巴拉海湾。 2 ADJ If someone makes a **sweeping** statement or generalization, they make a statement which applies to all things of a particular kind, although they have not considered all the relevant facts carefully. 笼统的 [DISAPPROVAL] ❑ *It is far too early to make sweeping statements about gene therapy.* 对基因疗法进行概括地说明还为时尚早。 3 ADJ **Sweeping** changes are large and very important or significant. (改变) 意义深远的 ❑ *The new government has started to make sweeping changes in the economy.* 新一届政府已经开始在经济领域进行意义深远的变革。 4 → see also **sweep**

sweet ♦◇◇ /swi̲t/ (**sweeter, sweetest, sweets**) 1 ADJ **Sweet** food and drink contains a lot of sugar. 甜的 ❑ *...a mug of sweet tea.* …一杯甜茶。 ❑ *If the sauce seems too sweet, add a dash of red wine vinegar.* 如果酱太甜，就加少许红酒醋。 ● **sweet·ness** N-UNCOUNT 甜味 ❑ *Florida oranges have a natural sweetness.* 佛罗里达柑桔有一种天然的甜味。 2 ADJ A **sweet** smell is a pleasant one, for example the smell of a flower. 芳香的 ❑ *...the sweet smell of her shampoo.* …她的洗发水芳香的味道。 3 ADJ A **sweet** sound is pleasant, smooth, and gentle. 悦耳的 ❑ *Her voice was as soft and sweet as a young girl's.* 她的声音和小女孩的一样温柔悦耳。 ● **sweet·ly** ADV 悦耳地 ❑ *He sang much more sweetly than he has before.* 他唱歌比以前悦耳多了。 4 ADJ If you describe something as **sweet**, you mean that it gives you great pleasure and satisfaction. 令人痛快的 [WRITTEN] ❑ *There are few things quite as sweet as revenge.* 几乎没有什么事情像复仇一样让人痛快。 5 ADJ If you describe someone as **sweet**, you mean that they are pleasant, kind, and gentle toward other people. 温柔的 ❑ *He was a sweet man but when he drank he tended to quarrel.* 他是个温柔的男人，但一喝酒他就爱吵架。 ● **sweet·ly** ADV 温柔地 ❑ *I just smiled sweetly and said no.* 我只是温和地笑了笑，说了声“不”。 6 ADJ If you describe a small person or thing as **sweet**, you mean that they are attractive in a simple or unsophisticated way. (小孩或小东西) 可爱的 [INFORMAL] ❑ *...a sweet little baby girl.* …一个可爱的小女婴。 7 N-PLURAL **Sweets** are foods that have a lot of sugar. 甜食 [AM] ❑ *To maintain her weight, she simply chooses fruits and vegetables over fats and sweets.* 为了保持自己的体重，她选择只吃水果和蔬菜而不吃肥肉和

甜食。 8 N-COUNT **Sweets** are small sweet things such as chocolates and mints. 糖果 [BRIT]

in AM, use **candy**

9 N-VAR A **sweet** is the same as a **dessert**. 餐后甜点 [BRIT] 10 → see also **sweetness** 11 **a sweet tooth** → see **tooth**
→ see **fruit, sugar, taste**

sweet·corn /swiːtkɔrn/ N-UNCOUNT **Sweetcorn** is a long rounded vegetable covered in small yellow seeds. It is part of the maize plant. The seeds themselves can also be referred to as **sweetcorn**. 甜玉米

sweet·en /swiːtᵊn/ (**sweetens, sweetening, sweetened**) 1 V-T If you **sweeten** food or drink, you add sugar, honey, or another sweet substance to it. 使变甜 ❑ *He liberally sweetened his coffee.* 他在咖啡里加了大量的糖。 2 V-T If you **sweeten** something such as an offer or a business deal, you try to make someone want it more by improving it or by increasing the amount you are willing to pay. (通过改善条件或提高价格等) 使(报价或交易等) 更有诱惑力 ❑ *Kalon Group has sweetened its takeover offer for Manders.* 卡隆集团已经在其收购曼德斯的报价上加了些好处。

sweet·en·er /swiːtᵊnər/ (**sweeteners**) 1 N-MASS **Sweetener** is an artificial substance that can be used in drinks instead of sugar. 甜味剂 2 N-COUNT A **sweetener** is something that you give or offer someone in order to persuade them to accept an offer or business deal. (为说服他人而提供的) 有利条件 ❑ *A corporation can buy back its bonds by paying investors the face value (plus a sweetener).* 公司可通过支付投资人债券票面价值 (外加甜头) 来买回自己的债券。

sweet·heart /swiːthɑrt/ (**sweethearts**) 1 N-VOC You call someone **sweetheart** if you are very fond of them. 亲爱的 ❑ *Happy birthday, sweetheart.* 生日快乐，亲爱的。 2 N-COUNT Your **sweetheart** is your boyfriend or your girlfriend. 恋人 [OLD-FASHIONED] ❑ *I married Shurla, my childhood sweetheart.* 我和我青梅竹马的恋人舒拉结了婚。

sweet·ness /swiːtnɪs/ 1 PHRASE If you say that a relationship or situation is not **all sweetness and light**, you mean that it is not as pleasant as it appears to be. (关系) 融洽的 ❑ *It has not all been sweetness and light between him and the mayor.* 他和市长之间的关系并不总是很融洽。 2 → see also **sweet**

swell /swɛl/ (**swells, swelling, swelled, swollen**)

The forms **swelled** and **swollen** are both used as the past participle.

1 V-T/V-I If the amount or size of something **swells** or if something **swells** it, it becomes larger than it was before. 使增大; 增大 ❑ *The human population swelled, at least temporarily, as migrants moved south.* 随着移民们南移，人口便增加了，至少是暂时增加了。 ❑ *His bank balance has swelled by $222,000 in the last three weeks.* 他的银行存款在过去的3周里增加了$222, 000。 2 V-I If something such as a part of your body **swells**, it becomes larger and rounder than normal. (身体部位等) 肿胀 ❑ *Do your ankles swell at night?* 你的脚踝晚上会肿吗？ ● PHRASAL VERB **Swell up** means the same as **swell**. 肿胀 ❑ *When you develop a throat infection or catch a cold the glands in the neck swell up.* 当你咽喉发炎或感冒时，脖子上的腺体会肿起来。 3 → see also **swollen**

swell·ing /swɛlɪŋ/ (**swellings**) N-VAR A **swelling** is a raised, curved shape on the surface of your body which appears as a result of an injury or an illness. (由于受伤或疾病导致的) 肿块 ❑ *His eye was partly closed, and there was a swelling over his lid.* 他一只眼睛半闭着，眼睑上有个肿块。

swel·ter·ing /swɛltərɪŋ/ ADJ If you describe the weather as **sweltering**, you mean that it is extremely hot and makes you feel uncomfortable. 酷热难耐的 ❑ *...the sweltering heat of the St. Petersburg summer.* …圣彼得堡夏季的酷热。

swept /swɛpt/ **Swept** is the past tense and past participle of **sweep**. **sweep** 的过去式和过去分词

▲ **swerve** /swɜrv/ (**swerves, swerving, swerved**) V-T/V-I If a vehicle or other moving thing **swerves** or if you **swerve** it, it suddenly changes direction, often in order to avoid hitting something. 使突然转向; 突然转向 ❑ *Drivers coming in the opposite direction swerved to avoid the bodies.* 从反方向过来的司机们突然转向以避开这些尸体。 ❑ *Her car swerved off the road into a 6 ft high brick wall.* 她的车突然转向冲出道路，撞上一面6英尺高的砖墙。 ● N-COUNT **Swerve** is also a noun. 转向 ❑ *He swung the car to the left and that swerve saved Malone's life.* 他把车猛转向左边，那一转救了马隆的命。

swift /swɪft/ (**swifter, swiftest, swifts**) 1 ADJ A **swift** event or process happens very quickly or without delay. 迅速的 ❑ *Our task is to challenge the U.N. to make a swift decision.* 我们的任务是敦促联合国做出迅速的决定。 ● **swift·ly** ADV 迅速地 ❑ *Wall Street reacted swiftly to yesterday's verdict.* 华尔街对昨天的裁决迅速地做出了反应。 2 ADJ Something that is **swift** moves very quickly. 快速移动的 ❑ *With a swift movement, Matthew Jerrold sat upright.* 马修・杰罗德迅速地坐直了。 ● **swift·ly** ADV 快速移动地 [ADV with v] ❑ *Lenny moved swiftly and silently across the front lawn.* 兰尼快速并且无声地穿过前面的草坪。 3 N-COUNT A **swift** is a small bird with long curved wings. 雨燕

swim ♦◇◇ /swɪm/ (**swims, swimming, swam, swum**) 1 V-T/V-I When you **swim**, you move through water by making movements with your arms and legs. 游泳 ❑ *She learned to swim when she was really tiny.* 她很小就学会了游泳。 ❑ *He was rescued only when an exhausted friend swam ashore.* 当一个精疲力尽的朋友游上岸时，他才得救。 ❑ *I swim a mile a day.* 我每天游一英里。 ● N-SING **Swim** is also a noun. 游泳 ❑ *When can we go for a swim?* 我们什么时候可以去游泳？ 2 V-T If you **swim** a race, you take part in a swimming race. 参加游泳比赛 ❑ *She swam the 400 meters medley.* 她参加了400米混合泳比赛。 3 V-T If you **swim** a stretch of water, you keep swimming until you have crossed it. 游过 (一段水域) ❑ *By the time we reached the other side, Maram vowed that he would never swim a river again.* 我们到河对岸时，马拉姆发誓说他再也不游泳渡河了。 4 V-I When a fish **swims**, it moves through water by moving its body. (鱼) 游水 ❑ *The barriers are lethal to fish trying to swim upstream.* 这些障碍物对于逆流而上的鱼来说是致命的。 5 V-I If your head **is swimming**, you feel unsteady and slightly ill. 头晕 ❑ *The musty aroma of incense made her head swim.* 熏香的霉味令她头晕。 6 **sink or swim** → see **sink**

swim·mer /swɪmər/ (**swimmers**) N-COUNT A **swimmer** is a person who swims, especially for sport or pleasure, or a person who is swimming. 游泳者 ❑ *You don't have to worry about me. I'm a good swimmer.* 你不必替我担心。我是一个游泳健将。

swim·ming /swɪmɪŋ/ N-UNCOUNT **Swimming** is the activity of swimming, especially as a sport or for pleasure. 游泳运动 ❑ *Swimming is probably the best form of exercise you can get.* 游泳可能是你能采取的最佳的锻炼方式。

swim·ming pool (**swimming pools**) N-COUNT A **swimming pool** is a large hole in the ground that has been made and filled with water so that people can swim in it. 游泳池

swim·ming trunks N-PLURAL **Swimming trunks** are the shorts that a man wears when he goes swimming. 男式泳裤 [also "a pair of" N]

swim·suit /swɪmsut/ (**swimsuits**) N-COUNT A **swimsuit** is a piece of clothing that is worn for swimming, especially by women and girls. 女式游泳衣 ❑ *...pictures of models in swimsuits.* …泳装模特的照片。

swin·dle /swɪndᵊl/ (**swindles, swindling, swindled**) V-T If someone **swindles** a person or an organization, they deceive them in order to get something valuable from them, especially money. 诈骗 (尤指钱财) ❑ *A businessman swindled investors out of millions of dollars.* 一位商人骗走了投资者数百万美元。 ● N-COUNT **Swindle** is also a noun. 诈骗 ❑ *He fled to Switzerland rather than face trial for a tax swindle.* 他不去面对骗税的审判而是逃到了瑞士。

swing ♦◇◇ /swɪŋ/ (**swings, swinging, swung**) 1 V-T/V-I If something **swings** or if you **swing** it, it moves repeatedly backward and forward or from side to side from a fixed point. 使摇摆; 摇摆 ❑ *The sail of the little boat swung crazily from one side to the other.* 这艘小船的船帆发疯似地左右摇晃着。 ❑ *She was swinging a bottle of wine by its neck.* 她当时正在握着瓶颈摇晃酒瓶。 ● N-COUNT **Swing** is also a noun. 摇摆 ❑ *...a woman in a tight red dress, walking with a slight swing to her hips.* …一位穿着紧身红色连衣裙、走路时轻扭臀部的女子。 2 V-T/V-I If something **swings** in a particular direction or if you **swing** it in that direction, it moves in that direction with a smooth, curving movement. 转动; 成弧线运动 ❑ *The torchlight swung across the little beach and out over the water, searching.* 手电筒的光旋转掠过这片小海滩，而后越到水面上搜寻着。 ❑ *The canoe found the current and swung around.* 独木舟遇上了急流，打着转。 ● N-COUNT **Swing** is also a noun. 转动 ❑ *When he's not on the tennis court, you'll find him practising his golf swing.* 当他不在网球场时，你会发现他在练高尔夫挥杆动作。 3 V-T/V-I If a vehicle **swings** in a particular direction, or if the driver **swings** it in a particular direction, they turn suddenly in that direction. 使急转向; 转向 ❑ *Joanna swung back on to the main approach and headed for the airport.* 乔安娜把车急转回主干道，

向机场开去。 **4** V-I If someone **swings around**, they turn around quickly, usually because they are surprised. (因惊讶而) 急转身 ❑ *She swung around to him, spilling her tea without noticing it.* 她急转过身来对着他，茶水洒了出来她都没注意到。 **5** V-I If you **swing at** a person or thing, you try to hit them with your arm or with something that you are holding. 击打 ❑ *Blanche swung at her but she moved her head back and Blanche missed.* 布兰奇向她打去，但她把头向后一闪，布兰奇没打中。 ● N-COUNT **Swing** is also a noun. 击打 ❑ *I often want to take a swing at someone to relieve my feelings.* 我老想打谁一顿来发泄我的情绪。 **6** N-COUNT A **swing** is a seat hanging by two ropes or chains from a metal frame or from the branch of a tree. You can sit on the seat and move forward and backward through the air. 秋千 ❑ *Go to the neighborhood park. Run around, push the kids on the swings.* 到附近的公园去吧。跑跑步，帮孩子们推一推秋千。 **7** N-COUNT A **swing** in people's opinions, attitudes, or feelings is a change in them, especially a sudden or big change. (突然的或大的) 改变 ❑ *Educational practice is liable to sudden swings and changes.* 教育实践活动易出现突然的转向和变化。 ❑ *Dieters suffer from violent mood swings.* 节食者们经受剧烈的情绪变化的折磨。 **8** V-I If people's opinions, attitudes, or feelings **swing**, they change, especially in a sudden or extreme way. 改变 ❑ *In two years' time there is a presidential election, and the voters could swing again.* 两年后有一次总统竞选，选民们有可能再次大转向。 **9** PHRASE If something is **in full swing**, it is operating fully and is no longer in its early stages. 正在热烈进行中 ❑ *When we returned, the party was in full swing and the dance floor was crowded.* 我们回来的时候，聚会正开得起劲，舞池里挤满了人。 **10** PHRASE If you **get into the swing of** something, you become very involved in it and enjoy what you are doing. 全力投入 ❑ *Everyone understood how hard it was to get back into the swing of things after such a long absence.* 每个人都明白离开这么长一段时间后要重新全力投入有多难。

Word Partnership *swing* 的常用搭配：

ADJ. **good** swing, **perfect** swing 2
big swing 2 5 7
in full swing 9

N. swing **a bat**, **golf** swing 2
swing **at a ball** 5
porch swing 6
voters swing 8

swipe /swaɪp/ (**swipes, swiping, swiped**) **1** V-I If you **swipe at** a person or thing, you try to hit them with a stick or other object, making a swinging movement with your arm. 抡打 ❑ *She swiped at Rusty as though he was a fly.* 她像在打一只苍蝇一样抡打拉斯蒂。 ● N-COUNT **Swipe** is also a noun. 抡打 ❑ *He took a swipe at Andrew that deposited him on the floor.* 他朝安德鲁一记抡打让他倒在地板上。 **2** V-T If you **swipe** something, you steal it quickly. 扒窃 [INFORMAL] ❑ *She was convicted of swiping more than $5,500 worth of goods from Saks Fifth Avenue.* 她从萨克斯第五大道百货公司扒窃了价值超过$5500的商品而被判有罪。 **3** N-COUNT If you take a **swipe at** a person or an organization, you criticize them, usually in an indirect way. (以间接的方式) 批评 ❑ *Genesis recorded a song which took a swipe at greedy property developers who bought up and demolished people's homes.* 吉尼西丝录制了一首歌曲，对买下并拆毁他人家园的贪婪房地产开发商进行抨击。 **4** V-T If you **swipe** a credit card or swipe card through a machine, you pass it through a narrow space in the machine so that the machine can read information on the card's magnetic strip. 刷 (卡) ❑ *Swipe your card through the phone, then dial.* 在电话机上刷卡，然后拨号。

swipe card (**swipe cards**) also **swipecard** N-COUNT A **swipe card** is a plastic card with a magnetic strip on it which contains information that can be read or transferred by passing the card through a special machine. 磁卡 ❑ *They use a swipe card to go in and out of their offices.* 他们使用磁卡进出办公室。

▲ **swirl** /swɜrl/ (**swirls, swirling, swirled**) V-T/V-I If you **swirl** something liquid or flowing, or if it **swirls**, it moves around and around quickly. 使 (液态、流动的物质) 快速旋流; (液态、流动的物质) 快速旋流 ❑ *She smiled, swirling the wine in her glass.* 她微笑了，旋动着玻璃杯里的葡萄酒。 ❑ *The black water swirled around his legs, reaching almost to his knees.* 黑水在他的双腿周围打转，差不多没到他的膝盖。 ❑ *She swirled the ice-cold liquid around her mouth.* 她含着冰冷的液体在口里打转。 ● N-COUNT **Swirl** is also a noun. 旋涡 ❑ *...small swirls of chocolate cream.* …小块旋涡形的奶油夹心巧克力。

swish /swɪʃ/ (**swishes, swishing, swished**) V-T/V-I If something **swishes** or if you **swish** it, it moves quickly through the air, making a soft sound. 使嗖地快速移动; 嗖地快速移动 ❑ *A car swished by steady and fast heading for the coast.* 一辆汽车又快又稳地嗖地驶过，朝海岸去。 ❑ *He swished his cape around his shoulders.* 他嗖地披上斗篷。 ● N-COUNT **Swish** is also a noun. 嗖嗖声 ❑ *She turned with a swish of her skirt.* 她转过身，裙子窸窣作响。

switch ♦◇◇ /swɪtʃ/ (**switches, switching, switched**) **1** N-COUNT A **switch** is a small control for an electrical device which you use to turn the device on or off. 开关 ❑ *Leona put some detergent into the dishwasher, shut the door, and pressed the switch.* 利昂娜在洗碗机里放了些清洁剂，关上门，然后按下开关。 **2** N-PLURAL On a railroad track, the **switches** are the levers and rails at a place where two tracks join or separate. The **switches** enable a train to move from one track to another. 转辙器 [AM]

in BRIT, use **points**

❑ *...a set of railroad tracks – including switches – and a model train.* …一套铁轨——含转辙器——和一个火车模型。 **3** V-T/V-I If you **switch to** something different, for example to a different system, task, or subject of conversation, you change to it from what you were doing or saying before. 转向 ❑ *Estonia is switching to a market economy.* 爱沙尼亚正在向市场经济转变。 ❑ *The law would encourage companies to switch from coal to cleaner fuels.* 法律会鼓励各公司从用煤转向使用更清洁的燃料。 ● N-COUNT **Switch** is also a noun. 转变 [usu with supp] ❑ *The spokesman implicitly condemned the United States policy switch.* 这位发言人含蓄地谴责了美国政策上的转变。 ● PHRASAL VERB **Switch over** means the same as **switch**. 转变 **4** V-T/V-I If you **switch** your attention from one thing **to** another or if your attention **switches**, you stop paying attention to the first thing and start paying attention to the second. 转移 (注意力) ❑ *My mother's interest had switched to my health.* 我母亲的兴趣已转移到我的健康上来了。 **5** V-T If you **switch** two things, you replace one with the other. 调换 ❑ *In half an hour, they'd switched the tags on every cable.* 半个小时内，他们换了每根电缆的标签。

▸ **switch off** **1** PHRASAL VERB If you **switch off** a light or other electrical device, you stop it working by operating a switch. 用开关关闭 ❑ *She switched off the coffee-machine.* 她关掉了咖啡机。 **2** PHRASAL VERB If you **switch off**, you stop paying attention or stop thinking or worrying about something. 不再注意; 不再担忧 [INFORMAL] ❑ *Thankfully, I've learned to switch off and let it go over my head.* 谢天谢地，我已经学会了不再烦恼，把它抛到脑后。

▸ **switch on** PHRASAL VERB If you **switch on** a light or other electrical device, you make it start working by operating a switch. 用开关开启 ❑ *She emptied both their mugs and switched on the electric kettle.* 她倒空了他们俩的杯子，然后打开了电水壶。

Word Partnership *switch* 的常用搭配：

V. **flick a** switch, **flip a** switch, **turn a** switch 1
make a switch 3

N. **ignition** switch, **light** switch, **power** switch 1
switch **sides** 3

switch·board /swɪtʃbɔrd/ (**switchboards**) N-COUNT A **switchboard** is a place in a large office or business where all the telephone calls are connected. 电话总机 ❑ *He asked to be connected to the central switchboard.* 他要求转接到电话总机。

swiv·el /swɪvᵊl/ (**swivels, swiveling** or **swivelling, swiveled** or **swivelled**) V-T/V-I If something **swivels** or if you **swivel** it, it turns around a central point so that it is facing in a different direction. 使旋转; 旋转 ❑ *She swiveled her chair and stared out the window.* 她把椅子转过来，向窗外凝视着。

swol·len /swoʊlᵊn/ **1** ADJ If a part of your body is **swollen**, it is larger and rounder than normal, usually as a result of injury or illness. 肿大的 ❑ *My eyes were so swollen I could hardly see.* 我的眼睛肿得很厉害，几乎看不见东西。 **2** ADJ A **swollen** river has more water in it and flows faster than normal, usually because of heavy rain. 上涨的 ❑ *The river, brown and swollen with rain, was running fast.* 这条河因下雨变成褐色，水位上涨，水流快速地流动。 **3** **Swollen** is the past participle of **swell**. swell的过去分词

swoop /swup/ (**swoops, swooping, swooped**) **1** V-I If police or soldiers **swoop on** a place, they go there suddenly and quickly, usually in order to arrest someone or to attack the place. 突袭 [JOURNALISM] ❑ *The terror ended when armed police swooped on the car.* 当武装警察突袭了这辆汽车时，这起恐怖活动就此结束。 ● N-COUNT

Swoop is also a noun. 突袭 ❑ *Police held 10 suspected illegal immigrants after a swoop on a Mexican truck.* 警方对一辆墨西哥卡车进行了突袭后扣留了10名非法移民嫌疑人。 **2** V-I When a bird or airplane **swoops**, it suddenly moves downwards through the air in a smooth curving movement. 俯冲 ❑ *More than 20 helicopters began swooping in low over the ocean.* 超过二十架直升飞机开始俯冲到贴着海平面。 **3** PHRASE If something is done **in one fell swoop**, it is done on a single occasion or by a single action. 一下子 ❑ *In one fell swoop the bank wiped away the tentative benefits of this policy.* 银行一下子就抹去了该政策带来的初步好处。

swop /swɒp/ [BRIT] → see **swap**

sword /sɔrd/ (**swords**) **1** N-COUNT A **sword** is a weapon with a handle and a long sharp blade. 剑 **2** PHRASE If you **cross swords with** someone, you disagree with them and argue with them about something. 争论 ❑ *...a candidate who's crossed swords with labor by supporting the free-trade pact.* …一位因支持自由贸易协定而与工党争论的候选人。 **3** PHRASE If you say that something is a **double-edged sword**, you mean that it has negative effects as well as positive effects. 双刃剑 ❑ *A person's looks are a double-edged sword. Sometimes it works in your favor, sometimes it works against you.* 一个人的相貌是一把双刃剑。有时它对你有利，有时又对你不利。
→ see **army**

swore /swɔr/ **Swore** is the past tense of **swear**. **swear**的过去式

sworn /swɔrn/ **1** **Sworn** is the past participle of **swear**. **swear**的过去分词 **2** ADJ If you make a **sworn** statement or declaration, you swear that everything that you have said in it is true. 宣过誓的 [ADJ n] ❑ *The allegations against them were made in sworn evidence to the inquiry.* 对他们的指控都是从调查中得到的宣过誓的证词中提出的。 **3** ADJ If two people or two groups of people are **sworn** enemies, they dislike each other very much. 不共戴天的 [ADJ n] ❑ *It somehow seems hardly surprising that Ms. Player is now his sworn enemy.* 看来，普莱耶女士现在成了他不共戴天的仇敌似乎不足为奇了。

swum /swʌm/ **Swum** is the past participle of **swim**. **swim**的过去分词

swung /swʌŋ/ **Swung** is the past tense and past participle of **swing**. **swing**的过去式和过去分词

▲ **syl·la·ble** /sɪləbᵊl/ (**syllables**) N-COUNT A **syllable** is a part of a word that contains a single vowel sound and that is pronounced as a unit. So, for example, "book" has one syllable, and "reading" has two syllables. 音节 ❑ *We children called her Oma, accenting both syllables.* 我们这些孩子叫她**Oma**，两个音节都重读。

syl·la·bus /sɪləbəs/ (**syllabuses**) **1** N-COUNT A **syllabus** is an outline or summary of the subjects to be covered in a course. 教学大纲 [mainly AM] ❑ *The course syllabus consisted mainly of novels by African-American authors, male and female.* 该课程的教学大纲主要包括了非裔美国男女作家的小说。 **2** N-COUNT You can refer to the subjects that are studied in a particular course as the **syllabus**. 课程 [mainly BRIT]

in AM, usually use **curriculum**

S

sym·bol ♦◇◇ /sɪmbᵊl/ (**symbols**) **1** N-COUNT Something that is a **symbol of** a society or an aspect of life seems to represent it because it is very typical of it. 象征 ❑ *To them, the monarchy is the special symbol of nationhood.* 对他们而言，君主政体是国家的特殊象征。 **2** N-COUNT A **symbol of** something such as an idea is a shape or design that is used to represent it. 象征物 ❑ *Later in this same passage Yeats resumes his argument for the Rose as an Irish symbol.* 后来在这同一篇文章里，叶芝再次提到把玫瑰作为爱尔兰象征的观点。 **3** N-COUNT A **symbol for** an item in a calculation or scientific formula is a number, letter, or shape that represents that item. 符号 ❑ *What's the chemical symbol for mercury?* 水银的化学符号是什么？ **4** → see also **sex symbol**
→ see **flag, myth**

sym·bol·ic /sɪmbɒlɪk/ **1** ADJ If you describe an event, action, or procedure as **symbolic**, you mean that it represents an important change, although it has little practical effect. 有象征意义的 ❑ *A lot of Latin-American officials are stressing the symbolic importance of the trip.* 许多拉丁美洲官员正在强调这次旅行在象征意义上的重要性。 ● **sym·boli·cal·ly** /sɪmbɒlɪkli/ ADV 有象征意义地 ❑ *It was a simple enough gesture, but symbolically important.* 这虽是个再简单不过的手势，但却有着重要的象征意义。 **2** ADJ Something that is **symbolic of** a person or thing is regarded or used as a symbol of them. 用作象征的 ❑ *Yellow clothes are worn as symbolic of spring.* 黄色衣服被穿着来象征春天。 ● **sym·boli·cal·ly** ADV 象征性地 [ADV with v] ❑ *Each circle symbolically represents the whole of humanity.* 每个圆圈都象征性地代表全人类。 **3** ADJ **Symbolic** is used to describe things involving or relating to symbols. 符号的 [ADJ n] ❑ *...symbolic representations of landscape.* …地形的符号表征。

sym·bol·ise /sɪmbəlaɪz/ [BRIT] → see **symbolize**

sym·bol·ism /sɪmbəlɪzəm/ **1** N-UNCOUNT **Symbolism** is the use of symbols in order to represent something. 象征手法 ❑ *The scene is so rich in symbolism that any explanation risks spoiling the effect.* 这个场景的象征手法非常丰富，任何解释都可能破坏其效果。 **2** N-UNCOUNT You can refer to the **symbolism** of an event or action when it seems to show something important about a situation. 象征意义 ❑ *The symbolism of every gesture will be of vital importance during the short state visit.* 这次短暂的国事访问中的一举一动都有极其重要的象征意义。

sym·bol·ize /sɪmbəlaɪz/ (**symbolizes, symbolizing, symbolized**)

in BRIT, also use **symbolise**

V-T If one thing **symbolizes** another, it is used or regarded as a symbol of it. 象征 ❑ *The fall of the Berlin Wall symbolized the end of the Cold War between East and West.* 柏林墙的倒塌象征着东西方冷战的结束。
→ see **flag**

★ **sym·met·ri·cal** /sɪmɛtrɪkᵊl/ ADJ If something is **symmetrical**, it has two halves which are exactly the same, except that one half is the mirror image of the other. 对称的 ❑ *...the neat rows of perfectly symmetrical windows.* …一排排整齐的完全对称的窗户。 ● **sym·met·ri·cal·ly** /sɪmɛtrɪkli/ ADV 对称地 [ADV with v] ❑ *The south garden was composed symmetrically.* 南面花园的布局很对称。

★ **sym·me·try** /sɪmɪtri/ (**symmetries**) **1** N-VAR Something that has **symmetry** is symmetrical in shape, design, or structure. 对称 ❑ *...the incredible beauty and symmetry of a snowflake.* …雪花令人难以置信的美丽和对称。 **2** N-UNCOUNT **Symmetry** in a relationship or agreement is the fact of both sides giving and receiving an equal amount. (关系或协议中双方) 平衡; 均等 ❑ *The superpowers pledged to maintain symmetry in their arms shipments.* 这些超级大国承诺要在其武器运载上保持数量相等。

sym·pa·thet·ic /sɪmpəθɛtɪk/ **1** ADJ If you are **sympathetic** to someone who is in a bad situation, you are kind to them and show that you understand their feelings. 同情的 ❑ *She was very sympathetic to the problems of adult students.* 她对成年学生的问题很同情。 ● **sym·pa·theti·cal·ly** /sɪmpəθɛtɪkli/ ADV 同情地 [ADV with v] ❑ *She nodded sympathetically.* 她同情地点了点头。 **2** ADJ If you are **sympathetic to** a proposal or action, you approve of it and are willing to support it. 赞同的 ❑ *Many of these early visitors were sympathetic to the Chinese socialist experiment.* 这些早期访问者中的很多人都赞同中国的社会主义实验。 ● **sym·pa·theti·cal·ly** ADV 赞同地 [ADV with v] ❑ *After a year we will sympathetically consider an application for reinstatement.* 一年以后我们会考虑赞同复职申请。

Do not confuse **sympathetic** and **friendly**. If you have a problem and someone is **sympathetic** or shows a **sympathetic** attitude, they show that they care and would like to help you. ❑ *My boyfriend was very sympathetic.* A person who is **friendly** or has a **friendly** attitude is kind and pleasant and behaves the way a friend would. ❑ *...a friendly woman who offered me a coffee. ...a pleasant, friendly smile.* Note that people sometimes refer to characters in a play or novel who are easy to like as **sympathetic.** ❑ *There were no sympathetic characters in my book.* You usually say that real people are "nice" or "likable."

sym·pa·thise /sɪmpəθaɪz/ [BRIT] → see **sympathize**

sym·pa·this·er /sɪmpəθaɪzəʳ/ [BRIT] → see **sympathizer**

sym·pa·thize /sɪmpəθaɪz/ (**sympathizes, sympathizing, sympathized**)

in BRIT, also use **sympathise**

1 V-I If you **sympathize** with someone who is in a bad situation, you show that you are sorry for them. 同情 ❑ *I must tell you how much I sympathize with you for your loss, Professor.* 教授，我必须告诉您我对您所受的损失深表同情。 **2** V-I If you **sympathize with** someone's feelings, you understand them and are not critical of them. 理解 ❑ *Some Europeans sympathize with the Americans over the issue.* 一些欧洲人在这个问题上对美国人表示理解。 **3** V-I If you **sympathize with** a proposal or action, you approve of it and are willing to support it. 支持 ❑ *Most of the people living there sympathized with the guerrillas.* 住在那儿的大部分人支持这些游击队员。

sym·pa·thiz·er /sɪmpəθaɪzər/ (**sympathizers**)
in BRIT, also use **sympathiser**
N-COUNT The **sympathizers** of an organization or cause are the people who approve of it and support it. 支持者 ❑ *Safta Hashmi was a well-known playwright and Communist sympathizer.* 萨夫塔·哈什米是一个著名的剧作家和共产主义的支持者。

Word Link *path ≈ feeling : apathy, empathy, sympathy*

Word Link *sym ≈ together : sympathy, symphony, symposium*

sym·pa·thy ♦◇◇ /sɪmpəθi/ (**sympathies**) **1** N-UNCOUNT If you have **sympathy** for someone who is in a bad situation, you are sorry for them, and show this in the way you behave toward them. 同情 [also N in pl] ❑ *We expressed our sympathy for her loss.* 我们对她的损失表示了同情。 ❑ *I have had very little help from doctors and no sympathy whatsoever.* 我从医生那儿得到的帮助极少，而且没得到任何同情。 **2** N-UNCOUNT If you have **sympathy** with someone's ideas or opinions, you agree with them. 赞同 [also N in pl, oft N "with/for" n] ❑ *I have some sympathy with this point of view.* 我对这一观点有些赞同。 ❑ *Lithuania still commands considerable international sympathy for its cause.* 立陶宛仍得到相当多对其事业的国际支持。 **3** N-UNCOUNT If you take some action **in sympathy with** someone else, you do it in order to show that you support them. 支持 ❑ *Several hundred workers struck in sympathy with their colleagues.* 几百名工人举行罢工以示对其工友们的支持。

Word Partnership *sympathy* 的常用搭配:
ADJ. **deep** sympathy, **great** sympathy, **public** sympathy **1**
V. **express** sympathy, **feel** sympathy, **gain** sympathy, **have** sympathy **1 2**

Word Link *phon ≈ sound : microphone, symphony, telephone*

★ **sym·pho·ny** /sɪmfəni/ (**symphonies**) N-COUNT; N-IN-NAMES A **symphony** is a piece of music written to be played by an orchestra. Symphonies are usually made up of four separate sections called movements. 交响乐 ❑ *...Beethoven's Ninth Symphony.* …贝多芬的第九交响曲。
→ see **music, orchestra**

sym·pho·ny or·ches·tra (**symphony orchestras**) N-COUNT; N-IN-NAMES A **symphony orchestra** is a large orchestra that plays classical music. 交响乐团

★ **sym·po·sium** /sɪmpoʊziəm/ (**symposia** /sɪmpoʊziə/ or **symposiums**) N-COUNT A **symposium** is a conference in which experts or academics discuss a particular subject. 专题研讨会 ❑ *He had been taking part in an international symposium on population.* 他那时在参加一个有关人口的国际研讨会。

symp·tom ♦◇◇ /sɪmptəm/ (**symptoms**) **1** N-COUNT A **symptom** of an illness is something wrong with your body or mind that is a sign of the illness. 症状 ❑ *One of the most common symptoms of schizophrenia is hearing imaginary voices.* 精神分裂症最常见的症状之一是幻听。 ❑ *...patients with flu symptoms.* …有流感症状的病人。 **2** N-COUNT A **symptom of** a bad situation is something that happens which is considered to be a sign of this situation. 征兆 ❑ *Your problem with keeping boyfriends is just a symptom of a larger problem: making and keeping friends.* 你无法留住男友的问题只是一个更大的问题的征兆：结交朋友并与其维持关系。
→ see **diagnosis, illness**

symp·to·mat·ic /sɪmptəmætɪk/ ADJ If something is **symptomatic of** something else, especially something bad, it is a sign of it. 作为征兆的 [v-link ADJ] [FORMAL] ❑ *The city's problems are symptomatic of the crisis that is spreading throughout the country.* 这个城市的问题是正在席卷全国的这场危机的征兆。

syna·gogue /sɪnəgɒg/ (**synagogues**) N-COUNT; N-IN-NAMES A **synagogue** is a building where Jewish people meet to worship or to study their religion. 犹太教堂

syn·chro·nise /sɪŋkrənaɪz/ [BRIT] → see **synchronize**

Word Link *chron ≈ time : chronic, chronicle, synchronize*

Word Link *syn ≈ together : synchronize, synergy, synopsis*

syn·chro·nize /sɪŋkrənaɪz/ (**synchronizes, synchronizing, synchronized**)
in BRIT, also use **synchronise**
V-RECIP If you **synchronize** two activities, processes, or movements, or if you **synchronize** one activity, process, or movement **with** another, you cause them to happen at the same time and speed as each other. 使同步 ❑ *It was virtually impossible to synchronize our lives so as to take vacations and weekends together.* 为了一起度假和过周末而要让我们的生活同步几乎是不可能的。 ❑ *Synchronize the score with the film action.* 让配乐和电影动作同步。

▲ **syn·di·cate** /sɪndɪkɪt/ (**syndicates, syndicating, syndicated**) **1** N-COUNT A **syndicate** is an association of people or organizations that is formed for business purposes or in order to carry out a project. 联合组织 ❑ *They formed a syndicate to buy the car in which they competed in the race.* 他们合伙买了参加赛车用的那部车。 ❑ *...a syndicate of 152 banks.* …一个由152家银行组成的联合集团。 **2** V-T When newspaper articles or television programs **are syndicated**, they are sold to several different newspapers or television stations, who then publish the articles or broadcast the programs. (将稿子或电视节目) 出售给多个媒体 [usu passive] ❑ *Today his program is syndicated to 500 stations.* 今天他的节目被出售给500家电台播出。 **3** N-COUNT A press **syndicate** is a group of newspapers or magazines that are all owned by the same person or company. (报业) 辛迪加

★ **syn·drome** /sɪndroʊm/ (**syndromes**) N-COUNT; N-IN-NAMES A **syndrome** is a medical condition that is characterized by a particular group of signs and symptoms. 综合症状 ❑ *Irritable bowel syndrome seems to affect more women than men.* 肠易激综合症对女性比对男性影响更大。

syn·er·gy /sɪnərdʒi/ (**synergies**) N-VAR If there is **synergy** between two or more organizations or groups, they are more successful when they work together than when they work separately. 协同作用 [BUSINESS] ❑ *Of course, there's quite obviously a lot of synergy between the two companies.* 当然，这两家公司之间显然有许多的协同作用。

Word Link *onym ≈ name : acronym, anonymous, synonym*

▲ **syno·nym** /sɪnənɪm/ (**synonyms**) N-COUNT A **synonym** is a word or expression which means the same as another word or expression. 同义词 ❑ *The term "industrial democracy" is often used as a synonym for worker participation.* "工业民主"这一词语常被用作"工人参与"的同义词。

syn·ony·mous /sɪnɒnɪməs/ ADJ If you say that one thing is **synonymous with** another, you mean that the two things are very closely associated with each other so that one suggests the other or one cannot exist without the other. 密不可分的 ❑ *Paris has always been synonymous with elegance, luxury and style.* 巴黎与优雅、华贵和时尚一直是密不可分的。

syn·op·sis /sɪnɒpsɪs/ (**synopses** /sɪnɒpsiz/) N-COUNT A **synopsis** is a summary of a longer piece of writing or work. 提要 ❑ *For each title there is a brief synopsis of the book.* 每本书都附有一个该书的简短提要。

★ **syn·the·sis** /sɪnθɪsɪs/ (**syntheses** /sɪnθɪsiz/) **1** N-COUNT A **synthesis of** different ideas or styles is a mixture or combination of these ideas or styles. 结合体 [FORMAL] ❑ *His novels are a rich synthesis of Balkan history and mythology.* 他的小说是一个巴尔干半岛的历史和神话的丰富结合。 **2** N-VAR The **synthesis** of a substance is the production of it by means of chemical or biological reactions. 合成 [TECHNICAL] ❑ *...the genes that regulate the synthesis of these compounds.* …控制这些化合物合成的基因。

S

syn·the·sise /sɪnθɪsaɪz/ [BRIT] → see **synthesize**

syn·the·sis·er /sɪnθɪsaɪzəʳ/ [BRIT] → see **synthesizer**

syn·the·size /sɪnθɪsaɪz/ (**synthesizes, synthesizing, synthesized**)
in BRIT, also use **synthesise**
1 V-T To **synthesize** a substance means to produce it by means of chemical or biological reactions. 合成 [TECHNICAL] ❑ *After extensive research, Albert Hoffman first succeeded in synthesizing the acid in 1938.* 经过大量研究之后，艾伯特·霍夫曼于1938年首次成功合成了迷幻剂。 **2** V-T If you **synthesize** different ideas, facts, or experiences, you combine them to form a single idea or impression. 综合 [FORMAL] ❑ *The movement synthesized elements of modern art that hadn't been brought together before, such as Cubism and Surrealism.* 这次运动综合了立体派和超现实主义等以前未曾同时出现的现代艺术元素。

syn·the·siz·er /sɪnθɪsaɪzər/ (**synthesizers**)
in BRIT, also use **synthesiser**
N-COUNT A **synthesizer** is an electronic machine that produces

speech, music, or other sounds, usually by combining individual syllables or sounds that have been previously recorded. 音响合成器 ❑ *Now he can only communicate through a voice synthesizer.* 如今他只能通过声音合成器来进行交流。

→ see **keyboard**

syn·thet·ic /sɪnθe̱tɪk/ ADJ **Synthetic** products are made from chemicals or artificial substances rather than from natural ones. 合成的 ❑ *Boots made from synthetic materials can usually be washed in a machine.* 用合成材料做成的靴子通常可以在机器里洗。

sy·phon /saɪfᵊn/ [mainly BRIT] → see **siphon**

sy·ringe /sɪrɪndʒ/ (**syringes**) N-COUNT A **syringe** is a small tube with a thin hollow needle at the end. Syringes are used for putting liquids into things and for taking liquids out, for example for injecting drugs or for taking blood from someone's body. 注射器 ❑ *As he reached over, Azrak slid a hypodermic syringe into his left arm.* 他把手臂伸过来时，阿兹拉克便将皮下注射器刺进他的左臂。

syr·up /sɪrəp, sɜr-/ (**syrups**) **1** N-MASS **Syrup** is a sweet liquid made by cooking sugar with water, and sometimes with fruit juice as well. 糖水 ❑ *...canned fruit with sugary syrup.* …糖水水果罐头。 **2** N-MASS **Syrup** is a medicine in the form of a thick, sweet liquid. 药用糖浆 ❑ *...cough syrup.* …止咳糖浆。

sys·tem ♦♦♦ /sɪstəm/ (**systems**) **1** N-COUNT A **system** is a way of working, organizing, or doing something which follows a fixed plan or set of rules. You can use **system** to refer to an organization or institution that is organized in this way. 体制 ❑ *The present system of funding for higher education is unsatisfactory.* 目前高等教育的经费体制并不令人满意。 ❑ *...a flexible and relatively efficient filing system.* …一个灵活且相对高效的文件归档方法。 **2** N-COUNT A **system** is a set of devices powered by electricity, for example a computer or an alarm. 系统 ❑ *Viruses tend to be good at surviving when a computer system crashes.* 病毒往往在电脑系统瘫痪时仍然存在。 **3** N-COUNT A **system** is a set of equipment or parts such as water pipes or electrical wiring, which is used to supply water, heat, or electricity. (水管或电线等的) 系统 ❑ *...a central heating system.* …一个中央供暖系统。 **4** N-COUNT A **system** is a network of things that are linked together so that people or things can travel from one place to another or communicate. 网络 ❑ *...Australia's road and rail system.* …澳大利亚的公路网和铁路网。 **5** N-COUNT Your **system** is your body's organs and other parts that together perform particular functions. 身体系统 ❑ *He had slept for over fourteen hours, and his system seemed to have recuperated admirably.* 他已睡了超过十四个小时，他的身体系统看起来已经恢复得很好了。 **6** N-COUNT A **system** is a particular set of rules, especially in mathematics or science, which is used to count or measure things. (计算或测量用的) 体系 ❑ *...the decimal system of metric weights and measures.* …公制度量衡的十进制体系。 **7** N-SING People sometimes refer to the government or administration of a country as **the system**. 政府 ❑ *These feelings are likely to make people attempt to overthrow the system.* 这些情绪可能促使人们试着去推翻政府。 **8** → see also **ecosystem, immune system, nervous system, solar system, sound system**

sys·tem·at·ic /sɪstəmæ̱tɪk/ ADJ Something that is done in a **systematic** way is done according to a fixed plan, in a thorough and efficient way. 有计划的 ❑ *They went about their business in a systematic way.* 他们按部就班地做生意。 ● **sys·tem·ati·cal·ly** /sɪstəmæ̱tɪkli/ ADV 有计划地 ❑ *The army has systematically violated human rights.* 军队已有计划地侵犯了人权。

sys·tem·ic /sɪste̱mɪk/ ADJ **Systemic** means affecting the whole of something. 影响全局的 [FORMAL] ❑ *The economy is locked in a systemic crisis.* 经济陷入全面的危机。

sys·tems ana·lyst (**systems analysts**) N-COUNT A **systems analyst** is someone whose job is to decide what computer equipment and software a company needs, and to provide it. 系统分析员

S

Tt

T also **t** /tiː/ (**T's, t's**) 1 N-VAR **T** is the twentieth letter of the English alphabet. 英语字母表的第20个字母 2 PHRASE You can use **to a T** or **to a tee** to mean perfectly or exactly right. For example, if something suits you **to a T**, it suits you perfectly. If you have an activity or skill **down to a T**, you have succeeded in doing it exactly right. 完美无缺；恰到好处 [INFORMAL] ❑ *Everything had to be rehearsed down to a T.* 一切都得排演得完美无缺。 ❑ *The description fits us to a tee.* 这个描述恰好符合我们的情况。

tab /tæb/ (**tabs**) 1 N-COUNT A **tab** is a small piece of cloth or paper that is attached to something, usually with information about that thing written on it. 标签 ❑ *A clerk had slipped the wrong tab on Tony's X-ray.* 一位职员失手把一个错误的标签贴到了托尼的X光片上。 2 N-COUNT A **tab** is the total cost of goods or services that you have to pay, or the bill or check for those goods or services. 总价钱；帐单 [mainly AM] ❑ *At least one estimate puts the total tab at $7 million.* 至少有一种估计认为总价达7百万美元。 3 PHRASE If someone **keeps tabs on** you, they make sure that they always know where you are and what you are doing, often in order to control you. 密切监视 [INFORMAL] ❑ *It was obvious Hill had come over to keep tabs on Johnson and make sure he didn't do anything drastic.* 显然，希尔是来严密监视约翰逊的，以确保他不做什么过激的事。 4 PHRASE If you **pick up the tab**, you pay a bill on behalf of a group of people or provide the money that is needed for something. (代表一群人) 付帐；承担全部费用 [INFORMAL] ❑ *Pollard picked up the tab for dinner that night.* 波拉德为那天的晚宴付了帐。

ta·ble ♦♦◊ /teɪbəl/ (**tables, tabling, tabled**) 1 N-COUNT A **table** is a piece of furniture with a flat top that you put things on or sit at. 桌子 ❑ *She was sitting at the kitchen table eating a peach.* 她正坐在餐桌旁吃着桃子。 2 V-T If someone **tables** a proposal or plan which has been put forward, they decide to discuss it or deal with it at a later date, rather than right away. 搁置 (提议或计划) [AM] ❑ *We will table that for later.* 我们将把那件事留到以后再讨论。 3 V-T If someone **tables** a proposal, they say formally that they want it to be discussed at a meeting. 正式提交 (议案) [BRIT] ❑ *They've tabled a motion criticizing the government for doing nothing about the problem.* 他们已经正式提交了批评政府对该问题不作为的动议。 4 N-COUNT A **table** is a written set of facts and figures arranged in columns and rows. 表格 [also N num] ❑ *Consult the table on page 104.* 查阅104页的表格。 5 → see also **negotiating table**

table·cloth /teɪbəlklɔθ/ (**tablecloths**) N-COUNT A **tablecloth** is a cloth used to cover a table. 桌布

table·spoon /teɪbəlspun/ (**tablespoons**) N-COUNT A **tablespoon** is a fairly large spoon used for serving food and in cooking. 大汤匙

★ **tab·let** /tæblɪt/ (**tablets**) 1 N-COUNT A **tablet** is a small solid mass of medicine which you swallow. 药片 ❑ *...half a tablet of aspirin.* …半片阿斯匹林。 2 N-COUNT Clay **tablets** or stone **tablets** are the flat pieces of clay or stone which people used to write on before paper was invented. (黏土或石头制的、用以铭刻文字的) 匾；碑 3 **tablets of stone** → see **stone**

tab·loid /tæblɔɪd/ (**tabloids**) N-COUNT A **tabloid** is a newspaper that has small pages, short articles, and a lot of photographs. Tabloids are usually considered to be less serious than other newspapers. Compare **broadsheet**. 通俗小报 ❑ *The tabloids speculated as to whether she was having an affair, and with whom.* 那些通俗小报猜测她是否正有风流韵事，以及跟谁有。

★ **ta·boo** /tæbuː/ (**taboos**) N-COUNT A **taboo** against a subject or activity is a social custom to avoid doing that activity or talking about that subject, because people find them embarrassing or offensive. 禁忌 ❑ *The topic of addiction remains something of a taboo in our family.* 毒瘾在我们家依然是个有些忌讳的话题。 ● ADJ **Taboo** is also an adjective. 禁忌的 ❑ *Cancer is a taboo subject and people are frightened or embarrassed to talk openly about it.* 癌症是个禁忌的话题，人们对公开谈论它感到害怕或尴尬。

▲ **tac·it** /tæsɪt/ ADJ If you refer to someone's **tacit** agreement or approval, you mean they are agreeing to something or approving it without actually saying so, often because they are unwilling to admit to doing so. 默许的 ❑ *The question was a tacit admission that a mistake had indeed been made.* 这个问题等于默认确实已犯了错误。 ● **tac·it·ly** ADV 默许地 [ADV with v] ❑ *He tacitly admitted that the government had breached regulations.* 他默认政府违反了规定。

★ **tack** /tæk/ (**tacks, tacking, tacked**) 1 N-COUNT A **tack** or a **thumbtack** is a short pin with a wide head that you can push with your thumb, especially for a bulletin board. 图钉 ❑ *...a box of carpet tacks.* …一盒地毯钉。 2 N-COUNT A **tack** is a short nail with a broad, flat head, especially one that is used for fastening carpets to the floor. 平头钉 ❑ *...a box of carpet tacks.* …一盒地毯钉。 3 → see also **thumbtack** 4 V-T If you **tack** something to a surface, you pin it there with tacks or thumbtacks. 用平头钉或图钉钉住 ❑ *He had tacked this note to her door.* 他已经把这张便条用图钉钉在了她的门上。 5 N-SING If you change **tack** or try a different **tack**, you try a different method for dealing with a situation. 方法 [also no det] ❑ *Seeing the puzzled look on his face, she tried a different tack.* 看到他脸上困惑的神情，她试了一个不同的方法。 6 V-T If you **tack** pieces of material together, you sew them together with big, loose stitches in order to hold them firmly or check that they fit, before sewing them permanently. 用粗线脚缝 ❑ *Tack them together with a 1 cm seam.* 用1厘米的针脚把它们粗缝上。

▸ **tack on** PHRASAL VERB If you say that something **is tacked on** to something else, you think that it is added in a hurry and in an unsatisfactory way. (匆忙且令人不满地) 附加 ❑ *The child-care bill is to be tacked on to the budget plan now being worked out in the Senate.* 儿童保育款项将被附加到参议院正在制定的预算计划中。

tack·le ♦◊◊ /tækəl/ (**tackles, tackling, tackled**) 1 V-T If you **tackle** a difficult problem or task, you deal with it in a very determined or efficient way. 处理 ❑ *The first reason to tackle these problems is to save children's lives.* 解决这些问题的首要原因是为了挽救孩子们的生命。 2 V-T If you **tackle** someone in a game such as football or rugby, you knock them to the ground. If you **tackle** someone in soccer or hockey, you try to take the ball away from them. (美式或英式橄榄球比赛中) 擒抱摔倒；(足球运动或曲棍球运动中) 抢断 ❑ *Foley tackled the quarterback.* 福利擒住并摔倒了四分卫。 ● N-COUNT **Tackle** is also a noun. 擒抱撞倒；抢断 ❑ *...a tackle by fullback Brian Burrows.* …后卫布赖恩•伯罗斯的阻截。 3 V-T If you **tackle** someone about a particular matter, you speak to them honestly about it, usually in order to get it changed or done. 坦率地与某人交谈 ❑ *I tackled him about how anyone could live amidst so much poverty.* 我坦率地与他谈论哪有人能在如此的极度贫困中生活。 4 V-T If you **tackle** someone, you attack them and fight them. 攻击 ❑ *Two security guards tackled and apprehended a man suspected of robbing 17 banks.* 两名保安与一名涉嫌抢劫17家银行的男子搏斗并逮捕了他。 5 N-UNCOUNT **Tackle** is the equipment that you need for a sport or activity, especially fishing. (尤指钓鱼等活动的) 器具 ❑ *...fishing tackle.* …渔具。

tacky /tæki/ (**tackier, tackiest**) 1 ADJ If you describe something as **tacky**, you dislike it because it is cheap and badly made or vulgar. 低劣的 [INFORMAL, DISAPPROVAL] ❑ *...a woman in a fake leopard-skin coat and tacky red sunglasses.* …一名穿着假豹皮大衣、戴着劣质红色太阳镜的女子。 2 ADJ If something such as paint or glue is **tacky**, it is slightly sticky and not yet dry. 发黏的 ❑ *Test to see if the finish is tacky, and if it is, leave it to harden.* 测试一下看看最后一道漆是否还发黏，如果是的话，就放着让它变硬。

▲ **tact** /tækt/ N-UNCOUNT **Tact** is the ability to avoid upsetting or offending people by being careful not to say or do things that would hurt their feelings. 得体 ❑ *Her tact and intuition never failed.* 她的得体和直觉从不出错。 ❑ *On this occasion, the media has shown great tact.* 在这个时候，媒体表现得十分老练。

★ **tact·ful** /tæktfəl/ ADJ If you describe a person or what they say as **tactful**, you approve of them because they are careful not to offend or upset another person. 有分寸的 [APPROVAL] ❑ *He had been extremely tactful in dealing with the financial question.* 他在处理这个财务问题时一直非常有分寸。 ● **tact·ful·ly** ADV 有分寸地 ❑ *Alex tactfully refrained from further comment.* 亚历克斯很有分寸地不多作评论。

▲ **tac·tic** ♦◇◇ /tæktɪk/ (**tactics**) N-COUNT **Tactics** are the methods that you choose to use in order to achieve what you want in a particular situation. 战术 ❑ *The rebels would still be able to use guerrilla tactics to make the country ungovernable.* 反叛者仍然可以用游击战术使国家难以统治。

Word Partnership *tactic* 的常用搭配:
ADJ. **effective** tactic, **similar** tactic
N. **scare** tactic

tac·ti·cal /tæktɪkəl/ **1** ADJ You use **tactical** to describe an action or plan which is intended to help someone achieve what they want in a particular situation. 战术上的 ❑ *It's not yet clear whether his resignation offer is a serious one, or whether it's simply a tactical move.* 还不清楚他的辞职请求是认真的，还是只是个策略上的举动。 ● **tac·ti·cal·ly** /tæktɪkli/ ADV 有策略地 ❑ *The electorate is astute enough to vote tactically against the government.* 全体选民非常精明，很有策略地投了政府的反对票。 **2** ADJ **Tactical** weapons or forces are those which a military leader can decide for themselves to use in a battle, rather than waiting for a decision by a political leader. (武器或军队) 战术性的 [ADJ n] ❑ *They have removed all tactical nuclear missiles that could strike Europe.* 他们已经拆走了所有可能攻击欧洲的战术性核导弹。

taf·fy /tæfi/ N-UNCOUNT **Taffy** is a sticky candy that you chew. It is made by boiling sugar and butter together with water. 太妃糖 [AM] in BRIT, use **toffee**

tag /tæg/ (**tags, tagging, tagged**) **1** N-COUNT A **tag** is a small piece of card or cloth which is attached to an object or person and has information about that object or person on it. 标签 ❑ *Staff wore name tags and called inmates by their first names.* 工作人员戴着姓名标签，对同僚直呼其名。 **2** → see also **price tag** **3** N-COUNT An electronic **tag** is a device that is firmly attached to someone or something and sets off an alarm if that person or thing moves away or is removed. (电子) 跟踪器 ❑ *Ranchers are testing electronic tags on animals' ears to create a national cattle-tracking system.* 牧场主正在检测动物耳朵上的跟踪器，以建立一个全国性的家畜跟踪系统。 **4** N-UNCOUNT **Tag** is a children's game where one child runs to touch or tag the others. (儿童玩的) 触碰捉人游戏 **5** V-T If you **tag** something, you attach something to it or mark it so that it can be identified later. 给…贴标签 ❑ *Professor Orr has developed interesting ways of tagging chemical molecules using existing laboratory lasers.* 奥尔教授已经研发出了用现有的实验室激光给化学分子贴标签的有趣方法。

▶ **tag along** PHRASAL VERB If someone goes somewhere and you **tag along**, you go with them, especially when they have not asked you to. (尤指未被邀请地) 跟随 ❑ *I let him tag along because he had not been too well recently.* 我让他跟着走，因为他最近一直感到不太舒服。

tail ♦◇◇ /teɪl/ (**tails, tailing, tailed**) **1** N-COUNT The **tail** of an animal, bird, or fish is the part extending beyond the end of its body. 尾巴 ❑ *...a black dog with a long tail.* …一只长尾巴的黑狗。 **2** N-COUNT You can use **tail** to refer to the end or back of something, especially something long and thin. (尤指细长物体的) 尾部 ❑ *...the horizontal stabilizer bar on the plane's tail.* …飞机尾部的水平稳定杆。 **3** N-PLURAL If a man is wearing **tails**, he is wearing a formal jacket which has two long pieces hanging down at the back. 燕尾服 ❑ *...men in tails and women in party dresses.* …穿燕尾服的男士和穿宴会礼服的女士。 **4** V-T To **tail** someone means to follow close behind them and watch where they go and what they do. 跟踪 [INFORMAL] ❑ *Officers had tailed the gang during a major undercover operation.* 警方在一次重大的秘密行动中跟踪过这个团伙。 **5** ADV If you toss a coin and it comes down **tails**, you can see the side of it that does not have a picture of a head on it. (硬币) 反面朝上地 [ADV after v] ❑ *"Heads or tails?"* "正面还是反面?" ❑ *The captain called heads as usual — and the coin came down tails.* 队长像以往一样叫了正面——可硬币反面朝上地落了下来。 **6** cannot **make head or tail of** something → see **head**

▶ **tail off** PHRASAL VERB When something **tails off**, it gradually becomes less in amount or value, often before coming to an end completely. 逐渐减少 ❑ *Last year, economic growth tailed off to below four percent.* 去年，经济增长率逐渐降到了4%以下。

tail·back /teɪlbæk/ (**tailbacks**) **1** N-COUNT In football, a **tailback** is the player furthest from the front line. The **tailback** often runs with the ball. (美式足球) 攻方尾后位 [AM] **2** N-COUNT A **tailback** is the same as a **backup**. 后援 [BRIT]

tai·lor /teɪlər/ (**tailors, tailoring, tailored**) **1** N-COUNT A **tailor** is a person whose job is to make men's clothes. (缝制男装的) 裁缝 **2** V-T If you **tailor** something such as a plan or system **to** someone's needs, you make it suitable for a particular person or purpose by changing the details of it. 调整 ❑ *We can tailor the program to the patient's needs.* 我们可以根据病人的需要调整这个方案。

tailor-made **1** ADJ If something is **tailor-made**, it has been specially designed for a particular person or purpose. 专门设计的 ❑ *Each client's portfolio is tailor-made.* 每一位客户的投资组合都是个别设计的。 **2** ADJ If you say that someone or something is **tailor-made for** a particular task, purpose, or need, you are emphasizing that they are perfectly suitable for it. 非常合适的 [EMPHASIS] ❑ *He was tailor-made, it was said, for the task ahead.* 据说他非常适合将来的任务。 **3** ADJ **Tailor-made** clothes have been specially made to fit a particular person. (衣服) 量身定做的 ❑ *He was wearing a suit that looked tailor-made.* 他穿着一套似乎是量身定做的西装。

tail·pipe /teɪlpaɪp/ (**tailpipes**) N-COUNT A **tailpipe** is the end pipe of a car's exhaust system. (汽车的) 排气管 [AM] ❑ *...a dramatic reduction in tailpipe emissions.* …汽车尾气排放量的急剧减少。

▲ **taint** /teɪnt/ (**taints, tainting, tainted**) **1** V-T If a person or thing **is tainted by** something bad or undesirable, their status or reputation is harmed because they are associated with it. 玷污 ❑ *Opposition leaders said that the elections had been tainted by corruption.* 反对派领导人说这些选举已被腐败玷污了。 ● **taint·ed** ADJ 受玷污的 ❑ *He came out only slightly tainted by telling millions of viewers he and his wife had had marital problems.* 他告诉上百万观众他和他的妻子已有婚姻问题，结果他只是略受影响。 **2** N-COUNT A **taint** is an undesirable quality which ruins the status or reputation of someone or something. 污点 ❑ *Her government never really shook off the taint of corruption.* 她的政府从未真正甩掉腐败的污点。 **3** V-T If an unpleasant substance **taints** food or medicine, the food or medicine is spoiled or damaged by it. 使 (食品或药品) 变坏 ❑ *Rancid oil will taint the flavor.* 变质的油会破坏味道。

take
❶ USED WITH NOUNS DESCRIBING ACTIONS
❷ OTHER USES

❶ **take** ♦♦♦ /teɪk/ (**takes, taking, took, taken**)

Take is used in combination with a wide range of nouns, where the meaning of the combination is mostly given by the noun. Many of these combinations are common idiomatic expressions whose meanings can be found at the appropriate nouns. For example, the expression **take care** is explained at **care**.

1 V-T You can use **take** followed by a noun to talk about an action or event, when it would also be possible to use the verb that is related to that noun. For example, you can say **"she took a shower"** instead of "she showered." 后接名词描述动作或事件 ❑ *She was too tired to take a shower.* 她累得不想淋浴了。 ❑ *Betty took a photograph of us.* 贝蒂给我们拍了一张照片。 **2** V-T In ordinary spoken or written English, people use **take** with a range of nouns instead of using a more specific verb. For example, people often say **"he took control"** or **"she took a positive attitude"** instead of "he assumed control" or "she adopted a positive attitude." 与许多名词连用，代替更具体的动词 ❑ *The Patriotic Front took power after a three-month civil war.* 爱国阵线经过3个月的内战后夺取了政权。 ❑ *I felt it was important for women to join and take a leading role.* 我感觉妇女参与并担任领导角色很重要。

❷ **take** ♦♦♦ /teɪk/ (**takes, taking, took, taken**)
➩ **Please look at meanings 44 – 50 to see if the expression you are looking for is shown under another headword.** **1** V-T If you **take** something, you reach out for it and hold it. 拿 ❑ *Here, let me take your coat.* 来，我帮你拿大衣。 ❑ *Colette took her by the shoulders and shook her.* 科利特抓住她的双肩，摇晃着她。 **2** V-T If you **take** something with you when you go somewhere, you carry it or

T

have it with you. 随身带着 ❑ *Mark often took his books to Bess's house to study.* 马克经常带着书去贝丝家学习。 ❑ *You should take your passport with you when changing money.* 你换汇时应该带着你的护照。 **3** V-T If a person, vehicle, or path **takes** someone somewhere, they transport or lead them there. 运送; 带领 ❑ *She took me to a Mexican restaurant.* 她带我去了一家墨西哥餐馆。 **4** V-T If something such as a job or interest **takes** you to a place, it is the reason for you going there. (工作或兴趣等) 使某人去 ❑ *He was a poor student from Madras whose genius took him to Stanford.* 他是个来自马德拉斯的穷学生，他的才华使他考上了斯坦福。 **5** V-T If you **take** something such as your problems or your business to someone, you go to that person when you have problems you want to discuss or things you want to buy. 请教 (问题); 洽谈 (生意) ❑ *You need to take your problems to a trained counselor.* 你需要向一位训练有素的顾问请教你的问题。 **6** V-T If one thing **takes** another **to** a particular level, condition, or state, it causes it to reach that level or condition. 使达到 (某种水平或状态) ❑ *A combination of talent, hard work and good looks have taken her to the top.* 天赋、勤奋和美貌的组合使她成了佼佼者。 **7** V-T If you **take** something from a place, you remove it from there. 拿走 ❑ *He took a handkerchief from his pocket and lightly wiped his mouth.* 他从口袋里拿出一块手帕，轻轻地擦了擦嘴。 **8** V-T If you **take** something from someone who owns it, you steal it or go away with it without their permission. 偷走; 擅自拿走 ❑ *He has taken my money, and I have no chance of getting it back.* 他偷了我的钱，我不可能把它要回来了。 **9** V-T If an army or political party **takes** something or someone, they win them from their enemy or opponent. 夺取 ❑ *A Serb army unit took the town.* 一支塞尔维亚部队夺取了这个镇。 **10** V-T If you **take** one number or amount from another, you subtract it or deduct it. 减去 ❑ *Take off the price of the house, that's another hundred thousand.* 减去房价，又是10万。 **11** V-T If you cannot **take** something difficult, painful, or annoying, you cannot tolerate it without becoming upset, ill, or angry. 忍受 [no passive, usu with brd-neg] ❑ *Don't ever ask me to look after those kids again. I just can't take it!* 不要再叫我照看那些孩子们了。我简直无法忍受！ **12** V-T If you **take** something such as damage or loss, you suffer it, especially in war or in a battle. (尤指在战争中) 遭受 ❑ *They have taken heavy casualties.* 他们遭受了惨重的伤亡。 **13** V-T If something **takes** a certain amount of time, that amount of time is needed in order to do it. 花费 (时间) [no passive] ❑ *Since the roads are very bad, the trip took us a long time.* 由于道路很差，这次旅程花费了我们很长时间。 ❑ *I had heard an appeal could take years.* 我已听说一项诉讼可能要花费好几年时间。 ❑ *The sauce takes 25 minutes to prepare and cook.* 从准备到烹制成这种调味汁需要25分钟。 ❑ *It takes 15 minutes to convert the plane into a car by removing the wings and the tail.* 拆除机翼和机尾，把那架飞机改成汽车需要15分钟的时间。 **14** V-T If something **takes** a particular quality or thing, that quality or thing is needed in order to do it. 需要 (某种品质或事物) [no passive] ❑ *At one time, walking across the room took all her strength.* 曾经有段时间，穿过这个房间得用尽她全部的力气。 ❑ *It takes courage to say what you think.* 说出你的想法需要勇气。 **15** V-T If you **take** something that is given or offered to you, you agree to accept it. 接受 ❑ *When I took the job I thought I could change the system, but it's hard.* 当我接受这份工作时我以为我能改变这种体制，但太难了。 **16** V-T If you **take** a feeling such as pleasure, pride, or delight in a particular thing or activity, it gives you that feeling. 感到 ❑ *They take great pride in their heritage.* 他们为自己的传统感到十分自豪。 **17** V-T If you **take** a prize or medal, you win it. 赢得 ❑ *"Poison" took first prize at the 1991 Sundance Film Festival.* 《毒药》在1991年的圣丹斯电影节上赢得一等奖。 **18** V-T If you **take** the blame, responsibility, or credit for something, you agree to accept it. 承担 ❑ *His brother Raoul did it, but Leonel took the blame and kept his mouth shut.* 莱昂内尔的兄弟拉乌尔做了这件事，但莱昂内尔承担了责任而且对此绝口不提。 **19** V-T If you **take** patients or clients, you accept them as your patients or clients. 接纳 ❑ *Some universities would be forced to take more students than they wanted.* 有些大学将被迫接纳比他们想要的更多的学生。 **20** V-T If you **take** a telephone call, you speak to someone who is telephoning you. 接听 (电话) ❑ *Douglas telephoned Catherine at her office. She refused to take his calls.* 道格拉斯把电话打到凯瑟琳的办公室。她拒绝接听他的电话。 **21** V-T If you **take** something in a particular way, you react in the way mentioned to a situation or to someone's beliefs or behavior. (以某种方式) 看待 ❑ *Unfortunately, no one took my opinion seriously.* 不幸的是，没有人严肃地看待我的意见。 **22** V-T You use **take** when you are discussing or explaining a particular question, in order to introduce an example or to say how the question is being considered. 举出… (为例) [usu imper] ❑ *There's confusion and resentment, and it's almost never expressed out in the open. Take this office, for example.* 混乱和怨恨是存在的，而几乎从没人公开表露出来过。就以这个办公室为例。 **23** V-T If you **take** someone's meaning or point, you understand and accept what they are saying. 理解 ❑ *I had made it as plain as I could so that he could not fail to take my meaning.* 我已经尽我所能地说明白，所以他不会不理解我的意思。 **24** V-T If you **take** someone **for** something, you believe wrongly that they are that thing. 把…错当成 ❑ *She had taken him for a journalist.* 她把他错当成记者了。 **25** V-T If you **take** a road or route, you choose to travel along it. 选择走 (某条路) ❑ *From the community college take Old Mill Road to the outskirts of town.* 从社区学院出发，走老磨坊路到达市郊。 **26** V-T If you **take** a car, train, bus, or plane, you use it to go from one place to another. 搭乘 ❑ *It's the other end of town so we should take the car.* 它在城镇的那头，因此我们应该乘车去。 **27** V-T If you **take** a subject or course at school or college, you choose to study it. 选修 ❑ *Students are allowed to take European history and American history.* 学生被允许选修欧洲史和美国史。 **28** V-T If you **take** a test or examination, you do it in order to show your knowledge or ability. 参加 (考试) ❑ *She took her driving test yesterday.* 她昨天参加了驾照考试。 **29** V-T If someone **takes** drugs, pills, or other medicines, they take them into their body, for example, by swallowing them. 服用 ❑ *She's been taking sleeping pills.* 她一直在服用安眠药。 **30** V-T If you **take** a note or a letter, you write down something you want to remember or the words that someone says. 写下 ❑ *She sat expressionless, carefully taking notes.* 她面无表情地坐着，仔细地记着笔记。 **31** V-T If you **take** a measurement, you find out what it is by measuring. 测量 ❑ *By drilling, geologists can take measurements at various depths.* 通过钻孔，地质学家可以在不同深度测量。 **32** V-T If a place or container **takes** a particular amount or number, there is enough space for that amount or number. 容纳 [no passive] ❑ *The place could just about take 2,000 people.* 这个地方只能容纳大约两千人。 **33** V-T If you **take** a particular size in shoes or clothes, that size fits you. 穿 (某个尺寸的鞋子或衣服) ❑ *"What size do you take?"—"I take a size 7."* "你穿多少号？" —— "我穿7号。" **34** N-SING You can use **take** to refer to the amount of money that a business such as a store or theater gets from selling its goods or tickets during a particular period. 营业收入 [mainly AM, BUSINESS]

in BRIT, usually use **takings**

❑ *It added another $11.8 million to the take, for a grand total of $43 million.* 它又增加了1180万美元的营业收入，总计为4300万美元。 **35** V-T If a store, restaurant, theater, or other business **takes** a certain amount of money, they get that amount from people buying goods or services. 赚得 [mainly BRIT, BUSINESS]

in AM, usually use **take in**

36 V-T If you **are taken by** someone, you are cheated or deceived by them. 欺骗 [INFORMAL] ❑ *They got taken by a scam artist.* 他们被一个假冒的艺术家骗了。 **37** N-COUNT A **take** is a short piece of action which is filmed in one continuous process for a movie. (电影中一次连续拍摄的) 镜头 ❑ *She couldn't get it right – she never knew the lines and we had to do several takes.* 她就是做不好——她一直不熟悉台词，我们只好一个镜头拍好几次。 **38** N-SING Someone's **take on** a particular situation or fact is their attitude to it or their interpretation of it. 态度; 解释 ❑ *What's your take on the new government? Do you think it can work?* 你对新政府持什么态度？你认为它能行吗？ **39** CONVENTION If you say to someone "**take it or leave it,**" you are telling them that they can accept something or not accept it, but that you are not prepared to discuss any other alternatives. 要么接受，要么走开 ❑ *A 72-hour week, 12 hours a day, six days a week, take it or leave it.* 1周72小时，每天12小时，每周6天，要么接受，要么走开。 **40** PHRASE If someone **takes** an insult or attack **lying down**, they accept it without protesting. 心甘情愿地忍受 ❑ *The government is not taking such criticism lying down.* 政府不会心甘情愿地忍受这种批评。 **41** PHRASE If something **takes a lot out of** you or **takes it out of** you, it requires a lot of energy or effort and makes you feel very tired and weak afterward. 使某人筋疲力尽 ❑ *He looked tired, as if the argument had taken a lot out of him.* 他看上去累了，似乎这场辩论已使他筋疲力尽。 **42** PHRASE If someone tells you to **take five** or to **take ten**, they are telling you to have a five- or ten-minute break from what you are doing. 休息5分钟; 休息10分钟 [mainly AM, INFORMAL] **43** PHRASE Someone who is **on the take** is receiving illegal income such as bribes. 受贿 [INFORMAL] ❑ *I can also name cops who are on the take.* 我也能说出受贿警察的名字。 **44** to **be taken aback** → see **aback** **45** to **take up arms** → see **arm** **46** to **take the cake** → see **cake**

t

47 to **take** your **hat off to** someone → see **hat** 48 to **be taken for a ride** → see **ride** 49 to **take** someone **by surprise** → see **surprise** 50 **take my word for it** → see **word**
→ see **photography**

Take and **bring** are both used to talk about carrying something or accompanying someone somewhere, but **take** is used to suggest movement away from the speaker, and **bring** is used to suggest movement toward the speaker. ❑ *Anna took the book to school with her... Bring your calculator to every lesson.* In the first sentence, **took** suggests that Anna left the speaker when she went to school. In the second sentence, **bring** suggests that the person and the calculator should come to the place where the speaker is. You could also say "Anna brought the book to school with her" to suggest that Anna and the speaker were both at school, and "Take your calculator to every lesson" to suggest that the speaker will not be present at the lesson. The difference between **take** and **bring** is equivalent to that between **go** and **come**. **Fetch** suggests that someone goes away to get something and comes back with it. ❑ *O'Leary went to fetch tickets and was soon back.*

▸ **take after** PHRASAL VERB If you **take after** a member of your family, you resemble them in your appearance, your behavior, or your character. (长相、举止或性格) 像 [no passive] ❑ *She was a smart, brave woman. You take after her.* 她是一名聪明、勇敢的女子。你像她。

▸ **take apart** PHRASAL VERB If you **take** something **apart**, you separate it into the different parts that it is made of. 拆开 ❑ *When the clock stopped, he took it apart, found what was wrong, and put the whole thing together again.* 当钟不走时，他把它拆了，找出毛病所在，然后再组装起来。

▸ **take away** 1 PHRASAL VERB If you **take** something **away from** someone, you remove it from them, so that they no longer possess it or have it with them. 夺走 ❑ *They're going to take my citizenship away.* 他们将夺走我的公民权。 ❑ *"Give me the toy," he said softly, "or I'll take it away from you."* "给我玩具，"他轻声说道，"否则我就把它从你身边夺走。" 2 PHRASAL VERB If you **take** one number or amount **away from** another, you subtract one number from the other. 减去 ❑ *Add up the bills for each month. Take this away from the income.* 把每个月的帐单加起来。从收入中减去这个。 3 PHRASAL VERB To **take** someone **away** means to bring them from their home to an institution such as a prison or hospital. 带走 (送到监狱或医院) ❑ *Two men claiming to be police officers went to the pastor's house and took him away.* 两个自称是警官的人去了牧师的房子，把他带走了。 4 → see also **takeaway**

▸ **take back** 1 PHRASAL VERB If you **take** something **back**, you return it to the place where you bought it or where you borrowed it from, because it is unsuitable or broken, or because you have finished with it. 退还 ❑ *If I buy something and he doesn't like it I'll take it back.* 如果我买了什么东西，他不喜欢，我就退掉它。 2 PHRASAL VERB If you **take** something **back**, you admit that something that you said or thought is wrong. 收回 (错话或错误的想法) ❑ *Take back what you said about Jeremy!* 收回你说的有关杰里米的话！ 3 PHRASAL VERB If you **take** someone **back**, you allow them to come home again, after they have gone away because of an argument or other problem. 允许…再回家 ❑ *Why did she take him back?* 她为什么又让他回家呢？ 4 PHRASAL VERB If you say that something **takes** you **back**, you mean that it reminds you of a period of your past life and makes you think about it again. 使回想起 ❑ *I enjoyed experimenting with colors – it took me back to being five years old.* 我喜欢尝试各种颜色——这使我回忆起5岁时的情景。

▸ **take down** 1 PHRASAL VERB If you **take** something **down**, you reach up and get it from a high place such as a shelf. (从高处) 取下 ❑ *Alberto took the portrait down from the wall.* 阿尔伯特从墙上取下那幅肖像画。 2 PHRASAL VERB If you **take down** a structure, you remove each piece of it. 拆除 ❑ *The Canadian army took down the barricades erected by the Indians.* 加拿大军队拆除了印度人设置的路障。 3 PHRASAL VERB If you **take down** a piece of information or a statement, you write it down. 记下 ❑ *We've been trying to get back to you, Tom, but we think we took your number down incorrectly.* 我们一直试着给你回复，汤姆，但我们觉得我们记错了你的号码。

▸ **take in** 1 PHRASAL VERB If you **take** someone **in**, you allow them to stay in your house or your country, especially when they do not have anywhere to stay or are in trouble. 收留 ❑ *He persuaded Jo to take him in.* 他说服乔收留了他。 2 PHRASAL VERB If the police **take** someone **in**, they remove them from their home in order to question them. (警察) 带走 ❑ *The police have taken him in for questioning in connection with the murder of a girl.* 警察把他带进去，以询问一女孩被杀的有关情况。 3 PHRASAL VERB If you **are taken in by** someone or something, you are deceived by them, so that you get a false impression of them. 欺骗 ❑ *I married in my late teens and was taken in by his charm – which soon vanished.* 我在十八九岁时结婚，被他的魅力给骗了——那种魅力很快就消失了。 4 PHRASAL VERB If you **take** something **in**, you pay attention to it and understand it when you hear it or read it. 领会 ❑ *Lesley explains possible treatments but you can tell she's not taking it in.* 莱斯莉解释了可行的治疗方法，但是你可以看得出她没有领会。 5 PHRASAL VERB If you **take** something **in**, you see all of it. 一眼看清 ❑ *The eyes behind the lenses were dark and quick-moving, taking in everything at a glance.* 镜片后的眼睛黑黑的且快速转动着，一眼就能看清一切。 6 PHRASAL VERB If people, animals, or plants **take in** air, drink, or food, they allow it to enter their body, usually by breathing or swallowing. 吸收 ❑ *They will certainly need to take in plenty of liquid.* 他们会肯定需要吸收大量液体。 7 PHRASAL VERB If a store, restaurant, theater, or other business **takes in** a certain amount of money, they get that amount from people buying goods or services. 收入 [mainly AM] ❑ *They plan to take in $1.6 billion.* 他们计划要收入16亿美元。

in BRIT, usually use **take**

→ see **calorie**

▸ **take off** 1 PHRASAL VERB When an airplane **takes off**, it leaves the ground and starts flying. (飞机) 起飞 ❑ *We eventually took off at 11 o'clock and arrived in Juneau at 1:30.* 我们终于在11点起飞，1:30到达朱诺。 2 PHRASAL VERB If something such as a product, an activity, or someone's career **takes off**, it suddenly becomes very successful. 突然成功 ❑ *In 1944, he met Edith Piaf, and his career took off.* 1944年，他遇到伊迪丝·琵雅芙，从此他的事业飞黄腾达。 3 PHRASAL VERB If you **take off** or **take yourself off**, you go away, often suddenly and unexpectedly. (常指突然且出人意料地) 离开 ❑ *He took off at once and headed back to the motel.* 他出人意料地立刻就离开了，然后回到了那家汽车旅馆。 4 PHRASAL VERB If you **take** a garment **off**, you remove it. 脱去 ❑ *He wouldn't take his hat off.* 他不愿脱下他的帽子。 5 PHRASAL VERB If you **take** time **off**, you obtain permission not to go to work for a short period of time. 休假 ❑ *Mitchel's schedule had not permitted him to take time off.* 米切尔的日程表已不允许他休假。

▸ **take on** 1 PHRASAL VERB If you **take on** a job or responsibility, especially a difficult one, you accept it. 承担 ❑ *No other organization was able or willing to take on the job.* 没有任何其他组织能够或愿意承担这项工作。 2 PHRASAL VERB If something **takes on** a new appearance or quality, it develops that appearance or quality. 呈现 [no passive] ❑ *Believing he had only a year to live, his writing took on a feverish intensity.* 他认为自己只有一年能活了，他的文字呈现出一种极度的狂热。 3 PHRASAL VERB If a vehicle such as a bus or ship **takes on** passengers, goods, or fuel, it stops in order to allow them to get on or to be loaded on. (交通工具) 停下装载 (乘客、货物、燃料) ❑ *This is a brief stop to take on passengers and water.* 这是一次短暂的停车以上客和装水。 4 PHRASAL VERB If you **take** someone **on**, you employ them to do a job. 聘用 ❑ *He's spoken to a publishing company. They're going to take him on.* 他已经跟一家出版公司谈过了。他们将聘用他。 5 PHRASAL VERB If you **take** someone **on**, you fight them or compete against them, especially when they are bigger or more powerful than you are. 与 (尤指强于自己的人) 较量 [no passive] ❑ *Democrats were reluctant to take on a president whose popularity ratings were historically high.* 民主党不愿意与一个支持率创历史新高的总统较量。 6 PHRASAL VERB If you **take** something **on** or **upon yourself**, you decide to do it without asking anyone for permission or approval. 擅自决定做 [no passive] ❑ *Knox had taken it on himself to choose the wine.* 诺克斯已擅自主张选了这种葡萄酒。 ❑ *He took upon himself the responsibility for protecting her.* 他自作主张承担起保护她的责任。

▸ **take out** 1 PHRASAL VERB If you **take** something **out**, you remove it permanently from its place. 除掉 ❑ *I got an abscess so he took the tooth out.* 我牙龈脓肿，所以他把那颗牙齿拔掉了。 2 PHRASAL VERB If you **take out** something such as a loan, a license, or an insurance policy, you obtain it by fulfilling the conditions and paying the money that is necessary. 取得 (贷款、许可、保险等) ❑ *I'll have to stop by the bank and take out a loan.* 我将不得不去一下那家银行领一笔贷款。 3 PHRASAL VERB If you **take** someone **out**, they go to something such as a restaurant or theater with you after you have invited them, and usually you pay for them. 带某人出去 (吃饭或看电影等) ❑ *Jessica's grandparents took her out for the day.* 杰茜卡的祖父母带她出去了一天。 ❑ *Sophia took me out to lunch.* 索菲娅请我出去吃午饭。

T

▸ **take over** 1 PHRASAL VERB If you **take over** a company, you get control of it, for example, by buying its shares. 接管(公司) [BUSINESS] ❑ *I'm going to take over the company one day.* 我总有一天会接管这家公司。 2 PHRASAL VERB If someone **takes over** a country or building, they get control of it by force, for example, with the help of the army. (用武力) 接管 ❑ *The Belgians took over Rwanda under a League of Nations mandate.* 比利时人在一项国际联盟的授权下接管了卢旺达。 3 PHRASAL VERB If you **take over** a job or role or if you **take over**, you become responsible for the job after someone else has stopped doing it. 接替 ❑ *His widow has taken over the running of his empire, including six theaters.* 他的遗孀已经接替了管理他的帝国的工作，包括6家剧院。 ❑ *In 2001, I took over from him as governing mayor.* 2001年我接替他担任了主管市长。 4 PHRASAL VERB If one thing **takes over** from something else, it becomes more important, successful, or powerful than the other thing, and eventually replaces it. 取代 ❑ *Cars gradually took over from horses.* 汽车逐渐取代了马。 5 → see also **takeover**

▸ **take to** 1 PHRASAL VERB If you **take to** someone or something, you like them, especially after knowing them or thinking about them for only a short time. (短时间内) 喜欢上 ❑ *Did the children take to him?* 孩子们喜欢上他了吗？ 2 PHRASAL VERB If you **take to** doing something, you begin to do it as a regular habit. 养成…的习惯 ❑ *They had taken to wandering through the streets arm-in-arm.* 他们已经养成了臂挽着臂漫步街头的习惯。

▸ **take up** 1 PHRASAL VERB If you **take up** an activity or a subject, you become interested in it and spend time doing it, either as a hobby or as a career. 开始从事 ❑ *He did not particularly want to take up a competitive sport.* 他并没有特别想要开始从事竞技性运动项目。 2 PHRASAL VERB If you **take up** a question, problem, or cause, you act on it or discuss how you are going to act on it. 着手处理；讨论如何处理 ❑ *If you have a problem with the law, take it up with your legislators.* 如果你有法律问题，去找你们的立法员讨论如何处理。 ❑ *She had taken up the cause of a generation of American youth.* 她已经开始着手一代美国年轻人的事业。 3 PHRASAL VERB If you **take up** a job, you begin to work at it. 开始工作 ❑ *He will take up his post as the head of the civil courts at the end of next month.* 他将于下个月底开始担任民事法庭的庭长。 4 PHRASAL VERB If you **take up** an offer or a challenge, you accept it. 接受(建议或挑战) ❑ *Increasingly, more winemakers are taking up the challenge of growing Pinot Noir.* 越来越多的葡萄酒商开始接受种植"黑比诺"葡萄的挑战。 5 PHRASAL VERB If something **takes up** a particular amount of time, space, or effort, it uses that amount. 占用(时间、空间或精力) ❑ *I know how busy you must be and naturally I wouldn't want to take up too much of your time.* 我知道你一定很忙，当然我不想占用你太多的时间。 ❑ *A good deal of my time is taken up with driving the children to soccer games.* 我的许多时间都用在开车送孩子们去参加足球比赛。

▸ **take upon** → see **take on 6**

Thesaurus *take* 另参见：

V.	grab, grasp, hold 2 1
	drive, escort, transport 2 3
	steal 2 8
	capture, seize 2 9

take·away /teɪkəweɪ/ (**takeaways**) 1 N-COUNT A **takeaway** is a store or restaurant which sells hot cooked food that you eat somewhere else. 外卖餐馆 [BRIT]

in AM, use **takeout**

2 N-COUNT A **takeaway** is hot cooked food that you buy from a store or restaurant and eat somewhere else. 外卖食品 [BRIT]

in AM, use **takeout**

take-home pay N-UNCOUNT Your **take-home pay** is the amount of your wages or salary that is left after income tax and other payments have been subtracted. 实得工资 [BUSINESS] ❑ *Her monthly take-home pay is $1,500 after taxes.* 扣除税款后，她每月的实得工资是$1500。

tak·en /teɪkən/ 1 **Taken** is the past participle of **take**. **take**的过去分词 2 ADJ If you are **taken with** something or someone, you are very interested in them or attracted to them. 对…很感兴趣的 [v-link ADJ] [INFORMAL] ❑ *She seems very taken with the idea.* 她好像对这个想法很感兴趣。

★ **take·off** /teɪkɔf/ (**takeoffs**) also **take-off** N-VAR **Takeoff** is the beginning of a flight, when an aircraft leaves the ground. (飞机) 起飞 ❑ *What time is takeoff?* 起飞时间是什么时候？

take·out /teɪkaʊt/ (**takeouts**) 1 N-COUNT A **takeout** is a store or restaurant which sells hot cooked food that you eat somewhere else. 外卖餐馆 [AM]

in BRIT, use **takeaway**

❑ *...a Chinese takeout restaurant.* …一家中餐外卖馆。 2 N-UNCOUNT **Takeout** or **takeout** food is hot cooked food which you buy from a store or restaurant and eat somewhere else. 外卖食品 [AM]

in BRIT, use **takeaway**

❑ *...a takeout pizza.* …一个外卖比萨。
→ see **restaurant**

take·over ♦◇◇ /teɪkoʊvər/ (**takeovers**) 1 N-COUNT A **takeover** is the act of gaining control of a company by buying more of its shares than anyone else. (公司的) 收购 [BUSINESS] ❑ *He lost his job in a corporate takeover.* 他在一次公司收购中丢掉了工作。 2 N-COUNT A **takeover** is the act of taking control of a country, political party, or movement by force. (用武力的) 接管 ❑ *There's been a military takeover of some kind.* 曾发生过一次类似军事接管的事情。

tak·ings /teɪkɪŋz/ N-PLURAL You can use **takings** to refer to the amount of money that a business such as a store or a movie theater gets from selling its goods or tickets during a particular period. (商店或电影院等某个时期的) 营业收入 [BUSINESS] ❑ *Their takings were fifteen to twenty thousand dollars a week.* 他们的营业收入是每周1.5万至2万美元之间。

tale ♦◇◇ /teɪl/ (**tales**) 1 N-COUNT; N-IN-NAMES A **tale** is a story, often involving magic or exciting events. 故事(常包含神奇的或令人激动的事件) ❑ *...a collection of stories, poems and folk tales.* …一部由故事、诗歌和民间传说构成的作品集。 2 N-COUNT You can refer to an interesting, exciting, or dramatic account of a real event as a **tale**. (对真实事件的有趣的、令人激动的、戏剧性的) 描述 ❑ *The media have been filled with tales of horror and loss resulting from Monday's earthquake.* 媒体上已充斥着对星期一地震造成的恐怖和损失的种种描述。 3 → see also **fairy tale**

tal·ent ♦◇◇ /tælənt/ (**talents**) N-VAR **Talent** is the natural ability to do something well. 天赋 ❑ *She is proud that both her children have a talent for music.* 她为自己的两个孩子都有音乐天赋感到自豪。 ❑ *He's got lots of talent.* 他有许多天赋。

Thesaurus *talent* 另参见：

N.	ability, aptitude, gift

Word Partnership *talent* 的常用搭配：

ADJ.	**great** talent, **musical** talent, **natural** talent
V.	**have (a)** talent, **have got** talent
N.	talent **pool**, talent **search**

tal·ent·ed /tæləntɪd/ ADJ Someone who is **talented** has a natural ability to do something well. 有天赋的 ❑ *Howard is a talented pianist.* 霍华德是一名有天赋的钢琴家。

talk ♦♦♦ /tɔk/ (**talks, talking, talked**) 1 V-I When you **talk**, you use spoken language to express your thoughts, ideas, or feelings. 说话 ❑ *He was too distressed to talk.* 他伤心得说不出话来。 ❑ *The boys all began to talk at once.* 男孩们都马上开始说话了。 ● N-UNCOUNT **Talk** is also a noun. 说话 ❑ *That's not the kind of talk one usually hears from accountants.* 那不是人们通常从会计人员那里听到的那种话。 2 V-RECIP If you **talk to** someone, you have a conversation with them. You can also say that two people **talk**. 交谈 ❑ *We talked and laughed a lot.* 我们畅怀说笑。 ❑ *I talked to him yesterday.* 我昨天和他谈过。 ❑ *When she came back, they were talking about American food.* 当她回来时，他们正在谈论美国食品。 ● N-COUNT **Talk** is also a noun. 交谈 ❑ *We had a long talk about her father, Tony, who was a friend of mine.* 关于她父亲托尼我们进行了一次长时间的交谈，托尼是我的一个朋友。 3 V-RECIP If you **talk to** someone, you tell them about the things that are worrying you. You can also say that two people **talk**. 诉说 ❑ *Your first step should be to talk to a teacher or school counselor.* 你第一步应该是去找个老师或学校辅导员谈谈。 ❑ *Do call if you want to talk about it.* 一定要打电话来，如果你想谈谈这件事。 ● N-COUNT **Talk** is also a noun. 谈话 ❑ *I think it's time we had a talk.* 我认为是我们进行一次谈话的时候了。 4 V-I If you **talk on** or **about** something, you make an informal speech telling people what you know or think about it. 发表(非正式的) 讲话 ❑ *She will talk on the issues she cares passionately about including education and nursery care.* 她将就她热切关注的问题发表讲话，包括教育和幼儿护理。 ● N-COUNT **Talk** is also a noun. 非正式的讲话 ❑ *A guide gives a brief talk on the history of the site.* 一位导游就这个遗址的历史作了一次简要的讲述。 5 N-PLURAL **Talks** are formal

t

discussions intended to produce an agreement, usually between different countries or between employers and employees. (通常指国家间或雇主和雇员间的) 谈判 ❑ *...the next round of Middle East peace talks.* …下一轮中东和平谈判。 6 V-RECIP If one group of people **talks to** another, or if two groups **talk**, they have formal discussions in order to do a deal or produce an agreement. 磋商 ❑ *We're talking to some people about opening an office in Boston.* 我们正与一些人磋商在波士顿设立办事处的事。 ❑ *It triggered speculation that GM and Jaguar might be talking.* 这引发了通用公司和捷豹公司可能正在进行磋商的猜测。 7 V-RECIP When different countries or different sides in a dispute **talk**, or **talk to** each other, they discuss their differences in order to try and settle the dispute. 和谈 ❑ *They are collecting information in preparation for the day when the two sides sit down and talk.* 他们正在收集信息，为双方坐下来和谈的那一天做准备。 8 V-I If people **are talking about** another person or **are talking**, they are discussing that person. 议论 ❑ *Everyone is talking about him.* 大家都在议论他。 ❑ *We'd better not be seen together. People will talk.* 我们最好不要被人看见在一起。人们会议论。 ● N-UNCOUNT **Talk** is also a noun. 议论 ❑ *There has been a lot of talk about me getting married.* 有很多关于我要结婚了的议论。 9 V-I If someone **talks** when they are being held by police or soldiers, they reveal important or secret information, usually unwillingly. 供出消息 ❑ *They'll talk, they'll implicate me.* 他们将招供，他们将把我牵连进去。 10 V-T/V-I If you **talk** a particular language or **talk** with a particular accent, you use that language or have that accent when you speak. 说 (某种语言); 带 (某种口音) [no passive] ❑ *You don't sound like a foreigner talking English.* 你听起来不像外国人在说英语。 11 V-T If you **talk** something such as politics or sports, you discuss it. 谈论 (政治、体育等) [no passive] ❑ *The guests were mostly middle-aged men talking business.* 客人们大多是谈生意的中年男人。 12 V-T You can use **talk** to say what you think of the ideas that someone is expressing. For example, if you say that someone **is talking sense**, you mean that you think the opinions they are expressing are sensible. 说话 (有道理或没道理) ❑ *You must admit George, you're talking absolute nonsense.* 你必须承认，乔治，你正在说废话。 13 V-T You can say that you **are talking** a particular thing to draw attention to your topic or to point out a characteristic of what you are discussing. 正在讨论 (的是) [no passive] [SPOKEN] ❑ *We're talking megabucks this time.* 我们这次正在讨论的可是一笔巨款。 14 N-UNCOUNT If you say that something such as an idea or threat is just **talk**, or **all talk**, you mean that it does not mean or matter much, because people are exaggerating about it or do not really intend to do anything about it. 空谈 ❑ *Has much of this actually been tried here? Or is it just talk?* 这其中有多少在这里真正被试过？或者这只是空谈？ 15 PHRASE You can say **talk about** before mentioning a particular expression or situation, when you mean that something is a very striking or clear example of that expression or situation. 这就叫… [INFORMAL, EMPHASIS] ❑ *Took us quite a while to get here, didn't it? Talk about fate moving in a mysterious way!* 用了我们好长一段时间才到这里，不是吗？这叫作命运难料啊！ 16 PHRASE You can use the expression **talking of** to introduce a new topic that you want to discuss, and to link it to something that has already been mentioned. (用于引出新话题) 说起 ❑ *I'll give a prize to the best idea. Talking of good ideas, here's one to break the ice at a wedding reception.* 我将奖励最佳主意。说起好主意，这里就有一个，能活跃婚礼气氛。 17 to **talk shop** → see **shop**

T

> There are some differences in the way the verbs **speak** and **talk** are used. When you **speak**, you could, for example, be addressing someone or making a speech. **Talk** is more likely to be used when you are referring to a conversation or discussion. ❑ *I talked about it with my family at dinner... Sometimes we'd talk all night.* **Talk** can also be used to emphasize the activity of saying things, rather than the words that are spoken. ❑ *She thought I talked too much.*

▸ **talk back** PHRASAL VERB If you **talk back** to someone in authority such as a parent or teacher, you answer them in a rude way. 顶嘴 ❑ *How dare you talk back to me!* 你竟敢和我顶嘴！

▸ **talk down** 1 PHRASAL VERB To **talk down** someone who is flying an aircraft in an emergency means to give them instructions so that they can land safely. 紧急引导 (飞行员) 安全着陆 ❑ *The pilot began to talk him down by giving instructions over the radio.* 飞行员开始通过无线电发出指令，引导他安全着陆。 2 PHRASAL VERB If someone **talks down** a particular thing, they make it less interesting, valuable, or likely than it originally seemed. 贬低 ❑ *They even blame the government for talking down the nation's fourth biggest industry.* 他们甚至指责政府贬低国家的第4大产业。 ❑ *Businessmen are tired of politicians talking the economy down.* 商人对政客贬低经济的行为感到厌倦。

▸ **talk into** PHRASAL VERB If you **talk** a person **into** doing something they do not want to do, especially something wrong or stupid, you persuade them to do it. 劝服 (尤指做错事或蠢事) ❑ *He talked me into marrying him. He also talked me into having a baby.* 他劝服我和他结了婚。他也劝服我生了个孩子。

▸ **talk out of** PHRASAL VERB If you **talk** someone **out of** doing something they want or intend to do, you persuade them not to do it. 说服…不做 ❑ *My mother tried to talk me out of getting a divorce.* 我妈妈试图说服我不要离婚。

▸ **talk over** PHRASAL VERB If you **talk** something **over**, you discuss it thoroughly and honestly. (详细坦诚地) 商谈 ❑ *He always talked things over with his friends.* 他总是和他的朋友们详细地商谈事情。 ❑ *We should go somewhere quiet, and talk it over.* 我们应该去个安静的地方好好谈谈这件事。

▸ **talk through** 1 PHRASAL VERB If you **talk** something **through** with someone, you discuss it with them thoroughly. 详细地讨论 ❑ *He and I have talked through this whole tricky problem.* 他和我已经详细讨论了这一整个棘手的问题。 ❑ *Now her children are grown-up and she has talked through with them what happened.* 现在她的孩子们长大了，因此她已向他们详述了所发生的事情。 2 PHRASAL VERB If someone **talks** you **through** something that you do not know, they explain it to you carefully. 向…详细解释 ❑ *Now she must talk her sister through the process a step at a time.* 现在她必须向她姐姐详细解释这个过程，一次只说一个步骤。

▸ **talk up** PHRASAL VERB If someone **talks up** a particular thing, they make it sound more interesting, valuable, or likely than it originally seemed. 夸大 ❑ *Politicians accuse the media of talking up the possibility of a riot.* 政客们谴责媒体夸大骚乱的可能性。 ❑ *He'll be talking up his plans for the economy.* 他将夸大他的经济计划。

Thesaurus *talk* 另参见:

V.	chat, discuss, gossip, say, share, speak, tell; (*ant.*) listen 2
N.	argument, conversation, dialogue, discussion, interview, negotiation; (*ant.*) silence 2 chatter, chitchat, conversation, gossip, rumor 8

talka·tive /tɔkətɪv/ ADJ Someone who is **talkative** talks a lot. 爱说话的 ❑ *He suddenly became very talkative, his face slightly flushed, his eyes much brighter.* 他突然变得很爱说话，他的脸颊稍微有点红，他的眼睛明亮多了。

talk show (**talk shows**) also **talk-show** N-COUNT A **talk show** is a television or radio show in which people talk to a host in an informal way. (电视或广播中的) 访谈节目

tall ♦◇◇ /tɔl/ (**taller, tallest**) 1 ADJ Someone or something that is **tall** has a greater height than is normal or average. 高的 ❑ *Being tall can make you feel incredibly self-confident.* 个子高能使你感觉极其自信。 2 ADJ You use **tall** to ask or talk about the height of someone or something. (有多) 高 ❑ *How tall are you?* 你有多高？ 3 PHRASE If something is **a tall order**, it is very difficult. 难办的事 ❑ *Financing your studies may seem like a tall order, but there is plenty of help available.* 资助你的学业似乎是一件难办的事，但有很多可利用的帮助。 4 PHRASE If you say that someone **walks tall**, you mean that they behave in a way that shows that they have pride in themselves and in what they are doing. 昂首阔步 ❑ *They shouldn't be disappointed or let their heads fall, but walk tall.* 他们不应该失望或垂头丧气，而应该昂首阔步。

tal·ly /tæli/ (**tallies, tallying, tallied**) 1 N-COUNT A **tally** is a record of amounts or numbers which you keep changing and adding to as the activity which affects it progresses. 记录 ❑ *They do not keep a tally of visitors to the palace, but it is very popular.* 他们没有对来宫殿的游客作一个记录，不过这个地方非常受欢迎的。 2 V-RECIP If one number or statement **tallies with** another, they agree with each other or are exactly the same. You can also say that two numbers or statements **tally**. 与…相符 ❑ *Its own estimate of three hundred tallies with that of another survey.* 它自己估计的300与另一项调查的结果相吻合。

tame /teɪm/ (**tames, taming, tamed, tamer, tamest**) 1 ADJ A **tame** animal or bird is one that is not afraid of humans. 驯服的 ❑ *They never became tame; they would run away if you approached them.* 它们从没有被驯服，如果你靠近，它们就跑开了。 2 ADJ If you say that something or someone is **tame**, you are criticizing them for being weak and uninteresting, rather than forceful or shocking.

软弱的；乏味的 [DISAPPROVAL] ❑ *These ideas may seem tame today, but they were inflammatory in his time.* 这些想法今天看来也许是平淡乏味的，但在他那个时代却是很有煽动性的。 **3** V-T If someone **tames** a wild animal or bird, they train it not to be afraid of humans and to do what they say. 驯化 ❑ *The Amazons were believed to have been the first to tame horses.* 亚马逊人被认为是最早驯化了马的人。

tam·per /tæmpər/ (**tampers, tampering, tampered**) V-I If someone **tampers with** something, they interfere with it or try to change it when they have no right to do so. 干涉；篡改 ❑ *I don't want to be accused of tampering with the evidence.* 我不想被指控篡改证据。

tam·pon /tæmpɒn/ (**tampons**) N-COUNT A **tampon** is a tube made of cotton that a woman puts inside her vagina in order to absorb blood during menstruation. 月经棉塞

★ **tan** /tæn/ (**tans, tanning, tanned**) **1** N-SING If you have a **tan**, your skin has become darker than usual because you have been in the sun. 晒黑的皮肤 ❑ *She is tall and blonde, with a permanent tan.* 她个子高，一头金发，皮肤黝黑。 **2** V-T/V-I If a part of your body **tans** or if you **tan** it, your skin becomes darker than usual because you spend a lot of time in the sun. 使晒黑；晒黑 ❑ *I have very pale skin that never tans.* 我肤色很白，永远晒不黑。● **tanned** ADJ 晒黑的 ❑ *Their skin was tanned and glowing from their weeks at the sea.* 他们在海上呆了几个星期，皮肤晒得黑里泛红。

tan·dem /tændəm/ (**tandems**) **1** N-COUNT A **tandem** is a bicycle designed for two riders, on which one rider sits behind the other. 前后双人自行车 **2** PHRASE If one thing happens or is done **in tandem with** another thing, the two things happen at the same time. 同时地 ❑ *...when literature is used in tandem with textbooks.* …当文学作品与教材同时被使用时。
→ see **bicycle**

Word Link *tang ≈ touching : entangle, intangible, tangible*

▲ **tan·gible** /tændʒɪbᵊl/ ADJ If something is **tangible**, it is clear enough or definite enough to be easily seen, felt, or noticed. 清晰明确的 ❑ *There should be some tangible evidence that the economy is starting to recover.* 应该有一些足够清晰的证据表明经济正开始复苏。

★ **tan·gle** /tæŋgᵊl/ (**tangles, tangling, tangled**) **1** N-COUNT A **tangle of** something is a mass of it twisted together in a messy way. 乱糟糟的一团 ❑ *A tangle of wires is all that remains of the computer and phone systems.* 乱糟糟的一团电线是电脑和电话系统留下来的全部。 **2** V-T/V-I If something **is tangled** or **tangles**, it becomes twisted together in a messy way. 使缠结；缠结 ❑ *Animals get tangled in fishing nets and drown.* 动物被缠在渔网里淹死了。 ❑ *Her hair tends to tangle.* 她的头发易打结。

tank ♦◇◇ /tæŋk/ (**tanks, tanking, tanked**) **1** N-COUNT A **tank** is a large container for holding liquid or gas. (盛放液体或气体的) 罐；箱；槽 ❑ *...an empty fuel tank.* …一个空的燃料罐。 ❑ *Two water tanks provide a total capacity of 400 liters.* 两个水箱的总容量为400升。 **2** N-COUNT A **tank** is a large military vehicle that is equipped with weapons and moves along on metal tracks that are fitted over the wheels. 坦克 **3** V-I If something such as a stock price or a movie **tanks**, it performs very badly, for example because it loses a lot of money. 表现得很糟糕 [AM, INFORMAL] ❑ *Tech stocks have tanked.* 科技股票已经表现得很糟糕了。 ❑ *The movie, which cost $137 million, tanked, grossing only $32 million.* 这部电影，花了1.37亿美元，表现得很糟糕，票房总收入只有3200万美元。 ❑ *His career tanked after the show left the air.* 这个节目不再播放后，他的事业就变得很糟糕。
→ see **scuba diving**

★ **tank·er** /tæŋkər/ (**tankers**) **1** N-COUNT A **tanker** is a very large ship used for transporting large quantities of gas or liquid, especially oil. 油轮 [oft supp N, also "by" N] ❑ *A Greek oil tanker has run aground.* 一艘希腊油轮已经搁浅了。 **2** N-COUNT A **tanker** is a large truck, railroad vehicle, or aircraft used for transporting large quantities of a substance. 大卡车；铁路货车；运输机 [usu supp N, also "by" N] ❑ *...aerial refueling tankers.* …空中加油飞机。
→ see **oil, ship**

tan·ta·lise /tæntəlaɪz/ [BRIT] → see **tantalize**

tan·ta·lize /tæntᵊlaɪz/ (**tantalizes, tantalizing, tantalized**)

in BRIT, also use **tantalise**

V-T If someone or something **tantalizes** you, they make you feel hopeful and excited about getting what you want, usually before disappointing you by not letting you have what they appeared to offer. (以可望而不可及之物) 逗引 ❑ *...the dreams of democracy that have so tantalized them.* …让他们可望而不可及的民主梦想。

● **tan·ta·liz·ing** ADJ 逗引性的 ❑ *A tantalizing aroma of roast beef fills the air.* 烤牛肉诱人的香味弥漫在空气中。

tan·ta·mount /tæntəmaʊnt/ ADJ If you say that one thing is **tantamount to** another, more serious thing, you are emphasizing how bad, unacceptable, or unfortunate the first thing is by comparing it to the second thing. 无异于的 [v-link ADJ "to" n/-ing] [FORMAL, EMPHASIS] ❑ *What Bracey is saying is tantamount to heresy.* 布里斯正在说的无异于异端邪说。

tan·trum /tæntrəm/ (**tantrums**) N-COUNT If a child has a **tantrum**, they lose their temper in a noisy and uncontrolled way. If you say that an adult is throwing a **tantrum**, you are criticizing them for losing their temper and acting in a childish way. 发脾气 [DISAPPROVAL] ❑ *He immediately threw a tantrum, screaming and stomping up and down like a child.* 他立刻发起脾气来，尖叫着，像孩子似的来回跺脚。 ❑ *...a temper tantrum.* …发了一顿脾气。

tap ♦◇◇ /tæp/ (**taps, tapping, tapped**) **1** N-COUNT A **tap** is a device that controls the flow of a liquid or gas from a pipe or container, for example, on a sink or on a cask or barrel. 阀门 [mainly BRIT]

in AM, usually use **faucet**

2 V-T/V-I If you **tap** something, you hit it with a quick light blow or a series of quick light blows. 轻敲 ❑ *He tapped the table nervously with his fingers.* 他紧张地用手指轻轻地敲打桌子。 ❑ *Grace tapped on the bedroom door and went in.* 格雷斯轻轻地敲卧室的门，然后进去了。 ● N-COUNT **Tap** is also a noun. 轻敲 ❑ *A tap on the door interrupted him and Sally Pierce came in.* 轻轻的敲门声打断了他，萨莉·皮尔斯进来了。 **3** V-T If you **tap** your fingers or feet, you make a regular pattern of sound by hitting a surface lightly and repeatedly with them, especially while you are listening to music. (随着音乐) 打拍子 ❑ *The song's so catchy it makes you bounce around the living room or tap your feet.* 这首歌很琅琅上口，它让你在客厅里跳跃或者用脚打拍子。 **4** V-T If someone **taps** your telephone, they attach a special device to the line so that they can secretly listen to your conversations. 窃听 (电话) ❑ *The government passed laws allowing the police to tap telephones.* 政府通过了允许警察窃听电话的法律。 ● N-COUNT **Tap** is also a noun. 电话窃听 ❑ *He assured us that we were not subjected to phone taps.* 他向我们保证我们不会遭到电话窃听。 **5** PHRASE If drinks are **on tap**, they come from a tap rather than from a bottle. 从阀门流出 [usu v-link PHR] ❑ *Filtered water is always on tap here.* 在这儿，过滤过的水随时可以从阀门流出。

Word Partnership *tap* 的常用搭配：

V.	**turn on a** tap **1**
N.	**cold/hot water** tap **1**
	tap **on a door**, tap ***someone*** **on the shoulder** **2**
	tap **your feet** **3**
	tap **a (tele)phone** **4**

tap danc·er (**tap dancers**) N-COUNT A **tap dancer** is a dancer who does tap dancing. 踢踏舞者

tap danc·ing also **tap-dancing, tap** N-UNCOUNT **Tap dancing** is a style of dancing in which the dancers wear special shoes with pieces of metal on the heels and toes. The shoes make loud sharp sounds as the dancers move their feet. 踢踏舞

tape ♦♦◇ /teɪp/ (**tapes, taping, taped**) **1** N-UNCOUNT **Tape** is a sticky strip of plastic used for sticking things together. 胶带 ❑ *...strong adhesive tape.* …黏性很强的胶带。 **2** N-UNCOUNT **Tape** is a narrow plastic strip covered with a magnetic substance. It is used to record sounds, pictures, and computer information. 磁带 ❑ *Tape is expensive and loses sound quality every time it is copied.* 磁带很贵，而且每被复制一次，音质就会有所降低。 **3** N-COUNT A **tape** is a cassette or spool with magnetic tape wound around it. 盒式磁带 ❑ *...a new cassette tape.* …一盘新的盒式磁带。 **4** V-T/V-I If you **tape** music, sounds, or television pictures, you record them using a tape recorder or a video recorder. (用磁带录音机或录像机) 录制 ❑ *She has just taped an interview.* 她刚刚录制了一次采访。 ❑ *He shouldn't be taping without the singer's permission.* 他不应该未经歌手允许就录音。 **5** V-T If you **tape** one thing to another, you attach it using adhesive tape. 用胶带粘贴 ❑ *I taped the base of the feather onto the velvet.* 我用胶带把羽毛的根部粘到天鹅绒上。 **6** N-COUNT A **tape** is a ribbon that is stretched across the finishing line of a race. (赛跑的) 终点线 ❑ *...the finishing tape.* …终点线。 **7** → see also **red tape, videotape**
→ see **office**

t

Word Partnership *tape* 的常用搭配：

N. **piece of** tape, **roll of** tape 1
reel of tape 2
cassette tape, **music** tape, tape **player** 3
tape **a conversation**, tape **an interview**, tape **a show** 4
V. **listen to a** tape, **make a** tape, **play a** tape, **watch a** tape 3

tape meas·ure (tape measures) N-COUNT A **tape measure** is a strip of metal, plastic, or cloth which has numbers marked on it and is used for measuring. 卷尺

ta·per /teɪpər/ (tapers, tapering, tapered) 1 V-T/V-I If something **tapers**, or if you **taper** it, it becomes gradually thinner at one end. 使逐渐变细；逐渐变细 ❑ *Unlike other trees, it doesn't taper very much. It stays fat all the way up.* 不像其他树，它不是越往上越细，而是自下往上一样粗。● **ta·pered** ADJ 锥形的 ❑ *...the elegantly tapered legs of the dressing-table.* …梳妆台那优美的锥形腿。 2 N-COUNT A **taper** is a long, thin candle or a thin wooden strip that is used for lighting fires. 细长的蜡烛；点火木条 ❑ *Taking up a candlestick, he touched the wick to a lighted taper.* 他举起烛台，触摸一根燃着的蜡烛的烛芯。

tape re·cord·er (tape recorders) also **tape-recorder** N-COUNT A **tape recorder** is a machine used for recording and playing music, speech, or other sounds. 磁带录放机

tap·es·try /tæpɪstri/ (tapestries) N-VAR A **tapestry** is a large piece of heavy cloth with a picture woven into it using colored threads. 织锦 ❑ *He stared in wonder at the tapestries on the walls.* 他惊奇地注视着墙上的织锦。

▲ **tar** /tɑr/ 1 N-UNCOUNT **Tar** is a thick black sticky substance that is used especially for making roads. 沥青 ❑ *The oil has hardened to tar.* 油已硬化成沥青了。 2 N-UNCOUNT **Tar** is one of the poisonous substances contained in tobacco. (烟草中的) 焦油 ❑ *...strict guidelines as to the amount of tar contained in cigarettes.* …关于香烟中焦油含量的严格的指导原则。

tar·get ♦♦◊ /tɑrgɪt/ (targets, targeting or targetting, targeted or targetted) 1 N-COUNT A **target** is something at which someone is aiming a weapon or other object. 靶；(攻击的) 目标 ❑ *The village lies beside a main road, making it an easy target for bandits.* 该村位于大路边，容易成为匪徒攻击的目标。 2 N-COUNT A **target** is a result that you are trying to achieve. (试图达成的) 目标 ❑ *She's won back her place too late to achieve her target of 20 goals this season.* 她赢回她的位置为时已晚，无法实现她本赛季打进20个球的目标。 3 V-T To **target** a particular person or thing means to decide to attack or criticize them. 把…作为攻击目标；把…作为批评对象 ❑ *Republicans targeted her as vulnerable in her bid for reelection this year.* 共和党人认为她在今年的再次参选中是不堪一击的攻击目标。● N-COUNT **Target** is also a noun. (攻击、批评的) 对象 [oft N "of/for" n] ❑ *In the past they have been the target of racist abuse.* 过去他们一直是种族虐待的对象。 4 V-T If you **target** a particular group of people, you try to appeal to those people or affect them. 以 (某特定人群) 为目标；针对 ❑ *The campaign will target American insurance companies.* 这场运动将以美国的保险公司为目标。● N-COUNT **Target** is also a noun. (针对的) 目标 ❑ *Yuppies are a prime target group for marketing strategies.* 雅皮士是市场营销策略的主要目标群体。 5 PHRASE If someone or something is **on target**, they are making good progress and are likely to achieve the result that is wanted. 有望达到目标 ❑ *We were still right on target for our deadline.* 我们那时仍然很有希望在最后期限之前完成目标。

T

Word Partnership *target* 的常用搭配：

V. **attack** a target 1
hit a target, **miss** a target 1 2
ADJ. **easy** target, **moving** target 1
intended target, **likely** target, **possible** target, **prime** target 1 – 4
N. target **practice** 1
target **date** 2
target **of criticism**, target **of an investigation** 3
target **audience**, target **group**, target **population** 4

★ **tar·iff** /tærɪf/ (tariffs) N-COUNT A **tariff** is a tax that a government collects on goods coming into a country. (政府对进口货物征收的) 关税 [BUSINESS] ❑ *America wants to eliminate tariffs on items such as electronics.* 美国想要取消电子类产品的关税。

tar·mac /tɑrmæk/ 1 N-UNCOUNT **Tarmac** is a material used for making road surfaces, consisting of crushed stones mixed with tar. (用来铺路面的) 柏油碎石 [BRIT, TRADEMARK]

in AM, usually use **blacktop**

2 N-SING **The tarmac** is an area with a surface made of tarmac, especially the area from which planes take off at an airport. 柏油碎石路面 (尤指飞机跑道) ❑ *Standing on the tarmac were two American planes.* 停在跑道上的是两架美国飞机。

tar·nish /tɑrnɪʃ/ (tarnishes, tarnishing, tarnished) 1 V-T If you say that something **tarnishes** someone's reputation or image, you mean that it causes people to have a worse opinion of them than they would otherwise have had. 玷污；损坏 (名声或形象) ❑ *The affair could tarnish the reputation of the senator.* 这一事件可能有损那位参议员的名声。● **tar·nished** ADJ 受玷污了的；受损了的 ❑ *He says he wants to improve the tarnished image of his country.* 他说想改善他的国家已受损的形象。 2 V-T/V-I If a metal **tarnishes** or if something **tarnishes** it, it becomes stained and loses its brightness. 玷污；变得有污迹 ❑ *It never rusts or tarnishes.* 它从不生锈，也没有污迹。

▲ **tart** /tɑrt/ (tarts) 1 N-VAR A **tart** is a shallow pastry case with a filling of food, especially sweet food. (尤指甜心) 馅饼 ❑ *...apple tarts.* …苹果馅饼。 2 ADJ If something such as fruit is **tart**, it has a sharp taste. (水果等) 味道浓烈的 ❑ *The blackberries were too tart on their own, so we stewed them gently with some apples.* 黑莓本身的味道太浓烈，所以我们加些苹果将其稍稍炖一下。 3 ADJ A **tart** remark or way of speaking is sharp and unpleasant, often in a way that is a little cruel. (言辞) 尖刻的 ❑ *The words were more tart than she had intended.* 这些话比她原本意欲表达的要尖刻。 4 N-COUNT If someone refers to a woman or girl as a **tart**, they are criticizing her because they think she is sexually immoral or dresses in a way that makes her look sexually immoral. 轻佻放荡的女人 [INFORMAL, OFFENSIVE, DISAPPROVAL]

tar·tan /tɑrtᵊn/ (tartans) N-VAR **Tartan** is a group of designs for cloth traditionally associated with Scotland. The design is made up of lines of different widths and colors crossing each other at right angles. **Tartan** is also used to refer to cloth which has this pattern. (苏格兰) 花格图案；格子呢 ❑ *...traditional tartan kilts.* …传统的格子呢褶裙。

task ♦♦◊ /tæsk/ (tasks, tasking, tasked) 1 N-COUNT A **task** is an activity or piece of work which you have to do, usually as part of a larger project. 任务 ❑ *Walker had the unenviable task of breaking the bad news to Mark.* 沃克得把这个坏消息告诉马克，这可不是什么美差。 2 V-T If you **are tasked with** doing a particular activity or piece of work, someone in authority asks you to do it. 委派任务 (给…) ❑ *Jen was tasked with running a charity basketball tournament.* 珍被委以举办一场慈善篮球赛的任务。

Thesaurus *task* 另参见：

N. assignment, job, responsibility 1

Word Partnership *task* 的常用搭配：

V. **accomplish** a task, **assign** *someone* a task, **complete** a task, **face** a task, **give** *someone* a task, **perform** a task 1
ADJ. **complex** task, **difficult** task, **easy** task, **enormous** task, **important** task, **impossible** task, **main** task, **simple** task 1

taste ♦♦◊ /teɪst/ (tastes, tasting, tasted) 1 N-UNCOUNT **Taste** is one of the five senses that people have. When you have food or drink in your mouth, your sense of taste makes it possible for you to recognize what it is. 味觉 ❑ *...a keen sense of taste.* …灵敏的味觉。 2 N-COUNT The **taste** of something is the individual quality that it has when you put it in your mouth and that distinguishes it from other things. For example, something may have a sweet, bitter, sour, or salty taste. 味道 ❑ *I like the taste of wine and enjoy trying different kinds.* 我喜欢葡萄酒的味道，喜欢品尝不同种类的葡萄酒。 3 N-SING If you have a **taste** of some food or drink, you try a small amount of it in order to see what the flavor is like. 尝 ❑ *Yves sometimes gives customers a taste of a wine before they order.* 伊维斯有时候会在顾客们点酒前让他们先尝一下。 4 V-I If food or drink **tastes of** something, it has that particular flavor, which you notice when you eat or drink it. 有…味道 [no cont] ❑ *I drank a cup of tea that tasted of diesel.* 我喝了一杯有柴油味的茶。 ❑ *It tastes like chocolate.* 它吃起来像巧克力。 5 V-T If you **taste** some food or drink, you eat or drink a small amount of it in order to try its flavor, for example, to see if

Word Web taste

What we think of as **taste** is mostly **odor**. The sense of **smell** accounts for about 80% of the experience. We actually taste only four **sensations: sweet, salty, sour,** and **bitter**. We experience sweetness and saltiness through taste buds near the tip of the **tongue**. We sense sourness at the sides and bitterness at the back of the tongue. Saltiness is felt all over the tongue. Some people have more taste buds than others. Scientists have discovered some "supertasters" with 425 taste buds per square centimeter. Most of us have about 184 and some "nontasters" have only about 96.

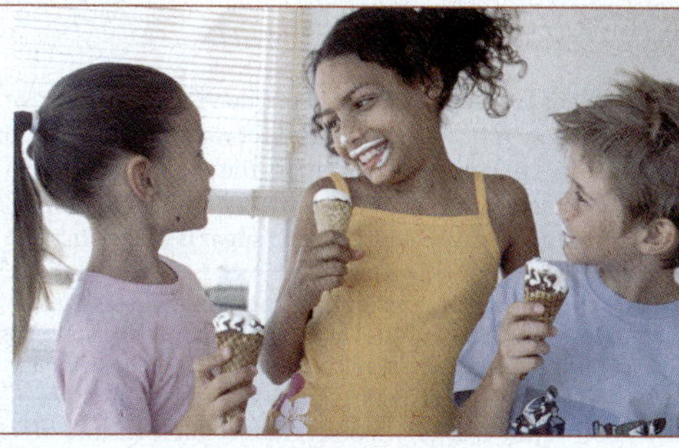

you like it or not. 品尝 ❑ *I tasted the wine the waiter had produced.* 我尝了尝服务员端上来的葡萄酒。 6 V-T If you can **taste** something that you are eating or drinking, you are aware of its flavor. 尝出…味道 [no passive] ❑ *You can taste the green chili in the dish but it is a little sweet.* 你能吃出菜里有青辣椒的味道，但它有点甜。 7 N-SING If you have a **taste of** a particular way of life or activity, you have a brief experience of it. (短暂的) 体验 ❑ *This voyage was his first taste of freedom.* 这次航行使他第一次体验到自由的滋味。 8 V-T If you **taste** something such as a way of life or a pleasure, you experience it for a short period of time. (短暂地) 体验 [no passive] ❑ *Once you have tasted the outdoor life in southern California, it's hard to return to Montana in winter.* 一旦你体验过南加州的户外生活，再要回到蒙大拿过冬就会感到很难。 9 N-SING If you have a **taste for** something, you have a liking or preference for it. 喜好 ❑ *That gave me a taste for reading.* 那使我有了读书的喜好。 10 N-UNCOUNT A person's **taste** is their choice **in** the things that they like or buy, for example, their clothes, possessions, or music. If you say that someone has good **taste**, you mean that you approve of their choices. If you say that they have bad **taste**, you disapprove of their choices. 品味 [also N in pl] ❑ *His taste in clothes is extremely good.* 他在服装上品味极好。 11 PHRASE If you say that something that is said or done is **in bad taste** or **in poor taste**, you mean that it is offensive, often because it concerns death or sex and is inappropriate for the situation. If you say that something is **in good taste**, you mean that it is not offensive and that it is appropriate for the situation. 品味低/高 ❑ *He rejects the idea that his film is in bad taste.* 他拒绝接受那种认为他的电影品味低的观点。

→ see Word Web: **taste**

→ see **sugar**

Word Partnership taste 的常用搭配：

N.	**sense of** taste 1
ADJ.	**bitter/salty/sour/sweet** taste 2
	taste **bitter/salty/sour/sweet**, taste **good** 4
	acquired taste 9
	bad/good/poor taste 10
	in bad/good/poor taste 11
V.	**like the** taste **of** *something* 2
	get a taste **of** *something* 7

taste·ful /teɪstfəl/ ADJ If you say that something is **tasteful**, you consider it to be attractive, elegant, and in good taste. 有品位的 ❑ *The decor is tasteful and restrained.* 该装饰有品位且不花哨。 ● **taste·ful·ly** ADV 有品位地 ❑ *...a large and tastefully decorated home.* …一座装饰很有品位的大宅邸。

taste·less /teɪstlɪs/ 1 ADJ If you describe something such as furniture, clothing, or the way that a house is decorated as **tasteless**, you consider it to be vulgar and unattractive. (家具、衣物、房屋装饰等) 没品位的 ❑ *...a house crammed with tasteless furniture.* …一座塞满了毫无品位的家具的房子。 2 ADJ If you describe something such as a remark or joke as **tasteless**, you mean that it is offensive. (言辞、笑话) 没品位的；低俗的 ❑ *I think that is the most vulgar and tasteless remark I have ever heard in my life.* 我认为那是我平生听到过的最庸俗没品位的话。 3 ADJ If you describe food or drink as **tasteless**, you mean that it has very little or no flavor. (食品、饮料) 没味的 ❑ *The fish was mushy and tasteless.* 这鱼烧得烂而无味。

tasty /teɪsti/ (**tastier, tastiest**) ADJ If you say that food is **tasty**, you mean that it has a fairly strong and pleasant flavor which makes it good to eat. 味美的 ❑ *Try this tasty dish for supper with a crispy salad.* 晚餐就着一道鲜脆色拉尝尝这道佳肴。

tat·tered /tætərd/ ADJ If something such as clothing or a book is **tattered**, it is damaged or torn, especially because it has been used a lot over a long period of time. (衣物、书籍等) 破旧的 ❑ *He fled wearing only a sarong and a tattered shirt.* 他逃跑时仅穿着一条莎笼和一件破衬衫。

tat·ters /tætərz/ 1 N-PLURAL Clothes that are **in tatters** are badly torn in several places, so that pieces can easily come off. (衣服) 破烂不堪 ❑ *His jeans were left in tatters.* 他的牛仔裤已破烂不堪。 2 N-PLURAL If you say that something such as a plan or a person's state of mind is **in tatters**, you are emphasizing that it is weak, has suffered a lot of damage, and is likely to fail completely. (计划、心情等) 千疮百孔的状态 [EMPHASIS]

tat·too /tætu/ (**tattoos, tattooing, tattooed**) 1 N-COUNT A **tattoo** is a design that is drawn on someone's skin using needles to make little holes and filling them with colored dye. 文身 ❑ *On the back of his neck he has a tattoo of a cross.* 他后脖子上有个十字文身。 2 V-T If someone **tattoos** you, they give you a tattoo. 给…文身 ❑ *In the old days, they would paint and tattoo their bodies for ceremonies.* 过去，他们会为了某些仪式而在身上绘图、文身。

taught /tɔt/ **Taught** is the past tense and past participle of **teach**. **teach**的过去式和过去分词

taunt /tɔnt/ (**taunts, taunting, taunted**) V-T If someone **taunts** you, they say unkind or insulting things to you, especially about your weaknesses or failures. 嘲笑；羞辱 ❑ *A gang taunted a disabled man.* 一帮混混儿羞辱了一个残疾人。 ● N-COUNT **Taunt** is also a noun. 嘲笑；羞辱 ❑ *For years they suffered racist taunts.* 多年来他们遭到了种族主义者的羞辱。

taut /tɔt/ (**tauter, tautest**) 1 ADJ Something that is **taut** is stretched very tight. 紧绷的 ❑ *The clothes line is pulled taut and secured.* 晾衣绳被拉紧系牢了。 2 ADJ If someone has a **taut** expression, they look very worried and tense. (神色) 紧张不安的 ❑ *Ben sat up quickly, his face taut and terrified.* 本迅速坐起来，神情紧张而恐惧。

▲ **tav·ern** /tævərn/ (**taverns**) N-COUNT; N-IN-NAMES A **tavern** is a bar. 酒吧 [OLD-FASHIONED] ❑ *Drinkers line the bar at Byrnes Tavern.* 酒客沿伯恩斯酒吧的吧台排成一行。

tax ◆◆◆ /tæks/ (**taxes, taxing, taxed**) 1 N-VAR **Tax** is an amount of money that you have to pay to the government so that it can pay for public services such as road and schools. 税 [BUSINESS] ❑ *No-one enjoys paying tax.* 没人喜欢缴税。 ❑ *...a pledge not to raise taxes on people below a certain income.* …一个对收入低于一定水平的人不提高税收的承诺。 2 V-T When a person or company **is taxed**, they have to pay a part of their income or profits to the government. When goods **are taxed**, a percentage of their price has to be paid to the government. (对个人、公司、货物) 征税 [BUSINESS] ❑ *Husband and wife may be taxed separately on their incomes.* 丈夫和妻子可能会分别被征收所得税。 3 → see also **taxing, income tax**

tax·able /tæksəbᵊl/ ADJ **Taxable** income is income on which you have to pay tax. 应纳税的 [BUSINESS] ❑ *It is worth consulting the guide to see whether your income is taxable.* 值得查一下这本手册看看你的收入是否该纳税。

taxa·tion /tækseɪʃᵊn/ 1 N-UNCOUNT **Taxation** is the system by which a government takes money from people and spends it on things such as education, health, and defense. 税制 [BUSINESS] ❑ *...the proposed reforms to taxation.* …拟议的税制改革。 2 N-UNCOUNT **Taxation** is the amount of money that people have to pay in taxes. 税额 [BUSINESS] ❑ *The result will be higher taxation.* 结果将是更高的税额。

tax break (**tax breaks**) N-COUNT If the government gives a **tax break** to a particular group of people or type of organization, it

t

Word Web tea

If you want to **brew** a good cup of **tea**, don't use a tea bag. For the best taste, try using fresh **tea leaves**. Begin by bringing a **teakettle** of water to a full boil. Use some of the water to warm the inside of a china **teapot**. Then empty the pot and add the tea leaves. Pour in more boiling water and let the tea steep for at least five minutes. Cover the pot with a tea cozy to keep it hot. Serve the tea in thin china teacups. Add milk and sugar if you wish.

reduces the amount of tax they have to pay or changes the tax system in a way that benefits them. 减税 [mainly AM, BUSINESS] ❑ *Today they'll consider tax breaks for businesses that create jobs in inner cities.* 今天他们将考虑对那些在市中心区创造就业机会的企业减税。

tax cred·it (**tax credits**) N-COUNT A **tax credit** is an amount of money on which you do not have to pay tax. 免税额度 [BUSINESS] ❑ *The president proposed tax credits for buying environmentally-friendly cars.* 总统提议对环保型汽车的购买者给予一定额度的免税。

tax-deductible /tæks dɪdʌktɪbᵊl/ ADJ If an expense is **tax-deductible**, it can be paid out of the part of your income on which you do not pay tax, so that the amount of tax you pay is reduced. (开销) 可在税前扣除的 [BUSINESS] ❑ *The cost of private childcare should be made tax-deductible.* 私人儿童保育费应做税前扣除。

tax eva·sion N-UNCOUNT **Tax evasion** is the crime of not paying the full amount of tax that you should pay. 逃税 [BUSINESS]

Word Link *free ≈ without : carefree, duty-free, tax-free*

tax-free ADJ **Tax-free** is used to describe income on which you do not have to pay tax. 免税的 [BUSINESS] ❑ *...a tax-free investment plan.* …一项免税投资计划。

tax ha·ven (**tax havens**) N-COUNT A **tax haven** is a country or place which has a low rate of tax so that people choose to live there or register companies there in order to avoid paying higher tax in their own countries. 避税地 (指税率较低的国家或地区) [BUSINESS] ❑ *The Caribbean has become an important location for international banking because it is a tax haven.* 加勒比海地区因其为避税安乐窝已成了国际银行业重地。

taxi /tæksi/ (**taxis, taxiing, taxied**) **1** N-COUNT A **taxi** is a car driven by a person whose job is to take people where they want to go in return for money. 出租车 [also "by" N] ❑ *The taxi drew up in front of the Riviera Club.* 该出租车在里维埃拉俱乐部前停了下来。 **2** V-T/V-I When an aircraft **taxis** along the ground or when a pilot **taxis** a plane somewhere, it moves slowly along the ground. 使 (飞机) 缓慢滑行; (飞机) 缓慢滑行 ❑ *She gave permission to the plane to taxi into position and hold for takeoff.* 她允许飞机滑行入位并准备起飞。

tax·ing /tæksɪŋ/ ADJ A **taxing** task or problem is one that requires a lot of mental or physical effort. 费劲的 ❑ *It's unlikely that you'll be asked to do anything too taxing.* 不大可能叫你去做任何太费劲的事。

taxi rank [BRIT] → see **taxi stand**

taxi stand (**taxi stands**) N-COUNT A **taxi stand** is a place where taxis wait for passengers, for example, at an airport or outside a station. 出租车候客区 [mainly AM]

in BRIT, usually use **taxi rank**

T

tax·payer /tækspeɪər/ (**taxpayers**) N-COUNT **Taxpayers** are people who pay a percentage of their income to the government as tax. 纳税人 [BUSINESS] ❑ *This is not going to cost the taxpayer anything. The company will bear the costs for the delay.* 这不会花纳税人的钱。公司将承担延误费用。

tax re·lief N-UNCOUNT **Tax relief** is a reduction in the amount of tax that a person or company has to pay, for example, because of expenses associated with their business or property. 税额减免 [BUSINESS] ❑ *...mortgage interest tax relief.* …抵押贷款利息款额减免。

tax re·turn (**tax returns**) N-COUNT A **tax return** is an official form that you fill in with details about your income and personal situation, so that the tax you owe can be calculated. 纳税申报表 [BUSINESS]

tax year (**tax years**) N-COUNT A **tax year** is a particular period of twelve months which is used by the government as a basis for calculating taxes and for organizing its finances and accounts. 税务年度 [BUSINESS]

TB /ti bi/ N-UNCOUNT **TB** is an extremely serious infectious disease that affects someone's lungs and other parts of their body. **TB** is an abbreviation for **tuberculosis**. 肺结核

TBA also **tba** **TBA** is sometimes written in announcements to indicate that something such as the place where something will happen or the people who will take part is not yet known and will be announced at a later date. **TBA** is an abbreviation for "to be announced." 待宣布 ❑ *When a manufacturer could not supply requested information, we have shown TBA.* 制造商不能提供所需信息时，我们已表示"有待宣布"。

tbc also **TBC** **Tbc** is sometimes written in announcements about future events to indicate that details of the event are not yet certain and will be confirmed later. **Tbc** is an abbreviation for "to be confirmed." 待定 [BRIT]

tea ♦♦◊ /ti/ (**teas**) **1** N-MASS **Tea** is a drink made by adding boiling water to tea leaves or tea bags. Tea usually refers to black tea from India or China. Herbal tea is made from various plants. 茶 ❑ *...a cup of tea.* …一杯茶。 ❑ *Would you like some tea?* 你想喝茶吗? ❑ *...chamomile tea.* …甘菊花茶。 ❑ *Four or five men were drinking tea from flasks.* 四五个男子在从瓶子里喝茶。 **2** N-MASS The chopped dried leaves of the plant that tea is made from is referred to as **tea**. 茶叶 ❑ *...a box of tea.* …一盒茶叶。
→ see Word Web: **tea**

teach ♦♦◊ /titʃ/ (**teaches, teaching, taught**) **1** V-T If you **teach** someone something, you give them instructions so that they know about it or how to do it. 教 ❑ *She taught me fractions and counting.* 他教我分数和计算。 ❑ *George had taught him how to ride a horse.* 乔治曾教过他骑马。 **2** V-T To **teach** someone something means to make them think, feel, or act in a new or different way. 教导 ❑ *Their daughter's death had taught him humility.* 他们女儿的死使他懂得了做人要谦逊。 ❑ *He taught his followers that they could all be members of the kingdom of God.* 他教导他的信徒说他们都会成为天国的成员。 **3** V-T/V-I If you **teach** or **teach** a subject, you help students to learn about it by explaining it or showing them how to do it, usually as a job at a school or college. 教 (某一科目); 教书 ❑ *Ingrid is currently teaching mathematics at the high school.* 英格丽德目前在那所中学教数学。 ❑ *She taught English to Japanese business people.* 她教日本商人英语。 ❑ *She has taught for 34 years.* 她教书已有34年。 **4** → see also **teaching** **5** to **teach** someone **a lesson** → see **lesson**

Thesaurus *teach* 另参见:
V. educate, school, train **1** – **3**

Word Partnership *teach* 的常用搭配:

ADV.	teach *someone* how **1**
N.	teach *someone* a skill, teach **students** **1**
	teach **children** **1** – **3**
	teach *someone* a lesson **2**
	teach **classes**, teach **courses**, teach **English/history/reading/science**, teach **school** **3**
V.	**try** to teach **1** – **3**

teach·er ♦♦◊ /titʃər/ (**teachers**) N-COUNT A **teacher** is a person who teaches, usually as a job at a school or similar institution. 教师 ❑ *I'm a teacher with 21 years' experience.* 我是一个有21年经验的教师。

Thesaurus *teacher* 另参见:
N. educator, instructor, professor, trainer

teach·ing ♦◊◊ /titʃɪŋ/ (**teachings**) **1** N-UNCOUNT **Teaching** is the work that a teacher does in helping students to learn. 教学 ❑ *The quality of teaching in the school is excellent.* 该校的教学质量非常好。 **2** N-COUNT The **teachings** of a particular person, school of thought, or religion are all the ideas and principles that they teach. 教导; 教义; 学说 ❑ *...the teachings of Jesus.* …耶稣的教义。

teak /tik/ N-UNCOUNT **Teak** is the wood of a tall tree with very hard, light-colored wood which grows in Southeast Asia. 柚木 ❑ *The door is beautifully made in solid teak.* 这扇门由纯柚木制成，做工精美。

tea·kettle /tikɛtᵊl/ (**teakettles**) also **tea kettle** N-COUNT A **teakettle** is a kettle that is used for boiling water to make tea. 烧水壶 [mainly AM]
→ see **tea**

team ◆◆◆ /tim/ (**teams, teaming, teamed**) 1 N-COUNT-COLL A **team** is a group of people who play a particular sport or game together against other similar groups of people. 运动队 ❑ *...a soccer team.* …一支足球队。 ❑ *...the swim team.* …那支游泳队。 2 N-COUNT-COLL You can refer to any group of people who work together as a **team**. 团队; 组 ❑ *Each specialist has a team of doctors under him or her.* 每位专家手下都有一组医生。
▸ **team up** PHRASAL VERB If you **team up with** someone, you join them in order to work together for a particular purpose. You can also say that two people or groups **team up**. (与某人) 组队; 合作 ❑ *Elton teamed up with Eric Clapton to wow thousands at the rock concert.* 埃尔顿与埃里克•克拉普顿在那场摇滚音乐会上联袂演出，博得了上千观众的喝彩。

team·mate /timmeɪt/ (**teammates**) also **team-mate** N-COUNT In a game or sport, your **teammates** are the other members of your team. 队友 ❑ *He was always a solid player, a hard worker, a great example to his teammates.* 他一直是实力派运动员，勤奋刻苦，是队友的好榜样。

team·work /timwɜrk/ N-UNCOUNT **Teamwork** is the ability a group of people have to work well together. 团队协作能力 ❑ *Today's complex buildings require close teamwork between the architect and the builders.* 当今复杂的建筑物需要建筑师和建筑工人的密切协作。

tea·pot /tipɒt/ (**teapots**) also **tea pot** 1 N-COUNT A **teapot** is a container with a lid, a handle, and a spout, used for making and serving tea. 茶壶 2 PHRASE If you describe a situation as **a tempest in a teapot**, you think that a lot of fuss is being made about something that is not important. 小题大做 [PHR after v, v-link PHR] [AM]

in BRIT, use **a storm in a teacup**

❑ *For some, it may seem silly, a tempest in a teapot.* 对有些人来说，这似乎很荒唐，是小题大做。
→ see **tea**

tear
1 CRYING
2 DAMAGING OR MOVING

❶ **tear** ◆◇◇ /tɪər/ (**tears**) 1 N-COUNT **Tears** are the drops of salty liquid that come out of your eyes when you are crying. 眼泪 ❑ *Her eyes filled with tears.* 她眼里噙满了泪水。 ❑ *I just broke down and wept with tears of joy.* 我实在控制不住，流下了高兴的眼泪。 2 N-PLURAL You can use **tears** in expressions such as **in tears, burst into tears**, and **close to tears** to indicate that someone is crying or is almost crying. 哭泣 ❑ *He was in floods of tears on the phone.* 他在电话里大哭。 ❑ *She burst into tears and ran from the kitchen.* 她突然哭了起来，跑出了厨房。
→ see **cry**

❷ **tear** ◆◆◇ /tɛər/ (**tears, tearing, tore, torn**)
➪ **Please look at meaning 8 to see if the expression you are looking for is shown under another headword.** 1 V-T/V-I If you **tear** paper, cloth, or another material, or if it **tears**, you pull it into two pieces or you pull it so that a hole appears in it. 撕破 (纸、布等); 撕开 ❑ *I tore my coat on a nail.* 我的外套在一个钉子上挂破了。 ● PHRASAL VERB **Tear up** means the same as **tear**. 撕破 ❑ *She tore the letter up.* 她把那封信撕了。 ❑ *Don't you dare tear up her ticket.* 你竟敢撕坏她的票。 2 N-COUNT A **tear** in paper, cloth, or another material is a hole that has been made in it. 破洞 ❑ *I peered through a tear in the van's curtains.* 我透过货车窗帘上的一个破洞偷偷窥视。 3 V-T/V-I If you **tear** one of your muscles or ligaments, or if it **tears**, you injure it by accidentally moving it in the wrong way. 拉伤 (肌肉或韧带); (肌肉或韧带) 拉伤 ❑ *He tore a muscle in his right thigh.* 他拉伤了右大腿的一块肌肉。 ❑ *If the muscle is stretched again it could even tear.* 这块肌肉再受到拉伸的话，它甚至可能会拉伤。 4 V-T To **tear** something from somewhere means to remove it roughly and violently. (猛烈地) 撕掉 ❑ *She tore the windscreen wipers from his car.* 她猛地扯掉了他车上的雨刮器。 5 V-I If a person or animal **tears at** something, they pull it violently and try to break it into pieces. 撕扯 ❑ *Female fans fought their way past bodyguards and tore at his clothes.* 女性仰慕者拼命绕过保镖，撕扯他的衣服。 6 V-I If you **tear** somewhere, you run, drive, or move there very quickly. 奔; 冲 ❑ *The door flew open and Miranda tore into the room.* 门猛地开了，米兰达冲进了房间。 7 V-T PASSIVE If you say that a place **is torn by** particular events, you mean that unpleasant events which cause suffering and division among people are happening there. 折磨 ❑ *...a country that has been torn by civil war and foreign invasion since its independence.* …一个自独立以来饱受内战外扰之苦的国家。 8 → see also **torn, wear and tear**
▸ **tear apart** 1 PHRASAL VERB If something **tears** people **apart**, it causes them to argue or to leave each other. 使 (人们) 不和; 使分裂 ❑ *Her pregnancy was tearing the family apart.* 她的怀孕引起了家庭的不和。 2 PHRASAL VERB If something **tears** you **apart**, it makes you feel very upset, worried, and unhappy. 使痛苦 ❑ *Don't think it hasn't torn me apart to be away from you.* 不要以为离开了你我并没有感到痛苦。
▸ **tear away** PHRASAL VERB If you **tear** someone **away from** a place or activity, you force them to leave the place or stop doing the activity, even though they want to remain there or carry on. 逼 (某人) 离开; 迫使停止 ❑ *He finally tore himself away from the table long enough to pour me a drink.* 他最终迫不得已离开了那张桌子片刻，给我倒了一杯饮料。
▸ **tear down** PHRASAL VERB If you **tear** something **down**, you destroy it or remove it completely. 拆除; 拆毁 ❑ *Angry Russians may have torn down the statue of Felix Dzerzhinsky.* 愤怒的俄罗斯人可能已经拆除了菲利克斯•捷尔任斯基的雕像。
▸ **tear off** PHRASAL VERB If you **tear off** your clothes, you take them off in a rough and violent way. 胡乱脱掉 ❑ *Totally exhausted, he tore his clothes off and fell into bed.* 由于疲惫不堪，他胡乱脱掉衣服就倒在了床上。
→ see **cut**
▸ **tear up** 1 PHRASAL VERB If something such as a road, railroad, or area of land **is torn up**, it is completely removed or destroyed. 拆除; 拆毁 ❑ *Dozens of miles of railroad track have been torn up.* 数十英里的铁轨已被拆除。 2 → see **tear** ❷ 1

tear·ful /tɪərfəl/ ADJ If someone is **tearful**, their face or voice shows signs that they have been crying or that they want to cry. 有泪的; 想哭的 ❑ *She became very tearful when pressed to talk about it.* 被逼谈论此事时，她眼泪汪汪。

tear gas /tɪər gæs/ N-UNCOUNT **Tear gas** is a gas that causes your eyes to sting and fill with tears so that you cannot see. It is sometimes used by the police or army to control crowds. 催泪瓦斯 ❑ *Police used tear gas to disperse the demonstrators.* 警察动用了催泪瓦斯来驱散示威人群。

★ **tease** /tiz/ (**teases, teasing, teased**) 1 V-T To **tease** someone means to laugh at them or make jokes about them in order to embarrass, annoy, or upset them. 嘲笑; 取笑 ❑ *He told her how the boys had set on him, teasing him.* 他告诉她那些男孩曾是如何攻击他、取笑他的。 ❑ *He teased me mercilessly about going Hollywood.* 他无情地取笑我想去好莱坞。 ● N-COUNT **Tease** is also a noun. 嘲笑; 取笑 ❑ *Calling her by her real name had always been one of his teases.* 称呼她的真名曾是他一贯的取笑方式之一。 2 N-COUNT If you refer to someone as a **tease**, you mean that they like laughing at people or making jokes about them. 爱嘲笑他人者; 爱取笑他人者 ❑ *My brother's such a tease.* 我弟弟就爱取笑他人。 3 V-T If someone **teases** their hair, they separate the individual strands from each other, for example by combing it. 梳理 ❑ *Her hair was teased until it stood out and around her face.* 她的头发被梳得直垂在脸旁。 ❑ *...two women in party dresses and teased hair.* …两位身着礼服、头发梳理整齐的妇女。

Thesaurus *tease* 另参见:
V. aggravate, bother, provoke 1

tea·spoon /tispun/ (**teaspoons**) N-COUNT A **teaspoon** is a small spoon used for putting sugar into tea or coffee, and in cooking. 茶匙 ❑ *Drop the dough onto a baking sheet with a teaspoon.* 用茶匙把面团舀到一张烘焙纸上。

Word Link *techn ≈ art, skill : biotechnology, technical, technician*

tech·ni·cal ◆◇◇ /tɛknɪkᵊl/ 1 ADJ **Technical** means involving the sorts of machines, processes, and materials that are used in industry, transportation, and communications. 技术的; 工艺的 ❑ *In order to reach this limit a number of technical problems will have to be solved.* 为了达到这个限度，有许多技术问题得解决。 ● **tech·ni·cal·ly** /tɛknɪkli/ ADV 技术上地; 工艺上地 [ADV adj] ❑ *...the largest and most technically advanced furnace company in the world.* …世界上规模最大、技术最先进的锅炉公司。 2 ADJ You use **technical** to describe the practical skills and methods used to do an activity such as an art, a craft, or a sport. 技巧的 ❏ *Their technical ability is exceptional.* 他们的技能是非凡的。 • **tech·ni·cal·ly** ADV 技巧上地 [ADV adj] ❏ *While Sade's voice isn't technically brilliant it has a quality which is unmistakable.* 虽然萨德的嗓音从技巧上讲不是很出色，但它有一种独特的音质。 **3** ADJ **Technical** language involves using special words to describe the details of a specialized activity. 专业的（语言）❏ *The technical term for sunburn is erythema.* 晒斑的专业术语是红斑。 **4** → see also **technically**

Word Partnership *technical* 的常用搭配：

N. technical **knowledge** **1**
technical **assistance**, technical **difficulties**, technical **expertise**, technical **experts**, technical **information**, technical **issues**, technical **problems**, technical **services**, technical **skills**, technical **support**, technical **training** **1** **2**

ADV. **highly** technical **1** **2**

tech·ni·cal·ity /tɛknɪkælɪti/ (**technicalities**) **1** N-PLURAL The **technicalities** of a process or activity are the detailed methods used to do it or to carry it out. (过程、活动的) 技术性细节 ❏ *...the technicalities of classroom teaching.* …课堂教学的技术性细节。 **2** N-COUNT A **technicality** is a point, especially a legal one, that is based on a strict interpretation of the law or of a set of rules but that may seem unimportant compared to a larger issue. (尤指法律的) 技术性细则 ❏ *The earlier verdict was overturned on a legal technicality.* 较早的裁决因法律上的一项技术性细则而遭到推翻。

tech·ni·cal·ly /tɛknɪkli/ **1** ADV If something is **technically** the case, it is the case according to a strict interpretation of facts, laws, or rules, but may not be important or relevant in a particular situation. 严格按照事实地；严格按照规定地 ❏ *More than a third of workers said they called into the office while technically on vacation.* 三分之一以上的员工说他们在按规定休假期间被召回过办公室。 **2** → see also **technical**

tech·ni·cal sup·port N-UNCOUNT **Technical support** is a repair and advice service that some companies such as computer companies provide for their customers, usually by telephone, fax, or e-mail. 技术支持 ❏ *...technical support for America Online users.* …对美国在线用户的技术支持。

Word Link *techn ≈ art, skill : biotechnology, technical, technician*

tech·ni·cian /tɛknɪʃ^{ə}n/ (**technicians**) **1** N-COUNT A **technician** is someone whose job involves skilled practical work with scientific equipment, for example, in a laboratory. 技术人员 ❏ *...a laboratory technician.* …一位实验室技术人员。 **2** N-COUNT A **technician** is someone who is very good at the detailed technical aspects of an activity. 精于某项技术的人 ❏ *...a versatile, veteran player, a superb technician.* …一个多才多艺、经验丰富、技能超凡的高手。

tech·nique ◆◆◇ /tɛknik/ (**techniques**) **1** N-COUNT A **technique** is a particular method of doing an activity, usually a method that involves practical skills. 技术 ❏ *...tests performed using a new technique.* …采用一种新技术做的试验。 **2** N-UNCOUNT **Technique** is skill and ability in an artistic, sporting, or other practical activity that you develop through training and practice. 技艺；技能 ❏ *He went off to the Amsterdam Academy to improve his technique.* 他去了阿姆斯特丹学院以提高技艺。

T

tech·no·logi·cal /tɛknəlɒdʒɪk^{ə}l/ ADJ **Technological** means relating to or associated with technology. 与技术有关的 [ADJ n] ❏ *...an era of very rapid technological change.* …一个技术飞速变革的时代。 • **tech·no·logi·cal·ly** /tɛknəlɒdʒɪkli/ ADV 技术上地 ❏ *...technologically advanced aircraft.* …技术先进的飞机。

tech·nol·ogy ◆◆◇ /tɛknɒlədʒi/ (**technologies**) N-VAR **Technology** refers to methods, systems, and devices which are the result of scientific knowledge being used for practical purposes. 技术 ❏ *Technology is changing fast.* 技术日新月异。 ❏ *They should be allowed to wait for cheaper technologies to be developed.* 他们应该被允许等待更廉价的技术开发出来。
→ see Word Web: **technology**

Word Partnership *technology* 的常用搭配：

ADJ. **advanced** technology, **available** technology, **educational** technology, **high** technology, **latest** technology, **medical** technology, **modern** technology, **new** technology, **sophisticated** technology, **wireless** technology

N. **computer** technology, **information** technology, **science and** technology

te·di·ous /tidiəs/ ADJ If you describe something such as a job, task, or situation as **tedious**, you mean it is boring and frustrating. 乏味烦人的 ❏ *Such lists are long and tedious to read.* 这种清单读起来既冗长又乏味烦人。 • **te·di·ous·ly** ADV 乏味烦人地 ❏ *...the most tediously boring aspects of international relations.* …国际关系中最乏味烦人的某些方面。

▲ **teem** /tim/ (**teems, teeming, teemed**) V-I If you say that a place **is teeming with** people or animals, you mean that it is crowded and the people and animals are moving around a lot. 挤满 [usu cont] ❏ *For most of the year, the area is teeming with tourists.* 一年的大部分时间里这个地方都挤满了游客。

teen /tin/ (**teens**) **1** N-PLURAL If you are a **teen** in your **teens**, you are between thirteen and nineteen years old. Teen is informal for teenager. 十几岁 (指13至19岁)；十几岁的人 ❏ *Most people who smoke began smoking in their teens.* 大多数吸烟的人都是在十几岁时开始吸的。 **2** ADJ **Teen** is used to describe things such as movies, magazines, bands, or activities that are aimed at or are done by people who are in their teens. 有关青少年的 [ADJ n] ❏ *...a new teen center.* …一个新的青少年中心。

teen·age /tineɪdʒ/ **1** ADJ **Teenage** children are aged between thirteen and nineteen years old. 十几岁 (指13至19岁) 的 [ADJ n] ❏ *She looked like any other teenage girl.* 她看上去和别的少女一样。 **2** ADJ **Teenage** is used to describe things such as movies, magazines, bands, or activities that are aimed at or are done by teenage children. 关于青少年的 [ADJ n] ❏ *..."Smash Hits," a teenage magazine.* …《流行金曲》，一本青少年杂志。

Word Link *teen ≈ plus ten, from 13-19 : eighteen, seventeen, teenager*

teen·ager ◆◇◇ /tineɪdʒər/ (**teenagers**) N-COUNT A **teenager** is someone who is between thirteen and nineteen years old. 十几岁 (指13至19岁) 的人 ❏ *As a teenager he attended Tulse Hill Senior High School.* 十几岁时，他上了塔尔斯山高级中学。
→ see **age, child**

tee·ter /titər/ (**teeters, teetering, teetered**) **1** V-I **Teeter** is used in expressions such as **teeter on the brink** and **teeter on the edge** to emphasize that something seems to be in a very unstable situation or position. 岌岌可危 [EMPHASIS] ❏ *The hotel is teetering on the brink of bankruptcy.* 这家旅馆正濒临破产。 **2** V-I If someone or something **teeters**, they shake in an unsteady way, and seem to be about to lose their balance and fall over. (人) 踉踉跄跄；(物) 摇摇欲坠 ❏ *Hyde shifted his weight and felt himself teeter forward, beginning to overbalance.* 海德挪了一下身子便感到自己往前晃动，开始失去平衡了。

teeth /tiθ/ **Teeth** is the plural of **tooth**. tooth的复数形式
→ see Word Web: **teeth**
→ see **face**

Word Web technology

Innovative technologies affect every aspect of our lives. **State-of-the-art** computer systems coordinate heating, lighting, communication, and entertainment systems in new homes. **Gadgets** such as **digital** music players the size of a pack of gum are common. The high-tech trend also has a more serious side. **Biotechnology** may help us find cures for diseases, but it also raises many ethical questions. **Cutting-edge** biometric technology is replacing old-fashioned security systems. Soon your ATM will check your identity by scanning the iris of your eye and your laptop will scan your fingerprint.

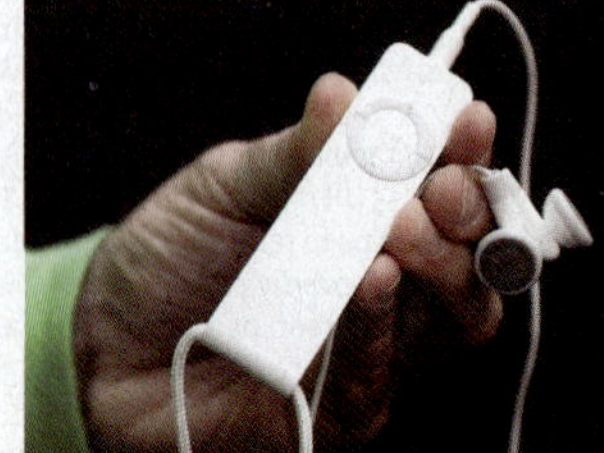

Word Web teeth

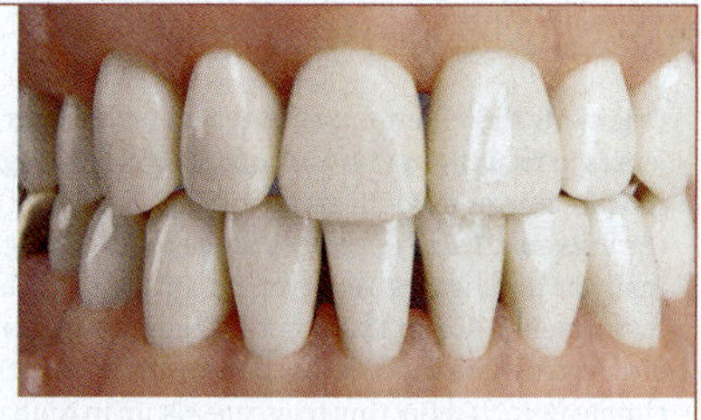

Dentists suggest **brushing** and flossing every day to help prevent **cavities**. Brushing removes food from the surface of the **teeth**. Flossing helps remove the **plaque** that forms between teeth and **gums**. In many places, the water supply contains **fluoride** which also helps keep teeth healthy. If **tooth decay** does develop, a dentist can use a metal or plastic **filling** to repair the tooth. A badly damaged or broken tooth may require a **crown**. Orthodontists use **braces** to straighten uneven rows of teeth. Occasionally, a dentist must remove all of a patient's teeth. Then **dentures** take the place of natural teeth.

★ **tele·com** /tɛlɪkɒm/ also **telecoms** N-UNCOUNT 1 **Telecom** is short for **telecommunications.** 电信 [N n] ❑ *The telecom industry in Australia is very small in comparison with the rest of the world.* 澳大利亚电信业与世界其他地区电信业相比规模很小。

tele·com·mu·ni·ca·tions /tɛlɪkəmyunɪkeɪʃᵊnz/

The form **telecommunication** is used as a modifier.

N-UNCOUNT **Telecommunications** is the technology of sending signals and messages over long distances using electronic equipment, for example, by radio and telephone. 电信 ❑ *...the telecommunications industry.* …电信业。

tele·com·mut·ing /tɛlɪkəmyutɪŋ/ N-UNCOUNT **Telecommuting** is working from home using equipment such as telephones, fax machines, and modems to contact people. 家庭远程办公 [BUSINESS] ❑ *There is also the potential to develop telecommuting and other more flexible working practices.* 也有发展家庭远程办公及其他更灵活的工作方式的可能性。

tele·con·fer·ence /tɛlɪkɒnfərəns, -frəns/ (**teleconferences**) N-COUNT A **teleconference** is a meeting involving people in various places around the world who use telephones or video links to communicate with each other. 电话会议；视频会议 [BUSINESS] ❑ *Managers at their factory hold a two-hour teleconference with head office every day.* 他们工厂的经理们每天与总部举行两小时的电话会议。 ● **tele·con·fer·enc·ing** N-UNCOUNT 电话会议；视频会议 ❑ *...teleconferencing facilities.* …电话会议设备。

Word Link *gram ≈ writing : diagram, program, telegram*

Word Link *tele ≈ distance : telegram, telepathy, telephone*

tele·gram /tɛlɪgræm/ (**telegrams**) N-COUNT A **telegram** is a message that is sent by telegraph and then printed and delivered to someone's home or office. 电报 [also "by" N] ❑ *The president received a briefing by telegram.* 总裁收到了一份电报简报。

tele·graph /tɛlɪgræf/ (**telegraphs, telegraphing, telegraphed**) 1 N-UNCOUNT **Telegraph** is a system of sending messages over long distances, either by means of electricity or by radio signals. Telegraph was used more often before the invention of telephones. 电报 [also "the" N] 2 V-T To **telegraph** someone means to send them a message by telegraph. 发电报给 ❑ *Churchill telegraphed an urgent message to Wavell.* 丘吉尔给韦维尔发了一个急电。 3 V-T If someone **telegraphs** something that they are planning or intending to do, they make it obvious, either deliberately or accidentally, that they are going to do it. 流露（要做某事） ❑ *The commission telegraphed its decision earlier this month by telling an official to prepare the order.* 该委员会本月早些时候通过让一个官员准备那项命令流露了其要做的决定。

tele·mar·ket·er /tɛlɪmɑrkɪtər/ (**telemarketers**) N-COUNT **Telemarketers** are salespeople who are employed by a company to telephone people in order to persuade them to buy the company's products or services. 电话营销员 ❑ *They found that 18 million people a day were being called by telemarketers.* 他们发现每天有1800万人接到电话营销员的来电。

tele·mar·ket·ing /tɛlɪmɑrkɪtɪŋ/ N-UNCOUNT **Telemarketing** is a method of selling in which someone employed by a company telephones people to try and persuade them to buy the company's products or services. 电话营销 [BUSINESS] ❑ *As postal rates go up, many businesses have been turning to telemarketing as a way of contacting new customers.* 随着邮资上涨，许多企业已经转而将电话营销作为一种联系新顾客的方法。

tele·path·ic /tɛlɪpæθɪk/ ADJ If you believe that someone is **telepathic**, you believe that they have mental powers which cannot be explained by science, such as being able to communicate with other people's minds, and know what other people are thinking. 有心灵感应能力的 ❑ *About half the subjects considered themselves to be telepathic.* 大约有一半的实验对象认为自己有心灵感应能力。

te·lepa·thy /tɪlɛpəθi/ N-UNCOUNT If you refer to **telepathy**, you mean the direct communication of thoughts and feelings between people's minds, without the need to use speech, writing, or any other normal signals. 心灵感应 ❑ *You never tell me what you're thinking. Am I supposed to use telepathy?* 你从来不告诉我你在想什么。我是不是该用心灵感应术呢？

Word Link *phon ≈ sound : microphone, symphony, telephone*

tele·phone ♦♦◇ /tɛlɪfoʊn/ (**telephones, telephoning, telephoned**) 1 N-UNCOUNT The **telephone** is the electrical system of communication that you use to talk directly to someone else in a different place. You use the telephone by dialing a number on a piece of equipment and speaking into it. 电话 ❑ *It's easier to reach her by telephone than by mail or email.* 打电话比写信或发电子邮件更容易联系上她。 ❑ *I hate to think what our telephone bill is going to be.* 我不愿去想我们的电话费将会是多少。 2 N-COUNT A **telephone** is the piece of equipment that you use when you talk to someone by telephone. 电话机 ❑ *He got up and answered the telephone.* 他站起来接了电话。 3 V-T/V-I If you **telephone** someone, you dial their telephone number and speak to them by telephone. 打电话给（某人）；打电话 ❑ *I felt so badly I had to telephone Owen to say I was sorry.* 我感到很糟糕，必须给欧文打电话道个歉。 ❑ *They usually telephone first to see if she's home.* 他们通常先打电话看她是否在家。 4 PHRASE If you are **on the telephone**, you are speaking to someone by telephone. 在通话中 ❑ *Linda remained on the telephone to the police for three hours.* 琳达和警察通了3个小时的电话。

tele·sales /tɛlɪseɪlz/ N-UNCOUNT **Telesales** is the selling of a company's products or services by telephone, either by phoning possible customers or by answering calls from customers. 电话销售 [BUSINESS] ❑ *Many people start their careers in telesales.* 很多人从电话销售开始他们的职业生涯。

Word Link *scope ≈ looking : horoscope, microscope, telescope*

tele·scope /tɛlɪskoʊp/ (**telescopes**) N-COUNT A **telescope** is a long instrument shaped like a tube. It has lenses inside it that make distant things seem larger and nearer when you look through it. 望远镜 ❑ *It's hoped that the telescope will enable scientists to see deeper into the universe than ever before.* 希望该望远镜能让科学家们比以往更深入地观察宇宙。

→ see Word Web: telescope

▲ **tele·vise** /tɛlɪvaɪz/ (**televises, televising, televised**) V-T If an event or program **is televised**, it is broadcast so that it can be seen on television. 在电视上播放 [usu passive] ❑ *His comeback fight will be televised on network TV.* 他的复出之战将在网络电视上播出。

tele·vi·sion ♦♦◇ /tɛlɪvɪʒᵊn, -vɪʒ-/ (**televisions**) 1 N-COUNT A **television** or **television set** is a piece of electrical equipment consisting of a box with a glass screen on it on which you can watch programs with pictures and sounds. 电视机 ❑ *She turned the television on and flicked around between news programs.* 她打开电视机，不停地在新闻节目间切换。 2 N-UNCOUNT **Television** is the system of sending pictures and sounds by electrical signals over a distance so that people can receive them on a television in their home. 电视 ❑ *Toy manufacturers began promoting some of their products on television.* 玩具制造商们开始在电视上促销他们的一些产品。

t

Word Web telescope

Originally there were only two types of **telescopes**. Refracting telescopes used lenses to **focus light rays** and produce a clear **image**. **Reflecting** telescopes used a concave **mirror** to do the same thing. Today scientists use **radio telescopes** to study the **universe**. These telescopes can detect **X-rays**, gamma rays, and other types of invisible light **waves**. However, important discoveries don't always require fancy instruments. Robert Evans is an amateur **astronomer** in Australia. He has discovered more supernovas than anyone else in the world. And he uses a very simple 16-inch reflecting telescope set up in his backyard.

3 N-UNCOUNT **Television** refers to all the programs that you can watch. 电视节目 ❑ *I don't have much time to watch very much television.* 我没有很多时间看很多电视节目。 4 N-UNCOUNT **Television** is the business or industry concerned with making programs and broadcasting them on television. 电视行业 ❑ *I'd like a job in television.* 我想有份电视行业的工作。
→ see Word Web: **television**
→ see **advertising**

tele·work·ing /tɛ̱liwɜrkɪŋ/ N-UNCOUNT **Teleworking** is the same as **telecommuting**. 家庭远程办公

tell ♦♦♦ /tɛ̱l/ (**tells, telling, told**) 1 V-T If you **tell** someone something, you give them information. 告诉（某人某事）❑ *In the evening I returned to tell Phyllis I got the job.* 晚上我回来告诉菲莉丝我得到了那份工作。 ❑ *I called Andie to tell her how spectacular the stuff looked.* 我打电话给安迪告诉她那东西看上去多么壮观。 ❑ *Claire had made me promise to tell her the truth.* 克莱尔已经逼我答应了告诉她真相。 2 V-T If you **tell** something such as a joke, a story, or your personal experiences, you communicate it to other people using speech. 讲述（笑话、故事、个人经历等）❑ *His friends say he was always quick to tell a joke.* 他的朋友们说他以前总是张口就能讲笑话。 ❑ *He told his story to The L.A. Times and produced photographs.* 他向《洛杉机时报》叙述了自己的故事，并提供了一些照片。 3 V-T If you **tell** someone **to** do something, you order or advise them to do it. 命令；建议（某人做某事）❑ *He said officers told him to get out of his car and lean against it.* 他说警官们命令他从他的车里出来并靠在车上。 4 V-T If you **tell yourself** something, you put it into words in your own mind because you need to encourage or persuade yourself about something. 叮嘱（自己）❑ *"Come on," she told herself.* "加油，"她叮嘱自己。 5 V-T If you can **tell** what is happening or what is true, you are able to judge correctly what is happening or what is true. 判断 [no cont, oft with brd-neg] ❑ *It was already impossible to tell where the bullet had entered.* 已经不可能判断子弹是从哪里射进来的。 6 V-T If you can **tell** one thing **from** another, you are able to recognize the difference between it and other similar things. 辨别 [no cont, oft with brd-neg] ❑ *I can't really tell the difference between their policies and ours.* 我真地看不出他们的政策和我们的政策有什么区别。 ❑ *How do you tell one from another?* 你怎么把它们区分开来？ 7 V-I If you **tell**, you reveal or give away a secret. 泄密 [INFORMAL] ❑ *Many of the children know who they are but are not telling.* 许多孩子知道他们是谁，但不愿泄露秘密。 8 V-T If facts or events **tell** you something, they reveal certain information to you through ways other than speech. （事实、事件）告诉（某人某事）❑ *The facts tell us that this is not true.* 事实告诉我们这不是真的。 ❑ *I don't think the unemployment rate ever tells us much about the future.* 我认为失业率不会告诉我们很多关于未来的东西。 9 V-I If an unpleasant or tiring experience begins to **tell**, it begins to have a serious effect. （让人不愉快或疲倦的经历）产生严重影响 ❑ *It wasn't long before the strain began to tell on our relationship.* 很快，这种极度的紧张就开始对我们的关系产生严重影响。 10 → see also **telling** 11 PHRASE You use **as far as I can tell** or **so far as I could tell** to indicate that what you are saying is based on the information you have, but that there may be things you do not know. 就某人判断 [VAGUENESS] ❑ *As far as I can tell, Jason is basically a nice guy.* 就我判断，杰森基本上是个好人。 12 CONVENTION You can say **"I tell you," "I can tell you,"** or **"I can't tell you"** to add emphasis to what you are saying. 我告诉你/我可以告诉你/我没法告诉你（用以强调）[INFORMAL, EMPHASIS] ❑ *I tell you this, I will not rest until that day has come.* 我告诉你，不到那天我不会休息。 13 CONVENTION If someone disagrees with you or refuses to do what you suggest and you are eventually proved to be right, you can say **"I told you so."** 我早跟你说过 [INFORMAL] ❑ *Her parents did not approve of her decision and, if she failed, her mother would say, "I told you so."* 她的父母没有同意她的决定，如果她失败了，她的母亲就会说，"我早跟你说过。" 14 CONVENTION You use **I'll tell you what** or **I tell you what** to introduce a suggestion or a new topic of conversation. 你听我说（用以引入建议或新话题）[SPOKEN] ❑ *I tell you what, I'll bring the beer over to your house.* 你听我的，由我带啤酒到你家来。 15 to **tell the time** → see **time** 16 **time will tell** → see **time**

Note that the verb **tell** is usually followed by a direct object indicating the person who is being addressed. ❑ *He told Alison he was suffering from leukemia... What did she tell you?* "What did she tell to you?" is wrong. With the verb **say**, however, if you want to mention the person who is being addressed, you should use the preposition **to**. "What did she say you?" is wrong. **"What did she say to you?"** is correct. **Tell** is used to report information that is given to someone. ❑ *The manufacturer told me that the product did not contain corn.* **Tell** can also be used with a "to" infinitive to report an order or instruction. ❑ *My mother told me to shut up and eat my dinner.* **Say** is the most general verb for reporting the words that someone speaks.

▸ **tell apart** PHRASAL VERB If you can **tell** people or things **apart**, you are able to recognize the differences between them and can therefore identify each of them. 区分 ❑ *It's easy to tell my pills apart because they're all different colors.* 我的药片很容易区分，因为它们的颜色不一样。

▸ **tell off** PHRASAL VERB If you **tell** someone **off**, you speak to them angrily or seriously because they have done something wrong. 训斥 ❑ *He never listened to us when we told him off.* 我们训斥他时，他从来都不听。 ❑ *I'm always being told off for being so awkward.* 我总因为手脚笨而受训斥。

Thesaurus *tell* 另参见：
v. communicate, declare, disclose, state 1 2
advise, order 3

tell·er /tɛ̱lər/ (**tellers**) N-COUNT A **teller** is a someone who works in a bank and who customers pay money to or get money from. （银行）出纳员 [mainly AM or SCOTTISH] ❑ *Every bank pays close attention to the speed and accuracy of its tellers.* 每家银行都密切关注其出纳员的速度和准确性。 ❑ *...a bank teller.* ……一位银行出纳员。

Word Web television

For many years, all **televisions** used cathode ray tubes to produce a picture. In the tube, a stream of

electrons from one end strikes a **screen** at the other end. This creates tiny lighted areas called **pixels**. The average cathode ray TV screen has about 200,000 pixels. Recently, however, **high definition** TV has become very popular. Ground **stations**, **satellites**, and **cables** still supply the TV **signal**. However, high definition television creates its picture using **digital** information on a flat screen. Digital **receivers** can display two million pixels per square inch. This produces an extraordinarily clear **image**.

tell·ing /tɛlɪŋ/ (**tellings**) **1** N-VAR The **telling** of a story or of something that has happened is the reporting of it to other people. 讲述 ❑ *Juan sat quietly through the telling of this saga.* 胡安安静地坐着听完了这个长篇故事。 **2** ADJ If something is **telling**, it shows the true nature of a person or situation. 显露真相的 ❑ *How a man shaves may be a telling clue to his age.* 一个男人如何刮脸也许会暴露他的实际年龄。 ● **tell·ing·ly** ADV 显露真相地 ❑ *Most tellingly, perhaps, chimpanzees do not draw as much information from the world around them as we do.* 也许最能说明问题的是，黑猩猩从周围的世界获取的信息不如我们获取的那么多。

tel·ly /tɛli/ (**tellies**) N-VAR A **telly** is a television. 电视(机) [BRIT, INFORMAL]

in AM, use **TV**

temp /tɛmp/ (**temps, temping, temped**) **1** N-COUNT A **temp** is a person who is employed by an agency that sends them to work in different offices for short periods of time, for example, to replace someone who is ill or on vacation. 临时雇员 [BUSINESS] ❑ *She began working for the company as a temp.* 她开始在这家公司做临时雇员。 **2** V-I If someone **is temping**, they are working as a temp. 做临时雇员 [only cont] [BUSINESS] ❑ *Like so many aspiring actresses, she ended up waiting tables and temping in office jobs.* 和众多曾经满怀抱负的女演员一样，她最终也只落得在餐厅端盘子、在办公室打临时工。

tem·per /tɛmpər/ (**tempers**) **1** N-VAR If you refer to someone's **temper** or say that they have a **temper**, you mean that they become angry very easily. 暴躁的脾气 ❑ *He had a temper and could be nasty.* 他脾气暴躁，会令人讨厌。 ❑ *His short temper had become notorious.* 他的急性子已臭名远扬。 **2** N-VAR Your **temper** is the way you are feeling at a particular time. If you are **in a good temper**, you feel cheerful. If you are **in a bad temper**, you feel angry and impatient. 情绪 ❑ *I was in a bad temper last night.* 我昨晚情绪不好。 **3** PHRASE If someone is **in a temper** or gets **into a temper**, the way that they are behaving shows that they are feeling angry and impatient. 在发脾气中 ❑ *She was still in a temper when Colin arrived.* 科林到的时候她还在发脾气。 **4** PHRASE If you **lose** your **temper**, you become so angry that you shout at someone or show in some other way that you are no longer in control of yourself. 发脾气 ❑ *I've never seen him get mad or lose his temper.* 我从未见过他发疯或发火。

Word Partnership *temper* 的常用搭配：

ADJ. **bad** temper, **explosive** temper, **quick** temper, **short** temper, **violent** temper **1**
N. temper **tantrum** **1**
V. **control your** temper, **have a** temper **1**
lose your temper **4**

★ **tem·pera·ment** /tɛmprəmənt/ (**temperaments**) **1** N-VAR Your **temperament** is your basic nature, especially as it is shown in the way that you react to situations or to other people. 性格 ❑ *His impulsive temperament regularly got him into difficulties.* 他容易冲动的性格经常使他陷入困境。 **2** N-UNCOUNT **Temperament** is the tendency to behave in an uncontrolled, bad-tempered, or unreasonable way. 喜怒无常的性情 ❑ *Some of the models were given to fits of temperament.* 模特中有些人喜怒无常。

tem·pera·men·tal /tɛmprəmɛntᵊl/ **1** ADJ If you say that someone is **temperamental**, you are criticizing them for not being calm or quiet by nature, but having moods that change often and suddenly. 喜怒无常的 [DISAPPROVAL] ❑ *He is very temperamental and critical.* 他喜怒无常，而且吹毛求疵。 **2** ADJ If you describe something such as a machine or car as **temperamental**, you mean that it often does not work well. (机器、汽车等) 性能不稳定的 ❑ *The boys couldn't start the temperamental motor.* 那些男孩子无法发动那辆性能不稳定的摩托车。

▲ **tem·per·ate** /tɛmpərɪt, -prɪt/ ADJ **Temperate** is used to describe a climate or a place which is never extremely hot or extremely cold. (气候或地区) 温和的 ❑ *The Nile Valley keeps a temperate climate throughout the year.* 尼罗河流域全年气候温和。

tem·pera·ture ♦◇◇ /tɛmprətʃər, -tʃʊər/ (**temperatures**) **1** N-VAR The **temperature** of something is a measure of how hot or cold it is. 温度 ❑ *Winter closes in and the temperature drops below freezing.* 冬天来临，气温降至冰点以下。 **2** N-UNCOUNT Your **temperature** is the temperature of your body. A normal temperature is about 98.6° Fahrenheit. 体温 ❑ *His temperature continued to rise and the cough worsened until Tania finally persuaded him to see a doctor.* 他的体温持续升高且咳嗽加重，直到塔妮娅最终说服了他去看医生。 **3** N-COUNT You can use **temperature** to talk about the feelings and emotions that people have in particular situations. (特定场合的) 氛围 ❑ *There's also been a noticeable rise in the political temperature.* 政治气氛也明显升温。 **4** PHRASE If you **are running a temperature** or if you **have a temperature**, your temperature is higher than it should be. 发烧 ❑ *He began to run an extremely high temperature.* 他开始发严重高烧。 **5** → see also **fever** **6** PHRASE If you **take** someone's **temperature** you use an instrument called a thermometer to measure the temperature of their body in order to see if they are ill. 量某人的体温 ❑ *He will probably take your child's temperature too.* 他可能也会量你孩子的体温。

→ see **calorie, climate, cooking, forecast, greenhouse effect, refrigerator, wind**

In the United States, two different scales are commonly used for measuring temperature. On the **Celsius** (formerly **Centigrade**) scale, used for scientific purposes, water freezes at zero degrees and boils at 100 degrees. On the **Fahrenheit** scale, used for everyday subjects such as the weather and cooking, water freezes at 32 degrees and boils at 212 degrees. In Britain, the Celsius scale is used for most things, including the weather, but some people use the Fahrenheit scale informally.

Word Partnership *temperature* 的常用搭配：

ADJ. **average** temperature, **high/low** temperature, **normal** temperature **1**
V. **reach a** temperature **1**
N. **changes in/of** temperature, temperature **increase**, **ocean** temperature, **rise in** temperature, **room** temperature, **surface** temperature, **water** temperature **1**
body temperature **2**

tem·plate /tɛmplɪt/ (**templates**) **1** N-COUNT A **template** is a thin piece of metal or plastic which is cut into a particular shape. It is used to help you cut wood, paper, metal, or other materials accurately, or to reproduce the same shape many times. (用于切割木材、纸、金属等的) 模板 ❑ *Trace around your template and transfer the design onto a sheet of card.* 沿着模板描摹，把设计图案描到一张薄纸板上。 **2** N-COUNT In computing, a **template** is a model of a document that you can use as a guide when creating a document of your own. (计算机中用于创建文档的) 模板 [COMPUTING] ❑ *Open any of the layout templates, insert your text, make any other changes, and print.* 打开任何一个设计模板，插入你的文本，做任何其他改动，然后打印。 **3** N-COUNT If one thing is a **template for** something else, the second thing is based on the first thing. 样板 ❑ *The template for Adair's novel is not somebody else's fiction, but fact.* 阿代尔长篇小说的样板不是别人的虚构故事，而是事实。

tem·ple ♦◇◇ /tɛmpᵊl/ (**temples**) **1** N-COUNT; N-IN-NAMES A **temple** is a building used for the worship of a god or gods, especially in the Buddhist, Jewish, Mormon, and Hindu religions, and in ancient Greek and Roman times. 神殿；寺庙 ❑ *...a small Hindu temple.* …一座小的印度教寺庙。 ❑ *We go to temple on Saturdays.* 我们每个星期六去寺庙。 **2** N-COUNT Your **temples** are the flat parts on each side of the front part of your head, near your forehead. 太阳穴 ❑ *Threads of silver ran through his beard and the hair at his temples.* 缕缕银丝已爬上了他的胡须和两鬓的头发。

★ **tem·po** /tɛmpoʊ/ (**tempos**)

Tempi can also be used as the plural form.

1 N-SING The **tempo** of an event is the speed at which it happens. (事件发展的) 速度 ❑ *...owing to the slow tempo of change in an overwhelmingly rural country.* …由于一个高度农业化国家变革的缓慢速度。 **2** N-VAR The **tempo** of a piece of music is the speed at which it is played. (音乐的) 节奏 ❑ *In a new recording, the Boston Philharmonic tried the original tempo.* 在一张新唱片中，波士顿爱乐乐团尝试了音乐原本的节奏。

Word Link *tempo ≈ time : contemporary, temporal, temporary*

★ **tem·po·ral** /tɛmpərəl/ **1** ADJ **Temporal** powers or matters relate to ordinary institutions and activities rather than to religious or spiritual ones. 凡尘的；普通的 [ADJ n] [FORMAL] ❑ *...the spiritual and temporal leader of the Tibetan people.* …西藏人民的宗教及凡尘领袖。 **2** ADJ **Temporal** means relating to time. 时间的 [ADJ n] [FORMAL] ❑ *One is also able to see how specific acts are related to a temporal and spatial context.* 人们也能看到具体的行为如何与时间和空间背景相关联。

t

Word Link *tempo ≈ time : contemporary, temporal, temporary*

tem·po·rary ♦◇◇ /tɛmpərɛri/ ADJ Something that is **temporary** lasts for only a limited time. 暂时的 ❑ *His job here is only temporary.* 他在这儿的工作只是暂时的。 ❑ *Most adolescent problems are temporary.* 多数青春期的问题都是暂时的。 ● **tem·po·rari·ly** /tɛmpərɛərɪli/ ADV 暂时地 ❑ *The peace agreement has at least temporarily halted the civil war.* 该和平协议至少已暂时中止了内战。

★ **tempt** /tɛmpt/ (**tempts, tempting, tempted**) **1** V-T Something that **tempts** you attracts you and makes you want it, even though it may be wrong or harmful. 引诱；吸引 ❑ *Cars like that may tempt drivers to speed.* 那样的汽车可能会引诱司机超速行驶。 ❑ *It is the fresh fruit that tempts me at this time of year.* 只有新鲜的水果才会在每年的这个时候吸引我。 **2** V-T If you **tempt** someone, you offer them something they want in order to encourage them to do what you want them to do. 诱使 ❑ *...a million-dollar marketing campaign to tempt American tourists back to Britain.* …旨在诱使美国游客回到英国的、耗资一百万美元的营销活动。 ❑ *Don't let credit tempt you to buy something you can't afford.* 不要让赊购诱使你去购买你支付不起的东西。 **3** → see also **tempted**

Word Link *tempt ≈ trying : attempt, temptation, tempted*

temp·ta·tion /tɛmpteɪʃ^ən/ (**temptations**) N-VAR If you feel you want to do something or have something, even though you know you really should avoid it, you can refer to this feeling as **temptation**. You can also refer to the thing you want to do or have as a **temptation**. 诱惑 ❑ *Will they be able to resist the temptation to buy?* 他们能抵抗得住购买的诱惑吗？

tempt·ed /tɛmptɪd/ ADJ If you say that you are **tempted to** do something, you mean that you would like to do it. 被引诱（而想做）的 [v-link ADJ] ❑ *I'm very tempted to sell my house.* 我很想卖掉我的房子。

tempt·ing /tɛmptɪŋ/ ADJ If something is **tempting**, it makes you want to do it or have it. 诱人的 ❑ *In the end, I turned down Raoul's tempting offer of the Palm Beach trip.* 最后，我拒绝了拉乌尔去棕榈海滩旅行的诱人提议。 ● **tempt·ing·ly** ADV 诱人地 ❑ *The good news is that prices are still temptingly low.* 好消息是价格仍然低得诱人。

ten ♦♦♦ /tɛn/ (**tens**) NUM **Ten** is the number 10. 10；十 ❑ *Over the past ten years things have changed.* 在过去的10年中，情况已经发生了变化。

ten·able /tɛnəb^əl/ ADJ If you say that an argument, point of view, or situation is **tenable**, you believe that it is reasonable and could be successfully defended against criticism.（论点、观点或形势）站得住脚的 ❑ *This argument is simply not tenable.* 这个论点简直无懈可击。

te·na·cious /tɪneɪʃəs/ ADJ If you are **tenacious**, you are very determined and do not give up easily. 执著的 ❑ *He is regarded as a tenacious and persistent interviewer.* 他被认为是个执著坚毅的采访者。 ● **te·na·cious·ly** ADV 执著地 ❑ *In spite of his illness, he clung tenaciously to his job.* 尽管有病，他仍顽强地坚持工作。

te·nac·ity /tɪnæsɪti/ N-UNCOUNT If you have **tenacity**, you are very determined and do not give up easily. 执著 ❑ *Talent, hard work and sheer tenacity are all crucial to career success.* 才能、勤奋和百分之百的执著对事业成功都是至关重要的。

ten·an·cy /tɛnənsi/ (**tenancies**) N-VAR **Tenancy** is the use that you have of land or property belonging to someone else, for which you pay rent.（土地、财产等的）承租；租用 ❑ *His father took over the tenancy of the farm 40 years ago.* 他父亲40年前承租了这个农场。

★ **ten·ant** /tɛnənt/ (**tenants**) N-COUNT A **tenant** is someone who pays rent for the place they live in, or for land or buildings that they use. 租户；佃户 ❑ *Regulations placed clear obligations on the landlord for the benefit of the tenant.* 为了租户的利益，条例给房东规定了明确的义务。

tend ♦♦◇ /tɛnd/ (**tends, tending, tended**) **1** V-T If something **tends to** happen, it usually happens or it often happens. 倾向于；往往会 ❑ *A problem for manufacturers is that lighter cars tend to be noisy.* 制造商遇到的一个问题是重量较轻的汽车往往噪音大。 **2** V-I If you **tend toward** a particular characteristic, you often display that characteristic. 趋向… ❑ *Artistic and intellectual people tend toward left-wing views.* 艺术人士和知识分子趋向左翼观点。 **3** V-T You can say that you **tend to** think something when you want to give your opinion, but do not want it to seem too forceful or definite. 倾向于（认为）[VAGUENESS] ❑ *I tend to think that our Representatives by and large do a good job.* 我倾向于认为我们的众议员们总体上干得不错。

Word Partnership *tend* 的常用搭配：

V. tend **to avoid**, tend **to become**, tend **to develop**, tend **to forget**, tend **to happen**, tend **to lose**, tend **to stay** **1** tend **to agree**, tend **to blame**, tend **to feel**, tend to **think** **1** **3**

N. **Americans** tend, **children/men/women** tend, **people** tend **1** **2**

ten·den·cy ♦◇◇ /tɛndənsi/ (**tendencies**) **1** N-COUNT A **tendency** is a worrying or unpleasant habit or action that keeps occurring. 倾向 ❑ *...the government's tendency to secrecy in recent years.* …近年来政府的保密倾向。 **2** N-COUNT A **tendency** is a part of your character that makes you often behave in an unpleasant or worrying way.（性格方面不好的）倾向 ❑ *He is spoiled, arrogant and has a tendency toward snobbery.* 他被宠坏了，很傲慢，而且有势利倾向。

Thesaurus *tendency* 另参见：

N. habit, inclination, predisposition, weakness **1** **2**

tender
❶ ADJECTIVE USES
❷ NOUN AND VERB USES

❶ **ten·der** /tɛndər/ (**tenderer, tenderest**) **1** ADJ Someone or something that is **tender** expresses gentle and caring feelings. 温柔的 ❑ *Her voice was tender, full of pity.* 她的声音很温柔，充满了怜悯。 ● **ten·der·ly** ADV 温柔地 [ADV with v] ❑ *Mr. White tenderly embraced his wife.* 怀特先生温柔地拥抱了妻子。 ● **ten·der·ness** N-UNCOUNT 温柔 ❑ *She smiled, politely rather than with tenderness.* 她微微一笑，是出于礼貌，而不是出于柔情。 **2** ADJ If you say that someone does something at a **tender** age, you mean that they do it when they are still young and have not had much experience. 幼小的 [ADJ n] ❑ *He took up the game at the tender age of seven.* 他在7岁的小小年纪就开始从事这项运动。 **3** ADJ Meat or other food that is **tender** is easy to cut or chew.（肉等食物）嫩的；易嚼的 ❑ *Cook for a minimum of 2 hours, or until the meat is tender.* 至少煮两个小时，或一直煮到肉软了为止。 **4** ADJ If part of your body is **tender**, it is sensitive and painful when it is touched.（身体部位）敏感的；易触痛的 ❑ *My tummy felt very tender.* 我的肚子一碰就痛。 ● **ten·der·ness** N-UNCOUNT 触痛 ❑ *There is still some tenderness in her ankle.* 她的脚踝还有些触痛。 → see **cooking**

❷ **ten·der** /tɛndər/ (**tenders, tendering, tendered**) **1** N-VAR A **tender** is a formal offer to supply goods or to do a particular job, and a statement of the price that you or your company will charge. If a contract is **put out to tender**, formal offers are invited. If a company **wins a tender**, their offer is accepted. 投标 [BUSINESS] ❑ *Builders will then be sent the specifications and asked to submit a tender for the work.* 然后建筑商们将会接到设计说明并被邀请参与此项工程的投标。 **2** V-I If a company **tenders for** something, it makes a formal offer to supply goods or do a job for a particular price. 投标 [BUSINESS] ❑ *The staff are forbidden to tender for private-sector work.* 员工们禁止投标私营部门的工程。 **3** → see also **legal tender**

ten·don /tɛndən/ (**tendons**) N-COUNT A **tendon** is a strong cord in a person's or animal's body which joins a muscle to a bone. 腱 ❑ *...a torn tendon in his right shoulder.* …他右肩一根被拉伤的腱。

ten·ement /tɛnəmənt/ (**tenements**) **1** N-COUNT A **tenement** is a large, old building which is divided into a number of individual apartments. 旧式公寓大楼 ❑ *...streets of low-cost tenements.* …低成本旧式公寓街。 ❑ *...elegant 19th-century tenement buildings.* …19世纪的典雅的公寓建筑群。 **2** N-COUNT A **tenement** is one of the apartments in a tenement.（公寓大楼里的）公寓 ❑ *He struggled to pay the rent on his $88-a-month tenement.* 他艰难地支付每月$88的公寓租金。

▲ **ten·et** /tɛnɪt/ (**tenets**) N-COUNT The **tenets** of a theory or belief are the main principles on which it is based.（理论、信仰的）基本原则 [FORMAL] ❑ *Non-violence and patience are the central tenets of their faith.* 非暴力和忍耐是他们信仰的基本原则。

ten·nis ♦◇◇ /tɛnɪs/ N-UNCOUNT **Tennis** is a game played by two or four players on a rectangular court. The players use an oval racket with strings across it to hit a ball over a net across the middle of the court. 网球运动
→ see Picture Dictionary: **tennis**
→ see **park**

T

Picture Dictionary tennis

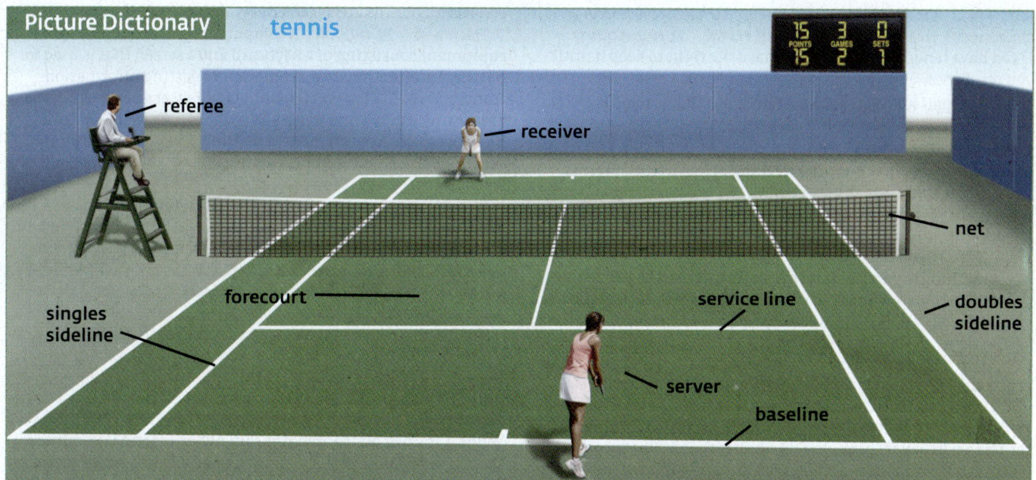

ten·or /tɛnər/ (**tenors**) 1 N-COUNT A **tenor** is a male singer whose voice is fairly high. 男高音歌唱家 ❑ *...a free, open-air concert given by the Italian tenor, Luciano Pavarotti.* …由意大利男高音歌唱家卢西亚诺•帕瓦罗蒂举行的一场免费的露天音乐会。 2 ADJ A **tenor** saxophone or other musical instrument has a range of notes that are of a fairly low pitch. 次中音的 ❑ *...one of the best tenor sax players ever.* …有史以来最好的次中音萨克斯管吹奏者之一。

tense /tɛns/ (**tenser, tensest, tenses, tensing, tensed**) 1 ADJ A **tense** situation or period of time is one that makes people anxious, because they do not know what is going to happen next. 令人紧张的（形势、时期等）❑ *This gesture of goodwill did little to improve the tense atmosphere at the talks.* 这一友好姿态对改善谈判的紧张气氛几乎没起什么作用。 2 ADJ If you are **tense**, you are anxious and nervous and cannot relax. （人）紧张的 ❑ *Mark, who had at first been very tense, at last relaxed.* 马克起初非常紧张，最后终于放松了。 3 ADJ If your body is **tense**, your muscles are tight and not relaxed. （肌肉）紧绷的 ❑ *A bath can relax tense muscles.* 泡个澡能放松紧绷的肌肉。 4 V-T/V-I If your muscles **tense**, if you **tense**, or if you **tense** your muscles, your muscles become tight and stiff, often because you are anxious or frightened. 使（肌肉）绷紧；绷紧 ❑ *Newman's stomach muscles tensed.* 纽曼的腹部肌肉绷紧了。 ● PHRASAL VERB **Tense up** means the same as **tense**. 绷紧 ❑ *When we are under stress our bodies tend to tense up.* 当我们处在压力之下时，我们的身体往往会绷紧。 5 N-COUNT The **tense** of a verb group is its form, which usually shows whether you are referring to past, present, or future time. （动词的）时态 ❑ *It was as though Corinne was already dead: they were speaking of her in the past tense.* 就好像科琳已经死了似的：他们当时在用过去时态谈起她。

Word Partnership *tense* 的常用搭配：

- N. tense **atmosphere**, tense **moment**, tense **situation** 1
  tense **mood** 2
  muscles tense 4
  future/past/perfect/present tense 5
- ADV. **very** tense 1 – 3
- V. **feel** tense 2 3

ten·sion ♦◇◇ /tɛnʃᵊn/ (**tensions**) 1 N-UNCOUNT **Tension** is a feeling of worry and anxiety which makes it difficult for you to relax. （精神上的）紧张 [also N in pl] ❑ *Smiling and laughing has actually been shown to relieve tension and stress.* 微笑和大笑确实已证明能缓解紧张和压力。 2 N-UNCOUNT **Tension** is the feeling that is produced in a situation when people are anxious and do not trust each other, and when there is a possibility of sudden violence or conflict. 紧张局面 [also N in pl] ❑ *The tension between the two countries is likely to remain.* 两国之间的紧张局面可能持续。 3 N-VAR If there is a **tension** between forces, arguments, or influences, there are differences between them that cause difficulties. 冲突 ❑ *The film explored the tension between public duty and personal affections.* 该片探讨了公共义务和个人情感之间的冲突。 4 N-UNCOUNT The **tension** in something such as a rope or wire is the extent to which it is stretched tight. 拉紧程度 ❑ *As the cable wraps itself around the wheel, there is provision for adjusting the tension of the cable.* 缆绳绕在轮子上时就留了调整缆绳松紧的余地。
→ see **anger**

Word Partnership *tension* 的常用搭配：

- V. **ease** tension, tension **grows**, tension **mounts**, **relieve** tension 1 – 3
- N. **source of** tension 1 – 4
- ADJ. **racial** tension 2 3

tent /tɛnt/ (**tents**) N-COUNT A **tent** is a shelter made of canvas or nylon which is held up by poles and ropes, and is used mainly by people who are camping. 帐篷

ten·ta·cle /tɛntəkᵊl/ (**tentacles**) 1 N-COUNT The **tentacles** of an animal such as an octopus are the long thin parts that are used for feeling and holding things, for getting food, and for moving. 触须 2 N-COUNT If you talk about the **tentacles** of a political, commercial, or social organization, you are referring to the power and influence that it has in the outside community. （政治、经济或社会组织的影响）触角 [DISAPPROVAL] ❑ *Free speech is being gradually eroded year after year by new tentacles of government control.* 言论自由正被政府控制的新触角逐渐侵蚀。

★ **ten·ta·tive** /tɛntətɪv/ 1 ADJ **Tentative** agreements, plans, or arrangements are not definite or certain, but have been made as a first step. 初步的 ❑ *Political leaders have reached a tentative agreement to hold a preparatory conference next month.* 政治领导人已经就下个月召开准备会达成初步协议。 ● **ten·ta·tive·ly** ADV 初步地 [ADV with v] ❑ *The next round of talks is tentatively scheduled to begin October 21st in Washington.* 下一轮谈判初步定在10月21日于华盛顿进行。 2 ADJ If someone is **tentative**, they are cautious and not very confident because they are uncertain or afraid. 犹豫的 ❑ *My first attempts at complaining were kind of tentative.* 我头几次的投诉尝试都有点儿犹豫。 ● **ten·ta·tive·ly** ADV 犹豫地 [ADV with v] ❑ *Perhaps, he suggested tentatively, they should send for Dr. Esteves.* 他犹犹豫豫地建议道，他们也许应该派人去请埃斯特维斯医生。

tenth ♦♦◇ /tɛnθ/ (**tenths**) 1 ORD The **tenth** item in a series is the one that you count as number ten. 第10 ❑ *...her tenth birthday.* …她的10岁生日。 2 FRACTION A **tenth** is one of ten equal parts of something. 1/10 ❑ *He finished three-tenths of a second behind Prost.* 他比普罗斯特迟0.3秒到达终点。

tenu·ous /tɛnyuəs/ ADJ If you describe something such as a connection, a reason, or someone's position as **tenuous**, you mean that it is very uncertain or weak. 脆弱的 ❑ *He did not speculate on the future of his tenuous career.* 他没有考虑到自己不稳定的职业前景。

▲ **ten·ure** /tɛnyər/ 1 N-UNCOUNT **Tenure** is the legal right to live in a particular building or to use a particular piece of land during a fixed period of time. 居住权；（土地的）使用权 ❑ *Lack of security of tenure was a reason for many families becoming homeless.* 居住权缺乏安全保障是许多家庭无家可归的一个原因。 2 N-UNCOUNT **Tenure** is the period of time during which someone holds an important

t

job. 任期 ❑ *...the challenges he faced during his tenure as chief executive officer.* …他在首席执行官任期内面临的种种挑战。 3 N-UNCOUNT If you have **tenure** in your job, you have the right to keep it until you retire. 终身职位

tep·id /tɛpɪd/ ADJ Water or another liquid that is **tepid** is slightly warm. 微温的

term ♦♦♦ /tɜrm/ (**terms, terming, termed**) 1 PHRASE If you talk about something **in terms of** something or **in particular terms**, you are specifying which aspect of it you are discussing or from what point of view you are considering it. 从…角度来看 ❑ *Our goods compete in terms of product quality, reliability and above all variety.* 我们的产品从质量、可靠性、尤其是多样性来看很有竞争力。 2 PHRASE If you say something **in particular terms**, you say it using a particular type or level of language or using language which clearly shows your attitude. 以某种语言 ❑ *The video explains in simple terms how the new tax works.* 该录像以浅显易懂的语言解释了新税法的运作方式。 3 N-COUNT A **term** is a word or expression with a specific meaning, especially one which is used in relation to a particular subject. 术语 ❑ *Myocardial infarction is the medical term for a heart attack.* 心肌梗塞是心脏病发作的医学术语。 4 V-T If you say that something **is termed** a particular thing, you mean that that is what people call it or that is their opinion of it. 把…称作 ❑ *He had been termed a temporary employee.* 他曾被称为临时工。 5 N-VAR A **term** is one of the periods of time that a school, college, or university divides the year into. 学期 ❑ *...the summer term.* …夏季学期。 6 N-COUNT A **term** is a period of time between two elections during which a particular party or government is in power. (政党或政府的) 任期 ❑ *Nixon never completed his term of office.* 尼克松没有完成自己的任期。 7 N-COUNT A **term** is a period of time that someone spends doing a particular job or in a particular place. (工作或居住) 期间 ❑ *...a 12-month term of service.* …12个月的任职期。 8 N-COUNT A **term** is the period for which a legal contract or insurance policy is valid. (合同或保险的) 有效期 ❑ *Premiums are guaranteed throughout the term of the policy.* 在保单的有效期内保证支付保险费。 9 N-UNCOUNT The **term** of a woman's pregnancy is the nine-month period that it lasts. **Term** is also used to refer to the end of the nine-month period. 怀孕期；临产 ❑ *That makes her the first TV presenter to work the full term of her pregnancy.* 那使她成了第一个在整个怀孕期间一直工作的电视节目主持人。 10 N-PLURAL The **terms** of an agreement, treaty, or other arrangement are the conditions that must be accepted by the people involved in it. 条款 ❑ *...the terms of the Helsinki agreement.* …《赫尔辛基协议》的各项条款。 11 PHRASE If you **come to terms with** something difficult or unpleasant, you learn to accept and deal with it. 接受 ❑ *She had come to terms with the fact that her husband would always be crippled.* 她已接受了丈夫将终生跛足这个事实。 12 PHRASE If two people or groups compete **on equal terms** or **on the same terms**, neither of them has an advantage over the other. 在同等条件下 ❑ *I had at last found a sport where I could compete on equal terms with able-bodied people.* 我终于找到一种体育运动，能和身体健全的人公平竞赛 13 PHRASE If two people are **on good terms** or **on friendly terms**, they are friendly with each other. 关系好 ❑ *Madeleine is on good terms with Sarah.* 马德琳和萨拉关系很好。 14 PHRASE You use the expressions **in the long term, in the short term**, and **in the medium term** to talk about what will happen over a long period of time, over a short period of time, and over a medium period of time. 从长远/短期/中期来看 ❑ *Organic fertilizers will have very positive results in the long term.* 有机肥料从长远来看将产生非常积极的效果。 15 PHRASE If you do something **on your terms**, you do it under conditions that you decide because you are in a position of power. 按照自己的意愿 ❑ *They will sign the union treaty only on their terms.* 他们在符合自己意愿的条件下才会签署联合条约。 16 PHRASE If you say that you **are thinking in terms of** doing a particular thing, you mean that you are considering it. 考虑 ❑ *You should be thinking in terms of graduating next year.* 你应该考虑明年毕业的事了。 17 **in no uncertain terms** → see **uncertain** 18 **in real terms** → see **real**

T

Word Link	*term, termin ≈ limit, end : determine, terminal, terminate*

ter·mi·nal /tɜrmɪnᵊl/ (**terminals**) 1 ADJ A **terminal** illness or disease causes death, often slowly, and cannot be cured. (疾病) 晚期的；致命的 ❑ *...terminal cancer.* …晚期癌症。 ● **ter·mi·nal·ly** ADV 致命地 [ADV adj] ❑ *The patient is terminally ill.* 这个病人病入膏肓。 2 N-COUNT A **terminal** is a place where vehicles, passengers, or goods begin or end a journey. 起点站；终点站 [usu supp N] ❑ *Plans are underway for a new terminal at Dulles airport.* 正计划在杜勒斯机场修建新的航站大楼。 3 N-COUNT A computer **terminal** is a piece of equipment consisting of a keyboard and a screen that is used for putting information into a computer or getting information from it. (计算机) 终端 [COMPUTING] ❑ *Carl sits at a computer terminal 40 hours a week.* 卡尔每周要在电脑前坐40小时。 4 N-COUNT On a piece of electrical equipment, a **terminal** is one of the points where electricity enters or leaves it. (电路的) 端头 ❑ *...the positive terminal of the battery.* …电池的正极。

★ **ter·mi·nate** /tɜrmɪneɪt/ (**terminates, terminating, terminated**) 1 V-T/V-I When you **terminate** something or when it **terminates**, it ends completely. 终止 [FORMAL] ❑ *Her next remark abruptly terminated the conversation.* 她接下来的言论使得谈话突然终止。 ● ★ **ter·mi·na·tion** /tɜrmɪneɪʃᵊn/ N-UNCOUNT 终止 ❑ *...a dispute which led to the abrupt termination of trade.* …一个导致贸易突然终止的争端。 2 V-T To **terminate** a pregnancy means to end it. 终止 (妊娠) [MEDICAL] ❑ *After a lot of agonizing she decided to terminate the pregnancy.* 在多次痛苦的考虑后，她决定终止妊娠。 ● **ter·mi·na·tion** ★ N-VAR (**terminations**) 终止妊娠 ❑ *You should also have a medical check-up after the termination of a pregnancy.* 你在终止妊娠后也应该做个体检。 3 V-I When a train or bus **terminates** somewhere, it ends its journey there. (火车或公共汽车) 到达终点 [FORMAL] ❑ *This train will terminate at Lamy.* 这列火车的终点站是拉米。

ter·mi·nol·ogy /tɜrmɪnɒlədʒi/ (**terminologies**) N-VAR The **terminology** of a subject is the set of special words and expressions used in connection with it. 术语 ❑ *...gastritis, which in medical terminology means an inflammation of the stomach.* …胃炎这个词在医学术语里的意思是胃部发炎。

★ **ter·race** /tɛrɪs/ (**terraces**) 1 N-COUNT A **terrace** is a flat area of stone or grass next to a building where people can sit. (房屋旁的) 露台；草坪 ❑ *Some guests recline in deck chairs on the sea-facing terrace.* 有些客人斜躺在朝海露台的躺椅上。 2 N-COUNT **Terraces** are a series of flat areas built like steps on the side of a hill so that crops can be grown there. 梯田 ❑ *...massive terraces of corn and millet carved into the mountainside like giant steps.* …山坡上开垦出来种玉米和小米的巨型台阶般的大块大块梯田。

ter·raced house /tɛrɪst haʊs/ (**terraced houses**) N-COUNT A **terraced house** or a **terrace house** is one of a row of similar houses joined together by their side walls. 一所排屋 [BRIT]

in AM, use **row house**

terra·cotta /tɛrəkɒtə/ also **terra cotta** N-UNCOUNT **Terracotta** is a brownish-red clay that has been baked and is used for making things such as flower pots, small statues, and tiles. 赤陶 ❑ *...plants in terracotta pots.* …赤陶花盆里的植物。

Word Link	*terr ≈ earth : subterranean, terrain, terrestrial*

★ **ter·rain** /tәreɪn/ (**terrains**) N-VAR **Terrain** is used to refer to an area of land or a type of land when you are considering its physical features. 地形 ❑ *The terrain changed quickly from arable land to desert.* 这里的地形很快由耕地变为沙漠。

ter·res·trial /tɪrɛstriəl/ 1 ADJ **Terrestrial** means relating to the planet Earth rather than to some other part of the universe. 地球的 [ADJ n] ❑ *...terrestrial life forms.* …地球上的生命形态。 2 → see also **extraterrestrial**

ter·ri·ble ♦♦◊ /tɛrɪbᵊl/ 1 ADJ A **terrible** experience or situation is very bad or very unpleasant. 可怕的 ❑ *Tens of thousands more suffered terrible injuries in the world's worst industrial disaster.* 还有数万人在这场世界最严重的工业灾难中受了重伤。 ❑ *I often have terrible nightmares.* 我经常做可怕的恶梦。 ● **ter·ri·bly** ADV 可怕地 [ADV after v] ❑ *My son has suffered terribly. He has lost his best friend.* 我儿子遭受了可怕的打击，失去了最好的朋友。 2 ADJ If something is **terrible**, it is very bad or of very poor quality. 糟糕的；劣质的 ❑ *She admits her French is terrible.* 她承认自己的法语很糟糕。 3 ADJ You use **terrible** to emphasize the great extent or degree of something. (程度) 十足的 [ADJ n] [EMPHASIS] ❑ *I was a terrible fool, you know.* 你知道，我那时是个十足的傻瓜。 ● **ter·ri·bly** ADV 非常 ❑ *I'm terribly sorry to bother you at this hour.* 我非常抱歉这个时候来打搅您。

★ **ter·rif·ic** /tərɪfɪk/ 1 ADJ If you describe something or someone as **terrific**, you are very pleased with them or very impressed by them. 极好的 [INFORMAL] ❑ *What a terrific idea!* 多好的主意啊！ 2 ADJ **Terrific** means very great in amount, degree, or intensity. 巨大的 [ADJ n] [EMPHASIS] ❑ *All of a sudden there was a terrific bang and a flash of smoke.* 忽然发出一声巨响，还冒出一股烟。

★ **ter·ri·fy** /tɛ̲rɪfaɪ/ (**terrifies, terrifying, terrified**) 1 V-T If something **terrifies** you, it makes you feel extremely frightened. 使非常害怕 ❑ *Flying terrifies him.* 坐飞机让他非常害怕。 ● **ter·ri·fied** ADJ 非常害怕的 ❑ *He was terrified of heights.* 他过去恐高。 2 → see also **terror**

ter·ri·fy·ing /tɛ̲rɪfaɪɪŋ/ ADJ If something is **terrifying**, it makes you very frightened. 令人恐惧的 ❑ *I still find it terrifying to find myself surrounded by large numbers of horses.* 我发现被一大群马包围着还是很吓人。

ter·ri·to·rial /tɛ̲rɪtɔ̲riəl/ 1 ADJ **Territorial** means concerned with the ownership of a particular area of land or water. 领土的 ❑ *It is the only republic which has no territorial disputes with the others.* 它是惟一一个和其他国家没有领土争端的共和国。 2 ADJ If you describe an animal or its behavior as **territorial**, you mean that it has an area which it regards as its own, and which it defends when other animals try to enter it. (动物) 有地盘意识的 ❑ *Two cats or more in one house will also exhibit territorial behavior.* 两只或更多的猫在同一所房子里，也会表现出领地意识行为。

ter·ri·tory ◆◆◇ /tɛ̲rətɔri/ (**territories**) 1 N-VAR **Territory** is land which is controlled by a particular country or ruler. 领土 ❑ *The government denies that any of its territory is under rebel control.* 该政府否认有任何领土被叛乱者控制。 ❑ *...the view that the US should use military force only when our borders or US territories are attacked.* …那种观点认为只有我们的边界或美国领土受到袭击时美国才应该使用武力。 2 N-COUNT A **territory** is a country or region that is controlled by another country. 属地 ❑ *He toured some of the disputed territories now under UN control.* 他巡访过一些现归联合国管辖的有争议的属地。 3 N-UNCOUNT You can use **territory** to refer to an area of knowledge or experience. 领域 [with supp] ❑ *Following the futuristic "The Handmaid's Tale," Margaret Atwood's seventh novel, "Cat's Eye," returns to more familiar territory.* 在推出具有未来主义色彩的《女仆的故事》之后，玛格丽特・阿特伍德的第7部小说《猫眼》返回了更为熟悉的领域。 4 **virgin territory** → see **virgin** 5 N-VAR An animal's **territory** is an area which it regards as its own and which it defends when other animals try to enter it. (动物的) 地盘 ❑ *The territory of a cat only remains fixed for as long as the cat dominates the area.* 猫的地盘只在它占据那个地方的时候才保持稳定不变。 6 N-UNCOUNT **Territory** is land with a particular character. (具有某种特征的) 地带 ❑ *...mountainous territory.* …多山地带。

Word Partnership *territory* 的常用搭配：

N. **enemy** territory, **part of a** territory 1 2

ADJ. **vast** territory 1 – 4

controlled territory, **disputed** territory 2

familiar territory, **uncharted** territory 3

ter·ror ◆◆◇ /tɛ̲rər/ (**terrors**) 1 N-UNCOUNT **Terror** is very great fear. 恐惧 ❑ *I shook with terror whenever I was about to fly in a plane.* 我每次要坐飞机时都害怕得发抖。 2 N-UNCOUNT **Terror** is violence or the threat of violence, especially when it is used for political reasons. 恐怖活动 ❑ *...the war on terror.* …反恐战争。 ❑ *The bomb attack on the capital could signal the start of a pre-election terror campaign.* 对首都的炸弹袭击可能标志着选举前的恐怖活动的开始。 3 N-COUNT A **terror** is something that makes you very frightened. 使人恐惧的事物 ❑ *As a boy, he had a real terror of facing people.* 他小时候其实非常害怕见人。

Word Partnership *terror* 的常用搭配：

N. **acts of** terror, terror **alert**, terror **attack**, terror **campaign**, **fight against** terror, **reign of** terror, terror **suspects** 2

ter·ror·ise /tɛ̲rəraɪz/ [mainly BRIT] → see **terrorize**

★ **ter·ror·ism** ◆◆◇ /tɛ̲rərɪzəm/ N-UNCOUNT **Terrorism** is the use of violence, especially murder and bombing, in order to achieve political goals or to force a government to do something. 恐怖主义 [DISAPPROVAL] ❑ *...the threat of global terrorism.* …全球恐怖主义的威胁。

★ **ter·ror·ist** ◆◇◇ /tɛ̲rərɪst/ (**terrorists**) N-COUNT A **terrorist** is a person who uses violence, especially murder and bombing, in order to achieve political aims. 恐怖分子 [DISAPPROVAL] ❑ *One American was killed and three were wounded in terrorist attacks.* 在几起恐怖袭击中，1名美国人被杀且有3人受伤。

ter·ror·ize /tɛ̲rəraɪz/ (**terrorizes, terrorizing, terrorized**)

in BRIT, also use **terrorise**

V-T If someone **terrorizes** you, they keep you in a state of fear by making it seem likely that they will attack you. 恐吓 ❑ *Bands of gunmen have hijacked food shipments and terrorized relief workers.* 几伙持枪歹徒劫持了运送的食物，并恐吓救援人员。

terse /tɜ̲rs/ (**terser, tersest**) ADJ A **terse** statement or comment is brief and unfriendly. 简短生硬的 ❑ *He issued a terse statement, saying he is discussing his future with colleagues before announcing his decision on Monday.* 他发表了简短生硬的声明，说他正和同事商讨自己的未来，并说将于星期一宣布他的决定。 ● **terse·ly** ADV 简短生硬地 [ADV with v] ❑ *"It's too late," he said tersely.* "太晚了，" 他生硬地说道。

▲ **ter·tiary** /tɜ̲rʃieri/ 1 ADJ **Tertiary** means third in order, third in importance, or at a third stage of development. 第三的 [FORMAL] ❑ *He must have come to know those philosophers through secondary or tertiary sources.* 他一定是通过第二手或第三手资料了解那些哲学家的。 2 ADJ **Tertiary education** is education at the university or college level. 大学的 (教育) [ADJ n] [mainly BRIT] ❑ *...institutions of tertiary education.* …提供大学教育的学院。

in AM, usually use **higher education**

→ see **primary, secondary**

test ◆◆◆ /tɛ̲st/ (**tests, testing, tested**) 1 V-T When you **test** something, you try it, for example, by touching it or using it for a short time, in order to find out what it is, what condition it is in, or how well it works. 试验 ❑ *Either measure the temperature with a thermometer or test the water with your wrist.* 要么用温度计测量水温，要么用你的手腕来试水温。 2 N-COUNT A **test** is a deliberate action or experiment to find out how well something works. 试验 ❑ *...the banning of nuclear tests.* …对核试验的禁止。 3 V-T If you **test** someone, you ask them questions or tell them to perform certain actions in order to find out how much they know about a subject or how well they are able to do something. 测试 ❑ *There was a time when each teacher spent an hour, one day a week, testing students in every subject.* 曾有一段时间，每个老师每周都花一小时来测验学生的各门功课。 ❑ *She decided to test herself with a training run in London.* 她想通过参加在伦敦举办的培训来挑战自己。 4 N-COUNT A **test** is a series of questions that you must answer or actions that you must perform in order to show how much you know about a subject or how well you are able to do something. 测试 ❑ *Out of a total of 25 students only 15 passed the test.* 所有25个学生中只有15个通过了测试。 ❑ *She sold her bike, took a driving test and bought a car.* 她卖了自行车，参加了驾驶测试然后买了辆车。 5 → see also **quiz** 6 V-T If you **test** someone, you deliberately make things difficult for them in order to see how they react. 考验 ❑ *From the first day, Rudolf was testing me, seeing if I would make him tea, bring him a Coke.* 从第一天起，鲁道夫就在考验我，看我会不会给他泡茶，给他拿可乐。 7 N-COUNT If an event or situation is a **test of** a person or thing, it reveals their qualities or effectiveness. 考验 ❑ *It is a fact that holidays are a major test of any relationship.* 这是事实，节假日是对任何情感关系的重大考验。 8 V-T If you **are tested for** a particular disease or medical condition, you are examined or go through various procedures in order to find out whether you have that disease or condition. 检查(身体) [usu passive] ❑ *My doctor wants me to be tested for diabetes.* 我的医生要我去做糖尿病检查。 9 N-COUNT A medical **test** is an examination of a part of your body in order to check that you are healthy or to find out what is wrong with you. (医疗) 检查 ❑ *If necessary, X-rays and blood tests will also be used to aid diagnosis.* 如有必要的话，X光检查和血液检查也会被用来帮助诊断。 ❑ *...a pregnancy test.* …妊娠检查。 10 PHRASE If you **put** something **to the test**, you find out how useful or effective it is by using it. 检验某物 ❑ *The team are now putting their theory to the test.* 该团队正在检验他们的理论。 11 PHRASE If new circumstances or events **put** something or someone **to the test**, they put a strain on it and indicate how strong or stable it really is. 考验某事/某人 ❑ *Multiple hijackings are putting air traffic controllers to the test.* 连环劫机案正在考验航空调度员。 12 PHRASE If you say that something **will stand the test of time**, you mean that it is strong or effective enough to last for a very long time. 经受时间的考验 ❑ *It says a lot for her cooking skills that so many of her recipes have stood the test of time.* 她的很多食谱经受了时间的考验，这很能证明她的厨艺。 13 **to test the waters** → see **water**

Student knowledge or skill can be measured by a **test**. If the test is not long or a significant share of the total grade, it may be called a **quiz**. An **examination** is a comprehensive test that contributes either all or a major portion of the final grade.

Word Partnership *test* 的常用搭配：

N. test **a drug**, test **a hypothesis** 1
crash test, test **drive**, **flight** test, **strength** test, **stress** test 2
achievement test, **aptitude** test, test **data/results**, **intelligence** test, test **items**, **math/reading** test, test **preparation**, test **scores**, **standardized** test, test **takers** 4
blood test, **drug** test, **HIV** test, **pregnancy** test 9
ADJ. **nuclear** test 2
diagnostic test 4 9
test **negative/positive** 8
V. **administer** a test, **fail** a test, **give** *someone* a test, **pass** a test, **study for** a test, **take** a test 4

tes·ta·ment /tɛstəmənt/ (**testaments**) 1 N-VAR If one thing is a **testament to** another, it shows that the other thing exists or is true. 证明 [FORMAL] ❑ *For him to win the game like that is a testament to his perseverance.* 他能赢得那样的比赛证明了他的毅力。 2 PHRASE Someone's **last will and testament** is the most recent will that they have made, especially the last will that they make before they die. 临终遗嘱 [LEGAL]

test case (**test cases**) N-COUNT A **test case** is a legal case which becomes an example for deciding other similar cases. (被其他类似案件援引的) 判例案件 ❑ *It is considered an important test case by both advocates and opponents of gun control.* 这在枪支管制的支持者和反对者双方看来都是一个重要的判例案件。

tes·ti·cle /tɛstɪkᵊl/ (**testicles**) N-COUNT A man's **testicles** are the two reproductive glands that produce sperm and are contained in the scrotum. 睾丸

★ **tes·ti·fy** /tɛstɪfaɪ/ (**testifies, testifying, testified**) V-T/V-I When someone **testifies** in a court of law, they give a statement of what they saw someone do or what they know of a situation, after having promised to tell the truth. (在法庭上) 作证 ❑ *Several eyewitnesses testified that they saw the officers hit Miller in the face.* 几个目击者证明他们看到那些警察们打了米勒的脸。 ❑ *Eva testified to having seen Herndon with his gun on the stairs.* 伊娃证明曾看见赫恩登在楼梯上拿着枪。

tes·ti·mo·nial /tɛstɪmoʊniəl/ (**testimonials**) 1 N-COUNT A **testimonial** is a written statement about a person's character and abilities, often written by their employer. (常指雇主证明某人品德和能力的) 证明书 ❑ *She could hardly expect her employer to provide her with testimonials to her character and ability.* 她几乎不指望老板会给她写证明她的人品和能力的证明书。 2 N-COUNT A **testimonial** is an event which is held to honor someone for their services or achievements. 表彰会 ❑ *...a testimonial dinner held in New York.* …在纽约举行的一个表彰晚宴。

Word Link *mony ≈ resulting state : ceremony, harmony, testimony*

★ **tes·ti·mo·ny** /tɛstɪmoʊni/ (**testimonies**) 1 N-VAR In a court of law, someone's **testimony** is a formal statement that they make about what they saw someone do or what they know of a situation, after having promised to tell the truth. (法庭上的) 证词 ❑ *His testimony was an important element of the prosecution's case.* 他的证词是本起公诉案中的一个重要因素。 2 N-UNCOUNT If you say that one thing is **testimony to** another, you mean that it shows clearly that the second thing has a particular quality. 明证 [also "a" N, usu N "to" n] ❑ *The environmental movement is testimony to the widespread feelings of support for nature's importance.* 环保运动是大自然重要性得到广泛认可的明证。
→ see **trial**

test·ing ♦◇◇ /tɛstɪŋ/ 1 ADJ A **testing** problem or situation is very difficult to deal with and shows a lot about the character of the person who is dealing with it. 考验人的 ❑ *The most testing time is undoubtedly in the early months of your return to work.* 最考验人的时候无疑是在你重返工作岗位的头几个月。 2 N-UNCOUNT **Testing** is the activity of testing something or someone in order to find out information. 检测 ❑ *...product testing and labeling.* …产品的检测与标贴。
→ see **experiment**

tes·tos·ter·one /tɛstɒstəroʊn/ N-UNCOUNT **Testosterone** is a hormone found in men and male animals, which can also be produced artificially. It is thought to be responsible for the male sexual instinct and other male characteristics. 睾丸素

teth·er /tɛðər/ (**tethers, tethering, tethered**) 1 PHRASE If you say that you are **at the end of** your **tether**, you mean that you are so worried, tired, and unhappy because of your problems that you feel you cannot cope. 束手无策；山穷水尽 ❑ *She was jealous, humiliated, and emotionally at the end of her tether.* 她觉得又嫉妒又屈辱，情绪低落至极。 2 N-COUNT A **tether** is a rope or chain which is used to tie an animal to a post or fence so that it can only move around within a small area. (拴动物的) 绳；链 ❑ *...a dog that choked to death on its tether.* …一条被拴绳勒死的狗。 3 V-T If you **tether** an animal or object **to** something, you attach it there with a rope or chain so that it cannot move very far. 拴住 ❑ *The officer dismounted, tethering his horse to a tree.* 这位军官下了马，把马拴在一棵树上。

text ♦◇◇ /tɛkst/ (**texts, texting, texted**) 1 N-SING **The text** of a book is the main part of it, rather than the introduction, pictures, or notes. 正文 ❑ *The text was informative and well written.* 正文信息量大，写得很好。 2 N-UNCOUNT **Text** is any written material. 文字材料；文本 ❑ *The machine can recognize handwritten characters and turn them into printed text.* 这台机器能识别手写的文字并将其转换为打印文本。 3 N-COUNT The **text** of a speech, broadcast, or recording is the written version of it. (演讲、广播或录音的) 文字稿 ❑ *The text of his recent speech was circulated among leading republicans.* 他新近演讲的文字稿在共和党领导人之间传阅。 4 N-COUNT A **text** is a book or other piece of writing, especially one connected with science or learning. (尤指与科学或学术相关的) 文稿 ❑ *Her text is believed to be the oldest surviving manuscript by a female physician.* 她的文稿被认为是女性内科医生写的现存最古老的手稿。 5 N-COUNT A **text** is the same as a **text message**. 短信 ❑ *The new system can send a text to a cellphone, or to another landline phone.* 新系统可以向手机或向另一台座机发短信。 6 V-T If you **text** someone, you send them a text message on a cellphone. (用手机) 给…发短信 ❑ *Mary texted me when she got home.* 玛丽到家时给我发了短信。
→ see **diary**

text·book /tɛkstbʊk/ (**textbooks**) also **text book** 1 N-COUNT A **textbook** is a book containing facts about a particular subject that is used by people studying that subject. 教科书 ❑ *She wrote a textbook on international law.* 她写了一本国际法的教科书。 2 ADJ If you say that something is a **textbook** case or example, you are emphasizing that it provides a clear example of a type of situation or event. 典型的 [ADJ n] [EMPHASIS] ❑ *The house is a textbook example of medieval domestic architecture.* 这座房子是中世纪民居建筑的典型范例。

tex·tile /tɛkstaɪl/ (**textiles**) 1 N-COUNT **Textiles** are types of cloth or fabric, especially ones that have been woven. 纺织品 ❑ *...decorative textiles for the home.* …家用的装饰性纺织品。 2 N-PLURAL **Textiles** are the industries concerned with the manufacture of cloth. 纺织业 [no det] ❑ *Another 75,000 jobs will be lost in textiles and clothing.* 纺织业和制衣业又将失去7.5万个就业机会。
→ see **cotton, industry, quilt**

text·ing /tɛkstɪŋ/ N-UNCOUNT **Texting** is the same as **text messaging**. 发短信

text mes·sage (**text messages**) N-COUNT A **text message** is a message that you send using a cellphone. 短信息 ❑ *She has sent text messages to her family telling them not to worry.* 她已发短信给家人，告诉他们不要担心。

text mes·sag·ing N-UNCOUNT **Text messaging** is the sending of written messages using a cellphone. 发短信 ❑ *...the popularity of text messaging.* …发短信的流行。

★ **tex·ture** /tɛkstʃər/ (**textures**) 1 N-VAR The **texture** of something is the way that it feels when you touch it, for example, how smooth or rough it is. 手感 ❑ *It is used in moisturizers to give them a wonderfully silky texture.* 它被用于各种保湿霜中，使之产生丝般的美妙手感。 2 N-VAR The **texture** of something, especially food or soil, is its structure, for example, whether it is light with lots of holes, or very heavy and solid. (尤指食品、土壤等的) 结构 ❑ *Matured over 18 months, this cheese has an open, crumbly texture with a strong flavor.* 这种奶酪18个月后发酵成熟，气孔多，组织松脆，味道浓郁。

than ♦♦♦ /ðən, STRONG ðæn/ 1 PREP You use **than** after a comparative adjective or adverb in order to link two parts of a comparison. (用于形容词或副词的比较级后，连接相比较的两个部分) 比 [compar PREP group] ❑ *Children learn faster than adults.* 孩子比大人学得快。 ❑ *The radio only weighs a few ounces and is smaller than a pack of* *cigarettes.* 这个收音机只有几盎司重，比一包香烟还小。● CONJ **Than** is also a conjunction. 比 ❑ *He wished he could have helped her more than he did.* 他希望自己当时能更多地帮帮她。 2 PREP You use **than** when you are stating a number, quantity, or value approximately by saying that it is above or below another number, quantity, or value. (数、量或价值) 高于；低于 ["more/less" PREP n] ❑ *They talked on the phone for more than an hour.* 他们在电话里聊了一个多小时。 3 CONJ You use **than** in order to link two parts of a contrast, for example, in order to state a preference. (连接相比较的两个部分，表优先选择) 与其说 ❑ *The arrangement was more a formality than a genuine partnership of two nations.* 这种安排与其说是两国间真正的伙伴关系的表现，还不如说是装样子。 4 **less than → see less** 5 **more than → see more** 6 **more often than not → see often** 7 **other than → see other** 8 **rather than → see rather**

thank ♦♦♦ /θæŋk/ (**thanks, thanking, thanked**) 1 CONVENTION You use **thank you** or, in more informal English, **thanks** to express your gratitude when someone does something for you or gives you what you want. 谢谢 (用于表示感谢别人所做之事或赠与所需之物) [FORMULAE] ❑ *Thank you very much for your call.* 非常感谢您打电话来。 ❑ *Thanks for the information.* 谢谢您告诉我这消息。 2 CONVENTION You use **thank you** or, in more informal English, **thanks** to politely accept something that has just been offered to you. 谢谢 (用于礼貌接受别人给与之物) [FORMULAE] ❑ *"Would you like a cup of coffee?"—"Thank you, I'd love one."* "你要喝杯咖啡吗？"——"谢谢，来一杯吧。" 3 CONVENTION You use **no thank you** or, in more informal English, **no thanks** to politely refuse something that has just been offered to you. 谢谢 (用于礼貌拒绝别人给与之物) [FORMULAE] ❑ *"Would you like a cigarette?"—"No thank you."* "你要来支香烟吗？"——"不了，谢谢。" 4 CONVENTION You use **thank you** or, in more informal English, **thanks** to politely acknowledge what someone has said to you, especially when they have answered your question or said something nice to you. 谢谢 (用于礼貌地感谢别人的回答或赞美) [FORMULAE] ❑ *"You look very nice indeed."—"Thank you."* "你看起来真漂亮。"——"谢谢。" 5 CONVENTION You use **thank you** or **thank you very much** in order to say firmly that you do not want someone's help or to tell them that you do not like the way that they are behaving toward you. 谢谢 (用于拒绝别人的帮助或告诉对方自己不喜欢这种对待方式) [EMPHASIS] ❑ *I can find my own way home, thank you.* 我自己能找到路回家，谢谢。 6 V-T When you **thank** someone **for** something, you express your gratitude to them for it. 感谢 ❑ *I thanked them for their long and loyal service.* 我感谢他们长期忠诚的效力。 7 N-PLURAL When you express your **thanks** to someone, you express your gratitude to them for something. 谢意 ❑ *They accepted their certificates with words of thanks.* 他们接过证书，同时表示了谢意。 8 PHRASE You say **"Thank God," "Thank Goodness,"** or **"Thank heavens"** when you are very relieved about something. 谢天谢地 [FEELINGS] ❑ *I was wrong, thank God.* 原来我错了，谢天谢地。 9 PHRASE If you say that you **have** someone **to thank for** something, you mean that they caused it to happen. 归因于某人 ❑ *I have her to thank for my life.* 我多亏她才保住性命。 ❑ *You have only yourself to thank for this mess.* 你只能怪你自己把事情弄得这么糟。 10 PHRASE If you say that something happens **thanks to** a particular person or thing, you mean that they are responsible for it happening or they caused it to happen. 归功于 ❑ *It is thanks to this committee that many new sponsors have come forward.* 多亏这个委员会，才来了这么多新的赞助商。

thank·ful /θæŋkfəl/ ADJ When you are **thankful**, you are very happy and relieved to have something, or that something has happened. 感到庆幸的 ❑ *Most of the time I'm just thankful that I've got a job.* 大部分时候我庆幸自己有了份工作。

thank·ful·ly /θæŋkfəli/ ADV You use **thankfully** in order to express approval or happiness about a statement that you are making. 万幸地 [ADV with cl/group] ❑ *Thankfully, she was not injured.* 万幸的是她没受伤。

★ **thanks·giving** /θæŋksgɪvɪŋ/ N-UNCOUNT **Thanksgiving** is the giving of thanks to God, especially in a religious ceremony. (对上帝) 感恩

★ **Thanks·giving** (**Thanksgivings**) 1 N-VAR In the United States, **Thanksgiving** or **Thanksgiving Day** is a public holiday on the fourth Thursday in November. On this day, people remember the first American thanksgiving, when the first European settlers had been taught how to grow food by the Native Americans, and they celebrated the successful harvest together. 感恩节 (在美国为11月的第4个星期四) ❑ *No matter where his business took him, he always managed to be home for Thanksgiving.* 无论因公务走到哪儿，他总是设法赶回家过感恩节。 2 N-VAR In Canada, **Thanksgiving** or **Thanksgiving Day** is a public holiday on the second Monday in October. On this day, people celebrate a successful harvest. 感恩节 (在加拿大为10月的第2个星期一)

> A national holiday in the US and a big family occasion, **Thanksgiving** falls on the fourth Thursday in November. It commemorates the first harvest reaped by the **Pilgrims**, the first English settlers, in 1621, for which they gave thanks to God – hence the name of the festival. The traditional meal centers around a roast turkey, followed by "pumpkin pie" for dessert.

that

1 DEMONSTRATIVE USES
2 CONJUNCTION AND RELATIVE PRONOUN USES

1 that ♦♦♦ /ðæt/

➪ **Please look at meanings 19 – 21 to see if the expression you are looking for is shown under another headword.** 1 PRON You use **that** to refer back to an idea or situation expressed in a previous sentence or sentences. 那 (指前面句子提过的想法或情形) ❑ *They said you particularly wanted to talk to me. Why was that?* 他们说你特别想和我谈谈。那是为什么？ ❑ *"There's a party tonight."—"Is that why you're phoning?"* "今晚有聚会。"——"那就是你打电话的原因吗？" ● DET **That** is also a determiner. 那 ❑ *She's away; for that reason I'm cooking tonight.* 她不在家，所以今晚我煮饭。 2 DET You use **that** to refer to someone or something already mentioned. 那 (指已提及的人或物) ❑ *The salespeople get between $50,000 and $60,000 a year but that amount can double with commission.* 推销员每年的收入在5万到6万美元之间，但是加上佣金，那数额能翻倍。 3 DET When you have been talking about a particular period of time, you use **that** to indicate that you are still referring to the same period. You use expressions such as **that morning** or **that afternoon** to indicate that you are referring to an earlier period of the same day. 那 (指前文提到的同一时期) ❑ *The story was published in a Sunday newspaper later that week.* 这个故事在那周晚些时候被刊登在一家星期日报纸上。 4 PRON You use **that** in expressions such as **that of** and **that which** to introduce more information about something already mentioned, instead of repeating the noun which refers to it. 那 (用于引入有关已提及的事物的更多信息，避免重复提及相关名词) [FORMAL] ❑ *A recession like that of 1973-74 could put one in ten American companies into bankruptcy.* 一场像1973到1974年那样的经济衰退会使1/10的美国公司破产。 5 PRON You use **that** in front of words or expressions which express agreement, responses, or reactions to what has just been said. 那 (用于对已说过的话表示同意或应答的词前) ❑ *"She said she'd met you in England."—"That's true."* "她说她在英格兰见过你。"——"没错。" 6 DET You use **that** when you are referring to someone or something which is a distance away from you in position or time, especially when you indicate or point to them. When there are two or more things near you, **that** refers to the more distant one. 那个 (指距离或时间上较远的人或事物) ❑ *Look at that guy. He's got red socks.* 看那家伙，他穿着红袜子。● PRON **That** is also a pronoun. 那个 ❑ *Leo, what's that you're writing?* 利奥，你写的那是什么呀？ 7 PRON You use **that** when you are identifying someone or asking about their identity. 那个 (用于识别或询问他人的身份) ❑ *That's my wife you were talking to.* 刚才和你说话的是我妻子。 ❑ *"Who's that with you?"—"A friend of mine."* "和你在一起的那个人是谁？"——"我的一位朋友。" 8 DET You can use **that** when you expect the person you are talking to to know what or who you are referring to, without needing to identify the particular person or thing fully. 那个 (不需明确指出，指代对方应该知道的人或物) [SPOKEN] ❑ *I really thought I was something when I wore that hat and my patent leather shoes.* 当我戴上那顶帽子，穿着我的漆皮鞋的时候，我还真以为自己是个人物。● PRON **That** is also a pronoun. 那 ❑ *That was a terrible case of blackmail in the paper today.* 那是今天报纸里刊登的一宗可怕的勒索案。 9 ADV If something is **not that** bad, funny, or expensive for example, it is not as bad, funny, or expensive as it might be or as has been suggested. 那么 [with brd-neg, ADV adj/adv] ❑ *Not even Gary, he said, was that stupid.* 他说，就是加里也没那么笨。 10 ADV You can use **that** to emphasize the degree of a feeling or quality. 那样

t

(用于强调感情或品质的程度) [ADV adj/adv] [INFORMAL, EMPHASIS] ❑ *I would have walked out, I was that angry.* 我本要走出去的，我是那样的生气。 11 → see also **those** 12 PHRASE You use **and all that** or **and that** to refer generally to everything else which is associated with what you have just mentioned. 诸如此类 [INFORMAL, VAGUENESS] ❑ *I'm not a cook myself but I am interested in nutrition and all that.* 我本人不是厨师，但我对营养之类的事感兴趣。 13 PHRASE You use **at that** after a statement which modifies or emphasizes what you have just said. 而且 [EMPHASIS] ❑ *Success never seems to come but through hard work, often physically demanding work at that.* 成功不通过努力工作似乎是无法取得的，而且往往是很耗费体力的工作。 14 PHRASE You use **that is** or **that is to say** to indicate that you are about to express the same idea more clearly or precisely. 也就是说 ❑ *I am a disappointing, though generally dutiful, student. That is, I do as I'm told.* 我是个令人失望的学生，尽管一般来说我很听话，也就是说，我按别人说的做。 15 PHRASE You use **that's it** to indicate that nothing more needs to be done or that the end has been reached. 就这样 ❑ *When he left the office, that was it, the workday was over.* 他一离开办公室，工作日就这样结束了。 16 CONVENTION You use **that's it** to express agreement with or approval of what has just been said or done. 没错 [FORMULAE] ❑ *"You got married, right?"—"Yeah, that's it."* "你结婚了，对吧？"——"是的，没错。" 17 PHRASE You use **just like that** to emphasize that something happens or is done immediately or in a very simple way, often without much thought or discussion. 就那样 [INFORMAL, EMPHASIS] ❑ *Just like that, I was in love.* 就那样，我恋爱了。 18 PHRASE You use **that's that** to say there is nothing more you can do or say about a particular matter. 就那样好了 [SPOKEN] ❑ *"Well, if that's the way you want it," he replied, tears in his eyes, "I guess that's that."* "哦，如果你要那样的话，"他泪汪汪地回答道，"我想就那样好了。" 19 **like that** → see **like** 20 **this and that** → see **this** 21 **this, that and the other** → see **this**

❷ **that** ♦♦♦ /ðət, STRONG ðæt/ 1 CONJ You can use **that** after many verbs, adjectives, nouns, and expressions to introduce a clause in which you report what someone has said, or what they think or feel. 用于某些动词、形容词、名词和短语后，引导从句来引述某人的话语、思想或感觉 ❑ *He called her up one day and said that he and his wife were coming to New York.* 他有一天给她打电话，说他和他妻子要来纽约。 2 CONJ You use **that** after "it" and a linking verb and an adjective to comment on a situation or fact. 用于**it**、系动词或形容词后来评论某种情况或事实 ❑ *It's interesting that you like him.* 很有意思，你喜欢他。 3 PRON-REL You use **that** to introduce a clause which gives more information to help identify the person or thing you are talking about. 用于引导定语从句来帮助说明所谈及的人或物 ❑ *...pills that will make the problem disappear.* …会消除该症状的药丸。 4 CONJ You use **that** after expressions with "so" and "such" in order to introduce the result or effect of something. 用于带**so**和**such**的短语后，引入某事的结果或影响 ❑ *She became so nervous that she shook violently.* 她紧张得全身猛烈颤抖。

▲ **thatch** /θætʃ/ (**thatches**) 1 N-COUNT A **thatch** or a **thatch roof** is a roof made from straw or reeds. 茅草屋顶 ❑ *They would live in a small house with a green door and a new thatch.* 他们会住在一座有一个绿门和新茅草屋顶的小房子里。 2 N-UNCOUNT **Thatch** is straw or reeds used to make a roof. 做屋顶用的稻草或芦苇 3 N-SING You can refer to someone's hair as their **thatch of** hair, especially when it is very thick and messy. 浓密蓬乱 [oft N "of" n] ❑ *Teddy ran thick fingers through his unruly thatch of hair.* 泰迪用粗大的手指拢他那不服贴的浓密蓬乱的头发。

thatched /θætʃt/ ADJ A **thatched** house or a house with a **thatched** roof has a roof made of straw or reeds. (屋顶) 用稻草盖的；用芦苇盖的 ❑ *...a 400-year-old thatched cottage.* …一座有400年历史的茅草屋。

that's /ðæts/ **That's** is a spoken form of "that is." **that is**的口语形式

▲ **thaw** /θɔ/ (**thaws, thawing, thawed**) 1 V-I When ice, snow, or something else that is frozen **thaws**, it melts. (冰雪等) 融化 ❑ *It's so cold the snow doesn't get a chance to thaw.* 天气太冷了，积雪都没机会融化。 2 N-COUNT A **thaw** is a period of warmer weather when snow and ice melt, usually at the end of winter. (通常指冬末的) 解冻期 ❑ *We slogged through the mud of an early spring thaw.* 我们在初春解冻期的泥泞里艰难跋涉。 3 V-T/V-I When you **thaw** frozen food or when it **thaws**, you leave it in a place where it can reach room temperature so that it is ready for use. 解冻 ❑ *Always thaw pastry thoroughly.* 一定要让油酥面团完全解冻。 ● PHRASAL VERB **Thaw out** means the same as **thaw**. 解冻 ❑ *Thaw it out completely before reheating in a saucepan.* 将之完全解冻后，放到平底锅里重新加热。

the ♦♦♦

The is the definite article. It is used at the beginning of noun groups. **The** is usually pronounced /ðə/ before a consonant and /ði/ before a vowel, but pronounced /ðiː/ when you are emphasizing it.

1 DET You use **the** at the beginning of noun groups to refer to someone or something that you have already mentioned or identified. 用于名词词组前，指前面已经提及的人或物 ❑ *Six of the 38 people were U.S. citizens.* 那38人中有6个是美国公民。 2 DET You use **the** at the beginning of a noun group when the first noun is followed by an "of" phrase or a clause which identifies the person or thing. 当名词后接**of**词组或表明身份的从句时，该名词前用**the** ❑ *There has been a slight increase in the consumption of meat.* 肉类消费略微增加。 3 DET You use **the** in front of some nouns that refer to something in our general experience of the world. 用于某些表示人们共同经历的名词前 ❑ *It's always hard to speculate about the future.* 推测未来总是很难的。 4 DET You use **the** in front of nouns that refer to people, things, services, or institutions that are associated with everyday life. 用于表示与日常生活有关的人、事物、服务或机构的名词前 ❑ *The doctor's on his way.* 医生正在路上。 5 DET You use **the** instead of a possessive determiner, especially when you are talking about a part of someone's body or a member of their family. 用于代替所有格限定词，尤其用于谈论身体部位或家庭成员 ❑ *"How's the family?"—"Just fine, thank you."* "家里人好吗？"——"很好，谢谢。" 6 DET You use **the** in front of a singular noun when you want to make a general statement about things or people of that type. 用于单数名词前，指某一类人或事物 ❑ *An area in which the computer has made considerable strides in recent years is in playing chess.* 近年来计算机取得重大进展的一个领域是国际象棋。 7 DET You use **the** with the name of a musical instrument when you are talking about someone's ability to play the instrument. 用于乐器名称前，谈论某人是否会演奏该乐器 ❑ *Did you play the piano as a child?* 你小时候弹钢琴吗？ 8 DET You use **the** with nationality adjectives and nouns to talk about the people who live in a country. 与表示国籍的形容词和名词连用，指该国国民 ❑ *The Japanese, Americans, and even the French and Germans, judge economic policies by results.* 日本人、美国人，甚至法国人和德国人，都是根据结果来评判经济政策的好坏。 9 DET You use **the** with words such as "rich," "poor," "old," or "unemployed" to refer to all people of a particular type. 表示一类人 ❑ *Conditions for the poor in Los Angeles have not improved.* 洛杉矶穷人的生活条件还未改善。 10 DET If you want to refer to a whole family or to a married couple, you can make their surname into a plural and use **the** in front of it. 用于姓氏的复数形式前，表示一家人或一对夫妇 ❑ *The Taylors decided that they would employ an architect to do the work.* 泰勒夫妇决定雇个建筑师来做这个工作。 11 DET You use **the** in front of an adjective when you are referring to a particular thing that is described by that adjective. 用于形容词前表示该形容词描绘的事物 ❑ *He knows he's wishing for the impossible.* 他知道自己在企盼不可能的事。 12 DET You use **the** to indicate whether or not you have enough of the thing mentioned for a particular purpose. 表示所提及的东西是否有足够的量 ❑ *She may not have the money to maintain or restore her property.* 她也许没有足够的钱来保留或维修自己的房产。 13 DET You use **the** with some titles, place names, and other names. 和称呼、地名等名称连用 ❑ *...the Seattle Times.* …《西雅图时报》。 ❑ *...the White House.* …白宫。 ❑ *...The Great Gatsby.* …《了不起的盖茨比》。 14 DET You use **the** in front of numbers such as first, second, and third. 用于序数词前 ❑ *The meeting should take place on the fifth of May.* 会议应于5月5日举行。 15 DET You use **the** in front of numbers when they refer to decades. 用于表示年代的数字前 ❑ *It's sometimes hard to imagine how bad things were in the thirties.* 有的时候很难想像三十年代的情况有多糟。 16 DET You use **the** in front of superlative adjectives and adverbs. 用于形容词或副词最高级前 ❑ *Brisk daily walks are still the best exercise for young and old alike.* 每天快步走对老老少少来说仍然是最好的锻炼方式。 17 DET You use **the** in front of each of two comparative adjectives or adverbs when you are describing how one amount or quality changes in relation to another. 用于两个形容词或副词的比较级前，表示其中一个随另一个发生数量或性质的变化 ❑ *The longer the therapy goes on, the more successful it will be.* 治疗的时间越长，疗效就越好。 18 DET When you express rates, prices, and measurements, you can use **the** to say how many units apply to each of the items being measured. (表示速度、价格或计量) 每

T

❑ ...*cars that get more miles to the gallon.* …每加仑汽油能多行驶几英里的汽车。 19 DET You use **the** to indicate that something or someone is the most famous, important, or best thing of its kind. In spoken English, you put more stress on it, and in written English, you often underline it or write it in capitals or italics. 表示某人或某物是最有名的、最重要的或最好的；口语中需要重读，书面语中常加下划线或用大写或斜体 ❑ *The circus is the place to be this Saturday or Sunday.* 马戏团是这周六或周日的最佳去处。

thea·ter ♦♦◇ /θi̯ətər/ (**theaters**)

in BRIT, use **theatre**

1 N-COUNT; N-IN-NAMES A **theater** is a building with a stage in it, on which plays, shows, and other performances take place. 剧院 ❑ *They brought her to the theater where their new musical was in production.* 他们带她到正确排新音乐剧的剧院。 2 N-SING You can refer to work in the theater such as acting or writing plays as **the theater.** 戏剧工作 ❑ *The story of her career in the theater is told in a new biography.* 她的戏剧生涯故事记载在新的传记中。 3 N-COUNT A **theater** or a **movie theater** is a place where people go to watch movies for entertainment. 电影院 [AM]

in BRIT, use **cinema**

❑ *A movie theater and roller rink attracted customers and profit.* 一家兼作溜冰场的电影院吸引了顾客，也招来了利润。 4 N-UNCOUNT **Theater** is entertainment that involves the performance of plays. 戏剧表演 ❑ ...*American musical theater.* …美国的音乐剧表演。

→ see Word Web: **theater**

→ see **city**

thea·tre /θi̯ətəʳ/ [BRIT] → see **surgery, theater**

▲ **the·at·ri·cal** /θiætrɪkᵊl/ 1 ADJ **Theatrical** means relating to the theater. 戏剧的 [ADJ n] ❑ ...*the most outstanding theatrical performances of the year.* …年度最杰出的戏剧表演。 ● **the·at·ri·cal·ly** /θiætrɪkli/ ADV 在戏剧上 ❑ *Shaffer's great gift lies in his ability to animate ideas theatrically.* 谢弗的天赋在于他能把想法在戏剧上表现出来。 2 ADJ **Theatrical** behavior is exaggerated and unnatural, and intended to create an effect. (行为) 夸张的 ❑ *In a theatrical gesture Jim clamped his hand over his eyes.* 以一个夸张的手势，吉姆用一只手紧紧捂住双眼。 ● **the·at·ri·cal·ly** ADV 夸张地 ❑ *He looked theatrically at his watch.* 他夸张地看了看表。

theft /θɛft/ (**thefts**) N-VAR **Theft** is the crime of stealing. 盗窃 ❑ *Over the last decade, auto theft has increased by over 56 percent.* 过去的10年来汽车盗窃案上升了56%以上。

their ♦♦♦ /ðɛər/

Their is the third person plural possessive determiner.

1 DET You use **their** to indicate that something belongs or relates to the group of people, animals, or things that you are talking about. 他们的；她们的；它们的 ❑ *Janis and Kurt have announced their engagement.* 贾尼斯和库尔特已宣布订婚。 2 DET You use **their** instead of "his or her" to indicate that something belongs or relates to a person without saying whether that person is a man or a woman. Some people think this use is incorrect. 用于代替"他的"或"她的"，不指明是男是女 ❑ *Each student determines their own pace in the yoga class.* 每个学生决定他们自己在这个瑜珈班的学习速度。

theirs /ðɛərz/

Theirs is the third person plural possessive pronoun.

1 PRON-POSS You use **theirs** to indicate that something belongs or relates to the group of people, animals, or things that you are talking about. 他们的；她们的；它们的 (东西) ❑ *There was a big group of a dozen people at the table next to theirs.* 他们旁边的那张桌坐了一大群人，有十几个。 2 PRON-POSS You use **theirs** instead of "his or hers" to indicate that something belongs or relates to a person without saying whether that person is a man or a woman. Some people think this use is incorrect. 用于代替"他的"或"她的"，不指明是男是女，有些人认为这种用法不正确 ❑ *He would leave the trailer unlocked. If there was something inside that someone wanted, it would be theirs for the taking.* 他不会锁活动房屋。如果屋里有别人想要的东西，他们就可以拿走。

them ♦♦♦ /ðəm, STRONG ðɛm/

Them is a third person plural pronoun. **Them** is used as the object of a verb or preposition.

1 PRON-PLURAL You use **them** to refer to a group of people, animals, or things. 他们；她们；它们 [V PRON, prep PRON] ❑ *The Beatles – I never get tired of listening to them.* 甲壳虫乐队——我百听不厌。 ❑ *Kids these days have no one to tell them what's right and wrong.* 现在的孩子们没人告诉他们什么是对什么是错。 2 PRON-PLURAL You use **them** instead of "him or her" to refer to a person without saying whether that person is a man or a woman. Some people think this use is incorrect. 用于代替宾格"他"或"她"，不指明是男是女，有些人认为这种用法不正确 [V PRON, prep PRON] ❑ *It takes great courage to face your child and tell them the truth.* 需要很大的勇气来面对你的孩子并告诉他们真相。

theme ♦◇◇ /θi̱m/ (**themes**) 1 N-COUNT A **theme** in a piece of writing, a talk, or a discussion is an important idea or subject that runs through it. (著作、谈话或讨论的) 主题 ❑ *The theme of the conference is renaissance Europe.* 该会议的主题是文艺复兴时期的欧洲。 2 N-COUNT A **theme** in an artist's work or in a work of literature is an idea in it that the artist or writer develops or repeats. (艺术品或文学作品的) 主题 ❑ *The novel's central theme is the ongoing conflict between men and women.* 这部小说的主题是男女之间永无休止的冲突。 3 N-COUNT A **theme** is a short simple tune on which a piece of music is based. (音乐的) 主旋律 ❑ ...*variations on themes from Mozart's The Magic Flute.* …莫扎特的《魔笛》中主旋律的变奏曲。 4 N-COUNT **Theme** music or a **theme** song is a piece of music that is played at the beginning and end of a movie or of a television or radio program. (电影、电视节目或广播节目的) 主题曲；主题歌 ❑ ...*the theme from Dr. Zhivago.* …《日瓦戈医生》的主题曲。

→ see **myth**

Word Partnership *theme* 的常用搭配:

N. **campaign** theme 1
theme **of a book/movie/story** 2
theme **and variations** 3
theme **music**, theme **song** 4

ADJ. **central** theme, **common** theme, **dominant** theme, **main** theme, **major** theme, **new** theme, **recurring** theme 1 2

them·selves ♦♦♦ /ðəmsɛlvz/

Themselves is the third person plural reflexive pronoun.

1 PRON-REFL You use **themselves** to refer to people, animals, or things when the object of a verb or preposition refers to the same people or things as the subject of the verb. 他们自己；她们自己；它们自己 [V PRON, prep PRON] ❑ *They all seemed to be enjoying themselves.* 他们看起来都玩得很愉快。 2 PRON-REFL-EMPH You use **themselves** to emphasize the people or things that you are referring to. **Themselves** is also sometimes used instead of "them" as the

t

Word Web theater

Plays in ancient Greece were very different from those of today. **Performances** happened outdoors in open air **theaters.** Two or three male **actors** played all of the **roles** in the **production.** Women could not appear onstage. The actors would go **backstage,** change their **masks** and **costumes,** and re-emerge as new **characters.** A group of people, called the chorus, explained what was happening to the **audience.** Traditional Greek **tragedies** came from stories of the distant past. **Comedies** often made fun of contemporary public figures. Several **plays** appeared together as a contest. The **audience** voted for their favorite **show.**

object of a verb or preposition. (用于强调，或代替宾格“他们”)他们自己；她们自己；它们自己 [EMPHASIS] ❑ *Many mentally ill people are themselves unhappy about the idea of community care.* 许多精神病患者自身不喜欢社区护理。 3 PRON-REFL You use **themselves** instead of “himself or herself” to refer back to the person who is the subject of the sentence without saying whether it is a man or a woman. Some people think this use is incorrect. 用于代替“他自己”或“她自己”，指代句子的主语，不指明是男是女，有些人认为这种用法不正确 [V PRON, prep PRON] ❑ *What can a patient with emphysema do to help themselves?* 肺气肿的病人能做些什么来自助？ 4 PRON-REFL-EMPH You use **themselves** instead of “himself or herself” to emphasize the person you are referring to without saying whether it is a man or a woman. **Themselves** is also sometimes used as the object of a verb or preposition. Some people think this use is incorrect. 用于代替“他自己”或“她自己”，强调所指代的人，不指明是男是女，有时也用作动词或介词的宾语。有些人认为这种用法不正确 [EMPHASIS] ❑ *Each student makes only one item themselves.* 每个学生自己只做一项。 5 → see also **ourselves**

then ♦♦♦ /ðɛn/ 1 ADV **Then** means at a particular time in the past or in the future. 那时 ❑ *He wanted to have a source of income after his retirement; until then, he wouldn't require additional money.* 他想在退休后有个收入来源，而这之前则不需要额外的钱。 ❑ *Executives pledged to get the company back on track. Since then, though, shares have fallen 30 per cent.* 主管们发誓要让公司重上轨道，不过从那以后股票价格还是下降了30%。 2 ADJ **Then** is used when you refer to something which was true at a particular time in the past but is not true now. 当时的 [ADJ n] ❑ *...a tour of the then new airport.* …在当时新机场的一次参观。 ● ADV **Then** is also an adverb. 当时 [ADV group] ❑ *Richard Strauss, then 76 years old, suffered through the war years in silence.* 理查德·斯特劳斯当时已76岁，默默地熬过了战争岁月。 3 ADV You use **then** to say that one thing happens after another, or is after another on a list. 然后 ❑ *Add the oil and then the scallops to the pan, leaving a little space for the garlic.* 往锅里倒入油，然后加入扇贝，再放一点大蒜。 4 ADV You use **then** in conversation to indicate that what you are about to say follows logically in some way from what has just been said or implied. 那么 [cl/group ADV] ❑ *"I wasn't a very good scholar in school."—"Then why did you become a teacher?"* “我在学校时成绩不是很好。”——“那你为什么当老师呢？” 5 ADV You use **then** to signal the end of a topic or the end of a conversation. 用于表示话题或谈话结束 [cl/group ADV] ❑ *"I'll talk to you on Friday anyway."—"Yep. Okay then."* “我星期五总归要和你谈谈的。”——“行，就这么定了。” 6 ADV You use **then** with words like “now,” “well,” and “okay,” to introduce a new topic or a new point of view. 用于引入新话题或新观点 [adv ADV] ❑ *Now then, I'm going to explain everything to you before we do it.* 嗯，我要在我们动手之前向你们把一切解释清楚。 7 ADV You use **then** to introduce the second part of a sentence which begins with “if.” The first part of the sentence describes a possible situation, and **then** introduces the result of the situation. (引导以“if”开头的句子，叙述可能的情况) 那么 [ADV cl] ❑ *If the answer is "yes," then we need to leave now.* 如果答案为“是”，那么我们现在就该离开了。 8 ADV You use **then** at the beginning of a sentence or after “and” or “but” to introduce a comment or an extra piece of information to what you have already said. (用于句首或“**and**”、“**but**”之后) 话说回来 [ADV cl] ❑ *He sounded sincere, but then, he always did.* 他听起来很诚恳，不过，话说回来，他一贯如此。 9 **now and then** → see **now** 10 **there and then** → see **there**

T

the·ol·ogy /θiɒlədʒi/ N-UNCOUNT **Theology** is the study of the nature of God and of religion and religious beliefs. 神学 ❑ *...questions of theology.* …神学上的问题。 ● **theo·logi·cal** /θiəlɒdʒɪkᵊl/ ADJ 神学的 ❑ *...theological books.* …神学书籍。

theo·reti·cal /θiərɛtɪkᵊl/ 1 ADJ A **theoretical** study or explanation is based on or uses the ideas and abstract principles that relate to a particular subject, rather than the practical aspects or uses of it. 理论的 ❑ *...theoretical physics.* …理论物理。 2 ADJ If you describe a situation as a **theoretical** one, you mean that although it is supposed to be true or to exist in the way stated, it may not in fact be true or exist in that way. 理论上的 ❑ *This is certainly a theoretical risk but in practice there is seldom a problem.* 这在理论上肯定有风险，但在实践中却很少出问题。

theo·reti·cal·ly /θiərɛtɪkli/ ADV You use **theoretically** to say that although something is supposed to be true or to happen in the way stated, it may not in fact be true or happen in that way. 从理论上说 [ADV with cl/group] ❑ *Theoretically, the price is supposed to be marked on the shelf.* 从理论上说，价格是要标在货架上的。

theo·rist /θiərɪst/ (**theorists**) N-COUNT A **theorist** is someone who develops an abstract idea or set of ideas about a particular subject in order to explain it. 理论家 ❑ *...theorists unaligned with any particular doctrine.* …不附和任何教条的理论家们。

theo·ry ♦♦◊ /θiəri/ (**theories**) 1 N-VAR A **theory** is a formal idea or set of ideas that is intended to explain something. 理论 ❑ *Marx produced a new theory about historical change based upon conflict between competing groups.* 马克思提出了一个新理论，认为历史变革是由于对立集团的冲突而产生的。 2 N-COUNT If you have a **theory** about something, you have your own opinion about it which you cannot prove but which you think is true. 观点 ❑ *There was a theory that he wanted to marry her.* 有种观点认为他想娶她。 3 N-UNCOUNT The **theory** of a practical subject or skill is the set of rules and principles that form the basis of it. 基础理论 ❑ *He taught us music theory.* 他教我们乐理。 4 PHRASE You use **in theory** to say that although something is supposed to be true or to happen in the way stated, it may not in fact be true or happen in that way. 从理论上说 ❑ *Achieving these goals is relatively easy in theory, yet quite difficult in practice.* 实现这些目标从理论上说比较容易，但在实践上却相当困难。 → see **experiment, science**

Word Partnership *theory* 的常用搭配：

N.	theory **and practice** 1 **evidence for a** theory, **support for a** theory 1 2 **conspiracy** theory 2 **learning** theory 3
V.	**advance a** theory, **develop a** theory, **propose a** theory, **test a** theory 1 2
ADJ.	**scientific** theory 1 3 **economic** theory, **literary** theory 3

thera·peu·tic /θɛrəpyutɪk/ ADJ If something is **therapeutic**, it helps you to relax or to feel better about things, especially about a situation that made you unhappy. (尤指不开心的情况下) 使人放松心情的 ❑ *Having a garden is therapeutic.* 有个花园能让人放松心情。

thera·pist /θɛrəpɪst/ (**therapists**) N-COUNT A **therapist** is a person who is skilled in a particular type of therapy, especially psychotherapy. (尤指心理疗法的) 治疗师 ❑ *My therapist helped me to deal with my anger.* 我的治疗师帮我消除怒气。

thera·py ♦◊◊ /θɛrəpi/ (**therapies**) 1 N-UNCOUNT **Therapy** is the process or talking to a trained counselor about your emotional and mental problems and your relationships in order to understand and improve the way you feel and behave. 心理治疗 ❑ *Children may need therapy to help them deal with grief and death.* 孩子可能需要心理治疗来帮助他们应对悲伤和死亡。 ❑ *Since I've been in therapy, I've grown to be a better husband and father.* 自从我接受心理治疗后，我成了个更称职的丈夫和父亲。 2 N-VAR **Therapy** or **a therapy** is a treatment for a particular illness or condition. (针对某种病情的) 治疗 [MEDICAL] ❑ *...hormonal therapies.* …激素疗法。 → see **cancer, illness**

there ♦♦♦

Pronounced /ðər, ʃRONG ðɛr/ for meanings 1 and 2, and /ðɛər/ for meanings 3 to 19.

义项1和2读作 /ðər, ʃRONG ðɛr/，义项3至19读作 /ðɛər/。

1 PRON **There** is used as the subject of the verb “be” to say that something exists or does not exist, or to draw attention to it. 用作动词**be**的主语，表示某物是否存在，或使人注意该物 [PRON “be” n] ❑ *There are temporary traffic lights now at the school.* 那所学校现在设有临时交通信号灯。 ❑ *Are there any cookies left?* 有剩下的曲奇饼吗？

> **There** is normally followed by a plural form of the verb **be** when it is used to introduce a count noun in the plural. ❑ *There were policemen everywhere.* However, when it introduces a series of nouns in the singular, linked by **and**, a singular form of the verb **be** is normally used. ❑ *There is a time and a place for everything... There was a street fair and an old-fashioned brass band.* Take care not to confuse **there** and **their**.

2 PRON You use **there** in front of certain verbs when you are saying that something exists, develops, or can be seen. Whether the verb is singular or plural depends on the noun which follows the verb. 用于某些动词前表示某物存在、发展或可见；动词的单复数形

式取决于其后的名词 [PRON V N] ❑ *There remains considerable doubt over when the road will be completed.* 对于道路何时能竣工，人们还有相当多的疑虑。 3 CONVENTION **There** is used after "hello" or "hi" when you are greeting someone. 表问候，用于**hello**或**hi**后 [INFORMAL] ❑ *"Hello there," said the woman, smiling at them.—"Hi!" they chorused.* "嗨，你们好！"那妇人朝他们笑着招呼道。——"你好！"他们齐声回答。 4 ADV If something is **there**, it exists or is available. 存在 ❑ *The group of old buildings is still there today.* 那个旧楼群如今还在。 5 ADV You use **there** to refer to a place which has already been mentioned. 在那儿 (指前面提到的地方) ❑ *The next day we drove 33 miles to Siena (the Villa Arceno is a great place to stay while you are there).* 第二天我们驱车33英里到了锡耶纳（在那儿，阿尔切诺别墅是个很不错的落脚之处）。❑ *"Come on over, if you want."—"How do I get there?"* "过来看看吧，如果你愿意。"——"我怎么到那儿？" 6 ADV You use **there** to indicate a place that you are pointing to or looking at, in order to draw someone's attention to it. (用来引起注意) 那儿 ❑ *There it is, on the corner over there.* 在那儿，在那边转角处。❑ *There she is on the left up there.* 她在那儿，在左边那儿。 7 ADV You use **there** in expressions such as "**there he was**" or "**there we were**" to sum up part of a story or to slow a story down for dramatic effect. (用于概括故事或放慢讲故事的速度) 就这样 [ADV cl] [SPOKEN] ❑ *So there he was all covered in mud, and still in a good mood.* 就这样他全身是泥，但仍然情绪高昂。 8 ADV You use **there** when speaking on the telephone to ask if someone is available to speak to you. (电话用语) …在吗 [ADV with "be"] ❑ *Hello, is Gordon there please?* 您好，请问戈登在吗？ 9 ADV You use **there** to refer to a point that someone has made in a conversation. 在那点上 [ADV after v] ❑ *I think you're right there John.* 我认为你在那一点上说对了，约翰。 10 ADV You use **there** to refer to a stage that has been reached in an activity or process. (指活动或过程已达到的阶段) 那里 ❑ *We are making further investigations and will take the matter from there.* 我们正在进一步调查，并将从那里入手。 11 ADV You use **there** to indicate that something has reached a point or level which is completely successful. 做成地；达成地 ❑ *We had hoped to fill the back page with extra news; we're not quite there yet.* 我们原本希望在最后一版面载满附加新闻；但我们现在还没真正做到。 12 ADV You can use **there** in expressions such as **there you go** or **there we are** when accepting that an unsatisfactory situation cannot be changed. 别无他法 [ADV cl] [SPOKEN] ❑ *This is a little cruel, but there you go.* 这是有点儿残忍，但也没办法。 13 ADV You can use **there** in expressions such as **there you go** and **there we are** when emphasizing that something proves that you were right. 我没说错吧 [ADV cl] [SPOKEN, EMPHASIS] ❑ *You see? There you go. That's why I didn't mention it earlier. I knew you'd take it the wrong way.* 瞧见了没？我没说错吧。这就是我没早说的原因，就知道你们会弄错的。 14 PHRASE Phrases such as **there you go again** are used to show anger at someone who is repeating something that has annoyed you in the past. 又来了 [SPOKEN] ❑ *"There you go again, upsetting the child!" said Shirley.* "你又来折腾孩子了！"雪莉说道。 15 PHRASE You can add "**so there**" to what you are saying to show that you have won an argument, or that you will not change your mind about a decision you have made, even though the person you are talking to disagrees with you. This is usually said by children or to be funny. 没错吧；就这么定了 [INFORMAL] ❑ *I think that's sweet, so there.* 我觉得那很好，就这么定了。❑ *You see? Mom said I could - so there!* 瞧见了没？妈妈说我能行-没错吧！ 16 PHRASE If something happens **there and then** or **then and there**, it happens immediately. 立即 ❑ *Many felt that he should have resigned there and then.* 很多人觉得他原本就应该立即辞职。 17 CONVENTION You say "**there there**" to someone who is very upset, especially a small child, in order to comfort them. (用来安慰别人，尤其是孩子) 好了，好了 [SPOKEN] ❑ *"There, there," said Mommy. "You've been having a bad dream."* "好了，好了，"妈妈说道。"你是在作恶梦。" 18 CONVENTION You say "**there you are**" or "**there you go**" when you are offering something to someone. 给你 [SPOKEN, FORMULAE] ❑ *"There you go, Mr. Walters," she said, giving him his documents.* "给你，沃尔特斯先生，"她边说边把文件给了他。 19 PHRASE If someone **is there for** you, they help and support you, especially when you have problems. (尤指在别人困难时) 帮助支持某人 [INFORMAL] ❑ *Despite what happened in the past I want her to know I am there for her.* 尽管过去发生了一些事，我仍希望她知道我支持她。

★ **there·after** /ðɛəræftər/ ADV **Thereafter** means after the event or date mentioned. 其后 [ADV with cl] [FORMAL] ❑ *The plan will help you lose 3-4 pounds the first week, and 1-2 pounds the weeks thereafter.* 该计划将帮助你在第1周减3到4磅，其后每周减1到2磅。

there·by /ðɛərbaɪ/ ADV You use **thereby** to introduce an important result or consequence of the event or action you have just mentioned. 由此 [ADV with cl] [FORMAL] ❑ *Our bodies can sweat, thereby losing heat by evaporation.* 我们的身体会流汗，由此能通过蒸发散热。

there·fore ♦♦◇ /ðɛərfɔr/ ADV You use **therefore** to introduce a logical result or conclusion. 因此 [ADV with cl/group] ❑ *Muscle cells need lots of fuel and therefore burn lots of calories.* 肌肉细胞需要很多"燃料"，并因此燃烧大量卡路里。

there·in /ðɛərɪn/ 1 ADV **Therein** means contained in the place that has been mentioned. 在那里 [n ADV] [LITERARY] ❑ *By burning tree branches, pine needles, and pine cones, many not only warm their houses but improve the smell therein.* 通过燃烧树枝、松针和松果，许多人不仅给屋子供暖，而且还改善里面的气味。 2 ADV **Therein** means relating to something that has just been mentioned. 在其中 (指与刚提及的事物相关) [n ADV] [FORMAL] ❑ *Afternoon groups relate to the specific addictions and problems therein.* 下午各小组谈到具体的成瘾病例和其中的问题。

★ **ther·mal** /θɜrməl/ (**thermals**) 1 ADJ **Thermal** means relating to or caused by heat or by changes in temperature. 热的；由热引起的；由温度变化引起的 [ADJ n] ❑ *...thermal power stations.* …热电站。 2 ADJ **Thermal** streams or baths contain water which is naturally hot or warm. 天然温热的 [ADJ n] ❑ *Volcanic activity has created thermal springs and boiling mud pools.* 火山活动产生了温泉和沸腾的泥浆池。 3 ADJ **Thermal** clothes are specially designed to keep you warm in cold weather. 保暖的 (衣服) [ADJ n] ❑ *...thermal underwear.* …保暖内衣 ❑ *My feet were like blocks of ice despite the thermal socks.* 我的双脚尽管穿着保暖袜，还是像冰块。● N-PLURAL **Thermals** are thermal clothes. 保暖衣 ❑ *Have you got your thermals on?* 你穿上保暖衣了吗？ 4 N-COUNT A **thermal** is a movement of rising warm air. 上升的暖气流 ❑ *Birds use thermals to lift them through the air.* 鸟类利用上升的暖气流升空。

→ see **solar system**

ther·mal im·ag·ing N-UNCOUNT **Thermal imaging** is the use of special equipment that can detect the heat produced by people or things and use it to produce images of them. 热成像 ❑ *He was found by a police helicopter using thermal imaging equipment.* 他被一架警用直升飞机用热成像设备找到了。

ther·mom·eter /θərmɒmɪtər/ (**thermometers**) N-COUNT A **thermometer** is an instrument for measuring temperature. It usually consists of a narrow glass tube containing a thin column of a liquid which rises and falls as the temperature rises and falls. 温度计

Ther·mos /θɜrməs/ (**Thermoses**) N-COUNT A **Thermos** is a container which is used to keep hot drinks hot or cold drinks cold. It has two thin shiny glass walls with no air between them. 保温瓶 [TRADEMARK]

the·sau·rus /θɪsɔrəs/ (**thesauruses**) N-COUNT A **thesaurus** is a reference book in which words with similar meanings are grouped together. 同义词汇编手册

these ♦♦♦

> The determiner is pronounced /ðiz/. The pronoun is pronounced /ðiz/.

> 限定词读作 /ðiz/。代词读作 /ðiz/。

1 DET You use **these** at the beginning of noun groups to refer to someone or something that you have already mentioned or identified. 这些 (用于名词前，指前文曾提到的人或物) ❑ *A committee has been formed. These people can make decisions in ten minutes which would take us months.* 委员会已经成立。这些人能在10分钟内做出决定，换作我们则要花几个月。● PRON **These** is also a pronoun. 这些 ❑ *"I have faith in these guys," the coach said. "These are good players."* "我相信这些人，"教练说道。"这些都是好球员。" 2 DET You use **these** to introduce people or things that you are going to talk about. 这些 (用于引出将要谈及的人或物) ❑ *Your camcorder should have these basic features: autofocus, playback facility, zoom lens.* 你的便携式摄像机应该具有这些基本特征：自动调焦、回放及变焦镜头。● PRON **These** is also a pronoun. 这些 ❑ *Take care of yourself while you are pregnant. These are some of the things you can do for yourself.* 怀孕期间要照顾好自己。这些是你自己可以做的事情。 3 DET In spoken English, people use **these** to introduce people or things into a story. 这些 (口语中用于引出故事中的人或物) ❑ *I was by myself and these guys suddenly came towards me.* 我独自一人时，这些人忽然向我走来。 4 PRON You use **these** when

you are identifying a group or asking about their identity. 这些(用于识别或询问身份) ❑ *These are my children.* 这些是我的孩子。 5 DET You use **these** to refer to people or things that are near you, especially when you touch them or point to them. 这些(尤指所碰触或指向的附近的人或物) ❑ *These scissors are awfully heavy.* 这几把剪刀非常重。 ● PRON **These** is also a pronoun. 这些 ❑ *These are the people who are helping us.* 这些是正在帮助我们的人。 6 DET You use **these** when you refer to something which you expect the person you are talking to to know about, or when you are checking that you are both thinking of the same person or thing. 这些(指双方均了解的事物) ❑ *You know these last few months when we've been expecting it to warm up a little bit?* 你知道最近这几个月我们一直盼望天气能暖和一些吗？ 7 DET You use **these** in the expression **these days** to mean "at the present time." 目前 ❑ *These days, people appreciate a chance to relax.* 目前人们很珍惜能放松的机会。

★ **the·sis** /θi̲sɪs/ (**theses** /θi̲siz/) 1 N-COUNT A **thesis** is an idea or theory that is expressed as a statement and is discussed in a logical way. 论点 ❑ *This thesis does not stand up to close inspection.* 这个论点经不起仔细推敲。 2 N-COUNT A **thesis** is a long piece of writing based on your own ideas and research that you do as part of a college degree, especially a higher degree such as a Ph.D. 学位论文

→ see **graduation**

they ♦♦♦ /ðeɪ/

> **They** is a third person plural pronoun. **They** is used as the subject of a verb.

1 PRON-PLURAL You use **they** to refer to a group of people, animals, or things. 他们；她们；它们 ❑ *Feed the dogs because they haven't eaten.* 喂喂这几条狗，因为它们还没吃呢。 ❑ *The two men were far more alike than they would ever admit.* 这两个男子非常相像，尽管他们可能不愿意承认。 ❑ *People matter because of what they are, not what they have.* 人重要的不在于他们拥有什么，而在于他们是什么样的人。 2 PRON-PLURAL You use **they** instead of "he or she" to refer to a person without saying whether that person is a man or a woman. Some people think this use is incorrect. 代替**he**或**she**，而不指明是男是女，有些人认为这种用法不正确 ❑ *The teacher is not responsible for the student's success or failure. They are only there to help the student learn.* 教师不为学生的成败负责。他们只是帮助学生学习而已。 3 PRON-PLURAL You use **they** in expressions such as "they say" or "they call it" to refer to people in general when you are making general statements about what people say, think, or do. 人们 [VAGUENESS] ❑ *They say there's plenty of opportunities out there, you just have to look carefully and you'll find them.* 人们说那里有很多机会，你只要仔细寻找就能发现机会。

they'd /ðeɪd/ 1 **They'd** is a spoken form of "they had," especially when "had" is an auxiliary verb. **they had**的口语形式，尤其当**had**为助动词时 ❑ *They'd both lived on this road all their lives.* 他们两个人一辈子都住在这条路上。 2 **They'd** is a spoken form of "they would." **they would**的口语形式 ❑ *He agreed that they'd visit her after they stopped at Jan's for coffee.* 他同意他们在简家喝了咖啡之后就去拜访她。

they'll /ðeɪl/ **They'll** is the usual spoken form of "they will." **they will**的口语形式 ❑ *They'll probably be here Monday and Tuesday.* 他们星期一和星期二可能会在这里。

T

they're /ðɛər/ **They're** is the usual spoken form of "they are." **they are**的口语形式 ❑ *People eat when they're depressed.* 人们会在沮丧时吃东西。

they've /ðeɪv/ **They've** is the usual spoken form of "they have," especially when "have" is an auxiliary verb. **they have**的口语形式，尤其当**have**为助动词时 ❑ *The worst thing is when you call friends and they've gone out.* 最糟糕的是，你给朋友们打电话时他们却出去了。

thick ♦◊◊ /θɪk/ (**thicker, thickest**) 1 ADJ Something that is **thick** has a large distance between its two opposite sides. 厚的 ❑ *For breakfast I had a thick slice of bread and butter.* 早餐我吃了一片厚厚的黄油面包。 ❑ *He wore thick glasses.* 他戴着厚厚的眼镜。 ● **thick·ly** ADV 厚厚地 [ADV with v] ❑ *Slice the meat thickly.* 把肉切成厚片。 2 ADJ You can use **thick** to talk or ask about how wide or deep something is. 有…厚的 ❑ *The folder was two inches thick.* 那个文件夹有两英寸厚。 ● COMB IN ADJ **Thick** is also a combining form. 用以构成复合词 [ADJ n] ❑ *His life was saved by a quarter-inch-thick bullet-proof vest.* 他被0.25英寸厚的防弹背心救了一命。 ● **thick·ness** N-VAR (**thicknesses**) 厚度 ❑ *The size of the fish will determine the thickness of the steaks.* 鱼的大小决定鱼排的厚度。 3 ADJ If something that consists of several things is **thick**, it has a large number of them very close together. 浓密的 ❑ *She inherited our father's thick, wavy hair.* 她继承了我们父亲浓密的卷发。 ● **thick·ly** ADV 浓密地 ❑ *I rounded a bend where the trees and brush grew thickly.* 我在一个林木茂密的地方绕了个弯。 4 ADJ If something is **thick with** another thing, the first thing is full of or covered with the second. 充满的 [v-link ADJ "with" n] ❑ *The air is thick with acrid smoke from the fires.* 空气中充满了火灾产生的刺鼻浓烟。 5 ADJ **Thick** clothes are made from heavy cloth, so that they will keep you warm in cold weather. (衣服等) 厚的 ❑ *In the winter she wears thick socks, boots and gloves.* 冬天她穿着厚袜和靴子，还戴着手套。 6 ADJ **Thick** smoke, fog, or cloud is difficult to see through. (烟、雾或云) 浓的 ❑ *The smoke was bluish-black and thick.* 这烟雾呈蓝黑色，而且很浓。 7 ADJ **Thick** liquids are fairly stiff and solid and do not flow easily. (液体) 浓稠的 ❑ *It had rained last night, so the garden was thick mud.* 昨晚下了雨，所以花园里全是浓稠的泥浆。

> **Word Partnership** *thick* 的常用搭配：
>
> N. thick **glass**, thick **ice**, thick **layer**, thick **lips**, thick **neck**, thick **slice**, thick **wall** 1
> thick **carpet**, **feet/inches** thick 2
> thick **beard**, thick **fur**, thick **grass**, thick **hair** 3
> thick **with smoke** 4
> thick **air**, thick **clouds**, thick **fog**, thick **smoke** 6
>
> ADV. **so** thick, **too** thick, **very** thick 1–7

thick·en /θɪkən/ (**thickens, thickening, thickened**) 1 V-T/V-I When you **thicken** a liquid or when it **thickens**, it becomes stiffer and more solid. 使变浓；变浓 ❑ *Thicken the broth with the mashed potato.* 加土豆泥使汤变浓。 2 V-I If something **thickens**, it becomes more closely grouped together or more solid than it was before. 变密集 ❑ *The dust behind us grew closer and thickened into a cloud.* 我们身后的尘土越来越密，变成了浓密的一团。

thief /θif/ (**thieves** /θi̲vz/) N-COUNT A **thief** is a person who steals something from another person. 小偷 ❑ *The thieves snatched the camera.* 那些小偷抢走了照相机。

> Anyone who steals can be called a **thief**. A **robber** often uses violence or the threat of violence to steal things from places such as banks or businesses. A **burglar** breaks into houses or other buildings and steals things.

★ **thigh** /θaɪ/ (**thighs**) N-COUNT Your **thighs** are the top parts of your legs, between your knees and your hips. 大腿 ❑ *The shorts are so small I can't fit my thighs into any of them.* 短裤太小了，我的大腿塞不进去。

→ see **body**

thin ♦◊◊ /θɪn/ (**thinner, thinnest, thins, thinning, thinned**) 1 ADJ Something that is **thin** is much narrower than it is long. 细的 ❑ *A thin cable carries the signal to a computer.* 一条细电缆把信号传给一台计算机。 2 ADJ A person or animal that is **thin** has no extra fat on their body. (人或动物) 瘦的 ❑ *He was a tall, thin man with gray hair that fell in a wild tangle to his shoulders.* 他个子瘦高，灰白的头发乱蓬蓬地散落在肩上。 3 ADJ Something such as paper or cloth that is **thin** is flat and has only a very small distance between its two opposite surfaces. (纸或布等) 薄的 ❑ *...a small, blue-bound book printed in fine type on thin paper.* …一本纸质轻薄、用细小字体印刷而成的蓝皮小书。 ● **thin·ly** ADV 薄薄地 [ADV with v] ❑ *Peel and thinly slice the onion.* 给洋葱剥皮，切成薄片。 4 ADJ Liquids that are **thin** are weak and watery. (液体) 稀的 ❑ *The soup was thin and clear, yet mysteriously rich.* 那汤既稀又清，但味道却出奇地足。 5 ADJ A crowd or audience that is **thin** does not have many people in it. 人数稀少的 ❑ *The crowd, which had been thin for the first half of the race, had now grown considerably.* 上半场比赛时观众稀稀拉拉的，现在则大大增多了。 ● **thin·ly** ADV 稀少地 [ADV -ed] ❑ *The island is thinly populated.* 这个岛人口稀少。 6 ADJ **Thin** clothes are made from light cloth and are not warm to wear. (衣服) 薄的 ❑ *Her gown was thin, and she shivered, partly from cold.* 她的礼服很薄，她浑身发抖，部分是由于寒冷所致。 7 ADJ If you describe an argument, an explanation, or evidence as **thin**, you mean that it is weak and difficult to believe. (论点、解释或证据) 难以令人信服的 ❑ *The DA was certain she had the right man, but the evidence was thin.* 这位地方检察官确信自己找对了人，但是证据却难以令人信服。 ● **thin·ly** ADV 难以令人信服地 ❑ *Much of the speech was a thinly disguised attack on environmentalists.* 演讲内容大多是对环保主义者几乎不加掩饰的攻击。 8 ADJ If someone's hair is described as **thin**, they do not have a lot of hair. (头发) 稀疏的 ❑ *She had pale thin yellow hair she pulled back into a bun.* 她的头发稀疏、淡黄，往后梳成了一个圆髻。 9 V-T/V-I When you **thin** something or when it **thins**, it becomes less crowded because people or things have been removed from it. 使变稀疏；变稀疏 ❑ *It would have been better to have thinned the trees over several winters rather than all at one time.* 当初要是分几个冬天来疏剪树木，会比一次性疏剪要更好些。 ● PHRASAL VERB **Thin out** means the same as **thin**. 使稀疏 ❑ *NATO will continue to thin out its forces.* 北约将继续裁军。 **10** PHRASE If someone's patience, for example, **is wearing thin**, they are beginning to become impatient or angry with someone. (耐心等) 消磨掉 ❑ *War has achieved little, and public patience is wearing thin.* 战争收获甚微，公众的耐心日渐消磨。 **11** **on thin ice** → see **ice** **12** **thin air** → see **air**

Thesaurus *thin* 另参见：

ADJ. flimsy, transparent, wispy; (*ant.*) dense, solid, thick **1**
lean, skinny, slender, slim, underweight; (*ant.*) fat, heavy **2**
watery, weak; (*ant.*) thick **4**

Word Partnership *thin* 的常用搭配：

N. thin **face**, thin **fingers**, thin **legs**, thin **line**, thin **lips**, thin **mouth**, thin **smile**, thin **strips** **1**
thin **body**, thin **man/woman** **2**
thin **film**, thin **ice**, thin **layer**, **razor** thin, thin **slice** **3**
ADJ. **long and** thin **1**
tall and thin **2**
ADV. **extremely** thin, **too** thin, **very** thin **1** – **8**

thing
❶ NOUN USES
❷ PHRASES

❶ **thing** ♦♦♦ /θɪŋ/ (**things**) **1** N-COUNT You can use **thing** to refer to any object, feature, or event when you cannot, need not, or do not want to refer to it more precisely. (不具体指称的) 东西；事情 ❑ *"What's that thing in the middle of the fountain?"—"Some kind of statue, I guess."* "喷泉中间那个东西是什么？"——"我想是雕像之类的吧。" ❑ *She was in the middle of clearing the breakfast things.* 她正忙着清理早餐后的那些东西。 **2** N-COUNT **Thing** is used in lists and descriptions to give examples or to increase the range of what you are referring to. (用于举例或扩大所指范围) 等事物 ❑ *They spend their money on things like rent and groceries.* 他们把钱花在房租和杂货之类的事情上。 **3** N-COUNT **Thing** is often used after an adjective, where it would also be possible just to use the adjective. For example, you can say **it's a different thing** instead of **it's different**. 东西(用于形容词后，单用该形容词也可表示相同的意思) ❑ *Of course, literacy isn't the same thing as intelligence.* 当然，识字与智力不是一回事。 **4** N-SING **Thing** is often used instead of the pronouns "anything," or "everything" in order to emphasize what you are saying. 任何事情(用于强调) [EMPHASIS] ❑ *I haven't done a thing all day.* 我一整天还没做任何事情。 ❑ *It isn't going to solve a single thing.* 这解决不了任何问题。 **5** N-COUNT **Thing** is used in expressions such as **such a thing** or **a thing like that**, especially in negative statements, in order to emphasize the bad or difficult situation you are referring back to. 这种事情(尤用于否定句，强调前面提到的糟糕或困难情况) [EMPHASIS] ❑ *I don't believe he would tell Leo such a thing.* 我不信他会告诉利奥这种事。 **6** N-COUNT You can use **thing** to refer in a vague way to a situation, activity, or idea, especially when you want to suggest that it is not very important. (尤指不重要的) 情形；活动；想法 [INFORMAL, VAGUENESS] ❑ *I'm a bit unsettled tonight. This war thing's upsetting me.* 我今晚有点儿不安，这种争斗很让我心烦。 **7** N-COUNT You often use **thing** to indicate to the person you are addressing that you are about to mention something important, or something that you particularly want them to know. 表示将要提及重要的事情或特别希望对方知道的事情 ❑ *One thing I am sure of was that she was scared.* 有一点我可以肯定的是她被吓坏了。 **8** N-COUNT A **thing** is often used to refer back to something that has just been mentioned, either to emphasize it or to give more information about it. 常指前面曾提到的内容，表示强调或提供更多信息 ❑ *Getting drunk is a thing all young men do.* 喝醉酒是所有小伙子都会干的事。 **9** N-COUNT A **thing** is a physical object that is considered as having no life of its own. (无生命的) 物体；东西 ❑ *It's not a thing. It's a human being!* 这不是一件东西，这是一个人！ **10** N-COUNT **Thing** is used to refer to something, especially a physical object, when you want to express contempt or anger toward it. (用于表示蔑视或愤怒) 东西 [SPOKEN, DISAPPROVAL] ❑ *Turn that thing off!* 把那个东西关掉！ **11** N-COUNT You can call a person or an animal a particular **thing** when you want to mention a particular quality that they have and express your feelings toward them, usually affectionate feelings. 东西(常指惹人怜爱的人或动物) [INFORMAL] ❑ *She is such a cute little thing.* 她是个非常可爱的小东西。 **12** N-PLURAL Your **things** are your clothes or possessions. 衣物；财物 ❑ *Sara told him to take all his things and not to return.* 萨拉叫他带上他的所有东西离开，别再回来。 **13** N-PLURAL **Things** can refer to the situation or life in general and the way it is changing or affecting you. 情况 ❑ *Everyone agrees things are getting better.* 大家都认为情况正在好转。

Thesaurus *thing* 另参见：

N. device, figure, gadget, item, object, tool ❶ **1** **9**

❷ **thing** ♦♦♦ /θɪŋ/ (**things**)

➪ **Please look at meaning 11 to see if the expression you are looking for is shown under another headword.** **1** PHRASE If, for example, you **do the** right **thing** or **do the** decent **thing** in a situation, you do something which is considered correct or socially acceptable in that situation. 做(正确、合宜) 的事 ❑ *People want to do the right thing and buy "green."* 人们想做正确的事，购买"绿色"商品。 **2** PHRASE If you do something **first thing**, you do it at the beginning of the day, before you do anything else. If you do it **last thing**, you do it at the end of the day, before you go to bed or go to sleep. 第一/最后一件事；一大早/临睡前 ❑ *I'll go see her, first thing.* 我一大早就去看她。 **3** PHRASE You say **it is a** good **thing to** do something to introduce a piece of advice or a comment on a situation or activity. …是件好/坏事 ❑ *Can you tell me whether it is a good thing to prune an apple tree?* 你能否告诉我，修剪苹果树是不是件好事？ **4** PHRASE You can say that the first of two ideas, actions, or situations **is one thing** when you want to contrast it with a second idea, action, or situation and emphasize that the second one is much more difficult, important, or extreme. …是一回事(用于两种想法、行动或局势的对比，以强调第二种情况更困难、重要或极端) [EMPHASIS] ❑ *It was one thing to talk about leaving; it was another to physically walk out the door.* 说要离开是一回事；真正走出门又是另一回事。 **5** PHRASE You can say **for one thing** when you are explaining a statement or answering a question, to suggest that you are not giving the whole explanation or answer, and that there are other points that you could add to it. 其一(用于引出更多的理由) ❑ *She was a monster. For one thing, she really enjoyed cruelty.* 她是个恶魔。其中之一就是，她真的以残忍为乐。 **6** PHRASE You can use the expression **"one thing and another"** to suggest that there are several reasons for something or several items on a list, but you are not going to explain or mention them all. 种种原因 [SPOKEN] ❑ *What with one thing and another, it was fairly late in the day when we got home.* 由于种种原因，我们回到家时已经相当晚了。 **7** PHRASE If you say **it is just one of those things** you mean that you cannot explain something because it seems to happen by chance. 这是无法解释的事情 ❑ *"I wonder why." Mr. Dambar shrugged. "It must be just one of those things, I guess."* "我想知道原因。"丹巴先生耸了耸肩说道。"我想这肯定是无法解释的事情。" **8** PHRASE If you say that someone **is seeing** or **hearing things**, you mean that they believe they are seeing or hearing something, but it is not really there. 幻视；幻听 ❑ *Dr. Payne led Lana back into the examination room and told her she was seeing things.* 佩恩医生把拉娜带回检查室并告诉她这是她的视觉幻象。 **9** PHRASE You can say there is **no such thing as** something to emphasize that it does not exist or is not possible. 没有这回事 [EMPHASIS] ❑ *There really is no such thing as a totally risk-free industry.* 完全没风险的行业实际上是不存在的。 **10** PHRASE You say **the thing is** to introduce an explanation, comment, or opinion, that relates to something that has just been said. **The thing is** is often used to identify a problem relating to what has just been said. 问题是 [SPOKEN] ❑ *"What does your market research consist of?"—"Well, the thing is, it depends on our target age group."* "你的市场研究包含什么内容？"——"哦，问题是，这取决于我们的目标年龄群体。" **11** **other things being equal** → see **equal**

think
❶ VERB AND NOUN USES
❷ PHRASES
❸ PHRASAL VERBS

❶ **think** ♦♦♦ /θɪŋk/ (**thinks, thinking, thought**) **1** V-T/V-I If you **think** that something is the case, you believe that it is the case.

t

认为 [no cont] ❑ *I certainly think there should be a ban on tobacco advertising.* 我确实认为应该禁止香烟广告。 ❑ *A generation ago, it was thought that babies born this small could not survive.* 在上一代以前，人们认为这么小的新生儿是没法存活的。 ❑ *Tell me, what do you think of my theory?* 告诉我，你认为我的理论怎么样？ 2 V-T If you say that you **think** that something is true or will happen, you mean that you have the impression that it is true or will happen, although you are not certain of the facts. 觉得 [no cont] ❑ *Nora thought he was seventeen years old.* 诺拉觉得他有17岁。 ❑ *The storm is thought to be responsible for as many as four deaths.* 这场暴风雨据信造成多达4人死亡。 3 V-T/V-I If you **think** in a particular way, you have those general opinions or attitudes. 考虑 [no cont, no passive] ❑ *You were probably brought up to think like that.* 你可能从小就被教成那样来考虑问题的。 ❑ *If you think as I do, vote as I do.* 如果你考虑问题和我一样，就和我投一样的票。 ❑ *I don't blame you for thinking that way.* 我不怪你那样想。 4 V-I When you **think** about ideas or problems, you make a mental effort to consider them. 思考 ❑ *She closed her eyes for a moment, trying to think.* 她闭了一会儿眼，想好好思考一下。 ❑ *I have often thought about this problem.* 我经常思考这个问题。 ● N-SING **Think** is also a noun. 思考 ["a" N] [mainly BRIT] ❑ *I'll have a think about that.* 我会就那件事有所考虑。 5 V-T/V-I If you **think** in a particular way, you consider things, solve problems, or make decisions in this way, for example, because of your job or your background. (以某种方式)考虑 [no passive] ❑ *To make the computer work at full capacity, the programmer has to think like the machine.* 为了使计算机能充分发挥作用，程序员必须像机器那样思考。 ❑ *Why do they think the way they do?* 为什么他们这么想？ 6 V-T/V-I If you **think of** something, it comes into your mind or you remember it. 想到 [no cont] ❑ *Nobody could think of anything to say.* 谁也想不出什么话说。 ❑ *I was trying to think what else we had to do.* 我在努力想我们还得做些什么。 7 V-I If you **think of** an idea, you make a mental effort and use your imagination and intelligence to create it or develop it. 想出 ❑ *He thought of another way of making electricity.* 他想出另一种发电的方法。 8 V-T If you **are thinking** something at a particular moment, you have words or ideas in your mind without saying them out loud. 心想 [no passive] ❑ *She must be sick, Tatiana thought.* 她一定是病了，塔蒂亚娜心想。 ❑ *I remember thinking how lovely he looked.* 我记得曾在心里想过他看起来有多么可爱。 9 V-T/V-I If you **think of** someone or something **as** having a particular quality or purpose, you regard them as having this quality or purpose. 认为 (某人或某物具有某种特性或功能) [no cont] ❑ *We all thought of him as a father.* 我们都当他是一位父亲。 ❑ *He thinks of it as his home.* 他把这儿当作自己的家。 ❑ *I wouldn't have thought him capable of it.* 我不会想到他能干这事。 10 V-T/V-I If you **think** a lot **of** someone or something, you admire them very much or think they are very good. 对…评价(高) [no cont] ❑ *To tell the truth, I don't think much of psychiatrists.* 说实话，我认为精神病医生不怎么样。 ❑ *Everyone in my family thought very highly of him.* 我们家的所有人都非常钦佩他。 11 V-I If you **think of** someone or **about** someone, you show consideration for them and pay attention to their needs. 为…着想 ❑ *I'm only thinking of you.* 我只是在为你着想。 12 V-I If you **are thinking of** or **are thinking about** taking a particular course of action, you are considering it as a possible course of action. 考虑 (采取某行动) ❑ *Martin was thinking of taking legal action against Zuckerman.* 马丁正考虑起诉朱克曼。 13 V-I You can say that you **are thinking of** a particular aspect or subject, in order to introduce an example or explain more exactly what you are talking about. 所指的是 (用于引出例子或进一步解释) [usu cont] ❑ *The parts of the enterprise which are scientifically the most exciting are unlikely to be militarily useful. I am thinking here of the development of new kinds of lasers.* 这份计划中，从科学角度看最让人兴奋的部分在军事上却可能无用。我指的是新型激光开发。 14 V-I You use **think** in questions where you are expressing your anger or shock at someone's behavior. 想 (用于问句，表示生气或震惊) [only interrog] [DISAPPROVAL] ❑ *What were you thinking of? You shouldn't steal.* 你当时在想什么？你不该偷东西。 15 V-T/V-I You use **think** when you are commenting on something which you did or experienced in the past and which now seems surprising, foolish, or shocking to you. 想想看 (用于评论过去做过或经历的事，现在看来令人惊讶、愚蠢或荒唐) [no cont, no passive] ❑ *To think I left you alone in a strange place.* 想想我居然把你留在一个陌生的地方。 ❑ *When I think of how you've behaved and the trouble you've caused!* 想想你的行为，还有你惹的麻烦！ 16 → see also **thinking**, **thought**

T

Thesaurus *think* 另参见:

v. believe, consider, feel, judge, understand ❶ 1
analyze, evaluate, meditate, reflect, study ❶ 4
recall, remember; (*ant.*) forget ❶ 6

❷ **think** ♦♦♦ /θɪŋk/ (**thinks, thinking, thought**)
➪ **Please look at meanings 8 – 11 to see if the expression you are looking for is shown under another headword.** 1 PHRASE You use expressions such as **come to think of it, when you think about it,** or **thinking about it**, when you mention something that you have suddenly remembered or realized. 想起来了 ❑ *He was her distant relative, as was everyone else on the island, come to think of it.* 想起来了，他和岛上的其他人一样都是她的远亲。 2 PHRASE You use "**I think**" as a way of being polite when you are explaining or suggesting to someone what you want to do, or when you are accepting or refusing an offer. 我想 (用于委婉地表达想法或表示接受或拒绝) [POLITENESS] ❑ *I think I'll go home and have a shower.* 我想我要回家冲澡了。 3 PHRASE You use "**I think**" in conversations or speeches to make your statements and opinions sound less forceful, rude, or direct. 我认为 (用于对话或演说中，使陈述听起来委婉些) [VAGUENESS] ❑ *Thanks, but I think I can handle it.* 谢谢，不过我认为我能处理这件事。 4 PHRASE You say **just think** when you feel excited, fascinated, or shocked by something, and you want the listener to feel the same. 想像一下 (用于表示兴奋、着迷或震惊，并想将这种感觉传给听者) ❑ *Just think; tomorrow we shall walk out of this place and leave it all behind us forever.* 想像一下，明天我们就要走出这地方，并且永远地离开。 5 PHRASE If you **think again about** an action or decision, you consider it very carefully, often with the result that you change your mind and decide to do things differently. 重新考虑 ❑ *It has forced politicians to think again about the wisdom of trying to evacuate refugees.* 这已迫使政客们重新考虑试图疏散难民是否明智。 6 PHRASE If you **think nothing of** doing something that other people might consider difficult, strange, or wrong, you consider it to be easy or normal. 觉得…没什么了不起 ❑ *I thought nothing of betting $1,000 on a horse.* 我觉得在一匹马上花$1000的赌注没什么了不起的。 7 PHRASE If something happens and you **think nothing of it**, you do not pay much attention to it or think of it as strange or important, although later you realize that it is. 对…不在意; 不觉得…奇怪 ❑ *When she went off to see her parents for the weekend, I thought nothing of it.* 她周末去看她的父母时，我没觉得有什么奇怪的。 8 **you can't hear yourself think** → see **hear** 9 **to think better of it** → see **better** 10 **to think big** → see **big** 11 **to think twice** → see **twice**

Note that when you are using the verb **think** with a "that"-clause in order to state a negative opinion or belief, you normally make **think** negative, rather than the verb in the "that"-clause. For instance, it is more usual to say "**I don't think he saw me**" than "I think he didn't see me." The same pattern applies to other verbs with a similar meaning, such as **believe**, **consider**, and **suppose**.

❸ **think** ♦♦♦ /θɪŋk/ (**thinks, thinking, thought**)
▶ **think back** PHRASAL VERB If you **think back**, you make an effort to remember things that happened to you in the past. 回想 ❑ *I thought back to the time in 1995 when my son was desperately ill.* 我回想起1995年我儿子病重的那段时间。
▶ **think over** PHRASAL VERB If you **think** something **over**, you consider it carefully before making a decision. 仔细考虑 ❑ *She said she needs time to think it over.* 她说她需要时间仔细考虑它。
▶ **think through** PHRASAL VERB If you **think** a situation **through**, you consider it thoroughly, together with all its possible effects or consequences. 充分考虑 ❑ *I didn't think through the consequences of promotion.* 我没有充分考虑到晋升带来的各种结果。 ❑ *The administration has not really thought through what it plans to do once the fighting stops.* 政府还没有真正充分考虑一旦战争结束它打算做什么。
▶ **think up** PHRASAL VERB If you **think** something **up**, for example, an idea or plan, you invent it using mental effort. 想出 (主意或计划) ❑ *Julian has been thinking up new ways of raising money.* 朱利安已经想出几个筹款的新办法。

think·er /θɪŋkər/ (**thinkers**) N-COUNT A **thinker** is a person who spends a lot of time thinking deeply about important things, especially someone who is famous for thinking of new or interesting ideas. 思想家 ❑ *...some of the world's greatest thinkers.* …一些世界上最伟大的思想家。

think·ing ♦♦◇ /θɪŋkɪŋ/ 1 N-UNCOUNT **Thinking** is the activity of using your brain by considering a problem or possibility or creating an idea. 思维 ❑ *This is a time of decisive action and quick thinking.* 这个时刻需要行动果断、思维敏捷。 2 N-UNCOUNT The general ideas or opinions of a person or group can be referred to as their **thinking**. 想法 ❑ *There was undeniably a strong theoretical dimension to his thinking.* 不可否认，他的想法很有理论深度。 3 → see also **wishful thinking** 4 to my **way of thinking** → see **way**

third ♦♦◇ /θɜrd/ (**thirds**) 1 ORD The **third** item in a series is the one that you count as number three. 第3 ❑ *I sleep on the third floor.* 我睡在3楼。 2 FRACTION A **third** is one of three equal parts of something. 1/3 ❑ *A third of the cost went into technology and services.* 1/3的成本用于技术和服务。 3 ADV You say **third** when you want to make a third point or give a third reason for something. 第三(点) ❑ *First, interest rates may take longer to fall than is hoped. Second, lending may fall. Third, bad loans could wipe out much of any improvement.* 首先，利率下调可能比预期的时间要久。第二，贷款可能下降。第三，坏帐可能抵消大部分的成效。 4 N-COUNT A **third** is the lowest honors degree that can be obtained from a British university. 三等学位(英国大学的最低荣誉学位) ❑ *...Ms. Hodge, who graduated in 2002 with a third in economics.* …霍奇小姐，2002年毕业并获得经济学三等学位。

third·ly /θɜrdli/ ADV You use **thirdly** when you want to make a third point or give a third reason for something. 第三(点) ❑ *First of all, there are not many of them, and secondly, they have little money and, thirdly, they're hungry.* 首先，他们人数不多；第二，他们没什么钱；第三，他们在挨饿。

Third World ♦◇◇ N-PROPER The countries of Africa, Asia, and Central and South America are sometimes referred to all together as **the Third World**, especially those parts that are poor, do not have much power, and are not considered to be highly developed. 第三世界 ❑ *...development in the Third World.* …第三世界的发展。

thirst /θɜrst/ (**thirsts**) 1 N-VAR **Thirst** is the feeling of wanting to drink something. 口渴 ❑ *Instead of tea or coffee, drink water to quench your thirst.* 别喝茶或者咖啡，喝水来解渴。 2 N-UNCOUNT **Thirst** is the condition of not having enough to drink. 缺水 ❑ *They died of thirst on the voyage.* 他们在旅行途中因缺水而死。

thirsty /θɜrsti/ (**thirstier, thirstiest**) ADJ If you are **thirsty**, you feel a need to drink something. 口渴的 ❑ *Drink whenever you feel thirsty during exercise.* 锻炼时一感到口渴就喝水。

thir·teen ♦♦♦ /θɜrtin/ (**thirteens**) NUM **Thirteen** is the number 13. 13

thir·teenth ♦♦◇ /θɜrtinθ/ ORD The **thirteenth** item in a series is the one that you count as number thirteen. 第13 ❑ *...his thirteenth birthday.* …他的13岁生日。

thir·ti·eth ♦♦◇ /θɜrtiəθ/ ORD The **thirtieth** item in a series is the one that you count as number thirty. 第30 ❑ *...the thirtieth anniversary of my parents' wedding.* …我父母的结婚30周年纪念日。

thir·ty ♦♦♦ /θɜrti/ (**thirties**) 1 NUM **Thirty** is the number 30. 30 2 N-PLURAL When you talk about the **thirties**, you are referring to numbers between 30 and 39. For example, if you are **in** your **thirties**, you are aged between 30 and 39. If the temperature is **in the thirties**, the temperature is between 30 and 39 degrees. 三十几(指30到39之间) ❑ *Mozart clearly enjoyed good health throughout his twenties and early thirties.* 莫扎特显然在二十几岁和三十刚出头时身体很好。 3 N-PLURAL **The thirties** is the decade between 1930 and 1939. 20世纪30年代 ❑ *She became quite a notable director in the thirties and forties.* 她在20世纪的三四十年代成为一位名导演。

this ♦♦♦

> The determiner is pronounced /ðɪs/. In other cases, **this** is pronounced /ðɪs/.

> 限定词读作/ðɪs/。其他情况下，**this**读作/ðɪs/。

1 DET You use **this** to refer back to a particular person or thing that has been mentioned or implied. 这(指前面曾提及或暗指的人或物) ❑ *The entire portfolio is worth $160,312. Of this amount, my investment is worth only $7,748.* 整个投资组合价值为$160312。在这当中，我的投资额仅为$7748。 ● PRON **This** is also a pronoun. 这 ❑ *I don't know how bad the injury is, because I have never had one like this before.* 我不知道伤势有多重，因为我以前从未受过这样的伤。 2 PRON You use **this** to introduce someone or something that you are going to talk about. 这(用于引出将要谈论的人或物) ❑ *This is what I will do. I will telephone Anna and explain.* 这就是我要做的。我会打电话向安娜解释。 ● DET **This** is also a determiner. 这 ❑ *This report is from our Science Unit.* 这份报告出自我们的科学部。 3 PRON You use **this** to refer back to an idea or situation expressed in a previous sentence or sentences. 这一点(指前文曾提到的观点或情况) ❑ *You feel that it's uneconomical. Why is this?* 你觉得这很不划算。这是为什么呢？ ● DET **This** is also a determiner. 这 ❑ *There have been continual demands to put an end to this situation.* 人们不断要求要结束这种局面。 4 DET In spoken English, people use **this** to introduce a person or thing into a story. 口语中用以引出故事里的人或物 ❑ *I came here by chance and was just watching what was going on, when this girl came up to me.* 我碰巧来到这里，正在看热闹，这时一个女孩向我走来。 5 PRON You use **this** to refer to a person or thing that is near you, especially when you touch them or point to them. When there are two or more people or things near you, **this** refers to the nearest one. 这个(用于指附近或最近的人或物) ❑ *I like this coat better than that one.* 我更喜欢这件大衣，而不是那件。 ❑ *"If you'd prefer something else, I'll gladly have it changed for you."—"No, this is great."* "如果您喜欢别的东西，我很乐意帮您调换一下。"——"不用，这个很好。" ● DET **This** is also a determiner. 这个 ❑ *This church was built by the Emperor Constantine Monomarchus in the eleventh century.* 这座教堂是11世纪时君主康斯坦丁・莫诺马库斯建造的。 6 PRON You use **this** when you refer to a general situation, activity, or event which is happening or has just happened and which you feel involved in. 这(指正在发生或刚发生的与自己有关的事) [PRON with "be"] ❑ *I thought, this is why I've traveled thousands of miles.* 我想，这就是我走了几千英里路的原因。 7 DET You use **this** when you refer to the place you are in now or to the present time. 这(指当前所处的地方或时间) ❑ *This country is weird.* 这个国家很怪。 ❑ *This place is run like a hotel ought to be run.* 这个地方经营得像一个酒店一样。 ● PRON **This** is also a pronoun. 这 ❑ *This is the worst place I've come across.* 这是我到过的最糟糕的地方。 8 DET You use **this** to refer to the next occurrence in the future of a particular day, month, season, or festival. 这(指即将要发生某事的时间) ❑ *...this Sunday's 7:45 performance.* …这个星期天7:45的演出。 9 ADV You use **this** when you are indicating the size or shape of something with your hands. 这么(用手表示物体的大小或形状时可说) [ADV adj] ❑ *"They'd said the wound was only about this big," and he showed me with his fingers.* "他们说伤口只有这么大。" 他用手指比划给我看。 10 ADV You use **this** when you are going to specify how much you know or how much you can tell someone. 这么(用于说明自己所知道或所能告知内容的多少) [ADV adv] ❑ *I don't know if it's the best team I've ever had, but I can tell you this much, they're incredible people to be around.* 我不知道这是否是我拥有过的最好的团队，但我可以这么告诉你，他们是非常棒的合作伙伴。 11 CONVENTION If you say **this is it**, you are agreeing with what someone else has just said. 是这样 [BRIT, FORMULAE] ❑ *"You know, people conveniently forget the things they say."—"Well this is it."* "你知道，人们会轻易地忘记自己说的话。"——"嗯，是这样。" 12 PRON You use **this is** in order to say who you are or what organization you are representing, when you are speaking on the telephone, radio, or television. 我是(用在电话、广播或电视中作自我介绍) ❑ *Hello, this is John Thompson.* 你好，我是约翰・汤普森。 13 DET You use **this** to refer to the medium of communication that you are using at the time of speaking or writing. 这个(指说话或写字时使用的媒介) ❑ *What I'm going to do in this lecture is focus on something very specific.* 我在这次讲座中将集中讲解非常具体的问题。 14 → see also **these** 15 PHRASE If you say that you are doing or talking about **this and that**, or **this, that, and the other**, you mean that you are doing or talking about a variety of things that you do not want to specify. 各种事情 ❑ *"And what are you doing now?"—"Oh this and that."* "那么你目前在做什么？"——"哦，各种事情。"

★ **thorn** /θɔrn/ (**thorns**) 1 N-COUNT **Thorns** are the sharp points on some plants and trees, for example, on a rose bush. 刺 ❑ *Roses will always have thorns but with care they can be avoided.* 玫瑰总有刺，但是只要小心，还是可以避开刺。 2 N-VAR A **thorn** or a **thorn bush** or a **thorn tree** is a bush or tree which has a lot of thorns on it. 带刺灌木丛；带刺的树 ❑ *...the shade of a thorn bush.* …一棵带刺灌木的树阴。

thorny /θɔrni/ (**thornier, thorniest**) 1 ADJ A **thorny** plant or tree is covered with thorns. 带刺的 ❑ *...thorny hawthorn trees.* …带刺的山楂树。 2 ADJ If you describe a problem as **thorny**, you mean that it is very complicated and difficult to solve, and that people are often unwilling to discuss it. 棘手的 ❑ *...the thorny issue of immigration policy.* …移民政策这个棘手的问题。

t

thor·ough ♦◇◇ /θɜroʊ/ **1** ADJ A **thorough** action or activity is one that is done very carefully and in a detailed way so that nothing is forgotten. 彻底的 ❑ *We are making a thorough investigation.* 我们正在进行彻底的调查。❑ *This very thorough survey goes back to 1784.* 这项非常彻底的调查可追溯到1784年。● **thor·ough·ly** ADV 彻底地 [ADV with v] ❑ *Food that is being offered hot must be reheated thoroughly.* 热熟食拿到手后必须重新热透。● **thor·ough·ness** N-UNCOUNT 彻底性 ❑ *The thoroughness of the evaluation process we went through was impressive.* 我们经历的评估过程非常彻底，给人深刻的印象。**2** ADJ Someone who is **thorough** is always very careful in their work, so that nothing is forgotten. 细心的 ❑ *Martin would be a good judge, I thought. He was calm and thorough.* 我想马丁会是个好法官。他既沉着又细心。● **thor·ough·ness** N-UNCOUNT 细心 ❑ *His thoroughness and attention to detail is legendary.* 他的细心和对细节的关注是很有名的。**3** ADJ **Thorough** is used to emphasize the large degree or extent of something. (用于强调程度或范围) 完全的 [det ADJ] [EMPHASIS] ❑ *To me, this seemed like a thorough waste of time.* 在我看来，这好像完全是浪费时间。● **thor·ough·ly** ADV 完全地 ❑ *I thoroughly enjoy your program.* 我非常喜欢你们的节目。

those ♦♦♦

The determiner is pronounced /ðoʊz/. The pronoun is pronounced /ðoʊz/.

限定词读作 /ðoʊz/。代词读作 /ðoʊz/。

1 DET You use **those** to refer to people or things which have already been mentioned. 那些 (指已提及的人或物) ❑ *Witnesses said that two people were killed, but those accounts could not be confirmed.* 目击者说两人遇害，但那些说法都没法得到证实。● PRON **Those** is also a pronoun. 那些 ❑ *I understand that there are a number of projects going on. Could you tell us a little bit about those?* 我知道有一些项目正在进行之中。你能给我们简单谈谈那些项目吗？**2** DET You use **those** when you are referring to people or things that are a distance away from you in position or time, especially when you indicate or point to them. 那些 (指在空间或时间上离说话者稍远的人或物) ❑ *What are those buildings?* 那些建筑物是什么？● PRON **Those** is also a pronoun. 那些 ❑ *I like these but not those.* 我喜欢这些，而不是那些。❑ *Those are nice shoes. Where'd you get them?* 那些鞋子很不错。你在哪儿买的？**3** DET You use **those** to refer to someone or something when you are going to give details or information about them. 那些 (指将要详细谈到的人或物) [FORMAL] ❑ *Those people who took up weapons to defend themselves are political prisoners.* 那些拿起武器自卫的人是些政治犯。**4** PRON You use **those** to introduce more information about something already mentioned, instead of repeating the noun which refers to it. 那些 (对已提及事物作补充说明以免重复) [FORMAL] ❑ *The interests he is most likely to enjoy will be those which enable him to show off himself or his talents.* 他最有可能感兴趣的，是那些能让他自我炫耀或卖弄才华的事情。**5** PRON You use **those** to mean "people." 人们 ❑ *A little selfish behavior is unlikely to cause real damage to those around us.* 有点儿自私的行为不太可能对我们周围的人们造成真正的伤害。**6** DET You use **those** when you refer to things that you expect the person you are talking to to know about or when you are checking that you are both thinking of the same people or things. 那些 (指双方均了解的人或事物) ❑ *He did buy me those daffodils a week or so ago.* 他确实在大约一周前给我买了那些水仙花。

T

though ♦♦♦ /ðoʊ/ **1** CONJ You use **though** to introduce a statement in a subordinate clause which contrasts with the statement in the main clause. You often use **though** to introduce a fact which you regard as less important than the fact in the main clause. 尽管 ❑ *Everything I told them was correct, though I forgot a few things.* 我告诉他们的全部正确，尽管我忘了几件事。❑ *I like him. Though he makes me angry sometimes.* 我喜欢他，尽管他有时惹我生气。**2** CONJ You use **though** to introduce a subordinate clause which gives some information that is relevant to the main clause and weakens the force of what it is saying. 不过 ❑ *He did reply, though not immediately.* 他确实回复了，不过不是立马回复。**3** **as though** → see **as** **4** **even though** → see **even**

thought ♦♦♦ /θɔt/ (**thoughts**) **1** **Thought** is the past tense and past participle of **think**. **think**的过去式和过去分词 **2** N-COUNT A **thought** is an idea that you have in your mind. 想法 ❑ *The thought of Nick made her throat tighten.* 一想到尼克就会让她的喉咙发紧。❑ *I've just had a thought.* 我刚刚有了个想法。**3** N-PLURAL A person's **thoughts** are their mind, or all the ideas in their mind when they are concentrating on one particular thing. 心思 ❑ *I jumped to my feet so my thoughts wouldn't start to wander.* 我猛地站了起来，这样我就不会走神了。❑ *Usually at this time our thoughts are on Christmas.* 通常在这种时候我们的心思都放在圣诞节上。**4** N-PLURAL A person's **thoughts** are their opinions on a particular subject. 看法 ❑ *Many of you have written to us to express your thoughts on the conflict.* 你们中的很多人已经写信给我们表达对这次冲突的看法。**5** N-UNCOUNT **Thought** is the activity of thinking, especially deeply, carefully, or logically. 思考 ❑ *Alice had been so deep in thought that she had walked past her car without even seeing it.* 爱丽斯陷入深深的思考之中，连经过自己的车都没看到。❑ *He had given some thought to what she had told him.* 他已对她告诉自己的话做了些思考。**6** N-COUNT A **thought** is an intention, hope, or reason for doing something. 意图；希望；理由 ❑ *Sarah's first thought was to run back and get Max.* 萨拉首先想到的是跑回去叫马克斯。**7** N-UNCOUNT **Thought** is the group of ideas and beliefs which belongs, for example, to a particular religion, philosophy, science, or political party. 思想体系 ❑ *Aristotle's scientific theories dominated Western thought for fifteen hundred years.* 亚里士多德的科学理论统治西方思想长达1500年之久。**8** → see also **second thought**

thought·ful /θɔtfəl/ **1** ADJ If you are **thoughtful**, you are quiet and serious because you are thinking about something. 沉思的 ❑ *Nancy, who had been thoughtful for some time, suddenly spoke.* 南希沉思半晌后，突然开口说话。● **thought·ful·ly** ADV 沉思地 [ADV with v] ❑ *Daniel nodded thoughtfully.* 丹尼尔若有所思地点点头。**2** ADJ If you describe someone as **thoughtful**, you approve of them because they remember what other people want, need, or feel, and try not to upset them. 考虑周到的 [APPROVAL] ❑ *...a thoughtful and caring man.* …一个考虑周到、关心体贴的男人。● **thought·ful·ly** ADV 考虑周到地 [ADV with v] ❑ *...the bottle of wine he had thoughtfully purchased for the celebrations.* …他为庆祝活动特地购买的这瓶葡萄酒。**3** ADJ If you describe something such as a book, film, or speech as **thoughtful**, you mean that it is serious and well thought out. (书籍、电影或讲话等) 有思想深度的 ❑ *...a thoughtful and scholarly book.* …一本既有思想深度又有学术价值的书。● **thought·ful·ly** ADV 有思想深度地 [ADV with v] ❑ *...these thoughtfully designed machines.* …这些经缜密思考而设计的机器。

thought·less /θɔtlɪs/ ADJ If you describe someone as **thoughtless**, you are critical of them because they forget or ignore other people's wants, needs, or feelings. 不顾及他人的 [DISAPPROVAL] ❑ *...a small minority of thoughtless and inconsiderate people.* …一小撮不顾及别人、不替别人着想的人。❑ *It was a thoughtless remark and I regretted it immediately.* 这是一句欠考虑的话，我马上就后悔了。● **thought·less·ly** ADV 不顾及他人地 [ADV with v] ❑ *They thoughtlessly planned a picnic without him.* 他们考虑不周，安排了一次野餐却没带上他。

thou·sand ♦♦♦ /θaʊzᵊnd/ (**thousands**)

The plural form is **thousand** after a number, or after a word or expression referring to a number, such as "several" or "a few."

1 NUM **A thousand** or **one thousand** is the number 1,000. 1000 ❑ *...five thousand acres.* …5000英亩。**2** QUANT If you refer to **thousands of** things or people, you are emphasizing that there are very many of them. 成千上万 [QUANT "of" pl-n] [EMPHASIS] ❑ *Thousands of refugees are packed into overcrowded towns and villages.* 成千上万的难民挤入拥挤不堪的城镇与村庄。● PRON You can also use **thousands** as a pronoun. 成千上万 ❑ *Hundreds have been killed in the fighting and thousands made homeless.* 数百人在战斗中丧生，成千上万的人无家可归。**3** **a thousand and one** → see **one**

thou·sandth /θaʊzᵊnθ/ (**thousandths**) **1** ORD The **thousandth** item in a series is the one that you count as number one thousand. 第一千 ❑ *The magazine has just published its six thousandth edition.* 这本杂志刚刚出版了第6000期。**2** ORD If you say that something has happened for the **thousandth** time, you are emphasizing that it has happened again and that it has already happened a large number of times. 第一千 (强调某事发生的次数非常多) [EMPHASIS] ❑ *The phone rings for the thousandth time.* 电话铃响了1千次了。**3** FRACTION A **thousandth** is one of a thousand equal parts of something. 1/1000 ❑ *...a dust particle weighing only a thousandth of a gram.* …重量仅为1/1000克的尘粒。

▲ **thrash** /θræʃ/ (**thrashes, thrashing, thrashed**) **1** V-T If one player or team **thrashes** another in a game or contest, they defeat them easily or by a large score. (在比赛或竞赛中) 轻松击败 [INFORMAL] ❑ *The Kings were thrashed by the Knicks last night.* 国王队昨晚被尼克斯队轻松击败。**2** V-T If you **thrash** someone, you hit them several times as a punishment. 揍(作为惩罚) ❑ *"Liar!" Sarah screamed, as she thrashed the child. "You stole it."* "说谎！"萨拉一边揍孩子，一边尖叫道，"你偷了那东西。" **3** V-T/V-I If someone **thrashes around** or **thrashes** their arms or legs **around**, they move in a wild or violent way, often hitting against something. You can also say that someone's arms or legs **thrash around**. 使剧烈扭动；剧烈扭动 ❑ *She would thrash around in her hospital bed and remove her intravenous line.* 她会在医院的病床上剧烈扭动并拔掉静脉注射管。 ❑ *Many of the crew died a terrible death as they thrashed about in shark-infested waters.* 许多船员在鲨鱼成群的水域拼命扭动挣扎，死得很惨。 **4** V-T/V-I If a person or thing **thrashes** something, or **thrashes at** something, they hit it continually in a violent or noisy way. 猛烈地连续击打 ❑ *...a magnificent paddle-steamer on the mighty Mississippi, her huge wheel thrashing the muddy water.* …航行在一望无际的密西西比河上的一艘华丽的明轮船，巨轮猛烈地拍打着浑浊的河水。 **5** → see also **thrashing**

▸ **thrash out** **1** PHRASAL VERB If people **thrash out** something such as a plan or an agreement, they decide on it after a lot of discussion. 反复讨论得出(计划或协议等) ❑ *John and Monica have thrashed out a divorce agreement.* 约翰和莫妮卡经反复讨论，已达成离婚协议。 **2** PHRASAL VERB If people **thrash out** a problem or a dispute, they discuss it thoroughly until they reach an agreement. 商讨解决(问题或争端) ❑ *...a sincere effort by two people to thrash out differences about which they have strong feelings.* …两人为解决双方的重大分歧而做出的真诚努力。

thrash·ing /θræʃɪŋ/ (**thrashings**) **1** N-COUNT If one player or team gives another one a **thrashing**, they defeat them easily or by a large score. 轻松击败 [INFORMAL] ❑ *She dropped only eight points in the 43-minute thrashing of the former champion.* 她在轻松击败前冠军的43分钟里，仅失掉8分。 **2** N-COUNT If someone gives someone else a **thrashing**, they hit them several times as a punishment. 揍(作为惩罚) ❑ *If Sarah caught her, she would get a terrible thrashing.* 如果萨拉抓到她，她会挨一顿痛揍。 **3** → see also **thrash**

thread /θrɛd/ (**threads, threading, threaded**) **1** N-VAR **Thread** or a **thread** is a long very thin piece of a material such as cotton, nylon, or silk, especially one that is used in sewing. (尤指用于缝纫的)线 ❑ *This time I'll do it right with a spool of thread.* 这次我会用一轴线把它弄好的。 **2** V-T When you **thread** a needle, you put a piece of thread through the hole in the top of the needle in order to sew with it. 穿(针) ❑ *I sit down, thread a needle, snip off an old button.* 我坐下来，穿好针，剪下了一粒旧钮扣。 **3** N-COUNT The **thread** of an argument, a story, or a situation is an aspect of it that connects all the different parts together. 主线 ❑ *The thread running through many of these proposals was the theme of individual power and opportunity.* 贯穿众多提案的主线，是个人权力与机遇的主题。 **4** N-COUNT A **thread of** something such as liquid, light, or color is a long thin line or piece of it. 线状物；一线 ❑ *A thin, glistening thread of moisture ran along the rough concrete sill.* 一条细细亮亮的水印爬过粗糙的水泥窗台。 **5** N-COUNT The **thread** on a screw, or on something such as a lid or a pipe, is the raised spiral line of metal or plastic around it which allows it to be fixed in place by twisting. 螺纹 ❑ *The screw threads will be able to get a good grip.* 这些螺纹可以咬合得很紧。 **6** V-T/V-I If you **thread** your **way** through a group of people or things, or **thread through** it, you move through it carefully or slowly, changing direction frequently as you move. 穿行 ❑ *Slowly she threaded her way back through the moving mass of bodies.* 她在行人中缓慢穿行，挤了回来。 **7** V-T If you **thread** a long thin object **through** something, you pass it through one or more holes or narrow spaces. 把(细长物体)穿进 ❑ *...threading the laces through the eyelets of his shoes.* …把鞋带穿进他的鞋眼。 **8** V-T If you **thread** small objects such as beads onto a string or thread, you join them together by pushing the string through them. 把(珠子等)串起来 ❑ *Wipe the mushrooms clean and thread them on a string.* 把蘑菇擦干净，然后把它们串在细绳上。 **9** N-COUNT On websites such as newsgroups, a **thread** is one of the subjects that is being written about. (新闻组等网站上的)话题 [COMPUTING] ❑ *The dialogues are organized by month so you can go back to previous threads and read them.* 这些对话是按月份编排的，所以你可以找以前的话题来读一读。
→ see **rope**

threat ♦♦◊ /θrɛt/ (**threats**) **1** N-VAR A **threat to** a person or thing is a danger that something bad might happen to them. A **threat** is also the cause of this danger. 威胁；造成威胁的原因 ❑ *Some couples see single women as a threat to their relationships.* 有些夫妇把单身女子看作是对他们夫妻关系的一种威胁。 **2** N-COUNT A **threat** is a statement by someone that they will hurt you in some way, especially if you do not do what they want. 威胁的言论 ❑ *He may be forced to carry out his threat to resign.* 他可能会迫不得已将自己扬言要辞职的威胁付诸实施。 **3** PHRASE If a person or thing is **under threat**, there is a danger that something bad might be done to them, or that they might cease to exist. 受到威胁 ❑ *His position as leader is under threat.* 他的领导职位受到威胁。

Word Partnership *threat* 的常用搭配：

ADJ.	**biggest** threat, **greatest** threat, **major** threat **1** **credible** threat, **potential** threat, **real** threat, **serious** threat, **significant** threat **1** **2**
N.	threat **to** ***someone's*** **health** **1** threat **of attack**, **death** threat, threat **to peace**, threat **to stability**, threat **of a strike**, **terrorist** threat, threat **of violence**, threat **of war** **1** **2**

threat·en ♦♦◊ /θrɛtᵊn/ (**threatens, threatening, threatened**) **1** V-T If a person **threatens to** do something bad to you, or if they **threaten** you, they say or imply that they will hurt you in some way, especially if you do not do what they want. 威胁 ❑ *He said army officers had threatened to destroy the town.* 他说军官们已威胁要摧毁这座小镇。 ❑ *He tied her up and threatened her with a six-inch knife.* 他把她绑起来，拿着一把6英寸长的刀威胁她。 **2** V-T If something or someone **threatens** a person or thing, they are likely to harm that person or thing. 威胁到 ❑ *The newcomers directly threaten the livelihood of the established workers.* 新来的人直接威胁到原有工人的生计。 **3** V-T If something bad **threatens to** happen, it seems likely to happen. (坏事)可能发生 ❑ *It's threatening to rain.* 天可能要下雨。 ❑ *The fighting is threatening to turn into full-scale war.* 这次冲突可能要演变成全面战争。 **4** → see also **threatening**

Word Partnership *threaten* 的常用搭配：

N.	threaten **safety**, threaten **security**, threaten **stability**, threaten **survival** **2**

threat·en·ing ♦◊◊ /θrɛtᵊnɪŋ/ **1** ADJ You can describe someone's behavior as **threatening** when you think that they are trying to harm you. (行为)威胁的 ❑ *People who engage in threatening behavior should expect to be arrested.* 有威胁行为的人应该被逮捕。 **2** → see also **threaten**

three ♦♦♦ /θri/ (**threes**) NUM **Three** is the number 3. 3 ❑ *We waited three months before going back to see the specialist.* 我们等了3个月后才回去见那位专家。

three-dimensional **1** ADJ A **three-dimensional** object is solid rather than flat, because it can be measured in three different directions, usually the height, length, and width. The abbreviation **3-D** can also be used. 三维的 ❑ *...a three-dimensional model.* …一个三维模型。 **2** ADJ A **three-dimensional** picture, image, or movie looks as though it is deep or solid rather than flat. The abbreviation **3-D** can also be used. (照片、图像或电影)三维的 ❑ *The software generates both two-dimensional drawings and three-dimensional images.* 这种软件既能生成二维图形也能生成三维图像。

three-quarters QUANT **Three-quarters** is an amount that is three out of four equal parts of something. 3/4 [QUANT "of" n] ❑ *Three-quarters of the students are African American.* 3/4的学生是非洲裔美国人。 ● PRON **Three-quarters** is also a pronoun. 3/4 ❑ *Applications have increased by three-quarters.* 求职信增加了3/4。 ● ADV **Three-quarters** is also an adverb. 3/4地 [ADV adj/-ed] ❑ *We were left with an open bottle of champagne three-quarters full.* 有人留给我们一瓶打开过的、还剩3/4的香槟酒。

★ **thresh·old** /θrɛʃhoʊld/ (**thresholds**) **1** N-COUNT The **threshold** of a building or room is the floor in the doorway, or the doorway itself. 门口 ❑ *He stopped at the threshold of the bedroom.* 他在卧室门口停了下来。 **2** N-COUNT A **threshold** is an amount, level, or limit on a scale. When the **threshold** is reached, something else happens or changes. 界限；临界点 ❑ *Moss has a high threshold for pain and a history of fast healing.* 莫斯的忍痛力很强，而且有迅速愈合的经历。 **3** PHRASE If you are **on the threshold of** something exciting or new, you are about to experience it. 即将经历 ❑ *We are on the threshold of a new era in astronomy.* 我们将迈入天文学的新时代。

threw /θru/ **Threw** is the past tense of **throw**. throw的过去式

▲ **thrift** /θrɪft/ (**thrifts**) **1** N-UNCOUNT **Thrift** is the quality and practice of being careful with money and not wasting things.

节俭 [APPROVAL] ❑ *They were rightly praised for their thrift and enterprise.* 他们因勤俭节约和开创精神而受到了应得的表扬。 **2** N-COUNT A **thrift** or a **thrift institution** is a kind of savings bank. 某种储蓄银行 [AM, BUSINESS]

> **Thrift stores** (or **charity shops** in the UK) are a great source of pleasure for the bargain-hunter. When people no longer need clothes, books, toys and other items, they may take them along to these shops, which rely on this type of donation. The proceeds all go to a particular charity.

thrill /θrɪl/ (**thrills, thrilling, thrilled**) **1** N-COUNT If something gives you a **thrill**, it gives you a sudden feeling of great excitement, pleasure, or fear. (突然的) 激动; 狂喜; 恐惧 ❑ *I can remember the thrill of not knowing what I would get on Christmas morning.* 我记得，在不知道圣诞节早上会收到何种礼物时自己的激动心情。 **2** V-T/V-I If something **thrills** you, or if you **thrill at** it, it gives you a feeling of great pleasure and excitement. 使激动; 感到激动 ❑ *The electric atmosphere both terrified and thrilled him.* 这种紧张的气氛使他既害怕又激动。 **3** → see also **thrilled, thrilling**

thrilled /θrɪld/ **1** ADJ If someone is **thrilled**, they are extremely happy and excited about something. 狂喜的 [v-link ADJ] ❑ *I was so thrilled to get a good grade from him.* 让我欣喜若狂的是能从他那儿得到好分数。 **2** → see also **thrill**

thrill·er /θrɪlər/ (**thrillers**) N-COUNT A **thriller** is a book, movie, or play that tells an exciting fictional story about something such as criminal activities or spying. 惊悚小说; 惊悚电影; 惊悚戏剧 ❑ *...a tense psychological thriller.* …一部紧张刺激的心理惊悚小说。

thrill·ing /θrɪlɪŋ/ **1** ADJ Something that is **thrilling** is very exciting and enjoyable. 激动人心的 ❑ *Our wildlife trips offer a thrilling encounter with wildlife in its natural state.* 我们的野生动植物之旅真是激动人心，使我们接触了自然状态下的野生动植物。 **2** → see also **thrill**

thrive /θraɪv/ (**thrives, thriving, thrived**) **1** V-I If someone or something **thrives**, they do well and are successful, healthy, or strong. 兴旺发达; 茁壮成长 ❑ *He appears to be thriving.* 他看起来兴旺发达蒸蒸日上。 ❑ *Today her company continues to thrive.* 如今，她的公司继续蓬勃发展。 **2** V-I If you say that someone **thrives on** a particular situation, you mean that they enjoy it or that they can deal with it very well, especially when other people find it unpleasant or difficult. 喜欢; 从容应对 (尤指别人不喜欢或认为困难的事) ❑ *Many people thrive on a stressful lifestyle.* 许多人喜欢有压力的生活方式。

throat ♦◇◇ /θroʊt/ (**throats**) **1** N-COUNT Your **throat** is the back of your mouth and the top part of the tubes that go down into your stomach and your lungs. 喉咙 ❑ *She had a sore throat.* 她喉咙痛。 **2** N-COUNT Your **throat** is the front part of your neck. 喉部 ❑ *His striped tie was loosened at his throat.* 他脖子上的条纹领带松开着。 **3** PHRASE If you **clear** your **throat**, you cough once either to make it easier to speak or to attract people's attention. 清喉咙 ❑ *Cross cleared his throat and spoke in low, polite tones.* 克罗斯清了清喉咙，低声礼貌地说起话来。 **4** PHRASE If you **ram** something **down** someone's **throat** or **force** it **down** their **throat**, you keep mentioning a situation or idea in order to make them accept it or believe it. 反复灌输以让人接受或相信 ❑ *I've always been close to my dad but he's never rammed his career down my throat.* 我和父亲一直很亲近，但是他从来没有强迫我继承他的事业。 **5** PHRASE If two people or groups are **at each other's throats**, they are arguing or fighting violently with each other. 激烈争吵; 激烈打斗 ❑ *The idea that we are at each other's throats couldn't be further from the truth.* 认为我们在激烈争吵的想法简直是无稽之谈。 **6** a **lump** in your **throat** → see **lump**

▲ **throb** /θrɒb/ (**throbs, throbbing, throbbed**) **1** V-I If part of your body **throbs**, you feel a series of strong and usually painful beats there. 阵痛 ❑ *His head throbbed.* 他的头一阵阵地痛。 **2** V-I If something **throbs**, it vibrates and makes a steady noise. (有规律地) 震动作响 [LITERARY] ❑ *The engines throbbed.* 发动机轰隆隆地震动。

★ **throne** /θroʊn/ (**thrones**) **1** N-COUNT A **throne** is a decorative chair used by a king, queen, or emperor on important official occasions. (君王的) 宝座 **2** N-SING You can talk about **the throne** as a way of referring to the position of being king, queen, or emperor. 王位; 皇位 ❑ *...the queen's 40th anniversary on the throne.* …女王登位40周年纪念日。

▲ **throng** /θrɔŋ/ (**throngs, thronging, thronged**) **1** N-COUNT A **throng** is a large crowd of people. 一大群人 [LITERARY] ❑ *An official pushed through the throng.* 一位官员从人群中挤过。 **2** V-I When people **throng** somewhere, they go there in great numbers. (人群) 涌向 [LITERARY] ❑ *The crowds thronged into the stadium.* 人群涌进了体育馆。

throt·tle /θrɒtᵊl/ (**throttles, throttling, throttled**) **1** V-T To **throttle** someone means to kill or injure them by squeezing their throat or tightening something around it and preventing them from breathing. 勒死; 使窒息 ❑ *The attacker then tried to throttle her with wire.* 那名袭击者然后试图用电线勒死她。 **2** N-COUNT The **throttle** of a motor vehicle or aircraft is the device, lever, or pedal that controls the quantity of fuel entering the engine which is used to control the vehicle's speed. (机动车、飞机的) 节流阀; 油门杆; 油门踏板 ❑ *He gently opened the throttle, and the ship began to ease forward.* 他轻轻地松开油门杆，船开始缓缓向前移动。

> **through**
> 1. ADVERBS AND PREPOSITIONS: PHYSICAL MOVEMENTS AND POSITIONS
> 2. ADVERBS AND PREPOSITIONS, ABSTRACT USES: TIMES, EXPERIENCES, CAUSES
> 3. ADJECTIVES

❶ **through** ♦♦♦ **1** PREP To move **through** something such as a hole, opening, or pipe means to move directly from one side or end of it to the other. 穿过 ❑ *The theater was evacuated when rain poured through the roof.* 雨水从屋顶灌下来，剧院就被撤空了。 ❑ *Go straight through that door under the EXIT sign.* 直着穿过那道上方有"安全出口"字样的门。 ● ADV **Through** is also an adverb. 穿过 [ADV after v] ❑ *There was a hole in the wall and water was seeping through.* 墙上有个洞，水正渗出来。 **2** PREP To cut **through** something means to cut it in two pieces or to make a hole in it. (切) 开; (钻) 透 ❑ *Use a genuine fish knife and fork if possible as they are designed to cut through the flesh but not the bones.* 如果可能的话，使用一副真正的鱼刀和鱼叉，因为它们是专门设计用来切鱼肉而非鱼骨的。 ● ADV **Through** is also an adverb. (切) 开; (钻) 透 [ADV after v] ❑ *Score lightly at first and then repeat, scoring deeper each time until the board is cut through.* 先轻轻地划一下，然后反复划，一次比一次划得深些，直到木板被完全割开。 **3** PREP To go **through** a town, area, or country means to travel across it or in it. 穿越 (城镇、地区或国家) ❑ *Go through North Carolina and into Virginia.* 穿越北卡罗来纳州进入弗吉尼亚州。 ● ADV **Through** is also an adverb. 穿越 [ADV after v] ❑ *Few know that the tribe was just passing through.* 几乎没人知道这个部落只是路过。 **4** PREP If you move **through** a group of things or a mass of something, it is on either side of you or all around you. 穿过 (人群或物体) ❑ *We made our way through the crowd to the river.* 我们穿过人群来到河边。 ● ADV **Through** is also an adverb. 穿过 [ADV after v] ❑ *He pushed his way through to the edge of the crowd where he waited.* 他挤到人群边上，在那里等候。 **5** PREP To get **through** a barrier or obstacle means to get from one side of it to the other. 越过 (障碍) ❑ *Allow twenty-five minutes to get through passport control and customs.* 留出25分钟通过护照检查处和海关。 ● ADV **Through** is also an adverb. 越过 [ADV after v] ❑ *...a maze of concrete and steel barriers, designed to prevent vehicles driving straight through.* …为防止车辆直接通过而设计的迷宫式钢筋混凝土障碍物。 **6** PREP If a driver goes **through** a red light, they keep driving even though they should stop. 闯 (红灯) ❑ *He was killed at an intersection by a driver who went through a red light.* 他在十字路口被一个闯红灯的司机撞死了。 **7** PREP If something goes into an object and comes out of the other side, you can say that it passes **through** the object. 穿过 (物体内部) ❑ *The ends of the net pass through a wooden bar at each end.* 这张网的两端各穿着一根木棒。 ● ADV **Through** is also an adverb. 穿过 [ADV after v] ❑ *I bored a hole so that the bolt would pass through.* 我钻了一个孔，这样门闩就能穿过去。 **8** PREP To go **through** a system means to move around it or to pass from one end of it to the other. 通过 (系统) ❑ *...electric currents traveling through copper wires.* …通过铜导线的电流。 ● ADV **Through** is also an adverb. 通过 [ADV after v] ❑ *Food should be allowed to go through immediately with fewer restrictions.* 食品应允许快速流通，少受限制。 **9** PREP If you see, hear, or feel something **through** a particular thing, that thing is between you and the thing you can see, hear, or feel. 透过 ❑ *Alice gazed pensively through the wet glass.* 艾丽斯透过湿漉漉的玻璃若有所思地凝视着。 **10** PREP If something such as a feeling, attitude, or quality happens **through** an area, organization, or a person's body, it happens everywhere in it or affects all of it. 贯穿; 遍布 ❑ *An atmosphere of anticipation vibrated through the crowd.* 人群中充满着期盼的气氛。

❷ **through** ◆◆◆ 1 PREP If something happens or exists **through** a period of time, it happens or exists from the beginning until the end. 从…的开始到结束 ❑ *She kept quiet all through breakfast.* 她吃早餐时始终保持沉默。● ADV **Through** is also an adverb. 自始至终 [ADV after v] ❑ *We'll be working right through to the summer.* 我们会一直工作到夏季。 2 PREP If something happens from a particular period of time **through** another, it starts at the first period and continues until the end of the second period. 直至 [AM] in BRIT, use **to** ❑ *...open Monday through Friday from 9 to 5.* …周一至周五9点到5点开放。 3 PREP If you go **through** a particular experience or event, you experience it, and if you behave in a particular way **through** it, you behave in that way while it is happening. (以某种行动方式) 经历 ❑ *Men go through a change of life emotionally just like women.* 男人就和女人一样会在情绪上经历更年期。 4 PREP You use **through** in expressions such as **half-way through** and **all the way through** to indicate to what extent an action or task is completed. 完成 [n PREP n] ❑ *A thirty-nine-year-old competitor collapsed half-way through the marathon.* 一位39岁的参赛者在马拉松赛跑的中途摔倒了。● ADV **Through** is also an adverb. 完成 [n ADV] ❑ *Stir the pork until it turns white all the way through.* 搅拌猪肉直到完全变白为止。 5 PREP If something happens because of something else, you can say that it happens **through** it. 因为 ❑ *I only succeeded through hard work.* 我就是因为努力工作才成功的。 6 PREP You use **through** when stating the means by which a particular thing is achieved. 凭借; 通过 ❑ *Those who seek to grab power through violence deserve punishment.* 那些想凭借暴力夺取权力的人应该受到惩罚。 7 PREP If you do something **through** someone else, they take the necessary action for you. 经由 (某人) ❑ *Do I need to go through my doctor to get an appointment?* 我需要通过我的医生来预约吗? 8 ADV If something such as a proposal or idea goes **through**, it is accepted by people in authority and is made legal or official. (提议或想法等) 得到批准 [ADV after v] ❑ *We're waiting for the building permit to go through.* 我们在等着工程许可证获得批准。● PREP **Through** is also a preposition. 得到…的批准 ❑ *They want to get the plan through Congress as quickly as possible.* 他们想让这个计划尽快获得国会的批准。 9 PREP If someone gets **through** an examination or a round of a competition, they succeed or win. 通过 (考试); (在比赛中) 胜出 ❑ *She was bright, learned languages quickly, and sailed through her exams.* 她聪明伶俐，学语言很快，顺利通过了各门考试。● ADV **Through** is also an adverb. 成功地 [ADV after v] ❑ *Only the top four teams go through.* 仅4个顶尖队伍胜出。 10 ADV When you get **through** while making a telephone call, the call is connected and you can speak to the person you are phoning. (电话) 接通 [ADV after v] ❑ *Telephones are down so he can't get through.* 电话出了故障，所以他打不通。 11 PREP If you look or go **through** a lot of things, you look at them or deal with them one after the other. 逐个 (浏览、处理) ❑ *Let's go through the numbers together and see if a workable deal is possible.* 让我们一起把这些数字过一遍，看能否找出一个可行的方案。 12 PREP If you read **through** something, you read it from beginning to end. 从头到尾 (阅读) ❑ *She read through pages and pages of the music I had brought her.* 她一页一页地翻看我带给她的乐谱。● ADV **Through** is also an adverb. 从头到尾 [ADV after v] ❑ *The article had been authored by Raymond Kennedy. He read it right through, looking for any scrap of information that might have passed him by.* 这篇文章是由雷蒙德·肯尼迪写的。他从头一直读到尾，寻找任何可能遗漏的点滴信息。 13 ADV If you say that someone or something is wet **through**, you are emphasizing how wet they are. (湿) 透 [adj ADV] [EMPHASIS] ❑ *I returned to the inn cold and wet, soaked through by the drizzling rain.* 我回到那家小客栈，被毛毛雨淋透了，又冷又湿。

❸ **through** ◆◆◆ 1 ADJ If you are **through with** something or if it is **through**, you have finished doing it. 完成的 [v-link ADJ] ❑ *We're through with dinner.* 我们吃完饭了。 ❑ *Are you through with this?* 你完成这个了吗? 2 ADJ If you are **through with** someone, you do not want to have anything to do with them again. 断绝关系的 [v-link ADJ] ❑ *I'm through with her; she's bad news!* 我和她断绝关系了；她是个讨厌鬼!

> The preposition is pronounced /θru/. In other cases, **through** is pronounced /θru̲/

> 介词读作/θru/。其余读作/θru̲/。

> In addition to the uses shown here, **through** is used in phrasal verbs such as "follow through," "see through," and "think through."

through·out ◆◆◇ /θruaʊ̲t/ 1 PREP If you say that something happens **throughout** a particular period of time, you mean that it happens during the whole of that period. 自始至终 ❑ *The national tragedy of rival groups killing each other continued throughout 1990.* 1990年全年，敌对组织互相残杀的民族悲剧持续不断。 ❑ *Movie music can be made memorable because its themes are repeated throughout the film.* 电影音乐可以制作得令人难忘，因为其主旋律在影片中反复出现。● ADV **Throughout** is also an adverb. 自始至终 [ADV with cl] ❑ *The first song, "Blue Moon," didn't go too badly except that everyone talked throughout.* 第一首歌《蓝月亮》效果还不算太差，只是所有的人自始至终都在说话。 2 PREP If you say that something happens or exists **throughout** a place, you mean that it happens or exists in all parts of that place. 遍及 ❑ *"Sight Savers," founded in 1950, now runs projects throughout Africa, the Caribbean and Southeast Asia.* 国际防盲救盲组织成立于1950年，如今在非洲、加勒比海和东南亚各地区开展项目。● ADV **Throughout** is also an adverb. 到处 [ADV with cl] ❑ *The route is well sign-posted throughout.* 这条路线全程设有路标。

throw ◆◆◇ /θroʊ̲/ (**throws, throwing, threw, thrown**) 1 V-T When you **throw** an object that you are holding, you move your hand or arm quickly and let go of the object, so that it moves through the air. 投; 扔 ❑ *He spent hours throwing a tennis ball against a wall.* 他花了数小时对着一堵墙扔网球。 ❑ *The crowd began throwing stones.* 那群人开始扔石头。● N-COUNT **Throw** is also a noun. 投; 扔 ❑ *That was a good throw.* 那是一次很棒的投掷。 ❑ *A throw of the dice allows a player to move himself forward.* 投掷一次骰子，玩家即可向前移动。 2 V-T If you **throw** your body or part of your body into a particular position or place, you move it there suddenly and with a lot of force. 猛然移动 (身体或身体部位) ❑ *She threw her arms around his shoulders.* 她猛地伸出双臂抱住他的肩膀。 ❑ *She threatened to throw herself in front of a train.* 她威胁说要卧轨。 3 V-T If you **throw** something into a particular place or position, you put it there in a quick and careless way. (漫不经心地) 扔下 ❑ *He struggled out of his bulky jacket and threw it on to the back seat.* 他用力脱下笨重的夹克，顺手把它扔到后座上。 4 V-T To **throw** someone into a particular place or position means to force them roughly into that place or position. 使摔倒 ❑ *He threw me to the ground.* 他把我摔倒在地。 5 V-T If you say that someone **is thrown into** prison, you mean that they are put there by the authorities. 把…关进 (监狱) ❑ *Those two should have been thrown in jail.* 那两个人当时就该被关进监狱。 6 V-T If a horse **throws** its rider, it makes him or her fall off, by suddenly jumping or moving violently. (马) 摔落 (骑手) ❑ *The horse reared, throwing its rider and knocking down a youth standing beside it.* 这匹马向后一仰，摔下骑手并撞倒站在它旁边的一个年轻人。 7 V-T If a person or thing **is thrown into** a bad situation or state, something causes them to be in that situation or state. 使陷入 (困境等) ❑ *Abidjan was thrown into turmoil because of a protest by taxi drivers.* 阿比让因计程车司机们的抗议而陷入了混乱。 8 V-T If something **throws** light or a shadow **on** a surface, it causes that surface to have light or a shadow on it. 投下 (光线或影子) ❑ *The sunlight is white and blinding, throwing hard-edged shadows on the ground.* 阳光亮白刺眼，在地上投下轮廓分明的影子。 9 V-T If something **throws** doubt **on** a person or thing, it causes people to doubt or suspect them. 使…产生怀疑 ❑ *This new information does throw doubt on their choice.* 这个新消息确实让人对他们的选择产生怀疑。 10 V-T If you **throw** a look or smile at someone or something, you look or smile at them quickly and suddenly. 猛然投以 (一瞥或一笑) [no cont] ❑ *Emily turned and threw her a suggestive grin.* 埃米莉转过身，猛然地向她投了个暗示性的微笑。 11 V-T If you **throw** yourself, your energy, or your money **into** a particular job or activity, you become involved in it very actively or enthusiastically. 投身于; 投入 ❑ *She threw herself into a modeling career.* 她投身于模特职业。 12 V-T If you **throw** a fit or a tantrum, you suddenly start to behave in an uncontrolled way. 爆发 (脾气); 耍 (性子) ❑ *I used to get very upset and scream and swear, throwing tantrums all over the place.* 我以前经常很不开心，喊叫骂人，到处乱发脾气。 13 V-T If something such as a remark or an experience **throws** you, it surprises you or confuses you because it is unexpected. 使吃惊; 使困惑 ❑ *Her sudden change in attitude threw me.* 她态度上的突然变化令我吃惊。 ❑ *This new confession threw me for a loop.* 这份新口供使我很震惊。 14 V-T If you **throw** a punch, you punch someone. 打 (一拳) ❑ *Everything was fine until someone threw a punch.* 一切都还好，直到有人动了拳头。 15 V-T When someone **throws** a party, they organize one, usually in their own home. (常指在家) 举行 (聚会) [INFORMAL] ❑ *Why not throw a party for your friends?* 为何不给你的朋友们搞一个聚会呢? 16 **to throw** someone **in at the deep end** → see **end** 17 **to throw**

t

down the gauntlet → see **gauntlet** 18 to **throw light on** something → see **light** 19 to **throw money at** something → see **money** 20 to **throw in the towel** → see **towel** 21 to **throw your weight around** → see **weight**

▸ **throw away** or **throw out** 1 PHRASAL VERB When you **throw away** or **throw out** something that you do not want, you get rid of it, for example, by putting it in the trash. 扔掉 ❑ *I never throw anything away.* 我从来不扔任何东西。 2 PHRASAL VERB If you **throw away** an opportunity, advantage, or benefit, you waste it, rather than using it sensibly. 浪费（机会、优势或好处）❑ *Failing to tackle the deficit would be throwing away an opportunity we haven't had for a generation.* 解决不了赤字问题将会浪费我们一整代人都不曾遇到的一个机会。

▸ **throw out** 1 → see **throw away** 1 2 PHRASAL VERB If a judge **throws out** a case, he or she rejects it and the accused person does not have to stand trial. 不受理（案件）❑ *The defense wants the district Judge to throw out the case.* 辩护律师想要区法官拒绝受理这个案子。 3 PHRASAL VERB If you **throw** someone **out**, you force them to leave a place or group. 撵走；开除 ❑ *He was thrown out of the Olympic team after testing positive for drugs.* 他在药检呈阳性后被逐出了奥林匹克运动队。 ❑ *I wanted to kill him, but instead I just threw him out of the house.* 我本想杀了他，但我只是把他撵出了家门。

▸ **throw up** 1 PHRASAL VERB When someone **throws up**, they vomit. 呕吐 ❑ *She said she had thrown up after reading reports of the trial.* 她说她看了有关该审讯的报告后呕吐了。 2 PHRASAL VERB If something **throws up** dust, stones, or water, when it moves or hits the ground, it causes them to rise up into the air. 扬起（灰尘）；溅起（石头、水）❑ *If it had hit the Earth, it would have made a crater 100 miles across and thrown up an immense cloud of dust.* 如果它撞上了地球，就会砸出一个100英里宽的大坑并扬起巨大的尘埃云团。

Word Partnership *throw* 的常用搭配:
N. throw **a ball**, throw **a pass**, throw **a pitch**, throw **a rock/stone**, throw **strikes** 1

thrown /θroʊn/ **Thrown** is the past participle of **throw**. throw 的过去分词

thrush /θrʌʃ/ (**thrushes**) 1 N-COUNT A **thrush** is a fairly small bird with a brown back and sometimes a spotted breast. There are several different kinds of **thrush**. 鸫 2 N-UNCOUNT **Thrush** is a medical condition caused by a fungus called Candida. It most often occurs in a baby's mouth or in a woman's vagina. 鹅口疮；念珠菌阴道炎 ❑ *...a medicine that's used to prevent and treat thrush and other fungal infections.* …一种用于预防和治疗鹅口疮及其他真菌感染的药物。

thrust /θrʌst/ (**thrusts, thrusting, thrust**) 1 V-T If you **thrust** something or someone somewhere, you push or move them there quickly with a lot of force. 猛推；猛塞；猛刺 ❑ *They thrust him into the back of a jeep.* 他们把他猛推入吉普车的后部。 ● N-COUNT **Thrust** is also a noun. 猛推；猛塞；猛刺 ❑ *Two of the knife thrusts were fatal.* 猛刺的其中两刀是致命的。 2 V-T If you **thrust** your **way** somewhere, you move there, pushing between people or things which are in your way. 挤；推 ❑ *She thrust her way into the crowd.* 她挤进了人群。 3 V-I If something **thrusts** up or out of something else, it sticks up or sticks out in a noticeable way. 竖起；挺出 [LITERARY] ❑ *...a seedling ready to thrust up into any available light.* …一株正要挺出来迎接光线的幼苗。 4 N-UNCOUNT **Thrust** is the power or force that is required to make a vehicle move in a particular direction. （车辆等的）推力 ❑ *It provides the thrust that makes the craft move forward.* 它提供了使飞机前进的推力。
→ see **flight**

T

Word Partnership *thrust* 的常用搭配:
N. thrust ***your* hands**, thrust ***your* head** 1
ADV. thrust ***someone/something* aside** 1
thrust ***something/yourself* forward** 1 2

thud /θʌd/ (**thuds, thudding, thudded**) 1 N-COUNT A **thud** is a dull sound, such as that which a heavy object makes when it hits something soft. 沉闷声 ❑ *She tripped and fell with a sickening thud.* 她绊倒了，发出一声吓人的闷响。 2 V-I If something **thuds** somewhere, it makes a dull sound, usually when it falls onto or hits something else. 发出沉闷声 ❑ *She ran up the stairs, her bare feet thudding on the wood.* 她跑上楼梯，光脚在木头上发出噔噔的声音。 3 V-I When your heart **thuds**, it beats strongly and somewhat quickly, for example, because you are very frightened or very happy. （因害怕或狂喜心脏）怦怦跳 ❑ *My heart had started to thud, and my mouth was dry.* 我的心开始怦怦跳，而且嘴巴发干。

thug /θʌg/ (**thugs**) N-COUNT You can refer to a violent person or criminal as a **thug**. 暴徒；罪犯 [DISAPPROVAL] ❑ *...the cowardly thugs who mug old people.* …那些抢劫老人的懦夫暴徒。

thumb /θʌm/ (**thumbs, thumbing, thumbed**) 1 N-COUNT Your hand has four fingers and one **thumb**. 大拇指 ❑ *She bit the tip of her left thumb, not looking at me.* 她咬着左手的大拇指头，也不看我。 2 V-T If you **thumb** a lift or **thumb** a ride, you stand by the side of the road holding out your thumb until a driver stops and gives you a lift. （站在公路边）竖起大拇指请求（搭便车）❑ *It may interest you to know that a boy answering Rory's description thumbed a ride to San Antonio.* 可能让你感兴趣的是，有个和罗里描述相符的男孩竖起大拇指请求搭便车到圣安东尼奥。 3 PHRASE If you are **under** someone's **thumb**, you are under their control, or very heavily influenced by them. 在…的控制下；深受…的影响 ❑ *I cannot tell you what pain I feel when I see how much my mother is under my father's thumb.* 我无法向你形容，当我看到母亲完全在父亲的控制之下时我有多么痛苦。 4 **green thumb** → see **green** 5 **rule of thumb** → see **rule**
→ see **hand**

thumb·tack /θʌmtæk/ (**thumbtacks**) N-COUNT A **thumbtack** is a short pin with a broad flat top which is used for fastening papers or pictures to a board, wall, or other surface. 图钉 [AM]
in BRIT, use **drawing pin**
→ see **office**

▲ **thump** /θʌmp/ (**thumps, thumping, thumped**) 1 V-T/V-I If you **thump** something, you hit it hard, usually with your fist. 捶（某物）❑ *He thumped my shoulder affectionately, nearly knocking me over.* 他亲热地捶了一下我的肩膀，差点把我打倒了。 ❑ *I heard you thumping on the door.* 我听到你在捶门了。 ● N-COUNT **Thump** is also a noun. 捶 ❑ *He felt a thump on his shoulder.* 他感到肩膀被捶了一下。 2 V-T If you **thump** someone, you attack them and hit them with your fist. 捶；揍（某人）[INFORMAL] ❑ *Don't say it serves me right or I'll thump you.* 别说我活该，否则我就揍你。 3 V-T/V-I If you **thump** something somewhere or if it **thumps** there, it makes a loud, dull sound by hitting something else. 使…沉闷地撞击；沉闷地撞击 ❑ *Their teacher thumped her pen on her book.* 他们的老师把她的钢笔重重地摔在她的书上。 ● N-COUNT **Thump** is also a noun. 沉闷的撞击声 ❑ *There was a loud thump as the horse crashed into the van.* 那匹马撞上那辆货车时发出巨大的一声闷响。 4 V-I When your heart **thumps**, it beats strongly and quickly, usually because you are afraid or excited. （常指因害怕或激动心脏）怦怦跳 ❑ *My heart was thumping wildly but I didn't let my face show any emotion.* 我的心在狂跳着，但我没在脸上流露出任何表情。

thun·der /θʌndər/ (**thunders, thundering, thundered**) 1 N-UNCOUNT **Thunder** is the loud noise that you hear from the sky after a flash of lightning, especially during a storm. 雷 ❑ *There was thunder and lightning, and torrential rain.* 雷电交加，暴雨倾盆而下。 2 V-I When **it thunders**, a loud noise comes from the sky after a flash of lightning. 打雷 ❑ *The day was heavy and still. It would probably thunder later.* 天阴沉沉的，一丝风也没有。等会儿可能会打雷。 3 N-UNCOUNT The **thunder of** something that is moving or making a sound is the loud deep noise it makes. 轰隆声 ❑ *The thunder of the sea on the rocks seemed to blank out other thoughts.* 海浪拍击礁石的轰隆声似乎要把其他的思绪都淹没。 4 V-I If something or someone **thunders** somewhere, they move there quickly and with a lot of noise. 轰隆隆地快速移动 ❑ *The horses thundered across the valley floor.* 马群轰隆隆地从谷底奔跑而过。

thun·der·ous /θʌndərəs/ ADJ If you describe a noise as **thunderous**, you mean that it is very loud and deep. 雷鸣般的 ❑ *The audience responded with thunderous applause.* 观众报以雷鸣般的掌声。

thunder·storm /θʌndərstɔrm/ (**thunderstorms**) N-COUNT A **thunderstorm** is a storm with thunder and lightning and a lot of heavy rain. 雷雨
→ see **erosion**

Thurs.

The spelling **Thur.** is also used.

Thurs. is a written abbreviation for **Thursday**. 星期四 [mainly BRIT]

Thurs·day ◆◆◆ /θɜrzdeɪ, -di/ (**Thursdays**) N-VAR **Thursday** is the day after Wednesday and before Friday. 星期四 ❑ *On Thursday Barrett invited me for a drink.* 星期四巴雷特请我喝了一杯。 ❑ *We go and do the weekly shopping every Thursday morning.* 我们每周四早上都去进行每周一次的采购。

thus ♦♦◇ /ðʌs/ 1 ADV You use **thus** to show that what you are about to mention is the result of something else that you have just mentioned. 因此 [ADV with cl/group] [FORMAL] ❑ *Neither of them thought of turning on the news. Thus Caroline didn't hear of John's death until Peter telephoned.* 他们俩都没想到要收看新闻。因此，直到彼得打来电话卡罗琳才获悉约翰的死讯。 2 ADV If you say that something is **thus** or happens **thus** you mean that it is, or happens, as you have just described or as you are just about to describe. 如此；那样 [FORMAL] ❑ *Joanna was pouring the wine. While she was thus engaged, Charles sat on one of the bar-stools.* 乔安娜在倒葡萄酒。就在她忙着时，查尔斯坐在了其中一张酒吧椅上。

thwart /θwɔrt/ (**thwarts, thwarting, thwarted**) V-T If you **thwart** someone or **thwart** their plans, you prevent them from doing or getting what they want. 阻挠；挫败 ❑ *The security forces were doing all they could to thwart terrorists.* 安全部队正尽其所能挫败恐怖分子。

thyme /taɪm/ N-UNCOUNT **Thyme** is a type of herb used in cooking. 百里香（一种烹饪调料）

tick /tɪk/ (**ticks, ticking, ticked**) 1 V-I When a clock or watch **ticks**, it makes a regular series of short sounds as it works. （钟表）嘀嗒作响 ❑ *A wind-up clock ticked busily from the kitchen counter.* 一个上了发条的时钟在厨房案台上不停地嘀嗒作响。 ● PHRASAL VERB **Tick away** means the same as **tick**. 嘀嗒作响 ❑ *A grandfather clock ticked away in a corner.* 一个落地式大钟在墙角嘀嗒作响。 ● **tick·ing** N-UNCOUNT 嘀嗒声 ❑ *...the endless ticking of clocks.* …时钟没完没了的嘀嗒声。 2 N-COUNT The **tick** of a clock or watch is the series of short sounds it makes when it is working, or one of those sounds. （钟表的）嘀嗒声 ❑ *He sat listening to the tick of the grandfather clock.* 他坐着倾听那个落地式大钟的嘀嗒声。 3 N-COUNT A **tick** is a written mark like a V: ✓. It is used to show that something is correct or has been selected or dealt with. 对勾 [BRIT]

in AM, use **check, checkmark**

4 N-COUNT A **tick** is a small creature which lives on the bodies of people or animals and uses their blood as food. 壁虱 ❑ *The company produces chemicals that destroy ticks and mites.* 该公司生产消灭壁虱和螨虫的化学品。 5 V-T If you **tick** something that is written on a piece of paper, you put a tick next to it. 在…旁打勾 [BRIT]

in AM, use **check**

▶ **tick off** 1 PHRASAL VERB If you **tick off** items on a list, you write a tick or other mark next to them, in order to show that they have been dealt with. 在…旁打勾；在…旁作记号 [BRIT]

in AM, usually use **check off**

2 PHRASAL VERB If you say that someone or something **ticks** you **off**, you mean that they annoy you. 使恼火 [AM, INFORMAL] ❑ *I can't lay blame anywhere and that ticks me off.* 我不能把责任推卸到任何地方，这令我很恼火。

tick·et ♦♦◇ /tɪkɪt/ (**tickets**) 1 N-COUNT A **ticket** is a small, official piece of paper or card which shows that you have paid to enter a place such as a theater or a sports stadium, or shows that you have paid for a trip. 入场券；票 [also "by" N] ❑ *He had a ticket for a flight on Friday.* 他有一张星期五的机票。 ❑ *...two tickets for the game.* …两张比赛入场券。 2 N-COUNT A **ticket** is an official piece of paper which orders you to pay a fine or to appear in court because you have committed a driving or parking offense. （交通）罚款通知单；违章传票 ❑ *Slow down or you'll get a ticket.* 开慢点儿，否则你会接到一张罚款通知单。 3 N-COUNT A **ticket** for a game of chance such as a raffle or a lottery is a piece of paper with a number on it. If the number on your ticket matches the number chosen, you win a prize. 彩票 ❑ *She bought a lottery ticket and won more than $33 million.* 她买了一张彩票，中了三千三百多万美元。 4 → see also **season ticket**

Word Partnership *ticket* 的常用搭配：

N.	ticket **agent**, ticket **booth**, ticket **counter**, ticket **holder**, **plane** ticket, ticket **price** 1
	parking ticket, **speeding** ticket 2
	lottery ticket 3
ADJ.	**free** ticket 1
	winning ticket 3
V.	**get a** ticket 1 2
	buy/pay for a ticket 1 3

★ **tick·le** /tɪkᵊl/ (**tickles, tickling, tickled**) 1 V-T When you **tickle** someone, you move your fingers lightly over a sensitive part of their body, often in order to make them laugh. 胳肢 ❑ *I was tickling him, and he was laughing and giggling.* 我在胳肢他，他咯咯笑起来。 2 V-T/V-I If something **tickles** you or **tickles**, it causes an irritating feeling by lightly touching a part of your body. 使发痒；发痒 ❑ *...a yellow hat with a great feather that tickled her ear.* …一顶黄帽子上饰有一根大羽毛，扎得她发痒。 ❑ *A beard doesn't scratch, it just tickles.* 胡子不扎人，但是可以使人痒。

tid·al /taɪdᵊl/ ADJ **Tidal** means relating to or produced by tides. 潮汐的；潮汐产生的 ❑ *The tidal stream or current gradually decreases in the shallows.* 浅滩上的潮水逐渐退去。
→ see **wetland**

tid·al wave (**tidal waves**) N-COUNT A **tidal wave** is a very large wave, often caused by an earthquake, that flows onto the land and destroys things. （常指地震引起的）潮波 ❑ *...a massive tidal wave swept the ship up and away.* …一股巨大的潮波把那只船掀起来，卷走了。

tide ♦◇◇ /taɪd/ (**tides**) 1 N-COUNT **The tide** is the regular change in the level of the ocean on the beach. You say the tide is in when water reaches a high point on the land or out when the water leaves the land. 潮水 ❑ *The tide was at its highest.* 潮水那时正处于最高位。 ❑ *The tide was going out, and the sand was smooth and glittering.* 潮水正在退去，沙滩平坦，闪闪发亮。 2 N-COUNT A **tide** is a current in the sea that is caused by the regular and continuous movement of large areas of water toward and away from the shore. （不断冲刷海岸的）海浪 ❑ *Roman vessels used to sail with the tide from Boulogne to Richborough.* 罗马的船只过去常常乘着海浪从布洛涅航行到里奇伯勒。 3 N-SING The **tide of** opinion, for example, is what the majority of people think at a particular time. （观点的）潮流 ❑ *The tide of opinion seems overwhelmingly in his favor.* 大部分人的观点似乎对他极为有利。
→ see Word Web: **tide**
→ see **ocean**

tidy /taɪdi/ (**tidier, tidiest, tidies, tidying, tidied**) 1 ADJ Someone who is **tidy** likes everything to be neat and arranged in an organized way. 爱整洁的 [mainly BRIT] ❑ *It is always important to have a tidy desk.* 有一张整洁的桌子总是很重要。

in AM, use **neat**

● **tidi·ness** N-UNCOUNT 整洁 ❑ *I'm very impressed by your tidiness and order.* 你的整洁和条理性给我留下了非常深刻的印象。 2 ADJ Something that is **tidy** is neat and is arranged in an organized way. 整洁的 [mainly BRIT]

in AM, use **neat**

● **tidi·ly** /taɪdɪli/ ADV 整洁地 ❑ *...books and magazines stacked tidily on shelves.* …整齐地摆放在架子上的书和杂志。 ● **tidi·ness** N-UNCOUNT 整洁 ❑ *Employees are expected to maintain a high standard of tidiness in their dress and appearance.* 雇员必须在着装和仪表上保持高度整洁。 3 V-T When you **tidy** a place such as a room or closet, you make it neat by putting things in their proper places. 整理（房间、橱柜等） [mainly BRIT]

in AM, use **clean, neaten**

Word Web tide

The **gravitational** pull of the **moon** on the earth's **oceans** causes **tides**. **High tides** occur twice a day at any given point on the earth's surface. During the next six hours, the water gradually **ebbs** away, producing a **low tide**. In some places tidal energy powers hydroelectric **plants**. Riptides are responsible for the deaths of hundreds of swimmers each year. However, a riptide is not really a tide. It is a strong ocean **current**.

▶ **tidy away** PHRASAL VERB When you **tidy** something **away**, you put it in something else so that it is not in the way. 把…收拾起来 [mainly BRIT]

in AM, use **put away**

▶ **tidy up** PHRASAL VERB When you **tidy up** or **tidy** a place **up**, you put things back in their proper places so that everything is neat. 收拾 [mainly BRIT]

in AM, use **clean up, neaten up**

tie ♦♦◇ /taɪ/ (**ties, tying, tied**) 1 V-T If you **tie** two things **together** or **tie** them, you fasten them together with a knot. 系；把…打成结 ❑ *He tied the ends of the plastic bag together.* 他把塑料袋的两头系在一起。 2 V-T If you **tie** something or someone in a particular place or position, you put them there and fasten them using rope or string. (用绳索) 捆绑；固定 ❑ *He had tied the dog to one of the trees near the canal.* 他已经把狗拴在运河边的一棵树上。 3 V-T If you **tie** a piece of string or cloth around something or **tie** something **with** a piece of string or cloth, you put the piece of string or cloth around it and fasten the ends together. (用绳子或布条) 捆 ❑ *She tied her scarf over her head.* 她把围巾围在头上。 ❑ *Roll the meat and tie it with string.* 把肉卷起来用线捆好。 4 V-T If you **tie** a knot or bow **in** something or **tie** something **in** a knot or bow, you fasten the ends together. 打 (结)；把…打成 (结) ❑ *He took a short length of rope and swiftly tied a slip knot.* 他拿了一小段绳子迅速打了个活结。 ❑ *She tied a knot in a cherry stem.* 她在樱桃梗上打了个结。 5 V-T/V-I When you **tie** something or when something **ties**, you close or fasten it using a bow or knot. 打结系牢 ❑ *He pulled on his heavy suede shoes and tied the laces.* 他穿上那双厚重的绒面革皮鞋并系好鞋带。 ❑ *...a long white thing around his neck that tied in front in a floppy bow.* …一条围着他脖子、前面打了个蓬松蝴蝶结的白色长东西。 6 N-COUNT A **tie** is a long narrow piece of cloth that is worn around the neck under a shirt collar and tied in a knot at the front. Ties are worn mainly by men. 领带 ❑ *Jason had taken off his jacket and loosened his tie.* 贾森已经脱下夹克，松开了领带。 7 V-T If one thing **is tied to** another or two things **are tied**, the two things have a close connection or link. 使…紧密联系 [usu passive] ❑ *Their cancers are not so clearly tied to radiation exposure.* 他们的癌症与接触辐射并没有太明显的联系。 8 V-T If you **are tied to** a particular place or situation, you are forced to accept it and cannot change it. 束缚 [usu passive] ❑ *They had children and were consequently tied to the school vacations.* 他们有几个孩子，因此被学校假期束缚住了。 9 N-COUNT **Ties** are the connections you have with people or a place. 联系 [usu pl, oft N prep] ❑ *Quebec has always had particularly close ties to France.* 魁北克一直都与法国有着特别密切的联系。 10 V-RECIP If two people **tie** in a competition or game or if they **tie with** each other, they have the same number of points or the same degree of success. (在竞赛或比赛中) 打成平局 ❑ *Ronan Rafferty had tied with Frank Nobilo.* 罗南·拉弗蒂与诺比罗打成了平局。 ● N-COUNT **Tie** is also a noun. 平局 ❑ *The first game ended in a tie.* 第一场比赛以平局结束。 11 N-COUNT In sports, a **tie** is a match that is part of a competition. The losers leave the competition and the winners go on to the next round. 淘汰赛 [BRIT] ❑ *They'll meet the winners of the first round tie.* 他们将迎战第一轮淘汰赛的胜出者。 12 **your hands are tied** → see **hand**
→ see **clothing**

▶ **tie down** PHRASAL VERB A person or thing that **ties** you **down** restricts your freedom in some way. 限制 ❑ *We'd agreed from the beginning not to tie each other down.* 我们从一开始就约定不限制对方。 ❑ *He didn't want a family because he didn't want to be tied down.* 他不想要家庭，因为他不想受限制。

▶ **tie up** 1 PHRASAL VERB When you **tie** something **up**, you fasten string or rope around it so that it is firm or secure. 系牢；扎紧 ❑ *He tied up the bag and took it outside.* 他把袋子扎紧，然后拿到了外面。 2 PHRASAL VERB If someone **ties** another person **up**, they fasten ropes around them so that they cannot move or escape. 捆绑 (某人) ❑ *Masked robbers broke in, tied him up, and made off with $8,000.* 蒙面劫匪破门而入，将他绑了起来，并抢走了$8000。 3 PHRASAL VERB If you **tie** an animal **up**, you fasten it to a fixed object with a piece of rope so that it cannot run away. 拴住 (动物) ❑ *Would you go and tie your horse up please?* 请你去拴住你的马好吗？

tier /tɪər/ (**tiers**) 1 N-COUNT A **tier** is a row or layer of something that has other layers above or below it. 排；层 ❑ *...the auditorium with the tiers of seats around and above it.* …周围和上方有一排排座位的礼堂。 ● COMB IN ADJ **Tier** is also a combining form. (用于构成合成形容词) …排的；…层的 ❑ *...a three-tier wedding cake.* …一个3层的结婚蛋糕。 2 N-COUNT A **tier** is a level in an organization or system. (组织或系统中的) 级 ❑ *Islanders have campaigned for the abolition of one of the three tiers of municipal power on the island.* 岛民们已经发起了运动，要废除该岛3级市政权力中的1级。 ● COMB IN ADJ **Tier** is also a combining form. (用于构成合成形容词) …级的 ❑ *...the possibility of a two-tier system of universities.* …大学双轨制的可能性。

ti·ger /taɪgər/ (**tigers**) N-COUNT A **tiger** is a large fierce animal belonging to the cat family. Tigers are orange with black stripes. 老虎

tight ♦◇◇ /taɪt/ (**tighter, tightest**) 1 ADJ **Tight** clothes or shoes are small and fit closely to your body. (衣服或鞋子) 紧贴的 ❑ *She walked off the plane in a miniskirt and tight top.* 她穿着迷你裙和紧身上衣走下飞机。 ● **tight·ly** ADV 紧贴地 [ADV with v] ❑ *He buttoned his collar tightly round his thick neck.* 他把衣领紧紧地扣在自己的粗脖子上。 2 ADV If you hold someone or something **tight**, you hold them firmly and securely. 紧紧地 [ADV after v] ❑ *She just fell into my arms, clutching me tight for a moment.* 她就倒在了我的怀里，一时间紧紧地抓着我。 ❑ *Just hold tight to my hand and follow along.* 只要紧紧地抓住我的手，跟着我。 ● ADJ **Tight** is also an adjective. 紧的 ❑ *As he and Hannah passed through the gate he kept a tight hold of her arm.* 他和汉娜经过大门时，他紧抓着她的胳膊。 ● **tight·ly** ADV 紧紧地 [ADV after v] ❑ *She climbed back into bed and wrapped her arms tightly around her body.* 她爬回床上，用双臂紧紧地抱住自己的身体。 3 ADJ **Tight** controls or rules are very strict. 严格的 ❑ *The measures include tight control of media coverage.* 这些措施包括对媒体报道的严格管理。 ❑ *The government was prepared to keep a tight hold on public sector pay rises.* 政府准备保持对公共部门薪资增长的严格控制。 ● **tight·ly** ADV 严格地 ❑ *The internal media was tightly controlled by the government during the war.* 国内媒体在战争期间被政府严格地控制着。 4 ADV Something that is shut **tight** is shut very firmly. 紧紧地 (关闭) ❑ *The baby lay on his back with his eyes closed tight.* 这个婴儿平躺着，两眼紧闭。 ❑ *I keep the flour and sugar in individual jars, sealed tight with their glass lids.* 我把面粉和糖分别放在罐子里，并用玻璃盖密封。 ● **tight·ly** ADV 紧紧地 ❑ *Pemberton frowned and closed his eyes tightly.* 彭伯顿皱着眉头，紧紧地闭上双眼。 5 ADJ Skin, cloth, or string that is **tight** is stretched or pulled so that it is smooth or straight. (皮肤、布或绳线等) 绷紧的 ❑ *My skin feels tight and lacking in moisture.* 我的皮肤感觉紧巴巴的，缺乏水分。 ● **tight·ly** ADV 绷紧地 [ADV with v] ❑ *Her sallow skin was drawn tightly across the bones of her face.* 她蜡黄的皮肤紧紧地绷在脸骨上。 6 ADJ **Tight** is used to describe a group of things or an amount of something that is closely packed together. 密集的；装得满满的 ❑ *She curled up in a tight ball, with her knees tucked up at her chin.* 她蜷缩成紧紧的一团，膝盖顶着下巴。 ● ADV **Tight** is also an adverb. 紧密地 ❑ *The people sleep on army cots packed tight, end to end.* 这些人睡在首尾紧挨着的行军床上。 ● **tight·ly** ADV 紧密地 ❑ *Many animals travel in tightly packed trucks and are deprived of food, water and rest.* 许多动物被装在拥挤不堪的卡车里运送，没吃没喝，也不能休息。 7 ADJ If a part of your body is **tight**, it feels uncomfortable and painful, for example, because you are sick, anxious, or angry. (身体部位因生病、焦虑或生气) 僵硬的 ❑ *It is better to stretch the tight muscles first.* 最好先舒展一下僵硬的肌肉。 8 ADJ A **tight** group of people is one whose members are closely linked by beliefs, feelings, or interests. 关系紧密的 ❑ *We're a tight group, so we do keep in touch.* 我们是一个亲密的团体，所以我们的确保持着联系。 9 ADJ A **tight** bend or corner is one that changes direction very quickly so that you cannot see very far around it. (弯道或拐角) 急转的 ❑ *They collided on a tight bend and both cars were extensively damaged.* 他们在一个急转弯处相撞，两辆车都严重受损。 10 ADJ A **tight** schedule or budget allows very little time or money for unexpected events or expenses. (日程或预算) 紧的 ❑ *It's difficult to cram everything into a tight schedule.* 难以把所有的事都排进一个紧张的日程。 ❑ *Emma is on a tight budget for clothes.* 埃玛手头很紧，没钱买衣服。 11 → see also **airtight** 12 to **keep a tight rein on** → see **rein** 13 to **sit tight** → see **sit**

Word Partnership *tight* 的常用搭配：

N.	tight **dress/jeans/pants** 1
	tight **grip**, tight **hold** 2
	tight **control**, tight **security** 3
	tight **fit**, tight **squeeze** 6
	tight **lips**, tight **muscles**, tight **smile** 7
ADV.	**extremely** tight, **a little** tight, **so** tight, **too** tight, **very** tight 1 – 10
ADJ.	**closed** tight, **locked** tight, **shut** tight 4
	tight **knit** 8

tight·en /taɪtᵊn/ (**tightens, tightening, tightened**) **1** V-T/V-I If you **tighten** your grip on something, or if your grip **tightens**, you hold the thing more firmly or securely. 抓紧 ❑ *Luke answered by tightening his grip on her shoulder.* 卢克回应了，紧紧抓住她的肩膀。 ❑ *Her arms tightened about his neck in gratitude.* 她的双臂紧紧搂住他的脖子，充满感激。 **2** V-T/V-I If you **tighten** a rope or chain, or if it **tightens**, it is stretched or pulled hard until it is straight. 使(绳或链)拉紧；拉紧 ❑ *The anchorman flung his whole weight back, tightening the rope.* 这位排尾压阵队员用尽全部的力气往后拽，把绳子拉紧。 **3** V-T/V-I If a government or organization **tightens** its grip on a group of people or an activity, or if its grip **tightens**, it begins to have more control over it. 对…加强控制；加强控制 ❑ *He knows he has considerable support for his plans to tighten his grip on the machinery of central government.* 他知道他那些对中央政府加强控制的计划拥有相当多的支持。 **4** V-T When you **tighten** a screw, nut, or other device, you turn it or move it so that it is more firmly in place or holds something more firmly. 拧紧(螺丝、螺帽等) ❑ *I used my thumbnail to tighten the screw on my lamp.* 我用拇指指甲拧紧了灯上的螺丝。 ● PHRASAL VERB **Tighten up** means the same as **tighten**. 拧紧(同 **tighten**) ❑ *It's important to tighten up the wheels properly, otherwise they vibrate loose and fall off.* 把车轮拧紧很重要，否则它们会振动而松脱。 **5** V-I If a part of your body **tightens**, the muscles in it become tense and stiff, for example, because you are angry or afraid. (身体部位因生气或害怕) 变得僵硬 ❑ *Sofia's throat had tightened and she couldn't speak.* 索菲娅的喉咙哽住了，说不了话。 **6** V-T If someone in authority **tightens** a rule, a policy, or a system, they make it stricter or more efficient. 使(规定、政策或制度) 更严格；使更有效 ❑ *The United States plans to tighten the economic sanctions currently in place.* 美国计划使现行的经济制裁更加严厉。 ● PHRASAL VERB **Tighten up** means the same as **tighten**. 使…更严格 ❑ *Until this week, every attempt to tighten up the law had failed.* 到本周为止，一切严格执法的努力都失败了。 **7** **to tighten** your **belt** → see **belt**

tights /taɪts/ **1** N-PLURAL **Tights** are a piece of clothing, worn by women and girls. They are usually made of nylon and cover the hips, legs, and feet. (女用) 紧身裤袜 [also "a pair of" N] [mainly BRIT]

in AM, also use **pantyhose**

2 N-PLURAL **Tights** are a piece of tight clothing, usually worn by dancers, acrobats, or people in exercise classes, that cover the hips and each leg. (舞蹈、杂技演员或健身者穿的) 紧身衣 [also "a pair of" N]

★ **tile** /taɪl/ (**tiles**) **1** N-VAR **Tiles** are flat, square pieces of baked clay, carpet, cork, or other substance, which are fixed as a covering onto a floor or wall. (贴墙或铺地用的) 瓷砖；地毯；地板 ❑ *Amy's shoes squeaked on the tiles as she walked down the corridor.* 埃米走过走廊时，鞋子在地砖上吱吱作响。 **2** N-VAR **Tiles** are flat pieces of baked clay which are used for covering roofs. (覆盖屋顶的) 瓦片 ❑ *...a fine building, with a neat little porch and ornamental tiles on the roof.* …一幢精致建筑，有个整洁的小门廊，屋顶上盖着装饰瓦。

till ♦◇◇ /tɪl/ (**tills**) **1** PREP In spoken English and informal written English, **till** is often used instead of **until**. 直到…为止 ❑ *They had to wait till Monday to phone the bank.* 他们不得不等到星期一才打电话给银行。 ● CONJ **Till** is also a conjunction. 直到…为止 ❑ *I hadn't left home till I was nineteen.* 我直到19岁才离开家门。 **2** N-COUNT A **till** is the drawer of a cash register, where the money is kept. (收银机中的) 钱柜 [AM] ❑ *He checked the register. There was money in the till.* 他检查了收银机。钱柜里有钱。 **3** N-COUNT In a store or other place of business, a **till** is a counter or cash register where money is kept, and where customers pay for what they have bought. (商店等的) 收银台；收银机 [BRIT]

in AM, use **cash register**

Note that you only use **until** or **till** when you are talking about time. You do not use these words to talk about place or position. Instead, you should use **as far as** or **up to**. ❑ *Then you'll be riding with us as far as the village?...We walked up to where his bicycle was.*

★ **tilt** /tɪlt/ (**tilts, tilting, tilted**) **1** V-T/V-I If you **tilt** an object or if it **tilts**, it moves into a sloping position with one end or side higher than the other. 使倾斜；倾斜 ❑ *She tilted the mirror and began to comb her hair.* 她把镜子斜放，开始梳头。 ❑ *Leonard tilted his chair back on two legs and stretched his long body.* 伦纳德把他的椅子向后斜着撑在两条脚上，然后舒展他修长的身躯。 ❑ *The boat instantly tilted when he got in, filled with water, and then sank.* 当他进去时船立即倾斜，灌入水，然后沉没了。 **2** V-T If you **tilt** part of your body, usually your head, you move it slightly upward or to one side. 使(常指头部) 侧倾；使微仰 ❑ *Mari tilted her head back so that she could look at him.* 玛丽把头向后仰了仰，以便能看着他。 ❑ *His wife tilted his head to the side and inspected the wound.* 他的妻子把他的头侧向一边，然后检查伤口。 ❑ *She tilted her face and kissed me quickly on the chin.* 她歪着脸迅速在我的下巴上亲了一下。 ● N-COUNT **Tilt** is also a noun. 倾斜 ❑ *He opened the rear door for me with an apologetic tilt of his head.* 他歉疚地歪着头为我打开了后门。 **3** N-COUNT The **tilt** of something is the fact that it tilts or slopes, or the angle at which it tilts or slopes. 倾斜；倾斜度 ❑ *...calculations based on our understanding of the tilt of the Earth's axis.* …基于我们对地球轴线倾斜度的理解的计算。 **4** V-I If a person or thing **tilts toward** a particular opinion or if something **tilts** them **toward** it, they change slightly so that they become more in agreement with that opinion or position. 倾向 ❑ *Political will might finally tilt toward some sort of national health plan.* 政治意愿可能最终会倾向于某种全民医疗方案。

tim·ber /tɪmbər/ N-UNCOUNT **Timber** is wood that is used for building houses and making furniture. You can also refer to trees that are grown for this purpose as **timber**. 木材 ❑ *These Michigan woods have been exploited for timber since the Great Fire of Chicago.* 自芝加哥大火灾之后，密歇根的森林一直被砍伐作木材用。 → see **forest**

time

❶ NOUN USES
❷ VERB USES
❸ PHRASES: GROUP 1
❹ PHRASES: GROUP 2
❺ PHRASES: GROUP 3

❶ **time** ♦♦♦ /taɪm/ (**times**) **1** N-UNCOUNT **Time** is what we measure in minutes, hours, days, and years. 时间 ❑ *...a two-week period of time.* …一段为期两周的时间。 ❑ *Time passed, and still Ma did not appear.* 时间一点点过去，可是玛还没有出现。 **2** N-SING You use **time** to ask or talk about a specific point in the day, which can be stated in hours and minutes and is shown on clocks. 钟点 ❑ *"What time is it?"—"Eight o'clock."* "几点了？" —— "8点。" ❑ *He asked me the time.* 他问了我时间。 **3** N-COUNT The **time** when something happens is the point in the day when it happens or is supposed to happen. (某事发生的) 时间 ❑ *Departure times are 08:15 from Baltimore, and 10:15 from Newark.* 从巴尔的摩的出发时间是08:15，从纽瓦克的出发时间是10:15。 **4** N-UNCOUNT You use **time** to refer to the system of expressing time and counting hours that is used in a particular part of the world. (世界某时区的) 时间 ❑ *The incident happened just after ten o'clock local time.* 该事件发生在当地时间刚过10点。 **5** N-UNCOUNT You use **time** to refer to the period that you spend

t

Word Web **time**

Before railroads began to move people rapidly over long distances, **time zones** were not an issue. The government of each community (or sometimes a local clockmaker) would set the "official" **time** and the citizens would adjust their **clocks** and **watches** accordingly. However, as long-distance railroad travel became more common in the 1800s, these disparate times created havoc with railroad schedules. In the 1840s, England, Scotland, and Wales adopted a "railway standard time," replacing several "local time" systems. In 1878, Sir Sanford Fleming, a Canadian railroad official, proposed the system of worldwide time zones that is still in use today.

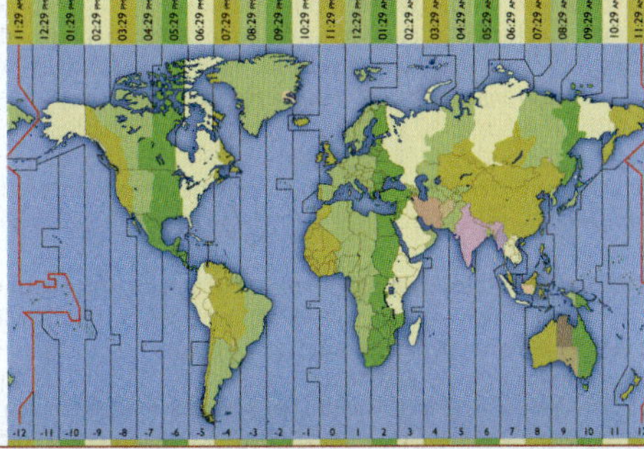

doing something or when something has been happening. 时间(段) [also "a" N] ❑ *Adam spent a lot of time in his grandfather's office.* 亚当在他祖父的办公室里度过了很多时间。 ❑ *He wouldn't have the time or money to take care of me.* 他不会有时间，也没有钱来照看我。 ❑ *Listen to me, I haven't got much time.* 听我说，我没有多少时间。 ❑ *It's obvious that you need more time to think.* 显然你需要更多的时间来思考。 **6** N-SING If you say that something has been happening for **a time**, you mean that it has been happening for a fairly long period of time. (相当长的) 一段时间 ❑ *He was also for a time an art critic.* 他曾有相当长的一段时间是一位艺术评论家。 ❑ *He stayed for quite a time.* 他呆了很长一段时间。 **7** N-COUNT You use **time** to refer to a period of time or a point in time, when you are describing what is happening then. For example, if something happened **at** a particular **time**, that is when it happened. If it happens **at all times**, it always happens. (某事发生的) 时期; 时刻 ❑ *We were in the same college, which was male-only at that time.* 我们当时在同一所学院，那时还是男子学院。 ❑ *By this time he was thirty.* 到这时他30岁了。 ❑ *It was a time of terrible uncertainty.* 那是一段非常不确定的时期。 **8** N-COUNT You use **time** or **times** to talk about a particular period in history or in your life. (历史上或一生中的特殊) 时期 ❑ *They were hard times and his parents had been struggling to raise their family.* 那是困难时期，他的父母一直挣扎着养家糊口。 ❑ *We'll be alone together, just like old times.* 我们会单独在一起，就像过去一样。 **9** N-PLURAL You can use **the times** to refer to the present time and to modern fashions, tastes, and developments. For example, if you say that someone **keeps up with the times**, you mean they are fashionable or aware of modern developments. If you say they are **behind the times**, you mean they are unfashionable or not aware of them. 时代潮流 ❑ *This approach is now seriously out of step with the times.* 这种方法如今与时代潮流严重脱节。 **10** N-COUNT When you describe the **time** that you had on a particular occasion or during a particular part of your life, you are describing the sort of experience that you had then. (经历的) 一段时光 ❑ *Sarah and I had a great time while the kids were away.* 萨拉和我在孩子们不在时度过了一段美好的时光。 **11** N-SING Your **time** is the amount of time that you have to live, or to do a particular thing. 生命期; 期限 ❑ *Now that Martin has begun to suffer the effects of AIDS, he says his time is running out.* 马丁已开始遭受艾滋病的折磨，他说自己时日不多了。 **12** N-UNCOUNT If you say it is **time for** something, **time to** do something, or **time** you did something, you mean that this thing ought to happen or be done now. (该做某事的) 合适时候 ❑ *Opinion polls indicated a feeling among the public that it was time for a change.* 民意测验表明，公众觉得该是改变的时候了。 ❑ *It was time for him to go to work.* 该是他去上班的时间了。 **13** N-COUNT When you talk about a **time** when something happens, you are referring to a specific occasion when it happens. 次 ❑ *Every time she travels on the bus, it's delayed by at least three hours.* 每次她坐公共汽车出行时，至少要耽搁3个小时。 **14** N-COUNT You use **time** after numbers to say how often something happens. (表示频率) 次 ❑ *It was her job to make tea three times a day.* 她的任务是每天泡3次茶。 **15** N-PLURAL You use **times** after numbers when comparing one thing to another and saying, for example, how much bigger, smaller, better, or worse it is. 倍 ❑ *Its profits are rising four times faster than the average company.* 其利润正以快于一般公司4倍的速度增长。 **16** CONJ You use **times** to show multiplication. Three times five is 3x5. 乘 ❑ *Four times six is 24.* 4乘以6等于24。 **17** N-COUNT Someone's **time** in a race is the amount of time it takes them to finish the race. 时间 (完成赛跑所用的) ❑ *He was over a second faster than his previous best time.* 他比自己以前的最好成绩快了一秒多。

→ see Word Web: time

T

❷ time ♦♦♦ /taɪm/ (**times, timing, timed**) **1** V-T If you **time** something **for** a particular hour, day, or period, you plan or decide to do it or cause it to happen at this time. 为…安排时间 ❑ *He timed the election to coincide with new measures to boost the economy.* 他把选举的时间安排在振兴经济的新措施出台的时候。 ❑ *I timed our visit for March 7.* 我把我们访问时间定在3月7日。 **2** V-T If you **time** an action or activity, you measure how long someone takes to do it or how long it lasts. 测量…所花的时间 ❑ *A radar gun timed the speed of the baseball.* 一支雷达枪测出了棒球的速度。 **3** → see also **timing**

❸ time ♦♦♦ /taɪm/ (**times**) **1** PHRASE If you say it is **about time** that something was done, you are saying in an emphatic way that it should happen or be done now, and really should have happened or been done sooner. 该是…的时候了 [EMPHASIS] ❑ *It's about time a few movie makers with original ideas were given a chance.* 该是给一些有创意的电影制作者一个机会的时候了。 **2** PHRASE If you do something **ahead of time**, you do it before a particular event or before you need to, in order to be well prepared. 提前 ❑ *Find out ahead of time what regulations apply to your situation.* 提前弄清楚什么规定适合你的情况。 **3** PHRASE If someone is **ahead of** their **time** or **before** their **time**, they have new ideas a long time before other people start to think in the same way. 思想先进 ❑ *He was indeed ahead of his time in employing women, ex-convicts, and the handicapped.* 他的确思想先进，雇用了女性、刑满释放犯和残疾人。 **4** PHRASE If something happens or is done **all the time**, it happens or is done continually. 一直 ❑ *We can't be together all the time.* 我们不能一直在一起。 **5** PHRASE You say **at a time** after an amount to say how many things or how much of something is involved in one action, place, or group. 一次 ❑ *Beat in the eggs, one at a time.* 把这些鸡蛋打破，一次一个。 **6** PHRASE If something could happen **at any time**, it is possible that it will happen very soon, though nobody can predict exactly when. 在任何时候 ❑ *Conditions are still very tense and the fighting could escalate at any time.* 形势依然很紧张，战斗随时可能升级。 **7** PHRASE If you say that something was the case **at one time**, you mean that it was the case during a particular period in the past. 曾经 ❑ *At one time 400 men, women and children lived in the village.* 曾一度有400个男人、女人和儿童住在这个村子。 **8** PHRASE If two or more things exist, happen, or are true **at the same time**, they exist, happen, or are true together although they seem to contradict each other. 同时 ❑ *I was afraid of her, but at the same time I really liked her.* 我害怕她，但同时我又实在喜欢她。 **9** PHRASE **At the same time** is used to introduce a statement that slightly changes or contradicts the previous statement. 然而 ❑ *I don't think I set out to come up with a different sound for each CD. At the same time, I do have a sense of what is right for the moment.* 我想我一开始就没打算为每张CD设计不同的声音。然而，我确实能感觉到目前什么是对的。 **10** PHRASE You use **at times** to say that something happens or is true on some occasions or at some moments. 有时 ❑ *The debate was highly emotional at times.* 辩论有时非常情绪化。 **11** PHRASE If you say that something will be the case **for all time**, you mean that it will always be the case. 永远 ❑ *He promised to love her for all time.* 他许诺要永远爱她。 **12** PHRASE If something is the case or will happen **for the time being**, it is the case or will happen now, but only until something else becomes possible or happens. 目前 ❑ *For the time being, however, immunotherapy is still in its experimental stages.* 然而，目前免疫疗法还处于试验阶段。 **13** PHRASE If you do something **from time to time**, you do it occasionally but not regularly. 不时地 ❑ *Her daughters visited him from time to time when he was bedridden.* 他卧床不起时她的女儿们不时地来探望他。

❹ time ♦♦♦ /taɪm/ (**times**) **1** PHRASE If you say that something is the case **half the time** you mean that it often is the case. 经常 [INFORMAL] ❑ *Half the time, I don't have the slightest idea what he's talking about.* 我常常对他所谈论的没有一丁点儿概念。 **2** PHRASE If you are **in time for** a particular event, you are not too late for it. 及时 ❑ *I arrived just in time for my flight to Hawaii.* 我正好及时赶上飞往夏威夷的航班。 **3** PHRASE If you say that something will happen **in time** or **given time**, you mean that it will happen eventually, when a lot of time has passed. 迟早 ❑ *He would sort out his own problems, in time.* 他迟早会解决自己的问题。 **4** PHRASE If you are playing, singing, or dancing **in time** with a piece of music, you are following the rhythm and speed of the music correctly. If you are **out of time** with it, you are not following the rhythm and speed of the music correctly. (演奏、唱歌或跳舞) 合拍/不合拍 ❑ *Her body swayed in time with the music.* 她的身体随着音乐节拍摇摆。 **5** PHRASE If you say that something will happen, for example, **in a week's time** or **in two years' time**, you mean that it will happen a week from now or two years from now. 在 (几分钟、几天、几周等) 之后 ❑ *Presidential elections are due to be held in ten days' time.* 总统竞选将在10天后如期举行。 **6** PHRASE If you arrive somewhere **in good time**, you arrive early so that there is time to spare before a particular event. 提早 ❑ *We got there in good time for the opening ceremony.* 我们提早到了那儿参加开幕式。 **7** PHRASE If something happens **in no time** or **in next to no time**, it happens almost immediately or very quickly. 立刻; 很快 ❑ *He's going to be just fine. At his age he'll heal in no time.* 他会好起来的。以他的年纪，会很快痊愈。 **8** PHRASE If you **keep time** when playing or singing music, you follow or play the beat, without going too fast or too slowly. 按节拍 ❑ *As he sang he kept time on a small drum.* 他唱歌时和着一面小鼓的节拍。 **9** PHRASE When you talk about how well a watch or clock **keeps time**, you are talking about how accurately it measures time. (钟表) 走得准

❑ *Some pulsars keep time better than the Earth's most accurate clocks.* 有些脉冲星表比地球上最精确的时钟还准。 **10** PHRASE If you **make time for** a particular activity or person, you arrange to have some free time so that you can do the activity or spend time with the person. 腾出时间 ❑ *Before leaving the city, be sure to make time for a shopping trip.* 在离开这个城市前，一定要腾出时间购一次物。 **11** PHRASE If you say that you **made good time** on a trip, you mean it did not take you very long compared to the length of time you expected it to take. (旅途耗时) 比预计时间少 ❑ *They had left early in the morning, on quiet roads, and made good time.* 他们一大早就出发了，路上行人稀少，所以旅途花的时间比预期要少。 **12** PHRASE If someone **is making up for lost time**, they are doing something actively and with enthusiasm because they have not had the opportunity to do it before or when they were younger. 弥补失去的时光 ❑ *Five years older than the majority of officers of his same rank, he was determined to make up for lost time.* 他比同级别的大多数官员大5岁，他决心弥补自己失去的时光。 **13** PHRASE If you say that something happens or is the case **nine times out of ten** or **ninety-nine times out of a hundred**, you mean that it happens on nearly every occasion or is almost always the case. 十之八九 ❑ *When they want something, nine times out of ten they get it.* 当他们想要什么时，十之八九都能得到。

❺ **time** ♦♦♦ /taɪm/ (**times**)
➪ **Please look at meaning 13 to see if the expression you are looking for is shown under another headword.** **1** PHRASE If you say that someone or something is, for example, the best writer **of all time**, or the most successful movie **of all time**, you mean that they are the best or most successful that there has ever been. 有史以来的 ❑ *"Monopoly" is one of the best-selling games of all time.* "大富翁"是有史以来最畅销的游戏之一。 **2** PHRASE If you are **on time**, you are not late. 准时 ❑ *Don't worry, she'll be on time.* 别担心，她会准时的。 **3** PHRASE If you say that it is **only a matter of time** or **only a question of time** before something happens, you mean that it cannot be avoided and will definitely happen at some future date. 只是时间问题 ❑ *It now seems only a matter of time before they resign.* 如今看来，他们辞职只是个时间问题。 **4** PHRASE If you do something to **pass the time**, you do it because you have some time available and not because you really want to do it. 消磨时间 ❑ *Without particular interest and just to pass the time, I read a story.* 没有特别的兴趣，只是为了消磨时间，我才读了一篇故事。 **5** PHRASE If you say that something will **take time**, you mean that it will take a long time. 需要很长时间 ❑ *Change will come, but it will take time.* 变化会有的，但需要很长时间。 **6** PHRASE If you **take** your **time** doing something, you do it slowly and do not hurry. 慢慢地；不着急 ❑ *"Take your time," Ted told him. "I'm in no hurry."* "慢慢来，"泰德告诉他说，"我不着急。" **7** PHRASE If a child can **tell the time**, they are able to find out what the time is by looking at a clock or watch. 认时间 ❑ *My four-year-old daughter cannot quite tell the time.* 我4岁的女儿不太会看时间。 **8** PHRASE If something happens **time after time**, it happens in a similar way on many occasions. 屡次 ❑ *Burns had escaped from jail time after time.* 伯恩斯屡次越狱逃跑。 **9** PHRASE If you say that **time flies**, you mean that it seems to pass very quickly. 时光飞逝 ❑ *Time flies when you're having fun.* 当你开心的时候，时光飞逝。 **10** PHRASE If you say there is **no time to lose** or **no time to be lost**, you mean you must hurry as fast as you can to do something. 必须尽快 ❑ *He rushed home, realizing there was no time to lose.* 他意识到时间紧迫，急忙赶回家去。 **11** PHRASE If you say that **time will tell** whether something is true or correct, you mean that it will not be known until some time in the future whether it is true or correct. 时间会证明 ❑ *Only time will tell whether Broughton's optimism is justified.* 只有时间能证明布劳顿的乐观有没有道理。 **12** PHRASE If you **waste no time in** doing something, you take the opportunity to do it immediately or quickly. 立即 ❑ *Tom wasted no time in telling me why he had come.* 汤姆立即告诉我他来的原因。 **13** **time and again** → see **again**

> You do not say "one time a year" or "two times a year"; you say **once a year** or **twice a year**. You also do not say "two times as much"; you say **twice as much**.

time-consuming also **time consuming** ADJ If something is **time-consuming**, it takes a lot of time. 耗时的 ❑ *It's just very time consuming to get such a large quantity of data.* 要收集这么多的数据就是非常耗时。

time·less /taɪmlɪs/ ADJ If you describe something as **timeless**, you mean that it is so good or beautiful that it cannot be affected by changes in society or fashion. 永恒的；不受时间影响的 ❑ *There is a timeless quality to his best work.* 他的最佳作品堪称永恒之作。

time·line /taɪmlaɪn/ (**timelines**) also **time line** **1** N-COUNT A **timeline** is a visual representation of a sequence of events, especially historical events. (尤指历史事件) 年表 ❑ *The timeline shows important events from the Earth's creation to the present day.* 该年表列出了从地球诞生迄今的重要事件。 **2** N-COUNT A **timeline** is the length of time that a project is expected to take. 限期 [BUSINESS] ❑ *Use your deadlines to establish the timeline for your research plan.* 根据最后期限为你的研究计划设定时间表。
→ see **history**

★ **time·ly** /taɪmli/ ADJ If you describe an event as **timely**, it happens exactly at the moment when it is most useful, effective, or relevant. 适时的 [APPROVAL] ❑ *The recent outbreaks of cholera are a timely reminder that this disease is still a serious health hazard.* 最近几次爆发的霍乱是一个适时的提醒，该疾病依然是个严重的健康危害。

time out (**time outs**) also **time-out** **1** N-VAR In basketball, football, ice hockey, and some other sports, when a team calls a **time out**, they call a stop to the game for a few minutes in order to rest and discuss how they are going to play. (篮球、足球、冰球等比赛中的) 暂停 ❑ *With 22.2 seconds to go before halftime, Brown wanted to call a time-out.* 距中场休息还有22.2秒时布朗想叫一次暂停。 **2** N-UNCOUNT If you take **time out from** a job or activity, you have a break from it and do something different instead. (工作或活动中的) 暂停时间；休息 [oft N "from" n, N to-inf] ❑ *He took time out from campaigning to accompany his mother to dinner.* 他暂停竞选活动陪她母亲吃晚饭。

time·scale /taɪmskeɪl/ (**timescales**) also **time scale** N-COUNT The **timescale** of an event is the length of time during which it happens or develops. 时段 ❑ *The likelihood is that these companies now will show excellent profits on a two-year timescale.* 这些公司现在很可能会在一个两年的时段内取得丰厚的收益。

time-share (**time-shares**) also **time share** N-VAR If you have **a time-share**, you have the right to use a particular property as vacation accommodations for a specific amount of time each year. (度假住房的) 分时享用权 ❑ *Other prizes include hotel discounts and a time-share at a resort in Palm Springs.* 其他奖励包括旅馆折扣和棕泉市内一处的度假房分时享用权。

time·table /taɪmteɪbᵊl/ (**timetables**) **1** N-COUNT A **timetable** is a plan of the times when particular events will take place. 时间表 ❑ *The timetable was hopelessly optimistic.* 这个时间表过于乐观。 **2** N-COUNT A **timetable** is a list of the times when trains, boats, buses, or airplanes are supposed to arrive at or leave from a particular place. (车、船或飞机等的) 时刻表 [mainly BRIT]

> in AM, usually use **schedule**

3 N-COUNT In a school or college, a **timetable** is a list that shows the times in the week at which particular subjects are taught. You can also refer to the range of subjects that a student learns or the classes that a teacher teaches as their **timetable**. 课程表 [BRIT]

> in AM, usually use **class schedule**

★ **tim·id** /tɪmɪd/ ADJ **Timid** people are shy, nervous, and lack courage or confidence in themselves. 羞怯的 ❑ *A timid child, Isabella had learned obedience at an early age.* 伊莎贝拉是一个羞怯的孩子，很小的时候就已经学会了顺从。 ● **ti·mid·ity** /tɪmɪdɪti/ N-UNCOUNT 羞怯 ❑ *She doesn't ridicule my timidity.* 她不会嘲笑我的羞怯。 ● **tim·id·ly** ADV 羞怯地 ❑ *The little boy stepped forward timidly and shook Leo's hand.* 这个小男孩羞怯地走上前去握了握里奥的手。

tim·ing /taɪmɪŋ/ **1** N-UNCOUNT **Timing** is the skill or action of judging the right moment in a situation or activity at which to do something. 时机掌握 ❑ *His photo is a wonderful happy moment caught with perfect timing.* 他的照片抓拍到的是开心一刻，时机掌握得很好。 **2** N-UNCOUNT **Timing** is used to refer to the time at which something happens or is planned to happen, or to the length of time that something takes. 时间安排 ❑ *They had concerns about the timing of the report.* 他们对这个报道的时间安排有担忧。 **3** → see also **time**

tin /tɪn/ (**tins**) **1** N-UNCOUNT **Tin** is a soft silvery-white metal. 锡 ❑ *...a factory that turns scrap metal into tin cans.* …一个将废金属制成马口铁罐的工厂。 **2** N-COUNT A **tin** is a metal container with a lid in which things such as cookies, cakes, or tobacco can be kept. 金属罐 ❑ *Store the cookies in an airtight tin.* 把这些饼干存放在一个密封的金属罐里。 **3** N-COUNT You can use **tin** to refer to a tin and its contents, or to the contents only. 罐；罐中之物 ❑ *...a tin of paint.* …一罐油漆。

4 N-COUNT A **tin** is a metal container which is filled with food and sealed in order to preserve the food for long periods of time. 罐头 [mainly BRIT] **5** N-COUNT You can use **tin** to refer to a tin and its contents, or to the contents only. 罐头; 罐中之物 [mainly BRIT]

in AM, usually use **can**

6 N-COUNT A baking **tin** is a metal container used for baking things such as cakes and bread in an oven. (蛋糕、面包等的) 烤模 [BRIT]

in AM, use **pan**

7 **to have a tin ear** → see **ear**

→ see **can, pan**

▲**tinge** /tɪndʒ/ (**tinges**) N-COUNT A **tinge** of a color, feeling, or quality is a small amount of it. 些许 (颜色、感情或性质) ❑ *His skin had an unhealthy grayish tinge.* 他的皮肤有些许不健康的淡灰色。

tinged /tɪndʒd/ **1** ADJ If something is **tinged with** a particular color, it has a small amount of that color in it. 略带 (某种颜色) 的 ❑ *His dark hair was just tinged with gray.* 他的黑发只是略带灰色。 **2** ADJ If something is **tinged with** a particular feeling or quality, it has or shows a small amount of that feeling or quality. 略带 (某种感情或性质) 的 ❑ *Her homecoming was tinged with sadness.* 她的返乡略带伤感。

▲**tin·gle** /tɪŋᵊl/ (**tingles, tingling, tingled**) **1** V-I When a part of your body **tingles**, you have a slight stinging feeling there. 略感刺痛 ❑ *The backs of his thighs tingled.* 他的两条大腿后侧略感刺痛。 ●**tin·gling** N-UNCOUNT 略微的刺痛感 ❑ *Its effects on the nervous system include weakness, paralysis, and tingling in the hands and feet.* 它对神经系统的影响包括虚弱、麻痹和手脚的略微刺痛感。 **2** V-I If you **tingle with** a feeling such as excitement, you feel it very strongly. 强烈感到 ❑ *She tingled with excitement.* 她感到非常兴奋。 ● N-COUNT **Tingle** is also a noun. 强烈的感受 ❑ *I felt a sudden tingle of excitement.* 我突然感到了一种强烈的兴奋。

tink·er /tɪŋkər/ (**tinkers, tinkering, tinkered**) V-I If you **tinker with** something, you make some small changes to it, in an attempt to improve it or repair it. 小修改 ❑ *Instead of the country admitting its error, it just tinkered with the problem.* 该国未承认自己的错误，只是对这个问题稍作修改。

tinned /tɪnd/ ADJ **Tinned** food is food that has been preserved by being sealed in a tin. 罐装的 [mainly BRIT]

in AM, usually use **canned**

tint /tɪnt/ (**tints, tinting, tinted**) **1** N-COUNT A **tint** is a small amount of color. 少许色彩 ❑ *Its large leaves often show a delicate purple tint.* 它的大叶子常现出一种柔和的淡紫色。 **2** V-T If something **is tinted**, it has a small amount of a particular color or dye in it. 使略有…色彩; 给…淡淡地染色 [usu passive] ❑ *Eyebrows can be tinted with the same dye.* 眉毛可淡淡地染成相同的颜色。

tiny ♦◇◇ /taɪni/ (**tinier, tiniest**) ADJ Something or someone that is **tiny** is extremely small. 极小的 ❑ *The living room is tiny.* 这间起居室极小。 ❑ *Though she was tiny, she had a very loud voice.* 虽然她个头很小，嗓门却很大。

tip ♦◇◇ /tɪp/ (**tips, tipping, tipped**) **1** N-COUNT The **tip** of something long and narrow is the end of it. 尖端 ❑ *The sleeves covered his hands to the tips of his fingers.* 衣袖遮住了他的手，一直盖到他的手指尖。 **2** V-T/V-I If you **tip** an object or part of your body or if it **tips**, it moves into a sloping position with one end or side higher than the other. 倾 ❑ *He leaned away from her, and she had to tip her head back to see him.* 他侧身避开她，她只得向后侧过头来看他。 **3** V-T If you **tip** something somewhere, you pour it there. 倾倒 ❑ *Tip the vegetables into a bowl.* 把这些蔬菜倒进一个碗里。 **4** V-T If you **tip** someone such as a waiter in a restaurant, you give them some money in order to thank them for their services. 给…小费 ❑ *We usually tip 18-20%.* 我们通常付18-20%的小费。 **5** N-COUNT If you give a **tip** to someone such as a waiter in a restaurant, you give them some money to thank them for their services. 小费 ❑ *I gave the barber a tip.* 我给了理发师小费。 **6** N-COUNT A **tip** is a useful piece of advice. 建议 ❑ *It shows how to prepare a resume, and gives tips on applying for jobs.* 它说明了如何准备一份简历，并提了一些有关求职的建议。 **7** N-COUNT A **tip** is the same as a **dump** or a **garbage dump**. 垃圾场 [BRIT] **8** PHRASE If you say that a problem is **the tip of the iceberg**, you mean that it is one small part of a much larger problem. (问题的) 冰山一角 ❑ *Unless we're all a lot more careful, the people who have died so far will be just the tip of the iceberg.* 除非我们大家都更加小心，否则迄今为止已经死去的人数将只是冰山一角。 **9** PHRASE If something **tips the scales** or **tips the balance**, it gives someone a slight advantage. 使稍占优势 ❑ *Today's slightly shorter race could well help to tip the scales in her favor.* 今日稍短程的比赛将很有可能使她稍占优势。

→ see **restaurant**

▸ **tip off** PHRASAL VERB If someone **tips** you **off**, they give you information about something that has happened or is going to happen. 向…通风报信 ❑ *Greg tipped police off about a drunk driver.* 格雷格向警方报告了一名酒后驾车司机。

▸ **tip over** PHRASAL VERB If you **tip** something **over** or if it **tips over**, it falls over or turns over. 翻倒 ❑ *He tipped the table over in front of him.* 他打翻了他前面的那张桌子。 ❑ *Don't tip over that glass.* 别打翻那个玻璃杯。

Word Partnership *tip* 的常用搭配：

N.	tip **of your finger/nose** **1**
	tip **your hat** **2**
ADJ.	**northern/southern** tip **of an island** **1**
	anonymous tip **6**

tip-off (**tip-offs**) N-COUNT A **tip-off** is a piece of information or a warning that you give to someone, often privately or secretly. 密告 ❑ *The man was arrested at his home after a tip-off to police from a member of the public.* 在警方收到一名平民的举报之后，这名男子在家被捕了。

tip·toe /tɪptoʊ/ (**tiptoes, tiptoeing, tiptoed**) **1** V-I If you **tiptoe** somewhere, you walk there very quietly without putting your heels on the floor when you walk. 踮着脚尖走 ❑ *She slipped out of bed and tiptoed to the window.* 她溜下床，踮起脚尖走向窗户。 **2** PHRASE If you do something **on tiptoe** or **on tiptoes**, you do it standing or walking on the front part of your foot, without putting your heels on the ground. 踮着脚 ❑ *She leaned her bike against the stone wall and stood on tiptoe to peer over it.* 她把自行车靠在石墙上，然后踮起脚从墙头望过去。

ti·rade /taɪreɪd/ (**tirades**) N-COUNT A **tirade** is a long angry speech in which someone criticizes a person or thing. 愤怒申讨 ❑ *She launched into a tirade against the policies that ruined her business.* 她针对毁掉她生意的那些政策发起了一番愤怒声讨。

tire /taɪər/ (**tires, tiring, tired**) **1** V-T/V-I If something **tires** you or you **tire**, you feel that you have used a lot of energy and you want to rest or sleep. 使感到疲倦; 感到疲倦 ❑ *If driving tires you, take the train.* 如果开车使你感到疲劳，那就坐火车吧。 **2** V-I If you **tire of** something, you no longer wish to do it, because you have become bored of it or unhappy with it. 厌倦 [no passive] ❑ *He felt he would never tire of listening to her stories.* 他觉得自己永远也不会厌倦听她的故事。 **3** N-COUNT A **tire** is a thick piece of rubber which is fitted onto the wheels of vehicles such as cars, buses, and bicycles. 轮胎

in BRIT, use **tyre**

→ see **bicycle**

tired ♦◇◇ /taɪərd/ **1** ADJ If you are **tired**, you feel that you want to rest or sleep. 疲倦的 ❑ *Michael is tired and he has to rest after his long trip.* 迈克尔累了，他在长途旅行之后不得不休息。 ●**tired·ness** N-UNCOUNT 疲倦 ❑ *He had to cancel some engagements because of tiredness.* 他由于疲劳不得不取消一些约会。 **2** ADJ You can describe a part of your body as **tired** if it looks or feels as if you need to rest it or to sleep. (身体部位) 疲劳的 ❑ *Cucumber is good for soothing tired eyes.* 黄瓜对缓解眼睛疲劳很有效。 **3** ADJ If you are **tired of** something, you do not want it to continue because you are bored of it or unhappy with it. 厌烦的 [v-link ADJ "of" n/-ing] ❑ *I am tired of all the speculation.* 我厌烦了所有这些猜测。

→ see **sleep**

Word Partnership *tired* 的常用搭配：

V.	**look** tired **1**
	feel tired **1** **2**
	be tired, **get** tired, **grow** tired **1** – **3**
ADJ.	tired **and hungry** **1**
	sick and tired **of** *something* **3**
ADV.	**a little** tired, **(just) too** tired, **very** tired **1** – **3**

tire·less /taɪərlɪs/ ADJ If you describe someone or their efforts as **tireless**, you approve of the fact that they put a lot of hard work into something, and refuse to give up or take a rest. 孜孜不倦的 [APPROVAL] ❑ *...Mother Teresa's tireless efforts to help the poor.* …特雷莎修女为帮助穷人所作的孜孜不倦的努力。 ●**tire·less·ly** ADV 孜孜不倦地 [ADV with v] ❑ *He worked tirelessly for the cause of health and safety.* 他为健康和安全事业孜孜不倦地工作。

T

▲ **tire·some** /taɪərsəm/ ADJ If you describe someone or something as **tiresome**, you mean that you find them irritating or boring. 讨厌的；无聊的 ❑ *...the tiresome old lady next door.* ···隔壁的那个讨厌的老妇人。

tir·ing /taɪərɪŋ/ ADJ If you describe something as **tiring**, you mean that it makes you tired so that you want to rest or sleep. 累人的 ❑ *It had been a long and tiring day.* 那是漫长而又累人的一天。

tis·sue ♦◇◇ /tɪʃu/ (**tissues**) **1** N-UNCOUNT In animals and plants, **tissue** consists of cells that are similar to each other in appearance and that have the same function. (动植物的) 组织 [also N in pl] ❑ *As we age, we lose muscle tissue.* 随着年纪的增大，我们会失去一些肌肉组织。 **2** N-UNCOUNT **Tissue paper** is thin paper that is used for wrapping things that are easily damaged, such as objects made of glass or china. (包装易碎物品的) 薄棉纸 ❑ *...a small package wrapped in tissue paper.* ···一个小包裹，用薄棉纸包着。 **3** N-COUNT A **tissue** is a piece of thin soft paper that you use to blow your nose. 面巾纸 ❑ *...a box of tissues.* ···一盒面巾纸。
→ see **cancer**

tit·il·late /tɪtᵊleɪt/ (**titillates, titillating, titillated**) V-T If something **titillates** someone, it pleases and excites them, especially in a sexual way. 挑逗 ❑ *The pictures were not meant to titillate audiences.* 这些图片并非为了挑逗观众。 ● **tit·il·lat·ing** ADJ 挑逗性的 ❑ *...deliberately titillating lyrics.* ···刻意挑逗的歌词。

ti·tle ♦♦◇ /taɪtᵊl/ (**titles, titling, titled**) **1** N-COUNT The **title** of a book, play, movie, or piece of music is its name. (书、戏剧、电影或乐曲的) 标题 ❑ *"Patience and Sarah" was first published in 1969 under the title "A Place for Us."* 《耐心与萨拉》于1969年以《我们的地方》为书名首次出版。 **2** V-T When a writer, composer, or artist **titles** a work, they give it a name. 给···加标题 ❑ *Pirandello titled his play "Six Characters in Search of an Author."* 皮兰德娄将其戏剧命名为《六个寻找作者的剧中人》。 ❑ *The single is titled "White Love."* 这支单曲名为《白色之恋》。 **3** N-COUNT Publishers and booksellers often refer to books or magazines as **titles**. (某种) 书刊 ❑ *The magazine has become the biggest publisher of new poetry, with 50 new titles a year.* 该杂志已成了最大的新诗出版商，每年出版50种杂志。 **4** N-COUNT Someone's **title** is a word such as "Mr," "Mrs," or "Doctor," that is used before their own name in order to show their status or profession. 称呼 ❑ *Please fill in your name and title.* 请填上你的名字和称呼。 **5** N-COUNT Someone's **title** is a name that describes their job or status in an organization. 职位名称 ❑ *He was given the title of assistant manager.* 他被授予经理助理的职位。 **6** N-COUNT If a person or team wins a particular **title**, they win a sports competition that is held regularly. Usually a person keeps a title until someone else defeats them. (体育比赛的) 冠军 ❑ *He became Jamaica's first Olympic gold medalist when he won the 400-meter title in 1948.* 他在1948年赢得400米赛跑冠军，成为牙买加首位奥运金牌得主。 **7** N-COUNT In Britain, and some other countries, a person's **title** is a word such as "Sir," "Lord," or "Lady" that is used in front of their name, or a phrase that is used instead of their name, and indicates that they have a high rank in society. 头衔 ❑ *Her husband was also honored with his title "Sir Denis."* 她的丈夫也被授予头衔，尊称为"丹尼斯爵士"。
→ see **graph**

to

❶ PREPOSITION AND ADVERB USES
❷ USED BEFORE THE BASE FORM OF A VERB

❶ **to** ♦♦♦

Usually pronounced /tə/ before a consonant and /tu/ before a vowel, but pronounced /tu/ when you are emphasizing it.

辅音前通常读作 /tə/，元音前通常读作 /tu/，但当重读时读作 /tu/。

In addition to the uses shown below, **to** is used in phrasal verbs such as "see to" and "come to." It is also used with some verbs that have two objects in order to introduce the second object.

1 PREP You use **to** when indicating the place that someone or something visits, moves toward, or points at. (表示方向、目的地) 向 ❑ *Two friends and I drove to Florida during spring break.* 我和两位朋友在春假期间开车去了佛罗里达州。 ❑ *She went to the window and looked out.* 她走到窗前向外望去。 **2** PREP If you go **to** an event, you go where it is taking place. 去 (参加) ❑ *We went to a party at the Kurt's house.* 我们去库尔特家参加了一个聚会。 ❑ *He came to dinner.* 他来吃晚饭。 **3** PREP If something is attached **to** something larger or fixed **to** it, the two things are joined together. 附着 ❑ *There was a piece of cloth tied to the dog's collar.* 有一条布系在狗项圈上。 **4** PREP You use **to** when indicating the position of something. For example, if something is **to** your left, it is nearer your left side than your right side. (表示方位) 在 ❑ *Hemingway's studio is to the right.* 海明威的工作室在右边。 **5** PREP When you give something **to** someone, they receive it. 给 [V n PREP n] ❑ *He picked up the knife and gave it to me.* 他捡起刀并拿给我。 **6** PREP You use **to** to indicate who or what an action or a feeling is directed toward. (表示行为或情感针对的目标) 对于 [adj/n PREP n] ❑ *Marcus has been really mean to me today.* 马库斯今天确实一直对我不友好。 ❑ *...troops loyal to the government.* ···忠于政府的军队。 **7** PREP **To** can show who is affected by something. 对 (表示受某事影响) [adj/n PREP n] ❑ *He is a witty man, and an inspiration to all of us.* 他是一个风趣的男人，对我们所有的人是一种鼓舞。 **8** PREP If you say something **to** someone, you want that person to listen and understand what you are saying. 对··· (说) ❑ *I will explain to them that I can't pay them.* 我会向他们解释说我无法付钱给他们。 **9** PREP You use **to** when showing someone's reaction to something or their feelings about a situation or event. For example, if you say that something happens **to** someone's surprise you mean that they are surprised when it happens. (表示反应或情感) 致使 ❑ *To his surprise, the bedroom door was locked.* 使他吃惊的是，卧室的门是锁着的。 **10** PREP **To** can show whose opinion is being stated. 在···看来 ❑ *It was clear to me that he respected his boss.* 在我看来，显然他尊重他的老板。 **11** PREP You use **to** when indicating what something or someone is becoming, or the state or situation that they are progressing toward. (表示状态或形势等的变化) 成为 ❑ *The shouts changed to laughter.* 叫喊声变成了笑声。 ❑ *...an old ranch house that has been converted to a nature center.* ···一幢破旧的牧场主住宅，已被改装成一个大自然中心。 **12** PREP **To** can be used as a way of introducing the person or organization you are employed by. (表示雇佣关系) 为···工作 [n PREP n] ❑ *Rickman worked as a dresser to Nigel Hawthorne.* 里克曼曾做过奈杰尔•霍索恩的服装师。 **13** PREP **To** can show a span of time. (表示时间跨度) 直到 ❑ *From 1977 to 1985 the United States gross national product grew 21 percent.* 从1977年至1985年，美国的国民生产总值增长了21%。 **14** PREP You use **to** to show two extreme examples of something. (从···) 到··· (用于举例) ["from" n PREP n] ❑ *I read everything from fiction to history.* 我从小说到历史书什么书都读。 **15** PREP If someone goes from place **to** place or from job **to** job, they go to several places, or work in several jobs, and spend only a short time in each one. (从···) 到··· (表示处所和工作的变换) ["from" n PREP n] ❑ *Larry and Andy had drifted from place to place, working at this and that.* 拉里和安迪四处漂泊，干了各种各样的活。 **16** PHRASE If someone moves **to and fro**, they move repeatedly from one place to another and back again, or from side to side. 来回地 ❑ *She stood up and began to pace to and fro.* 她站起来开始来回地踱步。 **17** PREP You use **to** when you are stating a time less than thirty minutes before an hour. For example, if it is "five **to** eight," it is five minutes before eight o'clock. (表示时间) 差···不到 [num/n PREP num] ❑ *At twenty to six I was waiting by the entrance to the station.* 6点差20分时，我在车站入口处等着。 **18** PREP You use **to** when giving ratios and rates. (表示比例) 每 ❑ *...engines that can run at 60 miles to the gallon.* ···发动机，每加仑油可行驶60英里。 **19** PREP You use **to** when indicating that two things happen at the same time. For example, if something is done **to** music, it is done at the same time as music is being played. 伴随着 ❑ *Romeo left the stage, to enthusiastic applause.* 罗密欧在热烈的掌声中离开了舞台。 **20** CONVENTION If you say **"There's nothing to it," "There's not much to it,"** or **"That's all there is to it,"** you are emphasizing how simple you think something is. (表示强调) 容易得很 [EMPHASIS] ❑ *"There is nothing to it," those I asked about it told me.* "那容易得很，"我问过的那些人告诉我说。 **21** → see also **according to** **22** → see also **too**

❷ **to** ♦♦♦

Pronounced /tə/ before a consonant and /tu/ before a vowel.

辅音前读作 /tə/，元音前读作 /tu/。

1 PREP You use **to** before the base form of a verb to form the to-infinitive. You use the to-infinitive after certain verbs, nouns, and adjectives, and after words such as "how," "which," and "where." 置于动词原形前构成不定式，该不定式结构可置于某些动词、名词和形容词以及如**how**，**which**和**where**等词之后 ❑ *The management wanted to know what I was doing there.* 管理层想知道我在那儿做什么。 ❑ *She told the family of her decision to resign.* 她告诉她家里人她要辞职的决定。 **2** PREP You use **to** before the base form of a verb to indicate the purpose or intention of an action. 用于动词原形前表示行为的目的或意图 ❑ *...using the experience of big companies to help small businesses.* …用大公司的经验来帮助小企业。 **3** PREP You use **to** before the base form of a verb when you are commenting on a statement that you are making, for example, when saying that you are being honest or brief, or that you are summing up or giving an example. 用于动词原形前表示对自己的话的评论 ❑ *I'm disappointed, to be honest.* 我很失望，说实在的。 **4** PREP You use **to** before the base form of a verb when indicating what situation follows a particular action. 用于动词原形前，表明某个动作之后的情况 ❑ *From the garden, you walk down to discover a large and beautiful lake.* 从花园往前走你会发现一个美丽的大湖。 **5** You use **to** with "too" and "enough" in expressions like **too much to** and **old enough to**; see **too** and **enough**. 用于短语**too much to**和**old enough to**中；见**too** 和 **enough**

▲ **toad** /toʊd/ (**toads**) N-COUNT A **toad** is a creature which is similar to a frog but which has a drier skin and spends less time in water. 蟾蜍

toast /toʊst/ (**toasts, toasting, toasted**) **1** N-UNCOUNT **Toast** is bread which has been cut into slices and made brown and crisp by cooking at a high temperature. 烤面包片 ❑ *...a piece of toast.* …一片烤面包片。 **2** V-T When you **toast** something such as bread, you cook it at a high temperature so that it becomes brown and crisp. 烤（面包等）❑ *Toast the bread lightly on both sides.* 把面包的两面稍微烤一下。 **3** N-COUNT When you drink a **toast to** someone or something, you drink some wine or another alcoholic drink as a symbolic gesture, in order to show your appreciation of them or to wish them success. 敬酒 ❑ *Eleanor and I drank a toast to the bride and groom.* 埃莉诺和我给新郎和新娘敬了酒。 **4** V-T When you **toast** someone or something, you drink a toast to them. 为…举杯祝酒 ❑ *We all toasted his health.* 我们大家为他的健康举杯祝酒。
→ see **cook**

toast·er /toʊstər/ (**toasters**) N-COUNT A **toaster** is a piece of electric equipment used to toast bread. 烤面包机

to·bac·co /təbækoʊ/ (**tobaccos**) **1** N-MASS **Tobacco** is dried leaves which people smoke in pipes, cigars, and cigarettes. You can also refer to pipes, cigars, and cigarettes as a whole as **tobacco**. 烟叶；烟草制品 ❑ *Try to do without tobacco and alcohol.* 尽量不要抽烟喝酒。 **2** N-UNCOUNT **Tobacco** is the plant from which tobacco is obtained. 烟草 ❑ *...Cuba's tobacco crop.* …古巴的烟草作物。

to·day ♦♦♦ /tədeɪ/ **1** ADV You use **today** to refer to this day on which you are speaking or writing. 今天 [ADV with cl] ❑ *How are you feeling today?* 你今天感觉怎么样？ ● N-UNCOUNT **Today** is also a noun. 今天 ❑ *Today is Friday, September 14th.* 今天是9月14日，星期五。 **2** → see also **yesterday, tomorrow** **3** ADV You can refer to the present period of history as **today**. 当今 ❑ *The United States is in a serious recession today.* 美国当今处于严重的经济萧条期。 ● N-UNCOUNT **Today** is also a noun. 当今 ❑ *In today's America, health care is one of the very biggest businesses.* 在当今的美国，医疗保健是几个最大的行业之一。

T

tod·dler /tɒdlər/ (**toddlers**) N-COUNT A **toddler** is a young child who has only just learned to walk or who still walks unsteadily with small, quick steps. 学步的儿童 ❑ *I had a toddler at home and two other children at school.* 我有一个刚学步的孩子在家中，另外两个孩子在学校。
→ see **age, child**

toe /toʊ/ (**toes**) **1** N-COUNT Your **toes** are the five movable parts at the end of each foot. 脚趾 ❑ *She wiggled her toes against the packed sand.* 她用脚趾拨弄着板结的沙子。 **2** PHRASE If you say that someone or something **keeps** you **on** your **toes**, you mean that they cause you to remain alert and ready for anything that might happen. 使保持警觉 ❑ *His fiery campaign rhetoric has kept opposition parties on their toes for months.* 他激烈的竞选言辞使反对党数月保持警觉。
→ see **foot**

toe·nail /toʊneɪl/ (**toenails**) N-COUNT Your **toenails** are the thin hard areas at the end of each of your toes. 脚趾甲
→ see **foot**

tof·fee /tɔfi/ (**toffees**) **1** N-VAR **Toffee** or **English toffee** is a hard brown candy made with butter and sugar. 乳脂糖 **2** N-VAR **Toffee** is a sticky candy that is very chewy. It is made by boiling sugar and butter together with water. 太妃糖 [BRIT]

in AM, use **taffy**

tof·fee ap·ple [BRIT] → see **candy apple**

to·geth·er ♦♦♦ /təgɛðər/

In addition to the uses shown below, **together** is used in phrasal verbs such as "piece together," "pull together," and "sleep together."

1 ADV If people do something **together**, they do it with each other. 在一起 ❑ *We went on long bicycle rides together.* 我们一起骑着自行车进行长途旅行。 ❑ *He and I worked together on a book.* 他和我合写了一本书。 **2** ADV If things are joined **together**, they are joined with each other so that they touch or form one whole. （物体结合）到一起 [ADV after v] ❑ *Mix the ingredients together thoroughly.* 把这些配料充分地混合到一起。 **3** ADV If things or people are situated **together**, they are in the same place and very near to each other. 紧挨着 [ADV after v] ❑ *The trees grew close together.* 这些树紧挨着一起成长。 ❑ *Ginette and I gathered our things together.* 吉内特和我把我们的东西集中到一起。 **4** ADV If a group of people are held or kept **together**, they are united with each other in some way. 一致地 [ADV after v] ❑ *He has done a lot to keep the family together.* 他做了很多努力来保持家庭和睦。 ● ADJ **Together** is also an adjective. 一致的 [v-link ADJ] ❑ *We are together in the way we're looking at this situation.* 我们对这种情况的看法一致。 **5** ADJ If two people are **together**, they are married or having a sexual relationship with each other. （因婚姻、性关系）在一起的 ❑ *We were together for five years.* 我们在一起5年了。 **6** ADV If two things happen or are done **together**, they happen or are done at the same time. 同时 [ADV after v] ❑ *Three horses crossed the finish line together.* 3匹马同时冲过终点线。 **7** ADV You use **together** when you are adding two or more amounts or things to each other in order to consider a total amount or effect. 总共 ❑ *Together we earn $60,000 per year.* 我们每年总共赚$60000。 **8** PHRASE If you say that two things **go together**, or that one thing **goes together with** another, you mean that they go well with each other or cannot be separated from each other. 相配；不可分割 ❑ *I can see that some colors go together and some don't.* 我能看出一些颜色相配，一些则不相配。 **9** PHRASE You use **together with** to mention someone or something else that is also involved in an action or situation. 加之 ❑ *Every month we'll deliver the very best articles, together with the latest fashion and beauty news.* 每个月我们都会刊登最好的文章，加之最新的时尚美容资讯。 **10** to **get** your **act together** → see **act** **11** to **put** your **heads together** → see **head** **12** **put together** → see **put**

Word Partnership *together* 的常用搭配：

V. **live** together, **play** together, **spend time** together, **work** together **1**
come together **1**–**4**
get together **1** **5**
act together, **go** together **1** **8**
bound together **2**
fit together, **glue** together, **join** together, **lump** together, **mix** together, **string** together, **stuck** together, **tied** together **2**
bring together, **keep** together, **stay** together **2** **4** **5**
gather together, **sit** together, **stand** together **3**
hold together **4**
stick together **4** **5**
ADJ. **close** together **3**

▲ **toil** /tɔɪl/ (**toils, toiling, toiled**) V-T/V-I When people **toil**, they work very hard doing unpleasant or tiring tasks. 辛苦工作 [LITERARY] ❑ *People who toiled in dim, dank factories were too exhausted to enjoy their family life.* 在阴暗潮湿的工厂里苦作的人们精疲力竭了，无法享受家庭生活。 ❑ *Workers toiled long hours.* 工人们长时间辛苦工作。 ● PHRASAL VERB **Toil away** means the same as **toil**. 辛苦工作 ❑ *He doesn't spend every minute toiling away at his desk.* 他并非每分钟都在伏案辛苦地工作。

toi·let /tɔɪlɪt/ (**toilets**) **1** N-COUNT A **toilet** is a large bowl with a seat, or a platform with a hole, which is connected to a water system and which you use when you want to get rid of urine or feces from your body. 抽水马桶 ❑ *She made Tina flush the pills down the* toilet. 她让蒂娜把药丸冲下抽水马桶。 2 N-COUNT A **toilet** is a room in a house or public building that contains a toilet. 厕所 [mainly BRIT]

in AM, usually use **bathroom, rest room**

3 PHRASE You can say that someone **goes to the toilet** to mean that they get rid of waste substances from their body, especially when you want to avoid using words that you think may offend people. 上厕所 [mainly BRIT]

in AM, usually use **go to the bathroom**

→ see **plumbing**

toi·let·ries /tɔɪlətriz/ N-PLURAL **Toiletries** are things that you use when washing or taking care of your body, for example, soap and toothpaste. 洗漱用具

to·ken /toʊkən/ (**tokens**) 1 ADJ You use **token** to describe things or actions which are small or unimportant but are meant to show particular intentions or feelings which may not be sincere. 装样子的 [ADJ n] ❑ *The announcement was welcomed as a step in the right direction, but was widely seen as a token gesture.* 这个通告受到欢迎，被认为是向正确方向迈进了一步，但也被普遍看作是装装样子。 2 N-COUNT A **token** is a round flat piece of metal or plastic that is sometimes used instead of money. 代用币 ❑ *...slot-machine tokens.* …自动贩卖机使用的代用币。 3 N-COUNT A **token** is a piece of paper or card that can be exchanged for goods, either in a particular store or as part of a special offer. 代金券; 购物卡 [BRIT]

in AM, use **coupon**

4 PHRASE You use **by the same token** to introduce a statement that you think is true for the same reasons that were given for a previous statement. 同样地 ❑ *If you give up exercise, your muscles shrink and fat increases. By the same token, if you expend more energy you will lose fat.* 如果你放弃锻炼，肌肉就会萎缩，脂肪会增多。同样地，如果你消耗较多的体能，你就会减掉脂肪。

told /toʊld/ 1 **Told** is the past tense and past participle of **tell**. **tell**的过去式和过去分词 2 PHRASE You can use **all told** to introduce or follow a summary, general statement, or total. 总共 ❑ *All told there were 104 people on the payroll.* 工资表上总共有104个人。

tol·er·able /tɒlərəbəl/ ADJ If you describe something as **tolerable**, you mean that you can bear it, even though it is unpleasant or painful. 可忍受的 ❑ *Our living conditions are tolerable, but I can't wait to leave.* 我们的居住条件还是可忍受的，但是我迫不及待地想离开。 ● **tol·er·ably** /tɒlərəbli/ ADV 可忍受地 ❑ *Their captors treated them tolerably well.* 俘获他们的人待他们勉强还过得去。

tol·er·ance /tɒlərəns/ (**tolerances**) 1 N-UNCOUNT **Tolerance** is the quality of allowing other people to say and do what they like, even if you do not agree with or approve of it. 宽容 [APPROVAL] ❑ *...his tolerance and understanding of diverse human nature.* …他对各种人性的宽容和理解。 2 N-UNCOUNT **Tolerance** is the ability to bear something painful or unpleasant. 忍耐力 ❑ *There is lowered pain tolerance, lowered resistance to infection.* 对痛苦的忍耐力和对感染的抵抗力下降了。

★ **tol·er·ant** /tɒlərənt/ 1 ADJ If you describe someone as **tolerant**, you approve of the fact that they allow other people to say and do as they like and that they are willing to accept different races, religions, and lifestyles. 宽容的 [APPROVAL] ❑ *They need to be tolerant of different points of view.* 他们需要容忍不同的观点。 2 ADJ If a plant, animal, or machine is **tolerant of** particular conditions or types of treatment, it is able to bear them without being damaged or hurt. 能耐…的 [v-link ADJ "of" n] ❑ *...plants which are more tolerant of dry conditions.* …更耐干旱的植物。

tol·er·ate /tɒləreɪt/ (**tolerates, tolerating, tolerated**) 1 V-T If you **tolerate** a situation or person, you accept them although you do not particularly like them. 容忍 ❑ *She can no longer tolerate the position that she's in.* 她再也无法容忍自己目前的处境了。 2 V-T If you can **tolerate** something bad or painful, you are able to bear it. 忍受(坏的或痛苦的事物) ❑ *The ability to tolerate pain varies from person to person.* 对疼痛的忍受力因人而异。

toll /toʊl/ (**tolls, tolling, tolled**) 1 V-T/V-I When a bell **tolls** or when someone **tolls** it, it rings slowly and repeatedly, often as a sign that someone has died. 敲(常指丧钟); (常指丧钟) 鸣响 ❑ *Church bells tolled and black flags fluttered.* 教堂丧钟敲响了，黑旗飘动着。 2 N-COUNT A **toll** is a sum of money that you have to pay in order to use a particular bridge or road. (桥梁或道路的)通行费 ❑ *You can pay a toll to drive on Pike's Peak Highway or relax and take the Pike's Peak Cog Railway.* 你可以付通行费开车上派克斯峰公路，或者放松一下，乘坐派克斯峰齿轨式火车。 3 N-COUNT A **toll** road or **toll** bridge is a road or bridge that you have to pay to use. (道路或桥梁) 收费 [N n] ❑ *Most people who drive the toll roads don't use them every day.* 大部分开车上收费公路的人不是每天都走公路。 4 N-COUNT A **toll** is a total number of deaths, accidents, or disasters that occur in a particular period of time. (死亡、事故或灾难的) 总数 [JOURNALISM] ❑ *There are fears that the casualty toll may be higher.* 人们担心伤亡人数可能会更多。 5 → see also **death toll** 6 PHRASE If you say that something **takes its toll** or **takes a heavy toll**, you mean that it has a bad effect or causes a lot of suffering. 造成坏影响 (或痛苦) ❑ *Winter takes its toll on your health.* 冬季影响你的健康。

toma·hawk /tɒməhɔk/ (**tomahawks**) N-COUNT A **tomahawk** is a small light ax that was used by Native American peoples. 又轻又小的斧头

to·ma·to /təmeɪtoʊ/ (**tomatoes**) N-VAR **Tomatoes** are soft, red fruit that you can eat raw in salads or cooked as a vegetable. 番茄; 西红柿

▲ **tomb** /tum/ (**tombs**) N-COUNT A **tomb** is a grave, especially one that is above ground and that usually has a sculpture or other decoration on it. 坟墓 (尤指地面以上的部分) ❑ *...the continuing excavation of the emperor's tomb.* …对这位皇帝的坟墓的不断挖掘。

tom·boy /tɒmbɔɪ/ (**tomboys**) N-COUNT If you say that a girl is a **tomboy**, you mean that she likes playing rough or noisy games, or doing things that were traditionally considered to be things that boys enjoy. 假小子

to·mor·row ♦♦◇ /təmɒroʊ/ (**tomorrows**) 1 ADV You use **tomorrow** to refer to the day after today. 明天 [ADV with cl] ❑ *Bye, see you tomorrow.* 再见，明天见。 ● N-UNCOUNT **Tomorrow** is also a noun. 明天 ❑ *What's on your agenda for tomorrow?* 你明天日程有什么安排？ 2 ADV You can refer to the future, especially the near future, as **tomorrow**. 在(尤指不久的) 将来 [ADV with cl] ❑ *What is education going to look like tomorrow?* 教育将来会是什么样子呢？ ● N-UNCOUNT **Tomorrow** is also a noun. 未来 [also N in pl] ❑ *...tomorrow's computer industry.* …未来的计算机业。

ton ♦◇◇ /tʌn/ (**tons**) 1 N-COUNT A **ton** is a unit of weight that is equal to 2,000 pounds. 吨 ❑ *Hundreds of tons of oil spilled into the ocean.* 数百吨石油溢出流入大海。 2 N-COUNT A **ton** is the same as a **tonne** or **metric ton**, which is 1,000 kilograms. 吨 [BRIT]

tone ♦◇◇ /toʊn/ (**tones, toning, toned**) 1 N-COUNT The **tone** of a sound is its particular quality. 音质 ❑ *Cross could hear him speaking in low tones to Sarah.* 克罗斯可以听到他在低声对萨拉说话。 2 N-COUNT Someone's **tone** is a quality in their voice which shows what they are feeling or thinking. 语气 ❑ *I still didn't like his tone of voice; he sounded angry and accusing.* 我仍然不喜欢他说话的语气：他的声音听起来好像是怒气冲冲地在指责人。 3 N-SING The **tone** of a speech or piece of writing is its style and the opinions or ideas expressed in it. 风格; (讲话或文章的) 口气 [also "in" N] ❑ *The tone of the letter was very friendly.* 这封信的语气相当友好。 4 N-SING The **tone** of a place or an event is its general atmosphere. 氛围 ❑ *There were no stores that would lower the tone of the area.* 没有一家商店会降低该地区的氛围。 5 N-UNCOUNT The **tone** of someone's body, especially their muscles, is its degree of firmness and strength. (尤指肌肉的) 结实度 ❑ *...stretch exercises that improve muscle tone.* …提高肌肉结实度的伸展锻炼。 6 V-T/V-I Something that **tones** your body makes it firm and strong. 使强健 ❑ *This movement lengthens your spine and tones the spinal nerves.* 该运动能伸展你的脊柱，强健脊髓神经。 ❑ *Try these toning exercises before you start the day.* 试着在开始新的一天前练练这些健身操。 ● PHRASAL VERB **Tone up** means the same as **tone**. 同**tone** ❑ *Exercise tones up your body.* 运动强健身体。 7 N-VAR A **tone** is one of the lighter, darker, or brighter shades of the same color. 色调 ❑ *Each brick also varies slightly in tone, texture and size.* 每块砖在色调、质地和尺寸上也略有不同。 8 N-SING A **tone** is one of the sounds that you hear when you are using a telephone, for example, the sound that tells you that a number is busy, or no longer exists. (电话的) 提示音 ❑ *I can't get a dial tone on this phone.* 我在这部电话上听不到拨号音。

→ see **drum**

▸ **tone down** 1 PHRASAL VERB If you **tone down** something that you have written or said, you make it less forceful, severe, or offensive. 使缓和 ❑ *The fiery right-wing leader toned down his militant statements after the meeting.* 这位言辞激烈的右翼领导人在会后缓和了他的好战言辞。 2 PHRASAL VERB If you **tone down** a color or a flavor, you make it less bright or strong. 使 (颜色或味道) 柔和 ❑ *He was asked to tone down the spices and garlic in his recipes.* 他被要求烹调时少放香料和大蒜。

Word Partnership *tone* 的常用搭配:

ADJ. **clear** tone, **low** tone 1
different tone 2
serious tone 2 3
V. **change your** tone 2
set a tone 4
N. tone **of voice** 2
muscle tone 5
skin tone 7

tongue /tʌŋ/ (tongues) 1 N-COUNT Your **tongue** is the soft movable part inside your mouth which you use for tasting, eating, and speaking. 舌头 ❑ *I walked over to the mirror and stuck my tongue out.* 我走到镜子前伸出舌头。 2 N-COUNT You can use **tongue** to refer to the kind of things that a person says. 话语 ❑ *She had a nasty tongue.* 她满口脏话。 3 N-COUNT A **tongue** is a language. 语言 [LITERARY] ❑ *The French feel passionately about their native tongue.* 法国人非常热爱他们的母语。 4 PHRASE A **tongue-in-cheek** remark or attitude is not serious, although it may seem to be. 无诚意的 ❑ *...a lighthearted, tongue-in-cheek approach.* …一种漫不经心、无诚意的态度。 5 to **bite** your **tongue** → see **bite**
→ see **face, taste**

Word Partnership *tongue* 的常用搭配:

V. **bite your** tongue, **stick out your** tongue 1
ADJ. **pink** tongue 1
sharp tongue 2
N. **native** tongue 3

ton·ic /tɒnɪk/ (tonics) 1 N-MASS **Tonic** or **tonic water** is a colorless carbonated drink that has a slightly bitter flavor and is often mixed with alcoholic drinks, especially gin. 奎宁水 ❑ *Keeler sipped at his gin and tonic.* 基勒小口呷着杜松子酒奎宁水。 2 N-MASS A **tonic** is a medicine that makes you feel stronger, healthier, and less tired. 补药 ❑ *People are spending twice as much on health tonics as they were five years ago.* 人们花在保健补药上的钱是5年前的两倍。

to·night ♦♦◊ /tənaɪt/ ADV **Tonight** is used to refer to the evening of today or the night that follows today. 在今晚 ❑ *I'm at home tonight.* 我今晚在家。 ❑ *Tonight he proved what a great player he was.* 今晚他证明了自己是一个多么了不起的选手。 ● N-UNCOUNT **Tonight** is also a noun. 今晚 ❑ *Tonight is the opening night of the opera.* 今晚是这部歌剧的首演之夜。

tonne /tʌn/ (tonnes) 1 N-COUNT A **tonne** is a metric unit of weight that is equal to 1,000 kilograms. 吨 [BRIT]
in AM, use **metric ton**
2 → see also **ton**

too
❶ ADDING SOMETHING OR RESPONDING
❷ INDICATING EXCESS

❶ **too** ♦♦♦ /tu/ 1 ADV You use **too** after mentioning another person, thing, or aspect that a previous statement applies to or includes. 也 [cl/group ADV] ❑ *"Nice to talk to you."—"Nice to talk to you too."* "和你交谈很高兴。"——"和你交谈我也很高兴。" ❑ *"I've got a great feeling about it."—"Me too."* "我对此感觉棒极了。"——"我也一样。" ❑ *He doesn't want to meet me. I, too, have been afraid to talk to him.* 他不想见我。我也是，我害怕跟他谈话。 ❑ *We talked to her agent. He's your agent, too, right?* 我们同她的代理人谈了。他也是你的代理人，对吧？ 2 ADV You use **too** after adding a piece of information or a comment to a statement, in order to emphasize that it is surprising or important. (用于补充信息或评论) 还 [cl/group ADV] [EMPHASIS] ❑ *We did learn to read, and quickly too.* 我们确实识了字，而且还很快。 ❑ *People usually think of it as a "boy's book," which of course it is, and a very good one too.* 人们通常把它看做一本"男孩"的书。当然如此，而且还是本很好的书。

❷ **too** ♦♦♦ /tu/
➪ **Please look at meaning 4 to see if the expression you are looking for is shown under another headword.** 1 ADV You use **too** in order to indicate that there is a greater amount or degree of something than is desirable, necessary, or acceptable. 太 ❑ *Leather jeans that are too big will make you look larger.* 皮仔裤太大会让你显得更胖。 ❑ *I'm turning up the heat, it's too cold.* 我在调高暖气，天太冷了。 ❑ *She was eating too much, drinking too much, and having too many late nights.* 她吃得太多，喝的太多，而且在太多晚上熬夜。 2 ADV You use **too** with a negative to make what you are saying sound less forceful or more polite or cautious. (与否定词连用以使语气更缓和、更礼貌或更谨慎) 非常 [with brd-neg, ADV adj] [VAGUENESS] ❑ *I wasn't too happy with what I'd written so far.* 我对自己到目前为止所写的东西还不是非常满意。 3 PHRASE You use **all too** or **only too** to emphasize that something happens to a greater extent or degree than is good or desirable. (用于强调程度之好) 极其 [EMPHASIS] ❑ *She remembered it all too well.* 她对这事记得极其清楚。 4 **none too** → see **none**

Too can be used to intensify the meaning of an adjective, an adverb, or a word like **much** or **many**. **Too**, however, also suggests an excessive or undesirable amount, often so much that a particular result does not or cannot happen. ❑ *She does wear too much makeup at times... He was too late to save her.* **Too** is not generally used to modify an adjective inside a noun group. For instance, you cannot say "the too heavy boxes" or "too expensive jewelry." There is one exception to this rule, which is when the noun group begins with **a** or **an**. Notice the word order in the following examples. ❑ *...if the products have been stored at too high a temperature... He found it too good an opportunity to miss... It was too long a drive for one day.*

took /tʊk/ **Took** is the past tense of **take**. **take**的过去式

tool ♦◊◊ /tul/ (tools) 1 N-COUNT A **tool** is any instrument or simple piece of equipment that you hold in your hands and use to do a particular kind of work. For example, spades, hammers, and knives are all tools. 工具 ❑ *I find the best tool for the purpose is a pair of shears.* 我发现达到这一目的的最好工具是一把大剪刀。 2 N-COUNT You can refer to anything that you use for a particular purpose as a particular type of **tool**. 方法 ❑ *Writing is a good tool for expressing feelings.* 写作是表达情感的一种好方法。
→ see Picture Dictionary: **tools**

Thesaurus *tool* 另参见:
N. appliance, device, instrument 1 2

T

Picture Dictionary **tools**

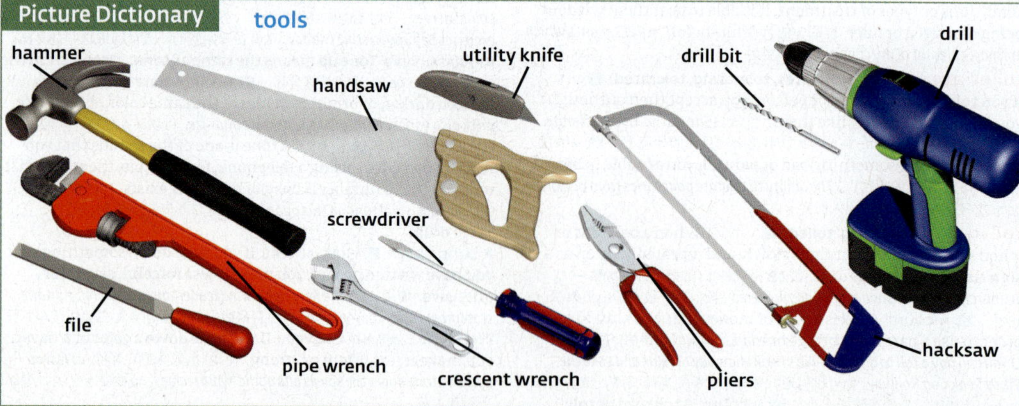

Word Partnership *tool* 的常用搭配：

N. tool **belt** 1
communication tool, **learning** tool, **management** tool, **marketing** tool, **teaching** tool 2
V. **use** a tool 1 2
ADJ. **effective** tool, **important** tool, **valuable** tool 1 2 **powerful** tool 2

tool·bar /tu̲lbɑr/ (**toolbars**) N-COUNT A **toolbar** is a narrow strip across a computer screen containing pictures, called icons, which represent different computer functions. When you want to use a particular function, you move the cursor onto its icon using a mouse and click. 工具栏 [COMPUTING]

tooth ♦◇◇ /tu̲θ/ (**teeth**) 1 N-COUNT Your **teeth** are the hard white objects in your mouth, which you use for biting and chewing. 牙齿 ❑ *She had very pretty straight teeth.* 她有非常漂亮整齐的牙齿。 2 N-PLURAL The **teeth** of something such as a comb, saw, cog, or zipper are the parts that stick out in a row on its edge. (梳子、锯子、齿轮或拉链等物的) 齿 ❑ *The front cog has 44 teeth.* 前齿轮有44个齿。 3 PHRASE If you have **a sweet tooth**, you like sweet food very much. 吃甜食的嗜好 ❑ *Add more honey if you have a sweet tooth.* 如果你嗜好甜食就多加些蜂蜜。 4 **to grit** your **teeth** → see **grit** 5 **a kick in the teeth** → see **kick**

Word Partnership *tooth* 的常用搭配：

N. tooth **decay**, tooth **enamel** 1
V. **lose** a tooth, **pull** a tooth 1

tooth·brush /tu̲θbrʌʃ/ (**toothbrushes**) N-COUNT A **toothbrush** is a small brush that you use for cleaning your teeth. 牙刷

tooth·paste /tu̲θpeɪst/ (**toothpastes**) N-MASS **Toothpaste** is a thick substance which you put on your toothbrush and use to clean your teeth. 牙膏 ❑ *Shaving supplies, toothpaste, and soap were found inside.* 在里面找到了剃须用品、牙膏和肥皂。

top
1 NOUN AND ADJECTIVE USES
2 VERB AND PHRASAL VERBS
3 PHRASES

1 **top** ♦♦♦ /tɒp/ (**tops**) 1 N-COUNT The **top** of something is its highest point or part. 顶端 ❑ *I waited at the top of the stairs.* 我在楼梯顶端上等着。 ❑ *...the picture at the top of the page.* …顶端的图片。 ● ADJ **Top** is also an adjective. 顶端的 [ADJ n] ❑ *...the top corner of the newspaper.* …报纸顶端的一角。 2 ADJ The **top** thing or layer in a series of things or layers is the highest one. 最上面的 [ADJ n] ❑ *I can't reach the top shelf.* 我够不着最上面的架子。 3 N-COUNT The **top** of something such as a bottle, jar, or tube is a cap, lid, or other device that fits or screws onto one end of it. (瓶、罐或软管等的) 盖子 ❑ *...the plastic tops from soda bottles.* …汽水瓶的塑料盖。 4 N-SING The **top** of a street, garden, bed, or table is the end of it that is farthest away from where you usually enter it or from where you are. 尽头 [BRIT]

in AM, use **end**

5 N-COUNT A **top** is a piece of clothing that you wear on the upper half of your body, for example, a blouse or shirt. 上衣 [INFORMAL] ❑ *Look at my new top.* 看看我的新上衣。 6 ADJ You can use **top** to indicate that something or someone is at the highest level of a scale or measurement. 最高的; 最快的 [ADJ n] ❑ *The vehicles have a top speed of 80 miles per hour.* 这些车的最高时速达80英里。 7 N-SING The **top** of an organization or career structure is the highest level in it. 最高层 ❑ *We started from the bottom and we had to work our way up to the top.* 我们从最底层做起，必须奋斗到最高层。 ❑ *...his dramatic rise to the top of the military hierarchy.* …他戏剧性地晋升到军队的最高层。 ● ADJ **Top** is also an adjective. 最高层的 [ADJ n] ❑ *I need to have the top people in this company pull together.* 我需要把这家公司最高层的人员团结在一起。 8 ADJ You can use **top** to describe the most important or famous people or things in a particular area of work or activity. 最重要的; 最著名的 [ADJ n] ❑ *So you want to be a top model.* 如此说来，你想成为一名顶级名模。 9 N-SING If someone is **at the top of**, for example, a table or league or is **the top of** the table or league, their performance is better than that of all the other people involved. 首位 ❑ *...the golfer at the top of the leaderboard.* …居积分榜首位的高尔夫球选手。 ● ADJ **Top** is also an adjective. 居首位的 ❑ *He was the top student in physics.* 他是物理学尖子生。 10 ADJ You can use **top** to indicate that something is the first thing you are going to do, because you consider it to be the most important. 最重要的 ❑ *Cleaning up the water supply is their top priority.* 清洗供水系统是他们的首要任务。 11 ADJ You can use **top** to indicate that someone does a particular thing more times than anyone else or that something is chosen more times than anything else. 居首位的 [ADJ n] ❑ *Jamillah Lang was Colorado's top scorer.* 贾米拉·兰是科罗拉多州得分最多的球员。

Thesaurus *top* 另参见：

N. peak, summit, zenith; (*ant.*) base, bottom 1 1
ADJ. best, finest, first-rate 1 8

2 **top** ♦♦♦ /tɒp/ (**tops, topping, topped**) V-T To **top** a list means to be mentioned or chosen more times than anyone or anything else. 位居…榜首 [JOURNALISM] ❑ *It was the first time in years that a Japanese manufacturer had not topped the list for imported vehicles.* 这是多年来日本厂商第一次未能位居进口汽车名单榜首。

▶ **top out** PHRASAL VERB If something such as a price **tops out at** a particular amount, that is the highest amount that it reaches. (价格等) 达到最高水平 [AM] ❑ *The stock topped out at more than $25.* 股票达到了最高价，超过$25。 ❑ *Last Friday was a warm day, topping out at 85 degrees.* 上周五天气很暖和，最高气温达85华氏度。

▶ **top up** PHRASAL VERB If you **top** something **up**, you make it full again when part of it has been used. 重新加足 [mainly BRIT] ❑ *We topped up the water tanks.* 我们重新把水箱添满了。

3 **top** ♦♦♦ /tɒp/ (**tops**) 1 PHRASE If you say that you clean or examine something **from top to bottom**, you are emphasizing that you do it completely and thoroughly. 彻底地 [EMPHASIS] ❑ *She would clean the house from top to bottom.* 她会彻底地打扫房子。 2 PHRASE You can use **from top to toe** to emphasize that the whole of someone's body is covered or dressed in a particular thing or type of clothing. 从头到脚 [mainly BRIT, EMPHASIS] ❑ *They were sensibly dressed from top to toe in rain gear.* 他们非常明智，从头到脚裹着雨具。 3 PHRASE When something **gets on top of** you, it makes you feel unhappy or depressed because it is very difficult or worrying, or because it involves more work than you can manage. 使沮丧 ❑ *Things have been getting on top of me lately.* 事情最近太多，令我很沮丧。 4 PHRASE If you **are on top of** or **get on top of** something that you are doing, you are dealing with it successfully. 成功处理 ❑ *...the government's inability to get on top of the situation.* …政府无力处理这种局面。 5 PHRASE If you say something **off the top of** your **head**, you say it without thinking about it much before you speak, especially because you do not have enough time. 不假思索地 ❑ *It was the best I could think of off the top of my head.* 这是我能马上想出的最好办法。 6 PHRASE If one thing is **on top** of another, it is placed over it or on its highest part. 在上面 ❑ *He was sound asleep on top of the covers.* 他在床单上睡得很香。 7 PHRASE You can use **on top** or **on top of** to indicate that a particular problem exists in addition to a number of other problems. 另外 ❑ *A stepfamily faces all the problems that a normal family has, with a set of additional problems on top.* 再婚家庭会面临正常家庭的所有问题，另外还有一系列其他问题。 8 PHRASE You say that someone is **on top** when they have reached the most important position in an organization or business. 处于显要职位 ❑ *In such a fast-changing business, it's hard to stay on top.* 在一个变化如此迅速的行业里，要保持显要地位很难。 9 PHRASE If you say that you feel **on top of the world**, you are emphasizing that you feel extremely happy and healthy. 极其幸福 [EMPHASIS] ❑ *Two months before she gave birth to Jason, she left work feeling on top of the world.* 在生下贾森的两个月前，她辞去了工作，感到极其幸福。 10 PHRASE If someone pays **top dollar** for something, they pay the highest possible price for it. 最高价格 [V PHR, PHR n] [INFORMAL] ❑ *People will always pay top dollar for something exclusive.* 人们总愿意为奢侈品付最高价。 11 PHRASE If one thing is **over the top** of another, it is placed over it so that it is completely covering it. 盖上 ❑ *I placed a sheet of plastic over the top of the container.* 我在容器的上面盖了一层塑料纸。 12 PHRASE You describe something as **over the top** when you think that it is exaggerated, and therefore unacceptable. 夸张的 [mainly BRIT, INFORMAL] ❑ *The special effects are a bit over the top but I enjoyed it.* 特技效果有点夸张，不过我很欣赏。 13 PHRASE If you say something **at the top of** your **voice**, you say it very loudly. 声嘶力竭地 ❑ *"Stephen, come back!" shouted Marcia at the top of her voice.* "斯蒂芬，回来！" 马西娅声嘶力竭地喊道。

t

top-end ADJ **Top-end** products are expensive and of extremely high quality. 价高质优的 [BUSINESS] ❑ *...top-end camcorders.* …价高质优的便携式摄像机。

top·ic /tɒpɪk/ (**topics**) N-COUNT A **topic** is a particular subject that you discuss, study, or write about. 话题 ❑ *The weather is a constant topic of conversation in Alaska.* 天气在阿拉斯加是一个永恒的交谈话题。

▲ **topi·cal** /tɒpɪkəl/ ADJ **Topical** is used to describe something that concerns or relates to events that are happening at the present time. 有关时事的 ❑ *The newscast covers topical events and entertainment.* 该新闻广播涉及时事和娱乐。

top·less /tɒplɪs/ ADJ If a woman is **topless**, she does not wear anything to cover her breasts. 袒胸的 ❑ *I wouldn't sunbathe topless if I thought I might offend anyone.* 如果我知道可能冒犯任何人，我就不会袒胸沐日光浴。

▲ **top·ple** /tɒpəl/ (**topples, toppling, toppled**) 1 V-T/V-I If someone or something **topples** somewhere or if you **topple** them, they become unsteady or unstable and fall over. 倒下 ❑ *He just released his hold and toppled slowly backwards.* 他就松手，慢慢地向后倒下了。 ● PHRASAL VERB **Topple over** means the same as **topple.** 同**topple** ❑ *The tree is so badly damaged they are worried it might topple over.* 这棵树损伤非常严重以至于他们担心它会倒下。 2 V-T To **topple** a government or leader, especially one that is not elected by the people, means to cause them to lose power. 推翻 [JOURNALISM] ❑ *...the revolution which toppled the regime.* …推翻了该政权的革命。

top se·cret ADJ **Top secret** information or activity is intended to be kept completely secret, for example, in order to prevent a country's enemies from finding out about it. 绝密的 ❑ *The top secret documents had to do with the most advanced military equipment.* 这些绝密文件涉及最先进的军事装备。

torch /tɔrtʃ/ (**torches**) 1 N-COUNT A **torch** is a long stick with burning material at one end, used to provide light or to set things on fire. 火把 ❑ *The shepherd followed, carrying a torch to light his way.* 牧羊人跟在后面，举着火把把路照亮。 2 N-COUNT A **torch** is a device that produces a hot flame and is used for tasks such as cutting or joining pieces of metal. 吹管 ❑ *The gang worked for up to ten hours with acetylene torches to open the vault.* 这帮强盗为了打开金库，用乙炔吹管干了长达10个小时。 3 N-COUNT A **torch** is a small electric light which is powered by batteries and which you can carry in your hand. 手电筒 [BRIT]

in AM, use **flashlight**

tore /tɔr/ **Tore** is the past tense of **tear**. **tear**的过去式

▲ **tor·ment** (**torments, tormenting, tormented**)

The noun is pronounced /tɔrmɛnt/. The verb is pronounced /tɔrmɛnt/.

名词读作 /tɔrmɛnt/，动词读作 /tɔrmɛnt/。

1 N-UNCOUNT **Torment** is extreme suffering, usually mental suffering. (常指精神上的) 极度痛苦 ❑ *After years of turmoil and torment, she is finally at peace.* 经历多年的动荡与痛苦后，她终于安心下来了。 2 N-COUNT A **torment** is something that causes extreme suffering, usually mental suffering. 烦恼事 ❑ *Sooner or later most writers end up making books about the torments of being a writer.* 迟早大多数作家最终都会写书诉说当一名作家的苦恼。 3 V-T If something **torments** you, it causes you extreme mental suffering. (精神上) 折磨 ❑ *At times the memories returned to torment her.* 有时这些记忆会又来折磨她。

torn /tɔrn/ 1 **Torn** is the past participle of **tear**. **tear**的过去分词 2 ADJ If you are **torn between** two or more things, you cannot decide which to choose, and so you feel anxious or troubled. 犹豫的 ❑ *Robb is torn between becoming a doctor and a career in athletics.* 罗布在成为医生和从事体育运动之间犹豫不决。

▲ **tor·na·do** /tɔrneɪdoʊ/ (**tornadoes** or **tornados**) N-COUNT A **tornado** is a violent wind storm consisting of a tall column of air which spins around very fast and causes a lot of damage. 龙卷风

tor·pe·do /tɔrpidoʊ/ (**torpedoes, torpedoing, torpedoed**) 1 N-COUNT A **torpedo** is a bomb that is shaped like a tube and that travels under water. 鱼雷 2 V-T If a ship **is torpedoed**, it is hit, and usually sunk, by a torpedo or torpedoes. (用鱼雷) 击中 [usu passive] ❑ *More than a thousand people died when the Lusitania was torpedoed.* 卢西塔尼亚号被鱼雷击沉，一千多人丧生。

▲ **tor·rent** /tɔrənt/ (**torrents**) 1 N-COUNT A **torrent** is a lot of water falling or flowing rapidly or violently. 急流 ❑ *Torrents of water gushed into the reservoir.* 急流涌进了水库。 2 N-COUNT A **torrent of** abuse or questions is a lot of abuse or questions directed continuously at someone. (漫骂或问题的) 迸发 ❑ *He turned around and directed a torrent of abuse at me.* 他转过身对我破口大骂了一通。

tor·ren·tial /tɔrɛnʃəl/ ADJ **Torrential** rain pours down very rapidly and in great quantities. (雨水) 倾盆的 ❑ *The storms and torrential rain caused traffic chaos across the country.* 暴风雨和倾盆大雨造成了全国的交通混乱。

tor·so /tɔrsoʊ/ (**torsos**) N-COUNT Your **torso** is the main part of your body, and does not include your head, arms, and legs. 躯干 [FORMAL] ❑ *The man had the bulky upper torso of a weightlifter.* 这名男子有着举重运动员的粗壮身躯。

▲ **tor·toise** /tɔrtəs/ (**tortoises**) N-COUNT A **tortoise** is a slow-moving animal with a shell into which it can pull its head and legs for protection. 龟

tor·tu·ous /tɔrtʃuəs/ 1 ADJ A **tortuous** road is full of bends and twists. 弯弯曲曲的 ❑ *The only road access is a tortuous mountain route.* 惟一的通路是一条弯弯曲曲的山路。 2 ADJ A **tortuous** process or piece of writing is very long and complicated. 冗长复杂的 ❑ *...these long and tortuous negotiations aimed at ending the conflict.* …这些漫长曲折的谈判旨在结束冲突。

tor·ture ♦◇◇ /tɔrtʃər/ (**tortures, torturing, tortured**) 1 V-T If someone **is tortured**, another person deliberately causes them terrible pain over a period of time, in order to punish them or to make them reveal information. 拷打；拷问 ❑ *Despite being tortured, she proclaimed her innocence.* 尽管受到拷打，她仍声称自己是清白的。 ● N-VAR **Torture** is also a noun. 拷打；拷问 ❑ *...alleged cases of torture and murder by the security forces.* …安全部队涉嫌严刑拷打与谋杀的案子。 2 V-T To **torture** someone means to cause them to suffer mental pain or anxiety. (精神上) 折磨 ❑ *He would not torture her further by trying to argue with her.* 他不会通过和她争吵而进一步折磨她。

toss /tɔs/ (**tosses, tossing, tossed**) 1 V-T If you **toss** something somewhere, you throw it there lightly, often in a careless way. 扔 ❑ *Just toss it in the trash.* 把它扔进垃圾桶就可以了。 2 V-T If you **toss** your head or **toss** your hair, you move your head backward, quickly and suddenly, often as a way of expressing an emotion such as anger or contempt. 甩 (表达愤怒、蔑视等情感) ❑ *"I'm sure I don't know." Deb tossed her head.* "我确实不知道。"德布甩头说道。 ● N-COUNT **Toss** is also a noun. 后甩 ❑ *With a toss of his head and a few hard gulps, Bob finished the last of his beer.* 鲍勃仰头咕咚咕咚几大口喝完了剩下的啤酒。 3 V-T In sports and informal situations, if you decide something by **tossing** a coin, you spin a coin into the air and guess which side of the coin will face upward when it lands. 抛 (硬币) ❑ *We tossed a coin to decide who would go out and buy the bagels.* 我们抛硬币来决定谁出去买百吉圈。 ● N-COUNT **Toss** is also a noun. 抛硬币的方法 ❑ *It would be better to decide it on the toss of a coin.* 最好用抛硬币的方式来对此事做决定。 4 PHRASE If you **toss and turn**, you keep moving around in bed and cannot sleep, for example, because you are sick or worried. 辗转反侧 ❑ *I try to go back to sleep and toss and turn for a while.* 我努力重新入睡，辗转反侧了一会儿。

→ see **sleep**

to·tal ♦♦♦ /toʊtəl/ (**totals, totaling** or **totalling, totaled** or **totalled**) 1 N-COUNT A **total** is the number that you get when you add several numbers together or when you count how many things there are in a group. 总数 ❑ *The companies have a total of 1,776 employees.* 这些公司总共有1776名雇员。 2 ADJ The **total** number or cost of something is the number or cost that you get when you add together or count all the parts in it. 总的 [ADJ n] ❑ *They said that the total number of cows dying from BSE would be twenty thousand.* 他们说死于疯牛病的奶牛总数会有2万头。 3 PHRASE If there are a number of things **in total**, there are that number when you count or add them all together. 总共 ❑ *I was with my husband for eight years in total.* 我和我丈夫在一起总共8年。 4 V-T If several numbers or things **total** a certain figure, that figure is the total of all the numbers or all the things. 总计为 ❑ *The unit's exports will total $85 million this year.* 今年该单位的出口总计将达8500万美元。 5 V-T If someone **totals** a vehicle, they are in a serious accident and the vehicle is so badly damaged that it is not worth repairing. 彻底撞毁 (车辆) [AM, INFORMAL] ❑ *Buddy totaled his car.* 巴迪彻底撞毁了他的车。 6 ADJ You can use **total** to emphasize that something is as great in extent, degree, or amount as it possibly can be. 完全的 [EMPHASIS] ❑ *You were a total failure if you hadn't married by the time you were about twenty-three.* 如果你在二十三岁左右还没结婚，就是一个彻底的失败者。 ● **to·tal·ly** ADV 完全地 ❑ *Young people want something totally different from the old ways.* 年轻人想要完全不同于老路子的东西。

Word Partnership *total* 的常用搭配：

N. total **area**, total **population**, **sum** total 1
total **amount**, total **cost**, total **expenses**, total **sales**, total **savings**, total **value** 2

ADJ. **grand** total 1 2

to·tali·tar·ian /toʊtælɪteəriən/ ADJ A **totalitarian** political system is one in which there is only one political party which controls everything and does not allow any opposition parties. 极权主义的 [DISAPPROVAL] ❑ *...a brutal totalitarian regime.* …一个残忍的极权主义政权。

tot·ter /tɒtər/ (**totters, tottering, tottered**) V-I If someone **totters** somewhere, they walk there in an unsteady way, for example, because they are drunk. 摇摇晃晃地走 ❑ *She came tottering in in her mother's high heels.* 她穿着她妈妈的高跟鞋摇摇晃晃地走进来。

touch
❶ VERB AND NOUN USES
❷ PHRASES AND PHRASAL VERBS

❶ **touch** ♦♦◊ /tʌtʃ/ (**touches, touching, touched**) 1 V-T/V-I If you **touch** something, you put your hand onto it in order to feel it or to make contact with it. 触摸；碰 ❑ *Her tiny hands gently touched my face.* 她的小手轻轻地触摸我的脸。 ❑ *Don't touch!* 请勿触摸！ ● N-COUNT **Touch** is also a noun. 触摸；接触 ❑ *Sometimes even a light touch on the face is enough to trigger off this pain.* 有时甚至在脸上轻摸一下也足以引发这种痛苦。 2 V-RECIP If two things **are touching**, or if one thing **touches** another, or if you **touch** two things, their surfaces come into contact with each other. 相碰 ❑ *Their knees were touching.* 他们的膝盖相碰。 ❑ *A cyclist crashed when he touched wheels with another rider.* 一名骑车人同另一名骑车人车轮相碰而摔倒。 3 N-UNCOUNT Your sense of **touch** is your ability to tell what something is like when you feel it with your hands. 触觉 ❑ *The evidence suggests that our sense of touch is programmed to diminish with age.* 该证据表明我们的触觉会随着年龄的增长而逐渐变弱。 4 V-T To **touch** something means to strike it, usually quite gently. 轻击 ❑ *He scored the first time he touched the ball.* 他第一次击球就得了分。 5 V-T If something **has** not **been touched**, nobody has dealt with it or taken care of it. 处理；照管 [usu passive, with brd-neg] ❑ *When John began to restore the house in the 1960s, nothing had been touched for 40 years.* 约翰在20世纪60年代开始重修这座房子时，它已经40年没有任何照管了。 6 V-T If you say that you did not **touch** someone or something, you are emphasizing that you did not attack, harm or destroy them, especially when you have been accused of doing so. 碰(指攻击、伤害、破坏等) [with brd-neg] [EMPHASIS] ❑ *Pearce remained adamant, saying "I didn't touch him."* 皮尔斯还是毫不动摇，说："我没碰他。" 7 V-T You say that you never **touch** something or that you have not **touched** something for a long time to emphasize that you never use it, or you have not used it for a long time. 碰(指使用) [no passive, with brd-neg] [EMPHASIS] ❑ *He doesn't drink much and doesn't touch drugs.* 他酒喝得不多，而且不碰毒品。 8 V-I If you **touch on** a particular subject or problem, you mention it or write briefly about it. 触及 ❑ *The film touches on these issues, but only superficially.* 这部电影触及了这些问题，但很肤浅。 9 V-T If something **touches** you, it affects you in some way for a short time. 影响到 ❑ *...a guilt that in some sense touches everyone.* …在某种意义上影响到每个人的内疚感。 10 V-T If something that someone says or does **touches** you, it affects you emotionally, often because you see that they are suffering a lot or that they are being very kind. 感动 ❑ *It has touched me deeply to see how these people live.* 我看到这些人如何生活而深受感动。 ● **touched** ADJ 受感动的 [v-link ADJ] ❑ *I was touched to find that he regards me as engaging.* 让我感动的是，他认为我很有魅力。 11 N-COUNT A **touch** is a detail which is added to something to improve it. 点睛之笔 [supp N] ❑ *They called the event "a tribute to heroes," which was a nice touch.* 他们把这次活动称为"向英雄致敬"，这是个点睛妙笔。 12 N-SING If someone has a particular kind of **touch**, they have a particular way of doing something. 风格 ❑ *The dishes he produces all have a personal touch.* 他做的菜都具有一种个人的风格。 13 QUANT **A touch of** something is a very small amount of it. 一点 [QUANT "of" n-uncount] ❑ *She thought she just had a touch of the flu.* 她觉得她只是有一点感冒。 14 → see also **touching**

Word Partnership *touch* 的常用搭配：

ADJ. **gentle** touch, **light** touch ❶ 1
finishing touch, **nice** touch ❶ 11
personal touch, **soft** touch ❶ 12

❷ **touch** ♦♦◊ /tʌtʃ/ (**touches, touching, touched**)
➪ **Please look at meanings 6 and 7 to see if the expression you are looking for is shown under another headword.** 1 PHRASE You use **at the touch of** in expressions such as **at the touch of a button** and **at the touch of a key** to indicate that something is possible by simply touching a switch or one of the keys of a keyboard. 一按 ❑ *Staff will be able to trace calls at the touch of a button.* 员工只要一按按钮就可以追踪电话。 2 PHRASE If you get **in touch with** someone, you contact them by writing to them or telephoning them. If you are, keep, or stay **in touch with** them, you write, phone, or visit each other regularly. 联系 ❑ *I will get in touch with my lawyer about this.* 我会就此与我的律师联系。 3 PHRASE If you are **in touch with** a subject or situation, or if someone keeps you **in touch with** it, you know the latest news or information about it. If you are **out of touch with** it, you do not know the latest news or information about it. 了解/不了解 ❑ *...keeping the unemployed in touch with the job market.* …让那些没有工作的人了解就业市场。 4 PHRASE If you **lose touch with** someone, you gradually stop writing, telephoning, or visiting them. 失去联系 ❑ *In my job one tends to lose touch with friends.* 从事我这种工作的人往往会与朋友们失去联系。 5 PHRASE If you **lose touch with** something, you no longer have the latest news or information about it. 不再了解 ❑ *Their leaders have lost touch with what is happening in the country.* 他们的领导人已不再了解国内正发生的事情。 6 **the finishing touch** → see **finish** 7 **touch wood** → see **wood**

▸ **touch down** PHRASAL VERB When an aircraft **touches down**, it lands. 着陆 ❑ *The space shuttle touched down yesterday.* 这架航天飞机昨日着陆。

▸ **touch off** PHRASAL VERB If something **touches off** a situation or series of events, it causes it to start happening. 引发 ❑ *The lightning could touch off wildfires in Eastern Washington.* 闪电可能引发华盛顿东部的野火。

▸ **touch up** PHRASAL VERB If you **touch** something **up**, you improve its appearance by covering up small marks with paint or another substance. 修饰 ❑ *...editing tools to help people touch up photos.* …一些帮助人们修饰照片的编辑工具。 ❑ *The painting has yellowed but the gallery has resisted pressure to touch it up.* 那幅画已经发黄了，但该画廊顶住了要对其进行修饰的压力。

touch·ing /tʌtʃɪŋ/ 1 ADJ If something is **touching**, it causes feelings of sadness or sympathy. 感人的 ❑ *Her story is the touching tale of a wife who stood by the husband she loved.* 她的故事感人肺腑，讲一个妻子支持她深爱的丈夫的经历。 2 → see also **touch**

touch·screen /tʌtʃskrin/ (**touchscreens**) also **touch-screen** N-COUNT A **touchscreen** is a computer screen that allows the user to give commands to the computer by touching parts of the screen rather than by using a keyboard or mouse. 触摸屏 [COMPUTING] ❑ *...touchscreen voting machines.* …一些触摸屏投票机。

touch-tone ADJ A **touch-tone** telephone has numbered buttons that make different sounds when you press them. Some automatic telephone services can only be used with this kind of telephone. (电话机) 塔奇通按钮式拨号的 [ADJ n]

touchy /tʌtʃi/ (**touchier, touchiest**) ADJ If you describe someone as **touchy**, you mean that they are easily upset, offended, or irritated. 敏感的；易生气的 [DISAPPROVAL] ❑ *She is very touchy about her past.* 她对自己的过去非常敏感。

tough ♦♦◊ /tʌf/ (**tougher, toughest**) 1 ADJ A **tough** person is strong and determined, and can tolerate difficulty or suffering. 坚强的 ❑ *He built up a reputation as a tough businessman.* 他树立起了一个坚强生意人的名声。 ● **tough·ness** N-UNCOUNT 坚强 ❑ *Ms. Potter has won a reputation for toughness and determination on her way to the top.* 波特小姐在奋斗到顶层的过程中赢得了坚强和果断的名声。 2 ADJ If you describe someone as **tough**, you mean that they are rough and violent. 粗暴的 ❑ *He had shot three people dead earning himself a reputation as a tough guy.* 他已开枪打死了3个人，为自己赢得了一个硬汉

t

的名声。 **3** ADJ A **tough** place or area is considered to have a lot of crime and violence. 治安很差的 ❑ *She doesn't seem cut out for this tough neighborhood.* 她似乎不适合这个治安很差的社区。 **4** ADJ A **tough** way of life or period of time is difficult or full of suffering. 艰苦的 ❑ *She had a pretty tough childhood.* 她度过了一个非常艰苦的童年。 **5** ADJ A **tough** task or problem is difficult to do or solve. 困难的 ❑ *It was a very tough decision but we feel we made the right one.* 这是一个非常困难的决定，但我们觉得自己做出了正确的选择。 **6** ADJ **Tough** policies or actions are strict and firm. (政策或行动)强硬的 ❑ *He is known for taking a tough line on security.* 他以在安全方面采取强硬路线而闻名。 **7** ADJ A **tough** substance is strong, and difficult to break, cut, or tear. (物质) 坚硬的 ❑ *In industry, diamond can form a tough, non-corrosive coating for tools.* 在工业中，钻石可以制成工具上的一层坚硬且耐腐蚀的涂层。 **8** ADJ **Tough** meat is difficult to cut and chew. (肉) 嚼不动的 ❑ *The steak was tough and the peas were like bullets.* 牛排硬得嚼不动，豌豆就像子弹。

Word Partnership *tough* 的常用搭配:

N. tough **guy** 2
tough **conditions**, tough **going**, tough **luck**, tough **situation**, tough **time** 4
tough **choices**, tough **competition**, tough **decision**, tough **fight**, tough **job**, tough **question**, tough **sell** 5
tough **laws**, tough **policy**, tough **talk** 6
V. **get** tough 2 4
make the tough **decisions** 5
talk tough 6

tough·en /tʌfᵊn/ (**toughens, toughening, toughened**) **1** V-T If you **toughen** something or if it **toughens**, you make it stronger so that it will not break easily. 使坚硬 ❑ *Months of walking barefoot had toughened his feet.* 数月的赤脚行走已使他的双脚变得坚硬。 **2** V-T If a person, institution, or law **toughens** its policies, regulations, or punishments, it makes them firmer or stricter. 加强(政策、规章或惩罚) ❑ *Talks are under way to toughen trade restrictions.* 加强贸易限制的会谈正在进行中。 ● PHRASAL VERB **Toughen up** means the same as **toughen**. 加强(政策、规章或惩罚) ❑ *The new law toughens up penalties for those that misuse guns.* 这部新法律加强了对滥用枪支者的惩处。 **3** V-T If an experience **toughens** you, it makes you stronger and more independent in character. (经历) 使坚强 ❑ *They believe that participating in fights toughens boys and shows them how to be men.* 他们认为参与打架可以使男孩们变得坚强，并且教会他们怎样成为男子汉。 ● PHRASAL VERB **Toughen up** means the same as **toughen**. (经历) 使坚强 ❑ *He thinks boxing is good for kids, that it toughens them up.* 他认为拳击对孩子们有好处，使他们变得坚强。

tour ♦♦◊ /tʊər/ (**tours, touring, toured**) **1** N-COUNT A **tour** is an organized trip that people such as musicians, politicians, or theater companies go on to several different places, stopping to meet people or perform. 巡回访问；巡回演出 ❑ *The band is currently on a two-month tour of Europe.* 这个乐队目前正在欧洲进行为期两个月的巡回演出。 ● PHRASE When people are traveling on a tour, you can say that they are **on tour**. 进行巡回访问；进行巡回演出 ❑ *The band will be going on tour.* 这个乐队将要进行巡回演出。 **2** V-T/V-I When people such as musicians, politicians, or theater companies **tour**, they go on a tour, for example, in order to perform or to meet people. 巡回演出 ❑ *A few years ago they toured the country with a roadshow.* 几年前他们在该国巡回流动演出。 **3** N-COUNT A **tour** is a trip during which you visit several places that interest you. 旅行 ❑ *It was week five of my tour of the major cities of Europe.* 这是我在欧洲主要城市旅行的第5周。 **4** N-COUNT A **tour** is a short trip that you make around a place, for example, around a historical building, so that you can look at it. 游览 ❑ *...a guided tour.* …一次有导游带领的游览。 **5** V-T If you **tour** a place, you go on a trip or journey around it. 游览 ❑ *You can also tour the site on bicycle.* 你也可以骑自行车游览那处遗址。

Word Partnership *tour* 的常用搭配:

N. **concert** tour, **farewell** tour 1
world tour 3
tour **bus**, tour **guide**, **walking** tour 3 4
museum tour 4
V. **begin a** tour, **finish a** tour 1 3 4
take a tour 3 4

tour·ism /tʊərɪzəm/ N-UNCOUNT **Tourism** is the business of providing services for people on vacation, for example, hotels, restaurants, and trips. 旅游业 ❑ *Tourism is vital for the economy.* 旅游业对于经济至关重要。
→ see **industry**

tour·ist ♦◊◊ /tʊərɪst/ (**tourists**) N-COUNT A **tourist** is a person who is visiting a place for pleasure and interest, especially when they are on vacation. 游客 ❑ *...a tourist attraction.* …一处旅游景点。
→ see **city**

▲**tour·na·ment** ♦◊◊ /tʊərnəmənt, tɜr-/ (**tournaments**) N-COUNT A **tournament** is a sports competition in which players who win a match continue to play further matches in the competition until just one person or team is left. 锦标赛 ❑ *...the biggest golf tournament to be held in Australia.* …即将在澳大利亚举行的最大规模的高尔夫球锦标赛。

tout /taʊt/ (**touts, touting, touted**) **1** V-T If someone **touts** something, they try to sell it or convince people that it is good. 兜售；吹嘘 [DISAPPROVAL] ❑ *...slick television ads touting the candidates.* …吹嘘那些候选人的华而不实的电视广告。 **2** V-T If someone **touts** tickets, they sell them outside a sports stadium or theater, usually for more than their original value. (在体育场或剧院外)高价倒卖(票) [BRIT]

in AM, use **scalp**

3 N-COUNT A **tout** is someone who sells things such as tickets unofficially, usually at prices which are higher than the official ones. 票贩子 [BRIT]

in AM, use **scalper**

★**tow** /toʊ/ (**tows, towing, towed**) V-T If one vehicle **tows** another, it pulls it along behind it. 拖 ❑ *He had been using the vehicle to tow his work trailer..* 他一直用那辆车来拖他的活动工作室。 ❑ *They threatened to tow away my car.* 他们威胁说要拖走我的车。

to·ward ♦♦♦ /tɔrd/ also **towards**

In addition to the uses shown below, **toward** is used in phrasal verbs such as "count toward" and "lean toward."

1 PREP If you move, look, or point **toward** something or someone, you move, look, or point in their direction. 向 ❑ *They were all moving toward him down the stairs.* 他们都正朝着他走下楼梯。 ❑ *When he looked toward me, I smiled and waved.* 他朝我看时，我微笑着挥了挥手。 **2** PREP If things develop **toward** a particular situation, that situation becomes nearer in time or more likely to happen. 趋向 [PREP n/-ing] ❑ *The agreement is a major step toward peace.* 这项协议是走向和平的一大步。 **3** PREP If you have a particular attitude **toward** something or someone, you have that attitude when you think about them or deal with them. 对 ❑ *My attitude toward religion has been shaped by this man.* 我对宗教的态度受到了这个男人的影响。 **4** PREP If something happens **toward** a particular time, it happens just before that time. 接近 (时间) ❑ *There was a forecast of cooler weather toward the end of the week.* 天气预报说接近周末时天气会更凉爽。 **5** PREP If something is **toward** part of a place or thing, it is near that part. 靠近 ❑ *Gulls are nesting on a small island toward the eastern shore.* 海鸥正在靠近东海岸的一个小岛上筑巢。 **6** PREP If you give money **toward** something, you give it to help pay for that thing. (钱) 用于 ❑ *Taxes only get part of the way toward a $50 billion deficit.* 税收只会部分解决500亿美元的赤字。

tow·el /taʊəl/ (**towels, toweling** or **towelling, toweled** or **towelled**) **1** N-COUNT A **towel** is a piece of thick soft cloth that you use to dry yourself. 毛巾 ❑ *...a bath towel.* …一条浴巾。 ❑ *...a hand towel.* …一块手巾。 ❑ *...a beach towel.* …一条沙滩浴巾。 **2** V-T If you **towel** something or **towel** it dry, you dry it with a towel. 用毛巾擦干 ❑ *James came out of his bedroom, toweling his wet hair.* 詹姆斯走出他的卧室，用毛巾擦干他那湿漉漉的头发。 ❑ *I toweled myself dry.* 我用毛巾把自己擦干。 **3** PHRASE If you **throw in the towel**, you stop trying to do something because you realize that you cannot succeed. 认输 [INFORMAL] ❑ *It seemed as if the police had thrown in the towel and were abandoning the investigation.* 看起来好象警察已经认输了，并且要放弃调查。

tow·er ♦◊◊ /taʊər/ (**towers, towering, towered**) **1** N-COUNT; N-IN-NAMES A **tower** is a tall, narrow building, that either stands alone or forms part of another building such as a church or castle. 塔 ❑ *...an eleventh-century castle with 120-foot high towers.* …一座11世纪的城堡，有着120英尺高的塔楼。 **2** V-I Someone or something that **towers over** surrounding people or things is a lot taller than they are. 高出许多 ❑ *He stood up and towered over her.* 他站起来，高出她许多。 **3** N-COUNT A **tower** is a tall structure that is used for sending radio or television signals. (无线电或电视信号的) 发射塔 ❑ *Troops are still in control of the television and radio tower.* 军队仍然控制着电视和无线电的发射塔。 **4** N-COUNT A **tower** is a tall box that contains the main parts of a computer, such as the hard disk and the drives. (计算机) 机箱 [COMPUTING]

tow·er·ing /taʊərɪŋ/ **1** ADJ If you describe something such as a mountain or cliff as **towering**, you mean that it is very tall and therefore impressive. 高耸的 [ADJ n] [LITERARY] ❑ *...towering cliffs of black granite which rise straight out of the sea.* …高耸的黑色花岗岩峭壁，从海里径直升起。 **2** ADJ If you describe someone or something as **towering**, you are emphasizing that they are impressive because of their importance, skill, or intensity. 杰出的 [ADJ n] [LITERARY, EMPHASIS] ❑ *He remains a towering figure in rock and roll.* 他仍是摇滚乐界的一位杰出人物。

town ◆◆◆ /taʊn/ (**towns**) **1** N-COUNT A **town** is a place with streets and buildings, where people live and work. Towns are larger than neighborhoods and smaller than cities. In informal English, cities are sometimes called towns. 城镇 ❑ *...the northern California town of Albany.* …加利福尼亚北部的奥尔巴尼镇。 ❑ *Parking can be difficult in the town centre.* 在市中心停车可能会困难。 ● N-COUNT You can use **the town** to refer to the people of a town. 某一城镇的居民 ❑ *The town takes immense pride in recent achievements.* 镇上的居民为最近的成就感到无比自豪。 **2** N-UNCOUNT You use **town** in order to refer to the town where you live. (自己居住的) 城镇 ❑ *He admits he doesn't even know when his brother is in town.* 他承认甚至不知道他的兄弟什么时候在镇上。 **3** N-UNCOUNT You use **town** in order to refer to the central area of a town where most of the stores and offices are. 市中心 ❑ *I walked into town.* 我走进了市中心。 **4** → see also **downtown, uptown**

town hall (**town halls**) also **Town Hall** N-COUNT A **town hall** is a building or hall used for local government business, usually a building which is the main office of a town council. 市政厅

★ **tox·ic** /tɒksɪk/ ADJ A **toxic** substance is poisonous. 有毒的 ❑ *...the cost of cleaning up toxic waste.* …清除有毒废弃物的成本。 ❑ *These products are not toxic to humans.* 这些产品对人类无毒。
→ see **cancer**

toy ◆◇◇ /tɔɪ/ (**toys, toying, toyed**) N-COUNT A **toy** is an object that children play with, for example, a doll or a model car. 玩具 ❑ *He was really too old for children's toys.* 他确实过了玩孩子的玩具的年纪了。

▸ **toy with** **1** PHRASAL VERB If you **toy with** an idea, you consider it casually without making any decisions about it. 不太认真地考虑 ❑ *He toyed with the idea of going to China.* 他没有太认真地考虑去中国的这个想法。 **2** PHRASAL VERB If you **toy with** food or drink, you do not eat or drink it with any enthusiasm, but only take a bite or a little drink from time to time. 摆弄 (食物或饮料) ❑ *She had no appetite, and merely toyed with the bread and cheese.* 她没有胃口，只是拨弄着那些面包和奶酪。

trace ◆◇◇ /treɪs/ (**traces, tracing, traced**) **1** V-T If you **trace** the origin or development of something, you find out or describe how it started or developed. 追溯 ❑ *The exhibition traces the history of graphic design in America from the 19th century to the present.* 这个展览会追溯了从19世纪到现在美国平面设计的历史。 ● PHRASAL VERB **Trace back** means the same as **trace**. 追溯 ❑ *...Bronx residents who trace their families back to Dutch settlers.* …将自己的家族追溯到荷兰移民者们的布朗克斯居民。 **2** V-T If you **trace** someone or something, you find them after looking for them. 找到 ❑ *Police are anxious to trace two men seen leaving the house just before 8am.* 警察急切想找到在接近早晨8点前被人看到离开那幢房子的两名男子。 **3** V-T If you **trace** something such as a pattern or a shape, for example, with your finger or toe, you mark its outline on a surface. 勾画出 (轮廓) ❑ *I traced the course of the river on the map spread out on my briefcase.* 我在自己公文包上铺展开的地图中勾画出了这条河的流向。 **4** V-T If you **trace** a picture, you copy it by covering it with a piece of transparent paper and drawing over the lines underneath. (用透明纸盖在底样上) 描摹 ❑ *She learned to draw by tracing pictures out of old storybooks.* 她通过描摹旧故事书上的图画来学绘画。 **5** N-COUNT A **trace of** something is a very small amount of it. 少许 ❑ *Wash them in cold water to remove all traces of sand.* 用冷水清洗它们以清除所有的沙子。 **6** PHRASE If you say that someone or something **disappears without a trace**, you mean that they stop existing or stop being successful very suddenly and completely. 消失得无影无踪 ❑ *One day he left, disappeared without a trace.* 有一天他离开了，消失得无影无踪。
→ see **fossil**

Word Partnership *trace* 的常用搭配:
N. trace ***your* ancestry/origins/roots**, trace **the history of *something***, trace **the origins/roots of *something*** **1**
trace **of an accent**, trace **amount**, trace **minerals** **5**

track ◆◆◇ /træk/ (**tracks, tracking, tracked**) **1** N-COUNT A **track** is a rough, unpaved road or path. (崎岖不平的) 小路 ❑ *We set off once more, over a rough mountain track.* 我们又一次出发了，走在一条崎岖不平的山间小路上。 **2** N-COUNT A **track** is a piece of ground, often oval-shaped, that is used for races involving running, cars, bicycles, horses, or dogs called greyhounds. 跑道 ❑ *...the athletics track.* …那条运动员跑道。 **3** N-COUNT Railroad **tracks** are the rails that a train travels along. 铁轨 ❑ *A cow stood on the tracks.* 一头奶牛站在铁轨上。 **4** N-COUNT A **track** is one of the songs or pieces of music on a CD, record, or tape. (录制在CD、唱片或磁带上的) 一首歌曲; 一首乐曲 ❑ *I only like two of the ten tracks on this CD.* 我只喜欢这张CD上的10首歌曲中的2首。 **5** N-PLURAL **Tracks** are marks left in the ground by the feet of animals or people. 足迹 ❑ *The only evidence of pandas was their tracks in the snow.* 有熊猫活动的惟一证据就是它们在雪中的足迹。 **6** V-T If you **track** animals or people, you try to follow them by looking for the signs that they have left behind, for example, the marks left by their feet. 跟踪 ❑ *He thought he had better track this wolf and see where it lived.* 他认为他最好跟踪这只狼，并看看它在哪儿生活。 **7** V-T To **track** someone or something means to follow their movements by means of a special device, such as a satellite or radar. (用卫星、雷达等特殊装置) 追踪 ❑ *Our radar began tracking the jets.* 我们的雷达开始追踪那些喷气式飞机。 **8** → see also **fast track, racetrack, soundtrack** **9** PHRASE If you **keep track of** a situation or a person, you make sure that you have the newest and most accurate information about them all the time. 了解…的动向 ❑ *With eleven thousand employees, it's very difficult to keep track of them all.* 有11000名员工，很难了解他们所有人的动向。 **10** PHRASE If you **lose track of** someone or something, you no longer know where they are or what is happening. 不了解…的进展 ❑ *You become so deeply absorbed in an activity that you lose track of time.* 你是那么专注于一项活动，以致忘了时间。 **11** PHRASE If someone or something is **on track**, they are acting or progressing in a way that is likely to result in success. 步入正轨 ❑ *It may take some time to get the economy back on track.* 可能要花一些时间使经济重回正轨。 **12** PHRASE If you are **on the right track**, you are acting or progressing in a way that is likely to result in success. If you are **on the wrong track**, you are acting or progressing in a way that is likely to result in failure. 做得正确/不正确 ❑ *Guests are returning in increasing numbers – a sure sign that we are on the right track.* 回头客越来越多——一个我们做得对的确凿迹象。 **13** PHRASE If someone or something **stops** you **in** your **tracks**, or if you **stop dead in** your **tracks**, you suddenly stop moving because you are very surprised, impressed, or frightened. (因吃惊、感动或惊恐) 突然停住脚步 ❑ *This magnificent church cannot fail to stop you in your tracks.* 这座宏伟的教堂一定会让你叹为观止。 **14** PHRASE If someone or something **stops** a process or activity **in its tracks**, or if it **stops dead in its tracks**, they prevent the process or activity from continuing. 中断 ❑ *Francis felt he would like to stop this conversation in its tracks.* 弗朗西斯觉得他想中断这次谈话。 **15** **off the beaten track** → see **beaten**
→ see **fossil, transportation**

▸ **track down** PHRASAL VERB If you **track down** someone or something, you find them, or find information about them, after a difficult or long search. (经过长时间艰难搜索后) 找到 ❑ *She had spent years trying to track down her parents.* 她已经花了多年试图找到她的父母。

Word Partnership *track* 的常用搭配:
N. **dirt** track **1** **2**
track **meet**, track **team** **2**
train track **3**

track and field N-UNCOUNT **Track and field** refers to sports that are played or performed on a racetrack and a nearby field, such as running, the high jump, and the javelin. 田径运动 ❑ *...events that range from track and field to soccer, rugby and hockey.* …比赛项目包括田径、足球、橄榄球和曲棍球。

track rec·ord (**track records**) N-COUNT If you talk about the **track record** of a person, company, or product, you are referring to their past performance, achievements, or failures in it. (个人、

公司或产品的）业绩记录 ❑ *The job needs someone with a good track record in investment.* 这份工作需要一个在投资方面有良好业绩的人。

track·suit /trӕksut/ (**tracksuits**) also **track suit** N-COUNT A **tracksuit** is a loose, warm suit consisting of pants and a top which people wear to relax and to do exercise. 运动服

★ **tract** /trӕkt/ (**tracts**) 1 N-COUNT A **tract of** land is a very large area of land. 大片 [usu N "of" n] ❑ *A vast tract of land is ready for development.* 一大片土地正待开发。 2 N-COUNT A **tract** is a short article expressing a strong opinion on a religious, moral, or political subject in order to try to influence people's attitudes. 短文 ❑ *She produced a feminist tract, "Comments on Birth-Control," in 1930.* 她1930年写了一篇女性主义短文《论计划生育》。 3 N-COUNT A **tract** is a system of organs and tubes in an animal's or person's body that has a particular function, especially the function of processing a substance in the body. （体内的）道 [usu supp N] [MEDICAL] ❑ *Foods are broken down in the digestive tract.* 食物在消化道内被分解。

Word Link *tract ≈ dragging, drawing : contract, subtract, tractor*

trac·tor /trӕktər/ (**tractors**) 1 N-COUNT A **tractor** is a farm vehicle that is used to pull farm machinery. 拖拉机 2 N-COUNT A **tractor** is a short vehicle with a powerful engine and a driver's cab. It is used to pull a trailer, such as in a tractor-trailer. 牵引车头 ❑ *The truck was an 18-wheeler with a white tractor.* 这辆卡车有18轮，还有一个白色牵引车头。

→ see **barn**

tractor-trailer (**tractor-trailers**) N-COUNT A **tractor-trailer** is a large truck that is made in two separate sections, a tractor and a trailer, which are joined together by metal bars. 牵引式挂车 [AM] ❑ *Driving a tractor-trailer is not an easy job.* 驾驶一辆牵引式挂车不是一项容易的工作。

trade ♦♦♦ /tre͟ɪd/ (**trades, trading, traded**) 1 V-RECIP If someone **trades** one thing **for** another or if two people **trade** things, they agree to exchange one thing for the other thing. 互相交换 [mainly AM] ❑ *They traded land for goods and money.* 他们用土地来换取商品和金钱。 ❑ *Kids used to trade baseball cards.* 孩子们过去常互相交换棒球卡片。 ● N-COUNT **Trade** is also a noun. 交易

in BRIT, usually use **exchange**

❑ *I am willing to make a trade with you.* 我愿意和你做个交易。 2 V-RECIP If you **trade** places **with** someone or if the two of you **trade** places, you move into the other person's position or situation, and they move into yours. 交换（位置）[mainly AM] ❑ *Mike asked George to trade places with him so he could ride with Tomas.* 迈克请乔治跟他交换位置，这样他就能和托马斯同车了。 3 V-RECIP If two people or groups **trade** something such as blows, insults, or jokes, they hit each other, insult each other, or tell each other jokes. 对打；互骂；互开玩笑 [mainly AM] ❑ *Children would settle disputes by trading punches or insults in the schoolyard.* 孩子们通过在校园里打架或对骂来解决争端。 4 N-UNCOUNT **Trade** is the activity of buying, selling, or exchanging goods or services between people, companies, or countries. 贸易；买卖 [BUSINESS] ❑ *Texas has a long history of trade with Mexico.* 得克萨斯与墨西哥有着悠久的贸易史。 ❑ *...negotiations on a new international trade agreement.* …关于一个新的国际贸易协定的谈判。 5 V-I When people, companies, or countries **trade**, they buy, sell, or exchange goods or services between themselves. 做生意 [BUSINESS] ❑ *They may refuse to trade, even when offered attractive prices.* 他们有可能拒绝做生意，即便是报价很有吸引力。 ❑ *They had years of experience of trading with the West.* 他们有数年与西方做生意的经验。 ● **trad·ing** N-UNCOUNT 交易 ❑ *Trading on the stock exchange may be suspended.* 股票交易可能被暂停。 6 N-COUNT A **trade** is a particular area of business or industry. 生意；行业 [BUSINESS] ❑ *They've ruined the tourist trade for the next few years.* 他们已经毁掉了以后几年的旅游生意。 7 N-COUNT Someone's **trade** is the kind of work that they do, especially when they have been trained to do it over a period of time. 职业；手艺 [oft poss N, also "by" N] [BUSINESS] ❑ *He learned his trade as a diver in the North Sea.* 他在北海当上了潜水员。 ❑ *Alicia was a jeweler by trade.* 艾丽西亚是个珠宝商。

→ see **company, stock market**

▸ **trade down** PHRASAL VERB If someone **trades down**, they sell something such as their car or house and buy a less expensive one. 卖掉（汽车、房子等）去买较便宜的东西 ❑ *They are selling their five-bedroom house and trading down to a two-bedroom apartment.* 他们正在变卖其五居室的房子，去买一处两居室的公寓。

▸ **trade up** PHRASAL VERB If someone **trades up**, they sell something such as their car or their house and buy a more expensive one. 卖掉（汽车、房子等）去买更贵的东西 ❑ *Gas prices are discouraging small car owners from trading up to SUV's.* 汽油的价格使得小车车主不敢卖掉小车购买运动型多用途汽车。

Thesaurus *trade* 另参见：
V. barter, exchange, swap 1 5
N. business, employment, profession 6 7

trade gap (**trade gaps**) N-COUNT A **trade gap** is the same as a **trade deficit**. 贸易逆差 [usu sing] [BUSINESS] ❑ *The trade gap surprised most analysts by shrinking, rather than growing.* 贸易逆差不增反减使得大多数分析家大吃一惊。

trade-in (**trade-ins**) N-COUNT A **trade-in** is an arrangement in which someone buys a new car at a reduced price by giving their old one, as well as money, in payment. （将旧车）折价换新 [BUSINESS] ❑ *...the trade-in value of the car.* …这辆汽车的以旧换新价。

Word Link *mark ≈ boundary, sign : benchmark, bookmark, trademark*

trade·mark /tre͟ɪdmɑrk/ (**trademarks**) also **trade mark** 1 N-COUNT A **trademark** is a name or symbol that a company uses on its products and that cannot legally be used by another company. 商标 [BUSINESS] ❑ *She has registered a trademark for a new range of perfumes.* 她已为一个新系列的香水注册了商标。 2 N-COUNT If you say that something is the **trademark** of a particular person or place, you mean that it is characteristic of them or typically associated with them. 标志 ❑ *...the spiky punk hairdo that became his trademark.* …刺猬式的朋克发型成了他的标志。

trade name (**trade names**) N-COUNT A **trade name** is the name which manufacturers give to a product or to a range of products. 品牌名称 [BUSINESS] ❑ *It's marketed under the trade name "Mirage."* 它使用"米拉日"这一品牌名称在市场上销售。

trad·er ♦◊◊ /tre͟ɪdər/ (**traders**) N-COUNT A **trader** is a person whose job is to trade in goods or stocks. 商人；证券交易人 [BUSINESS] ❑ *Market traders display an exotic selection of the island's produce.* 市场商家们展示了该岛具有异国情调的农产品系列。

trade se·cret (**trade secrets**) N-COUNT A **trade secret** is information that is known, used, and kept secret by a particular company, for example, about a method of production or a chemical process. 行业秘密 [BUSINESS] ❑ *The nature of the polymer is currently a trade secret.* 该聚合物的属性目前是个行业秘密。

trades·man /tre͟ɪdzmən/ (**tradesmen**) N-COUNT A **tradesman** is a person, usually a man, who is a skilled worker. 技工（通常为男性）[BUSINESS] ❑ *...tradesmen such as electricians or plumbers.* …技工们，例如电工或管子工。

trade sur·plus (**trade surpluses**) N-COUNT If a country has a **trade surplus**, it exports more than it imports. 贸易顺差 [BUSINESS] ❑ *The country's trade surplus widened to 16.5 billion dollars.* 这个国家的贸易顺差增加到了165亿美元。

trade un·ion [mainly BRIT] → see **union, labor union**

tra·di·tion ♦◊◊ /trədɪʃᵊn/ (**traditions**) N-VAR A **tradition** is a custom or belief that has existed for a long time. 传统 ❑ *...the rich traditions of Afro-Cuban music and dance.* …非裔古巴人多姿多彩的音乐和舞蹈传统。

Thesaurus *tradition* 另参见：
N. culture, custom, practice, ritual

tra·di·tion·al ♦♦◊ /trədɪʃənᵊl/ 1 ADJ **Traditional** customs, beliefs, or methods are ones that have existed for a long time without changing. 传统的 ❑ *Traditional teaching methods sometimes only succeeded in putting students off learning.* 传统的教学方法有时只会使学生们厌学。 ● **tra·di·tion·al·ly** ADV 传统地 [ADV with cl/group] ❑ *Married women have traditionally been treated as dependent on their husbands.* 已婚妇女传统上被认为是依附于其丈夫的。 2 ADJ A **traditional** organization or person prefers older methods and ideas to modern ones. 守旧的 ❑ *We're still a traditional school in a lot of ways.* 我们在很多方面仍然是一所守旧的学校。 ● **tra·di·tion·al·ly** ADV 守旧地 ❑ *He is loathed by some of the more traditionally minded officers.* 他被一些思想更为守旧的官员所厌恶。

Word Link *tra ≈ across : traffic, travel, travesty*

traf·fic ♦◊◊ /trӕfɪk/ (**traffics, trafficking, trafficked**)

Word Web traffic

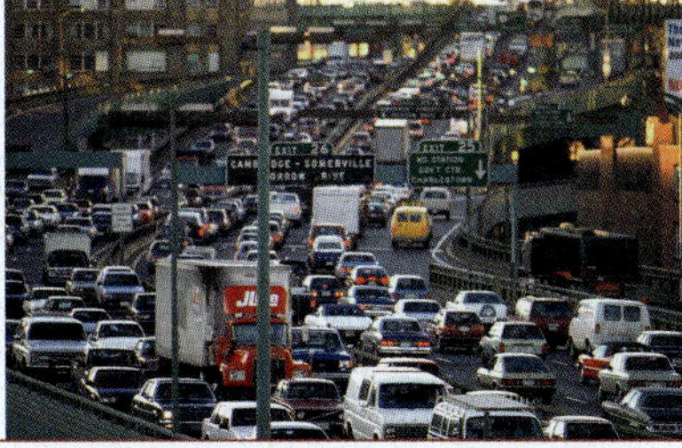

Boston's Southeast Expressway was built to handle 75,000 **vehicles** a day. But from the day it opened in 1959, **commuter traffic** crawled. Sometimes it **stalled** completely. The 27 entrance **ramps** and lack of **breakdown lanes** caused frequent **gridlock**. By the 1990s, **traffic congestion** was even worse. Nearly 200,000 cars a day were using the **highway** and there were constant **traffic jams**. In 1994, a ten-year **road** construction project called the Big Dig began. The project built underground roadways, six-**lane** bridges, and improved **tunnels**. As a result of the project traffic **flows** more smoothly through the city.

1 N-UNCOUNT **Traffic** refers to all the vehicles that are moving along the roads in a particular area. 交通 [also "the" N] ❑ *There was heavy traffic on the roads.* 路上的交通很拥挤。 ❑ *Traffic was unusually light for that time of day.* 交通在白天的那个时段有些异常地顺畅。 2 N-UNCOUNT **Traffic** refers to the movement of ships, trains, or aircraft between one place and another. **Traffic** also refers to the people and goods that are being transported. 运输；人流；货流 ❑ *Air traffic had returned to normal.* 空中交通已恢复正常。 3 N-UNCOUNT **Traffic in** something such as drugs or stolen goods is an illegal trade in them. (毒品或赃物等的) 非法买卖 ❑ *...the widespread traffic in stolen cultural artifacts.* …被盗文物非法买卖泛滥。 4 V-I Someone who **traffics in** something such as drugs or stolen goods buys and sells them even though it is illegal to do so. 从事(毒品或赃物等的) 非法买卖 ❑ *The president said illegal drugs are hurting the entire world and anyone who traffics in them should be brought to justice.* 总统说毒品正在危害全世界，毒品非法交易者都应该绳之以法。
● **traf·fick·ing** N-UNCOUNT 非法买卖 ❑ *He was sentenced to ten years in prison on charges of drug trafficking.* 他被指控贩毒，被判10年徒刑。
→ see Word Web: **traffic**

Word Partnership *traffic* 的常用搭配：

ADJ. **heavy** traffic, **light** traffic, **oncoming** traffic, **stuck in** traffic 1
N. traffic **accident**, **city** traffic, traffic **congestion**, traffic **flow**, traffic **pollution**, traffic **problems**, **rush hour** traffic, traffic **safety**, traffic **signals**, traffic **violation** 1
air traffic 2
drug traffic 3

traf·fic cir·cle (**traffic circles**) N-COUNT A **traffic circle** is a circular structure in the road at a place where several roads meet. You drive around it until you come to the road that you want. 环型交通枢纽 [AM]
in BRIT, use **roundabout**

traf·fick·er /trǽfɪkər/ (**traffickers**) N-COUNT A **trafficker** in particular goods, especially drugs, is a person who illegally buys or sells these goods. (尤指毒品的) 非法买卖者 ❑ *They have been arrested as suspected drug traffickers.* 他们因涉嫌贩毒而被捕。

traf·fic light (**traffic lights**) 1 N-COUNT **Traffic lights** are sets of red, yellow, and green lights at the places where roads meet. They control the traffic by signaling red when vehicles have to stop and green when they can go. 交通信号灯 2 → see also **stoplight**

trag·edy ♦◇◇ /trǽdʒɪdi/ (**tragedies**) 1 N-VAR A **tragedy** is an extremely sad event or situation. 灾难 ❑ *They have suffered an enormous personal tragedy.* 他们遭受了一场巨大的个人灾难。 2 N-VAR **Tragedy** is a type of literature, especially drama, that is serious and sad, and often ends with the death of the main character. 悲剧 ❑ *The story has elements of tragedy and farce.* 这个故事含有悲剧和闹剧的成分。
→ see **theater**

★ **trag·ic** /trǽdʒɪk/ 1 ADJ A **tragic** event or situation is extremely sad, usually because it involves death or suffering. 悲惨的；不幸的 ❑ *It was just a tragic accident.* 这只是一场悲惨的事故。 ❑ *...the tragic loss of so many lives.* …如此多人的不幸丧生。
● **tragi·cal·ly** /trǽdʒɪkli/ ADV 悲惨地；不幸地 ❑ *Tragically, she never saw the completed building because she died before it was finished.* 不幸的是，她未能见到完工的大楼，因为她在大楼竣工前就去世了。 2 ADJ **Tragic** is used to refer to tragedy as a type of literature. 悲剧的 [ADJ n] ❑ *...Shakespeare's tragic hero, Hamlet.* …莎士比亚的悲剧主人公哈姆雷特。

trail ♦◇◇ /treɪl/ (**trails, trailing, trailed**) 1 N-COUNT A **trail** is a rough path across open country or through forests. (乡间或林中的) 崎岖小路 ❑ *He was following a trail through the trees.* 他正沿着一条崎岖小路穿过树林。 2 N-COUNT A **trail** is a route along a series of paths or roads, often one that has been planned and marked out for a particular purpose. (有特定目的的) 路线；路径 ❑ *...a large area of woodland with hiking and walking trails.* …有徒步旅行和散步路线的大片林区。 3 N-COUNT A **trail** is a series of marks or other signs of movement or other activities left by someone or something. 痕迹 ❑ *Everywhere in the house was a sticky trail of orange juice.* 房子里到处都是粘乎乎的橙汁印迹。 4 V-T If you **trail** someone or something, you follow them secretly, often by finding the marks or signs that they have left. 跟踪 ❑ *Two detectives were trailing him.* 两个侦探正在跟踪他。 5 N-COUNT You can refer to all the places that a politician visits in the period before an election as their campaign **trail**. (竞选巡回宣传) 路线 ❑ *During a recent speech on the campaign trail, he was interrupted by hecklers.* 在最近的一次竞选巡回演讲中，他被诘问者打断了。 6 V-T/V-I If you **trail** something or it **trails**, it hangs down loosely behind you as you move along. 拖 ❑ *She came down the stairs slowly, trailing the coat behind her.* 她慢慢地走下楼梯，身后拖着大衣。 7 PHRASE If you are **on the trail of** a person or thing, you are trying hard to find them or find out about them. 追踪 ❑ *The police were hot on his trail.* 警方正紧紧跟踪他。

Word Partnership *trail* 的常用搭配：

V. **follow** a trail 1 – 3
leave a trail, **pick up** a trail 3
N. **hiking** trail 2
campaign trail 5

trail·er /treɪlər/ (**trailers**) 1 N-COUNT A **trailer** is a long narrow house made to be delivered to a home site, where it becomes a permanent home. (一种长而狭窄的造好后可送货上门的) 房屋 2 N-COUNT A **trailer** is a temporary vacation home that is pulled by a car to each vacation spot. (汽车拖行的) 临时度假屋
in BRIT, use **caravan**
3 N-COUNT A **trailer** is a container on wheels which is pulled by a car or other vehicle and which is used for transporting large or heavy items. 拖车 4 N-COUNT A **trailer** for a movie or television program is a set of short extracts which are shown to advertise it. (电影或电视节目的) 预告片 ❑ *...a misleadingly violent trailer for the movie.* …一个让人误以为充斥暴力的电影预告片。

trail·er park (**trailer parks**) N-COUNT A **trailer park** is an area where people can pay to park their trailers and live in them. 拖车式活动房屋停车场 [AM]
in BRIT, use **caravan site**

train
❶ NOUN USES
❷ VERB USES

❶ **train** ♦♦◇ /treɪn/ (**trains**) 1 N-COUNT A **train** is a number of containers on wheels which are all connected together and which are pulled by an engine along a railroad. Trains carry people and goods from one place to another. 火车 [also "by" N] ❑ *The train pulled into a station.* 那列火车驶入了一个车站。 ❑ *We can catch the early morning train.* 我们能赶上清晨的那班火车。 2 N-COUNT A **train of** vehicles, people, or animals is a long line of them traveling slowly in the same direction. (行进中的) 队列 ❑ *In the old days this used to be done with a baggage train of camels.* 在古时候，这常常由一队拉行李的骆驼来完成。 3 N-COUNT A **train of** thought or a

t

Word Web train

In sixteenth-century Germany, a **railway** was a **horse-drawn wagon** traveling along wooden **rails**. By the 19th century, **steam locomotives** and **steel rails** had replaced the older system. At first, railroads operated only **freight lines**. Later, they began to run **passenger** trains. And soon Pullman cars were added to make overnight trips more comfortable. Today, Japan's bullet trains carry people at speeds up to 300 miles per hour. This type of train doesn't have an engine or use tracks. Instead, an electromagnetic field allows the **cars** to float just above the ground. This electromagnetic field also propels them ahead.

A Japanese Bullet Train

train of events is a connected sequence, in which each thought or event seems to occur naturally or logically as a result of the previous one. (一) 连串 (想法或事件) ❑ *He lost his train of thought for a moment, then recovered it.* 他一时断了思路，接着又重新想起来了。
→ see Word Web: **train**
→ see **transportation**

❷ **train** ◆◆◇ /treɪn/ (**trains, training, trained**) 1 V-T/V-I If someone **trains** you **to** do something, they teach you the skills that you need in order to do it. If you **train to** do something, you learn the skills that you need in order to do it. 培训；接受培训 ❑ *He was training us to be soldiers.* 他正把我们训练成士兵。 ● **-trained** COMB IN ADJ 受过培训的 ❑ *Michael is a professionally-trained chef.* 迈克尔是受过职业培训的厨师。 ● **train·er** N-COUNT (**trainers**) 培训者 ❑ *...a book for both teachers and teacher trainers.* …一本适合教师和教师培训者看的书。 2 V-T To **train** a natural quality or talent that someone has, for example, their voice or musical ability, means to help them to develop it. 开发 (天生的素质或才能) ❑ *I see my degree as something which will train my mind and improve my chances of getting a job.* 我把我的学历视为开发心智、增加就业机会的东西。 3 V-T/V-I If you **train for** a physical activity such as a race or if someone **trains** you **for** it, you prepare for it by doing particular physical exercises. (为体育比赛等) 训练 ❑ *Strachan is training for the new season.* 斯特罗恩正在为新赛季进行训练。 ● **train·er** N-COUNT 教练员 ❑ *She went to the gym with her personal trainer.* 她和她的私人教练一起去了健身房。 4 V-T If an animal or bird **is trained to** do particular things, it is taught to do them, for example, in order to be able to work for someone or to be a good pet. 训练 (动物或鸟类) ❑ *Sniffer dogs could be trained to track them down.* 可以训练嗅探犬来追捕他们。 ● **train·er** N-COUNT 驯兽师 ❑ *The horse made a winning start for his new trainer.* 这匹马让它的新驯马师旗开得胜。 5 → see also **training**

Thesaurus *train* 另参见：
N. caravan, procession, series ❶ 2
V. coach, educate, guide, prepare ❷ 1

trainee /treɪniː/ (**trainees**) N-COUNT A **trainee** is someone who is employed at a low level in a particular job in order to learn the skills needed for that job. 实习生 [oft N n] [BUSINESS] ❑ *He is a 24-year-old trainee reporter.* 他是一个24岁的实习记者。

train·er /treɪnər/ (**trainers**) 1 N-COUNT **Trainers** are shoes that people wear, especially for running and other sports. 运动鞋 [BRIT]
in AM, use **sneakers, running shoes, tennis shoes**
2 → see also **train**

T

train·ing /treɪnɪŋ/ 1 N-UNCOUNT **Training** is the process of learning the skills that you need for a particular job or activity. 培训 [BUSINESS] ❑ *He called for much higher spending on education and training.* 他呼吁在教育和培训上投入更多的资金。 ❑ *Kennedy had no formal training as a decorator.* 肯尼迪没有接受过油漆工的正式培训。 2 N-UNCOUNT **Training** is physical exercise that you do regularly in order to keep fit or to prepare for an activity such as a race. (体育) 锻炼；(为参加赛跑等的) 训练 ❑ *The emphasis is on developing fitness through exercises and training.* 重点放在通过运动和锻炼来促进健康。

trait /treɪt/ (**traits**) N-COUNT A **trait** is a particular characteristic, quality, or tendency that someone or something has. 特征 ❑ *The study found that some alcoholics had clear personality traits showing up early in childhood.* 这项研究发现一些酗酒者早在孩童时就表现出明显的个性特征。
→ see **culture, gene**

trai·tor /treɪtər/ (**traitors**) 1 N-COUNT If you call someone a **traitor**, you mean that they have betrayed beliefs that they used to hold, or that their friends hold, by their words or actions. 背叛者 [DISAPPROVAL] ❑ *Some say he's a traitor to the peace movement.* 一些人说他是和平运动的背叛者。 2 N-COUNT If someone is a **traitor**, they betray their country, friends, or a group of which they are a member by helping its enemies, especially during time of war. (尤指战争期间的) 卖国贼；叛徒 ❑ *...rumors that there were traitors among us who were sending messages to the enemy.* …谣言说我们中有正给敌人送信的叛徒。

▲ **tram** /træm/ (**trams**) 1 N-COUNT A **tram** is a public transportation vehicle, usually powered by electricity from wires above it, which travels along rails laid in the surface of a street. 有轨电车 [also "by" N] ❑ *You can get to the beach easily from the center of town by tram.* 你可以很容易地在市中心坐有轨电车到达海滩。
in AM, use **streetcar**
2 N-COUNT A **tram** is the same as a **cable car**. 缆车 [AM]
→ see **transportation**

▲ **tramp** /træmp/ (**tramps, tramping, tramped**) 1 N-COUNT A **tramp** is a person who has no home or job, and very little money. Tramps go from place to place, and get food or money by asking people or by doing casual work. 流浪汉 ❑ *Hypothermia is common among tramps sleeping outdoors.* 体温过低症在那些露宿户外的流浪汉中很普遍。 2 V-T/V-I If you **tramp** somewhere, you walk there slowly and with regular, heavy steps, for a long time. 脚步沉重地缓缓行走；踏 ❑ *They put on their coats and tramped through the falling snow.* 他们穿上大衣，在落雪中脚步沉重地缓缓走着。 3 N-UNCOUNT The **tramp** of people is the sound of their heavy, regular walking. 沉重的脚步声 ❑ *He heard the slow, heavy tramp of feet on the stairs.* 他听见楼梯上缓慢而沉重的脚步声。 4 N-COUNT If someone refers to a woman as a **tramp**, they are insulting her, because they think that she is immoral in her sexual behavior. 荡妇 [mainly AM, OFFENSIVE, DISAPPROVAL] ❑ *He'd think I was a tramp, a cheap slut, and he'd lose all respect for me.* 他会认为我是个荡妇，一个低贱的妓女，不会对我有丝毫尊重。

▲ **tram·ple** /træmpᵊl/ (**tramples, trampling, trampled**) 1 V-T/V-I To **trample on** someone's rights or values or to **trample** them means to deliberately ignore them. 无视 ❑ *They say loggers are destroying rain forests and trampling on the rights of natives.* 他们说伐木工正在破坏雨林，无视当地人的权利。 2 V-T If someone **is trampled**, they are injured or killed by being stepped on by animals or by other people. 踩伤；踩死 [usu passive] ❑ *Many people were trampled in the panic that followed.* 很多人在随后的恐慌中被踩伤。 3 V-T/V-I If someone **tramples** something or **tramples on** it, they step heavily and carelessly on it and damage it. 践踏；踩坏 ❑ *They don't want people trampling the grass, pitching tents or building fires.* 他们不想让人们践踏草地、搭帐篷或生火。

trance /træns/ (**trances**) N-COUNT A **trance** is a state of mind in which someone seems to be asleep and to have no conscious control over their thoughts or actions, but in which they can see and hear things and respond to commands given by other people. 催眠状态 ❑ *Like a man in a trance, Blake found his way back to his rooms.* 像一个处于催眠状态的人，布莱克回到了自己的房间。
→ see **hypnosis**

tranche /trɑnʃ/ (**tranches**) 1 N-COUNT In economics, a **tranche** of shares in a company, or a **tranche** of a company, is a number of shares in that company. (股票的) 一部分 [usu N "of" n] [BUSINESS] ❑ *On February 12th he put up for sale a second tranche of 32 state-owned companies.* 2月12号，他售出了第2部分32家国有公司的股票。 2 N-COUNT A **tranche** of something is a piece, section, or part of it. A **tranche** of things is a group of them. (一) 片；(一) 部分；(一) 群 [usu N "of" n] [FORMAL] ❑ *They risk losing the next tranche of funding.* 他们冒着失去下一批资金的风险。

▲ **tran·quil** /træŋkwɪl/ ADJ Something that is **tranquil** is calm and peaceful. 宁静的 ❑ *The tranquil atmosphere of the inn allows guests to feel totally at home.* 这家客栈的宁静氛围让客人们感到宾至如归。 ● **tran·quil·lity** /træŋkwɪlɪti/ N-UNCOUNT 宁静 ❑ *The hotel is a haven of peace and tranquillity.* 这个旅馆是一个宁静的好去处。

tran·quil·ize /træŋkwɪlaɪz/ (**tranquilizes, tranquilizing, tranquilized**) V-T To **tranquilize** a person or an animal means to make them become calm, sleepy, or unconscious by means of a drug. (用药物) 使镇静; 使失去知觉 ❑ *This powerful drug is used to tranquilize patients undergoing surgery.* 这种强效的药物用于使手术中的病人失去知觉。

tran·quil·iz·er /træŋkwɪlaɪzər/ (**tranquilizers**) N-COUNT A **tranquilizer** is a drug that makes people feel calmer or less anxious. Tranquilizers are sometimes used to make people or animals become sleepy or unconscious. 镇静剂 ❑ *If a tranquilizer is prescribed, be sure your physician informs you of its possible side effects, such as addiction.* 如果开了镇静剂，一定要让医生告诉你它可能带来的副作用，例如上瘾。

trans·ac·tion ♦◇◇ /trænzækʃᵊn/ (**transactions**) N-COUNT A **transaction** is a piece of business, for example, an act of buying or selling something. 交易 [FORMAL, BUSINESS] ❑ *The transaction is completed by payment of the fee.* 交易在支付费用之后就完成了。
→ see **bank**

Word Partnership *transaction* 的常用搭配:
N. **cash** transaction, transaction **costs**, transaction **fee**
V. **complete a** transaction

trans·at·lan·tic /trænzətlæntɪk/ ADJ **Transatlantic** flights or signals go across the Atlantic Ocean, usually between the United States and Britain. 横跨大西洋的 [ADJ n] ❑ *Many transatlantic flights land there.* 很多飞越大西洋的航班都在那里着陆。

★ **trans·cend** /trænsɛnd/ (**transcends, transcending, transcended**) V-T Something that **transcends** normal limits or boundaries goes beyond them, because it is more significant than them. 超越 ❑ *...issues like disaster relief that transcend party loyalty.* …诸如超越党派忠诚的灾后救济的问题。

★ **trans·con·ti·nen·tal** /trænskɒntɪnɛntᵊl/ ADJ A **transcontinental** journey or route goes from one side of a continent to the other. **Transcontinental** usually means from one side of the United States to the other, not including Alaska and Hawaii. 横跨大陆的 [usu ADJ n] ❑ *...in mid-nineteenth-century America, before the transcontinental railroad was built.* …在美洲大铁路修建以前19世纪中期的美国。

Word Link *scrib ≈ writing : inscribe, scribble, transcribe*

★ **tran·scribe** /trænskraɪb/ (**transcribes, transcribing, transcribed**) V-T If you **transcribe** a speech or text, you write or type it out, for example, from notes or from a tape recording. (根据笔记或磁带录音等) 写下; 用打字机打出 ❑ *She is transcribing, from his dictation, the diaries of Simon Forman.* 她正在根据他的口述记录西蒙·福曼的日记。

Word Link *script ≈ writing : manuscript, scripture, transcript*

▲ **tran·script** /trænskrɪpt/ (**transcripts**) N-COUNT A **transcript of** a conversation or speech is a written text of it, based on a recording or notes. (根据录音或笔记整理的) 文字本 ❑ *A transcript of this PBS program is available through our website, pbs.com.* 这个公共广播公司节目的文字本可通过我们的网址**pbs.com**查阅。

Word Link *trans ≈ across : transfer, transition, translate*

trans·fer ♦♦◇ (**transfers, transferring, transferred**)

The verb is pronounced /trænsfɜr/. The noun is pronounced /trænsfɜr/.

动词读作 /trænsfɜr/。名词读作 /trænsfɜr/。

1 V-T/V-I If you **transfer** something or someone **from** one place **to** another, or they **transfer from** one place **to** another, they go from the first place to the second. 转移 ❑ *Transfer the meat to a platter and leave in a warm place.* 把肉转到一个大浅盘中，然后搁在一个温暖的地方。 ● N-VAR **Transfer** is also a noun. 转移 [oft N "of" n] ❑ *Arrange for the transfer of medical records to your new doctor.* 安排把医疗记录转给你的新医生。 2 V-T/V-I If something **is transferred**, or **transfers, from** one person or group of people **to** another, the second person or group gets it instead of the first. 移交 ❑ *The decision to transfer the investigation from the police to the district attorney's office is a mutual one.* 将调查从警方移交到区律师办公室的决定是共同做出的。 ● N-VAR **Transfer** is also a noun. 移交 ❑ *...the transfer of power from the old to the new regimes.* …从旧政权到新政权的权力移交。 3 V-T/V-I If you **are transferred**, or if you **transfer, to** a different job or place, the company moves you to a different job or you start working in a different part of the same company or organization. 调动 ❑ *I was transferred to the book department.* 我被调到了图书部。 ❑ *I suspect that she is going to be transferred to Fort Meyer.* 我怀疑她将被调到迈耶堡。 ● N-VAR **Transfer** is also a noun. 调动 [oft N "to" n] ❑ *They will be offered transfers to other locations.* 他们将得到去其他地方的调动令。 4 V-T When information **is transferred onto** a different medium, it is copied from one medium to another. 转录 (信息) ❑ *Such information is easily transferred onto microfilm.* 这样的信息很容易被转录到微缩胶片上。 ● N-UNCOUNT **Transfer** is also a noun. 转录 ❑ *It can be connected to a PC for the transfer of information.* 它可以连接到个人电脑上进行信息转录。

Word Partnership *transfer* 的常用搭配:
N. **balance** transfer, transfer **funds**, transfer **money** 1
transfer **ownership**, transfer **of power** 2
transfer **schools, students** transfer 3
transfer **data**, transfer **information** 4

trans·fer·able /trænsfɜrəbᵊl/ ADJ If something is **transferable**, it can be passed or moved from one person or organization to another and used by them. 可转让的; 可转移的 ❑ *Use the transferable skills acquired from your previous working background.* 利用你以前工作经历中获得的可转移性技能。

trans·form ♦◇◇ /trænsfɔrm/ (**transforms, transforming, transformed**) 1 V-T To **transform** something **into** something else means to change or convert it into that thing. 使改变; 使转换 ❑ *Your metabolic rate is the speed at which your body transforms food into energy.* 你的新陈代谢率就是你身体将食物转换成能量的速度。 ● **trans·for·ma·tion** /trænsfərmeɪʃᵊn/ N-VAR (**transformations**) 改变; 转换 ❑ *Norah made plans for the transformation of an attic room into a study.* 诺拉制订了将阁楼间改造为书房的几个方案。 ❑ *Chemical transformations occur.* 化学变化发生。 2 V-T To **transform** something or someone means to change them completely and suddenly so that they are much better or more attractive. 彻底改变 (使更好、更有吸引力) ❑ *Industrialization transformed the world.* 工业化彻底改变了世界。 ● **trans·for·ma·tion** N-VAR 彻底改变 ❑ *In the last five years he's undergone a personal transformation.* 在过去的5年里，他完全变了个人。

Thesaurus *transform* 另参见:
V. alter, change, convert 1 2

▲ **trans·fu·sion** /trænsfyuʒᵊn/ (**transfusions**) N-VAR A **transfusion** is the same as a **blood transfusion**. 输血

★ **tran·si·ent** /trænʃənt/ (**transients**) 1 ADJ **Transient** is used to describe a situation that lasts only a short time or is constantly changing. 短暂的 [FORMAL] ❑ *...the transient nature of high fashion.* …最新时尚转瞬即逝的特点。 2 N-COUNT **Transients** are people who stay in a place for only a short time and then move somewhere else. 流动人员 [usu pl] [FORMAL] ❑ *...a dormitory for transients.* …一个流动人员的宿舍。

★ **tran·sis·tor** /trænzɪstər/ (**transistors**) 1 N-COUNT A **transistor** is a small electronic part in something such as a television or radio, which controls the flow of electricity. 晶体管 2 N-COUNT A **transistor** or a **transistor radio** is a small portable radio. 晶体管收音机 [OLD-FASHIONED]

★ **trans·it** /trænzɪt/ 1 N-UNCOUNT **Transit** is the carrying of goods or people by vehicle from one place to another. 运输 ❑ *During their talks, the two presidents discussed the transit of goods between the two countries.* 在会谈中，两位总统讨论了两国之间货物的运输。 ❑ *...a transit time of about 42 minutes.* …大约42分钟的运输时间。 ● PHRASE If people or things are **in transit**, they are traveling or being taken from one place to another. 在途中; 在被运送中 2 ADJ A **transit** area is an area where people wait or where goods are kept between different stages of a journey. 中转的 (地方) [ADJ n] ❑ *...refugees arriving at the two transit camps.* …到达两个中转难民营的难民。 3 N-UNCOUNT A **transit system** is a system for moving people or goods from one place to another, for example, using buses or trains. 交通系统 [AM]

in BRIT, use **transport system**

❏ *The president wants to improve the nation's highways and mass transit systems.* 总统想要改善国家的公路和公共交通系统。

→ see **transportation**

Word Link *trans ≈ across : transfer, transition, translate*

★ **tran·si·tion** ♦◇◇ /trænzɪʃ^ə^n/ (**transitions, transitioning, transitioned**) **1** N-VAR **Transition** is the process in which something changes from one state to another. 转型 ❏ *The transition from a dictatorship to a multi-party democracy is proving to be difficult.* 从专政国家到多党民主国家的转型证明是很艰难的。 **2** V-I If someone **transitions from** one state or activity to another, they move gradually from one to the other. (逐渐地) 转向 [BUSINESS] ❏ *Most of the discussion was on what needed to be done now as we transitioned from the security issues to the challenging economic issues.* 大多数讨论都集中在目前需要做什么，因为我们已从安全问题逐渐转到具有挑战性的经济问题上。

tran·si·tion·al /trænzɪʃən^ə^l/ **1** ADJ A **transitional** period is one in which things are changing from one state to another. 过渡的 [ADJ n] ❏ *...a transitional period following more than a decade of civil war.* …十多年内战之后的一个过渡时期。 **2** ADJ **Transitional** is used to describe something that happens or exists during a transitional period. 过渡时期的 [ADJ n] ❏ *The main rebel groups have agreed to join in a meeting to set up a transitional government.* 主要的叛乱团体已同意参加会议来建立一个过渡政府。

tran·si·tive /trænzɪtɪv/ ADJ A **transitive** verb has a direct object. (动词) 及物的

trans·late /trænzleɪt/ (**translates, translating, translated**) **1** V-T/V-I If something said or written **is translated from** one language **into** another, it is said or written again in the second language. 翻译 ❏ *Only a small number of Kadare's books have been translated into English.* 卡达莱的书只有一小部分被翻译成了英文。 ❏ *The Spanish word "acequia" is translated as "irrigation ditch."* 西班牙语中的 "**acequia**" 一词被译为 "灌溉渠"。 ❏ *The girls waited for Mr. Esch to translate.* 这些女孩们等着埃施先生来翻译。 ● **trans·la·tion** N-UNCOUNT 翻译 ❏ *The papers have been sent to Saudi Arabia for translation.* 这些文件已被送往沙特阿拉伯进行翻译。 **2** V-I If a name, a word, or an expression **translates as** something in a different language, that is what it means in that language. (翻译过来) 意思是 ❏ *His family's Cantonese nickname for him translates as Never Sits Still.* 他家人为他起的广东话绰号翻译过来意思是 "永远坐不住"。 **3** V-T/V-I If one thing **translates** or **is translated into** another, the second happens or is done as a result of the first. 转变 ❏ *Reforming the stagnant economy requires harsh measures that would translate into job losses.* 改革停滞的经济需要严厉措施，而这将造成失业。

Thesaurus *translate* 另参见:

v. alter, change, transform **3**

trans·la·tion /trænzleɪʃ^ə^n/ (**translations**) **1** N-COUNT A **translation** is a piece of writing or speech that has been put into a different language. 译文 [also "in" N] ❏ *...a translation of the Iliad.* …《伊利亚特》的一种译本。 **2** → see also **translate**

trans·la·tor /trænzleɪtər/ (**translators**) N-COUNT A **translator** is a person whose job is translating writing or speech from one language to another. 译员

Word Link *luc ≈ light : hallucinate, lucid, translucent*

trans·lu·cent /trænzlus^ə^nt/ ADJ If a material is **translucent**, some light can pass through it. 半透明的 ❏ *The building is roofed entirely with translucent corrugated plastic.* 这座建筑全部都是用半透明的波纹状塑料封顶。

→ see **pottery**

trans·mis·sion /trænzmɪʃ^ə^n/ (**transmissions**) **1** N-UNCOUNT The **transmission** of something is the passing or sending of it to a different person or place. 传送; 传播 ❏ *Heterosexual contact is responsible for the bulk of HIV transmission.* 异性间的性接触是造成大多数艾滋病病毒传播的原因。 **2** N-UNCOUNT The **transmission** of television or radio programs is the broadcasting of them. (电视或广播节目的) 播送 ❏ *The transmission of the program was brought forward due to its unexpected topicality.* 该节目提前播送是因有出人意料的热门话题。 **3** N-COUNT A **transmission** is a broadcast. 广播节目; 电视节目 ❏ *...foreign television transmissions.* …外国的电视节目。

trans·mit /trænzmɪt/ (**transmits, transmitting, transmitted**) **1** V-T/V-I When radio and television programs, computer data, or other electronic messages **are transmitted**, they are sent from one place to another, using wires, radio waves, or satellites. 传播 (广播电视节目、计算机信息等) ❏ *The game was transmitted live.* 这场比赛被现场直播。 ❏ *This is currently the most efficient way to transmit certain types of data like electronic mail.* 这是目前传输电子邮件等某类数据最有效的方法。 **2** V-T If one person or animal **transmits** a disease to another, they have the disease and cause the other person or animal to have it. 传播 (疾病) [FORMAL] ❏ *...mosquitoes that transmit disease to humans.* …向人类传播疾病的蚊子。 **3** V-T If an object or substance **transmits** something such as sound or electrical signals, the sound or signals are able to pass through it. 传导 (声音、电子信号等) ❏ *These thin crystals transmit much of the power.* 这些薄薄的晶体能传导大部分的能量。

▲ **trans·mit·ter** /trænzmɪtər/ (**transmitters**) N-COUNT A **transmitter** is a piece of equipment that is used for broadcasting television or radio programs. (电视信号或无线电的) 发射机 ❏ *...a homemade radio transmitter.* …一台自制的无线电发射机。

→ see **cellphone, radio**

trans·par·en·cy /trænspɛərənsi, -pær-/ (**transparencies**) **1** N-COUNT A **transparency** is a small piece of photographic film with a frame around it which can be projected onto a screen so that you can see the picture. 幻灯片 ❏ *...transparencies of masterpieces from Lizzie's art collection.* …莉齐艺术收藏品中一些杰作的幻灯片。 **2** N-UNCOUNT **Transparency** is the quality that an object or substance has when you can see through it. 透明性 ❏ *Cataracts affect the transparency of the eye's lenses.* 白内障影响眼睛晶状体的透明度。

trans·par·ent /trænspɛərənt, -pær-/ **1** ADJ If an object or substance is **transparent**, you can see through it. 透明的 ❏ *...a sheet of transparent colored plastic.* …一片透明的彩色塑料。 **2** ADJ If a situation, system, or activity is **transparent**, it is easily understood or recognized. 易懂的; 显而易见的 ❏ *The company has to make its accounts and operations as transparent as possible.* 该公司不得不尽力使它的帐目和运作一目了然。 **3** ADJ You use **transparent** to describe a statement or action that is obviously dishonest or wrong, and that you think will not deceive people. If a person is transparent, you can see their true bad motives. 易识破的 ❏ *He thought he could fool people with transparent deceptions.* 他以为他能用易识破的骗术愚弄人。 ❏ *He's so transparent.* 他很容易被识破。

→ see **glass**

tran·spire /trænspaɪər/ (**transpires, transpiring, transpired**) **1** V-T When **it transpires that** something is the case, people discover that it is the case. (人们) 发现 [FORMAL] ❏ *It transpired that Kareem had left his driver's license at home.* 人们发现卡里姆把驾照落在家里了。 **2** V-I When something **transpires**, it happens. 发生 ❏ *Nothing is known as yet about what transpired at the meeting.* 没有人知道会上发生了什么事。

trans·plant (**transplants, transplanting, transplanted**)

The noun is pronounced /trænsplænt/. The verb is pronounced /trænsplænt/.

名词读作 /trænsplænt/，动词读作 /trænsplænt/。

1 N-VAR A **transplant** is a medical operation in which a part of a person's body is replaced because it is diseased. (器官) 移植 ❏ *He was recovering from a heart transplant operation.* 他正从心脏移植手术中康复。 **2** V-T If doctors **transplant** an organ such as a heart or a kidney, they use it to replace a patient's diseased organ. 移植 ❏ *The operation to transplant a kidney is now fairly routine.* 移植肾脏的手术如今相当常见。 **3** V-T To **transplant** a plant, person, or thing means to move them to a different place. 移种; 转移 ❏ *I have to transplant the begonias.* 我得移种那些秋海棠。

→ see **donor, hospital**

trans·port ♦♦◇ (**transports, transporting, transported**)

The verb is pronounced /trænspɔrt/. The noun is pronounced /trænspɔrt/.

动词读作 /trænspɔrt/。名词读作 /trænspɔrt/。

1 V-T To **transport** people or goods somewhere is to take them from one place to another in a vehicle. 运送 ❏ *They are banned from launching any flights except to transport people.* 他们被禁止飞行任何航班，

运送人除外。 2 N-UNCOUNT **Transport** refers to any vehicle that you can travel in or carry goods in. 交通工具 [mainly BRIT]

in AM, usually use **transportation**

3 N-UNCOUNT **Transport** is a system for taking people or goods from one place to another, for example, using buses or trains. 交通运输系统 [mainly BRIT]

in AM, usually use **transportation**

4 N-UNCOUNT **Transport** is the activity of taking goods or people from one place to another in a vehicle. 运输 [mainly BRIT]

in AM, usually use **transportation**

trans·por·ta·tion ♦♦◇ /trænspərteɪʃ[ə]n/ 1 N-UNCOUNT **Transportation** refers to any type of vehicle that you can travel in or carry goods in. 交通工具 [mainly AM]

in BRIT, usually use **transport**

❑ *The company will provide transportation.* 这家公司将提供交通工具。 2 N-UNCOUNT **Transportation** is a system for taking people or goods from one place to another, for example, using buses or trains. 交通运输系统 [mainly AM]

in BRIT, usually use **transport**

❑ *Campuses are usually accessible by public transportation.* 到校园通常可以乘坐公交。 3 N-UNCOUNT **Transportation** is the activity of taking goods or people from one place to another in a vehicle. 运输 [mainly AM]

in BRIT, usually use **transport**

❑ *The baggage was being rapidly stowed away for transportation.* 行李正迅速被装好收起以便运输。

→ see Word Web: **transportation**

trans·port sys·tem [BRIT] → see **transit**

trap ♦◇◇ /træp/ (**traps, trapping, trapped**) 1 N-COUNT A **trap** is a device which is placed somewhere or a hole which is dug somewhere in order to catch animals or birds. (捉捕动物或鸟类的)捕捉器；陷阱 ❑ *Nathan's dog got caught in a trap.* 内森的狗被捕捉器夹住了。 2 V-T If a person **traps** animals or birds, he or she catches them using traps. 用捕捉器捕捉；设陷阱捕捉 ❑ *The locals were encouraged to trap and kill mice to stop the spread of the virus.* 当地人被鼓励用捕捉器捕杀老鼠以阻止病毒的传播。 3 N-COUNT A **trap** is a trick that is intended to catch or deceive someone. 圈套 ❑ *He failed to keep a rendezvous after sensing a police trap.* 他觉察到是警察的圈套后，就未去赴约。 4 V-T If you **trap** someone **into** doing or saying something, you trick them so that they do or say it, although they did not want to. 诱骗 ❑ *Were you just trying to trap her into making some admission?* 你仅仅是在试图诱骗她招供吗？ 5 V-T To **trap** someone, especially a criminal, means to capture them. 抓捕 ❑ *The police knew they had to trap the killer.* 警察知道他们得抓住那个凶手。 6 N-COUNT A **trap** is an unpleasant situation that you cannot easily escape from. 困境 ❑ *The government has found that it's caught in a trap of its own making.* 政府已经发现其陷入了自己造成的困境中。 7 V-T If you **are trapped** somewhere, something falls onto you or blocks your way and prevents you from moving or escaping. 困住 ❑ *The train was trapped underground by a fire.* 列车被一场大火困在了地下。 ❑ *The light aircraft then cartwheeled, trapping both men.* 那架轻型飞机随后侧翻，把两个人困住了。 8 V-T When something **traps** gas, water, or energy, it prevents it from escaping. 留住(气体、水或能量) ❑ *Wool traps your body heat, keeping the chill at bay.* 羊毛织物能留住你的身体热量，阻挡寒气。 9 → see also **trapped**, **deathtrap**

→ see **golf**

Word Partnership *trap* 的常用搭配：

V. **avoid a trap, caught in a trap, fall into a trap, set a trap** 1 3 6

trapped /træpt/ 1 ADJ If you feel **trapped**, you are in an unpleasant situation in which you lack freedom, and you feel you cannot escape from it. 受困的 ❑ *...people who think of themselves as trapped in mundane jobs.* …认为自己受平庸工作束缚的人们。 2 → see also **trap**

trap·pings /træpɪŋz/ N-PLURAL The **trappings** of power, wealth, or a particular job are the extra things, such as decorations and luxury items, that go with it. 装饰 [DISAPPROVAL] ❑ *The family ruled for several generations and evidently loved the trappings of power.* 那个家族统治了好几代，他们显然喜爱权力带来的虚饰。

trash /træʃ/ 1 N-UNCOUNT **Trash** consists of unwanted things or waste material such as used paper, empty containers and bottles, and waste food. 垃圾；废物 [also "the" N] [AM]

in BRIT, use **rubbish**

❑ *The yards are overgrown and cluttered with trash.* 院子杂草丛生，堆满了垃圾。 ❑ *Would you take out the trash?* 你可以把垃圾带出去吗？ 2 N-UNCOUNT If you say that something such as a book, painting, or movie is **trash**, you mean that it is of very bad quality. 劣质的东西 [INFORMAL] ❑ *Pop music doesn't have to be trash; it can be art.* 流行音乐并不一定是劣质的东西，它可以是艺术。 3 N-SING **The trash** means the trash can. 垃圾桶 ❑ *I threw it in the trash.* 我把它扔进了垃圾桶。

Thesaurus *trash* 另参见：

N. debris, garbage, junk, litter 1

In American English, the words **trash** and **garbage** are most commonly used to refer to waste material that is thrown away. ❑ *...the smell of rotting garbage... She threw the bottle into the trash.* In British English, **rubbish** is the usual word. **Trash** and **garbage** are sometimes used in British English, but only informally and metaphorically. ❑ *I don't have to listen to this garbage... The book was trash.*

trash can (**trash cans**) N-COUNT A **trash can** is a large round container where people put their trash. 垃圾桶 [AM]

trashed /træʃt/ ADJ If someone is **trashed**, they are very drunk. 酩酊大醉的 ❑ *They get trashed and act totally out of character, shouting and swearing.* 他们酩酊大醉，行为异常，大喊大骂。

trau·ma /traʊmə, trɔ-/ (**traumas**) N-VAR **Trauma** is a very severe shock or very upsetting experience, which may cause psychological damage. (精神上的) 创伤；痛苦经历 ❑ *I'd been through the trauma of losing a house.* 我已经历过失去房子的痛苦。

trau·mat·ic /trəmætɪk/ ADJ A **traumatic** experience is very shocking and upsetting, and may cause psychological damage. (精神上) 令人痛苦的 ❑ *I suffered a nervous breakdown. It was a traumatic experience.* 我遭受过一回精神崩溃，那是一次痛苦的经历。

trau·ma·tise /trɔːmətaɪz/ [BRIT] → see **traumatize**

trau·ma·tize /traʊmətaɪz, trɔ-/ (**traumatizes, traumatizing, traumatized**)

in BRIT, also use **traumatise**

V-T If someone **is traumatized** by an event or situation, it shocks or upsets them very much, and may cause them psychological damage. 使…(精神) 痛苦 ❑ *My wife was traumatized by the experience.* 我妻子因那次经历而痛苦。 ● **trau·ma·tized** ADJ 痛苦的 ❑ *He left her in the middle of the road, shaking and deeply traumatized.* 他把她留在路中间，浑身发抖，痛苦万分。

t

Word Link *tra ≈ across : traffic, travel, travesty*

trav·el ♦♦◇ /træv[ə]l/ (**travels, traveling** or **travelling, traveled** or **travelled**) 1 V-T/V-I If you **travel**, you go from one place to

Word Web **transportation**

Urban **mass transportation** began more than 200 years ago. By 1830, there were **horse-drawn streetcars** in New York City and New Orleans. They ran on **rails** built into the right of way of city streets. The first electric **tram** opened in Berlin in 1881. Later on, **buses** became more popular because they didn't require **tracks**. Today, **commuter trains** link **suburbs** to cities everywhere. Many large cities also have an underground train system. It's called the **subway, metro,** or **tube** depending on where you live. In cities with steep hills, cable cars are a popular form of mass **transit**.

another, often to a place that is far away. 旅行 ❑ *You had better travel to Nova Scotia tomorrow.* 你最好明天去新斯科舍。 ❑ *I've been traveling all day.* 我一整天都在旅行。 ❑ *Students often travel hundreds of miles to get here.* 学生们常常要旅行数百英里才能到这儿。 **2** N-UNCOUNT **Travel** is the activity of traveling. 旅行 ❑ *Information on travel in New Zealand is available at the hotel.* 新西兰的旅游信息在该酒店可以查到。 ❑ *He detested air travel.* 他厌恶空中旅行。 **3** V-T If you **travel** the world, the country, or the area, you go to many different places in the world or in a particular country or area. 游历 ❑ *He was a very wealthy man who had traveled the world.* 他是个非常富有的人，曾经周游过世界。 **4** V-I When light or sound from one place reaches another, you say that it **travels** to the other place. (光或声音) 传播 ❑ *When sound travels through water, strange things can happen.* 当声音在水中传播时，奇怪的事情会发生。 **5** V-I When news becomes known by people in different places, you can say that it **travels** to them. (消息) 流传 ❑ *News of his work traveled all the way to Asia.* 有关他工作的消息一直传到了亚洲。 **6** N-PLURAL Someone's **travels** are the trips that they make to places a long way from their home. 旅游 ❑ *He also collects things for the house on his travels abroad.* 他在国外旅游时也为家人收集些东西。 **7** PHRASE If you **travel light**, you travel without taking much luggage. 轻装旅行 ❑ *It would be good to be able to travel light, but I end up taking too many clothes.* 能够轻装旅行再好不过，但我最终还是带了太多衣服。

> The noun **travel** is used to talk about the general activity of traveling. It is either uncount or plural. You cannot say "a travel;" you would use the word **trip** or **journey** instead.
> ❑ *First-class rail travel to Paris or Brussels is included... We were going to go on a trip to Florida together.*

Thesaurus *travel* 另参见：

V. explore, trek, visit **1** **3**
N. expedition, journey, trip **2**

Word Partnership *travel* 的常用搭配：

ADV. travel **abroad** **1** – **3**
N. **air** travel, travel **arrangements**, travel **books**, **car** travel, travel **delays**, travel **expenses**, travel **guide**, travel **industry**, travel **insurance**, travel **plans**, travel **reports**, travel **reservations** **2**
travel **the world** **3**

trav·el agent (**travel agents**) **1** N-COUNT A **travel agent** or **travel agent's** is a store or office where you can go to arrange a vacation or trip. 旅行社 ❑ *He worked in a travel agent's.* 他在一家旅行社工作。 **2** N-COUNT A **travel agent** is a person or business that arranges people's vacations and trips. 旅行代理商

trav·el·er ♦◇◇ /trævələr/ (**travelers**) also **traveller** N-COUNT A **traveler** is a person who is on a trip or a person who travels a lot. 旅客; 旅行者 ❑ *Airline travelers need to be confident that their bookings will be honored.* 航空公司的旅客可以放心，他们的预订会得到兑现。

trav·el·er's check (**traveler's checks**) N-COUNT **Traveler's checks** are checks that you buy at a bank and take with you when you travel, for example, so that you can exchange them for the currency of the country that you are in. 旅行支票

★ **tra·verse** /trævɜrs, trəvɜrs/ (**traverses, traversing, traversed**) V-T If someone or something **traverses** an area of land or water, they go across it. 走过 [LITERARY] ❑ *I traversed the narrow pedestrian bridge.* 我走过了那座狭窄的步行桥。

Word Link *tra ≈ across : traffic, travel, travesty*

trav·es·ty /trævəsti/ (**travesties**) N-COUNT If you describe something as a **travesty of** another thing, you mean that it is a very bad representation of that other thing. 嘲弄 ❑ *Her research suggests that Smith's reputation today is a travesty of what he really stood for.* 她的研究表明，史密斯如今的声誉是对他原本立场的嘲弄。

trawl /trɔl/ (**trawls, trawling, trawled**) **1** V-T/V-I If you **trawl through** a large number of similar things, you search through them looking for something that you want or something that is suitable for a particular purpose. 搜索 ❑ *A team of officers is trawling through the records of thousands of petty thieves.* 一队警察正在数千名小偷的记录中搜索。 ❑ *Petra trawled the aisles of the Europa supermarket.* 佩特拉搜索了欧罗巴超市的各个通道。 **2** V-T/V-I When fishermen **trawl for** fish, they pull a wide net behind their ship in order to catch fish. 用拖网捕 (鱼); 拖网捕鱼 ❑ *They had seen him trawling and therefore knew that there were fish.* 他们看见他正用拖网捕鱼，因此他们知道那里有鱼。 ❑ *She would walk on to the beach and watch the night fishermen trawl the shallow waters.* 她会步行到海滩去看夜间工作的渔民在浅水中拖网捕鱼。
→ see **fish**

trawl·er /trɔlər/ (**trawlers**) N-COUNT A **trawler** is a fishing boat that is used for trawling. 拖网渔船
→ see **fish**

tray /treɪ/ (**trays**) N-COUNT A **tray** is a flat piece of wood, plastic, or metal, which usually has raised edges and which is used for carrying things, especially food and drinks. 托盘

treach·er·ous /trɛtʃərəs/ **1** ADJ If you describe someone as **treacherous**, you mean that they are likely to betray you and cannot be trusted. 背信弃义的 [DISAPPROVAL] ❑ *He publicly left the party and denounced its treacherous leaders.* 他公开脱离了该党，并谴责党内那些背信弃义的领导人们。 **2** ADJ If you say that something is **treacherous**, you mean that it is very dangerous and unpredictable. 危险的; 变化莫测的 ❑ *The current of the river is fast flowing and treacherous.* 河水的水流湍急而且变化莫测。

▲ **treach·ery** /trɛtʃəri/ N-UNCOUNT **Treachery** is behavior or an action in which someone betrays their country or betrays a person who trusts them. 背叛 ❑ *He was deeply wounded by the treachery of close aides and old friends.* 他被亲密助手和老朋友的背叛深深地伤害了。

▲ **tread** /trɛd/ (**treads, treading, trod, trodden**) **1** N-VAR The **tread** of a tire or shoe is the pattern of thin lines cut into its surface that stops it from slipping. (鞋底或轮胎上的) 花纹 ❑ *The fat, broad tires had a good depth of tread.* 鼓鼓的宽轮胎上有一道很深的花纹。 **2** V-I If you **tread** in a particular way, you walk that way. 行走 [LITERARY] ❑ *She trod casually, enjoying the touch of the damp grass on her feet.* 她随意行走，享受着脚底接触着湿草的感觉。 **3** V-I If you **tread** carefully, you behave in a careful or cautious way. (小心) 行事 ❑ *If you are hoping to form a new relationship, tread carefully and slowly to begin with.* 如果你希望建立一种新的关系，开始时就要小心缓慢行事。 **4** V-I If you **tread on** something, you put your foot on it when you are walking or standing. 踩 [mainly BRIT]

> in AM, usually use **step**

5 PHRASE If you **tread** a particular **path**, you take a particular course of action or do something in a particular way. 以…方式行事 ❑ *He continues to tread an unconventional path.* 他继续以一种不合常规的方式行事。

tread·mill /trɛdmɪl/ (**treadmills**) **1** N-COUNT You can refer to a task or a job as a **treadmill** when you have to keep doing it although it is unpleasant and exhausting. 单调的工作 ❑ *He exhausted himself on an endless treadmill to pay for rent and food.* 为了支付房租和食物，他精力全都耗在了一份没完没了的单调工作上。 **2** N-COUNT A **treadmill** is a piece of equipment, for example, an exercise machine, consisting of a wheel with steps around its edge or a continuous moving belt. The weight of a person or animal walking on it causes the wheel or belt to turn. 踏车

▲ **trea·son** /triz°n/ N-UNCOUNT **Treason** is the crime of betraying your country, for example, by helping its enemies or by trying to remove its government using violence. 叛国罪 ❑ *They were tried and found guilty of treason.* 他们受到了审判并被处以叛国罪。

treas·ure /trɛʒər/ (**treasures, treasuring, treasured**) **1** N-UNCOUNT **Treasure** is a collection of valuable old objects such as gold coins and jewels that has been hidden or lost. 财宝 [LITERARY] ❑ *It was here, the buried treasure, she knew it was.* 那些埋藏的珍宝就在这儿，她知道就在这儿。 **2** N-COUNT **Treasures** are valuable objects, especially works of art and items of historical value. 珍品 (尤指艺术品和有历史价值的物品) ❑ *The house was large and full of art treasures.* 那栋房子很大，里面满是艺术珍品。 **3** V-T If you **treasure** something that you have, you keep it or care for it carefully because it gives you great pleasure and you think it is very special. 珍惜 ❑ *She treasures her memories of those joyous days.* 她珍惜那些快乐时光的记忆。 ● N-COUNT **Treasure** is also a noun. 珍爱之物 ❑ *His greatest treasure is his collection of rock records.* 他最珍爱的东西就是他收藏的摇滚唱片。 ● **treas·ured** ADJ 珍贵的 [ADJ n] ❑ *These books are still among my most treasured possessions.* 这些书仍然是我最珍贵的财产之一。

treas·ure chest (**treasure chests**) 1 N-COUNT A **treasure chest** is a box containing treasure. 财宝箱 2 N-COUNT If you describe something as a **treasure chest of** a particular thing, you mean that it is very good source of that thing. 是…的好资源 [usu N "of" n] ❑ *This book is a treasure chest of information.* 这本书是信息的好资源。

treas·ur·er /trɛʒərər/ (**treasurers**) N-COUNT The **treasurer** of a society or organization is the person who is in charge of its finances and keeps its accounts. (团体或组织的) 财务主管

▲ **treas·ury** ♦◊◊ /trɛʒəri/ (**treasuries**) 1 N-COUNT-COLL In the United States and some other countries, **the Treasury** is the government department that deals with the country's finances. 财政部 ❑ *...a senior official at the Treasury.* …财政部的一位高级官员。 2 N-PLURAL **Treasuries** are financial bonds that are issued by the United States government in order to raise money. (美国政府发行的) 国库券 [AM] ❑ *...people who invest in 10- and 20- and 30-year Treasuries.* …10年、20年和30年期国库券的投资者。

treat ♦♦◊ /trit/ (**treats, treating, treated**) 1 V-T If you **treat** someone or something in a particular way, you behave toward them or deal with them in that way. 对待；处理 ❑ *Artie treated most women with indifference.* 阿蒂对待大多数女性颇为冷淡。 ❑ *Police say they're treating it as a case of attempted murder.* 警方说他们正将其作为谋杀未遂案件来处理。 2 V-T When a doctor or nurse **treats** a patient or an illness, he or she tries to make the patient well again. 治疗 ❑ *Doctors treated her with aspirin.* 医生用阿斯匹林给她治疗。 ❑ *The boy was treated for a minor head wound.* 那个男孩因头部轻伤而接受治疗。 3 V-T If something **is treated with** a particular substance, the substance is put onto or into it in order to clean it, to protect it, or to give it special properties. (用某种物质) 处理 ❑ *About 70% of the cocoa acreage is treated with insecticide.* 大约70%的可可豆种植区都用杀虫剂处理过。 4 V-T If you **treat** someone **to** something special which they will enjoy, you buy it or arrange it for them. 款待 ❑ *She was always treating him to ice cream.* 她总请他吃冰淇淋。 ❑ *Tomorrow I'll treat myself to a day's gardening.* 明天我要好好享受一天的园艺活儿。 5 N-COUNT If you give someone a **treat**, you buy or arrange something special for them which they will enjoy. 款待 ❑ *Lettie had never yet failed to return from town without some special treat for him.* 莱蒂每次从城里回来都要带一些特别的礼物送给他。

Word Partnership *treat* 的常用搭配：

ADV. treat **differently**, treat **equally**, treat **fairly**, treat **well** 1

N. treat **with contempt/dignity/respect** 1
treat **people**, treat **women** 1 2
treat **AIDS**, treat **cancer**, treat **a disease**, **doctors** treat 2

treat·ment ♦♦◊ /tritmənt/ (**treatments**) 1 N-VAR **Treatment** is medical attention given to a sick or injured person or animal. 治疗 ❑ *Many patients are not getting the medical treatment they need.* 许多病人都没有得到他们需要的医疗。 ❑ *...a veterinary surgeon who specializes in the treatment of caged birds.* …一个专长治疗笼养鸟的兽医。 2 N-UNCOUNT Your **treatment** of someone is the way you behave toward them or deal with them. 对待；处理 ❑ *We don't want any special treatment.* 我们不需要任何特殊待遇。 3 N-VAR **Treatment** of something involves putting a particular substance onto or into it, in order to clean it, to protect it, or to give it special properties. (采用某种物质的) 处理 ❑ *There should be greater treatment of sewage before it is discharged.* 污水排放前应该进行更充分的处理。

→ see **cancer, illness**

Word Partnership *treatment* 的常用搭配：

V. **get/receive** treatment, **give** treatment, **undergo** treatment 1

ADJ. **effective** treatment, **medical** treatment 1
better treatment, **equal/unequal** treatment, **fair** treatment, **humane** treatment 2
special treatment 2 3

N. treatment **of addiction, AIDS** treatment, **cancer** treatment, treatment **center**, treatment **of an illness** 1
treatment **of prisoners** 2
treatment **plant, water** treatment 3

trea·ty ♦♦◊ /triti/ (**treaties**) N-COUNT A **treaty** is a written agreement between countries in which they agree to do a particular thing or to help each other. 条约 ❑ *...negotiations over a treaty on global warming.* …关于全球变暖条约的谈判。

tre·ble /trɛbᵊl/ (**trebles, trebling, trebled**) 1 N-COUNT On a stereo system or radio, the **treble** is the ability to reproduce the higher musical notes. The **treble** is also the knob which controls this. (立体声音响或收音机的) 高音；高音调节旋钮 2 V-T/V-I If something **trebles** or if you **treble** it, it becomes three times greater in number or amount than it was. 使增加两倍；增加两倍 [mainly BRIT]

in AM, use **triple**

❑ *They will have to pay much more when rents treble in January.* 房租1月份时将增加两倍，他们得付多得多的钱。 3 PREDET If one thing is **treble** the size or amount of another thing, it is three times greater in size or amount. 3倍的 [mainly BRIT, FORMAL]

in AM, use **triple**

tree ♦♦◊ /tri/ (**trees**) N-COUNT A **tree** is a tall plant that has a hard trunk, branches, and leaves. 树 ❑ *I planted those apple trees.* 我种了那些苹果树。

→ see Word Web: **tree**
→ see **forest, mountain, plant**

▲ **trek** /trɛk/ (**treks, trekking, trekked**) 1 V-I If you **trek** somewhere, you go on a journey across difficult country, usually on foot. (艰难地) 徒步旅行 ❑ *...trekking through the jungles.* …徒步穿越丛林。 ● N-COUNT **Trek** is also a noun. 徒步旅行 ❑ *He is on a trek through the South Gobi desert.* 他正徒步穿越南戈壁沙漠。 2 V-I If you **trek** somewhere, you go there heavily and unwillingly, usually because you are tired. 疲惫地行走 ❑ *They trekked from shop to shop in search of white knee-high socks.* 他们疲惫地奔波于一家又一家商店，寻找高到膝盖的白色长筒袜。

Word Link *trem ≈ shaking : tremble, tremendous, tremor*

trem·ble /trɛmbᵊl/ (**trembles, trembling, trembled**) 1 V-I If you **tremble**, you shake slightly because you are frightened or cold. 颤抖 ❑ *His mouth became dry, his eyes widened, and he began to tremble all over.* 他嘴巴干涩，眼睛睁大，而且开始全身发抖。 ❑ *Lisa was white and trembling with anger.* 莉萨气得脸色发白，身体颤抖。 ● N-SING **Tremble** is also a noun. 颤抖 ❑ *I will never forget the look on the patient's face, the tremble in his hand.* 我将永远不会忘记那病人脸上的表情和他颤抖的手。 2 V-I If something **trembles**, it shakes slightly. (轻微地) 颤动 [LITERARY] ❑ *He felt the earth tremble under him.* 他感觉大地在脚下颤动。 3 V-I If your voice **trembles**, it sounds unsteady and uncertain, usually because you are upset or nervous. (声音) 发颤 [LITERARY] ❑ *His voice trembled, on the verge*

Word Web tree

Trees are one of the oldest living things. They are also the largest **plant**. Some scientists believe that the largest living thing on Earth is a coniferous giant redwood tree named General Grant. Other scientists point to a huge grove of deciduous aspen trees known as Pando. This grove is a single plant because all of the trees grow from the root system of just one tree. Pando covers more than 106 acres. Some aspen trees **germinate** from seeds, but most result from natural cloning. In this process the parent tree sends up new **sprouts** from its root system. Fossil records show tree clones may live up to a million years.

t

of tears. 他的声音颤抖着，就要落下泪来。● N-SING **Tremble** is also a noun. (声音的) 发颤 ❑ *"Please understand this," she began, a tremble in her voice.* "请理解这个"，她开始用颤抖的声音说道。

Word Link *trem ≈ shaking : tremble, tremendous, tremor*

tre·men·dous ♦◇◇ /trɪmɛndəs/ **1** ADJ You use **tremendous** to emphasize how strong a feeling or quality is, or how large an amount is. 非常的；巨大的 [EMPHASIS] ❑ *I felt a tremendous pressure on my chest.* 我感到胸口有股巨大的压力。● **tre·men·dous·ly** ADV 非常地；极大地 ❑ *I thought they played tremendously well, didn't you?* 我认为他们表演得非常好，你不觉得吗？ **2** ADJ You can describe someone or something as **tremendous** when you think they are very good or very impressive. 极好的；精彩的 ❑ *I thought it was absolutely tremendous.* 我觉得它绝对精彩。

trem·or /trɛmər/ (**tremors**) **1** N-COUNT A **tremor** is a small earthquake. 小地震 ❑ *The earthquake sent tremors through the region.* 这次地震的震感传遍了整个地区。 **2** N-COUNT If an event causes a **tremor** in a group or organization, it threatens to make the group or organization less strong or stable. (团体或组织内的) 波动 ❑ *News of 160 lay-offs had sent tremors through the community.* 裁员160人的消息在社区中引起了波动。 **3** N-COUNT A **tremor** is a shaking of your body or voice that you cannot control. (身体或声音的) 颤抖 ❑ *The old man has a tremor in his hands.* 那位老人的双手颤抖着。

★ **trench** /trɛntʃ/ (**trenches**) **1** N-COUNT A **trench** is a long narrow channel that is cut into the ground, for example, in order to lay pipes or get rid of water. 沟渠 **2** N-COUNT A **trench** is a long narrow channel in the ground used by soldiers in order to protect themselves from the enemy. People often refer to the battlegrounds of the First World War in Northern France and Belgium as **the trenches**. 战壕 ❑ *We fought with them in the trenches.* 我们在战壕里与他们作战。

trend ♦◇◇ /trɛnd/ (**trends**) **1** N-COUNT A **trend** is a change or development toward something new or different. 趋势 ❑ *This is a growing trend.* 这是一个不断增长的趋势。 ❑ *...a trend toward part-time employment.* …非全日制就业的趋势。 **2** N-COUNT To set a **trend** means to do something that becomes accepted or fashionable, and that a lot of other people copy. 时尚 ❑ *The latest trend is gardening.* 最新的时尚是园艺。

→ see **population**

Thesaurus *trend* 另参见：

N. craze, fad, style **2**

Word Partnership *trend* 的常用搭配：

ADJ. **overall** trend, **upward** trend, **warming** trend **1**
current trend, **disturbing** trend, **growing** trend, **latest** trend, **new** trend, **recent** trend **1** **2**
V. **continue a** trend, **reverse a** trend, **start a** trend **1** **2**

trendy /trɛndi/ (**trendier, trendiest**) ADJ If you say that something or someone is **trendy**, you mean that they are very fashionable and modern. 时髦的 [INFORMAL] ❑ *...a trendy Seattle night club.* …一家时髦的西雅图夜总会。

trepi·da·tion /trɛpɪdeɪʃən/ N-UNCOUNT **Trepidation** is fear or anxiety about something that you are going to do or experience. 惊恐；焦虑 [FORMAL] ❑ *It was with some trepidation that I viewed the prospect of cycling across Uganda.* 想到要骑自行车穿越乌干达，我感到有点惊恐不安。

tres·pass /trɛspəs, -pæs/ (**trespasses, trespassing, trespassed**) V-I If someone **trespasses**, they go onto someone else's land without their permission. 擅自进入 ❑ *They were trespassing on private property.* 他们正在擅自闯入私人领地。● N-VAR **Trespass** is the act of trespassing. 擅自进入 [LEGAL] ❑ *You could be prosecuted for trespass.* 你可能会因擅自闯入而被起诉。

tri·al ♦♦◇ /traɪəl/ (**trials**) **1** N-VAR A **trial** is a formal meeting in a law court, at which a judge and jury listen to evidence and decide whether a person is guilty of a crime. 审判 ❑ *New evidence showed the police lied at the trial.* 新的证据表明警方在审判时撒了谎。 ❑ *I have the right to a trial with a jury of my peers.* 我有权要求由和我一样的平民组成的陪审团参加审判。 **2** N-VAR A **trial** is an experiment in which you test something by using it or doing it for a period of time to see how well it works. If something is **on trial**, it is being tested in this way. 试验 ❑ *They have been treated with this drug in clinical trials.* 他们在临床试验中一直接受这种药物的治疗。 ❑ *I took the car out for a trial on the roads.* 我把车开出去在公路上试了一下。 **3** N-COUNT If you refer to the **trials of** a situation, you mean the unpleasant things that you experience in it. 磨难 ❑ *...the trials of adolescence.* …青春期的磨难。 **4** PHRASE If you do something **by trial and error**, you try several different methods of doing it until you find the method that works best. 反复试验 ❑ *Many drugs were found by trial and error.* 许多药物都是经过反复试验后才被发现的。 **5** PHRASE If someone is **on trial**, they are being tried in a court of law. 在受审 ❑ *He is currently on trial for drunk driving.* 他目前因酒后驾车而受审。 **6** PHRASE If you say that someone or something is **on trial**, you mean that they are in a situation where people are observing them to see whether they succeed or fail. 在试验中；在考验中 ❑ *The president will be drawn into a damaging battle in which his credentials will be on trial.* 总统将被拖入一场破坏性的斗争，他正陷入信任危机。 **7** PHRASE If someone **stands trial**, they are tried in court for a crime they are accused of. 受审判 ❑ *He was found to be mentally unfit to stand trial.* 发现他精神状况不适合接受审判。

→ see Word Web: **trial**

Word Partnership *trial* 的常用搭配：

ADJ. **civil** trial, **fair** trial, **federal** trial, **speedy** trial, **upcoming** trial **1**
clinical trial **2**
N. trial **date**, **jury** trial, **murder** trial, **outcome of a** trial **1**
trial **and error** **4**
V. **await** trial, **bring** *someone* **to** trial, **face** trial, **go on** trial, **put on** trial **5**

Word Link *tri ≈ three : triangle, trilogy, triplet*

tri·an·gle /traɪæŋgəl/ (**triangles**) **1** N-COUNT A **triangle** is an object, arrangement, or flat shape with three straight sides and three angles. 三角形 ❑ *This design is in pastel colors with three rectangles and three triangles.* 这个图案色彩柔和淡雅，有3个长方形和3个三角形。 ❑ *Its outline roughly forms an equilateral triangle.* 它的大致轮廓是一个等边三角形。 **2** N-COUNT The **triangle** is a musical instrument that consists of a piece of metal shaped like a triangle. You play it by hitting it with a short metal bar. 三角铁 (一种打击乐器) ❑ *My musical career consisted of playing the triangle in kindergarten.* 我的音乐生涯包括在幼儿园演奏三角铁。

→ see **circle, shape**

tri·an·gu·lar /traɪæŋgyələr/ ADJ Something that is **triangular** is in the shape of a triangle. 三角形的 ❑ *...a triangular roof.* …一个三角形的屋顶。

trib·al /traɪbəl/ ADJ **Tribal** is used to describe things relating to or belonging to tribes and the way that they are organized. 部落的 ❑ *...tribal warfare.* …部落战争。 ❑ *...the Navajo Tribal Council.* …纳瓦霍人的部落会。

Word Web trial

Many countries guarantee the right to a **trial** by jury. The **judge** begins by explaining the **charges** against the **defendant**. Next the defendant **pleads guilty** or not guilty. Then the **lawyers** for the **plaintiff** and the defendant present **evidence**. Both **attorneys** interview **witnesses**. They can also question each other's **clients**. Sometimes the lawyers go back and **cross-examine** witnesses about **testimony** they gave earlier. When they finish, the **jury** meets to **deliberate**. They deliver their **verdict** and the judge **pronounces** the **sentence**. At this point, the defendant may be able to **appeal** the verdict and request a new trial.

T

★ **tribe** /traɪb/ **(tribes)** N-COUNT-COLL **Tribe** is sometimes used to refer to a group of people of the same race, language, and customs, especially in a developing country. Some people disapprove of this use. 部落 ❑ *...three-hundred members of the Xhosa tribe.* …科萨族部落的3百名成员。
→ see **society**

tribu·la·tion /trɪbyəleɪʃən/ **(tribulations)** N-VAR You can refer to the suffering or difficulty that you experience in a particular situation as **tribulations.** 苦难；艰难 [FORMAL] ❑ *...the trials and tribulations of everyday life.* …日常生活的磨练与艰难。

★ **tri·bu·nal** /traɪbyunəl/ **(tribunals)** N-COUNT-COLL A **tribunal** is a special court or committee that is appointed to deal with particular problems. 特别法庭；特别委员会 ❑ *His case comes before an industrial tribunal in March.* 他的案子将于3月在产业法庭审判。

★ **trib·ute** /trɪbyut/ **(tributes)** 1 N-VAR A **tribute** is something that you say, do, or make to show your admiration and respect for someone. 称赞；敬意 ❑ *The song is a tribute to Roy Orbison.* 这首歌是敬献给罗伊・奥比森的。 2 N-SING If one thing is **a tribute to** another, the first thing is the result of the second and shows how good it is. 有成效的结果 ❑ *His success has been a tribute to hard work, to professionalism.* 他的成功是辛勤工作和兢兢业业的结果。

trick ♦◇◇ /trɪk/ **(tricks, tricking, tricked)** 1 N-COUNT A **trick** is an action that is intended to fool or deceive someone. 捉弄；诡计 ❑ *We are playing a trick on a man who keeps bothering me.* 我们正要弄着一个人，因为他一直烦扰我。 2 V-T If someone **tricks** you, they deceive you, often in order to make you do something. 欺骗 ❑ *Stephen is going to be pretty upset when he finds out how you tricked him.* 当斯蒂芬发现你是如何欺骗他时，他会非常不高兴的。 ❑ *His family tricked him into going to Pakistan, and once he was there, they took away his passport.* 他的家人骗他去了巴基斯坦，他一到那里，他们便拿走了他的护照。 3 N-COUNT A **trick** is a clever or skillful action that someone does in order to entertain people. 戏法 ❑ *...magic tricks.* …魔术戏法。 ❑ *He shows me card tricks.* 他向我表演纸牌戏法。 4 N-COUNT A **trick** is a clever way of doing something. 窍门 ❑ *Everything I cooked was a trick of my mother's.* 我烹饪都是沿用了我母亲的诀窍。 5 → see also **hat trick** 6 PHRASE If something **does the trick**, it achieves what you wanted. 达到目的 [INFORMAL] ❑ *Sometimes a few choice words will do the trick.* 有时斟酌得当的只言片语就能达到目的。 7 PHRASE If someone tries **every trick in the book**, they try every possible thing that they can think of in order to achieve something. 浑身解数 [INFORMAL] ❑ *Companies are using every trick in the book to stay one step in front of their competitors.* 各公司正用尽浑身解数想领先竞争对手一步。 8 PHRASE **The tricks of the trade** are the quick and clever ways of doing something that are known by people who regularly do a particular activity. 行业诀窍 ❑ *To get you started, we have asked five successful writers to reveal some of the tricks of the trade.* 为了帮你起步，我们请了5位成功作家来揭示一些诀窍。

Word Partnership *trick* 的常用搭配：

ADJ.	**cheap** trick 1
	old trick 1 3
	clever trick, **neat** trick 1 3 4
V.	**play** a trick, **pull** a trick 1
	try to trick *someone* 2
	do the trick 6
N.	**card** trick 3
	every trick **in the book** 7

▲ **trick·le** /trɪkəl/ **(trickles, trickling, trickled)** 1 V-T/V-I When a liquid **trickles**, or when you **trickle** it, it flows slowly in a thin stream. 使细流；细流 ❑ *A tear trickled down the old man's cheek.* 一滴泪水顺着老人的面颊流了下来。 ● N-COUNT **Trickle** is also a noun. 细流 ❑ *There was not so much as a trickle of water.* 一点儿细流的水也没有。 2 V-I When people or things **trickle** in a particular direction, they move there slowly in small groups or amounts, rather than all together. (陆续地) 慢慢移动 ❑ *Some donations are already trickling in.* 一些捐款已经陆续到了。 ● N-COUNT **Trickle** is also a noun. 慢慢移动 ❑ *The flood of cars has now slowed to a trickle.* 洪水般的车流现已减缓为慢慢移动了。

▸ **trickle down** PHRASAL VERB If benefits given to people at the top of a society or system **trickle down**, they are eventually passed on to people lower down the society or system. 渗漏 (利益在社会阶层或体制中从上往下传递) ❑ *...the failure of the prosperity of Las Vegas' casinos to trickle down to poor neighborhoods.* …拉斯维加斯赌场的繁荣向贫穷街区渗漏的失败。

tricky /trɪki/ **(trickier, trickiest)** ADJ If you describe a task or problem as **tricky**, you mean that it is difficult to do or deal with. 难对付的 ❑ *Parking can be tricky downtown.* 在市中心停车会很难。

tried /traɪd/ 1 ADJ **Tried** is used in the expressions **tried and tested, tried and trusted,** and **tried and true,** which describe a product or method that has already been used and has been found to be successful. 经过检验的 [ADJ "and" adj] ❑ *...over 1,000 tried-and-tested recipes.* …经过检验的一千多种配方。 2 → see also **try**

tri·fle /traɪfəl/ **(trifles)** 1 PHRASE You can use **a trifle** to mean slightly or to a small extent, especially in order to make something you say seem less extreme. 有点儿 [OLD-FASHIONED, VAGUENESS] ❑ *As a photographer, he'd found both locations just a trifle disappointing.* 作为一名摄影师，他发现这两个地方都有点儿令人失望。 2 N-COUNT A **trifle** is something that is considered to have little importance, value, or significance. 琐事；微不足道的东西 ❑ *He had no money to spare on trifles.* 他没钱花在琐碎的东西上。 3 N-VAR **Trifle** is a cold dessert made of layers of sponge cake, fruit gelatin, fruit, and custard, and usually covered with cream. 屈莱弗甜食 (由蛋糕、果冻、水果、蛋奶沙司做成，上浇鲜奶油。) ❑ *...a bowl of trifle.* …一碗屈莱弗甜食。

★ **trig·ger** ♦◇◇ /trɪgər/ **(triggers, triggering, triggered)** 1 N-COUNT The **trigger** of a gun is a small lever which you pull to fire it. 扳机 ❑ *A man pointed a gun at them and pulled the trigger.* 一名男子把枪对着他们并扣动了扳机。 2 N-COUNT The **trigger** of a bomb is the device which causes it to explode. (炸弹的) 引爆装置 ❑ *...trigger devices for nuclear weapons.* …核武器的引爆装置。 3 V-T To **trigger** a bomb or system means to cause it to work. 引爆；触发 ❑ *The thieves must have deliberately triggered the alarm and hidden inside the house.* 那些小偷一定是故意触发了报警器，然后藏在屋子里。 4 V-T If something **triggers** an event or situation, it causes it to begin to happen or exist. 引起 ❑ *...the incident which triggered the outbreak of the First World War.* …引起第一次世界大战爆发的事件。 ● PHRASAL VERB **Trigger off** means the same as **trigger.** 引起 ❑ *It is still not clear what events triggered off the demonstrations.* 还不清楚是什么事件引发了示威。 5 N-COUNT If something acts as a **trigger for** another thing such as an illness, event, or situation, the first thing causes the second thing to begin to happen or exist. 引发…的原因 ❑ *Stress may act as a trigger for these illnesses.* 压力也许是引发这些疾病的一个原因。

★ **tril·lion** /trɪlyən/ **(trillions)**

The plural form is **trillion** after a number, or after a word or expression referring to a number, such as "several" or "a few."

1 NUM A **trillion** is 1,000,000,000,000. 万亿 [AM]
in BRIT, use **billion**
❑ *...a 4 trillion dollar debt.* …一笔4万亿美元的债务。 2 NUM A **trillion** is 1,000,000,000,000,000,000. 百万兆 [BRIT]
in AM, use **quintillion**

tril·ogy /trɪlədʒi/ **(trilogies)** N-COUNT A **trilogy** is a series of three books, plays, or movies that have the same subject or the same characters. (书、戏剧或电影的) 三部曲 ❑ *...Tolkien's trilogy, The Lord of the Rings.* …托尔金的三部曲《指环王》。

trim /trɪm/ **(trimmer, trimmest, trims, trimming, trimmed)** 1 ADJ Something that is **trim** is neat, and attractive. 整洁美观的 ❑ *The neighbors' gardens were trim and neat.* 邻居们的花园既整洁又美观。 2 ADJ If you describe someone's figure as **trim**, you mean that it is attractive because there is no extra fat on their body. 苗条的 [APPROVAL] ❑ *The driver was a trim young woman of perhaps thirty.* 驾车者是一位大约三十来岁的苗条年轻女子。 3 V-T If you **trim** something, for example, someone's hair, you cut off small amounts of it in order to make it look neater. 修剪 ❑ *My friend trims my hair every eight weeks.* 我朋友每隔8周就为我修剪一次头发。 ● N-SING **Trim** is also a noun. 修剪 ❑ *His hair needed a trim.* 他的头发需要修剪了。 4 V-T If a government or other organization **trims** something such as a plan, policy, or amount, they reduce it slightly in extent or size. 削减 ❑ *American companies looked at ways they could trim these costs.* 美国公司研究了他们可能削减成本的方案。 5 V-T If something such as a piece of clothing **is trimmed with** a type of material or design, it is decorated with it, usually along its edges. 镶边于 [usu passive] ❑ *...jackets, which are then trimmed with crocheted flowers.* …镶着钩针编织花边的夹克。 6 N-VAR The **trim** on something such as a piece of clothing is a decoration, for example, along its edges, that is in a different color or material. 镶边 ❑ *...a white satin scarf with black trim.* …一条镶着黑边的白色绸缎围巾。

trim·ming /trɪmɪŋ/ (**trimmings**) 1 N-VAR The **trimming** on something such as a piece of clothing is the decoration, for example, along its edges, that is in a different color or material. 镶边装饰 ❑ *...the lace trimming on her satin nightgown.* …她的绸缎睡衣上的花边装饰。 2 N-PLURAL **Trimmings** are pieces of something, usually food, which are left over after you have cut what you need. (通常指食物切割后剩下的) 零头碎片 ❑ *Use the pastry trimmings to decorate the pie.* 用油酥的零头碎片来装饰馅饼。

trio /triou/ (**trios**) N-COUNT-COLL A **trio** is a group of three people together, especially musicians or singers, or a group of three things that have something in common. (尤指演奏或演唱的) 三人小组; 三件套 ❑ *...classy American songs from a Texas trio.* …来自德克萨斯州三重唱小组的时髦的美国歌曲。

trip ♦♦◊ /trɪp/ (**trips, tripping, tripped**) 1 N-COUNT A **trip** is a journey that you make to a particular place. 旅行 ❑ *We're taking a trip to Montana.* 我们要去一趟蒙大拿州。 ❑ *On Thursday we went out on a day trip.* 周四我们出去旅行了一天。 2 → see also **round trip**
3 V-I If you **trip** when you are walking, you knock your foot against something and fall or nearly fall. 绊倒; 绊 ❑ *She tripped and fell last night and broke her hip.* 她昨晚绊倒了，摔断了髋关节。
● PHRASAL VERB **Trip up** means the same as **trip**. 绊倒; 绊 ❑ *I tripped up and hurt my foot.* 我绊倒了，弄伤了脚。 4 V-T If you **trip** someone who is walking or running, you put your foot or something else in front of them, so that they knock their own foot against it and fall or nearly fall. 绊倒; 绊 (某人) ❑ *One guy stuck his foot out and tried to trip me.* 有个家伙伸出他的脚试图绊倒我。 ● PHRASAL VERB **Trip up** means the same as **trip**. 绊倒; 绊 (某人) ❑ *He made a sudden dive for Uncle Jim's legs to try to trip him up.* 他突然扑向吉姆大叔的双腿，试图把他绊倒。

> The noun **travel** is used to talk about the general activity of traveling. It is either uncount or plural. You cannot say "a travel;" you would use the word **trip** or **journey** instead.
> ❑ *First-class rail travel to Paris or Brussels is included... We were going to go on a trip to Florida together.*

Thesaurus *trip* 另参见:

N.	excursion, expedition, jaunt, journey, voyage 1
V.	fall, slip, stumble 3

Word Partnership *trip* 的常用搭配:

N.	**boat** trip, **bus** trip, **business** trip, **camping** trip, **field** trip, trip **home**, **return** trip, **shopping** trip, **train** trip, **vacation** trip 1
V.	**cancel** a trip, **make** a trip, **plan** a trip, **return from** a trip, **take** a trip 1
ADJ.	**free** trip, **last** trip, **long** trip, **next** trip, **recent** trip, **safe** trip, **short** trip 1

★ **tri·ple** /trɪpᵊl/ (**triples, tripling, tripled**) 1 ADJ **Triple** means consisting of three things or parts. 三个的; 三部分的 [ADJ n] ❑ *...a triple somersault.* …连续三个筋斗。 2 V-T/V-I If something **triples** or if you **triple** it, it becomes three times as large in size or number. 使成为三倍; 变成三倍 ❑ *I got a fantastic new job and my salary tripled.* 我得到了一份极好的新工作，我的薪水是原来的三倍。 ❑ *The exhibition has tripled in size from last year.* 这个展览会面积是去年的三倍。
3 PREDET If something is **triple the** amount or size of another thing, it is three times as large. 3倍的 [PREDET "the" n] ❑ *The mine reportedly had an accident rate triple the national average.* 据报道，那个矿的事故发生率是全国平均水平的三倍。

T

Word Link *tri* ≈ *three* : *triangle, trilogy, triplet*

tri·plet /trɪplɪt/ (**triplets**) N-COUNT **Triplets** are three children born at the same time to the same mother. 三胞胎 ❑ *"Guess what? Katinka had triplets–all healthy."* "你猜怎么着？卡金卡生了三胞胎——全都健健康康的。"

tri·pod /traɪpɒd/ (**tripods**) N-COUNT A **tripod** is a stand with three legs that is used to support something such as a camera or a telescope. 三脚架

tri·umph ♦◊◊ /traɪʌmf/ (**triumphs, triumphing, triumphed**)
1 N-VAR A **triumph** is a great success or achievement, often one that has been gained with a lot of skill or effort. 胜利; 成就 ❑ *The championships proved to be a personal triumph for the coach, Dave Donovan.* 那些冠军称号证明了教练戴夫・多诺万的个人成就。 2 N-UNCOUNT **Triumph** is a feeling of great satisfaction and pride resulting from a success or victory. (成功或胜利的) 喜悦 ❑ *Her sense of triumph was short-lived.* 她喜悦的感觉是短暂的。 3 V-I If someone or something **triumphs**, they gain complete success, control, or victory, often after a long or difficult struggle. 成功; 获胜 ❑ *All her life, Kelly had stuck with difficult tasks and challenges, and triumphed.* 凯利在一生中遭遇了种种艰巨任务与挑战，但成功了。 ❑ *The whole world looked to her as a symbol of good triumphing over evil.* 整个世界把她看作是正义战胜邪恶的象征。

tri·um·phant /traɪʌmfənt/ ADJ Someone who is **triumphant** has gained a victory or succeeded in something and feels very happy about it. (因胜利或成功而) 得意洋洋的 ❑ *The captain's voice was triumphant.* 船长的声音听起来得意洋洋的。 ● **tri·um·phant·ly** ADV 得意洋洋地 ❑ *They marched triumphantly into the capital.* 他们得意洋洋地列队进入首都。

trivia /trɪviə/ N-UNCOUNT **Trivia** is unimportant facts or details that are considered to be interesting rather than serious or useful. 琐事 ❑ *The two men chatted about such trivia as their favorite kinds of fast food.* 那两位男子聊着诸如他们最喜欢的快餐之类的琐事。

★ **triv·ial** /trɪviəl/ ADJ If you describe something as **trivial**, you think that it is unimportant and not serious. 无关紧要的 ❑ *The director tried to wave aside these issues as trivial details that could be settled later.* 那位主任对这些问题置之不理，视它们为可以后解决的无关紧要的细节。

trivi·al·ise /trɪviəlaɪz/ [BRIT] → see **trivialize**

trivi·al·ize /trɪviəlaɪz/ (**trivializes, trivializing, trivialized**)
in BRIT, also use **trivialise**
V-T If you say that someone **trivializes** something important, you disapprove of them because they make it seem less important, serious, and complex than it is. 贬低; 简化 [DISAPPROVAL] ❑ *It never ceases to amaze me how the business world continues to trivialize the world's environmental problems.* 工商界继续轻视世界的环境问题，这一直令我感到惊讶。

trod /trɒd/ **Trod** is the past tense of **tread**. **tread**的过去式

trod·den /trɒdᵊn/ **Trodden** is the past participle of **tread**. **tread** 的过去分词

▲ **trol·ley** /trɒli/ (**trolleys**) 1 N-COUNT A **trolley** or **trolley car** is an electric vehicle for carrying people which travels on rails in the streets of a city or town. 有轨电车 [AM]
in BRIT, use **tram**
❑ *He took a northbound trolley on State Street.* 他在州大街坐上了一辆北行的有轨电车。 2 N-COUNT A **trolley** is an object with wheels that you use to transport heavy things such as shopping or luggage. 手推车 [BRIT]
in AM, use **cart**
3 N-COUNT A **trolley** is a small table on wheels which is used for serving drinks or food. (送饮料或食品的) 小车 [BRIT]
in AM, use **cart**
4 N-COUNT A **trolley** is a bed on wheels for moving patients in a hospital. (医院用的) 担架车 [BRIT]
in AM, use **gurney**

trom·bone /trɒmboun/ (**trombones**) N-VAR A **trombone** is a large musical instrument of the brass family. It consists of two long oval tubes, one of which can be pushed backward and forward to play different notes. 长号 [oft "the" N] ❑ *Her husband had played the trombone in the band for a decade.* 她丈夫已在这支乐队吹了十年的长号。
→ see **orchestra**

troop ♦♦◊ /trup/ (**troops, trooping, trooped**) 1 N-PLURAL **Troops** are soldiers, especially when they are in a large organized group doing a particular task. 士兵 ❑ *The next phase of the operation will involve the deployment of more than 35,000 troops from a dozen countries.* 下阶段的行动包括部署来自12个国家的三万五千多名士兵。
2 N-COUNT-COLL A **troop** is a group of soldiers. 一群士兵 ❑ *...a troop of American Marines.* …一群美国海军陆战队士兵。 3 N-COUNT A **troop** of people or animals is a group of them. (一) 群 ❑ *The whole troop of men and women wore their hair fairly short.* 那一整群男女都留着相当短的头发。 4 V-I If people **troop** somewhere, they walk there in a group, often in a sad or tired way. (尤指悲伤或疲惫地) 成群结队地走 [INFORMAL] ❑ *They all trooped back to the house for a rest.* 他们都成群结队地回房子里休息。
→ see **army**

troop·er /trupər/ (**troopers**) **1** N-COUNT In the United States, a **trooper** is a police officer in a state police force. (美国的) 州警察 ❑ *Once long ago he had considered becoming a state trooper.* 很久以前他曾考虑过当一名州警官。 **2** N-COUNT; N-TITLE A **trooper** is a soldier of low rank in the cavalry or in an armored regiment in the army. 骑兵; 装甲兵 ❑ *...a trooper from the 7th Cavalry.* …第7骑兵团的1名士兵。

▲ **tro·phy** /troʊfi/ (**trophies**) **1** N-COUNT A **trophy** is a prize, for example, a silver cup, that is given to the winner of a competition or race. 奖品 ❑ *The special trophy for the best rider went to Chris Read.* 最佳骑手的特别奖给了克里斯·里德。 **2** N-COUNT A **trophy** is something that you keep in order to show that you have done something very difficult. 战利品 ❑ *His office was lined with animal heads, trophies of his hunting hobby.* 他的办公室排列着动物的头颅，都是他业余狩猎的战利品。

trop·i·cal /trɒpɪkəl/ **1** ADJ **Tropical** means belonging to or typical of the tropics. 热带的 [ADJ n] ❑ *...tropical diseases.* …热带疾病。 **2** ADJ **Tropical** weather is hot and damp weather typical of the tropics. 湿热的 ❑ *The cool, sweet milk is just what you need in the tropical heat.* 清凉的甜牛奶正是你在湿热的高温中所需要的。
→ see **disaster, hurricane**

▲ **trop·ics** /trɒpɪks/ N-PLURAL **The tropics** are the parts of the world that lie between two lines of latitude, the tropic of Cancer, 23½° north of the equator, and the tropic of Capricorn, 23½° south of the equator. 热带 ❑ *Being in the tropics meant that insects formed a large part of our life.* 身处热带地区意味着昆虫成了我们生活的一大部分。
→ see **globe**

▲ **trot** /trɒt/ (**trots, trotting, trotted**) **1** V-I If you **trot** somewhere, you move fairly fast at a speed between walking and running, taking small quick steps. 小跑 ❑ *I trotted down the steps and out to the shed.* 我小步跑下台阶去棚屋。 ● N-SING **Trot** is also a noun. 小跑 ❑ *He walked briskly, but without breaking into a trot.* 他轻快地走着，但没有小跑起来。 **2** V-I When an animal such as a horse **trots**, it moves fairly fast, taking quick small steps. You can also say that the rider of the animal **is trotting**. (马等) 小跑 ❑ *Alan took the reins and the small horse started trotting.* 艾伦抓住缰绳，小马开始小跑起来。 ● N-SING **Trot** is also a noun. (马等的) 小跑 ❑ *As they started up again, the horse broke into a brisk trot.* 当他们又出发时，那匹马便轻快地小跑起来。

trou·ble ♦♦◊ /trʌbəl/ (**troubles, troubling, troubled**)
1 N-UNCOUNT You can refer to problems or difficulties as **trouble**. 麻烦; 困难 [oft "in" N, also N in pl] ❑ *I had trouble parking.* 我停车有困难。 ❑ *You've caused us a lot of trouble.* 你已经给我们造成了很多麻烦。 **2** N-SING If you say that one aspect of a situation is **the trouble**, you mean that it is the aspect which is causing problems or making the situation unsatisfactory. 问题 (指引起麻烦的事情) ❑ *The trouble is that these restrictions have remained while other things have changed.* 问题是，虽然其他事情已经改变，这些限制却依旧存在。 **3** N-PLURAL Your **troubles** are the things that you are worried about. 烦恼 ❑ *She tells me her troubles. I tell her mine.* 她告诉了我她的烦恼，我也把我的告诉了她。 **4** N-UNCOUNT If you have kidney **trouble** or back **trouble**, for example, there is something wrong with your kidneys or your back. 疾病 ❑ *An old bed is the most likely cause of back trouble.* 旧床最有可能导致背部疾病。 ❑ *Her husband had never before had any heart trouble.* 她丈夫以前从未得过任何心脏疾病。 **5** N-UNCOUNT If there is **trouble** somewhere, especially in a public place, there is fighting or rioting there. 骚乱 [also N in pl] ❑ *Riot police are being deployed throughout the city to prevent any trouble.* 防暴警察正部署至全城以防止骚乱。 ❑ *Fans who make trouble during the World Cup will be arrested.* 在世界杯期间捣乱的球迷将被逮捕。 **6** N-UNCOUNT If you tell someone that it is **no trouble** to do something for them, you are saying politely that you can or will do it, because it is easy or convenient for you. 麻烦 [POLITENESS] ❑ *It's no trouble at all; on the contrary, it will be a great pleasure to help you.* 这根本不麻烦。相反，我很乐意帮助你。 **7** N-UNCOUNT If you say that a person or animal is **no trouble**, you mean that they are very easy to look after. 令人操心的人 (或动物) ❑ *My little grandson is no trouble at all, but his 6-year-old sister is a handful.* 我的小孙子一点不用人操心，但他6岁的姐姐却很难管教。 **8** V-T If something **troubles** you, it makes you feel worried. 使烦恼 ❑ *Is anything troubling you?* 有什么事使你烦恼吗？ ● **trou·bling** ADJ 令人烦恼的 ❑ *But most troubling of all was the simple fact that nobody knew what was going on.* 但是最令人烦恼的就是没人知道正发生什么事。 **9** V-T If a part of your body **troubles** you, it causes you physical pain or discomfort. 使疼痛; 使不适 ❑ *The ulcer had been troubling her for several years.* 溃疡已经折磨她好几年了。 **10** V-T If you say that someone does **not trouble to** do something, you are critical of them because they do not do something that they should, and you think that this would require very little effort. 费力 [DISAPPROVAL] ❑ *He burps, not troubling to cover his mouth.* 他打嗝连嘴巴都懒得捂住。 **11** V-T You use **trouble** in expressions such as **I'm sorry to trouble you** when you are apologizing to someone for disturbing them in order to ask them something. 打扰 [FORMULAE] ❑ *I'm sorry to trouble you, but I wondered if by any chance you know where he is.* 对不起打扰您了，我想问问您是否碰巧知道他在哪里。 **12** PHRASE If someone is **in trouble**, they are in a situation in which a person in authority is angry with them or is likely to punish them because they have done something wrong. 受训斥; 惹上麻烦 ❑ *He was in trouble with his teachers.* 他受到了他的老师们的训斥。 **13** PHRASE If you **take the trouble to** do something, you do something which requires a small amount of additional effort. 费神; 费力 ❑ *He did not take the trouble to see the movie before he attacked it.* 他在抨击那部电影前并没有费心去看看电影。

Word Partnership *trouble* 的常用搭配：

V.	**run into** trouble **1**
	have trouble **1 4**
	cause trouble, **make** trouble, **spell** trouble, **start** trouble **1 5**
	get in/into trouble, **get out of** trouble, **stay out of** trouble **12**
N.	**engine** trouble **1**
	sign of trouble **1 4 5**
ADJ.	**financial** trouble **1**
	big trouble, **deep** trouble, **real** trouble, **serious** trouble **1 5**
	heart trouble **4**
PREP.	trouble **with 1 2 5**
	in trouble **12**
ADV.	trouble **ahead 1 5**

trou·bled /trʌbəld/ **1** ADJ Someone who is **troubled** is worried because they have problems. 苦恼的 ❑ *Rose sounded deeply troubled.* 罗斯听上去极为烦恼。 **2** ADJ A **troubled** place, situation, organization, or time has many problems or conflicts. 麻烦一大堆的 ❑ *There is so much we can do to help this troubled country.* 我们可做很多事来帮助这个骚乱的国家。

trouble·maker /trʌbəlmeɪkər/ (**troublemakers**) N-COUNT If you refer to someone as a **troublemaker**, you mean that they cause unpleasantness, quarrels, or fights, especially by encouraging people to oppose authority. 闹事者 [DISAPPROVAL] ❑ *The fair coordinator has been given powers to expel suspected troublemakers.* 那位公正的协调员已被赋予权力，以驱逐涉嫌闹事者。

trouble·shooter /trʌbəlʃutər/ (**troubleshooters**) also **trouble-shooter** N-COUNT A **troubleshooter** is a person whose job is to solve major problems or difficulties that occur in a company or government. (公司或政府中的) 排解纠纷者 ❑ *The United Nations dispatched a team of troubleshooters to Somalia today.* 联合国今天派遣了一队纠纷人员到索马里。

Word Link *some ≈ causing : awesome, fearsome, troublesome*

trou·ble·some /trʌbəlsəm/ ADJ You use **troublesome** to describe something or someone that causes annoying problems or difficulties. 令人烦恼的 ❑ *He needed surgery to cure a troublesome back injury.* 他需要动手术来医治烦人的背部伤痛。

trough /trɔf/ (**troughs**) **1** N-COUNT A **trough** is a long narrow container from which farm animals drink or eat. 饮水槽; 饲料槽 ❑ *The old stone cattle trough still sits by the main entrance.* 那尊古老的石制牛食槽依旧位于主要入口处。 **2** N-COUNT A **trough** is a low area between two big waves on the sea. (波浪间的) 波谷 ❑ *The boat rolled heavily in the troughs between the waves.* 小船在海浪间的波谷中剧烈地摇晃着。 **3** N-COUNT A **trough** is a low point in a process that has regular high and low points, for example, a period in business when people do not produce as much as usual. 低谷 ❑ *...recovery from the industry's worst-ever trough in 2001 and 2002.* …从2001和2002年工业的最低谷复苏。 **4** N-COUNT A **trough of** low pressure is a long narrow area of low air pressure between two areas of higher pressure. (低气压) 槽 [TECHNICAL] ❑ *The trough of low pressure extends over 1,000 miles.* 低气压槽延伸一千多英里。
→ see **sound**

troupe /trup/ (**troupes**) N-COUNT-COLL A **troupe** is a group of actors, singers, or dancers who work together and often travel around together, performing in different places. 剧团 ❑ *...troupes of traveling actors.* …巡回演出的演员剧团。

trou·sers /traʊzərz/

The form **trouser** is used as a modifier.

N-PLURAL **Trousers** are a piece of men's clothing that cover the body from the waist downward, and that cover each leg separately. 裤子 [also "a pair of" N] [FORMAL] ❑ *He was dressed in a shirt, dark trousers and boots.* 他穿着衬衣、深色裤子和靴子。

trou·ser suit (**trouser suits**) N-COUNT A **trouser suit** is women's clothing consisting of a pair of trousers and a jacket which are made from the same material. (上衣与裤子搭配的) 女长裤套装 [BRIT]

in AM, use **pantsuit, pants suit**

trout /traʊt/ (**trout** or **trouts**)

The plural can be either **trout** or **trouts**.

N-VAR A **trout** is a fairly large fish that lives in rivers and streams. 鳟鱼; 鲑鱼 ● N-UNCOUNT **Trout** is this fish eaten as food. 鳟鱼肉; 鲑鱼肉 ❑ *Grilled trout needs only a squeeze of lemon.* 烤鳟鱼只需要一点柠檬榨汁。

tru·ant /truənt/ (**truants**) **1** N-COUNT A **truant** is a student who stays away from school without permission. 逃学者 ❑ *The parents of persistent truants can be put in jail.* 那些长期逃学学生的家长会被监禁。 **2** PHRASE If a student **plays truant**, he or she stays away from school without permission. 逃学 [BRIT] ❑ *She was getting into trouble over playing truant from school.* 她由于逃学而遇到了麻烦。

truce /trus/ (**truces**) N-COUNT A **truce** is an agreement between two people or groups of people to stop fighting or arguing for a short time. 停战协议 ❑ *The fighting of recent days has given way to an uneasy truce between the two sides.* 最近几天的交战已结束，双方好不容易达成了休战协议。

truck ♦◇◇ /trʌk/ (**trucks, trucking, trucked**) **1** N-COUNT A **truck** is a large vehicle that is used to transport goods by road. 卡车 [mainly AM]

in BRIT, usually use **lorry**

❑ *Now and then they heard the roar of a heavy truck.* 他们不时听见一辆重型卡车的轰响声。 ❑ *My dad is a truck driver.* 我的父亲是个卡车司机。 **2** N-COUNT A **truck** is a vehicle with a large area in the back for carrying things with low sides to make it easy to load and unload. A **truck** is the same as a **pickup**. 敞篷货车 [mainly AM] ❑ *We can only seat two in the truck.* 我们的敞篷货车里只能坐两个人。 ❑ *Throw the dogs in the back of the truck.* 把狗都扔到敞篷车的后面去。 **3** N-COUNT A **truck** is an open vehicle used for carrying goods on a railroad. 敞篷货运火车 [BRIT]

in AM, use **freight car**

4 V-T When something or someone **is trucked** somewhere, they are driven there in a truck. 用卡车运送 [usu passive] [mainly AM] ❑ *The liquor was sold legally and trucked out of the state.* 这种酒合法出售，由卡车运出该州。

truck·er /trʌkər/ (**truckers**) N-COUNT A **trucker** is someone who drives a truck as their job. 卡车司机 [mainly AM]

T

in BRIT, use **lorry driver**

❑ *...the type of place where truckers and farmers stopped for coffee and pie.* …卡车司机们和农民们停下来喝咖啡和吃馅饼的那种地方。

▲ **trudge** /trʌdʒ/ (**trudges, trudging, trudged**) V-I If you **trudge** somewhere, you walk there slowly and with heavy steps, especially because you are tired or unhappy. 步履艰难地走 ❑ *We had to trudge up the track back to the station.* 我们不得不沿着铁轨步履艰难地走回车站。 ● N-SING **Trudge** is also a noun. 艰难的步行 ❑ *We were reluctant to start the long trudge home.* 我们不情愿的开始长途跋涉回家。

true ♦♦◇ /tru/ (**truer, truest**) **1** ADJ If something is **true**, it is based on facts rather than being invented or imagined, and is accurate and reliable. 真实的 ❑ *Everything I had heard about him was true.* 我所听到的关于他的一切都是真的。 ❑ *He said it was true that a collision had happened.* 他说碰撞真的发生了一次。 **2** ADJ You use **true** to emphasize that a person or thing is sincere or genuine, often in contrast to something that is pretended or hidden. (人或物品) 真实的 [ADJ n] [EMPHASIS] ❑ *I allowed myself to acknowledge my true feelings.* 我愿意承认自己的真实感情。 **3** ADJ If you use **true** to describe something or someone, you approve of them because they have all the characteristics or qualities that such a person or thing typically has. 真正的 [ADJ n] [APPROVAL] ❑ *This country professes to be a true democracy.* 该国宣称自己是一个真正的民主国家。 ❑ *Maybe one day you'll find true love.* 也许有一天你会找到真爱。 **4** ADJ If you say that a fact is **true of** a particular person or situation, you mean that it is valid or relevant for them. 确实的; 符合的 [v-link ADJ "of/for" n] ❑ *I accept that the romance may have gone out of the marriage, but surely this is true of many couples.* 我承认浪漫可能已从婚姻中消失，但许多夫妻的确都是如此。 **5** ADJ If you are **true to** someone, you remain committed and loyal to them. If you are **true to** an idea or promise, you remain committed to it and continue to act according to it. 忠诚的 [v-link ADJ "to" n] ❑ *David was true to his wife.* 大卫忠于他的妻子。 ❑ *India has remained true to democracy.* 印度一直恪守民主。 **6** PHRASE If a dream, wish, or prediction **comes true**, it actually happens. (梦想、愿望或预测) 成为现实 ❑ *Many of his predictions are coming true.* 他的许多预言都在成为现实。 **7** PHRASE If a general statement **holds true** in particular circumstances, or if your previous statement **holds true** in different circumstances, it is true or valid in those circumstances. 同样适用 [FORMAL] ❑ *This law is known to hold true for galaxies at a distance of at least several billion light years.* 这个定律被普遍认为同样适用于至少数十亿光年之远的星系。 **8** PHRASE If you say that something seems **too good to be true**, you are suspicious of it because it seems better than you had expected, and you think there may be something wrong with it that you have not noticed. 好得令人难以置信 ❑ *On the whole the celebrations were remarkably good-humored and peaceful. It seemed almost too good to be true.* 大体上说，庆祝活动非常快乐祥和，似乎好得令人难以置信。 **9** **to ring true** → see **ring** **10** **tried and true** → see **tried**

tru·ly ♦◇◇ /truli/ **1** ADV You use **truly** to emphasize that something has all the features or qualities of a particular thing, or is the case to the fullest possible extent. 真正地; 完全地 [EMPHASIS] ❑ *...a truly democratic system.* …一个真正民主的体制。 ❑ *Not all doctors truly understand the reproductive cycle.* 并非所有的医生都完全地了解生育周期。 **2** ADV You can use **truly** in order to emphasize your description of something. 非常 [ADV adj] [EMPHASIS] ❑ *...a truly splendid man.* …一个非常好的男人。 **3** ADV You use **truly** to emphasize that feelings are genuine and sincere. 由衷地; 真诚地 [EMPHASIS] ❑ *Believe me, Susan, I am truly sorry.* 相信我，苏珊，我由衷地感到愧疚。 **4** **well and truly** → see **well** **5** CONVENTION You write **Yours truly** at the end of a formal letter, and before signing your name, to someone you do not know very well. 你忠诚的 (用于正式信件的信末署名前) [OLD-FASHIONED] ❑ *Yours truly, Phil Turner.* 你忠诚的菲尔・特纳。

trump /trʌmp/ (**trumps, trumping, trumped**) **1** N-UNCOUNT-COLL In a game of cards, **trumps** is the suit which is chosen to have the highest value in one particular game. (牌戏中的) 王牌 ❑ *Hearts are trumps.* 红桃牌是王牌。 **2** N-COUNT In a game of cards, a **trump** is a playing card which belongs to the suit which has been chosen as trumps. (一张) 王牌 ❑ *He played a trump.* 他打了一张王牌。 **3** V-T If you **trump** what someone has said or done, you beat it by saying or doing something else that seems better. (因说或做得更好而) 胜过 ❑ *The Republicans tried to trump this with their slogan.* 共和党人试图用他们的口号来胜出。 **4** PHRASE Your **trump card** is something powerful that you can use or do, which gives you an advantage over someone. 某人的王牌 ❑ *The administration knows that's their trump card and will keep playing it as long as they can.* 政府知道那是他们的王牌，会尽可能长久地使用它。

trum·pet /trʌmpɪt/ (**trumpets**) N-VAR A **trumpet** is a musical instrument of the brass family which plays comparatively high notes. 小号 [oft "the" N] ❑ *I played the trumpet in the school orchestra.* 我在学校管弦乐队吹小号。
→ see **orchestra**

trun·dle /trʌndᵊl/ (**trundles, trundling, trundled**) **1** V-I If a vehicle **trundles** somewhere, it moves there slowly, often with difficulty or an irregular movement. (车辆) 缓慢行进 ❑ *The truck was trundling along the escarpment of the Zambesi valley.* 卡车正沿着赞比西山谷的悬崖缓慢行驶。 **2** V-T If you **trundle** something somewhere, especially a small, heavy object with wheels, you move or roll it along slowly. 使缓慢移动; 使缓慢滚动 ❑ *The old man lifted the wheelbarrow and trundled it away.* 老人抬起手推车，慢慢地推走了。

trunk /trʌŋk/ (**trunks**) 1 N-COUNT The **trunk** of a tree is the large main stem from which the branches grow. 树干 ❑ *...the gnarled trunk of a birch tree.* …一棵长满节瘤的桦树的树干。 2 N-COUNT A **trunk** is a large, strong case or box used for storing things or for taking on a trip. 大箱子 ❑ *Maloney unlocked his trunk and took out some coveralls.* 马洛尼把他的大箱子的锁打开了，拿出了一些工作服。 3 N-COUNT An elephant's **trunk** is its very long nose that it uses to lift food and water to its mouth. 象鼻 ❑ *Manfred the elephant reached out with his trunk and gently scooped up the baby.* 大象曼弗雷德伸出它的鼻子，轻轻地抱起了幼仔。 4 N-COUNT The **trunk** of a car is a covered space at the back or front in which you put luggage or other things. (汽车的) 行李箱 [AM]

in BRIT, use **boot**

❑ *She opened the trunk of the car and started to take out a bag of groceries.* 她打开汽车的行李箱，开始拿出一袋杂货。 5 N-PLURAL **Trunks** are shorts that a man wears when he goes swimming. 男式游泳裤 6 N-COUNT Your **trunk** is the central part of your body, from your neck to your waist. (人体的) 躯干 [usu sing] [FORMAL] ❑ *The leg to be stretched should be positioned behind your trunk with your knee bent.* 要伸展的那条腿应该放在躯干的后面并弯曲膝盖。

trust ♦♦◇ /trʌst/ (**trusts, trusting, trusted**) 1 V-T If you **trust** someone, you believe that they are honest and sincere and will not deliberately do anything to harm you. 信任 ❑ *"I trust you completely," he said.* "我完全信任你。"他说。 2 N-UNCOUNT Your **trust in** someone is your belief that they are honest and sincere and will not deliberately do anything to harm you. 信任 ❑ *He destroyed me and my trust in men.* 他毁了我，也毁了我对男人的信任。 ❑ *You've betrayed their trust.* 你辜负了他们的信任。 3 V-T If you **trust** someone **to** do something, you believe that they will do it. 相信 (某人会做某事) ❑ *That's why I must trust you to keep this secret.* 这就是我一定相信你会保守此秘密的原因。 4 V-T If you **trust** someone **with** something important or valuable, you allow them to look after it or deal with it. 托付 ❑ *This could make your superiors hesitate to trust you with major responsibilities.* 这可能会使你的上司犹豫着不愿把重大职责托付给你。 ● N-UNCOUNT **Trust** is also a noun. 托付 [also "a" N] ❑ *She was organizing and running a large household, a position of trust which was generously paid.* 她那时正在照管一个大家庭，那是一个报酬优厚的要职。 5 V-T If you do not **trust** something, you feel that it is not safe or reliable. (不) 相信 (某物安全或可靠) ❑ *She nodded, not trusting her own voice.* 她点了点头，无法相信自己的声音。 ❑ *For one thing, he didn't trust his legs to hold him up.* 首先，他不相信自己的腿能站起来。 6 V-T If you **trust** someone's judgment or advice, you believe that it is good or right. 相信 (某人的判断或建议) ❑ *Jake has raised two incredible kids and I trust his judgement.* 杰克已经抚养了两个极好的孩子，我相信他的判断。 7 V-T If you say you **trust that** something is true, you mean you hope and expect that it is true. 相信 (某事的真实性) [FORMAL] ❑ *I trust you will take the earliest opportunity to make a full apology.* 我相信你会抓住最早的机会来一次彻底的道歉。 8 V-I If you **trust in** someone or something, you believe strongly in them, and do not doubt their powers or their good intentions. 信任 [FORMAL] ❑ *For a believer, replies to all the questions about life and work are far different because he trusts in God.* 对一个信徒来说，对所有生活和工作问题的回答是大不一样的，因为他相信上帝。 9 N-COUNT A **trust** is a financial arrangement in which a group of people or an organization keeps and invests money for someone. 信托 [also "in" N] [BUSINESS] ❑ *You could also set up a trust so the children can't spend any inheritance until they are a certain age.* 你也可以建立信托，那样孩子们到了一定的年龄以后才可以用任何遗产。 10 N-COUNT A **trust** is a group of people or an organization that has control of an amount of money or property and invests it on behalf of other people or as a charity. 信托人员；信托机构 [BUSINESS] ❑ *He had set up two charitable trusts.* 他已经成立了两家慈善信托机构。 11 → see also **unit trust** 12 **tried and trusted** → see **tried**

Word Partnership *trust* 的常用搭配：

V.	**learn to** trust 1
	build trust, **create** trust, **place** trust **in** ***someone*** 2
ADJ.	**mutual** trust 2
	charitable trust 10
N.	trust ***your*** **instincts**, trust ***someone's*** **judgment** 6
	investment trust 9

▲ **trus·tee** /trʌsti/ (**trustees**) N-COUNT A **trustee** is someone with legal control of money or property that is kept or invested for another person, company, or organization. 受托人 [BUSINESS] ❑ *The trustees of your pension fund decide which fund manager will invest some or all of your future income.* 你的养老基金的受托人决定哪一位基金经理将投资你部分或所有的未来收入。

trust fund (**trust funds**) N-COUNT A **trust fund** is an amount of money or property that someone owns, usually after inheriting it, but which is kept and invested for them. 信托基金 [BUSINESS] ❑ *The money will be placed in a trust fund for her daughter.* 这笔钱将投入到为她女儿设立的信托基金里。

Word Link ***worthy*** ***≈ deserving, suitable : creditworthy, trustworthy, unworthy***

trust·worthy /trʌstwɜrði/ ADJ A **trustworthy** person is reliable, responsible, and can be trusted completely. 可信赖的；可靠的 ❑ *He is a trustworthy and level-headed leader.* 他是个可信赖的、头脑冷静的领导。

truth ♦♦◇ /truθ/ (**truths**) 1 N-UNCOUNT **The truth** about something is all the facts about it, rather than things that are imagined or invented. 实情；真相 ❑ *Is it possible to separate truth from fiction?* 有可能区分事实和谎言吗？ ❑ *I must tell you the truth about this business.* 我必须告诉你这桩交易的真相。 2 N-UNCOUNT If you say that there is some **truth in** a statement or story, you mean that it is true, or at least partly true. 真实性 ❑ *There is no truth in this story.* 这个故事不具备真实性。 ❑ *Is there any truth to the rumors?* 这些谣传有事实根据吗？ 3 N-COUNT A **truth** is something that is believed to be true. 真理 ❑ *It is an almost universal truth that the more we are promoted in a job, the less we actually exercise the skills we initially used to perform it.* 一个几乎普遍的真理是，工作上提升得越高，我们最初的那些工作技能实际上就用得越少。 4 PHRASE You say **to tell you the truth** or **truth to tell** in order to indicate that you are telling someone something in an open and honest way, without trying to hide anything. 跟你说实话 ❑ *To tell you the truth, I was afraid to see him.* 跟你说实话，我怕见到他。

Word Partnership *truth* 的常用搭配：

N.	**a grain of** truth, **the** truth **of the matter** 1
ADJ.	**the awful** truth, **the plain** truth, **the sad** truth, **the simple** truth, **the whole** truth 1
	absolute truth 1 3
V.	**accept the** truth, **find the** truth, **know the** truth, **learn the** truth, **search for the** truth, **tell the** truth 1
	to tell you the truth 4

★ **truth·ful** /truθfəl/ ADJ If a person or their comments are **truthful**, they are honest and do not tell any lies. 诚实的 ❑ *Most religions teach you to be truthful.* 大多数宗教都教你要诚实。 ❑ *We've all learned to be fairly truthful about our personal lives.* 我们都已学会了对我们的个人生活要相当诚实。 ● **truth·ful·ly** ADV 诚实地 [ADV with v] ❑ *I answered all their questions truthfully.* 我如实地回答了他们的所有问题。 ● **truth·ful·ness** N-UNCOUNT 诚实 ❑ *I can say, with absolute truthfulness, that I did my best.* 我可以绝对诚实地说我已尽力了。

try ♦♦♦ /traɪ/ (**tries, trying, tried**) 1 V-T/V-I If you **try** to do something, you want to do it, and you take action which you hope will help you to do it. 试图 ❑ *He secretly tried to help her at work.* 他试图悄悄地在工作上帮助她。 ❑ *Does it annoy you if others don't seem to try hard enough?* 如果其他人做得似乎不够努力，这会使你烦恼吗？ ● N-COUNT **Try** is also a noun. 尝试 ❑ *It wasn't that she'd really expected to get any money out of him; it had just seemed worth a try.* 并非是她真的期望从他那里弄到一些钱；只是似乎值得一试。 2 V-T To **try and** do something means to try to do it. 设法 [INFORMAL] ❑ *I must try and see him.* 我必须设法见到他。 3 V-I If you **try for** something, you make an effort to get it or achieve it. 试图 (获得) ❑ *My partner and I have been trying for a baby for two years.* 我和我的配偶两年来一直试着生个孩子。 4 V-T If you **try** something new or different, you use it, do it, or experience it in order to discover its qualities or effects. 试用 ❑ *It's best not to try a new recipe for the first time on such an important occasion.* 在这样的重要场合，最好不要首次试用新的食谱。 ● N-COUNT **Try** is also a noun. 试用 ❑ *If you're still skeptical about exercising, we can only ask you to trust us and give it a try.* 如果你仍对锻炼持怀疑态度，我们只能请你相信我们，试一试。 5 V-T If you **try** a particular place or person, you go to that place or person because you think that they may be able to provide you with what you want. 试试 (去某处或找某人) ❑ *Have you tried the local music shops?* 你试过当地的音乐商店吗？ 6 V-T If you **try** a door or window, you try to open it. 试着 (开门、窗) ❑ *Bob tried the door. To his surprise it opened.* 鲍勃试着推推门。令他吃惊

的是门开了。 **7** V-T When a person **is tried**, he or she has to appear in a law court and is found innocent or guilty after the judge and jury have heard the evidence. When a legal case **is tried**, it is considered in a court of law. 审讯；审理 ❑ *He suggested that those responsible should be tried for crimes against humanity.* 他建议那些责任人应该以反人类罪受审。 ❑ *Whether he is innocent or guilty is a decision that will be made when the case is tried in court.* 他有罪还是无罪要等案子经由法庭审理后才能做出判决。 **8** N-COUNT In the game of rugby, a **try** is the action of scoring by putting the ball down behind the goal line of the opposing team. (橄榄球运动中在对方球门线后) 带球触地得分 ❑ *The French, who led 21-3 at half time, scored eight tries.* 法国队在上半场结束时以21比3领先，他们有8次带球触地得分。 **9** → see also **tried, trying** **10** to **try** your **best** → see **best** **11** to **try** your **hand** → see **hand** **12** to **try** someone's **patience** → see **patience**

> **Try and** is often used instead of **try to** in spoken English, but you should avoid it in writing. ❑ *Just try and stop me!* Notice also the difference between **try to** and **try** with the "-ing" form of the verb, which often suggests doing something. ❑ *I'm going to try to open a jammed door... Try opening the windows to freshen the air.*

▶ **try on** PHRASAL VERB If you **try on** a piece of clothing, you put it on to see if it fits you or if it looks nice. 试穿 ❑ *Try on clothing and shoes to make sure they fit.* 衣服和鞋要试穿以确保它们合适。

▶ **try out** PHRASAL VERB If you **try** something **out**, you test it in order to find out how useful or effective it is or what it is like. 测试 (性能) ❑ *I wanted to try the boat out next weekend.* 我想下个周末去试一下这艘船。 ❑ *Some owners wish they could try out the car in a race track.* 一些车主希望他们能在一条跑道上试一下那辆车。

> **Thesaurus** *try* 另参见：
> V. attempt, endeavor, risk, venture **1** **3** **4**
> N. attempt, effort, shot **1** **4**

try·ing /traɪɪŋ/ **1** ADJ If you describe something or someone as **trying**, you mean that they are difficult to deal with and make you feel impatient or annoyed. 难对付的；令人厌烦的 ❑ *Support from those closest to you is vital in these trying times.* 在这些难熬的日子里，你最亲近的人的支持是极其重要的。 **2** → see also **try**

T-shirt (T-shirts) also **tee-shirt** N-COUNT A **T-shirt** is a cotton shirt with no collar or buttons. T-shirts usually have short sleeves. T恤衫 → see **clothing**

▲ **tsu·na·mi** /tsʊnɑmi/ (**tsunamis**) N-COUNT A **tsunami** is a very large wave, often caused by an earthquake, that flows onto the land and can cause widespread deaths and destruction. 海啸

★ **tub** /tʌb/ (**tubs**) **1** N-COUNT A **tub** is the same as a **bathtub**. 浴缸 [AM] ❑ *She lay back in the tub.* 她仰靠在浴缸里。 **2** N-COUNT A **tub** is a deep container of any size. 深的容器 ❑ *He peeled the paper top off a little white tub and poured the cream into his coffee.* 他撕去一个白色小杯的纸盖子，把奶油倒进他的咖啡。 **3** N-COUNT You can use **tub** to refer to a tub and its contents, or to the contents only. (一) 容器 ❑ *She would eat four tubs of ice cream in one sitting.* 她会一口气吃下4杯冰淇淋。 → see **soap**

tube ♦◇◇ /tub/ (**tubes**) **1** N-COUNT A **tube** is a long hollow object that is usually round, like a pipe. 管子 ❑ *He is fed by a tube that enters his nose.* 他通过一根插入鼻子的管子进食。 **2** N-COUNT A **tube of** something such as paste is a long, thin container which you squeeze in order to force the paste out. (装膏状物体的) 管子 ❑ *I went out today and bought a tube of toothpaste.* 我今天出去买了一管牙膏。 **3** N-COUNT Some long, thin, hollow parts in your body are referred to as **tubes**. (人体内的) 管状器官 ❑ *The lungs are in fact constructed of thousands of tiny tubes.* 肺其实是由数千个细小管状器官构成的。 **4** N-COUNT You can refer to the television as **the tube**. 电视机 [AM, INFORMAL]

> in BRIT, use **the box**

❑ *The only baseball he saw was on the tube.* 他只在电视上看过棒球比赛。 **5** N-SING **The tube** is the underground railway system in London. 伦敦地铁 [BRIT] → see **transportation**

tu·ber·cu·lo·sis /tubɜrkyəloʊsɪs/ N-UNCOUNT **Tuberculosis** is a serious infectious disease that affects someone's lungs and other parts of their body. The abbreviation **TB** is also used. 肺结核

tub·ing /tubɪŋ/ N-UNCOUNT **Tubing** is plastic, rubber, or another material in the shape of a tube. 管子 ❑ *...metres of plastic tubing.* …几米塑料管。

★ **tuck** /tʌk/ (**tucks, tucking, tucked**) **1** V-T If you **tuck** something somewhere, you put it there so that it is safe, comfortable, or neat. (为舒服或整齐) 把…塞入；把…夹入 ❑ *He tried to tuck his flapping shirt inside his trousers.* 他试图把飘动的衬衫塞进他的裤子里。 **2** N-COUNT You can use **tuck** to refer to a form of plastic surgery which involves reducing the size of a part of someone's body. 减脂手术 ❑ *She'd undergone 13 operations, including a tummy tuck.* 她做过13次手术，包括1次腹部减脂。

▶ **tuck away** **1** PHRASAL VERB If you **tuck away** something such as money, you store it in a safe place. 把…藏于安全处 ❑ *The extra income has meant Phillippa can tuck away the rent.* 这笔额外的收入意味着菲利帕可以把租金藏起来。 **2** PHRASAL VERB If someone or something **is tucked away**, they are well hidden in a quiet place where very few people go. 躲藏 ❑ *We were tucked away in a secluded corner of the room.* 我们被藏在那房间的一个隐蔽角落里。

▶ **tuck in** **1** PHRASAL VERB If you **tuck in** a piece of material, you keep it in position by placing one edge or end of it behind or under something else. For example, if you **tuck in** your shirt, you place the bottom part of it inside your pants or skirt. 把…塞进 **2** PHRASAL VERB If you **tuck** a child **in** bed or **tuck them in**, you make them comfortable by straightening the sheets and blankets and pushing the loose ends under the mattress. (为小孩) 盖好 (被子) ❑ *I read Lili a story and tucked her in.* 我给莉莉读了一篇故事，然后给她盖好被子。

Tues.

> The spelling **Tue.** is also used.

Tues. is a written abbreviation for **Tuesday**. 星期二

Tues·day ♦♦♦ /tuzdeɪ, -di/ (**Tuesdays**) N-VAR **Tuesday** is the day after Monday and before Wednesday. 星期二 ❑ *He phoned on Tuesday, just before you came.* 他星期二打了电话，刚好在你来之前。 ❑ *Talks are likely to start next Tuesday.* 会谈可能在下星期二开始。

★ **tug** /tʌg/ (**tugs, tugging, tugged**) **1** V-T/V-I If you **tug** something or **tug at** it, you give it a quick and usually strong pull. 猛拉；拽 ❑ *A little boy came running up and tugged at his sleeve excitedly.* 一个小男孩跑了过来，兴奋地拽着他的袖子。 ● N-COUNT **Tug** is also a noun. 猛拉；拽 ❑ *I felt a tug at my sleeve.* 我感觉我的袖子被拽了一下。 **2** N-COUNT A **tug** or a **tug boat** is a small powerful boat which pulls large ships, usually when they come into a port. 拖船 ❑ *...a 76,000-ton barge pulled by five tug boats.* …被5艘拖船拖拉着的一艘76000吨的驳船。

> **Word Link** *tu ≈ watching over : tuition, tutor, tutorial*

★ **tui·tion** /tuɪʃən/ **1** N-UNCOUNT You can use **tuition** to refer to the amount of money that you have to pay for being taught in a university, college, or private school. 学费 ❑ *Angela's $7,000 tuition at university this year will be paid for with scholarships.* 安吉拉今年$7000的大学学费将用奖学金来支付。 **2** N-UNCOUNT If you are given **tuition** in a particular subject, you are taught about that subject. 指导 [mainly BRIT]

> in AM, usually use **instruction**

▲ **tu·lip** /tulɪp/ (**tulips**) N-COUNT **Tulips** are flowers that grow in the spring from bulbs, and have oval or pointed petals packed closely together. 郁金香

★ **tum·ble** /tʌmbəl/ (**tumbles, tumbling, tumbled**) **1** V-I If someone or something **tumbles** somewhere, they fall there with a rolling or bouncing movement. 摔倒 ❑ *A small boy tumbled off the porch.* 一个小男孩从门廊上摔了下去。 ● N-COUNT **Tumble** is also a noun. 摔 [usu sing] ❑ *He injured his ribs in a tumble from his horse.* 他从马上摔下来伤了肋骨。 **2** V-I If prices or levels of something **are tumbling**, they are decreasing rapidly. (价格或水平) 暴跌 [JOURNALISM] ❑ *Profit after taxes tumbled by half to $15.8 million.* 税后利润猛降了一半，跌到了1580万美元。 ❑ *Share prices continued to tumble today on the Tokyo stock market.* 东京股市今天的股票价格继续暴跌。 ● N-COUNT **Tumble** is also a noun. (价格或水平的) 暴跌 ❑ *Oil prices took a tumble yesterday.* 石油价格昨天一阵暴跌。 **3** V-I If water **tumbles**, it flows quickly over an uneven surface. (水流) 翻滚 ❑ *Waterfalls crash and tumble over rocks.* 瀑布在岩石上撞击翻滚。

tum·ble dry·er (**tumble dryers**) also **tumble drier** N-COUNT A **tumble dryer** is an electric machine which dries washing by turning it over and over and blowing warm air onto it. 滚筒式烘干机 [mainly BRIT]

> in AM, use **dryer**

T

tum·my /tʌmi/ (**tummies**) 1 N-COUNT Your **tummy** is the part of the front of your body below your waist. **Tummy** is often used by children or by adults talking to children. 肚子(儿童化用语) ❑ *Your baby's tummy should feel warm, but not hot.* 你宝宝的肚子摸起来应该是温的，而不是热的。 2 N-COUNT You can use **tummy** to refer to the parts inside your body where food is digested. **Tummy** is often used by children or by adults talking to children. 胃(儿童化用语) ❑ *I've got a sore tummy.* 我胃痛。 ❑ *...a tummy ache.* …胃痛。

▲ **tu·mor** /tumər/ (**tumors**)

in BRIT, use **tumour**

N-COUNT A **tumor** is a mass of diseased or abnormal cells that has grown in a person's or animal's body. 肿瘤 ❑ *...a malignant brain tumor.* …一个恶性脑瘤。

▲ **tu·mour** /tjuːməʳ/ [BRIT] → see **tumor**

tu·mul·tu·ous /tumʌltʃuəs/ 1 ADJ A **tumultuous** event or period of time involves many exciting and confusing events or feelings. 激动的；混乱的 ❑ *...the tumultuous changes in Eastern Europe.* …东欧的剧变。 2 ADJ A **tumultuous** reaction to something is very noisy, because the people involved are very happy or excited. 欢腾的；喧哗的 ❑ *A tumultuous welcome from a 2,000-strong crowd greeted the champion.* 多达2千之众的人群热闹欢腾地迎接冠军。

tuna /tunə/ (**tuna** or **tunas**)

The plural can be either **tuna** or **tunas**.

N-VAR **Tuna** or **tuna fish** are large fish that live in warm seas and are caught for food. 金枪鱼 ❑ *...a shoal of tuna.* …一群金枪鱼。 ● N-UNCOUNT **Tuna** or **tuna fish** is this fish eaten as food. 金枪鱼肉 ❑ *She began opening a can of tuna.* 她开始打开一罐金枪鱼。

tune ♦◇◇ /tun/ (**tunes, tuning, tuned**) 1 N-COUNT A **tune** is a series of musical notes that is pleasant and easy to remember. 曲调 ❑ *She was humming a merry little tune.* 她正哼着一曲欢快的小调。 2 N-COUNT You can refer to a song or a short piece of music as a **tune**. 歌曲；乐段 ❑ *She'll also be playing your favorite pop tunes.* 她也将演奏你最喜欢的流行歌曲。 3 V-T When someone **tunes** a musical instrument, they adjust it so that it produces the right notes. 为(乐器)调音 ❑ *"We do tune our guitars before we go on," he insisted.* "我们继续演奏之前一定要为吉他定音，"他坚持说。 ● PHRASAL VERB **Tune up** means the same as **tune**. 调音 ❑ *Others were quietly tuning up their instruments.* 其他人正安静地为他们的乐器调音。 4 V-T When an engine or machine **is tuned**, it is adjusted so that it works well. 调整(发动机或机器) [usu passive] ❑ *Drivers are urged to make sure that car engines are properly tuned.* 司机们被要求要确保把汽车发动机调整好。 ● PHRASAL VERB **Tune up** means the same as **tune**. 调整 ❑ *The shop charges up to $500 to tune up a Porsche.* 该店调试一辆保时捷的收费高达$500。 5 V-T If your radio or television **is tuned to** a particular channel or broadcasting station, you are listening to or watching the programs being broadcast by that station. 调整(频道或频率) [usu passive] ❑ *A small color television was tuned to an afternoon soap opera.* 一台小彩电被调到了一个午后肥皂剧频道。 6 → see also **fine-tune** 7 PHRASE If you say that a person or organization **is calling the tune**, you mean that they are in a position of power or control in a particular situation. 定调子；发号施令 ❑ *It is Coulthard who is calling the tune so far this season.* 本赛季到目前为止一直是库特哈德发号施令。 8 PHRASE If you say that someone **has changed** their **tune**, you are criticizing them because they have changed their opinion or way of doing things. 改变调子(指改变态度) [DISAPPROVAL] ❑ *You've changed your tune since this morning, haven't you?* 自从今天早上起你就改变了调子，不是吗？ 9 PHRASE A person or musical instrument that is **in tune** produces exactly the right notes. A person or musical instrument that is **out of tune** does not produce exactly the right notes. 合调的；不合调的 ❑ *It was just an ordinary voice, but he sang in tune.* 嗓音只是一般，但他唱得很合调。

▸ **tune in** 1 PHRASAL VERB If you **tune in** to a particular television or radio station or program, you watch or listen to it. 收看；收听 ❑ *All over the country, youngsters tune in to Sesame Street every day.* 全国各地的儿童每天都收看"芝麻街"。 2 PHRASAL VERB If you **tune in to** something such as your own or other people's feelings, you become aware of them. 了解(感情等) ❑ *You can start now to tune in to your own physical, social and spiritual needs.* 你可以现在开始了解你自己身体、社交和精神方面的需要了。

▸ **tune out** PHRASAL VERB If you **tune out**, you stop listening or paying attention to what is being said. 不听；不注意 ❑ *Children rapidly tune out if you go beyond them.* 如果你的话超出了孩子们的理解力，他们很快就不听了。 ❑ *Rose heard the familiar voice, but tuned out the words.* 罗斯听到了那熟悉的声音，但却没有注意说的是什么话。

tu·nic /tunɪk/ (**tunics**) N-COUNT A **tunic** is a long sleeveless garment that is worn on the top part of your body. 无袖上装 ❑ *...a cotton tunic.* …一件棉的无袖上装。

tun·nel ♦◇◇ /tʌnᵊl/ (**tunnels, tunneling, tunneled**)

in BRIT, use **tunnelling, tunnelled**

1 N-COUNT A **tunnel** is a long passage which has been made under the ground, usually through a hill or under the sea. 隧道 ❑ *Boston drivers love the tunnel.* 波士顿的司机们喜欢那条隧道。 2 V-I To **tunnel** somewhere means to make a tunnel there. 挖掘隧道 ❑ *The thieves tunneled under all the security devices.* 小偷们在所有的那些安全装置下面都挖了地道。

→ see Word Web: **tunnel**

→ see **traffic**

▲ **tur·bine** /tɜrbɪn, -baɪn/ (**turbines**) N-COUNT A **turbine** is a machine or engine which uses a stream of air, gas, water, or steam to turn a wheel and produce power. 涡轮机 ❑ *The new ship will be powered by two gas turbines and four diesel engines.* 那艘新轮船将由2台燃气涡轮机和4台柴油机驱动。

→ see **electricity, wheel**

★ **tur·bu·lence** /tɜrbyələns/ 1 N-UNCOUNT **Turbulence** is a state of confusion and disorganized change. 动荡；骚乱 ❑ *The 1960s and early 1970s were a time of change and turbulence.* 20世纪60年代和70年代初期是个变革和动荡的年代。 2 N-UNCOUNT **Turbulence** is violent and uneven movement within a particular area of air, liquid, or gas. 湍流；紊流 ❑ *The plane encountered severe turbulence and winds of nearly two-hundred miles an hour.* 那架飞机遇到了强湍流和时速近二百英里的强风。

★ **tur·bu·lent** /tɜrbyələnt/ 1 ADJ A **turbulent** time, place, or relationship is one in which there is a lot of change, confusion, and disorder. 动荡的 ❑ *They had been together for five or six turbulent years of break-ups and reconciliations.* 他们在一起度过了分分合合动荡不定的五六年。 2 ADJ **Turbulent** water or air contains strong currents which change direction suddenly. (水流或气体)湍急的 ❑ *I had to have a boat that could handle turbulent seas.* 我必须有一条能应付汹涌海浪的船。

t

Word Web **tunnel**

The Egyptians built the first **tunnels** as entrances to tombs. Later the Babylonians* built a tunnel under the Euphrates River*. It linked the royal palace with the Temple of Jupiter*. The Romans **dug** tunnels when **mining** for gold. By the late 1600s, **explosives** had replaced **digging**. Gunpowder was used to build the **underground** section of a canal in France in 1679. Nitroglycerin explosions helped create a railroad tunnel in Massachusetts in 1867. The longest continuous tunnel in the world is the Delaware Aqueduct. It carries water from the Catskill Mountains* to New York City and is 105 miles long.

Babylonians: people who lived in the ancient city of Babylon.
Euphrates River: a large river in the Middle East.
Temple of Jupiter: a religious building.
Catskill Mountains: a mountain range in the northeastern U.S.

turf /tɜrf/ **1** N-UNCOUNT **Turf** is short, thick, even grass. 草皮 [also "the" N] ❑ *They shuffled slowly down the turf toward the cliff's edge.* 他们在草地上拖着脚步慢慢走向悬崖边。 **2** N-UNCOUNT Someone's **turf** is the area which is most familiar to them or where they feel most confident. 地盘; 活动范围 ❑ *Their turf was St. Louis: its streets, theaters, homes, and parks.* 他们的地盘是圣路易斯：它的街道、剧院、住宅和公园。

▲**tur·key** /tɜrki/ (**turkeys**) N-COUNT A **turkey** is a large bird that is kept on a farm for its meat. 火鸡 ● N-UNCOUNT **Turkey** is the meat of this bird eaten as food. 火鸡肉 ❑ *They will sit down to a traditional turkey dinner early this afternoon.* 他们今天下午早些时候将坐下来吃一顿传统的火鸡宴。

▲**tur·moil** /tɜrmɔɪl/ (**turmoils**) N-VAR **Turmoil** is a state of confusion, disorder, uncertainty, or great anxiety. 混乱; 骚乱

turn

❶ VERB AND NOUN USES
❷ PHRASES
❸ PHRASAL VERBS

❶ **turn** ♦♦♦ /tɜʳn/ (**turns, turning, turned**) **1** V-T/V-I When you **turn** or when you **turn** part of your body, you move your body or part of your body so that it is facing in a different or opposite direction. 转动 (身体); 转身 ❑ *He turned abruptly and walked away.* 他突然转身走开了。 ❑ *He sighed, turning away and surveying the sea.* 他叹了口气，转过身去，眺望着大海。 ● PHRASAL VERB **Turn around** means the same as **turn**. 转身 ❑ *I felt a tapping on my shoulder and I turned around.* 我感到有人拍了一下我的肩膀，于是转过身去。 **2** V-T When you **turn** something, you move it so that it is facing in a different or opposite direction, or is in a very different position. 使转向 ❑ *They turned their telescopes toward other nearby galaxies.* 他们把望远镜转向附近的其他星系。 ❑ *She had turned the bedside chair to face the door.* 她已经把那张床边的椅子转过来对着门。 **3** V-T/V-I When something such as a wheel **turns**, or when you **turn** it, it continually moves around in a particular direction. 转动 ❑ *As the wheel turned, the potter shaped the clay.* 随着轮子的转动，制陶工人给黏土塑形。 **4** V-T/V-I When you **turn** something such as a key, knob, or switch, or when it **turns**, you hold it and twist your hand, in order to open something or make it start working. 转动 (开启) ❑ *Turn the key three times to the right.* 把那钥匙向右转3次。 ❑ *Turn the heat to very low and cook for 20 minutes.* 把炉火转到很低，煮上20分钟。 **5** V-T/V-I When you **turn** in a particular direction or **turn** a corner, you change the direction in which you are moving or traveling. 转向; 拐弯 ❑ *He turned into the narrow street where he lived.* 他拐进了他住的那条狭窄的街道。 ❑ *Now turn right to follow West Ferry Road.* 现在向右转沿着西渡口路走。 ● N-COUNT **Turn** is also a noun. 转向; 拐弯 ❑ *You can't do a right-hand turn here.* 你不能在这里右转弯。 **6** V-I The point where a road, path, or river **turns** is the point where it has a bend or curve in it. (路或河流) 转弯 ❑ *...the corner where Tenterfield Road turned into the main road.* …坦特菲尔德路转向主干道的那个拐角。 ● N-COUNT **Turn** is also a noun. 转弯 ❑ *...a sharp turn in the road.* …公路上的一个急转弯。 **7** V-I When the tide **turns**, it starts coming in or going out. (潮水) 涨; 落 ❑ *There was not much time before the tide turned.* 没过多少时间就退潮了。 **8** V-T When you **turn** a page of a book or magazine, you move it so that it is flat against the previous page, and you can read the next page. 翻动 (书页) ❑ *He turned the pages of a file in front of him.* 他翻着面前的一份档案。 **9** V-T If you **turn** a weapon or an aggressive feeling **on** someone, you point it at them or direct it at them. 把 (武器或挑衅的情绪) 指向 ❑ *He tried to turn the gun on me.* 他试图把枪对着我。 **10** V-I If you **turn to** a particular page in a book or magazine, you open it at that page. 翻到 (某页) ❑ *To order, turn to page 236.* 要订货，请翻到第236页。 **11** V-T/V-I If you **turn** your attention or thoughts **to** a particular subject or if you **turn to** it, you start thinking about it or discussing it. (注意力) 转向 ❑ *We turned our attention to the practical matters relating to forming a company.* 我们把注意力转向了与组建公司有关的实际问题上。 ❑ *We turn now to our primary question.* 我们现在转到我们的主要问题上。 **12** V-I If you **turn to** someone, you ask for their help or advice. 求助于 ❑ *For assistance, they turned to one of the city's most innovative museums.* 为了寻求帮助，他们求助于该市最具创新精神的博物馆中的一座。 **13** V-I If you **turn to** a particular activity, job, or way of doing something, you start doing or using it. 开始做; 开始用 ❑ *These communities are now turning to recycling as a cheaper alternative to landfills.* 这些社区现正开始用回收这种较为廉价的方法替代废物填埋法。 **14** V-T/V-I To **turn** or **be turned into** something means to become that thing. 变成 (某物) ❑ *A prince turns into a frog in this cartoon fairytale.* 在这部卡通童话片里，一位王子变成了一只青蛙。 **15** V-LINK You can use **turn** before an adjective to indicate that something or someone changes by acquiring the quality described by the adjective. 变得 (接形容词) ❑ *If the bailiff thinks that things could turn nasty he will enlist the help of the police.* 如果司法官认为情况可能会变糟，他会寻求警方帮助。 **16** V-LINK If something **turns** a particular color or if something **turns** it a particular color, it becomes that color. 变成 (某种颜色) ❑ *The sea would turn pale pink and the sky blood red.* 大海将变成浅粉色，而天空将变成血红色。 **17** V-LINK You can use **turn** to indicate that there is a change to a particular kind of weather. For example, if it **turns** cold, the weather starts being cold. (天气) 变得 ❑ *If it turns cold, cover the plants.* 如果天气变冷，就把植物盖起来。 **18** N-COUNT If a situation or trend takes a particular kind of **turn**, it changes so that it starts developing in a different or opposite way. (情况的) 变化 ❑ *The scandal took a new turn over the weekend.* 这一丑闻在周末时发生了新的变化。 **19** V-T If a business **turns** a profit, it earns more money than it spends. 赚取 [no passive] [BUSINESS] ❑ *The firm will be able to pay off its debts and still turn a modest profit.* 该公司将能够还清其债务，而且还会稍有赢利。 **20** V-T When someone **turns** a particular age, they pass that age. When it **turns** a particular time, it passes that time. 达到 (一定的年龄或时间) ❑ *It was his ambition to accumulate a million dollars before he turned thirty.* 他的雄心是在30岁以前积攒100万美元。 **21** N-SING **Turn** is used in expressions such as **the turn of the century** and **the turn of the year** to refer to a period of time when one century or year is ending and the next one is beginning. (世纪或年代的) 交替时期 ❑ *They fled to South America around the turn of the century.* 他们在世纪之交时逃往南美。 **22** N-COUNT If it is your **turn to** do something, you now have the duty, chance, or right to do it, when other people have done it before you or will do it after you. (多人依次) 轮到的机会 ❑ *Tonight it's my turn to cook.* 今晚轮到我做饭。 **23** → see also **turning**

Thesaurus *turn* 另参见：

V.	bend, pivot, revolve, rotate, spin, twist ❶ 1 – 4; become ❶ 14 – 17
N.	chance, opportunity ❶ 22

❷ **turn** ♦♦♦ /tɜʳn/ (**turns**) **1** PHRASE If there is a particular **turn of events**, a particular series of things happen. 形势的变化 ❑ *They were horrified at this unexpected turn of events.* 他们对出乎意料的形势变化感到震惊。 **2** PHRASE If you say that something happens **at every turn**, you are emphasizing that it happens frequently or all the time, usually so that it prevents you from achieving what you want. 常常; 总是 [EMPHASIS] ❑ *Its operations were hampered at every turn by inadequate numbers of trained staff.* 它的运转常常因受过培训的员工人数不够而受到限制。 **3** PHRASE If you do someone **a good turn**, you do something that helps or benefits them. 有利的事 ❑ *He did you a good turn by resigning.* 他辞职对你有利。 **4** PHRASE You use **in turn** to refer to actions or events that are in a sequence one after the other, for example, because one causes the other. 转而 ❑ *One of the members of the surgical team leaked the story to a fellow physician who, in turn, confided in a reporter.* 该外科小组的一名成员把此事泄露给一个同行医生，而后者转而又将此透露给了一位记者。 **5** PHRASE If each person in a group does something **in turn**, they do it one after the other in a fixed or agreed order. 依次地 ❑ *There were cheers for each of the women as they spoke in turn.* 女士们依次发言时，每一位都得到了喝彩。 **6** PHRASE If two or more people **take turns to** do something, they do it one after the other several times, rather than doing it together. 轮流 ❑ *We took turns driving.* 我们轮流驾驶。 **7** PHRASE If a situation **takes a turn for the worse**, it suddenly becomes worse. If a situation **takes a turn for the better**, it suddenly becomes better. 突然变坏; 突然变好 ❑ *Her condition took a sharp turn for the worse.* 她的病情突然急剧恶化。

❸ **turn** ♦♦♦ /tɜʳn/ (**turns, turning, turned**)

▸ **turn against** PHRASAL VERB If you **turn against** someone or something, or if you **are turned against** them, you stop supporting them, trusting them, or liking them, and sometimes you work against them. 转而反对 ❑ *A kid I used to be friends with turned against me after being told that I'd been insulting him.* 一个与我曾经是朋友的年轻人在被告知我一直在污蔑他后就和我反目成仇了。

T

▸ **turn around**
in BRIT, also use **turn round**
1 → see **turn** ❶ 1 2 PHRASAL VERB If you **turn** something **around**, or if it **turns around**, it is moved so that it faces the opposite direction. 转向反方向 ❑ *Bud turned the truck around, and started back for Dalton Pond.* 巴德把卡车调了个头，开始返回道尔顿池塘。 ❑ *He had reached over to turn around a bottle of champagne so that the label didn't show.* 他伸过手把一瓶香槟酒转过去，使它的标签显露不出来。
3 PHRASAL VERB If something such as a business or economy **turns around**, or if someone **turns** it **around**, it becomes successful, after being unsuccessful for a period of time. (生意或经济) 好转 [BUSINESS] ❑ *Turning the company around won't be easy.* 使公司好转不容易。 ❑ *In his long career, Horton turned around two entire divisions.* 在他漫长的职业生涯中，霍顿曾使整整两个分部扭亏为盈。
▸ **turn away** 1 PHRASAL VERB If you **turn** someone **away**, you do not allow them to enter your country, home, or other place. 把…拒之门外 ❑ *Turning Cuban boat people away would be an inhumane action.* 不准这些古巴船民入境将是一种不人道的行为。 2 PHRASAL VERB To **turn away from** something such as a method or an idea means to stop using it or to become different from it. 不再使用 ❑ *Japanese companies have been turning away from production and have moved into real estate.* 日本公司一直以来都在退出制造业而转入房地产业。
▸ **turn back** 1 PHRASAL VERB If you **turn back** or if someone **turns** you **back** when you are going somewhere, you change direction and go toward where you started from. 往回走 ❑ *She turned back toward home.* 她折了回来往家走去。 ❑ *Police attempted to turn back.* 警察试图往回走。 2 PHRASAL VERB If you **cannot turn back**, you cannot change your plans and decide not to do something, because the action you have already taken makes it impossible. (无法) 回头 [with brd-neg] ❑ *The Senate has now endorsed the bill and can't turn back.* 参议院现已同意了该议案，无法回头了。
▸ **turn down** 1 PHRASAL VERB If you **turn down** a person or their request or offer, you refuse their request or offer. 拒绝 ❑ *I thanked him for the offer but turned it down.* 我感谢他的好意，但拒绝了他。
2 PHRASAL VERB When you **turn down** a radio, heater, or other piece of equipment, you reduce the amount of sound or heat being produced, by adjusting the controls. 调低 (音量或热度) ❑ *He kept turning the central heating down.* 他不断地调低中央暖气系统的温度。
▸ **turn off** 1 PHRASAL VERB If you **turn off** the road or path you are going along, you start going along a different road or path which leads away from it. 离开 (道路) ❑ *The truck turned off the main road, and went along the gravelly track which led to the farm.* 卡车离开主路，沿着通向农场的碎石路行驶。 2 PHRASAL VERB When you **turn off** a piece of equipment or a supply of something, you stop heat, sound, or water from being produced by adjusting the controls. 关掉 ❑ *The light's a bit too harsh. You can turn it off.* 那灯光有点太刺眼。你可以关掉它。 3 PHRASAL VERB If something **turns** you **off** a particular subject or activity, it makes you have no interest in it. 对…失去兴趣 ❑ *What turns teenagers off science?* 是什么使青少年们对科学失去了兴趣？ ❑ *Greed on the part of owners and athletes turns fans off completely.* 球队老板和运动员的贪婪使球迷们对其完全失去了兴趣。
▸ **turn on** 1 PHRASAL VERB When you **turn on** a piece of equipment or a supply of something, you cause heat, sound, or water to be produced by adjusting the controls. 打开 ❑ *I want to turn on the television.* 我想打开电视机。 2 PHRASAL VERB If someone or something **turns** you **on**, they attract you and make you feel sexually excited. 激发性欲 [INFORMAL] ❑ *The body that turns men on doesn't have to be perfect.* 激发男人们性欲的身体不一定要完美。
3 PHRASAL VERB If someone **turns on** you, they suddenly attack you or speak angrily to you. 突然袭击；突然斥责 ❑ *Demonstrators turned on police, overturning vehicles and setting fire to them.* 示威者们突然袭击了警察，掀翻车辆并将其放火焚烧。
▸ **turn out** 1 PHRASAL VERB If something **turns out** a particular way, it happens in that way or has the result or degree of success indicated. 结果为 ❑ *If I had known my life was going to turn out like this, I would have let them kill me.* 如果我知道我的一生会是这样的结果，我早就该让他们杀了我。 ❑ *I was positive things were going to turn out fine.* 我当时就确信事情最终会好起来。 2 PHRASAL VERB If something **turns out to** be a particular thing, it is discovered to be that thing. 被发现是 ❑ *Cosgrave's forecast turned out to be completely wrong.* 科斯格累夫的预测被发现是完全错误的。 3 PHRASAL VERB When you **turn out** something such as a light, you move the switch or knob that controls it so that it stops giving out light or heat. 关掉 ❑ *The janitor comes around to turn the lights out.* 那个看门人会过来把灯关掉。
4 → see also **turnout**
▸ **turn over** 1 PHRASAL VERB If you **turn** something **over**, or if it **turns over**, it is moved so that the top part is now facing downward. 翻转 ❑ *Liz picked up the blue envelope and turned it over curiously.* 莉兹捡起那个蓝色的信封，好奇地把它翻过来。 ❑ *The buggy turned over and Nancy was thrown out.* 那辆婴儿车翻倒了，南希被甩了出来。 2 PHRASAL VERB If you **turn over**, for example, when you are lying in bed, you move your body so that you are lying in a different position. 翻身 ❑ *Ann turned over in her bed once more.* 安在床上又翻了一次身。 3 PHRASAL VERB If you **turn** something **over in** your mind, you think carefully about it. 仔细考虑 ❑ *Even when she didn't say anything you could see her turning things over in her mind.* 即使在她什么也不说时，你也能看得出她脑子里在考虑事情。 4 PHRASAL VERB If you **turn** something **over to** someone, you give it to them when they ask for it, because they have a right to it. 交；移交 ❑ *I would have to turn the evidence over to the police.* 我将不得不把证据交给警察。
5 → see also **turnover**
▸ **turn round** [BRIT] → see **turn around**
▸ **turn up** 1 PHRASAL VERB If you say that someone or something **turns up**, you mean that they arrive unexpectedly or after you have been waiting a long time. (意外地或终于) 出现 ❑ *They finally turned up at nearly midnight.* 他们终于在近午夜时出现了。 ❑ *Richard had turned up on Christmas Eve with Tony.* 理查德在圣诞前夜与托尼一起出现。
2 PHRASAL VERB If you **turn** something **up** or if it **turns up**, you find, discover, or notice it. 找到；发现 ❑ *Investigations have never turned up any evidence.* 调查从未发现过任何证据。 3 PHRASAL VERB When you **turn up** a radio, heater, or other piece of equipment, you increase the amount of sound, heat, or power being produced, by adjusting the controls. 调高 (音量或热度) ❑ *Can you turn up the TV?* 你能把电视机的声音调大点吗？ ❑ *I turned the volume up.* 我把音量调大了。

Turn is used in a large number of other expressions which are explained under other words in the dictionary. For example, the expression "turn over a new leaf" is explained at **leaf**.

turn·ing /tɜrnɪŋ/ (**turnings**) N-COUNT If you take a particular **turning**, you go along a road which leads away from the side of another road. 拐弯处 [mainly BRIT]
in AM, usually use **turn**
turn·ing point (**turning points**) N-COUNT A **turning point** is a time at which an important change takes place which affects the future of a person or thing. 转折点 ❑ *The vote yesterday appears to mark a turning point in the war.* 昨天的投票似乎标志着这场战争的一个转折点。
tur·nip /tɜrnɪp/ (**turnips**) N-VAR A **turnip** is a round root vegetable with a cream-colored skin. 芜菁
★ **turn·out** /tɜrnaʊt/ (**turnouts**) N-COUNT The **turnout** at an event is the number of people who go to it or take part in it. 参加人数 ❑ *On the big night there was a massive turnout.* 在那个重要的夜晚，出席的人数很多。
★ **turn·over** /tɜrnoʊvər/ (**turnovers**) 1 N-VAR The **turnover** of a company is the value of the goods or services sold during a particular period of time. 营业额 [BUSINESS] ❑ *The company had a turnover of $3.8 million.* 那个公司拥有380万美元的营业额。 2 N-VAR The **turnover** of people in an organization or place is the rate at which people leave and are replaced. 人员流动率 [BUSINESS] ❑ *Short-term contracts increase staff turnover.* 短期合同会增加员工的流动率。
turn sig·nal (**turn signals**) N-COUNT A car's **turn signals** are the flashing lights that tell you it is going to turn left or right. (汽车的) 转向灯 [AM]
in BRIT, use **indicators**
❑ *He flipped his turn signal, and took a left.* 他打开汽车方向灯，向左转了弯。
turn-up [BRIT] → see **cuff** 2
tur·quoise /tɜrkwɔɪz/ (**turquoises**) 1 COLOR **Turquoise** or **turquoise blue** is used to describe things that are of a light greenish-blue color. 青绿色 (的) ❑ *...a clear turquoise sea.* …一片清澈的碧蓝色大海。 2 N-VAR **Turquoise** is a bright blue stone that is often used in jewelry. 绿松石 [oft N n] ❑ *...beautiful silver and turquoise jewelry.* …漂亮的银首饰和绿松石首饰。

t

▲**tur·tle** /tɜrtᵊl/ (**turtles**) N-COUNT A **turtle** is any reptile that has a thick shell around its body, for example a tortoise or terrapin, and can pull its whole body into its shell. 龟 [AM] ❑ *...a pet turtle.* …一只宠物龟。 ❑ *...the giant sea turtle.* …那只巨大的海龟。

tusk /tʌsk/ (**tusks**) N-COUNT The **tusks** of an elephant, wild boar, or walrus are its two very long, curved, pointed teeth. (大象等的)长牙

tus·sle /tʌsᵊl/ (**tussles, tussling, tussled**) V-RECIP If one person **tussles with** another, or if they **tussle**, they get hold of each other and struggle or fight. 扭打 ❑ *They ended up ripping down perimeter fencing and tussling with the security staff.* 他们最终扯掉了周边的栅栏，并和保安人员扭打起来。 ❑ *He grabbed my microphone and we tussled over that.* 他抓住我的话筒，我们为此扭打起来。 ● N-COUNT **Tussle** is also a noun. 扭打 ❑ *Two players were ejected after a tussle on the field.* 两名球员在场上扭打后被罚出场。

Word Link *tu ≈ watching over : tuition, tutor, tutorial*

tu·tor /tutər/ (**tutors**) **1** N-COUNT A **tutor** is someone who gives private lessons to one student or a very small group of students. 家庭教师 ❑ *...a Spanish tutor.* …一位西班牙语家庭教师。 **2** N-COUNT In some American universities or colleges, a **tutor** is a teacher of the lowest rank. (一些美国大学或学院的) 助教

★**tu·to·rial** /tutɔriəl/ (**tutorials**) **1** N-COUNT In a university or college, a **tutorial** is a regular meeting between a tutor or professor and one or several students, for discussion of a subject that is being studied. (大学里师生之间定期的) 辅导班 ❑ *The methods of study include lectures, tutorials, case studies and practical sessions.* 学习的方法包括讲课、辅导课、案例研究和实践课。 **2** N-COUNT A **tutorial** is part of a book or a computer program which helps you learn something step-by-step without a teacher. 学习指南；使用说明 ❑ *There is an excellent tutorial section, which carefully walks you through how to play.* 有一个非常好的使用指南，它仔细地教你怎么玩。 **3** ADJ **Tutorial** means relating to a tutor or tutors, especially one at a university or college. 助教的 [ADJ n] ❑ *Students may decide to seek tutorial guidance.* 学生们可以决定寻求助教的指导。

tux·edo /tʌksidoʊ/ (**tuxedos**) **1** N-COUNT A **tuxedo** is a suit, usually black, that is worn by men for formal social events. 男式礼服 [mainly AM] **2** N-COUNT A **tuxedo** is a jacket, usually black or white, that is worn by men for formal social events. 男式无尾礼服上装 [mainly AM]

in BRIT, usually use **dinner jacket**

TV ♦♦◇ /ti vi/ (**TVs**) also **T.V.** N-VAR **TV** means the same as **television.** 电视 ❑ *The TV was on.* 电视开着。 ❑ *What's on TV?* 电视上有什么节目？ ❑ *They watch too much TV.* 他们看电视看得太多了。

tweed /twid/ (**tweeds**) N-MASS **Tweed** is a thick woolen cloth, often woven from different colored threads. 粗花呢 ❑ *...a tweed jacket.* …一件粗花呢上衣。

twelfth ♦♦◇ /twɛlfθ/ (**twelfths**) **1** ORD The **twelfth** item in a series is the one that you count as number twelve. 第12 ❑ *...the twelfth anniversary of the April revolution.* …四月革命的12周年纪念日。 **2** FRACTION A **twelfth** is one of twelve equal parts of something. 1/12 ❑ *She is entitled to a twelfth of the cash.* 她有权得到那笔现金的1/12。

twelve ♦♦♦ /twɛlv/ (**twelves**) NUM **Twelve** is the number 12. 12

T

twen·ti·eth ♦♦◇ /twɛntiəθ/ (**twentieths**) **1** ORD The **twentieth** item in a series is the one that you count as number twenty. 第12 ❑ *...the twentieth century.* …20世纪。 **2** FRACTION A **twentieth** is one of twenty equal parts of something. 1/20 ❑ *A few twentieths of a gram can be critical.* 二十分之几克可能是关键的。

twen·ty ♦♦♦ /twɛnti/ (**twenties**) **1** NUM **Twenty** is the number 20. 20 **2** N-PLURAL When you talk about the **twenties**, you are referring to numbers between 20 and 29. For example, if you are **in your twenties**, you are aged between 20 and 29. If the temperature is **in the twenties**, the temperature is between 20 and 29 degrees. 二十几 ❑ *They're both in their twenties and both married with children of their own.* 他们俩都二十几岁了，都已结婚有了自己的孩子。 **3** N-PLURAL **The twenties** is the decade between 1920 and 1929. 20世纪20年代 ❑ *It was written in the Twenties, but it still really stands out.* 它写于20世纪20年代，但现在仍很引人注目。

24-7 /twɛntifɔrsɛvᵊn/ also **twenty-four seven** ADV If something happens **24-7**, it happens all the time without ever stopping. **24-7** means twenty-four hours a day, seven days a week. (每周7天、每天24小时) 一直不停地 [ADV after v] [mainly AM, INFORMAL] ❑ *I feel like sleeping 24-7.* 我每时每刻都想睡觉。 ● ADJ **24-7** is also an adjective. 一直不停的 [ADJ n] ❑ *Now it is a 24-7 radio station that generates $30 million a year in advertising revenue.* 现在它是一家24小时广播的电台，每年创造3000万美元的广告收入。

Word Link *twi ≈ two : twice, twilight, twin*

twice ♦♦♦ /twaɪs/ **1** ADV If something happens **twice**, it happens two times, or there are two actions or events of the same kind. 两次 ❑ *He visited me twice that fall and called me on the telephone often.* 他那年秋天两次来看我，并经常给我打电话。 ❑ *The government has twice declined to back the scheme.* 政府已经两次拒绝支持该计划。 **2** ADV You use **twice** in expressions such as **twice a day** and **twice a week** to indicate that something happens two times in each day or week. 两次 [ADV "a" n] ❑ *I phoned twice a day, leaving messages with his wife.* 我一天打了两次电话，留言给他妻子。 **3** ADV If one thing is, for example, **twice as** big or old **as** another, the first thing is double the size or age of the second. People sometimes say that one thing is **twice as** good or hard **as** another when they want to emphasize that the first thing is much better or harder than the second. 两倍 [ADV "as" adj/adv] ❑ *The figure of seventy-million dollars was twice as big as expected.* 7千万美元这个数字是预计的两倍。 ● PREDET **Twice** is also a predeterminer. 两倍 [PREDET "the" n] ❑ *Unemployment here is twice the national average.* 这儿的失业率是全国平均数的两倍。 **4** PHRASE If you **think twice** about doing something, you consider it again and decide not to do it, or decide to do it differently. 三思 ❑ *From now on, think twice before saying stupid things.* 从现在起，说蠢话前要三思。 **5** **once or twice** → see **once** **6** **twice over** → see **over**

▲**twig** /twɪg/ (**twigs**) N-COUNT A **twig** is a very small thin branch that grows out from a main branch of a tree or bush. 细枝 ❑ *There is the bird, sitting on a twig halfway up the tree.* 鸟儿在那里，栖息在树中段的一根细枝上。

▲**twi·light** /twaɪlaɪt/ N-UNCOUNT **Twilight** is the time just before night when the daylight has almost gone but when it is not completely dark. 黄昏 ❑ *They returned at twilight.* 他们在黄昏时返回。

twin ♦◇◇ /twɪn/ (**twins**) **1** N-COUNT **Twins** are two people who were born at the same time from the same mother. 双胞胎 ❑ *Sarah was looking after the twins.* 萨拉当时正在照看双胞胎。 ❑ *I think there are many positive aspects to being a twin.* 我认为作为双胞胎之一有很多积极的方面。 **2** ADJ **Twin** is used to describe a pair of things that look the same and are close together. 成对的；成双的 [ADJ n] ❑ *...the twin spires of the cathedral.* …那座大教堂的双尖顶。 **3** ADJ **Twin** is used to describe two things or ideas that are similar or connected in some way. 相似的；相关的 [ADJ n] ❑ *...the twin concepts of liberty and equality.* …自由和平等这两个相关的概念。
→ see **clone**

twin·kle /twɪŋkᵊl/ (**twinkles, twinkling, twinkled**) **1** V-I If a star or a light **twinkles**, it shines with an unsteady light which rapidly and constantly changes from bright to faint. 闪烁 ❑ *At night, lights twinkle in distant cabins across the valleys.* 晚上，灯光在山谷对面远处的小木屋里闪烁。 **2** V-I If you say that someone's eyes **twinkle**, you mean that their eyes express good humor or amusement. (眼睛) 闪烁 ❑ *She saw her mother's eyes twinkle with amusement.* 她看到她母亲的双眸愉快地闪烁着。 ● N-SING **Twinkle** is also a noun. 闪烁 ❑ *A kindly twinkle came into her eyes.* 她的眼睛里闪烁着亲切的光芒。

twirl /twɜrl/ (**twirls, twirling, twirled**) **1** V-T/V-I If you **twirl** something or if it **twirls**, it turns around and around with a smooth, fast movement. 旋转 ❑ *Bonnie twirled her empty glass in her fingers.* 邦妮用手指转动着她的空杯子。 **2** V-I If you **twirl**, you turn around and around quickly, for example, when you are dancing. (跳舞等时) 旋转 ❑ *Several hundred people twirl around the ballroom dance floor.* 几百人在舞厅的舞池里旋转着。

twist ♦◇◇ /twɪst/ (**twists, twisting, twisted**) **1** V-T If you **twist** something, you turn it to make a spiral shape, for example, by turning the two ends of it in opposite directions. 扭曲；拧 ❑ *Her hands began to twist the handles of the bag she carried.* 她的双手开始拧她拎着的那个包的拎柄。 **2** V-T/V-I If you **twist** something, especially a part of your body, or if it **twists**, it moves into an unusual, uncomfortable, or bent position, for example, because of being hit or pushed, or because you are upset. 扭弯；扭曲 ❑ *He twisted her arms behind her back and clipped a pair of handcuffs on her wrists.* 他把她的双臂扭到她的背后，把一副手铐扣在她的手腕上。 ❑ *Sophia's face twisted* *in perplexity.* 索菲娅的脸因困惑而扭曲着。 **3** V-T/V-I If you **twist** part of your body such as your head or your shoulders, you turn that part while keeping the rest of your body still. 转动（身体某部分） ❑ *She twisted her head sideways and looked toward the door.* 她把头转向一边，朝门口看去。 ❑ *Susan twisted round in her seat until she could see Graham behind her.* 苏珊在她的座位上转过身去，直到她能看见她身后的格雷厄姆。 **4** V-T If you **twist** a part of your body such as your ankle or wrist, you injure it by turning it too sharply, or in an unusual direction. 扭伤（脚踝或手腕等） ❑ *He fell and twisted his ankle.* 他摔了一跤，扭伤了脚踝。 **5** V-T If you **twist** something, you turn it so that it moves around in a circular direction. 旋转 ❑ *She was staring down at her hands, twisting the ring on her finger.* 她往下盯着自己的手，旋转着手指上的戒指。 ● N-COUNT **Twist** is also a noun. 旋转 ❑ *Just a twist of the handle is all it takes to wring out the mop.* 只需旋转一下那个手柄就可以拧干拖把。 **6** V-I If a road or river **twists**, it has a lot of sudden changes of direction in it. （道路或河流）迂回曲折 ❑ *The roads twist around hairpin bends.* 那些道路有很多险弯。 ● N-COUNT **Twist** is also a noun. （道路或河流的）迂回曲折 [usu pl] ❑ *It allows the train to maintain a constant speed through the twists and turns of existing track.* 它可以让火车在现有蜿蜒盘旋的轨道上保持匀速。 **7** V-T If you say that someone **has twisted** something that you have said, you disapprove of them because they have repeated it in a way that changes its meaning, in order to harm you or benefit themselves. 歪曲 [DISAPPROVAL] ❑ *It's a shame the way the media can twist your words and misrepresent you.* 媒体歪曲人们的话语及误传人们的本意的作风是可耻的。 **8** N-COUNT A **twist** in something is an unexpected and significant development. 意外进展 ❑ *The battle of the sexes also took a new twist.* 性别之战也有了意想不到的新进展。 **9** to **twist** someone's **arm** → see **arm** **10** to **twist the knife** → see **knife**

Word Partnership *twist* 的常用搭配：

ADV.	twist **around** 1 3 5
V.	twist **and turn** 6
N.	**plot** twist, **story** twist 8
ADJ.	**added** twist, **bizarre** twist, **interesting** twist, **latest** twist, **new** twist, **unexpected** twist 8

twist·er /twɪstər/ (**twisters**) N-COUNT A **twister** is the same as a **tornado**. 龙卷风 [AM, INFORMAL] ❑ *The park was devastated by the twister.* 公园被龙卷风摧毁了。

▲ **twitch** /twɪtʃ/ (**twitches, twitching, twitched**) V-T/V-I If something, especially a part of your body, **twitches** or if you **twitch** it, it makes a little jumping movement. （身体等）抽动 ❑ *When I stood up to her, her right cheek would begin to twitch.* 每当我直面她时，她的右脸颊就会开始抽动。 ● N-COUNT **Twitch** is also a noun. 抽动 ❑ *He developed a nervous twitch and began to blink constantly.* 他患上了一种神经痉挛病，开始不停地眨眼睛。

two ♦♦♦ /tuː/ (**twos**) **1** NUM **Two** is the number 2. 2 **2** PHRASE If you say **it takes two** or **it takes two to tango**, you mean that a situation or argument involves two people and they are both therefore responsible for it. 一个巴掌拍不响 ❑ *Divorce is never the fault of one partner; it takes two.* 离婚从来就不是哪一方的错；双方都有责任。 **3** PHRASE If you **put two and two together**, you work out the truth about something for yourself, by using the information that is available to you. 根据已知信息分析 ❑ *Putting two and two together, I assume that this was the car he used.* 根据所掌握的信息判断，我认为这就是他用的那辆车。 **4** to **kill two birds with one stone** → see **bird**

two-faced ADJ If you describe someone as **two-faced**, you are critical of them because they say they do or believe one thing when their behavior or words show that they do not do it or do not believe it. 两面派的；言行不一致的 [DISAPPROVAL] ❑ *The scientists saw the public as being particularly two-faced about animal welfare in view of the way domestic animals are treated.* 考虑到他们对待家畜的方式，科学家们认为公众在动物福利方面特别言行不一致。

two·fold /tuːfoʊld/ also **two-fold** ADJ You can use **twofold** to introduce a topic that has two equally important parts. 有两部分的 [FORMAL] ❑ *The reason for the interview is twofold: we want to find out what he can tell us, plus we also want to find out what condition he is in.* 这一采访的原因有两个：我们既想看看他能告诉我们些什么，也想弄清他的处境如何。

two-way **1** ADJ **Two-way** means moving or working in two opposite directions or allowing something to move or work in two opposite directions. 双向的 ❑ *The bridge is now open to two-way traffic.* 这座桥现在可以双向行驶。 **2** ADJ A **two-way** radio can send and receive signals. （无线电设备）收发两用的 [ADJ n] ❑ *Each squad has a two-way radio to stay in touch.* 每个小组都有一台收发两用的无线电通信设备以保持联系。

ty·coon /taɪkuːn/ (**tycoons**) N-COUNT A **tycoon** is a person who is successful in business and so has become rich and powerful. （工商界的）大亨 ❑ *...a self-made Irish-American property tycoon.* …一个靠自己奋斗成功的爱尔兰裔美国房地产大亨。

type
❶ SORT OR KIND
❷ WRITING AND PRINTING

❶ **type** ♦♦◊ /taɪp/ (**types**) **1** N-COUNT A **type of** something is a group of those things that have particular features in common. 类型；种类 ❑ *...several types of lettuce.* …生菜的几个品种。 ❑ *There are various types of the disease.* 该疾病有各种类型。 **2** N-COUNT If you refer to a particular thing or person as a **type of** something more general, you are considering that thing or person as an example of that more general group. 某类（人或事物） ❑ *Have you done this type of work before?* 你以前做过这种工作吗？ ❑ *Rates of interest for this type of borrowing can be high.* 这种贷款的利率可能会很高。 **3** N-COUNT If you refer to a person as a particular **type**, you mean that they have that particular appearance, character, or type of behavior. 具有某种特点的人 ❑ *It's the first time I, a fair-skinned, freckly type, have sailed in the sun without burning.* 这是第一次，我这样一个皮肤白皙、有雀斑的人，顶着太阳航海而没有晒伤。

The **brand** of a product such as jeans, tea, or soap is its name, which can also be the name of the company that makes or sells it. The **make** of a car or electrical appliance such as a radio or washing machine is the name of the company that produces it. If you talk about what **type** of product or service you want, you are talking about its quality and what features it should have. You can also talk about **types** of people or of abstract things. ❑ *...which type of coffeemaker to choose. ...a new type of bank account. ...looking for a certain type of actor.* A **model** of car or of some other devices is a name that is given to a particular **type**, for example, a Ford Escort. Note that **type** can also be used informally to mean either **make** or **model**. For example, if someone asks what **type** of car you have got, you could reply "an SUV," "a Ford," or perhaps "an Escort."

❷ **type** ♦♦◊ /taɪp/ (**types, typing, typed**) **1** V-T/V-I If you **type** something, you use a typewriter or computer keyboard to write it. 打字 ❑ *I can type your essays for you.* 我可以为你打文章。 ❑ *I had never really learned to type properly.* 我从未真正地学会正确地打字。 **2** N-UNCOUNT **Type** is printed text as it appears in a book or newspaper, or the small pieces of metal that are used to create this. 印刷文字；铅字 ❑ *The correction had already been set in type.* 校正稿已经排好版了。 ❑ *I can't read this small type.* 我无法读这种小号字体。 **3** → see also **typing**
→ see **printing**

▸ **type in** or **type into** PHRASAL VERB If you **type** information **into** a computer or **type** it **in**, you press keys on the keyboard so that the computer stores or processes the information. 键入 ❑ *Officials type each passport number into a computer.* 官员们把每份护照的号码输入一台电脑。 ❑ *You have to type in commands, such as "help" and "print."* 你必须键入指令，如"帮助"和"打印"。

▸ **type up** PHRASAL VERB If you **type up** a text that has been written by hand, you produce a typed copy of it. 把（手写稿）打出来 ❑ *When the first draft was completed, Nichols typed it up.* 当初稿完成时，尼科尔斯把它打了出来。

Thesaurus *type* 另参见：

N.	class, kind, sort ❶ 1 – 3
	print ❷ 2
V.	transcribe, write ❷ 1

type·face /taɪpfeɪs/ (**typefaces**) N-COUNT In printing, a **typeface** is a set of alphabetical characters, numbers, and other characters that all have the same design. There are many different typefaces. 字体 ❑ *...the ubiquitous Times New Roman typeface.* …普遍使用的泰晤士新罗马字体。

type·writ·er /taɪpraɪtər/ (**typewriters**) N-COUNT A **typewriter** is a machine with keys which are pressed in order to print letters, numbers, or other characters onto paper. 打字机

▲**ty·phoon** /taɪfuːn/ (**typhoons**) N-COUNT A **typhoon** is a very violent tropical storm. 台风
→ see **disaster, hurricane**

typi·cal ♦◇◇ /tɪpɪkᵊl/ **1** ADJ You use **typical** to describe someone or something that shows the most usual characteristics of a particular type of person or thing, and is therefore a good example of that type. (某人或某物) 有典型性的; 有代表性的 ❑ *Cheney is everyone's image of a typical cop: a big white guy, six feet, 220 pounds.* 切尼是每个人心目中典型的警察形象：高大的白人，身高6英尺，体重220磅。 **2** ADJ If a particular action or feature is **typical of** someone or something, it shows their usual qualities or characteristics. (行为或特征) 典型的 ❑ *This reluctance to move toward a democratic state is typical of totalitarian regimes.* 这种不愿朝民主国家迈进的态度是极权主义政体的典型特征。 **3** ADJ If you say that something is **typical of a** person, situation, or thing, you are criticizing them or complaining about them and saying that they are just as bad or disappointing as you expected them to be. 一贯的 (用于批评或抱怨) [FEELINGS] ❑ *She threw her hands into the air. "That is just typical of you, isn't it?"* 她往空中挥挥双手说，"你一贯就是这个样子，是不是？"

typi·cal·ly /tɪpɪkli/ **1** ADV You use **typically** to say that something usually happens in the way that you are describing. 通常 [ADV with cl/group] ❑ *It typically takes a day or two, depending on size.* 这通常需要一天或两天，依大小而定。 **2** ADV You use **typically** to say that something shows all the most usual characteristics of a particular type of person or thing. 典型地 [ADV adj] ❑ *Philip paced the floor, a typically nervous expectant father.* 菲利普在地板上踱来踱去，一个典型紧张的准爸爸。 **3** ADV You use **typically** to indicate that someone has behaved in the way that they normally do. 一贯地 ❑ *Typically, the Norwegians were on the mountain two hours before anyone else.* 挪威人一贯比其他人早两个小时到山上。

typi·fy /tɪpɪfaɪ/ (**typifies, typifying, typified**) V-T If something or someone **typifies** a situation or type of thing or person, they have all the usual characteristics of it and are a typical example of it. 是…的典型; 代表 ❑ *These two buildings typify the rich extremes of local architecture.* 这两座建筑物代表着当地建筑风格的迥异。

typ·ing /taɪpɪŋ/ **1** N-UNCOUNT **Typing** is the work or activity of typing something by means of a typewriter or computer keyboard. 打字 ❑ *I'm taking a typing class.* 我在上一个打字班。 **2** N-UNCOUNT **Typing** is the skill of using a typewriter or keyboard quickly and accurately. 打字技术 ❑ *My typing is hideous.* 我打字很糟。

typ·ist /taɪpɪst/ (**typists**) N-COUNT A **typist** is someone who works in an office typing letters and other documents. 打字员

▲**tyr·an·ny** /tɪrəni/ (**tyrannies**) **1** N-VAR A **tyranny** is a cruel, harsh, and unfair government in which a person or small group of people have power over everyone else. 专制暴政 ❑ *Self-expression and individuality are the greatest weapons against tyranny.* 自我表达和个性是对抗专制暴政的最强武器。 **2** N-UNCOUNT If you describe someone's behavior and treatment of others that they have authority over as **tyranny**, you mean that they are severe with them or unfair to them. 专横暴虐 ❑ *I'm the sole victim of Mother's tyranny.* 我是母亲专横暴虐的惟一受害者。

ty·rant /taɪrənt/ (**tyrants**) N-COUNT You can use **tyrant** to refer to someone who treats the people they have authority over in a cruel and unfair way. 暴君 ❑ *...households where the father was a tyrant.* …有暴君之父的家庭。

tyre /taɪər/ [mainly BRIT] → see **tire**

T

Uu

U /yu/ also **u** (**U's, u's**) N-VAR **U** is the twenty-first letter of the English alphabet. 英语字母表的第21个字母

ubiqui·tous /yubɪkwɪtəs/ ADJ If you describe something or someone as **ubiquitous**, you mean that they seem to be everywhere. 无所不在的 [FORMAL] ❑ *Sugar is ubiquitous in the diet.* 糖在饮食中到处可见。

ugly /ʌgli/ (**uglier, ugliest**) **1** ADJ If you say that someone or something is **ugly**, you mean that they are very unattractive and unpleasant to look at. 难看的；丑的 ❑ *...an ugly little hat.* …一顶丑陋的小帽子。 ● **ug·li·ness** N-UNCOUNT 丑陋 ❑ *Dekkeret found the landscape startling in its ugliness.* 德克雷特发现那风景难看得惊人。 **2** ADJ If you refer to an event or situation as **ugly**, you mean that it is very unpleasant, usually because it involves violent or aggressive behavior. 丑恶的 ❑ *There have been some ugly scenes.* 出现了一些丑恶的场面。 ❑ *The confrontation turned ugly.* 冲突变得丑恶了。 ● **ug·li·ness** N-UNCOUNT 丑恶 ❑ *...the ugliness of sexual harassment.* …性骚扰的丑恶。 **3** **to rear its ugly head** → see **head**

Thesaurus *ugly* 另参见：
ADJ. hideous, unattractive; *(ant.)* beautiful **1**
disagreeable, offensive, unpleasant **2**

U.K. ♦♦◇ /yu keɪ/ also **UK** N-PROPER **The U.K.** is England, Wales, Scotland, and Northern Ireland. **U.K.** is an abbreviation for **United Kingdom**. (英格兰、威尔士、苏格兰和北爱尔兰) 联合王国；英国 ["the" N]

★ **ul·cer** /ʌlsər/ (**ulcers**) N-COUNT An **ulcer** is a sore area on the outside or inside of your body which is very painful and may bleed or produce a poisonous substance. 溃疡 ❑ *In addition to headaches, you may develop stomach ulcers as well.* 除了头痛，你还可能患上胃溃疡。

ul·te·ri·or /ʌltɪəriər/ ADJ If you say that someone has an **ulterior** motive for doing something, you believe that they have a hidden reason for doing it. 暗藏的 [ADJ n] ❑ *Sheila had an ulterior motive for trying to help Stan.* 希拉设法帮助斯坦是别有用心。

Word Link *ultim ≈ end, last : penultimate, ultimate, ultimatum*

ul·ti·mate ♦◇◇ /ʌltɪmɪt/ **1** ADJ You use **ultimate** to describe the final result or aim of a long series of events. 最终的 [ADJ n] ❑ *He said it is still not possible to predict the ultimate outcome.* 他说现在还不可能预测最终的结果。 **2** ADJ You use **ultimate** to describe the original source or cause of something. 最终的；根本的 [ADJ n] ❑ *Plants are the ultimate source of all foodstuffs.* 植物是所有食物的最终来源。 **3** ADJ You use **ultimate** to describe the most important or powerful thing of a particular kind. 终极的 (指最重要或最强大的) [ADJ n] ❑ *My experience as player, coach and manager has prepared me for this ultimate challenge.* 我做球员、教练和经理人的经历已经使我为这终极挑战作好了准备。 **4** ADJ You use **ultimate** to describe the most extreme and unpleasant example of a particular thing. 终极的 (指最极端、最恶劣的) [ADJ n] ❑ *Bringing back the death penalty would be the ultimate abuse of human rights.* 恢复死刑将是对人权最极端恶劣的践踏。 ❑ *Treachery was the ultimate sin.* 背叛曾是弥天大罪。 **5** ADJ You use **ultimate** to describe the best possible example of a particular thing. 终极的 (指最好的) [ADJ n] ❑ *Experience the ultimate adventure!* 去体验最有刺激的冒险吧！ **6** PHRASE **The ultimate in** something is the best or most advanced example of it. 极致；最佳典范 ❑ *Ballet is the ultimate in human movement.* 芭蕾舞是人类动作的至美。 ❑ *This hotel is the ultimate in luxury.* 这家酒店为豪华之典范。

Word Partnership *ultimate* 的常用搭配：
N. ultimate **aim/goal/objective**, ultimate **outcome** **1**
ultimate **authority**, ultimate **decision**, ultimate **power**, ultimate **weapon** **3**
ultimate **experience** **3** **5**

ul·ti·mate·ly ♦◇◇ /ʌltɪmɪtli/ **1** ADV **Ultimately** means finally, after a long and often complicated series of events. 最终 ❑ *Whatever the scientists ultimately conclude, all of their data will immediately be disputed.* 无论科学家们最终得出什么结论，他们的所有数据将随即受到质疑。 **2** ADV You use **ultimately** to indicate that what you are saying is the most important point in a discussion. 最重要地 [ADV with cl] ❑ *Ultimately, Judge Lewin has the final say.* 最重要地，卢因法官有最终发言权。

Thesaurus *ultimately* 另参见：
ADV. eventually, finally **1**

▲ **ul·ti·ma·tum** /ʌltɪmeɪtəm/ (**ultimatums**) N-COUNT An **ultimatum** is a warning to someone that unless they act in a particular way, action will be taken against them. 最后通牒 ❑ *They issued an ultimatum to the police to rid the area of racist attackers, or they will take the law into their own hands.* 他们向警方发出了最后通牒，要他们清除掉该地区的种族主义袭击者，否则他们就要自行采取行动。

▲ **ultra-** /ʌltrə-/ PREFIX **Ultra-** is added to adjectives to form other adjectives that emphasize that something or someone has a quality to an extreme degree. 极其… [EMPHASIS] ❑ *...a wide range of ultramodern equipment.* …一系列极其现代的仪器。

ultra·sound /ʌltrəsaʊnd/ N-UNCOUNT **Ultrasound** is sound waves which travel at such a high frequency that they cannot be heard by humans. Ultrasound is used in medicine to get pictures of the inside of people's bodies. 超声波 ❑ *I had an ultrasound scan to see how the pregnancy was progressing.* 我做了超声波扫描，检查妊娠进展情况。

★ **ultra·vio·let** /ʌltrəvaɪəlɪt/ ADJ **Ultraviolet** light or radiation is what causes your skin to become darker in color after you have been in sunlight. In large amounts ultraviolet light is harmful. 紫外的 ❑ *The sun's ultraviolet rays are responsible for both tanning and burning.* 太阳的紫外线是皮肤晒黑和晒伤的原因。
→ see **skin, sun, wave**

um **Um** is used in writing to represent a sound that people make when they are hesitating, usually while deciding what they want to say next. 嗯 (表示迟疑) ❑ *She felt her face going red. "I'm sorry Rob, it's just that I'm, um, overwhelmed."* 她感到自己的脸变红了。"对不起罗伯，只是我，嗯，太惊讶了。"

um·brel·la /ʌmbrɛlə/ (**umbrellas**) **1** N-COUNT An **umbrella** is an object which you use to protect yourself from the rain or hot sun. It consists of a long stick with a folding frame covered in cloth. 伞 ❑ *Harry held an umbrella over Denise.* 哈里为丹尼斯撑着伞。 **2** N-SING **Umbrella** is used to refer to a single group or description that includes a lot of different organizations or ideas. 总组织；总称 ❑ *The country's blood banks are under the umbrella of the American Red Cross.* 该国的血库均属于美国红十字会。

um·pire /ʌmpaɪər/ (**umpires, umpiring, umpired**) **1** N-COUNT An **umpire** is a person whose job is to make sure that a sports contest or game is played fairly and that the rules are not broken. (体育比赛或竞赛的) 裁判 ❑ *The umpire's decision is final.* 裁判的判决是不可更改的。 **2** V-T/V-I To **umpire** means to be the umpire in a sports contest or game. (在体育比赛或竞赛中) 担任裁判 ❑ *He umpired baseball games.* 他过去担任棒球比赛的裁判。

U.N. ♦♦◇ /yu ɛn/ also **UN** N-PROPER The **U.N.** is the same as the **United Nations**. 联合国 ❑ *...a U.N. peacekeeping mission.* …一项联合国维和使命。

un·able ♦◇◇ /ʌneɪbᵊl/ ADJ If you are **unable to** do something, it is impossible for you to do it, for example because you do not have the necessary skill or knowledge, or because you do not have enough time or money. 不能做到的 [v-link ADJ to-inf] ❑ *The military may feel unable to hand over power to a civilian president next year.* 军方可能觉得无法在明年把政权移交给一位民选总统。

Word Partnership *unable* 的常用搭配:
V. unable **to afford**, unable **to agree**, unable **to attend**, unable **to control**, unable **to cope**, unable **to decide**, unable **to explain**, unable **to find**, unable **to hold**, unable **to identify**, unable **to make**, unable **to move**, unable **to pay**, unable **to perform**, unable **to reach**, unable **to speak**, unable **to walk**, unable **to work**
ADV. **physically** unable

un·ac·cep·table /ʌnəksɛptəbᵊl/ ADJ If you describe something as **unacceptable**, you strongly disapprove of it or object to it and feel that it should not be allowed to continue. 不能接受的 ❑ *It is totally unacceptable for children to swear.* 小孩子骂人是完全不能接受的。

Word Partnership *unacceptable* 的常用搭配:
ADV. **absolutely** unacceptable, **completely** unacceptable, **simply** unacceptable, **socially** unacceptable, **totally** unacceptable
N. unacceptable **behavior**, unacceptable **conditions**

un·af·fect·ed /ʌnəfɛktɪd/ 1 ADJ If someone or something is **unaffected by** an event or occurrence, they are not changed by it in any way. 未受影响的 [v-link ADJ] ❑ *She seemed totally unaffected by what she'd drunk.* 她似乎完全没有受到所喝的东西的影响。 2 ADJ If you describe someone as **unaffected**, you mean that they are natural and genuine in their behavior, and do not act as though they are more important than other people. 质朴的 [APPROVAL] ❑ *...this unaffected, charming couple.* …这对质朴、可爱的夫妇。

Thesaurus *unaffected* 另参见:
ADJ. unaltered, unchanged 1
genuine, honest, natural 2

una·nim·ity /yunənɪmɪti/ N-UNCOUNT When there is **unanimity** among a group of people, they all agree about something or all vote for the same thing. 一致同意 ❑ *All decisions would require unanimity.* 所有决定都需要全体一致同意。

Word Link *anim ≈ alive, mind : animal, animated, unanimous*

★ **unani·mous** /yunænɪməs/ 1 ADJ When a group of people are **unanimous**, they all agree about something or all vote for the same thing. 一致同意的 ❑ *Editors were unanimous in their condemnation of the proposals.* 编辑们一致谴责这些提议。 ● **unani·mous·ly** ADV 一致同意地 [ADV with v] ❑ *The board unanimously approved the project last week.* 董事会上周一致同意批准了这个项目。 2 ADJ A **unanimous** vote, decision, or agreement is one in which all the people involved agree. 全体同意的 (投票、决定、协议等) ❑ *Their decision was unanimous.* 他们的决定是全体同意的。

un·an·nounced /ʌnənaʊnst/ ADJ If someone arrives or does something **unannounced**, they do it unexpectedly and without anyone having been told about it beforehand. 未事先通知的 ❑ *He had just arrived unannounced from South America.* 他刚从南美来，事先也没通知。

un·an·swered /ʌnænsərd/ ADJ Something such as a question or letter that is **unanswered** has not been answered. 未被答复的 ❑ *Some of the most important questions remain unanswered.* 一些最重要的问题仍未被答复。 ❑ *The report of the judges leaves a lot of unanswered questions.* 法官们的报告留下了许多没有回答的问题。

U

un·ap·pe·tis·ing /ʌnæpɪtaɪzɪŋ/ [BRIT] → see **unappetizing**

un·ap·pe·tiz·ing /ʌnæpɪtaɪzɪŋ/
in BRIT, also use **unappetising**
ADJ If you describe food as **unappetizing**, you think it will be unpleasant to eat because of its appearance. 引不起食欲的 ❑ *...cold and unappetizing chicken.* …凉的、引不起食欲的鸡肉。

un·armed /ʌnɑrmd/ ADJ If a person or vehicle is **unarmed**, they are not carrying any weapons. 未武装的 ❑ *The soldiers concerned were unarmed at the time.* 有关士兵当时未携带武器。 ● ADV **Unarmed** is also an adverb. 未武装地 [ADV after v] ❑ *He says he walks inside the prison without guards, unarmed.* 他说他没带警卫、没带武器走进那个监狱。

un·ashamed /ʌnəʃeɪmd/ ADJ If you describe someone's behavior or attitude as **unashamed**, you mean that they are open and honest about things that other people might find embarrassing or shocking. 不害臊的; 不觉难堪的 ❑ *I grinned at him in unashamed delight.* 我高兴地朝他咧嘴笑了笑，一点儿也不觉得难为情。

● **un·asham·ed·ly** /ʌnəʃeɪmɪdli/ ADV 不害臊地; 不觉难堪地 ❑ *Drugs are sold unashamedly in broad daylight.* 毒品在光天化日之下公然被出售。

un·at·tend·ed /ʌnətɛndɪd/ ADJ When people or things are left **unattended**, they are not being watched or taken care of. 无人照管的 ❑ *Never leave young children unattended near any pool or water tank.* 千万别把小孩留在水池或水箱旁而无人看管。 ❑ *An unattended backpack was found in a garbage pail.* 在垃圾桶里发现了一个无人看管的背包。

un·at·trac·tive /ʌnətræktɪv/ 1 ADJ **Unattractive** people and things are unpleasant in appearance. (外表) 不吸引人的 ❑ *I felt lonely and unattractive.* 我感到孤独、长得也不好看。 ❑ *...an unattractive shade of orange.* …一种难看的橙色。 2 ADJ If you describe something as **unattractive**, you mean that people do not like it and do not want to be involved with it. 不招人喜爱的; 没有吸引力的 ❑ *The market is still unattractive to many insurers.* 这个市场仍然不受许多保险公司青睐。

un·author·ised /ʌnɔːθəraɪzd/ [BRIT] → see **unauthorized**

un·author·ized /ʌnɔθəraɪzd/
in BRIT, also use **unauthorised**
ADJ If something is **unauthorized**, it has been produced or is happening without official permission. 未经授权的; 未经许可的 ❑ *...a new unauthorized biography of the Russian president.* …一本新的未经授权的俄罗斯总统传记。 ❑ *It has also been made quite clear that the trip was unauthorized.* 这次旅行是未经过批准的，这一点也已经非常清楚了。

un·avail·able /ʌnəveɪləbᵊl/ ADJ When things or people are **unavailable**, you cannot obtain them, meet them, or talk to them. 得不到的; 见不到的; 不能交谈的 ❑ *Mr. Hicks is out of the country and so unavailable for comment.* 希克斯先生在国外，所以不能发表评论。

Word Link *able ≈ able to be : incurable, portable, unavoidable*

un·avoid·able /ʌnəvɔɪdəbᵊl/ ADJ If something is **unavoidable**, it cannot be avoided or prevented. 不可避免的; 无法防止的 ❑ *Managers said the job losses were unavoidable.* 经理们说失业是不可避免的。

Word Link *un ≈ not : unaware, uncommon, undecided*

un·aware /ʌnəwɛər/ ADJ If you are **unaware of** something, you do not know about it. 不知道的 [v-link ADJ] ❑ *Many people are unaware of just how much food and drink they consume.* 许多人不知道自己到底消耗掉多少食物和饮料。

Word Partnership *unaware* 的常用搭配:
ADV. **apparently** unaware, **blissfully** unaware, **completely** unaware, **totally** unaware

un·bal·anced /ʌnbælənst/ 1 ADJ If you describe someone as **unbalanced**, you mean that they appear disturbed and upset or they seem to be slightly crazy. 心神不定的; 精神有些失常的 ❑ *I knew how unbalanced Paula had been since my uncle Peter died.* 我知道葆拉自彼得叔叔去世以来有多么心神不定。 2 ADJ If you describe something such as a report or argument as **unbalanced**, you think that it is unfair or inaccurate because it emphasizes some things and ignores others. 不公正的; 片面的 ❑ *UN officials argued that the report was unbalanced.* 联合国官员们辩称那份报告有失公正。

un·bear·able /ʌnbɛərəbᵊl/ ADJ If you describe something as **unbearable**, you mean that it is so unpleasant, painful, or upsetting that you feel unable to accept it or deal with it. 无法忍受的 ❑ *War has made life almost unbearable for the civilians remaining in the capital.* 对留在首都的市民来说，战争已使得生活几乎无法忍受了。

● **un·bear·ably** /ʌnbɛərəbli/ ADV 无法忍受地 ❑ *By the evening it had become unbearably hot.* 到了晚上天气已热得无法忍受。

un·beat·able /ʌnbitəbᵊl/ 1 ADJ If you describe something as **unbeatable**, you mean that it is the best thing of its kind. 无可匹敌的; 无与伦比的 [EMPHASIS] ❑ *These resorts remain unbeatable in terms of price.* 这些度假胜地在价格上仍是无可匹敌的。 2 ADJ In a game or competition, if you describe a person or team as **unbeatable**, you mean that they win so often, or perform so well that they are unlikely to be beaten by anyone. 无敌手的 ❑ *With two more days of competition to go China is in an unbeatable position.* 比赛进行到最后两天时，中国队已处于无敌手的地位。

un·beat·en /ʌnbitᵊn/ ADJ In sports, if a person or their performance is **unbeaten**, nobody else has performed well enough to beat them. 未被击败过的; 未曾被超越的 ❑ *He's unbeaten in 20 fights.* 他在20场拳击赛中没有被击败过。

un·be·liev·able /ʌnbɪliːvəbᵊl/ 1 ADJ If you say that something is **unbelievable**, you are emphasizing that it is very good, impressive, intense, or extreme. (好得、强得、极端得) 令人难以置信的 [EMPHASIS] ❑ *His guitar solos are just unbelievable.* 他的吉他独奏简直妙得令人难以置信。 ❑ *The pressure they put us under was unbelievable.* 他们让我们承受的压力大得令人难以置信。 ● **un·be·liev·ably** /ʌnbɪliːvəbli/ ADV 令人难以置信地 [ADV with cl/group] ❑ *It was unbelievably dramatic as lightning crackled all around the van.* 闪电在货车周围炸开时，场面异常壮观。 ❑ *Our car was still going unbelievably well.* 我们的汽车当时仍然运行得让人难以相信地好。 2 ADJ You can use **unbelievable** to emphasize that you think something is very bad or shocking. (糟糕得) 令人难以置信的 [EMPHASIS] ❑ *I find it unbelievable that people can accept this sort of behavior.* 人们竟然能接受这种行为，我感到难以相信。 ● **un·be·liev·ably** ADV 令人难以置信地 [ADV with cl/group] ❑ *What you did was unbelievably stupid.* 你所做的愚蠢至极。 3 ADJ If an idea or statement is **unbelievable**, it seems so unlikely to be true that you cannot believe it. (主意、陈述) 令人难以相信的 ❑ *I still find this story both fascinating and unbelievable.* 我仍然觉得这个故事非常有趣和难以置信。 ● **un·be·liev·ably** ADV 令人难以相信地 [ADV with cl/group] ❑ *Lainey was, unbelievably, pregnant again.* 莱内令人难以相信地再次怀孕了。

Thesaurus *unbelievable* 另参见：

ADJ. astounding, incredible, remarkable 1
inconceivable, preposterous, unimaginable 3

un·born /ʌnbɔrn/ ADJ An **unborn** child has not yet been born and is still inside its mother's uterus. 未出世的 ❑ *...her unborn baby.* …她未出世的婴儿。 ● N-PLURAL **The unborn** are children who are not born yet. 未出世的孩子 ❑ *...a law that protects the lives of pregnant women and the unborn.* …一项保护孕妇和未出世孩子的生命的法律。

un·bro·ken /ʌnbroʊkən/ ADJ If something is **unbroken**, it is continuous or complete and has not been interrupted or broken. 连续的；完整的 ❑ *...an unbroken string of victories.* …接连不断的一连串胜利。 ❑ *We've had ten days of almost unbroken sunshine.* 我们已经有10天几乎完全没有中断过的艳阳天。

★ **un·but·ton** /ʌnbʌtᵊn/ (**unbuttons, unbuttoning, unbuttoned**) V-T If you **unbutton** an item of clothing, you undo the buttons fastening it. 解开…的钮扣 ❑ *She had begun to unbutton her blouse.* 她开始解她衬衫的钮扣。

un·can·ny /ʌnkæni/ ADJ If you describe something as **uncanny**, you mean that it is strange and difficult to explain. 出奇的 ❑ *The hero, Danny, bears an uncanny resemblance to Kirk Douglas.* 主人翁丹尼与柯克·道格拉斯出奇地相像。 ● **un·can·ni·ly** /ʌnkænɪli/ ADV 出奇地 ❑ *They have uncannily similar voices.* 他们有着出奇相似的嗓音。

un·cer·tain /ʌnsɜrtᵊn/ 1 ADJ If you are **uncertain about** something, you do not know what you should do, what is going to happen, or what the truth is about something. 不确定的 ❑ *He was uncertain about his brother's intentions.* 他对他兄弟的意图心中无数。 ❑ *They were uncertain of the total value of the transaction.* 他们不清楚这笔交易的总额。 ● **un·cer·tain·ly** ADV 不确定地 ❑ *He entered the hallway and stood uncertainly.* 他走进门厅，站在那儿不知道做什么好。 2 ADJ If something is **uncertain**, it is not known or definite. 未知的；不明确的 ❑ *How much practical help they can give us is uncertain.* 他们能给我们多少实际帮助还是个未知数。 ❑ *It's uncertain whether they will accept the plan.* 他们会不会接受这项计划现在还不清楚。 3 PHRASE If you say that someone tells a person something **in no uncertain terms**, you are emphasizing that they say it strongly and clearly so that there is no doubt about what they mean. 非常明确地 [EMPHASIS] ❑ *She told him in no uncertain terms to go away.* 她非常明确地叫他走开。

Word Partnership *uncertain* 的常用搭配：

PREP. uncertain **about** *something* 1
V. **be** uncertain, **remain** uncertain 1 2
ADV. **highly** uncertain, **still** uncertain 1 2

un·cer·tain·ty /ʌnsɜrtᵊnti/ (**uncertainties**) N-VAR **Uncertainty** is a state of doubt about the future or about what is the right thing to do. 不确定状态 ❑ *...a period of political uncertainty.* …一段政治不稳定时期。

Word Partnership *uncertainty* 的常用搭配：

ADJ. **economic** uncertainty, **great** uncertainty, **political** uncertainty

un·chal·lenged /ʌntʃælɪndʒd/ 1 ADJ When something goes **unchallenged** or is **unchallenged**, people accept it without asking questions about whether it is right or wrong. 未受到过质疑的 ❑ *These views have not gone unchallenged.* 这些观点并非没有受到过质疑。 ❑ *His integrity was unchallenged.* 他的诚实正直未受到过质疑。 2 ADJ If you say that someone's position of authority is **unchallenged**, you mean that it is strong and no one tries to replace them. (地位、权威等) 未受到过挑战的 ❑ *He is the unchallenged leader of the chess club.* 他是该国际象棋俱乐部未受到过挑战的领导人。

un·changed /ʌntʃeɪndʒd/ ADJ If something is **unchanged**, it has stayed the same for a particular period of time. 未改变过的 ❑ *For many years prices have remained virtually unchanged.* 多年来价格几乎没变过。

un·char·ac·ter·is·tic /ʌnkærɪktərɪstɪk/ ADJ If you describe something as **uncharacteristic of** someone, you mean that it is not typical of them. 非(某人) 特征性的 ❑ *It was uncharacteristic of her father to disappear like this.* 就这样消失不是她父亲的风格。 ● **un·char·ac·ter·is·ti·cal·ly** /ʌnkærɪktərɪstɪkli/ ADV 非特征性地 ❑ *Owen has been uncharacteristically silent.* 欧文一反常态地保持着沉默。 ❑ *Uncharacteristically for Keegan, he decided to have a snooze.* 基根一反常态，他决定打个盹。

un·checked /ʌntʃɛkt/ ADJ If something harmful or undesirable is left **unchecked**, nobody controls it or prevents it from growing or developing. 未受遏制的；未加制止的 ❑ *If left unchecked, weeds will flourish.* 如果不加遏制，杂草就会疯长。 ❑ *...a world in which brutality and lawlessness are allowed to go unchecked.* …一个野蛮与无法无天横行无阻的世界。

un·civi·lised /ʌnsɪvɪlaɪzd/ [BRIT] → see **uncivilized**

un·civi·lized /ʌnsɪvɪlaɪzd/

in BRIT, also use **uncivilised**

ADJ If you describe someone's behavior as **uncivilized**, you find it unacceptable, for example because it is very cruel or very rude. 不文明的 [DISAPPROVAL] ❑ *I think any sport involving harm to animals is barbaric and uncivilized.* 我认为，任何伤害到动物的体育运动都是野蛮的、不文明的。

un·cle ♦♦◊ /ʌŋkᵊl/ (**uncles**) N-FAMILY; N-TITLE Someone's **uncle** is the brother of their mother or father, or the husband of their aunt. 舅父；伯父；叔父；姨父；姑父 ❑ *My uncle was the mayor of Memphis.* 我叔叔是孟菲斯市市长。 ❑ *An e-mail from Uncle Fred arrived.* 来自弗雷德叔叔的电子邮件到了。
→ see **family**

un·clear /ʌnklɪər/ 1 ADJ If something is **unclear**, it is not known or not certain. 未知的；不确定的 ❑ *It is unclear how much popular support they have among the island's population.* 不知道他们在该岛居民中有多少民众支持。 ❑ *Just what the soldier was doing there is unclear.* 那个士兵在那儿到底在干什么不得而知。 2 ADJ If you are **unclear** about something, you do not understand it well or are not sure about it. 不明白的；不清楚的 [v-link ADJ] ❑ *He is still unclear about his own future.* 他对自己的未来仍不清楚。

un·com·fort·able /ʌnkʌmftəbᵊl, -kʌmfərtə-/ 1 ADJ If you are **uncomfortable**, you are slightly worried or embarrassed, and not relaxed and confident. 不自在的；尴尬的 ❑ *The request for money made them feel uncomfortable.* 要钱的事使他们感到很尴尬。 ❑ *If you are uncomfortable with your therapist, you must discuss it.* 如果你在自己的治疗师面前不自在，你必须提出来。 ● **un·com·fort·ably** /ʌnkʌmftəbli, -kʌmfərtə-/ ADV 不自在地；尴尬地 ❑ *Sandy leaned across the table, his face uncomfortably close to Brad's.* 桑迪将身体探过桌子，他的脸贴近布拉德的脸，使布拉德感觉很不自在。 ❑ *I became uncomfortably aware that the people at the next table were watching me.* 我意识到旁桌的人在看我，感到很不自在。 2 ADJ Something that is **uncomfortable** makes you feel slight pain or physical discomfort when you experience it or use it. 令人不舒服的 ❑ *Wigs are hot and uncomfortable to wear constantly.* 假发常戴让人感到又热又不舒服。 ❑ *The ride back to the center of the town was hot and uncomfortable.* 乘车返回市中心一路上又热又不舒服。 ● **un·com·fort·ably** ADV 令人不舒服地 [ADV adj] ❑ *The water was uncomfortably cold.* 水冷得让人不舒服。 3 ADJ If you are **uncomfortable**, you are not physically content and relaxed, and feel slight pain or discomfort. 不舒服的 ❑ *I sometimes feel uncomfortable after eating in the evening.* 我晚上吃过饭后有时会感到不舒服。 ● **un·com·fort·ably** ADV 不舒服地 ❑ *He felt uncomfortably hot.* 他感到热得难受。

u

Thesaurus *uncomfortable* 另参见：
ADJ. awkward, embarrassed, troubled; (*ant.*) comfortable 1
irritating, painful 2

Word Link *un ≈ not : unaware, uncommon, undecided*

un·com·mon /ʌnkɒmən/ ADJ If you describe something as **uncommon**, you mean that it does not happen often or is not often seen. 不常发生的；不常见的 ❑ *Fortunately, cancer of the breast in young women is uncommon.* 幸运的是，年轻妇女患乳腺癌的情况不常见。

un·com·pli·cat·ed /ʌnkɒmplɪkeɪtɪd/ ADJ If you describe someone or something as **uncomplicated**, you approve of them because they are easy to deal with or understand. 不复杂的 [APPROVAL] ❑ *She is a beautiful, uncomplicated girl.* 她是个漂亮、单纯的女孩。

un·com·pro·mis·ing /ʌnkɒmprəmaɪzɪŋ/ 1 ADJ If you describe someone as **uncompromising**, you mean that they are determined not to change their opinions or aims in any way. 不妥协的；坚定的 ❑ *Voters have elected an uncompromising nationalist as their new president.* 选民们已选出一位坚定的民族主义者作为他们的新总统。 2 ADJ If you describe something as **uncompromising**, you mean that it does not attempt to make something that is shocking or unpleasant any more acceptable to people. 顽固不化的 ❑ *...a movie of uncompromising brutality.* …一部描写残暴不化的电影。

un·con·cerned /ʌnkənsɜrnd/ ADJ If a person is **unconcerned about** something, usually something that most people would care about, they are not interested in it or worried about it. 不在意的 ❑ *Paul was unconcerned about what he had done.* 保罗对自己所做过的事情并不在意。

★ **un·con·di·tion·al** /ʌnkəndɪʃənəl/ ADJ If you describe something as **unconditional**, you mean that the person doing or giving it does not require anything to be done by other people in exchange. 无条件的 ❑ *Children need unconditional love from their parents.* 孩子们需要父母无条件的爱。 ● **un·con·di·tion·al·ly** ADV 无条件地 [ADV with v] ❑ *The hostages were released unconditionally.* 那些人质被无条件地释放了。

un·con·firmed /ʌnkənfɜrmd/ ADJ If a report or a rumor is **unconfirmed**, there is no definite proof as to whether it is true or not. 未证实的 ❑ *There are unconfirmed reports of several small villages buried by mudslides.* 有未经证实的报道称几个小村庄被泥石流淹没了。

un·con·nect·ed /ʌnkənɛktɪd/ ADJ If one thing is **unconnected with** another or the two things are **unconnected**, the things are not related to each other in any way. 无关联的 ❑ *She had personal problems unconnected with her marriage.* 她有过一些与婚姻无关的个人问题。

Word Link *sci ≈ knowing : conscience, science, unconscious*

un·con·scious /ʌnkɒnʃəs/ 1 ADJ Someone who is **unconscious** is in a state similar to sleep, usually as the result of a serious injury or a lack of oxygen. 不清醒的 ❑ *By the time the ambulance arrived he was unconscious.* 救护车赶到时他已神志不清。 ● **un·con·scious·ness** N-UNCOUNT 不清醒 ❑ *He knew that he might soon lapse into unconsciousness.* 他知道他可能很快就会陷入昏迷状态。 2 ADJ If you are **unconscious of** something, you are unaware of it. 未意识到的 [v-link ADJ "of" n] ❑ *He himself seemed totally unconscious of his failure.* 他本人似乎完全没意识到自己的失败。 ● **un·con·scious·ly** ADV 未意识到地 ❑ *"I was very unsure of myself after the divorce," she says, unconsciously sweeping back the curls from her forehead.* "离婚后我对自己很没有信心，"她边说边无意识地把前额上的几绺鬈发往后捋。 3 ADJ If feelings or attitudes are **unconscious**, you are not aware that you have them, but they show in the way that you behave. 无意中显示出的 ❑ *...my unconscious ambivalence about becoming a mother.* …我无意中显示出的对于做母亲的矛盾心理。 ● **un·con·scious·ly** ADV 无意中显示出地 ❑ *Many women whose fathers left home unconsciously expect to be betrayed by their own mates.* 许多父亲弃家出走的妇女会在无意中料想她们会被自己的配偶所背叛。
→ see dream

Thesaurus *unconscious* 另参见：
ADJ. comatose; (*ant.*) conscious 1
subconscious, subliminal; (*ant.*) conscious 3

▲ **un·con·sti·tu·tion·al** /ʌnkɒnstɪtuʃənəl/ ADJ If something is **unconstitutional**, it breaks the rules of a constitution. 违反宪法的 ❑ *Lincoln decided that seceding from the Union was unconstitutional.* 林肯判定退出联邦是违反宪法的。 ● **un·con·sti·tu·tion·al·ly** ADV 违反宪法地 [ADV with v] ❑ *They claimed that he acted unconstitutionally when he banned their party.* 他们声称他取缔他们政党的做法是违反宪法的。 ● **un·con·sti·tu·tion·al·ity** /ʌnkɒnstɪtuʃənælɪti/ N-UNCOUNT 违反宪法 ❑ *...the unconstitutionality of such legislation.* …这种立法的违宪。

un·con·trol·lable /ʌnkəntroʊləbəl/ 1 ADJ If you describe a feeling or physical action as **uncontrollable**, you mean that you cannot control it or prevent yourself from feeling or doing it. (情感、动作) 无法控制的 ❑ *It had been a time of almost uncontrollable excitement.* 那曾是个激动时刻，那激动几乎无法控制。 ❑ *William was seized with uncontrollable rage.* 威廉怒不可遏。 ● **un·con·trol·lably** /ʌnkəntroʊləbli/ ADV 无法控制地 ❑ *I started shaking uncontrollably and began to cry.* 我开始不由自主地颤抖，而后哭了起来。 2 ADJ If you describe a person as **uncontrollable**, you mean that their behavior is bad and that nobody can make them behave more sensibly. 无法管束的 ❑ *Mark was withdrawn and uncontrollable.* 马克性格孤僻，无法管束。 3 ADJ If you describe a situation or series of events as **uncontrollable**, you believe that nothing can be done to control them or to prevent things from getting worse. (局势、事件) 无法控制的 ❑ *If political problems are not resolved, the situation may become uncontrollable.* 如果政治问题得不到解决，局势可能变得无法控制。

un·con·trolled /ʌnkəntroʊld/ 1 ADJ If you describe someone's behavior as **uncontrolled**, you mean they appear unable to stop it or to make it less extreme. (行为) 不加约束的 ❑ *His uncontrolled behavior disturbed the entire class.* 他不加约束的行为扰乱了全班。 2 ADJ If a situation or activity is **uncontrolled**, no one is controlling it or preventing it from continuing or growing. (形势、活动) 未受控制的 ❑ *The capital, Nairobi, is choking on uncontrolled immigration.* 首都内罗毕因未受控制的移民而拥挤不堪。

un·con·ven·tion·al /ʌnkənvɛnʃənəl/ 1 ADJ If you describe a person or their attitude or behavior as **unconventional**, you mean that they do not behave in the same way as most other people in their society. (人、态度、行为等) 非传统的 ❑ *Linus Pauling is an unconventional genius.* 莱纳斯·鲍林是个奇才。 ❑ *He was known for his unconventional behavior.* 他曾因另类行为而出名。 2 ADJ An **unconventional** way of doing something is not the usual way of doing it, and may be surprising. (做法) 非常规的 ❑ *The vaccine had been produced by an unconventional technique.* 这种疫苗是用非常规的技术生产出来的。 ❑ *Despite his unconventional methods, he has inspired students more than anyone else.* 虽然用的是非常规的方法，他却比其他人更多地启发了学生。

un·con·vinc·ing /ʌnkənvɪnsɪŋ/ 1 ADJ If you describe something such as an argument or explanation as **unconvincing**, you find it difficult to believe because it does not seem real. (论辩、解释等) 难以令人信服的 ❑ *Mr. Patel phoned the university for an explanation, and he was given the usual unconvincing excuses.* 帕特尔先生给那个大学打了电话要个解释，得到的是贯用的难以令人信服的托词。 ● **un·con·vinc·ing·ly** ADV 难以令人信服地 [ADV with v] ❑ *"It's not that I don't believe you, Meg," Jack said, unconvincingly.* "并不是我不相信你，梅格，"杰克说，语气难以令人信服。 2 ADJ If you describe a story or a character in a story as **unconvincing**, you think they do not seem likely or real. (故事或故事中的人物) 难以令人相信的 ❑ *...an unconvincing love story.* …一个难以令人相信的爱情故事。

un·count·able noun /ʌnkaʊntəbəl naʊn/ (**uncountable nouns**) N-COUNT An **uncountable noun** is a noun such as "gold," "information," or "furniture" which has only one form and can be used without a determiner. 不可数名词

un·count noun /ʌnkaʊnt naʊn/ (**uncount nouns**) N-COUNT An **uncount noun** is the same as an **uncountable noun**. 不可数名词

un·cov·er /ʌnkʌvər/ (**uncovers, uncovering, uncovered**) 1 V-T If you **uncover** something, especially something that has been kept secret, you discover or find out about it. 找出 ❑ *Auditors said they had uncovered evidence of fraud.* 审计员们说他们已找到了诈骗的证据。 2 V-T To **uncover** something means to remove something that is covering it. 移去(某物的) 遮盖物 ❑ *When the seedlings sprout, uncover the tray.* 幼苗发芽后，揭开盘上的遮盖物。

Word Partnership *uncover* 的常用搭配：
N. uncover **evidence**, uncover **a plot**, uncover **the truth** 1
V. **help** uncover *something* 1 2

un·daunt·ed /ʌndɔntɪd/ ADJ If you are **undaunted**, you are not at all afraid or worried about dealing with something, especially

U

something that would frighten or worry most people. 未被吓倒的 ❑ *Undaunted by the scale of the job, Lesley set about planning how each room should look.* 莱斯利没有被该工程的规模所吓倒，开始规划每个房间的陈设。

Word Link *un ≈ not : unaware, uncommon, undecided*

un·de·cid·ed /ʌndɪsaɪdɪd/ ADJ If someone is **undecided**, they cannot decide about something or have not yet decided about it. 无法决定的；未决定的 ❑ *After college she was still undecided as to what career she wanted to pursue.* 大学毕业后她仍无法决定自己要追求什么事业。

Word Link *demo ≈ people : democracy, demographic, undemocratic*

un·demo·crat·ic /ʌndeməkrætɪk/ ADJ A system, process, or decision that is **undemocratic** is one that is controlled or made by one person or a small number of people, rather than by all the people involved. 不民主的 ❑ *...the undemocratic rule of the former political establishment.* …前政权的不民主统治。 ❑ *Opponents denounced the law as undemocratic and unconstitutional.* 反对者们抨击这项法律是不民主的、是违反宪法的。

un·de·ni·able /ʌndɪnaɪəbᵊl/ ADJ If you say that something is **undeniable**, you mean that it is definitely true. 无可否认的 ❑ *Her charm is undeniable.* 她的魅力无可否认。 ● **un·de·ni·ably** /ʌndɪnaɪəbli/ ADV 无可否认地 ❑ *Bringing up a baby is undeniably hard work.* 抚养一个孩子无可否认地是项艰苦的工作。

un·der ♦♦♦ /ʌndər/

In addition to the uses shown below, **under** is also used in phrasal verbs such as "go under" and "knuckle under."

1 PREP If a person or thing is **under** something, they are at a lower level than that thing, and may be covered or hidden by it. 在…下面 ❑ *They found a labyrinth of tunnels under the ground.* 他们发现了地下一处迷宫似的地道。 ❑ *...swimming in the pool or lying under an umbrella.* …在池里游泳或躺在遮阳伞下。 ❑ *A path runs under the trees.* 一条小路在树下延伸。 **2** PREP In a place such as an ocean, river, or swimming pool, if someone or something is **under** the water, they are fully in the water and covered by it. 在（水）下 ❑ *She held her breath for three minutes under the water.* 她在水下屏息了3分钟。 ● ADV **Under** is also an adverb. 在水下 [ADV after v] ❑ *He took a deep breath before he went under.* 他在钻下水前深深地吸了口气。 **3** PREP If you go **under** something, you move from one side to the other of something that is at a higher level than you. 从（较高物）下面 ❑ *He went under a brick arch.* 他从一座砖拱门下面走过。 **4** PREP Something that is **under** a layer of something, especially clothing, is covered by that layer. 在（一层衣服等）里面 ❑ *I was wearing two sweaters under the green army jacket.* 我那时在绿色的军上衣里面穿着两件毛衣。 ❑ *...a faded striped shirt under a knit sweater.* …穿在一件针织毛衣里边的一件褪了色的条纹衬衫。 **5** PREP You can use **under** before a noun to indicate that a person or thing is being affected by something or is going through a particular process. 在（…的影响或过程）中 ❑ *...fishermen whose livelihoods are under threat.* …生计受到威胁的渔民们。 ❑ *Firemen said they had the blaze under control.* 消防员们说他们已控制住了火势。 **6** PREP If something happens **under** particular circumstances or conditions, it happens when those circumstances or conditions exist. 在（…情况或条件）下 ❑ *His best friend died under questionable circumstances.* 他最好的朋友在不明的情况下死了。 ❑ *Under normal conditions, only about 20 to 40 percent of vitamin E is absorbed.* 在正常情况下，只有约百分之二十到百分之四十的维生素E被吸收。 **7** PREP If something happens **under** a law, agreement, or system, it happens because that law, agreement, or system says that it should happen. 在（法律、协议、制度等的规定）下 ❑ *Under law, your employer has the right to hire a temporary worker to replace you.* 按法律规定，你的雇主有权聘用临时工来代替你。 ❑ *Under the new regulations, one in five cars may need repairs costing as much as $120.* 在新的规定下，1/5的车可能需要费用高达$120的维修。 **8** PREP If something happens **under** a particular person or government, it happens when that person or government is in power. 在（…的领导或统治）下 ❑ *There would be no new taxes under his leadership.* 在他的领导下不会有新的税项。 ❑ *...the realities of life under a brutal dictatorship.* …在残酷的独裁统治下的生活现实。 **9** PREP If you study or work **under** a particular person, that person teaches you or tells you what to do. 在（…的指导或带领）下 ❑ *Kiefer was just one of the artists who had studied under Beuys in the early Sixties.* 基弗只是60年代初期在博伊斯指导下学艺的艺术家之一。 ❑ *General Lewis Hyde had served under General Mitchell.* 刘易斯・海德将军曾在米切尔将军麾下服役。 **10** PREP If you do something **under** a particular name, you use that name instead of your real name. 以（…名） ❑ *Were any of your books published under the name Amanda Fairchild?* 你的书有以阿曼达・费尔柴尔德的名字出版的吗？ **11** PREP You use **under** to say which section of a list, book, or system something is in. 在（…部分）下 ❑ *The "General Diseases of the Eye" study is filed under E.* "普通眼病"研究归在E下。 **12** PREP If something or someone is **under** a particular age or amount, they are less than that age or amount. 在（某年龄或数量）以下 [PREP amount] ❑ *...jobs for those under 65.* …适合65岁以下人士的工作。 ❑ *Nearly half of mothers with children under five have a job.* 孩子不足5岁的母亲中近一半有工作。 ● ADV **Under** is also an adverb. 在（某年龄或数量）以下 [amount "and" ADV] ❑ *...free or subsidized health insurance for children 13 and under.* …13岁及13岁以下儿童的免费的或给予补助的健康保险。 **13** **under wraps** → see **wrap**

under·arm /ʌndərɑrm/ (**underarms**) **1** ADJ **Underarm** means in or for the areas under your arms, where they are joined to your body. 腋下的 [ADJ n] ❑ *...underarm deodorants.* …腋下除臭剂。 ● N-COUNT **Underarm** is also a noun. 腋下 [usu pl] ❑ *Wash the feet, underarms and body surface using a soap.* 用一块肥皂洗脚、腋下和身体表面。 **2** ADJ You use **underarm** to describe actions, such as throwing a ball, in which you do not raise your arm above your shoulder. 低手的 [ADJ n] [BRIT] ❑ *...an underarm throw.* …一记低手抛球。 ● ADV **Underarm** is also an adverb. 低手地 [ADV after v]

in AM, use **underhand**, **underhanded**

❑ *Practice throwing a ball underarm.* 练习低手抛球。

under·brush /ʌndərbrʌʃ/ N-UNCOUNT **Underbrush** consists of bushes and plants growing close together under the trees in a forest. （森林里树木下的）下层灌丛 [AM]

in BRIT, use **undergrowth**

❑ *...the cool underbrush of the rain forest.* …雨林中使人感觉凉爽的下层灌丛。

▲ **under·cov·er** /ʌndərkʌvər/ ADJ **Undercover** work involves secretly obtaining information for the government or the police. 秘密的 ❑ *...an undercover operation designed to catch drug smugglers.* …一次为抓捕毒品走私贩而策划的秘密行动。 ❑ *...undercover FBI agents.* …联邦调查局的密探。 ● ADV **Undercover** is also an adverb. 秘密地 [ADV after v] ❑ *Swanson persuaded Hubley to work undercover to capture the killer.* 斯旺森说服了赫布利秘密工作以捕获凶手。

under·cur·rent /ʌndərkɜrənt/ (**undercurrents**) **1** N-COUNT If there is an **undercurrent of** a feeling, you are hardly aware of the feeling, but it influences the way you think or behave. 潜在（情感）倾向 ❑ *...the strong undercurrent of pro-business sentiment in Congress.* …国会中强烈亲商的潜在感情倾向。 **2** N-COUNT An **undercurrent** is a strong current of water that is moving below the surface current and in a different direction to it. 暗流 ❑ *Karen tried to swim after him but the strong undercurrent swept them apart.* 卡伦试图跟在他后面游，但强大的暗流把他们冲开了。

under·cut /ʌndərkʌt/ (**undercuts, undercutting**)

The form **undercut** is used in the present tense and is also the past tense and past participle.

V-T If you **undercut** someone or **undercut** their prices, you sell a product more cheaply than they do. 以低于…的价格出售 [BUSINESS] ❑ *Subsidies allow growers to undercut competitors and depress world prices.* 补贴使得种植者能以低于竞争对手的价格出售并压低世界价格。 ❑ *...promises to undercut air fares on some routes by 40 percent.* …将一些航线的票价降低40%出售的承诺。

★ **under·de·vel·oped** /ʌndərdɪvɛləpt/ ADJ An **underdeveloped** country or region does not have modern industries and usually has a low standard of living. Some people dislike this term and prefer to use **developing**. 不发达的 ❑ *Underdeveloped countries should be assisted by allowing them access to modern technology.* 应该通过允许不发达国家使用现代技术来帮助它们。

under·dog /ʌndərdɔg/ (**underdogs**) N-COUNT **The underdog** in a competition or situation is the person who seems least likely to succeed or win. 处于劣势者 ❑ *Most of the crowd were cheering for the underdog to win just this one time.* 人群中大多数人在为那位处于劣势者赢得一次比赛而加油鼓劲。

★ **under·es·ti·mate** /ʌndərɛstɪmeɪt/ (**underestimates, underestimating, underestimated**) **1** V-T If you **underestimate** something, you do not realize how large or great it is or will be.

低估（某事）❏ *None of us should ever underestimate the degree of difficulty women face in career advancement.* 我们谁都不应低估妇女在职业发展中所面临的困难程度。 2 V-T If you **underestimate** someone, you do not realize what they are capable of doing. 低估（某人）❏ *I think a lot of people still underestimate him.* 我认为许多人仍然低估了他。

under·fund·ed /ʌndərfʌndɪd/ ADJ An organization or institution that is **underfunded** does not have enough money to spend, and so it cannot function properly. 经费不足的 ❏ *For years we have argued that the FDA is underfunded.* 数年来我们一直在讲食品及药物管理局经费不足。

under·go /ʌndərgoʊ/ (**undergoes, undergoing, underwent, undergone**) V-T If you **undergo** something necessary or unpleasant, it happens to you. 经历；经受 ❏ *New recruits have been undergoing training in recent weeks.* 新兵们最近几周一直在接受训练。

under·gradu·ate /ʌndərgrædʒuɪt/ (**undergraduates**) N-COUNT An **undergraduate** is a student at a university or college who is studying for a bachelor's or associate's degree. 大学本科生 ❏ *Economics undergraduates are probably the brightest in the university.* 经济学本科生很可能是该大学里最聪明的学生。

under·ground ♦◇◇

The adverb is pronounced /ʌndərgraʊnd/. The noun and adjective are pronounced /ʌndərgraʊnd/.

副词读作 /ʌndərgraʊnd/。名词和形容词读作 /ʌndərgraʊnd/。

1 ADV Something that is **underground** is below the surface of the ground. 在地下 [ADV after v] ❏ *Solid low-level waste will be disposed of deep underground.* 低放射性固体废物将被弃置在地下深处。● ADJ **Underground** is also an adjective. 地下的 [ADJ n] ❏ *...an underground parking garage for 2,100 vehicles.* …一座能停放2100辆车的地下停车库。 2 N-SING **The underground** in a city is the railroad system in which electric trains travel below the ground in tunnels. 地铁 ["the" N, also "by" N] [BRIT]

in AM, use **subway**

3 ADJ **Underground** groups and activities are secret because their purpose is to oppose the government and they are illegal. 秘密的；地下的 [ADJ n] ❏ *...the underground Kashmir Liberation Front.* 秘密的克什米尔解放阵线。 4 ADV If you go **underground**, you hide from the authorities or the police because your political ideas or activities are illegal. 秘密地；在地下 [ADV after v] ❏ *After the violent clashes of 1981 they either went underground or left the country.* 1981年的暴力冲突之后，他们要么转入地下了，要么离开了这个国家。

→ see **tunnel**

under·growth /ʌndərgroʊθ/ also **underbrush** N-UNCOUNT **Undergrowth** consists of bushes and plants growing together under the trees in a forest. 下层灌丛 ❏ *...plunging through the undergrowth.* …冲过那片下层灌丛。

under·hand /ʌndərhænd/ or **underhanded** 1 ADJ If an action is **underhand** or if it is done in an **underhand** way, it is done secretly and dishonestly. 秘密的；不诚实的 [usu ADJ n] [DISAPPROVAL] ❏ *...underhand financial deals.* …秘密的金融交易。 ❏ *...a list of the underhanded ways in which their influence operates in the United States.* …他们的势力在美国运作的一系列不正当手段。 2 ADJ You use **underhand** or **underhanded** to describe actions, such as throwing a ball, in which you do not raise your arm above your shoulder. （投球等）低手的（指手不过肩）[ADJ n] [AM] ❏ *...an underhand pitch.* …一次低手投球。● ADV **Underhand** is also an adverb. 低手地 [ADV after v]

in BRIT, use **underarm**

❏ *In softball, pitches are tossed underhand.* 垒球运动中投球均是低手式投。

▲ **under·lie** /ʌndərlaɪ/ (**underlies, underlying, underlay, underlain**) 1 V-T If something **underlies** a feeling or situation, it is the cause or basis of it. 是…的原因；是…的基础 ❏ *Try to figure out what feeling underlies your anger.* 设法找出什么情绪是你生气的原因。 2 → see also **underlying**

under·line /ʌndərlaɪn/ (**underlines, underlining, underlined**) 1 V-T If one thing, for example an action or an event, **underlines** another, it draws attention to it and emphasizes its importance. 突出显示；强调 ❏ *The report underlined his concern that standards were at risk.* 该报告强调了他对于标准被降低的担忧。 ❏ *This incident underlines the danger of traveling in the border area.* 这一事件突出显示了在边界地区旅行的危险。 2 V-T If you **underline** something such as a word or a sentence, you draw a line underneath it in order to make people notice it or to give it extra importance. 在…下面划线 ❏ *Underline the following that apply to you.* 在以下适用于你的部分下面划线。

Word Partnership *underline* 的常用搭配：

N. underline **the need for *something*** 1
underline **passages**, underline **text**, underline **titles**, underline **words** 2

★ **un·der·ly·ing** /ʌndərlaɪɪŋ/ 1 ADJ The **underlying** features of an object, event, or situation are not obvious, and it may be difficult to discover or reveal them. 潜在的 [ADJ n] ❏ *To stop a problem you have to understand its underlying causes.* 要解决问题，你得了解其潜在原因。 2 ADJ You describe something as **underlying** when it is below the surface of something else. 在下面的 [ADJ n] ❏ *...hills with the hard underlying rock poking through the turf.* …从被草覆盖的地面下突出来的坚硬岩石的山峦。 3 → see also **underlie**

under·mine ♦◇◇ /ʌndərmaɪn/ (**undermines, undermining, undermined**) 1 V-T If you **undermine** something such as a feeling or a system, you make it less strong or less secure than it was before, often by a gradual process or by repeated efforts. 逐渐削弱；逐渐动摇 ❏ *Offering advice on each and every problem will undermine her feeling of being adult.* 每个问题都为她提出忠告会逐渐削弱她的成年意识。 2 V-T If you **undermine** someone or **undermine** their position or authority, you make their authority or position less secure, often by indirect methods. （通常以间接方式）动摇（某人的地位或权威）❏ *She undermined him and destroyed his confidence in his own talent.* 她动摇了他的地位，摧毁了他对自己才能的信心。 3 V-T If you **undermine** someone's efforts or **undermine** their chances of achieving something, you behave in a way that makes them less likely to succeed. 破坏；损害（某人的努力或成功的机会）❏ *The continued fighting threatens to undermine efforts to negotiate an agreement.* 持续的战斗有可能破坏通过谈判达成协议的努力。

Word Partnership *undermine* 的常用搭配：

N. undermine **confidence**, undermine **government**, undermine **peace**, undermine **security** 1
undermine **authority** 1 2
V. **threaten to** undermine, **try to** undermine 1 - 3

under·neath /ʌndərniθ/ 1 PREP If one thing is **underneath** another, it is directly under it, and may be covered or hidden by it. 在…下面；在…底下 ❏ *The device exploded underneath a van.* 那个装置在一辆面包车底下爆炸了。 ❏ *...using dogs to locate people trapped underneath collapsed buildings.* …利用狗来寻找困在倒塌楼房下面的人。● ADV **Underneath** is also an adverb. 在下面；在底下 ❏ *He has on his jeans and a long-sleeved blue denim shirt with a white T-shirt underneath.* 他身穿牛仔裤和一件蓝色长袖粗斜纹棉布衬衫，里面还有件白色T恤衫。 ❏ *The shooting-range is lit from underneath by rows of ruby-red light fixtures.* 射击场被一排排宝石红照明装置从下面照亮。 2 ADV The part of something which is **underneath** is the part which normally touches the ground or faces toward the ground. 在下面；在底部 ❏ *Check the actual construction of the chair by looking underneath.* 看一下椅子的底部来检查它的实际结构。 ❏ *The sand martin is a brown bird with white underneath.* 崖沙燕是一种腹部为白色的褐色的鸟。● N-SING **Underneath** is also a noun. 下面；底部 ❏ *Now I know what the underneath of a car looks like.* 现在我知道汽车的底部是什么样子了。 3 ADV You use **underneath** when talking about feelings and emotions that people do not show in their behavior. 在内心 [ADV with cl] ❏ *He was as violent as Nick underneath.* 他在内心和尼克一样暴烈。● PREP **Underneath** is also a preposition. 在…内 ❏ *Underneath his outgoing behavior Luke was shy.* 卢克表面外向、内心羞怯。

under·paid /ʌndərpeɪd/ ADJ People who are **underpaid** are not paid enough money for the job that they do. 所得报酬过低的 ❏ *Women are frequently underpaid for the work that they do.* 妇女们所付出的劳动常常没有得到足额的报酬。

under·pants /ʌndərpænts/ N-PLURAL **Underpants** are a piece of underwear which have two holes to put your legs through and elastic around the top to hold them up around your waist or hips. 内裤 [also "a pair of" N] ❏ *Half of men admit that their underpants are their oldest item of clothing.* 一半的男人承认他们的内裤是他们最旧的衣物。

under·pass /ʌndərpæs/ (**underpasses**) N-COUNT An **underpass** is a road or path that goes underneath a railroad or another road. （铁路、公路等下的）下穿通道 ❏ *The underpass was closed through flooding.* 下穿通道在洪水期被封闭。

U

under·rate /ʌndərreɪt/ (**underrates, underrating, underrated**) V-T If you **underrate** someone or something, you do not recognize how intelligent, important, or significant they are. 低估；看轻 ❑ *We women have a lot of good business skills, although we tend to underrate ourselves.* 我们女性有许多好的商业技能，只是我们往往低估自己。 ● **under·rat·ed** ADJ 被低估了的；被看轻了的 ❑ *He is a very underrated poet.* 他是个严重被低估了的诗人。

★ **under·score** /ʌndərskɔr/ (**underscores, underscoring, underscored**) 1 V-T If something such as an action or an event **underscores** another, it draws attention to the other thing and emphasizes its importance. 突出显示；强调 [mainly AM]

in BRIT, usually use **underline**

❑ *The Labor Department figures underscore the shaky state of the economic recovery.* 劳工部的数字突出显示了经济复苏的不稳定。 2 V-T If you **underscore** something such as a word or a sentence, you draw a line underneath it in order to make people notice it or give it extra importance. 在…下面划线 [mainly AM]

in BRIT, usually use **underline**

❑ *He heavily underscored his note to Shelley.* 他在写给谢利的短笺下重重地划了线。

under·shirt /ʌndərʃɜrt/ (**undershirts**) N-COUNT An **undershirt** is a piece of clothing that you wear on the top half of your body next to your skin and under your regular shirt, in order to keep warm. 汗衫；背心 [AM]

in BRIT, use **vest**

❑ *He put on a pair of boxer shorts and an undershirt.* 他穿上一条平腿短裤和一件背心。

under·side /ʌndərsaɪd/ (**undersides**) N-COUNT The **underside** of something is the part of it which normally faces towards the ground. 下面；底部 ❑ *...the underside of the car.* …汽车的底部。

under·spend /ʌndərspɛnd/ (**underspends, underspending, underspent**) V-I If an organization or country **underspends**, it spends less money than it plans to or less money than it can afford. (比计划的或能支付的) 少花费 [BUSINESS] ❑ *...a country that underspends on health and overspends on statisticians.* …一个在医疗卫生上支出不足而在统计员身上支出过多的国家。 ● N-COUNT **Underspend** is also a noun. 支出不足 ❑ *There has been an underspend in the department's budget.* 该部门的预算中出现了支出不足。

under·stand ♦♦♦ /ʌndərstænd/ (**understands, understanding, understood**) 1 V-T If you **understand** someone or **understand** what they are saying, you know what they mean. 明白 (某人的话的意思) [no cont] ❑ *I think you heard and also understand me.* 我想你听到了我的话，而且也明白我的意思。 ❑ *I don't understand what you are talking about.* 我不明白你在说什么。 2 V-T If you **understand** a language, you know what someone is saying when they are speaking that language. 懂 (某种语言) [no cont] ❑ *I couldn't read or understand a word of Yiddish, so I asked him to translate.* 我完全不懂意第绪语，所以请他翻译。 3 V-T To **understand** someone means to know how they feel and why they behave in the way that they do. 理解 (某人) [no cont] ❑ *It would be nice to have someone who really understood me, a friend.* 有个真正理解我的人，一个朋友，就太好啦。 ❑ *Trish had not exactly understood his feelings.* 特里希并没有确切地理解他的感受。 4 V-T You say that you **understand** something when you know why or how it happens. 明白 (某事) [no cont] ❑ *They are too young to understand what is going on.* 他们太小，不明白在发生什么事。 ❑ *She didn't understand why the TV was kept out of reach of the patients.* 她那时不明白为什么不让病人看电视。 5 V-T If you **understand** that something is the case, you think it is true because you have heard or read that it is. You can say that something **is understood** to be the case to mean that people generally think it is true. 知道；听说；获悉 [no cont] ❑ *We understand that she's in the studio recording her second album.* 我们得知她正在录音室里录制她的第2张专辑。 ❑ *As I understand it, she has a house in the city.* 据我所知，她在市里有座房子。 ❑ *The management is understood to be very unwilling to agree to this request.* 据说管理层很不愿意答应这项要求。

→ see **philosophy**

Thesaurus *understand* 另参见：

V. catch on, comprehend, get, grasp; (*ant.*) misunderstand 1

under·stand·able /ʌndərstændəbᵊl/ 1 ADJ If you describe someone's behavior or feelings as **understandable**, you think that they have reacted to a situation in a natural way or in the way you would expect. 可以理解的 ❑ *His unhappiness was understandable.* 他的不高兴是可以理解的。 ● **under·stand·ably** /ʌndərstændəbli/ ADV 可以理解地 ❑ *Officials are understandably nervous about the tense situation in the neighborhood.* 官员们对这个地区的紧张局势很感不安，这是可以理解的。 2 ADJ If you say that something such as a statement or theory is **understandable**, you mean that people can easily understand it. (陈述、理论等) 易懂的 ❑ *Roger Neuberg writes in a simple and understandable way.* 罗杰・纽伯格的作品简单易懂。

under·stand·ing ♦◊◊ /ʌndərstændɪŋ/ (**understandings**) 1 N-VAR If you have an **understanding of** something, you know how it works or know what it means. 了解 ❑ *They have to have a basic understanding of computers in order to use the advanced technology.* 为了利用这一先进技术他们必须对计算机有基本的了解。 2 ADJ If you are **understanding** toward someone, you are kind and forgiving. 能理解的；体谅的 ❑ *Her boss, who was very understanding, gave her time off.* 她的老板很体谅她，给她放了假。 3 N-UNCOUNT If you show **understanding**, you show that you realize how someone feels or why they did something, and are not hostile toward them. 理解；谅解 ❑ *We would like to thank them for their patience and understanding.* 我们要为他们的耐心和理解而感谢他们。 4 N-UNCOUNT If there is **understanding between** people, they are friendly toward each other and trust each other. 相互理解；信任 ❑ *There was complete understanding between Wilson and myself.* 威尔逊和我彼此完全理解与信任。 5 N-COUNT An **understanding** is an informal agreement about something. (非正式的) 协议 ❑ *We had not set a date for marriage but there was an understanding between us.* 我们还没有确定结婚日期，不过我们已有了一致意见。 6 N-SING If you say that it is your **understanding that** something is the case, you mean that you believe it to be the case because you have heard or read that it is. 理解；了解 ❑ *It is my understanding that the meeting is Thursday.* 据我了解，会议是在星期四。 7 PHRASE If you agree to do something **on the understanding that** something else will be done, you do it because you have been told that the other thing will definitely be done. 在得知…一定会发生的条件下 ❑ *Poverty forced her to surrender him to foster families, but only on the understanding that she could eventually regain custody.* 贫困迫使她把他交给了寄养家庭，但她是在明确她最终一定能重新获得抚养权的条件下才这样做的。

Word Partnership *understanding* 的常用搭配：

V. **develop** understanding, **have trouble** understanding, **lack** understanding 1
difficulty understanding 1 3 4

ADJ. **basic** understanding, **clear** understanding, **complete** understanding 1
deep/deeper understanding, **greater** understanding 1 – 4
better understanding 1 4
mutual understanding 3 4

under·state /ʌndərsteɪt/ (**understates, understating, understated**) V-T If you **understate** something, you describe it in a way that suggests that it is less important or serious than it really is. 不充分陈述 ❑ *The government chooses deliberately to understate the increase in prices.* 政府有意选择对价格的上涨轻描淡写。

under·stat·ed /ʌndərsteɪtɪd/ ADJ If you describe a style, color, or effect as **understated**, you mean that it is simple and plain, and does not attract attention to itself. 简朴的；不惹眼的 [ADJ n] ❑ *I have always liked understated clothes.* 我一向喜欢简朴的衣服。

under·state·ment /ʌndərsteɪtmənt/ (**understatements**) 1 N-COUNT If you say that a statement is an **understatement**, you mean that it does not fully express the extent to which something is true. 不充分的陈述 ❑ *To say I'm disappointed is an understatement.* 说我很失望是很轻的说法。 2 N-UNCOUNT **Understatement** is the practice of suggesting that things have much less of a particular quality than they really have. 低调说法；轻描淡写 ❑ *...typical British understatement.* …典型的英国式低调语言。

un·der·stood /ʌndərstʊd/ **Understood** is the past tense and past participle of **understand**. **understand**的过去式和过去分词

under·take /ʌndərteɪk/ (**undertakes, undertaking, undertook, undertaken**) 1 V-T When you **undertake** a task or job, you start doing it and accept responsibility for it. 从事；承担 ❑ *She undertook the task of monitoring the elections.* 她承担了监督选举的任务。 2 V-T If you **undertake to** do something, you promise that you will do it. 承诺 ❑ *He undertook to edit the text himself.* 他承诺亲自编辑正文。

Word Partnership *undertake* 的常用搭配：

N. undertake **an action**, undertake **a project**, undertake **reforms**, undertake **a task**, undertake **work** 1

under·tak·er /ʌndərteɪkər/ (**undertakers**) N-COUNT An **undertaker** is a person whose job is to deal with the bodies of people who have died and to arrange funerals. 殡仪员 ❑ *An undertaker had already taken the body to be embalmed.* 一位殡仪员已把尸体运去进行防腐处理。

under·tak·ing /ʌndərteɪkɪŋ/ (**undertakings**) N-COUNT An **undertaking** is a task or job, especially a large or difficult one. (尤指艰巨的) 任务; 工作 ❑ *Organizing the show has been a massive undertaking.* 组织这场演出是一项巨大的任务。

un·der·took /ʌndərtʊk/ **Undertook** is the past tense of **undertake**. **undertake**的过去式

under·value /ʌndərvælyu/ (**undervalues, undervaluing, undervalued**) V-T If you **undervalue** something or someone, you fail to recognize how valuable or important they are. 低估…的价值 ❑ *We must never undervalue freedom.* 我们决不可低估自由的价值。

under·wa·ter /ʌndərwɔtər/ 1 ADV Something that exists or happens **underwater** exists or happens below the surface of the ocean, a river, or a lake. 在水面下 ❑ *...giant submarines able to travel at high speeds underwater.* …能在水下高速行驶的巨型潜艇。 ❑ *Some stretches of beach are completely underwater at high tide.* 有些沙滩在涨潮时会完全被水淹没。 ● ADJ **Underwater** is also an adjective. 在水下的 [ADJ n] ❑ *...underwater exploration.* …水下勘探。 ❑ *...underwater fishing with harpoons.* …使用鱼叉的水下捕鱼。 ❑ *...a retired underwater photographer.* …一名退休的水下摄影师。 2 ADJ **Underwater** devices are specially made so that they can work in water. 水下用的 [ADJ n] ❑ *...underwater camera equipment.* …水下摄影设备。

★ **under·way** /ʌndərweɪ/ ADJ If an activity is **underway**, it has already started. If an activity gets **underway**, it starts. 进行中的 [V-link ADJ] ❑ *An investigation is underway to find out how the disaster happened.* 一项调查正在进行，以查明这场灾难是如何发生的。 ❑ *It was a cold evening, winter well underway.* 那是个寒冷的夜晚，冬天早已来临。

▲ **under·wear** /ʌndərwɛər/ N-UNCOUNT **Underwear** is items of clothing that you wear next to your skin and under your other clothes. 内衣 ❑ *For Christmas my brother and I got new underwear, one toy and one book.* 作为圣诞礼物，我弟弟和我得到了新内衣、一件玩具和一本书。

un·der·went /ʌndərwɛnt/ **Underwent** is the past tense of **undergo**. **undergo**的过去式

under·world /ʌndərwɜrld/ N-SING The **underworld** in a city is the organized crime there and the people who are involved in it. 黑社会 ❑ *...a Spanish Harlem underworld of gangs, drugs and violence.* …一个成群结帮、贩毒施暴的西班牙哈莱姆黑社会。 ❑ *Some claim that she still has connections to the criminal underworld.* 一些人声称她仍与犯罪的黑社会有联系。

under·write /ʌndərraɪt/ (**underwrites, underwriting, underwrote, underwritten**) V-T If an institution or company **underwrites** an activity or **underwrites** the cost of it, they agree to provide any money that is needed to cover losses or buy special equipment, often for an agreed-upon fee. 为…提供经济担保; 同意资助 [BUSINESS] ❑ *The government will have to create a special agency to underwrite small business loans.* 政府将不得不建立一个专门机构来为小额企业贷款提供担保。

U

under·writ·er /ʌndərraɪtər/ (**underwriters**) 1 N-COUNT An **underwriter** is someone whose job involves agreeing to provide money for a particular activity or to pay for any losses. 资助人; 担保人 [BUSINESS] ❑ *If the market will not buy the shares, the underwriter buys them.* 如果市场不买这些股票，包销商就会买。 2 N-COUNT An **underwriter** is someone whose job is to judge the risks involved in certain activities and decide how much to charge for insurance. 核保人 [BUSINESS] ❑ *AIG is an organization of insurance underwriters.* 美国国际集团是一家保险核保人机构。

un·de·sir·able /ʌndɪzaɪərəbᵊl/ ADJ If you describe something or someone as **undesirable**, you think they will have harmful effects. 不受欢迎的; 不利的 ❑ *Inflation is considered to be undesirable because of its adverse effects on income distribution.* 通货膨胀因其对收入分配的反作用而被认为是不利的。

un·did /ʌndɪd/ **Undid** is the past tense of **undo**. **undo**的过去式

un·dis·closed /ʌndɪsklouzd/ ADJ **Undisclosed** information is not revealed to the public. 保密的; 未公开的 ❑ *The company has been sold for an undisclosed amount.* 该公司已经以一笔未公开的价钱被出售。

un·dis·put·ed /ʌndɪspyutɪd/ 1 ADJ If you describe a fact or opinion as **undisputed**, you are trying to persuade someone that it is generally accepted as true or correct. (事实、观点等) 无需争议的 ❑ *...an undisputed fact.* …无需争议的事实。 ❑ *...his undisputed genius.* …他那无需争议的天才。 2 ADJ If you describe someone as the **undisputed** leader or champion, you mean that everyone accepts their position as leader or champion. 公认的; 无异议的 (领袖、冠军等) ❑ *Seles won 10 tournaments, and was the undisputed world champion.* 塞莱斯赢了10次锦标赛，是无异议的世界冠军。 ❑ *At 78 years of age, he's still undisputed leader of his country.* 78岁时，他仍是他的国家公认的领袖。

un·dis·turbed /ʌndɪstɜrbd/ 1 ADJ Something that remains **undisturbed** is not touched, moved, or used by anyone. 未触及的; 未动用过的 ❑ *The desk looked undisturbed.* 那张书桌子看上去没有被动过。 2 ADJ A place that is **undisturbed** is peaceful and has not been affected by changes that have happened in other places. 平静的; 未被扰乱的 ❑ *It was one of the most peaceful and undisturbed places she had found.* 这是她发现的最安宁平静的地方之一。 3 ADJ If you are **undisturbed** in something that you are doing, you are able to continue doing it and are not affected by something that is happening. 未受干扰的 ❑ *I can spend the whole day undisturbed at the warehouse.* 我可以不受干扰地在仓库里呆上一整天。 ❑ *There was a small restaurant on Sullivan Street where we could talk undisturbed.* 沙利文街上曾有一家小餐馆，我们可以在那里不受干扰地交谈。 4 ADJ If someone is **undisturbed by** something, it does not affect, bother, or upset them. 不受…影响的; 不受…烦扰的 ❑ *Victoria was strangely undisturbed by this symptom, even though her husband and family were frightened.* 维多利亚奇怪地没有因这种症状而感到不安，尽管她的丈夫和家人都吓坏了。

undo /ʌndu/ (**undoes, undoing, undid, undone**) 1 V-T If you **undo** something that is closed, tied, or held together, or if you **undo** the thing holding it, you loosen or remove the thing holding it. 打开; 解开; 松开 ❑ *I managed secretly to undo a corner of the parcel.* 我设法偷偷地打开包裹的一角。 ❑ *I undid the bottom two buttons of my yellow and gray shirt.* 我解开了我黄灰色相间衬衫最下面的两个钮扣。 2 V-T To **undo** something that has been done means to reverse its effect. 使无效 ❑ *A heavy-handed approach from the police could undo that good impression.* 警察的专制手段能使那个好印象化为乌有。 ❑ *She knew it would be difficult to undo the damage that had been done.* 她知道难以挽回已造成的损失。 3 → see also **undoing**

un·do·ing /ʌnduɪŋ/ N-SING If something is someone's **undoing**, it is the cause of their failure. 失败的原因 ❑ *His lack of experience may prove to be his undoing.* 缺乏经验可能就是他失败的原因。

un·doubt·ed /ʌndaʊtɪd/ ADJ You can use **undoubted** to emphasize that something exists or is true. 无疑的 [EMPHASIS] ❑ *The event was an undoubted success.* 这次活动是一个无可置疑的成功。 ❑ *...a man of your undoubted ability.* …一个拥有你这样无可置疑的能力的人。 ● **un·doubt·ed·ly** ADV 无疑地 ❑ *Undoubtedly, political and economic factors have played their part.* 毫无疑问，政治和经济因素起了作用。

▲ **un·dress** /ʌndrɛs/ (**undresses, undressing, undressed**) V-T/V-I When you **undress** or **undress** someone, you take off your clothes or someone else's clothes. 使脱去衣服; 脱衣服 ❑ *She went out, leaving Rachel to undress and take a shower.* 她出去了，留下雷切尔脱衣淋浴。

un·dressed /ʌndrɛst/ ADJ If you are **undressed**, you are wearing no clothes or your underwear or pajamas. If you get **undressed**, you take off your clothes. 不穿衣服的 ❑ *Fifteen minutes later he was undressed and in bed.* 15分钟后，他已脱掉衣服上了床。

un·due /ʌndu/ ADJ If you describe something bad as **undue**, you mean that it is greater or more extreme than you think is reasonable or appropriate. 过分的 [ADJ n] ❑ *This would help the families to survive the drought without undue suffering.* 这将有助于这些家庭免受过多痛苦而度过这次旱灾。 ❑ *It is unrealistic to put undue pressure on ourselves by saying we are the best.* 说我们是最好的来给我们自己施加过多的压力是不现实的。

Word Partnership *undue* 的常用搭配：

N. undue **attention**, undue **burden**, undue **delay**, undue **emphasis**, undue **hardship**, undue **influence**, undue **interference**, undue **pressure**, undue **risk**

un·du·ly /ʌnduli/ ADV If you say that something does not happen or is not done **unduly**, you mean that it does not happen or is not done to an excessive or unnecessary extent. 过分地 ❑ *"But you're not unduly worried about doing this report?"—"No."* "但你没有过分担心作这个报告？"——"没有。" ❑ *This will achieve greater security without unduly burdening the consumers or the economy.* 这将获得更大的安全而没有给消费者或经济过度增加负担。

★ **un·du·ti·ful** /ʌndutɪfəl/ ADJ If you say that someone is **undutiful**, you mean that they do not show respect or behave as they are expected to. 不恭敬的；不本分的 [DISAPPROVAL, FORMAL] ❑ *They were looking into the King's coach in a most undutiful manner.* 他们极其没有礼貌地向那位国王的车厢里观望。

un·earned in·come /ʌnɜrnd ɪnkʌm/ N-UNCOUNT **Unearned income** is money that people gain from interest or profit from property or investment, rather than money that they earn from a job. (地产或投资所得的) 非劳动收入 [BUSINESS] ❑ *Your IRA deduction cannot be taken from unearned income.* 你的个人退休账户的扣税不可能从非劳动收入中减去。

un·earth /ʌnɜrθ/ (**unearths, unearthing, unearthed**) **1** V-T If someone **unearths** facts or evidence, they discover them with difficulty. (经努力) 发现 ❑ *Researchers have unearthed documents from the 1600s.* 研究人员已发现了17世纪的文件。 ❑ *Other financial scandals are out there waiting to be unearthed.* 其他金融丑闻正有待于被揭发。 **2** V-T If someone **unearths** something that is buried, they find it by digging in the ground. 挖掘出土 ❑ *Fossil hunters have unearthed the bones of an elephant believed to be 500,000 years old.* 化石寻找者们挖掘出了一头被认为有50万年之久的大象遗骨。 ❑ *More human remains have been unearthed in the north.* 更多人类遗骸在北方挖掘出土。 **3** V-T If you say that someone **has unearthed** something, you mean that they have found it after it had been hidden or lost for some time. 找出 ❑ *From somewhere, he had unearthed a black silk suit.* 他已从某处找出了一套黑色丝绸套装。 ❑ *Today I unearthed a copy of "90 Minutes" and had a chuckle at your article.* 今天，我找到了一册《90分钟》，并暗笑你的文章。

un·ease /ʌniz/ **1** N-UNCOUNT If you have a feeling of **unease**, you feel anxious or afraid, because you think that something is wrong. 不安 ❑ *Sensing my unease about the afternoon ahead, he told me, "These men are pretty easy to talk to."* 觉察到我对要来临的下午心神不安，他告诉我，"这些人很容易交谈。" ❑ *We left with a deep sense of unease, because we knew something was being hidden from us.* 我们深感不安地离开了，因为我们知道有事瞒着我们。 **2** N-UNCOUNT If you say that there is **unease** in a situation, you mean that people are dissatisfied or angry, but have not yet started to take any action. 不安 ❑ *He faces growing unease among the Democrats about the likelihood of war.* 他面对着民主党人对战争可能性的日益增加的不安。 ❑ *...the depth of public unease about the economy.* …公众对经济忧虑的深度。

un·easy /ʌnizi/ **1** ADJ If you are **uneasy**, you feel anxious, afraid, or embarrassed, because you think that something is wrong or that there is danger. 不安的 ❑ *He said nothing but gave me a sly grin that made me feel terribly uneasy.* 他什么也没说，只朝我狡黠地咧嘴一笑，令我感到极为不安。 ❑ *He looked uneasy and refused to answer questions.* 他看起来心神不安，并且拒绝回答问题。 ● **un·easi·ly** /ʌnizɪli/ ADV 不安地 ❑ *Meg shifted uneasily on her chair.* 梅格在她椅子上不安地动来动去。 ● **un·easi·ness** N-UNCOUNT 不安 ❑ *With a small degree of uneasiness, he pushed it open and stuck his head inside.* 带着些许不安，他把它打开，把头伸了进去。 **2** ADJ If you are **uneasy about** doing something, you are not sure that it is correct or wise. 不确信的 ❑ *Richard was uneasy about how best to approach his elderly mother.* 理查德对如何最好地向年迈的母亲开口没有把握。 ● **un·easi·ness** N-UNCOUNT 不确信 ❑ *I felt a certain uneasiness about meeting her again.* 我对再次见她感到有些拿不准。 **3** ADJ If you describe a situation or relationship as **uneasy**, you mean that the situation is not settled and may not last. 不稳定的 [JOURNALISM] ❑ *An uneasy calm has settled over Los Angeles.* 一种暂时的平静笼罩了洛杉矶。 ❑ *There is an uneasy relationship between us and the politicians.* 我们与政客之间有种不稳定的关系。 ● **un·easi·ly** ADV 不稳定地 ❑ *...a country whose component parts fit uneasily together.* …组成部分不稳定地结合在一起的国家。

un·em·ployed /ʌnɪmplɔɪd/ ADJ Someone who is **unemployed** does not have a job. 失业的 ❑ *The problem is millions of people are unemployed.* 问题是成百万的人失业。 ❑ *This workshop helps young unemployed people.* 这个讲习班帮助失业的年轻人。 ● N-PLURAL **The unemployed** are people who are unemployed. 失业者 ❑ *We want to create jobs for the unemployed.* 我们想为失业者创造更多的工作。

un·em·ploy·ment ♦◇◇ /ʌnɪmplɔɪmənt/ **1** N-UNCOUNT **Unemployment** is the fact that people who want jobs cannot get them. 失业 ❑ *The state's unemployment rate rose slightly to 7.1 percent last month.* 该国的失业率上个月略微上升到7.1%。 **2** N-UNCOUNT **Unemployment** is the same as **unemployment compensation.** 失业救济金 [AM] ❑ *He worked most of the year. Now he's getting unemployment.* 他一年的大部分时间都在工作。现在他将得到失业救济金。

un·em·ploy·ment com·pen·sa·tion N-UNCOUNT **Unemployment compensation** is money that some people receive from the state, usually for a limited time after losing a job, when they do not have a job and are unable to find one. 失业救济金 [AM] ❑ *He has to get by on unemployment compensation.* 他不得不靠失业救济金勉强度日。

un·equivo·cal /ʌnɪkwɪvək^əl/ ADJ If you describe someone's attitude as **unequivocal**, you mean that it is completely clear and very firm. 明确的 [FORMAL] ❑ *...Richardson's unequivocal commitment to fair play.* …理查森对公平竞赛的明确承诺。 ● **un·equivo·cal·ly** /ʌnɪkwɪvəkli/ ADV 明确地 ❑ *He stated unequivocally that the forces were ready to go to war.* 他明确表示部队已经作好准备去打仗。

un·ethi·cal /ʌnɛθɪk^əl/ ADJ Behavior that is **unethical** is wrong and unacceptable according to rules or beliefs about morality. 不道德的 ❑ *It's simply unethical to promote and advertise such a dangerous product.* 给这样一个危险的产品做宣传广告是极不道德的。 ❑ *I thought it was unethical for doctors to operate upon their families.* 我认为让医生给他们的家人动手术是不道德的。

un·even /ʌniv^ən/ **1** ADJ An **uneven** surface or edge is not smooth, flat, or straight. 不平坦的；不直的 ❑ *He staggered on the uneven surface.* 他摇摇晃晃地走在高低不平的表面上。 ❑ *The pathways were uneven, broken and dangerous.* 道路不平坦、被损坏，而且危险。 **2** ADJ Something that is **uneven** is not regular or consistent. 不规则的；不一致的 ❑ *He could hear that her breathing was uneven.* 他能听到她的呼吸不均匀。 **3** ADJ An **uneven** system or situation is unfairly arranged or organized. 不均衡的 ❑ *Some of the victims are complaining loudly about the uneven distribution of emergency aid.* 一些受害者正大声地抱怨紧急援助的不均衡分配。

Thesaurus *uneven* 另参见：
ADJ. jagged, rough; (*ant.*) even **1**
inconsistent, irregular **2**

un·event·ful /ʌnɪvɛntfəl/ ADJ If you describe a period of time as **uneventful**, you mean that nothing interesting, exciting, or important happened during it. 平静无事的 ❑ *The return trip was uneventful, the car running perfectly.* 返程平安无事，汽车运行得很好。

un·ex·pec·ted ♦◇◇ /ʌnɪkspɛktɪd/ ADJ If an event or someone's behavior is **unexpected**, it surprises you because you did not think that it was likely to happen. 出人意料的 ❑ *His death was totally unexpected.* 他的死完全出人意料。 ❑ *He made a brief, unexpected appearance at the office.* 他在办公室短暂、出人意料地露了一面。 ● **un·ex·pect·ed·ly** ADV 出人意料地 ❑ *Moss had clamped an unexpectedly strong grip on his arm.* 莫斯出乎意料地牢牢抓住他的手臂。

Thesaurus *unexpected* 另参见：
ADJ. startling, surprising

un·ex·plained /ʌnɪkspleɪnd/ ADJ If you describe something as **unexplained**, you mean that the reason for it or cause of it is unclear or is not known. 原因不明的 ❑ *An unexplained death is difficult to come to terms with.* 原因不明的死亡是难以接受的。 ❑ *The city's water supply has been cut for unexplained reasons.* 城市的供水被莫名其妙地切断了。

un·fair ♦◇◇ /ʌnfɛər/ ADJ An **unfair** action or situation is not right or fair. 不公平的 ❑ *She was awarded $5,000 in compensation for unfair dismissal.* 她因不公平的解雇获得了$5000的补偿。 ❑ *It was unfair that he should suffer so much.* 他遭受这么多痛苦是不公平的。 ● **un·fair·ly** ADV 不公平地 ❑ *He unfairly blamed Frances for the failure.* 他不公平地把失败归咎于弗朗西丝。

Thesaurus *unfair* 另参见：
ADJ. unjust, unreasonable, unwarranted; (*ant.*) fair

un·faith·ful /ʌnfeɪθfəl/ ADJ If someone is **unfaithful to** their lover or to the person they are married to, they have a sexual relationship with someone else. (对恋人或配偶) 不忠诚的 ❑ *James had been unfaithful to Christine for the entire four years they'd been together.* 詹姆斯在与克里斯蒂娜一起的整整4年里一直是不忠的。

un·fa·mil·iar /ʌnfəmɪlyər/ **1** ADJ If something is **unfamiliar to** you, you know nothing or very little about it, because you have not seen or experienced it before. 不太了解的 ❑ *She grew many wonderful plants that were unfamiliar to me.* 她种了很多我从未见过的奇异植物。 **2** ADJ If you are **unfamiliar with** something, you know nothing or very little about it. 对…不熟悉的 [v-link ADJ "with" n] ❑ *She speaks no Japanese and is unfamiliar with Japanese culture.* 她不说日语并且不熟悉日本文化。

un·fash·ion·able /ʌnfæʃənəbᵊl/ ADJ If something is **unfashionable**, it is not approved of or done by most people because it is out of style. 不流行的 ❑ *Wearing fur has become unfashionable.* 穿裘皮服装已经变得不流行了。

un·fa·vor·able /ʌnfeɪvərəbᵊl/
in BRIT, use **unfavourable**

1 ADJ **Unfavorable** conditions or circumstances cause problems for you and reduce your chances of success. 不利的 ❑ *The decision to delay the launch stems from unfavorable weather conditions.* 推迟发射的决定源于不利的天气情况。 ❑ *The whole international economic situation is very unfavorable for the countries in the south.* 整个国际经济形势非常不利于南部国家。 **2** ADJ If you have an **unfavorable** reaction to something, you do not like it. 不赞同的 ❑ *The president is drawing unfavorable comments on his new forest policy.* 总统正招致对他的新森林政策的异议。 ❑ *...views unfavorable to the capitalist system.* …不赞同资本主义制度的观点。 ● **un·fa·vor·ably** /ʌnfeɪvərəbli/ ADV 不赞同地 [ADV after v] ❑ *Other medications or foods may react unfavorably with it.* 其他药物或食物可能会与之起不良反应。 **3** ADJ If you make an **unfavorable** comparison between two things, you say that one thing seems worse than the other. 相形见绌的 [ADJ n] ❑ *I didn't expect unfavorable comparisons between my sons and their friends.* 我没料到我的儿子们和他们的朋友们相比有相形见绌之处。 ● **un·fa·vor·ably** ADV 相形见绌地 [ADV with v] ❑ *Tax rates compare unfavorably with the less heavy-handed North American agreement.* 税率比起较为宽松的北美协议更糟。

un·fa·vour·able /ʌnfeɪvᵊrəbᵊl/ [BRIT] → see **unfavorable**

un·fin·ished /ʌnfɪnɪʃt/ ADJ If you describe something such as a work of art or a piece of work as **unfinished**, you mean that it is not complete, for example because it was abandoned or there was no time to complete it. 未完成的 ❑ *...Jane Austen's unfinished novel.* …简・奥斯汀未写完的小说。 ❑ *The cathedral was eventually completed in 1490, though the Gothic facade remains unfinished.* 大教堂在1490年终于完工，虽然哥特式的正面仍未建好。

un·fit /ʌnfɪt/ **1** ADJ If you are **unfit**, your body is not in good condition because you have not been getting regular exercise. (缺乏常规锻炼而) 不健康的 ❑ *Many children are so unfit they are unable to do even basic exercises.* 许多孩子很不强健，他们甚至不能做基本的运动。 **2** ADJ If someone is **unfit** for something, he or she is unable to do it because of injury or illness. (因受伤或生病) 不适合做…的 ❑ *He had a third examination and was declared unfit for duty.* 他做了第3次检查，被宣布不适合上班。 **3** ADJ If you say that someone or something is **unfit** for a particular purpose or job, you are criticizing them because they are not good enough for that purpose or job. 不能胜任的 [DISAPPROVAL] ❑ *Existing houses are becoming totally unfit for human habitation.* 现存的房子正变得完全不适合人居住。 ❑ *They were utterly unfit to govern.* 他们完全不胜任管理。

★ **un·fold** /ʌnfoʊld/ (**unfolds, unfolding, unfolded**) **1** V-I If a situation **unfolds**, it develops and becomes known or understood. 逐渐明朗 ❑ *The outcome depends on conditions as well as how events unfold.* 结果取决于条件以及事件如何发展。 **2** V-T/V-I If a story **unfolds** or if someone **unfolds** it, it is told to someone else. 使 (事情等) 传开; 传开 ❑ *Don's story unfolded as the cruise got under way.* 唐的故事随着航游的开始而漫漫展开了。 **3** V-T/V-I If someone **unfolds** something which has been folded or if it **unfolds**, it is opened out and becomes flat. 展开 ❑ *He quickly unfolded the blankets and spread them on the mattress.* 他迅速摊开毯子，铺在褥垫上。

U

un·fore·seen /ʌnfɔrsin/ ADJ If something that has happened was **unforeseen**, it was not expected to happen or known about beforehand. 未预见的 ❑ *Radiation may damage cells in a way that was previously unforeseen.* 辐射也许会以以前未预见的方式损坏细胞。 ❑ *Unfortunately, due to unforeseen circumstances, this year's show has been cancelled.* 遗憾的是，由于意外情况，今年的演出已被取消了。

un·for·get·table /ʌnfərgɛtəbᵊl/ ADJ If you describe something as **unforgettable**, you mean that it is, for example, extremely beautiful, enjoyable, or unusual, so that you remember it for a long time. You can also refer to extremely unpleasant things as **unforgettable**. 令人难忘的 ❑ *A visit to the museum is an unforgettable experience.* 对该博物馆的参观是一次难忘的经历。 ❑ *...the outdoor activities that will make your vacation unforgettable.* …将使你的假期难忘的户外活动。

un·for·tu·nate /ʌnfɔrtʃənɪt/ (**unfortunates**) **1** ADJ If you describe someone as **unfortunate**, you mean that something unpleasant or unlucky has happened to them. You can also describe the unpleasant things that happen to them as **unfortunate**. 不幸的; 令人不愉快的 ❑ *Some unfortunate person passing below could all too easily be seriously injured.* 某个正好从下面路过的倒霉的人会太容易严重受伤。 ❑ *Apparently he had been unfortunate enough to fall victim to a gang of thugs.* 显然他曾够不幸的，遭遇了一伙恶棍。 **2** ADJ If you describe something that has happened as **unfortunate**, you think that it is inappropriate, embarrassing, awkward, or undesirable. 令人遗憾的 ❑ *It is unfortunate that your flight was canceled.* 遗憾的是，你的航班被取消了。 ❑ *...the unfortunate incident of the upside-down Canadian flag.* …颠倒了加拿大旗帜这件憾事。 **3** ADJ You can describe someone as **unfortunate** when they are poor or have a difficult life. (生活穷困而) 不幸的 ❑ *Every year we have fundraisers to raise money for unfortunate people.* 每年我们有募捐会为不幸的人筹集钱款。 ● N-COUNT An **unfortunate** is someone who is unfortunate. 不幸的人 ❑ *Dorothy was another of life's unfortunates.* 多萝西是又一个生活不幸的人。

un·for·tu·nate·ly ◆◇◇ /ʌnfɔrtʃənɪtli/ ADV You can use **unfortunately** to introduce or refer to a statement when you consider that it is sad or disappointing, or when you want to express regret. 遗憾地 [FEELINGS] ❑ *Unfortunately, my time is limited.* 遗憾的是，我的时间有限。 ❑ *Unfortunately for him, his title brought obligations as well as privileges.* 对他来说遗憾的是，他的头衔既带来了特权也带来了义务。

un·found·ed /ʌnfaʊndɪd/ ADJ If you describe a rumor, belief, or feeling as **unfounded**, you mean that it is wrong and is not based on facts or evidence. 无根据的 ❑ *Unfounded rumors of accounting problems hit stocks of other companies.* 有关账目问题的无根据的谣言打击了其他公司的股票。 ❑ *The allegations were totally unfounded.* 指控是完全无根据的。

un·friend·ly /ʌnfrɛndli/ ADJ If you describe a person, organization, or their behavior as **unfriendly**, you mean that they behave toward you in an unkind or slightly hostile way. 不友好的 ❑ *Some people were unfriendly to the new recruit.* 一些人对新成员不友好。 ❑ *People always complain that the big banks and big companies are unfriendly and unhelpful.* 人们总抱怨大银行和大公司不友好，也不予帮助。

Thesaurus	*unfriendly* 另参见:
ADJ.	cold, unkind, unsociable; (*ant.*) friendly

un·ful·filled /ʌnfʊlfɪld/ **1** ADJ If you use **unfulfilled** to describe something such as a promise, ambition, or need, you mean that what was promised, hoped for, or needed has not happened. 未实现的 ❑ *Do you have any unfulfilled ambitions?* 你有未实现的抱负吗？ ❑ *...angry at unfulfilled promises of jobs and decent housing.* …对未兑现的、有关工作和像样住房的诺言的气愤。 **2** ADJ If you describe someone as **unfulfilled**, you mean that they feel dissatisfied with life or with what they have done. 不满意的 ❑ *You must let go of the idea that to be single is to be unhappy and unfulfilled.* 你必须放弃单身就不快乐不满足的想法。

un·furl /ʌnfɜrl/ (**unfurls, unfurling, unfurled**) **1** V-T/V-I If you **unfurl** something rolled or folded such as an umbrella, sail, or flag, you open it, so that it is spread out. You can also say that it **unfurls**. 展开 (伞、帆或旗帜) ❑ *Once outside the inner breakwater, we began to unfurl all the sails.* 一出内防波堤，我们就开始展开所有的风帆。 **2** V-I If you say that events, stories, or scenes **unfurl** before you, you mean that you are aware of them or can see them as they happen or develop. (事件、故事、场景等) 逐渐展开 ❑ *The dramatic changes in Europe continue to unfurl.* 剧变在欧洲继续呈现。

un·grate·ful /ʌngreɪtfəl/ ADJ If you describe someone as **ungrateful**, you are criticizing them for not showing thanks or for being unkind to someone who has helped them or done them a favor. 不感激的 [DISAPPROVAL] ❑ *I thought it was ungrateful of her.* 我认为她这是不知好歹。

un·hap·pi·ly /ʌnhæpɪli/ ADV You use **unhappily** to introduce or refer to a statement when you consider it to be sad and wish that it were different. 不幸地 [ADV with cl] ❑ *On May 23rd, unhappily, the* little boy died. 在5月23日，小男孩不幸死了。 ❑ *Unhappily the facts do not wholly bear out the theory.* 遗憾的是，事实不完全证实该理论。

un·hap·py ♦◇◇ /ʌnhæpi/ (**unhappier, unhappiest**) 1 ADJ If you are **unhappy**, you are sad and depressed. 不幸福的 ❑ *Her marriage is in trouble and she is desperately unhappy.* 她的婚姻出了问题，她极不快乐。 ❑ *He was a shy, sometimes unhappy man.* 他是一个害羞、有时不快乐的人。 ● **un·hap·pi·ly** ADV 不快乐地 ❑ *"I don't have your imagination," Kevin said unhappily.* "我没有你的想像力，"凯文不快地说。 ● **un·hap·pi·ness** N-UNCOUNT 不幸 ❑ *There was a lot of unhappiness in my adolescence.* 我的青春期有许多不幸。 2 ADJ If you are **unhappy about** something, you are not pleased about it or not satisfied with it. 对…不高兴的; 对…不满意的 [v-link ADJ] ❑ *He has been unhappy with his son's political leanings.* 他一直不满于儿子的政治倾向。 ❑ *College students are unhappy with their school bookstores.* 大学生们对学校的书店不满意。 ❑ *A lot of republicans are unhappy that the government isn't doing more.* 许多共和党人对政府不做更多感到不满。 ● **un·hap·pi·ness** N-UNCOUNT 不高兴; 不满意 ❑ *He has, by submitting his resignation, signaled his unhappiness with the government's decision.* 他通过递交辞呈已表明对政府决定的不满。 3 ADJ An **unhappy** situation or choice is not satisfactory or desirable. 不令人满意的; 不理想的 [ADJ n] ❑ *It is our hope that this unhappy chapter in the history of relations between our two countries will soon be closed.* 我们希望我们两国关系史上这一不愉快的阶段将很快过去。 ❑ *The legislation represents in itself an unhappy compromise.* 这项立法本身就是不可取的妥协 ❑ *...unhappy experiences of writing for television.* …给电视撰稿的不愉快经历。

Thesaurus *unhappy* 另参见:
ADJ. depressed, miserable, sad; *(ant.)* happy 1

un·harmed /ʌnhɑrmd/ ADJ If someone or something is **unharmed** after an accident or violent incident, they are not hurt or damaged in any way. 未受伤的 [ADJ after v, v-link ADJ] ❑ *They both escaped unharmed.* 他们俩都逃脱了，没有受伤。

un·healthy /ʌnhɛlθi/ (**unhealthier, unhealthiest**) 1 ADJ Something that is **unhealthy** is likely to cause illness or bad health. (物) 不利健康的 ❑ *Avoid unhealthy foods such as hamburgers and fries.* 避免不健康的食物，如汉堡包和炸薯条。 2 ADJ If you are **unhealthy**, you are sick or not in good physical condition. (人) 不利健康的 ❑ *...a pale, unhealthy looking man.* …一个面色苍白、看上去不健康的男人。 3 ADJ An **unhealthy** economy or company is financially weak and unsuccessful. (经济或公司) 不景气的 ❑ *If you have an unhealthy economy, the poor will get hurt worst because they are the weakest.* 如果经济不景气，穷人将遭受最大打击，因为他们是最弱的群体。 4 ADJ If you describe someone's behavior or interests as **unhealthy**, you do not consider them to be normal and think they may involve mental problems. (行为、兴趣) 不正常的 ❑ *Frank has developed an unhealthy relationship with these people.* 弗兰克和这些人发展了不正常的关系。

un·heard of /ʌnhɜrd ʌv/ ADJ An event or situation that is **unheard of** never happens. 没发生过的 [v-link ADJ] ❑ *Riots are almost unheard of in Japan.* 暴乱在日本几乎是闻所未闻的。

un·help·ful /ʌnhɛlpfəl/ ADJ If you say that someone or something is **unhelpful**, you mean that they do not help you or improve a situation, and may even make things worse. 不帮忙的; 无益的 ❑ *The criticism is both unfair and unhelpful.* 这种批评不合理且无益。

un·hurt /ʌnhɜrt/ ADJ If someone who has been attacked, or involved in an accident, is **unhurt**, they are not injured. 未受伤的 [ADJ after v, v-link ADJ] ❑ *The driver escaped unhurt, but a pedestrian was injured.* 司机逃脱了没有受伤，但一个行人受伤了。

Word Link *ident ≈ same : identical, identification, unidentified*

un·iden·ti·fied ♦◇◇ /ʌnaɪdɛntɪfaɪd/ 1 ADJ If you describe someone or something as **unidentified**, you mean that nobody knows who or what they are. 身份不明的; 未知的 ❑ *He was shot this morning by unidentified intruders at his house.* 他今天早晨在家里遭到身份不明的闯入者枪击。 2 ADJ If you use **unidentified** to describe people, groups, and organizations, you do not want to give their names. 不愿透露姓名的 [JOURNALISM] ❑ *His claims were based on the comments of anonymous and unidentified sources.* 他的主张基于匿名及未知出处的资料的评论。

★ **uni·fi·ca·tion** /yunɪfɪkeɪʃən/ N-UNCOUNT **Unification** is the process by which two or more countries join together and become one country. 统一 ❑ *...the process of European unification.* …欧洲统一进程。

Word Link *uni ≈ one : uniform, unilateral, union*

uni·form ♦◇◇ /yunɪfɔrm/ (**uniforms**) 1 N-VAR A **uniform** is a special set of clothes which some people, for example soldiers or the police, wear to work in and which some children wear in school. 制服 ❑ *The police wear dark blue uniforms.* 警察穿深蓝色制服。 ❑ *Felipe was in uniform for the parade.* 费利佩穿着游行服装。 2 ADJ If something is **uniform**, it does not vary, but is even and regular throughout. 一致的 ❑ *Cut down between the bones so that all the chops are of uniform size.* 在骨头之间砍削，使所有的排骨大小一致。 ❑ *All flowing water, though it appears to be uniform, is actually divided into extensive inner surfaces, or layers, moving against one another.* 所有流水尽管看起来是一样的，实际上是分成了大量相互碰撞的内在表层。 ● **uni·form·ity** /yunɪfɔrmɪti/ N-UNCOUNT 一致性 ❑ *...the caramel that was used to maintain uniformity of color in the brandy.* …为保持白兰地色泽一致而添加的焦糖。 ● **uni·form·ly** ADV 一致地 ❑ *Beyond the windows, a November midday was uniformly gray.* 窗外，11月的正午是一片灰色。 3 ADJ If you describe a number of things as **uniform**, you mean that they are all the same. 同样的 ❑ *Along each wall stretched uniform green metal filing cabinets.* 沿每堵墙摆放着清一色的绿色金属档案柜。 ● **uni·form·ity** N-UNCOUNT 相同性 ❑ *...the dull uniformity of the houses.* …那些房子的单调雷同。 ● **uni·form·ly** ADV 相同地 ❑ *They are all about twenty years old, serious, smart, a bit conventional perhaps, but uniformly pleasant.* 他们全都大约二十来岁，严肃、聪明，也许有点传统，但全都很愉快。
→ see **football, soccer**

uni·formed /yunɪfɔrmd/ ADJ If you use **uniformed** to describe someone who does a particular job, you mean that they are wearing a uniform. 穿制服的 ❑ *...uniformed policemen.* …穿制服的警察。

uni·form·ity /yunɪfɔrmɪti/ 1 N-UNCOUNT If there is **uniformity** in something such as a system, organization, or group of countries, the same rules, ideas, or methods are applied in all parts of it. 统一性 ❑ *He argues that we need statewide uniformity.* 他辩称我们需要全州统一。 2 → see also **uniform**

★ **uni·fy** /yunɪfaɪ/ (**unifies, unifying, unified**) V-T/V-I If someone **unifies** different things or parts, or if the things or parts **unify**, they are brought together to form one thing. 使成一体; 成为一体 ❑ *He pledged to unify the city's political factions.* 他保证要统一全市的政治小集团。 ❑ *...constitutional reforms designed to unify the country.* …旨在统一国家的宪法改革。 ● **uni·fied** ADJ 统一的 ❑ *...a unified system of taxation.* …统一的税制。

★ **uni·lat·er·al** /yunɪlætərəl/ ADJ A **unilateral** decision is made by only one of the groups, organizations, or countries that are involved in a particular situation, without the agreement of the others. 单方面的 ❑ *...unilateral nuclear disarmament.* …单方面的核裁军。

un·im·agi·nable /ʌnɪmædʒɪnəbəl/ ADJ If you describe something as **unimaginable**, you are emphasizing that it is difficult to imagine or understand well, because it is not part of people's normal experience. 难以想像的 [EMPHASIS] ❑ *The scale of the fighting is almost unimaginable.* 战斗的规模几乎难以想像。 ● **un·im·agi·nably** /ʌnɪmædʒɪnəbli/ ADV 难以想像地 [ADV adj] ❑ *Conditions in prisons out there are unimaginably bad.* 那里各监狱的条件难以想像地恶劣。

un·im·por·tant /ʌnɪmpɔrtənt/ ADJ If you describe something or someone as **unimportant**, you mean that they do not have much influence, effect, or value, and are therefore not worth serious consideration. 不重要的 ❑ *When they had married, six years before, the difference in their ages had seemed unimportant.* 他们6年前结婚时，年龄上的差别似乎并不重要。

Thesaurus *unimportant* 另参见:
ADJ. frivolous, insignificant, trivial; *(ant.)* important

un·im·pressed /ʌnɪmprɛst/ ADJ If you are **unimpressed by** something or someone, you do not think they are very good, intelligent, or useful. 未被…留下深刻印象 [v-link ADJ] ❑ *He was also very unimpressed by his teachers.* 他也没觉得他的老师们有多好。

un·in·hib·it·ed /ʌnɪnhɪbɪtɪd/ ADJ If you describe a person or their behavior as **uninhibited**, you mean that they express their opinions and feelings openly, and behave as they want to, without worrying what other people think. 不受约束的 ❑ *...a bold and uninhibited entertainer.* …一位大胆且豪放不羁的艺人。 ❑ *The dancing is uninhibited and as frenzied as an aerobics class.* 跳舞都放开了，像健身课那样尽情。

un·in·stall /ʌnɪnstɔ̲l/ (**uninstalls, uninstalling, uninstalled**) V-T If you **uninstall** a computer program, you remove it permanently from your computer. 卸载(电脑程序) [COMPUTING] ❑ *If you don't like the program, just uninstall it and forget it.* 如果你不喜欢这个程序，就卸载掉算了。

un·in·tel·li·gible /ʌnɪntɛ̲lɪdʒɪbᵊl/ ADJ **Unintelligible** language is impossible to understand, for example because it is not written or pronounced clearly, or because its meaning is confused or complicated. 令人费解的 ❑ *He muttered something unintelligible.* 他喃喃些莫名其妙的话 ❑ *...the unintelligible phrases and images of his earlier poems.* …他早期诗歌中的让人难以理解的短语和想象。

un·in·ten·tion·al /ʌnɪntɛ̲nʃənᵊl/ ADJ Something that is **unintentional** is not done deliberately, but happens by accident. 非故意的 ❑ *Perhaps he had slightly misled them, but it was quite unintentional.* 或许他有一点误导他们了，但完全是无意的。● **un·in·ten·tion·al·ly** ADV 无意地 ❑ *...an overblown and unintentionally funny adaptation of "Dracula."* …对《吸血鬼德古拉》的一种夸大且无意中显得滑稽的改编。

un·in·ter·rupt·ed /ʌnɪntərʌ̲ptɪd/ **1** ADJ If something is **uninterrupted**, it is continuous and has no breaks or interruptions in it. 不间断的 ❑ *This enables the healing process to continue uninterrupted.* 这能使愈合进程连续不断。❑ *His hearing remained good, so that his contact with the world was uninterrupted.* 他的听力仍然良好，因此他与世界的接触没有间断。**2** ADJ An **uninterrupted** view of something is a clear view of it, without any obstacles in the way. 一览无遗的 ❑ *Diners can enjoy an uninterrupted view of the gardens.* 就餐者能欣赏到花园一览无余的景色。

Word Link *uni ≈ one : uniform, unilateral, union*

un·ion ♦♦♦ /yu̲nyən/ (**unions**) **1** N-COUNT A **union** is a workers' organization which represents its members and which tries to improve things such as their working conditions and pay. 工会 ❑ *Do all teachers have a right to join a union?* 所有的教师都有权利加入工会吗？**2** N-UNCOUNT When the **union** of two or more things occurs, they are joined together and become one thing. 合并 ❑ *In 1918 the Romanian majority in this former czarist province voted for union with Romania.* 1918年，这个前沙俄省份的大多数罗马尼亚人投票支持与罗马尼亚合并。**3** N-SING When two or more things, for example countries or organizations, have been joined together to form one thing, you can refer to them as a **union**. 联盟 ❑ *Tanzania is a union of the states of Tanganyika and Zanzibar.* 坦桑尼亚是坦噶尼喀州和桑给巴尔州的联盟。
→ see Word Web: union
→ see **empire, factory**

unique ♦◇◇ /yuni̲k/ **1** ADJ Something that is **unique** is the only one of its kind. 惟一的 ❑ *Each person's signature is unique.* 每个人的签名是独一无二的。● **unique·ly** ADV 惟一地 ❑ *Because of the extreme cold, the Antarctic is a uniquely fragile environment.* 由于极端寒冷，南极州的生态环境尤其脆弱。● **unique·ness** N-UNCOUNT 独特性 ❑ *...the uniqueness of China's own experience.* …中国自身经验的独特性。**2** ADJ You can use **unique** to describe things that you admire because they are very unusual and special. 极不寻常的；独特的 [APPROVAL] ❑ *She was a woman of unique talent and determination.* 她是一个有独特天赋和决心的女人。● **unique·ly** ADV 极不寻常地；独特地 ❑ *There'll never be a shortage of people who consider themselves uniquely qualified to be president of the United States.* 从不缺乏那种自认为特有资格成为美国总统的人。**3** ADJ If something is **unique to** one thing, person, group, or place, it concerns or belongs only to that thing, person, group, or place. 独有的 [v-link ADJ "to" n] ❑ *No one knows for sure why adolescence is unique to humans.* 没人确切知道为什么青春期是人类独有的。● **unique·ly** ADV 独有地 [ADV adj] ❑ *The problem isn't uniquely American.* 该问题并非美国独有。

Thesaurus *unique* 另参见：
ADJ. different, one-of-a-kind, special, uncommon; *(ant.)* common, standard, usual **1**

uni·sex /yu̲nisɛks/ ADJ **Unisex** is used to describe things, usually clothes or places, which are designed for use by both men and women rather than by only one sex. 男女都适用的 ❑ *...the classic unisex hair salon.* …古典的男女通用发廊。

uni·son /yu̲nɪsən, -zən/ **1** PHRASE If two or more people do something **in unison**, they do it together at the same time. 一起 ❑ *Every morning the kids say the Pledge of Allegiance in unison.* 每天早晨孩子们齐声进行效忠宣誓。**2** PHRASE If people or organizations act **in unison**, they act the same way because they agree with each other or because they want to achieve the same goals. 一致地 ❑ *The international community is ready to work in unison against him.* 国际社会准备齐心协力对付他。

unit ♦♦◇ /yu̲nɪt/ (**units**) **1** N-COUNT If you consider something as a **unit**, you consider it as a single, complete thing. 单元 ❑ *Agriculture was based in the past on the family as a unit.* 农业过去以一个家庭单元为基础。**2** N-COUNT A **unit** is a group of people who work together at a specific job, often in a particular place. (工作) 单位 ❑ *...the environmental research unit.* …环境研究单位。**3** N-COUNT A **unit** is a group within an armed force or police force, whose members fight or work together or carry out a particular task. 分队 ❑ *...a firefighting unit.* …一个消防分队。**4** N-COUNT A **unit** is a small machine which has a particular function, often part of a larger machine. 部件 ❑ *The unit plugs into any TV set.* 该部件可接入任何电视机。**5** N-COUNT A **unit** of measurement is a fixed standard quantity, length, or weight that is used for measuring things. The quart, the inch, and the ounce are all units. (计量用的) 单位 **6** N-COUNT A **unit** is one of the parts that a textbook is divided into. (教科书的) 单元 ❑ *Unit V of this book explains those errors in detail and shows you ways to correct them.* 这本书的第5单元详细解释那些错误并且教你改正的方法。
→ see **graph**

▲ **uni·tary** /yu̲nɪtɛri/ ADJ A **unitary** country or organization is one in which two or more areas or groups have joined together, have the same aims, and are controlled by a single government. 一元化的 [ADJ n] ❑ *...a call for the creation of a single unitary state.* …一个建立一元化国家的呼吁。

unit cost (**unit costs**) N-COUNT **Unit cost** is the amount of money that it costs a company to produce one article. 单位成本 [BUSINESS] ❑ *They hope to reduce unit costs through extra sales.* 他们希望通过额外销售降低单位成本。

unite /yunaɪ̲t/ (**unites, uniting, united**) V-T/V-I If a group of people or things **unite** or if something **unites** them, they join together and act as a group. 使联合；联合 ❑ *We need to unite against terrorism.* 我们需要团结起来反对恐怖主义。

Thesaurus *unite* 另参见：
V. blend, combine, incorporate; *(ant.)* separate

unit·ed ♦◇◇ /yunaɪ̲tɪd/ **1** ADJ When people are **united** about something, they agree about it and act together. 团结的 ❑ *The entire Brazilian people are united by their love of soccer.* 整个巴西民族由其对足球的热爱团结在一起。**2** ADJ **United** is used to describe a country which has been formed from two or more states or countries. 联盟的 ❑ *...the first elections to be held in a united Germany for fifty eight years.* …在统一的德国将举行58年来的第一次竞选。

Unit·ed Na·tions ♦♦◇ N-PROPER **The United Nations** is an organization which most countries belong to. Its role is to encourage international peace, cooperation, and friendship. 联合国

Word Web union

In some places, **laborers** work long hours with little chance for a **raise** in **wages**. **Workdays** of 10 to 12 hours are not uncommon. Some people even work seven days a week. Conditions like this lead to unrest among **workers**. At that point, **organizers** can sometimes get them to join a **union**. Union leaders engage in **collective bargaining** with business owners. They try to win a shorter workday or better working conditions for workers. If the **employees** are not satisfied with the results, they may **strike**. In Sweden, 85% of laborers and 75% of **white-collar** employees belong to unions.

U

unit sales N-PLURAL **Unit sales** refers to the number of individual items that a company sells. 单位销售量 [BUSINESS] ❑ *Unit sales of T-shirts increased 6%.* T恤衫的单位销售增加了6%。

unit trust (**unit trusts**) N-COUNT **Unit trust** means the same as **mutual fund**. 单位信托投资公司 [BRIT, BUSINESS]

unity ♦◇◇ /yu̲nɪti/ **1** N-UNCOUNT **Unity** is the state of different areas or groups being joined together to form a single country or organization. 统一 ❑ *We have to act to preserve the unity of this nation.* 我们必须行动起来以维护这个国家的统一。 **2** N-UNCOUNT When there is **unity**, people are in agreement and act together for a particular purpose. 团结; 一致 ❑ *...a renewed unity of purpose.* …目的的重新统一。 ❑ *Speakers at the rally expressed sentiments of unity.* 集会上的发言者们表达了团结的观点。

Word Partnership *unity* 的常用搭配:

ADJ. **economic** unity, **national** unity, **political** unity **1** **2**
V. **maintain** unity, **promote** unity **1** **2**
N. **party** unity, unity **of purpose**, **sense of** unity, **show of** unity, **spirit of** unity **2**

uni·ver·sal /yu̲nɪvɜ̲rsᵊl/ **1** ADJ Something that is **universal** relates to everyone in the world or everyone in a particular group or society. 全世界的; 普遍的 ❑ *The insurance industry has produced its own proposals for universal health care.* 保险业为全民保健提出了自己的建议。 ❑ *The desire to look attractive is universal.* 爱美之心人皆有之。 **2** ADJ Something that is **universal** affects or relates to every part of the world or the universe. 全世界的; 普遍存在的 ❑ *...universal diseases.* …世界性的疾病。

uni·ver·sal bank (**universal banks**) N-COUNT A **universal bank** is a bank that offers both banking and stockbroking services to its clients. (提供银行业务和股票经纪业务的) 全能银行 [BUSINESS] ❑ *...universal banks offering a wide range of services.* …提供广泛服务的全能银行。

uni·ver·sal·ly /yu̲nɪvɜ̲rsəli/ **1** ADV If something is **universally** believed or accepted, it is believed or accepted by everyone with no disagreement. 普遍 (相信、接受) 地 ❑ *...a universally accepted point of view.* …一个被普遍接受的观点。 **2** ADV If something is **universally** true, it is true everywhere in the world or in all situations. 普遍 (真实) 地 ❑ *The disadvantage is that it is not universally available.* 不利之处是它并非到处都能找到。

uni·verse ♦◇◇ /yu̲nɪvɜrs/ (**universes**) **1** N-COUNT **The universe** is the whole of space and all the stars, planets, and other forms of matter and energy in it. 宇宙 ❑ *Einstein's equations showed the universe to be expanding.* 爱因斯坦的方程式表明宇宙正在扩大。 **2** N-COUNT If you talk about someone's **universe**, you are referring to the whole of their experience or an important part of it. (某人的) 经历 ❑ *Good writers suck in what they see of the world, re-creating their own universe on the page.* 好的作家吸收他们所看到的世界，在书里重新创造自己的世界。

→ see **galaxy**, **telescope**

uni·ver·sity ♦♦♦ /yu̲nɪvɜ̲rsɪti/ (**universities**) N-VAR; N-IN-NAMES A **university** is an institution where students study for degrees and where academic research is done. 大学 ❑ *Offenbacker earned an education degree at the University of Washington and taught elementary school.* 奥芬巴克在华盛顿大学获得了教育学位，教了小学。 ❑ *She goes to Duke University.* 她上杜克大学。

un·just /ʌndʒʌ̲st/ ADJ If you describe an action, system, or law as **unjust**, you think that it treats a person or group badly in a way that they do not deserve. 不公正的 ❑ *The attack on Charles was unjust.* 对查尔斯的攻击是不公正的。 ● **un·just·ly** ADV 不公正地 ❑ *She was unjustly accused of stealing money, and then fired.* 她被不公正地指控窃取了金钱，然后被解雇了。

un·jus·ti·fied /ʌndʒʌ̲stɪfaɪd/ ADJ If you describe a belief or action as **unjustified**, you think that there is no good reason for having it or doing it. 无正当理由的 ❑ *Your report last week was unfair. It was based upon wholly unfounded and totally unjustified allegations.* 你上周的报告是不公正的，它基于毫无事实根据和完全无正当理由的指控。

un·kind /ʌnka̲ɪnd/ (**unkinder**, **unkindest**) **1** ADJ If someone is **unkind**, they behave in an unpleasant, unfriendly, or slightly cruel way. You can also describe someone's words or actions as **unkind**. 不友好的 ❑ *All last summer he'd been unkind to her.* 去年整个夏天他都对她不友好。 ❑ *No one has an unkind word to say about him.* 没人用不善之辞谈论过他。 ● **un·kind·ly** ADV 不友好地 ❑ *Several viewers commented unkindly on her costumes.* 几个观众恶评了她的戏装。 ● **un·kind·ness** N-UNCOUNT 不友好 ❑ *He realized the unkindness of the remark and immediately regretted having hurt her with it.* 他意识到了所说之话的刻薄，立刻后悔用这样的话伤害了她。 **2** ADJ If you describe something bad that happens to someone as **unkind**, you mean that they do not deserve it. 不仁慈的 [WRITTEN] ❑ *The weather was unkind to those pipers who played in the morning.* 天气对那些早晨吹奏管乐器者来说并不妙。

Thesaurus *unkind* 另参见:

ADJ. harsh, mean, unfriendly; *(ant.)* kind **1**

un·know·able /ʌnno̲ʊəbᵊl/ ADJ If you describe something as **unknowable**, you mean that it is impossible for human beings to know anything about it. 不可知的 [WRITTEN] ❑ *The specific impact of the greenhouse effect is unknowable.* 温室效应的确切影响是不可知的。

un·know·ing /ʌnno̲ʊɪŋ/ ADJ If you describe a person as **unknowing**, you mean that they are not aware of what is happening or of what they are doing. 不知情的 [usu ADJ n] ❑ *Some governments have been victims and perhaps unknowing accomplices in the bank's activities.* 有些政府是银行活动的受害者，也或许是不知情的同犯。

un·know·ing·ly /ʌnno̲ʊɪŋli/ ADV If someone does something **unknowingly**, they do it without being aware of it. 不知情地

un·known ♦◇◇ /ʌnno̲ʊn/ (**unknowns**) **1** ADJ If something is **unknown** to you, you have no knowledge of it. 不了解的 ❑ *An unknown number of demonstrators were arrested.* 不知多少示威者被逮捕了。 ❑ *The motive for the killing is unknown.* 杀人的动机不明。 ● N-COUNT An **unknown** is something that is unknown. 未知的事物 ❑ *The length of the war is one of the biggest unknowns.* 战争的持续时间是其中一个最大的未知数。 **2** ADJ An **unknown** person is someone whose name you do not know or whose character you do not know anything about. (姓名或性格) 未知的 ❑ *...the tomb of the unknown soldier.* …那名无名士兵的墓。 **3** ADJ An **unknown** person is not famous or publicly recognized. 不出名的 ❑ *He was an unknown writer.* 他是个没有名气的作家。 ● N-COUNT An **unknown** is a person who is unknown. 不为人知的人 ❑ *Within a short space of time a group of complete unknowns had established a wholly original form of humor.* 在短短的一段时间内，一群完全不为人知的人已始创了一种新式幽默。 **4** ADJ If you say that a particular problem or situation is **unknown**, you mean that it never occurs. 从未发生过的 ❑ *A hundred years ago coronary heart disease was virtually unknown in America.* 100年前，冠心病在美国几乎从未有过。 **5** N-SING **The unknown** refers generally to things or places that people do not know about or understand. 未知事物 ❑ *Ignorance of people brings fear, fear of the unknown.* 人的无知带来了恐惧，对未知事物的恐惧。

★ **un·law·ful** /ʌnlɔ̲fəl/ ADJ If something is **unlawful**, the law does not allow you to do it. 不合法的 [FORMAL] ❑ *...employees who believe their dismissal was unlawful.* …认为其被解雇不合法的雇员们。 ● **un·law·ful·ly** ADV 不合法地 [ADV with v] ❑ *The government acted unlawfully in imposing the restrictions.* 政府不合法地采取行动强加制约。

un·lead·ed /ʌnlɛ̲dɪd/ ADJ **Unleaded** fuel contains a smaller amount of lead than most fuels so that it produces less harmful substances when it is burned. (燃料) 无铅的 ❑ *He filled up his Toyota with regular unleaded gas.* 他把自己的丰田车加满了普通无铅汽油。 ● N-UNCOUNT **Unleaded** is also a noun. 无铅汽油 ❑ *All its V8 engines will run happily on unleaded.* 所有其V8引擎将靠无铅汽油良好运转。

▲ **un·leash** /ʌnli̲ʃ/ (**unleashes**, **unleashing**, **unleashed**) V-T If you say that someone or something **unleashes** a powerful force, feeling, activity, or group, you mean that they suddenly start it or send it somewhere. 释放 ❑ *The announcement unleashed a storm of protest from the public.* 公告引发了一场公众的抗议风暴。 ❑ *The officers were still reluctant to unleash their troops in pursuit of a defeated enemy.* 军官们仍不愿发兵追击溃敌。

un·less ♦♦◇ /ʌnlɛ̲s/ CONJ You use **unless** to introduce the only circumstances in which an event you are mentioning will not take place or in which a statement you are making is not true. 除非; 如果不 ❑ *Unless you are trying to lose weight to please yourself, it's going to be tough to keep your motivation level high.* 除非你在为了让自己开心而努力减肥，否则要保持驱动力很高将很难。 ❑ *We cannot understand disease unless we understand the person who has the disease.* 除非我们了解有某种疾病的人，否则我们不会了解疾病。

u

Do not confuse **unless**, **except**, **except for**, and **besides**. **Unless** is used to introduce the only situation in which something will take place or be true. ❑ *In the 1940s, unless she wore gloves a woman was not properly dressed... You must not give compliments unless you mean them.* You use **except** to introduce the only things, situations, people, or ideas that a statement does not apply to. ❑ *All of his body relaxed except his right hand... Traveling was impossible, except in the cool of the morning.* You use **except for** before something that prevents a statement from being completely true. ❑ *The classrooms were silent, except for the scratching of pens on paper... I had absolutely no friends except for Tom.* You use **besides** to introduce extra things in addition to the ones you are mentioning already. ❑ *Fruit will give you, besides enjoyment, a source of vitamins.* However, note that if you talk about "the only thing" or "the only person **besides**" a particular person or thing, **besides** means the same as "apart from." ❑ *He was the only person besides Gertrude who talked to Guy.*

un·like ♦◇◇ /ʌnlaɪk/ **1** PREP If one thing is **unlike** another thing, the two things have different qualities or characteristics from each other. 不像 ❑ *This was a foreign country, so unlike San Jose.* 这是异国，因而不像圣何塞。 **2** PREP You can use **unlike** to contrast two people, things, or situations, and show how they are different. 和…不同 ❑ *Unlike aerobics, walking entails no expensive fees for classes or clubs.* 不像有氧运动，散步不需要昂贵的课时费或俱乐部费。 **3** PREP If you describe something that a particular person has done as being **unlike** them, you mean that you are surprised by it because it is not typical of their character or normal behavior. 不像是… ❑ *It was so unlike him to say something like that, with such intensity, that I was astonished.* 那样激烈地说那样的话真不像是他，以至我很惊讶。

un·like·ly ♦♦◇ /ʌnlaɪkli/ (**unlikeliest**) ADJ If you say that something is **unlikely to** happen or **unlikely to** be true, you believe that it will not happen or that it is not true, although you are not completely sure. 未必发生的；不太可能的 ❑ *A military coup seems unlikely.* 一场兵变似乎不太可能。 ❑ *As with many technological revolutions, you are unlikely to be aware of it.* 正如很多技术革命一样，你不太可能意识到它。

Word Partnership *unlikely* 的常用搭配：

V.	unlikely **to change**, unlikely **to happen**, **seem** unlikely
N.	unlikely **event**
ADV.	**extremely** unlikely, **highly** unlikely, **most** unlikely, **very** unlikely

un·lim·it·ed /ʌnlɪmɪtɪd/ ADJ If there is an **unlimited** quantity of something, you can have as much or as many of that thing as you want. 无限制的 ❑ *An unlimited number of copies can still be made from the original.* 无限量的复制品依然能从原物制作出来。 ❑ *You'll also have unlimited access to the swimming pool.* 你将还可以无限制地进入该游泳池。

un·list·ed /ʌnlɪstɪd/ **1** ADJ If a person or their telephone number is **unlisted**, the number is not listed in the telephone book, and the telephone company will refuse to give it to people who ask for it. 未列入名单的 [mainly AM]

in BRIT, usually use **ex-directory**

❑ *Mr. Marra, whose New York telephone number is unlisted, could not be contacted yesterday.* 马拉先生在纽约的电话号码没列入电话簿，昨天联系不上他。 **2** ADJ An **unlisted** company or **unlisted** stock is not listed officially on a stock exchange. (公司或公司股票) 未上市的 [BUSINESS] ❑ *Its shares are traded on the Unlisted Securities Market.* 它的股票在未上市证券交易市场上交易。

U

un·load /ʌnloʊd/ (**unloads, unloading, unloaded**) V-T If you **unload** goods from a vehicle, or you **unload** a vehicle, you remove the goods from the vehicle, usually after they have been transported from one place to another. 从…卸下 ❑ *Unload everything from the boat and clean it thoroughly.* 从小船上卸下所有的货物并彻底地清洗。

un·lock /ʌnlɒk/ (**unlocks, unlocking, unlocked**) **1** V-T If you **unlock** something such as a door, a room, or a container that has a lock, you open it using a key. 用钥匙打开 ❑ *He unlocked the car and threw the coat on to the back seat.* 他启动汽车，将外套扔到了后座。 **2** V-T If you **unlock** the potential or the secrets of something or someone, you release them. 发掘 (潜力)；揭开 (秘密) ❑ *The point of the competition is to encourage all people to unlock their hidden potential.* 竞赛的目的是鼓励所有人发掘其隐藏的潜力。

un·lucky /ʌnlʌki/ (**unluckier, unluckiest**) **1** ADJ If someone is **unlucky**, they have bad luck. 不幸的 ❑ *You certainly were unlucky to get that horrible illness.* 你得了那种可怕的病当然是很不幸。 **2** ADJ You can use **unlucky** to describe unpleasant things which happen to someone, especially when you feel that the person does not deserve them. 倒霉的 ❑ *...Argentina's unlucky defeat by Ireland.* …阿根廷倒霉地败给爱尔兰。 **3** ADJ **Unlucky** is used to describe something that is thought to cause bad luck. 招致霉运的 ❑ *Some people think it is unlucky to walk under a ladder.* 一些人认为在梯子下走会倒霉。

un·marked /ʌnmɑrkt/ **1** ADJ Something that is **unmarked** has no marks on it. 无记号的 ❑ *Her shoes are still white and unmarked.* 她的鞋子仍是白色、无记号的。 **2** ADJ Something that is **unmarked** has no marking on it which identifies what it is or whose it is. 没有标志的 ❑ *He had seen them come out and get into the unmarked police car.* 他看见他们出来了，进了没有标志的警车。

un·me·tered /ʌnmiːtərd/ ADJ An **unmetered** service for something such as water supply is one that allows you to use as much as you want for a basic cost, instead of paying for the amount you use. 不用表计量的 ❑ *Clients are not charged by the minute but given unmetered access to the Internet for a fixed fee.* 客户不按分钟付费，而以某固定费用无限上网。

un·mis·tak·able /ʌnmɪsteɪkəbᵊl/ also **unmistakeable** ADJ If you describe something as **unmistakable**, you mean that it is so obvious that it cannot be mistaken for anything else. 不会弄错的 ❑ *He didn't give his name, but the voice was unmistakable.* 他没有给出其名，但其声错不了。 ● **un·mis·tak·ably** /ʌnmɪsteɪkəbli/ ADV 不会弄错地 ❑ *It's still unmistakably a Minnelli movie.* 这显然还是一部明尼里电影。 ❑ *...an unmistakably American accent.* …明显的美国口音。

un·miti·gat·ed /ʌnmɪtɪgeɪtɪd/ ADJ You use **unmitigated** to emphasize that a bad situation or quality is totally bad. 全然的 (强调糟糕程度) [ADJ n] [EMPHASIS] ❑ *Last year's cotton crop was an unmitigated disaster.* 去年的棉花收成是场十足的灾难。

Word Link *mov ≈ moving : movement, movie, unmoved*

un·moved /ʌnmuːvd/ ADJ If you are **unmoved by** something, you are not emotionally affected by it. 无动于衷的 [v-link ADJ] ❑ *Mr. Bird remained unmoved by the corruption allegations.* 伯德先生对贪污指控仍无动于衷。

un·named /ʌnneɪmd/ **1** ADJ **Unnamed** people or things are talked about but their names are not mentioned. 未提及名字的 ❑ *Perot accused unnamed U.S. officials of covering up the facts.* 佩罗未指名地谴责美国官员掩盖了事实。 **2** ADJ **Unnamed** things have not been given a name. 未取名字的 ❑ *...unnamed comets and asteroids.* …未命名的彗星和小行星。

un·natu·ral /ʌnnætʃərᵊl/ **1** ADJ If you describe something as **unnatural**, you mean that it is strange and often frightening, because it is different from what you normally expect. 异常的 ❑ *The aircraft rose with unnatural speed on takeoff.* 飞机以异常之速起飞升空。 ● **un·natu·ral·ly** ADV 异常地 [ADV adj] ❑ *The house was unnaturally silent.* 房子异常地寂静。 **2** ADJ Behavior that is **unnatural** seems artificial and not normal or genuine. 不自然的；不正常的；不真实的 ❑ *She gave him a bright, determined smile which seemed unnatural.* 她给了他一个快乐、坚定、看似不自然的微笑。 ● **un·natu·ral·ly** ADV 做作地；不正常地；不真实地 [ADV with v] ❑ *Try to avoid shouting or speaking unnaturally.* 尽量避免做作地喊叫或讲话。

un·natu·ral·ly /ʌnnætʃərəli/ **1** PHRASE You can use **not unnaturally** to indicate that the situation you are describing is exactly as you would expect in the circumstances. 异常地 ❑ *The result, not unnaturally, was that he became more tense and increasingly frustrated.* 结果自然是他变得更加紧张和日益沮丧。 **2** → see also **unnatural**

un·nec·es·sary /ʌnnɛsəsɛri/ ADJ If you describe something as **unnecessary**, you mean that it is not needed or does not have to be done. 不必要的 ❑ *The slaughter of whales is unnecessary and inhuman.* 对鲸的屠宰是不必要且不人道的。 ● **un·nec·es·sari·ly** /ʌnnɛsəsɛərɪli/ ADV 不必要地 ❑ *I didn't want to upset my husband or my daughter unnecessarily.* 我不想不必要地让我的丈夫或女儿不开心。

Thesaurus *unnecessary* 另参见：

ADJ. dispensable, superfluous, useless; (*ant.*) necessary

un·nerve /ʌnnɜrv/ (**unnerves, unnerving, unnerved**) V-T If you say that something **unnerves** you, you mean that it worries or troubles you. 使不安 ❑ *The news about Dermot had unnerved me.* 有关德莫特的消息已让我不安了。

un·nerv·ing /ʌnnɜrvɪŋ/ ADJ If you describe something as **unnerving**, you mean that it makes you feel worried or uncomfortable. 使人不安的；使人不舒服的 ❑ *It is very unnerving to find out that someone you see every day is carrying a potentially deadly virus.* 发现你每天都见的人携带着可能致命的病毒让人不安。

un·no·ticed /ʌnnoʊtɪst/ ADJ If something happens or passes **unnoticed**, it is not seen or noticed by anyone. 未被看见的；未被注意到的 ❑ *I tried to slip up the stairs unnoticed.* 我试图神不知鬼不觉地溜上楼梯。

un·ob·tru·sive /ʌnəbtrusɪv/ ADJ If you describe something or someone as **unobtrusive**, you mean that they are not easily noticed or do not draw attention to themselves. 不引人注目的 [FORMAL] ❑ *The coffee table is glass, to be as unobtrusive as possible.* 咖啡茶几是玻璃制的，尽可能地不引人注目。 ● **un·ob·tru·sive·ly** ADV 不引人注目地 ❑ *They slipped away unobtrusively.* 他们神不知鬼不觉地溜走了。

un·of·fi·cial /ʌnəfɪʃᵊl/ ADJ An **unofficial** action or statement is not organized or approved by a person or group in authority. 非官方的；未经官方批准的 ❑ *Staff voted to continue an unofficial strike in support of seven colleagues who were dismissed last week.* 全体职员投票继续非正式罢工以支持上星期被解雇的7个同事。 ● **un·of·fi·cial·ly** ADV 非官方地；未经官方批准地 ❑ *Some workers are legally employed, but the majority work unofficially with neither health insurance nor wage security.* 一些工人合法受雇用，但大多数人是非正式的，既没有健康保险，也没有工资保障。

> **Word Link** dox ≈ opinion : orthodoxy, paradox, unorthodox

un·ortho·dox /ʌnɔrθədɒks/ ADJ If you describe someone's behavior, beliefs, or customs as **unorthodox**, you mean that they are different from what is generally accepted. 非正统的；另类的 ❑ *The reality-based show followed the unorthodox lives of Ozzy, his wife Sharon, daughter Kelly, and son, Jack.* 这个写实剧取材于奥兹、其妻莎伦、女儿凯莉和儿子杰克的另类生活。

un·pack /ʌnpæk/ (**unpacks, unpacking, unpacked**) V-T/V-I When you **unpack** a suitcase, box, or similar container, or you **unpack** the things inside it, you take the things out of the container. 打开（箱子或盒子）取出 ❑ *He unpacked his bag.* 他打开了他的包。

un·paid /ʌnpeɪd/ **1** ADJ If you do **unpaid** work or are an **unpaid** worker, you do a job without receiving any money for it. 无报酬的 [ADJ n] ❑ *Even unpaid work for charity is better than nothing.* 甚至无偿的慈善工作也好过没事可做。 **2** ADJ **Unpaid** taxes or bills, for example, are taxes or bills which have not been paid yet. （税收或帐单）未缴纳的 ❑ *...millions of dollars in unpaid taxes.* …所欠的数百万美元的税款。

un·pal·at·able /ʌnpælɪtəbᵊl/ **1** ADJ If you describe an idea as **unpalatable**, you mean that you find it unpleasant and difficult to accept. 令人不愉快的；使人难以接受的 ❑ *It was only then that I began to learn the unpalatable truth about John.* 直到那时我才开始了解到有关约翰的令人难以接受的真相。 **2** ADJ If you describe food as **unpalatable**, you mean that it is so unpleasant that you can hardly eat it. 难以下咽的 ❑ *...a lump of dry, unpalatable cheese.* …一块干巴巴的、难以下咽的乳酪。

un·par·al·leled /ʌnpærəleld/ ADJ If you describe something as **unparalleled**, you are emphasizing that it is, for example, bigger, better, or worse than anything else of its kind, or anything that has happened before. 无比的 [EMPHASIS] ❑ *...a period of unparalleled economic growth.* …空前的经济增长时期。

un·pleas·ant /ʌnplɛzᵊnt/ **1** ADJ If something is **unpleasant**, it gives you bad feelings, for example by making you feel upset or uncomfortable. 使人不愉快的 ❑ *The symptoms can be uncomfortable, unpleasant and serious.* 其症状会是令人不舒服、不愉快且严重的。 ❑ *The vacuum has an unpleasant smell.* 这个真空吸尘器有股难闻的气味。 ● **un·pleas·ant·ly** ADV 令人不愉快地 ❑ *The water moved around the body, unpleasantly thick and brown.* 水在尸体周围流动，浓稠且呈褐色，令人恶心。 ❑ *The smell was unpleasantly strong.* 气味浓得令人难受。 **2** ADJ An **unpleasant** person is very unfriendly and rude. 不友好的；粗鲁的 ❑ *She thought he was an unpleasant man.* 她曾认为他是个令人不愉快的人。 ● **un·pleas·ant·ly** ADV 不友好地；粗鲁地 ❑ *Melissa laughed unpleasantly.* 梅利莎令人不愉快地笑着。

> **Thesaurus** *unpleasant* 另参见：
> ADJ. irksome, troublesome; (*ant.*) pleasant **1**
> mean, rude, unkind **2**

un·plug /ʌnplʌg/ (**unplugs, unplugging, unplugged**) V-T If you **unplug** an electrical device or telephone, you pull a wire out of an outlet so that it stops working. 拔去…的电源插头 ❑ *Whenever there's a storm, I unplug my computer.* 一有暴雨，我就拔掉电脑插头。

un·popu·lar /ʌnpɒpyʊlər/ ADJ If something or someone is **unpopular**, most people do not like them. 不受欢迎的 ❑ *It was a painful and unpopular decision.* 这是一个痛苦且不受欢迎的决定。 ❑ *In high school, I was very unpopular, and I did encounter a little prejudice.* 在中学，我很不受欢迎，确实遇到了一点偏见。 ● **un·popu·lar·ity** /ʌnpɒpyəlærɪti/ N-UNCOUNT 不受欢迎 ❑ *...his unpopularity among his colleagues.* …他在同事中不受欢迎。

★ **un·prec·edent·ed** /ʌnprɛsɪdɛntɪd/ **1** ADJ If something is **unprecedented**, it has never happened before. 史无前例的 ❑ *Such a move is rare, but not unprecedented.* 这样的举动少见，但并非从来没有过。 **2** ADJ If you describe something as **unprecedented**, you are emphasizing that it is very great in quality, amount, or scale. （质量、数量或规模）空前的 [EMPHASIS] ❑ *The mission has been hailed as an unprecedented success.* 这次使命已被宣布为一次空前的成功。

un·pre·dict·able /ʌnprɪdɪktəbᵊl/ ADJ If you describe someone or something as **unpredictable**, you mean that you cannot tell what they are going to do or how they are going to behave. 不可预测的 ❑ *He is utterly unpredictable.* 他这个人完全让人捉摸不透。 ● **un·pre·dict·abil·ity** /ʌnprɪdɪktəbɪlɪti/ N-UNCOUNT 不可预测性 [oft with poss] ❑ *...the unpredictability of the weather.* …天气的不可预测性。

un·pre·pared /ʌnprɪpɛərd/ **1** ADJ If you are **unprepared for** something, you are not ready for it, and you are therefore surprised or at a disadvantage when it happens. 无准备的 ❑ *I was totally unprepared for the announcement on the next day.* 我对次日的通告毫无准备。 ❑ *Faculty members complain that their students are unprepared to do college-level work.* 大学教师们抱怨他们的学生对大学阶段的学习没有做好准备。 **2** ADJ If you are **unprepared to** do something, you are not willing to do it. 不愿意的 [v-link ADJ to-inf] ❑ *They are unprepared to accept the real reasons for their domestic and foreign situation.* 他们不愿接受导致其国内外处境的真正原因。

un·pro·duc·tive /ʌnprədʌktɪv/ ADJ Something that is **unproductive** does not produce any good results. 没有效果的 ❑ *Research workers are well aware that much of their time and effort is unproductive.* 研究工作者们很清楚他们的大部分时间和努力都不会有成果。

un·pro·fes·sion·al /ʌnprəfɛʃənᵊl/ ADJ If you use **unprofessional** to describe someone's behavior at work, you are criticizing them for not behaving according to the standards that are expected of a person in their profession. 不专业的；（工作中的行为）未达到专业标准的 [DISAPPROVAL] ❑ *He was fired for unprofessional conduct.* 他因不专业的操作而被解雇。

un·prof·it·able /ʌnprɒfɪtəbᵊl/ **1** ADJ An industry, company, or product that is **unprofitable** does not make any profit or does not make enough profit. 不赢利的 [BUSINESS] ❑ *...unprofitable, badly-run industries.* …不赢利、经营不善的各企业 **2** ADJ **Unprofitable** activities or efforts do not produce any useful or helpful results. （活动或努力）无益的 ❑ *...an endless, unprofitable argument.* …一场没完没了、没有意义的争论。

un·pro·tect·ed /ʌnprətɛktɪd/ **1** ADJ An **unprotected** person or place is not watched over or defended, and so they may be harmed or attacked. （人或地方）未受保护的；未设防的 ❑ *The landing beaches would be unprotected.* 登陆的海滩可能没有设防。 **2** ADJ If something is **unprotected**, it is not covered or treated with anything, and so it may easily be damaged. 无保护的 ❑ *Exposure of unprotected skin to the sun carries the risk of developing skin cancer.* 无保护的皮肤在太阳暴晒下有患皮肤癌的危险。 **3** ADJ If two people have **unprotected** sex, they do not use a condom to protect against sexually-transmitted diseases and pregnancy. 未用避孕套的 [ADJ n] ❑ *...the dangers of unprotected sex.* …未用避孕套的性行为的危险。

un·pub·lished /ʌnpʌblɪʃt/ ADJ An **unpublished** book, letter, or report has never been published. An **unpublished** writer has never had his or her work published. 从未发表过的（书、信、报告）；从未发表过作品的（作者） ❑ *Much of his writing remains unpublished.* 他的许多作品仍未发表。

u

un·quali·fied /ʌnkwɒlɪfaɪd/ **1** ADJ If you are **unqualified**, you do not have any qualifications, or you do not have the right qualifications for a particular job. 无资格的 ❑ *She was unqualified for the job.* 她无资格做这份工作。 **2** ADJ **Unqualified** means total or unlimited. 完全的；不受限制的 [EMPHASIS] ❑ *The event was an unqualified success.* 这项活动取得了极大的成功。

un·ques·tion·able /ʌnkwɛstʃənəbᵊl/ ADJ If you describe something as **unquestionable**, you are emphasizing that it is so obviously true or real that nobody can doubt it. 无可置疑的 [EMPHASIS] ❑ *He inspires affection and respect as a man of unquestionable integrity.* 作为一个无可争议的正直的人，他赢得了人们的爱戴与尊敬。 ● **un·ques·tion·ably** /ʌnkwɛstʃənəbli/ ADV 毫无疑问地 [ADV with cl/group] ❑ *They have seen the change as unquestionably beneficial to the country.* 他们认为这场变革对该国无疑是很有益的。

un·rav·el /ʌnrævᵊl/ (**unravels, unraveling, unraveled**)

in BRIT, and sometimes in AM, use **unravelling, unravelled**

1 V-T/V-I If you **unravel** something that is knotted, woven, or knitted, or if it **unravels**, it becomes one straight piece again or separates into its different threads. 解开；拆散 ❑ *He could unravel a knot that others wouldn't even attempt.* 他能解开其他人甚至不敢尝试的绳结。 **2** V-T/V-I If you **unravel** a mystery or puzzle, or it **unravels**, it gradually becomes clearer until you can work out the answer to it. 揭开 ❑ *A young mother has flown to Iceland to unravel the mystery of her husband's disappearance.* 一个年轻母亲已飞到冰岛，去揭开她丈夫失踪之谜。

→ see **rope**

un·real /ʌnrɪl/ **1** ADJ If you say that a situation is **unreal**, you mean that it is so strange that you find it difficult to believe it is happening. 很奇异的 [v-link ADJ] ❑ *Then we won our next 10 games, which remains a record. It was unreal.* 接着我们赢了后面的10场比赛，而且到现在这仍然是最高纪录，真太神奇了。 ● **un·re·al·ity** /ʌnriælɪti/ N-UNCOUNT 奇异 ❑ *To his surprise he didn't feel too weak. Light-headed certainly, and with a sense of unreality, but able to walk.* 令他惊讶的是，他并没有感觉太虚弱，虽然头晕，并有些不真实感，但能走路。 **2** ADJ If you use **unreal** to describe something, you are critical of it because you think that it is not like, or not related to, things you expect to find in the real world. 虚构的 [DISAPPROVAL] ❑ *Almost all fictional detectives are unreal.* 几乎所有小说里的侦探都是虚构的。

un·re·al·is·tic /ʌnriəlɪstɪk/ ADJ If you say that someone is being **unrealistic**, you mean that they do not recognize the truth about a situation, especially about the difficulties involved in something they want to achieve. 不切实际的 ❑ *There are many who feel that the players are being completely unrealistic in their demands.* 许多人都觉得那些运动员的要求是完全不切实际的。 ❑ *It would be unrealistic to expect such a process ever to be completed.* 期望完成这样一个过程是不现实的。

un·rea·son·able /ʌnrizənəbᵊl/ **1** ADJ If you say that someone is being **unreasonable**, you mean that they are behaving in a way that is not fair or sensible. 不公平的；不明理的 ❑ *The strikers were being unreasonable in their demands, having rejected the deal two weeks ago.* 罢工者两周前拒绝接受协议，他们的要求变得不合理。 ❑ *It was her unreasonable behavior with a Texan playboy which broke up her marriage.* 她和一个得克萨斯的花花公子的不明智行为导致了她的婚姻破裂。 ● **un·rea·son·ably** /ʌnrizənəbli/ ADV 不公平地；不明理地 ❑ *We unreasonably expect near perfect behavior from our children.* 我们很不理智地期望孩子们有近乎完美的行为。 **2** ADJ An **unreasonable** decision, action, price, or amount seems unfair and difficult to justify. 不合理的；不讲道理的 ❑ *...unreasonable increases in the price of gas.* …汽油价格的不合理上涨。 ● **un·rea·son·ably** ADV 不合理地；不讲道理地 ❑ *The banks' charges are unreasonably high.* 银行的收费高得离谱。

un·rec·og·nis·able /ʌnrɛkəgnaɪzəbl, -naɪz-/ [BRIT] → see **unrecognizable**

Word Link *cogn ≈ knowing : cognitive, recognize, unrecognizable*

un·rec·og·niz·able /ʌnrɛkəgnaɪzəbl, -naɪz-/

in BRIT, also use **unrecognisable**

ADJ If someone or something is **unrecognizable**, they have become impossible to recognize or identify, for example because they have been greatly changed or damaged. 无法辨认的 [oft ADJ "to" n] ❑ *Today that same hotel is almost unrecognizable.* 如今那同一家旅馆几乎无法辨认了。

un·re·lat·ed /ʌnrɪleɪtɪd/ **1** ADJ If one thing is **unrelated to** another, there is no connection between them. You can also say that two things are **unrelated**. 不相关的 ❑ *My line of work is entirely unrelated to politics.* 我的职业与政治完全无关。 **2** ADJ If one person is **unrelated to** another, they are not members of the same family. You can also say that two people are **unrelated**. 无亲属关系的 [WRITTEN] ❑ *Jimmy is adopted and thus unrelated to Beth by blood.* 吉米是收养的，因此和贝丝无血缘关系。

un·re·lent·ing /ʌnrɪlɛntɪŋ/ **1** ADJ If you describe someone's behavior as **unrelenting**, you mean that they are continuing to do something in a very determined way, often without caring whether they hurt or embarrass other people. 不留情面地坚持的 ❑ *She established her authority with unrelenting thoroughness.* 她以彻底的一丝不苟树立了自己的权威。 **2** ADJ If you describe something unpleasant as **unrelenting**, you mean that it continues without stopping. 无休止的 (不愉快的事情) ❑ *...an unrelenting downpour of rain.* …一场下不停的倾盆大雨。

un·re·li·able /ʌnrɪlaɪəbᵊl/ ADJ If you describe a person, machine, or method as **unreliable**, you mean that you cannot trust them. 不可靠的 ❑ *Diplomats can be a notoriously unreliable and misleading source of information.* 外交官可能会提供不可靠的误导性信息，这是众所周知的。 ❑ *His judgment was unreliable.* 他的判断是不可靠的。

un·re·mark·able /ʌnrɪmɑrkəbᵊl/ ADJ If you describe someone or something as **unremarkable**, you mean that they are very ordinary, without many exciting, original, or attractive qualities. 普通的 ❑ *...a tall, lean man, with an unremarkable face.* …一个又高又瘦、长相普通的男子。

un·re·pent·ant /ʌnrɪpɛntənt/ ADJ If you are **unrepentant**, you are not ashamed of your beliefs or actions. 不感到羞愧的 ❑ *Pamela was unrepentant about her strong language and abrasive remarks.* 帕梅拉对自己激烈粗暴的言论不感到羞愧。

un·re·solved /ʌnrɪzɒlvd/ ADJ If a problem or difficulty is **unresolved**, no satisfactory solution has been found to it. 尚未解决的 ❑ *The murder remains unresolved.* 这宗谋杀案还没有侦破。

un·rest /ʌnrɛst/ N-UNCOUNT If there is **unrest** in a particular place or society, people are expressing anger and dissatisfaction about something, often by demonstrating or rioting. 骚乱 [JOURNALISM] ❑ *The real danger is civil unrest in the east of the country.* 真正的危险是该国东部的民众骚乱。

un·re·strict·ed /ʌnrɪstrɪktɪd/ **1** ADJ If an activity is **unrestricted**, you are free to do it in the way that you want, without being limited by any rules. 不受限制的 ❑ *Freedom to pursue extracurricular activities is totally unrestricted.* 参加课外活动的自由完全不受限制。 **2** ADJ If you have an **unrestricted** view of something, you can see it fully and clearly, because there is nothing in the way. 无遮拦的；(视线) 完全清楚的 ❑ *Nearly all seats have an unrestricted view.* 几乎所有的座位都没有任何东西阻挡视线。

un·ri·valed /ʌnraɪvᵊld/

in BRIT, use **unrivalled**

ADJ If you describe something as **unrivaled**, you are emphasizing that it is better than anything else of the same kind. 无与伦比的 [EMPHASIS] ❑ *He acquired unrivaled knowledge of party affairs.* 他掌握的党务工作知识无人可比。

un·ru·ly /ʌnruli/ **1** ADJ If you describe people, especially children, as **unruly**, you mean that they behave badly and are difficult to control. 难管教的 (尤指儿童) ❑ *...unruly behavior.* …不守规矩的行为。 **2** ADJ **Unruly** hair is difficult to keep tidy. 难梳理的 (头发) ❑ *The man had remarkably black, unruly hair.* 那个男子有一头不同寻常的乱蓬蓬的黑发。

un·safe /ʌnseɪf/ **1** ADJ If a building, machine, activity, or area is **unsafe**, it is dangerous. 危险的 ❑ *Critics claim the trucks are unsafe.* 批评者声称这些卡车很危险。 **2** ADJ If you are **unsafe**, you are in danger of being harmed. 不安全的 [v-link ADJ] ❑ *In the larger neighborhood, I felt very unsafe.* 在较大的街区，我感到非常不安全。

un·sat·is·fac·tory /ʌnsætɪsfæktəri/ ADJ If you describe something as **unsatisfactory**, you mean that it is not as good as it should be, and cannot be considered acceptable. 不能令人满意的 ❑ *He asked a few more questions, to which he received unsatisfactory answers.* 他又问了一些问题，没有得到满意的答案。

Thesaurus *unsatisfactory* 另参见：

ADJ. inadequate, insufficient, unacceptable; (*ant.*) satisfactory

U

un·sa·vory /ʌnseɪvəri/
in BRIT, use **unsavoury**
ADJ If you describe a person, place, or thing as **unsavory**, you mean that you find them unpleasant or morally unacceptable. 令人讨厌的；不道德的 [DISAPPROVAL] ❑ *Police officers meet more unsavory characters in a week than most of us do in a lifetime.* 警察在一个星期内遇到的令人厌恶的人比我们大多数人一生中遇见的还多。

un·sa·voury /ʌnseɪvəri/ [BRIT] → see **unsavory**

un·scathed /ʌnskeɪðd/ ADJ If you are **unscathed** after a dangerous experience, you have not been injured or harmed by it. 未受伤的；未受伤害的 [ADJ after v, v-link ADJ] ❑ *Tony emerged unscathed apart from a severely bruised finger.* 托尼结果除了一个手指严重淤青外，没受别的伤。 ❑ *East Los Angeles was left relatively unscathed by the riots.* 相对来说，洛杉矶东部没有受到骚乱的损害。

un·scru·pu·lous /ʌnskrupyələs/ ADJ If you describe a person as **unscrupulous**, you are critical of the fact that they are prepared to act in a dishonest or immoral way in order to get what they want. 不诚实的；不道德的 [DISAPPROVAL] ❑ *These kids are being exploited by very unscrupulous people.* 这些孩子正被极不道德的人利用。

un·secured /ʌnsɪkyʊərd/ ADJ **Unsecured** is used to describe loans or debts that are not guaranteed by a particular asset such as a person's home. 无担保的(贷款或债务) [BUSINESS] ❑ *Sam received an unsecured loan of $282,000.* 山姆接受了一笔28.2万的无担保贷款。

un·seen /ʌnsin/ **1** ADJ If you describe something as **unseen**, you mean that it has not been seen for a long time. 久未见过的 ❑ *...a spectacular ballroom, unseen by the public for over 30 years.* …公众三十多年未见过的一个豪华舞厅。 **2** ADJ You can use **unseen** to describe things which people cannot see. 看不见的 [ADJ n, ADJ after v] ❑ *For me, a performance is in front of a microphone, over the radio, to an unseen audience.* 对我来说，表演就是在麦克风前，通过无线电，传播给看不见的听众。

★ **un·set·tle** /ʌnsɛtᵊl/ (**unsettles, unsettling, unsettled**) V-T If something **unsettles** you, it makes you feel rather worried or uncertain. 使不安 ❑ *The presence of the two policemen unsettled her.* 两名警察的出现令她不安。

un·set·tled /ʌnsɛtᵊld/ **1** ADJ In an **unsettled** situation, there is a lot of uncertainty about what will happen. 动荡不安的 ❑ *The developments leave the airline with several problems, including an unsettled labor situation.* 事情的发展给航空公司带来了一些问题，其中包括不安定的劳工状况。 **2** ADJ If you are **unsettled**, you cannot concentrate on anything because you are worried. (因担忧) 不能集中精力的 [v-link ADJ] ❑ *To tell the truth, I'm a bit unsettled tonight.* 说实话，今晚我有点心神不安。 **3** ADJ An **unsettled** argument or dispute has not yet been resolved. 未解决的(争论) ❑ *They were in the process of resolving all the unsettled issues.* 他们正在解决所有未解决的问题。 **4** ADJ **Unsettled** weather is unpredictable and changes a lot. 变化莫测的(天气) ❑ *Despite the unsettled weather, we had a marvelous weekend.* 尽管天气多变，我们还是度过了一个精彩的周末。

un·set·tling /ʌnsɛtəlɪŋ/ ADJ If you describe something as **unsettling**, you mean that it makes you feel worried or uncertain. 令人担忧的；令人不安的 ❑ *Phil had several unsettling dreams every night.* 菲尔每晚都做好几个令他不安的梦。

un·sight·ly /ʌnsaɪtli/ ADJ If you describe something as **unsightly**, you mean that it is ugly. 难看的 ❑ *...an unsightly pile of garbage right in front of the restaurant.* …就在餐馆前面的一堆很不雅观的垃圾。

un·skilled /ʌnskɪld/ **1** ADJ People who are **unskilled** do not have any special training for a job. 未经专门训练的 ❑ *He worked as an unskilled laborer.* 他是一个未经专门训练的工人。 **2** ADJ **Unskilled** work does not require any special training. 无需专门技能的 ❑ *In the U.S., minorities and immigrants have generally gone into low-paid, unskilled jobs.* 在美国，少数民族和移民通常从事低报酬、无需专门技能的工作。

un·so·lic·it·ed /ʌnsəlɪsɪtɪd/ ADJ Something that is **unsolicited** has been given without being asked for and may not have been wanted. 未被请求的；主动提供的 ❑ *She's always full of unsolicited advice.* 她总是未被请求即提供一大堆建议。

un·solved /ʌnsɒlvd/ ADJ An **unsolved** mystery or problem has never been solved. 未解决的 ❑ *...America's unsolved problems of poverty and racism.* …美国尚未解决的贫穷和种族问题。

un·speak·able /ʌnspikəbᵊl/ ADJ If you describe something as **unspeakable**, you are emphasizing that it is extremely unpleasant. 糟到无法形容的 [EMPHASIS] ❑ *...the unspeakable horrors of chemical weapons.* …对化学武器难以名状的恐惧。 ❑ *The pain is unspeakable.* 这种痛苦是无法形容的。 ● **un·speak·ably** /ʌnspikəbli/ ADV 糟到无法形容地 ❑ *The novel was unspeakably boring.* 这部小说无聊得无法形容。

un·speci·fied /ʌnspɛsɪfaɪd/ ADJ You say that something is **unspecified** when you are not told exactly what it is. 未指明的 ❑ *The company said that an unspecified number of people were offered jobs.* 该公司说若干人得到了工作。

un·spoiled /ʌnspɔɪld/
in BRIT, also use **unspoilt** /ʌnspɔɪlt/
ADJ If you describe a place as **unspoiled**, you think it is beautiful because it has not been changed or built on for a long time. (地方因保持原样而) 有自然美的 ❑ *The port is quiet and unspoiled.* 这个港口很安静，有未受破坏的自然美。

un·spoilt /ʌnspɔɪlt/ [BRIT] → see **unspoiled**

un·spo·ken /ʌnspoʊkən/ **1** ADJ If your thoughts, wishes, or feelings are **unspoken**, you do not speak about them. 未说出的(想法、愿望或感情) ❑ *His face was expressionless, but Alex felt the unspoken criticism.* 他面无表情，但亚历克斯感觉到了他无言的批评。 **2** ADJ When there is an **unspoken** agreement or understanding between people, their behavior shows that they agree about something or understand it, even though they have never spoken about it. 有默契的 [ADJ n] ❑ *There was an unspoken agreement that he and Viv would look after the frail old couple.* 他和维夫有一个默契，一起照顾那对年老体弱的夫妇。

un·sta·ble /ʌnsteɪbᵊl/ **1** ADJ You can describe something as **unstable** if it is likely to change suddenly, especially if this creates difficulty or danger. 不稳定的 ❑ *The situation is unstable and potentially dangerous.* 情况不稳定，可能有危险。 **2** ADJ **Unstable** objects are likely to move or fall. 不牢固的 ❑ *Both clay and sandstone are unstable rock formations.* 黏土和砂岩都是不坚固的岩石构造。 **3** ADJ If people are **unstable**, their emotions and behavior keep changing because their minds are disturbed or upset. 多变的(情绪或行为) ❑ *He was emotionally unstable.* 他情绪多变。

un·steady /ʌnstɛdi/ **1** ADJ If you are **unsteady**, you have difficulty doing something, for example walking, because you cannot completely control your legs or your body. (走路等) 不稳的 ❑ *The boy was very unsteady and had staggered around when he got up.* 那男孩很难站稳，起身时摇摇晃晃。 ● **un·steadi·ly** /ʌnstɛdᵊli/ ADV 不稳地 [ADV with v] ❑ *She pulled herself unsteadily from the bed to the dresser.* 她拖着身子摇摇晃晃地从床走到梳妆台。 **2** ADJ If you describe something as **unsteady**, you mean that it is not regular or stable, but unreliable or unpredictable. 不规则的；无法捉摸的 ❑ *His voice was unsteady and only just audible.* 他的声音颤抖，只能勉强听清。 **3** ADJ **Unsteady** objects are not held, attached, or balanced securely. 不牢固的 ❑ *...a slightly unsteady table.* …一张有点不牢固的桌子。

un·sub·scribe /ʌnsəbskraɪb/ (**unsubscribes, unsubscribing, unsubscribed**) V-I If you **unsubscribe** from an online service, you send a message saying that you no longer wish to receive that service. 退订(网上服务) [COMPUTING] ❑ *Go to the website today and you can unsubscribe online.* 今天上网就能在线退订。

un·sub·stan·ti·at·ed /ʌnsəbstænʃieɪtɪd/ ADJ A claim, accusation, or story that is **unsubstantiated** has not been proven to be valid or true. 未经证实的 ❑ *I do object to their claim, which I find totally unsubstantiated.* 我确实反对他们的说法，我发现那是完全没有根据的。

un·suc·cess·ful /ʌnsəksɛsfəl/ **1** ADJ Something that is **unsuccessful** does not achieve what it was intended to achieve. 不成功的 ❑ *His efforts were unsuccessful.* 他的努力没有成功。 ❑ *...a second unsuccessful operation on his knee.* …他膝盖的第2次不成功手术。 ● **un·suc·cess·ful·ly** ADV 不成功地 [ADV with v] ❑ *He has been trying unsuccessfully to sell the business in one piece since early last year.* 自去年年初起，他一直没法成功地把整个企业一起卖掉。 **2** ADJ Someone who is **unsuccessful** does not achieve what they intended to achieve, especially in their career. (尤指事业上) 不成功的 ❑ *The difference between successful and unsuccessful people is that successful people put into practice the things they learn.* 成功者和失败者之间的区别是成功者将他们所学的东西付诸于实践。

un·suit·able /ʌnsutəbᵊl/ ADJ Someone or something that is **unsuitable for** a particular purpose or situation does not have the right qualities for it. 不合适的 ❑ *Amy's shoes were unsuitable for walking any distance.* 埃米的鞋根本不适合走路。

un·sure /ʌnʃʊər/ **1** ADJ If you are **unsure of yourself**, you lack confidence. 缺乏信心的 ❑ *The evening show was terrible, with hesitant unsure performances from all.* 晚上的演出很糟糕，所有人的表演都犹豫不决，缺乏信心。 **2** ADJ If you are **unsure about** something, you feel uncertain about it. 无把握的 [v-link ADJ] ❑ *Fifty-two percent were unsure about the idea.* 52%的人对这个想法都没有把握。

un·sus·pect·ing /ʌnsəspɛktɪŋ/ ADJ You can use **unsuspecting** to describe someone who is not at all aware of something that is happening or going to happen. 不知情的 ❑ *She threw a surprise party for her unsuspecting husband.* 她为她毫不知情的丈夫举办了一个惊喜聚会。

un·sym·pa·thet·ic /ʌnsɪmpəθɛtɪk/ **1** ADJ If someone is **unsympathetic**, they are not kind or helpful to a person in difficulties. 无同情心的 ❑ *Her husband was unsympathetic and she felt she had no one to turn to.* 她丈夫没有同情心，她感到无人可以求助。 **2** ADJ An **unsympathetic** person is unpleasant and difficult to like. 不讨人喜欢的 ❑ *...a very unsympathetic main character.* …一个很不讨人喜欢的主角。 **3** ADJ If you are **unsympathetic to** a particular idea or aim, you are not willing to support it. 对(某个想法或目标)不愿支持 [v-link ADJ "to" n] ❑ *I'm highly unsympathetic to what you are trying to achieve.* 我很不愿意支持你正在极力追求的目标。

un·ten·able /ʌntɛnəbəl/ ADJ An argument, theory, or position that is **untenable** cannot be defended successfully against criticism or attack. 不堪一击的(观点、理论或立场) ❑ *This argument is untenable from an intellectual, moral and practical standpoint.* 从知识、道德和现实的角度来看，这种论点是站不住脚的。

un·think·able /ʌnθɪŋkəbəl/ ADJ If you say that something is **unthinkable**, you are emphasizing that it cannot possibly be accepted or imagined as a possibility. 无法接受的；难以想像的 [EMPHASIS] ❑ *Her strong Catholic beliefs made abortion unthinkable.* 笃信天主教使她无法接受堕胎。 ● N-SING **The unthinkable** is something that is unthinkable. 无法接受的事物；难以想像的事物 ["the" N] ❑ *Teresa Zapata told her family the unthinkable; she was going to work in the United States.* 特雷莎・扎帕塔告诉了那件她的家人很难想像的事实，她打算到美国工作。

un·ti·dy /ʌntaɪdi/ [mainly BRIT] → see **messy**

Word Link	*un ≈ reversal : untie, unusual, unwrap*

un·tie /ʌntaɪ/ (**unties, untying, untied**) **1** V-T If you **untie** something that is tied to another thing or if you **untie** two things that are tied together, you remove the string or rope that holds them or that has been tied around them. 松开；解开 ❑ *Nicholas untied the boat from her mooring.* 尼古拉斯解开泊船的缆绳。 ❑ *Just untie my hands.* 快松开我的双手。 **2** V-T If you **untie** something such as string or rope, you undo it so that there is no knot or so that it is no longer tying something. 解开(绳结等) ❑ *She hurriedly untied the ropes binding her ankles.* 她赶紧解开绑着自己双脚的绳子。 **3** V-T When you **untie** your shoelaces or your shoes, you loosen or undo the laces of your shoes. 解开(鞋带等) ❑ *She untied the laces on one of her sneakers.* 她解开了她一只运动鞋的鞋带。

un·til ♦♦♦ /ʌntɪl/ **1** PREP If something happens **until** a particular time, it happens during the period before that time and stops at that time. 直到…为止 [PREP n/prep] ❑ *Until 2004, she lived in Canada.* 到2004年为止，她一直住在加拿大。 ● CONJ **Until** is also a conjunction. 直到…为止 ❑ *I waited until it got dark.* 我一直等到天黑。 **2** PREP You use **until** with a negative to emphasize the moment in time after which the rest of your statement becomes true, or the condition which would make it true. 直到…才 [PREP after neg] ❑ *The traffic laws don't take effect until the end of the year.* 交通法要到年底才生效。 ● CONJ **Until** is also a conjunction. 直到…才 ❑ *The government said that it has suspended all aid to Haiti until that country's legitimate government is restored.* 政府说它已经暂停对海地的所有援助，直到海地恢复合法政府为止。 **3** **up until** → see **up**

> Note that you only use **until** or **till** when you are talking about time. You do not use these words to talk about place or position. Instead, you should use **as far as** or **up to**. ❑ *Then you'll be riding with us as far as the village?... We walked up to where his bicycle was.*

un·told /ʌntoʊld/ **1** ADJ You can use **untold** to emphasize how bad or unpleasant something is. 不可名状的(用于强调事情的糟糕程度) [ADJ n] [EMPHASIS] ❑ *Landmines have caused untold misery to thousands of innocent people.* 地雷已给成千上万无辜的人带来了不可名状的苦难。 **2** ADJ You can use **untold** to emphasize that an amount or quantity is very large, especially when you are not sure how large it is. 难以计数的 [ADJ n] [EMPHASIS] ❑ *...the nation's untold millions of anglers.* …该国数百万的钓鱼爱好者。

un·touched /ʌntʌtʃt/ **1** ADJ Something that is **untouched by** something else is not affected by it. 不受影响的 [v-link ADJ, ADJ after v] ❑ *Asian airlines remain untouched by the deregulation that has swept the U.S.* 亚洲的航空公司没有受到已席卷美国的撤销管制的影响。 **2** ADJ If something is **untouched**, it is not damaged in any way, although it has been in a situation where it could easily have been damaged. 未受损害的 [v-link ADJ, ADJ after v] ❑ *Michael pointed out to me that in all the rubble, there was one building that remained untouched.* 迈克尔指给我看，在那一大片瓦砾中有一幢楼依然完好无损。 **3** ADJ An **untouched** area or place is thought to be beautiful because it is still in its original state and has not been changed or damaged in any way. 保持原样的；未受破坏的 ❑ *Ducie is one of the world's last untouched islands.* 迪西是世界上最后几个未受破坏的岛屿之一。 **4** ADJ If food or drink is **untouched**, none of it has been eaten or drunk. 未被吃过的；未被喝过的 ❑ *The coffee was untouched, the toast was cold.* 咖啡未被动过，吐司是冷的。

un·trained /ʌntreɪnd/ ADJ Someone who is **untrained** has not been taught the skills that they need for a particular job, activity, or situation. 未经培训的 ❑ *It is nonsense to say we have untrained staff dealing with emergencies.* 说我们让未经培训的员工去处理紧急情况，真是胡说八道。

un·treat·ed /ʌntritɪd/ **1** ADJ If an injury or illness is left **untreated**, it is not given medical treatment. 未经治疗的 ❑ *If left untreated, the condition may become chronic.* 如果得不到治疗，此病可能会转成慢性。 **2** ADJ **Untreated** materials, water, or chemicals are harmful and have not been made safe. 未经处理的(有害的材料、水或化学品) ❑ *...the dumping of nuclear waste and untreated sewage.* …核废料和未经处理的污水的倾倒。 **3** ADJ **Untreated** materials are in their natural or original state, often before being prepared for use in a particular process. 未经加工的 ❑ *All the bedding is made of simple, untreated cotton.* 所有的床上用品都是由未经加工的普通棉布制成的。

un·true /ʌntru/ ADJ If a statement or idea is **untrue**, it is false and not based on facts. 不真实的；没有事实根据的 ❑ *The allegations were completely untrue.* 这些指控完全没有事实根据。 ❑ *It was untrue to say that all political prisoners have been released.* 说所有的政治犯已被释放，这不是事实。

un·used

> Pronounced /ʌnyuzd/ for meaning **1**, and /ʌnyust/ for meaning **2**.

> 义项**1**读作 /ʌnyuzd/，义项**2**读作 /ʌnyust/。

1 ADJ Something that is **unused** has not been used or is not being used at the moment. 未用过的；目前不被使用的 ❑ *...unused containers of food.* …未用过的食物容器。 **2** ADJ If you are **unused to** something, you have not often done it or experienced it before, so it feels unusual and unfamiliar to you. 不习惯的 [v-link ADJ "to" n] ❑ *My mother was entirely unused to such hard work.* 我母亲完全不习惯这样的艰苦工作。

un·usual ♦◇◇ /ʌnyuʒuəl/ **1** ADJ If something is **unusual**, it does not happen very often or you do not see it or hear it very often. 不寻常的；不常见的 ❑ *They have replanted many areas with rare and unusual plants.* 他们在很多地方重新种上了稀有罕见的植物。 **2** ADJ If you describe someone as **unusual**, you think that they are interesting and different from other people. 与众不同的 ❑ *He was an unusual man with great business talents.* 他是一个与众不同的人，极具高超的商业才能。

> **Thesaurus** *unusual* 另参见：
> ADJ. abnormal, strange, uncommon; (*ant.*) usual **1**
> different, interesting, unconventional **2**

un·usu·al·ly /ʌnyuʒuəli/ **1** ADV You use **unusually** to emphasize that someone or something has more of a particular quality than is usual. 不寻常地 [ADV adj] [EMPHASIS] ❑ *He was an unusually complex man.* 他是个异常复杂的人。 **2** ADV You can use **unusually** to suggest that something is not what normally happens. 异常地 ❑ *Unusually, for a Japanese politician, he's a fluent English speaker.* 不同寻常的是，作为一位日本政府官员，他能讲流利的英语。

★ **un·veil** /ʌnveɪl/ (**unveils, unveiling, unveiled**) **1** V-T If someone formally **unveils** something such as a new statue or

U

painting, they draw back the curtain which is covering it. 为…揭幕 ❑ *...a ceremony to unveil a monument to the victims.* …死难者纪念碑揭幕仪式。 **2** V-T If you **unveil** a plan, new product, or some other thing that has been kept secret, you introduce it to the public. 公布 ❑ *Mr. Werner unveiled his new strategy this week.* 沃纳先生本周公布了他的新策略。 ❑ *Companies from across Europe are here to unveil their latest models.* 全欧洲的公司来到这里公布他们最新的模型。

un·want·ed /ʌnwɒntɪd/ ADJ If you say that something or someone is **unwanted**, you mean that you do not want them, or that nobody wants them. 不想要的；无人要的 ❑ *...the misery of unwanted pregnancies.* …意外怀孕的痛苦。 ❑ *She felt unwanted.* 她感到没人要她。 ❑ *Every year, thousands of unwanted animals are abandoned.* 每年，成千上万没人要的动物被遗弃。

un·war·rant·ed /ʌnwɔrəntɪd/ ADJ If you describe something as **unwarranted**, you are critical of it because there is no need or reason for it. 不必要的；无端的 [FORMAL, DISAPPROVAL] ❑ *Any attempt to discuss the issue of human rights was rejected as an unwarranted interference in the country's internal affairs.* 任何希望讨论人权问题的要求都被视为对该国内政的无端干涉而被拒绝了。

un·wel·come /ʌnwɛlkəm/ **1** ADJ An **unwelcome** experience is one that you do not like and did not want. 不喜欢的；不想要的 ❑ *The mayor delivered the unwelcome news that city employees may have to take unpaid time off.* 市长宣布了人们不想听到的消息，所有城市雇员可能不得不进行不带薪休工。 **2** ADJ If you say that a visitor is **unwelcome**, you mean that you did not want them to come. 不受欢迎的（来访者） ❑ *...an unwelcome guest.* …一个不受欢迎的客人。

un·well /ʌnwɛl/ ADJ If you are **unwell**, you are sick. 不舒服的；生病的 [V-LINK ADJ] ❑ *Their grandmother was feeling unwell and had to stay at home.* 他们的祖母感觉不舒服，只好呆在家里。

un·wieldy /ʌnwildi/ **1** ADJ If you describe an object as **unwieldy**, you mean that it is difficult to move or carry because it is so big or heavy. 笨重的 ❑ *They came panting up to his door with their unwieldy baggage.* 他们带着笨重的行李，气喘吁吁地来到他的门口。 **2** ADJ If you describe a system as **unwieldy**, you mean that it does not work very well as a result of it being too large or badly organized. 庞大而难以控制的（体制）

un·will·ing /ʌnwɪlɪŋ/ **1** ADJ If you are **unwilling** to do something, you do not want to do it and will not agree to do it. 不愿意的 ❑ *Initially the government was unwilling to accept the defeat.* 最初，政府不愿意接受失败。 ● **un·will·ing·ness** N-UNCOUNT 不愿意 ❑ *...their unwillingness to accept responsibility for mistakes.* …他们不愿意承担出错的责任。 **2** ADJ You can use **unwilling** to describe someone who does not really want to do the thing they are doing. 不情愿的 ❑ *A youthful teacher, he finds himself an unwilling participant in school politics.* 作为一位青年教师，他发现自己很不情愿地卷入了学校的权术之争。 ● **un·will·ing·ly** ADV 不情愿地 ❑ *He accepted his orders very unwillingly.* 他非常不情愿地接受了他的命令。

un·wind /ʌnwaɪnd/ (**unwinds, unwinding, unwound**) **1** V-I When you **unwind**, you relax after you have done something that makes you tense or tired. 放松 ❑ *It helps them to unwind after a busy day at work.* 这有助于他们在一天繁忙的工作后放松一下。 **2** V-T/V-I If you **unwind** a length of something that is wrapped around something else or around itself, you loosen it and make it straight. You can also say that it **unwinds**. 解开 ❑ *One of them unwound a length of rope from around his waist.* 他们中的一个人解开绕在他腰间的一条绳子。

un·wise /ʌnwaɪz/ ADJ If you describe something as **unwise**, you think that it is foolish and likely to lead to a bad result. 不明智的 ❑ *It would be unwise to expect too much.* 期望太多是不明智的。 ❑ *I think this is extremely unwise.* 我认为这是极端不明智的。 ● **un·wise·ly** ADV 不明智地 ❑ *She accepted that she had acted unwisely.* 她承认自己做得不明智。

un·wit·ting /ʌnwɪtɪŋ/ ADJ If you describe a person or their actions as **unwitting**, you mean that the person does something or is involved in something without realizing it. 无意的 ❑ *We were unwitting collaborators in his plan.* 我们无意中成为他的计划的协作者。 ● **un·wit·ting·ly** ADV 无意地 ❑ *He was unwittingly caught up in the confrontation.* 他无意中陷入了这场冲突。

★ **un·work·able** /ʌnwɜrkəbᵊl/ ADJ If a plan, law, or system is **unworkable**, it cannot be successful. 不可行的 ❑ *There is the strong possibility that such cooperation will prove unworkable.* 这种合作很有可能行不通。

Word Link	*worthy ≈ deserving, suitable : creditworthy, trustworthy, unworthy*

un·wor·thy /ʌnwɜrði/ ADJ If a person or thing is **unworthy of** something good, they do not deserve it. 不值得的 ❑ *You may feel unworthy of the attention and help people offer you.* 你可能觉得自己不值得别人的关心和帮助。

un·wound /ʌnwaʊnd/ **Unwound** is the past tense and past participle of **unwind**. **unwind**的过去式和过去分词

Word Link	*un ≈ reversal : untie, unusual, unwrap*

un·wrap /ʌnræp/ (**unwraps, unwrapping, unwrapped**) V-T When you **unwrap** something, you take off the paper, plastic, or other covering that is around it. 拆开（包装） ❑ *I untied the bow and unwrapped the small box.* 我解开蝴蝶结，拆开那个小盒子的包装。

un·writ·ten /ʌnrɪtᵊn/ **1** ADJ Something such as a book that is **unwritten** has not been printed or written down. 未付印的；未写好的 ❑ *Universal has agreed to pay $5 million for Grisham's next, as yet unwritten, novel.* 环球公司已同意给格里森姆的下一部还未完稿的小说支付500万美元。 **2** ADJ An **unwritten** rule, law, or agreement is one that is understood and accepted by everyone, although it may not have been formally or officially established. 不成文的 ❑ *They obey the one unwritten rule that binds them all—no talking.* 他们遵守那条约束他们所有人的不成文规定——不许说话。

un·zip /ʌnzɪp/ (**unzips, unzipping, unzipped**) **1** V-T/V-I When you **unzip** something which is fastened by a zipper or when it **unzips**, you open it by pulling open the zipper. 拉开（拉链）；（拉链）拉开 ❑ *James unzipped his bag.* 詹姆斯拉开他袋子的拉链。 **2** V-T To **unzip** a computer file means to open a file that has been compressed. 给（文档）解压缩 [COMPUTING] ❑ *Unzip the icons into a subdirectory.* 把图标解压到一个子目录。

up

❶ PREPOSITION, ADVERB, AND ADJECTIVE USES
❷ USED IN COMBINATION AS A PREPOSITION
❸ VERB USES

❶ **up** ♦♦♦

The preposition is pronounced /ʌp/. The adverb and adjective are pronounced /ʌp/.

介词读作 /ʌp/。副词和形容词读作 /ʌp/。

Up is often used with verbs of movement such as "jump" and "pull," and also in phrasal verbs such as "give up" and "wash up."

➪ **Please look at meaning 16 to see if the expression you are looking for is shown under another headword.** **1** PREP If a person or thing goes **up** something such as a slope, ladder, or chimney, they move away from the ground or to a higher position. 向上 ❑ *They were climbing up a narrow mountain road.* 他们正爬上一条狭窄的山路。 ❑ *I ran up the stairs and saw Alison lying at the top.* 我跑上楼梯，看见艾莉森躺在顶上。 ● ADV **Up** is also an adverb. 向上地 ❑ *Finally, after an hour, I went up to Jeremy's room.* 一个小时后，我终于上楼去了杰里米的房间。 ❑ *Intense balls of flame rose up into the sky.* 炙热的火球冲上天空。 **2** PREP If a person or thing is **up** something such as a ladder or a mountain, they are near the top of it. 靠近…顶端 ❑ *He was up a ladder sawing off the tops of his apple trees.* 他在梯子上锯苹果树的树冠。 ● ADV **Up** is also an adverb. 靠近顶端 [ADV after V] ❑ *...a research station perched 4,000 meters up on the lip of the crater.* …位于海拔4000米，靠近火山口的一个研究站。 **3** ADV You use **up** to indicate that you are looking or facing in a direction that is away from the ground or toward a higher level. 朝上 [ADV after V] ❑ *Keep your head up, and look around you from time to time.* 抬起头来，不时地环顾四周。 **4** ADV If someone stands **up**, they move so that they are standing. 起来 [ADV after V] ❑ *He stood up and went to the window.* 他站了起来，走向窗户。 **5** PREP If you go or look **up** something such as a road or river, you go or look along it. If you are **up** a road or river, you are somewhere along it. 沿着 [V PREP n] ❑ *A line of tanks came up the road from the city.* 一排坦克由市里沿路开过来了。 ❑ *We leaned on the wooden rail of the bridge and looked up the river.* 我们靠在桥的

u

木栏杆上，沿河望去。 **6** ADV If you are traveling to a particular place, you can say that you are going **up** to that place, especially if you are going toward the north or to a higher level of land. If you are already in such a place, you can say that you are **up** there. 向上(尤指向北方或向高处); 在(北方或高处) [mainly SPOKEN] ❑ *I'll be up to see you tomorrow.* 我明天上来看你。 ❑ *He was living up North.* 他当时正住在北方。 **7** ADV If you go **up** to something or someone, you move to the place where they are and stop there. 往 ❑ *The girl ran the rest of the way across the street and up to the car.* 那个女孩穿过街道，跑完剩下的一段路，来到那辆车旁。 ❑ *On the way out a boy of about ten came up on roller skates.* 在出去的路上，一个大约十岁的男孩穿着旱冰鞋滑了过来。 **8** ADV If an amount of something goes **up**, it increases. If an amount of something is **up**, it has increased and is at a higher level than it was. 增多; 上涨 ❑ *The total budget went up almost $300 million.* 总预算几乎增加了3亿美元。 ❑ *Tourism is up, jobs are up, individual income is up.* 旅游火了，职位多了，个人收入涨了。 **9** ADJ If you are **up**, you are not in bed. 起床的 [v-link ADJ] ❑ *Are you sure you should be up?* 你肯定你该起床了吗? ❑ *These days they were up at the crack of dawn.* 这些天他们在破晓时就起床。 **10** ADJ If a period of time is **up**, it has come to an end. (时间) 到点的 [v-link ADJ] ❑ *The moment the half-hour was up, Brooks rose.* 半小时一到，布鲁克斯就起来了。 **11** ADJ If a computer or computer system is **up**, it is working. Compare **down**. (计算机或计算机系统) 工作的 [v-link ADJ] ❑ *The new system is up and ready to run.* 新系统工作了，可以开始运行了。 **12** PHRASE If someone who has been in bed for some time, for example because they have been sick, is **up and about**, they are now out of bed and living their normal life. 已下床从事正常活动的 ❑ *How are you Lennox? Good to see you up and about.* 伦诺克斯你好吗? 真高兴看到你恢复正常活动了。 **13** PHRASE If you say that **something is up**, you mean that something is wrong or that something worrying is happening. 出问题 [INFORMAL] ❑ *What is it then? Something's up, isn't it?* 那么这是怎么回事? 出问题了，是不是? **14** PHRASE If you say to someone **"What's up?"** or if you tell them **what's up**, you are asking them or telling them what is wrong or what is worrying them. 出了什么事? [INFORMAL] ❑ *"What's up?" I said to him.—"Just tired," he answered.* "出了什么事?" 我对他说。—— "只是累了，" 他答道。 **15** PHRASE If you move **up and down** somewhere, you move there repeatedly in one direction and then in the opposite direction. 上下地; 来来回回 ❑ *I used to jump up and down to keep warm.* 我过去常常上下跳动来保暖。 ❑ *I strolled up and down thoughtfully before calling a taxi.* 叫出租车前，我若有所思地来回踱步。 **16** **up in arms** → see **arm**

❷ up ♦♦♦ /ʌp/

➪ **Please look at meaning 9 to see if the expression you are looking for is shown under another headword.** **1** PHRASE If you feel **up to** doing something, you are well enough to do it. 能胜任 ❑ *Those patients who were up to it could move to the adjacent pool.* 身体状况允许的病人可以到旁边的那个游泳池去。 ❑ *His fellow directors were not up to running the business without him.* 没有他，其他主管管理不了这家企业。 **2** PHRASE To be **up to** something means to be secretly doing something that you should not be doing. 捣鬼 [INFORMAL] ❑ *Why did you need a room unless you were up to something?* 除非你要捣什么鬼，不然为什么需要一个房间呢? ❑ *They must have known what their father was up to.* 他们一定已经知道他们的父亲在暗地里做什么。 **3** PHRASE If you say that it is **up to** someone to do something, you mean that it is their responsibility to do it. 是…的责任 ❑ *It was up to him to make it right, no matter how long it took.* 不管需要花多长时间，把事情摆平是他的责任。 ❑ *I'm sure I'd have spotted him if it had been up to me.* 要是换了我，我肯定已经认出他了。 **4** PHRASE **Up until** or **up to** are used to indicate the latest time at which something can happen, or the end of the period of time that you are referring to. 直至 ❑ *Please feel free to call me any time up until 9:30 at night.* 晚上9:30之前随时都可以给我打电话。 **5** PHRASE You use **up to** to say how large something can be or what level it has reached. 多达; 高达 ❑ *Up to twenty thousand students paid between five and six thousand dollars.* 多达2万名学生支付了5000到6000美元。 **6** PHRASE If someone or something is **up for** election, review, or discussion, they are about to be considered. 将被考虑 ❑ *A third of the Senate and the entire House are up for re-election.* 1/3的参议员和全体众议员将重新选举。 **7** PHRASE If you are **up for** something, you are willing or eager to do it. 愿意做; 急于做 [INFORMAL] ❑ *I'm starved. Who's up for pizza?* 我快饿死了。谁想吃比萨饼? **8** PHRASE If you are **up against** something, you have a very difficult situation or problem to deal with. 面临(困境或困难) ❑ *The chairwoman is up against the greatest challenge to her position.* 女主席面临她职位的最大挑战。 **9** **up to par** → see **par**

❸ up /ʌp/ (**ups, upping, upped**) **1** V-T If you **up** something such as the amount of money you are offering for something, you increase it. 增加; 提高 ❑ *He upped his offer for the company.* 他提高了对该公司的出价。 ❑ *Drug stores upped sales by 63 percent.* 药店的销售额增加了63%。 **2** V-I If you **up** and leave a place, you go away from it, often suddenly or unexpectedly. 突然行动 ❑ *One day he just upped and left.* 有一天他突然离开了。

up-and-coming ADJ **Up-and-coming** people are likely to be successful in the future. 有望成功的 [ADJ n] ❑ *...his readiness to share the limelight with young, up-and-coming stars.* …他愿意与年轻有为的明星们一起成为公众关注的焦点。

up·beat /ʌpbit/ ADJ If people or their opinions are **upbeat**, they are cheerful and hopeful about a situation. 乐观的 [INFORMAL] ❑ *The Defense Secretary gave an upbeat assessment of the war so far.* 国防部长对迄今为止的战事进行了乐观的评价。 ❑ *Neil's colleagues said he was actually in a joking, upbeat mood in spite of the bad news.* 尼尔的同事说，尽管有这样的坏消息，他居然还有心情嬉笑、逗乐。

up·bring·ing /ʌpbrɪŋɪŋ/ N-UNCOUNT Your **upbringing** is the way that your parents treat you and the things that they teach you when you are growing up. 教养 ❑ *Martin's upbringing shaped his whole life.* 马丁的教养影响了他的一生。

★ **up·com·ing** /ʌpkʌmɪŋ/ ADJ **Upcoming** events will happen in the near future. 即将发生的 [ADJ n] ❑ *We'll face a tough fight in the upcoming election.* 我们在即将到来的竞选中将面临一场恶战。

★ **up·date** /ʌpdeɪt/ (**updates, updating, updated**)

> The verb is pronounced /ʌpdeɪt/. The noun is pronounced /ʌpdeɪt/.

> 动词读作 /ʌpdeɪt/。名词读作 /ʌpdeɪt/。

1 V-T/V-I If you **update** something, you make it more modern, usually by adding new parts to it or giving new information. 更新 ❑ *He was back in the office, updating the work schedule on the computer.* 他回到办公室，在计算机上更新了工作日程。 ❑ *Airlines would prefer to update rather than retrain crews.* 航空公司宁愿增添新机组人员而不愿对老的机组人员进行再培训。 **2** N-COUNT An **update** is a news item containing the latest information about a particular situation. 最新消息; 快讯 ❑ *She had heard the newsflash on a TV channel's news update.* 她在电视频道的新闻快讯里听到了这条简短报道。 ❑ *...a weather update.* …最新天气预报。 **3** V-T If you **update** someone **on** a situation, you tell them the latest developments in that situation. 给…提供最新信息 ❑ *We'll update you on the day's top news stories.* 我们将向你提供当天的头条新闻。

★ **up front** also **up-front** **1** ADJ If you are **up front about** something, you act openly or publicly so that people know what you are doing or what you believe. 坦率的 [INFORMAL] ❑ *You can't help being biased so you may as well be up front about it.* 你阻止不了别人对你的偏见，因此你还不如就大大方方地接受。 **2** ADV If a payment is made **up front**, it is made in advance and openly, so that the person being paid can see that the money is there. 预付地 [ADV after v] ❑ *Some companies charge a fee up front, but we don't think that's right.* 一些公司预先收费，但我们不认为这是对的。 ● ADJ **Up front** is also an adjective. 预付的 [ADJ n] ❑ *The eleven percent loan has no up-front costs.* 11%的那笔贷款没有预付费用。

★ **up·grade** /ʌpgreɪd, -greɪd/ (**upgrades, upgrading, upgraded**) **1** V-T If equipment or services **are upgraded**, they are improved or made more efficient. 使升级 [usu passive] ❑ *Helicopters have been upgraded and modernized.* 直升机已经升级并且装上现代化设备。 ❑ *Medical facilities are being reorganized and upgraded.* 医疗设施正在进行重组和升级。 ● N-COUNT **Upgrade** is also a noun. 升级 ❑ *...equipment which needs expensive upgrades.* …需要进行昂贵升级的设备。 **2** V-T If someone **is upgraded**, their job or status is changed so that they become more important or receive more money. 提升 [usu passive] ❑ *He was upgraded to security guard.* 他被提升为保安。 **3** V-T/V-I If you **upgrade** or **are upgraded**, you change something such as your plane ticket or your hotel room to one that is more expensive. 使升舱; 使(旅馆房间等) 升级; 升舱; 升级 ❑ *His family was upgraded from economy to business class.* 他的家人从经济舱升到了商务舱。 → see **hotel**

up·heav·al /ʌphivəl/ (**upheavals**) N-COUNT An **upheaval** is a big change which causes a lot of trouble, confusion, and worry. 动乱 ❑ *Algeria has been going through political upheaval for the past two months.* 在过去的两个月里，阿尔及利亚一直经历着政治动乱。

up·held /ʌphɛld/ **Upheld** is the past tense and past participle of **uphold**. **uphold**的过去式和过去分词

up·hill /ʌphɪl/ **1** ADV If something or someone is **uphill** or is moving **uphill**, they are near the top of a hill or are going up a slope. 靠近山顶；上坡地；在高处 ❑ *He had been running uphill a long way.* 他向上坡跑了很长的一段路。 ❑ *The man was no more than ten yards away and slightly uphill.* 那个男子就在不到10码远、位置稍高一点的地方。 ● ADJ **Uphill** is also an adjective. 在高处的；上坡的 ❑ *...a long, uphill journey.* …一段漫长的上坡路。 **2** ADJ If you refer to something as an **uphill** battle or an **uphill** struggle, you mean that it requires a lot of effort and determination, but it should be possible to achieve it. (战斗或斗争) 艰难的 [ADJ n] ❑ *It had been an uphill battle to achieve what she had wanted.* 她经过艰难的奋斗才达到她想要的目标。

★ **up·hold** /ʌphoʊld/ (**upholds, upholding, upheld**) **1** V-T If you **uphold** something such as a law, a principle, or a decision, you support and maintain it. 维护 ❑ *Our policy has been to uphold the law.* 我们的政策一直是维护法律。 ❑ *It is the responsibility of every government to uphold certain basic principles.* 每个政府都有责任维护某些基本原则。 **2** V-T If a court of law **upholds** a legal decision that has already been made, it decides that it was the correct decision. 维持 (原判) ❑ *The State Supreme Court upheld the Superior Court judge's decision.* 国家最高法院维持了高级法院法官的判决。

up·hol·stery /ʌphoʊlstəri, əpoʊl-/ N-UNCOUNT **Upholstery** is the soft covering on chairs and seats that makes them more comfortable to sit on. 座套 ❑ *...white leather upholstery.* …白色皮座套。

up·keep /ʌpkip/ **1** N-UNCOUNT The **upkeep** of a building or place is the work of keeping it in good condition. 维护 ❑ *The money will be used for the upkeep of the park.* 这些钱将用于该公园的维护。 **2** N-UNCOUNT The **upkeep** of a group of people or services is the process of providing them with the things that they need. 供养；维持 ❑ *He offered to pay $250 a month toward his son's upkeep.* 他提出每月支付$250作为儿子的抚养费。

up·lift·ing /ʌplɪftɪŋ/ ADJ You describe something as **uplifting** when it makes you feel very cheerful and happy. 令人振奋的 ❑ *...a charming and uplifting love story.* …一个引人入胜、令人振奋的爱情故事。

up·load /ʌploʊd/ (**uploads, uploading, uploaded**) V-T If you **upload** data, you transfer it from a disk to your computer or from your computer to another computer. 上传 [COMPUTING] ❑ *All you need to do is upload the files on to your web space.* 你所需要做的只是把文件上传到你的网络空间。

up·market /ʌpmɑrkɪt/ also **up-market** ADJ **Upmarket** products or services are expensive, of good quality, and intended to appeal to people with money and education. 高端的 (产品或服务) [mainly BRIT]

in AM, usually use **upscale**

upon ♦♦◊ /əpɒn/

In addition to the uses shown below, **upon** is used in phrasal verbs such as "come upon" and "look upon," and after some other verbs such as "decide" and "depend."

1 PREP If one thing is **upon** another, it is on it. 在…上 [LITERARY] ❑ *He set the tray upon the table.* 他把盘子放在桌上。 ❑ *He bent forward and laid a kiss softly upon her forehead.* 他俯下身，在她的前额温柔地吻了一下。 **2** PREP You use **upon** when mentioning an event that is followed immediately by another event. 一…就 [PREP -ing/n] [FORMAL] ❑ *The door on the left, upon entering the church, leads to the Crypt of St. Issac.* 一进入教堂，左侧的门就通往圣以撒之墓。 **3** PREP You use **upon** between two occurrences of the same noun in order to say that there are large numbers of the thing mentioned. …又… [n PREP n] ❑ *Row upon row of women surged forwards.* 一排又一排的妇女向前涌去。 **4** PREP If an event is **upon** you, it is just about to happen. 即将发生 [PREP pron] [LITERARY] ❑ *The long-threatened storm was upon us.* 那场预示已久的暴风雨即将来临。 ❑ *The wedding season is upon us.* 婚礼旺季即将来临。

up·per ♦◊◊ /ʌpər/ **1** ADJ You use **upper** to describe something that is above something else. 上面的 [ADJ n, "the" ADJ] ❑ *There is a good restaurant on the upper floor.* 楼上有一家很好的餐馆。 **2** ADJ You use **upper** to describe the higher part of something. 较高的 (部位) [ADJ n] ❑ *...the upper part of the foot.* …脚面。 ❑ *...the muscles of the upper back and chest.* …上背部和胸部的肌肉。 **3** PHRASE If you have **the upper hand** in a situation, you have an advantage over other people involved, for example because you have more power or success. 优势 ❑ *The home team was beginning to gain the upper hand.* 主队正开始占上风。

upper·case /ʌpərkeɪs/ also **upper case** ADJ **Uppercase** letters are capital letters. 大写的 (字母) ❑ *Most schools teach children lowercase letters first, and uppercase letters later.* 大多数学校先教孩子们小写字母，后教大写字母。 ● N-UNCOUNT **Uppercase** is also a noun. 大写字母 ❑ *They should use uppercase.* 他们应该使用大写字母。

up·per class (**upper classes**) also **upper-class** N-COUNT-COLL The **upper class** or the **upper classes** are the group of people in a society who own the most property and have the highest social status, and who may not need to work for money. 上层阶级 ❑ *...goods specifically designed to appeal to the tastes of the upper class.* …为迎合上层阶级的品味而专门设计的商品。 ● ADJ **Upper class** is also an adjective. 上层阶级的 ❑ *All of them came from wealthy, upper class families.* 他们所有人都来自富裕的上层阶级家庭。

up·right /ʌpraɪt/ (**uprights**) **1** ADJ If you are sitting or standing **upright**, you are sitting or standing with your back straight, rather than bending or lying down. 笔直的 ❑ *Helen sat upright in her chair.* 海伦笔直地坐在椅子上。 ❑ *He moved into an upright position.* 他换成了一个挺直的姿势。 **2** ADJ An **upright** vacuum cleaner or freezer is tall rather than wide. 立式的 (吸尘器或冰箱) [ADJ n] **3** ADJ An **upright** chair has a straight back and no arms. 有靠背无扶手的 (椅子) ❑ *He was sitting on an upright chair beside his bed, reading.* 他正坐在床边一把有靠背无扶手的椅子上阅读。 **4** N-COUNT You can refer to vertical posts or the vertical parts of an object as **uprights**. 立柱 ❑ *...the uprights of a canopy bed.* …一张顶篷床的立柱。 **5** ADJ You can describe people as **upright** when they are careful to follow acceptable rules of behavior and behave in a moral way. 正直的 ❑ *...a very upright, trustworthy man.* …一个非常正直、值得信任的人。

▲ **up·ris·ing** /ʌpraɪzɪŋ/ (**uprisings**) N-COUNT When there is an **uprising**, a group of people start fighting against the people who are in power in their country, because they want to bring about a political change. 起义 ❑ *...an uprising against the government.* …反对政府的一次起义。

▲ **up·roar** /ʌprɔr/ **1** N-UNCOUNT If there is **uproar**, there is a lot of shouting and noise because people are very angry or upset about something. 骚动 [also "a" N, oft "in" N] ❑ *The announcement caused an uproar in the crowd.* 公告在人群中引起了一阵骚动。 **2** N-UNCOUNT You can also use **uproar** to refer to a lot of public criticism and debate about something that has made people angry. 哗然 [also "a" N] ❑ *The town is in an uproar over the dispute.* 该城对此争端一片哗然。

▲ **up·root** /ʌprut/ (**uproots, uprooting, uprooted**) **1** V-T If you **uproot yourself** or if you **are uprooted**, you leave, or are made to leave, a place where you have lived for a long time. 使…离开家园 ❑ *...the trauma of uprooting themselves from their homes.* …他们背井离乡的痛苦经历。 ❑ *He had no wish to uproot Dena from her present home.* 他没想让德娜搬离她现在的家。 **2** V-T If someone **uproots** a tree or plant, or if the wind **uproots** it, it is pulled out of the ground. 把…连根拔起 ❑ *They had been forced to uproot their vines and plant wheat.* 他们早已被迫把葡萄藤连根拔起，种上小麦。 ❑ *...fallen trees which have been uprooted by the storm.* …被暴风连根拔起而倒下的树。

up·scale /ʌpskeɪl/ ADJ **Upscale** is used to describe products or services that are expensive, of good quality, and intended to appeal to people with a lot of money and education. 高档的 (产品和服务) [usu ADJ n] [AM] ❑ *...upscale department-store chains such as Bloomingdale's and Saks Fifth Avenue.* …如布卢明代尔百货和萨克斯第五大街这样的高档连锁百货商店。 ● ADV **Upscale** is also an adverb. 向高档地 [ADV after v]

in BRIT, use **upmarket**

❑ *T-shirts, the epitome of American casualness, have moved upscale.* T恤，美国人的随意的标志，已提升至高档商品之列。

up·set ♦◊◊ (**upsets, upsetting, upset**)

The verb and adjective are pronounced /ʌpsɛt/. The noun is pronounced /ʌpsɛt/.

动词和形容词读作 /ʌpsɛt/。名词读作 /ʌpsɛt/。

1 ADJ If you are **upset**, you are unhappy or disappointed because something bad has happened to you. 难过的；沮丧的 ❑ *After she died I felt very, very upset.* 她死后，我感觉非常非常难过。 ❑ *Marta looked*

U

upset. 玛尔塔看起来很沮丧。● N-COUNT **Upset** is also a noun. 烦恼；失望 ❑ *...stress and other emotional upsets.* …压力和其他情感上的烦恼。 **2** V-T If something **upsets** you, it makes you feel worried or unhappy. 使…烦恼；使…不高兴 ❑ *The whole incident had upset me and my fiancee terribly.* 整个事件已使我和我的未婚妻非常烦恼。 ❑ *She warned me not to say anything to upset him.* 她警告我不要说任何让他心烦的话。● **up·set·ting** ADJ 令人烦恼的；使人不高兴的 ❑ *Childhood sickness can be upsetting for children and parents alike.* 童年的疾病能使孩子和父母同样苦恼。 **3** V-T If events **upset** something such as a procedure or a state of affairs, they cause it to go wrong. 搅乱 ● N-COUNT **Upset** is also a noun. 混乱 ❑ *Markets are very sensitive to any upsets in the Japanese economic machine.* 市场对日本经济机器里的任何混乱都是非常敏感的。 **4** V-T If you **upset** an object, you accidentally knock or push it over so that it scatters over a large area. 弄翻 ❑ *Don't upset the piles of sheets under the box.* 别碰乱了盒子下面的那几摞纸。 **5** N-COUNT A stomach **upset** is a slight sickness in your stomach caused by an infection or by something that you have eaten. (胃) 不舒服 ❑ *Paul was unwell last night with a stomach upset.* 保罗昨晚胃不舒服。● ADJ **Upset** is also an adjective. 不舒服的 [ADJ n] ❑ *Larry has an upset stomach.* 拉里肠胃不适。 **6** to **upset the applecart** → see **applecart**

→ see **anger**

Thesaurus *upset* 另参见：

ADJ.	disappointed, hurt, unhappy; *(ant.)* happy **1**
	ill, sick, unsettled **5**
V.	overturn, spill, topple **4**

Word Partnership *upset* 的常用搭配：

PREP.	upset **about/by/over** *something* **1**
ADV.	**so** upset, **very** upset, **visibly** upset **1**
	really upset **1 2**
V.	**become** upset, **feel** upset, **get** upset **1 5**
N.	**stomach** upset (*or* upset **stomach**) **5**

up·shot /ʌpʃɒt/ N-SING **The upshot** of a series of events or discussions is the final result of them, usually a surprising result. (通常指出乎意外的) 结果 ❑ *The upshot is that we have lots of good but not very happy employees.* 令人意想不到的结果是，我们有许多优秀但却不快乐的雇员。

★ **up·side** /ʌpsaɪd/ (**upsides**) N-COUNT The **upside** of an unpleasant situation is the aspect of it that is more pleasant or positive. 好的方面 ❑ *Residents said the only upside would be a boost to the island's economy.* 居民们说唯一好的方面会是对该岛经济的促进。

up·side down /ʌpsaɪd daʊn/ also **upside-down** ADV If something is or has been turned **upside down**, it has been turned around so that the part that is usually lowest is above the part that is usually highest. 倒置地 ❑ *The painting was hung upside down.* 这幅画挂颠倒了。● ADJ **Upside down** is also an adjective. 颠倒的 ❑ *...chandeliers that resemble upside-down wedding cakes.* …酷似倒置的婚礼蛋糕形状的吊灯。

up·stage /ʌpsteɪdʒ/ (**upstages, upstaging, upstaged**) V-T If someone **upstages** you, they draw attention away from you by being more attractive or interesting. 抢…的风头 ❑ *He had a younger brother who always publicly upstaged him.* 他有个弟弟，总是公开抢他的风头。

up·stairs /ʌpstɛərz/ **1** ADV If you go **upstairs** in a building, you go up a staircase toward a higher floor. 往楼上 [ADV after v] ❑ *He went upstairs and changed into clean clothes.* 他上楼换了干净的衣裳。 **2** ADV If something or someone is **upstairs** in a building, they are on a floor that is higher than the ground floor. 在楼上 ❑ *The restaurant is upstairs and consists of a large, open room.* 餐馆在楼上，是一个宽敞的大开间。 **3** ADJ An **upstairs** room or object is situated on a floor of a building that is higher than the ground floor. 楼上的 [ADJ n] ❑ *Marsani moved into the upstairs apartment.* 玛萨妮搬进了楼上的公寓。 **4** N-SING **The upstairs** of a building is the floor or floors that are higher than the ground floor. 一楼以上的楼层 ❑ *Together we went through the upstairs.* 我们一起走过上面各楼层。

up·start /ʌpstɑrt/ (**upstarts**) N-COUNT You can refer to someone as an **upstart** when they behave as if they are important, but you think that they are too new in a place or job to be treated as important. 自命不凡的新手 [DISAPPROVAL] ❑ *Many prefer a familiar authority figure to a young upstart.* 许多人更喜欢熟悉的权威人物而不喜欢自命不凡的年轻新贵。

U

up·stream /ʌpstrim/ ADV Something that is moving **upstream** is moving toward the source of a river against the current, from a point further down the river. Something that is **upstream** is toward the source of a river. 向上游 ❑ *Salmon manage to swim upstream to lay their eggs.* 三文鱼设法游到上游产卵。 ❑ *...the river police, whose headquarters are just upstream of the Ile St. Louis.* …总部就设在圣路易斯岛上游的水警。● ADJ **Upstream** is also an adjective. 上游的 [ADJ n] ❑ *We'll go to the upstream side of that big rock.* 我们将去那块大岩石的上游一侧。

up·surge /ʌpsɜrdʒ/ N-SING If there is an **upsurge in** something, there is a sudden, large increase in it. 剧增 ❑ *...the upsurge in oil prices.* …油价的暴涨。

up·tight /ʌptaɪt/ ADJ Someone who is **uptight** is tense, nervous, or annoyed about something and so is difficult to be with. 紧张不安的 [INFORMAL] ❑ *Penny never got uptight about exams.* 彭尼从未对考试感到紧张。

up-to-date also **up to date** **1** ADJ If something is **up-to-date**, it is the newest thing of its kind. 最新的 ❑ *...the most up-to-date information available on foods today.* …今日有关食物的最新消息。 ❑ *Web services are always up-to-date and available.* 网络服务总是最新的且随时可用。 **2** ADJ If you are **up-to-date** about something, you have the latest information about it. 掌握最新信息的 ❑ *We'll keep you up to date with any news.* 我们将让你了解最新消息。

up·town /ʌptaʊn/ ADV If you go **uptown**, or go to a place **uptown**, you go away from the center of a city or town toward the edge. **Uptown** sometimes refers to a part of the city other than the main business district. 在市郊；非商业区 [ADV after v] [mainly AM] ❑ *He rode uptown and made his way to Bob's apartment.* 他骑车到市郊，来到鲍勃的公寓。 ❑ *Susan continued to live uptown.* 苏珊继续住在市郊。● ADJ **Uptown** is also an adjective. 市郊的 [ADJ n] ❑ *...uptown clubs.* …市郊的俱乐部。 ❑ *...a small uptown radio station.* …市郊的一个小电台。

up·trend /ʌptrend/ N-SING An **uptrend** is a general improvement in something such as a market or the economy. (市场、经济等的) 上升趋势 ❑ *Racal Electronics shares have been in a strong uptrend.* 瑞卡尔电子公司的股票已处在强劲上升趋势中。

up·turn /ʌptɜrn/ (**upturns**) N-COUNT If there is an **upturn** in the economy or in a company or industry, it improves or becomes more successful. (经济、公司或行业的) 好转 [BUSINESS] ❑ *They do not expect an upturn in the economy until the end of the year.* 他们预计经济要到年底才可能好转。

up·ward /ʌpwərd/

The form **upwards** is also used for the adverb.

1 ADJ An **upward** movement or look is directed towards a higher place or a higher level. 向上的 [ADJ n] ❑ *She started once again on the steep upward climb.* 她再次沿着峭壁开始向上攀爬。 ❑ *She gave him a quick, upward look, then lowered her eyes.* 她飞速地抬眼看了看他，然后又垂下双眼。 **2** ADJ If you refer to an **upward** trend or an **upward** spiral, you mean that something is increasing in quantity or price. 上升的 (趋势、螺旋) [ADJ n] ❑ *...the Army's concern that the upward trend in the numbers avoiding military service may continue.* …军方对逃避服兵役者数量的上升趋势可能继续下去的担忧。 **3** ADV If someone moves or looks **upward**, they move or look up toward a higher place. 向上 ❑ *They climbed upward along the steep cliffs surrounding the village.* 他们沿着环绕村庄的陡峭悬崖向上爬。 ❑ *"There," said Jack, pointing upwards.* "那儿，"杰克往上指着说。 **4** ADV If an amount or rate moves **upward**, it increases. (数量、比率) 向上 (增涨) [ADV after v] ❑ *...with prices soon heading upward in stores.* …随着商店里价格迅速上涨。 ❑ *Unemployment will continue upward for much of this year.* 失业率今年大部分时间将继续上升。 **5** PHRASE A quantity that is **upwards of** a particular number is more than that number. (某数字) 以上 ❑ *It costs upwards of $40,000 a year to keep some prisoners in prison.* 关押一些囚犯每年要花费4万美元以上。

up·wards /ʌpwərdz/ → see **upward**

▲ **ura·nium** /yʊreɪniəm/ N-UNCOUNT **Uranium** is a naturally occurring radioactive metal that is used to produce nuclear energy and weapons. 铀

ur·ban ◆◇◇ /ɜrbən/ ADJ **Urban** means belonging to, or relating to, a city or town. 城市的 ❑ *For a small state it has a large urban population.* 作为一个小州，其城市人口算是很多了。 ❑ *Most urban areas are close to a park.* 大多数城区都靠近公园。

→ see **city**

urge ♦♦◇ /ɜrdʒ/ (**urges, urging, urged**) **1** V-T If you **urge** someone **to** do something, you try hard to persuade them to do it. 敦促(某人做某事) ❑ *They urged Congress to approve plans for their reform program.* 他们敦促国会批准他们有关改革项目的计划。 **2** V-T If you **urge** someone somewhere, you make them go there by touching them or talking to them. 鼓动(某人去某地) ❑ *He slipped his arm around her waist and urged her away from the window.* 他悄悄用一只手臂揽住她的腰，劝她离开了窗口。 **3** V-T If you **urge** a course of action, you strongly advise that it should be taken. 竭力主张 ❑ *He urged restraint on the security forces.* 他竭力主张限制安全部队。 **4** N-COUNT If you have an **urge to** do or have something, you have a strong wish to do or have it. 强烈欲望 ❑ *He had an urge to open a shop of his own.* 他很想开一家自己的商店。

Word Partnership *urge* 的常用搭配:
N. urge **people**, urge **voters** **1**
leaders/officials urge **1** **3**
urge **action**, urge **caution**, urge **restraint**, urge **support** **3**
ADV. **strongly** urge **1** **3**
V. **feel an** urge, **fight an** urge, **get an** urge, **resist an** urge **4**

ur·gent ♦◇◇ /ɜrdʒᵊnt/ **1** ADJ If something is **urgent**, it needs to be dealt with as soon as possible. 紧急的; 迫切的 ❑ *There is an urgent need for food and water.* 有着对食品和水的迫切需要。 ● **ur·gen·cy** ★ N-UNCOUNT 紧急性; 迫切性 ❑ *The urgency of finding a cure attracted some of the best minds in medical science.* 因迫切需要找到一种治疗方法，医学界的一些最优秀的人才前仆后继。 ● **ur·gent·ly** ADV 紧急地; 迫切地 [ADV with v] ❑ *Red Cross officials said they urgently needed bread and water.* 红十字会官员们说他们迫切需要面包和水。 **2** ADJ If you speak in an **urgent** way, you show that you are anxious for people to notice something or to do something. 急切的 ❑ *His voice was low and urgent.* 他的声音低沉而急切。 ● **ur·gen·cy** ★ N-UNCOUNT 急切 ❑ *She was surprised at the urgency in his voice.* 她对他声音的急切感到吃惊。 ● **ur·gent·ly** ADV 急切地 [ADV with v] ❑ *They hastened to greet him and asked urgently, "Did you find it?"* 他们赶紧去迎接他，急切地问，"你找到它了吗？"

Word Partnership *urgent* 的常用搭配:
N. urgent **action**, urgent **business**, urgent **care**, urgent **matter**, urgent **meeting**, urgent **mission**, urgent **need**, urgent **problem** **1**
urgent **appeal**, urgent **message** **2**

uri·nate /yʊərɪneɪt/ (**urinates, urinating, urinated**) V-I When someone **urinates**, they get rid of urine from their body. 排尿; 小便

▲ **urine** /yʊərɪn/ N-UNCOUNT **Urine** is the liquid that you get rid of from your body when you go to the toilet. 尿 ❑ *The doctor took a urine sample and a blood sample.* 医生取了尿样和血样。

URL /yu̲ ɑr ɛ̲l/ (**URLs**) N-COUNT A **URL** is an address that shows where a particular page can be found on the World Wide Web. **URL** is an abbreviation for "Uniform Resource Locator." 统一资源定位器; 网址 [COMPUTING] ❑ *The URL for the Lonely Planet travel center is http://www.lonelyplanet.com.* "孤独行星"旅行中心的网址是 **http://www.lonelyplanet.com**。

urn /ɜrn/ (**urns**) **1** N-COUNT An **urn** is a container in which a dead person's ashes are kept. 骨灰瓮 ❑ *...a funeral urn.* …一个骨灰瓮。 **2** N-COUNT An **urn** is a metal container used for making a large quantity of tea or coffee and keeping it hot. (用于泡茶或咖啡并保温的金属) 大壶 ❑ *...the ten-gallon coffee urn.* …那只10加仑的咖啡壶。

us ♦♦♦ /əs, STRONG ʌs/

Us is the first person plural pronoun. **Us** is used as the object of a verb or a preposition.

1 PRON-PLURAL A speaker or writer uses **us** to refer both to himself or herself and to one or more other people. You can use **us** before a noun to make it clear which group of people you are referring to. 我们 [V PRON, prep PRON] ❑ *Neither of us forgot about it.* 我俩都没忘记它。 ❑ *Heather went to the kitchen to get drinks for us.* 希瑟去厨房给我们拿饮料。 ❑ *They don't like us much.* 他们不大喜欢我们。 **2** PRON-PLURAL **Us** is sometimes used to refer to people in general. 我们(泛指人们) [V PRON, prep PRON] ❑ *All of us will struggle fairly hard to survive if we are in danger.* 我们所有人如果遇到危险都会竭力挣扎着活下来。 **3** PRON-PLURAL A speaker or writer may use **us** instead of "me" in order to include the audience or reader in what they are saying. 我们(指演讲者及其听众或作者及其读者) [V PRON, prep PRON] [mainly FORMAL] ❑ *This brings us to the second question I asked.* 这就将我们引入了我提出的第2个问题。

U.S. ♦♦♦ /yu̲ ɛ̲s/ also **US** N-PROPER **The U.S.** is an abbreviation for **the United States**. 美国 ["the" N, N n] ❑ *The first time I saw TV was when I arrived in the U.S. in 1956.* 我第一次看到电视是我1956年到达美国的时候。 ❑ *He inherited 10,000 U.S. dollars.* 他继承了1万美元。

U.S.A. ♦◇◇ /yu̲ ɛs e̲ɪ/ also **USA** N-PROPER **The U.S.A.** is an abbreviation for **the United States of America**. 美国 ["the" N]

us·able /yu̲zəbᵊl/ ADJ If something is **usable**, it is in a good enough state or condition to be used. (指某物) 可用的; 能用的 ❑ *It's been reported that no usable fingerprints were found at the scene.* 据报道，现场没有发现任何可用的指纹。

us·age /yu̲sɪdʒ/ (**usages**) **1** N-UNCOUNT **Usage** is the way in which words are actually used in particular contexts, especially with regard to their meanings. (词在特定语境中的) 使用 ❑ *He was a stickler for the correct usage of English.* 他是一个坚持英语的正确使用的人。 **2** N-COUNT A **usage** is a meaning that a word has or a way in which it can be used. (词的) 意义; 用法 ❑ *It's very definitely a usage which has come over to Britain from America.* 这肯定是从美国传至英国的一种用法。 **3** N-UNCOUNT **Usage** is the degree to which something is used or the way in which it is used. (指某物的) 利用度; 使用 ❑ *Parts of the motor wore out because of constant usage.* 发动机的一些部件由于不断使用而磨损了。

USB /yu̲ ɛs bi̲/ (**USBs**) N-COUNT A **USB** or **USB port** on a computer is a place where you can attach another piece of equipment, for example a printer. **USB** is an abbreviation for "Universal Serial Bus." 通用串行总线 [COMPUTING] ❑ *The device plugs into one of the laptop's USB ports.* 该装置可插入笔记本电脑的一个USB接口。

use
❶ VERB USES
❷ NOUN USES

❶ **use** ♦♦♦ /yu̲z/ (**uses, using, used**) **1** V-T If you **use** something, you do something with it in order to do a job or to achieve a particular result or effect. 使用 ❑ *Trim off the excess pastry using a sharp knife.* 用一把锋利刀削掉过多的油酥面团。 ❑ *The U.S. has used ships to bring most of its heavy material, like tanks, to the region.* 美国已用船把坦克等大多数重型物资运到了该地区。 **2** V-T If you **use** a supply of something, you finish it so that none of it is left. 用光 ❑ *You used all the ice cubes and didn't put the ice trays back.* 你用光了所有的冰块，也没有把冰格盘放回去。 ● PHRASAL VERB **Use up** means the same as **use**. 用光 ❑ *It isn't animals who use up the world's resources.* 不是动物耗尽了世界资源。 **3** V-T If someone **uses** drugs, they take drugs regularly, especially illegal ones. 服; 吸食(药、毒品) ❑ *He denied he had used drugs.* 他否认吸食过毒品。 **4** V-T You can say that someone **uses** the toilet or bathroom as a polite way of saying that they go to the toilet. 用(厕所、卫生间) [POLITENESS] ❑ *Wash your hands after using the bathroom.* 如厕后请洗手。 **5** V-T If you **use** a particular word or expression, you say or write it, because it has the meaning that you want to express. 用(某词语或表达方式) ❑ *The judge liked using the word "wicked" of people he had sent to jail.* 那位法官喜欢用"邪恶的"这个词来形容他判决入狱的人。 **6** V-T If you **use** a particular name, you call yourself by that name, especially when it is not the name that you usually call yourself. 用(某个名字) ❑ *Now I use a false name if I'm meeting people for the first time.* 现在我和素未谋面的人见面都用假名。 **7** V-T If you say that someone **uses** people, you disapprove of them because they make others do things for them in order to benefit or gain some advantage from it, and not because they care about the other people. 利用(人) [DISAPPROVAL] ❑ *Why do I have the feeling I'm being used again?* 为什么我觉得自己又在被人利用呢? **8** → see also **used**

❷ **use** ♦♦◇ /yu̲s/ (**uses**) **1** N-UNCOUNT Your **use** of something is the action or fact of your using it. 使用 [also "a" N, usu N "of" n] ❑ *The treatment does not involve the use of any artificial drugs.* 这种疗法不涉及任何人造药物的使用。 ❑ *...research related to microcomputers and their use in classrooms.* …有关微型计算机及其在课堂中的使用的研究。 **2** N-SING If you have **a use for** something, you need it or can find something to do with it. 用处 ❑ *You will no longer have a use for the magazines.* 你将不再用得着这些杂志了。 **3** N-VAR If something has a particular **use**, it is intended for a particular purpose. 用途

❑ *Infrared detectors have many uses.* 红外探测器有多种用途。 ❑ *It's an interesting scientific phenomenon, but of no practical use whatever.* 这是一种有趣的科学现象，但没有什么实际用途。 ❑ *The report outlined possible uses for the new weapon.* 该报告勾画了这种新武器的可能用途。 **4** N-UNCOUNT If you have the **use of** something, you have the permission or ability to use it. (对某物的) 使用权；使用能力 [also "the" N, usu N "of" n] ❑ *She will have the use of the car one night a week.* 她每周可以有一个晚上使用这辆车。 ❑ *...young people who at some point in the past have lost the use of their limbs.* …在过去某个时刻丧失了肢体使用能力的年轻人。 **5** N-COUNT A **use** of a word is a particular meaning that it has or a particular way in which it can be used. (词的) 意义；用法 ❑ *There are new uses of words coming in and old uses dying out.* 词语的新用法在涌现，旧用法在消亡。 **6** N-UNCOUNT Your **use of** a particular name is the fact of your calling yourself by it. (某名字的) 使用 ❑ *Police have been hampered by Mr. Urquhart's use of bogus names.* 厄克特先生使用假名，警察的调查受阻。 **7** PHRASE If something is **for the use of** a particular person or group of people, it is for that person or group to use. 以供 (某人、某些人) 使用 ❑ *The facilities are there for the use of guests.* 那些设施摆在那儿以供客人们使用。 **8** PHRASE If you say that being something or knowing someone **has** its **uses**, you mean that it makes it possible for you to do what you otherwise would not be able to do. 有其用途 [INFORMAL] ❑ *It wasn't a life she particularly enjoyed, but it had its uses.* 这不是她特别喜欢的一种生活，但有它的用处。 **9** PHRASE If something such as a technique, building, or machine is **in use**, it is used regularly by people. If it has gone **out of use**, it is no longer used regularly by people. 在用/不再用 ❑ *...the methods of making champagne which are still in use today.* …今天仍在使用的酿造香槟的方法。 **10** PHRASE If you **make use of** something, you do something with it in order to do a job or achieve a particular result or effect. 利用；发挥 [WRITTEN] ❑ *Few found jobs in which they could make use of their new skills.* 几乎无人找得到能发挥自己新技能的工作。 **11** PHRASE If you say **it's no use**, you mean that you have failed to do something and realize that it is useless to continue trying because it is impossible. 没有用；不奏效 ❑ *It's no use. Let's hang up and try for a better line.* 没用。我们挂断电话试打更好的线路吧。 **12** PHRASE If something or someone is **of use**, they are useful. If they are **no use**, they are not at all useful. 有用/无用 ❑ *The contents of this booklet should be of use to all students.* 这本小册子的内容应该对所有的学生都有用。

Thesaurus *use* 另参见：

V.	utilize ❶ **1**
N.	application, function ❷ **3**

used

❶ MODAL USES AND PHRASES
❷ ADJECTIVE USES

❶ **used** ♦♦◊ /yust/ **1** PHRASE If something **used to** be done or **used to** be the case, it was done regularly in the past or was the case in the past. 过去惯常 ❑ *People used to come and visit him every day.* 过去人们每天都来看他。 ❑ *He used to be one of my professors.* 他过去是我的一个教授。 **2** PHRASE If something **did not use to** be done, **used to not** be done or **used not to** be done, it was not done in the past. 过去不曾 ❑ *Borrowing used to not be recommended.* 借东西在过去是不提倡的。 ❑ *At some point kids start doing things they didn't use to do. They get more independent.* 从某时起孩子们开始做他们过去没做过的事情。他们变得更独立。 **3** PHRASE If you **are used to** something, you are familiar with it because you have done it or experienced it many times before. 习惯于 ❑ *I'm used to having my sleep interrupted.* 我习惯了睡觉时被吵醒。 **4** PHRASE If you **get used to** something or someone, you become familiar with it or get to know them, so that you no longer feel that the thing or person is unusual or surprising. 变得习惯于 ❑ *This is how we do things here. You'll soon get used to it.* 这是我们这里的做事风格。你很快就会习惯的。 ❑ *You quickly get used to using the brakes.* 你很快会习惯用刹车。

U

❷ **used** /yuzd/ **1** ADJ A **used** object is dirty or spoiled because it has been used, and usually needs to be thrown away or washed. 用过的 ❑ *...a used cotton ball stained with makeup.* …一个用过的棉花球，沾着化妆品。 **2** ADJ A **used** car has already had one or more owners. 二手的 ❑ *Would you buy a used car from this man?* 你会向这个人买辆二手车吗？

use·ful ♦♦◊ /yusfəl/ **1** ADJ If something is **useful**, you can use it to do something or to help you in some way. 有用的 ❑ *The pressure cooker is very useful for people who go out all day.* 压力锅对整天外出的人非常有用。 ❑ *Hypnotherapy can be useful in helping you give up smoking.* 催眠疗法在帮助你戒烟方面可能有用。● **use·ful·ly** ADV 有用地 [ADV with v] ❑ *...the problems to which computers could be usefully applied.* …可以应用计算机来解决的问题。● **use·ful·ness** N-UNCOUNT 有用性；实用性 ❑ *His interest lay in the usefulness of his work, rather than in any personal credit.* 他的兴趣在于自己工作的实用性，而不在于个人的任何荣誉。 **2** PHRASE If an object or skill **comes in useful**, it can help you achieve something in a particular situation. 有用 ❑ *Extra blank paper will probably come in useful.* 额外的空白纸可能用得着。

Word Partnership *useful* 的常用搭配：

ADV.	**also** useful, **especially** useful, **extremely** useful, **less/more** useful, **particularly** useful, **very** useful **1**
N.	useful **information**, useful **knowledge**, useful **life**, useful **purpose**, useful **strategy**, useful **tool** **1**

use·less /yuslɪs/ **1** ADJ If something is **useless**, you cannot use it. (指某物) 不能用的 ❑ *He realized that their money was useless in this country.* 他意识到他们的货币在这个国家不能用。 **2** ADJ If something is **useless**, it does not achieve anything helpful or good. 没用的；不起作用的 ❑ *She knew it was useless to protest.* 她知道抗议是没用的。 **3** ADJ If you say that someone or something is **useless**, you mean that they are no good at all. (人或物) 不行的 ❑ *Their education system is useless.* 他们的教育制度一点儿也不好。 **4** ADJ If someone feels **useless**, they feel bad because they are unable to help someone or achieve anything. (某人感到) 没用的 ❑ *She sits at home all day, watching TV and feeling useless.* 她整天坐在家里，看电视、感到自己没用。

user ♦◊◊ /yuzər/ (**users**) N-COUNT A **user** is a person or thing that uses something such as a place, facility, product, or machine. 使用者；使用物 ❑ *Beach users have complained that the bikes are noisy.* 去海滩的人已在抱怨那些自行车太吵。 ❑ *...a regular user of the subway.* …一个定期乘坐地铁的人。

→ see **Internet**

user-friendly ADJ If you describe something such as a machine or system as **user-friendly**, you mean that it is well designed and easy to use. 为用户着想的；好用的 ❑ *This is an entirely computer-operated system which is very user-friendly.* 这是一个完全由计算机操作的系统，非常好用。

▲ **ush·er** /ʌʃər/ (**ushers, ushering, ushered**) **1** V-T If you **usher** someone somewhere, you show them where they should go by going with them. 引领 [FORMAL] ❑ *I ushered him into the office.* 我领他进了办公室。 **2** N-COUNT An **usher** is a person who shows people where to sit, for example at a wedding or at a concert. (婚礼、音乐会等的) 引座员 ❑ *He did part-time work as an usher in a theater.* 他曾在一家剧院做兼职引座员。

USP /yu ɛs pi/ (**USPs**) N-COUNT The **USP** of a product or service is a particular feature of it which can be used in advertising to show how it is different from, and better than, other similar products or services. **USP** is an abbreviation for "Unique Selling Point." 独特卖点 [BUSINESS] ❑ *With Volvo, safety was always the USP.* 沃尔沃的安全性能一向是其独特卖点。

usu·al ♦♦◊ /yuʒuəl/ **1** ADJ **Usual** is used to describe what happens or what is done most often in a particular situation. 常见的；平常的 ❑ *It is a neighborhood beset by all the usual inner-city problems.* 这是个受所有常见市中心区问题所困扰的市区。 ❑ *After lunch there was a little more clearing up to do than usual.* 午餐之后有比平常多的清扫工作要做。● N-SING **Usual** is also a noun. 往常的 (饭食、饮料等) ❑ *The stout barman in a bow tie presented himself to take their order. "Good morning, sir. The usual?"* 那位系着领结的粗壮的酒吧男招待走过来请他们点菜。"早上好，先生。跟以往一样？" **2** PHRASE You use **as usual** to indicate that you are describing something that normally happens or that is normally the case. 和往常一样 ❑ *As usual there will be the local and regional elections on June the twelfth.* 和往常一样，6月12日将举行地方及地区选举。 **3** PHRASE If something happens **as usual**, it happens in the way that it normally does, especially when other things have changed. 照常 ❑ *Surgery was scheduled, but life went on as usual.* 手术定好了时间，而生活照常继续。 **4** **business as usual** → see **business**

Word Partnership *usual* 的常用搭配：

ADV.	**less/more than** usual, **longer than** usual **1**
N.	usual **place**, usual **routine**, usual **self**, usual **stuff**, usual **suspects**, usual **way** **1**

usu·al·ly ♦♦◇ /yuʒuəli/ **1** ADV If something **usually** happens, it is the thing that most often happens in a particular situation. 通常 ❑ *The best information about hotels usually comes from friends and acquaintances who have been there.* 有关旅馆的最佳信息通常来自曾经去过那儿的朋友和熟人。❑ *Usually, the work is boring.* 通常这种工作很乏味。 **2** PHRASE You use **more than usually** to show that something shows even more of a particular quality than it normally does. 比平常更甚地 ❑ *She felt more than usually hungry after her excursion.* 远足后她感到非同寻常地饥饿。

usurp /yusɜrp, -zɜrp/ (**usurps, usurping, usurped**) V-T If you say that someone **usurps** a job, role, title, or position, they take it from someone when they have no right to do this. 篡夺; 夺取 [FORMAL] ❑ *Did she usurp his place in his mother's heart?* 她夺取了他在他母亲心目中的地位吗?

▲ **uten·sil** /yutɛnsᵊl/ (**utensils**) N-COUNT **Utensils** are tools or objects that you use in order to help you to cook, serve food, or eat. 器皿; 用具 ❑ *...utensils such as bowls, steamers and frying pans.* …碗、蒸锅、平底锅等用具。

uter·us /yutərəs/ (**uteruses**) N-COUNT The **uterus** of a woman or female mammal is the part of her body where babies develop. 子宫 [MEDICAL] ❑ *...an ultrasound scan of the uterus.* …一次对子宫的超声波扫描。

uti·lise /yutɪlaɪz/ [BRIT] → see **utilize**

utili·tar·ian /yutɪlɪtɛəriən/ (**utilitarians**) **1** ADJ **Utilitarian** objects and buildings are designed to be useful rather than attractive. (物体、建筑等) 实用的 ❑ *Bruce's office is utilitarian and unglamorous.* 布鲁斯的办公室实用而素淡。 **2** ADJ **Utilitarian** means based on the idea that the morally correct course of action is the one that produces benefit for the greatest number of people. 功利主义的 [TECHNICAL] ❑ *It was James Mill who was the best publicist for utilitarian ideas on government.* 詹姆斯·米尔才是政府功利主义思想的最佳宣传家。● N-COUNT A **utilitarian** is someone with utilitarian views. 功利主义者 ❑ *One of the greatest utilitarians was Claude Helvetius.* 最伟大的功利主义者之一是克劳德·爱尔维修。

util·ity /yutɪlɪti/ (**utilities**) N-COUNT A **utility** is an important service such as water, electricity, or gas that is provided for everyone, and that everyone pays for. 公用事业 ❑ *...public utilities such as gas, electricity and phones.* …煤气、电和电话等公用事业。

uti·lize /yutɪlaɪz/ (**utilizes, utilizing, utilized**)

in BRIT, also use **utilise**

V-T If you **utilize** something, you use it. 利用 [FORMAL] ❑ *Sound engineers utilize a range of techniques to enhance the quality of the recordings.* 音响工程师利用一系列的技术来提高录音质量。
● **uti·li·za·tion** ★ /yutɪlɪzeɪʃᵊn/ N-UNCOUNT 利用 ❑ *...the utilization of human resources.* …人力资源的利用。

ut·most /ʌtmoʊst/ **1** ADJ You can use **utmost** to emphasize the importance or seriousness of something or to emphasize the way that it is done. 最大的; 极度的 [ADJ n] [EMPHASIS] ❑ *It is a matter of the utmost urgency to find out what has happened to these people.* 当务之急是弄清楚这些人出了什么事。 ❑ *Security matters are treated with the utmost seriousness.* 安全问题受到极为严肃的对待。 **2** N-SING If you say that you are doing your **utmost to** do something, you are emphasizing that you are trying as hard as you can to do it. 最大努力 [EMPHASIS] ❑ *He would have done his utmost to help her.* 他本来会尽最大努力帮助她。

★ **uto·pia** /yutoʊpiə/ (**utopias**) N-VAR If you refer to an imaginary situation as a **utopia**, you mean that it is one in which society is perfect and everyone is happy. 理想社会; 乌托邦 ❑ *We weren't out to design a contemporary utopia.* 我们不想去设计一个当代乌托邦。

uto·pian /yutoʊpiən/ **1** ADJ If you describe a plan or idea as **utopian**, you are criticizing it because it is unrealistic and shows a belief that things can be improved much more than is possible. (计划、主意等) 空想的; 不切合实际的 [DISAPPROVAL] ❑ *He was pursuing a utopian dream of world prosperity.* 他那时在追求一个不切实际的世界繁荣之梦。 **2** ADJ **Utopian** is used to describe political or religious philosophies which claim that it is possible to build a new and perfect society in which everyone is happy. (政治或宗教思想) 空想的; 乌托邦式的 [FORMAL] ❑ *His was a utopian vision of nature in its purest form.* 他对大自然的看法是一种最纯粹的乌托邦式看法。

ut·ter /ʌtər/ (**utters, uttering, uttered**) **1** V-T If someone **utters** sounds or words, they say them. 发出 (声音); 说 [LITERARY] ❑ *He uttered a snorting laugh.* 他扑哧一声笑了。 **2** ADJ You use **utter** to emphasize that something is great in extent, degree, or amount. 完全的; 彻底的 [ADJ n] [EMPHASIS] ❑ *This, of course, is utter nonsense.* 这当然纯属胡言乱语。 ❑ *...this utter lack of responsibility.* …如此彻底地缺乏责任心。

ut·ter·ance /ʌtərəns/ (**utterances**) N-COUNT Someone's **utterances** are the things that they say. 言辞; 话语 [FORMAL] ❑ *These two utterances communicate the same message.* 这两句话传递同样的信息。

ut·ter·ly /ʌtərli/ ADV You use **utterly** to emphasize that something is very great in extent, degree, or amount. 完全地; 彻底地 [EMPHASIS] ❑ *China is utterly different.* 中国完全不一样。 ❑ *The new laws coming in are utterly ridiculous.* 即将实施的新法律荒唐至极。

U-turn (**U-turns**) **1** N-COUNT If you make a **U-turn** when you are driving or riding a bicycle, you turn in a half circle in one movement, so that you are then going in the opposite direction. U形转弯; 掉头 ❑ *Dave made a U-turn on North Main and drove back to Depot Street.* 戴夫在北干道掉头，把车开回了第伯街。 **2** N-COUNT If you describe a change in someone's policy, plans, or actions as a **U-turn**, you mean that it is a complete change. (政策、计划、行动等) 180度大转弯; 彻底转变 [DISAPPROVAL] ❑ *He's doing a U-turn and forecasting 1% growth this year after earlier predicting a 2% drop.* 他来了个180度大转弯，早先预言今年会有2%的下降，现在又预言会有1%的增长。

Vv

V also **v** /vi/ (**V's, v's**) N-VAR **V** is the twenty-second letter of the English alphabet. 英语字母表中的第22个字母

★ **va·can·cy** /veɪkənsi/ (**vacancies**) **1** N-COUNT A **vacancy** is a job or position that has not been filled. 职位空缺 ❑ *Most vacancies are at the senior level, requiring appropriate qualifications.* 大多数空缺在高层，要求适当的资历。 **2** N-COUNT If there are **vacancies** at a building such as a hotel, some of the rooms are available to rent. (酒店等的) 空房间 ❑ *This year hotels that usually are jammed had vacancies all summer.* 今年那些通常爆满的旅馆整个夏天都有空房。

Word Link *vac ≈ empty : evacuate, vacant, vacate*

va·cant /veɪkənt/ **1** ADJ If something is **vacant**, it is not being used by anyone. 空着的 ❑ *Halfway down the bus was a vacant seat.* 这辆公共汽车中部有个空座。 **2** ADJ If a job or position is **vacant**, no one is doing it or in it at present, and people can apply for it. 空缺的 ❑ *The position of chairman has been vacant for some time.* 主席的职位已经空缺一段时间了。 **3** ADJ A **vacant** look or expression is one that suggests that someone does not understand something or that they are not thinking about anything in particular. 茫然的 ❑ *She had a kind of vacant look on her face.* 在她脸上有一种茫然的表情。 ● **va·cant·ly** ADV 茫然地 [ADV after v] ❑ *He looked vacantly out of the window.* 他茫然地望着窗外。

va·cate /veɪkeɪt/ (**vacates, vacating, vacated**) V-T If you **vacate** a place or a job, you leave it or give it up, making it available for other people. 离开; 辞去 [FORMAL] ❑ *He quickly vacated the gym after the workout.* 锻炼完他很快离开了健身房。

va·ca·tion /veɪkeɪʃən/ (**vacations, vacationing, vacationed**) **1** N-COUNT A **vacation** is a period of time during which you relax and enjoy yourself away from home. 休假 [also "on/from" N] [AM]

in BRIT, use **holiday**

❑ *They planned a late summer vacation in Europe.* 他们计划了一个夏末在欧洲的休假。

> American workers generally get 2 weeks a year of paid **vacation**. Most people take their vacation time in the summer when their children are not in school. In the UK, workers usually get 4-5 weeks of paid vacation per year.

2 N-COUNT A **vacation** is a period of the year when schools, universities, and colleges are officially closed. (学校的) 假期 ❑ *During his summer vacation he visited Russia.* 暑假期间他游览了俄罗斯。 **3** N-UNCOUNT If you have a particular number of days' or weeks' **vacation**, you do not have to go to work for that number of days or weeks. (工作中的) 假期 [AM]

in BRIT, use **holiday**

❑ *The French get five to six weeks' vacation a year.* 法国人一年有5到6周的假期。 **4** V-I If you **are vacationing** in a place away from home, you are on vacation there. 度假 [AM]

in BRIT, use **holiday**

va·ca·tion·er /veɪkeɪʃənər/ (**vacationers**) N-COUNT **Vacationers** are people who are on vacation in a particular place. 度假者 [usu pl] [mainly AM]

in BRIT, usually use **holidaymakers**

❑ *Camping, biking, hiking and swimming are all available for the vacationer.* 露营、骑车、远足和游泳都是可供度假者选择的。

★ **vac·ci·nate** /væksɪneɪt/ (**vaccinates, vaccinating, vaccinated**) V-T If a person or animal **is vaccinated**, they are given a vaccine, usually by injection, to prevent them from getting a disease. 给…接种疫苗 [usu passive] ❑ *Dogs must be vaccinated against distemper.* 犬类必须接种疫苗以防犬热病。 ❑ *Have you had your child vaccinated against whooping cough?* 你给你的孩子接种预防百日咳的疫苗了吗？ ● **vac·ci·na·tion** /væksɪneɪʃən/ N-VAR (**vaccinations**) 疫苗的接种 ❑ *Anyone who wants to avoid the flu should consider getting a vaccination.* 任何希望避免患流感的人都应该考虑接种疫苗。

★ **vac·cine** /væksin/ (**vaccines**) N-MASS A **vaccine** is a substance containing a harmless form of the germs that cause a particular disease. It is given to people, usually by injection, to prevent them from getting that disease. 疫苗 ❑ *Anti-malarial vaccines are now undergoing trials.* 抗疟疾疫苗现在正处于试验阶段。 → see **hospital**

vacuum /vækyum, -yuəm/ (**vacuums, vacuuming, vacuumed**) **1** N-COUNT If someone or something creates a **vacuum**, they leave a place or position that then needs to be filled by another person or thing. 空缺 ❑ *His presence should fill the power vacuum that has been developing over the past few days.* 他的出现应该能填补过去几天中形成的权力空缺。 **2** PHRASE If something is done **in a vacuum**, it is not affected by any outside influences or information. 在与世隔绝的状态中 ❑ *Moral values cannot be taught in a vacuum.* 道德价值观不能在与世隔绝的状态中进行传授。 **3** N-COUNT A **vacuum** is a space that contains no air or other gas. 真空 ❑ *Wind is a current of air caused by a vacuum caused by hot air rising.* 风是由热空气上升产生真空而引起的空气流动。 **4** N-COUNT A **vacuum** is the same as a **vacuum cleaner**. 真空吸尘器 **5** V-T/V-I If you **vacuum** something, you clean it using a vacuum cleaner. 用真空吸尘器清洁 ❑ *I vacuumed the carpets today.* 我今天用吸尘器清洁地毯了。 ❑ *It's important to vacuum regularly.* 定期用吸尘器清洁是很重要的。

vacuum clean·er (**vacuum cleaners**) N-COUNT A **vacuum cleaner** or a **vacuum** is an electric machine that sucks up dust and dirt from carpets. 真空吸尘器

va·gi·na /vədʒaɪnə/ (**vaginas**) N-COUNT A woman's **vagina** is the passage connecting her outer sex organs to her uterus. 阴道

vagi·nal /vædʒɪnᵊl/ ADJ **Vaginal** means relating to or involving the vagina. 阴道的 [ADJ n] ❑ *The creams have been used to reduce vaginal infections.* 这些乳膏一直被用来减轻阴道感染。

vague /veɪg/ (**vaguer, vaguest**) **1** ADJ If something written or spoken is **vague**, it does not explain or express things clearly. 含糊的 ❑ *A lot of the talk was apparently vague and general.* 这次会谈的许多内容显然是含糊而笼统的。 ❑ *The description was pretty vague.* 这项描述是相当含糊的。 ● **vague·ly** ADV 含糊地 ❑ *"I'm not sure," Liz said vaguely.* "我不能肯定，" 莉兹含糊地说。 **2** ADJ If you have a **vague** memory or idea of something, the memory or idea is not clear. 模糊的 ❑ *They have only a vague idea of the amount of water available.* 他们对于可用水量只有一点模糊的了解。 ● **vague·ly** ADV 模糊地 [ADV with v] ❑ *Judith could vaguely remember her mother lying on the sofa.* 朱迪斯能够模糊地记得她母亲当时正躺在沙发上。 **3** ADJ If you are **vague** about something, you deliberately do not tell people much about it. 含糊其辞的 ❑ *He was vague, however, about just what U.S. forces might actually do.* 然而，他对于美国军队真正可能做什么却含糊其辞。 **4** ADJ If something such as a feeling is **vague**, you experience it only slightly. (感觉等) 轻微的 ❑ *He was conscious of that vague feeling of irritation again.* 他又一次感到微微有些恼火。 **5** ADJ A **vague** shape or outline is not clear and is therefore not easy to see. 模糊不清的 ❑ *The bus was a vague shape in the distance.* 远处的那辆公共汽车只是一个模糊不清的轮廓。

Word Partnership *vague* 的常用搭配：

N.	vague **references**, vague **terms** **1**
	vague **idea/notion/sense** **2**
ADV.	**deliberately** vague **1** **3**
	a little vague, **rather** vague, **too** vague, **very** vague **1**–**5**
V.	**have (only) a** vague **idea/notion/sense of** *something* **2**

vague·ly /veɪgli/ **1** ADV **Vaguely** means to some degree but not to a very large degree. 有点儿 [ADV adj] ❑ *The voice on the line was vaguely familiar, but Crook couldn't place it at first.* 电话中的声音有点儿熟悉，但一开始克鲁克却听不出是谁。 **2** → see also **vague**

vain /veɪn/ (vainer, vainest) 1 ADJ A **vain** attempt or action is one that fails to achieve what was intended. 徒劳的 [ADJ n] ❑ *The drafting committee worked through the night in a vain attempt to finish on schedule.* 起草委员会徒劳地通宵工作想按期完成工作。 ● **vain·ly** ADV 徒劳地 [ADV with v] ❑ *He hunted vainly through his pockets for a piece of paper.* 他徒劳地摸索着自己的口袋想找到一张纸。 2 ADJ If you describe a hope that something will happen as a **vain** hope, you mean that there is no chance of it happening. 徒然的 [ADJ n] ❑ *He married his fourth wife, Susan, in the vain hope that she would improve his health.* 他怀着她能改善自己健康的徒然希望娶了第4个妻子苏珊。 ● **vain·ly** ADV 徒然地 [ADV with v] ❑ *He then set out for Virginia for what he vainly hoped would be a peaceful retirement.* 于是他出发前往弗吉尼亚，徒然地希望这会是一次平静的引退。 3 ADJ If you describe someone as **vain**, you are critical of their extreme pride in their own beauty, intelligence, or other good qualities. 自负的 [DISAPPROVAL] ❑ *He wasn't so vain as to think he was smarter than his boss.* 他还没有自负到以为他比自己的上司还精明。 ❑ *I think he is shallow, vain, and untrustworthy.* 我认为他浅薄、自负而且不可靠。 4 PHRASE If you do something **in vain**, you do not succeed in achieving what you intend. 徒然 ❑ *He stopped at the door, waiting in vain for her to acknowledge his presence.* 他停在门口，徒然地等着她跟自己打招呼。 5 PHRASE If you say that something such as someone's death, suffering, or effort was **in vain**, you mean that it was useless because it did not achieve anything. 无意义的 ❑ *He wants the world to know his son did not die in vain.* 他想让世人知道他儿子的死不是毫无意义的。

val·iant /vælyənt/ ADJ A **valiant** action is very brave and determined, though it may lead to failure or defeat. 顽强的 ❑ *Despite valiant efforts by the finance minister, inflation rose to 36%.* 尽管这位财政部长作了顽强的努力，通货膨胀率还是升到了36%。 ● **val·iant·ly** ADV 顽强地 [ADV with v] ❑ *He suffered further heart attacks and strokes, all of which he fought valiantly.* 他又发作过几次心脏病并中过几次风，他与这一切都作了顽强的斗争。

val·id /vælɪd/ 1 ADJ A **valid** argument, comment, or idea is based on sensible reasoning. 有根据的 ❑ *They put forward many valid reasons for not exporting.* 他们提出了许多有根据的理由来反对出口。 ● **va·lid·ity** ★ /vəlɪdɪti/ N-UNCOUNT 合理性 ❑ *The editorial says this argument has lost much of its validity.* 这篇社论说该论点已失去了其许多合理性。 2 ADJ Something that is **valid** is important or serious enough to make it worth saying or doing. 重要的 ❑ *Most designers share the unspoken belief that fashion is a valid form of visual art.* 大多数设计师都有一种心照不宣的信念，即时尚是视觉艺术的一种重要形式。 ● **va·lid·ity** ★ N-UNCOUNT 重要性 ❑ *...the validity of making children wear bicycle helmets.* …让孩子们戴自行车头盔的重要性。 3 ADJ If a ticket or other document is **valid**, it can be used and will be accepted by people in authority. 有效的 ❑ *All tickets are valid for two months.* 所有的票在两个月内有效。 4 → see also **validity**

★ **vali·date** /vælɪdeɪt/ (validates, validating, validated) 1 V-T To **validate** something such as a claim or statement means to prove or confirm that it is true or correct. 证实 [FORMAL] ❑ *This discovery seems to validate the claims of popular astrology.* 这一发现似乎证实了流行占星术的一些观点。 ● **vali·da·tion** /vælɪdeɪʃən/ N-VAR (validations) 确认 ❑ *When we want validation for our decisions we often turn to friends for advice and approval.* 当我们想要获得对我们的决定的确认时，我们经常向朋友们求得建议和认可。 2 V-T To **validate** a person, state, or system means to prove or confirm that they are valuable or worthwhile. 证实…有价值 ❑ *The Academy Awards appear to validate his career.* 这些奥斯卡金像奖看来证实了他的职业生涯的价值。 ● **vali·da·tion** N-VAR 认可 ❑ *I think the film is a validation of our lifestyle.* 我想这部电影是对我们的生活方式的一种认可。

★ **va·lid·ity** /vəlɪdɪti/ 1 N-UNCOUNT **The validity of** something such as a result or a piece of information is whether it can be trusted or believed. 可信性 ❑ *Shocked by the results of the elections, they now want to challenge the validity of the vote.* 震惊于这些选举的结果，他们现在想质疑投票的可信性。 ❑ *Some people, of course, denied the validity of any such claim.* 当然，一些人否认任何此类说法的可信性。 2 → see also **valid**

Va·lium /væliəm/ (Valium)

Valium is both the singular and the plural form.

N-VAR **Valium** is a drug given to people to calm their nerves when they are very depressed or upset. 安定 (药名) [TRADEMARK] ❑ *Do you have any Valium?* 你有安定片吗？

val·ley ◆◇◇ /væli/ (valleys) N-COUNT; N-IN-NAMES A **valley** is a low stretch of land between hills, especially one that has a river flowing through it. 山谷 ❑ *...a wooded valley set against the backdrop of Monte Rosa.* …罗莎峰前一个林木繁茂的山谷。 → see **river**

valu·able ◆◇◇ /vælyuəbəl/ 1 ADJ If you describe something or someone as **valuable**, you mean that they are very useful and helpful. 有益的 ❑ *Many of our teachers also have valuable academic links with Heidelberg University.* 我们的许多教师也和海德堡大学保持着有价值的学术联系。 2 ADJ **Valuable** objects are objects that are worth a lot of money. 值钱的 ❑ *Just because a camera is old does not mean it is valuable.* 并不能因为照相机样式老就以为它是值钱的。

Thesaurus *valuable* 另参见:

ADJ.	helpful, important, useful; *(ant.)* useless 1
	costly, expensive, priceless; *(ant.)* worthless 2

Word Partnership *valuable* 的常用搭配:

V.	**learn a** valuable **lesson** 1
N.	valuable **experience**, valuable **information**, valuable **lesson**, **time is** valuable 1
	valuable **asset**, valuable **resource** 1 2
	valuable **property** 2
ADV.	**extremely** valuable, **less** valuable, **very** valuable 1 2

valu·ables /vælyuəbəlz/ N-PLURAL **Valuables** are things that you own that are worth a lot of money, especially small objects such as jewelry. 贵重物品 ❑ *Leave your valuables in the hotel safe behind the reception desk.* 将您的贵重物品寄放在前台后的宾馆保险箱中。

▲ **valua·tion** /vælyueɪʃən/ (valuations) N-VAR A **valuation** is a judgment that someone makes about how much money something is worth. 估价 ❑ *Valuation lies at the heart of all takeovers.* 估价是一切收购活动的核心。

value ◆◆◆ /vælyu/ (values, valuing, valued) 1 N-UNCOUNT The **value** of something such as a quality, attitude, or method is its importance or usefulness. If you place a particular **value** on something, that is the importance or usefulness you think it has. 重要性；益处 [also "a" N] ❑ *The value of this work experience should not be underestimated.* 这项工作经验的重要性不应该被低估。 ● PHRASE If something is **of value**, it is useful or important. If it is **of no value**, it has no usefulness or importance. 重要的/不重要的 ❑ *This weekend course will be of value to everyone interested in the Pilgrim Route.* 这个周末课程对于每一个对朝圣路线感兴趣的人来说都将是重要的。 2 V-T If you **value** something or someone, you think that they are important and you appreciate them. 重视 ❑ *I value the opinion of my husband and we agree on most things.* 我重视我丈夫的意见，而且我们在大多数事情上看法一致。 3 N-VAR The **value** of something is how much money it is worth. 价值 ❑ *The value of his investment has risen by more than $50,000.* 他的投资价值已经增长$50000多。 ● PHRASE If something is **of value**, it is worth a lot of money. If it is **of no value**, it is worth very little money. 值钱的/不值钱的 ❑ *...a brooch that is really of no value.* …一枚根本不值钱的胸针。 4 V-T When experts **value** something, they decide how much money it is worth. 为…估价 ❑ *The school board valued the property at $130,000.* 这所学校的董事会将这项财产估价为$130000。 ❑ *I asked him to have my jewelry valued.* 我请求他为我的珠宝估价。 5 N-UNCOUNT You use **value** in certain expressions to say whether something is worth the money that it costs. For example, if something is **good value**, or if you get **good value** for your money when you buy something, then it is worth the money that it costs. (与价格相比的) 合算程度 ❑ *We believe that is good value for money for our customers.* 我们认为我们顾客的钱在那上面花得很值。 6 N-PLURAL The **values** of a person or group are the moral principles and beliefs that they think are important. 价值观念 ❑ *The countries of South Asia also share many common values.* 南亚各国也有许多共同的价值观念。 7 N-UNCOUNT **Value** is used after another noun when mentioning an important or noticeable feature about something. 特色 ❑ *The script has lost all of its shock value over the intervening 24 years.* 在这期间的24年中，该剧本已完全失去了它惊世骇俗的特色。

Thesaurus *value* 另参见:

N.	importance, merit, usefulness 1
	cost, price, worth 3
V.	admire, honor, respect 2
	appraise, estimate, price 4

Word Partnership *value* 的常用搭配：

ADJ. **artistic** value 1
actual value, **equal** value, **great** value 1 3
estimated value 3
V. **decline in** value, **increase in** value, **lose** value 1 3
N. **cash** value, **dollar** value, value **of an investment, market** value 3

★ **valve** /vælv/ (**valves**) N-COUNT A **valve** is a device attached to a pipe or a tube that controls the flow of air or liquid through the pipe or tube. 阀门
→ see **engine**

vam·pire /væmpaɪər/ (**vampires**) N-COUNT A **vampire** is a creature in legends and horror stories. Vampires are said to come out of graves at night and suck the blood of living people. 吸血鬼
→ see **bat**

van ◆◇◇ /væn/ (**vans**) 1 N-COUNT A **van** is a small or medium-sized road vehicle with one row of seats at the front and a space for carrying goods behind. 中小型货车 2 → see also **baggage car**
→ see **car**

van·dal /vænd^əl/ (**vandals**) N-COUNT A **vandal** is someone who deliberately damages things, especially public property. (尤指公共财产的）故意破坏者 ❑ *The street lights were out, smashed by vandals.* 那些路灯不亮了，是被破坏分子们打碎的。

van·dal·ise /vændəlaɪz/ [BRIT] → see **vandalize**

van·dal·ism /vænd^əlɪzəm/ N-UNCOUNT **Vandalism** is the deliberate damaging of things, especially public property. (尤指对公共财产的）故意破坏 ❑ *...a 13-year-old boy whose crime file includes violence, theft, vandalism and bullying.* …一个犯罪档案中包括暴力、偷窃、破坏公物和恃强凌弱的13岁男孩。

van·dal·ize /vænd^əlaɪz/ (**vandalizes, vandalizing, vandalized**)
in BRIT, also use **vandalise**
V-T If something such as a building or part of a building **is vandalized** by someone, it is damaged on purpose. 故意破坏 ❑ *The walls had been horribly vandalized with spray paint.* 这些墙壁已被人用喷漆破坏得一塌糊涂。 ❑ *About 1,000 rioters vandalized buildings and looted stores.* 大约一千个暴徒故意破坏了建筑、抢劫了商店。

van·guard /vængɑrd/ N-SING If someone is **in the vanguard of** something such as a revolution or an area of research, they are involved in the most advanced part of it. You can also refer to the people themselves as **the vanguard**. 先锋 ❑ *Students and intellectuals have been in the vanguard of revolutionary change in China.* 学生和知识分子一直是中国革命变革的先锋。

★ **va·nil·la** /vənɪlə/ N-UNCOUNT **Vanilla** is a flavoring used in ice cream and other sweet food. 香草 ❑ *I added a dollop of vanilla ice cream to the pie.* 我在馅饼中加了一块香草冰淇淋。

van·ish /vænɪʃ/ (**vanishes, vanishing, vanished**) 1 V-I If someone or something **vanishes**, they disappear suddenly or in a way that cannot be explained. 突然消失；神秘失踪 ❑ *He just vanished and was never seen again.* 他就这么突然消失了，再也没有人见到过他。 ❑ *Anne vanished from outside her home last Wednesday.* 上周三安妮在自己家门外神秘失踪了。 2 V-I If something such as a species of animal or a tradition **vanishes**, it stops existing. 消亡 ❑ *Many of these species have vanished or are facing extinction.* 这些物种中的许多已经消亡或是正濒临灭绝。

▲ **van·ity** /vænɪti/ N-UNCOUNT If you refer to someone's **vanity**, you are critical of them because they take great pride in their appearance or abilities. 虚荣 [DISAPPROVAL] ❑ *Men who use steroids are motivated by sheer vanity.* 服用类固醇的男人们纯粹是受了虚荣心的驱使。

van·tage point /væntɪdʒ pɔɪnt/ (**vantage points**) 1 N-COUNT A **vantage point** is a place from which you can see a lot of things. (便于观察的）有利位置 ❑ *From a concealed vantage point, he saw a car arrive.* 从一个隐蔽的有利位置，他看到一辆车到了。 2 N-COUNT If you view a situation **from** a particular **vantage point**, you have a clear understanding of it because of the particular period of time you are in. (某一时期的）观点 ❑ *From today's vantage point, the 1987 crash seems just a blip in the upward progress of the market.* 从今天的观点来看，1987年的暴跌似乎只是市场上扬进程中一次短暂的下挫。

va·por /veɪpər/ (**vapors**)
in BRIT, use **vapour**
N-VAR **Vapor** consists of tiny drops of water or other liquids in the air, that appear as mist. 蒸汽 ❑ *...water vapor.* …水蒸气。
→ see **greenhouse effect, water**

va·pour /veɪpə^r/ [BRIT] → see **vapor**

vari·able /vɛəriəb^əl/ (**variables**) 1 ADJ Something that is **variable** changes quite often, and there usually seems to be no fixed pattern to these changes. 多变的 ❑ *The potassium content of foodstuffs is very variable.* 食品中钾的含量是多变的。 ● **vari·abil·ity** /vɛəriəbɪlɪti/ N-UNCOUNT 可变性 ❑ *There's a great deal of variability between individuals.* 个体之间存在着很大的可变性。 2 N-COUNT A **variable** is a factor that can change in quality, quantity, or size, that you have to take into account in a situation. 可变因素 ❑ *Decisions could be made on the basis of price, delivery dates, after-sales service or any other variable.* 决定可以基于价格、送货日期、售后服务或是任何其他可变因素而做出。
→ see **experiment**

vari·ance /vɛəriəns/ PHRASE If one thing is **at variance with** another, the two things seem to contradict each other. 与…相矛盾 [FORMAL] ❑ *Many of his statements were at variance with the facts.* 他的许多陈述都与事实相矛盾。

▲ **vari·ant** /vɛəriənt/ (**variants**) N-COUNT A **variant** of a particular thing is something that has a different form from that thing, although it is related to it. 变体；变种 ❑ *The quagga was a strikingly beautiful variant of the zebra.* 白氏斑马是一种极其美丽的斑马变种。

vari·ation /vɛərieɪʃ^ən/ (**variations**) 1 N-COUNT A **variation on** something is the same thing presented in a slightly different form. (某一事物）略有变化的形式 ❑ *This delicious variation on an omelette is quick and easy to prepare.* 这种略有变化的美味煎蛋饼做起来又快又容易。 2 N-VAR A **variation** is a change or slight difference in a level, amount, or quantity. 变化；差别 ❑ *The survey found a wide variation in the prices charged for canteen food.* 这项调查发现不同的餐厅出售食物的价格存在很大的差别。

var·ied /vɛərid/ 1 ADJ Something that is **varied** consists of things of different types, sizes, or qualities. 各种各样的 ❑ *It is essential that your diet is varied and balanced.* 重要的是你的饮食应当是多样而平衡的。 2 → see also **vary**

va·ri·ety ◆◆◇ /vəraɪɪti/ (**varieties**) 1 N-UNCOUNT If something has **variety**, it consists of things that are different from each other. 多样化 ❑ *Susan's idea of freedom was to have variety in her life style.* 苏珊对自由的理解就是拥有生活方式的多样化。 2 N-SING A **variety of** things is a number of different kinds or examples of the same thing. (同一事物的）一些不同种类 ❑ *West Hampstead has a variety of good stores and supermarkets.* 西汉普斯特德有几家不同的高品质商店和超市。 ❑ *The island offers such a wide variety of scenery and wildlife.* 这座岛屿有如此丰富多样的景色和野生动植物。 3 N-COUNT A **variety** of something is a type of it. 品种 ❑ *I'm always pleased to try out a new variety.* 我一直乐于尝试新的品种。

Thesaurus *variety* 另参见：

N. diversity, variation; (*ant.*) uniformity 1
assortment 2
breed, sort, type 3

Word Partnership *variety* 的常用搭配：

N. variety **of activities**, variety **of colors**, variety **of foods**, variety **of issues**, variety **of problems**, variety **of products**, variety **of reasons**, variety **of sizes**, variety **of styles**, variety **of ways** 2
V. **choose a** variety, **offer a** variety, **provide a** variety 2

vari·ous ◆◆◇ /vɛəriəs/ 1 ADJ If you say that there are **various** things, you mean there are several different things of the type mentioned. 各种不同的 ❑ *His plan is to spread the capital between various building society accounts.* 他的计划是把资金分散到类型不同的建房互助会的账户中。 2 ADJ If a number of things are described as **various**, they are very different from one another. 非常不同的 ❑ *The methods are many and various.* 方法很多而且各不相同。

vari·ous·ly /vɛəriəsli/ ADV You can use **variously** to introduce a number of different ways that something can be described. 不同地 ❑ *...the crowds, which were variously estimated at two to several thousand.* …估计从两千人到几千人不等的人群。

V

Word Web vegetables

Fresh vegetables are good for you! They're low in fat and calories so they may help you lose weight. **Broccoli** contains vitamin C. It can help you avoid colds and other infections. **Carrots** are a good source of vitamin A, which is good for the eyes. Because they grow in soil, vegetables also contain minerals such as calcium and iron. These substances help keep bones, teeth, and hair healthy. **Leafy** green vegetables like **cabbage** contain antioxidants. These natural chemicals may help prevent cancer. Vegetables also contain **fiber**. This aids digestion and helps carry toxins out of the body quickly.

▲ **var·nish** /vɑrnɪʃ/ **(varnishes, varnishing, varnished)** **1** N-MASS **Varnish** is an oily liquid that is painted onto wood or other material to give it a hard, clear, shiny surface. 清漆 ❑ *The varnish comes in six natural wood shades.* 这种清漆有6种天然木材的色泽可选。 **2** V-T If you **varnish** something, you paint it with varnish. 给…涂上清漆 ❑ *Varnish the table with two or three coats of water-based varnish.* 给桌子涂上2到3层水性清漆。

vary ♦◇◇ /vɛəri/ **(varies, varying, varied)** **1** V-I If things **vary**, they are different from each other in size, amount, or degree. 各不相同 ❑ *As they're handmade, each one varies slightly.* 由于它们是手工制作的，每一件都会略有不同。 ❑ *The text varies from the earlier versions.* 这一文本有别于那些早期的版本。 **2** V-T/V-I If something **varies** or if you **vary** it, it becomes different or changed. 变化；使变化 ❑ *The cost of the alcohol duty varies according to the amount of wine in the bottle.* 这项酒税的额度根据瓶中酒量的不同而变化。 **3** → see also **varied**

Word Partnership *vary* 的常用搭配：

N. prices vary, rates vary, styles vary **1**
vary **by location**, vary **by size**, vary **by state**, vary **by store** **1** **2**
ADV. vary **considerably**, vary **greatly**, vary **slightly**, vary **widely** **1** **2**

▲ **vase** /veɪs, vɑz/ **(vases)** N-COUNT A **vase** is a jar, usually made of glass or pottery, used for holding cut flowers or as an ornament. 花瓶 ❑ *...a vase of red roses.* …一个插着红玫瑰的花瓶。 → see **glass**

vast ♦◇◇ /væst/ **(vaster, vastest)** ADJ Something that is **vast** is extremely large. 巨大的 ❑ *...Afrikaner farmers who own vast stretches of land.* …拥有广阔土地的南非白人农场主们。

Thesaurus *vast* 另参见：

ADJ. broad, endless, massive; *(ant.)* limited

Word Partnership *vast* 的常用搭配：

N. vast **amounts**, vast **distance**, vast **expanse**, vast **knowledge**, vast **majority**, vast **quantities**

vast·ly /væstli/ ADV **Vastly** means to an extremely great degree or extent. 极其 ❑ *The jury has heard two vastly different accounts.* 陪审团听到了两种极为不同的陈述。

Vati·can /vætɪkən/ N-PROPER **The Vatican** is the city state in Rome ruled by the pope that is the center of the Roman Catholic Church. You can also use **the Vatican** to refer to the pope or his officials. 梵蒂冈；教皇或其政府 ❑ *The president had an audience with the pope in the Vatican.* 该总统在梵蒂冈拜会了教皇。

▲ **vault** /vɔlt/ **(vaults, vaulting, vaulted)** **1** N-COUNT A **vault** is a secure room where money and other valuable things can be kept safely. 保险库 ❑ *Most of the money was in storage in bank vaults.* 这笔钱的一大部分是存放在银行保险库中的。 **2** N-COUNT A **vault** is a room underneath a church or in a cemetery where people are buried, usually the members of a single family. 家族墓穴 ❑ *He ordered that Matilda's body should be buried in the family vault.* 他下命令说玛蒂尔达的尸体要埋葬在家族墓穴中。 **3** V-T/V-I If you **vault** something or **vault over** it, you jump quickly onto or over it, especially by putting a hand on top of it to help you balance while you jump. (尤指以手支撑的) 跃过；跳跃 ❑ *He could easily vault the wall.* 他可以轻而易举地跃过这堵墙。

VCD /vi si di/ **(VCDs)** N-COUNT A **VCD** is a computer disc that is used to store video and audio data, especially movies for watching at home. **VCD** is an abbreviation for "video compact disc." VCD盘

VCR /vi si ɑr/ **(VCRs)** N-COUNT A **VCR** is a machine that can be used to record television programs or movies onto videotapes, so that people can play them back and watch them later on a television set. **VCR** is an abbreviation for "video cassette recorder." 卡式录像机 ❑ *Panasonic's Program Director lets you program your VCR so easily!* 松下的程序设置指南让你如此轻松地设置自己的卡式录像机！

veal /vil/ N-UNCOUNT **Veal** is meat from a calf. 小牛肉 ❑ *...a veal cutlet.* …一块小牛排。

veer /vɪər/ **(veers, veering, veered)** **1** V-I If something **veers** in a certain direction, it suddenly moves in that direction. 突然转向 ❑ *The plane veered off the runway and crashed through the perimeter fence.* 这架飞机突然偏离了跑道并且冲断了周边的护栏。 **2** V-I If someone or something **veers** in a certain direction, they change their position or direction in a particular situation. 改变立场 ❑ *He is unlikely to veer from his boss's strongly held views.* 他是不大可能在他的上司强烈坚持的观点上改变立场的。

ve·gan /vigən/ **(vegans)** ADJ Someone who is **vegan** never eats meat or any animal products such as milk, butter, or cheese. 严格的素食主义的 ❑ *The menu changes weekly and usually includes a vegan option.* 这份菜单每周变化，而且通常包括纯素菜肴供选择。 ● N-COUNT A **vegan** is someone who is vegan. 严格的素食主义者 ❑ *...vegetarians and vegans.* …素食者和严格的素食主义者。 → see **vegetarian**

veg·eta·ble ♦◇◇ /vɛdʒtəbᵊl, vɛdʒɪ-/ **(vegetables)** **1** N-COUNT **Vegetables** are plants such as cabbages, potatoes, and onions that you can cook and eat. 蔬菜 ❑ *A good general diet should include plenty of fresh vegetables.* 一份良好的日常饮食应当包括大量的新鲜蔬菜。 **2** ADJ **Vegetable** matter comes from plants. 植物的 [FORMAL] ❑ *...compounds of animal, vegetable or mineral origin.* …来自动物、植物或矿物的化合物。 **3** N-COUNT If someone refers to a brain-damaged person as a **vegetable**, they mean that the person cannot move, think, or speak. 植物人 [usu sing] [INFORMAL, OFFENSIVE]
→ see Word Web: **vegetables**
→ see **vegetarian**

V

Word Web vegetarian

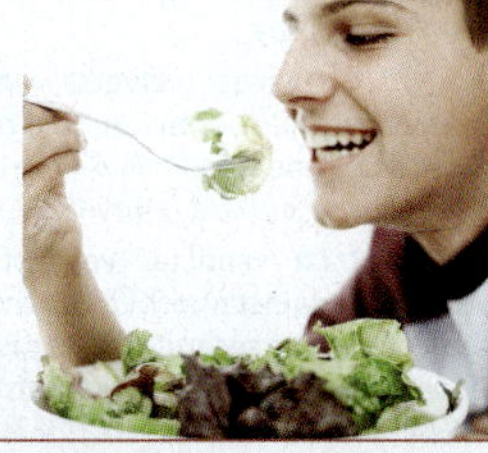

The Greek philosopher Pythagoras was a **vegetarian**. He believed that as long as humans kept killing animals, they would keep killing each other. He decided not to eat **meat**. Vegetarians eat more than just **vegetables**. They also eat fruits, grains, oils, fats, and sugar. **Vegans** are vegetarians who don't eat eggs or dairy products. Some people choose this **diet** for health reasons. A well-balanced veggie diet can be healthy. Some people choose this diet for religious reasons. Others want to make the world's **food** supply go further. It takes fifteen pounds of grain to produce one pound of meat.

> **Word Link** *arian ≈ believing in, having : authoritarian, humanitarian, vegetarian*

veg·etar·ian /vɛdʒɪtɛəriən/ (**vegetarians**) 1 ADJ Someone who is **vegetarian** never eats meat or fish. 素食的 ❑ *Yasmin sticks to a strict vegetarian diet.* 亚斯敏坚持一种严格的纯素饮食。 ● N-COUNT A **vegetarian** is someone who is vegetarian. 素食者 ❑ *...a special menu for vegetarians.* …一份针对素食者的特殊菜单。 2 ADJ **Vegetarian** food does not contain any meat or fish. 素的 ❑ *...vegetarian lasagnes.* …素意式宽面条。
→ see Word Web: **vegetarian**

★ **veg·eta·tion** /vɛdʒɪteɪʃᵊn/ N-UNCOUNT Plants, trees, and flowers can be referred to as **vegetation**. 植物 [FORMAL] ❑ *The inn has a garden of semi-tropical vegetation.* 这家小旅馆拥有一个亚热带植物园。
→ see **erosion**

ve·he·ment /viəmənt/ ADJ If a person or their actions or comments are **vehement**, the person has very strong feelings or opinions and expresses them forcefully. (人) 激动的; (行为或评论) 激烈的 ❑ *She suddenly became very vehement and agitated, jumping around and shouting.* 她突然变得十分激动和不安，四处暴跳并大喊大叫。 ● **ve·he·mence** N-UNCOUNT 激烈 ❑ *He spoke more loudly and with more vehemence than he had intended.* 他演讲得比自己预想的声音更响亮，语调也更激烈。 ● **ve·he·ment·ly** ADV 激烈地 ❑ *Krabbe has always vehemently denied using drugs.* 克拉贝一直激烈地否认服用过毒品。

ve·hi·cle ◆◆◇ /viɪkᵊl/ (**vehicles**) 1 N-COUNT A **vehicle** is a machine with an engine, such as a bus, car, or truck, that carries people or things from place to place. 机动车辆 ❑ *...a vehicle that was somewhere between a tractor and a truck.* …一辆介于拖拉机和卡车之间的机动车。 2 N-COUNT You can use **vehicle** to refer to something that you use in order to achieve a particular purpose. 媒介
→ see **car, traffic**

veil /veɪl/ (**veils**) 1 N-COUNT A **veil** is a piece of thin soft cloth that women sometimes wear over their heads and that can also cover their face. 面纱 ❑ *She's got long fair hair but she's got a veil over it.* 她有长长的金发，却把面纱罩于其上。 2 N-COUNT You can refer to something that hides or partly hides a situation or activity as a **veil**. 掩饰物 ❑ *The country is ridding itself of its disgraced prime minister in a veil of secrecy.* 该国正在暗地里将其名誉扫地的首相赶下台。 3 N-COUNT You can refer to something that you can partly see through, such as a mist, as a **veil**. (薄雾等) 半透明物 [LITERARY] ❑ *The eruption has left a thin veil of dust in the upper atmosphere.* 这次火山喷发在上层大气中留下了一个薄薄的尘土层。

veiled /veɪld/ 1 ADJ A **veiled** comment is expressed in a disguised form rather than directly and openly. 含蓄的 [ADJ n] ❑ *He made only a veiled reference to international concerns over human rights issues.* 他只是含蓄地提及对人权问题的国际关注。 2 ADJ A woman or girl who is **veiled** is wearing a veil. 戴面纱的 ❑ *A veiled woman gave me a kindly smile.* 一位戴面纱的女子给了我一个友好的微笑。

★ **vein** /veɪn/ (**veins**) 1 N-COUNT Your **veins** are the thin tubes in your body through which your blood flows toward your heart. Compare **artery**. 静脉 ❑ *Many veins are found just under the skin.* 许多静脉就在皮肤下面。 2 N-COUNT Something that is written or spoken **in** a particular **vein** is written or spoken in that style or mood. 风格; 语气 ❑ *It is one of his finest works in a lighter vein.* 这是他使用了较为轻盈的风格的最佳作品之一。 3 N-COUNT A **vein of** a particular quality is evidence of that quality that someone often shows in their behavior or work. 迹象 ❑ *A rich vein of humor runs through the book.* 幽默的痕迹遍布全书。 4 N-COUNT The **veins** on a leaf are the thin lines on it. 叶脉 ❑ *...the serrated edges and veins of the feathery leaves.* …这些羽状树叶的锯齿形边缘和叶脉。

★ **ve·loc·ity** /vəlɒsɪti/ (**velocities**) N-VAR **Velocity** is the speed at which something moves in a particular direction. (沿某一方向运动的) 速度 [TECHNICAL] ❑ *...the velocities at which the stars orbit.* …恒星绕轨道运行的速度。

★ **vel·vet** /vɛlvɪt/ (**velvets**) N-MASS **Velvet** is soft material made from cotton, silk, or nylon, that has a thick layer of short cut threads on one side. 天鹅绒 ❑ *...a charcoal-gray overcoat with a velvet collar.* …一件带天鹅绒衣领的深灰色大衣。

ven·det·ta /vɛndɛtə/ (**vendettas**) N-VAR If one person has a **vendetta against** another, the first person wants revenge for something the second person did to them in the past. 宿怨 ❑ *The vice president said the cartoonist has a personal vendetta against him.* 这位副总统说那个漫画家同他有个人宿怨。

vend·ing ma·chine /vɛndɪŋ məʃin/ (**vending machines**) N-COUNT A **vending machine** is a machine from which you can get things such as cigarettes, chocolate, or coffee by putting in money and pressing a button. 投币式自动售货机

▲ **ven·dor** /vɛndər/ (**vendors**) 1 N-COUNT A **vendor** is someone who sells things such as newspapers, cigarettes, or food from a small stall or cart. 小贩 ❑ *...ice cream vendors.* …卖冰淇淋的小贩们。 2 N-COUNT A **vendor** is a company or person that sells a product or service, especially one who sells to other companies that sell to the public. 卖主 [LEGAL] ❑ *Tour America acts as an agent for other vendors and cannot be held responsible for any delays.* "巡游美国"充当其他卖主的代理商，它对任何延误不承担责任。

ve·neer /vɪnɪər/ (**veneers**) 1 N-SING If you refer to the pleasant way that someone or something appears as a **veneer**, you are critical of them because you believe that their true, hidden nature is not good. 虚饰 [DISAPPROVAL] ❑ *He was able to fool the world with his veneer of education.* 他能够通过对自己的教育背景加以虚饰来愚弄世人。 2 N-VAR **Veneer** is a thin layer of wood or plastic that is used to improve the appearance of something. 饰面薄板 ❑ *The wood was cut into large sheets of veneer.* 这些木料被切割成了大块的饰面薄板。

★ **ven·er·able** /vɛnərəbᵊl/ 1 ADJ A **venerable** person deserves respect because they are old and wise. (因年高或睿智) 令人尊敬的 ❑ *Her Chinese friends referred to the empress as their venerable ancestor.* 她的中国朋友们称那位皇后是令他们尊敬的祖先。 2 ADJ Something that is **venerable** is impressive because it is old or important historically. (因历史悠久而) 神圣庄严的 ❑ *May Day has become a venerable institution.* 国际劳动节已经成为一个神圣庄严的既定节日。

▲ **venge·ance** /vɛndʒᵊns/ 1 N-UNCOUNT **Vengeance** is the act of killing, injuring, or harming someone because they have harmed you. 复仇 ❑ *He swore vengeance on everyone involved in the murder.* 他发誓要向每一个与此谋杀案有关联的人复仇。 2 PHRASE If you say that something happens **with a vengeance**, you are emphasizing that it happens to a much greater extent than was expected. 猛烈地 [EMPHASIS] ❑ *It began to rain again with a vengeance.* 天又开始大雨滂沱了。

veni·son /vɛnɪsᵊn, -zᵊn/ N-UNCOUNT **Venison** is the meat of a deer. 鹿肉 ❑ *They had a wonderful lunch of salmon salad and roast venison.* 他们吃了一顿很棒的午餐，有鲑鱼沙拉和烤鹿肉。

ven·om /vɛnəm/ (**venoms**) 1 N-UNCOUNT You can use **venom** to refer to someone's feelings of great bitterness and anger toward someone. 怨恨 ❑ *He reserved particular venom for critics of his foreign policy.* 他对批评他的外交政策的人怀有特别的怨恨。 2 N-MASS The **venom** of a creature such as a snake or spider is the poison that it puts into your body when it bites or stings you. (蛇或蜘蛛等分泌的) 毒液 ❑ *...snake handlers who grow immune to snake venom.* …对蛇毒已产生免疫力的训蛇者们。

ven·om·ous /vɛnəməs/ 1 ADJ If you describe a person or their behavior as **venomous**, you mean that they show great bitterness and anger toward someone. 恶毒的 ❑ *...his terrifying and venomous Aunt Bridget.* …他那可怕而恶毒的布丽奇特姑妈。 2 ADJ A **venomous** snake, spider, or other creature uses poison to attack other creatures. 有毒的 ❑ *He had been bitten by a venomous snake.* 他被一条毒蛇咬了。

★ **vent** /vɛnt/ (**vents, venting, vented**) 1 N-COUNT A **vent** is a hole in something through which air can come in and smoke, gas, or smells can go out. 通风孔; 排放口 ❑ *A lot of steam escaped from the vent at the front of the machine.* 大量蒸汽从机器前端的排气孔冒了出来。 2 V-T If you **vent** your feelings, you express your feelings forcefully. 发泄 ❑ *She telephoned her best friend to vent her frustration.* 她打电话给自己最好的朋友来发泄她的沮丧。 3 PHRASE If you **give vent to** your feelings, you express them forcefully. 发泄 [FORMAL] ❑ *She gave vent to her anger and jealousy.* 她发泄了自己的怨怒和嫉妒。

★ **ven·ti·late** /vɛntᵊleɪt/ (**ventilates, ventilating, ventilated**) V-T If you **ventilate** a room or building, you allow fresh air to get into it. 使通风 ❑ *Ventilate the room properly when stripping paint.* 在刮漆的时候要适当地使房间通风。 ● **ven·ti·la·tion** /vɛntᵊleɪʃᵊn/ N-UNCOUNT 通风 ❑ *The only ventilation comes from tiny sliding windows.* 惟一的通风来自几扇小小的推拉窗。

ven·ture ◆◇◇ /vɛntʃər/ (**ventures, venturing, ventured**) 1 N-COUNT A **venture** is a project or activity that is new, exciting,

V

and difficult because it involves the risk of failure. 风险项目；冒险活动 ❑ *...a Russian-American joint venture.* …一个俄美合资的风险项目。 **2** V-I If you **venture** somewhere, you go somewhere that might be dangerous. 冒险去（某处）[LITERARY] ❑ *People are afraid to venture out for fear of sniper attacks.* 人们不敢冒险外出，害怕狙击手的袭击。 **3** V-T If you **venture** a question or statement, you say it in an uncertain way because you are afraid it might be stupid or wrong. 试探地提出（问题或观点）[WRITTEN] ❑ *"So you're Leo's girlfriend?" he ventured.* "那么你就是利奥的女朋友了？"他小心地问道。 ❑ *He ventured that plants draw part of their nourishment from the air.* 他试探着提出了植物从空气中吸取它们的部分养分的观点。 **4** V-T If you **venture to** do something that requires courage or is risky, you do it. 冒险（做某事）❑ *"Don't ask," he said, whenever Ginny ventured to raise the subject.* 每当金尼冒险提起这个话题时，他总是说："你不要问了。" **5** V-I If you **venture into** an activity, you do something that involves the risk of failure because it is new and different. 冒险（从事活动）❑ *He enjoyed little success when he ventured into business.* 他在冒险涉足生意时很少成功。

ven·ture capi·tal N-UNCOUNT **Venture capital** is capital that is invested in projects that have a high risk of failure, but that will bring large profits if they are successful. 风险资本 [BUSINESS] ❑ *Successful venture capital investment is a lot harder than it sometimes looks.* 成功的风险资本投资有时候比它看上去的情况要复杂得多。

ven·ture capi·tal·ist (**venture capitalists**) N-COUNT A **venture capitalist** is someone who makes money by investing in high risk projects. 风险投资者 [BUSINESS]

★ **venue** ♦◇◇ /vɛnyu/ (**venues**) N-COUNT The **venue** for an event or activity is the place where it will happen. 举办场所 ❑ *The International Convention Centre is the venue for a three-day arts festival.* 国际会议中心是为期3天的艺术节的举办场所。
→ see **concert**

ve·ran·da /vərændə/ (**verandas**) also **verandah** N-COUNT A **veranda** is a roofed platform along the outside of a house. 阳台 ❑ *They had their coffee and tea on the veranda.* 他们在阳台上享用了自己的咖啡和茶。

verb /vɜrb/ (**verbs**) **1** N-COUNT A **verb** is a word such as "sing," "feel," or "die" that is used with a subject to say what someone or something does or what happens to them, or to give information about them. 动词 **2** → see also **phrasal verb**

Word Link *verb ≈ word : proverb, verbal, verbatim*

★ **ver·bal** /vɜrbəl/ **1** ADJ You use **verbal** to indicate that something is expressed in speech rather than in writing or action. 口头的 ❑ *They were jostled and subjected to a torrent of verbal abuse.* 他们被推来搡去，并受到了潮水般的辱骂。 ● **ver·bal·ly** ADV 口头地 ❑ *Dave drank heavily and became verbally abusive.* 戴夫喝多了，嘴里脏话连篇。 **2** ADJ You use **verbal** to indicate that something is connected with words and the use of words. 词语的；文字的 [ADJ n] ❑ *The test has scores for verbal skills, mathematical skills, and abstract reasoning skills.* 该项测试对文字表达技能、数学技能和抽象推理技能进行记分。 **3** ADJ In grammar, **verbal** means relating to a verb. 动词的 ❑ *...a verbal noun.* …一个动名词。

Word Link *ver ≈ truth : verbatim, verdict, verify*

ver·ba·tim /vərbeɪtɪm/ ADV If you repeat something **verbatim**, you use exactly the same words as were used originally. 一字不差地 [ADV after v] ❑ *The president's speeches are regularly reproduced verbatim in the state-run newspapers.* 这位总统的演讲经常会一字不差地被刊登在那些国有报纸上。 ● ADJ **Verbatim** is also an adjective. 一字不差的 [ADJ n] ❑ *I was treated to a verbatim report of every conversation she's taken part in over the past week.* 有人给了我一份报告，上面一字不差地记录了她在过去的一周中参与的每一次谈话。

★ **ver·dict** ♦◇◇ /vɜrdɪkt/ (**verdicts**) **1** N-COUNT In a court of law, the **verdict** is the decision that is given by the jury or judge at the end of a trial. 裁决 ❑ *The jury returned a unanimous guilty verdict.* 该陪审团作出了一份一致通过的有罪裁决。 **2** N-COUNT Someone's **verdict** on something is their opinion of it, after thinking about it or investigating it. 判断 ❑ *The doctor's verdict was that he was entirely healthy.* 这名医生的判断是他完全是健康的。
→ see **trial**

★ **verge** /vɜrdʒ/ (**verges, verging, verged**) **1** PHRASE If you are **on the verge of** something, you are going to do it very soon or it is likely to happen or begin very soon. 即将 ❑ *The country was on the verge of becoming prosperous and successful.* 这个国家即将变得繁荣昌盛。 **2** N-COUNT The **verge** of a road is a narrow piece of ground by the side of a road, which is usually covered with grass or flowers. （通常种有花草的）路边 [BRIT]

in AM, use **shoulder**

▶ **verge on** PHRASAL VERB If someone or something **verges on** a particular state or quality, they are almost the same as that state or quality. 接近 ❑ *...a fury that verged on madness.* …一种近乎疯狂的暴怒。

veri·fy /vɛrɪfaɪ/ (**verifies, verifying, verified**) **1** V-T If you **verify** something, you check that it is true by careful examination or investigation. 核实 ❑ *I verified the source from which I had that information.* 我核实了我获知那条信息的来源。 ● **veri·fi·ca·tion** /vɛrɪfɪkeɪʃən/ N-UNCOUNT 核实 ❑ *All charges against her are dropped pending the verification of her story.* 在她的陈述得到证实前，所有针对她的指控都被撤回。 **2** V-T If you **verify** something, you state or confirm that it is true. 证实 [no cont] ❑ *The government has not verified any of those reports.* 该政府尚未证实那些报道中的任何一个。

veri·table /vɛrɪtəbəl/ ADJ You can use **veritable** to emphasize the size, amount, or nature of something. 名副其实的 [EMPHASIS] ❑ *...a veritable feast of pre-game entertainment.* …一场名副其实的赛前娱乐盛宴。

ver·nacu·lar /vərnækyələr/ (**vernaculars**) N-COUNT **The vernacular** is the language or dialect that is most widely spoken by ordinary people in a region or country. 方言 ❑ *...books or plays written in the vernacular.* …用此方言写的一些书或剧本。

Word Link *vers ≈ turning : subversion, versatile, version*

★ **ver·sa·tile** /vɜrsətəl/ **1** ADJ If you say that a person is **versatile**, you approve of them because they have many different skills. 多才多艺的 [APPROVAL] ❑ *He had been one of the game's most versatile athletes.* 他是这次运动会中最有才能的运动员之一。 ● **ver·sa·til·ity** /vɜrsətɪlɪti/ N-UNCOUNT 多才多艺 ❑ *Aileen stands out for her incredible versatility as an actress.* 作为一名女演员，艾琳以其难以置信的多才多艺而出类拔萃。 **2** ADJ A tool, machine, or material that is **versatile** can be used for many different purposes. 用途广泛的 ❑ *Never before has computing been so versatile.* 计算机技术从未像现在这样用途广泛。 ● **ver·sa·til·ity** N-UNCOUNT 用途广泛 ❑ *Velvet as a fabric is not known for its versatility.* 天鹅绒作为一种织物并非以其用途广泛而闻名。

★ **verse** /vɜrs/ (**verses**) **1** N-UNCOUNT **Verse** is writing arranged in lines that have rhythm and that often rhyme at the end. 诗；韵文 ❑ *I have been moved to write a few lines of verse.* 我曾经被感动得写了几行诗。 **2** N-COUNT A **verse** is one of the parts into which a poem, a song, or a chapter of the Bible or the Koran is divided. 诗节；歌曲的段落；（《圣经》、《古兰经》的）节 ❑ *This verse describes three signs of spring.* 这节诗描述了春天的3个征兆。

ver·sion ♦♦◇ /vɜrʒən/ (**versions**) **1** N-COUNT A **version of** something is a particular form of it in which some details are different from earlier or later forms. 版本；变体 ❑ *...an updated version of his bestselling book.* …他这本畅销书的一个最新版本。 ❑ *Ludo is a version of an ancient Indian racing game.* "鲁多游戏"是一种古代印度竞赛游戏的变体。 **2** N-COUNT Someone's **version of** an event is their own description of it, especially when it is different from other people's. （某人对某事有别于他人的）说法 ❑ *Some former hostages contradicted the official version of events.* 一些以前的人质反驳了官方对这些事件的说法。

★ **ver·sus** /vɜrsəs/ **1** PREP You use **versus** to indicate that two figures, ideas, or choices are opposed. 与…相对 ❑ *Only 18.8% of the class of 1982 had some kind of diploma four years after high school, versus 45% of the class of 1972.* 相对于1972届学生中有45%在中学毕业4年后获得了某种文凭来说，1982届学生的这一比例只有18.8%。 **2** PREP **Versus** is used to indicate that two teams or people are competing against each other in a sports event. （体育比赛中）…对… ❑ *Italy versus Japan is turning out to be a surprisingly well matched competition.* 意大利对日本队的比赛结果是一场出人意料地势均力敌的比赛。 **3** PREP **Versus** is used in a court of law to indicate that two people or organizations are involved in a law suit. The abbreviation **v** is also used. （在法庭上）…诉… ❑ *That case became known as Healey versus Jones.* 那起讼案被称作"希利诉琼斯案"。

ver·te·bra /vɜrtɪbrə/ (**vertebrae** /vɜrtɪbreɪ, -bri/) N-COUNT **Vertebrae** are the small circular bones that form the spine of a human being or animal. 椎骨

ver·ti·cal /vɜrtɪkᵊl/ ADJ Something that is **vertical** stands or points straight up. 垂直的 ❑ *The climber inched up a vertical wall of rock.* 那名登山者一点点爬上了一处垂直的岩石峭壁。● **ver·ti·cal·ly** ADV 垂直地 [ADV after v] ❑ *Cut each bulb in half vertically.* 将每一个球茎垂直切成两半。
→ see **graph**

very ♦♦♦ /vɛri/ **1** ADV **Very** is used to give emphasis to an adjective or adverb. 很 [ADV adj/adv] [EMPHASIS] ❑ *The problem and the answer are very simple.* 这个问题及其答案都很简单。❑ *I'm very sorry.* 我很抱歉。❑ *They are getting the hang of it very quickly.* 他们会很快地掌握它的窍门。**2** PHRASE **Not very** is used with an adjective or adverb to say that something is not at all true, or that it is true only to a small degree. 一点儿也不；不太… ❑ *She's not very impressed with them.* 她对他们没有什么印象。❑ *"How well do you know her?"—"Not very."* "你对她有多了解？"——"不是很多。" **3** ADV You use **very** to give emphasis to a superlative adjective or adverb. For example, if you say that something is **the very best**, you are emphasizing that it is the best. 最（在形容词或副词最高级前表示强调）[ADV superl] [EMPHASIS] ❑ *They will be helped by the very latest in navigation aids.* 他们将得到最新的导航设备的帮助。❑ *I am feeling in the very best of spirits.* 我感觉自己正处于最佳的精神状态。**4** ADJ You use **very** with certain nouns in order to specify an extreme position or extreme point in time. （置于某些名词前表示极限）最 [ADJ n] [EMPHASIS] ❑ *At the very back of the yard was a wooden shack.* 在院子的最后面是一间小木屋。❑ *I turned to the very end of the book, to read the final words.* 我翻到书的最后面，读了最后的那些话。**5** ADJ You use **very** with nouns to emphasize that something is exactly the right one or exactly the same one. （置于名词前表示强调）最佳的；最合适的 [ADJ n] [EMPHASIS] ❑ *Everybody says he is the very man for the case.* 人人都说他是这件案子的最佳人选。**6** ADJ You use **very** with nouns to emphasize the importance or seriousness of what you are saying. （置于名词前表示重要性）甚至 [ADJ n] [EMPHASIS] ❑ *At one stage his very life was in danger.* 有一个阶段甚至连他的生命都处于危险之中。❑ *History is taking place before your very eyes.* 历史甚至就在你的眼前发生着。**7** PHRASE The expression **very much so** is an emphatic way of answering "yes" to something or saying that it is true or correct. 确实如此 [EMPHASIS] ❑ *"Are you enjoying your vacation?"—"Very much so."* "你假期过得愉快吗？"——"非常愉快。" **8** CONVENTION **Very well** is used to say that you agree to do something or you accept someone's answer, even though you might not be completely satisfied with it. （表示勉强同意或接受）好吧 [FORMULAE] ❑ *"We need proof, sir." Another pause. Then, "Very well."* "我们需要证据，先生。" 又顿了一下。然后说道，"好吧。" **9** PHRASE If you say that you **cannot very well** do something, you mean that it would not be right or possible to do it. 不可能（做某事）❑ *I said yes. I can't very well say no under the circumstances.* 我答应了。在当时那种情形下我不可能不答应。

> **Very, so,** and **too** can all be used to intensify the meaning of an adjective, an adverb, or a word like **much** or **many**. However, they are not used in the same way. **Very** is the simplest intensifier. It has no other meaning beyond that. **So** can suggest an emotional reaction on the part of the speaker, such as pleasure, surprise, or disappointment. ❑ *John makes me so angry!... Oh thank you so much!* **So** can also refer forward to a result clause introduced by **that**. ❑ *The procession was forced to move so slowly that he arrived three hours late.* **Too** suggests an excessive or undesirable amount, often so much that a particular result does not or cannot happen. ❑ *She does wear too much makeup at times... He was too late to save her.*

V

> **Thesaurus** *very* 另参见：
> ADV. absolutely, extremely, greatly, highly **1**

ves·sel ♦◇◇ /vɛsᵊl/ (**vessels**) **1** N-COUNT A **vessel** is a ship or large boat. 船；舰 [FORMAL] ❑ *...a New Zealand navy vessel.* …一艘新西兰海军舰艇。**2** → see also **blood vessel**
→ see **ship**

▲ **vest** /vɛst/ (**vests**) **1** N-COUNT A **vest** is a sleeveless piece of clothing with buttons that people usually wear over a shirt. 马甲 [AM]

in BRIT, use **waistcoat**

2 N-COUNT A **vest** is a piece of underwear that you can wear on the top half of your body in order to keep warm. 背心 [BRIT]

in AM, use **undershirt**

vest·ed in·ter·est (**vested interests**) N-VAR If you have a **vested interest in** something, you have a very strong reason for acting in a particular way, for example, to protect your money, power, or reputation. 既得利益 ❑ *The administration has no vested interest in proving public schools good or bad.* 该行政部门在证明公立学校的好坏方面没有什么既得利益。

ves·tige /vɛstɪdʒ/ (**vestiges**) N-COUNT A **vestige of** something is a very small part that still remains of something that was once much larger or more important. 残留部分；遗迹 [FORMAL] ❑ *We represent the last vestige of what made this nation great – hard work.* 我们代表了曾经使这个国家伟大的仅存的品质——勤奋。

vet /vɛt/ (**vets, vetting, vetted**) **1** N-COUNT A **vet** is someone who is qualified to treat sick or injured animals. **Vet** is an abbreviation for **veterinarian**. 兽医 [INFORMAL] ❑ *She's at the vet, with her dog, right now.* 她此刻正带着自己的狗在兽医那里。**2** N-COUNT A **vet** is someone who has served in the armed forces of their country, especially during a war. **Vet** is an abbreviation for **veteran**. （尤指曾在战争中服役的）退伍军人 [AM, INFORMAL] ❑ *The New England Shelter in Boston will serve Christmas dinner for 200 vets.* 位于波士顿的新英格兰收容所将为200名老兵提供圣诞晚餐。**3** V-T If someone **is vetted**, they are investigated fully before being given a particular job, role, or position, especially one that involves military or political secrets. （尤指将要从事军事或政治机密的工作人员）受审查 [usu passive] [mainly BRIT] ❑ *She was secretly vetted before she ever undertook any work for me.* 她在为我承担任何工作之前受到了秘密审查。● **vet·ting** N-UNCOUNT 审查 ❑ *The government is to make major changes to the procedure for carrying out security vetting.* 该政府将对执行安全审查的程序作出重大调整。

vet·er·an ♦◇◇ /vɛtərən/ (**veterans**) **1** N-COUNT A **veteran** is someone who has served in the armed forces of their country, especially during a war. 退伍军人 ❑ *They approved a $1.1 billion package of pay increases for the veterans of the Persian Gulf War.* 他们批准了为参加过波斯湾战争的退伍军人增付11亿美元的一揽子计划。**2** N-COUNT You use **veteran** to refer to someone who has been involved in a particular activity for a long time. 经验丰富的人 ❑ *...Annette Michelson, the veteran critic and professor of cinema studies at New York University.* …安妮特·米切尔森，这位纽约大学电影研究的教授和资深影评人。

vet·eri·nar·ian /vɛtərɪnɛəriən/ (**veterinarians**) N-COUNT A **veterinarian** is a person who is qualified to treat sick or injured animals. 兽医 [mainly AM]

vet·eri·nary /vɛtərənɛri/ ADJ **Veterinary** is used to describe the work of a person whose job is to treat sick or injured animals, or to describe the medical treatment of animals. 兽医的 [ADJ n] ❑ *It was decided that our veterinary screening of horses at events should be continued.* 已经决定，我们对参赛马匹的疾病检查将继续进行。

★ **veto** /vitoʊ/ (**vetoes, vetoing, vetoed**) **1** V-T If someone in authority **vetoes** something, they forbid it, or stop it from being put into action. 否决 ❑ *The president vetoed the economic package passed by Congress.* 总统否决了国会通过的一揽子经济计划。● N-COUNT **Veto** is also a noun. 否决 ❑ *They need 12 votes to override his veto.* 他们需要12票来推翻他的否决。**2** N-UNCOUNT **Veto** is the right that someone in authority has to forbid something. 否决权 ❑ *...the president's power of veto.* …总统的否决权。

vex /vɛks/ (**vexes, vexing, vexed**) **1** V-T If someone or something **vexes** you, they make you feel annoyed, puzzled, and frustrated. 使烦恼；使迷惑；使沮丧 ❑ *It vexed me to think of others gossiping behind my back.* 想到别人在我背后说闲话让我很恼火。● **vexed** ADJ 烦恼的 ❑ *Exporters, farmers and industrialists alike are vexed and blame the government.* 出口商、农场主和工业家们同样恼火，都谴责政府。● **vex·ing** ADJ 令人烦恼的 ❑ *There remains, however, another and more vexing problem.* 然而还剩下另外一个更令人烦恼的问题。**2** → see also **vexed**

vexed /vɛkst/ **1** ADJ A **vexed** problem or question is very difficult and causes people a lot of trouble. 棘手的 ❑ *Ministers have begun work on the vexed issue of economic union.* 部长们已经开始着手处理这个棘手的经济联盟问题。**2** → see also **vex**

via ♦◇◇ /vaɪə, viə/ **1** PREP If you go somewhere **via** a particular place, you go through that place on the way to your destination. 经由 ❑ *We drove via Lovech to the old Danube town of Ruse.* 我们驱车经由

洛维奇去了多瑙河畔的古城鲁塞。 2 PREP If you do something **via** a particular means or person, you do it by making use of that means or person. 通过 ❑ *The technology to allow relief workers to contact the outside world via satellite already exists.* 允许救援人员通过卫星与外界取得联系的技术已经存在。

▲ **vi·able** /vaɪəbᵊl/ ADJ Something that is **viable** is capable of doing what it is intended to do. 可行的 ❑ *Cash alone will not make Eastern Europe's banks viable.* 单靠现金不可能使东欧的银行维持下去。 ● **vi·abil·ity** /vaɪəbɪlɪti/ N-UNCOUNT 可行性 ❑ *...the shaky financial viability of the nuclear industry.* …核工业不可靠的财政可行性。

vibe /vaɪb/ (**vibes**) N-COUNT **Vibes** are the good or bad atmosphere that you sense with a person or in a place. 感应；气氛 [INFORMAL] ❑ *Sorry, Chris, but I have bad vibes about this guy.* 对不起，克里斯，但我对这家伙感觉不太好。

vi·brant /vaɪbrənt/ 1 ADJ Someone or something that is **vibrant** is full of life, energy, and enthusiasm. 充满活力的 ❑ *Tom felt himself being drawn toward her vibrant personality.* 汤姆感到自己正被她充满活力的个性所吸引。 ❑ *...Shakespeare's vibrant language.* …莎士比亚那充满活力的语言。 ● **vi·bran·cy** /vaɪbrənsi/ N-UNCOUNT 活力 ❑ *She was a woman with extraordinary vibrancy and extraordinary knowledge.* 她是一个活力四射、知识渊博的女性。 2 ADJ **Vibrant** colors are very bright and clear. (色彩) 鲜亮的 ❑ *Horizon blue, corn yellow and pistachio green are just three of the vibrant colors in this range.* 天际蓝、玉米黄和淡草绿只是这一色域中的3种鲜亮色彩。 ● **vi·brant·ly** ADV 鲜亮地 [ADV adj] ❑ *...a selection of vibrantly colored French cast-iron saucepans.* …一套精选的色彩鲜亮的法国铸铁炖锅。

vi·brate /vaɪbreɪt/ (**vibrates, vibrating, vibrated**) V-T/V-I If something **vibrates** or if you **vibrate** it, it shakes with repeated small, quick movements. 使颤动；颤动 ❑ *The ground shook and the cliffs seemed to vibrate.* 大地摇晃，那些悬崖似乎在颤动。 ● **vi·bra·tion** /vaɪbreɪʃᵊn/ N-VAR (**vibrations**) 颤动 ❑ *The vibrations of the vehicles rattled the store windows.* 那些车辆的颤动使得商店的窗户咯咯作响。
→ see **ear, sound**

vic·ar /vɪkər/ (**vicars**) N-COUNT; N-VOC A **vicar** is a priest who is in charge of a chapel that is associated with a parish church in the Episcopal Church in the United States. (美国新教圣公会教区中掌管一座小教堂的) 牧师 [AM]

vice ◆◇◇ /vaɪs/ (**vices**) 1 N-COUNT A **vice** is a habit that is regarded as a weakness in someone's character, but not usually as a serious fault. 不良习惯 ❑ *His only vice is to get drunk on champagne after concluding a successful piece of business.* 他惟一的不良习惯就是在成功做成一笔生意之后喝香槟酒至大醉。 2 N-UNCOUNT **Vice** refers to criminal activities, especially those connected with pornography or prostitution. (尤指与色情、卖淫等有关的) 犯罪活动 ❑ *He said those responsible for offences connected with vice, gaming and drugs should be deported on conviction.* 他说那些跟卖淫、赌博、贩毒有关的罪犯应在判罪后被驱逐出境。 3 N-COUNT A **vice** is a tool with a pair of parts that hold an object tightly while you do work on it. 虎钳 [BRIT]

in AM, use **vise**

vice ver·sa /vaɪsə vɜrsə, vaɪs/ PHRASE **Vice versa** is used to indicate that the reverse of what you have said is true. For example, "women may bring their husbands with them, and vice versa" means that men may also bring their wives with them. 反之亦然 ❑ *They want to send students from low-income homes into more affluent neighborhoods and vice versa.* 他们想把来自低收入家庭的学生送到较为富裕的地区，反之亦然。

★ **vi·cin·ity** /vɪsɪnɪti/ N-SING If something is **in the vicinity of** a particular place, it is near it. (在…) 附近 [FORMAL] ❑ *There were a hundred or so hotels in the vicinity of the station.* 在车站附近有大约一百家左右的旅馆。

★ **vi·cious** /vɪʃəs/ 1 ADJ A **vicious** person or a **vicious** blow is violent and cruel. 凶残的 ❑ *He was a cruel and vicious man.* 他是一个残忍而凶恶的人。 ❑ *He suffered a vicious attack by a gang of white youths.* 他遭到了一帮白人青年凶残的攻击。 ● **vi·cious·ly** ADV 凶残地 ❑ *She had been viciously attacked with a hammer.* 她曾被人用锤子凶残地袭击过。 ● **vi·cious·ness** N-UNCOUNT 凶残 ❑ *...the intensity and viciousness of these attacks.* …这些袭击的激烈和凶残。 2 ADJ A **vicious** remark is cruel and intended to upset someone. 恶毒的 ❑ *It is a deliberate, nasty and vicious attack on a young man's character.* 这是对一位青年的人格蓄意的、下流的和恶毒的攻击。 ● **vi·cious·ly** ADV 恶毒地 [ADV with v] ❑ *"He deserved to die," said Penelope viciously.* "他该死，" 佩内洛普恶毒地说道。

> **Thesaurus** *vicious* 另参见：
> ADJ. brutal, cruel, violent; (*ant.*) nice 1 2

vi·cious cir·cle (**vicious circles**) also **vicious cycle** N-COUNT A **vicious circle** is a problem or difficult situation that has the effect of creating new problems that then cause the original problem or situation to occur again. 恶性循环 ❑ *The more pesticides are used, the more resistant the insects become so the more pesticides have to be used. It's a vicious circle.* 杀虫剂使用得越多，那些昆虫的抵抗力越强，因此就要使用更多的杀虫剂。这是一个恶性循环。

vic·tim ◆◆◇ /vɪktəm/ (**victims**) 1 N-COUNT A **victim** is someone who has been hurt or killed. 受害者 ❑ *Statistically our chances of being the victims of violent crime are remote.* 从统计上来看，我们成为暴力犯罪受害者的可能性是微乎其微的。 2 N-COUNT A **victim** is someone who has suffered as a result of someone else's actions or beliefs, or as a result of unpleasant circumstances. 牺牲品 ❑ *He was a victim of racial prejudice.* 他是种族偏见的一个牺牲品。 ❑ *He described himself and Altman as victims rather than participants in the scandal.* 他把自己和奥尔特曼描述成这一丑闻的受害者，而不是参与者。

vic·tim·ise /vɪktɪmaɪz/ [BRIT] → see **victimize**

vic·tim·ize ◆◇◇ /vɪktəmaɪz/ (**victimizes, victimizing, victimized**)

in BRIT, also use **victimise**

V-T If someone **is victimized**, they are deliberately treated unfairly. 受迫害 ❑ *He felt the students had been victimized because they'd voiced opposition to the government.* 他认为学生们因发表反对政府的言论而受到了迫害。 ● **vic·timi·za·tion** /vɪktəmɪzeɪʃᵊn/ N-UNCOUNT 迫害 ❑ *...society's cruel victimization of women.* …社会对妇女的残酷迫害。

vic·tor /vɪktər/ (**victors**) N-COUNT The **victor** in a battle or contest is the person who wins. 胜利者 [LITERARY] ❑ *Oliver Townsend and co-driver Kirk Lee eventually emerged as victors after five different cars had led the event.* 5辆车相继领先，最终奥利佛・汤森和副驾驶员柯克・李成为胜利者。

Vic·to·rian /vɪktɔriən/ (**Victorians**) 1 ADJ **Victorian** means belonging to, connected with, or typical of Britain in the middle and last parts of the 19th century, when Victoria was Queen. 维多利亚时代的 ❑ *We have a lovely old Victorian house.* 我们有一幢可爱的维多利亚时代的老房子。 ❑ *...a Victorian-style family portrait.* …一幅维多利亚时代风格的家族画像。 2 ADJ You can use **Victorian** to describe people who have old-fashioned attitudes, especially about good behavior and morals. 维多利亚时代的 ❑ *Victorian values are much misunderstood.* 维多利亚时代的价值观被极大地误解了。 3 N-COUNT The **Victorians** were the British people who lived in the time of Queen Victoria. 维多利亚时代的人 ❑ *The Victorians were the last people to invest properly in the railways.* 维多利亚时代的人是恰当投资铁路的最后一代人。

★ **vic·to·ri·ous** /vɪktɔriəs/ ADJ You use **victorious** to describe someone who has won a victory in a struggle, war, or competition. 胜利的 ❑ *In 1978 he played for the victorious Argentinian side in the World Cup.* 1978年，他为世界杯上获胜的阿根廷队踢球。

vic·to·ry ◆◆◇ /vɪktəri, vɪktri/ (**victories**) 1 N-VAR A **victory** is a success in a struggle, war, or competition. 胜利 ❑ *Union leaders are heading for victory in their battle over workplace rights.* 工会领袖们在争取工作场所权利的斗争中正迈向胜利。 2 PHRASE If you say that someone has won a **moral victory**, you mean that although they have officially lost a contest or dispute, they have succeeded in showing they are right about something. 精神胜利 ❑ *She said her party had won a moral victory.* 她说她的党已赢得了精神上的胜利。

> **Thesaurus** *victory* 另参见：
> N. conquest, success, win; (*ant.*) defeat 1

video ◆◆◇ /vɪdioʊ/ (**videos, videoing, videoed**) 1 N-COUNT A **video** is a movie or television program recorded on tape for people to watch on a television set. 录像带 ❑ *...sports and exercise videos.* …体育和运动录像带。 2 N-UNCOUNT **Video** is the system of recording movies and events on tape so that people can watch them on a television set. 录像 ❑ *She has watched the race on video.* 她已观看了比赛的录像。 ❑ *...manufacturers of audio and video equipment.* …录音和录像设备制造商。 3 N-COUNT A **video** is a machine that you can use to record television programs and play videotapes on a television set. 录像机 [mainly BRIT]

in AM, usually use **VCR**

V

4 V-T If you **video** a television program or event, you record it on tape using a VCR or video camera, so that you can watch it later. 录制 [mainly BRIT]

in AM, usually use **tape, videotape**

→ see **DVD**

video cas·sette (**video cassettes**) also **videocassette** N-COUNT A **video cassette** is a cassette containing videotape, on which you can record or watch moving pictures and sounds. 盒式录像带

video-conference (**video-conferences**) also **videoconference** N-COUNT A **video-conference** is a meeting that takes place using video conferencing. 电视会议 [BUSINESS] ❑ *It is now possible to hold a video conference in real time on a cellphone.* 现在有可能在移动电话上举行实时电视会议。

video con·fer·enc·ing /vɪdioʊ kɒnfrənsɪŋ/ also **video-conferencing, videoconferencing** N-UNCOUNT **Video conferencing** is a system that enables people in various places around the world to have a meeting by seeing and hearing each other on a screen. 电视会议系统 [BUSINESS] ❑ *We also hope to use video conferencing to train and supervise staff.* 我们还希望能用电视会议系统来培训和指导员工。

video game (**video games**) N-COUNT A **video game** is an electronic or computerized game that you play on your television or on a computer screen. 电子游戏

video·phone /vɪdioʊfoʊn/ (**videophones**) also **video phone** N-COUNT A **videophone** is a telephone that has a camera and screen so that people who are using the phone can see and hear each other. 可视电话

video re·cord·er (**video recorders**) N-COUNT A **video recorder** or a **video cassette recorder** is the same as a **VCR**. 盒式磁带录像机

Word Link *vid, vis ≈ seeing : audiovisual, videotape, visible*

video·tape /vɪdioʊteɪp/ (**videotapes, videotaping, videotaped**) also **video tape** **1** N-UNCOUNT **Videotape** is magnetic tape that is used to record moving pictures and sounds to be shown on television. 录像带 ❑ *...the use of videotape in criminal court rooms.* …录像带在刑事法庭上的使用。 **2** N-COUNT A **videotape** is the same as a **video cassette**. 盒式录像带 **3** V-T If you **videotape** a television program or event, you record it on tape using a video recorder or video camera, so that you can watch it later. 录制 [mainly AM] ❑ *She videotaped the entire trip.* 她录下了整个旅程。

vie /vaɪ/ (**vies, vying, vied**) V-RECIP If one person or thing **is vying** with another for something, the people or things are competing for it. 竞争 [FORMAL] ❑ *California is vying with other states to capture a piece of the growing communications market.* 加州正在与各州竞争，以求在不断扩大的通讯市场上获得份额。 ❑ *The two are vying for the support of New York voters.* 两人正在争夺纽约选民的支持。

view ♦♦♦ /vyu/ (**views, viewing, viewed**) **1** N-COUNT Your **views** on something are the beliefs or opinions that you have about it, for example,whether you think it is good, bad, right, or wrong. 观点 ❑ *Washington and Moscow are believed to have similar views on Kashmir.* 华盛顿和莫斯科被认为在克什米尔问题上持有相似的观点。 ❑ *You should also make your views known to your congressperson.* 你们的观点也应该让国会议员们知道。 **2** N-SING Your **view of** a particular subject is the way that you understand and think about it. 看法 ❑ *The whole point was to get away from a Christian-centered view of religion.* 整个核心问题是要摆脱以基督教为中心的宗教观。 **3** V-T If you **view** something in a particular way, you think of it in that way. 看待 ❑ *First-generation Americans view the United States as a land of golden opportunity.* 第一代美国人把美国看成一个充满良机的大陆。 ❑ *Abigail's mother Linda views her daughter's talent with a mixture of pride and worry.* 阿比盖尔的母亲琳达看待女儿的天赋时既骄傲又担忧。 **4** N-COUNT The **view** from a window or high place is everything that can be seen from that place, especially when it is considered to be beautiful. 景色 ❑ *The view from our window was one of beautiful green countryside.* 从我们窗口可以看到一片绿色乡村的美景。 **5** N-SING If you have a **view of** something, you can see it. 看到 ❑ *He stood up to get a better view of the blackboard.* 他站了起来，以便能更清楚地看黑板。 **6** N-UNCOUNT You use **view** in expressions to do with being able to see something. For example, if something is **in view**, you can see it. If something is **in full view of everyone**, everyone can see it. 在视线内 ❑ *She was lying there in full view of anyone who walked by.* 她躺在那儿，任何路过的人都能看到她。 **7** V-T If you **view** something, you look at it for a particular purpose. 察看 [FORMAL] ❑ *They came back to view the house again.* 他们又回来察看了一下房子。 **8** V-T If you **view** a television program, video, or movie, you watch it. 观看 [FORMAL] ❑ *We have viewed the video recording of the incident.* 我们已观看了该事件的录像。 **9** N-SING **View** refers to the way in which a piece of text or graphics is displayed on a computer screen. (文本或图表在计算机屏幕上的) 显示方式 [COMPUTING] ❑ *To see the current document in full-page view, click the Page Zoom Full button.* 要全页显示来察看当前文件，请点击全屏显示按钮。 **10** PHRASE You use **in my view** when you want to indicate that you are stating a personal opinion, that other people might not agree with. 在我看来 ❑ *In my view things won't change.* 在我看来形势不会改变。 **11** PHRASE You use **in view of** when you are taking into consideration facts that have just been mentioned or are just about to be mentioned. 鉴于; 考虑到 ❑ *In view of the fact that Hobson was not a trained economist, his achievements were remarkable.* 鉴于霍布森非科班出身的经济学家这一事实，他的成就是很了不起的。 **12** PHRASE If something such as a work of art is **on view**, it is shown in public for people to look at. 在展出 ❑ *A significant exhibition of contemporary sculpture will be on view at the Portland Gallery.* 一场意义重大的当代雕塑展将在波特兰美术馆展出。 **13** PHRASE If you do something **with a view to** doing something else, you do it because you hope it will result in that other thing being done. 目的在于 ❑ *He has called a meeting of all parties tomorrow, with a view to forming a national reconciliation government.* 他已召集各派于明天会谈，目的在于组建一个民族和解政府。

view·er /vyuər/ (**viewers**) **1** N-COUNT **Viewers** are people who watch television, or who are watching a particular program on television. 电视观众 ❑ *These programs are each watched by around 19 million viewers every week.* 这些电视节目中，每个每周都有约一千九百万观众收看。 **2** N-COUNT A **viewer** is someone who is looking carefully at a picture or other interesting object. 观赏者 ❑ *...the relationship between the art object and the viewer.* …艺术品和观赏者之间的关系。

→ see **photography**

view·point /vyupɔɪnt/ (**viewpoints**) **1** N-COUNT Someone's **viewpoint** is the way that they think about things in general, or the way they think about a particular thing. 视点 ❑ *The novel is shown from the girl's viewpoint.* 这部小说是从那个女孩儿的视点展开的。 **2** N-COUNT A **viewpoint** is a place from which you can get a good view of something. 视角 ❑ *You have to know where to stand for a good viewpoint.* 你得知道站在哪儿才会有好的视角。

Word Link *vig ≈ awake, strong : invigorating, vigil, vigilant*

vig·il /vɪdʒɪl/ (**vigils**) N-COUNT A **vigil** is a period of time when people remain quietly in a place, especially at night, for example,because they are praying or are making a political protest. (尤指夜间的) 值班; (祈祷或政治抗议的) 守夜 ❑ *Protesters are holding a twenty-four hour vigil outside the socialist party headquarters.* 抗议者正在社会党总部外面举行24小时的静坐示威。 ● PHRASE If someone **keeps a vigil** or **keeps vigil** somewhere, they remain there quietly for a period of time, especially at night, for example,because they are praying or are making a political protest. 守夜

vigi·lant /vɪdʒɪlənt/ ADJ Someone who is **vigilant** gives careful attention to a particular problem or situation and concentrates on noticing any danger or trouble that there might be. 警惕的 ❑ *He warned the public to be vigilant and report anything suspicious.* 他告诫公众要保持警惕，报告任何可疑情况。 ● **vigi·lance** N-UNCOUNT 警惕 ❑ *Constant vigilance is needed to combat this evil.* 同这种邪恶作斗争需要时刻保持警惕。

vigi·lan·te /vɪdʒɪlænti/ (**vigilantes**) N-COUNT **Vigilantes** are people who organize themselves into an unofficial group to protect their community and to catch and punish criminals. (自发组织维持社区治安的) 联防队员 ❑ *The vigilantes dragged the men out.* 联防队员们把那些男子拖了出来。

vig·or /vɪgər/

in BRIT, use **vigour**

N-UNCOUNT **Vigor** is physical or mental energy and enthusiasm. 活力 ❑ *He has approached his job with renewed vigor.* 他已带着重新焕发的活力投入了工作。

vig·or·ous /vɪgərəs/ **1** ADJ **Vigorous** physical activities involve using a lot of energy, usually to do short and repeated actions. 用力的 ❑ *Very vigorous exercise can increase the risk of heart attacks.* 耗费

大量体力的运动会增加心脏病发作的风险。● **vig·or·ous·ly** ADV 用力地 [ADV after v] ❑ *He shook his head vigorously.* 他用力地摇了摇头。**2** ADJ A **vigorous** person does things with great energy and enthusiasm. A **vigorous** campaign or activity is done with great energy and enthusiasm. 精力充沛的(人)；强有力的(运动、活动) ❑ *Theodore Roosevelt was a strong and vigorous politician.* 西奥多·罗斯福是一位身体强壮、精力充沛的政治家。● **vig·or·ous·ly** ADV 强烈地 [ADV with v] ❑ *The police vigorously denied that excessive force had been used.* 警方坚决否认曾过度使用武力。

vig·our /vɪgər/ [mainly BRIT] → see **vigor**

▲ **vile** /vaɪl/ (**viler, vilest**) ADJ If you say that someone or something is **vile**, you mean that they are very unpleasant. 令人不快的 ❑ *The weather was consistently vile.* 天气一直很恶劣。

vil·la /vɪlə/ (**villas**) N-COUNT A **villa** is a fairly large house, especially one in a hot country or a resort. (尤指热带国家或风景区的) 别墅 ❑ *He lives in a secluded five-bedroom luxury villa.* 他住在一幢僻静的、有5间卧室的豪华别墅里。

vil·lage ♦♦◊ /vɪlɪdʒ/ (**villages**) N-COUNT A **village** consists of a group of houses, together with other buildings such as a church and a school, in a country area. 村庄 ❑ *He lives quietly in the country in a village near Lahti.* 他在乡下拉赫蒂附近的一个村庄里过着平静的生活。

▲ **vil·lain** /vɪlən/ (**villains**) **1** N-COUNT A **villain** is someone who deliberately harms other people or breaks the law in order to get what he or she wants. 恶棍 ❑ *I left the room, feeling like a villain and a murderer.* 我离开了那个房间，感觉自己就像一个恶棍，一个杀人犯。**2** N-COUNT The **villain** in a novel, movie, or play is the main bad character. (小说、电影、戏剧中的) 反面主角 ❑ *He also played a villain opposite Sylvester Stallone in Demolition Man (1992).* 他在1992年的影片《超级战警》中扮演了一个与西尔维斯特·史泰龙敌对的反面主角。

vin·di·cate /vɪndɪkeɪt/ (**vindicates, vindicating, vindicated**) V-T If a person or their decisions, actions, or ideas **are vindicated**, they are proved to be correct, after people have said that they were wrong. 证明是正确的 [FORMAL] ❑ *The director said he had been vindicated by the experts' report.* 主任说专家们的报告证明他是正确的。● **vin·di·ca·tion** /vɪndɪkeɪʃən/ N-UNCOUNT 证明正确 [also "a" N, usu N "of" n] ❑ *He called the success a vindication of his party's free-market economic policy.* 他称这次成功证明了他的政党的自由市场经济政策是正确的。

vin·dic·tive /vɪndɪktɪv/ ADJ If you say that someone is **vindictive**, you are critical of them because they deliberately try to upset or cause trouble for someone who they think has done them harm. 想复仇的 [DISAPPROVAL] ❑ *...a vindictive woman desperate for revenge against the man who loved and left her.* …一个想复仇的女人，要报复那个爱过她又离开她的男人。● **vin·dic·tive·ness** N-UNCOUNT 报复 ❑ *...a dishonest person who is operating completely out of vindictiveness.* …一个完全出于报复而行事的不诚实的人。

vine /vaɪn/ (**vines**) N-VAR A **vine** is a plant that grows up or over things, especially one that produces grapes. (尤指葡萄的) 藤 ❑ *Every square meter of soil was used, mainly for olives, vines, and almonds.* 每一平方米的土壤都用上了，主要是种植橄榄、葡萄藤和杏树。

vin·egar /vɪnɪgər/ (**vinegars**) N-MASS **Vinegar** is a sharp-tasting liquid, usually made from sour wine or malt, that is used in cooking to make things such as salad dressing. 醋

vine·yard /vɪnyərd/ (**vineyards**) N-COUNT A **vineyard** is an area of land where grape vines are grown in order to produce wine. You can also use **vineyard** to refer to the set of buildings in which the wine is produced. 葡萄园；葡萄酒厂

vin·tage /vɪntɪdʒ/ (**vintages**) **1** N-COUNT The **vintage** of a good quality wine is the year and place that it was made before being stored to improve it. You can also use **vintage** to refer to the wine that was made in a certain year. (优质葡萄酒的) 生产年份和地点；(特定年份酿造的) 葡萄酒 ❑ *This wine is from one of the two best vintages of the decade in this region.* 这种葡萄酒是这一地区近十年来葡萄产量最好的两个年份之一生产的佳酿。**2** ADJ **Vintage** wine is good quality wine that has been stored for several years in order to improve its quality. 优质的(葡萄酒) [ADJ n] ❑ *If you can buy only one case at auction, it should be vintage port.* 如果你在拍卖会上只能买一箱酒，那就应该是优质的波尔图葡萄酒。**3** ADJ **Vintage** cars or airplanes are old but are admired because they are considered to be the best of their kind. 老式的(汽车或飞机) [ADJ n] ❑ *The museum will have a permanent exhibition of 60 vintage and racing cars.* 这家博物馆将永久展出60辆老式汽车和赛车。**4** ADJ **Vintage** clothing and furniture is old or secondhand, but usually of good quality. 古旧而优质的 (衣物或家具) ❑ *...collectors of vintage clothing.* …古装收藏者。

vi·nyl /vaɪnɪl/ (**vinyls**) **1** N-MASS **Vinyl** is a strong plastic used for making things such as floor coverings and furniture. 乙烯基塑料 ❑ *...a modern vinyl floor covering.* …一种现代乙烯基塑料地板。**2** N-UNCOUNT You can use **vinyl** to refer to records, especially in contrast to cassettes or compact discs. (尤指区别于磁带和激光唱片的) 乙烯基塑料唱片 ❑ *This compilation was first issued on vinyl in 1984.* 这一辑于1984年首次以乙烯基塑料唱片形式发行。

vio·la /vioʊlə/ (**violas**) N-VAR A **viola** is a musical instrument with four strings that is played with a bow. It is like a violin, but is slightly larger and can play lower notes. 中提琴 ❑ *She also played the viola in some amateur orchestras.* 她也曾在一些业余管弦乐队拉过中提琴。

→ see **orchestra, string**

vio·late ♦◊◊ /vaɪəleɪt/ (**violates, violating, violated**) **1** V-T If someone **violates** an agreement, law, or promise, they break it. 违反 [FORMAL] ❑ *They went to prison because they violated the law.* 他们因犯法而入狱。● **vio·la·tion** /vaɪəleɪʃən/ N-VAR (**violations**) 违反 ❑ *To deprive the boy of his education is a violation of state law.* 剥夺这个男孩的受教育权是一种违反州法律的行为。**2** V-T If you **violate** someone's privacy or peace, you disturb it. 侵犯 [FORMAL] ❑ *These men were violating her family's privacy.* 这些男人在侵犯她的家庭隐私。**3** V-T If someone **violates** a special place such as a grave, they damage it or treat it with disrespect. 亵渎 ❑ *Detectives are still searching for those who violated the graveyard.* 侦探们还在查找那些亵渎了墓地的家伙。● **vio·la·tion** N-UNCOUNT 亵渎 ❑ *The violation of the graves is not the first such incident.* 亵渎墓地的事件这已不是第一回。

Word Partnership *violate* 的常用搭配：

N. violate **an agreement**, violate **the Constitution**, violate **the law**, violate **rights**, violate **rules** **1**
violate ***someone's* privacy** **2**

vio·lence ♦♦◊ /vaɪələns/ **1** N-UNCOUNT **Violence** is behavior that is intended to hurt, injure, or kill people. 暴力行为 ❑ *Twenty people were killed in the violence.* 有20人在这起暴力事件中被杀害。❑ *...domestic violence between husband and wife.* …夫妻间的家庭暴力。**2** N-UNCOUNT If you do or say something with **violence**, you use a lot of force and energy in doing or saying it, often because you are angry. 激烈 [LITERARY] ❑ *The violence in her tone gave Tyler a shock.* 她语气激烈，使泰勒大为震惊。

Word Partnership *violence* 的常用搭配：

N. **acts of** violence, **outbreak of** violence, **victims of** violence, violence **against women** **1**
V. **condemn** violence, violence **erupts**, **prevent** violence, **resort to** violence, **stop** violence **1**
ADJ. **ethnic** violence, **increasing** violence, **physical** violence, **racial** violence, **widespread** violence **1**

vio·lent ♦◊◊ /vaɪələnt/ **1** ADJ If someone is **violent**, or if they do something that is **violent**, they use physical force or weapons to hurt, injure, or kill other people. 暴力的 ❑ *A quarter of current inmates have committed violent crimes.* 四分之一的在押囚犯实施过暴力犯罪。❑ *...violent anti-government demonstrations.* …反政府的暴力示威。● **vio·lent·ly** ADV 暴力地 [ADV with v] ❑ *Some opposition activists have been violently attacked.* 一些反对派激进分子遭到了暴力袭击。**2** ADJ A **violent** event happens suddenly and with great force. 猛烈的 ❑ *A violent impact hurtled her forward.* 一股剧烈的冲击力将她猛地向前抛了出去。● **vio·lent·ly** ADV 剧烈地 [ADV with v] ❑ *A nearby volcano erupted violently, sending out a hail of molten rock and boiling mud.* 一座附近的火山猛烈爆发，喷出大量熔岩和沸腾的泥浆。**3** ADJ If you describe something as **violent**, you mean that it is said, done, or felt very strongly. 强烈的 ❑ *Violent opposition to the plan continues.* 对该计划的强烈反对在持续。❑ *He had violent stomach pains.* 他有过剧烈的胃痛。● **vio·lent·ly** ADV 强烈地 ❑ *He was violently scolded.* 他受到了严厉叱责。**4** ADJ A **violent** death is painful and unexpected, usually because the person who dies has been murdered. 暴力引起的 ❑ *...an innocent man who had met a violent death.* …一名遭暴力致死的无辜男子。● **vio·lent·ly** ADV 谋杀性地 [ADV with v] ❑ *...a girl who had died violently nine years earlier.* …9年前暴亡的一个女孩。**5** ADJ A **violent** movie or television program contains a lot of scenes that show violence. 多暴力场景的 (电影或电视节目) ❑ *It was the most violent movie that I have ever seen.* 这是我看过的最暴力的电影。

Word Partnership *violent* 的常用搭配:

N. violent **acts**, violent **attacks**, violent **behavior**, violent **clash**, violent **conflict**, violent **confrontations**, violent **crime**, violent **criminals**, violent **demonstrations**, violent **incidents**, violent **offenders** 1
violent **protests**, violent **reaction** 1 3
violent **death** 4
violent **films/movies** 5

ADV. **extremely** violent, **increasingly** violent 1 3

vio·let /vaɪəlɪt/ (**violets**) 1 N-COUNT A **violet** is a small plant that has purple or white flowers in the spring. 紫罗兰 2 COLOR Something that is **violet** is a bluish-purple color. 紫罗兰色的 ❑ *The light was beginning to drain from a violet sky.* 光线正开始从紫罗兰色的天空中渐渐消失。 3 PHRASE If you say that someone is no **shrinking violet**, you mean that they are not at all shy. 羞涩的人 ❑ *When it comes to expressing himself he is no shrinking violet.* 他表达自己看法时一点都不羞涩。
→ see **rainbow**

vio·lin /vaɪəlɪn/ (**violins**) N-VAR A **violin** is a musical instrument. Violins are made of wood and have four strings. You play the violin by holding it under your chin and moving a bow across the strings. 小提琴 ❑ *Lizzie used to play the violin.* 莉齐过去常拉小提琴。
→ see **orchestra, string**

vio·lin·ist /vaɪəlɪnɪst/ (**violinists**) N-COUNT A **violinist** is someone who plays the violin. 小提琴手 ❑ *Rose's father was a talented violinist.* 罗斯的父亲是一位天才的小提琴手。

VIP /vi aɪ pi/ (**VIPs**) N-COUNT A **VIP** is someone who is given better treatment than ordinary people because they are famous, influential, or important. **VIP** is an abbreviation for "very important person." 贵宾 ❑ *...such VIPs as Prince Charles and Richard Nixon.* …像查尔斯王子和理查德·尼克松这样的贵宾。

Word Link *vir ≈ poison : viral, virulent, virus*

vi·ral /vaɪrəl/ ADJ A **viral** disease or infection is caused by a virus. 病毒性的 ❑ *...a 65-year-old patient suffering from severe viral pneumonia.* …一位65岁患有严重病毒性肺炎的病人。

★ **vir·gin** /vɜrdʒɪn/ (**virgins**) 1 N-COUNT A **virgin** is someone, especially a woman or girl, who has never had sex. 处女 ❑ *I was a virgin until I was thirty years old.* 我到30岁时还是个处女。 2 ADJ You use **virgin** to describe something such as land that has never been used or spoiled. (土地等) 未使用过的 ❑ *Within 40 years there will be no virgin forest left.* 过不了40年原始森林将所剩无几。 3 PHRASE If you say that a situation is **virgin territory**, you mean that you have no experience of it and it is completely new for you. 处女地; 全新领域 ❑ *The World Cup is virgin territory for Ecuador.* 世界杯对厄瓜多尔来说尚为一片全新的领域。 4 N-COUNT You can use **virgin** to describe someone who has never done or used a particular thing before. 生手 ❑ *Until he appeared in "In the Line of Fire" Malkovich had been an action-movie virgin.* 在出演《火线》之前，马尔科维奇还是一个动作片的生手。

vir·ile /vɪrᵊl/ ADJ If you describe a man as **virile**, you mean that he has the qualities that a man is traditionally expected to have, such as strength and sexual power. 有男子气概的; 有男性生殖力的 ❑ *He wanted his sons to become strong, virile, and athletic like himself.* 他希望他的儿子们变得像他一样身强力壮、充满阳刚之气，并擅长体育运动。 ● **vi·ril·ity** /vɪrɪlɪti/ N-UNCOUNT 男子气概; 男性生殖能力 ❑ *Children are also considered proof of a man's virility.* 儿女也被视为男子生殖力的证明。

V

vir·tual /vɜrtʃuəl/ 1 ADJ You can use **virtual** to indicate that something is so nearly true that for most purposes it can be regarded as true. 事实上的 [ADJ n] ❑ *Argentina came to a virtual standstill while the game was being played.* 阿根廷在比赛进行期间全国上下事实上进入了停顿状态。 2 ADJ **Virtual** objects and activities are generated by a computer to simulate real objects and activities. (计算机仿真) 虚拟的 [ADJ n] [COMPUTING] ❑ *Up to four players can compete in a virtual world of role playing.* 最多能有4个人可以在虚拟世界中扮演角色进行角逐。 ● **vir·tu·al·ity** N-UNCOUNT 虚拟性 ❑ *People speculate about virtuality systems, but we're already working on it.* 人们对虚拟系统尚存疑虑，而我们已经在开发了。

vir·tu·al·ly ♦◇◇ /vɜrtʃuəli/ ADV You can use **virtually** to indicate that something is so nearly true that for most purposes it can be regarded as true. 事实上 [ADV with group] ❑ *Virtually all cooking was done over coal-fired ranges.* 事实上所有的烹饪都是在烧煤的炉灶上完成的。

vir·tual memo·ry N-UNCOUNT **Virtual memory** is a computing technique in which you increase the size of a computer's memory by arranging or storing the data in it in a different way. 虚拟内存 [COMPUTING] ❑ *...with 512mb RAM and 768mb virtual memory.* …有512mb的随机内存和768mb的虚拟内存。

vir·tual re·al·ity N-UNCOUNT **Virtual reality** is an environment that is produced by a computer and seems very like reality to the person experiencing it. 虚拟现实 [COMPUTING] ❑ *One day virtual reality will revolutionize the entertainment industry.* 有朝一日虚拟现实将给娱乐业带来一场革命。

vir·tual stor·age N-UNCOUNT **Virtual storage** is the same as **virtual memory**. 虚拟内存 [COMPUTING]

vir·tue /vɜrtʃu/ (**virtues**) 1 N-UNCOUNT **Virtue** is thinking and doing what is right and avoiding what is wrong. 正直的品性 ❑ *Virtue is not confined to the Christian world.* 正直的品性并不限于基督教世界。 2 N-COUNT A **virtue** is a good quality or way of behaving. 美德 ❑ *His virtue is patience.* 他的美德就是耐心。 3 N-COUNT The **virtue** of something is an advantage or benefit that it has, especially in comparison with something else. 优势; 益处 ❑ *There was no virtue in returning to Calvi the way I had come.* 按我来的路线返回卡尔维并不可取。 4 PHRASE You use **by virtue of** to explain why something happens or is true. 因为 [FORMAL] ❑ *The article stuck in my mind by virtue of one detail.* 该文章因一细节而印入我脑海。

vir·tuo·so /vɜrtʃuoʊsoʊ/ (**virtuosos** or **virtuosi** /vɜrtʃuoʊsi/) 1 N-COUNT A **virtuoso** is someone who is extremely good at something, especially at playing a musical instrument. 大师 (尤指乐器演奏高手) ❑ *...one of the nation's leading violin virtuosos.* …该国最杰出的小提琴大师之一。 2 ADJ A **virtuoso** performance or display shows great skill. 技艺精湛的 [ADJ n] ❑ *The game was a triumph; the team gave a virtuoso performance.* 比赛大获全胜; 该队表演精彩。

★ **vir·tu·ous** /vɜrtʃuəs/ 1 ADJ A **virtuous** person behaves in a moral and correct way. 品德高尚的 ❑ *Louis was shown as an intelligent, courageous and virtuous family man.* 路易斯看上去是一个聪明、勇敢而且品德高尚的顾家男人。 2 ADJ If you describe someone as **virtuous**, you mean that they have done what they ought to do and feel very pleased with themselves, perhaps too pleased. 自鸣得意的 ❑ *I cleaned the apartment, which left me feeling virtuous.* 我打扫了整个公寓，这让我感到自己很了不起。 ● **vir·tu·ous·ly** ADV 自鸣得意地 ❑ *"I've already done that," said Ronnie virtuously.* "那事儿我已经做完了，" 罗尼自鸣得意地说。

Word Link *ulent ≈ full of : fraudulent, opulent, virulent*

viru·lent /vɪryələnt/ 1 ADJ **Virulent** feelings or actions are extremely bitter and hostile. 恶毒的 [FORMAL] ❑ *Now he faces virulent attacks from the Italian media.* 现在他面临着意大利媒体的恶毒攻击。 ● **viru·lent·ly** ADV 恶毒地 ❑ *The talk was virulently hostile to the leadership.* 这次谈话对领导层充满了恶毒的敌意。 2 ADJ A **virulent** disease or poison is extremely powerful and dangerous. 致命的 ❑ *A very virulent form of the disease appeared in Belgium.* 该疾病的一种极其致命形式在比利时出现。

vi·rus ♦◇◇ /vaɪrəs/ (**viruses**) 1 N-COUNT A **virus** is a kind of germ that can cause disease. 病毒 ❑ *There are many different strains of flu virus.* 有许多不同类型的流感病毒。 2 N-COUNT In computer technology, a **virus** is a program that introduces itself into a system, altering or destroying the information stored in the system. (计算机) 病毒 [COMPUTING] ❑ *Hackers are said to have started a computer virus.* 据说黑客们已开始传播一种计算机病毒。
→ see **illness**

visa /vizə/ (**visas**) N-COUNT A **visa** is an official document, or a stamp put in your passport, that allows you to enter or leave a particular country. 签证 ❑ *His visitor's visa expired.* 他的访问签证过期了。 ❑ *...an exit visa.* …一张出境签证。

vise /vaɪs/ (**vises**) N-COUNT A **vise** is a tool with a pair of parts that hold an object tightly while you do work on it. 钳子 [AM]
in BRIT, use **vice**

★ **vis·ibil·ity** /vɪzɪbɪlɪti/ 1 N-UNCOUNT **Visibility** means how far or how clearly you can see in particular weather conditions. 能见度 ❑ *Visibility was poor.* 能见度差。 2 N-UNCOUNT If you refer to the **visibility** of something such as a situation or problem, you mean how much it is seen or noticed by other people. 关注程度 ❑ *The plight of the Kurds gained global visibility.* 库尔德人的困境受到了全球的关注。

Word Link *vid, vis ≈ seeing : audio**vis**ual, **vid**eotape, **vis**ible*

vis·ible ♦◇◇ /vɪzɪbəl/ **1** ADJ If something is **visible**, it can be seen. 可见的 ❑ *The warning lights were clearly visible.* 警示灯清晰可见。 **2** ADJ You use **visible** to describe something or someone that people notice or recognize. 明显的 ❑ *The most visible sign of the intensity of the crisis is unemployment.* 危机加剧的最明显迹象是失业情况。 ● **vis·ibly** /vɪzɪbli/ ADV 明显地 ❑ *The Russians were visibly wavering.* 俄国人显然犹豫不决。

→ see **wave**

Word Partnership *visible* 的常用搭配：

N. visible **to the naked eye** **1**
ADV. **barely** visible, **clearly** visible, **highly** visible, **less** visible, **more** visible, **still** visible, **very** visible **1** **2**
V. **become** visible **1** **2**

vi·sion ♦◇◇ /vɪʒən/ (**visions**) **1** N-COUNT Your **vision of** a future situation or society is what you imagine or hope it would be like, if things were very different from the way they are now. 憧憬 ❑ *I have a vision of a society that is free of exploitation and injustice.* 我憧憬一个没有剥削和不公的社会。 ❑ *That's my vision of how the world could be.* 那就是我对这个世界未来的憧憬。 **2** N-COUNT If you have a **vision of** someone in a particular situation, you imagine them in that situation, for example because you are worried that it might happen, or hope that it will happen. 想像 ❑ *He had a vision of Cheryl, slumped on a plastic chair in the waiting room.* 他想像谢丽尔跌坐在候诊室的一把塑料椅子上。 **3** N-COUNT A **vision** is the experience of seeing something that other people cannot see, for example in a religious experience or as a result of madness or taking drugs. 幻觉 ❑ *It was on June 24, 1981 that young villagers first reported seeing the Virgin Mary in a vision.* 那是在1981年的6月24日，年轻的村民们首次报告说在幻觉中看到了圣母玛利亚。 **4** N-UNCOUNT Your **vision** is your ability to see clearly with your eyes. 视力 ❑ *It causes blindness or serious loss of vision.* 这会引起失明或严重的视力衰退。 **5** N-UNCOUNT Your **vision** is everything that you can see from a particular place or position. 视野 ❑ *Jane blocked Craig's vision and he could see nothing.* 简挡住了克雷格的视线，他什么也看不见了。

Word Partnership *vision* 的常用搭配：

V. **share** a vision **1**
have a vision **1**–**3**
see a vision **3**
N. vision **of the future**, vision **of peace**, vision **of reality** **1**
color vision **4**
field of vision **5**
ADJ. **clear** vision **1** **2** **4**
blurred vision **4**

★ **vi·sion·ary** /vɪʒənɛri/ (**visionaries**) **1** N-COUNT If you refer to someone as a **visionary**, you mean that they have strong, original ideas about how things might be different in the future, especially about how things might be improved. 有远见的人 ❑ *An entrepreneur is more than just a risk taker. He is a visionary.* 企业家不仅是个冒险者，还是一个有远见的人。 **2** ADJ You use **visionary** to describe the strong, original ideas of a visionary. 有创见的 ❑ *...the visionary architecture of Etienne Boullée.* …艾蒂安·布雷设计的创见性建筑。

vis·it ♦♦♦ /vɪzɪt/ (**visits, visiting, visited**) **1** V-T/V-I If you **visit** someone, you go to see them and spend time with them. 拜访 ❑ *He wanted to visit his brother in Worcester.* 他想去拜访住在伍斯特的兄弟。 ❑ *In the evenings, friends would visit.* 晚上朋友们会来拜访。 ● N-COUNT **Visit** is also a noun. 拜访 ❑ *Helen had recently paid him a visit.* 海伦最近拜访了他。 **2** V-T/V-I If you **visit** a place, you go there for a short time. 访问 ❑ *He'll be visiting four cities including Cagliari in Sardinia.* 他将访问4座城市，包括撒丁岛的卡利亚里。 ❑ *...a visiting family from Texas.* …一个从得克萨斯来访的家庭。 ● N-COUNT **Visit** is also a noun. 访问 ❑ *...the pope's visit to Canada.* …教皇对加拿大的访问。 **3** V-T If you **visit** a website, you look at it. 浏览 [COMPUTING] ❑ *For details visit our website at www.harpercollins.com.* 欲知详情请浏览我们的网站www.harpercollins.com。 **4** V-T If you **visit** a professional person such as a doctor or lawyer, you go and see them in order to get professional advice. If they **visit** you, they come to see you in order to give you professional advice. 上门咨询；(专业人士) 上门服务 ❑ *If necessary the patient can then visit his doctor for further advice.* 如果必要的话，病人可向自己的医生咨询以得到更多的建议。 ● N-COUNT **Visit** is also a noun. 咨询；上门服务 ❑ *You may have regular home visits from a neonatal nurse.* 你可以让育婴护士定期上门服务。

▸ **visit with** PHRASAL VERB If you **visit with** someone, you go to see them and spend time talking with them. 看望 [AM] ❑ *I visited with him in San Francisco.* 我去旧金山看望了他。

Word Partnership *visit* 的常用搭配：

N. visit **family/relatives**, visit **friends**, visit *your* **mother** **1**
weekend visit **1** **2**
visit **a museum**, visit **a restaurant** **2**
visit **a website** **3**
visit **a doctor** **4**
V. **come to** visit, **go to** visit, **invite** *someone* **to** visit, **plan to** visit **1** **2**
ADJ. **brief** visit, **last** visit, **next** visit, **recent** visit, **short** visit, **surprise** visit **1** **2**
foreign visit, **official** visit **2**

visi·tor ♦◇◇ /vɪzɪtər/ (**visitors**) N-COUNT A **visitor** is someone who is visiting a person or place. 访问者 ❑ *The other day we had some visitors from Switzerland.* 前几天我们接待了一些瑞士的来访者。

vis·ta /vɪstə/ (**vistas**) N-COUNT A **vista** is a view from a particular place, especially a beautiful view from a high place. (尤指从高处看到的) 景色 [WRITTEN] ❑ *From my bedroom window I looked out on a crowded vista of hills and rooftops.* 我从自己卧室的窗口向外眺望远处密集的山峦和屋顶。

vis·ual /vɪʒuəl/ (**visuals**) **1** ADJ **Visual** means relating to sight, or to things that you can see. 视觉的 ❑ *...the graphic visual depiction of violence.* …对暴力生动的视觉描绘。 ● **visu·al·ly** ADV 视觉地 ❑ *...visually handicapped boys and girls.* …有视力障碍的男孩女孩。 **2** N-COUNT A **visual** is something such as a picture, diagram, or piece of film that is used to show or explain something. 视觉资料 (展示或解释用的图画、图表或电影片段等) ❑ *Remember you want your visuals to reinforce your message, not detract from what you are saying.* 要记住，你是要用视觉资料来强化你的信息，而不是削弱你所讲述的内容。

Word Partnership *visual* 的常用搭配：

N. visual **arts**, visual **effects**, visual **information**, visual **memory**, visual **perception** **1**

vis·ual aid (**visual aids**) N-COUNT **Visual aids** are things that you can look at, such as a film, model, map, or slides, to help you understand something or to remember information. 直观教具

★ **visu·al·ise** /vɪʒuəlaɪz/ [BRIT] → see **visualize**

★ **visu·al·ize** /vɪʒuəlaɪz/ (**visualizes, visualizing, visualized**)

in BRIT, also use **visualise**

V-T If you **visualize** something, you imagine what it is like by forming a mental picture of it. 想像 ❑ *Susan visualized her wedding day and saw herself walking down the aisle on her father's arm.* 苏珊想像着自己婚礼那天，挽着父亲的手臂沿着教堂过道走过来。 ❑ *He could not visualize her as old.* 他无法想像她年老的样子。

Word Link *vita ≈ life : re**vita**lize, **vita**l, **vita**lity*

vi·tal ♦◇◇ /vaɪtəl/ ADJ If you say that something is **vital**, you mean that it is necessary or very important. 至关重要的 ❑ *The port is vital to supply relief to millions of drought victims.* 这个港口至关重要，给数百万旱灾民提供救济物资。 ❑ *It is vital that parents give children clear and consistent messages about drugs.* 至关重要的是，父母们给子女提供关于毒品明确一致的观点。 ● **vi·tal·ly** ADV 至关重要地 ❑ *Lesley's career in the church is vitally important to her.* 莱斯利的教会生涯对于她而言至关重要。

Thesaurus *vital* 另参见：

ADV. absolutely vital
ADJ. crucial, essential, necessary; (*ant.*) unimportant

Word Partnership *vital* 的常用搭配：

ADV. **absolutely** vital
N. vital **importance**, vital **information**, vital **interests**, vital **link**, vital **organs**, vital **part**, vital **role**

vi·tal·ity /vaɪtælɪti/ N-UNCOUNT If you say that someone or something has **vitality**, you mean that they have great energy and liveliness. 活力 ❑ *Without continued learning, graduates will lose* *their intellectual vitality.* 如果不继续学习，毕业生们就会失去他们的思维活力。

vi·ta·min ♦◇◇ /vaɪtəmɪn/ (**vitamins**) N-COUNT **Vitamins** are substances that you need in order to remain healthy, which are found in food or can be eaten in the form of pills. 维生素 ❑ *Lack of vitamin D is another factor to consider.* 缺乏维生素D是另一个需要考虑的因素。

Word Link *viv ≈ living : revival, survive, vivacious*

vi·va·cious /vɪveɪʃəs/ ADJ If you describe someone, usually a woman, as **vivacious**, you mean that they are lively, exciting, and attractive. (常指女性) 活泼的 [WRITTEN, APPROVAL] ❑ *She's beautiful, vivacious, and charming.* 她美丽、活泼、迷人。

viv·id /vɪvɪd/ **1** ADJ If you describe memories and descriptions as **vivid**, you mean that they are very clear and detailed. (记忆和描写) 清晰的; 生动逼真的 ❑ *People of my generation who lived through World War II have vivid memories of confusion and incompetence.* 我们这一代经历过第二次世界大战的人都还清晰地记得当时的混乱和无能为力。 ●**viv·id·ly** ADV 清晰地 ❑ *I can vividly remember the feeling of panic.* 我能清晰地回忆起那恐慌感。 **2** ADJ Something that is **vivid** is very bright in color. (颜色) 鲜艳的 ❑ *...a vivid blue sky.* …碧蓝的天空。 ●**viv·id·ly** ADV 鲜艳地 [ADV -ed/adj] ❑ *...vividly colored birds.* …色彩艳丽的鸟儿。

vivi·sec·tion /vɪvɪsɛkʃən/ N-UNCOUNT **Vivisection** is the practice of using live animals for scientific experiments. 活体解剖 ❑ *...a fierce opponent of vivisection.* …一个活体解剖的激烈反对者。

viz. **viz.** is used in written English to introduce a list of specific items or examples. 即 ❑ *The school offers two modules in Teaching English as a Foreign Language, viz. Principles and Methods of Language Teaching and Applied Linguistics.* 该校提供两个模块用于英语作为外语的教学，即语言教学的原理方法和应用语言学。

Word Link *voc ≈ speaking : advocate, vocabulary, vocal*

vo·cabu·lary /voʊkæbyəlɛri/ (**vocabularies**) **1** N-VAR Your **vocabulary** is the total number of words you know in a particular language. 词汇量 ❑ *His speech is immature, his vocabulary limited.* 他讲话不成熟，词汇量也有限。 **2** N-SING The **vocabulary** of a language is all the words in it. 某一语言的总词汇量 ❑ *...a new word in the German vocabulary.* …德语词汇中的一个新词。 **3** N-VAR The **vocabulary** of a subject is the group of words that are typically used when discussing it. (某学科的) 专门词汇 ❑ *...the vocabulary of natural science.* …自然科学词汇。

→ see **English**

Word Partnership *vocabulary* 的常用搭配:

N. **part of** ***someone's*** vocabulary **1**
vocabulary **development** **1** **2**
V. **learn** vocabulary **2** **3**
ADJ. **specialized** vocabulary, **technical** vocabulary **3**

★ **vo·cal** /voʊkᵊl/ **1** ADJ You say that people are **vocal** when they speak forcefully about something that they feel strongly about. 直言不讳的 ❑ *He has been very vocal in his displeasure over the results.* 他直言不讳地说出了对结果的不满。 **2** ADJ **Vocal** means involving the use of the human voice, especially in singing. 嗓音的 [ADJ n] ❑ *...a wider range of vocal styles.* …更多样的嗓音风格。

vo·cal·ist /voʊkəlɪst/ (**vocalists**) N-COUNT A **vocalist** is a singer who sings with a group. 歌手 ❑ *He and Carla Torgerson take turns as the band's lead vocalist.* 他和卡拉·托格森轮流担任乐队的领唱。

vo·cals /voʊkᵊlz/ N-PLURAL In a pop song, the **vocals** are the singing, in contrast to the playing of instruments. 歌唱 ❑ *Johnson now sings backing vocals for Mica Paris.* 约翰逊现在为迈卡·帕里斯伴唱。

vo·ca·tion /voʊkeɪʃᵊn/ (**vocations**) **1** N-VAR If you have a **vocation**, you have a strong feeling that you are especially suited to do a particular job or to fulfill a particular role in life, especially one that involves helping other people. 使命感 ❑ *It could well be that he has a real vocation.* 他很可能有种真正的使命感。 **2** N-VAR If you refer to your job or profession as your **vocation**, you feel that you are particularly suited to it. 适合的职业 ❑ *Her vocation is her work as an actress.* 她适合的职业就是当演员。

★ **vo·ca·tion·al** /voʊkeɪʃənᵊl/ ADJ **Vocational** training and skills are the training and skills needed for a particular job or profession. 职业的 ❑ *...a course designed to provide vocational training in engineering.* …为提供工程学职业培训而设计的一门课程。

vo·cif·er·ous /voʊsɪfərəs/ ADJ If you describe someone as **vociferous**, you mean that they speak with great energy and determination, because they want their views to be heard. 大声疾呼的 ❑ *He was a vociferous opponent of Conservatism.* 他是保守主义的强烈反对者。 ●**vo·cif·er·ous·ly** ADV 大声疾呼地 ❑ *He vociferously opposed the state of emergency imposed by the government.* 他大声疾呼反对政府强行宣布紧急状态。

vod·ka /vɒdkə/ (**vodkas**) N-MASS **Vodka** is a strong, clear, alcoholic drink. 伏特加 (一种烈性酒)

▲ **vogue** /voʊg/ **1** N-SING If there is a **vogue for** something, it is very popular and fashionable. 时尚 ❑ *Despite the vogue for so-called health teas, there is no evidence that they are any healthier.* 尽管所谓的保健茶成了时尚，但并没有证据表明这种茶更有益于健康。 **2** PHRASE If something is **in vogue**, it is very popular and fashionable. If it comes **into vogue**, it becomes very popular and fashionable. 正在流行; 变得流行 ❑ *Pale colors are much more in vogue than autumnal bronzes and coppers.* 浅色比秋季的古铜色和紫铜色更为流行。

voice ♦♦◇ /vɔɪs/ (**voices, voicing, voiced**) **1** N-COUNT When someone speaks or sings, you hear their **voice**. 嗓音 ❑ *Miriam's voice was strangely calm.* 米里亚姆的声音出奇地平静。 ❑ *"The police are here," she said in a low voice.* "警察在这儿，"她低声说。 **2** N-COUNT Someone's **voice** is their opinion on a particular topic and what they say about it. 意见 ❑ *What does one do when a government simply refuses to listen to the voice of the opposition?* 当政府完全拒绝倾听反对意见时，那该怎么办? **3** V-T If you **voice** something such as an opinion or an emotion, you say what you think or feel. 表达 ❑ *Some scientists have voiced concern that the disease could be passed on to humans.* 一些科学家已经表示，担心这种疾病可能会传染给人类。 **4** PHRASE If you **give voice to** an opinion, a need, or a desire, you express it aloud. 大声表达 ❑ *...a community radio run by the Catholic Church that gave voice to the protests of the slum-dwellers.* …一家由天主教教会开办的、表达贫民窟居民抗议之声的社区电台。 **5** PHRASE If someone tells you to **keep** your **voice down**, they are asking you to speak more quietly. 放低嗓门 ❑ *Keep your voice down, for goodness sake.* 看在上帝的份上，把你的嗓门放低点。 **6** PHRASE If you **lose** your **voice**, you cannot speak for a while because of an illness. 失声 ❑ *I had to be careful not to get a sore throat and lose my voice.* 我必须小心，不要患上咽喉炎而哑了嗓子。 **7** PHRASE If you **raise** your **voice**, you speak more loudly. If you **lower** your **voice**, you speak more quietly. 提高嗓门; 压低嗓门 ❑ *He raised his voice for the benefit of the other two women.* 他提高了嗓门，以便让另两个女人听得到。 **8** PHRASE If you say something **at the top of** your **voice**, you say it as loudly as possible. 用最大的音量 [EMPHASIS] ❑ *"Damn!" he yelled at the top of his voice.* "该死!"他声嘶力竭地喊道。

voice mail N-UNCOUNT **Voice mail** is a system of sending messages over the telephone. Calls are answered by a machine that connects you to the person you want to leave a message for, and they can listen to their messages later. 语音信箱 ❑ *He was on a call, so I left a message on his voice mail.* 他正在通话，我就在他的语音信箱留了言。

voice-over (**voice-overs**) also **voiceover** N-COUNT The **voice-over** of a film, television program, or advertisement consists of words spoken by someone who is not seen. (电影、电视节目或广告的) 画外音 ❑ *89% of advertisements had a male voice-over.* 89%的广告都用男声画外音。

★ **void** /vɔɪd/ (**voids, voiding, voided**) **1** N-COUNT If you describe a situation or a feeling as a **void**, you mean that it seems empty because there is nothing interesting or worthwhile about it. 空白; 空虚感 ❑ *His death has left a void in the entertainment world that can never be filled.* 他的去世在娱乐界留下了一个永远无法填补的空白。 **2** N-COUNT You can describe a large or frightening space as a **void**. (空间) 大而恐怖的 ❑ *He stared into the dark void where the battle had been fought.* 他凝望着那一大片黑洞洞的空地，那里曾是战斗的地方。 **3** ADJ Something that is **void** or **null and void** is officially considered to have no value or authority. 无效的 [v-link ADJ] ❑ *The original elections were declared void by the former military ruler.* 原来的选举被前军事首领宣布为无效。 **4** ADJ If you are **void of** something, you do not have any of it. 没有…的 [v-link ADJ "of" n] [FORMAL] ❑ *He rose, his face void of emotion as he walked toward the door.* 他站了起来，面无表情地朝门口走去。 **5** V-T To **void** something means to officially say that it is not valid. 正式宣布…无效 [FORMAL] ❑ *The Supreme Court threw out the confession and voided his conviction for murder.* 最高法院驳回供状，宣布他的谋杀罪判决无效。

Word Web volcano

The most famous **volcano** in the world is Mount Vesuvius, near Naples, Italy. This mountain sits in the middle of the much older **volcanic cone** of Mount Somma. In 79 AD the sleeping volcano **erupted** and magma surged to the surface. The people of the nearby city of Pompeii were terrified. Soon huge black clouds of **ash** and pumice came rushing toward them. The clouds blocked out the sun and smothered thousands of people. Pompeii was buried under hot ash and **molten lava**. Centuries later the remains of the people and town were exposed. The discovery made this active volcano world famous.

vol. ♦◇◇ (**vols.**) **Vol.** is used as a written abbreviation for **volume** when you are referring to one or more books in a series of books. 卷

▲ **vola·tile** /vɒlətᵊl/ **1** ADJ A situation that is **volatile** is likely to change suddenly and unexpectedly. 变化无常的 ❑ *There have been riots before and the situation is volatile.* 先前一直就有暴乱，局势变化无常。 **2** ADJ If someone is **volatile**, their mood often changes quickly. 情绪不稳定的 ❑ *He accompanied the volatile actress to Hollywood the following year.* 他次年陪那个情绪反复无常的女演员去了好莱坞。 ❑ *He has a volatile temper.* 他的脾气反复无常。 **3** ADJ A **volatile** liquid or substance is one that will quickly change into a gas. 易挥发的 [TECHNICAL] ❑ *The blast occurred when volatile chemicals exploded.* 冲击波是在易挥发的化学品爆炸时产生的。

vol·can·ic /vɒlkænɪk/ ADJ **Volcanic** means coming from or created by volcanoes. 火山的 ❑ *Over 200 people have been killed by volcanic eruptions.* 已有两百多人死于火山喷发。

vol·ca·no /vɒlkeɪnoʊ/ (**volcanoes**) N-COUNT A **volcano** is a mountain from which hot melted rock, gas, steam, and ash from inside the earth sometimes burst. 火山 ❑ *The volcano erupted last year killing about 600 people.* 去年那座火山喷发导致大约六百人丧生。
→ see Word Web: **volcano**
→ see **rock**

▲ **vol·ley** /vɒli/ (**volleys, volleying, volleyed**) **1** V-T/V-I In sports, if someone **volleys** the ball or if they **volley**, they hit the ball before it touches the ground. 截击空中球 ❑ *He volleyed the ball spectacularly into the far corner of the net.* 他一个精彩的凌空抽射，将球踢进了球网的远角。 ● N-COUNT **Volley** is also a noun. 截击空中球 ❑ *She hit most of the winning volleys.* 大多数得分的拦击球都是她击出的。 **2** N-COUNT A **volley of** gunfire is a lot of bullets that travel through the air at the same time. (炮火的) 齐发 ❑ *It's still not known how many died in the volleys of gunfire.* 尚不知道有多少人死于齐发的炮火中。

volley·ball /vɒlibɔl/ N-UNCOUNT **Volleyball** is a game in which two teams hit a large ball with their hands back and forth over a high net. If you allow the ball to touch the ground, the other team wins a point. 排球

volt /voʊlt/ (**volts**) N-COUNT A **volt** is a unit used to measure the force of an electric current. 伏特 (电压单位)

volt·age /voʊltɪdʒ/ (**voltages**) N-VAR The **voltage** of an electrical current is its force measured in volts. 电压 ❑ *The systems are getting smaller and using lower voltages.* 这些系统正变得更小而且使用更低的电压。

vol·ume ♦♦◇ /vɒlyum/ (**volumes**) **1** N-COUNT The **volume of** something is the amount of it that there is. 量 ❑ *Senior officials will be discussing how the volume of sales might be reduced.* 高级官员们将讨论如何才能减少销售量。 **2** N-COUNT The **volume** of an object is the amount of space that it contains or occupies. 容积 ❑ *When egg whites are beaten, they can rise to seven or eight times their original volume.* 打过的蛋清，体积可以涨到原来的七八倍。 **3** N-COUNT A **volume** is one book in a series of books. (书籍的) 卷 ❑ *...the first volume of his autobiography.* …他自传的第一卷。 **4** N-COUNT A **volume** is a collection of several issues of a magazine, for example, all the issues for one year. 合订本 ❑ *...bound volumes of the magazine.* …杂志的合订本。 **5** N-UNCOUNT **The volume** of a radio, television, or sound system is the loudness of the sound it produces. (收音机、电视机或音响系统的) 音量 ❑ *He turned down the volume.* 他调低了音量。 **6** PHRASE If something such as an action **speaks volumes about** a person or thing, it gives you a lot of information about them. 充分表明 ❑ *What you wear speaks volumes about you.* 你的穿戴能充分表明你的方方面面。
→ see Picture Dictionary: **volume**

vol·un·tary ♦◇◇ /vɒlənteri/ **1** ADJ **Voluntary** actions or activities are done because someone chooses to do them and not because they have been forced to do them. 自愿的 ❑ *Attention is drawn to a special voluntary course in Commercial French.* 注意力被吸引到一门特别的商务法语选修课上。 ● **vol·un·tar·ily** /vɒlənteərɪli/ ADV 自愿地 [ADV with v] ❑ *I would never leave here voluntarily.* 我永远不会自愿地离开这里。 **2** ADJ **Voluntary** work is done by people who are not paid for it, but who do it because they want to do it. 义务的 ❑ *In her spare time she does voluntary work.* 她在业余时间做义工。

Picture Dictionary volume

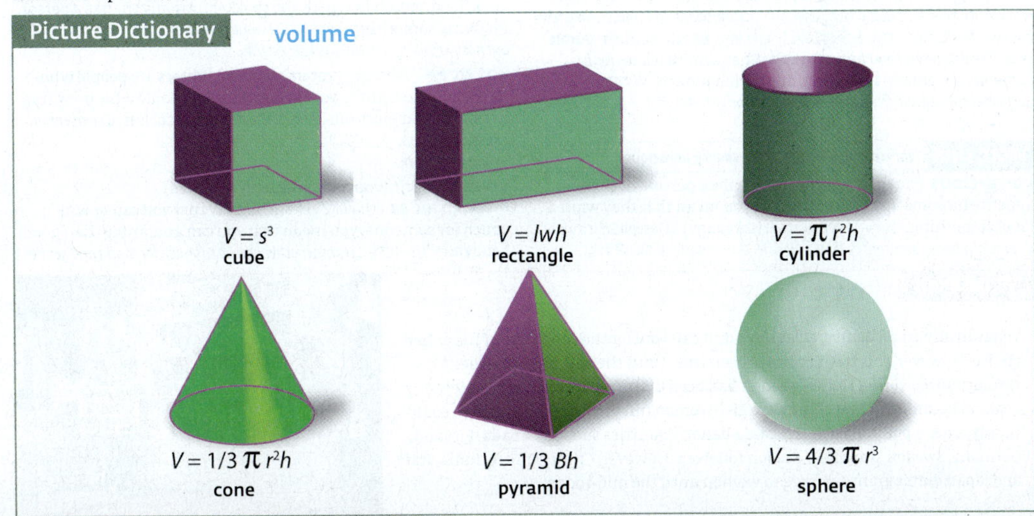

V

3 ADJ A **voluntary** organization is controlled and organized by the people who have chosen to work for it, often without being paid, rather than receiving help or money from the government. 志愿的 [ADJ n] ❑ *Some voluntary organizations run workshops for disabled people.* 一些志愿组织为残障人士开办讲习班。
→ see **muscle**

Word Partnership *voluntary* 的常用搭配:
N. voluntary **action**, voluntary **basis**, voluntary **compliance**, voluntary **contributions**, voluntary **program**, voluntary **retirement**, voluntary **test** 1
voluntary **organizations** 3

Word Link *eer ≈ one who does : auctioneer, mountaineer, volunteer*

Word Link *vol ≈ will : benevolent, involuntary, volunteer*

vol·un·teer ♦◇◇ /vɒləntɪər/ (**volunteers, volunteering, volunteered**) 1 N-COUNT A **volunteer** is someone who does work without being paid for it, because they want to do it. 志愿者 ❑ *She now helps in a local school as a volunteer three days a week.* 她现在作为一名志愿者每周3天在当地一所学校帮忙。 2 N-COUNT A **volunteer** is someone who offers to do a particular task or job without being forced to do it. 自告奋勇者 ❑ *Right. What I want now is two volunteers to come down to the front.* 对了。我现在需要的就是两个自告奋勇者到前面来。 3 V-I If you **volunteer** to do something, you offer to do it without being forced to do it. 主动要求做 ❑ *Aunt Mary volunteered to clean up the kitchen.* 玛丽姨妈主动要求打扫厨房。 ❑ *He volunteered for the army in 1939.* 他在1939年自愿参军。 4 V-T If you **volunteer** information, you tell someone something without being asked. 主动提供(信息) [FORMAL] ❑ *The room was quiet; no one volunteered any further information.* 房间里很安静；没有人主动提供更多的信息。 ❑ *"They were both great supporters of Franco," Ryle volunteered.* "他们俩都是佛朗哥的坚定支持者，"赖尔主动说道。 5 N-COUNT A **volunteer** is someone who chooses to join the armed forces, especially during a war, as opposed to someone who is forced to join by law. 志愿兵 ❑ *They fought as volunteers with the Afghan guerrillas.* 他们作为志愿兵与阿富汗游击队一起战斗。

Word Partnership *volunteer* 的常用搭配:
N. **community** volunteer, **Red Cross** volunteer 1
volunteer **organization**, volunteer **program**, volunteer **work** 1 2
volunteer **for service**, volunteer **for the army** 3
volunteer **information** 4
V. **need a** volunteer 1 2 5
volunteer **to help**, volunteer **to work** 3

▲ **vom·it** /vɒmɪt/ (**vomits, vomiting, vomited**) 1 V-T/V-I If you **vomit**, food and drink comes back up from your stomach and out through your mouth. 呕吐 ❑ *Any product made from cow's milk made him vomit.* 任何牛奶制品都会让他呕吐。 ❑ *She began to vomit blood a few days before she died.* 她在去世前几天开始吐血。 2 N-UNCOUNT **Vomit** is partly digested food and drink that has come back up from someone's stomach and out through their mouth. 呕吐物 ❑ *Zimmer slipped and nearly fell on a pool of vomit.* 齐默滑了一跤，差点儿摔倒在一滩呕吐物上。

Word Link *vor ≈ eating : herbivorous, savory, voracious*

vo·ra·cious /vɔreɪʃəs/ ADJ If you describe a person, or their appetite for something, as **voracious**, you mean that they want a lot of something. 贪婪的；如饥似渴的 [LITERARY] ❑ *Joseph Smith was a voracious book collector.* 约瑟夫·史密斯是一个如饥似渴的藏书家。 ❑ *All otters have a voracious appetite.* 所有的水獭都有一个贪吃的胃口。

vote ♦♦♦ /voʊt/ (**votes, voting, voted**) 1 N-COUNT A **vote** is a choice made by a particular person or group in a meeting or an election. 选票 ❑ *He walked to the local polling place to cast his vote.* 他走到当地的投票点去投票。 ❑ *Mr. Reynolds was re-elected by 102 votes to 60.* 雷诺兹先生以102票对60票再次当选。 2 N-COUNT **A vote** is an occasion when a group of people make a decision by each person indicating his or her choice. The choice that most people support is accepted by the group. 投票表决 ❑ *Why do you think we should have a vote on that?* 你为什么认为我们应该对那件事进行投票表决？ 3 N-SING **The vote** is the total number of votes or voters in an election, or the number of votes received or cast by a particular group. 投票总数；得票总数 ❑ *Opposition parties won about fifty-five percent of the vote.* 反对党赢得大约55%的选票。 4 N-SING If you have **the vote** in an election, or have **a vote** in a meeting, you have the legal right to indicate your choice. 选举权 ❑ *Before that, women did not have a vote at all.* 在那之前，妇女根本就没有选举权。 5 V-T/V-I When you **vote**, you indicate your choice officially at a meeting or in an election, for example, by raising your hand or writing on a piece of paper. 投票；表决 ❑ *Two-thirds of the national electorate had the chance to vote in these elections.* 全国2/3的选民有机会在这些选举中投票。 ❑ *Nearly two-thirds of this group voted for Buchanan.* 这一组几乎2/3的人将票投给了布坎南。 ❑ *The residents of Leningrad voted to restore the city's original name of St. Petersburg.* 列宁格勒的居民投票赞成恢复该市原来的名字圣彼得堡。 ● **vot·ing** N-UNCOUNT 投票 ❑ *Voting began about two hours ago.* 投票开始于约两个小时前。 6 V-T If you **vote** a particular political party or leader, or **vote yes** or **no**, you make that choice with the vote that you have. 投票支持 ❑ *52.5% of those questioned said they'd vote Republican.* 52.5%的受访者说他们将投票支持共和党。 7 V-T If people **vote** someone a particular title, they choose that person to have that title. 投票授予…称号 ❑ *His class voted him the man "who had done the most for Yale."* 他所在的班级投票授予他"耶鲁最大贡献者"称号。 8 PHRASE If you **vote with** your **feet**, you show that you do not support something by leaving the place where it is happening or leaving the organization that is supporting it. (以离去或退出的方式) 反对 ❑ *Thousands of citizens are already voting with their feet, and leaving the country.* 成千上万的公民已表明了他们的反对意见，要离开这个国家。 9 PHRASE If you say, for example, "**I vote that** we go" or "**I vote** we stay," you are suggesting that you should go or stay. 我建议 [INFORMAL] ❑ *I vote that we all go to Houston immediately.* 我建议我们都马上去休斯敦。 10 PHRASE **One man one vote** or **one person one vote** is a system of voting in which every person in a group or country has the right to cast their vote, and in which each individual's vote is counted and has equal value. 一人一票制 ❑ *Mr. Gould called for a move toward "one man one vote."* 古尔德先生要求向"一人一票"制迈出一步。
→ see Word Web: **vote**
→ see **election**

vote of thanks (**votes of thanks**) N-COUNT A **vote of thanks** is an official speech in which the speaker formally thanks a person for doing something. 致谢词 ❑ *I would like to propose a vote of thanks to our host.* 我提议向我们的主人表示感谢。

vot·er ♦♦◇ /voʊtər/ (**voters**) N-COUNT **Voters** are people who have the legal right to vote in elections, or people who are voting in a particular election. 选民 ❑ *The turnout was at least 62 percent of registered voters.* 至少有62%的登记选民参加了投票。
→ see **election**

vouch /vaʊtʃ/ (**vouches, vouching, vouched**)
▸ **vouch for** 1 PHRASAL VERB If you say that you can or will **vouch for** someone, you mean that you can guarantee their good behavior. 为…担保 ❑ *Kim's mother agreed to vouch for Maria and get her*

V

Word Web vote

Today in almost all **democracies** any adult can **vote** for the **candidate** of his or her choice. However, this hasn't always been true. Until the suffrage movement revolutionized voting rights, women had been **disenfranchised**. In 1893, New Zealand became the first country to give women full voting rights. Women could finally enter a **polling place** and **cast a ballot**. Countries such as Canada, Finland, Germany, Sweden, and the U.S. soon followed. However, China, France, India, Italy, and Japan didn't grant suffrage to women until the mid-1900s.

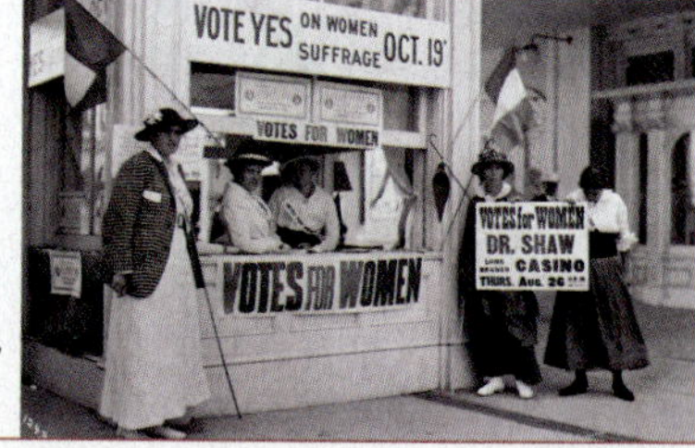

a job. 金的母亲同意为玛丽亚担保，好让她找到一份工作。 2 PHRASAL VERB If you say that you can **vouch for** something, you mean that you have evidence from your own personal experience that it is true or correct. 证明 ❑ *He cannot vouch for the accuracy of the story.* 他不能证明报道的准确性。

★ **vouch·er** /vaʊtʃər/ (**vouchers**) N-COUNT A **voucher** is a ticket or piece of paper that can be used instead of money to pay for something. 代币券；购物券 ❑ *The winners will each receive a voucher for a pair of movie tickets.* 获胜者每人将获得一张代币券，可换取两张电影票。

★ **vow** /vaʊ/ (**vows, vowing, vowed**) 1 V-T If you **vow** to do something, you make a serious promise or decision that you will do it. 发誓 ❑ *While many models vow to go back to college, few do.* 很多模特儿发誓要重返大学，但几乎无人做到。 ❑ *I solemnly vowed that someday I would return to live in Europe.* 我郑重起誓总有一天我要重回欧洲生活。 2 N-COUNT A **vow** is a serious promise or decision to do a particular thing. 誓言 ❑ *I made a silent vow to be more careful in the future.* 我默默发誓今后要更加小心。 3 N-COUNT **Vows** are a particular set of serious promises, such as the promises two people make when they are getting married. 誓约 ❑ *I took my marriage vows and kept them.* 我结婚时立下了誓言而且一直信守诺言。

vow·el /vaʊəl/ (**vowels**) N-COUNT A **vowel** is a sound such as the ones represented in writing by the letters **a, e, i, o** and **u**, that you pronounce with your mouth open, allowing the air to flow through it. Compare **consonant**. 元音 ❑ *The vowel in words like "my" and "thigh" is not very difficult.* 在 "**my**" 和 "**thigh**" 这样的单词中的元音并不难发。

voy·age /vɔɪɪdʒ/ (**voyages**) N-COUNT A **voyage** is a long journey on a ship or in a spacecraft. 航程 ❑ *He aims to follow Columbus's voyage to the West Indies.* 他打算沿着哥伦布的航程到达西印度群岛。

vs. **vs.** is a written abbreviation for **versus**. 对 ❑ *We were watching the Yankees vs. the Red Sox.* 我们当时在观看扬基队对红袜队的比赛。

★ **vul·gar** /vʌlgər/ 1 ADJ If you describe something as **vulgar**, you think it is in bad taste or of poor artistic quality. 粗俗的 [DISAPPROVAL] ❑ *I think it's a very vulgar house.* 我认为这是一栋很俗气的房子。 ● **vul·gar·ity** /vʌlgærɪti/ N-UNCOUNT 粗俗 ❑ *I hate the vulgarity of the bright colors in this room.* 我不喜欢这个房间里艳丽而俗气的色调。 2 ADJ If you describe pictures, gestures, or remarks as **vulgar**, you dislike them because they refer to sex or parts of the body in an offensive way that you find unpleasant. 下流的 [DISAPPROVAL] ❑ *The women laughed coarsely at the comedian's vulgar jokes.* 那些女人们听到滑稽演员的下流笑话后都放荡地大笑起来。 ● **vul·gar·ity** N-UNCOUNT 下流 ❑ *Charles was a complete gentleman, incapable of rudeness or vulgarity.* 查尔斯完完全全是个绅士，无粗鲁下流之举。 3 ADJ If you describe a person or their behavior as **vulgar**, you mean that they lack taste or behave offensively. 粗鲁的 [DISAPPROVAL] ❑ *He was a vulgar old man, but he never swore in front of a woman.* 他是个粗鲁的老头，但他从来没有在女人面前说过脏话。 ● **vul·gar·ity** N-UNCOUNT 粗鲁 ❑ *It's his vulgarity that I can't take.* 我不能忍受的正是他的粗鲁。

★ **vul·ner·able** ♦◇◇ /vʌlnərəbəl/ 1 ADJ Someone who is **vulnerable** is weak and without protection, with the result that they are easily hurt physically or emotionally. 易受伤害的 ❑ *Old people are particularly vulnerable members of our society.* 老人是我们社会中特别容易受到伤害的成员。 ● **vul·ner·abil·ity** /vʌlnərəbɪlɪti/ N-VAR (**vulnerabilities**) 脆弱 ❑ *David accepts his own vulnerability.* 戴维承认自己的脆弱。 2 ADJ If a person, animal, or plant is **vulnerable to** a disease, they are more likely to get it than other people, animals, or plants. 容易患…病的 ❑ *People with high blood pressure are especially vulnerable to diabetes.* 血压高的人尤其容易患糖尿病。 ● **vul·ner·abil·ity** N-UNCOUNT 患病的可能性 ❑ *Taking long-term courses of certain medicines may increase vulnerability to infection.* 长期服用某些药物可能会增加受感染的几率。 3 ADJ Something that is **vulnerable** can be easily harmed or affected by something bad. 易受损害的 ❑ *Their tanks would be vulnerable to attack from the air.* 他们的坦克将易受空袭。 ● **vul·ner·abil·ity** N-UNCOUNT 易受攻击性 ❑ *...anxieties about the country's vulnerability to invasion.* …对国家易受侵略的忧虑。

Word Partnership *vulnerable* 的常用搭配：

V.	**feel** vulnerable 1 **become** vulnerable, **remain** vulnerable 1 – 3
N.	vulnerable **children/people/women** 1 2 vulnerable **to attack** 3
ADV.	**especially** vulnerable, **extremely** vulnerable, **highly** vulnerable, **particularly** vulnerable, **so** vulnerable, **too** vulnerable, **very** vulnerable 1 – 3

vul·ture /vʌltʃər/ (**vultures**) 1 N-COUNT A **vulture** is a large bird that eats the flesh of dead animals. 秃鹫 2 N-COUNT If you describe a person as a **vulture**, you disapprove of them because you think they are trying to gain from another person's troubles. 趁火打劫的人 [JOURNALISM, DISAPPROVAL] ❑ *With no buyer in sight for the company as a whole, the vultures started to circle.* 因为眼下没有买家要买整个公司，趁火打劫的人开始打他们的主意。

vy·ing /vaɪɪŋ/ **Vying** is the present participle of **vie**. **vie**的现在分词

Ww

W also **w** /dʌbəlyu/ (**W's, w's**) N-VAR **W** is the twenty-third letter of the English alphabet. 英语字母表的第23个字母

wacko /wækoʊ/ ADJ If you say that someone is **wacko**, you are saying in an unkind way that they are strange and eccentric. 古怪的 [INFORMAL, DISAPPROVAL] ❑ *Lampley was obviously completely wacko.* 兰普利显然是个十足的怪胎。

wacky /wæki/ (**wackier, wackiest**) also **whacky** ADJ If you describe something or someone as **wacky**, you mean that they are eccentric, unusual, and often funny. 古怪的; 滑稽的 [INFORMAL] ❑ *...a wacky new television comedy series.* …一部新的电视系列滑稽喜剧。

wad /wɒd/ (**wads**) N-COUNT A **wad of** something such as paper or cloth is a tight bundle or ball of it. (一) 团; (一) 叠; (一) 卷 ❑ *...a wad of banknotes.* …一沓钞票。

▲ **wade** /weɪd/ (**wades, wading, waded**) **1** V-I If you **wade** through something that makes it difficult to walk, usually water or mud, you walk through it. 蹚 (过水、泥等) ❑ *Her mother came to find them, wading across a river to reach them.* 她的母亲蹚过河来找他们。 **2** V-I To **wade through** a lot of documents or pieces of information means to spend a lot of time and effort reading them or dealing with them. 费时费力地啃读 ❑ *It has taken a long time to wade through the "incredible volume" of evidence.* 已经花费了很长时间来研读这宗 "卷帙浩瀚" 的证据。

▸ **wade in** or **wade into** PHRASAL VERB If someone **wades in** or **wades into** something, they get involved in a very determined and forceful way, often without thinking enough about the consequences of their actions. 介入 ❑ *They don't just listen sympathetically, they wade in with remarks like, "If I were you..."* 他们不仅同情地倾听着，还不时地插话说，"如果我是你的话…"。

wad·dle /wɒdəl/ (**waddles, waddling, waddled**) V-I To **waddle** somewhere means to walk there with short, quick steps, swinging slightly from side to side. A person or animal that waddles usually has short legs and a fat body. 摇摇摆摆地走 ❑ *McGinnis pushed himself laboriously out of the chair and waddled to the window.* 麦克尼费力地从椅子上挪起来，摇摇摆摆地走向窗户。

waf·fle /wɒfəl/ (**waffles, waffling, waffled**) V-I If someone **waffles** on an issue or question, they cannot decide what to do or what their opinion is about it. 含糊其辞 [AM] ❑ *He has waffled on abortion and gay rights.* 他在人工流产和同性恋者的权利问题上含糊其辞。

waft /wɒft, wæft/ (**wafts, wafting, wafted**) V-T/V-I If sounds or smells **waft** through the air, or if something such as a light wind **wafts** them, they move gently through the air. 随风飘荡 ❑ *The scent of climbing roses wafts through the window.* 蔷薇的香味随风从窗户飘进来。

▲ **wag** /wæg/ (**wags, wagging, wagged**) **1** V-T When a dog **wags** its tail, it repeatedly waves its tail from side to side. (狗) 摇摆 (尾巴) ❑ *The dog was biting, growling and wagging its tail.* 那条狗咬着叫着，还摇着尾巴。 **2** V-T If you **wag** your finger, you shake it repeatedly and quickly from side to side, usually because you are annoyed with someone. 摇晃 (手指) ❑ *He wagged a disapproving finger.* 他摇摇手指表示不赞成。

wage ◆◇◇ /weɪdʒ/ (**wages, waging, waged**) **1** N-COUNT Someone's **wages** are the amount of money that is regularly paid to them for the work that they do. 工资 ❑ *His wages have gone up.* 他的工资涨了。 **2** V-T If a person, group, or country **wages** a campaign or a war, they start it and continue it over a period of time. 发动 (运动或战争) ❑ *The government, along with the three factions that had been waging a civil war, signed a peace agreement.* 政府和发动了内战的3方一起签订了1份和平协议。

→ see **factory, union**

Thesaurus *wage* 另参见:

N. earnings, pay, salary **1**

When used as a noun, **pay** is a general word which you can use to refer to the money you get from your employer for doing your job. Manual workers are paid **wages**, or **a wage**. The plural is more common than the singular, especially when you are talking about the actual cash that someone receives. ❑ *Every week he handed all his wages in cash to his wife.* Wages are usually paid, and quoted, as a weekly sum. ❑ *...a starting wage of five dollars an hour.* Professional people and office workers receive a **salary**, which is paid monthly. However, when talking about someone's salary, you usually give the annual figure. ❑ *I'm paid a salary of $29,000 a year.* Your **income** consists of all the money you receive from all sources, including your pay.

Word Partnership *wage* 的常用搭配:

ADJ. **average** wage, **high/higher** wage, **hourly** wage, **low/lower** wage **1**

V. **offer a** wage, **pay a** wage, **raise a** wage **1**

N. wage **cuts**, wage **earners**, wage **increases**, wage **rates** **1**
wage **a campaign**, wage **war** **2**

wage pack·et (**wage packets**) N-COUNT People's wages can be referred to as their **wage packet**. 工资 [mainly BRIT]

in AM, usually use **paycheck**

wa·ger /weɪdʒər/ (**wagers, wagering, wagered**) V-T/V-I If you **wager on** the result of a horse race, baseball game, or other event, you give someone a sum of money which they give you back with extra money if the result is what you predicted, or which they keep if it is not. 下赌注 [JOURNALISM] ❑ *Just because people wagered on the Yankees did not mean that they liked them.* 虽然人们在北方佬身上下赌注，但并不意味着他们喜欢北方佬。 ❑ *They wagered a lot of money on the race.* 他们在这次赛跑上押了很多钱。 ● N-COUNT **Wager** is also a noun. 赌注; 打赌 ❑ *There have been various wagers on certain candidates since the senator announced his retirement.* 自从那位参议员宣布引退之后，对某些候选人的打赌猜测纷纷出现。

wag·on /wægən/ (**wagons**) **1** N-COUNT A **wagon** is a strong vehicle with four wheels, usually pulled by horses or oxen and used for carrying heavy loads. 四轮运货马 (或牛) 车 **2** N-COUNT A **wagon** is a large container on wheels which is pulled by a train. (火车的) 货车车厢 [BRIT]

in AM, use **freight car**

→ see **train**

▲ **wail** /weɪl/ (**wails, wailing, wailed**) **1** V-I If someone **wails**, they make long, loud, high-pitched cries which express sorrow or pain. 哀号 ❑ *The women began to wail in mourning.* 女人们开始大放悲声。 ● N-COUNT **Wail** is also a noun. 悲鸣声 ❑ *Wails of grief were heard as visitors filed past the site of the disaster.* 当来访者们列队走过灾难现场时听见阵阵悲痛的哀号声。 **2** V-T If you **wail** something, you say it in a loud, high-pitched voice that shows that you are unhappy or in pain. 高声数落 ❑ *"Now look what you've done!" Shirley wailed.* "现在，看看你干了什么！" 雪莉高声数落道。 **3** V-I If something such as a siren or an alarm **wails**, it makes a long, loud, high-pitched sound. (汽笛、警报等) 长鸣 ❑ *Police cars, their sirens wailing, accompanied the trucks.* 警车警笛长鸣，与卡车相随。 ● N-UNCOUNT **Wail** is also a noun. 长鸣声 ❑ *The wail of the bagpipe could be heard in the distance.* 老远就可听到风笛悠长的奏鸣声。

waist /weɪst/ (**waists**) **1** N-COUNT Your **waist** is the middle part of your body where it narrows slightly above your hips. 腰部 ❑ *Ricky kept his arm around her waist.* 里基搂着她的腰。 **2** N-COUNT The **waist** of a garment such as a dress, coat, or pair of pants is the part of it which covers the middle part of your body. (衣服的) 腰部 ❑ *She tucked her thumbs into the waist of her trousers.* 她把拇指插进裤腰里。

→ see **body**

waist·coat /weɪstkoʊt, wɛskət/ (**waistcoats**) N-COUNT A **waistcoat** is a sleeveless piece of clothing with buttons that people usually wear over a shirt. (西装) 背心；马甲 [BRIT]

in AM, use **vest**

wait ♦♦♦ /weɪt/ (**waits, waiting, waited**) 1 V-T/V-I When you **wait** for something or someone, you spend some time doing very little, because you cannot act until that thing happens or that person arrives. 等候 [no passive] ❑ *I walk to a street corner and wait for the school bus.* 我走到一个街道拐角处等校车。 ❑ *I waited to see how she responded.* 我等着看她如何反应。 ❑ *We had to wait a week before we got the results.* 我们不得不等候一个星期才拿到了结果。 ● **wait·ing** N-UNCOUNT 等候 ❑ *The waiting became almost unbearable.* 等待变得几乎令人难以忍受了。 2 N-COUNT A **wait** is a period of time in which you do very little, before something happens or before you can do something. 等待的时间 ❑ *…the four-hour wait for the organizers to declare the result.* …组织者们宣布结果前4个小时的等待。 3 V-T/V-I If something **is waiting for** you, it is ready for you to use, have, or do. 等 (你) 使用；等 (你) 去做 [usu cont] ❑ *There'll be a car waiting for you.* 将会有辆车等着你。 ❑ *When we came home we had a meal waiting for us.* 我们回到家时，有一顿饭正等着我们去享用。 ❑ *He had a car waiting to take him back to the office.* 有一辆车等着送他回办公室。 4 V-I If you say that something can **wait**, you mean that it is not important or urgent and so you will deal with it or do it later. 延缓 [no cont] ❑ *I want to talk to you, but it can wait.* 我想和你谈谈，但可以等会儿再说。 5 V-I You can use **wait** when you are trying to make someone feel excited, or to encourage or threaten them. 等着吧 (期望引起对方兴奋之情，或鼓励对方)；等着瞧 (表示威胁) [only imper] ❑ *If you think this all sounds very exciting, just wait until you read the book.* 如果你觉得所有这些听起来令人兴奋，那就等你看了书之后再说吧。 6 V-T **Wait** is used in expressions such as **wait a minute, wait a second**, and **wait a moment** to interrupt someone when they are speaking, for example, because you object to what they are saying or because you want them to repeat something. 等一下 (用以打断对方的谈话，或要求对方重复)；且慢 [only imper] [SPOKEN] ❑ *"Wait a minute!" he broke in. "This is not giving her a fair hearing!"* "且慢！"他插话道。"这没有给她一个公平的辩解机会。" 7 V-I If an employee **waits on** you, for example, in a restaurant or hotel, they take orders from you and bring you what you want. 服侍；招待 ❑ *There were plenty of servants to wait on her.* 有许多佣人服侍她。 8 PHRASE If you say that you **can't wait** to do something or **can hardly wait** to do it, you are emphasizing that you are very excited about it and eager to do it. 急于要 (做某事) [SPOKEN, EMPHASIS] ❑ *We can't wait to get started.* 我们迫不及待地想要开始了。 9 PHRASE If you tell someone to **wait and see**, you tell them that they must be patient or that they must not worry about what is going to happen in the future because they have no control over it. 等着瞧 ❑ *We'll have to wait and see what happens.* 我们只有等着看将会发生什么事情。

Do not confuse **wait for, expect**, and **look forward to**. When you **wait for** someone or something, you stay in the same place until the person arrives or the thing happens. ❑ *Soft drinks were served while we waited for him… We got off the plane and waited for our luggage.* When you are **expecting** someone or something, you think that the person or thing is going to arrive or that the thing is going to happen. ❑ *I sent a postcard, so they were expecting me… We are expecting rain.* When you **look forward to** something that is going to happen, you feel happy because you think you will enjoy it. ❑ *I'll bet you're looking forward to your holidays… I always looked forward to seeing her.*

▸ **wait around** PHRASAL VERB If you **wait around**, you stay in the same place, usually doing very little, because you cannot act before something happens or before someone arrives. (无所事事地) 等待 ❑ *The attacker may have been waiting around for an opportunity to strike.* 袭击者可能一直在等待着一个下手的机会。 ❑ *I waited around to speak to the doctor.* 我一直等着去和医生谈话。

▸ **wait up** PHRASAL VERB If you **wait up**, you deliberately do not go to bed, especially because you are expecting someone to return home late at night. 熬夜等待 ❑ *I hope he doesn't expect you to wait up for him.* 我希望他不要指望着你熬夜等他回来。

Thesaurus *wait* 另参见：

V. anticipate, expect, hold on, stand by; *(ant.)* carry out, go ahead 1

N. delay, halt, hold-up, pause 2

Word Partnership *wait* 的常用搭配：

V. (can't) afford to wait 1
can/can't/couldn't wait, have to wait, will/won't/wouldn't wait 1 4
wait to hear, wait to say 1 4 8
can hardly wait, can't wait 8
wait and see 9

N. wait for an answer, wait days/hours, wait a long time, wait *your* turn 1
wait a minute, wait until tomorrow 1 4 6

ADV. wait forever, wait here, wait outside, wait patiently 1
just wait 1 5

ADJ. worth the wait 2

wait·er /weɪtər/ (**waiters**) N-COUNT A **waiter** is a man who works in a restaurant, serving people food and drink. 男侍者
→ see **restaurant**

Waiter and waitress are used less often in the U.S. these days, although they are still the usual terms in the U.K. Restaurant staff, especially in the U.S., can be called **servers** or **waitpersons**, and these terms are used to refer to both men and women.

wait·ing list (**waiting lists**) N-COUNT A **waiting list** is a list of people who have asked for something that cannot be given to them immediately, such as medical treatment, housing, or training, and who must therefore wait until it is available. 等候者名单 ❑ *There were 20,000 people on the waiting list for a home.* 有2万人列在等候解决住房的名单上。

wait·ress /weɪtrɪs/ (**waitresses**) N-COUNT A **waitress** is a woman who works in a restaurant, serving people food and drink. 女侍者 ❑ *She has been working in a restaurant as a waitress since she graduated from college.* 她从大学毕业之后就一直在一家餐馆做服务员。
→ see **restaurant**

waive /weɪv/ (**waives, waiving, waived**) 1 V-T If you **waive** your right to something, such as legal representation, you choose not to have it or do it. 放弃 (权利) ❑ *He pleaded guilty to the murders of three boys and waived his right to appeal.* 他对杀害了3个男孩的罪行表示认罪伏法，并放弃上诉的权利。 2 V-T If someone **waives** a rule, they say that people do not have to obey it in a particular situation. 放弃 (规则) ❑ *The art gallery waives admission charges on Sundays.* 美术馆星期天免费开放。

waiv·er /weɪvər/ (**waivers**) N-COUNT A **waiver** is when a person, government, or organization agrees to give up a right or says that people do not have to obey a particular rule or law. 弃权者 ❑ *…a waiver of constitutional rights.* …一位放弃宪法权利者。

Word Link *wak ≈ being awake : awake, awakening, wake*

wake ♦◇◇ /weɪk/ (**wakes, waking, woke, woken** or **waked**) 1 V-T/V-I When you **wake** or when someone or something **wakes** you, you become conscious again after being asleep. 醒来；唤醒 ❑ *It was cold and dark when I woke at 6:30.* 我6点30分醒来时，天又冷又黑。 ❑ *She went upstairs to wake Milton.* 她上楼去叫醒米尔顿。 ❑ *Bob woke slowly to sunshine pouring in his window.* 鲍勃在窗户撒射进来的阳光中慢慢醒来。 ● PHRASAL VERB **Wake up** means the same as **wake**. 醒来；唤醒 ❑ *One morning I woke up and felt something was wrong.* 一天早上我醒来时感到有些不对劲。 2 N-COUNT The **wake** of a boat or other object moving in the water is the track of waves it makes behind it as it moves through the water. (船只或其他物体在水中前行时留下的) 尾波 [usu sing, with poss] ❑ *Dolphins sometimes play in the wake of the boats.* 海豚有时跟着船只的尾波戏水。 3 N-COUNT A **wake** is a gathering or social event that is held before or after someone's funeral. 守灵 ❑ *A funeral wake was in progress.* 葬礼前在守灵。 4 PHRASE If one thing follows **in the wake of** another, it happens after the other thing is over, often as a result of it. 紧随…之后 ❑ *The governor has enjoyed a huge surge in the polls in the wake of last week's convention.* 州长在上周大会之后的民意测验中支持率激增。
→ see **funeral**

▸ **wake up** 1 PHRASAL VERB If something such as an activity **wakes** you **up**, it makes you more alert and ready to do things after you have been lazy or inactive. 使振奋 ❑ *A cool shower wakes up the body and boosts circulation.* 冷水浴使身体振奋，促进血液循环。
2 → see also **wake 1**

Word Partnership *wake* 的常用搭配：

ADV. wake *(someone)* up 1
PREP-P. wake **up during the night**, wake **up in the middle of the night**, wake **up in the morning** 1

wak·en /weɪkən/ (**wakens, wakening, wakened**) V-T/V-I When you **waken**, or when someone or something **wakens** you, you wake from sleep. 使醒来；醒来 [LITERARY] ❑ *The noise outside wakened her.* 那外面的噪声吵醒了她。❑ *Women are much more likely than men to waken because of noise.* 女性比男性更容易被噪音吵醒。● PHRASAL VERB **Waken up** means the same as **waken**. 使醒来；醒来 ❑ *Drink this coffee – it will waken you up.* 喝了这咖啡——它会让你清醒。❑ *If you do waken up during the night, start the exercises again.* 如果你的确在夜里醒来，重新开始做那些运动。

wake-up call (**wake-up calls**) 1 N-COUNT A **wake-up call** is a telephone call that you can arrange through an operator or at a hotel to make sure that you wake up at a particular time. (总机、宾馆等提供的) 叫醒电话 ❑ *I book a wake-up call for 4:45 a.m.* 我预订了凌晨4点45分的叫醒电话。 2 N-COUNT If you describe something bad that happens as a **wake-up call**, you mean that it acts as a warning that action needs to be taken to prevent something even worse from happening. 警钟 ❑ *He urged her to treat the arrest as a wake-up call.* 他力劝她把这次拘捕当作一次警钟。

walk ♦♦♦ /wɔk/ (**walks, walking, walked**) 1 V-T/V-I When you **walk**, you move forward by putting one foot in front of the other in a regular way. 行走；步行 ❑ *Rosanna and Forbes walked in silence.* 罗莎娜与福布斯默默地走着。❑ *We walked into the foyer.* 我们走进前厅。❑ *I walked a few steps toward the fence.* 我向栅栏走了几步。 2 N-COUNT A **walk** is a trip that you make by walking, usually for pleasure. 散步 ❑ *I went for a walk.* 我去散步了。 3 N-SING A **walk** of a particular distance is the distance that a person has to walk to get somewhere. 步行的距离 ❑ *It was only a three-mile walk to Kabul from there.* 从那里到喀布尔只有3英里的步行路程。 4 N-COUNT A **walk** is a route suitable for walking along for pleasure. (适宜散步的) 人行道 ❑ *...a 2-mile coastal walk.* …一条2英里长的海边人行道。 5 N-SING A **walk** is a paved pathway. 小径；走道 ❑ *She started up the walk toward the front door.* 她踏上了通向前门的小路。 6 N-SING A **walk** is the action of walking rather than running. 行走 ❑ *She slowed to a steady walk.* 她慢下来，稳步行走。 7 N-SING Someone's **walk** is the way that they walk. 步态 ❑ *George, despite his great height and gangling walk, was a great dancer.* 尽管乔治身材高大，步态笨拙，舞却跳得好极了。 8 V-T If you **walk** someone somewhere, you walk there with them in order to show politeness or to make sure that they get there safely. 陪伴护送 ❑ *She walked me to my car.* 她陪我走到我的汽车旁。 9 **to walk tall** → see **tall**

▸ **walk away** PHRASAL VERB If you **walk away** from a problem or a difficult situation, you do nothing about it or do not face any bad consequences from it. 脱身 ❑ *The most appropriate strategy may simply be to walk away from the problem.* 最恰当的策略也许就是回避这个问题。

▸ **walk away with** PHRASAL VERB If you **walk away with** something such as a prize, you win it or get it very easily. 轻松赢得 [JOURNALISM] ❑ *Enter our competition and you could walk away with $10,000.* 参加我们的竞赛，你就可以轻松赢得$10000。

▸ **walk into** PHRASAL VERB If you **walk into** an unpleasant situation, you become involved in it without expecting to, especially because you have been careless. (不慎) 陷入 ❑ *He's walking into a situation that he absolutely can't control.* 他正不知不觉地陷入他完全无法控制的局面中。

▸ **walk off with** PHRASAL VERB If you **walk off with** something such as a prize, you win it or get it very easily. 轻松赢得 [JOURNALISM] ❑ *We'd like nothing better than to see him walk off with the big prize.* 没有什么能比他轻而易举地获得大奖而更令我们欢喜的了。

▸ **walk out** 1 PHRASAL VERB If you **walk out of** a meeting, a performance, or an unpleasant situation, you leave it suddenly, usually in order to show that you are angry or bored. (通常表示气愤或厌烦) 退出 (会议)；(演出中途) 退场 ❑ *Several dozen councillors walked out of the meeting in protest.* 几十位议员中途愤然退出会议，以示抗议。 2 PHRASAL VERB If someone **walks out on** their family or their partner, they leave them suddenly and go to live somewhere else. 突然离开 (亲人或伴侣)；出走 ❑ *Her husband walked out on her.* 她的丈夫弃她而走。 3 PHRASAL VERB If workers **walk out**, they stop doing their work for a period of time, usually in order to try to get better pay or conditions for themselves. 罢工 ❑ *The miners were furious and threatened to walk out.* 矿工们很愤怒，威胁要罢工。

W

Thesaurus *walk* 另参见：

V. amble, hike, stroll 1
N. hike, jaunt, march, parade, stroll 2

Word Partnership *walk* 的常用搭配：

ADV. walk **alone**, walk **away**, walk **back**, walk **home**, walk **slowly** 1
V. **begin to** walk, **start to** walk 1
go for a walk, **take a** walk 2
ADJ. **(un)able to** walk 1
brisk walk, **long** walk, **short** walk 2

walk·ing /wɔkɪŋ/ N-UNCOUNT **Walking** is the activity of taking walks for exercise or pleasure, especially in the country. 郊游；远足 ❑ *Recently I've started to do a lot of walking and cycling.* 最近我开始进行大量的远足和骑车运动。

Walk·man /wɔkmən/ (**Walkmans**) N-COUNT A **Walkman** is a small cassette player with headphones which people carry around so that they can listen to music, for example, while they are traveling. 随身听 [TRADEMARK]

walk of life (**walks of life**) N-COUNT The **walk of life** that you come from is the position that you have in society and the kind of job you have. 行业；职业 ❑ *One of the greatest pleasures of this job is meeting people from all walks of life.* 这份工作最大的乐趣之一就是结识来自各行各业的人。

walk·out /wɔkaʊt/ (**walkouts**) 1 N-COUNT A **walkout** is a strike. 罢工 ❑ *But union leaders are holding off on calling the walkout while talks are showing progress.* 然而，工会领袖们在会谈正取得进展时却暂停了罢工号召。 2 N-COUNT If there is a **walkout** during a meeting, some or all of the people attending it leave in order to show their disapproval of something that has happened at the meeting. (为表示反对的) 退场；退席 ❑ *The commission's proceedings have been wrecked by tantrums and walkouts.* 委员会的议程由于不时有人发火和中途退席而无法进行下去。

walk·way /wɔkweɪ/ (**walkways**) N-COUNT A **walkway** is a passage or path for people to walk along. Walkways are often raised above the ground. 走道 ❑ *...a new concrete walkway between two rows of apartment blocks.* …一条贯穿于两排公寓大楼之间的新混凝土走道。

wall ♦♦♦ /wɔl/ (**walls**) 1 N-COUNT A **wall** is one of the vertical sides of a building or room. 墙；墙壁 ❑ *Kathryn leaned against the wall of the church.* 凯瑟琳倚靠在教堂的墙壁上。❑ *The bedroom walls would be papered with chintz.* 卧室的墙上将会贴上印花棉布。 2 N-COUNT A **wall** is a long narrow vertical structure made of stone or brick that surrounds or divides an area of land. 围墙 ❑ *He sat on the wall in the sun.* 他坐在围墙上晒太阳。 3 N-COUNT The **wall** of something that is hollow is its side. (中空物体的) 壁 ❑ *He ran his fingers along the inside walls of the box.* 他用手摸了摸箱子的内壁。 4 → see also **off-the-wall** 5 PHRASE If you say that something or someone **is driving** you **up the wall**, you are emphasizing that they annoy and irritate you. 惹恼 [INFORMAL, EMPHASIS] ❑ *The heat is driving me up the wall.* 我热得快疯了。

Word Partnership *wall* 的常用搭配：

PREP. **against a** wall, **along a** wall, **behind a** wall, **near a** wall, **on a** wall 1 2
N. **back to the** wall, **brick** wall, **concrete** wall, **glass** wall, **stone** wall 1 2
V. **lean against/on a** wall, **build a** wall, **climb a** wall 1 2

walled /wɔld/ ADJ If an area of land or a city is **walled**, it is surrounded or enclosed by a wall. 用墙围起来 ❑ *The city was walled and built upon a rock.* 这座城有城墙围着，而且建在岩石上。

wal·let /wɒlɪt/ (**wallets**) N-COUNT A **wallet** is a small flat folded case, usually made of leather or plastic, in which you can keep money and credit cards. 钱包

wal·low /wɒloʊ/ (**wallows, wallowing, wallowed**) 1 V-I If you say that someone **is wallowing in** an unpleasant situation, you are criticizing them for being deliberately unhappy. 沉溺 [DISAPPROVAL] ❑ *His tired mind continued to wallow in self-pity.* 他疲惫的心灵继续沉溺于自怜之中。 2 V-I If a person or animal **wallows in** water or mud, they lie or roll about in it slowly for pleasure. 休闲浸泡 (在水中或泥中) ❑ *Never have I had such a good excuse for wallowing in deep warm baths.* 我从不曾有过这样一个好理由，可以好好地享受个热水澡。

wall·paper /wɔlpeɪpər/ (**wallpapers, wallpapering, wallpapered**) 1 N-MASS **Wallpaper** is thick colored or patterned paper that is used for covering and decorating the walls of rooms. 墙纸 ❑ *...the wallpaper in the bedroom.* …卧室里的墙纸。 2 V-T If someone **wallpapers** a room, they cover the walls with wallpaper. 贴墙纸于 ❑ *We were going to wallpaper that room anyway.* 反正我们也打算给那个房间贴墙纸的。 3 N-UNCOUNT **Wallpaper** is the background on a computer screen. (电脑桌面的) 背景 [COMPUTING] ❑ *...preinstalled wallpaper images.* …预先安装的电脑背景图。

Wall Street ♦◇◇ N-PROPER **Wall Street** is a street in New York where the Stock Exchange and financial businesses are located. **Wall Street** is often used to refer to the financial business carried out there and to the people who work there. 华尔街 (纽约金融街，常借指金融业界) [BUSINESS] ❑ *On Wall Street, stocks closed at their second highest level today.* 华尔街股市今天在第二高位上收盘。

▲ **wal·nut** /wɔlnʌt, -nət/ (**walnuts**) N-VAR **Walnuts** are edible nuts that have a wrinkled shape and a hard round shell that is light brown in color. 胡桃；核桃 ❑ *...chopped walnuts.* …砸碎了的核桃。

waltz /wɔlts, wɔls/ (**waltzes, waltzing, waltzed**) 1 N-COUNT; N-IN-NAMES A **waltz** is a piece of music with a rhythm of three beats in each bar, which people can dance to. 华尔兹舞曲 ❑ *...Tchaikovsky's "Waltz of the Flowers."* …柴可夫斯基的《花之圆舞曲》。 2 N-COUNT A **waltz** is a dance in which two people hold each other and move around the floor doing special steps in time to waltz music. 华尔兹舞 ❑ *Arthur Murray taught the foxtrot, the tango and the waltz.* 亚瑟・默里教过狐步舞、探戈舞和华尔兹舞。 3 V-RECIP If you **waltz** with someone, you dance a waltz with them. 跳华尔兹舞 ❑ *"Waltz with me," he said, taking her hand.* "和我跳华尔兹舞吧！" 他拉起她的手说。

wan·der /wɒndər/ (**wanders, wandering, wandered**) 1 V-T/V-I If you **wander** in a place, you walk around there in a casual way, often without intending to go in any particular direction. 漫步 ❑ *When he got bored he wandered around the fair.* 烦闷时，他便在集市上四处闲逛。 ❑ *They wandered off in the direction of the nearest store.* 他们朝着最近那家店铺的方向闲逛去了。 ❑ *People wandered the streets aimlessly.* 人们在街上漫无目的地闲逛。 ● N-SING **Wander** is also a noun. 漫步 ❑ *A wander around any market will reveal stalls piled high with vegetables.* 在哪个市场上闲逛都会发现高高堆着蔬菜的摊子。 2 V-I If a person or animal **wanders** from a place where they are supposed to stay, they move away from the place without going in a particular direction. 走开 ❑ *Because Mother is afraid we'll get lost, we aren't allowed to wander far.* 母亲因为害怕我们走丢了，不准我们走远。 3 V-I If your mind **wanders** or your thoughts **wander**, you stop concentrating on something and start thinking about other things. 心不在焉 ❑ *His mind would wander, and he would lose track of what he was doing.* 他会心不在焉起来，忘了自己刚才正在干什么。 4 V-I If your eyes **wander**, you stop looking at one thing and start looking around at other things. (目光) 无目的地移动 ❑ *His eyes wandered restlessly around the room.* 他的眼睛不停地打量着房间。

wane /weɪn/ (**wanes, waning, waned**) V-I If something **wanes**, it becomes gradually weaker or less, often so that it eventually disappears. 减弱；减少 ❑ *While his interest in these sports began to wane, a passion for lacrosse developed.* 他对这些运动项目的兴趣开始减退的同时，对长曲棍球的兴趣却浓厚起来。

want ♦♦♦ /wɒnt/ (**wants, wanting, wanted**) 1 V-T If you **want** something, you feel a desire or a need for it. 想要 [no cont, no passive] ❑ *I want a drink.* 我想要点喝的。 ❑ *People wanted to know who this talented designer was.* 人们想知道这位天才的设计者是谁。 ❑ *They began to want their father to be the same as other daddies.* 他们开始想要自己的爸爸和别人的爸爸一样。 ❑ *They didn't want people staring at them as they sat on the lawn, so they put up high walls.* 他们不想自己坐在草坪时被人盯着看，所以修筑了高墙。

> Note that **want** and **wish** have similar meanings, but are used differently. If you **want** something, you feel a need for it or a desire to have it. You can say that you **want** to do something, that you **want** someone to do something, or that you **want** something to happen. If you use **wish** with a "to" infinitive, this has the same meaning as **want** but is more formal.
> ❑ *I want to get out of here... She wished to consult him about her future.*

2 V-T You can say that you **want to** say something to indicate that you are about to say it. 想要 (说) [no cont, no passive] ❑ *I want to say how delighted I am that you're having a baby.* 我想要说，你怀孕了我是多么高兴啊。 3 V-T If you say to someone that you **want** something, or ask them if they **want to** do it, you are firmly telling them what you want or what you want them to do. 想要得到；想做 [no cont, no passive] ❑ *I want an explanation from you, Jeremy.* 我要你给我一个解释，杰里米。 ❑ *Do you want to tell me what all this is about?* 你是否想告诉我这究竟是怎么回事？ 4 V-T If you tell someone that they **want to** do a particular thing, you are advising them to do it. 必须 [no cont, no passive] [INFORMAL] ❑ *You want to be very careful not to have a man like Crevecoeur for an enemy.* 你必须非常小心，不要与像克雷弗克那样的人为敌。 5 V-T If someone **is wanted** by the police, the police are searching for them because they are thought to have committed a crime. 通缉 [usu passive] ❑ *He was wanted for the murder of a judge.* 他因谋杀一位法官而被通缉。 ● **want·ed** ADJ 被通缉的 [ADJ n] ❑ *He is one of the most wanted criminals in Europe.* 他是欧洲的头号通缉犯之一。 6 N-PLURAL Your **wants** are the things that you want. 想要的东西 ❑ *She couldn't lift a spoon without a servant anticipating her wants and getting it for her.* 若没有佣人揣摩她想要什么而且递给她，她连个汤勺都举不起来。 7 PHRASE If you do something **for want of** something else, you do it because the other thing is not available or not possible. 由于缺少 ❑ *The factories shut down for want of fuel and materials.* 这家工厂由于缺少燃料和原料而停产。

Thesaurus *want* 另参见：
v. covet, desire, long for, need, require, wish 1

want·ing /wɒntɪŋ/ ADJ If you find something or someone **wanting**, they are not of as high a standard as you think they should be. 不够应有水准的 [v-link ADJ] ❑ *He analyzed his game and found it wanting.* 他分析了自己的比赛，发现还有待提高。

WAP /wæp/ N-UNCOUNT **WAP** is a system that allows devices such as cellphones to connect to the Internet. **WAP** is an abbreviation for **Wireless Application Protocol**. 无线应用协议 ❑ *...a WAP phone.* …无线应用协议手机。

war ♦♦♦ /wɔr/ (**wars**) 1 N-VAR A **war** is a period of fighting or conflict between countries or states. 战争 ❑ *He spent part of the war in the National Guard.* 他战时在国民警卫队服役了一段时间。 ❑ *...matters of war and peace.* …战争与和平的问题。 2 N-VAR **War** is intense economic competition between countries or organizations. 激烈竞争 ❑ *The most important thing is to reach an agreement and to avoid a*

Word Web war

The Hague Conventions* and the Geneva Convention* attempt to provide humane guidelines for **war**. First of all, they advise avoiding **armed conflict**. The regulations suggest using of a **neutral mediator** or setting up a 30-day "time out." Before **combat** can begin, a country must formally **declare** war. Sneak **attacks** are prohibited. The rules governing the use of **firearms** are quite simple. One regulation states it is illegal to **kill** or **injure** a person who has **surrendered**. **Wounded soldiers, prisoners,** and **civilians** must receive immediate medical care. The rules also prohibit the use of **biological** and **chemical weapons**.

Hague Conventions: agreements between many nations on rules to limit warfare and weapons.
Geneva Convention: an agreement between most nations on treatment of prisoners of war and the sick, injured, or dead.

W

trade war. 最重要的就是达成协议，避免贸易战。 3 N-VAR If you make **war on** someone or something that you are opposed to, you do things to stop them from succeeding. 斗争 ❑ *She has been involved in the war against organized crime.* 她参与了打击有组织犯罪的斗争。 4 → see also **civil war, warring** 5 PHRASE If a country **goes to war**, it starts fighting a war. 开战 ❑ *Do you think this crisis can be settled without going to war?* 你认为不发动战争就能解决这场危机吗？

→ see Word Web: **war**

→ see **army, history**

war·ble /wɔrbᵊl/ (**warbles, warbling, warbled**) 1 V-T/V-I When a bird **warbles**, it sings pleasantly. (鸟) 鸣啭；啁啾 ❑ *The bird continued to warble.* 鸟儿继续啁啾。 ❑ *...birds warbling a morning chorus.* …鸟儿们齐唱晨曲。 2 V-T/V-I If someone **warbles**, they sing in a high-pitched, rather unsteady voice. 用颤音高唱 ❑ *She warbled as she worked.* 她一边干活一边颤声高唱。 ❑ *...singers warbling "Over the Rainbow."* …歌手们颤声高唱着《彩虹那一端》。

ward /wɔrd/ (**wards, warding, warded**) N-COUNT A **ward** is a room in a hospital which has beds for many people, often people who need similar treatment. 病房 ❑ *They transferred her to the psychiatric ward.* 他们把她转移到了精神病病房。

→ see **hospital**

▸ **ward off** PHRASAL VERB To **ward off** a danger or illness means to prevent it from affecting you or harming you. 阻挡 (危险、疾病等) ❑ *She may have put up a fight to try to ward off her assailant.* 她可能进行过一场搏斗，试图击退袭击者。

▲ **war·den** /wɔrdᵊn/ (**wardens**) 1 N-COUNT A **warden** is a person who is responsible for a particular place or thing, and for making sure that the laws or regulations that relate to it are obeyed. (法律、法规) 督察员 ❑ *He was a warden at the local parish church.* 他是本地教区教堂的监察员。 2 N-COUNT The **warden** of a prison is the person in charge of it. 监狱长；看守长 [AM]

in BRIT, use **governor**

❑ *A new warden took over the prison.* 新一任狱长接管了这所监狱。

war·der /wɔrdər/ (**warders**) N-COUNT A **warder** is someone who works in a prison supervising the prisoners. 看守 [BRIT]

in AM, use **guard**

★ **ward·robe** /wɔrdroʊb/ (**wardrobes**) 1 N-COUNT Someone's **wardrobe** is the total collection of clothes that they have. (某人的) 全部服装 ❑ *Her wardrobe consists primarily of huge cashmere sweaters and tiny Italian sandals.* 她的衣服主要是宽大的开司米毛衣和纤小的意大利凉鞋。 2 N-COUNT A **wardrobe** is a tall closet or cabinet in which you can hang your clothes. 衣柜

★ **ware·house** /wɛərhaʊs/ (**warehouses**) N-COUNT A **warehouse** is a large building where raw materials or manufactured goods are stored until they are exported to other countries or distributed to stores to be sold. 仓库；货栈

▲ **wares** /wɛərz/ N-PLURAL A person's or a company's **wares** are the things that they are selling. 商品 ❑ *Many companies are choosing to display their wares online.* 许多公司正选择在网上展示其产品。

★ **war·fare** /wɔrfɛər/ 1 N-UNCOUNT **Warfare** is the activity of fighting a war. 作战；战争 ❑ *...the threat of chemical warfare.* …化学战的威胁。 2 N-UNCOUNT **Warfare** is sometimes used to refer to any violent struggle or conflict. 打斗；冲突 ❑ *Much of the violence is related to drugs and gang warfare.* 很多暴力行为都与毒品和帮派冲突有关。

war·head /wɔrhɛd/ (**warheads**) N-COUNT A **warhead** is the front part of a bomb or missile where the explosives are carried. (炸弹或导弹的) 弹头 ❑ *...nuclear warheads.* …核弹头。

warm ♦♦◇ /wɔrm/ (**warmer, warmest, warms, warming, warmed**) 1 ADJ Something that is **warm** has some heat but not enough to be hot. 温暖的 ❑ *Wheat is grown in places which have cold winters and warm, dry summers.* 小麦生长在冬季寒冷、夏季温暖干燥的地方。 ❑ *Because it was warm, David wore only a white cotton shirt.* 因为天气暖和，戴维只穿了一件白色棉衬衫。

W

> In informal English, if you want to emphasize how hot the weather is, you can say that it is **boiling** or **scorching**. In winter, if the temperature is above average, you can say that it is **mild**. In general, **hot** suggests a higher temperature than **warm**, and **warm** things are usually pleasant. ❑ *...a warm evening.*

2 ADJ **Warm** clothes and blankets are made of a material such as wool that protects you from the cold. 保暖的 ❑ *They have been forced to sleep in the open without food or warm clothing.* 他们被迫睡在露天里，没有食物也没有保暖的衣服。 ● **warm·ly** ADV 保暖地 ❑ *Remember to wrap up warmly on cold days.* 记得天冷时穿暖和些。 3 ADJ **Warm** colors have red or yellow in them rather than blue or green, and make you feel comfortable and relaxed. 暖色调的；有暖感的 ❑ *The basement hallway is painted a warm yellow.* 地下室的走廊被涂成暖色调的黄色。 4 ADJ A **warm** person is friendly and shows a lot of affection or enthusiasm in their behavior. 热心的 ❑ *She was a warm and loving mother.* 她是位既热心又慈爱的母亲。 ● **warm·ly** ADV 热情地；热烈地 [ADV with V] ❑ *New members are warmly welcomed.* 新成员受到热烈欢迎。 5 V-T If you **warm** a part of your body or if something hot **warms** it, it stops feeling cold and starts to feel hotter. 使…暖和 ❑ *The sun had come out to warm his back.* 太阳出来了，把他的背晒得暖暖的。 6 V-I If you **warm to** a person or an idea, you become fonder of the person or more interested in the idea. (对某人) 产生好感；(对某事) 开始感兴趣 ❑ *Those who got to know him better warmed to his openness and honesty.* 那些逐渐了解了他的人对他的率真与坦诚产生了好感。

▸ **warm up** 1 PHRASAL VERB If you **warm** something **up** or if it **warms up**, it gets hotter. 加热；变暖和 ❑ *He blew on his hands to warm them up.* 他哈气暖手。 ❑ *All that she would have to do was warm up the pudding.* 她所需要做的只是加热布丁。 2 PHRASAL VERB If you **warm up** for an event such as a race, you prepare yourself for it by doing exercises or by practicing just before it starts. 热身；做准备活动 ❑ *In an hour the drivers will be warming up for the main event.* 一小时后车手们要为主赛做热身运动。 3 PHRASAL VERB When a machine or engine **warms up** or someone **warms it up**, it becomes ready for use a little while after being switched on or started. (机器或引擎) 预热 ❑ *He waited for his car to warm up.* 他等着车预热起来。

→ see **greenhouse effect**

Word Partnership *warm* 的常用搭配：

ADJ.	warm **and sunny** 1
	warm **and cozy**, warm **and dry** 1 2
	soft and warm 2
	warm **and friendly** 4
N.	warm **air**, warm **bath**, warm **breeze**, warm **hands**, warm **water**, warm **weather** 1
	warm **clothes** 2
	warm **smile**, warm **welcome** 4

warmth /wɔrmθ/ 1 N-UNCOUNT The **warmth** of something is the heat that it has or produces. 温暖 ❑ *She went further into the room, drawn by the warmth of the fire.* 她被火的温暖吸引着，走进了房间。 2 N-UNCOUNT The **warmth** of something such as a garment or blanket is the protection that it gives you against the cold. 保暖 ❑ *The blanket will provide additional warmth and comfort in bed.* 毯子能让你睡觉时感觉更温暖更舒适。

warm-up (**warm-ups**) N-COUNT A **warm-up** is something that prepares you for an activity or event, usually because it is a short practice or example of what the activity or event will involve. 热身；(赛前的) 准备活动 ❑ *The exercises can be fun and a good warm-up for the latter part of the program.* 这些练习很有趣，还可以为后面的课程做热身准备。

warn ♦♦◇ /wɔrn/ (**warns, warning, warned**) 1 V-T/V-I If you **warn** someone about something such as a possible danger or problem, you tell them about it so that they are aware of it. 警告；提醒 ❑ *When I had my first baby friends warned me that children were expensive.* 当我有了第一个孩子时，朋友们提醒我说养小孩是很花钱的。 ❑ *They warned him of the dangers of sailing alone.* 他们警告他独自航行的重重危险。 ❑ *He warned of a possibility of a new terrorist attack.* 他警告说可能会有一次新的恐怖袭击。 2 V-T/V-I If you **warn** someone not to do something, you advise them not to do it so that they can avoid possible danger or punishment. 告诫 ❑ *Mrs. Blount warned me not to interfere.* 布朗特太太告诫我不要插手。 ❑ *"Don't do anything yet," he warned. "Too risky."* "先别行动，"他警告道，"太冒险了。"

Thesaurus *warn* 另参见：

V.	alert, caution, notify 1 2

warn·ing ♦◇◇ /wɔrnɪŋ/ (**warnings**) 1 N-COUNT A **warning** is something said or written to tell people of a possible danger, problem, or other unpleasant thing that might happen. 警告；警报 ❑ *The minister gave a warning that if war broke out, it would be catastrophic.* 大臣警告说战争一旦爆发，将会是灾难性的。 ❑ *He was killed because he ignored a warning to put stronger cords on his parachute.*

他死了，因为他忽视了要给降落伞装上更结实的绳索的警告。 2 N-VAR A **warning** is an advance notice of something that will happen, often something unpleasant or dangerous. 预告 ❑ *The soldiers opened fire without warning.* 士兵们未发警告就开了火。 3 ADJ **Warning** actions or signs give a warning. 警告性的 [ADJ n] ❑ *She ignored the warning signals and did not check the patient's medical notes.* 她忽视了一些先兆症状，也没有检查病人的病历。

Word Partnership *warning* 的常用搭配:
ADJ. **stern** warning 1
advance warning, **early** warning 1 2
N. warning **of danger**, **hurricane** warning, **storm** warning 1
warning **labels**, warning **signs** 3
V. **give (a)** warning, **ignore a** warning, **receive (a)** warning, **send a** warning 1 2

▲ **warp** /wɔrp/ (**warps, warping, warped**) V-T/V-I If something **warps** or **is warped**, it becomes damaged by bending or curving, often because of the effect of heat or water. (尤指因受潮、受热而)翘曲 ❑ *Left out in the heat of the sun, tapes easily warp or get stuck in their cases.* 放在太阳底下暴晒后，磁带容易翘曲变形或卡带。

★ **war·rant** /wɔrənt/ (**warrants, warranting, warranted**) 1 V-T If something **warrants** a particular action, it makes the action seem necessary or appropriate for the circumstances. 使…显得必要; 使…显得适当 ❑ *The allegations are serious enough to warrant an investigation.* 指控已严重得有必要进行一番调查。 2 N-COUNT A **warrant** is a legal document that allows someone to do something, especially one that is signed by a judge or magistrate and gives the police permission to arrest someone or search their house. 搜查令; 拘捕令 [oft N "for" n, also "by" N] ❑ *Police confirmed that they had issued a warrant for his arrest.* 警方证实他们已对他签发了拘捕令。

▲ **war·ran·ty** /wɔrənti/ (**warranties**) N-COUNT A **warranty** is a written promise by a company that, if you find a fault in something they have sold you within a certain time, they will repair it or replace it free of charge. 保修单 [also "under" N] ❑ *...a twelve-month warranty.* …为期12个月的保修单。

war·ring /wɔrɪŋ/ ADJ **Warring** is used to describe groups of people who are involved in a conflict or quarrel with each other. 交战的; 敌对的 [ADJ n] ❑ *An official said the warring factions have not yet turned in all their heavy weapons.* 一位官员说交战方还未全部上缴重武器。

▲ **war·ri·or** /wɔriər/ (**warriors**) N-COUNT A **warrior** is a fighter or soldier, especially one in former times who was very brave and experienced in fighting. 武士; 勇士 ❑ *...the tale of Bima, the great warrior of Indonesian folklore.* …印度尼西亚民间传说中大勇士毕马的故事。

war·ship /wɔrʃɪp/ (**warships**) N-COUNT A **warship** is a ship with guns that is used for fighting in wars. 战舰; 军舰
→ see **ship**

wart /wɔrt/ (**warts**) N-COUNT A **wart** is a small lump that grows on your skin. 疣

war·time /wɔrtaɪm/ N-UNCOUNT **Wartime** is a period of time when a war is being fought. 战争时期 ❑ *The government will commandeer ships only in wartime.* 政府只在战争时期征用船只。

Word Link *war ≈ watchful : aware, beware, wary*

▲ **wary** /wɛəri/ (**warier, wariest**) ADJ If you are **wary of** something or someone, you are cautious because you do not know much about them and you believe they may be dangerous or cause problems. 小心的; 提防的 ❑ *People did not teach their children to be wary of strangers.* 人们以前没教过自己的孩子们要提防陌生人。
● **wari·ly** /wɛərɪli/ ADV 小心地; 谨慎地 ❑ *She studied me warily, as if I might turn violent.* 她警惕地盯着我，好像我会变得很粗暴似的。

was /wəz, STRONG wʌz, wɒz/ **Was** is the first and third person singular of the past tense of **be**. 动词**be**的第一、第三人称单数过去式

wash ♦◇◇ /wɒʃ/ (**washes, washing, washed**) 1 V-T If you **wash** something, you clean it using water and usually a substance such as soap or detergent. 洗涤 ❑ *We did odd jobs like farm work and washing dishes.* 我们做了一些诸如干农活儿和洗盘子之类的零活儿。 ❑ *It took a long time to wash the mud out of his hair.* 花了很长时间才把泥从他头发上洗掉。 2 V-T/V-I If you **wash** or if you **wash** part of your body, especially your hands and face, you clean part of your body using soap and water. 洗; 盥洗 ❑ *They looked as if they hadn't washed in days.* 他们看起来好像有好几天没洗澡了。 ❑ *She washed her face with cold water.* 她用冷水洗脸。 3 V-T/V-I If a sea or river **washes** somewhere, it flows there gently. You can also say that something carried by a sea or river **washes** or **is washed** somewhere. 缓缓流向; (被) 冲走 ❑ *The sea washed against the shore.* 海水冲刷着海岸。 4 V-I If a feeling **washes over** you, you suddenly feel it very strongly and cannot control it. (情绪) 冲击 [WRITTEN] ❑ *A wave of self-consciousness can wash over her when someone new enters the room.* 当有陌生人进入房间时，她会感到不自在。 5 → see also **washing** 6 PHRASE If you say that something such as an item of clothing **is in the wash**, you mean that it is being washed, is waiting to be washed, or has just been washed and should therefore not be worn or used. 待洗; 正洗; 刚洗 [INFORMAL] ❑ *Your jeans are in the wash.* 你的牛仔裤正在洗呢。 7 **to wash** your **hands of** something → see **hand**
→ see **dry-cleaning, soap**

▸ **wash away** PHRASAL VERB If rain or floods **wash away** something, they destroy it and carry it away. 冲垮; 冲走 ❑ *Flood waters washed away one of the main bridges in Pusan.* 洪水冲垮了釜山的一座主要桥梁。

▸ **wash down** 1 PHRASAL VERB If you **wash** something, especially food, **down** with a drink, you drink the drink after eating the food, especially to make the food easier to swallow or digest. (以水或者饮料) 冲咽 ❑ *He took two aspirin immediately and washed them down with three cups of water.* 他立刻服用了两粒阿斯匹林，用了3杯水冲服下去。 2 PHRASAL VERB If you **wash down** an object, you wash it all, from top to bottom. 彻底冲洗 ❑ *The prisoner started to wash down the walls of his cell.* 犯人开始彻底冲洗囚室的墙壁。

▸ **wash up** 1 PHRASAL VERB If you **wash up**, you clean part of your body with soap and water, especially your hands and face. 洗(手或脸) [AM] ❑ *He headed to the bathroom to wash up.* 他去盥洗室洗漱。 2 PHRASAL VERB If something **is washed up on** a piece of land, it is carried by a river or sea and left there. (被) 冲上岸 ❑ *Thousands of herring and crab are washed up on the beaches during every storm.* 成千上万的鲱鱼和螃蟹每逢暴风雨都会被冲上岸。 3 PHRASAL VERB If you **wash up**, you wash the plates, cups, flatware, and pans that have been used for cooking and eating a meal. 洗餐具 [BRIT]
in AM, use **wash the dishes**

Thesaurus *wash* 另参见:
V. clean, rinse, scrub 1
bathe, clean, soap 2

Word Partnership *wash* 的常用搭配:
N. wash **a car**, wash **clothes**, wash **dishes** 1
wash ***your* face/hair/hands** 2

wash·able /wɒʃəbᵊl/ ADJ **Washable** clothes or materials can be washed in water without being damaged. 可水洗的 ❑ *Choose washable curtains.* 选择可水洗的窗帘。

wash·cloth /wɒʃklɔθ/ (**washcloths**) N-COUNT A **washcloth** is a small cloth that you use for washing yourself. 洗脸毛巾 [AM]
in BRIT, use **flannel, facecloth**

wash·er /wɒʃər/ (**washers**) 1 N-COUNT A **washer** is a thin flat ring of metal or rubber that is placed over a bolt before the nut is screwed on. (金属或橡胶制的) 垫圈 2 N-COUNT A **washer** is the same as a **washing machine**. 洗衣机 [INFORMAL]

wash·ing /wɒʃɪŋ/ N-UNCOUNT **Washing** is a collection of clothes, sheets, and other things that are waiting to be washed, are being washed, or have just been washed. 待洗的衣物; 正在洗的衣物; 刚洗了的衣物 ❑ *...plastic bags full of dirty washing.* …装满要洗的脏衣物的塑料袋。

wash·ing ma·chine (**washing machines**) N-COUNT A **washing machine** is a machine that you use to wash clothes in. 洗衣机

wasn't /wʌzᵊnt, wɒz-/ **Wasn't** is the usual spoken form of "was not." **was not**的常用口语形式

wasp /wɒsp/ (**wasps**) N-COUNT A **wasp** is an insect with wings and yellow and black stripes across its body. Wasps have a painful sting like a bee but do not produce honey. 黄蜂

wast·age /weɪstɪdʒ/ N-UNCOUNT **Wastage** of something is the act of wasting it or the amount of it that is wasted. 浪费 ❑ *There was a lot of wastage and many wrong decisions were hastily taken.* 浪费很大，又仓促地作了许多错误决定 ❑ *...measures to prevent the wastage of water.* …一些预防浪费水的措施。

waste ♦♦◇ /weɪst/ (**wastes, wasting, wasted**) 1 V-T If you **waste** something such as time, money, or energy, you use too much of it doing something that is not important or necessary, or is unlikely to succeed. 浪费 ❑ *There could be many reasons and he was not going to waste time speculating on them.* 原因可能很多，而他不打算浪费时间猜测这些原因。 ❑ *I resolved not to waste money on a hotel.* 我决定不把钱白白浪费在旅馆住宿上。 ● N-SING **Waste** is also a noun. (时间、金钱等的) 浪费 ❑ *It is a waste of time going to the doctor with most mild complaints.* 为了种种小毛病去看医生是浪费时间。 2 N-UNCOUNT **Waste** is the use of money or other resources on things that do not need it. 浪费 ❑ *The packets are measured to reduce waste.* 测量包裹尺寸以减少浪费。 3 N-UNCOUNT **Waste** is material that has been used and is no longer wanted, for example, because the valuable or useful part of it has been taken out. 废物；废水 [also N in pl] ❑ *Congress passed a law that regulates the disposal of waste.* 国会通过了一条管理废物处理的法律。 ❑ *...the dangers posed by toxic waste.* …有毒废弃物造成的危险。 4 V-T If you **waste** an opportunity for something, you do not take advantage of it when it is available. 错过 (机会) ❑ *Let's not waste an opportunity to see the children.* 我们别错过看看孩子们的机会。 5 ADJ **Waste** land is land, especially in or near a city, that is not used or taken care of by anyone, and so is covered by wild plants and garbage. 荒芜的；废弃的 [BRIT]

in AM, use **vacant land**

6 PHRASE If something **goes to waste**, it remains unused or has to be thrown away. 被浪费掉 ❑ *So much of his enormous effort and talent will go to waste if we are forced to drop one hour of the film.* 如果我们被迫删减一小时的电影，就会浪费掉他的非凡努力和才华。 7 **to waste no time** → see **time**

→ see **dump**

▸ **waste away** PHRASAL VERB If someone **wastes away**, they become extremely thin or weak because they are ill or worried and they are not eating properly. 变消瘦；变衰弱 ❑ *Persons dying from cancer grow thin and visibly waste away.* 身患癌症濒临死亡的人会变得消瘦，并明显地衰弱下去。

Thesaurus *waste* 另参见:

V.	misuse, squander 1 4
N.	garbage, junk, trash 3

Word Partnership *waste* 的常用搭配:

N.	waste **energy**, waste **money**, waste **time**, waste **water** 1
V.	**reduce** waste 2
	recycle waste 3
ADJ.	**hazardous** waste, **human** waste, **industrial** waste, **nuclear** waste, **toxic** waste 3

★ **waste·ful** /weɪstfəl/ ADJ Action that is **wasteful** uses too much of something valuable such as time, money, or energy. 浪费的 ❑ *This kind of training is ineffective, and wasteful of scarce resources.* 这种训练没有效果，浪费了稀有资源。

▲ **waste·land** /weɪstlænd/ (**wastelands**) 1 N-VAR A **wasteland** is an area of land on which not much can grow or which has been spoiled in some way. 荒地 ❑ *The pollution has already turned vast areas into a wasteland.* 污染已使大片地区变为荒原。 2 N-COUNT If you refer to a place, situation, or period in time as a **wasteland**, you are criticizing it because you think there is nothing interesting or exciting in it. (精神上或文化上的) 荒原 [DISAPPROVAL] ❑ *...the cultural wasteland of Franco's repressive rule.* …佛朗哥残暴统治下的文化荒原。

watch
❶ LOOKING AND PAYING ATTENTION
❷ INSTRUMENT THAT TELLS THE TIME

❶ **watch** ♦♦♦ /wɒtʃ/ (**watches, watching, watched**)
➩ **Please look at meaning 11 to see if the expression you are looking for is shown under another headword.** 1 V-T/V-I If you **watch** someone or something, you look at them, usually for a period of time, and pay attention to what is happening. 观看 ❑ *The man was standing in his doorway watching him.* 那个男人正站在自家门道里看着他。 ❑ *He seems to enjoy watching me work.* 他似乎喜欢看我干活。 ❑ *Here, now watch how I cut this, OK?* 嘿，现在看我怎样切，好吗？ ❑ *He watched as the Yankees rallied for a second comeback victory.* 他看着北方佬为了又一次东山再起而集结。 2 V-T If you **watch** something on television or an event such as a sports contest, you spend time looking at it, especially when you see it from the beginning to the end. 观看 (电视节目、比赛等) ❑ *I'd stayed up late to watch the movie.* 我熬夜看了那部电影。 3 V-T/V-I If you **watch** a situation or event, you pay attention to it or you are aware of it, but you do not influence it. 关注 ❑ *Human rights groups have been closely watching the case.* 人权组织一直在密切关注着这件案子。 ❑ *He watched as nine people were swept into the crevasse.* 他眼看着9个人被卷入冰缝中。 4 V-T If you **watch** people, especially children or animals, you are responsible for them, and make sure that they are not in danger. 照看 ❑ *Parents can't be expected to watch their children 24 hours a day.* 不能指望父母全天24小时都照看自己的孩子。 5 V-T If you tell someone to **watch** a particular person or thing, you are warning them to be careful that the person or thing does not get out of control or do something unpleasant. 当心；留神 ❑ *You really ought to watch these quiet types.* 你真该当心这类不声不响的人。 6 PHRASE If someone **keeps watch**, they look and listen all the time, while other people are asleep or doing something else, so that they can warn them of danger or an attack. 守望；放哨 ❑ *Jose, as usual, had climbed a tree to keep watch.* 乔斯一如往常地爬到树上放哨。 7 PHRASE If you **keep watch** on events or a situation, you pay attention to what is happening, so that you can take action at the right moment. 注意；关注 (事态发展，以便适时采取行动) ❑ *U.S. officials have been keeping close watch on the situation.* 美国官员们一直密切关注着事态的发展。 8 PHRASE You say "**watch it**" in order to warn someone to be careful, especially when you want to threaten them about what will happen if they are not careful. 当心；留神 ❑ *"Now watch it, Patsy," the sergeant told her.* "当心，帕齐，"警官提醒她说。 9 PHRASE If someone is being kept **under watch**, they are being guarded or observed all the time. 受到保卫；受到监视 ❑ *Doctors confirmed how serious Josephine's condition was, and she is still being kept under watch.* 医生证实了约瑟芬的情况很糟糕，她仍被留床观察。 10 PHRASE You say to someone "**you watch**" or "**just watch**" when you are predicting that something will happen, and you are very confident that it will happen as you say. 你瞧着吧 ❑ *You watch. Things will get worse before they get better.* 你瞧着吧。事情会先变糟，然后再好转。 11 **to watch your step** → see **step**

▸ **watch for** or **watch out for** PHRASAL VERB If you **watch for** something or **watch out for** it, you pay attention so that you notice it, either because you do not want to miss it or because you want to avoid it. 密切注视；提防 ❑ *We'll be watching for any developments.* 我们会密切注视任何进展。

▸ **watch out** PHRASAL VERB If you tell someone to **watch out**, you are warning them to be careful, because something unpleasant might happen to them or they might get into difficulties. (提醒别人) 小心 ❑ *You have to watch out because there are land mines all over the place.* 你必须要小心，因为这里到处都是地雷。

▸ **watch out for** → see **watch for**

If you want to say that someone is paying attention to something they can see, you say that they **are watching** or **looking at** it. In general, you **watch** something that is moving or changing, and you **look at** something that is not moving. ❑ *I asked him to look at the picture above his bed... He watched Blake run down the stairs.* You use **see** to talk about things that you are aware of because a visual impression reaches your eyes. You often use **can** in this case. ❑ *I can see the fax here on the desk.*

Word Partnership *watch* 的常用搭配:

ADV.	watch **carefully**, watch **closely** ❶ 1 3 5
N.	watch **a DVD**, watch **a film/movie**, watch **fireworks**, watch **a game**, watch **the news**, watch **people**, watch **television/TV**, watch **a video** ❶ 2
	watch **children** ❶ 4
V.	**check** *your* watch, **glance at** *your* watch, **look at** *your* watch ❷

❷ **watch** ♦◇◇ /wɒtʃ/ (**watches**) N-COUNT A **watch** is a small clock that you wear on a strap on your wrist, or on a chain. 表；手表
→ see **jewelry, time**

★ **watch·dog** /wɒtʃdɔg/ (**watchdogs**) 1 N-COUNT A **watchdog** is a person or committee whose job is to make sure that companies do not act illegally or irresponsibly. 监察员；监察委员会

❑ ...*an anticrime watchdog group funded by New York businesses.* …一个由纽约商界资助的反犯罪监察组织。 2 N-COUNT A **watchdog** is a fierce dog that has been specially trained to protect a particular place. 看门狗 [mainly AM]

watch·ful /wɒtʃfəl/ ADJ Someone who is **watchful** notices everything that is happening. 警觉的 ❑ *The best thing is to be watchful and see the family doctor for any change in your normal health.* 最好的做法就是保持警惕，身体一有变化就去看家庭医生。

watch·word /wɒtʃwɜrd/ (**watchwords**) N-COUNT Someone's **watchword** is a word or phrase that sums up their attitude or approach to a particular subject or to things in general. 口号；格言 ❑ *Caution has been one of Mr. Allan's watchwords.* "谨慎"是艾伦先生的格言之一。

wa·ter ◆◆◆ /wɔtər/ (**waters, watering, watered**) 1 N-UNCOUNT **Water** is a clear thin liquid that has no color or taste when it is pure. It falls from clouds as rain and enters rivers and seas. All animals and people need water in order to live. 水 ❑ *Get me a glass of water.* 给我一杯水。 ❑ ...*the sound of water hammering on the metal roof.* …雨水敲打着金属屋顶的声音。 2 N-PLURAL You use **waters** to refer to a large area of sea, especially the area of sea that is near to a country and that is regarded as belonging to it. 海域；(尤指) 领海 ❑ *The ship will remain outside Chinese territorial waters.* 这艘船将继续停留在中国领海之外。 3 V-T If you **water** plants, you pour water over them in order to help them to grow. 浇水 ❑ *He went out to water the plants.* 他出去给植物浇水。 4 V-I If your eyes **water**, tears build up in them because they are hurting or because you are upset. 流泪 ❑ *His eyes watered from cigarette smoke.* 他的眼睛被香烟烟雾呛出了泪水。 5 V-I If you say that your mouth **is watering**, you mean that you can smell or see some nice food that makes you want to eat it. 流口水 ❑ ...*cookies to make your mouth water.* …令你流口水的曲奇饼。 6 PHRASE If you say that an event or incident is **water under the bridge**, you mean that it has happened and cannot now be changed, so there is no point in worrying about it anymore. 桥下水 (比喻无需再挂怀的往事) ❑ *He was relieved his time in jail was over and regarded it as water under the bridge.* 他对自己的刑期已满而感到如释重负，把那视为桥下之水过往之事而不再挂怀。 7 PHRASE If you are **in deep water**, you are in a difficult or awkward situation. 陷入困境 ❑ *You certainly seem to be in deep water.* 你的确看起来像是陷入了困境中。 8 PHRASE If an argument or theory does not **hold water**, it does not seem to be reasonable or be in accordance with the facts. (理论或论点) 符合逻辑；与事实相符 ❑ *This argument simply cannot hold water in Europe.* 这种论点在欧洲根本就说不通。 9 PHRASE If you are **in hot water**, you are in trouble. 陷入困境 [INFORMAL] ❑ *The company has already been in hot water over high prices this year.* 该公司今年已陷入了高价的困境中。 10 PHRASE If you **pour cold water on** an idea or suggestion, you show that you have a low opinion of it. (对想法或建议) 泼冷水 ❑ *University economists pour cold water on the idea that the economic recovery has begun.* 大学的经济学家们对经济已经开始复苏的观点泼冷水。 11 PHRASE If you **test the water** or **test the waters**, you try to find out what reaction an action or idea will get before you do it or tell it to people. 试探 ❑ *You should be cautious when getting involved and test the water before committing yourself.* 当你涉足其中时你应该小心谨慎，在表态之前要先行试探。 12 **like water off a duck's back** → see **duck** 13 to **take to** something **like a duck to water** → see **duck** 14 to **keep** your **head above water** → see **head**

▸ **water down** 1 PHRASAL VERB If you **water down** a substance, such as food or drink, you add water to it to make it weaker. 掺水稀释 ❑ *You can water down a glass of wine and make it last twice as long.* 你可以在一杯葡萄酒中掺水，这样就能当两杯喝。 2 PHRASAL VERB If something such as a proposal, speech, or statement is **watered down**, it is made much weaker and less forceful, or less likely to make people angry. 降低声调；缓和语气 ❑ *Proposed legislation affecting bird-keepers has been watered down.* 事关养鸟人的立法提案已作了缓和修改。

→ see Word Web: **water**

→ see **erosion, glacier, greenhouse effect, lake, ocean, plumbing, wetland**

water·color /wɔtərkʌlər/ (**watercolors**)

in BRIT, use **watercolor**

1 N-VAR **Watercolors** are colored paints, used for painting pictures, which you apply with a wet brush or dissolve in water first. 水彩 ❑ *Oil paints can be replaced with watercolors.* 油彩可以用水彩来替代。 2 N-COUNT A **watercolor** is a picture that has been painted with watercolors. 水彩画 ❑ ...*a lovely watercolor by J. M. W. Turner.* …J. M. W. 特纳的一幅漂亮的水彩画。

water·colour /wɔːtəʳkʌləʳ/ [BRIT] → see **watercolor**

water·fall /wɔtərfɔl/ (**waterfalls**) N-COUNT A **waterfall** is a place where water flows over the edge of a steep, high cliff in hills or mountains, and falls into a pool below. 瀑布 ❑ ...*Angel Falls, the world's highest waterfall.* …安赫尔瀑布，世界上最高的瀑布。

water·front /wɔtərfrʌnt/ (**waterfronts**) N-COUNT A **waterfront** is a street or piece of land next to an area of water, such as a harbor or the sea. 滨水地区 ❑ *They went for a stroll along the waterfront.* 他们沿着滨水区漫步。

water·melon /wɔtərmɛlən/ (**watermelons**) N-VAR A **watermelon** is a large, heavy fruit with green skin, pink flesh, and black seeds. 西瓜

water·proof /wɔtərpruf/ ADJ Something that is **waterproof** does not let water pass through it. 防水的 ❑ *Take waterproof clothing – Oregon weather is unpredictable.* 带上防水的衣物吧——俄勒冈州的天气总是难以预测。

▲ **water·shed** /wɔtərʃɛd/ (**watersheds**) N-COUNT If something such as an event is a **watershed in** the history or development of something, it is very important because it represents the beginning of a new stage in it. 分水岭；转折点 ❑ *The election of Mary Robinson in 1990 was a watershed in Irish politics.* 1990年玛丽·鲁滨逊的当选是爱尔兰政治的分水岭。

★ **water·tight** /wɔtərtaɪt/ also **water-tight** 1 ADJ Something that is **watertight** does not allow water to pass through it, for example, because it is tightly sealed. 不透水的 ❑ *The flask is completely watertight, even when laid on its side.* 这水瓶即使平放也不漏一滴水。 2 ADJ A **watertight** case, argument, or agreement is one that has been so carefully put together that nobody will be able to find a fault in it. (事实、论点、协议等) 严密的；无懈可击的 [mainly BRIT]

in AM, usually use **airtight**

water·way /wɔtərweɪ/ (**waterways**) N-COUNT A **waterway** is a canal, river, or narrow channel of sea which ships or boats can sail along. 航道 ❑ *There are more than 400 miles of waterways to explore in the area.* 此地有400多英里的航道有待勘察。

wa·tery /wɔtəri/ 1 ADJ Something that is **watery** is weak or pale. 微弱的；淡薄的 ❑ *A watery light began to show through the branches.* 一缕微弱的光线从树枝间透射过来。 2 ADJ If you describe food or drink as **watery**, you dislike it because it contains too much water, or has no flavor. 像水一样稀的；淡而无味的 [DISAPPROVAL] ❑ ...*a bowl of watery soup.* …一碗淡而无味的汤。 3 ADJ Something that is **watery** contains, resembles, or consists of water. 含水的；似水的；由水组成的 ❑ *There was a watery discharge from her ear.* 她的耳朵里有水状物流出。

★ **watt** /wɒt/ (**watts**) N-COUNT A **watt** is a unit of measurement of electrical power. 瓦特 (电的功率单位) ❑ *Use a 3 amp fuse for equipment up to 720 watts.* 在达到720瓦特的设备上要用3安培的保险丝。

Word Web water

Water changes its form in the **hydrologic cycle**. The sun warms oceans, lakes, and rivers. This causes some water to **evaporate**. Evaporation creates a gas called **water vapor**. Plants also give off water vapor through transpiration. Water vapor rises into the **atmosphere**. When it hits cooler air, it **condenses** into drops of water and forms **clouds**. When these drops get heavy enough, they begin to fall. They form different types of precipitation. Rain forms in warm air. Cold air creates **freezing rain, sleet,** and **snow**.

Word Web wave

As **wind** blows across water, it creates **waves**. It does this by transferring energy to the water. If the waves encounter an object, they bounce off it. Light also travels in waves and behaves the same way. We are able to see an object only if light waves bounce off it. Light waves can be categorized by their **frequency**. Wave frequency is usually the measure of the number of waves per second. **Radio waves** and **microwaves** are examples of low-frequency light waves. **Visible light** consists of medium-frequency light waves. **Ultraviolet radiation** and **X-rays** are high-frequency light waves.

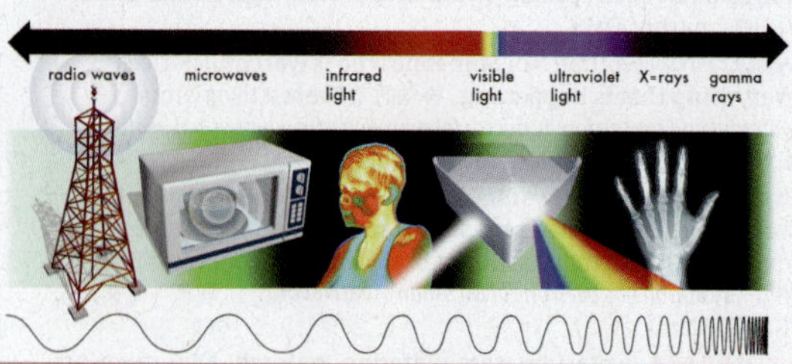

wave ♦♦◇ /weɪv/ (**waves, waving, waved**) **1** V-T/V-I If you **wave** or **wave** your hand, you move your hand from side to side in the air, usually in order to say hello or goodbye to someone. 挥(手以示意) ❑ *Jessica caught sight of Lois and waved to her.* 杰茜卡看到洛伊丝，向她挥了挥手。 ❑ *He grinned, waved, and said, "Hi!"* 他咧嘴笑笑，挥挥手，说道："嗨！" ● N-COUNT **Wave** is also a noun. 挥(手) ❑ *Steve stopped him with a wave of the hand.* 史蒂夫把手一挥，制止了他。 **2** V-T If you **wave** someone away or **wave** them on, you make a movement with your hand to indicate that they should move in a particular direction. 挥手(示意某人离开、前进等) ❑ *Leshka waved him away with a show of irritation.* 廖什卡生气地挥手示意他离开。 ❑ *He waited for a policeman to stop the traffic and wave the people on.* 他等着一位警察来让车辆停下，挥手让众人前行。 **3** V-T If you **wave** something, you hold it up and move it rapidly from side to side. 挥舞 ❑ *Hospital staff were outside to welcome him, waving flags and applauding.* 医院工作人员在院外迎接他，一边挥舞旗帜一边鼓掌。 **4** V-I If something **waves**, it moves gently from side to side or up and down. 飘扬；摆动 ❑ *...grass and flowers waving in the wind.* …随风摆动的花草。 **5** N-COUNT A **wave** is a raised mass of water on the surface of water, especially the sea, which is caused by the wind or by tides making the surface of the water rise and fall. 波浪；(尤指) 海浪 ❑ *...the sound of the waves breaking on the shore.* …波浪拍打海岸的声响。 **6** N-COUNT If someone's hair has **waves**, it curves slightly instead of being straight. (头发的) 波浪卷；鬈曲 ❑ *Her blue eyes shone and caught the light, and so did the platinum waves in her hair.* 她蓝色的眼睛闪闪发光，白金色的波浪发卷也闪闪发光。 **7** N-COUNT A **wave** is a sudden increase in heat or energy that spreads out from an earthquake or explosion. (地震、爆炸的) 冲击波 ❑ *The shock waves of the earthquake were felt in Teheran.* 在德黑兰感觉到了地震的震波。 **8** N-COUNT **Waves** are the form in which things such as sound, light, and radio signals travel. (光、声、无线电等的) 波 ❑ *Regular repeating actions such as sound waves, light waves, or radio waves have a certain frequency, or number of waves per second.* 有规律的重复活动如声波、光波、无线电波都有一个特定的频率，或者说是每秒的波动次数。 **9** N-COUNT If you refer to a **wave of** a particular feeling, you mean that it increases quickly and becomes very intense, and then often decreases again. (情绪的) 波动 ❑ *She felt a wave of panic, but forced herself to leave the room calmly.* 她感到一阵惊慌，但是强迫自己镇静地离开了房间。 **10** N-COUNT A **wave** is a sudden increase in a particular activity or type of behavior, especially an undesirable or unpleasant one. (活动或行为的) 突然爆发；浪潮 ❑ *...the current wave of violence.* …当前的暴力浪潮。 **11** → see also **new wave**, **tidal wave**

→ see Word Web: **wave**

→ see **beach, ear, earthquake, echo, ocean, radio, sound, telescope, weather**

Word Partnership *wave* 的常用搭配：

N. wave *your* hand **1**
wave a flag **3**
crest of a wave **5**
radio wave **8**
wave of attacks/bombings, wave of violence **10**

V. smile and wave **1**
ride a wave **5** **9**

wave·length /weɪvlɛŋθ/ (**wavelengths**) **1** N-COUNT A **wavelength** is the distance between a part of a wave of energy such as light or sound and the next similar part. (光波、音波等的) 波长 ❑ *Sunlight consists of different wavelengths of radiation.* 阳光由波长不同的射线组成。 **2** N-COUNT A **wavelength** is the size of radio wave that a particular radio station uses to broadcast its programs. (广播的) 波段 ❑ *She found the wavelength of their broadcasts, and left the radio tuned to their station.* 她找到了他们广播的波段，把收音机调到他们的电台上。 **3** PHRASE If two people are **on the same wavelength**, they find it easy to understand each other and they tend to agree, because they share similar interests or opinions. 志趣相投 ❑ *We could complete each other's sentences because we were on the same wavelength.* 我们可以彼此把没说完的句子接完整，因为我们志趣相投。

▲ **wa·ver** /weɪvər/ (**wavers, wavering, wavered**) **1** V-I If you **waver**, you cannot decide about something or you consider changing your mind about something. 犹豫不决；踌躇 ❑ *Some military commanders wavered over whether to support the coup.* 一些军队指挥官对是否支持政变犹豫不决。 **2** V-I If something **wavers**, it shakes with very slight movements or changes. 摇摆 ❑ *The shadows of the dancers wavered continually.* 舞者的身影摇摆不停。

wavy /weɪvi/ (**wavier, waviest**) **1** ADJ **Wavy** hair is not straight or curly, but curves slightly. (指头发) 波浪形的；鬈曲的 ❑ *She had short, wavy brown hair.* 她有一头又短又卷的褐发。 **2** ADJ A **wavy** line has a series of regular curves along it. 波纹状的 ❑ *The boxes were decorated with a wavy gold line.* 这些盒子上装饰了一条波纹状的金边。

wax /wæks/ (**waxes, waxing, waxed**) **1** N-MASS **Wax** is a solid, slightly shiny substance made of fat or oil that is used to make candles and polish. It melts when it is heated. 蜡 ❑ *There were colored candles which had spread pools of wax on the furniture.* 彩色蜡烛在家具上留下了一摊摊的蜡油。 **2** → see also **beeswax** **3** V-T If you **wax** a surface, you put a thin layer of wax onto it, especially in order to polish it. 给…上蜡 ❑ *We'd have long talks while she helped me wax the floor.* 她帮我给地板上蜡时，我们闲聊了很长时间。 **4** N-UNCOUNT **Wax** is the sticky yellow substance found in your ears. 耳垢 ❑ *Use a Q-Tip to remove the wax from your ears.* 用棉花棒挖掉你耳朵里的耳垢。 **5** V-T If you have a part of your body **waxed**, for example your legs, you have the hair removed from the area by having wax put on it and then pulled off quickly. (用蜡) 去毛 ❑ *She has just had her legs waxed at the local beauty parlor.* 她刚在当地的美容院用蜡去了腿毛。

way

1 NOUN AND ADVERB USES
2 PHRASES: GROUP 1
3 PHRASES: GROUP 2
4 PHRASES: GROUP 3
5 PHRASES: GROUP 4

❶ **way** ♦♦♦ /weɪ/ (**ways**) **1** N-COUNT If you refer to a **way** of doing something, you are referring to how you can do it, for example, the action you can take or the method you can use to achieve it. 方式；方法 ❑ *Freezing isn't a bad way of preserving food.* 冷冻不失为保存食品的一种好方法。 ❑ *I worked myself into a frenzy plotting ways to make him jealous.* 我绞尽脑汁，处心积虑，就是为了让他嫉妒。 ❑ *There just might be a way.* 可能会有个办法的。 **2** N-COUNT If you talk about the **way** someone does something, you are talking about the qualities their action has. 态度；样子 ❑ *She smiled in a friendly way.* 她友好地笑了笑。 ❑ *He had a strange way of talking.* 他说话的样子很奇怪。 **3** N-COUNT If a general statement or description is true **in** a particular **way**, this is the form of it that is true in a particular case. 形式；方面 ❑ *Computerized reservation systems help airline profits in several ways.* 电子订票系统让航空公司在好几个方面获利。

W

❑ *She was afraid in a way that was quite new to her.* 她感到害怕，而这种害怕是以前不曾有过的。 4 N-COUNT You use **way** in expressions such as **in some ways**, **in many ways**, and **in every way** to indicate the degree or extent to which a statement is true. 某方面；某点 ❑ *In some ways, the official opening is a formality.* 从某些方面来说，官方开幕仪式是个形式而已。 5 N-PLURAL The **ways** of a particular person or group of people are their customs or their usual behavior. 习俗；习惯 ❑ *He denounces people who urge him to alter his ways.* 他指责那些敦促他改变习惯的人们。 ❑ *She began to study the ways of the Native Americans.* 她开始研究土著印第安人的习俗。 6 N-SING If you refer to someone's **way**, you are referring to their usual or preferred type of behavior. 习惯；作风 ❑ *She is now divorced and, in her usual resourceful way, has started her own business.* 她现在离婚了，并以她一贯机敏能干的作风开始自己创业。 7 N-COUNT You use **way** to refer to one particular opinion or interpretation of something, when others are possible. 看法 ❑ *I suppose that's one way of looking at it.* 我想那是其中的一种看法。 ❑ *With most of Dylan's lyrics, however, there are other ways of interpreting the words.* 然而，迪伦的大多数歌词都有其他的解读方法。 8 N-COUNT You use **way** when mentioning one of a number of possible, alternative results or decisions. 结果；决定 ❑ *There is no indication which way the vote could go.* 没有迹象表明投票的结果会怎么样。 9 N-SING The **way** you feel about something is your attitude to it or your opinion about it. 态度；观点 ❑ *I'm so sorry – I had no idea you felt that way.* 我很抱歉——我不知道你是那样想的。 10 N-SING If you mention **the way** that something happens, you are mentioning the fact that it happens. 情形 ❑ *I hate the way he manipulates people.* 我讨厌他摆布人。 11 N-SING You use **way** in expressions such as **push your way**, **work your way**, or **eat your way**, followed by a prepositional phrase or adverb, in order to indicate movement, progress, or force as well as the action described by the verb. 用于**push your way**、**work your way**或者**eat your way**等词组中，表示运动、进程、力量以及所用动词所表示的动作 ❑ *She thrust her way into the crowd.* 她挤进了人群。 12 N-COUNT **The way** somewhere consists of the different places that you go through or the route that you take in order to get there. 路径 ❑ *Does anybody know the way to the bathroom?* 有没有人知道到卫生间的路怎么走？ ❑ *I'm afraid I can't remember the way.* 恐怕我不记得路了。 13 N-SING If you go or look a particular **way**, you go or look in that direction. 方向 ❑ *As he strode into the kitchen, he passed Pop coming the other way.* 他大步走进厨房，同迎面过来的爸爸擦肩而过。 ❑ *They paused at the top of the stairs, doubtful as to which way to go next.* 他们在楼梯的顶头停了下来，不知道下一步朝哪个方向走。 14 N-SING You can refer to the direction you are traveling in as your **way**. 行进方向 [SPOKEN] ❑ *She would say she was going my way and offer me a lift.* 她会说和我同路，可以载我一程。 15 N-SING If you lose your **way**, you take a wrong or unfamiliar route, so that you do not know how to get to the place that you want to go to. If you find your **way**, you manage to get to the place that you want to go to. 路途 ❑ *The men lost their way in a sandstorm and crossed the border by mistake.* 这些男人在沙尘暴中迷了路，误越了边境。 16 N-COUNT You talk about people going their different **ways** in order to say that their lives develop differently and they have less contact with each other. 生活道路 ❑ *It wasn't until we each went our separate ways that I began to learn how to do things for myself.* 直到我们各奔东西后，我才开始学会如何自己做事情。 17 N-SING If something comes your **way**, you get it or receive it. 获得 ❑ *Take advantage of the opportunities coming your way in a couple of months.* 把握住这几个月之内你可能获得的机会。 18 N-SING You use **way** in expressions such as **the right way up** and **the other way around** to refer to one of two or more possible positions or arrangements that something can have. 可能的位置 ❑ *Books have a right and a wrong way up.* 书可以正着放，也可以反着放。 19 ADV You can use **way** to emphasize, for example, that something is a great distance away or is very much below or above a particular level or amount. 大大地；远远地 [ADV adv/prep] [EMPHASIS] ❑ *Way down in the valley to the west is the town of Freiburg.* 远远的西边山谷中坐落着弗赖堡镇。 ❑ *You've waited way too long.* 你们已经等了太久了。 20 N-PLURAL If you split something a number of **ways**, you divide it into a number of different parts or quantities, usually fairly equal in size. (分成的通常大小相同的) 部分 ❑ *The region was split three ways, between Greece, Serbia and Bulgaria.* 该地区被希腊、塞尔维亚和保加利亚一分为三。 ● COMB IN ADJ **Way** is also a combining form. 部分 (用于构成合成词) [ADJ n] ❑ *...a simple three-way division.* …一种简单的3分法。 21 N-SING **Way** is used in expressions such as **a long way**, **a little way**, and **quite a way**, to say how far away something is or how far you have traveled. 距离 ❑ *Some of them live in places quite a long way from here.* 他们当中一些人住在离这儿相当远的地方。 ❑ *A little way further down the lane we passed the driveway to a house.* 我们沿着小巷又走了一小段距离，穿过车道来到一幢房子前。 22 N-SING **Way** is used in expressions such as **a long way**, **a little way**, and **quite a way**, to say how far away in time something is. (时间的) 距离 ❑ *Success is still a long way off.* 离成功还远着呢。 23 N-SING You use **way** in expressions such as **all the way**, **most of the way** and **half the way** to refer to the extent to which an action has been completed. (行为完成的) 程度 ❑ *He had unscrewed the caps most of the way.* 他已经快要把瓶盖拧开了。

Thesaurus *way* 另参见：
N. method, practice, style, technique ❶ 1 6
behavior, characteristic, habit, personality ❶ 2

❷ **way** ♦♦♦ /weɪ/ (**ways**) 1 PHRASE You use **all the way** to emphasize how long a distance is. 一路 [EMPHASIS] ❑ *He had to walk all the way home.* 他不得不一路步行回家。 2 PHRASE You can use **all the way** to emphasize that your remark applies to every part of a situation, activity, or period of time. 一直 [EMPHASIS] ❑ *Having started a revolution we must go all the way.* 既然我们已经开始革命了，就必须一直坚持下去。 3 PHRASE If someone says that you **can't have it both ways**, they are telling you that you have to choose between two things and cannot do or have them both. 二者不能兼得 ❑ *Countries cannot have it both ways: the cost of a cleaner environment may sometimes be fewer jobs in dirty industries.* 各国不能二者兼得：环境更为洁净的代价有可能是污染工业的减少。 4 PHRASE You say **by the way** when you add something to what you are saying, especially something that you have just thought of. 顺便提一下 [SPOKEN] ❑ *The name Latifah, by the way, means "delicate."* 顺便提一下，Latifah这个名字有"精致"之意。 5 PHRASE If you **clear the way**, **open the way**, or **prepare the way** for something, you create an opportunity for it to happen. (为某事) 创造机会；扫清道路 ❑ *The talks are meant to clear the way for formal negotiations on a new constitution.* 会谈旨在为新宪法的正式协商扫清道路。 6 PHRASE If you say that someone takes **the easy way out**, you disapprove of them because they do what is easiest for them in a difficult situation, rather than dealing with it properly. 走捷径 [DISAPPROVAL] ❑ *As soon as things got difficult he took the easy way out.* 事情刚变得有些棘手他就走捷径脱身。 7 PHRASE You use **either way** in order to introduce a statement that is true in each of the two possible or alternative cases that you have just mentioned. (两种情况中) 不论发生哪种情况 ❑ *The sea may rise or the land may fall; either way the sand dunes will be gone in a short time.* 海平面可能会升高，或者陆地可能会下降；不论发生哪种情况，沙丘都将很快消失。 8 PHRASE If you say that a particular type of action or development is **the way forward**, you approve of it because it is likely to lead to success. 进步 [APPROVAL] ❑ *...people who genuinely believe that anarchy is the way forward.* …真正相信无政府状态是一种进步的人。 9 PHRASE If someone **gets** their **way** or **has** their **way**, nobody stops them from doing what they want to do. You can also say that someone **gets** their **own** way or **has** their **own way**. 随心所欲 ❑ *She is very good at using her charm to get her way.* 她非常擅长利用自己的魅力来为所欲为。 10 PHRASE If one thing **gives way to** another, the first thing is replaced by the second. 被…取代 ❑ *First he had been numb. Then the numbness gave way to anger.* 一开始他只是麻木。后来麻木被愤怒代替。 11 PHRASE If an object that is supporting something **gives way**, it breaks or collapses, so that it can no longer support that thing. 断裂；倒塌 ❑ *The hook in the ceiling had given way and the lamp had fallen blazing on to the table.* 天花板上的钩子脱落，结果挂灯大亮着掉到了桌子上。

❸ **way** ♦♦♦ /weɪ/ (**ways**) 1 PHRASE You use **in no way** or **not in any way** to emphasize that a statement is not at all true. 决不 [EMPHASIS] ❑ *In no way am I going to adopt any of his methods.* 我决不会采用他的任何一个方法。 2 PHRASE If you say that something is true **in a way**, you mean that although it is not completely true, it is true to a limited extent or in certain respects. You use **in a way** to reduce the force of a statement. 在某种程度上 [VAGUENESS] ❑ *In a way, I suppose I'm frightened of failing.* 我想，从某种程度上来说我害怕失败。 3 PHRASE If you say that someone **gets in the way** or **is in the way**, you are annoyed because their presence or their actions stop you from doing something properly. 妨碍 ❑ *"We wouldn't get in the way," Suzanne promised. "We'd just stand quietly in a corner."* "我们不会妨碍你的，"苏珊保证说，"我们就在角落里安安静静地站着。" 4 PHRASE To **get in the way of** something means to make it difficult for it to happen, continue, or be appreciated properly. 阻碍 ❑ *She had a job which never got in the way of her leisure interests.* 她有一份工作，但丝毫不妨碍她的个人爱好。 **5** PHRASE If you **know** your **way around** a particular subject, system, or job, you know all the procedures and facts about it. 通晓 ❑ *He knows his way around the intricate maze of patent law.* 他通晓错综复杂的专利法。 **6** PHRASE If you **lead the way** along a particular route, you go along it in front of someone in order to show them where to go. 领路 ❑ *She grabbed his suitcase and led the way.* 她抓过他的手提箱，在前面带路。 **7** PHRASE If a person or group **leads the way in** a particular activity, they are the first person or group to do it or they make the most new developments in it. 领先 ❑ *Sony has also led the way in shrinking the size of compact-disc players.* 索尼公司在缩小CD播放机尺寸方面也处于领先地位。 **8** PHRASE If you say that someone or something **has come a long way**, you mean that they have developed, progressed, or become very successful. 取得了长足进步 ❑ *He has come a long way since the days he could only afford one meal a day.* 和以前那种一天只吃得起一顿饭的日子相比他取得了很大的成就。 **9** PHRASE If you say that something is **a long way from** being true, you are emphasizing that it is definitely not true. 还差很远 [EMPHASIS] ❑ *She is a long way from being the richest person in Florida.* 她远远算不上是佛罗里达最富有的人。 **10** PHRASE If you say that something **goes a long way toward** doing a particular thing, you mean that it is an important factor in achieving that thing. 是…的重要因素 ❑ *Being respectful and courteous goes a long way toward building a relationship.* 对人恭谨、彬彬有礼是建立关系的重要因素。

❹ **way** ♦♦♦ /weɪ/ (**ways**) **1** PHRASE If you say that someone has **lost** their **way**, you are criticizing them because they do not have any good ideas anymore, or seem to have become unsure about what to do. 不知所措 [DISAPPROVAL] ❑ *Why has the White House lost its way on tax and budget policy?* 为什么白宫在税收和预算政策方面会不知所措呢？ **2** PHRASE When you **make** your **way** somewhere, you walk or travel there. 前往 ❑ *He made his way to the marketplace.* 他去了市场。 **3** PHRASE If one person or thing **makes way for** another, the first is replaced by the second. 让位 ❑ *He said he was prepared to make way for younger people in the party.* 他说他准备让位于党内的年轻人。 **4** PHRASE If you say **there's no way** that something will happen, you are emphasizing that you think it will definitely not happen. 没有可能 [EMPHASIS] ❑ *There was absolutely no way that we were going to be able to retrieve it.* 我们绝对不可能把它找回来。 **5** PHRASE You can say **no way** as an emphatic way of saying no. 绝不 [INFORMAL, EMPHASIS] ❑ *Mike, no way am I playing cards with you for money.* 迈克，我是决不会和你玩牌赌钱的。 **6** PHRASE If you **are on** your **way**, you have started your trip somewhere. 在路途中 ❑ *He has been allowed to leave the country and is on his way to Hawaii.* 他已获准离开该国，现正在前往夏威夷的途中。 **7** PHRASE If something happens **on the way** or **along the way**, it happens during the course of a particular event or process. 在过程中 ❑ *You may have to learn a few new skills along the way.* 你也许还得在这个过程中学习一些新的技能。 **8** PHRASE If you are **on** your **way** or **well on** your **way** to something, you have made so much progress that you are almost certain to achieve that thing. 大有进展 ❑ *I am now out of the hospital and well on the way to recovery.* 我现已出院，很快就会康复。 **9** PHRASE If something is **on the way**, it will arrive soon. 即将到来 ❑ *The forecasters say more snow is on the way.* 天气预报员说不久还将有更多降雪。 **10** PHRASE You can use **one way or another** or **one way or the other** when you want to say that something definitely happens, but without giving any details about how it happens. 无论怎样 [VAGUENESS] ❑ *You know pretty well everyone here, one way or the other.* 你不管怎么说肯定非常了解这里的每个人。 **11** PHRASE You use **one way or the other** or **one way or another** to refer to two possible decisions or conclusions that have been previously mentioned, without stating which one is reached or preferred. (两种可能的决定或结论中) 无论哪个 ❑ *We've got to make our decision one way or the other.* 我们无论如何都得作出决定。

W

❺ **way** ♦♦♦ /weɪ/ (**ways**) **1** PHRASE You use **the other way around** to refer to the opposite of what you have just said. 相反地 ❑ *You'd think you were the one who did me the favor, and not the other way around.* 你会认为是你帮助了我，而不是我帮助了你。 **2** PHRASE If something or someone is **on the way out** or **on** their **way out**, they are likely to disappear or to be replaced very soon. 行将消失；即将被取代 ❑ *There are encouraging signs that cold war attitudes are on the way out.* 令人欣慰的是有迹象表明冷战思维行将消失。 **3** PHRASE If you **go out of** your **way to** do something, for example, to help someone, you make a special effort to do it. 特地 ❑ *He was very kind to me and seemed to go out of his way to help me.* 他对我非常友善，好像是在特意帮我的忙。 **4** PHRASE If you **keep out of** someone's **way** or **stay out of** their **way**, you avoid them or do not get involved with them. 躲避某人 ❑ *I'd kept out of his way as much as I could.* 我一直尽量躲避着他。 **5** PHRASE When something is **out of the way**, it has finished or you have dealt with it, so that it is no longer a problem or needs no more time spent on it. 结束；得到解决 ❑ *The plan has to remain confidential at least until the local elections are out of the way.* 此项计划至少得保密到地方选举结束为止。 **6** PHRASE If you **go** your **own way**, you do what you want rather than what everyone else does or expects. 自行其是 ❑ *In school I was a loner. I went my own way.* 在学校里我是个不合群的人，自行其是。 **7** PHRASE You use **in the same way** to introduce a situation that you are comparing with one that you have just mentioned, because there is a strong similarity between them. 同样地 ❑ *There is no reason why an aircraft designer should also be a good pilot. In the same way, a good pilot can be a bad driver.* 没有理由期待一个飞机设计师同时也是一个优秀的飞行员。同样的道理，优秀的飞行员可能是个糟糕的汽车驾驶员。 **8** PHRASE You can use **that way** and **this way** to refer to a statement or comment that you have just made. 那样；这样 ❑ *We have a beautiful city and we pray it stays that way.* 我们拥有一个漂亮的城市，并祈祷永远如此。 **9** PHRASE You can use **that way** or **this way** to refer to an action or situation that you have just mentioned, when you go on to mention the likely consequence or effect of it. 那样；这样 (用于引出结果) ❑ *Keep the soil moist. That way, the seedling will flourish.* 保持土壤湿润，那样小苗就会茁壮成长。 **10** → see also **underway**

way of life (**ways of life**) **1** N-COUNT A **way of life** is the behavior and habits that are typical of a particular person or group, or that are chosen by them. 生活方式 ❑ *Mining activities have totally disrupted the traditional way of life of the Yanomami Indians.* 采矿活动已经完全扰乱了亚诺马米印第安人的传统生活方式。 **2** N-COUNT If you describe a particular activity as **a way of life** for someone, you mean that it has become a very important and regular thing in their life, rather than something they do or experience occasionally. 生活的一部分 ❑ *She likes traveling so much it's become a way of life for her.* 她如此喜欢旅游，以至于旅游已经成为她生活的一部分。

way·side /weɪsaɪd/ (**waysides**) **1** N-COUNT **The wayside** is the side of the road. 路边 [usu "the" N in sing] [LITERARY] **2** PHRASE If a person or plan **falls by the wayside**, they fail or stop before they complete what they set out to do. 半途而废 ❑ *Amateurs fall by the wayside when the going gets tough.* 初学者们遇到困难就半途而废。

▲ **way·ward** /weɪwərd/ ADJ If you describe a person or their behavior as **wayward**, you mean that they behave in a selfish, bad, or unpredictable way, and are difficult to control. 任性的 ❑ *...wayward children with a history of severe emotional problems.* …曾出现过严重情感问题的任性的孩子们。

we ♦♦♦ /wɪ, STRONG wi/

> **We** is the first person plural pronoun. **We** is used as the subject of a verb.

1 PRON-PLURAL A speaker or writer uses **we** to refer both to himself or herself and to one or more other people as a group. You can use **we** before a noun to make it clear which group of people you are referring to. 我们 ❑ *We both swore we'd be friends ever after.* 我们俩人都发誓从此以后永为朋友。 ❑ *We ordered another bottle of champagne.* 我们又点了一瓶香槟酒。 **2** PRON-PLURAL **We** is sometimes used to refer to people in general. 我们 (泛指人们) ❑ *We need to take care of our bodies.* 我们需要照顾好自己的身体。 **3** PRON-PLURAL A speaker or writer may use **we** instead of "I" in order to include the audience or reader in what they are saying, especially when discussing how a talk or book is organized. 我们 (作者或说话者使用，指读者或听众以及自己，尤其用于报告中或书中) [FORMAL] ❑ *We will now consider the raw materials from which the body derives energy.* 我们现在来细想一下为身体提供能量的原料。

weak ♦♦◊ /wik/ (**weaker, weakest**) **1** ADJ If someone is **weak**, they are not healthy or do not have good muscles, so that they cannot move quickly or carry heavy things. 虚弱的 ❑ *I was too weak to move or think or speak.* 我太虚弱了，不能动、不能思维、不能说话。 ● **weak·ly** ADV 虚弱地 [ADV with v] ❑ *"I'm all right," Max said weakly, but his breathing came in jagged gasps.* "我没事，"马克斯虚弱地说，但是他呼吸艰难，长短不均。 ● **weak·ness** N-UNCOUNT 虚弱 ❑ *Symptoms of anemia include weakness, fatigue and iron deficiency.* 贫血的症状包括虚弱、

疲惫和缺铁。 **2** ADJ If someone has an organ or sense that is **weak**, it is not very effective or powerful, or is likely to fail. (人的器官、感官) 衰弱的 ❑ *She tired easily and had a weak heart.* 她容易疲劳，心脏也比较弱。 **3** ADJ If you describe someone as **weak**, you mean that they are not very confident or determined, so that they are often frightened or worried, or easily influenced by other people. 懦弱的 ❑ *He was a nice doctor, but a weak man who wasn't going to stick his neck out.* 他是个好医生，但为人懦弱，遇事不敢出头。 ●**weak·ness** N-UNCOUNT 懦弱 ❑ *Many people felt that admitting to stress was a sign of weakness.* 很多人认为，承认压力是懦弱的表现。 **4** ADJ If you describe someone's voice or smile as **weak**, you mean that it not very loud or big, suggesting that the person lacks confidence, enthusiasm, or physical strength. (声音、微笑等) 微弱的 ❑ *His weak voice was almost inaudible.* 他声音微弱得几乎听不到。 ●**weak·ly** ADV 微弱地 [ADV after v] ❑ *He smiled weakly at reporters.* 他朝记者们淡淡一笑。 **5** ADJ If an object or surface is **weak**, it breaks easily and cannot support a lot of weight or resist a lot of strain. 易碎的; 薄弱的 ❑ *The owner said the bird may have escaped through a weak spot in the aviary.* 主人说那只鸟可能是从鸟舍的一个薄弱处逃出去的。 **6** ADV A **weak** physical force does not have much power or intensity. (力量) 微弱的 ❑ *The molecules in regular liquids are held together by relatively weak bonds.* 常规液体中的分子被相对较弱的结合物聚合在一起。 ❑ *Strong winds can turn boats when the tide is weak.* 潮汐微弱时，强风可以掀翻船只。 ●**weak·ly** ADV 微弱地 ❑ *The mineral is weakly magnetic.* 这种矿石有轻微的磁性。 **7** ADJ If individuals or groups are **weak**, they do not have any power or influence. (个人或团体) 弱小的; 缺少力量和影响力的 ❑ *The council was too weak to do anything about it.* 理事会软弱无能，对此无能为力。 ●N-PLURAL **The weak** are people who are weak. 弱势群体 ❑ *He voiced his solidarity with the weak and defenseless.* 他表示自己站在弱势无助群体一边。 ●**weak·ness** N-UNCOUNT 软弱无能 ❑ *It made me feel patronized, in a position of weakness.* 这让我感到受惠于人，处于弱势。 **8** ADJ A **weak** government or leader does not have much control, and is not prepared or able to act firmly or severely. (政府或领导人) 软弱无力的 ❑ *The changes come after mounting criticism that the government is weak and indecisive.* 随着对政府软弱无能、优柔寡断的批评不断高涨，情况终于有了变化。 ●**weak·ly** ADV 软弱无力地 ❑ *...the weakly-led movement for reform.* …领导乏力的改革运动。 ●**weak·ness** N-UNCOUNT 软弱无力 ❑ *Officials fear that he might interpret the emphasis on diplomacy as a sign of weakness.* 官员们担心，他可能会把对外交的重视理解为软弱无能的表现。 **9** ADJ If you describe something such a country's currency, economy, industry, or government as **weak**, you mean that it is not successful, and may be likely to fail or collapse. (货币、经济、工业、政府等) 疲软的 ❑ *The weak dollar means American goods are relative bargains for foreigners.* 美元疲软意味着美国产品对外国顾客来说是相对便宜的。 ●**weak·ness** N-UNCOUNT 疲软 ❑ *The weakness of his regime is showing more and more.* 他政权的疲弱性日益显露。 **10** ADJ If something such as an argument or case is **weak**, it is not convincing or there is little evidence to support it. (论点) 没有说服力的; (案例) 缺少证据的 ❑ *Do you think the prosecution made any particular errors, or did they just have a weak case?* 你认为控方是真的出了纰漏，还是只是证据不足？ ●**weak·ly** ADV 没有说服力地 [ADV before v] ❑ *Bush listened to that statement and responded rather weakly.* 布什听了那个声明，做的回应却相当没有说服力。 ●**weak·ness** N-VAR (**weaknesses**) 说服力的缺乏; 证据的不足 ❑ *Critical thinking requires that you examine the weaknesses of any argument.* 批判性思维要求你分析任何论点的不足之处。 **11** ADJ A **weak** drink, chemical, or drug contains very little of a particular substance, for example, because a lot of water has been added to it. 稀薄的 ❑ *Grace poured a cup of weak tea.* 格莱斯倒了一杯淡茶。 **12** ADJ Your **weak** points are the qualities or talents you do not possess, or the things you are not very good at. 弱的 ❑ *Geography was my weak subject.* 地理课是我的弱项。 ●**weak·ness** N-VAR 弱点 ❑ *His only weakness is his temperament.* 他惟一的弱点是他的脾气。 **13** → see also **weakness**
→ see **muscle**

Thesaurus *weak* 另参见:
ADJ. feeble, frail, puny; (*ant.*) strong **1**
cowardly, insecure, wimpy; (*ant.*) strong **3**

Word Partnership *weak* 的常用搭配:
ADV. **relatively** weak, **still** weak, **too** weak, **very** weak **1**–**12**
N. weak **dollar**, weak **economy**, weak **sales**, weak **spending** **9**

weak·en ♦◇◇ /wikən/ (**weakens, weakening, weakened**) **1** V-T/V-I If you **weaken** something or if it **weakens**, it becomes less strong or less powerful. 使虚弱; 变得虚弱 ❑ *The recession has weakened so many businesses that many can no longer survive.* 经济衰退削弱了很多企业的实力，以至于很多无法再生存下去。 ❑ *Family structures are weakening and breaking up.* 家庭结构正在弱化、崩溃。 **2** V-T/V-I If your resolve **weakens** or if something **weakens** it, you become less determined or less certain about taking a particular course of action that you had previously decided to take. 动摇 ❑ *I looked at the list and felt my resolve weakening.* 我看着那张单子，感到我的决心开始动摇。 ❑ *Jennie weakened, and finally relented.* 珍妮犹豫一下，最终不再拒绝了。 **3** V-T If something **weakens** you, it causes you to lose some of your physical strength. 使虚弱 ❑ *Malnutrition obviously weakens the patient.* 营养不良明显使病人虚弱无力。 **4** V-T If something **weakens** an object, it does something to it that causes it to become less firm and more likely to break. 使松动 ❑ *A bomb blast had weakened an area of brick on the back wall.* 炸弹爆炸使后墙的块砖都松动了。

Word Partnership *weaken* 的常用搭配:
N. weaken **the economy** **1**
weaken ***someone's* ability**, weaken ***someone's* resolve** **2**

weak·ling /wiklɪŋ/ (**weaklings**) N-COUNT If you describe a person or an animal as a **weakling**, you mean that they are physically weak. 体质孱弱的人 (或动物) [DISAPPROVAL] ❑ *You were never a ninety-eight pound weakling.* 你从来就不是一个体重98磅、体质孱弱的人。

weak·ness /wiknɪs/ (**weaknesses**) **1** N-COUNT If you have a **weakness for** something, you like it very much, although this is perhaps surprising or undesirable. 癖好 ❑ *Stephen himself had a weakness for cats.* 史蒂芬自己偏爱猫。 **2** → see also **weak**

wealth ♦◇◇ /wɛlθ/ **1** N-UNCOUNT **Wealth** is the possession of a large amount of money, property, or other valuable things. You can also refer to a particular person's money or property as their **wealth**. 财富 ❑ *Economic reform has brought relative wealth to peasant farmers.* 经济改革使农民相对富裕起来。 **2** N-SING If you say that someone or something has **a wealth of** good qualities or things, you are emphasizing that they have a very large number or amount of them. 大量的 ["a" N "of" n] [FORMAL, EMPHASIS] ❑ *Their websites contain a wealth of information on the topic.* 他们的网站上有大量与该主题相关的信息。 ❑ *The city boasts a wealth of beautiful churches.* 该城引以为荣的是有大量漂亮的教堂。
→ see **economics**

Thesaurus *wealth* 另参见:
N. affluence, funds, money; (*ant.*) poverty **1**

wealthy /wɛlθi/ (**wealthier, wealthiest**) ADJ Someone who is **wealthy** has a large amount of money, property, or valuable possessions. 富有的 ❑ *...a wealthy international businessman.* …一个富有的跨国商人。 ●N-PLURAL **The wealthy** are people who are wealthy. 富人 ❑ *The best education should not be available only to the wealthy.* 不应该只有富人才能得到最好的教育。

wean /win/ (**weans, weaning, weaned**) **1** V-T When a baby or baby animal **is weaned**, its mother stops feeding it milk and starts giving it other food, especially solid food. 使断奶 ❑ *When would be the best time to start weaning my baby?* 什么时候开始给我的孩子断奶最好呢？ **2** V-T If you **wean** someone **off** a habit or something they like, you gradually make them stop doing it or liking it, especially when you think it is bad for them. 使戒除 (尤指恶习) ❑ *You are given capsules or pills with small quantities of nicotine to wean you from the habit.* 会给你一些含有少量尼古丁的胶囊或药片帮你戒瘾。

weap·on ♦♦◇ /wɛpən/ (**weapons**) N-COUNT A **weapon** is an object such as a gun, a knife, or a missile, which is used to kill or hurt people in a fight or a war. 武器 ❑ *...nuclear weapons.* …核武器。
→ see **army, war**

wea·pon·ry /wɛpənri/ N-UNCOUNT **Weaponry** is all the weapons that a group or country has or that are available to it. (一个团体、国家所拥有或可供使用的) 所有武器 ❑ *...rich nations, armed with superior weaponry.* …装备着尖端武器的富国。

wear ♦♦◇ /wɛər/ (**wears, wearing, wore, worn**) **1** V-T When you **wear** something such as clothes, shoes, or jewelry, you have them on your body or on part of your body. 穿; 戴 ❑ *He was wearing a brown uniform.* 他穿着一件棕色制服。 ❑ *I sometimes wear contact lenses.* 我有时候戴隐形眼镜。

W

After you get up in the morning, you **get dressed**, or you **dress**, by **putting on** your clothes. ❑ *He put on his shoes and socks.* Small children and sick people may be unable to **dress themselves**, so someone else has to **dress** them. When you **are dressed**, you **are wearing** your clothes, or you **have** them **on**. ❑ *Edith had her hat on... They ought to stop walking around the house with nothing on.* During the day you might want to **get changed**, or to **change** your clothes. ❑ *She returned having changed from pants into a skirt... Adams changed his shirt a couple of times a day.* Before you go to bed, you **get undressed**, or you **undress**, by **taking off** your clothes. ❑ *He won't take his clothes off in front of me.* See also note at **clothes**.

2 V-T If you **wear** your hair or beard in a particular way, you have it cut or styled in that way. 留着(某种样式的头发或胡须) ❑ *She wore her hair in a long braid.* 她留着长辫子。 **3** N-UNCOUNT You use **wear** to refer to clothes that are suitable for a certain time or place. For example, **evening wear** is clothes suitable for the evening. (在特定时间或场合穿戴的)服装 ❑ *The shop stocks an extensive range of beach wear.* 这家商店备有品种繁多的沙滩服装。 **4** N-UNCOUNT **Wear** is the amount or type of use that something has over a period of time. 耐用性；经久性 ❑ *You'll get more wear out of a hat if you choose one in a neutral color.* 如果选择中性颜色的帽子，戴的时间会更久一些。 **5** N-UNCOUNT **Wear** is the damage or change that is caused by something being used a lot or for a long time. 磨损 ❑ *...a large, well-upholstered armchair which showed signs of wear.* …一张宽大、装饰精美的有些磨损的扶手椅。 **6** V-I If something **wears**, it becomes thinner or weaker because it is constantly being used over a long period of time. 磨损 ❑ *The stone steps, dating back to 1855, are beginning to wear.* 这些可以追溯到1855年的石阶开始出现磨损。 **7** V-I You can use **wear** to talk about how well something lasts over a period of time. For example, if something **wears well**, it still seems quite new or useful after a long time or a lot of use. 耐用 ❑ *Ten years on, the original concept was wearing well.* 十年过去，最初的观念依然适用。

▸ **wear away** PHRASAL VERB If you **wear** something **away** or if it **wears away**, it becomes thin and eventually disappears because it is used a lot or rubbed a lot. 使磨损 ❑ *It had a saddle with springs sticking out, which wore away the seat of my pants.* 马鞍上的弹簧翘了出来，磨坏了我臀部的裤子。

▸ **wear down** **1** PHRASAL VERB If you **wear** something **down** or if it **wears down**, it becomes flatter or smoother as a result of constantly rubbing against something else. 使磨平 ❑ *Pipe smokers sometimes wear down the tips of their teeth where they grip their pipes.* 抽烟斗的人用牙齿咬住烟斗，有时会把牙齿尖磨平。 ❑ *The heels on his shoes had worn down.* 他鞋子的后跟磨平了。 **2** PHRASAL VERB If you **wear** someone **down**, you make them gradually weaker or less determined until they eventually do what you want. 消磨(某人)斗志 ❑ *None can match your sheer will-power and persistence in wearing down the opposition.* 在消磨反对派的意志方面，没有人能比得上你那惊人的毅力和恒心。 ❑ *They hoped the waiting and the uncertainty would wear down my resistance.* 他们希望这种等待和不确定性会削弱我的抵抗。

▸ **wear off** PHRASAL VERB If a drug, sensation, or feeling **wears off**, it disappears slowly until it no longer exists or has any effect. (药性、感觉、感情等)逐渐消失 ❑ *For many the philosophy was merely a fashion, and the novelty soon wore off.* 对很多人而言这种哲学只是一时时髦，新鲜感很快就消失了。

▸ **wear out** **1** PHRASAL VERB When something **wears out** or when you **wear** it **out**, it is used so much that it becomes thin or weak and unable to be used anymore. 用坏；用尽 ❑ *Every time she consulted her watch, she wondered if the batteries were wearing out.* 每次看手表的时候，她都会想是不是电池没电了。 ❑ *Horses used for long-distance riding tend to wear their shoes out more quickly.* 用来作长途跋涉的马匹会很快就磨破铁掌。 **2** PHRASAL VERB If something **wears** you **out**, it makes you feel extremely tired. 使筋疲力尽 [INFORMAL] ❑ *The past few days had really worn him out.* 过去几天真让他筋疲力尽了。 ❑ *The young people run around kicking a ball, wearing themselves out.* 这些年轻人四处跑动踢球，把自己弄得筋疲力尽。 **3** → see also **worn out**
→ see **makeup**

Word Partnership *wear* 的常用搭配:

N. wear **black/red/white**, wear **clothes**, wear **contact lenses**, wear **glasses**, wear **gloves**, wear **a hat/helmet**, wear **a jacket**, wear **jeans**, wear **makeup**, wear **a mask**, wear **a suit**, wear **a uniform** **1**
ADJ. **casual** wear, **day** wear, **evening** wear **3**

wear and tear /wɛər ən tɛər/ N-UNCOUNT **Wear and tear** is the damage or change that is caused to something when it is being used normally. 损耗 ❑ *...the problem of wear and tear on the equipment in the harsh desert conditions.* …在恶劣的沙漠环境下设备损耗的问题。

★ **wea·ry** /wɪəri/ (**wearier, weariest**) **1** ADJ If you are **weary**, you are very tired. 疲惫的 ❑ *Rachel looked pale and weary.* 雷切尔看起来苍白而疲惫。 **2** ADJ If you are **weary of** something, you have become tired of it and have lost your enthusiasm for it. 对…感到厌倦 [v-link ADJ "of" n/-ing] ❑ *They're getting awfully weary of this silly war.* 他们对这场愚蠢的战争感到极其厌倦。

weath·er ◆◆◇ /wɛðər/ (**weathers, weathering, weathered**) **1** N-UNCOUNT The **weather** is the condition of the atmosphere in one area at a particular time, for example, if it is raining, hot, or windy. 天气 ❑ *The weather was bad.* 天气恶劣。 ❑ *I like cold weather.* 我喜欢寒冷的天气。 **2** V-T/V-I If something such as wood or rock **weathers** or **is weathered**, it changes color or shape as a result of the wind, sun, rain, or cold. 风化；褪色 ❑ *Unpainted wooden furniture weathers to a gray color.* 没有上漆的木质家具会褪成灰色。 **3** V-T If you **weather** a difficult time or a difficult situation, you survive it and are able to continue normally after it has passed or ended. 经受住 ❑ *The company has weathered the recession.* 公司度过了萧条期。 **4** PHRASE If you say that you are **under the weather**, you mean that you feel slightly ill. 身体不适 ❑ *I was still feeling a bit under the weather.* 我依然感觉有些不适。
→ see Word Web: **weather**
→ see **forecast, storm**

Word Partnership *weather* 的常用搭配:

ADJ. **bad** weather, **clear** weather, **cold** weather, **cool** weather, **dry** weather, **fair** weather, **good** weather, **hot** weather, **inclement** weather, **mild** weather, **nice** weather, **rainy** weather, **rough** weather, **severe** weather, **stormy** weather, **sunny** weather, **warm** weather, **wet** weather **1**
N. weather **conditions**, weather **prediction**, weather **report**, weather **service** **1**
V. weather **permitting** **1**

Word Web **weather**

Researchers believe the **weather** affects our bodies and minds. When **barometric pressure** drops before a **storm**, some people get migraine headaches. The difference in pressure may change the blood flow in the brain. **Damp**, **humid** weather leads to increased problems with arthritis. A sudden heat wave can produce heatstroke. Seasonal affective disorder or SAD occurs during the short, **gloomy** days of winter. As the word "sad" suggests, people with this condition feel depressed. The bitter cold of a **blizzard** can cause frostbite. The **hot, dry** Santa Ana winds* in southern California create confusion and depression in some people.

Santa Ana winds: strong, hot, dry winds that blow in southern California in fall and early spring.

weath·er fore·cast (**weather forecasts**) N-COUNT A **weather forecast** is a statement saying what the weather will be like the next day or for the next few days. 天气预报

weave /wiv/ (**weaves, weaving, wove, woven**)

The form **weaved** is used for the past tense and past participle for meaning 3.

1 V-T/V-I If you **weave** cloth or a carpet, you make it by crossing threads over and under each other using a frame or machine called a loom. 织 ❑ *They would spin and weave cloth, cook and attend to the domestic side of life.* 他们纺纱、织布、做饭，还料理家务。 ❑ *She sat at her loom and continued to weave.* 她坐在织布机前，继续织布。 ● **wo·ven** ADJ 编织的 ❑ *...woven cotton fabrics.* …棉织物。 ● **weav·ing** N-UNCOUNT 编织 ❑ *When I studied weaving, I became intrigued with natural dyes.* 在我学习编织的时候，对天然染料发生了兴趣。 2 V-T If you **weave** something such as a basket, you make it by crossing long plant stems or fibers over and under each other. 编织（篮子等） ❑ *Jenny weaves baskets from willow she grows herself.* 珍妮用自己栽种的柳树的枝条编织篮子。 ● **wo·ven** ADJ 编织的 ❑ *The floors are covered with woven straw mats.* 地板上铺着用草编织的垫子。 3 V-T/V-I If you **weave** your way somewhere, you move between and around things as you go there. 迂回行进 ❑ *The cars then weaved in and out of traffic at top speed.* 汽车然后在车流中高速穿梭前进。 ❑ *He weaved around the tables to where she sat with Bob.* 他在桌子间穿梭走动，来到她和鲍勃坐的地方。
→ see **industry**

weav·er /wivər/ (**weavers**) N-COUNT A **weaver** is a person who weaves cloth, carpets, or baskets. 织工

web ♦♦♦ /wɛb/ (**webs**) 1 N-PROPER **The Web** is a computer system that links documents and pictures into a database that is stored in computers in many different parts of the world and that people everywhere can use. It is also referred to as the **World Wide Web**. 互联网 [oft N n] [COMPUTING] ❑ *The handbook is available on the Web.* 这本手册互联网上有。 ❑ *She recommended the service on her Web journal after trying it out.* 在经过试用后，她在自己的网络杂志中推荐了这项服务。 2 N-COUNT A **web** is a complicated pattern of connections or relationships, sometimes considered as an obstacle or a danger. 错综复杂的事物 ❑ *He's forced to untangle a complex web of financial dealings.* 他被迫去理顺一大堆错综复杂的金融交易。 3 N-COUNT A **web** is the thin net made by a spider from a sticky substance that it produces in its body. 蜘蛛网 ❑ *...the spider's web in the window.* …窗户上的蜘蛛网。
→ see **blog**

web·cam /wɛbkæm/ (**webcams**) also **Webcam** N-COUNT A **webcam** is a video camera that takes pictures that can be viewed on a website. The pictures are often of something that is happening while you watch. 网络摄像头 [COMPUTING]

web·cast /wɛbkæst/ (**webcasts**) also **Webcast** N-COUNT A **webcast** is an event such as a musical performance that you can listen to or watch on the Internet. 网络广播 [COMPUTING] ❑ *...a Webcast of the Saturday and Sunday concerts.* …周六和周日音乐会的网上播放。

web·master /wɛbmæstər/ (**webmasters**) N-COUNT A **webmaster** is someone who is in charge of a website, especially someone who does that as their job. 网站管理员 [COMPUTING]
→ see **Internet**

web page (**web pages**) also **Web page** N-COUNT A **web page** is a set of data or information that is designed to be viewed as part of a website. 网页 [COMPUTING] ❑ *The company also has a Web page for small businesses and a hotline.* 公司还有针对小企业的网页和一条服务热线。
→ see **Internet**

web ring (**web rings**) also **Web ring, webring** N-COUNT A **web ring** is a set of related websites that you can visit one after the other. 网络环（指连接起来的一组相关网站） [COMPUTING] ❑ *Log on to the HammerWeb ring, with 12 more sites devoted to macabre movies.* 登录哈默的相关系列网站，就会找到另外12个专门提供恐怖电影的网站。

Word Link *site, situ ≈ position, location : campsite, situation, website*

web·site ♦♦◇ /wɛbsaɪt/ (**websites**) also **Web site, web site** N-COUNT A **website** is a set of data and information about a ❑ *...a website devoted to hip-hop music.* …一个嬉蹦乐专门网站。
→ see **blog, Internet**

web·zine /wɛbzin/ (**webzines**) N-COUNT A **webzine** is a website that contains the kind of articles, pictures, and advertisements that you would find in a magazine. 网络杂志 [COMPUTING] ❑ *The Dismal Scientist, a webzine dedicated to economic news, is fun.* 经济新闻网络杂志《忧郁科学家》趣闻十足。

wed /wɛd/ (**weds, wedded**)

The form **wed** is used in the present tense and is the past tense. The past participle can be either **wed** or **wedded**.

V-RECIP If one person **weds** another or if two people **wed** or **are wed**, they get married. 结婚 [no cont] [OLD-FASHIONED, JOURNALISM] ❑ *In 1952 she wed film director Roger Vadim.* 1952年，她嫁给了电影导演罗杰·瓦丹。

Wed.

The spelling **Weds.** is also used.

Wed. is a written abbreviation for **Wednesday**. 星期三

we'd /wid, STRONG wid/ 1 **We'd** is the usual spoken form of "we had," especially when "had" is an auxiliary verb. **we had**的常用口语形式，尤**had**为助动词时 ❑ *Come on, George, we'd better get back now.* 快点，乔治，我们最好现在就回去。 2 **We'd** is the usual spoken form of "we would." **we would**的常用口语形式 ❑ *If we smoked, we'd light a cigarette and let her try it out.* 如果我们吸烟，也会点一支让她试试。

wed·ding ♦◇◇ /wɛdɪŋ/ (**weddings**) N-COUNT A **wedding** is a marriage ceremony and the party or special meal that often takes place after the ceremony. 婚礼 ❑ *Most couples want a traditional wedding.* 多数情侣希望举办一个传统的婚礼。 ❑ *...the couple's 22nd wedding anniversary.* …这对夫妇的第22个结婚纪念日。
→ see Word Web: **wedding**

Do not confuse **wedding** and **marriage**. A **wedding** is a ceremony in which a man and woman get married. It usually includes a meal or other celebration that takes place after the ceremony itself. ❑ *It wasn't a formal wedding.* This ceremony can also be called a **marriage**. ❑ *...the day of my marriage.* **Marriage** can also be used to refer to the relationship between a husband and wife. ❑ *It has been a happy marriage.*

★ **wedge** /wɛdʒ/ (**wedges, wedging, wedged**) 1 V-T If you **wedge** something, you force it to remain in a particular position by holding it there tightly or by sticking something next to it to prevent it from moving. 把…楔住；把…抵牢 ❑ *I shut the shed door and wedged it with a log of wood.* 我关上小屋的门，然后用一根圆木将它抵牢。 2 V-T If you **wedge** something somewhere, you fit it there tightly. 将…塞入 ❑ *Wedge the plug into the hole.* 把塞子塞进洞里。 3 N-COUNT A **wedge** of something such as fruit or cheese is a piece of it that has a thick triangular shape. 楔形物 ❑ *Serve with a wedge of lime.* 和一块楔形酸橙一起端上桌。

Word Web **wedding**

Some **weddings** are fancy, like the one in this picture. Most ceremonies include a similar group of attendants. The maid of honor or matron of honor helps the **bride** get ready for the ceremony. She also signs the **marriage certificate** as a legal **witness**. The **bridesmaids** plan the bride's wedding **shower**. The best man arranges for the bachelor party the night before the wedding. He also helps the groom dress for the wedding. After the **ceremony**, the guests gather for a **reception**. When the party is over, many couples leave on a **honeymoon** trip.

Wednes·day ♦♦♦ /wɛnzdeɪ, -di/ (**Wednesdays**) N-VAR **Wednesday** is the day after Tuesday and before Thursday. 星期三 ❑ *Come and have supper with us on Wednesday, if you're free.* 星期三过来和我们一起吃晚饭，如果有空的话。 ❑ *Did you happen to see her leave last Wednesday?* 上星期三你正好碰巧看见她离开？

wee /wi/ ADJ **Wee** means small in size or extent. (尺寸、程度)小的 [ADJ n] [mainly SCOTTISH, INFORMAL] ❑ *He just needs to calm down a wee bit.* 他只是需要稍微冷静一点。

weed /wid/ (**weeds, weeding, weeded**) **1** N-COUNT A **weed** is a wild plant that grows in gardens or fields of crops and prevents the plants that you want from growing properly. 杂草 ❑ *With repeated applications of weedkiller, the weeds were overcome.* 通过反复使用除草剂，杂草终于根除了。 **2** V-T/V-I If you **weed** an area, you remove the weeds from it. 除草 ❑ *Caspar was weeding the garden.* 卡斯帕正在给花园除草。 ❑ *Try not to walk on the flowerbeds while weeding.* 除草的时候尽量不要在花坛上走。

▸ **weed out** PHRASAL VERB If you **weed out** things or people that are useless or unwanted in a group, you find them and get rid of them. 剔除（无用的人和物）❑ *He is eager to weed out the many applicants he believes may be frauds.* 他急于剔除那些他认为可能是行骗的申请人。

week ♦♦♦ /wik/ (**weeks**) **1** N-COUNT A **week** is a period of seven days. Some people consider that a week starts on Monday and ends on Sunday. 星期 ❑ *I had a letter from my mother last week.* 我上星期收到了母亲的一封信。 ❑ *This has been on my mind all week.* 我整个星期都在想这件事。 **2** N-COUNT A **week** is a period of about seven days. 一周时间 ❑ *Her mother stayed for another two weeks.* 她母亲又呆了两周时间。 ❑ *Only 12 weeks ago he underwent major heart transplant surgery.* 仅仅12周之前，他接受了一次心脏移植的大手术。 **3** N-COUNT Your working **week** is the hours that you spend at work during a week. 工作周（指一周的工作时数）❑ *It is not unusual for women to work a 40-hour week.* 女性1周工作40小时并不少见。 **4** N-SING **The week** is the part of the week that does not include Saturday and Sunday. (除星期六和星期日以外的）周工作日 ❑ *...the hard work of looking after the children during the week.* …除周末外每天都照看孩子的辛苦活。 **5** N-COUNT You use **week** in expressions such as "a week last Monday," "a week ago this Tuesday," and "a week ago yesterday" to mean exactly one week before the day that you mention. 用于**a week last Monday**、**a week ago this Tuesday**以及**a week ago yesterday**等词组中，表示前一星期的该日 ❑ *"That's the time you weren't well, wasn't it?"—"Yes, that's right, that was a week ago last Monday."* "就是那个时候你不舒服，是吗？"—"是的，就是一周前的星期一。"
→ see **year**

week·day /wikdeɪ/ (**weekdays**) N-COUNT A **weekday** is any of the days of the week except Saturday and Sunday. 工作日（指星期一至星期五的任何一天）❑ *If you want to avoid the crowds, it's best to come on a weekday.* 如果你想避开人流，最好在工作日来。

week·end ♦♦◊ /wikɛnd/ (**weekends**) N-COUNT A **weekend** is Saturday and Sunday. 周末 ❑ *She had agreed to have dinner with him in town the following weekend.* 她同意下周末和他一起到城里吃晚饭。

week·ly ♦◊◊ /wikli/ (**weeklies**) **1** ADJ A **weekly** event or publication happens or appears once a week or every week. 一周一次的；每周的 [ADJ n] ❑ *Each course comprises 10-12 informal weekly meetings.* 每门课程包括10至12次每周1次的非正式见面会。 ❑ *We go and do the weekly shopping every Thursday.* 我们每星期四采购一次。 ● ADV **Weekly** is also an adverb. 每周一次地 [ADV after v] ❑ *The group meets weekly.* 小组每周见面一次。 **2** ADJ **Weekly** quantities or rates relate to a period of one week. 按周计算的 [ADJ n] ❑ *Of course, in addition to my weekly pay, I got a lot of tips.* 当然，除了周薪外，我还得到很多小费。 **3** N-COUNT A **weekly** is a newspaper or magazine that is published once a week. 周报；周刊 ❑ *Two of the four national daily papers are to become weeklies.* 4家全国性的日报中有2家要改为周报。

weep /wip/ (**weeps, weeping, wept**) V-T/V-I If someone **weeps**, they cry. 哭泣 [LITERARY] ❑ *She wanted to laugh and weep all at once.* 她哭笑不得。 ❑ *The weeping family hugged and comforted each other.* 一家人相拥而泣，互相安慰着。 ❑ *She wept tears of joy.* 她喜极而泣。
→ see **cry**

weigh ♦◊◊ /weɪ/ (**weighs, weighing, weighed**) **1** V-T If someone or something **weighs** a particular amount, this amount is how heavy they are. 重量为 [no cont] ❑ *It weighs nearly 27 kilos (about 65 pounds).* 它重量接近27公斤（约65磅）。 ❑ *This little ball of gold weighs a quarter of an ounce.* 这个小金球重0.25盎司。 **2** V-T If you **weigh** something or someone, you measure how heavy they are. 称（重量）❑ *The scales can be used to weigh other items such as parcels.* 这台秤可以用来称量包裹等其他物品。 **3** V-T If you **weigh** the facts about a situation, you consider them very carefully before you make a decision, especially by comparing the various facts involved. 权衡 ❑ *She weighed her options.* 她在各种选择间权衡斟酌。 ❑ *He is weighing the possibility of filing criminal charges against the doctor.* 他在权衡向这位医生提起刑事诉讼的可能性。

▸ **weigh down** PHRASAL VERB If something that you are wearing or carrying **weighs** you **down**, it stops you moving easily by making you heavier. 使负荷太重 ❑ *He wrenched off his sneakers. If he had to swim, he didn't want anything weighing him down.* 他猛地蹬掉运动鞋。如果不得不游泳的话，他不想让自己负荷太重。 ❑ *These nests increase in size each year, and can eventually weigh down the branch.* 这些巢每年都会变大，最终会把树枝压弯。

> **Word Partnership** *weigh* 的常用搭配：
> ADV. weigh **less**, weigh **more** **1**
> weigh **carefully** **2** **3**
> N. weigh **ten pounds** **1**
> weigh **alternatives**, weigh **benefits**, weigh **costs**, weigh **the evidence**, weigh **risks** **3**

weight ♦♦◊ /weɪt/ (**weights, weighting, weighted**) **1** N-VAR The **weight** of a person or thing is how heavy they are, measured in units such as kilograms, pounds, or tons. 重量 ❑ *What is your height and weight?* 你的身高和体重是多少？ ● PHRASE If someone **loses weight**, they become lighter. If they **gain weight** or **put on weight**, they become heavier. 体重减轻；体重增加 ❑ *I'm lucky really as I never put on weight.* 我真的很幸运，体重从未增加过。 ❑ *The boy appeared anxious, had lost weight and was not sleeping well.* 那个男孩显得很焦虑，体重减轻了，觉也睡不好。 **2** N-UNCOUNT A person's or thing's **weight** is the fact that they are very heavy. 分量重 ❑ *His weight was harming his health.* 他沉重的体重正危害着他的健康。 **3** N-SING If you move your **weight**, you change position so that most of the pressure of your body is on a particular part of your body. (身体的)重心 ❑ *He shifted his weight from one foot to the other.* 他将身体的重心从一只脚挪到另一只脚上。 **4** N-COUNT **Weights** are objects that weigh a known amount and that people lift as a form of exercise. 哑铃 ❑ *I was in the gym lifting weights.* 我正在健身房举哑铃。 **5** N-COUNT **Weights** are metal objects that weigh a known amount and that are used on a set of scales to weigh other things. 砝码 **6** N-COUNT You can refer to a heavy object as a **weight**, especially when you have to lift it. (尤其指必须举起的）重物 ❑ *Straining to lift heavy weights can lead to a rise in blood pressure.* 用尽全身力气举起重物会导致血压升高。 **7** V-T If you **weight** something, you make it heavier by adding something to it, for example, in order to stop it from moving easily. 加重量于 ❑ *It can be sewn into curtain hems to weight the curtain and so allow it to hang better.* 可以把它缝在窗帘的摺边里以增加窗帘的重量，使之更有下垂感。 **8** N-VAR If something is given a particular **weight**, it is given a particular value according to how important or significant it is. 权重 ❑ *The scientists involved put different weight on the conclusions of different models.* 相关科学家们对不同模型的结论赋予的权重各不相同。 **9** N-UNCOUNT If someone or something gives **weight** to what a person says, thinks, or does, they emphasize its significance. 分量 ❑ *The fact that he is gone has given more weight to fears that he may try to launch a civil war.* 他已离开这一事实让人更加担心他可能要发动一场内战。 **10** N-UNCOUNT If you give something or someone **weight**, you consider them to be very important or influential in a particular situation. 重视 ❑ *Consumers generally place more weight on negative information than on the positive when deciding what to buy.* 消费者在决定购买的时候，一般更看重负面信息而不是正面信息。 **11** → see also **weighting** **12** PHRASE If a person or their opinion **carries weight**, they are respected and are able to influence people. 有影响力 ❑ *Senator Kerry carries considerable weight in Washington.* 参议员克里在华盛顿举足轻重。 **13** PHRASE If you say that someone or something is **worth** their **weight in gold**, you are emphasizing that they are so useful, helpful, or valuable that you feel you could not manage without them. 极有价值 [EMPHASIS] ❑ *Any successful manager is worth his weight in gold.* 任何成功的经理都非常有价值。 **14** PHRASE If you **pull** your **weight**, you work as hard as everyone else who is involved in the same task or activity. 尽本分 ❑ *He accused the team of not pulling their weight.* 他指责队员们没有尽到自己的本分。 **15** **a weight off** your **mind** → see **mind**
→ see **diet**

W

Word Partnership *weight* 的常用搭配：

V. add weight, **gain/lose** weight, **put on** weight 1
N. body weight, weight **gain/loss**, **height and** weight 1
size and weight 1 2
weight **training** 4
ADJ. **excess** weight, **healthy** weight, **ideal** weight, **normal** weight 1
heavy weight, **light** weight 4 6

weight·ed /weɪtɪd/ ADJ A system that is **weighted** in favor of a particular person or group is organized so that this person or group has an advantage. 有(有利)倾向的 ❑ *The current electoral law is still heavily weighted in favor of the ruling party.* 目前的选举法依然非常有利地倾向于执政党。

weight·ing /weɪtɪŋ/ (**weightings**) N-COUNT A **weighting** is a value given to something according to how important or significant it is. 权重 ❑ *...an index formed of equal weightings of three statistics.* …对3份统计结果进行平均加权而形成的指数。

★ **weight·lifting** /weɪtlɪftɪŋ/ N-UNCOUNT **Weightlifting** is a sport in which the competitor who can lift the heaviest weight wins. 举重

weight train·ing N-UNCOUNT **Weight training** is a kind of physical exercise in which people lift or push heavy weights with their arms and legs in order to strengthen their muscles. 举重训练 ❑ *I used to do weight training years ago.* 我多年前曾进行过举重训练。

weighty /weɪti/ (**weightier, weightiest**) ADJ If you describe something such as an issue or a decision as **weighty**, you mean that it is serious or important. 严重的; 重要的 [FORMAL] ❑ *Surely such weighty matters merit a higher level of debate?* 这样重要的事情值得进行更高级别的讨论吧？

weir /wɪər/ (**weirs**) N-COUNT A **weir** is a low barrier built across a river in order to control or direct the flow of water. 堰

weird /wɪərd/ (**weirder, weirdest**) ADJ If you describe something or someone as **weird**, you mean that they are strange. 奇怪的 [INFORMAL] ❑ *That first day was weird.* 第一天很奇怪。 ❑ *Drugs can make you do all kinds of weird things.* 毒品可以让你做出各种各样奇怪的事情来。

wel·come ♦♦◊ /wɛlkəm/ (**welcomes, welcoming, welcomed**) 1 V-T If you **welcome** someone, you greet them in a friendly way when they arrive somewhere. 欢迎 ❑ *Several people came by to welcome me.* 几个人走过来欢迎我。 ❑ *She was there to welcome him home from war.* 她在那里欢迎他从战场回家。 ❑ *...a welcoming speech.* …欢迎辞。 ● N-COUNT **Welcome** is also a noun. 欢迎 ❑ *There would be a fantastic welcome awaiting him back here.* 会有一场热烈的欢迎仪式迎接他回来。 2 CONVENTION You use **welcome** in expressions such as **welcome home**, **welcome to Boston**, and **welcome back** when you are greeting someone who has just arrived somewhere. 欢迎来到… [FORMULAE] ❑ *Welcome to Washington.* 欢迎来到华盛顿。 3 V-T If you **welcome** an action, decision, or situation, you approve of it and are pleased that it has occurred. 欣然接受 ❑ *She welcomed this move but said that overall the changes didn't go far enough.* 她欣然接受了这一举措，但又说总体上改变还不彻底。 ● N-COUNT **Welcome** is also a noun. 欢迎 ❑ *Environmental groups have given a guarded welcome to the prime minister's proposal.* 环保组织对首相的提议表示了谨慎的欢迎。 4 ADJ If you describe something as **welcome**, you mean that people wanted it and are happy that it has occurred. 受欢迎的 ❑ *Any progress in reducing chemical weapons is welcome.* 削减化学武器的任何进展都是受欢迎的。 5 V-T If you say that you **welcome** certain people or actions, you are inviting and encouraging people to do something, for example, to come to a particular place. 欢迎 ❑ *We would welcome your views about the survey.* 我们欢迎你们对这项调查提出意见。 6 ADJ If you say that someone is **welcome** in a particular place, you are encouraging them to go there by telling them that they will be liked and accepted. 受欢迎的 ❑ *New members are always welcome.* 新成员欢迎加入。 7 ADJ If you tell someone that they are **welcome** to do something, you are encouraging them to do it by telling them that they are allowed to do it. 可任意的 [v-link ADJ] ❑ *You are welcome to visit the hospital at any time.* 你可随时来医院参观。 8 ADJ If you say that someone is **welcome to** something, you mean that you do not want it yourself because you do not like it and you are very willing for them to have it. 尽管…好了 [v-link ADJ "to" n] ❑ *If women want to take on the business world they are welcome to it as far as I'm concerned.* 就我而言，如果妇女想承担起商业领域的重任，她们尽管这样做好了。 9 → see also **welcoming** 10 PHRASE If you **make** someone **welcome** or **make** them **feel welcome**, you make them feel happy and accepted in a new place. 使受欢迎 ❑ *Here are six Mexican hotels where children are made to feel welcome.* 这里有6家墨西哥旅馆，孩子们觉得在那儿颇受欢迎。 11 CONVENTION You say **"You're welcome"** to someone who has thanked you for something in order to acknowledge their thanks in a polite way. 不用客气 (对别人为某事表示感谢时所作的礼貌回答) [FORMULAE] ❑ *"Thank you for the information."—"You're welcome."* "谢谢你提供的信息。"——"不客气。"

Word Partnership *welcome* 的常用搭配：

ADJ. **warm** welcome 1 3
N. welcome **guests**, welcome **visitors** 1 6
ADV. welcome **home** 2
always welcome 3 – 7

wel·com·ing /wɛlkəmɪŋ/ ADJ If someone is **welcoming** or if they behave in a **welcoming** way, they are friendly to you when you arrive somewhere, so that you feel happy and accepted. 热情的 ❑ *When we arrived at her house Susan was very welcoming.* 当我们到达苏珊家时，她非常热情。

weld /wɛld/ (**welds, welding, welded**) V-T/V-I To **weld** one piece of metal to another means to join them by heating the edges and putting them together so that they cool and harden into one piece. 焊接 ❑ *It's possible to weld stainless steel to ordinary steel.* 将不锈钢和普通钢焊接在一起是可能的。 ❑ *Where did you learn to weld?* 你在哪里学会的焊接技术？

wel·fare ♦◊◊ /wɛlfɛər/ 1 N-UNCOUNT The **welfare** of a person or group is their health, comfort, and happiness. 健康; 幸福; 福利 ❑ *I do not think he is considering Emma's welfare.* 我认为他没有考虑到艾玛的幸福。 2 ADJ **Welfare** services are provided to help with people's living conditions and financial problems. 福利的 ❑ *Child welfare services are well established and comprehensive.* 儿童福利机构发展成熟、体系完善。 3 N-UNCOUNT **Welfare** is money that is paid by the government to people who are unemployed, poor, or sick. 社会保障金 ❑ *States such as Michigan are making deep cuts in welfare.* 密西根等州正在大幅度削减社会保障金。

The American government has a variety of programs to help people who are poor. They may receive a monthly unemployment check, food stamps, subsidized housing, health care, and other services. This system is called **welfare** and is funded by taxes.

Word Partnership *welfare* 的常用搭配：

ADJ. **social** welfare 1
N. **animal** welfare, **health and** welfare 1
child welfare, welfare **programs**, **public** welfare, welfare **reform**, welfare **system** 2
welfare **benefits**, welfare **checks** 3

wel·fare state N-SING In some countries, the **welfare state** is a system in which the government provides free social services such as health and education and gives money to people when they are unable to work, because they are old, unemployed, or sick. 福利制度 ❑ *...the future of the welfare state.* …福利制度的未来。

well

1. DISCOURSE USES
2. ADVERB USES
3. PHRASES
4. ADJECTIVE USE
5. NOUN USES
6. VERB USES

W

❶ **well** ♦♦♦ /wɛl/

Well is used mainly in spoken English.

➪ **Please look at meaning** 9 **to see if the expression you are looking for is shown under another headword.** 1 ADV You say **well** to indicate that you are about to say something. 哦 (用于将要说的话之前) [ADV cl] ❑ *Well, it's a pleasure to meet you.* 哦，很高兴见到你。 2 ADV You say **well** just before or after you pause, especially to give yourself time to think about what you are going to say.

(用于说话停顿的前后，尤用于给自己考虑的时间) 嗯 [ADV cl] ❑ *Look, I'm really sorry I woke you, and, well, I just wanted to tell you I was all right.* 你看，我真抱歉吵醒了你，嗯，我只是想告诉你我一切都很好。 3 ADV You say **well** when you are correcting something that you have just said. (用于更正刚说过的话) 哦 [ADV cl/group] ❑ *The comet is going to come back in 2061 and we are all going to be able to see it. Well, our offspring are, anyway.* 这颗彗星将于2061年返回，到时我们都可以看到它。哦，无论如何，我们子孙是可以看到的。 4 ADV You say **well** to express your doubt about something that someone has said. (用于表示对别人说过的话的怀疑) 啊 [ADV cl] [FEELINGS] ❑ *"But finance is far more serious."—"Well I don't know really."* "但是财政形势更加严峻了。" ——"啊，我真的不知道。" 5 EXCLAM You say **well** to express your surprise or anger at something that someone has just said or done. (用于表达惊讶或气愤) 哎呀 [FEELINGS] ❑ *She beamed at Patty. "Well! That was a bit of unexpected excitement."* 她对帕蒂灿烂地一笑。"哎呀，那真是有些出人意料，叫人兴奋哦。" 6 CONVENTION You say **well** to indicate that you are waiting for someone to say something and often to express your irritation with them. (用于等待别人回应，常表示不耐烦) 嗯 [FEELINGS] ❑ *"Well?" asked Barry, "What does it tell us?"* "嗯？" 巴里问道，"这到底告诉我们什么呢？" ❑ *"Well, why don't you ask me?" he said finally.* "嗯，那你为什么不问我呢？" 他最后说了一句。 7 CONVENTION You use **well** to indicate that you are amused by something you have heard or seen, and often to introduce a comment on it. (表示高兴并常引出评价) 好啊 [FEELINGS] ❑ *Well, well, well. How quickly things change.* 好啊，好啊，好啊。变化真快啊。 8 CONVENTION You say **oh well** to indicate that you accept a situation or that someone else should accept it, even though you or they are not very happy about it, because it is not too bad and cannot be changed. (表示勉强接受) 算了 [FEELINGS] ❑ *Oh well, it could be worse.* 哎，算了，情况本可能会更糟的。 ❑ *"I called her and she said no."—"Oh well."* "我给她打过电话，但她拒绝了。" ——"唉，那就算了吧。" 9 **very well** → see **very**

❷ **well** ♦♦♦ /wɛl/ (**better, best**) 1 ADV If you do something **well**, you do it to a high standard or to a great extent. (标准或程度) 出色地 [ADV after v] ❑ *It's important that we play well at home.* 重要的是我们应该打好国内的比赛。 ❑ *He speaks English better than I do.* 他英语比我讲得好。 2 ADV If you do something **well**, you do it thoroughly and completely. 完全地 [ADV after v] ❑ *Mix all the ingredients well.* 把所有配料搅拌均匀。 3 ADV If you speak or think **well of** someone, you say or think favorable things about them. (评价) 令人满意地 [ADV after v] ❑ *"He speaks well of you."—"I'm glad to hear that."* "他对你评价很高。" ——"很高兴听见这话。" 4 COMB IN ADJ **Well** is used in front of past participles to indicate that something is done to a high standard or to a great extent. 用于过去分词之前，表示高水准或高程度 ❑ *Helen is a very well-known novelist in Australia.* 海伦是澳大利亚著名的小说家。 ❑ *People live longer nowadays, and they are better educated.* 如今，人们越来越长寿，受教育程度也提高了。 5 ADV You use **well** to ask or talk about the extent or standard of something. (程度或标准) 怎样 ❑ *How well do you remember your mother, Franzi?* 关于你的母亲你还记得多少，弗兰齐？ ❑ *He wasn't dressed any better than me.* 他穿得并不比我好多少。 6 ADV You use **well** in front of a prepositional phrase to emphasize it. For example, if you say that one thing happened **well before** another, you mean that it happened a long time before it. (用于介词短语之前，表示强调) 远远地；很久地 [ADV prep] [EMPHASIS] ❑ *Franklin did not turn up until well after midnight.* 富兰克林直到午夜过后很久才露面。 ❑ *...a war in which well over a million people died.* …一场死亡人数远远超过一百万人的战争。 7 ADV You use **well** before certain adjectives to emphasize them. (用于某些形容词之前，表示强调) 很 [ADV adj] [EMPHASIS] ❑ *She has a close group of friends who are very well aware of what she has suffered.* 她有一群密友，十分了解她的遭遇。 8 ADV You use **well** after adverbs such as "perfectly," "jolly," or "damn" in order to emphasize an opinion or the truth of what you are saying. 用于**perfectly**，**jolly**，**damn**副词之后，强调观点或真相 [EMPHASIS] ❑ *You know perfectly well I can't be blamed for the failure of that mission.* 你非常清楚这次任务的失败不该怪我。 9 ADV You use **well** after verbs such as "may" and "could" when you are saying what you think is likely to happen. (用于**may**，**could**等词的后面) 很可能 [modal ADV] [EMPHASIS] ❑ *Ours could well be the last generation for which moviegoing has a sense of magic.* 我们很可能是感到去电影院看电影很神奇的最后一代人。

❸ **well** ♦♦♦ /wɛl/

➪ **Please look at meaning** 7 **to see if the expression you are looking for is shown under another headword.** 1 PHRASE You use **as well** when mentioning something that happens in the same way as something else already mentioned, or that should be considered at the same time as that thing. 也 ❑ *It is most often diagnosed in women in their thirties and forties, although I've seen it in many younger women, as well.* 这种病多发于三四十岁女性的身上，不过我见过很多更年轻的女性也患了此症。 2 PHRASE You use **as well as** when you want to mention another item connected with the subject you are discussing. 除了…外(还)；和 ❑ *The movie will appeal to adults as well as children.* 这部电影除了将吸引儿童外，还会吸引成年人。 3 PHRASE If you say that something that has happened **is just as well**, you mean that it is fortunate that it happened in the way it did. 幸好 ❑ *Blue asbestos is far less common in buildings, which is just as well because it's more dangerous than white asbestos.* 蓝色的石棉在建筑中要少见得多，幸好是这样，因为它比白色石棉更危险。 4 PHRASE If you say that something, usually something bad, **might as well** be true or **may as well** be true, you mean that the situation is the same or almost the same as if it were true. 简直就像…一样 (常指不好的事情) ❑ *The couple might as well have been strangers.* 这对夫妇简直就像是陌路人。 5 PHRASE If you say that you **might as well** do something, or that you **may as well** do it, you mean that you will do it although you do not have a strong desire to do it and may even feel slightly unwilling to do it. (做…) 也无妨 ❑ *If I've got to go somewhere I may as well go to Tulsa.* 如果我必须去一个地方的话，我就去塔尔萨吧。 ❑ *Anyway, you're here; you might as well stay.* 无论如何你已在这里，你就留下来吧。 6 PHRASE If you say that something is **well and truly** finished, gone, or done, you are emphasizing that it is completely finished or gone, or thoroughly done. 彻底地 [mainly BRIT, EMPHASIS] ❑ *The war is well and truly over.* 战争彻底结束了。 7 **all very well** → see **all** 8 **to know full well** → see **full**

❹ **well** ♦♦♦ /wɛl/ ADJ If you are **well**, you are healthy and not ill. 健康的 ❑ *I'm not very well today, I can't come in.* 我今天身体不太舒服，不能参加了。

❺ **well** /wɛl/ (**wells**) 1 N-COUNT A **well** is a hole in the ground from which a supply of water is extracted. 水井 ❑ *I had to fetch water from the well.* 我得去从水井里打水。 2 N-COUNT A **well** is an oil well. 油井 ❑ *About 650 wells are on fire.* 约六百五十口油井在燃烧。 → see **oil**

❻ **well** /wɛl/ (**wells, welling, welled**) V-I If liquids **well**, they come to the surface and form a pool. (液体) 涌出 ❑ *Tears welled in her eyes.* 泪水从她的眼中涌出。 ● PHRASAL VERB **Well up** means the same as **well**. 涌出 ❑ *Tears welled up in Anni's eyes.* 泪水从安妮的眼中涌出。

we'll /wɪl, STRONG wil/ **We'll** is the usual spoken form of "we shall" or "we will." **we shall**或**we will**的常用口语形式 ❑ *Whatever you want to chat about, we'll do it tonight.* 不管你想聊什么，我们今晚谈。

well-balanced 1 ADJ If you describe someone as **well-balanced**, you mean that they are sensible and do not have many emotional problems. 明智的；情绪稳定的 ❑ *...a fun-loving, well-balanced individual.* …一个风趣而明智的人。 2 ADJ If you describe something that is made up of several parts as **well-balanced**, you mean that the way that the different parts are put together is good, because there is not too much or too little of any one part. 均衡的 ❑ *...a well-balanced diet.* …一份均衡的饮食。

well-behaved ADJ If you describe someone, especially a child, as **well-behaved**, you mean that they behave in a way that adults generally like and think is correct. (尤指小孩) 行为规矩的 ❑ *...well-behaved little boys.* …行为规矩的小男孩们。

★ **well-being** N-UNCOUNT Someone's **well-being** is their health and happiness. 健康快乐 ❑ *Singing can create a sense of well-being.* 唱歌能产生一种幸福感。

well-built ADJ A **well-built** person, especially a man, has big and strong muscles. (尤指男人) 强壮的 ❑ *Mitchell is well-built, of medium height, with a dark complexion.* 米切尔身体强壮，中等个子，面色黝黑。

well-connected ADJ Someone who is **well-connected** has important or influential relatives or friends. 社会关系优越的 ❑ *Mr. Guber and Mr. Peters aren't universally loved in Hollywood but they are well-connected.* 古贝尔先生和彼得斯先生在好莱坞并不普遍受人爱戴，但他们有着良好的社会关系。

well-defined ADJ Something that is **well-defined** is clear and precise and therefore easy to recognize or understand. 明确的 ❑ *Today's pawnbrokers operate within well-defined financial regulations.* 现今的当铺老板按照明确的金融法规来经营。

well done 1 CONVENTION You say **Well done** to indicate that you are pleased that someone has done something good. 做得好 [FEELINGS] ❑ *"Daddy! I came second in history"—"Well done, sweetheart!"* "爸爸！我历史得了第二名"——"做得好，宝贝儿！" 2 ADJ If something that you have cooked, especially meat, is **well done**, it has been cooked thoroughly. (尤指肉类) 烧得烂的 ❑ *Allow an extra 10-15 min if you prefer lamb well done.* 如果你想要小羊肉烧得烂些，就再烧10-15分钟。

well-dressed ADJ Someone who is **well-dressed** is wearing fashionable or elegant clothes. 衣着入时的；衣着讲究的 ❑ *She's always well-dressed.* 她总是衣着讲究。

well-established ADJ If you say that something is **well-established**, you mean that it has been in existence for a long time and is successful. 确立已久的 ❑ *The university has a well-established tradition of welcoming postgraduate students from overseas.* 该大学有由来已久的接收海外研究生的传统。

well-informed (**better-informed**) ADJ If you say that someone is **well-informed**, you mean that they know a lot about many different subjects or about one particular subject. 见多识广的；知识渊博的 ❑ *...a lending library to encourage members to become as well-informed as possible.* …一个鼓励会员尽量变得见多识广的公共图书馆。

well-intentioned also **well intentioned** ADJ If you say that a person or their actions are **well-intentioned**, you mean that they intend to be helpful or kind but they are unsuccessful or cause problems. 用意良好的 (但却常事与愿违) ❑ *He is well-intentioned but a poor administrator.* 他用意良好，但却是位糟糕的管理者。

well-known ♦◇◇ 1 ADJ A **well-known** person or thing is known about by a lot of people and is therefore famous or familiar. If someone is **well-known** for a particular activity, a lot of people know about them because of their involvement with that activity. 有名的；熟悉的 ❑ *Hubbard was well known for his work in the field of drug rehabilitation.* 哈伯德因在戒毒领域的工作而出名。

> A **famous** person or thing is known to more people than a **well-known** one. A **notorious** person or thing is famous because they are connected with something bad or undesirable. **Infamous** is not the opposite of **famous**. It has a similar meaning to **notorious**, but is a stronger word.

2 ADJ A **well-known** fact is a fact that is known by people in general. 众所周知的 ❑ *It is well-known that bamboo shoots are a panda's staple diet.* 众所周知，竹笋是熊猫的主要食物。

well-meaning ADJ If you say that a person or their actions are **well-meaning**, you mean that they intend to be helpful or kind but they are unsuccessful or cause problems. 善意的 (但却常事与愿违) ❑ *He is a well-meaning but ineffectual leader.* 他是位有善意却没有效率的领导。

★ **well-off** ADJ Someone who is **well-off** is rich enough to be able to do and buy most of the things that they want. 富裕的 [INFORMAL] ❑ *My grandparents were quite well-off.* 我的祖父母生活很富裕。

well-paid ADJ If you say that a person or their job is **well-paid**, you mean that they receive a lot of money for the work that they do. 薪水高的 ❑ *Kate was well-paid and enjoyed her job.* 凯特薪水很高，工作很开心。

well-to-do ADJ A **well-to-do** person is rich enough to be able to do and buy most of the things that they want. 富裕的 ❑ *...a well-to-do family of diamond cutters.* …一个富裕的钻石切割匠之家。

well-wisher (**well-wishers**) N-COUNT **Well-wishers** are people who hope that a particular person or thing will be successful, and who show this by their behavior. 表示良好祝愿的人 ❑ *The main street was lined with well-wishers.* 大街两旁站满了祝愿的人们。

went /wɛnt/ **Went** is the past tense of **go**. **go**的过去式

wept /wɛpt/ **Wept** is the past tense and past participle of **weep**. **weep**的过去式和过去分词

were /wər, STRONG wɜr/ 1 **Were** is the plural and the second person singular of the past tense of **be**. **be**的复数形式和第二人称单数过去式 2 **Were** is sometimes used instead of "was" in certain structures, for example, in conditional clauses or after the verb "wish." 有时代替**was**，如在条件从句中或动词**wish**之后 [FORMAL] ❑ *He told a diplomat that he might withdraw if he were allowed to keep part of a disputed oil field.* 他对一名外交官说，如果允许他保留一个有争议的油田的一部分，他可能会撤出。 3 **as it were** → see **as**

we're /wɪər/ **We're** is the usual spoken form of "we are." **we are**的常用口语形式 ❑ *I'm married, but we're separated.* 我已婚，但是我们分居了。

weren't /wɜrnt, wɜrənt/ **Weren't** is the usual spoken form of "were not." **were not**的常用口语形式

west ♦♦♦ /wɛst/ also **West** 1 N-UNCOUNT The **west** is the direction you look toward in the evening in order to see the sun set. 西方 [also "the" N] ❑ *I pushed on toward Flagstaff, a hundred miles to the west.* 我继续向西边100英里处的弗拉格斯塔夫市前进。 2 N-SING **The west of** a place, country, or region is the part of it which is in the west. 西部 ❑ *Many of the buildings in the west of the city are on fire.* 该城西部的许多建筑都着火了。 3 ADV If you go **west**, you travel toward the west. 往西边 [ADV after V] ❑ *We are going west to California.* 我们将往西去加利福尼亚。 4 ADV Something that is **west of** a place is positioned to the west of it. …以西 ❑ *Penryn is about 60 miles west of Philadelphia.* 彭林位于费城以西60英里的地方。 5 ADJ The **west** part of a place, country, or region is the part which is toward the west. 西部的 [ADJ n] ❑ *...a small island off the west coast of South Korea.* …韩国西海岸外的一个小岛。 6 ADJ **West** is used in the names of some countries, states, and regions in the west of a larger area. (用于国家、州和地区的名称中) 西部的 [ADJ n] ❑ *Mark has been working in West Africa for about six months.* 马克已在西非工作了大约六个月。 ❑ *...his West Hollywood home.* …他在西好莱坞的家。 7 ADJ A **west** wind blows from the west. 从西边吹来的 (风) [ADJ n] ❑ *...the warm west wind.* …和煦的西风。 8 N-SING **The West** is used to refer to the United States, Canada, and the countries of Western, Northern, and Southern Europe. 西方国家 (指美国、加拿大以及西欧、北欧和南欧诸国) ❑ *...relations between Iran and the West.* …伊朗和西方国家之间的关系。

west·er·ly /wɛstərli/ 1 ADJ A **westerly** point, area, or direction is to the west or toward the west. 西边的；朝西的 ❑ *...Finisterre, Spain's most westerly point.* …菲尼斯泰尔，西班牙的最西端。 2 ADJ A **westerly** wind blows from the west. 从西边吹来的 (风) ❑ *...a prevailing westerly wind.* …一股盛行的西风。

west·ern ♦♦◇ /wɛstərn/ (**westerns**) also **Western** 1 ADJ **Western** means in or from the west of a region, state, or country. 西部的 [ADJ n] ❑ *...hand-made rugs from Western and Central Asia.* …来自西亚和中亚的手工地毯。 2 ADJ **Western** is used to describe things, people, ideas, or ways of life that come from or are associated with the United States, Canada, and the countries of Western, Northern, and Southern Europe. 西方国家的 (指与北美、西欧、北欧、南欧各国相关的) ❑ *Mexico had the support of the big western governments.* 墨西哥得到了西方大国政府的支持。 3 N-COUNT A **western** is a book or movie about life in the western United States and territories in the nineteenth century, especially the lives of cowboys. (有关19世纪美国西部的生活，尤指牛仔生活的) 西部小说；西部影片 ❑ *John Agar starred in westerns, war films and low-budget science fiction pictures.* 约翰·阿加出演过西部片、战争片和低投入的科幻片。 → see **genre**

west·ern·er /wɛstərnər/ (**westerners**) also **Westerner** N-COUNT A **westerner** is a person who was born in or lives in the United States, Canada, or Western, Northern, or Southern Europe. 西方人 (指生活在美国、加拿大或西欧、北欧或南欧的人) ❑ *It's the first time a Westerner has been convicted for a drug-related offense in recent years in China.* 这是近年来第一次有西方人在中国被判犯有与毒品有关的罪行。

west·erni·sa·tion /wɛstərnaɪzeɪʃən/ [BRIT] → see **westernization**

west·ern·ised /wɛstərnaɪzd/ [BRIT] → see **westernized**

west·erni·za·tion /wɛstərnɪzeɪʃən/

> in BRIT, also use **westernisation**

N-UNCOUNT The **westernization** of a country, place, or person is the process of them adopting ideas and behavior that are typical of Europe and North America, rather than preserving the ideas and behavior traditional in their culture. 西方化 ❑ *...fundamentalists unhappy with the westernization of Afghan culture.* …不满阿富汗文化被西化的原教旨主义者。

west·ern·ized /wɛstərnaɪzd/

> in BRIT, also use **westernised**

ADJ A **westernized** country, place, or person has adopted ideas and behavior typical of Europe and North America, rather than preserving the ideas and behavior that are traditional in their

W

Word Web wetlands

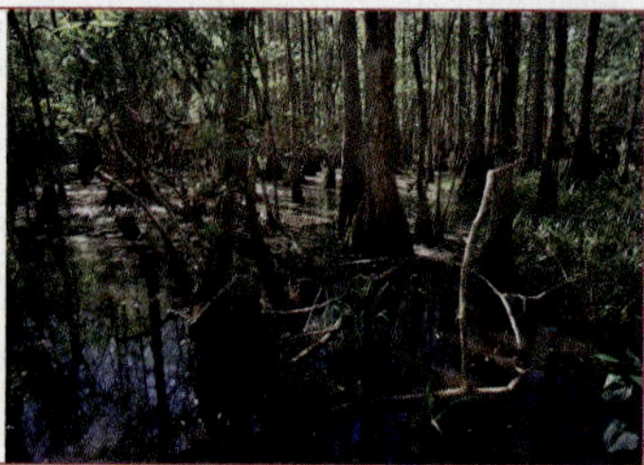

Salt water wetlands protect beaches from erosion. These **tidal flats** also provide homes for shellfish and migrating birds. In some areas, mangrove **swamps** form along the shore. They shelter many species of fish and help filter groundwater before it reaches the ocean. Inland wetlands also form along rivers and streams. They become **marshes** and **freshwater** swamps. A **bog** is an unusual type of freshwater wetland. In a bog, a layer of **peat** forms on the surface of the water. This layer can support shrubs, trees, and small animals. In some places people dry peat and use it for cooking and heating.

culture. 西方化的 ❑ *Rapid urbanization brings with it a more westernized and generally more sugary diet.* 迅速的城市化带来了一种更为西方化的、普遍摄入更多食糖的饮食习惯。

west·ward /wɛstwərd/

The form **westwards** is also used.

ADV **Westward** or **westwards** means toward the west. 向西 ❑ *He sailed westward from Palos de la Frontera.* 他从帕洛斯·德拉·弗龙特拉港出发向西航行。 ● ADJ **Westward** is also an adjective. 向西的 [ADJ n] ❑ *...the one-hour westward flight over the Andes to Lima.* …越过安第斯山脉到利马一小时的向西飞行。

wet ♦◇◇ /wɛt/ (**wetter, wettest, wets, wetting, wet** or **wetted**) **1** ADJ If something is **wet**, it is covered in water, rain, sweat, tears, or another liquid. 湿的 ❑ *He toweled his wet hair.* 他用毛巾将湿头发擦干。 ❑ *I lowered myself to the water's edge, getting my feet wet.* 我俯下身子靠近水边，把双脚弄湿。 **2** V-T To **wet** something means to get water or some other liquid over it. 弄湿 ❑ *When assembling the pie, wet the edges where the two crusts join.* 包馅儿饼的时候，要把两张馅饼皮捏合的地方弄湿。 **3** ADJ If the weather is **wet**, it is raining. 下雨的 ❑ *If the weather is wet or cold choose an indoor activity.* 如果下雨或是天气寒冷，就选择室内活动。 ● N-SING **The wet** is used to mean wet weather. 雨天 ❑ *They had come in from the cold and the wet.* 他们从寒冷又下着雨的外面走了进来。 **4** ADJ If something such as paint, ink, or cement is **wet**, it is not yet dry or solid. (油漆、墨水、水泥等) 未干的 ❑ *...leaves dipped in wet paint then pressed on white paper.* …浸上未干的油漆然后又按压在白纸上的树叶。 **5** V-T If people, especially children, **wet** their beds or clothes or **wet** themselves, they urinate in their beds or in their clothes because they cannot stop themselves. (尤指孩子) 尿湿 ❑ *A quarter of 4-year-olds frequently wet the bed.* 4岁的孩子中有1/4经常性尿床。

Word Partnership *wet* 的常用搭配：

V.	get wet **1**
ADJ.	soaking wet **1**
	cold and wet **1** **3**
N.	wet **clothes**, wet **feet**, wet **grass**, wet **hair**, wet **sand** **1**
	wet **snow**, wet **weather** **3**
	wet **the bed** **5**

wet·land /wɛtlænd/ (**wetlands**) N-VAR A **wetland** is an area of very wet, muddy land with wild plants growing in it. You can also refer to an area like this as **wetlands**. 湿地 ❑ *...a plan that aims to protect the wilderness of the wetlands.* …一项旨在保护湿地荒原的计划。
→ see Word Web: **wetlands**

we've /wiv, STRONG wiv/ **We've** is the usual spoken form of "we have," especially when "have" is an auxiliary verb. **we have** 的常用口语形式，尤当**have**为助动词时 ❑ *It's the first time we've been to the cinema together as a family.* 这是我们一家人第一次一起去看电影。

whack /wæk/ (**whacks, whacking, whacked**) **1** V-T If you **whack** someone or something, you hit them hard. 重击 [INFORMAL] ❑ *You really have to whack the ball.* 你真得重击这个球。 ● N-COUNT; SOUND **Whack** is also a noun. 重击 ❑ *He gave the donkey a whack across the back with his stick.* 他用棍子在驴背上狠狠打了一下。 **2** PHRASE If something is **out of whack**, it is not working properly, often because its natural balance has been upset. (常因天然的平衡被打乱而) 出问题 [PHR after v, oft v-link PHR] [mainly AM, INFORMAL] ❑ *The ecosystem will be thrown out of whack.* 生态系统将出现问题。

whacky /wæki/ → see **wacky**

whale /weɪl/ (**whales**) **1** N-COUNT **Whales** are very large mammals that live in the sea. 鲸鱼 **2** PHRASE If you say that someone **is having a whale of a time**, you mean that they are enjoying themselves very much. 玩得非常愉快 [INFORMAL] ❑ *I had a whale of a time in Fargo.* 我在法戈过得非常快乐。
→ see Word Web: **whale**
→ see **arctic**

whal·ing /weɪlɪŋ/ N-UNCOUNT **Whaling** is the activity of hunting and killing whales. 捕鲸 ❑ *...a ban on commercial whaling.* …一项有关商业性捕鲸的禁令。

▲ **wharf** /wɔrf/ (**wharves** or **wharfs**) N-COUNT A **wharf** is a platform by a river or the sea where ships can be tied up. 码头

what ♦♦♦ /wʌt, wɒt/

Usually pronounced /wɒt/ for meanings **2**, **4** and **5**.

义项**2**、**4**和**5**通常读作 /wɒt/。

1 QUEST You use **what** in questions when you ask for specific information about something that you do not know. 什么 (用于疑问句，就所不知道的事询问具体信息) ❑ *What do you want?* 你要什么？ ❑ *What did she tell you, anyway?* 她到底对你说了什么？ ❑ *"Has something happened?"—"It certainly has."—"What?"* "发生了什么事吗？" —— "是的。" —— "是什么事？" ● DET **What** is also a determiner. 什么 ❑ *What time is it?* 现在几点钟？ ❑ *What crimes are the defendants being charged with?* 被告被控何罪？ ❑ *"The heater works."—"What heater?"* "加热器可以用。" —— "什么加热器？" **2** CONJ You use **what** after certain words, especially verbs and adjectives, when you are referring to a situation that is unknown or has not been specified. 什么 (用在某些词后，尤其是动词和形容词后，指未知或不确定的情形) ❑ *You can imagine what it would be like driving a car into a brick wall at 30 miles an hour.* 你可以想像以每小时30英里的速度，开车向一面砖墙撞去会是什么样子。 ❑ *I want to know what happened to Norman.* 我想知道诺曼出什么事了。 ● DET **What** is also a determiner. 什么 ❑ *I didn't know what college I wanted to go to.* 我不知道我想上什么样的大学。 ❑ *I didn't know what else to say.* 我不知道还能再说点什么。 **3** CONJ You use **what** at the beginning of a clause in structures where you are changing the order of the information to give special emphasis to something. 用于某些从句之首，表示强调 [EMPHASIS] ❑ *What precisely triggered off yesterday's riot is still unclear.* 具体是什么引发了昨天的暴乱仍然不清楚。 ❑ *What I wanted, more than anything, was a few days' rest.* 我最想要的是休息几天。 **4** CONJ You use **what** in expressions

Word Web whale

Whales are part of a group of animals called cetaceans. This group also includes **dolphins** and porpoises. Although whales live in the water, they are **mammals**. They breathe air and are warm-blooded. Whales have adapted to life in the open **ocean**. They have a 2-inch thick layer of blubber just under their skin. This insulates them from the cold ocean water. They sing beautiful songs that can be heard miles away. Blue whales are the largest animals in the world. They can become almost 100 feet long and weigh up to 145 tons.

such as **what is called** and **what amounts to** when you are giving a description of something. …那样的 ❑ *She had been in what doctors described as an irreversible vegetative state for five years.* 她陷入医生们所说的一种不可逆转的植物人状态已达5年之久。 **5** CONJ You use **what** to indicate that you are talking about the whole of an amount that is available to you. 所有的（指所能获得的全部） ❑ *He drinks what is left in his glass as if it were water.* 他把杯子里所剩下的全部喝光，好像那是水一样。 ● DET **What** is also a determiner. 所有的 ❑ *They had used what money they had.* 他们用尽了所有的钱。 **6** CONVENTION You say **"What?"** to tell someone who has indicated that they want to speak to you that you have heard them and are inviting them to continue. 什么？（表示听到对方的话，请对方继续说下去）[SPOKEN, FORMULAE] ❑ *"Dad?"—"What?"—"Can I have the car tonight?"* "爸爸？"——"什么？"——"我今晚可以用车吗？" **7** CONVENTION You say **"What?"** when you ask someone to repeat the thing that they have just said because you did not hear or understand it properly. "What?" is more informal and less polite than expressions such as "Pardon?" and "Excuse me?" 什么（表示没听清楚或没听明白而请别人重复刚说过的话，没有**pardon**和**excuse me**正式和礼貌）[SPOKEN, FORMULAE] ❑ *"They could paint this place," she said. "What?" he asked.* "他们可以把这个地方油漆一下，"她说。"什么？"他问。 **8** CONVENTION You say **"What"** to express surprise. 表示吃惊 [FEELINGS] ❑ *"Adolphus Kelling, I arrest you on a charge of trafficking in narcotics."—"What?"* 阿道弗斯・克林，我现在以贩毒的罪名逮捕你。"——"什么？" **9** PREDET You use **what** in exclamations to emphasize an opinion or reaction. 多么（用于感叹句，强调某种看法或反应）[EMPHASIS] ❑ *What a horrible thing to do.* 做这样的事多可怕！ ● DET **What** is also a determiner. 多么 ❑ *What pretty hair she has, nice and thick.* 她的头发多漂亮啊，好看又浓密。 **10** ADV You use **what** to indicate that you are making a guess about something such as an amount or value. 嗯（表示对数量或价值等的猜测）[ADV n] ❑ *It's, what, eleven years or more since he's seen her.* 自从他上次见到她，已经有，嗯，11年甚至更久了。 **11** CONVENTION You say **guess what** or **do you know what** to introduce a piece of information that is surprising, that is not generally known, or that you want to emphasize. 你知道吗（用于讲述让人吃惊的、不为人知的消息，或表示强调） ❑ *Guess what? I'm going to dinner at Mrs. Chang's tonight.* 你知道吗？我今晚要去常太太家吃晚饭啦。 **12** PHRASE In conversation, you say **or what?** after a question as a way of stating an opinion forcefully and showing that you expect other people to agree. 不然又是什么（用于问句末尾，更有力地陈述观点，并期待别人同意自己的看法）[EMPHASIS] ❑ *Look at that moon. Is that beautiful or what?* 看那月亮。很美，不是吗？ **13** CONVENTION You say **so what?** or **what of it?** to indicate that the previous remark seems unimportant, uninteresting, or irrelevant to you. 那又怎么样呢（表示别人刚说的话对自己不重要、没意思或不相干）[FEELINGS] ❑ *"What if there is no kerosene this winter?" said Al.—"So what?" she said. "We still have electricity."* "今年冬天如果没有煤油可怎么办呢？"阿尔说。——"那又怎么样？"她说。"我们还有电呢。" ❑ *"You're talking to yourself."—"Well, what of it?"* "你在自言自语。"——"呵，那又怎么样？" **14** PHRASE You say **"Tell you what"** to introduce a suggestion or offer. 你听我说（表示提出建议） ❑ *Tell you what, let's stay here another day.* 你听我说，咱们在这儿再住一天吧。 **15** PHRASE You use **what about** at the beginning of a question when you make a suggestion, offer, or request. …怎么样（用于问句句首，表示提建议或要求） ❑ *What about going out with me tomorrow?* 明天和我一块出去怎么样？ **16** PHRASE You use **what about** or **what of** when you introduce a new topic or a point that seems relevant to a previous remark. …又怎么样（用于引入与刚说过的话相关的新话题或观点） ❑ *Now you've talked about work on daffodils, what about other commercially important flowers, like roses?* 既然你谈到了种植水仙，那么其他有重要商业价值的花卉，如玫瑰，又怎么样呢？ **17** PHRASE You say **what about** a particular person or thing when you ask someone to explain why they have asked you about that person or thing. …怎么了（用于请别人解释提问的原因） ❑ *"This thing with the Corbett woman."—"Oh, yeah. What about her?"* "与那个姓科比特的女人有关的那件事。"——"噢，是啊，她怎么了？" **18** PHRASE You say **what if** at the beginning of a question when you ask about the consequences of something happening, especially something undesirable. 如果…怎样（用于疑问句之首，询问某事尤其是不希望发生的事的后果） ❑ *What if this doesn't work out?* 如果这行不通怎么办呢？ **19** **what's more → see more**

what·ev·er ♦♦◇ /wʌtɛvər, wɒt-/ **1** CONJ You use **whatever** to refer to anything or everything of a particular type. 任何事物 ❑ *Franklin was free to do pretty much whatever he pleased.* 富兰克林几乎可以做他想做的任何事情。 ❑ *When you're older I think you're better equipped mentally to cope with whatever happens.* 当你年龄再大一点儿，我想你在心理上就更有能力去应对所发生的任何事情。 ● DET **Whatever** is also a determiner. 任何 ❑ *Whatever doubts he might have had about Ingrid were all over now.* 他对英格丽德可能有过的任何疑问现在都烟消云散了。 **2** CONJ You use **whatever** to say that something is the case in all circumstances. 不管情况怎样 ❑ *We shall love you whatever happens, Diana.* 黛安娜，不管发生什么事我们都会爱你的。 ❑ *She runs on average about 15 miles a day every day, whatever the circumstances, whatever the weather.* 她坚持每天平均跑15英里左右，不论什么情况，不论什么天气。 **3** ADV You use **whatever** after a noun group in order to emphasize a negative statement. 任何（用于名词词组后，强调否定陈述）[with brd-neg, n ADV] [EMPHASIS] ❑ *There is no evidence whatever that competition in broadcasting has ever reduced costs.* 没有任何证据证明广播行业的竞争曾经使成本降低。 **4** QUEST You use **whatever** to ask in an emphatic way about something which you are very surprised about. 究竟（表示对让自己感动吃惊的事的强调）[EMPHASIS] ❑ *Whatever can you mean?* 你究竟是什么意思？ **5** CONJ You use **whatever** when you are indicating that you do not know the precise identity, meaning, or value of the thing just mentioned. 不管什么（表示不知道所谈论事物的确切身份、意义或价值）[VAGUENESS] ❑ *I thought that my upbringing was "normal," whatever that is.* 我曾以为我的成长过程是"正常"的，不管"正常"是什么意思。 **6** PHRASE You say **or whatever** to refer generally to something else of the same kind as the thing or things that you have just mentioned. 诸如此类 [INFORMAL] ❑ *They're always protesting about something or saving the trees or whatever.* 他们总是在抗议一些事情，或是在拯救树木或诸如此类的事情。 **7** PHRASE You say **whatever** you **do** when giving advice or warning someone about something. 不管做什么（用于给出建议或警告）[EMPHASIS] ❑ *Whatever you do, don't ask for a pay increase.* 你不管做什么，就是别要求涨工资。

what's /wʌts, wɒts/ **What's** is the usual spoken form of "what is" or "what has," especially when "has" is an auxiliary verb. **what is**或**what has**的常用口语形式，尤当**has**为助动词时

what·so·ev·er /wʌtsoʊɛvər, wɒt-/ ADV You use **whatsoever** after a noun group in order to emphasize a negative statement. 任何（用于名词词组之后，强调否定陈述）[EMPHASIS] ❑ *My school did nothing whatsoever in the way of athletics.* 我的学校就体育运动而言没有任何作为。

wheat /wit/ (**wheats**) N-MASS **Wheat** is a cereal crop grown for food. **Wheat** is also used to refer to the grain of this crop, which is usually ground into flour and used to make bread. 小麦 ❑ *…farmers growing wheat, corn, or other crops.* …种小麦、玉米或其他农作物的农民们。 **→ see grain**

wheel ♦◇◇ /wil/ (**wheels, wheeling, wheeled**) **1** N-COUNT The **wheels** of a vehicle are the circular objects that are attached underneath it and that enable it to move along the ground. 车轮

Word Web wheel

The **wheel** was invented about 5000 BC in Mesopotamia, part of modern-day Iraq. That's when someone first **spun** a potter's wheel to make a clay jar. About 1500 years later, people put wheels on an axle and created the chariot. These first wheels were solid wood and were very heavy. However, in about 2000 BC the Egyptians introduced much lighter wheels with **spokes**. The wheel has driven the development of all kinds of modern technology. The waterwheel, spinning wheel, and **turbine** played an important part in the Industrial Revolution. Even the propeller and jet engine are descendants of the wheel.

❑ *The car wheels spun and slipped on some oil on the road.* 小汽车的车轮在路面的油迹上空转打了滑。 **2** N-COUNT A **wheel** is a circular object that forms a part of a machine, usually a moving part. 机轮 ❑ *The wheels are usually fairly large.* 该机轮通常相当大。 **3** N-COUNT **The wheel** of a car or other vehicle is the circular object that is used to steer it. **The wheel** is used in expressions to talk about who is driving a vehicle. For example, if someone is **at the wheel** or **behind the wheel** of a car, they are driving it. 方向盘 ❑ *My co-pilot suddenly grabbed the wheel.* 我的副驾驶突然抢过了方向盘。 ❑ *Curtis got behind the wheel and they started back toward the cottage.* 柯蒂斯开车，他们启程返回小屋。 **4** V-T If you **wheel** an object that has wheels somewhere, you push it along. 推(带轮子的物体) ❑ *He wheeled his bike into the alley at the side of the house.* 他把自行车推进了房屋一侧的胡同里。 **5** N-PLURAL People talk about **the wheels of** an organization or system to mean the way in which it operates. (组织或系统的) 运作方式 ❑ *He knows the wheels of administration turn slowly.* 他知道行政机构运作缓慢。 **6** → see also **steering wheel**
→ see Word Web: **wheel**
→ see **bicycle, color, skateboarding**

Word Partnership *wheel* 的常用搭配:
N. wheel **of a car/truck/vehicle** **1** **3**
V. **grip the** wheel, **slide behind the** wheel, **spin the** wheel, **turn the** wheel **3**

wheel and deal (**wheels and deals, wheeling and dealing, wheeled and dealed**) V-I If you say that someone **wheels and deals**, you mean that they use a lot of different methods and contacts to achieve what they want in business or politics, often in a way which you consider dishonest. (生意场或政治中的) 钻营谋取 ❑ *He still wheels and deals around the globe.* 他仍在世界各地钻营谋取。 ● **wheel·ing and deal·ing** N-UNCOUNT (生意场或政治中的) 钻营谋取 ❑ *He hates the wheeling and dealing associated with conventional political life.* 他痛恨传统政治生活中的钻营谋取。

wheel·chair /wiltʃɛər/ (**wheelchairs**) N-COUNT A **wheelchair** is a chair with wheels that you use in order to move around in if you cannot walk properly, for example, because you are disabled or sick. 轮椅
→ see **disability**

wheeze /wiz/ (**wheezes, wheezing, wheezed**) V-I If someone **wheezes**, they breathe with difficulty and make a whistling sound. 气喘 ❑ *He had serious problems with his chest and wheezed and coughed all the time.* 他胸部有严重问题，总是不停地气喘和咳嗽。

when ♦♦♦ /wɛn/ **1** QUEST You use **when** to ask questions about the time at which things happen. 什么时候 (用于疑问句，询问某事发生的时间) ❑ *When are you going home?* 你什么时候回家？ ❑ *When did you get married?* 你是什么时候结婚的？ **2** CONJ If something happens **when** something else is happening, the two things are happening at the same time. (表示两件事同时发生) 当…的时候 ❑ *When eating a whole cooked fish, you should never turn it over to get at the flesh on the other side.* 吃一整条做熟的鱼时，你永远都不要把鱼翻过来吃另一边的肉。 **3** CONJ You use **when** to introduce a clause in which you mention something that happens at some point during an activity, event, or situation. 当…时 (引导从句，表示从句中提到的事发生在另一活动、事件或情况期间) ❑ *When I met the Gills, I had been gardening for nearly ten years.* 我结识吉尔一家时，我已经几乎做了十年的园艺。 **4** CONJ You use **when** to introduce a clause where you mention the circumstances under which the event in the main clause happened or will happen. 在…情况下 (引导从句，表示从句中提到的情况是主句中已经发生或即将发生的事的前提) ❑ *When he brought Imelda her drink she gave him a genuine, sweet smile of thanks.* 当他给艾梅尔达拿来一杯饮料时，她给了他一个真诚、甜美、表示谢意的微笑。 **5** CONJ You use **when** after certain words, especially verbs and adjectives, to introduce a clause where you mention the time at which something happens. 什么时候 (用在某些词尤其是动词和形容词后，引导从句说明某事发生的时间) ❑ *I asked him when he'd be back to pick me up.* 我问他什么时候回来接我。 **6** PRON-REL You use **when** to introduce a clause that specifies or refers to the time at which something happens. 当…的时候 (引导表示某事发生的具体时间的从句) ❑ *He could remember a time when he had worked like that himself.* 他还记得当他自己也像那样工作的那段时间。 **7** CONJ You use **when** to introduce the reason for an opinion, comment, or question. 既然 (用于引入观点、评论、或问题的原因) ❑ *How can I love myself when I look like this?* 既然我这么一副样子，我怎么能爱我自己？ **8** CONJ You use **when** in order to introduce a fact or comment which makes the other part of the sentence rather surprising or unlikely. 而 (引出令人吃惊的事实或评论) ❑ *Our mothers sat us down to read and paint, when all we really wanted to do was to make a mess.* 我们的妈妈们让我们坐下读书、画画，而我们真正想要做的却是胡闹一阵。

when·ever ♦◇◇ /wɛnɛvər/ **1** CONJ You use **whenever** to refer to any time or every time that something happens or is true. 无论什么时候 ❑ *Whenever I talked to him, he seemed like a pretty regular guy.* 我无论什么时候同他讲话，他都好像是个很正常的人。 ❑ *You can stay at my cottage in the country whenever you like.* 只要你愿意，无论什么时候都可以住在我乡下的小屋里。 **2** CONJ You use **whenever** to refer to a time that you do not know or are not sure about. 什么时候 (表示不知道或不确定的时间) ❑ *He married Miss Vancouver in 1963, or whenever it was.* 他在1963年或什么时候娶了温哥华小姐。

where ♦♦♦ /wɛər/

Usually pronounced /wɛər/ for meanings **2** and **3**.

义项**2**和**3**通常读作 /wɛər/。

1 QUEST You use **where** to ask questions about the place something is in, or is coming from or going to. 哪里 (用于就地点提问) ❑ *Where did you meet him?* 你在哪里见到他的？ ❑ *Where's Anna?* 安娜在哪里？ **2** CONJ You use **where** after certain words, especially verbs and adjectives, to introduce a clause in which you mention the place in which something is situated or happens. 哪里 (用于某些词特别是动词和形容词后，引导从句表示某物所处或发生的地点) ❑ *People began looking across to see where the noise was coming from.* 人们开始望过去，看响声是从哪里发出的。 ❑ *He knew where Henry Carter had gone.* 他知道亨利·卡特去了哪里。 ● PRON-REL **Where** is also a relative pronoun. …的地方 (用作关系代词) ❑ *The area where the explosion occurred was closed off by police.* 爆炸发生的地方被警察封锁起来了。 **3** QUEST You use **where** to ask questions about a situation, a stage in something, or an aspect of something. 哪里 (在疑问句中，就某一情况、某事所处的阶段或方面等提问) ❑ *If they get their way, where will it stop?* 如果他们说了算，那么哪里才是尽头？ **4** CONJ You use **where** after certain words, especially verbs and adjectives, to introduce a clause in which you mention a situation, a stage in something, or an aspect of something. 哪里 (用于某些词特别是动词和形容词后，引导从句表示某一情况、某事所处的阶段或方面等) ❑ *It's not hard to see where she got her feelings about herself.* 不难看出她从何处获得了对自己的那种感觉。 ❑ *She had a feeling she already knew where this conversation was going to lead.* 她感觉到她已经知道这次谈话将导向何处。 ● PRON-REL **Where** is also a relative pronoun. 用作关系代词 ❑ *The government is at a stage where it is willing to talk to almost anyone.* 政府已经到了几乎愿意与任何人对话的地步。

▲ **where·abouts**

Pronounced /wɛərəbaʊts/ for meaning **1**, and /wɛərəbaʊts/ for meaning **2**.

义项**1**读作 /wɛərəbaʊts/，义项**2**读作 /wɛərəbaʊts/。

1 N-SING-COLL If you refer to the **whereabouts** of a particular person or thing, you mean the place where that person or thing may be found. 下落 ❑ *The police are anxious to hear from anyone who may know the whereabouts of the firearms.* 警察急于从任何可能知道那些枪支下落的人那里得到消息。 **2** QUEST You use **whereabouts** in questions when you are asking precisely where something is. (用在疑问句中) 确切在哪里 ❑ *"Whereabouts in France?"—"Normandy," I said.* "在法国的确切位置？"——"诺曼底，"我说。 ❑ *Whereabouts are you living?* 你居住的确切地点是哪里？

where·as ♦◇◇ /wɛəræz/ CONJ You use **whereas** to introduce a comment that contrasts with what is said in the main clause. 而 (引导与主句内容相对比的评论) ❑ *Benefits are linked to inflation, whereas they should be linked to the cost of living.* 救济金与通货膨胀联系了起来，而它们应该与生活费用挂钩。

★ **where·by** /wɛərbaɪ/ PRON-REL A system or action **whereby** something happens is one that makes that thing happen. 凭借 [FORMAL] ❑ *The company operates an arrangement whereby employees may select any 8-hour period between 6 a.m. to 8 p.m. to go to work.* 该公司做出了一种安排，据此员工可以在上午6点到晚上8点之间任意选择8个小时去上班。

▲ **where·in** /wɛərɪn/ **1** PRON **Wherein** means in which place or thing. 在此 [FORMAL, LITERARY or OLD-FASHIONED] ❑ *...a riding*

W

school wherein we could learn the art of horsemanship. …一所我们在此可以学习马术的骑术学校。 **2** QUEST **Wherein** means in which part or respect. 在此方面 [FORMAL] ❑ *Wherein lies the truth?* 在哪方面是真的？

where·upon /wɛərəpɒn/ CONJ You use **whereupon** to say that one thing happens immediately after another thing, and usually as a result of it. 于是（表示某事紧接着另一件事之后发生，通常为结果）[FORMAL] ❑ *Mr. Jones refused to talk to them except in the company of his legal colleagues, whereupon the police officers departed.* 琼斯先生拒绝在没有法律界同事们的陪同下和他们谈话，于是警官们离开了。

wher·ever /wɛrɛvər/ **1** CONJ You use **wherever** to indicate that something happens or is true in any place or situation. 无论哪里 ❑ *Some people enjoy themselves wherever they are.* 有些人无论在哪里都很开心。 **2** CONJ You use **wherever** when you indicate that you do not know where a person or place is. 不管哪里（表示不知道在哪里）❑ *I'd like to leave as soon as possible and join my children, wherever they are.* 我想尽快离开这里，去和我的孩子们团聚，不管他们在哪里。 **3** QUEST You use **wherever** in questions as an emphatic form of "where," usually when you are surprised about something. 究竟在哪里（在疑问句中作为where的强调形式，通常表示对某事感到吃惊）[EMPHASIS] ❑ *Wherever did you get that idea?* 你究竟从哪得来的那个想法？

where·with·al /wɛrwɪðɔl, -wɪθ-/ N-SING If you have **the wherewithal** for something, you have the means, especially the money, that you need for it. 所需物资（尤指资金）❑ *Some of the companies illegally sent the wherewithal for making chemical weapons.* 有些公司非法寄去了生产化学武器所需的资金。

wheth·er ♦♦♦ /wɛðər/ **1** CONJ You use **whether** when you are talking about a choice or doubt between two or more alternatives. 是否 ❑ *To this day, it's unclear whether he shot himself or was murdered.* 直到今天，他是自杀还是被谋杀仍然不清楚。 ❑ *Whether it turns out to be a good idea or a bad idea, we'll find out.* 最终这个点子是好还是坏，我们会搞清楚的。 **2** CONJ You use **whether** to say that something is true in any of the circumstances that you mention. 无论 ❑ *This happens whether the children are in two-parent or one-parent families.* 这种情况无论在双亲家庭还是单亲家庭的孩子身上都会发生。 ❑ *Whether they say it aloud or not, most men expect their wives to be faithful.* 无论他们是否说出来，大部分男人都希望他们的妻子忠贞不渝。

which ♦♦♦ /wɪtʃ/

Usually pronounced /wɪtʃ/ for meanings **2**, **3** and **4**.

义项**2**、**3**和**4**，通常读作 /wɪtʃ/。

1 QUEST You use **which** in questions when there are two or more possible answers or alternatives. 哪一个（用于疑问句，表示选择）❑ *"You go down that passageway over there."—"Which one?"* "你顺着那边的过道走。"——"哪个过道？" ❑ *Which vitamin supplements are good for you?* 哪种维生素补品对你有好处？ **2** DET You use **which** to refer to a choice between two or more possible answers or alternatives. 哪个（指所做出的那个选择）❑ *I wanted to know which school it was you went to.* 我想知道你就读的是哪所学校。 ❑ *I can't remember which teachers I had.* 我不记得哪些老师教过我。 ● CONJ **Which** is also a conjunction. 哪个 ❑ *In her panic she couldn't remember which was Mr. Grainger's cabin.* 慌乱中，她不记得哪间是格兰杰先生的船舱。 **3** PRON-REL You use **which** at the beginning of a relative clause when specifying the thing that you are talking about. In such clauses, **which** has the same meaning as **that**. 引导关系从句，具体说明所谈论的事，此时与**that**意思相同 ❑ *Soldiers opened fire on a car which failed to stop at an army checkpoint.* 士兵们向一辆没在军事检查站停下来的汽车开了火。 **4** PRON-REL You use **which** to refer back to an idea or situation expressed in a previous sentence or sentences, especially when you want to give your opinion about it. 这个（指前面所说过的内容，尤其要发表个人意见时）❑ *They ran out of drink. Which actually didn't bother me because I wasn't drinking.* 他们没有酒了，这个其实对我倒无所谓，因为我当时没在喝酒。 ● DET **Which** is also a determiner. 这个 ❑ *The chances are you haven't fully decided what you want from your career at the moment, in which case you're definitely not cut out to be a boss yet!* 很可能你目前没有完全确定要从职业中得到什么，在这种情况下，你肯定还没有具备做老板的素质。 **5** PHRASE If you cannot tell the difference between two things, you can say that you do not know **which is which**. 哪个是哪个（指无法区分两者的不同）❑ *They all look so alike to me that I'm never sure which is which.* 它们在我看来简直一模一样，我永远分不清哪个是哪个。

which·ever /wɪtʃɛvər/ **1** DET You use **whichever** in order to indicate that it does not matter which of the possible alternatives happens or is chosen. 无论哪个 ❑ *Whichever way you look at it, nuclear power is the energy of the future.* 无论你从哪个方面看，核能都是未来的能源。 ● CONJ **Whichever** is also a conjunction. 无论哪个 ❑ *If you are unhappy with anything you have bought from us, we will gladly exchange your purchase, or refund your money, whichever you prefer.* 如果您对从我们这里买到的任何商品不满意，我们将乐意为您更换或办理退货，您愿意哪种方式都行。 **2** DET You use **whichever** to specify which of a number of possibilities is the right one or the one you mean. 无论哪个（用以具体说明几种可能性中正确的或所特指的那个）❑ *Learning to relax by whichever method suits you best is a positive way of contributing to your overall good health.* 学会以最适合你的方法来放松是改善身体整体健康状况的一个积极办法。 ● CONJ **Whichever** is also a conjunction. 无论哪个 ❑ *He has been extraordinarily fortunate or clever, whichever is the right word.* 他一直格外幸运或者特别聪明，不管是其中的哪一个。

whiff /wɪf/ (**whiffs**) N-COUNT If there is a **whiff of** a particular smell, you smell it only slightly or only for a brief period of time, for example, as you walk past someone or something. （气味等）微弱的一阵 ❑ *He caught a whiff of her perfume.* 他闻到了她身上的一丝香水味。

while

❶ CONJUNCTION USES
❷ NOUN AND VERB USES

❶ **while** ♦♦♦ /waɪl/

Usually pronounced /waɪl/ for meaning **4**.

1 CONJ If something happens **while** something else is happening, the two things are happening at the same time. 当…的时候（表示两事同时发生）❑ *They were grinning and watching while one man laughed and poured beer over the head of another.* 当一个男人大笑着将啤酒倒在另一个男人头上时，他们正边看边咧着嘴笑。 ❑ *I sat on the chair to unwrap the package while he stood behind me.* 我坐在椅子上打开包裹，当时他就站在我身后。 **2** CONJ If something happens **while** something else happens, the first thing happens at some point during the time that the second thing is happening. 正值…之时（表示一件事是在另一件事发生过程中的某个时间发生的）❑ *The two ministers have yet to meet, but may do so while in New York.* 两位部长还未会面，但他们在纽约期间可能会见面。 **3** CONJ You use **while** at the beginning of a clause to introduce information that contrasts with information in the main clause. 而（用于从句之首，引出与主句内容相对比的信息）❑ *Most digital camera owners are male, while women prefer film.* 大部分数码相机的主人都是男性，而女性偏爱用胶卷。 **4** CONJ You use **while**, before making a statement, in order to introduce information that partly conflicts with your statement. 虽然（用于发表陈述之前，引入和陈述内容部分矛盾的信息）❑ *While the news, so far, has been good, there may be days ahead when it is bad.* 虽然到目前为止都是好消息，但是可能过几天就有坏消息了。

❷ **while** ♦♦◇ /waɪl/ (**whiles, whiling, whiled**)

➪ **Please look at meaning 3 to see if the expression you are looking for is shown under another headword.** **1** N-SING **A while** is a period of time. 一段时间 ❑ *They walked on in silence for a while.* 他们默默地走了一会儿。 ❑ *He was married a little while ago.* 他前不久刚结了婚。 **2** PHRASE You use **all the while** in order to say that something happens continually or that it happens throughout the time when something else is happening. 一直 ❑ *All the while the people at the next table watched me eat.* 邻桌的人一直在看着我吃东西。 **3** **once in a while** → see **once** **4** **worth your while** → see **worth**

▸ **while away** PHRASAL VERB If you **while away** the time in a particular way, you spend time in that way, because you are waiting for something else to happen, or because you have nothing else to do. 消磨（时间）❑ *Craig had been whiling away his spare time in our basement.* 克雷格一直在我们的地下室里消磨他的业余时间。

whilst ♦◇◇ /waɪlst/ CONJ **Whilst** means the same as the conjunction **while**. 同连词**while** [mainly BRIT]

whim /wɪm/ (**whims**) N-VAR A **whim** is a wish to do or have something that seems to have no serious reason or purpose behind it, and often occurs suddenly. 突发的念头 ❑ *We decided, more or less on a whim, to sail to Morocco.* 我们多少有些心血来潮地决定乘船去摩洛哥。

whim·per /wɪmpər/ (**whimpers, whimpering, whimpered**) V-I If someone **whimpers**, they make quiet unhappy or frightened sounds, as if they are about to start crying. 抽泣；呜咽 ❑ *She lay*

W

at the bottom of the stairs, whimpering in pain. 她躺在楼梯的下面，痛苦地抽泣。● N-COUNT **Whimper** is also a noun. 抽泣；呜咽 ❑ *David's crying subsided to a whimper.* 戴维的大声哭叫减弱为抽泣。

whim·si·cal /wɪmzɪkᵊl/ ADJ A **whimsical** person or idea is unusual, playful, and unpredictable, rather than serious and practical. 异想天开的 ❑ *McGrath remembers his offbeat sense of humor, his whimsical side.* 麦格拉思记得他非同寻常的幽默感，和他异想天开的一面。

whine /waɪn/ (**whines, whining, whined**) **1** V-I If something or someone **whines**, they make a long, high-pitched noise, especially one that sounds sad or unpleasant. 哀鸣 ❑ *He could hear her dog barking and whining in the background.* 他能听到她的狗在远处吠叫哀鸣。● N-COUNT **Whine** is also a noun. 哀鸣 ❑ *...the whine of air-raid sirens.* …空袭警报的尖叫。**2** V-T/V-I If someone **whines**, they complain in an annoying way about something unimportant. (为小事) 令人厌烦地抱怨 [DISAPPROVAL] ❑ *They come to me to whine about their troubles.* 他们到我这里来絮絮叨叨地抱怨他们的烦恼。❑ *...children who whine that they are bored.* …哼哼唧唧地抱怨无聊的孩子们。

whip ♦◇◇ /wɪp/ (**whips, whipping, whipped**) **1** N-COUNT A **whip** is a long thin piece of material such as leather or rope, fastened to a stiff handle. It is used for hitting people or animals. 鞭子 **2** V-T If someone **whips** a person or animal, they beat them or hit them with a whip or something like a whip. 鞭打 ❑ *Eye-witnesses claimed Mr. Melton whipped the horse up to 16 times.* 目击者声称梅尔顿先生抽打那匹马达16鞭之多。● **whip·ping** N-COUNT (**whippings**) 鞭打 ❑ *He threatened to give her a whipping.* 他威胁要鞭打她一顿。**3** V-T If someone **whips** something out or **whips** it off, they take it out or take it off very quickly and suddenly. 猛地拿出；猛地脱掉 ❑ *Bob whipped out his notebook.* 鲍勃猛地拿出他的笔记本。❑ *Players were whipping their shirts off.* 选手们正麻利地脱掉衬衣。**4** V-T When you **whip** something liquid such as cream or an egg, you stir it very fast until it is thick or stiff. 搅打 (奶油或鸡蛋等液体使粘稠) ❑ *Whip the cream until thick.* 将奶油打稠。❑ *Whip the eggs, oils and honey together.* 将鸡蛋、油和蜂蜜搅打在一起。**5** V-T If you **whip** people **into** an emotional state, you deliberately cause and encourage them to be in that state. 怂恿 ❑ *He could whip a crowd into hysteria.* 他可以怂恿一群人，使他们变得歇斯底里。

▶ **whip up** PHRASAL VERB If someone **whips up** an emotion, especially a dangerous one such as hatred, or if they **whip** people **up** into an emotional state, they deliberately cause and encourage people to feel that emotion. 煽动 ❑ *He accused politicians of whipping up antiforeign sentiments in order to win right-wing votes.* 他谴责政客们煽动排外情绪以赢得右翼选票。

whip·lash /wɪplæʃ/ N-UNCOUNT **Whiplash** is a neck injury caused by the head suddenly moving forward and then back again, for example, in a car accident. (如车祸中，头部突然向前又向后动而造成的) 颈部扭伤 ❑ *His wife suffered whiplash and shock.* 他的妻子颈部扭伤且受到了惊吓。

whir /wɜr/ (**whirs, whirring, whirred**) also **whirr** V-I When something such as a machine or an insect's wing **whirs**, it makes a series of low sounds so quickly that they seem like one continuous sound. 发出嗡嗡声 ❑ *The camera whirred and clicked.* 相机发出嗡嗡声和咯嚓声。● N-COUNT; SOUND **Whir** is also a noun. 嗡嗡声 ❑ *He could hear the whir of a vacuum cleaner.* 他能听到吸尘器的嗡嗡声。

★ **whirl** /wɜrl/ (**whirls, whirling, whirled**) **1** V-T/V-I If something or someone **whirls** around or if you **whirl** them around, they move around or turn around very quickly. 使快速旋转；快速旋转 ❑ *Not receiving an answer, she whirled around.* 没有得到答复，她猛地转过身来。❑ *He was whirling Anne around the floor.* 他正与安妮旋转起舞。● N-COUNT **Whirl** is also a noun. 快速旋转 ❑ *...the barely audible whirl of wheels.* …几乎听不见的轮子转动声。**2** N-COUNT You can refer to a lot of intense activity as a **whirl** of activity. 紧张激烈的一连串 ❑ *In half an hour's whirl of activity she does it all.* 在半个小时马不停蹄的忙碌中，她做完了这一切。**3** PHRASE If you decide to **give** an activity **a whirl**, you do it even though it is something that you have never tried before. 试一试 [INFORMAL] ❑ *Why not give acupuncture a whirl?* 为什么不试试针灸？

W

whirl·wind /wɜrlwɪnd/ (**whirlwinds**) **1** N-COUNT A **whirlwind** is a tall column of air that spins around and around very fast and moves across the land or sea. 旋风 **2** N-COUNT You can describe a situation in which a lot of things happen very quickly and are very difficult for someone to control as a **whirlwind**. 众多事情一下子发生令人难以招架的局面 ❑ *I had been running around southern California in a whirlwind of activity.* 我一直在南加州辗转奔走，穷于处理应接不暇的事务。**3** ADJ A **whirlwind** event or action happens or is done much more quickly than normal. 闪电式的 (形容事件或行动发生迅速) [ADJ n] ❑ *He got married after a whirlwind romance.* 他在一场闪电式恋爱之后结婚了。

whirr /wɜr/ → see **whir**

▲ **whisk** /wɪsk/ (**whisks, whisking, whisked**) **1** V-T If you **whisk** someone or something somewhere, you take them or move them there quickly. 迅速带走 ❑ *He whisked her across the dance floor.* 他带她迅速穿过舞池。**2** V-T If you **whisk** something such as eggs or cream, you stir it very fast, often with an electric device, so that it becomes full of small bubbles. (常指用搅打器) 快速搅打 (鸡蛋、奶油等) ❑ *Just before serving, whisk the cream.* 在端上桌之前，要搅打一下奶油。**3** N-COUNT A **whisk** is a kitchen tool used for whisking eggs or cream. 搅拌器 ❑ *Using a whisk, mix the yolks and sugar to a smooth paste.* 用搅拌器将蛋黄和糖搅打成均匀的糊状。

whisk·er /wɪskər/ (**whiskers**) **1** N-COUNT The **whiskers** of an animal such as a cat or a mouse are the long stiff hairs that grow near its mouth. (猫、鼠等动物的) 须 **2** N-PLURAL You can refer to the hair on a man's face, especially on the sides of his face, as his **whiskers**. 络腮胡子 ❑ *...wild, savage-looking fellows, with large whiskers and dirty faces.* …一些狂野、面相凶恶的家伙，留着满脸的络腮胡子，蓬头垢面。

whis·key /wɪski/ (**whiskeys**) N-MASS **Whiskey** is a strong alcoholic drink made, especially in the United States and Ireland, from grain such as barley or rye. 威士忌酒 (尤指产于美国和爱尔兰，由大麦或黑麦等酿成的烈性酒) ❑ *...a tumbler with about an inch of whiskey in it.* …一个装了大约一英寸高的威士忌酒的大玻璃杯。● N-COUNT A **whiskey** is a glass of whiskey. (一) 杯威士忌酒 ❑ *Stark took two whiskeys from a tray.* 斯塔克从托盘里拿了两杯威士忌。

▲ **whis·ky** /wɪski/ (**whiskies**) N-MASS **Whisky** is whiskey that is made especially in Scotland and Canada. (尤指产于苏格兰和加拿大的) 威士忌酒 ● N-COUNT A **whisky** is a glass of whisky. (一) 杯威士忌酒

whis·per ♦◇◇ /wɪspər/ (**whispers, whispering, whispered**) V-T/V-I When you **whisper**, you say something very quietly, using your breath rather than your throat, so that only one person can hear you. 悄声说出；悄声说 ❑ *"Keep your voice down," I whispered.* "小声点，"我悄声说。❑ *She sat on Rossi's knee as he whispered in her ear.* 她坐在罗西的膝盖上，罗西在对她嘀嘀耳语。❑ *He whispered the message to David.* 他悄声把消息告诉了戴维。● N-COUNT **Whisper** is also a noun. 悄声说话 ❑ *Men were talking in whispers in every office.* 男人们在每个办公室里悄声交谈着。

whis·tle /wɪsᵊl/ (**whistles, whistling, whistled**) **1** V-T/V-I When you **whistle** or when you **whistle** a tune, you make a series of musical notes by forcing your breath out between your lips, or your teeth. 用口哨吹出；吹口哨 ❑ *He whistled and sang snatches of songs.* 他边用口哨吹边唱了几个歌曲的片段。❑ *He was whistling softly to himself.* 他自娱自乐地轻声吹着口哨。**2** V-I When someone **whistles**, they make a sound by forcing their breath out between their lips or their teeth. People sometimes whistle when they are surprised, or to call a dog, to get someone's attention, or to show that they are impressed. 吹口哨 (表示吃惊、呼唤小狗、引人注意或表示欣赏) ❑ *He whistled, surprised but not shocked.* 他吹了声口哨，有些惊讶，但并不震惊。❑ *Jenkins whistled through his teeth, impressed at last.* 詹金斯从齿间吹了一声口哨，总算被打动了。● N-COUNT **Whistle** is also a noun. 口哨 ❑ *Jackson gave a low whistle.* 杰克逊低声地吹了一下口哨。**3** V-I If something such as a train or a kettle **whistles**, it makes a loud, high sound. (火车等) 鸣汽笛；(水开时水壶) 发出尖啸声 ❑ *Somewhere a train whistled.* 某个地方响起了火车的鸣笛声。**4** V-I If something such as the wind or a bullet **whistles** somewhere, it moves there, making a loud, high sound. (风、子弹等) 呼啸而过 ❑ *The wind was whistling through the building.* 风呼啸着穿过那座大楼。**5** N-COUNT A **whistle** is a loud sound produced by air or steam being forced through a small opening, or by something moving quickly through the air. (某物在空中疾驰而过的) 呼啸声；(空气、蒸汽通过狭小孔道时的) 尖啸声 ❑ *...the whistle of the wind.* …风的呼啸声。❑ *...a shrill whistle from the boiling kettle.* …烧开的水壶发出的刺耳的尖啸声。**6** N-COUNT A **whistle** is a small metal tube that you blow in order to produce a loud sound and attract someone's attention. 哨子 ❑ *On the platform, the guard blew his whistle.* 站台上，警卫吹响了他的哨子。**7** PHRASE If you **blow the whistle on** someone, or on something secret or illegal, you tell another person, especially a person in authority, what is happening. (尤指向当局) 揭发 ❑ *Companies should protect employees who blow the whistle on dishonest workmates and work practices.* 公司应该保护那些揭发不诚实的同事和不良工作行为的员工。 **8** PHRASE If you describe something as **clean as a whistle**, you mean that it is completely clean. 一尘不染 ❑ *The kitchen was clean as a whistle.* 厨房里一尘不染。

whistle-blowing also **whistleblowing** N-UNCOUNT **Whistle-blowing** is the act of telling the authorities or the public that the organization you work for is doing something immoral or illegal. (向当局或公众) 检举(自己所工作的机构或组织) ❑ *It took internal whistle-blowing and investigative journalism to uncover the rot.* 通过来自内部的检举和调查性报道才揭露出了这一腐败现象。

white ♦♦♦ /waɪt/ (**whiter, whitest, whites**) **1** COLOR Something that is **white** is the color of snow or milk. 白色 ❑ *He had nice square white teeth.* 他有整齐洁白的漂亮牙齿。 ❑ *Issa's white beach hat gleamed in the harsh lights.* 伊萨的白色沙滩帽在刺目的灯光下闪闪发光。 **2** ADJ A **white** person has a pale skin and belongs to a race of European origin. 白色人种的 ❑ *Working with white people hasn't been a problem for me or for them.* 和白种人在一起工作对我或对他们来说一直都不是个问题。 ● N-COUNT **Whites** are white people. 白种人 ❑ *It's a school that's brought blacks and whites and Hispanics together.* 这是一所让黑人、白种人和西班牙裔人走到了一起的学校。 **3** ADJ **White** wine is pale yellow in color. 白葡萄酒 ❑ *Gregory poured another glass of white wine and went back to his bedroom.* 格雷戈里又倒了一杯白葡萄酒，回卧室去了。 **4** ADJ **White** blood cells are the cells in your blood your body uses to fight infection. 白(细胞) [ADJ n] ❑ *...an AIDS drug that helps restore a patient's white blood cells.* …帮助修复病人白细胞的一种治疗艾滋病的药。 **5** N-VAR The **white** of an egg is the transparent liquid that surrounds the yellow part called the yolk. 蛋清 ❑ *As soon as the whites of the eggs have set, remove the cover.* 蛋清一凝固，就把盖子揭开。 **6** N-COUNT The **white** of someone's eye is the white part that surrounds the colored part called the iris. 眼白(指眼球中的白色部分) ❑ *Susanne stared at me, the whites of her eyes gleaming in the streetlight.* 苏珊娜盯着我看，她的眼白在街灯下发亮。 → see **color**

white·board /waɪtbɔrd/ (**whiteboards**) N-COUNT A **whiteboard** is a shiny white board on which people draw or write using special pens. Whiteboards are often used for teaching or giving talks. 白板(可用特殊的笔在上面书写，常用于教学或讲座)

white-collar also **white collar** **1** ADJ **White-collar** workers work in offices rather than doing physical work such as making things in factories or building things. 白领的 [ADJ n] ❑ *White-collar workers now work longer hours.* 白领工人现在工作的时间更长了。 **2** ADJ **White-collar** crime is committed by people who work in offices, and involves stealing money secretly from companies or the government, or getting money in an illegal way. (非法窃取公司或政府钱财的) 白领(犯罪) [ADJ n] ❑ *...a New York lawyer who specializes in white-collar crime.* …纽约的一位专门处理白领犯罪案的律师。 → see **union**

white goods N-PLURAL People in business sometimes refer to refrigerators, washing machines, and other large pieces of electrical household equipment as **white goods**. (电冰箱、洗衣机等) 大件家用电器 ❑ *...the third largest manufacturer of white goods in the South.* …南部大件家用电器的第三大生产商。

White House ♦◇◇ N-PROPER **The White House** is the official home in Washington DC of the president of the United States. You can also use **the White House** to refer to the president of the United States and his or her officials. 白宫(美国总统官邸，也可指美国总统及其官员) ❑ *He drove to the White House.* 他开车去白宫。 ❑ *The White House has not participated in any talks.* 白宫方面没有参与任何会谈。

white knight (**white knights**) N-COUNT A **white knight** is a person or an organization that rescues a company from difficulties such as financial problems or an unwelcome takeover bid. 救星(指帮助公司度过财政难关或避免公司被收购的人或机构) [BUSINESS] ❑ *...a white-knight bid.* …一次救援性的竞标。

white·wash /waɪtwɒʃ/ (**whitewashes, whitewashing, whitewashed**) **1** N-UNCOUNT **Whitewash** is a mixture of lime or chalk and water that is used for painting walls white. (将墙壁刷成白色的) 石灰水 **2** V-T If a wall or building **has been whitewashed**, it has been painted white with whitewash. (用石灰水) 刷白 ❑ *The walls had been whitewashed.* 墙壁被粉刷成白色。 **3** V-T If you say that people **whitewash** something, you are accusing them of hiding the unpleasant facts or truth about it in order to make it acceptable. 粉饰 [DISAPPROVAL] ❑ *The administration is whitewashing the regime's actions.* 政府正在粉饰该政权的行为。

whit·tle /wɪtᵊl/ (**whittles, whittling, whittled**) V-T If you **whittle** something from a piece of wood, you carve it by cutting pieces off the wood with a knife. 削(木头) ❑ *He whittled a new handle for his ax.* 他为自己的斧头削了一个新斧柄。

▸ **whittle away** PHRASAL VERB To **whittle away** something or **whittle away** at it means to gradually make it smaller, weaker, or less effective. 逐渐削减 ❑ *...the plight of monkeys and other primates as people whittle away their habitat.* …由于人们日益缩小它们的栖息地而导致的猴子和其他灵长目动物的生存困境。

whiz /wɪz/ (**whizzes, whizzing, whizzed**) also **whizz** **1** V-I If something **whizzes** somewhere, it moves there very fast. 嗖嗖地快速移动 [INFORMAL] ❑ *They heard bullets continue to whiz over their heads.* 他们听到子弹不断在他们头顶上嗖嗖飞过。 **2** N-COUNT If you are a **whiz** at something, you are very good at it. 高手 [INFORMAL] [oft "a" N "at/with/on" n] ❑ *Simon's a whiz at card games.* 西蒙是纸牌游戏的高手。

who ♦♦♦ /hu/

Usually pronounced /hu/ for meanings **2** and **3**.

义项**2**和**3**通常读作 /hu/。

Who is used as the subject or object of a verb. See entries at **whom** and **whose**.

1 QUEST You use **who** in questions when you ask about the name or identity of a person or group of people. 谁(用于疑问句，询问姓名和身份) ❑ *Who's there?* 那是谁？ ❑ *Who is the least popular man around here?* 谁是这里最不受欢迎的人？ ❑ *"You reminded me of somebody."—"Who?"* "你让我想起了一个人。" —— "谁？" **2** CONJ You use **who** after certain words, especially verbs and adjectives, to introduce a clause where you talk about the identity of a person or a group of people. 谁(用于特别是动词和形容词之后，引导从句，说明人的身份) ❑ *Police have not been able to find out who was responsible for the forgeries.* 警察还未能发现谁是那些伪造案的元凶。 ❑ *I went over to start up a conversation, asking her who she knew at the party.* 我走过去攀谈起来，问她在聚会上都认识谁。 **3** PRON-REL You use **who** at the beginning of a relative clause when specifying the person or group of people you are talking about or when giving more information about them. …的人(用于关系从句句首，具体说明所谈论的人或给出更多相关信息) ❑ *There are those who eat out for a special occasion, or treat themselves.* 有那么一些在特殊日子到饭馆吃饭或犒劳自己的食客。

Who is now commonly used where it used only to be considered to be correct to use **whom**. **Who**, however, cannot be used directly after a preposition, for example, you cannot say "...the woman to who I spoke." Instead you can say "**...the woman to whom I spoke**" or "**...the woman I spoke to**." There are some types of sentence in which **who** cannot be used, for example when you are talking about quantities. ❑ *...twenty masked prisoners, many of whom are armed with makeshift weapons.*

who'd /hud, hud/ **1** **Who'd** is the usual spoken form of "who had," especially when "had" is an auxiliary verb. **who had**的常用口语形式，尤当**had**为助动词时 **2** **Who'd** is a spoken form of "who would." **who would**的口语形式

who·ever /huɛvər/ **1** CONJ You use **whoever** to refer to someone when their identity is not yet known. 无论谁(表示不确切知道是谁) ❑ *Whoever did this will sooner or later be caught and will be punished.* 无论是谁干的，迟早都会被抓住并被惩罚。 ❑ *Whoever wins the election is going to have a tough job getting the economy back on its feet.* 无论谁在选举中取胜都将面临使经济复苏的艰巨任务。 **2** CONJ You use **whoever** to indicate that the actual identity of the person who does something will not affect a situation. 无论谁(表示做某件事的人的身份无关紧要) ❑ *You can have whoever you like to visit you.* 你可以让任何你想见的人拜访你。 **3** QUEST You use **whoever** in questions as an emphatic way of saying "who," usually when you are surprised about something. 究竟谁(用于疑问句中，是who的强调形式，通常表示对某事感到惊讶) [EMPHASIS] ❑ *Whoever thought up that joke?* 究竟是谁想出那个笑话的？

whole ♦♦♦ /hoʊl/ (**wholes**) **1** QUANT If you refer to **the whole of** something, you mean all of it. 整个 [QUANT "of" def-n] ❑ *He has* *said he will make an apology to the whole of Asia for his country's past behavior.* 他说过他将为他的国家在过去的所作所为向全体亚洲人民道歉。❑ *I was cold throughout the whole of my body.* 我浑身冰冷。● ADJ **Whole** is also an adjective. 整个的 [ADJ n] ❑ *We spent the whole summer in Italy that year.* 我们那一年在意大利度过了整个夏天。**2** N-COUNT A **whole** is a single thing that contains several different parts. (包含几个不同部分的) 整体 ❑ *An atom itself is a complete whole, with its electrons, protons and neutrons and other elements.* 原子本身是个整体，含电子、质子、中子以及其他组成部分。**3** ADJ If something is **whole**, it is in one piece and is not broken or damaged. 完整的 [v-link ADJ, v n ADJ] ❑ *I struck the glass with my fist with all my might; yet it remained whole.* 我使尽全力用拳头砸那块玻璃，但它却完好无损。**4** ADV You use **whole** to emphasize what you are saying. (表强调) 完全地 [ADV adj] [INFORMAL, EMPHASIS] ❑ *It was like seeing a whole different side of somebody.* 这就像见到了某个人完全不同的一面。● ADJ **Whole** is also an adjective. 完全的 [ADJ n] ❑ *That saved me a whole bunch of money.* 那给我节省下一大笔钱。**5** PHRASE If you refer to something **as a whole**, you are referring to it generally and as a single unit. 总体上 ❑ *He described the move as a victory for the people of South Africa as a whole.* 他把这一行动描述成全体南非人民的一次胜利。**6** PHRASE You use **on the whole** to indicate that what you are saying is true in general but may not be true in every case, or that you are giving a general opinion or summary of something. 大体上说 ❑ *On the whole, people miss the opportunity to enjoy leisure.* 大体上说，人们都渴望享受休闲时光的机会。

> **Whole** is often used to mean the same as **all** but when used in front of plurals, **whole** and **all** have different meanings. For example, if you say "**Whole buildings have been destroyed**", you mean that some buildings have been destroyed completely. If you say "**All the buildings have been destroyed**," you mean that every building has been destroyed.

whole·hearted /hoʊlhɑrtɪd/ ADJ If you support or agree to something in a **wholehearted** way, you support or agree to it enthusiastically and completely. 全心全意的 [EMPHASIS] ❑ *The governor deserves our wholehearted support for having taken a step in this direction.* 州长已朝这个方向迈进了一步，值得我们全心全意的支持。
● **whole·hearted·ly** ADV 全心全意地 ❑ *That's exactly right. I agree wholeheartedly with you.* 那是完全正确的。我全心全意地支持你。

★ **whole·ness** /hoʊlnɪs/ N-UNCOUNT **Wholeness** is the quality of being complete or a single unit and not broken or divided into parts. 完整性 ❑ *...the need for wholeness and harmony in mind, body and spirit.* …心理、生理和精神完整和谐的需要。

★ **whole·sale** /hoʊlseɪl/ **1** N-UNCOUNT **Wholesale** is the activity of buying and selling goods in large quantities and therefore at cheaper prices, usually to stores who then sell them to the public. Compare **retail**. 批发 [BUSINESS] ❑ *Warehouse clubs allow members to buy goods at wholesale prices.* 仓储式会所允许会员以批发价购买商品。**2** ADV If something is sold **wholesale**, it is sold in large quantities and at cheaper prices, usually to stores. 批发地 [ADV after v] [BUSINESS] ❑ *The fabrics are sold wholesale to retailers, fashion houses, and other manufacturers.* 这些纺织品批发给零售商、时装店和其他厂家。**3** ADJ You use **wholesale** to describe the destruction, removal, or changing of something when it affects a very large number of things or people. (破坏、迁移或变动) 大规模的 [ADJ n] [EMPHASIS] ❑ *They are only doing what is necessary to prevent wholesale destruction of vegetation.* 他们只是在做为防止植被遭大规模破坏而必须做的事情。

whole·sal·er /hoʊlseɪlər/ (**wholesalers**) N-COUNT A **wholesaler** is a person whose business is buying large quantities of goods and selling them in smaller amounts, for example, to stores. 批发商 [BUSINESS] ❑ *Under state law, bar owners must buy their liquor from wholesalers.* 依照州法律，酒吧经营者们必须从批发商们那儿购买酒。

W

whole·sal·ing /hoʊlseɪlɪŋ/ N-UNCOUNT **Wholesaling** is the activity of buying or selling goods in large amounts, especially in order to sell them in stores or supermarkets. Compare **retailing**. 批发 [BUSINESS] ❑ *The business thrived and he turned to wholesaling.* 生意做得红火，他就转做批发。

▲ **whole·some** /hoʊlsəm/ **1** ADJ If you describe something as **wholesome**, you approve of it because you think it is likely to have a positive influence on people's behavior or mental state, especially because it does not involve anything sexually immoral. 有益身心的 (尤指不涉及非道德的性内容) [APPROVAL] ❑ *The Dove Foundation aims to promote wholesome family entertainment.* 达夫基金会旨在倡导有益身心的家庭娱乐。**2** ADJ If you describe food as **wholesome**, you approve of it because you think it is good for your health. (食物) 有益健康的 [APPROVAL] ❑ *...fresh, wholesome ingredients.* …有益健康的新鲜配料。

who'll /hul, hul/ **Who'll** is a spoken form of "who will" or "who shall." **who will**或**who shall**的口语形式

> **Word Link** *hol ≈ whole : holistic, holocaust, wholly*

whol·ly /hoʊlli/ ADV You use **wholly** to emphasize the extent or degree to which something is the case. 完全地 [EMPHASIS] ❑ *While the two are only days apart in age they seem to belong to wholly different generations.* 虽然这两位年龄上只有几天之差，但他们好像属于完全不同年代的人。

wholly-owned sub·sidi·ary (**wholly-owned subsidiaries**) N-COUNT A **wholly-owned subsidiary** is a company whose shares are all owned by another company. 全资子公司 (指其全部股份由另一家公司所有) [BUSINESS] ❑ *The Boston-owned software company became a wholly-owned subsidiary of IBM.* 这家波士顿所有的软件公司成了IBM的一家全资子公司。

whom ♦♦◇ /hum/

> **Whom** is used in formal or written English instead of "who" when it is the object of a verb or preposition.

1 QUEST You use **whom** in questions when you ask about the name or identity of a person or group of people. 谁 (用于询问姓名或身份) ❑ *"I want to send a telegram."—"Fine, to whom?"* "我想发个电报。"——"好的，给谁？" ❑ *Whom did he expect to answer his phone?* 他原来以为谁会接他的电话？**2** CONJ You use **whom** after certain words, especially verbs and adjectives, to introduce a clause where you talk about the name or identity of a person or a group of people. 尤用在动词和形容词后，引导用来谈论人的姓名或身份的从句 ❑ *He asked whom I'd told about his having been away.* 他问我对谁说过他不在的事。**3** PRON-REL You use **whom** at the beginning of a relative clause when specifying the person or group of people you are talking about or when giving more information about them. 用在关系从句的句首，具体指明被谈论者或给出更多相关信息等 ❑ *One writer in whom I had taken an interest was Immanuel Velikovsky.* 一位令我产生兴趣的作家是伊曼纽尔・韦利科夫斯基。

whoop /hup/ (**whoops, whooping, whooped**) V-I If you **whoop**, you shout loudly in a very happy or excited way. 欢呼 [WRITTEN] ❑ *She whoops with delight at a promise of money.* 她一听到答应给她钱就兴高采烈地欢呼起来。● N-COUNT **Whoop** is also a noun. 欢呼声 ❑ *Scattered groans and whoops broke out in the crowd.* 人群中发出零星的懊恼声和欢呼声。

who're /huər, huər/ **Who're** is a spoken form of "who are." **who are**的口语形式 ❑ *I've got loads of friends who're unemployed.* 我有许多失业的朋友。

who's /huz, huz/ **Who's** is the usual spoken form of "who is" or "who has," especially when "has" is an auxiliary verb. **who is**或**who has**的口语形式，尤当**has**为助动词时

whose ♦♦♦ /huz/

> Usually pronounced /huz/ for meanings **2** and **3**.

> 义项**2**和**3**通常读作 /huz/。

1 PRON-REL You use **whose** at the beginning of a relative clause where you mention something that belongs to or is associated with the person or thing mentioned in the previous clause. 用在关系从句的句首，表示某事与前面分句中提到人或事有所属关系或相关联 ❑ *I saw a man shouting at a driver whose car was blocking the street.* 我看见一个人正冲着一个司机大喊，那个司机的车挡住了街道。❑ *...a speedboat, whose fifteen-strong crew claimed to belong to China's navy.* … 一艘快艇，其船员超过15人，声称自己属于中国海军。**2** QUEST You use **whose** in questions to ask about the person or thing that something belongs to or is associated with. 用在疑问句中，询问某物所属或与之有关联的人或事 ❑ *"Whose is this?"—"It's mine."* "这是谁的？"——"是我的。" ❑ *"It wasn't your fault, John."—"Whose, then?"* "这并非你的错，约翰。"——"那么，是谁的呢？" ❑ *Whose car were they in?* 他们坐在谁的车里？❑ *Whose daughter is she?* 她是谁的女儿？**3** DET You use **whose** after certain words, especially verbs and adjectives, to introduce a clause where you talk about the person or thing that something belongs to or is associated with. 尤用在动词和形容词后，引导谈论某物所属或与何人

何事有关的从句 ❑ *I'm wondering whose mother she is then.* 我想知道她又会是谁的母亲呢。 ❑ *I can't remember whose idea it was.* 我记不得这是谁的主意了。 ● CONJ **Whose** is also a conjunction. 谁的 ❑ *I wondered whose the coat was.* 我思忖着那件大衣是谁的。

who've /huv, huv/ **Who've** is the usual spoken form of "who have," especially when "have" is an auxiliary verb. **who have**的口语形式，尤当**have**为助动词时

why ♦♦♦ /waɪ/

The conjunction and the pronoun are usually pronounced /waɪ/.

连词和代词通常读作 /waɪ/。

1 QUEST You use **why** in questions when you ask about the reasons for something. 为什么 (用于提问原因) ❑ *Why hasn't he brought the whiskey?* 为什么他还没把威士忌酒带来？ ❑ *Why didn't he stop me?* 为什么他没有阻止我？ 2 CONJ You use **why** at the beginning of a clause in which you talk about the reasons for something. …的原因 (用在从句开头) ❑ *He still could not throw any further light on why the elevator could have become jammed.* 他对电梯为什么会卡住仍给不出更多解释。 ❑ *Experts wonder why the U.S. government is not taking similarly strong actions against AIDS in this country.* 专家们想弄明白为什么美国政府没有对该国的艾滋病采取类似的强硬举措。 ● ADV **Why** is also an adverb. 为什么 ❑ *I don't know why.* 我不知道为什么。 ❑ *It's obvious why.* 很明显是为什么。 3 PRON-REL You use **why** to introduce a relative clause after the word "reason." 用在**reason**后面，引导关系从句 ❑ *There's a reason why women don't read this stuff; it's not funny.* 妇女们不读这种东西是有原因的：它并不逗趣。 ● ADV **Why** is also an adverb. 为什么 [n ADV] ❑ *He confirmed that the city had been closed to foreigners, but gave no reason why.* 他证实这座城市已经禁止外国人进入，但没有给出原因。 4 QUEST You use **why** with "not" in questions in order to introduce a suggestion. (问句中与**not**连用，引入建议) 为什么 ❑ *Why not give Charmaine a call?* 为什么不给莎梅因打个电话呢？ 5 QUEST You use **why** with "not" in questions in order to express your annoyance or anger. (在问句中与**not**连用，表达懊恼或愤怒) 为什么 [FEELINGS] ❑ *Why don't you look where you're going?* 为什么你不看看自己在往哪儿走？ 6 CONVENTION You say **why not** in order to agree with what someone has suggested. (表示赞同某人的建议) 为什么不呢 [FORMULAE] ❑ *"Want to spend the afternoon with me?"—"Why not?"* "想和我一起度过这个下午吗？" —— "为什么不呢？" 7 EXCLAM People say **"Why!"** at the beginning of a sentence when they are surprised, shocked, or angry. (用于句首表达惊讶、震惊或愤怒) 哎呀！ [mainly AM, FEELINGS] ❑ *Why hello, Tom.* 哎呀，你好，汤姆。

wick·ed /wɪkɪd/ ADJ You use **wicked** to describe someone or something that is very bad and deliberately harmful to people. 邪恶的 ❑ *She described the shooting as a wicked attack.* 她把那次射击描述成一次邪恶的攻击。

wick·et ♦◇◇ /wɪkɪt/ (**wickets**) 1 N-COUNT In cricket, a **wicket** is a set of three upright sticks with two small sticks on top of them at which the ball is bowled. (板球比赛中的) 三柱门 2 N-COUNT In cricket, a **wicket** is the area of grass in between the two wickets on the field. (板球中) 两个三柱门之间的场地 3 N-COUNT In cricket, when a **wicket** falls or is taken, a batsman is out. (板球中击球手) 出球的一轮 ❑ *Matthew Hoggard took three wickets in six balls.* 马修·霍加德在6个投球中使3个击球手出局。

wide ♦♦♦ /waɪd/ (**wider, widest**) 1 ADJ Something that is **wide** measures a large distance from one side or edge to the other. 宽的 ❑ *All worktops should be wide enough to allow plenty of space for food preparation.* 所有的厨房操作台都必须足够宽，以便有充足的空间准备食物。 2 ADJ If you open or spread something **wide**, you open or spread it as far as possible or to the fullest extent. 完全张开的 ❑ *"It was huge," he announced, spreading his arms wide.* "它大极了，" 他大张开双臂比划着说。 3 ADJ You use **wide** to talk or ask about how much something measures from one side or edge to the other. …宽的 ❑ *...a corridor of land four miles wide.* …一条4英里宽的陆地走廊。 ❑ *The road is only one lane wide.* 这条路只有一个车道那么宽。 4 ADJ You use **wide** to describe something that includes a large number of different things or people. 范围广的 ❑ *The brochure offers a wide choice of hotels, apartments and vacation homes.* 这本手册提供了选择范围很广的旅馆、公寓及度假屋。 ● **wide·ly** ADV 范围广地 ❑ *He published widely in scientific journals.* 他在科学期刊上广泛地发表各类文章。 5 ADJ You use **wide** to say that something is found, believed, known, or supported by many people or throughout a large area. 广泛的 ❑ *The case has attracted wide publicity.* 这个案件得到了广泛的关注。 ● **wide·ly** ADV 广泛地 [ADV with v] ❑ *At present, no widely approved vaccine exists for malaria.* 目前没有被广泛认可的疟疾疫苗。 6 ADJ A **wide** difference or gap between two things, ideas, or qualities is a large difference or gap. (不同或差距) 很大的 ❑ *Research shows a wide difference in tastes around the country.* 研究表明全国各地的口味大不相同。 ● **wide·ly** ADV 很大地 ❑ *The treatment regime may vary widely depending on the type of injury.* 治疗方法可能会因受伤类型的不同而有很大差别。 7 ADJ **Wider** is used to describe something that relates to the most important or general parts of a situation, rather than to the smaller parts or to details. 更大的 [ADJ n] ❑ *He emphasized the wider issue of superpower cooperation.* 他强调超级大国合作这个更大的话题。 8 **wide awake** → see **awake** 9 **wide of the mark** → see **mark** 10 **wide open** → see **open**
→ see **ratio**

Thesaurus *wide* 另参见：
ADJ. broad, large; *(ant.)* narrow 1 4 6

Word Partnership *wide* 的常用搭配：
N. wide **grin/smile**, wide **shoulders** 1
arms/eyes/mouth open wide 2
wide **array**, wide **audience**, wide **margin**, wide **selection**, wide **variety** 4

wid·en /waɪdᵊn/ (**widens, widening, widened**) 1 V-T/V-I If you **widen** something or if it **widens**, it becomes greater in measurement from one side or edge to the other. 使变宽；变宽 ❑ *He had an operation last year to widen a heart artery.* 他去年动了一次扩张心脏动脉的手术。 2 V-T/V-I If you **widen** something or if it **widens**, it becomes greater in range or it affects a larger number of people or things. 扩大 ❑ *U.S. prosecutors have widened a securities-fraud investigation.* 美国检察官已经扩大了一个证券欺诈案的调查范围。 3 V-T/V-I If a difference or gap **widens** or if something **widens** it, it becomes greater. 拉大 (不同或差距) ❑ *Wage differences in the two areas are widening.* 两个地区之间的工资差距正在拉大。

wide-ranging ADJ If you describe something as **wide-ranging**, you mean it deals with or affects a great variety of different things. 广泛的 ❑ *...a package of wide-ranging economic reforms.* …一整套内容广泛的经济改革。

wide·screen /waɪdskrin/ ADJ A **widescreen** television has a screen that is wide in relation to its height. (电视机) 宽屏的

Word Link *wide ≈ extending throughout : nationwide, widespread, worldwide*

wide·spread ♦◇◇ /waɪdsprɛd/ ADJ Something that is **widespread** exists or happens over a large area, or to a great extent. 广泛的 ❑ *There is widespread support for the new proposals.* 这些新提案得到了广泛的支持。

wid·ow /wɪdoʊ/ (**widows**) N-COUNT A **widow** is a woman whose husband has died and who has not married again. 寡妇 ❑ *She became a widow a year ago.* 她一年前成了寡妇。

wid·owed /wɪdoʊd/ V-T PASSIVE If someone **is widowed**, their husband or wife dies. 丧偶的 ❑ *More and more young men are widowed by cancer.* 越来越多的男青年被癌症夺去妻子。

wid·ow·er /wɪdoʊər/ (**widowers**) N-COUNT A **widower** is a man whose wife has died and who has not married again. 鳏夫 ❑ *He is a widower and lives in Durango.* 他是一个鳏夫，住在杜兰戈。

width /wɪdθ, wɪtθ/ (**widths**) N-VAR The **width** of something is the distance it measures from one side or edge to the other. 宽度 ❑ *Measure the full width of the window.* 测量一下窗户的总宽度。 ❑ *The road was reduced to 18 ft in width by adding parking bays.* 这条路增加了停车区域后，宽度减少为18英尺。
→ see **ratio**

▲ **wield** /wild/ (**wields, wielding, wielded**) 1 V-T If you **wield** a weapon, tool, or piece of equipment, you carry and use it. 拿着 (武器、工具或设备) ❑ *He was attacked by a man wielding a knife.* 他遭到一名持刀男子的袭击。 2 V-T If someone **wields** power, they have it and are able to use it. 掌握 (权力) ❑ *He remains chairman, but wields little power at the company.* 他还是主席，但在公司内没有什么权力。

wife ♦♦♦ /waɪf/ (**wives**) N-COUNT A man's **wife** is the woman he is married to. 妻子 ❑ *He married his wife Jane 37 years ago.* 他和妻子简37年前结婚。
→ see **family, love**

▲ wig /wɪg/ (**wigs**) N-COUNT A **wig** is a covering of false hair that you wear on your head, for example, because you have little hair of your own or because you want to cover up your own hair. 假发 ❑ *Jo wore a long wig that made her look very sexy.* 乔带着一头长长的假发，使她看起来很性感。

wig·gle /wɪgᵊl/ (**wiggles, wiggling, wiggled**) V-T/V-I If you **wiggle** something or if it **wiggles**, it moves up and down or from side to side in small quick movements. 摆动；扭动 ❑ *She wiggled her finger.* 她摆动着手指头。 ● N-COUNT **Wiggle** is also a noun. 摆动；扭动 ❑ *...a wiggle of the hips.* …臀部的扭动。

wi·ki //wɪki// (**wikis**) N-COUNT A **wiki** is a website that allows anyone visiting it to change or add to the material in it. 维基网站 ❑ *...wiki technology.* …维基技术。 ❑ *Most wikis are collaborative websites.* 大多数维基网站是合作网站。

wild ◆◆◇ /waɪld/ (**wilds, wilder, wildest**) **1** ADJ **Wild** animals or plants live or grow in natural surroundings and are not taken care of by people. (动物或植物) 野生的 ❑ *We saw two more wild cats creeping toward us in the darkness.* 我们看见还有两只野猫在黑暗中向我们爬来。 **2** ADJ **Wild** land is natural and is not used by people. 荒芜的 ❑ *...a wild area of woods and lakes.* …一片荒芜的森林和湖泊区域。 **3** N-PLURAL **The wilds** of a place are the natural areas that are far away from cities and towns. 荒野 ❑ *They went canoeing in the wilds of Canada.* 他们在加拿大的荒野地区划独木舟。 **4** ADJ **Wild** is used to describe the weather or the sea when it is stormy. (天气或海面) 狂风暴雨的 ❑ *The wild weather did not deter some people from taking an unseasonable dip in the sea.* 狂风暴雨的天气并没有使一些不合时宜地到海里游泳的人却步。 **5** ADJ **Wild** behavior is uncontrolled, excited, or energetic. (行为) 狂热的 ❑ *The children are wild with joy.* 孩子们欣喜若狂。 ❑ *As George himself came on stage they went wild.* 当乔治本人登上舞台的时候，他们都发狂了。 ● **wild·ly** ADV 狂热地 [ADV with v] ❑ *As she finished each song, the crowd clapped wildly.* 她每唱完一首歌，人群就狂热地鼓起掌来。 **6** ADJ If you describe someone or their behavior as **wild**, you mean that they behave in a very uncontrolled way. (指人或其行为) 疯狂的 ❑ *The house is in a mess after a wild party.* 一次疯狂的聚会之后，房子里一片狼藉。 ● **wild·ly** ADV 疯狂地 [ADV with v] ❑ *Five people were injured as Reynolds slashed out wildly with a kitchen knife.* 五个人因雷诺兹拿着菜刀疯狂乱砍而受伤。 **7** ADJ A **wild** idea is unusual or extreme. A **wild** guess is one that you make without much thought. 不寻常的 (想法)；胡乱的 (猜测) [ADJ n] ❑ *Browning's prediction is no better than a wild guess.* 布朗宁的预言只不过是胡乱猜测而已。 ● **wild·ly** ADV 不寻常地；胡乱地 ❑ *"Thirteen?" he guessed wildly.* "十三？" 他胡乱猜道。 **8** → see also **wildly** **9** PHRASE Animals that live **in the wild** live in a free and natural state and are not taken care of by people. 处于野生状态 ❑ *Fewer than a thousand giant pandas still live in the wild.* 不到1000只的大熊猫还处于野生状态。 **10** **beyond your wildest dreams** → see **dream** **11** **in your wildest dreams** → see **dream** **12** **to sow your wild oats** → see **oats**

Thesaurus *wild* 另参见：

ADJ. feral, untamed **1**
desolate, natural, overgrown **2**
choppy, stormy, tempestuous **4**
excited, rowdy, uncontrolled **5** **6**

Word Partnership *wild* 的常用搭配：

N. wild **animal**, wild **beasts/creatures**, wild **game**, wild **horse**, wild **mushrooms** **1**
wild **pitch**, wild **swing** **5**
ADJ. **wild-eyed** **5**
V. **run** wild **5**
go wild **5** **6**

W

wild card (**wild cards**) also **wildcard** **1** N-COUNT If you refer to someone or something as a **wild card** in a particular situation, you mean that they cause uncertainty because you do not know how they will behave. 未知因素 ❑ *The wild card in the picture is eastern Europe.* 局势中的未知因素在东欧。 **2** N-COUNT A **wildcard** is a symbol such as * or ? used in some computing commands or searches in order to represent any character or range of characters. 通配符 (计算机指令中如*或?的符号，用于替代任一字符或系列字符) [COMPUTING] **3** N-COUNT In card games, if a particular card is named as a **wild card**, the player who holds it may give it any value he chooses. 百搭牌 (牌戏中由持牌人决定牌值的牌) ❑ *Look. I have a straight of 3, 4, 6, 7 and the wild card for the 5.* 看，我有连着的3，4，6，7，还有一张百搭牌作5。

wil·der·ness /wɪldərnɛs/ (**wildernesses**) N-COUNT A **wilderness** is a desert or other area of natural land which is not used by people. 荒野 ❑ *...the icy Canadian wilderness.* …冰封的加拿大荒野。

wild·fire /waɪldfaɪər/ (**wildfires**) **1** N-COUNT A **wildfire** is a fire that starts, usually by itself, in a wild area such as a forest, and spreads rapidly, causing great damage. 野火 ❑ *...a wildfire in Montana that's already burned thousands of acres of rich grassland.* …已经烧毁几千英亩肥沃草地的蒙大拿州野火。 **2** PHRASE If something, especially news or a rumor, **spreads like wildfire**, it spreads extremely quickly. (尤指消息或谣言) 快速传播 ❑ *These stories are spreading like wildfire through the city.* 这些故事正迅速传遍整座城市。 → see **fire**

wild·life /waɪldlaɪf/ N-UNCOUNT You can use **wildlife** to refer to the animals and other living things that live in the wild. 野生生物 ❑ *People were concerned that pets or wildlife could be affected by the pesticides.* 人们担心宠物或野生生物会受到杀虫剂的影响。 → see **zoo**

wild·ly /waɪldli/ **1** ADV You use **wildly** to emphasize the degree, amount, or intensity of something. 非常 [EMPHASIS] ❑ *Here again, the community and police have wildly different stories of what happened.* 这里同样，社区和警察对所发生的事又有着非常不同的说法。 **2** → see also **wild**

will
❶ MODAL VERB USES
❷ WANTING SOMETHING TO HAPPEN

❶ will ◆◆◆ /wɪl/

Will is a modal verb. It is used with the base form of a verb. In spoken English and informal written English, the form **won't** is often used in negative statements.

1 MODAL You use **will** to indicate that you hope, think, or have evidence that something is going to happen or be the case in the future. 将会 ❑ *I'm sure we will find a wide variety of choices available in school cafeterias.* 我相信我们将会发现学校的自助餐厅里有多种多样的选择。 ❑ *Will you ever feel at home here?* 你在这儿会感到自在吗？ ❑ *The ship will not be ready for a month.* 这艘船一个月内将不会准备就绪。 **2** MODAL You use **will** in order to make statements about official arrangements in the future. 表示将来的正式安排 ❑ *The show will be open to the public at 2 pm; admission will be $5.* 展览将于下午2点对公众开放；入场费为$5。 **3** MODAL You use **will** in order to make promises and threats about what is going to happen or be the case in the future. (表示承诺或威胁) 将 ❑ *I'll call you tonight.* 我今晚将会打电话给你。 ❑ *Price quotes on selected product categories will be sent on request.* 所选产品类型的报价将索要即寄。 **4** MODAL You use **will** to indicate someone's intention to do something. 想要 ❑ *I will say no more on these matters, important though they are.* 我不想对这些事再说些什么，尽管它们很重要。 ❑ *In this section we will describe common myths about cigarettes, alcohol, and marijuana.* 在这一节我们想讲述有关香烟、酒和大麻的一些常见的错误认识。 ❑ *"Dinner's ready."—"Thanks, Carrie, but we'll have a drink first."* "晚饭做好了。"——"谢谢，卡丽，但是我们想先喝一杯。" ❑ *Will you be remaining in the city?* 你想留在这座城市里吗？ **5** MODAL You use **will** in questions in order to make polite invitations or offers. …好吗 (用在问句中，表示礼貌的邀请或提议) [POLITENESS] ❑ *Will you stay for supper?* 你留下来吃晚饭好吗？ ❑ *Will you join me for a drink?* 和我喝一杯好吗？ **6** MODAL You use **will** in questions in order to ask or tell someone to do something. 好吗 (用在问句中，表示请人或告诉某人做某事) ❑ *Will you drive me home?* 你开车送我回家好吗？ ❑ *Will you listen again, Andrew?* 再听一遍好吗，安德鲁？ **7** MODAL You use **will** to say that someone is willing to do something. You use **will not** or **won't** to indicate that someone refuses to do something. 愿意 ❑ *All right, I'll forgive you.* 好吧，我愿意原谅你。 **8** → see also **willing** **9** MODAL You use **will** to say that a person or thing is able to do something in the future. 表示将来能做某事 ❑ *How the country will defend itself in the future has become increasingly important.* 这个国家将来如何防御已经变得越来越重要。 **10** MODAL You use **will** to indicate that an action usually happens in the particular way mentioned. 通常会 (用于表明某动作通常以特定方式发生) ❑ *The thicker the material, the less susceptible the garment will be to wet conditions.* 布料越厚，衣服通常就越不容易浸湿。 **11** MODAL You use **will** in the main clause of some "if" and "unless" sentences to indicate something that you consider to be fairly likely to happen. 会(用在if和unless引导的从句的主句中，表示某事很可能发生) ❑ *If you overcook the meat it will be dry.* 你如果煮过头，肉会很干。 **12** MODAL You use **will** to say that someone insists on behaving or doing something in a particular way and you cannot change them. You emphasize **will** when you use it in this way. 总是要 ❑ *He will leave his socks lying all over the place and it drives me crazy.* 他总是把袜子丢得到处都是，这简直让我发疯。 **13** MODAL You use **will have** with a past participle when you are saying that you are fairly certain that something will be true by a particular time in the future. (与过去分词连用，表示某事将来肯定如此) 将已经 ❑ *As many as ten-million children will have been infected with the virus by the end of the decade.* 多达1千万的儿童到这个时代末将已染上这种病毒。 **14** MODAL You use **will have** with a past participle to indicate that you are fairly sure that something is the case. (与过去分词连用，表示相当肯定) 将 ❑ *Jack will have been very upset by all this.* 这一切肯定会让杰克非常难过。

❷ will ♦♦◇ /wɪl/ (**wills, willing, willed**) **1** N-VAR **Will** is the determination to do something. 意志 ❑ *He was said to have lost his will to live.* 据说他已经丧失了活下去的意志。 **2** → see also **free will** **3** N-SING If something is **the will of** a person or group of people with authority, they want it to happen. 意愿 ❑ *He has submitted himself to the will of God.* 他已经让自己听从上帝的意旨。 **4** V-T If you **will** something **to** happen, you try to make it happen by using mental effort rather than physical effort. 希望(某事发生) ❑ *I looked at the telephone, willing it to ring.* 我看着电话，希望它响起来。 **5** N-COUNT A **will** is a document in which you declare what you want to happen to your money and property when you die. 遗嘱 ❑ *Attached to his will was a letter he had written to his wife just days before his death.* 他遗嘱中附带的是他去世前几天写给妻子的一封信。 **6** PHRASE If something is done **against** your **will**, it is done even though you do not want it to be done. 违背某人的意愿 ❑ *No doubt he was forced to leave his family against his will.* 毫无疑问，他是被迫违心地离开家人的。

will·ful /wɪlfəl/ **1** ADJ If you describe actions or attitudes as **willful**, you are critical of them because they are done or expressed deliberately, especially with the intention of causing someone harm. (旨在造成伤害) 故意的 [ADJ n] ❑ *The sergeant faces a lesser charge of willful neglect of duty.* 这位军士面临着一个较轻的故意玩忽职守指控。 **2** ADJ If you describe someone as **willful**, you mean that they are determined to do what they want to do, even if it is not sensible. 任性的 ❑ *Molly was at times impatient and willful.* 莫莉有时很没耐心，而且任性。

will·ing ♦♦◇ /wɪlɪŋ/ **1** ADJ If someone is **willing to** do something, they are fairly happy about doing it and will do it if they are asked or required to do it. 乐意的 [v-link ADJ to-inf] ❑ *There are, of course, questions which she will not be willing to answer.* 当然，有些问题她不乐意回答。 **2** ADJ **Willing** is used to describe someone who does something fairly enthusiastically and because they want to do it rather than because they are forced to do it. 心甘情愿的 ❑ *Have the party on a Saturday, when you can get your partner and other willing adults to help.* 把聚会安排在某个星期六吧，到时你就可以找你的伙伴以及其他愿意相助的人帮忙。 **3** **God willing** → see **god**

▲ **wil·low** /wɪloʊ/ (**willows**) N-COUNT A **willow** or a **willow tree** is a type of tree with long branches and long narrow leaves that grows near water. 柳树

will·power /wɪlpaʊər/ also **will-power, will power** N-UNCOUNT **Willpower** is a very strong determination to do something. 毅力 ❑ *He came in for help after his attempts to stop smoking by willpower alone failed.* 他仅靠毅力戒烟失败后到这里来求助。

wilt /wɪlt/ (**wilts, wilting, wilted**) V-I If a plant **wilts**, it gradually bends downward and becomes weak because it needs more water or is dying. 枯萎 ❑ *The roses wilted the next day.* 这些玫瑰花第二天就枯萎了。

wily /waɪli/ (**wilier, wiliest**) ADJ If you describe someone or their behavior as **wily**, you mean that they are clever at achieving what they want, especially by tricking people. 狡猾的 ❑ *This is a wily politician.* 这是一个狡猾的政客。

wimp /wɪmp/ (**wimps**) N-COUNT If you call someone a **wimp**, you disapprove of them because they lack confidence or determination, or because they are often afraid of things. 懦弱的人 [INFORMAL, DISAPPROVAL] ❑ *I was a wimp, because I had spent my life being bullied by my Dad.* 我是一个懦弱的人，因为我一生都受我父亲的欺凌。

win ♦♦♦ /wɪn/ (**wins, winning, won**) **1** V-T/V-I If you **win** something such as a competition, battle, or argument, you defeat those people you are competing or fighting against, or you do better than everyone else involved. 赢得(比赛、战争或辩论等); 赢 ❑ *He does not have any realistic chance of winning the election.* 他没有任何赢得这次选举的实际机会。 ❑ *The top four teams all won.* 排名最靠前的4支队伍都赢了。 ● N-COUNT **Win** is also a noun. 赢 ❑ *The voters gave a narrow win to Vargas Llosa.* 选民们使瓦尔加斯・略萨取得险胜。 **2** V-T If something **wins** you something such as an election, competition, battle, or argument, it causes you to defeat the people competing with you or fighting you, or to do better than everyone else involved. 使…赢得(选举、比赛、战争或辩论等) ❑ *The Democrats had found a message that could win them the White House.* 民主党人已找到了一条可以使他们赢得总统选举的口号。 **3** V-T If you **win** something such as a prize or medal, you get it because you have defeated everyone else in something such as an election, competition, battle, or argument, or have done very well in it. 赢得(奖或奖牌) ❑ *Trent Dimas won gold in the final men's gymnastic event.* 特伦特・迪马斯在男子体操决赛中赢得了金牌。 **4** V-T If you **win** something that you want or need, you succeed in getting it. 赢得(想要或需要的事物)

in BRIT, also use **win round**

❑ *...moves to win the support of the poor.* …赢得穷人支持的举措 ❑ *British Aerospace has won an order worth 340 million dollars.* 英国航空公司争取到了价值3亿4千万美元的订单。 **5** → see also **winning** **6** **to win hands down** → see **hand**

▸ **win over** PHRASAL VERB If you **win** someone **over**, you persuade them to support you or agree with you. 赢得…的支持; 使…与自己的观点一致 ❑ *He has won over a significant number of the left-wing deputies.* 他已赢得相当一部分左翼代表的支持。 ❑ *They still hope to win him over.* 他们还是希望获得他的支持。

Thesaurus *win* 另参见:

V.	conquer, succeed, triumph; *(ant.)* lose **1**
N.	conquest, success, victory; *(ant.)* defeat **1**

wince /wɪns/ (**winces, wincing, winced**) V-I If you **wince**, the muscles of your face tighten suddenly because you have felt a pain or because you have just seen, heard, or remembered something unpleasant. (由于疼痛或看见、听到或记起某些不愉快的事而) 龇牙咧嘴 ❑ *Every time he put any weight on his left leg he winced in pain.* 每当他的左腿受力时，他就会疼得龇牙咧嘴。

winch /wɪntʃ/ (**winches, winching, winched**) **1** N-COUNT A **winch** is a machine that is used to lift heavy objects or people who need to be rescued. It consists of a cylinder around which a rope or chain is wound. 绞车 **2** V-T If you **winch** an object or person somewhere, you lift or lower them using a winch. 用绞车吊起; 用绞车放下 ❑ *He would attach a cable around the chassis of the car and winch it up on to the canal bank.* 他会在汽车底盘上拴一条缆绳，然后用绞车把汽车吊到运河岸边。

wind

❶ AIR
❷ TURNING OR WRAPPING

❶ wind ♦♦◇ /wɪnd/ (**winds, winding, winded**) **1** N-VAR A **wind** is a current of air that is moving across the earth's surface. 风 ❑ *There was a strong wind blowing.* 正刮着一阵大风。 **2** N-COUNT Journalists often refer to a trend or factor that influences events as a **wind of** a particular kind. (影响事态发展的) 趋势; 因素 ❑ *The winds of change are blowing across the country.* 转变之风正吹遍全国。 **3** V-T If you **are winded** by something such as a blow, the air is suddenly knocked out of your lungs so that you have difficulty breathing for a short time. 呼吸困难 ❑ *He was winded and shaken.* 他呼吸困难，身体发抖。 **4** PHRASE If someone **breaks wind**, they release gas from their intestines through their anus. 放屁 ❑ *If I break wind at dinner, should I say "Pardon," or pretend nothing has happened?* 如果我在用餐的时候放屁，我是应该说"对不起"，还是假装什么事情都没发生？ **5** PHRASE If you **get wind of** something, you hear about it, especially when someone else did not want you to know about it. 听到…的消息 (尤指在别人不想让知道的情况下) [INFORMAL] ❑ *I don't want the public, and especially not the press, to get wind of it at this stage.* 我不想让公众，尤其是新闻界，在这个阶段听到什么消息。

→ see Word Web: **wind**

→ see **beach, electricity, erosion, storm, wave**

W

Word Web wind

The earth's surface **temperature** isn't the same everywhere. This temperature difference causes **air** to flow from one area to another. We call this airflow **wind**. As warm air expands and rises, air pressure goes down. Then denser cool air **blows** in. The amount of difference in air pressure determines how strong the wind will be. It can be anything from a **breeze** to a **gale**. The earth's geography creates **prevailing winds**. For example, air in the warmer areas near the Equator is always rising, and cooler air from polar regions is always flowing in to take its place.

Word Partnership *wind* 的常用搭配：

ADJ. **cold** wind, **hot** wind, **howling** wind, **icy** wind, **warm** wind ❶ 1
N. **desert** wind, **gust of** wind, **wind** power, **winter** wind ❶ 1
V. wind **blows**, **blown/driven by the** wind, wind **whips** ❶ 1
get wind **of** ***something*** ❶ 5

❷ **wind** ♦♦◇ /waɪnd/ (**winds, winding, wound**) 1 V-T/V-I If a road, river, or line of people **winds** in a particular direction, it goes in that direction with a lot of bends or twists in it. (路、河流或一行人) 蜿蜒而行 ❑ *Quiet mountain roads wind through groves of bamboo and cedar.* 幽静的山路蜿蜒穿过竹林和雪松林。 ❑ *...a narrow winding road.* …一条狭窄蜿蜒的道路。 ❑ *We wound our way southeast.* 我们向东南方向蜿蜒前行。 2 V-T When you **wind** something flexible around something else, you wrap it around it several times. 缠绕 ❑ *The horse jumped forward and around her, winding the rope around her waist.* 那匹马向前一跳，然后围着她把绳子缠在她的腰际。 3 V-T When you **wind** a mechanical device, for example, a watch or a clock, you turn a knob, key, or handle on it several times in order to make it operate. 给(钟表等) 上发条 ❑ *I still hadn't wound my watch so I didn't know the time.* 我还没给手表上发条，所以我不知道时间。 ● PHRASAL VERB **Wind up** means the same as **wind**. 给(钟表等) 上发条 ❑ *I wound up the watch and listened to it tick.* 我给手表上好发条，听着它滴答作响。 4 V-T To **wind** a tape or film **back** or **forward** means to make it move toward its starting or ending position. 倒/快进 (磁带或胶卷) ❑ *The camcorder winds the tape back or forward at high speed.* 便携式摄像机可以高速度倒带或快进。

▶ **wind down** 1 PHRASAL VERB When you **wind down** something such as the window of a car, you make it move downwards by turning a handle. 摇下(车窗等) ❑ *Glass motioned to him to wind down the window.* 格拉斯示意他摇下车窗。 2 PHRASAL VERB If you **wind down**, you relax after doing something that has made you feel tired or tense. (疲劳或紧张后) 放松一下 [INFORMAL] ❑ *I regularly have a drink to wind down.* 我经常喝点酒来放松一下。 3 PHRASAL VERB If someone **winds down** a business or activity, they gradually reduce the amount of work that is done or the number of people that are involved, usually before closing or stopping it completely. 逐步减少(业务或活动等直至停止) ❑ *Aid workers have begun winding down their operation.* 援助工作人员已开始逐步减少他们的工作。

▶ **wind up** 1 PHRASAL VERB When you **wind up** an activity, you finish it or stop doing it. 完成；停止(活动) ❑ *The president is about to wind up his visit to Somalia.* 总统即将结束对索马里的访问。 2 PHRASAL VERB When you **wind up** something such as the window of a car, you make it move upwards by turning a handle. 摇上(车窗等) ❑ *He started winding the window up but I grabbed the door and opened it.* 他开始摇上车窗，但是我抓住车门，把它打开。 3 → see also **wind** ❷ 3

→ see also **wound up**

Thesaurus *wind* 另参见：

N. air, current, gust ❶ 1
V. bend, loop, twist; (*ant.*) straighten ❷ 2

W

wind·fall /wɪndfɔl/ (**windfalls**) N-COUNT A **windfall** is a sum of money that you receive unexpectedly or by luck, for example, if you win a lottery. 意外之财 ❑ *...the man who received a $250,000 windfall after a banking error.* …因银行失误得到25万美元意外之财的那位男子。 ❑ *...windfall profits.* …意外横利。

wind·mill /wɪndmɪl/ (**windmills**) N-COUNT A **windmill** is a building with long pieces of wood on the outside that turn around as the wind blows and provide energy for a machine that crushes grain. A **windmill** is also a similar structure that uses the power of the wind to pump water or make electricity. 风车房；风车

win·dow ♦♦◇ /wɪndoʊ/ (**windows**) 1 N-COUNT A **window** is a space in the wall of a building or in the side of a vehicle, which has glass in it so that light can come in and you can see out. 窗户 ❑ *He stood at the window, moodily staring out.* 他站在窗旁，忧郁地盯着外面。 ❑ *The room felt very hot and she wondered why someone did not open a window.* 房间里感觉非常热，她纳闷为什么没人打开一扇窗。 2 N-COUNT A **window** is a glass-covered opening above a counter, for example, in a bank, post office, train station, or museum, which the person serving you sits behind. (银行、邮局、火车站、博物馆等提供服务的) 窗口 ❑ *The woman at the ticket window told me that the admission fee was $17.50.* 售票窗口的那位女士告诉我入场费为$17.50。 3 N-COUNT On a computer screen, a **window** is one of the work areas that the screen can be divided into. (电脑屏幕上的) 视窗 [COMPUTING] ❑ *Yahoo! Pager puts a small window on your screen containing a list of your "friends."* 雅虎通在您的屏幕上弹出一个包含您的"朋友"名单的小视窗。 4 PHRASE If you say that something such as a plan or a particular way of thinking or behaving **has gone out of the window** or **is out the window**, you mean that it has disappeared completely. (计划或某种思维或行为方式) 完全消失 ❑ *By now all logic had gone out of the window.* 到此时，已没有什么道理可讲。

→ see **glass**

Word Partnership *window* 的常用搭配：

N. **car** window, window **curtains**, window **display**, **kitchen** window, window **screen**, **shop** window, **store** window, window **treatment** 1
V. **close/open a** window 1
look in/out a window, **peer in/into/out/through a** window, **watch through a** window 1 2
ADJ. **open** window 1
broken window, **dark** window, **large/small** window, **narrow** window 1 2

wind·screen /wɪnʔdskriːn/ [BRIT] → see **windshield**

wind·shield /wɪndʃild/ (**windshields**) N-COUNT The **windshield** of a car or other vehicle is the glass window at the front through which the driver looks. (机动车辆的) 挡风玻璃 [AM]

in BRIT, use **windscreen**

wind·shield wip·er (**windshield wipers**) N-COUNT A **windshield wiper** is a device that wipes rain from a vehicle's windshield. 风挡雨刷 [AM]

wind·surf·ing /wɪndsɜrfɪŋ/ N-UNCOUNT **Windsurfing** is a sport in which you move along the surface of the sea or a lake on a long narrow board with a sail on it. 风帆冲浪运动

windy /wɪndi/ (**windier, windiest**) ADJ If it is **windy**, the wind is blowing a lot. 风大的 ❑ *It was windy and Jake felt cold.* 风很大，杰克觉得很冷。

wine ♦♦◇ /waɪn/ (**wines**) N-MASS **Wine** is an alcoholic drink made from grapes. You can also refer to alcoholic drinks made from other fruits or vegetables as **wine**. 葡萄酒；果酒 ❑ *...a bottle of white wine.* …一瓶白葡萄酒。

wine bar (**wine bars**) N-COUNT A **wine bar** is a place where people can buy and drink wine, and sometimes eat food as well. 酒吧

wing ♦♦◇ /wɪŋ/ (**wings**) 1 N-COUNT The **wings** of a bird or insect are the two parts of its body that it uses for flying. 翅膀 ❑ *The bird flapped its wings furiously.* 那只鸟使劲地拍打着翅膀。 2 N-COUNT The **wings** of an airplane are the long flat parts sticking out of its side which support it while it is flying. 机翼 ❑ *The plane made one pass, dipped its wings, then circled back.* 飞机掠过去，垂下机翼，然后盘旋而回。 3 N-COUNT A **wing** of a building is a part of it that sticks out from the main part. (建筑的) 侧翼 ❑ *We were given an office in the empty west wing.* 我们在空荡荡的西侧厅得到了一间

办公室。 4 N-COUNT A **wing** of an organization, especially a political organization, is a group within it which has a particular function or particular beliefs. (尤指政治组织中有某种作用或信仰的) 派系 ❑ *...the military wing of the African National Congress.* …非洲国民大会的武装派。 5 → see also **left-wing, right-wing** 6 N-PLURAL In a theater, **the wings** are the sides of the stage that are hidden from the audience by curtains or scenery. (舞台被帘幕或布景遮挡的) 侧面 ❑ *Most nights I watched the start of the play from the wings.* 大多数晚上，我都从舞台的侧面观看演出的开场。 7 PHRASE If you say that someone is waiting **in the wings**, you mean that they are ready and waiting for an opportunity to take action. 准备就绪 ❑ *There are now more than 20 big companies waiting in the wings to take over some of its business.* 现在有二十多家大公司正等着随时接手它的一些业务。 8 PHRASE If you **spread** your **wings**, you do something new and somewhat difficult or move to a new place, because you feel more confident in your abilities than you used to and you want to gain wider experience. (在陌生领域或到新的地方) 施展身手 ❑ *I led a very confined life in my village so I suppose that I wanted to spread my wings.* 我在自己的村庄里过着非常封闭的生活，所以我觉得我想要出去施展一下身手。 9 PHRASE If you **take** someone **under** your **wing**, you look after them, help them, and protect them. 把某人置于自己的保护之下 ❑ *Her boss took her under his wing after fully realizing her potential.* 她的老板充分意识到她的潜力后就把她招到自己的旗下。
→ see **bird**

Word Partnership *wing* 的常用搭配:
N. aircraft wing 2
ADJ. military/political wing 4

winged /wɪŋd/ ADJ A **winged** insect or other creature has wings. (昆虫或其他生物) 有翼的 ❑ *Flycatchers feed primarily on winged insects.* 鹟主要捕食有翼昆虫。

▲ **wink** /wɪŋk/ (**winks, winking, winked**) 1 V-I When you **wink at** someone, you look toward them and close one eye very briefly, usually as a signal that something is a joke or a secret. 眨眼示意 ❑ *Brian winked at his bride-to-be.* 布赖恩向他的准新娘眨眼示意。 ● N-COUNT **Wink** is also a noun. 眨眼 ❑ *I gave her a wink.* 我向她眨了眨眼。 2 PHRASE If you say that you **did not sleep a wink** or **did not get a wink of sleep**, you mean that you tried to go to sleep but could not. 没合一下眼 [INFORMAL] ❑ *I didn't get a wink of sleep on the flight.* 我在飞行过程中没有合一下眼。

win·ner ♦♦◊ /wɪnər/ (**winners**) N-COUNT The **winner** of a prize, race, or competition is the person, animal, or thing that wins it. 获胜者 ❑ *She will present the trophies to the award winners.* 她将给获胜者颁奖。
→ see **lottery**

win·ning ♦◊◊ /wɪnɪŋ/ 1 ADJ You can use **winning** to describe a person or thing that wins something such as a competition, game, or election. 获胜的 [ADJ n] ❑ *...the winning lotto ticket.* …中奖的乐透彩票。 2 ADJ You can use **winning** to describe actions or qualities that please other people and make them feel friendly toward you. 迷人的 [ADJ n] ❑ *She gave him another of her winning smiles.* 她又给了他一个迷人的微笑。 3 → see also **win**
→ see **lottery**

win·nings /wɪnɪŋz/ N-PLURAL You can use **winnings** to refer to the money that someone wins in a competition or by gambling. (比赛或赌博中) 赢得的钱 ❑ *I have come to collect my winnings.* 我来领取我赢得的钱。
→ see **lottery**

win·ter ♦◊◊ /wɪntər/ (**winters**) N-VAR **Winter** is the season between fall and spring. In the winter the weather is usually cold. 冬季 ❑ *In winter the nights are long and cold.* 冬季的夜晚又长又冷。 ❑ *...the late winter of 1941.* …1941年的晚冬。

win-win ADJ A **win-win** situation is certain to bring good results, sometimes for two people or groups. 双赢的 [ADJ n] ❑ *It is surprising that it has taken people so long to take advantage of what is a win-win opportunity.* 令人惊讶的是，人们花了那么长的时间才把一个双赢的机会利用起来。

wipe ♦◊◊ /waɪp/ (**wipes, wiping, wiped**) 1 V-T If you **wipe** something, you rub its surface to remove dirt or liquid from it. 擦拭 ❑ *I'll just wipe the table.* 我只擦擦桌子。 ❑ *When he had finished washing he began to wipe the basin clean.* 他洗漱完后开始把水盆擦干净。 ● N-COUNT **Wipe** is also a noun. 擦拭 ❑ *Tomorrow I'm going to give the toys a good wipe as some seem a bit greasy.* 明天我会把那些玩具好好擦拭一番，因为有些看上去有点油腻了。 2 V-T If you **wipe** dirt or liquid from something, you remove it by using a cloth or your hand. (用布或手) 擦去 ❑ *Gleb wiped the sweat from his face.* 格莱布擦去了脸上的汗水。 3 N-COUNT A **wipe** is a small moist cloth for cleaning things and is designed to be used only once. 一次性湿巾 ❑ *...antiseptic wipes.* …一次性杀菌湿巾。

▶ **wipe out** PHRASAL VERB To **wipe out** something such as a place or a group of people or animals means to destroy them completely. 摧毁；使灭绝 ❑ *Experts say if the island is not protected, the spill could wipe out the gulf's turtle population.* 专家们说如果那座小岛得不到保护，此次泄露有可能使该海湾地区的海龟灭绝。

Word Partnership *wipe* 的常用搭配:
N. wipe *your* **eyes**, wipe *someone's* **face** 1
wipe **blood**, wipe **tears** 2

wip·er /waɪpər/ (**wipers**) N-COUNT A **wiper** is a device that wipes rain from a vehicle's windshield. 风挡雨刷

wire ♦◊◊ /waɪər/ (**wires, wiring, wired**) 1 N-VAR A **wire** is a long thin piece of metal that is used to fasten things or to carry electric current. (用以绑东西或导电的) 金属丝 ❑ *...fine copper wire.* …细铜丝。 2 N-COUNT A **wire** is a cable that carries power or signals from one place to another. 电线；电缆 ❑ *I ripped out the telephone wire that ran through to his office.* 我拔掉连接到他办公室的电话线。 3 V-T If you **wire** something such as a building or piece of equipment, you put wires inside it so that electricity or signals can pass into or through it. 在…里装设电线 ❑ *...learning to wire and plumb the house herself.* …她学会自己在房子里装设电线和水管。 ❑ *Each of the homes has a security system and is wired for cable television.* 每一家都有安全系统，并装设了有线电视线。 ● PHRASAL VERB **Wire up** means the same as **wire**. 在…里装设电线 ❑ *Wire the thermometers up to trigger off an alarm bell if the temperature drops.* 把温度计的电线连接上，当温度下降时，就会触发警报。 4 PHRASE If something goes **to the wire**, it continues until the last possible moment. 直至最后一刻 [mainly JOURNALISM] ❑ *Negotiators again worked right down to the wire to reach an agreement.* 谈判者们再次一直工作到最后达成协议为止。 5 → see also **barbed wire**
→ see **metal**

wire·less ♦♦◊ /waɪərlɪs/ ADJ **Wireless** technology uses radio waves rather than electricity and therefore does not require any wires. 无线电的 ❑ *...the fast-growing wireless communication market.* …快速增长的无线通讯市场。
→ see **cellphone**

wir·ing /waɪərɪŋ/ N-UNCOUNT The **wiring** in a building or machine is the system of wires that supply electricity to the different parts of it. 供电线路 ❑ *Faulty wiring is the major cause of house fires.* 错误的供电线路是房屋火灾的主要原因。

wiry /waɪəri/ 1 ADJ Someone who is **wiry** is somewhat thin but is also strong. (人) 瘦而结实的 ❑ *His body is wiry and athletic.* 他的身体精瘦结实而且健壮。 2 ADJ Something such as hair or grass that is **wiry** is stiff and rough to touch. (毛发或草等) 硬而粗糙的 ❑ *Her wiry hair was pushed up on top of her head in an untidy bun.* 她那硬直的头发被向上梳起，在头顶盘成一个乱蓬蓬的髻。

Word Link *dom ≈ state of being : boredom, freedom, wisdom*

wis·dom /wɪzdəm/ 1 N-UNCOUNT **Wisdom** is the ability to use your experience and knowledge in order to make sensible decisions or judgments. 智慧 ❑ *...the patience and wisdom that comes from old age.* …老年的耐心和智慧。 2 N-SING If you talk about **the wisdom of** a particular decision or action, you are talking about how sensible it is. 明智 ❑ *Many Lithuanians have expressed doubts about the wisdom of the decision.* 许多立陶宛人都已经对这个决定是否明智表示了怀疑。

wise ♦◊◊ /waɪz/ (**wiser, wisest**) 1 ADJ A **wise** person is able to use their experience and knowledge in order to make sensible decisions and judgments. 有智慧的 ❑ *She has the air of a wise woman.* 她有才女的气质。 ● **wise·ly** ADV 英明地 [ADV with v] ❑ *The three of us stood around the machine nodding wisely.* 我们3个人站在机器周围，明白地点点头。 2 ADJ A **wise** action or decision is sensible. (行动或决定) 明智的 ❑ *It's never wise to withhold evidence.* 隐瞒证据绝不明智。 ❑ *She had made a very wise decision.* 她作出了一个非常明智的决定。 ● **wise·ly** ADV 明智地 ❑ *They've invested their money wisely.* 他们明智地把钱做了投资。

wish ♦♦◊ /wɪʃ/ (**wishes, wishing, wished**) 1 N-COUNT A **wish** is a desire or strong feeling that you want to have something or do something. 愿望 ❑ *She was sincere and genuine in her wish to make amends for the past.* 她诚恳而真心地希望弥补过去的错误。 ❑ *The decision was made against the wishes of the party leader.* 这项决定是在违背该党领袖愿望的情况下作出的。 **2** V-T/V-I If you **wish** to do something or to have it done for you, you want to do it or have it done. 想要 [FORMAL] ❑ *If you wish to go away for the weekend, our office will be delighted to make hotel reservations.* 如果您想在周末外出，我们的办事处将很高兴为您预定旅馆。 ❑ *We can dress as we wish now.* 我们如今想穿什么就可以穿什么。 **3** V-T If you **wish** something were true, you would like it to be true, even though you know that it is impossible or unlikely. 但愿 (表某事不可能成为现实) [no cont] ❑ *I wish I could do that.* 我但愿我能做那件事。 ❑ *Pa, I wish you wouldn't shout.* 爸，我但愿你不要嚷嚷了。 **4** V-I If you **wish for** something, you express the desire for that thing silently to yourself. In fairy tales, when a person wishes for something, the thing they wish for often happens by magic. 默默期盼 ❑ *Be careful what you wish for. You might get it!* 留意你所期盼的。你可能会得到它！ ● N-COUNT **Wish** is also a noun. 祈愿 ❑ *The custom is for people to try and eat 12 grapes as the clock strikes midnight. Those who are successful can make a wish.* 这个习俗是让人们在午夜钟声敲响时试着吃12颗葡萄。那些成功做到这一点的人就可以许个愿。 **5** V-T If you say that you would not **wish** a particular thing **on** someone, you mean that the thing is so unpleasant that you would not want them to be forced to experience it. (不) 希望 (不愉快的事会发生在某人身上) [no cont, with brd-neg] ❑ *It's a horrid experience and I wouldn't wish it on my worst enemy.* 这是一次可怕的经历，我甚至不希望它发生在我仇敌的身上。 **6** V-T If you **wish** someone something such as luck or happiness, you express the hope that they will be lucky or happy. 祝愿 ❑ *I wish you both a good trip.* 我祝你们俩旅途愉快。 **7** N-PLURAL If you express your good **wishes** toward someone, you are politely expressing your friendly feelings toward them and your hope that they will be successful or happy. 祝福 [POLITENESS] ❑ *I found George's story very sad. Please give him my best wishes.* 我觉得乔治的经历很可怜。请向他表达我最好的祝福。

Word Partnership *wish* 的常用搭配：

V. **get your** wish, **grant a** wish, **have a** wish, **make a** wish **1** **4**
I wish **I knew** **3**
wish **come true** **4**
N. wish ***someone*** **the best**, wish ***someone*** **luck** **6**

Note that **wish** and **want** have similar meanings, but are used differently. If you **want** something, you feel a need for it or a desire to have it. You can say that you **want** to do something, that you **want** someone to do something, or that you **want** something to happen. If you use **wish** with a "to" infinitive, this has the same meaning as **want** but is more formal. ❑ *I want to get out of here... She wished to consult him about her future.* **Wish** is normally followed by a "that"-clause, although the word "that" is often omitted from the clause. If you **wish** that something was the case, you would like it to be the case, even though this is unlikely or impossible. ❑ *I wish I lived near Miami... He wished he had phoned for a cab.* Note the use of the tenses in the examples; when **wish** is in the present tense, the past tense is used in the clause, and when **wish** is in the past tense, the past perfect tense is used in the clause.

wish·ful think·ing N-UNCOUNT If you say that an idea, wish, or hope is **wishful thinking**, you mean that it has failed to come true or is unlikely to come true. 痴心妄想 ❑ *It is wishful thinking to expect deeper change under his leadership.* 指望在他领导下有更深刻的变化是痴心妄想。

W

wist·ful /wɪstfəl/ ADJ Someone who is **wistful** is sad because they want something and know that they cannot have it. 依依不舍的 ❑ *I can't help feeling slightly wistful about the perks I'm giving up.* 我对自己将放弃的外快不由感到有点依依不舍。

wit /wɪt/ (**wits**) **1** N-UNCOUNT **Wit** is the ability to use words or ideas in an amusing, clever, and imaginative way. 风趣；机智 ❑ *Boulding was known for his biting wit.* 博尔丁以其嘲讽式的风趣而出名。 **2** N-SING If you say that someone has **the wit to** do something, you mean that they have the intelligence and understanding to make the right decision or take the right action in a particular situation. 才智 ❑ *The information is there and waiting to be accessed by anyone with the wit to use it.* 信息是现成的，等着有头脑的人去获取和利用。 **3** N-PLURAL You can refer to your ability to think quickly and effectively in a difficult situation as your **wits**. 机智 ❑ *She has used her wits to progress to the position she holds today.* 她用她的机智攀升到今天的这个位置。 **4** N-PLURAL You can use **wits** in expressions such as **frighten** someone **out of their wits** and **scare the wits out of** someone to emphasize that a person or thing worries or frightens someone very much. 神志 [EMPHASIS] ❑ *You scared us out of our wits. We heard you had an accident.* 你把我们吓坏了。我们听说你出事了。

▲ **witch** /wɪtʃ/ (**witches**) **1** N-COUNT In fairy tales, a **witch** is a woman, usually an old woman, who has evil magic powers. Witches often wear a pointed black hat. (童话中的) 女巫 **2** N-COUNT A **witch** is a man or woman who claims to have magic powers and to be able to use them for good or bad purposes. 巫师

witch·craft /wɪtʃkræft/ N-UNCOUNT **Witchcraft** is the use of magic powers, especially evil ones. 巫术 ❑ *This week Sabrina uses witchcraft to overcome her fear of giving a speech.* 这一周萨布丽娜用巫术来克服对发表演说的恐惧。

witch-hunt (**witch-hunts**) N-COUNT A **witch-hunt** is an attempt to find and punish a particular group of people who are being blamed for something, often simply because of their opinions and not because they have actually done anything wrong. (因所持观点而遭受的) 追查迫害 [DISAPPROVAL] ❑ *...Senator Joe McCarthy, who led the witch-hunt against alleged communists in the 1950s.* … 参议员乔・麦卡锡，他在20世纪50年代领导了对所谓共产党员的追查迫害。

with
❶ IN THE SAME PLACE AT THE SAME TIME
❷ OTHER USES: METHODS, FEATURES, QUALITIES

❶ **with** ♦♦♦ /wɪð, wɪθ/ **1** PREP If one person is **with** another, they are together in one place. 和…一起 (指在同一个地点) ❑ *With her were her son and daughter-in-law.* 和她在一起的是她儿子和儿媳。 **2** PREP If something is put **with** or is **with** something else, they are used at the same time. 和…同时用 ❑ *Serve hot, with pasta or rice and French beans.* 趁热端上，与意大利面或米饭和四季豆一起享用。 **3** PREP If you do something **with** someone else, you both do it together or are both involved in it. 与…一起 (做或参与某事) ❑ *Parents will be given reports on their child's progress and the right to discuss it with a teacher.* 家长将收到关于他们孩子进步的报告，并有权就此与老师一起进行探讨。

❷ **with** ♦♦♦ /wɪð, wɪθ/

Pronounced /wɪð/ for meanings **17** and **18**.

义项**17**和**18**读作 /wɪð/。

1 PREP If you fight, argue, or compete **with** someone, you oppose them. 和 (某人争斗、争论或竞争) ❑ *About a thousand students fought with riot police in the capital.* 约一千名学生在首都和防暴警察发生冲突。 **2** PREP If you do something **with** a particular tool, object, or substance, you do it using that tool, object, or substance. 用 (某种工具、物品或材料) ❑ *Remove the meat with a fork and divide it among four plates.* 用叉把肉移开，分到4个盘里。 ❑ *Pack the fruits and nuts into the jars and cover with brandy.* 把水果和坚果装进罐子，用白兰地浸没。 **3** PREP If someone stands or goes somewhere **with** something, they are carrying it. 带着 ❑ *A young woman came in with a cup of coffee.* 一个年轻女子端着一杯咖啡走了进来。 **4** PREP Someone or something **with** a particular feature or possession has that feature or possession. 具有 (某种特征) ❑ *He was in his early forties, tall and blond with bright blue eyes.* 他四十出头，高个，长着一头金发和一双明亮的蓝眼睛。 **5** PREP Someone **with** an illness has that illness. 患 (病) ❑ *I spent a week in bed with flu.* 我患了流感卧床一个星期。 **6** PREP If something is filled or covered **with** a substance or **with** things, it has that substance or those things in it or on it. 用… (充满或覆盖) ❑ *His legs were caked with dried mud.* 他的双腿结着干泥巴。 **7** PREP If you are, for example, pleased or annoyed **with** someone or something, you have that feeling toward them. 对 (某人或某事有某种感情) [adj/n PREP n] ❑ *He was still a little angry with her.* 他还是对她有点生气。 **8** PREP You use **with** to indicate what a state, quality, or action relates to, involves, or affects. 在…方面 ❑ *Our aim is to* *allow student teachers to become familiar with the classroom.* 我们的目的是让实习老师熟悉课堂。 ❑ *He still has a serious problem with money.* 他在金钱方面还存在着严重问题。 **9** PREP You use **with** when indicating the way that something is done or the feeling that a person has when they do something. 用(某种方式); 带(某种感情) ❑ *...teaching her to read music with skill and sensitivity.* …教她熟练而敏锐地识乐谱。 **10** PREP You use **with** when indicating a sound or gesture that is made when something is done, or an expression that a person has on their face when they do something. 伴着(声音或手势); 带着(表情) ❑ *With a sigh, she leant back and closed her eyes.* 伴着一声叹息，她往后一靠，闭上了眼睛。 **11** PREP You use **with** to indicate the feeling that makes someone have a particular appearance or type of behavior. 由于(某种感情而使某人有某种表现或行为) ❑ *Gil was white and trembling with anger.* 吉尔由于生气，脸色煞白，浑身发抖。 **12** PREP You use **with** when mentioning the position or appearance of a person or thing at the time that they do something, or what someone else is doing at that time. 在…同时 [PREP n prep/-ing] ❑ *Joanne stood with her hands on the sink, staring out the window.* 乔安妮站着，同时双手放在水槽上，眼睛盯着窗外。 **13** PREP You use **with** to introduce a current situation that is a factor affecting another situation. 在…情况下 ❑ *With all the night school courses available, there is no excuse for not getting some sort of training.* 在夜校有那么多课程可供选择的条件下，就没有理由不去接受一些培训。 **14** PREP You use **with** when making a comparison or contrast between the situations of different people or things. 与(表示比较或对比) ❑ *We're not like them. It's different with us.* 我们不像他们。这对我们来说是不同的。 **15** PREP If something increases or decreases **with** a particular factor, it changes as that factor changes. 随着 [V PREP n] ❑ *The risk of developing heart disease increases with the number of cigarettes smoked.* 患心脏病的风险随着吸烟数量的增多而加大。 **16** PREP If something moves **with** a wind or current, it moves in the same direction as the wind or current. 与(风或水流)同向 ❑ *...a piece of driftwood carried down with the current.* …顺流而下的一块浮木。 **17** PREP If someone says that they are **with** you, they mean that they understand what you are saying. 理解 [v-link PREP n] [INFORMAL] ❑ *Yes, I know who you mean. Yes, now I'm with you.* 是的，我知道你指的是谁。是的，我现在理解你的意思了。 **18** PREP If someone says that they are **with** you, they mean that they support or approve of what you are doing. 支持 [v-link PREP n] ❑ *"I'm with you all the way."—"Thank you."* "我一直都支持你。"——"谢谢你。" **19** → see also **with it**

> In addition to the uses shown here, **with** is used after some verbs, nouns and adjectives in order to introduce extra information. **With** is also used in most reciprocal verbs, such as "agree" or "fight," and in some phrasal verbs, such as "deal with" and "dispense with."

Word Link *with ≈ against, away : withdraw, withhold, withstand*

with·draw ♦♦◇ /wɪðdrɔ, wɪθ-/ (**withdraws, withdrawing, withdrew, withdrawn**) **1** V-T If you **withdraw** something from a place, you remove it or take it away. 移开; 拿走 [FORMAL] ❑ *He reached into his pocket and withdrew a sheet of notepaper.* 他把手伸进口袋，拿出一张便签。 **2** V-T/V-I When groups of people such as troops **withdraw** or when someone **withdraws** them, they leave the place where they are fighting or where they are based and return nearer home. 使撤退; 撤退 ❑ *He stated that all foreign forces would withdraw as soon as the crisis ended.* 他声明危机一结束所有外国军队就会撤退。 ❑ *The United States has announced it is to withdraw forty-thousand troops from Western Europe in the next year.* 美国已经宣布第2年将从西欧撤回4万军队。 **3** V-T If you **withdraw** money from a bank account, you take it out of that account. (从银行)取(钱) ❑ *Open a savings account that does not charge ridiculous fees to withdraw money.* 开立一个取钱时不荒唐地收取费用的储蓄账户。 ❑ *They withdrew hundreds of dollars from their bank account.* 他们从他们的银行账户中提取了数百美元。 **4** V-I If you **withdraw from** an activity or organization, you stop taking part in it. (从活动或组织中)退出 ❑ *The African National Congress threatened to withdraw from the talks.* 非洲国民大会威胁要从会谈中退出。

Word Partnership *withdraw* 的常用搭配：

N. withdraw **an offer**, withdraw **support** **1**
decision to withdraw **1**–**4**
deadline to withdraw, **forces/troops** withdraw **2**
withdraw **money** **3**

▲ **with·draw·al** ♦◇◇ /wɪðdrɔəl, wɪθ-/ (**withdrawals**) **1** N-VAR The **withdrawal** of something is the act or process of removing it, or ending it. 去除; 结束 [FORMAL] ❑ *If you experience any unusual symptoms after withdrawal of the treatment then contact your doctor.* 如果在治疗结束后感到有任何异常症状，请和您的医生联系。 **2** N-UNCOUNT Someone's **withdrawal from** an activity or an organization is their decision to stop taking part in it. 退出 ❑ *...his withdrawal from government in 1946.* …1946年他从政府的退出。 **3** N-COUNT A **withdrawal** is an amount of money that you take from your bank account. 所取钱款 ❑ *I went to the machine to make the withdrawal and it told me to see someone inside the bank.* 我到取款机前取款，而机器则指示我找银行里的人。 **4** N-UNCOUNT **Withdrawal** is the period during which someone feels ill after they have stopped taking a drug they were addicted to. 戒毒过程 ❑ *Withdrawal from heroin is actually like a severe attack of gastric flu.* 戒除海洛因瘾的过程实际上就像是患了严重的胃肠性感冒。

with·drawn /wɪðdrɔn, wɪθ-/ **1** **Withdrawn** is the past participle of **withdraw**. **withdraw**的过去分词 **2** ADJ Someone who is **withdrawn** is very quiet, and does not want to talk to other people. 沉默寡言的 [v-link ADJ] ❑ *Her husband had become withdrawn and moody.* 她的丈夫变得沉默寡言而且喜怒无常。
→ see **bank**

with·drew /wɪðdru, wɪθ-/ **Withdrew** is the past tense of **withdraw**. **withdraw**的过去式

▲ **with·er** /wɪðər/ (**withers, withering, withered**) **1** V-I If someone or something **withers**, they become very weak. 变虚弱 ❑ *When he went into retirement, he visibly withered.* 到了退休年龄时，他明显变得虚弱了。 ● PHRASAL VERB **Wither away** means the same as **wither**. 变虚弱 ❑ *To see my body literally wither away before my eyes was exasperating.* 看着我的身体在自己的眼前日渐虚弱真是让人恼火。 **2** V-I If a flower or plant **withers**, it dries up and dies. (花朵或植物)枯萎 ❑ *The flowers in Isabel's room had withered.* 伊莎贝尔房间里的花朵已经枯萎了。

with·ered /wɪðərd/ ADJ If you describe a person or a part of their body as **withered**, you mean that they are thin and their skin looks old. (指人或其身体的部位)枯槁的 ❑ *Diana grasped his face in her withered hands.* 黛安娜用她枯槁的双手紧抓住他的脸。

★ **with·hold** /wɪðhoʊld, wɪθ-/ (**withholds, withholding, withheld** /wɪðhɛld, wɪθ-/) V-T If you **withhold** something that someone wants, you do not let them have it. 拒绝给 [FORMAL] ❑ *Police withheld the dead boy's name yesterday until relatives could be told.* 警察昨天拒绝在通知亲属前透露死去男孩的名字。

with·hold·ing tax (**withholding taxes**) N-VAR A **withholding tax** is an amount of money that is taken in advance from someone's income, in order to pay some of the tax they will owe. 代扣的所得税 [mainly AM, BUSINESS]

with·in ♦♦♦ /wɪðɪn, wɪθ-/ **1** PREP If something is **within** a place, area, or object, it is inside it or surrounded by it. 在…里 [FORMAL] ❑ *Clients are entertained within private dining rooms.* 客户们在私人餐厅里受到款待。 ● ADV **Within** is also an adverb. 在里面 ❑ *A small voice called from within. "Yes, just coming."* 从里面传出一个很小的声音："是的，就来了。" **2** PREP Something that happens or exists **within** a society, organization, or system, happens or exists inside it. 在(社会、组织或体系)中 ❑ *...the spirit of self-sacrifice within an army.* …军队里的自我牺牲精神。 ● ADV **Within** is also an adverb. 在内部 ❑ *The real dangers to these rebels came from within.* 对于这些叛乱分子真正的危险来自内部。 **3** PREP If something is **within** a particular limit or set of rules, it does not go beyond it or is not more than what is allowed. 在(某一限制或规则)之内 ❑ *Troops have agreed to stay within specific boundaries to avoid confrontations.* 部队已同意驻扎在特定地界内，以避免冲突。 **4** PREP If you are **within** a particular distance of a place, you are less than that distance from it. 在(一定距离)之内 ❑ *The man was within a few feet of him.* 那名男子离他只有几英尺。 **5** PREP **Within** a particular length of time means before that length of time has passed. 在(一定时间)之内 [PREP amount] ❑ *About 40% of all students entering as freshmen graduate within 4 years.* 所有新入学的学生中大约有40%在4年内毕业。 **6** PREP If something is **within sight, within earshot**, or **within reach**, you can see it, hear it, or reach it. 在(视线、听力、手臂所及的范围)之内 ❑ *His twenty-five-foot boat was moored within sight of his house.* 他那只25英尺长的小船停在他房子的视野范围之内。 **7** **within reason** → see **reason**

with·out ♦♦♦ /wɪðaʊt, wɪθ-/

In addition to the uses shown below, **without** is used in the phrasal verbs "do without," "go without," and "reckon without."

1 PREP You use **without** to indicate that someone or something does not have or use the thing mentioned. 没有 ❑ *I don't like myself without a beard.* 我不喜欢自己一根胡子没有。 ❑ *She wore a brown shirt pressed without a wrinkle.* 她穿了一件熨得没有一丝皱褶的棕色衬衫。 **2** PREP If one thing happens **without** another thing, or if you do something **without** doing something else, the second thing does not happen or occur. 没有 [PREP n/-ing] ❑ *He was offered a generous pension provided he left without a fuss.* 只要他毫无怨言地离开，他就会得到一笔丰厚的退休金。 ❑ *They worked without a break until about eight in the evening.* 他们不停地工作到大约晚上8点。 **3** PREP If you do something **without** a particular feeling, you do not have that feeling when you do it. 没有(某种感觉) ❑ *Janet Magnusson watched his approach without enthusiasm.* 珍尼特·马格努森毫无热情地看着他走近。 **4** PREP If you do something **without** someone else, they are not in the same place as you are or are not involved in the same action as you. 无(某人)在场 ❑ *I told Franklin he would have to start dinner without me.* 我告诉富兰克林他得撇下我开饭了。

Word Link *with ≈ against, away : withdraw, withhold, withstand*

with·stand /wɪðstænd, wɪθ-/ (**withstands, withstanding, withstood** /wɪðstʊd, wɪθ-/) V-T If something or someone **withstands** a force or action, they survive it or do not give in to it. 抵御 [FORMAL] ❑ *...armored vehicles designed to withstand chemical attack.* …设计来抵御化学攻击的装甲车。

wit·ness ♦◊◊ /wɪtnɪs/ (**witnesses, witnessing, witnessed**) **1** N-COUNT A **witness** to an event such as an accident or crime is a person who saw it. 目击者 ❑ *Witnesses to the crash say they saw an explosion just before the disaster.* 这起坠机事故的目击者说，在灾难发生之前他们看到了爆炸。 **2** V-T If you **witness** something, you see it happen. 目击 ❑ *Anyone who witnessed the attack should call the police.* 任何目睹了那场攻击的人都应该报警。 **3** N-COUNT A **witness** is someone who appears in a court of law to say what they know about a crime or other event. 证人 ❑ *In the next three or four days, eleven witnesses will be called to testify.* 在随后的三四天里，11名证人将传唤来作证。 **4** N-COUNT A **witness** is someone who writes their name on a document that you have signed, to confirm that it really is your signature. 连署人 ❑ *The codicil must first be signed and dated by you in the presence of two witnesses.* 该遗嘱附件必须首先由你当着两个连署人的面签名并写上日期。 **5** V-T If someone **witnesses** your signature on a document, they write their name after it, to confirm that it really is your signature. 连署 ❑ *Ask a friend, (not your spouse), to witness your signature.* 请一位朋友（不可以是你的配偶），来连署你的签名。 **6** V-T If you say that a place, period of time, or person **witnessed** a particular event or change, you mean that it happened in that place, during that period of time, or while that person was alive. 见证 ❑ *India has witnessed many political changes in recent years.* 印度近些年见证了许多政治变革。

→ see **trial, wedding**

Word Partnership *witness* 的常用搭配:

V. **call a** witness, witness **tells**, witness **testifies** **3**
N. **defense** witness, **key** witness, **material** witness, **prosecution** witness, **star** witness **3**

wit·ty /wɪti/ (**wittier, wittiest**) ADJ Someone or something that is **witty** is amusing in a clever way. 诙谐的 ❑ *His plays were very good, very witty.* 他的那些剧作非常好，非常诙谐。

wives /waɪvz/ **Wives** is the plural of **wife**. **wife**的复数形式

▲ **wiz·ard** /wɪzərd/ (**wizards**) **1** N-COUNT In legends and fairy tales, a **wizard** is a man who has magic powers. 男巫 **2** N-COUNT If you admire someone because they are very good at doing a particular thing, you can say that they are a **wizard**. 奇才 [APPROVAL] ❑ *...a financial wizard.* …一位金融奇才。 **3** N-COUNT A **wizard** is a computer program that guides you through the stages of a particular task. 向导程序 [COMPUTING] ❑ *Wizards and templates can help you create brochures, calendars, and Web pages.* 各向导程序和模板可以帮助你创建指南、日历和网页。

→ see **fantasy**

wk (**wks**) **wk** is a written abbreviation for **week**. 星期

wob·ble /wɒbᵊl/ (**wobbles, wobbling, wobbled**) V-I If something or someone **wobbles**, they make small movements from side to side, for example, because they are unsteady. 摇晃 ❑ *Some of the tables wobble.* 有的桌子摇晃。 ● N-VAR **Wobble** is also a noun. 晃动 ❑ *We might look for a tiny wobble in the position of a star.* 我们可以期待在一颗恒星位置上的一个微小晃动。

wob·bly /wɒbli/ ADJ Something that is **wobbly** moves unsteadily from side to side. 摇晃的 ❑ *I was sitting on a wobbly plastic chair.* 我当时正坐在一把摇摇晃晃的塑料椅子上。 ❑ *...a wobbly green dessert.* …一块颤动的绿色甜点。

▲ **woe** /woʊ/ N-UNCOUNT **Woe** is great sadness. 悲伤 [LITERARY] ❑ *He listened to my tale of woe.* 他听了我悲伤的故事。

woe·ful /woʊfəl/ **1** ADJ If someone or something is **woeful**, they are very sad. 悲伤的 ❑ *...a woeful ballad.* …一支悲伤的歌谣。 ● **woe·ful·ly** ADV 悲伤地 [ADV with v] ❑ *He said woefully: "I love my country, but it does not give a damn about me."* 他悲伤地说："我爱我的国家，但是它压根就不在乎我。" **2** ADJ You can use **woeful** to emphasize that something is very bad or undesirable. 糟糕透顶的 [JOURNALISM, EMPHASIS] ❑ *...the woeful state of the economy.* …这种糟糕透顶的经济状况。 ● **woe·ful·ly** ADV 糟糕透顶地 ❑ *Public expenditure on the arts is woefully inadequate.* 艺术上的公共支出严重不足。

woke /woʊk/ **Woke** is the past tense of **wake**. **wake**的过去式

wok·en /woʊkən/ **Woken** is the past participle of **wake**. **wake**的过去分词

wolf /wʊlf/ (**wolves, wolfs, wolfing, wolfed**) **1** N-COUNT A **wolf** is a wild animal that looks like a large dog. 狼 **2** V-T If someone **wolfs** their food, they eat it all very quickly and greedily. 狼吞虎咽 [INFORMAL] ❑ *Hotels were full of rich people wolfing expensive meals.* 酒店满是狼吞虎咽昂贵饭菜的有钱人。 ● PHRASAL VERB **Wolf down** means the same as **wolf**. 狼吞虎咽 ❑ *He wolfed down the rest of the biscuit and cheese.* 他狼吞虎咽地吃下了剩余的饼干和奶酪。

Word Link *man ≈ human being : foreman, humane, woman*

wom·an ♦♦♦ /wʊmən/ (**women**) **1** N-COUNT A **woman** is an adult female human being. 成年女子 ❑ *...a young Lithuanian woman named Dayva.* …一个名叫戴瓦的年轻立陶宛女子。 ❑ *...men and women over 75 years old.* …75岁以上的男女。 **2** N-UNCOUNT You can refer to women in general as **woman**. 女性 ❑ *...the oppression of woman.* …对女性的压迫。 **3** → see also **career woman**

→ see **age**

wom·an·hood /wʊmənhʊd/ **1** N-UNCOUNT **Womanhood** is the state of being a woman rather than a girl, or the period of a woman's adult life. 女子成年的状态；女子成年期 ❑ *Pregnancy is a natural part of womanhood.* 怀孕是女子成年期的一个自然部分。 **2** N-UNCOUNT You can refer to women in general or the women of a particular country or community as **womanhood**. 女性 ❑ *She symbolized for me the best of Indian womanhood.* 对我来说，她代表着最杰出的印度女性。

womb /wum/ (**wombs**) N-COUNT A woman's **womb** is the part inside her body where a baby grows before it is born. 子宫 ❑ *...the development of the fetus in the womb.* …胎儿在子宫里的发育。

wom·en /wɪmɪn/ **Women** is the plural of **woman**. **woman**的复数形式

won /wʌn/ **Won** is the past tense and past participle of **win**. **win**的过去式和过去分词

→ see **election**

won·der ♦♦◊ /wʌndər/ (**wonders, wondering, wondered**) **1** V-T/V-I If you **wonder** about something, you think about it, either because it interests you and you want to know more about it, or because you are worried or suspicious about it. 想知道 ❑ *I wondered what that noise was.* 我想知道那噪音是什么。 ❑ *"He claims to be her father," said Max. "We've been wondering about him."* "他声称是她的父亲，"马克斯说，"我们一直想知道是否如此。" **2** V-T/V-I If you **wonder at** something, you are very surprised about it or think about it in a very surprised way. 对…感到惊讶 ❑ *I could only wonder at how far this woman had come.* 我只能对这名妇女远道而来感到惊讶。 ❑ *I wonder you don't feel it too.* 我惊讶于你也感觉不到它。 **3** N-SING If you say that it is a **wonder that** something happened, you mean that it is very surprising and unexpected. 奇事 ❑ *It's a wonder that it took almost ten years.* 花了几乎十年时间，真是桩奇事。 **4** N-UNCOUNT **Wonder** is a feeling of great surprise and pleasure that you have, for example, when you see something that is very beautiful, or when something happens that you thought was impossible. 惊奇 ❑ *"That's right!" Bobby exclaimed in wonder. "How did you remember*

W

that?" "对呀！"鲍勃惊奇地喊道，"你怎么记得那件事？" 5 N-COUNT A **wonder** is something that causes people to feel great surprise or admiration. 奇迹 ❑ *...a lecture on the wonders of space and space exploration.* …一个关于太空奇迹和太空探险的讲座。 6 ADJ If you refer, for example, to a young man as a **wonder** boy, or to a new product as a **wonder** drug, you mean that they are believed by many people to be very good or very effective. 神奇的 [ADJ n] ❑ *Mickelson was hailed as the wonder boy of American golf.* 米克尔森被称颂为美国高尔夫球界的神奇男孩。 7 PHRASE You can say "**I wonder**" if you want to be very polite when you are asking someone to do something, or when you are asking them for their opinion or for information. 不知(表示礼貌地提问或求助) [POLITENESS] ❑ *I was just wondering if you could help me.* 不知你是否能帮助我。 8 PHRASE If you say "**no wonder**," "**little wonder**," or "**small wonder**," you mean that something is not surprising. 难怪(表示某事不足为奇) ❑ *No wonder my brother wasn't feeling well.* 难怪我兄弟当时感觉不舒服。 9 PHRASE You can say "**No wonder**" when you find out the reason for something that has been puzzling you for some time. (表示弄清了困惑已久的事) 难怪 ❑ *Brad was Jane's brother! No wonder he reminded me so much of her!* 布拉德是简的哥哥！难怪他很多方面使我想起她！ 10 PHRASE If you say that a person or thing **works wonders** or **does wonders**, you mean that they have a very good effect on something. 产生奇效 ❑ *A few moments of relaxation can work wonders.* 短暂的放松能产生奇效。

Word Partnership *wonder* 的常用搭配：

V.	**begin to** wonder, wonder **what happened**, **make** ***someone*** wonder 1
CONJ.	wonder **how**, wonder **what**, wonder **when**, wonder **where**, wonder **whether**, wonder **who**, wonder **why** 1 wonder **that** 3

won·der·ful ♦♦◇ /wʌndərfəl/ ADJ If you describe something or someone as **wonderful**, you think they are extremely good. 极好的 ❑ *The cold, misty air felt wonderful on his face.* 那凉凉的雾气使他脸上感觉好极了。 ❑ *It's wonderful to see you.* 见到你好极了。 ● **won·der·ful·ly** ADV 极好地 ❑ *It's a system that works wonderfully well.* 它是一个运行极好的系统。

won't /woʊnt/ **Won't** is the usual spoken form of "will not." **will not**的常用口语形式 ❑ *The space shuttle won't lift off the launch pad until Sunday at the earliest.* 这架航天飞机最早要到星期天才会发射升空。

woo /wu/ (**woos, wooing, wooed**) V-T If you **woo** people, you try to encourage them to help you, support you, or vote for you, for example, by promising them things which they would like. 争取 ❑ *They wooed customers by offering low interest rates.* 他们通过提供低利率来争取顾客。
→ see **love**

wood ♦♦◇ /wʊd/ (**woods**) 1 N-MASS **Wood** is the material that forms the trunks and branches of trees. 木头 ❑ *Their dishes were made of wood.* 他们的盘子是用木头制成的。 ❑ *There was a smell of damp wood and machine oil.* 有一股湿木头和机油的气味。 2 N-COUNT A **wood** or **woods** is a fairly large area of trees growing near each other. 树林 ❑ *After dinner Alice slipped away for a walk in the woods with Artie.* 晚饭后，艾丽斯悄悄溜到树林里与阿迪散步。 3 PHRASE If something or someone is **not out of the woods** yet, they are still having difficulties or problems. 尚未摆脱困境 [INFORMAL] ❑ *The nation's economy is not out of the woods yet.* 该国的经济尚未摆脱困境。 4 CONVENTION You can say "**knock on wood**" to indicate that you hope to have good luck in something you are doing, usually after saying that you have been lucky with it so far. 但愿好运仍在 ❑ *I got it all taken care of, knock on wood.* 我把它各个方面都照顾到了，但愿好运仍在。
→ see **energy, fire, forest**

wood·ed /wʊdɪd/ ADJ A **wooded** area is covered in trees. 树木覆盖的 ❑ *...a wooded valley.* …树木覆盖的山谷。

wood·en ♦◇◇ /wʊdᵊn/ ADJ **Wooden** objects are made of wood. 木制的 [ADJ n] ❑ *...the shop's bare brick walls and faded wooden floorboards.* …那家商店光秃秃的砖墙和褪了色的木地板。

wood·land /wʊdlənd/ (**woodlands**) N-VAR **Woodland** is land with a lot of trees. 林地 ❑ *...an area of dense woodland.* …一片茂密的林区。

wood·work /wʊdwɜrk/ 1 N-UNCOUNT You can refer to the doors and other wooden parts of a house as the **woodwork**. 木构件 ❑ *I love the living room, with its dark woodwork, oriental rugs, and chunky furniture.* 我喜欢这间起居室，它有着深色的木构件、东方地毯和厚实的家具。 2 N-UNCOUNT **Woodwork** is the activity or skill of making things out of wood. 木工活；木工手艺 ❑ *I have done woodwork for many years.* 我做过许多年木工活。

wool /wʊl/ (**wools**) 1 N-UNCOUNT **Wool** is the hair that grows on sheep and on some other animals. (羊等动物的) 毛 ❑ *A new invention means sheep do not have to be sheared – the wool just falls off.* 一项新的发明意味着羊不必被剪毛——羊毛就会脱落下来。 2 N-MASS **Wool** is a material made from animal's wool that is used to make things such as clothes, blankets, and carpets. 毛料 ❑ *...a wool overcoat.* …一件毛料大衣。

wool·en /wʊlən/
in BRIT, use **woollen**
ADJ **Woolen** clothes or materials are made from wool or from a mixture of wool and artificial fibers. 羊毛的；毛纺的 ❑ *...thick woolen socks.* …厚羊毛袜。

wool·len /wʊlən/ [BRIT] → see **woolen**

wool·ly /wʊli/ also **wooly** ADJ Something that is **woolly** is made of wool or looks like wool. 羊毛的；像羊毛的 ❑ *She wore this woolly hat with pompoms.* 她戴着这顶带绒球的羊毛帽。

word
❶ NOUN AND VERB USES
❷ PHRASES

❶ **word** ♦♦♦ /wɜrd/ (**words, wording, worded**) 1 N-COUNT A **word** is a single unit of language that can be represented in writing or speech. In English, a word has a space on either side of it when it is written. 单词 ❑ *The words stood out clearly on the page.* 这些单词清晰地呈现在页面上。 ❑ *The word "ginseng" comes from the Chinese word "Shen-seng."* **ginseng**这个词来自中文的"人参"。 2 N-PLURAL Someone's **words** are what they say or write. 话 ❑ *I was devastated when her words came true.* 她的话应验时，我感到震惊。 3 N-PLURAL **The words** of a song consist of the text that is sung, in contrast to the music that is played. 歌词 ❑ *Can you hear the words on the album?* 你能听清那张专集里的歌词吗？ 4 N-SING If you have **a word** with someone, you have a short conversation with them. 简短的交谈 [SPOKEN] ❑ *I think it's time you had a word with him.* 我认为该是你和他谈一谈的时候了。 5 N-COUNT If you offer someone **a word of** something such as warning, advice, or praise, you warn, advise, or praise them. (警告、建议、赞扬等的) 话语 ❑ *A word of warning. Don't stick too precisely to what it says in the book.* 一句警告的话。不要对书上所说的抠得太死。 6 N-SING If you say that someone does **not** hear, understand, or say **a word**, you are emphasizing that they hear, understand, or say nothing at all. (说的) 话 [EMPHASIS] ❑ *I can't understand a word she says.* 她说的我一个字也听不懂。 7 N-UNCOUNT If there is **word** of something, people receive news or information about it. 消息；信息 ❑ *There is no word from the authorities on the reported attack.* 没有任何来自当局的有关攻击报道的消息。 8 N-SING If you give your **word**, you make a sincere promise to someone. 诺言 ❑ *...an adult who gave his word the boy would be supervised.* …许诺这个男孩将受到监督的一个成年人。 9 N-SING If someone gives **the word** to do something, they give an order to do it. 命令 ❑ *I want nothing said about this until I give the word.* 没有我的命令，谁对此都别发表任何议论。 10 V-T To **word** something in a particular way means to choose or use particular words to express it. 措辞 ❑ *If I had written the letter, I might have worded it differently.* 如果是我写这封信，我可能会措辞不同。 ● **-worded** COMB IN ADJ 措辞…的 ❑ *...a strongly-worded statement.* …一份措辞强硬的声明。 11 → see also **wording**
→ see **English**

❷ **word** ♦♦♦ /wɜrd/ (**words**) 1 PHRASE If you say that people consider something to be a **dirty word**, you mean that they disapprove of it. 引起反感的词 ❑ *So many people think feminism is a dirty word.* 那么多的人认为女权主义是一个令人反感的词。 2 PHRASE If you do something **from the word go**, you do it from the very beginning of a period of time or situation. 从一开始 ❑ *It's essential you make the right decisions from the word go.* 重要的是你从一开始就要做出正确的决定。 3 PHRASE You can use **in their words** or **in their own words** to indicate that you are reporting what someone said using the exact words that they used. 用某人自己的话说 ❑ *Even the Assistant Secretary of State had to admit that previous policy did not, in his words, produce results.* 就连这位国务卿助理也不得不承认以前的政策，用他本人的话说，没有产生效果。 4 PHRASE If someone has **the last**

word or **the final word** in a discussion, argument, or disagreement, they are the one who wins it or who makes the final decision. 最终意见；最终决定 ❑ *She does like to have the last word in any discussion.* 她的确喜欢在任何讨论中发表最终意见。 5 PHRASE If news or information passes by **word of mouth**, people tell it to each other rather than it being printed in written form. 口头 ❑ *The story has been passed down by word of mouth.* 这个故事是口头流传下来的。 6 PHRASE You say **in other words** in order to introduce a different, and usually simpler, explanation or interpretation of something that has just been said. 换句话说 ❑ *...coronary heart disease, in other words, heart attacks and strokes.* …冠心病，换句话说，心脏病和中风。 7 PHRASE If you say something **in your own words**, you express it in your own way, without copying or repeating someone else's description. 用某人自己的话说 ❑ *Now tell us in your own words about the events of Saturday.* 现在用你自己的话告诉我们关于星期六的事情。 8 PHRASE If you say to someone "**take my word for it**," you mean that they should believe you because you are telling the truth. 相信我的话 ❑ *You'll buy nothing but trouble if you buy that house, take my word for it.* 你如果买了那幢房子，买到的只有麻烦，相信我的话。 9 PHRASE If you repeat something **word for word**, you repeat it exactly as it was originally said or written. 逐字地 ❑ *I don't try to memorize speeches word for word.* 我不会尝试去逐字地背那些演说。 10 **the operative word** → see **operative**

★ **word·ing** /wɜrdɪŋ/ N-UNCOUNT The **wording** of a piece of writing or a speech are the words used in it, especially when these are chosen to have a particular effect. 措辞 ❑ *The two sides failed to agree on the wording of a final report.* 双方未能就一份总结报告的措辞达成一致。

word pro·cess·ing also **word-processing** N-UNCOUNT **Word processing** is the work or skill of producing printed documents using a computer. 文字处理 [COMPUTING] ❑ *Many temp agencies offer word processing courses to those with rusty office skills.* 许多临时工中介机构为那些办公技能不熟练的人开设文字处理课程。

word pro·ces·sor (**word processors**) N-COUNT A **word processor** is a computer program or a computer which is used to produce printed documents. 文字处理程序；文字处理机 [COMPUTING]

word wrap·ping N-UNCOUNT In computing, **word wrapping** is a process by which a word that comes at the end of a line is automatically moved onto a new line in order to keep the text within the margins. (文字处理中的) 自动换行 [COMPUTING]

wore /wɔr/ **Wore** is the past tense of **wear**. **wear**的过去式

work
1 VERB USES AND PHRASES
2 NOUN USES AND PHRASES
3 PHRASAL VERBS

1 **work** ◆◆◆ /wɜrk/ (**works, working, worked**) 1 V-I People who **work** have a job, usually one which they are paid to do. 工作 ❑ *I started working in a recording studio.* 我开始在一个录音棚里工作。 ❑ *He worked as a teacher for 50 years.* 他从事教师工作50年了。 ❑ *I want to work, I don't want to be on welfare.* 我想工作，我不想依靠救济。 2 V-T/V-I When you **work**, you do the things that you are paid or required to do in your job. 工作 ❑ *I can't talk to you right now – I'm working.* 我这会儿不能和你说话——我正在工作。 ❑ *He was working at his desk.* 他正在伏案工作。 ❑ *They work forty hours a week.* 他们一周工作40个小时。 3 V-I When you **work**, you spend time and effort doing a task that needs to be done or trying to achieve something. 努力从事 ❑ *Linda spends all her time working on the garden.* 琳达用所有的时间在那座花园里劳作。 ❑ *The government expressed hope that all the sides will work toward a political solution.* 该政府希望所有各方致力于一个政治解决方案。 4 V-I If someone **is working on** a particular subject or question, they are studying or researching it. 研究 ❑ *Professor Bonnet has been working for many years on molecules of this type.* 博内特教授多年来一直在研究这类分子。 5 V-I If you **work with** a person or a group of people, you spend time and effort trying to help them in some way. 帮助 ❑ *She spent a period of time working with people dying of cancer.* 她用一段时间帮助即将死于癌症的人们。 6 V-I If a machine or piece of equipment **works**, it operates and performs a particular function. (机器或设备) 运转 ❑ *The pump doesn't work and we have no running water.* 这个水泵不运转了，我们没有自来水。 7 V-I If an idea, system, or way of doing something **works**, it is successful, effective, or satisfactory. (想法、系统或方法) 奏效 ❑ *95 percent of these diets do not work.* 这些节食方法中的95%都不奏效。 8 V-I If a drug or medicine **works**, it produces a particular physical effect. (药物) 起作用 ❑ *I wake up at 6 a.m. as the sleeping pill doesn't work for more than nine hours.* 我早上6点醒来，因为这种安眠药作用不会超过9个小时。 9 V-I If your mind or brain **is working**, you are thinking about something or trying to solve a problem. (脑子或思想) 运转 ❑ *My mind was working frantically, running over the events of the evening.* 我的脑子疯狂地运转着，将那天晚上发生的事情过了一遍。 10 V-I If you **work on** an assumption or idea, you act as if it were true or base other ideas on it, until you have more information. 基于 (一个假设) 而行动 ❑ *We are working on the assumption that it was a gas explosion.* 我们正依据它是一起燃气爆炸的假设而行动。 11 V-T If you **work** someone, you make them spend time and effort doing a particular activity or job. 使干活 ❑ *They're working me too hard. I'm too old for this.* 他们让我干得太苦。我干这个年纪太大了。 12 V-T When people **work** the land, they do all the tasks involved in growing crops. 开垦 ❑ *Farmers worked the fertile valleys.* 农民们开垦了这个肥沃的山谷。 13 V-T If you **work** a machine or piece of equipment, you use or control it. 操作 (机器或设备) ❑ *Many adults still depend on their children to work the video.* 许多成年人仍依靠他们的孩子来操作录像机。 14 V-I If something **works** into a particular state or condition, it gradually moves so that it is in that state or condition. 逐渐变成 ❑ *It's important to put a lock washer on that last nut, or it can work loose.* 重要的是要在最后一个螺母上安装一个防松垫圈，否则它会逐渐变松。 15 → see also **working** 16 PHRASE If you **work** your **way** somewhere, you move or progress there slowly, and with a lot of effort or work. 逐渐移动到某处 ❑ *Rescuers were still working their way toward the trapped men.* 救援人员仍在慢慢地挪近那些被困人员。

2 **work** ◆◆◆ /wɜrk/ (**works**) 1 N-UNCOUNT People who have **work** or who are **in work** have a job, usually one which they are paid to do. 工作 ❑ *Fewer and fewer people are in work.* 越来越少的人有工作。 ❑ *I was out of work at the time.* 那时我失业了。 2 N-UNCOUNT Your **work** consists of the things you are paid or required to do in your job. 工作 ❑ *We're supposed to be running a business here. I've got work to do.* 我们本应该在这做生意。我有工作要做。 ❑ *I used to take work home, but I don't do it any more.* 我过去常把工作带回家，但现在再也不那样做了。 3 N-UNCOUNT **Work** is tasks that need to be done or things that need to be achieved. 活计 ❑ *There was a lot of work to do on their house.* 他们的房子有很多活要干。 4 N-UNCOUNT **Work** is the place where you do your job. 工作单位 ❑ *Many people travel to work by car.* 许多人乘车去工作单位。 5 N-UNCOUNT **Work** is something that you produce as a result of an activity or as a result of doing your job. 工作成果 ❑ *It can help to have an impartial third party look over your work.* 让中立的第3方来检查你的工作会有所帮助。 6 N-COUNT A **work** is something such as a painting, book, or piece of music produced by an artist, writer, or composer. 作品；著作 ❑ *In my opinion, this is Rembrandt's greatest work.* 在我看来，这是伦勃朗最伟大的作品。 7 N-UNCOUNT Someone's **work** is the study or research that they have done on a particular subject or question. 研究 ❑ *Their work shows that one-year-olds are much more likely to have allergies if either parent smokes.* 他们的研究显示，如果父母任何一方吸烟，1岁的婴儿更有可能患过敏。 8 N-UNCOUNT **Work** with a particular person or a group of people is time and effort spent trying to help them in some way. (帮助他人的) 工作 ❑ *She became involved in social and relief work among the refugees.* 她参加了针对难民的社会救济工作。 9 N-COUNT-COLL A **works** is a place where something is manufactured or where an industrial process is carried out. **Works** is used to refer to one or to more than one of these places. 工厂 ❑ *...the steelworks in Gary, Indiana.* …在印第安纳州盖瑞市的那家钢厂。 10 N-PLURAL **Works** are activities such as digging the ground or building on a large scale. 施工 ❑ *...six years of disruptive building works, road construction and urban development.* …6年混乱的建筑施工、路政和城市开发。 11 PHRASE If someone is **at work** they are doing their job or are busy doing a particular activity. 在工作；在从事某种活动 ❑ *The salvage teams are already hard at work trying to deal with the spilled oil.* 那些救援队已在拼命工作，设法处理泄漏的油。 12 PHRASE If a force or process is **at work**, it is having a particular influence or effect. 正起作用 ❑ *It is important to understand the powerful economic and social forces at work behind our own actions.* 重要的是要理解在我们自己的行动背后起作用的那些强大的经济和社会力量。 13 PHRASE If you **put** someone **to work** or **set** them **to work**, you give them a job or task to do. 给某人工作 ❑ *By stimulating the economy, we're going to put people to work.* 通过刺激经济，我们将给人们工作。 14 PHRASE If you **get to work**, **go to work**, or **set to work** on a job, task, or problem,

W

you start doing it or dealing with it. 开始工作；着手处理 ❑ *He promised to get to work on the state's massive deficit.* 他承诺着手处理该国严重的赤字问题。
→ see **book, drawing, factory, gallery**

> The verb **work** has a different meaning in the continuous tenses than it does in the simple tenses. You use the continuous tenses, with the "-ing" form, to talk about a temporary job, but the simple tenses to talk about a permanent job. For example, if you say "**I'm working in Boston**," this suggests that the situation is temporary and you may soon move to a different place. If you say "**I work in Boston**", this suggests that Boston is your permanent place of work.

Thesaurus *work* 另参见：
V. labor ❶ 1 – 3
function, go, operate, perform, run ❶ 6 7
N. business, craft, job, occupation, profession, trade, vocation; *(ant.)* entertainment, fun, pastime ❷ 1 2

❸ **work** ♦♦♦ /wɜrk/ (**works, working, worked**)
▸ **work off** PHRASAL VERB If you **work off** energy, stress, or anger, you get rid of it by doing something that requires a lot of physical effort. 发泄 ❑ *Cleaning my kitchen really works off frustration if I've had a fight with someone.* 假如我与人发生了争执，打扫厨房的确会消除沮丧。
▸ **work out** 1 PHRASAL VERB If you **work out** a solution to a problem or mystery, you manage to find the solution by thinking or talking about it. 找到（解决办法等）❑ *Negotiators are due to meet later today to work out a compromise.* 谈判者们预定在今天晚些时候会面以找到一个折中的办法。 ❑ *It took me some time to work out what was causing this.* 它花了我一些时间，找到导致这种状况的原因。 2 PHRASAL VERB If you **work out** the answer to a mathematical problem, you calculate it. 计算 ❑ *It is proving hard to work out the value of bankrupt companies' assets.* 经证明，计算破产公司的资产较难。 3 PHRASAL VERB If something **works out** at a particular amount, it is calculated to be that amount after all the facts and figures have been considered. 总计为 ❑ *The price per pound works out at $3.20.* 每磅的价格总计为$3.20。 4 PHRASAL VERB If a situation **works out** well or **works out**, it happens or progresses in a satisfactory way. 进展顺利 ❑ *Things just didn't work out as planned.* 事情没有像计划的那样进展顺利。 ❑ *The deal just isn't working out the way we were promised.* 这项交易并不如承诺我们的那样进展顺利。 5 PHRASAL VERB If a process **works itself out**, it reaches a conclusion or satisfactory end. 有满意的结果 ❑ *People involved in it think it's a nightmare, but I'm sure it will work itself out.* 参与其中的人们认为它是一场噩梦，但我确信它会有满意的结果。 6 PHRASAL VERB If you **work out**, you do physical exercises in order to make your body fit and strong. 锻炼 ❑ *Work out at a gym or swim twice a week.* 每周两次在健身房锻炼或游泳。 7 → see also **workout**
▸ **work up** 1 PHRASAL VERB If you **work** yourself **up**, you make yourself feel very upset or angry about something. 使烦恼；使发怒 ❑ *She worked herself up into a bit of a state.* 她把自己搞得有点动肝火。 2 → see also **worked up** 3 PHRASAL VERB If you **work up** the enthusiasm or courage to do something, you succeed in making yourself feel it. 激发 ❑ *Your creative talents can also be put to good use, if you can work up the energy.* 如果你能激发自己的能量，你的创新才能也能派上好用场。 4 PHRASAL VERB If you **work up** a sweat or an appetite, you make yourself sweaty or hungry by doing exercise or hard work. 通过锻炼或高强度工作而产生 ❑ *Even if you are not prepared to work up a sweat three times a week, any activity is better than none.* 即使你不准备1周流3次汗，任何活动总比没有要好。

work·able /wɜrkəbᵊl/ ADJ A **workable** idea or system is realistic and practical, and likely to be effective. 切实可行的 ❑ *Investors can simply pay cash, but this isn't a workable solution in most cases.* 投资者可以仅付现金，但这在多数情况下不是一种切实可行的解决办法。

worka·hol·ic /wɜrkəhɔlɪk/ (**workaholics**) N-COUNT A **workaholic** is a person who works most of the time and finds it difficult to stop working in order to do other things. 工作狂 [INFORMAL] ❑ *Eighteen percent of 30-year-olds claim they are workaholics.* 18%的30岁的人声称他们是工作狂。

work·book /wɜrkbʊk/ (**workbooks**) N-COUNT A **workbook** is a book to help you learn a particular subject that has questions in it with spaces for the answers. 练习册 ❑ *Just do one more exercise in this workbook.* 就再做一道这本练习册中的练习吧。

work·day /wɜrkdeɪ/ (**workdays**) also **work day** 1 N-COUNT A **workday** is the amount of time during a day that you spend doing your job. 一天的工作时间 [mainly AM] ❑ *His workday starts at 3:30 a.m. and lasts 12 hours.* 他每天的工作时间从早上3:30开始，持续12个小时。 2 N-COUNT A **workday** is a day on which people go to work. 工作日 ❑ *What's he doing home on a workday?* 工作日他在家里干什么？
→ see **union**

worked up ADJ If someone is **worked up**, they are angry or upset. 生气的；烦恼的 [v-link ADJ] ❑ *Steve shouted at her. He was really worked up now.* 斯蒂夫朝她大吼。他现在真的生气了。

work·er ♦♦♦ /wɜrkər/ (**workers**) 1 N-COUNT A particular kind of **worker** does the kind of work mentioned. 人员 ❑ *She ate her sandwich alongside several other office workers taking their break.* 她在其他几位正在休息的办公室人员旁边吃自己的三明治。 2 N-COUNT **Workers** are people who are employed in industry or business and who are not managers. 工人；员工 ❑ *Wages have been frozen and workers laid off.* 工资已被冻结，员工们下岗了。 3 N-COUNT You can use **worker** to say how well or badly someone works. 工作（好或坏）的人 ❑ *He is a hard worker and a skilled gardener.* 他是一个工作努力的人，一个技艺娴熟的园艺工。 4 → see also **social worker**
→ see **factory, union**

Thesaurus *worker* 另参见：
N. employee, help, laborer 2

work·force /wɜrkfɔrs/ (**workforces**) 1 N-COUNT The **workforce** is the total number of people in a country or region who are physically able to do a job and are available for work. 劳动力 ❑ *...a country where half the workforce is unemployed.* …一个半数劳动力无业的国家。 2 N-COUNT The **workforce** is the total number of people who are employed by a particular company. 雇员总数 ❑ *...an employer of a very large workforce.* …一个拥有大批雇员的雇主。

work·ing ♦♦♦ /wɜrkɪŋ/ (**workings**) 1 ADJ **Working** people have jobs that they are paid to do. 有工作的 [ADJ n] ❑ *Like working women anywhere, Asian women are buying convenience foods.* 像其他地方的职业妇女一样，亚洲的妇女们在购买方便食品。 2 ADJ **Working** people are ordinary people who do not have professional or very highly paid jobs. 从事普通工作的 [ADJ n] ❑ *The needs and opinions of ordinary working people were ignored.* 那些从事一般工作的普通人的需求和观点被忽视了。 3 ADJ Your **working** life is the period of your life in which you have a job or are of a suitable age to have a job. 工作的 [ADJ n] ❑ *He started his working life as a truck driver.* 他开始工作时是一名卡车司机。 4 ADJ The **working** population of an area consists of all the people in that area who have a job or who are of a suitable age to have a job. 有工作的；达到工作年龄的 [ADJ n] ❑ *Almost 13 percent of the working population is already unemployed.* 几乎13%的劳动人口已经失业。 5 ADJ **Working** conditions or practices are ones that you have in your job. 工作的（条件等）[ADJ n] ❑ *The strikers are demanding higher pay and better working conditions.* 这些罢工者正在要求更高的工资和更好的工作条件。 6 ADJ A **working** farm or business exists to do normal work and make a profit, and not only for tourists or as someone's hobby. 经营性的；赢利性的 [ADJ n] ❑ *...a vacation spent on a working farm.* …在一家赢利性农场度过的一个假期。 7 ADJ The **working** parts of a machine are the parts that move and operate the machine, in contrast to the outer case or container in which they are enclosed. 运行的（机器零部件）[ADJ n] ❑ *The reel comes complete with a set of spares for all the working parts.* 那个卷轴配有一套所有运行部件的备用件。 8 ADJ A **working** knowledge or majority is not very great, but is enough to be useful. 基本的（知识）[ADJ n] ❑ *This book was designed in order to provide a working knowledge of finance and accounts.* 本书是为提供金融和会计的基本知识而编写的。 9 N-PLURAL **The workings of** a piece of equipment, an organization, or a system are the ways in which it operates and the processes which are involved in it. 运行方式 ❑ *Neural networks are computer systems which mimic the workings of the brain.* 神经网络是模仿大脑运行的计算机系统。 10 **in working order** → see **order**

work·ing capi·tal N-UNCOUNT **Working capital** is money available for use immediately, rather than money invested in land or equipment. 周转资金 [BUSINESS] ❑ *He borrowed a further $1.5 m from conventional sources to provide working capital.* 他通过常规渠道又借了150万美金，用作周转资金。

work·ing class (**working classes**) N-COUNT-COLL **The working class** or **the working classes** are the group of people in a society who do not own much property, who have low social status, and who do jobs that involve using physical skills rather than intellectual skills. 工人阶级 ❑ *A quarter of the working class voted for him.* 1/4的工人阶级给他投了票。● ADJ **Working class** is also an adjective. 工人阶级的 ❑ *...a self-educated man from a working class background.* …一个来自工人阶级背景的自学成才的人。

work·load /wɜrkloʊd/ (**workloads**) N-COUNT The **workload** of a person or organization is the amount of work that has to be done by them. 工作量 ❑ *You need someone to bounce ideas off and share your workload.* 你需要有人和你探讨想法并分担你的工作量。

work·man /wɜrkmən/ (**workmen**) N-COUNT A **workman** is a man who works with his hands, for example, building or repairing houses or roads. 工匠；工人 ❑ *In University Square workmen are building a steel fence.* 在大学广场工人们正在筑一个钢栅栏。

work·man·ship /wɜrkmənʃɪp/ N-UNCOUNT **Workmanship** is the skill with which something is made and which affects the appearance and quality of the finished object. 工艺 ❑ *The problem may be due to poor workmanship.* 问题可能是出在拙劣的工艺上。

work·mate /wɜrkmeɪt/ (**workmates**) N-COUNT Your **workmates** are the people you work with. 同事 [mainly BRIT, INFORMAL]

work of art (**works of art**) N-COUNT A **work of art** is a painting or piece of sculpture of high quality. 艺术品 ❑ *...a collection of works of art of international significance.* …一组具有国际意义的艺术品收藏。

work·out /wɜrkaʊt/ (**workouts**) N-COUNT A **workout** is a period of physical exercise or training. 体育锻炼；体育训练 ❑ *Give your upper body a workout by using handweights.* 用哑铃锻炼一下你的上半身。 → see **muscle**

work·place /wɜrkpleɪs/ (**workplaces**) also **work place** N-COUNT Your **workplace** is the place where you work. 工作场所 ❑ *...the difficulties facing women in the workplace.* …妇女在工作场所中面临的困难。

work·sheet /wɜrkʃit/ (**worksheets**) N-COUNT A **worksheet** is a specially prepared page of exercises designed to improve your knowledge or understanding of a particular subject. 活页练习题 ❑ *Complete this worksheet before you decide on the model you want.* 在你确定课程之前，先完成这个活页练习题。

work·shop /wɜrkʃɒp/ (**workshops**) **1** N-COUNT A **workshop** is a period of discussion or practical work on a particular subject in which a group of people share their knowledge or experience. 讨论会 ❑ *Trumpeter Marcus Belgrave ran a jazz workshop for young artists.* 鼓手马库斯马贝尔格瑞夫为年轻艺术家们举办了一场爵士乐研讨会。 **2** N-COUNT A **workshop** is a building that contains tools or machinery for making or repairing things, especially using wood or metal. 车间 ❑ *...a modestly equipped workshop.* …一个装备普通的车间。

work·station /wɜrksteɪʃən/ (**workstations**) also **work station** N-COUNT A **workstation** is a screen and keyboard that are part of an office computer system. (计算机系统的) 工作站 ❑ *Or you can set up databases on any number of servers and access them from particular workstations.* 或者你可以在任意数目的服务器上建立数据库，并从特定的工作站获取数据。

work·week /wɜrkwik/ (**workweeks**) N-COUNT A **workweek** is the amount of time during a normal week that you spend doing your job. 一周工作时间 [mainly AM] ❑ *The union had sought a wage increase, a shorter workweek.* 该工会已经请求增加工资并缩短一周工作时间。

world ♦♦♦ /wɜrld/ (**worlds**) **1** N-SING **The world** is the planet that we live on. 地球 ❑ *The satellite enables us to calculate their precise location anywhere in the world.* 这颗卫星使得我们可以计算他们在地球上的任何准确位置。 **2** N-SING **The world** refers to all the people who live on this planet, and our societies, institutions, and ways of life. 世人 ❑ *The world was, and remains, shocked.* 世人震惊了，并且仍然震惊。 ❑ *He wants to show the world that anyone can learn to be an ambassador.* 他想向世人展示，任何人都能够学做一名大使。 **3** ADJ You can use **world** to describe someone or something that is one of the most important or significant of its kind on earth. 世界性的 [ADJ n] ❑ *China has once again emerged as a world power.* 中国再次成为一个世界性的强国。 **4** N-SING You can use **world** in expressions such as **the Arab world**, **the Western world**, and **the ancient world** to refer to a particular group of countries or a particular period in history. 世界 (指某些国家或时期) ❑ *Athens had strong ties to the Arab world.* 雅典与阿拉伯世界有着紧密的联系。 **5** N-COUNT Someone's **world** is the life they lead, the people they have contact with, and the things they experience. 生活世界；生活圈子 ❑ *His world seemed so different from mine.* 他的生活圈子与我的似乎是那么的不同。 **6** N-SING You can use **world** to refer to a particular field of activity, and the people involved in it. 界 ❑ *The publishing world had certainly never seen an event quite like this.* 出版界当然从未见过类似这样的事情。 **7** N-SING You can use **world** to refer to a particular group of living things, for example, **the animal world**, **the plant world**, and **the insect world**. (某生物) 界 ❑ *When it comes to dodging disaster, the champions of the insect world have to be cockroaches.* 谈到躲避灾难，昆虫界的冠军非蟑螂莫属。 **8** → see also **real world**, **Third World** **9** PHRASE If you say that someone has **the best of both worlds**, you mean that they have only the benefits of two things and none of the disadvantages. 两全其美 ❑ *Her living room provides the best of both worlds, with an office at one end and comfortable sofas at the other.* 她的起居室两全其美，一端是个办公室，另一端有舒服的沙发。 **10** PHRASE If you say that something **has done** someone **a world of good**, you mean that it has made them feel better or improved their life. 对…大有好处 [INFORMAL] ❑ *Just sit for a while and relax. It will do you a world of good.* 就坐一会儿，放松放松。这将对你大有好处。 **11** PHRASE You can use **in the world** in expressions such as **what in the world** and **who in the world** to emphasize a question, especially when expressing surprise or anger. 到底 (表示强调) [EMPHASIS] ❑ *What in the world is he doing?* 他到底在干什么呢？ **12** PHRASE You can use **in an ideal world** or **in a perfect world** when you are talking about things that you would like to happen, although you realize that they are not likely to happen. 在理想状态下 ❑ *In an ideal world Karen Stevens says she would love to stay at home with her two-and-half-year-old son.* 卡林·斯蒂芬斯说，她愿意和两岁半的儿子待在家里，但那只是理想状态。 **13** PHRASE You can use **the outside world** to refer to all the people who do not live in a particular place or who are not involved in a particular situation. 外界 ❑ *For many, the post office is the only link with the outside world.* 对许多人来说，邮局是与外界联系的惟一纽带。 **14** **not be the end of the world** → see **end** **15** **the world is your oyster** → see **oyster** **16** **on top of the world** → see **top**

Word Partnership *world* 的常用搭配：

PREP.	**all over the** world, **anywhere in the** world, **around the** world **1**
V.	**travel the** world **1**
N.	world **history**, world **peace**, world **premiere** **2**
	world **of *something*** **2** **5** **6**
	world **record** **3**

world-class ADJ A **world-class** athlete, performer, or organization is one of the best in the world. 世界级的 [JOURNALISM] ❑ *He was determined to become a world-class player.* 他下决心要成为一名世界级选手。

world-famous ADJ Someone or something that is **world-famous** is known about by people all over the world. 举世闻名的 ❑ *...the world-famous Hollywood Bowl.* …举世闻名的好莱坞露天剧场。

world·ly /wɜrldli/ **1** ADJ Someone who is **worldly** is experienced and knows about the practical or social aspects of life. 老于世故的 ❑ *He was different from anyone I had known, very worldly, everything that Duane was not.* 他不同于我认识的任何人，老于世故，与杜安完全不一样。 **2** ADJ You can refer to someone's possessions as their **worldly** goods or possessions. 物质的 [ADJ n] [LITERARY] ❑ *...a man who had given up all his worldly goods.* …一个放弃了他所有物质财产的人。

world view (**world views**) also **world-view** N-COUNT A person's **world view** is the way they see and understand the world, especially regarding issues such as politics, philosophy, and religion. 世界观 ❑ *...their Christian world view.* …他们的基督教世界观。

world war ♦◇◇ (**world wars**) N-VAR A **world war** is a war that involves countries all over the world. 世界大战 ❑ *Many senior citizens have been through two world wars.* 许多年长的公民经历了两次世界大战。

Word Link ***wide** ≈ extending throughout : nationwide, widespread, worldwide*

world·wide ♦◇◇ /wɜrldwaɪd/ ADV If something exists or happens **worldwide**, it exists or happens throughout the world. 在全世界 ❑ *His books have sold more than 20 million copies worldwide.* 他的书在全世界卖出了两千多万本。● ADJ **Worldwide** is also an adjective. 全世界的 ❑ *Today, doctors are fearing a worldwide epidemic.* 如今，医生们在担心一次世界性的流行。

W

World-Wide Web N-PROPER **The World Wide Web** is a computer system that links documents and pictures into a database that is stored in computers in many different parts of the world and that people everywhere can use. The abbreviations **WWW** and the **Web** are often used. 万维网 [COMPUTING]
→ see **Internet**

worm /wɜrm/ (**worms, worming, wormed**) 1 N-COUNT A **worm** is a small animal with a long thin body, no bones, and no legs. 蠕虫 2 V-T If you say that someone **is worming** their **way** to success, or **is worming** their **way** into someone else's affection, you disapprove of the way that they are gradually making someone trust them or like them, often in order to deceive them or gain some advantage. 赢得(欢心等) [DISAPPROVAL] ❑ *She never misses a chance to worm her way into the public's hearts.* 她从不错过任何讨公众喜爱的机会。 3 N-COUNT A **worm** is a computer program that contains a virus which duplicates itself many times in a network. 蠕虫病毒 [COMPUTING] ❑ *...a new computer worm that disables security software.* …一种使安全软件失灵的新型计算机蠕虫病毒。 4 PHRASE If you say that someone is opening **a can of worms**, you are warning them that they are planning to do or talk about something that is much more complicated, unpleasant, or difficult than they realize and that might be better left alone. 马蜂窝 ❑ *Introducing this legislation would be like opening a can of worms.* 提出这项法规会像捅了马蜂窝一样。

worm·hole /wɜrmhoul/ (**wormholes**) N-COUNT In physics, a **wormhole** is a tunnel in space that is believed to connect different parts of the universe. 蛀洞 [TECHNICAL]

worn /wɔrn/ 1 **Worn** is the past participle of **wear**. **wear**的过去分词 2 ADJ **Worn** is used to describe something that is damaged or thin because it is old and has been used a lot. 用旧的; 用坏的 ❑ *Worn rugs increase the danger of tripping.* 用旧的地毯增加了绊跌的危险。 3 ADJ If someone looks **worn**, they look tired and old. 疲倦的; 衰老的 [V-link ADJ] ❑ *She was looking very haggard and worn.* 她看上去非常憔悴而疲倦。

worn out also **worn-out** 1 ADJ Something that is **worn out** is so old, damaged, or thin from use that it cannot be used anymore. 破旧不堪的; 报废的 ❑ *Car buyers tend to replace worn-out tires with the same brand.* 汽车的买主们倾向于用同一品牌的轮胎更换废旧轮胎。 2 ADJ Someone who is **worn out** is extremely tired after hard work or a difficult or unpleasant experience. 疲惫不堪的 ❑ *Before the race, he is fine. But afterwards he is worn out.* 比赛前，他状态良好。但在赛后，他就疲惫不堪了。

wor·ried ♦◇◇ /wɜrid/ ADJ When you are **worried**, you are unhappy because you keep thinking about problems that you have or about unpleasant things that might happen in the future. 担忧的 ❑ *He seemed very worried.* 他似乎非常担忧。

wor·ri·some /wɜrisəm/ ADJ Something that is **worrisome** causes people to worry. 令人担心的 [mainly AM]
in BRIT, usually use **worrying**
❑ *It's Houston's injury that is now the most worrisome.* 休斯顿的伤现在是最令人担心的。

wor·ry ♦♦◇ /wɜri/ (**worries, worrying, worried**) 1 V-T/V-I If you **worry**, you keep thinking about problems that you have or about unpleasant things that might happen. 担心 ❑ *Don't worry, your luggage will come on afterwards by taxi.* 不要担心，你的行李随后将由出租车送到。 ❑ *I worry about her constantly.* 我一直在为她担心。 ❑ *They worry that high interest rates are keeping the dollar too high.* 他们担心高利率会使美元比值过高。 2 V-T If someone or something **worries** you, they make you anxious because you keep thinking about problems or unpleasant things that might be connected with them. 使担心 ❑ *I'm still in the early days of my recovery and that worries me.* 我仍处于恢复期的初始阶段，这使我担心。 3 V-T If someone or something does not **worry** you, you do not dislike them or you are not annoyed by them. 使烦恼(用于否定句中) [oft with neg] [SPOKEN] ❑ *The cold doesn't worry me.* 寒冷不会使我烦恼。 4 N-UNCOUNT **Worry** is the state or feeling of anxiety and unhappiness caused by the problems that you have or by thinking about unpleasant things that might happen. 忧虑 ❑ *Modern American life is full of worry: the job, the kids, money, the stock market.* 现代美国生活充满了忧虑：工作、孩子、金钱、股市。 5 N-COUNT A **worry** is a problem that you keep thinking about and that makes you unhappy. 令人烦恼的事 ❑ *My main worry was that Madeleine Johnson would still be there.* 我的主要烦恼是玛得琳•约翰逊还会在那里。

Word Partnership *worry* 的常用搭配：
N. **analysts** worry, **experts** worry, **people** worry, **no need** to worry 1
V. **begin to** worry, **don't** worry, **have things/nothing to** worry **about**, **not going to** worry 1 2

wor·ry·ing /wɜriɪŋ/ ADJ If something is **worrying**, it causes people to worry. 令人担忧的 [mainly BRIT]
in AM, usually use **worrisome**

worse /wɜrs/ 1 **Worse** is the comparative of **bad**. **bad**的比较级 2 **Worse** is the comparative of **badly**. **badly**的比较级 3 PHRASE If a situation changes **for the worse**, it becomes more unpleasant or more difficult. 更糟糕的情况 ❑ *The grandparents sigh and say how things have changed for the worse.* 祖父母叹着气然后说事情是如何变得更糟糕的。

wors·en /wɜrsən/ (**worsens, worsening, worsened**) V-T/V-I If a bad situation **worsens** or if something **worsens** it, it becomes more difficult, unpleasant, or unacceptable. 使变得更糟; 变得更糟 ❑ *The security forces had to intervene to prevent the situation worsening.* 那些安全部队不得不干预以阻止形势变得更糟。

wor·ship /wɜrʃɪp/ (**worships, worshiping, worshiped**)
in BRIT, sometimes AM use **worshipping, worshipped**
1 V-T/V-I If you **worship** a god, you show your respect to the god, for example, by saying prayers. 敬奉 ❑ *..disputes over ways of life and ways of worshiping God.* …一些在生活方式和敬奉上帝方式上的争论。 ❑ *He prefers to worship in his own home.* 他更喜欢在自己的家里敬奉神明。 ● N-UNCOUNT **Worship** is also a noun. 敬奉 ❑ *...the worship of the ancient Roman gods.* …对古罗马众神的敬奉。 ● **wor·ship·er** N-COUNT (**worshipers**) 敬神者 ❑ *She burst into tears and loud sobs that disturbed the other worshipers.* 她突然哭起来，大声抽噎，干扰了其他拜神者。 2 V-T If you **worship** someone or something, you love them or admire them very much. 爱慕 ❑ *She had worshiped him for years.* 她爱慕他已有好多年了。

worst /wɜrst/ 1 **Worst** is the superlative of **bad**. **bad**的最高级 2 **Worst** is the superlative of **badly**. **badly**的最高级 3 N-SING **The worst** is the most unpleasant or unfavorable thing that could happen or does happen. 最糟糕的情况 ❑ *Though mine safety has much improved, miners' families still fear the worst.* 虽然矿井安全已极大改善，矿工的家属们仍然担心发生最糟糕的事情。 4 **Worst** is used to form the superlative of compound adjectives beginning with "bad" and "badly." For example, the superlative of "badly-affected" is "worst-affected." 最糟糕地(以**bad**或**badly**开头的复合形容词的最高级) ❑ *The worst-affected areas were in Jefferson Parish.* 影响最严重的地区是在杰斐逊教区。 5 PHRASE You say **worst of all** to indicate that what you are about to mention is the most unpleasant or has the most disadvantages out of all the things you are mentioning. 最糟糕的是 ❑ *The people most closely affected are the passengers who were injured and, worst of all, those who lost relatives.* 受影响最严重的是那些受伤的乘客，最糟糕的是其中那些失去亲人的。 6 PHRASE You use **at worst** or **at the worst** to indicate that you are mentioning the worst thing that might happen in a situation. 最糟糕的情况是 ❑ *At best Nella would be an invalid; at worst she would die.* 最好的情况是内纳会成为一个残疾人，最糟糕的情况是她会死亡。 7 PHRASE When someone is **at their worst**, they are as unpleasant, bad, or unsuccessful as it is possible for them to be. 最糟糕的 ❑ *This was their mother at her worst. Her voice was strident, she was ready to be angry at anyone.* 这是他们的母亲最糟糕的情形。她声音刺耳，随时会对人发脾气。 8 PHRASE You use **if worst comes to worst** or **if the worst comes to the worst** to say what you might do if a situation develops in the most unfavorable way possible. 如果最糟的情形产生 ❑ *If worst comes to worst, Europe could withstand a trade war.* 如果最糟的情形产生，欧洲可以顶住一场贸易战。

worth ♦♦◇ /wɜrθ/ 1 V-T If something is **worth** a particular amount of money, it can be sold for that amount or is considered to have that value. 值…钱 [V-link "worth" amount] ❑ *A local jeweler says the pearl is worth at least $500.* 一位本地珠宝商说这颗珍珠至少值$500。 ❑ *His mother inherited a business worth 15,000 dollars a year.* 他的母亲继承了一个每年盈利15000美元的商行。 2 COMB IN QUANT **Worth** combines with amounts of money, so that when you talk about a particular amount of money**'s worth of** something, you mean the quantity of it that you can buy for that amount of money. 价值…的 [QUANT "of" n] ❑ *I went and bought about six dollars' worth of potato chips.* 我去买了价值约六美元的土豆片。 ● PRON **Worth** is also a pronoun. 价值…的 ❑ *Gold reserves had fallen to less than $3 billion worth.* 黄金储备已经降价至30亿美元以下。 **3** COMB IN QUANT **Worth** combines with time expressions, so you can use **worth** when you are saying how long an amount of something will last. For example, a week's **worth of** food is the amount of food that will last you for a week. 可维持（一段时间）的东西 [QUANT "of" n] ❑ *You've got three years' worth of research money to do what you want with.* 你有可维持3年的研究经费来做你想做的事情。 ● PRON **Worth** is also a pronoun. 可维持（一段时间）的… ❑ *There's really not very much food down there. About two weeks' worth.* 那里真的没什么食物了。大约能维持两周的。 **4** V-T If you say that something is **worth** having, you mean that it is pleasant or useful, and therefore a good thing to have. 值得（拥有）[v-link "worth" -ing] ❑ *He's decided to get a look at the house and see if it might be worth buying.* 他已经决定去看一下那所房子，看看是否值得买。 ❑ *Most things worth having never come easy.* 大多数值得拥有的东西一向来之不易。 **5** V-T If something is **worth** a particular action, or if an action is **worth** doing, it is considered to be important enough for that action. 值得（做…）[v-link "worth" n/-ing] ❑ *I am spending a lot of money and time on this boat, but is it worth it?* 我正把大量的金钱和时间花在这艘船上，但这样做值得。 ❑ *This restaurant is well worth a visit.* 这家饭店很值得光顾。 **6** PHRASE If an action or activity is **worth** someone's **while**, it will be helpful, useful, or enjoyable for them if they do it, even though it requires some effort. 值得（花某人精力）的 ❑ *It might be worth your while to go to court and ask for the agreement to be changed.* 你花精力上法庭请求更改协议可能会是值得的。 **7** **worth your weight in gold** → see **weight**

Word Partnership *worth* 的常用搭配：

N. worth **five dollars**, worth **a fortune**, worth **money**, worth **the price** **1**
worth **the effort**, worth **the risk**, worth **the trouble**, worth **a try** **5**

V. worth **buying**, worth **having** **4**
worth **fighting for**, worth **remembering**, worth **saving**, worth **watching** **5**

Word Link *less ≈ without : aimless, harmless, worthless*

worth·less /wɜ̲rθləs/ **1** ADJ Something that is **worthless** is of no real value or use. 无价值的 ❑ *The guarantee could be worthless if the store goes out of business.* 如果商店倒闭，这张保修单可能就没有价值了。 ❑ *Training is worthless unless there is proof that it works.* 训练并无价值，除非证明其有效。 **2** ADJ Someone who is described as **worthless** is considered to have no good qualities or skills. 一无是处的 ❑ *You feel you really are completely worthless and unlovable.* 你觉得你真的是一无是处、不讨人喜欢。

worth·while /wɜ̲rθwa̲ɪl/ ADJ If something is **worthwhile**, it is enjoyable or useful, and worth the time, money, or effort that is spent on it. 值得的 ❑ *The president's trip to Washington this week seems to have been worthwhile.* 该总统本周的华盛顿之行似乎是值得的。

Thesaurus *worthwhile* 另参见：

ADJ. beneficial, helpful, useful; *(ant.)* worthless

wor·thy /wɜ̲rði/ (**worthier, worthiest**) ADJ If a person or thing is **worthy of** something, they deserve it because they have the qualities or abilities required. 应得的 [FORMAL] ❑ *The bank might think you're worthy of a loan.* 这家银行可能认为你应该得到一笔贷款。

would ◆◆◆ /wəd, STRONG wʊd/

Would is a modal verb. It is usually used with the base form of a verb. In spoken English, **would** is often abbreviated to **'d**.

1 MODAL You use **would** when you are saying what someone believed, hoped, or expected to happen or be the case. 会（表示相信或期待）❑ *No one believed the soldiers stationed at the border would actually open fire.* 没人相信驻扎在边境的士兵们会真的开火。 ❑ *Would he always be like this?* 他会总像这样吗？ **2** MODAL You use **would** when saying what someone intended to do. 要（表示想要做）❑ *The statement added that although there were a number of differing views, these would be discussed by both sides.* 该声明补充说，尽管存在着许多不同的观点，但这些要由双方来讨论。 **3** MODAL You use **would** when you are referring to the result or effect of a possible situation. 会（表示可能的结果或影响）❑ *Ordinarily it would be fun to be taken to fabulous restaurants.* 被人带到豪华饭店去通常会很开心。 ❑ *It would be wrong to suggest that police officers were not annoyed by acts of indecency.* 错误的是认为警官不会为无礼行为所恼。 **4** MODAL You use **would**, or **would have** with a past participle, to indicate that you are assuming or guessing that something is true, because you have good reasons for thinking it. 一定（表示假设或猜测）❑ *You wouldn't know him.* 你一定不认识他。 ❑ *His fans would already be familiar with Caroline.* 他的崇拜者们一定已熟悉卡罗琳。 **5** MODAL You use **would** in the main clause of some "if" and "unless" sentences to indicate something you consider to be fairly unlikely to happen. 就会（同**if**和**unless**引导的从句连用，表示某事极不可能发生）❑ *If only I could get some sleep, I would be able to cope.* 要是我能睡一会儿，就可以应付。 **6** MODAL You use **would** to say that someone was willing to do something. You use **would not** to indicate that they refused to do something. 愿意 ❑ *They said they would give the police their full cooperation.* 他们说他们愿意同警方通力合作。 ❑ *He wouldn't say where he had picked up the information.* 他不愿意说出他是在哪里得到这个消息的。 **7** MODAL You use **would not** to indicate that something did not happen, often in spite of a lot of effort. 就不 ❑ *He kicked, pushed, and hurled his shoulder at the door. It wouldn't open.* 他又踢又推，还用肩膀撞门。它就是不开。 **8** MODAL You use **would**, especially with "like," "love," and "wish," when saying that someone wants to do or have a particular thing or wants a particular thing to happen. 想要 ❑ *She asked me what I would like to do and mentioned a particular job.* 她问我想做什么，而且提到了一份特别的工作。 ❑ *Ideally, she would love to become pregnant again.* 按理想来说，她想要再次怀孕。 **9** **would rather** → see **rather** **10** MODAL You use **would** with "if" clauses in questions when you are asking for permission to do something. 会（同**if**引导的从句连用，表示请求允许）❑ *Do you think it would be all right if I smoked?* 你觉得我可以吸烟吗？ **11** MODAL You use **would**, usually in questions with "like," when you are making a polite offer or invitation. 想要（在疑问句中同**like**连用，表示邀请）[POLITENESS] ❑ *Would you like a drink?* 你想喝一杯吗？ ❑ *Would you like to stay?* 你想留下来吗？ **12** MODAL You use **would**, usually in questions, when you are politely asking someone to do something. 能（表示请求）[POLITENESS] ❑ *Would you do me a favor and get rid of this letter I've just received?* 你能帮我个忙把我刚收到的这封信处理掉吗？ ❑ *Would you come in here a moment, please?* 能请你进来待一会吗？ **13** MODAL You say that someone **would** do something when it is typical of them and you are critical of it. You emphasize the word **would** when you use it in this way. 总是（表示批评）[DISAPPROVAL] ❑ *Well, you would say that: you're a man.* 哎，你总是说：你是个男人。 **14** MODAL You use **would**, or sometimes **would have** with a past participle, when you are expressing your opinion about something or seeing if people agree with you, especially when you are uncertain about what you are saying. 可能会 [VAGUENESS] ❑ *I think you'd agree he's a very respected columnist.* 我想你可能会同意，他是个十分受人尊敬的专栏作家。 ❑ *I would have thought he was too old to do that job.* 我可能会认为他年纪太大不适合做那份工作。 **15** MODAL You use **I would** when you are giving someone advice in an informal way. 会（指非正式提出建议）❑ *If I were you I would simply ring your friend's doorbell and ask for your bike back.* 如果我是你，我会按你朋友的门铃，索回自己的自行车。 **16** MODAL You use **you would** in negative sentences with verbs such as "guess" and "know" when you want to say that something is not obvious, especially something surprising. 会（用在否定句中表示吃惊）❑ *Chris is so full of artistic temperament you'd never think she was the daughter of a banker.* 克里丝如此充满艺术家的气质，你绝不会想到她是一位银行家的女儿。 **17** MODAL You use **would have** with a past participle when you are saying what was likely to have happened by a particular time. 可能会（表示过去时态的虚拟语气）❑ *Within ten weeks of the introduction, 34 million people would have been reached by our television commercials.* 在10周的宣传期内，3400万人可能会看到我们的电视广告。 **18** MODAL You use **would have** with a past participle when you are referring to the result or effect of a possible event in the past. 就会（表示过去时态的虚拟语气）❑ *My daughter would have been 17 this week if she had lived.* 我的女儿如果还活着，这个星期就满17岁了。 **19** MODAL If you say that someone **would have** liked or preferred something, you mean that they wanted to do it or have it but were unable to. 本想 ❑ *I would have liked a life in politics.* 我本想从事政治。

would-be ADJ You can use **would-be** to describe someone who wants or attempts to do a particular thing. For example, a **would-be** writer is someone who wants to be a writer. 想要成为…的；试图做…的 [ADJ n] ❑ *...a book that provides encouragement for would-be writers who cannot get their novel into print.* …一本给不能使自己的小说出版而又想当作家的人提供鼓励的书。

W

wouldn't /wʊdᵊnt/ **Wouldn't** is the usual spoken form of "would not." **would not**的常用口语形式 ❏ *They wouldn't allow me to smoke.* 他们不会允许我抽烟。

would've /wʊdəv/ **Would've** is a spoken form of "would have," when "have" is an auxiliary verb. **would have**的口语形式，其中**have**为助动词 ❏ *I knew deep down that my mom would've loved one of us to go to college.* 我深知我妈妈本希望我们中的一个上大学。

wound
❶ VERB FORM OF "WIND"
❷ INJURY

❶ **wound** /waʊnd/ **Wound** is the past tense and past participle of **wind**. **wind**的过去式和过去分词 → see **wind** ❷

❷ **wound** ♦♦◊ /wund/ (**wounds, wounding, wounded**) 1 N-COUNT A **wound** is damage to part of your body, especially a cut or a hole in your flesh, which is caused by a gun, knife, or other weapon. 伤口 ❏ *The wound is healing nicely and the patient is healthy.* 伤口在很好地愈合，病人情况良好。 2 V-T If a weapon or something sharp **wounds** you, it damages your body. 使受伤 ❏ *A bomb exploded in a hotel, killing six people and wounding another five.* 一颗炸弹在一家旅馆爆炸，致6人死亡、另5人受伤。 ● N-PLURAL **The wounded** are people who are wounded. 受伤的人 ❏ *Hospitals said they could not cope with the wounded.* 各医院说他们不能处理伤员。 3 V-T If you **are wounded** by what someone says or does, your feelings are deeply hurt. 伤害（感情） ❏ *He was deeply wounded by his son's comments.* 他被他儿子的评论深深地刺伤了。
→ see **war**

Note that when someone is hurt accidentally, for example, in a car crash or when they are playing sports, you do not use the word **wound**. You use **injury** instead. ❏ *A man and his baby were injured in the explosion... Many of the deaths that occur in cycling are due to head injuries.* In more formal English, **injury** can also be an uncount noun. ❏ *Two teenagers escaped serious injury when their car rolled down an embankment.* **Wound** is normally restricted to soldiers who are injured in battle, or to deliberate acts of violence against a particular person. ❏ *...stab wounds*

Word Partnership *wound* 的常用搭配：
N. **bullet** wound, **chest** wound, **gunshot** wound, **head** wound ❷ 1
V. **die from a** wound, wound **heals**, **inflict** a wound ❷ 1
ADJ. **fatal** wound, **open** wound ❷ 1

wound up /waʊnd ʌp/ ADJ If someone is **wound up**, they are very tense and nervous or angry. 很紧张的；生气的 ❏ *"My caddie got so wound up I had to calm him down," Lancaster said.* "我的球童很紧张，我不得不去安抚他，"兰开斯特说。

wove /woʊv/ **Wove** is the past tense of **weave**. **weave**的过去式

wo·ven /woʊvᵊn/ **Woven** is a past participle of **weave**. **weave**的过去分词

wow /waʊ/ EXCLAM You can say "**wow**" when you are very impressed, surprised, or pleased. 哇（用于表示感叹、惊讶或高兴） [INFORMAL, FEELINGS] ❏ *I thought, "Wow, what a good idea."* 我想："哇，多妙的一个主意。"

wran·gle /ræŋgᵊl/ (**wrangles, wrangling, wrangled**) V-RECIP If you say that someone **is wrangling with** someone **over** a question or issue, you mean that they have been arguing angrily for a long time about it. （长时间的）争吵 ❏ *The two sides have spent most of their time wrangling over procedural problems.* 双方花了大部分的时间争论程序上的一些问题。

wrap ♦◊◊ /ræp/ (**wraps, wrapping, wrapped**) 1 V-T When you **wrap** something, you fold paper or cloth tightly around it to cover it completely, for example, in order to protect it or so that you can give it to someone as a present. 包 ❏ *Harry had carefully bought and wrapped presents for Mark to give the children.* 哈里已精心为马克买好、包好那些给孩子们的礼物。 ● PHRASAL VERB **Wrap up** means the same as **wrap**. 包 ❏ *Diana is taking the opportunity to wrap up the family presents.* 戴安娜正在利用这个机会包装给家人的礼物。 2 V-T When you **wrap** something such as a piece of paper or cloth around another thing, you put it around it. 用…包裹 ❏ *She wrapped a handkerchief around her bleeding palm in an effort to protect it.* 她用手帕包扎她那流血的手掌来保护它。 3 → see also **wrapping** 4 PHRASE If you keep something **under wraps**, you keep it secret, often until you are ready to announce it at some time in the future. 保密 ❏ *The bids were submitted in May and were kept under wraps until October.* 标书是5月递交的，直到10月都秘而不宣。

▸ **wrap up** 1 PHRASAL VERB If you **wrap up**, you put warm clothes on. 穿上暖和的衣服 ❏ *She wrapped up in her mother's red shawl.* 她裹上妈妈的红披肩取暖。 ❏ *Kids just love being able to romp around in the fresh air without having to wrap up warm.* 孩子们就是喜欢在新鲜的空气里嬉闹，无须穿得太暖和。 2 PHRASAL VERB If you **wrap up** something such as a job or an agreement, you complete it in a satisfactory way. 圆满完成（工作）；达成（协议） ❏ *NATO defense ministers wrap up their meeting in Brussels today.* 北约国防部长们今天在布鲁塞尔圆满结束了他们的会议。 3 → see also **wrap 1**, **wrapped up**

wrapped up ADJ If someone is **wrapped up in** a particular person or thing, they spend nearly all their time thinking about them, so that they forget about other things that may be important. 专心致志的 [v-link ADJ "in/with" n] ❏ *He's too serious and dedicated, wrapped up in his career.* 他太认真、专注，一心扑在事业上。

wrap·per /ræpər/ (**wrappers**) N-COUNT A **wrapper** is a piece of paper, plastic, or thin metal that covers and protects something that you buy, especially food. （尤指食品的）外包装 ❏ *I emptied the candy wrappers from the ashtray.* 我从那个烟灰缸里倒出了那些糖纸。

wrap·ping /ræpɪŋ/ (**wrappings**) N-VAR **Wrapping** is something such as paper or plastic that is used to cover and protect something. 包装材料 ❏ *Nick asked for the tile to be delivered in waterproof wrapping.* 尼克要求这块砖放被在防水包装材料里寄送。

▲ **wrath** /ræθ/ N-UNCOUNT **Wrath** means the same as anger. 愤怒 [LITERARY] ❏ *He incurred the wrath of the authorities in speaking out against government injustices.* 他因为公开反对政府的不公正而引起当局的愤怒。

wreak /rik/ (**wreaks, wreaking, wreaked**)

Some people use the form **wrought** as the past tense and past participle of **wreak**, but many people consider this to be wrong.

V-T Something or someone that **wreaks** havoc or destruction causes a great amount of disorder or damage. 造成（混乱或严重破坏） [LITERARY, JOURNALISM] ❏ *Violent storms wreaked havoc on the French Riviera, leaving three people dead and dozens injured.* 强风暴对法国里维埃拉造成严重破坏，致使3人死亡、数十人受伤。

▲ **wreath** /riθ/ (**wreaths**) 1 N-COUNT A **wreath** is an arrangement of flowers and leaves in the shape of a circle, which you put on a grave or by a statue to show that you remember a person who has died or people who have died. 花圈 ❏ *The coffin lying before the altar was bare, except for a single wreath of white roses.* 摆在圣坛前的棺材上光秃秃的，只有一个白玫瑰花圈。 2 N-COUNT A **wreath** is a circle of leaves that some people hang somewhere in their house or on the front door as decoration. （装饰用的）花环 ❏ *A Christmas wreath exclaiming PEACE ON EARTH hangs on the restaurant door.* 一个写着"世界和平"的圣诞花环悬挂在饭店的门上。

wreck /rɛk/ (**wrecks, wrecking, wrecked**) 1 V-T To **wreck** something means to completely destroy or ruin it. 摧毁 ❏ *He wrecked the garden.* 他毁掉了那个花园。 ❏ *His life has been wrecked by the tragedy.* 他的生活被这场悲剧毁了。 2 N-COUNT A **wreck** is something such as a ship, car, plane, or building that has been destroyed, usually in an accident. （轮船、汽车、飞机或房屋失事后的）残骸 ❏ *...the wreck of a sailing ship.* …一艘帆船的残骸。 ❏ *The car was a total wreck.* 这辆车完全报废了。 3 N-COUNT A **wreck** is an accident in which a moving vehicle hits something and is damaged or destroyed. 撞车事故 [mainly AM]
in BRIT, usually use **crash**
❏ *He was killed in a car wreck.* 他在一场车祸中丧生。 4 N-COUNT If you say that someone is a **wreck**, you mean that they are very exhausted or unhealthy. 疲惫不堪的人；不健康的人 [INFORMAL] ❏ *You look a wreck.* 你看起来极度疲惫。

★ **wreck·age** /rɛkɪdʒ/ N-UNCOUNT When something such as a plane, car, or building has been destroyed, you can refer to what remains as **wreckage** or **the wreckage**. （飞机、汽车失事或房屋遭损毁后的）残骸 [also "the" N] ❏ *Mark was dragged from the burning wreckage of his car just before it exploded.* 马克刚被人从他的燃烧着的汽车残骸里拉了出来，车就爆炸了。

★ **wrench** /rɛntʃ/ (**wrenches, wrenching, wrenched**) **1** V-T If you **wrench** something that is fixed in a particular position, you pull or twist it violently, in order to move or remove it. 猛拽；猛扭 ❑ *He felt two men wrench the suitcase from his hand.* 他感觉有两个人在猛拽他手里的手提箱。 **2** V-T If you **wrench** yourself free from someone who is holding you, you get away from them by suddenly twisting the part of your body that is being held. 挣脱 ❑ *She wrenched herself from his grasp.* 她挣脱了他的把持。 ❑ *He wrenched his arm free.* 他把手臂挣脱开来。 **3** N-COUNT A **wrench** is an adjustable metal tool used for tightening or loosening metal nuts of different sizes. 活动扳手 **4** → see also **monkey wrench** **5** V-T If you **wrench** your neck, you hurt it by pulling or twisting it in an unusual way. 扭伤 ❑ *She was involved in a car accident and she wrenched her neck.* 她被卷入一场车祸，扭伤了脖子。 **6** PHRASE If someone **throws a wrench** or **throws a monkey wrench** into a process, they prevent something happening smoothly by deliberately causing a problem. 阻挠 [AM] ❑ *The decision will throw a monkey wrench into our efforts to develop a national broadband policy.* 这一决定将妨碍我们制定一个全国性宽带政策的努力。
→ see **tool**

▲ **wres·tle** /rɛsᵊl/ (**wrestles, wrestling, wrestled**) **1** V-I When you **wrestle with** a difficult problem, you try to deal with it. 试图解决 ❑ *Delegates wrestled with the problems of violence and sanctions.* 代表们试图解决暴力和制裁问题。 **2** V-I If you **wrestle** with someone, you fight them by forcing them into painful positions or throwing them to the ground, rather than by hitting them. Some people wrestle as a sport. 摔跤 ❑ *They taught me to wrestle.* 他们教我去摔跤。 **3** V-T If you **wrestle** a person or thing somewhere, you move them there using a lot of force, for example, by twisting a part of someone's body into a painful position. 费力地拉 ❑ *We had to physically wrestle the child from the man's arms.* 我们只得用力地从那个男子怀里把孩子夺过来。 **4** → see also **wrestling**

wres·tler /rɛslər/ (**wrestlers**) N-COUNT A **wrestler** is someone who wrestles as a sport. 摔跤运动员

wres·tling /rɛslɪŋ/ N-UNCOUNT **Wrestling** is a sport in which two people wrestle and try to throw each other to the ground. 摔跤运动 ❑ *...a championship wrestling match.* …一项摔跤锦标赛。

★ **wretch·ed** /rɛtʃɪd/ **1** ADJ You use **wretched** to describe someone or something that you dislike or feel angry with. 讨厌的 [ADJ n] [INFORMAL, FEELINGS] ❑ *Wretched woman, he thought, why the hell can't she wait?* 讨厌的女人，他想，她怎么就不能等等呢？ **2** ADJ Someone who feels **wretched** feels very unhappy. 极不愉快的 [FORMAL] ❑ *I feel really confused and wretched.* 我真的感到迷惑和难过。

wrig·gle /rɪgᵊl/ (**wriggles, wriggling, wriggled**) V-T/V-I If you **wriggle** or **wriggle** part of your body, you twist and turn with quick movements, for example, because you are uncomfortable. 扭来扭去 ❑ *The babies are wriggling on their tummies.* 婴儿们趴着扭来扭去。

▸ **wriggle out of** PHRASAL VERB If you say that someone has **wriggled out of** doing something, you disapprove of the fact that they have managed to avoid doing it, although they should have done it. 设法摆脱(应做的事) [DISAPPROVAL] ❑ *He's wriggled out of doing the dishes again.* 他又逃避了洗碗。

▲ **wring** /rɪŋ/ (**wrings, wringing, wrung**) **1** V-T If you **wring** something **out of** someone, you manage to make them give it to you even though they do not want to. 设法获取 ❑ *Buyers use different ruses to wring free credit out of their suppliers.* 买主们想方设法从他们那些供应商那里获取无息赊购。 **2** PHRASE If someone **wrings** their **hands**, they hold them together and twist and turn them, usually because they are very worried or upset about something. You can also say that someone is **wringing** their **hands** when they are expressing sorrow that a situation is so bad but are saying that they are unable to change it. (因焦虑、悲伤或无计可施) 纽绞双手 ❑ *We can't simply stand by wringing our hands. We have to do something.* 我们不能只站着搓手，我们得做点什么。

▸ **wring out** PHRASAL VERB When you **wring out** a wet cloth or a wet piece of clothing, you squeeze the water out of it by twisting it strongly. 拧干 ❑ *He turned away to wring out the wet shirt.* 他转身去拧干那件湿衬衫。

wrin·kle /rɪŋkᵊl/ (**wrinkles, wrinkling, wrinkled**) **1** N-COUNT **Wrinkles** are lines that form on someone's face as they grow old. 皱纹 ❑ *His face was covered with wrinkles.* 他的脸布满了皱纹。 **2** V-T/V-I When someone's skin **wrinkles** or when something **wrinkles** it, lines start to form in it because the skin is getting old or damaged. 使起皱纹；起皱纹 ❑ *The skin on her cheeks and around her eyes was beginning to wrinkle.* 她脸颊上和眼睛周围的皮肤开始起皱纹了。

● **wrin·kled** ADJ 有皱纹的 ❑ *I did indeed look older and more wrinkled than ever.* 我看起来确实比以前老了，皱纹也多了。 **3** N-COUNT A **wrinkle** is a raised fold in a piece of cloth or of paper that spoils its appearance. (布或纸上的) 皱褶 ❑ *Ben brushed smooth a wrinkle in his pants.* 本把他裤子上的一个皱褶刷平了。 **4** V-T/V-I If cloth **wrinkles**, or if someone or something **wrinkles** it, it gets folds or lines in it. 使起皱褶；起皱褶 ❑ *Her stockings wrinkled at the ankles.* 她的长袜在脚踝处起皱褶了。

● **wrin·kled** ADJ 起皱褶的 ❑ *His suit was wrinkled and he looked very tired.* 他的外套皱巴巴的，他看上去非常疲惫。 **5** V-T/V-I When you **wrinkle** your nose or forehead, or when it **wrinkles**, you tighten the muscles in your face so that the skin folds. 皱起 ❑ *Donna wrinkled her nose at her daughter.* 多娜对她的女儿皱起鼻子。
→ see **skin**

wrist /rɪst/ (**wrists**) N-COUNT Your **wrist** is the part of your body between your hand and your arm that bends when you move your hand. 手腕 ❑ *He broke his wrist climbing rocks for a cigarette ad.* 他为了一个香烟广告攀岩折断了手腕。
→ see **body, hand**

writ /rɪt/ (**writs**) N-COUNT A **writ** is a legal document that orders a person to do a particular thing. 传票 ❑ *He issued a writ against one of his accusers.* 他向其中一位指控者发出了传票。

write ♦♦♦ /raɪt/ (**writes, writing, wrote, written**) **1** V-T/V-I When you **write**, you use something such as a pen or pencil to produce words, letters, or numbers. 写 ❑ *Simply write your name and address on a postcard and send it to us.* 只要在明信片上写下你的名字和地址，然后寄给我们。 ❑ *They were still trying to teach her to read and write.* 他们当时仍在试图教她读书写字。 **2** V-T If you **write** something such as a book, a poem, or a piece of music, you create it and record it on paper or perhaps on a computer. 创作 ❑ *I had written quite a lot of orchestral music in my student days.* 我在学生时代创作了许多管弦乐曲。 ❑ *Thereafter she wrote articles for papers and magazines in Paris.* 从那以后，她为巴黎的报纸和杂志撰稿。 **3** V-I Someone who **writes** creates books, stories, or articles, usually for publication. 创作 ❑ *Jay wanted to write.* 杰伊那时想搞创作。 **4** V-T/V-I When you **write** someone or **to** someone or **write** them a letter, you give them information, ask them something, or express your feelings in a letter. 写 (信) ❑ *Apparently she had written to her aunt in Holland asking for advice.* 显然，她已给她荷兰的姑妈写信征求意见了。 ❑ *She had written him a note a couple of weeks earlier.* 两周前她曾给他写过一张便条。 ❑ *I wrote a letter to the car rental agency, explaining what had happened.* 我给汽车出租代理机构写了一封信，解释所发生的事情。 **5** **nothing to write home about** → see **home** **6** V-T When someone **writes** something such as a check, receipt, or prescription, they put the necessary information on it and usually sign it. 填写 (支票、收据或处方) ❑ *Snape wrote a receipt with a gold fountain pen.* 斯内普用自来水金笔填写了一张收据。 **7** V-I If you **write** to a computer or a disk, you record data on it. (在电脑或磁盘上) 写入 (数据) [COMPUTING] ❑ *You should write-protect all disks that you do not usually need to write to.* 你应该对你通常不需要写入内容的磁盘进行写保护。 **8** → see also **writing, written**

▸ **write back** PHRASAL VERB If you **write back** to someone who has sent you a letter, you write them a letter in reply. 回信 ❑ *Macmillan wrote back saying that he could certainly help.* 麦克米伦回信说他肯定能帮忙。

▸ **write down** PHRASAL VERB When you **write** something **down**, you record it on a piece of paper using a pen or pencil. 写下 ❑ *On the morning before starting a diet, write down your starting weight.* 早上开始节食前，记下你的起始体重。

▸ **write in** PHRASAL VERB If you **write in** to an organization, you send them a letter. (给某组织) 发函 ❑ *What's the point in writing in when you only print half the letter anyway?* 你只打印了信件的一半就寄走了，有什么用呢？

▸ **write into** PHRASAL VERB If a rule or detail **is written into** a contract, law, or agreement, it is included in it when the contract, law, or agreement is made. 写入 (合同或规定中) ❑ *They insisted that a guaranteed supply of Chinese food was written into their contracts.* 他们坚持要将保证供应中餐写入他们的那些合同中。

▸ **write off** **1** PHRASAL VERB If someone **writes off** a debt or an amount of money that has been spent on a project, they accept that they are never going to get the money back. 勾销 (债款等) [BUSINESS] ❑ *It was the president who persuaded the West to write off Polish debts.* 是总统说服西方国家勾销波兰债务的。 **2** PHRASAL VERB

W

If you **write** someone or something **off**, you decide that they are unimportant or useless and that they are not worth further serious attention. 摒弃 ❑ *He is fed up with people writing him off because of his age.* 他受够了人们因其年龄而摒弃他。 ❑ *His critics write him off as too cautious to succeed.* 评论他的人认为他不值得重视，说他太谨慎以致难以成功。 **3** PHRASAL VERB If you **write off** a plan or project, you accept that it is not going to be successful and do not continue with it. 放弃（计划或项目等）❑ *We decided to write off the rest of the day and go shopping.* 我们决定放弃那天余下的时间而去购物。 **4** PHRASAL VERB If you **write off** something such as a living expense, you deduct it from your taxes. 从税中扣除 ❑ *Teachers are still entitled to write off business expenses.* 教师仍然享有从税中扣除商业开支的权利。 **5** PHRASAL VERB If you **write off** to a company or organization, you send them a letter, usually asking for something. 发函 **6** [BRIT] → see also **write-off**

▸ **write out** **1** PHRASAL VERB When you **write out** something fairly long such as a report or a list, you write it on paper. 写出 ❑ *We had to write out a list of ten jobs we'd like to do.* 我们得列个单子，写出我们想做的10项工作。 **2** PHRASAL VERB If a character in a drama series **is written out**, he or she is taken out of the series. 取消（某一角色）❑ *Terry's character has been written out of the show.* 特里的角色已从演出中取消了。

▸ **write up** PHRASAL VERB If you **write up** something that has been done or said, you record it on paper in a neat and complete form, usually using notes that you have made. （根据笔记）整理成文 ❑ *He wrote up his visit in a report of over 600 pages.* 他把他的访问整理成了六百多页的一份报告。

Thesaurus	*write* 另参见：
V.	jot down, note down, scribble **1** author, compose, draft **2**

write-off (**write-offs**) **1** N-SING If you describe a plan or period of time as a **write-off**, you mean that it has been a failure and you have achieved nothing. 白费时间 [INFORMAL] ❑ *Today was really a write-off for me.* 今天我真是白忙了。 **2** N-COUNT A **write-off** is something, such as a living expense, that can be deducted from your taxes. 从税中扣除的费用 ❑ *She got a nice $20,000 tax write-off for 2004.* 她2004年从税中扣了可观的2万美金。

Word Link	*er, or ≈ one who does, that which does : astronomer, author, writer*

writ·er ◆◆◇ /raɪtər/ (**writers**) **1** N-COUNT A **writer** is a person who writes books, stories, or articles as a job. 作家 ❑ *Turner is a writer and critic.* 特纳是一位作家和评论家。 ❑ *...detective stories by American writers.* …美国作家们的那些侦探故事。 **2** N-COUNT The **writer** of a particular article, report, letter, or story is the person who wrote it. 撰写者 ❑ *No one is to see the document without the permission of the writer of the report.* 任何人没有报告撰写者的允许不得看这份文件。

writhe /raɪð/ (**writhes, writhing, writhed**) V-I If you **writhe**, your body twists and turns violently backward and forward, usually because you are in great pain or discomfort. （因痛苦或不适）扭动身体 ❑ *He was writhing in agony.* 他痛得直打滚。

writ·ing ◆◆◇ /raɪtɪŋ/ **1** N-UNCOUNT **Writing** is something that has been written or printed. 书面形式 ❑ *If you have a complaint about your vacation, please inform us in writing.* 如果你对你的假期有意见，请以书面形式告知我们。 **2** N-UNCOUNT You can refer to any piece of written work as **writing**, especially when you are considering the style of language used in it. 文字作品 ❑ *The writing is brutally tough and savagely humorous.* 该作品文笔痛快地犀利和极端地幽默。 **3** N-UNCOUNT **Writing** is the activity of writing, especially of writing books for money. 写作 ❑ *She had begun to be a little bored with novel writing.* 她已经开始对小说写作有点厌倦了。 **4** N-UNCOUNT Your **writing** is the way that you write with a pen or pencil, which can usually be recognized as belonging to you. 笔迹 ❑ *It was a little difficult to read your writing.* 辨认你的笔迹有点难。

writ·ten ◆◇◇ /rɪtᵊn/ **1** **Written** is the past participle of **write**. **write**的过去分词 **2** ADJ A **written** test or piece of work is one that involves writing rather than doing something practical or giving spoken answers. 书面的 ❑ *...knowledge that can be assessed in a short written test.* …用简短的书面测试可以评估的知识。 **3** ADJ A **written** agreement, rule, or law has been officially written down. 正式写成的（协议、规定、法律）[ADJ n] ❑ *The newspaper broke a written agreement not to sell certain photographs.* 该报纸违反了不出售某些摄影作品的书面协议。

wrong ◆◆◇ /rɔŋ/ (**wrongs**) **1** ADJ If you say there is something **wrong**, you mean there is something unsatisfactory about the situation, person, or thing you are talking about. 有毛病的 [v-link ADJ] ❑ *Pain is the body's way of telling us that something is wrong.* 疼痛是身体在告诉我们有地方出毛病了。 ❑ *Nobody seemed to notice anything wrong.* 似乎没人注意到有什么问题。 ❑ *What's wrong with him?* 他怎么啦？ **2** ADJ If you choose the **wrong** thing, person, or method, you make a mistake and do not choose the one that you really want. 错误的 ❑ *He went to the wrong house.* 他走错了房子。 ❑ *The wrong man had been punished.* 罚错了人。 ● ADV **Wrong** is also an adverb. 错误地 [ADV after v] ❑ *You've done it wrong.* 你做错了。 **3** ADJ If something such as a decision, choice, or action is **the wrong** one, it is not the best or most suitable one. 不恰当的 [ADJ n] ❑ *I really made the wrong decision there.* 在那一点上我的决定确实不恰当。 ❑ *The wrong choice of job might limit your chances of success.* 工作选择不当可能会限制你成功的机会。 **4** ADJ If something is **wrong**, it is incorrect and not in accordance with the facts. 错的 ❑ *How do you know that this explanation is wrong?* 你怎么知道这个解释错了？ ❑ *...a clock which showed the wrong time.* …一座时间不准的钟。 ● ADV **Wrong** is also an adverb. 错地 [ADV after v] ❑ *I must have added it up wrong, then.* 那我一定是加错了。 ❑ *It looks like it's spelled wrong.* 看起来像是拼错了。

● **wrong·ly** ADV 错地 [ADV with v] ❑ *A child was wrongly diagnosed as having a bone tumor.* 一个孩子被误诊为有骨瘤。 **5** ADJ If something is **wrong** or goes **wrong with** a machine or piece of equipment, it stops working properly. （机器或设备）有问题的 [v-link ADJ] ❑ *We think there's something wrong with the computer.* 我们认为计算机出了问题。 **6** ADJ If you are **wrong** about something, what you say or think about it is not correct. 错的 [v-link ADJ] ❑ *I was wrong about it being a casual meeting.* 我错认为那是一次非正式的会面。 ❑ *I'm sure you've got it wrong. Kate isn't like that.* 我确信你错了，凯特不像那样。 **7** ADJ If you think that someone was **wrong to** do something, you think that they should not have done it because it was bad or immoral. 不应该的 [ADJ to-inf] ❑ *She was wrong to leave her child alone.* 她丢下孩子是不应该的。 ● N-UNCOUNT **Wrong** is also a noun. 错事 ❑ *...a man who believes that he has done no wrong.* …一个相信自己没做错什么的男子。 **8** ADJ **Wrong** is used to refer to activities or actions that are considered to be morally bad and unacceptable. 不道德的 [v-link ADJ] ❑ *Is it wrong to try to save the life of someone you love?* 尽力挽救你爱的人的生命错了吗？ ❑ *They thought slavery was morally wrong.* 他们当时认为奴隶制是不道义的。 ● N-UNCOUNT **Wrong** is also a noun. 不道德 ❑ *Johnson didn't seem to be able to tell the difference between right and wrong.* 约翰逊似乎不能明辨是非。 **9** N-COUNT A **wrong** is an unfair or immoral action. 不公正的行为；不道德的行为 ❑ *No matter how difficult it might be, she had to right the terrible wrong she'd done to him.* 不管有多难，她都得纠正她对他犯下的可怕错误。 **10** ADJ You use **wrong** to describe something that is not thought to be socially acceptable or desirable. 不被认可的 [ADJ n] ❑ *If you went to the wrong school, you won't get the job.* 如果你上了一个不被认可的学校，你就会找不到工作。 **11** PHRASE If a situation **goes wrong**, it stops progressing in the way that you expected or intended, and becomes much worse. 出问题 ❑ *We should investigate what happened, what went wrong.* 我们应该调查发生了什么事情，什么地方出了问题。 **12** PHRASE If someone who is involved in an argument or dispute has behaved in a way which is morally or legally wrong, you can say that they are **in the wrong**. （道义或法律上）错的 ❑ *He didn't press charges because he was in the wrong.* 他没有提起诉讼，因为是他不对。 **13** **to get off on the wrong foot** → see **foot** **14** **to get hold of the wrong end of the stick** → see **stick**

Thesaurus	*wrong* 另参见：
ADJ.	incorrect; (*ant.*) right **4** corrupt, immoral, unjust **8**
N.	abuse, offense, sin **9**

wrong·doing /rɔŋduɪŋ/ (**wrongdoings**) N-VAR **Wrongdoing** is behavior that is illegal or immoral. 违法行为；不道德行为 ❑ *The city attorney's office hasn't found any evidence of criminal wrongdoing.* 市律师事务所还没有发现任何犯罪行为的证据。

wrong·ful /rɔŋfəl/ ADJ A **wrongful** act is one that is illegal, immoral, or unjust. 违法的；不道德的；不公正的 ❑ *He is on hunger strike in protest at what he claims is his wrongful conviction for murder.* 他正绝食抗议，声称对他谋杀罪的判决不公正。 ● **wrong·ful·ly** ADV 不公正地 [ADV with v] ❑ *The criminal justice system is in need of urgent reform to prevent more people being wrongfully imprisoned.* 刑事司法体制急需改革，以防更多的人被不公正地监禁。

wrote /roʊt/ **Wrote** is the past tense of **write**. **write**的过去式

wrought /rɔt/ V-T If something has **wrought** a change, it has made it happen. 使发生 [only past] [LITERARY, JOURNALISM] ❑ *Nuclear weapons have wrought a revolution in international relations.* 核武器已经使国际关系发生了变革。

wrung /rʌŋ/ **Wrung** is the past tense of **wring**. **wring**的过去式

wry /raɪ/ **1** ADJ If someone has a **wry** expression, it shows that they find a bad situation or a change in a situation slightly amusing. 啼笑皆非的 ❑ *Matthew allowed himself a wry smile.* 马休露出了一丝苦笑。 **2** ADJ A **wry** remark or piece of writing refers to a bad situation or a change in a situation in an amusing way. (话语或文章) 讽刺的 ❑ *There is a wry sense of humor in his work.* 他的作品里有一种讽刺的幽默。

WTO /dʌbəlyu ti oʊ/ N-PROPER **WTO** is an abbreviation for "World Trade Organization." 世界贸易组织 ❑ *The world desperately needs an effective WTO.* 世界急切需要一个有效的世贸组织。

wuss /wʊs/ (**wusses**) N-COUNT If you call someone a **wuss**, you are criticizing them for being afraid. 胆小鬼 [INFORMAL, DISAPPROVAL] ❑ *"I confess to being a big wuss," she admitted.* "我承认我是个胆小鬼。" 她实话实说。

WWW /dʌbəlyu dʌbəlyu dʌbəlyu/ **WWW** is an abbreviation for **World-Wide Web**. It appears at the beginning of website addresses in the form **www**. 万维网 [COMPUTING] ❑ *Check our website at www.harpercollins.com.* 查看我们的网站**www.harpercollins.com**。

WYSIWYG /wɪziwɪg/ **WYSIWYG** is used to refer to a computer screen display that exactly matches the way that a document will appear when it is printed. **WYSIWYG** is an abbreviation for "what you see is what you get." 所见即所得 [COMPUTING] ❑ *WYSIWYG editing makes your word processing smoother and more flexible.* "所见即所得"编辑使你的文字信息处理更加顺畅和灵活。

X also **x** /e̲ks/ (**X's, x's**) N-VAR **X** is the twenty-fourth letter of the English alphabet. 英语字母表中的第24个字母

Word Link *phob ≈ fear : homophobic, phobia, xenophobia*

xeno·pho·bia /ze̲nəfo̲u̲biə/ N-UNCOUNT **Xenophobia** is strong and unreasonable dislike or fear of people from other countries. 排外情绪; 恐外症 [FORMAL] ❑ *...a just and tolerant society which rejects xenophobia and racism.* …一个不容排外情绪和种族歧视的公正宽容的社会。

xeno·pho·bic /ze̲nəfo̲u̲bɪk/ ADJ If you describe someone as **xenophobic**, you disapprove of them because they show strong dislike or fear of people from other countries. 排外的; 有恐外症的 [FORMAL, DISAPPROVAL] ❑ *Service in the armed forces gave many Americans a less xenophobic view of the world.* 在武装部队的服役使得许多美国人有了较不排外的世界观。

Xer·ox /zɪ̲ərɒks/ (**Xeroxes, Xeroxing, Xeroxed**) **1** N-COUNT A **Xerox** is a machine that can make copies of pieces of paper which have writing or other marks on them. 施乐复印机 [TRADEMARK] ❑ *The rooms are crammed with humming Xerox machines.* 那些房间里摆满了嗡嗡作响的施乐复印机。 **2** N-COUNT A **Xerox** is a copy of something written or printed on a piece of paper, which has been made using a Xerox machine. 施乐复印件 ❑ *I got a Xerox of the lyrics, handed them out, and then we had the rehearsals.* 我得到了那些歌词的施乐复印件，发给了大家，而后我们进行了排练。 **3** V-T If you **Xerox** a document, you make a copy of it using a Xerox machine. 用施乐复印机复印 ❑ *I should have simply Xeroxed this sheet for you.* 我本应该只为你复印这张。

Xmas **Xmas** is used in informal written English to represent the word Christmas. 圣诞节 (非正式书面形式) ❑ *It would be nice to have my Dad home for Xmas.* 圣诞节有爸爸在家就好了。

X-ray (**X-rays, X-raying, X-rayed**) also **x-ray** **1** N-COUNT **X-rays** are a type of radiation that can pass through most solid materials. X-rays are used by doctors to examine the bones or organs inside your body and are also used at airports to see inside people's luggage. X射线 **2** N-COUNT An **X-ray** is a picture made by sending X-rays through something, usually someone's body. X光片 ❑ *She was advised to have an abdominal X-ray.* 她被建议拍个腹部X光片。 **3** V-T If someone or something **is X-rayed**, an X-ray picture is taken of them. 给…拍摄X光片 ❑ *All hand baggage would be x-rayed.* 所有手提行李都要拍X光片。

→ see **telescope, wave**

Yy

Y also **y** /waɪ/ (**Y's, y's**) N-VAR **Y** is the twenty-fifth letter of the English alphabet. 英语字母表中的第25个字母

★ **yacht** ♦◇◇ /yɒt/ (**yachts**) N-COUNT A **yacht** is a large boat with sails or a motor, used for racing or pleasure trips. 赛艇；游艇 ❑ *His 36 ft yacht sank suddenly last summer.* 他的36英尺游艇去年夏天突然沉没了。

yacht·ing /yɒtɪŋ/ N-UNCOUNT **Yachting** is the sport or activity of sailing a yacht. 帆船运动；驾驶游艇 ❑ *...the joys of yachting.* …帆船运动的种种乐趣。

yank /yæŋk/ (**yanks, yanking, yanked**) V-T/V-I If you **yank** someone or something somewhere, you pull them there suddenly and with a lot of force. 猛拉 ❑ *She yanked open the drawer.* 她猛地拉开了抽屉。 ❑ *She couldn't open the door no matter how hard she yanked.* 她无论怎么用力猛拽都不能打开那个门。 ❑ *A quick-thinking ticket inspector yanked an emergency cord.* 一名思维敏捷的检票员猛拉了救生索。 ● N-COUNT **Yank** is also a noun. 猛拉 ❑ *Grabbing his ponytail, Shirley gave it a yank.* 雪莉抓住他的马尾辫猛地一拉。

★ **Yan·kee** /yæŋki/ (**Yankees**) **1** N-COUNT A **Yankee** is a person from a northern or northeastern state of the United States. 美国北方人 [mainly AM] **2** N-COUNT Some speakers of British English refer to anyone from the United States as a **Yankee**. This use could cause offense. 美国佬 [INFORMAL]

yard ♦♦◇ /yɑrd/ (**yards**) **1** N-COUNT A **yard** is a unit of length equal to thirty-six inches or approximately 91.4 centimeters. 码 ❑ *The incident took place about 500 yards from where he was standing.* 该事件发生在距他所站位置约五百码处。 ❑ *...a long narrow strip of linen two or three yards long.* …一条两三码长的细长亚麻布条。 **2** N-COUNT A **yard** is a flat area of concrete or stone that is next to a building and often has a wall around it. 院子 ❑ *I saw him standing in the yard.* 我看见他站在院子里。 **3** N-COUNT You can refer to a large open area where a particular type of work is done as a **yard**. (进行某种作业的)场地 ❑ *...a rail yard.* …一个铁路调车场。 **4** N-COUNT A **yard** is a piece of land next to someone's house, with grass and plants growing in it. 庭院 [AM]

in BRIT, use **garden**

❑ *He dug a hole in our yard on Edgerton Avenue to plant a maple tree when I was born.* 他在我出生时在埃杰顿大道我家的院子里挖了个坑，种了一棵枫树。

→ see **barn**

In the USA and Australia, when people need to clear out their cupboards, basements or attics (for example if they are moving house), they sometimes hold **yard sales** or **garage sales**, where they set up stalls in the yard or garage and sell unwanted items. In the UK, **car boot sales** are a very popular way of selling unwanted items. The organizers charge a small fee and in return, sellers come together, usually in a car park or a field to set out their goods in the open trunks of their cars.

yard·stick /yɑrdstɪk/ (**yardsticks**) N-COUNT If you use someone or something as a **yardstick**, you use them as a standard for comparison when you are judging other people or things. 准绳 ❑ *The book gives a yardstick for measuring assets.* 该书为评估资产提供了一种标准。

▲ **yarn** /yɑrn/ (**yarns**) N-MASS **Yarn** is thread used for knitting or making cloth. 纱线 ❑ *She still spins the yarn and knits sweaters for her family.* 她仍在为她的家人纺线织毛衣。

yawn /yɔn/ (**yawns, yawning, yawned**) V-I If you **yawn**, you open your mouth very wide and breathe in more air than usual, often when you are tired or when you are not interested in something. 打哈欠 ❑ *She yawned, and stretched lazily.* 她打了个哈欠，伸了个懒腰。 ● N-COUNT **Yawn** is also a noun. 哈欠 ❑ *Rosanna stifled a huge yawn.* 罗莎娜忍住了一个大哈欠。

→ see **sleep**

yd. (**yds.**) **yd.** is a written abbreviation for **yard**. **yard**的缩写 ❑ *The entrance is on the left 200 yds. further on up the road.* 入口在前方路左200码处。

yeah ♦♦♦ /yɛə/ **1** CONVENTION **Yeah** means yes. 是 [INFORMAL, SPOKEN] ❑ *"Bring us something to drink."—"Yeah, yeah."* "给我们拿点儿喝的来。"——"好，好。" **2** → see also **yes**

year ♦♦♦ /yɪər/ (**years**) **1** N-COUNT A **year** is a period of twelve months or 365 or 366 days, beginning on the first of January and ending on the thirty-first of December. 年 ❑ *The year was 1840.* 那是1840年。 ❑ *We had an election last year.* 我们去年进行了一次选举。 **2** → see also **leap year** **3** N-COUNT A **year** is any period of twelve months. 1年时间 ❑ *The museums attract more than two and a half million visitors a year.* 这些博物馆一年吸引二百五十多万参观者。 ❑ *She's done quite a bit of work this past year.* 她在这过去的一年里做了很多工作。 **4** N-COUNT **Year** is used to refer to the age of a person. For example, if someone or something is twenty **years** old or twenty **years** of age, they have lived or existed for twenty years. 年龄 ❑ *He's 58 years old.* 他58岁。 ❑ *I've been in trouble since I was eleven years of age.* 我从11岁以后一直处于麻烦中。 **5** N-COUNT A school **year** or academic **year** is the period of time in each twelve months when schools or colleges are open and students are studying there. The school year starts in August or September. 学年 ❑ *...the 1990/91 academic year.* …1990/91学年。 **6** N-COUNT A financial or business **year** is an exact period of twelve months which businesses or institutions use as a basis for organizing their finances. (财政) 年度 [BUSINESS] ❑ *He announced big tax increases for the next two financial years.* 他宣布了下两个财政年度的大幅税收增加。 **7** N-PLURAL You can use **years** to emphasize that you are referring to a long time. 很久 [EMPHASIS] ❑ *I haven't laughed so much in years.* 我很久没有笑这么多了。 **8** → see also **calendar year, fiscal year** **9** PHRASE If something happens **year after year**, it happens regularly every year. 年复一年 ❑ *Regulars return year after year.* 常客年年都回来。 **10** PHRASE If something changes **year by year**, it changes gradually each year. 一年一年地 ❑ *This problem has increased year by year.* 这个问题一年年地加重。 **11** PHRASE If you say something happens **all year round** or **all the year round**, it happens continually throughout the year. 全年地 ❑ *Town gardens are ideal because they produce flowers nearly all year round.* 城市花园是理想的，因为它们几乎全年都开花。

→ see Word Web: **year**

→ see **season**

Word Web year

A **year** is the time it takes the earth to orbit around the sun—about 365 **days**. The exact time is 365.242199 days. To adjust for this, every four years there is a **leap year** with 366 days. The **months** on a **calendar** were inspired by the phases of the moon. The Greeks had a 10-month calendar, but there were about 60 days left over. So the Romans added two months. The idea of seven-day **weeks** came from the Bible. The Romans named the days. We still use three of these names: Sunday (sun day), Monday (moon day), and Saturday (Saturn day).

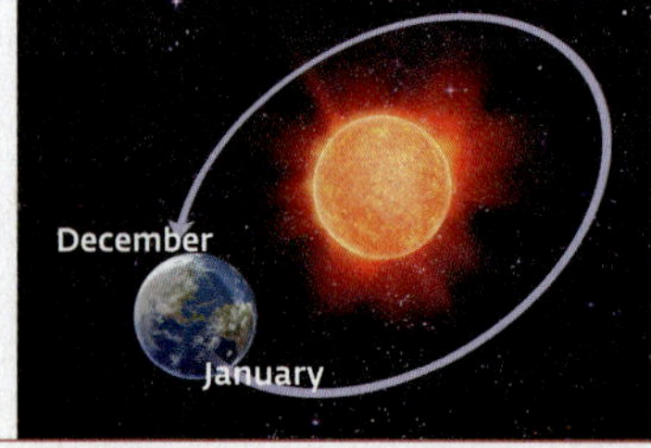

year·ly /yɪərli/ **1** ADJ A **yearly** event happens once a year or every year. 一年一度的 [ADJ n] ❑ *The two sisters looked forward to their yearly meetings.* 姐妹俩期盼着她们一年一度的会面。 ● ADV **Yearly** is also an adverb. 一年一度地 [ADV after v] ❑ *Clients normally pay fees in advance, monthly, quarterly, or yearly.* 客户们通常提前付费，或按月，或按季度，或按年。 **2** ADJ You use **yearly** to describe something such as an amount that relates to a period of one year. 年度的 [ADJ n] ❑ *In Holland, the government sets a yearly budget for health care.* 在荷兰，政府设有一个保健年度预算。 ● ADV **Yearly** is also an adverb. 年度地 [ADV after v] ❑ *Novello says college students will spend $4.2 billion yearly on alcoholic beverages.* 诺韦洛说大学生每年会在各种酒精饮料上花费42亿美元。

Thesaurus *yearly* 另参见：
ADJ. annual **1 2**

▲ **yearn** /yɜrn/ (**yearns, yearning, yearned**) V-T/V-I If someone **yearns for** something that they are unlikely to get, they want it very much. 渴望 ❑ *He yearned for freedom.* 他曾渴望自由。 ❑ *I yearned to be an actor.* 我曾渴望成为一名演员。

-year-old /-yɪər-oʊld/ (**-year-olds**) COMB IN ADJ **-year-old** combines with numbers to describe the age of people or things. (与数字合用) …岁的；…年的 [ADJ n] ❑ *She has a six-year-old daughter.* 她有个6岁的女儿。 ● COMB IN N-COUNT **-year-old** also combines to form nouns. (数字) …岁的人；…年的事物 ❑ *Snow Puppies is a ski school for 3 to 6-year-olds.* "雪小狗"是一所为3至6岁的儿童开办的滑雪学校。

yeast /yist/ (**yeasts**) N-MASS **Yeast** is a kind of fungus which is used to make bread rise, and in making alcoholic drinks such as beer. 酵母
→ see **fungus**

yell /yɛl/ (**yells, yelling, yelled**) **1** V-T/V-I If you **yell**, you shout loudly, usually because you are excited, angry, or in pain. (因兴奋、生气或痛苦) 大声叫喊 ❑ *"Eva!" he yelled.* "伊娃！"他大声叫道。 ❑ *I'm sorry I yelled at you last night.* 很抱歉我昨晚对你大喊大叫了。 ● PHRASAL VERB **Yell out** means the same as **yell**. 大声叫 ❑ *"Are you coming or not?" they yelled out after him.* "你来还是不来？"他们在他身后大声叫喊。 **2** N-COUNT A **yell** is a loud shout given by someone who is afraid or in pain. (恐惧或痛苦中的人发出的) 大声叫喊 ❑ *Something brushed past Bob's face and he let out a yell.* 什么东西擦过了鲍勃的脸，他发出了一声大叫。

Thesaurus *yell* 另参见：
V. cry, scream, shout; (*ant.*) whisper **1**

yel·low ♦♦♦ /yɛloʊ/ (**yellows**) COLOR Something that is **yellow** is the color of lemons, butter, or the middle part of an egg. 黄色 (的) ❑ *The walls have been painted bright yellow.* 这些墙壁已被漆成亮黄色。
→ see **color, rainbow**

yel·low card (**yellow cards**) N-COUNT In soccer, if a player is shown the **yellow card**, the referee holds up a yellow card to indicate that the player has broken the rules, and that if they do so again, they will be ordered to leave the field. 黄牌 ❑ *Sheringham was then shown a yellow card for dissent.* 谢林汉姆当时因不服判罚被亮了黄牌。

yen ♦◇◇ /yɛn/ (**yen**)

Yen is both the singular and the plural form.

N-COUNT The **yen** is the unit of currency used in Japan. 日元 (货币单位) ❑ *She's got a part-time job for which she earns 2,000 yen a month.* 她得到了一份每月挣2000日元的兼职工作。 ● N-SING **The yen** is also used to refer to the Japanese currency system. 日元 (货币体系) …*sterling's devaluation against the dollar and the yen.* …英镑对美元和日元的贬值。

yep /yɛp/ CONVENTION **Yep** means yes. 是 [INFORMAL, SPOKEN] ❑ *"Did you like it?"—"Yep."* "你喜欢过它吗？"——"是啊。"

yes ♦♦♦ /yɛs/

In informal English, **yes** is often pronounced in a casual way that is usually written as **yeah**.

1 CONVENTION You use **yes** to give a positive response to a question. 是的 (用以对问题作肯定回答) ❑ *"Are you a friend of Nick's?"—"Yes."* "你是尼克的朋友吗？"——"是的。" ❑ *"You actually wrote it down, didn't you?"—"Yes."* "你实际上把它写下来了，不是吗？"——"是的。"

There are many other informal ways of expressing agreement. **Yeah** is common in everyday speech. People also say **Yep, Yup, Uh-huh**, and **Mm-hmm** in informal situations. Body language for agreement is a forward nod of the head. This gesture is different in other cultures.

2 CONVENTION You use **yes** to accept an offer or request, or to give permission. 好的 (用以接受提议、要求或给予许可) ❑ *"More wine?"—"Yes please."* "再要点儿葡萄酒？"——"好的，请来点。" ❑ *"Will you take me there?"—"Yes, I will."* "你带我去那儿吗？"——"好的，我会的。" **3** CONVENTION You use **yes** to tell someone that what they have said is correct. 对 (用以告诉某人他所说的是正确的) ❑ *"Well I suppose it is based on the old lunar months, isn't it?"—"Yes, that's right."* "嗯，我想它是基于旧的阴历月份的，不是吗？"——"对，是那样的。" **4** CONVENTION You use **yes** to show that you are ready or willing to speak to the person who wants to speak to you, for example when you are answering a telephone or a knock at your door. 请讲；请进 (用于表示准备好或愿意跟想跟自己说话的人说话) ❑ *He pushed a button on the intercom. "Yes?" came a voice.* 他按了对讲机的一个按钮。"什么事？"传来一个声音。 **5** CONVENTION You use **yes** to indicate that you agree with, accept, or understand what the previous speaker has said. (用以表示同意、接受或理解前一说话者的话) 是的 ❑ *"A lot of people find it very difficult indeed to give up smoking."—"Oh yes. I used to smoke three packs a day."* "许多人发现戒烟确实很难。"——"噢，是的。我过去1天抽3包。" **6** CONVENTION You use **yes** to encourage someone to continue speaking. (用以鼓励某人继续说) 嗯哼 ❑ *"I remembered something funny today."—"Yes?"* "我今天想起件有趣的事。"——"是吗？" **7** CONVENTION You use **yes**, usually followed by "but," as a polite way of introducing what you want to say when you disagree with something the previous speaker has just said. 不错 (后接**but**，礼貌地引出反对意见) [POLITENESS] ❑ *"She is entitled to her personal allowance which is three thousand dollars of income."—"Yes, but she doesn't earn any money."* "她享有她3000美元收入的个人免税额。"——"不错，不过她根本不挣钱。" **8** CONVENTION You use **yes** to say that a negative statement or question that the previous speaker has made is wrong or untrue. 不 (用以说明前一说话人的否定陈述或问题是不正确或不真实的) ❑ *"That is not possible," she said.—"Oh, yes, it is!" Mrs. Gruen insisted.* "那是不可能的，"她说。——"哦，不，那是可能的！"格伦太太坚持道。 **9** CONVENTION You can use **yes** to suggest that you do not believe or agree with what the previous speaker has said, especially when you want to express your annoyance about it. 是吗 (用以暗示不相信或不同意前一说话人的话，尤用于想表达厌烦时) [FEELINGS] ❑ *"There was no way to stop it."—"Oh yeah? Well, here's something else you won't be able to stop."* "没法阻止它。"——"哦，是吗？那么，这儿还有别的你无法阻止的事。" **10** CONVENTION You use **yes** to indicate that you had forgotten something and have just remembered it. (表示忘了某事又刚想起来) 对了 ❑ *What was I going to say. Oh yeah, we've finally got our second computer.* 我想说什么来着？噢，对了，我们终于有了我们的第二台电脑。 **11** CONVENTION You use **yes** to emphasize and confirm a statement that you are making. 没错 (用以强调并确认所作的陈述) [EMPHASIS] ❑ *He collected the $10,000 first prize. Yes, $10,000.* 他获得了1万美元的一等奖。没错，1万美元。 **12** CONVENTION You say **yes and no** in reply to a question when you cannot give a definite answer, because in some ways the answer is yes and in other ways the answer is no. 说不好 (用以作不可断言是或不是的回答) [VAGUENESS] ❑ *"Was it strange for you, going back after such a long absence?"—"Yes and no."* "这对你来讲奇怪吗，这么长时间不在之后又回去？"——"不好说。"

yes·ter·day ♦♦♦ /yɛstərdeɪ, -di/ (**yesterdays**) **1** ADV You use **yesterday** to refer to the day before today. 昨天 [ADV with cl] ❑ *She left yesterday.* 她昨天离开了。 ● N-UNCOUNT **Yesterday** is also a noun. 昨天 ❑ *In yesterday's games, Switzerland beat the United States two to one.* 在昨天的比赛中，瑞士队2比1打败了美国队。 **2** N-UNCOUNT You can refer to the past, especially the recent past, as **yesterday**. (尤指不久前的) 过去 [also N in pl] ❑ *The worker of today is different from the worker of yesterday.* 如今的工人跟过去的工人不一样了。

yet ♦♦♦ /yɛt/ **1** ADV You use **yet** in negative statements to indicate that something has not happened up to the present time, although it probably will happen. You can also use **yet** in questions to ask if something has happened up to the present time. 尚 (用于否定句)；已经 (用于疑问句) ❑ *They haven't finished yet.* 他们还没有结束。 ❑ *No decision has yet been made.* 尚未作出决定。 ❑ *She hasn't yet set a date for her marriage.* 她尚未定下她结婚的日子。

2 ADV You use **yet** with a negative statement when you are talking about the past, to report something that was not the case then, although it became the case later. (当时) 还 (用于否定句) ❑ *There was so much that Sam didn't know yet.* 有那么多萨姆当时还不知道的。

> In British English, **yet** and **already** are usually used with the present perfect tense. ❑ *Have they said sorry or not yet?... I have already started knitting baby clothes.* In American English, a past tense is commonly used. ❑ *I didn't get any sleep yet... She already told the neighbors not to come.*

3 ADV If you say that something should not or cannot be done **yet**, you mean that it should not or cannot be done now, although it will have to be done at a later time. (此时) 还 (用于否定句) [with brd-neg, ADV with v] ❑ *Don't get up yet.* 还别起床。❑ *The hostages cannot go home just yet.* 人质们这时还不能回家。 4 ADV You use **yet** after a superlative to indicate, for example, that something is the worst or the best of its kind up to the present time. 迄今 (最…) ❑ *This is the network's worst idea yet.* 这是到目前为止该网络最糟糕的点子。❑ *Her latest novel is her best yet.* 她的最新小说是到目前为止她的最好的小说。 5 ADV You can use **yet** to say that there is still a possibility that something will happen. 仍 (用以表示某事仍有发生的可能性) [ADV before v] ❑ *Like the best stories, this one may yet have a happy ending.* 像那些最好的故事一样，这个故事可能仍有个幸福的结局。 6 ADV You can use **yet** after expressions that refer to a period of time, when you want to say how much longer a situation will continue for. 还 (会继续某段时间) [n ADV] ❑ *Unemployment will go on rising for some time yet.* 失业人数还会继续增长一段时间。❑ *Nothing will happen for a few years yet.* 几年内还不会发生什么事。 7 ADV If you say that you have **yet to** do something, you mean that you have never done it, especially when this is surprising or bad. 还 (不曾做某事) [ADV to-inf] ❑ *She has yet to spend a Christmas with her husband.* 她还不曾跟丈夫一起度过一个圣诞节。 8 CONJ You can use **yet** to introduce a fact that is rather surprising after the previous fact you have just mentioned. 然而 ❑ *I don't eat much, yet I am a size 16.* 我吃得不多，然而我是个穿16号的人。 9 ADV You can use **yet** to emphasize a word, especially when you are saying that something is surprising because it is more extreme than previous things of its kind, or a further case of them. 还 (尤用以强调令人吃惊的事物) [EMPHASIS] ❑ *I saw yet another doctor.* 我还看了另一位医生。❑ *They would criticize me, or worse yet, pay me no attention.* 他们会批评我，甚或更糟，会不理我。 10 PHRASE You use **as yet** with negative statements to describe a situation that has existed up until the present time. 迄今还 (用于否定陈述句中) [FORMAL] ❑ *As yet it is not known whether the crash was the result of an accident.* 迄今尚不知该撞击是否是由于一起事故。

yield ♦◇◇ /yild/ (**yields, yielding, yielded**) 1 V-I If you **yield to** someone or something, you stop resisting them. 屈服 [FORMAL] ❑ *Carmen yielded to general pressure and grudgingly took the child to a specialist.* 卡门屈服于普遍的压力，不得已带孩子去看了位专科大夫。 2 V-T If you **yield** something that you have control of or responsibility for, you allow someone else to have control or responsibility for it. 放弃 [FORMAL] ❑ *He may yield control.* 他可能放弃控制权。 3 V-I If a moving person or a vehicle **yields**, they slow down in order to allow other people or vehicles to pass in front of them. 让行 [AM] ❑ *When entering a trail or starting a descent, yield to other skiers.* 进入滑道或开始下滑时，给其他滑雪者们让行。❑ *...examples of common signs like No Smoking and Yield.* …像"禁止吸烟"和"让行"这样的常见标志例子。 4 V-I If something **yields**, it breaks or moves position because force or pressure has been put on it. (因受力或受压而) 破碎；断裂；移位 ❑ *He reached the massive door of the barn and pushed. It yielded.* 他够着了畜棚厚重的大门推了推。门开了。 5 V-T If an area of land **yields** a particular amount of a crop, this is the amount that is produced. You can also say that a number of animals **yield** a particular amount of meat. 产 ❑ *Last year 400,000 acres of land yielded a crop worth $1.75 billion.* 去年40万英亩的土地出产了价值17.5亿美元的粮食。 6 N-COUNT A **yield** is the amount of food produced on an area of land or by a number of animals. 产量 ❑ *...improving the yield of the crop.* …增加农作物的产量。 7 V-T If a tax or investment **yields** an amount of money or profit, this money or profit is obtained from it. 产生 (收益) [BUSINESS] ❑ *It yielded a profit of at least $36 million.* 它带来了至少三千六百万美元的利润。 8 N-COUNT A **yield** is the amount of money or profit produced by an investment. (投资的) 利润；收益 [BUSINESS] ❑ *...a yield of 4%.* …4%的收益。❑ *The high yields available on the dividend shares made them attractive to private investors.* 股息股能获得的高收益使它们对私人投资者们很有吸引力。 9 V-T If something **yields** a result or piece of information, it produces it. 产生 (结果)；制造 (消息) ❑ *This research has been in progress since 1961 and has yielded a great number of positive results.* 这项研究自1961年以来一直在开展，已经取得了大量的积极成果。

Thesaurus *yield* 另参见：

V. give in, submit, succumb, surrender; (*ant.*) resist 1 2 4
bear, produce, supply 5 7

Word Partnership *yield* 的常用搭配：

N. yield **to pressure**, yield **to temptation** 1
yield **a profit** 7
yield **information**, yield **results** 9
V. **refuse** to yield 1 – 4
ADJ. **annual** yield, **expected** yield, **high/higher** yield 6 8

yoga /yoʊgə/ N-UNCOUNT **Yoga** is a type of exercise in which you move your body into various positions in order to become more fit or flexible, to improve your breathing, and to relax your mind. 瑜伽 ❑ *I do yoga twice a week.* 我一周做两次瑜伽。

yo·ghurt /yoʊgərt/ → see **yogurt**

yo·gurt /yoʊgərt/ (**yogurts**) also **yoghurt** N-VAR **Yogurt** is a food in the form of a thick, slightly sour liquid that is made by adding bacteria to milk. A **yogurt** is a small container of yogurt. 酸奶；小包装酸奶

▲ **yolk** /yoʊk/ (**yolks**) N-VAR The **yolk** of an egg is the yellow part in the middle. 蛋黄 ❑ *Only the yolk contains cholesterol.* 只有蛋黄含胆固醇。

you ♦♦♦ /yu/

> **You** is the second person pronoun. **You** can refer to one or more people and is used as the subject of a verb or the object of a verb or preposition.

1 PRON A speaker or writer uses **you** to refer to the person or people that they are talking or writing to. It is possible to use **you** before a noun to make it clear which group of people you are talking to. 你；你们 ❑ *When I saw you across the room I knew I'd met you before.* 当看见房间对面的你时，我知道我以前曾见过你。❑ *You two seem very different to me.* 你们俩在我看来似乎很不同。 2 PRON In spoken English and informal written English, **you** is sometimes used to refer to people in general. 你 (在口语及非正式书面语中用以泛指人) ❑ *Getting good results gives you confidence.* 得到好的结果给你信心。❑ *In those days you did what you were told.* 在那些日子里你做别人让你做的事。

you'd /yud/ 1 **You'd** is the usual spoken form of "you had," when "had" is an auxiliary verb. **you had**的常用口语形式，其中**had**为助动词 ❑ *I think you'd better tell us why you're asking these questions.* 我想你最好告诉我们你为什么问这些问题？ 2 **You'd** is the usual spoken form of "you would." **you would**的常用口语形式 ❑ *With your hair and your beautiful skin, you'd look good in red and other bright colors.* 有你这样的头发和美丽的皮肤，你穿上红色和其它亮色会好看。

you'll /yul/ **You'll** is the usual spoken form of "you will." **you will**的常用口语形式 ❑ *Promise me you'll take very special care of yourself.* 答应我你会特别照顾自己。

young ♦♦♦ /yʌŋ/ (**younger** /yʌŋgər/, **youngest** /yʌŋgɪst/) 1 ADJ A **young** person, animal, or plant has not lived or existed for very long and is not yet mature. 年轻的；幼小的 (人、动物、植物等) ❑ *...sex information written for young people.* …为年轻人写的性知识。❑ *I crossed the hill, and found myself in a field of young barley.* 我翻过那座山，发现自己来到了一块大麦苗地。● N-PLURAL **The young** are people who are young. 年轻人 ❑ *The association is advising pregnant women, the very young and the elderly to avoid such foods.* 该协会在建议孕妇、幼儿和老人避免这类食品。 2 ADJ You use **young** to describe a time when a person or thing was young. 幼小的；年轻的 (时期) [ADJ n] ❑ *In her younger days my mother had been a successful saleswoman.* 在年轻的时侯，我母亲曾是位成功的推销员。 3 ADJ Someone who is **young** in appearance or behaves as if they are young. (外表、行为) 显得年轻的 ❑ *I was twenty-three, I suppose, and young for my age.* 我想我那时是23岁，看起来比我实际年龄小。 4 N-PLURAL The **young** of an animal are its babies. 幼崽；幼禽

❑ *The hen may not be able to feed its young.* 这只母鸡也许不能喂它的幼雏。
→ see **age, mammal**

Thesaurus *young* 另参见：
ADJ. childish, immature, youthful; *(ant.)* mature, old 1
N. family, litter 4

Word Link *ster ≈ one who does : barrister, gangster, youngster*

young·ster ♦◇◇ /yʌŋstər/ (**youngsters**) N-COUNT Young people, especially children, are sometimes referred to as **youngsters**. 年轻人（尤指小孩）❑ *Other youngsters are not so lucky.* 其他的年轻人没有这么幸运。

your ♦♦♦ /yɔr, yʊər/

Your is the second person possessive determiner. **Your** can refer to one or more people.

1 DET A speaker or writer uses **your** to indicate that something belongs or relates to the person or people that they are talking or writing to. 你的；你们的 ❑ *Emma, I trust your opinion a great deal.* 埃玛，我非常相信你的观点。 ❑ *I left all of your messages on your desk.* 我把你的所有便条都放到你的书桌上了。 2 DET In spoken English and informal written English, **your** is sometimes used to indicate that something belongs to or relates to people in general. 你的（口语中用于泛指属于或有关任何人的）❑ *Painkillers are very useful in small amounts to bring your temperature down.* 小剂量的止痛药对于降低体温非常有用。 3 DET In spoken English, a speaker sometimes uses **your** before an adjective such as "typical" or "normal" to indicate that the thing referred to is a typical example of its type. 人们所认为的（口语中用于形容词前，表示所指事物为某类事物的典型）❑ *This isn't your typical economics class.* 这不是人们所认为的典型的经济学课。

you're /yɔr, yʊər/ **You're** is the usual spoken form of "you are." **you are**的常用口语形式 ❑ *Go to him, tell him you're sorry.* 去找他，告诉他你很抱歉。

yours ♦◇◇ /yɔrz, yʊərz/

Yours is the second person possessive pronoun. **Yours** can refer to one or more people.

1 PRON-POSS A speaker or writer uses **yours** to refer to something that belongs or relates to the person or people that they are talking or writing to. 你的；你们的（东西）❑ *I'll take my coat upstairs. Shall I take yours, Roberta?* 我将把我的外套拿到楼上去。要我把你的拿上去吗，罗伯塔？ ❑ *I believe Paul was a friend of yours.* 我相信保罗曾是你的一个朋友。 2 CONVENTION People write **yours, yours sincerely, sincerely yours,** or **yours truly** at the end of a letter before they sign their name. 你…的（常与**truly**或**sincerely**等词连用写于信末签名前）❑ *With best regards, Yours, George.* 谨致问候。你真诚的：乔治。

your·self ♦♦◇ /yɔrsɛlf, yʊər-/ (**yourselves**)

Yourself is the second person reflexive pronoun.

1 PRON-REFL A speaker or writer uses **yourself** to refer to the person that they are talking or writing to. **Yourself** is used when the object of a verb or preposition refers to the same person as the subject of the verb. 你自己；你们自己（用于某动作的宾语和主语是同一人时）[V PRON, prep PRON] ❑ *Have the courage to be honest with yourself and about yourself.* 有勇气对自己诚实并对别人诚实。 ❑ *Your baby depends on you to look after yourself properly while you are pregnant.* 你的宝宝靠你怀孕时好好照顾你自己。 2 PRON-REFL-EMPH You use **yourself** to emphasize the person that you are referring to. 你自己（用以强调所指之人）[EMPHASIS] ❑ *You can't convince others if you yourself aren't convinced.* 如果你没有使你自己信服你就不能使别人信服。 3 PRON-REFL-EMPH You use **yourself** instead of "you" for emphasis or in order to be more polite when "you" is the object of a verb or preposition. 你自己（代替**you**作动词或介词的宾语以表示强调或更礼貌）[V PRON, prep PRON] [POLITENESS] ❑ *A wealthy man like yourself is bound to make an enemy or two along the way.* 像你自己这样的一个有钱人注定会在前进的路上树一两个敌人。 4 **by yourself** → see **by**

youth ♦♦◇ /yuθ/ (**youths** /yuðz/) 1 N-UNCOUNT Someone's **youth** is the period of their life during which they are a child, before they are a fully mature adult. 年轻时期 ❑ *In my youth my ambition had been to be an inventor.* 在我年轻时我的抱负曾是当一名发明家。 2 N-UNCOUNT **Youth** is the quality or state of being young. 年轻 ❑ *The team is now a good mixture of experience and youth.* 这支队伍现在正是经验与年轻的一个良好结合体。 3 N-COUNT Journalists often refer to young men as **youths**, especially when they are reporting that the young men have caused trouble. 年轻人（尤用于新闻报道中指惹了麻烦的年轻人）❑ *A 17-year-old youth was arrested yesterday.* 一个17岁的年轻人昨天被逮捕了。 4 N-PLURAL **The youth** are young people considered as a group. 青年人 ❑ *He represents the opinions of the youth of today.* 他代表了如今的青年人的意见。

Word Partnership *youth* 的常用搭配：
N. youth **center**, youth **culture**, youth **groups**, youth **organizations**, youth **programs**, youth **services** 4

youth·ful /yuθfəl/ ADJ Someone who is **youthful** behaves as if they are young or younger than they really are. 显得年轻的 ❑ *I'm a very youthful 50.* 我是个显得很年轻的50岁的人。 ❑ *...youthful enthusiasm and high spirits.* …青春的激情和昂扬的情绪。

youth hos·tel (**youth hostels**) N-COUNT A **youth hostel** is a place where people can stay cheaply when they are traveling. 青年旅社

you've /yuv/ **You've** is the usual spoken form of "you have," when "have" is an auxiliary verb. **you have**的常用口语形式，其中**have**为助动词 ❑ *You've got to see it to believe it.* 你要看见了才能相信。

yo-yo (**yo-yos**) N-COUNT A **yo-yo** is a toy made of a round piece of wood or plastic attached to a piece of string. You play with the yo-yo by letting it rise and fall on the string. 悠悠 ❑ *...a competition to find the boy or girl who could do the most tricks with a yo-yo.* …一场找出能用一副悠悠玩出最多花样的男孩或女孩的竞赛。

yr. (**yrs.**) **yr.** is a written abbreviation for **year**. **year**的缩写 ❑ *Their imaginations are quite something for 2 yr. olds.* 他们的想像力对于2岁的孩子而言真是了不起的东西。

yuan /yuɑn/ (**yuan**) N-COUNT The **yuan** is the unit of money used in the People's Republic of China. 元（指中国的货币单位）❑ *For most events, tickets cost one, two or three yuan.* 对于多数比赛项目而言，门票要1元、2元或3元。 ● N-SING **The yuan** is also used to refer to the Chinese currency system. 元（指中国的货币体系）["the" N] ❑ *The yuan recovered a little; it now hovers around 6.8 to the dollar.* 人民币复苏了点；它现在对美元徘徊在6.8左右。

yum·my /yʌmi/ ADJ **Yummy** food tastes very good. 好吃的 [INFORMAL] ❑ *I'll bet they have yummy ice cream.* 我打赌他们有好吃的冰激淋。 ❑ *It smells yummy.* 闻着好香。

yup·pie /yʌpi/ (**yuppies**) N-COUNT A **yuppie** is a young person who has a well-paid job and likes to show that they have a lot of money by buying expensive things and living in an expensive way. 雅皮士 [DISAPPROVAL] ❑ *The Porsche 911 reminds me of the worst parts of the yuppie era.* 这辆保时捷911使我想起了雅皮士时代最糟糕的日子。

Zz

Z also **z** /ziː/ (**Z's, z's**) N-VAR **Z** is the twenty-sixth and last letter of the English alphabet. 英语字母表中的第26个字母

zap /zæp/ (**zaps, zapping, zapped**) 1 V-T To **zap** someone or something means to kill, destroy, or hit them, for example, with a gun or in a computer game. (用枪或在电脑游戏中) 杀死; 摧毁; 击中 [INFORMAL] ❑ *A guard zapped him with the stun gun.* 一名警卫用眩晕枪击中了他。 2 V-T To **zap** something such as a computer file or document means to delete it from the computer memory or to clear it from the screen. 清除(电脑文件、文档等) [INFORMAL, COMPUTING] ❑ *"We zap millions and millions of spam mails a day from our servers," AOL spokesman Nicholas Graham said.* "我们一天要从我们的服务器上清除数以百万计的垃圾邮件,"美国在线公司发言人尼古拉斯·格雷厄姆说。

▲ **zeal** /ziːl/ N-UNCOUNT **Zeal** is great enthusiasm, especially in connection with work, religion, or politics. (尤指对工作、宗教或政治的) 热衷 ❑ *...his zeal for teaching.* …他对教学的热衷。

zeal·ous /zɛləs/ ADJ Someone who is **zealous** spends a lot of time or energy in supporting something that they believe in very strongly, especially a political or religious ideal. (尤指对政治或宗教理想) 热衷的 ❑ *She was a zealous worker for charity.* 她是个热衷于慈善事业的工作者。

Thesaurus *zealous* 另参见:
ADJ. eager, enthusiastic, gung-ho

▲ **zeb·ra** /ziːbrə/ (**zebras** or **zebra**) N-COUNT A **zebra** is an African wild horse that has black and white stripes. 斑马

zen·ith /ziːnɪθ/ N-SING The **zenith** of something is the time when it is most successful or powerful. 鼎盛时期 ❑ *His career is now at its zenith.* 他的事业现在正处于巅峰时期。

zero /zɪəroʊ/ (**zeros** or **zeroes**) 1 NUM **Zero** is the number 0. 零 ❑ *Visibility at the city's airport came down to zero, bringing air traffic to a standstill.* 这个城市机场的能见度下降到了零,使航空运输陷入停顿状态。 2 N-UNCOUNT **Zero** is a temperature of 0°. It is freezing point on the centigrade and Celsius scales, and 32° below freezing point on the Fahrenheit scale. (摄氏) 零度 ❑ *It's a sunny late winter day, just a few degrees above zero.* 这是晚冬晴朗的一天,只有零上几度。 3 ADJ You can use **zero** to say that there is none at all of the thing mentioned. 为零的 ❑ *This new ministry was being created with zero assets and zero liabilities.* 这个新部门当时是以零资产零负债进行创建。
→ see Word Web: zero

Thesaurus *zero* 另参见:
NUM. none, nothing, zilch 1

As a number, **zero** is used mainly in scientific contexts, or when you want to be precise. In spoken American English, different informal words stand for **zero**, such as **zip**. ❑ *...from zip to 60 in a fraction of one second.* However, when you are stating a telephone number, you say **o** (/oʊ/). In some sports contexts, especially in football scores, **nothing** is used. ❑ *Dallas beat San Diego 18 to nothing.* In tennis, **love** is the usual word. ❑ *...a two-games-to-love lead.*

zero-sum game N-SING If you refer to a situation as a **zero-sum game**, you mean that if one person gains an advantage from it, someone else involved must suffer an equivalent disadvantage. 零和游戏(指一方得利另一方相应失利的情形) ❑ *They believe they're playing a zero-sum game, where both must compete for the same resources.* 他们认为他们在玩一场零和游戏,双方必须争夺同样的资源。

zero tol·er·ance N-UNCOUNT If a government or organization has a policy of **zero tolerance** of a particular type of behavior or activity, they will not tolerate it at all. 零容忍 ❑ *They have a policy of zero tolerance for sexual harassment.* 他们对性骚扰采取零容忍态度。

zest /zɛst/ (**zests**) 1 N-UNCOUNT **Zest** is a feeling of pleasure and enthusiasm. 热情 [also "a" N, oft N "for" n] ❑ *He has a zest for life and a quick intellect.* 他有生活的热情和机敏的头脑。 2 N-UNCOUNT **Zest** is a quality in an activity or situation which you find exciting. 兴奋点 ❑ *Live interviews add zest and a touch of the unexpected to any piece of research.* 现场采访给任何一份研究增添兴奋点和些许意外。

★ **zig·zag** /zɪgzæg/ (**zigzags, zigzagging, zigzagged**) also **zig-zag** 1 N-COUNT A **zigzag** is a line that has a series of angles in it like a continuous series of Ws. 之字线 ❑ *They staggered in a zigzag across the road.* 他们东倒西歪地踉踉跄跄穿过了公路。 2 V-T/V-I If you **zigzag**, you move forward by going at an angle first to one side then to the other. 作之字形前移 ❑ *I zigzagged down a labyrinth of alleys.* 我在如迷宫般的小巷里拐来拐去。 ❑ *He zigzagged his way across the field.* 他东拐西拐穿过了田野。

★ **zinc** /zɪŋk/ N-UNCOUNT **Zinc** is a bluish-white metal which is used to make other metals such as brass, or to cover other metals such as iron to stop rust from forming. 锌

▲ **zip** /zɪp/ (**zips, zipping, zipped**) 1 V-T When you **zip** something, you fasten it using a zipper. 用拉锁系上 ❑ *She zipped her jeans.* 她拉上了她的牛仔裤拉锁。 2 V-T To **zip** a computer file means to compress it so that it needs less space for storage on disk and can be transmitted more quickly. 压缩(电脑文件) [COMPUTING] ❑ *If you zipped the files first, they did not become read-only when written to the CD.* 如果你先压缩了这些文件,写入光盘时它们就不变成只读文件。 3 N-COUNT A **zip** or **zip fastener** is the same as a **zipper**. 拉锁 [mainly BRIT] ❑ *He pulled the zip of his leather jacket down slightly.* 他稍稍拉下了他皮夹克的拉锁。

▸ **zip up** 1 PHRASAL VERB If you **zip up** something such as a piece of clothing or if it **zips up**, you are able to fasten it using its zipper. 拉上拉锁 ❑ *He zipped up his jeans.* 他拉上了他的牛仔裤拉锁。 2 PHRASAL VERB To **zip up** a computer file means to compress it so that it needs less space for storage on disk and can be transmitted more quickly. 压缩(电脑文件) [COMPUTING] ❑ *These files have been zipped up to take up less disk space so they take less time to download.* 这些文件已被压缩以占用更少的磁盘空间,这样它们需要更短的时间下载。

zip code (**zip codes**) also **ZIP code** N-COUNT Your **zip code** is a short sequence of letters and numbers at the end of your address, which helps the post office to sort the mail. 邮政编码 [AM]
in BRIT, use **postcode**
❑ *Type your street address and zip code.* 键入你的街道地址和邮政编码。

Word Web zero

The **number zero** developed after the other numbers. Ancient peoples first used numbers in concrete situations—to **count** two children or four sheep. It took a while to move from "four sheep" to "four things" to the abstract concept of "four." The use of a **place** holder like zero came from the Babylonians*. Originally, they wrote numbers like 23 and 203 the same way. The reader had to figure out the difference based on the context. The use of zero later came to include the concept of **null** value. It shows that there is no amount of something.

Babylonians: people who lived in the ancient city of Babylon.

Word Web zoo

Zoos are not just places where people enjoy looking at animals. They perform another very important function. As increasing numbers of **species** become extinct, zoos help preserve **biological diversity**. They do this through educational programs, **breeding** programs, and **research** studies. The Smithsonian National Zoological Park in Washington, DC, provides training for **wildlife** managers from 80 different countries. A breeding program at the Wolong Reserve in China has produced 38 **pandas** since 1991. And the Tama Zoo in Hino, Japan, is conducting research studies of **chimpanzee** behavior. Surprisingly, one chimp has learned to use a vending machine.

zip disk (**zip disks**) N-COUNT A **zip disk** is a removable computer disk that is capable of storing great amounts of data. 电脑压缩盘 [COMPUTING] ❑ *Zip disks could be used to store the equivalent of three music CDs.* 压缩盘能用以存储相当于3张音乐CD容量的内容。

zip drive (**zip drives**) N-COUNT A **zip drive** is a piece of computer equipment that reads and writes to zip disks. 压缩驱动器 [COMPUTING] ❑ *Zip drives help people to organize their important information.* 压缩驱动器帮助人们管理他们的重要信息。

zip file (**zip files**) N-COUNT A **zip file** is a computer file containing data that has been compressed. 压缩文件 [COMPUTING] ❑ *When you download the font it may be in a compressed format, such as a zip file.* 下载这种字体时它可能是压缩格式的，例如压缩文件。

▲ **zip·per** /zɪpər/ (**zippers**) N-COUNT A **zipper** is a device used to open and close parts of clothes and bags. It consists of two rows of metal or plastic teeth which separate or fasten together as you pull a small handle along them. 拉锁 [mainly AM]

in BRIT, usually use **zip**

❑ *...the metal zipper on his jacket.* …他的夹克上的金属拉锁。

zo·di·ac /zoʊdiæk/ N-SING **The zodiac** is a diagram used by astrologers to represent the positions of the planets and stars. It is divided into twelve sections, each of which has its own name and symbol. The zodiac is used to try to calculate the influence of the planets on people's lives. (占星中的) 黄道带 ❑ *...the twelve signs of the zodiac.* …黄道12宫。

zone ♦◇◇ /zoʊn/ (**zones, zoning, zoned**) **1** N-COUNT A **zone** is an area that has particular features or characteristics. (有某些特征或特点的) 地带 ❑ *Many people have stayed behind in the potential war zone.* 许多人留在了可能交战的地带。 ❑ *The area has been declared a disaster zone.* 该地区已被宣布为灾难带。 **2** V-T If an area of land **is zoned**, it is formally set aside for a particular purpose. 将…划为特殊区域 [usu passive] ❑ *The land was not zoned for commercial purposes.* 这块地未被划为商业用地。 ● **zon·ing** N-UNCOUNT 分区制 ❑ *...the use of zoning to preserve agricultural land.* …使用分区制以保留农业用地。

→ see **football, time**

Thesaurus *zone* 另参见:
N. area, region, section **1**

zoo /zu/ (**zoos**) N-COUNT; N-IN-NAMES A **zoo** is a park where live animals are kept so that people can look at them. 动物园 ❑ *He took his son Christopher to the zoo.* 他带儿子克里斯托弗去了动物园。

→ see Word Web: **zoo**

→ see **park**

zo·ol·ogy /zoʊɒlədʒi/ N-UNCOUNT **Zoology** is the scientific study of animals. 动物学 ● **zoo·logi·cal** ★ /zoʊəlɒdʒɪkəl/ 动物学的 [ADJ n] ❑ *...zoological specimens.* …动物学标本。

▲ **zoom** /zum/ (**zooms, zooming, zoomed**) V-I If you **zoom** somewhere, you go there very quickly. 赶往 [INFORMAL] ❑ *We zoomed through the gallery.* 我们快速穿过了画廊。

▸ **zoom in** PHRASAL VERB If a camera **zooms in on** something that is being filmed or photographed, it gives a close-up picture of it. (像机镜头) 拉近 ❑ *...a tracking system which can follow a burglar around a building and zoom in on his face.* …一套可以在楼里追踪窃贼并将镜头拉近到他面部的跟踪系统。

Thesaurus *zoom* 另参见:
V. dart, rush, speed; (*ant.*) slow

zuc·chi·ni /zukini/ (**zucchini** or **zucchinis**) N-VAR **Zucchini** are long thin vegetables with a dark green skin. 深绿皮密生西葫芦 [mainly AM]

in BRIT, usually use **courgette**

Index

This is an index of the translations found in this dictionary ordered according to pinyin. English references in the text are given in alphabetical order following the Chinese word or phrase. If the translation relates to a run-on or phrase, the headword under which the run-on or phrase appears is given in brackets. For example, 按节拍 to keep time (at **time**).

The order of the English words does not imply any order of importance and words with similar senses are not grouped together.

The index directs you to the relevant English entry in the dictionary through the medium of Chinese. The index is **not** a dictionary as such, although the English words to which you are referred can function as translations of the Chinese in many cases.

摆架子 pomposity
摆弄 play, toy
摆脱 break, dig, emerge, fight off (at **fight**), out of (at **out**), pull, shake off (at **shake**), shed
摆脱掉某人 get rid of sb (at **rid**)
摆姿势 pose
败坏名声的 compromising
拜访 come, look, see, visit
拜访地 around
扳机 trigger
扳手 spanner
班 class
颁发 present, presentation (at **present**)
颁奖仪式 presentation
斑 spot
斑点 fleck, mark, spot
斑迹 speck
斑马 zebra
搬动 removal
搬进 move in (at **move**)
搬迁 move
搬迁费 relocation expenses
搬运 removal
搬运工 porter
搬运者 bearer
搬走 move out (at **move**)
板 board, panel
板擦 eraser
板球 cricket
板球员 cricketer
版 book, page
版本 edition, version
版次 edition
版画 print
版权 copyright, right
版税 royalty
办公场所 premise
办公时间 office hours
办公时间之外 after hours (at **hour**)
办公室 office
办公桌 desk
办理 see
半…的 half
半场 half
半导体 semiconductor
半岛 peninsula
半独立式的 semi-detached
半价 half-price
半径 radius
半决赛 semi, semifinal
半年的 half-yearly
半球 hemisphere
半身像 bust
半熟的 rare
半熟练的 semiskilled
半天 half-day
半透明的 translucent
半透明物 veil
半途而废 wayside
半心半意的 halfhearted
半圆 semicircle
伴唱 backup
伴娘 bridesmaid
伴随…而有 go with (at **go**)
伴着 with
伴奏 accompaniment, backup
扮…玩 play
扮怪相 grimace
扮演 play, portray, portrayal
扮演小丑 clown
扮演主角的演员 lead
扮演主要角色 star
绊 trip
绊倒 trip
绊脚 stumble
绊脚石 stumbling block
绊住 catch
瓣 segment
帮派 clan
帮助 aid, assist, assistance, hand, help, oblige, support, work
帮助…摆脱困境 bail out (at **bail**)
帮助…做事 help out (at **help**)
帮助某人 lend sb a hand (at **hand**)
帮助支持某人 be there for someone (at **there**)
绑架 abduct, abduction (at **abduct**), kidnap, kidnapping (at **kidnap**)
绑架者 kidnapper (at **kidnap**)
榜样 example, poster child
膀胱 bladder
傍晚 evening
棒打 flog
棒极了的 awesome
棒球 baseball
棒球场 ballpark, diamond
棒球队球童 batboy
棒球帽 baseball cap
磅 lb, pound
镑制 pound
包 bundle, encase, pack, packet, wrap
包庇 cover
包袱 baggage
包裹 package, packet, parcel, pkg.
包裹住 envelop
包含 comprise, contain, embody, encompass, inc., incl., incorporate
包价 package
包括 contain, extend, include, including, inclusion, span
包皮割除 circumcision (at **circumcise**)
包围 close in (at **close**), enclose, lay siege (at **siege**), siege, surround
包围层 cocoon
包厢 box
包装 pack, package, packaging, packing (at **pack**), sex up (at **sex**)
包装材料 packing, wrapping
包装袋 packet
包租 charter
剥去…的壳 shell
剥去…的皮 skin
宝贝 jewel
宝贝儿 baby
宝贵的 dear, precious, priceless
宝库 goldmine
宝马 Beemer
宝石 gem, jewel, stone
宝座 throne
饱 fullness (at **full**)
饱的 full, full up
饱和 saturation
饱经曲折的 beleaguered
饱受折磨 jump through hoops (at **hoop**)
饱胀的 bloated
保安 bouncer
保安措施 security
保安人员 security guard
保镖 bodyguard, heavy
保藏 preserve
保持平衡 keep your balance (at **balance**)
保持 hold, keep, maintain, remain, stay, sustain
保持不变 hold
保持不变的 constant, even
保持沉默 keep your mouth shut (at **shut**)
保持健康 keep
保持距离 keep one's distance (at **distance**)
保持原样的 untouched
保持中立 sit on the fence (at **fence**)
保存 keep
保管箱 safe deposit box
保护 conservation, conserve, defend, defense, guard, preservation (at **preserve**), preserve, protect, protection, safeguard, shield
保护层 covering, lining
保护区 reserve
保护人 protector, shield
保护色 camouflage
保护者 guardian
保护装置 protector
保皇党人 royalist
保皇主义者 royalist
保健的 lifestyle
保龄球 bowling
保龄球道 lane
保龄球手 bowler
保留 hang, keep, retain, retention, save
保留备用 in reserve (at **reserve**)
保留权利 reserve the right (at **right**)
保留地 reservation
保留剧目 repertoire
保留剧目轮演 repertory
保留看法 reserve judgment (at **judgment**)
保留意见 reservation
保密 confidence, keep your mouth shut (at **shut**), secrecy, under wraps (at **wrap**)
保密的 confidential, secret, undisclosed
保密信托 blind trust
保密性 confidentiality (at **confidential**)
保姆 nanny
保暖 warmth
保暖的 thermal, warm
保释 bail
保释金 bail
保释释放 make bail (at **bail**)
保释许可 bail
保守 guard, insularity (at **insular**)
保守党的 conservative
保守的 conservative, insular, reactionary
保守秘密 keep a secret (at **secret**), keep quiet about sth/keep sth quiet (at **quiet**), keep sth under your hat (at **hat**)
保守思想 reaction
保守主义 conservatism
保卫 safeguard
保温瓶 Thermos
保鲜 keep
保鲜膜 clingfilm, plastic wrap
保险 cover, insurance, protection
保险单 policy
保险的 safe
保险费 premium
保险杠 bumper
保险公司 insurer
保险柜 safe
保险库 vault
保险理赔人 claims adjuster
保险理算员 insurance adjuster
保险丝 fuse
保修单 guarantee, warranty
保养 maintain, service
保障 cover, indemnify, indemnity
保证 assurance, assure, guarantee, indemnity, pledge
保证给予 pledge
保证金 deposit, surety
保证赔偿 indemnify
保质期 expiration date
保住 hold down (at **hold**)
堡垒 bastion, fort
报 gazette, quote
报酬 recompense, remuneration
报春花 primrose
报答 repay
报到 report
报道 account, coverage, report
报废的 worn out
报复 pay, reprisal, retaliate, retaliation (at **retaliate**), revenge, settle a score (at **score**), to get your own back (at **own**), vindictiveness (at **vindictive**)
报告 report
报价 quotation, quote
报名参加 sign
报社 newspaper
报销 reimburse, reimbursement
报应 retribution
报纸 newspaper, paper, press
刨花 shaving
抱 carry
抱紧 clasp
抱满的 full
抱起来 scoop up (at **scoop**)
抱歉 excuse me (at **excuse**), sorry
抱太大希望 get/build your hopes up (at **hope**)
抱一线希望 hope against hope (at **hope**)
抱怨 complain, gripe, griping (at **gripe**), groan, grumble, moan
抱怨的缘由 complaint
抱住 hold, hug, scoop
抱着 cradle
抱子甘蓝 brussels sprout, sprout
豹 leopard
暴跌 nosedive, plummet, slump, tumble
暴动 insurgency
暴发 explosion
暴风雪 blizzard
暴风雨 storm
暴风雨般的声音 storm
暴君 tyrant
暴力的 violent
暴力行为 violence
暴露 come to light/bring sth to light (at **light**), exposure, give
暴乱 riot
暴民 mob
暴虐的 heavy-handed
暴徒 thug
暴行 atrocity, savagery
暴饮暴食 pig out (at **pig**)
暴躁的 foul, hot, quick
暴躁的脾气 temper
暴增 explosion
暴涨 explode, explosion
暴涨的 explosive

爆发 bout, break out (at **break**), erupt, eruption (at **erupt**), explosion, flare, outbreak, outburst, strike, throw
爆发期 outburst
爆发骚乱 erupt
爆裂 burst, rupture
爆裂声 crack, pop
爆满 bursting at the seams (at **seam**)
爆米花 popcorn
爆炸 blow up (at **blow**), detonate, explode, explosion, go, go off (at **go**)
爆炸物 explosive
爆炸性的 explosive
爆炸性消息 bombshell
卑鄙到… stoop
卑鄙的 dirty, grubby, sordid
卑鄙小人 rat
卑躬屈膝 grovel
卑微的 lowly, menial, small
杯威士忌酒 whisky
杯状物 cup
杯子 cup
悲哀 sadness (at **sad**)
悲惨的 deplorable, tragic
悲观 doom
悲观的 dark, dim, pessimistic
悲观主义 pessimism
悲观主义者 pessimist
悲剧 tragedy
悲剧的 tragic
悲伤 dismay, sorrow, woe
悲伤的 dismay, mournful, sad, saddened (at **sadden**), sorry, woeful
悲痛 distress, grief
碑 tablet
碑文 inscription
北 north
北部 north
北大西洋公约组织 NATO
北方 north
北方的 northerly
北方发达国家 north
北极 arctic
北美大草原 prairie
贝壳 shell
备份 back
备忘录 memorandum
备用的 auxiliary, spare
备用零件 spare part
备用物 backup, standby
背包 knapsack
背部 back
背衬 backing
背带 brace, harness, sash
背带裤 dungarees
背地里 behind sb's back (at **back**)
背黑锅 take the rap (at **rap**)
背景 background, beginning, context, pedigree, setting, wallpaper
背景声音 background
背靠 back
背离 departure, go back on (at **go**)
背面 back, reverse
背叛 betray, defect, defection (at **defect**), sell, sell-out, treachery
背叛行为 betrayal
背叛者 traitor
背心 undershirt, vest, waistcoat
背信 renege
背信弃义的 treacherous
背阴 shadow
背阴的 shady
倍 time
倍数 factor, multiple
悖论 paradox
被...严重影响 be hard hit (at **hard**)
被 by
被…覆盖的 clad
被…领导 report
被…迷住的 hooked
被…取代 give way to (at **way**)
被…所震惊 taken aback (at **aback**)
被安排做 down
被裁减的 redundant
被采访者 interviewee
被彻底摧毁 oblivion
被称为…的 so-called
被单 sheet
被淡忘状态 oblivion
被当作 pass
被盗的 stolen (at **steal**)
被低估了的 underrated (at **underrate**)
被调查人 respondent
被动的 passive
被动语态 passive
被分开 part
被腐蚀了的 corroded (at **corrode**)
被感动的 moved (at **move**)
被高估的 overrated (at **overrate**)
被告 accused, defendant
被告律师 defense
被告席 dock
被公开的 out
被忽视 escape, invisibility (at **invisible**)
被忽视的 invisible, neglected (at **neglect**)
被激怒的 incensed (at **incense**), irritated (at **irritate**)
被忌讳的 forbidden
被寄予希望的 hopeful
被寄予希望的人 hope
被揭露 light
被解雇 get/be given the boot (at **boot**)
被解雇人群 scrapheap
被禁止的 forbidden
被拘留者 detainee
被拒绝 go by the board (at **board**)
被卷入 catch
被卷入的 entangled
被开除 expulsion
被砍掉 ax
被看待 stand
被看轻了的 underrate
被看作 rate
被困住的 stuck
被理解 get across (at **get**)
被领会 sink
被垄断的 captive
被录取 get
被冒犯了的 offended (at **offend**)
被面试者 interviewee
被铭记于心 to stick in your mind (at **mind**)
被溺爱的 pampered (at **pamper**)
被拍卖 auction
被抛弃 boot
被骗 fall
被评定为 rate
被评价 rate
被迫放弃 forfeit
被迫认错 eat crow (at **crow**)
被谴责 stand accused (at **accuse**)
被囚禁的 captive
被圈养的 captive
被人唾弃的 disgraced
被深刻领会 hit/strike home (at **home**)
被授予 award
被水覆盖的 awash
被淘汰的 obsolete
被讨论 come
被提及 come
被提交到 come
被提名 nominate
被通过 get
被通缉的 wanted (at **want**)
被同化 assimilate
被推崇的 recommended (at **recommend**)
被退学 flunk out (at **flunk**)
被忘掉 escape
被侮辱的 insulted (at **insult**)
被误解的 misunderstood
被吸引的 attracted (at **attract**)
被细心照顾的 pamper
被吓倒的 intimidated
被泄露的秘密 revelation
被询问者 interviewee
被压迫的 oppressed
被压抑的 pent-up
被淹没 inundate
被遗弃的 deserted (at **desert**)
被遗忘 slip your mind (at **slip**)
被引见给… meet
被引诱的 tempted
被用于 intend
被征入伍者 conscript
被证实了的 established (at **establish**)
被逐出 expulsion
被子 quilt
奔 tear
奔波 on the move (at **move**)
奔忙 bustle
奔跑 scamper
奔涌 rush
本地的 local
本地人 native
本国产的 homegrown
本国的 home
本国人 native
本金 capital, principal
本来可能 might
本来应有的 rightful
本能 instinct
本能的 instinctive
本能的反应 instinct
本钱 capital, seed money
本人 in the flesh (at **flesh**), person
本人直接地 personally
本身 itself, per se
本土的 indigenous
本性 self
本意为 mean
本应该 ought, supposed
本质 essence, nature
本质的 intrinsic
本质上 by its nature (at **nature**), essentially, in essence (at **essence**), per se
笨蛋 dummy, fool, idiot
笨重的 cumbersome, unwieldy
笨拙 clumsiness (at **clumsy**)
笨拙的 awkward, bungling (at **bungle**), clumsy
崩溃 collapse, crumble, go to pieces (at **piece**), seam
崩溃边缘 breaking point
崩塌 crumble
绷带 bandage
绷紧 brace, tense
绷紧的 tight
绷着的脸 a straight face (at **face**)
绷着脸 scowl
泵 pump
迸发 explode, gust, rush, spurt, torrent
蹦跳 bounce, jig, skip
蹦跳着走 bounce, skip
逼近 move
逼离开 tear away (at **tear**)
逼迫 compulsion, push
逼迫卸职 chase
逼向 come at (at **come**)
逼真的 authentic, gritty, real, realistic
鼻孔 nostril
鼻梁架 bridge
鼻烟 snuff
鼻子 nose
匕首 dagger
比 in proportion to (at **proportion**), than
比…更重要 override
比…好的 superior
比…活得长 outlive, survive
比…经久 outlive
比…领先一圈 lap
比…少地 less
比得上 compare, equal, like, match
比分 score
比基尼泳装 bikini
比较 compare, comparison
比较的 comparative
比较而言的 relative
比较级 comparative
比较级的 comparative
比例 proportion
比例尺 scale
比例大小 dimension
比例代表制 proportional representation
比率 ratio
比起来 compare
比如说 say
比萨饼 pizza
比赛 contest, game, match, race
比赛场地 pitch
比赛项目 event
比特/秒 bps
比特 bit
比喻的 figurative
比喻意义上的 metaphorical
比照 against
比值 proportion
比重 outweigh
彼此协调 harmonize
笔 sum
笔法 handwriting
笔画 stroke
笔迹 handwriting, writing
笔记 note
笔记本 notebook
笔记本电脑 laptop
笔名 pseudonym
笔友 pen-friend
笔直的 straight, upright
笔直地 bolt upright (at **bolt**)
笔直向前地 ahead
鄙视 despise, scorn
币制 coinage
必备条件 requirement
必不可少的 basic, indispensable
必不可少的事物 must
必定 must, without fail (at **fail**)
必定地 surely
必然的 necessary
必然的事 certainty
必然地 necessarily
必然发生的 inevitable
必然会 bound
必然性 inevitability

鳖脚货 dog
瘪的 flat
瘪胎 flat
宾戈游戏 bingo
宾语 object
彬彬有礼 courtesy, refinement
彬彬有礼的 courteous, refined
滨海区 seafront
滨水地区 waterfront
濒临消亡的 dying
摈弃 reject, rejection (at **reject**), scorn
殡仪员 undertaker
殡葬承办者 mortician
冰 ice
冰棒 ice lolly
冰雹 hail
冰川 glacier
冰刀 skate
冰的 glacial
冰点 freezing, freezing point
冰冻的 frozen
冰棍 Popsicle
冰河的 glacial
冰激凌 ice cream
冰冷的 freezing, icy
冰球 hockey
冰山 iceberg
冰山一角 the tip of the iceberg (at **tip**)
冰上曲棍球 ice hockey
冰箱 fridge, refrigerator
冰鞋 skate
冰镇的 iced
冰锥 icicle
兵 pawn
兵役 service
丙烯酸纤维 acrylic
柄 handle, shaft, stalk
饼分图 pie chart
饼状食物 cake
并发症 complication
并非 exactly, no, not
并列 juxtaposition
并排 side by side (at **side**)
并排地 abreast
并且 and
并吞 annex, annexation (at **annex**)
病床边 bedside
病的 poorly
病毒 virus
病毒携带者 carrier
病毒性的 viral
病房 ward
病假 sick leave
病假工资 sick pay
病菌 germ
病理的 pathological
病理学 pathology
病理学的 pathological
病理学家 pathologist
病人 invalid, patient
病弱的 delicate
病态的 morbid, pathological
病危 at death's door (at **death**)
病危的 critical
摒弃 write
拨 pluck, set
拨号 dial
拨号音 dial tone, dialling tone
拨火棍 poker
拨款 appropriation
拨浪鼓 rattle
波 wave
波长 wavelength
波动 fluctuate, fluctuation (at **fluctuate**), tremor, wave
波段 channel, wavelength
波谷 trough
波浪 wave
波浪卷 wave
波浪形的 wavy
波纹状的 wavy
波状的 corrugated
玻璃 glass
玻璃杯 glass
玻璃罐 jar
玻璃制品 glass
剥夺 deprivation, deprive, strip
剥夺权利 disenfranchise
剥离 strip
剥落 flake, peel
剥削 exploit
菠菜 spinach
菠萝 pineapple
播 sow
播报 on the air (at **air**)
播放 air, airing (at **air**), broadcast, play, put, run, screen, show
播客 podcast
播送 beam, transmission
播音 sound
播音员 announcer
伯父 uncle
伯爵 count, earl
伯母 aunt, auntie
驳倒 demolish, refute
泊位 berth, dock
勃起 erection
勃然大怒 see red (at **red**)
铂 platinum
博爱 humanity
博得 command
博得全场喝彩 bring the house down (at **house**)
博客 blog
博客空间 blogosphere
博览会 expo
博若莱葡萄酒 Beaujolais
博士 doctor, Dr., Ph.D.
博士学位 doctorate, Ph.D.
博物馆 museum
博物学家 naturalist
博学的 learned, scholarly
搏斗 combat
箔纸 foil
薄层 film, skin
薄脆饼干 cracker
薄得透明的 see-through
薄的 flimsy, slim, thin
薄荷 mint
薄荷糖 mint
薄煎饼 pancake
薄棉布 muslin
薄棉纸 tissue
薄膜 film
薄皮 skin
薄片 slice
薄弱的 weak
薄雾 haze
跛行 hobble, limp
补 fill
补笔 postscript
补编 supplement
补偿 compensate, compensation, recompense, satisfaction
补偿金 compensation
补充 add, complement, put, restock, supplement
补充的 supplementary
补充剂 refill
补充说明 footnote
补充物 complement
补丁 patch
补给品 supply
补救 redeem, redress, remedy, repair
补救的 remedial
补考 make
补缺选举 by-election
补贴 allowance, subsidize
补贴金 subsidy
补习的 remedial
补修 make
补药 tonic
补助 credit
补助金 grant
补足 make
补做 catch
哺乳动物 mammal
捕获 capture, catch
捕鲸 whaling
捕捞 net
捕食 prey
捕鱼 fishing
捕捉器 trap
不 never, no, nope, not, yes
不安 discomfort, unease, uneasiness (at **uneasy**)
不安的 disturbed, uneasy
不安全 insecurity (at **insecure**)
不安全的 insecure, unsafe
不帮忙的 unhelpful
不包括 exclude
不包括…的 exclusive
不保密 make no secret (at **secret**)
不被接受的 not on/just not on (at **on**)
不被认可的 wrong
不本分的 undutiful
不必多言 suffice it to say (at **suffice**)
不必客气 don't mention it (at **mention**)
不必要的 gratuitous, needless, unnecessary, unwarranted
不便的 awkward
不变的 static
不变地 invariably
不参与 stay
不常 seldom
不常发生的 uncommon
不常见的 uncommon, unusual
不称职的 incompetent
不成比例的 disproportionate
不成功的 barren, dud, unsuccessful
不成熟 immaturity
不成熟的 immature
不成文的 unwritten
不诚恳的 insincere
不诚实的 dishonest, improper, sordid, underhand, unscrupulous
不诚实行为 dishonesty
不充分的 insufficient
不充分的陈述 understatement
不出错 not put a foot wrong (at **foot**)
不出名的 unknown
不出牌 pass
不出声的 quiet
不出问题的 foolproof
不穿衣服的 undressed
不纯的 impure
不存在 absence, lack, nil
不存在的 nonexistent
不错的 okay
不打扰 leave
不打算 have no intention (at **intention**)
不打自招的 self-confessed
不大可能的 doubtful, improbable
不带电的 neutral
不当班的 off-duty
不道德的 immoral, scandalous, unethical, unsavory, unscrupulous, wrong, wrongful
不道德的行为 wrong
不道德行为 wrongdoing
不得不 have to do (at **have**)
不得当 clumsy
不得当的 clumsy
不得体 have the decency (at **decency**)
不得体的 improper
不定冠词 indefinite article
不定式 infinitive
不动 hold still (at **hold**)
不动产 real estate, real property
不动的 inert
不动声色 neutrality (at **neutral**)
不动声色的 neutral
不端行为 misconduct
不断出现的 perennial
不断打扰 besiege
不断的 running
不断发生的 permanent
不断供给 ply
不断批评 bombard
不断骚扰 barrage
不对外公开的 in camera (at **camera**)
不对外开放的 private, restricted
不多 little
不多的 low
不发达的 underdeveloped
不法的 shady
不方便 inconvenience
不方便的 cumbersome, inconvenient
不妨 do no/little harm; no harm in doing (at **harm**)
不费劲的 painless
不费力的 effortless
不费力地讲出 reel off (at **reel**)
不锋利的 blunt
不服从 disobedience, disobey
不负责任 irresponsibility (at **irresponsible**)
不负责任的 irresponsible
不复存在 bite the dust (at **dust**)
不复存在的 extinct, lost
不复杂的 uncomplicated
不甘落后 not to be outdone (at **outdo**)
不敢想 dread to think (at **dread**)
不感到羞愧的 unrepentant
不感激的 ungrateful
不感兴趣的 disinterested, lukewarm
不高兴 unhappiness (at **unhappy**)
不公的待遇 deal
不公平 inequality
不公平的 unfair, unreasonable
不公平的待遇 a raw deal (at **raw**)
不公平的评论 injustice
不公平对待 discriminate
不公正 injustice
不公正的 below the belt (at **belt**), unbalanced, unjust, wrongful
不公正的行为 injustice, wrong
不恭的 impudent
不恭敬的 undutiful
不共戴天的 sworn
不苟言笑的 sedate
不够的 pushed
不够好 inadequacy
不够好的 inadequate
不够应有水准的 wanting
不顾 bypass
不顾后果的 reckless

不停的 nonstop
不停地 on and on (at **on**)
不停地抱怨 gripe
不停地移动 flit
不停顿的 seamless
不同 differ
不同的 different, dissimilar, divergent, diverse, separate
不同地 variously
不同寻常的 quite, remarkable, striking
不同意 disagree, reject, won't/wouldn't hear of sth (at **hear**)
不透明的 opaque
不透水的 watertight
不退却 stand one's ground/hold one's ground (at **ground**)
不褪色的 fast
不妥协的 uncompromising
不完美的 imperfect
不完全的 incomplete, sketchy
不完全是 exactly
不文明的 uncivilized
不稳的 unsteady
不稳定 instability
不稳定的 erratic, inconsistent, precarious, rocky, uneasy, unstable
不稳固的 precarious, rickety
不吸烟的人 nonsmoker
不吸引人的 unattractive
不希望 hate
不惜任何代价 at any price (at **price**)
不惜任何代价地 at all costs (at **cost**)
不习惯的 unused
不喜爱 dislike
不喜欢 disapprove
不喜欢的 disapproving, unwelcome
不喜欢的事物 dislike
不显眼的 discreet
不相关 irrelevance
不相关的 beside the point (at **point**), irrelevant, meaningless, unrelated
不相容 incompatibility (at **incompatible**)
不相容的 incompatible
不祥的 ominous, sinister
不想 hate
不想要的 unwanted, unwelcome
不像 unlike
不协调 clash
不协调的 incompatible, incongruous
不屑一顾的 dismissive
不屑于 above
不新鲜的 stale
不信 doubt
不信任 distrust, mistrust
不行 dice, no
不行的 useless
不幸 misfortune, unhappiness (at **unhappy**)
不幸的 bad, hapless, regrettable, sad, tragic, unfortunate, unlucky
不幸地 unhappily
不幸福的 unhappy
不朽 immortality (at **immortal**)
不朽的 immortal, monumental
不锈钢 stainless steel
不许干涉 hand
不许碰 keep one's hands off sth/take one's hands off sth (at **hand**)
不寻常的 curious, different, freak, odd, out of the ordinary (at **ordinary**), peculiar, unusual, wild
不寻常地 unusually
不逊色的 favorable
不雅的 gross
不严格的 lax
不严重的 light, minor
不言而喻 goes without saying (at **say**)
不言而喻的 self-evident
不要 no
不一定 not necessarily (at **necessarily**)
不一致 inconsistency
不一致的 inconsistent, uneven
不依赖的 independent
不易察觉的 subtle
不易动怒的 quiet
不易弯曲的 stiff
不淫秽的 clean
不引起变化的 neutral
不引人注目的 unobtrusive
不应该 can
不应该的 wrong
不赢利的 unprofitable
不用 no
不用客气 you're welcome (at **welcome**)
不用谢 it's nothing (at **nothing**), not
不由自主的 involuntary
不由自主地 spite
不友好 cold, unkindness (at **unkind**)
不友好的 cold, distant, mean, miserable, sour, unfriendly, unkind, unpleasant
不友善地 badly
不予理睬 brush off (at **brush**)
不予理会 dismiss
不愉快的 disturbed
不愉快的事 evil
不育 infertility (at **infertile**), sterility (at **sterile**)
不育的 sterile
不愿 dream, hate
不愿谈及的 coy
不愿透露姓名的 unidentified
不愿意 hesitate, hesitation, reluctance (at **reluctant**), unwillingness (at **unwilling**)
不愿意的 reluctant, unprepared, unwilling
不悦 displeasure
不运转的 dead
不再 cease, no longer/any longer (at **long**)
不再抱幻想的 disenchanted
不再产油的 dry
不再存在的 defunct, finished
不再担忧 switch
不再发生的 finished
不再负责 hand
不再考虑 dismiss
不再了解 lose touch (at **touch**)
不再起作用的 defunct
不再使用 turn
不再谈论 leave
不再喜欢 off
不再重要的 dead
不再注意 switch
不在 out
不在的 gone
不在工地上 off site (at **site**)
不在工作中地 off
不在乎 couldn't care less, could care less (at **care**)
不在家过夜 sleep over (at **sleep**), sleepover
不在拍摄中 off camera (at **camera**)
不在适宜状态 not in a fit state (at **state**)
不在现场 site
不在现场证明 alibi
不在一起地 apart
不在意的 careless, unconcerned
不赞成 disagree, disapproval, frown upon (at **frown**)
不赞同 disapprove
不赞同的 disapproving, unfavorable
不择手段的 deadly
不择手段地谋取 jockey for (at **jockey**)
不怎么样 of sorts/a sort (at **sort**)
不粘食物的 nonstick
不招人喜爱的 unattractive
不真诚的 false
不真实 nothing to it (at **nothing**)
不真实的 incorrect, unnatural, untrue
不正常的 unhealthy, unnatural
不正当 irregularity (at **irregular**)
不正当的 illicit
不正当关系 affair
不正规的 irregular
不正确的 incorrect, spurious
不证自明的 self-evident
不知 I don't suppose (at **suppose**), I wonder (at **wonder**)
不知道 dunno
不知情的 unaware, unsuspecting
不知所措 be at a loss (at **loss**), floor, flounder, lose one's way (at **way**)
不知所措的 bewildered
不知怎地 somehow
不直的 uneven
不值得的 unworthy
不只是 more than (at **more**)
不至于 above
不忠 disloyalty
不忠诚的 disloyal, unfaithful
不忠实于 cheat on (at **cheat**)
不重要 insignificance
不重要的 insignificant, irrelevant, meaningless, petty, small, unimportant
不属于 out of place (at **place**)
不注意 tune
不专业的 unprofessional
不准确 inaccuracy
不准确的 inaccurate, out
不准许 disallow
不着急 there's no hurry (at **hurry**), time
不自然的 plastic, unnatural
不自信 insecurity (at **insecure**)
不自信的 insecure
不自在 ease
不自在的 self-conscious, uncomfortable
不奏效 use
不足 deficiency, inadequacy, shortfall
不足的 deficient, inadequate, scant, skimpy
不尊敬 irreverence (at **irreverent**)
不尊敬的 irreverent
不作为 inaction, inactivity (at **inactive**)
不作为的 inactive
不做 go, skip
布 cloth, preach
布道 preach, sermon
布道所 mission
布道坛 pulpit
布丁 pudding
布告 placard
布告栏 board, bulletin board
布告牌 noticeboard
布谷鸟 cuckoo
布景 set
布局 configuration, layout
布雷 mine
布料 material
布满 drip
布满…的 scattered
布满的 dotted, riddled
布置 arrange, arrangement, assign, furnish
步兵 infantry
步伐 step
步伐一致 in/out of step (at **step**)
步距 pace
步履艰难地走 trudge
步枪 rifle
步入正轨 on track (at **track**)
步速 pace
步态 gait, walk
步行 on foot (at **foot**), walk
步行的 foot
步行的距离 walk
步骤 step
钚 plutonium
部 department, ministry
部长 secretary
部长的 ministerial
部分 centerpiece, end, part, portion, proportion, section, sector, segment, slice, tranche, way
部分的 partial
部分地 half
部分时间的 part-time
部分支付 down
部件 piece, unit
部落 tribe
部落的 tribal
部门 arm, department, division, sector
部门的 departmental
部门经理 line manager
部署 deploy, deployment
部位 area, region
簿记 bookkeeping
簿记员 bookkeeper
擦 rub, strike
擦掉 erase, rub out (at **rub**)
擦干 dry, mop up (at **mop**)
擦过 graze
擦肩而过 brush
擦亮 polish
擦亮的 polished (at **polish**)
擦破皮 graze
擦去 wipe
擦伤 graze, scrape
擦拭 mop, wipe
擦洗 scour
猜测 guess, speculate, speculation (at **speculate**), surmise
猜测性的 speculative
猜忌 jealousy
猜想 gather, guess, idea, imagine
猜疑 suspicion
猜中 guess
才干 caliber
才华 flair
才能 ability, capability, order
才智 brilliance (at **brilliant**), intellect, mind, wit

充实 enrich, enrichment, flesh out (at **flesh**)
充实的 full
充盈 brim
充裕的 plenty
充足的 ample
冲 at, charge, chase, flush, make a dash (at **dash**), rush, tear
冲刺 sprint, spurt
冲掉 flush
冲动 compulsion, impulse
冲昏…的头脑 go to one's head (at **head**)
冲击 wash
冲击波 shock wave, wave
冲击力 shock
冲垮 wash away (at **wash**)
冲浪 surf
冲浪运动 surfing
冲浪者 surfer (at **surf**)
冲泡 brew
冲破 break through (at **break**)
冲上岸 wash
冲突 collision, conflict, strife, tension, warfare
冲洗 develop, flush, rinse
冲向 dive
冲咽 wash down (at **wash**)
冲印 print
冲走 wash
憧憬 vision
重播 repeat
重叠 overlap
重订…的时间表 reschedule
重返 resume
重逢 reunion
重复 duplication, repeat, repetitive
重复的 repetitive
重复的呼声 chanting (at **chant**)
重复的话语 chant
重复的语句 repetition
重复性劳损 RSI
重回 revert
重建 rebuild, reconstruct, reconstruction, recreate, recreation, redevelopment, regenerate, regeneration (at **regenerate**)
重聚 reunite
重聚会 reunion
重赛 rematch
重申 reaffirm, reassert, reiterate, restate
重述 retell
重说 repeat
重塑 rebrand, rebranding
重提 dredge
重温 relive
重现 recreation
重写 repeat, rework, rewrite
重新 over again (at **over**)
重新安排 rearrange, rearrangement, reorganize
重新安置 relocate
重新变成 reclaim
重新播放 replay
重新部署 regroup
重新充满 replenish
重新地 afresh, anew
重新分配 redistribute, redistribution (at **redistribute**)
重新获得 regain
重新集合 reconvene
重新计票 recount
重新加足 top up (at **top**)
重新建构 restructure, restructuring (at **restructure**)
重新进货 restock
重新举行 replay
重新开发 redevelopment, relaunch
重新开始 back to square one (at **square**), get back to (at **get**), kick, relaunch, renew, renewal, resume, resumption (at **resume**), return, start over (at **start**)
重新考虑 reconsider, rethink, revisit, think again (at **think**)
重新联合 reunite
重新评价 reassess, reassessment
重新上演 revive
重新审视 reexamination (at **reexamine**), reexamine
重新适应 readjust, readjustment
重新讨论 revisit
重新统一 reunification
重新引发 rekindle
重新占领 recapture
重新找回 recover
重新召集 reconvene
重新振作 bounce back (at **bounce**)
重新振作起来 pull
重新整理 rearrange, rearrangement
重新装满 refill
重修 reconstruction
重演 repeat, repetition, reproduce
重印 reprint
重印本 reprint
重游 revisit
重振 kick-start
重置 readjust
重组 reorganization (at **reorganize**), reorganize
重组家庭 stepfamily
重做 repeat
崇拜 idolize
崇高的 lofty, noble
崇高地位 pedestal
崇敬 homage, revere
宠爱 fuss
宠物 pet
抽 draw, puff, suck
抽鼻子 sniff
抽出 set, spare
抽出时间做 get around to (at **get**)
抽搐 convulsion
抽打 flick, swat
抽动 twitch
抽筋 cramp
抽泣 whimper
抽签 draw lots (at **lot**)
抽丝 run
抽送 pump
抽屉 drawer
抽象的 abstract
抽象概念 abstraction
抽象作品 abstract
抽样 sample, specimen
抽噎 sob, sobbing (at **sob**)
抽走 siphon
仇敌 enemy
仇恨 hate
稠密的 dense
筹措 raise
筹划 arrange
筹码 chip
筹募 raise
酬金 fee, remuneration
踌躇 waver
踌躇不前 hang
丑的 ugly
丑恶 ugliness (at **ugly**)
丑恶的 ugly
丑陋 ugliness (at **ugly**)
丑陋的 grotesque
丑闻 scandal
臭迹 scent
臭味 stench
臭小子 brat
臭氧 ozone
臭氧层 ozone layer
出 break, out
出版 appear, publication, publish
出版公司 publisher
出版社 publishing house
出版物 publication
出版业 publishing
出版者 publisher
出差错 slip
出差错的 amiss
出场 entrance
出发 move, set
出发点 starting point
出故障 break down (at **break**), go, malfunction
出故障的 down, faulty
出汗 sweat, sweating (at **sweat**)
出汗的 sweaty
出乎意料的 dream
出价 bid, offer
出价高于… outbid
出价者 bidder
出借 lend, lending (at **lend**)
出境签证 exit visa
出局的 out
出口 exit, export
出口公司 exporter
出口国 exporter
出口品 export
出口商 exporter
出来 come, emerge, forth, forward
出冷汗 in a cold sweat/in a sweat (at **sweat**)
出卖 betray, sell, sell-out
出卖灵魂 sell one's soul (at **sell**)
出卖肉体 sell one's body (at **sell**)
出门 go out (at **go**)
出纳员 cashier, teller
出奇的 uncanny
出奇地 suspiciously
出勤 attendance
出人意料的 unexpected
出色 go places (at **place**), magnificence (at **magnificent**)
出色的 beautiful, magnificent
出色地 well
出身 background, beginning, birth, descent, origin, parentage, pedigree
出神的 dreamy
出生 birth, born
出生地 birthplace, of one's birth (at **birth**)
出生率 birth rate
出生日期 date of birth
出生于 hail
出生证 birth certificate
出声背诵 recite
出声地 out loud (at **loud**)
出声地喝着 slurp
出师不利 get off on the wrong foot (at **foot**)
出示 produce
出售 on sale (at **sale**), sell, sell-off
出售权 option
出售物 offering
出水口 outlet
出问题 go wrong (at **wrong**), out of whack (at **whack**), sth is up (at **up**)
出席 appear, attend, attendance, present
出席人数 attendance
出现 advent, appear, appearance, arise, come, emerge, figure, go, occur, open, show, turn up (at **turn**)
出现故障 out of order (at **order**)
出现了 here
出行 pilgrimage, run
出血 bleeding (at **bleed**)
出洋相 have egg on one's face/ have egg all over one's face (at **egg**)
出于 out of (at **out**)
出于礼节的 courtesy
出众的 quite
出众的女子 queen
出走 run away (at **run**), walk
出租 hire out (at **hire**), let, rent, rental
出租车 hack, taxi
出租车候客区 taxi stand
出租的 rental
出租汽车 cab
初步的 preliminary, tentative
初步的感受 glimpse
初次抵达 arrive
初次接触 introduction (at **introduce**)
初稿 draft
初级的 primary
初级入门的 entry-level
初级水平的 entry-level
初级中学 junior high school
初期 beginning, infancy
初期的 early, infant
初选 primary
初学者 beginner
除 divide, go
除…外 bar, excepted, excepting, short
除…之外 apart, aside, barring, except, excluding, over
除草 weed
除臭剂 deodorant
除此以外 otherwise
除掉 take out (at **take**)
除法 division
除非 unless
除尽 divide
除了 aside, besides, beyond, but
除了… except for (at **except**)
除了…都 all but (at **all**)
除了…外 as well as (at **well**)
除了…之外 other than (at **other**)
除外 with the exception of (at **exception**)
厨房 galley, kitchen
厨师 chef, cook
厨灶 cooker
锄 hoe
锄头 hoe
雏菊 daisy
雏鸟 chick
橱柜 cupboard
储备 hold, reserve, stock, store up (at **store**)
储备物资 stockpile
储藏室 closet
储存 hold, store
储存处 store
储户 saver
储物箱 chest
储蓄 save

打架 fight, scrap
打交道 deal
打结系牢 tie
打卡上班 clock in (at **clock**), clock on (at **clock**), punch
打卡下班 clock off (at **clock**), clock out (at **clock**)
打开 open, put, turn on (at **turn**), undo
打开取出 unpack
打瞌睡 doze off (at **doze**), nod off (at **nod**)
打孔器 punch
打雷 thunder
打了就跑的 hit-and-run
打猎 hunt
打趔趄 lurch
打乱 derail, play havoc with sth/wreak havoc on sth (at **havoc**)
打拍子 tap
打喷嚏 sneeze
打平 draw
打平地 all
打破 beat, break
打破沉默 break your silence (at **silence**)
打破僵局 breaks the ice (at **ice**)
打扰 bother, disturb, intrusion, trouble
打扰的 intrusive
打扰一下 excuse me (at **excuse**)
打入 penetrate, penetration (at **penetrate**)
打扫 clean, sweep
打扫卫生 clean
打扫卫生的工作 cleaning (at **clean**)
打上 stamp
打手 heavy
打手势 gesture, sign
打算 aim, be going to (at **going**), idea, intend, mean, plan on (at **plan**), propose
打算做…的 out
打算做某事 to have sth in mind (at **mind**)
打碎 bust
打听 inquire
打退 repel
打退堂鼓 pull back (at **pull**)
打下基础 prepare the ground (at **ground**)
打响指 snap
打印出来 print out (at **print**)
打印机 printer
打印件 printout
打中目标 strike home (at **home**)
打字 type, typing
打字机 typewriter
打字技术 typing
打字员 typist
大巴 coach
大堡垒 fortress
大爆炸 blast
大本营 base, stronghold
大比分的 emphatic
大比例尺的 large-scale
大笔钱 fortune
大不列颠 G.B.
大步 stride
大步走 stride
大部分 bulk, most
大部分地 mainly
大层 sheet
大臣 secretary
大大地 way
大大增加 multiply
大胆 bold
大胆猜测 hazard
大胆的 audacious, bold, daring
大胆行为 audacity
大得骇人的 horrific
大的 big, grand, great, large
大的程度 magnitude
大调的 major
大都会 metropolis
大都会的 metropolitan
大堆 mountain
大多地 mostly
大多数 at large (at **large**), mass, most
大多数人 multitude
大而笨重的 bulky
大而厚的 chunky
大而恐怖的 void
大发牢骚 make a fuss (at **fuss**)
大发雷霆 do one's nut/go nuts (at **nut**)
大发脾气 blow, fit
大方的 expansive
大方地 naturally
大风 gale
大幅度削减 slash
大概 doubtless
大概的 approximate, ballpark
大公司 corporation
大功告成 home and dry, home free (at **home**)
大功率的 high-powered
大关 barrier
大规模的 large-scale, wholesale
大规模计划 scheme
大规模屠杀 massacre
大锅 cauldron
大国 giant
大海 ocean
大喊 shout, shout out (at **shout**)
大好人 angel
大亨 baron, fat cat, magnate, tycoon
大壶 urn
大会 assembly
大混乱 havoc
大火 blaze
大货箱 crate
大获全胜 sweep the board (at **board**)
大剪刀 shear
大件家用电器 white goods
大教堂 cathedral
大教堂教士 canon
大街 avenue
大卡车 tanker
大开的 wide open (at **open**)
大开眼界的事物 eye-opener
大坑 crater, pit
大口杯 beaker
大口地吸 gulp
大口烧杯 beaker
大口吞下 gulp
大块 block, bulk, hunk
大捆 bale
大理石 marble
大理石雕像 marble
大力改进 blitz
大力宣传 plug
大量 array, blaze, body, cascade, diet, heaviness (at **heavy**), host, lot, mass, million, multiplicity, multitude, myriad, onslaught, quantity, score
大量储备 reservoir, stock up (at **stock**), stockpile
大量的 copious, galore, generous, heavy, large, liberal, mountainous, myriad, plenty, profuse, substantial, wealth
大量地 freely
大量地给予 heap
大量繁殖 multiply
大量毁灭 decimate
大量获得 rack up (at **rack**)
大量击中 pepper
大量射出 spray
大量下落 shower
大量消耗 absorb
大量涌进 roll in (at **roll**)
大量涌入 influx
大量涌至 pour
大量用品 paraphernalia
大量装入 load, load up (at **load**)
大裂口 chasm
大楼 block
大陆 mainland
大陆的 continental
大陆军士兵 continental
大旅行袋 holdall
大律师 barrister
大麻 cannabis, marijuana, pot
大麻袋 sack
大麻烟卷 joint
大麦 barley
大门 gate
大门入口 gateway
大名鼎鼎的 legendary
大拇指 thumb
大牧场 ranch, range
大男子气的 macho
大脑的 cerebral
大鸟笼 aviary
大炮 artillery, cannon
大陪审团 grand jury
大批出没的 infested (at **infest**)
大批出没于 infest
大批地 bulk, in force (at **force**)
大批离开 exodus
大批量生产 mass production, mass-produce
大批量生产的 mass-produced (at **mass-produce**)
大批流动 stream
大片 blockbuster, tract
大企业 big business, giant
大气层 atmosphere
大气层的 atmospheric
大浅盘 platter
大权在握 rule the roost (at **roost**)
大群 army, swarm
大群移动 swarm
大群涌入 invasion
大人 honor, Lordship
大人物 great
大赛 major
大生意 big business
大声表达 give voice to (at **voice**)
大声播放 blast
大声的 loud
大声地 aloud
大声点说 speak
大声读出 read out (at **read**)
大声放 blast
大声喊叫 bawl
大声疾呼的 vociferous
大声叫喊 cry, cry out (at **cry**), yell
大声叫骂 hurl
大声咀嚼 munch
大声猛击 bang
大声演唱 belt out (at **belt**)
大声演奏 belt
大师 virtuoso
大使 ambassador
大使馆 embassy
大手提包 carryall
大肆宣传 build, build-up, hype
大蒜 garlic
大汤匙 tablespoon
大提琴 cello
大提琴手 cellist
大体的 general
大体上 broadly, in the main (at **main**)
大体上说 on the whole (at **whole**)
大铁桶 skip
大厅 hall, lobby
大桶 butt
大屠杀 carnage, genocide, holocaust, massacre
大腿 thigh
大腿部 lap
大腿上部 knee
大为吃惊的 off-balance
大为赞叹 marvel
大西洋 pond
大厦 edifice, mansion
大箱子 trunk
大象 elephant
大小 proportion, size
大笑 laugh one's head off (at **head**)
大写的 uppercase
大写字母 capital
大猩猩 gorilla
大型超市 superstore
大型的 great
大型购物区 mall
大型购物中心 shopping mall
大型会议 convention
大型机械设备 plant
大熊猫 panda
大选 general election
大学 college, school, university
大学本科生 undergraduate
大学的 tertiary
大学教授 chair
大学校长 chancellor
大摇大摆地走 swagger
大一统的 monolithic
大衣 overcoat
大意是 to this/that effect (at **effect**)
大有进展 on one's way/well on one's way (at **way**)
大有前途 sb will go far (at **far**)
大约 about, around about (at **around**), circa, in/of the order of sth (at **order**), maybe, or so (at **so**), some, something like (at **like**), somewhere
大约地 around
大约为 in the neighborhood of (at **neighborhood**)
大约一打 dozen
大灾难 holocaust
大张旗鼓的宣传 fanfare
大致 more
大致的 rough
大致的信息 idea
大致说来 basically
大致印象 snapshot
大致知道 hear
大众传媒 mass media
大众市场 mass market
大众市场的 mass market
大洲 continent
大主教 archbishop, primate
大自然 nature
大醉的 plastered
大作 blow
呆在家里 stay in (at **stay**)
呆在外面 stay out (at **stay**)
呆在原地不动 stick around (at **stick**)
呆滞的 glazed
呆住不动 freeze

呆着不动的 rooted
代 generation
代币券 voucher
代表 delegate, denote, envoy, figure, for, in the name of sb/ in sb's name (at **name**), indicate, on sb's behalf/ on behalf of sb (at **behalf**), rep, represent, representation, representative, stand, typify
代表…发言 speak
代表大会 congress
代表个人行事的 private
代表团 contingent, delegation
代表制的 representative
代表作 masterpiece
代词 pronoun
代价 cost, price
代金券 token
代课教师 sub, substitute teacher, supply teacher
代理 act, represent
代理公司 agency
代理权 proxy
代理人 deputy, representative
代理商 agent
代码 code
代人临时照看 babysit
代数 algebra
代替 cover, replace, replacement, substitute, substitution (at **substitute**)
代为处理事务 hold the fort (at **fort**)
代言 endorse, endorsement
代言人 mouthpiece
代议制的 representative
代用币 token
代孕母亲 surrogate mother
带 band, in, talk, with
带…姿态 carry
带鼻音的 nasal
带刺的 thorny
带刺的树 thorn
带刺灌木丛 thorn
带刺铁丝网 barbed wire
带电的 electric, live
带发条装置的 clockwork
带扣 buckle
带宽 bandwidth
带来 bring, pay, present
带来耻辱的人 disgrace
带来好结果 pay
带来钱 pay
带来生机 bring sth to life/come to life (at **life**)
带来新气象 be a breath of fresh air (at **breath**)
带领 lead, take
带螺旋的 screw
带某人出去 take
带黏性的 adhesive
带球 dribble
带球触地得分 try
带入 bring
带薪的 paid
带有 bear, carry
带有…迹象 smack
带浴室的 en suite
带在…身上 on
带脏字的 bad
带状疱疹 shingle
带状物 band
带着 with
带子 band, strap
带走 take
待处理的 pending
待定 tbc
待发生 pending
待售 up for sale (at **sale**)
待洗 be in the wash (at **wash**)
待洗的衣物 washing
待宣布 TBA
待租的 for rent (at **rent**)
待做 remain
怠工 go-slow
怠工抗议 slowdown
怠慢 slight, snub
贷方 lender
贷方款额 credit
贷款 lend, loan
贷款利率 lending rate
袋鼠 kangaroo
袋子 bag
逮捕 apprehend, arrest, bust, catch up with (at **catch**), pick, round up (at **round**), seize
逮个正着 catch sb in the act (at **act**)
戴 wear
戴面纱的 veiled
戴水肺潜水 scuba diving
戴头罩的 hooded
戴着面具的 masked
丹佛锁扣 Denver boot
单程的 one-way, single
单程票 single
单词 word
单打比赛 single
单单 alone
单单的 mere
单的 odd
单调的 monotonous, mundane
单调的工作 treadmill
单调乏味 drabness (at **drab**)
单调乏味的 drab, mindless
单独的 individual, separate, solo
单独地 in isolation (at **isolation**), single-handed
单独考虑 isolate
单方面的 unilateral
单干 go it alone (at **alone**)
单个的 single
单簧管 clarinet
单间附加费 single supplement
单间公寓 studio
单件衣服 separate
单脚跳行 hop
单据 note
单利 simple interest
单排滚轴旱冰鞋 Rollerblade
单亲 single parent
单曲唱片 single
单人表演的喜剧 stand-up
单人的 single
单人喜剧表演的 stand-up
单人喜剧演员 stand-up
单身的 single
单身汉 bachelor
单声道的 mono
单数的 singular
单数形式 singular
单位 unit
单位成本 unit cost
单位销售量 unit sales
单位信托投资公司 unit trust
单向行驶的 one-way
单一的 single-
单一配偶的 monogamous
单一配偶制 monogamy
单一性伴侣的 monogamous
单元 unit
担保 guarantee
担保金 collateral
担保人 guarantor, underwriter
担保物 guarantee, surety
担当职员 staff
担架 stretcher
担架车 trolley
担任 act, fill, hold
担任…的成员 sit
担任裁判 referee, umpire
担任主席 chair
担任主演 feature
担任主要角色的 leading
担心 fear, fret, lose sleep (at **sleep**), worry
担心得要命 worried sick (at **sick**)
担心的 afraid, apprehensive, scared
担忧 brood, concern, dread, fear, shudder
担忧的 worried
耽搁 delay, detain, hold, keep
耽误 leave sth too late (at **leave**)
胆固醇 cholesterol
胆量 daring, gut
胆囊 gall bladder
胆怯的 daunted (at **daunt**)
胆小 cowardice
胆小的 cowardly
胆小鬼 chicken, coward, wuss
但是 but
但愿 hopefully, I hope (at **hope**), wish
诞生 born
弹弓 catapult, slingshot
弹身 fuselage
弹头 warhead
弹药 ammunition
弹药筒 cartridge
弹子 marble
弹子游戏 marble
淡薄的 watery
淡的 pastel, subtle
淡而无味的 bland, watery
淡绿褐色 hazel
淡水的 freshwater
淡紫粉色的 lilac
淡棕色的 beige
蛋 egg
蛋白质 protein
蛋糕 cake
蛋糕烤盘 cake pan
蛋黄 yolk
蛋黄酱 mayonnaise
蛋卷冰淇淋 cone
蛋奶糕 custard
蛋奶沙司 custard
蛋清 white
氮 nitrogen
当…的时候 when, while
当场 spot
当船员 crew
当代的 contemporary
当地的 indigenous, local
当地土生的 native
当即 on the spot (at **spot**)
当即死亡 be killed outright (at **outright**)
当季期 season
当今 today
当局 authority
当面 person
当面地 personally
当模特儿 model, modeling (at **model**)
当前的 current
当权者 establishment
当然 certainly, course, of course, sure
当然不 certainly
当然可以 by all means (at **means**), of course
当日交易者 day trader
当时的 then
当心 beware, mind, watch, watch it (at **watch**)
当心的 careful
当选 election, get in (at **get**)
当真 seriously
当中 midway
当中的 middle
当众 in public (at **public**)
当众吵闹 scene
当众批评 put
当着…的面 in front of (at **front**), under sb's nose (at **nose**)
当着某人的面 to sb's face (at **face**)
挡 bar
挡风玻璃 windshield
挡泥板 fender
挡位 setting
挡住 block, fend
荡妇 tramp
档案 archive
档案馆 archive
刀 knife
刀具 cutlery
导出 export
导弹 missile
导航 navigate, navigation (at **navigate**)
导火线 fuse
导盲犬 guide dog, Seeing Eye dog
导入 import
导师 mentor
导体 conductor
导线 lead
导向 home
导演 direct, director
导游 guide
导致 account, dictate, entail, lead, lead up to (at **lead**), mean
导致定罪的 damning
岛 island, isle
岛民 islander
倒进 wind
倒 back, pour, reverse
倒闭 closure, fail, failure, go bust (at **bust**), go under (at **go**)
倒车 back
倒出 pour, pour out (at **pour**)
倒带 rewind
倒档 reverse
倒过来 reverse
倒计时 countdown
倒空 empty
倒立 stand on one's head (at **head**)
倒卖 scalp
倒霉的 ill-fated, unlucky
倒票者 scalper
倒数第二的 penultimate
倒塌 way
倒退 back, setback
倒退地 backward
倒吸气 gasp, gulp
倒下 collapse, fall over (at **fall**), keel over (at **keel**), over, topple
倒下的 fallen (at **fall**)
倒叙 flashback
倒置地 upside down
倒着地 backward
捣蛋鬼 rogue
捣鬼 up
捣毁 smash
捣乱 mischief
捣碎 pound
祷词 prayer
到 get
到… over, to
到…程度 far, insofar (at

发出回声 echo
发出火花 spark
发出尖而刺耳的叫声 screech
发出尖啸声 whistle
发出警报 raise/sound the alarm (at **alarm**)
发出咔嚓声 click
发出连续低沉的声音 hum
发出连续急促刺耳的声音 crackle
发出啪的一声 snap
发出劈啪声 crackle, splutter
发出声音 sound
发出咝咝声 sizzle
发出微光 shimmer
发出微弱稳定的光 glow
发出翁翁声 purr
发出嗡嗡声 whir
发出响亮刺耳的声音 blare
发出嘘声 boo, booing (at **boo**)
发出吱嘎声 groan
发出吱吱嘎嘎的摩擦声 grate
发传真 fax
发慈悲 relent
发达 develop
发达的 advanced, developed, developed (at **develop**)
发大财 make a killing (at **killing**)
发电报给 telegraph
发电机 dynamo, generator
发电站 power plant, power station
发动 fire up (at **fire**), mount, start, wage
发动机 motor
发动机防盗锁装置 immobilizer
发抖 quake, quake in one's boots/shoes (at **quake**), shudder
发短信 message, text messaging, texting
发放 release
发疯 out of your mind (at **mind**)
发疯的 crazy, loony, manic, nut
发光 burn, glisten, shine
发光小饰物 glitter
发函 write, write in (at **write**)
发号施令 call the shots (at **shot**), tune
发呼噜声 purr
发挥 carry, realize, use
发挥作用 fit
发夹 bobby pin, hairgrip
发僵 seize up (at **seize**)
发酵 ferment, fermentation (at **ferment**)
发卷 roller
发觉 catch, discover, find
发掘 unlock
发狂 beside oneself (at **beside**)
发狂的 frantic, giddy
发牢骚 bitch
发亮 shine
发亮的 luminous
发令枪 gun
发落 consign
发明 invent, invention
发明物 invention
发明者 father, inventor
发黏的 tacky
发怒 boil, flare, rage
发怒的 in a huff (at **huff**)
发脾气 lose one's temper (at **temper**), scene, tantrum
发票 invoice
发起 initiate, initiation, instigate, launch
发球 serve, service
发球失误 fault
发球员 server
发人深思的事 food for thought (at **food**)
发散出 emanate
发烧 fever, run a temperature (at **temperature**)
发烧的 feverish
发射 launch
发射机 transmitter
发射升空 blast off (at **blast**)
发射塔 tower
发射台 pad
发射线 line of fire (at **fire**)
发生 come, develop, enact, go, happen, occur, occurrence, take place (at **place**), transpire
发生冲突 clash
发生的事情 occurrence
发生联系 relate
发生率 incidence
发生小冲突 skirmish
发生性关系 go to bed (at **bed**)
发生于其间的 intervening
发誓 swear, vow
发嘶嘶声 hiss
发送 dispatch, mail, send
发现 catch, detection, discover, discovery, find, identify, pick, revelation, spot, strike, transpire, turn, unearth
发泄 to give vent to (at **vent**), vent, work off (at **work**)
发泄途径 outlet
发薪日 payday
发信号 signal
发行 release
发行价 issue price
发行量 circulation
发行物 release
发型 haircut, hairstyle
发嘘声 hiss
发芽 germinate, germination (at **germinate**), sprout
发言 have the floor (at **floor**), speak
发言权 say
发言人 spokesperson
发言者 speaker
发炎的 inflamed
发痒 itch, tickle
发痒的 itchy
发音 pronounce, pronunciation
发音不清 slur
发荧光的 fluorescent
发育 development
发育成熟 mature, maturity
发育的 develop
发源地 birthplace, home, matrix
发展 advance, develop, development, evolution, expand, expansion, growth
发展的 developed (at **develop**), growth, onward
发展方向 direction
发展为 grow
发展中的 developing
发自内心地 from the heart/from the bottom of one's heart (at **heart**)
发作 attack, bout
乏味 dull
乏味的 boring, dull, slow, tame
乏味烦人的 tedious
罚款 fine
罚款通知单 ticket
罚球 penalty
阀门 faucet, tap, valve
筏 raft
法案 act, initiative
法典 code
法定的 mandatory, statutory
法定货币 legal tender
法定假日 bank holiday
法官 bench, judge, justice
法规 code, law, ordinance, regulation
法警 bailiff
法兰绒 flannel
法郎 franc
法老 pharaoh
法令 decree, statute
法律 law
法律的 legal
法律行业 law
法律制定 enactment
法庭 court, courtroom
法庭科学取证 forensic
法庭科学取证的 forensic
法西斯主义 fascism
法西斯主义的 fascist
法学 law
法院大楼 courthouse
法则 rule
砝码 weight
珐琅质 enamel
帆 sail
帆布 canvas
帆布油画 canvas
帆船运动 sailing, yachting
番茄 tomato
翻 root
翻版 clone
翻倍 double
翻边 cuff
翻倒 overturn, tip over (at **tip**)
翻到 turn
翻动 flip, turn
翻滚 tumble
翻过来 roll over (at **roll**)
翻筋斗 roll, somersault
翻领 lapel
翻身 turn
翻腾 buzz
翻新 facelift, refurbish
翻译 translate, translation (at **translate**)
翻阅 leaf through (at **leaf**)
翻找 burrow, rummage
翻折 fold
翻转 roll, turn over (at **turn**)
翻转倒置 over
凡尘的 temporal
凡人 mortal
烦乱 disturbance
烦恼 bother, care, trouble
烦恼的 bothered (at **bother**), vexed (at **vex**), worked up
烦恼事 torment
烦请 kindly
烦扰 eat, hassle, hound, nag
烦人的 annoying
烦人的事物 annoyance
烦人之人或物 menace
烦心事 pain
烦躁 fray
繁忙 hum
繁忙的 busy, heavy
繁荣 boom, buoyancy, flourish, prosperity
繁荣的 buoyant, flourishing (at **flourish**), healthy
繁荣-萧条周期 boom-bust cycle
繁盛的 flourishing (at **flourish**)
繁文缛节 red tape
繁殖 breed, breeding (at **breed**), propagate, reproduce
繁殖的 reproductive
繁重的 burdensome, heavy, onerous
繁重费力的 punishing
反 back to front (at **back**)
反驳 contradict, dispute, retort
反常 deviance (at **deviant**)
反常的 deviant, perverted
反常的事物 anomaly
反导弹 antimissile
反导弹的 antimissile
反动的 reactionary
反动力 dynamic
反对 against, disagreement, hostility, object, objection, oppose, rebel, vote with one's feet (at **vote**)
反对党 opposition
反对的 hostile, opposed
反对意见 criticism, objection
反对者 enemy, opponent, rebel
反而 only
反复不断的 perpetual
反复出现的 recurrent
反复的 repeated
反复地 over and over (at **over**), persistently, repeatedly
反复地讲 repeat
反复地说 chant
反复灌输 drum into (at **drum**)
反复回想 replay
反复啮咬 gnaw
反复试验 trial and error (at **trial**)
反复讨论得出 thrash out (at **thrash**)
反复无常 blow hot and cold (at **hot**), inconsistency
反复无常的 inconsistent
反复袭击 buffet
反感 distaste, exception
反感的 repel
反击 counterattack
反抗 react, reaction, rebellion, resist, revolt
反恐的 counterterrorist (at **counterterrorism**)
反恐行动 counterterrorism
反馈 feedback
反垄断的 antitrust
反面 reverse
反面朝上地 tail
反面主角 villain
反叛 mutiny
反叛的 rebellious
反叛者 rebel
反射 bounce, reflect, reflection
反射的 reflective
反射动作 reflex
反问的 rhetorical
反向地 reverse
反义词 antonym
反应 reaction, response
反应迟钝的 insensitive
反应过激 overreact
反应能力 reaction
反应神速地 quick as a flash (at **flash**)
反应时间 response time
反映 echo, mirror, reflect, reflection, represent
反映的 reflective
反战的 pacifist
反战者 pacifist
反正 anyhow, anyway
反之亦然 vice versa (at **vice versa**)
反作用于 rebound
返程的 return
返还部分 rebate
返回 return
返利 return
犯 commit, perpetrate
犯错误 err, put your foot in it (at **foot**)

割破 cut, gash
割去包皮 circumcise
割让 cede
搁 prop
搁浅 ground
搁浅地 aground
搁物架 rack
搁置 shelve, table
搁置一段时间 stand
歌唱 singing, song, vocals
歌唱家 singer
歌词 lyric, rap, word
歌剧 opera
歌剧的 operatic
歌曲 song, tune
歌曲的段落 verse
歌手 singer, vocalist
阁楼 attic, loft
革命 revolution
革命的 revolutionary
革命性的 revolutionary
革命者 revolutionary
革新 innovate, innovation
革新的 innovative
革新者 innovator
格 case
格调 style
格林尼治标准时间 GMT
格式 format
格外 particularly
格外地 extra
格言 maxim, motto, saying, watchword
格状结构 lattice
格子间 cubicle
格子呢 tartan
格子图案 check
蛤蜊 clam
隔壁 next door
隔断 partition
隔阂 barrier
隔护层 cocoon
隔间 compartment
隔绝 insulation (at **insulate**)
隔绝的 cut off (at **cut**)
隔开 partition
隔开的用餐区 booth
隔离 cut, isolate, isolation (at **isolate**), quarantine, segregate, segregation, separation
隔离的 segregated
隔区 bay
隔热材料 insulation
隔条箱 crate
嗝 hiccup
个案研究 case study
个别的 isolated, single
个人 individual
个人财物 effect
个人的 intimate, personal
个人电脑 PC, personal computer
个人数字助理 PDA, personal digital assistant
个体经营的 self-employed
个位数字 figure
个性 personality, quality, self, soul
个性化设置 customize
各 apiece
各半的 even
各不相同 vary
各不相同的 different
各处 about
各地 everywhere
各式各样的 assorted, miscellaneous
各位 folk
各异的 sundry
各种 array
各种各样 all sorts (at **sort**), diversity, myriad
各种各样的 all kinds of (at **kind**), diverse, myriad, rich, varied, various
各种事情 this and that/this, that, and the other (at **this**)
各自的 respective
铬 chromium
铬合金 chrome
给 dose, for, here, to
给你 there you are/go (at **there**)
给养 ration
给予 accord, award, concede, deal out (at **deal**), deliver, dish, hand, impart, lend, offer, pay
给予帮助的 supportive
给予荣幸 honor
给作解说 narrate
根 root
根本 at all (at **all**), by a long shot (at **shot**), earthly, keystone, on earth (at **earth**), remotely
根本不 exactly, less than (at **less**)
根本的 fundamental, ultimate
根本原因 rationale
根除 eliminate, elimination (at **eliminate**), eradicate, eradication (at **eradicate**), root
根据 according to (at **according to**), by, case, foundation, from, ground, in the light of sth (at **light**)
根据…而定 depend
根据…判断 judging by/judging from/to judge from (at **judge**)
根据法律 by law (at **law**)
根深蒂固的 deep-seated, embedded (at **embed**), ingrained, institutional, rooted
根源 root, source
跟…调情 flirt
跟…一样 same
跟别人一样 as the next (at **next**)
跟唱 sing along (at **sing**)
跟某人过不去 to have it in for sb (at **have**)
跟你说实话 to tell you the truth (at **truth**)
跟上 keep, keep up (at **keep**)
跟随 follow, tag along (at **tag**)
跟着做 follow suit (at **suit**)
跟踪 follow, tail, track, trail
跟踪器 tag
更 more
更不用说 let alone (at **let**), much less (at **much**), never mind sth (at **mind**)
更大程度地 better, more
更大的 wide
更多的 further, more
更改 alter, move
更高标准 better
更好 be better doing sth/it is better doing sth (at **better**)
更好的 better
更合心意的 preferable
更换 change, exchange, replacement
更加 all, even, more, still
更坚定 harden
更进一步地 further
更经常地 more
更年期 menopause
更年期的 menopausal (at **menopause**)
更强硬 harden
更确切地说 rather, specifically
更少的 less
更深入地 further
更适合的 preferable
更喜欢 favor, prefer
更新 update
更新的 new
更衣 change
更优的 favorable
更有生气 liven
更有头脑 better
更远地 further
更糟糕的情况 for the worse (at **worse**)
更糟糕的是 add insult to injury (at **insult**)
耕地 farmland
耕种 farm, farming
耕种的 arable
梗 stalk
梗阻 obstruction
工厂 factory, mill, plant, work
工程 engineering
工程师 engineer
工程学 engineering
工会 labor union, union
工匠 craftsman, workman
工具 tool
工具栏 toolbar
工人 worker, workman
工人阶级 working class
工时 man-hour
工头 foreman
工薪 pay packet, paycheck
工薪袋 pay envelope, pay packet
工业 industry
工业的 industrial
工业废料 sludge
工业化 industrialization (at **industrialize**)
工业家 industrialist
工业品 manufacture
工业园区 industrial estate, industrial park
工艺 craft, workmanship
工艺的 technical
工装裤 overall
工资 wage, wage packet
工资级别 scale
工资条 payslip, paystub
工资支票 paycheck
工作 business, duty, employment, job, labor, undertaking, work
工作报告 report card
工作场所 shop floor, workplace
工作成果 work
工作单位 work
工作的 up, working
工作的人 worker
工作过度 overwork
工作狂 workaholic
工作量 load, workload
工作日 weekday, workday
工作时间 hour
工作室 studio
工作台 bench
工作台面 countertop
工作站 workstation
工作周 week
工作着 on
弓 arch, bow
弓着 arch
弓着的 bowed
公报 communiqué
公布 publicize, unveil
公车 company car
公道的 reasonable
公地 homestead
公告 announcement, bulletin, pronouncement
公公 father-in-law
公共厕所 restroom
公共储金 kitty
公共的 public
公共服务机构 service
公共服务系统 service
公共汽车 bus
公共汽车站 depot
公共卫生 sanitation
公共卫生的 sanitary
公关 PR
公关工作 public relations
公关形象 public relations
公鸡 cock, rooster
公斤 kg, kilo, kilogram
公爵 duke
公爵夫人 duchess
公开 disclosure, publication, publish
公开表明身份 come
公开承认的 self-confessed
公开的 in the open/out in the open (at **open**), open, overt, public
公开地 openly
公开肯定 affirm, affirmation (at **affirm**)
公开请求 call
公开市场 open market
公开说出 speak out (at **speak**)
公开显露的 explicit
公开性 openness (at **open**)
公开支持 endorse
公里 kilometer, km
公里每小时 kph
公立学校 public school, state school
公路 highway, Rd., road, route
公路车赛 rally
公路货运商 hauler
公民 citizen
公民的 civic, civil
公民身份 citizenship
公民投票 referendum
公民义务和责任 citizenship
公牛 bull
公平的 fair
公平合理的 equitable
公顷 hectare
公然的 blatant, naked, open
公认 be meant to (at **meant**)
公认的 accepted, known, undisputed
公使 envoy, minister
公式 formula
公司 Co., company, concern, Corp., enterprise, firm, operation
公司的 corporate
公司收购 buyout
公司税 corporation tax
公文 document
公文包 briefcase
公务 civil service
公务的 official
公务员 civil servant
公学 public school
公羊 ram
公益服务 public service
公营部分 public sector
公用电话 payphone
公用电话亭 phone booth, phone box
公用事业 public service, public utility, utility
公寓 apartment, tenement
公寓楼 apartment building

payments
国际跳棋 draughts
国际象棋 chess
国际制裁 sanction
国家 country, land, nation, state
国家的 state
国家公园 national park
国家或组织 flag
国家首脑 head of state
国界 frontier
国库券 treasury
国民 country, national, people
国民的 civil, national
国民生产总值 GNP, gross national product
国内的 domestic, internal
国内货物税 excise
国内生产总值 GDP, gross domestic product
国内税务署 IRS
国旗 color
国旗色 color
国事的 state
国王 king
国务卿 Secretary of State
国务院 State Department
国有化 nationalization (at **nationalize**)
掴 slap
腘绳肌腱 hamstring
果冻 Jell-O, jelly
果断 decision, decisiveness (at **decisive**)
果断的 decisive
果核 stone
果酱 jam, jelly, preserve
果酒 wine
果岭 green
果皮 skin
果然 sure enough (at **sure**)
果肉 flesh, pulp
果园 orchard
果真 really
裹尸布 shroud
过 across, after, past
过…的生活 lead
过程 means, process, road
过错 fault
过道 hall, hallway, passage, passageway
过度 heavy
过度从事 overdose
过度的 excessive, heavy
过度地 overly, to excess (at **excess**)
过度地做 overdo
过度工作的 overworked (at **overwork**)
过度拥挤 overcrowding
过度拥有 overdose
过渡 passage
过渡贷款 bridge loan
过渡的 transitional
过多的 excessive
过多地 excess
过分 go overboard (at **overboard**)
过分的 extravagant, undue
过分活跃的 hyperactive
过分简单化的 simplistic
过分认真 intensity (at **intense**)
过分渲染的 noisy
过分耀眼的 garish
过分在乎琐事的 petty
过分赞扬的 gushing (at **gush**)
过高的 exorbitant
过激的 extreme
过量 excess, overdose
过量的 excess
过量服用 overdose
过滤 filter, sieve, strain
过滤器 filter, sieve
过路人 passerby
过敏 allergy
过敏的 allergic
过气的人物 has-been
过桥贷款 bridge loan
过去 past, yesterday
过去的好时光 the good old days (at **old**)
过去惯常 used
过热 overheat
过热的 overheated (at **overheat**)
过山车 roller coaster
过剩 plethora, surplus
过剩的 surplus
过失 fault
过失杀人 manslaughter
过时 date
过时的 antiquated, dated, dead, old, old-fashioned, out, out of date, outdated, staid
过稀的 runny
过一遍 run through (at **run**)
过于矮小的 dwarf
过于的 indecent
过于夸张的 melodramatic
过于严格 rigid
过于严格的 rigid
过于拥挤的 overcrowded
过早的 premature
过早行动 jump the gun (at **gun**)
哈哈大笑 crack
嗨 hi
孩子 family, kid, son
孩子的 childish
孩子们 children
孩子气的人 baby
孩子特有的 childish
骸骨的 skeletal
海 sea
海岸 coast
海岸边 seashore
海岸警卫队 coast guard
海岸线 coastline
海拔 elevation
海拔高度 altitude
海报 poster
海报上的性感男女 pin-up
海豹 seal
海贝壳 seashell
海边 seaside
海草 seaweed
海产食品 seafood
海床 bed, seabed
海盗 pirate
海盗行为 piracy
海关 customs
海关部门 customs
海关的 customs
海关检查处 control
海角 cape
海军 navy
海军的 naval
海军军官 commander
海军陆战队士兵 marine
海军上将 admiral
海军上尉 lieutenant
海浪 tide, wave
海狸 beaver
海狸毛皮 beaver
海洛因 heroin, smack
海绵 foam, sponge
海绵块 sponge
海鸥 seagull
海平面 sea level
海上的 offshore
海上航游 cruise
海事的 marine, maritime
海滩 beach
海滩装 beachwear
海图 chart
海豚 dolphin
海外的 overseas
海湾 bay, gulf
海峡 strait
海啸 tsunami
海洋 sea
海洋的 marine
海域 water
海员 seaman
骇人的 horrendous
骇人听闻的 appalling, monstrous
害虫 pest
害怕 dread, fear, foot, shudder
害怕的 afraid, fearful, frightened, scared
害怕的感觉 chill
害羞的 shy
酣的 sound
含大量奶油的 creamy
含二氧化碳的 carbonated
含否定词的 negative
含糊不清的 murky
含糊不清地说 babble
含糊的 vague
含糊地说 slur
含糊其辞 waffle
含糊其辞的 vague
含金属的 metallic
含酒精的 alcoholic
含量 content
含量低的 low
含量高的 strong
含氯氟烃 CFC
含水的 watery
含碳水化合物的食物 carbohydrate
含蓄的 implicit, veiled
含盐的 salty
含义 meaning, sense
含意 implication
含油的 oily
含有 contain
含有…意味 smack
含脂肪的 fatty
函件 circular
函授课程 correspondence course
涵盖不全面的 incomprehensive
寒冷 cold, coldness (at **cold**)
寒冷的 chill, chilly, cold
寒冷而清新的 brisk
罕见的 few, rare
罕见之人 rarity
喊 call
喊叫 holler
喊叫声 cry
喊某人过来 call
汉堡 burger
汉堡包 hamburger
汗 sweat
汗毛 hair
汗衫 undershirt
汗水 perspiration
旱冰场 rink
旱冰鞋 skate
捍卫 champion, stand up for (at **stand**), stick
捍卫者 champion, defender
焊接 weld
航班 flight
航程 passage, voyage
航道 channel, waterway
航海的 nautical
航空 aviation
航空公司 airline
航空航天 aerospace
航空器 craft
航空小姐 air hostess
航空邮递 airmail
航天飞机 shuttle, space shuttle
航天器 craft, spacecraft
航线 lane, route
航行 navigate, navigation, sail
航运业 shipping
毫不 none too (at **none**)
毫不迟疑的 quick
毫不迟疑地 shot
毫不耽搁地 fast
毫不费力地得到 hand sth to sb on a platter (at **platter**)
毫不留情的 relentless
毫不犹豫 have no hesitation (at **hesitation**)
毫不犹豫地 without hesitation (at **hesitation**)
毫不在乎 do not give a hoot (at **hoot**), not give a damn (at **damn**)
毫克 mg, milligram
毫米 millimeter, mm
毫升 milliliter, ml
毫无 imaginable
毫无变化的 same
毫无睡意的 wide awake (at **awake**)
毫无头绪 haven't a clue (at **clue**)
毫无希望 not a hope in hell (at **hope**)
毫无效果 like water off a duck's back (at **duck**)
毫无遗漏地 fully
毫无疑问地 evidently, no doubt (at **doubt**)
毫无怨言 without a murmur (at **murmur**)
嗥叫 howl
豪华 opulence (at **opulent**)
豪华的 lush, luxurious, opulent, posh, sleek
豪华轿车 limousine
豪华舒适的 plush
嚎叫 bay, howl
嚎叫声 cry
好 away, done, right
好啊 hip hip hooray/hurrah (at **hip**), well
好吧 all right, okay, very well (at **very**)
好办的 simple
好猜忌的 jealous
好吃的 yummy
好处 benefit, merit, mileage
好得令人难以置信 too good to be true (at **true**)
好的 fine, long, yes
好的方面 upside
好的选择 bet
好的做法 a good bet (at **bet**)
好动的 active
好斗的 aggressive, belligerent, combative
好斗性 belligerence (at **belligerent**)
好好表现 shape
好家伙 boy/oh boy (at **boy**)
好交际的 sociable
好看的 nice
好客的 hospitable
好了 anyway, now, okay, right
好朋友 buddy
好奇的 curious, inquisitive
好奇心 curiosity
好强的 aggressive
好胜 competitiveness (at **competitive**)
好胜的 competitive
好似 seemingly
好问的 inquiring

好像 as, if
好像是 as it were (at **as**)
好像总是不能 cannot seem (at **seem**)
好笑的 funny
好心的 good
好学的 scholarly
好言说服 nudge
好意 kindness
好意地 kindly
好用的 user-friendly
好运 fortune
好战性 militancy (at **militant**)
好支使人的 bossy
好转 mend, rally, recede, recover, recovery, turn, upturn
号 horn
号码 number
耗费 eat into (at **eat**), exert, exertion (at **exert**), soak
耗费…的 heavy
耗费过多的 extravagant
耗尽 drain, run, stretch
耗尽的 depleted (at **deplete**)
耗时的 time-consuming
呵气 blow
喝 consume, drink
喝光 finish
喝酒 booze, drink, drinking (at **drink**)
喝完 finish
喝下 down
喝醉的 intoxicated, loaded
喝醉了的 high
合并 amalgamate, amalgamation (at **amalgamate**), combine, consolidate, merge, merger, union
合唱队的 choral
合唱曲 chorus
合唱团 choir, chorus
合成 synthesis, synthesize
合成的 composite, synthetic
合成树脂 resin
合尺寸的 fitted
合调的 in tune/out of tune (at **tune**)
合订本 volume
合法的 lawful, legal, legitimate
合法化 legalization (at **legalize**)
合法性 legality, legitimacy (at **legitimate**)
合格 eligible
合格证明 certification (at **certify**)
合乎道德的 ethical
合乎逻辑的 logical
合乎情理 add
合乎情理的 sane
合乎语法的 grammatical
合伙人 partner
合集 compilation
合计达 come
合计的 aggregate
合金 alloy
合理 fairness
合理的 fair, good, justified, legitimate, logical, reasonable
合理行事 shape
合理性 legitimacy (at **legitimate**), validity (at **valid**)
合谋 conspiracy, conspire
合拍 in of time (at **time**)
合情合理的 within reason (at **reason**)
合身 fit
合身的 fitted
合适 fit
合适的 correct, cut out, fitting, satisfactory
合适的活动 niche
合适的职位 niche
合适时候 time
合适于 fit
合算程度 value
合算的 good
合同 contract
合同的 contractual
合为一体 combine
合心意 suit
合宜的 decent
合宜地 properly
合住 room
合住一套公寓房的人 flatmate
合作 collaborate, collaboration, cooperate, cooperation (at **cooperate**), team
合作成果 collaboration
合作的 collaborative, cooperative
合作关系 linkup
合作性企业 cooperative
合作性组织 cooperative
合作者 collaborator
和 and, sum, well, with
和…不同 unlike
和…共舞 dance
和…交朋友 befriend
和…类似的 in the nature of sth (at **nature**)
和…签约 sign up (at **sign**)
和…同时用 with
和…相关 correlate
和…相配 match
和…相似 the same as (at **same**)
和…一道 join
和…一起 with
和蔼 kindness
和蔼的 affable, kind
和蔼可亲的 amiable, gracious
和好 make
和解 conciliation, reconciliation, settle, settlement
和睦相处 side by side (at **side**)
和平的 peaceful
和平鸽 dove
和平问题 peace
和平运动 peace
和平主义 pacifism
和平主义的 pacifist
和平主义者 pacifist
和平状态 peace
和善的 benign
和声 harmony
和声的 harmonic
和声演唱或演奏 harmonize
和谈 talk
和往常一样 as usual (at **usual**)
和弦 chord
和谐 harmony
河 river
河边 riverside
河床 bed
河道 course
河口 estuary, mouth
河流水浅处 ford
河鲈 perch
核 core, nucleus, pit
核保人 underwriter
核的 nuclear
核对 check off (at **check**)
核反应堆 nuclear reactor, reactor
核辐射 fallout
核聚变 fusion
核实 check, make sure (at **sure**), verification (at **verify**), verify
核桃 walnut
核武器 bomb
核武器的 nuclear
核心 core, heart, nucleus, pillar
核心集团 inner circle
核心组织 caucus
荷尔蒙 hormone
荷尔蒙的 hormonal
盒 carton, case, pack
盒饭 box lunch
盒式磁带 tape
盒式磁带录像机 video recorder
盒式录像带 video cassette, videotape
盒装午餐 box lunch
盒装物 carton
盒子 box
颌骨 jaw
贺卡 card
喝倒彩 hiss
褐黄色 mustard
褐色的 brown
赫然出现 loom
鹤 crane
黑暗 dark, darkness (at **dark**)
黑暗的 dark, dim
黑白的 black and white
黑白分明的 black and white
黑白图像的 black and white
黑板 blackboard, board, chalkboard
黑鬼 Negro
黑客 hacker
黑麦 rye
黑麦面包 rye
黑莓果 blackberry
黑莓手机 blackberry
黑名单 blacklist
黑人 black
黑人家园 homeland
黑色的 black, dark
黑色礼袍 gown
黑色轮廓 silhouette
黑色人种的 black
黑社会 underworld
黑市 black market
黑桃 spade
黑线鳕 haddock
黑猩猩 chimpanzee
嘿 hey
痕迹 trail
很 as hell (at **hell**), much, only, very, well
很棒的 cool, great, neat
很差的 low
很长久地 forever
很长时间 age
很大程度的 substantial
很大程度上 much
很大的 wide
很大的希望 high/great hopes (at **hope**)
很大数额的钱 fortune
很多 a hundred and one/a thousand and one/a million and one (at **one**)
很费劲的事 struggle
很高的 exalted
很高兴的 nice
很高兴见到你 pleased to meet you (at **pleased**)
很乖的 as good as gold (at **gold**)
很好 good
很好的 bad
很紧张的 wound up
很久 year
很久地 well
很久没见的 long-lost
很久以前的 bygone
很可能 easily, in all probability (at **probability**), presumably, well
很可能的 calculated
很可能地 likely
很可能发生 in the cards (at **card**)
很可能由于…导致的 attributable
很快 time
很快发生的 quick
很快就来 won't be long (at **long**)
很快转变 flit
很没意思的事 drag
很难 hardly
很难的 hard-pressed
很难地 hardly
很难过 sorry
很难说 you never know (at **know**)
很奇异的 unreal
很认真的 intense
很少 few, seldom
很吸引人的 gorgeous
很喜欢 adore, fond, sb wouldn't mind sth/doing sth (at **mind**)
很险的 narrow
很想购买 in the market for something (at **market**)
很小的 minimum
很性感的 gorgeous
很遗憾 I'm sorry to say (at **sorry**)
很有可能的 liable
很远的距离 mile
很远地 far
很愿意 love, mind
很重要 mean
狠打 club
狠批 crucify
狠揍 belt
哼 hum
横冲直撞 go on a/the rampage (at **rampage**), rampage
横穿全国的 cross-country
横传 cross
横的 horizontal
横渡 crossing
横断面 cross-section
横幅 banner
横杆 rail
横膈膜 diaphragm
横跨 cross, span, straddle
横跨大陆的 transcontinental
横跨大西洋的 transatlantic
横排格式 landscape
横向的 lateral
衡量基准 benchmark
轰动 sensation, stir
轰动性的 sensational
轰轰烈烈地 with a bang (at **bang**)
轰击 bombardment
轰隆的雷声 clap
轰隆隆地快速移动 thunder
轰隆隆地慢慢停下 grind to a halt (at **grind**)
轰隆声 thunder
轰隆着缓慢行进 rumble
轰鸣 roar
轰炸 bomb, bombardment, bombing (at **bomb**)
轰炸机 bomber
哄 coax
哄骗 con, delude
哄然 roar
烘烤 bake, baking (at **bake**), grill
烘烤用具 broiler
红宝石 ruby
红的 ruddy

桦树 birch
怀 conceive
怀抱 cuddle
怀敌意的 hostile
怀旧 nostalgia
怀旧的 nostalgic
怀念 memory, remembrance
怀疑 cynicism, disbelief, distrust, doubt, question, skepticism, suspect, suspicion
怀疑的 cynical, incredulous, suspicious
怀疑论者 skeptic
怀有 nurse
怀孕 conceive, expect, pregnancy
怀孕的 pregnant
怀孕期 pregnancy, term
怀着…的希望 in the hope of/that (at **hope**)
坏的 bad
坏的影响 reflection
坏疽 gangrene
坏脾气的 morose
坏事 bad news (at **news**)
坏习惯 habit
坏账 bad debt
欢呼 cheer, ovation, whoop
欢快的 merry
欢快活泼的 bright
欢乐 amusement, gaiety
欢闹的 boisterous
欢庆 festivity
欢腾的 tumultuous
欢欣 exhilaration
欢欣鼓舞的 jubilant
欢迎 fete, welcome
獾 badger
还 also, still, supposed, too, yet
还差很远 a long way from/some way from (at **way**)
还成的 all right
还击 fight back (at **fight**), return fire (at **fire**)
还清 pay off (at **pay**)
还清债务 debt
还是 or
还算好的 reasonable
环 hoop, link
环保 greenness (at **green**)
环保的 eco-friendly, environmental, green
环保运动的成员 green
环保主义者 environmentalist
环岛 roundabout
环礁湖 lagoon
环境 condition, environment, ground, milieu, surroundings
环境保护主义者 conservationist
环扣 eye
环路 ring road
环绕 circle, encircle, frame, hem in (at **hem**), loop
环绕…的轨道运行 orbit
环绕着的 edged
环行的 circular
环形公路 beltway
环型交通枢纽 traffic circle
环状物 ring
缓冲 cushion
缓冲区 buffer
缓冲物 buffer
缓过气来 get one's breath back (at **breath**)
缓和 defuse, lighten, moderation (at **moderate**), smooth over (at **smooth**), soothe
缓和的 soothing (at **soothe**)
缓和语气 water
缓缓流向 wash
缓缓升起的大团 billow
缓解 cushion, diffuse, kill, loosen, mitigate, relieve, remission
缓解物 cushion
缓慢 slowness (at **slow**)
缓慢笨拙地移动 lumber
缓慢沉重地走 plod
缓慢但确实地 slowly but surely (at **surely**)
缓慢的 slow, sluggish
缓慢地 slow
缓慢地移动 drift, inch
缓慢滑行 taxi
缓慢或艰难地前进 limp
缓慢行进 crawl, trundle
缓慢行驶 nose
缓慢移动 draw
缓刑 reprieve
缓刑监助官 probation officer
缓刑期 probation
缓行 roll
幻灯片 slide, transparency
幻觉 hallucination, vision
幻觉的 phantom, psychedelic
幻灭 disillusion, disillusionment
幻灭的 disillusioned
幻视 seeing/hearing things (at **thing**)
幻听 thing
幻想 daydream, fantasize, fantasy, illusion, imagine
唤起 evoke, inspire, raise, rouse
唤起回忆的 evocative
唤起某人的记忆 jog sb's memory (at **jog**)
唤醒 wake
换 change, shift
换班人 relief
换成 change over (at **change**)
换乘 change
换个环境 a change of scene (at **scene**), a change of scenery (at **scenery**)
换句话说 in other words (at **word**)
换零钱 make change (at **change**)
换取 buy
换上 replace
换算 convert
换下 replace
患 get, have, run, with
患病的 diseased, ill
患病的可能性 vulnerability (at **vulnerable**)
患癫痫的 epileptic
患感冒 catch cold/catch a cold (at **cold**)
患关节炎的 arthritic
患上 catch
患妄想狂的 paranoid
患厌食症的 anorexic
荒地 wasteland
荒废的 ruined
荒凉 desolation
荒凉的 bleak, desolate
荒谬的 absurd, improbable, ludicrous, preposterous
荒谬可笑的 cockamamie
荒谬性 absurdity (at **absurd**)
荒僻处 backwater
荒唐的 farcical, grotesque, sad, silly
荒唐的决定 insanity
荒唐可笑的 ridiculous
荒唐事 farce
荒芜的 barren, waste, wild
荒野 moor, wild, wilderness
荒原 moorland, wasteland
慌张的 flustered (at **fluster**)
皇帝 emperor
皇后 empress
皇家的 royal
皇位 throne
黄道带 zodiac
黄蜂 wasp
黄瓜 cucumber
黄褐色的 olive
黄昏 dusk, twilight
黄昏以后 after dark (at **dark**)
黄昏以前 before dark (at **dark**)
黄金 gold
黄金般的 golden
黄金法则 golden rule
黄金降落伞 golden parachute
黄金女郎 golden girl (at **golden**)
黄金时段 prime time
黄牌 yellow card
黄色 amber, yellow
黄铜 brass
黄杨 box
黄油 butter
黄油奶糖 caramel
蝗虫 locust
簧片 reed
恍惚的 distant, dreamy
恍然大悟 click
谎报 hoax
谎话 story
谎言 falsehood, lie
幌子 cloak
灰 ash
灰暗的 somber
灰白的 pale
灰尘 dirt, dust
灰狗巴士 greyhound
灰浆 mortar
灰泥 plaster
灰色的 gray
灰色区域 gray area
灰市 gray market
灰心的 disheartened
灰心丧气 lose heart (at **heart**)
诙谐的 witty
恢复 bring, get back (at **get**), on your feet (at **foot**), recover, recovery, reinstate, reinstatement, renew, renewal, restoration (at **restore**), restore, return, revert, revive
恢复过来 get over (at **get**)
恢复健康 pull through (at **pull**), rally, recover
恢复理智 come to one's senses/bring sb to their senses (at **sense**)
恢复生机 come/bring alive (at **alive**)
恢复原状 back
挥 wave
挥动 sweep
挥霍 blow
挥霍的 lavish
挥手 wave
挥手招 hail
挥舞 brandish, flourish, shake, wave
挥舞击打 slash
辉煌 dazzle
辉煌成就 glory
辉煌的 glorious
徽章 badge, emblem
回 back
回报 reciprocate, repay, return, reward
回报率 rate of return
回避 evade, sidestep, skirt
回答 answer, reply
回荡 ring
回到 back, get, go, go back to (at **go**), return
回到现实 back/down to earth (at **earth**)
回电话 ring back (at **ring**)
回放 play back (at **play**)
回复 answer
回购 buy-back
回顾 look back (at **look**)
回顾的 retrospective
回顾展 retrospective
回锅肉丁 hash
回国 homecoming
回合 round
回火 backfire
回击 reply
回家 home, homecoming
回扣 rake-off
回来 come back (at **come**)
回落 subside
回声 echo
回收利用 recycle, recycling (at **recycle**)
回天无力的 far
回头 turn
回头的 repeat
回头见 see
回头客的 repeat
回向后 back
回味 relive
回响 echo, reverberate
回想 in retrospect (at **retrospect**), think back (at **think**)
回想起 cast your mind back (at **mind**), remember
回信 answer, write back (at **write**)
回信信封 s.a.e., SASE, stamped addressed envelope
回形针 clip, paper clip
回忆 recall
回忆道 recall
回忆录 memoirs, reminiscence
回忆起 come, recollect
回应 answer, receive, respond, return
悔恨 remorse, repent, repentance
悔恨的 repentant
悔悟 repent, repentance
悔悟的 repentant
汇 remit
汇报 report
汇编 compilation, compile
汇合 join
汇合点 junction
汇集 compile
汇款 remittance
汇款单 money order
汇率 exchange rate
汇票 draft, money order
会 can, could, should, will, would
会飞的 flying
会歌 anthem
会合 converge
会话 discourse
会见 meet, see
会面 rendezvous
会面地点 rendezvous
会期 session
会社 club
会说话 speak
会算计的 calculating

搅拌 stir
搅拌机 mixer
搅拌器 whisk
搅打 beat, whip
搅动 agitate, stir
搅浑水 muddy the waters (at **muddy**)
搅乱 muddy, upset
搅乳器 churn
缴获 seizure
叫…来 call, call in (at **call**)
叫花子 panhandler
叫声 call
叫停 to call it quits (at **quit**)
叫外卖 send out for (at **send**)
叫醒电话 wake-up call
较差的 inferior
较高的 upper
较量 battle
较年幼者 junior
较轻的 lesser
较少的 less, lesser
较小的 lesser, modest
较远一端的 far
教鞭 pointer
教长 dean
教导 teach, teaching
教化 civilize
教皇的 papal
教皇或其政府 Vatican
教皇训谕 bull
教科书 course book, textbook
教练 coach, instructor, manager
教练员 trainer (at **train**)
教派 church, denomination
教区 parish
教区的 parochial
教师 instructor, schoolteacher, teacher
教士 clergy, cleric
教士的 clerical
教士身份 priesthood
教室 classroom
教授 professor
教堂 church
教条 dogma
教条主义 dogmatism
教训 lesson
教养 breeding, upbringing
教义 teaching
教义的 doctrinal
教育 educate, education, school
教育的 educational
酵母 yeast
阶层 echelon
阶段 phase, point, rung, stage, step
阶级 class
阶梯 ladder
疖子 boil
接 pick
接触 contact, meet
接触传染的 contagious
接触的机会 access
接触的权利 access
接待 receive, reception, serve
接待处 reception
接待员 clerk, desk clerk, receptionist
接到 hear, receive
接点 point
接管 take, take over (at **take**), takeover
接合 join
接近 close, level, near, proximity, toward, verge on (at **verge**)
接近底部的 low
接近地 at close quarters (at **quarter**)
接近地面的 low
接近海平面的 low
接近于 close to/on (at **close**), near
接近终了 late
接力棒 baton
接力赛 relay
接连相继地 back to back (at **back**)
接纳 accept, acceptance, take
接起 pick
接取 pickup
接任 fill, inherit
接收 admit, pick, receive
接收效果 reception
接手 inherit
接受 accept, acceptance, agree, assume, come to terms with (at **term**), recognition, take, take on board (at **board**)
接受量 intake
接受培训 train
接受挑战 pick/take up the gauntlet (at **gauntlet**)
接受再培训 retrain
接受者 recipient
接替 relieve, succeed, take
接替某人的位置 fill sb's shoes/ step into sb's shoes (at **shoe**)
接替者 relief, replacement
接听 take
接通 through
接下来 and, follow
接踵而至 hard on the heels of/ hot on the heels of (at **heel**)
接住 catch
接着 proceed
接着…发生 follow
揭穿 strip away (at **strip**)
揭发 blow the whistle (at **whistle**), exposure
揭开 unlock, unravel
揭露 expose, out, outing (at **out**), reveal, revelation
揭幕的 inaugural
揭伤疤 rub sb's nose in sth (at **nose**)
街 St.
街边小餐馆 café
街道 street
街垒 barricade
街区 block
街头 street
节 episode, festival, knot, verse
节疤 knot
节俭 thrift
节俭的 economical
节流阀 throttle
节目 act, program, show
节目单 program
节目主持人 anchor, host, presenter
节拍 beat, pulse
节日 festival
节日庆典的 festive
节日盛会 gala
节省 conserve, economy, saving
节省的 economical
节省开支 economize
节食 diet
节选 excerpt
节育 birth control
节约 conservation, save
节约的 sparing
节制 moderation
节奏 beat, pace, rhythm, tempo
劫持 hijack, hijacking (at **hijack**)
劫持者 hijacker
杰出 preeminence (at **preeminent**)
杰出的 outstanding, phenomenal, preeminent, shining, towering
杰出的技能 prowess
杰出典范 paragon
杰作 masterpiece
洁净 purity (at **pure**)
洁净的 pure
洁面乳 cleanser
结 bear, knot
结冰 freeze
结冰的 icy
结肠 colon
结成 enter, make
结成晶体 crystallize
结成块的 lumpy
结成群 cluster
结构 construction, fabric, organization, structure, texture
结构工程师 structural engineer
结构上的 structural
结构体 structure
结果 and, come, consequence, consequently, in consequence, as a consequence (at **consequence**), outcome, result, upshot, way
结果成为 culminate
结果实 fruit
结果是 come
结果为 turn out (at **turn**)
结合 bridge, combine, fuse, integrate
结合体 synthesis
结合在一起 fusion, integrate
结婚 marriage, marry, wed
结伙 gang up (at **gang**)
结交 hook
结结巴巴地说话 splutter, stutter
结晶体 crystal
结局 conclusion, culmination, ending
结论 conclusion
结盟 alignment, alliance
结盟的 allied
结清 close
结石 stone
结识 acquaintance
结实的 firm, stout, sturdy
结实度 tone
结实耐用的 heavy-duty, rugged
结束 be out of the way (at **way**), break, breakdown, close, conclude, conclusion, draw to an end/draw to a close (at **draw**), end, finish, passing, scotch, stop, withdrawal
结束的 dead, over
结束工作 call it a day (at **day**)
结束了 at an end (at **end**)
结算清单 statement
结算所 clearinghouse
结尾 end, finish
结尾的 closing
结业证书 certificate
结余 balance
捷径 fast track, shortcut
睫毛 eyelash, lash
睫毛膏 mascara
截 amputate
截点 cutoff
截击空中球 volley
截面图 cross-section
截然相反的 opposite, poles apart (at **pole**)
截然相反的两极 pole
截肢 amputation (at **amputate**)
竭尽全力的 all-out
竭尽全力地 flat out (at **flat**), with all one's might (at **might**)
竭力说 make
竭力维持 struggle
竭力争取 drum up (at **drum**), press
竭力主张 urge
她 her, she
她的 her, hers
她们 them, they
她们的 their, theirs
她们自己 themselves
她自己 herself
姐 sister
姐夫 brother-in-law
姐妹 sister
姐妹般的 sister
解 quench
解除 dislodge, dissolution, dissolve, lift, release, relief, relieve
解除管制 deregulate, deregulation
解除武装 disarm
解答 answer
解冻 thaw
解冻期 thaw
解毒药 antidote
解放 emancipate, emancipation (at **emancipate**), free, liberate, liberation (at **liberate**)
解雇 can, dismiss, fire, firing (at **fire**), lay off (at **lay**), layoff
解雇某人 let someone go (at **let**)
解救 free, salvation
解救物 salvation
解决 clear, clinch, contend, cure, get, get around (at **get**), iron out (at **iron**), remove, resolve, settle, smooth out (at **smooth**), solve, sort
解决办法 answer, cure, fix, remedy, solution
解开 open, undo, unravel, untie, unwind
解开…的钮扣 unbutton
解码 decode
解剖 dissect, dissection (at **dissect**)
解剖学 anatomy
解散 break, disband, dissolution, dissolve
解释 account, comment, define, explain, explanation, interpret, interpretation, put, take
解释明白 put
解释性的 explanatory
解说 commentate, narration (at **narrate**)
解说员 commentator, narrator (at **narrate**)
解体 breakup, disintegration (at **disintegrate**)
解脱的 liberating (at **liberate**)
介词 preposition
介乎…之间 between
介入 foot, move, wade in (at **wade**)
介绍 brief, introduce, introduction (at **introduce**), refer
介绍人 referee
介绍说明文件 prospectus
介意 mind
介于中间的 intervening

经期 period
经受 suffer, undergo
经受得住检验 hold
经受苦难 go through hell (at **hell**)
经受时间的考验 stand the test of time (at **test**)
经受突变 mutate
经受住 stand, stand up to (at **stand**), weather
经销 sell
经验 experience
经验法则 rule of thumb (at **rule**)
经验丰富的 seasoned
经验丰富的人 veteran
经遗传而得 inherit
经营 deal, manage, operation (at **operate**), run, running
经营场所 premise
经营二手货的 secondhand
经营性的 working
经营者 operator
经由 through, via
茎 cane, stem
惊呆的 numbed (at **numb**), stunned (at **stun**)
惊动 start
惊骇的 aghast
惊慌 panic
惊慌失措 lose one's nerve (at **nerve**)
惊叫 exclaim, exclamation
惊恐 alarm, trepidation
惊奇 wonder
惊扰 catch
惊人的 dazzling, startling
惊悚电影 thriller
惊悚戏剧 thriller
惊悚小说 thriller
惊喜 surprise
惊吓 fright, scare, shock
惊险故事 melodrama
惊讶 astonishment, surprise
晶体管 transistor
晶体管收音机 transistor
晶质玻璃 crystal
晶状体 lens
精彩的 tremendous
精彩片段 cameo
精萃 distillation (at **distill**)
精打细算的 careful
精华 pick
精力 energy
精力充沛 ebullience (at **ebullient**)
精力充沛的 ebullient, energetic, fresh, great, vigorous
精力过人的人 demon
精力恢复的 rested
精力旺盛的 energetic
精力旺盛的人 dynamo
精炼厂 refinery
精炼的 refined
精美的 delicate, exquisite
精密的 refined
精妙的 elegant, subtle
精妙之处 subtlety
精明 acumen
精明的 astute, calculating, shrewd, smooth
精明的交易 horse-trading
精明圆滑的人 operator
精疲力竭 exhaustion
精疲力竭的 exhausted (at **exhaust**)
精巧的 artful, delicate
精确 accuracy
精确的 accurate, exact, fine, precise
精确地 dead
精神 spirit
精神崩溃 breakdown, fall
精神变态者 psychopath
精神病的 insane, psychiatric
精神病患者 lunatic
精神病学 psychiatry
精神病医生 psychiatrist, shrink
精神病院 asylum
精神不健全的 sick
精神承受力 nerve
精神错乱 insanity, psychosis
精神错乱的 deranged, psychotic, raving
精神的 spiritual
精神分裂症 schizophrenia
精神分裂症患者 schizophrenic
精神分析 psychoanalysis
精神分析学家 psychoanalyst
精神领袖 guru
精神胜利 moral victory (at **victory**)
精神失常的 insane, unbalanced
精神性 spirituality (at **spiritual**)
精神压力 stress
精神振作的 refresh
精神支柱 bastion
精神状态 humor
精通的 accomplished, intimate, proficient
精心安排 lay on (at **lay**), structure
精心安排的 calculated
精心的安排 orchestration (at **orchestrate**)
精心呵护的 loving
精心制作 craft
精心组织 orchestrate
精选的 select
精液 semen, sperm
精英 elite, pick
精英的 elite
精英主义 elitism
精英主义的 elitist
精英主义者 elitist
精油 essence
精于…之道 have got something down to a fine art (at **fine art**)
精于某项技术的人 technician
精致 delicacy
精致的 fine
精装书 hardback
精准的 accurate
精子 sperm
鲸鱼 whale
井号键 hash
颈 neck
颈部的 cervical
颈部扭伤 whiplash
颈状部位 neck
景观美化 landscaping (at **landscape**)
景色 scenery, view, vista
景象 scene, sight
警报 warning
警报器 alarm, siren
警察 cop, officer, police, police officer, policeman
警察部队 police force
警察部门 force
警察分队 squad
警察局 police station
警察局长 marshal
警察局副巡官 captain
警长 superintendent
警车 cruiser
警方 police
警告 advisory, caution, warn, warning
警告的 cautionary, warning
警官 constable, deputy, lieutenant, officer, sergeant
警棍 baton, billy
警戒线 cordon
警句 phrase
警觉的 alert, watchful
警觉性 alertness (at **alert**)
警区 precinct
警惕 on your guard (at **guard**), vigilance (at **vigilant**)
警惕的 vigilant
警卫 sentry
警钟 wake-up call
净的 net, real
净化 purification (at **purify**), purify
净数的 net
净赚 net
径直 right
径直地 full, straight
胫 shin
痉挛 fit, knot, spasm
竞技场 arena
竞技状态 form
竞赛 competition, contest
竞选 run
竞选伙伴 running mate
竞争 compete, competition, race, rivalry, vie
竞争的 competitive
竞争对手 competition, competitor
竞争服务 competition
竞争力 competitiveness (at **competitive**)
竞争者 contender
竟然 after all (at **all**)
敬奉 worship
敬酒 toast
敬启者 sir
敬请赐复 RSVP
敬神者 worshiper (at **worship**)
敬畏 awe, overawe
敬意 tribute
敬重 deference, esteem, respect
境况 circumstance
静电 static
静电噪音 static
静脉 vein
静脉输入的 intravenous
静物画 still life
静止的 motionless, static, stationary, still
静坐示威 sit-in
镜头 lens, take
镜子 mirror
迥然不同的 disparate
窘迫的 hard-pressed
纠察线 picket line
纠缠 badger, pester, stalk
纠缠者 stalker
纠出 root out (at **root**)
纠错 debug
纠葛 entanglement
纠正 correct, redress, remedy, right
纠正的 corrective, remedial
纠正某事 to put sth right (at **right**)
究竟 anyway, earth, ever, the hell (at **hell**), whatever
究竟如何 however
究竟谁 whoever
究竟在哪 wherever
揪紧 knot
九 nine
九分之一 ninth
九十 ninety
九十几 ninety
九十年代 ninety
九月 Sept., September
久经世故的 sophisticated
久未见过的 unseen
久闻 by reputation (at **reputation**)
久远的 distant, far off, remote
久远地 far
酒 alcohol, booze, drink
酒吧 bar, tavern, wine bar
酒吧间 bar, barroom
酒吧间男招待 barman
酒吧间女招待 barmaid
酒吧侍者 bartender
酒馆 pub, saloon
酒鬼 lush
酒后驾车 drink-driving
酒窖 cellar
酒精 alcohol
酒徒 drinker
酒席承办 catering
酒席承办者 caterer
旧报纸 newspaper
旧式的 old-fashioned, primitive
旧式公寓大楼 tenement
救护车 ambulance
救济金 charity, handout, relief
救济品 charity, handout
救济物资 relief
救命 help
救生船 lifeboat
救生圈 float
救生艇 lifeboat
救生员 lifeguard
救赎 redeem, redemption
救星 salvation, savior, white knight
救醒 resuscitate, resuscitation (at **resuscitate**)
救援者 rescuer (at **rescue**)
救助 save
就… as
就…而言 by
就餐时段 sitting
就此一次 for once (at **once**)
就某人而言 for sb's part (at **part**), for one (at **one**)
就某人判断 as far as one can tell/ so far as one can tell (at **tell**)
就那样 just like that (at **that**)
就那样好了 that is that (at **that**)
就视线所能及 as far as the eye can/could see (at **eye**)
就是 just
就是这样 so, that's all (at **all**)
就业 employment
就业的 career
就业市场 market
就在 right
就这么定了 there
就这样 that is it (at **that**), there
就这样吧 all right
就职的 inaugural
就职典礼 inauguration (at **inaugurate**)
就职仪式 induction, install
舅父 uncle
舅妈 auntie
舅母 aunt
居…之首 head
居次要地位 take second place (at **place**)
居家购物 home shopping
居民 inhabitant, resident
居首位的 top
居无定所的 no fixed address (at **fixed**)
居用者 occupant
居于首要地位 come first (at **first**)
居中心地位的人或物 center
居住 live, people, reside,

哭泣 tear, weep
苦差事 grind
苦的 bitter
苦干 plod, slave, slog
苦苦思念 pine
苦难 misery, tribulation
苦恼的 pained, troubled
库 bank
库存 stocktaking
库存管理 stock control
库房 depot
裤裆 crotch
裤腿 leg
裤子 trousers
裤子的前开口 fly
酷爱 passion
酷的 cool
酷热的 blistering, scorching
酷热难耐的 sweltering
酷似某人 be the image of sb (at **image**)
夸大 blow, exaggerate, exaggeration (at **exaggerate**), inflate, magnify, overstate, talk up (at **talk**)
夸大了的 exaggerated
夸夸其谈 rant
夸脱 quart
夸耀 parade
夸张的 over the top (at **top**), theatrical
夸张的描述 caricature
夸张地演绎 parody
夸张地赞扬 gush
垮掉 crack
垮台 downfall, fall
胯部 crotch
跨国的 multinational
跨国公司 multinational
跨栏赛跑 hurdle
跨越 across, hurdle, straddle
跨着地 astride
跨坐 straddle
会计 accounting
会计师 accountant
会计学 accountancy
块 lump, mass, patch, piece, sheet
块根的 root
快 quickness (at **quick**)
快步走 march
快餐 fast food, snack
快餐店 snack bar
快车道 fast lane
快到 near
快的 quick
快递的 express
快活的 buoyant
快捷方式 shortcut
快捷键 hot key, shortcut
快进 fast forward
快乐 happiness (at **happy**), happy
快乐的 happy, jolly
快乐和痛苦 highs and lows (at **high**)
快门 shutter
快跑 sprint
快速 rapidity (at **rapid**), speed
快速摆动 flap
快速奔跑 sprint
快速拨号 speed dial
快速成长 shoot up (at **shoot**)
快速传播 spread like wildfire (at **wildfire**)
快速的 rapid
快速地 at a gallop (at **gallop**), on the double (at **double**)
快速地按动 flip
快速地带到 sweep
快速发展 race
快速翻看 flick
快速翻阅 flip
快速剪 snip
快速搅打 whisk
快速列车 express
快速猛击 jab
快速轻吻 peck
快速丸 speed
快速行进 hustle
快速旋流 swirl
快速旋转 spin, whirl
快速移动 bob, hop
快速移动的 swift
快速运动 race
快速振动 flap
快速重新启动 jumpstart
快速转换 skip
快讯 update
快要消亡的 dying
快游 dip
快照 snapshot
筷子 chopstick
宽敞的 roomy, spacious
宽敞的空间 space
宽大 fullness (at **full**)
宽大的 lenient
宽大多褶的 full
宽带 broadband
宽的 broad, fat, wide
宽度 breadth, width
宽泛的 broad
宽厚的 generous
宽距 span
宽屏的 widescreen
宽刃大刀 machete
宽容 permissiveness (at **permissive**), tolerance
宽容的 forgiving, permissive, tolerant
宽恕 forgiveness, let, mercy
宽松的 baggy, loose
宽慰 relief
宽裕的 comfortable
髋 hip
款待 fete, host, treat
款式 style
款项 money
匡正 corrective
筐 basket
狂爱的 crazy
狂奔 stampede
狂风暴雨的 wild
狂欢会 orgy
狂欢节 carnival
狂欢聚会 rave
狂乱地说 rave
狂怒 furor, fury, rage
狂怒的 fierce, furious, livid, mad
狂犬病 rabies
狂热 furor, mania
狂热爱好者 fan, freak
狂热崇拜 cult
狂热的 fanatic, fanatical, fierce, manic, passionate, rapturous, wild
狂热分子 fanatic, maniac
狂热于…的 nut
狂热者 nut
狂喜 ecstasy, euphoria, rapture, thrill
狂喜的 euphoric, overjoyed, rapturous, thrilled
狂笑 hysterics
狂躁不安 fit
狂躁症 mania
旷工 ditch
矿 mine
矿场 quarry
矿床 deposit
矿工 miner
矿井 pit
矿泉疗养地 spa
矿泉水 mineral water
矿石 ore
矿田 field
矿物 mineral
矿业 mining
框架 frame, shape, shell, skeleton
亏本出售的商品 loss leader
亏本地 at a loss (at **loss**)
亏待 short-change
亏空 in the hole (at **hole**)
亏损 deficit, lose, loss
亏损的 in deficit (at **deficit**)
盔甲 armor
窥探 pry, snoop
窥探者 snooper (at **snoop**)
奎宁水 tonic
魁梧的 burly
傀儡 figurehead, puppet
匮乏 deprivation
溃决 burst
溃疡 ulcer
昆虫 insect
捆 bundle, tie
捆绑 bind, tie
捆绑销售 bundle
捆紧 lash
困惑 boggle
困惑不解的 bemused, perplexed
困惑的 confused
困境 adversity, hardship, mess, plight, predicament, strait, trap
困境中救助人的勇士 knight in shining armor (at **knight**)
困窘的 sheepish
困倦的 sleepy
困难 a mountain to climb (at **mountain**), difficulty, hurdle, trouble
困难的 difficult, hard, tough
困扰 affect, afflict, beset, gnaw, overcome, prey
困住 trap
扩大 amplify, dilate, enlarge, enlargement, extend, widen
扩大的 dilated (at **dilate**)
扩建 add
扩建部分 addition
扩宽 broaden
扩散 diffuse, diffusion (at **diffuse**), disperse, spread
扩散全身 ripple
扩延 extend
扩音 amplification (at **amplify**)
扩音器 amp, amplifier, bullhorn
扩展 develop, spread
扩张 expansion
括号 bracket, parenthesis
括弧 brace
蛞蝓 slug
阔气的 fancy
垃圾 garbage, litter, refuse, rubbish, trash
垃圾场 dump, garbage dump, tip
垃圾车 garbage truck
垃圾焚化炉 incinerator
垃圾食品 junk food
垃圾填埋场 landfill
垃圾填埋法 landfill
垃圾桶 garbage can, trash, trash can
垃圾箱 bin, dustbin
垃圾邮件 junk mail
垃圾债券 junk bond
拉 draw, haul, heave, pull
拉…来帮忙 rope in (at **rope**)
拉比 rabbi
拉长 pad
拉长声调说话 drawl
拉大 widen
拉丁美洲的 Latin American
拉丁语 Latin
拉丁语国家的 Latin
拉丁语系的 Latin
拉紧 tighten
拉紧程度 tension
拉近 zoom in (at **zoom**)
拉开 unzip
拉客 solicit, soliciting (at **solicit**)
拉美裔美国籍的 Hispanic
拉皮条 pimp
拉起 hoist
拉伤 tear
拉上拉锁 zip up (at **zip**)
拉屎 shit
拉锁 zip, zipper
拉选票 canvass
邋遢的 dingy, messy
喇叭 horn, loudspeaker
落下 break, come, fall, set
腊肠 sausage
蜡 wax
蜡烛 candle
辣椒 chili
来 come
来吧 come on (at **come**)
来潮 menstruation (at **menstruate**)
来到 finds its/their way (at **find**)
来电参与互动的节目 call-in
来访 come around (at **come**)
来访者 caller
来复枪 rifle
来回地 back and forth (at **back**), backward and forward (at **backward**), to and fro (at **to**)
来客 caller
来来回回 up
来历不明的 mystery
来了 set in (at **set**)
来临 arrival, come, coming (at **come**), draw close/draw near (at **draw**)
来援助某人 come to sb's assistance (at **assistance**)
来源 source
来自 come, from, hail
来自北部的 northern
来自北方的 north
来自东北部的 northeastern
来自东南方的 southeast
来自可靠人士 from the horse's mouth (at **horse**)
来自某地的人 son
来自南方的 south, southerly
来自西北部的 northwestern
来自西南方的 southwest
兰科植物 orchid
拦截 intercept, interception (at **intercept**)
栏杆 rail, railing
阑尾 appendix
蓝宝石 sapphire
蓝筹股 blue chip
蓝调音乐 blue
蓝领的 blue-collar
蓝莓 blueberry
蓝色的 blue
蓝色阵营的 blue
蓝图 blueprint
蓝牙 Bluetooth
篮 basket

露齿嗥叫 snarl
露出 peep, poke
露出吃惊的表情 light
露出马脚 game
露出喜色 light
露口风 drop a hint (at **drop**)
露面 appear, appearance, show, to show your face (at **face**)
露水 dew
露台 patio, terrace
露天广场 plaza
露营 camp
露营地 campsite
露营者 camper
芦笋 asparagus
芦苇 reed
炉 stove
炉火 fire
炉火纯青的 consummate
炉盘 hob
炉灶 burner, range
炉栅 grate
颅骨 skull
鲈鱼 bass
鲁莽 daring, recklessness (at **reckless**)
鲁莽的 reckless
陆地 earth, land
陆军 army
陆军中尉 lieutenant
陆路的 overland
陆桥 bridge
录像 record, recording, video
录像带 recording, video, videotape
录像机 recorder, video
录音 record, recording
录音磁带 audiotape
录音带 recording
录音的 audio
录音公司 studio
录音机 recorder
录制 record, tape, video, videotape
鹿 deer
鹿肉 venison
滤除 filter out (at **filter**)
滤光器 filter
滤声器 filter
路边 curb, roadside, verge, wayside
路标 signpost
路径 approach, pathway, trail, way
路面 pavement
路途 way
路线 course, line, path, route, trail
路障 barricade
驴 ass, donkey
旅 brigade
旅伴 companion
旅程 ride
旅馆 hotel, lodge
旅馆经营者 hotelier
旅客 traveler
旅客的 passenger
旅行 journey, tour, travel, trip
旅行代理商 travel agent
旅行队 caravan, expedition
旅行房车 RV
旅行计划 itinerary
旅行轿车 station wagon
旅行社 travel agent
旅行拖车 caravan
旅行拖车停车场 caravan site
旅行小轿车 estate car
旅行者 traveler
旅行支票 traveler's check
旅行指南 guide, guidebook
旅游 travel
旅游业 tourism
铝 aluminum
屡次 time after time (at **time**)
屡次的 repeated
屡次发生 recur
缕 strand
履历 history, record
履行 deliver, discharge, honor, make good (at **good**)
律师 attorney, lawyer
律师事务所 practice
律师职业 bar
绿地 green
绿化地带 green belt
绿卡 green card
绿票讹诈 greenmail
绿色的 green
绿色植物覆盖的 green
绿松石 turquoise
绿洲 oasis
绿洲般的地方 oasis
氯气 chlorine
卵 egg
卵巢 ovary
卵石 pebble
卵状物 egg
卵子 egg
乱打 bash
乱的 rough
乱花钱 money
乱伦 incest
乱弄 mess
乱七八糟 clutter
乱塞 shove
乱涂乱画 scribble
乱糟糟的一团 tangle
掠夺 loot, plunder
掠夺性的 predatory
掠夺者 predator
掠过 run, skim
略带的 tinged
略低的 minus
略读 skim
略多一些的 plus
略感不适的 run-down
略感刺痛 tingle
略过 skip
略好一些的 plus
略胜某人一筹 be one up on sb (at **one**)
略图 sketch
略微的刺痛感 tingling (at **tingle**)
略微地 marginally
略微改动 fiddle
略微降低 shave
略微松开 loosen
略有变化的形式 variation
略有差异的形式 shade
抡打 swipe
伦敦地铁 tube
伦理学 ethic
轮 round
轮班 shift
轮船 ship
轮次 go
轮毂 hub
轮机师 engineer
轮廓 contour, outline, silhouette
轮廓线 contour
轮流 rotate, rotation, take turns (at **turn**)
轮盘赌 roulette
轮胎 tire
轮椅 wheelchair
论点 thesis
论及 cover
论据 ammunition, argument
论坛 forum
论文 dissertation, paper
论战 controversy
论证 reasoning
罗马的 Roman
罗马数字 Roman numeral
罗马天主教教皇 pope
罗盘 compass
罗网 net, snare
逻辑 logic
逻辑的 logical
逻辑炸弹 logic bomb
锣 gong
骡 mule
螺钉 bolt, screw
螺母 nut
螺丝刀 screwdriver
螺纹 thread
螺旋桨 propeller
螺旋式生长或移动 spiral
螺旋形 spiral
螺旋形开瓶器 corkscrew
裸体 nakedness (at **naked**), nudity
裸体的 naked, nude
裸体雕像 nude
裸体画 nude
裸体中 in the nude (at **nude**)
络腮胡子 whisker
骆驼 camel
落 shed, turn
落成典礼 inaugurate
落袋弹子戏 billiards
落到…身上 fall to (at **fall**)
落后 lag, leave
落后的 backward
落后于 fall behind (at **fall**)
落井下石 kick you when you are down (at **kick**)
落空 board, fall through (at **fall**)
落在 fall
摞 pile, stack
摞起 stack
妈妈 mom, mum
妈咪 mommy, mummy
麻烦 bother, hassle, trouble
麻烦的 troubled
麻烦的人或事情 nuisance
麻烦事 matter
麻木 numbness (at **numb**)
麻木不仁 callousness (at **callous**), insensitivity (at **insensitive**)
麻木不仁的 callous, insensitive
麻木的 asleep, numb
麻雀 sparrow
麻疹 measles
麻醉的 narcotic
麻醉剂 narcotic
麻醉科医师 anesthesiologist
麻醉师 anaesthetist, anesthetist
麻醉药 anesthetic
马 horse, knight
马背 horseback
马车 carriage
马蜂窝 a can of worms (at **worm**)
马夫 groom
马虎的 sloppy
马甲 vest, waistcoat
马厩 stable
马驹 foal
马克思主义 Marxism
马克思主义的 Marxist
马克思主义者 Marxist
马拉松赛跑 marathon
马勒 bridle
马力 horsepower
马前卒 pawn
马球 polo
马赛克 mosaic
马上 momentarily, now, off hand (at **hand**), quick, right away/off (at **right**), right off the bat (at **bat**)
马上想到 to come/spring to mind (at **mind**)
马蹄铁 horseshoe, shoe
马蹄型吉祥物 horseshoe
马尾发型 ponytail
马戏团 circus
码 yard
码头 dock, jetty, quay, wharf
蚂蚁 ant
吗啡 morphine
埋 bury
埋藏 bury
埋设 plant
埋葬 burial, bury
买不到的 inaccessible
买彩票抽奖 raffle
买得到 buy
买得合算的东西 buy
买断 buy out (at **buy**)
买方市场 a buyer's/seller's market (at **market**), buyer's market
买价 bid price
买进一部分 buy into (at **buy**)
买空的人 bull
买卖 trade
买主 buyer
迈着重重的脚步走 stomp
麦秆 straw
麦克风 megaphone, microphone, mike
麦片 cereal
麦片粥 porridge
麦乳精饮料 malt
麦芽 malt
麦芽酒 ale
卖 sell
卖得 fetch, get
卖的比…好 outsell
卖点 selling point
卖掉 part
卖掉去买更贵的东西 trade up (at **trade**)
卖掉去买较便宜的东西 trade down (at **trade**)
卖方 seller
卖方市场 market, seller's market
卖方要价 offer price
卖国贼 traitor
卖酒的商店 liquor store
卖空的人 bear
卖弄 show off (at **show**)
卖淫 prostitution
卖者 seller
卖主 vendor
脉搏 pulse
脉冲 impulse, pulse
鳗肉 eel
鳗鱼 eel
满的 full, full up
满怀希望的 hopeful
满怀着的 bursting
满满地 to overflowing (at **overflow**)
满塞 squeeze
满身汗 sweat
满意 satisfaction
满意的 content, contented, pleased, satisfied
满员 full strength (at **strength**)
满足 contentment, fill, gratification (at **gratify**), gratify, meet, satisfy, serve
满足…需要 cater

抛接杂耍表演者 juggler
抛开… to the exclusion of (at **exclusion**)
抛锚 anchor
抛弃 abandon, abandonment, desert, ditch, dump
抛撒 shower
刨 plane
刨掉 shave
刨子 plane
咆哮 bark, rant, ranting (at **rant**), roar
炮 firearm
炮兵部队 artillery
炮弹 shell
炮管 barrel
炮火 fire, gunfire
炮击 shell, shelling (at **shell**)
跑 run, running
跑步 run
跑步者 runner
跑车 sports car
跑道 course, lane, runway, track
跑马场 course
跑腿 to run an errand (at **errand**)
泡菜 pickle
泡菜酱 pickle
泡沫 foam, froth
泡澡 bath
泡状框 bubble
胚胎 embryo
陪伴 accompany, companionship, company
陪伴护送 walk
陪审团 jury
陪审团团长 foreman
陪审员 juror
陪同 see
培训 groom, training
培训者 trainer (at **train**)
培养 cultivate, cultivation (at **cultivate**), nurture
培育 nurture
培育者 breeder
赔偿 recompense, redress, satisfaction
赔偿金 damage
赔款 redress
赔礼道歉 eat humble pie (at **humble**)
赔率 odds
配备 equip
配备的职员人数 staffing
配备了职员的 staffed (at **staff**)
配备装甲车的 armored
配不上 beneath
配额 quota
配发 dispense
配方 formulation
配给量 ration
配给品 ration
配给制 rationing
配合 cooperate
配合融洽 gel
配件 fitting
配乐 score
配偶 mate, partner, spouse
配饰 accessory
配手势语 sign
配售 dispense
配套组件 kit
配销 distribute
配销权 distributorship
配销商 distributor, distributorship
配音 soundtrack
配有 complete with (at **complete**)
配有字幕的 subtitled
配制 make
配制品 preparation
配置 allocation, configuration, configure
喷 puff, spray, squirt
喷鼻息 snort
喷出 belch, puff, spew, spray, spurt, squirt
喷发 erupt, eruption (at **erupt**)
喷剂 spray
喷漆 spray
喷气发动机 jet engine
喷气式飞机 jet
喷气式滑水 jet skiing (at **Jet Ski**)
喷气式滑艇 Jet Ski
喷泉 fountain
喷射 fountain, spout
喷射流 jet
喷雾罐 aerosol
喷雾器 aerosol, spray
喷药 spray
喷涌 pour
盆 basin
盆地 basin
盆浴 bath
盆栽的 potted (at **pot**)
怦怦跳 pound, thud, thump
抨击 attack, come, flak, pan, snipe
砰地关上 bang, slam
砰砰敲击 hammer
砰然作响 bang
烹调 cook
烹调的 culinary
烹调风格 cuisine
烹饪 cookery, cooking, cooking (at **cook**)
烹煮 poaching (at **poach**)
朋客青年 punk
朋客摇滚乐 punk
朋友 friend, pal
棚式建筑 shed
棚屋 shed
蓬勃发展 bloom
膨胀 expand
碰 touch
碰壁 hit/come up against a brick wall (at **brick**)
碰到 meet
碰见 bump into (at **bump**), meeting
碰巧 as it happens (at **happen**), happen
碰伤 bruise
碰运气 take a chance (at **chance**)
碰运气地 on spec (at **spec**)
碰撞 bump, collide, collision, knock, strike
碰撞声 bump
批 batch, consignment, contingent
批发 wholesale, wholesaling
批发地 wholesale
批发商 distributor, wholesaler
批改 correct, correction
批量 run
批判 repudiate, repudiation (at **repudiate**)
批判性的 critical
批评 criticism, criticize, fault, knock, lecture, pan, rap, swipe
批评的 critical
批评者 critic
批准 approval, approve, authorization (at **authorize**), authorize, okay, pass, ratification, ratify, sanction
批准离开 discharge
批准下达 come
披垂 hang
披肩 cape, shawl
披散的 loose
劈 hack, slash
皮 peel, pelt
皮带 belt
皮带或链条 leash
皮肤 skin
皮革 leather
皮毛 coat
皮条客 pimp
皮下脂肪团 cellulite
皮下注射器 hypodermic
疲惫 fatigue
疲惫不堪的 harassed, worn out
疲惫不堪的人 wreck
疲惫的 run-down, weary
疲惫地行走 trek
疲乏 fatigue
疲倦 tiredness (at **tired**)
疲倦的 tired, worn
疲劳 fatigue
疲劳的 tired
疲软 weakness (at **weak**)
疲软的 weak
啤酒 beer
啤酒厂 brewery
啤酒花 hop
啤酒酿造公司 brewer
啤酒酿造者 brewer
脾气暴躁的 explosive
脾气坏的 bad-tempered, grumpy, miserable, sour
脾气极坏的 mean
癖好 weakness
屁股 arse, ass, backside, bum, bun, butt
僻静的 secluded
片 patch, piece, tranche
片段 fragment, snippet
片段镜头 footage
片断 clip, scene, snatch
片刻 minute, sec, second
片面的 one-sided, unbalanced
偏爱 preference
偏爱的 partial
偏激的 extreme
偏见 bias, prejudice, slant
偏离 depart, deviate, deviation, drift
偏僻的 isolated, lonely, remote
偏偏 of all (at **all**)
偏袒 favor, favoritism
偏袒的 one-sided, partial
偏头痛 migraine
偏向 slant
偏要 must
偏远的 remotely
偏执的 bigoted
偏执的人 bigot
偏执狂 paranoia
偏执态度 bigotry
偏执行为 bigotry
偏重于…的 biased
篇幅 length, space
骗 scam
骗过 outwit
骗局 con, scam
骗取 defraud
骗人的 deceptive
骗人的东西 fraud
骗子 fake, fraud
剽窃 plagiarism, plagiarize, steal
漂白 bleach
漂白剂 bleach
漂泊 drift
漂浮 float
漂浮着的 adrift
漂浮着地 afloat
漂亮 loveliness (at **lovely**)
漂亮的 good-looking, pretty
漂流 drift
飘动 flutter
飘浮 float
飘舞 flutter
飘扬 fly, wave
瓢泼大雨 downpour
票 ticket
票贩子 tout
票房 box office
票根 stub
票面上的 nominal
撇号 apostrophe
撇去 skim
瞥 glance, shoot
瞥见 catch, glimpse
瞥一眼 peek, peep
拼车 carpool
拼车旅行的人 carpool
拼凑 piece
拼凑的 ramshackle
拼读 spell
拼缝的 patchwork
拼命工作 work your guts out (at **gut**)
拼死搏斗 fight to the death (at **death**)
拼贴法 collage
拼贴画 collage
拼图游戏 jigsaw
拼写 spell, spelling
拼写检查 spell-check
拼写检查程序 spell-checker
拼写能力 spelling
贫乏 poverty
贫乏的 lean, poor
贫瘠的 barren, infertile
贫困的 deprived, impoverished (at **impoverish**), needy, poor
贫民窟 gutter
贫民区 ghetto, slum
贫穷 poverty
贫穷的 poor
贫血的 anemic
贫血症 anemia
频繁的 continual, frequent
频繁地 lot
频率 frequency, rate
频频往返于两地之间 shuttle
品尝 sample, savor, taste
品德高尚的 fine, virtuous
品牌 brand
品牌产品 brand-name product
品牌名称 trade name
品牌先锋 brand leader
品牌形象 brand image
品牌专卖的 proprietary
品评 size
品脱 pint
品位 class
品味 taste
品味低 in bad taste (at **taste**)
品性 personality
品质上的 qualitative
品种 breed, strain, variety
聘 engage
聘请 invite
聘用 take
乒乓球拍 paddle
平安 safety
平安的 safe
平常的 normal, usual
平淡的 routine
平淡乏味 routine
平淡乏味的 bland
平淡无趣的 colorless, flat
平的 flat
平等 equality, parity

平等的 equal
平等化 equalization (at **equalize**)
平等竞争环境 a level playing field (at **playing field**)
平底的 flat
平底锅 pan
平底载货船 barge
平凡的 mundane
平方 square
平方的 sq., square
平方根 square root
平房 bungalow
平放在 lie
平和 peace
平衡 balance, equilibrium, symmetry
平衡能力 balance
平滑的 even
平缓的 gentle
平级地 sideways
平交道口 crossing, grade crossing
平静 equilibrium, quietness (at **quiet**), serene
平静的 calm, placid, quiet, relaxed, undisturbed
平静无波的 calm
平静无事的 uneventful
平静下来 calm, cool down (at **cool**), settle
平均为 average
平均值 average, mean
平面 flat, plane
平面交叉处 level crossing
平面设计 graphic design
平民 populace
平民的 civilian
平平常常 nothing to write home about (at **home**)
平平的 average
平权举措 affirmative action
平台 deck, platform
平坦的 flat, level
平躺 stretch out (at **stretch**)
平头钉 tack
平稳 steady
平稳的 steady
平稳地 on an even keel (at **keel**)
平稳地前进 draw
平息 blow over (at **blow**), calm, die, patch up (at **patch**), quash, quiet, subside
平息下来 calm
平行的 parallel
平庸 mediocrity
平庸的 indifferent, mediocre, middle-of-the-road
平庸乏味的 banal, pedestrian
平邮 surface mail
平原 plain
平装书 paperback
平足的 flat
评定 place
评分 rating
评估 appraisal, assess, assessment, evaluate, measurement
评价 appraise, estimation, evaluate, evaluation (at **evaluate**), mark, opinion
评论 comment, commentary, criticism, notice, pass, remark, review
评论家 critic
评论文章 commentary, critique
评论员 commentator, reviewer
评判 judge
评述 observe
评委会 jury
评议会 Senate
凭猜测 at a guess (at **guess**)
凭处方 on prescription (at **prescription**)
凭记忆 from memory (at **memory**)
凭记忆演奏 play (a piece of music) by ear (at **ear**)
凭借 on the strength of (at **strength**), through, whereby
凭空设想出 dream
凭空想像 in the mind (at **mind**)
凭良知行事 conscience
凭某物的出示 on production of something/on the production of something (at **production**)
凭一时冲动 on impulse (at **impulse**)
凭直觉行事 follow one's nose (at **nose**)
凭自身努力获得 carve out (at **carve**)
苹果 apple
苹果酒 cider
苹果汁 cider
屏蔽 screen
屏风 screen
屏幕 display, screen
屏幕保护程序 screensaver
屏幕上的 on-screen
屏障 barrier
瓶 bottle
瓶盖 cap
瓶塞 cork
瓶装的 bottled
瓶子 bottle, flask
坡度 slope
泼打戏水 splash
泼妇 bitch
泼冷水 pour cold water on sth (at **water**)
颇 pretty, quite
婆婆 mother-in-law
迫不得已的 forced
迫不得已的话 if all else fails (at **fail**)
迫不及待地接受 jump
迫害 persecute, persecution, victimization (at **victimize**)
迫击炮 mortar
迫切的 burning, urgent
迫切性 urgent
迫切需要 cry out for (at **cry**)
迫使 compel, condemn, constrain, drive, force, make, oblige, reduce
迫使…明确表态 pin
迫使…同行 march
迫使进入 pitch
迫使离开 hound
迫使某人做某事 railroad
迫使停止 tear
破败的 run-down
破产 bankruptcy, insolvency, ruin, to go broke (at **broke**)
破产的 bankrupt, bust, insolvent
破产管理 receivership
破产接管人 receiver
破产者 bankrupt
破除 break
破洞 tear
破坏 damage, knock, mar, ravages, screw, scuttle, spoil, undermine
破坏性极强的 devastating
破解 break, crack
破旧 have seen better days (at **day**)
破旧不堪的 worn out
破旧的 dilapidated, old, ragged, shabby, tattered
破烂不堪 tatters
破烂的 shabby, sleazy
破烂衣服 rag
破裂 break, breakup, crack, rupture
破裂的 broken
破裂地 apart
破门而入 break in (at **break**)
破碎 break, come, disintegrate, disintegration (at **disintegrate**), fall apart (at **fall**), smash, yield
破碎物品 breakage
破晓 break
破译 decipher
破折号 dash
剖面图 section
剖析 dissect, dissection (at **dissect**)
仆人 servant
扑救 save
扑克牌 playing card
扑克牌游戏 poker
铺 make, pave
铺床 make the bed/make sb's bed/make a bed (at **bed**)
铺地毯 carpet
铺盖 cover
铺开 spread
铺设 lay, run
铺位 bunk
铺张的 ostentatious
葡萄 grape
葡萄干 raisin
葡萄酒 vintage, wine
葡萄酒厂 vineyard
葡萄糖 glucose
葡萄柚 grapefruit
葡萄园 vineyard
蒲公英 dandelion
朴素的 austere, plain, simple
普遍存在 prevail
普遍存在的 prevalent, universal
普遍的 broad, common, general, rife, universal
普遍地 popularly, universally
普及 generalize
普拉提 Pilates
普通百姓 mass
普通成员 rank, rank and file
普通的 average, common, humble, ordinary, regular, stark, temporal, unremarkable
普通股 common stock, equities, ordinary shares
普通名词 common noun
瀑布 fall, waterfall
七 seven
七分之一 seventh
七十 seventy
七十分之一 seventieth
七十几 seventy
七十年代 seventy
七月 Jul., July
妻子 wife
妻子的姐妹 sister-in-law
凄凉 desolation
栖木 perch
栖息 perch, populate, roost, settle
栖息处 roost
期 issue
期待 anticipation, bet, expect, expectancy, look forward to (at **look**)
期待的 expectant
期货 future
期间 term
期刊 journal, periodical
期盼 expectation
期票 promissory note
期权 option
期望 expectation, hope
期限 time
欺负 bully, pick
欺凌行为 bullying (at **bully**)
欺骗 deceit, deceive, deception, delude, dupe, false pretenses (at **pretense**), fool, kid, take, trick
欺骗的 deceitful
欺骗性的 fraudulent
欺诈 scam
漆 lacquer
齐发 volley
齐声 chorus
齐足跳行 hop
其次 second, secondly
其后 thereafter
其后的 following
其实 actually, indeed
其他的 else, other
其一 for one thing (at **thing**)
其余部分 rest
其余的 other
奇才 prodigy, wizard
奇怪 strangeness (at **strange**)
奇怪的 funny, queer, strange, weird
奇怪地 oddly
奇观 spectacle
奇迹 marvel, miracle, wonder
奇迹般的 miraculous
奇妙的感受 blast
奇事 wonder
奇数的 odd
奇异 unreality (at **unreal**)
奇异的 exotic, improbable
奇珍异宝 curiosity
歧视 discrimination
歧视性的 discriminatory
祈祷 pray, prayer
祈祷室 oratory
祈祷仪式 prayer
祈福祷告 blessing
祈求 prayer
祈求好运 cross one's fingers/keep one's fingers crossed (at **finger**)
祈求上帝祝福 bless
祈使语气 imperative
祈使语气动词 imperative
崎岖不平的 bumpy
崎岖多岩的 rugged
崎岖小路 trail
骑 ride
骑兵 trooper
骑兵团 cavalry
骑车 ride
骑的人 rider
骑马 ride, riding
骑马的 equestrian
骑马的人 horseman
骑马疾驰 gallop
骑马执勤的 mounted
骑摩托车的人 biker, motorcyclist
骑上 mount
骑士 knight
骑手 horseman, rider
骑自行车 bike, cycle, cycling (at **cycle**)
骑自行车的人 biker
骑自行车者 cyclist
棋子 counter, piece
旗 flag
旗舰 flagship

清算 liquidate, liquidation (at **liquidate**)
清算人 liquidator
清晰 clarity, in focus (at **focus**)
清晰的 bold, vivid
清晰地表达 lay
清晰度 definition
清晰简明 lucidity (at **lucid**)
清晰简明的 lucid
清晰可辨的 sharp
清晰明确的 tangible
清晰易见的 evident
清新的 fresh
清醒的 clear, sober
清淤 dredge
清真寺 mosque
蜻蜓 dragonfly
鲭鱼 mackerel
情报 intelligence
情报处 secret service
情妇 mistress
情感 emotion
情感表现 expression
情感的 sentimental
情感上的 emotional
情节 plot
情况 picture, situation, thing
情况不妙时 push comes to shove (at **shove**)
情况不同 a different story (at **story**)
情况介绍 orientation
情况糟糕的 bad off
情人 lover, partner
情形 circumstance, thing, way
情绪 feeling, mood, sentiment, spirit, temper
情绪不高的 down
情绪不稳定的 volatile
情绪低落的 low
情绪稳定的 well-balanced
情愿 choose
晴的 fair
晴朗的 clear, fine, sunny
氰化物 cyanide
请 please
请便 be my guest (at **guest**)
请教 take
请来 bring, send
请求 ask, request, seek
请求给予 solicit, solicitation
请恕冒昧 with due respect (at **due**)
请贴 invitation, invite
请原谅 forgive
请愿书 petition
请愿者 petitioner
请转交 c/o
庆典 festivity
庆祝 celebrate, observe
庆祝会 fete
庆祝活动 celebration
亲家 in-laws
穷困 misery
穷困的 bad off
穷困潦倒的 down-and-out
穷途末路 the end of the road (at **end**)
穹顶 dome
丘陵 foothills
秋季 fall
秋千 swing
秋天 autumn
囚犯 convict, prisoner
囚禁 captivity
囚禁某人 take sb captive/hold sb captive (at **captive**)
求购公司 suitor
求婚 pop the question (at **question**), proposal, propose
求婚者 suitor
求之难得 at a premium (at **premium**)
求助热线 helpline
求助于 invoke, turn
酋长 sheikh
球 ball
球棒 bat, stick
球场 court
球洞 hole
球杆 cue
球果 cone
球茎 bulb
球门 goal
球门柱 goalpost, post
球拍 racket
球体 sphere
球鞋 court shoe
球形把手 knob
球状部位 ball
球状物 ball, globe
区别 distinction, split
区分 differentiate, discriminate, distinguish, draw/make a distinction (at **distinction**), separate, split, tell apart (at **tell**)
区分开地 apart
区号 dialling code
区域 area, subdivision
区域代码 area code
曲柄 crank
曲柄手杖 crook
曲调 tune
曲棍球 field hockey, hockey
曲解 distort, distortion, misrepresent, misrepresentation (at **misrepresent**), skew
曲径 maze
曲线 curve
驱虫剂 repellent
驱动 drive
驱动程序 driver
驱动装置 drive
驱赶 drive, herd
驱使 drive
驱逐 banish, chase, evict, eviction, oust
驱逐出境 deportation (at **deport**)
屈从 bow, submit
屈服 cave, submission, succumb, surrender, yield
屈莱弗甜食 trifle
屈伸 flex
屈尊 condescend
屈尊的 patronizing
屈尊对待 patronize
蛆 maggot
躯干 body, torso, trunk
趋势 trend, wind
趋同性 convergence
趋向 tend, toward
趋向稳定 level off (at **level**)
趋于激化 simmer
渠道 channel
蠼螋 earwig
取 pick, withdraw
取保候审 remand
取保候审期 remand
取出 extract
取出…的内脏 gut
取代 displace, replace, replacement, supersede, take
取得 boast, chalk up (at **chalk**), draw, take
取得成功 pay
取得进展 get, make headway (at **headway**)
取得了长足进步 have come a long way (at **way**)
取得名次 place
取得资格 qualify
取缔 clamp down (at **clamp**)
取回 get, retrieval, retrieve
取决于 dependent, hang, rest, ride, subject to sth (at **subject**)
取款机 cash dispenser, cashpoint
取下 take down (at **take**)
取向 orientation
取消 call, call off (at **call**), cancel, cancellation (at **cancel**), off, scrap, write
取消赎回权 foreclose
取笑 tease
取悦 charm, court
取之不尽的事物 bottomless
龋洞 cavity
去 attend, go, to
去别处地 elsewhere
去除 removal, remove, shed, withdrawal
去除灰尘 dust
去掉…外层 pare
去掉杂质的 refined
去骨或刺 bone
去骨鱼片 fillet
去核 core
去核的 pitted
去毛 wax
去拿 fetch
去世 pass, pass away (at **pass**), passing
去世的 deceased
去往某地的 destined
去污粉 cleanser
去污剂 cleaner
去洗手间 go to the bathroom (at **bathroom**)
趣事 quirk
趣味 color
趣闻轶事 anecdote
圈 circle, coil, cycle, loop, pen, ring
圈内人 insider
圈起 fence
圈套 setup, trap
圈养 captivity
圈子 circle
全… all-
全部 entirety, lot, sum
全部的 complete, entire, every, full
全部地 in full (at **full**)
全部赌注 kitty
全部服装 wardrobe
全部理由 rationale
全部买下 buy up (at **buy**)
全部曲目 repertoire
全程的 from door to door/door to door (at **door**)
全国的 national
全国国民 nation
全国性的 nationwide
全家用的 family
全景 panorama
全景的 panoramic
全科医师 general practitioner, GP
全力投入 get into the swing of (at **swing**)
全力以赴地做 work overtime (at **overtime**)
全貌 panorama
全面的 all-, all-around, comprehensive, full-scale, global
全面地 full
全面发展的 rounded
全面公正的 balanced
全面规划 master plan
全面检修 overhaul
全面清理 clean out (at **clean**)
全面体检 medical
全面透彻地 in depth (at **depth**)
全面细致的 close
全面影响 permeate
全民公决 referendum
全能的 all-around
全能银行 universal bank
全年 all year round (at **round**)
全年地 all year round (at **year**)
全盘衡量过的 calculated
全凭自己地 in one's own right (at **right**)
全球 globe
全球变暖 global warming
全球的 global
全球化 globalization (at **globalize**), globalize
全球移动通信系统 GSM
全权 carte blanche
全然的 dead, unmitigated
全然地 altogether
全身的 full-length
全身性的 generalized
全神贯注的 busy, engrossed
全盛时期 heyday
全世界的 universal
全速地 flat
全速推进 full steam ahead (at **steam**)
全套服装 outfit
全体 lot
全体成员 membership
全体出席的 plenary
全体船员 crew
全体地 across the board (at **board**)
全体工人 shop floor
全体机务人员 crew
全体教士 priesthood
全体教员 faculty
全体审判人员 court
全体同意的 unanimous
全体选民 electorate
全体演员 cast
全体一起地 en masse
全体职员 staff
全无的 devoid
全校师生 school
全心全意的 wholehearted
全新的 brand-new
全新领域 virgin
全宇宙 creation
全职的 full-time
权衡 balance, weigh
权力 power
权力分享 power-sharing
权力经纪人 power broker
权利 entitlement, right
权利法案 Bill of Rights
权利赋予 empowerment
权势 influence
权术 politics
权威 pundit
权威的 standard
权威人士 authority
权威性的 authoritative, definitive
权宜的 Band-Aid, expedient
权宜之计 expediency, quick fix
权宜之举 expedient
权重 weight, weighting
诠释 construe, read, reading
诠释与宣传 spin

烧水壶 teakettle
烧死 burn
烧制 fire
稍等片刻 hold
稍微 slightly, some, somewhat
稍微的 certain
稍微改变 shift
稍微移动 shift
稍有不适的 funny
稍有点大 on the big side (at **side**)
勺 scoop, spoon
少到只有 as few as (at **few**)
少得可怜的 miserable
少的 light
少花费 underspend
少见地 rarely
少量 dab, dash, drop, fraction, lick, sliver
少量吃的东西 bite
少量的 scant
少量削减 shave
少年犯罪 delinquency
少年时代 boyhood
少女 maiden
少数 handful, minority
少数的 few
少数民族 minority
少数民族的 ethnic
少数人 few
少校 major
少许 trace
少许色彩 tint
少于 less
少找零钱给… short-change
少脂肪的 lean
哨兵 sentry
哨子 whistle
奢侈 extravagance, luxury
奢侈的 extravagant, luxury
奢侈品 extravagance, luxury
奢华的 deluxe, sumptuous
赊购 credit
舌头 tongue
蛇 serpent, snake
舍弃 sacrifice
设备 apparatus, equipment
设备或服装 gear
设备处 installation
设定程序 program
设法 manage, seek, try
设法摆脱 wriggle out of (at **wriggle**)
设法获得 court
设法获取 wring
设法与…联络 get hold of sb (at **hold**)
设法做 get
设计 create, design, devise, map out (at **map**), spec
设计师 architect, designer
设计式样 style
设计图 design, plan
设计舞蹈动作 choreograph
设计制造 engineer, put
设立 set
设施 facility
设陷阱捕捉 trap
设想 envisage, envision, scenario
设有账户 bank
设在海外的 offshore
设置 set, setting up (at **set**)
设置版式 format
社会 society
社会保险号码 Social Security number
社会保障金 welfare
社会保障制度 Social Security
社会的 social
社会的缩影 microcosm
社会地位 rank, status
社会福利部门 social services
社会福利工作 social work
社会福利工作者 social worker
社会福利机构 institution
社会福利机构的 institutional
社会关系优越的 well-connected
社会或文明 culture
社会经济的 socioeconomic
社会科学 social science
社会科学学科 social science
社会学 sociology
社会学的 sociological (at **sociology**)
社会学家 sociologist (at **sociology**)
社会政治的 sociopolitical
社会秩序 law and order, order
社会主义 socialism
社会主义的 socialist
社会主义者 socialist
社交 socialize
社交的 social
社交聚会 function, get-together
社交陪同 escort
社论 editorial
社论的 editorial
社区 community
社区服务 community service
社区活动中心 community center
社团 society
射 fire
射出的子弹 gunshot
射击 firing (at **fire**), shoot
射击场 range
射击手 shot
射击一次的量 round
射门 shoot, shot
射伤 shoot
射死 shoot
涉过 ford
涉及 about, extend, involve, stretch
涉及丑闻的 scandalous
涉及的 involved
涉及多人的 multiple
涉及私生活地 personally
涉猎 dabble
涉外的 external, foreign
涉足 foray, hook, set foot (at **foot**)
赦免 amnesty, pardon
赦免时段 amnesty
摄取量 intake
摄氏的 Celsius, centigrade
摄影 photography
摄影爱好者 photographer
摄影的 photographic
摄影机 camera
摄影棚 set
摄影师 cameraman, photographer
摄影术 photography
摄制人员名单 credit
申报 declare
申购 subscribe
申请 application, apply, petition, subscribe
申请加入 subscribe
申请人 applicant
申诉 appeal
伸 put
伸长 crane
伸出 extend, hold out (at **hold**), jut, poke, stick, stick out (at **stick**), stretch
伸开四肢坐着 sprawl
伸入 dip
伸手去 reach
伸展开 spread
伸展开的 outstretched
伸直 stretch
身边 side
身材 figure
身份 capacity, identity, status
身份不明的 unidentified
身份证 identity card
身份证件 ID, paper
身份证明 identification
身份证明卡 card
身高 stature
身居高位 highly, in high places (at **place**)
身居要职的 high-powered
身躯 frame
身体 anatomy, body, person
身体不适 under the weather (at **weather**)
身体的 bodily, physical
身体的前部 front
身体结构的 anatomical
身体系统 system
身体语言 body language
身无分文的 penniless
身陷困境 in a hole (at **hole**)
身心退化 rot
身心正常的 normal
身影 figure
身着…服装的 -coated, clad
呻吟 groan, moan
呻吟着说 groan
绅士 gentleman
深爱的 beloved
深奥难懂的 esoteric
深不见底的 bottomless
深长的 deep
深长的切口 gash
深处 depth, recess
深的 deep
深的容器 tub
深度 depth
深谷 ravine
深褐色 chocolate
深红色 ruby
深红色的 crimson
深厚 depth
深静脉血栓症 DVT
深刻的 incisive, intimate, profound, strong
深刻见解 insight
深蓝色的 navy
深切的 deep
深入的 deep
深入了解 insight
深入人心 take root (at **root**)
深色的 dark, deep
深深打动 blow
深深地 dearly
深深发出 heave
深深切入 sink
深受…的影响 thumb
深思 meditate, reflect
深陷地 deep
深陷困境 up to the eyeballs (at **eyeball**)
深陷情网 be head over heels/be head over heels in love (at **head**)
深渊 abyss
深远影响 imprint
深重 depth, enormity
神 deity, god
神的 divine
神殿 temple
神父 priest
神话 myth, mythology
神话中的 mythical, mythological (at **mythology**)
神经 nerve
神经崩溃 nervous breakdown
神经过敏的 neurotic
神经紧张 nerve, nervousness (at **nervous**)
神经紧张的 nervous
神经系统 nervous system
神经性的 nervous
神经质的 nervous, squeamish
神秘 mystery
神秘的 dark, mysterious, mystic, mystical, shadowy
神秘感 mystique
神秘难解的 enigmatic
神秘失踪 vanish
神秘学 occult
神秘之处 magic
神秘主义 mysticism
神秘主义者 mystic
神奇的 magical, miracle, wonder
神奇功能 magic
神气十足 panache
神情 expression
神圣 sanctity
神圣的 divine, hallowed, holy, sacred, saintly
神圣庄严的 venerable
神态 look
神像 idol
神学 theology
神学的 theological (at **theology**)
神一般的人物 god
神韵 atmosphere
神志 wit
神志不清 oblivion
神志清醒 lucidity (at **lucid**)
神志清醒的 conscious, lucid
神志正常 sanity
神志正常的 sane
神智恍惚的 stoned
神智昏迷的 delirious
神智正常 nobody in their right mind (at **mind**)
审裁 review
审查 censor, censorship, examination (at **examine**), examine, review, screen, vetting (at **vet**)
审查员 censor
审度 review
审计 audit
审计官 comptroller
审计员 auditor, controller
审理 try
审美的 aesthetic
审判 trial
审判的 judicial
审判室 courtroom
审慎 discretion
审视 survey
审问 interrogate, interrogation
审讯 try
审议 deliberation
婶母 aunt
婶娘 auntie
肾上腺素 adrenalin
肾脏 kidney
甚至 even, very
渗出 exude
渗开 run
渗漏 leak, trickle down (at **trickle**)
渗入 infiltrate, into
渗透 infiltration (at **infiltrate**), seep, soak
升 fly, liter
升半音 sharp
升舱 upgrade
升的 ascending
升高 rise
升级 upgrade

市民 citizen
市民的 civic
市内有轨电车 streetcar
市政的 civic, municipal
市政规划 planning
市政厅 town hall
市中心 town
市中心的 downtown
市中心区 inner city
示威集会 demonstration
示威抗议者 picket
示威游行 demonstration
示意 motion
示意图 diagram
事 affair
事出必然 in the nature of things (at **nature**)
事故 accident, incident
事后调查 postmortem
事件 affair, business, episode, event, happening, incident, scene
事例 case
事情 affair, matter, proposition, thing
事实 case, fact, the fact of the matter/the truth of the matter (at **matter**)
事实存在 reality
事实的 factual
事实上 actually, fact, in actuality (at **actuality**), in reality (at **reality**), virtually
事实上的 virtual
事态 matter, state of affairs
事务 affair, business
事先 beforehand
事先的 advance, prior
事先交代 prime
事先通知 notice
事先准备 prime
事业 cause, enterprise
事与愿违 backfire
侍者 server
势必 of necessity (at **necessity**)
势均力敌 neck and neck (at **neck**)
势均力敌的 close, matched
势力 force
势头 momentum
视察 inspect, inspection (at **inspect**)
视窗 window
视点 viewpoint
视而不见 turn a blind eye (at **blind**)
视而不见的 blind
视角 angle, viewpoint
视觉的 optic, visual
视觉资料 visual
视力 eyesight, sight, vision
视力的 optic, optical
视频会议 teleconference
视听的 audiovisual
视网膜 retina
视为 see
视野 field, vision
试 audition
试穿 fit, fitting, try on (at **try**)
试试 try
试试看 see
试探 test the water/test the waters (at **water**)
试探地提出 venture
试题 question
试图 attempt, try
试图解决 wrestle
试图抹掉 black
试图掩盖某事 sweep sth under the carpet/sweep sth under the rug (at **sweep**)
试销的 introductory
试行 pilot
试验 test, trial
试验性的 experimental, pilot
试样 sample
试样唱片 demo
试一试 give it a whirl (at **whirl**)
试用 try
试用期 probation
饰边 border
饰有流苏的 fringed
饰有图案的 patterned
饰章 crest
饰针 brooch
室内陈设 furnishings
室内的 indoor
室内地面材料 flooring
室内装修设计师 decorator
室友 roommate
恃强凌弱者 bully
是 are, go, make, yeah, yep
是的 yes
是否 if, whether
适当的 appropriate, due, right
适当位置 position
适度的 modest
适逢 fall
适合 become, befit, fit, suit, suitability (at **suitable**)
适合的 adapted, fit, suitable, suited
适合的职业 vocation
适合某人的口味 to sb's liking (at **liking**)
适合于 lend
适合正式场合的 formal
适配 square
适时的 timely
适宜的 hospitable, proper
适应 acclimate, acclimation (at **acclimate**), adapt, adaptation, adjust, orient
适应的 accustomed
适应下来 settle in (at **settle**)
适应性 adaptability (at **adaptable**)
适用 apply
适用的 applicable
适用于 cover, go
适用于全体的 blanket
适于 pertain
适于成人的 grown-up
适中的 moderate
舐食 lap
逝去的 lost
释放 free, release, unleash
释义 paraphrase
嗜杀成性的 homicidal
誓言 oath, pledge, vow
誓约 vow
收并 absorption
收藏 stow
收藏家 collector
收藏品 collection, library
收成 crop, harvest
收到 get, receipt, receive
收到成效 have something to show for sth (at **show**)
收费 charge, toll
收割 harvest
收割机 mower
收工 day
收购 acquisition, takeover
收购方 acquirer
收回 reclaim, recoup, recover, repossess, repossession, retraction (at **retract**), take
收获 crop
收集 collect, collecting (at **collect**), collection, garner, gather
收监 committal
收件箱 inbox
收据 receipt
收看 catch, tune in (at **tune**)
收看付费 pay-per-view
收款人 payee
收款台 checkout
收留 take in (at **take**)
收拢地 back
收录 embody
收买 buy
收盘 close
收盘价 closing price
收取人 collector
收容所 refuge, shelter
收入 income, proceed, receipt, revenue, take
收拾 bus, clear away (at **clear**), clear up (at **clear**), tidy up (at **tidy**)
收拾干净 clean up (at **clean**)
收拾整洁 spruce up (at **spruce**)
收视率 rating
收缩 constrict, contraction (at **contract**)
收听 catch, tune
收尾 shake out (at **shake**)
收文篮 in tray, inbox
收效 fruition, payback
收养 adopt, adoption (at **adopt**), foster
收养的 adoptive, foster
收益 payback, payoff, return, yield
收音机 radio
收银处 point of sale
收银机 cash register, till
收银台 cashier's desk, POS, till
收银员 cashier
收汁 reduce
手 hand
手臂 arm
手边的 handy
手表 watch
手册 handbook
手持式的 handheld
手电筒 flash, flashlight, torch
手段 instrument, means, ploy
手感 texture
手稿 manuscript
手工 by hand (at **hand**)
手工的 manual
手工艺 handicraft
手工艺品 artifact, handicraft
手工制作的 handmade
手铐 handcuff
手拉手 hand in hand (at **hand**), hold hands (at **hand**)
手榴弹 grenade
手帕 handkerchief
手枪 pistol
手势 gesture, motion, sign
手势语 sign language
手势语的使用 signing
手术 operation
手术刀 scalpel
手术服 scrub
手术室 operating room, operating theatre, surgery
手提包 bag
手提式扩音喇叭 loudhailer
手提箱 suitcase
手提行李 hand luggage
手推车 trolley
手腕 wrist
手写的 handwritten
手艺 craftsmanship, trade
手艺人 craftsman
手淫 masturbate
手掌 palm
手杖 cane
手指 finger
手指甲 fingernail
手中的牌 hand
手中的王牌 ace in the hole (at **ace**)
手镯 bracelet
手足情谊 brotherhood
守场员 fielder
守法的 law-abiding
守规矩 conform, in line/into line (at **line**)
守旧的 conservative, old-fashioned, provincial, traditional
守旧性 conservatism
守口如瓶 keep your mouth shut (at **mouth**)
守灵 wake
守门员 goalie, goalkeeper
守球 keeper
守望 keep watch (at **watch**)
守卫 guard
守夜 keep vigil (at **vigil**), vigil
守则 law
守住 hang
首次 for the first time (at **for**)
首次的 maiden
首次登台 debut
首次上演 premiere
首都 capital
首付 pay
首付款 down payment
首领 chief
首尾颠倒 back
首尾相接 nose to tail (at **nose**)
首尾相接的 bumper to bumper (at **bumper**)
首位 top
首席的 chief
首席法官 chief justice
首席法律官员 solicitor
首席执行官 CEO, chief executive officer
首先 above all (at **all**), first, first and foremost (at **foremost**), first of all (at **first**), firstly, for a start/to start with (at **start**), in the first instance (at **instance**), in the first place (at **place**), to begin with (at **begin**)
首相 prime minister
首要的 cardinal, central, chief, first, high, paramount, premier, primary
首要手段 the first line of (at **line**)
寿命 life, lifespan
受 carry
受…管辖 come
受…困扰的 burdened
受…灵感启示的 -inspired (at **inspire**)
受…影响的 subject
受…支配的 subject
受保护 buffer
受到 come in for (at **come**), receive
受到…的限制 hostage
受到保卫 under watch (at **watch**)
受到高度赞扬的 acclaimed (at **acclaim**)
受到鼓舞的 encouraged (at **encourage**), heartened (at **hearten**)
受到广泛尊重的 respected
受到监视 watch

水库 reservoir
水雷 mine
水雷区 minefield
水流 current
水泥 cement
水牛 buffalo
水暖工 plumber
水暖设备 plumbing
水疱 blister
水平 league, level, proficiency, standard
水平的 flat, horizontal
水平飞行 level
水平高度 level
水平仪 level
水渠 channel
水溶性的 soluble
水生的 aquatic
水湾 inlet
水位 level
水位浅的 low
水雾 spray
水下用的 underwater
水仙花 daffodil
水箱 radiator
水循环 hydrologic cycle
水银 mercury
水运航班 sailing
水藻 algae
水闸 lock
税 duty, tax
税额 taxation
税额减免 tax relief
税款 levy
税率 rate
税前的 pretax
税前收入赚得 gross
税务年度 tax year
税制 taxation
睡袋 sleeping bag
睡觉 sleep
睡懒觉 sleep in (at **sleep**)
睡眠 sleep, slumber
睡眠时间 sleep
睡眠者 sleeper
睡袍 dressing gown, robe
睡衣 pajamas
睡衣晚会 slumber party
睡意 drowsiness (at **drowsy**)
睡着 drop off (at **drop**), sleep
睡着的 asleep
吮吸 suck
顺便 in passing (at **passing**)
顺便的 passing
顺便看望 look in (at **look**)
顺便说及地 incidentally
顺便说一下 for the record (at **record**)
顺便提一下 by the way (at **way**)
顺差 surplus
顺畅地 freely
顺从 obedience (at **obedient**), subservience (at **subservient**)
顺从的 dutiful, obedient, submissive, subservient
顺道拜访 drop in (at **drop**), stop by (at **stop**)
顺服 obey
顺口溜 patter
顺理成章 fall into place (at **place**)
顺利的 downhill, smooth
顺利通过 sail
顺利无阻的事 a free ride (at **ride**)
顺时针地 clockwise
顺势疗法 homeopathy
顺势疗法的 homeopathic
顺序 order, sequence
瞬间 instant, moment, split second
说 crack, go, remark, say, speak, talk, utter
说…作为开场白 preface
说不出话的 dumb
说不好 yes and no (at **yes**)
说不清的 indeterminate
说唱乐手 rapper
说唱音乐 rap
说出 break, recite
说出…的名称 name
说出爆炸性消息 drop a bombshell (at **bombshell**)
说出心中所想 to speak your mind (at **mind**)
说得过去 fair enough (at **fair**)
说得太对了 you can say that again (at **say**)
说得委婉些 put it mildly (at **mildly**)
说得有理 talk sense (at **sense**)
说法 version
说服 cajole, convince, get, persuade, persuasion, reason with (at **reason**)
说服…不做 talk out of (at **talk**)
说服力 eloquent
说服力的缺乏 weakness (at **weak**)
说服某人 twist sb's arm (at **arm**)
说话 mouth, speak, speak up (at **speak**), speech, talk
说话…的 -mouthed (at **mouth**)
说话兑现 put your money where your mouth is (at **money**)
说话方式 speech
说话者 speaker
说谎的人 liar
说教 preach
说尽 exhaust
说来也怪 funnily enough (at **funnily**)
说明 direction, say, state
说明书 direction
说明文字 caption
说明问题的 significant
说某人好话 speak well/highly of sb (at **speak**)
说起 talking of (at **talk**)
说人人皆知的事 state the obvious (at **obvious**)
说实话 actually
说完 finish
说笑话 joke
说真的 seriously
说着玩 joke
硕士学位 master, master's degree
丝绸 silk
丝毫 remotely
丝毫的 faintest
丝线 silk
丝质的 silky
司法 justice
司法部 judiciary
司法部长 Attorney General
司法的 judicial
司法权 jurisdiction
司令官 commander
私奔 run, run off (at **run**)
私立学校 private school
私立学校校长 headmaster
私立预科学校 prep school
私立专科学校 school
私人财产 goods
私人车道 driveway
私人持股公司 privately held corporation
私人的 personal, private
私人空间 privacy
私人司机 chauffeur
私人助理 personal assistant
私人字画店 gallery
私生的 illegitimate
私生子 bastard
私事 business
私事假 compassionate leave
私室 den
私通 infidelity
私下传播途径 grapevine
私下的 intimate, private
私下地 in private (at **private**), privately
私下劝告某人 take/draw sb to one side (at **side**)
私营部分 private sector
私有的 private
私有化 privatization (at **privatize**)
私有企业 private enterprise
思考 think, thought
思路 line
思维 thinking
思维方式 mind, perspective
思想家 thinker
思想开明 open-mindedness (at **open-minded**)
思想开明的 open-minded
思想偏狭的 parochial
思想体系 thought
思想头脑 consciousness
思想先进 ahead of/before one's time (at **time**)
斯诺克 snooker
嘶嘶地冒泡 fizz
嘶嘶冒气泡的 fizzy
嘶嘶声 hissing (at **hiss**)
嘶哑的 hoarse
撕 rip
撕扯 tear
撕掉 tear
撕开 slit, tear
撕裂 rip
撕破 tear
撕碎 rip up (at **rip**), shred
死产的 stillborn
死的 dead, extinct
死胡同 dead end
死灰复燃 where you left off (at **leave**)
死机 crash
死机的 down
死囚区 death row
死伤者 casualty
死亡 death, demise, die, fatality, loss, perish
死亡率 death rate
死亡人数 death toll, mortality
死刑 capital punishment, death penalty, death sentence
死刑电椅 chair
死一般的 deafening, deathly
死者 deceased
四 four
四倍的 quadruple
四重唱曲 quartet
四重唱小组 quartet
四重奏乐团 quartet
四重奏曲 quartet
四处 around, near and far (at **near**)
四处打电话 call around (at **call**)
四处搜索 scour
四处行走 get
四处寻找 look high and low (at **high**)
四分之三 three-quarters
四分之一 fourth, quarter
四分之一决赛 quarterfinal
四个一组 foursome
四轮马车 coach
四轮驱动车 four-wheel drive
四轮运货马车 wagon
四舍五入 round
四十 forty
四十几 forty
四月 April
四肢 limb
寺庙 temple
伺机而动 move in for the kill/ close in for the kill (at **kill**)
似乎 appear, seem, seemingly
似乎没完没了地 forever
似是而非的 spurious
似水的 watery
似银的 silvery
似油的 oily
饲料 feed, fodder
饲料槽 trough
饲养 keep, raise, rear
饲养的 domestic
饲养员 keeper
饲养者 breeder
肆虐 rage
肆无忌惮的 deadly
肆意驰骋 run riot (at **riot**)
肆意撒野 run riot (at **riot**)
松弛的 slack
松的 loose
松紧带 elastic
松劲 ease
松开 relax, slacken, undo, untie
松了口气 sigh of relief (at **sigh**)
松软布丁 sponge
松软蛋糕 sponge
松软的 fluffy
松散的 loose, slack
松鼠 squirrel
松树 pine
松懈 laxity (at **lax**)
松懈的 lax, slack
怂恿 egg on (at **egg**), entice, whip
耸肩 shrug
耸肩弓身 hunch
耸立 rise
耸人听闻的 lurid, sensational
诵读困难 dyslexia
送 run
送…住院治疗 hospitalize
送达 arrive
送掉 part with (at **part**)
送货的 delivery
送货费 carriage
送交 commit, commitment, referral, serve
送礼会 shower
送葬者 mourner
送至门口 see someone to the door (at **door**)
颂歌 hymn
颂扬 celebration, extol
嗖地快速移动 swish, whiz
搜 root
搜查 search, sweep
搜查令 warrant
搜查证 search warrant
搜集 gather
搜身 search
搜索 browse, probe, search, trawl
搜索引擎 search engine
搜寻 grub, hunt, hunting, quest, scout, search
搜寻队 search party
搜寻者 hunter
馊的 sour
苏打水 soda, soda water
苏丹 sultan
苏格兰或爱尔兰的 Gaelic

苏格兰威士忌 Scotch
苏醒 come, come to (at **come**), revive
诉求点 focus
诉说 talk
诉讼 action, case, litigation, proceeding, sue
诉讼案 lawsuit, suit
诉讼费用 cost
诉诸 resort
诉状 petition
素材 fodder, material
素淡的 sober
素的 vegetarian
素净的 restrained
素描 drawing, sketch
素食的 vegetarian
素质 qualification
速度 pace, rate, speed, tempo, velocity
速度计 speedometer
速记法 shorthand
宿舍 dormitory
宿舍楼 dormitory
宿营 camp, camping (at **camp**)
宿怨 vendetta
宿醉 hangover
塑料 plastic
塑造 form, model, mold, shape
酸 acid
酸橙 lime
酸的 sour
酸辣酱 chutney
酸奶 yogurt
酸葡萄 sour grapes (at **grape**)
酸痛的 stiff
酸性 acidity (at **acid**)
酸性的 acid, acidic
酸雨 acid rain
蒜瓣 clove
算了 oh well (at **well**)
算命 tell your fortune (at **fortune**)
算盘 abacus
算清 settle
算术 arithmetic
虽然 although, while
随…而移动 follow
随便 familiarity (at **familiar**)
随便的 any old (at **old**), familiar
随从 entourage
随大流 conformity
随风飘荡 waft
随和的 easygoing
随后的 ensuing, subsequent
随后做 follow
随机存取存贮器 RAM
随机的 random
随机地 at random (at **random**)
随即发生 ensue
随叫随到 on call (at **call**)
随身带着 take
随身听 personal stereo, Walkman
随时 (at) any minute (now) (at **minute**), (at) any moment (now) (at **moment**)
随时关注 follow
随时准备行动的 poised
随喜欢 as you please/whatever you please (at **please**)
随心所欲 get one's way/have one's way/get one's own way/have one's own way (at **way**)
随心所欲的人 loose cannon (at **cannon**)
随意 feel free (at **free**), informal
随意的 arbitrary, random
随意地 at random (at **random**)
随意丢弃 chuck
随意翻阅 browse
随意放置 stick
随着 with
随自己 on one's own account (at **account**)
岁数为…的 aged
碎步疾跑 scuttle
碎成片 splinter
碎掉一小块 chip
碎裂 crumble, fragment
碎片 debris, fragment, scrap, shrapnel, shred
碎石 rubble
碎石滩 shingle
碎屑 chip, crumb
碎砖 rubble
隧道 tunnel
穗 ear
孙女 grandchild, granddaughter
孙子 grandchild, grandson
损害 blemish, damage, harm, impair, injury, inroads, jeopardize, prejudice, undermine
损耗 wear and tear
损坏 break, breakage, damage, tarnish
损毁 lose
损毁的内部 gut
损人利己的 cheap
损伤 impairment, strain
损失 lose out (at **lose**), loss
损失控制 damage control
损失者 loser
唆使者 instigator
缩短 contract, shorten
缩回 retract
缩减 curtail, narrow down (at **narrow**), reduction, run, scale, slim
缩水 shrink
缩小 contract, dwindle, narrow, narrowing (at **narrow**), scale down (at **scale**), shrink
缩小规模 downsizing (at **downsize**)
缩写 abbreviate, abbreviation, shorten
缩写形式 contraction
缩影 in miniature (at **miniature**)
所到之处 everywhere
所得报酬过低的 underpaid
所得税 income tax
所订的货 order
所见即所得 WYSIWYG
所取钱款 withdrawal
所容之物 content
所剩无几 run short/run low (at **run**)
所挑选的人或物 choice
所谓的 so-called, supposed
所需物资 wherewithal
所有 belong
所有参赛者 field
所有的 all, what
所有地方 everywhere
所有可能的 every
所有其他的 every other (at **other**)
所有权 ownership
所有人 everyone
所有事物 everything
所有武器 weaponry
所有物 belongings, possession
所有者 owner
所做 belong
索具 rigging
索赔 claim
索求权 claim
索取 claim
索取人 claimant
索要 ask, claim
索引 index
琐事 chore, trifle, trivia
锁 lock
锁定 lock
锁骨 collarbone
锁柜 locker
锁好 close up (at **close**), lock
锁扣 boot
锁牢了的 secure
锁起 screw up (at **screw**)
他 he, him
他本人 himself
他的 hers, his
他们 'em, them, they
他们的 their, theirs
他们自己 themselves
他人的 other
它 him, it
它本身 itself
它的 his, its
它们 them, they
它们的 their, theirs
它们自己 themselves
塔 tower
踏 tramp
踏板 pedal
踏板车 scooter
踏车 treadmill
踏脚石 stepping stone
胎儿 fetus
台 desk, station
台词 line
台风 typhoon
台阶 step
台面 surface
台球戏 billiards
台式的 desktop
台式电脑 desktop
抬高 elevate, inflate
抬起 jut, lift
抬头 rise
太 only too (at **only**), too
太棒了 excellent
太迟的 too late (at **late**)
太多的物质 overdose
太妃糖 taffy, toffee
太过分 a bit much (at **bit**)
太好了 excellent
太空 space
太空舱 capsule
太空站 space station
太平梯 fire escape
太太 Mrs.
太阳 sun
太阳产生的 solar
太阳的 solar
太阳镜 sunglasses
太阳系 solar system
太阳穴 temple
态度 attitude, demeanor, feeling, position, posture, spirit, stance, take, way, where someone is coming from (at **come**)
态度的改变 change of heart (at **heart**)
泰然自若的 philosophical
坍塌 cave in (at **cave**), collapse, give
坍塌的 ruined
贪得无厌的 insatiable
贪婪 greed
贪婪的 greedy, voracious
贪食症 bulimia
贪食症的 bulimic
摊 spread
摊开四肢躺着 sprawl
摊位 stand
瘫倒 collapse, slump
瘫痪 break, paralysis
瘫痪的 paralyzed (at **paralyze**)
瘫痪状态 paralysis
瘫下 drop
瘫坐 collapse
谈到 come
谈话的 conversational
谈及 refer, speak
谈恋爱 court
谈论 talk
谈论本行工作 to talk shop (at **shop**)
谈判 bargain, bargaining (at **bargain**), negotiate, negotiation, talk
谈判人 negotiator
谈判桌 negotiating table
谈正题 come/get to the point (at **point**)
弹 pluck, spring
弹出的 pop-up
弹掉 flick
弹簧 spring
弹簧锁 latch
弹回 rebound
弹力大的 bouncy
弹起 bounce
弹起立体图片的 pop-up
弹射 catapult
弹射出来 eject
弹性 elasticity, resilience (at **resilient**)
弹性工作时间制 flextime
弹性针织布料 jersey
弹奏 strum
弹奏吉他的人 guitarist
坦白地说 in all honesty (at **honesty**)
坦诚的 honest, open
坦克 tank
坦率 frankness (at **frank**), openness (at **open**)
坦率的 candid, frank, straightforward, up front
坦率地说 frankly
坦率地与某人交谈 tackle
袒胸的 topless
毯子 blanket
叹气 sigh
探测 detect
探测器 detector
探查 nose around (at **nose**)
探查的 exploratory
探出 peep, poke
探得 elicit
探求 quest
探取 extract
探索 delve
探索性的 exploratory
探讨 exploration (at **explore**), explore
探险者 adventurer, explorer
探寻 probe
探寻的 searching
探询 sound out (at **sound**)
探询的 inquiring
探照灯 searchlight
探针 probe
碳 carbon
碳排放量 carbon footprint
碳排放权交易 carbon trading
碳水化合物 carbohydrate
碳中和的 carbon neutral
碳足迹 carbon footprint
汤 soup
蹚 wade

行走 tread, walk
形成 develop, form, formation, germinate
形成的 formative
形成物 formation
形成一组 group
形成阴蔽 shade
形成中的 in the making (at **making**)
形容词 adjective
形式 way
形势 climate, situation
形势的变化 turn of events (at **turn**)
形势对某人不利 the odds are stacked against sb/things are stacked against sb (at **stack**)
形象 figurative, image
形象化描述 imagery
形影不离的 inseparable
形状 form, shape
型号 model
醒酒 sober up (at **sober**)
醒来 rouse, wake, waken
醒目的 bold
醒目刊载的 plastered
醒着的 awake
擤 blow
杏 apricot
杏仁 almond
杏色的 apricot
杏树 almond
姓 surname
幸存 survive
幸存者 survivor
幸福 welfare
幸好 be just as well (at **well**), fortunately
幸事 blessing
幸运 mercy
幸运的 blessed, fortunate, lucky
幸运的是 happily
幸运地 luckily, mercifully
幸灾乐祸 gloat
幸灾乐祸的 gleeful
幸灾乐祸地笑 smirk
性 gender, sex
性爱的 erotic
性伴侣 mate, partner
性变态 perversion
性别 gender, sex
性别歧视 sexism
性别歧视的 sexist
性的 physical
性感 desirability (at **desirable**), sensuality (at **sensual**)
性感的 cute, desirable, hot, luscious, seductive, sensuous, sexy
性感偶像 sex symbol
性高潮 orgasm
性格 character, makeup, nature, personality, temperament
性格特征 streak
性关系 intimacy
性交 intercourse, make, screw, sexual intercourse
性命 life
性能 performance
性能不稳定的 temperamental
性虐待 sexual abuse
性倾向 sexuality
性情 disposition
性情温和的 good-natured, mild
性骚扰 sexual harassment
性受虐狂 masochism
性受虐狂的 masochistic
性受虐狂者 masochist (at **masochism**)
性兴奋 arousal
性行为 sex
性欲 desire, sexuality
性欲强的 passionate
性质 character
凶残 ferocity, viciousness (at **vicious**)
凶残的 ferocious, vicious
凶恶的 evil
凶猛的 fierce
凶猛地攻击 savage
兄弟 brother
兄弟般的 brotherly
兄弟会 brotherhood
兄弟姐妹 sibling
兄弟情谊 brotherhood
兄或弟的妻子 sister-in-law
汹涌的 raging
胸部 breast, bust, chest
胸部厚实发达的 barrel-chested
胸脯 breast
胸脯肉 breast
胸罩 bra
胸针 pin
雄辩的 eloquent
雄辩力 eloquence (at **eloquent**)
雄厚的财力 deep pockets (at **pocket**)
雄伟 majesty
雄伟的 majestic
雄心 ambition
雄心勃勃的 ambitious
雄性 male
雄性动物 buck
雄有成竹的 assured
熊 bear
熊市 bear market
熊市的 bearish
熊熊燃烧 blaze
熊熊燃烧的 ablaze, fiery, raging, roaring
休假 leave, sabbatical, take, vacation
休克 shock
休眠的 dormant
休庭 recess
休息 break, recess, relaxation, rest, time out
休息日 day off
休息室 lounge
休闲的 casual, informal
休闲浸泡 wallow
休想 forget
休养处 retreat
休战 ceasefire
修补 mend, patch, repair
修船厂 shipyard
修辞上的 rhetorical
修辞性的 rhetorical
修辞艺术 rhetoric
修道会 order
修道院 abbey, monastery
修订 overhaul, revise
修复 reconstruct, reconstruction, renovate, renovation (at **renovate**), restoration (at **restore**), restore
修复的 restored (at **restore**)
修改 amendment, modification (at **modify**), modify, revamp, revise, revision, rework
修剪 clip, cut, prune, trim
修剪整齐的 clipped
修理 fix, mend, patch, repair
修理工 repairer (at **repair**)
修女 nun, sister
修缮 rehab
修士 brother
修饰 dress, finish, touch up (at **touch**)
修整 fix up (at **fix**)
修正 amend, revise, revision
修正案 amendment
羞耻 shame
羞愧 shame
羞怯 diffidence (at **diffident**), timidity (at **timid**)
羞怯的 diffident, timid
羞辱 taunt
羞涩 shyness (at **shy**)
羞涩的人 (no) shrinking violet (at **violet**)
绣 embroider
袖口 cuff
袖手旁观 sit back (at **sit**), stand
袖珍的 pocket
袖珍画像 miniature
袖子 arm, sleeve
锈 rust
须 whisker
须后水 aftershave
须有 call for (at **call**)
虚报 pad
虚的 broken
虚度 misspend
虚构 fiction, invent, invention
虚构出 dream up (at **dream**)
虚构的 fictional, fictitious, made-up, mythical, unreal
虚华词藻 rhetoric
虚幻的 fictitious
虚幻的故事 fantasy
虚假 falsehood
虚假的 fictitious
虚假人为的 contrived
虚假消息 misinformation
虚惊 false alarm
虚拟的 virtual
虚拟内存 virtual memory, virtual storage
虚拟现实 virtual reality
虚拟性 virtuality (at **virtual**)
虚荣 vanity
虚弱 frailty, weakness (at **weak**)
虚弱的 feeble, frail, weak
虚弱晕眩的 faint
虚饰 show, veneer
虚伪 hypocrisy
虚伪的 hollow, hypocritical, insincere, sly
虚张声势 bluff
虚张声势的 idle
嘘 hush, shh
嘘嘘声 Bronx cheer
需求 call
需求量 demand, market
需要 call, claim, could do with sth (at **do**), demand, in need of (at **need**), involve, need, require, requirement, take
需要帮助的 in need (at **need**)
需要的 ready
需要的话 if need be (at **need**)
需要抚养的人 mouth to feed (at **mouth**)
需要久坐的 sedentary
需要熟练能力的 skilled
需要小心处理的 delicate
需要专门技术的 skilled
许多 a/one hell of a lot (at **hell**), dozen, heap, load, many, mass, no end (at **end**), number
许多的 many, numerous
许多人 many
许可 agreement, go-ahead, permission
许可证 license, pass, permit
许许多多 hundred
序 introduction
序列号 serial number
序曲 beginning, overture
叙旧 catch, reminisce
叙事 narrative
叙事歌 ballad
叙述 narrate, narration (at **narrate**), recount, story
叙述人 narrator (at **narrate**)
畜群 herd
续发性的 secondary
续集 sequel
续篇 sequel
续期 roll
酗酒 alcoholism, drunken
酗酒者 alcoholic, drunk
嗅 smell
嗅出 sniff
嗅到 scent
嗅觉 nose, smell
蓄电池 battery
蓄意破坏 sabotage
蓄意收购公司者 corporate raider
宣布 announce, announcement, come, give, pass, proclaim, pronounce, return
宣布…合格 pass
宣布…为非法 outlaw
宣布…无效 annul
宣布放弃 renounce
宣布支持 come down on (at **come**)
宣称 say
宣传 advertise, advertisement, bill, exposure, herald, propaganda, propagate, propagation (at **propagate**), publicity, publicize
宣传单 flyer
宣传品 handout
宣传员 publicist
宣告 declare, sound
宣过誓的 sworn
宣判 sentence
宣判…无罪 acquit
宣判无罪 clear
宣誓 oath
宣言 declaration, manifesto
宣扬 preach
喧哗的 tumultuous
喧闹 racket
喧闹的 boisterous, noisy
喧闹活泼的 hearty
喧嚣 bustle, din
悬摆 dangle
悬带 sling
悬浮 hang
悬挂 dangle, hang, sling, suspend
悬挂着 hang
悬架 suspension
悬铃木 plane
悬念 suspense
悬起 sling
悬殊的 one-sided
悬崖 cliff
悬疑故事 mystery
悬于…之上 overhang
旋风 cyclone, whirlwind
旋律 melody
旋钮 knob
旋塞 faucet
旋转 revolve, rotate, rotation, swivel, twirl, twist
旋转的 rotary
旋转木马 carousel, merry-go-round, roundabout
选…扮演角色 cast

选出 single out (at **single**)
选定 select, settle on (at **settle**), slate
选段 extract
选集 anthology
选举 elect, election
选举权 franchise, vote
选举人 elector
选美大赛 pageant
选民 constituent, voter
选民阵营 constituency
选派 draft
选票 vote
选区 constituency
选人接任 fill
选手 player
选修 take
选修课 option
选择 choice, choose, elect, go for (at **go**), opt, select, selection
选择权 option
选择性的 selective
选址 siting (at **site**)
炫示 dangle
炫耀 flaunt, show
炫耀的 ostentatious
绚烂 dazzle
绚丽多彩的 colorful
眩晕 dizziness (at **dizzy**), spin
眩晕的 dizzy, giddy
渲染 dramatize, embroider
靴子 boot
学…的样 imitate
学步的儿童 toddler
学费 tuition
学分 credit
学会 learn, pick
学究气的 pedantic
学科 discipline, science, study
学历 qualification
学年 year
学派 school
学期 semester, term
学生 pupil, student
学生时代 schooldays
学生宿舍 hall of residence
学生宿舍楼 residence hall
学识 knowledge
学术的 academic, scholarly, scholastic
学术上的 academic
学术性的 scholarly
学术研究 scholarship
学说 doctrine, teaching
学徒 apprentice
学徒期 apprenticeship
学徒制 apprenticeship
学位 degree
学位论文 thesis
学问成就 scholarship
学习 backward, learn, learning, learning (at **learn**), study
学习好的 academic
学习曲线 learning curve
学习者 learner
学习指南 tutorial
学校 school
学校的 academic
学校教育 schooling
学业的 scholastic
学员 cadet
学院 college, school
学院院长 dean
学者 academic, scholar, student
学做某事 turn one's hand to sth (at **hand**)
雪 snow
雪崩 avalanche
雪堆 drift
雪纺绸 chiffon
雪利酒 sherry
雪泥 slush
雪橇 sled, sledge, sleigh
雪茄烟 cigar
雪球 snowball
雪人 snowman
雪松 cedar
雪松木 cedar
鳕鱼 cod
鳕鱼肉 cod
血管 blood vessel
血浆 plasma
血淋淋的 gory
血流 bloodstream
血清 serum
血肉之躯 flesh and blood (at **flesh**)
血统 blood, origin, side
血腥的 bloody
血压 blood pressure
血液 blood
血液循环 circulation
血友病 hemophilia
血友病患者 hemophiliac
熏倒 overcome
熏死 overcome
熏衣草 lavender
熏制 smoke
熏猪肉 bacon
寻呼机 beeper, pager
寻欢作乐者 player
寻求 look, quest
寻求避难者 asylum seeker
寻找 grope, in quest of (at **quest**), in search of (at **search**), look, seek
寻找…的来源 source
巡 round
巡访 make the rounds (at **round**), round, route
巡官 inspector
巡航 cruise
巡回访问 tour
巡回演出 tour
巡逻队 patrol
巡洋舰 cruiser
驯服的 tame
驯化 tame
驯鹿 reindeer
驯兽师 trainer (at **train**)
询问 inquiry, interview, query, question, questioning (at **question**), quiz
询问的 questioning
询问者 interviewer
循规蹈矩者 straight arrow
循环 circulate, circulation (at **circulate**)
循环使用 recycle
训 bawl out (at **bawl**)
训斥 rap sb's knuckles, rap sb on/over the knuckles (at **rap**), reprimand, tell off (at **tell**)
训练 coach, discipline, equip, orientation, school, train, training
训练有素的 crack
讯问 inquest
迅猛的 furious
迅猛地 headlong
迅速 quick, rapidity (at **rapid**), shoot
迅速传播 sweep
迅速带走 whisk
迅速的 fast, little, prompt, quick, rapid, speedy, swift
迅速低头 duck
迅速地 readily
迅速地走 rush
迅速发展 mushroom
迅速反应能力 reflex
迅速放置 pop
迅速积极的反应 responsiveness (at **responsive**)
迅速积极反应的 responsive
迅速疾驰 speed
迅速记录 note down (at **note**)
迅速扩散的 invasive
迅速拿走 snatch
迅速轻松地穿上 slip
迅速轻松地脱下 slip
迅速去做 dash off (at **dash**)
迅速生长 burgeon
迅速送 rush
迅速下降 drop
迅速增长 snowball
迅速占领 overrun
殉教者 martyr
压扁 crush, squash
压倒性的 overwhelming
压倒性优势的胜利 landslide
压倒一切的 overpowering
压低 muffle
压低嗓门 voice
压根儿不知道 not have the foggiest/not have the foggiest idea (at **foggy**)
压过 overpower
压力 load, pressure, strain
压力大的 stressful
压迫 oppress, oppression
压迫的 oppressive, repressive
压碎 crush, scrunch up (at **scrunch**), squash
压缩 compress, compression (at **compress**), zip
压缩驱动器 zip drive
压缩文件 zip file
压抑 repression, smother
压印 impression, imprint
压榨 squeeze
压制 hold, keep, repress, repression, stifle, stranglehold, suppress
压制言论自由 gag
压着不办 sit
押金 deposit
押韵 rhyme
押韵词 rhyme
押韵短诗 rhyme
鸦片 opium
鸭 duck
牙齿 tooth
牙齿的 dental
牙膏 toothpaste
牙箍 brace
牙菌斑 plaque
牙科的 dental
牙科医生 dentist
牙刷 toothbrush
牙医诊所 dentist's office
芽 bud
哑的 dumb, mute
哑剧表演 mime
哑铃 weight
哑谜猜字游戏 charade
雅皮士 yuppie
亚军 runner-up
亚麻布 linen
亚麻织品 linen
亚文化 subculture
亚洲的 Asian
烟 smoke
烟草 tobacco
烟草制品 tobacco
烟囱 chimney, funnel
烟蒂 butt
烟斗 pipe
烟花 firework
烟灰缸 ashtray
烟气 fume
烟雾 haze, smog
烟雾弥漫的 smoky
烟雾状的 smoky
烟熏味的 smoky
烟叶 tobacco
胭脂 rouge
淹没 flood, inundate, submerge, swamp
淹没于 drown
阉割 castrate, castration (at **castrate**)
阉公牛 ox
腌泡 marinade, marinate
腌汁 marinade
腌制 pickle
腌制的 pickled
腌猪肉 bacon
延长 extend, lengthen, prolong, renewal
延长的期限 extension
延长了的 prolonged
延长路段 extension
延长期限 extend
延长有效期 renew
延迟 hold
延搁 holdup
延缓 suspension, wait
延期 postponement
延期的 postdated
延伸 extend, reach, run, sprawl, spread, stretch
延伸部分 extension
延伸建筑 extension
延误 delay, set back (at **set**)
延续 continuation, endure, run
延展 extension
严惩措施 crackdown
严惩以警告他人 make an example of someone (at **example**)
严格按照规定地 technically
严格按照事实地 technically
严格的 strict, stringent, tight
严格控制 keep a tight rein on (at **rein**), rein back (at **rein**)
严格意义上的 proper
严格缜密的 rigorous
严管 ride
严寒刺骨的 biting
严寒的 bitter
严加管制 crack down (at **crack**)
严加限制 clamp
严加治理 crack
严谨 rigor
严峻的 acute
严酷 rigor
严酷的 cruel, draconian, grim, harsh, stark
严厉惩罚 hammer
严厉的 austere, hard, severe, sharp, stern, strict
严厉批评 hammer, slam
严厉性 severity (at **severe**)
严密保护的 secure
严密的 watertight
严肃 gravity, solemnity (at **solemn**)
严肃呆板的 staid
严肃的 deep, grave, meaningful, serious, sober, solemn
严肃地 earnest, earnestly
严重错误 crime
严重错误的 criminal
严重打击 shatter
严重的 appalling, bad, big, chronic, dire, grave, grievous, gross, large, massive, nasty, raging,

用右手的 right-handed
用于 toward
用于烹饪的 cooking
用于皮下注射的 hypodermic
用于战争的 assault
用鱼钩钓住 hook
用钥匙打开 unlock
用韵 rhyme
用凿子雕切 chisel
用炸药炸 blast
用真空吸尘器清洁 vacuum
用作象征的 symbolic
优待 spoil
优等的 first-class, preferential
优点 beauty, merit
优惠券 coupon
优良品质 quality
优美 grace
优美的 graceful, slender
优柔寡断的 indecisive
优势 advantage, benefit, dominance, edge, ground, plus, superiority, supremacy, the upper hand (at **upper**), virtue
优先处理的事 priority
优先的 prior
优先购买权 first refusal (at **refusal**)
优先股 preference shares, preferred stock
优先考虑 give priority (at **priority**), preference, prioritize
优先认股权 share option
优先性 precedence
优秀 excellence
优秀的 excellent, sterling, strong
优雅 elegance (at **elegant**)
优雅的 elegant, ethereal, graceful
优雅流畅的 fluid
优于 surpass
优越 superiority (at **superior**)
优越性 superiority (at **superior**)
优质 quality
优质的 choice, high-class, vintage
忧虑 apprehension, dread, worry
忧虑不安 disquiet
忧虑的 distressed
忧伤的 gloomy
忧郁 gloom
忧郁的 melancholy
幽灵 ghost, phantom, spirit
幽灵的 ghostly
幽默 humor
幽默的 humorous
幽默短剧 sketch
幽默感 sense of humor
幽默性 humor
幽雅的 polished
悠懒的 lazy
悠闲 ease
悠闲地 at leisure/at sb's leisure (at **leisure**)
悠着点 take it easy (at **easy**)
尤其 especially, notably
由… for, from
由…付费 at someone's expense (at **expense**)
由…紧接着 followed by (at **follow**)
由…康复 pull
由…联袂主演 costar
由…主演 feature, star
由…组成 comprise
由爆炸引起 blast
由表象 by the look of/by the looks of (at **look**)
由此 thereby
由此导致的 resultant
由癫痫引起的 epileptic
由点构成的 dotted
由电产生的 electric
由很多种类组成的 heterogeneous
由花组成的 floral
由某人处理 on one's hands (at **hand**)
由热引起的 thermal
由水组成的 watery
由温度变化引起的 thermal
由于 as, because, by, due, on account of (at **account**), owe, since, with
由于缺少 for want of (at **want**)
由于自身原因 for it's/their own sake (at **sake**)
由脂肪组成的 fatty
由直线组成的 linear
由衷地 truly
犹太教 Judaism
犹太教的 Jewish
犹太教堂 synagogue
犹太教徒 Jew
犹太人的 Jewish
犹豫 dither, falter, hold back (at **hold**)
犹豫不决 of two minds (at **mind**), waver
犹豫的 tentative, torn
邮包 parcel
邮递员 mailman, postman
邮购 mail order
邮购商品 mail order
邮寄 mail, mailing, post, send
邮寄的 postal
邮寄名单 mailing list
邮件 mail, mailing, post
邮件合并 mail merge
邮局 post office
邮票 stamp
邮筒 mailbox
邮箱 box, postbox
邮政 mail
邮政编码 postcode, zip code
邮政的 postal
邮政汇票 postal order
邮政信箱 PO Box, post office box
邮政信箱号码 box number
邮资 postage
油菜 rape
油画 oil painting
油画布 canvas
油画颜料 oil paint
油迹 smear
油井 well
油轮 tanker
油门 accelerator
油门杆 throttle
油门踏板 throttle
油墨 ink
油腻 richness (at **rich**)
油腻的 rich
油漆 paint
油漆层 paint
油漆工 painter
油漆刷 paintbrush
油酥糕点 pastry
油酥面团 pastry
油桃 nectarine
油脂 grease
油状的 oily
油嘴滑舌的 glib
柚木 teak
柚子酱 marmalade
疣 wart
铀 uranium
游过 swim
游击队员 guerrilla, partisan
游客 tourist
游览 look around (at **look**), tour
游览胜地 attraction
游历 travel
游猎 safari
游牧的 nomadic
游说 advocacy, lobby
游说团体 lobby
游艇 cruiser, yacht
游戏 game
游戏场 playground
游戏厅 arcade
游戏组 playgroup
游行 march, parade
游行彩车 float
游行示威 demonstrate
游行者 demonstrator, marcher (at **march**)
游泳 bathing (at **bathe**), swim
游泳池 pool, swimming pool
游泳运动 swimming
游泳者 swimmer
游泳姿势 stroke
游园会 fete
鱿鱼 squid
友爱 fraternity
友好 goodwill
友好的 amicable, expansive, friendly, nice, outgoing
友好对待 befriend
友好关系 friendship
友情 friendship
友情链接 hot link
友善 friendliness (at **friendly**), geniality (at **genial**)
友善的 cordial, genial, pleasant, sociable
友谊 friendship
友谊赛 friendly
友谊赛的 friendly
有心情 in the mood for/to (at **mood**)
有 get, have, you get (at **get**)
有…存货 stock
有…的才能 a head for sth (at **head**)
有…的气味 smell
有…的想法 flirt
有…方面的问题 have issues with (at **issue**)
有…看法的 disposed
有…倾向的 predisposed (at **predispose**)
有…体格的 built
有…天赋的 inclined
有…味道 taste
有…形状的 shaped
有…意向的 inclined
有…在里面 contain
有暧昧关系的 involved
有凹陷的 pitted
有把握得到的 assured
有把握的 certain, safe
有帮助 be of help (at **help**)
有帮助的 beneficial, helpful
有保留的 qualified
有暴风雨的 stormy
有悖常理的 perverse
有本领 to have it in you (at **have**)
有必要 occasion
有辨别力的 discerning
有别于 distinguish
有病的 sick
有才干的 capable
有才能的 able, capable
有才智的人 mind
有偿债能力的 solvent
有朝一日 one day/some day/one of these days (at **day**)
有衬垫的 pad
有成本效益的 cost-effective
有成效 bear fruit (at **fruit**)
有成效的 successful
有成效的结果 tribute
有臭味 smell
有臭味的 smelly
有创见的 visionary
有创新精神的 enterprising
有创新思维的 dynamic
有创造才能的 inventive
有创造力的 creative
有磁的 magnetic
有磁力的 magnetic
有磁性的 magnetic
有催眠作用的 hypnotic
有代表性的 representative, typical
有担保的 bonded
有弹性 stretch
有弹性的 elastic, resilient
有道德的 good, moral
有道理 something
有道理的 reasonable
有抵抗力的 resistant
有地盘意识的 territorial
有点 kind of (at **kind**), little
有点儿 a bit (at **bit**), a bit of a (at **bit**), a trifle (at **trifle**), half, something, vaguely
有洞察力的 perceptive
有毒的 poisonous, toxic, venomous
有独特氛围的 atmospheric
有发动机的 motorized
有反映的 receptive
有分寸的 tactful
有分歧 disagree, diverge
有分歧的 apart, divergent
有盖容器 canister
有感染力的 contagious, infectious, powerful
有感知力的 sensitive
有格调的 stylish
有格子图案的 checked
有根据的 informed, valid
有工作的 working
有关的 concerned (at **concern**), interested, question
有关个人的 personal
有关骨盆的 pelvic
有关建筑的 architectural
有关联的 allied, connected
有关两者的 straight
有关青少年的 teen
有关上帝的 holy
有关时事的 topical
有关通货膨胀的 inflationary
有关戏剧的 dramatic
有关宪法的 constitutional
有关刑罚的 penal
有关性爱的 romantic
有关性繁殖的 sexual
有关性取向的 sexual
有关性行为的 sexual
有关性欲的 sexual
有关于…的 concerned (at **concern**)
有关章程的 constitutional
有关职业的 professional
有光涂料 gloss, gloss paint
有轨电车 tram, trolley
有过错 at fault (at **fault**)
有过失的 guilty
有害的 detrimental, harmful, ill
有害的事 evil
有害的小动物 pest

有好处 pay
有很多优点 to be said for sth (at **say**)
有胡须的 bearded
有花边的 lacy
有花不完的钱 have money to burn (at **money**)
有花的 floral
有花卉图案的 floral
有回报 pay dividends (at **dividend**)
有活力的 alive, bouncy, dynamic
有货 in stock (at **stock**)
有机的 organic
有机会 have occasion (at **occasion**)
有机会获得 in the hunt (at **hunt**)
有机会做 get
有机种植的 organic
有积极性的 motivated (at **motivate**)
有计划的 systematic
有纪律的 disciplined
有技术的 skilled
有价证券 security
有价值 count
有价值之人 prize
有价值之物 prize
有驾驭力的 masterful
有尖端的 spiky
有监护权的 custodial
有教养的 civilized, cultivated, genteel, polished
有教养的人 gentleman
有教育意义的 educational
有节制的 low-key
有节制地 in moderation (at **moderation**)
有节奏的 rhythmic
有节奏地跳动 pulsate, pulse
有金属光泽的 metallic
有锦囊妙计 have sth up one's sleeve (at **sleeve**)
有经验的 experienced
有竞争力的 competitive
有距离的 distance
有聚合力的 cohesive
有开拓精神的 enterprising
有可读性的 readable
有可能 stand, stand a chance (at **chance**)
有可能成功 credible
有可能的 set
有可能会 might
有客人 have company (at **company**)
有空的 available
有空气调节设备的 air-conditioned
有恐外症的 xenophobic
有浪漫情调的 romantic
有泪的 tearful
有棱角的 angular
有礼貌的 civilized, gracious, polite
有力陈述 press
有力的 hefty
有利的 advantageous, favorable
有利的事 a good turn (at **turn**)
有利条件 advantage, sweetener
有利位置 vantage point
有利有弊的 double-edged
有利于 favor
有联系的 related
有恋爱关系的 intimate
有毛病的 wrong
有冒险精神的 adventurous
有美术才能的 artistic
有魅力的 attractive, charismatic
有迷幻色彩的 psychedelic
有名的 famous, note, well-known
有名望的 eminent, renowned
有名无实的 phantom
有名之地 capital
有魔力的 magic
有默契的 unspoken
有男性生殖力的 virile
有男子气概的 manly, virile
有能力的 capable, competent
有偏见的 biased, prejudiced
有偏向的 loaded
有品牌的 branded
有品位的 classy, tasteful
有魄力的 forceful
有启发性的 instructive
有前途的 high-flying
有墙裙的 paneled
有亲属关系的 related
有倾向的 weighted
有请 please
有区别的 distinct
有趣的 colorful, interesting, notable
有趣的人 fun
有趣的事 a good laugh/a bit of a laugh (at **laugh**)
有趣动人的 racy
有权势的 influential
有权势的人 movers and shakers (at **mover**)
有权威的 authoritative
有权做 qualify
有缺口的 chipped (at **chip**)
有缺损的 chip
有缺陷的 defective, flawed
有辱人格的 degrade
有色的 colored, of color (at **color**)
有深意的 loaded
有生命的 animate
有声望的 prestigious
有声誉的 renowned
有施虐狂的 sadistic
有时 at times (at **time**), maybe, off and on (at **off**), sometimes
有实力的 strong
有实效的 practical
有史以来的 of all time (at **time**)
有势力的 important
有霜的 frosty
有说服力的 convincing, eloquent, forceful, persuasive, strong
有思想深度的 thoughtful
有损害性的 damaging (at **damage**)
有损于 detriment (at **detriment**)
有特权的 privileged
有特色的 distinctive
有特异功能的 psychic
有天赋的 gifted, talented
有条不紊的 methodical
有条理 in order (at **order**)
有条理的 organized
有条纹的 striped
有同情心的 compassionate, soft
有瓦楞的 corrugated
有望成功的 promising, up-and-coming
有望成为…的事 candidate
有望达到目标 on target (at **target**)
有望获胜 in the running (at **running**)
有望做…的人 candidate
有危害的 hazardous
有危险的 risky
有文凭的 qualified
有问题的 doubtful, problematic, wrong
有雾的 foggy, misty
有吸收力的 absorbent
有吸引力 appeal
有吸引力的 magnetic
有吸引力的事物 magnet
有线电视 cable
有线广播系统 PA
有限的 confined, finite, limited
有限度的 qualified
有限责任的 limited
有乡村特色的 rural
有象征意义的 symbolic
有销路 sell
有效的 effective, good, valid
有效地 to (good) effect (at **effect**)
有效期 term
有效性 effectiveness (at **effective**)
有些进展 be getting somewhere (at **somewhere**)
有心灵感应能力的 telepathic
有薪酬的 paid
有信心的 confident
有信用的 creditworthy
有形的 physical
有幸具有的 blessed
有性关系的 intimate
有修养的 cultured
有选举权的人 elector
有严格道德原则的 puritanical
有研磨作用的 abrasive
有氧运动 aerobics
有疑虑的 dubious
有艺术性的 artistic
有异议 differ
有益的 good, valuable
有益健康的 healthy, sanitary, wholesome
有益身心的 wholesome
有意 make a point of (at **point**), mean
有意安排的 calculated
有意避开某人 steer clear of sb (at **steer**)
有意回避 shun
有意利用 play on (at **play**)
有意图的 purposeful
有意义 make sense (at **sense**)
有翼的 winged
有音乐天赋的 musical
有营养的 nourishing (at **nourish**), nutritious
有影响 make a difference (at **difference**)
有影响的人 influence
有影响力 carry weight (at **weight**)
有影响力的 big, dominating, influential, powerful
有用 be of use (at **use**), come in useful (at **useful**)
有用的 handy, helpful, meaningful, useful
有用性 usefulness (at **useful**)
有优先性 take priority/has priority (at **priority**)
有优越感的 superior
有油脂的 greasy
有诱惑力的 attractive
有羽毛的 feathered
有预见性的 prophetic
有原则的 principled
有远见的 farsighted
有远见的人 visionary
有约束力的 binding
有噪音的 noisy
有责任心的 responsible
有罩的 hooded
有褶的 pleated
有争议的 controversial, debatable, in dispute (at **dispute**)
有志向的 aspiring
有秩序的 orderly
有智慧的 intelligent, wise
有智能的 intelligent
有重大历史意义的 historic
有重大影响的 fateful, seminal
有重要性 resonate
有重要意义 count
有皱纹的 creased (at **crease**), wrinkled (at **wrinkle**)
有主见 to know your own mind (at **mind**)
有助益 assist, be of assistance (at **assistance**)
有助益的 conducive, helpful
有助于 aid, help, in sb's favor (at **favor**)
有专长 specialize
有追溯力的 retrospective
有资格的 eligible, qualified
有资格拥有 qualify
有自然美的 unspoiled
有自尊心的 proud
有组织的 organized
有组织的活动 effort
有组织的旅行 expedition
有尊严的 dignified
又 again
又长又乱的 shaggy
又及 PS
又来了 here we go again (at **here**), there you go again (at **there**)
又一次 all over again (at **over**)
又一次地 around
又一的 another
又一个 again
又脏又臭的 foul
右边 right
右边的 right
右侧 right
右侧的 right-hand
右击 right-click
右派 right-wing, rightist
右派的 right-wing, rightist
右派分子 right-winger
右舷的 starboard
右翼 right-wing
右翼的 right-wing
右翼分子 right, right-winger
幼虫 grub, larva
幼儿 infant
幼儿便盆 potty
幼儿园 kindergarten, nursery, nursery school
幼鹿 fawn
幼苗 seedling
幼禽 young
幼犬 pup, puppy
幼兽 calf, pup
幼小的 small, tender, young
幼崽 baby, offspring, young
幼稚 immaturity, naivety (at **naive**)
幼稚的 childish, naive, silly
幼仔 cub
诱饵 bait, carrot, decoy, lure
诱惑 seduce, seduction (at **seduce**), temptation
诱惑力 lure
诱奸 seduce
诱骗 trap
诱人的 enticing, inviting, seductive, tempting
诱使 tempt
诱因 inducement

战利品 trophy
战列舰 battleship
战略 strategy
战略家 strategist
战略上的 strategic
战略性的 strategic
战前的 prewar
战胜 beat
战术 tactic
战术上的 tactical
战术性的 tactical
战役 battle, campaign
战争 war, warfare
战争时期 wartime
战争状态 hostilities
站 station
站不住脚的 flimsy, invalid, lame
站出来 come forward (at **come**)
站得住脚 hold
站岗 stand guard (at **guard**)
站立 raise, stand
站起来 get up (at **get**), stand, to your feet (at **foot**)
站台 platform
站稳 footing
站住脚 find your feet (at **foot**)
站着 on your feet (at **foot**)
站着的脚来回挪动 shuffle
站姿 stance
绽开笑容 beam
蘸 dip
张 sheet
张皇失措 head
张开 open
张开双臂 with open arms (at **arm**)
张贴 post, put
张扬 glare
章 chapter
章程 constitution
章节 passage
章鱼 octopus
章鱼肉 octopus
彰显 assert
樟脑草 catnip
蟑螂 cockroach, roach
涨 come, turn
涨高 inflate
涨价 markup
掌管 charge, head, in control (at **control**)
掌控 clutch, grasp, grip, hand, have sth at one's command (at **command**), master
掌权 rein
掌上的 handheld
掌上电脑 palmtop, personal digital assistant
掌声 applause
掌握 command, hold, master, mastery, wield
掌握…的窍门 get the hang of sth (at **hang**)
掌握最新信息的 up-to-date
丈夫 husband
丈夫的姐妹 sister-in-law
帐簿 book
帐单 tab
帐篷 tent
账单 bill, check
账户 account
账面价值 book value
账目 account, entry
障碍 bar, barrier, drawback, hurdle, impediment, obstacle, obstruction
障碍物 fence, hindrance, impediment, obstacle
招待 entertaining (at **entertain**), wait
招待会 reception
招募 recruit
招聘 recruitment
招惹 invitation
招人恨的 in the doghouse (at **doghouse**)
招收 recruit, recruiting (at **recruit**)
招贴 poster
招摇的 ostentatious
招摇撞骗 bluff
招致 court, incur, invite
招致霉运的 unlucky
朝霞 sunrise
找不到的 missing
找出 dig, sniff out (at **sniff**), uncover, unearth
找到 come, discover, find, find one's way (at **find**), locate, seek, strike, trace, track down (at **track**), turn, work out (at **work**)
找到了 here we are (at **here**)
找得出 find
找回 get, retrieval, retrieve
找回的钱 change
找人算命 have one's cards read (at **card**)
沼泽 bog, marsh
沼泽地 swamp
召唤 beckon, summon
召回 recall
召集 call out (at **call**), convene, marshal
召见令 summons
召开 convene
兆字节 megabyte
照常 as usual (at **usual**)
照单全收 lap up (at **lap**)
照顾 care, hand, look after (at **look**)
照顾某人 take care of sb (at **care**)
照管 look, touch
照管的 custodial
照看 keep your eye on something (at **eye**), mind, watch
照例地 routinely
照亮 illuminate, light, light up (at **light**)
照料 attend, attention, fend, see to (at **see**)
照明 illumination, lighting
照片 photo, photograph, picture, portrayal, shot
照片的 photographic
照射 stream
照射于 catch
照相机 camera
照样地 likewise
照这样下去 at this rate (at **rate**)
照着说 repeat
照着写 repeat
罩 canopy
遮蔽 overshadow, shade, shelter
遮挡 block, blot out (at **blot**), cut, screen, shield
遮盖 canopy, conceal, hide
遮盖层 covering
遮帘 shade
遮掩 mask, obscure
遮住 interrupt, shadow
折叠 fold
折叠床 cot
折断 fracture
折返 retrace
折痕 crease, fold
折价换新 trade-in
折扣 discount
折磨 grind down (at **grind**), martyr, scourge, tear, torment, torture
折磨人的 harrowing
折磨人的事物 affliction
折叶 hinge
折衷 compromise
哲人 philosopher
哲学 philosophy
哲学的 philosophical
哲学家 philosopher
哲学思想 philosophy
蛰刺 sting
褶 pleat
褶边 frill, ruffle
褶皱 fold
褶皱的 crumpled (at **crumple**)
这个 one, this, which
这会儿 now
这就叫… talk about sth (at **talk**)
这就是 here
这里 over here (at **over**)
这么 this
这么多 so much/so many (at **so**)
这山望着那山高 the grass is greener (at **grass**)
这些 these
这样 so, way
这样的 such
这样好多了 that's better (at **better**)
这样一来 now
这一点 this
这种事情 thing
针 needle
针对 about, aim, direct, level, target
针对…的 specific
针脚 stitch
针灸 acupuncture
针线活 sewing
针叶 needle
针织套衫 jersey, jumper
侦察 reconnaissance
侦察员 scout
侦探 detective
侦探的 detective
珍爱 cherish
珍爱的 cherished (at **cherish**)
珍藏 cherish
珍藏的 cherished (at **cherish**)
珍贵的 precious, treasured (at **treasure**)
珍品 gem, treasure
珍视 cherish
珍视的 cherished (at **cherish**), dear
珍惜 treasure
珍珠 pearl
珍珠般的 pearl
真… enough
真棒的 brilliant
真不错 something
真诚 sincerity (at **sincere**)
真诚的 genuine, real, sincere
真诚地 sincerely, truly
真的 honest, honestly, really
真地 literally, really
真空 vacuum
真空吸尘器 vacuum, vacuum cleaner
真理 truth
真没想到 fancy
真品 the genuine article (at **article**)
真人秀 reality TV
真实的 actual, authentic, raw, real, true
真实发生的事 reality
真实可靠的 solid
真实情形 reality
真实性 authenticity (at **authentic**), truth
真相 truth
真心 seriousness (at **serious**)
真心的 serious
真心实意地 in good faith (at **faith**), with all one's heart (at **heart**)
真正的 genuine, real, true
真正地 indeed, positively, real, really, truly
真挚的 earnest
真作全集 canon
斟酌 mull, mull over (at **mull**)
榛树 hazel
诊察 examination (at **examine**), examine
诊察台 couch
诊断 diagnose, diagnosis
诊断的 diagnostic
诊疗时间 surgery
诊室 doctor's office, doctor's surgery, surgery
诊所 clinic, doctor, doctor's office, doctor's surgery, office
枕头 pillow
疹子 rash
缜密的 reasoned, rigorous
阵 round
阵列 lineup
阵容 lineup
阵痛 throb
阵营 bloc, camp
阵雨 shower
振翅 flutter
振作 perk
振作起来 cheer up (at **cheer**)
镇定 composure, poise
镇定的 poised, steady
镇定自若 keep one's head/lose one's head (at **head**)
镇静 poise
镇静剂 sedative, tranquilizer
镇静状态 sedation
镇压 crackdown, crush, crushing (at **crush**), put, quash, quell, repress, repression, squash, suppress, suppression (at **suppress**)
镇压的 repressive
震动 jar, rock, shake
震动作响 throb
震耳欲聋的 deafening
震惊 horror, jolt, rock, shake, shock
震惊的 shocked (at **shock**), staggered (at **stagger**)
震怒 outrage
震怒的 outraged (at **outrage**)
争辩 argue, argument, quibble
争吵 argue, argument, exchange, quarrel, squabble, squabbling (at **squabble**), wrangle
争吵不休 feud
争端 quarrel
争夺 compete, contend, contest, dispute, jostle, scramble
争夺赛 stake
争分夺秒 against the clock (at **clock**)
争购 snap up (at **snap**)
争论 contention, cross swords (at **sword**), dispute, haggle, lock horns (at **horn**), quarrel
争论的问题 battlefield
争论中的 at issue (at **issue**)

直到…为止 till, until
直到另行通知 until further notice (at **notice**)
直观教具 visual aid
直角 right angle
直接宾语 direct object
直接的 direct, first hand
直接地 first, immediately
直接税 direct tax
直接相关的 direct
直接引语 direct discourse, direct speech
直截了当的 straight
直截了当地 point-blank
直径 caliber, diameter
直觉 hunch, instinct, intuition
直觉的 gut, intuitive
直觉决断力 common sense
直立的 erect
直率 candor, directness (at **direct**)
直率的 direct, forthright, outright
直三角形 right triangle
直射的 direct
直升飞机 chopper
直升机 helicopter
直升机升降坪 helipad
直系的 close, immediate
直线 linear
直销店 outlet
直言不讳 candor, outspokenness (at **outspoken**)
直言不讳的 blunt, candid, explicit, outspoken, vocal
直至 through, up
直至最后一刻 to the wire (at **wire**)
直着往前走 follow one's nose (at **nose**)
值…钱 worth
值班 vigil
值得 rate, worth
值得帮助的 deserving
值得保留的东西 keeper
值得保留的人 keeper
值得称道的 creditable
值得称赞的 commendable
值得的 worth sb's while (at **worth**), worthwhile
值得关注的 noteworthy
值得记住的 memorable
值得敬仰的 honorable
值得钦佩的 admirable, fine
值得拥有的 desirable
值得赞扬 to sb's credit (at **credit**)
值得注意的 notable
值得尊敬的 salt
值得做的 desirable
值钱的 of value (at **value**), valuable
值勤表 roster
值守 on guard (at **guard**)
职权 authority, responsibility
职位 appointment, hat, position, post, rank
职位空缺 vacancy
职位名称 title
职务 appointment, post
职务高于…的 senior
职业 career, craft, occupation, profession, trade, walk of life
职业棒球总会的 major league
职业的 occupational, pro, professional, vocational
职业地位 status
职业介绍所 employment agency
职业女性 career woman
职业生涯 career
职业文人 hack
职业总会 major, major league
职责 brief, duty, job, portfolio, responsibility
植入式广告 product placement
植入物 implant
植物 growth, plant, vegetation
植物的 vegetable
植物群 flora
植物人 vegetable
植物学 botany
植物学的 botanical
植物学家 botanist
植物油 oil
殖民地 colony
殖民地的 colonial
殖民地居民 colonist
殖民地时期风格的 colonial
殖民者 colonist
殖民主义 colonialism
殖民主义的 colonial
止痛药 painkiller
只 only
只不过 just, mere, merely, simply
只读存储器 ROM
只读光盘 CD-ROM
只会 all sb ever does (at **ever**), just
只能责怪自己 have only oneself to blame/have no one but oneself to blame (at **blame**)
只剩下 down
只是 all, just, only
只是部分情况 only part of the story/not the whole story (at **story**)
只是时间问题 only/just etc a question/matter of time (at **time**)
只适合成人的 adult
只输无赢的情况 no-win situation
只限于的 confined
只要 as long as/so long as (at **long**)
只要…即可 only have to (at **only**)
只有 alone, no/nothing other than (at **other**), only
只有…才 only
旨在 about, aim, design
纸 paper
纸板 book
纸币 bill
纸尿裤 nappy
纸尿片 diaper
纸牌 card
纸牌游戏 card
纸条 slip
纸页 page
指标 mark
指称 allege
指称的 alleged
指出 point, point out (at **point**)
指导 guidance, guide, instruction, mentor, tuition
指导…的行动 guide
指导方针 guideline
指导原则 guide
指导者 supervisor
指定 designate
指定的 appointed, set
指给…看 show
指关节 knuckle
指挥 captain, command, conduct, conductor, direct, direction (at **direct**), director
指挥棒 baton
指挥部 command
指挥官 commandant, commander
指挥台 podium
指甲 nail
指尖 fingertip
指控 accusation, accuse, allegation, charge, cite, rap
指令 command, edict, injunction
指路 direct
指路人 beacon
指明 point
指南 guide
指派 designate
指示 dictate, indicate, instruct, instruction
指示棒 pointer
指示传达会 briefing
指示的 indicative
指示牌 sign
指示物 indicator
指示转向 indicate
指数 index
指套 finger
指头肚 pad
指望 bank on (at **bank**), count on (at **count**), expect, hope, look to (at **look**)
指望得过早 chicken
指纹 fingerprint
指向 point
指印 print
指责 accusation, accuse, blame, fault, knock, point the finger at/point an accusing finger at (at **finger**), reproach
指针 hand, needle, pointer
指针式的 analog
指状物 finger
趾高气扬地走 strut
趾甲 nail
至多 at most/at the most (at **most**)
至高无上的 sovereign
至关重要 of the essence (at **essence**)
至关重要的 crucial, essential, imperative, vital
至关重要的事情 big deal
至今 to this day (at **day**)
至今为止 to date (at **date**)
至少 at least (at **least**), if nothing else (at **else**), minimum
至少目前 for the moment (at **moment**)
至于 as, for, regard, regarding, respect
志趣相同的人 birds of a feather (at **bird**)
志趣相投 on the same wavelength (at **wavelength**)
志趣相投者 fraternity
志向 aspiration
志愿兵 volunteer
志愿的 voluntary
志愿者 volunteer
志在必得的 purposeful
志在取得某事 have something/someone in your sights (at **sight**)
制成的 made
制订 formulation, plot, set
制定 institute, lay, make, set down (at **set**)
制定出 hammer out (at **hammer**)
制度 institution
制服 overpower, subdue, uniform
制服帽 cap
制码法 coding
制陶 pottery
制陶厂 pottery
制陶艺术 ceramic
制图 graphic
制药的 pharmaceutical
制药业 pharmacy
制约 rule
制造 construction, yield
制造麻烦 mischief
制造麻烦者 offender
制造商 maker
制止 restrain, scotch, silence
制止某事 put a stop to sth (at **stop**)
制作 make, making, produce, production
制作人 producer
制作室 studio
制作者 maker
治安 order
治安法官 magistrate
治安官 constable
治安很差的 tough
治理 clean, government
治疗 remedy, therapy, treat, treatment
治疗精神病的 psychiatric
治疗师 therapist
治愈 clear, cure
炙热的 boiling, burning
炙手可热的 red-hot
质的 qualitative
质地如沙砾般的 gritty
质量 caliber, mass, quality
质量等级 grade
质量低劣的 dire
质量低劣的报纸 rag
质量高的 good
质量管理 quality control
质量控制 quality control
质朴的 raw, rustic, unaffected
质疑 challenge
挚爱的 devoted
桎梏 shackle
秩序 order
致残 maim
致残的 crippling
致命的 deadly, fatal, lethal, mortal, terminal, virulent
致命的事物 killer
致使 leave, make, put, result, to
致死的 deadly
致死的危险 deathtrap
致谢词 vote of thanks
致谢辞 acknowledgment
致意 acknowledgment
掷镖游戏 dart
痔疮 pile
窒息 choke, suffocation (at **suffocate**)
窒息而死 suffocate
智慧 wisdom
智慧结晶 brainchild
智力 intellect
智力的 intellectual, mental
智力问题 puzzle
智囊 brain
智能 intelligence
智能卡 smart card
智商 IQ
智胜 outwit
滞胀 stagflation
痣 mole
置…于…之上 place sth above sth (at **place**)
置身事外 sideline, stand back (at **stand**)
置于一旁地 aside
中部的 central

自行其是 go one's own way (at **way**)
自诩的 self-styled
自学 self-study
自以为 flatter
自以为是 self-righteousness (at **self-righteous**)
自以为是的 brash, cocky, dogmatic, self-righteous
自以为是的人 know-all, know-it-all
自由 freedom, liberty
自由处理权 blank check
自由党的 liberal
自由的 free, liberal, loose
自由度 latitude
自由放任的政策 laissez-faire
自由企业制度 free enterprise
自由市场 free market
自由意志 free will
自由泳 crawl
自由职业的 freelance
自有品牌商品 own brand, own label
自愿承担的 self-imposed
自愿的 voluntary
自愿地 freely, of one's own accord (at **accord**), of your own free will (at **free will**)
自愿放弃 forfeit
自在的 comfortable, ease
自责 remorse
自粘的 self-adhesive
自找麻烦 be asking for trouble/ be asking for it (at **ask**)
自制力 self-control
自治 autonomy
自治的 autonomous
自治区 borough
自治市 borough, municipality
自主沉浮 sink or swim (at **sink**)
自助餐 buffet
自助餐厅 cafeteria
自助的 self-service
自尊 dignity, self-esteem, self-respect
宗教 faith, religion
宗教的 religious, sacred, spiritual
宗教节庆时期 feast
宗教节日 feast
宗教信徒 believer
宗教信仰 faith
宗教仪式 ritual, service
宗旨 spirit
宗旨声明 mission statement
综合 synthesize
综合业务数字网 ISDN
综合症状 syndrome
综述 roundup
棕榈树 palm
棕色或黑色的 dark
鬃毛 mane
总罢工 general strike
总部 headquarters, HQ
总称 umbrella
总的 collective, gross, overall, total
总的来看 considering
总的来说 in general (at **general**), on balance (at **balance**)
总督 governor
总而言之 the fact is (at **fact**)
总负责人 director general
总共 all told (at **told**), in all (at **all**), in total (at **total**), together
总共的 gross
总共地 altogether
总管道 main
总管的 general
总计 amount, number
总计的 grand
总计为 add up to (at **add**), total, work
总价钱 tab
总结 summarize, summary
总经理 managing director
总课程 curriculum
总理 chancellor, premier, prime minister
总理任期 premiership
总是 always, turn, would
总数 toll, total
总体的 collective
总体上 as a whole (at **whole**), in general (at **general**)
总体上讲 altogether
总统 president
总之 all in all (at **all**), in summary (at **summary**)
总组织 umbrella
纵火罪 arson
纵容 condone, indulge, indulgence, sponsor
纵容的 indulgent
纵身跳向 plunge
纵深的 deep
纵向地 lengthwise
走道 walk, walkway
走读学校 day school
走过 cover, traverse
走后门地 by/through the back door (at **door**)
走极端 go/take/carry (sth) to extremes (at **extreme**)
走捷径 cut corners (at **corner**), the easy way out (at **way**)
走近 approach
走开 wander
走廊 corridor, passage, passageway, porch
走廊地带 corridor
走强 strength, strengthen
走上前来 come up (at **come**)
走神 lapse
走失 stray
走失的 stray
走私 smuggle, smuggling (at **smuggle**)
走私者 runner, smuggler
走形式 formality
走运 land on your feet (at **foot**)
走在…的前面 precede
奏鸣曲 sonata
奏响 play
奏效 come, work
揍 thrash, thrashing, thump
租 rent
租出 lease
租的 leasehold
租给 rent
租户 tenant
租借 rent, rental
租金 rent, rental
租进 lease
租赁业的 rental
租用 hire, tenancy
租约 lease
租住 lodge
足不出户的 armchair
足够 adequacy, suffice
足够的 adequate, enough, sufficient
足够好的 acceptable
足够支付 cover
足迹 track
足球运动 football
足球运动员 footballer
足以供…人食用 serve
足智多谋 ingenuity, resourcefulness (at **resourceful**)
足智多谋的 resourceful
足足有 all of (at **all**)
卒 pawn
诅咒 curse
阻碍 drag, get in the way (at **way**), hinder, impede, inhibit, shackle, stunt
阻挡 block, exclude, obstruct, ward off (at **ward**)
阻断 interdict
阻拦 discourage, obstruct
阻力 resistance
阻挠 obstruct, sabotage, throw a wrench (at **wrench**), thwart
阻气门 choke
阻塞 obstruct
阻止 block, contain, deter, hold, inhibit, keep, preclude, prevent, stem, stop, suppress
阻止…的言论 muzzle
阻止…发生 rule
阻止某事物 stand in the way of sth (at **stand**)
阻滞 block
组 group, party, team
组成 compose, makeup
组成部分 component, element
组成的 component
组队 team up (at **team**)
组合式的 modular
组件 module
组件的 modular
组建 form, put
组群 collection
组织 body, curate, get, mount, organization, organize, tissue
组织…进行秘密投票 ballot
组织并实施 conduct
组织方面的 organizational
组织方式 setup
组织和运作方式 apparatus
组织结构方面的 organizational
组织内部的 internal
组织上的 organizational
组织网络 network
组织者 organizer, steward
组装 assemble, assembly
祖父 grandfather, grandparent
祖国 home, homeland
祖母 grandmother
祖先 ancestor, family
祖先的 ancestral
钻 bore, drill
钻进 burrow
钻孔机 drill
钻石 diamond
钻塔 rig
钻探 drill
钻研 bone up on (at **bone**), dig, read up on (at **read**)
嘴 mouth, spout
嘴…的 -mouthed (at **mouth**)
嘴唇 lip
最 most, most of all (at **most**), very
最不可能的 last
最不想要的 last
最畅销的唱片 number one
最畅销的歌手 number one
最迟销售日期 sell-by date
最初 first, in the first place (at **place**), initially
最初的 initial, primary, real
最大程度地 best, furthest, most
最大的 full, max., maximum, utmost
最大的一份 lion's share
最大范围 range
最大距离的 far
最大努力 best, utmost
最大限量 blast
最大音量 full blast (at **blast**)
最得意之物 jewel
最低标准额的 basic
最低程度地 least
最低贷款利率 prime rate
最低点 low
最低工资 minimum wage
最低谷 rock bottom
最低限度的 minimal, minimum
最底层 bottom
最典型的 prime, real
最多 maximum
最多的 most
最高层 top
最高的 supreme, top
最高点 high
最高级 superlative
最高级别的 big time
最高级的 superlative
最高价格 top dollar (at **top**)
最高权力人 president
最高权力人的 presidential
最高职位 presidency
最高职位任期 presidency
最好 better
最好的 best, first, foremost, premier, right
最好的东西 best
最好的事物 best
最好的是 best of all (at **best**)
最好是 be better off (at **better**)
最合适的 very
最后 finally, in conclusion (at **conclusion**), lastly
最后得到 finish
最后的 final, last
最后的人 last
最后阶段 finish
最后来到 end up (at **end**)
最后期限 deadline
最后时刻 last gasp (at **gasp**)
最后通牒 ultimatum
最后修饰 the finishing touch (at **finish**)
最后一次 last
最后一刻 last minute (at **minute**), the last moment (at **moment**)
最后一名 bottom
最基本的 rudimentary
最激烈的时刻 heat
最佳的 optimum, prime, very
最佳典范 ultimate
最佳状态 best
最简要的 bare
最接近的 near
最近 lately, recently
最近的 first, last, latest, recent
最近一次 last
最精彩的部分 highlight
最快的 top
最频繁地 most
最起码的 skeleton
最恰当的 right
最前面的 first
最强的 full
最强烈的 ruling
最亲爱的 dearest
最上层 apex
最上面的 top
最少的 least
最适合的 perfect
最晚 at the latest (at **latest**)
最微不足道的 least

SIMPLE PRESENT TENSE

A. With states, feelings, and perceptions

The simple present tense describes states, feelings, and perceptions that are true at the moment of speaking.

- The box *contains* six cans. (state)
- Jenny *feels* tired. (feeling)
- I *see* three stars in the sky. (perception)

B. With situations that extend before and after the present moment

The simple present tense can also describe ongoing activities, or things that happen all the time.

- Tina *works* for a large corporation.
- She *lives* in California.
- Jim *goes* to San Francisco State College.

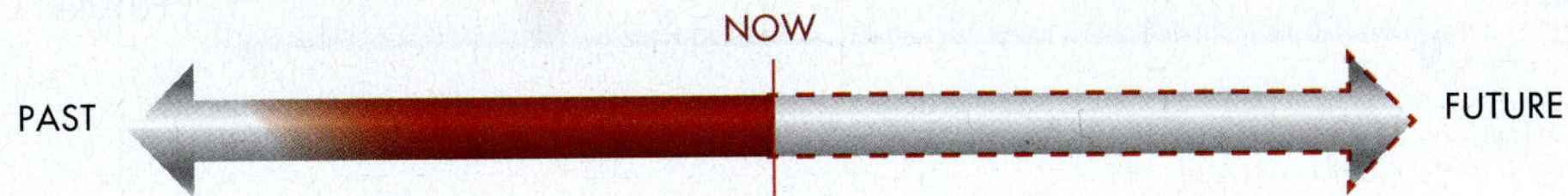

The simple present tense can also describe repeated activities that occur at regular intervals, including people's habits or customs.

- I *exercise* every morning.
- Peter usually *walks* to work.
- Anna often *cooks* dinner.

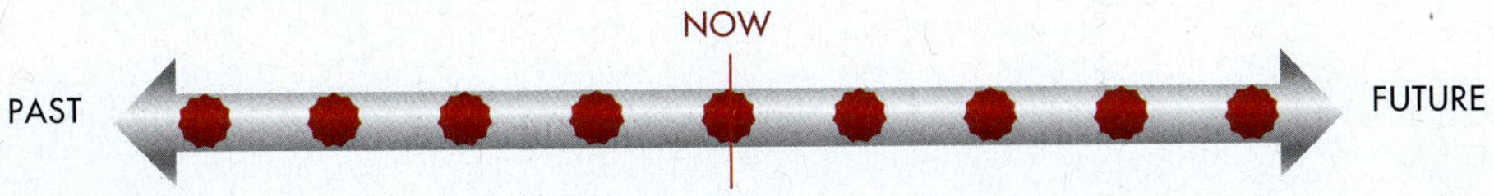

NOTE: Notice the adverbs of frequency *every morning*, *usually*, and *often* in these sentences. Other adverbs of frequency used this way include *always*, *sometimes*, *rarely*, and *never*.

C. With general facts

The simple present tense describes things that are always true.

- The Empire State Building *is* in New York City.
- The heart *pumps* blood throughout the body.
- Water *boils* at 100° Celsius.

D. With future activities

The simple present tense is sometimes used to talk about scheduled events in the future.

- The train *arrives* at 8:00 tonight.
- We *leave* at 10:00 tomorrow morning.
- The new semester *begins* in September.

Present continuous tense

A. For actions that are happening right now

The present continuous tense describes an action that is happening at the moment of speaking. These activities started a short time before and will probably end in the near future.

- Ali *is watching* television right now.
- Frank and Lisa *are doing* homework in the library.
- It *is raining*.

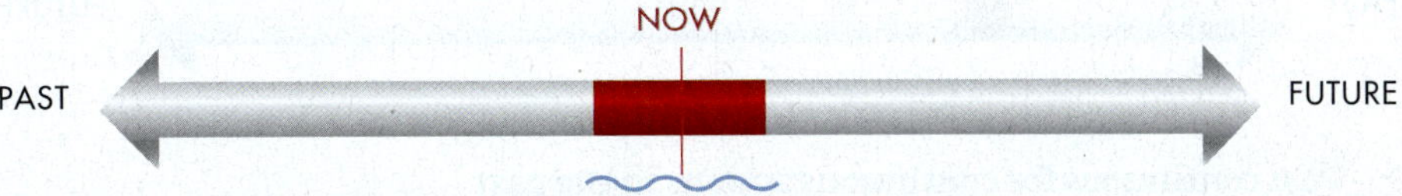

B. For ongoing activities that aren't necessarily happening at this moment

The present continuous tense can describe a continuing action that started in the past and will probably continue into the future. However, the action may not be taking place at the exact moment of speaking.

- Mr. Chong *is teaching* a Chinese cooking course.
- We *are practicing* for the soccer championships.
- My sister *is making* a quilt.

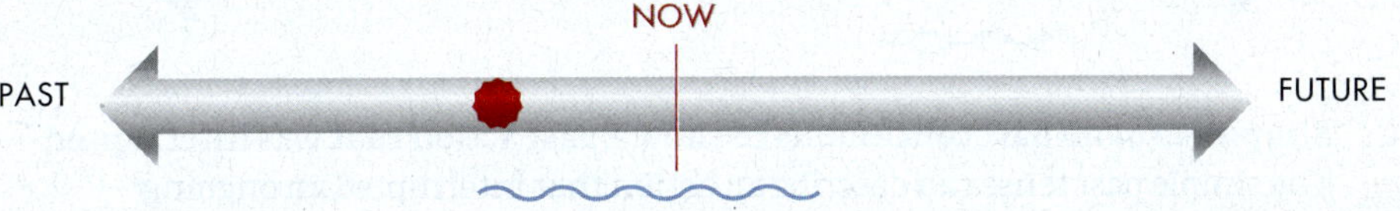

C. With situations that will happen in the future

The present continuous tense can also describe planned activities that will happen in the future.

- I *am studying* French next semester.
- We *are having* a party Friday night.
- Raquel *is taking* her driver's test on Saturday.

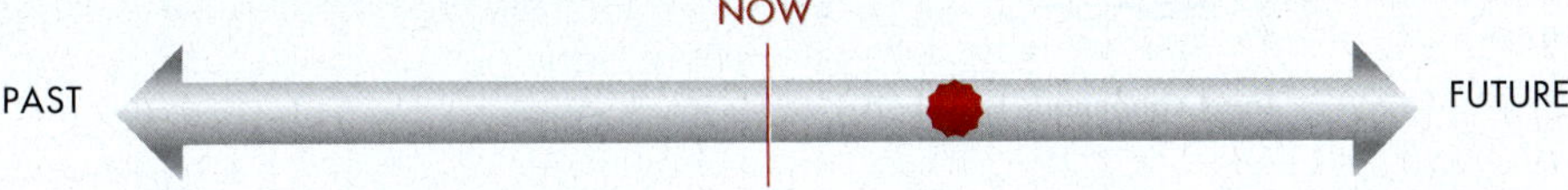

NOTE: The use of expressions like *next semester*, *Friday night*, and *on Saturday* help make it clear that the activity is planned and is not happening at the present moment, but will happen in the future.

Simple past and past continuous

A. Simple past for one-time and repeated activities that happened in the past

The simple past tense can describe single or repeated occurrences in the past.

- I *saw* Linda at the post office yesterday.
- Alex *visited* Paris last year.
- We *played* tennis every day last summer. (repeated activity)

B. Past continuous for continuous actions in the past

The past continuous tense can describe ongoing activities that went on for a period of time in the past.

- Anna *was living* in Mexico.
- The baby *was sleeping*.
- Snow *was falling*.

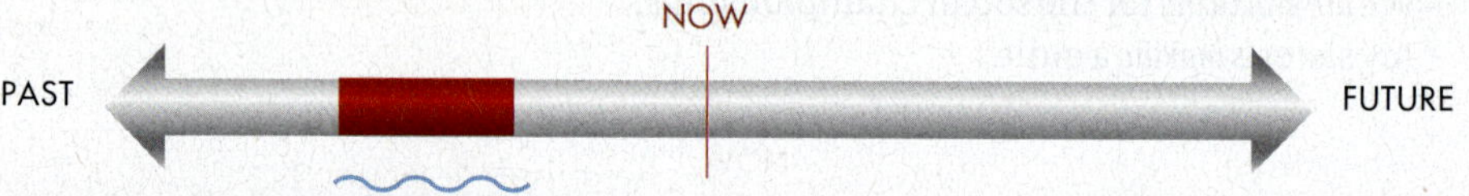

C. Simple past and past continuous to show a past action that was interrupted

The simple past tense can describe an action that interrupted an ongoing (past continuous) activity.

- I *met* Alice while I *was living* in New York.
- I *dropped* my purse while I *was crossing* the street.
- The phone *rang* while I *was studying*.

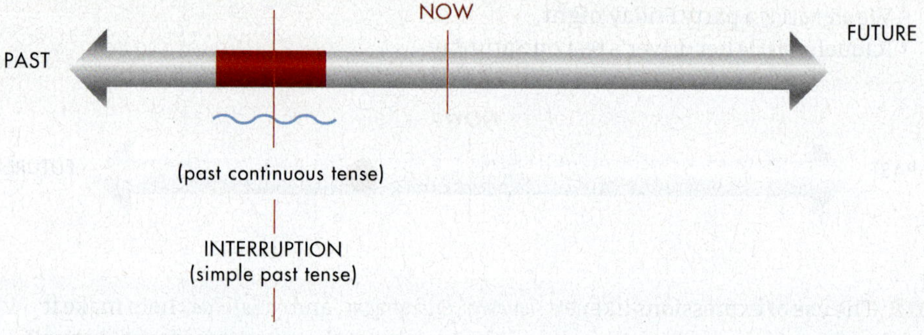

PRESENT PERFECT AND PRESENT PERFECT CONTINUOUS

A. Present perfect for actions or situations that started in the past and continue in the present and possibly the future

The present perfect tense describes an action that started in the past, continues up to the present, and may continue into the future.

- Lee *has collected* stamps for ten years.
- Carmen *has lived* in this country since 1995.
- Yukio *has played* piano since she was four years old.

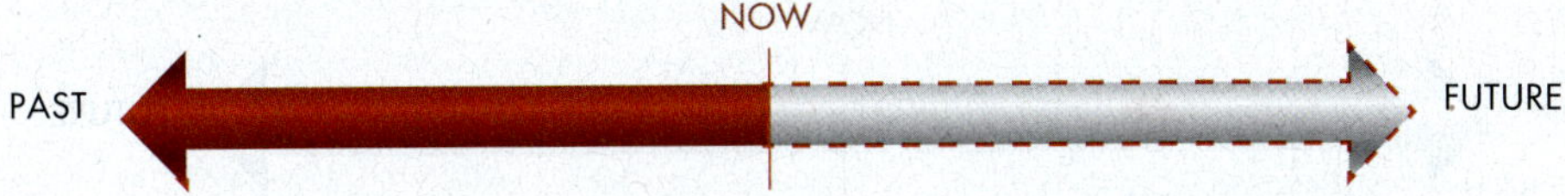

B. Present perfect for experience in general, without mentioning when something occurred

The present perfect tense can show that something happened in the past and the results can be seen in the present.

- We *have caught* several big fish. (they are on the table/in the boat)
- Larry *has met* my family. (they know each other)
- I *have seen* that movie twice. (I can tell you the plot)

C. Present perfect continuous for ongoing actions that started in the past and continue in the present

The present perfect continuous tense describes an ongoing activity that went on for a period of time in the past and is still going on.

- It *has been raining* for three days. (it's raining now)
- The baby *has been crying* for ten minutes. (she is still crying)
- We *have been waiting* for the bus since 9:00. (we're still waiting)

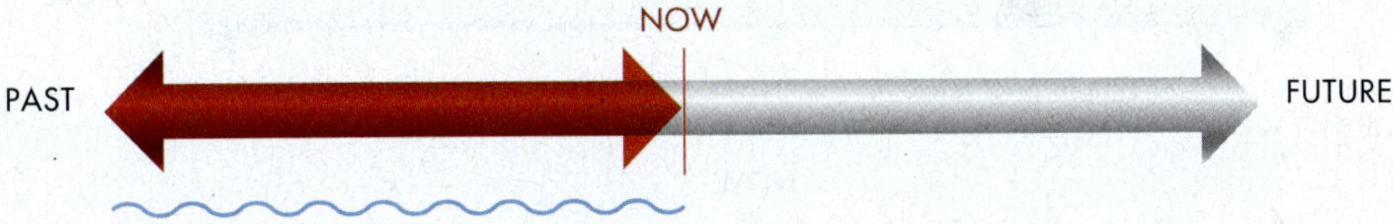

SIMPLE PAST VS. PRESENT PERFECT

A. Simple past for situations that started and ended in the past vs. present perfect for things that started in the past but continue in the moment

The simple past tense describes an action that started and ended in the past, while the present perfect tense describes situations that started in the past but continue up to the present and maybe into the future.

Past: John *worked* as a waiter for two years when he was in college.
Present perfect: Carol *has worked* as an engineer since 1998.

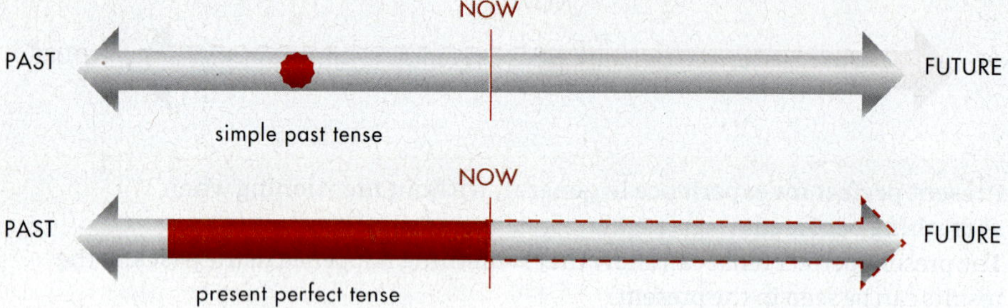

B. Simple past to emphasize when something happened vs. present perfect to emphasize that something happened, without indicating when

The simple past emphasizes when something happened, and the present perfect emphasizes its impact on the present.

Past: Peter *graduated* from college in 2007. (at a known point in the past: 2007)
Present perfect: Alice *has graduated* from college, and is working in the city. (exactly when is unknown)

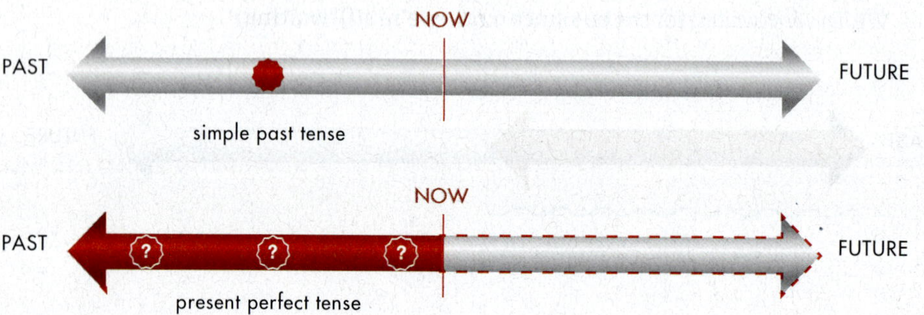

Simple past, past perfect, and past perfect continuous

A. Past and past perfect tenses with an activity that occurred before another activity in the past

Two simple past tenses are used to show a sequence of events in the past.

Simple past + simple past: Ali *said* goodbye before he *left*.
I *closed* the door and then *locked* it.

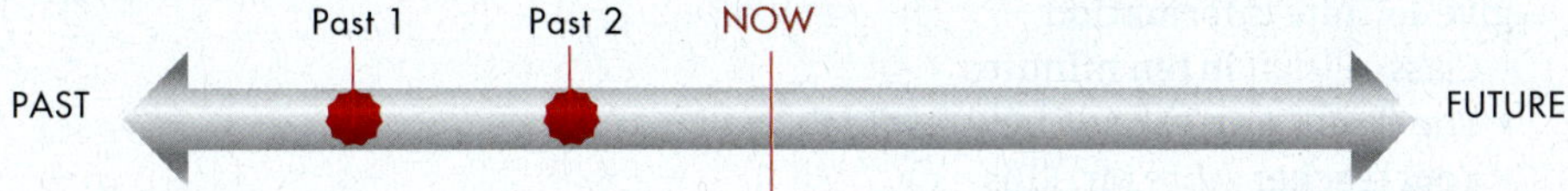

B. Past perfect continuous and simple past for a continuous activity that occurred before another event in the past

The past perfect continuous tense followed by the simple past tense shows that an ongoing activity in the past came before another past event.

- We *had been waiting* for two hours when the bus finally *arrived*.
- I *had been thinking* about the problem for days when the answer suddenly *occurred* to me.
- Terry *had been hoping* for the answer that he *got*.

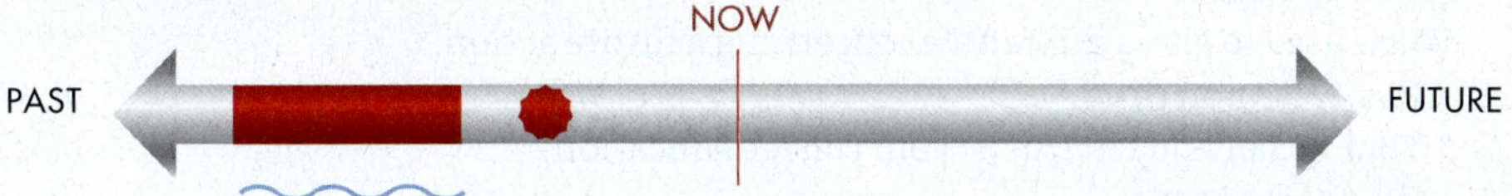

FUTURE WITH *will* AND *going to*

A. *Will* or *going to* for simple facts

Either *will* or *going to* can be used to give information about the future. *Will* is used to give definite information.

- Class *will start* in ten minutes.
- The class *is going* to use a new textbook.
- Your teacher *will be* Mr. Ellis.
- There *is going to* be a final exam.

B. *Will* or *going to* for prediction

Either *will* or *going to* can be used to describe things that are likely to happen in the future. *Will* is used when there is evidence that things are likely to happen.

- It *will rain* this afternoon.
- You *are going to love* that movie!
- They *are going to study* a lot the night before the exam.
- They *will* probably *stay up* all night.

C. *Will* for promises

Will is used to give a guarantee concerning a future action.

- I *will be there* on time.
- Your father and I *will pay for* your college education.
- I *won't tell* anyone.
- I *will save* you a seat.

D. *Will* for decisions made at the time of speaking

Will is used for decisions made at the time of speaking.

- I *will help* you with your homework.
- We're out of milk. I'*ll go* to the store on my way home.
- I can't talk right now, but I'*ll call* you later.
- Danny *will be* happy to wash your car.

MODALS *can*, *should/ought to*, *must*, AND *have to*

A. *Can* and *can't* for ability, permission, and requests

Can and *can't* are used to:

- make statements about things people are and are not able to do.
- describe what people are allowed or not allowed to do.
- make requests.

***Can/can't* for ability:**	Alan *can swim* very well. I *can't run* very fast.
***Can/can't* for permission:**	You *can leave* whenever you want. We *can't use* our dictionaries during the test.
***Can/can't* for requests:**	*Can I* borrow your laptop? *Can't you* turn down the TV?

B. *Should* and *ought to* for advice and warnings

Should and *ought to* are used to tell people what to do or what to avoid doing.

***Should/shouldn't* for advice/warnings:**	What *should* I *do*? You *should ask* questions in class. You *shouldn't drive* so fast.
***Ought to* for advice/warnings:**	You *ought to save* more money. He *ought to buy* some new clothes.

NOTE: *Ought to* is almost never used in questions or negative statements.

~~Ought I to go?~~ ~~You ought not see that movie.~~

C. *Must* and *mustn't* for rules and laws

Must and *mustn't* are used in formal situations to show that something is necessary or prohibited.

***Must* for necessity:**	My doctor told me that I *must lose* weight.
***Must* for obligation:**	Swimmers *must shower* before entering the pool.
***Mustn't* for prohibition:**	You *mustn't be* late to class.

Must and *mustn't* are not always opposites. *Needn't (need not)* expresses a lack of obligation to do something, whereas *mustn't* expresses an obligation not to do something.

D. *Have to* and *don't have to* for personal obligations

Have to and *don't have to* are used in informal or personal situations to show that something is necessary or not necessary.

***Have to* for necessity:**	I *have to call* my mother tonight. We *have to remember* to buy Jimmy a birthday present.
***Don't/doesn't have to* for lack of necessity:**	You *don't have to return* the pen. You can keep it. Grandpa *doesn't have to comb* his hair. He doesn't have any.

GRAMMAR

MODALS *may*, *might*, *could*, AND *would*

A. *May* and *might* to discuss possibility and permission

May and *might* are used to describe future possibilities. *May* is used to give permission in formal situations.

***May* for possibility:** We're not sure yet, but we *may leave* tomorrow.
The weather *may not be* good this weekend.

***Might* for possibility:** I *might fly* to Florida this weekend, but I probably won't.
We both *might get* 100 on the test.

NOTE: Sentences with *might* are less definite than sentences with *may*.

***May* for permission:** *May I call* you Jimmy?
You *may turn in* your paper Monday if it's not ready today.
No, you *may not have* my telephone number.

***Might* for permission:** I wonder if I *might leave* early.
When *might* I *need* to see the doctor again?

NOTE: *Can* also works in these sentences, but *may* is more polite and formal. Sentences with *might* are often indirect questions.

B. *Could* to show possibility, past ability, and to make requests

Could is used to indicate future possibilities, past abilities, and to ask for things.

***Could* for future possibilities:** The dog *could have* six or seven puppies.
The movie *could make* a million dollars if it's really popular.

***Could* for past ability:** When I was six, I *could* already *speak* two languages.
Tina *could walk* when she was only eight months old.

***Could* for requests:** *Could* you *give* me the remote control?
Could I *have* another cookie?

C. *Would* to ask permission and to make requests

Would is used to request permission and to ask for things.

***Would* to ask permission:** *Would* you *mind* if I asked your age?
Would he *mind* if I borrowed his book?

***Would* to make requests:** *Would* you *give* me a ride home?
I *would like* two tickets for the 7:00 show.

Used to

A. ***Used to*** **for statements and questions about past habits or customs**

Used to shows that something that was true in the past is no longer true.

- Years ago, children *used to be* more polite.
- I *used to hate* broccoli, but now I like it.
- Children *didn't use to have* TVs in their bedrooms.
- Did girls *use to play* on high school football teams?

NOTE: When using the negative and question forms with *used to*, drop the past tense *-d* from the word *used*.

B. ***Used to*** **for repeated past events**

Used to also shows that something that happened regularly in the past no longer does.

- We *used to go* to the movies every Friday night.
- Taylor *used to visit* his grandmother every Sunday.
- I didn't *use to sleep* late on Saturday, but now I do.
- Did you *use to walk* home every day?

C. ***Be used to*** **for statements and questions about things people have become accustomed to**

Be used to statements and questions discuss how strange or normal something feels.

- Gail has lived in Chicago and New York. She is *used to living* in big cities.
- I have six brothers and sisters. I *am used to sharing* everything with them.
- Pete *isn't used to doing* homework every night.
- *Are* you *used to* drinking black coffee yet?

NOTE: When using the negative and question forms with *be used to*, don't drop the past tense *-d* from the word *used*.

D. ***Get used to*** **for statements and questions about becoming accustomed to something new**

Get used to statements and questions focus on the process of becoming accustomed to something.

- After three weeks, I *got used to* the noise outside my apartment.
- I *am getting used to* living with three roommates.

NOTE: The negative form of *get used to* usually employs the modal *can't* or *couldn't*.

I *can't get used to* getting up at 6:00 AM.

Ellen *couldn't get used to* the cold weather in Chicago.

GRAMMAR

CONDITIONALS

A. Unreal conditions in the present

To describe a conditional situation that is unlikely to happen, use a past form in the conditional clause and the modal *would* or *could* in the main clause.

Conditional clause	Main clause
If I *had* enough money,	I *would buy* a boat.
If we *went* to Paris,	we *could visit* the Eiffel Tower.
If the traffic *got* any worse,	I *wouldn't drive* my car every day.
If Shelia *knew* the answer,	she *would tell* us.

B. Possible conditions in the future

To describe a conditional situation that is likely to happen, use a present form in the conditional clause and the future with *will* or the modal *can* in the main clause.

Conditional clause	Main clause
If I *have* enough money,	I *will buy* a boat.
If we *go* to Paris,	we *can visit* the Eiffel Tower.
If the traffic *gets* any worse,	I *won't drive* my car every day.
If Shelia *knows* the answer,	she *will tell* us.

C. Unreal conditions in the past

To describe a situation from a future point of view, use the past perfect in the conditional clause and *would have* + the past participle in the main clause.

Conditional clause	Main clause
If we *had known* it was raining,	we *would have taken* our umbrellas.
If Roberto *had been* home,	he *would have answered* the phone.
If you *had known* my grandmother,	you *would have loved* her.
If the movie *hadn't been* boring,	I *wouldn't have fallen* asleep.

D. Unreal conditions in the present

When discussing unreal conditions, the *if* clause is sometimes not stated; it is implied.

Conditional statement or question	Implied statement
I *would* never *borrow* money from a friend.	(if I had the opportunity)
Would you *want* to visit the moon?	(if you had the chance)
That *wouldn't work*.	(if you tried it)
Would he *borrow* your car without telling you?	(if he had the opportunity)

Passive voice

A. Passive statements and questions with *be* + past participle

The passive voice is used when it is not important (or we don't know) who performs the action. The passive can be used with any tense as well as with modals.

Sentence with passive voice	Verb form
The winner *was chosen* last night.	past tense
New cures *are being discovered* every day.	present continuous
Will the renovations *be finished* by next week?	future
Aspirin *should be taken* with a full glass of water.	modal *should*

B. Passives with an agent

To put the emphasis on the subject of the sentence and also tell who performed the action, use *by* followed by the agent at the end of the sentence.

- The missing girl was finally found *by her older brother.*
- The theory of relativity was discovered *by Albert Einstein.*
- The modern movie camera was invented *by Thomas Edison.*

C. Passives with *get*

In everyday speech, *get* instead of *be* is often used to form the passive. The verb *do* (instead of the verb *be*) is used for questions and negatives with the *get* passive.

- Most hourly workers *get paid* on Thursday or Friday.
- I *got caught* going 40 miles per hour in a 25 mile per hour zone.
- *Did* anyone *get killed* in the accident?
- Roger *didn't get hired* for the job.

Reported speech

A. Shifting verb tenses in reported speech

When reporting someone's exact words, the verb in the noun clause usually moves back one tense. Only the past perfect tense remains the same in reported speech.

Exact quote	Reported speech	Change in verb tense
I *am* tired.	He said that he *was* tired.	Simple present to simple past
We *are waiting.*	They told me that they *were waiting*.	Present continuous to past continuous
I *finished* the book last night.	She said that she *had finished* the book the night before.	Simple past to past perfect
We *are enjoying* the good weather.	They reported that they *were enjoying* the good weather.	Past continuous to past perfect continuous
I *have lived* here for two years.	He added that he *had lived* here for two years.	Present perfect to past perfect
We *had eaten* breakfast before we left the house.	They said that they *had eaten* breakfast before they left the house.	Past perfect remains the same

B. Shifting modals in reported speech

Many modals change form in reported speech.

Exact quote	Reported speech	Change in modal form
I *can speak* French.	She said that she *could speak* French.	*Can* to *could*
We *may need* help.	They said that they *might need* help.	*May* (for possibility) to *might*
You *may use* my pencil.	She said that I *could use* her pencil.	*May* (for permission) to *could*
I *must make* a phone call.	He said that he *had to make* a phone call.	*Must* to *had to*
We *will help* you.	They said that they *would help* me.	*Will* to *would*
I *should stop* smoking.	He said that he *should stop* smoking.	*Should* (no change)
We *should have left* at 9:00.	They said that they *should have left* at 9:00.	*Should have* (no change)
I *could have saved* money with a coupon.	She said that she *could have saved* money with a coupon.	*Could have* (no change)
She *must have gone* to bed early.	He said that she *must have gone* to bed early.	*Must have* (no change)

C. *Say* vs. *tell* in reported speech

The passive voice is used when it is not important (or we don't know) who performs the action. The passive can be used with any tense as well as with modals.

- When using *say* with reported speech, an object is not required. (Other verbs that work this way are *add*, *answer*, *explain*, and *reply*.)
- When using *tell* with reported speech, there is always a direct object. (Other verbs that work this way are *inform*, *notify*, *remind*, and *promise*.)

Exact quote	Reported speech	Direct object
It is raining.	He *said* that it was raining.	No
I was late to class.	She *explained* that she had been late to class.	No
I bought a camera at the mall.	He *told me* that he had bought a camera at the mall.	Yes
There is a test on Friday.	She *informed the students* that there was a test on Friday.	Yes

Comparatives and Superlatives

Comparatives and superlatives have several different forms.

A. With one-syllable adjectives and adverbs

Add *-er* or *-est*.

Adjective / Adverb	Comparative / superlative form	Example
cold	colder	December is *colder* than November.
hard	harder	The wind blows *harder* in winter than in summer.
short	shortest	December 21 is *the shortest* day of the year.
fast	fastest	Summer passes *the fastest* of any season.

B. With two-syllable adjectives ending in *-y*

Change the *-y* to *-i* and add *-er* or *-est*.

Adjective / Adverb	Comparative / superlative form	Example
easy	easier	Yesterday's assignment was *easier* than today's.
busy	busiest	This is the *busiest* shopping day of the year.

C. With most adjectives of two or more syllables not ending in *-y*

Use *more* + adjective for comparatives and *the most* + adjective for superlatives.

Adjective / Adverb	Comparative / superlative form	Example
famous	more famous	Amy's Pizza is *more famous* than Bennie's Pizza.
frequent	most frequent	Amy's has the *most frequent* specials of any pizzeria.
expensive	more expensive	Bennie's pizza is *more expensive* than Amy's.
delicious	most delicious	Bennie's makes the *most delicious* pizza in town.

D. Irregular comparatives and superlatives

Some adjectives and superlatives have irregular forms.

Adjective / Adverb	Comparative / superlative form	Example
bad	worse, worst	SUVs have *worse* safety records than sedans.
good	better, best	Sedans drive *better* than SUVs.
much	more, most	An SUV can carry *the most* people.
far	farther, farthest	A sedan can go *the farthest* on a tank of gas.

E. Comparisons with *as...as*

Use *as . . . as* + adjective or adverb to describe things that are equal, and *not as . . . as* + adjective or adverb to describe inequalities.

Adjective	Algebra was *as difficult as* geometry for me.
Adjective with negative	However, geometry was*n't as interesting as* algebra.
Adverb	I worked *as hard as* anyone else, but I got a C in algebra.
Adverb with negative	I did*n't* do *as well as* many other students.

Infinitives and gerunds

A verb (or sometimes an adjective) near the beginning of a sentence determines whether a second verb form should be an infinitive or a gerund. Below are lists of some common main verbs (and adjectives) and the type of verb form that follows each.

NOTE: Each list contains several high-frequency items, but the lists are not comprehensive.

A. Verb + infinitive

These verbs are followed by an infinitive, not a gerund: *ask*, *attempt*, *begin*, *decide*, *expect*, *hope*, *like*, *plan*, *promise*, *start*.

I *attempted* to start the car.

They *decided* to stay home last night.

We *hope* to save at least $1000 by the end of the year.

WRONG: She plans ~~giving~~ a party this weekend.

B. Causatives + infinitives

When a person causes something to happen, the causative verb is followed by a direct object plus an infinitive, not a gerund. These causative verbs are followed by an infinitive: *allow*, *convince*, *encourage*, *get*, *force*, *persuade*, *require*.

We *convinced* the teacher to postpone the test until Monday.

The teacher *encouraged* us to study over the weekend.

I *got* my brother to help me with the grammar.

WRONG: The teacher required us ~~leaving~~ our dictionaries at home.

C. Verb + gerund

These verbs are followed by a gerund, not an infinitive: *avoid*, *discuss*, *dislike*, *enjoy*, *finish*, *imagine*, *practice*, *quit*, *recommend*, *suggest*.

The couple *discussed* having another child.

The children *enjoy* going to the park.

The couple *can't imagine* having four children.

WRONG: They avoided ~~to talk~~ about it for a few days.

D. Preposition + infinitive and preposition + gerund

An infinitive is the preposition *to* and the base of a verb: *to speak*. Gerunds can be used with other prepositions such as *about*, *at*, *for*, *in*, *of*, and *on*.

I want *to go* on vacation in August.

I never even think *about swimming* in the winter.

This organization plans *on having* a fundraising drive.

WRONG: They are responsible for ~~help~~ thousands of animals.
The guests are sorry to ~~leaving~~ the party so early.

PUNCTUATION

Apostrophe

- The apostrophe + *s* is used with singular and plural nouns to show possession.

  Jim's computer — the children's toys

  my boss' file — the Smiths' house [Only the apostrophe is needed when a word ends in *s*.]

- The apostrophe + *s* is used to show ownership.

  Pedro and Ana**'s** CDs [The *'s* on the second name shows they own the CDs together.]

  Pedro**'s** and Ana**'s** hats [The *'s* on both names shows they each own different hats.]

- The apostrophe is used in contractions.

  I'm (= I am) — they'll (= they will)

Brackets

- Brackets are used to add your own information in quoted material.

  Jason said, "This is a good time [meaning today] for us to start looking for a new apartment."

- Brackets with three dots are used when you omit words from a quotation.

  Jason said, "This is a good time [. . .] for a new apartment."

Colon

- The colon is used with clock time.

  11:30 — 9:45

- The colon is used to introduce a list.

  Jean enjoys all kinds of physical activity: hiking, playing tennis, and even cleaning house.

- The colon is used in the salutation of a business letter.

  Dear Ms. Mansfield:

Comma

- Commas are used with dates and addresses.

  Monday, December 1, 1964 — 16 Terhune Street, Teaneck, NJ 07666

- Commas are used after introductory phrases or clauses.

  After finishing school, she joined the Navy.

- Commas are used to set off items in a series.

  They served pizza, pasta, lasagna, and salad at the party.

- Commas are used to set off added information in nonrestrictive phrases or clauses.

  Mr. Karas, my sister's teacher, comes from Greece.

  Rita, who almost never misses class, is absent today.

- Commas are used in the salutation in informal correspondence and at the close of a letter.

  Dear Grace, — Sincerely yours,

Dash

- Dashes are used instead of commas when the added information contains commas.

  The school offers several math courses—algebra, geometry, and trigonometry—as well as a wide variety of science classes.

Exclamation Point

- An exclamation point is used after a word or group of words to show strong feeling.

  Stop! Don't run over that cat!

Hyphen

- Hyphens appear in compound words or numbers.

  mother-in-law twenty-one

- Hyphens are used to divide words at the end of a line.

  After Mrs. Leander finished exploring all her options, she decided the best plan was to return home and start out tomorrow.

Parentheses

- Parentheses are used with nonessential information and with numbers and letters in lists.

  We left the party (which started at 7:00 P.M.) sometime after midnight.

  My requirements are (1) a room with a view and (2) a working air conditioner.

Period

- A period is used at the end of any sentence that is not a question or an exclamation.

  Rutgers University offers a wide variety of social science courses.

- A period is used after many abbreviations.

  Mr. etc. P.M. Jr. i.e.

Question Mark

- A question mark is used after a word or sentence that asks a question.

  What? Did you say you don't have a ride home?

Quotation Marks

- Quotation marks are used to set off a direct quotation but not an indirect quotation.

  Smithers said, "Homer, you must go home now."

  Smithers said Homer must go home.

- Quotation marks are used with the titles of short written material such as poems, short stories, chapters in books, songs, and magazine articles.

  My favorite poem is "A Spider Sewed at Night" by Emily Dickinson.

Semicolon

- The semicolon is used to link independent clauses when there is no coordinating conjunction (such as *and, but, or, nor,* or *for*) between them.

  Some people like country music; some people don't.

- The semicolon is also used to link independent clauses before a conjunctive adverb (such as *however, furthermore*).

  Some people like country music; however, other people dislike it intensely.

Slash

- The slash separates alternatives.

  and/or
- The slash divides numbers in dates, and divides numerators and denominators in fractions.

  the memorable date 9/11/01 Ten and 50/100 dollars
- The slash is used when quoting lines of poetry to show where each line ends.

  My favorite lines from this poem are, "She slept beneath a tree / remembered but by me."

CAPITALIZATION

Capitalize proper nouns and proper adjectives.

- Main words in titles: **G**one with the **W**ind
- People: **J**ohn **L**ennon, **P**elé
- Cities, nations, states, nationalities, and languages: **I**stanbul, **T**urkey, **C**alifornia, **B**razil, **A**merican, **S**panish
- Geographical items: **M**ekong **R**iver, **M**ount **O**lympus, **C**entral **P**ark
- Companies and organizations: **F**ord **M**otor **C**ompany, **H**arvard **U**niversity, **N**ational **O**rganization for **W**omen
- Departments and government offices: **E**nglish **D**epartment, **I**nternal **R**evenue **S**ervice
- Buildings: the **E**mpire **S**tate **B**uilding
- Trademarked products: **K**leenex tissue, **S**cotch tape
- Days, months, and holidays: **T**uesday, **J**anuary, **R**amadan
- Some abbreviations without periods: **AT&T, UN, YMCA**
- Religions and related words: **H**indu, **B**ible, **M**uslim
- Historical periods, events, and documents: **C**ivil **W**ar, **D**eclaration of **I**ndependence
- Titles of people: **S**enator Kennedy, **P**resident Lincoln, **M**s. Tanaka, **D**r. Lee
- Titles of printed matter: *Collins COBUILD Advanced Dictionary of American English, English/Chinese*

ITALICIZATION

In handwritten or typed copy, italics are shown by underlining.

Use italics for the following types of material.

- Words or phrases you wish to emphasize.

  Is this *really* your first time in an airplane?

  She feeds her dog *T-bone steak*. [It's best not to use italics for emphasis very often.]

- A publication that is not part of a larger publication.
  The Daily News (newspaper)
  The Sun Also Rises (book)
  Newsweek (magazine)
  Titanic (movie)
- Foreign words in an English sentence.
  The first four numbers in Turkish are *bir, iki, üc, dört.*
  The French have a saying: *Plus ça change . . .*
- Letters used in algebraic equations.
  $E = mc^2$

SPELLING

Frequently Misspelled Words

People sometimes confuse the spelling of the following words:

accept, except	conscience, conscious	lay, lie
access, excess	council, counsel	lead, led
advice, advise	diary, dairy	lessen, lesson
affect, effect	decent, descent, dissent	lightning, lightening
aisles, isles	desert, dessert	lose, loose
alley, ally	device, devise	marital, martial
already, all ready	discreet, discrete	maybe, may be
altar, alter	dyeing, dying	miner, minor
altogether, all together	elicit, illicit	moral, morale
always, all ways	emigrate, immigrate	of, off
amoral, immoral	envelop, envelope	passed, past
angel, angle	fair, fare	patience, patients
ask, ax	faze, phase	peace, piece
assistance, assistants	fine, find	personal, personnel
baring, barring, bearing	formerly, formally	plain, plane
began, begin	forth, fourth	pray, prey
believe, belief	forward, foreword	precede, proceed
board, bored	gorilla, guerrilla	presence, presents
break, brake	have, of	principle, principal
breath, breathe	hear, here	prophecy, prophesy
buy, by, bye	heard, herd	purpose, propose
capital, capitol	heroin, heroine	quiet, quit, quite
censor, censure, sensor	hole, whole	raise, rise
choose, chose	holy, wholly	respectfully, respectively
cite, site, sight	horse, hoarse	right, rite, write
clothes, cloths	human, humane	road, rode
coarse, course	its, it's	sat, set
complement, compliment	later, latter	sense, since

shown, shone
stationary, stationery
straight, strait
than, then
their, there, they're, there're
threw, through, thorough
throne, thrown
to, too, two
tract, track
waist, waste
weak, week
weather, whether
were, wear, where, we're
which, witch
who's, whose
your, you're

NOTE: The following summary will answer many spelling questions. However, there are many more rules and also many exceptions. Always check your dictionary if in doubt.

Ei and *ie*

There is an old saying that says: "I before *e*, except after *c*, or when pronounced like *ay* as in *neighbor* and *weigh*."

- *I* before *e*: br**ie**f, n**ie**ce, f**ie**rce
- *E* before *i* after the letter *c*: rec**ei**ve, conc**ei**t, c**ei**ling
- *E* before *i* when pronounced like *ay*: **ei**ght, w**ei**ght, th**ei**r

Prefixes

A prefix changes the meaning of a word but no letters are added or dropped.

- usual, **un**usual
- interested, **dis**interested
- use, **re**use

Suffixes

- Drop the final *e* on the base word when a suffix beginning with a vowel is added.
  drive, driv**ing**　　combine, combin**ation**
- Keep the silent *e* on the base word when a suffix beginning with a consonant is added.
  live, live**ly**　　safe, safe**ly** [Exceptions: truly, ninth]
- If the base word (1) ends in a final consonant, (2) is a one-syllable word or a stressed syllable, and (3) the final consonant is preceded by a vowel, double the final consonant.
  hit, hitting　　drop, dro**pp**ing
- Change a final *y* on a base word to *i* when adding any suffix except *-ing*.
  day, daily　　try, tried　　BUT: play, pla**ying**

GRAMMAR

Conjunctions

Conjunctions are words that connect words, phrases, or clauses.

Coordinating Conjunctions

The coordinating conjunctions are: *and, but, for, nor, or, so, yet*

- Sarah **and** Michael
- on vacation **for** three weeks
- You can borrow the book from a library **or** you can buy it at a bookstore.

Correlative Conjunctions

Correlative conjunctions are used in pairs.

The correlative conjunctions are: *both . . . and, either . . . or, neither . . . nor, not only . . . but also, whether . . . or*

- **Neither** Sam **nor** Madeleine could attend the party.
- The singer was **both** out of tune **and** too loud.
- Oscar **not only** ate too much, **but also** fell asleep at the table.

Subordinating Conjunctions

Subordinating conjunctions are used to connect a subordinate clause to a main clause.

- Antonia sighed loudly **as if** she were really exhausted.
- Uri arrived late **because** his car broke down.

Here is a list of subordinating conjunctions:

after	before	no matter how	than	where
although	even if	now that	though	wherever
as far as	even though	once	till	whether
as if	how	provided that	unless	while
as soon as	if	since	until	why
as though	in as much as	so that	when	
because	in case	supposing that	whenever	

Conjunctive Adverbs

Two independent clauses can be connected using a semicolon, plus a conjunctive adverb and a comma. The conjunctive adverb often comes right after the semicolon.

- Kham wanted to buy a car; **however,** he hadn't saved up enough money.
- Larry didn't go right home; **instead,** he stopped at the health club.

Some conjunctive adverbs can appear in different positions in the second clause.

- Kham wanted to buy a car; he hadn't, **however,** saved up enough money.
- Larry didn't go right home; he stopped at the health club **instead.**

Here is a list of conjunctive adverbs:

also	finally	indeed	nevertheless	then
anyhow	furthermore	instead	next	therefore
anyway	hence	likewise	otherwise	thus
besides	however	meanwhile	similarly	
consequently	incidentally	moreover	still	

Transitional Phrases

If all the sentences in a passage begin with subject + verb, the effect can be boring. To add variety, use a transitional phrase, followed by a comma, at the beginning of some sentences.

- Rita needed to study for the test. **On the other hand,** she didn't want to miss the party.
- Yuki stayed up all night studying. **As a result,** he overslept and missed the test.

Here is a list of transitional phrases:

after all	for example
as a result	in addition
at any rate	in fact
at the same time	in other words
by the way	on the contrary
even so	on the other hand

Common Prepositions

A preposition describes a relationship to another part of speech; it is usually used before a noun or pronoun.

- Sancho was waiting **outside** the club.
- I gave the money **to** him.

Here is a list of common prepositions:

about	by	out
above	concerning	outside
across	despite	over
after	during	past
against	down	regarding
among	except	round
around	for	since
as	from	through
at	in	to
before	inside	toward
behind	into	under
below	lie	unlike
beneath	near	until
beside	of	up
between	off	upon
beyond	on	with

Phrasal Prepositions

Here is a list of phrasal prepositions:

according to	by way of	in spite of
along with	due to	instead of
apart from	except for	on account of
as for	in addition to	out of
as regards	in case of	up to
as to	in front of	with reference to
because of	in lieu of	with regard to
by means of	in place of	with respect to
by reason of	in regard to	with the exception of

DOCUMENTATION

College instructors usually require one of three formats (APA, Chicago, or MLA) to document the information you use in research papers and essays. The following pages compare and contrast the highlights of these three styles.

APA Style (American Psychological Association style)

1. General Endnote Format

   Title the page "References." Double-space the page and arrange the names alphabetically by authors' last names, the date in parentheses, followed by the rest of the information about the publication.

2. Citation for a Single Author

   Moore, (1992). *The care of the soul*. New York: HarperPerennial.

3. Citation for Multiple Authors

   List the last names first followed by initials and use the "&" sign before the last author.

   Spinosa, C., Flores, F., & Dreyfus, H.L. (1997). *Disclosing new worlds: Entrepreneurship, democratic action, and the cultivation of solidarity*. Cambridge, MA: MIT Press.

4. Citation for an Editor as Author

   Wellwood, J. (Ed.). (1992). *Ordinary magic: Everyday life as a spiritual path*. Boston: Shambhala Publications.

5. Citation for an Article in a Periodical

   List the author, last name first, the year and month (and day if applicable) of the publication. Then list the title of the article (not underlined), the name of the publication (followed by the volume number if there is one) and the page number or numbers.

   Gibson, S. (2001, November). Hanging wallpaper. *This Old House*, 77.

6. Citation of Online Materials

   Provide enough information so that readers can find the information you refer to. Try to include the date on the posting, the title, the original print source (if any), a description of where you found the information, and the date you found the material.

   Arnold, W. (April 26, 2002). "State senate announces new tax relief." *Seattle Post-Intelligencer*. Retrieved May 1, 2002, from http://seattle.pi.nwsource.com/printer2/index.asp?ploc=b

7. General In-text Citation Format

   Include two pieces of information: the last name of the author or authors of the work cited in the References and the year of publication.
   (Moore, 1992).

Chicago Style (from *The Chicago Manual of Style*)

1. General Endnote Format

   Title the page "Notes." Double-space the page. Number and indent the first line of each entry. Use full author's names, not initials. Include page references at the end of the entry.

2. Citation for a Single Author

   Thomas Moore, *The Care of the Soul* (New York: HarperPerennial, 1992), 7–9.

3. Citation for Multiple Authors

   Charles Spinosa, Ferdinand Flores, and Hubert L. Dreyfus, *Disclosing New Worlds: Entrepreneurship, Democratic Action, and the Cultivation of Solidarity* (Cambridge: MIT Press, 1997), 66.

4. Citation for an Editor as Author

   John Wellwood, ed. 1992. *Ordinary Magic: Everyday Life as Spiritual Path* (Boston: Shambhala Publications).

5. Citation for an Article in a Periodical

   List the author, last name first. Then put the title of the article in quotation marks, the name of the publication, the volume number (if one is given), the month, and the page number or numbers.

   Gibson, Stephen, "Hanging Wallpaper," *This Old House* 53 (2001): 77.

6. Citation of Online Materials

   Number and indent each entry and provide enough information so that readers can find the information you refer to. Try to include the author (first name first), the date on the posting (in parentheses), the title, the original print source (if any), a description of where you found the information, the URL, and the date you found the material (in parentheses).

1. William Arnold, "State Senate Announces New Tax Relief, "*Seattle Post-Intelligencer*, April 26, 2002, http://seattle.pi.nwsource.com/printer2/index.asp?ploc=b

7. General In-text Citation Format

   Number all in-text notes. The first time you cite a work within the text, use all the information as shown in 2. above. When citing the same work again, include only the last name of the author or authors and the page or pages you refer to.

   (Moore, 8)

MLA Style (Modern Language Association style)

1. General Endnote Format

   Title the page "Works Cited." Double-space the page and arrange the names alphabetically by authors' last names, followed by the rest of the information about the publication as shown below.

2. Citation for a Single Author

   Moore, Thomas. *The Care of the Soul*. New York: HarperPerennial, 1992.

3. Citation for Multiple Authors

   List the first author's names in the same order as on the title page. List only the first author's last name first.

   Spinosa, Charles, Ferdinand Flores, and Hubert L. Dreyfus. *Disclosing New Worlds: Entrepreneurship, Democratic Action, and the Cultivation of Solidarity.* Cambridge: MIT, 1997.

4. Citation for an Editor as Author

   Wellwood, John, ed. *Ordinary Magic: Everyday Life as Spiritual Path*. Boston; Shambhala, 1992.

5. Citation for an Article in a Periodical

   List the author (last name first), the title of the article (using quotation marks), the title of the magazine (with no period), the volume number, the date (followed by a colon), and the page number.

   Gibson, Stephen. "Hanging Wallpaper." *This Old House* 53 (2001): 77.

6. Citation of On-line Materials

   Provide enough information so that readers can find the information you refer to. Try to include the date on the information, the title, the original print source (if any), the date you found the material, and the URL (if possible).

   Arnold, William. "State Senate Announces New Tax Relief. "*Seattle Post-Intelligencer* 26 Apr. 2002 http://seattle.pi.nwsource.com/printer2/index.asp?ploc=b

7. General In-text Citation Format

   Do not number entries. When citing a work listed in the "Works Cited" section, include only the last name of the author or authors and the page or pages you refer to.
   (Moore 7-8)

BLOCK LETTER FORMAT

Using the block letter format, there are no indented lines.

Return address	77 Lincoln Avenue Wellesley, MA 02480
Date	May 10, 2009
Inside address	Dr. Rita Bennett Midland Hospital Senior Care Center 5000 Poe Avenue Dayton, OH 45414
Salutation	Dear Dr. Bennett:
Body of the letter	I am responding to your advertisement for a dietitian in the May 5 edition of the *New York Times*. I graduated from Boston University two years ago. Since graduation, I have been working at Brigham and Women's Hospital and have also earned additional certificates in nutritional support and diabetes education. I am interested in locating to the Midwest and will be happy to arrange for an interview at your convenience.
Complimentary close	Sincerely,
Signature	*Daniel Chin*
Typed name	Daniel Chin

INDENTED LETTER FORMAT

Using the indented format, the return address, the date, and the closing appear at the far right side of the paper. The first line of each paragraph is also indented.

Return address	77 Lincoln Avenue Wellesley, MA 02480
Date	May 15, 2009
Inside address	Dr. Rita Bennett Senior Care Center 5000 Poe Avenue Dayton, OH 45414
Salutation	Dear Dr. Bennett:
Body of the letter	It was a pleasure to meet you and learn more about the programs offered at the Senior Care Center. I appreciate your taking time out to show me around and introduce me to the staff. I am excited about the possibility of working at the Senior Care Center and I look forward to talking with you again soon.
Complimentary close	Sincerely,
Signature	*Daniel Chin*
Typed name	Daniel Chin

RESUMES

Successful resume strategies

- **Length:** One page
- **Honesty:** Never say something that is untrue
- **Inclusiveness:** Include information about your experience and qualifications. You do not have to include your age, religion, marital status, race, or citizenship. It is not necessary to include a photo.

Heading

Include name, address, e-mail, and phone number.

Objective

Include your goals or skills or both.

Skills

Include any skills that you have that may be helpful in the job that you are applying for.

Experience

Describe the jobs you've held. Include your accomplishments and awards. Use positive, action-oriented words with strong verbs. Use present-tense verbs for your current job and past-tense verbs for jobs you've had in the past. Include the job titles that you've held.

Education

Include schools attended. If you are a college graduate, don't include high school. List degrees with most recent first.

Interests

This is not required, but can help a potential employer see you as a well-rounded person.

Sample Resume

There are several different acceptable resume formats. Here is one example.

Maria Gonzales
9166 Main Street, Apartment 3C
Los Angeles, CA 93001
gonzales@email.com
213-555-9878

OBJECTIVE: Experienced manager seeks a management position in retail sales

EXPERIENCE:

Assistant Director of Retail

2005 – Present — Shopmart, Los Angeles, CA
Manage relationships with vendors to complete orders, create accounts, and resolve issues. Maintain inventory and generate monthly inventory reports. Plan weekly promotions. Communicate with all retail employees to improve product knowledge and selling techniques. Implemented new customer service procedures.

Server

2005 – Present — Chuy's Grill, Santa Monica, CA
Greet and seat guests. Bus tables. Answer phones and take and prepare in-house, phone, or fax orders. Train new and existing employees. Awarded Employee of the Month five times for exceeding company expectations for quality and service.

Store Supervisor

1999 – 2005 — Impact Photography Systems, Waco, TX
Oversaw daily operations, including customer and employee relations, counter sales, inventory management, maintaining store appearance, banking transactions, and equipment maintenance. Managed, trained, and scheduled staff of 35.

SKILLS: Fluent in English and Spanish. Expert in MS Word and Excel.

EDUCATION:

Associate of Arts Degree

1997 – 2000 — Los Angeles Community College, Los Angeles, CA
Coursework in business management, marketing, studio art, communication, psychology, and sociology.

Study Abroad

2000 – 2001 — University of Valencia, Valencia, Spain
Coursework in Spanish and international business.

INTERESTS: Backpacking, playing softball, and volunteering as a tutor for Literacy First.

PROOFREADING MARKS

Teachers often use the following correction abbreviations and symbols on students' papers.

Problem area	Symbol	Example
agreement	**agr**	He **go** to work at 8:00.
capital letters	**cap**	the United states
word division or hyphenation	**div** **hy**	disorientati -on
sentence fragment	**frag**	**Where she found the book.**
grammar	**gr**	It's the **bigger** house on the street.
need italics	**ital**	I read it in **The Daily News**.
need lower case	**lc**	I don't like **P**eanut **B**utter.
punctuation error	**p**	Where did you find that coat.
plural needed	**pl**	I bought the **grocery** on my way home.
spelling error	**sp**	Did you recieve my letter yet?
wrong tense	**t**	I **see** her yesterday.
wrong word	**ww**	My family used to **rise** corn and wheat.
need an apostrophe	ˇ	I **don't** know her name.
need a comma	ˆ	However, we will probably arrive on time.
delete something		We had the most best meal of our lives.
start a new paragraph	¶	... since last Friday. ¶ Oh, by the way ...
transpose words		They live on the floor first.

1. GREETINGS, INTRODUCTIONS, AND LEAVE-TAKING

Greeting someone you know

Hello.
Hi.
Hey.
Morning.
How's it going? [Informal]
What's up? [Informal]

Greeting someone you haven't seen for a while

It's good to see you again.
It's been a long time.
How long has it been?
Long time no see! [Informal]
You look great! [Informal]
So what have you been up to? [Informal]

Greeting someone you don't know

Hello.
Good morning.
Good afternoon.
Good evening.
Hi, there! [Informal]

Saying goodbye

Goodbye.
Bye.
Bye-bye.
See you.
See you later.
Have a good day.
Take care.
Good night. [Only when saying goodbye]

Introducing yourself

Hi, I'm Tom.
Hello, my name is Tom.
Excuse me.
We haven't met.
My name is Tom. [Formal]
I saw you in (science) class.
I met you at Jane's party.

Introducing other people

Have you two met?
Have you met Maria?
I'd like you to meet Maria.
There's someone I'd like you to meet.
Let me introduce you to Maria.

You: This is my friend Maria.
Ali: Glad to meet you, Maria.
You: Maria, this is Ali.
Maria: Nice to meet you, Ali.

I've been wanting to meet you.
Tom has told me a lot about you.

Greeting guests

Welcome.
Oh, hi.
How are you?
Please come in.
Glad you could make it.
Did you have any trouble finding us?
Can I take your coat?
Have a seat.
Please make yourself at home.

You: Can I get you something to drink?
Guest: Yes, please.
You: What would you like?
Guest: I'll have some orange juice.

What can I get you to drink?
Would you like some . . . ?

Saying goodbye to guests

Thanks for coming.
Thanks for joining us.
I'm so glad you could come.
It wouldn't have been the same without you.
Let me get your things.
Stop by anytime.

2. Having a Conversation

Starting a conversation
Nice weather, huh?
Aren't you a friend of Jim's?
Did you see last night's game?
What's your favorite TV show?
So, what do you think about (the situation in Europe)?
So how do you like (your new car)?
Guess what I did last night.

Showing that you are listening
Uh-huh.
Right.
Exactly.
Yeah.
OK...
I know what you mean.

Giving yourself time to think
Well...
Um...
Uh...
Let me think.
Just a minute.

Other: We should ride our bikes.
You: It's too far. And, I mean..., it's raining and we're already late.

Checking for comprehension
Do you see what I mean?
Are you with me?
Does that make sense?

Checking for agreement
Don't you agree?
So what do you think?
We have to (act fast), you know?

Expressing agreement
You're right.
I couldn't agree with you more.
Good thinking! [Informal]
You said it! [Informal]
You're absolutely right.
Absolutely! [Informal]

Expressing disagreement
I'm afraid I disagree.
Yeah, but...
I see your point, but...
That's not true.
You must be joking! [Informal]
No way! [Informal]

Asking someone to repeat something
Excuse me?
Sorry?
I didn't quite get that.
Could you repeat that?
Could you say that again?
Say again? [Informal]

Interrupting someone
Excuse me.
Yes, but (we don't have enough time).
I know, but (that will take hours).
Wait a minute. [Informal]
Just hold it right there! [Impolite]

Changing the topic
By the way, what do you think about (the new teacher)?
Before I forget, (there's a free concert on Friday night).
Whatever... (Did you see David's new car?)
Enough about me. Let's talk about you.

Ending a conversation
It was nice talking with you.
Good seeing you.
Sorry, I have to go now.

3. Using the Telephone

Making personal calls

Hi, this is David.
Is this Alice?
Is Alice there?
May I speak with Alice, please? [Formal]
I work with her.
We're in the same science class.
Could you tell her I called?
Would you ask her to call me?

Answering personal calls

Hello?
Who's calling, please?
Oh, hi David. How are you?
I can't hear you.
Sorry, we got cut off.
I'm in the middle of something.
Can I call you back?
What's your number again?
Listen. I have to go now.
It was nice talking to you.

Answering machine greetings

You've reached 212-555-6701.
Please leave a message after the beep.
Hi, this is Carlos.
I can't take your call right now.
Sorry I missed your call.
Please leave your name and number.
I'll call you back as soon as I can.

Answering machine messages

This is Magda. Call me back when you get a chance. [Informal]
Call me back on my cell.
I'll call you back later.
Talk to you later.
If you get this message before 11:00, please call me back.

Making business calls

Hello. This is Andy Larson.
I'm calling about . . .
Is this an OK time?

Answering business calls

Apex Electronics. Rosa Baker speaking. [Formal]
Hello, Rosa Baker.
May I help you?
Who's calling, please?

Caller: May I speak with Mr. Hafner, please?
Businessperson: This is he.

Caller: Mr. Hafner, please.
Businessperson: Speaking.

Talking to an office assistant

Extension 716, please.
Customer Service, please.
May I speak with Sheila Spink, please?
She's expecting my call.
I'm returning her call.
I'd like to leave a message for Ms. Spink.

Making appointments on the phone

You: I'd like to make an appointment to see Ms. Spink.
Assistant: How's 11:00 on Wednesday?
You: Wednesday is really bad for me.
Assistant: Can you make it Thursday at 9:00?
You: That would be perfect!
Assistant: OK. I have you down for Thursday at 9:00.

Special explanations

I'm sorry. She's not available.
Is there something I can help you with?
Can I put you on hold?
I'll transfer you to that extension.
If you'll leave your number, I'll have Ms. Spink call you back.
I'll tell her you called.

4. Interviewing for a Job

Small talk by the interviewer

Thanks for coming in today.

Did you have any trouble finding us?

How was the drive?

Would you like a cup of coffee?

Do you happen to know (Terry Mendham)?

Small talk by the candidate

What a great view!

Thanks for arranging to see me.

I've been looking forward to meeting you.

I spent some time exploring the company's web site.

My friend, Dale, has worked here for several years.

Getting serious

OK, shall we get started?

So, anyway . . .

Let's get down to business.

General questions for a candidate

Tell me a little about yourself.

How did you get into this line of work?

How long have you been in this country?

How did you learn about the opening?

What do you know about this company?

Why are you interested in working for us?

General answers to an interviewer

I've always been interested in (finance).

I enjoy (working with numbers).

My (uncle) was (an accountant) and encouraged me to try it.

I saw your ad in the paper.

This company has a great reputation in the field.

Job-related questions for a candidate

What are your qualifications for this job?

Describe your work experience.

What were your responsibilities on your last job?

I'd like to hear more about (your supervisory experience).

Interviewer: Have you taken any courses in (bookkeeping)?

You: Yes, I took two courses in business school and another online course last year.

What interests you about this particular job?

Why do you think it's a good fit?

Why did you leave your last job?

Do you have any experience with (HTML)?

Would you be willing to (travel eight weeks a year)?

What sort of salary are you looking for?

Describing job qualifications to an interviewer

In (2000), I started working for (Booker's) as a (sales rep).

After (two years), I was promoted to (sales manager).

You'll notice on my resume that (I supervised six people).

I was responsible for (three territories).

I was in charge of (planning sales meetings).

I have experience in all areas of (sales).

I helped implement (online sales reports).

I had to (contact my reps) on a daily basis.

I speak (Spanish) fluently.

I think my strong points are (organization and punctuality).

Ending the interview

I'm impressed with your experience.

I'd like to arrange a second interview.

When would you be able to start?

You'll hear from us by (next Wednesday).

We'll be in touch.

5. Presentations

Introducing yourself

Hello, everyone. I'd like to thank you all for coming.
Let me tell you a little bit about myself.
My name is (Rita Nazario).
I am president of (Catco International).
Hi. I'm (Ivan Wolf) from (Peekskill Incorporated).
Two years ago (I started out as a salesperson at Peekskill).
Today (I supervise the West Coast sales team).

Introducing someone else

This is (Tina Gorman), a (woman) who needs no introduction.
(Tina) is one of America's best-known (lawyers).
(She) is going to talk to us about (car insurance).
Let's give (her) a warm welcome.
We are lucky to have with us today (Barry Rogers).
As you know, (he) is (the president of Ranger Incorporated).
It gives me great pleasure to present (Barry Rogers).
And so without further ado, I'd like to present (Barry Rogers).

Stating the purpose

Today I'd like to talk to you about (managing your money).
Today I'm going to show you how to (save a lot of money).
I'll begin by (outlining the basics).
Then I'll (go into more detail).
I'll tell you (everything you need to know about savings accounts).
I'll provide an overview of (different types of investments).
I also hope to interest you in (some safe investments).
I'll list (the three biggest mistakes people make).
By the end, you'll (feel like an expert).

Relating to the audience

Can everyone hear me?
Raise your hand if you need me to repeat anything.
Please stop me at any point if you have a question.
How many people here (plan to continue their education)?
If you're like me, (you haven't saved up enough money).
We all know what that's like, don't we?
Does this ring a bell?
Don't you hate it when (people tell you what you should do)?

Citing sources

According to the *New York Times*, ...
A study conducted by Harvard University showed that ...
Recent research shows that ...
Medical researchers have discovered that ...
Peter Butler said, and I quote, "..."
I read somewhere that ...
(The federal government) released a report stating that ...

Making transitions

I'd like to expand on that before we move on.
The next thing I'd like to talk about is ...
Now let's take a look at ...
Moving right along ...
To sum up what I've said so far, ...
Now let's move on to the question of ...
Now that you have an overview, let's look at some of the specifics.
Recapping the main points, ...
I'm afraid we have to move on.

Emphasizing important points

I'd like to emphasize that ...
Never forget that ...
This is a key concept.
The bottom line is ...
If you remember only one thing I've said today, ...
I can't stress enough the importance of ...

Using visuals

Take a look at (the chart on the screen).
I'd like to draw your attention to (the poster over there).
You'll notice that ...
Pay special attention to the ...
If you look closely, you'll see that ...
So what does this tell us?

Closing

And in conclusion, ...
Let's open the floor to questions.
It's been a pleasure being with you today.

6. Agreeing and Disagreeing

Agreeing

Yeah, that's right.
I know it.
I agree with you.
You're right.
That's true.
I think so, too.
That's what I think.
Me, too.
Me neither.

Agreeing strongly

You're absolutely right!
Definitely!
Certainly!
Exactly!
Absolutely!
Of course!
I couldn't agree more.
You're telling me! [Informal]
You said it! [Informal]

Agreeing weakly

I suppose so.
Yeah, I guess so.
It would seem that way.

Remaining neutral

I see your point.
You have a point there.
I understand what you're saying.
I see what you mean.
I'd have to think about that.
I've never thought about it that way before.
Maybe yes, maybe no.
Could be.

Disagreeing

No, I don't think so.
I agree up to a point.
I really don't see it that way.
That's not what I think.
I agree that (going by car is faster), but . . .
But what about (the expense involved)?
Yes, but . . .
I know, but . . .
No, it wasn't. / No, they don't. / etc.

Other person: We could save a lot of money by taking the bus.
You: Not really. It would cost almost the same as driving.

Disagreeing strongly

I disagree completely.
That's not true.
That is not an option.
Definitely not!
Absolutely not!
You've made your point, but . . .
No way! [Informal]
You can't be serious. [Informal]
You've got to be kidding! [Informal]
Where did you get that idea? [Impolite]
Are you out of your mind! [Impolite]

Disagreeing politely

I'm afraid I have to disagree with you.
I'm not so sure.
I'm not sure that's such a good idea.
I see what you're saying, but . . .
I'm sure many people feel that way, but . . .
But don't you think we should consider (other alternatives)?

7. Interrupting, Clarifying, Checking for Understanding

Informal interruptions

Ummm.
Sir? / Ma'am?
Just a minute.
Can I stop you for a minute?
Wait a minute! [Impolite]
Hold it right there! [Impolite]

Formal interruptions

Excuse me, sir / ma'am.
Excuse me for interrupting.
Forgive me for interrupting you, but . . .
I'm sorry to break in like this, but . . .
Could I interrupt you for a minute?
Could I ask a question, please?

Asking for clarification—Informal

What did you say?
I didn't catch that.
Sorry, I didn't get that.
I missed that.
Could you repeat that?
Could you say that again?
Say again?
I'm lost.
Could you run that by me one more time?
Did you say . . . ?
Do you mean . . . ?

Asking for clarification—Formal

I beg your pardon?
I'm not sure I understand what you're saying.
I can't make sense of what you just said.
Could you explain that in different words?
Could you please repeat that?
Could you go over that again?

Giving clarification—Informal

I'll go over it again.
I'll take it step by step.
I'll take a different tack this time.
Stop me if you get lost.
OK, here's a recap.
Maybe this will clarify things.
To put it another way, . . .
In other words, . . .

Giving clarification—Formal

Let me put it another way.
Let me give you some examples.
Here are the main points again.
I'm afraid you didn't understand what I said.
I'm afraid you've missed the point.
What I meant was . . .
I hope you didn't think that . . .
I didn't mean to imply that . . .
I hope that clears things up.

Checking for understanding

Do you understand now?
Is it clearer now?
Do you see what I'm getting at?
Does that help?
Is there anything that still isn't clear?
What other questions do you have?

Speaker: What else?
Listener: I'm still not clear on the difference between a preposition and a conjunction.

Now explain it to me in your own words.

8. Apologizing

Apologizing for a small accident or mistake

Sorry.
I'm sorry.
Excuse me.
It was an accident.
Pardon me. [Formal]
Oops! [Informal]
My mistake. [Informal]
I'm terrible with (names).
I've never been good with (numbers).
I can't believe I (did) that.

Apologizing for a serious accident or mistake

I'm so sorry.
I am really sorry that I (damaged your car).
I am so sorry about (damaging your car).
I feel terrible about (the accident).
I'm really sorry but (I was being very careful).
I'm sorry for (causing you a problem).
Please accept my apologies for . . . [Formal]
I sincerely apologize for . . . [Formal]

Apologizing for upsetting someone

I'm sorry I upset you.
I didn't mean to make you feel bad.
Please forgive me. [Formal]
I just wasn't thinking straight.
That's not what I meant to say.
I didn't mean it personally.
I'm sorry. I'm having a rough day.

Apologizing for having to say *no*

I'm sorry. I can't.
Sorry, I never (lend anyone my car).
I wish I could say *yes*.
I'm going to have to say *no*.
I can't. I have to (work that evening).
Maybe some other time.

Responding to an apology

Don't worry about it.
Oh, that's OK.
Think nothing of it. [Formal]
Don't mention it. [Formal]

Other person: I'm afraid I lost the pen you lent me.
You: No big thing.

It doesn't matter.
It's not important.
Never mind.
No problem.
It happens.
Forget it.
Don't sweat it. [Informal]
Apology accepted. [Formal]

Showing regret

I feel really bad.
It won't happen again.
I wish I could go back and start all over again.
I don't know what came over me.
I don't know what to say.
Now I know better.
Too bad I didn't . . .
It was inexcusable of me. [Formal]
It's not like me to . . .
I hope I can make it up to you.
That didn't come out right.
I didn't mean to take it out on you.

Sympathizing

This must be very difficult for you.
I know what you mean.
I know how you're feeling.
I know how upset you must be.
I can imagine how difficult this is for you.

9. Suggestions, Advice, Insistence

Making informal suggestions

Here's what I suggest.
I know what you should do.
Why don't you (go to the movies with Jane)?
What about (having lunch with Bob)?
Try (the French fries next time).
Have you thought about (riding your bike to work)?

Accepting suggestions

Thanks, I'll do that.
Good idea!
That's a great idea.
Sounds good to me.
That's a plan.
I'll give it a try.
Guess it's worth a try.

Refusing suggestions

No. I don't like (French fries).
That's not for me.
I don't think so.
That might work for some people, but . . .
Nawww. [Informal]
I don't feel like it. [Impolite]

Giving serious advice—Informal

Listen!
Here's the plan.
Take my advice.
Take it from one who knows.
Take it from someone who's been there.
Here's what I think you should do.
Hey! Here's an idea.
How about (waiting until you're 30 to get married)?
Don't (settle down too quickly).
Why don't you (see the world while you're young)?
You can always (settle down later).
Don't forget—(you only live once).

Giving serious advice—formal

Have you ever thought about (becoming a doctor)?
Maybe it would be a good idea if you (went back to school).
It looks to me like (Harvard) would be your best choice.
If I were you, I'd study (medicine).
In my opinion, you should (consider it seriously).
Be sure to (get your application in early).
I always advise people to (check that it was received).
The best idea is (to study hard).
If you're really smart, you'll (start right away).

Accepting advice

You're right.
Thanks for the advice.
That makes a lot of sense.
I see what you mean.
That sounds like good advice.
I'll give it a try.
I'll do my best.
You've given me something to think about.
I'll try it and get back to you.

Refusing advice

I don't think that would work for me.
That doesn't make sense to me.
I'm not sure that would be such a good idea.
I could never (become a doctor).
Thanks for the input.
Thanks, but no thanks. [Informal]
You don't know what you're talking about. [Impolite]
I think I know what's best for myself. [Impolite]
Back off! [Impolite]

Insisting

You have to (become a doctor).
Try to see it my way.
I know what I'm talking about.
If you don't (go to medical school), I won't (pay for your college).
I don't care what you think. [Impolite]

10. Describing Feelings

Happiness
I'm doing great.
This is the best day of my life.
I've never been so happy in my life.
I'm so pleased for you.
Aren't you thrilled?
What could be better?
Life is good.

Sadness
Are you OK?
Why the long face?
I'm not doing so well.
I feel awful.
I'm devastated.
I'm depressed.
I'm feeling kind of blue.
I just want to crawl in a hole.
Oh, what's the use?

Fear
I'm worried about (money).
He dreads (going to the dentist).
I'm afraid to (drive over bridges).
She can't stand (snakes).
This anxiety is killing me.
He's scared of (big dogs).
How will I ever (pass Friday's test)?
I have a phobia about (germs).

Anger
I'm really mad at (you).
They resent (such high taxes).
How could she (do) that?
I'm annoyed with (the neighbors).
(The noise of car alarms) infuriates her.
He was furious with (the children).

Boredom
I'm so bored.
There's nothing to do around here.
What a bore!
Nothing ever happens.
She was bored to tears.
They were bored to death.
I was bored stiff.
It was such a monotonous (movie).
(That TV show) was so dull.

Disgust
That's disgusting.
Eeew! Yuck! [Informal]
I hate (raw fish).
How can you stand it?
I almost vomited.
I thought I'd puke. [Impolite]
I don't even like to think about it.
How can you say something like that?
I wouldn't be caught dead (wearing that dirty old coat).

Compassion
I'm sorry.
I understand what you're going through.
Tell me about it.
How can I help?
Is there anything I can do?
She is concerned about him.
He worries about the children.
He cares for her deeply.
My heart goes out to them. [Old-fashioned]

Guilt
I feel terrible that I (lost your mother's necklace).
I never should have (borrowed it).
I feel so guilty!
It's all my fault.
I blame myself.
I make a mess of everything.
I'll never forgive myself.

Words That Frequently Appear on TOEFL® and TOEIC®

abate
abbreviate
above
abroad
abrupt
absence
absolute
absurd
abuse
abyss
accelerate
accentuate
accept
acceptable
access
accident
acclaim
accord
account
accounting
accredited
accretion
accurate
acknowledge
acquiesce
acquire
active
actually
addict
adept
adhere
adjacent
adjust
admiration
admit
admonish
adopt
advance
advanced
advantage
advent
adverse
advertisement
advice
affable
affliction
affluent
afford
affordable
agenda
agent
aggravating
aggregate
agile
agitate
agnostic
agoraphobia
aim
albeit
alleviate
allocation
allow
allowance
alter
amaze
ambiguous
ambivalence
amenity
amiable
amicable
amorous
ample
amplify
amusement
analogous
analogy
analyze
anchor
ancient
animal
animate
animosity
annals
annex
anniversary
annoying
annual
annuity
antecedent
anterior
anthropology
anticipate
antipathy
antiquated
antisocial
apart
apathy
apology
apparel
apparent
appeal
appealing
apprehensive
appropriate
approximately
aptly
aqueous
arbiter
arbitrary
archaic
arduous
arid
aroma
arrest
arrival
article
ascend
ascertain
aspect
assert
assimilate
assortment
assume
assure
astounding
astute
atom
atone
attendance
attest
attract
attractive
auction
audacious
audible
auditorium
augment
auspicious
author
authorize
autograph
autonomous
avail
avarice
average
avoid
background
backup
baffle
baked
balanced
bankrupt
barometer
bear
become
bellicose
benefit
benevolent
benign
bibliography
bill
biology
bisect
blame
bland
blind
block
bloom
blossom
blur
bold
bond
book
boorish
border
bothersome
bottom
boundary
brand
break
breakthrough
brevity
brief
brilliant
brink
broaden
bud
budget
bulk
burgeon
cabinet
caliber
calisthenics
callous
candid
capable
capital
captive
capture
card
career
carpet
carry
categorize
caution
celebrated
cement
certificate
challenge
chaotic
characteristic
charisma
chiefly
chilly
chore
chronic
chronicle
chronological
circle
circulate
circumstance
citizenship
clamor
clarify
classify
clear
clerk
clever

clock
coarse
code
coherent
collateral
colleague
collect
collection
college
colloquial
colonist
command
commemorate
commonplace
compatible
compel
complex
comply
conceal
concede
conceive
concept
concoct
condense
condition
conducive
conduct
confide
confidential
confirm
conform
conjure
conscientious
conscious
consecutive
consent
conservation
consider
considerate
consideration
consistently
consortium
constant
constraint
constrict
construe
consumption
contact
contemplate
contemporary
contend
content
contentment
contingent
continue
contort
contradictory
controversial
convene
convenience
convenient
conventional
convert
convey
convince
cook
copy
core
corner
corporate
corpse
corrupt
cost
counsel
couple
courageous
courier
course
court
cowardly
crack
crate
create
credible
credit
creed
creep
crescent
critical
criticize
crop
crucial
crush
cultivate
curb
curious
currency
current
custom
cyclone
damp
dangle
dash
deadline
deceased
deceive
decent
declare
decline
decompose
decorate
deduce
deduct
deep
default
deflate
defy
degenerate
degree
dehydrate
delegate
delicate
delighted
deluge
demand
demolish
demonstration
demure
dense
dentistry
dependent
depict
deplete
depreciate
deprive
describe
description
desiccated
despise
destroy
destruction
detail
detect
determined
develop
deviate
diagnose
dial
dichotomy
dictate
dictionary
diet
difficult
diffident
dignitary
dignity
diligent
dim
diminish
diminutive
direct
disapproval
discard
discernible
discount
discourse
discreditable
discuss
disguise
disintegrate
dismiss
disorient
disparate
disparity
disperse
display
dispose
disregard
disrobe
disruptive
dissimilar
dissociate
dissuade
distinct
distinguish
distort
distribute
disturb
disturbing
diverse
docile
doctor
doctrine
document
dogma
doleful
domestic
dominant
dormant
download
downturn
drab
dramatic
drastic
draw
droop
drought
dubious
due
dumbfound
dweller
dwelling
dwindle
dynamic
dysentery
dysfunction
dyslexia
dyspepsia
dystrophy
eager
earnest
educate
efface
effect
effective
effigy
egregious
eject

elaborate
elect
election
element
elementary
elevator
elicit
eligible
eliminate
elucidate
elude
emit
empathy
emphasize
employee
employment
emulate
enact
enchant
encircle
encompass
encourage
endeavor
endorse
endorsement
endure
energetic
engine
enhance
enormous
enrich
ensue
enthrall
enthuse
entirely
envision
equal
equity
equivalent
erode
erratic
espionage
essence
essential
establish
eternal
eugenics
eulogize
euphemism
euthanasia
evade
evaporate
even
eventually
evident
evolution
exaggerate
examiner
exceed
exceedingly
exceptional
exchange
excite
exclaim
exclude
exclusively
excursion
exemplify
exhaust
exhibit
exit
expand
expansion
expel
experience
explain
exploit
export
express
exquisite
extensive
extent
exterminate
extol
extract
extradite
extremely
fabricate
face
facet
facsimile
fact
factory
fail
faint
fallacy
familiar
famous
fantasy
fare
fashion
fathom
feasible
feature
fee
feign
fertile
fiction
fidelity
figment
figure
final
finance
finite
firm
flaw
flimsy
floor
florist
flourish
fluctuate
fluent
fluid
forbearance
forbid
forecast
forfeit
formal
format
formerly
formidable
formulate
fortify
fortune
found
founder
fracture
fragment
frail
frame
fraud
freezing
frequently
freshly
frigid
frontier
fulfillment
function
fundamental
further
gain
gather
gaudy
generally
generous
geography
get
ghastly
gigantic
gingerly
glove
goal
good
government
grade
gradually
graffiti
grant
graphic
gratitude
grimace
grumble
guess
harass
harmful
harmless
harvest
hasten
hazardous
haze
head
heave
heighten
henceforth
heretic
hero
hesitate
hidden
highlight
hit
homophone
honor
host
hue
humane
humid
hyperactive
hyperbole
hypersensitive
hypertension
ideal
identical
illuminate
illustrate
illustration
immense
immigrant
impact
impede
impediment
implicate
import
impossible
impressive
improper
inaccessible
inactive
inconvenience
incorporate
increase
incredible
incredulity
incredulous
incumbent
indeed
indicate
indigenous
indiscriminate

indispensable
indivisible
induce
induct
inert
inevitable
infancy
infant
infer
influence
inhabitant
initiate
injury
innovate
innovative
inordinate
inquire
insensitive
insipid
inspire
institution
instrument
intensify
intent
intentionally
interact
intercept
interchangeable
intermediate
intermittent
interpret
interrelate
interrupt
intersperse
intervene
intolerable
intrepid
intricate
intrigue
intrinsic
introduction
intrude
inundate
invent
invention
investment
involuntarily
involve
irate
irrelevant
irritation
isolate
itinerant
jeopardy
jettison
judge
junction
know
labor
lachrymose
lack
lasting
launch
lawyer
layman
lead
league
lease
leash
leather
legal
legible
legitimate
library
likelihood
limber
limit
litter
loafer
lobotomy
logic
logo
loom
lose
lounge
lucrative
luggage
lustrous
macrocosm
macroeconomics
magnificent
magnitude
mail
maintain
malign
manage
management
manhood
manly
manual
manufacture
margin
marvel
maternity
matriarch
maximum
mayor
mean
meanwhile
meddle
medieval
mediocre
memory
mend
mental
mention
merchandise
merciless
metropolitan
microbe
microcosm
microfilm
micrometer
microscope
microsecond
microwave
midday
mild
miniature
minimal
minimum
ministry
minor
minuscule
minute
mirror
mirth
misanthropy
misconstrue
misogyny
missive
mistake
misunderstand
mobile
moist
monotone
morphology
mortgage
motion
motivate
multiply
must
mutable
naïve
narrate
narrow
nascent
native
nausea
necessarily
neglect
negligible
neurology
nevertheless
nocturnal
nominal
nonsense
normally
note
notion
novel
novelty
novice
nuance
number
obese
oblige
observe
obsolete
obstruct
obtain
obviously
occasion
occupancy
occur
odd
offense
offensive
offer
office
omit
ongoing
operate
opposition
opus
order
orthodox
otherwise
outlandish
overcome
overlook
owner
ownership
package
pad
page
paradox
parallel
parched
partially
participate
particle
particular
partisan
party
pass
passage
passion
patch
paternal
pathetic
pathological
pathology
patient
patriarch
pattern
peace
peculiar

pedal
pedestal
pedestrian
pedicure
perceive
percent
perch
perennial
perfect
persistent
perspective
persuade
pervade
petition
petrified
petty
petulant
phantom
pharmacist
phenomena
philanthropic
philanthropy
philharmonic
philology
philosopher
philosophy
phobia
photograph
pier
pillage
pioneer
place
placid
plaid
plentiful
ply
pocket
podiatrist
podium
point
policy
poll
pollution
polygamy
polytechnic
ponder
population
portray
position
post
postpone
postscript
posture
potent
practical
practice
precarious
precede
precedent
precious
preconception
precondition
predecessor
predict
predictably
predominant
preference
pregnant
prestige
presumably
presumptuous
pretense
prevail
prevalent
prevent
previously
primary
prime
privacy
procedure
process
proclaim
produce
production
proficient
programmer
progress
prohibit
project
proliferate
prolong
prominent
promise
promontory
promote
prompt
prone
propel
prophetic
propose
prospective
prosperous
protection
protrude
provision
proximity
psychology
psychopathic
publication
publisher
pulse
pungent
query
quest
radiant
raise
range
rate
react
reaction
readily
reason
rebellion
rebound
recede
receive
receptionist
recess
recession
recognize
record
recover
reduce
refer
refine
reflect
reflection
refurbish
regard
regulate
reject
rejoicing
relate
relation
release
reliable
relinquish
remarkable
remind
reminisce
remove
renew
renown
repel
replace
replay
reply
reportedly
representative
requisite
rescue
research
resident
resilient
resource
respected
respiration
restore
restrain
retain
reticent
retrieve
retrospect
reveal
reverberate
reverse
revert
review
revive
revoke
revolt
revolve
rhythm
ridge
rigid
rigor
rivalry
robust
route
routine
routinely
rudimentary
rupture
rush
ruthless
sacrifice
salvage
saturated
savory
scarce
scarcely
scattered
scene
scenic
science
scorching
score
scribble
script
scrupulous
scrutinize
season
security
seduce
seedling
segment
selective
selfish
seminar
senior
sensation
sense
sensitive
sentimental
sequence
serve
settle
settler

severe
shallow
shatter
shed
shelf
sheltered
shift
ship
shipment
shipping
shoot
shortage
shrink
sideways
significance
significant
signify
sinecure
singular
site
situated
sketchy
skin
soaked
society
sociology
solid
solitary
soluble
solve
sometimes
somewhat
sound
source
spacious
span
specimen
spectator
spectrum
speculate
spiteful
spontaneous
sporadic
spread
sprout
spurn
square
stack
stagnant
stake
stance
static
stationary
stature
steady
stem
step
stipulate
stock
store
stream
strengthen
stress
stretch
strike
striking
stringent
strive
submit
subscribe
subsequent
subside
subsidize
substantiate
succeed
successive
succumb
suffer
suitable
sum
superficial
superfluous
superior
supervise
supplement
supply
supposition
surmise
surveillance
suspect
suspend
swift
switch
symbols
sympathetic
sympathy
synonym
synthesis
taciturn
talk
tangible
task
teacher
technology
tedious
telegram
telepathy
temper
temporize
tempt
tenacious
tentative
terminal
terrain
terrifying
territory
testify
theology
theoretically
thermal
thermometer
thrive
thrust
ticket
timid
title
topic
torment
torpid
torsion
total
tour
toxic
tradition
trail
train
transcend
translucent
transmit
transport
trap
trash
treacherous
treasury
treaty
tremor
tremulous
triangle
triple
tripod
triumph
trivial
trouble
truculent
tyro
ultrasonic
unbiased
undeniable
undercut
underestimated
underline
unfavorably
uniform
unique
unison
unite
unlikely
unmistakable
unravel
unwarranted
update
uproar
vacancy
vacant
vacuum
value
vanity
varied
vast
vegetable
vehemence
veil
veracity
verbalize
verify
versatile
verve
vibrant
viewpoint
vigorous
vindicate
virtual
visible
vital
vivid
vocal
vogue
volume
voluptuous
wait
wane
wanton
weak
weakness
wealth
weapon
weigh
wide
widespread
wilt
wisdom
wither
withstand
witticism
woo
worthwhile
wrinkle
xenophobia
zenith

Text Messaging and Emoticons

Texting Abbreviations

1 used to replace "*-one*": *NE1* = anyone

2 **to or too**: *it's up 2 U* = it's up to you; *me 2* = me too
used to replace "**to-**": *2day* = today

2DAY **today**

2MORO **tomorrow**

2NITE **tonight**

4 **for**: *4 U* = for you
used to replace "**-fore**": *B4* = before

411 **information**: *TNX 4 the 411*

8 used to replace "**-ate**" or "**-eat**": *GR8* = great; *C U L8R* = see you later

86 discard, get rid of

AFAIK **as far as I know**

B **be**: used to replace "**be-**" in other words: *B4* = before

B4 **before**

B4N **bye for now**

BRB **be right back**

BTW **by the way**

C **see**: *C U 2moro* = see you tomorrow

CID **consider it done**

CU **see you**

CUL8R **call you later**

D8 **date**

EZ **easy**

FWIW **for what it's worth**: used for saying that someone may or may not be interested in what you have to say

FYI **for your information**: used as a way of introducing useful information

GR8 **great**

G2G **got to go**

HHIS **hanging head in shame**: used for showing that you are embarassed

IB **I'm back**

IYSS **if you say so**

K **OK**

L8 **late**

L8R **later**: *CUL8R* = see you later

LOL **laughing out loud**: used for showing that you think something is funny

MSG **message**

MYOB **mind your own business**: for telling people not to ask questions about something that you do not want them to know about

NE **any**

NE1 **anyone**

NO1 **no one**

NETHING **anything**

OIC **Oh, I see**

OTOH **on the other hand**

PCM **please call me**

PLS **please**

prolly **probably**

R **are**: *RU free 2nite* = Are you free tonight?

RUCMNG **Are you coming?**

RUOK? **Are you OK?**

SPK **speak**

SRY **sorry**

THNQ **thank you**: *THNQ for visiting my home page.*

THX/TX **thanks**: *THX 4 the info.*

TTUL/TTYL **talk to you later**

U **you**: *CUL8R* = see you later

URW **You're welcome.**

W8 **wait**

WAN2 **want to**

WRK **work**

XLNT **excellent**

YR **your**

ZZZZ **sleeping**

Emoticons Horizontal →

`:-)` smiling; agreeing
`:-D` laughing
`|-)` hee hee
`|-D` ho ho
`‘-) or ;-)` winking; just kidding
`:*)` clowning
`:-(` frowning; sad
`:(` sad
`:’-(` crying and really sad
`>:-< or :-||` angry
`:-@` screaming
`:-V` shouting
`:-p or :-r` sticking tongue out
`|-O` yawning
`: *` kiss
`((((name))))` hug
`@-{----` rose
`<3` heart
`</3` broken heart

Emoticons Vertical ↓

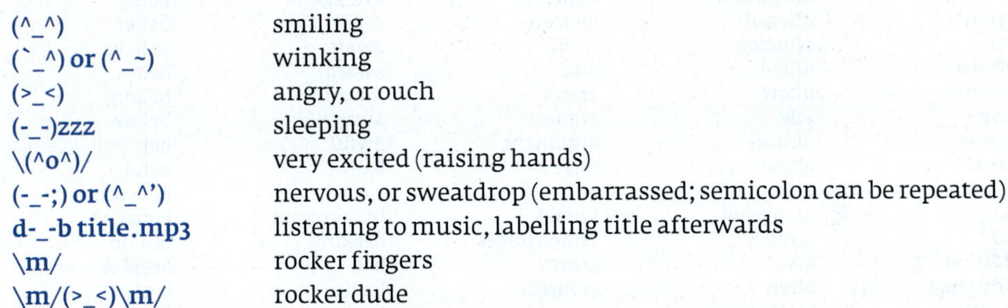

`(^_^)` smiling
`(`_^) or (^_~)` winking
`(>_<)` angry, or ouch
`(-_-)zzz` sleeping
`\(^o^)/` very excited (raising hands)
`(-_-;) or (^_^’)` nervous, or sweatdrop (embarrassed; semicolon can be repeated)
`d-_-b title.mp3` listening to music, labelling title afterwards
`\m/` rocker fingers
`\m/(>_<)\m/` rocker dude

DEFINING VOCABULARY

a
abandon
abandoned
ability
able
abortion
about
above
abroad
absence
absolute
absolutely
abuse
academic
accept
acceptable
accepted
access
accident
accompany
accord
according to
account
accurate
accuse
achieve
achievement
acid
acknowledge
acquire
acquisition
acre
across
act
action
active
activist
activity
actor
actress
actual
actually
ad
add
addition
additional
address
adequate
adjust
administration
admire
admit
adopt
adult
advance
advanced
advantage
advertise
advice
advise
adviser
advocate
affair
affect
afford
afraid
after
afternoon
afterward
again
against
age
agency
agenda
agent
aggressive
ago
agree
agreement
agricultural
agriculture
ah
ahead
aid
aim
air
air force
aircraft
airline
airport
alarm
album
alcohol
alert
alive
all
all right
allegation
alleged
alliance
allied
allow
ally
almost
alone
along
alongside
already
also
alter
alternative
although
altogether
always
amateur
amazing
ambassador
ambition
amendment
amid
among
amount
analysis
analyst
ancient
and
anger
angle
angry
animal
anniversary
announce
announcement
annual
another
answer
antique
anxiety
anxious
any
anybody
anymore
anyone
anything
anyway
anywhere
apart
apartment
apparent
apparently
appeal
appear
appearance
apple
application
apply
appoint
appointment
appreciate
approach
appropriate
approval
approve
April
area
aren't
argue
argument
arise
arm
armed
armed forces
army
around
arrange
arrangement
arrest
arrival
arrive
art
article
artist
as
Asian
aside
ask
aspect
assault
assembly
assess
assessment
asset
assist
assistance
assistant
associate
associated
association
assume
assumption
assured
at
athlete
atmosphere
attach
attack
attempt
attend
attention
attitude
attorney
attract
attractive
auction
audience
audio
August
aunt
author
authority
auto
automatic
autumn
available
avenue
average
avoid
await
award
aware
away
awful
baby
back
background
backing
bad
badly
bag
bake
balance
ball
ballot
ban
band
bank
banker
banking
bar
bare
barely
bargain
barrel
barrier
base
baseball
based
basic
basically
basis
basketball
bass
bat
bath
bathroom
battle
bay
be
beach
bean
bear
bearing
beat
beaten
beating
beautiful
beauty
because
become
bed
bedroom
beer
before
begin
beginning
behalf
behave
behavior
behind
being
belief
believe
bell
belong
below
belt
bend
beneath
benefit
beside
besides
best
bet
better
between
beyond
bid
big
bike
bill
billion
bird
birth
birthday
bit
bite
bitter
black
blame
blast

blind
block
blood
bloody
blow
blue
board
boat
body
boil
bomb
bond
bone
book
boom
boost
boot
border
bore
born
borrow
boss
both
bother
bottle
bottom
bound
bowl
box
boy
brain
branch
brand
brave
bread
break
breakfast
breast
breath
breathe
breed
bridge
brief
bright
brilliant
bring
broad
broadcast
broadcasting
broker
brother
brown
brush
budget
build
building
bunch
burden
burn
burst
bury
bus
business
businessman

busy
but
butter
button
buy
buyer
by
bye
cabinet
cable
cake
call
calm
camera
camp
campaign
can
cancel
cancer
candidate
cap
capable
capacity
capital
captain
caption
capture
car
carbon
card
care
career
careful
Caribbean
caring
carrier
carry
case
cash
cast
castle
casualty
cat
catch
category
Catholic
cause
cautious
cave
cease
ceasefire
celebrate
celebration
cell
center
central
century
ceremony
certain
certainly
chain
chair
chairman
challenge

chamber
champion
championship
chance
chancellor
change
channel
chaos
chapter
character
characteristic
charge
charity
chart
charter
chase
chat
cheap
check
cheer
cheese
chemical
chest
chicken
chief
child
childhood
chip
chocolate
choice
choose
chop
Christian
Christmas
church
cigarette
cinema
circle
circuit
circumstance
cite
citizen
city
civil
civil war
civilian
claim
clash
class
classic
classical
clean
clear
clever
client
climate
climb
clinic
clock
close
clothes
clothing
cloud
club

coach
coal
coalition
coast
coat
code
coffee
cold
collapse
colleague
collect
collection
collective
college
colonel
color
colored
column
combat
combination
combine
come
comedy
comfort
comfortable
coming
command
commander
comment
commentator
commerce
commercial
commission
commissioner
commit
commitment
committee
common
communicate
communication
communist
community
company
compare
compared
comparison
compensation
compete
competition
competitive
competitor
complain
complaint
complete
complex
complicated
component
comprehensive
compromise
computer
concede
concentrate
concentration
concept

concern
concerned
concert
concession
conclude
conclusion
concrete
condemn
condition
conduct
conference
confidence
confident
confirm
conflict
confront
confrontation
Congress
congressional
connection
conscious
consciousness
consequence
conservative
consider
considerable
consideration
considering
consist
consistent
constant
constitution
constitutional
construction
consult
consultant
consumer
contact
contain
contemporary
content
contest
context
continent
continue
contract
contrast
contribute
contribution
control
controversial
controversy
convention
conventional
conversation
convert
convict
conviction
convince
convinced
cook
cooking
cool
cooperate

cope
copy
core
corner
corporate
corporation
correct
correspondent
corruption
'cos
cost
cottage
cotton
cough
could
council
counsel
count
counter
counterpart
country
countryside
county
coup
couple
courage
course
court
cousin
cover
coverage
cow
crack
craft
crash
crazy
cream
create
creative
credit
crew
cricket
crime
criminal
crisis
critic
critical
criticism
criticize
crop
cross
crowd
crown
crucial
cruise
cry
crystal
cue
cultural
culture
cup
cure
curious
currency
current
curtain
customer
cut
cutting
cycle
dad
daily
damage
dance
dancing
danger
dangerous
dare
dark
data
date
daughter
day
dead
deadline
deal
dealer
dear
death
debate
debt
debut
decade
December
decide
decision
deck
declaration
declare
decline
decorate
deep
defeat
defend
defense
deficit
define
definitely
definition
degree
delay
delegate
delegation
deliberate
delight
delighted
deliver
delivery
demand
democracy
democrat
democratic
demonstrate
demonstration
demonstrator
deny
department
departure
depend
deposit
depression
depth
deputy
describe
description
desert
deserve
design
designer
desire
desk
desperate
despite
destroy
destruction
detail
detailed
detective
determine
determined
develop
development
device
dialogue
diary
didn't
die
diet
difference
different
difficult
difficulty
dig
digital
dinner
diplomat
diplomatic
direct
direction
director
dirty
disappear
disappointed
disaster
discipline
discount
discover
discovery
discuss
discussion
disease
dish
dismiss
display
dispute
distance
distribution
district
divide
dividend
division
divorce
do
doctor
document
doesn't
dog
dollar
domestic
dominate
done
door
double
doubt
down
downtown
dozen
draft
drag
drain
drama
dramatic
draw
dream
dress
dressed
drift
drink
drive
driver
drop
drug
drum
dry
due
dump
during
dust
duty
each
eager
ear
earlier
early
earn
earnings
earth
ease
easily
east
eastern
easy
eat
echo
economic
economics
economist
economy
edge
edit
edition
editor
editorial
education
educational
effect
effective
efficient
effort
egg
eight
eighteen
eighteenth
eighth
eightieth
eighty
either
elderly
elect
election
electoral
electric
electricity
electronic
elegant
element
eleven
eleventh
eliminate
else
elsewhere
embassy
emerge
emergency
emotion
emotional
emphasis
emphasize
empire
employ
employee
employer
employment
empty
enable
encounter
encourage
end
enemy
energy
enforcement
engage
engine
engineer
engineering
English
enhance
enjoy
enormous
enough
ensure
enter
enterprise
entertain
entertainment
enthusiasm
entire
entirely
entitle
entrance

entry
environment
environmental
equal
equally
equipment
equity
equivalent
era
error
escape
especially
essential
essentially
establish
establishment
estate
estimate
ethnic
European
even
evening
event
eventually
ever
every
everybody
everyone
everything
everywhere
evidence
evil
exact
exactly
examination
examine
example
excellent
except
exception
excerpt
excess
exchange
exchange rate
exciting
excuse
execute
executive
exercise
exhaust
exhibition
exile
exist
existence
existing
expand
expansion
expect
expectation
expense
expensive
experience
experiment
expert
explain
explanation
explode
exploit
explore
explosion
export
expose
exposure
express
expression
extend
extensive
extent
extra
extraordinary
extreme
extremely
eye
fabric
face
facility
fact
faction
factor
factory
fade
fail
failure
fair
fairly
faith
fall
false
familiar
family
famous
fan
fancy
fantasy
far
fare
farm
farmer
fashion
fast
fat
fate
father
fault
favor
favorite
fear
feature
February
federal
federation
fee
feed
feel
feeling
fellow
female
fence
festival
few
field
fierce
fifteen
fifteenth
fifth
fiftieth
fifty
fight
fighter
figure
file
fill
film
final
finally
finance
financial
find
fine
finger
finish
fire
firm
first
fiscal
fish
fishing
fit
five
fix
fixed
flag
flash
flat
flavor
flee
fleet
flexible
flight
float
flood
floor
flow
flower
fly
focus
fold
folk
follow
following
food
fool
foot
football
for
force
forecast
foreign
foreigner
forest
forget
form
formal
former
formula
forth
fortieth
fortune
forty
forward
found
foundation
founder
four
fourteen
fourteenth
fourth
frame
fraud
free
freedom
freeze
frequent
fresh
Friday
friend
friendly
friendship
from
front
fruit
frustrate
fry
fuel
fulfill
full
fully
fun
function
fund
fundamental
funding
funny
furniture
further
future
gain
gallery
game
gang
gap
garden
gas
gate
gather
gay
gear
gene
general
general election
generally
generate
generation
generous
gentle
gentleman
genuine
gesture
get
giant
gift
girl
give
given
glad
glance
glass
global
go
goal
god
going
gold
golden
golf
gone
good
goods
got
govern
government
governor
grab
grade
gradually
graduate
grain
grand
grant
grass
grave
gray
great
green
grip
gross
ground
group
grow
growth
guarantee
guard
guerrilla
guess
guest
guide
guilty
guitar
gun
guy
habit
hair
half
hall
halt
hand
handle
hang
happen
happy

DEFINING VOCABULARY

harbor
hard
hardly
harm
hat
hate
have
he
head
headline
headquarters
heal
health
health care
healthy
hear
hearing
heart
heat
heaven
heavy
height
helicopter
hell
hello
help
her
here
hero
herself
hi
hide
high
high school
highlight
highly
highway
hill
him
himself
hint
hip
hire
his
historic
historical
history
hit
hold
holder
hole
holiday
holy
home
homeless
homosexual
honest
honor
hook
hope
horror
horse
hospital
host
hostage
hot
hotel
hour
house
household
housing
how
however
huge
human
human rights
humor
hundred
hundredth
hunt
hunter
hurt
husband
I
ice
idea
ideal
identify
identity
if
ignore
ill
illegal
illness
illustrate
illustration
image
imagination
imagine
immediate
immediately
immigrant
immigration
immune
impact
implement
implication
imply
import
importance
important
impose
impossible
impress
impression
impressive
improve
improvement
in
inch
incident
include
included
including
income
increase
increasingly
incredible
indeed
independence
independent
index
indicate
indication
individual
industrial
industry
inevitable
infect
infection
inflation
influence
inform
information
ingredient
initial
initially
initiative
injured
injury
inner
innocent
inquiry
inside
insist
inspect
inspector
install
instance
instant
instead
institute
institution
instruction
instrument
insurance
integrate
intellectual
intelligence
intelligent
intend
intense
intention
interest
interested
interesting
interim
interior
internal
international
Internet
intervention
interview
into
introduce
invasion
invest
investigate
investment
investor
invitation
invite
involve
involved
involvement
iron
Islam
Islamic
island
issue
IT
it
item
its
itself
jacket
jail
January
jazz
jersey
Jesus
jet
Jew
Jewish
job
join
joint
joke
journal
journalist
journey
joy
judge
judgment
juice
July
jump
June
junior
jury
just
justice
justify
keen
keep
key
kick
kid
kill
killer
killing
kilometer
kind
king
kiss
kitchen
knee
knife
knock
know
know-how
knowledge
label
labor
laboratory
lack
lad
lady
lake
land
landscape
lane
language
lap
large
largely
last
late
later
latest
Latin
latter
laugh
laughter
launch
law
lawsuit
lawyer
lay
layer
lead
leader
leadership
leading
leaf
league
leak
lean
leap
learn
lease
least
leather
leave
lecture
left
leg
legal
legislation
lend
length
lens
lesbian
less
lesson
let
let's
letter
level
liberal
liberate
liberty
library
license
lie
life
lift
light
like
likely

limit
limited
line
link
lip
list
listen
literary
literature
little
live
live-in
living
load
loan
lobby
local
local authority
location
lock
long
long-term
long-time
look
loose
lord
lose
loss
lost
lot
loud
love
lovely
lover
low
lower
luck
lucky
lunch
luxury
machine
mad
made-up
magazine
magic
mail
main
mainly
maintain
major
majority
make
maker
make-up
male
man
manage
management
manager
manner
manufacture
manufacturer
many
map

March
march
margin
marine
mark
marked
market
marketing
marriage
married
marry
mask
mass
massive
master
match
mate
material
matter
maximum
May
may
maybe
mayor
me
meal
mean
meaning
means
meanwhile
measure
meat
mechanism
medal
media
medical
medicine
medium
meet
meeting
member
membership
memory
mental
mention
merchant
mere
merely
merger
mess
message
metal
method
metre
middle
middle class
Middle East
midnight
might
mild
mile
militant
military
milk

mill
million
millionth
mind
mine
miner
minimum
minister
ministry
minor
minority
minute
mirror
Miss
miss
missile
missing
mission
mistake
mix
mixed
mixture
mobile
model
moderate
modern
modest
mom
moment
Monday
monetary
money
monitor
month
monthly
mood
moon
moral
more
moreover
morning
mortgage
most
mostly
mother
motion
motivate
motor
mount
mountain
mouth
move
movement
movie
Mr.
Mrs.
Ms.
much
mum
murder
muscle
museum
music
musical

musician
Muslim
must
mutual
my
myself
mystery
myth
name
narrow
nation
national
nationalist
native
natural
naturally
nature
naval
navy
Nazi
near
nearby
nearly
neat
necessarily
necessary
neck
need
negative
negotiate
negotiation
neighbor
neighborhood
neither
nerve
nervous
net
network
never
nevertheless
new
newly
news
news agency
newscaster
newspaper
next
nice
night
nightmare
nine
nineteen
nineteenth
ninetieth
ninety
ninth
no
no one
nobody
nod
noise
none
nor
normal

normally
north
northeast
northern
northwest
nose
not
note
noted
nothing
notice
notion
novel
November
now
nowhere
nuclear
number
numerous
nurse
object
objective
observe
observer
obtain
obvious
obviously
occasion
occasional
occupation
occupy
occur
ocean
o'clock
October
odd
of
of course
off
offense
offensive
offer
offering
office
officer
official
often
oh
oil
okay
old
Olympic
on
once
one
one's
online
only
onto
open
opening
opera
operate
operation

operator
opinion
opponent
opportunity
oppose
opposed
opposite
opposition
opt
optimistic
option
or
orange
order
ordinary
organization
organize
organized
organizer
origin
original
originally
other
otherwise
ought
our
ourselves
out
outcome
outline
output
outside
outstanding
over
overall
overcome
overnight
overseas
overwhelming
owe
own
owner
ownership
pace
pack
package
pact
page
pain
painful
paint
painting
pair
palace
pale
pan
panel
panic
paper
parent
park
parliament
parliamentary
part
participate
particular
particularly
partly
partner
partnership
party
pass
passage
passenger
passion
past
path
patient
pattern
pause
pay
payment
peace
peaceful
peak
peer
peg
pen
penalty
penny
pension
people
pepper
per
percent
percentage
perfect
perfectly
perform
performance
perhaps
period
permanent
permission
permit
person
personal
personality
personally
personnel
perspective
persuade
pet
phase
philosophy
phone
photo
photograph
photographer
phrase
physical
pick
pickup
picture
piece
pile
pill
pilot
pin
pink
pipe
pit
pitch
place
plain
plan
plane
planet
planning
plant
plastic
plate
platform
play
player
playoff
pleasant
please
pleased
pleasure
pledge
plenty
plot
plunge
plus
pocket
poem
poet
poetry
point
point of view
pole
police
police officer
policeman
policy
political
politician
politics
poll
pollution
pool
poor
pop
popular
population
port
portrait
pose
position
positive
possibility
possible
possibly
post
pot
potato
potential
pound
pour
poverty
power
powerful
pp.
practical
practice
praise
precisely
predict
prefer
pregnancy
pregnant
premier
premium
preparation
prepare
prepared
presence
present
preserve
presidency
president
presidential
press
pressure
presumably
pretty
prevent
previous
previously
price
pride
priest
primary
prime
prime minister
prince
princess
principal
principle
print
prior
priority
prison
prisoner
private
privatize
prize
probably
problem
procedure
proceed
process
produce
producer
product
production
profession
professional
professor
profile
profit
program
progress
project
prominent
promise
promote
promotion
prompt
proof
proper
properly
property
proportion
proposal
propose
prosecution
prospect
protect
protection
protein
protest
proud
prove
provide
province
provision
provoke
psychological
pub
public
publication
publicity
publish
publisher
publishing
pull
pump
punch
pupil
purchase
pure
purple
purpose
pursue
push
put
qualified
qualify
quality
quantity
quarter
queen
question
quick
quiet
quite
quote
race
racial
racing
radical
radio
rage
raid
rail
railway
rain
raise

rally
range
rank
rape
rapid
rare
rarely
rate
rather
rating
raw
ray
reach
react
reaction
read
reader
reading
ready
real
real estate
reality
realize
really
rear
reason
reasonable
rebel
recall
receive
recent
recently
recession
reckon
recognition
recognize
recommend
recommendation
record
recording
recover
recovery
recruit
red
reduce
reduction
reel
refer
reference
referendum
reflect
reform
refugee
refuse
regard
regime
region
regional
register
regret
regular
regulation
regulator
reject
relate
related
relation
relationship
relative
relatively
relax
release
reliable
relief
religion
religious
reluctant
rely
remain
remaining
remark
remarkable
remember
remind
remote
remove
renew
rent
repair
repeat
replace
replacement
reply
report
reporter
reporting
represent
representative
republic
republican
reputation
request
require
requirement
rescue
research
reserve
resident
resign
resignation
resist
resistance
resolution
resolve
resort
resource
respect
respond
response
responsibility
responsible
rest
restaurant
restore
restriction
result
resume
retail
retain
retire
retirement
retreat
return
reveal
revenue
reverse
review
revolution
revolutionary
reward
rhythm
rice
rich
rid
ride
rider
right
right-wing
ring
riot
rise
risk
rival
river
road
rock
rocket
role
roll
Roman
romantic
roof
room
root
rose
rough
round
route
routine
row
royal
rugby
ruin
rule
ruling
rumor
run
runner
running
rural
rush
sack
sacrifice
sad
safe
safety
sail
saint
sake
salary
sale
salt
same
sample
sanction
sand
satellite
satisfied
Saturday
sauce
save
saving
say
scale
scandal
scene
schedule
scheme
school
science
scientific
scientist
score
scream
screen
script
sea
seal
search
season
seat
second
secret
secretary
Secretary of State
secretary-general
section
sector
secure
security
Security Council
see
seed
seek
seem
segment
seize
select
selection
self
sell
Senate
senator
send
senior
sense
sensible
sensitive
sentence
separate
September
series
serious
seriously
servant
serve
service
session
set
settle
settlement
setup
seven
seventeen
seventeenth
seventh
seventieth
seventy
several
severe
sex
sexual
shade
shadow
shake
shall
shame
shape
shaped
share
shareholder
sharp
she
shed
sheet
shell
shelter
shift
ship
shirt
shock
shoe
shoot
shop
shopping
shore
short
shortage
shortly
short-term
shot
should
shoulder
shout
show
shut
sick
side
sigh
sight
sign
signal
significant
silence
silent
silver
similar
simple
simply
since

sing
singer
single
sink
sir
sister
sit
site
situation
six
sixteen
sixteenth
sixth
sixtieth
sixty
size
ski
skill
skin
sky
sleep
slice
slide
slight
slightly
slim
slip
slow
small
smart
smash
smell
smile
smoke
smoking
smooth
snap
snow
so
so-called
soccer
social
socialist
society
soft
software
soil
soldier
solicitor
solid
solution
solve
some
somebody
somehow
someone
something
sometimes
somewhat
somewhere
son
song
soon
sophisticated
sorry
sort
soul
sound
source
south
southeast
southern
southwest
space
spare
spark
speak
speaker
speaking
special
specialist
specialize
species
specific
specifically
spectacular
speculate
speech
speed
spell
spend
spin
spirit
spiritual
spite
split
spokesman
spokeswoman
sponsor
sport
spot
spray
spread
spring
spur
squad
square
squeeze
stable
stadium
staff
stage
stake
stamp
stand
standard
star
stare
start
state
State Department
statement
station
statistic
status
stay
steady
steal
steam
steel
stem
step
sterling
stick
still
stimulate
stir
stock
stock exchange
stock market
stomach
stone
stop
store
storm
story
straight
strain
strange
strategic
strategy
stream
street
strength
strengthen
stress
stretch
strict
strike
striking
string
strip
stroke
strong
structure
struggle
student
studio
study
stuff
stupid
style
subject
subsequent
subsidy
substance
substantial
substitute
succeed
success
successful
such
sudden
suddenly
suffer
sufficient
sugar
suggest
suggestion
suicide
suit
suitable
sum
summer
summit
sun
Sunday
super
superb
superior
supply
support
supporter
suppose
supposed
supreme
sure
surely
surface
surgery
surplus
surprise
surprised
surprising
surrender
surround
survey
survival
survive
suspect
suspend
suspicion
sustain
sweep
sweet
swim
swing
switch
symbol
sympathy
symptom
system
table
tackle
tactic
tail
take
takeover
tale
talent
talk
tall
tank
tap
tape
target
task
taste
tax
tea
teach
teacher
teaching
team
tear
technical
technique
technology
teenager
telephone
television
tell
temperature
temple
temporary
ten
tend
tendency
tennis
tension
tenth
term
terrible
territory
terror
terrorism
terrorist
test
testing
text
than
thank
that
the
theater
their
them
theme
themselves
then
theory
therapy
there
therefore
these
they
thick
thin
thing
think
thinking
third
Third World
thirteen
thirteenth
thirtieth
thirty
this
thorough
those
though
thought
thousand
threat
threaten
threatening
three
throat
through
throughout

throw
Thursday
thus
ticket
tide
tie
tight
till
time
tiny
tip
tired
tissue
title
to
today
together
tomorrow
ton
tone
tonight
too
tool
tooth
top
torture
total
touch
tough
tour
tourist
tournament
toward
tower
town
toy
trace
track
trade
trader
tradition
traditional
traffic
tragedy
trail
train
transaction
transfer
transform
transition
transport
transportation
trap
travel
traveler
treasury
treat
treatment
treaty
tree
tremendous
trend
trial
trick
trigger
trip
triumph
troop
trouble
truck
true
truly
trust
truth
try
tube
Tuesday
tune
tunnel
turn
TV
twelfth
twelve
twentieth
twenty
twice
twin
twist
two
type
typical
ultimate
ultimately
U.N.
unable
uncle
under
underground
undermine
understand
understanding
unemployment
unexpected
unfair
unfortunately
unhappy
unidentified
uniform
union
unique
unit
united
United Nations
unity
universe
university
unknown
unless
unlike
unlikely
until
unusual
up
upon
upper
upset
urban
urge
urgent
us
use
used
useful
user
usual
usually
valley
valuable
value
van
variety
various
vary
vast
vegetable
vehicle
venture
venue
verdict
version
very
vessel
veteran
via
vice
victim
victimize
victory
video
view
village
violate
violence
violent
virtually
virus
visible
vision
visit
visitor
vital
vitamin
voice
volume
voluntary
volunteer
vote
voter
vulnerable
wage
wait
wake
walk
wall
Wall Street
want
war
warm
warn
warning
wash
waste
watch
water
wave
way
we
weak
weaken
wealth
weapon
wear
weather
web
website
wedding
Wednesday
week
weekend
weekly
weigh
weight
welcome
welfare
well
well-known
west
western
wet
what
whatever
wheel
when
whenever
where
whereas
whether
which
while
whilst
whip
whisper
white
White House
who
whole
whom
whose
why
wicket
wide
widespread
wife
wild
will
willing
win
wind
window
wine
wing
winner
winning
winter
wipe
wire
wireless
wise
wish
with
withdraw
withdrawal
within
without
witness
woman
wonder
wonderful
wood
wooden
word
work
worker
working
world
world war
worldwide
worried
worry
worth
would
wound
wrap
write
writer
writing
written
wrong
yacht
yard
yeah
year
yellow
yen
yes
yesterday
yet
yield
you
young
youngster
your
yours
yourself
youth
zone

Academic Word List

This list contains the head words of the families in the Academic Word List. The numbers indicate the sublist of the Academic Word List, with Sublist 1 containing the most frequent words, Sublist 2 the next most frequent and so on. For example, *abandon* and its family members are in Sublist 8 of the Academic Word List.

Word	Sublist
abandon	8
abstract	6
academy	5
access	4
accommodate	9
accompany	8
accumulate	8
accurate	6
achieve	2
acknowledge	6
acquire	2
adapt	7
adequate	4
adjacent	10
adjust	5
administrate	2
adult	7
advocate	7
affect	2
aggregate	6
aid	7
albeit	10
allocate	6
alter	5
alternative	3
ambiguous	8
amend	5
analogy	9
analyze	1
annual	4
anticipate	9
apparent	4
append	8
appreciate	8
approach	1
appropriate	2
approximate	4
arbitrary	8
area	1
aspect	2
assemble	10
assess	1
assign	6
assist	2
assume	1
assure	9
attach	6
attain	9
attitude	4
attribute	4
author	6
authority	1
automate	8
available	1
aware	5
behalf	9
benefit	1
bias	8
bond	6
brief	6
bulk	9
capable	6
capacity	5
category	2
cease	9
challenge	5
channel	7
chapter	2
chart	8
chemical	7
circumstance	3
cite	6
civil	4
clarify	8
classic	7
clause	5
code	4
coherent	9
coincide	9
collapse	10
colleague	10
commence	9
comment	3
commission	2
commit	4
commodity	8
communicate	4
community	2
compatible	9
compensate	3
compile	10
complement	8
complex	2
component	3
compound	5
comprehensive	7
comprise	7
compute	2
conceive	10
concentrate	4
concept	1
conclude	2
concurrent	9
conduct	2
confer	4
confine	9
confirm	7
conflict	5
conform	8
consent	3
consequent	2
considerable	3
consist	1
constant	3
constitute	1
constrain	3
construct	2
consult	5
consume	2
contact	5
contemporary	8
context	1
contract	1
contradict	8
contrary	7
contrast	4
contribute	3
controversy	9
convene	3
converse	9
convert	7
convince	10
cooperate	6
coordinate	3
core	3
corporate	3
correspond	3
couple	7
create	1
credit	2
criteria	3
crucial	8
culture	2
currency	8
cycle	4
data	1
debate	4
decade	7
decline	5
deduce	3
define	1
definite	7
demonstrate	3
denote	8
deny	7
depress	10
derive	1
design	2
despite	4
detect	8
deviate	8
device	9
devote	9
differentiate	7
dimension	4
diminish	9
discrete	5
discriminate	6
displace	8
display	6
dispose	7
distinct	2
distort	9
distribute	1
diverse	6
document	3
domain	6
domestic	4
dominate	3
draft	5
drama	8
duration	9
dynamic	7
economy	1

edit	6	flexible	6	infer	7	logic	5
element	2	fluctuate	8	infrastructure	8	maintain	2
eliminate	7	focus	2	inherent	9	major	1
emerge	4	format	9	inhibit	6	manipulate	8
emphasis	3	formula	1	initial	3	manual	9
empirical	7	forthcoming	10	initiate	6	margin	5
enable	5	foundation	7	injure	2	mature	9
encounter	10	found	9	innovate	7	maximize	3
energy	5	framework	3	input	6	mechanism	4
enforce	5	function	1	insert	7	media	7
enhance	6	fund	3	insight	9	mediate	9
enormous	10	fundamental	5	inspect	8	medical	5
ensure	3	furthermore	6	instance	3	medium	9
entity	5	gender	6	institute	2	mental	5
environment	1	generate	5	instruct	6	method	1
equate	2	generation	5	integral	9	migrate	6
equip	7	globe	7	integrate	4	military	9
equivalent	5	goal	4	integrity	10	minimal	9
erode	9	grade	7	intelligence	6	minimize	8
error	4	grant	4	intense	8	minimum	6
establish	1	guarantee	7	interact	3	ministry	6
estate	6	guideline	8	intermediate	9	minor	3
estimate	1	hence	4	internal	4	mode	7
ethic	9	hierarchy	7	interpret	1	modify	5
ethnic	4	highlight	8	interval	6	monitor	5
evaluate	2	hypothesis	4	intervene	7	motive	6
eventual	8	identical	7	intrinsic	10	mutual	9
evident	1	identify	1	invest	2	negate	3
evolve	5	ideology	7	investigate	4	network	5
exceed	6	ignorance	6	invoke	10	neutral	6
exclude	3	illustrate	3	involve	1	nevertheless	6
exhibit	8	image	5	isolate	7	nonetheless	10
expand	5	immigrate	3	issue	1	norm	9
expert	6	impact	2	item	2	normal	2
explicit	6	implement	4	job	4	notion	5
exploit	8	implicate	4	journal	2	notwithstanding	10
export	1	implicit	8	justify	3	nuclear	8
expose	5	imply	3	label	4	objective	5
external	5	impose	4	labor	1	obtain	2
extract	7	incentive	6	layer	3	obvious	4
facilitate	5	incidence	6	lecture	6	occupy	4
factor	1	incline	10	legal	1	occur	1
feature	2	income	1	legislate	1	odd	10
federal	6	incorporate	6	levy	10	offset	8
fee	6	index	6	liberal	5	ongoing	10
file	7	indicate	1	license	5	option	4
final	2	individual	1	likewise	10	orient	5
finance	1	induce	8	link	3	outcome	3
finite	7	inevitable	8	locate	3	output	4

overall	4	protocol	9	scheme	3	team	9
overlap	9	psychology	5	scope	6	technical	3
overseas	6	publication	7	section	1	technique	3
panel	10	publish	3	sector	1	technology	3
paradigm	7	purchase	2	secure	2	temporary	9
paragraph	8	pursue	5	seek	2	tense	8
parallel	4	qualitative	9	select	2	terminate	8
parameter	4	quote	7	sequence	3	text	2
participate	2	radical	8	series	4	theme	8
partner	3	random	8	sex	3	theory	1
passive	9	range	2	shift	3	thereby	8
perceive	2	ratio	5	significant	1	thesis	7
percent	1	rational	6	similar	1	topic	7
period	1	react	3	simulate	7	trace	6
persist	10	recover	6	site	2	tradition	2
perspective	5	refine	9	so-called	10	transfer	2
phase	4	regime	4	sole	7	transform	6
phenomenon	7	region	2	somewhat	7	transit	5
philosophy	3	register	3	source	1	transmit	7
physical	3	regulate	2	specific	1	transport	6
plus	8	reinforce	8	specify	3	trend	5
policy	1	reject	5	sphere	9	trigger	9
portion	9	relax	9	stable	5	ultimate	7
pose	10	release	7	statistic	4	undergo	10
positive	2	relevant	2	status	4	underlie	6
potential	2	reluctance	10	straightforward	10	undertake	4
practitioner	8	rely	3	strategy	2	uniform	8
precede	6	remove	3	stress	4	unify	9
precise	5	require	1	structure	1	unique	7
predict	4	research	1	style	5	utilize	6
predominant	8	reside	2	submit	7	valid	3
preliminary	9	resolve	4	subordinate	9	vary	1
presume	6	resource	2	subsequent	4	vehicle	8
previous	2	respond	1	subsidy	6	version	5
primary	2	restore	8	substitute	5	via	8
prime	5	restrain	9	successor	7	violate	9
principal	4	restrict	2	sufficient	3	virtual	8
principle	1	retain	4	sum	4	visible	7
prior	4	reveal	6	summary	4	vision	9
priority	7	revenue	5	supplement	9	visual	8
proceed	1	reverse	7	survey	2	volume	3
process	1	revise	8	survive	7	voluntary	7
professional	4	revolution	9	suspend	9	welfare	5
prohibit	7	rigid	9	sustain	5	whereas	5
project	4	role	1	symbol	5	whereby	10
promote	4	route	9	tape	6	widespread	8
proportion	3	scenario	9	target	5		
prospect	8	schedule	8	task	3		

USA States, Abbreviations, and Capitals

State	Capital
Alabama (AL)	Montgomery
Alaska (AK)	Juneau
Arizona (AZ)	Phoenix
Arkansas (AR)	Little Rock
California (CA)	Sacramento
Colorado (CO)	Denver
Connecticut (CT)	Hartford
Delaware (DE)	Dover
Florida (FL)	Tallahassee
Georgia (GA)	Atlanta
Hawaii (HI)	Honolulu
Idaho (ID)	Boise
Illinois (IL)	Springfield
Indiana (IN)	Indianapolis
Iowa (IA)	Des Moines
Kansas (KS)	Topeka
Kentucky (KY)	Frankfort
Louisiana (LA)	Baton Rouge
Maine (ME)	Augusta
Maryland (MD)	Annapolis
Massachusetts (MA)	Boston
Michigan (MI)	Lansing
Minnesota (MN)	Saint Paul
Mississippi (MS)	Jackson
Missouri (MO)	Jefferson City
Montana (MT)	Helena
Nebraska (NE)	Lincoln
Nevada (NV)	Carson City
New Hampshire (NH)	Concord
New Jersey (NJ)	Trenton
New Mexico (NM)	Santa Fe
New York (NY)	Albany
North Carolina (NC)	Raleigh
North Dakota (ND)	Bismarck
Ohio (OH)	Columbus
Oklahoma (OK)	Oklahoma City
Oregon (OR)	Salem
Pennsylvania (PA)	Harrisburg
Rhode Island (RI)	Providence
South Carolina (SC)	Columbia
South Dakota (SD)	Pierre
Tennessee (TN)	Nashville
Texas (TX)	Austin
Utah (UT)	Salt Lake City
Vermont (VT)	Montpelier
Virginia (VA)	Richmond
Washington (WA)	Olympia
West Virginia (WV)	Charleston
Wisconsin (WI)	Madison
Wyoming (WY)	Cheyenne
Capital of the United States of America (USA)	
District of Columbia (DC)	Washington (commonly abbreviated: Washington, D.C.)

Geographical Places and Nationalities

This list shows the spelling and pronunciation of geographical names. If a country has different words for the country, adjective, and person, these are all shown. Inclusion in this list does not imply status as a sovereign nation.

Af|ghan|i|stan /æfgænɪstæn/; Af|ghan, Af|ghani /æfgæn/, /æfgæni, -gani/

Af|ri|ca /æfrɪkə/; Af|ri|can /æfrɪkən/

Al|ba|nia /ælbeɪniə/; Al|ba|ni|an /ælbeɪniən/

Al|ge|ria /ældʒɪəriə/; Al|ge|ri|an /ældʒɪəriən/

An|dor|ra /ændɔrə/; An|dor|ran /ændɔrən/

An|go|la /æŋgoʊlə/; An|go|lan /æŋgoʊlən/

Ant|arc|ti|ca /æntarktɪkə, -artɪ-/; Ant|arc|tic /æntarktɪk, -artɪk/

An|ti|gua and Bar|bu|da /æntigə ən barbudə/; An|ti|guan, Bar|bu|dan /æntigən/, /barbudən/

(the) Arc|tic Ocean /(ði) arktɪk oʊʃən, artɪk/; Arc|tic /arktɪk, artɪk/

Ar|gen|ti|na /arjəntinə/; Ar|gen|tine, Ar|gen|tin|ian, or Ar|gen|tin|ean /arjəntin, -taɪn/, /arjəntɪniən/

Ar|me|nia /arminiə/; Ar|me|nian /arminiən/

A|sia /eɪʒə/; A|sian /eɪʒən/

(the) At|lan|tic Ocean /(ði) ætlæntɪk oʊʃən/

Aus|tra|lia /ɔstreɪlyə/; Aus|tra|lian /ɔstreɪlyən/

Aus|tria /ɔstriə/; Aus|tri|an /ɔstriən/

Azer|bai|jan /æzərbaɪdʒan, azər-/; Azer|bai|ja|ni, Azeri /æzərbaɪdʒani, azər-/, /əzɛri/

(the) Ba|ha|mas /(ðə) bəhaməz/; Ba|ha|mian /bəheɪmiən, -ha-/

Bah|rain /bareɪn/; Bah|raini /bareɪni/

Ban|gla|desh /baŋglədɛʃ, bæŋ-/; Ban|gla|deshi/baŋglədɛʃi, bæŋ-/

Bar|ba|dos /barbeɪdoʊs/; Bar|ba|di|an /barbeɪdiən/

Be|la|rus /bɛlərus, byɛl-/; Be|la|ru|si|an /bɛlərʌʃən, byɛl-/

Bel|gium /bɛldʒəm/; Bel|gian /bɛldʒən/

Be|lize /bəliz/; Be|liz|ean /bəliziən/

Be|nin /bənin/; Be|ni|nese /benɪniz/

Bhu|tan /butan, -tæn/; Bhu|tani, Bhu|ta|nese /butani, -tæni/, /butᵊniz/

Bo|liv|ia /bəlɪviə/; Bo|liv|i|an /bəlɪviən/

Bos|nia and Her|ze|go|vi|na /bɒzniə ən hɛrtsəgoʊvinə/; Bos|ni|an, Her|ze|go|vi|ni|an /bɒzniən/, /hɛrtsəgoʊviniən/

Bo|tswa|na /bɒtswanə/; Ba|tswa|nan/bɒtswanən/; Mo|tswan|a (person), Ba|tswa|na (people) /mɒtswanə/, /batswanə/

Bra|zil /brəzɪl/; Bra|zil|ian /brəzɪlyən/

Bru|nei Da|rus|sa|lam /brunaɪ darusaləm/; Bru|nei, Bru|nei|an /brunaɪ/, /brunaɪən/

Bul|gar|ia /bʌlgɛəriə/; Bul|gar|i|an /bʌlgɛəriən/

Bur|ki|na Fa|so /bərkinə fasoʊ/; Bur|kin|abe, Bur|kin|ese /bɜrkɪnabeɪ/, /bɜrkɪniz/

Bur|ma—See Myanmar /bɜrmə/; Bur|mese—/bɜrmiz/

Bu|run|di /burʊndi/; Bu|run|di|an /burʊndiən/

Cam|bo|dia /kæmboʊdiə/; Cam|bo|di|an /kæmboʊdiən

Cam|er|oon /kæmərun/; Cam|er|oo|ni|an /kæməruniən/

Can|a|da /kænədə/; Ca|na|di|an /kəneɪdiən/

Cape Verde /keɪp vɜrd/; Cape Verd|ean /keɪp vɜrdiən/

Cen|tral Af|ri|can Re|pub|lic /sɛntrəl æfrɪkən rɪpʌblɪk/; Cen|tral Af|ri|can /sɛntrəl æfrɪkən/

Chad /tʃæd/; Chad|ian /tʃædiən/

Chi|le /tʃɪli, -leɪ/; Chil|ean /tʃɪliən, tʃɪleɪ-/

Chi|na /tʃaɪnə/; Chi|nese /tʃaɪniz/

Co|lom|bia /kəlʌmbiə/; Co|lom|bi|an /kəlʌmbiən/

Com|o|ros /kɒmərouz/; Com|or|an /kɒmərən/

Cos|ta Ri|ca /kɒstə rikə/; Cos|ta Ri|can /kɒstə rikən/

Côte d'Ivoire /koʊt divwar/; Ivoir|i|an /ivwariən/

Cro|a|tia /kroʊeɪʃə/; Cro|a|tian /kroʊeɪʃən/

Cu|ba /kyubə/; Cu|ban /kyubən/

Cy|prus /saɪprəs/; Cyp|riot /sɪpriət/

(the) Czech Re|pub|lic /(ðə) tʃɛk rɪpʌblɪk/; Czech /tʃɛk/

Dem|o|crat|ic Re|pub|lic of the Con|go, or (the) Con|go /dɛməkrætɪk rɪpʌblɪk əv ðə kɒŋgoʊ/, /(ðə) kɒŋgoʊ/; Con|go|lese /kɒŋgəliz, -lis/

Den|mark /dɛnmark/; Dan|ish, Dane /deɪnɪʃ/, /deɪn/

Dji|bou|ti /dʒɪbuti/; Dji|bou|tian /dʒɪbutiən/

Dom|i|ni|ca /dɒmɪnikə, dəmɪnɪkə/; Do|mi|ni|can /dɒmɪnikən/

(the) Do|min|i|can Re|pub|lic /(ðə) dəmɪnɪkən rɪpʌblɪk; Do|mi|ni|can /dəmɪnɪkən/

East Ti|mor /ist timɔr/; East Ti|mor|ese /ist timɔriz/

Ec|ua|dor /ɛkwədɔr/; Ec|ua|dor|ian /ɛkwədɔriən/

Egypt /idʒɪpt/; Egyp|tian /ɪdʒɪpʃən/

El Sal|va|dor /ɛl sælvədɔr/; Sal|va|do|ran, Sal|va|do|rean /sælvədɔrən/, /sælvədɔriən/

Eng|land /ɪŋglənd/; Eng|lish /ɪŋglɪʃ/

Equi|to|ri|al Guinea /ɛkwɪtɔriəl gɪni/; Equi|to|ri|al Guin|ean, Equi|to|guinean /ɛkwɪtɔriəl gɪniən/, /ɛkwɪtoʊgɪniən/

Er|i|trea /ɛrɪtriə/; Er|i|tre|an /ɛrɪtriən/

Es|to|nia /ɛstoʊniə/; Es|to|ni|an /ɛstoʊniən/

Ethi|o|pia /iθioʊpiə/; Ethi|o|pi|an /iθioʊpiən/

Eu|rope /yʊərəp/; Eu|ro|pe|an /yʊərəpiən/

Fi|ji /fidʒi/; Fi|ji|an /fidʒiən, fiji-/

Fin|land /fɪnlənd/; Fin|nish, Finn, Fin|land|er /fɪnɪʃ/, /fɪn/, /fɪnləndər, -lændər/

France /fræns/; French /frɛntʃ/

Ga|bon /gaboʊn/; Gab|o|nese /gæbəniz/

(the) Gam|bia /(ðə) gæmbiə/; Gam|bi|an /gæmbiən/

Geor|gia /dʒɔrdʒə/; Geor|gian /dʒɔrdʒən/

Ger|ma|ny /dʒɜrməni/; Ger|man /dʒɜrmən/

Gha|na /ganə/; Gha|na|ian /ganiən, gəneɪən/

Greece /gris/; Greek /grik/

Gre|na|da /grɪneɪdə/; Gre|na|di|an /grɪneɪdiən/

Gua|te|ma|la /gwatəmalə/; Gua|te|ma|lan /gwatəmalən/

Guin|ea /gɪni/; Guin|ean /gɪniən/

Guin|ea-Bis|sau /gɪni bɪsaʊ/; Guin|ean /gɪniən/

Guy|ana /gaɪænə, -anə/; Guy|a|nese /gaɪəniz/

Hai|ti /heɪti/; Hai|tian /heɪʃən/

Hon|du|ras /hɒndʊərəs/; Hon|du|ran /hɒndʊərən/

Hun|ga|ry /hʌŋgəri/; Hun|gar|i|an /hʌŋgɛəriən/

Ice|land /aɪslənd/; Ice|lan|dic, Ice|land|er /aɪslændɪk/, /aɪsləndər, -lændər/

In|dia /ɪndiə/; In|di|an /ɪndiən/

(the) In|di|an Ocean /(ði) ɪndiən oʊʃən/

In|do|ne|sia /ɪndəniʒə/; In|do|ne|sian /ɪndəniʒən/

Iran /ɪran, ɪræn, aɪræn/; Ira|ni|an, Iran|i /ɪreɪniən, ɪra-, aɪreɪ-/, /ɪrani/

I|raq /ɪræk, ɪrak/; I|raq|i /ɪræki, ɪraki/

Ire|land /aɪərlənd/; Ir|ish /aɪrɪʃ/

Is|ra|el /ɪzriəl, -reɪəl/; Is|rae|li /ɪzreɪli/

It|a|ly /ɪtəli/; Ital|ian /ɪtælyən/

Ja|mai|ca /dʒəmeɪkə/; Ja|mai|can /dʒəmeɪkən/

Ja|pan /dʒəpæn/; Jap|a|nese /dʒæpəniz/

Jor|dan /dʒɔrdən/; Jor|da|ni|an /dʒɔrdeɪniən/

Ka|zakh|stan /kazakstan, -stæn/; Ka|zakh|stan|i, Ka|zakh /kazakstani, -stæni/, /kazak, kəzæk/

Ken|ya /kɛnyə, kin-/; Ken|yan /kɛnyən, kin-/

Ki|ri|bati /kɪərəbati, -bæs/; I-Ki|ri|bati /i kɪərəbati, -bæs/

Ko|rea, South Ko|rea, North Ko|rea /kəriə, kɔ-/, /soʊθ kəriə, kɔ-/, /nɔrθ kəriə, kɔ-/; Ko|rean /kəriən, kɔ-/, /soʊθ kəriən, kɔ-/, /nɔrθ kəriən, kɔ/

Ku|wait /kuweɪt/; Ku|wai|ti /kuweɪti/

Kyr|gyz|stan /kɪərgɪstan, -stæn/; Kyr|gyz|sta|ni /kɪərgɪstani, -stæni/

Laos /laoʊs, laʊs/; Lao, Lao|tian /laoʊ, laʊ/, /leɪoʊʃən/

Lat|via /lætviə, lat-/; Lat|vi|an /lætviən, lat-/

Leb|a|non /lɛbənən, -nɒn/; Leb|a|nese /lɛbəniz/

Le|so|tho /ləsoʊtoʊ, -sutu/ So|tho, Mo|so|tho (person), Ba|so|tho (people) /soʊtoʊ, sutu/, /məsoʊtoʊ, -sutu/, /basoʊtoʊ, -sutu/

Li|be|ria /laɪbɪəriə/; Li|be|ri|an /laɪbɪəriən/

Lib|ya /lɪbiə/; Lib|y|an /lɪbiən/

Liech|ten|stein /lɪktənstaɪn/; Liech|ten|stein, Liech|ten|stein|er /lɪktənstaɪn/, /lɪktənstaɪnər/

Lith|u|a|nia /lɪθueɪniə/; Lith|u|a|ni|an /lɪθueɪniən/

Lux|em|bourg /lʌksəmbɜrg/; Lux|em|bourger, |/lʌksəmbɜrgər/

Mac|e|do|nia /mæsɪdoʊniə/; Mac|e|do|ni|an /mæsɪdoʊniən/

Mad|a|gas|car /mædəgæskər/; Mad|a|gas|can, Mala|gasy /mædəgæskən/, /mæləgæsi/

Ma|la|wi /məlawi/; Ma|la|wi|an /məlawiən/

Ma|lay|sia /məleɪʒə/; Ma|lay|sian /məleɪʒən/

Mal|dives /mɔldivz, -daɪvz/; Mal|div|ian /mɔldɪviən/

Ma|li /mali/; Ma|lian /maliən/

Mal|ta /mɔltə/; Mal|tese /mɔltiz/

(the) Mar|shall Is|lands /(ðə) marʃəl aɪləndz/; Mar|shall|ese /marʃəliz/

Mau|ri|ta|nia /mɔrɪteɪniə/; Mau|ri|ta|ni|an /mɔrɪteɪniən/

Mau|ri|ti|us /mɔrɪʃəs/; Mau|ri|tian /mɔrɪʃən/

Mex|i|co /mɛksɪkoʊ/; Mex|i|can /mɛksɪkən/

Mi|cro|ne|sia /maɪkrəniʒə/; Mi|cro|ne|sian /maɪkrəniʒən/

Mol|do|va /mɔldoʊvə/; Mol|do|van /mɔldoʊvən/

Mo|na|co /mɒnəkoʊ/; Mo|na|can, Mon|e|gasque /mɒnəkən/, /mɒnɪgæsk/

Mon|go|lia /mɒŋgoʊliə/; Mon|go|li|an /mɒŋgoʊliən/

Mo|roc|co /mərɒkoʊ/; Mo|roc|can /mərɒkən/

Mo|zam|bique /moʊzæmbik, -zəm-/; Mo|zam|bi|can /moʊzæmbikən, -zəm-/

Myan|mar (Burma) /myanmar (bɜrmə)/; Bur|mese /bərmiz/

Na|mib|ia /nəmɪbiə/; Na|mib|ian /nəmɪbiən/

Na|u|ru /nauru/; Na|u|ru|an /nauruən/

Ne|pal /nəpɔl/; Nep|a|lese /nɛpəliz/

(the) Neth|er|lands /(ðə) nɛðərləndz/; Dutch /dʌtʃ/

New Zea|land /nu zilənd/; New Zea|land, New Zea|land|er /nu zilənd/, /nu ziləndər/

Nic|a|ra|gua /nɪkəragwə/; Nic|a|ra|guan /nɪkəragwən/

Ni|ger /naɪdʒər, niʒɛər/; Ni|ge|rien, Ni|ger|ois /naɪdʒɪəriən, niʒeryen/, /niʒɛrwa/

Ni|ge|ria /naɪdʒɪəriə/; Ni|ge|ri|an /naɪdʒɪəriən/

Nor|way /nɔrweɪ/; Nor|we|gian /nɔrwidʒən/

Oman /oʊman/; Omani /oʊmani/

(the) Pa|cif|ic Ocean /(ðə) pəsɪfɪk oʊʃən/

Pa|ki|stan /pækɪstæn, pakɪstan/; Pa|ki|sta|ni /pækɪstæni, pakɪstani/

Pa|lau /palaʊ, pə-/; Pa|lau|an /palaʊən, pə-/

Pan|a|ma /pænəma, -mɔ/; Pan|a|ma|ni|an /pænəmeɪniən/

Pap|ua New Guin|ea /pæpyuə nu gɪni, papuə/; Pa|p|ua New Guin|ean, Pap|uan /pæpyuə nu gɪniən, papuə/, pæpyuən, papuən/

Par|a|guay /pærəgwaɪ, -gweɪ/; Par|a|guay|an /pærəgwaɪən, -gweɪən/

Pe|ru /pəru/; Pe|ru|vi|an /pəruviən/

(the) Phil|ip|pines /(ðə) fɪlɪpinz/; Phil|ip|pine, Fi|li|pi|no, Fi|li|pi|na /fɪlɪpin/, /fɪlɪpinoʊ/, /fɪlɪpinə/

Po|land /poʊlənd/; Po|lish, Pole /poʊlɪʃ/, /poʊl/

Por|tu|gal /pɔrchəgəl/; Por|tu|guese /pɔrchəgiz/

Qa|tar /kətɑr/; Qa|tari /kətɑri/

Ro|ma|nia /roʊmeɪniə/; Ro|ma|nian /roʊmeɪniən/

Rus|sia /rʌʃə/; Rus|sian /rʌʃən/

Rwan|da /ruɑndə/; Rwan|dan /ruɑndən/

Saint Kitts–Ne|vis /seɪnt kɪts nivɪs/; Kit|ti|tian, Ne|vis|ian /kɪtɪʃən/, /nɪvɪʒən/

Saint Lu|cia /seɪnt luʃə/; Saint Lu|cian /seɪnt luʃən/

Saint Vin|cent and the Gren|a|dines /seɪnt vɪnsənt ən ðə grɛnədinz/; Saint Vin|cen|tian, Vin|cen|tian /seɪnt vɪnsɛnʃən/, /vɪnsɛnʃən/

Sa|moa /səmoʊə/; Sa|mo|an /səmoʊən/

San Ma|ri|no /sæn məriṉoʊ/; Sam|ma|ri|nese, San Ma|ri|nese /sæmmærɪniz/, /sæn mærɪniz/

São To|mé and Prin|ci|pe /soʊn tɔmeɪ ən prɪnsɪpi/; Sao To|me|an /soʊn tɔmeɪən/

Sau|di Ara|bia /soʊdi əreɪbiə/; Sau|di Ara|bi|an /soʊdi əreɪbiən/

Scot|land /skɒtlənd/; Scot|tish, Scot(s) /skɒtɪʃ/, /skɒts/

Sen|egal /sɛnɪgɔl, -gɑl/; Sen|e|gal|ese /sɛnɪgəliz/

Ser|bia and Mon|te|negro /sɜrbiə ən mɒntɪnegroʊ/ Ser|bi|an, Serb, Mon|te|ne|grin /sɜrbiən/, /sɜrb/, /mɒntɪnegrɪn/

(the) Sey|chelles /(ðə) seɪʃɛlz/; Sey|chel|lois /seɪʃɛlwɑ/

Sier|ra Le|one /siɛrə lioʊn/; Sier|ra Le|on|ean /siɛrə lioʊniən/

Sin|ga|pore /sɪŋəpɔr, sɪŋgə-/; Sin|ga|por|ean /sɪŋəpɔriən, sɪŋgə-/

Slo|va|kia /sloʊvɑkiə, -vækiə/; Slo|vak, Slo|va|ki|an /sloʊvæk/, /sloʊvɑkiən, -væk-/

Slo|ve|nia /sloʊviniə/; Slo|vene /sloʊvin/; Slo|ve|nian /sloʊviniən/

Sol|o|mon Is|lands /sɒləmən aɪləndz/; Sol|o|mon Is|land|er /sɒləmən aɪləndər/

So|ma|lia /səmɑliə, soʊ-/; So|ma|li, So|ma|lian /səmɑli, soʊ-/, /səmɑliən, soʊ-/

South Af|rica /soʊθ æfrɪkə/; South Af|ri|can /soʊθ æfrɪkən/

(the Re|pub|lic of) Spain (ðə rɪpʌblɪk əv) speɪn/; Span|ish, Span|iard /spænɪʃ/, /spænyərd/

Sri Lan|ka /sri lɑŋkə, ʃri/; Sri Lan|kan /sri lɑŋkən, ʃri/

Su|dan /sudæn, -dɑn/; Su|da|nese /sudᵊniz/

Su|ri|na|me /sʊərɪnɑm/; Su|ri|na|mer, Su|ri|na|mese / sʊərɪnɑmər/, /sʊərɪnəmiz/

Swa|zi|land /swɑzilænd/; Swazi /swɑzi/

Swe|den /swidᵊn/; Swe|dish, Swede /swidɪʃ/, /swid/

Swit|zer|land /swɪtsərlənd/; Swiss /swɪs/

Syr|ia /sɪəriə/; Syr|ian /sɪəriən/

Tai|wan /taɪwɑn/; Tai|wan|ese /taɪwɑniz/

Ta|jik|i|stan /tɑdʒɪkɪstæn, -stɑn/; Ta|jik|i|stan|i, Ta|jik /tɑdʒɪkɪstæni, -stɑni/, /tɑdʒɪk, -dʒik/

Tan|za|nia /tænzəniə/; Tan|za|nian /tænzəniən/

Thai|land /taɪlænd, -lənd/; Thai /taɪ/

To|go /toʊgoʊ/; To|go|lese /toʊgəliz/

Ton|ga /tɒŋgə/; Ton|gan /tɒŋgən/

Trin|i|dad and To|ba|go /trɪnɪdæd ən təbeɪgoʊ/; Trin|i|da|di|an, To|ba|go|ni|an /trɪnɪdeɪdiən/, /toʊbəgoʊniən/

Tu|ni|sia /tuniʒə/; Tu|ni|sian /tuniʒən/

Tur|key /tɜrki/; Turk|ish, Turk /tɜrkɪʃ/, /tɜrk/

Turk|men|i|stan /tɜrkmɛnɪstæn, -stɑn/; Turk|men /tɜrkmɛn, -mən/

Tu|va|lu /tuvɑlu, tuvəlu/; Tu|va|luan /tuvəluən/

Ugan|da /yugændə, ugɑn-/; Ugan|dan /yugændən, ugɑn-/

Ukraine /yukreɪn/; Ukrai|ni|an /yukreɪniən/

(the) Unit|ed Ar|ab Emir|ates /(ðə) yunaɪtɪd ærəb ɛmərɪts, -əreɪts/; Emir|ati /ɛmərɑti/

(the) Unit|ed King|dom of Great Brit|ain and North|ern Ire|land /(ðə) yunaɪtɪd kɪŋdəm əv greɪt brɪtᵊn ən nɔrðərn aɪərlənd/; Brit|ish /brɪtɪʃ/

(the) Unit|ed States of Amer|i|ca /(ðə) yunaɪtɪd steɪts əv əmɛrɪkə/; Amer|i|can /əmɛrɪkən/

Uru|guay /yʊərəgweɪ, -gwaɪ/; Uru|guay|an /yʊərəgweɪən, -gwaɪən/

Uz|bek|i|stan /ʊzbɛkɪstæn, -stɑn, uz-/; Uz|bek|i|stani,

Uz|bek /ʊzbɛkɪstæni, -stɑni, uz-/, /ʊzbɛk, uz-/

Va|nua|tu /vænwɑtu/; Ni-Va|nua|tu /ni vænwɑtu/

Vat|i|can City /vætɪkən sɪti/

Ven|e|zue|la /vɛnɪzweɪlə/; Ven|e|zue|lan /vɛnɪzweɪlən/

Vi|et|nam /viɛtnɑm, vyɛt-/; Vi|et|nam|ese /viɛtnəmiz, vyɛt-/

Wales /weɪlz/; Welsh /wɛlʃ/

Ye|men /yɛmən/; Ye|meni, Ye|men|ite /yɛməni/, /yɛmənaɪt/

Zam|bia /zæmbiə/; Zam|bi|an /zæmbiən/

Zim|ba|bwe /zɪmbɑbweɪ, -wi/; Zim|ba|bwe|an /zɪmbɑbweɪən, -wiən/

Credits

Illustrations

Richard Carbajal: pp. 41, 203, 344, 393, 423, 682, 726, 798, 1024, 1101, 1113, 1227 (bottom); © Richard Carbajal/illustrationOnLine.com
Ron Carboni: pp. 1155; © Ron Carboni/Anita Grien
Todd Daman: pp. 27, 95; © Todd Daman/illustrationOnLine.com
Dick Gage: pp. 81, 128, 348 (top), 587; © Dick Gage/illustrationOnLine.com
Patrick Gnan: pp. 53 (top), 365 (top) 602, 720, 764 (right), 951, 1162; © Patrick Gnan/illustrationOnLine.com
Sharon and Joel Harris: pp. 118, 119, 267, 299, 436, 505, 739, 936; © Sharon and Joel Harris/illustrationOnLine.com
Philip Howe: pp. 153, 194, 395, 728, 799, 979, 1258; © Philip Howe/illustrationOnLine.com
Robert Kayganich: pp. 85, 88, 108, 296, 348 (bottom), 354, 461, 474, 530, 696 (bottom), 1072, 1104, 1274; © Robert Kayganich/illustrationOnLine.com
Robert Kemp: pp. 233, 248, 349, 360, 488, 760; © Robert Kemp/illustrationOnLine.com
Stephen Peringer: pp. 196, 238, 293, 341, 352, 436, 468, 660; © Stephen Peringer/illustrationOnLine.com
Mark Ryan: pp. 1007, 1047, 1227 (top); © Mark Ryan/illustrationOnLine.com
Simon Shaw: pp. 105, 115, 355, 466, 643 (top), 894; © Simon Shaw/illustrationOnLine.com
Daniel M. Short: pp. 365; © Daniel M. Short
Gerard Taylor: pp. 24, 92, 402, 589, 1052, 1237, 1238; © Gerard Taylor/illustrationOnLine.com
Ralph Voltz: pp. 55, 87, 403, 438, 482, 544, 683, 689, 777, 956, 1030, 1044 (bottom), 1135; © Ralph Voltz/illustrationOnLine.com
Cam Wilson: pp. 242, 313, 364, 433, 446, 476, 491, 611, 624, 672, 917, 1045, 1047 (top), 1091; © Cam Wilson/illustrationOnLine.com

Photos

19: ImageState / Alamy; **58:** (right) © Burstein Collection/CORBIS, (left) © Archivo Iconografico, S.A./CORBIS; **65:** © Louie Psihoyos/CORBIS; **134:** AM Corporation / Alamy; **155:** Craig Lovell / Eagle Visions Photography / Alamy; **159:** (left) Phil Talbot / Alamy; **187:** © William Manning/Corbis; **192:** © Jonathan Blair/CORBIS; **199:** Holt Studios International Ltd / Alamy; **213:** © Royalty-Free/Corbis; **220:** Redferns Music Picture Library / Alamy; **239:** Imageshop / Alamy; **241:** ImageSource / Alamy; **253:** © Tim Wright/CORBIS; **261:** Blend Images / Alamy; **263:** (right) BananaStock / Alamy, (center) Kimball Hall / Alamy, (left) Digital Archive Japan / Alamy; **270:** © Bettmann/CORBIS; **300:** Dinodia Images / Alamy; **302:** BananaStock / Alamy; **307:** Frances Roberts / Alamy; **309:** Dinodia Images / Alamy; **325:** Owe Andersson / Alamy; **333:** © Alinari Archives/CORBIS; **338:** Adams Picture Library t/a apl / Alamy; **339:** Dynamic Graphics Group / Creatas / Alamy; **346:** David Butow/CORBIS SABA; **353:** David Turnley / Corbis; **372:** © Herbert Spichtinger/zefa/Corbis; **397:** © CORBIS; **425:** Pam Fraser / Alamy; **441:** Dennis MacDonald / Alamy; **442:** Bill Marsh Royalty Free Photography / Alamy; **458:** (top) © Jean Louis Atlan/Sygma/Corbis, (bottom) nagelestock.com / Alamy; **475:** Janine Wiedel Photolibrary / Alamy; **487:** Medioimages / Alamy; **503:** Image Source / Alamy; **524:** © Alexander Burkatovski/CORBIS; **541:** BananaStock / Alamy; **543:** Jeff Greenberg / Alamy; **550:** Bubbles Photolibrary / Alamy; **571:** (left) image100 / Alamy, (right top) Trevor Smithers ARPS / Alamy; **593:** © Alinari Archives/CORBIS; **614:** © CORBIS; **619:** © Bettmann/CORBIS; **621:** MONSERRATE J. SCHWARTZ / Alamy; **639:** Dynamic Graphics Group / IT Stock Free / Alamy; **661:** © Royalty-Free/Corbis; **667:** ImageState / Alamy; **713:** (right) Craig Lovell/ Eagle Visions Photography / Alamy; **715:** © NASA/Roger Ressmeyer/CORBIS; **718:** numb / Alamy; **725:** BananaStock / Alamy; **734:** (right) Comstock Images / Alamy; **812:** Nikreates / Alamy; **822:** (left) foodfolio / Alamy; **823:** (left) © Araldo de Luca/CORBIS; (center) © The Art Archive/Corbis; (right) © Bettmann/CORBIS ; **824:** Stockbyte Platinum / Alamy; **839:** © Royalty-Free/Corbis; **845:** oote boe / Alamy; **863:** © Bettmann/CORBIS; **865:** © Bettmann/CORBIS; **891:** © Bohemian Nomad Picturemakers/CORBIS; **896:** AM Corporation / Alamy; **901:** (left) nagelestock.com / Alamy, (right) © Gianni Dagli Orti/CORBIS; **938:** Brand X Pictures /

CREDITS

Alamy; **945**: Food Features / Alamy; **970**: PHOTOTAKE Inc. / Alamy; **1009**: ImageState / Alamy; **1012**: Stock Connection Distribution / Alamy; **1025**: © Mark Peterson/CORBIS; **1034**: Blend Images / Alamy; **1082**: AGStockUSA, Inc. / Alamy; **1084**: Jon Arnold Images / Alamy; **1127**: STOCK IMAGE/ PIXLAND / Alamy; **1130**: (top) © Kim Kulish/Corbis; **1132**: (top) Mark Hamilton / Alamy, (bottom, right) Rex Argent / Alamy, (bottom left) Leslie Garland Picture Library / Alamy; **1141**: North Wind Picture Archives / Alamy; **1153**: © Richard T. Nowitz/CORBIS; **1170**: © HASHIMOTO NOBORU/ CORBIS SYGMA; **1173**: © Bettmann/CORBIS; **1176**: Comstock Images / Alamy; **1183**: Digital Archive Japan / Alamy; **1200**: © Robert Galbraith/Reuters/Corbis; **1217**: Stockbyte Platinum / Alamy; **1228**: Bettmann/CORBIS; **1233**: © Stapleton Collection/CORBIS; **1243**: Purestock / Alamy; **1248**: (bottom) Stephen Frink Collection / Alamy; **1279**: John Sturrock / Alamy

Photos on the following pages are from JUPITER IMAGES. © 2006 Jupiter Images Corporation: 40, 89, 155, 181, 245, 262, 271, 301, 334, 343, 359, 422, 429, 432, 455, 549, 626, 643, 671, 685, 688, 692, 696 (top), 713 (left), 734 (left, center), 742, 764 (left), 766, 797, 802, 822 (right), 851, 924, 973, 984, 1039, 1044, 1046, 1060, 1128, 1169, 1217

Photos on the following pages are from IndexOpen. © 2006 IndexOpen: 52, (bottom), 159 (right), 169, 180, 218, 333, 421, 688, 703, 984, 1242, 1249

Words to Remember

Word: ____________________

Definition: ____________________

____

Sentence: ____________________

Word: ____________________

Definition: ____________________

____

Sentence: ____________________

Word: ____________________

Definition: ____________________

____

Sentence: ____________________

Word: ____________________

Definition: ____________________

____

Sentence: ____________________

Word: ____________________

Definition: ____________________

____

Sentence: ____________________

Words to Remember

Word: ______________________

Definition: ______________________

____

Sentence: ______________________

Word: ______________________

Definition: ______________________

____

Sentence: ______________________

Word: ______________________

Definition: ______________________

____

Sentence: ______________________

Word: ______________________

Definition: ______________________

____

Sentence: ______________________

Word: ______________________

Definition: ______________________

____

Sentence: ______________________

Words to Remember

Word: ______________________

Definition: ______________________________________

____

Sentence: _______________________________________

Word: ______________________

Definition: ______________________________________

____

Sentence: _______________________________________

Word: ______________________

Definition: ______________________________________

____

Sentence: _______________________________________

Word: ______________________

Definition: ______________________________________

____

Sentence: _______________________________________

Word: ______________________

Definition: ______________________________________

____

Sentence: _______________________________________

Words to Remember

Word: ____________________

Definition: ____________________

____

Sentence: ____________________

Word: ____________________

Definition: ____________________

____

Sentence: ____________________

Word: ____________________

Definition: ____________________

____

Sentence: ____________________

Word: ____________________

Definition: ____________________

____

Sentence: ____________________

Word: ____________________

Definition: ____________________

____

Sentence: ____________________